Full pronunciation key

The pronunciation of each word is shown just after the word, in this way:
ab bre vi ate (ə brē′vē āt).
The letters and signs used are pronounced as in the words below.
The mark ′ is placed after a syllable with primary or heavy accent, as in the example above.
The mark ′ after a syllable shows a secondary or lighter accent, as in **ab bre vi a tion** (ə brē′vē ā′shən).

at, cap	i	it, pin	p	paper, cup	v	very, save
ge, face	ī	ice, five	r	run, try	w	will, woman
ther, far			s	say, yes	y	young, yet
	j	jam, enjoy	sh	she, rush	z	zero, breeze
ad, rob	k	kind, seek	t	tell, it	zh	measure, seizure
hild, much	l	land, coal	th	thin, both		
id, red	m	me, am	ŦH	then, smooth		
	n	no, in			ə	represents:
t, best	ng	long, bring	u	cup, butter		a in about
qual, be			ù	full, put		e in taken
rm, learn	o	hot, rock	ü	rule, move		i in pencil
	ō	open, go				o in lemon
t, if	ô	order, all				u in circus
o, bag	oi	oil, voice				
e, how	ou	house, out				

Grammatical key

adj.	adjective	*n.*	noun
adv.	adverb	*prep.*	preposition
conj.	conjunction	*pron.*	pronoun
interj.	interjection	*v.*	verb
sing.	singular	*pl.*	plural

Thorndike
Barnhart
intermediate
dictionary

SECOND EDITION

by E.L. THORNDIKE / CLARENCE L. BARNHART

Scott, Foresman and Company

Cover symbols for Thorndike Barnhart Dictionaries

for the INTERMEDIATE DICTIONARY
is the letter **I** from an alphabet
designed by Albrecht Dürer in 1525.

for the BEGINNING DICTIONARY
is the letter **B** from the Persian cuneiform
alphabet used between the
sixth and fourth centuries B.C.

for the ADVANCED DICTIONARY
is the letter **A** from
the Hebrew alphabet.

ISBN: 0-673-04800-4

Regional offices of Scott, Foresman and Company are located in Dallas, Texas; Glenview, Illinois
    Oakland, New Jersey; Palo Alto, California; Tucker, Georgia; and Brighton, England.

CONTENTS

1-985 Your Dictionary

Introduction

The Thorndike-Barnhart Intermediate Dictionary is a revision of the Thorndike-Barnhart Junior Dictionary, first published in 1935 as the Thorndike-Century Junior Dictionary. This revision is in an entirely new format from the Junior, in line with the design of modern textbooks. The greatly expanded content includes hundreds of entries reflecting the increased technical and scientific vocabulary of our time.

Dr. Edward L. Thorndike's fundamental principle of explaining the meaning of words in terms that pupils can understand has been faithfully adhered to in this book. A trained editorial staff has screened citation files for new entries and meanings and has carefully examined the definitions and sentences to make sure that the dictionary gives explanations of hard words in terms that pupils understand. Many additional illustrative sentences have been added to clarify the definitions. These sentences have been written to reflect the pluralism of our society, and at the same time to avoid unfortunate stereotypes that abound in many textbooks and reference works.

Before the dictionary proper there are 34 pages of lessons that teach specific skills in the use of the dictionary, accompanied by exercises that help the pupil test his or her own progress. These lessons and exercises will enable pupils to use this dictionary, or any dictionary, more profitably.

It is hoped that this dictionary will continue to be a standard source of reference for schoolchildren and that they will find that it answers the questions they ask about the words they use and read.

The Editors

HOW TO USE THIS DICTIONARY

There are words to name almost everything you have seen or can imagine. Words name animals, people, parts of the body, places, machines, and ideas. There are words to tell almost everything that you can do. There are words to describe how things look or feel or act.

A dictionary is a book that tells about words. The words are listed so that you can find them when you need them. The boy in the picture above needs to know how to spell *hippopotamus.* In a dictionary you can find how to spell a word. The other boy in the picture wants to know how to pronounce *hors d'oeuvre.* In a dictionary you can find how to pronounce a word. And in a dictionary you can find what a word means. The girl at the table can look up the meaning of *ambidextrous* in a dictionary. You'll notice that the girl at the bookcase has found her own use for a dictionary.

A dictionary has to give many different kinds of information about thousands of words. All of this information has to be organized so that you can find it when you need it. These lessons will help you learn how to find words and understand what the dictionary says about them.

HOW TO FIND WORDS

Entry words

Ia., Iowa.

i am bic (ī am′bik), 1 a foot or measure in poetry consisting of two syllables, an unaccented followed by an accented. 2 of or containing iambic measures. Much English poetry is iambic. EXAMPLE:

"The sún|that bríef|De cém|ber dáy
Rose chéer|less ó|ver hílls|of gráy."

1 *n., 2 adj.*

-ian, suffix meaning the same as **-an,** as in *mammalian, Italian,* etc. [from Latin *-ianus*]

I ber i a (ī bir′ē ə), peninsula in SW Europe, containing Spain and Portugal. *n.*

i bex (ī′beks), a wild goat of Europe, Asia, and Africa. The male has very large horns which curve backward. *n., pl.* **i bex es** or **i bex.**

i bis (ī′bis), a large, long-legged wading bird of warm regions, related to the heron, and having a long, downward-curving bill. The ancient Egyptians regarded the ibis as sacred. *n., pl.* **i bis es** or **i bis.**

-ible, *suffix added to verbs to form adjectives.* that can be _____ed: *Perfectible = that can be perfected. Reducible = that can be reduced.* [from Latin *-ibilis*]

Ib sen (ib′sən), **Henrik,** 1828-1906, Norwegian dramatist. *n.*

The words that a dictionary explains are called entry words. Entry words are easy to find. They are printed in heavy black type and start at the left of each column. The section of the dictionary above has eight entry words. Read them and their definitions. Then answer the following questions.

TEACH YOURSELF

1. Which entry word is the name of a person?
2. Which is the name of a bird?
3. Which is an abbreviation?
4. Which is the name of an animal?
5. How many entry words are suffixes?
6. Which entry word is the name of a place?

You have learned from reading the entries above and from answering the questions that a dictionary explains different kinds of words. Some are the names of people, places, or things. Others are abbreviations or suffixes. Look through your dictionary. You will see many other kinds of entry words, too.

Alphabetical order

From *A* on page 1 to *zygote* on page 985, the entry words in this dictionary are in alphabetical order.

a b c d e f g h i j k l m n o p q r s t u v w x y z

A dictionary has a section for each letter of the alphabet. These 26 sections are different sizes. More words start with *s* than with any other letter of the alphabet. This dictionary has 122 pages of entry words starting with *s*. Few English words begin with *x*. That letter takes up less than a page. Words beginning with *a* take up 60 pages.

The first letter of a word tells you which section of the dictionary to look in. Next you must look at the second letter, because words are then alphabetized by their second letters, then their third, and so on.

TEACH YOURSELF

List A	List B	List C
abandon	alarm	water
accident	albatross	watercress
adapt	alfalfa	waterfall
aerial	alike	water line

1. In list A why does *adapt* come before *aerial?*
2. If you wanted to add *after* to List A, where would you put it?
3. In List B the third letters are used to alphabetize the words. Why?
4. If you added *alibi* to list B, where would you put it?
5. What letter did you have to look at to find where to put it?

An entry may be written as two or more words. Such entries are alphabetized like single words. In list C *water line* is two words. It follows *waterfall,* because *w-a-t-e-r-l* follows *w-a-t-e-r-f.*
6. If you added *water hole* to list C, where would you put it?

EXERCISE

Turn to pages 320-321. Decide where each nonsense word below would be listed if you added it to the dictionary. Tell which word in the dictionary would come before it and which would come after it.

1. fim	3. film-up	5. fintle	7. finalry
2. filt	4. firb	6. fire bloop	8. fiptious

Guide words

At the top of the outside column of every page in this dictionary is a word printed in heavy black type. It is called a guide word. Guide words make it easier for you to find entry words. Below are the guide words for pages 386 and 387. Open your dictionary to those pages.

harass   **hart**

TEACH YOURSELF

1. What is the first entry word on page 386?
2. What is the last entry word on page 387?

Whenever you open your dictionary, guide words tell you the first and last entry words on the pages you have opened to.

Hare follows *harass* in alphabetical order, and it is an entry word on page 386. *Harp* comes before *hart* in alphabetical order. It is an entry word on page 387. On these two pages you will also find the entry words *hardly, harebell, harmony,* and *harpoon.*

3. Tell why they are listed on pages 386 and 387.
4. Is *happy* listed on these pages? Why or why not?
5. Can you find *Hartford* there? Why or why not?

EXERCISES

1. Use the guide words to find each of the following entry words in your dictionary. Between which two guide words did you find each word?

   a. demolish   f. register
   b. consistent   g. remote
   c. handspring   h. shortcake
   d. confident   i. misfortune
   e. intersect   j. declare

2. The guide words for pages 402 and 403 are *hobby* and *home.* Copy the following words and circle those that you would find on pages 402 and 403. Then write the circled words in alphabetical order. Check your list with the dictionary.

hollow	hockey	hog	holding
hobo	holly	Holland	hoe
home base	hoarse	holy day	homely

Homographs

The boy and girl in the cartoon are not talking about the same thing.

cob bler[1] (kob′lər), person whose work is mending shoes. *n.* [Middle English *cobeler*]

cob bler[2] (kob′lər), a fruit pie baked in a deep dish, usually with a crust only on top. *n.* [origin unknown]

Sometimes two or more words have the same spelling but different origins and meanings. They are called homographs. A small raised number after an entry word tells you that at least one other entry word has the same spelling. If the first word is not the one you want, the number reminds you to look at the next one.

TEACH YOURSELF

1. In the cartoon above, which homograph is the girl talking about?
2. Which one does the boy think she means?

EXERCISES

1. How many homographs do you find in your dictionary for each of the following spellings?

a. sole	c. port	e. spat	g. mew
b. rose	d. bark	f. flag	h. bit

2. For each sentence below, decide which homograph of *bay* is used.
   a. We were awakened by the *bay* of the neighbor's dog.
   b. The *bay* was quite skittish and threw its rider.
   c. We planted a *bay* in our backyard.
   d. The *bays* of the cathedral are Gothic in style.
   e. The village is situated on a small *bay*.

Words that aren't entry words

When we speak and write, we automatically add the endings -s, -es, -ed, -ing, -er, and -est to words. We use the endings to show such things as whether we mean more than one or whether something has already happened. Words that have these endings are called inflected forms. Many of them are not entry words in your dictionary. To find them, you have to look up the root word to which the ending was added.

TEACH YOURSELF

1. To find *flogged* or *flogging,* look up *flog.* Notice that the inflected forms are given in heavy type after the definition. What letter is added to *flog* before the endings?
2. To find *pushier* or *pushiest,* look up *pushy.* What letter of *pushy* changes when -er or -est is added?
3. To find *rarer* or *rarest,* look up *rare.* What letter is dropped from *rare* before the endings?
4. To find *gullies,* look up *gully.* What letter of *gully* changes when -es is added?
5. To find *opted* or *opting,* look up *opt.* Notice that the inflected forms are not listed after the definition. Do you know why?

In answering the last question, you were right if you said that the inflected forms are not listed because the spelling of *opt* does not change when you add the endings. This dictionary gives inflected forms for a word only if its spelling changes when you add an ending.

EXERCISE

To look up each word listed below, what entry word do you have to find in your dictionary?

1. evading	4. nicer	7. pygmies	10. descended
2. fogies	5. carried	8. hoariest	11. marred
3. knotted	6. glibber	9. beckoning	12. pausing

Many words are formed by adding either prefixes or suffixes to other words. The prefixes and suffixes add new meaning to the basic word. Some of these words with prefixes and suffixes are not entry words in your dictionary. You will be able to find them if you look at the entry for the basic word. For example, look up the word *jocular.* After the definition you will see the word *jocularly* printed in heavy type. Words listed in this way are called run-on entries. To get the meaning of a run-on entry, combine the meaning of the entry word with the meaning of the suffix.

joc u lar (jok′yə lər), funny; joking. *adj.* —**joc′u lar ly,** *adv.*

-ly[1], *suffix added to adjectives to form adverbs.* 1 in a _____ manner. . . .

You can now see that *jocularly* means "in a joking manner."

Sometimes words formed by adding prefixes or suffixes to other words are not listed in your dictionary at all. It is simple to figure out the meaning of these words. *Repave* is not entered anywhere in your dictionary. To understand its meaning, you have to look at the following two entries.

⑪

re-, *prefix.* 1 again; anew; once more: *Reappear = appear again.* . . .

pave (pāv), 1 cover (a street, sidewalk, etc.) with a pavement: *pave a road with concrete.* . . .

EXERCISE

To find the meaning of each word listed below, what entry words do you have to look up? Write down the number of each word and after it write your answer. Do it like this: 1. non-, legal.

1. nonlegal	4. forklike	7. flourless
2. despoiler	5. sourish	8. curtness
3. redraw	6. counterplot	9. misdate

Word combinations and names

Sometimes two or more words together are an entry word. Examples of such entry words are *battle royal* and *parlor car.*

Knowing the meaning of the words *battle* and *royal* does not make clear the meaning of *battle royal.* Knowing what *parlor* and *car* mean tells you little about *parlor car.* When a combination of words like these puzzles you, look to see if the combined form is an entry word.

Some entries of more than one word are names of places. These are easy to recognize because they are capitalized. On page 371 there are several such entry words: *Great Lakes, Great Plains, Great Salt Lake.*

Names of people are capitalized too. People are usually listed under their family names, not under their first names. For example, you will find *Marie Curie* in the *c's*, not in the *m's.*

EXERCISE

Look up each entry word printed in italics below. Answer each question yes or no and give the reason for your answer. Do it like this: 1. No, it's a muscle cramp.

    1. Could you ride a *charley horse?*
    2. Would a fisherman catch a *red herring?*
    3. Does the postman deliver *chain mail?*
    4. Can a person be a *lame duck?*
    5. Is *aqueous humor* a kind of joke?
    6. Does a *sea dog* bark?
    7. Can a person be a *black sheep?*
    8. Would a kitten sleep in a *cat's cradle?*
    9. Would you eat an *honor roll* for breakfast?

Idioms

Suppose you are reading a newspaper story about local politics. You come to the following sentence: "The mayor had little support at the start of his reelection campaign, but now many people are beginning to climb on the bandwagon."

The phrase *climb on the bandwagon* may be a little puzzling to you. It is called an idiom. An idiom is a phrase or expression whose meaning cannot be understood from the ordinary meanings of the words in it. An idiom is not always given in the dictionary under its first word. To find it you must look under its most important word. In this case the word is *bandwagon.* Idioms are listed at the end of an entry, each on a separate line. They are in heavy black type.

If you look in your dictionary for the idiom *climb on the bandwagon,* you will find the following:

> **band wag on** (band′wag′ən), wagon that carries a musical band in a parade. *n.*
> **climb on the bandwagon,** INFORMAL. join what appears to be a winning or successful group, movement, fashion, etc.

Climb on the bandwagon has nothing to do with climbing. It has nothing to do with a bandwagon. Now you understand what the newspaper story was telling you. It was telling you that many people are beginning to join the mayor's campaign because he seems to be winning.

EXERCISE

Look up each of the following idioms in your dictionary. Write each number. After it write the entry word under which you found the idiom.

1. see red
2. no great shakes
3. up a tree
4. bottle up
5. rub the wrong way
6. place on a pedestal
7. call it quits
8. laugh up one's sleeve
9. keep one's eyes peeled
10. eat crow

Test yourself

1. Suppose you had a friend named Winifred G. Whizdom who became famous and had her name added to the dictionary.

   a. Between what two entry words would her name be?
   b. Between what guide words would her name be?

2. For each of the following sentences, look up all the entries spelled the same as the word in italics. Decide which entry is used in the sentence. Write each letter, and after it write your answer.

   a. My best friend has two hundred dollars in the *bank*.
   b. We had *squash* for dinner.
   c. The teacher was *stern* but fair.
   d. Fishmongers used to *hawk* their fish in the street.
   e. The *patter* of the rain woke me up early.
   f. The coin collection was kept in a *vault*.
   g. The boat was *bound* for the open sea.

3. Find the plural forms of the following nouns in your dictionary. Copy the letters *a* through *f,* and write the plural forms you found.

a. knife	c. thesis	e. goose
b. patty	d. mouse	f. symphony

4. The following paragraphs contain fourteen idioms that include parts of the body. Write down each idiom you find and look it up in your dictionary. Then underline the word under which you found the idiom. Do it like this: twiddle his <u>thumbs</u>.

   John couldn't decide if he should twiddle his thumbs and hope for a miracle or rack his brains for the right answers to the science test. He really had his hands full. He had passed the last test by the skin of his teeth, and the teacher had turned a cold shoulder to his excuses. "If you would take to heart my reading assignments, hold your tongue when I explain the lessons, and keep on your toes during class, you wouldn't lose your head every time we have a test," she said.

   John made no bones about the fact that he was in trouble. After this he would be all ears in science class. He would really knuckle down. But on this test he was risking his neck making wild guesses, even though he was trying to keep a stiff upper lip.

HOW TO USE THE PRONUNCIATIONS

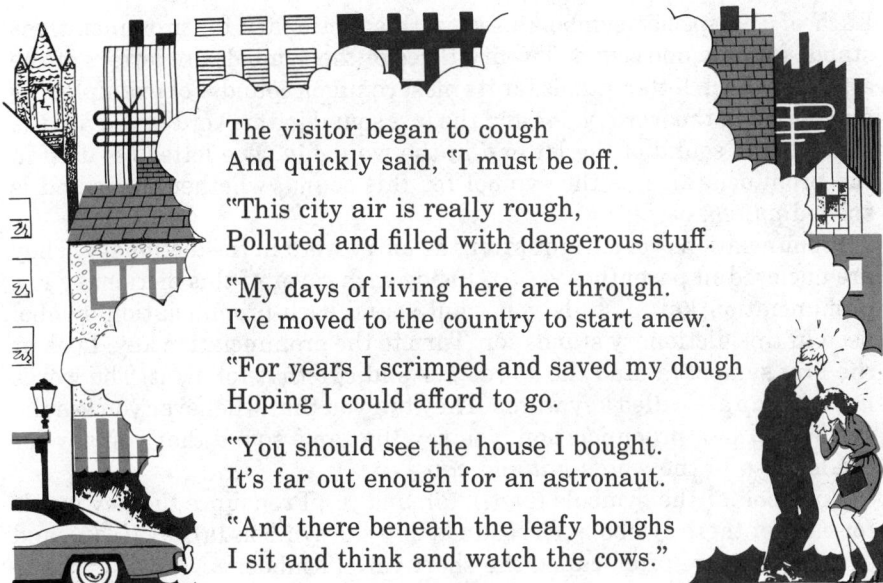

The visitor began to cough
And quickly said, "I must be off.

"This city air is really rough,
Polluted and filled with dangerous stuff.

"My days of living here are through.
I've moved to the country to start anew.

"For years I scrimped and saved my dough
Hoping I could afford to go.

"You should see the house I bought.
It's far out enough for an astronaut.

"And there beneath the leafy boughs
I sit and think and watch the cows."

When you read the poem above, did you notice that it contains six words spelled with the combination of letters *ough?* If you did not already know how to pronounce these words, you might think that they rhyme. But in each word the letters *ough* are pronounced in a different way. Because you cannot always tell how to pronounce a word just by looking at its spelling, this dictionary gives pronunciations for its entry words.

It would be easy to pronounce words if each letter of the alphabet stood for only one sound. But that is not the case. All the vowel letters and many of the consonant letters stand for more than one sound.

TEACH YOURSELF

How many different sounds does the letter *o* stand for in the words *hot, go, women, move,* and *other?*

Many words, such as *hot,* give an idea of how they are pronounced by the way they are spelled. Many others, such as *women,* do not.

Not only can one letter stand for more than one sound, but one sound can be spelled in more than one way. You hear the same sound (long *a*) in the words *age, pain, weigh, say, break, vein,* and *they.* But notice the different ways this one sound is spelled.

The pronunciation key and vowel sounds

Each of the special symbols used in this dictionary for pronunciations stands for only one sound. Twenty-three of the symbols are letters of the alphabet. Each letter stands for its most common sound. For example, the first sound in the word *phone* and the last sound in the word *laugh* are the same as the sound of the letter *f* in the word *fun.* The letter *f* is used in the pronunciations as the symbol for this sound, whether the sound is spelled *ph, gh,* or *f.*

Pronunciations come right after the entry word in the dictionary. They are enclosed in parentheses ( ). Inside each cover of this dictionary is a pronunciation key. It tells you what sound each pronunciation symbol used in this dictionary stands for. Turn to the pronunciation key. Look at the first symbol (a) and the words *hat* and *cap* that follow it. The words *hat* and *cap* are called key words. They tell you that whenever you see the symbol (a) in a pronunciation, you say the same sound that you say for the letter *a* in the words *hat* and *cap.*

Now look at the symbols (e), (i), (o), and (u). Pronounce the key words for each of these symbols. The sounds that the symbols (a), (e), (i), (o), and (u) stand for are often called the short vowel sounds.

TEACH YOURSELF

Pronounce the key words that tell you what to say when you see the pronunciation symbol (s). Now pronounce the following words: *sand, circle, silly, can, city, scene, psalm, coat, sugar.* Which of these words begin with the sound that you heard when you pronounced the key words for the symbol (s)?

EXERCISE

Each of the numbered pronunciations below stands for one of the words in the list on the right. Using the pronunciation key, match each word to its pronunciation. Do it like this: 1. cup.

1. (kup)	6. (frend)	has	edge
2. (laf)	7. (haz)	laugh	give
3. (dred)	8. (ej)	class	cup
4. (klas)	9. (juj)	dread	judge
5. (giv)	10. (duk)	friend	duck

dart (därt) **kite** (kīt) **pull** (pùl)
seed (sēd) **call** (kôl) **pool** (pül)

Each of the pronunciations above has a symbol in it that
stands for a vowel sound. These symbols are vowel letters
with special marks above them called diacritical marks.
Find each of these vowel symbols and its key words in
the pronunciation key. After you pronounce the key
words for a symbol, pronounce the word above that
has the same symbol in its pronunciation. You
should hear the same vowel sound in the word above
as you heard in the key words.

TEACH YOURSELF A

1. There are two other symbols in the pronunciation key that are vowel
   letters with diacritical marks. What are they?
2. Which of these two symbols would be used in the pronunciation of the
   word *though?* Which would be used in the pronunciation of *bait?*

17

EXERCISE

Using the pronunciation key, say each of the numbered words pronounced below. From the words on the right, choose the one you have just
pronounced. Write each number and after it write the word you chose.

1. (fāz)	3. (bird)	bird	car	bold	phase
2. (kär)	4. (bôld)	face	bald	care	beard

Listen to the vowel sound in each of the following words as you say
them: *herd, earn, bird, work, turn.* A two-letter symbol stands for this
sound. It is the symbol (ėr). Find it and the key words for it in the
pronunciation key.

There are two more two-letter symbols for vowel sounds in the
pronunciation key. They are the symbols (oi) and (ou). Say the key words
for these two symbols.

TEACH YOURSELF B

1. Tell which of the following words have the vowel sound (ou) in them:
   loud, crowd, bought, now, grow, group.
2. Tell which of the following words have the vowel sound (oi) in them:
   coin, aisle, toy, count, noise.

More two-letter symbols

chance (chans)   **shop** (shop)   **breathe** (brēᴛH)
sing (sing)   **breath** (breth)   **rouge** (rüzh)

All the rest of the two-letter symbols used in this dictionary are in the pronunciations of the words above. These symbols all stand for consonant sounds. They are the symbols (ch), (ng), (sh), (th), (ᴛH), and (zh). Find them in the pronunciation key and pronounce their key words.

TEACH YOURSELF

1. In which of the following words do you hear the sound (th)? In which do you hear the sound (ᴛH)?

this	bath	there	thought
bathe	faith	though	their

2. In which of the following words do you hear the sound (ch)? In which do you hear the sound (sh)? In which do you hear the sound (zh)?

chin	shin	cheap
beige	sure	sheep

EXERCISE

Pick a word from the list on the right which is pronounced with each numbered sound on the left. Do it like this: 1. cow

1. (ou)	think	chair
2. (ch)	word	choir
3. (oi)	cow	these
4. (th)	chord	weird
5. (ᴛH)	pour	boil
6. (ėr)	chef	Thames

18

Syllables and accent

I (ī)   **in vite** (in vīt′)   **in sin cere** (in′sin sir′)
blank (blangk)   **cup cake** (kup′kāk′)   **ath let ic** (ath let′ik)

Say the two words in the first list above. Notice that in these words you hear only one vowel sound.

TEACH YOURSELF

1. Say the words in the second list. How many vowel sounds do you hear in each word? Into how many parts is each word divided?
2. How many vowel sounds do you hear in each word in the third list? Into how many parts is each of these words divided?

Each part of a word in which we hear one vowel sound is called a syllable. In the pronunciations, words are divided into syllables by a space. The words in the first list have only one syllable. Those in the second list have two. Those in the third list have three.

When we say a word having two or more syllables, we accent at least one of the syllables. That is, we say it with more force or stress than we do the others. In the pronunciations above, some syllables are followed by the marks (′) and (′). The darker mark (′), called a primary accent, follows the syllable we say with the most force. The lighter mark (′), a secondary accent, follows the syllable we say with medium force. Syllables which are not followed by marks are unaccented or unstressed syllables. We say them with the least force.

EXERCISE

The words below are divided into syllables for you. Say each word, noticing where the stress falls. Then copy the words putting accent marks after the stressed syllable or syllables. (If a word has two stressed syllables, both primary and secondary accents will be needed.)

1. em ploy   3. laugh ing stock   5. ra di a tor   7. chem is try
2. chick en   4. pas sen ger   6. so lid i ty   8. tor na do

Sometimes in an unaccented syllable we do not say a vowel sound. Instead we say the sound (l) or (n). In these syllables (l) and (n) are called syllabic consonants. Here are some words that have syllables without vowel sounds.

lit tle (lit′l)   **jour nal** (jėr′nl)   **re cent** (rē′snt)
hast i ly (hā′stl ē)   **cot ton** (kot′n)   **sea son** (sē′zn)

The schwa

There is one more pronunciation symbol used in this dictionary. It is called schwa and looks like this: (ə). It is a vowel sound heard only in unaccented syllables. Find the symbol (ə) and its five key words in the pronunciation key. When you pronounce the key words, you hear the same sound for the *a* in *about* (ə bout′), the *e* in *taken* (tā′kən), the *i* in *pencil* (pen′səl), the *o* in *lemon* (lem′ən), and the *u* in *circus* (sėr′kəs). In an unaccented syllable, any of the five vowel letters can have the sound represented by (ə). Some combinations of vowel letters can have the sound (ə) too.

TEACH YOURSELF

e nor mous (i nôr′məs)   **tor toise** (tôr′təs)
bar gain (bär′gən)   **fash ion** (fash′ən)

In each word above, what combination of vowel letters has the sound represented by (ə)?

EXERCISE

The symbol (ə) is used in pronouncing each of the following words. Write each word, and circle the vowel letter or letters in each which have the sound represented by (ə).

batter	villain	furious
forum	awake	garland
obsess	grateful	mistake

Variant pronunciations

Most entries in this dictionary give only one pronunciation. It is the pronunciation you will almost always hear. Some entries, however, give more than one pronunciation. For example, two pronunciations are given for *rodeo* (rō′dē ō *or* rō dā′ō). The pronunciation (rō′dē ō) is given first, not because it is more correct than (rō dā′ō), but because scholars think it is used by more people than (rō dā′ō). If you are one of the people who says (rō dā′ō), you are just as correct as those who say (rō′dē ō).

Sometimes when the meaning of a word changes, its pronunciation changes too. The word *separate* is pronounced one way when it is used as a verb and another way when it is used as an adjective. Here is the way this is shown in the pronunciation of *separate.*

sep a rate (sep′ə rāt′ *for 1-4;* sep′ər it
for 5-7)

TEACH YOURSELF

Look at the entry *separate* and read the definitions. Tell whether *separate* is pronounced (sep′ə rāt′) or (sep′ər it) in the following sentences.
1. My brother and I have separate rooms.
2. Walls separate the rooms in a house.

EXERCISE

The pronunciation of each of the following words in italics changes when its meaning changes. Read the entry for each word and decide how it is pronounced in the sentence below. Write the number of each sentence and after it the pronunciation you decided on.
1. She never seems rushed; even her speech is *deliberate.*
2. Our dog always stays within the *confines* of our yard.
3. Would you *object* if I painted my room purple?
4. I heard her *conduct* the orchestra last week.

Test yourself

1. Use your dictionary to answer these questions:
   a. Does *campanile* rhyme with *crocodile, repeal,* or *steely?*
   b. Does *bury* rhyme with *hurry, ferry,* or *fury?*
   c. Does *faille* rhyme with *mile, fail,* or *pal?*
   d. Does *coup* rhyme with *stoup, who,* or *taupe?*
   e. Does *chamois* rhyme with *tortoise, mammy,* or *patois?*

2. The clues for this crossword puzzle are the pronunciations of common words. Copy the puzzle or get a copy from your teacher. Fill in the puzzle with the words that the pronunciations stand for.

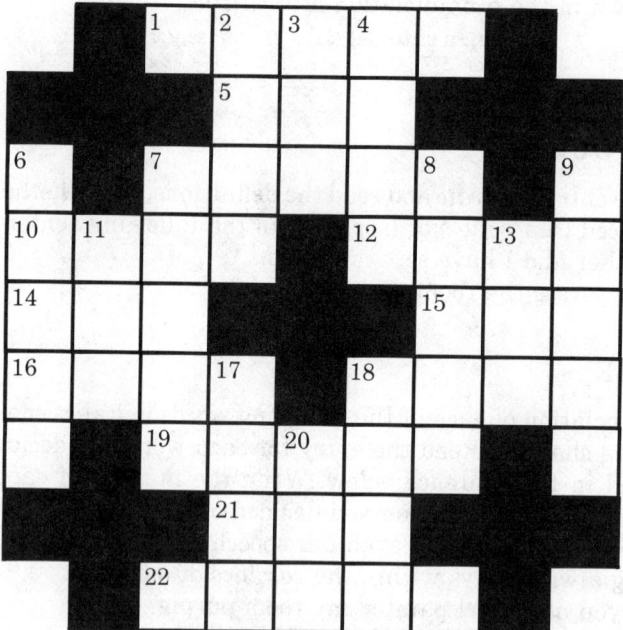

ACROSS
1. (spend)
5. (āj)
7. (krôs)
10. (rer *or* rar)
12. (thin)
14. (yü)
15. (ôr)
16. (els)
18. (ren)
19. (tas′it)
21. (rod)
22. (ang′gər)

DOWN
2. (per *or* par)
3. (ē′gō)
4. (nest)
6. (grēk)
7. (krest)
8. (shôrt)
9. (ə nent′)
11. (ôl)
13. (īr)
17. (ėrn)
18. (wīd)
20. (kog)

The crossword puzzle on this page may be reproduced for classroom use.

Test yourself

In *The Canterville Ghost,* a story by Oscar Wilde, an American diplomat named Mr. Otis buys a historic house in England. When he and his family move in, the scary spook who has been living there for over three hundred years soon becomes only a ghost of his former self.

In the following sentences, which describe how Mr. Otis first meets the ghost, some of the words are written in pronunciation symbols. Read the sentences, using the pronunciation key whenever you need help. Then rewrite the story spelling out the words written in symbols.

Mr. Otis was (ə wā′kənd) by a curious (noiz) in the (hôl), (out′sīd′) his (rüm). It sounded (līk) the (klangk) of (met′l), and (sēmd) to be coming (nir′ər) every (mō′mənt). He (pùt) on his (slip′ərz), (tùk) a small (ob′lông) phial from his (dres′ər), and (ō′pənd) the (dôr). Right in (frunt) of him he (sô) an (ōld) man of (ter′ə bəl) aspect. Long (grā) (her) fell (ō′vər) his (shōl′dərz) in matted (koilz). His (gär′mənts) were of antique (kut), and from his (rists) and (ang′kəlz) hung (hev′ē) manacles and (rus′tē) fetters.

QUESTION: What kind of hair did the ghost have?

23

"My (dir) (sėr)," said Mr. Otis, "I really must insist on (yùr) oiling those (chānz) and have (brôt) you for (т̄Hat) purpose a small (bot′l) of (lü′brə-kā′ting) oil."

QUESTION: Was Mr. Otis afraid of the ghost?

For a (mō′mənt) the (kan′tər vil) (gōst) stood (kwīt) motionless in natural (in′dig nā′shən). Then, dashing the bottle (vī′ə lənt lē) upon the (pol′isht) floor, he fled. On (rē′ching) the west wing, he (lēnd) up (ə genst′) a (mün′bēm′) to recover his (breth). Never, in a (bril′yənt) and (un′in tə-rup′tid) career of (thrē) hundred (yirz), had he (bin) so grossly (in sul′tid).

QUESTION: Did the ghost like Mr. Otis's gift?

HOW TO FIND A MEANING

Context

Jane is reading a suspense story. She is at a very exciting point when she comes to the following paragraph:

> "Lots of people here are not what they seem," he whispered. "That woman claims to be a pilot, but her real work is espionage. She spies on secret defense sites, taking aerial pictures of them. Then she sells the pictures for the highest price she can get."

Jane does not know the word *espionage.* But as she continues reading, she realizes that she will not need to look it up. The words used with it, which are called its context, have made its meaning clear to her. The woman's real work is said to be espionage. She spies on defense sites and sells aerial pictures of them. Jane decides, therefore, that espionage has something to do with spying.

If you look up *espionage* in your dictionary, you can see that Jane was right. She had found the word's meaning from its context.

Jane continues reading the story. The next sentence is:

> The woman he pointed out did not look wily to me.

Jane does not know the meaning of *wily,* and nothing in the sentence gives her a clue. When the context does not help to explain a word, you need to look it up in the dictionary. The definition you find for an entry word can often be used in place of the word in a sentence. A definition is a substitute for an entry word. Jane found the following definition for the word *wily:*

> **wil y** . . . using subtle tricks to deceive; crafty; cunning; sly: *a wily thief. The wily fox got away.*

In the definition are the three words *crafty, cunning,* and *sly.* They are all synonyms of *wily.* A synonym is a word that means the same as another word. When synonyms are included in the definition of a word, it is easy to substitute them for the word in a sentence. Jane was able to substitute *crafty, cunning,* and *sly* for *wily* in the sentence she was reading. Now she understood that the woman whose work was spying did not look crafty, cunning, or sly.

EXERCISES

1. Read each of the following sentences, trying to figure out the meaning of the word in italics from its context. Choose the meaning below which is closest to the one you figured out.

   a. When a *noxious* chemical polluted the lake, all the fish died.

      poisonous   dirty   liquid

   b. Her fine collection of old maps revealed her interest in *cartography*.

      transportation   pictures of carts   map making

   c. Since he was known to be *choleric,* we avoided telling him anything that might anger him.

      sad   irritable   suffering from cholera

   d. She *reiterated* her story, saying time after time that she was innocent of the theft.

      changed   continued   repeated

   e. No one noticed him until his books became popular, but after that he was *lionized* by the literary world.

      hunted   treated as important   made wild

   f. Anyone who writes about "leperds, elefants, and jeraffs" after visiting a zoo is no expert in *orthography*.

      spelling   animals   writing letters

2. Look up the word in italics in each of the following sentences. Then rewrite each sentence, substituting the definition for the word in italics.

   a. After dinner a *lethargic* feeling came over him.

   b. Her *intrepidity* during the hurricane impressed all of us.

   c. His selfish behavior filled us with *ire*.

   d. The party was so enjoyable I wished I could *prolong* it.

   e. My *vivacious* friend is quite popular.

   f. The *ferocity* of the crime stunned the police.

   g. The senator's Fourth of July speech was *fervid*.

More than one meaning and part of speech

Ruth said that a blacksnake was a harmless black snake. Bill said it was a leather whip. They looked up the word *blacksnake* in the dictionary and found that they were both right. *Blacksnake* has two meanings:

> 1 a harmless dark or black snake of North America. 2 a heavy whip made of braided leather.

Many words have more than one meaning. The meanings are numbered in your dictionary so you can find them easily.

Many words also have more than one use or function in a sentence. That is, they can be used as more than one part of speech. The parts of speech are summarized by definition number after the last definition. The abbreviations used for the parts of speech are shown in the upper left-hand corner of every left-hand page.

TEACH YOURSELF

26

Read the entry for *slow.* Notice the part-of-speech summary after definition ten.

1. How many different adjective meanings does *slow* have? How many adverb meanings? How many verb meanings?
2. In *We walked at a slow pace, slow* has the meaning given in the first definition. What part of speech is *slow* in this sentence?
3. In *Slow down so I can keep up, slow* has the meaning given in the sixth definition. What part of speech is *slow* in this sentence?
4. What part of speech is *slow* in *Let's walk slow?*

EXERCISE

Each word below in italics is used in two sentences. In each sentence it has a different meaning and part of speech. Tell which definition and part of speech is used. Do it like this: 1. definition 3, verb.

1. An abandoned shack *harbored* the hikers during the snowstorm.
2. We sailed the boat right into the *harbor.*
3. I stayed home because I had a bad *cold.*
4. The *cold* lemonade was very refreshing.
5. A *fast* train will get you there in an hour.
6. You certainly can run *fast.*
7. We *panned* for gold on our trip to Colorado last year.
8. He fried the fish in a *pan* over the open fire.

Hidden entries

You have just overheard some people talking about a young man who always wants to be in the swim. You know they don't mean that he wants to go to the beach to go swimming, but you don't know what they do mean. You look in your dictionary to find out what *the swim* means. You find the following:

> **swim** . . . . **7 the swim,** the current
> of affairs, activities, etc.: *An active and*
> *sociable person likes to be in the swim.*

The swim is called a hidden entry. Hidden entries are printed in heavy type slightly smaller than the entry word. They show special meanings that certain forms of the entry word have. Often they are either capitalized, uncapitalized, or plural forms of the entry word. Sometimes they are the word *the* plus the entry word, as *the swim*.

TEACH YOURSELF A

Read the entry for *room*. Pick out the sentence below in which *rooms* has its hidden-entry meaning.
1. The palace has many *rooms.*
2. We found *rooms* at the big house on the corner.
3. She *rooms* with her best friend.

Variant spellings

Some words have more than one spelling. The different spellings often have to be entered in different places in the dictionary to be in alphabetical order. When this happens, the definition is given under the more common spelling. Look up the word *britches.* Instead of a definition, you will find "breeches." This means that *breeches* is the more common spelling of the word. If you look under *breeches,* you will find two meanings. These are the meanings of *britches* as well as *breeches.*

TEACH YOURSELF B

Under what entry word will you find the meaning of each word below?
1. sirup   2. syphon   3. intrust   4. wilful

Labels

Some words or meanings of words are labeled to tell you how, when, or where they are used. Look at the following entries. In each of them you will see a label.

> **couldst** (kůdst), OLD USE. could.
> "Thou couldst" means "You could." *v.*

The label OLD USE means that the word or meaning is not used much today. You may see it in stories or poems written long ago or about the past.

> **stuck-up** (stuk′up′), INFORMAL. too
> proud; conceited; haughty. *adj.*

The label INFORMAL means that you might use the word or meaning in everyday talk. But you probably wouldn't use it in formal writing.

> **slob** (slob), SLANG. a stupid, untidy, or
> clumsy person. *n.*

The label SLANG means that you might use the word or meaning in familiar talk with your friends. But it is not considered good English by educated people.

> **bairn** (bern *or* barn), SCOTTISH.
> child. *n.*

Language labels, such as SCOTTISH, mean that a word or meaning is used chiefly in certain countries or by people from those countries. The label LATIN means, simply, that the word is a Latin word.

> **poke²** (pōk), DIALECT. bag; sack. *n.*

The label DIALECT means that the word or meaning is used by people in a certain region, or by a certain group of people.

EXERCISE

For each of the following sentences, look up the word in italics in your dictionary. Then give its meaning and tell how it is labeled.
1. We saw a *cool* movie last night.
2. He thought I wouldn't know him, but I *minded* seeing him before.
3. She is a real hockey *buff*.
4. The knight was *yclept* Lancelot.
5. He is *auld* now, but fifty years ago he was a bonny lad.
6. Your friend has a lot of *zing*.
7. "*Yon* peasant may be one of Robin Hood's men," said the sheriff.
8. We had a *horrid* time at the party.

prairie dog
about 15 in. long
with the tail

If you live in the eastern United States and have never seen a prairie dog, it might be hard for you to imagine what one looks like just from reading the definition.

prairie dog, a burrowing animal like a woodchuck but smaller, found on the Great Plains and in the Rocky Mountain region. Prairie dogs bark.

There are many pictures and diagrams in this dictionary to show you what things look like or how they are used. Every picture and diagram has a caption with it that gives the name of the entry. Many captions also give additional information about the entry. They tell you such things as the size of an animal or how something works.

microscope
There are magnifying lenses in the eyepiece and objective. The mirror reflects light up through the platform, which has an opening in it or is made of glass.

EYEPIECE
FOCUS ADJUSTER
OBJECTIVE
PLATFORM
MIRROR

Many maps are included in this dictionary. Some of them are of places that no longer exist but that you will read about in history books. Many of these historical places are shown as shaded areas on maps having present-day boundaries.

Roman Empire
The shaded area shows the Empire at its greatest extent in A.D. 117.

Etymologies

Histories of words are called etymologies. Etymologies are given for some of the entry words in this dictionary. They follow the definitions and are enclosed in brackets [ ]. Etymologies tell what language the word came from, how it was spelled in that language, and what it meant. If the original word was spelled as it is in English, the spelling is not given in the etymology. If its meaning was the same, the meaning is not given.

bridge[1] . . . . [Old English *brycg*]

Some words started as English words. But over the years they may have changed. Notice above how the spelling of *bridge* has changed.

clove[1] . . . 1 a strong, fragrant spice . . . . [from French of the 1300's *clou*, from Latin *clavus* a nail]

Au gust . . . the eighth month of the year. . . . [from the Roman emperor *Augustus*]

English has borrowed many of its words from other languages. Notice in the etymology of *clove* that French borrowed its word from Latin. Many words pass from language to language, often changing spelling and meaning as they go.

Some words are derived from the names of persons or places, as *August*.

All the homographs in this dictionary have etymologies to help explain why words spelled the same way can have very different meanings:

bat[1] . . . a stout wooden stick or club . . . . [Old English *batt* cudgel]

bat[2] . . . a flying mammal. . . . [perhaps from a Scandinavian word of the 1200's]. . . .

bat[3] . . . wink. . . . [from French of the 1200's *batre* beat]

It is impossible to be sure where some words come from. That is why the etymology of *bat*[2] has the word *perhaps* in it. Sometimes it is not even possible to make a good guess:

cob bler[2] . . . a fruit pie. . . . [origin unknown]

EXERCISE

Read the etymologies of the following words. Then write each number and after it write the language from which the word came.

1. villa
2. aloha
3. pit[2]
4. video
5. panic
6. adios
7. babushka
8. debris
9. hamburger
10. fiord
11. kosher
12. chop suey

Test yourself

1. Each numbered clue for the crossword puzzle below is a definition of one of these words:

arena	era	eland	pinnate
polyp	lob	Nubia	placard

   Look up each word in your dictionary. Match it to its definition below and fill in a copy of the puzzle.

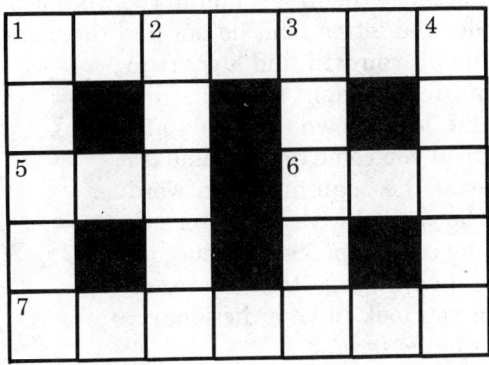

ACROSS
1. like a feather
5. to hit a ball in a high arc
6. an age in history
7. a posted notice; poster

DOWN
1. a small water animal
2. a region in northeast Africa
3. a place where contests took place
4. a large African antelope

2. Look up the clue word or the important word in each clue below. In its definition you will find a word that means the same thing as the clue. That word will be spelled using letters from the word *vocabulary.* Do it like this: Look up *kingly.* In its definition you will find the word *royal.* Write: a. royal.

a. kingly	d. kind of crustacean	g. caboose
b. laurel	e. kind of reef	h. rod
c. kinky	f. lad	i. ringlet

3. Look up each of the following words in your dictionary and read the etymology. Tell what person or place each word is derived from. Do it like this: a. Tulle, a town in France.

a. tulle	d. Queen Anne's lace	g. champagne	j. martinet
b. denim	e. Becquerel rays	h. dahlia	k. jersey
c. lynch	f. silhouette	i. sandwich	l. Chihuahua

The crossword puzzle on this page may be reproduced for classroom use.

HOW TO USE THIS DICTIONARY
FOR SPELLING

Sometimes you want to look up a word in the dictionary that you know how to pronounce but do not know how to spell. If you know just the first letter of the word, you will often be able to find it.

Suppose you hear someone say "Mr. Jones hunted (tär/mə gən) today." You want to look up (tär/mə gən) to find out what it means. You think it is spelled *tarmigan* because the first sound in the word is the sound (t) as in *tell.* You look under the letter *t* but do not find the word.

On pages 34 and 35 you will find a chart to help you spell initial consonant sounds. Turn to this chart and look down the columns headed "Sound" until you come to the sound (t). You will see that at the beginning of a word the sound (t) can be spelled with the letter *t* or with the letters *tw, th,* or *pt.* So (tär/mə gən) might be spelled *twarmigan, tharmigan,* or *ptarmigan.* When you look in your dictionary, you find that it is *ptarmigan.*

TEACH YOURSELF

Turn to the chart on pages 34 and 35. Read the instructions for using the chart. Then answer the following questions.
1. What consonant sounds that begin a word have only one spelling?
2. How many words are there in this dictionary that begin with the sound (l) spelled *ll?* What are they?
3. What is the spelling of the initial sound (r) in the word pronounced (rat)? What is it in the word pronounced (rench)? What is it in the word pronounced (rīn)?

After you found out that the initial consonant sound (t) was spelled *pt* in the word *ptarmigan* (tär/mə gən), it was easy to find the word in the dictionary. The vowel sound (ä) in the first syllable was spelled *a* as you expected. But sometimes the spelling of vowel sounds is not what you expect. This is because we have only five vowel letters, *a, e, i, o,* and *u,* which we combine many ways to spell seventeen different sounds. These seventeen vowel sounds, along with words showing their different spellings, are in a chart on page 36. This chart will help you find the spellings of vowels that begin words, or vowels that come in the first syllables of words.

Spelling (continued)

TEACH YOURSELF

Turn to the chart for the spellings of vowel sounds on page 36. Read the instructions for using the chart. Use the chart to find how the first sound in the word pronounced (es thet′ik) is spelled. Then find the entry for this word in your dictionary.

1. How is (es thet′ik) spelled?
2. Read through the entry you found. Can (es thet′ik) be spelled another way? What is it?

You may spell (es thet′ik) either *aesthetic* or *esthetic*. Both are correct. Since *aesthetic* is the more common spelling, the full definition is at that entry.

EXERCISES

1. Each of the following words is used as an example in the spelling charts. But in the list below the first letter or letters of each word is replaced by the symbol for the first sound in the word. Use the charts to find out how to spell this initial sound. Then spell out the complete word. Do it like this: a. phrase.

   a. (f)rase   d. (n)ife   g. (ou)l   j. (r)ong
   b. (z)ylophone   e. (ē)ch   h. (k)aki   k. (ə)ccur
   c. (i)nough   f. (sh)ef   i. (n)aw   l. (yü)se

2. Use the chart for the spelling of vowel sounds to find how the sound (ō) is spelled in each of the words pronounced below. Find each word in your dictionary. Then spell out the word you found.

   a. Please (hōld) my books while I tie my shoe.
   b. Turn right on that gravel (rōd).
   c. Let's go (bō′ling) on Saturday night.
   d. The color (tōp) is a dark brownish-gray.
   e. Loosen the soil in the garden with this (hō).
   f. An (ōm) is a measure of electrical resistance.
   g. I like the stories about the famous detective Sherlock (hōmz).

3. Use the spelling charts to find each word pronounced below in your dictionary. Spell out the word you found. Do it like this: a. gnat.

   a. (nat)   d. (ket säl′)   g. (säm)   j. (rī nos′ər əs)
   b. (flem)   e. (zē′bek)   h. (bāzh)   k. (pô′pər)
   c. (skēm)   f. (bə ler′ō)   i. (rīŦH)   l. (jėr′fôl′kən)

Spellings of initial consonant sounds

Each consonant sound that can begin a word appears with its spelling in this chart. Very common spellings are in boldface type: **boldface.** Spellings used in eleven to thirty entry words are in roman type: roman. Spellings used in only one to ten entry words are in italic type: *italic.* The spellings of each sound are arranged so that the first spelling is the one that occurs most often. The last spelling is the one that occurs least often.

If a word starts with a consonant sound, use this chart to find out how the sound is spelled. The chart will tell you which letter to look under in the dictionary to find the word. Remember that a consonant sound is sometimes spelled with a vowel letter. An example is the sound (y) spelled with *e* as in *Europe* or *ewe.*

Some of the spellings are followed by starred examples. The star (*) means that the examples given in the chart are the only words in this dictionary with that initial spelling. See, for example, the spelling *psh* for the sound (sh). The star before the example *pshaw* tells you that *pshaw* is the only word in this dictionary that has the initial spelling *psh* for the sound (sh).

The chart includes five combinations of sounds: (hw), (kw), (wu), (yü), and (yu). Look at the chart to see how these common combinations are spelled. You will find them in their proper alphabetical order.

Initial consonant sounds

Sound	Spellings	Examples	Sound	Spellings	Examples
(b)	**b**	bad	(r)	**r**	run
	bh	*Bhutan		**wr**	wrong
(ch)	**ch**	child		**rh**	rhythm
	c	cello	(s)	**s**	say
	cz	Czech		**c**	cent
	tch	*Tchaikovsky		ps	psalm
(d)	**d**	do		sc	scent
(f)	**f**	fat		*sch*	*schism,
	ph	phrase			schismatic
	v	*verboten		*z*	*zwieback
(g)	**g**	go	(sh)	**sh**	she
	gu	guest		**ch**	chef
	gh	ghost		su	sugar
(h)	**h**	he		*sch*	schwa
	wh	who		*psh*	*pshaw
	g	*Gila monster	(t)	**t**	tell
(hw)	**wh**	wheat		tw	two
(j)	**j**	jam		*th*	Thomas
	g	gem		*pt*	ptomaine
	ch	*Chou En-lai	(th)	**th**	thin
(k)	**c**	coat		*phth*	*phthisis
	k	kind	(ŦH)	**th**	then
	ch	chemist		*y*	*ye
	qu	quay	(v)	**v**	very
	kh	khaki	(w)	**w**	will, won
	x	*Xmas	(wu)	*o*	one, once
(kw)	**qu**	quick	(y)	**y**	you
(l)	**l**	land		*e*	Europe, ewe
	ll	*llama, llano	(yü)	**u**	use
	lh	*Lhasa	(yu̇)	u	uranium
(m)	**m**	me	(z)	**z**	zero
(n)	**n**	no		x	xylophone
	kn	knife		*cz*	*czar, czarina
	gn	gnaw	(zh)	*g*	*gendarme,
	pn	pneumonia			genre
(p)	**p**	pay		*j*	*jabot

35

*The only words in this dictionary with this initial spelling.

Spellings of vowel sounds

In this chart each vowel sound is followed by a list of words showing the different spellings of the sound. The part of each word that spells the sound is in heavy black type. Common spellings come before rare spellings.

Some of the words used as examples are in more than one list. This is because the words are pronounced in more than one way.

The symbols used in this chart for the vowel sounds are the same as those used in the pronunciation key.

36

Sound	Spellings and examples
(a)	**a**nd, pl**ai**d, h**a**lf, l**au**gh, **ae**rial, **ey**rie, **Aa**ron, **e**re pr**ay**er, th**ei**r, p**ea**r, h**ei**r
(ā)	**a**ge, **ai**d, s**ay**, **eigh**t, th**ey**, br**ea**k, str**aigh**t, bouqu**et**, **é**lite, su**è**de, v**ei**n, **eh**, g**ao**l, g**au**ge
(ä)	**a**rt, **ah**, c**a**lm, s**er**geant, h**ea**rt
(e)	**e**nd, s**ai**d, a**e**rial, **a**ny, br**ea**d, s**ay**s, h**ei**fer, l**eo**pard, fri**e**nd, b**u**ry, **ey**rie, **e**'er, h**ei**r, **Oe**dipus, **Aa**ron
(ē)	**e**ve, **ea**ch, b**ee**, **ei**ther, k**ey**, l**ie**ge, C**ae**sar, qu**ay**, pian**o**, ph**oe**nix, p**eo**ple
(ėr)	st**er**n, **ear**l, t**ur**n, f**ir**st, w**or**d, j**our**ney, m**yr**tle, **err**, wh**irr**, p**urr**
(i)	**i**n, en**ou**gh, **ear**, h**y**mn, b**ee**n, s**ie**ve, w**o**men, b**u**sy, b**ui**ld, w**ei**rd, A**e**gean, ycl**e**pt, **ey**rie
(ī)	**i**ce, l**ie**, sk**y**, r**ye**, **eye**, **i**sland, h**igh**, **Ei**senhower, **Ai**nu, **ai**sle, bay**ou**, **aye**, h**eigh**t, b**uy**

Sound	Spellings and examples
(o)	**o**dd, w**a**tch, h**o**nest, y**a**cht
(ō)	**o**ld, **oa**k, t**oe**, **ow**n, **oh**, **ow**e, f**o**lk, th**ou**gh, b**eau**, y**eo**man, s**ew**, br**oo**ch, s**ou**l, m**au**ve, S**eou**l
(ô)	**o**ff, **a**ll, **au**tomobile, **aw**ful, **aw**e, **oa**r, **ough**t, w**a**lk, **o**'er, t**augh**t, c**ough**, **U**tah
(oi)	**oi**l, b**oy**
(ou)	**ou**t, **ow**l, b**ou**gh, h**ou**r, a**ou**dad
(u)	**u**nder, **o**ther, tr**ou**ble, d**oe**s, fl**oo**d, **u**gh
(ù)	f**u**ll, g**oo**d, w**o**lf, sh**ou**ld
(ü)	f**oo**d, r**u**le, bl**ue**, m**o**ve, thr**ew**, s**ou**p, thr**ough**, sh**oe**, tw**o**, fr**ui**t, man**eu**ver, li**eu**tenant
(ə)	**a**bout, occ**u**r, eff**e**ct, **au**thority, barg**ai**n, Apr**i**l, cauti**ou**s, circ**u**s, raj**ah**, page**a**nt, dunge**o**n, tort**oi**se

HOW TO USE THIS DICTIONARY
FOR WRITING

---

bi og ra phy   i de a   **flight**

Suppose you are writing a book report on a book you read about the inventors Orville and Wilbur Wright. You begin by saying that the book is a biography. As you get to the end of the first line, you realize that you cannot get all the letters of the word *biography* on that line. A word like *biography* that has more than one syllable can be divided between syllables. Part of the word can go on one line, and part can go on the next line. Spaces between syllables in the entry word show you where to divide the word. You can divide *biography* after the *i,* after the *g,* or after the *a.* When you divide a word, you should put a hyphen at the end of the line to show that part of the word is on the next line. In your book report you decide to put *biog-* on the first line and *raphy* on the next line.

Now you are telling about the Wright brothers' idea for an airplane. Even though the entry word *idea* shows three syllables, it should not be divided. Do not divide a word so that a single letter is separated from the rest of the word. You should not put *i-* on one line and *dea* on the next, or *ide-* on one line and *a* on the next.

Further on you say, "The brothers flipped a coin for the first fli-ght." This last word looks strange. You check your dictionary and find that *flight* has only one syllable. One-syllable words are shown in the dictionary without spaces between letters. They should never be divided at the end of a line. You move *flight* to the next line before writing, "Orville won the flip and piloted the first successful airplane."

37

EXERCISES

1. The words below are divided into syllables for you. Copy each word, leaving spaces between the syllables. In each word circle the letter or letters after which you can divide the word at the end of a line.

   cu cum ber   na ture   a ne mi a
   e nam el   brav er y   ge o graph i cal

2. Look up the following words. Rewrite each word, leaving spaces between the syllables of those words having more than one syllable. Then for each word write "yes" if you would divide it at the end of a line, or "no" if you would not. Do it like this: a dult, no.

   adult   ever   prism   adjust
   funny   hilly   event   prison

THE PARTS OF A DICTIONARY ENTRY

(1) **The entry word** is printed in bold-face type. It shows how the word is spelled and how it may be divided in writing.

(2) **The homograph number** appears when successive entries are spelled the same way.

(3) **The pronunciation** is enclosed in parentheses. Letters used in the respelling for pronunciation have special sounds assigned to them. These are explained in the pronunciation key.

(4) **A restrictive label** shows that use of a word or meaning is limited to a particular region or level of usage.

(5) **The definition** of a word tells its meaning. A word with several different meanings has numbered definitions, one for each meaning.

(6) **An illustrative sentence** is printed in italic type following the definition. It shows how the entry word may be used with that particular meaning in a sentence.

(7) **The part-of-speech label** is an abbreviation in italic type naming the function of the entry word. When the word may function as more than one part of speech, definition numbers are added to each label.

(8) **Inflected forms,** in small boldface type, are given whenever their spelling or form might give you trouble.

(9) **The etymology** appears in square brackets. It tells the language where the English word came from and, if its form or meaning was different, how it was spelled or what it meant there.

(10) **A run-on entry,** in small boldface type, is an undefined word. Its meaning combines the meaning of the entry word with that of its suffix. Each run-on entry has a part-of-speech label.

(11) **Idioms,** in small boldface type, follow the rest of an entry. Such word combinations have special definitions.

38

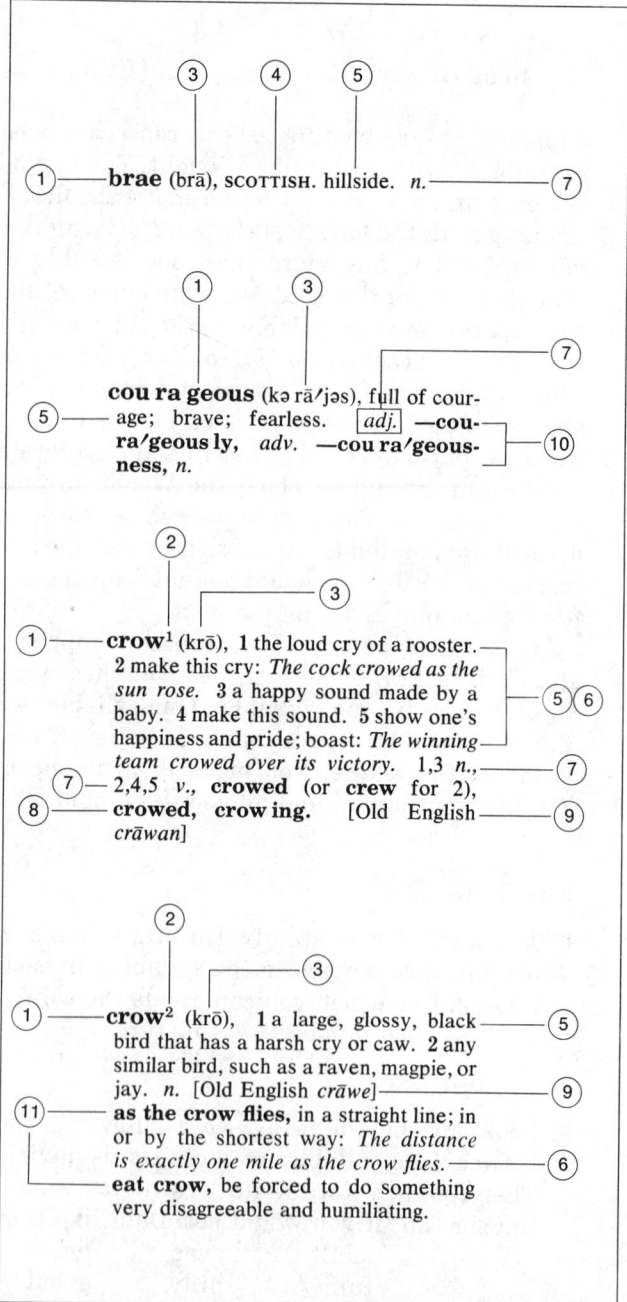

A a

A or **a¹** (ā), the first letter of the alphabet. *n., pl.* **A's** or **a's.**

a² (ə; *stressed* ā), 1 any: *A tree has leaves.* 2 one: *Buy a dozen eggs and a pound of butter.* 3 every: *Thanksgiving comes once a year. He earns ten dollars a day.* 4 one kind of: *Chemistry is a science. adj. or indefinite article.*

Aar on (er′ən *or* ar′ən), (in the Bible) the brother of Moses and the first high priest of the Hebrews. *n.*

ab a ca (ab′ə kä′), 1 a strong fiber made from the leaves of a Philippine banana plant, used for making ropes and fabrics; Manila hemp. 2 the plant itself. *n.*

a back (ə bak′). **taken aback,** suddenly surprised: *I was taken aback by my friend's angry reply. adv.*

ab a cus (ab′ə kəs), frame with rows of counters or beads that slide back and forth. Abacuses are used in China, Japan, Korea, etc., for adding and other tasks in arithmetic. *n., pl.* **ab a cus es, ab a ci** (ab′ə sī).

abacus—beads above middle bar,
5 each when lowered toward bar;
beads below middle bar,
1 each when raised toward bar.
Beads above and below the middle bar
are totaled in each row.
Numbers are shown below each wire
for the setting of 1,352,964,708.

a baft (ə baft′), 1 at or toward the back of a ship; aft. 2 back of; behind. 1 *adv.,* 2 *prep.*

ab a lo ne (ab′ə lō′nē), mollusk that can be eaten, with a large, rather flat shell lined with mother-of-pearl. *n.*

a ban don (ə ban′dən), 1 give up entirely: *We abandoned the idea of a picnic because of the rain.* 2 leave without intending to return to; desert: *The crew abandoned the ship before it sank.* 3 give (oneself) up completely (to a feeling, impulse, etc.): *The lost child abandoned himself to despair.* 4 freedom from restraint; carefree manner: *The students on the winning side cheered with abandon.* 1-3 *v.,* 4 *n.*

a ban doned (ə ban′dənd), 1 deserted. 2 wicked; immoral: *an abandoned life.* 3 unrestrained: *abandoned glee. adj.*

a ban don ment (ə ban′dən mənt), an abandoning or a being abandoned. *n.*

a base (ə bās′), make lower in rank, condition, or character; degrade: *A student who cheats abases himself. v.,* **a based, a bas ing.**

a base ment (ə bās′mənt), an abasing or a being abased; degradation. *n.*

a bash (ə bash′), make uneasy, shy, and somewhat ashamed; embarrass and confuse: *I was not abashed by the laughter of my classmates. v.*

a bate (ə bāt′), 1 make less; decrease: *Her confidence helped to abate my fear.* 2 become less; diminish: *Although the rain has abated somewhat the wind is still blowing very hard. v.,* **a bat ed, a bat ing.**

a bate ment (ə bāt′mənt), 1 a decrease; lessening. 2 amount abated; reduction. *n.*

ab at toir (ab′ə twär), slaughterhouse. *n.* [from French]

ab bé (ab′ā), a title used in France and Quebec for any clergyman, especially a priest. *n., pl.* **ab bés.** [from French]

ab bess (ab′is), woman who is the head of an abbey of nuns. *n., pl.* **ab bess es.**

ab bey (ab′ē), 1 the building or buildings where monks or nuns live a religious life ruled by an abbot or abbess; monastery or convent. 2 the monks or nuns living there. 3 church or building that was once an abbey or part of an abbey: *Westminster Abbey. n., pl.* **ab beys.**

ab bot (ab′ət), man who is the head of an abbey of monks. *n.*

ab bre vi ate (ə brē′vē āt), 1 make (a word or phrase) shorter so that a part stands for the whole: *We can abbreviate "hour" to "hr."* 2 make briefer. *v.,* **ab bre vi at ed, ab bre vi at ing.**

ab bre vi a tion (ə brē′vē ā′shən), 1 a shortened form of a word or phrase standing for the whole: *"Dr." is an abbreviation for "Doctor."* 2 a making briefer. *n.*

A B C (ā′bē′sē′), 1 facts or skills to be learned first; elementary principles: *We learned the ABC of swimming this summer at camp.* 2 **ABC's,** *pl.* the alphabet. *n., pl.* **ABC's** or **ABCs.**

ab di cate (ab′də kāt), give up or renounce (office, power, or authority) formally; resign: *When the king abdicated his throne, his brother became king. v.,* **ab di cat ed, ab di cat ing.**

ab di ca tion (ab′də kā′shən), an abdicating; resigning: *The abdication of King Edward VIII took place in 1936. n.*

ab do men (ab′də mən *or* ab dō′mən),

---

hat, āge, fär; let, ēqual, tėrm;
it, īce; hot, ōpen, ôrder;
oil, out; cup, pùt, rüle; ch, child;
ng, long; sh, she; th, thin;
ŦH, then; zh, measure;

ə represents *a* in about,
e in taken, *i* in pencil,
o in lemon, *u* in circus.

HEAD
THORAX
ABDOMEN

1 the part of the body containing the stomach, the intestines, and other important organs; belly. 2 the last of the three parts of the body of an insect or a crustacean. *n.*

ab dom i nal (ab dom′ə nəl), of, in, or for the abdomen: *Bending the body exercises the abdominal muscles. adj.* **—ab dom′i nal ly,** *adv.*

ab duct (ab dukt′), carry off (a person) by force or by trickery; kidnap: *The police are looking for the person who abducted the baby from its crib. v.*

ab duc tion (ab duk′shən), a kidnaping. *n.*

ab duc tor (ab duk′tər), kidnaper. *n.*

a beam (ə bēm′), directly opposite the middle of a ship's side: *Flash them a signal before their ship comes abeam of ours. adv.*

a bed (ə bed′), in bed. *adv.*

A bel (ā′bəl), (in the Bible) the second son of Adam and Eve. Abel was killed by his older brother Cain. *n.*

Ab er deen (ab′ər dēn′), city in E Scotland. *n.*

ab er ra tion (ab′ə rā′shən), 1 a wandering from the right path or usual course: *A lie is an aberration from the truth.* 2 an abnormal structure or development. 3 a wandering of the mind: *His peculiarities are no more than harmless aberrations.* 4 failure of a lens or mirror to bring to a single focus the rays of light coming from one point: *Aberration in the mirror caused a blurred and crooked image. n.*

a bet (ə bet′), encourage or help, especially in doing something wrong: *One man did the actual stealing, but two others abetted him by attracting the attention of the storekeeper. v.,* **a bet ted, a bet ting.**

a bey ance (ə bā′əns), a temporary stopping of activity; state of suspended

1

adj.	adjective	*n.* noun
adv.	adverb	*prep.* preposition
conj.	conjunction	*pron.* pronoun
interj.	interjection	*v.* verb
sing.	singular	*pl.* plural

action: *Let's hold that question in abeyance until we know more about it. n.*

ab hor (ab hôr′), shrink away from with horror; feel disgust or hate for; detest: *Most people abhor the thought of war. v.*, **ab horred, ab hor ring.**

ab hor rence (ab hôr′əns), 1 a feeling of very great hatred; horror; disgust: *I have an abhorrence of snakes.* 2 something hated or detested. *n.*

ab hor rent (ab hôr′ənt), causing horror; disgusting; hateful: *Lying and stealing are abhorrent to someone who is honest. adj.*

a bide (ə bīd′), 1 put up with; endure: *I can't abide their always being late.* 2 stay; remain: *Abide with me for a time.* 3 dwell; reside. 4 OLD USE. wait for. *v.*, **a bode** or **a bid ed, a bid ing.**

abide by, 1 accept and follow out: *Both teams will abide by the umpire's decision.* 2 remain faithful to; fulfill: *You must abide by your promise.*

a bid ing (ə bī′ding), permanent; lasting: *The old sailor had an abiding love of the sea. adj.*

Ab i djan (ab′i jän′), capital of the Ivory Coast, in the SE part. *n.*

Ab i lene (ab′ə lēn′), 1 city in central Texas. 2 town in central Kansas. *n.*

a bil i ty (ə bil′ə tē), 1 power to do or act: *A horse has the ability to work.* 2 power to do some special thing; skill: *Both Grant and Lee had great ability as generals.* 3 special natural gift; talent: *Musical ability often shows itself early in life. n., pl.* **a bil i ties.**

ab ject (ab′jekt), 1 so low or degraded as to be hopeless; wretched; miserable: *Many people in Asia still live in abject poverty.* 2 deserving contempt; despicable: *abject fear, abject flattery. adj.* —**ab ject′ly,** *adv.* —**ab ject′ness,** *n.*

ab ju ra tion (ab′jə rā′shən), an abjuring; renunciation on oath. *n.*

ab jure (ab jür′), swear to give up; renounce on oath: *An alien must abjure his foreign citizenship before he can become an American citizen. v.*, **ab jured, ab jur ing.**

ab la tion (ab lā′shən), disintegration of part of the nose cone on a missile or spacecraft when it reenters the atmosphere. Ablation usually occurs as melting or vaporizing of an outer surface to protect the rest of the structure from excessive heat. *n.*

a blaze (ə blāz′), 1 on fire: *The forest was set ablaze by lightning.* 2 shining brightly: *The hotel was ablaze with lights.* 3 in great excitement: *I was ablaze with anger when he kicked my dog. adj.*

a ble (ā′bəl), 1 having enough power, skill, or means to do something; capable: *A cat is able to see in the dark.* 2 having more power or skill than usual; skillful: *She is an able teacher.* 3 done with skill: *The audience applauded her able speech. adj.*, **a bler, a blest.**

-able suffix forming adjectives. 1 (added to verbs) that can be _____ed: *Enjoyable = that can be enjoyed.* 2 (added to nouns) suitable for _____: *Comfortable = suitable for comfort.* 3 (added to nouns) inclined to _____: *Peaceable = inclined to peace.* [from French before the 1400's *-able,* from Latin *-abilem*]

a ble-bod ied (ā′bəl bod′ēd), strong and healthy; physically fit. *adj.*

able-bodied seaman or **able seaman,** an experienced seaman who can perform all the duties required of a seaman.

a bloom (ə blüm′), in bloom; blossoming. *adj.*

ab lu tion (ab lü′shən). Often, **ablutions,** *pl.* a washing or cleansing of one's person, especially as part of a religious ceremony. *n.*

a bly (ā′blē), in an able manner; with skill; capably. *adv.*

ab ne ga tion (ab′nə gā′shən), a giving up of one's own interests and desires; self-denial; self-sacrifice: *A nun's life is one of abnegation. n.*

ab nor mal (ab nôr′məl), different from the ordinary conditions, the standard, or a type; unusual: *an abnormal amount of rain. It is abnormal for a person to have six fingers on each hand. adj.* —**ab nor′mal ly,** *adv.*

ab nor mal i ty (ab′nôr mal′ə tē), 1 an abnormal thing or happening. 2 an abnormal condition. *n., pl.* **ab nor mal i ties.**

a board (ə bôrd′), on board; in or on a ship, train, bus, airplane, etc.: *"All aboard!" shouted the conductor, and everyone rushed for the train (adv.). Everybody was soon aboard the train (prep.). adv., prep.*

a bode (ə bōd′), 1 place to live in; dwelling; house: *A simple hut was their abode.* 2 a past tense and a past participle of abide. *He abode there one year.* 1 *n.,* 2 *v.*

a bol ish (ə bol′ish), do away with completely; put an end to: *Many people wish that nations would abolish war. v.*

ab o li tion (ab′ə lish′ən), a putting an end to; an abolishing: *The abolition of slavery in the United States occurred in 1865. n.*

ab o li tion ist (ab′ə lish′ə nist), person who wishes to abolish something. The people who wished to put an end to Negro slavery in the United States were called **Abolitionists.** *n.*

A-bomb (ā′bom′), an atomic bomb. *n.*

a bom i na ble (ə bom′ə nə bəl), 1 arousing disgust and hatred; loathsome: *Kidnaping is an abominable act.* 2 very unpleasant; disagreeable: *The weather for the picnic was abominable—rainy, windy, and cold. adj.*

Abominable Snowman, an ape-like creature supposed to inhabit the higher parts of the Himalayas.

a bom i na bly (ə bom′ə nə blē), in an abominable manner. *adv.*

a bom i nate (ə bom′ə nāt), 1 feel disgust and hatred for; loathe: *Players abominate unfairness in an umpire.* 2 dislike: *She abominates hot, humid weather. v.*, **a bom i nat ed, a bom i nat ing.**

a bom i na tion (ə bom′ə nā′shən), 1 a disgusting or loathsome thing. 2 a feeling of disgust; loathing. *n.*

ab o rig i nal (ab′ə rij′ə nəl), 1 existing from the beginning; original; native: *the aboriginal inhabitants of a continent.* 2 of the earliest known inhabitants: *an aboriginal custom. adj.*

ab o rig i nes (ab′ə rij′ə nēz′), the earliest known inhabitants of a country or area: *The Eskimos are among the aborigines of North America. n. pl. of* **aborigine.**

a bort (ə bôrt′), fail to develop or come to completion: *The rocket flight aborted. v.*

a bor tion (ə bôr′shən), 1 birth that occurs before the embryo has developed enough to live. 2 failure to develop or to be completed. *n.*

a bor tive (ə bôr′tiv), 1 coming to nothing; unsuccessful; fruitless: *Early attempts to make airplanes fly proved abortive.* 2 born before the right time; born prematurely. *adj.* —**a bor′tive ly,** *adv.*

a bound (ə bound′), 1 be plentiful: *Fish abound in the ocean. Rock abounds under the soil.* 2 be well supplied; be filled; be rich: *The ocean abounds with fish. America abounds in natural resources. v.*

a bout (ə bout′), 1 of; having something to do with: *"Black Beauty" is a story about a horse.* 2 nearly; almost: *I have about finished my work.* 3 all around; around: *A collar goes about the neck (prep.). Look about and tell me what you see (adv.).* 4 in the opposite direction: *You are going the wrong way. Face about!* 5 one after another; by turns: *Turn about is fair play.* 6 moving around; active: *He is able to be up and about.* 1,3 *prep.,* 2-6 *adv.*

about to, on the point of; going to; ready to: *The plane is about to take off.*

a bout-face (ə bout′fās′ *for 1,2;* ə bout′fās′ *for 3*), 1 a turning or going in the opposite direction. 2 a shift to the opposite attitude or opinion. 3 turn or go in the opposite direction. 1,2 *n.,* 3 *v.,* **a bout-faced, a bout-fac ing.**

a bove (ə buv′), 1 in or at a higher place; overhead: *The sky is above.* 2 to or in a higher place than: *This elevator does not go above the third floor.* 3 higher than; over: *Look above the tall building to see the sun. A captain is above a sergeant.* 4 more than: *Our club has above thirty members—thirty-five, to be exact.* 5 beyond: *Turn at the first corner above the school.* 6 too great in importance for; superior to: *be above acting in such a childish manner.* 7 earlier in a book or article: *See what is written above (adv.). The above definition contains six words (adj.).* 8 above zero: *The temperature is five above.* 1,7,8 *adv.,* 2-6 *prep.,* 7 *adj.*

a bove board (ə buv′bôrd′), in open sight; without tricks or concealment: *Everything that the mayor did was open and aboveboard (adj.). His campaign was run aboveboard (adv.).* *adj., adv.*

ab ra ca dab ra (ab′rə kə dab′rə), 1 word supposed to have magic power. 2 meaningless talk; gibberish. *n.*

a brade (ə brād′), wear down or away by rubbing; scrape off: *The skin on her knees was abraded by her fall.* *v.,* **a brad ed, a brad ing.**

A bra ham (ā′brə ham), (in the Bible) the ancestor of the Hebrews. *n.*

a bra sion (ə brā′zhən), 1 place scraped or worn by rubbing: *He had an abrasion on his knee from falling on gravel.* 2 a wearing down or away by rubbing; scraping off: *Coins become thinner by constant abrasion.* *n.*

a bra sive (ə brā′siv), 1 substance used for grinding, smoothing, or polishing. Sandpaper, pumice, and emery are abrasives. 2 wearing away by rubbing; causing abrasion. 1 *n.,* 2 *adj.*

a breast (ə brest′), 1 side by side: *The soldiers marched four abreast (adv.). The airplane had four seats, two abreast on each side of the aisle (adj.).* 2 up with; alongside of; even with: *Read the newspapers to keep abreast of what is going on. Keep abreast with the flow of events.* *adv., adj.*

a bridge (ə brij′), 1 make shorter, especially by using fewer words: *A long story can be abridged by leaving out unimportant parts.* 2 make less: *The rights of citizens must not be abridged without proper cause.* *v.,* **a bridged, a bridg ing.**

a bridg ment or **a bridge ment** (ə brij′mənt), 1 a shortened form of a book, long article, etc.: *That one book is an abridgment of a three-volume history.* 2 a making shorter; an abridging. *n.*

a broad (ə brôd′), 1 outside one's country; to a foreign land: *I am going abroad next year to study in Italy.* 2 out in the open air; outdoors: *My grandfather walks abroad only on warm days.* 3 far and wide; widely: *The news that the astronaut was coming quickly spread abroad.* 4 going around; in motion; current: *A rumor is abroad that school will close.* *adv.*

ab ro gate (ab′rə gāt), do away with; repeal; cancel: *When war broke out, our government abrogated its trade agreements with the enemy country.* *v.,* **ab ro gat ed, ab ro gat ing.**

ab ro ga tion (ab′rə gā′shən), a doing away with; an abrogating. *n.*

a brupt (ə brupt′), 1 showing sudden change; unexpected: *I made an abrupt turn to avoid another car.* 2 very steep: *The road made an abrupt rise up the hill.* 3 short or sudden in speech or manner; blunt: *He had a gruff, abrupt way of speaking.* *adj.* **—a brupt′ly,** *adv.* **—a brupt′ness,** *n.*

Ab sa lom (ab′sə ləm), (in the Bible) David's favorite son. He rebelled against his father and was later killed in battle. *n.*

ab scess (ab′ses), a collection of pus in the tissues of some part of the body. An abscess results from an infection and usually makes a painful sore. *n., pl.* **ab scess es.**

abreast—soldiers marching abreast

ab scessed (ab′sest), having an abscess: *A dentist treated my abscessed tooth.* *adj.*

ab scond (ab skond′), go away suddenly and secretly, especially to avoid punishment; go off and hide: *The dishonest cashier absconded with the bank's money.* *v.*

ab sence (ab′səns), 1 a being away: *His absence from school was caused by illness.* 2 time of being away: *I returned to school after an absence of two days.*

hat, āge, fär; let, ēqual, tėrm;
it, īce; hot, ōpen, ôrder;
oil, out; cup, pùt, rüle; ch, child;
ng, long; sh, she; th, thin;
ᴛH, then; zh, measure;

ə represents *a* in about,
e in taken, *i* in pencil,
o in lemon, *u* in circus.

3 a being without; lack: *Darkness is the absence of light.* *n.*

ab sent (ab′sənt *for 1,3,4;* ab sent′ *for 2*), 1 away; not present: *Three members of the class are absent today.* 2 keep or take (oneself) away: *He absented himself from school on the day the test was given.* 3 lacking; not existing: *In certain fishes the ribs are entirely absent.* 4 absent-minded: *I knew you were daydreaming from your absent look.* 1,3,4 *adj.,* 2 *v.*

ab sen tee (ab′sən tē′), person who is away or remains away. *n.*

ab sent ly (ab′sənt lē), in an absent-minded manner; inattentively. *adv.*

ab sent-mind ed (ab′sənt mīn′did), not paying attention to what is going on around one; forgetful; inattentive: *The absent-minded man put salt in his coffee and sugar on his egg.* *adj.* **—ab′sent-mind′ed ly,** *adv.* **—ab′sent-mind′ed ness,** *n.*

ab so lute (ab′sə lüt), 1 free from any imperfection or lack; complete; whole; entire: *Try to tell the absolute truth.* 2 with no limits or restrictions: *The dictator had absolute power.* 3 certain; positive: *I had absolute proof that I was not present when the accident occurred.* *adj.* **—ab′so lute′ness,** *n.*

ab so lute ly (ab′sə lüt′lē *or* ab′sə lüt′lē), 1 completely; entirely: *My broken bicycle was absolutely useless.* 2 without doubt; certainly: *He is absolutely the finest boy I know.* *adv.*

absolute zero, temperature at which substances would have no heat whatever, and all molecules would stop moving. Theoretically, it is –273.16 degrees centigrade or –459.69 degrees Fahrenheit.

ab so lu tion (ab′sə lü′shən), a freeing from guilt or punishment for sin, guilt, or blame; forgiveness; an absolving. *n.*

ab solve (ab solv′), 1 declare free from sin, guilt, or blame: *The priest absolved the man after he confessed his sin and did penance.* 2 set free; release: *I absolve you from your promise to go.* *v.,* **ab solved, ab solv ing.**

ab sorb (ab sôrb′), 1 take in or suck

adj. adjective	*n.* noun
adv. adverb	*prep.* preposition
conj. conjunction	*pron.* pronoun
interj. interjection	*v.* verb
sing. singular	*pl.* plural

up (liquids): *The sponge absorbed the spilled milk.* 2 take in and make part of itself; assimilate: *The United States has absorbed millions of immigrants. Digested food is absorbed into the bloodstream in the intestines.* 3 take in without reflecting: *Rugs absorb sounds and make a house quieter.* 4 take up all the attention of; interest very much: *Building a dam in the brook absorbed the children completely. v.*

ab sorbed (ab sôrbd′), very much interested; completely occupied: *I was so absorbed that I did not hear the bell ring. adj.*

ab sorb en cy (ab sôr′bən sē), absorbent quality or condition. *n.*

ab sorb ent (ab sôr′bənt), 1 able to absorb moisture, light, or heat: *Absorbent paper is used to dry the hands.* 2 substance that absorbs moisture, light, or heat. 1 *adj.*, 2 *n.*

ab sorb ing (ab sôr′bing), extremely interesting: *The explorers told us the absorbing story of their adventures. adj.*

ab sorp tion (ab sôrp′shən), 1 act or process of absorbing: *A blotter dries ink by absorption.* 2 a being absorbed; great interest: *The absorption of the children in their game was so complete that they did not notice the first few drops of rain. n.*

ab stain (ab stān′), 1 do without something; hold oneself back; refrain: *If you want to lose weight, abstain from eating candy and rich foods.* 2 refrain from voting: *Six members voted in favor of the motion, five members voted against it, and four members abstained. v.*

ab ste mi ous (ab stē′mē əs), sparing in eating, drinking, etc.; moderate; temperate: *My father is abstemious in his eating habits; he never eats too much. adj.*

ab sten tion (ab sten′shən), 1 an abstaining; abstinence. 2 fact of not voting: *There were five votes in favor, four against, and three abstentions. n.*

ab sti nence (ab′stə nəns), partly or entirely giving up certain pleasures, food, drink, etc.: *His doctor recommended abstinence from coffee and tobacco. n.*

ab stract (ab′strakt *or* ab strakt′ *for*

1,3,7; ab strakt′ *for* 2,4; ab′strakt *for* 5,6), 1 thought of apart from any particular object or real thing; not concrete: *Sweetness is abstract; a lump of sugar is concrete.* 2 think of (a quality) apart from any object or real thing having that quality: *We can abstract the idea of redness from the color of all red objects.* 3 hard to understand; difficult: *The atomic theory of matter is so abstract that it can be fully understood only by advanced students.* 4 take away; remove: *Iron is abstracted from ore.* 5 a brief statement of the main ideas in an article, book, case in court, etc.; summary. 6 make an abstract of; summarize: *Try to abstract this story for a book report.* 7 not representing any actual object or concrete thing; having little or no resemblance to real or material things: *We saw many abstract paintings in the Museum of Modern Art.* 1,3,7 *adj.*, 2,4,6 *v.*, 5 *n.* —**ab′stract ly,** *adv.* —**ab′stract ness,** *n.*

ab stract ed (ab strak′tid), absentminded. *adj.* —**ab stract′ed ly,** *adv.*

ab strac tion (ab strak′shən), 1 the idea of a quality thought of apart from any particular object or real thing having that quality; abstract idea or term: *Whiteness, bravery, and length are abstractions.* 2 a taking away; removal: *After the abstraction of the juice from an orange, only the pulp and peeling are left.* 3 a being lost in thought; absent-mindedness. 4 a work of abstract art. *n.*

ab struse (ab strüs′), hard to understand: *If you do not master arithmetic, you will find algebra complicated and abstruse. adj.* —**ab struse′ly,** *adv.* —**ab struse′ness,** *n.*

ab surd (ab serd′), plainly not true or sensible; foolish; ridiculous: *The idea that the number 13 brings bad luck is absurd. adj.* —**ab surd′ly,** *adv.*

ab surd i ty (ab ser′də tē), 1 absurd quality or condition; lack of sense; foolishness: *the absurdity of superstition.* 2 something absurd; something unreasonable or ridiculous: *Your explanation is an absurdity. n., pl.* **ab surd i ties.**

a bun dance (ə bun′dəns), quantity that is more than enough; great plenty: *There is such an abundance of apples this year that many are not being picked. n.*

a bun dant (ə bun′dənt), 1 more than enough; very plentiful: *The trapper had an abundant supply of food for the winter.* 2 having more than enough; abounding: *The fishermen found a river abundant in salmon. adj.* —**a bun′dant ly,** *adv.*

a buse (ə byüz′ *for* 1,3,6; ə byüs′ *for* 2,4,5,7), 1 make wrong or bad use of; misuse: *By not coming home before*

dark *you have abused your privilege of playing outside after dinner.* 2 a wrong or bad use; misuse: *Talking aloud is an abuse of your library privileges.* 3 treat roughly or cruelly; mistreat: *abuse an animal by beating it.* 4 rough or cruel treatment: *abuse of a helpless animal.* 5 a bad practice or custom: *Slavery is an abuse.* 6 use harsh and insulting language about or to; scold severely: *Instead of debating the issues the candidates abused each other.* 7 harsh and insulting language; severe scolding. 1,3,6 *v.*, **a bused, a bus ing;** 2,4,5,7 *n.*

a bu sive (ə byü′siv), 1 using harsh and insulting language; scolding severely. 2 containing abuse. *adj.* —**a bu′sive ly,** *adv.* —**a bu′sive ness,** *n.*

a but (ə but′), touch at one end or edge; border; end: *Our property abuts on the street. The shed abuts against a stone wall. v.*, **a but ted, a but ting.**

abutments
These abutments support the arches and turn aside strong currents that might weaken the structure.

ABUTMENTS

a but ment (ə but′mənt), a support for an arch or bridge. *n.*

a bys mal (ə biz′məl), too deep to be measured; bottomless. *adj.* —**a bys′mal ly,** *adv.*

a byss (ə bis′), 1 a bottomless or very great depth; a very deep crack in the earth: *The mountain climber stood at the edge of a cliff overlooking an abyss four thousand feet deep.* 2 anything too deep or great to be measured; lowest depth: *an abyss of despair. n., pl.* **a byss es.**

Ab ys sin i a (ab′ə sin′ē ə), Ethiopia. *n.* —**Ab′ys sin′i an,** *adj., n.*

a.c. or **A.C.,** alternating current.

a ca cia (ə kā′shə), 1 tree or shrub with finely divided leaves that grows in tropical or warm regions. 2 a locust tree of North America. *n., pl.* **a ca cias.**

ac a dem ic (ak′ə dem′ik), 1 of or having to do with schools, colleges, and their studies: *The academic year begins when school opens in September.* 2 concerned with general education rather than commercial, technical, or professional education: *History and French are academic subjects; typewriting and bookkeeping are commercial subjects.* 3 theoretical; not practical: *"Which came first, the chicken or the egg?" is an academic question. adj.*

ac a dem i cal (ak′ə dem′ə kəl), academic. *adj.*

ac a dem i cal ly (ak/ə dem/ik lē), in an academic manner. *adv.*

a cad e my (ə kad/ə mē), 1 place for instruction. 2 a private high school. 3 school where some special subject can be studied: *West Point is a military academy.* 4 group of authors, scholars, scientists, artists, etc., organized to encourage literature, science, or art. *n., pl.* **a cad e mies.**

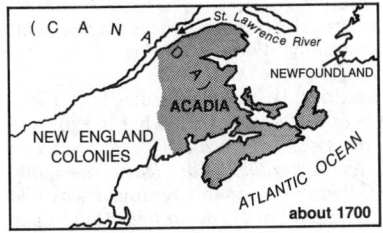
about 1700

A ca di a (ə kā/dē ə), former French colony, from 1604 until 1713, in SE Canada, including what is now Nova Scotia. *n.* —**A ca/di an,** *adj., n.*

a cap pel la (ä/ kə pel/ə), (in music) without instrumental accompaniment. [from Italian]

A ca pul co (ä/kə púl/kō), winter resort and port in SW Mexico, on the Pacific Ocean. *n.*

ac cede (ak sēd/), 1 give in; agree: *Please accede to my request.* 2 come or attain: *When the king died, his oldest son acceded to the throne.* *v.,* **ac ced ed, ac ced ing.**

ac cel e ran do (ak sel/ə rän/dō), (in music) gradually increasing in speed. *adv., adj.* [from Italian]

ac cel e rate (ak sel/ə rāt/), 1 go or cause to go faster; increase in speed; speed up: *The engineer accelerates a train by turning on more power. The more power he turns on, the more the train accelerates.* 2 cause to happen sooner; hasten: *Rest often accelerates a person's recovery from sickness.* *v.,* **ac cel e rat ed, ac cel e rat ing.**

ac cel e ra tion (ak sel/ə rā/shən), 1 a speeding up or hastening: *Acceleration of tooth decay is caused by lack of care.* 2 a change in velocity. *n.*

ac cel e ra tor (ak sel/ə rā/tər), 1 thing that causes an increase in the speed of anything. 2 pedal or lever that controls the speed of an automobile engine. 3 particle accelerator. *n.*

ac cent (ak/sent *for 1,2,4-6;* ak/sent *or* ak sent/ *for 3,7),* 1 greater force or stronger tone of voice used in pronouncing some syllables or words: *In "letter," the accent is on the first syllable.* 2 a mark (/) written or printed to show the spoken force of a syllable, as in *to day* (tə dā/). Some words have two accents, a primary or stronger accent (/) and a secondary or weaker accent (/),

as in *ac cel e ra tor* (ak sel/ə rā/tər). 3 pronounce or mark with an accent: *Is "acceptable" accented on the first or second syllable?* 4 a characteristic manner of pronunciation heard in different parts of the same country, or in the speech of a person speaking a language not his own: *My father was born in Germany and still speaks English with a German accent.* 5 **accents,** *pl.* tone of voice: *We soothed the child by speaking in tender accents.* 6 emphasis on certain musical notes or chords. 7 emphasize; accentuate. 1,2,4-6 *n.,* 3,7 *v.*

ac cen tu ate (ak sen/chü āt), 1 call special attention to; emphasize: *Her black hair accentuated the whiteness of her skin.* 2 pronounce with an accent. 3 mark with an accent. *v.,* **ac cen tu at ed, ac cen tu at ing.**

ac cen tu a tion (ak sen/chü ā/shən), an accentuating; emphasis. *n.*

ac cept (ak sept/), 1 take what is offered or given to one; consent to take: *The teacher accepted our gift.* 2 agree to; consent to: *The United States accepted Japan's proposal for a conference on fishing rights.* 3 say yes to an invitation, offer, etc.: *They asked me to go along and I accepted.* 4 take as true or satisfactory; believe: *The teacher accepted our excuse.* 5 receive with liking and approval; approve: *Our new neighbors have been accepted by everyone. The design of the new car was not accepted by the public.* *v.*

ac cept a bil i ty (ak sep/tə bil/ə tē), quality of being acceptable or satisfactory. *n.*

ac cept a ble (ak sep/tə bəl), 1 likely to be gladly received; agreeable: *Flowers are an acceptable gift to a sick person.* 2 good enough but not outstanding; satisfactory: *I received an acceptable mark on the test but my sister won honors.* *adj.* —**ac cept/a ble ness,** *n.*

ac cept a bly (ak sep/tə blē), in a way that pleases. *adv.*

ac cept ance (ak sep/təns), 1 act of taking something offered or given: *The teacher's acceptance of the flowers they brought delighted the children.* 2 favorable reception; approval: *She was thrilled by her acceptance into the club.* 3 the taking of something as true and satisfactory; belief: *The acceptance of the atomic theory by physicists has led to many scientific discoveries.* *n.*

ac cess (ak/ses), 1 right to approach, enter, or use; admittance: *All students have access to the library during the afternoon.* 2 approach to places, persons, or things; accessibility: *Access to mountain towns is often difficult because of poor roads.* 3 way or means of approach; entrance: *A ladder pro-*

hat, āge, fär; let, ēqual, tėrm;
it, īce; hot, ōpen, ôrder;
oil, out; cup, pùt, rüle; ch, child;
ng, long; sh, she; th, thin;
ᴙH, then; zh, measure;

ə represents *a* in about,
e in taken, *i* in pencil,
o in lemon, *u* in circus.

vided the only access to the attic. *n.*

ac ces si bil i ty (ak ses/ə bil/ə tē), condition of being easy to reach or get at. *n.*

ac ces si ble (ak ses/ə bəl), 1 easy to get at; easy to reach or enter: *A telephone should be put where it will be accessible.* 2 that can be entered or reached: *This rocky island is accessible only by helicopter.* 3 that can be obtained: *Not many facts about the kidnaping were accessible.* *adj.*

ac ces si bly (ak ses/ə blē), so as to be accessible. *adv.*

ac ces sion (ak sesh/ən), 1 act of attaining to a right, office, etc.: *The king's death was followed by the prince's accession to the throne.* 2 addition: *The school was increased by the accession of forty new pupils.* 3 thing added: *There are many new novels in the accessions to the library.* *n.*

ac ces sor y (ak ses/ər ē), 1 an extra thing added to help something of more importance; subordinate part or detail: *All the accessories to her costume—gloves, shoes, and purse—were perfectly matched.* 2 added; extra: *His tie supplied an accessory bit of color.* 3 person who has helped in a crime or who has helped to hide it: *By not reporting the theft he became an accessory.* 1,3 *n., pl.* **ac ces sor ies;** 2 *adj.*

ac ci dent (ak/sə dənt), 1 something harmful or unlucky that happens: *She was hurt in an automobile accident.* 2 something that happens without being planned, intended, wanted, or known in advance: *A series of lucky accidents led the explorer to his discovery.* *n.*

by accident, by chance; not on purpose: *I cut my foot by accident.*

ac ci den tal (ak/sə den/tl), 1 happening by accident; not planned; unexpected: *Our accidental meeting led to our becoming friends. Breaking the new dish was accidental; I did not mean to do it.* 2 a sign used in music to show a change of pitch. 1 *adj.,* 2 *n.*

ac ci den tal ly (ak/sə den/tl ē), in an accidental manner; by chance. *adv.*

ac claim (ə klām/), 1 welcome with loud approval; praise highly; applaud:

5

adj.	adjective	*n.*	noun
adv.	adverb	*prep.*	preposition
conj.	conjunction	*pron.*	pronoun
interj.	interjection	*v.*	verb
sing.	singular	*pl.*	plural

The crowd acclaimed the winning team. 2 announce with signs of approval; hail: *The newspapers acclaimed the results of the election.* 3 a shout or show of approval; applause: *The astronaut was welcomed with great acclaim.* 1,2 *v.*, 3 *n.*

ac cla ma tion (ak/lə mā/shən), a shout of welcome or show of approval by a crowd; applause: *When the President stood up to speak, he was greeted by the acclamation of the crowd.* *n.*

by acclamation, with an overwhelming oral vote of approval in which the votes are not counted: *All the club members said "Aye," and so the chairman was elected by acclamation.*

ac cli mate (ə kli/mit *or* ak/lə māt), accustom or become accustomed to a new climate, surroundings, or conditions: *The penguin has acclimated itself to antarctic conditions.* *v.*, **ac climat ed, ac cli mat ing.**

ac cli ma tize (ə kli/mə tīz), acclimate. *v.*, **ac cli ma tized, ac cli ma tiz ing.**

ac co lade (ak/ə lād), something awarded as an honor; praise or recognition. *n.*

ac com mo date (ə kom/ə dāt), 1 have room for; hold comfortably: *This airplane is large enough to accommodate 120 passengers.* 2 help out; oblige: *I want another color, but the store cannot accommodate me.* 3 supply with a place to sleep or live for a time: *Tourists are accommodated here.* 4 make fit; make suitable; adjust: *My eyes soon accommodated themselves to seeing objects in the darkness.* *v.*, **ac com mo dat ed, ac com mo dat ing.**

ac com mo dat ing (ə kom/ə dā/ting), willing to do favors; obliging: *My teacher was accommodating enough to lend me a dollar.* *adj.* —**ac com/mo dat/ing ly,** *adv.*

ac com mo da tion (ə kom/ə dā/shən), 1 anything that supplies a want or gives aid; a help, favor, or convenience: *It will be an accommodation to me if you will meet me tomorrow instead of today.* **2 accommodations,** *pl.* lodging and sometimes food as well: *Can we find accommodations at a motel for tonight?* 3 the fitting of something to a purpose or situation; adjustment: *The accommodation of our desires to a smaller income took some time.* 4 the automatic adjustment of the lens of the eye to see objects at various distances. *n.*

accommodation (def. 4) in a human eye. The eye muscles change the thickness of the eye lens to adjust the focus of near or far points in an image on the retina.

ac com pa ni ment (ə kum/pə nē-mənt), 1 anything that goes along with something else: *The rain was an unpleasant accompaniment to our ride.* 2 a part in music that helps or enriches the main part: *She sang with piano accompaniment.* *n.*

ac com pa nist (ə kum/pə nist), person who plays a musical accompaniment. *n.*

ac com pa ny (ə kum/pə nē), 1 go along with: *May we accompany you on your walk?* 2 be or happen in connection with: *The rain was accompanied by a high wind.* 3 play a musical accompaniment for: *She accompanied the singer on the piano.* *v.*, **ac com pa nied, ac com pa ny ing.**

ac com plice (ə kom/plis), person who knowingly aids another in committing a crime or other wrong act: *Without an accomplice to open the door the thief could not have got into the building so easily.* *n.*

ac com plish (ə kom/plish), succeed in completing; carry out; finish: *Did you accomplish your purpose? He can accomplish more in a day than anyone else in his class.* *v.*

ac com plished (ə kom/plisht), 1 carried out; completed; done: *The division of Germany is an accomplished fact.* 2 expert; skilled: *Only an accomplished dancer can perform with this ballet company.* *adj.*

ac com plish ment (ə kom/-plish mənt), 1 something that has been done with knowledge, skill, or ability; achievement: *The teacher was proud of her pupils' accomplishments.* 2 skill in some social art or grace: *In Grandmother's day playing the piano and speaking some French were considered necessary accomplishments for a young woman.* 3 a carrying out; completion: *The accomplishment of his purpose took two months.* *n.*

ac cord (ə kôrd/), 1 be in harmony; agree: *His account of the accident accords with yours.* 2 agreement; harmony: *Most people are in accord in their desire for peace.* 3 grant (a favor, request, etc.): *accord praise for good work.* 1,3 *v.*, 2 *n.*

of one's own accord, without being asked; without suggestion from another: *We didn't even have to ask for their help; they helped of their own accord.*

ac cord ance (ə kôrd/ns), agreement; harmony: *What he did was in accordance with what he said.* *n.*

ac cord ing ly (ə kôr/ding lē), 1 in a way that agrees with what is expected or stated: *These are the rules; you can act accordingly or leave the club.* 2 therefore; for this reason: *I was told to speak briefly; accordingly I cut short my talk.* *adv.*

ac cord ing to (ə kôr/ding), 1 in agreement with: *He came according to his promise.* 2 in proportion to; on the basis of: *You will be ranked according to the work you do.* 3 on the authority of: *According to this book a tiger is really a big cat.*

accordion (def. 1) The right hand plays the melody on the keys; the left plays chords by pushing buttons. The bellows force air through the reeds.

ac cor di on (ə kôr/dē ən), 1 a portable musical wind instrument with a bellows, metallic reeds, and keys. 2 having folds like the bellows of an accordion: *a skirt with accordion pleats.* 1 *n.*, 2 *adj.*

ac cost (ə kôst/), speak to first; come up and speak to: *A stranger accosted him asking for directions.* *v.*

ac count (ə kount/), 1 statement telling in detail about an event or thing; explanation: *We gave them an account of everything that had happened.* 2 value; worth: *This torn notebook is of little account.* 3 statement of money received and spent: *He keeps a written account of the way he spends his money.* 4 record of business dealings: *Businesses and factories keep accounts.* 5 statement of money due: *The office settles its accounts on the tenth of each month.* 6 hold to be; consider: *Solomon was accounted wise.* 1-5 *n.*, 6 *v.*

account for, 1 tell what has been done with; answer for: *The treasurer of the club had to account for the money paid to him and spent by him.* 2 explain: *Late frosts accounted for the poor fruit crop.* 3 cause the death or capture of:

The soldiers accounted for two enemy snipers.

call to account, 1 demand an explanation of: *The treasurer was called to account for the shortage of funds.* **2** scold; rebuke; reprimand: *We were called to account for our bad behavior in class.*

on account, as part payment: *I bought my new camera by paying a dollar a week on account.*

on account of, because of: *The game was put off on account of rain.*

on any account, under any conditions; for any reason: *We were brought up not to lie on any account.*

on no account, under no conditions; for no reason: *On no account should you lie.*

on one's account, for one's sake: *Don't wait on my account.*

on one's own account, for one's own purposes and at one's own risk: *The repairman left his regular job and has gone into business on his own account.*

take into account or **take account of,** make allowance for; consider: *You must take into account the wishes of all the class in planning a picnic.*

turn to account, get advantage or profit from: *The new pitcher turned the coach's advice to good account in the next game.*

ac count a bil i ty (ə koun′tə bil′-ə tē), state of being held responsible for carrying out one's obligations; responsibility. *n.*

ac count a ble (ə koun′tə bəl), **1** liable to be called to account; responsible: *Each person is accountable for his own work.* **2** explainable: *His bad temper is easily accountable; he has had a toothache all day. adj.*

ac count a bly (ə koun′tə blē), in a manner that can be accounted for. *adv.*

ac count ant (ə koun′tənt), person who examines or manages business accounts. *n.*

ac count ing (ə koun′ting), **1** system or practice of keeping, analyzing, and interpreting business accounts. **2** statement of accounts. *n.*

ac cou ter (ə kü′tər), furnish with clothing or equipment; equip; outfit: *Knights were accoutered in armor. v.*

ac cou ter ments (ə kü′tər mənts), **1** a soldier's equipment with the exception of his weapons and clothing. A blanket and knapsack are parts of a soldier's accouterments. **2** clothes; outfit. *n.pl.*

ac cou tre (ə kü′tər), accouter. *v.*, **ac cou tred, ac cou tring.**

ac cou tre ments (ə kü′tər mənts), accouterments. *n.pl.*

Ac cra (ə krä′), seaport in W Africa, capital of Ghana. *n.*

ac cred it (ə kred′it), **1** give authority to: *The president will accredit you as his representative.* **2** recognize as coming up to an official standard. **3** accept as true; believe; trust: *My sister is always truthful and anything she says will be accredited. v.*

ac cred i ted (ə kred′ə tid), **1** recognized as coming up to an official standard: *Some colleges will accept without examination the graduates of accredited high schools.* **2** worthy of acceptance, belief, or trust: *Einstein was an accredited authority in mathematics. adj.*

ac cre tion (ə krē′shən), **1** a growing together of separate things: *A glacier is formed by the accretion of many particles of frozen packed snow.* **2** something formed in this way. *n.*

ac cru al (ə krü′əl), **1** an accruing: *Money left in a savings bank increases by the accrual of interest.* **2** amount accrued or accruing. *n.*

ac crue (ə krü′), come as a growth or result: *Ability to think clearly will accrue from good habits of study. v.,* **ac crued, ac cru ing.**

acct., 1 account. **2** accountant.

ac cu mu late (ə kyü′myə lāt), collect little by little; pile up; gather: *Through the years he accumulated enough money to buy a farm when he retired. Dust and cobwebs had accumulated in the empty house. v.,* **ac cu mu lat ed, ac cu mu lat ing.**

ac cu mu la tion (ə kyü′myə lā′shən), **1** material collected; mass: *His accumulation of old papers filled the attic.* **2** a collecting together; an amassing: *The accumulation of useful knowledge is one result of reading. n.*

ac cu ra cy (ak′yər ə sē), a being without errors or mistakes; correctness; exactness: *Arithmetic problems must be solved with accuracy. n.*

ac cu rate (ak′yər it), without errors or mistakes; precisely correct; exact: *You must take care to be accurate in arithmetic. An airplane pilot must have an accurate watch. adj.* —**ac′cur ate ly,** *adv.*

ac cur sed (ə ker′sid *or* ə kerst′), **1** annoying and troublesome; detestable; hateful. **2** under a curse; doomed. *adj.*

ac cu sa tion (ak′yə zā′shən), a charge of having done something wrong, of being something bad, or of having broken the law: *The accusation against him was that he had stolen ten dollars from the store. n.*

ac cu sa tive (ə kyü′zə tiv), **1** showing the direct object; objective. *Me, us, him,* and *them* are in the accusative case, or, as usually said for English words, the objective case. **2** the objective case. **3** word used as the object

of a verb or preposition. **1** *adj.,* **2,3** *n.*

ac cuse (ə kyüz′), **1** charge with having done something wrong, with being something bad, or with having broken the law: *The driver was accused of speeding.* **2** place the blame on: *The President accused Congress for the delay in passing his program. v.,* **ac cused, ac cus ing.**

ac cus er (ə kyü′zər), person who accuses another. *n.*

ac cus ing ly (ə kyü′zing lē), in an accusing manner. *adv.*

ac cus tom (ə kus′təm), make familiar by use or habit; get used: *A good traveler can accustom himself to almost any kind of food. v.*

ac cus tomed (ə kus′təmd), usual; customary: *By Monday I was well again and was back in my accustomed seat in class. adj.*

accustomed to, used to; in the habit of: *The farmer was accustomed to hard work.*

ace (ās), **1** a playing card, domino, or side of a die having one spot. **2** (in tennis, handball, etc.) a point won on a serve which the opponent fails to return. **3** person expert at something: *He is an ace at basketball.* **4** very skilled; expert. **5** a combat pilot who has shot down five or more enemy planes. **1-3,5** *n.,* **4** *adj.*

ac et an i lide (as′ə tan′l id), drug used in medicines to lessen pain and fever. *n.*

ac e tate (as′ə tāt), a salt or ester of acetic acid. **Cellulose acetate** is used in making imitation leather, phonograph records, rayon, cellophane, etc. *n.*

a ce tic acid (ə sē′tik), a very sour, colorless acid present in vinegar. It is a compound of hydrogen, carbon, and oxygen.

a cet y lene (ə set′l ēn′), a colorless gas that burns with a bright light and very hot flame. It is used for lighting or, combined with oxygen, for welding metals. *n.*

ache (āk), **1** a dull, continuous pain: *Muscular aches often follow hard exercise.* **2** suffer continuous pain; be in pain; hurt: *My arm aches.* **3** INFORMAL.

---

hat, āge, fär; let, ēqual, tėrm;
it, īce; hot, ōpen, ôrder;
oil, out; cup, pùt, rüle; ch, child;
ng, long; sh, she; th, thin;
ŦH, then; zh, measure;

ə represents *a* in about,
e in taken, *i* in pencil,
o in lemon, *u* in circus.

adj.	adjective	*n.* noun
adv.	adverb	*prep.* preposition
conj.	conjunction	*pron.* pronoun
interj.	interjection	*v.* verb
sing.	singular	*pl.* plural

be eager; wish very much: *During the hot days of August we all ached to go swimming.* 1 *n.,* 2,3 *v.,* **ached, ach ing.**

a chieve (ə chēv′), 1 carry out to a successful end; accomplish; do: *Did you achieve your purpose?* 2 reach by one's own efforts; get by effort: *achieve high grades in mathematics.* *v.,* **a chieved, a chiev ing.**

a chieve ment (ə chēv′mənt), 1 thing achieved; some plan or action carried out with courage or unusual ability; accomplishment; feat: *Sailing a submarine under the North Pole was a great achievement.* 2 an achieving: *the achievement of success, the achievement of good grades. n.*

A chil les (ə kil′ēz), (in Greek legends) a hero of the Greeks at the siege of Troy. No weapon could injure Achilles anywhere, except in the heel. *n.*

ac id (as′id), 1 any of a class of chemical compounds that are sour or bitter to the taste and turn blue litmus paper red in water solution. Acids yield hydrogen ions when dissolved in water and usually react with a base to form a salt. Hydrochloric acid and sulfuric acid are two common acids. 2 of acids; having the properties of an acid: *Blue litmus paper turns red in an acid solution.* 3 sharp or biting to the taste; sour: *Lemons are an acid fruit.* 4 sharp in manner or temper; caustic: *an acid comment.* 1 *n.,* 2-4 *adj.* —**ac′id ly,** *adv.*

a cid i fy (ə sid′ə fī), 1 make or become sour. 2 change into an acid. *v.,* **a cid i fied, a cid i fy ing.**

a cid i ty (ə sid′ə tē), acid quality or condition; sourness. *n.*

ac knowl edge (ak nol′ij), 1 admit to be true: *He acknowledges his own faults.* 2 recognize the authority or claims of: *The boys acknowledged the pitcher to be the best player on the baseball team.* 3 make known that one has received (a service, favor, gift, message, etc.): *I acknowledged her letter at once. v.,* **ac knowl edged, ac knowl edg ing.**

ac knowl edg ment or **ac knowl edge ment** (ak nol′ij mənt), 1 something given or done to show that one has received a service, favor, gift, message, etc.: *The winner waved in acknowledg-*

ment of the crowd's cheers. 2 act of admitting that something is true: *acknowledgment of a mistake.* 3 recognition of authority, claims, or merit. *n.*

ac me (ak′mē), the highest point: *The acme of the development of spaceships probably lies in the future. n.*

ac ne (ak′nē), a skin disease in which the oil glands in the skin become clogged and inflamed, often causing pimples. *n.*

ac o lyte (ak′ə līt), 1 person who helps a priest during certain religious services: *The acolyte lit the candles on the altar.* 2 attendant; assistant. *n.*

A con ca gua (ä′kông kä′gwə), mountain in the Andes, in W Argentina, the highest mountain in the Western Hemisphere. *n.*

ac o nite (ak′ə nīt), 1 a poisonous plant with blue, purple, or yellow flowers shaped like hoods. Monkshood is one kind of aconite. 2 drug used to relieve inflammation and pain, obtained from monkshood. *n.*

a corn (ā′kôrn *or* ā′kərn), the nut of an oak tree. *n.*

a cous tic (ə kü′stik), 1 having to do with the sense or the organs of hearing. 2 having to do with the science of sound. *adj.*

a cous ti cal (ə kü′stə kəl), having to do with the science of sound. *adj.*

a cous tics (ə kü′stiks), 1 *pl. in form and use.* the qualities of a room, hall, auditorium, etc., that determine how well sounds can be heard in it: *The acoustics were so good that people in the last row could hear the speaker well.* 2 *pl. in form, sing. in use.* the science of sound: *Acoustics is taught in some colleges. n.*

ac quaint (ə kwānt′), make aware; let know; inform: *Acquaint me with your plans for next summer. v.*

be acquainted with, have personal knowledge of; know: *I have heard about your friend, but I am not acquainted with him.*

ac quaint ance (ə kwān′təns), 1 person known to one, but not a close friend: *We have many acquaintances in our neighborhood.* 2 knowledge of persons or things gained from experience

acre (def. 1)
The amount of space on a football field covered by one acre is shaded above.

with them: *I have some acquaintance with French, but I do not know it well. n.*

make someone's acquaintance, get to know someone: *We soon made the acquaintance of our new neighbors.*

ac quaint ance ship (ə kwān′təns ship), 1 relation between acquaintances: *Their acquaintanceship lasted many years.* 2 personal knowledge; acquaintance. *n.*

ac qui esce (ak′wē es′), give consent by keeping silent or by not making objections; agree or submit quietly: *We acquiesced in their plan because we could not suggest a better one. v.,* **ac qui esced, ac qui esc ing.**

ac qui es cence (ak′wē es′ns), an agreeing or submitting quietly; consent given without objections. *n.*

ac qui es cent (ak′wē es′nt), quietly consenting or agreeing; acquiescing. *adj.*

ac quire (ə kwīr′), come to have; get as one's own; obtain: *He acquired a strong liking for sports at camp. I acquired the money for a college education by working summers. v.,* **acquired, ac quir ing.**

ac quire ment (ə kwīr′mənt), 1 act of acquiring: *the acquirement of wealth.* 2 something acquired; attainment: *Her musical acquirements are remarkable for a girl of her age. n.*

ac qui si tion (ak′wə zish′ən), 1 an acquiring; getting as one's own: *the acquisition of skill by practicing.* 2 something acquired: *The gallery's new acquisitions included two paintings by Picasso. n.*

ac quis i tive (ə kwiz′ə tiv), fond of acquiring; eager to get wealth, power, knowledge, etc.: *My acquisitive friend is too fond of money. adj.* —**ac quis′ i tive ly,** *adv.* —**ac quis′ i tive ness,** *n.*

ac quit (ə kwit′), declare not guilty; exonerate: *The jury acquitted the man who had been accused of stealing the money. v.,* **ac quit ted, ac quit ting.**

acquit oneself, do one's part; behave: *You acquitted yourself well during the debate.*

ac quit tal (ə kwit′l), a setting free by declaring not guilty; discharge; release: *The jury brought in a verdict of acquittal. n.*

a cre (ā′kər), 1 measure of land, 160 square rods or 43,560 square feet. 2 **acres,** *pl.* lands; property. *n.*

a cre age (ā′kər ij), 1 number of acres: *The acreage of a square mile is 640.* 2 piece of land sold by the acre. *n.*

ac rid (ak′rid), 1 sharp, bitter, or stinging to the mouth, eyes, skin, or nose: *Smoke from a bonfire feels acrid when you breathe it in.* 2 irritating in manner; sharp in temper; acrimonious: *an*

8

acrid disposition. *adj.* —**ac′rid ly**, *adv.*

Ac ri lan (ak′rə lan), trademark for a synthetic fiber that resembles wool and resists wrinkling. *n.*

ac ri mo ni ous (ak′rə mō′nē əs), sharp or bitter in temper, language, or manner; caustic: *An acrimonious dispute broke out between the drivers who had the accident. adj.* —**ac′ri mo′ni ous ly**, *adv.* —**ac′ri mo′ni ous ness**, *n.*

ac ri mo ny (ak′rə mō′nē), sharpness or bitterness in temper, language, or manner. *n.*

ac ro bat (ak′rə bat), person who can swing on a trapeze, turn handsprings, walk a tightrope, or perform other feats of bodily skill and strength. *n.*

ac ro bat ic (ak′rə bat′ik), 1 of an acrobat: *Walking a tightrope is an acrobatic feat.* 2 like an acrobat's: *With an acrobatic leap, he picked the apple off the tree. adj.*

ac ro bat i cal ly (ak′rə bat′ik lē), with acrobatic skill or dexterity: *She bounced acrobatically and turned a handspring. adv.*

ac ro bat ics (ak′rə bat′iks), 1 tricks or performances of an acrobat; gymnastic feats. 2 feats like those of an acrobat: *a monkey's acrobatics. n., pl. in form, sometimes sing. in use.*

a crop o lis (ə krop′ə lis), the high, fortified part of an ancient Greek city. The Parthenon was built on **the Acropolis** of Athens. *n.*

a cross (ə krôs′), 1 from one side to the other of; over: *The cat walked across the street.* 2 from one side to the other: *What is the distance across?* 3 on the other side of; beyond: *The woods are across the river.* 4 on or to the other side: *When are you going across?* 1,3 *prep.,* 2,4 *adv.*

come across or **run across**, meet or fall in with; find: *We come across hard words in some books.*

North
East
West
South

acrostic
with first letters
forming the word
"news" in a column

a cros tic (ə krôs′tik), composition in verse or arrangement of words in which the first, last, or certain other letters in each line, taken in order, spell a word or phrase. *n.*

act (akt), 1 something done; deed: *Slapping his face was a childish act.* 2 process of doing: *I was caught in the act of hiding the gifts.* 3 do something: *The firemen acted promptly and saved the burning house.* 4 have effect: *The medicine failed to act.* 5 behave: *I apologize for acting badly.* 6 behave like: *Most people act the fool now and then.* 7 perform on the stage, in motion pictures, on television, or over the radio; play a part: *He acts the part of the district attorney. She acts very well.* 8 a main division of a play or opera: *Most modern plays have three acts.* 9 one of several performances on a program: *We stayed to see the comedian's act.* 10 a legislative decision; decree. An act of Congress is a bill that has been passed by Congress. 1,2,8-10 *n.,* 3-7 *v.*

act for or **act as**, take the place of; do the work of: *While the principal was gone, the assistant principal acted for her.*

act on or **act upon**, 1 follow; obey: *I will act on your suggestion.* 2 have an effect or influence on: *Yeast acted on the dough and made it rise.*

act up, INFORMAL. 1 behave badly: *The children began to act up when company came.* 2 play tricks; make mischief: *Children often act up on Halloween.*

act ing (ak′ting), temporarily taking another's place and doing his duties: *While the principal was sick, one of the teachers was acting principal. adj.*

ac tin ic (ak tin′ik), producing chemical changes by radiation. **Actinic rays** are important in photography. *adj.*

ac tin i um (ak tin′ē əm), a radioactive chemical element somewhat like radium, found in pitchblende. *n.*

ac tion (ak′shən), 1 process of acting; doing something: *The quick action of the firemen saved the building from being burned down.* 2 physical activity: *An athlete is a man of action.* 3 something done; act: *Helping a small child to cross the street was a kind action.* 4 **actions**, *pl.* conduct; behavior: *Her actions revealed her thoughtfulness.* 5 effect or influence of one thing on another: *The action of wind on the ship's sails moved the ship over the water.* 6 way of moving or working; movement: *A child can push our lawn mower, because it has such an easy action.* 7 battle; part of a battle: *My uncle was wounded in action in Vietnam.* 8 series of events in a story or play. 9 lawsuit. *n.*

in action, 1 active; taking part: *All the players stayed in action through the entire game.* 2 working: *The machine is now in action.*

take action, 1 begin to do something: *We decided to take action to raise money for the class party.* 2 start working: *We had to take quick action to finish on time.* 3 start a lawsuit; sue: *The man hurt in the accident has taken*

hat, āge, fär; let, ēqual, tėrm;
it, īce; hot, ōpen, ôrder;
oil, out; cup, pùt, rüle; ch, child;
ng, long; sh, she; th, thin;
ŦH, then; zh, measure;

ə represents *a* in about,
e in taken, *i* in pencil,
o in lemon, *u* in circus.

action to recover damages for his injury.

ac ti vate (ak′tə vāt), 1 make active. 2 make radioactive. *v.,* **ac ti vat ed**, **ac ti vat ing.**

ac ti va tion (ak′tə vā′shən), an activating. *n.*

ac tive (ak′tiv), 1 showing much action; moving rather quickly much of the time; lively: *The baby is as active as a kitten. Children are more active than old people.* 2 acting; working: *An active volcano may erupt at any time.* 3 working hard or with energy; busy and energetic: *We took an active part in organizing the stamp club.* 4 showing the subject of a verb as acting. In "He broke the window," *broke* is in the active voice. 5 a verb form that does this. 1-4 *adj.,* 5 *n.* —**ac′tive ly**, *adv.*

ac tiv i ty (ak tiv′ə tē), 1 a being active; use of power; movement: *Children engage in more physical activity than old people.* 2 action; doing: *the activities of enemy spies.* 3 vigorous action; liveliness: *The activity of the children disturbed the sleeping man.* 4 thing to do: *A student who has too many outside activities may find it hard to keep up with his studies. n., pl.* **ac tiv i ties.**

ac tor (ak′tər), person who acts on the stage, in motion pictures, on television, or over the radio. *n.*

ac tress (ak′tris), girl or woman actor. *n., pl.* **ac tress es.**

Acts (akts), the fifth book of the New Testament. Acts tells about the beginnings of the Christian church. *n.*

Acts of the Apostles, Acts.

ac tu al (ak′chü əl), existing as a fact; real: *What he told us was not a dream but an actual happening. adj.*

ac tu al i ty (ak′chü al′ə tē), 1 an actual thing; fact: *A trip to the moon is now an actuality.* 2 actual existence; reality. *n., pl.* **ac tu al i ties.**

ac tu al ly (ak′chü ə lē), really; in fact: *Are you actually going to camp this summer or just wishing to go? adv.*

ac tu ate (ak′chü āt), 1 put into action: *This pump is actuated by a belt driven by an electric motor.* 2 influence to act: *Kindness actuated him to help the old*

adj. adjective	*n.* noun
adv. adverb	*prep.* preposition
conj. conjunction	*pron.* pronoun
interj. interjection	*v.* verb
sing. singular	*pl.* plural

woman with the heavy bundle. v., **ac tu at ed, ac tu at ing.**

a cu men (ə kyü′mən), sharpness and quickness in seeing and understanding; keen insight; discernment. *n.*

ac u punc ture (ak′yu pungk′chər), an ancient Chinese practice of inserting needles into certain parts of the body. Acupuncture is used to treat some diseases and to relieve pain. *n.*

a cute (ə kyüt′), 1 sharp and severe: *A toothache can cause acute pain.* 2 brief and severe: *An acute disease like pneumonia reaches a crisis within a short time.* 3 threatening; critical: *The long drought caused an acute shortage of water in the city.* 4 quick in perceiving and responding to impressions; keen: *Dogs have an acute sense of smell.* 5 high in pitch; shrill: *Some sounds are so acute that we cannot hear them.* 6 having a sharp point. *adj.* —**a cute′ly,** *adv.* —**a cute′ness,** *n.*

acute accent, mark (ˊ) placed over a vowel letter to show the kind of sound, as in French *attaché,* or place of the accent, as in Spanish *Asunción.*

acute angle, angle less than a right angle.

ad (ad), INFORMAL. advertisement. *n.*

A.D., in the year of our Lord; after the birth of Christ. From 63 B.C. to A.D. 14 is 77 years. [abbreviation of Latin *Anno Domini* in the year of our Lord]

ad age (ad′ij), a wise saying that has been much used; proverb. "Haste makes waste" is a well-known adage. *n.*

a da gio (ə dä′jō), in music: 1 slowly. 2 slow. 3 a slow part. 1 *adv.,* 2 *adj.,* 3 *n., pl.* **a da gios.** [from Italian *ad agio* at ease]

Ad am (ad′əm), (in the Bible) the first man; father of the human race. *n.*

ad a mant (ad′ə mənt), not giving in readily; firm and unyielding: *Columbus was adamant in refusing the requests of his sailors to turn back.* *adj.* —**ad′a mant ly,** *adv.*

Ad ams (ad′əmz), 1 **John,** 1735-1826, the second president of the United States, from 1797 to 1801. 2 **John Quincy,** 1767-1848, the sixth president of the United States, from 1825 to 1829, son of John Adams. 3 **Samuel,** 1722-1803, a leader of the American colonists' resistance to Eng-

land at the time of the Revolutionary War. *n.*

Adam's apple, the slight lump in the front of a person's throat formed by the thyroid cartilage.

a dapt (ə dapt′), 1 make fit or suitable; adjust: *Can you adapt your way of working to the new job?* 2 change to fit different conditions or different use: *Cats seem to adapt themselves very well to indoor life.* *v.* —**a dapt′er,** *n.*

a dapt a bil i ty (ə dap′tə bil′ə tē), power to change easily to fit different conditions. *n.*

a dapt a ble (ə dap′tə bəl), easily changed or changing easily to fit different conditions: *an adaptable person. My schedule is adaptable; I can see you anytime.* *adj.*

ad ap ta tion (ad′ap tā′shən), 1 a changing to fit different conditions; an adapting: *He made a good adaptation to high school.* 2 a being adapted or made to fit: *Mother's adaptation of an old bottle to a table lamp was clever.* 3 something made by changing to fit different conditions: *A motion picture is often an adaptation of a novel.* 4 a change in structure, form, or habits to fit different conditions: *Wings are adaptations of the upper limbs for flight.* *n.*

a dapt ed (ə dap′tid), fitted; suitable: *Florida has a climate adapted to the growing of oranges.* *adj.*

ACUTE ANGLE   RIGHT ANGLE

add (ad), 1 find the sum of: *Add 73 and 27 and you have 100.* 2 say further; go on to say or write: *She said good-by and added that she had had a pleasant visit.* 3 join (one thing to another): *Add another stone to the pile. She tasted her lemonade, then added more sugar.* *v.*

add to, make greater; increase: *The fine day added to our pleasure.*

add up to, amount to: *What do the profits add up to?*

ad dend (ad′end *or* ə dend′), a number or quantity to be added to another number or quantity: *In the problem "421 + 365 =?" 365 is the addend.* *n.*

ad den da (ə den′də), plural of **addendum.** *n.*

ad den dum (ə den′dəm), thing added; appendix. *n., pl.* **ad den da.**

ad der (ad′ər), 1 a small, poisonous snake of Europe. 2 hognose snake. 3 puff adder. *n.*

ad dict (ad′ikt), person who is a slave to a habit: *A drug addict finds it almost impossible to stop using drugs.* *n.*

ad dict ed (ə dik′tid), slavishly following a habit or practice; strongly inclined: *He was so addicted to the use of tobacco that he smoked ten cigars a day.* *adj.*

ad dic tion (ə dik′shən), condition of being a slave to a habit. *n.*

Ad dis Ab a ba (ad′is ab′ə bə), capital of Ethiopia, in the central part.

ad di tion (ə dish′ən), 1 an adding of one number or quantity to another: *2 + 3 = 5 is a simple addition.* 2 an adding of one thing to another: *The addition of flour will thicken gravy.* 3 thing added: *Cream is a tasty addition to many desserts.* 4 part added to a building. *n.*

in addition or **in addition to,** besides; also: *In addition to her work in school, our teacher gives music lessons after school hours.*

ad di tion al (ə dish′ə nəl), added; extra; more: *Can you give me the additional information I need?* *adj.* —**ad di′tion al ly,** *adv.*

ad di tive (ad′ə tiv), 1 substance added to gasoline, fuel oil, etc., to improve its efficiency. 2 involving addition. 1 *n.,* 2 *adj.*

ad dled (ad′ld), 1 muddled; confused: *an addled brain.* 2 rotten: *addled eggs.* *adj.*

ad dress (ə dres′; *also* ad′res *for 4*), 1 a speech, especially a formal one: *The President gave an address to the nation over television.* 2 make an address to: *The speaker addressed the organization on the subject of ecology.* 3 direct speech or writing to: *She addressed me as though we were old friends. The king was addressed as "Your Majesty."* 4 the place to which one's mail is directed; place of residence or of business: *Write your name and address on this envelope.* 5 write on (a letter, package, etc.) where it is to be sent: *Address this letter to Alaska.* 6 manner in conversation: *A salesman should be a man of pleasant address.* 7 apply or devote (oneself); direct one's energies: *She addressed herself to the task of learning French.* 1,4,6 *n.,* 2,3,5,7 *v.*
ad dress es; 2,3,5,7 *v.*

ad dress ee (ə dre sē′), person to whom a letter, package, etc., is addressed. *n.*

ad duce (ə düs′ *or* ə dyüs′), offer as a reason; give as proof or evidence; bring up as an example: *The principal adduced the boy's long record of good marks to show he deserved a scholarship.* *v.,* **ad duced, ad duc ing.**

Ad e laide (ad′l ād), city in S Australia. *n.*

A den (äd′n *or* ād′n), 1 former British protectorate in SW Arabia, now Southern Yemen. 2 **Gulf of,** part of the

Arabian Sea between S Arabia and E Africa. *n.*

ad e noids (ad′n oidz), growths of glandular tissue in the upper part of the throat, just back of the nose. Adenoids can swell up and hinder natural breathing and speaking. *n.pl.*

a dept (ə dept′), thoroughly skilled; expert: *She is adept in music. adj.* —**a dept′ly,** *adv.* —**a dept′ness,** *n.*

ad e qua cy (ad′ə kwə sē), a being adequate; as much as is needed for a particular purpose; sufficiency. *n.*

ad e quate (ad′ə kwit), 1 as much as is needed for a particular purpose; sufficient; enough: *To be healthy one must have an adequate diet.* 2 suitable; competent: *He is barely adequate for the job. adj.* —**ad′e quate ly,** *adv.* —**ad′e quate ness,** *n.*

ad here (ad hir′), 1 stick fast; remain attached: *Mud adheres to your shoes.* 2 hold closely or firmly: *The principal adhered to the plan for dropping Latin in spite of the opposition of some teachers.* 3 be a follower or upholder; give allegiance: *adhere to a political party. v.,* **ad hered, ad her ing.**

ad her ence (ad hir′əns), a holding to and following closely; faithfulness; *The coach insisted on rigid adherence to the rules. n.*

ad her ent (ad hir′ənt), 1 a faithful supporter; follower: *He was an adherent of the conservative party.* 2 sticking fast; attached. 1 *n.,* 2 *adj.*

ad he sion (ad hē′zhən), a sticking fast; attachment; an adhering. *n.*

ad he sive (ad hē′siv), 1 gummed tape used to hold bandages in place. 2 glue, paste, or other substance for sticking things together. 3 holding fast; adhering easily; sticky. 1,2 *n.,* 3 *adj.*

a dieu (ə dü′ *or* ə dyü′), good-by. *interj., n., pl.* **a dieus** *or* **a dieux** (ə düz′ *or* ə dyüz′). [from French of the 1300's *a Dieu* to God]

a di os (ä′dē ōs′ *or* ad′ē ōs′), good-by. *interj., n.* [from Spanish *a Dios* to God]

ad i pose (ad′ə pōs), fat. *adj.*

Ad i ron dack Mountains (ad′ə ron′dak), mountains of a large area in NE New York State.

Ad i ron dacks (ad′ə ron′daks), Adirondack Mountains. *n.pl.*

adj., adjective.

ad ja cent (ə jā′snt), lying near or close; adjoining; next: *The house adjacent to ours has been sold. adj.* —**ad ja′cent ly,** *adv.*

ad jec ti val (aj′ik tī′vəl), 1 of an adjective. 2 used as an adjective. *adj.* —**ad′jec ti′val ly,** *adv.*

ad jec tive (aj′ik tiv), 1 one of a class of words that qualify, limit, or add to the meaning of a noun or pronoun. In "a tiny brook," "The day is warm," "great

ADENOIDS

happiness," and "this pencil," *tiny, warm, great,* and *this* are adjectives. 2 of an adjective. 3 used as an adjective. 1 *n.,* 2,3 *adj.*

ad join (ə join′), be next to; be close to; be side by side: *Canada adjoins the United States. v.*

ad join ing (ə joi′ning), being next to or in contact with; bordering: *The twins have adjoining rooms. adj.*

ad journ (ə jėrn′), 1 put off until a later time: *The members of the club voted to adjourn the meeting until two o'clock.* 2 stop activity for a time: *The court adjourned from Friday until Monday.* 3 go (to another place): *After the meeting we adjourned to the cafeteria to eat. v.*

ad journ ment (ə jėrn′mənt), 1 an adjourning or a being adjourned. 2 time during which a court, lawmaking body, etc., is adjourned. *n.*

adjutant bird
about 5 ft. high;
the heavy bill is
about 1 ft. long.

ad judge (ə juj′), 1 decree or decide by law: *The accused man was adjudged guilty.* 2 award by law: *The property was adjudged to the rightful owner. v.,* **ad judged, ad judg ing.**

ad junct (aj′ungkt), something added that is less important or not necessary, but helpful: *A spare tire is a more important adjunct to a car than a radio. n.*

ad ju ra tion (aj′ə rā′shən), an earnest or solemn appeal. *n.*

ad jure (ə jur′), ask earnestly or solemnly: *I adjure you on your honor to tell the truth. v.,* **ad jured, ad jur ing.**

ad just (ə just′), 1 change to make fit: *These desks and seats can be adjusted to the height of any child.* 2 put in proper order, position, or relation; arrange: *Please adjust the TV so that it is not so loud.* 3 arrange satisfactorily; right; settle: *The girls adjusted their difference of opinion and were friends*

again. 4 accommodate oneself; get used: *Some wild animals never adjust to life in a zoo. v.*

ad just a ble (ə jus′tə bəl), that can be adjusted: *The adjustable electric lamp on my desk can be placed in various positions. adj.*

ad just er or **ad jus tor** (ə jus′tər), 1 thing that adjusts something else. 2 person who adjusts claims. *n.*

ad just ment (ə just′mənt), 1 act or process of adjusting: *The adjustment of seats to the right height for children is necessary for their comfort.* 2 a means of adjusting: *Our TV has an adjustment so that we can make the volume loud or soft.* 3 settlement of a dispute, a claim, etc. *n.*

ad ju tant (aj′ə tənt), 1 an army officer who assists a commanding officer by sending out orders, writing letters, etc. 2 assistant. 3 adjutant bird. *n.*

adjutant bird or **adjutant stork,** a very large species of stork of India, southeastern Asia, and Africa.

ad lib (ad lib′), 1 make up as one goes along; improvise: *The actor forgot some of his lines and had to adlib his part.* 2 on the spur of the moment; freely: *The orchestra played adlib.* 3 music or words made up as one goes along. 1 *v.,* **ad libbed, ad lib bing;** 2 *adv.,* 3 *n.*

ad min is ter (ad min′ə stər), 1 manage the affairs of; direct: *The Secretary of Defense administers a department of the government. A housekeeper administers a household.* 2 give out; apply: *The coach administered first aid to the injured player. Judges administer justice and punishment.* 3 offer formally: *The witness could not testify until the judge had administered an oath to him to tell the truth.* 4 settle or take charge of (an estate). 5 be helpful; contribute: *The government administered to the needs of the flood victims. v.*

ad min is tra tion (ad min′ə strā′shən), 1 the managing of the affairs of a business, an office, etc.: *The administration of a big business requires skill in dealing with people.* 2 group of persons in charge: *The principal and teachers of a school are part of the adminis-*

hat, āge, fär; let, ēqual, tėrm;
it, īce; hot, ōpen, ôrder;
oil, out; cup, pùt, rüle; ch, child;
ng, long; sh, she; th, thin;
ŦH, then; zh, measure;

ə represents *a* in about,
e in taken, *i* in pencil,
o in lemon, *u* in circus.

adj. adjective	*n.* noun
adv. adverb	*prep.* preposition
conj. conjunction	*pron.* pronoun
interj. interjection	*v.* verb
sing. singular	*pl.* plural

tration of the school. 3 management of public affairs by government officials: *He is experienced in city administration.* 4 officials as a group; the government. 5 **the Administration,** the President of the United States, his cabinet, and the departments of the government run by the members of the cabinet or by other persons appointed by the President. 6 the period of time during which a government holds office: *The Liberal administration in Canada lasted many years.* 7 a giving out or applying: *The Red Cross handled the administration of aid to the refugees. n.*

ad min is tra tive (ad min′ə strā′tiv), having to do with administration; executive. *adj.* **—ad min′is tra′tive ly,** *adv.*

ad min is tra tor (ad min′ə strā′tər), 1 person who administers; manager. 2 person appointed to settle or take charge of an estate. *n.*

ad mir a ble (ad′mər ə bəl), 1 worth admiring: *Lincoln had an admirable character.* 2 very good; excellent: *What an admirable party! adj.* **—ad′mir a ble ness,** *n.*

ad mir a bly (ad′mər ə blē), in an admirable manner; excellently. *adv.*

ad mir al (ad′mər əl), 1 a naval officer having the highest rank. 2 officer in the United States Navy ranking next below a fleet admiral. 3 commander of a fleet of fishing or merchant ships. *n.*

ad mir al ty (ad′mər əl tē), branch of law dealing with affairs of the sea and of ships. *n., pl.* **ad mir al ties.**

ad mi ra tion (ad′mə rā′shən), 1 a feeling of wonder, pleasure, and approval: *The beauty of the sunset and the view excited our admiration.* 2 person or thing that is admired: *My new bicycle is the admiration of my friends. n.*

ad mire (ad mīr′), regard with wonder, pleasure, and approval; show admiration for: *admire someone's new car. I admire your courage. v.,* **ad mired, ad mir ing.**

ad mir er (ad mī′rər), person who admires: *The pretty girl had many admirers. n.*

ad mir ing ly (ad mī′ring lē), with admiration: *I looked at the new bicycle admiringly. adv.*

ad mis si ble (ad mis′ə bəl), 1 capable or worthy of being admitted: *Any student is admissible to this club.* 2 permitted by a person in authority or by the rules; allowable: *Is it admissible to play here? adj.*

ad mis sion (ad mish′ən), 1 an allowing to enter; entrance: *His admission into the hospital was delayed for lack of beds.* 2 right of entering or using a place, an office, etc.; permission to enter: *Every elementary school graduate has admission to high school.* 3 price paid for the right to enter: *Admission to the show is one dollar.* 4 an admitting to be true; acknowledging: *Their admission that they were to blame kept others from being punished. n.*

ad mit (ad mit′), 1 say (something) is real or true; acknowledge: *She admits now that she made a mistake. His opponent had to admit defeat.* 2 allow to enter; let in: *He was admitted to school this year. Windows admit light and air to the room.* 3 have room for; be large enough for: *This garage door will admit two cars abreast. v.,* **ad mit ted, ad mit ting.**

admit of, give allowance for; leave room for: *His answer admits of no reply.*

ad mit tance (ad mit′ns), right to enter; permission to enter: *She had admittance to all the theaters free of charge. n.*

ad mit ted ly (ad mit′id lē), without denial; by general consent: *Admittedly the rules are strict. adv.*

ad mix (ad miks′), add to something else; mix in; mingle. *v.*

ad mix ture (ad miks′chər), 1 a mixing; mixture: *The admixture of flour and water forms a paste.* 2 anything added in mixing; ingredient. *n.*

ad mon ish (ad mon′ish), 1 advise (a person) against something in order that he may be guided to improve; warn: *The policeman admonished him not to drive so fast.* 2 scold gently; reprove: *The teacher admonished the student for his careless work. v.*

ad mon ish ment (ad mon′ish mənt), admonition. *n.*

ad mo ni tion (ad′mə nish′ən), an admonishing; gentle reproof or warning: *I received an admonition from my teacher for not doing my homework. n.*

ad mon i to ry (ad mon′ə tôr′ē), admonishing; warning: *The librarian raised an admonitory finger. adj.*

a do (ə dü′), 1 noisy activity; bustle: *There was much ado about the party by all the family.* 2 trouble; difficulty. *n.*

a do be (ə dō′bē), 1 brick made of clay baked in the sun. 2 built or made of adobe: *Our friends in Arizona live in an adobe house.* 3 a building made of adobe. 1,3 *n.,* 2 *adj.*

ad o les cence (ad′l es′ns), period of growth from childhood to adulthood; youth. *n.*

ad o les cent (ad′l es′nt), 1 person growing up from childhood to adulthood, especially a person from about 12 to about 20 years of age. 2 growing up from childhood to adulthood; youthful: *He is still in the adolescent stage of development.* 3 of adolescents; characteristic of adolescents: *Adolescent friendships often do not last.* 1 *n.,* 2,3 *adj.*

A don is (ə don′is *or* ə dō′nis), 1 (in Greek and Roman myths) a handsome young man who was loved by Aphrodite (Venus). 2 any handsome young man. *n.*

a dopt (ə dopt′), 1 take as one's own choice: *I liked your idea and adopted it. Few Americans would find it easy to adopt Japanese customs.* 2 accept formally; approve: *The club adopted the motion by a vote of 20 to 5.* 3 take (a child of other parents) and bring up as one's own child: *The judge permitted the family to adopt both of the children. v.*

a dop tion (ə dop′shən), 1 an adopting: *Our club voted for the adoption of some new rules.* 2 a being adopted: *The children were offered for adoption. n.*

a dor a ble (ə dôr′ə bəl), 1 worthy of being adored. 2 INFORMAL. attractive; delightful: *an adorable kitten. adj.* **—a dor′a ble ness,** *n.*

a dor a bly (ə dôr′ə blē), in an adorable manner. *adv.*

ad o ra tion (ad′ə rā′shən), 1 devoted love and admiration. 2 worship. *n.*

a dore (ə dôr′), 1 love and admire very greatly: *We adore our family.* 2 INFORMAL. like very much: *I just adore that dress!* 3 worship: *"O! Come, let us adore Him," sang the choir at Christmas. v.,* **a dored, a dor ing.**

a dor er (ə dôr′ər), 1 a devoted admirer. 2 worshiper. *n.*

a dor ing ly (ə dôr′ing lē), with adoration. *adv.*

a dorn (ə dôrn′), add beauty to; put ornaments on; decorate: *She adorned her hair with flowers. v.*

a dorn ment (ə dôrn′mənt), 1 something that adds beauty; ornament; decoration: *The park is an adornment to the neighborhood.* 2 an adorning: *They are busy with the adornment of the room for the party. n.*

ad re nal gland (ə drē′nl), one of the two ductless glands, one on the upper part of each kidney, that secrete adrenaline; suprarenal gland.

Ad ren a lin (ə dren′l ən), trademark for adrenaline which is artificially produced. *n.*

ad ren a line (ə dren′l ən), hormone secreted by the adrenal glands. Adrenaline speeds up the heartbeat and increases bodily energy and resistance to fatigue. *n.*

A dri at ic Sea (ā′drē at′ik), sea between Italy and Yugoslavia. It is an arm of the Mediterranean.

a drift (ə drift′), 1 floating without being guided; drifting: *During the storm our boat was adrift on the lake.* 2 without guidance or direction; aimless: *The basketball team was adrift while the coach was sick. adj.*

a droit (ə droit′), 1 having or showing skill in using the hands or the body; skillful: *Monkeys are adroit climbers.* 2 having or showing skill in using the mind; clever: *A good teacher is adroit in asking questions. adj.* —**a droit′ly,** *adv.* —**a droit′ness,** *n.*

ad sorb (ad sôrb′), hold (a gas, liquid, or dissolved substance) spread out on a surface in a thin layer of molecules: *Dyes are adsorbed on fibers of cloth. v.*

ad sorp tion (ad sôrp′shən), an adsorbing; condensation of gases, liquids, or dissolved substances on the surface of solids. *n.*

ad u la tion (aj′ə lā′shən), too much praise; slavish flattery. *n.*

a dult (ə dult′ *or* ad′ult), 1 having full size and strength; fully developed; grown-up; mature: *an adult person.* 2 person who has reached full growth and development; grown-up person. 3 plant or animal grown to full size and development. 4 of, for, or by adults: *adult education, adult behavior.* 1,4 *adj.,* 2,3 *n.*

a dul ter ant (ə dul′tər ənt), substance used to adulterate something. *n.*

a dul te rate (ə dul′tə rāt′), make lower in quality by adding an inferior, impure, or improper substance: *It is against the law to adulterate milk with water. v.,* **a dul te rat ed, a dul te rat ing.**

a dul te ra tion (ə dul′tə rā′shən), 1 an adulterating: *We have laws against the adulteration of coffee and tea.* 2 product that has been adulterated. *n.*

a dul ter er (ə dul′tər ər), person guilty of adultery. *n.*

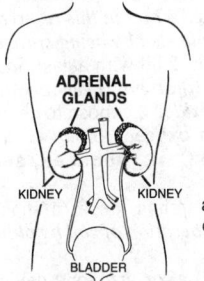

ADRENAL GLANDS

KIDNEY   KIDNEY

BLADDER

adrenal glands of a person

a dul ter ous (ə dul′tər əs), guilty of adultery. *adj.*

a dul ter y (ə dul′tər ē), unfaithfulness of a married man to his wife or of his wife to him. *n., pl.* **a dul ter ies.**

a dult hood (ə dult′hůd), condition of being an adult. *n.*

adv., 1 adverb. 2 advertisement.

ad vance (ad vans′), 1 move forward; push forward: *The troops advanced. The general advanced the troops.* 2 movement forward; progress: *The army's advance was very slow. We have made great advances in airplane design.* 3 ahead of time: *The teacher gave advance notice of the change of the date of our test.* 4 help forward; further: *The President's speech advanced the cause of peace.* 5 put forward; suggest: *What plan to win the game can you advance?* 6 raise to a higher rank; promote: *The colonel advanced him from lieutenant to captain. He advanced from vice-president to president of the company.* 7 raise (prices); increase: *The grocer advanced the price of milk by two cents. Milk advanced two cents a quart.* 8 a rise in price or value: *There was an advance of two cents a quart in the price of milk.* 9 pay (money) before it is due or as a loan: *The company advanced the salesman funds for expenses.* 10 money paid before it is due or as a loan: *May I have an advance on next week's allowance?* 11 **advances,** *pl.* attempts or offers to another or others to settle a difference, to make an acquaintance, etc.: *She made the first advances toward making up her quarrel with me.* 1,4-7,9 *v.,* **ad vanced, ad vanc ing;** 2,8,10,11 *n.,* 3 *adj.*

in advance, 1 in front; ahead: *The leader of the band marched in advance.* 2 ahead of time: *I paid for my ticket in advance.*

ad vanced (ad vanst′), 1 in front of others; forward: *Our army is in an advanced position.* 2 ahead of most others in progress, ideas, etc.: *an advanced class in science, an advanced aircraft design.* 3 far along in life; very old: *Her grandmother lived to the advanced age of ninety years. adj.*

ad vance ment (ad vans′mənt), 1 advance; improvement: *Loyalty and hard*

hat, āge, fär; let, ēqual, tėrm;
it, īce; hot, ōpen, ôrder;
oil, out; cup, pùt, rüle; ch, child;
ng, long; sh, she; th, thin;
ŦH, then; zh, measure;

ə represents *a* in about,
e in taken, *i* in pencil,
o in lemon, *u* in circus.

work brought him an advancement in pay. 2 promotion: *Good work won her advancement to a higher position. n.*

ad van tage (ad van′tij), anything that is in one's favor, or is a benefit; a help in getting something desired: *Good health is always a great advantage. n.*

take advantage of, 1 use to help or benefit oneself: *take advantage of a beautiful day by working in the garden.* 2 use unfairly; impose upon: *Don't take advantage of me by asking me to run errands on such a hot day.*

to advantage, to a good effect; with a useful effect; favorably: *That frame sets off the painting to advantage.*

to one's advantage, to one's benefit or help: *It will be to your advantage to study Spanish before you visit Mexico.*

ad van ta geous (ad′vən tā′jəs), giving advantage; favorable; helpful: *From our advantageous position we were able to see the whole valley. adj.* —**ad′van ta′geous ly,** *adv.* —**ad′van ta′geous ness,** *n.*

ad vent (ad′vent), 1 a coming or arrival, especially of someone or something infrequent or unusually important. 2 **Advent, a** the season of devotion including the four Sundays before Christmas. **b** the coming of Christ into the world. *n.*

ad ven ti tious (ad′ven tish′əs), coming from outside; additional; accidental: *The romantic life of the artist gives his painting an adventitious interest. adj.*

ad ven ture (ad ven′chər), 1 an unusual or exciting experience: *The trip to Alaska was quite an adventure for her.* 2 a bold and difficult undertaking, usually exciting and somewhat dangerous: *Sailing across the Pacific on a raft was a daring adventure.* 3 readiness to take part in exciting or dangerous undertakings: *An explorer must have a spirit of adventure.* 4 dare to do; risk. 1-3 *n.,* 4 *v.,* **ad ven tured, ad ven tur ing.**

ad ven tur er (ad ven′chər ər), 1 person who has or seeks adventures. 2 person who schemes for money or social position. *n.*

ad ven ture some (ad ven′chər səm),

adj. adjective	*n.* noun
adv. adverb	*prep.* preposition
conj. conjunction	*pron.* pronoun
interj. interjection	*v.* verb
sing. singular	*pl.* plural

bold and daring; adventurous. *adj.*

ad ven tur ess (ad ven/chər is), woman who schemes for money or social position. *n., pl.* **ad ven tur ess es.**

ad ven tur ous (ad ven/chər əs), 1 fond of adventures; ready to take risks; daring: *Magellan was a bold, adventurous explorer.* 2 full of risk; dangerous: *An expedition to the North Pole is an adventurous undertaking.* adj. —**ad ven/tur ous ly,** *adv.* —**ad ven/tur ous ness,** *n.*

ad verb (ad/verb/), one of a class of words that extend or limit the meaning of verbs (She sings *well*) but are also used to qualify adjectives (She is *very* pretty) or other adverbs (She sings *quite* well), usually to express time, place, manner, degree, or circumstance. Words like *soon, here, very, gladly,* and *not* are adverbs. Most adverbs are made up of adjectives or participles plus the ending *-ly,* like *badly* in "He rowed badly" and *deservedly* in "She was deservedly popular." *n.*

ad ver bi al (ad ver/bē əl), 1 used as an adverb. In the sentence, "He worked as quickly as possible," *as quickly as possible* is an adverbial phrase. 2 of an adverb; forming adverbs: *"-ly" is an adverbial suffix. adj.* —**ad ver/bi al ly,** *adv.*

ad ver sar y (ad/vər ser/ē), 1 person or group opposing or hostile to another person or group; enemy: *The United States and Japan were adversaries in World War II.* 2 person or group on the other side in a game or contest; opponent: *Which school is our adversary in this week's football game? n., pl.* **ad ver sar ies.**

ad verse (ad/vers/ *or* ad vers/), 1 unfriendly in purpose; hostile: *Adverse criticism discouraged me.* 2 acting against one's interests; unfavorable; harmful: *Dirt and disease are adverse to the best growth of children.* 3 coming from or acting in a contrary direction; opposing: *Adverse winds hinder planes. adj.* —**ad/verse/ly,** *adv.* —**ad/verse/ness.** *n.*

ad ver si ty (ad ver/sə tē), 1 condition of unhappiness, misfortune, or distress. 2 stroke of misfortune; unfavorable or harmful thing or event. *n., pl.* **ad ver si ties.**

ad vert (ad vert/), refer to in speaking or writing; direct attention: *The speaker adverted to the need for more parks. v.*

ad ver tise (ad/vər tīz), 1 give public notice of in a newspaper, on the radio or television, etc.: *When people lose something valuable, they advertise it in the newspaper.* 2 ask for by public notice: *He advertised for a job.* 3 praise the good qualities of (something) in order to create a demand or promote sales: *Manufacturers advertise products that they wish to sell.* 4 seek to sell goods, etc., by advertising: *It pays to advertise. v.,* **ad ver tised, ad ver tis ing.**

ad ver tise ment (ad/vər tīz/mənt *or* ad ver/tis mənt), a public notice or announcement recommending some product or service, or informing of some need: *The furniture store has an advertisement in the newspaper of a special sale. n.*

ad ver tis er (ad/vər tī/zər), person, organization, or business firm that advertises. *n.*

ad ver tis ing (ad/vər tī/zing), 1 business of preparing, publishing, or circulating advertisements. 2 advertisements: *Billboards carry advertising.* 3 a bringing to public notice by radio or television announcements, published notices, posters, or other means: *The store attracted many customers by advertising. n.*

ad vice (ad vīs/), 1 opinion about what should be done; counsel; suggestion: *To keep well, follow the doctor's advice.* 2 Often, **advices,** *pl.* information; news: *Advices from the battlefront were incomplete. n.*

ad vis a bil i ty (ad vī/zə bil/ə tē), a being advisable; fitness: *I asked about the advisability of buying a used car. n.*

ad vis a ble (ad vī/zə bəl), to be advised or recommended; wise; sensible; suitable: *It is not advisable for you to go to school while you are still sick. adj.*

ad vis a bly (ad vī/zə blē), wisely; sensibly. *adv.*

ad vise (ad vīz/), 1 give advice to; offer an opinion to; counsel: *Advise him to be cautious. I shall act as you advise.* 2 give notice; inform: *We were advised of the dangers before we began our trip.* 3 talk over plans; consult: *Before buying a house, they advised with friends who own houses. v.,* **ad vised, ad vis ing.**

ad vis ed ly (ad vī/zid lē), after careful consideration; deliberately. *adv.*

ad vise ment (ad vīz/mənt), careful consideration: *The lawyer took our case under advisement and said she would give us an answer in two weeks. n.*

ad vis er *or* **ad vi sor** (ad vī/zər), 1 person who gives advice. 2 teacher appointed to advise students. *n.*

ad vi sor y (ad vī/zər ē), 1 having power to advise: *an advisory committee.* 2 containing an advice: *an advisory opinion.* 3 bulletin or report to advise of developments: *An advisory by the Weather Bureau warned of a hurricane.* 1,2 *adj.,* 3 *n., pl.* **ad vi sor ies.**

ad vo ca cy (ad/və kə sē), a speaking in favor; public recommendation; support: *The senator's advocacy of the plan won votes for it. n.*

ad vo cate (ad/və kāt *for 1;* ad/və kit *or* ad/və kāt *for 2,3),* 1 speak or write in favor of; recommend publicly; support: *He advocates building more good roads.* 2 person who pleads or argues for; supporter: *She is an advocate of better school buildings.* 3 lawyer who pleads in a court of law. 1 *v.,* **ad vo cat ed, ad vo cat ing;** 2,3 *n.*

adz
man using an adz
to shape and smooth
a log

adz *or* **adze** (adz), a cutting tool for shaping heavy timbers. It is somewhat like an ax but with a blade set across the end of the handle and curving inward. *n., pl.* **adz es.**

AEC, Atomic Energy Commission.

Ae ge an Sea (i jē/ən), sea between Greece and Turkey. It is an arm of the Mediterranean. See **Adriatic Sea** for map.

ae gis (ē/jis), protecting influence or care; sponsorship: *The conference on world health was held under the aegis of the United Nations. n.* Also, **egis.**

Ae ne as (i nē/əs), (in Greek and Roman legends) a Trojan hero who after the fall of Troy and years of wandering reached Italy, where his descendants supposedly founded Rome. *n.*

Ae ne id (i nē/id), a long poem by Vergil telling the story of the wanderings of Aeneas. *n.*

Ae o lus (ē/ə ləs), (in Greek myths) the god of the winds. *n.*

ae on (ē/ən *or* ē/on), eon. *n.*

aer ate (er/āt *or* ar/āt), 1 expose to and mix with air: *Water in this reservoir is aerated and purified by being sprayed high into the air.* 2 fill with a gas: *Soda water is water that has been aerated with carbon dioxide.* 3 expose to chemical action with oxygen: *Blood is aerated in the lungs. v.,* **aer at ed, aer at ing.**

aer a tion (er/ā/shən *or* ar/ā/shən), an aerating: *the aeration of soil by plowing. n.*

aer a tor (er/ā tər *or* ar/ā tər), device

or apparatus that charges or supplies with air. *n.*

aer i al (er′ē əl *or* ar′ē əl), **1** a long wire or set of wires or rods used in television or radio for sending out or receiving electromagnetic waves; antenna. **2** having to do with or done by aircraft: *aerial photography, aerial warfare.* **3** growing in air instead of in soil: *The banyan tree has aerial roots.* **4** of or having to do with the air; atmospheric: *aerial currents.* **5** like air; as thin and light as air; airy: *dancing with aerial grace.* **1** *n.,* **2-5** *adj.* —**aer′i al ly,** *adv.*

aer i al ist (er′ē ə list *or* ar′ē ə list), acrobat who performs feats on a trapeze, tightrope, etc. *n.*

aer ie (er′ē, ar′ē, *or* ir′ē), the lofty nest of an eagle, hawk, or other bird of prey. *n.* Also, **eyrie** or **eyry.**

aer o dy nam ics (er′ō dī nam′iks *or* ar′ō dī nam′iks), branch of physics that deals with the forces exerted by air or other gases in motion on both flying and wind-blown bodies. *n.*

aer o nau tic (er′ə nô′tik *or* ar′ə-nô′tik), aeronautical. *adj.*

aer o nau ti cal (er′ə nô′tə kəl *or* ar′ə nô′tə kəl), of or having to do with aeronautics. *adj.* —**aer′o nau′ti cal ly,** *adv.*

aer o nau tics (er′ə nô′tiks *or* ar′ə-nô′tiks), science or art having to do with the design, manufacture, and operation of aircraft. *n.*

aer o plane (er′ə plān *or* ar′ə plān), airplane. *n.*

aer o sol (er′ə sol *or* ar′ə sol), very fine particles of a solid or liquid substance suspended in the air or in some other gas. Smoke and fog are common aerosols. *n.*

aerosol bomb, container from which an insecticide, paint, cosmetic, etc., can be released as a spray or mist.

aer o space (er′ō spās *or* ar′ō spās), the earth's atmosphere and the space beyond it, especially the space in which rockets, satellites, and other spacecraft operate. *n.*

Ae sop (ē′səp *or* ē′sop), Greek writer of fables who lived about 600 B.C. *n.*

aes thet ic (es thet′ik), **1** having to do with the beautiful, as distinguished from the useful, scientific, etc. **2** having an appreciation of beauty in nature or art: *an aesthetic person.* **3** showing good taste; artistic: *an aesthetic wallpaper. adj.* Also, **esthetic.**

aes thet i cal ly (es thet′ik lē), in an aesthetic manner. *adv.* Also, **esthetically.**

ae ther (ē′thər), ether (defs. 2 and 3). *n.*

ae ther e al (i thir′ē əl), ethereal. *adj.*

Aet na (et′nə), **Mount.** See **Etna.** *n.*

a far (ə fär′), at a great distance; far away: *a place afar off. adv.*

from afar, from a distance: *I saw him from afar.*

a feard or **a feared** (ə fird′), OLD USE. frightened; afraid. *adj.*

af fa bil i ty (af′ə bil′ə tē), quality that makes a person easy to talk to; courteous and pleasant ways. *n.*

af fa ble (af′ə bəl), easy to talk to; courteous and pleasant: *Our principal is very affable. adj.*

af fa bly (af′ə blē), in an affable manner; courteously. *adv.*

af fair (ə fer′ *or* ə far′), **1** thing to do; matter of business; job; task: *Such a large project is a time-consuming affair.* **2** any thing or matter or happening: *The party was a jolly affair. n.*

af fect[1] (ə fekt′), **1** produce a result on; have an effect on; influence: *The small amount of rain last year affected the growth of crops. Overwork has affected his health so that he must rest.* **2** touch the heart of; stir the feelings of: *The stories of starving children so affected him that he gave all his spare money to their aid. v.* [from Latin *affectum* acted on]

af fect[2] (ə fekt′), **1** pretend to have or feel: *He affected ignorance of the fight, but we knew that he had seen it.* **2** use because one prefers to; choose: *affect carelessness in dress. v.* [from French of the 1400's *affecter* strive for]

af fec ta tion (af′ek tā′shən), an artificial way of talking or acting put on to impress others; pretense: *Her roughness is an affectation; she really is a quiet, gentle girl. n.*

af fect ed[1] (ə fek′tid), **1** acted upon; influenced. **2** influenced injuriously: *She froze her feet and the affected toes were numb.* **3** moved in feeling; stirred up. *adj.* [*affect*[1] + *-ed*]

af fect ed[2] (ə fek′tid), put on for effect; not natural; artificial: *an affected tone of voice, an affected welcome. adj.* [*affect*[2] + *-ed*] —**af fect′ed ly,** *adv.* —**af fect′ed ness,** *n.*

af fect ing (ə fek′ting), touching the heart; moving the feelings: *The refugee told an affecting story of hunger and suffering. adj.* —**af fect′ing ly,** *adv.*

af fec tion (ə fek′shən), **1** friendly feeling; tenderness; love: *the affection of parents for their children.* **2** an unhealthy condition; disease: *He is suffering from an affection of the ear. n.*

af fec tion ate (ə fek′shə nit), showing or having affection; loving and tender: *an affectionate letter, an affectionate farewell. adj.* —**af fec′tion ate ly,** *adv.*

af fer ent (af′ər ənt), carrying inward to a central organ or point: *afferent nerves, afferent blood vessels. adj.*

hat, āge, fär; let, ēqual, tėrm;
it, īce; hot, ōpen, ôrder;
oil, out; cup, pùt, rüle; ch, child;
ng, long; sh, she; th, thin;
ŦH, then; zh, measure;

ə represents *a* in about,
e in taken, *i* in pencil,
o in lemon, *u* in circus.

af fi ance (ə fī′əns), promise in marriage; engage; betroth: *James and Beth are affianced to each other. v.,* **af fi anced, af fi anc ing.**

af fi da vit (af′ə dā′vit), statement written down and sworn to be true. An affidavit is usually made before a judge or notary public. *n.*

af fil i ate (ə fil′ē āt *for 1;* ə fil′ē it *or* ə fil′ē āt *for 2),* **1** join in close association; connect: *Though the two clubs did not have the same members, they were affiliated with each other.* **2** organization or group associated with another or larger organization or group: *Our local automobile club is an affiliate of the national automobile club.* **1** *v.,* **af fil i at ed, af fil i at ing;** **2** *n.*

af fil i a tion (ə fil′ē ā′shən), association; connection: *Our hospital has an affiliation with the medical school of the university. n.*

af fin i ty (ə fin′ə tē), **1** a natural attraction to a person or liking for a thing: *She has an affinity for science.* **2** relationship; connection: *There is an affinity between Swedes and Norwegians. n., pl.* **af fin i ties.**

af firm (ə ferm′), **1** declare to be true; say firmly; assert: *The prisoner affirmed his innocence.* **2** confirm; ratify: *The higher court affirmed the lower court's decision. v.*

af fir ma tion (af′ər mā′shən), positive statement; assertion. *n.*

af firm a tive (ə fer′mə tiv), **1** stating that a fact is so; saying yes: *The principal's answer to my question was affirmative.* **2** word or statement that says yes or agrees: *"I will" is an affirmative.*

Afferent nerves carry a stimulus, such as a burn, from nerves in the skin to the spinal cord. Efferent nerves carry impulses back to muscles which jerk the part away from the heat.

adj. adjective	*n.* noun
adv. adverb	*prep.* preposition
conj. conjunction	*pron.* pronoun
interj. interjection	*v.* verb
sing. singular	*pl.* plural

3 the side arguing in favor of a question being debated: *The affirmative presented a strong argument, but the negative won the debate.* 1 *adj.,* 2,3 *n.*
—af firm′a tive ly, *adv.*

in the affirmative, expressing agreement by saying yes: *The principal replied in the affirmative when we requested that we have an afternoon off for a class picnic.*

af fix (ə fiks′ *for* 1,2; af′iks *for* 3), 1 stick on; fasten to; attach: *She affixed an airmail stamp to her letter.* 2 add at the end: *The President affixed his signature to the bill.* 3 a sound or group of sounds added to a word to change its meaning or use. Affixes are either prefixes like *un-* and *re-* or suffixes like *-ly, -ness, -s,* or *-ed.* 1,2 *v.,* 3 *n., pl.* **af fix es.**

af flict (ə flikt′), cause pain to; trouble greatly; distress: *My grandfather is afflicted with arthritis.* *v.*

af flic tion (ə flik′shən), 1 state of pain, trouble, or distress; misery: *the affliction of war.* 2 a cause of pain, trouble, or distress; misfortune: *His blindness is an affliction.* *n.*

af flu ence (af′lü əns), 1 wealth; riches: *The United States is a country of great affluence.* 2 an abundant supply; great abundance: *We have had an affluence of rain this month.* *n.*

af flu ent (af′lü ənt), 1 having wealth; rich. 2 abundant; plentiful. 3 stream flowing into a larger stream or body of water; tributary. 1,2 *adj.,* 3 *n.* **—af′flu ent ly,** *adv.*

af ford (ə fôrd′), 1 spare the money for: *Can we afford a new car?* 2 manage to give, spare, or have: *A busy man cannot afford delay. He cannot afford to waste so much time.* 3 be able without difficulty or harm: *I can't afford to take the chance.* 4 give as an effect or a result; provide; yield: *Our own garden affords fresh vegetables for the family. Reading affords real pleasure.* *v.*

af fray (ə frā′), a noisy quarrel; fight in public; brawl. *n.*

af fright (ə frīt′), OLD USE. excite with sudden fear; frighten. *v.*

af front (ə frunt′), 1 word or act intended to show disrespect; open insult: *To be called a coward is an affront.* 2 insult openly; offend purposely: *The*

boy affronted his teacher by making a face at her. 1 *n.,* 2 *v.*

Af ghan (af′gən), 1 person born or living in Afghanistan. 2 of Afghanistan or its people. 3 **afghan,** blanket or shawl made of knitted or crocheted wool, nylon, etc. 1,3 *n.,* 2 *adj.*

Af ghan i stan (af gan′ə stan), country in SW Asia, between Pakistan and Iran. *Capital:* Kabul. *n.*

a field (ə fēld′), 1 away from home; away: *She wandered far afield in foreign lands.* 2 out of the right way; astray: *We seem to have gone far afield; we are lost.* 3 in or on the field; to the field: *The general decided to put another army afield.* *adv.*

a fire (ə fīr′), 1 on fire; burning. 2 enthusiastic. *adv., adj.*

a flame (ə flām′), 1 in flames; on fire. 2 in a glow; glowing. *adv., adj.*

AFL-CIO, a labor organization formed by the merger in 1955 of the craft unions of the American Federation of Labor (**AFL**) and the industrial unions of the Congress of Industrial Organizations (**CIO**).

a float (ə flōt′), 1 floating on the water or in the air. 2 on shipboard; at sea. 3 flooded. 4 being spread; going around. *adv., adj.*

aft (def. 2)

a flut ter (ə flut′ər), 1 fluttering or waving: *The flags were aflutter in the breeze.* 2 in a flutter; excited: *The town was aflutter at the news.* *adv., adj.*

a foot (ə fût′), 1 on foot; by walking. 2 going on; in progress. *adv., adj.*

a fore (ə fôr′), OLD USE. before. *prep., adv., conj.*

a fore men tioned (ə fôr′men′shənd), spoken of before; mentioned earlier. *adj.*

a fore said (ə fôr′sed′), spoken of before; mentioned earlier. *adj.*

a fore thought (ə fôr′thôt′), thought out beforehand; deliberately planned: *The evil deed was planned with malice aforethought.* *adj.*

a foul (ə foul′), in a tangle; in a collision; entangled: *Raising the sail was*

impossible with the lines afoul. *adj.*
run afoul of, get into trouble with: *He will run afoul of the law if he steals.*

a fraid (ə frād′), 1 feeling fear; frightened: *afraid of the dark.* 2 sorry to have to say: *I'm afraid you are wrong about that.* *adj.*

a fresh (ə fresh′), once more; again: *If you spoil your drawing, start afresh.* *adv.*

Af ri ca (af′rə kə), continent south of Europe. It is the second largest continent. *n.*

Af ri can (af′rə kən), 1 of or having to do with Africa, its peoples, their languages, or their ways of life. 2 Negro. 3 native of Africa, especially a person belonging to one of the native tribes of Africa. 4 a Negro. 1,2 *adj.,* 3,4 *n.*

African violet, a tropical plant with violet, white, or pink flowers, often grown as a house plant.

Af ri kaans (af′rə käns′ *or* af′rə känz′), dialect of Dutch spoken in South Africa; South African Dutch. *n.*

Af ro (af′rō), a bushy hairdo like that worn in parts of Africa. *n.*

Af ro-A mer i can (af′rō ə mer′ə kən), 1 of or having to do with American Negroes. 2 an American Negro. 1 *adj.,* 2 *n.*

aft (aft), 1 at the stern; toward the stern; abaft. 2 in or near the stern. 1 *adv.,* 2 *adj.*

af ter (af′tər), 1 later in time than: *After dinner we can go.* 2 following; I ran so hard I panted for five minutes after (*adv.*). *In after years she did not come to see us so often (adj.). Day after day I hoped to get a letter from my friend (prep.).* 3 later than the time that: *After he goes, we shall eat.* 4 behind: *The soldiers marched in line one after another (prep.). Jill came tumbling after (adv.).* 5 in search of; in pursuit of: *The dog ran after the rabbit.* 6 about; concerning: *Your aunt asked after you.* 7 because of; as a result of: *After such a big dinner, I couldn't finish my dessert.* 8 in spite of: *After all her suffering she is still cheerful.* 9 in imitation of; imitating: *He wrote a fable after the manner of Aesop.* 10 nearer or toward the stern of a ship: *the after sails.* 1,2,4-9 *prep.,* 2,4 *adv.,* 2,10 *adj.,* 3 *conj.*

af ter deck (af′tər dek′), part of a

16

deck at or near the stern of a ship. *n.*

af ter ef fect (af′tər i fekt′), 1 result or effect that follows later: *The aftereffect of the explosion was a great fire.* 2 secondary effect of a drug or disease. *n.*

af ter glow (af′tər glō′), 1 glow remaining after something bright has gone. 2 glow in the sky after sunset. 3 a pleasurable feeling following something greatly enjoyed. *n.*

af ter life (af′tər līf′), life after death. *n.*

af ter math (af′tər math), a result or consequence: *The aftermath of war is hunger and disease. n.*

af ter noon (af′tər nün′), the part of the day between noon and evening. *n.*

af ter thought (af′tər thôt′), 1 thought that comes too late to be used. 2 a second or later thought or explanation. *n.*

af ter ward (af′tər wərd), afterwards; later. *adv.*

af ter wards (af′tər wərdz), later: *The bud was small at first, but afterwards it became a large flower. adv.*

a gain (ə gen′), 1 another time; once more: *Come again to play. Say that again.* 2 on the other hand; yet: *It may rain, and again it may not.* 3 moreover; besides: *Again, I must say that you are wrong. adv.*

again and again, many times over; often: *I telephoned again and again before I finally reached them.*

as much again, as much as has already been spent, accounted for, etc.: *It will cost you not only all you have spent but also as much again to do the job right.*

a gainst (ə genst′), 1 in opposition to: *Our team will debate against yours. It is against the rules of the game.* 2 in the opposite direction to, so as to meet; upon or toward: *We will sail against the wind. Rain beats against the window.* 3 in contact with: *The ladder is leaning against the wall.* 4 in preparation for: *Squirrels store up nuts against the winter.* 5 so as to defend or protect from: *An umbrella is a protection against rain. prep.*

Ag a mem non (ag′ə mem′non), (in Greek legends) the leader of the Greeks in the Trojan War. He was the husband of Clytemnestra, the brother of Menelaus, and the father of Orestes. *n.*

a gape (ə gāp′), with the mouth wide open in wonder or surprise; gaping. *adj.*

a gar (ä′gər), a jellylike extract obtained from certain seaweeds, used in making cultures for bacteria and fungi. *n.*

Ag as siz (ag′ə sē), **Louis,** 1807-1873, American zoologist and geologist, born in Switzerland. *n.*

ag ate (ag′it), 1 variety of quartz with variously colored stripes or clouded colors. 2 a playing marble that looks like this. *n.*

a ga ve (ə gä′vē), any of a group of American desert plants having a dense cluster of rigid, fleshy leaves with spines along the edges and at the tips. Soap, alcoholic drinks, and rope are made from some kinds of agave. *n.*

age (āj), 1 length of life from birth on: *He has reached the age of fourteen.* 2 length of time that anything has existed: *A species of pine in California is said to have the greatest age of any living thing.* 3 a particular period or stage in life: *old age, middle age.* 4 the latter part of life; old age: *the wisdom of age.* 5 period in history: *the Bronze Age. This is the age of supersonic jets.* **6 ages,** pl. **a** INFORMAL. a long time: *I haven't seen you for ages.* **b** hundreds of years: *the work of ages.* 7 grow old: *to age fast.* 8 make old: *Worry can age you.* 9 bring or come to full growth: *This cheese must be aged for a year. Wine is put in casks to age.* 1-6 *n.,* 7-9 *v.,* **aged, ag ing** or **age ing.**

of age, at the time of life when a person is considered ready for adult rights and responsibilities, either 18 or 21 years old under the varying laws of the states of the United States.

-age, suffix forming nouns from other nouns or from verbs. 1 act of _____ing: *Breakage = act of breaking.* 2 group of _____s: *Baggage = a group of bags.* 3 condition or rank of _____: *Peerage = rank of peers.* 4 cost of or fee for _____ing: *Postage = cost of posting* (mailing). 5 home for _____s: *Orphanage = home for orphans.* [from French before the 1400's *-age,* from Latin *-aticum*]

a ged (ā′jid *for 1;* ājd *for 2,3*), 1 having lived a long time; old: *The aged woman was wrinkled and bent.* 2 having the age of: *She was aged six when she first went to school.* 3 improved by aging: *aged meat, aged cheese. adj.*

age less (āj′lis), never growing old; never coming to an end: *the ageless wisdom of the Bible. adj.*

age long (āj′lông′), lasting a long time; everlasting. *adj.*

a gen cy (ā′jən sē), 1 a person or company that has the authority to act for another: *An agency rented our house for us. Employment agencies help workers to get jobs.* 2 office of such a person or

agate (def. 1) polished, showing stripes

aggrandizement

hat, āge, fär; let, ēqual, tėrm; it, īce; hot, ōpen, ôrder; oil, out; cup, pùt, rüle; ch, child; ng, long; sh, she; th, thin; ŦH, then; zh, measure;

ə represents *a* in about, *e* in taken, *i* in pencil, *o* in lemon, *u* in circus.

company. 3 a special department of the government concerned with the administration of affairs within a specific field: *The agency in charge of intelligence activities in the United States is the Central Intelligence Agency.* 4 means of producing effects; action: *Snow is drifted by the agency of the wind. Through the agency of friends I learned of the job opening. n., pl.* **a gen cies.**

a gen da (ə jen′də), list of things to be dealt with or done: *The agenda for today's club meeting includes reading of committee reports, admission of new members, and planning of the month's activities. n. pl. or sing.*

a gent (ā′jənt), 1 person or company having the authority to act for another: *I made my brother my agent while I was out of the city.* 2 any power or cause that produces an effect by its action: *Yeast is an important agent in causing bread to rise.* 3 means; instrument: *Graphite is used as a lubricating agent.* 4 a law enforcement officer. 5 member of the government secret service. *n.*

age-old (āj′ōld′), having existed for a very long time; very old; ancient: *age-old customs. adj.*

ag glom e ra tion (ə glom′ə rā′shən), mass of things gathered or clustered together: *an agglomeration of stars. n.*

ag glu ti nate (ə glüt′n āt), stick together; join together. *v.,* **ag glu ti nat ed, ag glu ti nat ing.**

ag glu ti na tion (ə glüt′n ā′shən), process of agglutinating, especially the clumping together of bacteria or blood cells caused by the introduction of antibodies to such cells. *n.*

ag glu ti nin (ə glüt′n ən), antibody that causes bacteria to stick together in clumps. *n.*

ag gran dize (ə gran′dīz *or* ag′rən dīz), make greater or larger in power; increase the rank or wealth of: *The dictator sought to aggrandize himself at the expense of his people. v.,* **ag gran dized, ag gran diz ing.**

ag gran dize ment (ə gran′diz mənt), 1 a making greater, larger, or more powerful. 2 an increase in power, rank, or wealth. *n.*

adj.	adjective	*n.*	noun
adv.	adverb	*prep.*	preposition
conj.	conjunction	*pron.*	pronoun
interj.	interjection	*v.*	verb
sing.	singular	*pl.*	plural

ag gra vate (ag′rə vāt), 1 make worse or more severe: *His bad temper was aggravated by his headache.* 2 annoy; irritate; exasperate: *She aggravated me by asking so many questions.* *v.,* **ag gra vat ed, ag gra vat ing.**

ag gra va tion (ag′rə vā′shən), 1 a making worse or more severe. 2 a being made worse or more severe. 3 something that aggravates. *n.*

ag gre gate (ag′rə git *or* ag′rə gāt *for 1,3;* ag′rə gāt *for 2,4*), 1 total amount; sum: *The aggregate of all the gifts was over $100.* 2 amount to; come to; total: *The money collected will aggregate $1000.* 3 mass of separate things joined together: *A lump of sugar is an aggregate of sugar crystals.* 4 gather into one mass or whole; unite: *Granite is made of small particles aggregated together.* 1,3 *n.,* 2,4 *v.,* **ag gre gat ed, ag gre gat ing.**

in the aggregate, taken together; considered as a whole: *The payments on our house amount in the aggregate to a big sum of money.*

ag gre ga tion (ag′rə gā′shən), 1 the collecting of separate things into one mass or whole. 2 the group or mass collected. *n.*

ag gres sion (ə gresh′ən), 1 the first step in an attack or a quarrel; unprovoked attack: *A country that sends its army to occupy another country is guilty of aggression.* 2 practice of making assaults or attacks on the rights or territory of others as a method or policy. *n.*

ag gres sive (ə gres′iv), 1 taking the first step in an attack or a quarrel; ready to attack others: *a warlike and aggressive nation.* 2 very active; energetic: *The police are making an aggressive campaign against driving too fast.* 3 too confident and certain; assertive: *An aggressive manner can be irritating to others.* *adj.* —**ag gres′sive ly,** *adv.* —**ag gres′sive ness,** *n.*

ag gres sor (ə gres′ər), one that begins an attack or a quarrel, especially a nation that starts a war. *n.*

ag grieved (ə grēvd′), 1 feeling injured or wronged: *to make amends to an aggrieved person.* 2 feeling troubled or distressed: *I was aggrieved at having lost their friendship.* *adj.*

a ghast (ə gast′), struck with surprise or horror; filled with terror: *I was aghast when I saw the destruction caused by the earthquake.* *adj.*

ag ile (aj′əl), 1 moving quickly and easily; nimble: *as agile as a cat.* 2 quick in thinking; alert: *You need an agile mind to solve puzzles.* *adj.* —**ag′ile ly,** *adv.*

a gil i ty (ə jil′ə tē), 1 ability to move quickly and easily; nimbleness: *He has the agility of a monkey.* 2 alertness: *He solved the complex problem with astounding agility.* *n.*

ag i tate (aj′ə tāt), 1 move or shake violently: *The slightest wind will agitate the leaves of some trees.* 2 disturb or excite very much: *She was agitated by the unexpected news of her friend's illness.* 3 argue about or discuss a matter vigorously to arouse public interest and feeling: *agitate for a shorter working day, agitate the question of gun control.* *v.,* **ag i tat ed, ag i tat ing.**

ag i ta tion (aj′ə tā′shən), 1 a moving or shaking violently to and fro: *The agitation of the sea almost turned over the little boat.* 2 a disturbed, upset, or troubled state: *Because of her agitation over the unexpected news of her friend's illness, she could not sleep.* 3 argument or discussion to arouse public interest and feeling: *There was much agitation for and against slavery before the Civil War.* *n.*

ag i ta tor (aj′ə tā′tər), 1 person who stirs up public feeling for or against something. 2 device or machine for shaking or stirring. *n.*

a gleam (ə glēm′), gleaming. *adj.*

a glit ter (ə glit′ər), glittering. *adj.*

a glow (ə glō′), glowing: *The baby's cheeks were aglow with health.* *adj.*

Ag new (ag′nü *or* ag′nyü), **Spiro T(heodore),** born 1918, vice-president of the United States from 1969 to 1973. *n.*

ag nos tic (ag nos′tik), person who believes that nothing is known or can be known about the existence of God. *n.*

a go (ə gō′), 1 gone by; past: *I met her two years ago.* 2 in the past: *He lived here long ago.* 1 *adj.,* 2 *adv.*

a gog (ə gog′), full of expectation or excitement; eager: *The children were all agog to see their presents.* *adj.*

ag o niz ing (ag′ə nī′zing), causing very great suffering. *adj.* —**ag′o niz′ing ly,** *adv.*

ag o ny (ag′ə nē), 1 very painful suffering; very great anguish: *the agony of a severe toothache. The loss of their child filled them with agony.* 2 the last struggle before death. *n., pl.* **ag o nies.**

a grar i an (ə grer′ē ən), 1 having to do with farming land, its use, or its ownership: *Most old countries had*

agrarian disputes between tenants and landlords. 2 for the support and advancement of farmers or farming: *an agrarian movement. adj.*

a gree (ə grē′), 1 have the same feeling or opinion: *We all agree in liking the teacher. I agree that we should try to be more careful.* 2 be in harmony; correspond: *All accounts of the accident seem to agree.* 3 get along well together: *Brothers and sisters don't always agree as well as they should.* 4 say that one is willing; consent: *He agreed to go with us.* 5 come to an understanding, especially in settling a dispute: *The workers and employers agreed on the terms for settling the strike.* 6 say (something) is real or true; admit: *We agreed that we had been careless.* 7 (in grammar) have the same number, case, gender, or person. In the sentences "The man is going," "The men are going," the subjects and the verbs agree in person and number. *v.,* **a greed, a gree ing.**

agree with, have a good effect on; suit: *This food does not agree with me; it makes me sick.*

a gree a ble (ə grē′ə bəl), 1 giving pleasure; pleasing: *The boy had an agreeable manner.* 2 ready to agree; willing: *If you are agreeable to our suggestion, we can see the show together this afternoon.* *adj.*

a gree a bly (ə grē′ə blē), in an agreeable manner; pleasingly. *adv.*

a gree ment (ə grē′mənt), 1 an understanding reached by two or more persons, groups of persons, or nations among themselves. Nations make treaties and individuals make contracts; both are agreements. 2 a coming to an understanding, especially in settling a dispute: *Every obstacle to agreement has been removed.* 3 harmony in feeling or opinion: *There was perfect agreement between the two friends.* 4 (in grammar) correspondence of words in number, case, gender, or person. There is agreement in "that man" but lack of agreement in "those man." *n.*

ag ri cul tur al (ag′rə kul′chər əl), having to do with farming; of agriculture: *The Middle West is an important agricultural region. adj.* —**ag′ri cul′tur al ly,** *adv.*

ag ri cul tur al ist (ag′rə kul′chər ə list), agriculturist. *n.*

ag ri cul ture (ag′rə kul′chər), science or art of cultivating the soil, including the production of crops and the raising of livestock; farming. *n.*

ag ri cul tur ist (ag′rə kul′chər ist), 1 farmer. 2 an expert in farming. *n.*

a ground (ə ground′), stranded on the shore or on the bottom in shallow water: *The ship ran aground and stuck* in the sand (adv.). It is still aground (adj.). adv., adj.

a gue (ā′gyü), 1 a malarial fever with alternating chills and sweating at regular intervals. 2 any fit of shaking or shivering; a chill. n.

ah (ä), exclamation of pain, sorrow, regret, pity, admiration, surprise, joy, dislike, contempt, etc. interj.

a ha (ä hä′), exclamation of triumph, satisfaction, surprise, joy, etc. interj.

A hab (ā′hab), king of Israel from about 873 to 853 B.C., who was led to the worship of idols by his wife Jezebel. n.

a head (ə hed′), 1 in front; before: Walk ahead of me. Breakers ahead! 2 forward; onward: Go ahead with this work for another week. 3 in advance; earlier: Columbus was ahead of his time in his belief that the world was round. adv.

be ahead, 1 be winning: Our team is ahead by 6 points. 2 have more than is needed: We're ahead $10 on the budget.

get ahead, succeed: I worked hard at my job in the hope that I would get ahead.

get ahead of, do or be better than; surpass: If she works hard she will get ahead of her sister in arithmetic.

a hem (ə hem′), a sound made by coughing or clearing the throat, sometimes used to attract attention, express doubt, or gain time. interj.

a hoy (ə hoi′), call used by sailors to attract the attention of persons at a distance: The sailors in the lifeboat shouted "Ship ahoy!" to the passing freighter. interj.

aid (ād), 1 give support to; help: The Red Cross aids flood victims. 2 a help; assistance: When my arm was broken, I could not dress without aid. 3 person or thing that helps; helper: She was a nurse's aid for a time. A dishwasher is an aid to housework. 1 v., 2,3 n.

aide (ād), 1 helper; assistant. 2 aide-de-camp.

aide-de-camp (ād′də kamp′), a military officer who acts as an assistant to a superior officer by taking and sending messages and acting as a secretary. n., pl. **aides-de-camp.**

aigrette

ai grette (ā′gret or ā gret′), tuft of feathers worn as an ornament on the head, on a helmet, etc.; egret. n.

ail (āl), 1 be the matter with; trouble: What ails the child? 2 be ill; feel sick: Our cat is ailing again. v.

ai le ron (ā′lə ron′), a hinged, movable part on the rear edge of an airplane wing, used for banking or balancing the airplane. n.

AILERON

WING

aileron in a raised position

ail ment (āl′mənt), disorder of the body or mind; illness: His ailment was only a headache. n.

aim (ām), 1 point or direct (a gun, blow, etc.) in order to hit a target: The hunter aimed at the lion but missed. 2 act of pointing or directing at something: Take careful aim. 3 ability to point or direct (a gun, blow, etc.): The hunter's aim was so poor that he missed the lion. 4 direct (words or acts) at someone or something: The coach aimed his talk at the boys who had not played fair. 5 direct one's efforts; try: She aimed to please her friends. 6 have in mind as a purpose; intend: I aim to go. 7 purpose; intention: Her aim was to do two years' work in time. 1,4-6 v., 2,3,7 n.

aim less (ām′lis), without purpose; pointless. adj. —**aim′less ly,** adv. —**aim′less ness,** n.

ain't (ānt), 1 am not; is not. 2 are not. 3 have not; has not. Careful speakers and writers do not use ain't.

Ai nu (ī′nü), member of an aboriginal, light-skinned people in northern Japan. n., pl. **Ai nu** or **Ai nus.**

air (er or ar), 1 the mixture of gases that surrounds the earth; atmosphere. Air consists chiefly of nitrogen and oxygen, along with argon, carbon dioxide, hydrogen, and small quantities of neon, helium, and other inert gases. We breathe air. 2 space overhead; sky: Birds fly in the air. 3 put out in the air: It is good to air your clothes often. 4 fresh air: He opened the window to let some air into the overheated room. 5 let fresh air in: Open the windows and air the room. 6 make known: Don't air your troubles too often. 7 a simple melody or tune: an old Scottish air. 8 general character or appearance of a person or thing: The president had an air of importance. An air of mystery surrounds the deserted house. 9 **airs,** pl. unnatural or showy manners: Your friends will laugh if you put on airs. 10 medium through which radio waves travel; airways: to fill the air with advertising. 11 of or having to do with avia-

hat, āge, fär; let, ēqual, tèrm;
it, īce; hot, ōpen, ôrder;
oil, out; cup, pùt, rüle; ch, child;
ng, long; sh, she; th, thin;
ᴛн, then; zh, measure;

ə represents a in about,
e in taken, i in pencil,
o in lemon, u in circus.

tion or aircraft: air safety. 1,2,4,7-10 n., 3,5,6 v., 11 adj.

in the air, 1 being spread; going around: Wild reports of revolt were in the air. 2 uncertain or unsettled: Plans for the picnic are still in the air.

off the air, 1 not engaged in broadcasting: This station is off the air from midnight to six in the morning. 2 not being broadcast: We used to watch that show, but it's off the air now.

on the air, 1 engaged in broadcasting: This station has been on the air since 1958. 2 being broadcast: Is that show still on the air?

up in the air, uncertain or unsettled: Plans for the picnic are still up in the air.

walk on air, be very gay or pleased: We were walking on air when everything worked out as we had planned.

air base, headquarters and airfield for military aircraft.

air borne (er′bôrn′ or ar′bôrn′), 1 supported by the air; off the ground: Within fifteen minutes the plane will be airborne. 2 carried in aircraft: airborne troops. 3 carried by air: airborne dust, airborne pollen. adj.

air brake, brake operated by forcing compressed air against a piston.

air cell, a tiny cavity for air in an organism. The air sacs of a bird are air cells.

air-con di tion (er′kən dish′ən or ar′kən dish′ən), 1 supply (a building, room, car, etc.) with air conditioning. 2 treat air by means of air conditioning. v.

air-con di tioned (er′kən dish′ənd or ar′kən dish′ənd), having air conditioning. adj.

air conditioner, equipment used to air-condition a building, room, car, etc.

air conditioning, means of treating and circulating air in a building, room, car, etc., to regulate its temperature and amount of moisture and to free it from dust.

air-cool (er′kül′ or ar′kül), 1 remove heat from (an internal-combustion engine) by forcing air on or around the cylinders. 2 remove heat from (a room) by blowing cool air in. v.

adj.	adjective	*n.*	noun
adv.	adverb	*prep.*	preposition
conj.	conjunction	*pron.*	pronoun
interj.	interjection	*v.*	verb
sing.	singular	*pl.*	plural

air craft (er′kraft′ *or* ar′kraft′), machine for flying in the air that is supported in flight by buoyancy (such as a balloon) or by the action of air (such as an airplane). Airplanes, airships, helicopters, and balloons are aircraft. *n., pl.* **air craft.**

aircraft carrier, warship designed as a base for aircraft, with a large, flat deck on which to land or take off.

air drome (er′drōm′ *or* ar′drōm′), airport. *n.*

air drop (er′drop′ *or* ar′drop′), a delivering of food, supplies, or persons by parachute from aircraft in flight. *n.*

Airedale
about 23 in. high
at the shoulder

Aire dale (er′dāl *or* ar′dāl), a large terrier having a wiry brown or tan coat with dark markings. *n.*

air field (er′fēld′ *or* ar′fēld′), the landing area of an airport or air base. *n.*

air flow (er′flō′ *or* ar′flō′), 1 a natural movement of air. 2 the flow of air around and relative to an object moving in air. 3 streamlined: *airflow* design. 4 that is produced by air currents: *airflow patterns around cumulus clouds.* 1,2 *n.,* 3,4 *adj.*

air foil (er′foil′ *or* ar′foil′), a wing, aileron, rudder, or other surface designed to help lift or control an aircraft. *n.*

air force, 1 branch of the military forces that uses aircraft. 2 **Air Force,** branch of the armed forces of the United States that includes aviation personnel, equipment, etc.

air gun, 1 air rifle. 2 device that uses compressed air to force grease, putty, etc., into or onto something.

air i ly (er′ə lē *or* ar′ə lē), in an airy manner. *adv.*

air i ness (er′ē nis *or* ar′ē nis), airy quality. *n.*

air ing (er′ing *or* ar′ing), 1 exposure to air for drying, warming, etc.: *Give the* rug a thorough airing. 2 a walk, ride, or drive outdoors. 3 exposure to public notice or discussion: *The new bill is due for an airing in Congress.* *n.*

air lane, a regular route used by aircraft; airway.

air less (er′lis *or* ar′lis), 1 without fresh air; stuffy. 2 without a breeze; still. *adj.*

air lift (er′lift′ *or* ar′lift′), 1 system of using aircraft to transport passengers and freight to a place when existing land routes are closed or inadequate: *Medical supplies were brought by airlift to the flooded villages.* 2 transport by airlift: *Enough planes were provided to airlift two army divisions.* 1 *n.,* 2 *v.*

air line (er′līn′ *or* ar′līn′), 1 system of transportation of people and freight by aircraft. 2 company owning or operating such a system. 3 route for aircraft; airway. *n.*

air lin er (er′lī′nər *or* ar′lī′nər), a large passenger airplane. *n.*

air lock (er′lok′ *or* ar′lok′), an airtight compartment between places where there is a difference in air pressure. The pressure in an airlock can be raised or lowered. *n.*

air mail (er′māl′ *or* ar′māl′), 1 send by air mail: *Please airmail this letter.* 2 sent or to be sent by aircraft: *an airmail letter.* 1 *v.,* 2 *adj.*

air mail, 1 mail sent by aircraft. 2 system for carrying mail by aircraft.

air man (er′mən *or* ar′mən), 1 pilot of an aircraft; aviator. 2 an enlisted man or woman of the lowest rank in the Air Force. *n., pl.* **air men.**

air mass, a large body of air within the atmosphere that has nearly uniform temperature and humidity at any given level and moves horizontally over great distances without changing.

air mattress, pad that can be inflated to serve as a mattress.

air plane (er′plān′ *or* ar′plān′), aircraft heavier than air, supported in flight by the action of the air flowing past or thrusting upward on its fixed wings and driven by propeller, jet propulsion, etc. Also, **aeroplane.**

air pocket, a downward current of air that causes an aircraft to lose altitude suddenly.

air pollution, the contamination of the air by waste gases from industry, fuel exhaust, and atomic fallout.

air port (er′pôrt′ *or* ar′pôrt′), area, especially on land, used regularly by aircraft to land or take off. An airport usually has buildings for passengers and aircraft and equipment for storing, repairing, and servicing aircraft. *n.*

air pressure, pressure caused by the weight of the air; atmospheric pressure. Winds are caused by the flow of air from an area of high air pressure to an area of low air pressure.

air pump, apparatus for forcing air into or drawing air out of something.

air raid, attack by enemy aircraft, especially by bombers.

air rifle, gun that uses compressed air to shoot a single pellet or dart; air gun.

air sac, an air-filled space in different parts of the body of a bird, connected with the lungs. It aids in breathing and in regulating body temperature.

air ship (er′ship′ *or* ar′ship′), balloon that can be steered; dirigible. An airship is filled with a gas that is lighter than air. *n.*

air sick (er′sik′ *or* ar′sik′), sick as a result of the motion of aircraft. *adj.* —**air′sick′ness,** *n.*

air space (er′spās′ *or* ar′spās′), space in the air over a particular section of the earth: *China protested that her airspace had been violated by our airplanes.* *n.*

air speed, speed of an aircraft in relation to the speed of the air.

airplane with jet engines

air stream (er′strēm′ *or* ar′strēm′), the relative flow of air around or against an object in flight, usually in a direction opposite to that of the object's flight. *n.*

air strip (er′strip′ *or* ar′strip′), a paved or cleared runway, often temporary, on which aircraft land and take off; landing strip. *n.*

air tight (er′tīt′ *or* ar′tīt′), 1 so tight that no air or gas can get in or out. 2 having no weak points open to an opponent's attack: *The team had an airtight defense.* *adj.*

air waves (er′wāvz′ *or* ar′wāvz′), radio or television broadcasting. *n.pl.*

air way (er′wā′ *or* ar′wā′), 1 route for aircraft; air lane; airline. 2 passage for air. 3 **airways,** *pl.* channels for radio or television broadcasting. *n.*

air y (er′ē *or* ar′ē), 1 light as air; graceful: *She sang an airy tune.* 2 lighthearted and gay: *airy laughter.* 3 open to currents of air; breezy: *a large, airy room.* 4 of air; in the air; aerial: *birds and other airy creatures.* 5 like air; not solid or substantial: *Such airy plans won't succeed. adj.,* **air i er, air i est.**

aisle (īl), 1 passage between rows of seats in a hall, theater, school, etc. 2 passage on either side of a church parallel to the nave, often set off by pillars. See **apse** for diagram. 3 any long, narrow passage. *n.*

a jar (ə jär/), slightly open: *Please leave the door ajar. adj.*

A jax (ā/jaks), (in Greek legends) a Greek hero at the siege of Troy, second to Achilles in strength and courage. *n.*

akimbo—
boy with
arms akimbo

a kim bo (ə kim/bō), with the hands on the hips and the elbows bent outward. *adj.*

a kin (ə kin/), 1 of the same kind; similar: *His tastes in music seem akin to mine.* 2 of the same family; related: *Your cousins are akin to you. adj.*

Ak ron (ak/rən), city in NE Ohio. *n.*

-al¹, *suffix added to nouns to form adjectives.* of; like; having the nature of: *Natural = of nature or like nature. Ornamental = having the nature of ornament.* [from Latin *-alem* having to do with]

-al², *suffix added to verbs to form nouns.* act of _____ing: *Refusal = act of refusing.* [from Latin *-alia,* a neuter form of *-alem*]

Ala., Alabama.

Al a bam a (al/ə bam/ə), one of the south central states of the United States. *Capital:* Montgomery. *n.* —**Al/a bam/an, Al/a bam/i an,** *adj., n.*

al a bas ter (al/ə bas/tər), 1 a smooth, white or delicately shaded, translucent stone, a variety of gypsum. Alabaster is often carved into ornaments and vases. 2 smooth and white like alabaster. 1 *n.,* 2 *adj.*

à la carte (ä/ lə kärt/ *or* al/ ə kärt/), with a stated price for each dish (instead of one price for the whole meal). [from French *à la carte* according to the bill of fare]

a lack (ə lak/), OLD USE. alas. *interj.*

a lac ri ty (ə lak/rə tē), brisk and eager action; liveliness: *She began making the arrangements for her trip with alacrity. n.*

A lad din (ə lad/n), a youth in *The Arabian Nights,* who found a magic lamp and a magic ring. By rubbing either one of them he could call either of two powerful spirits to do whatever he asked. *n.*

Al a mo (al/ə mō), a mission building in San Antonio, Texas, used as a fort by a band of Texas rebels fighting for inde-

pendence from Mexico. Besieged by an army of Mexicans, the Texans were overwhelmed and killed on March 6, 1836. *n.*

à la mode or **a la mode** (ä/ lə mōd/ *or* al/ ə mōd/), 1 in style; fashionable. 2 served with ice cream: *pie à la mode.* 3 cooked with vegetables: *beef à la mode.* [from French *à la mode* in the fashion]

a larm (ə lärm/), 1 sudden fear of danger; fright: *The deer darted off in alarm.* 2 fill with sudden fear; frighten: *The breaking of a branch under my foot alarmed the deer.* 3 a warning of approaching danger: *This is no false alarm.* 4 signal giving such a warning: *a fire alarm.* 5 device that makes noise to warn or awaken people: *a burglar alarm.* 6 warn (anyone) of approaching danger: *Alarm everyone quickly; the house is full of smoke.* 7 call to arms or action: *Paul Revere gave the alarm to the towns near Boston.* 1,3-5,7 *n.,* 2,6 *v.*

alarm clock, clock that can be set to ring or sound at any fixed time.

a larm ing (ə lär/ming), causing alarm; frightening. *adj.* —**a larm/ing ly,** *adv.*

a larm ist (ə lär/mist), person who is easily alarmed or alarms others needlessly or on very slight grounds. *n.*

a lar um (ə lar/əm *or* ə lär/əm), OLD USE. alarm. *n.*

a las (ə las/), exclamation of sorrow, grief, regret, pity, or dread. *interj.*

Alas., Alaska.

A las ka (ə las/kə), one of the Pacific states of the United States, in the NW part of North America. *Capital:* Juneau. *n.* —**A las/kan,** *adj., n.*

alb (alb), a white linen robe worn by Roman Catholic and some Anglican priests at the Communion service. *n.*

al ba core (al/bə kôr), a large fish with long fins related to the tuna. It has light-colored flesh valued for canning. *n., pl.* **al ba cores** or **al ba core.**

Al ba ni a (al bā/nē ə), country in SE Europe, between Yugoslavia and Greece. *Capital:* Tirana. See **Adriatic Sea** for map. *n.* —**Al ba/ni an,** *adj., n.*

Al ba ny (ôl/bə nē), capital of New York State, on the Hudson River. *n.*

al ba tross (al/bə trôs), a very large

albatross
30 in. long, wingspread up to 11½ ft.

hat, āge, fär; let, ēqual, tėrm;
it, īce; hot, ōpen, ôrder;
oil, out; cup, pu̇t, rüle; ch, child;
ng, long; sh, she; th, thin;
ŦH, then; zh, measure;

ə represents *a* in about,
e in taken, *i* in pencil,
o in lemon, *u* in circus.

web-footed sea bird related to petrels, that can fly long distances. *n., pl.* **al ba tross es** or **al ba tross.**

al be it (ôl bē/it), even though; even if; although: *Albeit we are late, we may be able to catch the bus if we hurry. conj.*

Al ber ta (al bėr/tə), province in W Canada. *Capital:* Edmonton. *n.* —**Al ber/tan,** *adj., n.*

al bi no (al bī/nō), 1 person or animal that from birth has a pale, milky skin, very light hair, and pink eyes. 2 plant with defective coloring. *n., pl.* **al bi nos.**

Al bi on (al/bē ən), England. *n.*

al bum (al/bəm), 1 book with blank pages for holding photographs, stamps, autographs, etc. 2 case for or containing a set of phonograph records. 3 a single long-playing phonograph record. *n.*

al bu men (al byü/mən), the white of an egg, consisting mostly of albumin dissolved in water. *n.*

al bu min (al byü/mən), protein found in the white of an egg, milk, blood serum, lymph, and in many other animal and plant tissues and juices. *n.*

Al bu quer que (al/bə kėr/kē), city in central New Mexico. *n.*

al che mist (al/kə mist), person who studied a combination of chemistry and magic in the Middle Ages. *n.*

al che my (al/kə mē), 1 combination of chemistry and magic studied in the Middle Ages. Alchemy tried to find or prepare a liquid which would turn cheaper metals into gold and silver and which would prolong human life. 2 magical or mysterious power or process of transforming one thing into another. *n.*

al co hol (al/kə hôl), 1 the colorless liquid in whiskey, gin, wine, beer, etc., that makes them intoxicating; grain alcohol; ethyl alcohol. Alcohol is used in medicines, in manufacturing, and as a fuel. 2 whiskey, gin, or any other intoxicating liquor containing this liquid. 3 any of a group of similar organic compounds, reacting with certain acids to form esters. Wood alcohol is very poisonous. *n.*

adj.	adjective	n.	noun
adv.	adverb	prep.	preposition
conj.	conjunction	pron.	pronoun
interj.	interjection	v.	verb
sing.	singular	pl.	plural

al co hol ic (al′kə hô′lik), 1 consisting of alcohol: *alcoholic fumes.* 2 containing alcohol: *alcoholic drinks.* 3 person who has the habit of drinking too much intoxicating liquor. 4 suffering from the excessive use of intoxicating liquor. 1,2,4 *adj.*, 3 *n.*

al co hol ism (al′kə hô liz′əm), a diseased condition caused by continually drinking too much alcoholic liquor. *n.*

Al cott (ôl′kət), **Louisa May,** 1832-1888, American author. Her most famous book is *Little Women. n.*

al cove (al′kōv), 1 a small room opening out of a larger room. 2 recess or large, hollow space in a wall. *n.*

al der (ôl′dər), tree or shrub that usually grows in wet land and has clusters of catkins that develop into small, woody cones. *n.*

al der man (ôl′dər mən), person elected to represent a certain district on a council that governs a city. *n., pl.* **al der men.**

Al der ney (ôl′dər nē), one of the Channel Islands. *n.*

ale (āl), a bitter alcoholic beverage fermented from malt and hops. Ale is similar to beer but contains more alcohol. *n.*

a lee (ə lē′), on or toward the side of a ship that is away from the wind. *adv.*

a lert (ə lėrt′), 1 keen and watchful; wide-awake: *A good hunting dog is alert to every sound and movement in the field.* 2 quick in action; nimble: *A sparrow is very alert in its movements.* 3 signal warning of an attack by approaching enemy aircraft, a hurricane, or other threatening danger. 4 period of time after this warning until the attack is over or the danger has passed: *The hurricane alert is over.* 5 warn against an attack by aircraft, a hurricane, or other threatening danger. 6 notify (troops) to get ready for action. 7 make alert; warn. 1,2 *adj.*, 3,4 *n.*, 5-7 *v.* —**a lert′ly,** *adv.* —**a lert′ness,** *n.*

on the alert, ready at any instant for what is coming; watchful: *A driver must be on the alert.*

A leu tian Islands (ə lü′shən), chain of about 150 small islands in the N Pacific, part of Alaska and extending southwest from the mainland for 1200 miles.

Al ex an der the Great (al′ig zan′-dər), 356-323 B.C., king of Macedonia from 336 to 323 B.C. He conquered the Greek city-states and the whole Persian empire, from the coasts of Asia Minor and Egypt to India.

Al ex an dri a (al′ig zan′drē ə), seaport in N Egypt, on the Mediterranean. Alexandria was famous in ancient times for its library and scholars. *n.*

al fal fa (al fal′fə), plant, somewhat like clover, that has three leaflets to each leaf, deep roots, and bluish-purple flowers. Alfalfa is grown as food for horses and cattle. *n.*

Al fred the Great (al′frid), A.D. 849-899, king of England from A.D. 871 to 899, who defeated the Danes, united southern England, and led a revival of learning and literature.

al fres co (al fres′kō), in the open air; outdoors: *They dined alfresco (adv.). We dined at an alfresco café (adj.). adv., adj.* [from Italian *al fresco* in the cool]

al ga (al′gə), one of the algae. *n., pl.* **al gae.**

al gae (al′jē), group of water plants that can make their own food. Algae contain chlorophyll but lack true stems, roots, or leaves. Some algae are one-celled and form scum on rocks; others, such as the seaweeds, are very large. *n.pl.*

al ge bra (al′jə brə), branch of mathematics which describes the relations between quantities. In algebra quantities are denoted by letters, negative numbers as well as ordinary numbers are used, and problems are solved in the form of equations. $x + y = x^2$ is a way of stating, by algebra, that the sum of two numbers equals the square of one of them. *n.*

al ge bra ic (al′jə brā′ik), of or having to do with algebra; used in algebra: $(a+b)\,(a-b) = a^2 - b^2$ *is an algebraic statement. adj.*

al ge bra i cal ly (al′jə brā′ik lē), by means of algebra or of algebraic processes. *adv.*

Al ger i a (al jir′ē ə), country in N Africa, on the Mediterranean, which became independent of France in 1962.

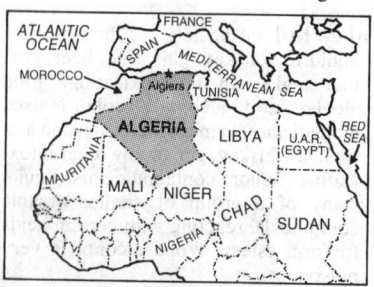

Capital: Algiers. *n.* —**Al ger′i an,** *adj., n.*

Al giers (al jirz′), capital of Algeria, on the Mediterranean. *n.*

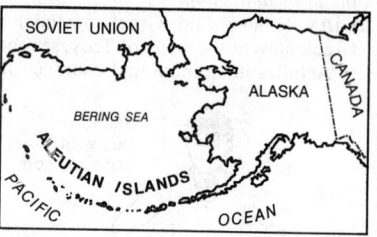

Al gon qui an (al gong′kē ən *or* al gong′kwē ən), 1 family of North American Indian languages, including the languages of the Arapaho, Blackfoot, Cheyenne, Ojibwa, Delaware, and Shawnee tribes. 2 of or having to do with this family of languages. 3 Indian belonging to an Algonquian tribe. 1,3 *n.*, 2 *adj.*

Al gon quin (al gong′kən *or* al gong′-kwən), member of a tribe of North American Indians that lived in eastern Canada. *n.*

Al ham bra (al ham′brə), palace of the Moorish kings at Granada, Spain. The Alhambra was the last stronghold of the Moors in Europe and was conquered in 1492. *n.*

a li as (ā′lē əs), 1 name used by a person instead of his real name to hide who he is; assumed name: *The spy's real name was Harrison, but he sometimes went by the alias of Johnson.* 2 otherwise called: *The thief's name was Jones, alias Williams.* 1 *n., pl.* **a li as es;** 2 *adv.*

A li Ba ba (ä′lē bä′bə *or* al′ē bab′ə), a poor woodcutter in *The Arabian Nights* who discovers a treasure hidden in a cave by forty thieves.

al i bi (al′ə bī), 1 the plea or the fact that an accused person was somewhere else when an offense was committed: *Immediately after the robbery the gang scattered to establish alibis.* 2 INFORMAL. an excuse: *What is your alibi for failing to do your homework?* 3 INFORMAL. make an excuse: *She alibied that she was very busy when they asked her why she didn't visit them.* 1,2 *n., pl.* **al i bis;** 3 *v.*, **al i bied, al i bi ing.**

al ien (ā′lyən), 1 foreigner. Aliens are not citizens of the country in which they live, and therefore owe their loyalty to another country. 2 of another country; foreign: *an alien language, alien conquerors.* 3 entirely different; not in agreement; strange: *Unkindness is alien to her nature.* 1 *n.*, 2,3 *adj.*

al ien ate (ā′lyə nāt), turn from affection to indifference, dislike, or hatred; make unfriendly: *The colonies were* alienated from England by disputes over trade and taxation. *v.*, **al ien at ed, al ien at ing.**

al ien a tion (ā′lyə nā′shən), 1 an alienating; making unfriendly. 2 a being alienated; not feeling interested in or involved with one's family, associates, or society. *n.*

a light[1] (ə līt′), 1 get down; get off; dismount: *She alighted from the bus.* 2 come down from the air and lightly settle; come down from flight: *The bird alighted on our window sill.* 3 come by chance; happen: *I alighted on just the book I needed in the library.* *v.*, **a light ed, a light ing.** [Old English ālīhtan get down]

a light[2] (ə līt′), 1 on fire; lighted: *Is the kindling alight?* 2 lighted up; aglow: *Her face was alight with happiness.* *adj.* [Old English ālīht lighted up]

a lign (ə līn′), 1 bring into line; arrange in a straight line: *The marksman aligned the sights of his gun with the target. The garage man aligned the front wheels of our car.* 2 form a line: *The troops aligned.* 3 join with others for or against a cause: *Germany was aligned with Japan in World War II.* *v.* Also, **aline.**

-○-○-○-○-○-○-○-○-
in ALIGNMENT

-○○○○○○○○-
out of ALIGNMENT
alignment (def. 1)

a lign ment (ə līn′mənt), 1 arrangement in a straight line: *The troops were in perfect alignment.* 2 a joining with others for or against a cause: *The establishment of the Common Market resulted in a new European alignment.* *n.* Also, **alinement.**

a like (ə līk′), 1 in the same way; similarly: *She and her sister think alike.* 2 like one another; similar: *These twins are very much alike.* 1 *adv.*, 2 *adj.* —**a like′ness,** *n.*

al i men tar y (al′ə men′tər ē), having to do with food and nutrition. *adj.*

alimentary canal, the parts of the body through which food passes as it is digested and from which wastes are eliminated.

al i mo ny (al′ə mō′nē), a fixed sum of money paid regularly by a husband to his wife or former wife, under orders from a court after a legal separation or after a divorce. *n.*

a line (ə līn′), align. *v.*, **a lined, a lin ing.**

a line ment (ə līn′mənt), alignment. *n.*

al i quot (al′ə kwət), dividing a number without leaving a remainder: *3 is an aliquot part of 12. adj.*

a lit (ə lit′), OLD USE. alighted. *v.*

a live (ə līv′), 1 having life; living: *Was the snake alive or dead?* 2 in continued activity; in full force; active: *We celebrate Memorial Day to keep alive the memory of soldiers and sailors who have died for their country.* 3 of all living: *I was the happiest person alive.* 4 full of energy; lively. *adj.* —**a live′ness,** *n.*

alive to, awake to; sensitive to: *Are you alive to what is going on?*

alive with, full of; swarming with: *The streets were alive with people.*

look alive! hurry up! be quick!

al ka li (al′kə lī), 1 any of a group of bitter-tasting substances that neutralize acids, form salts with them, and turn red litmus paper blue. Alkalis are soluble in water and often produce caustic solutions. Lye and ammonia are two common alkalis. 2 any salt or mixture of salts found in some desert soils, usually harmful to crops. *n., pl.* **al ka lis** or **al ka lies.**

al ka line (al′kə līn *or* al′kə lən), 1 of or like an alkali: *an alkaline reaction.* 2 containing alkali. *adj.*

al ka lin i ty (al′kə lin′ə tē), alkaline quality or condition. *n.*

al ka loid (al′kə loid), any of a group of alkaline substances that contain nitrogen and are found in or obtained from plants. Many alkaloids are drugs, such as cocaine, strychnine, morphine, and quinine. *n.*

all (ôl), 1 every one of: *All the children came. You all know the teacher.* 2 everyone: *All of us are going.* 3 everything: *All is well.* 4 the whole of: *The mice ate all the cheese.* 5 the whole amount: *All of the bread has been eaten.* 6 wholly; entirely: *I was all tired out and decided to go to bed early. The cake is all gone.* 7 the greatest possible: *I made all haste to reach home in time.* 8 nothing but; only: *This plane carries all cargo and no passengers.* 9 each; apiece: *The score was even at forty all.* 1,4,7,8 *adj.*, 2,3,5 *prep.*, 6,9 *adv.*

above all, before everything else: *Above all, he loves his work.*

after all, when everything has been

considered; nevertheless: *I see that you came after all.*

all but, nearly; almost: *She is all but nine years old.*

all in, INFORMAL. worn out; weary: *After the race, the horse was all in.*

all in all, when everything has been taken into account: *All in all, I think you did a good job.*

all over, 1 everywhere: *I looked all over for your glasses.* 2 done with; finished: *The game is all over.*

at all, 1 under any conditions: *I was surprised that he came at all, considering the hard storm.* 2 in any way: *The teacher was not at all disturbed by the interruption.*

for all that, in spite of that; notwithstanding: *The price was high, but for all that he bought the gift.*

in all, counting every person or thing; altogether: *There were five of us in all.*

Al lah (al′ə *or* ä′lə), the Moslem name for God. *n.*

all-A mer i can (ôl′ə mer′ə kən), 1 selected as the best of its class in the United States: *He was chosen as the quarterback on this year's all-American football team.* 2 made up entirely of Americans or American elements: *The ship had an all-American crew.* 3 player selected as one of the best in the United States at his position. 1,2 *adj.*, 3 *n.*

all-a round (ôl′ə round′), able to do many things; not limited or specialized: *He is an all-around football player—he runs, passes, and punts. adj.*

al lay (ə lā′), 1 put at rest; quiet: *His fears were allayed by the news that his family was safe.* 2 make less; weaken or relieve: *Her fever was allayed by the medicine. v.*

al le ga tion (al′ə gā′shən), a positive statement, especially one without proof; assertion: *Everyone knows better than to believe the allegations made against you. n.*

al lege (ə lej′), 1 state positively; assert: *Although he has no proof, this man alleges that the janitor stole his watch.* 2 give or bring forward as a reason, excuse, or argument: *He was tardy this*

alimentary canal of a person— a 30 ft. tube beginning at the mouth, where food enters, and ending at the anus, where undigested solids leave the body.

ESOPHAGUS
STOMACH
SMALL INTESTINE
LARGE INTESTINE
ANUS

adj.	adjective	*n.*	noun
adv.	adverb	*prep.*	preposition
conj.	conjunction	*pron.*	pronoun
interj.	interjection	*v.*	verb
sing.	singular	*pl.*	plural

morning, and alleges that his bus was late. *v.*, **al leged, al leg ing.**

al leg ed ly (ə lej′id lē), according to what is alleged. *adv.*

Al le ghe nies (al′ə gā′nēz), Allegheny Mountains. *n.pl.*

Al le ghe ny Mountains (al′ə-gā′nē), mountain range of the Appalachian Mountain system, in Pennsylvania, Maryland, Virginia, and West Virginia.

Allegheny River, river in W Pennsylvania. It joins the Monongahela at Pittsburgh to form the Ohio River.

al le giance (ə lē′jəns), 1 the loyalty owed by a citizen to his country or government: *I pledge allegiance to the flag.* 2 loyalty to any person or thing: *We owe allegiance to our friends. n.*

al le gor i cal (al′ə gôr′ə kəl), explaining or teaching something by a story; using allegory. *adj.* —**al′le go′ri cal ly,** *adv.*

al le go ry (al′ə gôr′ē), a story that is told to explain and teach something. The parables in the Bible are allegories. *n., pl.* **al le go ries.**

al le gro (ə leg′rō *or* ə lā′grō), in music: 1 quick; lively. 2 in quick time. 3 a quick, lively part in a piece of music. 1 *adj.,* 2 *adv.,* 3 *n., pl.* **al le gros.** [from Italian]

al le lu ia (al′ə lü′yə), hallelujah. *interj., n., pl.* **al le lu ias.**

Al len (al′ən), **Ethan,** 1737-1789, American officer in the Revolutionary War. *n.*

al ler gic (ə ler′jik), 1 having an allergy: *Some people who are allergic to eggs cannot eat them without breaking into a rash.* 2 of or caused by allergy: *Hay fever is an allergic reaction. adj.*

al ler gy (al′ər jē), unusual sensitiveness to certain substances such as particular kinds of pollen, food, hair, or cloth. Hay fever, asthma, headaches, and hives are common signs of allergy. *n., pl.* **al ler gies.**

al le vi ate (ə lē′vē āt), make easier to endure; relieve; lessen: *Heat often alleviates pain. v.,* **al le vi at ed, al le-vi at ing.**

al le vi a tion (ə lē′vē ā′shən), 1 an alleviating: *the alleviation of taxes.* 2 thing that alleviates: *Lower taxes were an alleviation to the taxpayers. n.*

al ley[1] (al′ē), 1 a narrow back street in a city or town. 2 path in a park or garden, bordered by trees. 3 a long, narrow lane along which the ball is rolled in bowling. 4 building having a number of alleys for bowling. *n., pl.* **al leys.** [from French of the 1300′s *alee* a going]

al ley[2] (al′ē), a large, white or colored marble used to shoot at other marbles. *n., pl.* **al leys.** [shortened from *alabaster*]

al ley way (al′ē wā′), 1 alley in a city or town. 2 a narrow passageway. *n.*

All Fools′ Day, April 1; April Fools′ Day.

All hal lows (ôl′hal′ōz), November 1; All Saints′ Day. *n.*

al li ance (ə lī′əns), 1 union formed by agreement; joining of interests. An alliance may be a joining of family interests by marriage or a joining of national interests by treaty. 2 the nations, persons, etc., that belong to such a union. *n.*

al lied (ə līd′ *or* al′īd), 1 united by agreement: *allied nations, allied armies.* 2 similar in structure or descent; related: *Allied animals, such as the dog and the wolf, look somewhat alike. adj.*

Al lies (al′īz *or* ə līz′), 1 the countries that fought against Germany, Austria-Hungary, Turkey, and Bulgaria in World War I. 2 the countries that fought against Germany, Italy, and Japan in World War II. *n.pl.*

al li ga tor (al′ə gā′tər), 1 a large reptile with a rather thick skin, similar to the crocodile but having a shorter and flatter head. Alligators live in the rivers and marshes of the warm parts of America and China. 2 leather prepared from its skin. *n.*

alligator pear, avocado.

al lit er a tion (ə lit′ə rā′shən), repetition of the same first sound or letter in a group of words or a line of poetry. EXAMPLE: "The sun sank slowly" contains alliteration of *s. n.*

al lo cate (al′ə kāt), set or lay aside for a special purpose; allot: *The federal government allocated millions of dollars for cancer research. v.,* **al lo cat ed, al lo cat ing.**

al lo ca tion (al′ə kā′shən), 1 an allocating; allotment. 2 share, portion, or thing allotted. *n.*

al lot (ə lot′), 1 divide and distribute in parts or shares: *The profits have been allotted among the owners of the company.* 2 give to as a share; assign: *The principal allotted each class a part in the school program. v.,* **al lot ted, al-lot ting.**

al lot ment (ə lot′mənt), 1 division and distribution in parts or shares: *The allotment of profits was made Monday.*

2 share allotted: *Your allotment was $4. n.*

all-out (ôl′out′), greatest possible; complete: *The team made an all-out effort to win. adj.*

all o ver (ôl′ō′vər), covering the whole surface: *an allover pattern. adj.*

al low (ə lou′), 1 let (someone) do something; permit (something) to be done or happen: *They do not allow swimming at this beach.* 2 let have; give: *My parents allowed me a dollar to spend as I wish.* 3 accept as true; acknowledge; recognize: *The judge allowed the claim of the man whose property was damaged.* 4 add or subtract to make up for something: *The trip will cost you only $20; but you ought to allow $5 more for extra expenses. v.* —**al low′er,** *n.*

allow for, take into consideration; provide for: *She made the dress a little large to allow for shrinking when it was washed.*

al low a ble (ə lou′ə bəl), allowed by law; permitted by the rules; not forbidden. *adj.*

al low a bly (ə lou′ə blē), in an allowable manner. *adv.*

al low ance (ə lou′əns), 1 a limited share set apart; definite portion or amount given out: *My weekly allowance is $1.* 2 amount added or subtracted to make up for something; discount: *The salesman offered us an allowance of $400 on our old car; so we got a $3000 car for $2600.* 3 an allowing; conceding: *allowance of a claim. n.*

make allowance for or **make allowances for,** take into consideration; allow for: *We made allowance for the heavy traffic by leaving half an hour early.*

al loy (al′oi *or* ə loi′ for 1,3; ə loi′ for 2,4), 1 metal made by mixing and fusing two or more metals or a metal and another substance. An alloy may be harder, lighter, and stronger than the metals of which it is composed. Brass is an alloy of copper and zinc. 2 make into an alloy. 3 an inferior metal mixed with a more valuable one: *Silver used in minting U.S. half dollars has 60 percent copper alloy in it.* 4 make lower or less valuable by mixing with something bad: *The travelers′ enthusiasm was alloyed by having a flat tire 10 miles outside of town.* 1,3 *n.,* 2,4 *v.*

all right, 1 without error; correct: *The answers were all right.* 2 satisfactory: *The work was not done very well; but it was all right.* 3 in a satisfactory way: *The engine seemed to be working all right.* 4 in good health: *The doctor says I am all right.* 5 yes: *"Will you come with me?" "All right."* 6 without doubt; certainly: *I am tired, all right!*

all-round (ôl/round/), all-around. *adj.*

All Saints' Day, November 1, a church festival honoring all the saints; Allhallows.

all spice (ôl/spīs/), 1 spice having a flavor suggesting a mixture of cinnamon, nutmeg, and cloves. 2 the berry of the West Indian pimento tree from which this spice is made. *n.*

all-star (ôl/stär/), made up of the best players or performers: *He has been named to the all-star team. adj.*

al lude (ə lüd/), refer indirectly to something; mention slightly in passing: *Don't tell them of our decision; don't even allude to it. v.,* **al lud ed, al lud ing.**

al lure (ə lùr/), 1 tempt or attract very strongly; fascinate; charm: *City life allured her with its action and excitement.* 2 attractiveness; fascination; charm: *the allure of the sea.* 1 *v.,* **al lured, al lur ing;** 2 *n.*

al lure ment (ə lùr/mənt), 1 attractiveness; fascination; charm. 2 thing that allures. *n.*

al lur ing (ə lùr/ing), strongly attracting; tempting: *an alluring advertisement. adj.* —**al lur/ing ly,** *adv.*

al lu sion (ə lü/zhən), slight mention made in passing; indirect reference: *Don't make any allusion to the surprise party while she is present. n.*

al lu vi al (ə lü/vē əl), consisting of or formed by sand or mud left by flowing water. A delta is an alluvial deposit at the mouth of a river. *adj.*

al ly (al/ī *or* ə lī/ *for 1,2;* ə lī/ *for 3,4*), 1 person, group, or nation united with another for some special purpose: *England and France were allies in some wars and enemies in others.* See also **Allies.** 2 helper; supporter. 3 combine for some special purpose; unite by agreement: *Our nation allies itself with England to protect our interests in Europe.* 4 relate by similarity of structure; connect by a common origin: *Dogs are allied to wolves.* 1,2 *n., pl.* **al lies;** 3,4 *v.,* **al lied, al ly ing.**

-ally, *suffix forming adverbs.* in a _____ic manner: *Basically = in a basic manner. Tragically = in a tragic manner.* [–al¹ + –ly¹]

al ma ma ter *or* **Al ma Ma ter** (al/mə mä/tər *or* äl/mə mä/tər), person's school, college, or university. [from Latin *alma mater* fostering mother]

al ma nac (ôl/mə nak), 1 table or book of tables published every year, containing a calendar and information about the weather, sun, moon, stars, tides, church days, and other facts. 2 reference book published every year, often containing summaries of information on particular subjects. *n.*

al might y (ôl mī/tē), 1 having supreme power; omnipotent. 2 the Almighty, God. 1 *adj.,* 2 *n.*

al mond (ä/mənd *or* am/ənd), 1 the oval-shaped nut of a peachlike fruit growing in warm regions. 2 tree that the fruit grows on. *n.*

al mon er (al/mə nər), person who distributes alms for a king, a monastery, or a person of rank. *n.*

al most (ôl/mōst), very near to; all but; nearly: *Nine is almost ten. I almost missed the train. adv.*

alms (ämz), money or gifts to help the poor: *The beggar's appeal for alms went unanswered. n. sing. or pl.*

alms house (ämz/hous/), home for very poor persons supported at public expense or by private charity. *n., pl.* **alms hous es** (ämz/ hou/ziz).

al ni co (al/nə kō), alloy of iron containing aluminum, nickel, cobalt, and other metals, used as a magnet. *n.*

al oe (al/ō), 1 plant related to the lily, having a long spike of flowers and thick, narrow leaves. It grows chiefly in South Africa. 2 **aloes,** *pl.* a bitter drug made from the dried juice of this plant's leaves, used as a laxative. 3 century plant. *n.*

a loft (ə lôft/), 1 far above the earth; up in the air; high up: *Some birds fly thousands of feet aloft.* 2 high up among the sails, rigging, or masts of a ship: *The sailor went aloft to get a better view of the distant shore. adv.*

a lo ha (ə lō/ə *or* ä lō/hä), 1 greetings; hello. 2 good-by; farewell. *n., pl.* **a lohas;** *interj.* [from Hawaiian]

a lone (ə lōn/), 1 apart from other persons or things: *He was alone (adj.). One tree stood alone on the hill (adv.).* 2 without anyone else: *One person alone can do this work.* 3 without anything more: *Meat alone is not adequate food.* 4 and nothing more; only; merely: *He did the job for money alone.* 1-3 *adj.,* 1,4 *adv.* —**a lone/ness,** *n.*

leave alone, not bother; not meddle with: *She's busy with her homework; you'd better leave her alone.*

let alone, 1 not bother; not meddle with: *If everyone will let him alone he will get his work done.* 2 not to mention: *It would have been a hot day for summer, let alone early spring.*

let well enough alone, be satisfied with conditions and not try to change them: *You have done what you can to help, so why not just let well enough alone?*

a long (ə lông/), 1 from one end to the other of; lengthwise of: *Trees are planted along the street.* 2 from one end to the other; lengthwise: *Cars are parked along by the stadium.* 3 forward; onward: *March along quickly.*

4 together with someone or something: *We took our dog along.* 5 INFORMAL. (of time) somewhere: *Be ready to leave along about four o'clock.* 1 *prep.,* 2-5 *adv.*

all along, all the time: *He knew the answer all along.*

along with, in company with; together with: *I'll go along with you.*

get along, 1 manage: *Can you get along without our help?* 2 agree: *They get along well as partners.* 3 go away: *Get along with you!* 4 move forward; advance: *Let's get along or we'll be late.* 5 succeed; prosper: *He is getting along in his new business.*

a long shore (ə lông/shôr/), near or along the shore. *adv.*

a long side (ə lông/sīd/), 1 at the side; side by side: *Anchor alongside.* 2 by the side of; side by side with: *The boat was alongside the wharf.* 1 *adv.,* 2 *prep.*

alongside of, beside; next to: *If you stay alongside of me, you won't get lost.*

a loof (ə lüf/), 1 at a distance or apart: *One boy stood aloof from all the others.* 2 withdrawn; reserved: *Her aloof manner kept her from making many friends.* 1 *adv.,* 2 *adj.* —**a loof/ly,** *adv.* —**a loof/ness,** *n.*

a loud (ə loud/), loud enough to be heard; not in a whisper: *He spoke aloud, although he was alone. She read the story aloud to the class. adv.*

alp (alp), a high mountain. See **Alps.** *n.*

alpaca (def. 1)
4½ ft. long;
5 ft. high
to top of head

al pac a (al pak/ə), 1 a sheeplike animal of South America with long, soft, silky hair or wool. It is closely related to but somewhat smaller than the llama. 2 its wool. 3 cloth made from this wool. 4 a glossy, wiry cloth made of wool and cotton. *n., pl.* **al pac as** *or* **al pac a.**

adj.	adjective	n.	noun
adv.	adverb	prep.	preposition
conj.	conjunction	pron.	pronoun
interj.	interjection	v.	verb
sing.	singular	pl.	plural

al pen stock (al′pən stok′), a strong staff with an iron point, used as an aid in climbing mountains. *n.*

al pha (al′fə), 1 the first letter of the Greek alphabet (A, α). 2 the first of a series. *n.*

alpha and omega, the beginning and the end.

al pha bet (al′fə bet), 1 the letters of a language arranged in their usual order, not as they are in words. 2 set of letters or characters representing sounds, used in writing a language. The English alphabet has only 26 letters to represent more than 40 sounds. *n.*

al pha bet ic (al′fə bet′ik), alphabetical. *adj.*

al pha bet i cal (al′fə bet′ə kəl), 1 arranged by letters in the order of the alphabet: *Dictionary entries are listed in alphabetical order.* 2 of the alphabet. *adj.* —**al′pha bet′i cal ly,** *adv.*

al pha bet ize (al′fə bə tīz), arrange in alphabetical order: *Alphabetize the words in your spelling lesson.* *v.,* **al pha bet ized, al pha bet iz ing.**

alpha particle, a positively charged particle consisting of two protons and two neutrons, released at a very high speed in the disintegration of radium and other radioactive substances.

alpha rays, stream of alpha particles.

al pine (al′pīn), 1 of or like high mountains: *alpine plants, alpine terrain.* 2 Alpine, of or like the Alps. *adj.*

Alps (alps), mountain system in S Europe, with ranges in France, Switzerland, Germany, Italy, Austria, and Yugoslavia. *n.pl.*

al read y (ôl red′ē), before this time; by this time; even now: *You are half an hour late already.* *adv.*

Al sace (al sās′), region in NE France, on the Rhine. *n.*

Al sace-Lor raine (al sās′lə rān′), Alsace and Lorraine, region in NE France. It formed a German province from 1871 to 1919 and from 1940 to 1945. *n.*

alternately
leaves spaced
alternately

Al sa tian (al sā′shən), 1 of Alsace or its people. 2 person born or living in Alsace. 3 a German shepherd dog. 1 *adj.,* 2,3 *n.*

al so (ôl′sō), in addition; besides; too: *That dress is pretty; it is also inexpensive.* *adv.*

al so-ran (ôl′sō ran′), an unsuccessful contestant; loser. *n.*

Alta., Alberta, a province in Canada.

al tar (ôl′tər), 1 table or stand in the most sacred part of a church or temple: *The worshipers received Communion from the priest at the altar.* 2 block of stone, mound of turf, etc., on which to place sacrifices or burn offerings to a god. *n.*

altar boy, man or boy who helps a priest during certain religious services; acolyte.

al tar piece (ôl′tər pēs′), a decorated panel or wall behind an altar. *n.*

al ter (ôl′tər), 1 make different; change; vary: *If this coat is too large, a tailor can alter it to fit you.* 2 become different: *Since her summer on the farm, her whole outlook has altered.* *v.*

al ter a ble (ôl′tər ə bəl), that can be altered. *adj.*

al ter a bly (ôl′tər ə blē), in a manner that can be altered. *adv.*

al ter a tion (ôl′tə rā′shən), 1 change in the appearance or form of anything; altered or changed condition: *I have made some alterations in my new dress.* 2 an altering: *The alteration of our house took three months.* *n.*

al ter ca tion (ôl′tər kā′shən), an angry dispute; noisy quarrel; wrangle: *The two teams had an altercation over the umpire's decision.* *n.*

al ter e go (ôl′tər ē′gō), a very intimate friend; close associate. [from Latin *alter ego* other self]

al ter nate (ôl′tər nāt *for 1-3;* ôl′tər nit *for 4-6),* 1 happen or be arranged by turns. Squares and circles alternate in this row: □○□○□○□○□○□○ 2 arrange by turns: *He alternated work and pleasure.* 3 take turns: *The two of us will alternate in setting the table.* 4 first one and then the other by turns: *The row has alternate squares and circles.* 5 every other: *Our dairy no longer delivers milk daily, but only on alternate days.* 6 person appointed to take the place of another if it should be necessary; substitute: *We have several alternates on our debating team.* 1-3 *v.,* **al ter nat ed, al ter nat ing;** 4,5 *adj.,* 6 *n.*

al ter nate ly (ôl′tər nit lē), by turns. *adv.*

alternating current, an electric current in which the electricity flows regularly in one direction and then the other, usually reversing 120 times per second.

al ter na tion (ôl′tər nā′shən), an alternating; occurring by turns, first one and then the other: *There is an alternation of red and white stripes in the flag of the United States.* *n.*

al ter na tive (ôl tér′nə tiv), 1 choice from among two or more things: *She had the alternative of going to summer school or finding a summer job.* 2 one of the things to be chosen: *She chose the former alternative and went to summer school.* 3 giving or requiring a choice between two or more things: *I offered the alternative suggestions of having a picnic or taking a trip on a boat.* 1,2 *n.,* 3 *adj.* —**al ter′na tive ly,** *adv.*

al though or **al tho** (ôl FHō′), in spite of the fact that; though: *Although it rained all morning, they went on the hike.* *conj.*

altimeter—As an airplane climbs, air pressure on the flexible, airtight metal box decreases and its sides expand, forcing the pointer to move up from zero. With a loss in altitude, air pressure on the box increases and its sides contract, forcing the pointer to move back toward zero.

POINTER

METAL BOX EXPANDED

METAL BOX CONTRACTED

al tim e ter (al tim′ə tər), instrument for measuring altitude. Altimeters are used in aircraft to indicate height above the earth's surface. *n.*

altitude (def. 4) of the triangle is the distance from A to B.

altitude (def. 5) of the star is 35°.

al ti tude (al′tə tüd *or* al′tə tyüd), 1 height above the earth's surface: *What altitude did the airplane reach?* 2 height above sea level: *The altitude of Denver is 5300 feet.* 3 a high place: *At some altitudes snow never melts.* 4 the vertical distance from the base of a geometrical figure to its highest point. 5 the angular distance of a star, planet, etc., above the horizon. *n.*

al to (al′tō), 1 the lowest female voice

or the highest male voice. 2 singer with such a voice. 3 part in music for such a voice or for an instrument of similar range. 4 instrument playing such a part. 5 for an alto part. 1-4 *n.*, *pl.* **al tos**; 5 *adj.*

alto clef, the C clef when the clef symbol is placed on the third line of the staff. See **clef** for diagram.

al to geth er (ôl′tə geŦH′ər), 1 to the whole extent; completely; entirely: *The house was altogether destroyed by fire.* 2 on the whole; considering everything: *Altogether, he was well pleased.* 3 all included: *Altogether there were 14 books. adv.*

al tru ism (al′trü iz′əm), unselfish devotion to the welfare of others; unselfishness. *n.*

al tru ist (al′trü ist), person who works for the welfare of others; unselfish person. *n.*

al tru is tic (al′trü is′tik), thoughtful of the welfare of others; unselfish. *adj.* —**al′tru is′ti cal ly,** *adv.*

al um (al′əm), 1 a white mineral salt used in medicine and in dyeing. Alum is sometimes used to stop the bleeding of a small cut. 2 a colorless, crystalline salt used in baking powder. *n.*

a lu mi num (ə lü′mə nəm), a very lightweight, silver-white, metallic element which does not readily tarnish. Aluminum is the most abundant metallic element in the earth's crust, of which it makes up about seven per cent. It occurs only in combination with other elements. Aluminum is used to make utensils, instruments, aircraft parts, etc. *n.*

a lum na (ə lum′nə), a woman graduate or former student of a school, college, or university. *n.*, *pl.* **a lum nae** (ə lum′nē).

a lum ni (ə lum′nī), graduates or former students of a school, college, or university. "Alumni" may mean either men graduates or both men and women. *n.pl.*

a lum nus (ə lum′nəs), graduate or former student of a school, college, or university. *n.*, *pl.* **a lum ni.**

al ve o lus (al vē′ə ləs), 1 a small cavity, pit, or cell. The air cells in the lung are alveoli. 2 socket of a tooth. *n.*, *pl.* **al ve o li** (al vē′ə lī).

al way (ôl′wā), OLD USE. always. *adv.*

al ways (ôl′wiz or ôl′wāz), 1 at all times; every time: *Night always follows day.* 2 all the time; continually: *Home is always a cheerful place at holiday time. adv.*

a lys sum (ə lis′əm), a plant of the same family as the mustard, having small white or yellow flowers. *n.*

am (am; *unstressed* əm), form of the verb **be** used with *I* in the present

tense. *The little boy said, "I am six years old. I am not too young, am I?" v.*

Am., 1 America. 2 American.

AM or **A.M.,** amplitude modulation.

a.m. or **A.M.,** the time from midnight to noon: *School begins at 9 a.m.* [abbreviation of Latin *ante meridiem* before noon]

a main (ə mān′), 1 at full speed. 2 with full force; violently. *adv.*

a mal gam (ə mal′gəm), 1 an alloy of mercury with some other metal or metals: *The dentist used silver amalgam to fill one of my teeth.* 2 mixture or blend of different things. *n.*

a mal gam ate (ə mal′gə māt), combine so as to form a whole; unite: *The two stores amalgamated to form one big store. The company amalgamated its three sales offices. v.*, **a mal gam at ed, a mal gam at ing.**

a mal gam a tion (ə mal′gə mā′shən), an amalgamating; mixture; combination; union: *Our nation is an amalgamation of many different peoples. n.*

a man u en sis (ə man′yü en′sis), person who writes down what another says or who copies what another has written. *n.*, *pl.* **a man u en ses** (ə man′yü en′sēz).

am a ranth (am′ə ranth′), plant with showy purple or crimson flowers. *n.*

Am a ril lo (am′ə ril′ō), city in NW Texas. *n.*

am a ryl lis (am′ə ril′is), a lilylike plant with clusters of large red, white, purple, or pink flowers. *n.*, *pl.* **am a ryl lis es.**

a mass (ə mas′), heap together; pile up; accumulate: *He invested wisely and amassed a fortune. v.*

am a teur (am′ə chər *or* am′ə tər), 1 person who does something for pleasure, not for money or as a profession: *Only amateurs can compete in Olympic games.* 2 person who does something unskillfully or in an inexpert way: *You can tell from his painting that he is an amateur, completely without training.* 3 of amateurs; by amateurs: *an amateur orchestra.* 4 being an amateur: *an amateur golfer.* 1,2 *n.*, 3,4 *adj.*

am a teur ish (am′ə tyúr′ish *or* am′ə tėr′ish), done as an amateur might do it; not expert; not very skillful. *adj.* —**am′a teur′ish ly,** *adv.* —**am′a teur′ish ness,** *n.*

am a to ry (am′ə tôr′ē), of love; expressing love: *Valentine cards often have amatory verses on them. adj.*

a maze (ə māz′), surprise greatly; strike with sudden wonder; astound: *She was so amazed by the surprise party that she could not think of a thing to say. v.*, **a mazed, a maz ing.**

a maz ed ly (ə mā′zid lē), with wonder or astonishment. *adv.*

hat, āge, fär; let, ēqual, tėrm;
it, īce; hot, ōpen, ôrder;
oil, out; cup, pùt, rüle; ch, child;
ng, long; sh, she; th, thin;
ŦH, then; zh, measure;

ə represents *a* in about,
e in taken, *i* in pencil,
o in lemon, *u* in circus.

a maze ment (ə māz′mənt), great surprise; sudden wonder; astonishment: *The girl was filled with amazement when she first saw the ocean. n.*

a maz ing (ə mā′zing), very surprising; wonderful; astonishing. *adj.* —**a maz′ing ly,** *adv.*

Am a zon (am′ə zon), 1 largest river in the world, in N South America. The Amazon flows from sources in the Andes Mountains of Peru across Brazil into the Atlantic. 2 one of a race of women warriors in Greek legends. 3 **amazon,** a tall, strong, aggressive woman. *n.*

Am a zo ni an (am′ə zō′nē ən), 1 of the Amazon River or the region it drains. 2 of the Amazons. 3 **amazonian,** (of a woman) aggressive or warlike. *adj.*

am bas sa dor (am bas′ə dər), 1 a representative of highest rank sent by one government or ruler to another: *Our ambassador to France lives in Paris, the capital of France, and speaks and acts in behalf of the government of the United States.* 2 any official messenger with a special errand; agent: *Miles Standish chose John Alden to be his ambassador. n.*

am bas sa do ri al (am bas′ə dôr′ē əl), of an ambassador or ambassadors. *adj.*

am bas sa dor ship (am bas′ə dər ship), 1 position or rank of an ambassador. 2 term of office of an ambassador. *n.*

am ber (am′bər), 1 a hard, translucent yellow or yellowish-brown gum, used for jewelry and in making stems of pipes. Amber is the resin of fossil pine trees. 2 made of amber: *amber beads.* 3 a yellow or yellowish brown: *Amber is her favorite color.* 4 yellow or yellowish-brown: *She has amber hair.* 1,3 *n.*, 2,4 *adj.*

am ber gris (am′bər grēs *or* am′bər gris), a waxlike, grayish substance secreted in the intestines of the sperm whale. Ambergris is used in making perfumes. *n.*

am bi dex trous (am′bə dek′strəs), able to use both hands equally well.

27

adj. adjective	*n.* noun
adv. adverb	*prep.* preposition
conj. conjunction	*pron.* pronoun
interj. interjection	*v.* verb
sing. singular	*pl.* plural

am bi ent (am′bē ənt), all around; surrounding: *The flowers made the ambient air fragrant. adj.*

am bi gu i ty (am′bə gyü′ə tē), 1 possibility of two or more meanings: *The ambiguity of the speaker's statement made it hard to tell which side he was on.* 2 word or expression that can have more than one meaning: *Answer me without ambiguities. n., pl.* **am bi gu i ties.**

am big u ous (am big′yü əs), 1 having more than one possible meaning. The sentence "After John hit Dick he ran away" is ambiguous because we cannot tell which boy ran away. 2 uncertain; doubtful; not clear: *He was left in an ambiguous position by his friend's failure to appear and help him. adj.* —**am big′u ous ly,** *adv.* —**am big′u ous ness,** *n.*

am bi tion (am bish′ən), 1 a strong desire for fame, honor, wealth, etc.; seeking after a high position or great power: *Because he was filled with ambition, he worked after school and on Saturdays.* 2 thing strongly desired or sought after: *Her ambition is to be an oceanographer. n.*

am bi tious (am bish′əs), 1 having or guided by ambition; desiring strongly: *He is ambitious to get through high school in three years.* 2 showing or arising from ambition: *He had an ambitious plan of building a rocket. adj.* —**am bi′tious ly,** *adv.*

am biv a lence (am biv′ə ləns), a being ambivalent. *n.*

am biv a lent (am biv′ə lənt), acting in opposite ways; having or showing conflicting feelings: *He has an ambivalent attitude toward his friend; he likes him but always quarrels with him. adj.*

am ble (am′bəl), 1 gait of a horse or mule when it lifts first the two legs on one side and then the two on the other side. 2 go with such a gait: *My horse can amble and trot.* 3 an easy, slow pace in walking. 4 walk at an easy, slow pace. 1,3 *n.,* 2,4 *v.,* **am bled, am bling.**

am bler (am′blər), 1 horse or mule that ambles. 2 person who ambles. *n.*

am bro sia (am brō′zhə), 1 (in Greek and Roman myths) the food of the gods. 2 anything especially delicious. *n.*

am bro sial (am brō′zhəl), like ambrosia; especially delicious. *adj.*

am bu lance (am′byə ləns), an automobile, boat, or aircraft equipped to carry sick, injured, or wounded persons. *n.*

am bu la to ry (am′byə lə tôr′ē), capable of walking; not bedridden: *an ambulatory patient. adj.*

am bus cade (am′bə skād′), ambush. *n., v.,* **am bus cad ed, am bus cad ing.**

am bush (am′bush), 1 soldiers or other persons hidden so that they can make a surprise attack on an approaching enemy. 2 a secret or hidden place where soldiers or others lie in wait to make such an attack: *The troops lay in ambush, waiting for the signal to open fire.* 3 attack unexpectedly from a hidden position: *Our men ambushed the retreating enemy.* 4 a lying in wait for the purpose of attacking by surprise: *The troops trapped the enemy by ambush.* 1,2,4 *n., pl.* **am bush es;** 3 *v.*

a me ba (ə mē′bə), amoeba. *n., pl.* **a me bas, a me bae** (ə mē′bē).

a me bic (ə mē′bik), amoebic. *adj.*

a mel io rate (ə mē′lyə rāt′), make or become better; improve: *New housing ameliorated living conditions in the slums. Living conditions in the city ameliorated with smoke control. v.,* **a mel io rat ed, a mel io rat ing.**

a mel io ra tion (ə mē′lyə rā′shən), an ameliorating; improvement. *n.*

a men (ā′men′ *or* ä′men′), so be it; may it become true. *Amen* is said after a prayer, a wish, or a statement with which one agrees. *interj.*

a me na bil i ty (ə mē′nə bil′ə tē *or* ə men′ə bil′ə tē), a being amenable. *n.*

a me na ble (ə mē′nə bəl *or* ə men′ə-bəl), 1 open to influence, suggestion, advice, etc.; responsive: *A reasonable person is amenable to persuasion.* 2 accountable; answerable: *People living in a country are amenable to its laws. adj.* —**a me′na ble ness,** *n.*

a me na bly (ə mē′nə blē *or* ə men′ə-blē), in an amenable manner. *adv.*

a mend (ə mend′), 1 change (a law, bill, or motion) by addition, omission, or alteration of language: *The Constitution of the United States was amended so that women could vote.* 2 change for the better; improve: *It is time we make a greater effort to amend conditions in the slums. v.*

a mend ment (ə mend′mənt), 1 change made in a law, bill, or motion by addition, omission, or alteration of language: *The Constitution of the United States has over twenty amend-*

ments. 2 a change for the better; improvement. *n.*

a mends (ə mendz′), something given or paid to make up for a wrong or an injury done; payment for loss; compensation: *If you carelessly took more than your share of the money, you should make amends at once by returning the extra amount. n. sing. or pl.*

a men i ty (ə men′ə tē *or* ə mē′nə tē), 1 amenities, *pl.* pleasant ways; polite acts. Saying "Thank you" and holding the door open for a person to pass through are amenities. 2 quality of being pleasant; agreeableness: *We went to Hawaii to enjoy the amenity of a warm climate. n., pl.* **a men i ties.**

Amer., 1 America. 2 American.

A mer i ca (ə mer′ə kə), 1 the United States of America. 2 North America. 3 Also, **the Americas.** North America and South America; the Western Hemisphere. 4 South America. *n.*

A mer i can (ə mer′ə kən), 1 of, having to do with, or in the United States: *Many immigrants become American citizens.* 2 person born or living in the United States; citizen of the United States: *The people of Alaska are Americans.* 3 native only to the Western Hemisphere: *Corn and tobacco are American plants.* 4 of or in the Western Hemisphere: *the Amazon and other American rivers.* 5 person born or living in the Western Hemisphere: *The citizens of Mexico, Canada, and Argentina are Americans.* 1,3,4 *adj.,* 2,5 *n.*

American eagle, bald eagle. The coat of arms of the United States has a design of the American eagle on it.

American Indian, member of one of the aboriginal peoples of North and South America; Indian.

A mer i can ism (ə mer′ə kə niz′əm), 1 devotion or loyalty to the United States and to its customs and traditions. 2 word, phrase, or meaning originating in the United States. 3 custom or trait peculiar to the United States. *n.*

A mer i can i za tion (ə mer′ə kə-nə zā′shən), an Americanizing. *n.*

A mer i can ize (ə mer′ə kə nīz), make or become American in habits, customs, or character: *Although she has lived in America for only a short time, she is already Americanized. v.,* **A mer i can ized, A mer i can iz ing.**

American Revolution, Revolutionary War.

a me ri ci um (am′ə rish′ē əm), a radioactive metallic element produced from plutonium. *n.* [from *America*]

am e thyst (am′ə thist), 1 a purple or violet variety of quartz, used for jewelry. 2 a purple or violet color. 3 purple; violet. 1,2 *n.,* 3 *adj.*

a mi a bil i ty (ā/mē ə bil/ə tē), a being amiable; good nature. *n.*

a mi a ble (ā/mē ə bəl), having a good-natured and friendly disposition; pleasant and agreeable: *She is an amiable girl who gets along with everyone.* *adj.* —**a/mi a ble ness,** *n.*

a mi a bly (ā/mē ə blē), in an amiable manner. *adv.*

am i ca bil i ty (am/ə kə bil/ə tē), a being amicable. *n.*

am i ca ble (am/ə kə bəl), having or showing a friendly attitude; peaceable: *Instead of fighting, the company and the union settled their quarrel in an amicable way by arbitration.* *adj.*

am i ca bly (am/ə kə blē), in an amicable manner. *adv.*

a mid (ə mid/), in the middle of; among: *One small house stood amid the tall buildings.* *prep.*

a mid ship (ə mid/ship), amidships. *adv.*

a mid ships (ə mid/ships), in or toward the middle of a ship; halfway between the bow and stern. *adv.*

a midst (ə midst/), amid. *prep.*

a mi go (ə mē/gō), friend. *n., pl.* **a mi gos.** [from Spanish]

a mi no acid (ə mē/nō *or* am/ə nō), any of a group of complex organic compounds of nitrogen, hydrogen, carbon, and oxygen that combine in various ways to form the proteins that make up living matter.

a mir (ə mir/), emir. *n.*

Am ish (am/ish *or* ä/mish), 1 a very strict Mennonite sect. 2 of this sect. 1 *n.,* 2 *adj.*

a miss (ə mis/), not the way it should be; out of order; wrong: *You must be tired; your work is going amiss today* (*adv.*). *It would not be amiss to offer an apology, even though you may not have intended harm* (*adj.*). *adv., adj.*

take amiss, be offended at (something not intended to offend): *Don't take it amiss if I reword some of the sentences you have written.*

am i ty (am/ə tē), peace and friendship; friendly relations: *If there were amity between nations, there would be no wars. n., pl.* **am i ties.**

Am man (ä/män *or* ä män/), capital of Jordan, in the NW part. *n.*

am me ter (am/ē/tər), instrument for measuring in amperes the strength of an electric current. *n.*

Am mon (am/ən), the sun god of ancient Egypt, represented with horns like a ram's. *n.*

am mo nia (ə mō/nyə), 1 a colorless gas, consisting of nitrogen and hydrogen, that has a pungent and suffocating smell and a strong alkaline reaction. 2 this gas dissolved in water. Ammonia is very useful for cleaning and for making fertilizers and other products. *n.*

am mu ni tion (am/yə nish/ən), 1 bullets, shells, gunpowder, bombs, etc., that can be exploded or fired from guns or other weapons; military explosives and missiles to be used against an enemy. 2 any means of attack or defense: *His most recent speech gave fresh ammunition to his opponents. n.*

am ne sia (am nē/zhə), loss of memory caused by injury to the brain, or by disease or shock. *n.*

am nes ty (am/nə stē), a general pardon for past offenses against a government: *After order was restored, the king granted amnesty to those who had rebelled against him. n., pl.* **am nes ties.**

am ni on (am/nē ən), a membrane forming the inner sac which encloses the embryos of reptiles, birds, and mammals. *n.*

am ni ot ic (am/nē ot/ik), 1 of or inside the amnion. 2 having an amnion. *adj.*

amoeba

a moe ba (ə mē/bə), an extremely small one-celled animal that moves by forming temporary projections that are constantly changing shape. Amoebas are so small that they can be examined only with a microscope. Many amoebas live in water; others live as parasites in other animals. *n., pl.* **a moe bas, a moe bae** (ə mē/bē). Also, **ameba.**

a moe bic (ə mē/bik), 1 of or like an amoeba or amoebas. 2 caused by amoebas: *amoebic dysentery. adj.* Also, **amebic.**

a mok (ə muk/ *or* ə mok/). **run amok** or **go amok,** 1 run about in a murderous frenzy: *The bull ran amok and tried to gore everyone in its way.* 2 behave wildly; disregard rules, instructions, etc.: *The boy ran amok, throwing his books all over the floor. adv.* Also, **amuck.**

a mong (ə mung/), 1 in the number or class of: *The United States and Russia are among the largest countries of the world.* 2 in the company of; in with: *spend time among one's friends.* 3 surrounded by: *a house among the trees.* 4 with a portion for each of: *Divide the fruit among all of us.* 5 by the combined action of: *You have, among you, done a good job.* 6 by, with, or through the whole of: *There was political unrest among the people. prep.*

hat, āge, fär; let, ēqual, tèrm; it, īce; hot, ōpen, ôrder; oil, out; cup, pùt, rüle; ch, child; ng, long; sh, she; th, thin; ₮H, then; zh, measure;

ə represents *a* in about, *e* in taken, *i* in pencil, *o* in lemon, *u* in circus.

among ourselves, among yourselves, or **among themselves,** each with all the others; as a group: *They agreed among themselves to have a party.*

a mongst (ə mungst/), among. *prep.*

am or ous (am/ər əs), 1 inclined to love; loving; fond: *an amorous disposition.* 2 having to do with love or courtship. *adj.* —**am/or ous ly,** *adv.* —**am/or ous ness,** *n.*

a mor phous (ə môr/fəs), 1 having no definite form; shapeless; formless: *An amoeba is amorphous.* 2 of no particular type or pattern; not classifiable. 3 not consisting of crystals: *Glass is amorphous; sugar is crystalline. adj.* —**a mor/phous ly,** *adv.* —**a mor/phous ness,** *n.*

am or ti za tion (am/ər tə zā/shən), 1 an amortizing of a debt, etc. 2 money regularly set aside for this purpose. *n.*

am or tize (am/ər tīz), set money aside regularly in a special fund for the future paying or settling of a debt. *v.,* **am or tized, am or tiz ing.**

A mos (ā/məs), 1 Hebrew prophet and social reformer who lived about 750 B.C. 2 book of the Old Testament containing his prophecies. *n.*

a mount (ə mount/), 1 the total of two or more numbers or quantities taken together; sum: *What is the amount of the bill for the groceries?* 2 the full value or extent: *The amount of evidence against him is great.* 3 portion or quantity: *No amount of coaxing would make the dog leave his master.* 4 add up; reach: *The loss from the flood amounts to ten million dollars.* 5 be equal: *Keeping what belongs to another amounts to stealing.* 6 the sum of the principal and interest due on a loan. 1-3,6 *n.,* 4,5 *v.*

a mour (ə mùr/), a love affair, especially a secret love affair. *n.*

amp., ampere.

am per age (am/pər ij), strength of an electric current measured in amperes. *n.*

am pere (am/pir), measure of the strength of an electric current. It is the amount of current one volt can send through a resistance of one ohm. Ordi-

adj. adjective	*n.* noun
adv. adverb	*prep.* preposition
conj. conjunction	*pron.* pronoun
interj. interjection	*v.* verb
sing. singular	*pl.* plural

nary light bulbs take from ¹/₄ to ¹/₂ ampere. *n.* [from André M. *Ampère,* 1775-1836, a French physicist]

am per sand (am′pər sand), the sign (&) meaning "and." It is often used in the titles of business firms. *n.*

am phib i an (am fib′ē ən), 1 one of a group of cold-blooded vertebrates with moist, scaleless skin, including frogs, toads, newts, salamanders, etc. Their young usually develop as tadpoles that have gills and live in water. 2 animal living both on land and in water but unable to breathe under water. Crocodiles, seals, and beavers are amphibians. 3 plant that grows on land or in water. 4 able to live both on land and in water. 5 aircraft that can take off from and land on either land or water. 6 able to start from and land on either land or water. 7 tank, truck, or other vehicle able to travel across land or water. 1-3,5,7 *n.,* 4,6 *adj.*

am phib i ous (am fib′ē əs), 1 able to live both on land and in water: *Frogs are amphibious.* 2 able to travel across land or water: *Some tanks are amphibious.* 3 by the combined action of land, sea, and air forces: *The enemy launched an amphibious attack. adj.* —**am phib′i ous ly,** *adv.* —**am phib′i ous ness,** *n.*

am phi the a ter or **am phi the a tre** (am′fə thē′ə tər), 1 a circular or oval building with rows of seats around a central open space. Each row is higher than the one in front of it. 2 something like an amphitheater in shape: *The town was set in an amphitheater of hills. n.*

am ple (am′pəl), 1 more than enough; abundant: *He has received ample praise for the work he did.* 2 as much as is needed; enough; sufficient: *My allowance is ample for carfare and lunches.* 3 having plenty of room; large; roomy: *A well-designed house has ample closets. adj.,* **am pler, am plest.**

am pli fi ca tion (am′plə fə kā′shən), 1 a making greater, stronger, or more extensive: *the amplification of knowledge.* 2 detail or example that amplifies: *Your argument needs amplification before I can understand and accept it.* 3 an increase in the strength of an electric current. *n.*

am pli fi er (am′plə fī′ər), 1 person or thing that amplifies. 2 a transistor, vacuum tube, or other device in a radio, phonograph, etc., for strengthening electrical impulses. 3 loudspeaker. *n.*

am pli fy (am′plə fī), 1 make greater; make stronger: *When sound is amplified, it can be heard a greater distance.* 2 make fuller and more extensive; expand; enlarge: *Please amplify your description of the accident by giving us more details. v.,* **am pli fied, am pli fy ing.**

am pli tude (am′plə tüd *or* am′plə tyüd), 1 quantity that is more than enough; abundance: *an amplitude of money.* 2 one half the range of a regular vibration. The distance between the position of rest and the highest position in the arc of a pendulum is its amplitude. 3 the peak strength of an alternating current in a given cycle. *n.*

amplitude (def. 2) of the 90° swing of the pendulum, 45°

amplitude modulation, deliberate change of the amplitude of radio waves in order to transmit sound. Ordinary broadcasting uses amplitude modulation.

am ply (am′plē), in an ample manner: *We were amply supplied with food. adv.*

am pu tate (am′pyə tāt), cut off (all or part of a leg, arm, etc.) by surgery. *v.,* **am pu tat ed, am pu tat ing.**

am pu ta tion (am′pyə tā′shən), a cutting off of all or a part of a leg, arm, etc. *n.*

am pu tee (am′pyə tē′), person who has had all or part of a leg or arm amputated. *n.*

Am ster dam (am′stər dam), the largest city and official capital of the Netherlands, on the North Sea. The unofficial capital is The Hague. *n.*

amt., amount.

a muck (ə muk′), amok. *adv.*

am u let (am′yə lit), some object worn as a magic charm against evil or harm. *n.*

A mund sen (ä′mən sən), **Roald,** 1872-1928, Norwegian explorer who discovered the South Pole in 1911. *n.*

A mur (ä mür′), river in E Asia flowing into the Sea of Okhotsk. *n.*

a muse (ə myüz′), 1 cause to laugh or smile: *The clown's jokes and antics amused everyone.* 2 keep pleasantly interested; cause to feel cheerful or happy; entertain: *The new toys amused the children. v.,* **a mused, a musing.**

a mus ed ly (ə myü′zid lē), in an amused manner. *adv.*

a muse ment (ə myüz′mənt), 1 condition of being amused: *The boy's amusement was so great that we all had to laugh with him.* 2 anything that amuses, such as an entertainment or sport: *When we go to the park we always enjoy the swings, slides, and other such amusements. n.*

a mus ing (ə myü′zing), 1 causing laughter or smiles: *an amusing joke.* 2 entertaining: *an amusing book. adj.* —**a mus′ing ly,** *adv.*

an (an; *unstressed* ən), 1 any: *Is there an apple in the box?* 2 one: *I'll have an egg for breakfast.* 3 every; each: *He earns two dollars an hour. adj.* or *indefinite article.*

-an, *suffix used to form adjectives and nouns, especially from proper nouns.* 1 of or having to do with _____: *Mohammedan = of or having to do with Mohammed.* 2 of or having to do with _____ or its people: *Asian = of or having to do with Asia or its people.* 3 person born or living in _____: *American = person born or living in America.* Also, **-ian.** [from Latin *-anum*]

a nach ro nism (ə nak′rə niz′əm), 1 a placing of a person, thing, or event in some time where he or it does not belong. It would be an anachronism to speak of George Washington riding in an automobile. 2 something placed or occurring out of its proper time. *n.*

a nach ro nis tic (ə nak′rə nis′tik), having or involving an anachronism. *adj.* —**a nach′ro nis′ti cal ly,** *adv.*

an a con da (an′ə kon′də), a very large South American snake related to the boa that crushes its prey in its coils. Anacondas live in tropical forests and rivers and are the longest snakes in America, sometimes over 30 feet. *n.,* *pl.* **an a con das.**

An a con da (an′ə kon′də), city in SW Montana, important for its copper mines and zinc smelting. *n.*

an ae ro bic (an′ə rō′bik), living or growing where there is no free oxygen. Anaerobic bacteria get their oxygen by decomposing compounds containing oxygen. *adj.*

an aes the sia (an′əs thē′zhə), anesthesia. *n.*

an aes thet ic (an′əs thet′ik), anesthetic. *adj.,* *n.*

an aes the tist (ə nes′thə tist), anesthetist. *n.*

an aes the tize (ə nes′thə tīz), anesthetize. *v.,* **an aes the tized, an aes the tiz ing.**

an a gram (an′ə gram), 1 word or

phrase formed from another by re-arranging the letters. EXAMPLE: lived—devil. **2 anagrams,** *pl.* game in which the players make words by changing and adding letters. *n.*

a nal (ā/nl), **1** of the anus. **2** near the anus. *adj.*

an al ge si a (an/l jē/zē ə), a deadening or absence of the sense of pain. *n.*

an al ge sic (an/l jē/zik), drug that relieves or lessens pain. *n.*

a nal o gous (ə nal/ə gəs), alike in some way; similar in the quality or feature that is being thought of; comparable: *The heart is analogous to a pump. adj.* **—a nal/o gous ly,** *adv.*

a nal o gy (ə nal/ə jē), likeness in some ways between things that are otherwise unlike; similarity: *There is an analogy between the heart and a pump. n., pl.* **a nal o gies.**

a nal y sis (ə nal/ə sis), **1** separation of anything into its parts or elements to find out what it is made of. A chemical analysis of ordinary table salt shows that it is made up of two elements, sodium and chlorine. **2** an examining carefully and in detail. An analysis can be made of a book, a person's character, etc. *n., pl.* **a nal y ses** (ə nal/ə-sēz/).

an a lyst (an/l ist), person who analyzes. *n.*

an a lyt ic (an/l it/ik), analytical. *adj.*

an a lyt i cal (an/l it/ə kəl), separating a whole into its parts; using analysis: *The methods of science are analytical. The detective had an analytical mind. adj.* **—an/a lyt/i cal ly,** *adv.*

an a lyze (an/l īz), **1** separate anything into its parts or elements to find out what it is made of: *The chemistry teacher analyzed water into two colorless gases, oxygen and hydrogen. Analyze this sentence by explaining the form and use of every word in it.* **2** examine carefully and in detail: *Analyze the situation before you act. The newspaper analyzed the results of the election. v.,* **an a lyzed, an a lyz ing.**

an ar chic (a när/kik), favoring anarchy; lawless: *an anarchic age. adj.*

an ar chism (an/ər kiz/əm), the political theory that all systems of government and law are harmful. *n.*

an ar chist (an/ər kist), **1** person who wants to overthrow established governments and have a world without laws. **2** person who promotes disorder and stirs up revolt. *n.*

an ar chis tic (an/ər kis/tik), of anarchism; like that of anarchists. *adj.*

an ar chy (an/ər kē), **1** absence of a system of government and law. **2** disorder and confusion; lawlessness. *n.*

a nath e ma (ə nath/ə mə), **1** a solemn curse by church authorities excommu-nicating some person from the church. **2** person or thing that has been cursed. **3** person or thing that is detested or condemned. *n., pl.* **a nath e mas.**

a nath e ma tize (ə nath/ə mə tīz), pronounce an anathema against; denounce; curse. *v.,* **a nath e ma tized, a nath e ma tiz ing.**

An a to li a (an/ə tō/lē ə), Asia Minor. *n.* **—An/a to/li an,** *adj., n.*

an a tom ic (an/ə tom/ik), anatomical. *adj.*

an a tom i cal (an/ə tom/ə kəl), of or having to do with anatomy. *adj.* **—an/a-tom/i cal ly,** *adv.*

a nat o mist (ə nat/ə mist), an expert in anatomy. *n.*

a nat o mize (ə nat/ə mīz), **1** divide (an animal, plant, etc.) into parts to study the structure of; dissect. **2** examine the parts of; analyze. *v.,* **a nat o-mized, a nat o miz ing.**

a nat o my (ə nat/ə mē), **1** science of the structure of animals and plants. Anatomy is a part of biology. **2** the dissecting of animals or plants to study their structure. **3** structure of an animal or plant: *The anatomy of an earthworm is much simpler than that of a human. n., pl.* **a nat o mies.**

-ance, *suffix forming nouns chiefly from verbs.* **1** act or fact of _____ing: *Avoidance = act or fact of avoiding.* **2** quality or state of being _____ed: *Annoyance = quality or state of being annoyed.* **3** thing that _____s: *Conveyance = thing that conveys.* **4** what is _____ed: *Contrivance = what is contrived.* **5** quality or state of being _____ant: *Importance = quality or state of being important.* [from French *-ance,* from Latin *-antia*]

an ces tor (an/ses/tər), **1** person from whom one is descended; forefather: *His ancestors came to America on the Mayflower.* **2** the early form from which a species or group is descended: *Dinosaurs and today's reptiles have the same ancestors. n.*

an ces tral (an ses/trəl), **1** of or having to do with ancestors: *England was the ancestral home of the Pilgrims.* **2** inherited from ancestors: *Black hair is an ancestral trait in that family. adj.* **—an ces/tral ly,** *adv.*

an ces tress (an/ses/tris), woman from whom one is descended. *n., pl.* **an ces tress es.**

an ces try (an/ses/trē), **1** ancestors: *Many of the early settlers in America had English ancestry.* **2** line of descent from ancestors; lineage: *The king was of noble ancestry. n., pl.* **an ces tries.**

an chor (ang/kər), **1** a shaped piece of iron attached to a chain or rope and used to hold a ship in place: *The anchor caught in the mud at the bottom of the* lake and kept the boat from drifting. See **fluke**[1] for picture. **2** hold in place with an anchor: *Can you anchor the boat in this storm?* **3** stop or stay in place by using an anchor: *The ship anchored in the bay.* **4** hold in place; fix firmly: *The scouts anchored the tent to the ground.* **5** something that makes a person feel safe and secure: *The weekly talks with an understanding counselor were an anchor to the troubled child.* **6** thing for holding something else in place: *The anchors of the cables of this suspension bridge are set in concrete.* 1,5,6 *n.,* 2-4 *v.*

at anchor, held by an anchor: *The ship was at anchor in the bay.*

cast anchor, drop the anchor: *The boat sailed to the other side of the island, where it cast anchor.*

weigh anchor, take up the anchor: *They weighed anchor and sailed away.*

an chor age (ang/kər ij), **1** place to anchor. **2** something on which to depend. *n.*

An chor age (ang/kər ij), seaport in S Alaska. *n.*

an cho rite (ang/kə rīt/), person who lives alone in a solitary place for religious meditation; hermit. *n.*

anchor man, 1 the last man to run or swim on a relay team. **2** person on a television or radio program who coordinates reports from correspondents in several different cities, countries, etc.

an cho vy (an/chō vē), a very small fish that looks somewhat like a herring. Anchovies are preserved by salting or drying, and may be packed in oil, made into a paste, or used in sauces. *n., pl.* **an cho vies.**

an cient (ān/shənt), **1** of or belonging to times long past: *In Egypt, we saw the ruins of an ancient temple built six thousand years ago.* **2 the ancients,** people who lived long ago, such as the ancient Greeks, Romans, and Egyptians. **3** of great age; very old: *Rome is an ancient city.* **4** a very old person. 1,3 *adj.,* 2,4 *n.*

ancient history, 1 history from the earliest times to the fall of the western part of the Roman Empire in A.D. 476.

adj. adjective	*n.* noun
adv. adverb	*prep.* preposition
conj. conjunction	*pron.* pronoun
interj. interjection	*v.* verb
sing. singular	*pl.* plural

2 INFORMAL. a well-known fact or event of the recent past.

an cient ly (ān′shənt lē), in ancient times. *adv.*

an cil lar y (an′sə ler′ē), 1 subordinate; dependent. 2 assisting; auxiliary: *an ancillary engine in a boat. adj.*

and (and; *unstressed* ənd *or* ən), 1 as well as: *You can come and go in the car.* 2 added to; with: *4 and 2 make 6. He likes ham and eggs.* 3 as a result: *The sun came out and the grass dried.* 4 INFORMAL. to: *Try and do better. conj.*

An da lu sia (an′də lü′zhə), region in S Spain, now divided into eight provinces. *n.* —**An′da lu′sian,** *adj., n.*

an dan te (än dän′tā *or* an dan′tē), in music: 1 moderately slow: *an andante movement (adj.). The movement was played andante (adv.).* 2 a moderately slow movement in a piece of music. 1 *adj., adv.,* 2 *n.*

An de an (an′dē ən *or* an dē′ən), of or having to do with the Andes Mountains. *adj.*

An der sen (an′dər sən), **Hans Christian,** 1805-1875, Danish writer of fairy tales. *n.*

An des Mountains (an′dēz), mountain range in W South America. It is the longest continuous mountain system in the world.

andirons

and i ron (and′ī′ərn), one of a pair of metal supports for wood in a fireplace; firedog. *n.*

and/or, both or either. "To earn money from stocks and/or bonds" means to earn it both from stocks and bonds or from either stocks or bonds.

An dor ra (an dôr′ə), 1 small country between France and Spain. 2 its capital. *n.* —**An dor′ran,** *adj., n.*

An dré (an′drā), **John,** 1751-1780, British major hanged as a spy during the Revolutionary War. *n.*

An dre a del Sar to (än drā′ə del sär′tō), 1486-1531, Italian painter.

An drew (an′drü), (in the Bible) one of Christ's twelve apostles. He is the patron saint of Greece, Russia, and Scotland. *n.*

An drom e da (an drom′ə də), (in Greek legends) a princess of Ethiopia who was chained to a rock as a sacrifice to a sea monster to save her country. Perseus killed the monster and married Andromeda. *n.*

an ec dot al (an′ik dō′tl), of anecdotes; containing anecdotes: *I think you will enjoy reading this anecdotal biography. adj.*

an ec dote (an′ik dōt), a short account of some interesting incident or event: *Many anecdotes are told about Abraham Lincoln. n.*

a ne mi a (ə nē′mē ə), a weak condition caused by not enough hemoglobin or red corpuscles in the blood or by a loss of blood. *n.*

a ne mic (ə nē′mik), 1 of anemia; having anemia: *anemic symptoms, an anemic patient.* 2 lacking in vigor, strength, or spirit; weak: *an anemic defense. adj.*

anemometer—Wind catches the cups and moves them around, causing the shaft below to turn. The speed of the turning is shown on the dial.

an e mom e ter (an′ə mom′ə tər), instrument for measuring the speed of wind. *n.*

a nem o ne (ə nem′ə nē), 1 plant with a slender stem and small white or colored flowers shaped like cups; windflower. It often blossoms early in the spring. 2 the sea anemone, a flowerlike polyp. *n.*

a nent (ə nent′), concerning; about. *prep.*

an e roid barometer (an′ə roid′), barometer worked by the pressure of air on the elastic lid of an airtight metal box from which the air has been pumped out.

an es the sia (an′əs thē′zhə), entire or partial loss of the feeling of pain, touch, cold, etc. *n.* Also, **anaesthesia.**

an es thet ic (an′əs thet′ik), 1 substance that causes entire or partial loss of the feeling of pain, touch, cold, etc. Chloroform and ether are two common anesthetics used by doctors so that patients will feel no pain. 2 causing anesthesia: *an anesthetic gas.* 1 *n.,* 2 *adj.* Also, **anaesthetic.** —**an′es thet′i cal ly,** *adv.*

an es the tist (ə nes′thə tist), person specially trained to give anesthetics. *n.* Also, **anaesthetist.**

an es the tize (ə nes′thə tīz), make unable to feel pain, touch, cold, etc.; make insensible. *v.,* **an es the tized, an es the tiz ing.** Also, **anaesthetize.**

a new (ə nü′ *or* ə nyü′), 1 once more; again: *He made so many mistakes he had to begin his work anew.* 2 in a new form or way: *The architect planned the building anew. adv.*

an gel (ān′jəl), 1 messenger from God: *The angels told the shepherds about the birth of Christ.* 2 person as good or as lovely as an angel. *n.*

an gel fish (ān′jəl fish′), any of several colorful tropical fishes with spiny fins. *n., pl.* **an gel fish es** *or* **an gel fish.**

an gel ic (an jel′ik), 1 of angels; heavenly: *an angelic vision.* 2 like an angel; pure, innocent, good, or lovely: *an angelic child. adj.*

an gel i cal (an jel′ə kəl), angelic. *adj.* —**an gel′i cal ly,** *adv.*

An gel i co (an jel′ə kō), **Fra,** 1387-1455, Italian painter. *n.*

an ge lus *or* **An ge lus** (an′jə ləs), 1 prayer said by Roman Catholics in memory of Christ's assuming human form. 2 the bell rung at morning, noon, and night to signal the times this prayer is said. *n.*

an ger (ang′gər), 1 the feeling that one has toward someone or something that hurts, opposes, offends, or annoys: *In a moment of anger, I hit my brother.* 2 make angry: *The girl's disobedience angered her parents.* 3 become angry: *He angers easily.* 1 *n.,* 2,3 *v.*

an gi o sperm (an′jē ō spėrm′), any plant having its seeds enclosed in an ovary or fruit; a flowering plant. Grasses, beans, strawberries, and oaks are angiosperms. *n.*

aneroid barometer—Rising air pressure forces down the elastic lid of the airtight box. This action lowers the spring and, by means of levers, moves the pointer on the dial. Falling air pressure reverses the movements.

an gle¹ (ang′gəl), 1 the space between two lines or surfaces that meet: *Angles are measured in degrees.* 2 the figure formed by two such lines or surfaces. 3 the difference in direction between two such lines or surfaces: *The two roads lie at an angle of about 45 de-*

grees. 4 move, turn, or bend at an angle: *The road angles to the right here.* 5 corner: *We took a picture of the northeast angle of the school.* 6 point of view: *We are treating the problem from a new angle.* 1-3,5,6 *n.,* 4 *v.,* **an gled, an gling.** [from French of the 1300's]

an gle² (ang′gəl), 1 fish with a hook and line. 2 try to get something by using tricks or schemes: *She angled for an invitation to his party by flattering him.* *v.,* **an gled, an gling.** [Old English *angel* fishhook]

An gle (ang′gəl), member of a Germanic tribe that, with the Jutes and Saxons, conquered England in the A.D. 400's and 500's. *n.*

an gler (ang′glər), person who fishes with a hook and line, especially one who does so for sport. *n.*

an gle worm (ang′gəl wėrm′), earthworm. *n.*

An gli can (ang′glə kən), 1 of or having to do with the Church of England or other churches of the same faith elsewhere. 2 member of an Anglican church. 1 *adj.,* 2 *n.*

An gli can ism (ang′glə kə niz′əm), the principles and beliefs of the Church of England or other churches of the same faith elsewhere. *n.*

An gli cize (ang′glə sīz), make or become English in form, pronunciation, habits, customs, or character. *Cajole, lace,* and *cousin* are French words that have been Anglicized. *v.,* **An gli cized, An gli ciz ing.**

an gling (ang′gling), act, art, or sport of fishing, especially with a hook and line. *n.*

An glo-Sax on (ang′glō sak′sən), 1 member of the Germanic tribes that invaded England in the A.D. 400's and 500's and ruled most of England until the Norman Conquest in 1066. 2 the language of these tribes; Old English. 3 of or having to do with the Anglo-Saxons or their language. 4 person who in any period of history has spoken English. 5 having to do with any English-speaking people. 6 person of English descent. 1,2,4,6 *n.,* 3,5 *adj.*

An go la (ang gō′lə), Portuguese colony in SW Africa. *Capital:* Luanda. See **Congo** for map. *n.*

An go ra (ang gôr′ə), 1 Angora cat. 2 Angora goat. 3 Angora rabbit. 4 Ankara. 5 **angora, a** mohair. **b** a very fluffy yarn made partly or entirely from the hair of Angora goats or Angora rabbits. *n., pl.* **An go ras** for 1-3.

ACUTE   RIGHT   OBTUSE

angle¹ (def. 2)—three kinds of angles

Angora cat, cat with long, silky hair.
Angora goat, goat with long, silky hair. This hair is used for wool and made into a cloth called angora or mohair.
Angora rabbit, rabbit with long, soft hair. This hair is used in making a very fluffy yarn or fabric.

an gri ly (ang′grə lē), in an angry manner; with anger. *adv.*

an gri ness (ang′grē nis), condition of being angry. *n.*

an gry (ang′grē), 1 feeling or showing anger: *I was very angry when you disobeyed. My friend's angry words hurt my feelings.* 2 stormy: *the dark clouds of an angry sky.* 3 inflamed and sore: *An infected cut looks angry.* *adj.,* **an gri er, an gri est.**

an guish (ang′gwish), very great pain or grief; great distress: *He was in anguish until the doctor set his broken leg.* *n.*

an guished (ang′gwisht), full of grief or distress; showing anguish: *He saw the anguished face of the mother whose child was lost.* *adj.*

angular (def. 3)
The angular distance of A from B, when measured from C, is the angle X.

an gu lar (ang′gyə lər), 1 having angles; having sharp corners: *an angular piece of rock.* 2 somewhat thin and bony; not plump: *Many basketball players have tall, angular bodies.* 3 measured by an angle: *angular distance.* *adj.* —**an′gu lar ly,** *adv.*

an gu lar i ty (ang′gyə lar′ə tē), condition of having sharp or prominent corners. *n.*

an i line or **an i lin** (an′l ən), a colorless, poisonous, oily liquid, obtained from coal tar. It is a compound of carbon, nitrogen, and hydrogen and is used in making dyes, medicines, plastics, etc. *n.*

aniline dye, 1 dye made from aniline. 2 any artificial dye.

an i mal (an′ə məl), 1 any living thing that is not a plant. Most animals can move about, feed upon other animals or plants, inhale oxygen and exhale carbon dioxide, and have a digestive cavity and a nervous system. A dog, a bird, a fish, a snake, a fly, and a worm are animals. 2 an animal other than man; beast. 3 any mammal, as distinguished from a bird, reptile, etc. Whales, apes, and horses are animals. 4 of animals: *the animal world.* 5 like that of animals: *animal cunning.* 6 person who is like a beast in the way that he acts or thinks. 1-3,6 *n.,* 4,5 *adj.*

animal kingdom, all animals.
animal spirits, natural liveliness.
an i mate (an′ə māt *for 1-4;* an′ə mit *for 5*), 1 make lively or vigorous: *His arrival animated the whole party.* 2 be a motive or a reason for; inspire: *Love for her job animated her work.* 3 put into action; cause to act or work: *Windmills are animated by the wind.* 4 cause to move as if alive: *a field of corn animated by the wind.* 5 living; having life. Animate nature means all living plants and animals. 1-4 *v.,* **an i mat ed, an i mat ing;** 5 *adj.*

an i mat ed (an′ə mā′tid), 1 lively; vigorous: *The children had an animated discussion about yesterday's field trip.* 2 seeming to be alive: *animated dolls.* *adj.* —**an′i mat′ed ly,** *adv.*

animated cartoon, series of drawings arranged to be photographed and shown as a motion picture. Each drawing shows a slight change from the one before it, so that when projected in rapid sequence the figures appear to move.

an i ma tion (an′ə mā′shən), 1 liveliness; vigor: *The boy acted his part as a pirate with great animation.* 2 an animating. 3 a being animated. *n.*

an i mos i ty (an′ə mos′ə tē), violent hatred; active dislike; ill will: *I have done nothing to earn your animosity. n., pl.* **an i mos i ties.**

an i mus (an′ə məs), violent hatred; active dislike; ill will; animosity. *n.*

an i on (an′ī′ən), 1 a negatively charged ion that moves toward the positive pole in electrolysis. 2 atom or group of atoms having a negative charge. *n.*

an ise (an′is), 1 a plant of the same family as the carrot, grown especially for its fragrant seeds. 2 the seed, used as a flavoring or in medicine. *n.*

An jou (an′jü), region in W France. *n.*

An kar a (ang′kər ə), capital since 1923 of Turkey, in the central part. *n.* Also, **Angora.**

an kle (ang′kəl), 1 joint that connects the foot with the leg; tarsus. 2 the slender part of the leg between this joint and the calf. *n.*

33

adj. adjective	n. noun
adv. adverb	prep. preposition
conj. conjunction	pron. pronoun
interj. interjection	v. verb
sing. singular	pl. plural

an klet (ang′klit), 1 a short sock. 2 band or bracelet worn around the ankle. An anklet may be an ornament, a brace, or a fetter. *n.*

an nal ist (an′l ist), 1 writer of annals. 2 historian. *n.*

an nals (an′lz), 1 historical records; history: *Marie Curie holds an important place in the annals of science.* 2 a written account of events year by year. *n.pl.*

An nam (ə nam′), former French protectorate in Indochina, now part of Vietnam. *n.*

An na mese (an′ə mēz′), 1 of or having to do with Annam, its people, or their language. 2 a native of Annam. 3 language spoken by the Annamese; Vietnamese. 1 *adj.*, 2,3 *n.*, *pl.* **An na mese.**

An na po lis (ə nap′ə lis), seaport and capital of Maryland. The United States Naval Academy is located there. *n.*

Anne (an), 1665-1714, queen of Great Britain and Ireland from 1702 to 1714. *n.*

an neal (ə nēl′), make (glass, metals, etc.) less brittle by heating and then gradually cooling. *v.*

an ne lid (an′l id), worm with a body composed of a series of similar ringlike segments. Earthworms, leeches, and various sea worms are annelids. *n.*

an nex (ə neks′ *for 1;* an′eks *for 2*), 1 join or add (a smaller thing) to a larger thing: *The United States annexed Texas in 1845.* 2 something annexed; an added part: *We are building an annex to the school.* 1 *v.*, 2 *n.*, *pl.* **an nex es.**

an nex a tion (an′ek sā′shən), 1 an annexing or a being annexed: *The annexation of Texas enlarged the United States.* 2 something annexed. *n.*

an ni hi late (ə nī′ə lāt), destroy completely; wipe out of existence: *An avalanche annihilated the village.* *v.*, **an ni hi lat ed, an ni hi lat ing.**

an ni hi la tion (ə nī′ə lā′shən), complete destruction. *n.*

an ni ver sar y (an′ə vėr′sər ē), 1 the yearly return of a special date: *Your birthday is an anniversary you like to have remembered.* 2 celebration of the yearly return of a special date. 3 having to do with an anniversary: *an anniver-*

sary dinner. 1,2 *n.*, *pl.* **an ni ver sa ries;** 3 *adj.*

an no Dom i ni (an′ō dom′ə nī), LATIN. in the year of our Lord; in the (specified) year since the birth of Christ. *Abbrev.:* A.D.

an no tate (an′ə tāt), 1 provide with notes or comments: *The Bible is often annotated so that the language used can be explained and the events described can be interpreted for a modern reader.* 2 write or insert notes or comments: *Some people annotate as they read.* *v.*, **an no tat ed, an no tat ing.**

an no ta tion (an′ə tā′shən), 1 a providing with notes or comments: *The annotation of this play by Shakespeare required the explanation of many words no longer used.* 2 note added to explain or criticize: *The editor's annotations were printed in small type at the bottom of the page.* *n.*

an nounce (ə nouns′), 1 give public or formal notice of: *Please announce to the children that there will be no school this afternoon.* 2 make known the presence or arrival of: *The loudspeaker announced each airplane as it landed at the airport.* 3 introduce programs, read news, etc., on the radio or television. *v.*, **an nounced, an nounc ing.**

an nounce ment (ə nouns′mənt), 1 an announcing; making known. We speak of the announcement of a speaker, a meeting, a wedding, a concert, etc. 2 what is announced or made known: *The chairman made two announcements. The announcement was published in the newspapers.* *n.*

an nounc er (ə noun′sər), 1 person or thing that announces. 2 person who announces on the radio or television. *n.*

an noy (ə noi′), make somewhat angry; disturb; trouble; vex: *The baby is always annoying his sister by pulling her hair.* *v.*

an noy ance (ə noi′əns), 1 a being annoyed; feeling of dislike or trouble; vexation: *He showed his annoyance at us by slamming the door.* 2 something that annoys; nuisance: *The heavy traffic on our street is an annoyance.* 3 an annoying. *n.*

an noy ing (ə noi′ing), disturbing; troublesome. *adj.* —**an noy′ing ly,** *adv.* —**an noy′ing ness,** *n.*

an nu al (an′yü əl), 1 coming once a year: *Your birthday is an annual event.* 2 in a year; for a year: *For the last two years his annual salary has been $9000.* 3 lasting for a whole year: *The earth makes an annual course around the sun.* 4 living but one year or season: *Corn and beans are annual plants.* 5 plant that lives but one year or season. 6 book, journal, etc., published once a year. 1-4 *adj.*, 5,6 *n.*

an nu al ly (an′yü ə lē), each year; year by year; yearly. *adv.*

an nu i ty (ə nü′ə tē *or* ə nyü′ə tē), 1 sum of money paid every year or at certain regular times: *Many businesses provide annuities for employees after they retire.* 2 the right to receive such a sum of money. 3 an investment that provides a fixed yearly income during one's lifetime or for a specified time. *n.*, *pl.* **an nu i ties.**

an nul (ə nul′), do away with; destroy the force of; make void; cancel: *The judge annulled the contract because one of the signers was too young.* *v.*, **an nulled, an nul ling.**

an nul ment (ə nul′mənt), an annulling or being annulled; declaring void; cancellation: *An annulment of the marriage was granted by the court because the marriage was illegal.* *n.*

an num (an′əm), LATIN. year. *Per annum* means for each year. *n.*

An nun ci a tion (ə nun′sē ā′shən), 1 (in the Bible) the announcement by the angel Gabriel to the Virgin Mary that she was to be the mother of Christ. 2 a church festival held on March 25 in memory of the Annunciation. *n.*

an ode (an′ōd), a positively charged electrode. Current flows from the cathode, a negatively charged electrode, to the anode. The carbon of a dry cell and the plate of a vacuum tube are anodes. *n.*

a noint (ə noint′), 1 put oil on; rub with a healing ointment; smear: *Anoint sunburned skin with cold cream.* 2 put oil on (a person) as part of a ceremony: *The bishop anointed the new king.* *v.*

a noint ment (ə noint′mənt), an anointing or being anointed. *n.*

a nom a lous (ə nom′ə ləs), departing from the common rule; irregular: *It would be anomalous for a principal to have no authority.* *adj.* —**a nom′a lous ly,** *adv.*

a nom a ly (ə nom′ə lē), 1 something abnormal: *A dog with six legs would be an anomaly.* 2 departure from the common rule; irregularity: *"A lamb in school is an anomaly,"* said the teacher to Mary. *n.*, *pl.* **a nom a lies.**

a non (ə non′), OLD USE. 1 in a little while; soon. 2 at another time; again. *adv.*

anon., anonymous.

an o nym i ty (an′ə nim′ə tē), condition of being anonymous. *n.*

a non y mous (ə non′ə məs), 1 by or from a person whose name is not known or given: *An anonymous book is one published without giving the name of the author.* 2 having no name; of unknown name; nameless: *This book was written by an anonymous author.* *adj.* —**a non′y mous ly,** *adv.*

an oth er (ə nuŦH′ər), 1 one more: *Have another glass of milk* (adj.). *He ate a bar of candy and then asked for another* (pron.). 2 a different: *Show me another kind of hat.* 3 a different one: *I don't like this book; give me another.* 1,2 adj., 1,3 pron.

ans., answer.

an swer (an′sər), 1 speak or write in return to a question: *I asked him a question, but he would not answer. He finally answered my question.* 2 words spoken or written in return to a question: *The boy gave a quick answer.* 3 gesture or act done in return: *A nod was her only answer.* 4 act in return to a call, signal, etc.; respond: *I knocked on the door, but no one answered. She answered the doorbell.* 5 solution to a problem: *What is the correct answer to this arithmetic problem?* 6 meet or satisfy a requirement, wish, etc.; serve: *On the picnic, a newspaper answered for a tablecloth.* 7 be responsible: *The bus driver must answer for the safety of the children in his bus.* 8 be similar to; agree with; correspond: *The dog we found answers to your description.* 1,4, 6-8 v., 2,3,5 n.

answer back, reply in a rude, impertinent way: *When the teacher scolded the pupil he answered back.*

an swer a ble (an′sər ə bəl), 1 responsible: *The club treasurer is held answerable to the club for the money given to her.* 2 that can be answered: *That question is easily answerable.* adj.

ant (ant), any of certain small insects that live together in tunnels in the ground or in wood in colonies of from dozens of individuals to half a million or more. Ants are black, brown, reddish, or yellowish. Ants, bees, and wasps belong to the same group of insects. n. —ant′like′, adj.

-ant, suffix added to verbs. 1 (to form adjectives) that _____s; _____ing: *Buoyant = that buoys or buoying. Compliant = that complies or complying.* 2 (to form nouns) one that _____s: *Assistant = one that assists.* [from French before the 1400's -ant, from Latin -antem]

ant ac id (ant′as′id), substance that

anteater—This species is about 3½ ft. long, including the tail.

neutralizes acids. Baking soda is an antacid. n.

an tag o nism (an tag′ə niz′əm), active opposition; hostility: *During the argument, the boy's antagonism showed plainly in his face.* n.

an tag o nist (an tag′ə nist), person who fights, struggles, or contends against another in a combat or contest of any kind; adversary; opponent: *The knight defeated each antagonist who came against him.* n.

an tag o nis tic (an tag′ə nis′tik), acting against each other; opposing; hostile: *Cats and dogs are antagonistic.* adj. —an tag′o nis′ti cal ly, adv.

an tag o nize (an tag′ə nīz), make an enemy of; arouse dislike in: *Her unkind remarks antagonized people who had been her friends.* v., an tag o nized, an tag o niz ing.

ant arc tic (ant′ärk′tik or ant′är′tik), 1 at or near the South Pole; of the south polar region. 2 **the Antarctic,** the south polar region. 1 adj., 2 n.

Ant arc ti ca (ant′ärk′tə kə or ant′-är′tə kə), continent around or near the South Pole. It is almost totally covered by ice and lies within the antarctic circle. n.

antarctic circle or **Antarctic Circle,** the imaginary boundary of the south polar region. It runs parallel to the equator at 23 degrees 30 minutes (23° 30′) north of the South Pole.

Antarctic Continent, Antarctica.

Antarctic Ocean, the ocean of the south polar region.

Antarctic Zone, region between the antarctic circle and the South Pole.

ante-, prefix. before; in front of: *Antedate = to date before. Anteroom = a room in front of (another).* [from Latin]

ant eat er (ant′ē′tər), any of various mammals that eat ants and termites which they catch with their long, sticky tongues. n.

an te-bel lum (an′ti bel′əm), 1 before the war. 2 before the American Civil War. adj. [from Latin ante bellum]

an te ced ent (an′tə sēd′nt), 1 the

hat, āge, fär; let, ēqual, tèrm; it, īce; hot, ōpen, ôrder; oil, out; cup, pùt, rüle; ch, child; ng, long; sh, she; th, thin; ŦH, then; zh, measure;

ə represents *a* in about, *e* in taken, *i* in pencil, *o* in lemon, *u* in circus.

noun or noun phrase to which a pronoun refers. In "The dog which killed the rat is brown," *dog* is the antecedent of *which.* 2 coming or happening before; previous: *The cavemen lived in a period of history antecedent to written records.* 3 a previous happening or event. 4 **antecedents,** pl. **a** past life or history: *No one knew the antecedents of the mysterious stranger.* **b** ancestors: *He has Scottish antecedents.* 1,3,4 n., 2 adj.

an te cham ber (an′ti chām′bər), anteroom. n.

an te date (an′ti dāt), 1 be or happen before; precede: *Radio antedated television.* 2 give an earlier date to: *Some states require a person to antedate legal papers to Saturday if they are signed on Sunday.* v., an te dat ed, an te dat ing.

an te di lu vi an (an′ti də lü′vē ən), 1 very old; old-fashioned. 2 a very old person; an old-fashioned person. 3 person who lived before the Flood. 4 before the Flood. 1,4 adj., 2,3 n.

an te lope (an′tl ōp), 1 any of certain hoofed mammals of Africa and Asia that belong to the same family as the goat and cow but resemble the deer in appearance, grace, and speed. Antelopes chew the cud and usually have a single pair of hollow horns that curve backward and do not fork or branch. 2 pronghorn. n., pl. an te lope or an te lopes.

antenna (def. 1)
antennae of a beetle

an ten na (an ten′ə), 1 one of the long, slender feelers on the head of an insect, scorpion, lobster, etc. 2 the aerial of a radio or television set. n., pl. an ten nae (an ten′ē) or an ten nas.

an ter i or (an tir′ē ər), 1 more to the front; fore: *The anterior part of a fish contains the head and gills.* 2 going

adj. adjective	*n.* noun
adv. adverb	*prep.* preposition
conj. conjunction	*pron.* pronoun
interj. interjection	*v.* verb
sing. singular	*pl.* plural

before; earlier: *events anterior to the last war. adj.*

an te room (an′ti rüm′ *or* an′ti rüm′), a small room leading to a larger one; waiting room. *n.*

an them (an′thəm), 1 song of praise, devotion, or patriotism: *"The Star-Spangled Banner" is the national anthem of the United States.* 2 piece of sacred music, usually with words from some passage in the Bible. *n.*

anther
The anther and filament together form the stamen.

—ANTHER
—FILAMENT

an ther (an′thər), the part of the stamen of a flower that bears the pollen. *n.*

ant hill, heap of dirt piled up by ants around the entrance to their tunnels.

an thol o gy (an thol′ə jē), collection of poems or prose selections, usually from various authors. *n., pl.* **an thol o gies.**

an thra cite (an′thrə sīt), coal that burns with very little smoke and flame; hard coal. It consists almost entirely of carbon. *n.*

an thrax (an′thraks), an often fatal disease of cattle, sheep, etc., that human beings may get from them. *n.*

an thro poid (an′thrə poid), 1 (of certain apes) manlike; resembling man. Anthropoid apes have no tail and lack cheek pouches. 2 a manlike ape. Gorillas, chimpanzees, orangutans, and gibbons are anthropoids; lemurs and most monkeys are not. 1 *adj.,* 2 *n.*

an thro po log i cal (an′thrə pə loj′ə kəl), of or having to do with anthropology. *adj.*

an thro pol o gist (an′thrə pol′ə jist), an expert in anthropology. *n.*

an thro pol o gy (an′thrə pol′ə jē), science of man, dealing with the origin, development, races, customs, and beliefs of mankind. *n.*

anti-, *prefix.* 1 against _____; opposed to _____: *Antiaircraft = against aircraft. Antislavery = opposed to slavery.* 2 preventing or counteracting _____: *Antirust = preventing or counteracting rust.* [from Greek]

an ti air craft (an′tē er′kraft′ *or* an′-

tē ar′kraft′), used in defense against enemy aircraft. *adj.*

an ti-A mer i can (an′tē ə mer′ə-kən), opposed to the interests or the people of the United States. *adj.*

an ti bi ot ic (an′ti bī ot′ik), substance produced by a living organism that destroys or weakens germs. Penicillin is an antibiotic useful in treating scarlet fever and common types of blood poisoning. *n.*

an ti bod y (an′ti bod′ē), a protein substance produced in the blood or tissues of animals or man that destroys or weakens bacteria or neutralizes poisons produced by them. *n., pl.* **an ti bod ies.**

an tic (an′tik), 1 a silly trick. See also **antics.** 2 grotesque; odd. 1 *n.,* 2 *adj.*

an tic i pate (an tis′ə pāt), 1 look forward to; expect: *We are anticipating a good time at your party.* 2 do before others do; be ahead of in doing: *The Chinese anticipated the European discovery of gunpowder.* 3 take care of ahead of time; consider in advance: *We anticipated hot weather and took our bathing suits with us. v.,* **an tic i-pat ed, an tic i pat ing.**

an tic i pa tion (an tis′ə pā′shən), act of anticipating; looking forward to; expectation: *In anticipation of a cold winter, the farmer cut more firewood than usual. n.*

an ti cli mac tic (an′ti klī mak′tik), of or like an anticlimax. *adj.*

an ti cli max (an′ti klī′maks), an abrupt descent from the important to the trivial or unimportant. EXAMPLE: "Alas! Alas! What shall I do? I've lost my wife and best hat, too!" *n., pl.* **an ti cli max es.**

an tics (an′tiks), funny gestures or actions; silly tricks; capers: *The antics of the clown amused us. n.pl.*

an ti cy clone (an′ti sī′klōn), winds moving around and away from a center of high pressure, which also moves. *n.*

an ti dote (an′ti dōt), 1 medicine or remedy that counteracts the harmful effects of a poison: *Milk is an antidote for some poisons.* 2 remedy for anything that is harmful: *Education is an antidote for ignorance. n.*

An tie tam (an tē′təm), small creek in NW Maryland. A major battle of the Civil War was fought near it in 1862 between Lee and McClellan which resulted in Lee's retreat. *n.*

an ti freeze (an′ti frēz′), substance added to a liquid to lower its freezing point. Alcohol is used as an antifreeze in automobile radiators because it prevents the water from freezing during cold weather. *n.*

an ti gen (an′tə jən), any protein substance that causes the body to produce

antibodies to counteract it. Bacteria are antigens. *n.*

an ti his ta mine (an′ti his′tə mēn′), medicine that helps to relieve the symptoms of colds and allergies. *n.*

an ti knock (an′ti nok′), substance added to the fuel of an internal-combustion engine to reduce noise caused by too rapid combustion. *n.*

An til les (an til′ēz), chain of islands in the West Indies. The **Greater Antilles** are Cuba, Hispaniola, Puerto Rico, and Jamaica; the **Lesser Antilles** are smaller islands southeast of Puerto Rico, including the Windward and Leeward Islands. See **Caribbean Sea** for map. *n.pl.*

an ti mis sile (an′ti mis′əl), used in defense against ballistic missiles, rockets, etc.: *antimissile missiles. adj.*

an ti mo ny (an′tə mō′nē), a brittle, silver-white, metallic element. It occurs chiefly in combination with other elements. Antimony is used to make alloys harder and its compounds are used to make medicines, pigments, and glass. *n.*

an tip a thy (an tip′ə thē), 1 a strong dislike; a feeling against: *He felt an antipathy to snakes.* 2 something or someone that arouses such a feeling. *n., pl.* **an tip a thies.**

an tip o des (an tip′ə dēz′), 1 two places on directly opposite sides of the earth: *The North Pole and the South Pole are antipodes.* 2 a place on the opposite side of the earth. 1 *n.pl.,* 2 *n. pl. or sing.*

an ti quar i an (an′tə kwer′ē ən), 1 of or having to do with antiques or antiquaries: *The antiquarian section of the museum was full of old furniture and dishes.* 2 antiquary. 1 *adj.,* 2 *n.*

an ti quar y (an′tə kwer′ē), student or collector of relics from ancient times. *n., pl.* **an ti quar ies.**

an ti quat ed (an′tə kwā′tid), 1 that has grown old but is no longer valued; old-fashioned; out-of-date: *Most science books written 20 years ago are now antiquated.* 2 too old for work or service: *This antiquated truck is ready for the junk heap. adj.*

an tique (an tēk′), 1 of times long ago; from times long ago: *This antique chair was made in 1750.* 2 something made long ago: *This carved chest is a genuine antique.* 1 *adj.,* 2 *n.*

an tiq ui ty (an tik′wə tē), 1 great age; oldness: *the antiquity of man.* 2 times long ago, especially the period of history between 5000 B.C. and A.D. 476: *Moses and Caesar were two great men of antiquity.* 3 the people of ancient times. 4 **antiquities,** *pl.* **a** things from times long ago: *We visited museums filled with antiquities.* **b** customs and anvil (def. 1)

life of olden times. *n., pl.* **an·tiq·ui·ties.**

an·ti-Se·mit·ic (an′ti sə mit′ik), prejudiced against Jews. *adj.*

an·ti-Sem·i·tism (an′ti sem′ə tiz′əm), dislike or hatred for Jews; prejudice against Jews. *n.*

an·ti·sep·tic (an′tə sep′tik), 1 substance that kills or prevents the growth of germs and thus prevents infection. Iodine, peroxide, Mercurochrome, alcohol, and boric acid are antiseptics. 2 preventing infection. 1 *n.,* 2 *adj.*

an·ti·sep·ti·cal·ly (an′tə sep′tik lē), by the use of antiseptics. *adv.*

an·ti·slav·er·y (an′ti slā′vər ē), opposed to slavery; against slavery. *adj.*

an·ti·so·cial (an′ti sō′shəl), 1 opposed to the principles upon which society is based: *Murder and stealing are antisocial acts.* 2 against the general welfare: *Spitting and littering in public places are forms of antisocial behavior.* 3 opposed to friendly relationship and normal companionship with others: *Hermits are antisocial. adj.*

an·tith·e·sis (an tith′ə sis), 1 the direct opposite: *Hate is the antithesis of love.* 2 contrast of ideas. EXAMPLE: "To err is human; to forgive, divine." 3 opposition; contrast: *the antithesis of theory and fact. n., pl.* **an·tith·e·ses** (an-tith′ə sēz′).

an·ti·tox·in (an′ti tok′sən), 1 antibody formed in response to the presence of a toxin to prevent or reduce the effects of that toxin. 2 serum containing antitoxin, injected into a person to make him immune to a disease. *n.*

an·ti·trust (an′ti trust′), opposed to large corporations that stifle competition and so control the trade practices of certain kinds of businesses. *adj.*

ant·ler (ant′lər), 1 horn of a deer, elk, or moose, usually having one or more branches. Antlers are shed once a year and grow back again during the next year. 2 branch of such a horn. *n.*

ant lion, insect whose larva digs a pit, where it lies in wait to catch ants and other insects as they fall in and are trapped.

An·toi·nette (an′twə net′), **Marie.** See **Marie Antoinette.** *n.*

An·to·ny (an′tə nē), **Mark,** 83?-30 B.C., Roman general and statesman. *n.*

an·to·nym (an′tə nim), word that means the opposite of another word. "Hot" is the antonym of "cold." *n.*

Ant·werp (ant′wərp), seaport in NW Belgium. *n.*

a·nus (ā′nəs), the opening at the lower end of the alimentary canal, through which solid waste material and undigested food pass. *n.*

an·vil (an′vəl), 1 an iron or steel block on which metals are hammered and shaped. 2 incus, a bone of the middle ear. *n.*

anx·i·e·ty (ang zī′ə tē), 1 uneasy thoughts or fears about what may happen; troubled, worried, or uneasy feeling: *We all felt anxiety when the airplane was caught in the storm.* 2 eager desire: *Her anxiety to succeed led her to work hard. n., pl.* **anx·i·e·ties.**

anx·ious (angk′shəs *or* ang′shəs), 1 uneasy because of thoughts or fears of what may happen; troubled; worried: *I felt anxious about my final exams.* 2 causing uneasy feelings or troubled thoughts; distressing: *The week of the flood was an anxious time for all of us.* 3 wishing very much; eager: *He was anxious for a bicycle. She was anxious to learn to play chess. adj.* —**anx′-ious·ly,** *adv.* —**anx′ious·ness,** *n.*

an·y (en′ē), 1 one out of many: *Choose any book you like from the books on the shelf.* 2 some: *Have you any fresh fruit? (adj.). I need more ink; have you any? (pron.).* 3 every: *Any child knows that.* 4 even a little; even one or two: *Because of an allergy, I can't eat any chocolate.* 5 to some extent or degree; at all: *Have I improved any?* 1-4 *adj.,* 2 *pron.,* 5 *adv.*

an·y·bod·y (en′ē bod′ē), 1 any person; anyone: *Has anybody been here?* 2 an important person: *Everybody who's anybody stays at that hotel.* 1 *pron.,* 2 *n., pl.* **an·y·bod·ies.**

an·y·how (en′ē hou), 1 in any case; at least: *I can see as well as you can, anyhow.* 2 in any way whatever: *The answer is wrong anyhow you look at it.* 3 carelessly: *He dumped the tools into the box just anyhow. adv.*

antler (def. 1)
antlers of a deer

an·y·one (en′ē wun), any person; anybody: *Can anyone go to this movie or is it just for adults? pron.*

an·y·place (en′ē plās), anywhere. *adv.*

an·y·thing (en′ē thing), 1 any thing:

hat, āge, fär; let, ēqual, tėrm;
it, īce; hot, ōpen, ôrder;
oil, out; cup, pu̇t, rüle; ch, child;
ng, long; sh, she; th, thin;
ᵞH, then; zh, measure;

ə represents *a* in about,
e in taken, *i* in pencil,
o in lemon, *u* in circus.

Do you have anything to eat? 2 a thing of any kind whatever: *My dog will eat almost anything.* 3 in any way; at all: *My bike isn't anything like yours.* 1 *pron.,* 2 *n.,* 3 *adv.*

anything but, not at all: *This old shack is anything but warm.*

an·y·time (en′ē tīm), at any time; no matter when: *You are welcome to visit us anytime. adv.*

an·y·way (en′ē wā), 1 in any case; at least: *I am coming anyway, no matter what you say.* 2 in any way whatever; carelessly; anyhow: *She stacked the books on the floor just anyway. adv.*

an·y·where (en′ē hwer), in, at, or to any place: *I'll meet you anywhere you say. adv.*

an·y·wise (en′ē wīz), in any way; to any degree; at all. *adv.*

A-OK (ā′ō′kā′), INFORMAL. OK. *adj., adv., interj.*

a·or·ta (ā ôr′tə), the main artery that carries the blood from the left side of the heart to all parts of the body except the lungs. *n., pl.* **a·or·tas, a·or·tae** (ā ôr′tē).

aou·dad (ou′dad), a wild sheep of northern Africa, found also in Texas, New Mexico, and California. *n.*

a·pace (ə pās′), very soon; swiftly; fast: *The summer flew by, and the time for school was coming on apace. adv.*

A·pach·e (ə pach′ē), member of a tribe of Indians living in the southwestern United States. They were formerly warlike and nomadic. *n., pl.* **A·pach·es** or **A·pach·e.**

a·part (ə pärt′), 1 to pieces; in pieces; in separate parts: *They took the watch apart to see how it runs.* 2 away from each other: *Keep the dogs apart.* 3 to one side; aside: *I set some money apart for a vacation each year.* 4 away from others; separately; independently: *View each idea apart. adv.*

apart from, besides: *Apart from that, it was a good plan.*

a·part·heid (ə pärt′hāt *or* ə pärt′hīt), racial segregation, especially as practiced in South Africa. *n.* [from Afrikaans]

a·part·ment (ə pärt′mənt), 1 room or

adj.	adjective	*n.*	noun
adv.	adverb	*prep.*	preposition
conj.	conjunction	*pron.*	pronoun
interj.	interjection	*v.*	verb
sing.	singular	*pl.*	plural

group of rooms to live in; flat: *The apartment for our family is in a building twenty stories high.* 2 apartment house. *n.*

apartment house, building with a number of apartments in it.

ap a thet ic (ap′ə thet′ik), 1 with little interest or desire for action; indifferent: *The student's apathetic attitude toward schoolwork annoyed the teacher.* 2 lacking in feeling; unemotional. *adj.*

ap a thet i cal ly (ap′ə thet′ik lē), in an apathetic manner. *adv.*

ap a thy (ap′ə thē), 1 lack of interest or desire for action; indifference: *The citizens' apathy to local affairs resulted in poor government.* 2 lack of feeling: *She reacted to her former friend's troubles with apathy.* *n., pl.* **ap a thies.**

ape (āp), 1 a large, tailless monkey with long arms, able to stand almost erect and walk on two feet. Chimpanzees, gorillas, orangutans, and gibbons are apes. 2 any monkey. 3 imitate; mimic: *They aped the mannerisms of their favorite TV star.* 4 person who imitates or mimics. 1,2,4 *n.,* 3 *v.,* **aped, ap ing.** **—ape′like′,** *adj.*

Ap en nines (ap′ə nīnz), the chief mountain range in Italy, extending north and south. *n.pl.*

ap er ture (ap′ər chər), an opening; gap; hole. A shutter regulates the size of the aperture through which light passes into a camera. *n.*

a pex (ā′peks), 1 the highest point; tip: *The apex of a triangle or of a leaf is the point opposite the base.* 2 climax: *Camping out on the last night and eating around the campfire was the apex of the children's vacation.* *n., pl.* **a pex es** or **ap i ces.**

aphelion—a planet in orbit around the sun shown at aphelion and perihelion

a phe li on (ə fē′lē ən), the point farthest from the sun in the orbit of a planet or comet. *n., pl.* **a phe li a** (ə fē′lē ə).

a phid (ā′fid *or* af′id), a very small insect that lives by sucking juices from plants; plant louse. *n.*

aph o rism (af′ə riz′əm), a short sen-

tence expressing a general truth or some practical wisdom; maxim; proverb. EXAMPLE: "A living dog is better than a dead lion." *n.*

Aph ro di te (af′rə dī′tē), (in Greek myths) the goddess of love and beauty. The Romans called her Venus. *n.*

a pi ar y (ā′pē er′ē), place where bees are kept; group of beehives. *n., pl.* **a pi ar ies.**

ap i ces (ap′ə sēz′ *or* ā′pə sēz′), a plural of **apex.** *n.*

a piece (ə pēs′), for each one; each: *These apples cost ten cents apiece.* *adv.*

ap ish (ā′pish), 1 foolish; silly: *I hid my embarrassment with an apish grin.* 2 like an ape. *adj.*

a plomb (ə plom′), self-possession; assurance; poise. *n.*

APO or **A.P.O.,** Army Post Office.

A poc a lypse (ə pok′ə lips), the last book of the New Testament; the book of Revelation. *n.*

A poc ry pha (ə pok′rə fə), fourteen books included in the Roman Catholic Bible but not generally found in Jewish or Protestant Bibles. *n.pl.*

a poc ry phal (ə pok′rə fəl), 1 of doubtful authorship or authority. 2 of doubtful genuineness; false: *There are always many apocryphal stories about a famous person.* 3 **Apocryphal,** of, having to do with, or from the Apocrypha. *adj.*

apogee—the moon in orbit around the earth shown at apogee and perigee

ap o gee (ap′ə jē), the point farthest from the earth in the orbit of the moon or any other earth satellite. *n.*

A pol lo (ə pol′ō), (in Greek and Roman myths) the god of the sun, poetry, music, prophecy, and healing. Apollo was the highest type of youthful, manly beauty to the Greeks and Romans. *n.*

a pol o get ic (ə pol′ə jet′ik), 1 making an excuse; expressing regret: *He sent me an apologetic note saying he was sorry for forgetting to come to my party.* 2 defending by speech or writing. *adj.*

a pol o get i cal ly (ə pol′ə jet′ik lē), in an apologetic manner. *adv.*

a pol o gist (ə pol′ə jist), person who defends an idea, belief, religion, etc., in speech or writing. *n.*

a pol o gize (ə pol′ə jīz), 1 make an apology; say one is sorry; offer an excuse: *She apologized for hurting my feelings.* 2 defend an idea, argument, belief, etc., in speech or writing. *v.,* **a pol o gized, a pol o giz ing.**

a pol o gy (ə pol′ə jē), 1 words saying one is sorry for an offense, fault, or

accident; explanation asking pardon: *Will you accept my apology for yelling at you? Make an apology to the teacher for your lateness.* 2 explanation of the truth or justice of something; defense: *Thomas Paine's "Common Sense" is a famous apology for American independence and democracy.* 3 a poor substitute; makeshift: *One piece of toast is a skimpy apology for a breakfast.* *n., pl.* **a pol o gies.**

ap o plec tic (ap′ə plek′tik), 1 of or causing apoplexy. 2 suffering from apoplexy. 3 showing symptoms of a tendency to apoplexy: *An apoplectic rage can increase one's blood pressure alarmingly.* *adj.*

ap o plex y (ap′ə plek′sē), a sudden loss of the power to feel or think or move; stroke. Apoplexy is caused by injury to the brain when a blood vessel breaks or the blood supply becomes obstructed. *n.*

a pos ta sy (ə pos′tə sē), a complete forsaking of one's religion, faith, political party, or principles. *n., pl.* **a pos ta sies.**

a pos tate (ə pos′tāt), person who completely forsakes his religion, faith, political party, or principles. *n.*

a pos tle or **A pos tle** (ə pos′əl), 1 one of the twelve disciples, **the Apostles,** chosen by Christ to preach the gospel to all the world. 2 any early Christian leader or missionary: *Paul was frequently called the "Apostle to the Gentiles."* 3 leader of any reform movement or new belief who shows great vigor in seeking to make it popular or to win converts. *n.*

ap os tol ic or **A pos tol ic** (ap′ə stol′ik), 1 of or having to do with the Apostles. 2 of or having to do with the Pope; papal. *adj.*

a pos tro phe (ə pos′trə fē), sign (′) used: 1 to show the omission of one or more letters in contractions, as in *o'er* for *over, thro'* for *through.* 2 to show the possessive forms of nouns or indefinite pronouns, as in *John's book, the lions' den,* and *everybody's business.* 3 to form plurals of letters and numbers: *There are two o's in apology and four 9's in 959,990.* *n.*

apothecaries' weight, system of weights in which a pound containing 12 ounces is used. Apothecaries' weight is used in mixing drugs and filling prescriptions.

a poth e car y (ə poth′ə ker′ē), person who prepares and sells drugs and medicines; druggist; pharmacist. *n., pl.* **a poth e car ies.**

ap o thegm (ap′ə them), a short, forceful saying; maxim. EXAMPLE: "Beauty is only skin deep." *n.*

Ap pa la chian Mountains (ap′ə-lā/chən), the chief mountain system in E North America, extending from Quebec Province in Canada to central Alabama.

Ap pa la chians (ap/ə lā/chəns), Appalachian Mountains. *n.pl.*

ap pall or **ap pal** (ə pôl/), fill with horror or fear; dismay; terrify: *The thought of another war appalled us. She was appalled when she saw the river had risen to the doorstep.* *v.,* **ap palled, ap pall ing.**

ap pall ing (ə pô/ling), causing horror; dismaying; terrifying. *adj.* —**ap pall/ing ly,** *adv.*

ap pa ra tus (ap/ə rā/təs *or* ap/ə-rat/əs), 1 the tools, machines, or other equipment necessary to carry out a purpose or for a particular use. Test tubes, beakers, and a Bunsen burner are part of the apparatus used in chemistry. 2 the organs of the body which together perform a particular function. The stomach and intestines are part of our digestive apparatus. *n., pl.* **ap pa ra tus** or **ap pa ra tus es.**

ap par el (ə par/əl), 1 clothing; dress: *Does this store sell women's apparel?* 2 clothe; dress up: *The horseback riders, gaily appareled, formed part of the circus parade.* 1 *n.,* 2 *v.,* **ap par eled, ap par el ing.**

ap par ent (ə par/ənt), 1 plain to see; so plain that one cannot help seeing it: *The stain is apparent from across the room.* 2 easily understood: *It is apparent that the days become shorter in October and November.* 3 that appears to be; seeming: *The apparent size of an airplane in the sky is smaller than the airplane's actual size.* *adj.* —**ap par/ent ness,** *n.*

ap par ent ly (ə par/ənt lē), 1 as far as one can judge by appearances; seemingly. 2 clearly; plainly. *adv.*

ap pa ri tion (ap/ə rish/ən), 1 ghost or phantom: *The apparition, clothed in white, glided through the wall.* 2 the appearance of something strange, remarkable, or unexpected. *n.*

ap peal (ə pēl/), 1 ask earnestly; ask for help, sympathy, etc.: *When the children were in trouble they appealed to their parents.* 2 a call for help, sympathy, etc.; earnest request: *an appeal for forgiveness, an appeal for money for the poor.* 3 call on some person to decide a matter in one's favor: *Everytime my mother answered "No," I appealed to my father.* 4 a call on some person to decide a matter in one's favor: *Sometimes his appeals for another chance were granted.* 5 ask that a case be taken to a higher court or judge to be heard again. 6 a request to have a case heard again before a higher court or judge. 7 be attractive, interesting, or enjoyable: *Blue and red appeal to me but I don't like gray or yellow.* 8 attraction or interest: *Television has a great appeal for most young people.* 1,3,5,7 *v.,* 2,4, 6,8 *n.*

ap peal ing (ə pē/ling), that appeals. *adj.* —**ap peal/ing ly,** *adv.*

ap pear (ə pir/), 1 be seen; come in sight: *One by one the stars appear.* 2 seem; look as if: *The apple appeared sound on the outside, but it was rotten inside.* 3 be published: *His latest book appeared a year ago.* 4 come before the public as a performer or author: *The singer will appear on the television program today.* 5 become known to the mind; be plain: *Their error appeared the next day.* 6 present oneself formally before an authority: *A person accused of a crime must appear before the court.* *v.*

ap pear ance (ə pir/əns), 1 act of coming in sight: *His appearance in the doorway was welcomed with shouts.* 2 a coming before the public as a performer or author: *The singer made her first appearance in a concert in San Francisco.* 3 outward look: *The appearance of the old gray house made us think that it was empty.* 4 outward show; pretense: *My aunt laughs a lot to keep up appearances so the neighbors won't think she is sick.* *n.*

ap pease (ə pēz/), 1 put an end to by satisfying an appetite or desire: *A good dinner will appease your hunger.* 2 make calm or quiet; pacify: *We tried to appease the crying child by giving him candy.* 3 give in to the demands of: *The boy appeased his parents and returned to finish school.* *v.,* **ap peased, ap peas ing.**

ap pease ment (ə pēz/mənt), an appeasing or being appeased; pacification; satisfaction. *n.*

ap peas er (ə pē/zər), person who appeases. *n.*

ap pel late court (ə pel/it), court having the power to examine again and reverse the decisions of a lower court.

ap pel la tion (ap/ə lā/shən), name or title describing some quality. In "John

the Baptist," the appellation of *John* is *the Baptist.* *n.*

ap pend (ə pend/), add to a larger thing; attach as a supplement: *The amendments to the Constitution of the United States are appended to it.* *v.*

ap pend age (ə pen/dij), thing attached to something larger or more important; addition. Arms, tails, fins, legs, etc., are appendages. *n.*

ap pen dec to my (ap/ən dek/tə mē), removal of the vermiform appendix by a surgical operation. *n., pl.* **ap pen dec to mies.**

ap pen di ces (ə pen/də sēz/), a plural of **appendix.** *n.*

ap pen di ci tis (ə pen/də sī/tis), inflammation of the vermiform appendix. *n.*

appendix (def. 2)

LIVER
STOMACH
APPENDIX
LARGE INTESTINE

ap pen dix (ə pen/diks), 1 addition at the end of a book or document. 2 a small saclike growth attached to the large intestine; vermiform appendix. *n., pl.* **ap pen dix es** or **ap pen di ces.**

ap per tain (ap/ər tān/), belong as a part; be connected; relate: *Forestry appertains to geography, to botany, and to agriculture.* *v.*

ap pe tite (ap/ə tīt), 1 desire for food: *Since I had no appetite, they had to coax me to eat.* 2 desire: *The lively children had a great appetite for excitement and amusement.* *n.*

ap pe tiz er (ap/ə tī/zər), something that arouses the appetite or gives relish to food. Pickles and olives are appetizers. *n.*

ap pe tiz ing (ap/ə tī/zing), arousing or exciting the appetite: *Appetizing food always smells delicious. adj.*

ap plaud (ə plôd/), 1 show approval

adj. adjective	*n.* noun
adv. adverb	*prep.* preposition
conj. conjunction	*pron.* pronoun
interj. interjection	*v.* verb
sing. singular	*pl.* plural

by clapping hands, shouting, etc.: *The audience applauds anything that pleases it in a play or concert.* 2 be pleased with; approve; praise: *My parents applauded my decision to remain in school.* *v.*

ap plause (ə plôz′), 1 approval shown by clapping the hands, shouting, etc.: *Applause for the singer's good performance rang out from the audience.* 2 approval; praise. *n.*

ap ple (ap′əl), 1 the firm, fleshy, somewhat round fruit of a tree widely grown in temperate regions. Apples have red, yellow, or green skin, and are eaten either raw or cooked. 2 the tree it grows on. Apples and pears are related to roses. *n.*

apple of one's eye, person or thing that is cherished or valued.

ap ple sauce (ap′əl sôs′), apples cut in pieces and cooked with sugar, spices, and water until soft. *n.*

ap pli ance (ə plī′əns), 1 instrument or machine designed for a particular purpose or operation. A can opener is an appliance for opening tin cans. Vacuum cleaners, washing machines, and refrigerators are household appliances. 2 a putting to use; application: *The appliance of electricity to household tasks made housework easier.* *n.*

ap pli ca bil i ty (ap′lə kə bil′ə tē), a being applicable. *n.*

ap pli ca ble (ap′lə kə bəl), capable of being applied; that can be put to practical use; appropriate; suitable: *The rule "Look before you leap" is almost always applicable.* *adj.*

ap pli cant (ap′lə kənt), person who applies (for a job, money, position, help, etc.). *n.*

ap pli ca tion (ap′lə kā′shən), 1 a putting to use; use: *the application of atomic energy to manufacturing. The application of what you know will help you solve new problems.* 2 way of using: *"Freedom" is a word of many applications.* 3 an applying; putting on: *The painter's careless application of paint spattered the floor.* 4 thing applied. Cold cream, ointments, and mustard plasters are applications. 5 a request (for employment, an award, tickets, etc.): *I filled out an application for the position of clerk.* 6 continued

effort; close attention: *By application to the study of geography, he has become a great geographer.* *n.*

ap pli ca tor (ap′lə kā′tər), instrument or device for applying a medicine, cosmetic, paint, etc. *n.*

ap plied (ə plīd′), put to practical use; used to solve actual problems: *The engineer used applied mathematics to solve the practical problems in building a bridge.* *adj.*

ap pli qué (ap′lə kā′), 1 ornament made of one material sewed or otherwise fastened on another. 2 trim or ornament with appliqué. 1 *n.*, 2 *v.*, **ap pli quéd, ap pli qué ing.** [from French *appliqué* applied]

ap ply (ə plī′), 1 put on; lay on or in contact with: *He applied two coats of paint to the table. Mother applied a wet cloth to the bump on my head.* 2 put to practical use; put into effect; use: *You know the rule but do not know how to apply it.* 3 use (a word or expression) to refer to a person or object: *The boys applied the nickname "Slowpoke" to the pet turtle.* 4 be useful or suitable: *When does this rule apply?* 5 make a request; ask: *He is applying for a job as clerk.* 6 set to work and stick to it: *She applied herself to learning to play the piano.* *v.*, **ap plied, ap ply ing.**

ap point (ə point′), 1 name for an office or position; choose: *The class president appointed five students to the clean-up committee.* 2 decide on; set: *The mayor appointed the town hall as the place for the meeting. We shall appoint eight o'clock as the hour to begin.* *v.*

ap point ee (ə poin′tē′), person who is appointed to an office or position. *n.*

ap poin tive (ə poin′tiv), filled by appointment: *Positions in the President's cabinet are appointive.* *adj.*

ap point ment (ə point′mənt), 1 act of naming for an office or position; choosing: *The appointment of several boys and girls to patrol duty was announced.* 2 office or position: *The Secretary of Commerce has a high government appointment.* 3 a meeting with someone at a certain time and place; engagement: *an appointment to see the doctor at four o'clock.* 4 **appointments,** *pl.* furniture; equipment: *an old hotel with shabby appointments.* *n.*

Ap po mat tox (ap′ə mat′əks), town in central Virginia. Lee surrendered to Grant there on April 9, 1865. *n.*

ap por tion (ə pôr′shən), divide and give out in fair shares; distribute according to some rule: *The father's property was apportioned among his children after his death.* *v.*

ap por tion ment (ə pôr′shən mənt), a dividing and giving out in fair shares;

distribution according to some rule. *n.*

ap po si tion (ap′ə zish′ən), the relation to a noun or pronoun of another noun or noun equivalent which is added to it as an explanation. In "Mr. Brown, our neighbor, has a new car," *Mr. Brown* and *our neighbor* are in apposition. *n.*

ap pos i tive (ə poz′ə tiv), noun or noun equivalent added to another noun or pronoun as an explanation; word, phrase, or clause in apposition. In the sentence, "Mr. Brown, our neighbor, has a new car," *our neighbor* is an appositive. *n.*

ap prais al (ə prā′zəl), 1 estimate of value, amount, quality, etc.: *The bank's appraisal of the worth of our house was $30,000.* 2 an appraising; evaluating: *The coach gave a frank appraisal of the runner's ability.* *n.*

ap praise (ə prāz′), 1 estimate the value, amount, quality, etc., of: *An employer should be able to appraise ability and character.* 2 set a price on; fix the value of: *Property is appraised for taxation.* *v.*, **ap praised, ap prais ing.**

ap prais er (ə prā′zər), 1 person authorized to fix the value of property, imported goods, etc. 2 person who appraises. *n.*

ap pre ci a ble (ə prē′shē ə bəl), enough to be felt or estimated; noticeable: *The slight hill made an appreciable difference in the ease of walking.* *adj.*

ap pre ci a bly (ə prē′shē ə blē), to an appreciable degree; noticeably. *adv.*

ap pre ci ate (ə prē′shē āt), 1 think highly of; recognize the worth or quality of; value; enjoy: *Almost everybody appreciates good food.* 2 be thankful for: *We appreciate your help.* 3 have an opinion of the value, worth, or quality of; estimate: *Most people can appreciate the contributions of medical research to good health.* 4 be fully aware of; recognize: *A musician is able to appreciate small differences in sounds.* 5 make or become greater in value: *New buildings appreciate the value of land.* *v.*, **ap pre ci at ed, ap pre ci at ing.**

ap pre ci a tion (ə prē′shē ā′shən), 1 a valuing highly; sympathetic understanding: *She has no appreciation of modern art.* 2 an appreciating; valuing: *He showed his appreciation of her help by sending flowers.* 3 a rise in value. *n.*

ap pre ci a tive (ə prē′shē ā′tiv or ə prē′shə tiv), having or showing appreciation; recognizing the value: *The lost child was appreciative of the smallest kindness.* *adj.* —**ap pre′ci a′tive ly,** *adv.*

ap pre hend (ap′ri hend′), 1 look forward to with fear; dread: *I apprehend a sharp decline in the value of the dollar.* 2 arrest; seize: *The thief was* apprehended and put in jail. **3** grasp with the mind; understand: *I apprehended his meaning more from his gestures than from the foreign words he used.* v.

ap pre hen sion (ap/ri hen/shən), **1** fear; dread: *The roar of the hurricane filled us with apprehension.* **2** a seizing or being seized; arrest: *The appearance of the thief's picture in all the papers led to his apprehension.* **3** a grasping by the mind; understanding: *I do not have a clear apprehension of fractions.* n.

ap pre hen sive (ap/ri hen/siv), feeling alarm; afraid, anxious, or worried: *The captain felt apprehensive for the safety of his passengers during the storm at sea.* adj. —**ap/pre hen/sive ly**, adv. —**ap/pre hen/sive ness**, n.

ap pren tice (ə pren/tis), **1** person learning a trade or art. In return for instruction the apprentice agrees to work for his employer a certain length of time with little or no pay. **2** bind or take as an apprentice: *Benjamin Franklin's father apprenticed him to a printer.* **3** beginner; learner. **1,3** n., **2** v., **ap pren ticed, ap pren tic ing.**

ap pren tice ship (ə pren/tis ship), **1** condition of being an apprentice. **2** time during which one is an apprentice. n.

ap prise (ə prīz/), give notice to; let know; inform: *Our teacher apprised us that there would be a test on Monday.* v., **ap prised, ap pris ing.**

ap proach (ə prōch/), **1** come near or nearer to: *Walk softly as you approach the baby's crib. Winter is approaching. The wind was approaching a gale.* **2** act of coming near or nearer: *Sunset announces the approach of night.* **3** way by which a place or person can be reached; access: *The approach to the house was a narrow path. Our best approach to the senator lay through a mutual friend.* **4** method of starting work on a task or problem: *She seems to have a good approach to the problem.* **5** make advances or overtures to: *He approached the general with the idea of arranging an armistice.* **1,5** v., **2-4** n., pl. **ap proach es.**

ap proach a ble (ə prō/chə bəl), **1** that can be approached; accessible: *The house on the mountain is approachable only on foot.* **2** easy to approach and talk to; friendly and sociable: *No matter how busy she was, she was always approachable.* adj.

ap pro ba tion (ap/rə bā/shən), favorable opinion; approval: *The teacher gave her approbation to the science committee's class report.* n.

ap pro pri ate (ə prō/prē it for 1; ə prō/prē āt for 2,3), **1** right for the

occasion; suitable; proper: *Plain, simple clothes are appropriate for school wear.* **2** set apart for some special use: *The state government appropriated money for a new road into our town.* **3** take for oneself; use as one's own: *You should not appropriate other people's belongings without their permission.* **1** adj., **2,3** v., **ap pro pri at ed, ap pro pri at ing.** —**ap pro/pri ate ly**, adv. —**ap pro/pri ate ness**, n.

ap pro pri a tion (ə prō/prē ā/shən), **1** sum of money or other thing appropriated: *Our town received a state appropriation of five thousand dollars for a new playground.* **2** act of appropriating: *The appropriation of the land made it possible to have a park.* n.

ap prov al (ə prü/vəl), **1** favorable opinion; approving; praise: *We all like others to show approval of what we do.* **2** permission; consent: *The principal gave her approval to our plan for a class picnic.* n.

on approval, so that the customer can inspect the item and decide whether to buy or return it: *We bought the television set on approval.*

ap prove (ə prüv/), **1** think or speak well of; be pleased with: *The teacher read my science report and approved it.* **2** give a favorable opinion: *I'm not sure I can approve of what you propose to do.* **3** authorize or make legal; consent to: *The school board approved the budget.* v., **ap proved, ap prov ing.**

ap prox i mate (ə prok/sə mit for 1; ə prok/sə māt for 2), **1** nearly correct: *The approximate length of a meter is 40 inches; the exact length is 39.37 inches.* **2** come near to; approach: *The crowd approximated a thousand people. Your account of what happened approximates the truth, but there are several small errors.* **1** adj., **2** v., **ap prox i mat ed, ap prox i mat ing.**

ap prox i mate ly (ə prok/sə mit lē), by a close estimate; nearly; about: *We are approximately 200 miles from home.* adv.

ap prox i ma tion (ə prok/sə mā/shən), **1** a nearly correct amount; close estimate: *25,000 miles is an approximation of the circumference of the earth.* **2** an approximating; approach: *Her story was a close approximation to the truth.* n.

ap pur te nance (ə pėrt/n əns), addition to something more important; accessory. A radio in a car is an appurtenance; an engine is a necessity. n.

Apr., April.

a pri cot (ā/prə kot or ap/rə kot), **1** a round, pale, orange-colored fruit, about the size of a plum. Apricots have a downy skin somewhat like that of a peach. **2** the tree it grows on. **3** a pale

orange yellow. **4** pale orange-yellow. **1-3** n., **4** adj.

A pril (ā/prəl), the fourth month of the year. It has 30 days. n.

April Fools' Day, April 1, a day observed by fooling people with tricks and jokes; All Fools' Day.

a pron (ā/prən), **1** garment worn over the front part of the body to cover or protect clothes: *a kitchen apron, a carpenter's apron.* **2** area in front of an airport terminal or hangar on which to park aircraft. **3** area of a stage in front of the curtain. n.

ap ro pos (ap/rə pō/), to the point; fitting; suitable: *Your remark is certainly apropos to what we are discussing.* adj. [from French *à propos* to the purpose]

apropos of, with regard to: *Apropos of the party, what are you going to wear?*

apse (aps), a semicircular or many-sided recess in a church, usually at the east end. The roof of an apse is arched or vaulted. n.

apt (apt), **1** fitted by nature; likely: *A careless person is apt to make mistakes.* **2** right for the occasion; suitable; fitting: *His apt reply to the question showed that he had understood it very well.* **3** quick to learn: *Some pupils in our class are more apt than others.* adj. —**apt/ly**, adv. —**apt/ness**, n.

apt., apartment. pl. **apts.**

ap ti tude (ap/tə tüd or ap/tə tyüd), **1** natural tendency or talent; ability; capacity: *Edison had a remarkable aptitude for inventing things.* **2** readiness in learning; quickness to understand: *She is a pupil of great aptitude.* n.

aq ua cade (ak/wə kād), a display of swimming, diving, and other aquatic skills before an audience. n.

Aqua-Lung (ak/wə lung/), trademark

adj. adjective	*n.* noun
adv. adverb	*prep.* preposition
conj. conjunction	*pron.* pronoun
interj. interjection	*v.* verb
sing. singular	*pl.* plural

for an underwater breathing device used in skin diving, consisting of one or more cylinders of compressed air strapped to the diver's back, a hose and mouthpiece through which the diver breathes, and sometimes a glass mask placed over the eyes and nose. The supply of air to the diver is regulated automatically by a valve. *n.*

aq ua ma rine (ak′wə mə rēn′), 1 a transparent, bluish-green, semiprecious stone that is a variety of beryl. 2 a light bluish green. 3 light bluish-green. 1,2 *n.*, 3 *adj.*

aq ua plane (ak′wə plān′), 1 a wide board on which a person rides as it is towed by a speeding motorboat. 2 ride on an aquaplane. 1 *n.*, 2 *v.*, **aq ua planed, aq ua plan ing.**

a quar i um (ə kwer′ē əm), 1 pond, tank, or glass bowl in which living fish, other water animals, and water plants are kept. 2 building used for showing collections of living fish, water animals, and water plants: *The aquarium had large tanks with glass fronts for different kinds of fish but kept crocodiles in a heated pool.* *n., pl.* **a quar i ums, a quar i a** (ə kwer′ē ə).

a quat ic (ə kwat′ik *or* ə kwot′ik), 1 growing or living in water: *Water lilies are aquatic plants.* 2 taking place in or on water: *Swimming and sailing are aquatic sports.* *adj.*

aqueduct (def. 2)

aq ue duct (ak′wə dukt), 1 an artificial channel or large pipe for bringing water from a distance. 2 structure that supports such a channel or pipe. *n.*

a que ous (ā′kwē əs), 1 of or made with water: *The druggist put the medicine in an aqueous solution.* 2 like water; watery: *Aqueous matter ran from the sore.* 3 produced by the action

of water. Aqueous rocks are formed of the sediment carried and deposited by water. *adj.*

aqueous humor, the watery liquid which fills the space in the eye between the cornea and the lens.

aq ui line (ak′wə līn *or* ak′wə lən), curved like an eagle's beak; hooked. *adj.*

A qui nas (ə kwī′nəs), **Saint Thomas,** 1225?-1274, Italian philosopher and theologian of the Roman Catholic Church. *n.*

Ar ab (ar′əb), 1 person born or living in Arabia. 2 member of a Semitic people now widely scattered over southwestern and southern Asia and northern Africa. 3 of or having to do with the Arabs or Arabia. 1,2 *n.*, 3 *adj.*

ar a besque (ar′ə besk′), 1 an elaborate and fanciful design of flowers, leaves, geometrical figures, etc. 2 carved or painted in arabesque. 3 a ballet pose in which the dancer stands on one leg, with the other at right angles to it, and with the arms held in any of various positions. 1,3 *n.*, 2 *adj.*

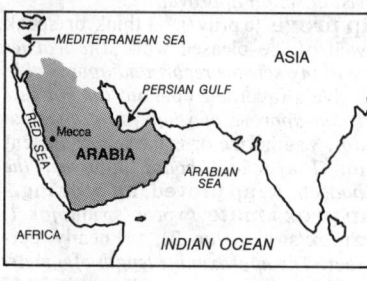

A ra bi a (ə rā′bē ə), large peninsula in SW Asia. *n.*

A ra bi an (ə rā′bē ən), 1 of Arabia or the Arabs. 2 person born or living in Arabia; Arab. 1 *adj.*, 2 *n.*

Arabian camel, dromedary.

Arabian horse, any of a breed of swift, graceful horses originally developed by the Arabs for use in the deserts of Arabia, now used as saddle horses.

Arabian Nights, The, collection of old tales from Arabia, Persia, and India, dating from the A.D. 900's. It contains tales of Ali Baba, Aladdin, and many others.

Arabian Sea, part of the Indian Ocean between Arabia and India.

Ar a bic (ar′ə bik), 1 the Semitic language of the Arabs, related to Hebrew. Arabic is now spoken chiefly in Arabia, Iraq, Syria, Jordan, Lebanon, and North Africa. 2 of or having to do with the language of the Arabs. 3 of or having to do with the Arabs or Arabia; Arabian. 1 *n.*, 2,3 *adj.*

Arabic numerals or **Arabic figures,** the figures 1, 2, 3, 4, 5, 6, 7, 8,

aquiline—An aquiline nose curves somewhat like an eagle's beak.

9, 0. They are called Arabic because they were introduced into western Europe by Arabian scholars, but most probably they were derived from India.

ar a ble (ar′ə bəl), fit for plowing: *There is not much arable land on the side of a rocky mountain.* *adj.*

Arab League, a group of Arab nations organized in 1945 to promote closer relations among its members. It includes Algeria, Egypt, Iraq, Jordan, Kuwait, Lebanon, Libya, Morocco, Saudi Arabia, Southern Yemen, Sudan, Syria, Tunisia, and Yemen.

Ar a by (ar′ə bē), OLD USE. Arabia. *n.*

a rach nid (ə rak′nid), any of a large group of animals that includes spiders, scorpions, mites, ticks, and daddylonglegs. An arachnid breathes air, has four pairs of walking legs, no antennae, and no wings. The body is usually divided into only two regions. *n.*

Ar a gon (ar′ə gon), region in NE Spain, formerly a kingdom. *n.*

Ar al Sea (ar′əl), inland sea in the SW Soviet Union, east of the Caspian Sea. See **Assyria** for map.

Ar a ma ic (ar′ə mā′ik), a Semitic language in which much Jewish and early Christian literature was written. *n.*

A rap a ho (ə rap′ə hō), member of a tribe of North American Indians that lived in Colorado and are now settled on reservations in Wyoming and Oklahoma. *n., pl.* **A rap a ho** or **A rap a hos.**

Ar a rat (ar′ə rat′), mountain in E Turkey. Noah's Ark is said to have grounded there after the Flood. *n.*

ar bi ter (är′bə tər), 1 person with full power to judge or decide: *an arbiter of good taste.* 2 person chosen to decide or settle a dispute; arbitrator. *n.*

ar bi trar i ly (är′bə trer′ə lē), in an arbitrary manner; at will. *adv.*

ar bi trar i ness (är′bə trer′ē nis), a being arbitrary. *n.*

ar bi trar y (är′bə trer′ē), 1 based on one's own wishes, notions, or will; not going by any rule or law: *The judge tried to be fair and did not make arbitrary decisions.* 2 fixed or determined by chance: *an arbitrary name.* 3 using or abusing unlimited power; tyrannical: *an arbitrary king.* *adj.*

ar bi trate (är′bə trāt), 1 give a decision in a dispute; act as arbitrator;

mediate: *The teacher arbitrated between the two boys in their quarrel.* 2 settle by arbitration; submit to arbitration: *The two nations finally agreed to arbitrate their dispute and war was avoided.* v., **ar bi trat ed, ar bi trat ing.**

ar bi tra tion (är/bə trā/shən), settlement of a dispute by the decision of a judge, umpire, or committee. *n.*

ar bi tra tor (är/bə trā/tər), 1 person chosen to decide or settle a dispute. 2 person with full power to judge or decide; arbiter. *n.*

ar bor (är/bər), a shaded place formed by trees or shrubs or by vines growing on a lattice. *n.*

Arbor Day, day set aside in many states of the United States for planting trees. The date varies in different states.

ar bo re al (är bôr/ē əl), 1 living in or among trees. A squirrel is an arboreal animal. 2 of trees; like trees. *adj.*

ar bo re tum (är/bə rē/təm), place where trees and shrubs are grown and exhibited for scientific and educational purposes. *n.*

ar bor vi tae (är/bər vī/tē), an evergreen tree often planted for ornament and for hedges. *n.* [from Latin *arbor vitae* tree of life]

ar bu tus (är byü/təs), a trailing plant of eastern North America that has clusters of fragrant, pink or white flowers that bloom very early in the spring; mayflower. *n., pl.* **ar bu tus es.**

arc (def. 1)
arcs of circles

arc (ärk), 1 any part of the circumference of a circle. 2 any part of any curved line. 3 a curved stream of brilliant light or sparks formed as a strong electric current jumps from one conductor to another. *n.* —**arc/like/,** *adj.*

Arc (ärk). See **Joan of Arc.** *n.*

ar cade (är kād/), 1 passageway with an arched roof. 2 any covered passageway: *This building has an arcade with small stores along either side.* 3 row of arches supported by columns. *n.*

arcade
(def. 1)

Ar ca di a (är kā/dē ə), 1 mountainous district in the S part of ancient Greece. It was famous for the simple, contented life of its people. 2 any region of simple, quiet contentment. *n.* —**Ar ca/di an,** *adj., n.*

arch[1]
(def. 1)

arch[1] (ärch), 1 a curved structure capable of bearing the weight of the material above it. Arches often form the tops of doors, windows, and gateways. 2 monument in the form of an arch or arches. 3 bend into an arch; curve: *The wind had arched the trees over the road.* 4 form an arch over; span: *A bridge arched the stream.* 5 archway. 6 instep: *Fallen arches cause flat feet.* 1,2,5,6 *n.,* *pl.* **arch es;** 3,4 *v.* [from French of the 1200's *arche,* from Latin *arcum* bow]

arch[2] (ärch), 1 playfully mischievous; saucy: *The little girl gave her mother an arch look and ran away.* 2 chief; principal; leading: *The arch rebel of all was Patrick Henry. adj.* [from Greek *archi-* chief, from *archein* be first, lead] —**arch/ly,** *adv.* —**arch/ness,** *n.*

ar chae o log i cal (är/kē ə loj/ə kəl), of or having to do with archaeology: *An archaeological expedition uncovered the lost city of Troy. adj.* Also, **archeological.** —**ar/chae o log/i cal ly,** *adv.*

ar chae ol o gist (är/kē ol/ə jist), an expert in archaeology. *n.* Also, **archeologist.**

ar chae ol o gy (är/kē ol/ə jē), the scientific study of the people, customs, and life of ancient times. Archaeologists excavate the remains of ancient cities and then classify and study tools, pottery, monuments, or any other remains in order to reconstruct a picture of life in the past when there were few or no written records. *n.* Also, **archeology.**

ar cha ic (är kā/ik), 1 no longer in general use. The words *forsooth* and *methinks* are archaic. 2 of an earlier time; out-of-date or ancient. *adj.*

ar cha ism (är/kē iz/əm), word or expression no longer in general use. *n.*

arch an gel (ärk/ān/jəl), angel of high rank. *n.*

Arch an gel (ärk/ān/jəl), seaport in NW Soviet Union, on the White Sea. *n.*

arch bish op (ärch/bish/əp), bishop having the highest rank. *n.*

arch di o cese (ärch/dī/ə sis *or* ärch/-

hat, āge, fär; let, ēqual, tėrm;
it, īce; hot, ōpen, ôrder;
oil, out; cup, pùt, rüle; ch, child;
ng, long; sh, she; th, thin;
ŦH, then; zh, measure;

ə represents *a* in about,
e in taken, *i* in pencil,
o in lemon, *u* in circus.

dī/ə sēs/), a church district governed by an archbishop. *n.*

arch duch ess (ärch/duch/is), 1 wife or widow of an archduke. 2 princess of the former ruling house of Austria-Hungary. *n., pl.* **arch duch ess es.**

arch duke (ärch/dük/ *or* ärch/dyük/), prince of the former ruling house of Austria-Hungary. *n.*

arch[1] (def. 6)

arched (ärcht), having an arch or arches. *adj.*

arch en e my (ärch/en/ə mē), a principal enemy. *n., pl.* **arch en e mies.**

ar che o log i cal (är/kē ə loj/ə kəl), archaeological. *adj.* —**ar/che o log/-i cal ly,** *adv.*

ar che ol o gist (är/kē ol/ə jist), archaeologist. *n.*

ar che ol o gy (är/kē ol/ə jē), archaeology. *n.*

arch er (är/chər), person who shoots with a bow and arrow; bowman. *n.*

arch er y (är/chər ē), 1 practice or sport of shooting with a bow and arrow. 2 archers: *The archery advanced, shooting steadily. n.*

ar che type (är/kə tīp), 1 the original model; prototype: *That little engine is the archetype of huge modern locomotives.* 2 pattern from which copies are made. *n.*

Ar chi me des (är/kə mē/dēz), 287?-212 B.C., Greek mathematician, physicist, and inventor. He discovered the principles of specific gravity and of the lever. *n.*

ar chi pel a go (är/kə pel/ə gō *or* är/-chə pel/ə gō), 1 group of many islands. The islands between southeast Asia and Australia form the Malay Archipelago. 2 sea having many islands in it. *n., pl.* **ar chi pel a gos** *or* **ar chi pel a goes.**

ar chi tect (är/kə tekt), 1 person who designs buildings, and then sees that his plans are followed by the contractors and workers who actually put up the

architectural

adj.	adjective	*n.*	noun
adv.	adverb	*prep.*	preposition
conj.	conjunction	*pron.*	pronoun
interj.	interjection	*v.*	verb
sing.	singular	*pl.*	plural

buildings. 2 maker; creator: *We are all the architects of our own fortunes. n.*

ar chi tec tur al (är′kə tek′chər əl), of or having to do with architecture. *adj.* —**ar′chi tec′tur al ly,** *adv.*

ar chi tec ture (är′kə tek′chər), 1 science or art of planning and designing buildings. 2 style or special manner of building: *Greek architecture made much use of columns.* 3 construction: *We admire the massive architecture of the Pyramids. n.*

CORNICE

FRIEZE

ARCHITRAVE

ar chi trave (är′kə trāv), the main beam resting on the top of a column or row of columns. *n.*

ar chives (är′kīvz), 1 place where public records or historical documents are kept. 2 the public records or historical documents kept in such a place. *n.pl.*

arch way (ärch′wā′), 1 entrance or passageway with an arch above it. 2 arch covering a passageway. *n.*

arc tic (ärk′tik *or* är′tik), 1 at or near the North Pole; of the north polar region: *They explored the great arctic wilderness of northern Canada.* 2 **the Arctic,** the north polar region. The Arctic has an extremely cold winter, but a comparatively warm summer with rich vegetation, and such animals as the reindeer, polar bear, and musk ox. 3 extremely cold; frigid. 4 **arctics,** *pl.* warm, waterproof overshoes. 1,3 *adj.,* 2,4 *n.*

arctic circle or **Arctic Circle,** the imaginary boundary of the north polar region. It runs parallel to the equator at 66 degrees 30 minutes (66°30′) north latitude.

Arctic Ocean, ocean of the north polar region.

Arctic Zone, region between the arctic circle and the North Pole.

Arc tur us (ärk tùr′əs *or* ärk tyúr′əs), the brightest star in the constellation Boötes, in the northern sky. *n.*

ar dent (ärd′nt), full of zeal; very enthusiastic; eager: *He is an ardent scout. adj.* —**ar′dent ly,** *adv.*

ar dor (är′dər), great enthusiasm; eagerness; zeal: *The politician spoke with patriotic ardor. n.*

ar du ous (är′jü əs), 1 hard to do; requiring much effort; difficult: *an arduous lesson.* 2 using up much energy; strenuous: *He enjoys an arduous workout in the gymnasium. adj.* —**ar′du ous ly,** *adv.* —**ar′du ous ness,** *n.*

are (är; *unstressed* ər), form of the verb **be** used with *we, you,* and *they* and any plural noun to indicate the present tense. *We are ready. You are next. They are waiting. v.*

ar e a (er′ē ə *or* ar′ē ə), 1 amount of surface; extent of surface: *The area of this floor is 600 square feet.* 2 range of knowledge or interest; sphere of activity; field: *Our science teacher is familiar with the areas of physics, chemistry, and related sciences.* 3 region or district: *The Rocky Mountain area is the most mountainous in the United States.* 4 a level, open space: *a playground area. n., pl.* **ar e as.**

area code, combination of three numerals used to dial directly by telephone from one region of the United States and Canada to another.

ar e a way (er′ē ə wä′ *or* ar′ē ə wä′), 1 a sunken area or court at the entrance to a cellar or basement. 2 area used as a passageway between buildings. *n.*

a re na (ə rē′nə), 1 space in an ancient Roman amphitheater in which contests or shows took place: *Gladiators fought with lions in the arena at Rome.* 2 a similar space, surrounded by seats, used today for contests or shows: *a boxing arena.* 3 building in which indoor sports are played. 4 any place of conflict and trial: *The United Nations is an arena for world debate.* 5 field of endeavor: *the political arena. n., pl.* **a re nas.**

ARCTIC CIRCLE · SOVIET UNION · ARCTIC · NORTH POLE · OCEAN · NORTH MAGNETIC POLE · GREENLAND · ALASKA · CANADA

aren't (ärnt), 1 are not. 2 am not. In this meaning, *aren't* is used only in questions. *Why aren't I allowed to stay?*

Ar es (er′ēz *or* ar′ēz), (in Greek myths) the god of war. The Romans called him Mars. *n.*

ar gent (är′jənt), OLD USE. silvery. *adj.*

Ar gen ti na (är′jən tē′nə), country in S South America. *Capital:* Buenos Aires. See **Chile** for map. *n.* —**Ar gen tin e an** (är′jən tin′ē ən), *adj., n.*

Ar gen tine (är′jən tēn′ *or* är′jən tīn), 1 of Argentina or its people. 2 person born or living in Argentina. 1 *adj.,* 2 *n.*

ar gon (är′gon), a colorless, odorless, inert gas that forms a very small part of the air. It is a chemical element. Argon is used in electric light bulbs and radio tubes. *n.*

Ar go naut (är′gə nôt), (in Greek legends) any of the men who sailed with Jason in search of the Golden Fleece. *n.*

ar go sy (är′gə sē), OLD USE. 1 a large merchant ship. 2 fleet of such ships. *n., pl.* **ar go sies.**

ar gue (är′gyü), 1 discuss with someone who disagrees: *He argued with his sister about who should wash the dishes.* 2 give reasons for or against something: *One side argued for a larger army and the other side argued against it.* 3 persuade by giving reasons: *They argued me into going along on the trip.* 4 try to prove by reasoning; maintain: *Columbus argued that the world was round.* 5 indicate; show; prove: *Her rich clothes argue her to be wealthy. v.,* **ar gued, ar gu ing.**

ar gu er (är′gyü ər), person who argues. *n.*

ar gu ment (är′gyə mənt), 1 discussion by persons who disagree; dispute: *She won the argument by producing facts to prove her point.* 2 reason or reasons offered for or against something: *His arguments in favor of a new school building are very persuasive. n.*

ar gu men ta tion (är′gyə men tā′shən), 1 process of arguing; reasoning. 2 discussion; debate: *A day was wasted in useless argumentation. n.*

ar gu men ta tive (är′gyə men′tiv), fond of arguing; quarrelsome: *an argumentative disposition. adj.* —**ar′gu men′ta tive ly,** *adv.*

Ar gus (är′gəs), 1 (in Greek myths) a giant with a hundred eyes. 2 a watchful guardian. *n.*

a ri a (är′ē ə, er′ē ə, *or* ar′ē ə), song for a single voice, with accompaniment, in an opera, oratorio, or cantata. *n., pl.* **a ri as.**

Ar i ad ne (ar′ē ad′nē), (in Greek legends) the daughter of Minos, king of Crete. She fell in love with Theseus and helped him escape from Crete after killing the Minotaur. *n.*

ar id (ar′id), **1** having very little rainfall; dry and barren: *Desert lands are arid.* **2** uninteresting and empty; dull: *an arid, boring speech. adj.* —**ar′id ly,** *adv.* —**ar′id ness,** *n.*

a rid i ty (ə rid′ə tē), **1** condition of dryness and barrenness. **2** lack of interest, life, or spirit; dullness. *n.*

Ar i el (er′ē əl *or* ar′ē əl), the airy spirit who helped Prospero in Shakespeare's play *The Tempest. n.*

a right (ə rīt′), correctly; rightly: *If I heard you aright, you said you would go. adv.*

a rise (ə rīz′), **1** rise up; get up: *The children arose from their seats to salute the flag.* **2** move upward; ascend: *Smoke arises from the chimney.* **3** come into being; come about: *A great wind arose. Accidents often arise from carelessness. v.,* **a rose, a ris en, a ris ing.**

a ris en (ə riz′n), past participle of **arise.** *Trouble had arisen over the ball game. v.*

ar is toc ra cy (ar′ə stok′rə sē), **1** class of people having a high position in society because of birth, rank, or title; nobility. Earls, dukes, and princes belong to the aristocracy. **2** class of people considered superior because of intelligence, culture, or wealth; upper class. **3** government in which the nobility or any privileged upper class rules. **4** country or state having such a government. *n., pl.* **ar is toc ra cies.**

a ris to crat (ə ris′tə krat), **1** person who belongs to the aristocracy; noble. **2** person like an aristocrat in tastes, opinions, and manners. *n.*

a ris to crat ic (ə ris′tə krat′ik), **1** belonging to the upper classes; superior in birth, intelligence, culture, or wealth. **2** like an aristocrat in manners; proud. **3** having to do with an aristocracy. *adj.* —**a ris to crat′i cal ly,** *adv.*

Ar is to te li an (ar′ə stə tē′lē ən *or* ə ris′tə tē′lyən), **1** of Aristotle or his philosophy. **2** follower or student of Aristotle or his philosophy. **1** *adj.,* **2** *n.*

Ar is tot le (ar′ə stot′l), 384-322 B.C., Greek philosopher and scientist. He was the pupil of Plato. *n.*

a rith me tic (ə rith′mə tik *for 1;* ar′ith met′ik *for 2*), **1** science or art of computing or calculating by means of numbers. When you study arithmetic, you learn to add, subtract, multiply, and divide. **2** arithmetical. **1** *n.,* **2** *adj.*

ar ith met i cal (ar′ith met′ə kəl), of or having to do with arithmetic. *adj.*

ar ith met i cal ly (ar′ith met′ik lē), according to arithmetic; by the use of arithmetic. *adv.*

arithmetical progression, series of numbers in which there is always the same difference between a number and the one next after it. 2, 4, 6, 8, 10 form an arithmetical progression; so do 8, 5, 2, −1.

a rith me ti cian (ə rith′mə tish′ən), an expert in arithmetic. *n.*

ar ith met ic mean (ar′ith met′ik), an average. *n.*

Ariz., Arizona.

Ar i zo na (ar′ə zō′nə), one of the southwestern states of the United States. *Capital:* Phoenix. *n.* —**Ar′i zo′nan, Ar′i zo′ni an,** *adj., n.*

ark (ärk), **1** (in the Bible) the large boat in which Noah saved himself, his family, and a pair of each kind of animal from the Flood. **2** the chest or box in which the Hebrews kept the two stone tablets containing the Ten Commandments. **3** a cabinet in a synagogue for housing scrolls of the Pentateuch. *n.*

Ark., Arkansas.

armadillo—total length 2½ ft.

Ar kan sas (är′kən sô *for 1;* är′kən sô *or* är kan′zəs *for 2*), **1** one of the south central states of the United States. *Capital:* Little Rock. **2** river flowing from central Colorado southeast into the Mississippi. *n.* —**Ar kan san** (är kan′zən), *adj., n.*

Ar ling ton (är′ling tən), the largest national cemetery in the United States, in NE Virginia, across the Potomac from Washington, D.C. *n.*

arm[1] (ärm), **1** the part of a person's body between the shoulder and the hand. **2** forelimb of an animal. The front legs of a bear are sometimes called arms. **3** something shaped or used like an arm: *the arm of a chair, an arm of the sea.* **4** power; authority: *The strong arm of the law keeps order in the city. n.* [Old English *earm*]

arm in arm, with arms linked: *She walked arm in arm with her sister.*

with open arms, in a warm, friendly way; cordially: *His friends welcomed him with open arms.*

arm[2] (ärm), **1** any weapon. A gun, a sword, an ax, or a stick—any of these might be an arm for defense or attack. See also **arms.** **2** supply with weapons: *In colonial days the French armed the Indians to attack the British.* **3** supply with any means of defense or attack: *Each lawyer entered court armed with the evidence he planned to use to support his case.* **4** take up weapons; prepare for war: *The soldiers armed for battle.* **5** a combat branch of one of the armed forces, such as the infantry or artillery. **6** one of the armed forces, such as the army, navy, or air force. **1,5,6** *n.,* **2-4** *v.* [from French of the 1200's *armer* to arm, from Latin *armare,* from *arma* weapons]

ar ma da (är mä′də), **1** a large fleet of warships. **2 the Armada,** the Spanish fleet that was sent to attack England in 1588 and was defeated in the English Channel. **3** any large group of military vehicles. *n., pl.* **ar ma das.**

ar ma dil lo (är′mə dil′ō), any of several small, burrowing mammals with a protective shell of bony plates. Armadillos are found in South America and some parts of southern North America. *n., pl.* **ar ma dil los.**

ar ma ment (är′mə mənt), **1** the weapons, ammunition, and equipment of a military force, vehicle, or installation; war equipment and supplies. **2** the army, navy, and other military forces of a country, including both men and equipment. **3** act or process of arming. *n.*

ar ma ture (är′mə chər), **1** a revolving part of an electric motor or dynamo, consisting of wire wound around an iron core placed between opposite poles of a magnet. **2** armor. **3** the protective covering of an animal or plant. A turtle's shell is an armature. *n.*

arm band (ärm′band′), band of cloth worn around the upper arm as a symbol or badge: *a mourning armband of black. n.*

arm chair (ärm′cher′ *or* ärm′char′), chair with sidepieces to support a person's arms or elbows. *n.*

armed forces, all the military, naval, and air forces of a country.

Ar me ni a (är mē′nē ə), **1** former country of SW Asia, now divided among Turkey, Iran, and the Soviet Union. See **Persia** for map. **2** republic in S Soviet Union, on the Black Sea. *n.* —**Ar me′ni an,** *adj., n.*

arm ful (ärm′fûl), as much as one arm or both arms can hold: *an armful of groceries. n., pl.* **arm fuls.**

arm hole (ärm′hōl′), hole for the arm or sleeve in a garment. *n.*

adj.	adjective	*n.*	noun
adv.	adverb	*prep.*	preposition
conj.	conjunction	*pron.*	pronoun
interj.	interjection	*v.*	verb
sing.	singular	*pl.*	plural

ar mi stice (är′mə stis), a stop in fighting; temporary peace; truce. *n.*

Armistice Day, November 11, the anniversary of the end of World War I, in 1918. As an official holiday it is now called Veterans Day, and is celebrated on the fourth Monday in October.

arm let (ärm′lit), an ornamental band or bracelet for the upper arm. *n.*

ar mor (är′mər), 1 a covering, usually of metal or leather, worn to protect the body in fighting. 2 any kind of protective covering. The steel plates of a warship and the scales of a fish are armor. 3 the armored forces and equipment, such as the tanks, of a military unit. *n.*

ar mored (är′mərd), 1 covered or protected with armor: *an armored car.* 2 using or equipped with armored vehicles: *He served in an armored division. adj.*

ar mor er (är′mər ər), 1 (in former times) a person who made or repaired armor. 2 soldier or sailor who takes care of revolvers, pistols, rifles, and other firearms. *n.*

ar mo ri al (är môr′ē əl), having to do with coats of arms or heraldry. *adj.*

armor plate, steel or iron plating to protect warships, tanks, forts, etc. Armor plate is now usually a specially toughened alloy of steel.

ar mor y (är′mər ē), 1 place where weapons are kept; arsenal. 2 place where weapons are manufactured. 3 a building with a drill hall, offices, etc., for militia. 4 OLD USE. armor; arms. *n., pl.* **ar mor ies.**

arm pit (ärm′pit), the hollow place under the arm at the shoulder. *n.*

arms (ärmz), 1 weapons: *The rebels did not have the arms they needed to fight.* 2 fighting; war: *A soldier is a man of arms.* 3 symbols and designs used in heraldry; coat of arms. *n.pl.*

bear arms, serve as a soldier; fight: *The soldier bore arms for his country.*

take up arms, arm for attack or defense: *take up arms against an enemy.*

under arms, having weapons; equipped for fighting: *The troops were under arms when war was declared.*

up in arms, very angry; in rebellion: *The students were up in arms when their holiday was canceled.*

Arm strong (ärm′strông′), **Neil A.,** born 1930, American astronaut. He was the first human being to walk on and explore the surface of the moon, on July 20, 1969. *n.*

ar my (är′mē), 1 a large, organized group of soldiers trained and armed for war: *American armies have fought in many lands.* 2 Often, **Army.** the military forces of a nation, exclusive of the naval forces and, in some countries, also exclusive of the air forces. 3 military unit made up of two or more corps plus supporting troops, commanded by a general. It is the largest tactical military unit. 4 any group of people organized for a purpose: *the Salvation Army.* 5 a very large number; multitude: *an army of ants. n., pl.* **ar mies.**

armor (def. 1) of the 1400's, consisting of seven major pieces with a total weight of about 65 pounds

ar ni ca (är′nə kə), 1 a healing liquid used on bruises and sprains, prepared from the dried flowers, leaves, or roots of a plant related to the aster. 2 the plant itself, which has showy, yellow flowers. *n., pl.* **ar ni cas** for 2.

Ar nold (är′nld), **Benedict,** 1741-1801, American general in the Revolutionary War who became a traitor. *n.*

a ro ma (ə rō′mə), spicy odor; fragrance: *Just smell the aroma of the cake baking in the oven. n., pl.* **a ro mas.**

ar o mat ic (ar′ə mat′ik), spicy; fragrant: *The cinnamon tree has an aromatic inner bark. adj.*

a rose (ə rōz′), past tense of **arise.** *She arose from her chair. v.*

a round (ə round′), 1 in a circle about: *She has traveled around the world.* 2 in a circle: *He spun around like a top.* 3 in circumference: *The tree measures four feet around.* 4 on all sides of: *Woods lay around the house.* 5 on all sides; in every direction: *A dense fog lay around.* 6 here and there; about: *We walked around to see the town (adv.). He leaves his books around the house (prep.).* 7 INFORMAL. somewhere about: *I waited around for an hour (adv.). Stay around the house (prep.).* 8 IN-FORMAL. near in amount or number to; approximately; about: *That hat cost around five dollars. I'll be home around*

six o'clock. 9 in the opposite direction: *Turn around! You are going the wrong way.* 10 from one to another: *If you pass the class roll around, everyone can sign his name.* 1,4,6-8 *prep.*, 2,3,5-7, 9,10 *adv.*

a rous al (ə rou′zəl), an arousing or a being aroused. *n.*

a rouse (ə rouz′), 1 stir to action; excite: *The attack on Pearl Harbor aroused the whole country.* 2 awaken: *The noise aroused the sleeping guard. v.,* **a roused, a rous ing.**

ar que bus (är′kwə bəs), harquebus. *n., pl.* **ar que bus es.**

ar raign (ə rān′), 1 bring before a court of law to answer a charge: *The cashier was arraigned on a charge of stealing.* 2 find fault with; accuse. *v.*

ar raign ment (ə rān′mənt), 1 a bringing before a court of law to answer a charge: *the arraignment of the suspects.* 2 unfavorable criticism; accusation. *n.*

ar range (ə rānj′), 1 put in the proper order: *Please arrange the books on the library shelf. I arranged my time so that I could work at my hobbies.* 2 form plans; prepare beforehand: *Can you arrange to meet me this evening?* 3 reach an understanding about; settle (a dispute): *The two neighbors have now arranged their differences.* 4 adapt (a piece of music) to voices or instruments for which it was not written: *This music for the violin is also arranged for the piano. v.,* **ar ranged, ar rang ing.**

ar range ment (ə rānj′mənt), 1 a putting or a being put in proper order: *Careful arrangement of books in a library makes them easier to find.* 2 way or order in which things or persons are put: *You can make six arrangements of the letters A, B, and C.* 3 something arranged in a particular way: *Make an arrangement of the chairs to form a circle.* 4 adjustment, settlement, or agreement: *No arrangement of the dispute could possibly please everybody.* 5 **arrangements,** *pl.* plans; preparations: *All arrangements have been made for our trip to Chicago.* 6 adaptation of a piece of music to voices or instruments for which it was not written. *n.*

ar rang er (ə rān′jər), person who arranges. *n.*

ar rant (ar′ənt), thoroughgoing; downright: *Nobody will believe such an arrant liar. adj.*

ar ras (ar′əs), a curtain, screen, or hangings of tapestry. *n., pl.* **ar ras.**

ar ray (ə rā′), 1 proper order; regular arrangement: *The troops were formed in battle array.* 2 put in order for some purpose: *The general arrayed his troops* for the battle. **3** display of persons or things: *The array of good players on the other team made our side look weak.* **4** clothes, especially for some special occasion: *bridal array.* **5** dress in fine clothes; adorn: *She was arrayed like a queen.* **6** (in mathematics) an orderly arrangement of objects or symbols in rows and columns. 1,3,4,6 *n.*, 2,5 *v.*

ar rears (ə rirz´), **1** money due but not paid; debts. **2** unfinished work; things not done on time. *n.pl.*

in arrears, behind in payments, work, etc.: *He is in arrears with his car payments.*

ar rest (ə rest´), **1** seize by authority of the law; take to jail or court: *A policeman arrested the thief.* **2** a seizing of a person by authority of the law; a taking to jail or court: *We saw the arrest of the burglar.* **3** stop; check: *Filling a tooth arrests decay. I grabbed the child in time to arrest her fall.* **4** a stopping; checking: *Machines can now take over after an arrest of the heart's function during an operation.* **5** catch and hold: *Our attention was arrested by the unusual sound.* 1,3,5 *v.*, 2,4 *n.*

under arrest, held by the police: *He was under arrest for stealing.*

ar rest ing (ə res´ting), that catches and holds the attention; striking. *adj.*

ar riv al (ə rī´vəl), **1** an arriving: *She is waiting for the arrival of the train.* **2** person or thing that arrives: *She greeted the new arrivals at the door. n.*

ar rive (ə rīv´), **1** reach the end of a journey; come to a place: *We arrived in Boston a week ago.* **2** come; occur: *The time has arrived for you to study.* **3** be successful: *It took years for Beethoven to arrive as a composer. v.,* **ar rived,** **ar riv ing.**

arrive at, come to; reach: *You should arrive at school before nine o'clock. We must arrive at a decision soon.*

ar ro gance (ar´ə gəns), a too great pride with contempt of others; haughtiness: *He was a talented actor, but his arrogance made him unpopular. n.*

ar ro gant (ar´ə gənt), too proud and contemptuous of others; haughty. *adj.* —**ar´ro gant ly,** *adv.*

ar ro gate (ar´ə gāt), claim or take without right: *The king arrogated to himself power that belonged to the nobles. v.,* **ar ro gat ed, ar ro gat ing.**

ar row (ar´ō), **1** a slender, pointed shaft or stick which is shot from a bow. **2** anything like an arrow in shape or speed. **3** a sign (→) used to show direction or position in maps, on road signs, and in writing. *n.*

ar row head (ar´ō hed´), head or tip of an arrow. An arrowhead is usually shaped like a wedge and made of harder

material than the shaft. The Indians made arrowheads of flint. *n.*

ar row root (ar´ō rüt´ *or* ar´ō rút´), **1** an easily digested starch made from the roots of a tropical American plant. **2** the plant itself. *n.*

ar roy o (ə roi´ō), in southwestern United States: **1** the dry bed of a stream; gully. **2** a small river. *n., pl.* **ar roy os.** [from Spanish]

ar se nal (är´sə nəl), **1** a building for storing or manufacturing military weapons and ammunition. **2** storehouse. *n.*

ar se nic (är´sə nik), **1** a very brittle, nonmetallic element which occurs chiefly in combination with other elements. It forms poisonous compounds with oxygen and is used to make insecticides, weed killers, certain medicines, etc. **2** a violent, tasteless poison that is a compound of this element. *n.*

ar son (är´sən), the crime of intentionally setting fire to a building or other property. *n.*

artesian well—Water, under pressure in the sandstone layer, rises in a pipe drilled through the seal of the rock layer above it.

art¹ (ärt), **1** a branch or division of learning. History is usually considered one of the arts; chemistry is one of the sciences. **2** a branch of learning that depends more on special practice than on general principles. Writing compositions is an art; grammar is a science. The fine arts include painting, drawing, sculpture, architecture, music, and dancing. **3** painting, drawing, and sculpture: *She is studying both art and music.* **4** paintings, sculptures, and other works of art: *We went to an exhibit at the museum of art.* **5** working principles; methods: *She understands the art of making friends.* **6** some kind of skill or practical application of skill. Cooking, sewing, and housekeeping are household arts. **7** human skill or effort: *This well-kept garden owes more to art than to nature.* **8** skillful act; cunning; trick: *The witch deceived the children by her arts. n.* [from French of the 1400's]

art² (ärt), OLD USE. are. "Thou art" means "You are." *v.* [Old English *eart*]

Ar te mis (är´tə mis), (in Greek myths) the goddess of the hunt and of the moon. She was the twin sister of Apollo and was called Diana by the Romans. *n.*

ar ter i al (är tir´ē əl), **1** of an artery or the arteries: *hardening of the arterial walls.* **2** contained in the arteries. Arterial blood is bright red because it has been purified by passing through the lungs. **3** serving as a major route of transportation, supply, or access: *an arterial highway. adj.*

ar ter i o scle ro sis (är tir´ē ō sklə rō´sis), a progressive thickening and hardening of the walls of the arteries, causing a decrease or loss of circulation. Arteriosclerosis usually occurs in elderly people. *n.*

ar ter y (är´tər ē), **1** any of the tubes that carry blood from the heart to all parts of the body. **2** a main road; important channel: *Main Street and Broadway are the two arteries of traffic in our city. n., pl.* **ar ter ies.**

ar te sian well (är tē´zhən), a deep, drilled well, especially one from which water gushes up without pumping.

art ful (ärt´fəl), **1** slyly clever; crafty; deceitful: *A swindler uses artful tricks to get people's money away from them.* **2** skillful; clever: *His artful handling of the situation won him the approval of the class. adj.* —**art´ful ly,** *adv.* —**art´ful ness,** *n.*

ar thrit ic (är thrit´ik), **1** of arthritis. **2** caused by arthritis. *adj.*

ar thri tis (är thrī´tis), inflammation of a joint or joints of the body. Rheumatism and gout are two kinds of arthritis. *n.*

ar thro pod (är´thrə pod), any of a large group of invertebrate animals having jointed bodies and legs. Insects (beetles, bees, etc.), arachnids (spiders, mites, etc.), and crustaceans (lobsters, crabs, etc.) are arthropods. *n.*

Ar thur (är´thər), **1** legendary king of ancient Britain who gathered about him the knights of the Round Table. The real Arthur was probably a British chieftain about A.D. 500. **2 Chester A.,** 1830-1886, the 21st president of the United States, from 1881 to 1885. *n.*

adj. adjective	*n.* noun
adv. adverb	*prep.* preposition
conj. conjunction	*pron.* pronoun
interj. interjection	*v.* verb
sing. singular	*pl.* plural

artichoke (def. 1)
above, bud
right, mature thistle-
like flower

ar ti choke (är′tə chōk), 1 a thistle-like plant with large prickly leaves. 2 its bud, which is cooked and eaten as a vegetable. *n.*

ar ti cle (är′tə kəl), 1 a written composition on a special subject, complete in itself, but forming part of a magazine, newspaper, or book: *This newspaper has a good article on gardening.* 2 a clause in a contract, treaty, statute, etc.: *When the Constitution of the United States was adopted it had seven articles.* 3 a particular thing; item: *Bread is an important article of food.* 4 one of the words *a*, *an*, or *the*, as in *a book, an egg, the boy. A* and *an* are indefinite articles; *the* is the definite article. *n.*

Articles of Confederation, the constitution adopted by the thirteen original states of the United States in 1781. It was replaced by the present Constitution in 1789.

ar tic u late (är tik′yə lit *for 1,3,4;* är-tik′yə lāt *for 2,5*), 1 spoken in distinct syllables or words: *A baby cries and gurgles, but does not use articulate sounds.* 2 speak distinctly; express in clear sounds and words: *The speaker was careful to articulate his words so that everyone in the room could understand him.* 3 able to put one's thoughts into words easily and clearly: *She is the most articulate of the sisters.* 4 having joints; jointed. The backbone is an articulate structure. 5 fit together in a joint: *After his knee was injured, he was lame because the bones did not articulate well.* 1,3,4 *adj.*, 2,5 *v.*, **ar tic u lat ed, ar tic u lat ing. —ar tic u late ly** (är tik′yə lit lē), *adv.* **—ar tic u late ness** (är tik′yə lit nis), *n.*

ar tic u la tion (är tik′yə lā′shən), 1 way of speaking; enunciation: *If you speak more slowly, your articulation will probably improve.* 2 a joint. 3 act or manner of connecting by a joint or joints: *The articulation of the bones of the hand is quite complex. n.*

ar ti fact (är′tə fakt), anything made by human skill or work, especially a tool or weapon: *Arrowheads and pottery were among the artifacts found at the site of the prehistoric village. n.*

ar ti fice (är′tə fis), 1 a clever device; trick; ruse: *She will use any artifice to get her own way.* 2 trickery; craft: *Her conduct is free from artifice.* 3 skill or ingenuity. *n.*

ar tif i cer (är tif′ə sər), a skilled workman; craftsman. *n.*

ar ti fi cial (är′tə fish′əl), 1 made by human skill or labor; not natural: *At night, you read by artificial light.* 2 made as a substitute or imitation; not real: *We made artificial paper flowers.* 3 put on for effect; affected; pretended: *When nervous, he had an artificial laugh. adj.* **—ar′ti fi′cial ly,** *adv.*

ar ti fi ci al i ty (är′tə fish′ē al′ə tē), 1 artificial quality or condition. 2 something unnatural or unreal. *n., pl.* **ar ti fi ci al i ties.**

artificial respiration, act or means of restoring normal breathing to a person who has stopped breathing by forcing air alternately into and out of his lungs.

ar til ler y (är til′ər ē), 1 mounted guns; cannon. 2 the part of an army that uses and manages cannon. *n.*

ar ti san (är′tə zən), workman skilled in some industry or trade; craftsman. Carpenters, masons, plumbers, and electricians are artisans. *n.*

art ist (är′tist), 1 person who paints pictures. 2 person who is skilled in any of the fine arts, such as sculpture, music, or literature. 3 a public performer, especially an actor or singer. 4 person who does work with skill and good taste. *n.*

ar tis tic (är tis′tik), 1 of art or artists: *artistic treasures.* 2 done with skill and good taste: *an artistic play or performance.* 3 having good color and design; pleasing to the senses: *an artistic wallpaper.* 4 having or showing appreciation of beauty: *You have an artistic way of arranging flowers. adj.*

ar tis ti cal ly (är tis′tik lē), 1 with skill and good taste. 2 from an artistic point of view. *adv.*

art ist ry (är′tə strē), artistic work; workmanship of an artist. *n., pl.* **art ist ries.**

art less (ärt′lis), 1 made or done without knowledge of social customs; simple and natural: *Small children ask many artless questions, such as, "Mother, did you want this lady to come to see you?"* 2 without art; unskilled; ignorant. *adj.* **—art′less ly,** *adv.* **—art′less ness,** *n.*

ar um (er′əm *or* ar′əm), any of a group of plants having a club-shaped spike of small flowers partly surrounded by a hooded sheath, such as the jack-in-the-pulpit. *n.*

as (az; *unstressed* əz), 1 to the same degree or extent; equally: *The son is as tall as his father.* 2 in the character of; doing the work of: *Who will act as teacher?* 3 during the time that; while: *As they were walking, it began to rain.* 4 in the same way that: *Treat others as you wish them to treat you.* 5 for example: *Some animals, as dogs and cats, eat meat.* 6 because: *As she was a skilled worker, she received good wages.* 7 though: *Brave as they were, the danger made them afraid.* 8 that: *Do the same thing as I do.* 1,5 *adv.*, 2 *prep.*, 3,4,6,7 *conj.*, 8 *pron.*

as for, about; concerning; referring to: *As for politics, I am indifferent.*

as if, similar to what it would be if: *You sound as if you were angry.*

as is, in the present condition; without a guarantee of good or perfect quality: *If you buy the car as is, it will cost you very little.*

as of, beginning on or at (a certain date or time): *The new contract becomes effective as of January 1st.*

as though, similar to what it would be if: *It looks as though it might rain.*

as to, about; concerning; referring to: *I'd like a cat, but I have no preference as to its color.*

as a fet i da (as′ə fet′ə də), gum resin that smells like garlic, formerly used in medicine to prevent spasms. *n.*

as bes tos (as bes′təs), 1 mineral that does not burn or conduct heat and that usually comes in fibers. 2 a fireproof fabric made of these fibers. Asbestos is used to make insulating and roofing materials, brake linings, and fire-resistant clothing. *n.*

as cend (ə send′), go up; rise; climb: *We watched the airplane ascend higher and higher. A small party is planning to ascend Mount Everest. v.*

as cend an cy or **as cend en cy** (ə sen′dən sē), controlling influence; domination; rule: *Hannibal and the Carthaginians challenged the ascendancy of Rome. n.*

as cend ant or **as cend ent** (ə sen′-dənt), 1 ascending; rising. 2 superior; dominant; controlling. *adj.*

in the ascendant, increasing in influence, popularity, etc.: *The study of science is in the ascendant in many schools.*

as cen sion (ə sen′shən), 1 an ascending; ascent. 2 **the Ascension,** (in the Bible) the ascent of Christ from earth to heaven after the Resurrection. *n.*

as cent (ə sent′), 1 a going up; upward

48

movement; rising: *The sudden ascent of the elevator made us dizzy.* 2 a climbing: *The ascent of Mount Everest is difficult.* 3 place or way that slopes up: *The gradual ascent of the hill made it easy to climb.* *n.*

as cer tain (as′ər tān′), find out; make sure of; determine: *The detective tried to ascertain the facts about the robbery.* *v.*

as cer tain a ble (as′ər tā′nə bəl), that can be ascertained. *adj.*

as cet ic (ə set′ik), 1 person who practices unusual self-denial or severe discipline over himself, especially for religious reasons. Fasting is a common practice of ascetics. 2 refraining from pleasures and comforts; practicing unusual self-denial. 1 *n.,* 2 *adj.*

as cet i cism (ə set′ə siz′əm), unusual or extreme self-denial. *n.*

a scor bic acid (ə skôr′bik), vitamin C.

as cribe (ə skrīb′), think of as caused by or coming from; attribute: *The police ascribed the automobile accident to fast driving. The author of this tale is unknown, but it is ascribed to the brothers Grimm.* *v.,* **as cribed, as crib ing.**

as crip tion (ə skrip′shən), 1 an ascribing: *the ascription of evil to the Devil.* 2 statement or words ascribing something. *n.*

a sep tic (ə sep′tik), free from the living germs causing infection: *Surgical instruments can be made aseptic by boiling them.* *adj.*

a sex u al (ā sek′shü əl), 1 having no sex. 2 independent of sexual processes. The division into two parts by an amoeba is a form of asexual reproduction. *adj.* **—a sex′u al ly,** *adv.*

As gard (as′gärd), home of the Norse gods and heroes. *n.*

ash¹ (ash), what remains of a thing after it has been thoroughly burned: *He flicked his cigarette ash into the fireplace.* See also **ashes.** *n., pl.* **ash es.** [Old English *æsce*]

ash² (ash), 1 a timber or shade tree that has a silver-gray bark, grayish twigs, and straight-grained wood. 2 its tough, springy wood. *n., pl.* **ash es.** [Old English *æsc*]

a shamed (ə shāmd′), 1 feeling shame; disturbed or uncomfortable because one has done something wrong, improper, or silly: *I was ashamed when I cried at the movies.* 2 unwilling because of fear of shame: *I failed math and was ashamed to tell my parents.* *adj.*

ash en¹ (ash′ən), 1 like ashes; pale as ashes. 2 of ashes. *adj.* [*ash¹*]

ash en² (ash′ən), made from the wood of the ash tree. *adj.* [*ash²*]

ash es (ash′iz), 1 what remains of a thing after it has thoroughly burned:

Ashes have to be removed from the fireplace to make room for more wood. 2 what remains of a dead body when burned. 3 a dead body; corpse. *n.pl.*

a shore (ə shôr′), 1 to the shore; to land: *The men rowed the captain ashore.* 2 on the shore; on land: *The sailor had been ashore for months.* *adv.*

ash tray (ash′trā′), a small dish to put tobacco ashes in. *n.*

Ash Wednesday, the first day of Lent; the seventh Wednesday before Easter.

ash y (ash′ē), 1 like ashes; pale as ashes; ashen. 2 consisting of ashes. 3 covered with ashes. *adj.,* **ash i er, ash i est.**

A sia (ā′zhə), the largest continent, separated from Europe by the Ural Mountains, Ural River, and Caspian Sea. China, India, and most of the Soviet Union are in Asia. *n.*

Asia Minor, peninsula of SW Asia, between the Black Sea and the Mediterranean Sea; Anatolia. It includes most of Asian Turkey.

A sian (ā′zhən), 1 person born or living in Asia. 2 of or having to do with Asia or its people. 1 *n.,* 2 *adj.*

A si at ic (ā′zhē at′ik), Asian. *adj., n.*

a side (ə sīd′), 1 on one side; to one side; away: *Help me move the table aside. She stood aside to let me pass.* 2 out of one's thoughts or consideration: *Swimming is easier if you can put your fears aside.* 3 words spoken to one side; remark that others who are present are not supposed to hear. An actor's asides are usually spoken to the audience. 1,2 *adv.,* 3 *n.*

aside from, 1 away from: *Your remark is aside from the question.* 2 except for: *Aside from arithmetic, I have finished my homework.*

as i nine (as′n īn), obviously silly; foolish and stupid. *adj.* **—as′i nine ly,** *adv.*

ask (ask), 1 try to find out by words; inquire: *Why don't you ask? She asked about our health. Ask the way.* 2 seek the answer to: *Ask any questions you wish.* 3 put a question to; inquire of: *Ask him how old he is.* 4 try to get by words; request: *Ask her to sing. Ask for help if you need it.* 5 invite: *She asked ten guests to the party.* *v.*

a skance (ə skans′), 1 with suspicion or disapproval: *The students looked askance at the plan to have classes on Saturday.* 2 to one side; sideways. *adv.*

a skew (ə skyü′), to one side; turned or twisted the wrong way; out of the proper position: *The wind blew her hat askew* (adv.). *Isn't that picture askew?* (adj.). *adv., adj.*

a slant (ə slant′), 1 in a slanting direc-

tion. 2 slantingly across. 3 slanting. 1 *adv.,* 2 *prep.,* 3 *adj.*

a sleep (ə slēp′), 1 not awake; sleeping: *The cat is asleep.* 2 into a condition of sleep: *The tired boy fell asleep.* 3 having lost the power of feeling; numb: *My foot is asleep.* 1,3 *adj.,* 2 *adv.*

asp (asp), any of several small, poisonous snakes of Africa. *n.*

as par a gus (ə spar′ə gəs), 1 plant with scalelike leaves. 2 its green, tender shoots, which are used as a vegetable. *n.*

as pect (as′pekt), 1 one of the ways in which a subject or situation may be looked at or thought about: *We must consider each aspect of this plan before we decide.* 2 look; appearance: *The judge has a solemn aspect.* 3 side fronting or facing in a given direction: *The southern aspect of the house is the warmest in winter.* *n.*

as pen (as′pən), 1 any of several popular trees of North America and Europe whose leaves tremble and rustle in the slightest breeze. 2 of this tree. 1 *n.,* 2 *adj.*

as per i ty (a sper′ə tē), 1 harshness or sharpness of temper or manner: *We grew quiet when we noticed the asperity in our teacher's voice.* 2 severity: *The settlers suffered the asperities of a very cold winter.* *n., pl.* **as per i ties.**

as per sion (ə spėr′zhən), a damaging or false statement; slander: *He was accused of casting aspersions on the reputation of an innocent person.* *n.*

as phalt (as′fôlt), 1 a dark substance much like tar, found in various parts of the world or obtained by refining petroleum. 2 a mixture of this substance with crushed rock or sand. Asphalt is used in surfacing roads. *n.*

as pho del (as′fə del), a plant of the same family as the lily, with spikes of white, pink, or yellow flowers. *n.*

as phyx i ate (a sfik′sē āt), suffocate because of lack of oxygen in the blood: *The men trapped in the coal mine were almost asphyxiated by carbon monoxide before help reached them.* *v.,* **as phyx i at ed, as phyx i at ing.**

hat, āge, fär; let, ēqual, tėrm; it, īce; hot, ōpen, ôrder; oil, out; cup, pùt, rüle; ch, child; ng, long; sh, she; th, thin; ₮H, then; zh, measure;

ə represents *a* in about, *e* in taken, *i* in pencil, *o* in lemon, *u* in circus.

adj. adjective	*n.* noun
adv. adverb	*prep.* preposition
conj. conjunction	*pron.* pronoun
interj. interjection	*v.* verb
sing. singular	*pl.* plural

as phyx i a tion (a sfik′sē ā′shən), suffocation caused by lack of oxygen in the blood. *n.*

as pic (as′pik), kind of jelly made from meat or fish stock, used as a garnish or in salads. *n.*

as pir ant (ə spī′rənt *or* as′pər ənt), person who aspires; person who seeks a position of honor: *There were many aspirants to the office of class president. n.*

as pi rate (as′pə rāt′ *for 1,2;* as′pər it *for 3,4*), **1** begin (a word or syllable) with a breathing or *h*-sound. *Hot* is aspirated; *honor* is not. **2** pronounce with such a sound. The *h* in *hot* is aspirated. **3** pronounced with a breathing or *h*-sound. The *h* in *here* is aspirate. **4** the sound of *h* in *hot.* 1,2 *v.,* **as pi rat ed, as pi rat ing;** 3 *adj.,* 4 *n.*

as pi ra tion (as′pə rā′shən), **1** earnest desire; longing; ambition: *She had aspirations to be a doctor.* **2** an aspirating: *Many people pronounce "where" with no aspiration.* **3** a drawing air into the lungs; breathing. *n.*

as pire (ə spīr′), have an ambition for something; desire earnestly; seek: *He aspired to be captain of the team. Scholars aspire after knowledge. v.,* **aspired, as pir ing.**

as pir in (as′pər ən), drug used to relieve headaches, colds, etc. It is prepared from salicylic acid. *n.*

ass (as), **1** donkey. **2** a stupid, silly, or stubborn person; fool. *n., pl.* **ass es.**

as sail (ə sāl′), **1** set upon with violence; attack: *The enemy assailed our fort.* **2** set upon vigorously with arguments or abuse: *The senators assailed the President on the subject of the treaty. v.*

as sail a ble (ə sā′lə bəl), that can be assailed. *adj.*

as sail ant (ə sā′lənt), person who attacks: *The injured man did not know who his assailant was. n.*

as sas sin (ə sas′n), murderer, especially one hired or chosen to murder by a sudden or secret attack. *n.*

as sas si nate (ə sas′n āt), murder by a sudden or secret attack: *President Kennedy was assassinated in 1963. v.,* **as sas si nat ed, as sas si nat ing.**

as sas si na tion (ə sas′n ā′shən), a murdering by a sudden or secret attack. *n.*

as sault (ə sôlt′), **1** a sudden, vigorous attack: *The enemy made an assault on our fort.* **2** make an assault on. **3** (in law) a threat or attempt to strike or otherwise harm a person. 1,3 *n.,* 2 *v.*

as say (ə sā′), **1** analyze (an ore or alloy) to find out the quantity of gold, silver, or other metal in it. **2** an analysis to find out the amount of metal in an ore or alloy by measuring, weighing, or calculating. **3** an analysis to determine the proportion of a certain ingredient in a drug. **4** try, test, or examine. **5** trial, test, or examination. 1,4 *v.,* 2,3,5 *n.* —**as say′er,** *n.*

as sem blage (ə sem′blij), **1** group of persons or things collected or gathered together; assembly. **2** process of putting together; fitting together: *The factory foreman supervised the assemblage of parts of the automobile engines. n.*

as sem ble (ə sem′bəl), **1** gather together; bring together: *The principal assembled all the students in the auditorium.* **2** come together; meet: *Congress assembles in January.* **3** put together; fit together: *Will you help me assemble my model airplane? v.,* **as sem bled, as sem bling.**

as sem bler (ə sem′blər), person or thing that assembles. *n.*

as sem bly (ə sem′blē), **1** a gathering of people for some purpose; meeting. A reception or a ball may be called an assembly. **2** a meeting of lawmakers. **3 Assembly,** the lower branch of the state legislature of some states of the United States. **4** a coming together; an assembling: *unlawful assembly.* **5** a putting together; fitting together: *In Detroit we saw the assembly of the parts which make up an automobile.* **6** the complete group of parts required to put something together: *the tail assembly of an airplane. n., pl.* **as sem blies.**

as sent (ə sent′), **1** express agreement; consent; agree: *Everyone assented to the plans for the dance.* **2** acceptance of a proposal, statement, etc; agreement: *She smiled her assent to the plan.* 1 *v.,* 2 *n.*

as sert (ə sėrt′), **1** state positively; declare firmly: *He asserts that he will go whether we do or not.* **2** defend or insist on (a right, a claim, etc.): *Assert your independence. v.*

assert oneself, put oneself forward; make demands: *A leader must assert himself in order to be followed.*

as ser tion (ə sėr′shən), **1** a positive statement; firm declaration: *His assertion of innocence was believed by the jury.* **2** an insisting on a right, a claim, etc. *n.*

as ser tive (ə sėr′tiv), too confident and certain; positive: *He is an assertive boy, always insisting on his rights and opinions. adj.* —**as ser′tive ly,** *adv.* —**as ser′tive ness,** *n.*

as sess (ə ses′), **1** estimate the value of (property or income) for taxation; value: *The town clerk has assessed our house at $20,000.* **2** fix the amount of (a tax, fine, damages, etc.): *Damages from last week's flood have been assessed at $150,000.* **3** put a tax on or call for a contribution from (a person, property, etc.): *Each member of the club will be assessed one dollar to pay for the trip. v.*

as sess ment (ə ses′mənt), **1** an assessing. **2** amount assessed. *n.*

as ses sor (ə ses′ər), person who estimates the value of property or income for taxation. *n.*

as set (as′et), **1** something having value: *Ability to get along with people is an asset in business.* **2 assets,** *pl.* **a** things of value; property: *His assets include a house, a car, stocks, bonds, and jewelry.* **b** property that can be used to pay debts. *n.*

as sev e rate (ə sev′ə rāt′), declare solemnly; state positively. *v.,* **as sev e rat ed, as sev e rat ing.**

as sev e ra tion (ə sev′ə rā′shən), a solemn declaration; positive statement. *n.*

as si du i ty (as′ə dü′ə tē *or* as′ə dyü′ə tē), careful and steady attention; diligence. *n., pl.* **as si du i ties.**

as sid u ous (ə sij′ü əs), careful and attentive; diligent. *adj.* —**as sid′u ous ly,** *adv.* —**as sid′u ous ness,** *n.*

as sign (ə sīn′), **1** give as a share; allot: *The teacher has assigned the next ten problems for today.* **2** appoint (to a post or duty): *We were assigned to decorate the room for the party.* **3** name definitely; fix; set: *The judge assigned a day for the trial.* **4** transfer or hand over (some property, right, etc.) legally: *Mr. Jones assigned his home and farm to his creditors. v.*

as sign ment (ə sīn′mənt), **1** something assigned, especially a piece of work to be done: *Today's assignment in arithmetic consists of ten examples.* **2** an assigning; appointment: *Homeroom assignments were made on the first day of school.* **3** the legal transfer of some property, right, etc. *n.*

as sim i late (ə sim′ə lāt), **1** take in and make part of oneself; absorb; digest: *She does so much reading that she cannot assimilate it all. The human body will not assimilate sawdust.* **2** become absorbed; be digested: *The woody fibers of plants will not assimilate into the human body.* **3** make or become like the people of a nation in customs, viewpoint, character, etc.: *By living a long* time with the Indians he was assimilated to them in his thinking and actions. *Many immigrants assimilate readily in this country.* v., **as sim i lat ed, as sim i lat ing.**

as sim i la tion (ə sim′ə lā′shən), 1 an absorbing or a being absorbed: *Life depends on the assimilation of food.* 2 a making or a becoming like. n.

as sist (ə sist′), 1 give aid to; help: *She assisted the science teacher with the experiment.* 2 INFORMAL. act of assistance; aid; help: *If you will give me an assist I think I can reach the branch.* 1 v., 2 n.

as sist ance (ə sis′təns), an assisting; aid; help: *I need your assistance.* n.

as sist ant (ə sis′tənt), 1 person who assists another; aid; helper: *He was my assistant in the library for a time.* 2 assisting; helping: *She is an assistant teacher.* 1 n., 2 adj.

as siz es (ə sī′ziz), the periodic sessions of a court of law held in each county of England. n.pl.

assn., ass'n, or **Assn.,** association.

as so ci ate (ə sō′shē āt for 1,3-5; ə sō′shē it or ə sō′shē āt for 2,6,7), 1 connect in thought: *We associate turkey with Thanksgiving.* 2 joined with another or others: *I am an associate editor of the school paper.* 3 join as a companion, partner, or friend: *He is associated with his brothers in business.* 4 be friendly; keep company: *He associated with interesting people.* 5 join; combine; unite: *The action of the stream had associated the gold particles with the sand.* 6 companion, partner, or friend: *I am one of his associates in this scheme.* 7 admitted to some, but not all, rights and privileges: *After being an associate member of the glee club for a year I became a full member.* 1,3-5 v., **as so ci at ed, as so ci at ing;** 2,7 adj., 6 n.

as so ci a tion (ə sō′sē ā′shən or ə sō′shē ā′shən), 1 group of people joined together for some purpose; society: *Will you join the young people's association at our church?* 2 an associating: *association of ideas.* 3 a being associated: *I look forward to my association with the counselors I will have at camp.* 4 companionship or friendship: *They had enjoyed a close association over many years.* 5 idea connected with another idea in thought: *Some people make the association of the color red with anger.* n.

as so ci a tive (ə sō′shē ā′tiv), 1 tending to associate. 2 having to do with association. 3 of or having to do with a rule that the combinations by which numbers are added or multiplied will not change their sum or product. EXAMPLE: (2×3)×5 will give the same

product as 2×(3×5). adj. —**as so′ci a′tive ly,** adv.

as so nance (as′n əns), 1 resemblance in sound of words or syllables. EXAMPLE: Wa ken lords and la dies ga y. 2 a substitute for rhyme in which the vowels are alike but the consonants are different. EXAMPLES: *brave—vain, lone—show, man—hat, penitent—reticence.* n.

as sort (ə sôrt′), arrange by kinds; sort out; classify: *He assorted the books in alphabetical order.* v.

as sort ed (ə sôr′tid), 1 selected so as to be of different kinds; various: *She served assorted cakes.* 2 arranged by kinds; classified: *There were socks assorted by size on the shelf.* 3 suited to one another; matched: *They are a poorly assorted couple, always quarreling.* adj.

as sort ment (ə sôrt′mənt), 1 a sorting out or classifying: *The assortment of so many books will take a long time.* 2 collection of various kinds: *These scarves come in an assortment of colors.* n.

asst. or **Asst.,** assistant.

as suage (ə swāj′), 1 calm or soothe: *Her words assuaged the child's fears.* 2 make milder or easier: *Aspirin assuages pain.* 3 satisfy; appease; quench: *She took a drink of water to assuage her thirst.* v., **as suaged, as suag ing.**

as sume (ə süm′), 1 take for granted without proof; suppose: *He assumed that the train would be on time.* 2 take upon oneself; undertake: *The class president assumed the leadership in planning the picnic.* 3 take on; put on: *The problem has assumed a new form.* 4 pretend: *Although she was afraid, she assumed an air of confidence.* 5 take for oneself; appropriate; usurp: *The king's wicked brother tried to assume the throne.* v., **as sumed, as sum ing.**

as sump tion (ə sump′shən), 1 an assuming: *The clerk bustled about with an assumption of authority. Her assumption of my chores enabled me to go to the movies.* 2 thing assumed: *His assumption that he won proved incorrect.* n.

as sur ance (ə shur′əns), 1 statement intended to make a person more sure or certain: *Do I have your assurance that you will not do it again?* 2 security, certainty, or confidence: *We have the assurance of final victory.* 3 confidence in one's own ability: *His careful preparation gave him assurance in reciting.* 4 too much boldness; impudence: *They had the assurance to walk right in without knocking.* 5 insurance. n.

as sure (ə shur′), 1 tell positively: *The captain of the ship assured the passengers that there was no danger.* 2 make

hat, āge, fär; let, ēqual, tėrm; it, īce; hot, ōpen, ôrder; oil, out; cup, pút, rüle; ch, child; ng, long; sh, she; th, thin; ŦH, then; zh, measure;

ə represents *a* in about, *e* in taken, *i* in pencil, *o* in lemon, *u* in circus.

sure or certain; convince: *She assured herself that the bridge was safe before she crossed it.* 3 make safe; secure: *Victory was assured when the team scored in the final seconds of the game.* 4 insure against loss. 5 give or restore confidence to; encourage: *The father assured his frightened son.* v., **assured, as sur ing.**

as sur ed ly (ə shur′id lē), 1 surely; certainly: *I will assuredly come.* 2 confidently; boldly: *He spoke more assuredly than he felt.* adv.

Assyria, 670 B.C.
shown by shaded area on a modern map

As syr i a (ə sir′ē ə), ancient country in SW Asia, once a great empire. The capital was Nineveh. n. —**As syr′i an,** adj., n.

as ta tine (as′tə tēn′), a radioactive nonmetallic element produced artificially from bismuth. n.

as ter (as′tər), 1 a common plant having daisylike flowers with white, pink, or purple petals around a yellow center. Some asters are very small; others are large with many petals. 2 its flower. n.

as ter isk (as′tə risk′), a star-shaped mark (*) used in printing and writing to call attention to a footnote, indicate the omission of words or letters, etc. n.

a stern (ə stėrn′), 1 at or toward the rear; aft: *The captain went astern.* 2 backward: *The boat moved slowly astern.* 3 behind: *Some yachts tow small boats astern.* adv.

adj. adjective   n. noun
adv. adverb   prep. preposition
conj. conjunction   pron. pronoun
interj. interjection   v. verb

sing. singular   pl. plural

---

as ter oid (as′tə roid′), any of the thousands of very small planets that revolve about the sun, chiefly between the orbits of Mars and Jupiter; planetoid. See **solar system** for diagram. *n.*

asth ma (az′mə), a chronic disease characterized by difficulty in breathing, a feeling of suffocation, and coughing. *n.*

a stig ma tism (ə stig′mə tiz′əm), defect of an eye or of a lens that makes objects look indistinct or gives imperfect images. *n.*

a stir (ə stėr′), in motion; up and about: *Although it was midnight, the whole town was astir. adj.*

as ton ish (ə ston′ish), surprise greatly; amaze: *We were astonished that she remembered the house she lived in as a child. v.*

as ton ish ing (ə ston′i shing), very surprising; amazing. *adj.* —**as ton′ish ing ly,** *adv.*

as ton ish ment (ə ston′ish mənt), great surprise; sudden wonder; amazement. *n.*

as tound (ə stound′), surprise greatly; amaze: *She was astounded by the news that she had won the contest. v.*

as tound ing (ə stound′ing), amazing. *adj.* —**as tound′ing ly,** *adv.*

a strad dle (ə strad′l), astride. *adv.*

as tra khan (as′trə kən), 1 the curly furlike wool on the skin of young caracul lambs. 2 a rough woolen cloth that looks like this. *n.* [from *Astrakhan,* district in the Soviet Union]

a stray (ə strā′), out of the right way; off: *Your reasoning is astray on that subject* (adj.). *The gate is open and all the cows have gone astray* (adv.). *adj., adv.*

a stride (ə strīd′), 1 with one leg on each side of: *He sits astride his horse.* 2 with one leg on each side: *The knight sat astride on his horse.* 3 with legs far apart. 1 *prep.,* 2,3 *adv.*

as trin gen cy (ə strin′jən sē), quality of being astringent. *n.*

as trin gent (ə strin′jənt), 1 substance that shrinks body tissues and thus checks the flow of blood or other secretions. Alum is an astringent. 2 having the property of shrinking tis-

sues. 1 *n.,* 2 *adj.* —**as trin′gent ly,** *adv.*

as tro labe (as′trə lāb), an astronomical instrument formerly used for measuring the altitude of the sun or stars. It has been replaced by the sextant. *n.*

as trol o ger (ə strol′ə jər), person who claims to know and interpret the supposed influence of the stars and planets on persons or events. *n.*

as tro log i cal (as′trə loj′ə kəl), of or having to do with astrology. *adj.*

as trol o gy (ə strol′ə jē), study of the stars and planets to reveal their supposed influence on persons or events, and to foretell what will happen. *n.*

as tro naut (as′trə nôt), pilot or member of the crew of a spacecraft. *n.*

as tro naut ics (as′trə nô′tiks), science or art having to do with the design, manufacture, and operation of spacecraft. *n.*

SYMMETRIC   ASYMMETRIC

as tron o mer (ə stron′ə mər), an expert in astronomy. *n.*

as tro nom ic (as′trə nom′ik), astronomical. *adj.*

as tro nom i cal (as′trə nom′ə kəl), 1 of or having to do with astronomy: *astronomical calculations.* 2 enormous; very great: *That trip will cost you an astronomical sum of money. adj.* —**as′tro nom′i cal ly,** *adv.*

as tron o my (ə stron′ə mē), science that deals with the sun, moon, planets, stars, and other heavenly bodies. It studies their composition, motions, positions, distances, sizes, etc. *n.*

as tro phys ics (as′trō fiz′iks), branch of astronomy that deals with the physical and chemical characteristics of heavenly bodies. *n.*

as tute (ə stüt′ *or* ə styüt′), shrewd with regard to one's own interests; clever: *He was an astute businessman. adj.* —**as tute′ly,** *adv.* —**as tute′ness,** *n.*

A sun ción (ä sün′syôn′), capital and a major port of Paraguay, on the Paraguay River. *n.*

a sun der (ə sun′dər), 1 in pieces; into separate parts: *Lightning split the tree asunder.* 2 apart or separate from each other: *The two armies were a mile asunder.* 1 *adv.,* 2 *adj.*

As wan Dam (ä swän′), large dam in SE Egypt, built to control the Nile for irrigation.

a sy lum (ə sī′ləm), 1 institution for the support and care of the insane,

astrolabe—A star is sighted along the length of the movable notched piece. The angle between the horizon and the star is read at the spot where the man's finger rests.

blind, orphans, or other groups of people who are unable to care for themselves. 2 refuge; shelter. In olden times a church might be an asylum for a debtor or a criminal, since no one was allowed to drag a person from the altar. Now asylum is sometimes given by one nation to persons of another nation who are accused of political crimes. *n.*

a sym met ric (ā′sə met′rik), not symmetrical; lacking symmetry. *adj.* —**a′sym met′ri cal ly,** *adv.*

a sym me try (ā sim′ə trē), lack of symmetry. *n.*

at (at; *unstressed* ət *or* it), 1 in; on; by; near: *There is someone at the front door. I will be at home.* 2 in the direction of; to; toward: *The dog ran at the cat.* 3 on or near the time of: *She goes to bed at nine o'clock.* 4 in a place or condition of: *England and France were at war.* 5 through; by way of: *Smoke came out at the chimney.* 6 doing; trying to do; engaged in: *He is at work on a new project.* 7 for: *We bought two books at a dollar each.* 8 because of; with: *The shipwrecked sailors were happy at the arrival of the rescuers.* 9 according to: *She can wiggle her ears at will.* 10 from: *The patient got good treatment at the hands of the doctor. prep.*

ate (āt), past tense of **eat.** *The boy ate his dinner. v.*

Ath a bas ka (ath′ə bas′kə), **Lake,** lake in central Canada. *n.*

a the ism (ā′thē iz′əm), belief that there is no God. *n.*

a the ist (ā′thē ist), person who believes that there is no God. *n.*

a the is tic (ā′thē is′tik), of atheism or atheists. *adj.*

A the na (ə thē′nə), (in Greek myths) the goddess of wisdom, arts, industries, and prudent warfare. The Romans called her Minerva. *n.*

A the ne (ə thē′nē), Athena. *n.*

A the ni an (ə thē′nē ən), 1 of Athens (especially ancient Athens) or its people. 2 person having the right of citizenship in ancient Athens. 3 person born or living in Athens. 1 *adj.*, 2,3 *n.*

Ath ens (ath′ənz), capital of Greece, in the SE part. Athens was famous in ancient times for its art and literature. *n.*

a thirst (ə thėrst′), 1 thirsty. 2 eager: *Most young people are athirst for new experiences. adj.*

ath lete (ath′lēt′), person trained in exercises of physical strength, speed, and skill. Baseball players, runners, boxers, and swimmers are athletes. *n.*

athlete's foot, a very contagious skin disease of the feet, which may be caused by any of various related fungi; ringworm of the feet.

ath let ic (ath let′ik), 1 of an athlete; like or suited to an athlete. 2 having to do with active games and sports: *join an athletic association.* 3 strong and active: *He is an athletic boy. adj.* —**ath let′i cal ly,** *adv.*

ath let ics (ath let′iks), 1 *pl. in form and use.* exercises of physical strength, speed, and skill; active games and sports. Athletics include baseball and basketball. 2 *pl. in form, sing. in use.* the practice and principles of physical training: *Athletics is recommended for every student. n.*

a thwart (ə thwôrt′), 1 across from side to side; crosswise. 2 across. 3 across the line or course of: *The tug steamed athwart the ship.* 4 in opposition to; against. 1 *adv.*, 2-4 *prep.*

a tilt (ə tilt′), at a tilt; tilted. *adj.*

a tin gle (ə ting′gəl), tingling. *adj.*

-ation, *suffix added mainly to verbs to form nouns.* 1 act or process of _____ing: *Preparation = act or process of preparing.* 2 condition or state of being _____ed: *Cancellation = condition or state of being canceled.* 3 result of _____ing: *Civilization = result of civilizing.* [from Latin *-ationem*]

-ative, *suffix added to verbs and nouns to form adjectives.* 1 tending to _____: *Talkative = tending to talk.* 2 having to do with _____: *Qualitative = having to do with quality.* [from Latin *-ativum*]

At lan ta (at lan′tə), capital of Georgia, in the NW part. *n.*

At lan tic (at lan′tik), 1 ocean east of North and South America. It extends to Europe and Africa. 2 of the Atlantic Ocean. 3 on, in, over, or near the Atlantic Ocean: *Atlantic air routes.* 4 of or on the Atlantic coast of the United States: *New Jersey is one of the Atlantic states.* 1 *n.*, 2-4 *adj.*

Atlantic City, seaside resort in SE New Jersey.

At lan tis (at lan′tis), legendary island in the Atlantic Ocean said to have sunk beneath the sea. *n.*

at las (at′ləs), 1 book of maps. 2 **Atlas,** (in Greek myths) a giant who sup-

ported the heavens on his shoulders. *n., pl.* **at las es** for 1.

Atlas Mountains, mountain range in NW Africa.

at mo sphere (at′mə sfir), 1 air that surrounds the earth. 2 mass of gases that surrounds any heavenly body: *the cloudy atmosphere of Venus.* 3 air in any given place: *the damp atmosphere of a cellar.* 4 mental and moral surroundings; surrounding influence: *Nuns live in a religious atmosphere.* 5 unit of pressure equal to 14.7 pounds per square inch. *n.*

at mo spher ic (at′mə sfir′ik *or* at′mə sfer′ik), 1 of or having to do with the atmosphere: *Normal atmospheric pressure on the earth's surface at sea level is 14.7 pounds to the square inch.* 2 in the atmosphere: *Atmospheric conditions often prevent observations of the stars. adj.* —**at′mo spher′i cal ly,** *adv.*

atoll

at oll (at′ol *or* ə tol′), a ring-shaped coral island or group of islands enclosing or partly enclosing a lagoon. *n.*

at om (at′əm), 1 the smallest particle of a chemical element that can take part in a chemical reaction without being permanently changed. An atom is made up of protons and neutrons in a central nucleus surrounded by electrons. A molecule of water consists of two atoms of hydrogen and one atom of oxygen. 2 a very small particle; tiny bit: *There is not an atom of truth in the whole story. n.*

atom (def. 1) of beryllium
The electrons orbit the nucleus.
In all elements the number of electrons equals the number of protons.

atom bomb, atomic bomb.

a tom ic (ə tom′ik), 1 of or having to do with atoms: *atomic research.* 2 using atomic energy: *an atomic submarine.* 3 extremely small; minute. *adj.*

atomic bomb, bomb in which the splitting of atomic nuclei results in an

hat, āge, fär; let, ēqual, tėrm;
it, īce; hot, ōpen, ôrder;
oil, out; cup, pùt, rüle; ch, child;
ng, long; sh, she; th, thin;
ᴛʜ, then; zh, measure;

ə represents *a* in about,
e in taken, *i* in pencil,
o in lemon, *u* in circus.

explosion of tremendous force and heat, accompanied by a blinding light; A-bomb.

atomic energy, energy that exists in atoms; nuclear energy. Some atoms can be made to release some of their energy, either slowly (in a reactor) or very suddenly (in a bomb), by the splitting or the fusion of their nuclei.

atomic number, the number of protons in the nucleus of an atom of an element: *The atomic number of hydrogen is 1, of uranium 92.*

atomic weight, the relative weight of an atom of a chemical element based on the weight of an atom of carbon, which is taken as 12. Formerly, atomic weights were based on the weight of an atom of oxygen, which was taken as 16: *The atomic weight of hydrogen is 1.00797, of uranium 238.03.*

at om ize (at′ə mīz), 1 change (a liquid) into a spray of very small drops. 2 reduce (anything) to small particles. 3 obliterate (anything) by an atomic explosion. *v.*, **at om ized, at om iz ing.**

at om iz er (at′ə mī′zər), apparatus used to blow a liquid in a spray of very small drops: *an atomizer for perfume. n.*

a ton al (ā tō′nl), (in music) having no key. *adj.* —**a ton′al ly,** *adv.*

a tone (ə tōn′), make up; make amends: *He atoned for his unkindness to his sister by taking her to the movies. v.*, **a toned, a ton ing.**

a tone ment (ə tōn′mənt), 1 a making up for something; giving satisfaction for a wrong, loss, or injury; amends. 2 **the Atonement,** the reconciliation of God with sinners through the sufferings and death of Christ. *n.*

a top (ə top′), on the top of: *He had a hat atop his head. prep.*

a tro cious (ə trō′shəs), 1 very wicked or cruel; very savage or brutal: *Kidnaping is an atrocious crime.* 2 INFORMAL. very bad or unpleasant: *The weather has been simply atrocious. adj.* —**a tro′cious ly,** *adv.* —**a tro′cious ness,** *n.*

a troc i ty (ə tros′ə tē), 1 very great wickedness or cruelty: *Many acts of*

adj.	adjective	n.	noun
adv.	adverb	prep.	preposition
conj.	conjunction	pron.	pronoun
interj.	interjection	v.	verb
sing.	singular	pl.	plural

atrocity are committed in war. 2 a very cruel or brutal act: *the atrocities of war.* 3 INFORMAL. a very bad blunder: *Her dress is an atrocity. n., pl.* **a troc i ties.**

at ro phy (at′rə fē), 1 a wasting away; withering: *Some diseases cause atrophy of the muscles in the legs.* 2 waste away: *An ability may atrophy if it is not used.* 1 *n.,* 2 *v.,* **at ro phied, at ro phy ing.**

at ro pine (at′rə pēn′), a poisonous drug obtained from belladonna and similar plants. Atropine relaxes muscles and dilates the pupil of the eye. *n.*

at tach (ə tach′), 1 fix in place; fasten: *We can attach the trailer to our car.* 2 add at the end; affix: *The signers attached their names to the Constitution.* 3 bind by affection: *She is very attached to her cousin.* 4 fasten itself; belong: *The blame for this accident attaches to the driver who did not stop.* 5 give to; attribute: *The world at first attached little importance to rockets.* 6 connect with for duty, etc.; assign: *He was attached as mate to the ship.* 7 take (a person or property) by order of a court of law: *If you owe money to a man, he can attach a part of your salary unless you pay him. v.*

at ta ché (at′ə shā′), person on the official staff of an ambassador or minister to a foreign country: *a naval attaché. n., pl.* **at ta chés.** [from French *attaché* attached]

at tach ment (ə tach′mənt), 1 an attaching or a being attached; connection: *the attachment of muscles to the bones of the jaw.* 2 thing attached, such as an additional device. Some sewing machines have attachments for making buttonholes. 3 means of attaching; fastening. 4 affection that binds a person to someone or something; devotion: *The children have a great attachment to their pets.* 5 the legal taking of a person or property. *n.*

at tack (ə tak′), 1 use force or weapons to hurt (an enemy); set upon to hurt; begin fighting against someone: *The dog attacked the cat. The enemy attacked at dawn.* 2 talk or write against: *The candidate angrily attacked his opponent's record as mayor.* 3 go at with vigor: *attack a hard lesson. The hungry hikers attacked dinner as soon*

as it was served. 4 an attacking: *The attack of the enemy took us by surprise.* 5 act harmfully on: *Locusts attacked the crops.* 6 a sudden occurrence of illness, discomfort, etc.: *an attack of flu.* 1-3,5 *v.,* 4,6 *n.* —**at tack′er,** *n.*

at tain (ə tān′), 1 arrive at; come to; reach: *Grandfather has attained the age of 80. She has attained to a position of great responsibility in the company.* 2 gain by effort; accomplish: *attain a goal. v.*

at tain a ble (ə tā′nə bəl), capable of being attained; that can be reached or achieved: *The office of President is the highest attainable in the United States. adj.*

at tain der (ə tān′dər), loss of property and civil rights as the result of being sentenced to death or being outlawed. *n.*

at tain ment (ə tān′mənt), 1 an attaining: *Her main goal was the attainment of a medical degree.* 2 accomplishment; ability: *Benjamin Franklin was a man of varied attainments; he was a diplomat, statesman, writer, and inventor. n.*

at taint (ə tānt′), 1 condemn by attainder. 2 taint; stain; disgrace. *v.*

at tar (at′ər), perfume made from the petals of roses or other flowers. *n.*

at tempt (ə tempt′), 1 make an effort; try: *I will attempt to reply to your question.* 2 a putting forth of effort to accomplish something; endeavor: *He made an attempt to climb Mount Everest.* 3 an attack: *an attempt upon someone's life.* 1 *v.,* 2,3 *n.*

at tend (ə tend′), 1 be present at: *Children must attend school.* 2 give care and thought; apply oneself: *Attend to the instructions.* 3 go with; accompany: *Noble ladies attended the queen.* 4 go with as a result: *Success often attends hard work.* 5 wait on; care for; tend: *Nurses attend the sick. v.*

at tend ance (ə ten′dəns), 1 act of being present at a place; an attending: *Our class had perfect attendance today.* 2 number of people present; persons attending: *The attendance at the meeting last night was over 200. n.*

dance attendance on, wait on often and with much care; be too polite and obedient to.

at tend ant (ə ten′dənt), 1 person who waits on another, such as a servant or follower. 2 employee who waits on customers. 3 waiting on another to help or serve: *An attendant nurse is at the sick man's bedside.* 4 going with as a result; accompanying: *Coughing and sneezing are some of the attendant discomforts of a cold.* 5 person who is present. 1,2,5 *n.,* 3,4 *adj.*

at ten tion (ə ten′shən), 1 act of at-

tending; heed: *The children paid attention to the teacher's explanation.* 2 power of attending; notice: *He called my attention to the cat trying to catch the mouse.* 3 care and thought; consideration: *Your letter will receive early attention.* 4 **attentions,** *pl.* acts of courtesy or devotion: *She received such attentions as invitations to parties, candy, and flowers from many young men.* 5 a military attitude of readiness: *The soldier came to attention when the officer addressed him. The private stood at attention during inspection. n.*

at ten tive (ə ten′tiv), 1 paying attention; observant: *The attentive pupil is most likely to learn.* 2 courteous; polite: *A good host and hostess are attentive to their guests. adj.* —**at ten′tive ly,** *adv.* —**at ten′tive ness,** *n.*

at ten u ate (ə ten′yü āt), 1 make or become thin or slender: *An earthworm's body alternately attenuates and thickens as it crawls. He was attenuated by hunger.* 2 weaken; reduce: *The authority of kings has been attenuated in modern times. v.,* **at ten u at ed, at ten u at ing.**

at ten u a tion (ə ten′yü ā′shən), an attenuating or a being attenuated. *n.*

at test (ə test′), 1 give proof of; certify: *Your good work attests the care you have taken.* 2 bear witness; testify: *The handwriting expert attested to the genuineness of the signature. v.*

at tic (at′ik), space in a house just below the roof; garret. *n.*

At ti ca (at′ə kə), district in SE Greece. Its chief city is Athens. Attica was famous in ancient times for its literature and art. *n.*

At ti la (at′l ə *or* ə til′ə), A.D. 406?-453, leader of the Huns in their invasions of Europe. He was defeated by the Romans and Goths in A.D. 451. *n.*

at tire (ə tīr′), 1 clothing or dress: *The queen wore rich attire to her coronation.* 2 clothe or dress; array: *She was attired in a cloak trimmed with ermine.* 1 *n.,* 2 *v.,* **at tired, at tir ing.**

at ti tude (at′ə tüd *or* at′ə tyüd), 1 way of thinking, acting, or feeling: *As the family next door got to know us better, their attitude changed from formality to friendliness.* 2 position of the body suggesting an action, purpose, emotion, etc.: *He raised his fists in the attitude of a boxer ready to fight. n.*

at tor ney (ə tėr′nē), 1 person who has power to act for another in business or legal matters. 2 lawyer. *n., pl.* **at tor neys.**

attorney general, 1 the chief law officer of a country, state, or province. 2 **Attorney General,** the head of the United States Department of Justice and the chief legal adviser of the President. *n., pl.* **attorneys general** or **attorney generals.**

at tract (ə trakt/), 1 draw to or toward oneself: *The magnet attracted the iron filings.* 2 be pleasing to; win the attention and liking of: *Bright colors attract children.* *v.*

at trac tion (ə trak/shən), 1 thing that delights or attracts people: *The elephants were the chief attraction at the circus.* 2 act or power of attracting: *the attraction of a magnet for iron filings. Sports have no attraction for him.* *n.*

at trac tive (ə trak/tiv), 1 winning attention and liking; pleasing: *She wore an attractive outfit to the party.* 2 attracting: *the attractive power of a magnet.* *adj.* —**at trac/tive ly,** *adv.* —**at trac/tive ness,** *n.*

at trib ut a ble (ə trib/yə tə bəl), that can be attributed: *Some diseases are attributable to lack of cleanliness.* *adj.*

at trib ute (ə trib/yüt *for 1,2;* at/rə byüt *for 3,4*), 1 regard as an effect of: *She attributes her good health to a carefully planned diet.* 2 think of as belonging to or appropriate to: *We attribute courage to the lion and cunning to the fox.* 3 object considered appropriate to a person, rank, or office; symbol: *The eagle was the attribute of Jupiter.* 4 a quality considered as belonging to a person or thing; characteristic: *Patience is an attribute of a good teacher.* 1,2 *v.,* **at trib ut ed, at trib ut ing;** 3,4 *n.*

at tri bu tion (at/rə byü/shən), 1 an attributing. 2 thing or quality attributed; an attribute. *n.*

at trib u tive (ə trib/yə tiv), 1 expressing a quality or attribute. An adjective used before or immediately after a noun is an attributive adjective, as in "a *white* shirt," "the ocean *blue*." 2 an attributive word. 1 *adj.,* 2 *n.* —**at trib/u tive ly,** *adv.*

at tri tion (ə trish/ən), a wearing away; gradual wearing down: *Pebbles become smooth by attrition. The long war of attrition exhausted the strength of both countries.* *n.*

at tune (ə tün/ *or* ə tyün/), put in tune or accord; tune: *Our ears became attuned to the noise of the city after several months.* *v.,* **at tuned, at tun ing.**

atty., attorney.

a typ i cal (ā tip/ə kəl), not typical; irregular. *adj.* —**a typ/i cal ly,** *adv.*

au burn (ô/bərn), 1 a reddish brown. 2 reddish-brown. 1 *n.,* 2 *adj.*

Auck land (ôk/lənd), important seaport in N New Zealand. *n.*

auc tion (ôk/shən), 1 a public sale in which each thing is sold to the person who offers the most money for it. 2 sell at an auction. 1 *n.,* 2 *v.*

auc tion eer (ôk/shə nir/), 1 person whose business is conducting auctions. 2 sell at an auction. 1 *n.,* 2 *v.*

au da cious (ô dā/shəs), 1 having the courage to take risks; bold; daring: *John Glenn was the audacious pilot of our first spacecraft.* 2 rudely bold; impudent: *The audacious waiter demanded a larger tip.* *adj.* —**au da/cious ly,** *adv.* —**au da/cious ness,** *n.*

au dac i ty (ô das/ə tē), 1 boldness; reckless daring: *The highest trapeze could not daunt the acrobat's audacity.* 2 rude boldness; impudence: *He had the audacity to go to the party without being invited.* *n., pl.* **au dac i ties.**

au di bil i ty (ô/də bil/ə tē), quality of being audible; distinctness to the hearing. *n.*

au di ble (ô/də bəl), that can be heard; loud enough to be heard: *She spoke in such a low voice that her remarks were barely audible.* *adj.*

au di bly (ô/də blē), in an audible manner; so as to be heard. *adv.*

au di ence (ô/dē əns), 1 people gathered in a place to hear or see: *The audience at the theater enjoyed the play.* 2 any persons within hearing: *The audience of this television program consists of over ten million people.* 3 the readers of a book, newspaper, or magazine. 4 chance to be heard; hearing: *The committee will give you an audience so you may present your plan.* 5 formal interview with a person of high rank: *The visiting students were granted an audience with the President.* *n.*

au di o (ô/dē ō), 1 using, involving, or having to do with audio frequencies. 2 involving, having to do with, or used in transmitting or receiving sound in television. An audio problem is a sound problem; a video problem involves the image that is supposed to appear on the screen. 3 sound reproduction: *Some of the audio for this film was very bad.* 1,2 *adj.,* 3 *n.*

audio frequency, frequency corresponding to audible sound vibrations, from about 20 to about 20,000 cycles per second for human beings.

au di om e ter (ô/dē om/ə tər), instrument for measuring the keenness and range of hearing. *n.*

au di o-vis u al (ô/dē ō vizh/ü əl), of or having to do with both hearing and sight. Motion pictures, slides, recordings, and other devices that help pupils to hear or see things directly are used as audio-visual aids by many teachers. *adj.*

au dit (ô/dit), 1 examine and check (business accounts). 2 an examination and check of business accounts. 3 statement of an account that has been examined and checked. 1 *v.,* 2,3 *n.*

au di tion (ô dish/ən), 1 a hearing to test the ability, quality, or performance of a singer, actor, or other performer. 2 give (a singer, actor, or other performer) such a hearing. 3 sing, act, or perform at such a hearing. 1 *n.,* 2,3 *v.*

au di tor (ô/də tər), 1 person who audits business accounts. 2 hearer; listener. *n.*

au di to ri um (ô/də tôr/ē əm), 1 large room for an audience in a church, theater, school, or the like; large hall. 2 a building especially designed for public meetings, concerts, lectures, etc. *n.*

au di to ry (ô/də tôr/ē), of or having to do with hearing: *The auditory nerve transmits impulses from the ear to the brain.* *adj.*

Au du bon (ô/də bon), **John James,** 1785-1851, American painter who made a study of birds. *n.*

Aug., August.

auger (def. 1)
Each turn
of the handle
makes the spiral
cutting edge
at the end
of the bit
bite deeper
into the wood.

au ger (ô/gər), 1 tool for boring holes in wood. 2 a large tool for boring holes in the earth. *n.*

aught¹ (ôt), anything: *Has she done aught to help you?* *n.* [Old English āwiht]

aught² (ôt), zero; cipher; nothing. *n.* [from *naught,* because *a naught* was read as *an aught* by mistake]

aug ment (ôg ment/), make or become greater in size, number, amount, or degree; increase: *The heat usually augments during the forenoon. The king augmented his power by taking over rights that had belonged to the nobles.* *v.*

aug men ta tion (ôg/men tā/shən), 1 an augmenting; increase. 2 thing that augments; addition. *n.*

hat, āge, fär; let, ēqual, tėrm; it, īce; hot, ōpen, ôrder; oil, out; cup, pùt, rüle; ch, child; ng, long; sh, she; th, thin; ŦH, then; zh, measure;

ə represents *a* in about, *e* in taken, *i* in pencil, *o* in lemon, *u* in circus.

adj. adjective	*n.* noun
adv. adverb	*prep.* preposition
conj. conjunction	*pron.* pronoun
interj. interjection	*v.* verb
sing. singular	*pl.* plural

au gur (ô′gər), 1 priest in ancient Rome who foretold future events and gave advice on the course of public business by interpreting such signs or omens as the flight of birds, thunder and lightning, etc. 2 soothsayer; fortune-teller. 3 guess from signs or omens; predict; foretell. 4 be a sign or promise of: *Those stormy clouds augur ill for our plans for a picnic.* 1,2 *n.*, 3,4 *v.*

au gur y (ô′gyər ē), 1 prediction; sign; omen. 2 art or practice of foretelling events by interpreting such signs and omens as the flight of birds, thunder and lightning, etc. *n., pl.* **au gur ies.**

au gust (ô gust′), inspiring reverence and admiration; majestic; venerable. *adj.* —**au gust′ly,** *adv.* —**au gust′ness,** *n.*

Au gust (ô′gəst), the eighth month of the year. It has 31 days. *n.* [from the Roman emperor *Augustus*]

Au gus ta (ô gus′tə), 1 capital of Maine, in the SW part. 2 city in E Georgia. *n.*

Au gus tine (ô′gə stēn′), **Saint,** A.D. 354-430, one of the leaders in the early Christian church. *n.*

Au gus tus (ô gus′təs), 63 B.C.-A.D. 14, the first emperor of Rome, who reigned from 27 B.C. to A.D. 14. He was the grandnephew and heir of Julius Caesar. *n.*

auk (ôk), any of several sea birds found in arctic regions, with legs set so far back that it stands like a penguin. It has short wings used chiefly as paddles in swimming. *n.*

auld (ôld), SCOTTISH. old. *adj.*

aunt (ant), 1 sister of one's father or mother. 2 wife of one's uncle. *n.*

aunt ie (an′tē), INFORMAL. aunt. *n.*

au ra (ôr′ə), something supposed to come from a person or thing and surround him or it as an atmosphere: *An aura of holiness enveloped the saint.* *n., pl.* **au ras.**

au ral (ôr′əl), of, having to do with, or perceived by the ear; auricular. *adj.* —**au′ral ly,** *adv.*

au re ole (ôr′ē ōl), ring of light surrounding a figure or object. *n.*

Au re o my cin (ôr′ē ō mī′sn), trademark for an antibiotic derived from a soil microorganism, used to check or kill certain bacterial infections and viruses. *n.*

au re voir (ō rə vwär′), FRENCH. good-by; till we see each other again.

au ri cle (ôr′ə kəl), 1 chamber of the heart that receives the blood from the veins and forces it into a ventricle. The heart of a bird, mammal, or reptile has two auricles. A fish has only one auricle. See **heart** for diagram. 2 the outer part of the ear. *n.*

au ric u lar (ô rik′yə lər), 1 having to do with an auricle of the heart. 2 of, having to do with, or perceived by the ear; aural. *adj.*

au rochs (ôr′oks), 1 bison of Europe. 2 an extinct wild ox of Europe. *n., pl.* **au rochs.**

Au ro ra (ô rôr′ə), (in Roman myths) the goddess of the dawn. *n.*

au ro ra bo re al is (ô rôr′ə bôr′ē al′is), streamers or bands of light appearing in the northern sky at night; northern lights. [from Latin]

aus pic es (ô′spə siz), 1 helpful influence; approval or support; patronage: *The school fair was held under the auspices of the Parents' Association.* 2 omens; signs. The ancient Romans used the flight of birds as auspices. *n.pl.*

aus pi cious (ô spish′əs), with signs of success; favorable: *The new boy had an auspicious first day in school.* *adj.* —**aus pi′cious ly,** *adv.*

aus tere (ô stir′), 1 stern in manner or appearance; harsh: *His father was a silent, austere man, very strict with his children.* 2 strict in morals: *Some of the ideas of the Puritans seem too austere to us.* 3 severely simple: *The tall, plain columns stood against the sky in austere beauty.* *adj.* —**aus tere′ly,** *adv.*

aus ter i ty (ô ster′ə tē), 1 sternness in manner or appearance; harshness; severity. 2 **austerities,** *pl.* severe practices, such as going without food. *n., pl.* **aus ter i ties.**

Aus tin (ô′stən), capital of Texas, in the central part. *n.*

Aus tral a sia (ô′strə lā′zhə), Australia, Tasmania, New Guinea, New Zealand, and other nearby islands. *n.* —**Aus′tral a′sian,** *adj., n.*

Aus tral ia (ô strā′lyə), 1 continent southeast of Asia. 2 **Commonwealth of,** country that includes this continent and Tasmania. It is a member of the Commonwealth of Nations. *Capital:* Canberra. *n.*

Aus tral ian (ô strā′lyən), 1 of Australia or its people. 2 person born or living in Australia. 1 *adj.*, 2 *n.*

Aus tri a (ô′strē ə), country in central Europe. Before World War I it was an empire. *Capital:* Vienna. *n.* —**Aus′tri an,** *adj., n.*

Aus tri a-Hun gar y (ô′strē ə hung′-gər ē), monarchy in central Europe from 1867 to 1918, composed of the Austrian empire and the kingdom of Hungary. *n.*

Austria-Hungary
Shaded area shows its extent in 1914.

au then tic (ô then′tik), 1 worthy of trust; reliable: *We heard an authentic account of the wreck, given by one of the ship's passengers.* 2 genuine; real: *We saw an authentic letter written by George Washington.* *adj.*

au then ti cal ly (ô then′tik lē), 1 reliably. 2 genuinely. *adv.*

au then ti cate (ô then′tə kāt), establish the truth of; show to be valid or genuine: *Handwriting experts authenticated the signature on the will.* *v.*, **au then ti cat ed, au then ti cat ing.**

au then ti ca tion (ô then′tə kā′shən), an authenticating or a being authenticated. *n.*

au then ti ca tor (ô then′tə kā′tər), person who authenticates. *n.*

au then tic i ty (ô′then tis′ə tē), 1 reliability: *The value of the evidence depends on its authenticity.* 2 genuineness: *The lawyer questioned the authenticity of the signature.* *n.*

au thor (ô′thər), 1 person who writes books, poems, stories, or articles; writer: *My little sister's favorite author is Dr. Seuss.* 2 person who creates or begins anything: *Are you the author of this scheme? n.*

au thor i tar i an (ə thôr′ə ter′ē ən), favoring obedience to authority instead of individual freedom: *An authoritarian government will often censor newspapers. adj.*

au thor i tar i an ism (ə thôr′ə ter′ē ə niz′əm), principle of obedience to authority. *n.*

au thor i ta tive (ə thôr′ə tā′tiv), 1 having authority; officially ordered: *Authoritative orders came from the general.* 2 commanding: *In authoritative tones the policeman shouted to us, "Keep back."* 3 having the authority of expert knowledge: *A doctor's statement concerning the cause of an illness is considered authoritative. adj.* —**au thor′i ta′tive ly,** *adv.* —**au thor′i ta′tive ness,** *n.*

au thor i ty (ə thôr′ə tē), 1 power to enforce obedience; right to command or act: *Parents have authority over their children. The police have the authority to arrest speeding drivers.* 2 person who has such power or right. 3 **the authorities,** the officials in control: *Who are the proper authorities to give permits to hunt or fish?* 4 source of correct information or wise advice: *A good dictionary is an authority on the meanings of words.* 5 an expert on some subject: *He is an authority on the Revolutionary War.* 6 a government body that runs some activity or business on behalf of the public. *Authorities provide electricity or housing, develop ports, build turnpikes, etc. n., pl.* **au thor i ties.**

au thor i za tion (ô′thər ə zā′shən), 1 an authorizing; giving legal power to: *The authorization of the police to give tickets to jaywalkers cut down on the number of accidents.* 2 legal right; official permission: *"What authorization have you for fishing in this pond?" asked the owner of the pond. n.*

au tho rize (ô′thə rīz′), 1 give power or right to: *The committee authorized her to proceed.* 2 give formal approval to; approve: *Congress authorized the spending of money for a new post-office building. This dictionary authorizes the two spellings "acknowledgment" and "acknowledgement." v.,* **au tho rized, au tho riz ing.**

au thor ship (ô′thər ship), 1 occupation of an author; writing: *She chose authorship as her work in life.* 2 origin as to author: *What is the authorship of that novel? n.*

au tism (ô′tiz əm), an escaping from reality by daydreaming and fantasy. *n.*

au tis tic (ô tis′tik), escaping from reality; indulging in daydreaming and fantasy. *adj.*

au to (ô′tō), automobile. *n., pl.* **au tos.**

au to bi o graph ic (ô′tə bī′ə graf′ik), autobiographical. *adj.*

au to bi o graph i cal (ô′tə bī′ə graf′ə kəl), 1 having to do with the story of one's own life. 2 telling or writing the story of one's own life. *adj.*

au to bi og ra phy (ô′tə bī og′rə fē), story of a person's life written by himself. *n., pl.* **au to bi og ra phies.**

au toc ra cy (ô tok′rə sē), 1 government by a single person having unrestricted power. 2 absolute authority. *n., pl.* **au toc ra cies.**

au to crat (ô′tə krat), 1 ruler having unrestricted power over his subjects. 2 person who uses his power over others in a harsh way: *A good teacher is never an autocrat. n.*

au to crat ic (ô′tə krat′ik), of or like an autocrat; having absolute power or authority; ruling without checks or limitations: *The principal's autocratic manner made him unpopular. adj.* —**au′to crat′i cal ly,** *adv.*

au to graph (ô′tə graf), 1 a person's name written by himself: *Many people collect the autographs of celebrities.* 2 write one's name in or on: *The movie star autographed my program.* 3 something written in a person's own handwriting. 1,3 *n.,* 2 *v.*

au to mat (ô′tə mat), restaurant in which food is obtained from compartments that open when coins are inserted in slots. *n.*

au to mate (ô′tə māt), convert to automation; operate by automation. *v.,* **au to mat ed, au to mat ing.**

au to mat ic (ô′tə mat′ik), 1 moving or acting by itself: *Our apartment house has an automatic elevator.* 2 done without thought or attention: *Breathing and swallowing are usually automatic.* 3 gun that throws out the empty shell and reloads by itself. An automatic continues to fire until the pressure on the trigger is released. 1,2 *adj.,* 3 *n.*

au to mat i cal ly (ô′tə mat′ik lē), in an automatic manner: *Electric refrigerators work automatically. adv.*

au to ma tion (ô′tə mā′shən), the use of automatic controls in the operation of a machine or group of machines. In automation, electronic or mechanical devices do many of the tasks formerly performed by people. *n.*

au tom a ton (ô tom′ə ton), 1 person or animal whose actions are entirely mechanical. 2 machine or toy that moves by itself. *n.*

au to mo bile (ô′tə mə bēl′), 1 a passenger vehicle, for use on roads and streets, that carries its own engine. 2 of or for automobiles: *an automobile mechanic.* 1 *n.,* 2 *adj.*

au to mo tive (ô′tə mō′tiv), 1 of or having to do with cars, trucks, and other self-moving vehicles. Automotive engineering deals with the design and construction of motor vehicles. 2 furnishing its own power; moving by itself: *A truck is one type of automotive vehicle. adj.*

au to nom ic (ô′tə nom′ik), 1 having to do with that part of the nervous system of vertebrates that controls digestive, reproductive, and other involuntary reactions. 2 autonomous. *adj.*

au ton o mous (ô ton′ə məs), self-governing; independent: *Many former African colonies have become autonomous nations. adj.* —**au ton′o mous ly,** *adv.*

au ton o my (ô ton′ə mē), 1 self-government; independence: *Algeria achieved autonomy in 1962.* 2 a self-governing state, community, etc. *n., pl.* **au ton o mies.**

au top sy (ô′top sē), medical examination of a dead body to find the cause of death; post-mortem: *The autopsy revealed that the man had been poisoned. n., pl.* **au top sies.**

au tumn (ô′təm), 1 season of the year between summer and winter; fall. 2 of autumn; coming in autumn: *autumn rains, autumn flowers.* 1 *n.,* 2 *adj.*

au tum nal (ô tum′nəl), of autumn; coming in autumn: *autumnal frosts. adj.*

aux il iar y (ôg zil′yər ē), 1 giving help or support; assisting: *Some sailboats have auxiliary engines.* 2 person or thing that helps; aid: *The microscope is a useful auxiliary to the human eye.* 3 additional; subsidiary: *The main library has several auxiliary branches.* 4 a subsidiary group: *a men's club with a women's auxiliary.* 5 auxiliary verb. 1,3 *adj.,* 2,4,5 *n., pl.* **aux il iar ies.**

auxiliary verb, verb used to form the tenses, moods, or voices of other verbs; helping verb. *Be, can, do, have, may, must, shall,* and *will* are auxiliary verbs. EXAMPLES: I *am* going; he *will* go; they *are* lost; they *were* lost.

---

adj.	adjective	*n.*	noun
adv.	adverb	*prep.*	preposition
conj.	conjunction	*pron.*	pronoun
interj.	interjection	*v.*	verb
sing.	singular	*pl.*	plural

av., 1 avenue. 2 average. 3 avoirdupois.

a vail (ə vāl/), 1 be of use or value to; help: *Money will not avail you after you are dead.* 2 be of use or value: *Talk will not avail without work.* v.

avail oneself of, take advantage of; profit by; make use of: *He availed himself of the opportunity to learn French.*

of no avail or **to no avail,** of no use or value: *Crying is of no avail now. I complained at being scolded, but to no avail.*

a vail a bil i ty (ə vā/lə bil/ə tē), a being available; being at hand; being ready: *The availability of water power helped make New England a manufacturing center.* n.

a vail a ble (ə vā/lə bəl), 1 that can be used: *She is not available for the job; she has other work now.* 2 that can be had: *All available tickets were sold.* adj.

a vail a bly (ə vā/lə blē), in an available manner; so as to be used or had readily. adv.

av a lanche (av/ə lanch), 1 a large mass of snow and ice, or of dirt and rocks, rapidly sliding or falling down the side of a mountain. 2 anything like an avalanche: *The reporters asked the governor an avalanche of questions.* n.

a vant-garde (ä/vänt gärd/), group of people, especially in the arts, who are ahead of all others in using or creating new ideas, methods, designs, etc. n. [from French *avant-garde* advance guard]

av ar ice (av/ər is), too great a desire to acquire money or property; greed for wealth. n.

av a ri cious (av/ə rish/əs), greatly desiring money or property; greedy for wealth. adj. —**av/a ri/cious ly,** adv. —**av/a ri/cious ness,** n.

a vast (ə vast/), stop! stay! "*Avast there!*" shouted the sailor. interj.

a vaunt (ə vônt/), OLD USE. begone! get out! go away! interj.

Ave., Avenue.

A ve Ma ri a (ä/vā mə rē/ə), 1 "Hail Mary!", the first words of the Latin form of a prayer of the Roman Catholic Church. 2 this prayer.

a venge (ə venj/), get revenge for: *He was determined to avenge the insult.*

They fought to avenge the enemy's invasion of their country. v., **a venged, a veng ing.**

a veng er (ə ven/jər), person who avenges. n.

av e nue (av/ə nü or av/ə nyü), 1 a wide street. 2 road or walk bordered by trees. 3 way of approach: *Hard work is one avenue to success.* n.

a ver (ə vėr/), state to be true; assert: *The man averred that he had nothing to do with breaking into the parked car.* v., **a verred, a ver ring.**

av er age (av/ər ij), 1 quantity found by dividing the sum of all the quantities by the number of quantities. The average of 3 and 5 and 10 is 6 ($3 + 5 + 10 = 18$; $18 \div 3 = 6$). 2 find the average of: *Will you average those numbers for me?* 3 obtained by averaging; being an average: *The average temperature for the week was 82.* 4 have as an average; amount on the average to: *The cost of our lunches at school averaged two dollars a week.* 5 usual sort or amount: *The amount of rain this year has been below average.* 6 usual; ordinary: *a child of average intelligence.* 7 do, get, yield, etc., on an average: *She averages six hours of work a day. The farmer averaged forty bushels of wheat to the acre.* 1,5 n., 2,4,7 v., **av er aged, av er ag ing;** 3,6 adj.

on the average or **on an average,** considered on the basis of the average: *I work six hours a day on the average. The farm produces, on an average, forty bushels to the acre.*

a verse (ə vėrs/), having a strong or fixed dislike; opposed or unwilling: *She was averse to fighting.* adj. —**a verse/ly,** adv.

a ver sion (ə vėr/zhən), 1 a strong or fixed dislike: *He has an aversion to tea.* 2 thing or person disliked: *Impoliteness is his special aversion.* n.

a vert (ə vėrt/), 1 keep from happening; prevent; avoid: *The driver averted an accident by a quick turn of the steering wheel.* 2 turn away: turn aside: *I averted my eyes from the wreck.* v.

a vi ar y (ā/vē er/ē), house, enclosure, or large cage in which many birds, especially wild birds, are kept. n., pl. **a vi ar ies.**

a vi a tion (ā/vē ā/shən or av/ē ā/shən), 1 art or science of operating and navigating aircraft. 2 the designing and manufacturing of aircraft, especially airplanes. n.

a vi a tor (ā/vē ā/tər or av/ē ā/tər), person who flies an aircraft; pilot. n.

a vi a trix (ā/vē ā/triks or av/ē ā/triks), a woman aviator. n., pl. **a vi a trix es.**

av id (av/id), extremely eager: *an avid*

desire for fame. She is an avid golfer. adj. —**av/id ly,** adv.

a vid i ty (ə vid/ə tē), 1 great eagerness: *The hungry campers looked at the food with avidity.* 2 greed for wealth; avarice. n.

av o ca do (av/ə kä/dō), 1 a tropical fruit shaped like a pear, with a dark-green skin and a very large seed; alligator pear. Its yellow-green pulp has a nutty flavor and is used in salads. 2 tree it grows on. n., pl. **av o ca dos.**

av o ca tion (av/ə kā/shən), something that a person does besides his regular business; minor occupation; hobby: *He is a lawyer, but writing stories is his avocation.* n.

a void (ə void/), keep away from; keep out of the way of: *We avoided driving through large cities on our trip.* v.

a void a ble (ə voi/də bəl), that can be avoided. adj.

a void ance (ə void/ns), an avoiding; keeping away from: *Avoidance of an infection is better than treatment after an infection.* n.

av oir du pois (av/ər də poiz/), system of weights in which a pound containing 16 ounces is used. The avoirdupois system is used to weigh everything except gems, precious metals, and drugs. n.

A von (ā/vən), name of several rivers in central and southern England. n.

a vouch (ə vouch/), 1 declare positively to be true; affirm. 2 guarantee; vouch for: *I can avouch for his honesty.* v.

a vow (ə vou/), declare frankly or openly; admit; acknowledge: *He avowed his opinions about the war with boldness.* v.

a vow al (ə vou/əl), a frank or open declaration; admission; acknowledgment: *She made a plain avowal of her opinions even though they were unpopular.* n.

a vowed (ə voud/), openly declared; admitted: *She is an avowed candidate for the office of class president.* adj.

a vow ed ly (ə vou/id lē), admittedly; openly. adv.

a wait (ə wāt/), 1 wait for; look forward to: *I shall await your answer to my letter with eagerness.* 2 be ready for; in store for: *Many pleasures await you on your trip.* v.

a wake (ə wāk/), 1 wake up; arouse: *I awoke from a sound sleep. The alarm clock awoke me.* 2 roused from sleep; not asleep: *She is always awake early.* 3 stir up: *My words awoke his anger.* 4 on the alert; watchful: *I am awake to potential danger.* 1,3 v., **a woke** or **a waked, a wak ing;** 2,4 adj.

a wak en (ə wā/kən), wake up; stir up; arouse: *The sun was shining when he* awakened. *I was awakened late this morning. v.*

a wak en ing (ə wā/kə ning), a waking up; arousing. *n.*

a ward (ə wôrd/), 1 give after careful consideration; grant: *A medal was awarded to the best speller in the class.* 2 something given after careful consideration; prize: *My dog won the highest award.* 3 decide upon by law; adjudge: *The court awarded damages of $5000 to the injured man.* 4 decision by a judge: *We all thought the award was fair.* 1,3 *v.,* 2,4 *n.*

a ware (ə wer/ *or* ə war/), having knowledge; realizing; conscious: *I was too sleepy to be aware how cold it was. She was not aware of her danger. adj.* —**a ware/ness,** *n.*

a wash (ə wosh/ *or* ə wôsh/), 1 level with the surface of the water; just covered with water: *The beach was awash with the flowing tide.* 2 carried about by water; floating: *The rising water set everything awash. adj.*

a way (ə wā/), 1 from a place; to a distance: *Stay away from the fire.* 2 at a distance; a way off: *The sailor was far away from home (adv.). His home is miles away (adj.).* 3 absent; gone: *My mother is away today.* 4 out of one's possession, notice, or use: *He gave his boat away.* 5 out of existence: *The sounds died away.* 6 in another direction; aside: *She turned her car away just in time to avoid an accident.* 7 without stopping; continuously: *She worked away at her job.* 8 without delay; at once: *Fire away!* 1,2,4-8 *adv.,* 2,3 *adj.*

away with, take (someone or something) away: *Away with him!*

do away with, 1 put an end to; get rid of: *The United States did away with slavery in 1865.* 2 kill: *They had to do away with the sick animal.*

awe (ô), 1 great fear and wonder; fear and reverence: *The sight of the great waterfall filled us with awe. The child stood in awe before the queen.* 2 cause to feel awe; fill with awe: *The majesty of the mountains awed us.* 1 *n.,* 2 *v.,* **awed, aw ing.**

a wear y (ə wir/ē), weary; tired. *adj.*

awe some (ô/səm), 1 causing awe: *The great fire was an awesome sight.* 2 showing awe; awed: *awesome admiration. adj.*

awe-strick en (ô/strik/ən), awe-struck. *adj.*

awe-struck (ô/struk/), filled with awe: *She was awe-struck by the mountain's grandeur. adj.*

aw ful (ô/fəl), 1 causing fear; dreadful; terrible: *An awful storm with thunder and lightning came up.* 2 deserving great respect and reverence: *He felt the awful power of God.* 3 filling with awe; impressive: *The mountains rose to awful heights.* 4 INFORMAL. very bad, great, ugly, etc.: *My room was in an awful mess. He is an awful nuisance.* 5 INFORMAL. very: *She was awful mad.* 1-4 *adj.,* 5 *adv.* —**aw/ful ness,** *n.*

aw ful ly (ô/flē *or* ô/fə lē), 1 dreadfully; terribly: *The broken leg hurt awfully.* 2 INFORMAL. very: *I'm awfully sorry that I hurt your feelings. adv.*

a while (ə hwīl/), for a short time: *He stayed awhile after dinner to talk. adv.*

awk ward (ôk/wərd), 1 not graceful or skillful in movement or shape; clumsy: *Seals are very awkward on land, but graceful in the water.* 2 not well suited to use: *The handle of this pitcher has an awkward shape.* 3 not easily managed: *This is an awkward corner to turn.* 4 inconvenient or embarrassing: *an awkward situation. He asked me such an awkward question that I did not know what to reply. adj.* —**awk/ward ly,** *adv.* —**awk/ward ness,** *n.*

awl being used to mark places for screws on a piece of wood

awl (ôl), a pointed tool used for making small holes in leather or wood. *n.*

awn ing (ô/ning), piece of canvas, metal, wood, or plastic spread over or before a door, window, porch, deck, or patio for protection from the sun or rain. *n.*

awnings

a woke (ə wōk/), a past tense and a past participle of **awake.** *She awoke at seven. He has not yet awoke. v.*

a wry (ə rī/), 1 with a twist or turn to one side: *Her hat was blown awry by the wind.* 2 wrong; out of order: *Our plans have gone awry. adv.*

ax or **axe** (aks), tool with a flat, sharp blade fastened on a handle, used for chopping, splitting, and shaping wood. *n., pl.* **ax es.**

ax es[1] (ak/siz), plural of **ax.** *n.*

ax es[2] (ak/sēz/), plural of **axis.** *n.*

ax i al (ak/sē əl), of, having to do with, or forming an axis: *The wheels turn on an axial rod. adj.* —**ax/i al ly,** *adv.*

BRANCH

AXIL

STEM

ax il (ak/səl), angle between the upper side of a leaf or stem and the supporting stem or branch. A bud is usually found in the axil. *n.*

ax i om (ak/sē əm), 1 statement taken to be true without proof; self-evident truth: *It is an axiom that if equals are added to equals the results will be equal.* 2 a well-established principle; rule or law. *n.*

ax i o mat ic (ak/sē ə mat/ik), accepted without proof; self-evident: *It is axiomatic that a whole is greater than any of its parts. adj.*

ax i o mat i cal ly (ak/sē ə mat/ik lē), 1 in an axiomatic manner; with axioms. 2 as an axiom; as an admitted truth. *adv.*

ax is (ak/sis), 1 a straight line about which an object turns or seems to turn. The axis of the earth is an imaginary line through the North Pole and the South Pole. 2 a central or principal line around which parts are arranged regularly: *The axis of a plant is the stem.* 3 one of the lines along which the coordinates of a point are measured. 4 **the Axis,** Germany, Italy, Japan, and their allies, during World War II. *n., pl.* **ax es.**

AXIS

axis (def. 1)

axle

axle
(def. 1)

ax le (ak′səl), 1 bar or shaft on which a wheel turns. Some axles turn with the wheel. 2 axletree. *n.*

ax le tree (ak′səl trē′), crossbar connecting two opposite wheels of a cart or wagon. The wheels turn on its ends. *n.*

ax on (ak′son), the long extension of a nerve cell that carries impulses away from the body of the cell. *n.*

ay[1] or **aye**[1] (ā), always; ever: *"There let it lie for ever and for ay."* *adv.* [from a Scandinavian word of the 1200's, such as Icelandic *ei* ever]

aye[2] or **ay**[2] (ī), 1 yes: *Aye, aye, sir.* 2 an affirmative answer, vote, or voter: *The ayes won when the vote was taken.* 1 *adv.*, 2 *n.* [apparently Old English *gī*]

Ayr shire (er′shər *or* ar′shər), 1 any of a breed of dairy cattle that are red and white or brown and white, originating in Scotland. 2 of or having to do with this breed. 1 *n.*, 2 *adj.*

a zal ea (ə zā′lyə), 1 any of a group of shrubs growing mainly in northeastern North America and in China. Azaleas are related to rhododendrons but are usually not evergreen. 2 its showy flower. *n.*, *pl.* **a zal eas.**

A zores (ə zôrz′ *or* ā′zôrz), group of islands in the Atlantic west of and belonging to Portugal. *n.pl.*

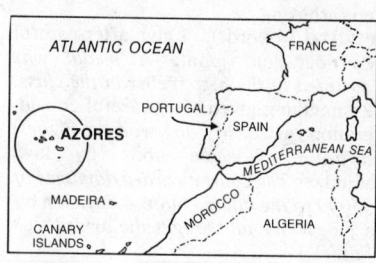

Az tec (az′tek), 1 member of a highly civilized American Indian people who ruled a large empire in central Mexico before its conquest by the Spaniards under Cortés in 1521. 2 their language; Nahuatl. 3 of the Aztecs or their language. 1,2 *n.*, 3 *adj.*

az ure (azh′ər), 1 the blue color of the unclouded sky. 2 having this color; sky-blue. 1 *n.*, 2 *adj.*

B b

B or **b** (bē), the second letter of the alphabet. *n., pl.* **B's** or **b's.**

baa (bä *or* ba), 1 the sound a sheep makes; bleat. 2 make this sound; bleat. *n., pl.* **baas;** 2 *v.,* **baaed, baa ing.**

Ba al (bā′əl), 1 the sun god of the Phoenicians. 2 a false god. *n.*

bab ble (bab′əl), 1 make sounds like a baby: *My baby brother babbles and coos in his crib.* 2 talk that cannot be understood: *A confused babble filled the room.* 3 talk foolishly: *They babbled on and on about the weather.* 4 foolish talk. 5 talk too much; tell secrets. 6 make a murmuring sound: *The little brook babbled away just behind our tent.* 7 a murmuring sound: *The babble of the brook put me to sleep.* 1,3,5,6 *v.,* **bab bled, bab bling;** 2,4,7 *n.*

bab bler (bab′lər), person or thing that babbles. *n.*

babe (bāb), baby. *n.*

Ba bel (bā′bəl *or* bab′əl), 1 (in the Bible) a city where a high tower, called the **Tower of Babel,** was built after the Flood to reach heaven. God punished its builders by changing their language into several new and different languages. Because they could not understand one another, they had to leave the tower unfinished. 2 **babel,** noise; confusion. *n.*

ba boon (ba bün′), kind of large, fierce monkey with a doglike face and a rather short tail. Baboons live in the rocky hills of Africa and Arabia in large troops. The mandrill is one kind of baboon. *n.*

ba bush ka (bə bush′kə), scarf worn on the head and tied under the chin. *n., pl.* **ba bush kas.** [from Russian *babushka* grandmother]

ba by (bā′bē), 1 child too young to walk or speak; infant. 2 the youngest of a family or group. 3 young: *a baby lamb.* 4 small for its kind; small: *my baby finger.* 5 of or for a baby: *baby shoes.* 6 childish: *baby talk.* 7 person who acts like a baby; childish person: *Don't be a baby.* 8 treat as a baby; pamper: *You are too old to be babied.* 1,2,7 *n., pl.* **ba bies;** 3-6 *adj.,* 8 *v.,* **ba bied, ba by ing.**

ba by hood (bā′bē hud), condition or time of being a baby. *n.*

ba by ish (bā′bē ish), like a baby; childish. *adj.* —**ba′by ish ly,** *adv.* —**ba′by ish ness,** *n.*

Bab y lon (bab′ə lən), ancient city in SW Asia, on the Euphrates, noted for its wealth, power, magnificence, and the wickedness of its people. Babylon was the capital of ancient Babylonia. *n.*

Bab y lo ni a (bab′ə lō′nē ə), ancient empire in SW Asia which reached its peak about 1800 B.C. The capital was Babylon. *n.* —**Bab′y lo′ni an,** *adj., n.*

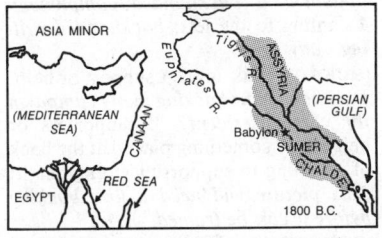

Babylonia—The shaded area shows the Babylonian Empire at its greatest extent.

ba by-sit (bā′bē sit′), take care of a child or children while the parents are away for a while. *v.,* **ba by-sat** (bā′bē-sat′), **ba by-sit ting.**

ba by-sit ter (bā′bē sit′ər), person who takes care of a child or children while the parents are away for a while. *n.*

baby teeth, the first set of teeth.

Bac chus (bak′əs), (in Roman and Greek myths) the god of wine. The Greeks also called him Dionysus. *n.*

Bach (bäk), **Johann Sebastian,** 1685-1750, German composer and organist. *n.*

bach e lor (bach′ə lər), 1 man who has not married. 2 person who has the first degree of a college or university. *n.*

bach e lor's-but ton (bach′ə lərz-but′n), 1 plant with a single, small, button-shaped flower having a blue, violet, pink, or white color; cornflower. 2 its flower. *n.*

ba cil lus (bə sil′əs), 1 any of the rod-shaped bacteria, especially one that forms spores: *the typhoid bacillus.* 2 any bacterium. See **bacteria** for picture. *n., pl.* **ba cil li** (bə sil′ī).

back (bak), 1 the part of a person's body opposite to his face or to the front part of his body. 2 the upper part of an animal's body from the neck to the end of the backbone. 3 the backbone; spine: *He fell off the ladder and broke his back.* 4 the side of anything away from one; rear, upper, or farther part: *Put the chair in the back of the room. I had a bruise on the back of my hand.* 5 opposite the front; away from one: *The box is in the back seat of the car.* 6 part of a chair, couch, bench, or the like, which supports the back of a person sitting down. 7 support or help: *Many of her friends backed her plan.* 8 move away from the front: *I backed the car out of the driveway. We backed away from the dog.* 9 behind in space or

hat, āge, fär; let, ēqual, tėrm;
it, īce; hot, ōpen, ôrder;
oil, out; cup, put, rüle; ch, child;
ng, long; sh, she; th, thin;
ᵺ, then; zh, measure;

ə represents *a* in about,
e in taken, *i* in pencil,
o in lemon, *u* in circus.

time: *Please walk back three steps* (*adv.*). *Have you read the back issues of this magazine?* (*adj.*) *Some years back this land was all in farms* (*adv.*). 10 in return: *They paid back what they borrowed.* 11 in the place from which something or someone came: *Put the books back.* 12 in check: *The police held the crowd back.* 13 (in football) a player whose position is behind the line of scrimmage. 1-4,6,13 *n.,* 5,9 *adj.,* 7,8 *v.,* 9-12 *adv.*

back and forth, first one way and then the other: *The dog ran back and forth across the field.*

back down, give up an attempt or claim; withdraw: *I said I would go swimming, but I backed down when I found out how cold the water was.*

back of, in the rear of; behind: *The barn is back of the house.*

back out or **back out of,** 1 break a promise: *I promised to buy everyone ice cream, but I backed out when I realized I had no money with me.* 2 withdraw from an undertaking: *The village backed out of building a pool when the cost got too high.*

behind one's back, without one's knowing it; secretly: *The cashier of the store stole money behind the owner's back.*

back ache (bak′āk′), a pain in the back. *n.*

back bite (bak′bīt′), speak evil of; slander (an absent person). *v.,* **back-bit** (bak′bit′), **back bit ten** (bak′bit′n) or **back bit, back bit ing.**

back bone (bak′bōn′), 1 the main bone along the middle of the back in man and other mammals, birds, reptiles, amphibians, and fishes; spine. The backbone consists of many separate bones, called vertebrae, held together by muscles and tendons. 2 the most important part; chief support; basis. 3 strength of character; firmness: *Although she is criticized, she has the backbone to stand up for her beliefs.* *n.*

back break ing (bak′brā′king), very exhausting or tiring; demanding great effort: *Shoveling snow all day is backbreaking work.* *adj.*

adj. adjective		*n.* noun
adv. adverb	*prep.* preposition	
conj. conjunction	*pron.* pronoun	
interj. interjection	*v.* verb	
sing. singular	*pl.* plural	

back drop (bak/drop/), 1 curtain at the back of a stage, often painted and used as part of the scenery. 2 background. *n.*

back er (bak/ər), person who supports another person, a plan, or an idea. *n.*

back field (bak/fēld/), (in football) the players whose position is behind the line of scrimmage. *n.*

back fire (bak/fīr/), 1 explosion of gas occurring at the wrong time or in the wrong place in a gasoline engine. 2 explode in this way. 3 fire set to check a forest or prairie fire by controlled burning off of the space in front of it. 4 have a result opposite to the expected result: *His scheme backfired, and instead of getting rich he lost all his money.* 1,3 *n.,* 2,4 *v.,* **back fired, back fir ing.**

back gam mon (bak/gam/ən), game for two played on a special board with 12 spaces on each side. Each player has 15 pieces, which are moved according to the throw of the dice. *n.*

back ground (bak/ground/), 1 the part of a picture or scene toward the back: *The cottage stands in the foreground with the mountains in the background.* 2 surface upon which things are made or placed: *Her dress had pink flowers on a white background.* 3 earlier conditions or events that help to explain some later condition or event: *This book gives the background of the Revolutionary War.* 4 past experience, knowledge, and training: *His early background included living on a farm.* *n.*

in the background, out of sight; not in clear view: *Stay in the background so you don't become involved in the dispute.*

backhand (def. 1)→

backhand writing

backhand (def. 2)

back hand (bak/hand/), 1 stroke in tennis and other games made with the back of the hand turned outward. 2 handwriting in which the letters slope to the left. 3 backhanded. 1,2 *n.,* 3 *adj.*

back hand ed (bak/han/did), 1 done or made with the back of the hand turned outward: *a backhanded stroke.* 2 indirect: *She means to help, even though she offers to do so in a backhanded way.* 3 sounding like praise but actually an insult; insincere: *He paid his opponent a backhanded compliment.* 4 slanting to the left: *backhanded writing.* *adj.*

back ing (bak/ing), 1 support or help: *Do I have your backing in my campaign for class president?* 2 supporters or helpers. 3 something placed at the back of anything to support or strengthen it: *This picture will need a firm backing before it can be framed.* *n.*

back log (bak/lôg/), 1 a reserve of orders, duties, etc., that have not yet been carried out: *He is working on the backlog of homework assignments that accumulated while he was sick.* 2 a large log at the back of a wood fire. *n.*

back slide (bak/slīd/), slide back into wrong ways, error, etc.; gradually return to old ways and practices. *v.,* **back slid** (bak/slid/), **back slid** or **back slid den** (bak/slid/n), **back slid ing.**

back slid er (bak/slī/dər), person who backslides. *n.*

back stage (bak/stāj/), in the part of a theater not seen by the audience; behind a backdrop, in the wings, or in a dressing room: *She went backstage (adv.). The star gave a backstage interview (adj.).* *adv., adj.*

back stop (bak/stop/), 1 wall, fence, or screen used in various games to keep the ball in the area of play. 2 INFORMAL. catcher in baseball. 3 anything that supports or reinforces. *n.*

back stroke (bak/strōk/), 1 a swimming stroke made by a swimmer lying on his back. 2 a backhanded stroke. *n.*

back talk, INFORMAL, impudent answers, especially by a younger person to an older one.

back track (bak/trak/), 1 go back over a course or path. 2 withdraw from an undertaking, position, etc.: *He backtracked on the promise he made last week.* *v.*

back ward (bak/wərd), 1 with the back first: *He tumbled over backward.* 2 toward the back: *He looked backward (adv.). She gave him a backward look (adj.).* 3 opposite to the usual way: *Can you read backward?* 4 from better to worse: *In some towns living conditions improved; in some they went backward.* 5 toward the past: *She looked backward forty years and talked about her childhood.* 6 slow in development: *Backward children need special help in school.* 7 behind time; late: *This is a backward season; spring is two weeks*

late. 8 shy; bashful: *Shake hands with her; don't be backward.* 1-5 *adv.,* 2,6-8 *adj.* —**back/ward ly,** *adv.* —**back/ward ness,** *n.*

back wards (bak/wərdz), backward (defs. 1-5). *adv.*

back wash (bak/wosh/ or bak/wôsh/), 1 water thrown back by oars, a passing ship, etc. 2 a backward current of air. 3 bad aftereffects: *the backwash of war.* *n., pl.* **back wash es.**

back wa ter (bak/wô/tər or bak/wot/ər), 1 stretch of water that is held, thrown, or pushed back. 2 a backward place. *n.*

back woods (bak/wüdz/), 1 uncleared forests or wild regions far away from towns. 2 a remote area; backward place. *n.pl.*

back woods man (bak/wüdz/mən), man who lives in the backwoods. *n., pl.* **back woods men.**

back yard (bak/yärd/), yard behind a house or building. *n.*

ba con (bā/kən), salted and smoked meat from the back and sides of a pig or hog. *n.*

Ba con (bā/kən), **Francis,** 1561-1626, English essayist, statesman, and philosopher. *n.*

COCCI   SPIRILLA   BACILLI

bacteria—the three main types: spherical, spiral, and rod-shaped

bac ter i a (bak tir/ē ə), very tiny and simple plants, so small that they can usually be seen only through a microscope. Bacteria consist of single cells that are rod-shaped, spherical, or spiral, and have no chlorophyll. Most bacteria multiply by splitting apart. Certain bacteria cause diseases such as pneumonia and typhoid fever; others do useful things, such as turning cider into vinegar. *n.pl. of* **bacterium.**

bac ter i al (bak tir/ē əl), 1 of bacteria: *bacterial life.* 2 caused by bacteria: *bacterial diseases.* *adj.*

bac ter i o log i cal (bak tir/ē ə loj/ə kəl), 1 of or having to do with bacteriology. 2 using bacteria: *bacteriological warfare.* *adj.*

bac ter i ol o gist (bak tir/ē ol/ə jist), an expert in bacteriology. *n.*

bac ter i ol o gy (bak tir/ē ol/ə jē), science that deals with bacteria. *n.*

bac ter i um (bak tir′ē əm), singular of **bacteria.** *n.*

Bac tri an camel (bak′trē ən), camel having two humps and long hair, found in central Asia.

bad (bad), 1 not good; not as it ought to be: *It is bad for your eyes to read in dim light.* 2 evil; wicked: *Only someone bad would hurt a helpless person.* 3 not friendly; cross; unpleasant: *a bad temper.* 4 unfavorable: *You have come at a bad time.* 5 severe: *A bad thunderstorm delayed the airplane.* 6 rotten; spoiled: *Don't use that egg; it's bad.* 7 sorry: *I feel bad about losing your baseball.* 8 sick: *Her cold made her feel bad.* 9 incorrect: *You made a bad guess.* 10 INFORMAL. badly. 11 something that is bad; bad condition or quality. 1-9 *adj.*, **worse, worst;** 10 *adv.*, 11 *n.* —**bad′ness,** *n.*

be in bad, INFORMAL. be in disfavor: *I'm in bad with the teacher, because I did not do my homework.*

not bad or **not half bad,** fairly good.

bad blood, unfriendly feeling; hate: *There is bad blood between the rival gangs.*

bade (bad), a past tense of **bid.** *The captain bade the soldiers go on. v.*

Ba den-Pow ell (bād′n pō′əl), **Sir Robert,** 1857-1941, English general who founded the Boy Scouts in 1908. *n.*

badge (baj), 1 something worn to show that a person belongs to a certain occupation, school, class, club, society, etc.: *Policemen wear badges. The Red Cross badge is a red cross on a white background.* 2 symbol or sign: *Chains are a badge of slavery. n.*

badg er (baj′ər), 1 a hairy, gray mammal that feeds at night and digs a hole in the ground to live in. Badgers are related to weasels but are larger and more heavily built. 2 its fur. 3 keep on annoying or teasing; bother or question persistently: *That salesman has been badgering my father for the last two weeks to buy a new car.* 1,2 *n.*, 3 *v.*

Bad lands (bad′landz′), 1 rugged, barren region in SW South Dakota and NW Nebraska in which erosion has produced unusual land formations. 2 **badlands,** any similar region. *n.pl.*

bad ly (bad′lē), 1 in a bad manner: *She sings badly.* 2 INFORMAL. very much: *He wants to go badly. adv.*

bad min ton (bad′min tən), game in which either two or four players use light rackets to keep a shuttlecock moving back and forth over a high net. Badminton is somewhat like tennis. *n.*

bad-tem pered (bad′tem′pərd), having a bad temper; cross; irritable. *adj.*

baf fle (baf′əl), 1 hinder (a person) by being too hard to understand or solve;

bewilder: *This puzzle baffles me. The absence of clues baffled the police.* 2 device for hindering or changing the flow of air, water, or sound waves: *a baffle for a jet engine.* 1 *v.*, **baf fled, baf fling;** 2 *n.*

bag (bag), 1 container made of paper, cloth, leather, etc., that can be pulled together to close at the top: *Fresh vegetables are sometimes sold in plastic bags.* 2 something like a bag in its use or shape; handbag, suitcase, etc.: *Mother calls her purse her bag.* 3 put into a bag or bags: *We bagged the cookies we had baked so we could sell them.* 4 bulge; swell: *The boy's trousers bag at the knees.* 5 game killed or caught at one time by a hunter. 6 kill or catch in hunting: *The hunter bagged many large ducks.* 7 base in baseball. 8 SLANG. something for which one has an interest, an ability, or a liking: *Tennis is my bag.* 1,2,5,7,8 *n.*, 3,4,6 *v.*, **bagged, bag ging.** —**bag′like′,** *adj.*

hold the bag, INFORMAL. 1 be left to take the blame. 2 be left empty-handed.

ba gasse (bə gas′), pulp of sugar cane after the juice has been extracted. *n.*

bag a telle (bag′ə tel′), a mere trifle; thing of no importance. *n.*

Bag dad (bag′dad), Baghdad. *n.*

ba gel (bā′gəl), a hard roll made of raised dough shaped into a ring. *n.*

bag gage (bag′ij), 1 the trunks, bags, suitcases, etc., that a person takes with him when he travels. 2 equipment that an army takes with it, such as tents, blankets, and dishes. *n.*

bag gi ness (bag′ē nis), baggy condition. *n.*

bag gy (bag′ē), hanging loosely; baglike: *The clown had baggy trousers. adj.*, **bag gi er, bag gi est.**

Bagh dad (bag′dad), capital of Iraq, on the Tigris in SW Asia. Baghdad is an ancient city mentioned many times in *The Arabian Nights. n.* Also, **Bagdad.**

bag pipe (bag′pīp′), a musical instrument made of a tube to blow through, a leather bag for air, and four sounding pipes. Bagpipes produce shrill tones and are used especially in Scotland and Ireland. *n.*

bag pip er (bag′pī′pər), person who plays the bagpipe. *n.*

bah (bä), exclamation of scorn, contempt, or impatience. *interj.*

Ba ha ma Islands (bə hä′mə or bə-hā′mə), country consisting of more than 700 islands in the West Indies, southeast of Florida. It is a member of the Commonwealth of Nations. *Capital:* Nassau. See **Caribbean Sea** for map.

Ba ha mas (bə hä′məz or bə hā′məz), Bahama Islands. *n.pl.*

Bah rein or **Bah rain** (bä rān′), island country in the Persian Gulf. *n.*

hat, āge, fär; let, ēqual, tèrm;
it, īce; hot, ōpen, ôrder;
oil, out; cup, pùt, rüle; ch, child;
ng, long; sh, she; th, thin;
ŦH, then; zh, measure;

ə represents *a* in about,
e in taken, *i* in pencil,
o in lemon, *u* in circus.

Bai kal (bī käl′), **Lake,** lake in S Siberia. It is the deepest freshwater lake in the world. *n.*

bail[1] (bāl), 1 guarantee of money necessary to release a person under arrest from jail or prison until he is to appear for trial: *The man put up bail for his son, who was accused of stealing.* 2 amount of money guaranteed. 3 obtain the release of (a person under arrest) by supplying bail: *The man bailed out his son.* 1,2 *n.*, 3 *v.* [from French of the 1300's *bail* custody]

go bail for, supply bail for.

bail[2] (bāl), the curved handle of a kettle or pail. *n.* [probably from a Scandinavian word of the 1400's, such as Icelandic *beygla*]

bail[3] (bāl), throw (water) out of a boat with a bucket, pail, or any other container: *The fisherman bailed water from the sinking boat. v.* [from French of the 1400's *baille* bucket]

bail out, jump from an airplane by parachute: *When the plane caught fire, the pilot bailed out.*

bail iff (bā′lif), 1 officer of a court of law who has charge of jurors and guards prisoners while they are in the courtroom. 2 assistant to a sheriff. 3 (in England) an overseer or steward of an estate: *The bailiff collected the rents from the tenants for the owner. n.*

bail i wick (bā′lə wik), 1 place over which a bailiff has authority. 2 a person's field of knowledge, work, or authority. *n.*

bairn (bern or barn), SCOTTISH. child. *n.*

bait (bāt), 1 anything, especially food, used to attract fish or other animals so that they may be caught. 2 put bait on (a hook) or in (a trap): *The hunter baited his traps.* 3 thing used to tempt or attract. 4 set dogs to attack: *Men used to bait bulls and bears for sport.* 5 torment or worry by unkind or annoying remarks: *A group of troublemakers kept baiting the speaker.* 1,3 *n.*, 2,4,5 *v.*

baize (bāz), a thick woolen or cotton cloth used for curtains, table covers, etc. *n.*

bake (bāk), 1 cook (food) by dry heat

adj.	adjective	n.	noun
adv.	adverb	prep.	preposition
conj.	conjunction	pron.	pronoun
interj.	interjection	v.	verb
sing.	singular	pl.	plural

without exposing it directly to the fire: *I am baking a cake in the oven. I bake every Saturday.* **2** dry or harden by heat: *Bricks and china are baked in a kiln.* **3** become baked: *Cookies bake quickly. v.,* **baked, baking.**

bak er (bā′kər), person who makes or sells bread, pies, cakes, etc. *n.*

baker's dozen, thirteen.

bak er y (bā′kər ē), store where bread, pies, cakes, etc., are made or sold; baker's shop. *n., pl.* **bak er ies.**

bak ing (bā′king), **1** a cooking in dry heat without exposing directly to the fire. **2** a drying or hardening by heat. **3** amount baked at one time; batch. *n.*

baking powder, mixture of sodium bicarbonate and cream of tartar, used instead of yeast to cause biscuits, cakes, etc., to rise.

baking soda, sodium bicarbonate.

Ba ku (bä kü′), seaport in S Soviet Union, on the Caspian Sea. *n.*

Ba laam (bā′ləm), (in the Bible) a heathen prophet who blessed the Israelites instead of cursing them after he was rebuked by the donkey he rode. *n.*

balance (def. 1)—Material on the right platform is weighed by adding weights of known value to the left platform. When the two platforms balance, the value of the weights is added up.

bal ance (bal′əns), **1** instrument for weighing. **2** weigh two things against each other on scales, in one's hands, or in one's mind to see which is heavier or more important: *She balanced a trip to the mountains against a chance to go to a summer camp.* **3** condition of being equal in weight, amount, etc.: *Keep the balance between the two sides of the scale.* **4** steady condition or position: *I lost my balance and fell off the ladder.* **5** put, keep, or be in a steady condition or position: *balance a coin on its edge.* **6** steadiness of character: *His balance*

kept him from losing his temper very often. **7** make up for the effect, influence, etc., of; counteract. **8** difference between the amount one owes or has withdrawn from an account and the amount one is owed or deposits in an account: *I have a balance of $20 in the bank.* **9** (in an account) make the amount one owes and the amount one is owed equal. **10** part that is left over; remainder: *I will be away for the balance of the week.* **11** wheel that regulates the rate of movement in a clock or watch. 1,3,4,6,8,10,11 *n.,* 2,5,7,9 *v.,* **bal anced, bal anc ing.**

in the balance, undecided: *The outcome of the baseball game was in the balance until the last inning.*

balance of payments, the net amount of money when all business between one country and another for a given period of time is balanced.

balance of power, an even distribution of military or economic power between nations or groups of nations to make sure that no one nation becomes strong enough to dominate the others.

balance of trade, the difference between the value of all the imports and that of all the exports of a country.

balance wheel, wheel for regulating motion. A clock or watch has a balance wheel that controls the movement of the hands.

bal bo a (bal bō′ə), a silver coin in Panama, worth about one U.S. dollar. *n., pl.* **bal bo as.** [from *Balboa*]

Bal bo a (bal bō′ə), **Vasco de,** 1475?-1517, Spanish explorer who discovered the Pacific Ocean in 1513. *n.*

bal brig gan (bal brig′ən), **1** a knitted cotton cloth, once used for stockings and underwear. **2 balbriggans,** *pl.* stockings and underwear made of this fabric. *n.* [from *Balbriggan,* a town in Ireland]

bal co ny (bal′kə nē), **1** an outside projecting platform with an entrance from an upper floor of a building. **2** a projecting upper floor in a theater, hall, or church with seats for part of the audience; gallery. *n., pl.* **bal co nies.**

bald (bôld), **1** wholly or partly without hair on the head. **2** without its natural covering: *A mountaintop with no trees or grass is bald.* **3** obvious; plain: *the bald truth, a bald lie. adj.* —**bald′ly,** *adv.* —**bald′ness,** *n.*

bald eagle, a large, powerful, North American eagle with white feathers on its head, neck, and tail; American eagle. It is the national emblem of the United States.

bal der dash (bôl′dər dash), nonsense; foolishness. *n.*

bal dric (bôl′drik), belt for a sword, horn, etc., hung from one shoulder

to the opposite side of the body. *n.*

bale (bāl), **1** a large bundle of merchandise or material securely wrapped or bound for shipping or storage: *a bale of cotton.* **2** make into bales: *We saw a big machine bale hay.* 1 *n.,* 2 *v.,* **baled, bal ing.**

Bal e ar ic Islands (bal′ē ar′ik), group of Spanish islands in the W Mediterranean.

ba leen (bə lēn′), whalebone. *n.*

bale ful (bāl′fəl), hostile; menacing: *The librarian gave the noisy children a baleful glance. adj.* —**bale′ful ly,** *adv.* —**bale′ful ness,** *n.*

bal er (bā′lər), person or machine that makes up bales or bundles. *n.*

Ba li (bä′lē), island in Indonesia, east of Java. *n.*

Ba li nese (bä′lə nēz′), **1** person born or living in Bali. **2** language of Bali. **3** of Bali, its people, or their language. 1,2 *n., pl.* **Ba li nese;** 3 *adj.*

balk (bôk), **1** stop short and stubbornly refuse to go on: *My horse balked at the fence.* **2** prevent from going on; hinder: *The police balked the robber's plans.* **3** hindrance. **4** (in baseball) an illegal motion made by a pitcher, especially one in which he fails to complete a throw he has started. 1,2 *v.,* 3,4 *n.* Also, **baulk.**

Bal kan (bôl′kən), **1 Balkans,** *pl.* Balkan States. **2** of the people living in the Balkan States. **3** of the Balkan Peninsula or the countries on it. 1 *n.,* 2,3 *adj.*

Balkan Peninsula, peninsula in SE Europe.

Balkan States, countries on the Balkan Peninsula; Yugoslavia, Romania, Bulgaria, Albania, Greece, and European Turkey.

Balkan States

balk y (bô′kē), stopping short and stubbornly refusing to go on; likely to balk: *Mules are balky animals. adj.* **balk i er, balk i est.**

ball[1] (bôl), **1** a roundish body thrown, hit, or kicked in various games. Different sizes and types of balls are used in tennis, golf, baseball, football, and soccer. **2** game in which some kind of ball is thrown, hit, or kicked, especially baseball. **3** anything round or roundish;

something that is somewhat like a ball: *Please get a ball of string. I have a blister on the ball of my thumb.* 4 baseball pitched too high, too low, or not over the plate, that the batter does not strike at. 5 bullet for firearms; a round, solid object to be shot from a gun. 6 form into a ball: *to ball string or yarn.* 1-5 *n.,* 6 *v.* [probably from a Scandinavian word of the 1200's, such as Icelandic *böllr*]

ball² (bôl), a large, formal party with dancing. *n.* [from French *bal*]

bal lad (bal′əd), 1 a simple song. 2 poem that tells a story in a simple verse form, especially one that tells a popular legend. Ballads are often sung. 3 a folk song. *n.*

ball-and-sock et joint (bôl′ənd-sok′it), joint formed by a ball or knob fitting into a socket, permitting motion in a rotary direction. The shoulder and hip joints are ball-and-socket joints.

bal last (bal′əst), 1 something heavy carried in a ship to steady it. 2 weight carried in a balloon or dirigible to steady it or regulate its ascent: *The balloon used bags of sand for ballast.* 3 anything which makes a person or thing steady. 4 gravel or crushed rock used in making the bed for a road or railroad track. 5 furnish or steady with ballast. 1-4 *n.,* 5 *v.*

BALL BEARING.

ball bearing
left, wheel cut away to show
ball bearing (def. 1); right, (def. 2)

ball bearing, 1 bearing in which the shaft turns upon a collar supported by a number of freely moving metal balls. Ball bearings are used to lessen friction. 2 one of the metal balls.

bal le ri na (bal′ə rē′nə), a woman ballet dancer. *n., pl.* **bal le ri nas.**

bal let (bal′ā *or* ba lā′), 1 an elaborate dance by a group on a stage. A ballet tells a story accompanied by music often written especially for it. 2 the dancers. *n.*

bal lis tic (bə lis′tik), having to do with the motion of projectiles. *adj.*

ballistic missile, missile aimed at or before the time of launching. It differs from a guided missile, which can be aimed during flight.

bal lis tics (bə lis′tiks), science that deals with the motion of projectiles, such as bullets, shells, or bombs, and also rockets after thrust has ended. *n.*

bal loon (bə lün′), 1 an airtight bag

filled with some gas lighter than air, so that it will rise and float in the air. Some balloons have a basket or container for carrying persons or instruments high up in the air. 2 a child's toy made of rubber that may be blown up by mouth or filled with gas. 3 swell out like a balloon: *The sails of the boat ballooned in the wind.* 1,2 *n.,* 3 *v.*

bal lot (bal′ət), 1 piece of paper or other object used in voting: *Have you cast your ballot?* 2 the total number of votes cast. 3 method of secret voting that uses paper slips, voting machines, etc. 4 vote or decide by using ballots: *We will now ballot for president of the club.* 1-3 *n.,* 4 *v.*

ball play er (bôl′plā′ər), person who plays ball, especially baseball. *n.*

ball-point pen (bôl′point′), pen that writes with a small metal ball which turns inside the end of a cartridge holding ink.

ball room (bôl′rüm′ *or* bôl′rùm′), a large room for dancing. *n.*

bal ly hoo (bal′ē hü), 1 sensational or noisy advertising. 2 uproar; outcry. 3 make exaggerated or false statements. 1,2 *n., pl.* **bal ly hoos;** 3 *v.*

balm (bäm *or* bälm), 1 a fragrant, oily, sticky substance obtained from certain kinds of trees, used to heal or to relieve pain. 2 an ointment or similar preparation that heals or soothes. 3 anything that heals or soothes: *Your kindness was balm to my wounded feelings. n.*

balm i ly (bä′mə lē *or* bäl′mə lē), in a balmy manner. *adv.*

balm i ness (bä′mē nis *or* bäl′mē nis), balmy condition or quality. *n.*

balm y (bä′mē *or* bäl′mē), 1 mild; gentle; soothing: *A balmy breeze blew across the lake.* 2 fragrant. *adj.,* **balm-i er, balm i est.**

bal sa (bôl′sə), 1 a tropical American tree with strong wood which is very light in weight. 2 its wood, used in making rafts, airplane models, etc. 3 raft, especially one made up of two or more floats fastened to a framework. *n., pl.* **bal sas** for 1 and 3.

bal sam (bôl′səm), 1 balsam fir. 2 balm. *n.*

balsam fir, 1 an evergreen tree of North America, of the same family as the pine, whose resin is used in making varnish and turpentine. Balsam firs are much used as Christmas trees. 2 its wood.

Bal tic (bôl′tik), 1 of or having to do with the Baltic Sea: *the Baltic coasts.* 2 of or having to do with the Baltic States. *adj.*

Baltic Sea, sea in N Europe, north of Poland and southeast of Sweden.

Baltic States, Estonia, Latvia, Lithuania, and sometimes Finland.

hat, āge, fär; let, ēqual, tèrm;
it, īce; hot, ōpen, ôrder;
oil, out; cup, pùt, rüle; ch, child;
ng, long; sh, she; th, thin;
₮H, then; zh, measure;

ə represents *a* in about,
e in taken, *i* in pencil,
o in lemon, *u* in circus.

Bal ti more (bôl′tə môr), city in N Maryland, near Chesapeake Bay. *n.*

bal us ter (bal′ə stər), one of the short posts or columns that support the railing of a staircase, balcony, etc. *n.*

baluster (left)
and balusters in a balustrade (right)

bal us trade (bal′ə strād), row of balusters and the railing on them. *n.*

Bam a ko (bäm′ə kō), capital of Mali, in the SW part. *n.*

bam bi no (bam bē′nō), 1 baby. 2 a little child. *n., pl.* **bam bi ni** (bam-bē′nē), **bam bi nos.** [from Italian]

bam boo (bam bü′), a woody or tree-like grass with a very tall, stiff, hollow stem that has hard, thick joints. Bamboo grows in warm regions. Its stems are used for making canes, fishing poles, furniture, and even houses. *n., pl.* **bam boos.**

bam boo zle (bam bü′zəl), INFORMAL. 1 impose upon; cheat; trick. 2 puzzle; perplex. *v.,* **bam boo zled, bam boo-zling.**

ban (ban), 1 forbid by law or authority; prohibit: *Swimming is banned in this lake.* 2 the forbidding of an act or speech by authority: *The city has a ban on parking cars in this busy street.* 3 a solemn curse by the church. 1 *v.,* **banned, ban ning;** 2,3 *n.*

ba nal (bā′nl *or* bə nal′), not new or interesting; commonplace; trite: *Their conversation was banal, full of uninteresting remarks such as "nice weather" and "slow traffic today." adj.* —ba′nal ly, *adv.*

ba nal i ty (bə nal′ə tē), 1 commonplaceness; triteness. 2 a banal remark, idea, etc. *n., pl.* **ba nal i ties.**

ba nan a (bə nan′ə), 1 a slightly

65

adj. adjective   *n.* noun
adv. adverb   *prep.* preposition
conj. conjunction   *pron.* pronoun
interj. interjection   *v.* verb

sing. singular   *pl.* plural

curved, yellow or red fruit with firm, creamy flesh. Bananas are five to eight inches long and grow in clusters two or three feet long. 2 the treelike, tropical plant on which bananas grow. It has great, long leaves. *n., pl.* **ba·nan·as.**

Ba·na·ras (bə när′əs), Benares. *n.*

band[1] (band), 1 number of persons or animals joined or acting together: *a band of robbers, a band of wild dogs.* 2 unite in a group: *The children banded together to buy a present for their teacher.* 3 group of musicians performing together, especially on wind and percussion instruments: *The school band played several marches.* 1,3 *n.,* 2 *v.* [from French of the 1400's *bande* troop]

band[2] (band), 1 a thin, flat strip of material for binding, trimming, or some other purpose: *The oak box was strengthened with bands of iron.* 2 put a band on: *Students of birds often band them in order to identify them later.* 3 a stripe: *The white cup has a gold band.* 4 a particular range of wavelengths or frequencies in radio broadcasting. 1,3,4 *n.,* 2 *v.* [from French of the 1100's *bande* flat strip]

band·age (ban′dij), 1 strip of cloth or other material used in binding up and dressing a wound or injury. 2 bind or dress with a bandage. 1 *n.,* 2 *v.,* **band·aged, band·ag·ing.**

ban·dan·a (ban dan′ə), bandanna. *n., pl.* **ban·dan·as.**

ban·dan·na (ban dan′ə), a large, gaily colored kerchief or handkerchief, often worn on the head or neck. *n., pl.* **ban·dan·nas.**

band·box (band′boks′), a light cardboard box to put hats, collars, etc., in. *n., pl.* **band·box·es.**

ban·deau (ban dō′), 1 a narrow band worn about the head. 2 any narrow band. *n., pl.* **ban·deaux** or **ban·deaus** (ban dōz′).

ban·dit (ban′dit), highwayman or robber. *n., pl.* **ban·dits, ban·dit·ti** (ban dit′ē).

ban·dit·ry (ban′də trē), 1 the work of bandits. 2 bandits. *n.*

band·mas·ter (band′mas′tər), leader of a band of musicians. *n.*

ban·do·leer or **ban·do·lier** (ban′-dl ir′), a broad belt worn over the shoulder and across the breast, often with loops for carrying cartridges or with small cases for bullets, gunpowder, etc. *n.*

band saw, saw in the form of an endless steel belt running over two pulleys. *n.*

band·stand (band′stand′), an outdoor platform for band concerts. It usually has a roof. *n.*

band·wag·on (band′wag′ən), wagon that carries a musical band in a parade. *n.*

climb on the bandwagon, INFORMAL. join what appears to be a winning or successful group, movement, fashion, etc.

banjo—Tightly stretched skin over the round body increases the sound made by plucking the strings.

ban·dy (ban′dē), 1 throw back and forth; toss about: *The team bandied the ball from player to player while waiting for the game to start.* 2 give and take; exchange: *bandy blows, bandy insults.* *v.,* **ban·died, ban·dy·ing.**

ban·dy-leg·ged (ban′dē leg′id), having legs that curve outward like a bow; bowlegged. *adj.*

bane (bān), cause of death, ruin, or harm: *Packs of wolves were the bane of the mountain village.* *n.*

bane·ful (bān′fəl), causing harm or destruction: *Air pollution has a baneful effect on trees in cities.* *adj.* —**bane′ful·ly,** *adv.* —**bane′ful·ness,** *n.*

bang[1] (bang), 1 a sudden, loud noise: *the bang of firecrackers.* 2 make or cause to make a sudden, loud noise: *The door banged as it blew shut. He banged the door.* 3 a violent, noisy blow: *She gave the drum a bang.* 4 strike noisily: *The baby was banging the pan with a spoon.* 5 violently and suddenly: *The bicyclist ran bang into a telephone pole.* 1,3 *n.,* 2,4 *v.,* 5 *adv.* [probably from a Scandinavian word of the 1500's, such as Icelandic *banga* to strike]

bang up, damage: *My car was banged up in the accident.*

bang[2] (bang), 1 **bangs,** *pl.* fringe of hair cut short and worn over the forehead. 2 cut squarely across: *She wears her hair banged.* 1 *n.,* 2 *v.* [origin uncertain]

Bang·kok (bang′kok), capital and chief port of Thailand. *n.*

Ban·gla·desh (bäng′glə desh′), country in S Asia, on the Bay of Bengal, a member of the Commonwealth of Nations. *Capital:* Dacca. *n.*

ban·gle (bang′gəl), 1 a small ornament suspended from a bracelet. 2 bracelet or anklet. *n.*

ban·ian (ban′yən), banyan. *n.*

ban·ish (ban′ish), 1 condemn (a person) to leave a country; exile: *The king banished some of his enemies.* 2 force to go away; drive away; expel: *The children banished him from their game for cheating. Now let's banish all our cares and have a happy time.* *v.*

ban·ish·ment (ban′ish mənt), 1 act of banishing. 2 condition of being banished; exile: *Their banishment made the patriots sick at heart.* *n.*

ban·is·ter (ban′ə stər), 1 **banisters,** *pl.* handrail of a staircase, balcony, etc., and its row of supports; balustrade. 2 one of the supports; baluster. *n.*

ban·jo (ban′jō), a musical instrument having four or five strings, played by plucking the strings with the fingers or a pick. *n., pl.* **ban·jos** or **ban·joes.**

bank[1] (bangk), 1 a long pile or heap: *There was a bank of snow over ten feet deep.* 2 pile up; heap up: *The tractors banked the snow by the side of the road.* 3 ground bordering a river, lake, etc.; shore: *We fished from the bank.* 4 a shallow place in a body of water; shoal: *the fishing banks of Newfoundland.* 5 cause to slope: *The bulldozers banked the curves of the new express highway.* 6 the sloping of an airplane to one side when making a turn. 7 make (an airplane) do this. 8 cover (a fire) with ashes or fresh fuel so that it will burn slowly: *The janitor banked the fire for the night.* 1,3,4,6 *n.,* 2,5,7,8 *v.* [probably from a Scandinavian word of the 1100's, such as Icelandic *bakki* ridge]

bank[2] (bangk), 1 place of business for keeping, lending, exchanging, and issuing money: *A bank pays interest on money deposited in a savings account.* 2 keep or put money in a bank: *We bank at the First National. I bank the money I earn baby-sitting.* 3 a small container with a slot through which coins can be dropped to save money. 4 any place where reserve supplies are kept: *a bank for blood plasma.* 1,3,4 *n.,* 2 *v.* [from French of the 1400's *banque,* from Italian *banca,* which originally meant counter or bench]

bank on, depend on: *I can bank on my teacher to help me.*

bank[3] (bangk), 1 row or close arrangement of things: *a bank of machines.* 2 row of keys on an organ, typewriter, etc. 3 row or tier of oars. 4 bench for rowers in a galley. *n.* [from French of the 1200's *banc* bench]

bank·er (bang′kər), person or company that manages a bank. *n.*

bank ing (bang′king), business of keeping, lending, exchanging, and issuing money. *n.*

bank rupt (bang′krupt), 1 person who is declared by a court of law to be unable to pay his debts, and whose property is distributed as far as it will go among the people to whom he owes money. 2 unable to pay one's debts. 3 make bankrupt: *Foolish expenditures will bankrupt him.* 1 *n.*, 2 *adj.*, 3 *v.*

bank rupt cy (bang′krupt sē), bankrupt condition. *n.*, *pl.* **bankrupt cies.**

ban ner (ban′ər), 1 flag: *The banners of many countries fly outside the headquarters of the United Nations.* 2 piece of cloth with some design or words on it: *The banner our school displays in parades is blue and white.* 3 leading; foremost: *Ours was the banner class in attendance.* 4 a newspaper headline extending across the top of a page. 1,2,4 *n.*, 3 *adj.*

ban nock (ban′ək), a flat cake made of oatmeal or barley flour, eaten in Scotland. *n.*

banns (banz), notice given three separate times in church that a certain man and woman are to be married. *n.pl.*

ban quet (bang′kwit), 1 an elaborate meal prepared for a special occasion or for many people; feast: *We went to the wedding banquet.* 2 a formal dinner with speeches. 3 give a banquet to: *The mayor banqueted the famous visitor.* 4 take part in a banquet. 1,2 *n.*, 3,4 *v.*

ban shee or **ban shie** (ban′shē), (in Irish and Scottish folklore) a female spirit whose wail means that there will soon be a death in the family. *n.*

ban tam or **Ban tam** (ban′təm), a small kind of domestic fowl. The roosters are often spirited fighters. *n.*

ban tam weight (ban′təm wāt′), boxer who weighs more than 112 and less than 118 pounds. *n.*

ban ter (ban′tər), 1 playful teasing; joking: *There was much banter going on at the party.* 2 tease playfully; make fun of. 3 talk in a joking way. 1 *n.*, 2,3 *v.*

Ban tu (ban′tü), 1 member of a large group of Negro tribes living in central and southern Africa. 2 any of the languages of these tribes. 3 of these tribes or their languages. 1,2 *n.*, *pl.* **Ban tu** or **Ban tus;** 3 *adj.*

ban yan (ban′yən), an East Indian fig tree whose branches have hanging roots that grow down to the ground and start new trunks. One tree may cover several acres. *n.* Also, **banian.**

ban zai (bän′zī′), a Japanese greeting, patriotic cheer, or battle cry. It means "May you live ten thousand years!" *interj.*

ba o bab (bā′ō bab), a tall, tropical tree of Africa, India, and Australia, with a very thick trunk and an oblong, gourd-like, woolly fruit. *n.*

bap tism (bap′tiz əm), 1 act of baptizing; rite or ceremony of dipping a person into water or sprinkling water on him, as a sign of washing away sin and admission to the Christian church. 2 an experience that tests a person or initiates him into a new kind of life. *n.*

bap tis mal (bap tiz′məl), of or having to do with baptism: *a baptismal ceremony.* *adj.*

Bap tist (bap′tist), member of a Christian church that believes in baptizing by dipping the whole person in water. *n.*

bap tis ter y (bap′tə stər ē), building or part of church where baptism is performed. *n.*, *pl.* **bap tis ter ies.**

bap tis try (bap′tə strē), baptistery. *n.*, *pl.* **bap tis tries.**

bap tize (bap tīz′ or bap′tīz), 1 dip (a person) into water or sprinkle with water as a sign of washing away sin and admission into the Christian church. 2 give a first name to (a person) at baptism; christen: *The baby was baptized Ann.* *v.*, **bap tized, bap tiz ing.**

bar (bär), 1 an evenly shaped piece of some solid, longer than it is wide or thick: *a bar of iron, a bar of soap, a bar of chocolate.* 2 pole or rod put across a door, gate, window, or across any opening: *Let down the pasture bars for the cows to come in.* 3 put bars across; fasten or shut off: *Bar the door.* 4 anything that blocks the way or prevents progress: *A bar of sand kept boats out of the harbor. Shyness can be a bar to making friends.* 5 block; obstruct: *Fallen trees bar the road.* 6 exclude or forbid: *All talking is barred during a study period. Dogs are barred from that store.* 7 except; excluding: *He is the best student, bar none.* 8 band of color; stripe: *a dark bar of cloud across the setting sun.* 9 mark with stripes: *a chicken with barred feathers.* 10 unit of rhythm in music. The regular accent falls on the first note of each bar. 11 the vertical line between two such units on a musical staff, dividing a composition into measures. A **double bar** marks

BAR BAR BAR

bar (def. 10)

BAR BAR

DOUBLE BAR

bar (def. 11)

the end of a movement or of an entire piece of music. 12 counter or place where drinks, usually alcoholic, and sometimes food are served to customers. 13 place where a prisoner stands in a court of law. 14 profession of a lawyer: *After you have passed your law examinations, you will be admitted to the bar.* 15 lawyers as a group: *Judges are chosen from the bar.* 16 court of law. 17 anything like a court of law; any place of judgment: *The bar of public opinion condemns dishonest people.* 1,2,4,8,10-17 *n.*, 3,5,6,9 *v.*, **barred, bar ring;** 7 *prep.*

BARB

barb (def. 1) on a fishhook to keep the hook from slipping out of the mouth of the fish

barb (bärb), 1 point sticking out and curving backward from the main point of an arrow, fishhook, etc. 2 something that wounds or stings: *the barb of sarcasm. n.*

Bar ba dos (bär bā′dōz), island country in the West Indies, a member of the Commonwealth of Nations. *n.*

bar bar i an (bär ber′ē ən or bär-bar′ē ən), 1 person belonging to a people or to a tribe that is not civilized: *The Roman Empire was conquered by barbarians.* 2 not civilized; cruel and coarse. 3 person who rejects or lacks interest in literature, the arts, etc. 4 of barbarians: *barbarian customs.* 1,3 *n.*, 2,4 *adj.*

bar bar ic (bär bar′ik), 1 like barbarians; suited to an uncivilized people; rough and rude. 2 rich or splendid in a crude way: *barbaric color, barbaric music. adj.*

bar ba rism (bär′bə riz′əm), 1 condition of uncivilized people: *People who have no form of writing live in barbarism.* 2 word or expression not in accepted use. EXAMPLE: "his'n" for "his." *n.*

bar bar i ty (bär bar′ə tē), 1 brutal cruelty; inhumanity. 2 a cruel act.

adj.	adjective	n.	noun
adv.	adverb	prep.	preposition
conj.	conjunction	pron.	pronoun
interj.	interjection	v.	verb
sing.	singular	pl.	plural

3 barbaric manner or style; gaudy taste. *n., pl.* **bar bar i ties.**

bar bar ous (bär′bər əs), 1 not civilized; savage. 2 savagely cruel; brutal: *Torture of prisoners is a barbarous custom.* 3 rough and rude; coarse; unrefined: *Many of the early fur trappers were barbarous men.* 4 (of a word or expression) not in accepted use. *adj.* —**bar′bar ous ly,** *adv.* —**bar′bar ous ness,** *n.*

Bar bar y (bär′bər ē), Moslem countries west of Egypt on the N coast of Africa. *n.*

bar be cue (bär′bə kyü), 1 an outdoor meal in which meat is roasted over an open fire. 2 grill or open fireplace for cooking meat, usually over charcoal. 3 meat roasted over an open fire. 4 roast (meat) over an open fire. 5 cook (meat or fish) in a highly flavored sauce. 6 an outdoor feast at which animals are roasted whole. 7 animal roasted whole. 1-3,6,7 *n.,* 4,5 *v.,* **bar be cued, bar be cu ing.**

barbed (bärbd), 1 having a barb or barbs: *A fishhook is barbed.* 2 sharply critical; cutting: *make a barbed remark. adj.*

barbed wire, wire with sharp points on it every few inches, used for fences.

bar bel (bär′bəl), a long, thin, fleshy growth on the mouths or nostrils of some fishes. *n.*

bar bell (bär′bel′), device like a dumbbell but with a much longer bar, to which weights may be added. *n.*

bar ber (bär′bər), person whose business is cutting hair and shaving or trimming beards. *n.*

bar ber ry (bär′ber′ē), 1 a low, thorny shrub with small, yellow flowers and sour, red berries. 2 its berry. *n., pl.* **bar ber ries.**

bar bi can (bär′bə kən), tower for defense built over a gate or bridge to a castle or city. *n.*

bar bit ur ate (bär bich′ər it *or* bär bich′ə rāt′), any of a group of drugs used in medicine to induce sleep. *n.*

bar ca role or **bar ca rolle** (bär′kə rōl′), 1 a Venetian boat song, sung by gondoliers. 2 music imitating such a song. *n.*

Bar ce lo na (bär′sə lō′nə), seaport in NE Spain, on the Mediterranean. *n.*

bard (bärd), 1 poet and singer of long ago: *The bard sang his own poems to the music of his harp.* 2 any poet. *n.*

bare[1] (ber *or* bar), 1 without covering; not clothed; naked: *The sun burned her bare shoulders. The top of the hill was bare, although trees grew part way up the hill.* 2 with the head uncovered; bareheaded. 3 not furnished; empty: *The room was bare of furniture.* 4 plain; not adorned: *We own a bare little cabin in the woods.* 5 just enough and no more; mere: *She earns only a bare living by her work.* 6 make bare; uncover; reveal: *The knight bared his sword. The dog bared its teeth.* 1-5 *adj.,* **bar er, bar est;** 6 *v.,* **bared, bar ing.** [Old English *bær*] —**bare′ness,** *n.*

lay bare, uncover; expose; reveal: *The police laid bare the plot to rob the bank.*

bare[2] (ber *or* bar), OLD USE. bore; past tense of **bear**[1]. *v.*

bare back (ber′bak′ *or* bar′bak′), without a saddle; on a horse's bare back: *The Indian rode bareback (adv.). You can see bareback riders at the circus (adj.). adv., adj.*

bare faced (ber′fāst′ *or* bar′fāst′), shameless; impudent: *a barefaced lie. adj.*

bare foot (ber′fut′ *or* bar′fut′), without shoes and stockings on: *A barefoot child played in the puddles (adj.). If you go barefoot, watch out for broken glass (adv.). adj., adv.*

bare foot ed (ber′fut′id *or* bar′fut′id), barefoot. *adj., adv.*

bare hand ed (ber′han′did *or* bar′han′did), 1 without any covering on the hands. 2 with no aid but one's own hands. *adj., adv.*

barbels
on a bullhead

bare head ed (ber′hed′id *or* bar′hed′id), wearing nothing on the head: *You shouldn't be bareheaded in such cold weather. adj.*

bare leg ged (ber′leg′id *or* bar′leg′id), without stockings on. *adj.*

bare ly (ber′lē *or* bar′lē), 1 with nothing to spare; only just; scarcely: *I have barely enough money to live on.* 2 poorly: *The hospital room was furnished barely but neatly.* 3 plainly; openly: *The facts are presented barely, without any comments. adv.*

bar gain (bär′gən), 1 an agreement to trade or exchange; deal: *If you will take fifty cents for your airplane, it's a bargain.* 2 something offered for sale cheap or bought cheap: *This hat is a bargain.* 3 try to get good terms; try to make a good deal: *For ten minutes she stood bargaining with the farmer for his vegetables.* 1,2 *n.,* 3 *v.* —**bar′gain er,** *n.*

bargain for, be ready for; expect: *I hadn't bargained for rain and have left my umbrella at home.*

into the bargain, besides; also: *My new dress shrank and it faded into the bargain.*

strike a bargain, make a bargain; reach an agreement: *They finally struck a bargain: a mitt for two baseballs and a bat.*

barge (bärj), 1 a large, strongly built, flat-bottomed boat for carrying freight on rivers, canals, etc.: *The grain barge was towed from Syracuse to Buffalo on the Erie Canal.* 2 a large boat used for excursions, pageants, and special occasions. 3 move clumsily like a barge: *He barged into the table and knocked the lamp over.* 4 INFORMAL. push oneself rudely: *Don't barge in where you're not wanted.* 1,2 *n.,* 3,4 *v.,* **barged, barging.**

bar graph, graph representing different quantities by rectangles of different lengths.

bar i tone (bar′ə tōn), 1 a man's voice between tenor and bass. 2 singer with such a voice. 3 part to be sung by such a voice. 4 of or for a baritone. 1-3 *n.,* 4 *adj.* Also, **barytone.**

bar i um (ber′ē əm *or* bar′ē əm), a soft, silvery-white metallic element which occurs only in combination with other elements. Barium compounds are used in making pigments, safety matches, radio tubes, etc. *n.*

bark[1] (bärk), 1 the tough outside covering of the trunk and branches of trees. 2 strip the bark from. 3 scrape the skin from: *I fell down the steps and barked my shins.* 1 *n.,* 2,3 *v.* [from a Scandinavian word of the 1200's, such as Icelandic *börkr*]

bark[2] (bärk), 1 the short, sharp sound that a dog makes. 2 a sound like this: *the bark of a fox, the bark of a gun, the bark of a cough.* 3 make this sound: *The dog barked. Rifles barked behind every tree.* 4 speak gruffly or sharply: *The policeman barked out his orders.* 1,2 *n.,* 3,4 *v.* [Old English *beorcan*]

bark[3] (bärk), 1 ship with three masts, square-rigged on the first two masts and fore-and-aft-rigged on the other. 2 OLD USE. boat; ship. *n.* Also, **barque.** [from French of the 1400's *barque*]

bar keep (bär′kēp′), barkeeper. *n.*

bar keep er (bär′kē′pər), bartender. *n.*

bark er (bär′kər), 1 one that barks. 2 person who stands in front of a store, show, etc., urging people to go in. *n.*

bar ley (bär'lē), 1 the seed or grain of a cereal grass that has compact spikes of flowers. Barley grows in cool climates and is used for food and for making malt. 2 plant yielding this grain. *n.*

bar magnet, a steel magnet in the shape of a bar or rod: *A bar magnet suspended from a string will serve as a simple compass.*

bar maid (bär'mād'), woman who serves alcoholic drinks to customers at a bar. *n.*

bar man (bär'mən), bartender. *n., pl.* **bar men.**

bar mitz vah (bär mits'və), 1 ceremony or celebration held when a Jewish boy becomes thirteen years old to affirm that he has reached the age of religious responsibility. 2 the boy himself. [from Hebrew]

barn (bärn), building for storing hay, grain, or other farm produce, and for sheltering cows, horses, and farm machinery. *n.*

bar na cle (bär'nə kəl), a small, salt-water animal with a shell, that attaches itself to rocks, the bottoms of ships, the timbers of wharves, etc. *n.*

barn dance, 1 an informal party for square dancing, formerly often held in a barn. 2 a lively square dance resembling a polka.

barn storm (bärn'stôrm'), travel from one small town or district to another, acting in plays, making political speeches, etc. *v.* —**barn'storm'er,** *n.*

barn swallow, a swallow that usually nests in barns. It has a reddish breast and a long, forked tail.

Bar num (bär'nəm), **P(hineas) T(aylor),** 1810-1891, American showman. *n.*

barn yard (bärn'yärd'), yard around or next to a barn for livestock. *n.*

ba rom e ter (bə rom'ə tər), 1 instrument for measuring the pressure of air, used in determining height above sea level and in predicting probable changes in the weather. 2 something that indicates changes: *Newspapers are often called barometers of public opinion. n.*

bar o met ric (bar'ə met'rik), 1 of a barometer. 2 indicated by a barometer: *Low barometric pressure is a sign of a possible storm. adj.*

bar on (bar'ən), 1 nobleman of the lowest hereditary rank. In Great Britain, a baron ranks next below a viscount and has "Lord" before his name instead of "Baron." In other European countries "Baron" is used before his name. 2 an English nobleman during the Middle Ages who held his lands directly from the king. *n.*

bar on ess (bar'ə nis), 1 wife or widow of a baron. 2 woman whose rank is equal to that of a baron. *n., pl.* **bar on ess es.**

bar on et (bar'ə nit), man in Great Britain ranking next below a baron and next above a knight. He has "Sir" before his name and "Bart." after it. EXAMPLE: Sir John Brown, Bart. *n.*

ba ro ni al (bə rō'nē əl), 1 of a baron or barons: *He gave her a family ring with a baronial crest on it.* 2 suitable for a baron; splendid, stately, and grand. *adj.*

bar on y (bar'ə nē), 1 lands of a baron. 2 rank or title of a baron. *n., pl.* **bar on ies.**

ba roque (bə rōk'), 1 having to do with a style of art or architecture characterized by the use of curved forms and lavish ornamentation. 2 having to do with a style of music characterized by complex rhythms and melodic ornamentation. 3 tastelessly odd; grotesque. 4 irregular in shape: *baroque pearls. adj.*

ba rouche (bə rüsh'), a four-wheeled carriage with a driver's seat, two passenger seats facing each other, and a folding top. *n.*

barque (bärk), bark³. *n.*

bar racks (bar'əks), a building or group of buildings for soldiers to live in, usually in a fort or camp. *n. pl. or sing.*

bar ra cu da (bar'ə kü'də), a large, fierce fish that looks somewhat like a pike. It sometimes attacks swimmers. *n., pl.* **bar ra cu das** or **bar ra cu da.**

bar rage (bə räzh'), 1 barrier of artillery fire to check the enemy or to protect one's own soldiers when advancing or retreating. 2 a large number of words, blows, etc., coming quickly one after the other: *The reporters kept up a barrage of questions for an hour. n.*

bar rel (bar'əl), 1 container with a round, flat top and bottom and sides that curve out slightly. Barrels are usually made of boards held together by hoops. 2 amount that a barrel can hold: *They picked a barrel of apples.* 3 unit of measure for liquids and dry things. Its exact amount is not the same for all commodities, and is often fixed by law. 4 put in barrels: *We plan to barrel the cider next Wednesday.* 5 the metal tube of a gun. The bullet is discharged through the barrel. 1-3,5 *n.,* 4 *v.*

barrel organ, hand organ.

bar ren (bar'ən), 1 not producing anything: *A desert is barren.* 2 not able to produce offspring: *Exposure to radioactivity may make animals and plants barren.* 3 without interest; unattractive; dull. 4 of no advantage; unprofitable: *the barren victories of modern war.* 5 **barrens,** *pl.* a barren stretch of land. 1-4 *adj.,* 5 *n.* —**bar'ren ness,** *n.*

bar rette (bə ret'), pin with a clasp,

used by women and girls for holding their hair in place. *n.*

bar ri cade (bar'ə kād' *or* bar'ə kād), 1 a rough, hastily made barrier for defense: *The soldiers cut down trees to make a barricade across the road.* 2 any barrier or obstruction. 3 block or obstruct with a barricade: *The soldiers barricaded the road with fallen trees.* 1,2 *n.,* 3 *v.,* **bar ri cad ed, bar ri cad ing.**

Bar rie (bar'ē), Sir **James Matthew,** 1860-1937, Scottish writer of novels and plays. *n.*

bar ri er (bar'ē ər), 1 something that stands in the way; something stopping progress or preventing approach; obstacle: *A dam is a barrier holding back water. Lack of water was a barrier to settling much of New Mexico.* 2 something that separates or keeps apart: *The Isthmus of Panama forms a barrier between the Atlantic and Pacific oceans. n.*

bar ring (bär'ing), leaving out of consideration; excepting: *Barring poor weather, the plane will leave Chicago at twelve. prep.*

bar ris ter (bar'ə stər), lawyer in England who can plead in any court. *n.*

bar room (bär'rüm' *or* bär'ru̇m'), room with a bar for the sale of alcoholic drinks. *n.*

bar row¹ (bar'ō), 1 frame with two short handles at each end, used for carrying a load. 2 wheelbarrow. 3 handcart. *n.* [Old English *bearwe*]

bar row² (bar'ō), mound of earth or stones over an ancient grave. *n.* [Old English *beorg*]

Bar row (bar'ō), **Point,** the northern tip of Alaska. It is the northernmost point of land in the United States. *n.*

bar sinister, a diagonal bar on a coat of arms wrongly supposed to indicate illegitimate descent.

Bart., Baronet.

bar tend er (bär'ten'dər), person who serves alcoholic drinks to customers at a bar. *n.*

bar ter (bär'tər), 1 to trade by exchanging one kind of goods for other goods without using money; exchange:

adj. adjective		*n.* noun
adv. adverb		*prep.* preposition
conj. conjunction		*pron.* pronoun
interj. interjection		*v.* verb
sing. singular		*pl.* plural

The Indians bartered furs for beads and guns. 2 a bartering; trading by exchanging goods: *Nations sometimes trade by barter instead of paying money for the things they need.* 1 *v.*, 2 *n.*

Bar tho lo mew (bär thol′ə myü), (in the Bible) one of Christ's twelve apostles. Saint Bartholomew's Day is August 24. *n.*

Bar tók (bär′tok), **Béla**, 1881-1945, Hungarian composer and pianist. *n.*

Bar ton (bärt′n), **Clara**, 1821-1912, American nurse who organized the American Red Cross in 1881. *n.*

bar y tone (bar′ə tōn), baritone. *n., adj.*

bas al (bā′səl), fundamental; basic. *adj.*

basal metabolism, amount of energy used by an animal or plant at rest.

ba salt (bə sôlt′), a hard, dark-colored rock of volcanic origin. It often occurs in a form resembling a group of columns. *n.*

base¹ (bās), 1 the part on which anything stands or rests; bottom: *This big machine has a wide steel base.* 2 a starting place; headquarters: *The base for our hiking trip was a camp beside a brook.* 3 set up and keep going; found: *Their large business was based on good service.* 4 thing or part on which something depends; basis; foundation: *The new law giving cities of our state more money was a base for new housing projects.* 5 the most important element of anything; essential part: *This paint has an oil base.* 6 place that is a station or goal in certain games, such as baseball or hide-and-seek: *His home run doesn't count because he failed to touch third base.* 7 any of a class of chemical compounds that are bitter to the taste, have a soapy feel, and turn red litmus paper blue in water solution. Bases yield ions composed of hydrogen and oxygen and will usually react with an acid to form a salt. Alkalis, such as sodium hydroxide, are bases. 8 line or surface on which a geometrical figure is supposed to rest. Any side of a triangle can be its base. 9 the number that is a definite starting point for a system of numbers. 10 is the base of the decimal system of arithmetic. 1,2,4-9 *n.*, 3 *v.*,

based, bas ing. [from French of the 1300's *base*, from Latin *basis*]

off base, INFORMAL. incorrect; wrong.

base² (bās), 1 morally low or mean; selfish and cowardly: *Betraying a friend is a base action.* 2 having little value when compared with something else; inferior: *Iron and lead are base metals; gold and silver are precious metals.* *adj.*, **bas er, bas est.** [from French of the 1300's *bas*, from Latin *bassus*] **—base′ly,** *adv.* **—base′ness,** *n.*

base ball (bās′bôl′), 1 game played with bat and ball by two teams of nine players each, on a field with four bases. A player making a complete circuit of the bases, under the rules, scores a run. 2 ball used in this game. *n.*

base board (bās′bôrd′), line of boards around the walls of a room, next to the floor. *n.*

base less (bās′lis), without foundation; groundless: *a baseless rumor.* *adj.*

base man (bās′mən), a baseball player guarding first, second, or third base. *n., pl.* **base men.**

base ment (bās′mənt), the lowest story of a building, partly or wholly below ground. *n.*

base runner, (in baseball) player on the team at bat who is on base or running between two bases.

bas es¹ (bā′siz), plural of **base¹.** *n.*

ba ses² (bā′sēz′), plural of **basis.** *n.*

bash (bash), INFORMAL. 1 strike with a smashing blow. 2 a smashing blow. 1 *v.*, 2 *n., pl.* **bash es.**

bash ful (bash′fəl), uneasy in the presence of strangers; easily embarrassed; shy: *The child was too bashful to greet us.* *adj.* **—bash′ful ly,** *adv.* **—bash′-ful ness,** *n.*

ba sic (bā′sik), 1 forming the basis; fundamental: *Addition, subtraction, multiplication, and division are the basic processes of arithmetic.* 2 (in chemistry) being, having the properties of, or containing a base; alkaline. *adj.*

ba si cal ly (bā′sik lē), as a basic principle; fundamentally. *adv.*

bas il (baz′əl), a sweet-smelling plant of the same family as mint, used in cooking. *n.*

ba sil i ca (bə sil′ə kə), 1 an oblong hall with a row of columns at each side and a structure in the shape of a half circle at one end. The Romans used such buildings for courts of law and

base (def. 8)—The base of figure A is a line; figure B, a triangle; figure C, a circle; figure D, a square.

public meetings. 2 church built in this form. *n., pl.* **ba sil i cas.**

bas i lisk (bas′ə lisk), 1 (in old stories) a reptile whose breath and look were thought to be fatal. It was supposed to be somewhat like a lizard and to have a black-and-yellow skin and fiery red eyes. 2 a tropical American lizard with a crest along its head and back which it can raise or lower. *n.*

ba sin (bā′sn), 1 a wide, shallow dish for holding liquids. 2 amount that a basin can hold: *They have used up a basin of water already.* 3 a shallow area containing water: *Part of the harbor is a basin for yachts.* 4 all the land drained by a river and the streams that flow into it: *The Mississippi basin extends from the Appalachians to the Rockies.* *n.*

ba sis (bā′sis), 1 thing or part on which anything is established or supported; foundation: *The basis of their friendship was a common interest in sports.* 2 the main part; base: *The basis of this medicine is an oil.* *n., pl.* **ba ses.**

bask (bask), 1 warm oneself pleasantly: *The cat basks before the fire.* 2 feel great pleasure: *He basked in the love of his family.* *v.*

bas ket (bas′kit), 1 container made of twigs, grasses, fibers, strips of wood, etc., woven together: *a clothes basket.* 2 amount that a basket holds: *We ate a basket of peaches.* 3 anything that looks like or is shaped like a basket: *This basket for waste paper is made of metal.* 4 net shaped like a basket open at the bottom, used as a goal in basketball. 5 score made in basketball by tossing the ball through the basket. *n.* **—bas′-ket like′,** *adj.*

bas ket ball (bas′kit bôl′), 1 game played with a large, round ball by two teams of five players each. The players try to toss the ball through a ring into a net shaped like a basket but open at the bottom. 2 ball used in this game. *n.*

bas ket ful (bas′kit ful), as much as a basket can hold. *n., pl.* **bas ket fuls.**

bas ket ry (bas′kə trē), 1 art of making baskets. 2 baskets. *n.*

bas-re lief (bä′ri lēf′), carving or sculpture in which the figures stand out only slightly from the background. *n.*

bass¹ (bās), 1 the lowest male voice in music. 2 singer with such a voice. 3 part in music for such a voice. 4 instrument playing such a part. 5 having a deep, low sound. 1-4 *n., pl.* **bass es;** 5 *adj.* [from *base²*, respelled under the influence of *basso*]

bass² (bas), any of various North American freshwater or saltwater fishes with spiny fins, used for food. *n., pl.* **bass es** or **bass.** [Old English *bærs* perch]

bass clef (bās), symbol in music

showing that the pitch of the notes on a staff is below middle C; F clef. See **clef** for diagram.

bass drum (bās), a large drum that makes a deep, low sound when struck on one or both of its heads.

bas set (bas′it), dog with short legs and a long body, like a dachshund, but larger and heavier. *n.*

bass horn (bās), tuba.

bas si net (bas′n et′), a baby's basket-like cradle, usually with a hood over one end. *n.*

bas so (bas′ō), singer with a bass voice. *n., pl.* **bas sos.** [from Italian]

bas soon (bə sün′), a deep-toned wind instrument with a doubled wooden body and a curved metal pipe to which a double reed is attached. *n.*

bass viol (bās), double bass.

bass wood (bas′wùd′), 1 the American linden tree. 2 its wood. *n.*

bast (bast), the tough fiber in the inner bark of certain trees, used in making rope, matting, etc. *n.*

bas tard (bas′tərd), child born of parents who are not married to each other. *n.*

baste[1] (bāst), drip or pour melted fat or butter on (meat, fowl, etc.) while roasting: *The cook basted the turkey to keep it from drying out. v.,* **bast ed, basting.** [origin unknown]

baste[2] (bāst), sew with long, loose stitches. These stitches are usually removed after the final sewing. *v.,* **basted, basting.** [from French of the 1400's *bastir*]

Bas tille (ba stēl′), an old fort in Paris used as a prison for enemies of the king. A mob captured and destroyed it on July 14, 1789, at the beginning of the French Revolution. *n.*

bas tion (bas′chən), 1 a part of a fortification that sticks out so that the defenders can fire at attackers from as many angles as possible. 2 stronghold; center of defense. *n.*

bat[1] (bat), 1 a stout wooden stick or club, used to hit the ball in baseball, cricket, etc. 2 hit with a bat; hit: *She bats well. I batted the balloon over to him with my hand.* 3 a turn at batting: *Who goes to bat first?* 4 a stroke; blow. 1,3,4 *n.,* 2 *v.,* **bat ted, bat ting.** [Old English *batt* cudgel]

at bat, in position to bat; having a turn at batting: *Our side is at bat.*

bat[2] (bat), a flying mammal with a body like that of a mouse and wings made of thin skin that are supported by the long, slim bones of the forelimbs. Bats fly at night. There are over 1000 species, with bodies varying in size from one and a half inches to twelve inches. Most of them eat insects but some live on fruit and a few suck the blood of other

mammals. *n.* [perhaps from a Scandinavian word of the 1200's] —**bat′-like′,** *adj.*

bat[3] (bat), INFORMAL. wink: *The ball nearly hit him, but he didn't bat an eye. v.,* **bat ted, bat ting.** [from French of the 1200's *batre* beat]

Ba taan (bə tan′), peninsula near Manila in the Philippines, where United States and Philippine troops surrendered to the Japanese in 1942. *n.*

batch (bach), 1 quantity of bread, cookies, etc., made at one baking. 2 quantity of anything made as one lot or set: *Our second batch of candy was better than the first.* 3 number of persons or things taken together: *We caught a fine batch of fish. n., pl.* **batch es.**

bat ed (bā′tid). **with bated breath,** holding the breath in great fear, wonder, interest, etc.: *We listened with bated breath to the exciting story. adj.*

bath (bath), 1 a washing of the body: *I took a hot bath.* 2 water in a tub for a bath: *Your bath is ready.* 3 tub, room, or other place for bathing. In ancient Rome, baths were often elaborate public buildings, which were also used as clubs. 4 liquid in which something is washed or dipped: *a bath for developing photographic film.* 5 container holding the liquid. *n., pl.* **baths** (baᵺz).

bathe (bāᵺ), 1 take a bath: *We wash our hair and bathe regularly.* 2 give a bath to: *He is bathing his dog.* 3 apply water to; wash or moisten with any liquid: *The doctor told her to bathe her eyes with the lotion.* 4 go swimming; go into a river, lake, ocean, etc., for pleasure or to get cool. 5 cover or surround: *The valley was bathed in sunlight. v.,* **bathed, bath ing.**

bath er (bā′ᵺər), 1 person who bathes. 2 swimmer. *n.*

bath house (bath′hous′), 1 house or building fitted out for bathing. 2 building containing dressing rooms for swimmers. *n., pl.* **bath hous es** (bath′hou′ziz).

bathing suit, garment worn for swimming.

bath robe (bath′rōb′), a long, loose garment worn to and from a bath or when resting or lounging. *n.*

bath room (bath′rüm′ or bath′rùm′), 1 room fitted out for taking baths, usually equipped with a sink and a toilet. 2 a room containing a toilet. *n.*

bath tub (bath′tub′), tub to bathe in, especially one permanently fixed in a bathroom. *n.*

bath y scaph (bath′ə skaf′), a diving craft consisting of a round steel chamber attached to a hull that can be navigated underwater to explore the depths of the sea. *n.*

hat, āge, fär; let, ēqual, tėrm;
it, īce; hot, ōpen, ôrder;
oil, out; cup, pùt, rüle; ch, child;
ng, long; sh, she; th, thin;
ᵺ, then; zh, measure;

ə represents *a* in about,
e in taken, *i* in pencil,
o in lemon, *u* in circus.

bath y sphere (bath′ə sfir′), a watertight steel ball with observation windows, lowered by cables from a ship to study the depths of the sea. *n.*

ba tik (bə tēk′), method of making designs on cloth by dyeing only a part at a time, the rest being protected by a removable coating of wax. *n.*

ba tiste (bə tēst′), a fine, thin cloth made of cotton, rayon, or wool. *n.*

ba ton (ba ton′), 1 the light stick or wand used by the leader of an orchestra, chorus, or band to indicate the beat and direct the performance. 2 staff or stick used as a symbol of office or authority. 3 a stick passed from runner to runner in a relay race. 4 a light, hollow metal rod twirled by a drum major or majorette as a showy display. *n.*

Bat on Rouge (bat′n rüzh′), capital of Louisiana, in the SE part.

ba tra chi an (bə trā′kē ən), a tailless amphibian. Frogs and toads are batrachians. *n.*

bats man (bats′mən), player whose turn it is to bat in cricket. *n., pl.* **bats men.**

bat tal ion (bə tal′yən), 1 military unit made up of two or more companies or batteries, usually commanded by a major or a lieutenant colonel. It is usually part of a group or a regiment. 2 any large group organized to act together: *A battalion of volunteers helped to rescue the flood victims. n.*

bat ten[1] (bat′n), 1 strip of wood: *The sailors nailed battens over the canvas on the ship's hatchway during the storm.* 2 fasten down with strips of wood. 1 *n.,* 2 *v.* [from French of the 1400's *batant,* from *batre* to beat]

bat ten[2] (bat′n), grow fat; thrive: *The cattle battened on the plentiful fodder. v.* [from a Scandinavian word of the 1200's, such as Icelandic *batna* improve]

bat ter[1] (bat′ər), strike with repeated blows so as to bruise, break, or get out of shape; pound: *The fireman battered down the door with a heavy ax. v.* [from French of the 1300's *batre* beat]

bat ter[2] (bat′ər), a liquid mixture of

adj. adjective		*n.* noun
adv. adverb		*prep.* preposition
conj. conjunction		*pron.* pronoun
interj. interjection		*v.* verb
sing. singular		*pl.* plural

flour, milk, eggs, etc., that becomes solid when cooked. Cakes, pancakes, and muffins are made from batter. *n.* [from French of the 1300's *bature* a beating]

bat ter³ (bat′ər), player whose turn it is to bat in baseball, cricket, etc. *n.* [*bat*¹ + *-er*¹]

bat tered (bat′ərd), damaged by hard use: *I found a battered old book in the office. The floor was worn and battered by many feet. adj.*

battlement (def. 1)

battering ram, 1 a heavy beam used in ancient warfare for battering down walls, gates, etc. Some battering rams had an iron piece in the shape of a ram's head mounted on a frame at one end. 2 any heavy object used to break down a door, wall, etc.

bat ter y (bat′ər ē), 1 container holding materials that produce electricity by chemical action; a single electric cell: *Most flashlights work on two batteries.* 2 set of two or more electric cells that produce electric current: *The car won't start because the battery is dead.* 3 any set of similar or connected things: *a battery of television cameras and microphones. If you want this job you will have to take a battery of tests.* 4 set of similar pieces of equipment, such as mounted guns, searchlights, mortars, etc., used as a unit. 5 a military unit of artillery, usually commanded by a captain. A battery corresponds to a company or troop in other branches of the army. 6 (in baseball) the pitcher and catcher together. 7 the unlawful beating of another person or any threatening touch to his clothes or body. *n., pl.* **bat ter ies.**

bat ting (bat′ing), cotton or wool pressed into thin layers, used to line comforters, quilts, etc. *n.*

bat tle (bat′l), 1 a fight between oppos-

ing armies, air forces, or navies: *The battle for the island lasted six months.* 2 fighting or warfare: *The soldier received his wounds in battle.* 3 any fight or contest: *The candidates fought a battle of words during the campaign.* 4 take part in a battle; fight; struggle; contend: *battle with wolves. The swimmer had to battle a strong current. Our team is battling for first place in hockey.* 1-3 *n.,* 4 *v.,* **bat tled, bat tling.**
join battle, begin to fight.

bat tle-ax or **bat tle-axe** (bat′l-aks′), ax with a broad blade, used in medieval times as a weapon in battle. *n., pl.* **bat tle-ax es.**

battle cry, 1 shout of soldiers rushing into or engaged in battle. 2 motto or slogan in any contest.

bat tle field (bat′l fēld′), place where a battle is fought or has been fought. *n.*

bat tle front (bat′l frunt′), place where the fighting between armies takes place; front. *n.*

bat tle ground (bat′l ground′), battlefield. *n.*

bat tle ment (bat′l mənt), 1 a low wall for defense at the top of a tower or wall having solid parts alternating with openings. Soldiers stood on a platform behind the wall and shot through the openings. 2 wall built like this for ornament. *n.*

bat tler (bat′lər), person who battles; warrior; fighter. *n.*

battle royal, 1 fight in which several take part; riot. 2 a long, hard fight. *pl.* **battles royal.**

bat tle ship (bat′l ship′), type of warship having the heaviest armor and the most powerful guns, last built during World War II. *n.*

bat ty (bat′ē), SLANG. crazy. *adj.,* **bat ti er, bat ti est.**

bau ble (bô′bəl), a showy trifle having no real value; trinket. *n.*

baulk (bôk), balk. *v., n.*

baux ite (bôk′sīt), a claylike mineral from which aluminum is obtained. *n.*

Ba var i a (bə ver′ē ə), state in S West Germany. In the past it has been a duchy, a kingdom, and a republic. *n.* —**Ba var′i an,** *n., adj.*

bawd y (bô′dē), not decent; lewd; obscene. *adj.,* **bawd i er, bawd i est.**

bawl (bôl), 1 shout or cry out in a noisy way: *a lost calf bawling for its mother.* 2 a shout at the top of one's voice. 3 weep loudly. 1,3 *v.,* 2 *n.*

bawl out, INFORMAL. scold loudly; reprimand: *She bawled me out for denting my bicycle.*

bay¹ (bā), part of a sea or lake extending into the land. A bay is usually smaller than a gulf and larger than a cove. *n.* [from French of the 1300's *baie,* from Latin *baia*]

bay² (bā), 1 a long, deep barking, especially by a large dog: *The hunters heard the distant bay of the hounds.* 2 to bark with long, deep sounds: *Dogs sometimes bay at the moon.* 3 a stand made to face or keep off an enemy or pursuers when escape is impossible: *The stag stood at bay against the hounds on the edge of the cliff.* 4 position of an enemy or pursuers thus faced or kept off: *The stag held the hounds at bay.* 1,3,4 *n.,* 2 *v.* [from French of the 1300's *abai* a barking]

bay³ (bā), a small evergreen tree with smooth, shiny leaves; laurel. Dried bay leaves are used for flavoring food. *n.* [from French of the 1300's *baie* berry, seed, from Latin *baca*]

bay⁴ (bā), 1 reddish-brown: *a bay horse.* 2 a reddish-brown horse with black mane and tail. 3 a reddish brown. 1 *adj.,* 2,3 *n.* [from French of the 1300's *bai* reddish brown, from Latin *badius*]

bay⁵ (bā), 1 space or division of a wall or building between columns, pillars, buttresses, etc. 2 bay window. 3 compartment in an airplane, especially one for carrying bombs. *n.* [from French of the 1300's *baée* an opening]

bay ber ry (bā′ber′ē), 1 a North American shrub with clusters of grayish-white berries coated with wax. Candles made from the wax of the berries burn with a pleasant fragrance. 2 one of the berries. *n., pl.* **bay ber ries.**

bay o net (bā′ə nit *or* bā′ə net′), 1 knife attached to the muzzle of a rifle. It may be detached and used as a separate hand weapon. 2 pierce or stab with a bayonet. 1 *n.,* 2 *v.*

bay ou (bī′ü), a marshy inlet or outlet of a lake, river, or gulf in the south central United States. The water in a bayou flows sluggishly and may even become stagnant. *n.*

bay window, window or set of windows projecting from a wall to form an alcove or small space in a room.

ba zaar or **ba zar** (bə zär′), 1 street or streets full of small shops and booths in Oriental countries. 2 place for the sale of many kinds of goods. 3 sale of things contributed by various people, held for some charity or other special purpose. *n.*

ba zoo ka (bə zü′kə), a portable gun for firing rockets at tanks. *n., pl.* **ba zoo kas.**

bbl., barrel. *pl.* **bbls.**

B.C., 1 before Christ. B.C. is used for times before the birth of Christ. A.D. is used for times after the birth of Christ. 350 B.C. is 100 years earlier than 250 B.C. From 20 B.C. to A.D. 50 is 70 years. 2 British Columbia.

be (bē). *He will be here all year. She tries*

to be good. *They will be punished.* v.,
was *or* were, been, be ing.

be-, *prefix.* **1** thoroughly; all around:
Bespatter = spatter thoroughly.
2 make; cause to seem: *Belittle = cause
to seem little.* **3** provide with: *Bespangle
= provide with spangles.* **4** at; on; to;
for; about; against: *Bewail = wail
about.* [Old English *be-,* a form of *bī*
by]

beach (bēch), **1** an almost flat shore of
sand or pebbles over which water
washes when high. **2** run (a boat)
ashore; pull up on the shore. **1** *n., pl.*
beach es; 2 *v.*

beach comb er (bēch′kō′mər), vagrant or loafer, especially on islands of
the Pacific. *n.*

beach head (bēch′hed′), the first position established by an invading army
on an enemy beach or shore to make
possible the landing of troops and supplies. *n.*

bea con (bē′kən), **1** fire or light used
as a signal to guide or warn. **2** marker,
signal light, or radio station that guides
aircraft and ships through fogs, storms,
etc. **3** a tall tower for a signal; lighthouse. *n.*

bead (bēd), **1** a small ball or bit of
glass, metal, etc., with a hole through it,
so that it can be strung on a thread with
others like it. **2 beads,** *pl.* **a** string of
beads. **b** string of beads for keeping
count in saying prayers; rosary. **3** put
beads on; ornament with beads. **4** any
small, round object like a drop or bubble: *Beads of sweat covered his forehead.* **5** piece of metal at the front end
of a gun to aim by. **1,2,4,5** *n.,* **3** *v.*
—bead′like′, *adj.*

draw a bead on, aim a gun at; take
aim at.

say one's beads, tell one's beads, *or*
count one's beads, say prayers, using
a rosary.

bead ed (bēd′id), **1** trimmed with
beads. **2** like beads. *adj.*

bead ing (bē′ding), **1** trimming made
of beads. **2** pattern or edge on woodwork, silver, etc., made of small
beads. *n.*

bea dle (bē′dl), a minor parish officer
whose duties include keeping order. *n.*

bead y (bē′dē), small, round, and
shiny: *The parakeet has beady eyes.*
adj., **bead i er, bead i est.**

bea gle (bē′gəl), a small hunting dog
with smooth hair, short legs, and drooping ears. *n.*

beak (bēk), **1** bill of a bird. Eagles and
hawks have strong, hooked beaks that
are useful in striking or tearing. **2** a
similar part in other animals. Turtles
and octopuses have beaks. **3** anything
shaped like a beak, such as the projecting prow of an ancient warship or the

spout of a pitcher, jug, etc. *n.* **—beak′-
like′,** *adj.*

beak er (bē′kər), **1** a large cup or
drinking glass with a wide mouth. **2** a
thin glass or metal cup used in laboratories. A beaker has a flat bottom, no
handle, and a small lip for pouring. *n.*

beam (bēm), **1** a large, long piece of
timber, iron, or steel, for use in building.
2 the main horizontal support of a
building or ship. **3** any long piece or
bar: *The beam of a balance supports a
pair of scales.* **4** ray or rays of light: *The
beam from the flashlight showed a
kitten.* **5** send out rays of light; shine.
6 a bright look or smile. **7** look or smile
brightly: *Her face beamed with delight.*
8 a radio signal directed in a straight
line, used to guide aircraft, ships, etc.
9 direct (a broadcast): *A program was
beamed at Russia.* **10** the widest part of
a ship: *This ship has a thirty-foot beam.*
1-4,6,8,10 *n.,* **5,7,9** *v.*

on the beam, 1 (of an aircraft) in the
right path, as indicated by the directing
radio signals: *The plane drifted off
course but very soon got back on the
beam.* **2** SLANG. just right: *Your answer
is on the beam.*

beam ing (bē′ming), **1** shining; bright.
2 looking or smiling brightly; cheerful.
adj. **—beam′ing ly,** *adv.*

bean (bēn), **1** a smooth, somewhat flat
seed used as a vegetable. Lima beans,
kidney beans, and navy beans are three
different varieties of beans. **2** the long
pod containing such seeds. The green or
yellow pods of some varieties are also
used as a vegetable. **3** plant that beans
grow on. **4** any seed shaped somewhat
like a bean. Coffee beans are seeds of
the coffee plant. *n.* **—bean′like′,** *adj.*

bean bag (bēn′bag′), a small bag
partly filled with dry beans, used to toss
in play. *n.*

bean stalk (bēn′stôk′), stem of a bean
plant. *n.*

bear¹ (ber *or* bar), **1** carry or support;
hold up: *It took two of us to bear that
stone. The ice is too thin to bear your
weight.* **2** put up with; endure: *She can't
bear the noise. He cannot bear any more
pain.* **3** bring forth; produce: *This tree
bears fine apples. That tree is too young
to bear.* **4** give birth to: *Our cat will
soon bear kittens. She was born on May
15.* **5** act in a certain way; behave;
conduct: *The President bore himself
with great dignity.* **6** hold in mind; hold:
bear a grudge, bear affection. **7** move;
go: *The ship bore north.* **8** take on
oneself as a duty: *bear the cost, bear the
responsibility.* *v.,* **bore, borne** *or*
born, bear ing. [Old English *beran*]

bear down *or* **bear down on, 1** put
pressure on; press down: *The lead will
break if you bear down too hard on your*

hat, āge, fär; let, ēqual, tėrm;
it, īce; hot, ōpen, ôrder;
oil, out; cup, pùt, rüle; ch, child;
ng, long; sh, she; th, thin;
ŦH, then; zh, measure;

ə represents *a* in about,
e in taken, *i* in pencil,
o in lemon, *u* in circus.

---

pencil. **2** put all one's efforts on; try
hard: *I bore down on my homework and
got it done on time.* **3** move toward;
approach: *The hunters bore down on the
wounded animal.*

bear on, have an effect on; have something to do with: *Your story does not
bear on the question.*

bear out, back up; support; prove: *The
facts bear out her claim.*

bear up, keep one's courage; not lose
hope or faith: *bear up under troubles.*

bear with, put up with; be patient
with: *Please bear with me while I ask
some questions.*

bear² (ber *or* bar), **1** a large mammal
with thick, coarse fur and a very short
tail. A bear walks flat on the soles of its
feet. The black bear, brown bear,
grizzly bear, and polar bear are four
kinds of bears. **2** a gruff or surly person. *n.* [Old English *bera*] **—bear′-
like′,** *adj.*

bear a ble (ber′ə bəl *or* bar′ə bəl), that
can be endured. *adj.*

bear a bly (ber′ə blē *or* bar′ə blē), in a
way that can be endured; tolerably.
adv.

bear bait ing (ber′bā′ting *or* bar′-
bā′ting), sport of setting dogs to fight a
chained bear, now forbidden by law. *n.*

beard (bird), **1** the hair growing on a
man's chin and cheeks. **2** something
resembling or suggesting this. The chin
tuft of a goat is a beard; so are the stiff
hairs around the beak of a bird, or hairs
on the heads of plants like oats, barley,
and wheat. **3** face boldly; defy: *beard
the lion in his den.* **1,2** *n.,* **3** *v.*
—beard′like′, *adj.*

Beard (bird), **Daniel Carter,** 1850-
1941, American naturalist who founded
the Boy Scouts of America in 1910. *n.*

beard ed (bir′did), having a beard.
adj.

beard less (bird′lis), **1** without a
beard. **2** young or immature. *adj.*

bear er (ber′ər *or* bar′ər), **1** person or
thing that carries. **2** person who holds
or presents a check, draft, or note for
payment. **3** tree or plant that produces
fruit or flowers. *n.*

bear ing (ber′ing *or* bar′ing), **1** way of

bearish

adj.	adjective	*n.*	noun
adv.	adverb	*prep.*	preposition
conj.	conjunction	*pron.*	pronoun
interj.	interjection	*v.*	verb
sing.	singular	*pl.*	plural

standing, sitting, walking, or behaving; manner: *A general should have a military bearing.* 2 connection in thought or meaning; relation: *His foolish question has no bearing on the problem.* 3 **bearings,** *pl.* position in relation to other things; direction: *Having no compass, we got our bearings from the stars.* 4 part of a machine on which another part moves. A bearing serves to support the moving part and to reduce friction by turning with the motion. See **ball bearing** for diagram. *n.*

bear ish (ber′ish *or* bar′ish), like a bear in manner or temper; rough or surly. *adj.* —**bear′ish ly,** *adv.* —**bear′ish ness,** *n.*

bear skin (ber′skin′ *or* bar′skin′), 1 the skin of a bear with the fur on it. 2 rug, blanket, or the like made from this. 3 a tall, black fur cap worn by some soldiers and drum majors, especially in the British Army. *n.*

beast (bēst), 1 any four-footed animal. Lions, bears, cows, and horses are beasts. 2 a coarse, dirty, or brutal person. *n.* —**beast′like′,** *adj.*

beast li ness (bēst′lē nis), beastly condition, behavior, or quality. *n.*

beast ly (bēst′lē), 1 like a beast; coarse, dirty, or brutal; vile. 2 INFORMAL. very bad or irritating; unpleasant: *I have a beastly headache.* 3 INFORMAL. very; unpleasantly. 1,2 *adj.,* **beast li er, beast li est;** 3 *adv.*

beast of burden, animal used for carrying or pulling heavy loads.

beast of prey, animal that kills other animals for food.

beat (bēt), 1 strike again and again: *I beat the rug to get the dust out.* 2 stroke or blow made again and again: *the beat of a drum.* 3 get the better of; defeat; overcome: *Their team beat ours by a huge score.* 4 make flat: *The jeweler beat gold into thin strips with a hammer.* 5 mix by stirring or striking with a fork, spoon, or other utensil: *I beat the eggs for a cake.* 6 move up and down; flap: *The bird beat its wings.* 7 to throb: *Her heart beats fast with joy.* 8 a throb: *the beat of the heart.* 9 make a sound by being struck: *The drums beat loudly.* 10 unit of time or accent in music: *three beats to a measure. The good dancer never missed a beat.* 11 mark time with

drumsticks or by tapping with the hands, fingers, or feet. 12 stroke of the hand, baton, etc., showing a musical beat. 13 a regular round or route taken by a policeman or watchman. 14 go through in a hunt: *The men beat the woods in search of the lost child.* 15 move against the wind by a zigzag course: *The sailboat beat along the coast.* 16 INFORMAL. worn out; tired; exhausted. 1,3-7,9,11,14,15 *v.,* beat, **beat en** or **beat, beat ing;** 2,8,10,12, 13 *n.,* 16 *adj.*

beat back, force or push back: *The policemen beat back the rioting crowd.*

beat down, INFORMAL. force to set a lower price.

beat off, drive away by blows: *He beat off the savage dog.*

beat en (bēt′n), 1 whipped; struck: *The beaten dog ran away from its master.* 2 much walked on or traveled: *a beaten path across the grass.* 3 defeated; overcome: *a beaten army.* 4 exhausted. 5 shaped by blows of a hammer: *This bowl is made of beaten silver.* 6 a past participle of **beat.** *Our team was beaten in football on Saturday.* 1-5 *adj.,* 6 *v.*

beat er (bē′tər), 1 person or thing that beats. 2 man hired to rouse game during a hunt. 3 device or utensil for beating eggs, cream, etc. *n.*

be a tif ic (bē′ə tif′ik), showing very great happiness; blissful. *adj.*

be at i fi ca tion (bē at′ə fə kā′shən), 1 a making or a being made blessed. 2 declaration by a decree of the pope that a dead person is among the blessed in heaven and deserves religious honor. *n.*

be at i fy (bē at′ə fī), 1 make supremely happy; bless. 2 declare by a decree of the pope that a dead person is among the blessed in heaven. *v.,* **be at i fied, be at i fy ing.**

beat ing (bē′ting), 1 act of one that beats; a striking. 2 punishment by blows; whipping; thrashing. 3 state of being beaten; defeat. 4 throbbing. *n.*

be at i tude (bē at′ə tüd *or* bē at′ə tyüd), 1 supreme happiness; bliss. 2 a blessing. 3 **the Beatitudes,** (in the Bible) the eight verses in the Sermon on the Mount which begin with "Blessed," as "Blessed are the poor in spirit." *n.*

beat nik (bēt′nik), a young person who rejects conventions and accepted standards by adopting unusual dress, speech, etc. *n.*

beau (bō), 1 a young man courting a young woman; suitor or lover. 2 man who pays much attention to the way he dresses and to the fashion of his clothes; dandy. *n., pl.* **beaus** or **beaux.**

Beau fort scale (bō′fərt), scale of

wind velocities, ranging from 0 (calm) to 17 (hurricane), used in weather maps. [from Sir Francis *Beaufort,* 1774-1857, British admiral who devised it]

beau geste (bō zhest′), FRENCH. a graceful or kindly act. *pl.* **beaux gestes** (bō zhest′).

beau te ous (byü′tē əs), beautiful. *adj.* —**beau′te ous ly,** *adv.* —**beau′te ous ness,** *n.*

beau ti fi ca tion (byü′tə fə kā′shən), a making beautiful or more beautiful; beautifying. *n.*

beau ti ful (byü′tə fəl), very pleasing to see or hear; delighting the mind or senses. *adj.* —**beau′ti ful ly,** *adv.* —**beau′ti ful ness,** *n.*

beau ti fy (byü′tə fī), make beautiful; make more beautiful: *Flowers beautify a room.* *v.,* **beau ti fied, beau ti fy ing.**

beau ty (byü′tē), 1 good looks: *The child had beauty and intelligence.* 2 quality that pleases in flowers, pictures, music, etc. 3 something beautiful: *the beauties of nature.* 4 a beautiful woman. *n., pl.* **beau ties.**

beauty shop or **beauty parlor,** place where women have their hair, skin, and nails cared for.

beaux (bōz), a plural of **beau.** *n.*

bea ver¹ (bē′vər), 1 a large rodent with soft fur, a broad, flat tail, and feet adapted to swimming. Beavers live both in water and on land and build dams across streams. 2 its soft brown fur. *n.* [Old English *beofor*] —**bea′ver like′,** *adj.*

beaver¹ (def. 1)   beaver²

bea ver² (bē′vər), the movable lower part of a helmet, protecting the chin and mouth. *n.* [from French of the 1400's *baviere* bib]

be calmed (bi kämd′ *or* bi kälmd′), kept from moving because there is no wind: *The sailboat lay becalmed on the lake. adj.*

be came (bi kām′), past tense of **become.** *The seed became a plant. v.*

be cause (bi kôz′), for the reason that; since: *Because we were late, we ran the whole way home. conj.*

because of, by reason of; on account of: *The game was called off because of rain.*

beck (bek), motion of the head or hand meant as a call or command. *n.*

74

at one's beck and call, 1 ready whenever wanted. **2** under one's complete control.

Beck et (bek/it), **Saint Thomas à,** 1118?-1170, archbishop of Canterbury. He was murdered in the cathedral for resisting the policies of Henry II of England. *n.*

beck on (bek/ən), signal by motion of the head or hand: *He beckoned me to follow him. v.*

be cloud (bi kloud/), **1** hide by a cloud or clouds. **2** make obscure; hide: *Too many big words becloud the meaning. v.*

be come (bi kum/), **1** come to be; grow to be: *It is becoming colder. I became tired and fell asleep.* **2** seem proper or fitting for: *It does not become you to brag about your grades.* **3** look well on; suit: *A white dress becomes her. v.,* **be came, be come, be com ing.**

become of, happen to: *What has become of the box of candy?*

be com ing (bi kum/ing), **1** fitting; suitable: *the high moral character becoming to a judge.* **2** pleasant to look at; attractive: *Her white dress is very becoming. adj.* —**be com/ing ly,** *adv.*

Becque rel rays (bek rel/), the invisible rays given off by radium, uranium, and other radioactive substances. [from Antoine *Becquerel,* 1852-1908, French physicist who first reported these rays]

bed (bed), **1** anything to sleep or rest on. A bed usually consists of a mattress raised upon a support and covered with sheets and blankets. **2** any place where people or animals sleep or rest: *The cat made his bed by the fireplace.* **3** provide with a bed; put to bed; go to bed: *The farmer bedded down his horse with straw.* **4** a flat base on which anything rests; foundation: *They set the pole in a bed of concrete.* **5** the ground under a body of water: *The bed of the river was muddy.* **6** piece of ground in a garden in which plants are grown: *a bed of tulips.* **7** plant in a garden bed: *These tulips should be bedded in rich soil.* **8** layer; stratum: *a bed of coal deep in the earth.* **1,2,4-6,8** *n.,* **3,7** *v.,* **bed ded, bed ding.**

be daub (bi dôb/), **1** smear with something dirty or sticky. **2** ornament in a gaudy or showy way. *v.*

be daz zle (bi daz/əl), dazzle completely; confuse by dazzling. *v.,* **be daz zled, be daz zling.**

bed bug (bed/bug/), a small, flat, reddish-brown insect that sucks blood, found in houses and especially in beds. Its bite is painful. *n.*

bed cham ber (bed/chām/bər), bedroom. *n.*

bed clothes (bed/klōz/ or bed/-klōŦHz/), sheets, blankets, quilts, etc. *n.pl.*

bed ding (bed/ing), **1** bedclothes. **2** material for beds: *Straw is used as bedding for cows and horses. n.*

be deck (bi dek/), adorn; decorate. *v.*

be dev il (bi dev/əl), **1** trouble greatly; torment: *Biting flies bedeviled the horses.* **2** confuse completely; muddle. *v.*

be dew (bi dü/ or bi dyü/), wet with dew or drops like dew: *cheeks bedewed with tears. v.*

bed fast (bed/fast/), confined to bed; bedridden. *adj.*

bed fel low (bed/fel/ō), **1** sharer of one's bed. **2** associate. *n.*

be di zen (bi dī/zn or bi diz/n), dress or ornament with showy finery. *v.*

bed lam (bed/ləm), **1** noisy confusion; uproar: *When our team won, there was bedlam in the gym.* **2** OLD USE. insane asylum; madhouse. *n.* [from *Bedlam,* old name for Saint Mary of *Bethlehem,* a hospital for the insane in London]

Bed ou in (bed/ü ən), **1** member of certain tribes of wandering Arabs who live in the deserts of Arabia, Syria, and northern Africa. **2** any wanderer or nomad. *n.*

be drag gled (bi drag/əld), **1** wet and hanging limp: *She tried to comb her bedraggled hair.* **2** soiled by being dragged in the dirt. *adj.*

bed rid den (bed/rid/n), compelled to stay in bed for a long time because of sickness or weakness. *adj.*

bed rock (bed/rok/), **1** the solid rock under the soil and under looser rocks. **2** the lowest level; bottom. *n.*

bed roll (bed/rōl/), blankets or a sleeping bag that can be rolled up and tied for carrying. *n.*

bed room (bed/rüm/ or bed/rum/), a room to sleep in. *n.*

bed side (bed/sīd/), side of a bed: *The nurse sat by the sick woman's bedside. n.*

bed spread (bed/spred/), cover for a bed that is spread over the blankets to make it look neater. *n.*

bed spring (bed/spring/), set of springs forming part of a bed and supporting a mattress. *n.*

bed stead (bed/sted/), the wooden or metal framework of a bed that supports the springs and mattress. *n.*

bed time (bed/tīm/), time to go to bed: *My regular bedtime is nine o'clock. n.*

bee (bē), **1** insect with four wings and a hairy body, that gathers nectar and pollen from flowers and makes honey and wax; honeybee. Bees live in large, permanent colonies containing a queen, many workers, and drones. Only the queen and the workers have stings. See **bumblebee** for picture. **2** any of various related insects. There are over 20,000 species of bees in the world. **3** a

hat, āge, fär; let, ēqual, tėrm;
it, īce; hot, ōpen, ôrder;
oil, out; cup, pùt, rüle; ch, child;
ng, long; sh, she; th, thin;
ŦH, then; zh, measure;

ə represents *a* in about,
e in taken, *i* in pencil,
o in lemon, *u* in circus.

gathering for work or amusement: *a spelling bee, a quilting bee. n.*

bee bread (bē/bred/), a brownish, bitter substance consisting of pollen, or pollen mixed with honey, used by bees as food for their larvae or young. *n.*

beech (bēch), **1** tree with smooth, gray bark and glossy leaves. It bears a sweet nut which is good to eat. **2** its wood. *n., pl.* **beech es** or **beech** for 1.

beech nut (bēch/nut/), the small, triangular nut of the beech tree. *n.*

beef (bēf), **1** meat from a steer, cow, or bull. **2** steer, cow, or bull when full-grown and fattened for food. **3** SLANG. complain. **4** SLANG. complaint. **1,2,4** *n., pl.* **beeves** for 2, **beefs** for 4; **3** *v.*

beef up, SLANG. make greater; enlarge; strengthen: *The company plans to beef up benefits to retired workers.*

beef cattle, cattle raised for meat.

beef steak (bēf/stāk/), slice of beef for broiling or frying. *n.*

beef y (bē/fē), strong, solid, and heavy. *adj.,* **beef i er, beef i est.**

bee hive (bē/hīv/), **1** hive or house for bees. **2** a busy, swarming place. *n.*

bee keep er (bē/kē/pər), person who raises bees for their honey. *n.*

bee line (bē/līn/), the straightest way between two places, like the flight of a bee to its hive. *n.*

Be el ze bub (bē el/zə bub), **1** (in the Bible) the Devil; Satan. **2** a devil. *n.*

been (bin), past participle of **be.** *He has been ill. The books have been read by everyone in the room. v.*

beep (bēp), **1** a sharp, short sound. **2** cause to make sharp, short sounds. **1** *n.,* **2** *v.*

beer (bir), **1** an alcoholic drink made from malted barley flavored with hops. **2** a soft drink made from roots or plants, such as root beer. *n.*

bees wax (bēz/waks/), wax given out by bees, from which they make their honeycomb. *n.*

beet (bēt), **1** plant grown for its thick, fleshy root. The leaves are sometimes eaten as greens. **2** its root. Red beets are eaten as vegetables. Sugar is made from white beets. *n.* —**beet/like/,** *adj.*

adj.	adjective	*n.*	noun
adv.	adverb	*prep.*	preposition
conj.	conjunction	*pron.*	pronoun
interj.	interjection	*v.*	verb
sing.	singular	*pl.*	plural

Bee tho ven (bā'tō vən), **Ludwig van,** 1770-1827, German composer. *n.*

bee tle (bē'tl), 1 insect that has its front pair of wings modified as hard, shiny cases that cover the delicate rear pair of wings when at rest. There are over 250,000 species of beetles, which vary in size from that of a pinhead to nearly that of a man's fist. 2 insect resembling a beetle. *n.*

beetle (def. 1)
three types at about life size:
A, ladybug; B, firefly; C, June bug

beet ling (bēt'ling), sticking out; projecting; overhanging: *the beetling edge of a cliff, beetling eyebrows. adj.*

beeves (bēvz), plural of **beef** (def. 2). *Beeves are shipped from the farm to the city. n.*

be fall (bi fôl'), 1 happen to: *Be careful that no harm befalls you.* 2 happen: *Whatever befell, the family held together. v.,* **be fell, be fall en, be fall ing.**

be fall en (bi fô'lən), past participle of **befall.** *An accident must have befallen them. v.*

be fell (bi fel'), past tense of **befall.** *Evil befell the knight upon his lonely trip. v.*

be fit (bi fit'), be suitable for; be proper for; suit: *He always wears clothes that befit the occasion. v.,* **be fit ted, be fit ting.**

be fog (bi fog'), 1 surround with fog; make foggy. 2 make obscure; confuse. *v.,* **be fogged, be fog ging.**

be fore (bi fôr'), 1 earlier than: *Come before five o'clock.* 2 earlier: *Come at five o'clock, not before.* 3 until now; in the past: *You were never late before.* 4 in front of; ahead of: *Walk before me.* 5 in front; ahead: *The scout went before to see if the trail was safe.* 6 rather than; sooner than: *I will starve before giving in* (prep.). *I will starve before I give in*

(conj.). 7 previous to the time when: *I would like to talk to her before she goes.* 1,4,6 prep., 2,3,5 adv., 6,7 conj.

be fore hand (bi fôr'hand), ahead of time; in advance: *I am going to get everything ready beforehand* (adv.). *Aren't you a little beforehand with your request for your allowance?* (adj.). adv., adj.

be friend (bi frend'), act as a friend to; help: *The policeman befriended the lost boy. v.*

be fud dle (bi fud'l), stupefy; confuse. *v.,* **be fud dled, be fud dling.**

be fud dle ment (bi fud'l mənt), a befuddling; confusion. *n.*

beg (beg), 1 ask for (food, money, clothes, etc.) as a charity: *The tramp begged his meals. Must I beg for a living?* 2 ask a favor; ask earnestly or humbly: *I beg you to forgive me. The children begged for a ride on the pony.* 3 ask politely and courteously: *I beg your pardon. v.,* **begged, beg ging.**

beg off, make an excuse for not being able to keep a promise: *Although he had promised to come to my party, he begged off because of a headache.*

go begging, find no one that will accept.

be gan (bi gan'), past tense of **begin.** *Snow began to fall early in the evening. v.*

be gat (bi gat'), OLD USE. begot; a past tense of **beget.** *v.*

be get (bi get'), 1 be the father of. 2 cause to be; produce: *Hate begets hate and love begets love. v.,* **be got, be got ten** or **be got, be get ting.**

beg gar (beg'ər), 1 person who lives by begging. 2 a very poor person; pauper. 3 bring to poverty: *Your reckless spending will beggar your family.* 4 go beyond; outdo: *The grandeur of Niagara Falls beggars description.* 1,2 n., 3,4 v.

beg gar ly (beg'ər lē), fit for a beggar; poor. *adj.*

be gin (bi gin'), 1 do the first part; make a start: *When shall we begin? I began reading the book yesterday.* 2 come or bring into being: *The club began two years ago. Five people began the club two years ago.* 3 be near; come near: *Your big brother's suit wouldn't even begin to fit you. v.,* **be gan, be gun, be gin ning.**

be gin ner (bi gin'ər), person who is doing something for the first time; person who lacks skill and experience: *You skate well for a beginner. n.*

be gin ning (bi gin'ing), 1 a start: *Make a good beginning.* 2 time when anything begins: *"In the beginning God created the heaven and the earth."* 3 first part: *I have enjoyed this book from beginning to end.* 4 first cause;

source; origin: *The idea of the airplane had its beginning in the flight of birds.* 5 that begins: *This is the beginning lesson of the spelling book.* 1-4 n., 5 adj.

be gone (bi gôn'), go away: *"Begone!" said the prince (interj.). The prince bade him begone (v.). interj., v.*

be go nia (bi gō'nyə), a tropical plant often grown for its large, richly colored leaves and waxy flowers. *n., pl.* **be go nias.**

be got (bi got'), past tense and a past participle of **beget.** *He begot a son. v.*

be got ten (bi got'n), a past participle of **beget.** *He has begotten two sons. v.*

be grudge (bi gruj'), 1 give or allow (something) unwillingly; grudge: *She is so stingy that she begrudges her dog a bone.* 2 envy: *The neighbors begrudge us our swimming pool. v.,* **be grudged, be grudg ing.** —**be grudg'ing ly,** adv.

be guile (bi gīl'), 1 trick or mislead (a person); deceive; cheat: *His flattery beguiled me into thinking that he was my friend.* 2 win the attention of; entertain; amuse: *The playful puppies beguiled the children with their antics.* 3 while away (time) pleasantly: *I read a book to beguile the hours on the long trip. v.,* **be guiled, be guil ing.**

be gun (bi gun'), past participle of **begin.** *It has begun to rain. v.*

be half (bi haf'), side, interest, or favor: *Her friends will act in her behalf. n.*

in behalf of or **on behalf of,** in the interest of; for: *I am speaking in behalf of my friend.*

be have (bi hāv'), 1 manage, handle, or conduct (oneself); act: *You behaved yourself well during the whole trip. The small ship behaved badly in the storm.* 2 act properly; do what is right: *If you behave today, we can come here again. v.,* **be haved, be hav ing.**

be hav ior (bi hā'vyər), manner of behaving; way of acting: *His sullen behavior showed that he was angry. The little boat's behavior was perfect on the trial trip. n.*

be head (bi hed'), cut off the head of. *v.*

be held (bi held'), past tense and past participle of **behold.** *The little child beheld the approaching storm with fear. You have all beheld beautiful sunsets. v.*

be he moth (bi hē'məth), 1 (in the Bible) a huge and powerful animal. It may have been the hippopotamus. 2 anything very large and powerful. *n.*

be hest (bi hest'), command; order: *I am ready to act at your behest. n.*

be hind (bi hīnd'), 1 at the back of; in the rear of: *Stand behind me.* 2 at the back; in the rear: *The dog's tail hung down behind.* 3 in support of; supporting: *Your friends are behind you.* **4** farther back: *The rest of the hikers are still quite a ways behind.* **5** later than: *The milkman is behind his usual time today.* **6** not on time; late: *The class is behind in its work.* **7** inferior to; less advanced than: *The boy who was sick is behind the others in his class in school.* 1,3,5,7 *prep.*, 2,4,6 *adv.*

be hind hand (bi hīnd′hand′), **1** behind time; late: *We can't wait for those who are behindhand* (adj.). *She handed her assignment in behindhand* (adv.). **2** behind others in progress: *She is behindhand in her schoolwork.* *adj., adv.*

be hold (bi hōld′), look at; see; observe: *They wanted to behold the sunrise* (v.). *Behold! the king!* (interj.). *v.,* **be held, be hold ing;** *interj.*

be hold en (bi hōl′dən), under obligation; in debt: *I am much beholden to you for your help.* *adj.*

be hold er (bi hōl′dər), onlooker; spectator. *n.*

be hoove (bi hüv′), **1** be necessary for: *It behooves you to work hard if you want to keep this job.* **2** be proper for: *It behooves a child to obey his parents.* *v.,* **be hooved, be hoov ing.**

beige (bāzh), **1** pale-brown. **2** a pale brown. 1 *adj.,* 2 *n.*

be ing (bē′ing), **1** present participle of **be.** *The dog is being fed. Being hungry, he eats much.* **2** person; living creature: *Men, women, and children are human beings.* **3** life; existence: *The world came into being long ago.* 1 *v.,* 2,3 *n.*

Bei rut (bā rüt′), capital and chief seaport of Lebanon, on the Mediterranean. *n.*

be la bor (bi lā′bər), **1** beat vigorously; thrash:*The rider belabored his tired horse with a stick.* **2** set upon with too much talk, advice, etc.: *Rip Van Winkle's wife belabored him for being lazy.* *v.*

be lat ed (bi lā′tid), happening or coming late; delayed: *Your belated letter has arrived at last.* *adj.* —**be lat′ed ly,** *adv.* —**be lat′ed ness,** *n.*

be lay (bi lā′), **1** fasten (a rope) by winding it around a pin or cleat. **2** "Belay!" is used by sailors to mean "stop!" "*Belay that and listen!*" *the first mate shouted.* *v.*

belaying pin, pin around which ropes on shipboard can be wound and fastened.

belch (belch), **1** throw out gas from the stomach through the mouth. **2** throw out with force: *The volcano belched fire, smoke, and ashes.* **3** a belching. 1,2 *v.,* 3 *n., pl.* **belch es.**

bel dam or **bel dame** (bel′dəm), an ugly old woman; hag; witch. *n.*

be lea guer (bi lē′gər), **1** surround with troops; besiege: *Cornwallis was*

beleaguered at Yorktown. **2** surround; beset: *Our cities are beleaguered by problems.* *v.*

Bel fast (bel′fast), capital of Northern Ireland, a seaport on the E coast. *n.*

bel fry (bel′frē), **1** tower for a bell or bells. **2** space in a tower in which a bell or bells may be hung. *n., pl.* **bel fries.**

belfry
(defs. 1 and 2)

Bel gian (bel′jən), **1** person born or living in Belgium. **2** of Belgium or its people. 1 *n.,* 2 *adj.*

Belgian hare, a large, reddish-brown, domestic rabbit.

Bel gium (bel′jəm), small country in W Europe, north of France. *Capital:* Brussels. *n.*

Bel grade (bel′grād), capital of Yugoslavia, on the Danube. *n.*

be lie (bi lī′), **1** give a false idea of; misrepresent: *Her frown belied her usual good nature.* **2** fail to come up to; disappoint: *He stole again, and so belied our hopes.* *v.,* **be lied, be ly ing.**

be lief (bi lēf′), **1** what is held to be true or real; thing believed; opinion: *It was once a common belief that the earth is flat.* **2** acceptance as true or real: *His belief in ghosts makes him afraid of the dark.* **3** confidence in any person or thing; faith; trust: *The judge expressed his complete belief in the boy's honesty.* **4** religious faith; creed: *Most children follow the belief of their parents.* *n.*

be liev a ble (bi lē′və bəl), that can be believed. *adj.*

be lieve (bi lēv′), **1** think (something) is true or real: *Who doesn't believe that the earth is round?* **2** think (somebody) tells the truth: *Her friends believe her.* **3** have faith; trust: *We believe in our friends.* **4** think; suppose: *I believe we are going to have a test soon.* *v.,* **be lieved, be liev ing.**

be liev er (bi lē′vər), **1** person who believes. **2** follower of some religion. *n.*

be like (bi līk′), OLD USE. perhaps. *adv.*

be lit tle (bi lit′l), cause to seem little or unimportant; make less important: *Jealous people belittled the explorer's great discoveries.* *v.,* **be lit tled, be lit tling.**

bell (bel), **1** a hollow metal cup that makes a musical sound when struck by

a clapper or hammer. **2** anything that makes a ringing sound as a signal: *Did I hear the bell at the front door?* **3** stroke or sound of a bell: *Our teacher dismissed us before the bell.* **4** stroke of a bell used on shipboard to indicate a half hour of time. 1 bell = 12:30, 4:30, or 8:30; 2 bells = 1:00, 5:00, or 9:00; and so on up to 8 bells = 4:00, 8:00, or 12:00. **5** put a bell on: *We belled the cat.* **6** anything shaped like a bell. The flaring end of a funnel or of a musical wind instrument is a bell. **7** swell out like a bell. 1-4,6 *n.,* 5,7 *v.*

Bell (bel), **Alexander Graham,** 1847-1922, American scientist who invented the telephone. *n.*

bel la don na (bel′ə don′ə), **1** a poisonous plant of Europe with black berries and red, bell-shaped flowers; deadly nightshade. **2** drug made from this plant; atropine. *n., pl.* **bel la don nas** for 1.

bell boy (bel′boi′), man or boy whose work is carrying baggage and doing errands for the guests of a hotel or club; bellhop. *n.*

belle (bel), **1** a beautiful woman or girl. **2** the prettiest or most admired woman or girl: *She was the belle of the ball.* *n.*

bell hop (bel′hop′), bellboy. *n.*

bel li cose (bel′ə kōs), fond of fighting; warlike. *adj.*

bel lig er ence (bə lij′ər əns), **1** fondness for fighting; being warlike. **2** act of fighting; being at war. *n.*

bel lig er en cy (bə lij′ər ən sē), belligerence. *n.*

bel lig er ent (bə lij′ər ənt), **1** at war; engaged in war; fighting: *Great Britain and Germany were belligerent powers in 1941.* **2** nation or state engaged in war: *France and Germany were belligerents in World War II.* **3** fond of fighting; quarrelsome: *a belligerent neighborhood gang.* **4** person engaged in fighting with another person. 1,3 *adj.,* 2,4 *n.* —**bel lig′er ent ly,** *adv.*

bell jar, a bell-shaped container or cover made of glass, used in laboratories.

bel low (bel′ō), **1** make a loud, deep noise; roar as a bull does. **2** a loud, deep

adj.	adjective	*n.*	noun
adv.	adverb	*prep.*	preposition
conj.	conjunction	*pron.*	pronoun
interj.	interjection	*v.*	verb
sing.	singular	*pl.*	plural

noise; roar. 3 shout loudly, angrily, or with pain. 1,3 *v.*, 2 *n.*

bel lows (bel′ōz), 1 instrument for producing a strong current of air, used for blowing fires or sounding an organ, accordion, etc. 2 the folding part of some cameras, behind the lens. *n. sing. or pl.*

bellows (def. 1)
Air is sucked into the bellows as the sides are pulled apart. When the sides are pushed together, the valve closes and air is forced out the nozzle.

bell weth er (bel′weᴛʜ/ər), a male sheep that leads the flock, wearing a bell. *n.*

bel ly (bel′ē), 1 the lower part of the human body, which contains the stomach and intestines; abdomen. 2 the underpart of an animal's body. 3 stomach. 4 bulging part of anything, or the hollow in it: *the belly of a sail.* 5 swell out; bulge: *The sails bellied in the wind.* 1-4 *n.*, *pl.* **bel lies**; 5 *v.*, **bel lied, belly ing.**

be long (bi lông′), have one's or its proper place: *That book belongs on this shelf. v.*

belong to, 1 be the property of: *Does this cap belong to you?* 2 be a part of: *That top belongs to this box.* 3 be a member of: *She belongs to the Girl Scouts.*

be long ings (bi lông′ingz), things that belong to a person; possessions. *n.pl.*

be lov ed (bi luv′id *or* bi luvd′), 1 dearly loved; dear. 2 person who is loved; darling. 1 *adj.*, 2 *n.*

be low (bi lō′), 1 in a lower place; to a lower place: *From the airplane we could see the fields below.* 2 on a lower floor or deck; downstairs: *The sailor went below.* 3 lower than; under: *The dining room is below my bedroom.* 4 less than: *four degrees below zero.* 5 un-

worthy of: *below contempt.* 6 after or later in a book or article: *See the note below.* 7 below zero: *The temperature was five below last night.* 1,2,6,7 *adv.*, 3-5 *prep.*

belt (belt), 1 strip of leather, cloth, etc., fastened around the waist to hold in or support clothes or weapons. 2 put a belt around: *She belted her dress.* 3 fasten on with a belt: *He belted his sword.* 4 beat with a belt. 5 hit suddenly and hard: *The hitter belted the ball over the fence.* 6 any broad strip or band: *A belt of trees grew between the two fields.* 7 region having distinctive characteristics: *The cotton belt is the region where cotton is grown.* 8 an endless band that transfers motion from one wheel or pulley to another: *A belt connected to the motor moves the fan in an automobile.* 1,6-8 *n.*, 2-5 *v.*

be moan (bi mōn′), moan about; weep for; bewail. *v.*

be mused (bi myüzd′), 1 confused; bewildered. 2 absorbed in thought or daydreaming. *adj.*

Be na res (bə när′ēz), city in E India, on the Ganges River. It is a sacred city of the Hindus. *n.* Also, **Banaras.**

bench (bench), 1 a long seat, usually of wood or stone. 2 a strong, heavy table used by a carpenter, or by any worker with tools and materials: *On Saturdays my father works at his bench in the cellar.* 3 seat where judges sit in a court of law. 4 judge or group of judges sitting in a court of law: *Bring the prisoner before the bench.* 5 position as a judge: *He was appointed to the bench last year.* 6 take (a player) out of a game. 1-5 *n.*, *pl.* **bench es**; 6 *v.*

bench mark, mark made on a rock, post, etc., in surveying. It is used as a starting point or guide in a line of levels to determine altitudes.

bend (bend), 1 part that is not straight; curve; turn: *There is a sharp bend in the road here.* 2 be crooked; curve: *The branch began to bend as I climbed along it.* 3 force out of a straight line; make crooked; curve: *The strong man bent the iron bar as if it had been made of rubber.* 4 turn or move in a certain direction; direct: *His steps were bent toward home now. She bent her mind to her homework.* 5 stoop; bow: *She bent down and picked up a stone.* 6 submit: *I bend to God's will.* 7 force to submit: *The spirit of the rebels could not be bent.* 8 **the bends,** INFORMAL. cramps caused by changing too suddenly from an environment of high pressure to ordinary air pressure. 1,8 *n.*, 2-7 *v.*, **bent, bend ing.**

bend ed (ben′did), OLD USE. 1 bent. 2 a past tense and a past participle of **bend.** 1 *adj.*, 2 *v.*

be neath (bi nēth′), 1 in a lower place; below; underneath; under: *What you drop will fall upon the spot beneath* (*adv.*). *The dog sat beneath the tree* (*prep.*). 2 not even worthy of: *A traitor is so low that he is beneath contempt.* 1 *adv.*, 1,2 *prep.*

Ben e dict (ben′ə dikt), **Saint,** A.D. 480?-543?, Italian monk who founded the order of monks called the Benedictine order. *n.*

Ben e dic tine (ben′ə dik′tən *or* ben′ə dik′tēn′), 1 monk or nun following the rules of the order founded by Saint Benedict. 2 of Saint Benedict or his order. 1 *n.*, 2 *adj.*

belts (def. 8)
belts used to transmit power in different directions.

be ne dic tion (ben′ə dik′shən), 1 the asking of God's blessing at the end of a religious service. 2 blessing. *n.*

ben e fac tion (ben′ə fak′shən), gift for charity; help given for any good purpose. *n.*

ben e fac tor (ben′ə fak′tər), person who has given money or kindly help. *n.*

ben e fac tress (ben′ə fak′tris), a woman benefactor. *n.*, *pl.* **ben e factress es.**

ben e fice (ben′ə fis), a permanent office or position in the church consisting of a sacred duty and the income that goes with it. *n.*

be nef i cence (bə nef′ə səns), 1 a doing of good; kindness. 2 a kindly act; gift. *n.*

be nef i cent (bə nef′ə sənt), doing good; kind. *adj.* —**be nef′i cent ly,** *adv.*

ben e fi cial (ben′ə fish′əl), producing good; favorable; helpful: *Sunshine is beneficial to plants. adj.* —**ben′e fi′cial ly,** *adv.*

ben e fi ci ar y (ben′ə fish′ē er′ē), 1 person who receives benefit: *All the children are beneficiaries of the new playground.* 2 person who receives money or property from an insurance policy, a will, etc. *n.*, *pl.* **ben e fi ci ar ies.**

ben e fit (ben′ə fit), 1 anything which is for the good of a person or thing; advantage: *Good roads are of great benefit to travelers.* 2 do good to; be good for: *Rest will benefit a sick person.* 3 receive good; profit: *I benefited from the medicine. Your grades would benefit from better study habits.* 4 performance at the theater, a game, etc., to raise money for a worthy cause or person. 5 money paid to a sick or disabled person by an insurance company, government agency, or the like. 1,4,5 *n*., 2,3 *v*.

Ben e lux (ben′ə luks), an economic union of Belgium, the Netherlands, and Luxembourg organized in 1948. *n*.

be nev o lence (bə nev′ə ləns), 1 desire to promote the happiness of others; good will; kindly feeling. 2 act of kindness; something good that is done. *n*.

be nev o lent (bə nev′ə lənt), having a desire to promote the happiness of others; kindly; charitable. *adj*. —**be nev′o lent ly,** *adv*.

Ben gal (beng gôl′), 1 former province of India, in the NE part. Bengal is now divided into **West Bengal,** a part of India, and **East Bengal,** the country of Bangladesh. 2 of or from Bengal: *a Bengal tiger.* 3 **Bay of,** bay between India and Burma, part of the Indian Ocean. 1,3 *n*., 2 *adj*.

Ben gha zi or **Ben ga si** (ben gä′zē), one of the two capitals of Libya, on the Mediterranean. The other is Tripoli. *n*.

be night ed (bi nī′tid), being in darkness; ignorant. *adj*.

be nign (bi nīn′), 1 having a kind disposition; gracious: *a benign old woman with a friendly smile.* 2 favorable; mild: *Hawaii has a benign climate.* 3 not dangerous to health; not malignant: *a benign tumor. adj.* —**be nign′ly,** *adv*.

be nig nant (bi nig′nənt), 1 having or showing a kindly feeling toward others; benevolent: *The benignant king tried to gain the good will of his subjects.* 2 having a good effect; beneficial. *adj*. —**be nig′nant ly,** *adv*.

be nig ni ty (bi nig′nə tē), 1 kindliness; graciousness. 2 a kind act; favor. *n*., *pl*. **be nig ni ties.**

ben i son (ben′ə zən), blessing. *n*.

Ben ja min (ben′jə mən), 1 (in the Bible) the youngest son of Jacob. 2 one of the twelve tribes of Israel. *n*.

bent (bent), 1 past tense and past participle of **bend.** *I bent the wire.* 2 not straight; crooked; curved: *The farmer's back was bent from years of toil.* 3 determined: *She is bent on being a doctor.* 4 a natural inclination; tendency: *He has a decided bent for drawing.* 1 *v*., 2,3 *adj*., 4 *n*.

be numb (bi num′), make numb; deaden: *My fingers were benumbed by the cold. I was benumbed with fright when I got up to give my speech. v*.

Ben ze drine (ben′zə drēn′), trademark for a drug that causes wakefulness. *n*.

ben zene (ben′zēn′), a colorless liquid easily set on fire, obtained chiefly from coal tar; benzol. It is used for removing grease stains and in making dyes. *n*.

ben zine (ben′zēn′), a colorless liquid easily set on fire, obtained in distilling petroleum. It is used in clean-

ing and dyeing and as a motor fuel. *n*.

ben zo ate of soda (ben′zō āt), a white, crystalline or powdery salt of benzoic acid, used in medicine and to preserve foods.

ben zo ic acid (ben zō′ik), acid occurring in benzoin, cranberries, etc., used in medicine and to preserve foods.

ben zo in (ben′zō ən), a fragrant resin obtained from certain species of trees of southeastern Asia, used in perfumes and medicine. *n*.

ben zol (ben′zōl), benzene. *n*.

be queath (bi kwēᴛʜ′), 1 give or leave by means of a will when one dies: *The farmer bequeathed the farm to his son.* 2 hand down; pass along: *One age bequeaths its knowledge to the next. v*.

be quest (bi kwest′), 1 something bequeathed; legacy: *When she died she left a bequest of ten thousand dollars to her niece.* 2 act of bequeathing. *n*.

be rate (bi rāt′), scold sharply; upbraid. *v*., **be rat ed, be rat ing.**

Ber ber (bėr′bər), 1 member of a group of Moslem tribes living in northern Africa, west of Egypt. 2 their language. *n*.

be reave (bi rēv′), leave desolate and alone; deprive: *The family was bereaved by the death of the father. v*., **bereaved** or **be reft, be reav ing.**

be reave ment (bi rēv′mənt), 1 loss of a relative or friend by death. 2 bereaved condition; great loss: *We sympathized with the widow in her bereavement. n*.

be reft (bi reft′), 1 deprived: *Bereft of hope and friends, the old man led a lonely life.* 2 a past tense and a past participle of **bereave.** *He was bereft by the loss of his son.* 1 *adj*., 2 *v*.

be ret (bə rā′), a soft, flat, round cap of wool, felt, etc., with no visor. *n*.

berg (bėrg), iceberg. *n*.

Ber gen (bėr′gən), seaport in SW Norway. *n*.

be rib boned (bi rib′ənd), decorated with many ribbons or medals. *adj*.

ber i ber i (ber′ē ber′ē), disease affecting the nervous system, accompanied by weakness and extreme loss of weight. It is caused by lack of vitamin B₁ in the diet. *n*.

Ber ing Sea (bir′ing or ber′ing), N portion of the Pacific, between Alaska and Siberia. See **Aleutian Islands** for map.

Bering Strait, strait between the Bering Sea and the Arctic Ocean.

Ber ke ley (bėr′klē), city in W California, near San Francisco. *n*.

ber ke li um (bėr′klē əm or bėr′kē′-lē əm), a metallic element produced artificially from americium, curium, or plutonium. *n*. [from *Berkeley,* California, where it was first produced]

hat, āge, fär; let, ēqual, tėrm;
it, īce; hot, ōpen, ôrder;
oil, out; cup, pût, rüle; ch, child;
ng, long; sh, she; th, thin;
ᴛʜ, then; zh, measure;

ə represents *a* in about,
e in taken, *i* in pencil,
o in lemon, *u* in circus.

Berk shires (bėrk′shərz), range of hills in W Massachusetts. *n.pl*.

Ber lin (bər lin′), former capital of Germany. Berlin is now divided into West Berlin, which belongs to West Germany, and East Berlin, the capital of East Germany. *n*.

Ber li oz (ber′lē ōz), **Hector,** 1803-1869, French composer. *n*.

Ber mu da (bər myü′də), group of British islands off the coast of the United States, in the N Atlantic. *n*.

Bermuda shorts, short trousers that end an inch or two above the knee.

Bern or **Berne** (bėrn), capital of Switzerland, in the W part. *n*.

ber ry (ber′ē), 1 any small, juicy fruit with many seeds. Strawberries and raspberries are berries. 2 a simple fruit having a skin or rind surrounding the seeds in the pulp. Botanists classify grapes, tomatoes, currants, and bananas as berries. 3 gather or pick berries: *During our vacation in Maine we went berrying one day.* 4 the dry seed or kernel of grain or other plants: *Coffee is made from the berries of the coffee plant.* 1,2,4 *n*., *pl*. **ber ries;** 3 *v*., **berried, ber ry ing.** —**ber′ry like′,** *adj*.

ber serk (bėr′sėrk′ or bər sėrk′). **go berserk** or **run berserk,** be carried away by madness or wild fury; become violently angry: *The sick dog went berserk and tried to bite everyone in its way. adv*.

berth (bėrth), 1 place to sleep on a ship, train, or airplane. 2 a ship's place at a wharf. 3 place for a ship to anchor conveniently or safely. 4 position; job: *My sister has a berth as lifeguard for the summer.* 5 to place in a berth; provide with a berth. 1-4 *n*., 5 *v*.
give a wide berth to, keep well away from: *Give a wide berth to her when she is angry.*

ber yl (ber′əl), a very hard mineral, usually green or blue-green, used as a gem and as a source of beryllium. The emerald is a variety of beryl. *n*.

be ryl li um (bə ril′ē əm), a hard, light, metallic element found in various minerals. Beryllium is used in various alloys and in controlling the speed

adj. adjective	*n.* noun
adv. adverb	*prep.* preposition
conj. conjunction	*pron.* pronoun
interj. interjection	*v.* verb
sing. singular	*pl.* plural

of neutrons in atomic reactors. *n.*

be seech (bi sēch′), ask earnestly; beg; implore: *I beseech you to listen to me.* *v.*, **be sought** or **be seeched, be seech ing.**

be seem (bi sēm′), OLD USE. seem proper for; befit; suit. *v.*

be set (bi set′), attack from all sides; attack so as to surround or hem in: *We were beset by mosquitoes in the swamp. In the darkness he was suddenly beset by fear.* *v.*, **be set, be set ting.**

be set ting (bi set′ing), habitually attacking: *Laziness is a loafer's besetting sin. adj.*

be shrew (bi shrü′), OLD USE. curse. *v.*

be side (bi sīd′), 1 by the side of; close to; near: *Grass grows beside the fence.* 2 compared with: *The wolf seems tame beside the tiger.* 3 away from; aside from: *That question is beside the point and shows that you were not listening.* 4 besides. 1-3 *prep.*, 4 *adv.*

beside oneself, out of one's mind; crazy: *He was beside himself with worry over his lost dog.*

be sides (bi sīdz′), 1 more than that; also; moreover: *I don't want to go shopping; besides, I have no money to spend.* 2 in addition to; over and above: *Others came to the school picnic besides our own class.* 3 in addition: *We tried two other ways besides.* 4 other than; except: *She spoke of no one besides you.* 1,3 *adv.*, 2,4 *prep.*

be siege (bi sēj′), 1 surround and try to capture: *For ten years the Greeks besieged the city of Troy.* 2 crowd around: *Hundreds of admirers besieged the famous astronaut.* 3 overwhelm with requests, questions, etc.: *During the flood, the Red Cross was besieged with calls for help.* *v.*, **be sieged, be sieg ing.**

be sieg er (bi sē′jər), person who besieges. *n.*

be smear (bi smir′), smear over. *v.*

be smirch (bi smėrch′), make dirty; soil; sully: *Her dishonesty has besmirched her family's good name.* *v.*

be som (bē′zəm), broom made of twigs. *n.*

be sought (bi sôt′), a past tense and a past participle of **beseech.** *She besought the doctor to stop the pain. v.*

be spake (bi spāk′), OLD USE. be-spoke; a past tense of **bespeak.** *v.*

be span gle (bi spang′gəl), adorn with spangles. *v.*, **be span gled, be span gling.**

be spat ter (bi spat′ər), spatter all over; soil by spattering. *v.*

be speak (bi spēk′), 1 ask for in advance; order; reserve: *We want to bespeak two tickets for the new play.* 2 be a sign of; show; indicate: *The neat appearance of the house bespeaks care.* *v.*, **be spoke, be spo ken** or **bespoke, be speak ing.**

be spec ta cled (bi spek′tə kəld), wearing glasses. *adj.*

be spoke (bi spōk′), a past tense and a past participle of **bespeak.** *We bespoke our tickets early. v.*

be spo ken (bi spō′kən), a past participle of **bespeak.** *Tickets have been bespoken for us at the theater. v.*

Bes se mer process (bes′ə mər), method of making steel by forcing a blast of air through molten iron in order to burn out carbon and other impurities. [from Sir Henry *Bessemer,* 1813-1898, English engineer who invented this method]

best (best) 1 most good, useful, desirable, etc.: *Her work is good; his work is better; but mine is best. We have the best food to eat. He is the best student in the class.* 2 in the most excellent way: *Who reads best?* 3 in or to the highest degree: *I like this book best.* 4 person or thing that is best: *Most parents want the best for their children. He is the best in the class.* 5 largest: *I spent the best part of the evening doing my homework.* 6 the most that is possible; utmost: *I did my best to finish the work on time.* 7 INFORMAL. outdo; defeat: *Our team was bested in the final game.* 1,5 *adj.,* superlative of **good;** 2,3 *adv.,* superlative of **well**[1]; 4,6 *n.,* 7 *v.*

all for the best, not so bad as it seems.

at best, under the most favorable circumstances: *Summer is at best very short.*

get the best of, defeat.

had best, ought to; will be wise to; should: *You had best leave before the storm breaks.*

make the best of, do as well as possible with: *Try to make the best of a bad job.*

bes tial (bes′chəl), like a beast; beastly; brutish. *adj.* —**bes′tial ly,** *adv.*

bes ti al i ty (bes′chē al′ə tē), bestial conduct. *n., pl.* **bes ti al i ties.**

be stir (bi stėr′), rouse to action; stir up; exert: *If we want to win this game we'll have to bestir ourselves. v.*, **be stirred, be stir ring.**

best man, the chief attendant of the bridegroom at a wedding.

be stow (bi stō′), give (something) as a gift; give: *Education bestows many benefits. The President bestowed a medal on the hero. v.*

be stow al (bi stō′əl), a bestowing: *the bestowal of his daughter in marriage. n.*

be strew (bi strü′), 1 strew; scatter; sprinkle: *The children bestrewed the path with flowers.* 2 lie scattered over: *Papers bestrewed the park. v.*, **bestrewed, be strewed** or **be strewn, be strew ing.**

be strewn (bi strün′), 1 scattered about. 2 bestrewed; a past participle of **bestrew.** 1 *adj.,* 2 *v.*

be strid den (bi strid′n), past participle of **bestride.** *The knight has bestridden the horse. v.*

be stride (bi strīd′), get on, sit on, or stand over (something) with one leg on each side; straddle. *You can bestride a horse, a chair, or a fence. v.*, **bestrode, be strid den, be strid ing.**

be strode (bi strōd′), past tense of **bestride.** *He bestrode his horse. v.*

best seller, anything, especially a book, that has a very large sale.

bet (bet), 1 promise (some money or a certain thing) to another if he is right and you are wrong; wager: *I bet her a nickel that she could not outrun me.* 2 a promise or pledge to give some money or a certain thing to another if he is right and you are wrong: *She made a bet that she would win the race.* 3 the money or thing promised: *I won the race; so she lost her bet.* 4 make a bet: *Which horse did you bet on?* 5 be very sure: *I bet you are wrong about that.* 6 thing to bet on: *Which horse is a good bet?* 1,4,5 *v.,* **bet** or **bet ted, bet ting;** 2,3,6 *n.*

be ta (bā′tə), the second letter of the Greek alphabet (B, β). *n.*

be take (bi tāk′). **betake oneself,** go: *They betake themselves to the mountains every summer. v.*, **be took, be tak en, be tak ing.**

be tak en (bi tā′kən), past participle of **betake.** *He has betaken himself to flight. v.*

beta particle, electron released by the nucleus of a radioactive substance in the process of disintegration.

be ta tron (bā′tə tron), particle accelerator that greatly increases the speed of electrons. *n.*

be tel (bē′tl), a climbing pepper plant of the East Indies. People in Asia chew its leaves. *n.*

Be tel geuse (bē′tl jüz), a very large red star in the constellation Orion. *n.*

bête noire (bāt′ nwär′), FRENCH. thing or person especially dreaded or detested.

Beth a ny (beth′ə nē), village near Jerusalem, now in NW Jordan. *n.*

be think (bi thingk′). **bethink oneself of,** think about; consider; remem-

ber: *I should bethink myself of the need to study.* v., **be thought, be think-ing.**

Beth le hem (beth/lə hem), the birth-place of Jesus, a town now in Jordan six miles south of Jerusalem. *n.*

be thought (bi thôt/), past tense and past participle of **bethink.** *I bethought myself of my duties.* v.

be tide (bi tīd/), 1 happen to: *Woe betide you if you dare break your promise.* 2 happen: *No matter what betides, the family will hold together.* v., **be tid ed, be tid ing.**

be times (bi tīmz/), OLD USE. early. *adv.*

be to ken (bi tō/kən), be a sign of; show: *His smile betokens his satisfac-tion. The dark clouds betoken a storm.* v.

be took (bi tuk/), past tense of **betake.** *The queen betook herself to her summer palace.* v.

be tray (bi trā/), 1 hand over or expose to the power of an enemy by being disloyal: *The traitor betrayed his coun-try.* 2 be unfaithful to: *She betrayed her friends by breaking her promise.* 3 mis-lead; deceive: *He was betrayed by his own enthusiasm.* 4 show signs of; re-veal: *The girl's wet shoes betrayed the fact that she had walked through pud-dles.* v. —**be tray/er,** *n.*

be tray al (bi trā/əl), act of betraying; violation of trust or confidence. *n.*

be troth (bi trōᴛн/ or bi trôth/), prom-ise in marriage; engage: *He betrothed his daughter to a rich man.* v.

be troth al (bi trō/ᴛнəl or bi trô/thəl), engagement to be married. *n.*

be trothed (bi trōᴛнd/ or bi trôtht/), 1 person engaged to be married: *The knight's betrothed was a lovely princess.* 2 engaged to be married: *James and Sue are now betrothed.* 1 *n.,* 2 *adj.*

bet ter[1] (bet/ər), 1 more good, useful, desirable, etc., than another: *She left her old job for a better one.* 2 in a more excellent way: *Try to read better next time.* 3 in a higher degree; more completely: *I know my old friend better than I know anyone else.* 4 more: *It is better than a mile to town.* 5 person or thing that is better: *Which is the better of these two dresses?* 6 **betters,** *pl.* one's superiors: *Listen to the advice of your elders and betters.* 7 make better; improve: *We can better that work by being more careful next time.* 8 do bet-ter than; surpass: *The other class can-not better our grades.* 9 larger: *Four days is the better part of a week.* 10 improved in health: *The sick child is better today.* 1,9,10 *adj.,* 2-4 *adv., comparative of* **good;** 2-4 *adv., comparative of* **well**[1]; 5,6 *n.,* 7,8 *v.* [Old English *betera*]

better off, in a better condition: *He is better off now that he has a new job.*

for the better, toward improvement or recovery: *The sick man took a turn for the better.*

get the better of or **have the better of,** be superior to; defeat: *The tortoise got the better of the hare.*

had better, ought to; will be wise to; should: *I had better go before it rains.*

think better of, think over and change one's mind about: *In the morning you will think better of your decision to go on such a long hike.*

bet ter[2] or **bet tor** (bet/ər), person who bets. *n.* [*bet* + *-er*[1] or *-or*]

bevel
(def. 1)

bevel
(def. 3)

bet ter ment (bet/ər mənt), a making better; improvement: *Doctors work for the betterment of their patients' health.* *n.*

be tween (bi twēn/), 1 in the space or time separating two points, objects, places, etc.: *Many cities lie between New York and Chicago* (prep.). *We could not see the moon, for a cloud came between* (adv.). 2 in the range or part separating: *She earned between ten and twelve dollars.* 3 from one to the other of; joining: *There is a new high-way between Chicago and Pittsburgh.* 4 having to do with: *A truce was ar-ranged between the two nations.* 5 in re-gard to one or the other of: *We must choose between the two books.* 6 by the joint action of: *They caught twelve fish between them.* 1-6 *prep.,* 1 *adv.*

between you and me, as a secret; confidentially: *This is between you and me; don't tell anyone else.*

in between, 1 in the middle: *He either studies very hard or not at all, never anything in between.* 2 in the midst of; among: *In between the rows of corn there was a scarecrow.*

be twixt (bi twikst/), between. *prep., adv.*

betwixt and between, in the middle; neither one nor the other.

Bev or **BeV** (bev), a billion electron volts, used as a measure of energy in nuclear physics. *n.*

hat, āge, fär; let, ēqual, tėrm;
it, īce; hot, ōpen, ôrder;
oil, out; cup, pu̇t, rüle; ch, child;
ng, long; sh, she; th, thin;
ᴛн, then; zh, measure;

ə represents *a* in about,
e in taken, *i* in pencil,
o in lemon, *u* in circus.

bev el (bev/əl), 1 a sloping edge. There is often a bevel on the frame of a picture, on a mirror, or on a piece of plate glass. 2 cut a square edge to a sloping edge; make slope: *The edges of the board have been beveled with a plane.* 3 instru-ment or tool for drawing or measuring angles. 1,3 *n.,* 2 *v.*

bev er age (bev/ər ij), liquid used or prepared for drinking. Milk, tea, coffee, beer, and wine are beverages. *n.*

bev y (bev/ē), a small group or flock: *a bevy of quail, a bevy of girls.* *n., pl.* **bev ies.**

be wail (bi wāl/), mourn for; weep for; bemoan: *The children bewailed the loss of their cat.* v.

be ware (bi wer/ or bi war/), be on one's guard against; be careful: *Beware! danger is here. You must beware of swimming in a strong current.* v.

be wil der (bi wil/dər), confuse com-pletely; puzzle; perplex: *The little girl was bewildered by the crowds.* v. —**be-wil/der ing ly,** *adv.*

be wil der ment (bi wil/dər mənt), a bewildered condition; complete confu-sion; perplexity. *n.*

be witch (bi wich/), 1 put under a spell; use magic on: *The wicked fairy bewitched the princess and made her fall into a long sleep.* 2 charm; fascinate; enchant: *We were all bewitched by our bright little cousin.* v. —**be witch/-ing ly,** *adv.*

bey (bā), governor of a Turkish province or district. *n., pl.* **beys.**

be yond (bi yond/), 1 on or to the farther side of: *He lives beyond the sea.* 2 farther on than: *The school is beyond the last house.* 3 farther away: *Beyond were the hills. Your ball did not fall here; look beyond for it.* 4 later than; past: *They stayed beyond the time set.* 5 out of the reach, range, or under-standing of: *This shirt is so worn that it is beyond repair. The meaning of this story is beyond him.* 6 more than: *The price of the suit was beyond what he could pay. The day at the beach was beyond all we had hoped.* 7 **the be-yond** or **the great beyond,** life after

bg.

adj.	adjective	*n.*	noun
adv.	adverb	*prep.*	preposition
conj.	conjunction	*pron.*	pronoun
interj.	interjection	*v.*	verb
sing.	singular	*pl.*	plural

death: *He has gone to the great beyond.* 1,2,4-6 *prep.*, 3 *adv.*, 7 *n.*

bg., bag. *pl.* **bgs.**

Bhu tan (bü tän′), country between Tibet and NE India. Bhutan's foreign affairs are partly under the control of the government of India. *n.*

bi-, *prefix.* 1 twice a _____: *Biannual = twice a year.* 2 two _____s: *Bisect = divide into two parts.* 3 having two _____: *Biped = having two feet.* 4 once every two _____: *Bimonthly = once every two months.* [from Latin *bi-,* from *bis* twice]

Bi a fra (bē ä′frə), region of Nigeria, in rebellion against the central government from 1967 to 1970. *n.*

bi an nu al (bī an′yü əl), occurring twice a year: *Our school nurse recommends a biannual visit to the dentist. adj.*

bi an nu al ly (bī an′yü ə lē), twice a year. *adv.*

bias (def. 1)
cloth cut on the bias

bi as (bī′əs), 1 a slanting or oblique line. 2 tendency to favor one side too much; prejudice: *An umpire should have no bias.* 3 give a bias to; influence, usually unfairly; prejudice: *The judge tried not to let his feelings bias his judgment.* 1,2 *n.*, *pl.* **bi as es;** 3 *v.*

on the bias, diagonally across the weave: *cloth cut on the bias.*

bi ased (bī′əst), favoring one side too much; prejudiced: *Parents are often biased where their children are concerned. adj.*

bib (bib), 1 cloth worn under the chin to protect clothing, especially at meals. 2 part of an apron or overalls above the waist. *n.*

Bi ble (bī′bəl), 1 the book of sacred writings of the Christian religion, comprising the Old Testament and the New Testament. 2 the form of the Old Testament accepted by the Jews. 3 book of the sacred writings of any religion. The Koran is the Bible of the Moslems. 4 **bible,** any book accepted as an authority. *n.*

bib li cal or **Bib li cal** (bib′lə kəl), 1 of the Bible: *biblical literature.* 2 according to the Bible: *biblical history.* 3 in the Bible: *a biblical reference to Solomon. adj.* —**bib′li cal ly, Bib′li cal ly,** *adv.*

bib li og ra pher (bib′lē og′rə fər), the compiler of a bibliography. *n.*

bib li o graph i cal (bib′lē ə graf′ə kəl), having to do with bibliography. *adj.* —**bib′li o graph′i cal ly,** *adv.*

bib li og ra phy (bib′lē og′rə fē), list of books or articles by a certain author or about a particular subject or person. *n.*, *pl.* **bib li og ra phies.**

bib li o phile (bib′lē ə fīl), lover of books, especially one who likes to collect books. *n.*

bi cam er al (bī kam′ər əl), having two legislative chambers. The Congress of the United States is a bicameral legislature; it consists of the Senate and the House of Representatives. *adj.*

bi car bo nate of soda (bī kär′bə nit), sodium bicarbonate.

bi cen ten ni al (bī′sen ten′ē əl), 1 having to do with a period of 200 years. 2 a 200th anniversary: *The town is celebrating its bicentennial.* 3 celebration of the 200th anniversary. 1 *adj.*, 2,3 *n.*

bi ceps (bī′seps), the large muscle in the front part of the upper arm. If you move your fist up to your shoulder, the biceps will stick out. *n.*, *pl.* **bi ceps** or **bi ceps es.**

bi chlo ride (bī klôr′īd), 1 compound containing two atoms of chlorine combined with another element or radical. 2 bichloride of mercury. *n.*

bichloride of mercury, an extremely poisonous, white substance, used in medicine as an antiseptic.

bick er (bik′ər), 1 take part in a petty, noisy quarrel; squabble: *The children bickered through the long, hot summer afternoon.* 2 a petty, noisy quarrel. 1 *v.*, 2 *n.*

bi cus pid (bī kus′pid), a double-pointed tooth that tears and grinds food; premolar. Adult human beings have eight bicuspids. *n.*

bi cy cle (bī′sik′əl), 1 a lightweight vehicle consisting of a metal frame with two wheels, one behind the other, handles for steering, and a seat for the rider. One rides a bicycle by pushing the two pedals with the feet. 2 ride a bicycle. 1 *n.*, 2 *v.*, **bi cy cled, bi cy cling.**

bi cy cler (bī′sik′lər), bicyclist. *n.*

bi cy clist (bī′sik′list), person who rides a bicycle. *n.*

bid (bid), 1 tell (someone) what to do, where to go, etc.; command: *We were bidden to assemble in the gym. Do as I bid you.* 2 say; tell: *His friends bade*

him good-by. 3 offer to pay (a certain price): *She bid $5 for the table. He then bid $7.* 4 an offer to pay a certain price: *She made a bid on the table.* 5 state one's price for doing a certain piece of work: *Several companies will bid for the contract.* 6 amount offered or stated: *My bid for the table was $7. The contractor's bid for building the new bridge was $300,000.* 7 invite: *The king bade the nobles stay for the feast.* 8 invitation: *a bid to join the honor society.* 9 an attempt to secure, achieve, or win: *The candidate made a bid for popular support.* 1-3,5,7 *v.*, **bade** or **bid, bid den** or **bid, bid ding;** 4,6,8,9 *n.*

bid den (bid′n), a past participle of **bid.** *Twelve guests were bidden to the feast. v.*

bid der (bid′ər), person who bids. The highest bidder at an auction is the person who offers to pay the highest price for something. *n.*

bid ding (bid′ing), 1 command; order: *We must heed the teacher's bidding.* 2 invitation. 3 the offering of a price for something: *The bidding was very slow at first. n.*

do one's bidding, obey one.

bid dy (bid′ē), hen. *n.*, *pl.* **bid dies.**

BICEPS

TRICEPS

bide (bīd), continue; wait; abide: *bide here awhile. v.*, **bode** or **bid ed, bid ing.**

bi en ni al (bī en′ē əl), 1 living two years or seasons. A biennial plant germinates in the first season, then flowers and produces fruit, and dies in the second season. 2 plant that lives two years or seasons. Carrots and onions are biennials. 3 occurring every two years. 4 event that occurs every two years. 1,3 *adj.*, 2,4 *n.*

bi en ni al ly (bī en′ē ə lē), once in two years. *adv.*

bier (bir), a movable stand or framework on which a coffin or dead body is placed before burial. *n.*

bi fo cal (bī fō′kəl), 1 having two focuses. The lenses of bifocal glasses have two sections of different focal lengths, the upper part for distant vision, the lower for close vision. 2 **bifocals,** *pl.* pair of glasses having bifocal lenses. 1 *adj.*, 2 *n.*

big (big), 1 great in amount or size;

large: *a big room, a big book. Making automobiles is a big business. An elephant is a big animal.* 2 grown up: *You are a big girl now.* 3 important; great: *The election of a president is big news.* 4 full; loud: *He has a big voice.* 5 generous: *His brother had a big heart and forgave him for breaking the model airplane.* 6 boastful: *big talk.* 7 INFORMAL. boastfully: *She talks big.* 1-6 adj., **big ger**, **big gest;** 7 adv. —**big′ness**, n.

big a my (big′ə mē), condition of having two wives or two husbands at the same time. Bigamy is unlawful in most countries. n.

Big Dipper, group of seven bright stars in the constellation Ursa Major.

big-heart ed (big′här′tid), kindly; generous. adj.

big horn (big′hôrn′), a wild, grayish-brown sheep of the Rocky Mountains, having large, curving horns. n., pl. **big horns** or **big horn.**

bight (bit), 1 a long curve in a coastline. 2 a bay formed by this curve. 3 a loop of rope. n.

big no ni a (big nō′nē ə), a tropical vine with clusters of large, orange-red flowers shaped like trumpets; trumpet creeper; trumpet vine. n., pl. **big no ni as.**

big ot (big′ət), an intolerant, prejudiced person; bigoted person. n.

big ot ed (big′ə tid), sticking to an opinion, belief, party, etc., without reason and not tolerating other views; intolerant; prejudiced. adj.

big ot ry (big′ə trē), bigoted conduct or attitude; intolerance; prejudice. n., pl. **big ot ries.**

big top, INFORMAL. circus.

big tree, 1 giant sequoia. 2 redwood.

bike (bik), INFORMAL. 1 bicycle. 2 ride a bicycle. 1 n., 2 v., **biked, bik ing.**

bi ki ni (bə kē′nē), a very scant bathing suit in two pieces for women and girls. n., pl. **bi ki nis.** [from *Bikini,* atoll in the western Pacific]

bi lat er al (bī lat′ər əl), 1 having two sides. 2 on two sides. 3 binding both sides or parties: *The two nations signed a bilateral treaty.* adj. —**bi lat′er al ly,** adv.

bile (bil), 1 a bitter, greenish-yellow liquid secreted by the liver and stored in the gall bladder; gall. It aids digestion in the small intestine by neutralizing acids and emulsifying fats. 2 ill humor; anger. n.

bilge (bilj), 1 the lowest part of a ship's hold; bottom of a ship's hull. 2 bilge water. 3 the widest part of a barrel. 4 INFORMAL. nonsense. n.

bilge water, dirty water that collects in the bottom of a ship's hold.

bi lin e ar (bī lin′ē ər), of or having to do with two lines. adj.

bi lin gual (bī ling′gwəl), 1 able to speak another language as well as or almost as well as one's own; knowing two languages. 2 containing or written in two languages: *a bilingual dictionary.* adj. —**bi lin′gual ly,** adv.

bil ious (bil′yəs), 1 suffering from or caused by some trouble with bile or the liver: *a bilious headache.* 2 peevish; cross; bad-tempered: *a bilious person.* adj. —**bil′ious ly,** adv. —**bil′ious ness,** n.

bilk (bilk), cheat; defraud. v. —**bilk′er,** n.

bill¹ (bil), 1 statement of money owed for work done or things supplied: *The garage sent us a $35 bill for repairing our car.* 2 send a bill to: *The dairy bills us on the first of each month.* 3 piece of paper money: *Do you have change for a five-dollar bill?* 4 a written or printed public notice, such as an advertisement, poster, or handbill: *Post no bills on this fence.* 5 announce by bills or public notice: *Many interesting television programs are billed for next week.* 6 a written or printed statement; list of items. 7 a proposed law presented to a lawmaking body for its approval: *This bill for gun control will be voted on by the Senate today.* 1,3,4,6,7 n., 2,5 v. [from Latin *billa* document, seal]
fill the bill, satisfy requirements.
foot the bill, pay or settle the bill.

bill² (def. 1)
left, bill adapted for pecking seeds;
right, bill adapted for tearing meat

bill² (bil), 1 the horny part of the jaws of a bird; beak. 2 anything shaped somewhat like a bird's bill: *the bill of a turtle.* 3 join beaks; touch bills. 1,2 n., 3 v. [Old English *bile*]

bill and coo, kiss and talk softly, as pigeons touch bills and coo.

bill board (bil′bôrd′), signboard, usually outdoors, on which to display advertisements or notices. n.

bil let¹ (bil′it), 1 a written order to provide board and lodging for a soldier. 2 place where a soldier is lodged. 3 assign to quarters by billet: *Soldiers were billeted in all the houses of the village.* 4 job; position. 1,2,4 n., 3 v. [from French of the 1400's *billette,* from *bille* document]

bil let² (bil′it), a thick stick of wood. n. [from French of the 1400's *billette,* from *bille* log, tree trunk]

bill fold (bil′fōld′), a folding pocketbook for carrying paper money, cards, etc.; wallet. n.

bil liards (bil′yərdz), game played with hard balls on a special table with a raised, cushioned edge. A long stick called a cue is used in hitting the balls. n.

Bil lings (bil′ingz), city in S Montana. n.

bil lings gate (bil′ingz gāt′), vulgar, abusive language. n. [from *Billingsgate,* a city gate and fish market in London]

bil lion (bil′yən), 1 (in the United States, Canada, and France) one thousand millions; 1,000,000,000. 2 (in Great Britain and Germany) one million millions; 1,000,000,000,000. n., adj.

bil lion aire (bil′yə ner′ or bil′yə nar′), an extremely wealthy person who has a billion or more dollars, francs, marks, pounds, etc. n.

bil lionth (bil′yənth), 1 last in a series of a billion. 2 one of a billion equal parts. 1 adj., 2 n.

bill of exchange, a written order to a person, bank, or firm to pay a stated sum of money to a specified person; draft.

bill of fare, menu.

bill of health, certificate stating whether or not there are infectious diseases on a ship or in a port. A bill of health is given to a captain when his ship sails.

bill of rights, 1 statement of the fundamental rights of the people of a state or nation. 2 **Bill of Rights,** the first ten amendments to the Constitution of the United States, adopted in 1791, which include a declaration of fundamental rights held by United States citizens.

bill of sale, a written statement transferring ownership of something from the seller to the buyer.

bil low (bil′ō), 1 a great, swelling wave or surge of the sea: *The billows of the Atlantic dash on these islands.* 2 any great wave or swelling mass of smoke, flame, sound, or the like: *Billows of smoke rose from the chimney.* 3 rise or

adj. adjective	*n.* noun
adv. adverb	*prep.* preposition
conj. conjunction	*pron.* pronoun
interj. interjection	*v.* verb
sing. singular	*pl.* plural

roll in big waves; surge: *The wind made the lake's surface billow.* 4 swell out; bulge: *The sheets on the clothesline billow in the wind.* 1,2 *n.,* 3,4 *v.*

bil low y (bil/ō ē), 1 rising or rolling in big waves; surging. 2 swelling out; bulging. *adj.,* **bil low i er, bil low i est.**

bil ly (bil/ē), a policeman's club or stick. *n., pl.* **bil lies.**

billy goat, a male goat.

Bi lox i (bə lok/sē), city in SE Mississippi. *n.*

bi month ly (bī munth/lē), 1 once every two months: *A bimonthly magazine is issued six times a year* (adj.). *The magazine is issued bimonthly* (adv.). 2 twice a month: *The bimonthly meetings are on the first and third Wednesdays of each month* (adj.). *The meetings are held bimonthly* (adv.). 3 newspaper or magazine published bimonthly. 1,2 *adj., adv.,* 3 *n., pl.* **bimonth lies.**

bin (bin), box or enclosed place for holding or storing grain, coal, etc. *n.*

bi nar y (bī/nər ē), consisting of two; involving two; dual. *adj.*

binary star, pair of stars that revolve around a common center of gravity.

binary system, system of numeration which counts only from 0 to 1 and then starts with a new place. In this system, the decimal number 1 is also noted as 1, but the decimal number 2 is noted as 10 (1 and 0), 3 as 11 (1 and 1), 4 as 100 (1 and 0 and 0), 5 as 101 (1 and 0 and 1), and so on.

bin au ral (bī nôr/əl), stereophonic: *binaural recording. adj.*

bind (bīnd), 1 tie together; hold together; fasten: *She bound the package with a bright ribbon.* 2 stick together: *Gravel or cinders can be bound by tar.* 3 hold by some force; restrain: *Vines are binding the flowers and choking their growth.* 4 fasten (sheets of paper) into a cover; put a cover on (a book): *The loose pages were bound into a small book.* 5 hold by a promise, duty, law, etc.; oblige: *A doctor is in duty bound to help the sick. Parents are bound to send their children to school.* 6 put a bandage on: *The nurse will bind up your cut.* 7 put a border or edge on to strengthen or ornament: *She bound the sleeves of*

her dress with red ribbon. *v.,* **bound, bind ing.**

bind er (bīn/dər), 1 person who binds books. 2 anything that ties or holds together. 3 cover for a loose-leaf notebook. 4 machine that cuts stalks of grain and ties them in bundles. *n.*

bind er y (bīn/dər ē), place where books are bound. *n., pl.* **bind er ies.**

bind ing (bīn/ding), 1 the covering of a book. 2 strip protecting or ornamenting an edge. Binding is used on the seams of dresses. 3 that binds, fastens, or connects. 4 having force or power to hold to a promise, duty, law, etc.; obligatory. A contract is a binding agreement. 1,2 *n.,* 3,4 *adj.* —**bind/ing ly,** *adv.*

binding energy, energy necessary to break a molecule, atom, or nucleus into its smaller component parts.

bind weed (bīnd/wēd/), plant with long stems that twine around fences, trees, or other plants. *n.*

bin go (bing/gō), game in which each player covers the numbers on his card as they are called out. The player who is first to cover a column of numbers is the winner. *n.*

bin na cle (bin/ə kəl), box or stand that contains a ship's compass. The binnacle is placed near the helm. *n.*

bi noc u lar (bə nok/yə lər), 1 for both eyes at once: *a binocular microscope.* 2 using both eyes at once: *Most animals have binocular vision. adj.*

bi noc u lars (bə nok/yə lərz), a double telescope joined as a unit for use with both eyes. Field glasses and opera glasses are binoculars. *n.pl.*

binoculars

bi no mi al (bī nō/mē əl), 1 expression in algebra consisting of two terms. $8a + 2b$ is a binomial. 2 the scientific name of a plant or animal, consisting of two terms. *Homo sapiens* is a binomial. 3 consisting of two terms. 1,2 *n.,* 3 *adj.*

bi o chem i cal (bī/ō kem/ə kəl), having to do with biochemistry. *adj.* —**bi/o chem/i cal ly,** *adv.*

bi o chem ist (bī/ō kem/ist), an expert in biochemistry. *n.*

bi o chem is try (bī/ō kem/ə strē), science that deals with the chemical processes of living animals and plants. *n.*

bi o de grad a ble (bī/ō di grā/də-

bəl), that is capable of being broken down by the action of bacteria: *a biodegradable detergent. adj.*

bi og ra pher (bī og/rə fər), person who writes someone's biography. *n.*

bi o graph i cal (bī/ə graf/ə kəl), 1 of a person's life: *biographical details.* 2 having to do with biography. *adj.* —**bi/o graph/i cal ly,** *adv.*

bi og ra phy (bī og/rə fē), an account of a person's life. *n., pl.* **bi og ra phies.**

bi o log i cal (bī/ə loj/ə kəl), 1 of plant and animal life; connected with the processes of life: *biological studies.* 2 having to do with biology: *a biological laboratory. adj.* —**bi/o log/i cal ly,** *adv.*

biological warfare, warfare in which disease germs are used against persons, animals, or crops.

bi ol o gist (bī ol/ə jist), an expert in biology. *n.*

bi ol o gy (bī ol/ə jē), the scientific study of plant and animal life, including its origin, structure, activities, and distribution. Botany, zoology, and ecology are branches of biology. *n.*

bi op sy (bī/op sē), 1 the surgical removal of a piece of tissue from a living body for examination. 2 medical examination of this tissue. *n., pl.* **bi op sies.**

bi par ti san (bī pär/tə zən), of, representing, or supported by two political parties: *a bipartisan foreign policy. adj.*

bi par tite (bī pär/tīt), 1 having to do with two peoples, nations, etc.: *a bipartite treaty between the United States and Canada.* 2 having two parts: *A clam has a bipartite shell. adj.*

bi ped (bī/ped), animal having two feet. Birds and men are bipeds. *n.*

bi plane (bī/plān/), airplane having two wings on each side of the fuselage, one above the other. *n.*

birch (bėrch), 1 a slender, hardy tree with a smooth bark that peels off in thin layers. 2 its hard, close-grained wood, often used in making furniture. 3 bundle of birch twigs or a birch stick used for whipping. 4 whip with a birch; flog. 1-3 *n., pl.* **birch es** for 1 and 3; 4 *v.*

birch bark (bėrch/bärk/), bark of a birch tree. Some Indians used birchbark to cover the framework of their canoes. *n.*

birch en (bėr/chən), 1 of a birch tree. 2 made of birch wood. *adj.*

bird (bėrd), 1 any of a group of vertebrates that lay eggs and have warm blood, a body covered with feathers, two legs, and wings. Most birds can fly. 2 shuttlecock. 3 SLANG. person: *He's an odd bird. n.* —**bird/like/,** *adj.*

bird bath (bėrd/bath/), a shallow

basin raised off the ground and filled with water for birds to bathe in or drink. *n., pl.* **bird baths** (bėrd′baᴛʜz′).

bird call, 1 sound that a bird makes. 2 instrument for imitating that sound.

bird dog, dog trained to find birds or bring back birds shot by hunters.

bird house (bėrd′hous′), a small box with a roof and one or more openings, raised off the ground for birds to nest in. *n., pl.* **bird hous es** (bėrd′hou′ziz).

bird ie (bėr′dē), 1 a little bird. 2 score of one stroke less than par for any hole on a golf course. *n.*

bird lime (bėrd′līm′), a sticky substance smeared on twigs to catch small birds that alight on it. *n.*

bird of paradise, bird of New Guinea noted for its magnificent plumage.

bird of passage, 1 bird that flies from one region to another as the seasons change. 2 person who roams from place to place.

bird of prey, any of a group of birds, including eagles, hawks, owls, and vultures, that hunt animals.

bird seed (bėrd′sēd′), mixture of small seeds often fed to caged birds. *n.*

bird's-eye (bėrdz′ī′), 1 seen from above or from a distance; general: *You can get a bird's-eye view of the city from an airplane.* 2 having markings somewhat like birds' eyes. **Bird's-eye maple** is a wood used in making furniture. *adj.*

bisect
The line DB
bisects the angle ADC.

bird watcher, person who observes and classifies wild birds in their natural environment.

bi ret ta (bə ret′ə), a stiff, square cap with three or four upright projecting pieces, worn by Roman Catholic or Episcopal clergymen on certain occasions. *n., pl.* **bi ret tas.**

Bir ming ham (bėr′ming ham), 1 city in central England. 2 city in central Alabama. *n.*

birth (bėrth), 1 a coming into life; being born: *the birth of a baby.* 2 a beginning; origin: *the birth of a nation.* 3 a bringing forth: *the birth of a plan, the birth of a new age.* 4 descent; family: *a person of Spanish birth. The queen was a woman of noble birth. n.* **give birth to,** 1 bring forth; bear: *The dog gave birth to four puppies.* 2 be the origin or cause of: *The scientist's experiments gave birth to a new drug.*

birth day (bėrth′dā′), 1 day on which a person was born. 2 day on which something began: *July 4, 1776, was the birthday of the United States.* 3 yearly return of the day on which a person was born, or on which something began: *Tomorrow is my birthday; I shall be ten years old. n.*

birth mark (bėrth′märk′), spot or mark on the skin that was there at birth. *n.*

birth place (bėrth′plās′), 1 place where a person was born. 2 place in which something began; place of origin: *Philadelphia is the birthplace of the United States. n.*

birth rate, relationship of the number of births in a year to the total population.

birth right (bėrth′rīt′), rights belonging to a person because he is the oldest son, or because he was born in a certain country, or because of any other fact about his birth: *According to the Bible story, when Esau sold his birthright to his younger brother Jacob, he forfeited all claim to property of his father Isaac. n.*

birth stone (bėrth′stōn′), gem associated with a certain month of the year. A birthstone is supposed to bring good luck when worn by a person born in its month. *n.*

Bis cay (bis′kā), **Bay of,** bay north of Spain and west of France. It is part of the Atlantic. *n.*

bis cuit (bis′kit), 1 soft bread dough baked in small shapes. 2 cracker. *n., pl.* **bis cuits** or **bis cuit.**

bi sect (bī′sekt), divide into two equal or almost equal parts: *You can bisect a 90 degree angle into two 45 degree angles. v.*

bi sec tion (bī sek′shən), 1 act of bisecting: *bisection of an angle.* 2 place of bisecting. 3 one of two equal parts. *n.*

bi sec tor (bī sek′tər), line that bisects something, especially an angle. *n.*

bish op (bish′əp), 1 clergyman of high rank who is the head of a church district or diocese. 2 one of the pieces in the game of chess that move diagonally. *n.*

bish op ric (bish′əp rik), 1 position, office, or rank of bishop. 2 church district under the charge of a bishop; diocese; see. *n.*

Bis marck (biz′märk), 1 **Otto von,** 1815-1898, German statesman who united the German states into an empire in 1871. 2 capital of North Dakota, in the S part. *n.*

bis muth (biz′məth), a brittle, reddish-white metallic element. Some of its compounds are used in medicine and in alloys. *n.*

bi son (bī′sn *or* bī′zn), 1 a wild ox of North America, the male of which has a big, shaggy head and strong front legs; buffalo. 2 the wild ox of Europe, slight-

ly larger than the American bison; aurochs. It is now almost extinct. *n., pl.* **bi son.**

bit¹ (bit), 1 a small piece; small amount: *bits of broken glass. A pebble is a bit of rock.* 2 INFORMAL. a short time: *Stay a bit.* 3 INFORMAL. 12½ cents. A quarter is two bits. *n.* [Old English *bita* piece bitten off]
a bit, 1 a little; slightly: *I am a bit tired.* 2 somewhat: *The children who hung around so much became a bit of a nuisance to the shopkeeper.*
bit by bit, little by little.
do one's bit, do one's share: *Each child did his bit toward getting the meal on the table.*

bit² (bit), past tense and a past participle of **bite.** *The strong trap bit the leg of the fox. The postman was bit by our dog. v.*

bit³ (def. 1)   BRACE   BIT

bit³ (bit), 1 tool for boring or drilling that fits into a brace, electric drill, etc. 2 the biting or cutting part of a tool. 3 the part of a bridle that goes in a horse's mouth. 4 the part of a key that goes into a lock and makes it turn. *n.* [Old English *bite* a bite]
champ at the bit, be restless or impatient.

bit⁴ (bit), the basic unit of information

bison (def. 1)
about 5½ ft. high at the shoulder

adj.	adjective	*n.*	noun
adv.	adverb	*prep.*	preposition
conj.	conjunction	*pron.*	pronoun
interj.	interjection	*v.*	verb
sing.	singular	*pl.*	plural

in an electronic computer. It is equivalent to a choice between two possibilities, such as "yes" or "no." *n.* [formed from *bi(nary) (digi)t*]

bitch (bich), a female dog, wolf, or fox. *n., pl.* **bitch es.**

bite (bīt), 1 seize, cut into, or cut off with the teeth: *She bit the apple. When I'm nervous I bite my fingernails.* 2 act of biting: *The dog gave a bite or two at the bone.* 3 a piece bitten off; mouthful: *Eat the whole apple, not just a bite.* 4 a light meal; snack: *Have a bite with me now or you'll get hungry later.* 5 wound with teeth, fangs, a sting, etc.: *My dog never bites. A mosquito bit me.* 6 a wound made by biting or stinging: *The man soon recovered from the snake's bite.* 7 a sharp, smarting pain: *We felt the bite of the cold wind.* 8 cause a sharp, smarting pain to: *Her fingers are bitten by frost.* 9 take a tight hold of; grip: *The jaws of a vise bite the wood they hold.* 10 take a bait; be caught: *The fish are biting well today.* 1,5,8-10 *v.*, **bit, bit ten** or **bit, bit ing;** 2-4,6.7 *n.*

bit er (bī′tər), person or animal that bites. *n.*

bit ing (bī′ting), 1 sharp; cutting: *Dress warmly before you go out in that biting wind.* 2 sarcastic; sneering: *Biting remarks hurt people's feelings. adj.* —**bit′ing ly,** *adv.*

bit ten (bit′n), a past participle of **bite.** *Finish the apple, now that you have bitten into it. v.*

bit ter (bit′ər), 1 having a sharp, harsh, unpleasant taste: *Quinine is bitter medicine.* 2 causing pain or grief; hard to admit or bear: *a bitter defeat. The death of his father was a bitter loss.* 3 showing pain or grief: *bitter tears.* 4 harsh or cutting: *a bitter remark, bitter enemies.* 5 very cold: *The bitter winter killed our apple tree. adj.* —**bit′ter ly,** *adv.* —**bit′ter ness,** *n.*

bit tern (bit′ərn), a wading bird which lives in marshes and has a peculiar booming cry. It is a small kind of heron. *n.*

bit ter root (bit′ər rüt′ or bit′ər rut′), a small plant with fleshy roots and pink flowers, found in the northern Rocky Mountains. *n.*

bit ters (bit′ərz), 1 liquid in which a bitter herb, bark, or root has been

steeped, used to flavor cocktails or foods. 2 a bitter, dark beer. *n.pl.*

bit ter sweet (bit′ər swēt′), 1 a climbing plant with purple flowers and poisonous, scarlet berries. 2 a climbing shrub of North America with greenish flowers and orange seedcases that open and show red seeds. 3 sweet and bitter mixed: *bittersweet chocolate.* 4 pleasant and painful at once: *The movie had a bittersweet ending which left her uncertain whether to laugh or cry.* 1,2 *n.*, 3,4 *adj.*

bi tu men (bə tü′mən *or* bə tyü′mən), any of a number of minerals that will burn, such as asphalt, petroleum, and naphtha. *n.*

bi tu mi nous coal (bə tü′mə nəs *or* bə tyü′mə nəs), coal that burns with much smoke and a yellow flame; soft coal.

bi va lent (bī vā′lənt), having a valence of two. *adj.*

bi valve (bī′valv′), any mollusk whose shell consists of two parts hinged together so that it will open and shut like a book. Oysters and clams are bivalves. *n.*

bivalve (left), an oyster with valves open, contrasted with a univalve (right), a whelk

biv ouac (biv′wak *or* biv′ü ak), 1 an outdoor camp usually without tents or with very small tents: *The soldiers made a bivouac for the night in a field.* 2 camp outdoors in this way: *They bivouacked there until morning.* 1 *n.*, 2 *v.*, **biv-ouacked, biv ouack ing.**

bi week ly (bī wēk′lē), 1 once every two weeks: *This magazine is a biweekly publication (adj.). The group meets biweekly (adv.).* 2 twice a week: *The teachers have a biweekly conference (adj.). That class is held biweekly (adv.).* 3 newspaper or magazine published biweekly. 1,2 *adj., adv.,* 3 *n., pl.* **bi-week lies.**

bi year ly (bī yir′lē), twice a year: *Their grandchildren make a biyearly visit (adj.). They pay taxes biyearly (adv.). adj., adv.*

bi zarre (bə zär′), strikingly odd or queer in appearance or style; fantastic; grotesque: *The frost made bizarre figures on the windowpanes. adj.* —**bi-zarre′ly,** *adv.* —**bi zarre′ness,** *n.*

Bi zet (bē zā′), **Georges,** 1838-1875, French composer. *n.*

bk., 1 bank. 2 book. *pl.* **bks.**

bkt., basket. *pl.* **bkts.**

blab (blab), tell (secrets); talk too much. *v.*, **blabbed, blab bing.**

blab ber (blab′ər), 1 person who blabs. 2 foolish talk. 3 blab. 1,2 *n.*, 3 *v.*

black (blak), 1 having the color of coal or soot; opposite of white: *This print is black.* 2 the color of coal or soot; the opposite of white: *The black shows up against the white.* 3 a black paint, dye, or pigment. 4 make black; blacken: *I blacked my shoes before going to the party.* 5 without any light; very dark: *The room was black as night.* 6 dirty; filthy: *Her hands were black with soot.* 7 dismal; gloomy: *a black day.* 8 sullen; angry: *She gave her brother a black look.* 9 evil; wicked: *a black lie.* 10 Also, **Black. a** having dark skin; Negro. **b** person who has dark skin; Negro. 1,5-10a *adj.*, 2,3,10b *n.*, 4 *v.* —**black′ly,** *adv.* —**black′ness,** *n.*

black out, 1 become temporarily blind or unconscious: *The pain was so intense that I blacked out for several minutes.* 2 darken completely: *black out the stage.* 3 suppress; withhold: *The general blacked out all news of the battle.*

black-and-blue (blak′ən blü′), discolored from a bruise. *adj.*

black art, evil magic; black magic.

black ball (blak′bôl′), 1 vote against; reject as a candidate for membership: *One member of the club blackballed him, so he could not become a member.* 2 a vote against a person or thing. 1 *v.*, 2 *n.*

black bear, a large North American bear that has dense black fur.

black ber ry (blak′ber′ē), 1 a small, black or dark purple fruit of certain bushes and vines that belong to the same family as the rose. It is sweet and juicy. 2 the thorny bush or vine that it grows on. *n., pl.* **black ber ries.**

black bird (blak′bėrd′), 1 any of various American birds so named because the male is mostly black. The cowbird, grackle, and redwing are blackbirds. 2 the European thrush. *n.*

black board (blak′bôrd′), a dark, smooth piece of slate, glass, or painted wood on which to write or draw with chalk. *n.*

black body, a theoretical surface or body capable of completely absorbing all the radiation falling on it.

Black Death, the bubonic plague that spread through Europe in the 1300's and destroyed one-fourth of its population.

black en (blak′ən), 1 make black: *Soot blackened the snow.* 2 become black: *The sky blackened and soon it began to rain.* 3 speak evil of: *blacken* someone's *reputation* by *spreading rumors about him.* v.

black eye, 1 a bruise around an eye. **2** INFORMAL. cause of disgrace or discredit.

black-eyed Su san (blak′īd′ sü′-zn), a yellow daisy with a black center.

Black foot (blak′fut′), member of a tribe of American Indians that formerly lived in northwestern United States and are now on reservations in Montana and in Alberta, Canada. *n.*, *pl.* **Black feet** (blak′fēt′), **Black foot.**

Black Forest, mountains covered with forests in SW West Germany.

black guard (blag′ärd), a low, contemptible person; scoundrel. *n.*

black head (blak′hed′), a small lump of dead cells and oil plugging a pore of the skin. *n.*

Black Hills, group of mountains in W South Dakota and NE Wyoming.

black ing (blak′ing), a black polish used on shoes, stoves, etc. *n.*

black ish (blak′ish), somewhat black. *adj.*

black jack (blak′jak′), **1** club with a flexible handle, used as a weapon. **2** hit with a blackjack. **3** the black flag of a pirate. **4** a card game in which the players draw cards face down from the dealer, trying for a score of not more than 21 points. 1,3,4 *n.*, 2 *v.*

black list (blak′list′), **1** list of persons who are believed to deserve punishment, blame, suspicion, etc.: *That store keeps a blacklist of persons who do not pay their bills.* **2** put on a blacklist. 1 *n.*, 2 *v.*

black magic, evil magic; sorcery. Witches were believed to practice black magic.

black mail (blak′māl′), **1** money obtained from a person by threatening to tell or reveal something bad about him. **2** get or try to get blackmail from. **3** an attempt to get money by threats. 1,3 *n.*, 2 *v.* —**black′mail er,** *n.*

black mark, mark of criticism or punishment made against a person.

black market, 1 the selling of goods at unlawful prices or in unlawful quantities. **2** place where such selling is done.

black out (blak′out′), **1** a turning off or going out of all the lights of a city, district, etc., as a protection against an air raid or as the result of power failure. **2** temporary blindness or loss of consciousness resulting from lack of blood circulation in the brain. **3** the withholding of information usually printed or broadcast: *a news blackout.* *n.*

Black Power, power of collective Negro action used to achieve equality.

Black Sea, large sea between Turkey and S Soviet Union.

black sheep, person considered by his group or family to be a disgrace.

black smith (blak′smith′), person who makes things out of iron by heating it in a forge and hammering it into shape on an anvil. Blacksmiths can mend tools and shoe horses. *n.*

black snake (blak′snāk′), **1** a harmless dark or black snake of North America. **2** a heavy whip made of braided leather. *n.*

black thorn (blak′thôrn′), a thorny European shrub of the same family as the rose, having white flowers and very small, dark-purple fruit. The fruit, and sometimes the shrub itself, is called sloe. *n.*

black top (blak′top′), **1** asphalt mixed with crushed rock, used as a pavement for highways, roads, and other surfaces. **2** surface covered with this substance. *n.*

black widow, a poisonous spider with a glossy black body which has a reddish mark in the shape of an hourglass on its underside. The black widow gets its name from its color and from the fact that the females sometimes eat their mates.

KIDNEY

bladder
(def. 1)

BLADDER

blad der (blad′ər), **1** a soft, thin bag in the body that receives urine from the kidneys. **2** anything like this. A football has a hollow rubber bladder that can be blown up with air. *n.*

blade (blād), **1** the cutting part of anything like a knife or sword: *A carving knife should have a very sharp blade. He had the blades of his skates sharpened.* **2** sword. **3** a smart, dashing fellow. **4** leaf of grass. **5** the flat, wide part of a leaf. **6** the flat, wide part of anything: *the blade of an oar or paddle, the shoulder blade.* *n.* —**blade′like′,** *adj.*

blad ed (blā′did), having a blade or blades. *adj.*

Blake (blāk), **William,** 1757-1827, English poet and artist. *n.*

blam a ble (blā′mə bəl), deserving blame; faulty. *adj.*

blame (blām), **1** hold responsible for something bad or wrong: *The driver blamed the fog for his accident.* **2** responsibility for something bad or

hat, āge, fär; let, ēqual, tėrm;
it, īce; hot, ōpen, ôrder;
oil, out; cup, pùt, rüle; ch, child;
ng, long; sh, she; th, thin;
ℱH, then; zh, measure;

ə represents *a* in about,
e in taken, *i* in pencil,
o in lemon, *u* in circus.

wrong: *Carelessness deserves the blame for many mistakes.* **3** find fault with: *The teacher will not blame us if we do our best.* **4** a finding fault; reproof. 1,3 *v.*, **blamed, blam ing;** 2,4 *n.*
be to blame, deserve to be blamed: *Each person said somebody else was to blame.*

blame less (blām′lis), not deserving blame; faultless: *The saint lived a blameless life.* *adj.* —**blame′less ly,** *adv.* —**blame′less ness,** *n.*

blame wor thy (blām′wėr′ℱHē), deserving blame; faulty. *adj.*

blanch (blanch), **1** make white; bleach. Almonds are blanched by soaking off their skins in boiling water. We blanch celery by keeping out the light. **2** turn white; become pale: *The boy blanched with fear when he saw the bear coming.* *v.*

bland (bland), **1** gentle; soothing; balmy: *a bland summer breeze.* **2** smoothly agreeable and polite: *a bland smile.* **3** mild; not irritating: *a bland diet of baby food.* *adj.* —**bland′ly,** *adv.* —**bland′ness,** *n.*

blan dish (blan′dish), persuade by gentle ways; coax; flatter. *v.*

blan dish ment (blan′dish mənt), a coaxing; flattery: *The princess did not yield to the sorcerer's blandishments.* *n.*

blank (blangk), **1** space left empty or to be filled in: *Leave a blank if you can't answer the question.* **2** not written or printed on: *blank paper.* **3** a paper with spaces to be filled in: *Fill out this application blank and return it at once.* **4** with spaces left for filling in: *a blank check, a blank form for you to fill in.* **5** an empty or vacant place: *When he read the hard questions his mind became a complete blank.* **6** empty; vacant: *There was a blank look on his face.* **7** cartridge containing gunpowder but no bullet or shot. 1,3,5,7 *n.*, 2,4,6 *adj.* —**blank′ly,** *adv.* —**blank′ness,** *n.*

draw a blank, be unsuccessful: *I drew a blank when I tried to recall her name.*

blan ket (blang′kit), **1** a soft, heavy covering woven from wool, cotton, nylon, or other material, used to keep

adj. adjective	*n.* noun
adv. adverb	*prep.* preposition
conj. conjunction	*pron.* pronoun
interj. interjection	*v.* verb
sing. singular	*pl.* plural

people or animals warm. 2 anything like a blanket: *A blanket of snow covered the ground.* 3 to cover with a blanket or anything like a blanket: *The snow blanketed the ground.* 4 covering several or all: *a blanket guarantee to repair defects of any kind.* 1,2 *n.*, 3 *v.*, 4 *adj.*

blank verse, 1 unrhymed poetry having five iambic feet in each line: *Shakespeare's "Julius Caesar" is written in blank verse.* 2 any unrhymed verse: *Walt Whitman wrote most of his poetry in blank verse.*

blare (bler *or* blar), 1 make a loud, harsh sound: *The trumpets blared, announcing the king's arrival.* 2 a loud, harsh sound. 1 *v.*, **blared, blaring;** 2 *n.*

blarney (blär′nē), 1 flattering, coaxing talk. 2 flatter; coax. 1 *n.*, 2 *v.*

Blarney Stone, a stone in a castle near Cork, Ireland. Anyone who kisses it is supposed to become skillful in flattering and coaxing people.

blasé (blä zā′), tired of pleasures; bored. *adj.* [from French]

blaspheme (bla sfēm′), speak about (God or sacred things) with abuse or contempt. *v.*, **blasphemed, blaspheming.**

blasphemer (bla sfē′mər), person who blasphemes. *n.*

blasphemous (blas′fə məs), speaking about God or sacred things with abuse or contempt. *adj.* —**blas′phemously,** *adv.*

blasphemy (blas′fə mē), abuse or contempt for God or sacred things. *n.*, *pl.* **blasphemies.**

blast (blast), 1 a strong, sudden rush of wind or air: *Last night we felt the icy blasts of winter.* 2 the blowing of a trumpet, horn, whistle, etc.: *The warning blast of a bugle aroused the camp.* 3 sound made by blowing a trumpet, horn, whistle, etc. 4 current of air used in smelting, etc. 5 blow up (rocks, earth, etc.) with dynamite, gunpowder, etc.: *The old building was blasted.* 6 a blasting; explosion: *We heard the blast a mile away.* 7 charge of dynamite, gunpowder, etc., that blows up rocks, earth, etc. 8 cause to wither; blight; destroy: *A disease has blasted our grapes. His conviction for theft blasted*

his reputation. 1-4,6,7 *n.*, 5,8 *v.* —**blast′er,** *n.*

blast off, take off into flight propelled by rockets: *All parts of the spacecraft are carefully checked before it blasts off.*

full blast, in full operation: *The carnival was going full blast.*

blast furnace, furnace in which ores are smelted by forcing a strong current of air into the furnace from the bottom to make a very great heat.

blast off (blast′ôf′), a launching or taking off into rocket-propelled flight: *The astronaut suffered no injury during blastoff and reentry.* *n.*

blatancy (blāt′n sē), noisy or unpleasant intrusion: *Viewers object to the blatancy of some television commercials.* *n.*

blatant (blāt′nt), 1 noisy; loud-mouthed: *a blatant fool.* 2 obvious; flagrant: *a blatant lie, a blatant disregard of others.* *adj.* —**bla′tantly,** *adv.*

blaze¹ (blāz), 1 a bright flame or fire: *We could see the blaze of the campfire across the beach.* 2 burn with a bright flame: *A fire was blazing in the fireplace.* 3 a glow of brightness; intense light; glare: *the blaze of the noon sun.* 4 show bright colors or lights: *On New Year's Eve the big house blazed with lights.* 5 bright display: *The tulips made a blaze of color in the garden.* 6 burst out in anger or excitement: *She blazed up at the insult.* 7 a sudden or violent outburst: *Her reaction to the insult was a blaze of temper.* 1,3,5,7 *n.*, 2,4,6 *v.*, **blazed, blazing.** [Old English *blæse*]

blaze² (blāz), 1 mark made on a tree by cutting off a piece of bark, to indicate a trail or boundary in a forest. 2 mark (a tree, trail, or boundary) with a blaze or by making blazes. 3 a white spot on the face of a horse, cow, etc. 1,3 *n.*, 2 *v.*, **blazed, blazing.** [perhaps from earlier German *bläse*]

blaze³ (blāz), make known; proclaim. *v.*, **blazed, blazing.** [from a Scandinavian word of the 1200's, such as Icelandic *blāsa*]

blazer (blā′zər), a distinctively colored or decorated jacket. Blazers are sometimes worn as part of the uniform of a team or school. *n.*

blazon (blā′zn), 1 make known; proclaim: *Big posters blazoned the wonders of the coming circus.* 2 decorate with designs, names, colors, etc. 3 coat of arms. 1,2 *v.*, 3 *n.*

blazonry (blā′zn rē), 1 bright decoration or display. 2 coat of arms. *n.*, *pl.* **blazonries.**

bldg., building. *pl.* **bldgs.**

bleach (blēch), 1 whiten by exposing to sunlight or by using chemicals: *We bleached the linen napkins in the wash.*

Bleached bones lay on the hot sands of the desert. 2 any chemical used in bleaching: *Laundries often use bleach to get dirty shirts clean.* 1 *v.*, 2 *n.*, *pl.* **bleaches.**

bleachers (blē′chərz), rows or tiers of low-priced seats, usually not covered by a roof, at an outdoor sports event. *n.pl.*

bleak (blēk), 1 swept by winds; bare: *The rocky peaks of high mountains are bleak.* 2 chilly; cold: *The bleak winter wind made us shiver.* 3 cheerless and depressing; dismal: *A prisoner's life is bleak.* *adj.* —**bleak′ly,** *adv.* —**bleak′ness,** *n.*

blear (blir), make dim or blurred: *The old dog's eyes were bleared by age.* *v.*

bleary (blir′ē), dim; blurred: *Her eyes were bleary from lack of sleep.* *adj.*, **blearier, bleariest.**

bleat (blēt), 1 cry made by a sheep, goat, or calf. 2 a sound like this: *a bleat of terror.* 3 make the cry of a sheep, goat, or calf. 4 make a sound like this. 1,2 *n.*, 3,4 *v.*

bled (bled), past tense and past participle of **bleed.** *The cut bled for ten minutes.* *v.*

bleed (blēd), 1 lose blood: *She is bleeding from a cut.* 2 suffer wounds or death: *He fought and bled for his country.* 3 take blood from: *Doctors used to bleed sick people.* 4 lose sap, juice, etc., from a surface that has been cut or scratched: *Trees bleed if they are pruned when the sap is rising in the spring.* 5 feel pity, sorrow, or grief: *My heart bleeds for the poor little orphan.* *v.*, **bled, bleeding.**

bleeder (blē′dər), person who bleeds excessively when injured, because the blood fails to clot. *n.*

blemish (blem′ish), 1 something that mars beauty, completeness, or perfection; defect; flaw: *A scar or a mole is a blemish on a person's skin.* 2 injure; mar: *Scandal blemished the mayor's good reputation.* 1 *n.*, *pl.* **blemishes;** 2 *v.*

blench (blench), draw back; shrink away. *v.*

blend (blend), 1 mix or become mixed so thoroughly that the things mixed cannot be distinguished or separated; mix together: *Even if you mix oil and water, they will not blend. Blend the butter and the sugar before adding the other ingredients of the cake.* 2 shade into each other, little by little; merge: *The colors of the rainbow blend into one another.* 3 go well together; harmonize. 4 a thorough mixture made by blending: *This coffee is a blend of three varieties.* 5 word made by combining two words, often with a syllable in common. EXAMPLE: *Motel* is a blend of *motor* and *hotel.* 1-3 *v.*, 4,5 *n.*

bless (bles), 1 make holy or sacred: *The bishop blessed the new church.* 2 ask God's favor for: *Bless these little children.* 3 wish good to; feel grateful to: *I bless her for her kindness.* 4 make happy or fortunate: *May this country always be blessed with freedom.* 5 praise; glorify: *Bless the Lord, O my soul.* v., **blessed** or **blest, bless ing.**

bless ed (bles′id *or* blest), 1 holy; sacred: *the blessed sacrament.* 2 happy; fortunate: *The birth of a baby is often called a blessed event.* adj. —**bless′ed ness,** n.

Bless ed Virgin (bles′id), the Virgin Mary.

bless ing (bles′ing), 1 prayer asking God to show His favor; benediction: *A religious service often ends with a blessing.* 2 a wish for happiness or success: *When I left home, I received my family's blessing.* 3 anything that makes one happy and contented; benefit: *A good temper is a great blessing.* 4 consent or approval: *The marriage had the blessing of the parents of the bride and groom.* n.

blest (blest), 1 a past tense and a past participle of **bless.** *He was blest with good health.* 2 blessed. 1 v., 2 adj.

blew (blü), past tense of **blow².** *All night long the wind blew.* v.

blight (blīt), 1 disease that causes plants or parts of plants to wither and die: *The apple crop was wiped out by blight.* 2 bacterium, fungus, or virus that causes such a disease. 3 anything that causes destruction or ruin. 4 cause to wither and die; destroy; ruin: *Mildew blighted the June roses. Rain blighted our hopes for a picnic.* 1-3 n., 4 v.

blimp (blimp), a small airship. n.

blimp—The gas-filled balloon provides lift. The motor behind the cabin moves the blimp forward.

blind (blīnd), 1 not able to see: *The woman with the white cane is blind.* 2 make unable to see: *The bright lights blinded me for a moment.* 3 hard to see; hidden: *There is a blind curve on the highway.* 4 make difficult to see; conceal: *Clouds blinded the stars from my view.* 5 without the help of sight; by means of instruments instead of the eyes: *blind flying of an aircraft at night* (adj.), *readings from instruments that enable pilots to fly blind* (adv.). 6 with-

out thought, judgment, or good sense: *He was in a blind fury. I made a blind guess.* 7 take away the power to understand or judge: *Her prejudices blinded her.* 8 something that keeps out light or hinders sight. A window shade or shutter is a blind. 9 anything that conceals an action or purpose: *Asking to see how fast his friend's bicycle would go was a blind to get to use it.* 10 with only one opening. A blind alley is a passageway closed at one end. 11 without an opening: *a blind wall.* 12 a hiding place for a hunter: *When he hunts ducks, he makes a blind of twigs, grass, and leaves so that he can keep out of sight.* 1,3,5,6,10,11 adj., 2,4,7 v., 5 adv., 8,9,12 n. —**blind′ly,** adv. —**blind′ness,** n.

blind er (blīn′dər), a leather flap on a horse's bridle to keep it from seeing sideways; blinker. n.

blinders—These prevent the horse from being distracted or frightened by objects to the side.

blind fold (blīnd′fōld′), 1 cover the eyes of: *We blindfolded her for a game of blindman's buff.* 2 with the eyes covered: *He said he could walk the line blindfold.* 3 thing covering the eyes: *After we put a blindfold on the horse, we led it from the blazing barn.* 1 v., 2 adj., 3 n.

blind man's buff (blīnd′manz buf′), game in which a blindfolded person tries to catch one of several other players and tell who he is.

blind spot, a point on the retina that is not sensitive to light. The optic nerve enters the eye there.

blink (blingk), 1 close the eyes and open them again quickly: *She blinked at the sudden light.* 2 shut the eyes to; look with indifference at; ignore: *You cannot blink the fact that time slips by.* 3 shine with an unsteady light: *A little lantern blinked through the darkness.* 4 a sudden flash of light; gleam. 1-3 v., 4 n.

on the blink, INFORMAL. not working properly: *My radio is on the blink.*

blink er (bling′kər), 1 blinder. 2 a warning signal with flashing lights. n.

blip (blip), image on a radar screen. n.

bliss (blis), great happiness; perfect joy: *What bliss it is to plunge into the cool waves on a hot day!* n.

bliss ful (blis′fəl), very happy; joyful: *blissful memories of a summer vacation.* adj. —**bliss′ful ly,** adv. —**bliss′ful ness,** n.

hat, āge, fär; let, ēqual, tėrm;
it, īce; hot, ōpen, ôrder;
oil, out; cup, pùt, rüle; ch, child;
ng, long; sh, she; th, thin;
ᴛʜ, then; zh, measure;

ə represents *a* in about,
e in taken, *i* in pencil,
o in lemon, *u* in circus.

blis ter (blis′tər), 1 a little baglike place in the skin filled with watery matter. Blisters are often caused by burns or rubbing. *My new shoes have made blisters on my heels.* 2 a similar swelling on the surface of a plant, on metal, on painted wood, or in glass. 3 raise a blister or blisters on: *Sunburn has blistered my back.* 4 become covered with blisters; have blisters: *People often blister when they get sunburned.* 1,2 n., 3,4 v.

blithe (blīᴛʜ *or* blīth), happy and cheerful; gay. adj., **blith er, blith est.** —**blithe′ly,** adv. —**blithe′ness,** n.

blithe some (blīᴛʜ′səm *or* blīth′-səm), blithe. adj. —**blithe′some ly,** adv.

blitz (blits), 1 a sudden, violent attack using many airplanes and tanks. 2 any sudden, violent attack. 3 to attack or overcome by a blitz. 1,2 n., pl. **blitz es;** 3 v. [from German *Blitzkrieg* lightning war]

bliz zard (bliz′ərd), a blinding snowstorm with a very strong wind and very great cold. n.

bloat (blōt), swell up; puff up: *Overeating bloated their stomachs.* v.

blob (blob), a small, soft drop; sticky lump: *Blobs of wax covered the candlestick.* n.

bloc (blok), group of persons, companies, or nations combined for a purpose: *The farm bloc in Congress is a group from different political parties that favors laws to help farmers.* n.

block (blok), 1 a solid piece of wood, stone, metal, ice, etc., usually with one

blip—The three blips on the radar screen indicate three objects. Distance from the radar is indicated by the circles. Those blips closest to the center are the nearest.

adj.	adjective	*n.* noun
adv.	adverb	*prep.* preposition
conj.	conjunction	*pron.* pronoun
interj.	interjection	*v.* verb
sing.	singular	*pl.* plural

or more flat sides: *The Pyramids are made of blocks of stone.* 2 fill up so as to prevent passage or progress: *The country roads were blocked with snow. The landslide blocked up the river bed.* 3 put things in the way of; obstruct; hinder: *Mother's illness blocked my plans for her birthday party.* 4 (in sports and games) hinder an opponent's play. 5 anything or any group of persons that keeps something from being done; obstruction; hindrance: *A block in traffic kept our car from moving on.* 6 space in a city or town enclosed by four streets; square. 7 length of one side of a block in a city or town: *Walk one block east.* 8 number of buildings close together. 9 group of things of the same kind: *We bought a block of ten tickets for a play.* 10 platform where things are put up for sale at an auction. 11 pulley or pulleys in a holder with a hook or eye by which it may be attached. 12 shape with a mold: *Felt hats are blocked.* 1,5-11 *n.,* 2-4,12 *v.*

block in or **block out,** plan or sketch roughly without filling in the details; outline: *The artist blocked in parts of a portrait. The committee blocked out its plan.*

on the block, up for sale: *A collection of paintings will go on the block at the auction.*

block ade (blo kād/), 1 a blocking of a place by military means to control who or what goes into or out of it: *A complete blockade of all the harbors and ports of the United States would require thousands of enemy warships.* 2 put under blockade. 3 anything that blocks up or obstructs. 4 block up; obstruct. 1,3 *n.,* 2,4 *v.,* **block ad ed, block-ad ing.**

run the blockade, sneak into or out of a port that is being blockaded.

block and tackle, combination of pulleys and ropes to lift or pull something.

block bust er (blok/bus/tər), INFORMAL. 1 a very destructive aerial bomb. 2 anything very large, forceful, or overwhelming. *n.*

block head (blok/hed/), a stupid person; fool. *n.*

block house (blok/hous/), a small fort or building with loopholes to shoot from. *n., pl.* **block hous es** (blok/-hou/ziz).

block y (blok/ē), 1 like a block; chunky: *a blocky pony.* 2 having patches of light and shade: *A photograph may be blocky.* adj., **block i er, block i est.**

blond or **blonde** (blond), 1 light in color: *blond hair, blond furniture.* 2 having yellow or light-brown hair, blue or gray eyes, and a fair skin. 3 person with such hair, eyes, and skin. A man or boy of this sort is usually referred to as a blond. A woman or girl of this sort is usually referred to as a blonde. 1,2 *adj.,* 3 *n.* —**blond/ness, blonde/ness,** *n.*

blood (blud), 1 the red liquid in the veins, arteries, and capillaries of vertebrates; the red liquid that flows from a cut. Blood is circulated by the heart, carrying oxygen and digested food to all parts of the body and carrying away waste materials. 2 the corresponding liquid in animals other than vertebrates. The blood of most insects looks yellowish or greenish. 3 relationship by descent from a common ancestor; family; parentage; descent: *Love of the sea runs in his blood.* 4 man of dash and spirit. *n.*

curdle one's blood, frighten very much; horrify; terrify: *The piercing scream curdled my blood.*

in cold blood, without feeling; cruelly and deliberately: *a crime committed in cold blood.*

blood bank, 1 place for storage of blood to be used in transfusions. 2 the blood kept in storage.

blood cur dling (blud/kėrd/ling), terrifying; horrible: *She read a blood-curdling story about a haunted house.* adj.

blood ed (blud/id), coming from good stock; of good breed: *a blooded stallion.* adj.

block and tackle

TACKLE BLOCKS

blood group, any one of the groups into which human blood may be divided on the basis of the presence or absence of certain substances that cause red cells to clump together; blood type. Blood groups are important in blood transfusions.

blood hound (blud/hound/), a large, powerful dog with a keen sense of smell. Bloodhounds are used to track criminals or find people who have become lost. *n.*

blood i ly (blud/l ē), in a bloody manner. *adv.*

blood i ness (blud/ē nis), condition of being bloody. *n.*

blood less (blud/lis), 1 without bloodshed: *By surrounding the city the enemy achieved a bloodless victory.* 2 without blood; pale: *a bloodless face.* 3 without energy; spiritless. *adj.* —**blood/less ly,** *adv.* —**blood/less ness,** *n.*

blood poisoning, a diseased condition of the blood caused by poisonous matter or germs.

blood pressure, pressure of the blood against the inner walls of the blood vessels. Blood pressure varies with exertion, excitement, health, and age.

blood root (blud/rüt/ or blud/rut/), a common wild plant that has a red root, red sap, and a white flower that blooms in early spring. It is related to the poppy. *n.*

blood shed (blud/shed/), the shedding of blood; slaughter: *There are no battles in war without bloodshed.* *n.*

blood shot (blud/shot/), red and sore from inflamed blood vessels: *A cinder in his eye made it bloodshot.* adj.

blood stained (blud/stānd/), stained with blood: *Her handkerchief was blood-stained from using it on a cut.* adj.

blood stream (blud/strēm/), blood as it flows through the body. *n.*

blood suck er (blud/suk/ər), 1 leech or other animal that sucks blood. 2 person who gets all he can from others in any way he can. *n.*

blood thirst i ly (blud/thėr/stl ē), in a bloodthirsty manner. *adv.*

blood thirst i ness (blud/thėr/-stē nis), eagerness for bloodshed. *n.*

blood thirst y (blud/thėr/stē), eager for bloodshed; cruel and murderous: *a bloodthirsty pirate.* adj.

blood type, blood group.

blood vessel, any tube in the body through which the blood circulates. Arteries, veins, and capillaries are blood vessels.

blood y (blud/ē), 1 covered with blood; bleeding: *He came home with a bloody nose.* 2 accompanied by much killing: *It was a bloody battle.* 3 cause to bleed. 4 stain with blood: *Her knee was bloodied by her fall.* 5 stained with blood: *The sword was bloody.* 6 eager for bloodshed; cruel. 1,2,5,6 *adj.,* **blood i er, blood i est;** 3,4 *v.,* **blood-ied, blood y ing.**

bloom (blüm), 1 have flowers; open into flowers; blossom: *Many plants* bloom in the spring. 2 a flower; blossom. 3 condition or time of flowering. 4 condition or time of greatest health, vigor, or beauty: *She was in the bloom of youth.* 5 be in the condition or time of greatest health, vigor, or beauty; flourish: *Only water can make the desert bloom.* 6 glow of health and beauty. 7 the powdery coating on some fruits and leaves. There is a bloom on grapes and plums. 1,5 *v.*, 2-4,6,7 *n.*

bloom ers (blü′mərz), 1 loose trousers, gathered at the knee, formerly worn by women and girls for physical training. 2 underwear made like these. *n.pl.* [from Amelia J. *Bloomer*, 1818-1894, who first referred to them]

blos som (blos′əm), 1 flower, especially of a plant that produces fruit: *apple blossoms.* 2 condition or time of flowering: *The cherry trees are in blossom.* 3 have flowers; open into flowers: *All the orchards blossom in spring.* 4 open out; develop: *She blossomed into a beautiful woman.* 1,2 *n.*, 3,4 *v.*

blot (blot), 1 a spot of ink or stain of any kind. 2 make blots on; stain; spot: *His pen slipped and blotted his paper in two places. This pen blots.* 3 dry with paper that soaks up ink: *Blot your page before you smear the ink.* 4 a spot upon one's character or reputation; blemish; disgrace. 1,4 *n.*, 2,3 *v.*, **blot ted, blot ting.**

blot out, 1 cover up entirely; hide: *He blotted out the mistake with ink.* 2 wipe out; destroy: *When the storm brought down all the electric lines, the lights were blotted out.*

blotch (bloch), 1 a large, irregular spot or stain. 2 place where the skin is red or broken out: *The fever made her face break out in blotches.* 3 cover or mark with spots or stains. 1,2 *n.*, *pl.* **blotch es;** 3 *v.*

blotch y (bloch′ē), having blotches. *adj.*, **blotch i er, blotch i est.**

blot ter (blot′ər), 1 piece of blotting paper. 2 book for recording happenings or transactions. A police station blotter is a record of arrests. *n.*

blotting paper, a soft paper used to dry writing by soaking up ink.

blouse (blous), 1 a loose upper garment worn by women and children as a part of their outer clothing: *She wore a white silk blouse with a blue skirt.* 2 a loosely fitting garment for the upper part of the body: *Sailors wear wool blouses as a part of their uniform.* 3 a short, fitted coat worn as part of a military uniform. *n.*

blow¹ (blō), 1 a hard hit; knock; stroke: *strike a blow with the fist, strike a blow with a hammer.* 2 a sudden happening that causes misfortune or loss; severe shock: *His mother's death*

was a great blow to him. 3 a sudden attack or assault: *The army struck a swift blow at the enemy.* n. [perhaps originally a special meaning of *blow²*]

come to blows, start fighting: *The two children came to blows.*

blow² (blō), 1 send forth a strong current of air: *Blow on the fire or it will go out.* 2 move in a current; move rapidly or with power: *The wind often blows in March.* 3 drive or carry by a current of air: *The wind blew the curtain.* 4 force a current of air into, through, or against: *The bellows blew the coals of the fire into flames.* 5 empty or clear by forcing air through: *The plumber blew the pipes.* 6 cause to pant: *He blew his horse by riding him hard.* 7 form or shape by air; swell with air: *blow glass, blow bubbles.* 8 make a sound by a current of air or steam: *The whistle blows at noon.* 9 break by an explosion: *The dynamite blew the wall to bits.* 10 melt: *The short circuit caused the fuse to blow.* 11 a blowing. 12 gale of wind: *Last night's big blow brought down several trees.* 13 spout water in the air: *"There she blows!" was the sailor's cry when he spotted the whale.* 1-10,13 *v.*, blew, blown, blow ing; 11,12 *n.* [Old English *blāwan*]

blow out, 1 put out or be put out by a current of air: *The candle blew out. I blew out the candle.* 2 have or cause a blowout in: *The worn tire blew out.*

blow over, 1 pass by or over: *The storm has blown over.* 2 be forgotten: *In time the scandal blew over.*

blow up, 1 explode: *The ammunition ship blew up and sank when it hit the rocks.* 2 fill with air: *blow up a bicycle tire.* 3 INFORMAL. become very angry: *I lost my patience and blew up at my sister for leaving our room in a mess.* 4 become stronger; arise: *A storm blew up suddenly.* 5 enlarge (a photograph).

blow er (blō′ər), 1 person or thing that blows: *a glass blower.* 2 fan or other machine for forcing air into a building, furnace, mine, or other enclosed area. *n.*

blow fly (blō′flī′), any of various two-winged flies that deposit their eggs on meat or in wounds. *n.*, *pl.* **blow flies.**

blow gun (blō′gun′), tube through which a person blows something, such as darts or dried beans; blowpipe. *n.*

blow hole (blō′hōl′), hole for breathing, in the top of the head of whales, porpoises, and dolphins. *n.*

blown (blōn), past participle of **blow².** *The wind has blown itself out.* *v.*

blow out (blō′out′), 1 the bursting of an automobile tire. 2 a sudden or violent escape of air, steam, or the like.

hat, āge, fär; let, ēqual, tèrm;
it, īce; hot, ōpen, ôrder;
oil, out; cup, pùt, rüle; ch, child;
ng, long; sh, she; th, thin;
ŦH, then; zh, measure;

ə represents *a* in about,
e in taken, *i* in pencil,
o in lemon, *u* in circus.

3 the melting of an electric fuse by a sudden overload in a circuit or line, causing a power failure. *n.*

blow pipe (blō′pīp′), 1 tube for blowing air or gas into a flame to increase the heat. 2 blowgun. *n.*

blow torch (blō′tôrch′), a small torch that shoots out a very hot flame under pressure. A blowtorch is used to melt metal and burn off paint. *n.*, *pl.* **blow torch es.**

blowtorch used to thaw a frozen water pipe

blow up (blō′up′), 1 explosion. 2 INFORMAL. outburst of anger. *n.*

blub ber (blub′ər), 1 fat of whales and some other sea animals. The oil obtained from whale blubber was formerly burned in lamps. 2 weep noisily. 1 *n.*, 2 *v.*

bludg eon (bluj′ən), 1 a short, heavy club. 2 strike with a bludgeon. 3 bully or threaten. 1 *n.*, 2,3 *v.*

blue (blü), 1 the color of the clear sky in daylight. 2 having this color. 3 something having this color. 4 **the blue, a** the sky: *A bolt of lightning struck from the blue.* **b** the sea: *Far out upon the blue sail many ships.* 5 having a dull-bluish color; livid: *Her hands were blue from cold.* 6 sad; gloomy; discouraged: *I felt blue when I failed.* See also **blues.** 7 use bluing on. 1,3,4 *n.*, 2,5,6 *adj.*, **blu er, blu est;** 7 *v.*, **blued, blu ing** or **blue ing.** —**blue′ness,** *n.*

out of the blue, completely unexpectedly: *His visit came out of the blue.*

blue bell (blü′bel′), any of various plants with blue flowers shaped like bells, such as the harebell. *n.*

blue ber ry (blü′ber′ē), 1 a small, round, sweet, blue berry which tastes like the huckleberry but has smaller seeds. 2 shrub that it grows on. *n.*, *pl.* **blue ber ries.**

adj. adjective	*n.* noun
adv. adverb	*prep.* preposition
conj. conjunction	*pron.* pronoun
interj. interjection	*v.* verb
sing. singular	*pl.* plural

blue bird (blü′bėrd′), a small thrush of North America that is related to the robin. The male usually has a bright blue back and wings and a chestnut-brown breast. *n.*

Blue Bird, member of the junior division of the Camp Fire Girls.

blue bon net (blü′bon′it), plant with blue flowers resembling sweet peas. *n.*

blue bot tle (blü′bot′l), a large blowfly that has a blue abdomen and a hairy body. *n.*

blue fish (blü′fish′), a saltwater fish, bluish or greenish above and silvery below, of the Atlantic coast of North America. It is valued as food. *n., pl.* **blue fish es** or **blue fish.**

blue grass (blü′gras′), grass with bluish-green stems. It is valuable for pasturage and hay. *n.*

blue ing (blü′ing), bluing. *n.*

blue jack et (blü′jak′it), sailor in the navy. *n.*

blue jay, a noisy, chattering North American bird with a crest and a blue back.

blue jeans, jeans, usually made of blue denim.

blue law, any very strict law regulating personal conduct. Laws prohibiting dancing or going to the theater on Sunday are blue laws.

blue print (blü′print′), 1 a photographic print that shows white outlines on a blue background. The process of making blueprints is used to copy original drawings of building plans, maps, etc. 2 a detailed plan for doing anything. *n.*

blue ribbon, the first prize; highest honor: *That sheep won a blue ribbon for best entry in its class at the fair.*

Blue Ridge, the SE range of the Appalachian Mountains, extending from NW Maryland to N Georgia.

blues (blüz), 1 a slow, melancholy song with jazz rhythm. 2 **the blues,** INFORMAL. low spirits: *A rainy day always gives me the blues. n.pl.*

blu et (blü′it), a small plant of North America, with pale blue flowers. *n.*

blue whale, a blue-gray whale with yellowish underparts, sometimes growing to over 100 feet in length. It is the largest living animal.

bluff[1] (bluf), 1 a high, steep bank or cliff. 2 rising with a straight, broad front: *a bluff headland.* 3 abrupt, frank, and hearty in manner. 1 *n.,* 2,3 *adj.* [probably from earlier Dutch *blaf* flat] —**bluff′ly,** *adv.* —**bluff′ness,** *n.*

bluff[2] (bluf), 1 show of pretended confidence put on to deceive or mislead others. We say it is a bluff when a person lets others think that he knows more than he really does, that he has more money than he really has, or that he holds better playing cards than he really holds. 2 deceive by a show of pretended confidence; fool: *By using logs for cannons the general bluffed the enemy so successfully that they retreated from their attack.* 3 threat that cannot be carried out: *The bully's attempt to scare us is merely a bluff.* 4 frighten with a threat that cannot be carried out: *He bluffed the robber with a toy gun.* 5 person who bluffs. 1,3,5 *n.,* 2,4 *v.* [probably from Dutch *bluffen* brag] —**bluff′er,** *n.*

call one's bluff, ask for proof or for action when pretense is suspected.

blu ing (blü′ing), a blue liquid or powder put in water when laundering clothes. It keeps white clothes from turning yellow. *n.* Also, **blueing.**

blu ish (blü′ish), somewhat blue. *adj.*

blun der (blun′dər), 1 a stupid mistake: *Misspelling the title of a book is a silly blunder to make in a book report.* 2 make a stupid mistake: *Someone blundered in sending you to the wrong address.* 3 move clumsily or blindly; stumble: *I blundered through the dark house.* 1 *n.,* 2,3 *v.* —**blun′der er,** *n.*

blun der buss (blun′dər bus), a short gun with a wide muzzle and large bore, formerly used to shoot balls or slugs a very short distance without exact aim. *n., pl.* **blun der buss es.**

blunt (blunt), 1 without a sharp edge or point; dull: *He sharpened the blunt knife.* 2 make less sharp; make less keen: *a knife blunted from use. A cold blunted my sense of smell.* 3 saying what one thinks very frankly, without trying to be tactful; outspoken: *Her blunt criticism of my work hurt my feelings.* 1,3 *adj.,* 2 *v.* —**blunt′ly,** *adv.* —**blunt′ness,** *n.*

blur (blėr), 1 make less clear in form or outline: *Mist blurred the hills.* 2 dim: *Tears blurred my eyes. My eyes blurred with tears.* 3 blurred condition; dimness: *The blur in his vision was caused by old age.* 4 thing seen dimly or indistinctly: *His face was just a blur without my glasses on.* 5 to smear; smudge: *He blurred the picture by touching it before the paint was dry.* 6 a smear; smudge: *The letter had many blots and blurs.* 1,2,5 *v.,* **blurred, blur ring;** 3,4,6 *n.*

blurb (blėrb), INFORMAL. advertisement or description, usually on the jacket of a book, album, etc., full of high praise. *n.*

blur ry (blėr′ē), 1 dim; indistinct: *The hills were a blurry outline in the dusk.* 2 full of smears and smudges. *adj.,* **blur ri er, blur ri est.**

blurt (blėrt), say suddenly or without thinking: *In his excitement he blurted out the secret. v.*

blush (blush), 1 become red in the face because of shame, confusion, or excitement: *The little girl was so shy that she blushed every time she was spoken to.* 2 a reddening of the face caused by shame, confusion, or excitement. 3 be ashamed: *I blushed at my brother's bad table manners.* 4 a rosy color: *The blush of dawn showed in the east.* 5 be or become red or rosy. 1,3,5 *v.,* 2,4 *n.,* *pl.* **blush es.**

at first blush, on first glance; at first thought: *At first blush, he thought the job would be easy.*

blus ter (blus′tər), 1 storm noisily; blow violently: *The wind blustered around the corner of the house.* 2 stormy noise and violence: *We heard the bluster of the wind and rain.* 3 talk noisily and violently: *He was very excited and angry and blustered for a while.* 4 noisy and violent talk: *angry bluster.* 1,3 *v.,* 2,4 *n.* —**blus′ter er,** *n.*

blus ter y (blus′tər ē), blustering. *adj.*

blvd., boulevard.

bo a (bō′ə), 1 any of various snakes which are not poisonous, but kill their prey by squeezing it in their coils. Most boas are found in tropical regions and are very large, ranging between 10 and 30 feet in length. Anacondas, pythons, and boa constrictors are boas. 2 a long scarf made of fur or feathers, worn around a woman's neck. *n., pl.* **bo as.**

boa constrictor, a large boa of the tropical parts of America, from 10 to 15 feet long.

boar (bôr), 1 a male pig or hog. 2 a wild pig or hog. *n.*

board (bôrd), 1 a broad, thin piece of wood for use in building, etc.: *We used boards 10 inches wide, 1 inch thick, and 3 feet long for shelves in our new bookcase.* 2 cover with boards: *We always board up the windows of our summer cottage when we leave in the fall.* 3 a flat piece of wood or other material used for one special purpose: *an ironing board, a drawing board, a bulletin board.* 4 table to serve food on; table. 5 meals provided for pay at a boardinghouse, etc.: *The landlady gives good board to her lodgers.* 6 provide with or get meals, or room and meals, for pay: *You will have to board elsewhere.* 7 group of persons managing something; council: *a school board, a board of directors.* 8 get on (a ship, train, bus, airplane, etc.): *We board the school bus at the corner every day.* 1,3-5,7 *n.*, 2,6,8 *v.*

on board, on a ship, train, bus, airplane, etc.: *When everybody was on board, the ship sailed.*

board er (bôr′dər), person who pays for meals, or for room and meals, at another's house. *n.*

board foot, unit of measure equal to a board one foot square and one inch thick; 144 cubic inches. It is used for measuring logs and lumber.

board ing (bôr′ding), 1 boards. 2 structure made of boards. *n.*

board ing house (bôr′ding hous′), house where meals, or room and meals, are provided for pay. *n., pl.* **board ing hous es** (bôr′ding hou′ziz).

boarding school, school with buildings where the pupils live during the school term.

board of health, department of a state or local government in charge of public health.

board walk (bôrd′wôk′), a wide sidewalk usually made of boards, near the water at a shore resort: *The boardwalk at Atlantic City is a famous promenade. n.*

boast (bōst), 1 speak too highly of oneself or what one owns; brag: *She boasts about her grades in school.* 2 statement speaking too highly of oneself or what one owns; bragging words: *I don't believe his boast that he can run faster than I can.* 3 something to be proud of: *The table she made by herself is her boast.* 4 have (something) to be proud of: *Our town boasts many fine parks.* 1,4 *v.*, 2,3 *n.* —**boast′er,** *n.*

boast ful (bōst′fəl), fond of bragging; boasting: *It is hard to listen very long to a boastful person. adj.* —**boast′ful ly,** *adv.* —**boast′ful ness,** *n.*

boat (bōt), 1 a small, open vessel for traveling on water, such as a motorboat or a rowboat. 2 a large vessel, such as a steamboat or ocean liner; ship. 3 go in a boat. 4 put or carry in a boat. 5 dish shaped somewhat like a boat for gravy or sauce. 1,2,5 *n.*, 3,4 *v.* —**boat′like′,** *adj.*

in the same boat, in the same position or condition; taking the same chances.

rock the boat, INFORMAL. disturb or upset the way things are: *Your refusal to obey the rules is rocking the boat.*

boat house (bōt′hous′), house or shed for sheltering a boat or boats. *n., pl.* **boat hous es** (bōt′hou′ziz).

boat man (bōt′mən), 1 man who rents out boats or takes care of them. 2 man who rows or sails boats for pay. 3 man who works on a boat. *n., pl.* **boat men.**

boat swain (bō′sn), a ship's officer in

charge of the anchors, ropes, and rigging. He directs some of the work of the crew. *n.* Also, **bo's'n** or **bosun.**

bob[1] (bob), 1 move up and down, or to and fro, with short, quick motions: *The pigeon bobbed its head as it picked up crumbs.* 2 a short, quick motion up and down, or to and fro. 1 *v.*, **bobbed, bob bing;** 2 *n.* [origin uncertain]

bob[2] (bob), 1 a child's or woman's haircut that is fairly short all around the head. 2 cut (hair) short. 3 weight on the end of a plumb line. 4 a float for a fishing line. 1,3,4 *n.*, 2 *v.*, **bobbed, bob bing.** [Middle English *bobbe* bunch]

bob bin (bob′ən), reel or spool for holding thread, yarn, etc. Bobbins are used in spinning, weaving, machine sewing, and making lace. Wire is also wound on bobbins. *n.*

bob by (bob′ē), INFORMAL. policeman (a term used in Great Britain). *n., pl.* **bob bies.**

bobby pin, a metal hairpin whose prongs close on and hold tightly to the hair.

bob by socks (bob′ē soks′), socks reaching just above the ankle, worn especially by girls. *n.pl.*

bobcat—23 in. high at the shoulder

bob cat (bob′kat′), a small lynx of North America, having a reddish-brown coat with black spots. *n.*

bob o link (bob′ə lingk), a common North American songbird which lives in fields and meadows and has a call that sounds somewhat like its name. It belongs to the same family as the blackbirds. *n.*

bob sled (bob′sled′), 1 a long sled with two sets of runners and a continuous seat. It has a steering wheel and brakes. 2 ride or coast on a bobsled. 1 *n.*, 2 *v.*, **bob sled ded, bob sled ding.**

bob stay (bob′stā′), rope or chain to hold a bowsprit down. *n.*

bob tail (bob′tāl′), 1 a short tail, or a tail cut short. 2 animal having such a tail. 3 having such a tail. 1,2 *n.*, 3 *adj.*

bob white (bob′hwīt′), an American quail that has a grayish body with brown and white markings. Its call sounds somewhat like its name. *n.*

bode[1] (bōd), be a sign of; indicate

beforehand; foreshadow: *The rumble of thunder boded rain. v.*, **bod ed, bod ing.** [Old English *bodian* announce, foretell]

bode ill, be a bad sign: *The dark clouds boded ill for the success of our picnic.*

bode well, be a good sign: *His good habits of study boded well for his success in school.*

bode[2] (bōd), a past tense of **bide.** *v.*

bod ice (bod′is), 1 the close-fitting upper part of a dress. 2 a wide girdle worn over a dress and laced up the front. *n.*

bod i less (bod′ē lis), without a body: *Spirits are bodiless. adj.*

bod i ly (bod′l ē), 1 of the body; in the body: *bodily pain.* 2 in person: *Although she cannot be with us bodily, she is here in spirit.* 3 as a whole; altogether; entirely: *The audience rose bodily to cheer the hero.* 1 *adj.*, 2,3 *adv.*

bod kin (bod′kən), 1 a large, blunt needle. 2 a long hairpin. 3 a pointed tool for making holes. *n.*

bod y (bod′ē), 1 the whole material or physical structure of a person, animal, or plant: *This boy has a strong, healthy body.* 2 the main part of an animal from which other parts, such as the head, limbs, or tail stick out. 3 the main or central part of anything, such as the hull of a ship or the part of a vehicle that holds the passengers or the load. 4 group of persons or things: *The student body of our school gathered for an assembly. Congress is the lawmaking body of our government.* 5 a dead person or animal; corpse. 6 portion of matter; mass: *A lake is a body of water. The moon, the sun, and the stars are heavenly bodies.* 7 matter; substance; density: *Thick soup has more body than thin soup. n., pl.* **bod ies.**

bod y guard (bod′ē gärd′), man or men who guard a person: *A bodyguard accompanies the President when he travels. n.*

Boer (bôr *or* bōr), 1 person of Dutch descent living in South Africa. 2 of or having to do with the Boers. 1 *n.*, 2 *adj.*

Boer War, war between Great Britain and the Boers, from 1899 to 1902.

adj. adjective	*n.* noun
adv. adverb	*prep.* preposition
conj. conjunction	*pron.* pronoun
interj. interjection	*v.* verb
sing. singular	*pl.* plural

bog (bog), 1 piece of soft, wet, spongy ground; marsh; swamp. 2 sink or get stuck in a bog. 1 *n.*, 2 *v.*, **bogged, bog ging.**

bog down, sink in or get stuck so that one cannot get out without help: *I am bogged down with my homework.*

bo gey (bō′gē *or* bŭg′ē for 1; bō′gē for 2), 1 bogy. 2 score of one stroke over par for any hole on a golf course. *n., pl.* **bo geys.**

bog gle (bog′əl), 1 hold back; hesitate: *Father boggled at the suggestion that we should help him paint the house.* 2 overwhelm or be overwhelmed with wonder, shock, etc.: *The vastness of the universe boggles the imagination. His mind boggled at the thought of his inheriting a million dollars.* *v.*, **bog gled, bog gling.**

bog gy (bog′ē), soft and wet like a bog; marshy; swampy: *boggy ground.* *adj.*, **bog gi er, bog gi est.**

bo gie (bō′gē *or* bŭg′ē), bogy. *n.*

Bo go tá (bō′gə tä′), capital of Colombia, in the central part. *n.*

bo gus (bō′gəs), not genuine; counterfeit; sham: *The man was arrested when he handed the cashier a bogus ten-dollar bill. adj.*

bo gy (bō′gē *or* bŭg′ē), 1 evil spirit; goblin. 2 person or thing, usually imaginary, that is feared without reason; bugbear; bugaboo. *n., pl.* **bo gies.** Also, **bogey** or **bogie.**

Bo he mi a (bō hē′mē ə), 1 former country in central Europe, now a region of Czechoslovakia. 2 Also, **bohemia.** an unconventional, carefree place or existence. *n.*

Bo he mi an (bō hē′mē ən), 1 of Bohemia, its people, or their language. 2 person born or living in Bohemia. 3 language of Bohemia; Czech. 4 Also, **bohemian. a** carefree and unconventional. **b** artist, writer, etc., who lives an unconventional, carefree sort of existence. 1,4a *adj.*, 2,3,4b *n.*

Bohr (bôr), **Niels,** 1855-1962, Danish physicist who studied the atom. *n.*

boil[1] (boil), 1 bubble up and give off steam or vapor: *Water boils when heated to 212 degrees Fahrenheit.* 2 cause (a liquid) to boil: *Boil some water for tea.* 3 cook by boiling: *We boil eggs four minutes.* 4 have its con-

tents boil: *The pot is boiling.* 5 be very excited; be stirred up: *I boiled with anger.* 6 a boiling condition: *Bring the water to a boil.* 1-5 *v.*, 6 *n.* [from French of the 1200's *boillir,* from Latin *bullire,* from *bulla* a bubble]

boil down, 1 make less by boiling: *Boil down the sauce to half the amount.* 2 shorten by getting rid of unimportant parts: *The notes for her oral report were so long that the teacher asked her to boil them down to a list of important facts.*

boil over, 1 come to the boiling point and overflow: *This pot of milk is boiling over.* 2 show excitement or anger: *I boiled over when someone took my bicycle without asking me first.*

boil[2] (boil), a painful, red swelling on the skin, formed by pus around a hard core. Boils are often caused by infection. *n.* [Old English *bȳle*]

boil er (boi′lər), 1 tank for making steam to heat buildings or drive engines. 2 tank for heating and holding hot water. 3 container for heating liquids. *n.*

boiling point, temperature at which a liquid boils. The boiling point of water at sea level is 212 degrees Fahrenheit or 100 degrees centigrade.

Boi se (boi′sē), capital of Idaho, in the SW part. *n.*

bois ter ous (boi′stər əs), 1 noisily cheerful: *The room was filled with boisterous laughter.* 2 violent; rough: *a boisterous wind. adj.* —**bois′ter ous ly,** *adv.* —**bois′ter ous ness,** *n.*

bo la (bō′lə), weapon consisting of stone or metal balls tied at the ends of long cords. South American cowboys throw it so that it winds around and entangles the animal aimed at. *n., pl.* **bo las.**

BOLT   **NUT**   **bolt**[1]
(top, def. 1)
(bottom, def. 2)

bold (bōld), 1 without fear; brave: *Lancelot was a bold knight.* 2 showing or requiring courage: *Climbing the steep mountain was a bold act.* 3 too free in manner; impudent: *The bold little boy made faces at us as we passed.* 4 sharp and clear to the eye; striking: *The mountains stood in bold outline against the sky.* 5 steep; abrupt: *Bold cliffs overlooked the sea. adj.* —**bold′ly,** *adv.* —**bold′ness,** *n.*

bold face (bōld′fās′), a heavy printing type that stands out clearly. **This sentence is in boldface.** *n.*

bole (bōl), stem or trunk of a tree. *n.*

bo ler o (bə ler′ō), 1 a lively Spanish dance in 3/4 time. 2 music for it. 3 a short, loose jacket coming barely to the waist. *n., pl.* **bo ler os.**

Bo lí var (bō lē′vär *or* bol′ə vər), **Simón,** 1783-1830, Venezuelan general and statesman, who led revolts against Spanish rule in South America. Bolivia is named after him. *n.*

Bo liv i a (bə liv′ē ə), country in W South America. *Capitals:* La Paz and Sucre. *n.* —**Bo liv′i an,** *adj., n.*

boll (bōl), the rounded seed pod of a plant, especially that of cotton or flax. *n.*

boll weevil, a small beetle with a long snout whose larva is hatched in and does great damage to young cotton bolls.

bo lo (bō′lō), a long, heavy knife, used in the Philippines. *n., pl.* **bo los.**

bo lo gna (bə lō′nē *or* bə lō′nə), a large sausage usually made of beef, veal, and pork. *n., pl.* **bo lo gnas.** [from *Bologna*]

Bo lo gna (bə lō′nyə), city in N Italy. *n.*

Bol she vik (bōl′shə vik), 1 member of a radical political party in Russia that seized power in November 1917. The Bolsheviks became the Communist Party in 1918. 2 member of any Communist Party. 3 of the Bolsheviks or Bolshevism. 4 Also, **bolshevik. a** any extreme radical. **b** extremely radical. 1,2,4a *n.*, 3,4b *adj.* [from Russian *bol'shevik,* from *bol'she* greater]

Bol she vism (bōl′shə viz′əm), 1 doctrines and methods of the Bolsheviks. 2 Also, **bolshevism.** extreme radicalism. *n.*

Bol she vist (bōl′shə vist), Bolshevik. *n., adj.*

bol ster (bōl′stər), 1 a long pillow for a bed. 2 a cushion or pad. 3 keep from falling; support; prop: *The walls of the church are bolstered up with buttresses. Her encouragement bolstered my confidence.* 1,2 *n.*, 3 *v.*

bolt[1] (bōlt), 1 rod with a head at one end and a screw thread for a nut at the other. Bolts are used to fasten things together or hold something in place. 2 bar slid or dropped into a bracket to lock a door, gate, etc. 3 part of a lock moved by a key. 4 fasten with a bolt: *Bolt the doors.* 5 a short arrow with a thick head. Bolts were shot from crossbows. 6 discharge of lightning. 7 a sudden start; a running away: *When the rabbit saw us, it made a bolt for safety.* 8 dash off; run away: *The horse bolted at the sight of the car.* 9 break away from one's party or its candidates. 10 roll of cloth or wallpaper. 11 swallow (food) quickly without chewing: *The dog bolted its food.*

1-3,5-7,10 *n.*, 4,8,9,11 *v.* [Old English *bolt* arrow]

bolt upright, stiff and straight: *A noise in the middle of the night made me sit bolt upright in bed.*

bolt[2] (bōlt), sift through a cloth or sieve: *Flour is bolted to remove the bran. v.* [from French of the 1200's *buleter*]

bomb (bom), 1 container filled with an explosive. A bomb is set off by a fuse, a timing device, or by the force with which it hits something. 2 attack with bombs; hurl bombs at; drop bombs on. 3 container filled with an insecticide, paint, or other liquid under pressure, that comes out as spray or foam. 1,3 *n.*, 2 *v.*

bom bard (bom bärd′), 1 attack with bombs or heavy fire of shot and shell from big guns: *The artillery bombarded the enemy all day.* 2 keep attacking vigorously: *The lawyer bombarded the witness with one question after another.* 3 strike (the nucleus of an atom) with a stream of fast-moving particles to change the structure of the nucleus. *v.*

bom bard ment (bom bärd′mənt), 1 an attack with bombs or with heavy fire of shot and shell. 2 a vigorous attack. 3 the striking of the nucleus of an atom with a stream of fast-moving particles. *n.*

bom bast (bom′bast), showy or high-flown language that is without much meaning: *A few plain facts are better than a lot of bombast. n.*

bom bas tic (bom bas′tik), using many showy or high-flown words with too little thought: *The speaker used bombastic language to cover up almost total ignorance of the subject. adj.*

bom bas ti cal ly (bom bas′tik lē), in a bombastic manner. *adv.*

Bom bay (bom bā′), seaport in W India, on the Arabian Sea. *n.*

bomb er (bom′ər), airplane used to drop bombs on enemy troops, factories, cities, etc. *n.*

bomb proof (bom′prüf′), strong enough to be safe from the effects of bombs and shells. *adj.*

bomb shell (bom′shel′), 1 bomb (def.1). 2 a sudden, unexpected happening; disturbing surprise: *The news of his dismissal from school was a bombshell to the family. n.*

bo na fide (bō′nə fīd′ or bō′nə fī′dē), in good faith; without make-believe or fraud; genuine: *a bona fide offer.* [from Latin]

bo nan za (bə nan′zə), 1 a rich mass of ore in a mine. 2 any rich source of profit: *Their farm has turned out to be a bonanza, for oil has been found on it. n., pl.* **bo nan zas.**

Bo na parte (bō′nə pärt), Napoleon. See **Napoleon I.** *n.*

bon bon (bon′bon′), piece of candy, usually soft and often having a fancy shape. *n.*

bond (bond), 1 anything that ties, binds, or unites: *a bond of affection between sisters.* 2 **bonds,** *pl.* a chains; shackles: *the bonds of slavery.* b OLD USE. imprisonment. 3 certificate issued by a government or private company which promises to pay back with interest the money borrowed from the buyer of the certificate: *The city issued bonds to raise money for building a new playground.* 4 a written agreement by which a person says he will pay a certain sum of money if he does not perform certain duties properly. 5 agree to pay a certain sum of money if a person does not perform certain duties properly: *An insurance company has bonded the city treasurer for one million dollars.* 6 bind together. 1-4 *n.*, 5,6 *v.*

bond age (bon′dij), a being held against one's will under the control or influence of some person or thing; lack of freedom; slavery. *n.*

bond ed (bon′did), 1 secured by bonds: *a bonded debt.* 2 put in a warehouse until taxes are paid: *bonded goods. adj.*

bonded warehouse, warehouse where bonded goods are kept.

bond man (bond′mən), 1 slave. 2 (in the Middle Ages) a person who belonged with the land and was sold with it; serf. *n., pl.* **bond men.**

bonds man (bondz′mən), 1 person who becomes responsible for another by giving a bond. 2 bondman. *n., pl.* **bonds men.**

bond wom an (bond′wùm′ən), a woman bondman. *n., pl.* **bond-wom en.**

bone (bōn), 1 one of the pieces of the skeleton of an animal with a backbone: *the bones of the hand, a beef bone for soup.* 2 take bones out of: *The waiter boned the fish before serving it.* 3 the hard substance of which bones are made. 4 something like bone. Ivory is sometimes called bone. 1,3,4 *n.*, 2 *v.*, **boned, bon ing. —bone′like′, adj.**

make no bones about, INFORMAL. show no hesitation about; acknowledge readily: *The tired children made no bones about wanting to go home.*

bone less (bōn′lis), 1 without bones. 2 without courage; cowardly. *adj.*

bon er (bō′nər), SLANG. a foolish mistake; stupid error; blunder. *n.*

bon fire (bon′fīr′), fire built outdoors: *We had to sit around the bonfire to keep warm. n.*

bon go (bong′gō), a small drum played with flattened hands, especially in Latin-American and African music. Bongos usually come in pairs and are

book

hat, āge, fär; let, ēqual, tèrm; it, īce; hot, ōpen, ôrder; oil, out; cup, pùt, rüle; ch, child; ng, long; sh, she; th, thin; ₮H, then; zh, measure;

ə represents *a* in about, *e* in taken, *i* in pencil, *o* in lemon, *u* in circus.

held between the knees. *n., pl.* **bongos.**

bongo drum, bongo.

bon i ness (bō′nē nis), quality of being bony. *n.*

Bonn (bon), capital of West Germany, in the W part, on the Rhine. *n.*

bon net (bon′it), 1 a covering for the head usually tied under the chin with strings or ribbons, worn by women and children. 2 cap worn by men and boys in Scotland. 3 headdress of feathers worn by North American Indians. *n.*

bon ny or **bon nie** (bon′ē), 1 fair to see; rosy and pretty: *What a bonny baby!* 2 gay or cheerful. *adj.*, **bon ni er, bon ni est.**

bo nus (bō′nəs), something extra, given in addition to what is due: *The company gave each worker a vacation bonus. n., pl.* **bo nus es.**

bon vo yage (bon′ vwä yäzh′), good-by; good luck; pleasant trip. [from French]

bon y (bō′nē), 1 of bone. 2 like bone. 3 full of bones: *bony fish.* 4 having big bones that stick out: *the bony hips of a thin horse.* 5 very thin: *bony, old hands. adj.*, **bon i er, bon i est.**

boo (bü), 1 sound made to show dislike or contempt, or to frighten: *Boos were heard from those who didn't like the concert* (n.). *We were frightened when he jumped from behind the door and shouted, "Boo!"* (interj.). 2 make such a sound; shout "boo" at: *He sang so badly that the audience booed him.* 1 *n., pl.* **boos;** 1 *interj.*, 2 *v.*, **booed, boo ing.**

boo by (bü′bē), 1 a stupid person; dunce. 2 kind of large tropical sea bird. *n., pl.* **boo bies.**

booby prize, prize given to the person or team that does the worst in a game or contest.

booby trap, 1 bomb arranged to explode when a harmless-looking object to which it is attached is touched or moved by an unsuspecting person. 2 trick arranged to annoy some unsuspecting person.

book (bùk), 1 a written or printed work of considerable length, especially

adj. adjective	*n.* noun
adv. adverb	*prep.* preposition
conj. conjunction	*pron.* pronoun
interj. interjection	*v.* verb
sing. singular	*pl.* plural

on sheets of paper bound together between covers: *She read the first two chapters of her book.* 2 blank sheets bound together: *You can keep a record of what you spend in this book.* 3 a main division of a book: *Genesis is the first book of the Old Testament.* 4 something fastened together like a book: *a book of tickets, stamps, or checks.* 5 **the Book,** the Bible. 6 make reservations to get tickets or to engage service: *He had booked passage by airplane from New York to London.* 7 enter a charge against (a person) in a police record. 1-5 *n.*, 6,7 *v.*

by the book, by rule; accurately: *She played the game carelessly and not by the book.*

keep books, keep a record of business accounts: *An accountant keeps books for the grocer.*

like a book, with fullness or accuracy; completely: *We are best friends; we know each other like a book.*

book case (bùk/kās/), piece of furniture with shelves for holding books. *n.*

book end, a prop or support placed at the end of a row of books to hold them upright.

book ish (bùk/ish), 1 fond of reading or studying; studious: *The bookish boy spent many hours in the library.* 2 knowing books better than real life: *The scholar was a bookish man who did not know the world of business.* 3 stiffly dignified or formal; scholarly in a dull and narrow way; stilted: *Her conversation was sprinkled with bookish phrases.* *adj.* —**book/ish ly,** *adv.* —**book/ish ness,** *n.*

book keep er (bùk/kē/pər), person who keeps a record of business accounts. *n.*

book keep ing (bùk/kē/ping), work of keeping a record of business accounts. *n.*

book let (bùk/lit), a little book; thin book. Booklets often have paper covers. *n.*

book mark (bùk/märk/), piece of cloth, paper, etc., put between the pages of a book to mark the reader's place. *n.*

book mo bile (bùk/mə bēl/), bus or truck that serves as a traveling branch of a library. *n.*

Book of Mormon, a sacred book of

the Church of Jesus Christ of Latter-day Saints.

book sell er (bùk/sel/ər), person whose business is selling books. *n.*

book shelf (bùk/shelf/), shelf for holding books. *n., pl.* **book shelves.**

book shop (bùk/shop/), bookstore. *n.*

book store (bùk/stôr/), store where books are sold. *n.*

book worm (bùk/wėrm/), 1 person who is very fond of reading and studying. 2 any insect larva that gnaws the bindings or leaves of books. *n.*

boom[1] (bùm), 1 a deep hollow sound like the roar of cannon or of big waves: *The big bell tolled with a loud boom.* 2 make a deep hollow sound: *The big man's voice boomed out above the rest.* 3 a sudden activity and increase in business, prices, or values of property; rapid growth: *Our town is having such a boom that it is likely to double its size in two years.* 4 increase suddenly in activity; grow rapidly: *Business is booming.* 5 push or urge to rapid progress: *Many citizens are booming the mayor for senator.* 1,3 *n.*, 2,4,5 *v.* [probably made up originally to imitate a loud sound]

boom[2] (bùm), 1 a long pole or beam, used to extend the bottom of a sail. 2 the lifting and guiding pole of a derrick. 3 chain, cable, or line of timbers that keeps logs from floating away. *n.* [from Dutch *boom* tree, pole]

boomerang (def. 1)
left, three types of boomerangs;
right, the path of a boomerang

boo me rang (bü/mə rang/), 1 a curved piece of wood, used as a weapon by Australian natives. It can be thrown so that it returns to the thrower. 2 anything that recoils or reacts to harm the doer or user. 3 act as a boomerang: *The evidence one member of the gang gave against the rest boomeranged when he was convicted with the rest.* 1,2 *n.*, 3 *v.*

boon[1] (bün), 1 a great benefit; blessing: *Those warm boots were a boon to me in the cold weather.* 2 OLD USE. something asked for or granted as a favor. *n.* [from a Scandinavian word of the 1100's, such as Icelandic *bôn* petition]

boon[2] (bün), jolly; gay; merry: *They are my boon companions. adj.* [from French of the 1300's *bon* good, from Latin *bonus*]

Boone (bün), **Daniel,** 1734-1820, American frontiersman who explored Kentucky. *n.*

boor (bür), a rude, bad-mannered person. *n.*

boor ish (bür/ish), having bad manners; rude. *adj.* —**boor/ish ly,** *adv.* —**boor/ish ness,** *n.*

boost (büst), 1 a push or shove that helps a person in rising or advancing: *Give me a boost over the fence.* 2 lift or push from below or behind. 3 help by speaking well of: *The manufacturers are boosting the new cereal in a series of TV ads.* 4 an increase in degree, amount, price, pay, etc.: *There has been a boost in prices at the supermarket.* 5 to raise; increase: *The supermarket has boosted its prices.* 1,4 *n.*, 2,3,5 *v.*

boost er (bü/stər), 1 person or thing that boosts. 2 any of various devices for increasing the power or thrust of an engine. 3 the first stage of a rocket, which provides all or part of the thrust needed for take-off. *n.*

booster (def. 3)

booster shot, an additional inoculation of a vaccine or serum to continue the effectiveness of a previous inoculation.

boot[1] (büt), 1 a leather or rubber covering for the foot and lower part of the leg. 2 put boots on; supply with boots: *The horseback rider was booted and spurred.* 3 a protective patch put inside an automobile tire. 4 (in Great Britain) an automobile trunk. 5 a kick: *He gave the ball a boot.* 6 give a kick to: *She booted the empty can off the sidewalk.* 1,3-5 *n.*, 2,6 *v.* [from French of the 1300's *bote*]

boot[2] (büt), OLD USE. profit; avail. *v.* [Old English *bôt* advantage]

to boot, in addition; besides: *For my knife she gave me a compass and a dime to boot.*

boot black (büt/blak/), person whose work is shining shoes and boots. *n.*

boot ee (bü/tē), a baby's soft shoe, often knitted. *n.*

Bo ö tes (bō ō/tēz), a northern constellation that includes the star Arcturus. *n.*

booth (büth), 1 a covered stall or similar place where goods are sold or shown at a fair, market, convention, etc. 2 a small, closed place for a telephone, motion-picture projector, etc. 3 a small, closed place for voting at elections. 4 a partly enclosed space in a restaurant or café, containing a table and seats for a few persons. *n., pl.* **booths** (büŦHz *or* büths).

Booth (büth), **William,** 1829-1912, English clergyman who founded the Salvation Army. *n.*

boot leg (büt′leg′), 1 sell, transport, or make unlawfully: *The police caught the truck driver who was bootlegging cigarettes into the state to avoid paying a tax.* 2 sold, transported, or made unlawfully. 1 *v.,* **boot legged, boot leg ging;** 2 *adj.*

boot leg ger (büt′leg′ər), person who bootlegs. *n.*

boot less (büt′lis), of no benefit or profit; useless. *adj.* —**boot′less ly,** *adv.*

boo ty (bü′tē), 1 things taken from the enemy in war. 2 things seized by violence and robbery; plunder: *The pirates fought over the booty from the town they raided.* 3 any valuable thing or things obtained; prize. *n., pl.* **booties.**

bo rax (bôr′aks), a white, crystalline powder used as an antiseptic, as a cleansing substance, in fusing metals, and in making heat-resistant glass. *n.*

Bor deaux (bôr dō′), 1 seaport in SW France. 2 a red or white wine made near Bordeaux. *n.*

bor der (bôr′dər), 1 the side, edge, or boundary of anything, or the part near it: *We pitched our tent on the border of the lake.* 2 form a boundary to; bound: *The Rio Grande borders part of Texas.* 3 line which separates one country, state, or province from another; frontier: *We crossed the border between France and Germany.* 4 a strip on the edge of anything for strength or ornament: *Her handkerchief has a blue border.* 5 put a border on; edge: *We have bordered our garden with shrubs.* 1,3,4 *n.,* 2,5 *v.*

border on or **border upon,** 1 touch at the border; be next to: *Canada borders on the United States.* 2 be close to; resemble: *Such silly behavior borders on the ridiculous.*

bor der land (bôr′dər land′), 1 land forming, or next to, a border. 2 an uncertain range, extent, or region: *the borderland between sleeping and waking. n.*

bor der line (bôr′dər līn′), 1 a dividing line; boundary. 2 on a border or boundary. 3 in between; uncertain: *I stayed home with a borderline case of mumps but didn't have to go to bed.* 1 *n.,* 2,3 *adj.*

bore[1] (bôr), 1 make a hole by means of a tool that keeps turning, or as a worm does in fruit: *The men dug the oil well by boring through the ground with huge drills.* 2 make (a hole, passage, etc.) by pushing through or digging out: *A mole has bored its way under the hedge.* 3 hole made by a revolving tool. 4 the hollow space inside a pipe, tube, or gun barrel: *He cleaned the bore of his gun.* 5 the distance across the inside of a hole or tube: *The bore of this pipe is two inches.* 1,2 *v.,* **bored, bor ing;** 3-5 *n.* [Old English *borian*]

bore[2] (bôr), 1 make weary by tiresome talk or by being dull: *This book bores me, so I shall not finish it.* 2 a dull, tiresome person or thing: *It is a bore to have to wash dishes three times a day.* 1 *v.,* **bored, bor ing;** 2 *n.* [origin unknown]

bore[3] (bôr), past tense of **bear**[1]. *She bore her loss bravely. v.*

Bo re as (bôr′ē əs), (in Greek myths) the north wind. *n.*

bore dom (bôr′dəm), a bored condition; weariness caused by dull, tiresome people or events. *n.*

bor er (bôr′ər), 1 insect or worm that bores into wood, fruit, etc. 2 tool for boring holes. *n.*

bo ric acid (bôr′ik), a white, crystalline substance used as a mild antiseptic. *n.*

born (bôrn), 1 brought into life; brought forth: *A baby born on Sunday is supposed to be lucky.* 2 by birth; by nature: *Most major league ballplayers are born athletes.* 3 a past participle of **bear**[1]. *She was born on December 30, 1900.* 1,2 *adj.,* 3 *v.*

borne (bôrn), a past participle of **bear**[1]. *I have borne the pack for three miles. She has borne three children. v.*

Bor ne o (bôr′nē ō), large island in the East Indies, between Java and the Philippines. Part of Borneo is a British protectorate, part belongs to the Federation of Malaysia, and part belongs to Indonesia. *n.*

bo ron (bôr′on), a nonmetallic element which occurs only in combination with other elements. It is present in borax. Boron is used in fuels, alloys, etc. *n.*

bor ough (bėr′ō), 1 (in some states of the United States) an incorporated town with certain privileges, smaller than a city. 2 one of the five divisions of New York City. 3 (in Alaska) a district similar to a county. *n.*

bor row (bor′ō), 1 get (something) from another person with the understanding that it must be returned: *If you lend your book to him, he has borrowed the book from you.* 2 take and use as one's own; adopt; take: *The word for the vegetable "squash" was borrowed from the Indians.* 3 (in subtraction) take (one) from the digit immediately to the left and add its place value to the digit being subtracted from: *In 46 − 19, borrow 10 from 40 to add to the 6,*

hat, āge, fär; let, ēqual, tėrm;
it, īce; hot, ōpen, ôrder;
oil, out; cup, pùt, rüle; ch, child;
ng, long; sh, she; th, thin;
ŦH, then; zh, measure;

ə represents *a* in about,
e in taken, *i* in pencil,
o in lemon, *u* in circus.

making the subtraction in the first digit 9 from 16. *v.* —**bor′row er,** *v.*

bosh (bosh), INFORMAL. foolish talk or ideas; nonsense: *She thought the new theories were bosh (n.). "Bosh," she responded when asked for an opinion (interj.). n., interj.*

bosk y (bos′kē), 1 wooded. 2 shady. *adj.,* **bosk i er, bosk i est.**

bos'n (bō′sn), boatswain. *n.*

bos om (bùz′əm), 1 the upper, front part of the human body; breast. 2 part of a garment covering this: *She wore a flower on the bosom of her dress.* 3 heart or feelings: *He kept the secret in his bosom.* 4 center or inmost part: *He did not mention it even in the bosom of his family.* 5 close and trusted: *Very dear friends are bosom friends.* 1-4 *n.,* 5 *adj.*

Bos por us (bos′pər əs), strait connecting the Black Sea and the Sea of Marmara. See **Dardanelles** for map. *n.*

boss[1] (bôs), INFORMAL. 1 person who hires workers or watches over or directs them; foreman; manager. 2 person who controls a political organization. 3 be the boss of; direct; control: *Who is bossing this job?* 1,2 *n., pl.* **boss es;** 3 *v.* [from Dutch *baas* master]

boss[2] (bôs), 1 a raised ornament of silver, ivory, or other material on a flat surface: *The boss on the knight's shield consisted of his coat of arms.* 2 decorate with ornamental nails, knobs, or studs. 1 *n.,* 2 *v.* [from French of the 1300's *boce* swelling, hump]

boss y (bô′sē), INFORMAL. fond of telling others what to do and how to do it; domineering. *adj.,* **boss i er, boss i est.**

Bos ton (bô′stən), seaport and capital of Massachusetts, on the Atlantic. *n.*

Bos to ni an (bô stō′nē ən), 1 of Boston. 2 person born or living in Boston. 1 *adj.,* 2 *n.*

bo sun (bō′sn), boatswain. *n.*

bo tan ic (bə tan′ik), botanical. *adj.*

bo tan i cal (bə tan′ə kəl), 1 having to do with plants and plant life. 2 having to do with botany. *adj.* —**bo tan′i cal ly,** *adv.*

adj. adjective	*n.* noun
adv. adverb	*prep.* preposition
conj. conjunction	*pron.* pronoun
interj. interjection	*v.* verb
sing. singular	*pl.* plural

bot a nist (bot′n ist), an expert in botany. *n.*

bot a ny (bot′n ē), science of plants; study of plants and plant life. Botany deals with the structure, growth, classification, diseases, etc., of plants. *n.*

botch (boch), 1 spoil by poor work; bungle: *I botched my essay and had to rewrite it.* 2 a poor piece of work. 1 *v.*, 2 *n.*, *pl.* **botch es.**

both (bōth), 1 the two; the one and the other: *Both houses are white.* 2 the two together: *Both belong to her.* 3 together; alike; equally: *She fears and hopes both at once (adv.). He is both strong and healthy (conj.).* 1 *adj.*, 2 *pron.*, 3 *adv.*, *conj.*

both er (boŦH′ər), 1 much fuss or worry about small matters; trouble: *What a lot of bother about nothing!* 2 take trouble; concern oneself: *Don't bother about my breakfast; I'll eat what is here.* 3 person or thing that causes worry, fuss, or trouble: *A door that will not shut is a bother.* 4 annoy; irritate: *Hot weather bothers me.* 1,3 *n.*, 2,4 *v.*

both er some (boŦH′ər səm), causing worry or fuss; troublesome. *adj.*

Bot swa na (bot swä′nə), country in S Africa, a member of the Commonwealth of Nations. See **South Africa** for map. *n.*

Bot ti cel li (bot′ə chel′ē), **Sandro,** 1444?-1510, Italian painter. *n.*

bot tle (bot′l), 1 container for holding liquids, made of glass, plastic, cardboard, etc. Bottles often have narrow necks fitted with caps or stoppers. 2 amount that a bottle can hold: *drink a bottle of milk.* 3 put into bottles: *Dairies bottle milk.* 1,2 *n.*, 3 *v.*, **bottled, bot tling. —bot′tle like′,** *adj.* **bottle up,** hold in; keep back; control: *I managed to bottle up my anger.*

bot tle neck (bot′l nek′), 1 a narrow passageway or street. 2 person, thing, or condition that hinders progress: *Heavy traffic caused a bottleneck at the narrow bridge. n.*

bot tom (bot′əm), 1 the lowest part: *These berries at the bottom of the basket are crushed.* 2 part on which anything rests: *The bottom of that glass is wet.* 3 ground under water: *Many wrecks lie at the bottom of the sea.* 4 Often, **bottoms,** *pl.* the low land along a river.

5 seat: *This chair needs a new bottom.* 6 basis; foundation; origin: *We will get to the bottom of the mystery.* 7 keel or hull of a ship; ship. 8 lowest or last: *I see a robin on the bottom branch of that tree. These are bottom prices. I have spent my bottom dollar.* 1-7 *n.*, 8 *adj.*

bot tom less (bot′əm lis), 1 without a bottom. 2 so deep that the bottom cannot be reached; extremely deep: *the bottomless depths of the sea. adj.*

bot u lism (boch′ə liz′əm), poisoning caused by eating food that has been spoiled by the action of certain bacteria. *n.*

bou doir (bü′dwär), a lady's private dressing room or sitting room. *n.*

bouf fant (bü fänt′), puffed out: *a bouffant hairdo. adj.* [from French]

bough (bou), 1 one of the main branches of a tree. 2 branch cut from a tree: *She held a blossoming bough from the apple tree in her hand. n.*

bought (bôt), past tense and past participle of **buy.** *We bought apples at the market. I have bought two new pencils. v.*

bouil lon (bül′yon), a clear, thin soup or broth. *n.*

boul der (bōl′dər), a large rock, rounded or worn by the action of water and weather. *n.*

Boulder Dam, Hoover Dam.

boul e vard (bül′ə värd), a broad street or avenue, often planted with trees. *n.*

bounce (bouns), 1 spring into the air like a ball: *The baby likes to bounce up and down on the bed.* 2 cause to bounce: *Bounce the ball to me.* 3 a bound; a spring; a bouncing: *I caught the ball on the first bounce.* 4 come or go noisily, angrily, etc.: *She bounced out of the room.* 1,2,4 *v.*, **bounced, bounc ing;** 3 *n.*

bounc ing (boun′sing), 1 that bounces: *a bouncing ball.* 2 big and strong. 3 vigorous; healthy: *a bouncing baby boy. adj.*

bound¹ (bound), 1 under some obligation; obliged: *I feel bound by my promise.* 2 certain; sure: *Everyone is bound to make a mistake sooner or later.* 3 INFORMAL. with one's mind firmly made up; determined; resolved: *He was bound to spend all of his allowance, though we did our best to stop him.* 4 past tense and past participle of **bind.** *She bound the package with string and tape. He has bound my hands.* 5 put in covers: *a bound book.* 1-3,5 *adj.*, 4 *v.* [Middle English *bounden*]

bound up in or **bound up with,** 1 closely connected with: *A farmer's life is bound up in his work.* 2 very devoted to: *The old friends are completely bound up in each other.*

bound² (bound), 1 spring back; bounce: *The ball bounded from the wall.* 2 a springing back; bounce: *I caught the ball on the first bound.* 3 leap or spring lightly along; jump: *Mountain goats can bound from rock to rock.* 4 a leaping or springing lightly along; jump: *With one bound the deer went into the woods.* 1,3 *v.*, 2,4 *n.* [from French of the 1500's *bondir* to leap]

bound³ (bound), 1 a limiting line; boundary; limit: *The king maintained peace and order within the bound of his realm.* 2 **bounds,** *pl.* area included within boundaries. 3 form the boundary of; limit: *Canada bounds the United States on the north.* 4 name the boundaries of: *Can you bound the state of Maine?* 1,2 *n.*, 3,4 *v.* [from French of the 1200's *bodne* or *bonde*]

out of bounds, outside the area allowed by rules, custom, or law: *I kicked the ball out of bounds. This town is out of bounds for the soldiers.*

bound⁴ (bound), on the way; going: *I am bound for home. adj.* [from a Scandinavian word of the 1200's, such as Icelandic *būinn* prepared]

bound ar y (boun′dər ē), a limiting line or thing; limit; border: *Lake Superior forms part of the boundary between Canada and the United States. n.*, *pl.* **bound ar ies.**

bound en (boun′dən), required: *It is our bounden duty as citizens to obey the laws. adj.*

bound less (bound′lis), 1 not limited; infinite: *Outer space is boundless.* 2 vast: *the boundless ocean. She has boundless energy. adj.* **—bound′less ly,** *adv.* **—bound′less ness,** *n.*

boun te ous (boun′tē əs), 1 given freely; generous: *The rich man gave bounteous gifts to the poor.* 2 plentiful; abundant: *Because of the spring rains, the farmer had a bounteous crop. adj.* **—boun′te ous ly,** *adv.* **—boun′te ous ness,** *n.*

boun ti ful (boun′tə fəl), 1 giving freely; generous: *the help of bountiful friends.* 2 more than enough; plentiful; abundant: *We put in so many plants that we have a bountiful supply of tomatoes. adj.* **—boun′ti ful ly,** *adv.* **—boun′ti ful ness,** *n.*

boun ty (boun′tē), 1 whatever is given freely; generous gift. 2 generosity in bestowing gifts and favors: *the bounty of Nature.* 3 reward; premium: *The state government used to give a bounty of one dollar for each coyote killed. n.*, *pl.* **boun ties.**

bou quet (bō kā′ *or* bü kā′ *for 1;* bü kā′ *for 2),* 1 bunch of flowers. 2 fragrance; aroma: *the bouquet of a wine. n.*

Bour bon (bùr′bən *for 1,2;* bėr′bən

bow² (def. 1)
bowman shooting
an arrow
from a bow

for 3), **1** a former royal family of France, Spain, Sicily, and Naples. The Bourbons were in power when the French Revolution begán. **2** person who clings to old ideas and opposes any change; extreme conservative. **3 bourbon,** kind of whiskey, distilled mainly from corn mash. *n.*

bour geois (bùr zhwä′), **1** person of the middle class, such as a merchant or professional person. **2** of the middle class. **3** like the middle class in way of thinking, appearance, etc.; ordinary: *bourgeois taste.* 1 *n., pl.* **bour geois;** 2,3 *adj.*

bour geoi sie (bùr′zhwä zē′), the middle class; people between the very wealthy class and the working class. *n.*

bourn¹ or **bourne¹** (bôrn), a small stream; brook. *n.* [Old English *burna*]

bourn² or **bourne²** (bôrn *or* bōrn), OLD USE. **1** boundary; limit. **2** goal. *n.* [from French of the 1500's *bourne*]

bout (bout), **1** trial of strength; contest: *Those are the two boxers who will appear in the main bout.* **2** period spent in some particular way; spell: *I have just had a long bout of illness. n.*

bou tique (bü tēk′), a small shop that specializes in stylish clothes and accessories for women or children. *n.*

bo vine (bō′vīn), **1** ox or cow. **2** of or like an ox or cow; slow; stupid: *a bovine stare.* **3** like that of an ox or cow; without emotion; stolid: *a bovine nature.* **4** any animal belonging to a group of mammals that chew the cud, including domestic cattle, bison, water buffaloes, and the like. **5** belonging to this group. 1,4 *n.,* 2,3,5 *adj.*

bow¹ (bou), **1** bend the head or body in greeting, respect, worship, or submission: *The people bowed before the king. Let us bow our heads in prayer.* **2** a bending of the head or body in this way: *She answered his bow with a curtsy.* **3** show by bowing: *The actors bowed their thanks at the end of the play.* **4** cause to stoop; bend: *The old man was bowed by age.* **5** submit; yield: *The boy bowed to his parents' wishes.* 1,3-5 *v.,* 2 *n.* [Old English *būgan*]
bow out, withdraw.
take a bow, accept praise or applause for something done.

bow² (bō), **1** weapon for shooting arrows. A bow usually consists of a strip of flexible wood bent by a string. **2** a slender rod with horsehairs stretched on it, for playing a violin, cello, etc. **3** play (a violin, cello, etc.) with a bow. **4** to curve; bend: *The branches of the young tree were bowed by the storm.* **5** something curved; curved part: *A rainbow is a bow.* **6** a looped knot: *She wears a bow of blue ribbon in her hair.* 1,2,5,6 *n.,* 3,4 *v.* [Old English *boga*] —**bow′like′,** *adj.*

bow³ (bou), the forward part of a ship, boat, or aircraft. See **aft** for picture. *n.* [probably from either Dutch of the 1500's *boech* or Danish *bov*]

bow el (bou′əl), **1** part of the bowels; intestine. **2 bowels,** *pl.* **a** the tube in the body into which food passes from the stomach; intestines. **b** the inner part of anything: *Miners dig for coal in the bowels of the earth. n.*

bow er (bou′ər), **1** shelter of leafy branches. **2** arbor. *n.*

bow ie knife (bō′ē *or* bü′ē), a long, single-edged hunting knife carried in a sheath. [from Colonel James *Bowie,* 1799-1836, an American pioneer who made it popular]

bowl¹ (bōl), **1** a hollow, rounded dish, usually without handles: *Cake batter was in the mixing bowl.* **2** amount that a bowl can hold: *She had a bowl of soup for lunch.* **3** the hollow, rounded part of anything: *The bowl of a pipe holds the tobacco.* **4** structure shaped somewhat like a bowl: *The Yale Bowl is a stadium used for football and other sports. n.* [Old English *bolla*] —**bowl′like′,** *adj.*

bowl² (bōl), **1** a large, heavy ball used in certain games. The balls used in bowls are wooden; those in bowling are made of hard rubber or plastic. **2** play the game of bowls or of bowling. **3** a throw or rolling of a ball in the game of bowls or in bowling. **4** roll or move along rapidly and smoothly: *Our car bowled along on the new highway.* 1,3 *n.,* 2,4 *v.* [from French of the 1400's *boule,* from Latin *bulla* bubble, knob] —**bowl′er,** *n.*

bowl over, 1 knock over: *The force of the wind nearly bowled me over.* **2** IN-FORMAL. make helpless and confused: *I was bowled over by the bad news.*

bow leg ged (bō′leg′id), having the legs curved outward: *a bowlegged cowboy. adj.*

bow line (bō′lən), knot used to tie a loop. *n.*

bowl ing (bō′ling), game played indoors, in which balls are rolled down an alley at bottle-shaped wooden pins; tenpins. *n.*

bowling alley, 1 a long, narrow lane for rolling the balls in bowling; alley.

hat, āge, fär; let, ēqual, tėrm; it, īce; hot, ōpen, ôrder; oil, out; cup, pùt, rüle; ch, child; ng, long; sh, she; th, thin; ŦH, then; zh, measure;

ə represents *a* in about, *e* in taken, *i* in pencil, *o* in lemon, *u* in circus.

2 building having a number of alleys for bowling.

bowling green, a smooth, flat stretch of grass for playing the game of bowls.

bowls (bōlz), game played on a lawn by rolling a slightly lopsided or weighted ball toward a stationary ball. *n.*

bow man (bō′mən), soldier armed with bow and arrows; archer. See **bow²** for picture. *n., pl.* **bow men.**

bow shot (bō′shot′), distance that a bow will shoot an arrow. *n.*

bow sprit (bou′sprit′), pole or spar projecting forward from the bow of a ship. Ropes attached to the bowsprit help to steady sails and masts and hold the jib. *n.*

bow string (bō′string′), a strong cord stretched from the ends of a bow, pulled back by the archer to send the arrow forward. *n.*

bow tie (bō), a small necktie tied in a bow.

box¹ (boks), **1** container, usually with four sides, a bottom, and a lid, to pack or put things in: *We packed the boxes full of books.* **2** amount that a box can hold: *Mother bought a box of soap.* **3** pack in a box; put into a box: *She boxed the candy before she sold it.* **4** a small enclosed space with chairs in a theater, stadium, etc. **5** an enclosed space in a courtroom for a jury, witnesses, newspaper reporters, etc. **6** the driver's seat on a coach, carriage, etc. **7** a small shelter: *a box for a sentry.* **8** (in baseball) place where the pitcher, batter, or catcher stands. 1,2,4-8 *n., pl.* **box es;** 3 *v.* [from Latin *buxis,* from Greek *pyxis*] —**box′like′,** *adj.*

box up or **box in,** shut in; keep in; confine: *The family was boxed up in a small shed on the hill during the flood.*

bowline

box² (boks), **1** a blow with the open hand or fist: *A box on the ear hurts.* **2** strike with such a blow: *I will box your ears if you yell at me again.* **3** fight with the fists as a sport: *He had not*

adj. adjective	*n.* noun
adv. adverb	*prep.* preposition
conj. conjunction	*pron.* pronoun
interj. interjection	*v.* verb
sing. singular	*pl.* plural

boxed since he left school. 1 *n., pl.* **box es;** 2,3 *v.* [origin unknown]

box³ (boks), an evergreen shrub or small, bushy tree, much used for hedges, borders, etc. *n., pl.* **box es.** [from Latin *buxus*, from Greek *pyxos*]

box car (boks/kär/), a railroad freight car enclosed on all sides. Most boxcars are loaded and unloaded through a sliding door on either side. *n.*

box elder, a North American maple tree, often grown for shade or ornament.

box er (bok/sər), 1 man who fights with his fists as a sport, usually in padded gloves and according to special rules. 2 a medium-sized dog with a smooth brown coat, related to the bulldog and terrier. *n.*

box ing (bok/sing), act or sport of fighting with the fists. *n.*

boxing gloves, padded leather gloves worn when boxing.

box office, office or booth in a theater, hall, etc., where tickets of admission are sold.

box wood (boks/wůd/), 1 the hard, fine-grained wood of the box tree. 2 the tree. *n.*

boy (boi), 1 a male child from birth to about eighteen. 2 bellboy. 3 a male servant. *n.*

boy cott (boi/kot), 1 join together against and have nothing to do with (a person, business, or nation) in order to coerce or punish. If people are boycotting someone, they do not associate with him, or buy from or sell to him, and they try to keep others from doing so. 2 refuse to buy or use (a product or service). 3 act of boycotting. 1,2 *v.*, 3 *n.* [from Captain Charles *Boycott*, 1832-1897, a manager of estates in Ireland whose tenants and neighbors would have nothing to do with him when he refused to lower rents in hard times]

boy friend (boi/frend/), INFORMAL. 1 a girl's sweetheart or steady male companion. 2 a male friend. *n.*

boy hood (boi/hůd/), 1 time or condition of being a boy. 2 boys: *the boyhood of the nation. n.*

boy ish (boi/ish), 1 of a boy: *boyish energy.* 2 like a boy: *a boyish young man.* 3 like a boy's; suitable for a boy:

boyish games. adj. —**boy/ish ly,** *adv.* —**boy/ish ness,** *n.*

boy scout, member of the Boy Scouts.

Boy Scouts, organization for boys that seeks to develop character, citizenship, usefulness to others, and outdoor skills.

boy sen ber ry (boi/zn ber/ē), 1 a purple berry like a blackberry in size and shape, and like a raspberry in flavor. 2 plant it grows on. *n., pl.* **boy sen ber ries.** [from Rudolph *Boysen*, 1895–1950, American botanist, who developed it]

brace (brās), 1 thing that holds parts together or in place, such as a timber used to strengthen a building or an iron frame to hold the ankle straight. 2 **braces,** *pl.* **a** metal wires used to straighten crooked teeth. **b** suspenders. 3 give strength or firmness to; support: *We braced the roof with four poles.* 4 prepare (oneself): *I braced myself for the crash.* 5 give strength and energy to; refresh: *The mountain air braced us after the long climb.* 6 a pair; couple: *a brace of ducks.* 7 handle for a tool or drill used for boring. See **bit³** for picture. 8 either of these signs { }, used to enclose words, figures, staffs in music, or a set in arithmetic. 1,2,6-8 *n.*, 3-5 *v.*, **braced, brac ing.**

brace up, gather one's strength or courage anew: *He braced up after his defeat and decided to run again in the next election.*

brace let (brās/lit), band or chain worn for ornament around the wrist or arm. *n.*

brac ing (brā/sing), giving strength and energy; refreshing. *adj.*

brack en (brak/ən), 1 a large, coarse fern common on hillsides, in woods, etc.; brake³. 2 thicket of these ferns. *n.*

brack et (brak/it), 1 a flat piece of stone, wood, or metal projecting from a wall as a support for a shelf, a statue, etc. 2 support with a bracket: *She bracketed the shelves to make them stronger.* 3 shelf supported by brackets. 4 a gas or electric fixture projecting from a wall. 5 either of these signs [ ], used to enclose words or figures: *In the article, he used brackets to show which parts expressed his own opinion.* 6 enclose within brackets: *The teacher bracketed the mistakes in my homework.* 7 think of or mention together; group in the same class or category: *Poets, artists, and musicians are often bracketed.* 8 any group thought of or mentioned together; class or category: *a family in a low income bracket.* 1,3-5,8 *n.*, 2,6,7 *v.*

brack ish (brak/ish), 1 slightly salty. Coastal marshes often have brackish

waters. 2 distasteful; unpleasant. *adj.* —**brack/ish ness,** *n.*

bract (brakt), a small leaf growing at the base of a flower or flower stalk. *n.*

BRACT

BRACT

brad (brad), a small, thin nail with a small head. *n.*

Brad dock (brad/ək), **Edward,** 1695-1755, British general, commander in America during the French and Indian War. *n.*

Brad ford (brad/fərd), **William,** 1590-1657, Pilgrim leader and second governor of Plymouth Colony. *n.*

brae (brā), SCOTTISH. hillside. *n.*

brag (brag), 1 praise oneself or what one has; boast: *He bragged about his new car.* 2 a boast. 3 boasting talk. 1 *v.*, **bragged, brag ging;** 2,3 *n.*

brag ga do ci o (brag/ə dō/shē ō), 1 a boasting; bragging. 2 a boaster; braggart. *n., pl.* **brag ga do ci os.** [from *Braggadocchio*, the name of a boastful character in Spenser's *The Faerie Queene*, made up from the word *brag*]

brag gart (brag/ərt), person who brags; boaster. *n.*

brag ger (brag/ər), person who brags; boaster. *n.*

Brah ma (brä/mə *for 1;* brä/mə *or* brä/mə *for 2*), 1 the Hindu god of creation. 2 kind of cattle, originally imported from India. *n.*

Brah man (brä/mən), member of the priestly caste, the highest caste in India. *n.*

Brah min (brä/mən), Brahman. *n., pl.* **Brah min.**

Brahms (brämz), **Johannes,** 1833-1897, German composer. *n.*

braid (brād), 1 band formed by weaving together three or more strands of hair, ribbon, straw, etc.: *She wore her hair in braids.* 2 weave or twine together (three or more strands of hair, ribbon, straw, etc.): *She can braid her own hair.* 3 a narrow band of fabric used to trim or bind clothing: *a uniform trimmed with gold braid.* 4 trim or bind with braid: *to braid an apron.* 1,3 *n.*, 2,4 *v.* —**braid/er,** *n.*

Braille or **braille** (brāl), system of writing and printing for blind people. The letters in Braille are represented by different arrangements of raised points and are read by touching them. *n.* [from Louis *Braille*, 1809-1852, a French teacher of the blind who invented this system]

brain (def. 1)—parts of the human brain

brain (brān), 1 the part of the central nervous system in man and other vertebrates that is enclosed in the skull or head and consists of a soft mass of nerve cells and nerve fibers. The brain controls almost all the functions of the body and with it we can learn, think, and remember. 2 kill by smashing the skull of: *The cave man brained the wolf with a large stone.* 3 a large electronic computer or an electronic device to control some mechanism. 4 Often, **brains,** *pl.* intelligence: *A dog has more brains than a worm.* 1,3,4 *n.,* 2 *v.*

cudgel one's brains or **rack one's brains,** try very hard to think: *He cudgeled his brains for his friend's phone number, but he couldn't remember it.*

brain less (brān'lis), without brains; stupid; foolish. *adj.* —**brain'less ly,** *adv.* —**brain'less ness,** *n.*

brain storm (brān'stôrm'), IN-FORMAL. a sudden inspiration. *n.*

brain wash (brān'wosh' or brān'-wôsh'), destroy or weaken a person's beliefs and ideas through torture or other methods, so that he becomes willing to accept different or opposite beliefs and ideas. *v.*

brain y (brā'nē), INFORMAL. intelligent; clever. *adj.,* **brain i er, brain i est.**

braise (brāz), brown quickly and then cook (meat or vegetables) long and slowly in a covered pan with very little water. *v.,* **braised, brais ing.**

brake[1] (brāk), 1 anything used to slow or stop the motion of a wheel or vehicle by pressing or scraping or by rubbing against. The brakes on a railroad train are blocks that press against the wheels. 2 slow or stop by using a brake: *He braked the speeding car and it slid to a stop.* 1 *n.,* 2 *v.,* **braked, brak ing.** [perhaps from French of the 1300's *brac* arm]

brake[2] (brāk), a thick growth of bushes; thicket. *n.* [probably from earlier German]

brake[3] (brāk), bracken, a large, coarse fern. *n.* [probably a changed form of *bracken*]

brake man (brāk'mən), man who helps the conductor of a railroad

train; trainman. *n., pl.* **brake men.**

bram ble (bram'bəl), shrub with slender, drooping branches covered with little thorns that prick. Blackberry and raspberry plants are brambles. *n.*

bram bly (bram'blē), 1 full of brambles: *a brambly field.* 2 like brambles; prickly: *a brambly bush. adj.,* **bram bli er, bram bli est.**

bran (bran), the broken covering of the grains of wheat, rye, etc., which is separated from the inner part that is made into flour. Bran is used as fodder and in cereal, bread, and other foods. *n.*

branch (branch), 1 part of a tree growing out from the trunk; any wood part of a tree above the ground except the trunk. A bough is a large branch. A twig is a very small branch. 2 division; part: *a branch of a river, a branch of a family.* History is a branch of learning. 3 a local office: *a branch of a bank, a branch of a library.* 4 divide into branches: *The road branches at the bottom of the hill.* 1-3 *n., pl.* **branch es;** 4 *v.*

branch off, go off (a main road or route) in a different direction: *The new route branches off to the left.*

branch out, 1 put out branches. 2 extend business interests or activities: *They used to be printers only; now they are branching out into publishing books.*

brand (brand), 1 a certain kind, grade, or make: *Do you like this brand of flour?* 2 a name or mark that a company uses to distinguish its goods from the goods of others; trademark. 3 an iron stamp for burning a mark. 4 a mark made by burning the skin with a brand: *The cattle on this big ranch are identified by a brand which shows who owns them.* 5 mark by burning the skin with a brand. In former times criminals were often branded. 6 a mark of disgrace: *He could never rid himself of the brand of coward.* 7 put a mark of disgrace on: *She has been branded as a traitor.* 8 piece of wood that is burning or partly burned. 9 OLD USE. a sword. 1-4,6,8,9 *n.,* 5,7 *v.* —**brand'er,** *n.*

branding iron, a brand used for branding cattle or horses.

bran dish (bran'dish), wave or shake in a threatening manner: *The knight brandished his sword at his enemy. v.*

brand-new (brand'nü' or brand'-nyü'), very new; entirely new. *adj.*

Brandt (brant), **Willy,** born 1913, chancellor of West Germany from 1969 to 1974. *n.*

bran dy (bran'dē), a strong alcoholic liquor distilled from wine or fermented fruit juice. *n., pl.* **bran dies.**

brant (brant), a small, dark, wild goose. It breeds in arctic regions and migrates

hat, āge, fär; let, ēqual, tėrm;
it, īce; hot, ōpen, ôrder;
oil, out; cup, pu̇t, rüle; ch, child;
ng, long; sh, she; th, thin;
ᴛH, then; zh, measure;

ə represents *a* in about,
e in taken, *i* in pencil,
o in lemon, *u* in circus.

south in the autumn. *n., pl.* **brants** or **brant.**

brash (brash), 1 showing lack of respect; impudent; saucy: *The brash boy contradicted his parents all the time.* 2 hasty; rash: *When I got over being angry, I regretted my brash act. adj.* —**brash'ness,** *n.*

Bra sí lia (brə zē'lyə), capital of Brazil since 1960, in the central part. *n.*

brass (bras), 1 a yellow metal that is an alloy of copper and zinc. 2 anything made of brass, such as a musical instrument, an ornament, or a dish: *She polished all the brass.* 3 made of brass: *brass candlesticks.* 4 Also, **brasses,** *pl.* musical instruments made of metal. The trumpet, trombone, and French horn are brasses. 5 INFORMAL. rude boldness; impudence: *She had the brass to go to the party uninvited.* 6 SLANG. military officers of high rank. 1,2,4-6 *n., pl.* **brass es;** 3 *adj.*

brass i ly (bras'ə lē), in a brassy manner. *adv.*

brass i ness (bras'ē nis), brassy quality or appearance. *n.*

brass y (bras'ē), 1 like brass: *a brassy green sky.* 2 loud and harsh: *The brassy music soon gave me a headache.* 3 IN-FORMAL. shameless; impudent: *a brassy manner. adj.,* **brass i er, brass i est.**

brat (brat), an unpleasant child. *n.*

Bra ti sla va (brä'ti slä'və), city in S Czechoslovakia, on the Danube. *n.*

bra va do (brə vä'dō), a great show of boldness without much real courage or real desire to fight. *n.*

brave (brāv), 1 without fear; having courage; showing courage: *The brave girl went into the burning house to save a baby.* 2 brave people: *The United States has been called "the land of the free and the home of the brave."* 3 meet without fear; defy: *The early settlers braved the hardships of life in a new land.* 4 a North American Indian warrior. 1 *adj.,* **brav er, brav est;** 2,4 *n.,* 3 *v.,* **braved, brav ing.** —**brave'ly,** *adv.* —**brave'ness,** *n.*

brav er y (brā'vər ē), 1 quality of being brave; fearlessness; courage: *The soldier was given a medal for bravery in*

adj. adjective	*n.* noun
adv. adverb	*prep.* preposition
conj. conjunction	*pron.* pronoun
interj. interjection	*v.* verb
sing. singular	*pl.* plural

battle. 2 fine appearance; finery: *They attended the prom in all the bravery of formal gowns and rented tuxedos. n., pl.* **brav er ies.**

bra vo (brä′vō), 1 well done! fine! excellent! 2 a cry of "bravo!" 1 *interj.*, 2 *n., pl.* **bra vos.**

bra vur a (brə vyur′ə), 1 display of daring; dash; spirit. 2 piece of music requiring great skill and spirit in the performer. *n.*

brawl (brôl), 1 a noisy and disorderly quarrel. 2 quarrel in a noisy and disorderly way. 1 *n.*, 2 *v.* —**brawl′er,** *n.*

brawn (brôn), 1 firm, strong muscles; muscle. 2 muscular strength: *Football requires brains as well as brawn. n.*

brawn i ness (brô′nē nis), brawny quality or condition. *n.*

brawn y (brô′nē), strong; muscular. *adj.*, **brawn i er, brawn i est.**

bray (brā), 1 the loud, harsh cry or noise made by a donkey. 2 a sound like this. 3 make this sound: *The trumpets brayed.* 1,2 *n.*, 3 *v.*

bra zen (brā′zn), 1 having no shame; shameless: *The brazen girl told lie after lie.* 2 loud and harsh; brassy: *the brazen bellow of a horn.* 3 made of brass. 4 like brass in color or strength. *adj.* —**bra′zen ly,** *adv.* —**bra′zen ness,** *n.*

brazen it out or **brazen it through,** act as if one did not feel ashamed of it: *Although he was caught lying, he tried to brazen it out by telling another lie.*

bra zier (brā′zhər), a large, metal pan or tray to hold burning charcoal or coal. *n.*

Bra zil (brə zil′), largest country in South America. *Capital:* Brasília. *n.*

Bra zil ian (brə zil′yən), 1 of Brazil or its people. 2 person born or living in Brazil. 1 *adj.*, 2 *n.*

Brazil nut, a large, triangular nut of a tree growing in Brazil. It is good to eat.

Braz za ville (braz′ə vil), capital of the Republic of Congo, in the S part. *n.*

breach (brēch), 1 an opening made by breaking down something solid; gap: *The cannon fire has made a breach in the wall of the enemy fort.* 2 break through; make an opening in: *The enemy's fierce attack finally breached our lines.* 3 a breaking or neglect: *For me to leave now would be a breach of duty.* 4 a breaking of friendly relations; quarrel: *There was never a breach between the two friends.* 1,3,4 *n., pl.* **breach es;** 2 *v.*

bread (bred), 1 food made of flour or meal mixed with milk or water and baked: *Buy a loaf of bread.* 2 means of keeping alive; food; livelihood: *How will you earn your daily bread?* 3 cover with bread crumbs before cooking: *She breaded the chicken before frying it.* 1,2 *n.*, 3 *v.*

break bread, share a meal.

bread and butter, 1 bread spread with butter. 2 things necessary to live; a living: *He earns his bread and butter by selling cars.*

bread fruit (bred′früt′), 1 a large, round, starchy fruit grown in the islands of the Pacific, much used for food. When it is baked, it tastes somewhat like bread. 2 tree that it grows on. *n.*

bread stuff (bred′stuf′), 1 grain, flour, or meal for making bread. 2 bread. *n.*

breadth (bredth), 1 how broad a thing is; distance across; width: *He has traveled the length and the breadth of this land.* 2 freedom from narrowness in outlook: *A tolerant person usually has breadth of mind. n.*

bread win ner (bred′win′ər), person who earns a living for himself and those dependent on him. *n.*

break (brāk), 1 make come to pieces by a blow or pull: *I broke the window with a ball.* 2 come apart; crack; burst: *The plate broke into pieces when it fell on the floor.* 3 a broken place; crack: *a break in the wall.* 4 damage; injure: *She broke her watch by winding it too tightly.* 5 crack or split the bone of: *break one's arm, break one's neck.* 6 fail to keep; act against: *He never breaks a promise. People who break the law are punished.* 7 force one's way: *The man broke loose from prison.* 8 a forcing one's way out: *The prisoners made a break for freedom.* 9 come suddenly: *The storm broke within ten minutes.* 10 change suddenly: *The spell of rainy weather has broken. His voice broke with emotion.* 11 an abrupt or marked change: *a break in the weather.* 12 a short interruption in work, athletic practice, etc.: *The teacher let us take a break from the test for five minutes.* 13 decrease the force of; lessen: *The bushes broke my fall from the tree.* 14 become weak; give way; fail: *The dog's heart broke when his master died.* 15 dawn; appear: *The day is breaking.* 16 put an end to; stop: *break one's fast, break a strike.* 17 train to obey; tame: *break a colt.* 18 go beyond; exceed: *The speed of the new train has broken all records.* 19 dig or plow: *The settlers on the prairies had to work hard to break the ground for the first crops.* 20 make known; reveal: *Someone must break the news of the girl's accident to her family.* 21 SLANG. chance; opportunity: *Finding that money was a lucky break.* 22 (in baseball) to curve or swerve abruptly: *The pitcher threw a ball that broke over the plate.* 23 act of breaking. 1,2,4-7,9,10,13-20,22 *v.*, **broke, bro ken, break ing;** 3,8,11, 12,21,23 *n.*

break away, 1 start before the signal: *The excited horse broke away at a gallop.* 2 pull or run away from; escape: *The rabbit broke away from the boy's arms.*

break down, 1 go out of order; fail to work: *The car's engine broke down.* 2 become weak; fail suddenly; collapse: *His health broke down.* 3 begin to cry: *She broke down when she heard the bad news.* 4 separate or divide into parts, steps, etc.: *break down a chemical, break down a process or operation.*

break in, 1 prepare for work or use; train: *He broke in the new office boy.* 2 enter by force: *The thieves broke in through the cellar.* 3 interrupt: *She broke in with a funny remark while the teacher was reading to us.*

break into, 1 enter by force: *A robber broke into the house.* 2 begin suddenly: *She broke into a run.* 3 interrupt: *He broke into their conversation.*

break off, 1 stop suddenly: *He broke off in the middle of his speech to clear his throat.* 2 stop being friends: *She broke off with the old crowd when she went away to college.*

break out, 1 start suddenly; begin: *War broke out. A fire broke out in the boiler house.* 2 have pimples, rashes, etc., appear on the skin: *The child broke out with measles.* 3 burst out: *A cry of horror broke out among the spectators when someone yelled "Fire!"* 4 leave by force; escape: *The thief broke out of jail.*

break up, 1 scatter: *The fog is breaking up.* 2 put an end to; stop: *The committee broke up its meeting early.* 3 disturb greatly; upset: *The news of his brother's death broke him up.*

break with, stop being friends with: *She broke with me after our fight.*

break a ble (brā′kə bəl), that can be broken. *adj.*

break age (brā′kij), 1 a breaking; break. 2 damage or loss caused by breaking. 3 allowance made for such damage or loss. *n.*

break down (brāk′doun′), 1 failure to work: *Lack of oil caused a breakdown in the motor.* 2 failure of health; collapse: *If you don't stop worrying, you will have a nervous breakdown.*

3 separation or division of anything into parts, steps, etc. *n.*

break er (brā′kər), 1 wave that breaks into foam on the beach or on rocks. 2 person or thing that breaks, crushes, or destroys something. *n.*

break fast (brek′fəst), 1 the first meal of the day. 2 eat breakfast: *I like to breakfast alone.* 1 *n.,* 2 *v.*

break neck (brāk′nek′), likely to cause a broken neck; very dangerous: *The car traveled at breakneck speed.* *adj.*

break of day, dawn.

break through (brāk′thrü′), 1 a military attack that gets through the enemy defense system into the area in the rear. 2 achievement or solution of some baffling or technical problem: *The development of the Salk vaccine against polio was an important breakthrough in medical research.* *n.*

break up (brāk′up′), 1 a scattering; separation. 2 a stopping; end. *n.*

break wa ter (brāk′wô′tər *or* brāk′-wot′ər), wall or barrier built to break the force of waves. *n.*

breakwater

bream (brēm), 1 carp of inland European waters. 2 the common freshwater sunfish of the United States. *n., pl.* **breams** or **bream.**

breast (brest), 1 the upper, front part of the body between the shoulders and the stomach; chest. 2 gland that gives milk. 3 heart or feelings: *Pity tore his breast.* 4 struggle with; face or oppose: *The swimmer breasted the waves with powerful strokes.* 1-3 *n.,* 4 *v.*

make a clean breast of, confess completely: *When he was shown proof that he broke the window, he made a clean breast of it.*

breast bone (brest′bōn′), the thin, flat bone in the front of the chest to which the ribs are attached by cartilages; sternum. *n.*

breast plate (brest′plāt′), piece of armor worn over the chest. *n.*

breast stroke, stroke in swimming in which the swimmer lies face downward and draws both arms at one time from in front of the head to the sides.

breast work (brest′werk′), a low, sometimes hastily built wall for defense. *n.*

breath (breth), 1 air drawn into and forced out of the lungs. 2 act of breath-ing: *Hold your breath a moment.* 3 moisture from breathing: *You can see your breath on a very cold day.* 4 ability to breathe easily: *Running fast made her lose her breath.* 5 a slight movement in the air; light breeze: *Not a breath was stirring.* 6 life. *n.*

below one's breath, in a whisper.

catch one's breath, 1 gasp; pant: *The dogs were catching their breath after a long chase.* 2 stop for breath; rest: *The hikers sat down to catch their breath.*

in the same breath, at the same time.

out of breath, short of breath; breathless: *At the end of the race the winner was out of breath.*

under one's breath, in a whisper: *She was talking under her breath so no one could hear.*

breathe (brēṮH), 1 draw air into the lungs and force it out. One breathes through the nose or through the mouth. 2 stop for breath; rest; allow to rest and breathe: *At last there is time to breathe. At the top of the hill the rider breathed his horse.* 3 say softly; whisper; utter: *Don't breathe a word of this to anyone.* 4 be alive; live: *As long as I breathe, I will remember all you've done for me.* 5 send out; give: *Her enthusiasm breathed new life into our club.* *v.,* **breathed, breath ing.**

breath er (brē′ṮHər), a short stop for breath; rest. *n.*

breath less (breth′lis), 1 out of breath: *Running upstairs very fast made me breathless.* 2 holding one's breath because of fear, amazement, excitement, etc.: *The beauty of the scenery left her breathless.* 3 without breath; dead. *adj.* —**breath′less ly,** *adv.* —**breath′less ness,** *n.*

breath tak ing (breth′tā′king), thrilling; exciting: *a breathtaking ride on a roller coaster.* *adj.* —**breath′-tak′ing ly,** *adv.*

Breck in ridge (brek′ən rij), **John C.,** 1821-1875, American statesman and Confederate general, vice-president of the United States from 1857 to 1861. *n.*

bred (bred), past tense and past participle of **breed.** *He bred cattle for market. Our parents have bred us to be honest.* *v.*

breech (brēch), 1 part of a gun behind the barrel. 2 the lower part; back part. *n., pl.* **breech es.**

breech cloth (brēch′klôth′), loincloth. *n., pl.* **breech cloths** (brēch′-klôṮHz′ *or* brēch′klôths′).

breech es (brich′iz *or* brē′chiz), 1 short trousers fastened below the knees. 2 trousers. *n.pl.*

breeches buoy, pair of short canvas trousers fastened to a belt or life preserver. A breeches buoy slides along a rope

hat, āge, fär; let, ēqual, tėrm; it, īce; hot, ōpen, ôrder; oil, out; cup, pùt, rüle; ch, child; ng, long; sh, she; th, thin; ṮH, then; zh, measure;

ə represents *a* in about, *e* in taken, *i* in pencil, *o* in lemon, *u* in circus.

on a pulley and is used to rescue people from sinking ships or to transfer people from one ship to another.

breech load ing (brēch′lō′ding), (of guns) loading from behind the barrel instead of at the muzzle. *adj.*

breed (brēd), 1 produce young: *Rabbits breed rapidly.* 2 raise or grow: *This farmer breeds cattle and hogs for market.* 3 be the cause of; produce: *Careless driving breeds accidents.* 4 bring up; train: *The captain bred his boy to be a sailor.* 5 group of animals or plants having the same ancestry; race or stock: *Terriers and spaniels are breeds of dogs.* 6 kind; sort: *The people of the early West were a hardy breed.* 1-4 *v.,* **bred, breed ing;** 5,6 *n.*

breed er (brē′dər), person who breeds animals: *a dog breeder.* *n.*

breeder reactor, reactor that produces at least as much fissionable material as it uses. In one type of reaction it consumes uranium and produces plutonium.

breed ing (brē′ding), 1 the producing of animals or new types of plants, especially to get improved kinds: *Breeding has produced types of wheat which can be grown in the far North.* 2 bringing up; training; behavior; manners: *Politeness is a sign of good breeding.* *n.*

breeze (brēz), 1 a light, gentle wind. 2 INFORMAL. move easily or briskly: *She breezed through her homework.* 1 *n.,* 2 *v.,* **breezed, breez ing.**

breeze way (brēz′wā′), a roofed passage open at the sides between a house and a garage. *n.*

breez i ly (brē′zə lē), in a breezy manner. *adv.*

breeches (def. 1)   breeches buoy

103

adj.	adjective	*n.*	noun
adv.	adverb	*prep.*	preposition
conj.	conjunction	*pron.*	pronoun
interj.	interjection	*v.*	verb
sing.	singular	*pl.*	plural

breez i ness (brē′zē nis), breezy condition. *n.*

breez y (brē′zē), 1 having many breezes; with light winds blowing: *It was a breezy day.* 2 lively and jolly: *We like his breezy, joking manner.* adj., **breez i er, breez i est.**

Brem en (brem′ən *or* brā′mən), city in N West Germany. *n.*

br'er (brér), DIALECT. brother: *Br'er Rabbit.*

breth ren (breᴛʜ′rən), 1 the fellow members of a church, society, or religious order. 2 OLD USE. brothers. *n.pl.*

Bret on (bret′n), 1 person born in Brittany. 2 language of Brittany. 3 having to do with Brittany, its people, or their language. 1,2 *n.*, 3 *adj.*

bre vi ar y (brē′vē er′ē), book of prescribed prayers to be said daily by clergymen of the Roman Catholic Church. *n.*, *pl.* **bre vi ar ies.**

brev i ty (brev′ə tē), shortness; briefness: *The brevity of such an exciting story disappointed the children.* *n.*, *pl.* **brev i ties.**

brew (brü), 1 make (beer, ale, etc.) by soaking, boiling, and fermenting malt, hops, etc. 2 make (a drink) by soaking, boiling, or mixing: *Tea is brewed in boiling water.* 3 a drink that is brewed: *The last brew of beer tasted bad.* 4 bring about; plan; plot: *The group whispering in the corner is brewing some mischief.* 5 begin to form; gather: *Dark clouds show that a storm is brewing.* 1,2,4,5 *v.*, 3 *n.*

brew er (brü′ər), person who brews beer, ale, etc. *n.*

brew er y (brü′ər ē), place where beer, ale, etc., is brewed. *n.*, *pl.* **brew er ies.**

Brezh nev (brezh′nef), **Leonid I.,** born 1906, Russian political leader, first secretary of the Soviet Communist Party since 1964. *n.*

bri ar¹ (brī′ər), brier¹. *n.*

bri ar² (brī′ər), brier². *n.*

bri ar wood (brī′ər wùd′), brierwood. *n.*

bribe (brīb), 1 money or other reward given or offered to a person to get him to do something dishonest, unlawful, etc.: *The thief offered the policeman a bribe to let him go.* 2 a reward for doing something that a person does not want

to do: *A child should not need a bribe to do well in school.* 3 give or offer a bribe to: *A gambler bribed one of the boxers to lose the fight.* 1,2 *n.*, 3 *v.*, **bribed, brib ing.**

brib er y (brī′bər ē), 1 the giving or offering of a bribe. 2 the taking of a bribe: *The dishonest policeman was arrested for bribery.* *n.*, *pl.* **brib er ies.**

bric-a-brac (brik′ə brak′), interesting or curious trinkets used as decorations; small ornaments, such as vases, old china, or small statues. *n.*

brick (brik), 1 block of clay baked by sun or fire. Bricks are used to build walls or houses, pave walks, etc. 2 bricks: *Chimneys are usually built of brick.* 3 made of bricks: *a brick house.* 4 anything shaped like a brick: *Ice cream is often sold in bricks.* 5 build or pave with bricks; cover or fill in with bricks: *He bricked up the old window.* 1,2,4 *n.*, 3 *adj.*, 5 *v.*

brick bat (brik′bat′), 1 piece of broken brick: *The speaker was injured by brickbats hurled from the crowd.* 2 INFORMAL. an insult. *n.*

brick lay er (brik′lā′ər), person whose work is building with bricks. *n.*

brick lay ing (brik′lā′ing), act or work of building with bricks. *n.*

brick work (brik′wèrk′), 1 wall, foundation, or other structure made of bricks. 2 the part of a building made of bricks. *n.*

brid al (brī′dl), of, or having to do with a bride or a wedding: *a bridal veil, the bridal cake.* adj.

bride (brīd), woman just married or about to be married. *n.*

bride groom (brīd′grüm′ *or* brīd′grùm′), man just married or about to be married; groom. *n.*

brides maid (brīdz′mād′), a young woman who attends the bride at a wedding. *n.*

bridge¹ (brij), 1 something built over a river, road, railroad, or anything that hinders the way, so that people, cars, trains, etc., can get across. 2 make a way over a river or anything that hinders; make or form a bridge over: *The engineers bridged the river. A log bridged the brook. Politeness will bridge many difficulties.* 3 platform above the deck of a ship for the officer in command: *The captain directed the course of his ship from the bridge.* 4 the upper, bony part of the nose. 5 the curved part of a pair of eyeglasses which rests on the nose. 6 bridgework. 7 a thin, arched piece over which the strings of a violin or some other stringed instrument are stretched. 1,3-7 *n.*, 2 *v.*, **bridged, bridg ing.** [Old English *brycg*] —**bridge′like′,** adj.

bridge² (brij), a card game for two

pairs of players played with 52 cards. *n.* [origin unknown]

bridge head (brij′hed′), position obtained and held by troops within enemy territory, used as a starting point for further attack. *n.*

Bridge port (brij′pôrt′), city in SW Connecticut, on Long Island Sound. *n.*

bridge work (brij′wèrk′), false teeth mounted and fastened to real teeth nearby. *n.*

bridle (def. 1)

bri dle (brī′dl), 1 the part of a harness that fits over a horse's head, used to hold him back or to control him. 2 put a bridle on: *I saddled and bridled my horse.* 3 anything that holds back or controls; curb. 4 hold back; bring under control; check: *Bridle your temper.* 5 hold the head up high with the chin drawn back to show pride, scorn, or anger: *She bridled when we criticized her ideas.* 1,3 *n.*, 2,4,5 *v.*, **bri dled, bri dling.**

brief (brēf), 1 lasting only a short time: *The meeting was brief. A brief shower fell in the afternoon.* 2 using few words: *He made a brief announcement. Be as brief as you can.* 3 a short statement; summary: *He read a brief of the debate. The lawyer prepared a brief of the facts and the points of law in the case.* 4 give detailed information to: *The park ranger briefed the boys on fire prevention.* 1,2 *adj.*, 3 *n.*, 4 *v.* —**brief′ly,** adv. —**brief′ness,** n.

hold a brief for, argue for; support; defend: *I hold no brief for cheating.*

in brief, in few words: *In brief, it has been an exciting day.*

brief case (brēf′kās′), a flat container for carrying loose papers, books, drawings, etc. A briefcase is often made of leather and has a handle like a suitcase does. *n.*

bri er¹ (brī′ər), bush that has a thorny or prickly, woody stem. The blackberry plant and rosebush are often called briers. *n.* Also, **briar.** [Old English *brēr*]

bri er² (brī′ər), 1 a white heath tree found in southern Europe. Its root is used in making tobacco pipes. 2 a tobacco pipe made of brierwood. *n.* Also, **briar.** [from French *bruyère* heath]

bri er wood (brī′ər wùd′), the wood of brier roots, used in making tobacco pipes. *n.* Also, **briarwood.**

brig (brig), 1 ship with two masts and

square sails set at right angles across the ship. **2** prison on a warship. *n.*

bri gade (bri gād'), **1** military unit made up of two or more regiments or groups, commanded by a brigadier general or a colonel. It is usually part of a division. **2** any group of people organized for some purpose. A fire brigade puts out fires. *n.*

brig a dier (brig'ə dir'), brigadier general. *n.*

brigadier general, a military officer next in rank above a colonel and below a major general.

brig and (brig'ənd), man who robs travelers on the road, especially one of a gang of robbers in mountain or forest regions; robber; bandit. *n.*

brig and age (brig'ən dij), robbery; plundering. *n.*

brig an tine (brig'ən tēn'), ship with two masts. The foremast is square-rigged; the mainmast is fore-and-aft-rigged. *n.*

bright (brīt), **1** giving much light; shining: *The stars are bright, but sunshine is brighter.* **2** very light or clear: *It is a bright day. Dandelions are bright yellow.* **3** clever; quick-witted: *A bright girl learns quickly.* **4** lively or cheerful: *Everybody was bright and gay at the party.* **5** likely to turn out well; favorable: *There is a bright outlook for the future.* **6** in a bright manner: *The fire shines bright.* **1-5** *adj.,* **6** *adv.* —**bright'ly,** *adv.* —**bright'ness,** *n.*

bright en (brīt'n), **1** become bright or brighter: *The sky brightened after the storm. Her face brightened as she read the good news.* **2** make bright or brighter: *Flowers brighten the fields in the spring. Hope brightens our outlook on life.* *v.*

brill (bril), a European flatfish related to the turbot. *n., pl.* **brills** or **brill.**

bril liance (bril'yəns), **1** great brightness; radiance; sparkle: *the blue brilliance of southern skies.* **2** splendor; magnificence: *the brilliance of the royal court.* **3** great ability: *His brilliance as a pianist was soon recognized. n.*

bril lian cy (bril'yən sē), brilliance. *n.*

bril liant (bril'yənt), **1** shining brightly; sparkling: *brilliant jewels, brilliant sunshine.* **2** splendid; magnificent: *The singer gave a brilliant performance.* **3** having great ability: *He is a brilliant musician.* **4** diamond or other gem cut to sparkle brightly. **1-3** *adj.,* **4** *n.* —**bril'liant ly,** *adv.*

brim (brim), **1** edge of a cup, bowl, etc.: *You have filled my glass to the brim.* **2** edge or border of anything; rim: *Deer drink at this lake's brim.* **3** fill to the brim; be full to the brim: *The pond was brimming with water after the heavy rain.* **4** the projecting edge of some-

thing: *The hat's wide brim shaded my eyes from the sun.* **1,2,4** *n.,* **3** *v.,* **brimmed, brim ming.**

brim ful (brim'fúl'), full to the brim; full to the very top. *adj.*

brim less (brim'lis), without a brim. *adj.*

brim stone (brim'stōn'), sulfur. *n.*

brin dle (brin'dl), **1** brindled. **2** a brindled color. **3** a brindled animal. **1** *adj.,* **2,3** *n.*

brin dled (brin'dld), gray, tan, or tawny with darker streaks and spots. *adj.*

brine (brīn), **1** very salty water. Some pickles are kept in brine. **2** a salt lake, sea, or ocean. *n.*

bring (bring), **1** carry (a thing or person) from another place; take along to a place or person: *The bus brought us home. Bring me a clean plate and take the dirty one away.* **2** cause to come: *What brings you into town today?* **3** win over to a belief or action; influence; persuade; convince: *The principal was brought to agree with us by our arguments.* **4** sell for: *Meat brings a high price this time of year.* **5** present before a court of law: *He brought a charge against us in a lawsuit.* *v.,* **brought, bring ing.** —**bring'er,** *n.*

bring about, cause; cause to happen: *The flood was brought about by a heavy rain.*

bring around or **bring round, 1** restore to consciousness: *When I fainted, they brought me around.* **2** win over to a belief or action; convince; persuade: *At first her parents refused to let her go to the party, but soon she brought them around and they let her go.*

bring forth, 1 give birth to; bear: *The trees in the orchard bring forth many apples.* **2** make known something that has been hidden; reveal; show: *New evidence was brought forth by the lawyer.*

bring off, carry out successfully: *He brought off a good business deal.*

bring on, cause; cause to happen: *My bad cold brought on pneumonia.*

bring out, 1 reveal; show: *The lawyer brought out new evidence at the trial.* **2** offer to the public: *The company is bringing out a new product.*

bring over, win over to do or believe; persuade: *Try to bring her over to our way of thinking.*

bring to, 1 restore to consciousness: *She fainted when she heard the news, but they finally brought her to.* **2** stop; check: *The captain brought the ship to.*

bring up, 1 care for in childhood: *Grandmother brought up four children.* **2** educate or train, especially in behavior or manners: *His good manners*

hat, āge, fär; let, ēqual, tėrm;
it, īce; hot, ōpen, ôrder;
oil, out; cup, pùt, rüle; ch, child;
ng, long; sh, she; th, thin;
ŦH, then; zh, measure;

ə represents *a* in about,
e in taken, *i* in pencil,
o in lemon, *u* in circus.

showed he was well brought up. **3** suggest for action or discussion: *Please bring your plan up at the meeting.* **4** stop suddenly: *Within seconds a policeman brought his car up at the scene of the accident.*

bring ing-up (bring'ing up'), care and training given to a child when growing up; upbringing. *n.*

brink (bringk), **1** edge at the top of a steep place: *the brink of the cliff.* **2** edge: *The business is on the brink of ruin. n.*

brin y (brī'nē), of or like brine; very salty: *Too much salt gives a briny taste. adj.,* **brin i er, brin i est.**

bri quette or **bri quet** (bri ket'), a molded block of coal dust or charcoal used for fuel. *n.*

Bris bane (briz'bān), seaport in E Australia. *n.*

brisk (brisk), **1** quick and active; lively: *Grandfather likes to take a brisk walk every morning.* **2** keen; sharp: *a brisk wind. Ginger has a brisk flavor. adj.* —**brisk'ly,** *adv.* —**brisk'ness,** *n.*

bris ket (bris'kit), meat from the breast of an animal. *n.*

bris tle (bris'əl), **1** the short, stiff hair of some animals or plants: *Brushes are often made of the bristles of hogs.* **2** stand up straight: *The dog growled and his hair bristled.* **3** have one's hair stand up straight: *The frightened kitten bristled when it saw the dog.* **4** show that one is aroused and ready to fight: *Don't bristle at me — I'm trying to help you.* **5** be thickly set: *The harbor bristled with boats and ships. His knowledge of arithmetic was so poor that he found algebra bristling with difficulties.* **1** *n.,* **2-5** *v.,* **bris tled, bris tling.**

bris tly (bris'lē), **1** rough with bristles or hair like bristles: *The trapper had a bristly chin after a week in the woods.* **2** like bristles: *bristly hair.* **3** likely to bristle: *a bristly temper. adj.,* **bris tli er, bris tli est.**

Bris tol (bris'tl), seaport in SW England, on the Avon River. *n.*

Bristol Channel, inlet of the Atlantic, between SW England and Wales.

adj. adjective	*n.* noun
adv. adverb	*prep.* preposition
conj. conjunction	*pron.* pronoun
interj. interjection	*v.* verb
sing. singular	*pl.* plural

Brit., 1 Britain. 2 British.

Brit ain (brit′n), England, Scotland, and Wales; Great Britain. *n.*

Bri tan ni a (bri tan′ē ə), Great Britain. *n.*

britch es (brich′iz), INFORMAL. breeches. *n.pl.*

Brit i cism (brit′ə siz′əm), word or phrase used especially by the British. *Lift* meaning *elevator* and *petrol* meaning *gasoline* are Briticisms. *n.*

Brit ish (brit′ish), 1 of Great Britain or its people. 2 the people of Great Britain. 3 the English spoken in Great Britain. 1 *adj.,* 2 *n.pl.,* 3 *n.sing.*

British Columbia, province in SW Canada, on the Pacific. *Capital:* Victoria.

British Commonwealth or **British Commonwealth of Nations,** Commonwealth of Nations.

British Empire, former empire consisting of all the countries and colonies owing allegiance to the British crown. At its height, in the late 1800's and early 1900's, it was the largest empire in the history of the world.

Brit ish er (brit′i shər), any British subject, especially an Englishman. *n.*

British Honduras, British colony in Central America, SE of Mexico.

British Isles

British Isles, Great Britain, Ireland, the Isle of Man, and other nearby islands.

British thermal unit, unit for measuring heat. It is the amount of heat necessary to raise the temperature of a pound of water one degree Fahrenheit.

British West Indies, British islands in the West Indies.

Brit on (brit′n), 1 person born or living in Great Britain. 2 one of the Celtic people who inhabited southern Britain before the Roman conquest of Britain. *n.*

Brit ta ny (brit′n ē), region in NW France. See **Burgundy** for map. *n.*

brit tle (brit′l), very easily broken; breaking with a snap; apt to break: *Thin glass is brittle. adj.* —**brit′tle ness,** *n.*

broach (brōch), 1 begin to talk about: *She broached the subject of a picnic to her parents.* 2 a pointed tool to make and shape holes with. 3 open by making a hole: *We broached a barrel of cider.* 1,3 *v.,* 2 *n., pl.* **broach es.**

broad (brôd), 1 large across; wide: *Many cars can go on that broad, new road.* 2 having wide range; extensive: *Our teacher has had broad experience with children.* 3 not limited or narrow; of wide range; liberal: *The police took a broad view of the boys' prank and sent them home with only a warning.* 4 including only the most important parts; not detailed; general: *Give the broad outlines of today's lesson.* 5 clear; full: *The theft was made in broad daylight.* 6 plain; plain-spoken: *He gave his parents broad hints of what he wanted for his birthday. adj.* —**broad′ly,** *adv.* —**broad′ness,** *n.*

broad ax or **broad axe** (brôd′-aks′), ax with a broad blade. *n., pl.* **broad ax es.**

broad cast (brôd′kast′), 1 something sent out by radio or television; a radio or television program of speech, music, etc.: *The President's broadcast was televised from Washington, D.C.* 2 send out by radio or television: *Some stations broadcast twenty-four hours a day.* 3 a sending out by radio or television: *a nation-wide broadcast.* 4 sent out by radio or television. 5 scatter or spread widely: *broadcast seed. Don't broadcast gossip.* 6 a scattering or spreading far and wide: *nature's broadcast of seed.* 7 scattered widely. 8 over a wide surface: *The seed was sown broadcast.* 1,3,6 *n.,* 2,5 *v.,* **broad cast** or **broad cast ed** for 2, **broad cast** for 5, **broad cast ing,** 4,7 *adj.,* 8 *adv.* —**broad′cast′er,** *n.*

broad cloth (brôd′klôth′), 1 a closely woven cotton or silk cloth with a smooth finish, used in making shirts, dresses, pajamas, etc. 2 a closely woven woolen cloth with a smooth finish, used in making men's suits. *n.*

broad en (brôd′n), become or make broad or broader; widen: *The river broadens at its mouth. Travel broadens a person's experience. v.*

broad jump, an athletic contest or event in which the contestants jump from a standing or running position to cover as much ground as possible.

broad loom (brôd′lüm′), 1 woven on a wide loom: *a broadloom carpet.* 2 material woven in this way: *gray broadloom.* 1 *adj.,* 2 *n.*

broad-mind ed (brôd′mīn′did), not prejudiced or bigoted; tolerant: *My grandparents have a broad-minded attitude toward today's young people. adj.* —**broad′-mind′ed ly,** *adv.* —**broad′-mind′ed ness,** *n.*

broad side (brôd′sīd′), 1 the whole side of a ship above the water. 2 the firing of all the guns on one side of a ship at the same time: *The broadside caught the pirates completely by surprise.* 3 with the side turned: *The ship drifted broadside to the wharf.* 4 a large sheet of paper printed on one or both sides: *broadsides announcing a big sale.* 1,2,4 *n.,* 3 *adv.*

broad sword (brôd′sôrd′), sword with a broad, flat cutting blade. *n.*

Broad way (brôd′wā′), street running northwest and southeast through New York City. Part of Broadway lies in the main theater district, and is gaily lighted. *n.*

bro cade (brō kād′), 1 an expensive cloth woven with raised designs on it, used for clothing or upholstery: *silk brocade, velvet brocade.* 2 weave or decorate with raised designs. 1 *n.,* 2 *v.,* **bro cad ed, bro cad ing.**

broc co li (brok′ə lē), 1 plant having green branching stems and flower heads. It belongs to the same family as the cabbage. 2 its heads and stems, which are eaten as a vegetable. *n., pl.* **broc co li.**

bro chure (brō shùr′), pamphlet. *n.*

bro gan (brō′gən), a strong work shoe made of heavy leather. *n.*

brogue[1] (brōg), a strongly marked pronunciation or accent peculiar to a dialect: *She speaks English with an Irish brogue. n.* [perhaps from *brogue[2]* in the sense of "the speech of those who call their shoes brogues"]

brogue[2] (brōg), a shoe made for comfort and long wear, often with decorative perforations. *n.* [from Irish Gaelic *bróg* shoe]

broil (broil), 1 cook by putting or holding directly over the fire or heat on a rack, or under it in a pan; grill: *We often broil steaks and chops.* 2 be or make very hot: *You will broil in this bright sunlight. v.*

broil er (broi′ler), 1 pan or rack for broiling. 2 a young chicken for broiling. *n.*

broke (brōk), 1 past tense of **break.** *She broke her doll.* 2 SLANG. without money. 1 *v.,* 2 *adj.*

bro ken (brō′kən), 1 past participle of **break.** *The window was broken by a ball.* 2 separated into parts by a break; in pieces: *a broken cup.* 3 not in working condition; damaged: *a broken* watch. **4** rough; uneven: *broken ground.* **5** acted against; not kept: *a broken promise.* **6** imperfectly spoken: *The French girl speaks broken English.* **7** weakened in strength, spirit, etc.; tamed; crushed: *broken by failure.* 1 *v.,* 2-7 *adj.* —**bro′ken ly,** *adv.* —**bro′ken ness,** *n.*

bro ken-down (brō′kən doun′), **1** shattered; ruined: *broken-down health.* **2** unfit for use: *broken-down furniture. adj.*

bro ken-heart ed (brō′kən här′tid), crushed by sorrow or grief; heart-broken. *adj.* —**bro′ken-heart′ed ly,** *adv.*

bro ker (brō′kər), person who buys and sells stocks, bonds, grain, cotton, etc., for other people. *n.*

bro ker age (brō′kər ij), **1** business of a broker. **2** money charged by a broker for his services. *n.*

bro mide (brō′mīd), any compound of bromine with another element or radical, especially, such a compound used as a drug to calm nervousness, cause sleep, etc. *n.*

bro mine (brō′mēn′), a dark, brownish-red, nonmetallic, liquid element. Bromine is somewhat like chlorine and iodine and gives off an irritating vapor. It is used in drugs and in photography. *n.*

bronchi (def. 1)

bron chi (brong′kī), **1** the two large, main branches of the windpipe, one going to each lung. **2** the smaller branching tubes in the lungs. *n.pl. of* **bronchus.**

bron chi al (brong′kē əl), having to do with the bronchi or with their many branching tubes. *adj.*

bronchial tubes, bronchi and their branching tubes.

bron chi ole (brong′kē ōl), a very small branch of the bronchi. *n.*

bron chi tis (brong kī′tis), inflammation of the mucous membrane that lines the bronchial tubes. Bronchitis is usually accompanied by a deep cough. *n.*

bron cho (brong′kō), bronco. *n., pl.* **bron chos.**

bron chus (brong′kəs), one of the bronchi. *n., pl.* **bron chi.**

bron co (brong′kō), a wild or partly tamed horse of the western United States. *n., pl.* **bron cos.** Also, **broncho.**

brontosaurus—60 ft. long; 14 ft. tall

bron to sau rus (bron′tə sôr′əs), a huge, extinct dinosaur of America. *n., pl.* **bron to sau ri** (bron′tə sôr′ī), **bron to sau rus es.**

Bronx (brongks), **The,** borough of New York City, the only one on the mainland. *n.*

bronze (bronz), **1** a brown alloy of copper and tin. **2** a similar alloy of copper and zinc or another metal. **3** a statue, medal, disk, etc., made of bronze: *A bronze went to the swimmer who came in third.* **4** made of bronze: *a bronze bell.* **5** color of bronze; a yellowish brown or reddish brown. **6** yellowish-brown or reddish-brown. **7** make or become bronze in color: *a lifeguard bronzed from the sun.* 1-3,5 *n.,* 4,6 *adj.,* 7 *v.,* **bronzed, bronz ing.**

Bronze Age, period after the Stone Age when bronze tools and weapons were used. It was followed by the Iron Age.

brooch (brōch *or* brüch), an ornamental pin having the point fastened by a catch. Brooches are often made of gold, silver, or jewels. *n., pl.* **brooch es.**

brood (brüd), **1** the young birds hatched at one time in the nest or cared for together: *a brood of chicks.* **2** young animals or humans who share the same mother or are cared for by the same person: *That father and mother have a brood of twelve children.* **3** sit on eggs in order to hatch; incubate. Hens and birds brood till the young are hatched. **4** worry a long time about some one thing: *He brooded over his lost dog.* 1,2 *n.,* 3,4 *v.*

brood er (brü′dər), **1** a closed place that can be heated, used in raising chicks, etc. **2** person who broods. *n.*

brook[1] (brůk), a natural stream of water smaller than a river. *n.* [Old English *brōc*]

brook[2] (brůk), put up with; endure; tolerate: *I will not brook any more of your insults. v.* [Old English *brūcan* to use]

brook let (brůk′lit), a little brook. *n.*

Brook lyn (brůk′lən), borough of New York City, on Long Island. *n.*

broom (brüm *or* brům), **1** brush with a long handle for sweeping. **2** shrub of the same family as the pea, with slender

hat, āge, fär; let, ēqual, tėrm; it, īce; hot, ōpen, ôrder; oil, out; cup, půt, rüle; ch, child; ng, long; sh, she; th, thin; ŦH, then; zh, measure;

ə represents *a* in about, *e* in taken, *i* in pencil, *o* in lemon, *u* in circus.

branches, small leaves, and yellow flowers. *n.*

broom corn (brüm′kôrn′ *or* brům′-kôrn′), a tall plant resembling corn, with seed clusters growing on long, stiff stems used for making brooms. *n.*

broom stick (brüm′stik′ *or* brům′-stik′), the long handle of a broom. *n.*

bros. *or* **Bros.,** brothers.

broth (brôth), a thin soup made from water in which meat or fish has been boiled. *n., pl.* **broths** (brôŦHz *or* brôths).

broth er (bruŦH′ər), **1** son of the same parents. A boy is a brother to the other children of his parents. **2** a close friend. **3** member of the same church, union, club, etc. **4** member of a religious order who is not a priest: *a lay brother. n., pl.* **broth ers** (*or* **breth ren** for 3,4).

broth er hood (bruŦH′ər hůd), **1** bond between brothers; feeling of brother for brother: *Soldiers who are fighting together often have a strong feeling of brotherhood.* **2** persons joined as brothers; association of men with some common aim or characteristic. *n.*

broth er-in-law (bruŦH′ər in lô′), **1** brother of one's husband or wife. **2** husband of one's sister. *n., pl.* **broth ers-in-law.**

broth er li ness (bruŦH′ər lē nis), brotherly affection or sympathy. *n.*

broth er ly (bruŦH′ər lē), **1** of a brother: *It is a brotherly trait to tease little sisters.* **2** like a brother; very friendly; kindly: *The scout gave the tenderfoot some brotherly advice. adj.*

brougham (brüm *or* brü′əm), a closed carriage having an outside seat for the driver. *n.* [from Lord *Brougham,* 1778-1868, a British statesman]

brought (brôt), past tense and past participle of **bring.** *He brought his lunch yesterday. She was brought to school in a bus. v.*

brow (brou), **1** part of the face above the eyes; forehead: *a wrinkled brow.* **2** arch of hair over the eye; eyebrow: *He has heavy brows over his eyes.* **3** edge of a steep place; top of a slope: *Our house is on the brow of a hill. n.*

brow beat (brou′bēt′), frighten into

adj. adjective	*n.* noun
adv. adverb	*prep.* preposition
conj. conjunction	*pron.* pronoun
interj. interjection	*v.* verb
sing. singular	*pl.* plural

doing something by overbearing looks or threats; bully. *v.*, **brow beat, brow-beat en, brow beat ing.**

brown (broun), 1 a dark color like that of toast, potato skins, or coffee. 2 having this color: *Many people have brown hair.* 3 make or become brown: *The cook browned the onions in hot butter.* 1 *n.*, 2 *adj.*, 3 *v.* —**brown′ness,** *n.*

Brown (broun), **John,** 1800-1859, American Abolitionist who attempted to incite a slave rebellion but was captured at Harpers Ferry, West Virginia. *n.*

brown bear, bear having brown fur that lives in northern Europe and North America, especially Alaska.

brown ie (brou′nē), 1 a good-natured elf or fairy, especially one supposed to help secretly at night. 2 **Brownie,** member of the junior division of the Girl Scouts. 3 a small, flat, sweet chocolate cake, often containing nuts. *n.*

Brown ing (brou′ning), **Robert,** 1812-1889, English poet. *n.*

brown ish (brou′nish), somewhat brown. *adj.*

brown rice, rice that is not polished.

brown stone (broun′stōn′), 1 a reddish-brown sandstone, used as a building material. 2 house with exterior walls built of this material. *n.*

brown sugar, sugar that is not refined or only partly refined.

browse (brouz), 1 feed on growing grass or the leaves and shoots of trees and bushes by nibbling and eating here and there; graze: *The sheep browsed in the meadow.* 2 read here and there in a book, library, etc.: *I spent the afternoon browsing in the bookstores.* *v.*, **browsed, brows ing.**

Bruce (brüs), **Robert the,** 1274-1329, king of Scotland from 1306 to 1329. *n.*

bru in (brü′ən), bear[2] (def. 1). *n.*

bruise (brüz), 1 injury to the body, caused by a fall or a blow, that breaks blood vessels without breaking the skin: *The bruise on my arm turned black and blue.* 2 injury to the outside of a fruit, vegetable, plant, etc. 3 injure the outside of: *Rough handling bruised the apples before they could be sold.* 4 hurt; injure: *Your harsh words bruised my feelings.* 5 become bruised: *Her flesh*

bruises easily. 1,2 *n.*, 3-5 *v.*, **bruised, bruis ing.**

bruit (brüt), spread a report or rumor of: *News of their engagement was bruited about.* *v.*

brunch (brunch), meal taken late in the morning and intended to combine breakfast and lunch. *n., pl.* **brunch es.**

bru nette or **bru net** (brü net′), 1 dark-colored: *brunette hair.* 2 having dark-brown or black hair, brown or black eyes, and dark skin. 3 person with such hair, eyes, and skin: *Many people of Spanish descent are brunettes; many people of Swedish descent are blonds.* 1,2 *adj.*, 3 *n.*

brunt (brunt), the main force or violence; hardest part: *The island felt the brunt of the hurricane. The infantry bore the brunt of the battle.* *n.*

brush[1] (brush), 1 tool for cleaning, sweeping, scrubbing, and for putting on paint. A brush is made of bristles, hair, or wire set in a stiff back or fastened to a handle. 2 clean, sweep, scrub, or paint with a brush; use a brush on: *She brushed her hair until it was shiny.* 3 a brushing; a rub with a brush: *I gave my puppy a good brush.* 4 wipe away; remove: *The child brushed the tears from his eyes.* 5 touch lightly in passing: *No harm was done—your bumper just brushed our fender.* 6 a light touch in passing: *Give the desk a brush with the cloth.* 7 a short, brisk fight or quarrel: *The trespassers had a brush with the farmer.* 8 the bushy tail of an animal, especially of a fox. 9 piece of carbon, copper, etc., used to connect the electricity from the revolving part of an electric motor or generator to the outside circuit. 1,3,6-9 *n., pl.* **brush es;** 2,4,5 *v.* [from French of the 1300's *broisse*]

brush aside, put aside; refuse to consider: *She brushed aside our offer of help, saying she could manage very well by herself.*

brush off, 1 refuse to see or listen to: *The mayor hurried into his office, brushing off the reporters.* 2 dismiss as unimportant; make light of: *The mayor brushed off the reporter's question with a joke.*

brush up on or **brush up,** refresh one's knowledge of: *I brushed up on fractions before the arithmetic test.*

brush[2] (brush), 1 branches broken or cut off; brushwood. 2 shrubs, bushes, and small trees growing thickly in the woods; brushwood. 3 thinly settled country; backwoods. *n.* [from French of the 1300's *brosse*]

brush off (brush′ôf′), INFORMAL. refusal or dismissal of a request, person, etc.: *The reporter got a polite brushoff when she asked the*

new mayor for an appointment. *n.*

brush wood (brush′wud′), brush[2] (defs. 1 and 2). *n.*

brush y (brush′ē), covered with bushes, shrubs, etc. *adj.*, **brush i er, brush i est.**

brusque (brusk), abrupt in manner or speech; blunt: *He was brusque in saying "I don't like it" when he could have said "No, thank you."* *adj.* —**brusque′ly,** *adv.* —**brusque′ness,** *n.*

Brus sels (brus′əlz), capital of Belgium, in the central part. *n.*

Brussels sprouts (def. 1) about 2½ ft. tall

Brussels sprouts, 1 plant having many small heads growing along a stalk. It belongs to the same family as the cabbage. 2 its heads, which are eaten as a vegetable.

bru tal (brü′tl), like a brute; coarse and savage; cruel: *The Vikings were brutal in battle.* *adj.* —**bru′tal ly,** *adv.*

bru tal i ty (brü tal′ə tē), 1 brutal conduct; cruelty. 2 a brutal act. *n., pl.* **bru tal i ties.**

bru tal ize (brü′tl īz), make brutal: *War brutalizes many people.* *v.*, **brutal ized, bru tal iz ing.**

brute (brüt), 1 an animal without power to reason. 2 like an animal; without power to reason. 3 a stupid, cruel, or coarse person. 4 stupid, cruel, or coarse. 5 without feeling: *We are often powerless against the brute forces of nature.* 1,3 *n.*, 2,4,5 *adj.*

brut ish (brü′tish), like a brute; stupid, cruel, or coarse. *adj.* —**brut′ish ly,** *adv.* —**brut′ish ness,** *n.*

Bru tus (brü′təs), **Marcus Junius,** 85-42 B.C., Roman political leader and one of the men who killed Julius Caesar. *n.*

Bry an (brī′ən), **William Jennings,** 1860-1925, American political leader and orator. *n.*

Bry ant (brī′ənt), **William Cullen,** 1794-1878, American poet. *n.*

Btu, B.t.u., or **B.T.U.,** British thermal unit or units.

bu., bushel or bushels.

bub ble (bub′əl), 1 a thin, round film of liquid enclosing air or gas. The surface of boiling water is covered with bubbles. 2 a round space filled with air in a liquid or solid. Sometimes there are bubbles in ice or in glass. 3 have bubbles; make bubbles; send up or rise in bubbles: *Water bubbled up between the stones.* 4 make sounds like water boiling; gurgle: *The baby bubbled and cooed.* 5 sound of bubbling. 6 plan or idea that looks good, but soon falls apart. 1,2,5,6 *n.,* 3,4 *v.,* **bub bled, bub bling. —bub′bling ly,** *adv.*

bubble over, 1 be very full; overflow: *The teakettle bubbled over on the stove.* 2 be very enthusiastic: *The children bubbled over at the idea of an overnight camping trip.*

bubble chamber, a small vessel filled with a very hot liquid, causing atomic particles to leave tracks of bubbles. In this way they can be examined and identified.

bubble gum, a chewing gum that can be blown out through the lips so as to form a large bubble.

bub bly (bub′lē), full of bubbles. *adj.*

bu bon ic plague (byü bon′ik), a very dangerous contagious disease, accompanied by fever, chills, and swelling of the lymph glands. It is carried to human beings by fleas from rats or squirrels.

buc ca neer (buk′ə nir′), pirate. *n.*

Bu chan an (byü kan′ən), **James,** 1791-1868, the 15th president of the United States, from 1857 to 1861. *n.*

Bu cha rest (bü′kə rest *or* byü′kə rest), capital of Romania, in the S part. *n.*

buck[1] (buk), 1 a male deer, goat, hare, rabbit, antelope, or sheep. 2 jump into the air with the back curved and come down with the front legs stiff: *My horse began to buck violently, but I managed to stay on.* 3 throw by bucking: *The cowboy was bucked by the bronco.* 4 a throw or attempt to throw by bucking. 5 charge against; work against: *The swimmer bucked the current with strong strokes.* 1,4 *n.,* 2,3,5 *v.* [Old English *buc* male deer, and *bucca* male goat]

buck up, INFORMAL. cheer up; be brave or energetic: *Buck up; everything will be all right.*

buck[2] (buk), SLANG. dollar. *n.* [origin uncertain]

buck board (buk′bôrd′), an open four-wheeled carriage having the seat fastened to a platform of long, springy boards instead of a body and springs. *n.*

buck et (buk′it), 1 pail made of wood, metal, or plastic. Buckets are used for carrying such things as water, milk, or coal. 2 bucketful: *Pour in about four buckets of water.* *n.*

buck et ful (buk′it ful′), amount that a bucket can hold. *n., pl.* **buck et fuls.**

bucket seat, a small, low, single seat with a rounded back, used in sports cars, small airplanes, etc.

buck eye (buk′ī′), 1 tree or shrub

closely related to the horse chestnut, with showy clusters of small flowers, large divided leaves, and large brown seeds. 2 its seed. *n.*

Buck ing ham Palace (buk′ing-əm), official London residence of all British sovereigns since 1837.

buck le (buk′əl), 1 catch or clasp used to hold together the ends of a belt, strap, or ribbon. 2 fasten together with a buckle: *buckle one's belt.* 3 a metal ornament for a shoe. 4 bend out of shape; bulge, kink, or wrinkle: *The heavy snowfall caused the roof of the building to buckle.* 5 a bend, bulge, kink, or wrinkle. 1,3,5 *n.,* 2,4 *v.,* **buck led, buck ling.**

buckle down to, work hard at: *I buckled down to my studies before the test.*

buck ler (buk′lər), a small, round shield. *n.*

buck ram (buk′rəm), a coarse cloth made stiff with glue or something like glue. *n.*

buck saw (buk′sô′), saw set in a light frame and held with both hands. *n.*

BUCKSAW

SAWHORSE

buck shot (buk′shot′), a large lead shot used to shoot large game, such as deer. *n.*

buck skin (buk′skin′), 1 a strong, soft leather, yellowish or grayish in color, made from the skins of deer or sheep. 2 buckskins, *pl.* clothing made of buckskin. *n.*

buck thorn (buk′thôrn′), a small, thorny tree or shrub with clusters of black berries. *n.*

buck toothed (buk′tütht′), having a protruding tooth or teeth. *adj.*

buck wheat (buk′hwēt′), 1 plant with black or gray, triangular seeds and fragrant white flowers. 2 its seeds, used as food for animals or ground into flour for pancakes, etc. 3 meal, flour, or batter made from buckwheat. *n.*

bu col ic (byü kol′ik), 1 of shepherds; pastoral. 2 rustic; rural. *adj.*

bud (bud), 1 a small swelling on a plant that will grow into a flower, leaf, or branch: *Buds on the trees are a sign of spring.* 2 a partly opened flower or leaf. 3 put forth buds: *The rosebush has budded.* 4 begin to grow or develop: *That student is budding into a scientist.*

hat, āge, fär; let, ēqual, tėrm; it, īce; hot, ōpen, ôrder; oil, out; cup, put, rüle; ch, child; ng, long; sh, she; th, thin; ∓H, then; zh, measure;

ə represents *a* in about, *e* in taken, *i* in pencil, *o* in lemon, *u* in circus.

5 anything in an undeveloped state or beginning stage. 6 a small swelling in certain plants and animals that grows into a new plant or animal: *The buds of new yeast plants grow very quickly.* 1,2,5,6 *n.,* 3,4 *v.,* **bud ded, bud ding.**

in bud, in the time or condition of budding: *In the spring the pear tree is in bud.*

nip in the bud, stop at the very beginning: *I tried to nip their argument in the bud before it turned into a fight.*

Bu da pest (bü′də pest), capital of Hungary, on the Danube. *n.*

Bud dha (bü′də *or* bud′ə), 563?-483? B.C., religious teacher of northern India, founder of Buddhism. *n.*

Bud dhism (bü′diz əm *or* bud′iz əm), religion based on the teachings of Buddha. It developed during his lifetime in northern India and spread widely after his death over central, southeastern, and eastern Asia. Buddhism teaches that right living will enable people to attain a condition free from all desire and pain. *n.*

Bud dhist (bü′dist *or* bud′ist), 1 believer in Buddhism. 2 having to do with Buddha or Buddhism. 1 *n.,* 2 *adj.*

bud dy (bud′ē), INFORMAL. a close friend; comrade; pal. *n., pl.* **bud dies.**

budge (buj), move even a little: *The stone was so heavy that the boy could not budge it. I was too tired to budge from my chair.* *v.,* **budged, budg ing.**

budg et (buj′it), 1 estimate of the amount of money that will probably be received and spent for various purposes in a given time. Governments, companies, schools, and persons make budgets: *The expenses for the school year are an important part of our city budget.* 2 make a plan for spending based on how much you have: *She budgeted her allowance so that she could save some money each week for a new tennis racket. Budget your time.* 3 put in a budget: *She budgeted fifty cents a week for candy and ice cream.* 1 *n.,* 2,3 *v.*

budg et ar y (buj′ə ter′ē), of a budget. *adj.*

Bue nos Ai res (bwā′nəs er′ēz *or*

buff

adj. adjective	*n.* noun
adv. adverb	*prep.* preposition
conj. conjunction	*pron.* pronoun
interj. interjection	*v.* verb
sing. singular	*pl.* plural

bwā′nəs ar′ēz), capital of Argentina, in the E part.

buff (buf), 1 dull-yellow. 2 a dull yellow. 3 a strong, soft, dull-yellow leather. Buff was formerly made from the skin of buffalo and is now made from the skin of oxen. 4 to polish with a wheel or stick covered with leather. 5 to polish; shine: *I buffed my shoes to make them shine.* 6 a polishing wheel or stick covered with leather. 7 IN-FORMAL. a fan or devotee: *a model-train buff.* 1 *adj.,* 2,3,6,7 *n.,* 4,5 *v.*

buf fa lo (buf′ə lō), 1 the bison of North America. Buffaloes used to graze on the plains of the United States. See **bison** for picture. 2 any of several kinds of oxen. The tame water buffalo of Asia and the wild Cape buffalo of Africa are two different kinds. *n., pl.* **buf fa loes, buf fa los,** or **buf fa lo.**

buffalo (def. 2)—water buffalo
5 ft. high at the shoulder

Buf fa lo (buf′ə lō), city in W New York State, a port on Lake Erie. *n.*
Buffalo Bill, 1846-1917, American frontier scout and showman. His real name was William F. Cody.
buff er¹ (buf′ər), anything that helps to soften the shock of a blow or to balance the effect of opposing forces: *She acted as a buffer between the quarreling children. n.* [from *buff,* an older word meaning to soften the shock of a blow]
buff er² (buf′ər), 1 stick or pad having a soft cloth or leather surface for polishing. 2 person who polishes. *n.* [from *buff,* from French *buffle* buffalo]
buffer state, a small country between two larger countries that are enemies or competitors.
buf fet¹ (buf′it), 1 a blow of the hand or fist. 2 strike with the hand or fist. 3 a knock, stroke, or hurt: *I withstood the buffets of the waves.* 4 knock about, strike, or hurt: *The waves buffeted me.* 5 fight or struggle against: *The boat*

buffeted the heavy waves caused by the storm. 1,3 *n.,* 2,4,5 *v.* [from French of the 1200's]
buf fet² (bu fā′ *or* bù fā′), 1 a low cabinet with a flat top for dishes and with shelves or drawers for silver and table linen; sideboard. 2 counter where food and drinks are served. 3 meal at which guests serve themselves from food laid out on a table or sideboard. *n.* [from French *buffet* piece of furniture]
buf foon (bu fün′), person who amuses people with tricks, pranks, and jokes; clown. *n.*
buf foon er y (bu fü′nər ē), 1 tricks, pranks, and jokes of a clown: *We enjoyed the buffoonery at the circus.* 2 undignified or rude joking. *n., pl.* **buf foon er ies.**
bug (bug), 1 insect without wings or with a front pair of wings thickened at the base, and a pointed beak for piercing and sucking. Bedbugs, lice, and chinch bugs are true bugs. 2 any insect or other invertebrate somewhat like an insect. Ants, spiders, beetles, and flies are often called bugs. 3 INFORMAL. a disease germ: *the flu bug.* 4 INFORMAL. mechanical defect or difficulty: *The new engine needed repair because of a bug in the design of the fuel system.* 5 IN-FORMAL. person who is very enthusiastic about something: *She is a basketball bug and goes to a lot of games.* 6 IN-FORMAL. a very small microphone hidden within a room, a telephone, etc., for overhearing a conversation. 7 IN-FORMAL. hide a small microphone within (a room, telephone, etc.): *The spy bugged enemy headquarters.* 1-6 *n.,* 7 *v.,* **bugged, bug ging. —bug′like′,** *adj.*
bug a boo (bug′ə bü), bogy. *n., pl.* **bug a boos.**
bug bear (bug′ber′ *or* bug′bar′), 1 bogy. 2 a difficulty, problem, or obstacle: *Out-of-date machinery is the chief bugbear of this old factory. n.*
bug gy (bug′ē), 1 a light carriage with or without a top, pulled by one horse and having a single large seat. 2 a baby's carriage. *n., pl.* **bug gies.**
bu gle (byü′gəl), a musical instrument like a small trumpet, made of brass or copper, and sometimes having keys or valves. Bugles are used in the army and navy for sounding calls and orders, and for playing band music. *n.*
bu gler (byü′glər), person who plays a bugle. *n.*
build (bild), 1 make by putting materials together; construct: *People build houses, bridges, and machines. Birds build nests.* 2 form or produce gradually; develop: *build a business. A lawyer builds his case on facts.* 3 form, style, or manner in which something is

put together; structure: *An elephant has a heavy build.* 1,2 *v.,* **built, build ing;** 3 *n.*
build up, 1 strengthen or develop: *When sick you must rest to build up your health.* 2 fill with houses: *The hill overlooking the town has been built up in the last five years.*
build er (bil′dər), 1 person or animal that builds. 2 person whose business is constructing buildings. *n.*
build ing (bil′ding), 1 thing built. Barns, factories, stores, houses, and hotels are all buildings. 2 business, art, or process of making houses, stores, bridges, ships, etc. *n.*
build-up (bild′up′), 1 an increasing of strength, size, rate, etc.: *a military build-up, a build-up of pressure.* 2 enhancement or promotion, especially by the use of publicity: *The play has had a big build-up in the press. n.*
built (bilt), past tense and past participle of **build.** *The bird built a nest. It was built of twigs. v.*
built-in (bilt′in′), included in or provided for as part of the plan or design of anything: *A built-in bookcase is fastened to the wall. adj.*

bulbs—lily bulb (def. 1); thermometer and electric light bulbs (def. 3)

bulb (bulb), 1 a round, underground bud from which certain plants grow. Onions, tulips, and lilies grow from bulbs. 2 the thick part of an underground stem resembling a bulb; tuber: *a crocus bulb.* 3 any object with a rounded end or swelling part: *an electric light bulb, the bulb of a thermometer. n.* **—bulb′like′,** *adj.*
bulb ous (bul′bəs), 1 shaped like a bulb; rounded and swelling: *The clown had a bulbous red nose.* 2 having bulbs; growing from bulbs: *Daffodils are bulbous plants. adj.*
Bul gar i a (bul ger′ē ə), country in SE Europe, on the Black Sea. *Capital:* Sofia. See **Balkan States** for map. *n.* **—Bul gar′i an,** *adj., n.*
bulge (bulj), 1 swell outward: *My pockets bulged with candy.* 2 an outward swelling: *When the man leaned against the tent, he made a bulge in the canvas.* 1 *v.,* **bulged, bulg ing;** 2 *n.*
bulk (bulk), 1 size, especially large size: *An elephant has great bulk.* 2 the largest part of: *The oceans form the bulk of the earth's surface.* 3 have size; be of importance: *The danger of*

drought bulks large in a farmer's life. 1,2 *n.,* 3 *v.*

in bulk, 1 lying loose in heaps, not in packages: *In most markets you can buy fresh fruit in bulk.* **2** in large quantities: *Grain goes to the mill in bulk.*

bulkhead (def. 1)
A, dividing
B, watertight

bulk head (bulk′hed′), **1** one of the upright partitions dividing a ship into compartments. **2** wall or partition built to hold back water, earth, rocks, air, etc. *n.*

bulk i ly (bul′kə lē), in a bulky manner. *adv.*

bulk i ness (bul′kē nis), bulky condition. *n.*

bulk y (bul′kē), **1** taking up much space; large: *Bulky shipments are often sent in freight cars.* **2** hard to handle; clumsy: *a bulky package of curtain rods. adj.,* **bulk i er, bulk i est.**

bull[1] (bul), **1** the full-grown male of cattle. **2** the male of the whale, elephant, seal, and other large mammals. **3** male: *a bull moose.* 1,2 *n.,* 3 *adj.* [Old English *bula*]

bull[2] (bul), a formal announcement or official order from the pope. *n.* [from Latin *bulla* document, seal]

bull dog (bul′dôg′), **1** a heavily built dog with a large head, very short nose, strong jaws, and short hair. Bulldogs are not large, but they are very muscular and courageous. **2** like a bulldog's: *bulldog courage, a bulldog grip.* **3** bring (a steer) to the ground by grasping its horns and twisting its neck. **1** *n.,* **2** *adj.,* **3** *v.,* **bull dogged, bull dog ging.**

bull doze (bul′dōz′), **1** INFORMAL. frighten, sometimes by violence or threats; bully: *The chairman bulldozed the whole committee into voting for his proposal.* **2** move, clear, dig, or level with a bulldozer. *v.,* **bull dozed, bull doz ing.**

bull doz er (bul′dō′zər), **1** a powerful crawler tractor with a wide steel blade that pushes rocks and earth, used for grading, road building, etc. **2** INFORMAL. person who bullies or frightens another, sometimes by violence or threats. *n.*

bul let (bul′it), piece of lead, steel, or other metal shaped to be fired from a pistol, rifle, or other small gun. *n.*

bul le tin (bul′ə tən), **1** a short statement of news: *Sports bulletins and weather bulletins are published in most*

newspapers. **2** magazine or newspaper appearing regularly, especially one published by a club or society for its members. *n.*

bulletin board, board on which notices are posted.

bull fight (bul′fīt′), fight between men and a bull in an arena. Bullfights are popular in Spain, Portugal, Mexico, and parts of South America. *n.*

bull fight er (bul′fī′tər), man who fights a bull in an arena. *n.*

bull fight ing (bul′fī′ting), act or sport of fighting a bull in an arena. *n.*

bull finch (bul′finch′), a European songbird with a blue and gray back and light-red breast, and a short, stout bill. *n., pl.* **bull finch es.**

bull frog (bul′frôg′), any of various large North American frogs that make a loud, croaking noise. *n.*

bull head (bul′hed′), any of various American catfishes which have large, broad heads. *n.*

bull head ed (bul′hed′id), stupidly stubborn; obstinate; headstrong. *adj.* —**bull′head′ed ness,** *n.*

bul lion (bul′yən), gold or silver in the form of lumps or bars. *n.*

bull ish (bul′ish), like a bull in manner or temper. *adj.* —**bull′ish ly,** *adv.* —**bull′ish ness,** *n.*

bull ock (bul′ək), ox; steer. *n.*

bull ring (bul′ring′), arena for bull-fights. *n.*

Bull Run, stream in NE Virginia where two Civil War battles took place in 1861 and 1862.

bull's-eye (bulz′ī′), **1** center of a target. **2** shot that hits it. **3** a thick piece of dome-shaped glass in the deck or side of a ship to let in light. **4** a small lantern with a dome-shaped lens in its side to concentrate light. *n.*

bul ly (bul′ē), **1** person who teases, frightens, threatens, or hurts smaller or weaker people. **2** frighten (into doing something) by noisy talk or threats: *Stop trying to bully me into doing what you want.* **3** INFORMAL. very good; excellent: *a bully plan. Bully for you!* **1** *n., pl.* **bul lies; 2** *v.,* **bul lied, bul ly ing; 3** *adj.,* **bul li er, bul li est; 3** *interj.*

bul rush (bul′rush′), a tall, slender

bulldozer (def. 1)

hat, āge, fär; let, ēqual, tėrm;
it, īce; hot, ōpen, ôrder;
oil, out; cup, put, rüle; ch, child;
ng, long; sh, she; th, thin;
ŦH, then; zh, measure;

ə represents *a* in about,
e in taken, *i* in pencil,
o in lemon, *u* in circus.

plant that grows in wet places. *n., pl.* **bul rush es.**

bul wark (bul′wərk), **1** person, thing, or idea that is a defense or a protection: *A free press and free speech are bulwarks of democracy.* **2** wall of earth or other material for defense against the enemy: *The city was protected by a moat and a bulwark surrounding it.* **3** breakwater for protection against the force of the waves. **4** Usually, **bulwarks,** *pl.* side of a ship above the deck. *n.*

bum (bum), INFORMAL. **1** an idle or good-for-nothing person; loafer; tramp. **2** get (food, money, etc.) by sponging on others; beg: *Let's try to bum a ride.* **3** loaf around; idle about.′ **4** of poor quality; worthless. **1** *n.,* 2,3 *v.,* **bummed, bum ming; 4** *adj.,* **bum mer, bum mest.**

bumblebee
about
life size

bum ble bee (bum′bəl bē′), a large bee with a thick, hairy body, usually banded with gold. Bumblebees make a loud, buzzing sound. They live in small colonies in underground nests, old logs, etc. *n.*

bump (bump), **1** push, throw, or strike against something large or solid: *She bumped against the table in the dark.* **2** hit or come against with heavy blows: *That truck bumped our car.* **3** a heavy blow or knock: *The bump knocked our car forward a few feet.* **4** move by bumping against things: *Our car bumped along the dirt road.* **5** a swelling caused by a bump: *He has a bump on his head from getting hit by a baseball.* **6** any swelling or lump: *She tried to avoid the bump in the road.* 1,2,4 *v.,* 3,5,6 *n.*

bump er (bum′pər), **1** bar or bars of metal across the front and back of a car or truck that protect it from being damaged if bumped. **2** unusually large: *The*

adj. adjective	*n.* noun
adv. adverb	*prep.* preposition
conj. conjunction	*pron.* pronoun
interj. interjection	*v.* verb
sing. singular	*pl.* plural

farmer raised a bumper crop of wheat last year. 3 cup or glass filled to the brim. 1,3 *n.*, 2 *adj.*

bump i ly (bum′pə lē), in a bumpy manner. *adv.*

bump i ness (bum′pē nis), bumpy condition. *n.*

bump kin (bump′kən), an awkward or simple person from the country. *n.*

bump tious (bump′shəs), unpleasantly forward or conceited. *adj.* —**bump′tious ly**, *adv.* —**bump′tious ness**, *n.*

bump y (bum′pē), 1 having bumps; full of bumps: *a bumpy road.* 2 causing bumps; rough: *a bumpy ride.* *adj.*, **bump i er, bump i est.**

bun (bun), 1 bread or cake in small shapes. Buns are often slightly sweetened and may contain spice, raisins, etc. 2 hair coiled at the back of the head in a knot. *n.*

bunch (bunch), 1 group of things of the same kind growing, fastened, placed, or thought of together: *a bunch of grapes, a bunch of flowers, a bunch of sheep.* 2 INFORMAL. group of people: *They are a friendly bunch.* 3 come together in one place: *The sheep were all bunched in the shed to keep warm.* 4 bring together and make into a bunch: *We have bunched the flowers for you to carry home.* 1,2 *n.*, *pl.* **bunch es**; 3,4 *v.*

Bunche (bunch), **Ralph,** 1904–1971, American educator and diplomat. He was the winner of the Nobel Peace Prize in 1950. *n.*

bun dle (bun′dl), 1 number of things tied or wrapped together: *We gave away several bundles of old newspapers and magazines.* 2 parcel; package: *We sent my uncle a large bundle on his birthday.* 3 tie or wrap together; make into a bundle: *We bundled all our old newspapers for the school's paper drive.* 4 send or go in a hurry; hustle: *They bundled me off to the hospital in an ambulance.* 1,2 *n.*, 3,4 *v.*, **bun dled, bun dling.**

bundle up, dress warmly: *You should bundle up on cold winter mornings.*

bung (bung), 1 stopper for closing the hole in the side or end of a barrel, keg, or cask. 2 bunghole. 3 close (a bunghole) with a stopper. 1,2 *n.*, 3 *v.*

bun ga low (bung′gə lō), a small one-story house. *n.*

bung hole (bung′hōl′), hole in the side or end of a barrel, keg, or cask through which it is filled and emptied. *n.*

bun gle (bung′gəl), 1 do or make in a clumsy, unskilled way: *I tried to make a birdhouse but bungled the job.* 2 a clumsy, unskilled performance or piece of work. 1 *v.*, **bun gled, bun gling;** 2 *n.*

bun gler (bung′glər), person who bungles. *n.*

bun ion (bun′yən), a painful, inflamed swelling on the foot, especially on the first joint of the big toe. *n.*

bunk¹ (bungk), 1 a narrow bed, one of two or more stacked one above another: *My sister and I sleep in bunks.* 2 sleep in a bunk; occupy a bunk. 3 any place to sleep. 4 sleep in rough quarters: *We bunked in a deserted house.* 1,3 *n.*, 2,4 *v.* [origin uncertain]

bunk² (bungk), SLANG. insincere talk; nonsense; humbug. *n.* [from *Buncombe,* a county in North Carolina whose congressman in 1819-1821 kept making long-winded and pointless speeches "for Buncombe"]

bunk er (bung′kər), 1 place or bin for coal on a ship. 2 a sandy hollow or mound of earth on a golf course, used as an obstacle. 3 a fortified shelter built partly or entirely below ground. *n.*

Bunker Hill, hill near Boston, Massachusetts. An early battle of the Revolutionary War was fought near there on June 17, 1775.

bunk house (bungk′hous′), a rough building with sleeping quarters or bunks: *The men at the lumber camp slept in bunkhouses.* *n.*, *pl.* **bunk hous es** (bungk′hou′ziz).

bun ny (bun′ē), a pet name for a rabbit. *n.*, *pl.* **bun nies.**

Bun sen burner (bun′sən), a gas burner with a very hot, blue flame, used in laboratories. Air is let in at the base and mixed with gas. [from Robert Bunsen, 1811-1899, German chemist who invented it]

bunt (bunt), 1 hit (a baseball) lightly so that the ball goes to the ground and rolls only a short distance. 2 act of bunting a baseball. 3 baseball that is bunted. 1 *v.*, 2,3 *n.* —**bunt′er,** *n.*

bun ting¹ (bun′ting), 1 a thin cloth used for flags. 2 long pieces of cloth having the colors and designs of a flag, used to decorate buildings and streets on holidays and special occasions. 3 a baby's warm, hooded, outer garment closed at the bottom. *n.* [perhaps from *bunt,* an older word meaning to sift (because cloth was used for sifting)]

bun ting² (bun′ting), any of several small, usually brightly colored birds

with stout bills, related to the finches. *n.* [origin unknown]

Bun yan (bun′yən), 1 **John,** 1628-1688, English religious writer who wrote *Pilgrim's Progress.* 2 **Paul,** (in American folklore) a giant lumberjack with amazing strength. *n.*

buoy (def. 1)
B, bell buoy
L, light buoy
W, whistle buoy

buoy (boi *or* bü′ē), 1 a floating object anchored on the water to warn against hidden rocks or shallows or to show the safe part of a channel. 2 life buoy. *n.*

buoy up, 1 hold up; keep from sinking: *Life jackets buoyed them up until rescuers came.* 2 support or encourage: *Hope buoys her up, even when something goes wrong.*

buoy an cy (boi′ən sē *or* bü′yən sē), 1 power to float: *Wood has more buoyancy than iron.* 2 power to keep things afloat: *Salt water has greater buoyancy than fresh water.* 3 tendency to be hopeful and cheerful: *Her buoyancy kept us from being downhearted.* *n.*

buoy ant (boi′ənt *or* bü′yənt), 1 able to float: *Wood and cork are buoyant in water; iron and lead are not.* 2 able to keep things afloat: *Balloons can float because air is buoyant.* 3 cheerful and hopeful; light-hearted: *Children are usually more buoyant than adults.* *adj.* —**buoy′ant ly,** *adv.*

bur (bėr), 1 a prickly, clinging seed case or flower of some plants. Burs stick to cloth and fur. 2 plant or weed that has burs. *n.* Also, **burr.**

Bur bank (bėr′bangk), **Luther,** 1849-1926, American naturalist who bred new varieties of fruit, flowers, and plants. *n.*

bur den¹ (bėrd′n), 1 something carried; load (of things, care, work, duty, or sorrow): *A light burden was laid on the mule's back. We have to carry each day's burden.* 2 a load too heavy to carry easily; heavy load: *His debts are a burden that will bankrupt him.* 3 put a burden on; load too heavily; weigh down; oppress: *The mule was burdened with heavy bags of ore. She was burdened with worries.* 4 quantity of freight that a ship can carry; weight of a ship's cargo. 1,2,4 *n.*, 3 *v.* [Old English *byrthen*]

bur den² (bėrd′n), 1 the main idea or

Burgundy (def. 1)

message: *The way to achieve peace was the burden of the President's speech.* 2 a repeated verse in a song; chorus; refrain. *n.* [from French of the 1300's *bourdon* a humming]

burden of proof, obligation to establish a fact by proof.

bur den some (bėrd'n səm), hard to bear; very heavy; oppressive: *The President's many duties are burdensome.* *adj.*

bur dock (bėr'dok'), a coarse weed with burs and broad leaves. *n.*

bur eau (byur'ō), 1 chest of drawers for clothes; dresser. It often has a mirror. 2 office: *We asked about the airplane fares at the travel bureau.* 3 a division within a government department: *The U.S. Weather Bureau makes daily reports on weather conditions.* *n.*

bu reauc ra cy (byu rok'rə sē), 1 system of government by groups of officials, each dealing with its own kind of business under the direction of its chief. 2 the officials running government bureaus. 3 too much insistence on rigid routine, resulting in delay in making decisions; red tape. *n., pl.* **bureauc ra cies.**

bur eau crat (byur'ə krat), 1 official in a bureaucracy. 2 a government official who insists on rigid routine. *n.*

bur eau crat ic (byur'ə krat'ik), having to do with a bureaucracy or a bureaucrat. *adj.*

burg (bėrg), INFORMAL. town or city. *n.*

bur geon (bėr'jən), grow or shoot forth; sprout: *New suburbs have burgeoned all around the city.* *v.*

bur gess (bėr'jis), member of the lower house of the colonial legislature in Virginia or Maryland. *n., pl.* **burgess es.**

burgh (bėrg *or* bėr'ō), a chartered town in Scotland. *n.*

burgh er (bėr'gər), citizen of a burgh or town; citizen. *n.*

bur glar (bėr'glər), person who breaks into a house or other building, usually at night, to steal. *n.*

bur glar y (bėr'glər ē), a breaking into a house or other building, usually at night, to steal. *n., pl.* **bur glar ies.**

bur go mas ter (bėr'gə mas'tər),

mayor of a town in Austria, Belgium, Germany, or the Netherlands. *n.*

Bur goyne (bər goin'), **John,** 1722-1792, English general. His defeat and surrender in 1777 marked the turning point of the Revolutionary War. *n.*

Bur gun di an (bər gun'dē ən), 1 of Burgundy or its people. 2 person born or living in Burgundy. 1 *adj.*, 2 *n.*

Bur gun dy (bėr'gən dē), 1 region in E France. Once an independent kingdom, it became a duchy and later a province of France. 2 a red or white wine first made there. *n., pl.* **Burgun dies.**

bur i al (bėr'ē əl), 1 act of putting a dead body in a grave, in a tomb, or in the sea; burying: *The sailor was given a burial at sea.* 2 having to do with burying: *a burial service.* 1 *n.*, 2 *adj.*

bur ied (bėr'ēd), past tense and past participle of **bury.** *The dog buried his bone. Many nuts were buried under the leaves.* *v.*

bur lap (bėr'lap), a coarse fabric made from jute or hemp, used to make bags. A finer grade of burlap is used for curtains, wall coverings, and upholstery. *n.*

bur lesque (bər lesk'), 1 a story, play, etc., that treats a serious subject ridiculously or a trivial subject as if it were important: *Mark Twain's story, "A Connecticut Yankee in King Arthur's Court," is a burlesque of the legends about King Arthur.* 2 imitate so as to make fun of. 3 a ridiculous imitation of something worthy or dignified; mockery: *By taking bribes the judge made a burlesque of his high office.* 1,3 *n.*, 2 *v.*, **bur lesqued, bur les quing.**

bur li ness (bėr'lē nis), condition of being burly. *n.*

bur ly (bėr'lē), big and strong; sturdy: *a burly wrestler. adj.*, **bur li er, burli est.**

Bur ma (bėr'mə), country in SE Asia, on the Indian Ocean. *Capital:* Rangoon. *n.*

Bur mese (bėr'mēz'), 1 person born in Burma. 2 language of Burma. 3 of Burma, its people, or their language. 1,2 *n., pl.* **Bur mese;** 3 *adj.*

burn[1] (bėrn), 1 be on fire; be very hot: *The campfire burned all night.* 2 set on fire; cause to burn: *They burned wood in the fireplace to keep warm.* 3 destroy or be destroyed by fire: *Please burn those old papers.* 4 injure or be injured by fire, heat, or acid: *The flame from the candle burned her finger. Your hand will burn if you touch that hot iron.* 5 injury caused by fire, heat, or acid; burned place: *She got a burn on her arm where she touched it with a hot pan. Don't lie too long in the sun or you will get a painful burn.* 6 make by fire, heat, acid,

etc.: *His cigar burned a hole in the rug. She burned designs on wood to make a picture.* 7 consume or change in chemical form by combining with oxygen: *The body makes energy by burning food.* 8 feel hot; give a feeling of heat to: *His forehead burns with fever. Mustard burns the tongue.* 9 be inflamed with anger, passion, etc.: *She burned with fury at the unkind remarks. We were burning with enthusiasm.* 10 give light: *Lamps were burning in every room.* 11 use to produce heat: *Our furnace burns oil.* 12 (of a rocket engine) fire or ignite. 1-4,6-12 *v.*, **burned** *or* **burnt, burn ing;** 5 *n.* [Old English *beornan* be on fire, and *bærnan* consume by fire]

burn[2] (bėrn), SCOTTISH. a small stream; brook. *n.* [Old English *burna*]

burn er (bėr'nər), 1 part of a lamp, stove, furnace, etc., where the flame is produced. 2 thing or part that burns or works by heat: *Some furnaces are oil burners; others are gas burners. n.*

bur nish (bėr'nish), 1 make shiny; polish: *burnish copper.* 2 a polish; shine. 1 *v.*, 2 *n.* —**bur'nish er,** *n.*

burnoose
The burnoose consists of a piece of cloth which is draped about the head and body.

bur noose *or* **bur nous** (bər nüs' *or* bėr'nüs), a cloak with a hood, worn by Moors and Arabs. *n.*

Burns (bėrnz), **Robert,** 1759-1796, Scottish poet. *n.*

burnt (bėrnt), burned; a past tense and a past participle of **burn[1].** *I don't like burnt toast. v.*

burp (bėrp), INFORMAL. belch. *n., v.*

burr[1] (bėr), 1 bur. 2 a rough ridge or edge left by a tool on metal, wood, etc., after cutting or drilling it. 3 tool with a head shaped like a bur, used by dentists in drilling. *n.* [probably from a Scandi-

---

Pronunciation key:

hat, āge, fär; let, ēqual, tėrm; it, īce; hot, ōpen, ôrder; oil, out; cup, pūt, rüle; ch, child; ng, long; sh, she; th, thin; ᴛʜ, then; zh, measure;

ə represents *a* in about, *e* in taken, *i* in pencil, *o* in lemon, *u* in circus.

adj. adjective   **n.** noun
adv. adverb   **prep.** preposition
conj. conjunction   **pron.** pronoun
interj. interjection   **v.** verb

sing. singular   **pl.** plural

navian word of the 1300's, such as Danish *borre* burdock]

burr[2] (bėr), 1 a rough pronunciation of r: *a Scottish burr.* 2 pronounce roughly: *He burrs his r's.* 3 a whirring sound. 4 make a whirring sound. 1,3 *n.*, 2,4 *v.* [probably an imitation of a rough pronunciation]

Burr (bėr), **Aaron**, 1756-1836, American political leader, vice-president of the United States from 1801 to 1805. *n.*

bur ro (bėr′ō *or* bùr′ō), a small donkey used to carry loads or packs in the southwestern United States. *n., pl.* **bur ros.**

burro
3 ft. high
at the
shoulder

bur row (bėr′ō), 1 hole dug in the ground by an animal for refuge or shelter. Rabbits live in burrows. 2 dig a hole in the ground: *The mole quickly burrowed out of sight.* 3 dig: *Rabbits have burrowed the ground for miles around.* 4 search: *She burrowed in the library for a book about Indian life.* 5 hide: *The runaway burrowed himself in the haystack.* 1 *n.*, 2-5 *v.* —**bur′row er,** *n.*

bur sa (bėr′sə), sac of the body, especially one containing a lubricating fluid. *n., pl.* **bur sae** (bėr′sē′), **bur sas.**

bur sar (bėr′sər), treasurer, especially of a college. *n.*

bur si tis (bər sī′tis), inflammation of a bursa, usually near the shoulder or hip. *n.*

burst (bėrst), 1 break open; break out suddenly: *They burst the lock. The trees had burst into bloom.* 2 fly apart or cause to fly apart suddenly with force; explode: *The balloon will burst.* 3 go, come, do, etc., by force or suddenly: *Don't burst into the room without knocking.* 4 be very full: *At the suggestion of a picnic, the class was bursting with enthusiasm.* 5 a bursting; out-

break: *There was a burst of laughter when the clown fell down.* 6 a sudden display of activity or energy: *In a burst of speed, she won the race at the last minute.* 1-4 *v.*, **burst, burst ing;** 5,6 *n.*

bur then (bėr′ᴛʜən), OLD USE. burden[1]. *n., v.*

Bu run di (bù rün′dē), country in central Africa. See **Congo** for map. *n.*

bur y (ber′ē), 1 put (a dead body) in the earth, in a tomb, or in the sea: *We buried the dead bird.* 2 cover up; hide: *The squirrels buried many nuts under the dead leaves.* 3 put or sink (oneself) deeply: *I buried myself in an interesting book.* 4 put far from one's mind: *I long ago buried any resentment caused by our argument.* *v.*, **bur ied, bur y ing.**

bus (bus), 1 a large motor vehicle with seats inside and formerly also on the roof. Buses are used to carry many passengers between fixed stations along a certain route. 2 take or go by bus: *The city bussed the children to school.* 1 *n., pl.* **bus es** *or* **bus ses;** 2 *v.*, **bused, bus ing** *or* **bussed, bus sing.**

bus boy (bus′boi′), a waiter's assistant. He brings bread and butter, fills glasses, and carries off empty dishes. *n.*

bush (bùsh), 1 a woody plant smaller than a tree, often with many separate branches starting from or near the ground. Some bushes are used as hedges; others are cultivated for their fruit. 2 open forest or wild, unsettled land: *The explorer went into the bush of Alaska. n., pl.* **bush es.**

beat around the bush, avoid coming straight to the point: *Tell me the truth right away, and don't beat around the bush.*

bush el (bùsh′əl), 1 measure for grain, fruit, vegetables, and other dry things. It is equal to 4 pecks or 32 quarts. 2 container that holds a bushel. *n.*

bush ing (bùsh′ing), a removable metal lining used to protect parts of machinery from wear. *n.*

Bush man (bùsh′mən), member of a tribe of roving hunters of southern Africa. *n., pl.* **Bush men.**

bush mas ter (bùsh′mas′tər), the largest poisonous snake of tropical America. *n.*

bush pilot, pilot who flies a small plane over unsettled country, such as parts of Alaska.

bush whack er (bùsh′hwak′ər), 1 person who lives or works in wooded areas. 2 person who clears out underbrush. 3 a guerrilla fighter. *n.*

bush y (bùsh′ē), 1 spreading out like a bush; growing thickly: *a bushy beard.* 2 overgrown with bushes: *a bushy ravine. adj.,* **bush i er, bush i est.**

bus i ly (biz′ə lē), in a busy manner;

actively: *Bees were busily collecting nectar in the clover. adv.*

busi ness (biz′nis), 1 thing that one is busy at; work; occupation: *A carpenter's business is building.* 2 matter; affair; concern: *Taking chances is sometimes risky business. I am tired of the whole business.* 3 buying and selling; commercial dealings; trade: *This hardware store does a big business in tools.* 4 of or having to do with business: *A business office usually has typewriters and other business machines.* 5 a store, factory, or other commercial enterprise; industrial establishment: *They sold the bakery business for a million dollars.* 6 right to act; responsibility: *Other people's business is not your business.* 1-3,5,6 *n., pl.* **busi ness es** for 5; 4 *adj.*

mean business, INFORMAL. be in earnest; be serious: *When he says he is going to get good marks, he means business.*

busi ness like (biz′nis līk′), having system and method; well-managed; practical: *They ran a prosperous store in a businesslike manner. adj.*

busi ness man (biz′nis man′), 1 man in business. A salesman is a businessman. 2 man who runs a business: *Some stores in our town are run by small businessmen. n., pl.* **busi ness men.**

busi ness wom an (biz′nis wùm′ən), 1 woman in business. 2 woman who runs a business: *The owner of our bakery is a good businesswoman. n., pl.* **busi ness wom en.**

bus kin (bus′kən), 1 boot reaching to the calf or knee, worn in olden times. 2 a high shoe with a very thick sole, worn by Greek and Roman actors of tragedy. 3 tragic drama; tragedy. *n.*

buskins (def. 2)

buss (bus), INFORMAL. kiss. *v., n., pl.* **buss es.**

bus ses (bus′iz), a plural of **bus.** *n.*

bust[1] (bust), 1 statue of a person's head, shoulders, and upper part of the chest. 2 the upper front part of the body, especially of a woman. *n.* [from French *buste*]

bust[2] (bust), SLANG. 1 burst; break. 2 punch; hit. 3 arrest or put in jail. *v.* [changed form of *burst*]

bus tle[1] (bus′əl), 1 be noisily busy and in a hurry: *The children bustled to get ready for the party. 2 noisy or excited activity: *There was a great bustle as the children got ready for the party.* 1 *v.,* **bus tled, bus tling;** 2 *n.* [perhaps an imitation of the sound of busy activity]

bus tle[2] (bus′əl), pad used to puff out the upper back part of a woman's skirt. *n.* [perhaps a special use of *bustle*[1]]

bus y (biz′ē), 1 having plenty to do; working; active; not idle: *The principal of our school is a busy person.* 2 full of work or activity: *Main Street is a busy place. Holidays are a busy time.* 3 make busy; keep busy: *The bees busied themselves at making honey.* 4 in use: *I tried to call her up, but her telephone line was busy.* 1,2,4 *adj.,* **bus i er, bus i est;** 3 *v.,* **bus ied, bus y ing.**

butte

bus y bod y (biz′ē bod′ē), person who pries into the affairs of others; meddler. *n., pl.* **bus y bod ies.**

but (but; *unstressed* bət), 1 on the other hand; yet: *You may go, but you must come home at six o'clock.* 2 except; save: *She works every day in the week but Sunday. You were right but for one thing.* 3 unless; except that: *It never rains but it pours.* 4 no more than; only; merely: *He is but a small boy. We can but try.* 5 other than; otherwise than: *We cannot choose but listen.* 6 who not; which not: *None come to his doors but are fed.* 7 that: *I don't doubt but she will come.* 1,3,5-7 *conj.,* 2 *prep.,* 4 *adv.*

bu tane (byü′tān), a colorless gas, a hydrocarbon, much used as a fuel. *n.*

butch er (bùch′ər), 1 man who cuts up and sells meat. 2 man whose work is killing animals for food. 3 kill (animals) for food. 4 kill (people, wild animals, or birds) needlessly, cruelly, or in large numbers. 5 a brutal killer; murderer. 6 spoil by poor work: *Don't butcher that song by singing off key.* 1,2,5 *n.,* 3,4,6 *v.*

butch er y (bùch′ər ē), brutal killing; murder in large numbers. *n., pl.* **butch er ies.**

but ler (but′lər), the head male servant in a household, in charge of the pantry and table service. *n.*

butt[1] (but), 1 the thicker end of a tool, weapon, ham, etc.: *the butt of a gun.* 2 end that is left; stub; stump: *a cigar butt. n.* [Middle English *but* (related to

Old English *buttuc* end) and French of the 1300's *bout* end]

butt[2] (but), 1 object of ridicule or scorn: *The new boy was the butt of many jokes.* 2 target. *n.* [from French of the 1300's *bout* end, and *but* aim]

butt[3] (but), 1 to strike or push by knocking hard with the head: *A goat butts.* 2 a push or blow with the head. 1 *v.,* 2 *n.* [from French of the 1200's *bouter* to thrust]

butt in, SLANG. meddle; interfere.

butte (byüt), (in the western United States) a steep hill standing alone. *n.*

but ter (but′ər), 1 the solid yellowish fat separated from cream by churning. 2 put butter on: *Please butter my bread.* 3 any of various foods like butter in looks or use: *apple butter, peanut butter.* 1,3 *n.,* 2 *v.*

butter up, INFORMAL. flatter.

but ter cup (but′ər kup′), a common plant with bright yellow flowers shaped like cups. *n.*

but ter fat (but′ər fat′), fat in milk. It can be made into butter. *n.*

but ter fin gers (but′ər fing′gərz), INFORMAL. a careless or clumsy person. *n.*

but ter fly (but′ər flī′), any of various insects with slender bodies and two pairs of large, usually brightly colored, overlapping wings. Butterflies fly mostly in the daytime. *n., pl.* **but ter flies.**

but ter milk (but′ər milk′), the sour liquid left after butter has been separated from cream. Milk can also be changed to buttermilk artificially. *n.*

but ter nut (but′ər nut′), 1 an oily kind of walnut grown in North America, which is good to eat. 2 tree that bears butternuts. *n.*

but ter scotch (but′ər skoch′), 1 candy made from brown sugar and butter. 2 flavored with brown sugar and butter: *butterscotch pudding.* 1 *n.,* 2 *adj.*

but ter y (but′ər ē), 1 like butter. 2 containing or spread with butter. *adj.*

but tocks (but′əks), the fleshy hind part of the body where the legs join the back; rump. *n.pl.*

but ton (but′n), 1 a round, flat piece of metal, bone, glass, plastic, etc., fastened on garments to hold them closed or to decorate them. 2 fasten the buttons of; close with buttons: *Please button my shirt for me.* 3 knob or disk pushed, turned, etc., to cause something to work: *Push the button of the elevator to make it go up.* 1,3 *n.,* 2 *v.*

but ton hole (but′n hōl′), 1 hole or slit through which a button is passed. 2 make buttonholes in. 3 hold in conversation or force to listen, as if holding someone by the buttonhole of his coat.

hat, āge, fär; let, ēqual, tėrm; it, īce; hot, ōpen, ôrder; oil, out; cup, pùt, rüle; ch, child; ng, long; sh, she; th, thin; ŦH, then; zh, measure;

ə represents *a* in about, *e* in taken, *i* in pencil, *o* in lemon, *u* in circus.

1 *n.,* 2,3 *v.,* **but ton holed, but ton hol ing.**

but ton wood (but′n wùd′), the sycamore tree of North America. *n.*

buttress (def. 1)
B, ordinary buttress
F, flying buttress

but tress (but′ris), 1 a support built against a wall or building to strengthen it. 2 a support like this; prop. 3 support and strengthen: *The pilot buttressed his report of the flight with photographs.* 1,2 *n., pl.* **but tress es;** 3 *v.*

bux om (buk′səm), plump and good to look at; healthy and cheerful. *adj.*

buy (bī), 1 get by paying a price; purchase: *You can buy a pencil for five cents.* 2 INFORMAL. a bargain: *That book was a real buy.* 3 bribe: *It was charged that two members of the jury had been bought by the defendant.* 1,3 *v.,* **bought, buy ing;** 2 *n.*

buy off, get rid of by paying money to; bribe: *The crook tried to buy off the policeman.*

buy out, buy all the shares, rights, merchandise, etc., of: *buy out a business.*

buy up, buy all one can of: *The little boy tried to buy up the candy in the store with his allowance.*

buy er (bī′ər), 1 person who buys. 2 person whose work is buying goods for a department store or other business. *n.*

buzz (buz), 1 the humming sound made by flies, mosquitoes, or bees. 2 the low, confused sound of many people talking quietly: *The buzz of whispers stopped when the teacher entered the room.* 3 make a steady, humming sound; hum loudly: *The radio should be fixed; it buzzes when you turn it on.* 4 talk

adj. adjective	*n.* noun
adv. adverb	*prep.* preposition
conj. conjunction	*pron.* pronoun
interj. interjection	*v.* verb
sing. singular	*pl.* plural

excitedly: *The whole class buzzed with the news of the holiday.* **5** fly an airplane very fast and low over (a place or person): *A pilot buzzed our school yesterday.* **6** to signal with a buzzer: *The editor buzzed her secretary.* 1,2 *n.*, 3-6 *v.*

buzz about, move about busily: *The children buzzed about the stage, getting ready to perform the play.*

buz zard (buz′ərd), **1** any of various large, heavy, slow-moving hawks. **2** turkey buzzard, a kind of vulture. *n.*

buzz er (buz′ər), **1** an electrical device that makes a buzzing sound as a signal. **2** thing that buzzes. *n.*

by (bī), **1** at the side or edge of; near; beside: *The garden is by the house. Sit by me.* **2** along; over; through: *They went by the main road.* **3** through the means or use of: *I travel by airplane. The house was destroyed by fire.* **4** in the measure of: *They sell eggs by the dozen.* **5** as soon as; not later than: *Try to be here by six o'clock.* **6** during: *The sun shines by day.* **7** past: *Julius Caesar lived in days gone by* (adv.). *A car raced by* (adv.). *They walked by our house* (prep.). **8** aside or away: *She puts money by every week to save for a new bicycle.* **9** according to: *They all work by the rules.* **10** in relation to; concerning: *They did well by their children.* 1-7,9,10 *prep.*, 7,8 *adv.*

by and by, after a while; before long; soon: *Summer vacation will come by and by.*

by and large, for the most part: *By and large it is a good book.*

by the by, by the way; incidentally: *By the by, here is the pen you lent me.*

by-and-by (bī′ən bī′), the future. *n.*

Byel o rus sia (byel′ə rush′ə), republic in the W Soviet Union, just east of Poland. *Capital:* Minsk. *n.* Also, **White Russia.** —**Byel′o rus′sian,** *adj., n.*

by gone (bī′gôn′), **1** gone by; past; former: *The ancient Romans lived in bygone days.* **2** bygones, *pl.* what is gone by and past: *Let bygones be forgotten.* 1 *adj.,* 2 *n.*

by law (bī′lô′), **1** law made by a city, company, club, etc., for the control of its own affairs. **2** a secondary law or rule; not one of the main rules: *Our club has a constitution and bylaws. n.*

by-line (bī′līn′), line at the beginning of a newspaper or magazine article giving the name of the writer. *n.*

by-pass (bī′pas′), **1** road, channel, pipe, etc., providing a secondary passage to be used instead of the main passage: *Drivers use the by-pass to avoid the city when there is a lot of traffic.* **2** go around: *The new highway by-passes the entire city.* 1 *n.,* pl. **by-pass es;** 2 *v.*

by-path (bī′path′), a side path; by-way. *n.,* pl. **by-paths** (bī′paᴛʜz′ or bī′paths′).

by-play (bī′plā′), action that is not part of the main action, especially on the stage. *n.*

by-prod uct (bī′prod′əkt), something of value produced in making the principal product or doing something else: *Kerosene is a by-product of petroleum refining. n.*

Byrd (bėrd), **Richard Evelyn,** 1888-1957, American naval officer, aviator, and polar explorer. *n.*

by-road (bī′rōd′), a side road. *n.*

By ron (bī′rən), **George Gordon,** Lord, 1788-1824, English poet. *n.*

by stand er (bī′stan′dər), person who stands near or looks on but does not take part; onlooker; spectator. *n.*

by way (bī′wā′), a side path or road; way which is little used. *n.*

by word (bī′wėrd′), **1** a common saying; proverb. **2** object of contempt; thing scorned: *Her cheating in class made her a byword to her classmates. n.*

Byz an tine (biz′n tēn′), **1** of the Byzantine Empire or Byzantium. **2** of or like a style of architecture developed in the Byzantine Empire, characterized by a circular dome over a square space, and the use of rich mosaics and frescoes. *adj.*

Byzantine Empire, E part of the Roman Empire after its division in A.D. 395. The Byzantine Empire ended with the capture of its capital, Constantinople, by the Turks in 1453.

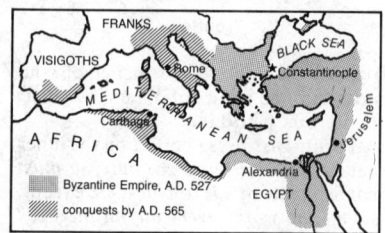

Byzantine Empire—The shaded areas show the Empire at its greatest extent.

By zan ti um (bi zan′shē əm or bi-zan′tē əm), ancient city where Istanbul (Constantinople) now is. It became the capital of the Roman Empire in A.D. 330. *n.*

C c

C or c (sē), 1 the third letter of the alphabet. 2 the Roman numeral for 100. *n., pl.* **C's** or **c's.**

c., 1 about; approximately. Also, **ca.** [abbreviation of Latin *circa*] 2 cent or cents. 3 centimeter. 4 cup or cups.

C., Centigrade.

ca., about; approximately. Also, **c.** [abbreviation of Latin *circa*]

cab (kab), 1 automobile that can be hired with driver; taxicab: *My father telephoned for a cab to take him to the airport.* 2 carriage that can be hired with driver, usually pulled by one horse: *We rode through the park in a cab.* 3 the enclosed part of a railroad engine where the engineer and fireman sit: *The engineer invited the boy to sit in the cab with him.* 4 the enclosed part of a truck, crane, or other machine, where the driver or operator sits. *n.*

ca bal (kə bal′), 1 a small group of people working or plotting in secret. 2 a secret scheme of such a group; plot. *n.*

cab al ler o (kab′ə ler′ō *or* kab′ə-lyer′ō), 1 (in Spain) a gentleman. 2 in southwestern United States: **a** horseman. **b** an ardent admirer. *n., pl.* **cab al-ler os.** [from Spanish]

ca ban a (kə ban′ə), shelter like a small tent or cabin, used on a beach or near a swimming pool for dressing or to provide shade. *n., pl.* **ca ban as.** [from Spanish *cabaña*]

cab a ret (kab′ə rā′), restaurant offering singing and dancing as entertainment. *n.*

cab bage (kab′ij), 1 plant whose thick leaves are closely folded into a round head that grows on a short stem. 2 its head, eaten either cooked or raw as a vegetable. *n.*

cab by or **cab bie** (kab′ē), INFORMAL. driver of a cab, especially a taxicab. *n., pl.* **cab bies.**

cab driv er (kab′drī′vər), person who drives a taxicab. *n.*

cab in (kab′ən), 1 a small, roughly built house; hut: *Last summer we stayed in a cabin in the Maine woods.* 2 a private room in a ship: *The 500 passengers occupied 200 cabins.* 3 a room on a small boat containing the bunks. 4 place for passengers in an aircraft: *Only the stewardess can go from the cabin to the cockpit. n.*

cabin boy, boy or man whose work is waiting on the officers and passengers on a ship.

cab i net (kab′ə nit), 1 piece of furni-ture with shelves or drawers, used to hold articles for use or display: *a medicine cabinet, a filing cabinet for letters. We keep our very best dishes in the china cabinet.* 2 Also, **Cabinet.** group of advisers chosen by the head of a nation, usually to administer particular departments of the government. The Attorney General and the Secretary of Defense are members of the cabinet of the President of the United States. *n.*

cab i net mak er (kab′ə nit mā′kər), person whose work is making fine furniture and woodwork. *n.*

ca ble (kā′bəl), 1 a strong, thick rope, usually made of wires twisted together: *The truck towed the automobile with a cable.* 2 tie or fasten with a cable: *The ship was cabled to the pier.* 3 an insulated bundle of wires which carries an electric current. Telegraph messages are sent across the ocean by underwater cable. 4 cablegram: *A transatlantic cable arrived from Paris.* 5 send (a message) across the ocean by underwater cable: *She cabled the good news of her safe arrival in Paris.* 1,3,4 *n.,* 2,5 *v.,* **ca bled, ca bling.**

cable car

cable car, car pulled by a moving cable that is operated by an engine.

ca ble gram (kā′bəl gram), message sent across the ocean by underwater cable. *n.*

ca boose (kə büs′), 1 a small car on a freight train in which trainmen can work, rest, and sleep. It is usually the last car. 2 kitchen on the deck of a ship. *n.*

caboose
(def. 1)

Cab ot (kab′ət), 1 **John,** 1450?-1498, English navigator and explorer, born in Italy, who reached North America in 1497. 2 his son, **Sebastian,** 1474?-1557, English navigator and explorer in the service of England and Spain, born in Italy. *n.*

ca ca o (kə kā′ō *or* kə kä′ō), 1 the

hat, āge, fär; let, ēqual, tèrm; it, īce; hot, ōpen, ôrder; oil, out; cup, pùt, rüle; ch, child; ng, long; sh, she; th, thin; ᴛʜ, then; zh, measure;

ə represents *a* in about, *e* in taken, *i* in pencil, *o* in lemon, *u* in circus.

seeds from which cocoa and chocolate are made. 2 the small, tropical American evergreen tree that they grow on. *n., pl.* **ca ca os.**

cach a lot (kash′ə lot), sperm whale. *n.*

cache (kash), 1 a hiding place to store food or other things: *The explorers dug a hole to serve as a cache for the supplies needed on the return trip.* 2 a hidden store of food or supplies: *Squirrels make caches of nuts for winter food.* 3 put in a cache; hide: *The bear had cached her cubs in a cave.* 1,2 *n.,* 3 *v.,* **cached, cach ing.**

cack le (kak′əl), 1 the shrill, broken sound that a hen makes, especially after laying an egg: *The cackle in the henhouse awoke the farmer.* 2 make this sound: *The hens started to cackle early in the morning.* 3 shrill, harsh, or broken laughter: *Before the comedian finished the joke, there were a few cackles from the audience.* 4 laugh in a shrill, harsh, or broken way: *The old man cackled at his own joke.* 5 noisy chatter; silly talk. 6 to chatter. 1,3,5 *n.,* 2,4,6 *v.,* **cack led, cack ling.**

ca coph o nous (kə kof′ə nəs), harsh and clashing in sound. *adj.* **—ca-coph′o nous ly,** *adv.*

cac tus (kak′təs), plant with a thick, fleshy stem that usually has spines but no leaves. Most cactuses grow in very hot, dry regions of America and often have brightly colored flowers. *n., pl.* **cac tus es, cac ti** (kak′tī).

cad (kad), boy or man who does not act like a gentleman. *n.*

ca dav er (kə dav′ər), a dead body; corpse. *n.*

ca dav er ous (kə dav′ər əs), 1 pale and ghastly. 2 thin and worn. *adj.*

cad die (kad′ē), 1 person who helps a golf player by carrying golf clubs, finding the ball, etc. 2 help a golf player in this way. 1 *n.,* 2 *v.,* **cad died, cad dy-ing.** Also, **caddy.**

cad dis fly (kad′is), insect somewhat like a moth. Its larva lives under water and forms for itself a case of sand, bits of leaves, or the like.

cad dish (kad′ish), like a cad; ungen-

adj. adjective	*n.* noun
adv. adverb	*prep.* preposition
conj. conjunction	*pron.* pronoun
interj. interjection	*v.* verb
sing. singular	*pl.* plural

tlemanly. *adj.* —**cad′dish ly**, *adv.* —**cad′dish ness**, *n.*

cad dy[1] (kad′ē), a small box, can, or chest, often used to hold tea. *n., pl.* **cad dies.** [from Malay *kati* a small weight]

cad dy[2] (kad′ē), caddie. *n., pl.* **cad dies;** *v.,* **cad died, cad dy ing.** [from French *cadet* younger brother]

ca dence (kād′ns), 1 the measure or beat of music, dancing, marching, or any movement regularly repeating itself; rhythm: *The cadence of the surf lulled us to sleep.* 2 fall of the voice: *the cadence at the end of a sentence.* 3 a rising and falling sound: *She speaks with a pleasant cadence.* 4 series of chords bringing part of a piece of music to an end: *He heard the cadence and realized that the concert was almost over.* *n.*

ca den za (kə den′zə), flourish or showy passage, often improvised, usually near the end of a section of a musical composition. *n., pl.* **ca den zas.**

ca det (kə det′), 1 a young man in training for service as an officer in the army, navy, or air force: *The cadets from West Point will graduate next week.* 2 student in a high-school or grade-school military academy. 3 a younger son or brother. *n.*

ca di (kä′dē), a minor Moslem judge, usually of a town or village. *n., pl.* **ca dis.**

cad mi um (kad′mē əm), a soft, bluish-white, metallic element resembling tin, used in plating to prevent corrosion and in making alloys. *n.*

ca du ce us (kə dü′sē əs *or* kə dyü′sē əs), staff of Mercury with two snakes twined around it and a pair of wings on top. The caduceus is often used as an emblem of the medical profession. *n., pl.* **ca du ce i** (kə dü′sē ī *or* kə dyü′sē ī).

Cae sar (sē′zər), 1 **Gaius Julius,** 102?-44 B.C., Roman general, statesman, and historian. 2 title of the Roman emperors from Augustus to Hadrian, and later of the heir to the throne. 3 emperor. 4 dictator or tyrant. *n.*

Cae sa re a (sē′zə rē′ə), small seaport in NW Israel. It was the ancient Roman capital of Judea. *n.*

cae sur a (si zhür′ə), a pause in a line of verse. EXAMPLE: "To err is human,| to forgive, divine." *n., pl.* **cae sur as, cae sur ae** (si zhür′ē).

ca fe (ka fā′), café. *n.*

ca fé (ka fā′), 1 place to buy and eat a meal; restaurant. 2 barroom. *n., pl.* **ca fés.** [from French *café* coffee, coffee house]

caf e ter i a (kaf′ə tir′ē ə), restaurant where people wait on themselves. *n., pl.* **caf e ter i as.**

caf feine *or* **caf fein** (kaf′ēn′), a slightly bitter, stimulating drug found in coffee and tea. *n.*

cage (kāj), 1 frame or place closed in with wires, strong iron bars, or wood. Birds and wild animals are kept in cages. 2 thing shaped or used like a cage. The car or closed platform of an elevator is a cage. Bank tellers often work in a cage. 3 put or keep in a cage: *After the lion was caught, it was caged.* 1,2 *n.,* 3 *v.,* **caged, cag ing.**

cag ey *or* **cag y** (kā′jē), INFORMAL. shrewd and cautious; sharp and wary: *The cagey fox could not be easily trapped by the farmer.* *adj.,* **cag i er, cag i est.**

cag i ly (kā′jə lē), in a cagey manner; warily. *adv.*

cag i ness (kā′jē nis), cagey quality; wariness. *n.*

ca hoots (kə hüts′), SLANG. **in cahoots,** in partnership: *She did the mischief in cahoots with another.* *n.*

cai man (kā′mən), a large reptile of tropical America, similar to an alligator. *n., pl.* **cai mans.** Also, **cayman.**

Cain (kān), 1 (in the Bible) the oldest son of Adam and Eve. He killed his brother Abel. 2 murderer. *n.*

raise Cain, SLANG. make a great disturbance: *When the teacher left the room, the students raised Cain.*

cairn (kern *or* karn), pile of stones heaped up as a memorial, tomb, or landmark. *n.*

Cai ro (kī′rō), capital of Egypt, in the NE part. *n.*

cais son (kā′sn *or* kā′son), 1 wagon to carry ammunition. 2 box for ammunition. 3 a watertight box or chamber in which men can work under ground or water to make foundations for buildings, tunnels, etc. 4 a watertight float used in raising sunken ships. *n.*

ca jole (kə jōl′), persuade by pleasant words, flattery, or false promises; coax: *He cajoled his friends into deciding in his favor.* *v.,* **ca joled, ca jol ing.**

ca jol er (kə jō′lər), person who cajoles. *n.*

ca jol er y (kə jō′lər ē), persuasion by pleasant words, flattery, or false promises; coaxing. *n., pl.* **ca jol er ies.**

Ca jun (kā′jən), person who is a descendant of the French who came to Louisiana from Acadia. *n.*

cake (kāk), 1 a baked mixture of flour, sugar, eggs, flavoring, and other things: *We baked a chocolate cake with white frosting for Mother's birthday.* 2 pancake. 3 a shaped mass of food or other substance: *That restaurant makes good fish cakes. She carved a cake of soap into the shape of a dog.* 4 form into a solid mass; harden: *Mud cakes as it dries.* 1-3 *n.,* 4 *v.,* **caked, cak ing.**

cake walk (kāk′wôk′), 1 a dance with prancing high steps that developed from an earlier march or promenade for couples. A cake was the prize for the most original steps. 2 do a cakewalk. 1 *n.,* 2 *v.*

Cal., California. The official abbreviation is **Calif.**

cal a bash (kal′ə bash), 1 gourd or gourdlike fruit whose dried shell is used to make bottles, bowls, drums, pipes, and rattles. 2 the tropical plant or tree that it grows on. 3 bottle, bowl, drum, pipe, or rattle made from such a dried shell. *n., pl.* **cal a bash es.**

Cal ais (ka lā′), seaport in N France that is nearest England. *n.*

cal a mine (kal′ə mīn), compound of zinc oxide and iron oxide used in lotions to relieve skin irritations or sunburn. *n.*

ca lam i tous (kə lam′ə təs), causing calamity; accompanied by calamity; disastrous. *adj.* —**ca lam′i tous ly,** *adv.*

ca lam i ty (kə lam′ə tē), 1 a great misfortune such as a flood, a fire, the loss of one's sight or hearing, or of much money or property; disaster. 2 serious trouble; misery: *Many people still suffer from the calamity of hunger and poverty.* *n., pl.* **ca lam i ties.**

caisson
(defs. 1 and 2)

caisson (def. 3)
The weight of the caisson forces it into sand and mud below the water. Air under pressure is then forced into the caisson, driving out the water and permitting workmen to enter through airtight compartments.

cal car e ous (kal ker′ē əs *or* kal kar′ē əs), of or containing lime, limestone, or calcium carbonate. *adj.*

cal ci fi ca tion (kal′sə fə kā′shən), 1 process of calcifying. 2 a calcified part. *n.*

cal ci fy (kal′sə fī), make or become hard or bony by the deposit of calcium salts: *Cartilage often calcifies in older people.* *v.,* **cal ci fied, cal ci fy ing.**

cal ci mine (kal′sə mīn), 1 a white or tinted lime solution used as a wash for walls, ceilings, etc. 2 cover with calcimine. 1 *n.,* 2 *v.,* **cal ci mined, cal ci min ing.**

cal cine (kal′sīn), burn (something) to ashes or powder: *calcine bones.* *v.,* **cal cined, cal cin ing.**

cal cite (kal′sīt), mineral made up of calcium carbonate. It is the chief substance in limestone, chalk, and marble. *n.*

cal ci um (kal′sē əm), a soft, silvery-white metallic element. It is a part of limestone, chalk, milk, bone, shells, teeth, etc. Calcium is used in alloys and its compounds are used in making plaster, in cooking, and as bleaching agents. *n.*

calcium carbonate, compound of calcium occurring in rocks such as marble and limestone, in animals' bones, shells, and teeth, and to some extent in plants.

calcium hydroxide, slaked lime.

calcium oxide, lime[1].

cal cu la ble (kal′kyə lə bəl), that can be calculated. *adj.*

cal cu la bly (kal′kyə lə blē), in a calculable manner. *adv.*

cal cu late (kal′kyə lāt), 1 find out by adding, subtracting, multiplying, or dividing; compute: *They calculated the cost of building a house.* 2 find out beforehand by any process of reasoning; estimate: *Calculate the day of the week on which New Year's Day will fall.* 3 rely; depend; count: *You can calculate on earning $50 a week if you take the job.* 4 plan or intend: *That remark was calculated to make me angry.* *v.,* **cal cu lat ed, cal cu lat ing.**

cal cu lat ing (kal′kyə lā′ting), 1 that calculates: *a calculating machine.* 2 shrewd and careful. 3 scheming and selfish. *adj.*

cal cu la tion (kal′kyə lā′shən), 1 act of adding, subtracting, multiplying, or dividing to find a result; computation. 2 result found by calculating. 3 careful thinking; deliberate planning: *The success of the expedition was the result of much calculation.* *n.*

cal cu la tor (kal′kyə lā′tər), 1 machine that calculates, especially one that solves difficult problems in calculation; computer. 2 person who calculates. *n.*

cal cu lus (kal′kyə ləs), 1 system of calculation in advanced mathematics, using algebraic symbols to solve problems dealing with changing quantities. 2 stone that has formed in the body because of a diseased condition. Gallstones are calculi. *n., pl.* **cal cu li** (kal′kyə lī), **cal cu lus es.**

Cal cut ta (kal kut′ə), seaport in E India. *n.*

cal dron (kôl′drən), a large kettle or boiler. *n.* Also, **cauldron.**

Cal e do ni a (kal′ə dō′nē ə), Scotland. *n.* —**Cal′e do′ni an,** *adj., n.*

cal en dar (kal′ən dər), 1 table showing the months, weeks, and days of the year. A calendar shows the day of the week on which each day of the month falls. *The calendar shows that Memorial Day will fall on a Monday.* 2 system by which the beginning, length, and divisions of the year are fixed: *The Julian calendar was established during the reign of Julius Caesar.* 3 a list or schedule; record; register: *The clerk of the court announced the next case on the calendar.* *n.*

cal en der (kal′ən dər), 1 machine in which cloth, paper, or similar material is smoothed and glazed by pressing between rollers. 2 make smooth and glossy by pressing in a calender. 1 *n.,* 2 *v.*

calf[1] (kaf), 1 a young cow or bull: *The calf stayed close behind its mother in the pasture.* 2 a young elephant, whale, deer, or seal: *The children saw the new seal calves at the zoo.* 3 calfskin: *The gloves she bought are made of calf.* *n., pl.* **calves** for 1 and 2. [Old English *cealf*]

calf[2] (kaf), the thick, fleshy part of the back of the leg below the knee. *n., pl.* **calves.** [from a Scandinavian word of the 1200's, such as Icelandic *kálfi*]

calf skin (kaf′skin′), 1 skin of a calf. 2 leather made from it. *n.*

Cal gar y (kal′gər ē), city in SW Canada. *n.*

Cal houn (kal hün′), **John Caldwell,** 1782-1850, American statesman, vice-president of the United States from 1825 to 1832. *n.*

cal i ber or **cal i bre** (kal′ə bər), 1 the inside diameter of the barrel of a gun. A .45-caliber revolver has a barrel with an inside diameter of 45/100 of an inch. 2 the diameter of a bullet or shell fired from a particular gun. 3 amount of ability: *We were able to find people of high caliber to fill the vacancies.* 4 quality: *We are always trying to improve the caliber of our schools.* *n.*

cal i brate (kal′ə brāt), 1 determine, check, or adjust the scale of (a thermometer, gauge, or other measuring instrument). Calibrating is usually done by comparison with a standard instrument. 2 find the caliber of. *v.,* **cal i brat ed, cal i brat ing.**

cal i bra tion (kal′ə brā′shən), a calibrating or a being calibrated. *n.*

hat, āge, fär; let, ēqual, tėrm;
it, īce; hot, ōpen, ôrder;
oil, out; cup, pùt, rüle; ch, child;
ng, long; sh, she; th, thin;
ŦH, then; zh, measure;

ə represents *a* in about,
e in taken, *i* in pencil,
o in lemon, *u* in circus.

cal i co (kal′ə kō), 1 a cotton cloth that usually has colored patterns printed on one side. 2 made of calico: *a calico dress.* 3 spotted in colors: *a calico cat.* 1 *n., pl.* **cal i coes** or **cal i cos;** 2,3 *adj.*

ca lif (kā′lif), caliph. *n.*

Calif., the official abbreviation of California.

cal if ate (kal′ə fāt), caliphate. *n.*

Cal i for nia (kal′ə fôr′nyə), 1 one of the Pacific states of the United States. *Capital:* Sacramento. 2 **Gulf of,** arm of the Pacific between Lower California and the mainland of Mexico. *n.* —**Cal′i for′nian,** *adj., n.*

cal i for ni um (kal′ə fôr′nē əm), a radioactive metallic element, produced artificially from curium, plutonium, or uranium. *n.* [from *California*]

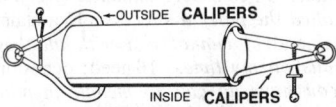

cal i pers (kal′ə pərz), instrument used to measure the diameter or thickness of something. *n.pl.* Also, **callipers.**

ca liph (kā′lif), the former title of religious and political heads of some Moslem states. *n.* Also, **calif.**

cal iph ate (kal′ə fāt), rank, reign, government, or territory of a caliph. *n.* Also, **califate.**

cal is then ics (kal′is then′iks), exercises to develop a strong and graceful body. Calisthenics are carried out simply by moving the body, without the use of special equipment. *n.pl.* Also, **callisthenics.**

calk[1] (kôk), a projecting piece on a horseshoe that catches in the ground or ice to prevent slipping. *n.* [from Latin *calx* heel or *calcar* spur]

calk[2] (kôk), caulk. *v.* [from French of the 1400's *cauquer,* from Latin *calcare* tread, press in, from *calx* heel]

call (kôl), 1 speak or say in a loud voice; shout or cry out: *He called from downstairs. The nurse called the names of the next three patients.* 2 a loud sound uttered by a person so as to be heard from a distance; shout: *I heard*

calla

adj. adjective	*n.* noun
adv. adverb	*prep.* preposition
conj. conjunction	*pron.* pronoun
interj. interjection	*v.* verb
sing. singular	*pl.* plural

the swimmer's call for help. **3** the special noise or cry an animal or bird makes: *The call of a moose came from the forest.* **4** make this noise or cry: *The crows called to each other from the trees around the meadow.* **5** give a signal to; arouse: *The bugle called the men to assemble. Call me at seven o'clock.* **6** command or ask to come; summon: *He called his dog with a loud whistle.* **7** invitation, command, or summons: *Every farmer in the neighborhood answered the firemen's call for volunteers.* **8** give a name to; name: *They called the new baby "Clara."* **9** read over aloud: *The teacher called the roll of the class.* **10** talk to by telephone: *Did anyone call today? Call me at the office.* **11** a telephone call: *I want to make a call to Chicago.* **12** make a short visit or stop: *Our pastor called yesterday.* **13** a short visit or stop: *The doctor had six calls to make.* **14** consider; estimate: *Everyone called the party a success.* **15** a claim; demand: *I cannot rest with all these calls on my time.* **16** need; occasion: *You have no call to meddle in other people's business.* **17** end; stop: *The ball game was called on account of rain.* **18** demand payment of: *The bank called their loan to my parents.* 1,4-6, 8-10,12,14,17,18 *v.,* 2,3,7,11,13,15, 16 *n.*

call back, 1 ask (a person) to return; recall: *Call back the postman.* **2** telephone to someone who has called earlier.

call down, scold: *Most people dislike being called down in front of others.*

call for, 1 go and get; stop and get: *The cab called for her at the hotel.* **2** need; require: *This recipe calls for two eggs.*

call in, 1 summon for advice or consultation: *Mother called in a doctor when I got a high fever.* **2** withdraw: *The library calls in books that are damaged.*

call off, 1 cancel: *We called off our trip.* **2** say or read over aloud in succession: *The teacher called off the names on the roll.* **3** order to withdraw: *Call off your dog.*

call on or **call upon, 1** pay a short visit to: *We must call on our new neighbors.* **2** appeal to: *He called upon his friends for help.*

call out, 1 say in a loud voice; shout:

She called out to the boys to stop quarreling. **2** summon into service: *The governor called out the National Guard to help with the rescue work during the flood.*

call up, 1 bring to mind; bring back: *The old friends called up childhood memories.* **2** telephone to: *He called me up at the office.* **3** draft into military service: *The army called him up when he finished school.*

on call, ready or available: *Doctors are expected to be on call day and night.*

within call, near enough to hear a call: *We are supposed to stay within call since supper is almost ready.*

cal la (kal′ə), plant with a large, white leaf like a petal around a thick spike of small yellow flowers. *n., pl.* **cal las.**

calla lily, 1 calla. **2** its blossom, formed of a white leaf around a yellow spike.

call er (kô′lər), **1** person who makes a short visit: *The doctor said that the patient was now able to receive callers.* **2** person who calls out names, steps at a square dance, etc. *n.*

cal lig ra phy (kə lig′rə fē), **1** handwriting. **2** beautiful handwriting: *Calligraphy is considered an art in China. n.*

call ing (kô′ling), **1** occupation, profession, or trade: *He chose to follow the calling of a teacher while his sister chose medicine as her calling.* **2** invitation, command, or summons: *the calling of the bells to prayer. He felt an inner calling to be a clergyman. n.*

cal li o pe (kə lī′ə pē), **1** a musical instrument having a series of steam whistles played by pressing keys on a keyboard. **2 Calliope,** (in Greek myths) the Muse of eloquence and heroic poetry. *n.*

cal li pers (kal′ə pərz), calipers. *n.pl.*

cal lis then ics (kal′is then′iks), calisthenics. *n.pl.*

call number, number put on a library book to enable the user to identify and find it.

cal lous (kal′əs), **1** having a callus; hard: *Going barefoot makes the bottoms of your feet callous.* **2** unfeeling; not sensitive: *Only a callous person can see suffering without trying to relieve it. adj.* —**cal′lous ly,** *adv.* —**cal′lous ness,** *n.*

cal loused (kal′əst), made callous; hardened. *adj.*

cal low (kal′ō), **1** not fully grown or developed; immature: *a callow youth.* **2** (of birds) without feathers sufficiently developed for flight. *adj.* —**cal′low ness,** *n.*

cal lus (kal′əs), a hard, thickened place on the skin. *n., pl.* **cal lus es.**

calm (käm *or* kälm), **1** not stormy or windy; not stirred up; quiet; still: *In fair*

weather, the sea is usually calm. **2** not excited; peaceful: *Although she was frightened, she answered with a calm voice.* **3** absence of wind or motion; quietness; stillness: *There was a sudden calm as the wind dropped.* **4** absence of excitement; peacefulness: *The activity of the game was followed by an unusual calm.* **5** make or become calm: *Father calmed the baby. The crying baby soon calmed down. The storm ceased and the sea calmed.* 1,2 *adj.,* 3,4 *n.,* 5 *v.* —**calm′ly,** *adv.* —**calm′ness,** *n.*

cal o mel (kal′ə mel), a white, tasteless, crystalline powder, a compound of mercury and chlorine, used in medicine as a laxative. *n.*

ca lo ric (kə lôr′ik), **1** heat. **2** having to do with heat or calories. 1 *n.,* 2 *adj.*

cal or ie or **cal or y** (kal′ər ē), **1** unit for measuring the amount of heat. It is the quantity of heat needed to raise by one degree centigrade the temperature of either a gram of water (**small calorie**) or a kilogram of water (**large calorie**). **2** unit of the energy supplied by food, corresponding to the large calorie. An ounce of sugar will produce about one hundred such calories. *n., pl.* **cal or ies.**

calumet

cal u met (kal′yə met), a long, ornamented tobacco pipe smoked by the American Indians in ceremonies as a symbol of peace. *n.*

ca lum ni ate (kə lum′nē āt), say false and harmful things about; slander. *v.,* **ca lum ni at ed, ca lum ni at ing.**

ca lum ni ous (kə lum′nē əs), slanderous. *adj.* —**ca lum′ni ous ly,** *adv.*

cal um ny (kal′əm nē), a false statement made on purpose to do harm to someone; slander. *n., pl.* **cal um nies.**

Cal var y (kal′vər ē), (in the Bible) a place near Jerusalem where Jesus died on the Cross; Golgotha. *n.*

calve (kav), give birth to a calf. *v.,* **calved, calv ing.**

Cal vert (kal′vərt), Sir **George,** 1580?-1632, the first Lord Baltimore, an English noble who was responsible for founding the colony of Maryland. *n.*

calves (kavz), plural of **calf¹** (defs. 1 and 2) and **calf².** *n.*

Cal vin (kal′vən), **John,** 1509-1564, French leader of the Protestant Reformation at Geneva. The Puritans and Huguenots followed the teachings of Calvin. *n.*

Cal vin ism (kal′və niz′əm), the religious teachings of Calvin and his followers. Calvin taught that only certain persons, the elect, were chosen by God to be saved and these could be saved only by God's grace. *n.*

Cal vin ist (kal′və nist), 1 person who follows the teachings of Calvin. 2 having to do with Calvinism or Calvinists. 1 *n.*, 2 *adj.*

calx (kalks), an ashy substance left after a metal or a mineral has been thoroughly roasted or burned. *n., pl.* **calx es.**

ca lyp so (kə lip′sō), type of improvised song, usually about some matter of current interest, that originated in the British West Indies. *n., pl.* **ca lyp sos.**

PETAL

SEPAL

calyx

ca lyx (kā′liks *or* kal′iks), the outer leaves that surround the unopened bud of a flower. The calyx is made up of sepals. *n., pl.* **ca lyx es, cal y ces** (kal′-ə sēz′ *or* kā′lə sēz′).

cam (kam), projection on a wheel or shaft that changes a regular circular motion into an irregular circular motion or into a back-and-forth motion. Cams are used to vary the speed of some mechanisms or change the direction of their movement. *n.*

ca ma ra der ie (kä′mə rä′dər ē), friendliness and loyalty among comrades; comradeship: *the cheerful cama-raderie of school days. n.*

cam bi um (kam′bē əm), layer of soft growing tissue between the bark and the wood of trees and shrubs. New bark and new wood grow from it. *n.*

Cam bo di a (kam bō′dē ə), country in SE Asia, formerly part of French Indochina. Its official name is **Khmer Republic.** *Capital:* Phnom Penh. See **Indochina** for map. *n.* —**Cam bo′di an,** *adj., n.*

cam bric (kām′brik), a fine, thin linen or cotton cloth. *n.*

cambric tea, drink made of hot water, milk, and sugar, sometimes flavored with a little tea.

Cam bridge (kām′brij), 1 city in SE England. 2 university located there. 3 city in E Massachusetts, near Boston. *n.*

Cam den (kam′dən), city in SW New Jersey, on the Delaware River. *n.*

came (kām), past tense of **come.** *He came to school early this morning. v.*

cam el (kam′əl), a large, four-footed, cud-chewing mammal with a long neck and cushioned feet. It is used as a beast of burden in the deserts of northern Africa and central Asia because it can go for a long time without drinking

water. The Arabian camel has one hump; the Bactrian camel has two humps. *n.*

ca mel lia (kə mē′lyə), 1 shrub or tree with glossy, evergreen leaves and waxy white, red, pink, or striped flowers shaped like roses. 2 its flower. *n., pl.* **ca mel lias.**

Cam e lot (kam′ə lot), legendary place in England where King Arthur had his palace and court. *n.*

Cam em bert (kam′əm ber), a rich, soft, ripened cheese. *n.* [from *Camembert,* a French village]

cam e o (kam′ē ō), a precious or semiprecious stone carved so that there is a raised design on a background usually of a different color. Agates, other stones with layers, and sometimes shells are used for cameos. *n., pl.* **cam e os.**

cam er a (kam′ər ə), 1 machine for taking photographs or motion pictures. 2 part of the transmitter which converts images into electronic impulses for television transmitting. *n., pl.* **cam er as.**

cam—As the cam turns with the shaft, the follower moves down (left) and up (right).

FOLLOWER

CAM

SHAFT

cam er a man (kam′ər ə man′), man who operates a camera, especially a motion-picture or television camera. *n., pl.* **cam er a men.**

Cam er oon *or* **Cam er oun** (kam′-ə rün′), country in W central Africa. See **Upper Volta** for map. *n.*

cam i sole (kam′ə sōl), a woman's undergarment that is like the top part of a slip. *n.*

cam o mile (kam′ə mīl), plant of the same family as the aster, with daisylike flowers. Its flowers and leaves are sometimes dried and used in medicine. *n.*

cam ou flage (kam′ə fläzh), 1 a disguise or false appearance serving to conceal. The white fur of a polar bear is a natural camouflage, for it prevents the bear's being easily seen against the snow. 2 the practice of giving soldiers, weapons, etc., a false appearance to conceal them from the enemy. 3 materials or other means by which this is done: *The guns were hidden by a camouflage of earth and branches.* 4 give a false appearance to in order to conceal; disguise: *The hunters were camouflaged with shrubbery so that they blended with the green landscape. The boy camouflaged his embarrassment by laughing.* 1-3 *n.,* 4 *v.,* **cam ou flaged, cam ou flag ing.**

hat, āge, fär; let, ēqual, tėrm;
it, īce; hot, ōpen, ôrder;
oil, out; cup, pùt, rüle; ch, child;
ng, long; sh, she; th, thin;
ᵺ, then; zh, measure;

ə represents *a* in about,
e in taken, *i* in pencil,
o in lemon, *u* in circus.

camp (kamp), 1 group of tents, huts, or other shelters where people live for a time: *A marching army usually makes camp every night. Many people live in the camp near that large lake during the summer.* 2 make a camp; put up tents, huts, or other shelters and stay for a time: *The Boy Scout troop camped at the foot of the mountain for two weeks.* 3 place where one lives in a tent or hut or outdoors: *There is a Girl Scout camp at the edge of the lake.* 4 area where an army sets up temporary shelter. 5 persons living in a camp: *The camp was awakened by the bugler.* 6 live simply, as one does in a tent: *We camped in the empty house until our furniture arrived.* 7 group of people who agree or work together: *The election of a new president divided the voters into two opposing camps.* 1,3-5,7 *n.,* 2,6 *v.*

break camp, pack up tents and equipment: *We broke camp early in the morning to return home.*

cam paign (kam pān′), 1 series of related military operations in a war which are aimed at some special purpose: *The general planned a campaign to capture the enemy's most important city.* 2 series of connected activities to do or get something: *Our town had a campaign to raise money for a new hospital.* 3 take part or serve in a campaign: *The candidates campaigned by giving speeches.* 1,2 *n.,* 3 *v.* —**cam paign′er,** *n.*

cam pa ni le (kam′pə nē′lē), tower built to contain a bell or bells. It may be a separate building. *n.*

camp er (kam′pər), 1 person who camps. 2 vehicle fitted out for camping, either self-propelled or pulled by an automobile. *n.*

camp fire (kamp′fīr′), 1 fire in a camp for cooking or warmth. 2 a social gathering of soldiers, scouts, etc. *n.*

campfire girl, member of the Camp Fire Girls.

Camp Fire Girls, organization for girls to help them develop character, health, and usefulness to others.

camp ground (kamp′ground′), 1 place for camping, especially a public park with campsites, fireplaces for cook-

adj. adjective	*n.* noun
adv. adverb	*prep.* preposition
conj. conjunction	*pron.* pronoun
interj. interjection	*v.* verb
sing. singular	*pl.* plural

ing, etc. **2** place where a camp meeting is held. *n.*

cam phor (kam′fər), a white, crystalline substance with a strong odor and a bitter taste, usually obtained from a laurel tree in eastern Asia. Camphor is used in medicine and to protect clothes from moths. *n.*

cam phor at ed (kam′fə rā′tid), containing camphor: *camphorated oil. adj.*

camp meeting, a religious gathering held outdoors or in a tent, sometimes lasting several days.

cam po ree (kam′pə rē′), a gathering or outing by boy scouts or girl scouts of a district. *n.*

camp site (kamp′sīt′), place where people camp. *n.*

cam pus (kam′pəs), grounds of a college, university, or school. *n., pl.* **cam pus es.**

can[1] (kan; *unstressed* kən), **1** be able to: *He can run fast.* **2** know how to: *She can speak Spanish.* **3** have the right to: *Anyone can cross the street here.* **4** IN-FORMAL. be allowed to; may: *Can I go now? You can go if you want to. v., past tense* **could.** [Old English *can* know, know how, can]

can[2] (kan), **1** a container of metal, usually with a cover or lid: *a trash can, a paint can, a can of peaches.* **2** amount that a can holds: *Add three cans of water to make the orange juice.* **3** put in an airtight can or jar to preserve: *Grandmother is canning fruit.* 1,2 *n.,* 3 *v.,* **canned, can ning.** [Old English *canne* vessel]

Can., **1** Canada. **2** Canadian.

Ca naan (kā′nən), (in the Bible) a region in Palestine between the Jordan River and the Mediterranean. God promised Canaan to Abraham and his descendants. *n.*

Ca naan ite (kā′nə nīt), inhabitant of Canaan before it was conquered by the Hebrews. *n.*

Can a da (kan′ə də), country in the N part of North America, consisting of ten provinces and two territories and extending from the Atlantic to the Pacific and from the United States to the Arctic Ocean. It is a member of the Commonwealth of Nations. *Capital:* Ottawa. *n.*

Canada goose, a large, wild goose of North America, having a black head and neck, white throat, and a brownish-gray body.

Ca na di an (kə nā′dē ən), **1** of Canada or its people. **2** person born or living in Canada. 1 *adj.,* 2 *n.*

ca nal (kə nal′), **1** waterway dug across land for ships or small boats to go through or to carry water for irrigation. **2** tube in the body of an animal that carries food, liquid, air, etc.: *The food that we eat goes through the alimentary canal. n.*

Canal Zone, the Panama Canal and the land five miles on each side, governed by the United States. Also, **Panama Canal Zone.**

can a pé (kan′ə pā *or* kan′ə pē), cracker or thin piece of toast or bread spread with olives, meat, fish, cheese, etc., and served as an appetizer. *n., pl.* **can a pés.** [from French *canapé* couch, sofa]

ca nard (kə närd′), a false rumor; exaggerated report; hoax. *n.*

ca nar y (kə ner′ē), **1** a small, yellow songbird, originally from the Canary Islands. It is a kind of finch and is often kept as a pet. **2** a light yellow. **3** lightyellow. 1,2 *n., pl.* **ca nar ies;** 3 *adj.*

Canary Islands, group of Spanish islands in the Atlantic, near the NW coast of Africa.

canary yellow, a light yellow.

Can ber ra (kan′ber ə), capital of Australia, in the SE part. *n.*

can cel (kan′səl), **1** put an end to, set aside, or withdraw; do away with; stop: *The teacher canceled his order for the books. She canceled her appointment with the doctor.* **2** make up for; compensate; balance: *The little boy's sweet smile canceled his mischief.* **3** cross out; mark, stamp, or punch so that it cannot be used again: *The post office cancels the stamp on a letter.* **4** in mathematics: **a** reduce (a fraction) by dividing both the numerator and the denominator by the same quantity. **b** reduce (an equation) by dividing both members by a common factor. *v.*

can cel la tion (kan′sə lā′shən), **1** a canceling or a being canceled: *cancellation of a baseball game because of rain.* **2** marks made when something is canceled or crossed out: *The cancellation*

of that check consists of small holes punched through it. **3** something that is canceled. *n.*

can cer (kan′sər), **1** a very harmful growth in the body; malignant tumor. Cancer tends to spread and destroy the healthy tissues and organs of the body. **2** an evil or harmful thing that tends to spread: *The existence of slums is a destructive cancer in many large cities.* **3 Cancer, a** tropic of Cancer. **b** group of stars shaped somewhat like a crab. *n.*

can cer ous (kan′sər əs), **1** like cancer: *a cancerous tumor.* **2** having cancer: *a cancerous liver. adj.*

can de la (kan dē′lə), unit for measuring the strength or intensity of light; candle. *n.*

can de la bra (kan′dl ä′brə *or* kan′dl ä′brə), candelabrum. *n., pl.* **can de la bras.**

can de la brum (kan′dl ä′brəm *or* kan′dl ä′brəm), an ornamental candlestick with several branches for candles. *n., pl.* **can de la bra** *or* **can de la brums.**

can did (kan′did), **1** saying openly what one really thinks; frank and sincere; outspoken: *a candid reply. Please be candid with me.* **2** fair; impartial: *a candid decision.* **3** not posed: *a candid photograph of children playing. adj.* —**can′did ly,** *adv.* —**can′did ness,** *n.*

can di da cy (kan′də də sē), fact or condition of being a candidate: *Please support my candidacy for class treasurer. n., pl.* **can di da cies.**

can di date (kan′də dāt), person who seeks, or is proposed for, some office or honor: *There are three candidates for president of the club. n.*

can died (kan′dēd), **1** cooked in sugar; glazed with sugar: *candied sweet potatoes.* **2** preserved or encrusted with sugar: *candied ginger.* **3** made sweet or agreeable: *candied words of praise. adj.*

can dle (kan′dl), **1** stick of wax or tallow with a wick in it, burned to give light: *There are ten candles on his birthday cake.* **2** test (eggs) for freshness by holding them in front of a light: *The farmer candled the eggs before he sold them.* **3** candela. 1,3 *n.,* 2 *v.,* **can dled, can dling.**

burn the candle at both ends, use up one's strength and resources rapidly.

not hold a candle to, not compare with: *The cake from the bakery did not hold a candle to the one we made at home.*

can dle light (kan′dl līt′), **1** light of a candle or candles. **2** time when candles are lighted; dusk; twilight; nightfall. *n.*

Can dle mas (kan′dl məs), February 2, a church festival in honor of the purification of the Virgin Mary. It is celebrated with lighted candles. *n.*

candle power, strength or intensity of light, measured in candelas.

can dler (kan′dlər), person who tests eggs for freshness by holding them in front of a light. *n.*

can dle stick (kan′dl stik′), holder for a candle, to make it stand up straight. *n.*

can dle wick (kan′dl wik′), wick of a candle. *n.*

can dor (kan′dər), 1 a saying openly what one really thinks; honesty in giving one's view or opinion; frankness and sincerity: *He expressed his views with great candor.* 2 fairness: *We must weigh each argument with candor before coming to a decision. n.*

can dy (kan′dē), 1 sugar or syrup, boiled with water and flavoring, then cooled and made into small pieces for eating. Chocolate, butter, milk, nuts, fruits, etc., are often added. 2 piece of this: *Take a candy from the box.* 3 turn into sugar: *This honey has candied.* 4 cook in sugar; preserve by boiling in sugar: *She candied the peaches before canning them.* 1,2 *n.,* pl. **can dies;** 3,4 *v.,* **can died, can dy ing.**

can dy tuft (kan′dē tuft′), plant of the same family as the mustard, with clusters of white, purple, or pink flowers. *n.*

cane (kān), 1 a slender stick used as an aid in walking: *On long walks the old man took along his cane.* 2 stick used to beat with: *A blow with a cane was an old form of punishment.* 3 beat with a cane: *Some schoolmasters used to cane boys when they did not obey.* 4 a long, jointed stem, such as that of the bamboo. 5 plant having such stems. Sugar cane, bamboo, and rattan are canes. 6 material made of such stems, used for furniture, chair seats, etc.: *Our porch chairs have cane seats.* 7 make or repair with this material: *We are having all our porch furniture caned.* 1,2,4-6 *n.,* 3,7 *v.,* **caned, can ing.**

cane brake (kān′brāk′), thicket of cane plants. *n.*

cane sugar, sugar made from sugar cane.

ca nine (kā′nīn), 1 dog. 2 of a dog: *canine faithfulness.* 3 like that of a dog; greedy: *The glutton had a canine appetite.* 4 any animal belonging to a group of meat-eating animals including dogs, foxes, and wolves. 5 belonging to this group. The coyote is a canine animal. 6 canine tooth. 1,4,6 *n.,* 2,3,5 *adj.*

canine tooth, one of the four pointed teeth next to the incisors; cuspid.

can is ter (kan′ə stər), a small box or can, especially for tea, coffee, flour, or sugar. *n.*

can ker (kang′kər), 1 a spreading sore, especially one in the mouth.

2 anything that causes rot or decay or destroys by a gradual eating away. *n.*

can ker ous (kang′kər əs), 1 of or like canker. 2 causing canker. *adj.*

can ker worm (kang′kər wèrm′), caterpillar that eats away the leaves of trees and plants. *n.*

can na (kan′ə), 1 a tropical plant with large, pointed leaves and large red, pink, or yellow flowers. 2 its flower. *n.,* pl. **can nas.**

canned (kand), 1 put in a can; preserved by being put in airtight cans or jars: *canned peaches.* 2 SLANG. preserved on a phonograph record; recorded: *canned music. adj.*

can nel coal (kan′l), bituminous coal in large lumps that burns with a bright flame.

can ner (kan′ər), person who cans food. *n.*

can ner y (kan′ər ē), factory where food is canned. *n.,* pl. **can ner ies.**

Cannes (kan), resort in SE France, on the Mediterranean. *n.*

can ni bal (kan′ə bəl), 1 person who eats human flesh: *Tribes of cannibals once lived on islands in the south Pacific ocean.* 2 animal that eats others of its own kind: *Many fishes are cannibals.* 3 of or like cannibals: *Cannibal ants help control ants that destroy crops.* 1,2 *n.,* 3 *adj.*

can ni bal ism (kan′ə bə liz′əm), act or habit of eating the flesh of one's own kind: *Most animals do not practice cannibalism. n.*

can ni bal is tic (kan′ə bə lis′tik), of cannibals; characteristic of cannibals. *adj.*

can ni ly (kan′l ē), in a canny manner. *adv.*

can ni ness (kan′ē nis), canny character or quality. *n.*

can ning (kan′ing), the preserving of meat, fish, fruit, etc., by cooking it and sealing it up in airtight cans or jars. *n.*

can non (kan′ən), a big gun, especially one that is too large to be carried by hand and is fixed to the ground or mounted on a carriage. Artillery consists of cannons, such as howitzers and mortars. The old-fashioned kind of cannon that fired cannonballs was much used during the Civil War. *n.,* pl. **cannons** or **can non.**

can non ade (kan′ə nād′), 1 a continued firing of cannons. 2 attack with cannons. 1 *n.,* 2 *v.,* **can non ad ed, can non ad ing.**

can non ball (kan′ən bôl′), a large iron or steel ball, formerly fired from cannons. *n.*

can non eer (kan′ə nir′), gunner. *n.*

can not (kan′ot *or* ka not′), can not. *v.*

can ny (kan′ē), shrewd and cautious in

dealing with others: *The canny trader made a large profit by buying goods when they were plentiful and selling them when they became scarce. adj.,* **can ni er, can ni est.**

canoe (def. 1)

ca noe (kə nü′), 1 a light boat moved with a paddle held in the hands without fixed supports: *The canoe was so light that the Indian could easily carry it.* 2 paddle a canoe; go in a canoe. 1 *n.,* 2 *v.,* **ca noed, ca noe ing.**

ca noe ist (kə nü′ist), person who paddles a canoe. *n.*

can on[1] (kan′ən), 1 rule by which a thing is judged; standard: *Your manners are in keeping with the canons of good taste.* 2 law of a church. 3 the official list of the books of the Bible accepted by the Christian church as genuine and inspired. 4 an official list of the saints. 5 any official list. *n.* [Old English *canon,* from Latin *canon,* from Greek *kanon* rule]

can on[2] (kan′ən), clergyman belonging to a cathedral or other church having more than one minister. *n.* [from French of the 1200's *canon,* from Latin *canonicus* clergyman, from Greek *kanon* rule]

ca ñon (kan′yən), canyon. *n.,* pl. **ca ñons.** [from Mexican Spanish]

ca non i cal (kə non′ə kəl), 1 according to church laws: *canonical dress.* 2 in the canon of the Bible. *adj.* —**ca non′i cal ly,** *adv.*

can on i za tion (kan′ə nə zā′shən), a canonizing or a being canonized. *n.*

can on ize (kan′ə nīz), declare (a dead person) to be a saint; place in the official list of saints: *Joan of Arc was canonized by the Roman Catholic Church in 1920. v.,* **can on ized, can on iz ing.**

can o py (kan′ə pē), 1 a covering fixed over a bed, throne, entrance, etc., or carried on poles over a person: *There is*

adj. adjective	*n.* noun
adv. adverb	*prep.* preposition
conj. conjunction	*pron.* pronoun
interj. interjection	*v.* verb
sing. singular	*pl.* plural

a striped canopy over the entrance to the hotel. **2** a rooflike covering; shelter or shade: *The trees formed a canopy over the old road.* **3** cover with a canopy. **1,2** *n., pl.* **can o pies; 3** *v.,* **can o pied, can o py ing.**

canst (kanst), OLD USE. **can**[1]. "Thou canst" means "you can." *v.*

cant[1] (kant), **1** talk that is not sincere; moral or religious statements that many people make, but few really believe or act upon. **2** the peculiar language of a special group, using many strange words; jargon: *"Jug" is one of the words for "jail" in thieves' cant.* *n.* [from Latin *cantus* song]

cant[2] (kant), **1** give a slant or slope to; bevel: *He canted the edges of the board.* **2** put into a slant; tip; tilt: *The wind canted the ship up to port.* **3** a sloping, slanting, or tilting; inclination: *The ship took on a dangerous cant to starboard.* **1,2** *v.,* **3** *n.* [from French of the 1300's *cant,* from Latin *cantus* corner, edge]

can't (kant), cannot or can not.

can ta loupe or **can ta loup** (kan'tl ōp), kind of muskmelon with a hard, rough rind and sweet, juicy, orange-colored flesh. *n.*

can tan ker ous (kan tang'kər əs), ready to make trouble and oppose anything suggested; ill-natured; quarrelsome. *adj.* —**can tan'ker ous ly,** *adv.* —**can tan'ker ous ness,** *n.*

can ta ta (kən tä'tə), musical composition consisting of a story or play which is sung by a chorus and soloists, but not acted. *n., pl.* **can ta tas.**

can teen (kan tēn'), **1** a small container for carrying water or other drinks. **2** a store in a school, camp, factory, etc., where food, drinks, and other articles are sold or given out. **3** recreation hall for servicemen. *n.*

can ter (kan'tər), **1** gallop gently: *She cantered her horse down the road. The horse cantered across the meadow.* **2** a gentle gallop. **1** *v.,* **2** *n.*

Can ter bur y (kan'tər ber'ē), city in SE England. Many pilgrims traveled there during the Middle Ages to visit the shrine of Saint Thomas à Becket. *n.*

Canterbury bell, plant with tall stalks of bell-shaped flowers, usually purplish-blue, pink, or white.

cant hook, pole with a movable hook at one end, used to grip and turn over logs.

can ti cle (kan'tə kəl), a short song, hymn, or chant used in church services. *n.*

can ti lev er (kan'tl ev'ər *or* kan'tl-ē'vər), a large, projecting bracket or beam that is supported at one end only. *n.*

cantilever bridge, bridge made of two cantilevers whose projecting ends meet but do not support each other.

cantilever bridge

can tle (kan'tl), the part of a saddle that sticks up at the back. *n.*

can to (kan'tō), one of the main divisions of a long poem. A canto of a poem is like a chapter of a novel. *n., pl.* **can tos.**

can ton (kan'tən *or* kan'ton), a small part or political division of a country. Switzerland is made up of 22 cantons. *n.*

Can ton (kan'ton for 1; kan'tən for 2), **1** city in S China. **2** city in NE Ohio. *n.*

Can ton ese (kan'tə nēz'), **1** person born or living in Canton, China. **2** the Chinese dialect spoken in or near Canton, China. **3** of Canton, China, its people, or their dialect. **1,2** *n., pl.* **Can ton ese; 3** *adj.*

can ton ment (kan ton'mənt), place where soldiers live; quarters for soldiers. *n.*

can tor (kan'tər), **1** man who leads the services in a synagogue. **2** man who leads the singing of a choir or congregation. *n.*

can vas (kan'vəs), **1** a strong cloth with a coarse weave made of cotton, flax, or hemp, used to make tents, sails, certain articles of clothing, etc., and for painting on: *The tops of my sneakers are made of canvas.* **2** made of canvas: *The boat had canvas sails.* **3** something made of canvas: *The artist painted on a large canvas. The sailors threw the canvas over the hatch and lashed it down.* **4** picture painted on canvas; oil painting: *The beautiful canvas was stolen from the art gallery.* **1,3,4** *n., pl.* **can vas es; 2** *adj.*

under canvas, 1 in tents: *The circus was held under canvas in an open field.* **2** with sails spread: *The schooner left the harbor under full canvas.*

can vas back (kan'vəs bak'), a large wild duck of North America with grayish feathers on its back. *n.*

can vass (kan'vəs), **1** go through a city, district, etc., asking for votes, orders, donations, etc.: *Salesmen can-* vassed the whole city for subscriptions to magazines. *The candidate canvassed right up to election day.* **2** an asking for votes, orders, donations, etc.: *During her canvass of the neighborhood, my mother collected $100 for the cancer fund.* **3** examine the parts of carefully; inspect: *He canvassed the papers, hunting for notices of after-school jobs.* **4** discuss: *The city council canvassed the mayor's plan thoroughly.* **5** discussion. **1,3,4** *v.,* **2,5** *n., pl.* **can vass es.** —**can'vass er,** *n.*

can yon (kan'yən), a narrow valley with high, steep sides, usually with a stream at the bottom. *n.* Also, **cañon.**

caou tchouc (kou chük'), the gummy, thickened juice of various tropical plants from which rubber is made; crude, natural rubber. *n.*

cap (kap), **1** a soft, close-fitting covering for the head, usually having little or no brim. Men and boys often wear caps instead of hats. **2** a special head covering worn to show rank or occupation: *a nurse's cap, a student's cap and gown.* **3** anything like a cap. The stopper or top of a jar, bottle, tube, or fountain pen is a cap. The top of a mushroom is called a cap. **4** the highest part; top: *the polar cap at the North Pole.* **5** put a cap on; cover the top of: *I capped the bottle. Whipped cream capped the dessert.* **6** do or follow up with something as good or better: *Each of the two clowns capped the other's last joke.* **7** a small amount of explosive in a wrapper or covering: *The boy used caps in his toy gun.* **1-4,7** *n.,* **5,6** *v.,* **capped, capping.** —**cap'like',** *adj.*

cap., capital letter. *pl.* **caps.**

ca pa bil i ty (kā'pə bil'ə tē), **1** ability to learn or do; power or fitness; capacity: *With her background in Latin, she has the capability to learn French.* **2 capabilities,** *pl.* undeveloped properties; potential uses: *Atomic energy has many unexplored capabilities.* *n., pl.* **ca pa bil i ties.**

ca pa ble (kā'pə bəl), having fitness, power, or ability; able; efficient; competent: *She was such a capable teacher that the school appointed her principal the next year. He did a very capable job and was rewarded with much praise.* *adj.*

cantilevers shown in a cross section of a football grandstand

capable of, 1 having ability, power, or fitness for: *Some airplanes are capable of going 1000 miles an hour.* 2 open to; ready for: *a statement capable of being misunderstood.*

ca pa bly (kā′pə blē), in a capable manner; with ability; ably: *a job capably done. adv.*

ca pa cious (kə pā′shəs), able to hold much; large and roomy; spacious: *a capacious closet. adj.* —**ca pa′cious ly,** *adv.* —**ca pa′cious ness,** *n.*

ca pac i tance (kə pas′ə təns), property of a capacitor that determines the amount of electrical charge it can receive and store; capacity. *n.*

ca pac i tor (kə pas′ə tər), device for receiving and storing a charge of electricity; condenser. *n.*

ca pac i ty (kə pas′ə tē), 1 amount of room or space inside; largest amount that can be held by a container: *A gallon can has a capacity of 4 quarts.* 2 ability to receive and hold: *the capacity of a metal for retaining heat. The theater has a seating capacity of 400.* 3 ability to learn or do; power or fitness: *an intelligent student with a capacity for learning.* 4 position or relation. A person may act in the capacity of guardian, trustee, voter, friend, etc. 5 capacitance. *n., pl.* **ca pac i ties.**

cap and bells, cap trimmed with bells, worn by a jester.

cap and gown, a flat cap and loose gown, worn by teachers and students on certain occasions, especially at commencement exercises.

ca par i son (kə par′ə sən), 1 an ornamental covering for a horse. 2 any rich dress or outfit. 3 dress richly. 1,2 *n.,* 3 *v.*

cape[1] (kāp), an outer garment, or part of one, without sleeves, worn falling loosely from the shoulders and often fastened at the neck. *n.* [from French *cape,* from Latin *cappa* hood]

cape[2] (kāp), point of land extending into the water. *n.* [from French of the 1300's *cap,* from Latin *caput* head]

Cape buffalo, a large, fierce buffalo of southern Africa.

Cape Ca nav er al (kə nav′ər əl), cape in E Florida from which the United States launches rockets.

Cape Horn, cape which forms the S tip of South America.

Cape of Good Hope, cape near the S tip of Africa.

ca per[1] (kā′pər), 1 leap or jump about playfully: *The children capered and laughed in the park.* 2 a playful leap or jump: *the shouts and capers of children playing tag.* 3 prank; trick: *The child's capers made his parents laugh.* 1 *v.,* 2,3 *n.* [perhaps short for *capriole* a leap, from Latin *caper* goat]

cut a caper or **cut capers,** 1 play or do a trick. 2 dance, leap, or jump about playfully.

ca per[2] (kā′pər), 1 a low, prickly shrub of the Mediterranean region. 2 capers, *pl.* the green flower buds and berries of this shrub, pickled and used for seasoning. *n.* [from Latin *capparis,* from Greek *kapparis*]

Cape town (kāp′toun′), Cape Town. *n.*

Cape Town, seaport near the S tip of Africa. The legislature for the Republic of South Africa meets there.

Cape Verde (vėrd), cape which is the westernmost point of Africa.

Cape Verde Islands, group of islands west of Cape Verde, belonging to Portugal.

cap il lar y (kap′ə ler′ē), 1 a blood vessel with a very slender, hairlike opening. Capillaries join the end of an artery to the beginning of a vein. 2 of or in such tubes. 3 like a hair; very slender. 1 *n., pl.* **cap il lar ies;** 2,3 *adj.*

capillary attraction, the force that causes a liquid to rise in a narrow tube or when in contact with a porous substance. A plant draws up water from the ground and a blotter absorbs ink by means of capillary attraction.

caparison (def. 1)

cap i tal (kap′ə təl), 1 city where the government of a country, state, or province is located. Toronto is the capital of Ontario. Lincoln is the capital of Nebraska. 2 capital letter. A capital is used at the beginning of a sentence or a proper name. 3 very important; leading; chief: *The invention of the telephone was a capital advance in communication.* 4 of the best kind; excellent: *A maple tree gives capital shade.* 5 punishable by death: *Murder is a capital crime in many countries.* 6 amount of money or property that a company or a person uses in carrying on a business: *The Smith Company has a capital of $30,000.* 7 the top part of a column or pillar. See **column** for diagram. 1,2, 6,7 *n.,* 3-5 *adj.*

make capital of, take advantage of: *He made capital of his father's fame to get the job.*

---

hat, āge, fär; let, ēqual, tėrm;
it, īce; hot, ōpen, ôrder;
oil, out; cup, pùt, rüle; ch, child;
ng, long; sh, she; th, thin;
ᴛH, then; zh, measure;

ə represents *a* in about,
e in taken, *i* in pencil,
o in lemon, *u* in circus.

---

cap i tal ism (kap′ə tə liz′əm), an economic system in which private individuals or groups of individuals own land, factories, and other means of production. They compete with one another, using the hired labor of other persons, to produce goods and services for profit. *n.*

cap i tal ist (kap′ə tə list), 1 person whose money and property are used in carrying on business. 2 a wealthy person. 3 person who favors or supports capitalism. *n.*

cap i tal is tic (kap′ə tə lis′tik), 1 of or having to do with capitalism or capitalists: *capitalistic production.* 2 favoring or supporting capitalism: *capitalistic policies. adj.* —**cap′i tal is′ti cal ly,** *adv.*

cap i tal i za tion (kap′ə tə lə zā′shən), 1 a capitalizing or a being capitalized. 2 amount at which a company is capitalized; capital stock of a business: *The company increased its capitalization to $10 million. n.*

cap i tal ize (kap′ə tə līz), 1 write or print with a capital letter: *She forgot to capitalize the first letter of the name Jackson.* 2 turn into capital; use as capital: *The company capitalized its reserve funds.* 3 provide or furnish with capital. *v.,* **cap i tal ized, cap i tal iz ing.**

capitalize on, take advantage of; use to one's own advantage: *The candidate capitalized on his opponent's mistake.*

capital letter, the large form of a letter; A, B, C, D, etc., as distinguished from a, b, c, d, etc.

cap i tal ly (kap′ə tə lē), very well; excellently: *He acted the part of the butler capitally. adv.*

capital punishment, the death penalty for a crime.

capital ship, a large warship, such as a battleship.

Cap i tol (kap′ə təl), 1 the building at Washington, D. C., in which Congress meets. 2 Also, **capitol.** the building in which a state legislature meets. *n.*

ca pit u late (kə pich′ə lāt), surrender on certain terms or conditions: *The men in the fort capitulated on condition that*

adj. adjective	*n.* noun
adv. adverb	*prep.* preposition
conj. conjunction	*pron.* pronoun
interj. interjection	*v.* verb
sing. singular	*pl.* plural

they be allowed to go away unharmed. *v.,* **ca pit u lat ed, ca pit u lat ing.**

ca pit u la tion (kə pich′ə lā′shən), a surrender on certain terms or conditions. *n.*

Cap'n (kap′ən), Captain. *n.*

ca pon (kā′pon), rooster specially raised to be eaten. It is castrated and fattened. *n.*

Ca pri (kə prē′), small island in W Italy, near Naples. *n.*

ca price (kə prēs′), a sudden change of mind without reason; unreasonable notion or desire; whim: *The child's refusal to wear red clothes was pure caprice. n.*

ca pri cious (kə prish′əs), likely to change suddenly without reason; changeable; fickle: *capricious weather. Children are often capricious. adj.* —**ca pri′cious ly,** *adv.* —**ca pri′cious ness,** *n.*

Cap ri corn (kap′rə kôrn), 1 tropic of Capricorn. 2 group of stars shaped somewhat like a goat. *n.*

caps., capital letters.

cap size (kap sīz′ or kap′sīz), turn bottom side up; upset; overturn: *The sailboat nearly capsized in the squall. The rough waves capsized the rowboat. v.,* **cap sized, cap siz ing.**

cap stan (kap′stən), machine for lifting or pulling that revolves on an upright shaft or spindle. Sailors on old sailing ships hoisted the anchor by turning the capstan. *n.*

cap stone (kap′stōn′), one of the stones along the top of a wall or of some other structure. *n.*

cap sule (kap′səl), 1 a small case or covering. Medicine is often given in capsules made of gelatin. 2 the enclosed front section of a rocket made to carry instruments, astronauts, etc., into space. In flight the capsule can separate from the rest of the rocket and go into orbit or be directed back to earth. 3 a dry seedcase that opens when ripe. 4 membrane enclosing an organ of the body. *n.*

Capt., Captain.

cap tain (kap′tən), 1 head of a group; leader or chief: *Robin Hood was captain of his band. He is captain of the football team.* 2 commander of a ship: *The captain refused to leave his sinking*

ship while there were others on board. 3 an army, air force, or marine officer ranking next below a major and next above a first lieutenant: *The captain led his company in the attack.* 4 a navy officer ranking next below a rear admiral and next above a commander. 5 a police officer or fire department officer ranking below a chief and above a lieutenant. 6 lead or command as captain: *She will captain the debating team next year.* 1-5 *n.,* 6 *v.*

cap tain cy (kap′tən sē), rank or authority of a captain. *n., pl.* **cap tain cies.**

cap tion (kap′shən), 1 title or heading at the beginning of a page, article, chapter, etc., or under a picture explaining it. 2 (in motion pictures) a subtitle. 3 put a caption on. 1,2 *n.,* 3 *v.*

cap tious (kap′shəs), hard to please; faultfinding. *adj.* —**cap′tious ly,** *adv.* —**cap′tious ness,** *n.*

cap ti vate (kap′tə vāt), hold captive by beauty or interest; charm; fascinate: *The children were captivated by the story of Peter Pan. The Pied Piper's beautiful music captivated the rats and the children. v.,* **cap ti vat ed, cap ti vat ing.** —**cap′ti vat′ing ly,** *adv.*

cap ti va tion (kap′tə vā′shən), 1 a captivating or a being captivated. 2 charm; fascination. *n.*

cap tive (kap′tiv), 1 person or animal captured and held against his will; prisoner: *The pirates took many captives during raids along the coast.* 2 made a prisoner; held against one's will: *a captive sparrow. The enemy released the captive soldiers.* 1 *n.,* 2 *adj.*

capstan on large sailing vessel.
As it is turned, it winds up the rope
that hoists the anchor, or unwinds it.

cap tiv i ty (kap tiv′ə tē), 1 condition of being in prison. 2 condition of being held against one's will: *Some animals cannot bear captivity, and die after a few weeks in a cage. n., pl.* **cap tiv i ties.**

cap tor (kap′tər), person who takes or holds a prisoner. *n.*

cap ture (kap′chər), 1 make a prisoner of; take by force, skill, or trickery; seize: *We captured butterflies with a net.* 2 person or thing taken in this way:

Captain Jones's first capture was an enemy ship. 3 a capturing or a being captured: *The capture of this ship took place on July 6.* 4 attract and hold; catch and keep: *The mystery story captured the girl's attention.* 1,4 *v.,* **captured, cap tur ing;** 2,3 *n.*

cap u chin (kap′yə shən or kə pyü′shən), 1 a South American monkey with black hair on its head that looks like a hood. 2 **Capuchin,** a Franciscan monk belonging to an order that wears a long, pointed hood or cowl. *n.*

cap y ba ra (kap′ə bär′ə), a tailless rodent of South America. It is the world's largest rodent. *n., pl.* **cap y ba ras.**

car (kär), 1 automobile: *They made the trip by car.* 2 any vehicle that moves on wheels. A carriage or cart is sometimes called a car. 3 a railroad car or streetcar. 4 the closed platform of an elevator, balloon, or airship for carrying passengers or cargo. *n.*

ca ra ba o (kär′ə bä′ō), water buffalo of the Philippines. *n., pl.* **ca ra ba os.**

Ca ra cas (kə rä′kəs or kə rak′əs), capital of Venezuela, in the N part. *n.*

car a cul (kar′ə kəl), 1 a short, flat, loose, curly fur made from the skin of newborn or very young lambs of a breed of Asian sheep. 2 this sheep. *n.* Also, **karakul.**

ca rafe (kə raf′), a glass bottle for holding water, wine, coffee, etc. *n.*

car a mel (kar′ə məl or kär′məl), 1 sugar browned or burned over heat, used for coloring and flavoring food. 2 a small block of chewy candy flavored with this sugar. *n.*

car a pace (kar′ə pās), shell or bony covering on the back of a turtle, armadillo, lobster, crab, etc. *n.*

car at (kar′ət), 1 unit of weight for precious stones, equal to 1/5 gram. 2 karat. *n.*

car a van (kar′ə van), 1 group of merchants, pilgrims, etc., traveling together for safety through difficult or dangerous country: *A caravan of Arab merchants and camels, laden with spices and silks, moved across the desert.* 2 a closed truck or trailer, or formerly a large, covered wagon, for moving people or goods; van. *n.*

car a van sar y (kar′ə van′sər ē), 1 inn or hotel in the Orient where caravans stop to rest. 2 any large inn or hotel. *n., pl.* **car a van sar ies.**

car a vel (kar′ə vel), a small, fast sailing ship of the type used by Columbus, with a broad bow and a high stern. *n.*

car a way (kar′ə wā), 1 plant that yields fragrant, spicy seeds which are used to flavor bread, rolls, or cakes. It is related to parsley. 2 its seeds. *n.*

car bide (kär′bīd), compound of carbon with another element, usually a metal. *n.*

car bine (kär′bīn *or* kär′bēn′), a short, light rifle or musket. *n.*

car bo hy drate (kär′bō hī′drāt), substance made from carbon dioxide and water by green plants in sunlight. Carbohydrates are composed of carbon, hydrogen, and oxygen. Sugar and starch are carbohydrates. *n.*

car bol ic acid (kär bol′ik), a very poisonous acid obtained from coal tar, used in solution as a disinfectant and antiseptic; phenol.

car bon (kär′bən), 1 a very common nonmetallic element which occurs in combination with other elements in all plants and animals. Diamonds and graphite are pure carbon in the form of crystals; coal and charcoal are mostly carbon in uncrystallized form. 2 piece of carbon paper: *I put a carbon between the two sheets of paper.* 3 copy made with carbon paper: *The secretary kept a carbon of each letter that she typed. n.*

carbon 12, the most common isotope of carbon, now used as the standard for measuring atomic weights.

carbon 14, a radioactive isotope of carbon produced by the bombardment of nitrogen atoms by neutrons; radiocarbon. Since carbon 14 gives off radioactivity at a uniform rate in all animals and plants that have died, scientists are able to find out the age of many ancient remains of living things by measuring the amount of carbon 14 left in them.

car bon ate (kär′bə nāt), 1 charge with carbon dioxide. Soda water is carbonated to make it bubble and fizz. 2 salt or ester of carbonic acid. 1 *v.*, **car bon at ed, car bon at ing; 2** *n.*

car bon a tion (kär′bə nā′shən), act of carbonating. *n.*

carbon dioxide, a heavy, colorless, odorless gas, present in the atmosphere or formed when any fuel containing carbon is burned. The air that is breathed out of an animal's lungs contains carbon dioxide. Plants absorb it from the air and use it to make plant tissue. Carbon dioxide is used in soda water, in fire extinguishers, etc.

car bon ic (kär bon′ik), of or containing carbon. *adj.*

carbonic acid, acid made when carbon dioxide is dissolved in water. It gives the sharp taste to soda water.

car bon if er ous (kär′bə nif′ər əs), containing or producing coal. *adj.*

car bon ize (kär′bə nīz), 1 change into carbon by burning; char. 2 cover or combine with carbon. *v.,* **car bon ized, car bon iz ing.**

carbon monoxide, a colorless, odorless, very poisonous gas, formed when carbon burns with an insufficient supply of air. It is part of the exhaust gases of automobile engines.

carbon paper, a thin paper having carbon or some other inky substance on one surface. It is used between sheets of paper to make a copy of what is written or typed on the upper sheet.

carbon tet ra chlo ride (tet′rə klôr′īd), a colorless liquid which does not burn, often used in fire extinguishers and in cleaning fluids.

car bun cle (kär′bung kəl), 1 a very painful, inflamed swelling under the skin. A carbuncle is larger than a boil and more serious in its effects. 2 a smooth, round garnet or other deep-red jewel. *n.*

carburetor—A float and valve control the flow of gasoline, which sprays into the pipe and is mixed with air.

car bu re tor (kär′bə rā′tər), device for mixing air with a liquid fuel to produce an explosive mixture. A carburetor is part of the gasoline engine of an automobile, lawn mower, etc. *n.*

car cass (kär′kəs), 1 body of a dead animal: *Steak is cut from a beef carcass.* 2 INFORMAL. a human body. *n., pl.* **car cass es.**

card¹ (kärd), 1 a flat piece of stiff paper or thin cardboard, usually small and rectangular: *The store sells post cards and birthday cards, but not report cards.* 2 playing card. 3 **cards,** *pl.* a game or games played with a pack of playing cards. b a playing such a game or games: *Many people at the party were busy at cards.* 4 INFORMAL. an odd or amusing person. *n.* [from French of the 1400's *carte,* from Latin *charta* chart]

in the cards, likely to happen.

put one's cards on the table, show what one has or can do; be frank about something.

card² (kärd), 1 a toothed tool or wire brush used to separate, clean, and straighten the fibers of wool, cotton, flax, etc., before spinning. 2 clean or comb with such a tool: *She carded wool for spinning.* 1 *n.,* 2 *v.* [from French of the 1400's *carde,* from Latin *carduus* thistle] —**card′er,** *n.*

card board (kärd′bôrd′), a stiff material made of layers of paper pressed together, used to make cards and boxes. *n.*

hat, āge, fär; let, ēqual, tèrm;
it, īce; hot, ōpen, ôrder;
oil, out; cup, pùt, rüle; ch, child;
ng, long; sh, she; th, thin;
ŦH, then; zh, measure;

ə represents *a* in about,
e in taken, *i* in pencil,
o in lemon, *u* in circus.

car di ac (kär′dē ak), of or having to do with the heart: *cardiac disease, cardiac arteries. adj.*

Car diff (kär′dif), seaport and capital of Wales, in the SE part. *n.*

car di gan (kär′də gən), a knitted jacket or sweater that buttons down the front. *n.* [from the Earl of *Cardigan,* 1797-1868, a famous British general]

car di nal (kärd′n əl), 1 of first importance; chief; principal: *The cardinal value of his plan is that it is simple.* 2 one of the high officials of the Roman Catholic Church, appointed by the pope as his advisers, and ranking next below him. Cardinals wear red robes and red hats. 3 bright, rich red. 4 a bright, rich red. 5 an American songbird. The male has bright-red feathers marked with a little gray and black. It is a kind of finch. 1,3 *adj.,* 2,4,5 *n.*

cardinal flower, 1 the bright-red flower of a North American plant. 2 plant that it grows on.

cardinal number, number which shows how many are meant. One, two, three, four, etc., are cardinal numbers; first, second, third, fourth, etc., are ordinal numbers.

cardinal points, the four main directions of the compass; north, south, east, and west.

card ing (kär′ding), the cleaning and straightening of the fibers of wool, cotton, flax, etc., before spinning. *n.*

car di o gram (kär′dē ə gram), electrocardiogram. *n.*

car di o graph (kär′dē ə graf), electrocardiograph. *n.*

cards (kärdz). See def. 3 under **card¹.** *n.pl.*

care (ker *or* kar), 1 a troubled state of mind because of fear of what may happen; worry: *Few people are completely free from care.* 2 serious attention; heed: *A pilot must do his work with great care.* 3 object of worry, concern, or attention: *The sick puppy was a care to its owners.* 4 be concerned; feel interest: *Musicians care about music.* 5 watchful keeping; charge: *The little girl was left in her older sister's care.* 6 food, shelter, and protection: *Your*

adj. adjective	*n.* noun
adv. adverb	*prep.* preposition
conj. conjunction	*pron.* pronoun
interj. interjection	*v.* verb
sing. singular	*pl.* plural

child will have the best of care. **7** like; want; wish: *A cat does not care to be washed.* 1-3,5,6 *n.,* 4,7 *v.,* **cared, car ing.**

care for, 1 be fond of; like: *I don't care for her friends.* **2** want; wish: *I don't care for any dessert tonight.* **3** take charge of; attend to: *The nurse will care for him now.*

in care of, at the address of: *All mail for the governor should be sent in care of the statehouse.*

take care, be careful: *Take care to be accurate.*

take care of, 1 take charge of; attend to: *Grandfather will take care of the children. My parents will take care of this bill.* **2** watch over; be careful with: *Take care of your money.*

ca reen (kə rēn′), lean to one side or sway sharply; tilt; tip: *The ship careened in the strong wind. The speeding taxi went careening around the corner. The gale careened the sailboat.* *v.*

ca reer (kə rir′), **1** a general course of action or progress through life: *It is exciting to read about the careers of explorers.* **2** way of living; occupation or profession: *The boy planned to make law his career.* **3** a run at full speed; going with force; speed: *The girls raced downhill in full career to see who could get to school first.* **4** rush along wildly; dash: *The runaway horse careered through the streets.* 1-3 *n.,* 4 *v.*

care free (ker′frē′ *or* kar′frē′), without worry; happy; gay: *The children spent a carefree summer sailing and swimming at the seashore.* *adj.*

care ful (ker′fəl *or* kar′fəl), **1** thinking what one says; watching what one does; taking pains; watchful; cautious: *She is a very careful driver. Please be careful with my new bicycle!* **2** showing care; done with thought or effort; exact; thorough: *Arithmetic requires careful work.* **3** full of care or concern; attentive: *Try to be careful of the feelings of others.* *adj.* —**care′ful ly,** *adv.* —**care′ful ness,** *n.*

care less (ker′lis *or* kar′lis), **1** not thinking what one says; not watching what one does; not careful: *I was careless and broke the cup.* **2** done without enough thought or effort; not exact or thorough: *careless work.* **3** not caring or

troubling; indifferent: *He has a careless attitude toward his homework, rarely getting it done on time.* *adj.* —**care′less ly,** *adv.* —**care′less ness,** *n.*

ca ress (kə res′), **1** a touch showing affection; tender embrace or kiss: *The little boy was embarrassed by his aunt's caresses.* **2** touch or stroke tenderly; embrace or kiss: *The mother caressed her baby.* **1** *n., pl.* **ca ress es; 2** *v.* —**ca ress′ing ly,** *adv.*

car et (kar′ət), a mark (∧) to show where something should be put in, used in writing or printing. *n.*

care tak er (ker′tā′kər *or* kar′tā′kər), person who takes care of another person, a place, or a thing, often for the owner or for another. *n.*

care worn (ker′wôrn′ *or* kar′wôrn′), showing signs of worry; tired or weary from care: *The old woman had a care-worn look on her face.* *adj.*

car fare (kär′fer′ *or* kär′far′), money paid for riding on a bus, subway, in a taxicab, etc. *n.*

car go (kär′gō), load of goods carried by a ship or plane: *The freighter had docked to unload a cargo of wheat.* *n., pl.* **car goes** *or* **car gos.**

car hop (kär′hop′), waiter or waitress who serves customers in their cars at a drive-in restaurant. *n.*

Car ib be an (kar′ə bē′ən *or* kə rib′ē-ən), of or having to do with the Caribbean Sea or the islands in it. *adj.*

Caribbean Sea, sea between Central America, the West Indies, and South America.

car i bou (kar′ə bü), any of several kinds of North American reindeer. *n., pl.* **car i bous** *or* **car i bou.**

car i ca ture (kar′ə kə chùr), **1** picture, cartoon, or description that exaggerates the peculiarities of a person or

caricature (def. 1)
caricature of
Abraham Lincoln

the defects of a thing. **2** art of making such pictures, cartoons, or descriptions: *His eye for detail made him a master of caricature.* **3** make a caricature of: *The artist caricatured the mayor.* 1,2 *n.,* 3 *v.,* **car i ca tured, car i ca tur ing.**

car i ca tur ist (kar′ə kə chúr′ist), person who makes caricatures. *n.*

car ies (ker′ēz *or* kar′ēz), decay of teeth, bones, or tissues. *n.*

car il lon (kar′ə lon), **1** set of bells arranged for playing melodies. **2** melody played on such bells. *n.*

car load (kär′lōd′), as much as a car can hold or carry. *n.*

Car lyle (kär līl′), **Thomas,** 1795-1881, Scottish essayist and historian. *n.*

Car mel (kär′məl), **Mount,** mountain in NW Israel. *n.*

Car mel ite (kär′mə līt), friar or nun of a Roman Catholic religious order founded in the 1100's. *n.*

car mine (kär′mən), **1** a deep red with a tinge of purple. **2** deep-red with a tinge of purple. **3** a light crimson. **4** light-crimson. 1,3 *n.,* 2,4 *adj.*

car nage (kär′nij), slaughter of a great number of people: *The battle resulted in frightful carnage.* *n.*

car nal (kär′nl), of or connected with the appetites and passions of the body; sensual. *adj.* —**car′nal ly,** *adv.*

car na tion (kär nā′shən), **1** a red, white, or pink flower with a spicy fragrance. **2** plant that it grows on. **3** rosy-pink. 1,2 *n.,* 3 *adj.*

Car ne gie (kär nā′gē *or* kär′nə gē), **Andrew,** 1835-1919, American steel manufacturer and philanthropist, born in Scotland. *n.*

car ni val (kär′nə vəl), **1** place of amusement or a traveling show having merry-go-rounds, games, sideshows, etc. **2** an organized program of events involving a particular sport, institution, etc.: *a water carnival, a school carnival.* **3** feasting and merrymaking; noisy and unrestrained revels. **4** time of feasting and merrymaking just before Lent. *n.*

car ni vore (kär′nə vôr), any animal that feeds chiefly on flesh. Carnivores have large, strong teeth with sharp cutting edges. *n.*

car niv or ous (kär niv′ər əs), feeding chiefly on flesh. Cats, dogs, lions, tigers, and bears are carnivorous animals. *adj.* —**car niv′or ous ly,** *adv.* —**car niv′-or ous ness,** *n.*

car ol (kar′əl), **1** song of joy. **2** hymn of joy sung at Christmas. **3** sing joyously; sing: *The birds carol in the early morning.* 1,2 *n.,* 3 *v.* —**car′ol er,** *n.*

Car o li na (kar′ə lī′nə), **1** an early American colony on the Atlantic coast, officially divided into North Carolina and South Carolina in 1729. **2** either North Carolina or South Carolina.

3 the Carolinas, North Carolina and South Carolina. *n.*

Car o line Islands (kar′ə līn), group of over 500 islands in the W Pacific, east of the Philippines.

Car o lin i an (kar′ə lin′ē ən), 1 of North Carolina and South Carolina, or either of them. 2 person born or living in North Carolina or South Carolina. 1 *adj.,* 2 *n.*

car om (kar′əm), 1 hit and bounce off: *The car went out of control and caromed off the wall.* 2 a hitting and bouncing off. 1 *v.,* 2 *n.*

ca rous al (kə rou′zəl), a noisy feast or drinking party. *n.*

ca rouse (kə rouz′), 1 drink heavily; take part in noisy feasts or merry-making. 2 a noisy feast or drinking party. 1 *v.,* **ca roused′, ca rous ing;** 2 *n.*

car ou sel (kar′ə sel′), carrousel. *n.*

carp¹ (kärp), find fault; complain. *v.* [from a Scandinavian word of the 1200's, such as Danish *karpa* to boast] —**carp′er,** *n.*

carp² (kärp), a bony, freshwater fish which lives in ponds and slow streams. It feeds mostly on plants and sometimes grows quite large. *n., pl.* **carps** or **carp.** [from French of the 1300's *carpe*]

Car pa thi an Mountains (kär-pā′thē ən), mountain system in central Europe, extending in an arc from central Czechoslovakia to SW Romania.

Car pa thi ans (kär pā′thē ənz), Carpathian Mountains. *n.pl.*

carpel of a compound pistil

CARPEL   PETAL
STAMEN

car pel (kär′pəl), a modified leaf which forms a pistil or part of a pistil of a flower. *n.*

car pen ter (kär′pən tər), person whose work is building and repairing the wooden parts of houses, barns, ships, etc. *n.*

car pen try (kär′pən trē), trade or work of a carpenter. *n.*

car pet (kär′pit), 1 a heavy, woven fabric for covering floors and stairs. 2 anything like a carpet: *He walked on a carpet of grass.* 3 cover with a carpet: *In the fall, the ground was carpeted with leaves.* 1,2 *n.,* 3 *v.*

on the carpet, INFORMAL. being scolded or rebuked: *I was on the carpet for being tardy too often.*

car pet bag (kär′pit bag′), a traveling bag made of carpet. *n.*

car pet bag ger (kär′pit bag′ər), Northerner who went to the South to get political or other advantages during the time of disorganization that followed the American Civil War. *n.*

car pet ing (kär′pə ting), 1 fabric for carpets. 2 carpets: *The carpeting was worn and frayed in spots. n.*

car port (kär′pôrt′), shelter for automobiles, usually attached to a house and open on at least one side. *n.*

car riage (kar′ij), 1 vehicle that moves on wheels. Some carriages are pulled by horses and are used to carry people. Baby carriages are small, light, and can often be folded. 2 frame on wheels that supports a gun. 3 a moving part of a machine that supports another part: *a typewriter carriage.* 4 manner of holding the head and body; bearing: *She has a queenly carriage.* 5 the taking of persons or goods from one place to another; carrying; transporting: *All carriage to that mountain town has to be done by animals.* 6 cost or price of carrying: *This will be $10 for the gift package plus a charge of 50 cents for carriage. n.*

car ri er (kar′ē ər), 1 person or thing that carries something. A postman is a mail carrier. A porter is a baggage carrier. Railroads, airlines, bus systems, and truck companies are common carriers. 2 person or thing that carries or transmits a disease. Carriers are often healthy persons who are immune to a disease, but carry its germs. 3 aircraft carrier. *n.*

carrier pigeon, homing pigeon.

carrier wave, a radio wave whose intensity and frequency are varied in order to transmit a signal, usually in broadcasting radio and television programs and sending telephone and telegraph messages.

car ri on (kar′ē ən), dead and decaying flesh: *Some crows feed largely on carrion. n.*

Car roll (kar′əl), **Lewis,** 1832-1898, English writer, author of *Alice in Wonderland.* His real name was **Charles L. Dodgson.** *n.*

car rot (kar′ət), 1 plant which has a long, tapering, orange-red root. 2 its root, which is eaten as a vegetable, either cooked or raw. *n.*

car rou sel (kar′ə sel′), merry-go-round. *n.* Also, **carousel.**

car ry (kar′ē), 1 take from one place to another: *Railroads carry coal from the mines to the factories. The man carried the child home. This story will carry your thoughts back to last winter.* 2 bear or have with one: *carry an umbrella in case of rain.* 3 hold up; support; sustain: *Rafters carry the weight of the roof.* 4 hold (one's body and) in

hat, āge, fär; let, ēqual, tėrm; it, īce; hot, ōpen, ôrder; oil, out; cup, pùt, rüle; ch, child; ng, long; sh, she; th, thin; ₮H, then; zh, measure;

ə represents *a* in about, *e* in taken, *i* in pencil, *o* in lemon, *u* in circus.

a certain way: *The dancer carried herself gracefully.* 5 capture or win: *Our congressman won the election by carrying seven out of the ten towns in the district.* 6 get (a motion or bill) passed or adopted: *The motion to adjourn the meeting was carried.* 7 cover the distance: *The opera singer's voice carried clear to the back rows of the theater.* 8 have as a result; involve: *The expert's judgment carried great weight.* 9 sing (a melody, theme, or part) with correct pitch: *The children in the glee club can all carry a tune.* 10 keep in stock: *This store carries clothing for men.* 11 transfer (a number) from one place or column in the sum to the next. *v.,* **car ried, car ry ing.**

carry away, arouse strong feeling in; influence beyond reason: *I was so carried away by the sad story that I began to cry.*

carry off, 1 win (a prize, honor, etc.): *The champion swimmer carried off two gold medals at the Olympic games.* 2 be the death of; kill: *Pneumonia carried him off.*

carry on, 1 do; manage; conduct: *She carried on a successful business.* 2 keep going; not stop; continue: *We must carry on in our effort to establish world peace.* 3 INFORMAL. behave wildly or foolishly: *A few of the younger children carried on at the party.*

carry out, get done; do; accomplish; complete: *He carried out his job well.*

car ry all¹ (kar′ē ôl′), a lightweight, covered, one-horse carriage. *n.* [from French *carriole*]

car ry all² (kar′ē ôl′), a large bag or basket. *n.* [*carry + all*]

car sick (kär′sik′), nauseated as a result of the motion of a car, train, etc. *adj.* —**car′sick′ness,** *n.*

Car son (kär′sən), **Kit,** 1809-1868, American frontiersman, scout, and guide in the Far West. *n.*

Carson City, capital of Nevada, in the W part.

cart (kärt), 1 vehicle with two wheels, used in farming and for carrying heavy loads. Horses, donkeys, and oxen are often used to draw carts. 2 a light

adj. adjective	*n.* noun
adv. adverb	*prep.* preposition
conj. conjunction	*pron.* pronoun
interj. interjection	*v.* verb
sing. singular	*pl.* plural

wagon, used to deliver goods or for general business. 3 a small vehicle on wheels, moved by hand: *a grocery cart.* 4 carry in a cart: *Cart away this rubbish.* 1-3 *n.,* 4 *v.*

put the cart before the horse, reverse the accepted or usual order of things: *The boy put the cart before the horse by starting off dinner with apple pie.*

cart age (kär′tij), 1 a carting or transporting. 2 cost or price of carting. *n.*

carte blanche (kärt′ blänsh′), freedom to use one's own judgment; full authority. [from French *carte blanche* blank paper]

car tel (kär tel′), a large group of business firms that agree to operate as a monopoly, especially to regulate prices and production. *n.*

cart er (kär′tər), man whose work is driving a cart or truck. *n.*

Car thage (kär′thij), ancient city and seaport in N Africa, founded by the Phoenicians. It was destroyed by the Romans in 146 B.C., rebuilt in 29 B.C., and finally destroyed by the Arabs in A.D. 698. See **Byzantine Empire** for map. *n.*

Car tha gin i an (kär′thə jin′ē ən), 1 of Carthage. 2 person who was born or lived in Carthage. 1 *adj.,* 2 *n.*

Car tier (kär tyā′), **Jacques,** 1491-1557, French navigator who discovered the St. Lawrence River. *n.*

car ti lage (kär′tl ij), a tough, elastic substance forming parts of the skeleton of vertebrates; gristle. Cartilage is more flexible than bone and not as hard. The external ear consists of cartilage and skin. *n.*

car ti lag i nous (kär′tl aj′ə nəs), 1 of or like cartilage; gristly. 2 having the skeleton formed mostly of cartilage: *Sharks are cartilaginous. adj.*

car tog ra pher (kär tog′rə fər), maker of maps or charts. *n.*

car tog ra phy (kär tog′rə fē), the making or study of maps or charts. *n.*

car ton (kärt′n), 1 box made of pasteboard or cardboard: *a candy carton. Pack the books in large cartons.* 2 amount that a carton holds: *He could drink a carton of milk at one meal. n.*

car toon (kär tün′), 1 sketch or drawing showing persons, things, or events

in an amusing way: *Political cartoons often represent the United States as a tall man with chin whiskers who is called Uncle Sam.* 2 animated cartoon. 3 comic strip. 4 a full-size drawing of a design or painting, used as a model for a fresco, mosaic, tapestry, etc. *n.*

car toon ist (kär tü′nist), person who draws cartoons. *n.*

cartridge (def. 1)

CARTRIDGE

car tridge (kär′trij), 1 case made of metal, plastic, or cardboard for holding gunpowder and a bullet or shot. 2 a small container holding a roll of photographic film, ink for a pen, etc. *n.*

cart wheel (kärt′hwēl′), 1 wheel of a cart. 2 a sideways handspring or somersault. *n.*

Cart wright (kärt′rīt), **Edmund,** 1743-1823, English clergyman, inventor of a power loom. *n.*

Ca ru so (kə rü′sō), **Enrico,** 1873-1921, Italian operatic tenor. *n.*

carve (kärv), 1 cut into slices or pieces: *I carved the meat at the dinner table.* 2 make by cutting; cut: *Statues are often carved from marble, stone, or wood.* 3 decorate with figures or designs cut on the surface: *The oak chest was carved with scenes from the Crusades. v.,* **carved, carv ing.**

carv er (kär′vər), 1 person who carves. 2 carving knife. *n.*

Car ver (kär′vər), **George Washington,** 1864?-1943, American botanist and chemist. *n.*

carv ing (kär′ving), carved work; carved decoration: *a wood carving. n.*

carving knife, knife for cutting meat.

car y at id (kar′ē at′id), statue of a woman used as a column. *n., pl.* **car y at ids, car y at i des** (kar′ē at′ə dēz′).

ca sa ba (kə sä′bə), kind of winter muskmelon with a yellow rind. *n., pl.* **ca sa bas.** Also, **cassaba.**

Cas a blan ca (kas′ə blang′kə), seaport in N Morocco, on the Atlantic. *n.*

cas cade (ka skād′), 1 a small waterfall. 2 anything like this: *A cascade of ivy was hanging from the flower box.* 3 fall, pour, or flow in a cascade: *The water cascaded off the roof in the thunderstorm.* 1,2 *n.,* 3 *v.,* **cas cad ed, cas cad ing.**

Cascade Range, mountain range in NW United States, extending from N California to British Columbia.

cas car a (ka sker′ə), 1 shrub or small tree of the northwestern United States. It belongs to the same family as the buckthorn. 2 medicine prepared from

the dried bark of this tree, used as a laxative. *n., pl.* **cas car as.**

case[1] (kās), 1 any special condition of a person or thing; instance; example: *a case of poverty. A case of chicken pox kept me away from school.* 2 the actual condition; real situation; true state: *She said the work was done, but that was not the case.* 3 person who is being treated by a doctor; patient: *Hospitals had many cases of polio each summer before a vaccine to prevent it was developed.* 4 matter for a court of law to decide: *The case will be brought before the court tomorrow.* 5 a convincing argument: *The agent made a good case for buying insurance.* 6 (in grammar) one of the forms of a noun, pronoun, or adjective used to show its relation to other words. *I* is in the nominative case; *me* is in the objective case; *my* is in the possessive case. *n.* [from French of the 1200's *cas,* from Latin *casus* a falling, chance]

in any case, no matter what happens; anyhow: *In any case, you should prepare for the worst.*

in case, if it should happen that; if; supposing: *What would you do in case fire broke out?*

in case of, if there should be: *In case of fire walk quietly to the nearest door.*

in no case, under no circumstances; never: *In no case should you panic.*

case[2] (kās), 1 thing to hold or cover something: *a typewriter case. Put the knife back in its case.* 2 box: *There is a big case full of books in the hall.* 3 amount that a case can hold: *The children drank a case of ginger ale at the party.* 4 frame. A window fits in a case. 5 put in a case; cover with a case: *He cased the books for shipping.* 6 SLANG. look over carefully; inspect or examine: *The thieves cased the bank before the robbery.* 1-4 *n.,* 5,6 *v.,* **cased, cas ing.** [from French of the 1200's *casse,* from Latin *capsa* box, container]

ca sein (kā′sēn′), protein present in milk, used in making plastics, adhesives, and certain kinds of paints. Cheese is mostly casein. *n.*

casement

case ment (kās′mənt), window which opens on hinges like a door. *n.*

cash (kash), 1 money in the form of coins and bills: *Mother didn't have enough cash with her to pay for the book, so she wrote a check.* 2 money paid at the time of buying something:

He paid cash for his new suit instead of charging it and paying later. **3** give cash for: *The bank will cash your five-dollar check.* **4** get cash for: *She cashed her check at the bank.* 1,2 *n.*, 3,4 *v.*

cash in, INFORMAL. change into cash: *I cashed in a savings bond at the bank.*

cash in on, INFORMAL. **1** make a profit from: *After holding the land till the city needed it, he finally cashed in on his real estate investment.* **2** take advantage of; use to advantage: *She cashed in on her love of travel by becoming a tour guide.*

cash ew (kash′ü), **1** a small, kidney-shaped nut which is good to eat. **2** the tropical American tree that it grows on. *n.*

cash ier[1] (ka shir′), person who has charge of money in a bank, or in any business. *n.* [from French *caissier* treasurer, from *caisse* money box, from Latin *capsa* box]

cash ier[2] (ka shir′), dismiss from service; discharge in disgrace: *The dishonest officer was deprived of his rank and cashiered.* *v.* [from Dutch *casseren*, from French of the 1300's *casser* or *quasser*, from Latin *quassare* break]

cash mere (kash′mir *or* kazh′mir), a fine, soft wool, used in making sweaters, coats, etc. The finest cashmere is obtained from a breed of long-haired goats of Tibet and Kashmir. *n.*

cash on delivery, payment when goods are delivered.

cash register, machine which records and shows the amount of a sale. It usually has a drawer to hold money.

cas ing (kā′sing), **1** thing put around something; covering; case. The outermost part of a tire and the skin of a sausage are kinds of casings. **2** frame. A window fits in a casing. *n.*

ca si no (kə sē′nō), **1** building or room for public shows, dancing, gambling, etc. **2** cassino. *n., pl.* **ca si nos.**

cask (kask), **1** barrel. A cask may be large or small, and is usually made to hold liquids. **2** amount that a cask holds. *n.*

cas ket (kas′kit), **1** coffin. **2** a small box or chest used to hold jewels, letters, or other valuables. *n.*

Cas pi an Sea (kas′pē ən), inland sea between Europe and Asia in the Soviet Union and Iran, east of the Black Sea. See Assyria for map.

casque (kask), helmet. *n.*

cas sa ba (kə sä′bə), casaba. *n., pl.* **cas sa bas.**

Cas san dra (kə san′drə), (in Greek legends) a daughter of King Priam of Troy. Apollo gave her the power to foretell the future, but later in anger punished her by ordering that no one should believe her prophecies. *n.*

cas sa va (kə sä′və), **1** a tropical plant with starchy roots; manioc. **2** starch made from its roots. Tapioca is made from cassava. *n., pl.* **cas sa vas.**

cas se role (kas′ə rōl′), **1** a covered baking dish in which food can be both cooked and served. **2** food cooked and served in such a dish. *n.*

cas sette (ka set′), **1** container holding magnetic tape for playing or recording sound automatically. **2** cartridge for film. *n.*

cas sia (kash′ə), **1** an inferior kind of cinnamon, made from the bark of a tree of southern China. **2** the tree. **3** plant yielding leaves and pods that are used in making senna. *n., pl.* **cas sias.**

cas si no (kə sē′nō), a card game in which cards in the hand are matched with cards on the table. *n. Also,* **casino.**

cas sock (kas′ək), a long outer garment, usually black, worn by a clergyman. *n.*

cas so war y (kas′ə wer′ē), a large bird of Australia and New Guinea like an ostrich, but smaller. Cassowaries run swiftly, but cannot fly. *n., pl.* **cas so war ies.**

cast (kast), **1** throw; fling or hurl: *cast a stone, cast a fishing line. The criminal was cast into jail.* **2** throw off; let fall; shed: *The snake cast its skin.* **3** the distance a thing is thrown; throw: *The fisherman made a long cast with his line.* **4** direct or turn: *He cast a glance of surprise at me.* **5** deposit (a ballot); give (a vote): *Voters cast their ballots for President of the United States in an election held every four years.* **6** to shape by pouring or squeezing into a mold to harden. Metal is first melted and then cast. **7** thing made by casting: *The sculptor made a cast of Lincoln.* **8** mold used in casting; mold: *Her broken arm is in a plaster cast.* **9** select for a part in a play: *Our teacher has cast my brother as Long John Silver in our school play.* **10** the actors in a play: *The cast was listed on the program.* **11** outward form or look; appearance: *His face had a gloomy cast.* **12** a slight amount of color; tinge: *a white dress with a pink cast.* **13** a slight squint. 1,2,4–6,9 *v.*, cast, **cast ing;** 3,7,8, 10–13 *n.*

cast about, search; look: *The company cast about for a long time until it found a good location for its new factory.*

cast aside, **1** throw or put away: *cast aside a stone in the road.* **2** throw aside from use; discard: *cast aside an old hat.*

cast away, **1** abandon: *He cast away the project as useless.* **2** shipwreck.

cast down, **1** turn downward; lower:

hat, āge, fär; let, ēqual, tėrm;
it, īce; hot, ōpen, ôrder;
oil, out; cup, pút, rüle; ch, child;
ng, long; sh, she; th, thin;
ŦH, then; zh, measure;

ə represents *a* in about,
e in taken, *i* in pencil,
o in lemon, *u* in circus.

Her head was cast down in thought. **2** make sad or discouraged: *She was cast down by the bad news.*

cast off, **1** let loose; set free: *cast off a boat from its moorings.* **2** abandon or discard: *He cast off his old friends as soon as he left the old neighborhood.*

castanets

cas ta net (kas′tə net′), one of a pair of instruments held in the hand and clicked together to beat time for dancing or music. Castanets are made of hard wood or ivory. *n.*

cast a way (kast′ə wā′), **1** thrown away; cast adrift. **2** a shipwrecked person: *The castaways swam to the island.* **3** outcast; rejected. **4** an outcast. 1,3 *adj.*, 2,4 *n.*

caste (kast), **1** one of the social classes into which Hindus are divided. By tradition, a Hindu is born into the caste of his father and cannot rise above it. **2** an exclusive social group; distinct class: *The priestly caste in ancient Egypt had great power.* **3** a social system having distinct classes separated by differences of rank, wealth, or position. *n.*

lose caste, lose social rank or position: *They had a fear of losing caste among their neighbors.*

cas tel lat ed (kas′tl ā′tid), built like a castle; having turrets and battlements. *adj.*

cast er (kas′tər), **1** a small wheel on a swivel set into the base of a piece of furniture or other heavy object to make it easier to move. **2** shaker or bottle containing seasoning for table use: *a pepper caster.* **3** stand or rack for such bottles. **4** person or thing that casts: *The inexperienced caster tangled her fishing line in a tree. n. Also,* **castor** for 1-3.

cas ti gate (kas′tə gāt), criticize

adj. adjective	*n.* noun
adv. adverb	*prep.* preposition
conj. conjunction	*pron.* pronoun
interj. interjection	*v.* verb
sing. singular	*pl.* plural

severely or punish. *v.*, **cas ti gat ed,
cas ti gat ing.**

cas ti ga tion (kas′tə gā′shən), severe criticism or punishment. *n.*

Cas tile (ka stēl′), 1 region in N and central Spain, formerly a kingdom. 2 Castile soap. *n.*

Castile soap, a pure, hard soap made from olive oil and sodium hydroxide.

Cas til ian (ka stil′yən), 1 of Castile, its people, or their language. 2 Castilian Spanish. 3 person born or living in Castile. 1 *adj.*, 2,3 *n.*

Castilian Spanish, the accepted standard form of the Spanish language.

cast ing (kas′ting), 1 thing shaped by being poured into a mold to harden. 2 act or process of shaping things by pouring into a mold: *Casting in bronze was practiced in ancient Greece. n.*

cast iron, a hard, brittle form of iron made by casting.

cast-i ron (kast′ī′ərn), 1 made of cast iron: *cast-iron parts of an automobile.* 2 not yielding; hard: *cast-iron policies.* 3 hardy; strong: *His cast-iron stomach could digest almost anything. adj.*

cas tle (kas′əl), 1 a large building or group of buildings with thick walls, turrets, battlements, and other defenses against attack: *The knight rode over the drawbridge into the castle.* 2 a large and stately residence. 3 rook². *n.*

castle in the air, something imagined but not likely to come true; daydream.

cast off (kast′ôf′), 1 thrown away; abandoned; discarded: *castoff clothes.* 2 person or thing that has been cast off. 1 *adj.*, 2 *n.*

cas tor (kas′tər), caster (defs. 1-3). *n.*

Cas tor (kas′tər), (in Greek and Roman myths) one of the twin sons of Zeus. Castor was mortal; his brother, Pollux, was immortal. *n.*

castor oil, a thick, yellow oil obtained from the beans of a tall, tropical plant, used as a laxative and as a lubricant for machines.

cas trate (kas′trāt), remove the testicles of; emasculate. An ox is a castrated bull. *v.*, **cas trat ed, cas trat ing.**

cas tra tion (ka strā′shən), a castrating or a being castrated. *n.*

Cas tro (kas′trō), **Fidel,** born

1927, premier of Cuba since 1959. *n.*

cas u al (kazh′ü əl), 1 happening by chance; not planned or expected; accidental: *Our long friendship began with a casual meeting at a party.* 2 without plan or method; careless: *I didn't read the newspaper but I did give it a casual glance.* 3 informal in manner; offhand: *Some people mistook his casual behavior for rudeness.* 4 occasional or irregular: *He employs casual labor on his farm but only at harvest time.* 5 designed for informal wear: *We dressed in casual clothes for the picnic. adj.* —**cas′u al ly,** *adv.* —**cas′u al ness,** *n.*

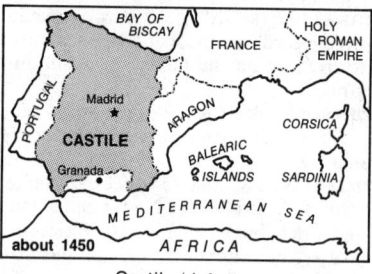

Castile (def. 1)

cas u al ty (kazh′ü əl tē), 1 member of the armed forces who has been wounded, killed, or captured as a result of enemy action: *The war produced many casualties.* 2 person injured or killed in an accident: *If drivers were more careful, there would be fewer casualties on the highways.* 3 accident, especially a fatal or serious one: *a casualty at sea. n., pl.* **cas u al ties.**

cas u ist (kazh′ü ist), person who reasons cleverly but falsely, especially in regard to right and wrong. *n.*

cas u ist ry (kazh′ü ə strē), clever but false reasoning, especially in regard to right and wrong. *n., pl.* **cas u ist ries.**

cat (kat), 1 a small, furry, flesh-eating mammal, often kept as a pet or for catching mice and rats. 2 any animal of the group including cats, lions, tigers, and leopards. 3 a mean, spiteful woman. 4 cat-o'-nine-tails. *n.*

let the cat out of the bag, tell a secret: *It was supposed to be a surprise party, but he let the cat out of the bag.*

catamaran
(def. 1)

rain cats and dogs, pour down rain very hard.

cat a clysm (kat′ə kliz′əm), 1 a great flood, earthquake, or any sudden, violent change in the earth. 2 any violent change or upheaval: *Atomic warfare between nations would be a cataclysm for all mankind. n.*

cat a clys mic (kat′ə kliz′mik), of or like a cataclysm; extremely sudden and violent. *adj.*

cat a comb (kat′ə kōm). Usually, **catacombs,** *pl.* an underground gallery forming a burial place, especially a network of such galleries with recesses in which to place the dead. *n.*

Cat a lan (kat′l ən), 1 of Catalonia, its people, or their language. 2 person born or living in Catalonia. 3 language spoken in Catalonia. 1 *adj.*, 2,3 *n.* Also, **Catalonian.**

cat a log (kat′l ôg), 1 list of items in some collection. A library has a catalog of its books, arranged in alphabetical order. A company sometimes prints a catalog with pictures and prices of the things that it sells. A college or university issues a catalog listing rules, courses to be given, etc. 2 make a catalog of; put in a catalog: *catalog an insect collection.* 1 *n.*, 2 *v.*

cat a log er (kat′l ô′gər), person who catalogs. *n.* Also, **cataloguer.**

cat a logue (kat′l ôg), catalog. *n., v.*, **cat a logued, cat a logu ing.**

cat a logu er (kat′l ô′gər), cataloger. *n.*

Cat a lo ni a (kat′l ō′nē ə), region in NE Spain. *n.*

Cat a lo ni an (kat′l ō′nē ən), Catalan. *adj., n.*

ca tal pa (kə tal′pə), tree of America and Asia with large, heart-shaped leaves, clusters of bell-shaped flowers, and long pods. *n., pl.* **ca tal pas.**

ca tal y sis (kə tal′ə sis), the causing or speeding up of a chemical reaction by the presence of a catalyst. *n., pl.* **ca tal y ses** (kə tal′ə sēz′).

cat a lyst (kat′l ist), 1 substance that causes or speeds up a chemical reaction while remaining practically unchanged itself. Enzymes are important catalysts in digestion. 2 anything that brings about some change or changes without being directly affected itself: *The first successful heart transplant was the catalyst that sparked widespread scientific work in this field. n.*

cat a lyt ic (kat′l it′ik), 1 of catalysis. 2 causing catalysis. *adj.*

cat a ma ran (kat′ə mə ran′), 1 boat with two hulls fitted side by side. 2 raft made of pieces of wood lashed together. *n.*

cat a mount (kat′ə mount), wildcat, such as a puma or lynx. *n.*

catapult (def. 1)—The very heavy bow was drawn by means of ropes and could send an arrow a great distance.

cat a pult (kat′ə pult), 1 weapon used in ancient times for shooting stones, arrows, etc. 2 slingshot. 3 device for launching an airplane from the deck of a ship. 4 throw; hurl: *He stopped his bicycle so suddenly that he was catapulted over the handlebars.* 5 shoot up suddenly; spring: *The frightened cat catapulted from the chair when the big dog came in.* 1-3 *n.*, 4,5 *v.*

cat a ract (kat′ə rakt′), 1 a large, steep waterfall. 2 a violent rush or downpour of water; flood: *Cataracts of rain flooded the streets.* 3 disease of the eye in which the lens develops a cloudy film, making a person partly or entirely blind. *n.*

ca tarrh (kə tär′), an inflamed condition of a mucous membrane, usually that of the nose or throat, causing a discharge of mucus. *n.*

ca tas tro phe (kə tas′trə fē), a sudden, widespread, or extraordinary disaster; great calamity or misfortune. A big earthquake, flood, or fire is a catastrophe. *n.*

cat a stroph ic (kat′ə strof′ik), of or caused by disaster; calamitous. *adj.* —**cat′a stroph′i cal ly,** *adv.*

cat bird (kat′bėrd′), a grayish North American songbird of the same family as the mockingbird. A catbird can make a sound like a cat mewing. *n.*

cat boat (kat′bōt′), sailboat with one mast set far forward and no jib. *n.*

cat call (kat′kôl′), 1 a shrill cry or whistle to express disapproval. Actors who perform poorly are sometimes greeted by catcalls from the audience. 2 make catcalls. 1 *n.*, 2 *v.*

catch (kach), 1 take and hold (something moving); seize: *Catch the ball with both hands. The policeman caught the thief. We were caught in the storm. Bright colors catch the baby's eye.* 2 take or get: *Paper catches fire easily. Put on a warm coat or you will catch cold. She caught a glimpse of her friend in the crowd.* 3 reach or get to in time: *You have just five minutes to catch your train.* 4 see, hear, or understand: *He spoke so rapidly that I didn't catch the meaning of what he said.* 5 become hooked or fastened: *My coat caught in the door.* 6 entangle or grip: *A nail caught her sleeve.* 7 come upon sudden-

ly; surprise: *Mother caught me just as I was hiding her birthday present.* 8 become lighted; burn: *Tinder catches easily.* 9 act as catcher in baseball: *He catches for our school team.* 10 act of catching: *She made a fine catch with one hand.* 11 thing that catches: *The catch on that door is broken.* 12 thing caught: *A dozen fish is a good catch.* 13 reach with a blow; hit; strike: *The stone caught him on the leg.* 14 game of throwing and catching a ball: *The children played catch on the lawn.* 15 (in music) a round. 16 check suddenly: *She caught her breath in surprise.* 17 a choking or stoppage of the breath: *He had a catch in his voice.* 18 INFORMAL. a hidden or tricky condition in a plan, etc.: *There is a catch to that question.* 1-9,13,16 *v.*, **caught, catch ing;** 10-12,14,15,17,18 *n.*, *pl.* **catch es.**

catch it, INFORMAL. be scolded or punished: *When the boy spilled the milk, he was afraid he would catch it.*

catch on, INFORMAL. 1 get the idea; understand: *The second time the teacher explained the problem, I caught on.* 2 become popular; be widely used or accepted: *That new song caught on quickly.*

catch up with, come up even with a person or thing while going the same way; overtake: *The dog ran as fast as he could to catch up with the car.*

catch er (kach′ər), 1 person or thing that catches. 2 a baseball player who stands behind the batter to catch the ball thrown by the pitcher. *n.*

catch ing (kach′ing), 1 likely to spread from one person to another; causing infection; contagious: *Colds are catching. Enthusiasm is catching.* 2 attractive or fascinating: *That singer has a catching style. adj.*

catch up (kech′əp *or* kach′əp), catsup. *n.*

catch word (kach′wėrd′), word or phrase used again and again for effect; slogan: *"No taxation without representation" was a political catchword during the Revolutionary War. n.*

catch y (kach′ē), 1 attractive and easy to remember: *The new musical play has several catchy tunes.* 2 tricky; misleading; deceptive: *The third question on the test was catchy; everyone in the class gave the wrong answer. adj.,* **catch i er, catch i est.**

cat e chism (kat′ə kiz′əm), 1 book of questions and answers about religion, used for teaching religious doctrine. 2 any long set of questions and answers about a subject. *n.*

cat e chist (kat′ə kist), person who catechizes. *n.*

cat e chize (kat′ə kīz), 1 teach by questions and answers. 2 question

hat, āge, fär; let, ēqual, tėrm; it, īce; hot, ōpen, ôrder; oil, out; cup, pùt, rüle; ch, child; ng, long; sh, she; th, thin; ᴛʜ, then; zh, measure;

ə represents *a* in about, *e* in taken, *i* in pencil, *o* in lemon, *u* in circus.

closely. *v.,* **cat e chized, cat e chiz ing.**

cat e gor i cal (kat′ə gôr′ə kəl), without conditions or qualifications; positive: *His categorical answer left no doubt about his opinion. adj.* —**cat′e gor′i cal ly,** *adv.*

cat e go ry (kat′ə gôr′ē), group or general division in classification; class: *She places all people into two categories: those she likes and those she dislikes. n., pl.* **cat e go ries.**

ca ter (kā′tər), 1 provide food, supplies, and sometimes service: *He runs a restaurant and also caters for weddings and parties.* 2 provide what is needed or wanted: *The new magazine caters to scouts by printing stories about camping, hiking, and nature. v.*

cat er-cor nered (kat′ər kôr′nərd), 1 diagonal: *a cater-cornered walk across the park.* 2 diagonally: *He walked cater-cornered across the park.* 1 *adj.,* 2 *adv.*

ca ter er (kā′tər ər), person who provides food, supplies, and sometimes service for parties, weddings, etc. *n.*

caterpillar about 2½ in. long

cat er pil lar (kat′ər pil′ər), the larva or wormlike form in which insects such as the butterfly and the moth hatch from the egg. *n.*

Cat er pil lar (kat′ər pil′ər), trademark for crawler tractors and other machinery. *n.*

cat er waul (kat′ər wôl), 1 howl like a cat; screech: *The bagpipes caterwauled.* 2 such a howl or screech. 1 *v.,* 2 *n.*

cat fish (kat′fish′), any of several fishes without scales and with long, slender feelers around the mouth that look somewhat like a cat's whiskers. *n., pl.* **cat fish es** *or* **cat fish.**

cat gut (kat′gut′), a tough string made from the dried and twisted intestines of sheep or other animals, used to string violins and tennis rackets. It was form-

133

adj. adjective	*n.* noun
adv. adverb	*prep.* preposition
conj. conjunction	*pron.* pronoun
interj. interjection	*v.* verb
sing. singular	*pl.* plural

erly used by surgeons for stitching wounds. *n.*

ca thar tic (kə thär′tik), 1 a strong laxative. Epsom salts and castor oil are cathartics. 2 strongly laxative. 1 *n.*, 2 *adj.*

Ca thay (ka thā′), OLD USE. China. *n.*

ca the dral (kə thē′drəl), 1 the official church of a bishop. The bishop of a district or diocese has a throne in the cathedral. 2 a large or important church. *n.*

Cath er ine the Great (kath′ər ən), 1729-1796, empress of Russia from 1762 to 1796.

cath ode (kath′ōd), a negatively charged electrode. Current flows from the cathode to the anode, a positively charged electrode. The zinc case of a dry cell and the filament of a vacuum tube are cathodes. *n.*

cathode rays, the invisible streams of electrons from the cathode in a vacuum tube. When cathode rays strike a solid substance, they produce X rays.

cath ode-ray tube (kath′ōd rā′), vacuum tube in which high-speed electrons are passed through magnetic fields in the form of a beam. Cathode-ray tubes are used in television receivers.

Cath o lic (kath′ə lik), 1 of the Christian church governed by the pope; Roman Catholic. 2 of the ancient, undivided Christian church, or of its present representatives, including the Anglican, Orthodox, and Roman Catholic Churches. 3 member of a Catholic church, especially the Roman Catholic. 4 **catholic,** of interest or use to all people; broad; universal: *Music has a catholic appeal to all ages, races, and classes of people.* 1,2,4 *adj.,* 3 *n.*

Ca thol i cism (kə thol′ə siz′əm), the faith, doctrine, and organization of the Roman Catholic Church. *n.*

cath o lic i ty (kath′ō lis′ə tē), broadness; universality: *the catholicity of an idea, a catholicity of taste in art.* *n.*

cat i on (kat′ī′ən), 1 a positively charged ion that moves toward the negative pole in electrolysis. 2 atom or group of atoms having a positive charge. *n.*

cat kin (kat′kən), the soft, downy or scaly, pointed cluster of flowers, having no petals, which grows on the willow or birch. *n.*

cat like (kat′līk′), 1 like a cat: *catlike in movement.* 2 like that of a cat: *catlike eyes.* *adj.*

cat nap (kat′nap′), a short nap. *n.*

cat nip (kat′nip), plant somewhat like mint, with strongly scented leaves that cats like. *n.*

Ca to (kā′tō), **Marcus Porcius,** 234-149 B.C., Roman statesman and writer. *n.*

cat-o'-nine-tails (kat′ə nīn′tālz′), whip consisting of nine pieces of knotted cord fastened to a handle. It was formerly used as a means of punishment in the navy. *n., pl.* **cat-o'-nine-tails.**

cat's cradle, a child's game played with a string looped over the fingers of both hands.

Cats kill Mountains (kats′kil), range of Appalachian Mountains in SE New York State.

Cats kills (kats′kilz), Catskill Mountains. *n.pl.*

cat's-paw or **cats paw** (kats′pô′), person used by another to do something unpleasant or dangerous. *n.*

cat sup (kech′əp *or* kat′səp), sauce made to use with meat, fish, etc. Tomato catsup is made of tomatoes, onions, salt, sugar, and spices. *n.* Also, **catchup** or **ketchup.**

cat tail (kat′tāl′), a tall marsh plant with flowers in long, round, furry, brown spikes. *n.*

cat ti ly (kat′l ē), in a catty manner. *adv.*

cat ti ness (kat′ē nis), catty quality. *n.*

cat tle (kat′l), 1 animals of the ox family raised for meat, milk, hides, etc.; cows, bulls, and steers. 2 (formerly) farm animals; livestock. *n.pl.*

cat tle man (kat′l mən), man who raises or takes care of cattle. *n., pl.* **cat tle men.**

cat ty (kat′ē), mean and spiteful: *Catty comments about your classmates will not help you make friends.* *adj.,* **cat ti er, cat ti est.**

cat walk (kat′wôk′), a narrow place to walk on a bridge, near the ceiling of a stage, in an airship, etc. *n.*

Cau ca sia (kô kā′zhə), region in the S Soviet Union, between the Black and Caspian Seas; Caucasus. *n.*

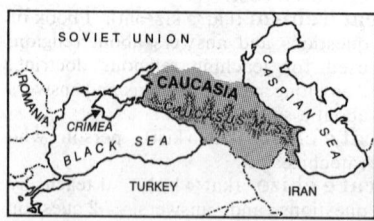

Cau ca sian (kô kā′zhən), 1 member of the so-called white race, including the chief peoples of Europe, southwestern Asia, northern Africa, the Western Hemisphere, and Australia. 2 of or having to do with the so-called white race. 3 person born or living in the Caucasus. 4 of or having to do with the Caucasus or its inhabitants. 1,3 *n.,* 2,4 *adj.*

Cau ca sus (kô′kə səs), 1 mountain range in S Soviet Union, extending from the Black Sea to the Caspian Sea. 2 Caucasia. *n.*

cau cus (kô′kəs), 1 meeting of members or leaders of a political party to make plans, choose candidates, or decide how to vote. 2 hold a caucus. 1 *n., pl.* **cau cus es;** 2 *v.*

cau dal (kô′dl), 1 of, at, or near the tail. 2 like a tail. *adj.*

caught (kôt), past tense and past participle of **catch.** *He caught the ball. The mouse was caught in a trap.* *v.*

caul dron (kôl′drən), caldron. *n.*

cau li flow er (kô′lə flou′ər), 1 plant having a solid, white head with a few leaves around it. It belongs to the same family as the cabbage. 2 its head, which is eaten as a vegetable. *n.*

caulk (kôk), fill up (a seam, crack, or joint) so that it will not leak; make watertight. Sailors caulk boats with oakum and tar. Plumbers caulk joints in pipe with lead. *v.* Also, **calk.** —**caulk′er,** *n.*

cause (kôz), 1 person, thing, or event that makes something happen: *The flood was the cause of much damage.* 2 make happen; make do; bring about: *The fire caused much damage. A loud noise caused me to jump.* 3 reason or occasion for action: *The hero's return was a cause for celebration. You have no cause to complain.* 4 subject or movement in which many people are interested and to which they give their support: *World peace is the cause she works for.* 1,3,4 *n.,* 2 *v.,* **caused, caus ing.**

cause less (kôz′lis), 1 without any known cause; happening by chance. 2 without good reason; not having reason enough: *causeless fear of the dark.* *adj.*

cause way (kôz′wā′), 1 a raised road or path, usually built across wet ground or shallow water: *A narrow causeway ran across the bog.* 2 a main road; highway: *The car followed the causeway over the hills.* *n.*

caus tic (kô′stik), 1 substance that burns or destroys flesh; corrosive substance: *My warts were burned away by the caustic put on them.* 2 that burns or destroys flesh; corrosive. Lye is caustic soda or caustic potash. 3 very critical or sarcastic; stinging; biting: *The coach's caustic remarks made the football players angry.* 1 *n.,* 2,3 *adj.*

caus ti cal ly (kô′stik lē), very critically or sarcastically. *adv.*

caustic potash, potassium hydroxide.

caustic soda, sodium hydroxide.

cau ter i za tion (kô′tər ə zā′shən), a cauterizing or a being cauterized. *n.*

cau ter ize (kô′tə rīz′), burn with a hot iron or a caustic substance. Doctors sometimes cauterize wounds to prevent bleeding or infection. *v.,* **cau ter ized, cau ter iz ing.**

cau tion (kô′shən), 1 great care; regard for safety; unwillingness to take chances: *Always use caution when crossing streets.* 2 a warning: *A sign with "Danger" on it is a caution.* 3 urge to be careful; warn: *My parents cautioned me against playing in that busy street.* 1,2 *n.,* 3 *v.*

cau tious (kô′shəs), very careful; taking care to be safe; not taking chances: *A cautious driver never drives his car too fast.* *adj.* —**cau′tious ly,** *adv.* —**cau′tious ness,** *n.*

cav al cade (kav′əl kād′), 1 procession of persons riding on horses, in carriages, or in automobiles. 2 series of scenes or events: *a cavalcade of sports.* *n.*

cav a lier (kav′ə lir′), 1 horseman, mounted soldier, or knight. 2 a courteous gentleman. 3 a courteous escort for a lady. 4 careless in manner; free and easy; offhand: *He did not take me seriously and gave a gay, cavalier reply.* 5 proud and scornful; haughty; arrogant: *People were often irritated by his cavalier attitude towards them.* 6 **Cavalier,** person who supported Charles I of England in his struggle with Parliament from 1640 to 1649. 1-3,6 *n.,* 4,5 *adj.* —**cav′a lier′ly,** *adv.*

cav al ry (kav′əl rē), 1 (formerly) soldiers who fought on horseback. 2 soldiers who fight from armored vehicles. *n., pl.* **cav al ries.**

cav al ry man (kav′əl rē mən), soldier in the cavalry. *n., pl.* **cav al ry men.**

cave (kāv), 1 a hollow space underground, especially one with an opening in the side of a hill or mountain. 2 **cave in,** fall in; sink: *The weight of the snow caused the roof of the cabin to cave in.* 1 *n.,* 2 *v.,* **caved, cav ing.** —**cave′like′,** *adj.*

cave-in (kāv′in′), 1 a caving in; collapse: *a tunnel cave-in, the cave-in of a mine.* 2 place where something has caved in. *n.*

cave man, man who lived in a cave in prehistoric times.

cav ern (kav′ərn), a large cave. *n.*

cav ern ous (kav′ər nəs), 1 like a cavern; large and hollow: *a cavernous cellar, cavernous eyes.* 2 full of caverns: *cavernous mountains.* *adj.*

cav i ar or **cav i are** (kav′ē är), a salty relish made from the eggs of sturgeon or of certain other large fish, eaten as an appetizer. *n.*

cav il (kav′əl), 1 find fault without good reason; raise trivial objections: *He cavils about minor points in the rules of the game.* 2 a trivial objection; petty criticism. 1 *v.,* 2 *n.* —**cav′il er,** *n.*

cav i ty (kav′ə tē), 1 hollow place; hole. Cavities in teeth are caused by decay. 2 an enclosed space inside the body: *the abdominal cavity.* *n., pl.* **cav i ties.**

ca vort (kə vôrt′), prance about; jump around: *The children cavorted about the field, racing and tumbling.* *v.*

ca vy (kā′vē), any of several South American rodents, the best known being the guinea pig. *n., pl.* **ca vies.**

caw (kô), 1 the harsh cry made by a crow or raven. 2 make this cry. 1 *n.,* 2 *v.*

Cax ton (kak′stən), **William,** 1422?-1491, first English printer. He was also an author and translator. *n.*

cay (kē *or* kā), a low island; reef; key. *n.*

cay enne (kī en′ *or* kā en′), a very hot, biting powder made from the seeds or fruit of a pepper plant; red pepper. *n.*

cay man (kā′mən), caiman. *n., pl.* **cay mans.**

Ca yu ga (kā yü′gə *or* kī yü′gə), 1 member of a tribe of Iroquois Indians formerly living in western New York State. 2 of this tribe. 1 *n., pl.* **Ca yu ga** or **Ca yu gas;** 2 *adj.*

cay use (kī yüs′ *or* kī′üs), in the western United States: 1 pony bred by Indians. 2 any pony or horse. *n.*

cc. or **c.c.,** cubic centimeter or cubic centimeters.

C clef, symbol in music that shows the position of middle C. It is called the alto clef when placed on the third line of the staff, and the tenor clef when placed on the fourth line of the staff. See **clef** for diagram.

cease (sēs), come to an end; put an end to; stop: *The music ceased suddenly. Cease trying to do more than you can.* *v.,* **ceased, ceas ing.**

cease-fire (sēs′fīr′), a halt in military operations, especially for the purpose of discussing peace. *n.*

cease less (sēs′lis), going on all the time; never stopping; continual: *the ceaseless roar of the falls.* *adj.* —**cease′less ly,** *adv.* —**cease′less ness,** *n.*

Ce ci lia (sə sē′lyə *or* sə sil′yə), **Saint,** died A.D. 230?, Roman Christian martyr, the patron saint of music. *n.*

hat, āge, fär; let, ēqual, tėrm; it, īce; hot, ōpen, ôrder; oil, out; cup, pùt, rüle; ch, child; ng, long; sh, she; th, thin; ŦH, then; zh, measure;

ə represents *a* in about, *e* in taken, *i* in pencil, *o* in lemon, *u* in circus.

Ce cro pi a moth (sə krō′pē ə), a large silkworm moth of the eastern United States. Its larvae feed on trees and shrubs.

ce dar (sē′dər), 1 an evergreen tree of the same family as the pine, with branches that spread widely, and fragrant, durable, reddish wood. 2 the wood of this tree, much used for lining clothes closets and making chests, cigar boxes, pencils, and posts. *n.*

ce dar bird (sē′dər bėrd′), cedar waxwing. *n.*

Cedar Rapids, city in E Iowa.

cedar waxwing, a small North American bird with a crest and small, red markings on its wings; cedarbird. *n.*

cede (sēd), hand over to another; give up; surrender: *Spain ceded the Philippines to the United States.* *v.,* **ced ed, ced ing.**

ce dil la (sə dil′ə), a mark somewhat like a comma (ç) put under *c* before *a, o,* or *u* in certain words to show that it has the sound of *s.* EXAMPLE: façade. *n., pl.* **ce dil las.**

ceil ing (sē′ling), 1 the inside, top covering of a room; surface opposite the floor. 2 the greatest height to which an airplane can go under certain conditions: *That new jet plane has a ceiling of more than 100,000 feet.* 3 distance between the earth and the lowest clouds: *The weather report said that the ceiling was only 300 feet.* 4 an upper limit set for prices, wages, rents, etc.: *There was a ceiling on the amount the candidate could spend for his election campaign.* *n.*

cel an dine (sel′ən dīn), plant with yellow flowers, belonging to the same family as the poppy. *n.*

Cel e bes (sel′ə bēz′), large island in Indonesia, between Borneo and New Guinea; Sulawesi. *n.*

cel e brant (sel′ə brənt), 1 person who performs a ceremony or rite. 2 priest who performs Mass. *n.*

cel e brate (sel′ə brāt), 1 observe (a special time or day) with the proper ceremonies or festivities: *We celebrated her birthday with cake, ice cream, and presents.* 2 perform publicly with the

adj.	adjective	*n.*	noun
adv.	adverb	*prep.*	preposition
conj.	conjunction	*pron.*	pronoun
interj.	interjection	*v.*	verb
sing.	singular	*pl.*	plural

proper ceremonies and rites: *The priest celebrates Mass in church.* 3 praise; honor: *Her books are celebrated all over the world.* 4 INFORMAL. have a gay time: *When the children saw the snow, they celebrated.* v., **cel e brat ed, cel e brat ing.**

cel e brat ed (sel′ə brā′tid), much talked about; famous; well-known: *Longfellow was a celebrated poet.* adj.

cel e bra tion (sel′ə brā′shən), 1 special services or activities in honor of a particular man, act, time, or day: *A Fourth of July celebration often includes a display of fireworks.* 2 act of celebrating: *celebration of a birthday.* n.

ce leb ri ty (sə leb′rə tē), 1 a famous person; person who is well known or much talked about: *Astronauts are celebrities around the world.* 2 a being well known or much talked about; fame: *His celebrity brought him riches.* n., pl. **ce leb ri ties.**

ce ler i ty (sə ler′ə tē), swiftness; speed: *celerity of flight, celerity of reply.* n.

cel er y (sel′ər ē), 1 plant having long, crisp stalks with leaves at the top. It belongs to the same family as the parsley. 2 its stalks, which are eaten either raw or cooked as a vegetable. n.

ce les ta (sə les′tə), a musical instrument with a keyboard, resembling a small, upright piano. The tones resemble the tinkle of small bells and are made by hammers hitting steel plates. n., pl. **ce les tas.**

ce les tial (sə les′chəl), 1 of the sky; having to do with the heavens: *The sun, moon, planets, and stars are celestial bodies.* 2 of or belonging to heaven as the place of God and the angels; heavenly; divine: *celestial joy.* 3 very good or beautiful. adj. —**ce les′tial ly,** adv.

celestial sphere, the imaginary sphere which appears to enclose the universe. To an observer on earth, the visible sky forms half of the celestial sphere.

cel i ba cy (sel′ə bə sē), unmarried state; single life. n.

cel i bate (sel′ə bit), 1 an unmarried person who takes a vow to lead a single life: *Nuns and priests are celibates.* 2 unmarried; single: *The monk led a celibate life.* 1 n., 2 adj.

cell (sel), 1 a small room in a prison, convent, or monastery. 2 any small, hollow place: *Bees store honey in the cells of a honeycomb.* 3 the basic unit of living matter of which all plants and animals are made. Cells vary in size and shape but are generally microscopic. Most cells consist of protoplasm, have a nucleus near the center, and are enclosed by a cell wall or cell membrane. The body has blood cells, nerve cells, muscle cells, etc. 4 container holding materials which produce electricity by chemical action. A battery consists of one or more cells. n.

cel lar (sel′ər), an underground room or rooms, usually under a building and often used for storing food or fuel. n.

Cel li ni (chə lē′nē), **Benvenuto,** 1500-1571, Italian sculptor and artist in metalwork. n.

cel list (chel′ist), person who plays the cello; violoncellist. n.

cell membrane, the thin membrane that forms the outer surface of the protoplasm of a cell.

cello
played with a bow
or by plucking strings
with the fingers

cel lo (chel′ō), a musical instrument like a violin, but very much larger and with a lower tone; violoncello. It is held between the knees while being played. n., pl. **cel los.**

cel lo phane (sel′ə fān), a transparent substance made from cellulose. It is used as a wrapping to keep food, candy, tobacco, etc., fresh and clean. n.

cel lu lar (sel′yə lər), 1 having to do with cells. 2 made up of cells. All animal and plant tissue is cellular. adj.

Cel lu loid (sel′yə loid), trademark for a hard, transparent substance made from cellulose and treated with camphor. It catches fire easily. Combs, toilet articles, camera films, etc., are often made of Celluloid. n.

cel lu lose (sel′yə lōs), substance that forms the walls of plant cells; the woody part of trees and plants. Wood, cotton, flax, and hemp are largely cellulose. Cellulose is used to make paper, rayon, plastics, explosives, etc. n.

cellulose acetate, any of several compounds, formed from cellulose in the presence of acetic acid. It is used in making textiles, camera films, lacquers, varnishes, etc.

cell wall, the hard outer covering of

cell (def. 3)—two types, greatly magnified

a plant cell, made up mostly of cellulose and surrounding the cell membrane.

Cel si us scale (sel′sē əs), the official name of the centigrade scale. [from Anders *Celsius,* 1701-1744, a Swedish astronomer, who invented it]

Celt (selt *or* kelt), member of a people to which the Irish, Scottish Highlanders, Welsh, Bretons, and Manx belong. The ancient Gauls and Britons were Celts. n.

Celt ic (sel′tik *or* kel′tik), 1 of the Celts or their language. 2 the group of languages spoken by the Celts, including Irish, Gaelic, Welsh, Breton, and Manx. 1 adj., 2 n.

ce ment (sə ment′), 1 a fine, gray powder made by burning clay and limestone. Cement mixed with water and such materials as sand and gravel becomes hard like stone when it dries and is used to make sidewalks, streets, floors, and walls, and to hold stones and bricks together in the walls of buildings. 2 anything applied soft which hardens to make things stick together: *rubber cement.* 3 substance used to fill cavities in teeth. 4 fasten together with cement: *A broken plate can be cemented.* 5 spread cement over: *The workmen were cementing the sidewalk.* 6 join firmly; unite: *The marriage of our son to their daughter cemented the friendship of our two families.* 1-3 n., 4-6 v.

cem e ter y (sem′ə ter′ē), place for burying the dead; graveyard. n., pl. **cem e ter ies.**

Cen o zo ic (sen′ə zō′ik), 1 the most recent era of geological history. The Cenozoic began about 60 or 70 million years ago, when mammals began to dominate the animal kingdom, and includes the present time. 2 of this era or its rocks. 1 n., 2 adj.

cen ser (sen′sər), container in which incense is burned, especially during religious ceremonies. n.

cen sor (sen′sər), 1 person who examines and, if necessary, changes letters, books, newspapers, plays, motion pictures, etc., so as to make their content satisfactory to the government or to some institution or organization. 2 examine or change as a censor; make changes in; take out part of (news reports, books, letters, motion pictures, etc.): *All letters from the battlefield were* censored to make sure military information did not fall into enemy hands. Two scenes in the movie had been censored for having too much violence. 3 a Roman magistrate who took the census and supervised the conduct of citizens. 4 person who tells others how they ought to behave. 1,3,4 *n.*, 2 *v.*

cen so ri ous (sen sôr′ē əs), too ready to find fault; severely critical. *adj.* —**cen so′ri ous ly,** *adv.* —**cen so′ri ous ness,** *n.*

cen sor ship (sen′sər ship), act or system of censoring: *Censorship of news is common in time of war. n.*

cen sure (sen′shər), 1 expression of disapproval; unfavorable opinion; criticism: *Censure is sometimes harder to bear than punishment.* 2 find fault with; criticize: *I was censured by the club for not paying my dues.* 1 *n.*, 2 *v.*, **censured, cen sur ing.**

cen sus (sen′səs), an official count of the people of a country or district. It is taken to find out the number of people, their age, sex, what they do to make a living, and many other facts about them. *n.*, *pl.* **cen sus es.**

cent (sent), coin of the United States and Canada, usually an alloy of copper; penny. 100 cents make one dollar. *n.*

centaur

cen taur (sen′tôr), (in Greek myths) a monster that had the head, arms, and chest of a man, and the body and legs of a horse. *n.*

cen ta vo (sen tä′vō), coin used in Mexico, Cuba, the Philippines, etc. 100 centavos make a peso. *n.*, *pl.* **cen ta vos.**

cen te nar i an (sen′tə ner′ē ən), person who is 100 years old or more. *n.*

cen ten ar y (sen ten′ər ē *or* sen′tə ner′ē), 1 a 100th anniversary: *The town was bustling with plans for its centenary.* 2 period of 100 years; century. 3 having to do with 100 years or a 100th anniversary: *a centenary celebration.* 1,2 *n.*, *pl.* **cen ten ar ies;** 3 *adj.*

cen ten ni al (sen ten′ē əl), 1 of or having to do with 100 years or the 100th anniversary. 2 100 years old: *centennial pines.* 3 a 100th anniversary: *The town is celebrating its centennial.* 4 celebration of the 100th anniversary: *I hope there will be a fair during our*

centennial. 1,2 *adj.*, 3,4 *n.* —**cen ten′ni al ly,** *adv.*

cen ter (sen′tər), 1 point within a circle or sphere equally distant from all points of the circumference or surface. 2 the middle point, place, or part: *the center of a room.* 3 person, thing, or group that is the central point of attraction: *The Egyptian mummy was the center of the exhibit.* 4 point toward which people or things go, or from which they come; main point: *New York City is one of the trade centers of the world.* 5 place in or at a center: *A bowl of fruit was centered on the kitchen table.* 6 concentrate; rest: *All his hopes are centered on being promoted.* 7 collect at a center: *The guests centered around the table.* 8 player who has the center position of a forward line in football, basketball, hockey, etc. 1-4, 8 *n.*, 5-7 *v.* Also, **centre.**

cen ter board (sen′tər bôrd′), a movable keel of a sailboat. It is lowered through a slot in the bottom of a boat to prevent drifting to leeward. *n.*

center field, (in baseball) the section of the outfield between left field and right field.

center of gravity, point in a body around which its weight is evenly balanced.

cen ter piece (sen′tər pēs′), an ornamental piece of glass, lace, etc., or an arrangement of flowers for the center of a dining table, buffet, mantel, etc. *n.*

cen ti grade (sen′tə grād), of, based on, or according to a scale for measuring temperature on which 0 degrees marks the freezing point of water and 100 degrees marks the boiling point. The **centigrade thermometer** is marked off according to this scale. *adj.*

cen ti gram (sen′tə gram), 1/100 of a gram. *n.*

cen ti li ter (sen′tə lē′tər), 1/100 of a liter. *n.*

cen time (sän′tēm′), coin used in France, Belgium, Switzerland, etc. 100 centimes make a franc. *n.*

cen ti me ter (sen′tə mē′tər), 1/100 of a meter; .3937 inch. *n.*

cen ti pede (sen′tə pēd′), a flat, wormlike animal with many pairs of legs, the front pair of which are clawlike and contain poison glands. Centipedes vary in length from an inch to nearly a foot. *n.*

cen tral (sen′trəl), 1 of the center; being or forming the center: *The sun is central in the solar system.* 2 at the center; near the center: *The park is in the central part of the city.* 3 from the center; head: *The central library sends books to its branches.* 4 equally distant from all points; easy to get to or from:

hat, āge, fär; let, ēqual, tėrm;
it, īce; hot, ōpen, ôrder;
oil, out; cup, půt, rüle; ch, child;
ng, long; sh, she; th, thin;
ŦH, then; zh, measure;

ə represents *a* in about,
e in taken, *i* in pencil,
o in lemon, *u* in circus.

We shop at a central market. 5 main; chief; principal: *What is the central idea in this story?* 6 a telephone exchange. 7 a telephone operator. 1-5 *adj.*, 6,7 *n.*

Central African Republic, country in central Africa, south of Chad, a member of the French Community. See Congo for map.

CENTERBOARD → RUDDER →

Central America, part of North America between Mexico and South America. Guatemala, El Salvador, Honduras, British Honduras, Nicaragua, Costa Rica, and Panama are the countries in Central America.

Central American, 1 having to do with Central America or its people. 2 person born or living in Central America.

cen tral i za tion (sen′trə lə zā′shən), 1 a coming or bringing to a center. 2 a gathering together at a center: *Centralization of medical services may prevent waste of effort.* 3 a bringing together under the control of a single authority: *the centralization of government under a dictator. n.*

cen tral ize (sen′trə līz), 1 bring to or toward a center; locate in a center. 2 gather together in a center; concentrate. 3 bring or come under the control of a single authority. *v.*, **cen tral ized, cen tral iz ing.**

cen tral ly (sen′trə lē), at the center; near the center: *The business district is centrally located. adv.*

central nervous system, part of the nervous system of vertebrates that consists of the brain and spinal cord. The nerves from the central nervous system control the muscles.

Central Standard Time, the standard time in the central part of the United States and Canada. It is six hours behind Greenwich Time.

cen tre (sen′tər), center (the spelling generally used in Great Britain and Canada). *n.*, *v.*, **cen tred, cen tring.**

cen trif u gal (sen trif′yə gəl), moving

137

adj.	adjective	*n.*	noun
adv.	adverb	*prep.*	preposition
conj.	conjunction	*pron.*	pronoun
interj.	interjection	*v.*	verb
sing.	singular	*pl.*	plural

away from the center. *adj.* —**cen trif′-
u gal ly,** *adv.*

cen tri fuge, the inertia, or
tendency to move in one direction,
which causes a body turning around a
center to move away from the center.

cen tri fuge (sen′trə fyüj), 1 machine
for separating two substances varying
in density, as cream from milk or
bacteria from a fluid, by means of centrifugal force. 2 separate with a centri-
fuge. 1 *n.,* 2 *v.,* **cen tri fuged, cen-
tri fug ing.**

cen trip e tal (sen trip′ə təl), moving
toward the center. *adj.* —**cen trip′-
e tal ly,** *adv.*

centripetal force, the force that
tends to move things toward the center
around which they are turning. Gravitation acts as a centripetal force. The
earth's gravity exerts a centripetal force
on an orbiting satellite and keeps it from
flying off into space.

cen tur i on (sen tùr′ē ən *or* sen-
tyùr′ē ən), commander of about 100
soldiers in the ancient Roman army. *n.*

cen tur y (sen′chər ē), 1 each 100
years, counting from some special time,
such as the birth of Christ. The first
century is 1 through 100; the nineteenth
century is 1801 through 1900; the
twentieth century is 1901 through 2000.
2 period of 100 years. From 1824 to
1924 is a century. *n., pl.* **cen tur ies.**

century plant, a large plant with
thick leaves, a kind of agave, growing in
Mexico and the southwestern United
States; aloe. It sometimes reaches thirty
feet in height and is often wrongly
supposed to bloom once every 100
years.

ce ram ic (sə ram′ik), 1 of or having to
do with pottery, earthenware, porcelain, etc., or with making them. 2 article
made of pottery, earthenware, porcelain, etc. 1 *adj.,* 2 *n.*

ce ram ics (sə ram′iks), art of making
pottery, earthenware, porcelain, etc. *n.,
pl. in form, sing. in use.*

Cer ber us (sèr′bər əs), (in Greek and
Roman myths) a dog with three heads
that guarded the entrance to Hades. *n.*

cer e al (sir′ē əl), 1 any grass that produces grain which is used as a food.
Wheat, rice, corn, oats, and barley are
cereals. 2 the grain. 3 food made from
the grain. Oatmeal and corn meal are
cereals. 4 of or having to do with grain
or the grasses producing it: *cereal
crops, cereal products.* 1-3 *n.,* 4 *adj.*
[from Latin *Cerealis* having to do with
Ceres]

cer e bel lum (ser′ə bel′əm), the part
of the brain that controls the coordination of the muscles. See **brain** for
diagram. *n., pl.* **cer e bel lums, cer-
e bel la** (ser′ə bel′ə).

ce re bral (sə rē′brəl *or* ser′ə brəl),
1 of the brain. 2 of the cerebrum.
3 characterized by thought and reason
rather than emotion or action: *Chess is
a cerebral game. adj.*

The tendency of the satellite A
to move in a straight line toward B
(centrifugal force) is overcome
by the force exerted by gravity
toward C (centripetal force),
resulting in motion toward D.

cerebral palsy, paralysis caused by
damage to the brain. Children suffering
from cerebral palsy have trouble coordinating their muscles.

ce re brum (sə rē′brəm *or* ser′ə-
brəm), the part of the human brain that
controls thought and voluntary muscular movements. See **brain** for diagram.
n., pl. **ce re brums, ce re bra** (sə rē′-
brə *or* ser′ə brə).

cere ment (sir′mənt), cloth or garment
in which a dead person is wrapped for
burial. *n.*

cer e mo ni al (ser′ə mō′nē əl), 1 of
or having to do with ceremony: *The
emperor's ceremonial costumes were
beautiful.* 2 very formal: *The ambassador receives guests in a ceremonial way.*
3 the formal actions proper to an occasion. Bowing the head and kneeling are
ceremonials of religion. 1,2 *adj.,* 3 *n.*
—**cer′e mo′ni al ly,** *adv.*

cer e mo ni ous (ser′ə mō′nē əs),
1 full of ceremony: *There was a ceremonious unveiling of the statue.* 2 very
formal; extremely polite: *a ceremonious
bow or curtsy. adj.* —**cer′e mo′ni-
ous ly,** *adv.* —**cer′e mo′ni ous-
ness,** *n.*

Cerberus

cer e mo ny (ser′ə mō′nē), 1 a special
act or set of acts to be done on special
occasions such as weddings, funerals,
graduations, or holidays: *The graduation ceremony was held in the gymnasium.* 2 very polite conduct; way of conducting oneself that follows all the rules
of polite social behavior: *The old gentleman showed us to the door with a
great deal of ceremony.* 3 attention to
forms and customs; formality: *The princess disliked the traditional ceremony
of the court. n., pl.* **cer e mo nies.**

stand on ceremony, be too polite; be
very formal: *He is a hospitable person
who does not stand on ceremony and so
makes everyone feel at ease in his home.*

Cer es (sir′ēz), (in Roman myths) the
goddess of agriculture. The Greeks
called her Demeter. *n.*

ce rise (sə rēs′), 1 bright pinkish-red.
2 a bright pinkish red. 1 *adj.,* 2 *n.*

cer i um (sir′ē əm), a grayish metallic
element which occurs only in combination with other elements. Cerium is
used in porcelain, glass, and alloys. *n.*

cer tain (sèrt′n), 1 without a doubt;
sure: *It is certain that 2 and 3 do not
make 6. I am certain that these are the
facts.* 2 known but not named; some;
particular: *Certain plants will not grow
in this country. A certain person gave
our organization $100.* 3 settled; fixed:
*I earn a certain amount of money each
week.* 4 that can be depended on; reliable: *Nothing is very certain in this
situation. I have certain information
that school will end a day earlier this
year. adj.* —**cer′tain ness,** *n.*

for certain, as a certainty; without a
doubt; surely: *She will be here for certain.*

cer tain ly (sèrt′n lē), without a doubt;
surely: *I will certainly be at the party.
adv.*

cer tain ty (sèrt′n tē), 1 a being certain; freedom from doubt: *The man's
certainty was amusing, for we could all
see that he was wrong.* 2 something
certain; a sure fact: *The coming of
spring and summer is a certainty. n., pl.*
cer tain ties.

cer tif i cate (sər tif′ə kit), an official
written or printed statement that de-
clares something to be a fact. A birth
certificate gives the date and place of a
person's birth and the names of his
parents. *n.*

cer ti fi ca tion (sèr′tə fə kā′shən),
1 a certifying or a being certified. 2 a
certified statement. *n.*

cer ti fied (sèr′tə fīd), 1 guaranteed:
certified Grade A milk. 2 having a certificate: *a certified public accountant.
adj.*

cer ti fy (sèr′tə fī), 1 declare (something) true or correct by an official

spoken, written, or printed statement: *This diploma certifies that you have completed high school.* **2** guarantee the quality or value of: *The fire inspector certified the school building as fireproof.* *v.,* **cer ti fied, cer ti fy ing.**

ce ru le an (sə rü′lē ən), **1** sky-blue. **2** a sky-blue color. **1** *adj.,* **2** *n.*

Cer van tes (sər van′tēz), **Miguel de,** 1547-1616, Spanish author who wrote *Don Quixote.* *n.*

ce si um (sē′zē əm), a soft, silvery, metallic element which occurs as a minute part of various minerals. Scientists use the rate of vibration of cesium atoms as a standard for measuring time. *n.*

ces sa tion (se sā′shən), a ceasing; a stopping: *Both armies agreed on a cessation of the fighting.* *n.*

cess pool (ses′pül′), a pool or pit for house drains to empty into. *n.*

Cey lon (si lon′), island country in the Indian Ocean, just off S India, a member of the Commonwealth of Nations. Its official name is **Sri Lanka.** *Capital:* Colombo. See **India** for map. *n.*

Cey lo nese (sē′lə nēz′), **1** of Ceylon or its people. **2** person born or living in Ceylon. **1** *adj.,* **2** *n., pl.* **Cey lo nese.**

Cé zanne (sā zan′), **Paul,** 1839-1906, French painter. *n.*

cf., compare.

ch., **1** chapter. **2** church.

Cha co (chä′kō), vast, low-lying plain in N Argentina, S Bolivia, and W Paraguay. *n.*

Chad (chad), **1 Lake,** lake in N central Africa. **2 Republic of,** country in central Africa south of Libya, a member of the French Community. See **Algeria** for map. *n.*

chafe (chāf), **1** rub so as to wear away, scrape, or make sore: *The stiff collar chafed my neck.* **2** rub to make warm: *The mother chafed her child's cold hands.* **3** make or become angry: *His big sister's teasing chafed him. He chafed under his big sister's teasing.* *v.,* **chafed, chaf ing.**

chaff[1] (chaf), **1** husks of wheat, oats, rye, etc., especially when separated from grain by threshing. **2** hay or straw cut fine for feeding cattle. **3** worthless stuff; rubbish. *n.* [Old English *ceaf*]

chaff[2] (chaf), **1** make fun of in a good-natured way to one's face: *Her friends chaffed the girl about her inability to sing the school song on key.* **2** good-natured joking about a person to his face: *She did not mind her friend's chaff.* **1** *v.,* **2** *n.* [origin unknown]

chaf finch (chaf′inch), a European songbird with a pleasant, short song, often kept as a cage bird. *n., pl.* **chaf finch es.**

chaf ing dish (chā′fing), pan with a

heater under it, used to cook food at the table or to keep it warm.

cha grin (shə grin′), **1** a feeling of disappointment, failure, or humiliation: *I felt chagrin because I did not pass the test.* **2** cause to feel chagrin: *He was chagrined by his failure.* **1** *n.,* **2** *v.*

chain (chān), **1** series of links joined together: *The dog is fastened to a post by a chain.* **2** series of things linked together: *a chain of mountains, a chain of restaurants, a chain of events.* **3** join together with a chain; fasten with a chain: *The dog was chained to a post.* **4** anything that binds or restrains: *the chains of duty.* **5** bind; restrain: *Work chained him to his desk.* **6** keep in prison; make a slave of. **7 chains,** *pl.* **a** bonds; fetters: *The rebels were brought back in chains.* **b** imprisonment or bondage: *Enemies of the government spent many years in chains.* **8** a measuring instrument like a chain. A surveyor's chain is 66 feet long; an engineer's chain is 100 feet long. **1,2,4,7,8** *n.,* **3,5,6** *v.* **—chain′like′,** *adj.*

chain letter, letter which each person receiving is asked to copy and send to several others.

chain mail, kind of flexible armor used in the Middle Ages, made of metal rings linked together.

chain reaction, 1 process of releasing atomic energy by a series of nuclear fissions that continues automatically once it has been started. In a chain reaction, some of the neutrons given off by a nucleus that has been split collide with other nuclei, which, in turn, give off neutrons that collide with more nuclei. **2** any series of events or happenings, each caused by the preceding one or ones.

chain store, one of a group of stores owned and operated by the same company.

chair (cher *or* char), **1** seat that has a back and, sometimes, arms, usually for one person. **2** seat of rank, dignity, or authority. **3** position or authority of a person who has such a seat: *Professor Smith has the chair of astronomy at this college.* **4** chairman: *The chair called the meeting to order.* **5** conduct as chairman: *chair a meeting.* **1-4** *n.,* **5** *v.*

take the chair, preside at a meeting: *The vice-president took the chair when the president was ill.*

chair man (cher′mən *or* char′mən), **1** person who is in charge of a meeting. **2** person at the head of a committee. *n., pl.* **chair men.**

chair man ship (cher′mən ship *or* char′mən ship), position of chairman. *n.*

chaise (shāz), **1** a light, open carriage,

hat, āge, fär; let, ēqual, tėrm;
it, īce; hot, ōpen, ôrder;
oil, out; cup, pùt, rüle; ch, child;
ng, long; sh, she; th, thin;
ᵺ, then; zh, measure;

ə represents *a* in about,
e in taken, *i* in pencil,
o in lemon, *u* in circus.

usually with a folding top. **2** chaise longue. *n.*

chaise longue (shāz′ lông′), chair with a long seat and a back at one end, somewhat like a couch. [from French *chaise longue* long chair]

Chal de a (kal dē′ə), ancient region in SW Asia, on the Tigris and Euphrates rivers. See **Babylonia** for map. *n.* **—Chal de′an,** *adj., n.*

cha let (sha lā′), **1** a herdsman's hut or cabin in the Swiss mountains. **2** a Swiss house with wide, overhanging eaves. **3** any house like this. *n.*

chal ice (chal′is), **1** cup or goblet. **2** cup that holds the wine used in the Communion service. *n.*

chalk (chôk), **1** a soft, white or gray limestone, made up mostly of very small fossil seashells. Chalk is used for making lime and for writing or drawing. **2** a white or colored substance like chalk, used for writing or drawing on a blackboard or chalkboard. **3** mark, write, or draw with chalk: *The new teacher chalked her name on the blackboard.* **1,2** *n.,* **3** *v.* **—chalk′like′,** *adj.*

chalk up, 1 write down; record: *You learned your lesson the hard way and you can chalk it up to experience.* **2** score: *Our team chalked up 10 points.*

chalk board (chôk′bôrd′), a smooth, hard surface, used for writing or drawing on with crayon or chalk. *n.*

chalk y (chô′kē), **1** of chalk; containing chalk. **2** like chalk; white as chalk: *The clown's face was chalky.* *adj.,* **chalk i er, chalk i est.**

chal lenge (chal′ənj), **1** a call to a game or contest: *The champions accepted our team's challenge.* **2** call to a game or contest; dare: *The champion swimmer challenged anyone in the world to beat him.* **3** call to fight: *The knight challenged his rival to a duel.* **4** a call to fight: *His rival accepted the challenge.* **5** a call to answer and explain: *"Who goes there?" was the challenge of the soldier on guard.* **6** stop a person and question his right to do what he is doing or to be where he is: *When I tried to enter the building, the guard at the door challenged me.* **7** call in question;

adj.	adjective	*n.*	noun
adv.	adverb	*prep.*	preposition
conj.	conjunction	*pron.*	pronoun
interj.	interjection	*v.*	verb
sing.	singular	*pl.*	plural

doubt; dispute: *The teacher challenged my statement that rice grows in Oregon.* **8** a demand for proof of the truth of a statement; a doubting or questioning of the truth of a statement: *Her challenge led me to read widely about Oregon.* **9** anything that claims or commands effort, interest, feeling, etc.: *Fractions are a real challenge to her.* **10** claim or command effort, interest, feeling, etc.: *How to prevent disease is a problem that challenges everyone's attention.* **11** object to: *The attorney for the defense challenged the juror.* **12** objection: *The judge upheld the challenge and dismissed the juror from duty.* 1,4,5, 8,9,12 *n.,* 2,3,6,7,10,11 *v.,* **challenged, chal leng ing.**

chal leng er (chal/ən jər), person who challenges another or others. *n.*

chal lis or **chal lie** (shal/ē), a lightweight printed cloth of cotton, wool, or rayon, used for dresses, blouses, etc. *n.*

cham ber (chām/bər), **1** a room, especially a bedroom. **2** hall where lawmakers meet: *the council chamber.* **3** group of lawmakers: *The Congress of the United States has two chambers, the Senate and the House of Representatives.* **4** an enclosed space in the body of an animal or plant, or in some kinds of machinery. The heart has four chambers. The part of a gun that holds the charge is called the chamber. **5 chambers,** *pl.* **a** office of a lawyer or judge: *The judge met the two lawyers in his chambers.* **b** set of rooms in a building arranged for living or for offices. *n.*

cham bered (chām/bərd), having a chamber or chambers; divided into compartments. *adj.*

cham ber lain (chām/bər lən), **1** person who manages the household of a king or great noble. **2** a high official of a royal court. **3** treasurer. *n.*

cham ber maid (chām/bər mād/), maid who takes care of bedrooms in a house, hotel, or motel. *n.*

chamber music, music suited for performance in a room or small hall, as music for a trio or quartet.

chamber of commerce, group of businessmen organized to protect and promote the business interests of a city, state, or country.

cham bray (sham/brā), a cotton cloth

woven from white and colored threads, used for dresses and men's shirts. It is a kind of gingham. *n.*

cha me le on (kə mē/lē ən), **1** a small lizard that can change the color of its skin to blend with the surroundings. **2** a changeable or fickle person. *n.*

cham ois (sham/ē), **1** a small, goatlike antelope that lives in the high mountains of Europe and southwestern Asia. **2** a soft leather made from its skin or the skin of sheep, goats, or deer. *n., pl.* **cham ois.**

chamois (def. 1)—2½ ft. high at shoulder

champ¹ (champ), **1** bite and chew noisily: *champ food.* **2** bite and chew on impatiently: *The race horse champed its bit.* *v.* [perhaps an imitation of the sound of chewing]

champ² (champ), INFORMAL. champion. *n.* [shortened from *champion*]

cham pagne (sham pān/), a sparkling, bubbling white wine, first made in France. *n.* [from *Champagne,* a region in northern France]

cham pi on (cham/pē ən), **1** person, animal, or thing that wins first place in a game or contest: *He is the swimming champion of our school.* **2** that has won first place; ahead of all others: *a champion runner. My sister is the champion reader in our house.* **3** person who fights or speaks for another; person who defends a cause: *That writer is a great champion of peace.* **4** fight for; speak in behalf of; defend: *All his life he has championed freedom.* 1,3 *n.,* 2 *adj.,* 4 *v.*

cham pi on ship (cham/pē ən ship), **1** position of a champion; first place: *Our school won the championship in baseball.* **2** defense; support: *She undertook the championship of our cause.* *n.*

Cham plain (sham plān/), **1 Lake,** long, narrow lake between New York and Vermont. **2 Samuel de,** 1567-1635, French explorer who founded Quebec. *n.*

chance (chans), **1** favorable time; opportunity: *Now is your chance. I saw a chance to earn some money selling newspapers.* **2** likelihood of anything happening; possibility or probability: *There's a good chance that you will be well enough to return to school next week. The chances are against snow in May.* **3** fate, fortune, or luck: *Chance*

chameleon (def. 1) up to 1 ft. long

led to the finding of gold in California. **4** have the fortune; happen: *I chanced to meet an old friend today.* **5** a risk; gamble: *He took a big chance when he swam the wide river.* **6** take the risk of: *I will not chance driving in this awful blizzard.* **7** not expected or planned; accidental: *We had a chance visit from Grandmother and Grandfather last week.* **8** ticket in a raffle or lottery: *She bought two chances in the car raffle at the fair.* 1-3,5,8 *n.,* 4,6 *v.,* **chanced, chanc ing;** 7 *adj.*

by chance, accidentally: *It was only by chance that I found the keys you lost.*

chance upon or **chance on,** happen to find or meet: *I chanced upon an old friend.*

chan cel (chan/səl), the space around the altar of a church, used by the clergy and the choir. *n.*

chan cel lor (chan/sə lər), **1** the prime minister or other very high official of some European countries. **2** the chief judge of a chancery. **3** president of some universities. *n.*

Chancellor of the Exchequer, the British cabinet minister responsible for financial affairs.

chan cel lor ship (chan/sə lər ship), **1** position of a chancellor. **2** term of office of a chancellor. *n.*

chan cer y (chan/sər ē), court of law that deals with cases in which fairness and justice require a settlement not covered by either common law or statute law. *n., pl.* **chan cer ies.**

chanc y (chan/sē), uncertain; risky. *adj.,* **chanc i er, chanc i est.**

chan de lier (shan/də lir/), fixture with branches for lights, usually hanging from the ceiling. *n.*

chand ler (chand/lər), **1** maker or seller of candles. **2** dealer in groceries and supplies: *The yachtsman bought his provisions from a ship chandler.* *n.*

change (chānj), **1** make or become different: *She changed the room by painting the walls green. The wind changed from east to west.* **2** put or take (something) in place of another; substitute or exchange: *change soiled clothes for clean ones. Can you change a dollar bill for ten dimes? I changed seats with my brother.* **3** a changing; a passing from one form or place to another: *The change from flower to fruit is interesting to watch. Vacationing in the country is a pleasant change from city life.* **4** a changed condition: *Do you see any* change in his behavior? **5** thing to be used in place of another of the same kind: *He brought along a change of clothes.* **6** money returned to a person when he has given a larger amount than the price of what he buys: *I handed the clerk a quarter for the candy bar, and he gave me fifteen cents in change.* **7** money of smaller denomination given in place of money of larger denomination: *Please give me four quarters in change for this dollar bill.* **8** coins of small denomination: *She was carrying a dollar and some change.* **9** change one's clothes: *After swimming we went to the cabin and changed.* **10** transfer from one aircraft, train, bus, etc., to another: *Passengers must change here for Chicago.* 1,2,9,10 *v.*, **changed, chang ing;** 3-8 *n.*

change a ble (chān′jə bəl), **1** that can change; likely to change; varying; fickle: *April weather is changeable.* **2** having a color or appearance that changes: *Silk is called changeable when it shows different colors in different lights. adj.* —**change′a ble ness,** *n.*

change a bly (chān′jə blē), in a changeable manner; with constant change or variety. *adv.*

change ful (chānj′fəl), full of changes; likely to change; changing: *the changeful color of the sky at sunset. adj.*

change less (chānj′lis), not changing; not likely to change; constant: *the changeless heat of the desert sun. adj.* —**change′less ly,** *adv.* —**change′less ness,** *n.*

change ling (chānj′ling), **1** child secretly left in the place of another. **2** (in fairy tales) a child left by fairies in place of a child carried off by them. *n.*

chang er (chān′jər), person or thing that changes something: *a phonograph record changer. n.*

chan nel (chan′l), **1** the bed of a stream, river, etc.: *Rivers cut their own channels to the sea.* **2** body of water joining two larger bodies of water: *The English Channel lies between the North Sea and the Atlantic Ocean.* **3** the deeper part of a waterway: *There is shallow water on both sides of the channel in this river.* **4** passage for liquids; groove or canal: *the poison channel in a snake's fangs.* **5** the means by which something moves or is carried: *The information came through secret channels.* **6** form a channel in; wear or cut into a channel: *The river had channeled its way through the rocks.* **7** a narrow band of frequencies that carries the programs of a television or radio station. **8** course of action; field of activity: *He tried to find a suitable channel for his abilities.* **9** direct into a particular course: *Chan-*nel all your efforts into this one project, and you will succeed. 1-5,7,8 *n.*, 6,9 *v.*

Channel Islands, British islands near the NW coast of France. The most important are Alderney, Guernsey, and Jersey.

chant (chant), **1** song: *an Indian war chant.* **2** sing: *chant a melody.* **3** a short, simple song in which several syllables or words are sung in one tone. Chants are sometimes used in religious services. **4** sing in this way. A choir chants psalms or prayers. **5** a singsong way of talking. **6** keep talking about; say over and over again: *The football fans chanted, "Go, team, go!"* 1,3,5 *n.*, 2,4,6 *v.* —**chant′er,** *n.*

chan tey (shan′tē *or* chan′tē), song chanted by sailors in rhythm with the motions of their work. *n., pl.* **chan teys.** Also, **chanty** or **shanty.**

chan ti cleer (chan′tə klir), rooster. *n.*

chan ty (shan′tē *or* chan′tē), chantey. *n., pl.* **chan ties.**

CHAPS

Cha nu kah (hä′nə kə), Hanukkah. *n.*

cha os (kā′os), very great confusion; complete disorder: *The tornado left the town in chaos. n.*

cha ot ic (kā ot′ik), very confused; completely disordered: *The town was in a chaotic condition after the flood. adj.* —**cha ot′i cal ly,** *adv.*

chap¹ (chap), crack open; make or become rough: *A person's lips or skin often chap in cold weather. Cold weather chaps his skin. v.,* **chapped, chap ping.** [Middle English *chappen* cut off, chop]

chap² (chap), INFORMAL. fellow; man or boy: *Hello, old chap! n.* [shortened from the old word *chapman* peddler, Old English *cǣpman* tradesman]

chap el (chap′əl), **1** a building for worship, not as large as a church. **2** a small place for worship in a larger building: *a hospital chapel.* **3** a religious service in a chapel, especially in a school or college: *There is chapel today. n.*

chap e ron or **chap e rone** (shap′ə rōn′), **1** a married or older woman who accompanies a young girl or unmarried woman in public for the sake of good form and protection. **2** an older person who is present at a party or other social activity of younger people to see that good taste is observed. **3** act as a chaperon to. 1,2 *n.,* 3 *v.,* **chape roned, chap e ron ing.**

chap lain (chap′lən), clergyman authorized or appointed to perform religious functions for a family, court, society, public institution, or unit in the armed forces: *a hospital chaplain, a prison chaplain. n.*

chap lain cy (chap′lən sē), position of a chaplain. *n., pl.* **chap lain cies.**

chap let (chap′lit), **1** wreath worn on the head. **2** string of beads. *n.*

chaps (shaps *or* chaps), strong leather trousers without a back, worn over other trousers by cowboys. *n.pl.*

chap ter (chap′tər), **1** a main division of a book or other writing, dealing with a particular part of the story or subject. **2** anything like a chapter; part; section: *The first moon flight is an interesting chapter in space travel.* **3** a local division of an organization, which holds its own meetings; branch of a club, society, etc. *n.*

Cha pul te pec (chə pul′tə pek), fort on a rocky hill in SW Mexico City. United States troops captured the fort in 1847 during the Mexican War. *n.*

char (chär), **1** burn to charcoal. **2** burn enough to blacken; scorch: *After the fire a carpenter replaced the badly charred floor. v.,* **charred, char ring.**

char ac ter (kar′ik tər), **1** all the qualities or features of anything; kind; sort; nature: *I dislike people of that character. The soil on the prairies is of a different character from that in the mountains.* **2** moral nature; moral strength or weakness; the special way in which any person feels, thinks, and acts, considered as good or bad: *She has an honest, dependable character.* **3** moral firmness, self-control, or integrity: *a person with no character whatever. It takes character to endure hardship for very long.* **4** the estimate formed of a person's qualities; reputation. **5** a special quality or feature; trait; characteristic: *The trunk is a character found only in elephants.* **6** position or condition: *The treasurer of the club also*

hat, āge, fär; let, ēqual, tėrm; it, īce; hot, ōpen, ôrder; oil, out; cup, pùt, rüle; ch, child; ng, long; sh, she; th, thin; ᵺ, then; zh, measure;

ə represents *a* in about, *e* in taken, *i* in pencil, *o* in lemon, *u* in circus.

adj. adjective	*n.* noun
adv. adverb	*prep.* preposition
conj. conjunction	*pron.* pronoun
interj. interjection	*v.* verb
sing. singular	*pl.* plural

serves in the character of secretary. **7** person or animal in a play, poem, story, or book: *His favorite character in "Charlotte's Web" is Wilbur, the pig.* **8** INFORMAL. person who attracts attention because he is different or odd: *The old captain was a character in the village.* **9** letter, mark, or sign used in writing or printing: *There are 52 characters in our alphabet, consisting of 26 small letters and 26 capital letters. n.*

in character, as expected; natural or usual: *It is in character for her to be on time.*

out of character, not as expected; not natural or usual: *It is out of character for small children to sit still for a long time.*

char ac ter is tic (kar/ik tə ris/tik), **1** marking off or distinguishing a certain person or thing from others; special: *Bananas have their own characteristic smell.* **2** a special quality or feature; whatever distinguishes one person or thing from others: *Cheerfulness is a characteristic that we admire in people. An elephant's trunk is its most noticeable characteristic.* **1** *adj.,* **2** *n.*

char ac ter is ti cal ly (kar/ik tə ris/tik lē), in a way that shows characteristics; specially; typically. *adv.*

char ac ter i za tion (kar/ik tər ə zā/shən), **1** a characterizing; description of characteristics. **2** creation of characters in a play or book. *n.*

char ac ter ize (kar/ik tə rīz/), **1** describe the special qualities or features of: *The story of "Red Riding Hood" characterizes the wolf as a cunning and savage beast.* **2** be a characteristic of; distinguish: *A camel is characterized by the humps on its back and its ability to go without water for several days. v.,* **char ac ter ized, char ac ter iz ing.**

cha rade (shə rād/). Often, **charades,** *pl.* game in which one player acts out a word or phrase and the others try to guess what it is. If the word he wants guessed is *penmanship,* the player might act out "pen," "man," and "ship." *n.*

char coal (chär/kōl/), a black, brittle form of carbon made by partly burning wood or bones in a place from which the air is shut out. Charcoal is used as fuel, in filters, and for drawing. *n.*

charge (chärj), **1** ask as a price; ask a price: *The grocer charged 75 cents a dozen for eggs. This store charges for delivery.* **2** price asked for or put on something: *The charge for delivery is $3.* **3** put down as a debt to be paid: *The dairy will charge for the milk delivered during the month and send a bill at the end of the month.* **4** a debt to be paid: *Taxes are a charge on property.* **5** load or fill: *He charged the gun with powder and shot. The battery in our car needs to be charged with electricity.* **6** amount needed to load or fill something. A gun is fired by exploding the charge of powder and shot. A car is started by drawing out a part of the charge of electricity accumulated in the battery. **7** give a task, duty, or responsibility to: *Mother charged me to take good care of my baby sister.* **8** task; duty; responsibility: *I accepted the charge to take good care of my baby sister.* **9** care; management: *Doctors and nurses have charge of sick people.* **10** person or thing under the care or management of someone: *Sick people are the charges of doctors and nurses.* **11** give an order or command to; direct: *She charged us to keep the plan secret. The judge charged the jury to come to a fair decision.* **12** an order; command; direction: *a judge's charge to the jury to arrive at a verdict.* **13** accuse: *The driver was charged with speeding.* **14** accusation: *He admitted the truth of the charge and paid a fine.* **15** rush with force; attack: *The soldiers charged the enemy. The captain gave the order to charge.* **16** an attack: *The charge drove the enemy back.* **1,3,5,7, 11,13,15** *v.,* **charged, charg ing; 2,4, 6,8-10,12,14,16** *n.*

charge off, 1 subtract as a loss: *The store owner charged off money which had been owed him for over three years as bad debts.* **2** put down as belonging: *A bad mistake must be charged off to experience.*

in charge, having the care or management: *The mate is in charge when the captain leaves the boat.*

in charge of, 1 having the care or management of: *My sister is in charge of the book department of the store.* **2** under the care or management of: *Furniture is in charge of another salesman.*

charge a ble (chär/jə bəl), **1** that can be charged: *The salesman's travel expenses are chargeable to the company.* **2** liable to be charged: *If a person steals he is chargeable with theft. adj.*

charge account, record kept at a store of things bought by a person on credit. A customer with a charge account receives and uses what he purchases and pays for it later.

charg er (chär/jər), **1** a war horse. **2** person or thing that charges. **3** device that gives an electrical charge to storage batteries. *n.*

char i ly (cher/ə lē *or* char/ə lē), **1** cautiously. **2** shyly. **3** stingily. *adv.*

char i ness (cher/ē nis *or* char/ē nis), **1** caution. **2** shyness. **3** stinginess. *n.*

Roman chariot

char i ot (char/ē ət), a two-wheeled carriage pulled by horses. The chariot was used in ancient times for fighting, for racing, and in processions. *n.*

char i ot eer (char/ē ə tir/), person who drives a chariot. *n.*

cha ris ma (kə riz/mə), a mysterious power to fascinate and attract; great personal magnetism or glamor: *the charisma of a popular leader. n.*

char i ta ble (char/ə tə bəl), **1** generous in giving to poor, sick, or helpless people; benevolent and kind: *He was a charitable man who used his wealth to give contributions to the relief of sickness and poverty.* **2** of or for charity: *The Salvation Army is a charitable organization.* **3** kindly in judging people and their actions; lenient: *Grandparents are usually charitable toward the mistakes of their grandchildren. adj.*

—char/i ta ble ness, *n.*

char i ta bly (char/ə tə blē), in a charitable manner; with charity. *adv.*

char i ty (char/ə tē), **1** generous giving to the poor, or to organizations which look after the sick, the poor, and the helpless: *The charity of our citizens enabled the hospital to purchase new beds.* **2** fund or organization for helping the sick, the poor, and the helpless: *She gives money regularly to the community chest and to other charities.* **3** kindness in judging people's faults. **4** love of one's fellow men: *The Bible says, "And now abideth faith, hope, and charity, and the greatest of these is charity." n., pl.* **char i ties.**

char la tan (shär/lə tən), person who pretends to have more knowledge or skill than he really has; quack. *n.*

Char le magne (shär/lə mān), A.D. 742?-814, king of the Franks from A.D. 768 to 814 and emperor of the Holy Roman Empire from A.D. 800 to 814. He made many reforms in government and education in western Europe. He was called "Charles the Great." *n.*

Charles I (chärlz), 1600-1649, king of England from 1625 until he was convicted of treason and executed in 1649.

Charles II, 1630-1685, king of England from 1660 to 1685. He was the son of Charles I.

Charles ton (chärlz′tən), 1 capital of West Virginia, in the W part. 2 seaport in SE South Carolina. 3 a lively ballroom dance, especially popular in the 1920's. *n.*

char ley horse (chär′lē), INFORMAL. stiffness or cramp in a muscle, especially of the leg or arm.

Char lotte town (shär′lət toun), capital of Prince Edward Island, Canada. *n.*

charm (chärm), 1 power of delighting or fascinating; attractiveness: *Our grandmother's house never lost its charm for our family.* 2 a pleasing quality or feature: *The book has many charms; the chief one is its delightful humor.* 3 please greatly; delight; fascinate; attract: *The children were charmed by the neighbor's pet raccoon.* 4 a small ornament or trinket worn on a bracelet, watch chain, etc. 5 word, verse, act, or thing supposed to have magic power to help or harm people. 6 act on as if by magic: *His grandchildren's laughter charmed away the old man's troubles.* 1,2,4,5 *n.,* 3,6 *v.*

charmed (chärmd), protected as by a charm: *The pilot led a charmed life in which he narrowly survived many accidents.* *adj.*

charm er (chär′mər), one that charms, delights, or fascinates. *n.*

charm ing (chär′ming), very pleasing; delightful; fascinating; attractive: *We saw a charming play. They are a charming couple.* *adj.* —**charm′ing ly,** *adv.*

char nel house (chär′nl), place where dead bodies or bones are laid.

Char on (ker′ən *or* kar′ən), (in Greek myths) the boatman who ferried the spirits of the dead across the river Styx to Hades. *n.*

chart (chärt), 1 map used by sailors to show the coasts, rocks, and shallow places of the sea. The course of a ship is marked on a chart. 2 an outline map showing special conditions or facts: *This weather chart shows where rain fell over the United States yesterday.* 3 sheet of information arranged in lists, pictures, tables, or diagrams: *Our history book has a chart of the Presidents of the United States.* 4 make a chart of; show on a chart: *The navigator charted the course of the ship.* 5 plan in detail: *The explorers charted their expedition with great care.* 1-3 *n.,* 4,5 *v.*

char ter (chär′tər), 1 a written grant by a government to a colony, a group of citizens, a corporation, etc., bestowing the right of organization, with other privileges, and specifying the form of organization: *The proposed new airline must obtain a government charter.* 2 a written order from the authorities of a society, giving to a group of persons the right to organize a new chapter, branch, or lodge. 3 document setting forth aims and purposes of a group of nations, organizations, or individuals in a common undertaking: *the Charter of the United Nations.* 4 give a charter to: *The government chartered the new airline.* 5 hire: *Our school chartered a bus to take the class to the zoo.* 1-3 *n.,* 4,5 *v.*

chassis (def. 1)

Char tres (shär′trə), city in N France. Its Gothic cathedral is over 700 years old. *n.*

char treuse (shär trüz′), 1 a light, yellowish green. 2 light yellowish-green. 1 *n.,* 2 *adj.*

char wom an (chär′wùm′ən), woman who is hired to clean and scrub homes, offices, and public buildings. *n., pl.* **char wom en.**

char y (cher′ē *or* char′ē), 1 showing caution; careful; wary: *The cat was chary of getting its paws wet.* 2 shy: *A bashful person is chary of strangers.* 3 sparing; stingy: *A jealous person is chary of praising those who do well.* *adj.,* **char i er, char i est.**

Cha ryb dis (kə rib′dis), 1 whirlpool supposedly located in the strait between Sicily and Italy, opposite the rock Scylla. 2 (in Greek myths) a monster that sucked down ships. *n.*

chase (chās), 1 run or follow after to catch or kill: *The cat chased the mouse.* 2 drive away: *The blue jay chased the squirrel from its nest.* 3 run after; follow; pursue: *The boys chased the ball as it rolled downhill.* 4 act of chasing: *We watched the children in their chase after butterflies.* 5 hunting as a sport; hunt: *The fox hunter was devoted to the chase.* 6 a hunted animal: *The chase escaped the hunter.* 1-3 *v.,* **chased, chas ing;** 4-6 *n.*

give chase, run after; pursue: *The fox gave chase as soon as it spotted the rabbit.*

chas er (chā′sər), person or thing that chases. *n.*

chasm (kaz′əm), 1 a deep opening or crack in the earth; gap. 2 a wide difference of feelings or interests between two persons or groups: *The chasm between England and the Ameri-*

can colonies finally led to the Revolutionary War. *n.*

chas sis (chas′ē *or* shas′ē), 1 the frame, wheels, and machinery of a motor vehicle that support the body. 2 the main landing gear that supports the body of an aircraft. 3 the base or frame for the parts of a radio or television set. *n., pl.* **chas sis** (chas′ēz *or* shas′ēz).

chaste (chāst), 1 pure; virtuous. 2 decent; modest. 3 simple in taste or style; not too much ornamented. *adj.* —**chaste′ly,** *adv.* —**chaste′ness,** *n.*

chas ten (chā′sn), 1 punish to improve; discipline: *chasten a child.* 2 restrain from excess or crudeness; moderate. 3 make chaste or pure; purify; refine. *v.* —**chas′ten er,** *n.*

chas tise (cha stīz′), 1 inflict punishment or suffering on to improve; punish. 2 criticize or rebuke severely. *v.,* **chas tised, chas tis ing.**

chas tise ment (cha stīz′mənt), 1 punishment. 2 a severe criticism or rebuke. *n.*

chas tis er (cha stī′zər), person who chastises. *n.*

chas ti ty (chas′tə tē), 1 purity; virtue. 2 decency; modesty. 3 simplicity of style or taste; absence of too much decoration. *n.*

chas u ble (chaz′yə bəl), a sleeveless outer vestment worn by the priest at Mass. *n.*

chat (chat), 1 easy, familiar talk: *The two friends had a pleasant chat about old times.* 2 talk in an easy, familiar way: *We sat chatting by the fire after supper.* 3 any of several birds with a chattering cry. 1,3 *n.,* 2 *v.,* **chat ted, chat ting.**

châ teau (sha tō′), 1 a large country house in France or elsewhere in Europe. 2 a French castle. *n., pl.* **châ teaux** (sha tōz′). [from French *château,* from Latin *castellum* castle]

Chat ta noo ga (chat′n ü′gə), city in SE Tennessee. *n.*

chat tel (chat′l), piece of property that is not real estate; any movable possession. Furniture, automobiles, and animals are chattels. *n.*

adj.	adjective	*n.*	noun
adv.	adverb	*prep.*	preposition
conj.	conjunction	*pron.*	pronoun
interj.	interjection	*v.*	verb
sing.	singular	*pl.*	plural

chat ter (chat/ər), 1 talk quickly and foolishly about unimportant things: *The children chattered about the circus.* 2 quick, foolish talk about unimportant things: *The pupils' chatter disturbed the classroom.* 3 make quick, indistinct sounds: *Monkeys chatter.* 4 quick, indistinct sounds: *The continual chatter of the sparrows annoyed her.* 5 rattle together: *Cold can make a person's teeth chatter.* 6 sound of rattling together: *the chatter of teeth.* 1,3,5 *v.,* 2,4,6 *n.* —**chat/ter er,** *n.*

chat ter box (chat/ər boks/), person who chatters. *n., pl.* **chat ter box es.**

chat ti ly (chat/l ē), in a chatty manner. *adv.*

chat ti ness (chat/ē nis), quality of being chatty; talkativeness. *n.*

chat ty (chat/ē), 1 fond of friendly, familiar talk about unimportant things. 2 having the style or manner of friendly, familiar talk: *a chatty article about current fashions in the newspaper.* *adj.,* **chat ti er, chat ti est.**

Chau cer (chô/sər), **Geoffrey,** 1340?-1400, English poet, author of *The Canterbury Tales.* *n.*

chauf feur (shō/fər *or* shō fèr/), 1 person whose work is driving an automobile. 2 act as a chauffeur to; drive around. 1 *n.,* 2 *v.*

chau vin ism (shō/və niz/əm), boastful, warlike patriotism; an unreasoning enthusiasm for the military glory of one's country. *n.* [from French *chauvinisme,* from Nicolas *Chauvin,* a very devoted soldier in Napoleon's army]

chau vin ist (shō/və nist), a boastful, warlike patriot. *n.*

cheap (chēp), 1 costing little: *Eggs are cheap out in the country.* 2 costing less than it is worth: *My new sweater will be cheap, because I am going to buy the yarn and knit it myself.* 3 charging low prices: *He bought that suit at a very cheap department store.* 4 costing little effort; easily obtained: *He thinks that the cheapest way to make friends is to give them presents.* 5 of little value; not worth respect; common: *cheap entertainment.* 6 at a low price; at small cost: *I sold the car cheap to get rid of it.* 1-5 *adj.,* 6 *adv.* —**cheap/ly,** *adv.* —**cheap/ness,** *n.*

feel cheap, feel inferior and ashamed: *I felt cheap about forgetting my best friend's birthday.*

cheap en (chē/pən), 1 make or become cheap; lower the price of. 2 cause to be thought little of. *v.*

cheap skate (chēp/skāt/), INFORMAL. person who is very stingy. *n.*

cheat (chēt), 1 play or do business in a way that is not honest; deceive or trick: *I hate to play games with a person who cheats. That cashier cheated me out of fifty-five cents in change.* 2 person who is not honest and does things to deceive or trick others. 3 fraud; trick. 1 *v.,* 2,3 *n.* —**cheat/er,** *n.*

check (chek), 1 stop suddenly: *The tennis player checked her swing as the ball went out of bounds.* 2 a sudden stop: *The storm warning put a check to our plans for a picnic.* 3 hold back; control; restrain: *check one's anger, check a forest fire.* 4 a holding back; control; restraint: *Keep a check on a child.* 5 any person, thing, or event that controls or holds back action. A rein used to prevent a horse from lowering his head is a check. 6 prove true or right by comparing or examining: *Check your watch with the school clock.* 7 examination or comparison to prove something true or right: *My work will be a check on yours.* 8 a mark (✔) to show that something has been examined or compared. Usually this mark indicates that the thing is true or right. Sometimes, as on examinations, it indicates something false or wrong. 9 to mark (something examined or compared) with a check: *How many answers did the teacher check as wrong?* 10 ticket or metal piece given in return for a coat, hat, baggage, package, etc., left for safekeeping, to show ownership or the right to claim again later: *Give your check to the man in the checkroom when you want your coat.* 11 leave or take for safekeeping: *He checked his hat at the door of the club. The hotel checked our baggage.* 12 a written order directing a bank to pay money to the person named; cheque: *My parents pay most of their bills by check.* 13 a written statement of the amount owed in a restaurant: *After our meal the waitress brought the check to our table.* 14 to mark in a pattern of squares. 15 a pattern made of squares: *Do you want a check or a stripe for your new suit?* 16 a single one of these squares: *The checks in this dress are big.* 17 in chess: **a** position of an opponent's king when it is in danger. A king in check must be moved, or the threatening piece must be blocked off or removed. **b** put (an opponent's king) in this position. 1,3,6,9,11,14,17b *v.,* 2,4, 5,7,8,10,12,13,15-17a *n.*

check in, arrive and register at a hotel, motel, etc.: *We checked in and were then shown to our rooms.*

check out, 1 pay one's bill at a hotel, motel, etc., when leaving: *We loaded the car while Father checked out at the desk.* 2 inspect or examine to see if in proper order, condition, etc.: *The mechanic checked out the plane before takeoff.* 3 prove right or true: *check out a fact or statement.*

check up, examine or compare to prove true or correct: *If you are not sure, you ought to check up on the facts.*

in check, held back; controlled: *He kept his temper in check.*

check book (chek/bùk/), book of blank checks on a bank. *n.*

check er¹ (chek/ər), 1 to mark in a pattern of squares of different colors. 2 pattern made of such squares. 3 one of these squares. 4 one of the flat, round pieces used in the game of checkers. 1 *v.,* 2-4 *n.* [from French of the 1200's *eschequier* chessboard]

check er² (chek/ər), person or thing that checks: *The checker in our supermarket checked out the merchandise at the counter.* *n.* [*check + -er¹*]

check er board (chek/ər bôrd/), board marked in a pattern of 64 squares of two alternating colors, used in playing checkers or chess; chessboard. *n.*

check ered (chek/ərd), 1 marked in a pattern of squares of different colors: *a checkered tablecloth.* 2 marked in patches. 3 often changing; varied; irregular: *a checkered career.* *adj.*

check ers (chek/ərz), game played by two people, each with 12 round, flat pieces to move on a checkerboard. The object of the game is to capture all the opponent's pieces or to prevent them from being able to move. *n.*

check list (chek/list/), list of names, titles, jobs, etc., arranged to form a ready means of reference, comparison, or checking: *The pilot went over the flight checklist before takeoff.* *n.*

check mate (chek/māt/), 1 in chess: **a** put (an opponent's king) in check from which his next move cannot free him, and so win the game. **b** a move that ends the game by putting the opponent's king in check so that he is unable to escape by his next move. 2 defeat completely. 3 a complete defeat. 1a, 2 *v.,* **check mat ed, check mat ing;** 1b, 3 *n.*

check point (chek/point/), place of inspection on a road, at a border, etc. *n.*

check rein (chek/rān/), 1 a short rein to keep a horse from lowering its head. 2 a short rein connecting the bit of one of a team of horses to the driving rein of the other. *n.*

check room (chek/rùm/ *or* chek/- rùm/), place where coats, hats, baggage, etc., can be left for safekeeping until called for later. *n.*

check up (chek′up′), 1 a careful inspection or examination: *The manager gave the store a final checkup before closing for the night.* 2 a thorough physical examination: *The doctor asked the patient to come to her office for a checkup.* *n.*

Ched dar (ched′ər), kind of hard, white or yellow cheese. *n.* [from *Cheddar,* a town in England, where it was first made]

cheek (chēk), 1 side of the face below either eye. 2 INFORMAL. saucy talk or behavior; impudence: *He had the cheek to tell the teacher she was completely wrong.* *n.*

cheek bone (chēk′bōn′), bone just below either eye. *n.*

cheek i ly (chē′kə lē), in a saucy, impudent manner. *adv.*

cheek i ness (chē′kē nis), cheeky quality; impudence. *n.*

cheek y (chē′kē), saucy; impudent. *adj.,* **cheek i er, cheek i est.**

cheep (chēp), 1 make a short, sharp sound such as a young bird makes; chirp; peep. 2 a young bird's cry. 1 *v.,* 2 *n.*

cheer (chir), 1 a shout of encouragement, approval, praise, etc.: *Give three cheers for the players who won the game.* 2 shout encouragement, approval, praise, etc.: *We all cheered loudly.* 3 urge on with cheers: *Everyone cheered our team.* 4 joy or gladness; comfort: *The warmth of the fire and a good meal brought cheer to our hearts again.* 5 give joy to; make glad; comfort: *It cheered our sick friend to have us visit him.* 6 state of mind; condition of feeling: *His friends encouraged him to be of good cheer.* 1,4,6 *n.,* 2,3,5 *v.* —**cheer′er,** *n.*

cheer up, brighten up; be or make glad; raise one's spirits: *The sick girl said that our visit cheered her up. Cheer up, perhaps we'll win the next game.*

cheer ful (chir′fəl), 1 full of cheer; joyful; glad: *She is a smiling, cheerful girl.* 2 filling with cheer; pleasant; bright: *This is a cheerful, sunny room.* 3 willing: *I appreciate a cheerful helper.* *adj.* —**cheer′ful ly,** *adv.* —**cheer′ful ness,** *n.*

cheer i ly (chir′ə lē), in a cheerful or cheery manner; cheerfully. *adv.*

cheer i ness (chir′ē nis), condition of being cheerful or cheery; cheerfulness. *n.*

cheer lead er (chir′lē′dər), person who leads a group in organized cheering, especially at high school or college athletic events. *n.*

cheer less (chir′lis), without joy or comfort; gloomy; dreary. *adj.*

—**cheer′less ly,** *adv.* —**cheer′less ness,** *n.*

cheer y (chir′ē), cheerful; pleasant; bright; gay: *a cheery smile. Sunshine and the singing of birds are cheery.* *adj.,* **cheer i er, cheer i est.**

cheese (chēz), a solid food made from the curds of milk. Most cheeses are pressed or molded into a shape and are often covered with a rind. *n.*

cheese burg er (chēz′ber′gər), a hamburger sandwich with a slice of melted cheese on top of the meat. *n.*

cheese cloth (chēz′klôth′), a thin, loosely woven cotton cloth, first used for wrapping cheese. *n., pl.* **cheese-cloths** (chēz′klôᴛнz′ or chēz′klôths′).

chees y (chē′zē), 1 of or like cheese. 2 SLANG. of low quality; inferior. *adj.,* **chees i er, chees i est.**

cheetah
2½ ft. high at the shoulder

chee tah (chē′tə), a flesh-eating mammal somewhat like a leopard, found in southern Asia and Africa. Cheetahs run very fast and can be trained to hunt deer and antelope. *n.*

chef (shef), 1 a head cook: *the chef of a large restaurant.* 2 any cook. *n.*

chem i cal (kem′ə kəl), 1 of, having to do with, or in chemistry: *Chemical research has made possible many new products.* 2 made by or used in chemistry: *The burning of coal is a process of chemical change in which oxygen in the air unites with carbon from the coal, giving off light and heat.* 3 any substance obtained by or used in a chemical process. Sulfuric acid, sodium bicarbonate, and borax are chemicals. 4 working, operated, or done by using chemicals: *a chemical fire extinguisher.* 1,2,4 *adj.,* 3 *n.*

chemical engineering, science or profession of using chemistry for industrial purposes.

chem i cal ly (kem′ik lē), 1 according to chemistry. 2 by chemical processes. *adv.*

che mise (shə mēz′), 1 a loose, shirt-like undergarment worn by women and girls. 2 a loosely fitting dress without a belt. *n.*

chem ist (kem′ist), 1 an expert in chemistry. 2 druggist (a term used in Great Britain). *n.*

chem is try (kem′ə strē), 1 science that deals with the characteristics of elements, the changes that take place when they combine to form substances, and the laws of their behavior under

hat, āge, fär; let, ēqual, tèrm;
it, īce; hot, ōpen, ôrder;
oil, out; cup, pút, rüle; ch, child;
ng, long; sh, she; th, thin;
ᴛн, then; zh, measure;

ə represents *a* in about,
e in taken, *i* in pencil,
o in lemon, *u* in circus.

various conditions. 2 the application of this science to a certain subject: *the chemistry of foods.* *n., pl.* **chem is tries.**

che nille (shə nēl′), 1 a velvety cord, used in embroidery, fringe, etc. 2 fabric woven from this cord, used for rugs, curtains, etc. *n.*

Che ops (kē′ops), 2600? B.C., king of Egypt who built the largest of the Pyramids. *n.*

cheque (chek), check (def. 12). *Cheque* is the spelling generally used in Great Britain and Canada. *n.*

Cher bourg (sher′bùrg), seaport in NW France, on the English Channel. *n.*

cher ish (cher′ish), 1 hold dear; treat with affection; care for tenderly: *Parents cherish their children.* 2 keep in mind; cling to: *We all cherished the hope of their safe return from the dangerous journey.* *v.*

Cher o kee (cher′ə kē), 1 member of a tribe of American Indians of the southern Appalachians, now living mostly in Oklahoma. 2 their language. *n., pl.* **Cher o kee** or **Cher o kees.**

cher ry (cher′ē), 1 a small, round, juicy fruit with a stone or pit in it. Cherries are good to eat. 2 the tree that it grows on. 3 the wood of this tree. 4 a bright red. 5 bright-red. 1-4 *n., pl.* **cher ries;** 5 *adj.* —**cher′ry like′,** *adj.*

cher ub (cher′əb), 1 angel. 2 picture or statue of a child with wings, or of a child's head with wings. 3 a beautiful, innocent, or good child. 4 person with a chubby face. *n., pl.* **cher u bim** for 1 and 2, **cher ubs** for 3 and 4.

che ru bic (chə rü′bik), 1 of or like a cherub; angelic. 2 innocent; good. 3 chubby. *adj.* —**che ru′bi cal ly,** *adv.*

cher u bim (cher′ə bim), 1 a plural of **cherub** (defs. 1 and 2). 2 (formerly) cherub. 1 *n.pl.,* 2 *n.sing.*

Ches a peake Bay (ches′ə pēk′), bay of the Atlantic, in Maryland and Virginia.

Chesh ire cat (chesh′ər), 1 the grinning cat in *Alice in Wonderland.* It faded away until finally only its grin was left. 2 any creature that grins fixedly. [from *Cheshire,* a county in England]

adj.	adjective	*n.*	noun
adv.	adverb	*prep.*	preposition
conj.	conjunction	*pron.*	pronoun
interj.	interjection	*v.*	verb
sing.	singular	*pl.*	plural

chess (ches), game played by two people, each with 16 pieces to move on a checkerboard. The object of the game is to checkmate the other's king. *n.*

chess board (ches′bôrd′), checkerboard. *n.*

chess man (ches′man′), one of the pieces used in playing chess. *n., pl.* **chess men.**

chest (chest), 1 part of a person's or an animal's body enclosed by ribs. 2 a large box with a lid, used for holding things: *a linen chest, a medicine chest, a tool chest.* 3 piece of furniture with drawers: *I put my new shirt in the clothes chest.* 4 place where money is kept; treasury. 5 the money itself. *n.*

ches ter field (ches′tər fēld′), 1 a single-breasted overcoat with the buttons hidden and a velvet collar. 2 sofa (a term used in Great Britain and Canada). *n.* [from the fourth Earl of *Chesterfield*, 1694-1773]

chest nut (ches′nut), 1 a large tree that bears nuts in prickly burs. The chestnut belongs to the same family as the beech. 2 the sweet nut of this tree. 3 the wood of this tree. 4 a reddish brown. 5 reddish-brown. 6 a reddish-brown horse. 1-4,6 *n.,* 5 *adj.*

chev a lier (shev′ə lir′), OLD USE. knight. *n.*

chev i ot (shev′ē ət), 1 a rough, woolen cloth. 2 a cotton cloth like it. *n.*

chev ron (shev′rən), a cloth design shaped like Λ or V, worn on the sleeve by noncommissioned officers, policemen, etc., as an indication of rank or length of service. *n.*

chew (chü), 1 crush or grind with the teeth: *We chew food.* 2 a chewing: *The puppy gave the rag a good chew.* 3 thing chewed; piece for chewing. 1 *v.,* 2,3 *n.*

chew i ness (chü′ē nis), chewy quality: *the chewiness of caramel. n.*

chewing gum, gum for chewing. It is usually chicle that has been sweetened and flavored.

che wink (chi wingk′), bird of eastern and central North America whose cry sounds somewhat like its name; towhee. The chewink is a kind of finch. *n.*

chew y (chü′ē), requiring much chewing: *chewy caramels. adj.,* **chew i er, chew i est.**

Chey enne (shī an′ *or* shī en′ *for 1,2;*

shī en′ *for 3,4),* 1 capital of Wyoming, in the SE part. 2 river flowing from E Wyoming into the Missouri River in South Dakota. 3 member of an Algonquian tribe of Indians, now living in Montana and Oklahoma. 4 their language. *n., pl.* **Chey enne** or **Chey ennes** for 3.

Chiang Kai-shek (chyäng′ kī′-shek′), born 1886, Chinese general and political leader, president of Nationalist China since 1948.

chic (shēk), 1 up-to-date in fashion; stylish: *a chic new suit.* 2 style: *She is famous for her chic.* 1 *adj.,* 2 *n.*

Chi ca go (shə kô′gō *or* shə kä′gō), city in NE Illinois, on Lake Michigan. Chicago is the second largest city in the United States. *n.*

chi can er y (shi kā′nər ē), low trickery; unfair practice: *He used chicanery to outwit his partner and take over the business. n., pl.* **chi can er ies.**

Chi ca no (chi kä′nō), an American of Mexican descent; Mexican American. *n.*

chick (chik), 1 a young chicken. 2 a young bird. 3 child. *n.*

chick a dee (chik′ə dē′), a small bird with black, white, and gray feathers, and usually a black head. Its cry sounds somewhat like its name. *n.*

Chick a mau ga (chik′ə mô′gə), a small creek flowing from NW Georgia into the Tennessee River. The Confederates defeated the Union army there in 1863. *n.*

Chick a saw (chik′ə sô), 1 member of a tribe of American Indians, now living in western Oklahoma. 2 their language. *n., pl.* **Chick a saw** or **Chick a saws.**

chick en (chik′ən), 1 a young hen or rooster. 2 any hen or rooster. 3 flesh of a chicken used for food: *fried chicken.* 4 any young bird. 5 SLANG. afraid of risk; cowardly. 1-4 *n.,* 5 *adj.*

chick en-heart ed (chik′ən här′tid), timid; cowardly. *adj.*

chicken pox, a mild, contagious disease of children, accompanied by a rash on the skin.

chick weed (chik′wēd′), a common weed with small white flowers. The leaves and seeds are eaten by birds. *n.*

chic le (chik′əl), a tasteless, gummy substance used in making chewing gum. It is the dried milky juice of a tree of tropical America. *n.*

chic or y (chik′ər ē), 1 plant with bright blue flowers whose leaves are used for salad. 2 its root, roasted and used as a substitute for coffee or for mixing with coffee. *n., pl.* **chic or ies.**

chid (chid), chided; a past tense and a past participle of **chide.** *v.*

chide (chīd), find fault with; blame; scold: *My uncle chided me for playing in

his flower garden. v.,* **chid ed** or **chid, chid ing.**

chief (chēf), 1 head of a group; person highest in rank or authority; leader: *the chief of an Indian tribe; a police chief.* 2 at the head; in authority; leading: *the chief engineer of a building project, the chief officer at an army post.* 3 most important; main: *the chief town in the county. The chief thing on my mind was dinner.* 1 *n.,* 2,3 *adj.*

in chief, at the head; of the highest rank or authority: *commander in chief of an army, editor in chief of a book.*

chief executive, 1 head of the executive branch of a government. 2 **Chief Executive,** the President of the United States or the governor of a state.

chief justice, 1 judge who acts as chairman of a group of judges in a court. 2 **Chief Justice,** the presiding judge of the United States Supreme Court.

chief ly (chēf′lē), 1 for the most part; mainly; mostly: *This juice is made up chiefly of tomatoes.* 2 first of all; above all: *We visited Washington chiefly to see the Capitol and the White House. adv.*

Chief of Staff, the senior officer of the Army or Air Force of the United States.

chief tain (chēf′tən), 1 chief of a clan or tribe: *a Highland chieftain.* 2 head of a group; leader. *n.*

chief tain cy (chēf′tən sē), position or rank of a chieftain. *n., pl.* **chief tain cies.**

chif fon (shi fon′), 1 a very thin silk or rayon cloth, used for dresses. 2 whipped light and fluffy: *lemon chiffon pie.* 1 *n.,* 2 *adj.*

chif fo nier (shif′ə nir′), a high chest of drawers, often having a mirror. *n.*

chig ger (chig′ər), larva of certain mites. Chiggers stick to the skin and suck the blood, causing severe itching. *n.*

chi gnon (shē′nyon), knot or roll of hair worn at the back of the head by women. *n.*

Chihuahua
7 in. high
at the shoulder

Chi hua hua (chi wä′wä), a very small dog of an ancient Mexican breed, usually weighing from one to six pounds. *n., pl.* **Chi hua huas.** [from *Chihuahua,* a state and city in Mexico]

chil blain (chil′blān′). Usually, **chil-**

blains, *pl.* an itching sore or redness on the hands or feet caused chiefly by exposure to cold. *n.*

child (chīld), 1 a young boy or girl: *games for children.* 2 son or daughter: *Parents love their children.* 3 baby; infant. *n., pl.* **chil dren.**

child birth (chīld/bėrth/), act of giving birth to a child. *n.*

child hood (chīld/hůd), 1 condition of being a child. 2 time during which one is a child. *n.*

child ish (chīl/dish), 1 of a child. 2 like a child. 3 not suitable for a grown person; weak; silly: *Crying for things you can't have is childish. adj.* —**child/ish ly,** *adv.* —**child/ish ness,** *n.*

child less (chīld/lis), having no child. *adj.* —**child/less ness,** *n.*

child like (chīld/līk/), like a child; innocent; frank; simple: *He has a child-like love of a circus. adj.*

chil dren (chil/drən), 1 plural of **child.** 2 members of a tribe or clan; descendants. *n.*

child's play, something very easy to do: *The carpenter found it child's play to repair the broken chair.*

Chil e (chil/ē), country in SW South America, on the Pacific coast. *Capital:* Santiago. *n.* —**Chil/e an,** *adj., n.*

chil i (chil/ē), 1 a hot-tasting pod of red pepper, used for seasoning. 2 plant that it grows on, a tropical American shrub grown in the southern part of the United States. 3 a highly seasoned Mexican dish of chopped meat cooked with red peppers and, usually, kidney beans. *n., pl.* **chil ies.** Also, **chilli.**

chili sauce, sauce made of red peppers, tomatoes, and spices, used on meat, fish, etc. Also, **chilli sauce.**

chill (chil), 1 unpleasant coldness: *feel a sudden chill. There was a chill in the air.* 2 unpleasantly cold: *A chill wind blew across the lake.* 3 make or become cold: *The icy wind chilled us to the bone. His blood chilled as he read the horror story.* 4 a sudden coldness of the body with shivering: *I caught a chill yester-*

day and today I have a fever. 5 cold in manner; unfriendly: *The old enemies gave each other a chill greeting.* 6 harden (metal) on the surface by rapid cooling. 1,4 *n.*, 2,5 *adj.*, 3,6 *v.*

chil li (chil/ē), chili. *n., pl.* **chil lies.**

chill i ness (chil/ē nis), chilly quality. *n.*

chilli sauce, chili sauce.

chill y (chil/ē), 1 unpleasantly cool; rather cold: *It is a rainy, chilly day. You'll feel chilly if you don't wear a coat.* 2 cold in manner; unfriendly: *We gave a chilly reception to the people who came to our party uninvited. adj.*, **chill i er, chill i est.**

chi maer a (kə mir/ə or kī mir/ə), chimera. *n., pl.* **chi maer as.**

chime (chīm), 1 set of bells tuned to a musical scale and played by hammers or simple machinery. 2 the musical sound made by a set of tuned bells. 3 ring out musically: *The bells of the town clock chime on the hour.* 1,2 *n.*, 3 *v.*, **chimed, chim ing.**

chime in, 1 be in harmony; agree: *Her ideas chimed in perfectly with mine.* 2 break into a conversation, especially to express one's agreement: *I said I would like to go to the circus and my brother chimed in.*

chi mer a (kə mir/ə or kī mir/ə), 1 Also, **Chimera.** (in Greek legends) a monster with a lion's head, a goat's body, and a serpent's tail, supposed to breathe out fire. 2 a horrible creature of the imagination. 3 an absurd or impossible idea; wild fancy: *The hope of changing dirt to gold was a chimera. n., pl.* **chi mer as.** Also, **chimaera.**

chi mer i cal (kə mer/ə kəl), 1 unreal; imaginary. 2 wildly fanciful; absurd; impossible: *Pay no attention to chimerical schemes for getting rich quick. adj.*

chim ney (chim/nē), 1 an upright structure of brick or stone, connected with a fireplace, furnace, etc., to make a draft and carry away smoke: *Her house has two chimneys.* 2 part of this that rises above a roof: *We could see the town's chimneys from afar.* 3 a glass tube placed around the flame of a lamp. *n., pl.* **chim neys.**

chimney sweep, person whose work is cleaning out chimneys.

chimney swift, bird of North America that often builds its nest in unused chimneys.

chimp (chimp), INFORMAL. chimpanzee. *n.*

chim pan zee (chim/pan zē/ or chim-pan/zē), a manlike ape of Africa, smaller than a gorilla. It is probably the most intelligent ape. *n.*

chin (chin), 1 the front of the lower jaw below the mouth. 2 **chin oneself,** hang by the hands from an overhead bar and

hat, āge, fär; let, ēqual, tėrm;
it, īce; hot, ōpen, ôrder;
oil, out; cup, půt, rüle; ch, child;
ng, long; sh, she; th, thin;
ŦH, then; zh, measure;

ə represents *a* in about,
e in taken, *i* in pencil,
o in lemon, *u* in circus.

pull up until one's chin reaches the bar. 1 *n.*, 2 *v.*, **chinned, chin ning.**

chi na (chī/nə), 1 a fine, white pottery baked by a special process, first used in China; porcelain. Colored designs can be baked into china. 2 dishes, vases, ornaments, etc., made of china. 3 pottery dishes of any kind. *n.*

China (def. 1)

Chi na (chī/nə), 1 **People's Republic of,** large country in E Asia, controlled by the Chinese Communists since 1949. *Capital:* Peking. 2 **Republic of,** the non-Communist Chinese government on Taiwan, established in 1949; Nationalist China. *Capital:* Taipei. *n.*

China Sea, part of the Pacific Ocean, east and southeast of Asia.

chi na ware (chī/nə wer/ or chī/nə-war/), china. *n.*

chinch (chinch), 1 bedbug. 2 chinch bug. *n., pl.* **chinch es.**

chinch bug, a small, black-and-white bug that does much damage to grain in dry weather.

chin chil la (chin chil/ə), 1 a South American rodent that looks somewhat

chimpanzee
4½ ft. tall
when standing

adj. adjective	*n.* noun
adv. adverb	*prep.* preposition
conj. conjunction	*pron.* pronoun
interj. interjection	*v.* verb
sing. singular	*pl.* plural

like a squirrel. 2 its very valuable soft, bluish-gray fur. 3 a thick woolen fabric woven in small, closely set tufts, used for overcoats. *n., pl.* **chin chil las.**

Chi nese (chī nēz'), 1 of China, its people, or their language. 2 person born or living in China. 3 person of Chinese descent. 4 language of China. 1 *adj.,* 2-4 *n., pl.* **Chi nese.**

Chinese Empire, China before it became a republic in 1912. It included Manchuria, Mongolia, Tibet, and Sinkiang.

Chinese lantern, lantern of thin colored paper that can be folded up like an accordion.

Chinese puzzle, something that is very complicated and hard to solve, like a kind of puzzle with interlocking pieces invented by the Chinese.

Chinese Wall, Great Wall of China.

chink[1] (chingk), 1 a narrow opening; crack: *Wind and snow came through the chinks between the logs of the cabin.* 2 fill up the chinks in: *The trapper chinked the cracks in the walls of the cabin with mud.* 1 *n.,* 2 *v.* [origin uncertain]

chink[2] (chingk), 1 a short, sharp, ringing sound like coins or drinking glasses hitting together. 2 make or cause to make such a sound: *I could hear the spoons chink in the glasses. He chinked the coins in his pocket.* 1 *n.,* 2 *v.* [an imitation of the sound]

chi nook (shə nūk' *or* chə nūk'), 1 a warm, moist wind blowing from the sea to the land in winter and spring in the northwestern United States. 2 a warm, dry wind that comes down the eastern slope of the Rocky Mountains. *n.* [from *Chinook*]

Chi nook (shə nūk' *or* chə nūk'), 1 member of a group of American Indian tribes living along the Columbia River in the northwestern United States. 2 language of these Indians. *n., pl.* **Chi nook** or **Chi nooks.**

chintz (chints), a cotton cloth printed in patterns of various colors and often glazed. *n., pl.* **chintz es.**

chip (chip), 1 a small, thin piece cut or broken off: *They used chips of wood to light a fire.* 2 place where a small, thin piece has been cut or broken off: *This plate has a chip on the edge.* 3 cut or

break off in small, thin pieces: *She chipped off the old paint. These cups chip if they are not handled carefully.* 4 shape by cutting at the surface or edge with an ax or chisel: *The Indians chipped flint arrowheads.* 5 a small, thin piece of food or candy. Potato chips are fried slices of potatoes. 6 a round, flat piece used for counting or to represent money in games: *poker chips.* 1,2,5,6 *n.,* 3,4 *v.,* **chipped, chip ping.**

chip in, INFORMAL. join with others in giving (money or help): *We all chipped in to buy our teacher a birthday present.*

chip off the old block, boy who is much like his father.

chip munk (chip'mungk), a small, striped, North American rodent of the same family as the squirrel; ground squirrel. *n.*

chip per (chip'ər), INFORMAL. lively and cheerful. *adj.*

Chip pe wa (chip'ə wä *or* chip'ə wā), Ojibwa. *n., pl.* **Chip pe wa** or **Chip pe was.**

chipping sparrow, a small sparrow of eastern and central North America.

Chi ron (kī'ron), (in Greek legends) a wise and kindly centaur, teacher of many Greek heroes. He was famous for his medical skill. *n.*

chi rop o dist (kə rop'ə dist), person who removes corns and treats other troubles of the feet. *n.*

chi ro prac tic (kī'rə prak'tik), 1 treatment of diseases by manipulating the spine. 2 having to do with the treatment of diseases by manipulating the spine. 1 *n.,* 2 *adj.*

chi ro prac tor (kī'rə prak'tər), person who treats diseases by manipulating the spine. *n.*

chirp (chėrp), 1 a short, sharp sound made by some small birds and insects: *the chirp of a sparrow.* 2 make a chirp: *The crickets chirped outside the house.* 1 *n.,* 2 *v.* —**chirp'er,** *n.*

chir rup (chir'əp *or* chėr'əp), 1 chirp again and again: *She chirruped to her horse to make it go faster.* 2 the sound of chirruping. 1 *v.,* 2 *n.*

chisel
(def. 1)

chis el (chiz'əl), 1 a cutting tool with a sharp edge at the end of a strong blade, used to cut or shape wood, stone, or metal. 2 cut or shape with a chisel: *The sculptor was at work chiseling a statue.*

3 SLANG. to cheat or swindle. 1 *n.,* 2,3 *v.*

chis el er (chiz'ə lər), 1 person or thing that chisels. 2 SLANG. a cheat. *n.*

Chis holm Trail (chiz'əm), famous western cattle trail from San Antonio, Texas, to Abilene, Kansas.

chit chat (chit'chat'), 1 friendly, informal talk; chat. 2 idle talk; gossip. *n.*

chi tin (kī'n), a horny substance forming the hard outer covering of beetles, lobsters, crabs, etc. *n.*

chit ter lings (chit'ər lingz), parts of the small intestines of pigs, cooked as food. *n.pl.*

chiv al rous (shiv'əl rəs), 1 having the qualities of an ideal knight; brave, courteous, helpful, and honorable. 2 having to do with the rules and customs of knights in the Middle Ages. *adj.* —**chiv'al rous ly,** *adv.* —**chiv'al rous ness,** *n.*

chiv al ry (shiv'əl rē), 1 the qualities of an ideal knight in the Middle Ages; bravery, honor, courtesy, protection of the weak, respect for women, and fairness to enemies. 2 rules and customs of knights in the Middle Ages. 3 knights as a group. *n.*

chive (chīv), plant of the same family as the onion, having a very small bulb. Its long, slender leaves are used as seasoning. *n.*

chlo ral (klôr'əl), 1 a colorless, oily liquid made from chlorine and alcohol, used in making chloral hydrate and DDT. 2 chloral hydrate. *n.*

chloral hydrate, a white, crystalline drug formerly much used to quiet nervousness and produce sleep.

chlo ride (klôr'īd), compound of chlorine with another element or radical. Sodium chloride is a compound of sodium and chlorine. *n.*

chlo rin ate (klôr'ə nāt), combine or treat with chlorine, especially to disinfect: *chlorinate water in a swimming pool.* *v.,* **chlo rin at ed, chlo rin at ing.**

chlo rin a tion (klôr'ə nā'shən), act or process of chlorinating. *n.*

chlo rine (klôr'ēn'), a greenish-yellow, bad-smelling, poisonous gas. It is a chemical element which occurs chiefly in combination with sodium as common salt. Chlorine is very irritating to the nose, throat, and lungs. It is used in bleaching and disinfecting, and in making plastics, explosives, and dyes. *n.*

chlo ro form (klôr'ə fôrm), 1 a colorless, volatile liquid with a sharp, sweetish smell and taste. When its vapor is inhaled, it makes a person unconscious or unable to feel pain. It is also used to dissolve rubber, resin, wax, and many other substances. 2 make unconscious or unable to feel pain by giving chloroform.   3 kill with chloroform.   1 *n.*, 2,3 *v.*

chlo ro phyll   or   **chlo ro phyl** (klôr′ə fil), the green coloring matter of plant cells. In the presence of light it makes carbohydrates, such as starch and sugar, from carbon dioxide and water.   *n.*

chlo ro plast (klôr′ə plast), a tiny body in the cells of green plants that contains chlorophyll.   *n.*

chock (chok), 1 block or wedge put under a barrel or wheel to keep it from rolling or under a boat to keep it in place.   2 provide or fasten with chocks: *chock a boat on a ship's deck.*   1 *n.*, 2 *v.*

chock-full (chok′fûl′), as full as can be; stuffed full: *The boy's pockets were chock-full of marbles.*   *adj.*   Also, **chuck-full.**

choc o late (chôk′lit *or* chôk′ə lit), 1 substance made by roasting and grinding cacao seeds. It has a strong, rich flavor and much value as food.   2 drink made of chocolate with hot milk or water and sugar.   3 candy made of chocolate.   4 made of or flavored with chocolate: *chocolate cake.*   5 a dark brown.   6 dark-brown.   1-3,5 *n.*, 4,6 *adj.*

Choc taw (chok′tô), 1 member of a tribe of American Indians, now living mostly in Oklahoma.   2 the language of these Indians.   *n., pl.* **Choc taw** or **Choc taws.**

choice (chois), 1 act of choosing: *She was careful in her choice of friends.*   2 power or chance to choose: *I have my choice between a radio and a camera for my birthday.*   3 person or thing chosen: *This hat is my choice.*   4 thing among several things to be chosen; alternative: *Their action left no choice but war.*   5 quantity and variety to choose from: *We found a wide choice of vegetables in the market.*   6 the best or finest part: *The flowers are the choice of my garden.*   7 of fine quality; excellent; superior: *The choicest fruit had the highest price.*   1-6 *n.*, 7 *adj.*, **choic er, choic est.**

choir (kwīr), 1 group of singers who sing together in a church service.   2 part of a church set apart for such a group.   3 any group of singers; chorus.   *n.*

choir boy (kwīr′boi′), boy who sings in a choir; chorister.   *n.*

choke (chōk), 1 stop the breath of (an animal or person) by squeezing or blocking up the throat; suffocate: *The smoke from the burning building almost choked the fireman.*   2 be unable to breathe: *I choked when a piece of meat stuck in my throat.*   3 act or sound of choking: *The man gave a few chokes and then got his breath.*   4 check or put out by cutting off air; smother: *A bucket of sand will choke a fire.*   5 control, hold,

or suppress: *She choked back a cry. He choked down his anger. She choked her laughter with a cough.*   6 fill up or block; clog: *Sand is choking the river.*   7 valve that reduces the supply of air to an internal-combustion engine.   8 reduce the supply of air to an internal-combustion engine.   9 kill or injure (a plant) by depriving it of air and light or of room to grow.   1,2,4-6,8,9 *v.*, **choked, chok ing;** 3,7 *n.*

choke off, put an end to; stop: *The break in the water main choked off the city's supply of water.*

choke up, 1 block up; fill up; clog up: *A traffic jam choked up the highway.*   2 fill with emotion; be or cause to be on the verge of tears: *The audience was choked up by the death of the hero in the last scene of the movie.*

choke cher ry (chōk′cher′ē), 1 a bitter wild cherry of North America.   2 tree that it grows on.   *n., pl.* **choke cher ries.**

chok er (chō′kər), 1 person or thing that chokes.   2 something that fits tightly around the neck, such as a necklace or high collar.   *n.*

chol er (kol′ər), an irritable disposition; anger.   *n.*

chol er a (kol′ər ə), an acute disease of the stomach and intestines, characterized by vomiting, cramps, and diarrhea. **Asiatic cholera** is infectious and often causes death.   *n.*

chol er ic (kol′ər ik), having an irritable disposition; easily made angry. *adj.*

cho les te rol (kə les′tə rol′ *or* kə-les′tə rōl′), a white, fatty substance, found in the blood and tissues of the body and also in foods such as eggs and meat. It is important in metabolism.   *n.*

choose (chüz), 1 pick out; select from a number: *She wants to choose a book from the library. She will probably choose wisely.*   2 prefer and decide; think fit: *The cat did not choose to go out in the rain.*   *v.*, **chose, cho sen, choos ing.**

choos er (chü′zər), person who chooses or has the right to choose.   *n.*

choos y (chü′zē), INFORMAL. particular or fussy: *They are so choosy about their food that no one invites them to dinner. adj.*, **choos i er, choos i est.**

chop[1] (chop), 1 cut by hitting with something sharp: *You can chop wood with an ax. We chopped down the dead tree.*   2 cut into small pieces: *chop up cabbage for coleslaw.*   3 a cutting blow or stroke: *He felled the tree with one chop of his ax.*   4 slice of meat, especially of lamb, pork, or veal on a piece of rib.   5 (in tennis, cricket, etc.) swing at or hit with a downward stroke: *The boy chopped at the ball with his bat.*

6 make by cutting: *The hikers had to chop their way through the bushes.*   7 a short, irregular, broken motion of waves.   1,2,5,6 *v.*, **chopped, chop ping;** 3,4,7 *n.* [Middle English *chop pen*]

chop[2] (chop), 1 jaw.   2 **chops,** *pl.* jaws or cheeks: *The cat is licking the milk off her chops. n.* [probably a special use of *chop*[1]]

chop[3] (chop), change suddenly; shift quickly; veer: *Watch the sails now that the wind is chopping.*   *v.*, **chopped, chop ping.** [probably a different form of *chap*, an old word meaning to exchange]

Cho pin (shō′pan), **Frédéric François,** 1810-1849, Polish pianist and composer who lived in France.   *n.*

chop per (chop′ər), 1 person who chops: *a chopper of wood.*   2 tool or machine for chopping. A short ax or a heavy knife are choppers.   3 SLANG. helicopter.   *n.*

chop py[1] (chop′ē), 1 making quick, sharp movements; jerky: *The speaker made nervous, choppy gestures.*   2 moving in short, irregular, broken waves: *The wind made the water choppy. adj.*, **chop pi er, chop pi est.**   [*chop*[1] + −*y*[1]]

chop py[2] (chop′ē), changing suddenly; shifting quickly: *A choppy wind tossed the ship about. adj.*, **chop pi er, chop pi est.**   [*chop*[3] + −*y*[1]]

chops (chops). See def. 2 under **chop**[2]. *n.pl.*

chopsticks held in one hand and used much like pliers to pick up food

chop sticks (chop′stiks′), pair of small, slender sticks used by the Chinese and Japanese to raise food to the mouth.   *n.pl.*

chop su ey (chop′ sü′ē), fried or

choral

adj. adjective	*n.* noun
adv. adverb	*prep.* preposition
conj. conjunction	*pron.* pronoun
interj. interjection	*v.* verb
sing. singular	*pl.* plural

stewed meat and vegetables cut up and cooked together in a sauce. It is usually served with rice. [from Chinese *tsap sui* odds and ends]

cho ral (kôr′əl *for 1,2;* kə ral′ *or* kôr′-əl *for 3*), 1 of a choir or chorus: *Our choral society meets on Wednesdays.* 2 sung by a choir or chorus: *a choral hymn.* 3 chorale. 1,2 *adj.,* 3 *n.*

cho rale (kə ral′), a simple hymn sung in unison. *n.*

chord¹ (kôrd), combination of two or more musical notes sounded together in harmony. *n.* [a different form of *cord,* shortened from *accord*]

chord² (def. 1)
AB and AC
are chords.

chord² (kôrd), 1 a straight line segment connecting two points on a curve. 2 cord (def. 4). 3 string of a harp or other musical instrument. 4 feeling or emotion: *The stray and hungry puppy touched a tender chord in him. n.* [from Latin *chorda,* from Greek *chorde* gut, string of a musical instrument]

chor date (kôr′dāt), one of the large group of animals that have backbones. Chordates include man and all other vertebrates. *n.*

chore (chôr), 1 an odd job; small task: *Feeding the dog is my daily chore.* 2 a difficult or disagreeable thing to do: *Painting the house is a real chore. n.*

cho re a (kô rē′ə), St. Vitus's dance. *n.*

cho re o graph (kôr′ē ə graf), arrange or design dancing for. *v.*

cho re og ra pher (kôr′ē og′rə fər), planner or creator of dances in a ballet, motion picture, or musical play. *n.*

cho re o graph ic (kôr′ē ə graf′ik), having to do with choreography. *adj.*

cho re og ra phy (kôr′ē og′rə fē), 1 art of planning or creating the dances in a ballet, motion picture, or musical play. 2 dancing, especially ballet dancing. *n.*

cho ris ter (kôr′ə stər), 1 singer in a choir. 2 choirboy. 3 leader of a choir. *n.*

chor tle (chôr′tl), 1 chuckle or snort

with glee: *He chortled at the joke.* 2 a gleeful chuckle or snort. 1 *v.,* **chor-tled, chor tling;** 2 *n.*

cho rus (kôr′əs), 1 group of singers who sing together, such as a choir: *Our school chorus gave a concert at the town hall.* 2 a musical composition to be sung by all singers together. A chorus is often a part of an opera or oratorio. 3 the repeated part of a song coming after each stanza: *Everybody knew the chorus by heart.* 4 sing or speak all at the same time: *The audience chorused its approval by loud cheering.* 5 anything sung by many people at once: *The children greeted the teacher with a chorus of "Happy Birthday."* 6 a saying all together at the same time: *My question was answered by a chorus of "no's."* 7 group of singers and dancers: *the chorus in a musical comedy.* 1-3, 5-7 *n., pl.* **cho rus es;** 4 *v.*

in chorus, all together at the same time: *The whole class replied in chorus to the teacher's questions.*

chose (chōz), past tense of **choose.** *She chose the red dress. v.*

cho sen (chō′zn), 1 past participle of **choose.** *Have you chosen a book from the library?* 2 picked out; selected from a group: *Six chosen scouts marched at the front of the parade.* 1 *v.,* 2 *adj.*

Cho sen (chō′sen′), Japanese name of **Korea.** *n.*

Chou En-lai (jō′ en′lī′), born 1898, premier of the People's Republic of China since 1949.

chow (chou), 1 a Chinese dog of medium size with a short, compact body, large head, and thick coat of one color, usually brown or black. 2 SLANG. food. *n.*

chow der (chou′dər), a thick soup or stew usually made of clams or fish with potatoes, onions, etc., and milk. *n.*

chow mein (chou′ mān′), a thickened stew of onions, celery, meat, etc., served with fried noodles. [from Chinese *ch'au min* fried noodles]

Christ (krīst), Jesus of Nazareth, whose life and teachings are the source of the Christian religion. *n.*

chris ten (kris′n), 1 give a first name to (a person) at baptism: *The child was christened Susan.* 2 give a name to: *The new ship was christened before it was launched.* 3 baptize as a Christian. *v.*

Chris ten dom (kris′n dəm), 1 Christian countries; the Christian part of the world: *Many of the monarchs of Christendom took part in the Crusades.* 2 all Christians: *Christendom everywhere celebrates Christmas. n.*

chris ten ing (kris′n ing), act or ceremony of baptizing and naming; baptism. *n.*

Chris tian (kris′chən), 1 person who

believes in Christ and follows His teachings; person belonging to the religion of Christ. 2 believing in or belonging to the religion of Christ: *the Christian church, the Christian gospel.* 3 showing a gentle, humble, helpful spirit: *Christian kindness.* 4 of Christians or Christianity: *the Christian faith.* 5 INFORMAL. decent; respectable: *Everyone deserves a Christian burial.* 1 *n.,* 2-5 *adj.*

Chris ti an i ty (kris′chē an′ə tē), 1 the religion taught by Christ and His followers; Christian religion. 2 condition of being a Christian; Christian spirit or character. 3 all Christians; Christendom. *n.*

Chris tian ize (kris′chə nīz), make Christian; convert to Christianity. *v.,* **Chris tian ized, Chris tian iz ing.**

Christian name, first name; given name: *"Mary" is the Christian name of "Mary Smith."*

Christian Science, religion and system of healing founded by Mary Baker Eddy in 1866. It treats disease by mental and spiritual means.

Christian Scientist, believer in Christian Science.

Christ like (krīst′līk′), like Christ; like that of Christ; showing the spirit of Christ. *adj.*

Christ mas (kris′məs), the yearly celebration of the birth of Christ; December 25. *n.*

Christmas Island, 1 island in the Indian Ocean, south of Java, governed by Australia. 2 British island in the central Pacific.

Christ mas tide (kris′məs tīd′), the Christmas season. *n.*

Christmas tree, an evergreen tree hung with decorations at Christmas time.

Chris to pher (kris′tə fər), **Saint,** died A.D. 250?, legendary Christian martyr. He is the patron saint of travelers. *n.*

chro mat ic (krō mat′ik), 1 of color or colors: *Most paint stores have chromatic charts.* 2 progressing only by half steps instead of by the regular intervals of the musical scale: *There are twelve chromatic tones. adj.* —**chro mat′i cal ly,** *adv.*

chromatic scale, a musical scale that progresses by half steps.

chro ma tin (krō′mə tən), a protein substance in the nucleus of an animal or plant cell. The chromosomes are made up in part of chromatin. *n.*

chro ma to graph ic (krō′mə tə-graf′ik), having to do with chromatography. *adj.*

chro ma tog ra phy (krō′mə tog′-rə fē), separation and analysis of mixtures of chemical compounds by the use of an adsorbing material, so that the different compounds become adsorbed in separate sections. *n.*

chrome (krōm), 1 chromium. 2 to cover or plate with chrome: *chromed steel.* 1 *n.*, 2 *v.*, **chromed, chrom ing.**

chro mi um (krō′mē əm), a grayish, hard, brittle metallic element that does not rust or become dull easily when exposed to air. Chromium occurs in compounds that are used as plating, as part of stainless steel and other alloys, for making dyes and paints, in photography, etc. *n.*

chro mo some (krō′mə sōm), any of the rod-shaped bodies found in the nucleus of a cell that appear when the cell divides. Chromosomes carry the genes that determine heredity. *n.*

chro mo sphere (krō′mə sfir), a red-hot layer of gas around the sun which can be seen only during a total eclipse. *n.*

chron ic (kron′ik), 1 lasting a long time: *Rheumatism is often a chronic disease.* 2 never stopping; constant; habitual: *a chronic tease.* *adj.* —**chron′ i cal ly,** *adv.*

chron i cle (kron′ə kəl), 1 record of events in the order in which they took place; history; story: *Columbus kept a chronicle of his voyages.* 2 write the history of; tell the story of: *Many of the old monks chronicled the Crusades.* 1 *n.*, 2 *v.*, **chron i cled, chron i cling.**

chron i cler (kron′ə klər), writer of a chronicle; recorder; historian. *n.*

Chron i cles (kron′ə kəlz), two books of the Old Testament, called I and II Chronicles. *n.*

chron o log i cal (kron′ə loj′ə kəl), arranged in the order in which the events happened: *In telling a story a person usually follows chronological order.* *adj.* —**chron′o log′i cal ly,** *adv.*

chro nol o gy (krə nol′ə jē), 1 science of measuring time and determining the proper order and dates of events. 2 table or list that gives the exact dates of events arranged in the order in which they happened. *n.*, *pl.* **chro nol o gies.**

chro nom e ter (krə nom′ə tər), clock or watch that keeps very accurate time. A ship's chronometer is used in determining longitude. *n.*

chrys a lid (kris′ə lid), chrysalis. *n.*

chrys a lis (kris′ə lis), 1 the stage in the development of moths, butterflies,

chrysalis
(defs. 1 and 2)
of a butterfly

and most other insects between the larva and the adult, when the larva lives in a hard case or cocoon; pupa. 2 the case or cocoon. *n.*, *pl.* **chrys a lis es, chry sal i des** (krə sal′ə dēz′).

chry san the mum (krə san′thə məm), 1 any of several cultivated plants of the same family as the aster, with round flowers that bloom in the fall. 2 its flower. Chrysanthemums have many petals and bloom in many shades, especially in white, yellow, red, and brown. *n.*

chrys o lite (kris′ə līt), a green or yellow semiprecious stone. *n.*

chub (chub), 1 a thick, freshwater fish of Europe, related to the carp. 2 any of various small, freshwater fishes of central and eastern United States and Canada. *n.*, *pl.* **chubs** or **chub.**

chub bi ness (chub′ē nis), a being chubby. *n.*

chub by (chub′ē), round and plump: *Most babies have chubby cheeks.* *adj.*, **chub bi er, chub bi est.**

chuck¹ (chuk), 1 give a slight blow or tap; pat: *He chucked the baby under the chin.* 2 a slight blow or tap: *He gave the baby a chuck under the chin.* 3 throw or toss: *She chucked the stones into the pond.* 4 a throw or toss. 1,3 *v.*, 2,4 *n.* [origin unknown]

CHUCK
chuck² (def. 1)
of an electric drill

chuck² (chuk), 1 device for holding a tool or piece of work in a machine. 2 cut of beef between the neck and the shoulder. *n.* [a different form of *chock*]

chuck-full (chuk′fùl′), chock-full. *adj.*

chuck le (chuk′əl), 1 laugh softly or quietly: *She kept chuckling to herself throughout the funny movie.* 2 a soft laugh; quiet laughter. 1 *v.*, **chuck led, chuck ling;** 2 *n.*

chuck wagon, (in the western United States) a wagon that carries food and cooking equipment for cowboys or harvest workers.

chug (chug), 1 a short, loud burst of sound: *We heard the chug of a steam engine.* 2 make such sounds. 3 INFORMAL. go or move with such sounds: *The old truck chugged along.* 1 *n.*, 2,3 *v.*, **chugged, chug ging.**

chum (chum), INFORMAL. 1 a very close friend. 2 be very close friends. 1 *n.*, 2 *v.*, **chummed, chum ming.**

chum my (chum′ē), INFORMAL. like a chum; very friendly; intimate. *adj.*, **chum mi er, chum mi est.**

chump (chump), INFORMAL. a foolish or stupid person; blockhead. *n.*

hat, āge, fär; let, ēqual, tėrm;
it, īce; hot, ōpen, ôrder;
oil, out; cup, pùt, rüle; ch, child;
ng, long; sh, she; th, thin;
ŦH, then; zh, measure;

ə represents *a* in about,
e in taken, *i* in pencil,
o in lemon, *u* in circus.

Chung king (chùng′king′), city in central China, on the Yangtze River. *n.*

chunk (chungk), a thick piece or lump: *Here's a chunk of wood for the fire.* *n.*

chunk y (chung′kē), 1 like a chunk; short and thick: *She threw a chunky log on the fire.* 2 INFORMAL. stocky: *The child had a chunky build.* *adj.*, **chunk i er, chunk i est.**

church (chėrch), 1 building for public Christian worship: *The church was full on Sunday morning.* 2 public worship of God in a church: *Don't be late for church.* 3 Usually, **Church.** group of Christians with the same beliefs and under the same authority; denomination: *the Methodist Church, the Presbyterian Church.* 4 **the Church,** all Christians. 5 profession of a clergyman: *He is going into the church as a career.* *n.*

church go er (chėrch′gō′ər), person who goes to church regularly. *n.*

Church ill (chėr′chil), 1 John. See Marlborough. 2 Sir **Winston,** 1874-1965, British statesman and writer, prime minister of Great Britain from 1940 to 1945 and 1951 to 1955. *n.*

church man (chėrch′mən), 1 clergyman. 2 member of a church. *n.*, *pl.* **church men.**

Church of England, the Episcopal Church in England that is recognized as a national institution by the government; Anglican Church.

Church of Jesus Christ of Latter-day Saints, the official name of the Mormon Church.

church ward en (chėrch′wôrd′n), a lay official in the Church of England or the Protestant Episcopal Church who manages the business, property, and money of a church. *n.*

church wom an (chėrch′wùm′ən), a woman member of a church. *n.*, *pl.* **church wom en.**

church yard (chėrch′yärd′), the ground around a church. Part of a churchyard is sometimes used as a burial ground. *n.*

churl (chėrl), 1 a rude, surly person. 2 person of low birth; peasant. *n.*

churl ish (chėr′lish), rude or surly;

151

adj.	adjective	*n.*	noun
adv.	adverb	*prep.*	preposition
conj.	conjunction	*pron.*	pronoun
interj.	interjection	*v.*	verb
sing.	singular	*pl.*	plural

bad-tempered. *adj.* —**churl′ish ly**, *adv.* —**churl′ish ness**, *n.*

churn (chėrn), 1 container or machine in which butter is made from cream or milk by beating and shaking. 2 beat and shake (cream) in a churn: *She made butter by churning the cream.* 3 stir violently; make or become foamy: *The ship's propeller churned the waves.* 4 move as if beaten and shaken: *The excited crowd churned about the speaker's platform. The water churns in the rapids.* 1 *n.,* 2-4 *v.* —**churn′er,** *n.*

chute (shüt), 1 a steep slide for dropping or sliding things down to a lower level. There are chutes for carrying mail, soiled clothes, coal, etc. A toboggan slide is called a chute. 2 rapids in a river; waterfall. 3 INFORMAL. parachute. *n.*

chut ney (chut′nē), a spicy sauce or relish made of fruits, herbs, pepper, etc. *n., pl.* **chut neys.**

chyme (kīm), a pulpy mass into which food is changed by the action of the stomach. Chyme passes from the stomach into the small intestine. *n.*

CIA, Central Intelligence Agency (an agency of the United States government that deals with matters involving national security).

ci ca da (sə kā′də), a large insect with two pairs of thin, transparent wings. The male makes a shrill sound in hot, dry weather. Cicadas are commonly called locusts. *n., pl.* **ci ca das.**

Cic e ro (sis′ə rō′), **Marcus Tullius,** 106-43 B.C., Roman orator, writer, and statesman. *n.*

Cid (sid), **the,** 1040?-1099, Spanish national hero who fought in the war against the Moors. *n.*

ci der (sī′dər), juice pressed out of apples, used as a drink and in making vinegar. *n.*

ci gar (sə gär′), a tight roll of tobacco leaves for smoking. *n.*

cig a rette or **cig a ret** (sig′ə ret′ or sig′ə ret′), a small roll of finely cut tobacco enclosed in a thin sheet of paper for smoking. *n.*

cil i a (sil′ē ə), very small, hairlike parts of leaves, wings, insects, etc. Some microscopic animals use cilia to move themselves. *n.pl. of* **cil i um** (sil′ē əm).

cinch (sinch), 1 a strong girth for fastening a saddle or pack on a horse. 2 fasten on with a cinch; bind firmly. 3 INFORMAL. a firm hold or grip. 4 INFORMAL. make certain of. 5 SLANG. something sure and easy: *It's a cinch to ride a bike once you know how.* 1,3,5 *n., pl.* **cinch es;** 2,4 *v.*

cin cho na (sin kō′nə), 1 an evergreen tree native to the Andes Mountains, now also grown in the East Indies. It is valuable for its bark. 2 its bitter bark, from which quinine and other drugs are obtained; Peruvian bark. *n., pl.* **cin cho nas.** [from Countess *Cinchón,* wife of a Spanish viceroy to Peru]

Cin cin nat i (sin′sə nat′ē), city in SW Ohio, on the Ohio River. *n.*

cinc ture (singk′chər), belt or girdle. *n.*

cin der (sin′dər), 1 piece of wood or coal that has burned up. 2 **cinders,** *pl.* wood or coal partly burned but no longer flaming. Cinders are made up of larger and coarser pieces than ashes are. *n.*

cinder block, a rectangular building block of cement and pressed coal cinders, usually hollow. It is used in walls and partitions.

Cin der el la (sin′də rel′ə), girl in a fairy tale who is forced by her cruel stepmother to work very hard, but is rescued by her fairy godmother and married to a prince. *n.*

cin e ma (sin′ə mə), 1 a motion picture. 2 a motion-picture theater. 3 **the cinema,** motion pictures. *n., pl.* **cin e mas.**

cin na bar (sin′ə bär), a reddish or brownish mineral that is the chief source of mercury. *n.*

cin na mon (sin′ə mən), 1 the dried, reddish-brown inner bark of a laurel tree or shrub of the East Indies, used as a spice and in medicine. 2 spice made from this bark. 3 tree or shrub yielding this bark. 4 light reddish-brown: *a cinnamon bear.* 5 a light, reddish brown. 1-3,5 *n.,* 4 *adj.*

CIO or **C.I.O.,** Congress of Industrial Organizations. It merged with the AFL in 1955. See **AFL-CIO.**

ci pher (sī′fər), 1 secret writing; code: *Part of his letter is in cipher.* 2 something in secret writing or code. 3 the key to a method of secret writing or a code. 4 zero; 0. 5 person or thing of no importance. 6 do arithmetic; use figures: *She can read, write, and cipher.* 1-5 *n.,* 6 *v.* Also, **cypher.**

cir ca (sėr′kə), about; approximately: *Mohammed was born circa* A.D. *570. prep.* [from Latin]

Cir cas sia (sər kash′ə), region in SW Soviet Union, on the NE shore of the Black Sea. *n.* —**Cir cas′sian,** *adj., n.*

Cir ce (sėr′sē), (in Greek legends) an enchantress who changed men into swine. Ulysses withstood her spell and forced her to set free his companions, whom she had changed to swine. *n.*

circle (def. 2)

cir cle (sėr′kəl), 1 a closed, curved line on which every point is equally distant from a point within called the center. 2 a plane figure bounded by such a line. 3 anything shaped like a circle or part of one: *a circle around the moon.* 4 ring: *We sat in a circle around the teacher.* 5 go around in a circle; revolve around: *The moon circles the earth. The airplane circled before it landed.* 6 form a circle around; surround; encircle: *A ring of trees circled the clearing.* 7 a complete series or course: *A year is a circle of twelve months.* 8 group of people held together by the same interests: *the family circle, a circle of friends.* 1-4,7,8 *n.,* 5,6 *v.,* **cir cled, cir cling.**

cir clet (sėr′klit), 1 a small circle. 2 a round ornament worn on the head, neck, arm, or finger. *n.*

cir cuit (sėr′kit), 1 a going around; a moving around: *It takes a year for the earth to make its circuit of the sun.* 2 route over which a person or group makes repeated journeys at certain times: *Some judges make a circuit, stopping at certain towns along the way to hold court.* 3 the part of the country through which such journeys are made. 4 distance around any space. 5 line enclosing any space. 6 the complete path over which an electric current flows. 7 arrangement of wiring, tubes, etc., forming electrical connections; hookup. 8 number of theaters under the same management and presenting the same shows. *n.*

circuit breaker, switch that automatically interrupts an electric circuit when the current gets too strong.

cir cu i tous (sər kyü′ə təs), not direct; roundabout: *We took a circuitous route home to avoid poor roads. adj.* —**cir cu′i tous ly,** *adv.* —**cir cu′i tous ness,** *n.*

circuit rider, preacher who rides from place to place over a circuit to preach. Methodist circuit riders were common in the 1800's.

cir cu lar (sėr′kyə lər), 1 round like a circle: *The full moon has a circular shape.* 2 moving in a circle; going around a circle: *A merry-go-round makes a circular trip.* **3** having to do with a circle. **4** sent to each of a number of people: *a circular letter.* **5** letter, notice, or advertisement sent to each of a number of people. **1-4** *adj.,* **5** *n.* —**cir′cu lar ly,** *adv.*

cir cu lar ize (sėr′kyə lə rīz′), send circulars to. *v.,* **cir cu lar ized, cir cu lar iz ing.**

cir cu late (sėr′kyə lāt), **1** go around; pass from place to place or from person to person: *Water circulates in the pipes of a building. Money circulates as it goes from person to person. A newspaper circulates among people who read it.* **2** send around from person to person or from place to place: *circulate news of a holiday. This book has been widely circulated among children.* **3** (of the blood) flow from the heart through the arteries and veins back to the heart. *v.,* **cir cu lat ed, cir cu lat ing.**

circulating library, library whose books can be rented or borrowed.

cir cu la tion (sėr′kyə lā′shən), **1** a going around; circulating: *Open windows increase the circulation of air in a room.* **2** flow of the blood from the heart through the arteries and veins back to the heart. **3** a sending around of books, papers, news, etc., from person to person or from place to place. **4** the number of copies of a book, newspaper, magazine, etc., that are sent out during a certain time: *That newspaper has a circulation of 500,000. n.*

cir cu la to ry (sėr′kyə lə tôr′ē), having to do with circulation. Arteries and veins are parts of the circulatory system of the human body. *adj.*

cir cum cise (sėr′kəm sīz), cut off the foreskin of. *v.,* **cir cum cised, cir cum cis ing.**

cir cum ci sion (sėr′kəm sizh′ən), act of circumcising. *n.*

cir cum fer ence (sər kum′fər əns), **1** the boundary line of a circle or of certain other surfaces. Every point in the circumference of a circle is at the same distance from the center. See **circle** for diagram. **2** the distance around: *The circumference of the earth at the equator is almost 25,000 miles. n.*

cir cum flex (sėr′kəm fleks), circumflex accent. *n., pl.* **cir cum flex es.**

circumflex accent, **1** (in the pronunciations in this book) a mark used over *o* to show that it is pronounced as in *order* (ôr′dər). **2** mark (ˆ or ˆ or ˜) placed over a vowel to tell something about its pronunciation, as in the French word *fête.*

cir cum lo cu tion (sėr′kəm lō kyü′shən), **1** the use of several or many words instead of one or a few: *The witness's account of the accident was so*

full of circumlocution that it was difficult to understand it. **2** a roundabout expression: *"The wife of your father's brother" is a circumlocution for "Your aunt." n.*

cir cum nav i gate (sėr′kəm nav′ə gāt), sail around: *Magellan's ship circumnavigated the earth. v.,* **cir cum nav i gat ed, cir cum nav i gat ing.**

cir cum nav i ga tion (sėr′kəm nav′ə gā′shən), act of sailing around. *n.*

cir cum nav i ga tor (sėr′kəm nav′ə gā′tər), person who has sailed around the earth. *n.*

cir cum po lar (sėr′kəm pō′lər), **1** around the North or South Pole. **2** around either pole of the heavens. *adj.*

circumscribe (def. 4)
circumscribed figures

cir cum scribe (sėr′kəm skrīb′), **1** draw a line around; mark the boundaries of; bound: *The horizon circumscribed my view of the sea.* **2** surround: *the atmosphere circumscribing the earth.* **3** put limits on; restrict: *Poor health circumscribes a person's activities.* **4** draw (a figure) around another figure so as to touch as many points as possible. **5** be so drawn around: *A circle that circumscribes a square touches the four corners of the square. v.,* **cir cum scribed, cir cum scrib ing.**

cir cum spect (sėr′kəm spekt), watchful on all sides; careful; cautious; prudent. *adj.* —**cir′cum spect′ly,** *adv.*

cir cum spec tion (sėr′kəm spek′shən), circumspect action or conduct; care; caution; prudence. *n.*

cir cum stance (sėr′kəm stans), **1** condition that accompanies an act or event: *Unfavorable circumstances such as fog and rain often delayed us on our trip to the mountains.* **2** fact or event: *It was a lucky circumstance that she found her money.* **3** full detail: *The speaker told of her adventures with great circumstance.* **4 circumstances,** *pl.* condition of a person with regard to the money or funds he has: *A rich person is in good circumstances; a poor person is in bad circumstances.* **5** ceremony; display: *The royal procession advanced with pomp and circumstance. n.*

under no circumstances, never: *Under no circumstances should you reveal that we are planning a surprise party.*

under the circumstances, because of these conditions: *Tickets to that show were sold out; under the circum-*

hat, āge, fär; let, ēqual, tėrm; it, īce; hot, ōpen, ôrder; oil, out; cup, pùt, rüle; ch, child; ng, long; sh, she; th, thin; ₮H, then; zh, measure;

ə represents *a* in about, *e* in taken, *i* in pencil, *o* in lemon, *u* in circus.

stances we had no choice but to go to another show.

cir cum stan tial (sėr′kəm stan′shəl), **1** depending on or based on circumstances: *Stolen jewels found on a person are circumstantial evidence that he stole them.* **2** not essential; not important; incidental: *Minor details are circumstantial compared with the main fact.* **3** giving full and exact details; complete: *a circumstantial report of an accident. adj.* —**cir′cum stan′tial ly,** *adv.*

cir cum vent (sėr′kəm vent′), **1** get the better of or defeat by trickery; outwit: *The dishonest merchant was always trying to circumvent the law.* **2** go around: *He took a roundabout route to circumvent the traffic. v.*

cir cum ven tion (sėr′kəm ven′shən), act of circumventing. *n.*

cir cus (sėr′kəs), **1** a traveling show of acrobats, clowns, horses, riders, and wild animals. The performers who give the show and the performances they give are both called the circus. **2** (in ancient Rome) an arena with seats around it in rows, each row higher than the one in front of it. *n., pl.* **cir cus es.**

cir rus (sir′əs), a thin, fleecy cloud of ice crystals formed very high in the air. *n., pl.* **cir ri** (sir′ī).

cis tern (sis′tərn), an artificial reservoir for storing water, especially a tank below ground. *n.*

cit a del (sit′ə dəl), **1** fortress, especially one in a city. **2** a strongly fortified place; stronghold. **3** a strong, safe place; refuge. *n.*

ci ta tion (sī tā′shən), **1** quotation or reference given as an authority for facts or opinions. **2** act of citing. **3** honorable mention for bravery in war: *The soldier received a citation from the President.* **4** official praise or commendation for public service: *The mayor gave her a citation for her role in planning the new museum.* **5** summons to appear before a court of law. *n.*

cite (sīt), **1** quote (a passage, book, or author), especially as an authority: *She cited the U.S. Constitution to prove her statement.* **2** refer to; mention as an

citizen

adj. adjective	*n.* noun
adv. adverb	*prep.* preposition
conj. conjunction	*pron.* pronoun
interj. interjection	*v.* verb
sing. singular	*pl.* plural

example: *The lawyer cited another case similar to the one being tried.* **3** give honorable mention for bravery in war. **4** commend publicly for service to the community. **5** summon to appear before a court of law. *v.,* **cit ed, cit ing.**

cit i zen (sit′ə zən), **1** person who by birth or by choice is a member of a state or nation which gives him certain rights and which claims his loyalty: *Many immigrants have become citizens of the United States.* **2** inhabitant of a city or town. **3** a civilian. *n.*

cit i zen ry (sit′ə zən rē), citizens as a group. *n., pl.* **cit i zen ries.**

cit i zen ship (sit′ə zən ship), **1** the duties, rights, and privileges of a citizen. **2** condition of being a citizen: *Voting is a right of citizenship. n.*

cit rate (sit′rāt), salt or ester of citric acid. *n.*

cit ric acid (sit′rik), a white, odorless acid with a sour taste, found in the juice of oranges, lemons, limes, and similar fruits. It is used as a flavoring, as a medicine, and in making dyes.

cit ron (sit′rən), **1** a pale-yellow fruit somewhat like a lemon but larger, with less acid, and a thicker rind. **2** the shrub or small tree that it grows on. **3** its rind, candied and used in fruit cakes, plum pudding, candies, etc. *n.*

cit ro nel la (sit′rə nel′ə), **1** oil used in making perfume, soap, liniment, etc., and for keeping mosquitoes away. **2** a fragrant grass of southern Asia and Central America from which this oil is made. *n.*

cit rus (sit′rəs), **1** any tree bearing lemons, grapefruit, limes, oranges, or similar fruits. Citruses usually grow in warm climates. **2** fruit of such a tree. **3** of such trees. Citrus fruits contain much vitamin C. **1,2** *n., pl.* **cit rus es; 3** *adj.*

cit y (sit′ē), **1** a large and important town. London, Tokyo, and Buenos Aires are three great cities. **2** division of local government in the United States having a charter from the state that fixes its boundaries and powers. A city is usually governed by a mayor and a board of aldermen or councilmen. **3** people living in a city: *The whole city was alarmed by the great fire.* **4** of or in a city. **1-3** *n., pl.* **cit ies; 4** *adj.*

city hall, the headquarters of the officials, bureaus, etc., of a city government: *The mayor's office is in city hall.*

city manager, person appointed by a city council or commission to manage the government of a city.

cit y-state (sit′ē stāt′), an independent state consisting of a city and the territories depending on it. Athens was a city-state in ancient Greece. *n.*

Ciu dad Tru jil lo (syü däd′ trü-hē′yō), former name of **Santo Domingo.**

civ et (siv′it), **1** a yellowish substance produced by certain glands of the civet cat. It has a musky odor and is used in making perfume. **2** civet cat. *n.*

civet cat—about 4 ft. long with tail

civet cat, a small, spotted mammal of Africa and Asia, having glands that produce civet.

civ ic (siv′ik), **1** of a city: *My aunt is interested in civic affairs and will be a candidate for mayor.* **2** of or having to do with citizens or citizenship. A person's civic duties include such things as obeying the laws, voting, and paying taxes. *adj.*

civ ics (siv′iks), study of the duties, rights, and privileges of citizens. *n.*

civ il (siv′əl), **1** of a citizen or citizens; having to do with citizens: *civil duties.* **2** of or having to do with the government, state, or nation: *Police departments are civil institutions to protect local citizens.* **3** occurring among citizens of one community, state, or nation: *civil strife.* **4** of a citizen in his ordinary capacity; not military, naval, or connected with the church: *The accused soldier was tried in a military rather than in a civil court. The couple had both a civil and a religious marriage ceremony.* **5** polite; courteous: *I pointed out the way in a very civil manner.* **6** having to do with the private rights of individuals and with laws protecting these rights. Civil lawsuits deal with such things as contracts, ownership of property, and payment for personal injury. *adj.*

civil defense, a civilian emergency program for protecting people and property from disasters such as fire, flood, or enemy attack.

civil disobedience, refusal on principle to obey a law of the country or state, especially by refusing to serve in the armed forces or not paying taxes.

civil engineering, the planning and directing of the construction of bridges, roads, harbors, canals, dams, and other public works.

ci vil ian (sə vil′yən), **1** person who is not enrolled in any of the armed forces. **2** of civilians; not military or naval: *Persons in the armed forces usually wear civilian clothes when on leave.* **1** *n.,* **2** *adj.*

ci vil i ty (sə vil′ə tē), **1** polite behavior; courtesy: *Thank you for your civility in replying to my letter so promptly.* **2** act or expression of politeness or courtesy. *n., pl.* **ci vil i ties.**

civ i li za tion (siv′ə lə zā′shən), **1** civilized condition; advanced stage in social development. **2** a civilizing or a becoming civilized: *The civilization of a primitive society is a gradual process which takes centuries.* **3** nations and peoples that have reached advanced stages in social development: *All civilization should be aroused against war.* **4** the ways of living of a people or nation: *There are differences between Chinese civilization and our own. n.*

civ i lize (siv′ə līz), bring out of a savage or barbarian condition; train in culture, science, and art: *The Romans civilized a great part of their world. v.,* **civ i lized, civ i liz ing.**

civ i lized (siv′ə līzd), **1** advanced in social customs, art, and science: *The ancient Greeks were a civilized people.* **2** showing culture and good manners; refined: *take a civilized attitude toward one's critics. adj.*

civil liberty, the freedom of a person to enjoy the rights guaranteed by the laws or constitution of a country without any undue restraint or interference by the government.

civ il ly (siv′ə lē), politely; courteously. *adv.*

civil rights, the rights of a citizen, especially the rights guaranteed to all U.S. citizens, regardless of race, color, or sex, by the 13th, 14th, 15th, 19th, and 24th amendments to the Constitution and certain acts of Congress.

civil servant, member of the civil service.

civil service, branch of government service concerned with affairs not military, naval, legislative, or judicial. It includes all civilian government workers who are appointed rather than elected. Forest rangers, Peace Corps workers, and post office employees belong to the United States civil service.

civil war, **1** war between opposing groups of citizens of one nation. **2 Civil War,** war between the northern and southern states of the United States from 1861 to 1865; War Between the States.

clab ber (klab/ər), 1 thick, sour milk. 2 become thick in souring; curdle. 1 *n.*, 2 *v.*

clack (klak), 1 make or cause to make a short, sharp sound: *The passenger train clacked over the rails.* 2 a short, sharp sound: *We heard the clack of the office typewriters.* 3 talk noisily; chatter. 4 the noise of continuous speech; senseless chatter. 1,3 *v.*, 2,4 *n.* —**clack′er,** *n.*

clad (klad), clothed; a past tense and a past participle of **clothe**. *v.*

claim (klām), 1 demand as one's own or one's right: *The prospector claimed the land beyond the river as his. Does anyone claim this pencil?* 2 such a demand: *She makes a claim to the pencil.* 3 a right or title to something; right to demand something: *have a legal claim to the property, too many claims on my time.* 4 something that is claimed, such as a piece of public land which a settler or prospector marks out for himself. 5 require; call for; deserve: *Your homework claims all of your attention.* 6 say strongly; declare as a fact; maintain: *She claimed that her answer was correct.* 7 declaration of something as a fact: *Careful study showed that the claims that Salk vaccine prevented polio were correct.* 1,5,6 *v.*, 2-4,7 *n.*

jump a claim, seize a piece of land claimed by another.

lay claim to, assert one's right to; claim: *The settlers laid claim to the piece of land they occupied.*

claim ant (klā/mənt), person who makes a claim. *n.*

clair voy ance (kler voi/əns or klar voi/əns), 1 the supposed power of seeing or knowing about things that are out of sight. 2 exceptional insight. *n.*

clair voy ant (kler voi/ənt or klar-voi/ənt), 1 supposedly having the power of seeing or knowing about things that are out of sight. 2 person who has, or claims to have, such power: *The clairvoyant claimed to be able to locate lost articles and to give news of faraway people.* 3 having exceptional insight. 1,3 *adj.*, 2 *n.* —**clair voy′-ant ly,** *adv.*

clam (klam), 1 mollusk somewhat like an oyster, with a soft body and a shell in two hinged halves. Clams burrow in sand along the seashore or at the edges of rivers, lakes, etc. Many kinds are good to eat. 2 go out after clams; dig for clams. 1 *n.*, 2 *v.*, **clammed, clamming.** —**clam′like′,** *adj.*

clam up, INFORMAL. stop talking.

clam bake (klam/bāk/), picnic where clams are baked or steamed. *n.*

clam ber (klam/bər), climb, using both hands and feet; climb awkwardly or

with difficulty; scramble: *The children clambered up the cliff.* *v.*

clam mi ly (klam/ə lē), in a clammy manner. *adv.*

clam mi ness (klam/ē nis), clammy condition or quality: *The damp air in the cellar had an uncomfortable clamminess about it.* *n.*

clam my (klam/ē), cold and damp: *A frog is a clammy creature.* *adj.*, **clam-mi er, clam mi est.**

clam or (klam/ər), 1 a loud noise, especially of voices; continual uproar: *The clamor of the crowd filled the air.* 2 make a loud noise or continual uproar; shout. 3 a noisy demand. 4 demand noisily: *The children were clamoring for candy.* 1,3 *n.*, 2,4 *v.*

clam or ous (klam/ər əs), 1 loud and noisy; shouting: *clamorous criticism.* 2 making noisy demands or complaints: *The mayor gave in to the clamorous parents and agreed to discuss building a new school with them.* *adj.* —**clam′-or ous ly,** *adv.* —**clam′or ous-ness,** *n.*

clamp (def. 1)

clamp (klamp), 1 brace, band, wedge, or other device for holding things tightly together: *She used a clamp to hold the arm on the chair until the glue dried.* 2 fasten together with a clamp; put in a clamp; strengthen with a clamp: *A picture frame must be clamped together while the glue is drying.* 1 *n.*, 2 *v.*

clamp down, INFORMAL. become more strict; impose strict control: *The police clamped down on speeders.*

clan (klan), 1 group of related families that claim to be descended from a common ancestor. 2 group of people closely joined together by some common interest: *The whole clan of writers was at the lecture.* *n.* —**clan′like′,** *adj.*

clan des tine (klan des/tən), arranged or made in a stealthy or underhanded manner; secret; concealed: *The spy's clandestine plans to enter the country went undetected.* *adj.* —**clan des′-tine ly,** *adv.*

clang (klang), 1 a loud, harsh, ringing sound like metal being hit: *The clang of the fire bell aroused the town.* 2 make a clang: *The fire bells clanged.* 3 cause to clang: *The firemen clanged the bell on the fire truck as it sped past us.* 1 *n.*, 2,3 *v.*

clan gor (klang/ər or klang/gər), 1 a continued clanging. 2 clang. *n.*

clan gor ous (klang/ər əs or klang/-gər əs), clanging. *adj.*

hat, āge, fär; let, ēqual, tėrm;
it, īce; hot, ōpen, ôrder;
oil, out; cup, pùt, rüle; ch, child;
ng, long; sh, she; th, thin;
ŦH, then; zh, measure;

ə represents *a* in about,
e in taken, *i* in pencil,
o in lemon, *u* in circus.

clank (klangk), 1 a sharp, harsh sound like the rattle of a heavy chain: *The clank of heavy machinery filled the factory.* 2 make a clank: *The old bridge rattled and clanked as we drove over it.* 3 cause to clank: *The dishwasher clanked the pots and pans.* 4 move with a clanking sound. 1 *n.*, 2-4 *v.*

clan nish (klan/ish), 1 having to do with a clan: *the clannish customs of the Scottish Highlanders.* 2 closely united; not liking outsiders: *The older settlers were clannish and afraid of their new neighbors.* *adj.* —**clan′nish ly,** *adv.* —**clan′nish ness,** *n.*

clans man (klanz/mən), member of a clan. *n.*, *pl.* **clans men.**

clap (klap), 1 strike together loudly: *clap the cymbals, clap one's hands.* 2 applaud by striking the hands together: *When the show was over, we all clapped.* 3 a sudden noise, such as a single burst of thunder, the sound of the hands struck together, or the sound of a loud slap. 4 strike with a quick blow; slap: *I clapped my friend on the back.* 5 a loud, quick blow; slap: *a clap on the shoulder.* 6 put or place quickly and effectively: *The police clapped the thief into jail.* 1,2,4,6 *v.*, **clapped, clapping;** 3,5 *n.*

clap board (klab/ərd or klap/bôrd/), 1 a thin board, thicker along one edge than along the other. Clapboards are used to cover the outer walls of wooden buildings. 2 cover with clapboards. 1 *n.*, 2 *v.*

clap per (klap/ər), 1 person or thing that claps. 2 the movable part inside a bell that strikes against and rings the outer part. *n.*

claret (klar/ət), 1 kind of red wine. 2 a dark purplish red. 3 dark purplish-red: *a claret coat.* 1,2 *n.*, 3 *adj.*

clar i fi ca tion (klar/ə fə kā/shən), act or process of clarifying. *n.*

clar i fy (klar/ə fī), 1 make clearer; explain: *The teacher's explanation clarified the difficult instructions.* 2 make or become clear; purify: *The cook clarified the fat by heating it in water and straining it through cloth.* *v.*, **clar-i fied, clar i fy ing.**

clarinet

adj. adjective	*n.* noun
adv. adverb	*prep.* preposition
conj. conjunction	*pron.* pronoun
interj. interjection	*v.* verb
sing. singular	*pl.* plural

clarinet
The player blows through. the mouthpiece and presses keys or covers holes to change pitch.

clar i net (klar/ə net/), a woodwind instrument, having a mouthpiece with a single reed and played by means of holes and keys. *n.*

clar i net ist (klar/ə net/ist), person who plays a clarinet. *n.*

clar i on (klar/ē ən), 1 a trumpet with clear, shrill tones. 2 sound made by this trumpet or a sound like it. 3 clear and shrill: *a clarion sound or call.* 1,2 *n.,* 3 *adj.*

clar i ty (klar/ə tē), clearness: *Her writing has great clarity of style. n.*

Clark (klärk), 1 **George Rogers,** 1752-1818, American soldier and frontiersman. 2 his brother, **William,** 1770-1838, American soldier and explorer of the American northwest together with Meriwether Lewis. *n.*

clash (klash), 1 a loud, harsh sound like that of two things running into each other, of striking metal, or of bells rung together but not in tune: *He heard the clash of cymbals.* 2 hit or strike with a clash: *In my haste I clashed my toolbox against the edge of the iron workbench. The metal gate clashed shut.* 3 a strong disagreement; conflict: *There are many clashes of opinion in that family, for no two of them think alike.* 4 come into conflict; disagree strongly: *The freshmen clashed with the sophomores. The purple house clashed with the red brick buildings next to it.* 1,3 *n., pl.* **clash es;** 2,4 *v.*

clasp (klasp), 1 thing to fasten two parts or pieces together. A buckle on a belt is one kind of clasp. 2 fasten together with a clasp. 3 hold closely with the arms; embrace: *I clasped the kitten gently to my breast.* 4 a close hold with the arms: *I was glad to escape from the bear's clasp.* 5 grip firmly with the hand; grasp: *I clasped a hammer in my hand.* 6 a firm grip with the hand: *She gave my hand a warm clasp.* 1,4,6 *n.,* 2,3,5 *v.*

class (klas), 1 group of persons or things alike in some way; kind; sort: *That magazine has an intelligent class of readers.* 2 group of students taught together: *The art class meets in room 202.* 3 a meeting of such a group: *When I was absent I missed a great many classes.* 4 group of pupils entering a school together and graduating in the same year: *The class of 1968 graduated in 1968.* 5 rank or division of society: *In the Middle Ages, kings and nobles belonged to the upper class, some tradesmen and merchants to the middle class, and peasants to the lower class.* 6 put or be in a class or group; classify: *She is classed with the best swimmers in the school.* 7 grade or quality: *First class is the best and most costly way to travel.* 8 SLANG. high quality; excellence; style: *That singer has never really shown much class.* 9 group of animals or plants ranking below a phylum and above an order. Crustaceans and insects are two classes in the phylum of arthropods. 1-5,7-9 *n., pl.* **class es;** 6 *v.*

clas sic (klas/ik), 1 author or artist of acknowledged excellence whose works serve as a standard, model, or guide: *Emily Dickinson is a classic.* 2 work of literature or art of the highest rank or quality: *Shakespeare's "Hamlet" is a classic.* 3 of the highest rank or quality; serving as a standard, model, or guide: *The "Mona Lisa" is a classic work of art. The Alhambra is a classic example of Moorish architecture.* 4 simple and fine in form: *the classic design of the Pyramids.* 5 contest of great importance: *The World Series is a baseball classic.* 6 of the literature, art, and life of ancient Greece and Rome. The classic orders of Greek architecture are the Doric, Ionic, and Corinthian. 7 **the classics,** the literature of ancient Greece and Rome. 1,2,5,7 *n.,* 3,4,6 *adj.*

clas si cal (klas/ə kəl), 1 of or having to do with the literature, art, and life of ancient Greece and Rome: *Classical languages include ancient Greek and the Latin of the ancient Romans.* 2 excellent; first-class. 3 simple and fine in form. 4 of high musical quality and enjoyed especially by serious students of music. Symphonies, concertos, and operas are considered classical music. *adj.* —**clas/si cal ly,** *adv.*

clas si fi a ble (klas/ə fī/ə bəl), that can be classified. *adj.*

clas si fi ca tion (klas/ə fə kā/shən), arrangement in classes or groups; grouping according to some system: *The classification of books in a library helps you to find the books you want. n.*

clas si fied (klas/ə fīd), 1 sorted or arranged in classes. A classified telephone directory lists names according to classes of business, services, and professions. 2 (of certain public documents of the United States) having a classification as secret, confidential, or restricted. 3 secret: *The airplane was on a classified flight. adj.*

clas si fi er (klas/ə fī/ər), person or thing that classifies. *n.*

clas si fy (klas/ə fī), arrange in classes or groups; group according to some system: *Employees in the post office classify letters and parcels according to the places where they are to go. v.,* **clas si fied, clas si fy ing.**

class less (klas/lis), without classes; not divided into classes: *a classless society. adj.*

class mate (klas/māt/), member of the same class in school. *n.*

class room (klas/rüm/ or klas/rum/), room in which classes are held; schoolroom. *n.*

clat ter (klat/ər), 1 a confused noise like that of many plates being struck together: *The clatter in the school cafeteria was so great that we could hardly hear one another talk.* 2 move or fall with confused noise; make a confused noise: *The horse's hoofs clattered over the stones.* 3 noisy talk. 4 talk fast and noisily. 1,3 *n.,* 2,4 *v.*

clause (klôz), 1 part of a sentence having a subject and predicate. In "He came before we left," "He came" is a main clause that can stand alone as a sentence, and "before we left" is a subordinate clause that depends upon the main clause for completion of its meaning. 2 a single provision of a law, treaty, or any other written agreement: *A clause in our lease says we may not keep a dog in this building. n.*

claus tro pho bi a (klô/strə fō/bē ə), an abnormal fear of enclosed spaces: *Elevators give me claustrophobia. n.*

clav i chord (klav/ə kôrd), a musical instrument with strings and a keyboard. The piano developed from it. *n.*

clav i cle (klav/ə kəl), collarbone. *n.*

cla vier (klə vir/), 1 keyboard or set of keys of a piano, organ, etc. 2 any musical instrument with a keyboard. The harpsichord and piano are two

clavichord
made in Germany about 1760

kinds of claviers. **3** a soundless keyboard used for practice. *n.*

claw (klô), **1** a sharp, hooked nail on a bird's or animal's foot. **2** foot with such sharp, hooked nails. **3** the pincers of a lobster, crab, etc. **4** anything like a claw. The part of a hammer used for pulling nails is the claw. **5** scratch, tear, seize, or pull with claws or hands: *The kitten was clawing the rug.* 1-4 *n.,* 5 *v.* —**claw′like′,** *adj.*

clay (klā), a stiff, sticky kind of earth, that can be easily shaped when wet and hardens when it is dried or baked. Bricks, dishes, and vases may be made from clay. *n.* —**clay′like′,** *adj.*

Clay (klā), Henry, 1777-1852, American statesman. *n.*

clay ey (klā′ē), **1** of, like, or containing clay. **2** covered or smeared with clay. *adj.,* **clay i er, clay i est.**

clay pigeon, a saucerlike clay target thrown in the air or released from the trap in trapshooting.

clean (klēn), **1** free from dirt or filth; not soiled or stained: *clean clothes. Soap and water make us clean.* **2** pure or innocent: *The saint had a clean heart.* **3** having clean habits: *Cats are clean animals.* **4** make clean: *clean a room. Washing cleans clothes.* **5** do cleaning: *I am going to clean this morning.* **6** clear, even, or regular: *a clean cut with no ragged edges, the clean features of a handsome face.* **7** well-shaped; trim: *an airplane with clean, sleek lines.* **8** clever; skillful: *a clean performance.* **9** complete; entire; total: *The new teacher made a clean sweep of the old textbooks, replacing them with brand-new ones.* **10** completely; entirely; totally: *The horse jumped clean over the brook.* 1-3,6-9 *adj.,* 4,5 *v.,* 10 *adv.*

clean out, 1 make clean by emptying: *Clean out your desk.* **2** empty; use up: *The children cleaned out a whole box of cookies.* **3** SLANG. deprive of money: *I was cleaned out in the card game.*

clean up, 1 make clean by removing dirt, rubbish, etc.: *clean up a campsite.* **2** put in order: *clean up a cluttered drawer.* **3** INFORMAL. finish; complete: *Let's clean up the plans for our trip.*

clean-cut (klēn′kut′), **1** having clear, sharp outlines; distinct; definite: *a clean-cut profile.* **2** having a neat and wholesome look: *a clean-cut young swimmer. adj.*

clean er (klē′nər), **1** person whose work is keeping buildings, windows, or other objects clean. **2** anything that removes dirt, grease, or stains. **3** dry cleaner. *n.*

clean li ness (klen′lē nis), a being always, or nearly always, clean; cleanness: *Cleanliness is good for health. n.*

clean ly¹ (klen′lē), clean; always, or

nearly always, clean: *Our cat is a cleanly animal.* adj., **clean li er, clean li est.** [Old English *clǣnlic,* from *clǣne* clean + -*līc* -ly²]

clean ly² (klēn′lē), in a clean manner: *The butcher's knife cut cleanly through the meat. adv.* [Old English *clǣnlīce,* from *clǣne* clean + -*līce* -ly¹]

clean ness (klēn′nis), clean condition or quality: *We judged the hotel by the cleanness of its rooms. n.*

cleanse (klenz), **1** make clean: *cleanse a wound before bandaging.* **2** make pure: *cleanse the soul. v.,* **cleansed, cleans ing.**

cleans er (klen′zər), substance that cleans. Soap and water are good cleansers. Detergents are chemical cleansers. *n.*

clear (klir), **1** not cloudy, misty, or hazy; bright; light: *A clear sky is free of clouds.* **2** easy to see through; transparent: *clear glass.* **3** easily heard, seen, or understood; plain; distinct: *The sound of the trumpet came loud and clear. There is a clear view of the sea from that hill. He gave a clear account of the accident.* **4** free from blemishes: *a clear skin.* **5** sure; certain: *It is clear that it is going to rain.* **6** make clean and free; get clear: *clear land of trees.* **7** become clear: *It rained and then it cleared.* **8** remove to leave a space clear: *clear the dishes from the table.* **9** pass by or over without touching: *The horse cleared the fence.* **10** free from blame or guilt; innocent: *a clear conscience.* **11** make free from blame or guilt; prove to be innocent: *The jury's verdict cleared the accused man.* **12** free from debts or charges: *He made a clear profit after taking money out to pay taxes and expenses.* **13** make as profit free from debts or charges: *The company cleared a million dollars last year.* **14** in a clear manner; completely; entirely: *The bullet went clear through the door.* **15** a clear space. 1-5,10,12 *adj.,* 6-9,11,13 *v.,* 14 *adv.,* 15 *n.* —**clear′ly,** *adv.* —**clear′ness,** *n.*

clear away or **clear off, 1** remove to leave a space clear: *I cleared away the snow with a shovel.* **2** disappear; go away: *The fog cleared away.*

clear out, 1 make clear by throwing out or emptying: *She cleared out her closet.* **2** INFORMAL. go away; leave: *The audience cleared out of the burning theater quickly.*

clear up, 1 make or become clear: *Stay indoors until the weather clears up.* **2** explain: *She cleared up our problems by telling us what we had done wrong.*

in the clear, INFORMAL. free of guilt or blame; innocent: *The testimony of the witness puts the suspect in the clear.*

clear ance (klir′əns), **1** act of clear-

hat, āge, fär; let, ēqual, tėrm;
it, īce; hot, ōpen, ôrder;
oil, out; cup, pùt, rüle; ch, child;
ng, long; sh, she; th, thin;
ᴛʜ, then; zh, measure;

ə represents *a* in about,
e in taken, *i* in pencil,
o in lemon, *u* in circus.

ing: *Clearance of the theater was quick and quiet during the fire.* **2** a clear space; distance between things that pass by each other without touching: *There was only a foot of clearance between the top of the truck and the roof of the tunnel.* **3** a certifying that a person considered for a position of trust is reliable. **4** sale of goods at reduced prices. *n.*

clear-cut (klir′kut′), **1** having clear, sharp outlines: *a face with clear-cut features.* **2** clear; definite; distinct: *Having planned carefully, she had clear-cut ideas about how to proceed. adj.*

clear ing (klir′ing), an open space of cleared land in a forest or in an area of dense undergrowth. *n.*

cleat
(def. 3)

cleat (klēt), **1** strip of wood or iron fastened across anything for support or for sure footing: *The gangway had cleats to keep the passengers from slipping.* **2** a small, wedge-shaped block fastened to a spar, etc., as a support, check, or the like. **3** piece of wood or iron used for securing ropes or lines to a flagpole, a dock, etc. **4** piece of metal, wood, or stiff leather attached to the sole or heel of a shoe to prevent slipping. *n.*

cleav age (klē′vij), **1** a cleaving or a being cleft; split; division. **2** the property of a crystal or rock of splitting along planes: *Slate shows a marked cleavage and can easily be separated into layers. n.*

cleave¹ (klēv), **1** cut, divide, or split open: *A blow of the whale's tail caused the whaling boat to cleave in two.* **2** pass through; pierce; penetrate: *The airplane swept across the sky, cleaving the clouds. v.,* **cleft** or **cleaved** or **clove, cleft** or **cleaved** or **clo ven, cleav ing.** [Old English *clēofan*]

cleave² (klēv), hold fast; cling; adhere: *cleave to an old-fashioned idea. v.,*

157

cleaver

adj. adjective	*n.* noun
adv. adverb	*prep.* preposition
conj. conjunction	*pron.* pronoun
interj. interjection	*v.* verb
sing. singular	*pl.* plural

cleaved, cleav ing. [Old English *cleofian*]

cleav er (klē′vər), a cutting tool with a heavy blade and a short handle. A butcher uses a cleaver to chop through meat or bone. *n.*

cleaver

clef (klef), symbol in music indicating the pitch of the notes on a staff. *n.*

cleft (kleft), **1** a past tense and a past participle of **cleave**[1]. *A blow of the ax cleft the log in two.* **2** split; divided: *a cleft stick.* **3** space or opening made by splitting; crack: *a cleft in the rocks.* **1** *v.,* **2** *adj.,* **3** *n.*

cleft palate, a narrow opening running lengthwise in the roof of the mouth, caused by failure of the two parts of the palate to join before birth.

clem a tis (klem′ə tis), a climbing vine with clusters of large white, red, pink, blue, or purple flowers. *n., pl.* **clem a tis es** or **clem a tis.**

clem en cy (klem′ən sē), **1** gentleness in the use of power or authority; mercy: *The government showed clemency to the defeated rebels.* **2** mildness: *The clemency of the weather allowed them to live outdoors. n., pl.* **clem en cies.**

Clem ens (klem′ənz), **Samuel Langhorne,** the real name of **Mark Twain.** *n.*

clem ent (klem′ənt), **1** merciful toward those in one's power. **2** mild: *Hawaii usually has clement weather. adj.* **—clem′ent ly,** *adv.*

clench (klench), **1** close tightly together: *clench one's teeth, a clenched fist.* **2** grasp firmly: *She clenched the handlebars as the bike went up over the curb.* **3** a firm grasp; tight grip: *the clench of a hand.* **4** clinch (a nail, staple, etc.). **1,2,4** *v.,* **3** *n., pl.* **clench es.**

Cle o pa tra (klē′ə pat′rə *or* klē′ə-pā′trə), 69?-30 B.C., last queen of an-

cient Egypt, from 47 to 30 B.C. *n.*

cler gy (klėr′jē), persons ordained for religious work; ministers, pastors, priests, and rabbis. *n., pl.* **cler gies.**

cler gy man (klėr′jē mən), member of the clergy; a minister, pastor, priest, or rabbi. *n., pl.* **cler gy men.**

cler ic (kler′ik), clergyman. *n.*

cler i cal (kler′ə kəl), **1** of a clerk or clerks; for clerks: *Keeping records and typing letters are clerical jobs in an office.* **2** of a clergyman or the clergy: *clerical duties, clerical robes. adj.* **—cler′i cal ly,** *adv.*

clerk (klėrk), **1** person employed in a store or shop to sell goods; salesman or saleswoman in a store. **2** person employed in an office to file records, type letters, etc. **3** work as a clerk: *I clerk in a drugstore after school.* **4** a public official who keeps the records and superintends the routine business of a court of law, legislature, town or county government, etc. **1,2,4** *n.,* **3** *v.*

Cleve land (klēv′lənd), **1** city in NE Ohio, on Lake Erie. **2 (Stephen) Grover,** 1837-1908, the 22nd and 24th president of the United States, from 1885 to 1889 and from 1893 to 1897. *n.*

clev er (klev′ər), **1** having a quick mind; bright; intelligent: *She is the cleverest girl in our class.* **2** skillful in doing some particular thing: *clever at working with wood.* **3** showing skill or intelligence: *The magician did a clever trick. Her answer to the riddle was clever. adj.* **—clev′er ly,** *adv.* **—clev′er ness,** *n.*

clew (klü), clue. *n.*

cli ché (klē shā′), expression or idea worn out by long use. "Father Time," "white as snow," and "cheeks like roses" are clichés. *n., pl.* **cli chés.**

click (klik), **1** a short, sharp sound like that of a key turning in a lock: *We heard a click as the dime went down the coin slot.* **2** make or cause to make such a sound: *The key clicked in the lock. I clicked my tongue.* **3** SLANG. come to an understanding; be in harmony: *I clicked with them from the start.* **4** SLANG. be successful: *The new play clicked with the critics.* **1** *n.,* **2-4** *v.*

cli ent (klī′ənt), **1** person for whom a lawyer, accountant, or other professional person acts. **2** customer. *n.*

cli en tele (klī′ən tel′), clients as a group: *a lawyer's clientele, the clientele of a theater. n.*

cliff (klif), a very steep slope of rock, clay, etc. *n.* **—cliff′like′,** *adj.*

cliff dweller, Indian in the southwestern United States who lived in a cave or house built in a cliff. The cliff dwellers were ancestors of the Pueblo Indians.

cli mate (klī′mit), **1** the kind of weather a place has over a long period of time, based on conditions of heat and cold, moisture and dryness, clearness and cloudiness, wind and calm. **2** region with certain conditions of heat and cold, rainfall, wind, sunlight, etc.: *The doctor ordered him to go to a drier climate to relieve his asthma.* **3** condition or feeling that exists, especially at some particular time: *The climate of public opinion just before the Revolutionary War was against new British taxes. n.*

cli mat ic (klī mat′ik), of or having to do with climate. *adj.*

cli max (klī′maks), **1** the highest point of interest; most exciting part: *A visit to the Grand Canyon was the climax of our vacation.* **2** bring or come to a climax: *Her election to the Senate climaxed a long career in politics.* **1** *n., pl.* **cli max es; 2** *v.*

climb (klīm), **1** go up, especially by using the hands or feet, or both; ascend: *The old man climbed the stairs slowly.* **2** go in any direction, especially with the help of the hands: *climb over a fence. The painter climbed down the ladder.* **3** move upward; rise: *Smoke climbed slowly from the chimney. The price of sugar has climbed during the past year.* **4** grow upward by holding on or twining around: *Ivy and honeysuckle climbed over the wall.* **5** a climbing: *Our climb up the mountain took ten hours.* **6** place to be climbed: *The path ended in a difficult climb.* **1-4** *v.,* **5,6** *n.*

climb er (klī′mər), **1** person or thing that climbs. **2** a climbing plant; vine. *n.*

clime (klīm), **1** region. **2** climate. *n.*

clinch (klinch), **1** fasten (a driven nail, a bolt, etc.) firmly by bending over the point that sticks out. **2** fix firmly; settle decisively: *A deposit of five dollars clinched our bargain.* **3** grasp one another tightly in boxing or wrestling; grapple. **4** act of clinching: *When the boxers went into a clinch, the crowd hissed.* **5** clench. **1-3,5** *v.,* **4** *n., pl.* **clinch es.**

clinch er (klin′chər), INFORMAL. a decisive argument, statement, etc. *n.*

cling (kling), stick or hold fast; adhere: *A vine clings to the wall. Wet clothes cling to the body. The child clung to its parent's hand. People sometimes cling to tradition. v.,* **clung, cling ing.**

clin ic (klin′ik), **1** place connected with a hospital or medical school where peo-

clipper
(def. 2)

(def. 3) →

[Old English *clyppan* encircle, embrace]

clip board (klip′bôrd′), board with a heavy spring clip at one end for holding papers while writing. *n.*

clip per (klip′ər), 1 person who clips or cuts. 2 Often, **clippers,** *pl.* tool for cutting: *hair clippers, a nail clipper.* 3 a large sailing ship built and rigged for speed: *American square-rigged clippers used to sail all over the world. n.*

clip ping (klip′ing), 1 article, picture, or advertisement cut out of a newspaper, magazine, etc. 2 piece cut off from or out of something else. *n.*

clique (klēk *or* klik), a small, exclusive group of people within a larger group. *n.*

cloak (klōk), 1 a loose outer garment with or without sleeves. 2 cover with a cloak. 3 anything that covers or conceals: *They hid their dislike of us behind a cloak of friendship.* 4 cover up; conceal: *I tried to cloak my fear by whistling and pretending to be unafraid.* 1,3 *n.,* 2,4 *v.*

cloak room (klōk′rüm′ *or* klōk′rüm′), room where coats, hats, etc., can be left for a time; coatroom. *n.*

clob ber (klob′ər), SLANG. 1 strike or beat heavily. 2 defeat severely. *v.*

clock[1] (klok), 1 instrument for measuring and showing time. A clock is not made to be carried around as a watch is. 2 measure or record the time of; time: *The teacher clocked the three girls with a stopwatch to see which was the fastest runner.* 1 *n.,* 2 *v.* [from Dutch of the 1300's *clocke* clock, bell] —**clock′-like′,** *adj.*

clock[2] (klok), an ornamental pattern on the side of a stocking or sock, extending from the ankle up. *n.* [origin uncertain]

clock wise (klok′wīz′), in the direction in which the hands of a clock move; from left to right: *Turn the key clockwise to unlock the door (adv.). He opened the faucet with a clockwise turn (adj.). adv., adj.*

clock work (klok′werk′), 1 the machinery by which a clock is run. 2 one form of such machinery, consisting of gears, wheels, and springs. Many toys that move are run by clockwork. *n.*

like clockwork, with great regularity and smoothness: *The launching of the rocket went off like clockwork.*

clod (klod), 1 lump of earth. 2 a stupid person; blockhead. *n.*

clog (klog), 1 fill up; choke up: *Grease clogged the drain. The expressway always clogs with heavy traffic during the rush hour.* 2 hinder; hold back: *Heavy clothes clogged the swimmer's progress.* 3 anything that hinders. 4 shoe with a thick, wooden sole. 1,2 *v.,* **clogged, clog ging;** 3,4 *n.*

ple can receive medical treatment, usually free or at low cost. 2 place for medical treatment or study of certain people or diseases: *The children's clinic is open during school hours.* 3 place where practical instruction on any subject is given: *a football clinic, a reading clinic.* 4 practical instruction of medical students by examining or treating patients in the presence of the students. *n.*

clin i cal (klin′ə kəl), 1 of or having to do with a clinic. 2 used or performed in a sickroom: *Doctors learn clinical procedure. adj.* —**clin′i cal ly,** *adv.*

clink (klingk), 1 a light, sharp, ringing sound like that of drinking glasses hitting together. 2 make or cause to make this sound: *The spoon clinked in the glass.* 1 *n.,* 2 *v.*

clink er (kling′kər), a large, rough cinder. *n.*

Clin ton (klin′tən), **De Witt,** 1769-1828, American political leader who promoted the building of the Erie Canal. *n.*

clip[1] (klip), 1 trim with shears, scissors, or clippers; cut short; cut: *A sheep's fleece is clipped off to get wool.* 2 cut the hair or fleece of: *Our dog is clipped every summer.* 3 act of clipping: *My hair needs a clip around the back of my neck.* 4 anything clipped off, especially wool clipped from sheep at one time. 5 cut out of a magazine, newspaper, etc.: *She clipped the cartoon and passed it around the class.* 6 INFORMAL. a fast motion: *Our bus passed through the village at quite a clip.* 7 INFORMAL. move fast: *The car clipped down the road at seventy miles an hour.* 8 INFORMAL. hit or punch sharply: *The boxer clipped his opponent on the jaw.* 9 INFORMAL. a sharp blow or punch. 1,2,5,7,8 *v.,* **clipped, clip ping;** 3,4,6,9 *n.* [probably from a Scandinavian word of the 1200's, such as Icelandic *klippa*]

clip[2] (klip), 1 hold tight; fasten: *The teacher clipped the papers together.* 2 something used for clipping things together. A clip for papers is often made of a piece of bent wire. 3 a metal holder for cartridges used in some firearms. 1 *v.,* **clipped, clip ping;** 2,3 *n.*

hat, āge, fär; let, ēqual, tėrm;
it, īce; hot, ōpen, ôrder;
oil, out; cup, pùt, rüle; ch, child;
ng, long; sh, she; th, thin;
ᵺ, then; zh, measure;

ə represents *a* in about,
e in taken, *i* in pencil,
o in lemon, *u* in circus.

cloister (def. 1)

clois ter (kloi′stər), 1 a covered walk, often along the wall of a building, with a row of pillars on the open side or sides. A cloister is sometimes built around the courtyard of monastery, church, or college buildings. 2 place of religious retirement; convent or monastery. 3 a quiet place shut away from the world. 4 shut away in a quiet place: *He cloistered himself in his room to work.* 1-3 *n.,* 4 *v.*

close[1] (klōz), 1 bring together or move the parts of so as to leave no opening; shut: *Close the door. The sleepy child's eyes are closing.* 2 stop up; fill; block: *close a crack in the wall with plaster.* 3 bring together; come together: *The troops closed ranks.* 4 bring or come to an end; finish: *The meeting closed with a speech by the president.* 5 an end; finish: *She spoke at the close of the meeting.* 1-4 *v.,* **closed, clos ing;** 5 *n.* [from French of the 1200's *clos-,* a form of *clore* to close, from Latin *claudere*]

close down, shut completely; stop: *The factory closed down because it had no orders from customers.*

close in, come near and shut in on all sides: *The zoo keepers closed in on the escaped tiger.*

close out, sell in order to get rid of: *The store closed out the old models in a special sale.*

clog (def. 4)

159

adj. adjective	n. noun
adv. adverb	prep. preposition
conj. conjunction	pron. pronoun
interj. interjection	v. verb
sing. singular	pl. plural

close up, 1 shut completely; stop up; block: *The windows of the warehouse were closed up with brick.* 2 bring or come nearer together: *The two divisions of the marching band closed up to form a single column.*

close[2] (klōs), 1 with little space between; near together; near: *These two houses are close. He has close teeth.* 2 fitting tightly; tight; narrow: *They live in very close quarters.* 3 having its parts near together; compact: *This sweater has a close weave.* 4 intimate; dear: *The two girls are close friends.* 5 careful; exact: *You need to take closer measurements before ordering the lumber.* 6 thorough; strict: *Pay close attention.* 7 having little fresh air; stuffy: *With the windows shut, the room was hot and close.* 8 near the surface; short: *a close haircut.* 9 stingy: *He is as close as a miser with his money.* 10 nearly equal: *The last game was a close contest.* 11 not fond of talking; not open; reserved: *She is very close about her own affairs.* 12 near: *The two farms lie close together. The end of the year is drawing close.* 1-11 *adj.,* **clos er, clos est;** 12 *adv.* [from French of the 1200's *clos,* from Latin *clausum* closed, from *claudere* to close] **—close′ly,** *adv.* **—close′ness,** *n.*

close call (klōs), INFORMAL. a narrow escape from danger or an accident.

close-fist ed (klōs′fis′tid), stingy; miserly. *adj.*

close-mouthed (klōs′mouᵀHd′ or klōs′moutht′), not fond of talking; reserved; reticent. *adj.*

clos et (kloz′it), 1 a small room for storing clothes or household supplies. 2 a small, private room for prayer or study. 3 shut up in a private room for a secret talk: *We were closeted with our lawyer for over an hour.* 1,2 *n.,* 3 *v.*

close-up (klōs′up′), 1 picture taken with a camera at close range. 2 a close view. *n.*

clo sure (klō′zhər), 1 a closing or a being closed: *the closure of a shop.* 2 thing that closes. 3 end; finish; conclusion. 4 cloture. *n.*

clot (klot), 1 a half-solid lump; thickened mass: *A clot of blood formed in the cut and stopped the bleeding.* 2 form into clots; coagulate: *Blood clots when it is exposed to the air.* 1 *n.,* 2 *v.,* **clot ted, clot ting.**

cloth (klôth), 1 material made from wool, cotton, silk, rayon, or other fiber, by weaving, knitting, or rolling and pressing. Cloth is used for clothing, curtains, bedding, and many other purposes. 2 piece of this material used for a special purpose: *a cloth for the table.* 3 profession of a clergyman. 4 **the cloth,** clergymen; the clergy. *n., pl.* **cloths** (klôᵀHz *or* klôths).

clothe (klōᵀH), 1 put clothes on; cover with clothes; dress: *We clothed the child warmly in a heavy sweater and pants.* 2 provide with clothes: *It costs quite a bit to clothe a family of six.* 3 cover: *The sun clothes the earth with light.* 4 provide; furnish; equip: *Congress is clothed with the authority to make laws.* 5 express: *Her ideas are clothed in simple words.* *v.,* **clothed** *or* **clad, cloth ing.**

clothes (klōz *or* klōᵀHz), 1 coverings for a person's body: *I gave the clothes I outgrew to my cousin.* 2 bedclothes. *n.pl.*

clothes line (klōz′līn′), rope or wire to hang clothes on to dry or air them. *n.*

clothes pin (klōz′pin′), a wooden or plastic clip to hold clothes on a clothesline. *n.*

cloth ier (klō′ᵀHyər), 1 seller or maker of clothing. 2 seller of cloth. *n.*

cloth ing (klō′ᵀHing), 1 clothes. 2 covering. *n.*

clo ture (klō′chər), a limiting of debate by a legislature in order to get an immediate vote on the question being discussed; closure. *n.*

cloud (kloud), 1 mass of tiny drops of water or ice particles floating in the air high above the earth. Clouds may be white, rounded heaps, fleecy streamers, or dark, almost black, masses. 2 mass of smoke or dust in the air. 3 cover with a cloud or clouds: *A mist clouded our view.* 4 grow or become cloudy: *The sky clouded over. My eyes clouded with tears.* 5 a great number of things moving close together: *A cloud of locusts descended upon the wheat field. Robin Hood's men sent the sheriff fleeing under a cloud of arrows.* 6 anything that darkens or dims: *A cloud of disappointment was reflected in his face.* 7 darken; dim; make or become gloomy: *a face clouded with anger.* 8 a cause of suspicion or disgrace: *The former convict found it hard to get a job because a cloud always hung over his reputation.* 9 bring under suspicion or disgrace. 1,2,5,6,8 *n.,* 3,4,7,9 *v.* **—cloud′like′,** *adj.*

in the clouds, 1 far above the earth. 2 unrealistic; not practical: *The inexperienced planners were completely in the* clouds. 3 daydreaming; absent-minded: *She is always up in the clouds; sometimes she even forgets to eat.*

cloud burst (kloud′bėrst′), a sudden, violent rainfall. *n.*

cloud i ly (kloud′l ē), in a cloudy manner. *adv.*

cloud i ness (kloud′ē nis), cloudy condition. *n.*

cloud less (kloud′lis), without a cloud; clear and bright; sunny: *a cloudless sky.* *adj.*

cloud y (kloud′ē), 1 covered with clouds; having clouds in it: *a cloudy sky.* 2 not clear: *The stream is cloudy with mud.* 3 not carefully thought out; confused; indistinct: *cloudy ideas.* 4 gloomy; frowning: *The unhappy child had a cloudy expression.* *adj.,* **cloud i er, cloud i est.**

clout (klout), 1 INFORMAL. hit with the hand; rap; knock. 2 INFORMAL. a rap or knock; cuff. 3 OLD USE. cloth or rag. 1 *v.,* 2,3 *n.*

clove[1] (klōv), 1 a strong, fragrant spice made from the dried flower buds of a tropical tree. 2 the dried flower bud. 3 the tree. *n.* [from French of the 1300's *clou,* from Latin *clavus* a nail]

clove[2] (klōv), a small, separate section of a bulb: *a clove of garlic.* *n.* [Old English *clufu*]

clove[3] (klōv), cleft; a past tense of **cleave**[1]. *v.*

clo ven (klō′vən), 1 cleft; a past participle of **cleave**[1]. 2 split; divided. Cows and sheep have cloven hoofs. 1 *v.,* 2 *adj.*

clo ver (klō′vər), a low plant with leaves having three leaflets and sweet-smelling rounded heads of small red, white, yellow, or purple flowers. Clover is grown as food for horses and cattle and to improve the soil. Clover belongs to the same family as the pea. *n.*

in clover, enjoying a life of pleasure and luxury without work or worry.

clo ver leaf (klō′vər lēf′), intersection of two highways, with one passing over the other, and with a series of curving ramps in the shape of a four-leaf clover that permit traffic to move from one highway to the other without having to cross in front of other traffic. *n., pl.*

cloverleaf

clo ver leafs, clo ver leaves (klō′vər lēvz′).

clown (kloun), 1 person in a circus, carnival, etc., who makes people laugh by wearing funny costumes and make-up and by playing tricks and jokes. 2 act like a clown; play tricks and jokes; act silly. 3 person who acts like a clown; silly person. 1,3 *n.,* 2 *v.*

clown ish (klou′nish), like a clown; like a clown's: *clownish behavior. adj.* —**clown′ish ly,** *adv.* —**clown′ish ness,** *n.*

cloy (kloi), 1 make weary by too much, too sweet, or too rich food: *His appetite was cloyed by all the candy he had eaten.* 2 make or become weary by too much of anything pleasant. *v.*

club (klub), 1 a heavy stick of wood, thicker at one end, used as a weapon. 2 stick or bat used in some games to hit a ball: *golf clubs.* 3 beat or hit with a club or something similar. 4 group of people joined together for some special purpose: *a tennis club, a yacht club, a nature-study club.* 5 building or rooms used by a club. 6 join together for some special purpose: *The children clubbed together to buy their parents an anniversary present.* 7 figure shaped like this: ♣. 8 a playing card with one or more black, club-shaped figures. 9 **clubs,** *pl.* suit of such playing cards. 1,2,4,5,7-9 *n.,* 3,6 *v.,* **clubbed, club bing.**

club foot (klub′fut′), 1 a deformed foot, short and distorted. 2 deformity of the foot caused by faulty development before birth. *n., pl.* **club feet** (klub′fēt′).

club moss, a flowerless plant that grows along the ground and looks much like a vine covered with pine needles.

cluck (kluk), 1 the sound that a hen makes in calling to her chickens. 2 make this sound. 1 *n.,* 2 *v.*

clue (klü), fact or object which aids in solving a mystery or problem: *The police could find no fingerprints or other clues to help them solve the robbery. n.* Also, **clew.**

clump (klump), 1 number of things of the same kind growing or grouped together; cluster: *The girl hid in a clump of bushes.* 2 lump or mass: *a clump of earth.* 3 sound of heavy, clumsy walking. 4 walk with a heavy, clumsy, noisy tread: *The weary hikers clumped along in their heavy boots.* 5 form a clump; form into a clump. 1-3 *n.,* 4,5 *v.*

clum si ly (klum′zə lē), in a clumsy manner; awkwardly. *adv.*

clum si ness (klum′zē nis), a being clumsy; awkwardness. *n.*

clum sy (klum′zē), 1 awkward in moving; not graceful or skillful: *The cast on my broken leg made me walk in a clumsy manner.* 2 awkwardly done; tactless: *a clumsy reply.* 3 not well shaped or well made: *The stage for the puppet show was a clumsy structure made out of old boxes. adj.,* **clum si er, clum si est.**

clung (klung), past tense and past participle of **cling.** *The child clung to his sister. The sticky mud had clung to my fingers. v.*

clus ter (klus′tər), 1 number of things of the same kind growing or grouped together: *a cluster of grapes, a little cluster of houses in the valley.* 2 any group of persons or things: *The citizens appeared in a cluster before the mayor's house.* 3 form into a cluster; gather in a group: *The students clustered around their teacher.* 1,2 *n.,* 3 *v.*

clutch (kluch), 1 a tight grasp; hold: *I lost my clutch on the rope and fell.* 2 grasp tightly: *I clutched the railing to keep my balance.* 3 seize eagerly; snatch: *clutch at an opportunity.* 4 Often, **clutches,** *pl.* **a** a grasping claw, paw, hand, etc.: *The fish wiggled out of the hungry bear's clutches and swam away.* **b** control; power: *That country is in the clutches of a dictator.* 5 device in a machine for transmitting motion from one shaft to another or for disconnecting related moving parts. The clutch in an automobile is used to connect the engine with the transmission or to disconnect it from the transmission. 6 lever or pedal that operates this device. 1,4-6 *n., pl.* **clutch es;** 2,3 *v.*

clut ter (klut′ər), 1 number of things scattered or left in disorder; litter: *It was hard to find the lost pen in the clutter of his room.* 2 litter with things in confusion: *Her desk drawer was cluttered with old papers, strings, and other odds and ends.* 1 *n.,* 2 *v.*

Cly tem nes tra (klī′təm nes′trə), (in Greek legends) the wife of Agamemnon. She killed him on his return from Troy and was afterwards slain by their son Orestes. *n.*

cm., centimeter or centimeters.

co-, *prefix.* 1 with; together: *Coexist = exist together or exist with.* 2 joint: *Coauthor = joint author.* 3 equally: *Coextensive = equally extensive.* [from Latin *co-,* a different form of *com-*]

Co., 1 Company. 2 County.

c/o or **c.o.,** in care of.

coach (kōch), 1 a large, usually closed carriage with seats inside and often on top, pulled by horses. In former times, most coaches carried passengers, and sometimes mail, along a regular route, stopping for meals and fresh horses. 2 a passenger car of a railroad train. 3 bus. 4 a class of coach accommodations on a commercial aircraft at lower rates than first class. 5 person who teaches

or trains athletic teams, singers, etc.: *a swimming coach, a drama coach.* 6 teach or train: *She coaches Olympic swimmers. He coaches at a university.* 1-5 *n., pl.* **coach es;** 6 *v.*

coach man (kōch′mən), man whose work is driving a coach or carriage. *n., pl.* **coach men.**

co ag u late (kō ag′yə lāt), change from a liquid to a thickened mass; thicken: *Cooking coagulates the whites of eggs. v.,* **co ag u lat ed, co ag u lat ing.**

co ag u la tion (kō ag′yə lā′shən), 1 act of coagulating. If coagulation of the blood does not take place in a cut or wound, the injured person may bleed to death. 2 a coagulated mass; clot. *n.*

coal (kōl), 1 a black mineral that burns and gives off heat, composed mostly of carbon. It is formed from partly decayed vegetable matter under great pressure in the earth. Anthracite and bituminous coal are two kinds of coal. 2 piece or pieces of this mineral for burning: *a bag of coal.* 3 supply or be supplied with coal: *The ship stopped just long enough to coal.* 4 piece of burning wood, coal, etc.; ember: *The big log had burned down to a few glowing coals.* 1,2,4 *n.,* 3 *v.*

co a lesce (kō′ə les′), 1 grow together. 2 unite into one body, mass, party, etc.; combine: *The thirteen colonies coalesced to form a nation. v.,* **co a lesced, co a lesc ing.**

co a les cence (kō′ə les′ns), 1 a growing together. 2 union; combination. *n.*

coal gas, 1 gas made from coal, used for heating and lighting. 2 gas given off by burning coal.

co a li tion (kō′ə lish′ən), 1 union; combination. 2 alliance of statesmen, political parties, etc., for some special

coach (def. 1)

adj.	adjective	*n.*	noun
adv.	adverb	*prep.*	preposition
conj.	conjunction	*pron.*	pronoun
interj.	interjection	*v.*	verb
sing.	singular	*pl.*	plural

purpose. In wartime several countries may form a temporary coalition against a common enemy. *n.*

coal oil, 1 kerosene. 2 petroleum.

coal scuttle, bucket for holding or carrying coal.

coal tar, a black, sticky substance left after bituminous coal has been distilled to make coal gas. Coal tar is used to make roofing and paving materials. Aniline dyes, flavorings, perfumes, benzene, etc., contain substances made from coal tar.

coarse (kôrs), 1 made up of fairly large parts; not fine: *coarse sand.* 2 heavy or rough in looks or texture: *The old fisherman had coarse, weathered features. Burlap is a coarse cloth.* 3 common; poor; inferior: *coarse food.* 4 not delicate or refined; crude; vulgar: *coarse manners. adj.,* **coars er, coars est.** —**coarse´ly,** *adv.* —**coarse´ness,** *n.*

coars en (kôr´sən), make or become coarse: *skin coarsened by wind and sun. His language coarsened while he was in the army.* *v.*

coast (kōst), 1 land along the sea; seashore: *Maine has a rocky coast.* 2 sail along or near the coast of: *The disabled ship coasted the island, looking for a harbor to make repairs.* 3 sail from port to port along a coast. 4 ride or slide without the use of effort or power: *You can coast downhill on a sled. She shut off the engine and the car coasted into the driveway.* 5 a ride or slide without the use of effort or power. 6 move or advance with little effort or exertion: *The test was so easy that I was able to just coast through it.* 1,5 *n.,* 2-4,6 *v.*

coast al (kō´stl), of the coast; near or along a coast: *coastal shipping. adj.*

coast er (kō´stər), 1 person or thing that coasts. 2 ship that sails or trades along a coast. 3 sled to coast on. 4 a little tray for holding a glass or bottle. A coaster protects surfaces of furniture from moisture. *n.*

coaster brake, brake in the hub of the rear wheel of a bicycle, worked by pushing back on the pedals.

coast guard, 1 group of men whose work is protecting lives and property and preventing smuggling along the coast of a country. 2 member of any

such group. **3 Coast Guard,** the government organization whose work is protecting lives and property and preventing smuggling along the coasts of the United States. It is under the Navy Department in wartime and under the Department of Transportation in peacetime.

coast line (kōst´līn´), outline of a coast. *n.*

coast wise (kōst´wīz´), along the coast: *travel coastwise (adv.), coastwise trade (adj.). adv., adj.*

coat (kōt), 1 an outer garment of cloth, fur, etc., with sleeves: *a winter coat. Father wears a coat and tie to work.* 2 a natural outer covering: *a dog's coat of hair, the silky coat of a kitten.* 3 a thin layer covering a surface: *a coat of paint.* 4 cover with a thin layer: *The old books were coated with dust. The floor is coated with varnish.* 1-3 *n.,* 4 *v.*

coat ing (kō´ting), 1 layer covering a surface: *a coating of dust.* 2 cloth for making coats. *n.*

coat of arms, shield, or drawing of a shield, bearing symbols or designs which show the marks of distinction of a noble family, a government, a city, etc. In the Middle Ages, each knight or lord had his own coat of arms. *pl.* **coats of arms.**

coat of arms
on the shield of a knight

coat of mail, garment made of metal rings or plates, worn as armor. See **mail**[2] for picture. *pl.* **coats of mail.**

coat room (kōt´rüm´ *or* kōt´rum´), cloakroom. *n.*

co au thor (kō ô´thər), a joint author. *n.*

coax (kōks), 1 persuade by soft words; influence by pleasant ways: *She coaxed me into letting her borrow my bicycle.* 2 get by coaxing: *The baby-sitter coaxed a smile from the baby.* *v.* —**coax´er,** *n.* —**coax´ing ly,** *adv.*

co ax i al cable (kō ak´sē əl), an electric cable consisting of a tube of conducting materials surrounding an insulated central conductor. It is used for transmitting many telegraph, telephone, and television signals at the same time.

cob (kob), 1 corncob. 2 a strong horse with short legs. 3 a male swan. *n.*

co balt (kō´bôlt), 1 a hard, silver-white metallic element with a pinkish tint which occurs only in combination with other elements. It is used in making alloys, paints, etc. 2 a dark-blue color-

ing matter made from cobalt. *n.* [from German *Kobold* goblin (because of miners' belief in the evil or mischievous effects of the substance)]

cob ble[1] (kob´əl), mend (shoes, etc.); repair; patch. *v.,* **cob bled, cob bling.** [probably from **cobbler**[1]]

cob ble[2] (kob´əl), cobblestone. *n.* [perhaps a form of Middle English *cobbe* lump]

cob bler[1] (kob´lər), person whose work is mending shoes. *n.* [Middle English *cobeler*]

cob bler[2] (kob´lər), a fruit pie baked in a deep dish, usually with a crust only on top. *n.* [origin unknown]

cob ble stone (kob´əl stōn´), a naturally rounded stone formerly much used in paving. *n.*

cobra
about 6 ft. long

co bra (kō´brə), a very poisonous snake of Asia and Africa. When excited, it flattens its neck so that the head takes on the appearance of a hood. *n., pl.* **co bras.**

cob web (kob´web´), 1 a spider's web, or the stuff it is made of. 2 anything thin and slight or entangling like a spider's web: *caught in a cobweb of lies. n.*

co caine or **co cain** (kō kān´ *or* kō´kān), drug used to deaden pain and as a stimulant. It is obtained from the dried leaves of a tropical shrub. When used in excess, it can cause addiction and poisoning. *n.*

coc cus (kok´əs), bacterium shaped like a sphere. *n., pl.* **coc ci** (kok´sī).

coch i neal (koch´ə nēl´), a bright-red dye made from the dried bodies of the females of a scale insect that lives on cactus plants of tropical America. *n.*

coch le a (kok´lē ə), a spiral-shaped cavity of the inner ear, containing the nerve endings that transmit sound impulses along the auditory nerve. *n., pl.* **coch le ae** (kok´lē ē´).

cock[1] (kok), 1 a male chicken; rooster. 2 the male of other birds: *a turkey cock.* 3 faucet used to turn the flow of a liquid or gas on or off. 4 hammer of a gun. 5 position of the hammer or firing pin of a gun when it is pulled back ready to fire. 6 pull back the hammer or firing pin of (a gun), ready to fire: *There was a click as the sheriff cocked his revolver.* 1-5 *n.,* 6 *v.* [Old English *cocc*]

cock² (kok), **1** turn or stick up, especially in a carefree, defiant, or inquiring manner: *The little bird cocked his eye at me. The dog cocked his ears when he heard the approaching footsteps. Uncle cocked his hat jauntily on the back of his head.* **2** an upward turn or bend of the eye, ear, hat, etc. **3** turn of the brim of a hat. **1** *v.,* **2,3** *n.* [probably from *cock¹*]

cock³ (kok), **1** a small, cone-shaped pile of hay, turf, etc., in a field. **2** to pile in cocks. **1** *n.,* **2** *v.* [Middle English *cocke*]

cock ade (ko kād′), knot of ribbon or a rosette worn on the hat as a badge. *n.*

cock-a-doo dle-doo (kok′ə dü′dl-dü′), imitation of the loud cry of a rooster. *n., pl.* **cock-a-doo dle-doos.**

cock a too (kok′ə tü′ *or* kok′ə tü′), a large, brightly colored parrot of Australia, the East Indies, etc., with a crest which it can raise and lower. Cockatoos are noisy but rarely learn to talk. *n., pl.* **cock a toos.**

cocked hat, **1** hat with the brim turned up. **2** hat pointed in front and in back.

cock er el (kok′ər əl), a young rooster, not more than one year old. *n.*

cocker spaniel
14 in. high
at the shoulder

cock er spaniel (kok′ər), one of a breed of small dogs with long, silky hair and drooping ears.

cock eyed (kok′īd′), **1** cross-eyed. **2** SLANG. tilted or twisted to one side. **3** SLANG. foolish; silly. *adj.*

cock horse (kok′hôrs′), rocking horse. *n.*

cock i ly (kok′ə lē), INFORMAL. in a cocky manner; cocksurely. *adv.*

cock i ness (kok′ē nis), INFORMAL. a cocky manner; cocksureness. *n.*

cock le¹ (kok′əl), **1** a small, saltwater shellfish that is good to eat. It has two ridged, heart-shaped shells. **2** cockleshell. **3** a wrinkle. *n.* [from French of the 1300's *coquille*]

warm the cockles of one's heart, make one feel much pleased and encouraged: *Her kind welcome into the new neighborhood warmed the cockles of her heart.*

cock le² (kok′əl), a weed that grows in grain fields, such as the cocklebur. *n.* [Old English *coccel*]

cock le bur (kok′əl bėr′), any of several weeds with spiny burs. *n.*

cock le shell (kok′əl shel′), **1** shell of the cockle. **2** a small, light, shallow boat. *n.*

cock ney (kok′nē), **1** person born or living in the eastern section of London who speaks a particular dialect of English. **2** this dialect. **3** of or like cockneys or their dialect. In cockney speech most *h*'s at the beginning of words are not pronounced. **1,2** *n., pl.* **cock neys;** **3** *adj.*

cock pit (kok′pit′), **1** place where the pilot sits in an airplane. **2** the open place in a boat where the pilot and passengers sit. **3** an enclosed space for fights between roosters or gamecocks. *n.*

cock roach (kok′rōch′), a small, brownish or yellowish insect often found in kitchens and around water pipes. Cockroaches usually come out at night. *n., pl.* **cock roach es.**

cocks comb (koks′kōm′), **1** the fleshy, red part on the top of a rooster's head. **2** plant with crested or feathery clusters of red or yellow flowers. *n.*

cock sure (kok′shūr′), **1** too sure; overly confident. **2** perfectly sure; absolutely certain. *adj.* —**cock′sure′ly,** *adv.* —**cock′sure′ness,** *n.*

cock tail (kok′tāl′), **1** a chilled alcoholic drink of gin, whiskey, rum, etc., mixed with vermouth, fruit juices, etc., and sometimes sugar or a dash of bitters. **2** an appetizing drink served just before a meal: *a tomato-juice cocktail.* **3** shellfish or mixed fruits served as an appetizer: *a shrimp cocktail.* *n.*

cock y (kok′ē), INFORMAL. conceited or swaggering; cocksure: *That bully is a cocky little fellow.* *adj.,* **cock i er,** **cock i est.**

co co (kō′kō), **1** coconut palm. **2** coconut. *n., pl.* **co cos.** Also, **cocoa.**

co coa¹ (kō′kō), **1** powder made by roasting and grinding the kernels of cacao seeds, and removing some of the fat. **2** drink made of this powder with milk or water and sugar. **3** a dull-brown color, lighter than chocolate. **4** dull-brown. **1-3** *n., pl.* **co coas;** **4** *adj.* [a different form of *cacao*, from Spanish]

co coa² (kō′kō), coco. *n., pl.* **co coas.** [from Portuguese *coco* grinning face]

co co nut or **co coa nut** (kō′kə-nut′), the large, round, hard-shelled fruit of the coconut palm that contains a sweet, white liquid called **coconut milk,** which is used as a drink. Coconuts have a brown shell with a sweet, white, pulpy meat which is often shredded for use in cakes, puddings, and pies. *n.*

coconut oil, oil obtained from coconuts, used for making soap, candles, etc.

coconut palm, a tall tropical palm tree on which coconuts grow; coco palm.

COCOON
cocoon (def. 1)

co coon (kə kün′), **1** case of silky thread spun by the larvae of various insects to live in while they are developing into adults. Most moth larvae form cocoons. Silk is obtained from the cocoons of silkworms. **2** any similar protective case or covering. *n.*

coco palm, coconut palm.

cod (kod), an important fish used for food, found in the cold parts of the northern Atlantic; codfish. It is usually between three and six feet long when fully grown. *n., pl.* **cods** or **cod.**

Cod (kod), **Cape,** hook-shaped peninsula in SE Massachusetts. *n.*

c.o.d. or **C.O.D.,** cash on delivery; collect on delivery.

cod dle (kod′l), **1** treat tenderly; pamper: *The mother coddled her sick child.* **2** cook in hot water without boiling: *coddle an egg.* *v.,* **cod dled,** **cod dling.**

code (kōd), **1** system of secret writing; arrangement of words, figures, etc., to keep a message short or secret: *The enemy could not decipher the code in which the general's letter was written.* **2** change into a code: *The spy coded a message to headquarters.* **3** a collection of laws arranged according to a system so that they can be understood and used: *The punishments for robbery and murder are prescribed in the penal code.* **4** any set of accepted manners or rules. A traffic code contains rules for driving. A moral code is made up of the notions of right and wrong conduct held by a person, a group of persons, or a society. **5** system of signals for sending messages by telegraph, flags, etc. The Morse code is used in telegraphy. **1,3-5** *n.,* **2** *v.,* **cod ed, cod ing.**

co deine (kō′dēn′), a white, crystalline drug obtained from opium, used to relieve pain and cause sleep. *n.*

cod fish (kod′fish′), cod. *n., pl.* **cod fish es** or **cod fish.**

163

adj.	adjective	*n.*	noun
adv.	adverb	*prep.*	preposition
conj.	conjunction	*pron.*	pronoun
interj.	interjection	*v.*	verb
sing.	singular	*pl.*	plural

codg er (koj′ər), INFORMAL. an odd or peculiar person. *n.*

cod i fi ca tion (kod′ə fə kā′shən *or* kō′də fə kā′shən), arrangement of laws, etc., according to a system. *n.*

cod i fy (kod′ə fī *or* kō′də fī), arrange (laws, etc.) according to a system: *The laws of France were codified by order of Napoleon I.* *v.*, **cod i fied, cod i fy ing.**

cod ling moth (kod′ling), a small moth whose larvae destroy apples, pears, etc.

cod-liv er oil (kod′liv′ər), oil extracted from the liver of cod or of related species, used in medicine as a source of vitamins A and D.

Co dy (kō′dē), **William F(rederick)**, the real name of **Buffalo Bill.** *n.*

co ed or **co-ed** (kō′ed′), INFORMAL. a girl or woman student at a coeducational school. *n.*

co ed u ca tion al (kō′ej ə kā′shə nəl), educating boys and girls or men and women together in the same school or classes. *adj.* —**co′ed u ca′tion al ly,** *adv.*

co ef fi cient (kō′ə fish′ənt), number or symbol put with and multiplying another. In *3x, 3* is the coefficient of *x,* and *x* is the coefficient of *3.* *n.*

co erce (kō ėrs′), compel; force: *The prisoner was coerced into confessing the crime.* *v.*, **co erced, co erc ing.**

co er cion (kō ėr′shən), use of force; compulsion: *Dictators rule by coercion.* *n.*

co er cive (kō ėr′siv), using force; compelling. *adj.* —**co er′cive ly,** *adv.*

co ex ist (kō′ig zist′), exist together or at the same time: *Orange trees have coexisting fruit and flowers.* *v.*

co ex ist ence (kō′ig zis′təns), existence together or at the same time. *n.*

cof fee (kô′fē), **1** a dark-brown drink made from the roasted and ground seeds of a tall, tropical tree or shrub. **2** coffee beans. **3** the plant itself. **4** the color of coffee; a dark brown, darker than chocolate. **5** having the color of coffee; dark-brown. 1-4 *n.,* 5 *adj.*

coffee bean, seed of the coffee plant. Coffee beans are roasted and ground to make coffee.

cof fee pot (kô′fē pot′), container for making or serving coffee. *n.*

coffee table, a low table for serving coffee and other refreshments. It is often placed in front of a sofa or chair.

cof fer (kô′fər), **1** box, chest, or trunk, especially one used to hold money or other valuable things. **2 coffers,** *pl.* treasury; funds: *The revenue from the sales tax goes into the city's coffers. n.*

cof fer dam (kô′fər dam′), a temporary dam, usually of wooden piles and earth, to enclose an underwater area so that it can be pumped dry to build a bridge, foundation, pier, or other structure. *n.*

cof fin (kô′fən), box into which a dead person is put to be buried; casket. *n.*

cog (kog), **1** one of a series of teeth on the edge of a cogwheel or gear. **2** cogwheel or gearwheel. *n.*

co gen cy (kō′jən sē), forcible quality; power of convincing: *The cogency of her argument helped her win the debate. n.*

co gent (kō′jənt), having the power to convince; forcible or convincing: *The lawyer used cogent arguments to persuade the jury that his client was innocent. adj.* —**co′gent ly,** *adv.*

cog i tate (koj′ə tāt), think over; consider with care; ponder; meditate: *The judge cogitated a long time before making any decision.* *v.*, **cog i tat ed, cog i tat ing.**

cog i ta tion (koj′ə tā′shən), deep thought; careful consideration; pondering; meditation. *n.*

co gnac (kō′nyak), a French brandy of superior quality. *n.* [from *Cognac,* a town and region in France]

cog nate (kog′nāt), **1** related by family or origin. English, Dutch, and German are cognate languages. **2** anything related to another by having a common source. The German word *Wasser* and the English word *water* are cognates. **1** *adj.,* **2** *n.*

cog ni zance (kog′nə zəns), knowledge obtained by observation or information; perception; awareness: *The queen had cognizance of plots against her. n.*

take cognizance of, take notice of; give attention to: *The judge took cognizance of the accused man's ill health in handing down the sentence.*

cog ni zant (kog′nə zənt), aware: *When the queen became cognizant of the plot to overthrow her, she acted swiftly to quash it. adj.*

cog wheel (kog′hwēl′), wheel with teeth cut in the rim for transmitting or receiving motion; gear; gearwheel. *n.*

co here (kō hir′), **1** stick together; hold together: *Brick and mortar cohere.* **2** be well connected; be consistent: *The various details of the witness's story failed to cohere.* *v.*, **co hered, co her ing.**

co her ence (kō hir′əns), **1** logical connection; consistency: *The excited girl's story lacked coherence.* **2** a sticking together; tendency to hold together; cohesion: *the coherence of atoms of the same element. n.*

co her ent (kō hir′ənt), **1** logically connected; consistent: *She was so excited that she could not give a coherent account of the accident.* **2** sticking together; holding together. *adj.* —**co her′ent ly,** *adv.*

co he sion (kō hē′zhən), **1** a sticking together; tendency to hold together: *Wet sand has more cohesion than dry sand.* **2** attraction between molecules of the same kind: *Drops of water are a result of cohesion. n.*

co he sive (kō hē′siv), sticking together; tending to hold together: *Magnetized iron filings form a cohesive mass. The members of a family are a cohesive unit in our society. adj.* —**co he′sive ly,** *adv.* —**co he′sive ness,** *n.*

co hort (kō′hôrt), **1** the tenth part of an ancient Roman legion. There were from 300 to 600 soldiers in each cohort. **2** any group, band, or company. **3** INFORMAL. associate or follower. *n.*

coif (koif), cap or hood that fits closely around the head. *n.*

coif fure (kwä fyúr′), style or manner of arranging a woman's hair. *n.*

coil (def. 4)
coils
in refrigerator

coil (def. 5)—coils
in electromagnet
of electric bell

coil (koil), **1** wind around and around in a circular or spiral shape: *A snake coiled around a branch. The sailor coiled the rope evenly.* **2** anything that is coiled: *a coil of rope.* **3** one wind or turn of a coil. **4** series of connected pipes arranged in a coil or row: *the coils in a radiator.* **5** wire wound round and round into a spiral for carrying electric current. **1** *v.,* **2-5** *n.*

coin (koin), **1** piece of metal stamped by the government for use as money.

cogwheels—As one wheel turns,
its teeth push against the teeth
of the other wheel, causing it to turn.

Pennies, nickels, dimes, and quarters are coins. 2 metal money. A government makes coin by stamping metal. 3 make (money) by stamping metal: *The mint coins millions of nickels and dimes each year.* 4 make (metal) into money: *coin silver into half dollars.* 5 make up; invent: *We often coin new words or phrases to name new products.* 1,2 *n.*, 3-5 *v.* —**coin′er,** *n.*

coin age (koi′nij), 1 the making of coins. The United States mint is in charge of coinage. 2 metal money; coins: *He is a collector of foreign coinage.* 3 system of coins. The United States has a decimal coinage. 4 a making up; inventing: *Travel in outer space has led to the coinage of many new words.* 5 word, phrase, etc., invented: *"Transistor" and "laser" are fairly new coinages.* *n.*

co in cide (kō′in sīd′), 1 occupy the same place in space: *If these two triangles △△ were placed one on top of the other, they would coincide.* 2 occupy the same time: *The working hours of the two friends coincide.* 3 be just alike; correspond exactly; agree: *Her answers are correct and coincide with the answers in the book.* *v.*, **co in cid ed, co in cid ing.**

co in ci dence (kō in′sə dəns), 1 the chance occurrence of two things at the same time or place in such a way as to seem remarkable, fitting, etc.: *It is a coincidence that my cousin and I were born on the very same day.* 2 a coinciding: *the coincidence of two triangles or circles.* *n.*

co in ci dent (kō in′sə dənt), 1 happening at the same time: *My twin's birthday is coincident with mine.* 2 in exact agreement: *My parents' views are often coincident.* *adj.*

co in ci den tal (kō in′sə den′tl), showing coincidence; occurring by chance. *adj.* —**co in′ci den′tal ly,** *adv.*

coke (kōk), fuel made from bituminous coal that has been heated in an oven from which most of the air has been shut out. Coke burns with much heat and little smoke, and is used in furnaces, for melting metal, etc. *n.*

col., column.

Col., 1 Colonel. 2 Colorado. The official abbreviation is **Colo.**

col an der (kul′ən dər *or* kol′ən dər), a wire or metal dish full of small holes for draining off liquids from foods. *n.*

cold (kōld), 1 much less warm than the body: *Snow and ice are cold.* 2 less warm than usual: *The weather is cold for April.* 3 feeling cold or chilly: *Put on a sweater, or you will be cold.* 4 coldness; being cold: *Warm clothes protect against the cold of winter.* 5 a

common illness that causes a running at the nose and a sore throat. 6 lacking in feeling; unfriendly: *Since our argument she has remained cold and aloof.* 7 faint; weak: *The hunting dogs could not trail the cold scent of the fox.* 8 (in games, treasure hunts, etc.) far from what one is searching for. 9 suggesting coolness. Blue, green, and gray are called cold colors. 1-3, 6-9 *adj.*, 4,5 *n.* —**cold′ly,** *adv.* —**cold′ness,** *n.*

catch cold, become ill with a cold: *I caught cold and stayed home from school.*

out in the cold, all alone; neglected.

cold-blood ed (kōld′blud′id), 1 having blood that is about the same temperature as the air or water around the animal. The blood of such animals is colder in winter than in summer. Turtles, snakes, and many other animals are cold-blooded; birds and mammals are warm-blooded. 2 lacking in feeling; cruel: *a cold-blooded murder.* 3 feeling the cold because of poor circulation. *adj.* —**cold′-blood′ed ly,** *adv.* —**cold′-blood′ed ness,** *n.*

cold cream, a creamy, soothing salve for the skin.

cold front, the advancing edge of a cold air mass as it overtakes and passes under a warmer one. Showers usually form along a cold front.

cold-heart ed (kōld′här′tid), lacking in feeling; unsympathetic; unkind. *adj.* —**cold′-heart′ed ly,** *adv.* —**cold′-heart′ed ness,** *n.*

cold sore, blister near or on the mouth, often accompanying a cold or a fever.

cold war, 1 a prolonged contest between nations or groups of nations, conducted by political, economic, and other means rather than by direct military action. 2 **Cold War,** the contest for world leadership between the communist and democratic nations that began after World War II.

cold wave, period of very cold weather.

Cole ridge (kōl′rij), **Samuel Taylor,** 1772-1834, English poet. *n.*

cole slaw (kōl′slô′), salad made of finely shredded raw cabbage; slaw. *n.*

col ic (kol′ik), severe pains in the stomach and intestines. *n.*

col ick y (kol′i kē), having colic. *adj.*

col i se um (kol′ə sē′əm), 1 a large building or stadium for games, contests, etc. 2 **Coliseum,** Colosseum. *n.*

col lab o rate (kə lab′ə rāt′), 1 work together: *The two authors collaborated in writing a history of the United States.* 2 aid or cooperate with enemies of one's country: *The traitor collaborated*

hat, āge, fär; let, ēqual, tėrm;
it, īce; hot, ōpen, ôrder;
oil, out; cup, pùt, rüle; ch, child;
ng, long; sh, she; th, thin;
ᵀH, then; zh, measure;

ə represents *a* in about,
e in taken, *i* in pencil,
o in lemon, *u* in circus.

with the enemy. *v.*, **col lab o rat ed, col lab o rat ing.**

col lab o ra tion (kə lab′ə rā′shən), 1 act of working together. 2 an aiding or cooperating with enemies of one's country. *n.*

col lab o ra tor (kə lab′ə rā′tər), 1 person who works with another, especially in writing a literary or scientific work. 2 person who aids or cooperates with enemies of his country. *n.*

col lage (kə läzh′), picture made by pasting on a background such things as parts of photographs and newspapers, fabric, and string. *n.* [from French *collage* pasting, gluing, from Greek *kolla* glue]

col lapse (kə laps′), 1 fall in; shrink together suddenly: *Sticking a pin into the balloon caused it to collapse.* 2 a falling in; sudden shrinking together: *A heavy flood caused the collapse of the bridge.* 3 break down; fail: *The business collapsed because it was run poorly.* 4 breakdown; failure: *She is suffering from a nervous collapse caused by overwork.* 5 fold or push together: *collapse a telescope.* 1,3,5 *v.*, **col lapsed, col laps ing;** 2,4 *n.*

col laps i ble (kə lap′sə bəl), made so that it can be folded or pushed together: *She put the collapsible table in the closet.* *adj.*

col lar (kol′ər), 1 the part of a coat, dress, or shirt that makes a band around the neck. 2 a separate band of linen, lace, or other material worn around the neck: *a fur collar.* 3 a leather or metal band for the neck of a dog or other pet animal. 4 a leather roll for a horse's neck to bear the weight of the loads he pulls. See **harness** for picture. 5 any of various kinds of rings, bands, or pipes in machinery. A collar on a shaft is a metal ring that keeps the shaft from moving sideways. Sometimes a collar is a short pipe connecting two other pipes. 6 put a collar on: *She collared the dog and took it for a walk on a leash.* 7 seize by the collar; capture: *The police collared the thief after a long chase.* 1-5 *n.*, 6,7 *v.* —**col′lar like′,** *adj.*

165

adj. adjective	*n.* noun
adv. adverb	*prep.* preposition
conj. conjunction	*pron.* pronoun
interj. interjection	*v.* verb
sing. singular	*pl.* plural

COLLARBONE

BREASTBONE

col lar bone (kol/ər bōn/), the bone connecting the breastbone and the shoulder blade; clavicle. *n.*

col lat er al (kə lat/ər əl), 1 aside from the main thing; secondary: *The teacher listed ten books about explorers as collateral reading for the chapter about discovering America.* 2 side by side; parallel. 3 descended from the same ancestors, but in a different line. Cousins are collateral relatives. 4 stocks, bonds, etc., pledged as security for a loan: *The bank will not make a loan without collateral.* 1-3 *adj.,* 4 *n.* —**col lat/er al ly,** *adv.*

col league (kol/ēg/), fellow worker; associate: *Our teacher's colleagues taught his classes while he was ill.* *n.*

col lect (kə lekt/), 1 bring or come together; gather together: *We collected sticks of wood to make a fire. A crowd soon collected at the scene of the accident.* 2 gather together for a set: *I collect stamps as a hobby.* 3 heap up; accumulate: *Dust is collecting under the bed.* 4 ask and receive payment of (bills, debts, dues, or taxes): *The milkman collects money from his customers each week.* 5 to be paid for at the place of delivery: *a collect telegram (adj.). Telephone me collect (adv.).* 6 regain control of: *We soon collected ourselves after the slight accident.* 1-4,6 *v.,* 5 *adj.,* 5 *adv.*

col lect ed (kə lek/tid), not confused or disturbed; calm: *Throughout all the excitement, she remained cool and collected.* *adj.* —**col lect/ed ly,** *adv.*

col lec tion (kə lek/shən), 1 a bringing together; coming together: *The collection of these stamps took ten years.* 2 group of things gathered from many places and belonging together: *Our library has a large collection of books.* 3 money gathered from people: *A church takes up a collection to help pay its expenses.* 4 a large quantity; mass or heap: *There is a collection of dust in the attic.* *n.*

col lec tive (kə lek/tiv), 1 of a group; as a group; taken all together: *Our fifth-grade class made a collective decision to write to a similar class in Italy.* 2 owned, worked, and managed by a group: *a collective farm.* 3 farm, factory, or other organization operated and worked by a group cooperatively: *There are many collectives in the Soviet Union.* 1,2 *adj.,* 3 *n.*

collective bargaining, negotiation about wages, hours, and working conditions between workers organized as a group and their employer or employers.

col lec tive ly (kə lek/tiv lē), 1 as a group; all together. 2 in a singular form, but with a plural meaning. In the sentence "We caught many fish," *fish* is used collectively. *adv.*

collective noun, noun that is singular in form, but plural in meaning. *Crowd, people, troop,* and *herd* are collective nouns.

col lec tor (kə lek/tər), 1 person or thing that collects: *I am a stamp collector.* 2 person hired to collect money owed: *a tax collector.* *n.*

col leen (kol/ēn/ or kə lēn/), IRISH. girl. *n.*

col lege (kol/ij), 1 school of higher learning that gives degrees or diplomas. A college is often a part of a university. *After I finish high school, I plan to go to college to become a doctor.* 2 school for special training: *I went to an agricultural college to learn about farming.* 3 group of persons with the same duties and privileges: *Many large hospitals have a college of surgeons.* *n.*

col le giate (kə lē/jit), 1 of, like, or belonging to a college: *a collegiate library.* 2 of or having to do with college students: *collegiate life.* *adj.*

col lide (kə līd/), 1 hit or strike violently together; crash: *Two ships collided in the harbor and sank.* 2 clash; conflict. *v.,* **col lid ed, col lid ing.**

col lie (kol/ē), one of a breed of large, intelligent, long-haired dogs used for tending sheep and as pets. *n.*

col lier (kol/yər), 1 ship for carrying coal. 2 a coal miner. *n.*

col lier y (kol/yər ē), a coal mine and its buildings and equipment. *n., pl.* **col lier ies.**

col li sion (kə lizh/ən), 1 a hitting or striking violently together; crash: *The car was badly damaged in the collision.* 2 clash; conflict: *There was a collision of interests on how to spend the club's money and some of the members quit the club.* *n.*

col loid (kol/oid), substance composed of particles that are extremely small but larger than most molecules. The particles in a colloid do not actually dissolve, but remain suspended in a suitable gas, liquid, or solid. *n.*

col loi dal (kə loi/dl), being, containing, or like a colloid. *adj.* —**col loi/dal ly,** *adv.*

col lo qui al (kə lō/kwē əl), used in common talk; belonging to everyday, familiar talk; informal. Such expressions as *clip* for *punch* and *close call* for *narrow escape* are colloquial. *adj.* —**col lo/qui al ly,** *adv.*

col lo qui al ism (kə lō/kwē ə liz/əm), a colloquial word or phrase. *n.*

col lo quy (kol/ə kwē), a talking together; conversation; conference. *n., pl.* **col lo quies.**

col lu sion (kə lü/zhən), secret agreement for some wrong or harmful purpose; secret or crafty understanding for the purposes of trickery or fraud. *n.*

Colo., the official abbreviation of Colorado.

co logne (kə lōn/), a fragrant liquid, not so strong as perfume. *n.*

Co logne (kə lōn/), city in W West Germany, on the Rhine. *n.*

Co lom bi a (kə lum/bē ə), country in NW South America. *Capital:* Bogotá. *n.* —**Co lom/bi an,** *adj., n.*

Co lom bo (kə lum/bō), seaport and capital of Ceylon, on the W coast. *n.*

co lon[1] (kō/lən), mark (:) of punctuation used before lists, explanations, long quotations, etc., to set them off from the rest of the sentence. An illustrative sentence or phrase in this dictionary usually has a colon before it. *n.* [from Latin *colon,* from Greek *kolon* limb, clause]

co lon[2] (kō/lən), the lower part of the large intestine. See **intestine** for diagram. *n.* [from Latin *colon,* from Greek *kolon* part of the large intestine]

Co lón (kō lōn/), seaport in N Panama near the Atlantic end of the Panama Canal. *n.*

colo nel (kėr/nl), officer ranking next below a brigadier general and next above a lieutenant colonel. The United States Army, Air Force, and Marine Corps all have colonels. *n.*

co lo ni al (kə lō/nē əl), 1 of or having to do with a colony or colonies: *Many European countries have lost or given up their colonial possessions since World War II.* 2 of or having to do with the thirteen British colonies which became the United States of America. 3 person who lives in a colony. 1,2 *adj.,* 3 *n.* —**co lo/ni al ly,** *adv.*

co lo ni al ism (kə lō/nē ə liz/əm), policy of a nation that rules or seeks to rule weaker or dependent nations. *n.*

col o nist (kol/ə nist), 1 person who lives in a colony; settler: *Early colonists* in New England suffered from cold and hunger. 2 person who helped to found a colony. *n.*

col o ni za tion (kol/ə nə zā/shən), establishment of a colony or colonies: *The English, French, Dutch, and Spanish took part in the colonization of North America. n.*

col o nize (kol/ə nīz), 1 establish a colony or colonies in: *The English colonized New England.* 2 form a colony; settle in a colony. *v.,* **col o nized, col o niz ing.**

col o niz er (kol/ə nī/zər), person who colonizes. *n.*

colonnade of an ancient Greek temple

col on nade (kol/ə nād/), series of columns set the same distance apart. *n.*

col o ny (kol/ə nē), 1 group of people who leave their own country and go to settle in another land, but who still remain citizens of their own country: *The Pilgrim colony came from England to America in 1620.* 2 the settlement made by such a group of people: *The Pilgrims founded a colony at Plymouth, Massachusetts.* 3 **the Colonies,** the thirteen British colonies that became the United States of America; New Hampshire, Massachusetts, Rhode Island, Connecticut, New York, New Jersey, Pennsylvania, Delaware, Maryland, Virginia, North Carolina, South Carolina, and Georgia. 4 territory distant from the country that governs it: *Hong Kong has been a British colony since 1842.* 5 group of people having the same background or occupation who live together in a certain part of a city: *a colony of artists, the Chinese colony in San Francisco.* 6 group of animals or plants of the same kind, living or growing together: *a colony of ants. Coral grows in colonies. n., pl.* **col o nies.**

col or (kul/ər), 1 sensation produced by the effect of waves of light striking the retina of the eye. Different colors are produced by rays of light having different wavelengths. 2 red, yellow, blue, or any combination of them except black, white, or gray. The color green is a mixture of yellow and blue. 3 give color to; put color on; change the color of: *My younger brother colored a picture with crayons.* 4 paint; dye; pig-

ment: *The color was so thick on the canvas that it began to peel off.* 5 coloring of the skin; complexion: *She has a healthy color.* 6 redness of the face; blush. 7 become or make red in the face; blush: *He colored when I teased him about having a girlfriend.* 8 an outward appearance; show: *Although she was not always honest, her story had some color of truth.* 9 change to give a wrong idea: *The fisherman colored the facts to make his catch seem the biggest of all.* 10 distinguishing quality; vividness: *The author's gift for description adds color to her stories.* 11 give a distinguishing or vivid quality to: *Love of nature colored our teacher's stories about camping.* 12 **the colors,** the flag of a nation, regiment, etc.: *Salute the colors.* 1,2,4-6,8,10,12 *n.,* 3,7,9,11 *v.*

change color, 1 turn pale: *She changed color and nearly fainted on hearing the bad news.* 2 blush: *The shy boy changed color when the teacher praised his work in front of the class.*

give color to, cause to seem true or likely.

show one's true colors, show oneself as one really is: *In the fight the bully showed his true colors and ran away.*

with flying colors, successfully; victoriously: *He passed the test with flying colors.*

Col o rad an (kol/ə rad/n *or* kol/ə-räd/n), 1 of or having to do with the state of Colorado. 2 person born or living in Colorado. 1 *adj.,* 2 *n.*

Col o ra do (kol/ə rad/ō *or* kol/ə-rä/dō), 1 one of the western states of the United States. *Capital:* Denver. 2 river flowing from N Colorado through Utah, Arizona, Nevada, California, and NW Mexico into the Gulf of California. *n.*

Colorado Springs, city in central Colorado. The United States Air Force Academy is located there.

col o ra tion (kul/ə rā/shən), way in which a person or thing is colored; coloring: *The coloration of some animals is like that of their surroundings. n.*

col o ra tur a (kul/ər ə tür/ə *or* kul/-ər ə tyur/ə), 1 ornamental passages in vocal music, such as trills or runs. 2 soprano who sings such passages. *n., pl.* **col o ra tur as.**

col or-blind (kul/ər blīnd/), unable to tell certain colors apart; unable to perceive certain colors. *adj.* —**col/or-blind/ness,** *n.*

col or cast (kul/ər kast/), a television broadcast in color. *n.*

col ored (kul/ərd), 1 having color; not black or white: *This book has colored pictures.* 2 having a certain kind of

hat, āge, fär; let, ēqual, tèrm;
it, īce; hot, ōpen, ôrder;
oil, out; cup, put, rüle; ch, child;
ng, long; sh, she; th, thin;
ŦH, then; zh, measure;

ə represents *a* in about,
e in taken, *i* in pencil,
o in lemon, *u* in circus.

color: *a green-colored leaf.* 3 of the black race or any race other than white. 4 tinged by prejudice, emotion, or desire for effect; biased: *The fisherman gave a highly colored description of the size of the fish he had caught. adj.*

col or ful (kul/ər fəl), 1 having excitement, variety, or interest; picturesque; vivid: *Her letters describe her colorful travel experiences.* 2 full of color. *adj.* —**col/or ful ly,** *adv.* —**col/or ful ness,** *n.*

col or ing (kul/ər ing), 1 way in which a person or thing is colored; coloration: *The fisherman had a ruddy coloring.* 2 substance used to color; pigment. 3 an outward or false appearance: *Her story had the coloring of truth, but we knew we could not believe her. n.*

col or less (kul/ər lis), 1 without color: *Her face was almost colorless from fright.* 2 without excitement or variety; uninteresting: *a colorless person, a colorless description. adj.* —**col/-or less ly,** *adv.* —**col/or less ness,** *n.*

co los sal (kə los/əl), of huge size; gigantic; vast: *The Empire State Building is a colossal structure. adj.* —**co los/-sal ly,** *adv.*

Col os se um (kol/ə sē/əm), a large amphitheater in Rome, completed in A.D. 80. The Colosseum was used for games and contests. *n. Also,* **Coliseum.**

co los sus (kə los/əs), 1 a huge statue. The **Colossus of Rhodes** was a huge statue of Apollo made at Rhodes about 280 B.C. It was one of the seven wonders of the ancient world. 2 anything huge; gigantic person or thing. Latin Americans have sometimes called the United States "the Colossus of the North." *n., pl.* **co los si** (kə los/ī), **co los sus es.**

colt (kōlt), a young horse, donkey, zebra, etc., especially a male less than four or five years old. *n.*

Co lum bi a (kə lum/bē ə), 1 capital of South Carolina, in the central part. 2 river flowing from British Columbia through E Washington and between Washington and Oregon into the Pacific. 3 a name for the United States

adj.	adjective	*n.*	noun
adv.	adverb	*prep.*	preposition
conj.	conjunction	*pron.*	pronoun
interj.	interjection	*v.*	verb
sing.	singular	*pl.*	plural

of America. Columbia is often represented as a woman dressed in red, white, and blue. *n.*

col um bine (kol′əm bīn), 1 plant whose flowers have petals shaped like hollow spurs. Wild columbines have red-and-yellow or blue-and-white flowers. 2 **Columbine,** a woman character in comedy and pantomime, the sweetheart of Harlequin. *n.*

Co lum bus (kə lum′bəs), 1 **Christopher,** 1451?-1506, Italian navigator in the service of Spain who discovered America in 1492. 2 capital of Ohio, in the central part. *n.*

Columbus Day, October 12, the anniversary of Columbus's discovery of America. It is observed as a legal holiday on the second Monday in October in most states of the United States.

CAPITAL

SHAFT

BASE

column
(def. 1)

column (def. 3)
column of ships

col umn (kol′əm), 1 a slender, upright structure; pillar. Columns are usually made of stone, wood, or metal, and are used as supports or ornaments to a building. Sometimes a column stands alone as a monument. 2 anything that seems slender and upright like a column: *the spinal column. A column of smoke rose from the fire. You add a column of figures.* 3 soldiers or ships following one another in a single line. 4 a narrow division of a page reading from top to bottom, kept separate by lines or by blank spaces. Some newspapers have eight columns on a page. 5 part of a newspaper used for a special subject or written by a special writer: *the sports column. n.*

col umn ist (kol′əm nist), person who writes a special column in a newspaper or magazine. *n.*

com-, *prefix.* with; together: *Commingle* = mingle with one another. *Compress* = *press together.* [from Latin *com-*]

co ma (kō′mə), a prolonged uncon-

sciousness caused by disease, injury, or poison. *n., pl.* **co mas.**

Co man che (kə man′chē), member of a tribe of American Indians that formerly roamed from Nebraska to northern Mexico and now live in Oklahoma. *n., pl.* **Co man che** or **Co man ches.**

comb (kōm), 1 piece of metal, plastic, rubber, bone, etc., with teeth, used to arrange or straighten the hair or to hold it in place. 2 anything shaped or used like a comb, especially an instrument for combing wool or flax. 3 arrange or straighten with a comb. 4 comb and take out tangles in (wool, flax, etc.) with a comb. 5 search through; look everywhere in: *We had to comb the whole playground before we found the lost ball.* 6 the red, fleshy piece on top of the head of chickens and some other fowls. 7 honeycomb. 1,2,6,7 *n.,* 3-5 *v.* —**comb′like′,** *adj.*

com bat (kəm bat′ *or* kom′bat *for 1;* kom′bat *for 2,3*), 1 fight against; struggle with: *Doctors combat disease.* 2 armed fighting between opposing forces; battle: *The soldier was wounded in combat.* 3 any fight or struggle; conflict. 1 *v.,* 2,3 *n.*

com bat ant (kəm bat′nt *or* kom′bə-tənt), 1 one that takes part in combat; fighter: *The chief combatants in World War II were Germany, Italy, and Japan on one side and the United States, Great Britain, and Russia on the other.* 2 fighting. 3 combative. 1 *n.,* 2,3 *adj.*

com bat ive (kəm bat′iv), ready to fight; fond of fighting: *A good football team has a combative spirit. adj.* —**com bat′ive ly,** *adv.* —**com-bat′ive ness,** *n.*

comb er (kō′mər), 1 breaker (def. 1). 2 person or thing that combs. *n.*

com bi na tion (kom′bə nā′shən), 1 one whole made by combining two or more different things: *The color purple is a combination of red and blue.* 2 persons or groups joined together for some common purpose: *The farmers formed a combination to sell their crops at better prices.* 3 series of numbers or letters dialed in opening a certain kind of lock: *Do you know the combination of the safe?* 4 a combining or a being combined; union: *The combination of flour and water makes paste. n.*

com bine (kəm bīn′ *for 1,2;* kom′bīn *for 3,4*), 1 join two or more things together; unite: *Our club combined the offices of secretary and treasurer so that one person could do the work of both.* 2 unite to form a chemical compound: *Two atoms of hydrogen combine with one of oxygen to form water.* 3 group of persons joined together for some common purpose; combination. 4 machine

for harvesting and threshing grain. 1,2 *v.,* **com bined, com bin ing;** 3,4 *n.*

com bus ti ble (kəm bus′tə bəl), 1 capable of taking fire and burning: *Gasoline is highly combustible.* 2 a combustible substance. Wood and coal are combustibles. 1 *adj.,* 2 *n.*

com bus tion (kəm bus′chən), act or process of burning. Many houses are heated by the rapid combustion of coal, oil, or gas. By slow combustion, the cells of the body transform food into energy and heat. *n.*

comb (def. 6)
of a rooster

come (kum), 1 move toward: *Come this way.* 2 get near; arrive: *The train comes at noon.* 3 reach; extend: *The drapes come to the floor.* 4 take place; happen: *Snow comes in winter.* 5 be born: *That girl comes from a poor family.* 6 turn out to be; become: *My wish came true.* 7 be obtainable or sold: *This soup comes in a can.* 8 be equal; amount: *The bill comes to $5.00. v.,* **came, come, com ing.**

come about, 1 take place; happen: *Many changes have come about in the past year.* 2 turn around; change direction: *The sailboat came about, heading back to the dock.*

come around, return to consciousness or health; recover: *He is coming around after his operation and will soon be back in school.*

come at, rush toward; attack: *The barking dog came at me and I ran away.*
come back, return: *Come back home.*
come by, get; obtain; acquire: *He came by the money honestly.*

come down, 1 be handed down: *Many fables have come down through the ages.* 2 become ill: *I came down with the measles.* 3 lose position, rank, money, etc.

come forward, offer oneself for work or duty; volunteer.

come in, 1 arrive: *When did you come in this morning?* 2 enter: *Come in, please.* 3 be brought into use; begin: *Fashions which come in this year may be out of style next year.*

come into, inherit: *She came into a great deal of money when her aunt died.*

come off, 1 take place; happen; occur: *The rocket launching comes off next week.* 2 turn out to be: *Our first meeting did not come off as I had expected.* 3 finish in a certain way: *Our team came* *off with a great victory in last week's game.*

come on, 1 find or meet by chance. 2 improve; progress: *She is coming on well and will be out of the hospital next week.*

come out, 1 be revealed or shown: *The sun came out from behind the clouds.* 2 take place in the end; result: *The ball game came out in our favor.* 3 be offered to the public: *The singer's new recording will come out next fall.* 4 put in an appearance: *How many boys came out for football this year?* 5 declare oneself: *One candidate came out for lower taxes.* 6 make a debut.

come to, return to consciousness: *He came to slowly after the accident.*

come up, come into being; arise: *The question is not likely to come up.*

come upon, find or meet by chance: *We came upon a rabbit in the woods.*

come back (kum′bak′), 1 INFORMAL. return to a former condition or position: *The team made a great comeback after losing several games.* 2 SLANG. a clever answer; sharp reply. *n.*

co me di an (kə mē′dē ən), 1 actor in comedies. 2 person who amuses others with his funny talk and actions. *n.*

come down (kum′doun′), INFORMAL. loss of position, rank, money, etc. *n.*

com e dy (kom′ə dē), 1 an amusing play or show having a happy ending. 2 an amusing happening. *n., pl.* **com e dies.**

come li ness (kum′lē nis), pleasant appearance; attractiveness. *n.*

come ly (kum′lē), pleasant to look at; attractive: *a comely girl. adj.,* **come li er, come li est.**

com er (kum′ər), 1 person who comes. 2 INFORMAL. person who seems likely to succeed or who shows promise. *n.*

com et (kom′it), a bright heavenly body with a starlike center and often with a cloudy tail of light which always points away from the sun. Comets move around the sun like planets, but in a long oval course. *n.*

com fort (kum′fərt), 1 ease the grief or sorrow of; cheer: *comfort a crying child.* 2 anything that makes trouble or sorrow easier to bear: *Your friendship brought me comfort while I was in the hospital.* 3 person or thing that makes life easier or takes away hardship: *The warm bonfire was a comfort to the cold campers.* 4 freedom from hardship; ease: *live in comfort.* 1 *v.,* 2-4 *n.*

com fort a ble (kum′fər tə bəl), 1 giving comfort: *A soft, warm bed is comfortable.* 2 in comfort; at ease: *The warmth of the house made me feel comfortable after a cold day outdoors.* 3 INFORMAL. enough for one's needs: *a comfortable income. adj.*

com fort a bly (kum′fər tə blē), in a comfortable manner. *adv.*

com fort er (kum′fər tər), 1 person or thing that gives comfort. 2 a padded or quilted covering for a bed. *n.*

com fort less (kum′fərt lis), 1 bringing no comfort or ease of mind. 2 having none of the comforts of life. *adj.*

com ic (kom′ik), 1 causing laughter or smiles; amusing; funny. 2 comedian. 3 of comedy; in comedies: *a comic actor.* 4 comic book. 5 **comics,** *pl.* comic strips; funnies. 1,3 *adj.,* 2,4, 5 *n.*

com i cal (kom′ə kəl), causing laughter or smiles; amusing; funny: *You look comical in that battered old hat. adj.* —**com′i cal ly,** *adv.*

comic book, magazine containing comic strips.

comic strip, series of drawings that tell a funny story, a series of happenings, or a story of adventure.

com ing (kum′ing), 1 a drawing near; approach; arrival: *the coming of summer.* 2 approaching; next: *this coming spring.* 1 *n.,* 2 *adj.*

com ma (kom′ə), mark (,) of punctuation that sets off or separates the parts of a sentence or the parts of an address, a date, or other series of words or numbers. *n., pl.* **com mas.**

com mand (kə mand′), 1 give an order to; direct: *The captain commanded the soldiers to fire.* 2 an order; direction: *The soldiers obeyed the captain's command.* 3 be in authority over; have power over; be master of: *The captain commands his ship.* 4 possession of authority; power; control: *The general is in command of the army.* 5 soldiers, ships, or region over which an officer has control or authority: *The captain knew every man in his command.* 6 position of control or authority: *The general has held several commands.* 7 control by position; rise high above; overlook: *The fortress stands on a hill that commands the sea.* 8 be able to have and use: *He cannot command such a large sum of money.* 9 ability to have and use: *A good storyteller has a good command of words.* 10 deserve and get: *Food commands a higher price when it is scarce.* 1,3,7,8,10 *v.,* 2,4-6, 9 *n.*

com man dant (kom′ən dant′), 1 commander. 2 officer in command of a fort, naval station, military school, etc. *n.*

com man deer (kom′ən dir′), seize (private property) for military or public use: *The police commandeered a taxicab to chase the bank robber. v.*

com mand er (kə man′dər), 1 person who commands: *a commander of rebel*

hat, āge, fär; let, ēqual, tėrm;
it, īce; hot, ōpen, ôrder;
oil, out; cup, pùt; rüle; ch, child;
ng, long; sh, she; th, thin;
ŦH, then; zh, measure;

ə represents *a* in about,
e in taken, *i* in pencil,
o in lemon, *u* in circus.

forces. 2 officer in the navy ranking next below a captain and above a lieutenant commander. *n.*

commander in chief, 1 person who has complete command of the armed forces of a country. In the United States, the President is the commander in chief. 2 officer in command of part of an army or navy. *pl.* **commanders in chief.**

com mand ing (kə man′ding), 1 in command: *a commanding officer.* 2 controlling; powerful: *commanding influences.* 3 authoritative; impressive: *a commanding voice. adj.* —**com mand′ing ly,** *adv.*

com mand ment (kə mand′mənt), 1 (in the Bible) one of the ten laws that God gave to Moses; one of the Ten Commandments. 2 any law or command. *n.*

com man do (kə man′dō), 1 soldier trained to make brief, daring, surprise raids upon enemy territory. 2 group of such soldiers. *n., pl.* **com man dos** or **com man does.**

com mem o rate (kə mem′ə rāt′), 1 preserve the memory of: *Roman emperors built arches to commemorate their victories.* 2 honor the memory of: *a stamp commemorating the landing of the Pilgrims. v.,* **com mem o rat ed, com mem o rat ing.**

com mem o ra tion (kə mem′ə rā′shən), 1 act of commemorating. 2 service or celebration in memory of some person or event. *n.*

in commemoration of, to honor the memory of: *Memorial Day is observed in commemoration of the American servicemen who died for their country.*

com mem o ra tive (kə mem′ə rā′tiv), preserving or honoring the memory of some person or event: *a commemorative postage stamp. adj.*

com mence (kə mens′), begin; start: *The boxers commenced fighting when the bell rang. v.,* **com menced, com menc ing.**

com mence ment (kə mens′mənt), 1 a beginning; start. 2 day when a school or college gives diplomas and degrees to students who have com-

adj. adjective	*n.* noun	
adv. adverb	*prep.* preposition	
conj. conjunction	*pron.* pronoun	
interj. interjection	*v.* verb	
sing. singular	*pl.* plural	

pleted the required course of study. 3 ceremonies on this day. *n.*

com mend (kə mend/), 1 speak well of; praise: *The teacher commended the pupils who studied for the test.* 2 hand over for safekeeping; entrust: *The child's parents commended her to her aunt's care until they returned from their trip. v.*

com mend a ble (kə men/də bəl), deserving praise or approval. *adj.*

com men da tion (kom/ən dā/shən), 1 praise; approval. 2 a handing over to another for safekeeping; entrusting. *n.*

com men sur ate (kə men/shər it *or* kə men/sər it), 1 in the proper proportion: *The pay should be commensurate with the work.* 2 of the same size or extent; equal: *The amount I earn and the amount I spend are nearly commensurate. adj.*

com ment (kom/ent), 1 a short statement, note, or remark that explains, praises, or finds fault with something that has been written, said, or done: *The teacher made some helpful comments about my work.* 2 make a comment or comments: *Everyone commented on her new hat.* 3 talk; gossip: *The scandal has been causing much comment.* 1,3 *n.,* 2 *v.*

com men tar y (kom/ən ter/ē), 1 series of notes explaining the hard parts of a book; explanation: *Some Bibles have commentaries at the back that give much information and help.* 2 series of comments: *a news or sports commentary on radio or television. n., pl.* **com men tar ies.**

com men ta tor (kom/ən tā/tər), 1 writer of comments. 2 person who reports and comments on news, sporting events, plays, concerts, etc.: *a radio or television commentator. n.*

com merce (kom/ərs), the buying and selling of goods, especially in large amounts between different places; business; trade. *n.*

com mer cial (kə mèr/shəl), 1 having to do with trade or business: *a store or other commercial establishment.* 2 made to be sold for a profit: *Anything you can buy in a store is a commercial product.* 3 supported by an advertiser or sponsor: *a commercial television program.* 4 an advertising message on

radio or television, broadcast between or during programs. 1-3 *adj.,* 4 *n.* —**com mer/cial ly,** *adv.*

com mer cial ize (kə mèr/shə līz), make a matter of business or trade: *Charging admission to church services would commercialize religion. v.,* **com mer cial ized, com mer cial iz ing.**

com min gle (kə ming/gəl), mingle with one another; blend. *v.,* **com mingled, com min gling.**

com mis e rate (kə miz/ə rāt/), feel or express sorrow for another's suffering or trouble; pity; sympathize. *v.,* **com mis e rat ed, com mis e rat ing.**

com mis e ra tion (kə miz/ə rā/shən), pity; sympathy. *n.*

com mis sar (kom/ə sär), (formerly) a head of a government department in the Soviet Union. *n.*

com mis sar i at (kom/ə ser/ē ət), the department of an army that provides food and daily supplies for soldiers. *n.*

com mis sar y (kom/ə ser/ē), store handling food and supplies in a mining camp, lumber camp, army camp, etc. *n., pl.* **com mis sar ies.**

com mis sion (kə mish/ən), 1 a written paper giving certain powers, rights, and duties: *Thomas Jefferson once held a commission as United States ambassador to France.* 2 give (a person) the power, right, or duty (to do something); give authority to: *My parents commissioned a real estate agent to sell our house.* 3 a written order giving rank or authority in the armed forces: *A captain in the United States Army has a commission signed by the President.* 4 give such a rank or authority to. 5 thing trusted to a person to do; errand: *The class gave me the commission of selecting a birthday present for our teacher.* 6 group of people appointed or elected with authority to do certain things: *The President appointed a commission to find out why food costs so much.* 7 a committing; doing; performance: *People are punished for the commission of crimes.* 8 a percentage of the amount of business done, paid to the agent who does it: *She gets a commission of 10 per cent on all the sales that she makes.* 9 working order; service; use: *A flat tire has put my bicycle out of commission.* 10 put into active service; make ready for use. A new warship is commissioned when it has the officers, sailors, and supplies needed for a sea trip. 1,3,5-9 *n.,* 2,4,10 *v.*

commissioned officer, officer holding the rank of second lieutenant or above in the United States Army, Air Force, or Marine Corps, or of ensign or above in the United States Navy.

com mis sion er (kə mish/ə nər), 1 member of a commission. 2 official in

charge of some department of a government: *a police commissioner. Our county has both road commissioners and health commissioners. n.*

com mit (kə mit/), 1 do or perform (usually something wrong): *commit a crime.* 2 hand over for safekeeping; deliver: *commit oneself to a doctor's care. The convicted thief was committed to the penitentiary.* 3 give over; carry over; transfer: *commit a poem to memory. She committed her thoughts to writing. The dead are committed to the grave.* 4 bind or involve (oneself); pledge: *I have committed myself now and must keep my promise.* 5 refer to a committee for consideration. *v.,* **com mit ted, com mit ting.**

com mit ment (kə mit/mənt), 1 a committing or a being committed: *the commitment of a prisoner to jail.* 2 a pledge; promise. *n.*

com mit tee (kə mit/ē), group of persons appointed or elected to do some special thing: *Our teacher appointed a committee of five pupils to plan the class picnic. n.*

com mode (kə mōd/), 1 chest of drawers. 2 washstand. *n.*

com mo di ous (kə mō/dē əs), having plenty of room; spacious; roomy. *adj.*

com mod i ty (kə mod/ə tē), anything that is bought and sold; article of trade or commerce: *Groceries are commodities. n., pl.* **com mod i ties.**

com mo dore (kom/ə dôr), 1 (formerly) an officer in the United States Navy ranking next below a rear admiral and next above a captain. 2 title given to the president of a yacht club. *n.*

com mon (kom/ən), 1 belonging equally to all; joint: *The house was the common property of the three sisters.* 2 of all; from all; by all; to all; general: *By common consent of the class, she was chosen president.* 3 often met with; ordinary; usual: *Snow is common in cold countries.* 4 having no special rank or position: *The common people do most of the work of the world. A common soldier is a private.* 5 below ordinary; having poor quality; inferior: *cloth of a common sort.* 6 coarse; vulgar: *His speech was very common.* 7 belonging to or representing the entire community; public: *A common council of twelve persons governs our city.* 8 Also, **commons,** *pl.* land owned or used by all the people of a town, village, etc. 1-7 *adj.,* 8 *n.* —**com/mon ness,** *n.*

in common, equally with another or others; owned, used, or done by both or all: *They have many interests in common.*

common carrier, company or person whose business is taking goods or people from one place to another for pay. Railroads, airlines, and bus lines are common carriers.

common denominator, a common multiple of the denominators of a group of fractions: *15 is the common denominator of* ³/₅ *and* ²/₃ *because these fractions can be expressed as* ⁹/₁₅ *and* ¹⁰/₁₅.

common divisor, number that will divide a group of two or more other numbers without a remainder: *2 is a common divisor of 4, 6, 8, and 10.*

com mon er (kom′ə nər), one of the common people; person who is not a nobleman. *n.*

common fraction, fraction expressed as the ratio of two whole numbers. ¹/₂ and ⁷/₈ are common fractions.

common law, law based on custom and usage.

com mon ly (kom′ən lē), usually; generally: *Arithmetic is commonly taught in elementary schools. adv.*

Common Market, an association established in 1958 to promote free trade among its members. It includes Belgium, Denmark, France, Great Britain, Ireland, Italy, Luxembourg, the Netherlands, and West Germany.

common multiple, number that can be divided by two or more other numbers without a remainder: *12 is a common multiple of 2, 3, 4, and 6.*

common noun, name for any one of a class. *Boy* and *city* are common nouns. *John* and *Boston* are proper nouns.

com mon place (kom′ən plās′), 1 an ordinary or everyday thing: *Forty years ago television was a novelty; today it is a commonplace.* 2 an ordinary statement; obvious remark: *boring talk full of commonplaces about the weather.* 3 not new or interesting; everyday; ordinary: *The plots of television movies are often commonplace.* 1,2 *n.,* 3 *adj.*

com mons (kom′ənz), 1 the common people; those who do not belong to the nobility or ruling class. 2 a dining hall or building where food is served to many at large tables. 3 **the Commons,** House of Commons. *n., pl. in form, sometimes sing. in use.*

common sense, good sense in everyday affairs; practical intelligence.

com mon weal (kom′ən wēl′), 1 the general welfare; public good. 2 OLD USE. commonwealth. *n.*

com mon wealth (kom′ən welth′), 1 the people who make up a nation; citizens of a state. 2 nation in which the people have the right to make the laws; republic. Brazil, Australia, and the United States are commonwealths. 3 any state of the United States, especially Kentucky, Massachusetts, Pennsylvania, and Virginia. 4 **the Commonwealth,** the Commonwealth of Nations. *n.*

Commonwealth of Nations, association of the United Kingdom, the independent member states (such as Canada, Australia, New Zealand, India, Ceylon, Ghana, Nigeria, Cyprus), and various associated states, dependent territories, protectorates, and protected states; the Commonwealth. It was formerly called **British Commonwealth of Nations** or **British Commonwealth.**

com mo tion (kə mō′shən), violent movement; confusion; disturbance; tumult: *Their fight caused quite a commotion in the hall. n.*

com mu nal (kə myü′nl *or* kom′yə-nəl), 1 of a community; public: *communal property.* 2 of or in a commune: *communal living. adj.* —**com mu′nal ly,** *adv.*

com mune¹ (kə myün′), 1 talk intimately. 2 receive Holy Communion. *v.,* **com muned, com mun ing.** [from French of the 1200′s *communer* make common, share]

com mune² (kom′yün), 1 the smallest division for local government in France, Belgium, and several other European countries. 2 group of people living together. *n.* [from French *commune*]

com mu ni ca ble (kə myü′nə kə-bəl), that can be transferred or passed along to others: *a communicable disease. Ideas are communicable by words. adj.*

com mu ni cant (kə myü′nə kənt), 1 person who receives Holy Communion. 2 person who informs or communicates. *n.*

com mu ni cate (kə myü′nə kāt), 1 give or exchange information or news by speaking, writing, etc.; send and receive messages: *She communicated her ideas to her friend. We communicate with them often by letter.* 2 pass along; transfer: *The stove communicated heat to the room.* 3 be connected: *The dining room communicates with the kitchen. v.,* **com mu ni cat ed, com mu ni cat ing.**

com mu ni ca tion (kə myü′nə kā′-shən), 1 a giving or exchanging information or news by speaking, writing, etc.; communicating: *Sign language is a means of communication.* 2 information or news given; letter, message, etc., which gives information or news: *Your communication came in time to change my plans.* 3 means of going from one place to another; passage; connection: *There is no communication between these two rooms.* 4 act or fact of passing along; transfer. 5 **communications,** *pl.* **a** system of communicating by telephone, telegraph, radio, television, etc.: *A network of communications links all parts of the civilized world.* **b** system of routes or facilities

community

hat, āge, fär; let, ēqual, tèrm; it, īce; hot, ōpen, ôrder; oil, out; cup, pùt, rüle; ch, child; ng, long; sh, she; th, thin; ŦH, then; zh, measure;

ə represents *a* in about, *e* in taken, *i* in pencil, *o* in lemon, *u* in circus.

for transporting military supplies, vehicles, and troops: *The enemy bombers broke up our line of communications. n.*

communications satellite, an artificial satellite that relays microwave signals between two points on earth.

com mu ni ca tive (kə myü′nə kā′-tiv), ready to give information; talkative. *adj.* —**com mu′ni ca′tive ly,** *adv.* —**com mu′ni ca′tive ness,** *n.*

com mun ion (kə myü′nyən), 1 a having in common; sharing: *The partners had a communion of interests.* 2 exchange of thoughts and feelings; fellowship. 3 group of people having the same religious beliefs. 4 **Communion,** Holy Communion. *n.*

com mu ni qué (kə myü′nə kā′), an official bulletin, statement, or other communication. *n., pl.* **com mu ni qués.** [from French]

com mu nism (kom′yə niz′əm), 1 an economic and social system in which most or all property is owned by the state or community as a whole and is supposed to be shared by all. 2 **Communism,** the principles and practices of members of a Communist Party. *n.*

com mu nist (kom′yə nist), 1 person who favors or supports communism. 2 communistic. 3 **Communist,** member of a Communist Party. 4 **Communist,** of or having to do with a Communist Party. 1,3 *n.,* 2,4 *adj.*

com mu nis tic (kom′yə nis′tik), 1 of or having to do with communists or communism. 2 favoring communism. *adj.*

Communist Party, a political party which supports communism.

com mu ni ty (kə myü′nə tē), 1 all the people living in the same place and subject to the same laws; people of any district or town: *This lake provides water for six communities.* 2 group of people living together or sharing common interests: *a monastery and its community of monks, the scientific community.* 3 **the community,** the public: *To be successful a new product needs the approval of the community.* 4 ownership together; sharing together: *community of food supplies.* 5 group of

adj.	adjective	*n.*	noun
adv.	adverb	*prep.*	preposition
conj.	conjunction	*pron.*	pronoun
interj.	interjection	*v.*	verb
sing.	singular	*pl.*	plural

animals or plants living together. 6 likeness; similarity: *community of interests.* *n., pl.* **com mu ni ties.**

community chest, fund of money given voluntarily by people to support charity and welfare in their community.

com mu ta tion (kom/yə tā/shən), 1 the changing (of a penalty, obligation, etc.) to a less severe one: *The prisoner obtained a commutation of his sentence from death to life imprisonment.* 2 regular travel to and from work by train, bus, automobile, etc. *n.*

com mu ta tive (kom/yə tā/tiv), of or having to do with a rule in mathematics that the order in which numbers are added or multiplied will not change the result. EXAMPLE: $2 + 3$ will give the same result as $3 + 2.$ *adj.*

com mu ta tor (kom/yə tā/tər), device for reversing the direction of an electric current. *n.*

com mute (kə myüt/), 1 change (a penalty, obligation, etc.) to a less severe one: *The governor commuted the prisoner's death sentence to life imprisonment.* 2 travel regularly to and from work by train, bus, automobile, etc. *v.,* **com mut ed, com mut ing.**

com mut er (kə myü/tər), person who travels regularly to and from work by train, bus, automobile, etc. *n.*

com pact[1] (kəm pakt/ *or* kom/pakt *for* 1,2,4; kəm pakt/ *for* 3; kom/pakt *for* 5,6), 1 firmly packed together; closely joined: *Cabbage leaves are folded into a compact head.* 2 having the parts neatly or tightly arranged within a small space; not scattered or sprawling: *a compact portable TV set.* 3 pack firmly together; compress. 4 using few words; brief: *Reporters usually write compact sentences.* 5 a small case containing face powder or rouge. 6 automobile smaller than most models. 1,2,4 *adj.,* 3 *v.,* 5,6 *n.* [from Latin *compactum* confined, from *com-* together + *pangere* fasten] —**com pact/ly,** *adv.* —**com pact/ness,** *n.*

com pact[2] (kom/pakt), agreement; contract: *The United Nations is a result of a compact among nations.* *n.* [from Latin *compactum* agreement, from *com-* together + *pacisci* make an agreement]

com pan ion (kəm pan/yən), 1 one who goes along with or accompanies another; one who shares in what another is doing; comrade: *The twins were companions in work and play.* 2 person paid to live or travel with another as a friend and helper. 3 anything that matches or goes with another in kind, size, and color: *I can't find the companion to this shoe.* *n.*

com pan ion a ble (kəm pan/yə nə-bəl), pleasant as a companion; agreeable. *adj.*

com pan ion a bly (kəm pan/yə nə-blē), in a companionable manner. *adv.*

com pan ion ship (kəm pan/yən-ship), a being a companion; fellowship: *the companionship of a friend.* *n.*

com pan ion way (kəm pan/yən-wā/), stairway from the deck of a ship down to the rooms or area below. *n.*

com pa ny (kum/pə nē), 1 group of people: *A great company came to church.* 2 group of people joined together for some purpose, such as carrying on a business or acting plays: *A band is a company of musicians.* 3 companion or companions: *You are known by the company you keep.* 4 companionship: *His dog provided the trapper with company during the long winters.* 5 one or more guests or visitors: *Are you expecting company for dinner?* 6 a military unit made up of two or more platoons, usually commanded by a captain. It is usually part of a battalion or a regiment. 7 a ship's crew. *n., pl.* **com pa nies.**

keep company, 1 go with; remain with for companionship: *My dog kept me company while you were away.* 2 go together.

part company, 1 go separate ways: *The friends parted company at the gate.* 2 end companionship: *They parted company forever.*

com pa ra ble (kom/pər ə bəl), 1 able to be compared: *A fire is comparable with the sun; both give light and heat.* 2 fit to be compared: *A cave is not comparable to a house for comfort.* *adj.*

com pa ra bly (kom/pər ə blē), in a comparable manner; to a comparable degree. *adv.*

com pa ra tive (kəm par/ə tiv), 1 that compares: *He made a comparative study of the habits of bees and wasps.* 2 measured by comparison with something else; relative: *Screens give us comparative freedom from flies.* 3 the second of three degrees of comparison of an adjective or adverb. *Fairer* is the comparative of *fair.* *More slowly* is the comparative of *slowly.* 4 showing the second degree of comparison of an adjective or adverb. *Better* is the comparative form of *good.* 1,2,4 *adj.,* 3 *n.*

com pa ra tive ly (kəm par/ə tiv lē),

by comparison; relatively; somewhat: *Mountains are comparatively free of mosquitoes.* *adv.*

com pare (kəm per/ *or* kəm par/), 1 find out or point out how persons or things are alike and how they are different: *I compared my answers with the teacher's and found I had made a mistake.* 2 say (two things) are alike; consider as similar; liken: *The fins of a fish may be compared to the wings of a bird; both are used in moving.* 3 be considered like or equal: *Canned fruit cannot compare with fresh fruit.* 4 name the positive, comparative, and superlative degrees of an adjective or adverb. *v.,* **com pared, com par ing.**

beyond compare, without an equal; most excellent: *The food at this restaurant is beyond compare.*

com par i son (kəm par/ə sən), 1 act or process of comparing; finding the likenesses and differences: *The comparison of the heart to a pump helped the students to understand how the heart works.* 2 likeness; similarity: *There is no comparison between these two cameras; one is much better than the other.* 3 change in an adjective or adverb to show degrees. The three degrees of comparison are positive, comparative, and superlative. EXAMPLE: cold, colder, coldest; helpful, more helpful, most helpful; good, better, best. *n.*

in comparison with, compared with: *Even a large lake is small in comparison with an ocean.*

com part ment (kəm pärt/mənt), a separate division or section of anything; part of an enclosed place set off by walls or partitions: *The ship's hold has watertight compartments so that a leak will fill up only part of the ship.* *n.*

compass (def. 1) Even though the dial may be turned, the needle remains fixed on north.

compass (def. 2) The sharply pointed arm remains fixed as the drawing arm revolves.

com pass (kum/pəs), 1 instrument for showing directions, especially one consisting of a needle that points to the North Magnetic Pole. 2 Also, **compasses,** *pl.* instrument consisting of two legs hinged together at one end, used for drawing circles and curved lines and for measuring distances. 3 boundary; circumference: *within the compass of four walls.* 4 space within limits; extent; range: *There have been many scientific discoveries within the compass of her lifetime.* 5 range of a voice or musical instrument. 6 go around; move around: *The astronaut compassed the earth in a space capsule.* 7 hem in; surround: *The lake is compassed by a ring of mountains.* 8 accomplish; obtain: *We compassed our goal.* 9 grasp with the mind; understand completely. 1-5 *n., pl.* **com pass es;** 6-9 *v.*

com pas sion (kəm pash′ən), feeling for another's sorrow or hardship that leads to help; sympathy; pity: *His compassion for the orphans caused him to give money for their support. n.*

com pas sion ate (kəm pash′ə nit), wishing to help those that suffer; sympathetic; pitying. *adj.* —**com pas′sion ate ly,** *adv.*

com pat i bil i ty (kəm pat′ə bil′ə tē), agreement; harmony. *n.*

com pat i ble (kəm pat′ə bəl), able to exist or get on well together; agreeing; in harmony: *Cats and birds are seldom compatible. adj.*

com pat i bly (kəm pat′ə blē), in a compatible manner; harmoniously. *adv.*

com pa tri ot (kəm pā′trē ət), a fellow countryman or countrywoman. *n.*

com peer (kəm pir′), 1 an equal; peer. 2 companion; comrade. *n.*

com pel (kəm pel′), 1 drive or urge with force; force: *Rain compelled us to stop our ball game.* 2 bring about by force; command: *A policeman can compel obedience to the law. v.,* **compelled, com pel ling.**

com pen sate (kom′pən sāt), 1 make an equal return to; give an equivalent to: *The children raised ten dollars to compensate us for the window they broke playing ball.* 2 balance by equal weight or power; make up: *Skill sometimes compensates for lack of strength.* 3 pay: *The company compensated her for her extra work. v.,* **com pen sat ed, com pen sat ing.**

com pen sa tion (kom′pən sā′shən), 1 something given to make up for something else; something which makes up for a loss, injury, etc.: *When he lost the knife I lent him, he gave me a new knife as compensation.* 2 pay: *Equal compensation should be given to men and women for equal work. n.*

com pete (kəm pēt′), 1 try hard to win or gain something wanted by others; be rivals; contend: *She competed against many fine athletes for the gold medal. It is difficult for a small grocery store to compete for trade with a supermarket.* 2 take part (in a contest): *Will you compete in the final race? v.,* **com pet ed, com pet ing.**

com pe tence (kom′pə təns), 1 a being competent; ability: *No one doubted the guide's competence.* 2 enough money to provide a comfortable living. *n.*

com pe ten cy (kom′pə tən sē), competence. *n.*

com pe tent (kom′pə tənt), properly qualified; able: *A competent cook gets high wages. A doctor should be competent to treat many diseases. adj.* —**com′pe tent ly,** *adv.*

com pe ti tion (kom′pə tish′ən), 1 a trying hard to win or gain something wanted by others; rivalry: *competition among businessmen for trade. There is competition in many games.* 2 contest: *She won first place in the swimming competition. n.*

com pet i tive (kəm pet′ə tiv), decided by competition; using competition: *He took a competitive examination for the job of postal clerk. adj.* —**com pet′i tive ly,** *adv.* —**com pet′i tive ness,** *n.*

com pet i tor (kəm pet′ə tər), person who competes; rival. *n.*

com pi la tion (kom′pə lā′shən), 1 act of compiling. 2 book, list, or table that has been compiled. *n.*

com pile (kəm pīl′), 1 collect and bring together in one list or account: *Mother compiled a list of the groceries we needed.* 2 make (a book, a report, etc.) out of various materials: *It takes many experts to compile an encyclopedia. v.,* **com piled, com pil ing.**

com pil er (kəm pī′lər), person who compiles. *n.*

com pla cence (kəm plā′sns), complacency. *n.*

com pla cen cy (kəm plā′sn sē), a being pleased with oneself or what one has; self-satisfaction: *She solved the difficult puzzle easily and smiled with complacency. n.*

com pla cent (kəm plā′snt), pleased with oneself or what one has; self-satisfied: *The winner's complacent smile annoyed the loser. adj.* —**com pla′cent ly,** *adv.*

com plain (kəm plān′), 1 say that something is wrong; find fault: *She complains that the room is cold.* 2 talk about one's pain, troubles, etc.: *He is always complaining.* 3 make an accusation or charge: *I complained to the police about the barking of my neighbor's dog. v.* —**com plain′er, n.**

com plain ant (kəm plā′nənt), person who brings a lawsuit against another. *n.*

com plaint (kəm plānt′), 1 a complaining; a voicing of dissatisfaction; finding fault: *His letter is filled with complaints about the food at camp.* 2 accusation; charge: *The judge heard the complaint and ordered an inves-*

hat, āge, fär; let, ēqual, tėrm;
it, īce; hot, ōpen, ôrder;
oil, out; cup, pùt, rüle; ch, child;
ng, long; sh, she; th, thin;
ŦH, then; zh, measure;

ə represents *a* in about,
e in taken, *i* in pencil,
o in lemon, *u* in circus.

tigation. 3 a cause for complaining: *Her main complaint is that she has too much work to do.* 4 illness; disease: *A cold is a very common complaint. n.*

com plai sance (kəm plā′zns), a being complaisant; obligingness; graciousness. *n.*

com plai sant (kəm plā′znt), inclined to do what is asked; obliging; gracious. *adj.* —**com plai′sant ly,** *adv.*

com ple ment (kom′plə mənt *for 1-3;* kom′plə ment *for 4*), 1 something that completes or makes perfect: *The teacher considers homework a necessary complement to classroom work.* 2 number required to complete or make perfect: *As the ship now has its full complement of men, no more can be taken on.* 3 word or group of words completing a predicate. In "The man is good" *good* is a complement. 4 supply a lack of any kind; complete: *My fishing poles complement his hooks and lines, so that together we can go fishing.* 1-3 *n.,* 4 *v.*

com ple men tar y (kom′plə men′tər ē), forming a complement; completing: *The four seasons are complementary parts of a year. adj.*

complementary angle
Angle ACB and angle BCD are complementary angles.

complementary angle, either of two angles which together form an angle of 90 degrees.

com plete (kəm plēt′), 1 with all the parts; whole; entire: *We have a complete set of garden tools.* 2 make whole or entire; make up the full number or amount of: *I completed the set of dishes by buying the cups and saucers.* 3 perfect; thorough: *a complete surprise.* 4 make perfect or thorough: *The good news completed my happiness.* 5 finished; done: *My homework is complete.* 6 get done; finish: *She completed her homework before dinner.* 1,3,5 *adj.,* 2,4,6 *v.,* **com plet ed, com plet ing.**

adj.	adjective	n.	noun
adv.	adverb	prep.	preposition
conj.	conjunction	pron.	pronoun
interj.	interjection	v.	verb
sing.	singular	pl.	plural

—**com plete′ly**, adv. —**com plete′ness**, n.

com ple tion (kəm plē′shən), 1 act of completing; finishing: *After the completion of the job, the workmen went home.* 2 condition of being completed: *The work is near completion.* n.

com plex (kəm pleks′ or kom′pleks *for 1,2;* kom′pleks *for 3-5*), 1 made up of a number of parts: *A watch is a complex device.* 2 hard to understand: *The instructions for building the radio were so complex we could not follow them.* 3 a complicated whole: *The assembly line handled a complex of 200 parts.* 4 group of related or connected buildings, structures, units, etc.: *The new complex built on the school grounds includes a library, a museum, and an auditorium.* 5 a strong prejudice; unreasonable dislike or fear: *He has a complex about cats.* 1,2 adj., 3-5 n., pl. **com plex es.** —**com plex′ly**, adv.

complex fraction, fraction having a fraction in the numerator, in the denominator, or in both; compound fraction. EXAMPLES: $\frac{1\frac{3}{4}}{3}$, $\frac{1}{3\frac{3}{4}}$, $\frac{\frac{3}{4}}{1\frac{7}{8}}$.

com plex ion (kəm plek′shən), 1 color, quality, and general appearance of the skin, particularly of the face. 2 general appearance of anything; nature; character: *The complexion of the little farm town was changed when two big factories were built nearby.* n.

com plex i ty (kəm plek′sə tē), 1 a complex quality or condition; intricacy: *The complexity of the road map puzzled me.* 2 something complex; complication. n., pl. **com plex i ties.**

complex sentence, sentence having one main clause and one or more subordinate clauses. EXAMPLE: When the traffic light turns red, traffic must stop.

com pli ance (kəm plī′əns), 1 a complying; yielding to a request or command: *I appreciated the clerk's ready compliance with my request to exchange the merchandise.* 2 tendency to yield to others: *Her refusal was all the more surprising in view of her usual compliance.* n.

in compliance with, complying with; according to: *He sent the package by air mail in compliance with the order to send it quickly.*

com pli ant (kəm plī′ənt), complying; yielding; obliging. adj. —**com pli′ant ly,** adv.

com pli cate (kom′plə kāt), 1 make hard to understand or settle; mix up; make complex; confuse: *Too many rules complicate a game.* 2 make worse or more mixed up: *a headache complicated by eye trouble.* v., **com pli cat ed, com pli cat ing.**

com pli cat ed (kom′plə kā′tid), hard to understand; involved; complex: *Many airplane models have very complicated directions for their assembly.* adj.

com pli ca tion (kom′plə kā′shən), 1 a complex or confused condition that is hard to understand or settle: *You never saw such a complication of little rules and restrictions.* 2 something that makes matters worse or harder to untangle or settle: *Pneumonia was the complication the doctor feared most after the operation.* 3 act of complicating. n.

com plic i ty (kəm plis′ə tē), a being an accomplice; partnership in wrongdoing: *Knowingly receiving stolen goods is complicity in theft.* n., pl. **com plic i ties.**

com pli ment (kom′plə mənt *for 1, 2,4;* kom′plə ment *for 3*), 1 something good said about one; something said in praise of one's work: *The famous actress was used to hearing many compliments.* 2 a courteous act: *The town paid the old artist the compliment of a large attendance at his exhibit.* 3 pay a compliment to; congratulate: *The principal complimented the boy on his good grades.* 4 **compliments,** pl. greetings: *In the box of flowers was a card saying "With the compliments of a friend."* 1,2,4 n., 3 v.

com pli men tar y (kom′plə men′tər ē), 1 expressing a compliment; praising: *a complimentary remark.* 2 given free: *a complimentary ticket to the circus.* adj.

com ply (kəm plī′), act in agreement with a request or a command: *I will comply with the doctor's orders.* v., **com plied, com ply ing.**

com po nent (kəm pō′nənt), 1 a necessary or essential part: *Quartz and feldspar are the chief components of granite.* 2 that composes; constituent: *Blade and handle are the component parts of a knife.* 1 n., 2 adj.

com port (kəm pôrt′), 1 conduct (oneself) in a certain manner; behave: *Judges should comport themselves with dignity.* 2 agree; suit: *Silliness does not comport with the position of judge.* v.

com pose (kəm pōz′), 1 make up; form: *The ocean is composed of salt water. Our party was composed of three grown-ups and four children.* 2 put together. To compose a story or poem is to construct it from words. To compose a piece of music is to invent the tune and write down the notes. To compose in a printing office is to set up type to form words or sentences. To compose a picture is to get an artistic arrangement of the things in it. 3 make calm: *Stop crying and compose yourself before the doctor gets here.* 4 settle; arrange: *The union and the company composed their differences and agreed on a contract.* v., **com posed, com pos ing.**

com posed (kəm pōzd′), calm; quiet. adj. —**com pos′ed ly,** adv.

com pos er (kəm pō′zər), 1 person who composes. 2 writer of music. n.

com pos ite (kəm poz′it), 1 made up of various parts; compound: *This composite photograph was made by putting together parts of several others.* 2 belonging to a group of plants having flower heads consisting of many very tiny flowers. Daisies and dandelions are composite flowers. 3 any composite thing. 1,2 adj., 3 n.

composite number, number exactly divisible by some counting number other than itself or one. 4,6, and 9 are composite numbers; 2,3,5 and 7 are prime numbers.

com po si tion (kom′pə zish′ən), 1 the make-up of anything; what is in it: *The composition of this candy includes sugar, chocolate, and milk.* 2 a putting together of a whole. Writing sentences, making pictures, and setting type in printing are all forms of composition. 3 thing composed. A symphony, poem, or painting is a composition. A piece of writing composed as a school exercise is also a composition. 4 mixture of substances; compound: *The dentist filled my tooth with a composition having silver and mercury in it.* n.

com post (kom′pōst), mixture of decaying leaves, manure, etc., for fertilizing soil. n.

com po sure (kəm pō′zhər), calmness; quietness; self-control: *She always keeps her composure, even during a crisis.* n.

com pound¹ (kom′pound *for 1-4;* kom pound′ *for 5,6*), 1 having more than one part: *Clover has compound leaves.* 2 something made by combining parts; mixture: *Many medicines are compounds.* 3 word made up of two or more words which keep their separate forms. *Steamship* is a compound made up of the two words *steam* and *ship.* 4 substance formed by chemical combination of two or more substances:

174

Water is a compound of hydrogen and oxygen. 5 mix; combine: *The druggist compounded several medicines to fill the prescription.* 6 add to; increase; multiply: *The naughty little boy compounded his troubles by kicking the teacher.* 1 *adj.*, 2-4 *n.*, 5,6 *v.* [from French of the 1300's *compondre* put together]

com pound² (kom′pound), an enclosed yard with buildings in it. *n.* [from Malay *kampong* village, enclosure]

compound eye, the eye of certain insects and crustaceans. It is composed of many tiny units, each of which receives part of the image.

compound fraction, complex fraction.

compound fracture, fracture in which a broken bone cuts through the flesh.

compound interest, interest paid on both the original sum of money borrowed or invested and the interest added to it.

compound leaf, leaf composed of two or more leaflets on a common stalk.

compound sentence, sentence made up of two or more main clauses. EXAMPLE: The winds blew, the rains fell, and the water covered the earth.

com pre hend (kom′pri hend′), 1 understand the meaning of: *If you can use a word correctly, you comprehend it.* 2 include; contain: *Your report comprehended all the facts.* *v.*

com pre hen si ble (kom′pri hen′sə bəl), understandable. *adj.*

com pre hen sion (kom′pri hen′shən), act or power of understanding: *Arithmetic is beyond the comprehension of a baby.* *n.*

com pre hen sive (kom′pri hen′siv), 1 of large scope or extent; including much: *The month's schoolwork ended with a comprehensive review.* 2 able to understand many things fully: *Benjamin Franklin had a comprehensive mind.* *adj.* —**com′pre hen′sive ly,** *adv.* —**com′pre hen′sive ness,** *n.*

com press (kəm pres′ for 1; kom′pres for 2), 1 squeeze together; make smaller by pressure: *compressed air. Cotton is compressed into bales. Can you compress the story into a few short sentences?* 2 pad of cloth applied to some part of the body to prevent bleeding, lessen inflammation, etc.: *Mother put a cold compress on my forehead to relieve my headache.* 1 *v.*, 2 *n.*, *pl.* **com press es.**

com press i bil i ty (kəm pres′ə bil′ə tē), compressible quality. *n.*

com press i ble (kəm pres′ə bəl), that can be compressed. *adj.*

com pres sion (kəm presh′ən), 1 act or process of compressing. 2 compressed condition. *n.*

com pres sor (kəm pres′ər), 1 person or thing that compresses. 2 machine for compressing air, gas, etc. *n.*

com prise (kəm prīz′), be made up of; consist of; include: *The United States comprises 50 states.* *v.*, **com prised, com pris ing.**

com pro mise (kom′prə mīz), 1 settle a quarrel or difference of opinion by agreeing that each will give up a part of what he demands: *A good politician knows how to compromise.* 2 settlement of a quarrel or difference of opinion in which both sides agree to give up a part of what each demands: *They both wanted the apple; their compromise was to share it.* 3 result of any such settlement. 4 put under suspicion; put in danger: *You will compromise your reputation if you go around with such a bad crowd.* 1,4 *v.*, **com pro mised, com pro mis ing;** 2,3 *n.*

comp trol ler (kən trō′lər), person employed to look after expenditures and accounts; controller. *n.*

com pul sion (kəm pul′shən), 1 a compelling or being compelled; use of force; force: *A contract signed under compulsion is not legal.* 2 impulse that is hard to resist: *A compulsion to steal is not normal.* *n.*

com pul sive (kəm pul′siv), of or having to do with an impulse that is hard to resist: *a compulsive desire for neatness.* *adj.* —**com pul′sive ly,** *adv.* —**com pul′sive ness,** *n.*

com pul sor y (kəm pul′sər ē), 1 compelled; required: *Attendance at school is compulsory for children over seven years old.* 2 compelling; using force. *adj.*

com punc tion (kəm pungk′shən), uneasiness of the mind because of wrongdoing; pricking of conscience; regret; remorse: *She had no compunction about copying her friend's work.* *n.*

com pu ta tion (kom′pyə tā′shən), a computing; calculation. Addition and subtraction are forms of computation. *n.*

com pute (kəm pyüt′), find out by arithmetical or other mathematical work; calculate: *When you know the distance across and the distance around a circle, you can compute its area.* *v.*, **com put ed, com put ing.**

com put er (kəm pyü′tər), 1 machine which computes, especially an electronic machine that either solves problems when given certain coded information or otherwise processes that information. 2 person skilled or trained in computing. *n.*

com rade (kom′rad), 1 a close companion and friend. 2 fellow worker; partner. *n.*

comrade in arms, a fellow soldier.

hat, āge, fär; let, ēqual, tėrm;
it, īce; hot, ōpen, ôrder;
oil, out; cup, pùt, rüle; ch, child;
ng, long; sh, she; th, thin;
ŦH, then; zh, measure;

ə represents *a* in about,
e in taken, *i* in pencil,
o in lemon, *u* in circus.

com rade ship (kom′rad ship), friendship; fellowship; companionship. *n.*

con¹ (kon), 1 against: *The two groups argued the question pro and con.* 2 a reason against: *The pros and cons of a question are the arguments for and against it.* 1 *adv.*, 2 *n.* [shortened from Latin *contra* against]

con² (kon), learn well enough to remember; study. *v.*, **conned, con ning.** [Old English *cunnian* test, examine]

concave lenses
A, concave surface
opposite plane surface
B, double concave
C, concave and convex

con cave (kon kāv′ *or* kon′kāv), hollow and curved like the inside of a circle or sphere: *The palm of one's hand is concave.* *adj.* —**con cave′ly,** *adv.*

con cav i ty (kon kav′ə tē), 1 concave condition or quality. 2 a concave surface or thing. *n.*, *pl.* **con cav i ties.**

con ceal (kən sēl′), 1 put out of sight; hide: *He concealed the surprise gift in the closet.* 2 keep secret: *She concealed her identity by wearing a mask.* *v.*

con ceal ment (kən sēl′mənt), 1 a concealing or keeping secret: *The witness's concealment of facts prevented a fair trial.* 2 means or place for concealing. *n.*

con cede (kən sēd′), 1 admit as true; acknowledge: *I conceded that I had made a mistake.* 2 allow (a person) to have; grant: *He conceded us the right to walk across his land.* *v.*, **con ced ed, con ced ing.**

con ceit (kən sēt′), 1 too much pride in oneself or in one's ability; vanity: *In his conceit, the track star thought that no one could outrun him.* 2 a pleasing fancy; a witty thought or expression. *n.*

con ceit ed (kən sē′tid), having too much pride in oneself or one's ability; vain. *adj.* —**con ceit′ed ly,** *adv.* —**con ceit′ed ness,** *n.*

con ceiv a ble (kən sē′və bəl), that can be conceived or thought of;

adj. adjective	*n.* noun
adv. adverb	*prep.* preposition
conj. conjunction	*pron.* pronoun
interj. interjection	*v.* verb
sing. singular	*pl.* plural

imaginable: *We take every conceivable precaution against fire. adj.*

con ceiv a bly (kən sē′və blē), in a conceivable manner. *adv.*

con ceive (kən sēv′), 1 form in the mind; think up; imagine: *The Wright brothers conceived the design of the first successful motor-powered airplane.* 2 have an idea or feeling; think: *Young children cannot conceive of life without automobiles and television.* 3 become pregnant with: *conceive a child. v.,* **con ceived, con ceiv ing.**

con cen trate (kon′sən trāt), 1 bring or come together in one place: *A magnifying glass can concentrate enough sunlight to scorch paper. The audience at the music festival concentrated around the stage.* 2 pay close attention; focus the mind: *He concentrated on his reading so that he would understand the story.* 3 make stronger. An acid solution is concentrated when it has very much acid in it. 4 something that has been concentrated: *Lemon juice with the water removed is a concentrate.* 1-3 *v.,* **con cen trat ed, con cen trat ing;** 4 *n.*

con cen tra tion (kon′sən trā′shən), 1 a concentrating or a being concentrated. 2 close attention: *When he gave the problem his full concentration, he figured out the answer.* 3 (of a solution) strength: *The acid solution was of weak concentration because so much water had been added. n.*

concentration camp, camp where political enemies, prisoners of war, and interned foreigners are held.

concentric circles

con cen tric (kən sen′trik), having the same center. *adj.*

con cept (kon′sept), idea of a thing or class of things; general notion; idea: *the concept that all men are equal. The concept of a triangle is different from the concept of a circle. n.*

con cep tion (kən sep′shən), 1 idea; thought; notion: *Her conception of the problem was different from mine.* 2 act

of forming an idea or thought. 3 a becoming pregnant. *n.*

con cern (kən sėrn′), 1 have to do with; be the business or affair of; belong to; interest: *This letter is private and concerns nobody but me. The school play concerns every member of the class.* 2 anything which touches or has to do with one's work or one's interests; business; affair: *The party decorations are my concern; you pay attention to refreshments.* 3 troubled interest; worry; anxiety: *Their concern over their sick child kept them awake all night.* 4 make anxious; cause to worry; trouble: *We didn't want to concern our parents with the news of the accident.* 5 a business company; firm: *We wrote to two big concerns for their catalogs.* 1,4 *v.,* 2,3,5 *n.*

con cerned (kən sėrnd′), 1 worried; anxious: *His parents are quite concerned about his poor health.* 2 interested: *Concerned citizens exercise their right to vote. adj.*

con cern ing (kən sėr′ning), having to do with; about: *The reporter asked many questions concerning the accident. prep.*

con cert (kon′sərt *for 1;* kən sėrt′ *for 2*), 1 a musical performance in which several musicians or singers take part: *The school orchestra gave a concert last night.* 2 arrange by agreement; plan or make together: *The children concerted a plan for raising money.* 1 *n.,* 2 *v.*

in concert, all together; in agreement: *The class worked in concert.*

con cert ed (kən sėr′tid), arranged by agreement; combined: *a concerted effort. adj.*

con cer ti na (kon′sər tē′nə), a small musical instrument somewhat like an accordion. *n., pl.* **con cer ti nas.**

con cer to (kən cher′tō), a long musical composition to be played by one or more principal instruments, such as a violin or piano, with the accompaniment of an orchestra. It usually has three movements. *n., pl.* **con cer tos.**

con ces sion (kən sesh′ən), 1 a conceding; granting: *As a concession to my pleas, I was allowed to stay up past my bedtime.* 2 anything conceded or granted; admission: *I have made all the concessions that I intend to make.* 3 something conceded or granted by a government or controlling authority; grant. Land or privileges given by a government to a business company are called concessions. A circus leases space for concessions selling food and drinks. *n.*

conch (kongk *or* konch), 1 mollusk of tropical waters having a large, spiral

shell. 2 its shell. *n., pl.* **conchs** (kongks), **conch es** (kon′chiz).

con cil i ate (kən sil′ē āt), 1 win over; soothe: *She conciliated her angry little sister with a candy bar.* 2 bring into harmony; reconcile. *v.,* **con cil i at ed, con cil i at ing.**

con cil i a tion (kən sil′ē ā′shən), 1 a winning over or soothing; reconciling. 2 a being won over or soothed; being reconciled. *n.*

con cil i a to ry (kən sil′ē ə tôr′ē), tending to win over, soothe, or reconcile: *Shaking hands after a fight is a conciliatory gesture. adj.*

con cise (kən sīs′), expressing much in few words; brief but full of meaning: *He gave a concise report of the meeting. adj.* —**con cise′ly,** *adv.* —**con cise′ness,** *n.*

con clave (kon′klāv), 1 a private meeting. 2 a private meeting of the cardinals for the election of a pope. *n.*

con clude (kən klüd′), 1 come or bring to an end; finish: *The play concluded with a happy ending and the curtain came down. We concluded the meeting at six o'clock.* 2 reach (certain decisions or opinions) by reasoning; infer: *From the large new marks we saw, we concluded that the animal must have been a bear.* 3 arrange; settle: *After the Revolutionary War the United States and Great Britain concluded a peace treaty.* 4 decide; resolve: *I concluded not to go. v.,* **con clud ed, con clud ing.**

con clu sion (kən klü′zhən), 1 final part; end: *The conclusion of the story was sad. The end of each chapter in our science book has a conclusion summing up all the important facts.* 2 decision or opinion reached by reasoning; inference: *She came to the conclusion that her skiing improved with practice.* 3 arrangement; settlement: *the conclusion of a peace treaty between two countries.* 4 a final result; outcome: *bring work to a good conclusion. n.*

in conclusion, finally; lastly; to conclude: *I will say, in conclusion, that it was an honor to be the speaker at this meeting.*

con clu sive (kən klü′siv), decisive; convincing; final: *The evidence against them was conclusive. adj.* —**con clu′sive ly,** *adv.* —**con clu′sive ness,** *n.*

con coct (kon kokt′), prepare; make up: *He concocted a drink made of grape juice and ginger ale. He concocted an*

conch (def. 1) with body and claw extended as when moving about excuse to explain why he came late to school. v.

con coc tion (kon kok′shən), 1 a concocting: *The concoction of the milk shake took several minutes.* 2 thing concocted. n.

con com i tant (kon kom′ə tənt), 1 accompanying: *a concomitant result.* 2 accompaniment: *Disease is a concomitant of poor sanitation.* 1 adj., 2 n. —**con com′i tant ly,** adv.

con cord (kon′kôrd or kong′kôrd), agreement; harmony; peace: *concord between friends.* n.

Con cord (kong′kərd), 1 town in E Massachusetts. The second battle of the Revolutionary War was fought there on April 19, 1775. 2 capital of New Hampshire, in the S part. n.

con cord ance (kon kôrd′ns), 1 an alphabetical list of the principal words of a book with references to the passages in which they occur. 2 concord; harmony. n.

con course (kon′kôrs), 1 a running, flowing, or coming together: *The fort was built on a wedge of land at the concourse of two rivers.* 2 a crowd. 3 a place where crowds come: *the main concourse of the railroad station.* 4 boulevard. n.

con crete (kon′krēt or kon krēt′), 1 existing as an actual object, not merely as an idea or as a quality; real. All actual objects are concrete. *A painting is concrete; its beauty is not.* 2 specific; particular; not general: *A daisy is a concrete example of a composite flower.* 3 mixture of crushed stone or gravel, sand, cement, and water that hardens as it dries. Concrete is used for foundations, whole buildings, sidewalks, roads, dams, and bridges. 4 made of this mixture: *a concrete sidewalk.* 1,2,4 adj., 3 n. —**con crete′ly,** adv. —**con crete′ness,** n.

con cu bine (kong′kyə bīn), 1 (in countries where one man can legally have many wives) a wife having inferior rank or rights. 2 woman who lives with a man without being legally married to him. n.

con cur (kən kėr′), 1 be of the same opinion; agree: *The judges all concurred in giving her the prize.* 2 happen at the same time; coincide: *This year two weeks of rain concurred with our vacation.* 3 work together: *The events of your life concur to make you what you are.* v., **con curred, con cur ring.**

con cur rence (kən kėr′əns), 1 agreement. 2 a happening at the same time. 3 a working together. n.

con cur rent (kən kėr′ənt), 1 happening at the same time: *The twins had* concurrent birthdays. 2 agreeing; harmonious: *concurrent ideas.* 3 working together. 4 coming together; meeting at a point. adj. —**con cur′rent ly,** adv.

con cus sion (kən kush′ən), 1 a sudden, violent shaking; shock: *The concussion caused by the explosion broke many windows.* 2 injury to the brain or spine caused by a blow, fall, etc.: *I suffered a severe concussion when I fell off the bicycle.* n.

con demn (kən dem′), 1 express strong disapproval of: *We condemn cruelty to animals.* 2 pronounce guilty of crime or wrong: *The accused man was condemned by the jury.* 3 sentence; doom: *condemned to death, condemned to a life of loneliness.* 4 declare not sound or suitable for use: *This bridge was condemned because it is no longer safe.* 5 take for public use under special provision of the law: *All these streets have been condemned to make room for the new expressway.* v.

con dem na tion (kon′dem nā′shən), 1 a condemning: *the condemnation of an unsafe bridge.* 2 a being condemned: *His condemnation made him an outcast.* n.

con den sa tion (kon′den sā′shən), 1 a condensing or a being condensed: *the condensation of milk, the condensation of steam into water.* 2 something condensed; condensed mass. A cloud is a condensation of water vapor in the atmosphere. n.

con dense (kən dens′), 1 make or become denser or more compact: *Milk is condensed by removing much of the water from it.* 2 make stronger; concentrate: *Light is condensed by means of lenses.* 3 change from a gas or vapor to a liquid. If steam touches cold surfaces, it condenses or is condensed into water. 4 put into fewer words; say briefly: *A long story can sometimes be condensed into a few sentences.* v., **con densed, con dens ing.**

con dens er (kən den′sər), 1 person or thing that condenses something. 2 capacitor. 3 apparatus for changing gas or vapor into a liquid. n.

con de scend (kon′di send′), 1 come down willingly or graciously to the level of one's inferiors in rank: *The king condescended to eat with the beggars.* 2 grant a favor with a haughty or patronizing attitude: *The little boy's older sister finally condescended to take him to the movies.* 3 stoop or lower oneself: *The policeman would not condescend to taking a bribe.* v. —**con′de scend′ing ly,** adv.

con de scen sion (kon′di sen′shən), 1 pleasantness to one's inferiors in rank. 2 a haughty or patronizing attitude. n.

hat, āge, fär; let, ēqual, tėrm;
it, īce; hot, ōpen, ôrder;
oil, out; cup, pùt, rüle; ch, child;
ng, long; sh, she; th, thin;
ŦH, then; zh, measure;

ə represents *a* in about,
e in taken, *i* in pencil,
o in lemon, *u* in circus.

con di ment (kon′də mənt), something used to give flavor and relish to food, such as mustard and spices. n.

con di tion (kən dish′ən), 1 state in which a person or thing is: *The condition of the house is better than when I bought it.* 2 good condition; good health: *People who take part in sports must keep in condition.* 3 put in good condition: *Exercise conditions your muscles.* 4 social position; rank: *Lincoln's parents were poor settlers of humble condition.* 5 thing on which something else depends; thing without which something else cannot be: *Ability and effort are conditions of success. Leases between landlords and tenants usually contain several conditions about the use of the property.* 6 **conditions,** pl. set of circumstances: *Icy roads make for poor driving conditions.* 7 shape the behavior of; accustom; habituate: *This dog has been conditioned to expect food when he hears a bell.* 8 a requirement that is expressed by an open mathematical sentence. 3 + x = 5 expresses the condition that a number you are to find, added to 3, must equal 5. 1,2,4-6,8 n., 3,7 v.

on condition that, with the understanding that; if: *I'll go on condition that you will go, too.*

con di tion al (kən dish′ə nəl), 1 depending on something else; limited: *When she said "I will come if the sun is shining" she was making a conditional promise.* 2 expressing or containing a condition: *Conditional statements in the sales agreement limited the use of the land.* adj.

con di tion al ly (kən dish′ə nə lē), under a condition or conditions: *He accepted the invitation conditionally, until he could check his calendar.* adv.

con di tion er (kən dish′ə nər), 1 device or substance that maintains or improves the quality of something: *water conditioner.* 2 air conditioner. n.

con dole (kən dōl′), express sympathy; grieve: *Friends condoled with the family at the funeral.* v., **con doled, con dol ing.**

con do lence (kən dō′ləns), a con-
doling; expression of sympathy: *Their
friends sent the family many condo-
lences. n.*

con done (kən dōn′), forgive or overlook: *Good friends will condone each
other's faults. v.,* **con doned, con-
don ing.**

con dor (kon′dər), a large vulture with
a ruffed neck and bare head. Condors
live on high mountains in South
America and California. *n.*

con duce (kən düs′ *or* kən dyüs′), be
favorable; lead; contribute: *Darkness
and quiet conduce to sleep. v.,* **con-
duced, con duc ing.**

con du cive (kən dü′siv *or* kən-
dyü′siv), favorable; helpful: *Exercise
and proper eating habits are conducive
to good health. adj.*

con duct (kon′dukt *for 1,4;* kən dukt′
for 2,3,5-7), 1 way of acting; behavior
thought of as good or bad: *Her conduct
was rude and inexcusable.* 2 act in a
certain way; behave: *At home he is
disorderly, but in company he conducts
himself well.* 3 direct; manage: *The
board of directors conducts the affairs
of this large business.* 4 direction;
management: *Conduct of such a large
office takes much planning.* 5 direct (an
orchestra, choir, etc.) as leader: *He
conducts a band of one hundred instruments.* 6 go along with and show
the way to; guide: *She conducted me
through the museum. Conduct me to
your teacher.* 7 transmit, transfer, or
convey: *Those pipes conduct steam to
the radiators upstairs. Metals conduct
heat and electricity.* 1,4 *n.,* 2,3,5-7 *v.*

con duc tion (kən duk′shən),
1 transmission of heat, electricity, etc.,
by the transferring of energy from one
particle to another. Radiators heat the
air in a room by conduction. 2 a conveying: *the conduction of water through
a pipe. n.*

con duc tiv i ty (kon′duk tiv′ə tē),
power of conducting heat, electricity,
sound, etc. *n.*

con duc tor (kən duk′tər), 1 person
who conducts; leader or guide: *the conductor of a tour.* 2 director of an orchestra, chorus, etc. 3 person in charge
of a train or bus and its passengers. The
conductor collects fares and enforces

regulations. 4 thing that transmits heat,
electricity, light, or sound. Copper is a
good conductor of heat and electricity. *n.*

con du it (kon′dü it *or* kon′dit),
1 channel or pipe for carrying liquids
long distances; aqueduct or canal. 2 a
specially made tube or underground
passage for electric wires or cables. *n.*

cone (kōn), 1 a solid object that has a
flat, round base that narrows to a point
at the top. 2 anything shaped like a
cone: *an ice-cream cone, the cone of a
volcano.* 3 a cone-shaped, scaly growth
that bears the seeds on pine, cedar, fir,
and other evergreen trees. 4 one of a
group of cells of the retina of the eye
that responds to light. *n.*

condor
4 ft. long,
wingspread up to
about 10 ft.

Con es to ga wagon (kon′ə-
stō′gə), a covered wagon with broad
wheels, used by the American pioneers
for traveling on soft ground or on the
prairie. [from *Conestoga* Valley, Pennsylvania, where they were first built]

co ney (kō′nē), cony. *n., pl.* **co neys.**

con fec tion (kən fek′shən), piece of
candy, candied fruit, jam, etc. *n.*

con fec tion er (kən fek′shə nər),
person who makes or sells candies, ice
cream, and cakes. *n.*

con fec tion er y (kən fek′shə-
ner′ē), 1 candies or sweets; confections. 2 place where confections, ice
cream, and cakes are made or sold. *n.,
pl.* **con fec tion er ies.**

con fed er a cy (kən fed′ər ə sē),
1 union of countries or states; group of
people joined together for a special
purpose; league. 2 **the Confederacy,**
group of eleven southern states that
seceded from the United States in 1860
and 1861. *n., pl.* **con fed er a cies.**

con fed er ate (kən fed′ər it *for 1,2,4;*
kən fed′ə rāt′ *for 3),* 1 country, person, etc., joined with another for a
special purpose; ally: *The hijacker told
his confederate to guard the passengers.*
2 joined together for a special purpose;
allied. 3 join together for a special
purpose; ally: *When the Civil War
began in 1861, only six states had con-
federated.* 4 **Confederate, a** of or
belonging to the Confederacy. **b** person
who lived in, supported, or fought for
the Confederacy. 1,4b *n.,* 2,4a *adj.,*

3 *v.,* **con fed er at ed, con fed er at-
ing.**

Confederate States of America,
the Confederacy.

con fed e ra tion (kən fed′ə rā′shən),
1 a joining together in a league or alliance: *The conference devised a plan for a
confederation of the colonies.* 2 league;
confederacy; alliance. *n.*

← cone (def. 1)
cones (def. 3) →
CLOSED   OPEN

con fer (kən fėr′), 1 talk things over;
consult together; exchange ideas: *My
parents conferred with the teacher about
my schoolwork.* 2 give; bestow: *The
President conferred a medal on each of
the astronauts. v.,* **con ferred, confer ring.**

con fer ence (kon′fər əns), 1 meeting
of interested persons to discuss a particular subject: *A conference was called
to discuss the best way of getting a
playground for the school.* 2 act of
consulting together: *The teacher was in
conference with parents after school.*
3 association of athletic teams,
churches, etc., joined together for some
special purpose. *n.*

con fess (kən fes′), 1 own up; acknowledge; admit: *I confess you are right
on one point.* 2 admit one's guilt: *The
thief decided to confess.* 3 tell one's sins
to a priest in order to obtain forgiveness. 4 hear (a person) tell his sins
in order to obtain forgiveness, as a
priest does. *v.*

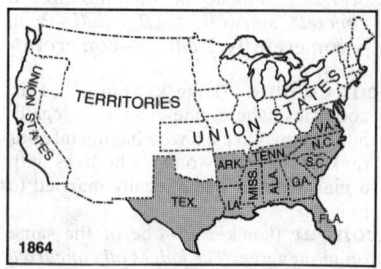
the Confederacy (def. 2)—the shaded area

con fess ed ly (kən fes′id lē), by acknowledgment; admittedly. *adv.*

con fes sion (kən fesh′ən), 1 act of
confessing; owning up; telling one's
mistakes or sins. 2 thing confessed. *n.*

con fes sion al (kən fesh′ə nəl), a
small booth in which a priest hears
confessions. *n.*

con fes sor (kən fes′ər), 1 person
who confesses. 2 priest who has

the authority to hear confessions. *n.*

con fet ti (kən fet′ē), bits of colored paper thrown about at carnivals, weddings, or parades. *n.* [from Italian]

con fi dant (kon′fə dant′), person trusted with one's secrets or private affairs; close friend. *n.*

con fide (kən fīd′), 1 tell as a secret: *He confided his troubles to his brother.* 2 show trust by telling secrets: *She always confided in her friend.* 3 put trust: *Confide in God.* 4 give to another to be kept safe; hand over: *She confides her baby to a day nursery while she is at work. v.,* **con fid ed, con fid ing.**

con fi dence (kon′fə dəns), 1 firm belief or trust: *We have no confidence in a liar.* 2 firm belief in oneself; self-confidence: *Years of experience at his work have given him great confidence.* 3 trust that a person will not tell others what is told to him: *The secret was told to me in strict confidence.* 4 thing told as a secret: *I would never reveal a confidence. n.*

con fi dent (kon′fə dənt), having confidence; firmly believing; certain; sure: *I feel confident that our team will win. adj.* —**con′fi dent ly,** *adv.*

con fi den tial (kon′fə den′shəl), 1 told or written as a secret: *a confidential report on the opposition's activities.* 2 showing confidence or intimacy: *She spoke in low, confidential tones.* 3 trusted with secrets or private affairs: *A confidential secretary should be discreet. adj.* —**con′fi den′tial ly,** *adv.*

con fid ing (kən fī′ding), trustful; trusting. *adj.* —**con fid′ing ly,** *adv.*

con fig u ra tion (kən fig′yə rā′shən), manner of arrangement; form; shape; outline: *Geographers study the configuration of the surface of the earth. n.*

con fine (kən fīn′ *for 1,2;* kon′fīn *for 3*), 1 keep within limits; restrict: *She confined her reading to biography.* 2 keep in; shut in: *A cold confined him to the house. For two years he was confined in prison.* 3 Often, **confines,** *pl.* boundary; border; limit: *I have never been beyond the confines of my own state.* 1,2 *v.,* **con fined, con fin ing;** 3 *n.*

con fine ment (kən fīn′mənt), 1 a confining or a being confined: *confinement indoors on account of a cold.* 2 period of childbirth. *n.*

con firm (kən fèrm′), 1 prove to be true or correct; make certain: *The news broadcast confirmed the rumor that a circus was coming to town.* 2 make more certain by putting in writing, by consent, or by encouragement: *He sent the written request to confirm his telephone order. The Senate confirmed the treaty.* 3 make firmer; strengthen: *A*

sudden storm confirmed my decision not to leave. 4 admit to full membership in a church or synagogue after required study and preparation. *v.*

con fir ma tion (kon′fər mā′shən), 1 a making certain by more information or evidence; a confirming: *She telephoned the store for confirmation that it was open Saturdays.* 2 thing that confirms; proof: *Don't believe rumors that lack confirmation.* 3 ceremony of admitting a person to full membership in a church or synagogue after required study and preparation. *n.*

con firmed (kən fèrmd′), 1 firmly established; proved: *a confirmed rumor.* 2 settled; habitual: *a confirmed bachelor. adj.*

con fis cate (kon′fə skāt), 1 seize for the public treasury: *The traitor's property was confiscated.* 2 seize by authority; take and keep: *The teacher confiscated my comic book. v.,* **con fis cat ed, con fis cat ing.**

con fis ca tion (kon′fə skā′shən), a confiscating or a being confiscated. *n.*

con fla gra tion (kon′flə grā′shən), a big and destructive fire: *A conflagration destroyed the whole neighborhood. n.*

con flict (kon′flikt *for 1,2;* kən flikt′ *for 3*), 1 a fight or struggle, especially a long one: *The conflict between Greece and Troy lasted for ten years.* 2 active opposition of persons or ideas; clash: *A conflict of opinion arose over what food was best for our rabbit.* 3 be actively opposed; differ in thought or action; clash: *The testimony of the witnesses conflicted on whether or not the robber had blond or dark hair.* 1,2 *n.,* 3 *v.*

con flu ence (kon′flü əns), 1 a flowing together: *the confluence of two streams to form a river.* 2 a coming together of people or things; throng. *n.*

con flu ent (kon′flü ənt), flowing or running together; blending into one: *confluent rivers. adj.*

con form (kən fôrm′), 1 act according to law or rule; be in agreement with generally accepted standards: *Members must conform to the rules of our club.* 2 be like; make similar; correspond: *Her dress conformed to the pattern. v.*

con form a ble (kən fôr′mə bəl), 1 similar. 2 in agreement; harmonious. 3 obedient; submissive. *adj.*

con for ma tion (kon′fôr mā′shən), manner in which a thing is formed; structure; form: *the conformation of a molecule, the conformation of a flower. n.*

con form ist (kən fôr′mist), person who conforms. *n.*

con form i ty (kən fôr′mə tē), 1 action in agreement with generally accepted standards. 2 likeness;

hat, āge, fär; let, ēqual, tèrm;
it, īce; hot, ōpen, ôrder;
oil, out; cup, pùt, rüle; ch, child;
ng, long; sh, she; th, thin;
ŦH, then; zh, measure;

ə represents *a* in about,
e in taken, *i* in pencil,
o in lemon, *u* in circus.

similarity; agreement. *n., pl.* **con form-i ties.**

con found (kon found′), confuse; perplex: *I was confounded by their rude behavior. v.*

con front (kən frunt′), 1 meet face to face; stand facing. 2 face boldly; oppose: *We crept downstairs with baseball bats in hand to confront the prowler.* 3 bring face to face; place before: *The teacher confronted the student with his failing grade. v.*

con fron ta tion (kon′frən tā′shən), a confronting or a being confronted. *n.*

Con fu cius (kən fyü′shəs), 551?-479 B.C., Chinese philosopher and moral teacher. *n.*

con fuse (kən fyüz′), 1 throw into disorder; mix up; bewilder: *So many people talking to me at once confused me.* 2 be unable to tell apart; mistake (one thing or person for another): *People often confuse this girl with her twin sister. v.,* **con fused, con fus ing.** —**con fus′ing ly,** *adv.*

con fu sion (kən fyü′zhən), 1 a disordered condition of things or of the mind: *the confusion in an untidy room, the confusion caused by an unexpected telegram.* 2 a mistaking one thing or person for another: *Words like "believe" and "receive" sometimes cause confusion in spelling.* 3 tumult: *the confusion in a busy street. n.*

con fu ta tion (kon′fyə tā′shən), 1 a confuting; disproving: *The lawyer's confutation of the witness's testimony helped him win his case.* 2 thing that confutes or disproves. *n.*

con fute (kən fyüt′), 1 prove (an argument, testimony, etc.) to be false or incorrect: *The lawyer confuted the testimony of the witness by showing actual photographs of the accident.* 2 prove (a person) to be wrong: *The speaker confuted her opponents by facts and logic. v.,* **con fut ed, con fut ing.**

con geal (kən jēl′), 1 harden or make solid by cold; freeze. 2 thicken; coagulate: *The pudding congealed as it cooled. v.*

con gen ial (kən jē′nyəl), 1 having similar tastes and interests; getting on

adj.	adjective	*n.*	noun
adv.	adverb	*prep.*	preposition
conj.	conjunction	*pron.*	pronoun
interj.	interjection	*v.*	verb
sing.	singular	*pl.*	plural

well together: *Congenial companions made the trip pleasant.* 2 agreeable; suitable: *The young scientist found laboratory work more congenial than teaching science.* *adj.* **—con gen′ial ly,** *adv.*

con gen i tal (kən jen′ə təl), present at birth: *The boy is lame because of a congenital defect in his foot.* *adj.* **—con gen′i tal ly,** *adv.*

conger
about 9 ft. long

con ger (kong′gər), a large ocean eel that is caught for food along the coasts of Europe. *n.*

con gest (kən jest′), 1 fill too full; overcrowd: *The streets of this city are often congested with traffic.* 2 become or cause to become too full of blood or mucus. The lungs are congested in pneumonia. *v.*

con ges tion (kən jes′chən), 1 an overcrowded or congested condition: *Many drivers were caught in Sunday's traffic congestion and were late getting home.* 2 too much blood or mucus in one part of the body: *Nose drops often relieve nasal congestion.* *n.*

con glom er ate (kən glom′ər it *for 1-4*; kən glom′ə rāt′ *for 5*), 1 made up of various parts or materials gathered into a mass: *a conglomerate rock.* 2 mass formed of fragments. 3 rock made up of pebbles, gravel, etc., held together by a cementing material. 4 group of unrelated corporations operating under a single ownership. 5 gather in a rounded mass; collect together. 1 *adj.*, 2-4 *n.*, 5 *v.*, **con glom er at ed, con glom er at ing.**

con glom e ra tion (kən glom′ə rā′shən), a mixed-up mass of various things or persons; mixture. *n.*

Con go (kong′gō), 1 river in central Africa, flowing from SE Zaïre to the Atlantic. Also, **Zaïre.** 2 former name of Zaïre, a country in central Africa. *Capital:* Kinshasa. 3 **Republic of,** country in central Africa on the Atlantic, a member of the French Community. *Capital:* Brazzaville. *n.*

con grat u late (kən grach′ə lāt), ex-

press one's pleasure at the happiness or good fortune of: *The judge congratulated the winner of the race.* *v.*, **con grat u lat ed, con grat u lat ing.**

con grat u la tion (kən grach′ə lā′-shən), 1 a congratulating; wishing a person joy. 2 **congratulations,** *pl.* expression of pleasure at another's happiness or good fortune: *Congratulations on your high grades.* *n.*

con gre gate (kong′grə gāt), come together into a crowd or mass; assemble: *The scouts congregated around the campfire.* *v.*, **con gre gat ed, con gre gat ing.**

con gre ga tion (kong′grə gā′shən), 1 act of coming together into a crowd or mass; an assembling. 2 group of people gathered together for religious worship or instruction: *The congregation joined together in prayer.* 3 a gathering of people or things; assembly. *n.*

con gre ga tion al (kong′grə gā′-shə nəl), 1 of a congregation: *congregational singing.* 2 **Congregational,** of or having to do with a form of church government in which each individual church governs itself. *adj.*

Con gre ga tion al ist (kong′grə-gā′shə nə list), member of a Congregational church. *n.*

con gress (kong′gris), 1 the lawmaking body of a nation, especially of a republic. 2 **Congress,** the national lawmaking body of the United States, consisting of the Senate and House of Representatives, with members elected from every state. 3 a meeting of representatives for the discussion of some subject; conference: *Doctors came from all over the world to the medical congress on heart transplants.* *n., pl.* **con gress es.**

con gres sion al (kən gresh′ə nəl), 1 of or having to do with a congress. 2 Often, **Congressional.** of or having to do with Congress. *adj.*

con gress man (kong′gris mən). Often, **Congressman.** member of Congress, especially of the House of Representatives. *n., pl.* **con gress-men.**

con gress wom an (kong′gris-wúm′ən). Often, **Congresswoman.** a woman member of Congress, especially

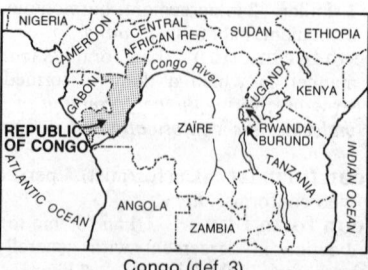
Congo (def. 3)

of the House of Representatives. *n., pl.* **con gress wom en.**

con gru ence (kən grü′əns *or* kong′-grü əns), a being congruent. *n.*

con gru ent (kən grü′ənt *or* kong′-grü ənt), 1 exactly coinciding: *Congruent triangles have the same size and shape.* 2 congruous. *adj.* **—con gru′-ent ly,** *adv.*

con gru ous (kong′grü əs), 1 in harmony; agreeing. 2 fitting; appropriate. *adj.*

con ic (kon′ik), conical. *adj.*

con i cal (kon′ə kəl), 1 shaped like a cone: *Volcanic mountains are conical.* 2 of a cone. *adj.* **—con′i cal ly,** *adv.*

con i fer (kon′ə fər *or* kō′nə fər), tree or shrub that bears cones. The pine, fir, spruce, hemlock, and larch are conifers. *n.*

co nif er ous (kō nif′ər əs), 1 bearing cones. 2 belonging to the conifers. *adj.*

conj., conjunction (def. 1).

con jec tur al (kən jek′chər əl), involving a guess; depending on conjecture: *His statement was merely conjectural, not proved.* *adj.* **—con jec′tur-al ly,** *adv.*

con jec ture (kən jek′chər), 1 conclusion reached by guessing: *Her estimate of the height of that mountain is only conjecture, not fact.* 2 make a conjecture; guess: *Weather forecasters often have to conjecture about the next day's weather conditions.* 1 *n.*, 2 *v.*, **con jec tured, con jec tur ing.**

con join (kən join′), join together; unite; combine. *v.*

con joint (kən joint′), united; combined. *adj.* **—con joint′ly,** *adv.*

con ju gal (kon′jə gəl), 1 of or having to do with marriage: *conjugal life.* 2 of husband and wife: *conjugal love.* *adj.*

con ju gate (kon′jə gāt), 1 give the forms of (a verb) in order: *The past tense of "to be" is conjugated: I was, you were, he was; we were, you were, they were.* 2 join together; couple. *v.*, **con ju gat ed, con ju gat ing.**

con ju ga tion (kon′jə gā′shən), 1 a systematic arrangement of the forms of a verb. 2 a joining together; coupling. Some one-celled animals reproduce by the conjugation of one cell with another. *n.*

con junc tion (kən jungk′shən), 1 word that connects words, phrases, clauses, or sentences. *And, but, or, though,* and *if* are conjunctions. 2 a joining together; union; combination: *Our school, in conjunction with two other schools, will hold a large bazaar next week.* *n.*

con ju ra tion (kon′jə rā′shən), 1 an invoking by a sacred name; conjuring: *conjuration of spirits.* 2 the practice of magic: *In the fairy tale, the princess was* changed to a toad by conjuration. **3** a magic form of words used in conjuring; magic spell. *n.*

con jure (kon′jər *or* kun′jər *for 1-3*; kən jür′ *for 4*), **1** compel to appear or disappear by a set form of words: *Nowadays we think it is useless to try to conjure spirits or devils.* **2** cause to appear as if by magic: *Grandmother conjured up a bag of old-fashioned toys from the attic to our delight.* **3** perform tricks by very quick, deceiving movements of the hands. **4** make a solemn appeal to: *I conjure you not to betray me. v.*, **con jured, con jur ing.**

con jur er *or* **con jur or** (kon′jər ər *or* kun′jər ər), **1** person who performs tricks with quick, deceiving movements of the hands; juggler. **2** magician. *n.*

conk (kongk), SLANG. **1** hit, especially on the head. **2** a blow on the head. **1** *v.*, **2** *n.*

conk out, SLANG. break down; stall: *The old car conked out.*

Conn., Connecticut.

con nect (kə nekt′), **1** join one thing to another; link two things together; join: *connect a hose to a faucet. The telephone operator connected us. These two rooms connect.* **2** think of one thing with another: *We usually connect spring with sunshine and flowers.* **3** join with others in some business or interest; bring into some relation: *This store is connected with a chain of stores. v.*

Con nect i cut (kə net′ə kət), one of the northeastern states of the United States. *Capital:* Hartford. *n.*

con nec tion (kə nek′shən), **1** act of connecting: *The connection of our telephone took several hours.* **2** a being joined together or connected; association: *His connection with our business firm has lasted over thirty years.* **3** thing that connects; connecting part: *The connection between the radiator and the pipe has become loose.* **4** any kind of relation with another: *I had no connection with that prank.* **5** a thinking of persons or things together; linking together of words or ideas in proper order: *His last remark had no connection with the earlier part of his talk.* **6** an influential, wealthy, or prominent associate or friend: *I got a summer job through my friend's connections.* **7** the meeting of trains, ships, etc., at definite times so that passengers can change from one to the other without delay: *The bus arrived late at the airport and we missed our airplane connection.* **8** a related person; relative: *My sister-in-law is a connection of mine by marriage. n.*

in connection with, in relation with; in regard to: *He read a biography of Booker T. Washington in connection with his study of American history.*

con nec tive (kə nek′tiv), **1** that connects. **2** anything that connects. Conjunctions and relative pronouns are connectives that join together words, phrases, or clauses. **1** *adj.*, **2** *n.*

connec'tive tissue, tissue that connects, supports, or encloses other tissues and organs in the body.

CONNING TOWER

con ning tower (kon′ing), tower on the deck of a submarine, used as an entrance and as a place for observation.

con niv ance (kə nī′vəns), a conniving; pretended ignorance or secret encouragement of wrongdoing. *n.*

con nive (kə nīv′), **1** avoid noticing what one might have to condemn; pretend not to see something wrong; give aid to wrongdoing by not telling of it: *The dishonest sheriff connived at gambling.* **2** cooperate secretly: *connive with the enemy. v.*, **con nived, con niv ing.**

con niv er (kə nī′vər), person who connives. *n.*

con nois seur (kon′ə sėr′), person competent to give critical judgments in art or in matters of taste; expert: *a connoisseur of antique furniture. n.*

con no ta tion (kon′ə tā′shən), what is suggested in addition to the simple or literal meaning. When Elaine is described in legends about King Arthur as "the lily maid," the connotation is that she was pale, delicate, and pure. *n.*

con note (kə nōt′), suggest in addition to the simple or literal meaning; mean besides; imply. Red is a color that can connote feelings of passion, anger, or hatred. *v.*, **con not ed, con not ing.**

con nu bi al (kə nü′bē əl *or* kə nyü′bē əl), of or having to do with marriage; conjugal. *adj.*

con quer (kong′kər), **1** get by fighting; win in war: *The Romans conquered much of the ancient world.* **2** overcome by force; get the better of; defeat: *conquer an enemy, conquer a bad habit.* **3** be victorious; be the conqueror: *The general said he would conquer or die. v.*

con quer or (kong′kər ər), person who conquers. *n.*

con quest (kon′kwest *or* kong′kwest), **1** act of conquering: *the conquest of a country, the conquest of disease.* **2** thing conquered; land, people, etc., conquered: *Troy was the Greeks' hardest conquest. n.*

con quis ta dor (kon kwis′tə dôr *or*

hat, āge, fär; let, ēqual, tėrm;
it, īce; hot, ōpen, ôrder;
oil, out; cup, půt, rüle; ch, child;
ng, long; sh, she; th, thin;
ŦH, then; zh, measure;

ə represents *a* in about,
e in taken, *i* in pencil,
o in lemon, *u* in circus.

kon kē′stə dôr), **1** a Spanish conqueror in North or South America during the 1500's. **2** conqueror. *n., pl.* **con quis ta dors, con quis ta do res** (kon kē′stə dôr′ēz).

Con rad (kon′rad), **Joseph,** 1857-1924, British novelist, born in Poland. *n.*

con science (kon′shəns), sense of right and wrong; ideas and feelings within a person that tell him when he is doing right and warn him of what is wrong. *n.*

con sci en tious (kon′shē en′shəs), **1** careful to do what one knows is right; controlled by conscience. **2** done with care to make it right: *Conscientious work is careful and exact. adj.* —**con′sci en′tious ly,** *adv.* —**con′sci en′tious ness,** *n.*

conscientious objector, person whose conscience does not let him take up arms in warfare.

con scious (kon′shəs), **1** having experience; aware; knowing: *He was conscious of a sharp pain.* **2** able to feel or perceive; awake: *About five minutes after fainting he became conscious again.* **3** known to oneself; felt: *The young woman had a conscious desire to see her family again.* **4** meant; intended: *He told a conscious lie when he denied that he had broken the vase. adj.* —**con′scious ly,** *adv.*

con scious ness (kon′shəs nis), **1** condition of being conscious; awareness: *The injured man did not regain consciousness for two hours.* **2** all the thoughts and feelings of a person. *n.*

con script (kən skript′ *for 1,3*; kon′skript *for 2*), **1** compel by law to serve in the armed forces; draft. **2** a conscripted soldier or sailor. **3** take for government use: *The dictator proposed to conscript the services of both business and labor.* **1,3** *v.*, **2** *n.*

con scrip tion (kən skrip′shən), **1** compulsory enlistment of men in the armed forces; draft. **2** act or system of forcing contributions of money, labor, or other service to the government. *n.*

con se crate (kon′sə krāt), **1** set apart

adj. adjective	*n.* noun
adv. adverb	*prep.* preposition
conj. conjunction	*pron.* pronoun
interj. interjection	*v.* verb
sing. singular	*pl.* plural

as sacred; make holy: *The new chapel in the church was consecrated by the bishop.* 2 devote to a purpose; dedicate: *The doctor consecrated his life to helping the sick.* *v.*, **con se crat ed, con se crat ing.**

con se cra tion (kon/sə krā/shən), 1 a consecrating or a being consecrated. 2 ordination to a sacred office, especially that of bishop. *n.*

con sec u tive (kən sek/yə tiv), following one right after another; successive: *Monday, Tuesday, and Wednesday are consecutive days of the week.* *adj.* —**con sec/u tive ly,** *adv.* —**con sec/u tive ness,** *n.*

con sen sus (kən sen/səs), general agreement; opinion of all or most of the people consulted: *The club members could not reach a consensus about adopting the proposal.* *n.*, *pl.* **con sen sus es.**

con sent (kən sent/), 1 give approval or permission; agree: *My father would not consent to my staying up past 10 p.m.* 2 approval; permission: *We have mother's consent to go swimming.* 1 *v.*, 2 *n.*

con se quence (kon/sə kwens), 1 a result or effect: *The consequence of his fall was a broken leg.* 2 importance: *The loss of her ring is a matter of great consequence to her.* *n.*

take the consequences, accept what happens because of one's action: *She did not study for the test, so she had to take the consequences.*

con se quent (kon/sə kwent), following as an effect; resulting; consequential: *His long illness and consequent absence put him far behind in his work.* *adj.*

con se quen tial (kon/sə kwen/shəl), 1 following as an effect; resulting; consequent. 2 self-important. *adj.*

con se quent ly (kon/sə kwent/lē), as a result; therefore: *He overslept and, consequently, he was late.* *adv.*

con ser va tion (kon/sər vā/shən), a preserving from harm or decay; protecting from loss or from being used up: *The conservation of our mineral resources is important because they can never be replenished.* *n.*

con ser va tion ist (kon/sər vā/shə nist), person who wants to preserve

and protect the forests, rivers, and other natural resources of a country. *n.*

con serv a tism (kən ser/və tiz/əm), inclination to keep things as they are or were in the past; opposition to change, especially any major change in established traditions. *n.*

con serv a tive (kən ser/və tiv), 1 inclined to keep things as they are or were in the past; opposed to change, especially any major change in established traditions: *Old people tend to be more conservative than young ones.* 2 person opposed to change. 3 not inclined to take risks; cautious; moderate: *This old, reliable company has conservative business methods.* 4 Often, **Conservative.** a of or belonging to a political party that is pledged to preserve established traditions and to oppose major changes in national institutions. b member of a conservative political party. 5 conserving; preserving. 1,3,4a,5 *adj.*, 2,4b *n.* —**con serv/a tive ly,** *adv.* —**con serv/a tive ness,** *n.*

con serv a to ry (kən ser/və tôr/ē), 1 school for instruction in music. 2 greenhouse for growing and displaying plants and flowers. *n.*, *pl.* **con serv a to ries.**

con serve (kən serv/ for 1; kon/serv/ for 2), 1 keep from harm or decay; keep from loss or from being used up; preserve: *Try to conserve your strength for the end of the race.* 2 fruit preserved in sugar, often as jam. 1 *v.*, **con served, con serv ing;** 2 *n.*

con sid er (kən sid/ər), 1 think about in order to decide; think about carefully: *Before you dash off an answer, take time to consider the problem.* 2 think to be; regard as: *I consider him a very able student.* 3 allow for; take into account: *This watch runs very well, if you consider how old it is.* 4 be thoughtful of: *A kind person considers the feelings of others.* *v.*

con sid er a ble (kən sid/ər ə bəl), 1 worth thinking about; important: *Pollution is a considerable problem.* 2 not a little; much: *$500 is a considerable sum of money.* *adj.*

con sid er a bly (kən sid/ər ə blē), a good deal; much: *The boy was considerably older than he looked.* *adv.*

con sid er ate (kən sid/ər it), thoughtful of others and their feelings: *She is considerate enough to tell her parents where she is going and with whom.* *adj.* —**con sid/er ate ly,** *adv.* —**con sid/er ate ness,** *n.*

con sid er a tion (kən sid/ə rā/shən), 1 a thinking about in order to decide: *Before writing your answers please give careful consideration to the questions on the test.* 2 something thought of

as a reason: *Price and quality are two considerations in buying anything.* 3 thoughtfulness for others and their feelings: *Playing the radio loud at night shows a lack of consideration for the neighbors.* 4 money or other payment: *I will do the work for you for a small consideration.* *n.*

in consideration of, 1 because of: *In consideration of my bad cold, the teacher let me leave school early.* 2 in return for: *The neighbor gave the girl a dollar in consideration of her helpfulness.*

take into consideration, allow for; take into account; consider: *The judge took the boy's age into consideration.*

under consideration, being thought about: *Her request for a higher salary is under consideration.*

con sid ered (kən sid/ərd), carefully thought out: *This is the judge's considered opinion.* *adj.*

con sid er ing (kən sid/ər ing), taking into account; making allowance for: *Considering her age, the little girl reads well.* *prep.*

con sign (kən sīn/), 1 hand over; deliver: *The dog was consigned to the pound. The parents consigned the child to its grandmother's care while they were away.* 2 send: *We will consign the goods to him by express.* *v.*

con sign ment (kən sīn/mənt), 1 a consigning: *The Red Cross ordered the consignment of food and clothing to the flooded area.* 2 something consigned. *n.*

con sist (kən sist/), be made up; be formed: *A week consists of seven days.* *v.*

consist in, be contained in; be made up of: *He believes that happiness consists in being easily pleased or satisfied.*

con sist ence (kən sis/təns), consistency. *n.*

con sist en cy (kən sis/tən sē), 1 degree of firmness or stiffness: *Frosting for a cake must be of the right consistency to spread easily without dripping.* 2 a keeping to the same principles, course, etc.: *He showed no consistency when he did excellent work the first part of the year and very poor work after that.* 3 agreement; accordance: *Her behavior is in consistency with her character.* *n.*, *pl.* **con sist en cies.**

con sist ent (kən sis/tənt), 1 keeping or inclined to keep to the same principles, course, etc.: *What a consistent person says or does today agrees with what he said or did yesterday.* 2 in agreement; in accord: *Driving an automobile at high speed on a rainy night is not consistent with safety.* *adj.* —**con sist/ent ly,** *adv.*

con sis to ry (kən sis/tər ē), court of

clergymen to decide church matters; church council. *n., pl.* **con sis tor ies.**

con so la tion (kon′sə lā′shən), 1 a consoling; comfort. 2 a comforting person, thing, or event. *n.*

con sole[1] (kən sōl′), ease the grief or sorrow of; comfort: *I tried to console the lost child.* *v.,* **con soled, con sol ing.** [from French *consoler*]

con sole[2] (kon′sōl), 1 part of an organ containing the keyboard, stops, and pedals. 2 a radio, television, or phonograph cabinet made to stand on the floor. 3 panel of buttons, switches, dials, etc., used to control electrical or electronic equipment in a computer, missile, etc. *n.* [from French *console* beam, support]

con sol i date (kən sol′ə dāt), 1 combine into one; unite; merge: *The three banks consolidated and formed a single large bank.* 2 make solid or firm; strengthen: *The Romans consolidated their conquest of Britain by building a wall to keep out the raiding Scots.* *v.,* **con sol i dat ed, con sol i dat ing.**

con sol i da tion (kən sol′ə dā′shən), a consolidating or a being consolidated. *n.*

con som mé (kon′sə mā′), a clear soup made by boiling meat in water. *n., pl.* **con som més.** [from French *consommé* consumed, finished]

con so nance (kon′sə nəns), 1 agreement; accordance. 2 harmony of sounds. *n.*

con so nant (kon′sə nənt), 1 a speech sound formed by completely or partially stopping the breath. The two consonants in *ship* are spelled by the letters *sh* and *p.* 2 any letter or combination of letters that stands for such a sound. *B, c, d,* and *f* are consonants. 3 in agreement; harmonious: *His action is consonant with his beliefs.* 1,2 *n.,* 3 *adj.*

con sort (kon′sôrt *for 1,3;* kən sôrt′ *for 2*), 1 husband or wife. The husband of a queen is sometimes called the prince consort. 2 keep company; associate: *I got a bad reputation by consorting with a rough gang.* 3 ship accompanying another. 1,3 *n.,* 2 *v.*

con spic u ous (kən spik′yü əs), 1 easily seen: *A traffic light should be placed where it is conspicuous.* 2 attracting notice; remarkable: *Abraham Lincoln is a conspicuous example of a poor boy who succeeded. adj.* —**con spic′u ous ly,** *adv.* —**con spic′u ous ness,** *n.*

con spir a cy (kən spir′ə sē), secret planning with others to do something unlawful or wrong; plot: *The leaders of the conspiracy against the government were caught. n., pl.* **con spir a cies.**

con spir a tor (kən spir′ə tər), person

who conspires; plotter: *A group of conspirators planned to overthrow the government. n.*

con spire (kən spīr′), 1 plan secretly with others to do something unlawful or wrong; plot: *The spies conspired to steal secret government documents.* 2 act together: *All things conspired to make her birthday a happy one.* *v.,* **con spired, con spir ing.**

con sta ble (kon′stə bəl *or* kun′stə-bəl), a police officer; policeman. *n.*

con stan cy (kon′stən sē), firmness in belief or feeling; steadfastness: *the constancy of Christopher Columbus in looking for a new route to India. n.*

con stant (kon′stənt), 1 going on without stopping: *Three days of constant rain made the field muddy.* 2 continually happening; repeated again and again: *The clock made a constant ticking sound.* 3 always the same; not changing: *If you walk due north, your direction is constant.* 4 thing that is always the same; value or quantity that does not change: *The speed of light is an important constant in physics.* 5 faithful; loyal; steadfast: *A constant friend helps you when you need help.* 1-3,5 *adj.,* 4 *n.*

Con stan tine the Great (kon′-stən tēn *or* kon′stən tīn), A.D. 288?-337, Roman emperor from A.D. 306 to 337, who granted liberty of worship to Christians and established the city of Constantinople.

Con stan ti no ple (kon′stan-tə nō′pəl), large city in SE Europe, now called **Istanbul.** It was the capital of the Byzantine Empire and later the capital of Turkey. See **Byzantine Empire** for map. *n.*

con stant ly (kon′stənt lē), 1 without change; always: *He is constantly late.* 2 without stopping: *If a clock is kept wound it runs constantly.* 3 often; again and again: *He has to be reminded constantly to pay attention to his homework. adv.*

two constellations

con stel la tion (kon′stə lā′shən), group of stars usually having a geometric shape. The Big Dipper is the easiest constellation to locate. *n.*

con ster na tion (kon′stər nā′shən), great dismay; paralyzing terror: *To our*

hat, āge, fär; let, ēqual, tèrm; it, īce; hot, ōpen, ôrder; oil, out; cup, pùt, rüle; ch, child; ng, long; sh, she; th, thin; ₮H, then; zh, measure;

ə represents *a* in about, *e* in taken, *i* in pencil, *o* in lemon, *u* in circus.

consternation the train rushed on toward the burning bridge. n.

con sti pate (kon′stə pāt), cause constipation in. *v.,* **con sti pat ed, con sti pat ing.**

con sti pa tion (kon′stə pā′shən), a condition in which it is difficult to empty the bowels. *n.*

con stit u en cy (kən stich′ü ən sē), 1 the voters in a district; constituents: *The congresswoman was reelected to office by her constituency.* 2 this district. *n., pl.* **con stit u en cies.**

con stit u ent (kən stich′ü ənt), 1 forming a necessary part: *Flour, water, salt, and yeast are constituent parts of bread.* 2 part of a whole; necessary part: *Sugar is the main constituent of candy.* 3 voter: *A congressman receives many letters from his constituents.* 4 appointing; electing: *The school board is the constituent body for the high school.* 1,4 *adj.,* 2,3 *n.*

con sti tute (kon′stə tüt *or* kon′stə-tyüt), 1 make up; form: *Seven days constitute a week.* 2 set up; establish: *Schools are constituted by law to teach boys and girls.* 3 appoint; elect: *The group constituted one member as its leader.* *v.,* **con sti tut ed, con sti tut ing.**

con sti tu tion (kon′stə tü′shən *or* kon′stə tyü′shən), 1 way in which a person or thing is organized; nature; make-up: *A person with a good constitution is strong and healthy.* 2 system of fundamental principles according to which a nation, state, or group is governed: *Great Britain does not have a written constitution.* 3 **the Constitution,** the written set of fundamental principles by which the United States is governed. 4 formation; establishment: *After the Revolutionary War, the Colonies undertook the constitution of a new nation. n.*

con sti tu tion al (kon′stə tü′shə nəl *or* kon′stə tyü′shə nəl), 1 of or in the constitution of a person or thing: *A constitutional weakness makes him catch a cold easily.* 2 of, in, or according to the constitution of a nation, state, or group: *The Supreme Court must*

adj.	adjective	*n.*	noun
adv.	adverb	*prep.*	preposition
conj.	conjunction	*pron.*	pronoun
interj.	interjection	*v.*	verb
sing.	singular	*pl.*	plural

decide whether this law is constitutional. **3** a walk taken for one's health: *After Sunday dinner my grandparents always take a constitutional.* **1,2** *adj.,* **3** *n.*

con sti tu tion al i ty (kon/stə tü/- shə nal/ə tē *or* kon/stə tyü/shə nal/- ə tē), accordance with the constitution of a nation, state, or group: *The constitutionality of freedom of speech has been upheld in the courts many times. n.*

con sti tu tion al ly (kon/stə tü/shə- nə lē *or* kon/stə tyü/shə nə lē), **1** in or by constitution; naturally. **2** according to the constitution. *adv.*

con strain (kən strān/), **1** force to do something; compel: *The principal was constrained to punish the rude child.* **2** confine; restrain: *The wild animal was bound and constrained. v.*

con straint (kən strānt/), **1** a holding back of natural feelings; embarrassment: *The new boy felt no constraint with the teacher since she was an old friend of the family.* **2** force; compulsion: *Are you staying home by choice or under constraint? n.*

con strict (kən strikt/), make smaller by squeezing; contract; compress: *A tourniquet stops the flow of blood by constricting the blood vessels. v.*

con stric tion (kən strik/shən), **1** a constricting; compression. **2** a feeling of tightness; constricted condition: *He coughed and complained of a constriction in his chest.* **3** a constricted part. *n.*

con stric tive (kən strik/tiv), contracting; compressing. *adj.*

con stric tor (kən strik/tər), any snake that kills its prey by squeezing it with its coils. The boa is a constrictor. *n.*

con struct (kən strukt/), put together; fit together; build: *The explorers constructed a raft of logs fastened with tough vines. v.*

con struc tion (kən struk/shən), **1** act of constructing; building: *The city council provided funds for the construction of a new gym.* **2** way in which a thing is constructed: *Cracks and leaks are signs of poor construction.* **3** thing built or put together; structure: *The doll's house was a construction of wood and cardboard.* **4** arrangement or relation of words in a sentence, phrase,

clause, etc. **5** meaning; interpretation: *You put an unfair construction on what I said. n.*

con struc tive (kən struk/tiv), **1** tending to construct; building up; helpful: *During the experiment the teacher gave some constructive suggestions that prevented accidents.* **2** having to do with construction; structural. *adj.* **—con struc/tive ly,** *adv.* **—con struc/tive ness,** *n.*

con strue (kən strü/), **1** show the meaning of; explain; interpret: *Different lawyers may construe the same law differently.* **2** analyze the arrangement or relation of words in (a sentence, etc.). *v.,* **con strued, con stru ing.**

con sul (kon/səl), **1** official appointed by a government to live in a foreign city to look after the business interests of his own country and protect citizens of his country who are traveling or living there. **2** either of two chief magistrates of the ancient Roman republic. *n.*

con su lar (kon/sə lər), **1** of or belonging to a consul. **2** serving as a consul: *the consular representative of the United States at Liverpool. adj.*

con su late (kon/sə lit), the official residence or the offices of a consul: *the Canadian consulate in New York. n.*

con sult (kən sult/), **1** seek information or advice from; refer to. You can consult persons, books, or maps to find out what you wish to know. **2** exchange ideas; talk things over: *He consulted with his lawyer before signing the contract.* **3** take into consideration; have regard for: *A good teacher consults the interests of the class. v.*

con sult ant (kən sult/nt), **1** person who gives professional or technical advice. **2** person who consults another. *n.*

con sul ta tion (kon/səl tā/shən), **1** act of consulting; seeking information or advice. **2** a meeting to exchange ideas or talk things over: *The three doctors held a consultation to determine the best way to cure the child. n.*

con sume (kən süm/), **1** use up; spend: *A student consumes much of his time in studying. He consumed almost all the money he earned last summer.* **2** eat or drink up: *We will each consume at least two sandwiches on our hike.* **3** destroy; burn up: *A huge fire consumed the entire forest. v.,* **consumed, con sum ing.**

consumed with, absorbed by curiosity, envy, etc.: *She was consumed with the desire to learn Russian.*

con sum er (kən sü/mər), **1** person who uses food, clothing, or anything grown or made by producers: *A low price for wheat should reduce the price of flour to the consumer.* **2** person or thing that consumes. *n.*

con sum mate (kon/sə māt *for* 1; kən sum/it *for* 2), **1** bring to completion; realize; fulfill: *His ambition was consummated when he won the first prize.* **2** in the highest degree; complete; perfect: *The pilot showed consummate skill in flying through the storm and landing in the fog.* **1** *v.,* **con sum mated, con sum mat ing; 2** *adj.* **—consum/mate ly,** *adv.*

con sum ma tion (kon/sə mā/shən), completion; fulfillment: *Winning first prize was the consummation of her ambition. n.*

con sump tion (kən sump/shən), **1** a using up; use: *We took along some food for consumption on our trip.* **2** amount used up: *In November the oil consumption of our furnace reached 200 gallons.* **3** tuberculosis of the lungs. *n.*

con sump tive (kən sump/tiv), **1** having or likely to have tuberculosis of the lungs. **2** person who has tuberculosis of the lungs. **3** tending to consume; destructive; wasteful. **1,3** *adj.,* **2** *n.*

con tact (kon/takt), **1** condition of touching; a touching together: *When two balls are in contact, one can be moved by touching the other. A magnet will draw iron filings into contact with it.* **2** condition of being in communication with: *The control tower lost radio contact with the airplane pilot.* **3** connection: *The insurance salesman tried to make contacts with wealthy people.* **4** INFORMAL. get in touch with: *I've been trying to contact you for two days.* **5** put or bring into contact. **1-3** *n.,* **4,5** *v.*

contact lens, a very small, thin, plastic lens fitted on the front of the eyeball. Contact lenses take the place of eyeglasses.

con ta gion (kən tā/jən), **1** the spreading of disease by contact: *Contagion is hard to prevent in crowded areas.* **2** disease spread in this way. **3** the spreading of any influence from one to another: *At the cry of "Fire!" a contagion of fear swept through the audience, causing a panic. n.*

con ta gious (kən tā/jəs), **1** spreading by contact: *Scarlet fever is a contagious disease.* **2** easily spreading from one person to another: *Yawning is often contagious. adj.* **—con ta/gious ly,** *adv.* **—con ta/gious ness,** *n.*

con tain (kən tān/), **1** have within itself; hold as contents: *Books contain information. My purse contains money.* **2** be capable of holding: *That pitcher will contain a quart of milk.* **3** be equal to: *A pound contains 16 ounces.* **4** control; hold back; restrain: *She could not contain her excitement over winning the contest.* **5** be divisible by (a number) without a remainder: *12 will contain 1, 2, 3, 4, 6, and 12. v.*

con tain er (kən tā′nər), 1 box, can, jar, etc., used to hold or contain something. 2 amount that a container can hold. *n.*

con tain ment (kən tān′mənt), the confinement of an unfriendly political or military force within existing geographical boundaries. *n.*

con tam i nate (kən tam′ə nāt), make impure by contact; defile; pollute: *The drinking water had been contaminated by sewage. v.,* **con tam i nat ed, con tam i nat ing.**

con tam i na tion (kən tam′ə nā′shən), a contaminating or being contaminated; pollution: *Surgical instruments must be free of contamination. n.*

contd., continued.

con temn (kən tem′), treat with contempt; despise; scorn. *v.*

con tem plate (kon′təm plāt), 1 look at or think about for a long time; study carefully: *I will contemplate your offer. We enjoyed contemplating the beautiful mountain landscape.* 2 have in mind; consider, intend, or expect: *She is contemplating a trip to Europe.* 3 meditate: *All day he did nothing but contemplate. v.,* **con tem plat ed, con tem plat ing.**

con tem pla tion (kon′təm plā′shən), 1 a looking at or thinking about something for a long time; deep thought: *He was sunk in contemplation and did not hear the doorbell.* 2 expectation or intention: *We are buying tents and other equipment in contemplation of a camping trip next summer. n.*

con tem pla tive (kon′təm plā′tiv), deeply thoughtful; meditative: *The monks lived a quiet, contemplative life in the monastery. adj.*

con tem po ra ne ous (kən tem′pə rā′nē əs), belonging to the same period of time; contemporary: *The lives of Thomas Jefferson and Betsy Ross were contemporaneous. adj.*

con tem po rar y (kən tem′pə rer′ē), 1 belonging to or living in the same period of time: *Dickinson and Whitman were contemporary poets. The telephone and the phonograph were contemporary inventions.* 2 person living in the same period of time: *Abraham Lincoln and Robert E. Lee were contemporaries.* 3 of or having to do with the present time; modern: *Our teacher reads the books of many contemporary authors to us.* 1,3 *adj.,* 2 *n., pl.* **con tem po rar ies.**

con tempt (kən tempt′), 1 the feeling that a person, act, or thing is mean, low, or worthless; despising; scorn: *feel contempt for a cheat.* 2 condition of

being despised or scorned; disgrace: *A patriot holds a traitor in contempt.* 3 disobedience to or open disrespect for the rules or decisions of a court of law or a lawmaking body. A person can be put in jail for contempt of court. *n.*

con tempt i ble (kən temp′tə bəl), deserving contempt: *a contemptible lie. adj.*

con tempt i bly (kən temp′tə blē), in a contemptible manner. *adv.*

con temp tu ous (kən temp′chü əs), showing contempt; scornful: *a contemptuous look. adj.* **—con temp′tu ous ly,** *adv.*

con tend (kən tend′), 1 work hard against difficulties; fight; struggle: *The first settlers in America had to contend with harsh winters, sickness, and lack of food.* 2 take part in a contest; compete: *Five runners were contending in the first race.* 3 argue: *We contended about whose turn it was. Columbus contended that the earth was round. v.* **—con tend′er,** *n.*

con tent¹ (kon′tent), 1 Often, **contents,** *pl.* what is contained in anything; all things inside: *An old chair, a desk, and a bed were the only contents of the room. The contents of the box fell out in her lap.* 2 facts and ideas stated; what is written in a book or said in a speech: *I didn't understand the content of his speech.* 3 amount contained: *The content of these apple boxes is six bushels. n.* [from Latin *contentum* something contained]

con tent² (kən tent′), 1 give satisfaction; please; make easy in mind: *Nothing contents me when I'm in a bad mood.* 2 satisfied; pleased; easy in mind; contented: *Will you be content to wait until tomorrow?* 3 contentment; satisfaction; ease of mind: *The cat lay stretched out beside the fire in complete content.* 1 *v.,* 2 *adj.,* 3 *n.* [from Latin *contentum* contained]

con tent ed (kən ten′tid), satisfied; pleased; easy in mind. *adj.* **—con tent′ed ly,** *adv.* **—con tent′ed ness,** *n.*

con ten tion (kən ten′shən), 1 statement or point that one has argued for; statement maintained as true: *Galileo's contention that the earth goes around the sun proved to be true.* 2 an arguing; disputing; quarreling: *There was some contention about the choice of a new captain of the baseball team. n.*

con ten tious (kən ten′shəs), fond of arguing; given to disputing; quarrelsome: *A contentious person argues about trifles. adj.* **—con ten′tious ly,** *adv.* **—con ten′tious ness,** *n.*

con tent ment (kən tent′mənt), a being satisfied or pleased; ease of mind. *n.*

hat, āge, fär; let, ēqual, tėrm; it, īce; hot, ōpen, ôrder; oil, out; cup, pùt, rüle; ch, child; ng, long; sh, she; th, thin; ŦH, then; zh, measure;

ə represents *a* in about, *e* in taken, *i* in pencil, *o* in lemon, *u* in circus.

con tents (kon′tents). See def. 1 of **content¹.** *n.pl.*

con test (kon′test *for* 1,2; kən test′ *for* 3,4), 1 trial of skill to see which can win. A game or race is a contest; so is a debate. 2 a fight, struggle, or dispute: *The contest between France and England for North America ended in a victory for England.* 3 fight for; struggle for: *The soldiers contested every inch of ground.* 4 argue against; dispute about: *The lawyer contested the claim and tried to prove that it was false.* 1,2 *n.,* 3,4 *v.*

con test ant (kən tes′tənt), person who contests; person who takes part in a contest: *My sister was a contestant in the 100-yard dash. n.*

con text (kon′tekst), the parts directly before and after a word or sentence that influence its meaning. You can often tell the meaning of a word from its use in context. *n.*

con ti gu i ty (kon′tə gyü′ə tē), 1 a being very close together; nearness: *The contiguity of the house and garage was a convenience in bad weather.* 2 contact. *n., pl.* **con ti gu i ties.**

con tig u ous (kən tig′yü əs), 1 in actual contact; touching: *A fence showed where the two farms were contiguous.* 2 very close together; near. *adj.* **—con tig′u ous ly,** *adv.*

con ti nence (kon′tə nəns), control of one's actions and feelings; self-restraint; moderation. *n.*

con ti nent¹ (kon′tə nənt), 1 one of the seven great masses of land on the earth. The continents are North America, South America, Europe, Africa, Asia, Australia, and Antarctica. 2 **the Continent,** the mainland of Europe. It does not include the British Isles. *n.* [from Latin *continentem* connected, continuous (land)]

con ti nent² (kon′tə nənt), having control of one's actions and feelings; using self-restraint; temperate. *adj.* [from Latin *continentem* holding together, refraining]

con ti nent al (kon′tə nen′tl), 1 of a continent; like a continent. 2 **Continental, a** belonging to or characteristic of the mainland of Europe: *Con-*

Continental Divide

adj. adjective	*n.* noun
adv. adverb	*prep.* preposition
conj. conjunction	*pron.* pronoun
interj. interjection	*v.* verb
sing. singular	*pl.* plural

---

tinental customs differ from those of England. **b** person living on the Continent; European. **c** of or having to do with the American colonies at the time of the Revolutionary War: *The Second Continental Congress adopted the Declaration of Independence in 1776.* **d** soldier of the American army during the Revolutionary War. 1,2a,2c *adj.,* 2b,2d *n.*

Continental Divide

Continental Divide, ridge in W North America which separates streams flowing toward the Pacific Ocean from those flowing toward the Atlantic or the Arctic Oceans; Great Divide. The Rocky Mountains form a major part of the Continental Divide.

con tin gen cy (kən tin′jən sē), **1** a happening or event depending on something that is uncertain; possibility: *The explorer carried supplies for every contingency.* **2** an accidental happening; chance. *n., pl.* **con tin gen cies.**

con tin gent (kən tin′jənt), **1** share of soldiers, laborers, etc., to be furnished: *The United States sent a large contingent of troops to Europe in World War II.* **2** group that is part of a larger group: *The New York contingent sat together at the national convention.* **3** depending on something not certain; conditional: *Our plans for a picnic are contingent upon fair weather.* **4** liable to happen or not to happen; possible; uncertain: *The traveler set aside five dollars a day for contingent expenses.* **5** happening by chance; accidental; unexpected. **6** something accidental or unexpected. 1,2,6 *n.,* 3-5 *adj.*

con tin u al (kən tin′yü əl), **1** never stopping: *the continual flow of the river.*

2 repeated many times; very frequent: *No one likes continual interruptions while reading. adj.*

con tin u al ly (kən tin′yü ə lē), **1** always; without stopping: *Time is continually passing.* **2** again and again; very frequently: *I am continually losing things. adv.*

con tin u ance (kən tin′yü əns), **1** a continuing; going on: *during the continuance of the war.* **2** act of remaining; stay: *His continuance in office depends on the voters.* **3** adjournment or postponement of legal proceedings until a future time. *n.*

con tin u a tion (kən tin′yü ā′shən), **1** act of going on with a thing after stopping; beginning again: *Continuation of the reading was difficult after so many interruptions.* **2** anything by which a thing is continued; added part: *The continuation of the story will appear in next month's issue of the magazine.* **3** act or fact of not stopping. *n.*

continuation school, an evening school for persons who have left elementary school or high school to go to work.

con tin ue (kən tin′yü), **1** keep up; keep on; go on; go on with: *The rain continued all day. The road continues for miles.* **2** go on after stopping; take up; carry on: *The story will be continued next month. The class begged the teacher to continue with the reading.* **3** last: *The king's reign continued for 20 years.* **4** stay: *The children must continue in school till the end of June.* **5** cause to stay; maintain: *The club members voted to continue the president in office for another term.* **6** put off until a later time; postpone; adjourn: *The judge continued the case until next month. v.,* **con tin ued, con tin u ing.**

con ti nu i ty (kon′tə nü′ə tē *or* kon′tə nyü′ə tē), **1** condition or quality of being continuous: *The continuity of her story was broken when the telephone rang.* **2** a continuous or connected whole; unbroken series. *n., pl.* **con ti nu i ties.**

con tin u ous (kən tin′yü əs), without a stop or break; connected; unbroken: *a continuous sound, a continuous line of cars. adj.* —**con tin′u ous ly,** *adv.*

con tort (kən tôrt′), twist or bend out of shape; distort: *The clown contorted his face. v.*

con tor tion (kən tôr′shən), **1** a twisting or bending out of shape. **2** twisted condition: *The acrobat went through various contortions. n.*

con tour (kon′tùr), **1** outline of a figure: *The contour of the Atlantic coast of America is very irregular.* **2** following natural ridges and furrows to avoid erosion: *contour plowing.* 1 *n.,* 2 *adj.*

contour line, line on a map, showing height above sea level. All points on a contour line have the same elevation.

contour map, map showing heights above sea level by means of contour lines.

contour map
Mountains in landscape sketch (above) appear on the contour map (below).

con tra band (kon′trə band), **1** goods imported or exported contrary to law; smuggled goods: *Customs officials went through each bag looking for contraband.* **2** a smuggling. **3** contraband of war. **4** against the law; prohibited: *to smuggle contraband drugs into a country.* 1-3 *n.,* 4 *adj.*

contraband of war, goods supplied by neutral nations to countries at war with one another which either warring country has the right to seize. Ammunition is always contraband of war.

con tra bass (kon′trə bās′), **1** the lowest bass instrument. **2** double bass. *n.*

con tract (kən trakt′ for 1-4; kon′trakt for 5,6,8; kon′trakt or kən trakt′ for 7), **1** draw together; make shorter: *Wrinkling your forehead contracts your brows.* **2** become shorter or smaller; shrink: *Wool fibers contract in hot water. Earthworms can contract.* **3** shorten (a word, etc.) by omitting some of the letters or sounds: *In talking we contract "do not" to "don't."* **4** bring on oneself; get; form: *Bad habits are easy to contract and hard to get rid of. His hoarseness and coughing showed that he had contracted a cold.* **5** agreement. In a contract two or more people agree to do or not to do certain things. **6** a written agreement that can be enforced by law. **7** make a contract: *The builder contracted to build the new house.* **8** one variety of the game of bridge. 1-4,7 *v.,* 5,6,8 *n.*

con trac tion (kən trak′shən), **1** process of contracting: *Cold causes the contraction of liquids, gases, metals, etc.; heat causes expansion.* **2** condition of being contracted: *The contraction of mercury by cold makes it go down in thermometers.* **3** something contracted; shortened form: *"Can't" is a contraction of "cannot."* *n.*

con trac tor (kon′trak tər *or* kən-trak′tər), person who agrees to furnish materials or to do a piece of work for a certain price: *a building contractor.* *n.*

con tra dict (kon′trə dikt′), 1 say that a statement is not true; deny: *He contradicted the rumor that he was moving to another town.* 2 say the opposite of what (a person) has said: *I seldom contradict my parents.* 3 be contrary to; disagree with: *Your story and her story contradict each other.* *v.*

con tra dic tion (kon′trə dik′shən), 1 a denying of what has been said; saying the opposite: *The expert spoke without fear of contradiction by his listeners.* 2 statement or act that contradicts another; denial. 3 disagreement. *n.*

con tra dic tor y (kon′trə dik′tər ē), in disagreement; contradicting; contrary: *First reports of the election were so contradictory we could not tell who won.* *adj.*

con tral to (kən tral′tō), 1 the lowest female voice; alto. 2 singer with such a voice. 3 part in music for such a voice. 4 of or for a contralto. 1-3 *n., pl.* **con tral tos;** 4 *adj.*

con trap tion (kən trap′shən), INFOR-MAL. device or gadget; contrivance. *n.*

con tra ri ly (kon′trer ə lē *or* kən-trer′ə lē), in a contrary manner; on the contrary. *adv.*

con tra ri ness (kon′trer ē nis *or* kən trer′ē nis), a being contrary. *n.*

con tra ri wise (kon′trer ē wīz′), 1 in the opposite way or direction. 2 on the contrary. *adv.*

con tra ry (kon′trer ē *for 1,2;* kən-trer′ē *for 3*), 1 completely different; opposed; opposite: *Your taste in clothes is just contrary to my own.* 2 the opposite: *After promising to stay and clean up, he did the contrary and went out.* 3 opposing others; stubborn: *The contrary boy often refused to do what was asked of him.* 1,3 *adj.,* 2 *n., pl.* **con tra ries.**
on the contrary, exactly opposite to what has been said: *He is not stingy; on the contrary, no one could be more generous.*

con trast (kon′trast *for 1,2;* kən trast′ *for 3,4*), 1 a great difference; difference: *Anybody can see the contrast between black and white. There is a great contrast between life now and life a hundred years ago.* 2 person, thing, event, etc., that shows differences when compared with another: *My dark hair is a sharp contrast to my sister's light hair.* 3 compare (two things) so as to show their differences: *Contrast birds with fishes.* 4 show differences when com-

pared or put side by side: *The black and the gold contrast well in that design.* 1,2 *n.,* 3,4 *v.*

con trib ute (kən trib′yüt), 1 give money or help along with others: *Will you contribute to the Red Cross? Everyone was asked to contribute suggestions for the party.* 2 write (articles, stories, etc.) for a newspaper or magazine. *v.,* **con trib ut ed, con trib ut ing.**
contribute to, help bring about: *A poor diet contributed to the child's bad health.*

con tri bu tion (kon′trə byü′shən), 1 act of contributing; giving of money or help along with others: *We felt that our contribution to the fund was both a duty and a pleasure.* 2 money or help contributed; gift: *Her contribution to the picnic was a basket of apples.* 3 article, story, etc., written for a newspaper or magazine. *n.*

con trib u tor (kən trib′yə tər), person or thing that contributes. *n.*

con trib u to ry (kən trib′yə tôr′ē), helping to bring about; contributing: *The worker's own carelessness was a contributory cause of the accident.* *adj.*

con trite (kən trīt′ *or* kon′trīt), 1 broken in spirit by a sense of guilt; penitent: *The boy felt contrite after he had hit his little sister.* 2 showing deep regret and sorrow: *He wrote an apology in contrite words.* *adj.* —**con trite′ly,** *adv.* —**con trite′ness,** *n.*

con tri tion (kən trish′ən), 1 sorrow for one's sins or guilt; being contrite; repentance. 2 deep regret. *n.*

con triv ance (kən trī′vəns), 1 thing invented; mechanical device: *A can opener is a handy contrivance.* 2 act or manner of contriving: *By careful contrivance she repaired the old clock and made it go.* 3 plan; scheme. *n.*

con trive (kən trīv′), 1 plan with cleverness or skill; design: *The inventor had contrived a new kind of engine.* 2 plan; scheme; plot: *contrive a robbery.* 3 arrange to have something happen; manage: *I will contrive to be there by ten o'clock.* *v.,* **con trived, con triv ing.**

con trol (kən trōl′), 1 have power or authority over; direct: *A captain controls his ship and its crew. The government controlled prices and wages during the war.* 2 power to direct or guide; authority: *A child is under its parents' control.* 3 hold back; keep down; restrain: *I was so upset by the accident that I couldn't control my tears.* 4 a holding back; a keeping down; restraint: *He lost control of his temper.* 5 means of restraint; check: *The President's power to veto is a control over the legislation passed by Congress.*

6 device that regulates the working of a machine: *The control of our furnace can be operated from the kitchen.* 7 **controls,** *pl.* the instruments and devices by which an aircraft, locomotive, car, etc., is operated: *The new pilot managed the controls better in taking off than in landing.* 8 individual or group serving as a standard of comparison for testing the results of a scientific experiment performed on a similar individual or group. 1,3 *v.,* **con trolled, con trol ling;** 2,4-8 *n.*

con trol ler (kən trō′lər), 1 person employed to supervise expenditures; comptroller: *The mayor directed the city controller to examine the expenses of the fire department.* 2 person who controls, directs, or restrains. *n.*

control tower, tower at an airfield for controlling the traffic of aircraft taking off and landing.

con tro ver sial (kon′trə vėr′shəl), 1 of or having to do with controversy: *controversial writing.* 2 open to controversy; debatable; disputed: *a controversial question.* 3 fond of disputing. *adj.* —**con′tro ver′sial ly,** *adv.*

con tro ver sy (kon′trə vėr′sē), act of arguing a question about which differences of opinion exist; debate; dispute; argument: *The long controversy over slavery was one of the causes of the Civil War.* *n., pl.* **con tro ver sies.**

con tro vert (kon′trə vėrt′), 1 dispute, deny, or oppose: *The statement of the last witness controverts the testimony of the first two.* 2 dispute about; discuss; debate. *v.*

con tu me ly (kən tü′mə lē *or* kən-tyü′mə lē), 1 insulting words or actions; humiliating treatment: *The nobles treated the peasants with contumely.* 2 a humiliating insult. *n., pl.* **con tu me lies.**

con tu sion (kən tü′zhən *or* kən-tyü′zhən), a bruise. *n.*

co nun drum (kə nun′drəm), 1 riddle whose answer involves a pun or play on words. EXAMPLE: "When is a door not a door?" ANSWER: "When it's ajar." 2 any puzzling problem. *n.*

convalesce

adj.	adjective	*n.*	noun
adv.	adverb	*prep.*	preposition
conj.	conjunction	*pron.*	pronoun
interj.	interjection	*v.*	verb
sing.	singular	*pl.*	plural

con va lesce (kon′və les′), recover health and strength after illness: *She convalesced at home for three weeks after her operation.* *v.,* **con va lesced, con va lesc ing.**

con va les cence (kon′və les′ns), 1 the gradual recovery of health and strength after illness. 2 time during which one is convalescing: *The doctor prescribed a three-week convalescence in bed.* *n.*

con va les cent (kon′və les′nt), 1 recovering health and strength after illness. 2 person recovering after illness. 1 *adj.,* 2 *n.*

con vec tion (kən vek′shən), the transfer of heat from one place to another by the movement of heated particles of a gas or liquid. *n.*

con vene (kən vēn′), 1 meet for some purpose; gather together; assemble: *Congress convenes in the Capitol at Washington, D.C., at least once a year.* 2 call together: *Any member may convene our club in an emergency.* *v.,* **con vened, con ven ing.**

con ven ience (kən vē′nyəns), 1 fact or quality of being convenient: *The convenience of packaged meats and other foods helps to increase their sales.* 2 comfort; advantage: *Many stores have a delivery service for the convenience of shoppers.* 3 anything handy or easy to use; thing that saves trouble or work: *A folding table is a convenience in a small room.* *n.*

at one's convenience, so as to suit one as to time, place, or other conditions: *Come by to pick me up at your convenience.*

con ven ient (kən vē′nyənt), 1 saving trouble; well arranged; easy to use: *use a convenient tool, live in a convenient house.* 2 easily done; not troublesome; suitable: *Will it be convenient for you to bring your lunch to school?* 3 within easy reach; handy: *meet at a convenient place.* *adj.* —**con ven′ient ly,** *adv.*

con vent (kon′vent), 1 group of nuns living together according to fixed rules and under religious vows. 2 building or buildings in which they live. *n.*

con ven tion (kən ven′shən), 1 a meeting arranged for some particular purpose; gathering; assembly: *The Democratic and Republican parties*

hold a convention every four years to choose candidates for President. 2 general agreement; common consent; custom: *Convention governs how we dress.* 3 custom or practice approved by general agreement: *Using the right hand to shake hands is a convention.* 4 agreement signed by two or more countries about matters less important than those in a treaty. *n.*

con ven tion al (kən ven′shə nəl), 1 depending on conventions; customary: *"Good morning" is a conventional greeting.* 2 acting or behaving according to commonly accepted and approved ways: *The people living next door are quiet, conventional people.* 3 of the usual type or design; commonly used or seen: *conventional furniture.* 4 (in the arts) following custom and traditional models; formal: *The ode and the sonnet are conventional forms of English poetry.* *adj.* —**con ven′tion al ly,** *adv.*

con ven tion al i ty (kən ven′shə nal′ə tē), 1 conventional quality or character; adherence to custom: *Conventionality requires people to wear shoes in public in most countries.* 2 a conventional custom, practice, or rule. *n., pl.* **con ven tion al i ties.**

converge (def. 1)
These lines
converge at C.

con verge (kən verj′), 1 tend to meet in a point: *The sides of a road seem to converge in the distance.* 2 turn toward each other: *If you look at the end of your nose, your eyes converge.* 3 come together; center: *A large group converged on the city hall. The attention of all the children converged upon the kitten I brought in.* *v.,* **con verged, con verg ing.**

con ver gence (kən ver′jəns), 1 act or process of converging; tendency to meet in a point. 2 point of converging. *n.*

con ver gent (kən ver′jənt), converging. *adj.*

con ver sant (kən ver′sənt), familiar by use or study; acquainted: *Our music teacher is conversant with all of the instruments of the orchestra.* *adj.*

con ver sa tion (kon′vər sā′shən), friendly talk; exchange of thoughts by talking informally together. *n.*

con ver sa tion al (kon′vər sā′shə nəl), 1 of or having to do with conversation. 2 fond of conversation; good at conversation. *adj.* —**con′ver sa′tion al ly,** *adv.*

con ver sa tion al ist (kon′vər sā′-

shə nə list), person who is fond of or who is good at conversation. *n.*

con verse[1] (kən vers′ *for 1;* kon′vers′ *for 2*), 1 talk together in an informal way. 2 conversation. 1 *v.,* **con versed, con vers ing;** 2 *n.* [from French of the 1300's *converser*]

con verse[2] (kən vers′ *or* kon′vers′ *for 1,2;* kon′vers′ *for 3*), 1 opposite or contrary in direction or action: *A converse wind slowed down the airplane.* 2 reversed in order; turned about: *The converse order of the alphabet is from "z" to "a."* 3 thing that is turned around, opposite, or contrary to something else: *The converse of a hamburger without onions is onions without a hamburger.* 1,2 *adj.,* 3 *n.* [from Latin *conversum* turned around]

con verse ly (kən vers′lē), if turned the other way around: *Six is more than five; conversely, five is less than six.* *adv.*

con ver sion (kən ver′zhən), 1 a converting; a changing or a turning; change: *Heat causes the conversion of water into steam.* 2 a change from unbelief to faith; change from one religion, party, etc., to another. 3 (in football) one or two extra points scored after a touchdown. *n.*

con vert (kən vert′ *for 1,2,4,5;* kon′-vert′ *for 3*), 1 turn to another or a particular use or purpose; change: *The generators at the dam convert water power into electricity. We converted old crates into furniture.* 2 cause to change from one belief to another or from lack of belief to faith: *French and Spanish missionaries tried to convert American Indians to the Christian religion.* 3 person who has been converted. 4 exchange for an equivalent: *She converted her dollars into pounds upon arriving in London.* 5 score a conversion: *convert after a touchdown.* 1,2,4,5 *v.,* 3 *n.*

con vert i ble (kən ver′tə bəl), 1 that can be converted: *A dollar bill is convertible into ten dimes. Wood is convertible into paper.* 2 automobile with a folding top. 1 *adj.,* 2 *n.*

convex lenses
A, convex surface
opposite plane surface
B, convex and concave
C, double convex

con vex (kon veks′ *or* kon′veks), curved out like the outside of a circle or sphere; curving out: *The lens of an automobile headlight is convex on the outside.* *adj.* —**con vex′ly,** *adv.*

con vex i ty (kon vek′sə tē), 1 convex condition or quality. 2 a convex surface or thing. *n., pl.* **con vex i ties.**

con vey (kən vā′), 1 take from one place to another; carry: *A bus conveyed the passengers from the city to the airport.* 2 transmit; conduct: *A wire conveys an electric circuit.* 3 make known; communicate: *Do the author's words convey any meaning to you?* 4 transfer ownership of; hand over; give: *convey property by a will.* v.

con vey ance (kən vā′əns), 1 a carrying; transmission: *Freighters engage in the conveyance of goods from one port to another. Books promote the conveyance of ideas.* 2 thing that carries people and goods; vehicle: *Railroad trains and buses are public conveyances.* 3 transfer of property from one person to another. n.

con vey or or **con vey er** (kən vā′ər), 1 person or thing that conveys. 2 a mechanical device that carries things from one place to another, especially by means of a moving, endless belt. n.

con vict (kən vikt′ for 1; kon′vikt for 2), 1 prove, find, or declare guilty: *The jury convicted the accused woman of stealing.* 2 person serving a prison sentence for some crime. 1 v., 2 n.

con vic tion (kən vik′shən), 1 act of proving or declaring guilty: *The trial resulted in the conviction of the guilty man.* 2 condition of being proved or declared guilty: *The thief's conviction meant two years in prison.* 3 firm belief: *It was President Lincoln's conviction that the Union must be preserved in order to survive.* n.

con vince (kən vins′), make (a person) feel sure; cause to believe; persuade by argument or proof: *The mistakes she made convinced me she had not studied her lesson.* v., **con vinced, con vinc ing.**

con vinc ing (kən vin′sing), that convinces: *The lawyer's convincing argument influenced the jury.* adj. —**convinc′ing ly,** adv.

con viv i al (kən viv′ē əl), 1 fond of eating and drinking with friends; sociable. 2 festive; gay. adj.

con vo ca tion (kon′və kā′shən), 1 a calling together. 2 assembly: *The convocation of clergymen passed a resolution condemning violence.* n.

con voke (kən vōk′), call together; summon to assemble. v., **con voked, con vok ing.**

con vo lu tion (kon′və lü′shən), 1 a coiling, winding, or twisting together: *the convolutions of a snake slithering through the grass.* 2 a coil; winding; twist. 3 an irregular fold or ridge on the surface of the brain. n.

con voy (kən voi′ or kon′voi for 1; kon′voi for 2-4), 1 go with in order to protect; escort: *Warships convoy unarmed merchant ships during time of war.* 2 an escort; protection: *The gold was moved from the truck to the bank's vault under convoy of armed guards.* 3 warships, soldiers, etc., that convoy. 4 ship, fleet, supplies, etc., that are convoyed. 1 v., 2-4 n.

con vulse (kən vuls′), 1 shake violently: *An earthquake convulsed the island.* 2 cause violent disturbance in: *His face was convulsed with rage.* 3 throw into convulsions; shake with muscular spasms: *The sick child was convulsed before the doctor came.* 4 throw into fits of laughter; cause to shake with laughter: *The clown convulsed the audience with his funny acts.* v., **con vulsed, con vuls ing.**

con vul sion (kən vul′shən), 1 a violent, involuntary contracting and relaxing of the muscles; spasm; fit: *The sick child's convulsions frightened her parents.* 2 a fit of laughter. 3 a violent disturbance: *Civil war causes a convulsion throughout a nation.* n.

con vul sive (kən vul′siv), 1 violently disturbing. 2 having convulsions. adj. —**con vul′sive ly,** adv. —**con vul′sive ness,** n.

co ny (kō′nē), 1 rabbit fur. 2 rabbit. n., pl. **co nies.** Also, **coney.**

coo (kü), 1 the soft, murmuring sound made by doves or pigeons. 2 make this sound. 3 murmur softly; speak in a soft, loving manner: *coo over a baby.* 1 n., pl. **coos;** 2,3 v.

cook (kuk), 1 prepare (food, etc.) by using heat. Boiling, frying, broiling, roasting, and baking are forms of cooking. 2 undergo cooking; be cooked: *Let the meat cook slowly.* 3 person who cooks. 1,2 v., 3 n.

cook up, INFORMAL. make up or prepare, especially falsely: *She cooked up an excuse for being late.*

cook book (kuk′buk′), book of directions for cooking various kinds of food; book of recipes. n.

cook er (kuk′ər), apparatus or container to cook things in: *a steam cooker.* n.

cook er y (kuk′ər ē), art or occupation of cooking. n.

cook ie (kuk′ē), a small, flat, sweet cake. n. Also, **cooky.**

cook out (kuk′out′), a picnic, etc., where the food is cooked outdoors on a grill, etc., and eaten outdoors. n.

cook y (kuk′ē), cookie. n., pl. **cookies.**

cool (kül), 1 somewhat cold; more cold than hot: *a cool, cloudy day.* 2 allowing or giving a cool feeling: *a cool, thin dress.* 3 not excited; calm: *Everyone kept cool when paper in the wastebasket caught fire.* 4 having little enthusiasm or interest; not cordial: *My old enemy*

hat, āge, fär; let, ēqual, tėrm;
it, īce; hot, ōpen, ôrder;
oil, out; cup, put, rüle; ch, child;
ng, long; sh, she; th, thin;
ŦH, then; zh, measure;

ə represents *a* in about,
e in taken, *i* in pencil,
o in lemon, *u* in circus.

gave me a cool greeting. 5 something cool; cool part, place, or time: *in the cool of the evening.* 6 make or become cool: *Ice cools water. He was cooled by the shade of the tree. The ground cools off after the sun goes down.* 7 bold or impudent in a calm way. 8 INFORMAL. without exaggeration: *a cool million dollars.* 9 SLANG. admirable; excellent. 10 SLANG. calm restraint; presence of mind. 1-4,7-9 adj., 5,10 n., 6 v. —**cool′ly,** adv. —**cool′ness,** n.

cool ant (kü′lənt), a cooling substance, used to reduce heat in machinery. n.

cool er (kü′lər), container that cools foods or drinks, or keeps them cool. n.

cool-head ed (kül′hed′id), not easily excited; calm. adj. —**cool′-head′ed ness,** n.

Coo lidge (kü′lij), (John) Calvin, 1872-1933, the 30th president of the United States, from 1923 to 1929. n.

coo lie or **coo ly** (kü′lē), an unskilled, native laborer in China, India, etc. n., pl. **coo lies.**

coon (kün), raccoon. n.

coop (küp or kup), 1 a small cage or pen for chickens, rabbits, etc. 2 keep or put in a coop. 3 confine, especially in a small space: *The children were cooped up indoors by the rain.* 1 n., 2,3 v.

co-op (kō′op), INFORMAL. cooperative. n.

coop er (kü′pər or kup′ər), man who makes or repairs barrels, casks, etc. n.

Coo per (kü′pər or kup′ər), James Fenimore, 1789-1851, American novelist who wrote stories about Indian and frontier life, and about the sea. n.

co op e rate (kō op′ə rāt′), work together: *The children cooperated with their teacher in helping to keep the classroom neat.* v., **co op e rat ed, co op e rat ing.**

co op e ra tion (kō op′ə rā′shən), a working together; united effort or labor: *Cooperation can accomplish many things which no individual could do alone.* n.

co op e ra tive (kō op′ə rā′tiv or kō op′ə rə tiv), 1 wanting or willing to work together with others: *Most of the pupils were helpful and cooperative.*

adj. adjective	*n.* noun
adv. adverb	*prep.* preposition
conj. conjunction	*pron.* pronoun
interj. interjection	*v.* verb
sing. singular	*pl.* plural

2 store where merchandise is sold to members who share in the profits and losses according to the amounts they buy. 3 union of farmers for buying and selling their produce at the best price. 4 an apartment house owned and operated by the tenants. 5 apartment in such a building. 1 *adj.*, 2-5 *n.* —**co op′e ra′tive ly**, *adv.* —**co op′e ra′tive ness**, *n.*

co or di nate (kō ôrd′n āt *for 1,3;* kō ôrd′n it *for 2,4-6*), 1 arrange in proper order; put in proper relation; harmonize; adjust: *Coordinating the movements of the arms and legs is the hardest part of learning to swim.* 2 equal in importance; of equal rank. 3 make equal in importance. 4 a co-ordinate person or thing; an equal. 5 joining words, phrases, or clauses of equal grammatical importance. *And and but* are coordinate conjunctions. 6 any of a set of numbers that give the position of a point by reference to fixed lines or axes. 1,3 *v.*, **co or di nat ed, co or di nat ing;** 2,5 *adj.*, 4,6 *n.* —**co or′di nate ly**, *adv.*

co or di na tion (kō ôrd′n ā′shən), 1 harmonious adjustment or working together: *Poor coordination in his hands made his drawing crude.* 2 arrangement in proper order or proper relation: *An outline often helps in the coordination of ideas. n.*

co or di na tor (kō ôrd′n ā′tər), person or thing that coordinates. *n.*

coot (küt), a wading and swimming bird with short wings and webbed feet. *n.*

coot ie (kü′tē), SLANG. louse. *n.*

cop (kop), INFORMAL. policeman. *n.*

cope[1] (kōp), struggle with some degree of success; struggle on even terms; deal successfully: *She was busy but she was still able to cope with the extra work. v.,* **coped, cop ing.** [from French of the 1300's *coper* to strike]

cope[2] (kōp), a long cape worn by priests during certain religious rites. *n.* [from Latin *capa* cloak]

Co pen ha gen (kō′pən hā′gən), capital of Denmark and its largest city, in the E part of Zealand. *n.*

Co per ni can (kə pėr′nə kən), of or having to do with Copernicus or his system of astronomy. *adj.*

Co per ni cus (kə pėr′nə kəs)

Nikolaus, 1473-1543, Polish astronomer who demonstrated that the earth rotates on its axis and that the planets revolve around the sun. *n.*

cop i er (kop′ē ər), 1 person who copies; imitator. 2 person who makes written copies. 3 machine that makes copies. *n.*

co pi lot (kō′pī′lət), the assistant or second pilot in an aircraft. *n.*

COPING▸

cop ing (kō′ping), the top layer of a brick or stone wall. It is usually built with a slope to shed water. *n.*

coping saw, a narrow saw in a U-shaped frame, used to cut curves.

co pi ous (kō′pē əs), more than enough; plentiful; abundant: *a copious harvest. adj.* —**co′pi ous ly**, *adv.* —**co′pi ous ness**, *n.*

Co pland (kō′plənd), **Aaron,** born 1900, American composer. *n.*

cop per (kop′ər), 1 a tough, reddish-brown metallic element which occurs in various ores. Copper resists rust and is easily shaped into thin sheets or fine wire. It is an excellent conductor of heat and electricity. 2 coin made of copper or bronze, especially a penny. 3 of copper: *a copper kettle.* 4 cover or coat with copper. 5 reddish-brown. 6 a reddish brown. 1,2,6 *n.*, 3,5 *adj.*, 4 *v.*

cop per as (kop′ər əs), compound of iron and sulfur which occurs in light-green crystals, used in making ink, in dyeing, as a disinfectant, and in photography. *n.*

cop per head (kop′ər hed′), 1 a poisonous snake with a copper-colored head, found in the eastern United States. It is related to the water moccasin and the rattlesnake. It grows to be about three feet long. 2 **Copperhead,** person in the North who sympathized with the South during the Civil War. *n.*

cop per plate (kop′ər plāt′), 1 a thin, flat piece of copper on which a design, writing, or the like is engraved or etched. 2 an engraving, picture, or print made from a copperplate. *n.*

cop per y (kop′ər ē), 1 of or containing copper. 2 like copper: *a coppery sky at sunset. adj.*

cop pice (kop′is), copse. *n.*

co pra (kō′prə), the dried meat of coconuts. Coconut oil is obtained from copra. *n.*

copse (kops), a number of small trees, bushes, or shrubs growing together; coppice. *n.*

cop ter (kop′tər), INFORMAL. helicopter. *n.*

cop y (kop′ē), 1 thing made to be just like another; thing made on the pattern or model of another. A written page, a picture, a dress, or a piece of furniture can be an exact copy of another. 2 make a copy of: *Copy this page. She copied my hat.* 3 be a copy of; be like; follow as a model or example; imitate: *The little boy copied his father's way of walking.* 4 one of a number of books, newspapers, magazines, etc., made at the same printing: *six copies of today's paper.* 5 material ready to be set in type for a newspaper, magazine, or book. 1,4,5 *n.*, *pl.* **copies;** 2,3 *v.*, **cop ied, cop y ing.**

cop y book (kop′ē bùk′), book with models of handwriting to be copied in learning to write. *n.*

cop y right (kop′ē rīt′), 1 the exclusive right to publish or sell a certain book, picture, etc., granted by a government for a certain number of years. 2 protect by getting a copyright. Books, pieces of music, plays, etc., are usually copyrighted. 1 *n.*, 2 *v.*

co que try (kō′kə trē *or* kō ket′rē), behavior of a coquette; flirting. *n.*, *pl.* **co que tries.**

co quette (kō ket′), woman who tries to attract men just to please her vanity; flirt. *n.*

co quet tish (kō ket′ish), 1 of a coquette. 2 like a coquette: *a coquettish smile. adj.* —**co quet′tish ly**, *adv.*

co qui na (kō kē′nə), a soft, porous, whitish rock composed of pieces of seashell and coral. *n.*, *pl.* **co qui nas.**

co ra cle (kôr′ə kəl), a small, light boat made by covering a wooden frame with waterproof material. *n.*

co ral (kôr′əl), 1 a stony substance consisting of the skeletons of certain kinds of very small sea animals called polyps. Reefs and small islands consisting of coral are common in tropical seas and oceans. Red, pink, and white coral are often used for jewelry. 2 polyp that secretes a skeleton of coral and forms large branching colonies by budding. 3 made of coral: *a coral reef.* 4 deep-pink or red. 5 a deep pink or red. 1,2,5 *n.*, 3,4 *adj.*

coral (def. 1), left—stony skeleton;
coral (def. 2), right—enlarged section
as it would appear with living polyps,
some expanded and others contracted

coral snake, a small, poisonous American snake whose body is banded with alternating rings of red, yellow, and black.

cord (kôrd), 1 a thick string; very thin rope: *She tied the bundle of papers with a cord.* 2 fasten or tie up with a cord: *She corded the bundle of papers.* 3 anything resembling a cord, such as an insulated cable fitted with a plug to connect a lamp or other electrical appliance with an electrical outlet. 4 nerve, tendon, or other structure in an animal body that is somewhat like a cord; chord. The spinal cord is in the backbone. The vocal cords are in the throat. 5 ridge or ridged pattern on cloth. 6 cloth with such ridges on it, especially corduroy. 7 measure of quantity for cut wood equal to 128 cubic feet. A pile of wood 4 feet wide, 4 feet high, and 8 feet long is a cord. 8 pile (wood) in cords. 1,3-7 *n.*, 2,8 *v.* —**cord'like'**, *adj.*

cord age (kôr'dij), 1 cords or ropes: *Most of the cordage on a sailing ship is in its rigging.* 2 quantity of wood measured in cords. *n.*

cord ed (kôr'did), 1 having ridges on it; ribbed: *corded cloth.* 2 fastened with a cord: *bound with cords: corded bundles of newspaper. adj.*

cor dial (kôr'jəl), 1 warm and friendly in manner; hearty: *My friends gave me a cordial welcome.* 2 food, drink, or medicine that strengthens or stimulates. 3 liqueur. 1 *adj.*, 2,3 *n.* —**cor'dial ly,** *adv.*

cor di al i ty (kôr'jē al'ə tē), cordial quality or feeling; heartiness: *The cordiality of our host's welcome made us feel at home. n., pl.* **cor di al i ties.**

cor dil ler a (kôr dil'ər ə), a long mountain range; chain of mountains. *n., pl.* **cor dil ler as.**

Cór do ba (kôr'də bə), 1 city in S Spain. 2 city in central Argentina. *n.* Also, **Cordova.**

cor don (kôrd'n), 1 line or circle of soldiers, policemen, forts, etc., enclosing or guarding a place: *A cordon of troops surrounded the burned-out area of the city.* 2 a cord, braid, or ribbon worn as an ornament or as a badge of honor. *n.*

Cor do va (kôr'də və), Córdoba. *n.*

cor do van (kôr'də vən), 1 kind of soft, fine-grained leather. 2 shoe made from this leather. *n.* [from Spanish *cordobán,* from *Córdoba,* Spain]

cor du roy (kôr'də roi'), 1 a thick, cotton cloth with close, velvetlike ridges. 2 made of corduroy: *a corduroy skirt.* 3 **corduroys,** *pl.* corduroy trousers. 1,3 *n.,* 2 *adj.*

corduroy road, road made of logs

laid crosswise, usually across low, wet land.

cord wood (kôrd'wùd'), 1 wood sold by the cord. 2 firewood piled in cords. 3 wood cut in 4-foot lengths. *n.*

core (kôr), 1 the hard, central part containing the seeds of fruits like apples and pears: *After eating the apple he threw the core away.* 2 the central or most important part. The core of an electromagnet is a soft iron bar. *He is honest to the core. The core of her argument against the plan is its costliness.* 3 take out the core of (fruit): *core apples for a pie.* 1,2 *n.,* 3 *v.,* **cored, cor ing.**

CORE (kôr), Congress of Racial Equality. *n.*

Cor inth (kôr'inth), seaport in S Greece. In ancient times, Corinth was a center of commerce noted for its art and luxury. *n.*

Co rin thi an (kə rin'thē ən), 1 of Corinth or its people. 2 person born or living in Corinth. 3 having to do with the most elaborate style of Greek architecture. 1,3 *adj.,* 2 *n.*

Co rin thi ans (kə rin'thē ənz), either of two books of the New Testament, consisting of letters written by Saint Paul to the Christians of Corinth. *n.*

cork (kôrk), 1 the light, thick, outer bark of the cork oak. Cork is used for bottle stoppers, floats for fishlines, inner soles of shoes, fillings for life preservers, and some floor coverings. 2 a shaped piece of cork: *the cork of a bottle.* 3 any stopper for a bottle, flask, etc., made of glass, rubber, etc. 4 stop up with a cork: *Fill these bottles and cork them tightly.* 1-3 *n.,* 4 *v.*

Cork (kôrk), 1 county in the S part of the Republic of Ireland. 2 city in this county. *n.*

cork oak, the oak tree from which cork is obtained.

cork screw (kôrk'skrü'), 1 tool used to pull corks out of bottles. 2 shaped like a corkscrew; spiral: *corkscrew curls.* 1 *n.,* 2 *adj.*

corm of a crocus partly cut away to show underlying layers

corm (kôrm), a fleshy, bulblike, underground stem of certain plants, such as the crocus and gladiolus, that produces leaves and buds on the upper surface and roots on the lower. *n.*

cor mor ant (kôr'mər ənt), a very large sea bird that has a pouch under its

hat, āge, fär; let, ēqual, tėrm; it, īce; hot, ōpen, ôrder; oil, out; cup, pùt, rüle; ch, child; ng, long; sh, she; th, thin; ŦH, then; zh, measure;

ə represents *a* in about, *e* in taken, *i* in pencil, *o* in lemon, *u* in circus.

beak for holding captured fish. *n.*

corn[1] (kôrn), 1 kind of grain that grows on large ears; maize; Indian corn. 2 plant that it grows on. 3 any small, hard seed or grain of wheat, barley, oats, etc.; kernel. 4 grain in general, especially wheat. 5 preserve (meat) with strong salt water or with dry salt. 6 SLANG. something trite, outdated, or sentimental. 1-4,6 *n.,* 5 *v.* [Old English *corn* grain, seed, wheat]

corn[2] (kôrn), a small, hard, shiny thickening of the outer layer of the skin: *The painful corns on his toes were caused by the pressure and rubbing of shoes that did not fit properly. n.* [from French of the 1400's *corn* horn]

corn bread, bread made of corn meal.

corn cob (kôrn'kob'), the central, woody part of an ear of corn, on which the kernels grow; cob. *n.*

corn crib (kôrn'krib'), bin or small, ventilated building for storing unshelled corn. *n.*

cor ne a (kôr'nē ə), the transparent part of the outer coat of the eyeball. The cornea covers the iris and the pupil. *n., pl.* **cor ne as.**

corned (kôrnd), preserved with strong salt water or with dry salt: *corned beef. adj.*

cor ner (kôr'nər), 1 place where two lines or surfaces meet: *the corner of a room.* 2 the place where two streets meet: *There is a traffic light at the corner.* 3 at or on a corner: *a corner house, a corner lot.* 4 for a corner: *a corner cupboard.* 5 piece to form, protect, or decorate a corner: *The leather pocketbook has gold corners.* 6 place away from crowds; secret place: *The money was hidden in odd corners all over the house.* 7 place that is far away; distant region or quarter: *People have searched in all the corners of the earth for gold.* 8 an awkward or difficult position; place from which escape is impossible: *His enemies had driven him into a corner.* 9 force into an awkward or difficult position; drive into a corner: *The police cornered the thief in the alley.* 10 a buying up of

adj. adjective	*n.* noun
adv. adverb	*prep.* preposition
conj. conjunction	*pron.* pronoun
interj. interjection	*v.* verb
sing. singular	*pl.* plural

large amounts of some stock or article to raise its price: *a corner in wheat.* 11 buy up large amounts of (some stock or article) to raise its price: *Some speculators have tried to corner wheat.* 1,2,5-8,10 *n.,* 3,4 *adj.,* 9,11 *v.*

cut corners, 1 shorten the way by going across corners. 2 save money by reducing effort, time, labor, etc.: *We had to cut corners to make a profit.*

turn the corner, pass the worst or most dangerous point.

cor nered (kôr′nərd), without hope of escape or relief: *A cornered animal will fight. adj.*

cor ner stone (kôr′nər stōn′), 1 stone at the corner of two walls that holds them together. 2 such a stone built into the corner of a building as its formal beginning. The laying of a cornerstone is often accompanied by ceremonies. 3 something of fundamental importance; foundation; basis: *The cornerstone of most religions is belief in God. n.*

cor net (kôr net′), a musical wind instrument somewhat like a trumpet, usually made of brass. It has three valves that control the pitch. *n.*

cor net tist or **cor net ist** (kôr-net′ist), person who plays a cornet. *n.*

corn field (kôrn′fēld′), field in which corn is grown. *n.*

corn flow er (kôrn′flou′ər), bachelor's-button. *n.*

corn husk (kôrn′husk′), husk of an ear of corn. *n.*

cor nice (kôr′nis), 1 an ornamental molding along the top of a wall, pillar, or side of a building. 2 a molding around the walls of a room just below the ceiling. *n.*

Cor nish (kôr′nish), 1 of or having to do with Cornwall, its people, or the language formerly spoken by them. 2 a Celtic language spoken in Cornwall until the late 1700's. 1 *adj.,* 2 *n.*

corn meal, meal made from ground-up corn. *n.*

corn stalk (kôrn′stôk′), stalk of corn. *n.*

corn starch (kôrn′stärch′), a starchy flour made from corn, used to thicken puddings, custard, etc. *n.*

corn sugar, sugar made from cornstarch.

corn syrup, syrup made from cornstarch.

cor nu co pi a (kôr′nə kō′pē ə), 1 horn-shaped container represented in art as overflowing with fruits, vegetables, and flowers; horn of plenty. It is a symbol of fruitfulness and plenty. 2 a horn-shaped ornament. Cornucopias are hung on Christmas trees. *n., pl.* **cor nu co pi as.**

Corn wall (kôrn′wôl), county in SW England. *n.*

Corn wal lis (kôrn wô′lis), **Charles,** 1738-1805, British general who surrendered to Washington at Yorktown on October 19, 1781. *n.*

corn y (kôr′nē), SLANG. trite, outdated, or sentimental: *corny jokes, corny music. adj.,* **corn i er, corn i est.**

co rol la (kə rol′ə), the petals of a flower. The petals which make up the corolla may be either separate from each other or fused together. *n., pl.* **co rol las.**

co rol lar y (kôr′ə ler′ē), 1 something proved by inference from something else already proved. 2 a natural consequence or result: *Destruction and suffering were corollaries of the war. n., pl.* **co rol lar ies.**

co ro na (kə rō′nə), 1 ring of light seen around the sun, moon, or other luminous body. 2 halo of light around the sun, seen only during an eclipse. *n., pl.* **co ro nas.**

Co ro na do (kôr′ə nä′dō), **Francisco Vásquez de,** 1510-1554, Spanish conquistador who explored the southwestern part of what is now the United States. *n.*

co ro nar y (kôr′ə ner′ē), 1 of or having to do with either of the two arteries (**coronary arteries**) that supply blood to the muscular tissue of the heart. 2 coronary thrombosis. 1 *adj.,* 2 *n., pl.* **co ro nar ies.**

coronary thrombosis, the stopping up of a branch of a coronary artery by a blood clot.

co ro na tion (kôr′ə nā′shən), ceremony of crowning a king, queen, emperor, etc. *n.*

co ro ner (kôr′ə nər), official of a local government who investigates any death not clearly due to natural causes. He may be assisted by a jury to determine the cause of death. *n.*

co ro net (kôr′ə net′), 1 a small crown worn as a mark of high rank: *The king wore a crown; the prince wore a coronet.* 2 a circle of gold, jewels, or flowers worn around the head as an ornament. *n.*

cor por al¹ (kôr′pər əl), of the body: *Spanking someone is corporal punishment. adj.* [from Latin *corporalem,*

cornucopia (def. 1)

from *corpus* body] —**cor′por al ly,** *adv.*

cor por al² (kôr′pər əl), the lowest-ranking noncommissioned officer in the army, ranking next below a sergeant and next above a private first class. He usually commands a squad. *n.* [from French *corporal,* from Italian *caporale,* from *capo* head]

cor por ate (kôr′pər it), 1 forming a corporation; incorporated: *Most car manufacturers are corporate companies.* 2 of a corporation: *corporate property.* 3 united; combined: *The corporate will of the majority prevailed. adj.*

cor po ra tion (kôr′pə rā′shən), 1 group of persons who obtain a charter giving them as a group the right to buy and sell, own property, manufacture and ship products, etc., as if it were one person. 2 group of persons with authority to act as a single person. The governing body of a college or the mayor and aldermen of a city are a corporation. *n.*

cor po re al (kôr pôr′ē əl), 1 of or for the body; bodily: *Food and water are corporeal nourishment.* 2 material; tangible: *Land, trees, and money are corporeal things. adj.* —**cor po′re al ly,** *adv.*

corps (kôr), 1 group of soldiers, trained for specialized military service: *the Medical Corps, the Signal Corps.* 2 a military unit made up of two or more divisions plus supporting troops, usually commanded by a lieutenant general. It is smaller than an army. 3 group of people with special training, organized for working together: *A large hospital has a corps of nurses. n., pl.* **corps** (kôrz).

corpse (kôrps), a dead human body. *n.*

cor pu lence (kôr′pyə ləns), fatness; stoutness. *n.*

cor pu lent (kôr′pyə lənt), fat; stout. *adj.*

cor pus cle (kôr′pus′əl), any of the cells that form a large part of the blood, lymph, etc. Red corpuscles carry oxygen to the tissues and remove carbon dioxide; some white corpuscles destroy disease germs. *n.*

cor ral (kə ral′), 1 pen for horses, cattle, etc. 2 drive into or keep in such a pen: *The cowhands corralled the herd of wild ponies.* 3 hem in; surround; capture: *The reporters corralled the candidate and asked him for a statement.* 4 a circular camp formed by wagons for defense against attack. 5 form (wagons) into such a circular camp. 1,4 *n.,* 2,3,5 *v.,* **cor ralled, cor ral ling.**

cor rect (kə rekt′), 1 free from mistakes; right: *He gave the correct answer.* 2 agreeing with a good standard of taste; proper: *correct manners, correct dress.* 3 change to what is right; remove mistakes or faults from: *Correct any misspellings that you find.* 4 alter or adjust to agree with some standard: *correct the reading of a barometer.* 5 point out or mark the errors of; check: *The teacher corrected our tests and returned them to us.* 6 set right by punishing; find fault with in order to improve; punish: *correct a child for misbehaving.* 1,2 *adj.,* 3-6 *v.* —**cor rect′ly,** *adv.* —**cor rect′ness,** *n.*

cor rec tion (kə rek′shən), 1 act or process of correcting; setting right: *The correction of all my mistakes took nearly an hour.* 2 a change to correct an error or mistake: *Write in your corrections neatly.* 3 punishment. A prison is sometimes called a house of correction. *n.*

cor rec tive (kə rek′tiv), 1 tending to correct; setting right; making better: *Corrective exercises can make weak muscles strong.* 2 something that corrects. 1 *adj.,* 2 *n.* —**cor rec′tive ly,** *adv.*

cor re late (kôr′ə lāt), 1 put in relation: *Try to correlate your knowledge of history with your knowledge of geography.* 2 be related one to the other: *The diameter and the circumference of a circle correlate.* *v.,* **cor re lat ed, cor re lat ing.**

cor re la tion (kôr′ə lā′shən), 1 the mutual relation of two or more things: *There is a close correlation between climate and crops.* 2 act or process of correlating. *n.*

cor rel a tive (kə rel′ə tiv), 1 having a mutual relation. Conjunctions used in pairs, such as *either...or,* are correlative. 2 either of two things having a mutual relation and commonly used together. Pairs of words like *husband* and *wife, father* and *mother,* are correlatives. 1 *adj.,* 2 *n.* —**cor rel′a tive ly,** *adv.*

cor re spond (kôr′ə spond′), 1 be in harmony; agree: *The answers she got on the test correspond with those I got.* 2 be similar: *The fins of a fish correspond to the wings of a bird.* 3 exchange letters; write letters to each other: *Will you correspond with me while I am away?* *v.*

cor re spond ence (kôr′ə spon′-

dəns), 1 a being in harmony; agreement: *Your account of the accident has little correspondence with the story the other driver told.* 2 similarity: *There is a correspondence of form in the skeletons of a lion and a tiger.* 3 exchange of letters; practice of letter writing: *The boy kept up a correspondence with his friend in Europe.* 4 letters: *Bring me the correspondence concerning that order.* *n.*

cor re spond ent (kôr′ə spon′dənt), 1 person who exchanges letters with another: *My mother and her sister have been regular correspondents for years, writing to each other weekly.* 2 person employed by a newspaper, magazine, radio or television network, etc., to send news from a particular place or region: *There were reports on the news tonight from correspondents in China and Great Britain.* 3 person or company that has regular business with another in a distant place: *Many American banks have correspondents in European cities.* 4 in agreement; corresponding. 1-3 *n.,* 4 *adj.*

cor re spond ing (kôr′ə spon′ding), similar: *The brigade's attack was met by a corresponding counterattack.* *adj.* —**cor′re spond′ing ly,** *adv.*

cor ri dor (kôr′ə dər), a long hallway; passage in a large building into which rooms open: *Our classroom is at the end of a corridor.* *n.*

cor rob o rate (kə rob′ə rāt′), make more certain; confirm: *Eyewitnesses corroborated the victim's statement to the police.* *v.,* **cor rob o rat ed, cor rob o rat ing.**

cor rob o ra tion (kə rob′ə rā′shən), additional proof; confirmation: *The police have an eyewitness's corroboration of the victim's statement.* *n.*

cor rob o ra tive (kə rob′ə rā′tiv), making more certain; corroborating; confirming. *adj.*

cor rode (kə rōd′), wear or eat away gradually: *Moist air corrodes iron. Acid caused the pipes to corrode.* *v.,* **cor rod ed, cor rod ing.**

cor ro sion (kə rō′zhən), 1 act or process of corroding. 2 a corroded condition. *n.*

cor ro sive (kə rō′siv), 1 eating away gradually; tending to corrode: *Most acids are corrosive.* 2 substance that corrodes. 1 *adj.,* 2 *n.* —**cor ro′sive ly,** *adv.* —**cor ro′sive ness,** *n.*

cor ru gate (kôr′ə gāt), bend or shape into wavy folds or ridges; wrinkle: *a carton made of corrugated cardboard.* *v.,* **cor ru gat ed, cor ru gat ing.**

cor ru ga tion (kôr′ə gā′shən), 1 a corrugating or a being corrugated. 2 one of a series of wavy folds or ridges; wrinkle. *n.*

hat, āge, fär; let, ēqual, tėrm; it, īce; hot, ōpen, ôrder; oil, out; cup, pùt, rüle; ch, child; ng, long; sh, she; th, thin; ᵺH, then; zh, measure;

ə represents *a* in about, *e* in taken, *i* in pencil, *o* in lemon, *u* in circus.

cor rupt (kə rupt′), 1 morally bad; evil; wicked: *Some people are so corrupt that they will lie against you in court.* 2 make evil or wicked: *Bad company may corrupt a good boy.* 3 influenced by bribes; dishonest: *a corrupt judge.* 4 influence by bribes: *That judge cannot be corrupted.* 5 changed for the worse by mistakes: *Constant copying of the manuscript resulted in a corrupt version of the original.* 6 change for the worse: *Careless scholars corrupted the original manuscript.* 7 make or become rotten or decayed. 8 OLD USE. rotten; decayed. 1,3,5,8 *adj.,* 2,4,6,7 *v.* —**cor rupt′er,** *n.* —**cor rupt′ly,** *adv.* —**cor rupt′ness,** *n.*

cor rupt i bil i ty (kə rup′tə bil′ə tē), corruptible quality; willingness to be corrupted. *n.*

cor rupt i ble (kə rup′tə bəl), that can be corrupted. *adj.*

cor rup tion (kə rup′shən), 1 a making or a being made evil or wicked. 2 evil conduct; wickedness. 3 a being influenced by bribes; dishonesty: *The police force must be kept free from corruption.* 4 a becoming less correct: *the corruption of a translated passage or text.* 5 rot; decay. *n.*

cor sage (kôr säzh′), bouquet to be worn on the waist or shoulder of a woman's dress. *n.*

cor sair (kôr′ser *or* kôr′sar), 1 pirate. 2 ship of a pirate. 3 privateer. *n.*

corse let (kôrs′lit), armor for the upper part of the body. *n.* Also, **corslet.**

cor set (kôr′sit), a woman's stiff, close-fitting undergarment, worn about the waist and hips to support or shape the body. *n.*

Cor si ca (kôr′sə kə), island in the Mediterranean, southeast of and belonging to France. *n.* —**Cor′si can,** *adj., n.*

cors let (kôrs′lit), corselet. *n.*

cor tege (kôr tezh′), 1 procession: *a funeral cortege.* 2 group of followers or attendants; retinue. *n.* [from French *cortège*]

cor tège (kôr tezh′), cortege. *n., pl.* **cor tèg es** (kôr tezh′iz).

Cor tés or **Cor tez** (kôr tez′), Her-

adj. adjective	*n.* noun
adv. adverb	*prep.* preposition
conj. conjunction	*pron.* pronoun
interj. interjection	*v.* verb
sing. singular	*pl.* plural

nando, 1485-1547, Spanish soldier who conquered Mexico. *n.*

cor tex (kôr′teks), 1 the layer of gray matter which covers most of the surface of the brain. 2 the outer layer of an internal organ: *the cortex of the kidney.* 3 the bark of a tree. *n., pl.* **cor ti ces** (kôr′tə sēz′).

cor ti cal (kôr′tə kəl), of or having to do with a cortex, especially of the brain or kidneys. *adj.*

cor ti sone (kôr′tə sōn), hormone obtained from the cortex of the adrenal glands or produced synthetically, used in the treatment of arthritis and other ailments. *n.*

co run dum (kə run′dəm), an extremely hard mineral. The dark-colored variety is used for polishing and grinding. Transparent varieties are sapphires and rubies. *n.*

cor vette or **cor vet** (kôr vet′), 1 a former warship with sails and only one tier of guns. 2 gunboat used against submarines and in convoy work. *n.*

co si ly (kō′zə lē), cozily. *adv.*

cosine

In a right triangle with hypotenuse BC, the cosine of angle ACB is $\frac{AC}{BC}$.

and the cosine of angle ABC is $\frac{AB}{BC}$.

co sine (kō′sīn), length of the side next to an acute angle of a right triangle divided by the length of the hypotenuse. *n.*

co si ness (kō′zē nis), coziness. *n.*

cos met ic (koz met′ik), 1 preparation for beautifying the skin, hair, nails, etc. Powder, rouge, lipstick, and face creams are cosmetics. 2 beautifying the skin, hair, nails, etc.: *a cosmetic cream.* 1 *n.,* 2 *adj.*

cos mic (koz′mik), 1 having to do with the whole universe: *Cosmic forces produce stars and meteors.* 2 vast: *a cosmic explosion. adj.*

cos mi cal ly (koz′mik lē), according to cosmic laws; on a vast or cosmic scale. *adv.*

cosmic dust, fine particles of matter in outer space.

cosmic rays, rays of very short wavelengths and very great penetrating power that come to the earth from beyond the earth's atmosphere.

cos mo naut (koz′mə nôt), a Soviet astronaut. *n.*

cos mo pol i tan (koz′mə pol′ə tən), 1 belonging to all parts of the world; not limited to any one country or its inhabitants; widely spread: *Music is a cosmopolitan art.* 2 free from national or local prejudices; feeling at home in all parts of the world: *Diplomats are usually cosmopolitan people.* 3 person who feels at home in all parts of the world. 1,2 *adj.,* 3 *n.*

cos mos (koz′məs), 1 the universe as an ordered whole; the opposite of chaos. 2 any complete, harmonious system. 3 a tall, tropical American plant with showy flowers of many colors, that blooms in the fall or late summer. It belongs to the same family as the aster. *n., pl.* **cos mos** or **cos mos es** for 2 and 3.

Cos sack (kos′ak), one of a people living in the southwestern Soviet Union, noted as horsemen. *n.*

cost (kôst), 1 price paid: *The cost of this watch was $10.* 2 be obtained at the price of: *This watch costs $10.* 3 loss or sacrifice: *The poor fox escaped from the trap at the cost of a leg.* 4 cause the loss or sacrifice of: *The school play had cost much time and effort.* 5 **costs,** *pl.* expenses of a lawsuit or case in court: *That man was found guilty and was ordered to pay a $1000 fine and $50 costs.* 1,3,5 *n.,* 2,4 *v.,* **cost, cost ing.**

at all costs or **at any cost,** regardless of expense; by all means; no matter what must be done: *Let's catch that bus at all costs; it's the last one today.*

Cos ta Ri ca (kos′tə rē′kə), country in Central America, northwest of Panama. *Capital:* San José. —**Cos′ta Ri′can.**

cos ter mon ger (kos′tər mung′gər), person who sells fruit, vegetables, fish, etc., in the street. *n.*

cost li ness (kôst′lē nis), great cost; expensiveness. *n.*

cost ly (kôst′lē), 1 of great value: *The queen had costly jewels.* 2 costing much: *He made a costly mistake and had to redo his work. adj.,* **cost li er, cost li est.**

cost of living, the average price paid for food, rent, clothing, transportation, and other necessities by a person, family, etc., within a given period.

cos tume (kos′tüm *or* kos′tyüm *for 1-3;* ko stüm′ *or* ko styüm′ *for 4*), 1 style of dress, outer clothing, etc.,

including the way the hair is worn, kind of jewelry worn, etc.: *The clown wore a funny costume. The kimono is part of the national costume of Japan.* 2 dress belonging to another time or place, worn on the stage, at masquerades, etc.: *The actors wore colonial costumes of breeches, long coats, and powdered wigs.* 3 a complete set of outer garments: *a street costume, a hunting costume.* 4 provide a costume for; dress: *One guest was costumed in Oriental style.* 1-3 *n.,* 4 *v.,* **cos tumed, cos tum ing.**

cos tum er (ko stü′mər *or* ko styü′mər), person who makes, sells, or rents costumes. *n.*

co sy (kō′zē), cozy. *adj.,* **co si er, co si est; n., pl.* **co sies.**

cot¹ (kot), a narrow bed. A cot is sometimes made of canvas stretched on a frame that folds together. *n.* [from Hindustani *khāt*]

cot² (kot), 1 cottage. 2 cote. *n.* [Old English *cot*]

cote (kōt), shelter or shed for small animals or birds. *n.*

co ter ie (kō′tər ē), set or circle of close acquaintances; group of people who often meet socially. *n.*

co til lion (kə til′yən), 1 a dance with complicated steps and much changing of partners, led by one couple. 2 any large, formal party for dancing. *n.*

Co to pax i (kō′tə pak′sē), volcano in the Andes Mountains in N Ecuador, the highest active volcano in the world. *n.*

cot tage (kot′ij), 1 a small house. 2 house at a summer resort. *n.*

cottage cheese, a soft, white cheese made from the curds of sour skim milk.

cot ter or **cot tar** (kot′ər), a Scottish peasant who works for a farmer and is allowed to use a small cottage and a plot of land. *n.*

cotter pin

cotter pin, a split pin inserted through a slot to hold small parts of machinery together. The ends are bent back to keep it in the slot.

cot ton (kot′n), 1 the soft, white fibers in a fluffy mass around the seeds of a tall plant, used in making fabrics, thread, etc. 2 the plant that produces these fibers. 3 thread or cloth made of cotton. 4 made of cotton: *She bought two cotton dresses.* 1-3 *n.,* 4 *adj.* —**cot′ton like′,** *adj.*

cotton cake, mass of cottonseed after the oil has been pressed out, used as feed for livestock.

cotton gin, machine for separating the fibers of cotton from the seeds; gin.

cot ton mouth (kot′n mouth′), water moccasin. *n.*

cot ton seed (kot′n sēd′), seed of cotton, used for making cottonseed oil, fertilizer, cattle food, etc. *n.*

cottonseed oil, oil pressed from cottonseed, used for cooking, for making soap, etc.

cot ton tail (kot′n tāl′), a common American wild rabbit with a fluffy, white tail. *n.*

cot ton wood (kot′n wùd′), 1 kind of American poplar tree with cottonlike tufts on the seeds. 2 its soft wood. *n.*

cot ton y (kot′n ē), 1 of cotton. 2 like cotton; soft; fluffy; downy. *adj.*

COTYLEDON COTYLEDON

cot y le don (kot′l ēd′n), the first leaf, or one of the first pair of leaves, growing from a seed; an embryo leaf in the seed of a plant. *n.*

couch (kouch), 1 piece of furniture to sit or lie on for rest or sleep. A bed or sofa is a couch. 2 any place for rest or sleep: *The deer sprang up from its grassy couch.* 3 lay or lie down on a couch. 4 put in words; express: *His thoughts were couched in beautiful poetry.* 5 lower into a level position ready to attack: *The knights couched their lances and prepared to charge.* 1,2 *n.,* pl. **couch es;** 3-5 *v.* —**couch′like′,** *adj.*

cou gar (kü′gər), puma. *n.*

cough (kôf), 1 force air from the lungs with sudden effort and noise. 2 act of coughing. 3 sound of coughing. 4 condition or symptom of repeated coughing: *Her cold had caused a bad cough.* 5 expel from the throat by coughing: *I coughed up the candy that was stuck in my throat.* 1,5 *v.,* 2-4 *n.*

could (kùd), 1 past tense of **can**[1]. *Years ago she could sing beautifully.* 2 might be able to: *Perhaps I could write a poem, but I doubt it.* *v.*

could n't (kùd′nt), could not.

couldst (kùdst), OLD USE. could. "Thou couldst" means "You could." *v.*

cou lee (kü′lē), 1 a deep ravine or gulch. A coulee is usually dry in summer. 2 a stream of lava. *n.*

cou lomb (kü′lom), measure of the quantity of electricity furnished by a current of one ampere in one second. *n.*

[from Charles A. de *Coulomb,* 1736-1806, a French physicist]

coun cil (koun′səl), 1 group of people called together to give advice and to discuss or settle questions. 2 group of persons elected by citizens to make laws for and manage a city or town. *n.*

coun cil lor (koun′sə lər), councilor. *n.*

coun cil man (koun′səl mən), member of the council of a city or town. *n.,* pl. **coun cil men.**

coun ci lor (koun′sə lər), member of a council. *n.* Also, **councillor.**

coun sel (koun′səl), 1 act of exchanging ideas; talking things over; consultation: *We benefited from our frequent counsel.* 2 advice: *A wise person gives good counsel.* 3 person or group that gives advice about the law; lawyer or group of lawyers: *Each side of a case in a court of law has its own counsel.* 4 give advice to: *She counsels sophomores to help them choose their courses.* 5 recommend: *The doctor counseled an operation.* 1-3 *n.,* 4,5 *v.*

take counsel, exchange ideas; talk things over; consult together: *I took counsel with my friends as to what I should do.*

coun se lor or **coun sel lor** (koun′sə lər), 1 person who gives advice; adviser. 2 lawyer. 3 instructor or leader in a summer camp. *n.*

count[1] (kount), 1 name numbers in order: *The child can count from one to ten.* 2 add up; find the number of: *I counted the books and found there were fifty.* 3 an adding up; a finding out how many: *The count showed that more than 5000 votes had been cast.* 4 the total number; amount: *The exact count was 5170 votes.* 5 include in counting; take into account: *There will be ten guests, not counting the family. Let's not count that practice game.* 6 be included in counting; be taken into account: *Your first race is only for practice; it won't count.* 7 have an influence; be of account or value: *Every vote counts in an election. Every penny counts.* 8 think of as; consider: *We count ourselves fortunate in having good health.* 9 depend; rely: *We count on your help.* 10 (in law) each charge in a formal accusation: *The thief was found guilty on all four counts.* 1,2,5-9 *v.,* 3,4,10 *n.* [from French of the 1300's *conter,* from Latin *computare* compute]

count in, INFORMAL. include: *Count me in on the list for the picnic.*

count off, divide into equal groups by counting: *For the spelling bee, you may count off from the left.*

count out, 1 fail to consider or include: *If you go skiing, count me out.* 2 declare (a fallen boxer) the loser when

hat, āge, fär; let, ēqual, tèrm; it, īce; hot, ōpen, ôrder; oil, out; cup, pùt, rüle; ch, child; ng, long; sh, she; th, thin; ŦH, then; zh, measure;

ə represents *a* in about, *e* in taken, *i* in pencil, *o* in lemon, *u* in circus.

he fails to rise after 10 seconds have been counted.

count[2] (kount), a European nobleman having a rank about the same as that of an English earl. *n.* [from French of the 1500's *conte,* from Latin *comitem* companion]

count down (kount′doun′), 1 period of time before the launching of a missile, rocket, etc. 2 the calling out of the passing minutes and seconds of this period as they pass. *n.*

coun te nance (koun′tə nəns), 1 expression of the face: *His angry countenance showed how he felt.* 2 face; features: *The king had a noble countenance.* 3 approve; support; encourage: *She will not countenance any dishonest schemes.* 4 approval; support; encouragement: *I gave countenance to the plan, but no active help.* 1,2,4 *n.,* 3 *v.,* **coun te nanced, coun te nanc ing.**

keep one's countenance, 1 be calm; not show feeling. 2 keep from smiling or laughing.

count er[1] (koun′tər), 1 a long table in a store, restaurant, bank, etc., on which money is counted out, and across which goods, food, or drinks are given to customers. 2 thing used for counting. Round, flat disks are often used as counters to keep score in card games. 3 an imitation coin. *n.* [from French of the 1300's *conteour,* from *conter* count[1]]

count er[2] (koun′tər), person or thing that counts. *n.* [count[1] + -er[1]]

coun ter[3] (koun′tər), 1 in the opposite direction; opposite; contrary: *He acted counter to his promise (adv.). Your plans are counter to ours (adj.).* 2 go or act counter to; oppose: *She countered my plan with one of her own.* 3 give a blow while receiving or blocking an opponent's blow: *The boxer countered with a right to the jaw.* 4 blow given while receiving or blocking an opponent's blow. 5 a stiff piece inside the back of a shoe around the heel. 1 *adv., adj.,* 2,3 *v.,* 4,5 *n.* [from French of the 1400's *countre,* from Latin *contra* against]

counter-

counter-, *prefix.* 1 in opposition to; against: *Counteract = act against.* 2 in return: *Counterattack = attack in return.* 3 corresponding: *Counterpart = corresponding part.* [from *counter³*]

coun ter act (koun′tər akt′), act against; neutralize the action or effect of: *A hot bath and a hot drink will sometimes counteract a chill. She tried to counteract her former rudeness by being especially polite now.* *v.*

coun ter at tack (koun′tər ə tak′), 1 attack made to counter another attack. 2 make an attack in return. 1 *n.,* 2 *v.*

coun ter bal ance (koun′tər bal′-əns *for 1,2;* koun′tər bal′əns *for 3*), 1 weight balancing another weight. 2 influence or power balancing or offsetting another: *The captain's good judgment was a counterbalance to the crew's panic in the gale.* 3 act as a counterbalance to; offset: *By studying hard, I was able to counterbalance my difficulty with arithmetic.* 1,2 *n.,* 3 *v.,* **coun ter bal anced,** **coun ter bal anc ing.**

coun ter check (koun′tər chek′), 1 check made upon a check; second check. 2 make a second check of; check again: *Before taking off the pilot counterchecked the course his copilot had charted.* 1 *n.,* 2 *v.*

coun ter claim (koun′tər klām′), an opposing claim; claim made by a person to offset a claim made against him: *A counterclaim for damages was filed by the other driver.* *n.*

counterclockwise

coun ter clock wise (koun′tər-klok′wīz′), in the direction opposite to that in which the hands of a clock go: *They danced counterclockwise around the maypole (adv.). The dance involved a counterclockwise movement around a central point (adj.).* *adv., adj.*

coun ter es pi o nage (koun′tər-es′pē ə nij *or* koun′tər es′pē ə näzh′), measures taken to prevent or confuse enemy espionage. *n.*

coun ter feit (koun′tər fit), 1 copy (money, handwriting, pictures, etc.) in order to deceive or defraud: *They were imprisoned for counterfeiting five-dollar bills.* 2 a copy made to deceive or defraud and passed as genuine: *This ten-dollar bill looks genuine, but it is a counterfeit.* 3 not genuine; sham: *a counterfeit coin.* 4 pretend: *She counterfeited interest to be polite.* 5 pretended; dissembled. 1,4 *v.,* 2 *n.,* 3,5 *adj.* —**coun′ter feit′er,** *n.*

coun ter in tel li gence (koun′tər-in tel′ə jəns), system or activity of counteracting the intelligence or spy activities of an enemy. *n.*

coun ter mand (koun′tər mand), withdraw or cancel (an order or command). *v.*

coun ter march (koun′tər märch′), 1 a march in the opposite direction; a march back. 2 to march in the opposite direction; march back. 1 *n., pl.* **coun ter march es;** 2 *v.*

coun ter of fen sive (koun′tər-ə fen′siv), an aggressive attack by a defending force against an attacking force. *n.*

coun ter pane (koun′tər pān′), an outer covering for a bed; bedspread. *n.*

coun ter part (koun′tər pärt′), 1 person or thing closely resembling another: *She is the counterpart of her twin sister.* 2 person or thing that complements or corresponds to another: *Night is the counterpart of day.* 3 copy; duplicate. *n.*

coun ter point (koun′tər point′), 1 melody added to another as an accompaniment. 2 art of adding melodies to a given melody according to fixed rules. *n.*

coun ter poise (koun′tər poiz′), 1 weight balancing another weight. 2 any equal and opposing power or force. 3 condition of being in balance; equilibrium. 4 act as a counterpoise to; offset. 1-3 *n.,* 4 *v.,* **coun ter poised,** **coun ter pois ing.**

coun ter rev o lu tion (koun′tər-rev′ə lü′shən), revolution against a government established by a previous revolution. *n.*

coun ter sign (koun′tər sīn′), 1 a secret signal; password; watchword: *The spy was caught when he could not give the countersign to the sentry.* 2 signature added to another signature to confirm it. 3 sign (something already signed by another) to confirm it: *The check was signed by the treasurer and countersigned by the president.* 1,2 *n.,* 3 *v.*

coun ter sink (koun′tər singk′), 1 enlarge the upper part of (a hole) to make room for the head of a screw or bolt. 2 sink the head of (a screw or bolt) into

such a hole so that it is even with or below the surface. *v.,* **coun ter sunk** (koun′tər sungk′), **coun ter sink ing.**

coun ter spy (koun′tər spī′), spy who works to uncover or oppose the activities of enemy spies. *n., pl.* **coun ter spies.**

coun ter weight (koun′tər wāt′), weight that balances another weight. *n.*

count ess (koun′tis), 1 wife or widow of a count or an earl. 2 lady whose rank is equal to that of a count or an earl. *n., pl.* **count ess es.**

count ing house (koun′ting hous′), building or office used for keeping accounts and doing business. *n., pl.* **count ing hous es** (koun′ting hou′-ziz).

counting number, any whole number except 0. The next counting number after 99 is 100.

count less (kount′lis), too many to count; very many; innumerable: *the countless sands of the seashore, the countless stars.* *adj.*

coun tri fied (kun′tri fīd), 1 looking or acting like a person from the country. 2 like the country; rural. *adj.*

coun try (kun′trē), 1 land, region, or district: *The country around the mining town was rough and hilly.* 2 all the land of a nation: *She came from France, a country across the sea.* 3 land where a person was born or where he is a citizen: *The United States is my country.* 4 people of a nation: *The whole country hated the dictator.* 5 land outside of cities and towns: *I like the farms and fields of the country better than the tall buildings and busy streets of the city.* 6 of the country; in the country; rural: *He likes hearty country meals and fresh country air.* 1-5 *n., pl.* **coun tries;** 6 *adj.*

coun try folk (kun′trē fōk′), people who live in the country. *n.pl.*

coun try man (kun′trē mən), 1 man of one's own country. 2 man who lives in the country. *n., pl.* **coun try-men.**

coun try side (kun′trē sīd′), 1 a rural area; country: *We saw many cows in the countryside.* 2 people of the countryside: *All the countryside is sure to be at the fair.* *n.*

coun try wom an (kun′trē wum′-ən), 1 woman of one's own country. 2 woman who lives in the country. *n., pl.* **coun try wom en.**

coun ty (koun′tē), 1 one of the districts into which a state, country, province, or other large political unit is divided for purposes of local government. The county officers collect taxes, hold court, keep county roads in repair, and maintain county schools. 2 people of a county: *The whole county voted* against the plan. 3 the officials of a county. *n., pl.* **coun ties.**

coup (kü), 1 a sudden, brilliant action; unexpected, clever move; master stroke. 2 coup d'état. *n., pl.* **coups** (küz).

coup d'é tat (kü′ dā tä′), a sudden, decisive act in politics, usually bringing about a change in government unlawfully or by force. *pl.* **coups d'é tat** (kü′ dā tä′). [from French *coup d'état* stroke of state]

coupe (küp), 1 a closed, two-door automobile, usually seating two to six people. 2 a four-wheeled, closed carriage with a seat for two people inside and a seat for the driver outside. *n., pl.* **coupes.**

cou pé (kü pā′), coupe. *n., pl.* **cou pés.**

cou ple (kup′əl), 1 two things of the same kind that go together; pair: *I bought a couple of tires for my bicycle.* 2 INFORMAL. a small number; a few: *Give me a couple of those apples— about four of them.* 3 man and woman who are married, engaged, or partners in a dance. 4 join together: *The brakeman coupled the freight cars.* 1-3 *n.,* 4 *v.,* **cou pled, cou pling.**

cou pler (kup′lər), 1 person or thing that couples. 2 device used to join two railroad cars; coupling. *n.*

cou plet (kup′lit), two successive lines of poetry, especially two that rhyme and have the same number of feet. EXAMPLE: "Whose woods these are I think I know,/His house is in the village though." *n.*

cou pling (kup′ling), 1 a joining together. 2 device for joining together parts of machinery. 3 coupler. *n.*

cou pon (kü′pon *or* kyü′pon), 1 part of a ticket, advertisement, package, etc., that gives the person who holds it certain rights: *If she saves the coupons that come with each box of soap, she can get a free camera.* 2 a printed statement of interest due on a bond, which can be cut from the bond and presented for payment. *n.*

cour age (kėr′ij), a meeting danger without fear; bravery; fearlessness: *The pioneer women faced the hardships of the westward trek with courage.* *n.*

cou ra geous (kə rā′jəs), full of courage; brave; fearless. *adj.* **—cou ra′geous ly,** *adv.* **—cou ra′geous ness,** *n.*

cour i er (kėr′ē ər *or* kūr′ē ər), 1 messenger sent in haste: *A courier was sent back to the fort for reenforcements.* 2 a secret agent who transfers information to and from other agents. *n.*

course (kôrs), 1 onward movement; forward progress; advance: *Our history book traces the course of human development from the cave to modern*

course (def. 2) of the above aircraft, approximately 210°

city living. 2 direction taken: *Our course was straight to the north.* 3 line of action; way of doing: *The only sensible course was to go home.* 4 way, path, track, or channel: *the winding course of the stream.* 5 number of like things arranged in some regular order: *a course of lectures.* 6 regular order: *In the course of nature spring always follows winter.* 7 series of studies in a school, college, or university. A student must complete a certain course in order to graduate. 8 one of the studies in such a series: *Each course in geography lasts one year.* 9 part of a meal served at one time: *Soup was the first course and dessert was the last course.* 10 area marked out for races or games: *a golf course, a race course.* 11 run: *The blood courses through the arteries.* 12 hunt with dogs. 13 row of brick or stones in a wall. 1-10,13 *n.,* 11,12 *v.,* **coursed, cours ing.**

in the course of, during; in the process of: *He mentioned you a few times in the course of our discussion.*

of course, 1 surely; certainly: *Of course you can go!* 2 naturally; as should be expected: *She gave me a gift, and, of course, I accepted it.*

cours er (kôr′sər), OLD USE. a swift horse. *n.*

court (kôrt), 1 space partly or wholly enclosed by walls or buildings: *The four apartment houses were built around a court of grass.* 2 a short street. 3 place marked off for a game: *a tennis court, a basketball court.* 4 place where a king, emperor, or other sovereign lives; royal palace. 5 establishment and followers of a king, emperor, or other sovereign: *The court of King Solomon was noted for its splendor.* 6 sovereign and his advisers as a ruling body or power: *"By order of the Court of St. James"* is by order of the British government. 7 assembly held by a king, emperor, or other sovereign: *The queen held court to hear from her advisers.* 8 place where justice is administered; law court: *The case will be heard in court next week.* 9 persons who are chosen to administer justice; judge or judges: *The court found her guilty.* 10 assembly of such persons to administer justice: *Court is now in session.* 11 seek the favor of; try to please: *The nobles courted the king to get power.* 12 pay loving attention to in order to marry; woo: *The young man*

courtyard

hat, āge, fär; let, ēqual, tėrm;
it, īce; hot, ōpen, ôrder;
oil, out; cup, pùt, rüle; ch, child;
ng, long; sh, she; th, thin;
ŦH, then; zh, measure;

ə represents *a* in about,
e in taken, *i* in pencil,
o in lemon, *u* in circus.

courted the girl by bringing her flowers every day. 13 try to get; seek: *court applause. It is foolish to court danger.* 1-10 *n.,* 11-13 *v.*

pay court to, pay attention to (a person) to get his favor; try to please: *pay court to a high official.*

cour te ous (kėr′tē əs), thoughtful of others; polite: *I shop at this store because the clerks are always courteous.* *adj.* **—cour′te ous ly,** *adv.* **—cour′te ous ness,** *n.*

cour te sy (kėr′tə sē), 1 polite behavior; thoughtfulness for others: *It is a sign of courtesy to give one's seat to an old person on a crowded bus.* 2 a courteous act or expression: *Thanks for all your courtesies.* *n., pl.* **cour te sies.**

court house (kôrt′hous′), 1 building in which courts of law are held. 2 building used for the government of a county. *n., pl.* **court hous es** (kôrt′hou′ziz).

cour ti er (kôr′tē ər), 1 person often present at the court of a king, emperor, etc.; court attendant. 2 person who tries to win the favor of another by flattering and pleasing him. *n.*

court li ness (kôrt′lē nis), a being courtly; politeness, elegance, or polish. *n.*

court ly (kôrt′lē), having manners fit for a king's court; polite, elegant, or polished: *The courtly gentleman was a favorite with the ladies.* *adj.,* **court li er, court li est.**

court-mar tial (kôrt′mär′shəl), 1 a military court for trying offenders against the laws of the armed forces. 2 trial by a military court. 3 try by a military court. 1,2 *n., pl.* **courts-mar tial;** 3 *v.*

court of law, place where justice is administered; law court.

court room (kôrt′rüm′ *or* kôrt′-rùm′), room where a court of law is held. *n.*

court ship (kôrt′ship), condition or time of courting in order to marry; wooing: *Their brief courtship was a very happy one.* *n.*

court yard (kôrt′yärd′), space en-

adj. adjective		*n.* noun	
adv. adverb		*prep.* preposition	
conj. conjunction		*pron.* pronoun	
interj. interjection		*v.* verb	
sing. singular		*pl.* plural	

closed by walls, in or near a large building. *n.*

cous in (kuz′n), 1 son or daughter of one's uncle or aunt. First cousins have the same grandparents; second cousins have the same great-grandparents; and so on for third and fourth cousins, etc. 2 a distant relative. 3 citizen of a related nation: *The British, Canadians, and Americans might be called cousins. n.*

cove (kōv), 1 a small, sheltered bay; inlet on the shore. 2 a sheltered place among hills or woods: *The bandits hid in a cove deep in the hills. n.*

cov e nant (kuv′ə nənt), 1 a solemn agreement between two or more persons or groups: *The rival nations signed a covenant to reduce their armaments.* 2 agree solemnly (to do certain things). 1 *n.,* 2 *v.*

Cov en try (kuv′ən trē), city in central England. *n.*

send to Coventry, refuse to associate with: *When the worker refused to join the strike, his fellow workers sent him to Coventry.*

cov er (kuv′ər), 1 put something over: *Pull the shade to cover the window.* 2 be over; occupy the surface of; spread over: *Snow covered the ground.* 3 anything that covers. Books have covers. A box, can, or jar usually has a cover. A blanket is a cover. 4 hide: *She tried to cover her mistake.* 5 protect; shelter: *Our insurance covers our belongings against loss by fire.* 6 protection; shelter: *We took cover in an old shed during the storm. The burglar escaped under cover of darkness.* 7 go over; travel: *The travelers covered 400 miles a day by car.* 8 take in; include: *The review covered everything we learned before Christmas.* 9 be enough for; provide for: *My allowance covers my lunch at school.* 10 (in sports) to protect on defense: *The shortstop covered second base on all throws from right field.* 11 report or photograph (events, meetings, etc.): *A reporter covered the fire for the newspaper.* 12 a place for one person at a table, set with a plate, knife, fork, spoon, napkin, etc. 13 an envelope or wrapper with stamp and any postal marking. 1,2,4,5,7-11 *v.,* 3,6,12,13 *n.*

cover up, 1 cover completely. 2 hide; conceal.

under cover, 1 hidden; secret: *He kept his activities under cover.* 2 secretly: *Spies work under cover.*

cov er age (kuv′ər ij), 1 risks covered by an insurance policy: *She has fire coverage on her belongings.* 2 scope or manner of presenting information by a reporter, newspaper, etc.: *The President's inauguration got broad coverage from all the radio and television stations. n.*

cov er all (kuv′ər ôl′). Often, **coveralls,** *pl.* a work garment that includes shirt and trousers in a single piece of clothing. *n.*

covered wagon, wagon having a canvas cover that can be taken off.

cov er ing (kuv′ər ing), thing that covers: *bed coverings. n.*

cov er let (kuv′ər lit), a covering, especially a covering for a bed. *n.*

cov ert (kuv′ərt *or* kō′vərt), 1 kept from sight; secret; hidden: *The children cast covert glances at the box of candy they were told not to touch.* 2 a hiding place; shelter. 3 thicket in which animals hide. 1 *adj.,* 2,3 *n.* —**cov′ert ly,** *adv.* —**cov′ert ness,** *n.*

cov et (kuv′it), desire eagerly (something that belongs to another): *Her friends coveted her new bat. v.*

cov et ous (kuv′ə təs), desiring things that belong to others. *adj.* —**cov′et ous ly,** *adv.* —**cov′et ous ness,** *n.*

cov ey (kuv′ē), 1 a small flock of partridges, quail, etc. 2 a small group: *a covey of girls. n., pl.* **cov eys.**

cow[1] (kou), 1 the full-grown female of domestic cattle that furnishes milk. 2 female of the buffalo, moose, etc. 3 female of various other large mammals: *an elephant cow. n.* [Old English *cū*]

cow[2] (kou), make afraid; frighten: *I was cowed by their threats and stayed out of their sight. v.* [from a Scandinavian word of the 1200's, such as Icelandic *kūga*]

cow ard (kou′ərd), person who lacks courage or is easily made afraid; person who runs from danger, trouble, etc. *n.*

cow ard ice (kou′ər dis), lack of courage; being easily made afraid: *The deserter was guilty of cowardice. n.*

cow ard li ness (kou′ərd lē nis), a being cowardly. *n.*

cow ard ly (kou′ərd lē), 1 lacking courage. 2 of a coward; suitable for a coward. 3 in a cowardly manner. 1,2 *adj.,* 3 *adv.*

cow bell (kou′bel′), bell hung around a cow's neck to indicate her whereabouts. *n.*

cow bird (kou′bèrd′), a small American blackbird that is often found with cattle. Most cowbirds lay their eggs in the nests of other birds. *n.*

cow boy (kou′boi′), man whose work is looking after cattle on a ranch. He rides horseback to do most of his work. *n.*

cow catch er (kou′kach′ər), a metal frame on the front of a locomotive, streetcar, etc., to clear the tracks of anything in the way. *n.*

cow er (kou′ər), crouch or draw back in fear or shame: *The dog cowered under the table after being scolded by its master. v.*

cow girl (kou′gèrl′), woman or girl who works on a ranch, at rodeos, etc. *n.*

cow hand (kou′hand′), person who works on a cattle ranch. *n.*

cow herd (kou′hèrd′), person whose work is looking after cattle at pasture. *n.*

cow hide (kou′hīd′), 1 the hide of a cow. 2 leather made from it. 3 a strong, heavy whip made of rawhide or braided leather. *n.*

cowl (def. 2)

cowl (koul), 1 a monk's cloak with a hood. 2 the hood itself. 3 the part of an automobile body that includes the windshield, the dashboard, and sometimes the hood. 4 cowling. *n.*

cow lick (kou′lik′), a small tuft of hair that will not lie flat. *n.*

cowl ing (kou′ling), a metal covering over the engine of an airplane; cowl. *n.*

co-work er (kō wèr′kər), person who works with another. *n.*

cow pox (kou′poks′), a contagious disease of cows. Vaccine for smallpox is obtained from cows that have cowpox. *n.*

cow punch er (kou′pun′chər), INFORMAL. cowboy. *n.*

cow rie *or* **cow ry** (kou′rē), the brightly colored, smooth shell of a tropical mollusk, used as money in some parts of Africa and Asia. *n., pl.* **cow ries.**

cow slip (kou′slip), 1 a wild plant with bright, yellow flowers that bloom in early spring. 2 marsh marigold. *n.*

cox comb (koks′kōm′), a vain, empty-headed man; conceited dandy. *n.*

cox swain (kok′sən *or* kok′swān′), person who steers a rowboat, racing boat, etc. *n.* Also, **cockswain.**

coy (koi), 1 shy or modest; bashful. 2 acting more shy than one really is.

adj. —**coy′ly**, *adv.* —**coy′ness**, *n.*

coy o te (kī ō′tē *or* kī′ōt), a small wolf living on the prairies of western North America. It is noted for loud howling at night. *n., pl.* **coy o tes** *or* **coy o te.**

coy pu (koi′pü), a large water rodent of South America; nutria. Its fur resembles beaver. *n., pl.* **coy pus** *or* **coy pu.**

coz en (kuz′n), deceive or trick; cheat; beguile. *v.* —**coz′en er,** *n.*

coz en age (kuz′n ij), practice of cozening; deception or trick; fraud. *n.*

co zi ly (kō′zə lē), in a cozy manner. *adv.* Also, **cosily.**

co zi ness (kō′zē nis), cozy condition or quality. *n.* Also, **cosiness.**

co zy (kō′zē), 1 warm and comfortable; snug: *The cat lay contented in a cozy corner near the fireplace.* 2 a padded cloth cover to keep a teapot warm. 1 *adj.,* **co zi er, co zi est;** 2 *n., pl.* **co zies.** Also, **cosy.**

C.P.A., Certified Public Accountant.

Cpl., corporal.

crab¹ (def. 1)—shell about 4 in. wide

crab¹ (krab), 1 a broad, flat crustacean that has four pairs of legs and one pair of claws. Many kinds of crabs are good to eat. 2 catch crabs for eating. 3 a cross, sour person. 4 INFORMAL. find fault; criticize: *Don't crab so much.* 1,3 *n.,* 2,4 *v.,* **crabbed, crab bing.** [Old English *crabba*] —**crab′like′,** *adj.*

crab² (krab), crab apple. *n.* [origin unknown]

crab apple, 1 a small, sour apple, used to make jelly. 2 tree on which it grows.

crab bed (krab′id), 1 hard to read or decipher because irregular: *Her handwriting is crabbed.* 2 crabby. *adj.*

crab by (krab′ē), INFORMAL. cross, peevish, or ill-natured; crabbed. *adj.,* **crab bi er, crab bi est.**

crab grass (krab′gras′), a coarse grass that spreads rapidly and spoils lawns. *n.*

crack (krak), 1 split or opening made by breaking without separating into parts: *There is a crack in this cup.* 2 break without separating into parts: *You have cracked the mirror. The glass cracked when I poured hot water into it.* 3 a narrow opening: *I can see between the cracks in the old floor boards.* 4 a sudden, sharp noise like that made by something breaking, by a whip, or by loud thunder. 5 make or cause to make a sudden, sharp noise: *The whip cracked. The stagecoach driver cracked the whip.* 6 break with a sudden, sharp noise: *The tree cracked and fell. We cracked the nuts.* 7 INFORMAL. a hard, sharp blow: *The falling branch gave me a crack on the head.* 8 INFORMAL. hit with a hard, sharp blow: *The falling branch cracked me on the head.* 9 make or become harsh, broken, or shrill: *His voice cracked with emotion.* 10 INFORMAL. give way; break down: *His mind cracked under the strain of working for three days without sleep.* 11 break into: *The burglar cracked the safe.* 12 INFORMAL. excellent; first-rate: *a crack train. Buffalo Bill was a crack shot.* 13 INFORMAL. a try; effort: *She took a crack at the job and succeeded.* 14 SLANG. a funny or clever remark; joke: *If you make another crack about my singing, you'll be sorry.* 15 SLANG. tell or say (something funny or clever): *She cracked a joke.* 16 figure out the meaning of (a code); decipher: *In wartime each enemy tries to crack the other's code.* 17 separate (petroleum, coal tar, etc.) into various substances: *This refinery cracks petroleum to make gasoline.* 1,3,4,7,13,14 *n.,* 2,5,6, 8-11,15-17 *v.,* 12 *adj.*

crack down, INFORMAL. take stern measures: *The police intend to crack down and haul cars away if drivers do not stop double-parking their cars.*

crack up, 1 crash; smash: *When the driver skidded off the road, he cracked up his car against a tree.* 2 suffer a mental or physical collapse: *She was in danger of cracking up under the strain of overworking.* 3 INFORMAL. praise: *That book is not what it is cracked up to be.*

cracked (krakt), 1 broken without separating into parts: *a cracked cup.* 2 having harsh notes; lacking evenness; broken: *The crying child spoke in a cracked voice.* 3 INFORMAL. crazy. *adj.*

crack er (krak′ər), 1 a thin, crisp biscuit. 2 firecracker. *n.*

crack er jack (krak′ər jak′), SLANG. 1 person or thing of superior ability or grade: *He is a crackerjack at dominoes.* 2 of superior ability or grade: *a crackerjack motorboat.* 1 *n.,* 2 *adj.*

crack ing (krak′ing), process of changing certain hydrocarbons in petroleum and other oils into lighter hydrocarbons by heat and pressure and a catalyst. Cracking is used in producing ordinary gasoline. *n.*

crack le (krak′əl), 1 make slight, sharp sounds: *A fire crackled in the fireplace. Twigs crackled beneath their feet.* 2 a slight, sharp sound, such as paper makes when crushed. 3 very small cracks on the surface of some kinds of china or glass. 4 craze (china

craftsman

hat, āge, fär; let, ēqual, tèrm; it, īce; hot, ōpen, ôrder; oil, out; cup, pùt, rüle; ch, child; ng, long; sh, she; th, thin; ŦH, then; zh, measure;

ə represents *a* in about, *e* in taken, *i* in pencil, *o* in lemon, *u* in circus.

or glass). 1,4 *v.,* **crack led, crack-ling;** 2,3 *n.*

crack ling (krak′ling), the crisp, browned skin of roasted pork. *n.*

crack pot (krak′pot′), SLANG. 1 a very eccentric or crazy person. 2 eccentric or impractical. 1 *n.,* 2 *adj.*

crack up (krak′up′), 1 a crash; smash-up: *That fast driver has been in more than one automobile crackup.* 2 INFORMAL. a mental or physical collapse; breakdown. *n.*

cra dle (krā′dl), 1 a small bed for a baby, usually mounted on rockers. 2 put or rock in a cradle; hold as in a cradle: *She cradled the baby in her arms.* 3 place where anything begins its growth: *The sea is thought to have been the cradle of life.* 4 shelter or train in early life: *The mother bear cradled her cub until he could take care of himself.* 5 frame to support a ship or other large object while it is being built, repaired, or lifted. 6 the part of the telephone that supports the receiver. 7 box on rockers to wash earth from gold or other metals. 8 wash (earth from gold or other metals) in a cradle. 9 frame fastened to a scythe for laying grain evenly as it is cut. 1,3,5-7,9 *n.,* 2,4,8 *v.,* **cra dled, cra dling.**

craft (kraft), 1 special skill: *The expert carpenter shaped and fitted the wood into a cabinet with great craft.* 2 trade or art requiring skilled work: *Carpentry is a craft.* 3 members of a trade requiring special skill: *She belongs to the craft of electricians.* 4 skill in deceiving others; slyness; trickiness: *By craft the gambler tricked them out of all their money.* 5 boats, ships, or aircraft: *Craft of all kinds come into New York every day.* 6 a boat, ship, or aircraft: *A strange craft sailed into the harbor.* *n.*

craft i ly (kraf′tə lē), in a crafty manner; cunningly. *adv.*

craft i ness (kraf′tē nis), skill in deceiving others; being crafty; cunning. *n.*

crafts man (krafts′mən), 1 a skilled workman: *The master shipbuilder was a real craftsman.* 2 artist. *n., pl.* **crafts-men.**

adj. adjective	n. noun
adv. adverb	prep. preposition
conj. conjunction	pron. pronoun
interj. interjection	v. verb
sing. singular	pl. plural

crafts man ship (krafts′mən ship), work or skill of a craftsman. *n.*

craft union, a labor union made up of persons in the same craft. Unions of carpenters, plumbers, or bricklayers are craft unions.

craft y (kraf′tē), skillful in deceiving others; sly; tricky: *crafty as a fox, a crafty schemer. adj.*, **craft i er, craft i est.**

crag (krag), a steep, rugged rock rising above others. *n.*

crag gi ness (krag′ē nis), quality of being craggy; ruggedness. *n.*

crag gy (krag′ē), 1 having many crags; steep and rugged: *The craggy hill was difficult to climb.* 2 rough; uneven: *The old fisherman had a craggy, weathered face. adj.*, **crag gi er, crag gi est.**

cram (kram), 1 force into; force down; stuff: *I crammed as many candy bars into my pockets as they would hold.* 2 fill too full; crowd: *The hall was crammed, with many people standing.* 3 eat too fast or too much: *She felt ill after she crammed down her lunch.* 4 INFORMAL. try to learn too much in a short time: *As he hasn't studied very hard during the year, he has to cram for his final tests. v.*, **crammed, cram ming.**

cramp (kramp), 1 shut into a small space: *The two of us were cramped in the telephone booth.* 2 a sudden, painful contracting or pulling together of muscles, often from chill or strain: *The swimmer was seized with a cramp and had to be helped from the pool.* 3 **cramps,** *pl.* very sharp pains in the abdomen. 4 cause to have a cramp: *The green apples she ate cramped her stomach.* 5 limit; restrict: *His work was cramped by the very short time he had left to spend on it.* 6 a metal bar bent at both ends. It is used for holding together blocks of stone, timbers, etc. 7 turn sharply to one side or the other; steer: *The driver had to cramp the front wheels to get out of the tight parking space.* 1,4,5,7 *v.*, 2,3,6 *n.*

cran ber ry (kran′ber′ē), 1 a firm, sour, dark-red berry, used for jelly and sauce. 2 the trailing vine that these berries grow on, found in marshes or bogs. *n., pl.* **cran ber ries.**

crane (krān), 1 machine with a long,

crane (def. 1)

swinging arm, for lifting and moving heavy weights. 2 a swinging metal arm in a fireplace, used to hold a kettle over the fire. 3 a large wading bird with long legs, neck, and bill. 4 stretch (the neck) as a crane does, in order to see better: *The little girl craned her neck to see the parade over the heads of the crowd.* 1-3 *n.*, 4 *v.*, **craned, cran ing.**

crane (def. 3)
about 4 ft. tall

cra ni al (krā′nē əl), of or having to do with the skull: *cranial nerves. adj.*

cra ni um (krā′nē əm), 1 the skull of a vertebrate. 2 the part of the skull that encloses the brain. *n., pl.* **cra ni ums, cra ni a** (krā′nē ə).

crank (krangk), 1 part or handle of a machine connected at right angles to a shaft to set it in motion: *I turned the crank of the sharpener to sharpen my pencil.* 2 work or start by means of a crank: *The engines of automobiles do not have to be cranked by hand any more.* 3 INFORMAL. person who has queer ideas or habits; odd person. 4 INFORMAL. a cross or ill-tempered person. 1,3,4 *n.*, 2 *v.*

crank case (krangk′kās′), a heavy, metal case forming the bottom of an internal-combustion engine. It contains lubricating oil and encloses the crank-shaft. *n.*

crank i ly (krang′kə lē), in a cranky manner. *adv.*

crank i ness (krang′kē nis), quality or condition of being cranky. *n.*

crank shaft (krangk′shaft′), shaft turning or turned by a crank. The crank-shaft of an automobile engine is connected to the pistons by piston rods. *n.*

crank y (krang′kē), cross, irritable, or ill-natured. *adj.*, **crank i er, crank i est.**

cran ny (kran′ē), a small, narrow opening; crack; crevice; chink: *I looked in all the nooks and crannies of our house for the misplaced book. n., pl.* **cran nies.**

crape (krāp), 1 crepe (def. 1). 2 piece of black crepe used as a sign of mourning. *n.*

crap pie (krap′ē), a small freshwater fish of North America, used for food. *n.*

crash (krash), 1 a sudden, loud noise like many dishes falling and breaking, or like sudden, loud band music: *The lightning was followed by a crash of thunder.* 2 make a sudden, loud noise: *The cymbals crashed.* 3 fall, hit, or break with force and a loud noise: *The dishes crashed to the floor.* 4 a falling, hitting, or breaking with force and a loud noise: *the crash of dishes on the floor.* 5 the violent striking of one thing against another; collision: *There was a crash of two cars at the corner.* 6 strike violently and shatter: *The baseball crashed through the window.* 7 fall to the earth in such a way as to be damaged or wrecked: *The airplane went out of control and crashed.* 8 such a fall or landing: *The skillful pilot brought down the damaged plane without a crash.* 9 sudden ruin; severe failure in business: *They lost their money in the stock market crash.* 10 INFORMAL. go to (a party or dance) without being invited. 1,4,5,8,9 *n.*, 2,3,6,7,10 *v.*

crash-land (krash′land′), land in an airplane so that a crash results; make an emergency landing. *v.*

crass (kras), gross or stupid: *crass ignorance, a crass person. adj.* —**crass′ly,** *adv.* —**crass′ness,** *n.*

crate (krāt), 1 a large frame or box made of strips of wood. Crates are used to pack furniture, glass, china, fruit, or household goods for shipping or storage. 2 pack in a crate: *crate a mirror for moving.* 1 *n.*, 2 *v.*, **crat ed, crat ing.**

CRATER

LAVA

crater (def. 1)
of an active
volcano

crater (def. 3)
cross sections
of three kinds

cra ter (krā′tər), 1 a bowl-shaped depression around the opening of a volcano. 2 hole in the ground shaped like this: *The meteor crashed to earth, forming a huge crater.* 3 a round, ringlike elevation on the surface of the moon, resembling the crater of a volcano. *n.*

cra vat (krə vat′), necktie, especially a wide one. *n.*

200

crave (krāv), 1 long for greatly; desire strongly: *The thirsty hiker craved water.* 2 ask earnestly for; beg: *He craved a favor of the king.* *v.,* **craved, crav ing.**

cra ven (krā′vən), 1 cowardly. 2 coward. 1 *adj.,* 2 *n.* —**cra′ven ly,** *adv.* —**cra′ven ness,** *n.*

crav ing (krā′ving), a strong desire; great longing; yearning: *a craving for alcohol. n.*

craw (krô), 1 crop of a bird or insect. 2 stomach of any animal. *n.*

craw fish (krô′fish′), crayfish. *n., pl.* **craw fish es** or **craw fish.**

crawl (krôl), 1 move slowly by pulling the body along the ground: *Worms and snakes crawl.* 2 creep on hands and knees: *We crawled through a hole in the fence.* 3 move slowly: *The heavy traffic crawled through the narrow tunnel.* 4 a crawling; slow movement: *The crawl of traffic annoyed the impatient driver.* 5 swarm with crawling things: *The ground under the garbage can was crawling with ants.* 6 feel creepy: *My flesh crawled when I saw a big snake.* 7 a fast way of swimming by overarm strokes and rapid kicking of the feet. 8 swim this way. 1-3,5,6,8 *v.,* 4,7 *n.*

crawler tractor, tractor that can travel over very rough ground on its two endless tracks.

crayfish (def. 1)—3 to 6 in. long

cray fish (krā′fish′), 1 any of numerous freshwater crustaceans looking much like a small lobster. 2 a similar but larger saltwater crustacean. *n., pl.* **cray fish es** or **cray fish.** Also, **crawfish.**

cray on (krā′on *or* krā′ən), 1 stick or pencil of chalk, charcoal, or a waxlike, colored substance, used for drawing or writing. 2 draw with a crayon or crayons. 3 drawing made with a crayon or crayons. 1,3 *n.,* 2 *v.*

craze (krāz), 1 a short-lived, eager interest in doing some one thing; fad: *The craze for flying kites was soon replaced by another for roller skating.* 2 make or become crazy: *The broken leg nearly crazed the horse with pain.* 3 make very small cracks on the surface of (a dish, vase, etc.); crackle. 1 *n.,* 2,3 *v.,* **crazed, craz ing.**

cra zi ly (krā′zə lē), in a crazy manner: *The driver zigzagged crazily through traffic. adv.*

cra zi ness (krā′zē nis), quality or condition of being crazy. *n.*

cra zy (krā′zē), 1 having a diseased or injured mind; mad; insane. A person who is crazy is not responsible for his actions and is often kept in an institution for the mentally ill. 2 greatly distressed or shaken by strong emotion: *The parents of the kidnaped child were nearly crazy with worry.* 3 unwise or senseless; foolish: *It was a crazy idea to jump out of such a high tree.* 4 IN-FORMAL. very eager or enthusiastic: *She is so crazy about cats that she brings home every stray she finds.* 5 not strong or sound; shaky: *That crazy light blinks on and off whenever anyone jiggles the table. adj.,* **cra zi er, cra zi est.**

like crazy, SLANG. like mad.

crazy quilt, quilt made of pieces of cloth of various shapes, colors, and sizes, sewed together with no definite pattern.

creak (krēk), 1 squeak loudly: *The hinges on the door creaked because they needed oiling.* 2 a creaking noise: *The creak of the stairs in the old house was spooky.* 1 *v.,* 2 *n.*

creak i ly (krē′kə lē), in a creaky manner. *adv.*

creak y (krē′kē), likely to creak; creaking: *a creaky floor. adj.,* **creak i er, creak i est.**

cream (krēm), 1 the oily, yellowish part of milk. Cream rises to the top when milk that is not homogenized is allowed to stand. Butter is made from cream. 2 take the cream from. 3 form a thick layer like cream on the top. 4 a fancy sweet dessert or candy made of cream: *chocolate creams.* 5 cook with cream, milk, or a sauce made of cream or milk with butter and flour. 6 make into a smooth mixture like cream: *I creamed the butter and sugar together for a cake.* 7 an oily preparation put on the skin to make it smooth and soft. 8 a yellowish white. 9 yellowish-white: *cream lace.* 10 the best or choicest part of anything: *the cream of the crop. The cream of a class is made up of the best students.* 1,4,7,8,10 *n.,* 2,3,5,6 *v.,* 9 *adj.*

cream cheese, a soft, white cheese made from cream, or milk and cream.

cream er (krē′mər), a small pitcher for holding cream. *n.*

cream er y (krē′mər ē), 1 place where butter and cheese are made. 2 place where cream, milk, and butter are bought and sold. *n., pl.* **cream er ies.**

cream i ness (krē′mē nis), creamy condition or quality. *n.*

cream of tartar, a very sour white powder used in cooking and in medicine.

cream y (krē′mē), 1 like cream;

hat, āge, fär; let, ēqual, tèrm; it, īce; hot, ōpen, ôrder; oil, out; cup, pùt, rüle; ch, child; ng, long; sh, she; th, thin; ᴛʜ, then; zh, measure;

ə represents *a* in about, *e* in taken, *i* in pencil, *o* in lemon, *u* in circus.

smooth and soft. 2 having much cream in it: *pie with a rich, creamy filling. adj.,* **cream i er, cream i est.**

crease (krēs), 1 line or mark made by folding or pressing cloth, paper, etc.; ridge; fold: *She likes a sharp crease in her slacks.* 2 a wrinkle: *The creases on his face showed that he was very old.* 3 make a crease or creases in: *Mother creased the pleats in her skirt with an iron.* 4 become creased: *Some cloth is too thick to crease well.* 1,2 *n.,* 3,4 *v.,* **creased, creas ing.**

cre ate (krē āt′), 1 make a thing which has not been made before; cause to be; bring into being; make: *She created a garden in the desert. Composers create music.* 2 be the cause of; cause: *The noise created a disturbance.* 3 make by giving a new character, function, or status to: *The queen created the man a knight. v.,* **cre at ed, cre at ing.**

cre a tion (krē ā′shən), 1 a creating; act of making a thing which has not been made before: *The gasoline motor led to the creation of the modern automobile.* 2 all things created; the world and everything in it; the universe: *Let all creation praise the Lord.* 3 thing produced by intelligence or skill, usually an important or original one: *Shakespeare's plays were great creations of the imagination.* 4 **the Creation,** the creating of the universe by God: *The Bible says the Creation took six days. n.*

cre a tive (krē ā′tiv), having the power to create; inventive; productive: *Sculptors are creative artists. adj.* —**cre a′tive ly,** *adv.*

cre a tor (krē ā′tər), 1 person who creates: *Leonardo da Vinci was the creator of many ideas for inventions.* 2 **the Creator,** God. *n.*

cre a ture (krē′chər), 1 any living person or animal: *Please let us keep the lost dog; the poor creature is starving.* 2 anything created: *Ghosts are creatures of the imagination.* 3 person who is strongly influenced or controlled by another person or thing. *n.*

crèche (kresh), model of the Christ child in the manger, with attending

adj. adjective   *n.* noun
adv. adverb   *prep.* preposition
conj. conjunction   *pron.* pronoun
interj. interjection   *v.* verb

sing. singular   *pl.* plural

figures, often displayed at Christmas. *n., pl.* **crèch es** (kresh′iz). [from French *crèche* manger, crib]

cre dence (krēd′ns), belief: *She seldom gives credence to gossip about her neighbors. n.*

cre den tials (kri den′shəlz), letters of introduction; references: *The new ambassador from England presented his credentials to the President. n.pl.*

cred i bil i ty (kred′ə bil′ə tē), quality of being believable. *n.*

cred i ble (kred′ə bəl), worthy of belief; believable: *Her excuse for being absent was hardly credible. adj.*

cred i bly (kred′ə blē), in a credible manner; so as to be believed. *adv.*

cred it (kred′it), 1 belief in the truth of something; faith; trust: *I know he is sure of his facts and put great credit in what he says.* 2 believe in the truth of something; have faith in; trust: *I can credit your story because I had a similar experience.* 3 a trust in a person's ability and intention to pay: *This store will extend credit to you by opening a charge account in your name.* 4 amount of money in a person's favor in an account: *When I deposit this check, I will have a credit of fifty dollars in my savings account.* 5 add to one's credit in a bank account, business record, etc.: *The bank credited fifty dollars to my savings account.* 6 delayed payment; time allowed for delayed payment: *The store allowed us six months' credit on our purchase.* 7 reputation in money matters: *If you pay your bills on time, your credit will be good.* 8 good reputation: *The mayor is a man of credit in the community.* 9 honor; praise: *The person who does the work should get the credit.* 10 person or thing that brings honor or praise: *Benjamin Franklin's great scientific achievements were a credit to his young country.* 11 entry on a student's record showing that he has passed a course of study: *You must pass the examination to get credit for the course.* 12 unit of work entered in this way: *She needs three credits to graduate.* 1,3,4,6-12 *n.*, 2,5 *v.*

credit with, attribute to: *I credit you with good sense for not panicking during the fire.*

do credit to, bring honor or praise to:

The winning team did credit to the school.

on credit, on a promise to pay later: *buy a car on credit.*

cred it a ble (kred′ə tə bəl), bringing credit or honor: *She has a creditable record as a senator. adj.*

cred it a bly (kred′ə tə blē), in a creditable manner; with credit to oneself. *adv.*

cred i tor (kred′ə tər), person to whom money or goods are due; one to whom a debt is owed. *n.*

cre do (krē′dō *or* krā′dō), creed. *n., pl.* **cre dos.** [from Latin *credo* I believe]

cre du li ty (krə dü′lə tē *or* krə dyü′lə tē), a too great readiness to believe. *n.*

cred u lous (krej′ə ləs), too ready to believe; easily deceived: *She was so credulous that the other children could easily fool her. adj.* —**cred′u lous ly,** *adv.*

Cree (krē), member of a tribe of American Indians living in Montana and in central and southern Canada. *n., pl.* **Cree** or **Crees.**

creed (krēd), 1 a brief statement of the essential points of religious belief as approved by some church. 2 any statement of faith, belief, or cherished opinions: *"Honesty is the best policy" was his creed in all his business dealings. n.*

creek (krēk *or* krik), 1 a small stream. 2 a narrow bay, running inland for some distance. *n.*

Creek (krēk), member of a group of American Indian tribes formerly living in Alabama and Georgia, and now living in Oklahoma. *n., pl.* **Creek** or **Creeks.**

creel (krēl), 1 basket for holding fish that have been caught. 2 a basketlike trap to catch fish or lobsters. *n.*

creep (krēp), 1 move slowly with the body close to the ground or floor; crawl: *The cat was creeping toward the mouse. A baby creeps on its hands and knees before it begins to walk.* 2 move slowly or little by little: *The traffic is creeping over the narrow bridge. The fog crept in while we were asleep.* 3 move in a timid or stealthy way: *They didn't see me creeping up on them. The dog crept into the room.* 4 grow along the ground or over a wall by means of clinging stems: *Ivy had crept up the wall of the old house.* 5 feel as if things were creeping over the skin: *It made my flesh creep to hear the wolves howl.* 6 a creeping; slow movement. **7 the creeps,** INFORMAL. a feeling of horror, as if things were creeping over one's skin: *Movies about werewolves give me the creeps.* 1-5 *v.*, **crept, creep ing;** 6,7 *n.*

creep er (krē′pər), 1 person or thing that creeps. 2 any plant that grows

along a surface, sending out rootlets from the stem, such as the Virginia creeper and ivy. 3 a small bird that creeps around on trees and bushes looking for food. *n.*

creep i ly (krē′pə lē), in a creepy manner. *adv.*

creep i ness (krē′pē nis), creepy quality or condition. *n.*

creep y (krē′pē), 1 having a feeling of horror, as if things were creeping over one's skin; frightened: *The ghost stories made the children creepy.* 2 causing such a feeling: *The wind howling through the old house was creepy. adj.,* **creep i er, creep i est.**

cre mate (krē′māt), burn (a dead body) to ashes instead of burying it. *v.,* **cre mat ed, cre mat ing.**

cre ma tion (kri mā′shən), the burning of a dead body to ashes instead of burying it. *n.*

cre ma to ry (krē′mə tôr′ē), 1 furnace for cremating. 2 building having such a furnace. *n., pl.* **cre ma to ries.**

Cre ole or **cre ole** (krē′ōl), 1 descendant of the early French or Spanish settlers in Louisiana. 2 the French language as spoken in Louisiana. 3 a French or Spanish person born in Latin America or the West Indies. 4 person who is part Negro and part Creole. 5 of or having to do with the Creoles: *Creole customs, Creole cooking.* 6 cooked in sauce made of stewed tomatoes, peppers, etc. 1-4 *n.*, 5,6 *adj.*

cre o sote (krē′ə sōt), 1 an oily liquid with a penetrating odor, obtained by distilling wood tar. It is used to preserve wood and in cough medicine. 2 a similar substance obtained from coal tar. *n.*

crepe or **crêpe** (krāp), 1 a thin, light cloth with a finely crinkled surface. 2 crepe paper. *n.* Also, **crape** for 1. [from French *crêpe,* from Latin *crispa* curled]

crepe paper, a thin, crinkled paper that looks like crepe, used for making decorations.

crepe rubber, a crude rubber with a crinkled surface, used for the soles of shoes.

crept (krept), past tense and past participle of **creep.** *We crept up on them from behind. v.*

cre scen do (krə shen′dō), 1 (in music) with a gradual increase in force or loudness: *a crescendo passage (adj.). Lullabies are not sung crescendo (adv.).* 2 a gradual increase in force or loudness, especially in music. 1 *adj., adv.,* 2 *n., pl.* **cre scen dos.**

cres cent (kres′nt), 1 shape of the moon in its first or last quarter. 2 anything that curves in a similar way. A curved street or row of houses is

WAXING MOON   WANING MOON

crescent (def. 1)

sometimes called a crescent. 3 shaped like the moon in its first or last quarter: *a crescent pin.* 4 growing; increasing: *the crescent darkness.* 1,2 *n.*, 3,4 *adj.* —**cres′cent like′**, *adj.*

cress (kres), any of various plants whose leaves have a peppery taste and are used as a garnish or in salad. *n., pl.* **cress es.**

cres set (kres′it), a metal container for burning oil, wood, etc., to give light. Cressets are mounted on poles or hung from above. *n.*

crest (krest), 1 tuft or comb on the head of a bird or other animal. 2 decoration of plumes or feathers worn on the top of a helmet. 3 decoration at the top of a coat of arms. A family crest is sometimes put on silverware, dishes, or letter paper. 4 the top part; peak; summit: *the crest of a wave, the crest of the hill.* *n.*

crest ed (kres′tid), having a crest: *a crested bird, a crested shield. adj.*

crest fall en (krest′fô′lən), dejected; discouraged: *Several students went home after school crestfallen because they had failed the examination. adj.*

Cret an (krēt′n), 1 of or having to do with Crete or its inhabitants. 2 person born or living in Crete. 1 *adj.*, 2 *n.*

Crete (krēt), Greek island in the Mediterranean, southeast of Greece. *n.*

cre tin (krēt′n), person in whom a deficiency in the thyroid gland has caused severe mental and physical retardation. The deficiency may be inborn or it may develop in infancy. *n.*

cre tonne (kri ton′ *or* krē′ton), a strong cotton, linen, or rayon cloth with designs printed in colors on one or both sides. Cretonne is used for curtains and furniture covers. *n.*

cre vasse (krə vas′), 1 a deep crack or split in the ice of a glacier, or in the ground after an earthquake. 2 a break in the levee of a river, dike, or dam. *n.*

crev ice (krev′is), a narrow split or crack; fissure: *Tiny ferns grew in crevices in the stone wall. n.*

crew[1] (krü), 1 the common sailors of a ship's company. 2 the group of persons manning an aircraft. 3 any group of people working or acting together: *a crew of loggers, a maintenance crew.* A train crew runs a railroad train. 4 a band or company; gang: *The boys on that street are a rough crew.* 5 the mem-

bers of a rowing team. *n.* [from French of the 1400's *creüe* increase, recruit, from *creistre* grow, from Latin *crescere*]

crew[2] (krü), crowed; a past tense of **crow**[1]. *The cock crew. v.*

crew cut, kind of very short haircut for men and boys.

crib (krib), 1 a small bed with high barred sides to keep a baby from falling out. 2 rack or manger for horses and cows to eat from. 3 building or box for storing grain, salt, etc.: *Rats damaged much of the corn in the crib.* 4 framework of logs or timbers used in building. The wooden lining inside a mine shaft is a crib. 5 INFORMAL. use (another's words or ideas) as one's own: *She cribbed from the encyclopedia to write her report.* 6 INFORMAL. notes or helps that are unfair to use in doing schoolwork. 7 INFORMAL. use notes or helps unfairly in doing schoolwork. 1-4,6 *n.*, 5,7 *v.*, **cribbed, crib bing.**

crest (def. 3)

crib bage (krib′ij) a card game for two, three, or four people. The players keep score on a narrow board into which movable pegs fit. *n.*

crick (krik), a muscular cramp; painful stiffness of muscles: *I got a crick in the neck from sleeping in the chair. n.*

crick et[1] (krik′it), a black insect related to the grasshopper. Male crickets make a chirping noise by rubbing their front wings together. *n.* [from French of the 1300's *criquet*, from *criquer* to creak]

crick et[2] (krik′it), 1 an outdoor game played by two teams of eleven players each, with a ball, bats, and wickets. Cricket is very popular in England. 2 INFORMAL. fair play; good sportsmanship: *It's not cricket to push ahead of others in line. n.* [from French of the 1500's *criquet* goal post, stick]

cried (krīd), past tense and past participle of **cry.** *He cried when he fell down. The baby has cried all day. v.*

cri er (krī′ər), 1 official who shouts out public announcements. 2 person who cries or shouts. *n.*

cries (krīz), 1 plural of **cry.** 2 a present tense of **cry.** *The baby cries when she is hungry.* 1 *n.*, 2 *v.*

crime (krīm), 1 a harmful or grave offense against the law. Theft, kidnaping, murder, and arson are crimes. 2 activity of criminals; violation of law:

Crime is increasing in the cities. 3 an evil or wrong act: *It is a crime to let people live without food and clothing and do nothing to help them. n.*

Cri me a (krī mē′ə), peninsula in the SW part of the Soviet Union in Europe, on the N coast of the Black Sea. See **Caucasia** for map. *n.* —**Cri me′an,** *adj., n.*

crim i nal (krim′ə nəl), 1 person who has committed a crime: *The criminal was sentenced to prison for theft.* 2 guilty of wrongdoing: *a criminal person.* 3 of or having to do with crime or its punishment: *A criminal court hears criminal cases.* 4 like crime; wrong: *It is criminal to let a dog out in this blizzard.* 1 *n.*, 2-4 *adj.* —**crim′i nal ly,** *adv.*

crimp (krimp), 1 press into small, regular, narrow folds; make wavy: *The children crimped tissue paper to make paper flowers.* 2 something crimped; fold or wave. 3 act of crimping. 1 *v.*, 2,3 *n.*

cricket[1]—about 1 in. long

crimp y (krim′pē), having small, narrow folds; wavy. *adj.*, **crimp i er, crimp i est.**

crim son (krim′zən), 1 a deep red. 2 deep-red. 3 turn deep red: *His face crimsoned with shame.* 1 *n.*, 2 *adj.*, 3 *v.*

cringe (krinj), 1 shrink from danger or pain; crouch in fear: *I cringed when the nurse gave me a shot.* 2 try to get favor by slavish attention or behavior: *The courtiers cringed before the king.* 3 act of cringing. 1,2 *v.*, **cringed, cring ing;** 3 *n.*

crin kle (kring′kəl), 1 wrinkle or ripple: *Crepe paper is crinkled.* 2 rustle: *Paper crinkles when it is crushed.* 3 a wrinkle or ripple: *There is a crinkle in the tablecloth.* 4 a rustle. 1,2 *v.*, **crinkled, crin kling;** 3,4 *n.*

adj. adjective	*n.* noun
adv. adverb	*prep.* preposition
conj. conjunction	*pron.* pronoun
interj. interjection	*v.* verb
sing. singular	*pl.* plural

crin kly (kring′klē), full of crinkles. *adj.*, **crin kli er, crin kli est.**

crin o line (krin′l ən), 1 a stiff cloth used as a lining to hold a skirt out, make a coat collar stand up, etc. 2 petticoat of crinoline to hold a skirt out. 3 a hoop skirt. *n.*

crip ple (krip′əl), 1 person or animal that cannot use his legs, arms, or body properly because of injury or lack; lame person or animal: *Long John Silver was a cripple who limped on a wooden leg.* 2 make a cripple of; make lame. 3 damage; disable; weaken: *The ship was crippled by the storm.* 1 *n.*, 2,3 *v.*, **crip pled, crip pling.**

cri sis (krī′sis), 1 an important or deciding event; point at which a change must come, either for the better or the worse: *The Battle of Waterloo was a crisis in Napoleon's career.* 2 time of difficulty, lack of security, and of anxious waiting: *The United States faced a crisis after the Japanese attack on Pearl Harbor.* 3 the turning point in a disease, toward life or death: *After his fever broke the doctor said he had passed the crisis and would recover.* *n.*, *pl.* **cri ses** (krī′sēz′).

crisp (krisp), 1 hard and thin; breaking easily with a snap: *Dry toast and fresh celery are crisp.* 2 make or become crisp: *Crisp the lettuce in cold water.* 3 sharp and clear; bracing: *The fresh air was cool and crisp.* 4 short and decisive; clear-cut: *a crisp manner.* "*Wait; I'll return,*" *was her crisp command.* 5 curly and wiry: *crisp hair.* 1,3-5 *adj.*, 2 *v.* —**crisp′ly**, *adv.* —**crisp′ness**, *n.*

crisp y (kris′pē), crisp. *adj.*, **crisp i er, crisp i est.**

criss cross (kris′krôs′), 1 mark or cover with crossed lines: *Little cracks crisscrossed the wall.* 2 come and go across: *Buses and cars crisscross the city.* 3 made or marked with crossed lines; crossed; crossing: *Plaids have a crisscross pattern.* 4 a mark or pattern of crossed lines: *The messy paper was a crisscross of lines and scribbles.* 1,2 *v.*, 3 *adj.*, 4 *n.*, *pl.* **criss cross es.**

cri ter i a (krī tir′ē ə), a plural of **criterion**. *n.*

cri ter i on (krī tir′ē ən), rule or standard for making a judgment; test: *Wealth is only one criterion of a person's worth. n.*, *pl.* **cri ter i a** or **cri ter i ons.**

crit ic (krit′ik), 1 person who makes judgments of the merits and faults of books, music, pictures, plays, acting, etc.: *We went to see the movie because we read that the critics liked it.* 2 person who disapproves or finds fault; fault-finder. *n.*

crit i cal (krit′ə kəl), 1 inclined to find fault or disapprove: *a critical disposition.* 2 of or having to do with a critic: *a critical judgment, critical essays.* 3 of a crisis: *the critical moment.* 4 important at a time of danger or difficulty: *His delay in getting a doctor was critical. adj.* —**crit′i cal ly**, *adv.*

crit i cism (krit′ə siz′əm), 1 unfavorable remarks or judgments; finding fault: *I cannot let her rudeness toward my guests pass without criticism.* 2 the making of judgments; analysis of merits and faults: *literary criticism, drama criticism.* 3 a critical comment, essay, review, etc.: *The editor wrote a criticism of the author's new book. n.*

crit i cize (krit′ə sīz), 1 find fault with; reprove; blame: *Do not criticize him until you know all the circumstances.* 2 judge or speak as a critic: *The editor criticized the author's new novel, comparing it with her last one. v.*, **crit i cized, crit i ciz ing.**

cri tique (kri tēk′), a critical essay or review: *Some magazines have critiques of new books. n.*

crit ter (krit′ər), DIALECT. creature. *n.*

croak (krōk), 1 the deep, hoarse sound made by a frog, crow, or raven. 2 make this sound. 3 utter in a deep, hoarse voice: *He croaked a reply.* 4 be dissatisfied; grumble. 1 *n.*, 2-4 *v.*

Cro at (krō′at), person born or living in Croatia. *n.*

Cro a tia (krō ā′shə), district in NW Yugoslavia. *n.* —**Cro a′tian**, *adj.*, *n.*

crochet (def. 1)

cro chet (krō shā′), 1 knit (sweaters, lace, etc.) with a single needle having a hook at one end. 2 knitting done in this way. 1 *v.*, **cro cheted** (krō shād′), **cro chet ing** (krō shā′ing); 2 *n.*

crock (krok), pot or jar made of baked clay. *n.*

crock er y (krok′ər ē), earthenware. *n.*

Crock ett (krok′it), **Davy**, 1786-1836, American hunter, scout, and Congress-man, killed at the defense of the Alamo. *n.*

croc o dile (krok′ə dīl), a large, lizard-like reptile with thick skin, a long narrow head, and webbed feet. Crocodiles live in the rivers and marshes of the warm parts of Africa, Asia, Australia, and America. *n.*

crocodile—20 to 30 ft. long

crocodile tears, pretended or insincere grief. It is so called because of the story that crocodiles shed tears while eating their victims.

cro cus (krō′kəs), 1 a small plant that grows from a bulblike base, having white, yellow, or purple flowers. Most crocuses bloom very early in the spring. 2 its flower. *n.*, *pl.* **cro cus es, cro ci** (krō′sī).

Croe sus (krē′səs), 1 king in Asia Minor from 560 to 546 B.C., famous for his great wealth. 2 any very rich person. *n.*

Cro-Mag non (krō mag′nən), 1 belonging to a group of prehistoric people who lived in southwestern Europe. They used stone and bone implements, and some of them were skilled artists. 2 person of this group. 1 *adj.*, 2 *n.*

Crom well (krom′wel), **Oliver**, 1599-1658, English general, statesman, and Puritan leader. *n.*

crone (krōn), a withered old woman. *n.*

cro ny (krō′nē), a very close friend; chum. *n.*, *pl.* **cro nies.**

crook (krúk), 1 make a hook or curve in; bend: *The hunter crooked his finger around the trigger of his gun.* 2 a hooked, curved, or bent part: *the crook of the elbow. There is a crook in the stream.* 3 a shepherd's hooked staff. Its upper end is curved or bent into a hook. 4 INFORMAL. a dishonest person; thief or swindler: *The crook stole all my money.* 1 *v.*, 2-4 *n.*

crook ed (krúk′id), 1 not straight; bent; curved; twisted: *a crooked toe.* 2 dishonest: *a crooked scheme. adj.* —**crook′ed ly**, *adv.* —**crook′ed ness**, *n.*

croon (krün), 1 hum, sing, or murmur in a low tone: *Father crooned a lullaby to the baby.* 2 sing in a low voice with exaggerated emotion. *v.* —**croon′er**, *n.*

crop (krop), 1 plants grown or gathered

by people for use as food: *Wheat, corn, and cotton are three main crops of the United States.* **2** the whole amount (of wheat, corn, or the produce of any plant or tree) that one season yields: *The drought made the potato crop very small this year.* **3** plant, cultivate, or yield a crop or crops. **4** anything like a crop; group; collection: *a crop of lies.* **5** cut or bite off the top of: *Sheep had cropped the grass very short.* **6** cut short; clip: *His hair was cropped in a crew cut.* **7** act or result of cropping. A short haircut is a crop. **8** a baglike swelling of a bird's or insect's food passage where food is prepared for digestion; craw. **9** a short whip with a loop instead of a lash: *a riding crop.* 1,2,4,7-9 *n.,* 3,5,6 *v.,* **cropped, cropping.**

crop out, appear or come to the surface: *Ridges of rock cropped out all over the hillside.*

crop up, turn up unexpectedly: *Unless you plan carefully, all sorts of difficulties may crop up.*

crop per (krop′ər). **come a cropper,** INFORMAL. meet with misfortune; fail or collapse. *n.*

cro quet (krō kā′), an outdoor game played by knocking wooden balls through small wire arches with mallets. *n.*

cro quette (krō ket′), a small mass of chopped meat, fish, or vegetables, coated with crumbs and fried. *n.*

cro sier (krō′zhər), an ornamental staff carried by or before bishops or certain abbots. *n.*

cross (krôs), **1** stick or post with another across it like a T or an X. **2** the **Cross,** the cross on which Jesus was crucified. **3** thing, design, or mark shaped like a cross. A cross is the symbol of the Christian religion. A person who cannot write his name makes a cross instead. A soldier is sometimes given a cross for bravery in war. **4** draw a line across: *In writing you cross the letter "t."* **5** cancel by marking with a cross or by drawing a line or lines across: *cross off a name on a list. I crossed out the wrong word.* **6** put or lay across: *He crossed his arms.* **7** lie across; intersect: *Main Street crosses Market Street. Parallel lines cannot cross.* **8** go across; move across: *Let's cross the street. The bridge crosses the river.* **9** meet and pass: *My letter to her and hers to me crossed in the mail.* **10** lying or going across; crossing: *We stood at the intersection of the cross streets.* **11** make the sign of the cross on or over: *The priest crossed himself before the altar.* **12** oppose; hinder: *If anyone crosses him, he gets very angry.* **13** in a bad temper;

peevish: *Children are sometimes cross when they feel sick.* **14** burden of duty or suffering; trouble: *bear one's cross without complaining.* **15** mix kinds, breeds, or races of: *A new plant is sometimes made by crossing two others.* **16** a mixing of kinds, breeds, or races. **17** result of such mixing: *A mule is a cross between a horse and a donkey.* 1-3,14,16,17 *n., pl.* **cross es;** 4-9,11, 12,15 *v.,* 10,13 *adj.* —**cross′ly,** *adv.* —**cross′ness,** *n.*

cross bar (krôs′bär′), bar, line, or stripe going crosswise. *n.*

cross bones (krôs′bōnz′), two bones placed crosswise, usually below a skull, to mean death: *Poisonous medicines are sometimes marked with a skull and crossbones. n.pl.*

crossbow

cross bow (krôs′bō′), a medieval weapon for shooting arrows, stones, etc., consisting of a bow fixed across a wooden stock, with a groove in the middle to direct the arrows, stones, etc. *n.*

cross breed (krôs′brēd′), **1** breed by mixing kinds, breeds, or races: *You can crossbreed a horse and a donkey to get a mule.* **2** individual or breed produced by crossbreeding. The loganberry is a crossbreed of the dewberry and the raspberry. 1 *v.,* **cross bred** (krôs′-bred′), **cross breed ing;** 2 *n.*

cross-coun try (krôs′kun′trē), **1** across fields or open country instead of by road: *a cross-country race.* **2** across an entire country, not merely a part: *a cross-country flight from New York to Seattle. adj.*

cross cut (krôs′kut′), **1** a cut, course, or path going across: *Take a crosscut through the field.* **2** used or made for cutting across. **3** to cut across: *Crosscut the field to take a short cut.* 1 *n.,* 2 *adj.,* 3 *v.,* **cross cut, cross cutting.**

crosscut saw, saw used or made for cutting across the grain of wood.

crosscut saw

hat, āge, fär; let, ēqual, tėrm; it, īce; hot, ōpen, ôrder; oil, out; cup, put, rüle; ch, child; ng, long; sh, she; th, thin; ŦH, then; zh, measure;

ə represents *a* in about, *e* in taken, *i* in pencil, *o* in lemon, *u* in circus.

cross-ex am i na tion (krôs′eg-zam′ə nā′shən), examination to check a previous examination, especially the questioning of a witness by the lawyer of the opposing side to test the truth of the witness's testimony. *n.*

cross-ex am ine (krôs′eg zam′ən), question closely (a witness of the opposing side) to check the truth of his testimony. *v.,* **cross-ex am ined, cross-ex am in ing.**

cross-eyed (krôs′īd′), having both eyes turned toward the nose, and unable to focus on the same point. *adj.*

cross-grained (krôs′grānd′), **1** having the grain arranged in crossing directions, or irregularly, instead of running straight: *cross-grained wood.* **2** hard to get along with; contrary. *adj.*

cross ing (krô′sing), **1** place where lines, tracks, etc., cross: *"Railroad crossing! Stop! Look! Listen!"* **2** place at which a street, river, etc., may be crossed: *White lines mark the crossing.* **3** a going across, especially a voyage across water: *The ocean liner makes a crossing from New York to England every two weeks. n.*

cross piece (krôs′pēs′), piece of wood, metal, etc., that is placed across something. *n.*

cross-pur pose (krôs′pėr′pəs), an opposing or contrary purpose. *n.*
at cross-purposes, misunderstanding each other's purpose: *We cannot accomplish anything while we are at cross-purposes.*

cross-ques tion (krôs′kwes′chən), question closely; cross-examine. *v.*

cross-ref er ence (krôs′ref′ər əns), reference from one part of a book, index, etc., to another. "See **harness** for diagram" under **crupper** is a cross-reference. *n.*

cross road (krôs′rōd′), **1** road that crosses another. **2** road that connects main roads. **3 crossroads,** *pl.* place where roads cross: *At the crossroads we stopped and read the signs. n.*

cross section, **1** act of cutting anything across: *She made cross sections of a carrot to use on slides for her microscope.* **2** piece cut in this way.

adj. adjective	*n.* noun
adv. adverb	*prep.* preposition
conj. conjunction	*pron.* pronoun
interj. interjection	*v.* verb
sing. singular	*pl.* plural

3 small selection of people, things, etc., with the same qualities as the entire group; sample: *They interviewed a cross section of the population in their survey of public opinion.*

cross tie (krôs′tī′), a heavy piece of timber or iron placed crosswise to form a foundation or support. The rails of a railroad track are fastened to crossties about a foot apart. *n.*

cross trees (krôs′trēz′), two horizontal bars of wood or metal near the top of a ship's mast. *n.pl.*

cross walk (krôs′wôk′), area marked with lines, used by pedestrians in crossing a street. *n.*

cross way (krôs′wā′), crossroad. *n.*

cross ways (krôs′wāz′), crosswise. *adv.*

cross wise (krôs′wīz′), 1 so as to cross; across: *The tree fell crosswise over the stream.* 2 in the form of a cross: *The streets come together crosswise at the intersection.* *adv.*

cross word puzzle (krôs′wėrd′), puzzle with sets of numbered squares to be filled in with words, one letter to each square, so that the words may be read both across and down. Synonyms, definitions, or other clues are given with numbers corresponding to the numbers in the squares.

crotch (kroch), 1 place where a tree, bough, etc., divides into two limbs or branches: *The bird's nest was in the crotch of a tree.* 2 place where the human body divides into the two legs. *n., pl.* **crotch es.**

crotch et (kroch′it), an odd notion; unreasonable whim: *The old woman had many crotchets.* *n.*

crotch et y (kroch′ə tē), full of odd notions or unreasonable whims. *adj.*

crouch (krouch), 1 stoop low with bent legs as though ready to spring: *The cat crouched in the corner, waiting for the mouse to come out of its hole.* 2 shrink down in fear: *The family crouched together in the basement waiting for the tornado to pass.* 3 a crouching. 4 a crouching position. 1,2 *v.*, 3,4 *n., pl.* **crouch es.**

croup[1] (krüp), inflammation or diseased condition of the throat and windpipe characterized by a hoarse cough and difficult breathing. *n.*

[imitating a croak or hoarse sound]

croup[2] (krüp), rump of a horse; crupper. *n.* [from French of the 1200's *croupe*]

croup y (krü′pē), 1 sick with croup. 2 hoarse and having difficulty in breathing: *the wheeze of a croupy baby.* *adj.*, **croup i er, croup i est.**

crou ton (krü′ton), a small piece of toasted or fried bread, often served in soup. *n.*

crow[1] (krō), 1 the loud cry of a rooster. 2 make this cry: *The cock crowed as the sun rose.* 3 a happy sound made by a baby. 4 make this sound. 5 show one's happiness and pride; boast: *The winning team crowed over its victory.* 1,3 *n.*, 2,4,5 *v.*, **crowed** (or **crew** for 2), **crowed, crow ing.** [Old English *crāwan*]

crow[2] (krō), 1 a large, glossy, black bird that has a harsh cry or caw. 2 any similar bird, such as a raven, magpie, or jay. *n.* [Old English *crāwe*]

as the crow flies, in a straight line; in or by the shortest way: *The distance is exactly one mile as the crow flies.*

eat crow, be forced to do something very disagreeable and humiliating.

Crow (krō), member of a tribe of American Indians who formerly lived in Montana and Wyoming and now live in Montana. *n., pl.* **Crow** or **Crows.**

crowbar

crow bar (krō′bär′), a strong iron or steel bar, used to lift things or pry them apart. *n.*

crowd (kroud), 1 a large number of people together: *A crowd gathered at the scene of the fire.* 2 people in general; the masses: *Advertisements seek to appeal to the crowd.* 3 INFORMAL. group; set: *Our crowd wasn't invited to the party.* 4 collect in large numbers: *crowd around a TV star.* 5 fill; fill too full: *Christmas shoppers crowded the store.* 6 push; shove: *The big man crowded the child out of his way.* 7 press forward; force one's way: *He crowded into the subway car.* 1-3 *n.*, 4-7 *v.*

crown (kroun), 1 a head covering of precious metal and jewels, worn by a king or queen. 2 **the Crown,** the governing power and authority in a monarchy; royal power: *The Crown granted lands in colonial America to William Penn.* 3 a king or queen: *Always address the crown respectfully.* 4 make king, queen, etc.: *The prince was crowned in London.* 5 of or having to do with a crown: *the crown jewels.* 6 wreath for the head: *The winner of the race received a crown.* 7 an honor; reward: *He won the amateur boxing crown in his last bout.* 8 to honor; reward: *His work was crowned with success.* 9 head: *"Jack fell down and broke his crown."* 10 the highest part; top: *the crown of the head, the crown of a hat. The Olympic victory was the crown of her athletic career.* 11 be on top of; cover the highest part of: *A fort crowns the hill.* 12 make perfect or complete; add the finishing touch to: *Success crowned her efforts.* 13 part of a tooth which appears above the gum, or an artificial substitute for it. 14 put a crown on (a tooth). 15 a British coin, worth 5 shillings. 1-3,6,7,9,10,13,15 *n.*, 4,8,11,12,14 *v.*, 5 *adj.*

crown prince, the oldest living son of a king or queen; the male heir to the throne.

crow's-feet (krōz′fēt′), the tiny wrinkles at the outer corners of the eyes. *n.pl.*

crow's-nest (krōz′nest′), a small, enclosed platform near the top of a ship's mast, used by the lookout. *n.*

cru cial (krü′shəl), very important or decisive; critical: *This is a crucial game, for it will decide the championship.* *adj.* —**cru′cial ly,** *adv.*

cru ci ble (krü′sə bəl), 1 container in which metals, ores, etc., can be melted. 2 a severe test or trial. *n.*

cru ci fix (krü′sə fiks), cross with a figure of the crucified Christ on it. *n., pl.* **cru ci fix es.**

cru ci fix ion (krü′sə fik′shən), 1 a crucifying or a being crucified. 2 **Crucifixion, a** the crucifying of Christ on the Cross. **b** picture, statue, etc., of this. *n.*

cru ci fy (krü′sə fī), 1 put to death by nailing or binding the hands and feet to a cross. 2 persecute or torture. *v.*, **cru ci fied, cru ci fy ing.**

crude (krüd), 1 in a natural or raw state. Crude oil is pumped from wells before it is refined and prepared for use. 2 rough; coarse: *a crude log cabin, a crude chair made out of a box.* 3 lacking finish, grace, taste, or refinement: *the crude manners of a rude person.* *adj.*, **crud er, crud est.** —**crude′ly,** *adv.* —**crude′ness,** *n.*

cru di ty (krü′də tē), 1 a being crude; lack of finish; roughness: *The crudity of the homemade furniture fit in with the rustic charm of the summer cabin.* 2 a crude action or thing. *n., pl.* **cru di ties.**

cru el (krü′əl), 1 ready to give pain to others or to delight in their suffering; hard-hearted: *The cruel man whipped* his horse. 2 causing pain and suffering: *cruel acts, a cruel war. Arthritis is a cruel disease of the joints.* adj. —**cru′el ly,** adv.

cru el ty (krü′əl tē), 1 readiness to give pain to others or to delight in their suffering. 2 a cruel act or acts: *I will never forgive his cruelty in kicking my little dog.* n., pl. **cru el ties.**

cru et (krü′it), a glass bottle to hold vinegar, oil, etc., for the table. n.

cruise (krüz), 1 sail about from place to place on pleasure or business; sail over or about: *We cruised to Bermuda on our vacation. Freighters and tankers cruise the oceans of the world. The coast guard cruised along the shore.* 2 act of sailing about from place to place on pleasure or business: *We went for a cruise on the Great Lakes last summer.* 3 to travel or journey from place to place: *The taxicab cruised the city streets in search of passengers.* 4 to travel in a car, airplane, boat, etc., at the speed at which it operates best. 1,3,4 v., **cruised, cruis ing;** 2 n.

cruis er (krü′zər), 1 warship with less armor and greater speed than a battleship. 2 airplane, taxicab, etc., that cruises. 3 motorboat having a cabin and equipped with facilities for living on board. 4 a police car used for patrolling streets and highways. n.

crul ler (krul′ər), piece of rich, sweet dough fried brown in deep fat. The dough is usually shaped in twists and cut in short pieces. n.

crumb (krum), 1 a very small piece of bread, cake, etc., broken from a larger piece: *I fed crumbs to the birds.* 2 break into crumbs; crumble. 3 cover with crumbs for frying or baking. 4 a little bit: *a crumb of comfort.* 5 the soft inside part of bread. 1,4,5 n., 2,3 v.

crum ble (krum′bəl), 1 break into very small pieces or crumbs: *I crumbled the bread for the birds.* 2 fall to pieces; decay: *The old wall was crumbling away at the edges.* v., **crum bled, crum bling.**

crum bly (krum′blē), tending to crumble; easily crumbled. adj., **crum bli er, crum bli est.**

crum pet (krum′pit), a round, flat cake, thicker than a pancake, baked on a griddle. Crumpets are usually toasted and eaten while hot. n.

crum ple (krum′pəl), 1 crush together; wrinkle: *He crumpled the paper into a ball.* 2 fall down: *He crumpled to the floor in a faint.* v., **crum pled, crum pling.**

crunch (krunch), 1 crush noisily with the teeth: *He was crunching celery.* 2 make or move with a crunching noise: *The frozen crust of snow crunched under our feet. The children crunched*

through the snow. 3 act or sound of crunching. 1,2 v., 3 n., pl. **crunch es.**

crunch y (krun′chē), INFORMAL. brittle and crackling: *crunchy peanut brittle.* adj., **crunch i er, crunch i est.**

crup per (krup′ər), 1 strap attached to the back of a harness and passed under a horse's tail to prevent the harness from slipping forward. See **harness** for diagram. 2 rump of a horse. n.

cru sade (krü sād′), 1 Often, **Crusade.** any one of the Christian military expeditions between the years 1096 and 1272 to recover the Holy Land from the Moslems. 2 a vigorous campaign against a public evil or in favor of some new idea: *Everyone was asked to join the crusade against littering the streets.* 3 take part in a crusade: *We crusaded against littering.* 1,2 n., 3 v., **cru sad ed, cru sad ing.**

cru sad er (krü sā′dər), person who takes part in a crusade. The **Crusaders** of the Middle Ages tried to recover the Holy Land from the Moslems. n.

cruse (krüz), OLD USE. jug, pot, or bottle made of earthenware. n.

crush (krush), 1 squeeze together violently so as to break or bruise: *The bear's squeeze crushed two of the hunter's ribs.* 2 wrinkle or crease by wear or rough handling: *My suitcase was so full that my clothes were crushed.* 3 break into fine pieces by grinding, pounding, or pressing: *The ore is crushed between steel rollers.* 4 act of crushing; violent pressure like grinding or pounding: *She pushed her way through the crush of the crowd.* 5 mass of people crowded close together: *There was a crush at the narrow exits after the football game.* 6 subdue; conquer: *The revolt was crushed and its leaders were imprisoned.* 7 INFORMAL. a sudden, strong liking for a person: *None of her crushes lasted very long.* 1-3,6 v., 4,5,7 n., pl. **crush es.** —**crush′er,** n.

Cru soe (krü′sō), **Robinson,** hero of Daniel Defoe's novel of the same name, a sailor shipwrecked on a desert island. n.

crust (krust), 1 the hard, outside part of bread. 2 piece of this. 3 any hard, dry piece of bread. 4 rich dough rolled out thin and baked for pies. 5 any hard outside covering: *The frozen crust on the snow was thick enough for us to walk on it.* 6 the solid outside part of the earth: *Volcanoes form below the crust of the earth.* 7 cover or become covered with a crust; form into a crust: *By the next day the snow had crusted over. The rocks were crusted with moss.* 1-6 n., 7 v. —**crust′like′,** adj.

crus ta cean (krus tā′shən), 1 any of a group of invertebrate animals with

hat, āge, fär; let, ēqual, tėrm; it, īce; hot, ōpen, ôrder; oil, out; cup, pùt, rüle; ch, child; ng, long; sh, she; th, thin; ŦH, then; zh, measure;

ə represents a in about, e in taken, i in pencil, o in lemon, u in circus.

hard shells and jointed bodies and appendages, living mostly in the water. Crabs, lobsters, and shrimps are crustaceans. 2 of or belonging to this group. 1 n., 2 adj.

crust i ly (krus′tl ē), in a crusty manner. adv.

crust y (krus′tē), 1 of or like a crust; having a crust; hard: *crusty bread.* 2 harsh in manner or speech: *The crusty sea captain has a quick temper.* adj., **crust i er, crust i est.**

crutch (kruch), 1 a support to help a lame person walk. It is a stick with a padded crosspiece at the top that fits under a lame person's arm and supports part of his weight in walking. 2 anything like a crutch in shape or use; support; prop: *She used her brother's answers as a crutch to get through her homework.* n., pl. **crutch es.**

crux (kruks), 1 the essential part; most important point: *the crux of an argument.* 2 a puzzling or perplexing question; difficult point to explain. n., pl. **crux es.**

cry (krī), 1 call loudly; shout: *"Wait!" she cried from behind me.* 2 a loud call; shout: *a cry of rage. We heard his cry for help.* 3 shed tears; weep: *The little girl cried when her doll was broken.* 4 spell of shedding tears; fit of weeping: *I feel better now that I have had a good cry.* 5 noise or call of an animal: *the cry of hounds, the hungry cry of the wolf.* 6 make such a noise: *The crows cried to one another from the treetops.* 7 a call to action; slogan: *"Forward" was the army's cry as it attacked.* 8 a call for help; appeal; entreaty. 9 sell by calling on the streets, etc.: *Peddlers cry their wares in the street.* 10 a call that means things for sale: *a peddler's cry.* 1,3,6,9 v., **cried, cry ing;** 2,4,5,7,8,10 n., pl. **cries.**

cry down, make little of; disparage.

cry for, 1 ask earnestly for; beg for: *The beggar cried for alms.* 2 need very much: *The run-down old house cried for a coat of paint.*

in full cry, in close pursuit: *The pack of hounds was in full cry after the fox.*

cry ba by (krī′bā′bē), person who

adj.	adjective	*n.*	noun
adv.	adverb	*prep.*	preposition
conj.	conjunction	*pron.*	pronoun
interj.	interjection	*v.*	verb
sing.	singular	*pl.*	plural

cries easily or pretends to be hurt. *n.,* *pl.* **cry ba bies.**

cry ing (krī′ing), 1 that cries. 2 demanding attention; very bad: *The slums in that city are a crying shame. adj.*

crypt (kript), an underground room or vault. The crypt beneath the main floor of a church was formerly often used as a burial place. *n.*

cryp tic (krip′tik), having a hidden meaning; secret; mysterious: *We could not fully understand his cryptic remark. adj.* —**cryp′ti cal ly,** *adv.*

cryp to gram (krip′tə gram), something written in secret code or cipher. *n.*

crys tal (kris′tl), 1 a clear, transparent mineral that looks like ice. It is a kind of quartz. 2 piece of crystal cut into form for use or ornament. Crystals may be hung around lights or worn as beads. 3 clear and transparent like crystal: *crystal spring water.* 4 a very transparent glass from which drinking glasses, serving dishes, etc., are made: *goblets of crystal.* 5 made of crystal: *crystal beads, crystal water goblets.* 6 the transparent glass or plastic cover of a watch dial. 7 a regularly shaped piece with angles and flat surfaces, into which many substances solidify. Crystals of sugar are different in form from crystals of snow. 1,2,4,6,7 *n.,* 3,5 *adj.* —**crys′tal like′,** *adj.*

crystal (def. 7)
crystal of
iron pyrites

crys tal line (kris′tl ən), 1 made of crystals: *Sugar and salt are crystalline.* 2 made of crystal. 3 clear and transparent like crystal: *A crystalline sheet of ice covered the pond. adj.*

crys tal li za tion (kris′tl ə zā′shən), 1 a crystallizing or a being crystallized: *the crystallization of water by freezing.* 2 a crystallized substance or formation. 3 the taking on of a real, concrete, or permanent form: *The meeting resulted in the crystallization of our plans. n.*

crys tal lize (kris′tl īz), 1 form into crystals; solidify into crystals: *Water crystallizes to form snow.* 2 form into definite shape: *After much thought her vague ideas crystallized into a clear plan. v.,* **crys tal lized, crys tal liz ing.**

CST or **C.S.T.,** Central Standard Time.

ct., cent. *pl.* **cts.**

cu., cubic.

cub (kub), 1 a young bear, fox, lion, etc. 2 an inexperienced or awkward boy. 3 a cub scout. *n.*

Cu ba (kyü′bə), country on the largest island in the West Indies, south of Florida. *Capital:* Havana. See **Caribbean Sea** for map. *n.*

Cu ban (kyü′bən), 1 of or having to do with Cuba or its inhabitants. 2 person born or living in Cuba. 1 *adj.,* 2 *n.*

cub by hole (kub′ē hōl′), a small, enclosed space. *n.*

cube (def. 1)

cube (kyüb), 1 a solid with 6 square faces or sides, all equal. 2 anything shaped like a cube: *ice cubes, a cube of sugar.* 3 make or form into the shape of a cube: *The beets we had for supper were cubed instead of sliced.* 4 use (a number) three times as a factor: *5 cubed is 125, because $5×5×5 = 125$. The teacher asked me to cube 25.* 5 product obtained when a number is cubed: *The cube of 4 is 64.* 1,2,5 *n.,* 3,4 *v.,* **cubed, cub ing.** —**cube′like′,** *adj.*

cube root, number that produces a given number when multiplied twice by itself: *The cube root of 27 is 3.*

cu bic (kyü′bik), 1 shaped like a cube: *the cubic form of a block of ice.* 2 having length, breadth, and thickness. A cubic inch is the volume of a cube whose edges are each one inch long. The cubic content of a room is the number of cubic feet it contains. 3 having to do with or involving cubes of numbers. *adj.*

cu bi cal (kyü′bə kəl), shaped like a cube; cubic. *adj.*

cu bi cle (kyü′bə kəl), a very small room or compartment. *n.*

cub ism (kyü′biz′əm), style of painting, drawing, and sculpture in which objects are represented by cubes and other geometric forms rather than by realistic details. *n.*

cub ist (kyü′bist), artist or sculptor whose art is based on cubism. *n.*

cu bit (kyü′bit), an ancient measure of length, about 18 to 22 inches. Once a cubit meant the length from the elbow to the tip of the middle finger. *n.*

cub scout, member of the junior division of the Boys Scouts. Cub scouts are 8 to 10 years of age.

cuck oo (kü′kü *or* kŭk′ü), 1 bird whose call sounds much like its name. The common European cuckoo lays its eggs in the nests of other birds instead of hatching them itself. The American cuckoo builds its own nest and has a call less like the name. 2 the call of the cuckoo. 3 SLANG. crazy; silly. 1,2 *n.,* *pl.* **cuck oos;** 3 *adj.*

cu cum ber (kyü′kum bər), 1 a long, green vegetable with firm flesh inside, used in salads and for pickles. 2 vine it grows on. *n.*

cud (kud), mouthful of food brought back from the first stomach of cattle or similar animals for a slow, second chewing in the mouth. *n.*

cud dle (kud′l), 1 hold closely and lovingly in one's arms or lap; hug tenderly: *The child cuddled the kittens.* 2 lie close and comfortably; curl up: *The two puppies cuddled together near the radiator. v.,* **cud dled, cud dling.**

cudg el (kuj′əl), 1 a short, thick stick used as a weapon; club. 2 beat with a cudgel. 1 *n.,* 2 *v.*

cue[1] (kyü), 1 action, word, or last part of a speech by an actor which serves as the signal for another actor to come on the stage or begin speaking. 2 a signal like this to a singer or musician. 3 hint or suggestion as to what to do or when to act: *Take your cue from me at the party about when it is time to leave.* 4 provide (a person) with a cue or hint: *During the rehearsal the director cued the actors.* 1-3 *n.,* 4 *v.,* **cued, cue ing** or **cu ing.** [perhaps a spelling for *q.,* abbreviation of Latin *quando* when (a word used in directions to actors)]

cue[2] (kyü), 1 a long, tapering stick used for striking the ball in the game of billiards or pool. 2 queue. *n.* [variant spelling of *queue*]

cuff[1] (kuf), 1 band around the wrist, either attached to a sleeve or separate: *My shirt cuffs got wet when I didn't pull my sleeves up to wash.* 2 a turned-up fold around the bottom of the legs of trousers. 3 handcuff. *n.* [Middle English *cuffe* glove]

cuff[2] (kuf), 1 hit with the hand; slap. 2 a hit with the hand; slap. 1 *v.,* 2 *n.* [origin unknown]

cubism

cuff link, link for the cuff of a shirt.

cui rass (kwi ras′), 1 piece of armor for the body made of a breastplate and a plate for the back fastened together. 2 the breastplate alone. *n., pl.* **cui rass es.**

cui ras sier (kwir′ə sir′), a cavalry soldier wearing a cuirass. *n.*

cui sine (kwi zēn′), 1 style of cooking or preparing food; cooking; cookery: *Italian cuisine.* 2 food: *The cuisine is excellent at that restaurant. n.*

cu li nar y (kyü′lə ner′ē), having to do with cooking or the kitchen: *After one of her meals, Mother is often praised for her culinary skill. adj.*

cull (kul), 1 pick out; select: *The lawyer culled important facts from the mass of evidence.* 2 pick over; make selections from: *We culled the berries, discarding the bad ones.* 3 something picked out as inferior or worthless. *Poor fruit, stale vegetables, and animals not up to standard are called culls.* 1,2 *v.,* 3 *n.*

cul mi nate (kul′mə nāt), reach its highest point; reach a climax: *The birthday party culminated in the opening of the presents. v.,* **cul mi nat ed, cul mi nat ing.**

cul mi na tion (kul′mə nā′shən), 1 the highest point; climax: *The fireworks display was the culmination of the Fourth of July celebration.* 2 a reaching of the highest point. *n.*

cul pa bil i ty (kul′pə bil′ə tē), fact or condition of being culpable. *n.*

cul pa ble (kul′pə bəl), deserving blame: *The policeman was dismissed for culpable neglect of duty. adj.*

cul pa bly (kul′pə blē), in a culpable manner. *adv.*

cul prit (kul′prit), 1 person guilty of a fault or crime; offender: *The person who broke the window is the culprit; he should pay for it.* 2 prisoner in court accused of a crime. *n.*

cult (kult), 1 system of religious worship: *Buddhism includes many cults.* 2 great admiration for a person, thing, or idea; worship. 3 group showing such admiration; worshipers. *n.*

cul ti vate (kul′tə vāt), 1 prepare and use (land) to raise crops by plowing it, planting seeds, and taking care of the growing plants; till. 2 help (plants) grow by labor and care. 3 loosen the ground around (growing plants) to kill weeds, etc. 4 improve or develop by study or training: *cultivate one's mind. He cultivated good manners.* 5 seek the friendship of: *She cultivated people who could help her. v.,* **cul ti vat ed, cul ti vat ing.**

cul ti vat ed (kul′tə vā′tid), 1 prepared and used to raise crops: *A field of wheat is cultivated land; a pasture is not.* 2 produce by cultivation; not wild:

a cultivated flower. 3 improved or developed. 4 cultured; refined: *cultivated tastes. adj.*

cul ti va tion (kul′tə vā′shən), 1 act of preparing land and growing crops by plowing, planting, and necessary care: *Better cultivation of soil will result in better crops.* 2 condition of being prepared by plowing, planting, etc.: *Only half the farm was under cultivation.* 3 act of giving time and thought to improving and developing (the body, mind, or manners): *She stressed the cultivation of good study habits.* 4 result of improvement or growth through education and experience; culture. *n.*

cul ti va tor (kul′tə vā′tər), 1 person or thing that cultivates. 2 tool or machine used to loosen the ground and destroy weeds. A cultivator is pulled or pushed between rows of growing plants. *n.*

cultivator (def. 2)—two types

cul tur al (kul′chər əl), of or having to do with culture: *Literature, art, and music are cultural studies. adj.* —**cul′tur al ly,** *adv.*

cul ture (kul′chər), 1 fineness of feelings, thoughts, tastes, manners, etc.; refinement: *He is a man of culture who has an appreciation of art, music, and literature.* 2 the customs, arts, and conveniences of a nation or people at a given time: *The culture of the ancient Incas is noted for its art, its fine buildings, and its religion.* 3 development of the mind or body by education or training: *a course in physical culture.* 4 preparation of land to raise crops by plowing, planting, and necessary care; cultivation. 5 the raising of bees, fish, silkworms, oysters, etc., by proper or special care. 6 growth of germs or bacteria in a special solution for scientific study or medicinal use. *n.*

cul tured (kul′chərd), 1 having or showing culture; refined. 2 produced or raised by culture: *cultured pearls. adj.*

cul vert (kul′vərt), a small channel or drain for water crossing under a road, railroad, etc. *n.*

cum ber (kum′bər), burden or hinder; encumber. *v.*

Cum ber land (kum′bər lənd), river

hat, āge, fär; let, ēqual, tėrm;
it, īce; hot, ōpen, ôrder;
oil, out; cup, pùt, rüle; ch, child;
ng, long; sh, she; th, thin;
ŦH, then; zh, measure;

ə represents *a* in about,
e in taken, *i* in pencil,
o in lemon, *u* in circus.

flowing from SE Kentucky through N Tennessee and W Kentucky into the Ohio River. *n.*

Cumberland Gap, a mountain pass in the Cumberland Mountains, where Virginia, Kentucky, and Tennessee meet.

Cumberland Mountains, plateau of the Appalachian Mountains, extending from S West Virginia to N Alabama.

cum ber some (kum′bər səm), hard to manage; clumsy, unwieldy, or burdensome: *The armor worn by knights was often so cumbersome they had to be helped onto their horses. adj.* —**cum′ber some ly,** *adv.* —**cum′ber some ness,** *n.*

cum brous (kum′brəs), cumbersome. *adj.* —**cum′brous ly,** *adv.* —**cum′brous ness,** *n.*

cum quat (kum′kwot), kumquat. *n.*

cu mu la tive (kyü′myə lə tiv), increasing or growing by additions; accumulated: *The cumulative effects of many illnesses made him a weak man. adj.* —**cu′mu la tive ly,** *adv.* —**cu′mu la tive ness,** *n.*

cu mu lus (kyü′myə ləs), cloud made up of rounded heaps with a flat bottom. *Cumuli are seen in fair weather. n., pl.* **cu mu li** (kyü′myə lī).

NUMERAL 1 10 TAP BE ME

cuneiform (def. 2)

cu ne i form (kyü nē′ə fôrm), 1 wedge-shaped. 2 the wedge-shaped characters used in the writing of ancient Babylonia, Assyria, Persia, etc. 3 composed of cuneiform inscriptions: *cuneiform tablets.* 1,3 *adj.,* 2 *n.*

cun ning (kun′ing), 1 clever in deceiving; sly: *The cunning fox outwitted the dogs and got away.* 2 slyness in getting what one needs or wants or in deceiving one's enemies: *The fox has a great deal of cunning.* 3 clever in doing; skillful: *With cunning hand the sculptor shaped the little statue.* 4 skill; cleverness: *The old sculptor's hand never lost its cunning.* 5 INFORMAL. pretty and dear; cute: *Kittens and babies are cun-*

adj.	adjective	*n.*	noun
adv.	adverb	*prep.*	preposition
conj.	conjunction	*pron.*	pronoun
interj.	interjection	*v.*	verb
sing.	singular	*pl.*	plural

ning. 1,3,5 *adj.,* 2,4 *n.* —**cun′ning ly,** *adv.*

cup (kup), 1 dish to drink from. Most cups have handles. 2 as much as a cup holds; cupful. In cooking, a cup equals a half pint. *She drank a cup of milk.* 3 thing shaped like a cup. The petals of some flowers form a cup. 4 shape like a cup: *She cupped her hands to catch the ball.* 5 take or put in a cup: *She cupped the flour from the bag and poured it into a mixing bowl.* 6 an ornamental cup, vase, etc., given to the winner of a contest. 7 something to endure or experience: *the bitter cup of defeat.* 1-3,6,7 *n.,* 4,5 *v.,* **cupped, cup ping.** —**cup′like′,** *adj.*

cup bear er (kup′ber′ər or kup′bar′-ər), (formerly) a person who filled and served cups of wine at banquets. *n.*

cup board (kub′ərd), 1 closet or cabinet with shelves, especially for dishes and food supplies. 2 any small closet. *n.*

cup cake (kup′kāk′), a small cake baked in a pan shaped like a cup. *n.*

cup ful (kup′fùl), as much as a cup holds. In cooking, a cupful equals a half pint. *n., pl.* **cup fuls.**

Cu pid (kyü′pid), 1 (in Roman myths) the god of love, son of Mercury and Venus. The Greeks called him Eros. Cupid is usually represented as a winged child with bow and arrows. 2 **cupid,** a winged child used as a symbol of love: *a valentine covered with little cupids. n.*

cu pid i ty (kyü pid′ə tē), eager desire to possess something; greed. *n.*

cupola (def. 2)

cu po la (kyü′pə lə), 1 a rounded roof; dome: *The Capitol at Washington, D.C., has a cupola.* 2 a small dome or tower on a roof. *n., pl.* **cu po las.**

cur (kėr), 1 a worthless dog of mixed breed; mongrel. 2 a bad-tempered, contemptible person. *n.*

cur a ble (kyùr′ə bəl), that can be cured: *With proper care and medicine tuberculosis is a curable disease. adj.*

cur ate (kyür′it), clergyman who assists a pastor, rector, or vicar. *n.*

cur a tive (kyür′ə tiv), 1 having the power to cure; tending to cure; curing. 2 means of curing; remedy. 1 *adj.,* 2 *n.*

cu ra tor (kyù rā′tər), person in charge of all or part of a museum, library, art gallery, zoo, etc. *n.*

curb (kėrb), 1 a raised border of concrete or stone along the edge of a pavement or sidewalk: *He parked his car close to the curb.* 2 hold in check; restrain: *I curbed my hunger by eating a piece of cheese.* 3 a check; restraint: *Put a curb on your temper.* 4 chain or strap fastened to a horse's bit and passed under its lower jaw. When the reins are pulled tight, the curb checks the horse. 1,3,4 *n.,* 2 *v.*

curb ing (kėr′bing), 1 material for making a curb. 2 a curb. *n.*

curb side (kėrb′sīd′), 1 area or sidewalk at or near a curb. 2 at or near a curb: *We went to a restaurant with curbside service.* 1 *n.,* 2 *adj.*

curb stone (kėrb′stōn′), stone or stones forming a curb along the edge of a pavement or sidewalk. *n.*

curd (kėrd). Often, **curds,** *pl.* the thick part of milk that separates from the watery part when milk sours. Cheese is made from curds. *n.*

cur dle (kėr′dl), 1 form into curds: *Milk curdles when it is kept too long in a warm place.* 2 thicken. *v.,* **cur dled, cur dling.**

cure (kyùr), 1 make well; bring back to health: *With penicillin the doctor cured several cases of pneumonia.* 2 get rid of: *Rest in bed will often cure a cold. Only great determination can cure a bad habit like smoking.* 3 means of curing; treatment intended to relieve or remove disease or any bad condition: *a cure for sore eyes, a cure for laziness.* 4 medicine that is a means of curing; remedy: *Quinine is a cure for malaria.* 5 a successful medical treatment; restoration to health. 6 preserve (bacon, fish, etc.) by drying, salting, smoking, pickling, etc. 7 be or become cured: *Tobacco leaves are often hung in barns to cure.* 1,2,6,7 *v.,* **cured, cur ing;** 3,4,5 *n.*

cu ré (kyù rā′), a parish priest. *n., pl.* **cu rés.** [from French]

cure-all (kyùr′ôl′), remedy supposed to cure all diseases or ills; panacea. *n.*

cur few (kėr′fyü), 1 rule requiring certain persons to be off the streets or at home before a fixed time: *The mayor has established a 10 p.m. curfew for children in our city.* 2 the ringing of a bell at a fixed time every evening as a signal. In the Middle Ages, it was a signal to put out lights and cover fires. 3 time when a curfew begins: *The curfew at our summer camp is ten o'clock. n.*

Cur ie (kyùr′ē or kyü rē′), 1 **Marie,** 1867-1934, French physicist and chemist, born in Poland. She and her husband discovered radium in 1898. 2 **Pierre,** 1859-1906, French physicist and chemist. 3 **curie,** unit for measuring radioactivity. *n.*

cur i o (kyür′ē ō), object valued as a curiosity: *My parents brought back many curios from the Orient. n., pl.* **cur i os.**

cur i os i ty (kyür′ē os′ə tē), 1 an eager desire to know: *He satisfied his curiosity about animals by visiting the zoo every week.* 2 a being too eager to know: *Curiosity got the better of her, and she opened the unmarked box.* 3 a strange, rare, or novel object: *One of his curiosities was a basket made from an armadillo's shell. n., pl.* **cur i os i ties.**

cur i ous (kyür′ē əs), 1 eager to know: *Small children are very curious and they ask many questions.* 2 too eager to know; prying: *Some people are always curious about their neighbors' business.* 3 strange, odd, or unusual: *I found a curious old box in the attic. adj.* —**cur′i ous ly,** *adv.* —**cur′i ous ness,** *n.*

cur i um (kyür′ē əm), a radioactive metallic element produced artificially from plutonium or uranium. *n.* [from Marie and Pierre *Curie*]

curl (kėrl), 1 twist into ringlets; roll into coils: *curl someone's hair. My sister's hair curls naturally.* 2 twist out of shape; bend into a curve: *Paper curls as it burns. She kept curling her handkerchief nervously around one finger.* 3 rise in rings: *Smoke is curling slowly from the chimney.* 4 a curled lock of hair. 5 anything curled or bent into a curve: *A carpenter's wood shavings form curls.* 6 a curling or a being curled: *keep one's hair in curl.* 1-3 *v.,* 4-6 *n.*

curl up, draw up one's legs: *She curled up on the sofa.*

curl er (kėr′lər), 1 person or thing that curls. 2 device on which hair is twisted or wound to make it curl. *n.*

cur lew (kėr′lü), a wading bird with a long, thin, curved bill. *n., pl.* **cur lews** or **cur lew.**

curl i cue (kėr′lə kyü), a fancy twist, curl, or flourish: *Curlicues in handwriting often make it hard to read. n.*

curl i ness (kėr′lē nis), curly quality or condition. *n.*

curl ing (kėr′ling), game in which large, smooth, rounded stones with handles are slid over ice at a target. *n.*

curl y (kėr′lē), 1 curling; wavy: *curly*

hair. 2 having curls or curly hair: *a curly head. adj.,* **curl i er, curl i est.**

cur rant (kėr′ənt), 1 a small raisin without seeds made from certain small, sweet grapes grown chiefly in the countries on the eastern Mediterranean Sea. Currants are used in puddings, cakes, and buns. 2 a small, sour, red, black, or white berry that grows in bunches and is used for jelly, jam, wine, and pies. 3 bush that this berry grows on. *n.*

cur ren cy (kėr′ən sē), 1 money in actual use in a country: *Coins and paper money are currency in the United States.* 2 a passing from person to person; circulation: *People who spread a rumor give it currency.* 3 general use or acceptance; common occurrence: *Words such as "couldst" and "thou" have little currency now. n., pl.* **cur ren cies.**

cur rent (kėr′ənt), 1 a flow of water, air, or any liquid; running stream: *The current swept the stick down the river. The draft created a current of cold air over my feet.* 2 flow of electricity through a wire, etc. Metals are good conductors of electric current. *The current went off when lightning hit the power lines.* 3 rate or amount of such a flow, usually expressed in amperes: *Heating requires much more current than lighting does.* 4 course or movement (of events or of opinions): *Newspapers influence the current of public opinion.* 5 of the present time. The current issue of a magazine is the latest one published. *We discuss current events in class whenever somebody reports on the news.* 6 generally used or accepted: *Long ago the belief was current that the earth was flat.* 7 going around; passing from person to person: *A rumor is current that school will close tomorrow.* 1-4 *n.,* 5-7 *adj.*

cur rent ly (kėr′ənt lē), 1 at the present time; now: *The flu is currently going around school and many people are absent.* 2 generally; commonly: *a currently held belief among the world's scientists. adv.*

cur ric u lar (kə rik′yə lər), having to do with a curriculum. *adj.*

cur ric u lum (kə rik′yə ləm), course of study: *At our school the curriculum in Grade 6 includes mathematics, science, geography, history, reading, and spelling. n., pl.* **cur ric u lums, cur ric u la** (kə rik′yə lə).

cur ry[1] (kėr′ē), rub and clean (a horse) with a brush or currycomb. *v.,* **cur ried, cur ry ing.** [from French of the 1200's *correier* put in order]

cur ry[2] (kėr′ē), 1 a peppery sauce or powder made from a mixture of spices, seeds, and vegetables. Curry is a popular seasoning in India. 2 food flavored with it. 3 prepare or flavor (food) with curry. 1,2 *n., pl.* **cur ries;** 3 *v.,* **cur ried, cur ry ing.** [from Tamil (language spoken in parts of India and Ceylon) *kari* sauce]

cur ry comb (kėr′ē kōm′), 1 a comb or brush with metal teeth for rubbing and cleaning a horse. 2 use a currycomb on; brush with a currycomb. 1 *n.,* 2 *v.*

curse (kėrs), 1 ask God to bring evil or harm on: *The evil witch cursed everyone she hated.* 2 the words that a person says when he asks God to curse someone or something: *Her curse was uttered against her enemies.* 3 bring evil or harm on; trouble greatly; torment: *cursed with blindness. He is cursed with a bad temper.* 4 trouble; harm: *My quick temper has been a curse to me all my life.* 5 use profane language; swear. 6 swear at. 7 words used in swearing: *His talk was full of vile curses.* 1,3,5,6 *v.,* **cursed** or **curst, curs ing;** 2,4,7 *n.*

curs ed (kėr′sid *or* kėrst), 1 under a curse. 2 deserving a curse; evil; hateful. *adj.*

cur sive (kėr′siv), written with the letters joined together. Ordinary handwriting is cursive. *adj.* —**cur′sive ly,** *adv.*

cur sor i ly (kėr′sər ə lē), in a cursory manner. *adv.*

cur sor y (kėr′sər ē), without attention to details; hasty and superficial: *She gave the lesson a cursory glance, expecting to study it later. adj.*

curst (kėrst), cursed; a past tense and past participle of **curse.** *v.*

curt (kėrt), rudely brief; short; abrupt: *a curt way of talking. A curt nod was the only notice he gave that he knew she was there. adj.* —**curt′ly,** *adv.* —**curt′ness,** *n.*

cur tail (kėr tāl′), cut short; cut off part of; reduce; lessen: *My parents curtailed my allowance from $1 to 50 cents. v.*

cur tail ment (kėr tāl′mənt), a curtailing; reduction; lessening: *The Bill of Rights forbids the curtailment of free speech. n.*

cur tain (kėrt′n), 1 cloth hung at windows or in doors for protection or ornament. 2 the drapery or hanging screen which separates the stage of a theater from the part where the audience sits. 3 the fall or closing of the curtain at the end of an act or scene. 4 provide or shut off with a curtain or curtains: *The boys took two sheets and curtained off a space in the corner.* 5 cover; hide: *Darkness curtained the entire winter countryside.* 6 thing that covers or hides: *A curtain of fog fell over the harbor.* 1-3,6 *n.,* 4,5 *v.*

cusp

hat, āge, fär; let, ēqual, tėrm;
it, īce; hot, ōpen, ôrder;
oil, out; cup, pùt, rüle; ch, child;
ng, long; sh, she; th, thin;
ŦH, then; zh, measure;

ə represents *a* in about,
e in taken, *i* in pencil,
o in lemon, *u* in circus.

curt sey (kėrt′sē), curtsy. *n., pl.* **curt seys;** *v.*

curt sy (kėrt′sē), 1 bow of respect or greeting by women and girls, made by bending the knees and lowering the body slightly. 2 make a curtsy: *The actress curtsied when the audience applauded.* 1 *n., pl.* **curt sies;** 2 *v.,* **curt sied, curt sy ing.**

curtsy (def. 1)

cur va ture (kėr′və chər), 1 a curving. 2 a curved conditon: *curvature of the spine. n.*

curve (kėrv), 1 line that has no straight part; a continuously bending line without angles. A circle is a closed curve. 2 something having the shape of a curve; bend: *The automobile had to slow down to go around the curves in the road.* 3 bend so as to form a curve; bend in a curve: *The strong man curved the iron bar. The highway curved to the right in a sharp turn.* 4 baseball thrown to swerve just before it reaches the batter. 5 throw a curve in baseball. 1,2,4 *n.,* 3,5 *v.,* **curved, curv ing.**

cush ion (kůsh′ən), 1 a soft pillow or pad used to sit, lie, or kneel on: *I rested my head by laying it on a cushion.* 2 anything that makes a soft place: *a cushion of moss under a tree.* 3 put or rest on a cushion: *The nurse cushioned the patient's head.* 4 provide with a cushion: *cushion a chair.* 5 anything that softens, lessens, or protects from a shock, jar, or jolt. Air or steam forms a protective cushion in some machines. *The bush acted as a cushion to my fall.* 6 soften or ease the effects of: *Nothing could cushion the shock of his father's death.* 1,2,5 *n.,* 3,4,6 *v.* —**cush′ion like′,** *adj.*

cusp (kusp), 1 a pointed end; point: *A*

211

adj. adjective	*n.* noun
adv. adverb	*prep.* preposition
conj. conjunction	*pron.* pronoun
interj. interjection	*v.* verb
sing. singular	*pl.* plural

crescent has two cusps. 2 a pointed end on the crown of a tooth. *n.*

cus pid (kus′pid) canine tooth. *n.*

cus pi dor (kus′pə dôr), spittoon, *n.*

cuss (kus), INFORMAL. curse. *v.*, *n.*

cus tard (kus′tərd), a baked, boiled, or frozen mixture of eggs, milk, and sugar. Custard is used as a dessert or as a food for sick people. *n.*

Cus ter (kus′tər), **George Armstrong**, 1839-1876, United States Army officer in the Civil War and in many Indian wars. *n.*

cus to di an (kus tō′dē ən), 1 person in charge; guardian; keeper: *When his father died his uncle became his legal custodian.* 2 person who takes care of a building or offices; janitor: *a school custodian. n.*

cus to dy (kus′tə dē), watchful keeping; charge; care: *Parents have the custody of their young children. All the important papers are in the lawyer's custody. n., pl.* **cus to dies.**

in custody, in the care of the police; under arrest: *The person accused of the murder will have to remain in custody until his trial.*

take into custody, arrest: *The suspect was taken into custody by the police.*

cus tom (kus′təm), 1 any usual action or practice; habit: *It was her custom to rise early every morning.* 2 a long-established habit having the force of law: *The social customs of many countries differ from ours.* 3 the regular business given by a customer to a particular store or shop: *The new gas station would like to have your custom.* 4 made to order; custom-made: *custom clothes.* 5 making things to order: *He had that suit made by a custom tailor.* **6 customs,** *pl.* **a** taxes paid to the government on things brought in from foreign countries: *I paid $4 in customs on the $100 Swiss watch.* **b** department of the government that collects these taxes. 1-3,6 *n.,* 4,5 *adj.*

cus tom ar i ly (kus′tə mer′ə lē), in a customary manner; usually: *He customarily walks to work. adv.*

cus tom ar y (kus′tə mer′ē), according to custom; usual: *Ten o'clock is her customary bedtime. adj.*

cus tom er (kus′tə mər), 1 person who buys, especially a regular shopper

at a particular store. 2 INFORMAL. person; fellow: *He can be a rough customer when he gets angry. n.*

custom house, a government building or office, usually at a seaport, airport, or border-crossing point, where taxes on things brought into a country are collected.

cus tom-made (kus′təm mād′), made to order; made specially for an individual customer; not ready-made: *a custom-made suit. adj.*

cut (kut), 1 divide, separate, open, or remove with a knife or any tool that has a sharp edge: *The butcher cut the meat with a knife. We cut a branch from the tree.* 2 pierce or wound with something sharp: *She cut her finger on the broken glass.* 3 opening made by something sharp: *bandage a cut.* 4 passage or channel that has been made by cutting or digging: *The train went through a deep cut in the side of the mountain.* 5 piece cut off or cut out: *A leg of lamb is a tasty cut of meat.* 6 make by cutting: *He cut a hole through the wall with an ax.* 7 be cut: *Cheese cuts easily.* 8 way in which a thing is cut; style; fashion: *the narrow, close-fitting cut of his coat.* 9 make a recording on: *cut a record, cut tape.* 10 have (teeth) grow through the gums. 11 reduce; decrease: *We must cut our expenses to save money.* 12 reduction; decrease: *The shopkeeper made a cut in his prices to attract more customers.* 13 shorten by removing a part or parts: *cut a speech, cut the hedge, cut one's hair.* 14 short cut. 15 go by a short cut: *He cut across the field to save time.* 16 divide by crossing: *A brook cuts through that field.* 17 hit or strike sharply: *The cold wind cut me to the bone.* 18 a sharp blow or stroke: *He took a cut at the ball and missed.* 19 hurt the feelings of: *His mean remark cut me.* 20 action or speech that hurts the feelings. 21 stop: *cut an engine. The cameraman said, "Cut!"* 22 INFORMAL. refuse to recognize (a person) on meeting or passing him: *No one in the class cut the new boy although he was very unfriendly.* 23 INFORMAL. be absent from (a class, lecture, etc.): *cut a history class.* 24 block or plate with a picture engraved on it, used in printing. 25 picture made from such a block or plate. 26 INFORMAL. **a** share: *Each partner has a cut of the profits.* 1,2,6,7,9-11,13,15-17,19,21-23 *v.,* **cut, cut ting;** 3-5,8,12,14,18,20,24-26 *n.*

cut and dried, dull; uninteresting: *Her speech was cut and dried.*

cut back, reduce or curtail: *The company had to cut back production because orders fell off.*

cut down, 1 cause to fall by cutting:

cut down a tree. 2 reduce; decrease: *cut down one's allowance.* 3 kill: *Hunters cut down most of the buffalo of our plains.*

cut in, 1 break in; interrupt: *She cut in suddenly with a remark while I was talking.* 2 interrupt a dancing couple to take the place of one of them. 3 move a vehicle suddenly into a line of moving traffic: *When the cab driver cut in he collided with another car.*

cut off, 1 remove by cutting: *Cut off that branch.* 2 shut off: *cut off the water.* 3 stop suddenly: *cut off all hope of success.* 4 break; interrupt: *cut off a conversation.* 5 disinherit: *The will cut her off without a cent.*

cut out, 1 remove by cutting: *He cut out the picture from a newspaper.* 2 take out; leave out: *Why did you cut out this part of the play?* 3 plan; map out: *She has her work cut out for her.* 4 stop doing, using, making, etc.: *Please cut out the noise.*

cut up, 1 cut to pieces. 2 SLANG. show off; play tricks.

cut a way (kut′ə wā′), 1 man's formal coat with the lower part cut back in a curve or slope from the waist in front to the tails in back. 2 object, or a model or drawing of an object, having part of its covering removed to show a section of its working parts for examination. 3 showing or representing an object in this way: *a cutaway drawing of an engine.* 1,2 *n.,* 3 *adj.*

cut back (kut′bak′), reduction: *a cutback in expenditures. The factory made a cutback in production when many of its orders were canceled. n.*

cute (kyüt), INFORMAL. 1 pretty and dear: *a cute baby.* 2 clever; shrewd: *a cute trick. adj.,* **cut er, cut est. —cute′ly,** *adv.* **—cute′ness,** *n.*

cu ti cle (kyü′tə kəl), 1 the outer layer of the skin of vertebrates. 2 the hard skin around the sides and base of a fingernail or toenail. *n.*

cut las (kut′ləs), cutlass. *n., pl.* **cut las es.**

cutlass
weight about
10 pounds

cut lass (kut′ləs), a short, heavy, slightly curved sword, used in former times especially by sailors. *n., pl.* **cutlass es.**

cut ler (kut′lər), person who makes, sells, or repairs knives, scissors, and other cutting instruments. *n.*

cut ler y (kut′lər ē), 1 cutting instruments, such as knives and scissors. 2 knives, forks, and spoons, for table use. *n.*

cut let (kut/lit), 1 slice of meat cut from the leg or ribs for broiling or frying: *a veal cutlet.* 2 a flat, fried cake of chopped meat or fish. *n.*

cut off (kut/ôf/), 1 a short way across or through; short cut: *We'll save time if we take the cutoff across the park.* 2 valve or other device that stops the passage of liquid, gas, etc., through a pipe or opening. 3 at or in which anything is cut off: *a cutoff period. A cutoff date ends this agreement.* 1,2 *n.,* 3 *adj.*

cut out (kut/out/), shape or design to be cut out: *Some books for children have cutouts.* *n.*

cutter (def. 3)

cut ter (kut/ər), 1 person who cuts: *A garment cutter cuts out pieces of fabric to be made into clothes.* 2 tool or machine for cutting: *The blade of a meat cutter is very sharp.* 3 a small, light sleigh, usually pulled by one horse. 4 a small, armed ship used for patrolling by the coast guard. 5 boat belonging to a ship, used to carry people and supplies to and from the ship. *n.*

cut throat (kut/thrōt/), 1 person who kills; murderer. 2 murderous: *a cutthroat band of pirates.* 3 without mercy; relentless or severe: *cutthroat competition.* 1 *n.,* 2,3 *adj.*

cut ting (kut/ing), 1 a small shoot cut from a plant to grow a new plant. 2 a newspaper or magazine clipping. 3 that cuts: *the cutting edge of a knife. A cutting wind whistled over the frozen lake.* 4 hurting the feelings: *He was offended by her cutting remark.* 1,2 *n.,* 3,4 *adj.* —**cut/ting ly,** *adv.*

cut tle bone (kut/l bōn/), the hard inside shell of cuttlefish. It is used for making polishing powder and as food for canaries, etc. *n.*

cut tle fish (kut/l fish/), a saltwater mollusk that has eight short arms with suckers, two long tentacles, and a hard inside shell. When frightened, cuttlefishes squirt out an inky fluid which is the source of sepia. *n., pl.* **cut tle fish es** or **cut tle fish.**

cut up (kut/up/), SLANG. person who shows off or plays tricks. *n.*

cut worm (kut/wėrm/), caterpillar that cuts off the stalks of young plants near or below the ground when feeding on them at night. *n.*

cwt., hundredweight. [from the abbreviations of Latin *centum* hundred and English *weight*]

-cy, *suffix added to nouns or adjectives to form nouns.* 1 office, position, or rank of _____: *Captaincy = rank of a captain.* 2 quality, condition, or fact of being _____: *Bankruptcy = condition of being bankrupt.* [from Latin *-cia, -tia*]

cy a nide (sī/ə nīd), any of various metal salts containing carbon and nitrogen. Cyanide is used in making plastics and insecticides, in extracting gold and silver from ores, and in treating metals. Some kinds of cyanide are extremely poisonous. *n.*

cy ber net ics (sī/bər net/iks), the comparative study of the nervous system and certain mechanical systems in order to understand better the communication and control of impulses and responses in both types of systems. *n.*

cyc la men (sik/lə mən), plant with heart-shaped leaves and showy white, purple, pink, or crimson flowers, whose five petals bend backward. It belongs to the same family as the primrose. *n.*

cy cle (sī/kəl), 1 period of time or complete process of growth or action that repeats itself in the same order. The seasons of the year — spring, summer, autumn, and winter — make a cycle. 2 a complete set or series: *a cycle of songs or of poems.* 3 all the stories or legends told about a certain hero or event: *There is a cycle of stories about the adventures of King Arthur and his knights.* 4 a very long period of time; age. 5 a complete or double alternation or reversal of an alternating electric current. The number of cycles per second is the measure of frequency. 6 bicycle, tricycle, or motorcycle. 7 ride a bicycle, tricycle, or motorcycle. 1-6 *n.,* 7 *v.,* **cy cled, cy cling.**

cy clic (sī/klik), 1 of a cycle: *the cyclic motion of a steam engine piston.* 2 moving in cycles; coming in cycles: *the cyclic nature of the seasons.* *adj.* —**cy/cli cal ly,** *adv.*

cy clist (sī/klist), rider of a bicycle, tricycle, or motorcycle. *n.*

cy clone (sī/klōn), 1 a very violent windstorm; tornado. 2 storm moving around and toward a calm center of low pressure, which also moves. *n.*

cy clon ic (sī klon/ik), 1 of a cyclone: *a cyclonic wind.* 2 like a cyclone. *adj.*

cy clo pae di a (sī/klə pē/dē ə), encyclopedia. *n., pl.* **cy clo pae di as.**

cy clo pae dic (sī/klə pē/dik), encyclopedic. *adj.*

cy clo pe di a (sī/klə pē/dē ə), encyclopedia. *n., pl.* **cy clo pe di as.**

hat, āge, fär; let, ēqual, tėrm;
it, īce; hot, ōpen, ôrder;
oil, out; cup, pùt, rüle; ch, child;
ng, long; sh, she; th, thin;
ᴛʜ, then; zh, measure;

ə represents *a* in about,
e in taken, *i* in pencil,
o in lemon, *u* in circus.

cy clo pe dic (sī/klə pē/dik), encyclopedic. *adj.*

Cy clops (sī/klops), (in Greek legends) one of a race of giants, each having only one eye in the center of his forehead. *n., pl.* **Cy clo pes** (sī klō/pēz).

cy clo tron (sī/klə tron), particle accelerator that greatly increases the speed and energy of protons and other atomic particles. *n.*

cyg net (sig/nit), a young swan. *n.*

cylinder (def. 1)   cylinder (def. 4)

cyl in der (sil/ən dər), 1 a solid bounded by two equal, parallel circles and by a curved surface, formed by moving a straight line of fixed length so that its ends always lie on the two parallel circles. 2 any long, round object, solid or hollow, with flat ends. Rollers and tin cans are cylinders. 3 the rotating part of a revolver that contains chambers for cartridges. 4 the piston chamber of an automobile engine. *n.*

cy lin dri cal (sə lin/drə kəl), shaped like a cylinder; having the form of a cylinder. Silos, candles, and water pipes are often cylindrical. *adj.* —**cy lin/dri cal ly,** *adv.*

cymbals

cym bal (sim/bəl), one of a pair of brass plates, used as a musical instrument. When cymbals are struck

213

adj.	adjective	*n.*	noun
adv.	adverb	*prep.*	preposition
conj.	conjunction	*pron.*	pronoun
interj.	interjection	*v.*	verb
sing.	singular	*pl.*	plural

together, they make a loud, ringing sound. *n.*

cyn ic (sin/ik), 1 person inclined to doubt the sincerity and goodness of human motives and to show this doubt by sneers and sarcasm. 2 cynical. 1 *n.*, 2 *adj.*

cyn i cal (sin/ə kəl), 1 doubting the sincerity and goodness of others. 2 sneering; sarcastic: *It is hard to befriend someone who is cynical about friendship. adj.* —**cyn/i cal ly,** *adv.*

cyn i cism (sin/ə siz/əm), 1 cynical disposition. 2 a cynical remark. *n.*

cy no sure (sī/nə shùr), center of attraction, interest, or attention. *n.*

cy pher (sī/fər), cipher. *n., v.*

cy press (sī/prəs), 1 an evergreen tree with hard wood and dark leaves. 2 its wood. Cypress is much used for boards and shingles and for doors. *n., pl.* **cy press es.**

Cyp ri ot (sip/rē ət), 1 person born or living in Cyprus. 2 of or having to do with Cyprus. 1 *n.*, 2 *adj.*

Cyp ri ote (sip/rē ōt), Cypriot. *n., adj.*

Cy prus (sī/prəs), island and country in the E Mediterranean, south of Turkey. Cyprus is a member of the Commonwealth of Nations. *n.*

Cy rus (sī/rəs), died 529 B.C., king of Persia and founder of the Persian empire. He was called "Cyrus the Great." *n.*

cyst (sist), a small sac in animals or plants, usually containing diseased matter. *n.*

cy tol o gist (sī tol/ə jist), an expert in cytology. *n.*

cy tol o gy (sī tol/ə jē), branch of biology that deals with the formation, structure, and function of cells. *n.*

cy to plasm (sī/tə plaz/əm), the living

substance or protoplasm of a cell, outside of the nucleus. *n.*

C.Z., Canal Zone.

czar (zär), 1 emperor. It was the title of the former emperors of Russia. 2 person having absolute power. *n.* Also, **tsar** or **tzar.**

cza ri na (zä rē/nə), wife of a czar; Russian empress. *n., pl.* **cza ri nas.** Also, **tsarina** or **tzarina.**

Czech (chek), 1 member of a branch of the Slavs. Bohemians, Moravians, and Silesians are Czechs. 2 their language; Bohemian. 3 of or having to do with Czechoslovakia, its people, or the language of the Czechs. 1,2 *n.*, 3 *adj.*

Czech o slo vak (chek/ə slō/vak *or* chek/ə slō/väk), 1 of or having to do with Czechoslovakia or its people. 2 person born or living in Czechoslovakia. 1 *adj.*, 2 *n.*

Czech o slo va ki a (chek/ə slō vä/kē ə), country in central Europe, surrounded by West Germany, Poland, the Soviet Union, Hungary, and Austria. *Capital:* Prague. *n.* —**Czech/o slo va/ki an,** *adj., n.*

Dd

D or **d** (dē), 1 the fourth letter of the alphabet. 2 the Roman numeral for 500. *n., pl.* **D's** or **d's.**

d., English penny; pence: *2d. = 2.3 cents.* [abbreviation of *denarius,* the name of an English penny, from Latin *denarius,* the name of an ancient Roman gold coin.]

D.A., District Attorney.

dab (dab), 1 touch lightly; pat with something soft or moist; tap: *dab a cut with alcohol.* 2 a quick, light touch or blow; pat or tap: *The cat made a dab at the butterfly with its paw.* 3 put on with light strokes: *She dabbed paint on the canvas.* 4 a small, soft or moist mass: *a dab of butter.* 5 a little bit: *This spot needs a dab of paint.* 1,3 *v.,* **dabbed, dab bing;** 2,4,5 *n.*

dab ble (dab'əl), 1 dip in and out of water; splash: *We sat and dabbled our feet in the pool.* 2 do anything in a slight or superficial manner; work at a little: *He dabbled at painting but soon gave it up. The businessman dabbled in the stock market.* *v.,* **dab bled, dab bling.**

dab bler (dab'lər), person who dabbles. *n.*

Dac ca (dak'ə), capital of Bangladesh. *n.*

dace (dās), any of several small freshwater fish, related to the carp. *n., pl.* **dac es** or **dace.**

dachs hund (däks'hunt' or daks'-hund'), a small hound with a long body and very short legs. *n.* [from German *Dachshund* badger dog (because it was used for hunting badgers)]

Da cron (dā'kron or dak'ron), trademark for an artificial fiber or fabric that does not wrinkle or fade easily. It is used for shirts, dresses, suits, etc. *n.*

dad (dad), INFORMAL. father. *n.*

dad dy (dad'ē), INFORMAL. father. *n., pl.* **dad dies.**

dad dy-long legs (dad'ē lông'legz'), animal that looks much like a spider, but does not bite. It has a small body and long, thin legs. *n., pl.* **dad dy-long legs.**

Daed a lus (ded'l əs), (in Greek legends) a skillful worker who made wings for flying and built the Labyrinth in Crete. *n.*

daf fo dil (daf'ə dil), 1 plant with long, slender leaves and yellow flowers that bloom in the spring. It grows from a bulb. 2 its flower. *n.*

daff y (daf'ē), INFORMAL. daft. *adj.* **daff i er, daff i est.**

daft (daft), 1 without sense or reason; silly; foolish. 2 crazy; insane. *adj.* —**daft'ly,** *adv.* —**daft'ness,** *n.*

da Gam a (də gam'ə or də gä'mə), Vasco, 1469?-1524, Portuguese navigator who discovered a route from Europe to India by sailing around southern Africa.

dag ger (dag'ər), 1 a small weapon with a short, pointed blade, used for stabbing. 2 sign (†) used in printing to refer the reader to a note someplace else in the book. *n.*

da guerre o type (də ger'ə tīp), 1 an early method of photography. The pictures were made on silvered metal plates made sensitive to light. 2 picture made in this way. *n.* [from French *daguerréotype,* from Louis *Daguerre,* 1789-1851, who invented it]

dahl ia (dal'yə), 1 a tall plant with large, showy flowers of many colors and varieties that bloom in autumn. It belongs to the same family as the aster. 2 its flower. *n., pl.* **dahl ias.** [from Anders *Dahl,* 1751-1789, a Swedish botanist]

Da ho mey (də hō'mē), country in W Africa on the Atlantic. See **Upper Vol ta** for map. *n.*

dai ly (dā'lē), 1 done, happening, or appearing every day, or every day but Sunday: *a daily paper, a daily visit.* 2 every day; day by day: *The bus runs daily.* 3 newspaper printed every day, or every day but Sunday. 1 *adj.,* 2 *adv.,* 3 *n., pl.* **dai lies.**

dain ti ly (dān'tl ē), in a dainty manner. *adv.*

dain ti ness (dān'tē nis), a being dainty. *n.*

dain ty (dān'tē), 1 having delicate beauty; fresh and pretty: *The violet is a dainty spring flower.* 2 delicate in tastes and feeling; particular: *a dainty eater, too dainty in one's choice of words.* 3 good to eat; delicious: *"Wasn't that a dainty dish to set before the king?"* 4 something very good to eat; delicious bit of food: *Candy and nuts are dainties.* 1-3 *adj.,* **dain ti er, dain ti est;** 4 *n., pl.* **dain ties.**

dair y (der'ē), 1 farm where milk and cream are produced and sometimes butter and cheese are made. 2 store or company that sells milk, cream, butter, and cheese. 3 room or building where milk and cream are kept and made into butter and cheese. *n., pl.* **dair ies.**

dairy cattle, cows kept for the milk they give.

dair y maid (der'ē mād'), girl or woman who works in a dairy. *n.*

dair y man (der'ē mən), 1 man who works in a dairy. 2 man who owns or manages a dairy. *n., pl.* **dair y men.**

da is (dā'is) a raised platform at one

hat, āge, fär; let, ēqual, tèrm; it, īce; hot, ōpen, ôrder; oil, out; cup, pùt, rüle; ch, child; ng, long; sh, she; th, thin; ғн, then; zh, measure;

ə represents *a* in about, *e* in taken, *i* in pencil, *o* in lemon, *u* in circus.

end of a hall or large room. A throne, seats of honor, a lecture desk, etc., may be set on a dais. *n., pl.* **da is es.**

dai sy (dā'zē), 1 plant whose flowers or petals are usually white or pink around a yellow center. It belongs to the same family as the aster. 2 its flower. *n., pl.* **dai sies.** —**dai'sy like',** *adj.*

Da kar (dä kär'), seaport and capital of Senegal, on the Atlantic. *n.*

Da ko ta (də kō'tə), 1 North Dakota or South Dakota. 2 the former territory of the United States that became North Dakota and South Dakota. *n., pl.* **Da ko tas.** —**Da ko'tan,** *adj., n.*

Da lai La ma (dä lī' lä'mə), the chief priest of the religion of the Buddhist priests in Tibet and Mongolia.

dale (dāl), valley. *n.*

Dal las (dal'əs), city in NE Texas. *n.*

dal li ance (dal'ē əns), a dallying; trifling. *n.*

dal ly (dal'ē), 1 act in a playful manner: *The spring breeze dallies with the flowers.* 2 flirt (with danger, temptation, a person, etc.); trifle: *He dallied with the offer for days, but finally refused it.* 3 linger idly; loiter: *She dallied along the way and was late for dinner.* 4 waste (time): *I dallied the afternoon away looking out the window and daydreaming.* *v.,* **dal lied, dal ly ing.**

Dal ma tia (dal mā'shə), region in W Yugoslavia, along the Adriatic. *n.*

Dal ma tian (dal mā'shən), a large, short-haired dog, usually white with black spots. *n.*

dam[1] (dam), 1 wall built to hold back the water of a stream or any flowing water: *There was a flood when the dam burst.* 2 provide with a dam; hold back or block up with anything: *Beavers had dammed the stream.* 1 *n.,* 2 *v.,* **dammed, dam ming.** [Middle English *dame*]

dam[2] (dam), the female parent of sheep, cattle, horses, and other four-footed animals. *n.* [a different form of *dame*]

dam age (dam'ij), 1 harm or injury that lessens value or usefulness: *The accident did some damage to the car.* 2 harm or injure so as to lessen value or

adj. adjective	*n.* noun
adv. adverb	*prep.* preposition
conj. conjunction	*pron.* pronoun
interj. interjection	*v.* verb
sing. singular	*pl.* plural

usefulness: *The wind blew the boat onto the rocks and damaged it.* 3 **damages,** *pl.* money claimed or paid by law to make up for some harm done to a person or his property: *The man who was hit by the car asked for $5000 in damages.* 1,3 *n.,* 2 *v.,* **dam aged, dam ag ing.**

Da mas cus (də mas′kəs), capital of Syria, in the SW part. It is one of the world's oldest cities. Damascus is famous for its fine metalwork and brocades. *n.*

dam ask (dam′əsk), 1 a firm, shiny, reversible linen, silk, or cotton fabric with woven designs: *hangings of damask.* 2 linen material of this type used especially for tablecloths and napkins. 3 made of damask. 4 a rose color; pink. 5 rose-colored; pink. 1,2,4 *n.,* 3,5 *adj.* [from *Damascus*]

dame (dām), 1 lady: *Dame Fortune, Dame Nature.* 2 title of honor given in Great Britain to a woman, corresponding to the rank of a knight. 3 an elderly woman. 4 SLANG. woman. *n.*

damn (dam), 1 declare (something) to be bad or inferior; condemn: *The critics damned the new book.* 2 doom to hell. 3 swear or swear at by saying "damn"; curse. 4 a saying of "damn"; curse. 5 SLANG. very. 1-3 *v.,* 4 *n.,* 5 *adv.*

dam na ble (dam′nə bəl), abominable or outrageous; detestable. *adj.*

dam na bly (dam′nə blē), in a damnable manner. *adv.*

dam na tion (dam nā′shən), a damning or a being damned; condemnation. *n.*

damned (damd), 1 cursed; abominable. 2 SLANG. very. 1 *adj.,* 2 *adv.*

Dam o cles (dam′ə klēz′), (in Greek legends) a courtier of the king of Syracuse who glorified the happiness and riches of kings. The king made Damocles aware of the constant dangers surrounding kings by seating him at a banquet under a sword suspended by a single hair. *n.*

Da mon (dā′mən), (in Roman legends) a man who pledged his life for his friend Pythias, who was sentenced to death. Because of their devotion, the lives of both were spared. *n.*

damp (damp), 1 slightly wet; moist: *My feet were damp from walking home in the rain.* 2 moisture: *When it's foggy you can feel the damp in the air.* 3 make moist or slightly wet; dampen: *Damp the cloth and wipe up the spilled milk.* 4 thing that checks or deadens; damper: *Our argument cast a damp over the evening.* 5 check or deaden: *Weariness damped the traveler's enthusiasm.* 6 any poisonous or explosive gas that collects in mines. Firedamp is one kind. 1 *adj.,* 2,4,6 *n.,* 3,5 *v.* —**damp′ly,** *adv.* —**damp′ness,** *n.*

damp en (dam′pən), 1 make or become damp; moisten: *I often sprinkle water over the clothes to dampen them before ironing. The camp supplies dampened and molded during the long rains.* 2 cast a damp over; depress; discourage: *The sad news dampened our spirits.* *v.* —**damp′en er,** *n.*

damp er (dam′pər), 1 person or thing that discourages or checks. 2 a movable plate to control the draft in a stove or furnace. *n.*

damper (def. 2)
Air flow into the furnace through openings in the front is controlled by the opening and closing of the carefully balanced damper.

dam sel (dam′zəl), OLD USE. a young girl; maiden. *n.*

dam son (dam′zən), 1 a small, dark-purple plum. 2 tree that it grows on. *n.*

Dan (dan), 1 (in the Bible) a Hebrew tribe that migrated to northern Palestine. 2 city in ancient Palestine. *n.*

dance (dans), 1 move in rhythm, usually in time with music: *The ballerina can dance very well.* 2 movement in rhythm, usually in time with music. 3 some special group of steps: *The waltz and polka are two different dances.* 4 party where people dance: *My older sister is going to the high-school dance.* 5 one round of dancing: *Will you be my partner in the next dance?* 6 do, perform, or take part in (a dance): *They danced a waltz.* 7 piece of music for dancing. 8 jump up and down; move in a lively way: *See that boat dancing over the waves. The little boy danced with delight.* 9 cause to dance: *He danced me around the room.* 1,6,8,9 *v.,* **danced, danc ing;** 2-5,7 *n.*

danc er (dan′sər), 1 person who dances. 2 person whose occupation is dancing. *n.*

dan de li on (dan′dl ī′ən), a common weed with deeply notched leaves and bright-yellow flowers that bloom in the spring. *n.*

dan dle (dan′dl), 1 move (a child) up and down on one's knees or in one's arms. 2 pet; pamper. *v.,* **dan dled, dan dling.**

dan druff (dan′drəf), small, whitish scales of dead skin that flake off the scalp. *n.*

dan dy (dan′dē), 1 man who is too careful about his dress and appearance; fop. 2 INFORMAL. an excellent or first-rate thing: *That new bike is a dandy.* 3 INFORMAL. excellent; first-rate: *She got a dandy new bike.* 1,2 *n.,* *pl.* **dandies;** 3 *adj.,* **dan di er, dan di est.**

Dane (dān), person born or living in Denmark. *n.*

dan ger (dān′jər), 1 chance of harm; nearness to harm; risk; peril: *A miner's work is full of danger.* 2 thing that may cause harm: *Hidden rocks are a danger to ships.* *n.*

dan ger ous (dān′jər əs), likely to cause harm; not safe; risky: *Shooting off firecrackers can be dangerous.* *adj.* —**dan′ger ous ly,** *adv.*

dan gle (dang′gəl), 1 hang and swing loosely: *The cord of the window shade dangled in the wind.* 2 hold or carry (a thing) so that it swings loosely: *The cat played with the string I dangled in front of it.* 3 hang about; follow: *The popular girl always had people dangling after her.* *v.,* **dan gled, dan gling.**

Dan iel (dan′yəl), 1 (in the Bible) a Hebrew prophet whose great faith in God kept him unharmed in a den of lions. 2 book in the Old Testament which tells about him. *n.*

Dan ish (dā′nish), 1 of or having to do with Denmark, its people, or their language. 2 people of Denmark. 3 language of Denmark. 4 kind of rich pastry. 1 *adj.,* 2 *n.pl.,* 3,4 *n.sing.*

dank (dangk), unpleasantly damp or moist: *The cave was dark, dank, and chilly.* *adj.* —**dank′ly,** *adv.* —**dank′ness,** *n.*

Dan te (dan′tē), 1265-1321, Italy's greatest poet. *n.*

Dan ube (dan′yüb), river flowing from S West Germany into the Black Sea. *n.*

Dan zig (dant′sig), seaport in N Poland, on the Baltic Sea. *n.*

Daph ne (daf′nē), (in Greek myths) a

nymph pursued by Apollo, from whom she was saved by being changed into a laurel tree. *n.*

dap per (dap′ər), 1 neat, trim, or spruce: *The dandy is very dapper about his clothes.* 2 small and active. *adj.*

dap ple (dap′əl), 1 marked with spots; spotted: *a dapple horse.* 2 mark or become marked with spots: *The bleach dappled the dark cloth. The dark cloth dappled in the bleach solution.* 1 *adj.,* 2 *v.,* **dap pled, dap pling.**

Dar da nelles (därd′n elz′), strait in NW Turkey which connects the Sea of Marmara with the Aegean Sea, and separates European from Asian Turkey. In ancient times it was called the Hellespont. *n.*

dare (der *or* dar), 1 have courage; be bold; be bold enough: *The children dared to explore the haunted house.* 2 have courage to try; not be afraid of; face or meet boldly: *The canoeist dared the dangers of the rapids.* 3 to challenge: *I dare you to jump the puddle.* 4 a challenge: *I took his dare to jump.* 1-3 *v.,* **dared, dar ing;** 4 *n.*

dare dev il (der′dev′əl *or* dar′dev′əl), 1 a reckless person. 2 recklessly daring: *The speeder's daredevil driving caused an accident.* 1 *n.,* 2 *adj.*

dare say (der′sā′ *or* dar′sā′), believe: *I daresay you will be late if you don't hurry. v.*

Dar es Sa laam (där es sə läm′), seaport and capital of Tanzania, on the Indian Ocean.

dar ing (der′ing *or* dar′ing), 1 courage to take risks; boldness: *The fireman's daring saved a life.* 2 bold; fearless; courageous: *Performing on a trapeze high above a crowd is a daring act.* 1 *n.,* 2 *adj.* —**dar′ing ly,** *adv.*

Da ri us I (də rī′əs), 558?-486? B.C., Persian emperor from 521 to 486? B.C., who was defeated by the Athenians at Marathon in 490 B.C. He was called "Darius the Great."

dark (därk), 1 without light; with very little light: *A night without a moon is dark.* 2 not light-colored; near to black in color: *She has dark-brown eyes and a dark complexion.* 3 gloomy; dull; dismal: *Rain and clouds make a dark day.* 4 absence of light; darkness: *Do not be afraid of the dark.* 5 night; nightfall: *The dark comes on early in the winter.*

6 a dark color. 7 secret or hidden: *The spy had a dark plan.* 8 without knowledge or culture; ignorant: *a dark period in history.* 9 evil; wicked: *The assassination of the ambassador was a dark deed.* 1-3,7-9 *adj.,* 4-6 *n.* —**dark′ly,** *adv.* —**dark′ness,** *n.*

in the dark, in ignorance; without knowledge or information: *She said nothing, leaving me in the dark about her plans.*

Dark Ages, the early part of the Middle Ages, from about A.D. 400 to about A.D. 1000, when learning and culture in western Europe were at a low ebb.

dark en (där′kən), make or become dark or darker: *We darkened the room by drawing the shades. As the storm approached, the sky darkened. v.*

dark horse, 1 an unexpected winner about whom little is known. 2 person who is unexpectedly nominated for a political office.

dark ish (där′kish), somewhat dark. *adj.*

dark ling (därk′ling), 1 in the dark. 2 dark. 1 *adv.,* 2 *adj.*

dark room (därk′rüm′ *or* därk′rüm′), room cut off from all outside light, arranged for developing photographs. It usually has a very dim, colored light. *n.*

dar ling (där′ling), 1 person or animal very dear to another; person or animal much loved: *The baby is the family darling.* 2 a favorite: *You are Grandfather's darling.* 3 very dear; much loved: *"My darling daughter," her letter began.* 4 INFORMAL. pleasing or attractive: *What a darling little house!* 1,2 *n.,* 3,4 *adj.*

darn[1] (därn), 1 mend by making rows of stitches back and forth across a hole or torn place. 2 place mended by darning. 1 *v.,* 2 *n.* [from French dialect *darner,* from *darne* piece]

darn[2] (därn), INFORMAL. damn. *v., n., adv.* [a different form of *damn*]

dar nel (där′nl), weed with poisonous seeds which looks somewhat like rye. Darnel often grows in grain fields. *n.*

dart (därt), 1 a slender, pointed weapon thrown by the hand or shot from a blowgun. 2 **darts,** *pl.* game in which darts are thrown at a target. 3 throw or shoot suddenly and quickly: *The Eskimos darted spears at the seal.* 4 a sudden, swift movement. 5 move suddenly and swiftly: *The deer saw us and darted away.* 6 send suddenly: *She darted an angry glance at her sister.* 1,2,4 *n.,* 3,5,6 *v.*

Dar win (där′wən), **Charles,** 1809-1882, English naturalist famous for his theory of evolution which maintains that present-day forms of plants and animals have developed from simpler

hat, āge, fär; let, ēqual, tėrm; it, īce; hot, ōpen, ôrder; oil, out; cup, pu̇t, rüle; ch, child; ng, long; sh, she; th, thin; ∓H, then; zh, measure;

ə represents *a* in about, *e* in taken, *i* in pencil, *o* in lemon, *u* in circus.

forms through slight variations, with the survival of those forms which are best adapted to their environment. *n.*

dash (dash), 1 throw, drive, or strike against: *In a fit of anger he dashed his ruler against the door. The waves dashed against the rocks.* 2 splash: *She dashed some paint on the canvas.* 3 a splash: *He was sprayed by a dash of mud.* 4 to rush: *They dashed by in a car.* 5 a rush: *We made a dash for safety.* 6 strike violently so as to break; smash: *He dashed the bowl to bits on a rock.* 7 a violent blow or stroke: *the dash of the oar against the water.* 8 ruin or destroy: *Our hopes were dashed by the bad news.* 9 a small amount: *More than a dash of pepper will make the meat too spicy.* 10 a short race: *the fifty-yard dash.* 11 energy; spirit; liveliness: *The winning team played with dash against the losers.* 12 a mark (—) used in writing or printing to show a break in sense, explanatory material, omitted letters or words, etc. 13 a long sound used in sending messages by telegraph or radiotelegraph. 14 dashboard. 1,2,4,6,8 *v.,* 3,5,7,9-14 *n.*

dash off, do, make, write, etc., quickly: *He dashed off a letter to his friend.*

dash board (dash′bôrd′), panel with instruments, gauges, and certain controls in front of the driver in an automobile, aircraft, etc. *n.*

dash er (dash′ər), 1 person or thing that dashes. 2 device for stirring the cream in a churn or in an ice-cream freezer. *n.*

dash ing (dash′ing), 1 full of energy and spirit; lively: *a dashing young man.* 2 showy: *The men in the band wore bright, dashing uniforms. adj.* —**dash′ing ly,** *adv.*

das tard (das′tərd), 1 a mean coward; sneak. 2 mean and cowardly; dastardly. 1 *n.,* 2 *adj.*

das tard ly (das′tərd lē), mean and cowardly: *Who was the dastardly person who put all the blame on me for breaking the window? adj.*

da ta (dā′tə *or* dat′ə), facts from which conclusions can be drawn; things known or admitted; information:

adj. adjective		*n.* noun
adv. adverb		*prep.* preposition
conj. conjunction		*pron.* pronoun
interj. interjection		*v.* verb
sing. singular		*pl.* plural

Names, ages, grades, and other data about the class are written in the teacher's notebook. **n.pl.** of **datum.**

date[1] (dāt), **1** time when something happens or happened; a particular day, month, or year: *Give the date of your birth. July 4, 1776 is the date of the signing of the Declaration of Independence.* **2** statement of time: *There is a date stamped on every piece of United States money.* **3** mark the time of; put a date on: *Please date your papers before handing them in.* **4** find out the date of; give a date to: *The historian was able to date the letter by its reference to Woodrow Wilson's election.* **5** be dated; have a date on it: *This letter dates from Paris.* **6** period of time: *At that date there were no airplanes.* **7** belong to a certain period of time; have its origin: *The oldest house in town dates from the 1800's.* **8** make old-fashioned or out of date: *Wearing a stiff collar dates Grandpa.* **9** INFORMAL. appointment for a certain time: *Don't forget to keep your Monday morning date with the dentist.* **10** INFORMAL. make a social appointment with (a person of the opposite sex): *My brother has been dating his girl friend regularly.* **11** INFORMAL. person of the opposite sex with whom a social appointment is made: *Will you be my date Friday for the school dance?* **1,2,6,9,11** *n.,* **3-5,7,8,10** *v.,* **dat ed, dat ing.** [from French *date,* from Latin *data* (*epistola Romae*) (letter) given, in the sense of "written" (at Rome)]

out of date, old-fashioned; not in present use: *I refused to wear the suit because it was out of date.*

up to date, 1 according to the latest style or idea; in fashion; modern: *Her clothes are always up to date.* **2** up to the present time: *The teacher entered our latest grades on our report cards to bring them up to date.*

date[2] (dāt), **1** the oblong, fleshy, sweet fruit of the date palm. **2** date palm. *n.* [from French of the 1200's *date,* from Latin *dactylus,* from Greek *daktylos* date, finger]

date less (dāt/lis), **1** without a date; not dated. **2** endless; unlimited. *adj.*

date palm, the palm tree on which dates grow.

da tive (dā/tiv), **1** showing the indirect object of a verb. Latin and some other languages have a dative case. **2** the dative case. **3** word in this case. **1** *adj.,* **2,3** *n.*

da tum (dā/təm *or* dat/əm), singular of **data.** *n.*

daub (dôb), **1** coat or cover with plaster, clay, mud, or any greasy or sticky material: *The mason filled the cracks in the wall by daubing them with cement.* **2** anything daubed on: *Just a few daubs of glue will mend the plate.* **3** make dirty; soil; stain: *Your skirt is daubed with mud.* **4** paint unskillfully: *She is no artist; she just daubs.* **5** a badly painted picture. **1,3,4** *v.,* **2,5** *n.* **—daub/er,** *n.*

daugh ter (dô/tər), **1** a female child or person in relation to her parent or parents. A girl is the daughter of her father and mother. **2** a female descendant. Women are sometimes called daughters of Eve. **3** girl or woman attached to a country, cause, etc., as a child is to its parents: *a daughter of France, daughters of liberty.* *n.*

daugh ter-in-law (dô/tər in lô/), wife of one's son. *n., pl.* **daugh ters-in-law.**

daugh ter ly (dô/tər lē), **1** of a daughter: *daughterly love toward her mother.* **2** like that of a daughter: *She had a daughterly relationship with the old couple next door.* **3** proper for a daughter: *daughterly duties.* *adj.*

daunt (dônt), frighten or discourage: *Rain did not daunt the campers.* *v.*

daunt less (dônt/lis), not to be frightened or discouraged; brave: *He is a dauntless mountain climber.* *adj.* **—daunt/less ly,** *adv.* **—daunt/less-ness,** *n.*

dau phin (dô/fən), title of the oldest son of the king of France, used from 1349 to 1830. *n.*

dav en port (dav/ən pôrt), a long couch with back and arms. *n.*

Da vid (dā/vid), died 970? B.C., Hebrew warrior, poet, and second king of Israel, who organized the Jewish tribes into a national state. According to tradition, he wrote many Psalms of the Bible. *n.*

da Vin ci (də vin/chē), **Leonardo,** 1452-1519, Italian painter, musician, sculptor, architect, engineer, and scientist.

Da vis (dā/vis), **Jefferson,** 1808-1889, president of the Confederacy from 1861 to 1865. *n.*

dav it (dav/it *or* dā/vit), one of a pair of metal or wooden arms at the side of a ship, used to hold or lower a small boat. *n.*

Da vy Jones (dā/vē), spirit of the sea.

Davy Jones's locker, grave of those who die at sea; bottom of the ocean.

daw (dô), jackdaw. *n.*

daw dle (dô/dl), waste time; idle; loiter: *Don't dawdle over your work. I dawdled the afternoon away.* *v.,* **daw dled, daw dling.**

daw dler (dô/dlər), person who dawdles; trifler; idler. *n.*

dawn (dôn), **1** beginning of day; the first light of the east: *The sun rose at dawn.* **2** beginning: *Dinosaurs roamed the earth before the dawn of man.* **3** grow bright or clear in the morning: *It was dawning when I awoke.* **4** grow clear to the eye or mind: *When they didn't leave, it dawned on me that they expected dinner. The ocean dawned on our view.* **5** begin; appear: *Day dawns in the east. A new era of progress is dawning in Africa.* **1,2** *n.,* **3-5** *v.*

day (dā), **1** time of light between sunrise and sunset: *Days are longer in summer than in winter.* **2** the period of 24 hours of day and night; time it takes for the earth to make one rotation on its axis. **3** day or date set aside for a particular purpose or celebration: *a school day, a feast day.* **4** hours for work; workday: *Our company has a seven-hour day.* **5** time; period: *the present day. In days of old they used candles instead of electric lights.* **6** period of life, activity, power, or influence: *Great Britain has had its day as a great colonial power.* **7** contest; conflict: *The debate was over; our side won the day.* *n.*

call it a day, INFORMAL. stop work: *After rehearsing the play for three hours, the director called it a day.*

day break (dā/brāk/), time when it begins to get light in the morning; dawn. *n.*

day dream (dā/drēm/), **1** dreamy thinking about pleasant things. **2** think dreamily about pleasant things. **3** something imagined but not likely to come true. **1,3** *n.,* **2** *v.* **—day/dream/er,** *n.*

day light (dā/līt/), **1** light of day: *It is easier to read by daylight than by lamplight.* **2** daytime. **3** dawn; daybreak: *We were up at daylight.* *n.*

see daylight, INFORMAL. get the meaning; understand.

day light-sav ing time (dā/līt/-sā/ving), time that is one hour ahead of standard time. It gives more daylight after working hours. Clocks are set

davits

ahead one hour when they are changed from standard to daylight-saving time.

Day of Atonement, Yom Kippur.

day school, 1 school held in the daytime. 2 a private school for students who live at home. 3 an elementary school held on weekdays.

day time (dā/tīm/), time when it is day and not night: *A baby sleeps even in the daytime. n.*

Day ton (dāt/n), city in SW Ohio. *n.*

daze (dāz), 1 make unable to think clearly; bewilder; stun: *The blow on his head dazed him so that he could not find his way home.* 2 hurt (one's eyes) with light; dazzle: *The child was dazed by the bright sun.* 3 a dazed condition: *I was in a daze from the accident and could not understand what was happening.* 1,2 *v.,* **dazed, daz ing;** 3 *n.*

daz zle (daz/əl), 1 hurt (the eyes) with too bright light or with quick-moving lights: *It dazzles the eyes to look straight at the sun.* 2 overcome the sight or the mind of with anything very bright or splendid: *The children were dazzled by the richness of the palace.* 3 a dazzling; bewildering brightness: *the dazzle of flashbulbs going off all around.* 1,2 *v.,* **daz zled, daz zling;** 3 *n.*

daz zler (daz/lər), person or thing that dazzles. *n.*

daz zling (daz/ling), that dazzles; brilliant or splendid: *the magician's dazzling display of skill. adj.* —**daz/zling-ly,** *adv.*

d.c., direct current.

D.C., 1 direct current. 2 District of Columbia.

DDT or **D.D.T.,** a very powerful, odorless insecticide.

de-, *prefix.* 1 do the opposite of: *Decentralize = do the opposite of centralize.* 2 down; lower: *Depress = press down.* 3 take away; remove: *Defrost = remove the frost.* [from Latin *de-,* from *de* away from]

dea con (dē/kən), 1 officer of a church who helps the minister in church duties not connected with preaching. 2 member of the clergy next below a priest in rank. *n.*

dead (ded), 1 no longer living: *The flowers in my garden are dead.* **2 the dead,** person or persons no longer living: *We remember the dead of our wars on Memorial Day.* 3 without life: *Stone and water are dead matter.* 4 like death: *I fell over in a dead faint.* 5 not active; dull or quiet: *Summer is never a dead season at camp.* 6 without force, power, spirit, or feeling: *The car won't start because the battery is dead.* 7 no longer in use: *The language of the ancient Romans is a dead language.* 8 INFORMAL. very tired; worn-out: *Dead from exhaustion, the children fell*

fast asleep. 9 sure: *Buffalo Bill was a dead shot with a rifle.* 10 complete; absolute: *There was dead silence in the library.* 11 completely; absolutely: *You are dead wrong. I was dead tired.* 12 directly; straight: *Don't take any side streets but walk dead ahead two miles.* 13 time when there is the least life stirring: *The plane landed in the dead of night.* 1,3-10 *adj.,* 2,13 *n.,* 11,12, *adv.* —**dead/ness,** *n.*

dead en (ded/n), 1 make dull or weak; lessen the force of: *Some medicines are given to deaden pain. The force of the blow was deadened by his heavy clothing.* 2 make soundproof: *The curtains, carpets, and thick walls deadened the room. v.*

dead end, street, passage, etc., closed at one end.

dead heat, race that ends in a tie.

dead letter, 1 letter that cannot be delivered or returned because of a wrong address, not enough stamps, etc. 2 law or rule that is no longer observed.

dead line (ded/līn/), the latest possible time to do something: *The teacher made Friday afternoon the deadline for handing in all book reports. n.*

dead li ness (ded/lē nis), deadly quality or character. *n.*

dead lock (ded/lok/), 1 a stopping of activity between two opposing sides because they are equally strong and neither one will give in; complete standstill: *Employers and strikers had reached a deadlock in their dispute over higher wages; neither group would give in to the other.* 2 bring or come to a complete standstill: *The two groups have been deadlocked for almost a week.* 1 *n.,* 2 *v.*

dead ly (ded/lē), 1 causing or likely to cause death; fatal: *a deadly wound, the deadly berries of a poisonous bush.* 2 like death; deathly: *deadly pale (adv.), deadly stillness (adj.).* 3 filled with hatred that lasts till death: *The warring Indian chiefs were deadly enemies.* 4 causing death of the soul: *Envy and pride are deadly sins.* 5 extremely: *"Washing dishes is deadly dull," she said.* 6 dull; boring: *a deadly lecture by a tiresome speaker.* 7 absolutely accurate: *Daniel Boone was a deadly shot.* 1-4,6,7 *adj.,* **dead li er, dead li est;** 2,5 *adv.*

deadly nightshade, belladonna.

dead reckoning, 1 calculation of the position of a ship or aircraft without observations of the sun, stars, etc., by using a compass and studying the navigator's record. 2 calculation of one's location by natural landmarks: *Daniel Boone made his way back to the settlement by dead reckoning.*

Dead Sea, a salt lake between Israel

hat, āge, fär; let, ēqual, tėrm;
it, īce; hot, ōpen, ôrder;
oil, out; cup, půt, rüle; ch, child;
ng, long; sh, she; th, thin;
ŦH, then; zh, measure;

ə represents *a* in about,
e in taken, *i* in pencil,
o in lemon, *u* in circus.

and Jordan. Its surface is the lowest on earth, almost 1300 feet below sea level.

Dead Sea Scrolls, collection of ancient scrolls discovered in several caves near the Dead Sea. They contain the oldest known copies of most of the books of the Bible.

dead weight, 1 the weight of anything lifeless, rigid, and unyielding. 2 a very great or oppressive burden.

dead wood (ded/wůd/), 1 dead branches or trees. 2 useless people or things. *n.*

deaf (def), 1 not able to hear: *The deaf man learned to read people's lips.* 2 not able to hear well. 3 not willing to hear: *The miser was deaf to all requests for money. adj.* —**deaf/ly,** *adv.* —**deaf/ness,** *n.*

deaf en (def/ən), 1 make deaf: *A hard blow on the ear deafened him for life.* 2 stun with noise: *A sudden explosion deafened us for a moment. v.*

deaf-mute (def/myüt/), person who is unable to hear and speak, usually because he has been deaf from birth or from childhood. *n.*

deal (dēl), 1 have to do: *Arithmetic deals with numbers.* 2 act; behave: *Deal kindly with them so you don't hurt their feelings.* 3 occupy oneself; take action: *The courts deal with those who break the laws.* 4 carry on a business; buy and sell: *A butcher deals in meat.* 5 INFORMAL. a business arrangement; bargain: *If you buy this television on sale you can get a good deal.* 6 give or deliver: *One fighter dealt the other a blow.* 7 give out among several; distribute: *The Red Cross dealt out food to the starving children.* 8 INFORMAL. arrangement; plan: *He is proposing that we substitute a new deal for the old one.* 9 a secret or underhanded agreement: *The corrupt mayor was caught in a deal to take public money.* 10 distribute playing cards: *It's your turn to deal.* 11 the distribution of playing cards. 1-4,6,7,10 *v.,* **dealt, deal ing;** 5,8,9, 11 *n.*

a good deal or **a great deal,** 1 a large part, portion, or amount: *She spends a great deal of her money on doctor's*

adj. adjective	*n.* noun
adv. adverb	*prep.* preposition
conj. conjunction	*pron.* pronoun
interj. interjection	*v.* verb
sing. singular	*pl.* plural

bills. 2 to a great extent or degree; much: *He is always going to the beach because he likes to swim a good deal.*

deal er (dē′lər), 1 person who makes his living by buying and selling: *a used-car dealer, a dealer in antique furniture.* 2 person who distributes the playing cards in a card game. *n.*

deal ing (dē′ling), 1 way of doing business: *The grocer is respected for her honest dealing.* 2 way of acting; behavior toward others: *The judge is known for his fair dealing.* 3 **dealings,** *pl.* **a** business relations: *That company has dealings with firms all over the world.* **b** friendly relations. *n.*

dealt (delt), past tense and past participle of **deal.** *The knight dealt his enemy a blow. The cards have been dealt. v.*

dean (dēn), 1 member of the faculty of a school, college, or university who has charge of the behavior or studies of the students: *the dean of women.* 2 head of a division or school in a college or university: *the dean of the law school.* 3 a high official of a church. A dean is often in charge of a cathedral. 4 member who has belonged to a group longest. *n.*

dear (dir), 1 much loved; precious: *His sister was very dear to him.* 2 dear one; darling: *"Come, my dear," said his grandmother.* 3 much valued; highly esteemed. *Dear* is used as a form of polite address at the beginning of letters: *Dear Sir.* 4 high in price; costly; expensive: *Fresh strawberries are dear in winter.* 5 at a high price; very much; much: *That mistake will cost you dear.* 6 exclamation of surprise, trouble, etc.: *Oh, dear! I lost my pencil.* 1,3,4 *adj.,* 2 *n.,* 5 *adv.,* 6 *interj.* —**dear′ness,** *n.*

dear ly (dir′lē), 1 fondly: *We love our parents dearly.* 2 at a high price: *She bought her new car quite dearly.* 3 very much: *You will regret your foolish behavior dearly in years to come. adv.*

dearth (dėrth), too small a supply; great scarcity or lack: *A dearth of food caused the prices to go up. The orphan suffered from a dearth of affection. n.*

dear y or **dear ie** (dir′ē), INFORMAL. a dear one; darling. *n., pl.* **dear ies.**

death (deth), 1 act or fact of dying; the ending of life: *The old man's death was*

calm and peaceful. 2 any ending that is like dying: *the death of an empire, the death of one's hopes.* 3 condition of being dead: *In death his heart was still.* 4 any condition like being dead. 5 cause of dying: *Her high blood pressure was her death. n.*

put to death, kill or execute.

to death, beyond endurance; excessively: *She was bored to death.*

death bed (deth′bed′), 1 bed on which a person dies. 2 the last hours of life. 3 during the last hours of life: *We tried to honor the patient's deathbed request.* 1,2 *n.,* 3 *adj.*

death blow (deth′blō′), 1 blow that kills: *He received a deathblow early in the battle.* 2 thing that puts an end (to something): *My illness was the death-blow to hopes for a trip to Europe. n.*

death less (deth′lis), never dying; living forever; immortal; eternal. *adj.*

death like (deth′līk′), like that of death: *There was a deathlike silence before the storm. adj.*

death ly (deth′lē), 1 like death: *Long illness had brought a deathly pallor to his face (adj.). The sick woman grew deathly pale (adv.).* 2 causing death; deadly: *The rats were killed with a deathly poison.* 3 extremely: *I am deathly afraid of deep water.* 1,2 *adj.,* 1,3 *adv.*

death rate, proportion of the number of deaths per year to the total population.

death's-head (deths′hed′), a human skull, used as a symbol of death. *n.*

Death Valley, valley in E California. It is the lowest land in the Western Hemisphere.

de ba cle (dā bä′kəl *or* di bak′əl), a sudden downfall or collapse; disaster; overthrow: *The election was a great debacle for the party in power since most of its candidates lost. n.*

de bar (di bär′), bar out; shut out; prevent; prohibit: *School rules debarred me from playing on the team until my grades improved. v.,* **de barred, de bar ring.**

de bark (di bärk′), go or put ashore from a ship; disembark: *After the passengers debarked in port, the captain debarked the crew. v.*

de base (di bās′), make low or lower; lessen the value of: *They debased themselves through greed. The nation's paper money was debased when the government could no longer give the full amount of gold or silver for it. v.,* **de based, de bas ing.**

de base ment (di bās′mənt), a debasing or a being debased: *the debasement of silver money by increasing the amount of alloy in it. n.*

de bat a ble (di bā′tə bəl), 1 capable

of being debated; open to debate. To be debatable a topic must have at least two sides. 2 not decided; in dispute; questionable: *The results of your experiment are debatable. adj.*

de bate (di bāt′), 1 talk about reasons for and against; consider; discuss: *I am debating buying a camera.* 2 discussion of reasons for and against: *There has been much debate about whose science project is best.* 3 a public argument for and against a question in a meeting. A formal debate is a contest between two sides to see which one has more skill in speaking and reasoning. 4 argue about (a question, topic, etc.) in a public meeting: *The two candidates debated the right of government employees to go out on strike for higher wages.* 1,4 *v.,* **de bat ed, de bat ing;** 2,3 *n.*

de bat er (di bā′tər), person who debates. *n.*

de bauch (di bôch′), 1 lead away from duty, virtue, or morality; corrupt or seduce: *Bad companions had debauched the boy.* 2 period of excessive eating, drinking, etc.: *One drunken debauch after another ruined his health.* 1 *v.,* 2 *n.*

de bauch er y (di bô′chər ē), 1 excessive eating, drinking, etc. 2 departure from duty, virtue, or morality. *n., pl.* **de bauch er ies.**

de bil i tate (di bil′ə tāt), make weak or feeble; weaken: *A hot, wet, tropical climate debilitates those who are not used to it. v.,* **de bil i tat ed, de bil i-tat ing.**

de bil i ty (di bil′ə tē), a being weak; weakness; feebleness: *His long illness caused him such debility that he even found it difficult to walk. n., pl.* **de bil i-ties.**

deb it (deb′it), 1 entry of something owed in an account. 2 charge with or as a debt: *The bank debited her account $500.* 1 *n.,* 2 *v.*

deb o nair or **deb o naire** (deb′ə-ner′ *or* deb′ə nar′), pleasant, courteous, and gay: *In spite of his carefree and debonair manner, he looked old. adj.* —**deb′o nair′ly,** *adv.* —**deb′o-nair′ness,** *n.*

de bris (də brē′), scattered fragments; ruins; rubbish: *The street was covered with broken glass, stone, and other debris from the explosion. n.* [from French *débris*]

debt (det), 1 something owed to another: *Having borrowed money a few times he had debts to pay back to several people. My debt for her kindness can never be repaid.* 2 condition of owing; indebtedness: *The loan from the bank has put her in debt.* 3 a sin; trespass: *Forgive us our debts against others. n.*

debt or (det′ər), person who owes something to another. *n.*

De bus sy (də byü′sē), **Claude,** 1862-1918, French composer. *n.*

de but (dā′byü *or* dā byü′), 1 a first public appearance: *a young actor's debut on the stage.* 2 the first formal appearance of a young woman in society. *n.* [from French *début*]

dé but (dā′byü *or* dā byü′), debut. *n., pl.* **dé buts.**

deb u tante (deb′yə tänt), a young woman during her first season in society. *n.* [from French *débutante*]

dé bu tante (deb′yə tänt), debutante. *n., pl.* **dé bu tantes.**

Dec., December.

dec ade (dek′ād), period of ten years: *The decade from 1908 to 1918 was one of great change. n.*

dec a dence (dek′ə dəns *or* di kād′ns), a falling off; growing worse; decline; decay: *a decadence in literature. The decadence of morals was one of the causes of the fall of Rome. n.*

dec a dent (dek′ə dənt *or* di kād′nt), 1 falling off; growing worse; declining; decaying: *a decadent nation.* 2 a decadent person. 1 *adj.,* 2 *n.*

dec a gon (dek′ə gon), a plane figure having 10 angles and 10 sides. *n.*

regular decagon   irregular decagon

de cal (dē′kal *or* di kal′), design or picture to be transferred to glass, wood, etc., treated so that it will stick fast. *n.*

Dec a logue *or* **Dec a log** (dek′ə lôg), (in the Bible) the Ten Commandments. *n.*

de camp (di kamp′), 1 leave quickly and secretly; run away; flee: *The strangers decamped during the night, taking two of our horses.* 2 leave a camp. *v.*

de cant (di kant′), 1 pour off (liquor or a solution) gently without disturbing the sediment: *The waiter decanted the wine.* 2 pour from one container to another. *v.*

de cant er (di kan′tər), a glass bottle with a stopper, used for serving wine or liquor. *n.*

de cap i tate (di kap′ə tāt), cut off the head of; behead. *v.,* **de cap i tat ed, de cap i tat ing.**

de cap i ta tion (di kap′ə tā′shən), a decapitating or a being decapitated. *n.*

de cath lon (di kath′lon), an athletic contest with ten different parts, such as racing, jumping, throwing the javelin,

etc. The person who scores the most points for all ten parts is the winner. *n.*

de cay (di kā′), 1 become rotten; rot: *The old apples got moldy and decayed. My teeth decayed because I ate too many sweets.* 2 a rotting: *The decay in the tree trunk proceeded so rapidly the tree fell over in a year.* 3 grow less in power, strength, wealth, or beauty: *Many nations have grown great and then decayed.* 4 a growing less in power, strength, wealth, or beauty: *the gradual decay of a person's health as one grows older.* 5 loss in quantity of a radioactive substance through disintegration of its component nuclei. 1,3 *v.,* 2,4,5 *n.*

de cease (di sēs′), 1 act or fact of dying; death: *the unexpected decease of a famous architect.* 2 die: *The queen deceased without leaving an heir.* 1 *n.,* 2 *v.,* **de ceased, de ceas ing.**

de ceased (di sēst′), 1 no longer living; dead. 2 **the deceased,** a (particular) dead person or persons: *The deceased had been a famous actor.* 1 *adj.,* 2 *n.*

de ce dent (di sēd′nt), (in law) a dead person. *n.*

de ceit (di sēt′), 1 a making a person believe as true something that is false; deceiving; lying: *An honest person is incapable of deceit.* 2 a dishonest trick; lie spoken or acted. 3 quality in a person that makes him tell lies or cheat; deceitfulness: *The dishonest trader was full of deceit. n.*

de ceit ful (di sēt′fəl), 1 ready or willing to deceive or lie: *a deceitful person.* 2 meant to deceive; deceiving; misleading: *a deceitful story. adj.* —**de ceit′ful ly,** *adv.* —**de ceit′ful ness,** *n.*

de ceive (di sēv′), 1 make (a person) believe as true something that is false; mislead: *The magician deceived her audience into thinking she had really pulled a rabbit from a hat.* 2 use deceit; lie. *v.,* **de ceived, de ceiv ing.**

de ceiv er (di sē′vər), person who deceives. *n.*

de cel e rate (dē sel′ə rāt′), decrease the velocity of; slow down: *By firing small rockets the astronauts decelerated the spaceship. v.,* **de cel e rat ed, de cel e rat ing.**

de cel e ra tion (dē sel′ə rā′shən), a decrease in velocity. *n.*

De cem ber (di sem′bər), the 12th and last month of the year. It has 31 days. *n.*

de cen cy (dē′sn sē), 1 a being decent; proper behavior: *Common decency requires that you pay for the window you broke.* 2 proper regard for modesty or delicacy; respectability. 3 **decencies,** *pl.* **a** suitable acts; proper observances: *courtesy, tolerance, kindness,*

and other decencies of life. **b** things required for a proper standard of living. *n., pl.* **de cen cies.**

de cent (dē′snt), 1 proper and right; respectable; modest: *It is not decent to laugh at another's troubles.* 2 good enough; fairly good; adequate: *He is not rich but he earns a decent living.* 3 not severe; rather kind: *The teacher was very decent to excuse my absence yesterday.* 4 dressed; not naked: *"Are you decent?" my sister called through the door. adj.* —**de′cent ly,** *adv.*

de cen tral i za tion (dē sen′trə lə zā′shən), a decentralizing or a being decentralized. *n.*

de cen tral ize (dē sen′trə līz), spread or distribute (authority, power, etc.) among more groups or local governments. *v.,* **de cen tral ized, de cen tral iz ing.**

de cep tion (di sep′shən), 1 a deceiving: *The twins' deception in exchanging places fooled everybody except their parents.* 2 a being deceived: *The deception of the magician's audience was almost complete.* 3 trick meant to deceive; fraud; sham: *The scheme is all a deception. n.*

de cep tive (di sep′tiv), 1 deceiving or misleading: *Travelers on the desert are often fooled by the deceptive appearance of trees and water.* 2 meant to deceive: *The deceptive friendliness of the fox fooled the rabbit. adj.* —**de cep′tive ly,** *adv.* —**de cep′tive ness,** *n.*

dec i bel (des′ə bəl), unit for measuring the relative loudness of sounds. *n.*

decibels	sounds
1	faintest sound heard
10	whisper, rustling of leaves
30	quiet conversation
50	quiet radio, average home
70	typewriter, average factory
90	police whistle, heavy traffic
110	deafening factory noise
130	sound vibrations *felt,* as with thunder or jet plane close by

de cide (di sīd′), 1 settle (a question, dispute, etc.): *Fighting is not the best*

decide

hat, āge, fär; let, ēqual, tèrm;
it, īce; hot, ōpen, ôrder;
oil, out; cup, pùt, rüle; ch, child;
ng, long; sh, she; th, thin;
ŦH, then; zh, measure;

ə represents *a* in about,
e in taken, *i* in pencil,
o in lemon, *u* in circus.

adj. adjective	*n.* noun	
adv. adverb	*prep.* preposition	
conj. conjunction	*pron.* pronoun	
interj. interjection	*v.* verb	
sing. singular	*pl.* plural	

way to decide an argument. 2 give judgment or decision: *The jury heard the evidence and decided in favor of the defendant.* 3 make up one's mind; resolve: *She decided to be a scientist.* 4 cause (a person) to reach a decision: *What decided you to vote for him? v.,* **de cid ed, de cid ing.**

de cid ed (di sī′did), 1 clear or definite; unquestionable: *The Olympic skier's strength gave her a decided advantage.* 2 firm; determined; resolute: *I studied hard because I had a decided wish to go to college. adj.*

de cid ed ly (di sī′did lē), without question; clearly; definitely: *Her work is decidedly better than his. It was a decidedly warm morning. adv.*

de cid u ous (di sij′ü əs), 1 shedding leaves each year. Maples, elms, and most oaks are deciduous trees. 2 falling off at a particular season or stage of growth: *Maples have deciduous leaves that fall in autumn. Antlers are deciduous horns. adj.*

dec i mal (des′ə məl), 1 decimal fraction. 2 number containing a decimal fraction. EXAMPLES: 75.24, 3.062, .091. 3 of tens; proceeding by tens. The metric system is a decimal system of measurement. 1,2 *n.,* 3 *adj.*

decimal fraction, fraction whose denominator is ten or a multiple of ten, expressed by placing a decimal point to the left of the numerator. EXAMPLES: $.04 = {}^4/_{100}, .2 = {}^2/_{10}.$

decimal point, period placed before a decimal fraction, as in 2.03, .623.

decimal system, system of numeration which is based on units of 10.

dec i mate (des′ə māt), 1 destroy much of; kill a large part of: *War decimated the tribe.* 2 take or destroy one tenth of. *v.,* **dec i mat ed, dec i mating.**

dec i ma tion (des′ə mā′shən), a decimating or a being decimated. *n.*

dec i me ter (des′ə mē′tər), measure of length equal to one tenth of a meter, or 3.937 inches. *n.*

de ci pher (di sī′fər), 1 make out the meaning of (something that is not clear): *I can't decipher this poor handwriting. We just couldn't decipher the mystery.* 2 change (something in cipher or code) to ordinary language; decode: *The spy deciphered the secret message. v.*

de ci sion (di sizh′ən), 1 a making up of one's mind; deciding: *I have not yet come to a decision about buying a new coat.* 2 judgment reached or given: *The jury brought in a decision of not guilty.* 3 firmness and determination: *She is a woman of decision who makes up her mind what to do and then does it.. n.*

de ci sive (di sī′siv), 1 having or giving a clear result; settling something beyond question: *The team won by 20 points, which was a decisive victory.* 2 having or showing decision: *When I asked for a decisive answer, he said flatly, "No." adj.* —**de ci′sive ly,** *adv.* —**de ci′sive ness,** *n.*

deck (dek), 1 one of the floors or platforms extending from side to side and often from end to end of a ship: *The main deck of this ship has no roof over it.* 2 part or floor resembling this: *the deck of an airplane.* 3 a pack of playing cards: *She shuffled the deck and dealt the cards.* 4 cover, dress, or adorn: *deck the halls with holly.* 1-3 *n.,* 4 *v.*

on deck, ready to do something.

deck hand (dek′hand′), sailor who works on deck; a common sailor. *n.*

de claim (di klām′), 1 recite in public; make a formal speech. 2 speak like an orator in a loud and emotional manner; speak for effect: *Everyone at the table listened as the old soldier declaimed against the lack of patriotism. v.*

dec la ma tion (dek′lə mā′shən), 1 act of declaiming; making formal speeches. 2 a formal speech or selection of poetry, prose, etc., for reciting: *He practiced his long declamation many times before giving it before an audience.* 3 loud and emotional talk. *n.*

dec la ra tion (dek′lə rā′shən), 1 a declaring: *rejoice at the declaration of a truce.* 2 thing declared; open or public statement: *The royal declaration was announced in every city and town.* 3 statement of goods, etc., for taxation: *The importer gave the customs agent a declaration showing what merchandise he was bringing into the country. n.*

Declaration of Independence, the public statement adopted by the Second Continental Congress on July 4, 1776, in which the American colonies declared themselves free and independent of Great Britain.

de clar a tive (di klar′ə tiv), making a statement; explaining. "I eat" and "The dog has four legs" are declarative sentences. *adj.*

de clare (di kler′ or di klar′), 1 announce publicly or formally; make known; proclaim: *Congress has the power to declare war.* 2 say openly; state strongly: *I declared that I would never do anything so foolish again.* 3 make a statement of (goods, etc.) for taxation: *Travelers returning to the United States must declare the things which they bought abroad. v.,* **de clared, de clar ing.**

de clas si fy (dē klas′ə fī), remove (documents, codes, etc.) from the list of restricted, confidential, or secret information. *v.,* **de clas si fied, de clas si fy ing.**

de clen sion (di klen′shən), 1 the giving of the different endings to nouns, pronouns, and adjectives according to their case or their relation to other words in the sentence. The declension of *who* is: nominative case, *who;* possessive case, *whose;* objective case, *whom.* 2 group of words whose endings for the different cases are alike. *n.*

dec li na tion (dek′lə nā′shən), 1 a downward bend or slope. 2 a polite refusal. 3 deviation of the needle of a compass from true north. *n.*

de cline (di klīn′), 1 turn away from doing; refuse (to do something): *The children declined to do as they were told.* 2 refuse politely: *I declined her offer of help.* 3 grow less in power, strength, wealth, beauty, etc.; grow worse; decay: *Great nations have risen and declined. A person's strength declines in old age.* 4 a losing of power, strength, wealth, beauty, etc.; growing worse: *Lack of money for books and equipment led to a decline in the condition of the school.* 5 a falling to a lower level; sinking: *a decline in prices, the decline of the sun as it nears the horizon.* 6 the last part of anything: *during the decline of a person's life.* 7 bend or slope down: *The hill declines to a fertile valley.* 8 a downward incline or slope: *The wagon rolled down the decline.* 9 give the different cases or case endings of (a noun, pronoun, or adjective). 1-3,7,9 *v.,* **de clined, de clin ing;** 4-6,8 *n.*

de cliv i ty (di kliv′ə tē), a downward slope. *n., pl.* **de cliv i ties.**

de code (dē kōd′), translate (secret writing) from code into ordinary language. *v.,* **de cod ed, de cod ing.**

de com pose (dē′kəm pōz′), 1 separate (a substance) into what it is made of: *The prism decomposed the sunlight into its many colors.* 2 rot or become rotten; decay: *The old fruits and vegetables decomposed quickly in the heat. v.,* **de com posed, de com posing.**

de com po si tion (dē′kom pə zish′ən), 1 act or process of decomposing: *fruit spoiled by decomposition, the decomposition of water into hydrogen and oxygen.* 2 decay; rot. *n.*

de com pres sion (dē′kəm-

222

presh/ən), removal or lessening of pressure, especially of air pressure: *Gradual decompression is necessary for deep-sea divers before they come up to the surface.* n.

dec o rate (dek/ə rāt/), 1 make beautiful; adorn; trim: *We decorated the school gymnasium with crepe paper for the spring festival.* 2 paint or paper (a room, etc.): *The old rooms looked like new after they had been decorated.* 3 give a medal, ribbon, or badge to (a person) as an honor: *The general decorated the soldier for bravery.* v., **dec o rat ed, dec o rat ing.**

dec o ra tion (dek/ə rā/shən), 1 thing used to decorate; ornament: *We put pictures and other decorations up in the classroom.* 2 medal, ribbon, or badge given as an honor. 3 act of decorating: *Decoration of the gymnasium took most of the day before the spring festival.* n.

Decoration Day, Memorial Day.

dec o ra tive (dek/ə rā/tiv), helping to adorn; ornamental; decorating: *The colored paper chains gave a decorative effect to the room.* adj. —**dec/o ra/tive ly,** adv. —**dec/o ra/tive ness,** n.

dec o ra tor (dek/ə rā/tər), 1 person who decorates. 2 interior decorator. n.

dec or ous (dek/ər əs *or* di kôr/əs), acting properly; in good taste; well-behaved; dignified: *Quiet, decorous behavior is requested in the library.* adj. —**dec/or ous ly,** adv.

de co rum (di kôr/əm), proper behavior; good taste in conduct, speech, dress, etc.: *act with decorum, observe decorum in a court of law.* n.

de coy (di koi/ *for 1,4;* dē/koi *or* di koi/ *for 2,3,5*), 1 lure (wild birds, animals, etc.) into a trap or near the hunter: *The farmer decoyed the rats with cheese.* 2 an artificial bird used to lure birds into a trap or near the hunter: *The duck hunter floated wooden decoys on the water.* 3 bird or other animal trained to lure others of its kind into a trap. 4 lead or tempt (a person) into danger by trickery; entice. 5 any person or thing used to lead or tempt into danger; lure. 1,4 v., 2,3,5 n.

de crease (di krēs/ *for 1;* dē/krēs/ *or* di krēs/ *for 2,3*), 1 make or become less; lessen: *Decrease the dose of medicine as you feel better. Hunger decreases as one eats.* 2 a growing less; lessening: *Toward night there was a decrease of heat.* 3 amount by which a thing becomes less or is made less: *The decrease in temperature was 10 degrees.* 1 v., **de creased, de creas ing;** 2,3 n.
on the decrease, decreasing.

de cree (di krē/), 1 something ordered or settled by authority; official decision; law: *The new state holiday was declared by a decree of the Governor.* 2 order or settle by authority: *The state legislature decreed that all dogs must be licensed.* 1 n., 2 v., **de creed, de cree ing.**

de crep it (di krep/it), broken down or weakened by old age; old and feeble: *He was too decrepit to climb stairs.* adj.

de crep i tude (di krep/ə tüd *or* di krep/ə tyüd), feebleness, usually from old age; decrepit condition; weakness. n.

de cre scen do (dē/krə shen/dō), in music: 1 a gradual decrease in force or loudness; diminuendo. 2 with a gradual decrease in force or loudness; diminuendo. 1 n., pl. **de cre scen dos;** 2 adj., adv. [from Italian *decrescendo* decreasing]

de cry (di krī/), 1 express strong disapproval of; condemn: *The taxpayers decried the increase in federal spending.* 2 make little of; try to lower the value of by slighting statements: *The librarian decried television as the only source of entertainment.* v., **de cried, de cry ing.**

ded i cate (ded/ə kāt), 1 set apart for a purpose; devote: *dedicate a national monument to the memory of a great civil rights leader. The doctor dedicated her life to improving hospital care in her community.* 2 address (a book, poem, etc.) to a friend or patron: *The author dedicated his book to his teacher as a mark of respect.* v., **ded i cat ed, ded i cat ing.**

ded i ca tion (ded/ə kā/shən), 1 a setting apart or a being set apart for a purpose: *the dedication of a park.* 2 words dedicating a book, poem, etc., to a friend or patron. n.

decoy (def. 2)
wooden decoy attracting wild ducks

ded i ca to ry (ded/ə kə tôr/ē), of dedication; as a dedication. adj.

de duce (di düs/ *or* di dyüs/), reach (a conclusion) by reasoning; infer: *Her instructions are so complicated I cannot deduce from them what she wants.* v., **de duced, de duc ing.**

de duct (di dukt/), take away; subtract: *When I broke the window, my parents deducted its cost from my allowance.* v.

de duct i ble (di duk/tə bəl), that can be deducted. adj.

de duc tion (di duk/shən), 1 a taking

hat, āge, fär; let, ēqual, tėrm;
it, īce; hot, ōpen, ôrder;
oil, out; cup, pùt, rüle; ch, child;
ng, long; sh, she; th, thin;
ŦH, then; zh, measure;

ə represents *a* in about,
e in taken, *i* in pencil,
o in lemon, *u* in circus.

away; subtraction: *No deduction from one's pay is made for absence due to illness.* 2 amount deducted: *There was a deduction of $50 from the bill for damage caused by the movers.* 3 a reaching of conclusions by reasoning; inference. A person using deduction reasons from general laws to particular cases. 4 thing deduced; conclusion: *The detective reached her clever deduction by careful study of the facts.* n.

de duc tive (di duk/tiv), of or using deduction; reasoning by deduction. adj. —**de duc/tive ly,** adv.

deed (dēd), 1 thing done; act; action: *a good deed. Deeds, not words, are needed.* 2 a written or printed statement of ownership. The buyer of real estate receives a deed to the property from the former owner. 3 transfer by deed: *She deeded her house to her only child.* 1,2 n., 3 v.

deem (dēm), think, believe, or consider: *The police deemed it necessary for the town's safety to arrest most speeders.* v.

deep (dēp), 1 going a long way down from the top or surface: *We had to dig a deep well to get pure water. The pond is deep in the middle.* 2 far down or back: *We dug deep before we could find water.* 3 going a long way back from the front: *The lot on which our house stands is 100 feet deep.* 4 a deep place. 5 low in pitch: *She heard the low tones of Father's deep voice.* 6 hard to understand: *a deep book.* 7 earnest; heartfelt: *deep sorrow. Deep feeling is hard to put into words.* 8 strong; great; intense; extreme: *I fell into a deep sleep after the exhausting hike.* 9 strong and dark in color: *a deep red.* 10 in depth: *a tank 8 feet deep.* 11 with the mind fully taken up: *deep in thought.* 12 well along in time; far on: *He studied deep into the night.* 13 the most intense part: *the deep of winter.* 14 **the deep,** the sea: *Frightened sailors thought they saw monsters from the deep.* 1,3,5-11 adj., 2,12 adv., 4,13,14 n. —**deep/ly,** adv. —**deep/ness,** n.

deep en (dē/pən), make or become deeper: *We deepened the hole. The*

adj. adjective	*n.* noun
adv. adverb	*prep.* preposition
conj. conjunction	*pron.* pronoun
interj. interjection	*v.* verb
sing. singular	*pl.* plural

water deepened as the tide came in. v.

deep-root ed (dēp′rü′tid *or* dēp′-rût′id), 1 deeply rooted: *a tall and deep-rooted tree.* 2 firmly fixed: *Many people have a deep-rooted fear of snakes. adj.*

deep-sea (dēp′sē′), of or in the deeper parts of the sea: *a deep-sea diver. adj.*

deep-seat ed (dēp′sē′tid), 1 far below the surface. 2 firmly fixed: *She has a deep-seated love of nature. adj.*

deep-set (dēp′set′), 1 set deeply: *He has deep-set eyes.* 2 firmly fixed. *adj.*

deer (dir), a swift, graceful mammal that has hoofs and chews the cud. All male deer and some female deer have antlers, which are shed and grow again every year. *n., pl.* **deer. —deer′like′,** *adj.*

deer—3½ ft. high at the shoulder

deer mouse, a small North American mouse with white feet and large ears.

deer skin (dir′skin′), 1 skin of a deer. 2 leather made from it. 3 clothing made of this leather. *n.*

def., definition.

de face (di fās′), spoil the appearance of; mar: *Scribbled pictures and notes defaced the pages of the book. v.,* **de faced, de fac ing.**

de face ment (di fās′mənt), 1 a defacing or a being defaced. 2 thing that defaces. *n.*

de fac to (di fak′tō), in fact; in reality; actually existing, whether lawful or not: *the dictator's de facto government.* [from Latin *de facto* from the fact]

def a ma tion (def′ə mā′shən), a defaming or a being defamed; slander or libel. *n.*

de fam a to ry (di fam′ə tôr′ē), that defames; slanderous or libelous. *adj.*

de fame (di fām′), attack the good name of; harm the reputation of; speak evil of; slander or libel: *Persons in public life are sometimes defamed by opponents. v.,* **de famed, de fam ing.**

de fault (di fôlt′), 1 failure to do something or to appear somewhere when due; neglect. If, in any contest, one side does not appear, it loses by default. 2 fail to do something or appear somewhere when due: *They defaulted in the tennis tournament. She defaulted in the payment of her debt.* 1 *n.,* 2 *v.* **—de fault′er,** *n.*

de feat (di fēt′), 1 win a victory over; overcome: *Washington defeated Cornwallis at Yorktown.* 2 cause to fail; frustrate: *defeat someone's plans.* 3 a defeating: *Washington's defeat of Cornwallis ended the Revolutionary War.* 4 a being defeated: *Cornwallis's defeat at Yorktown marked the end of British power in the United States.* 1,2 *v.,* 3,4 *n.*

de feat ism (di fē′tiz′əm), attitude or behavior of a defeatist. *n.*

de feat ist (di fē′tist), person who expects or admits defeat. *n.*

def e cate (def′ə kāt), discharge intestinal waste from the body. *v.,* **def e-cat ed, def e cat ing.**

de fect (dē′fekt *or* di fekt′ *for 1,2;* di fekt′ *for 3*), 1 a shortcoming or failing in a person or thing; fault or blemish: *The cloth had holes and other defects. Her bad temper was a defect in her kind and generous nature.* 2 lack of something necessary for completeness: *an error caused by a defect in reasoning.* 3 forsake one's own country, group, etc., for another, especially another that is opposed to it: *The traitor defected to the enemy.* 1,2 *n.,* 3 *v.*

de fec tion (di fek′shən), a falling away from loyalty, duty, etc.; desertion. *n.*

de fec tive (di fek′tiv), having a flaw or blemish; not perfect; not complete; faulty: *A watch with defective parts will not keep time. adj.*

de fec tor (di fek′tər), person who defects. *n.*

de fence (di fens′), defense (the spelling generally used in Great Britain and Canada). *n.*

de fend (di fend′), 1 guard from attack or harm; keep safe; protect: *defend a fort.* 2 act, speak, or write in favor of: *The newspapers defended the governor's action. Lawyers were hired to defend the people charged with crimes.* 3 fight or contest (a claim or a lawsuit). *v.* **—de fend′er,** *n.*

de fend ant (di fen′dənt), person accused or sued in a court of law: *This defendant is charged with theft. n.*

de fense (di fens′), 1 thing that defends or protects; thing to guard against attack or harm: *A wall around the city was a defense against enemies.* 2 a guarding against attack or harm; defending or protecting: *The armed forces are responsible for the defense of the country.* 3 action, speech, or writing in favor of something. 4 team or players defending a goal in a game. 5 a defendant and his lawyers. *n.* Also, **defence.**

de fense less (di fens′lis), helpless against attack or harm; having no defense; unprotected: *a defenseless village, a defenseless child. adj.*

de fen si ble (di fen′sə bəl), that can be defended or justified. *adj.*

de fen sive (di fen′siv), 1 ready to defend; intended to defend; defending: *A driver who is careful and prepared for the mistakes of others is a defensive driver.* 2 position or attitude of defense. 3 thing that defends. 1 *adj.,* 2,3 *n.* **—de fen′sive ly,** *adv.* **—de fen′sive ness,** *n.*

on the defensive, ready to defend, apologize, or explain.

de fer[1] (di fèr′), put off; delay: *Examinations were deferred because so many children were sick. v.,* **de ferred, de fer ring.** [from Latin *differre* set apart]

de fer[2] (di fèr′), yield in judgment or opinion: *The children deferred to their parents' wishes. v.,* **de ferred, de fer ring.** [from French of the 1400's *déférer*]

def er ence (def′ər əns), 1 a yielding to the judgment, opinion, wishes, etc., of another. 2 great respect: *show deference to persons who are much older and wiser. n.*

in deference to, out of respect for the wishes or authority of.

def er en tial (def′ə ren′shəl), showing deference; respectful. *adj.* **—def′er en′tial ly,** *adv.*

de fer ment (di fèr′mənt), a putting off; delay: *My uncle was given a deferment from military service until he finished college. n.*

de fi ance (di fī′əns), a defying; standing up against authority and refusing to recognize or obey it; open resistance to power: *Robin Hood shouted his defiance at the sheriff. n.*

in defiance of, without regard for; in spite of: *She wore a light jacket all winter in defiance of the cold weather.*

de fi ant (di fī′ənt), showing defiance; openly resisting: *She told us in a defiant manner that she was against our plans. adj.* **—de fi′ant ly,** *adv.*

de fi cien cy (di fish′ən sē), 1 lack of something needed or required; incompleteness: *A deficiency of calcium in your diet can cause weak teeth.* 2 amount by which something is not sufficient; shortage: *If a bill to be paid is*

$10 and you have only $6, the deficiency is $4. *n., pl.* **de fi cien cies.**

de fi cient (di fish′ənt), 1 not complete; defective: *The child's knowledge of arithmetic is deficient.* 2 not sufficient in quantity, force, etc.; lacking: *This milk is deficient in fat. adj.*

def i cit (def′ə sit), amount by which a sum of money falls short; shortage: *Since the club owed $15 and had only $10 in the treasury, there was a deficit of $5 to be made up by the members. n.*

de file[1] (di fīl′), 1 make filthy or dirty; make disgusting in any way. 2 destroy the purity or cleanness of (anything sacred); desecrate: *The barbarians defiled the church by using it as a stable. v.,* **de filed, de fil ing.** [from French of the 1300's *defouler* trample down or violate]

de file[2] (di fīl′), 1 march in single file or a narrow column. 2 a narrow place through which troops can march only in narrow columns; steep and narrow valley. 1 *v.,* **de filed, de fil ing;** 2 *n.* [from French *défiler*]

de file ment (di fīl′mənt), a defiling or a being defiled; pollution: *The defilement of the air by industrial wastes is a growing problem. n.*

de fine (di fīn′), 1 make clear the meaning of; explain: *A dictionary defines words.* 2 make clear; make distinct: *The shadow defined the shape of the building.* 3 fix; settle: *The powers of the courts are defined by law.* 4 settle the limits of: *The boundary between the United States and Canada is defined by treaty. v.,* **de fined, de fin ing.**

def i nite (def′ə nit), 1 clear or exact; not vague: *definite proof. I expect a definite answer, either yes or no.* 2 having settled limits: *a definite boundary line. adj.* —**def′i nite ness,** *n.*

definite article, the article *the.* "A dog" means "any dog"; "the dog" means "a certain or particular dog."

def i nite ly (def′ə nit lē), 1 in a definite manner: *Say definitely what you have in mind.* 2 certainly: *Will you go? Definitely. adv.*

def i ni tion (def′ə nish′ən), 1 an explaining of the nature of a thing; making clear the meaning of a word. 2 statement in which the nature of a thing is explained or the meaning of a word is made clear. One definition of "home" is "the place where a person or family lives." 3 clearness; distinctness. *Good photographs have definition. n.*

de fin i tive (di fin′ə tiv), that decides or settles a question; conclusive; final: *Mother's definitive answer was that we could not go unless we finished our homework first. adj.*

de flate (di flāt′), 1 let air or gas out of (a balloon, tire, football, etc.): *We*

found that a nail had deflated the tire. 2 reduce (prices or currency) from an inflated condition. 3 injure or destroy the conceit or confidence of: *Our laughter soon deflated him. v.,* **de flat ed, de flat ing.**

de fla tion (di flā′shən), 1 a letting the air or gas out: *the deflation of a tire.* 2 reduction of the amount of available money in circulation so that the value of money increases and prices go down. *n.*

de flect (di flekt′), bend or turn aside; change the direction of: *The wind deflected the arrow's flight. v.*

de flec tion (di flek′shən), 1 a bending or turning aside: *Strong winds caused some deflection from the plane's charted course.* 2 amount of bending or turning. *n.*

De foe (di fō′), **Daniel,** 1660?-1731, English author who wrote *Robinson Crusoe. n.*

de fo rest (dē fôr′ist), remove the trees from; clear of trees: *The land had to be deforested before the settlers could farm it. v.*

de for es ta tion (dē fôr′ə stā′shən), a deforesting or a being deforested. *n.*

de form (di fôrm′), 1 spoil the form or shape of: *Wearing shoes that are too tight may deform the feet.* 2 make ugly: *a face deformed by hate and anger. v.*

de for ma tion (dē′fôr mā′shən), 1 act of deforming. 2 deformed condition; disfigurement: *A crippling disease caused deformation of his body. n.*

de formed (di fôrmd′), not properly formed: *The baby's deformed foot was corrected by surgery. adj.*

de form i ty (di fôr′mə tē), 1 part that is not properly formed, such as a hump on the back. 2 condition of being improperly formed: *Doctors can now cure many deformities. n., pl.* **de form i ties.**

de fraud (di frôd′), take money, rights, etc., away from by fraud; cheat: *The company was accused of defrauding the government of millions of dollars in taxes. v.*

de fray (di frā′), pay (costs or expenses): *The expenses of national parks are defrayed by the taxpayers. v.*

de frost (di frôst′), 1 remove frost or ice from: *defrost the refrigerator.* 2 thaw out: *Cooking defrosts frozen foods. v.*

de frost er (di frôs′tər), device that removes frost or ice. *n.*

deft (deft), quick and skillful in action; nimble: *The fingers of a violinist must be deft. adj.* —**deft′ly,** *adv.* —**deft′ness,** *n.*

de funct (di fungkt′), no longer in existence; dead; extinct: *A business that fails is defunct. adj.*

hat, āge, fär; let, ēqual, tėrm;
it, īce; hot, ōpen, ôrder;
oil, out; cup, pùt, rüle; ch, child;
ng, long; sh, she; th, thin;
ᵬH, then; zh, measure;

ə represents *a* in about,
e in taken, *i* in pencil,
o in lemon, *u* in circus.

de fy (di fī′), 1 set oneself openly against (authority); resist boldly: *Now that I am earning my own living I can defy my stepmother's strict rules. The rebels openly defied the law.* 2 withstand; resist: *The beauty of the forest defies description.* 3 challenge (a person) to do or prove something; dare: *We defy you to show that our game is not fair. v.,* **de fied, de fy ing.**

de Gaulle (də gōl′), **Charles,** 1890-1970, French general and political leader, president of France from 1959 to 1969.

de gen er a cy (di jen′ər ə sē), degenerate condition or character. *n.*

de gen e rate (di jen′ə rāt′ *for 1,2;* di jen′ər it *for 3,4*), 1 grow worse; decline in physical, mental, or moral qualities: *His health degenerated with disease and old age.* 2 (in biology) sink to a lower type; lose the normal or more highly developed characteristics of one's race or kind. 3 that has degenerated; showing a decline in physical, mental, or moral qualities: *The thief was a degenerate member of a fine family.* 4 person having an evil and unwholesome character. 1,2 *v.,* **de gen e rat ed, de gen e rat ing;** 3 *adj.,* 4 *n.*

de gen e ra tion (di jen′ə rā′shən), 1 process of degenerating. 2 a degenerate condition. *n.*

deg ra da tion (deg′rə dā′shən), 1 a degrading: *A poor diet may cause a gradual degradation of health.* 2 a being degraded: *Failure to obey orders caused the corporal's degradation to the rank of private.* 3 a degraded condition: *While the trash collectors were on strike, we lived amid the degradation of an unclean neighborhood. n.*

de grade (di grād′), 1 reduce in rank as a punishment; take away a position, rank, or honor from: *The corporal was degraded to private for disobeying orders.* 2 make worse; lower; debase: *I degraded myself by cheating on the test. v.,* **de grad ed, de grad ing.**

de gree (di grē′), 1 a step in a scale; stage in a process: *By degrees I improved my ability to swim and dive.*

adj.	adjective	*n.*	noun
adv.	adverb	*prep.*	preposition
conj.	conjunction	*pron.*	pronoun
interj.	interjection	*v.*	verb
sing.	singular	*pl.*	plural

2 amount; extent: *To what degree are you interested in reading?* 3 unit for measuring temperature: *The freezing point of water is 32 degrees (32°) Fahrenheit, or 0 degrees (0°) centigrade.* 4 unit for measuring an angle or an arc of a circle. A degree is ¹/₉₀ of a right angle or ¹/₃₆₀ of the circumference of a circle. 45 degrees (45°) is half a right angle or one eighth of the line bounding a circle. 5 rank: *A noble is a person of high degree.* 6 rank or title given by a college or university to a student whose work fulfills certain requirements, or to a noted person as an honor: *a bachelor's degree, a master's degree.* 7 (in grammar) one of the three stages in the comparison of adjectives or adverbs. The positive degree of *fast* is *fast;* the comparative degree is *faster;* the superlative degree is *fastest.* 8 (in law) a relative measure of the seriousness of a crime: *murder in the first degree. n.*

de hu mid i fy (dē′hyü mid′ə fī), remove moisture from. *v.,* **de hu mid i fied, de hu mid i fy ing.**

de hy drate (dē hī′drāt), 1 take water or moisture from; dry: *dehydrate vegetables. High fever dehydrates the body.* 2 lose water or moisture. *v.,* **de hy drat ed, de hy drat ing.**

de hy dra tion (dē′hī drā′shən), removal of water or moisture from the body or from vegetables, fruits, etc. *n.*

de i fi ca tion (dē′ə fə kā′shən), 1 a deifying: *The deification of the emperor was customary in ancient Rome.* 2 a being deified: *After the emperor's deification, altars were erected to him throughout the empire. n.*

de i fy (dē′ə fī), 1 make a god of: *Many American Indians deified and worshiped streams, trees, animals, and other objects of nature.* 2 worship or regard as a god: *Some people deify wealth. v.,* **de i fied, de i fy ing.**

deign (dān), think fit; condescend: *So great a novelist would never deign to quarrel with such trifling critics. v.*

de ist (dē′ist), person who believes in God on the evidence of reason and nature, and without accepting any particular religion. *n.*

de i ty (dē′ə tē), 1 god or goddess: *Juno was the queen of the ancient*

Roman deities. 2 divine nature; being a god: *Christians believe in the deity of Christ.* 3 **the Deity,** God. *n., pl.* **de i ties.**

de ject ed (di jek′tid), in low spirits; sad; discouraged: *She was feeling dejected and unhappy until the good news cheered her up. adj.* —**de ject′ed ly,** *adv.*

de jec tion (di jek′shən), lowness of spirits; sadness; discouragement: *Her face showed her dejection at missing the airplane. n.*

Del., Delaware.

degree
(def.4)

Del a ware (del′ə wer *or* del′ə war), 1 one of the southeastern states of the United States. *Capital:* Dover. 2 river flowing from SE New York State between Pennsylvania and New Jersey into the Atlantic. 3 member of a tribe of American Indians, most of whom formerly lived in the valley of the Delaware River. *n.*

de lay (di lā′), 1 put off till a later time: *We will delay the party for a week and hold it next Saturday.* 2 a putting off till a later time: *The delay upset our plans.* 3 make late; keep waiting; hinder the progress of: *The accident delayed the train for two hours.* 4 be late; go slowly; stop along the way: *Do not delay on this errand.* 5 a stopping along the way; wait; hindering: *We were so late we could afford no further delay.* 1,3,4 *v.,* 2,5 *n.*

de lec ta ble (di lek′tə bəl), very pleasing; delightful: *the delectable taste of freshly baked bread. adj.*

del e gate (del′ə gāt *or* del′ə git *for 1;* del′ə gāt *for 2,3*), 1 person given power or authority to act for others; representative: *Our club sent two delegates to the meeting.* 2 appoint or send (a person) as a representative: *The club delegated her to buy the equipment.* 3 give over (one's power or authority) to another so that he may act for one: *The teacher delegated the task of keeping order to the class president.* 1 *n.,* 2,3 *v.,* **del e gat ed, del e gat ing.**

del e ga tion (del′ə gā′shən), 1 act of delegating. 2 fact of being delegated. 3 group of delegates: *Each state sent a delegation to the national convention. n.*

de lete (di lēt′), strike out or take out (anything written or printed); cross out: *I deleted the·unnecessary words from*

my theme. *v.,* **de let ed, de let ing.**

del e ter i ous (del′ə tir′ē əs), causing harm; injurious. *adj.*

Del hi (del′ē), city in N India, former capital of India. *n.*

de lib er ate (di lib′ər it *for 1-3;* di lib′ə rāt′ *for 4,5*), 1 carefully thought out beforehand; made or done on purpose; intended: *Their excuse was a deliberate lie.* 2 slow and careful in deciding what to do: *Deliberate persons do not make up their minds quickly.* 3 not hurried; slow: *The old man walked with deliberate steps.* 4 think over carefully; consider: *I am deliberating where to put up my new picture. He was slow to answer, deliberating over each question.* 5 talk over reasons for and against; discuss; debate: *In a long session, Congress deliberated the question of raising taxes.* 1-3 *adj.,* 4,5 *v.,* **de lib er at ed, de lib er at ing.** —**de lib′er ate ly,** *adv.* —**de lib′er ate ness,** *n.*

de lib e ra tion (di lib′ə rā′shən), 1 careful thought: *After long deliberation she decided not to go.* 2 a talking about reasons for and against something; discussion; debate: *the deliberations of Congress over raising taxes.* 3 slowness and care: *She drove the car over the icy bridge with great deliberation. n.*

de lib e ra tive (di lib′ə rā′tiv), for deliberation; having to do with deliberation: *Congress is a deliberative body. adj.*

del i ca cy (del′ə kə sē), 1 fineness of weave, quality, or make; slightness and grace: *the delicacy of lace, the delicacy of a flower, the delicacy of a baby's skin.* 2 fineness of feeling for small differences: *The watchmaker had great delicacy of touch.* 3 need of care, skill, or tact: *His refusal required great delicacy, since he did not wish to hurt his friend's feelings.* 4 thought for the feelings of others. 5 a shrinking from what is offensive or not modest. 6 a being easily hurt or made ill; weakness: *The parents often worried about their child's delicacy.* 7 a choice kind of food; dainty. Nuts and candy are delicacies. *n., pl.* **del i ca cies.**

del i cate (del′ə kit), 1 pleasing to the taste; lightly flavored; mild or soft: *delicate foods, delicate colors. Roses have a delicate fragrance.* 2 of fine weave, quality, or make; easily torn; thin: *A spider's web is very delicate.* 3 requiring care, skill, or tact: *a delicate situation, a delicate question.* 4 very quickly responding to slight changes of condition; finely sensitive: *delicate instruments, a delicate sense of touch.* 5 easily hurt or made ill: *a weak and delicate child.* 6 hard to appreciate;

subtle: *a delicate point in reasoning.* *adj.* —**del′i cate ly,** *adv.* —**del′i cate- ness,** *n.*

del i ca tes sen (del′ə kə tes′n), 1 store that sells prepared foods, such as cooked meats, smoked fish, cheese, salads, pickles, sandwiches, etc. 2 the foods sold at such a store. *n.* [from German *Delikatessen* delicacies]

de li cious (di lish′əs), very pleasing or satisfying, especially to the taste or smell; delightful: *delicious cake. adj.* —**de li′cious ly,** *adv.* —**de li′cious- ness,** *n.*

de light (di līt′), 1 great pleasure; joy: *The children took delight in their toys.* 2 something which gives great pleasure: *Astronomy is her delight.* 3 please greatly: *The circus delighted the children.* 4 have great pleasure: *Children delight in surprises.* 1,2 *n.,* 3,4 *v.*

de light ed (di lī′tid), greatly pleased; very glad: *I am delighted to be here. adj.* —**de light′ed ly,** *adv.*

de light ful (di līt′fəl), very pleasing; giving joy: *a delightful visit from an old friend. adj.* —**de light′ful ly,** *adv.*

de lin e ate (di lin′ē āt), 1 trace the outline of: *The map clearly delineated the boundary between Mexico and Texas.* 2 draw; sketch. 3 describe in words; portray: *He delineated his plan in a thorough report. v.,* **de lin e at ed, de lin e at ing.**

de lin e a tion (di lin′ē ā′shən), 1 act of delineating. 2 thing delineated; diagram, sketch, portrait, or description. *n.*

de lin quen cy (di ling′kwən sē), 1 failure in a duty; neglect of an obligation. 2 fault; offense; guilt; shortcoming. 3 condition or habit of behaving unlawfully: *We can curb juvenile delinquency by education. n., pl.* **de lin quen cies.**

de lin quent (di ling′kwənt), 1 failing in a duty; neglecting an obligation: *He was delinquent in paying his overdue taxes.* 2 guilty of a fault or an offense: *The delinquent children had to pay for the windows they broke.* 3 due and unpaid; overdue: *The owner lost her house when it was sold for delinquent taxes.* 4 a delinquent person; offender. 1-3 *adj.,* 4 *n.* —**de lin′quent ly,** *adv.*

de lir i ous (di lir′ē əs), 1 out of one's senses for a short time; wandering in mind; raving: *The patient's high fever made him delirious.* 2 wildly excited: *The students were delirious with joy when their team won the tournament. adj.* —**de lir′i ous ly,** *adv.*

de lir i um (di lir′ē əm), 1 a temporary disorder of the mind that occurs during fevers, insanity, drunkenness, etc. Delirium is characterized by restless-

ness, excitement, wild talk, and hallucinations. 2 wild excitement. *n.*

de liv er (di liv′ər), 1 carry and give out; distribute: *deliver mail.* 2 hand over; give up: *The badly defeated army delivered the fort to the enemy.* 3 give forth in words: *deliver a talk. The jury delivered its verdict.* 4 strike; throw: *The boxer delivered a blow.* 5 set free; rescue; save: *A passing ship delivered the shipwrecked passengers from a certain death at sea.* 6 help a woman give birth to a child. *v.* —**de liv′er er,** *n.*

de liv er ance (di liv′ər əns), 1 a setting free or a being set free; rescue; release: *deliverance from captivity.* 2 a formal opinion or judgment. *n.*

de liv er y (di liv′ər ē), 1 a carrying and giving out of letters, goods, etc.: *There is one delivery of mail a day in our city.* 2 a giving up; handing over: *The captive was released upon the payment of the ransom.* 3 manner of speaking; way of giving a speech or lecture: *Our congressman is an orator with an excellent delivery.* 4 act or way of striking, throwing, etc.: *That pitcher has a fast delivery.* 5 a rescue; release. 6 a giving birth to a child; childbirth. *n., pl.* **de liv er ies.**

dell (del), a small, sheltered glen or valley, usually with trees in it. *n.*

Del phi (del′fī), town in ancient Greece where a famous oracle of Apollo was located. *n.*

Del phic (del′fik), 1 having to do with the oracle of Apollo at Delphi. 2 having a double meaning; obscure. *adj.*

delta (def. 1) of the Mississippi River

del ta (del′tə), 1 deposit of earth and sand that collects at the mouths of some rivers and is usually three-sided. 2 the fourth letter of the Greek alphabet (Δ or δ). 3 anything shaped like Δ : *delta-wing aircraft. n., pl.* **del tas.**

de lude (di lüd′), mislead the mind or judgment of; trick or deceive: *He deluded me into thinking he was on my side. v.,* **de lud ed, de lud ing.**

del uge (del′yüj), 1 a great flood: *After the dam broke, the deluge washed away the bridge.* 2 **the Deluge,** (in the Bible) the great flood in the days of Noah; the Flood. 3 a heavy fall of rain: *We were caught in a deluge on the way home.* 4 flood or overflow: *Water deluged our cellar.* 5 overwhelm: *The folk singer*

hat, āge, fär; let, ēqual, tėrm; it, īce; hot, ōpen, ôrder; oil, out; cup, pùt, rüle; ch, child; ng, long; sh, she; th, thin; ŦH, then; zh, measure;

ə represents *a* in about, *e* in taken, *i* in pencil, *o* in lemon, *u* in circus.

was deluged with requests for her autograph. 6 any overwhelming rush: *Most stores have a deluge of orders just before Christmas.* 1-3,6 *n.,* 4,5 *v.,* **del uged, del ug ing.**

de lu sion (di lü′zhən), 1 a false belief or opinion: *She was under the delusion that she could pass any test without studying for it.* 2 a deluding or a being deluded. *n.*

de lu sive (di lü′siv), misleading the mind or judgment; deceptive; false. *adj.* —**de lu′sive ly,** *adv.*

de luxe (də lùks′ *or* də luks′), of exceptionally good quality; elegant. *adj.* [from French *de luxe* of luxury]

delve (delv), 1 search carefully for information: *The scholar delved into many books for facts to support her theory.* 2 OLD USE. dig. *v.,* **delved, delv ing.**

Dem., 1 Democrat. 2 Democratic.

de mag net ize (dē mag′nə tīz), deprive of magnetism. *v.,* **de mag net- ized, de mag net iz ing.**

dem a gogue *or* **dem a gog** (dem′- ə gog), a popular leader who stirs up the people by appealing to their emotions and prejudices. The chief aim of most demagogues is to get power and money for themselves alone. *n.*

de mand (di mand′), 1 ask for as a right: *demand a trial by jury.* 2 ask for with authority: *The teacher demanded the name of the student who rang the fire alarm.* 3 call for; require; need: *Training a puppy demands patience.* 4 act of demanding: *a demand for a bigger allowance.* 5 thing demanded; claim: *A mother has many demands upon her time.* 6 desire and ability to buy: *Because of the large crop, the supply of apples is greater than the demand.* 1-3 *v.,* 4-6 *n.* —**de mand′- er,** *n.*

in demand, wanted: *Taxicabs are much in demand on rainy days.*

de mar ca tion (dē′mär kā′shən), 1 a setting and marking the limits: *the demarcation of a country's authority.* 2 separation; distinction: *the demarcation of infancy from childhood. n.*

de mean[1] (di mēn′), lower in dignity or

adj.	adjective	*n.*	noun
adv.	adverb	*prep.*	preposition
conj.	conjunction	*pron.*	pronoun
interj.	interjection	*v.*	verb
sing.	singular	*pl.*	plural

standing; humble; degrade: *They demeaned themselves by insulting their friend.* v. [*de-* down + *mean²*]

de mean² (di mēn′), behave or conduct (oneself): *He demeans himself well.* v. [from French of the 1300's *demener*]

de mean or (di mē′nər), way a person looks and acts; behavior; manner: *He has a quiet, modest demeanor.* n.

de ment ed (di men′tid), mentally ill; insane; crazy. *adj.* —**de ment′ed ly,** *adv.*

de mer it (di mer′it), 1 fault or defect. 2 a mark against a person's record for bad behavior or poor work. n.

de mesne (di mān′ *or* di mēn′), 1 house and land belonging to a lord and used by him. 2 domain; realm. 3 district; region. n.

De me ter (di mē′tər), (in Greek myths) the goddess of agriculture, fruitfulness, and marriage. The Romans called her Ceres. n.

dem i god (dem′i god′), one who is partly divine and partly human. Hercules was a demigod. n.

dem i john (dem′i jon), a large bottle of glass or earthenware enclosed in wicker. n.

de mil i tar i za tion (dē mil′ə tər ə zā′shən), a demilitarizing or a being demilitarized. n.

de mil i ta rize (dē mil′ə tə rīz′), to free from military control: *demilitarize a zone or boundary between enemy countries.* v., **de mil i ta rized, de mil i ta riz ing.**

de mise (di mīz′), death. n.

dem i tasse (dem′i tas′), 1 a very small cup of black coffee. 2 a small cup for serving black coffee. n.

de mo bi li za tion (dē mō′bə lə zā′shən), a demobilizing or a being demobilized. n.

de mo bi lize (dē mō′bə līz), remove or disband from military service, status, or control: *When a war is over, the soldiers are demobilized and sent home.* v., **de mo bi lized, de mo bi liz ing.**

de moc ra cy (di mok′rə sē), 1 government that is run by the people who live under it. In a democracy the people rule either directly through meetings that all may attend, such as the town meetings in New England, or indirectly through the election of certain rep-

resentatives to attend to the business of government. 2 country, state, or community having such a government. 3 treatment of other people as one's equals: *The teacher's democracy made her popular among her pupils.* n., pl. **de moc ra cies.**

dem o crat (dem′ə krat), 1 person who believes that a government should be run by the people who live under it. 2 person who treats other people as his equals. 3 **Democrat,** member of the Democratic Party. n.

dem o crat ic (dem′ə krat′ik), 1 of a democracy; like a democracy. 2 treating other people as one's equals: *The queen's democratic ways made her dear to her people.* 3 **Democratic,** of the Democratic Party. *adj.*

dem o crat i cal ly (dem′ə krat′ik lē), in a democratic manner. *adv.*

Democratic Party, one of the two main political parties in the United States. The other is the Republican Party.

de moc ra tize (di mok′rə tīz), make or become democratic. v., **de moc ra tized, de moc ra tiz ing.**

de mol ish (di mol′ish), pull or tear down; destroy: *Shells and bombs demolished the fortress.* v.

dem o li tion (dem′ə lish′ən), a destroying; destruction: *The demolition of several buildings with explosives was necessary to clear the land for a new highway.* n.

de mon (dē′mən), 1 an evil spirit; devil; fiend. 2 a very wicked or cruel person. 3 person who has great energy or vigor: *My music teacher is a demon for practicing.* 4 an inferior or minor Greek god. n. —**de′mon like′,** *adj.*

de mo ni ac (di mō′nē ak), 1 of or like demons. 2 devilish; fiendish: *Burning people at the stake was a demoniac custom.* 3 raging; frantic. 4 person supposed to be possessed by an evil spirit. 1-3 *adj.,* 4 n.

de mo ni a cal (dē′mə nī′ə kəl), demoniac. *adj.*

de mon stra ble (di mon′strə bəl), that can be shown or proved. *adj.*

de mon stra bly (di mon′strə blē), 1 in a manner that can be proved; clearly. 2 by demonstration. *adv.*

dem on strate (dem′ən strāt), 1 show clearly; prove: *Magellan's voyage around the world demonstrated that the earth is round.* 2 explain by carrying out experiments, or by using samples or specimens; show how (a thing) is done: *The science teacher demonstrated the use of a magnet in class.* 3 show the merits of (a thing for sale); advertise or make known by carrying out a process in public: *The saleswoman computed some figures to demonstrate her adding*

machine to us. 4 show (feeling) openly: *I hugged the puppy to demonstrate my affection for it.* 5 take part in a parade or meeting to protest or to make demands: *An angry crowd demonstrated in front of the mayor's office for more police protection.* 6 display military strength to frighten or deceive an enemy. v., **dem on strat ed, dem on strat ing.**

dem on stra tion (dem′ən strā′shən), 1 clear proof: *The ease with which she solved the hard problem was a demonstration of her ability in math.* 2 a showing or explaining something by carrying out experiments or by using samples or specimens: *A compass was used in a demonstration of the earth's magnetism.* 3 a showing of the merits of a thing for sale; advertising or making known by carrying out a process in a public place: *the demonstration of a new vacuum cleaner.* 4 an open show or expression of feeling: *We greeted our returning sister with a demonstration of affection.* 5 parade or meeting to protest or make demands: *The tenants held a demonstration against the raise in rent.* 6 display of military strength to frighten or deceive an enemy. n.

de mon stra tive (di mon′strə tiv), 1 expressing one's affections freely and openly: *The girl's demonstrative greetings embarrassed her shy brother.* 2 pointing out. *This* and *that* are demonstrative pronouns. *adj.*

dem on stra tor (dem′ən strā′tər), 1 person or thing that demonstrates. 2 person who takes part in a demonstration. n.

de mor al i za tion (di môr′ə lə zā′shən), a demoralizing or a being demoralized. n.

de mor al ize (di môr′ə līz), 1 lower the morals of; corrupt: *The drug habit demoralizes its victims.* 2 lower the morale of; weaken the spirit, courage, or discipline of; dishearten: *The villagers were demoralized by the long famine.* v., **de mor al ized, de mor al iz ing.**

De mos the nes (di mos′thə nēz′), 384?-322 B.C., the most famous orator of ancient Greece. n.

de mote (di mōt′), put back to a lower grade; reduce in rank: *The student who had trouble doing fourth-grade work was demoted to third grade.* v., **de mot ed, de mot ing.**

de mo tion (di mō′shən), a demoting or a being demoted. n.

de mur (di mėr′), 1 show disapproval or dislike; object: *The clerk demurred at working overtime without extra pay.* 2 a demurring; objection; exception: *The clerk's demur was ignored by the boss.*

1 *v.*, **de murred, de mur ring;** 2 *n.*
de mure (di myùr′), 1 seeming more modest and proper than one really is; coy: *the demure smile of a flirt.* 2 serious; thoughtful; sober: *their restrained and demure conduct.* *adj.*, **de mur er, de mur est.** **—de mure′ly,** *adv.* **—de mure′ness,** *n.*

den (den), 1 place where a wild animal lives; lair: *The bear's den was in a cave.* 2 place where thieves or the like have their headquarters. 3 a small, dirty room. 4 one's private room for reading and work, usually small and cozy. 5 group of eight to ten cub scouts. *n.*

de na ture (dē nā′chər), 1 change the nature of. 2 make unfit for eating or drinking without destroying its usefulness for other purposes: *denatured alcohol.* *v.*, **de na tured, de na tur ing.**

den drite (den′drīt), the branching part at the receiving end of a nerve cell. *n.*

dendrites—A nerve impulse is received by the dendrites and travels through the cell body and axon to another cell.

de ni al (di nī′əl), 1 a saying that something is not true: *a denial of the existence of ghosts.* 2 a saying that one does not hold to or accept a belief: *Galileo was forced to make a public denial of his belief that the earth goes around the sun.* 3 a refusing: *Her denial of our request seemed very unkind.* 4 a refusing to acknowledge; disowning. *n.*

den im (den′əm), 1 a heavy, coarse cotton cloth with a diagonal weave, used for overalls, upholstery, etc. 2 **denims,** *pl.* overalls or pants made of this cloth. *n.* [from French (*serge*) *de Nîmes* (serge) from Nimes, town in France]

den i zen (den′ə zən), person or animal that lives in a place; inhabitant; occupant: *Fish are denizens of the sea.* *n.*

Den mark (den′märk), small country in N Europe, between the Baltic Sea and the North Sea. *Capital:* Copenhagen. *n.*

de nom i nate (di nom′ə nāt *for 1;* di nom′ə nit *for 2*), 1 give a name to; name. 2 called by a specific name. 6 ft., 4 oz., 10 in., and 9 lbs. are **denominate numbers.** 1 *v.*, **de nom i nat ed, de nom i nat ing;** 2 *adj.*

de nom i na tion (di nom′ə nā′shən), 1 name for a group or class of things; name. 2 a religious group or sect: *Methodists and Baptists are two large Protestant denominations.* 3 class or kind of units: *Reducing* ⁵/₁₂, ¹/₃, *and*

¹/₆ *to the same denomination gives* ⁵/₁₂, ⁴/₁₂, *and* ²/₁₂. *The United States coin of lowest denomination is a cent.* *n.*

de nom i na tion al (di nom′ə nā′shə nəl), having to do with or controlled by some religious denomination; sectarian: *a denominational school.* *adj.*

de nom i na tor (di nom′ə nā′tər), the number below the line in a fraction, stating the size of the parts in their relation to the whole: *In* ³/₄, *4 is the denominator, and 3 is the numerator.* *n.*

de no ta tion (dē′nō tā′shən), 1 meaning, especially the exact, literal meaning. The denotation of *home* is "place where one lives," but it has many connotations. 2 a denoting or marking out; indication. *n.*

de note (di nōt′), 1 be the sign of; indicate: *A fever usually denotes sickness. If the teacher puts an "A" on your paper, it denotes very good work.* 2 be a name for; mean: *The word "stool" denotes a small chair without a back.* *v.*, **de not ed, de not ing.**

de noue ment (dā′nü män′), solution of a plot in a story, play, situation, etc.; outcome; end. *n.* [from French *dénouement*]

de nounce (di nouns′), 1 speak against; express strong disapproval of: *In his speech the mayor denounced crime in the streets.* 2 give information against; accuse: *denounce someone to the FBI as a spy.* 3 give formal notice of the termination of (a treaty, etc.). *v.*, **de nounced, de nounc ing.**

dense (dens), 1 closely packed together; thick: *a dense fog. Dense patches of briers are difficult to walk through.* 2 stupid: *The dense looks of the students showed that they did not understand.* *adj.*, **dens er, dens est.** **—dense′ly,** *adv.* **—dense′ness,** *n.*

den si ty (den′sə tē), 1 a being dense; having parts very close together; compactness; thickness: *The density of the forest prevented us from seeing more than a little way ahead.* 2 the quantity of matter in a unit of volume or of area: *The density of lead is greater than the density of wood.* 3 stupidity. *n., pl.* **den si ties.**

dent (dent), 1 a hollow made by a blow or pressure: *The fall put a dent in my bicycle fender.* 2 make a dent in: *The movers dented the top of the table when they banged it against the doorknob.* 3 become dented: *Soft wood dents easily.* 1 *n.*, 2,3 *v.*

den tal (den′tl), 1 of or for the teeth: *Proper dental care can prevent tooth decay.* 2 of or for a dentist's work: *a dental drill.* *adj.* **—den′tal ly,** *adv.*

den ti frice (den′tə fris), paste, powder, or liquid for cleaning the teeth. *n.*

hat, āge, fär; let, ēqual, tėrm;
it, īce; hot, ōpen, ôrder;
oil, out; cup, pùt, rüle; ch, child;
ng, long; sh, she; th, thin;
ŦH, then; zh, measure;

ə represents *a* in about,
e in taken, *i* in pencil,
o in lemon, *u* in circus.

den tin (den′tən), dentine. *n.*

den tine (den′tēn′), the hard, bony material beneath the enamel of a tooth. It forms the main part of a tooth. *n.*

DENTINE — dentine shown in a cross section of a molar

den tist (den′tist), doctor whose work is the care of teeth. A dentist fills cavities in teeth, cleans, straightens, or extracts them, and supplies artificial teeth. *n.*

den tist ry (den′tə strē), work, art, or profession of a dentist. *n.*

den ture (den′chər), set of artificial teeth. *n.*

de nude (di nüd′ *or* di nyüd′), make bare; strip (something) of its clothing or covering: *Most trees are denuded of their leaves in winter.* *v.*, **de nud ed, de nud ing.**

de nun ci a tion (di nun′sē ā′shən), 1 expression of strong disapproval; condemnation; denouncing: *the mayor's denunciation of crime.* 2 an informing against; accusation: *The denunciation of our neighbor as a foreign spy shocked everyone.* *n.*

Den ver (den′vər), capital of Colorado, in the central part. *n.*

de ny (di nī′), 1 say (something) is not true: *deny the existence of slums in a city. I was jailed even though I denied the charges against me.* 2 say that one does not hold to or accept: *Even on Halloween she denies a belief in ghosts and witches.* 3 refuse to give or grant: *I could not deny the stray cat some milk.* 4 refuse to acknowledge; disown: *They denied their debts and refused to pay their bills.* *v.*, **de nied, de ny ing.**

deny oneself, do without the things one wants: *A person who diets to lose weight has to deny himself candy, cake, and other rich foods.*

de o dor ant (dē ō′dər ənt), preparation that destroys bad odors. *n.*

de o dor ize (dē ō′də rīz′), destroy the odor of. *v.*, **de o dor ized, de o dor iz ing.**

deoxyribonucleic acid

de ox y ri bo nu cle ic acid (dē-ok′sə rī′bō nü klē′ik), acid found in the nuclei of all living cells. It is the substance of which most genes are made and is chiefly responsible for the transmission of inherited characteristics.

de part (di pärt′), 1 go away; leave: *The train departs at 6:15.* 2 turn away; change: *He became very sloppy, departing from his usual neat ways.* 3 die. *v.*

de part ment (di pärt′mənt), 1 a separate part of some whole; special branch; division: *the toy department of a store. Our city government has a fire department, a police department, and a sanitation department.* 2 one of the administrative districts into which France is divided. *n.*

de part men tal (dē′pärt men′tl), 1 having to do with a department: *departmental policies.* 2 divided into departments: *Their business is so large that it must be handled on a departmental basis. adj.*

department store, store that sells many different kinds of articles arranged in separate departments.

de par ture (di pär′chər), 1 act of going away; leaving: *a sudden departure. The airplane's departure for New York was delayed by a blizzard.* 2 a turning away; change: *a departure from our old custom.* 3 a starting on a course of action or thought: *Attending this dancing class will be a new departure for me, for I have never done anything like it.* 4 OLD USE. death. `*n.*

de pend (di pend′), 1 be a result of; be controlled or influenced by something else: *The success of our picnic will depend partly upon the weather.* 2 get support; rely for help: *Children depend on their parents for food and clothing.* 3 rely; trust: *You can depend on the timetable to tell you when the airplanes leave. v.*

de pend a bil i ty (di pen′də bil′ə tē), reliability; trustworthiness. *n.*

de pend a ble (di pen′də bəl), that can be depended on; reliable; trustworthy: *Almanacs have fairly dependable information. adj.*

de pend a bly (di pen′də blē), in a dependable manner. *adv.*

de pend ence (di pen′dəns), 1 fact or condition of being dependent: *the dependence of crops on good weather.* 2 a trusting or relying on another for support or help: *I am going to work so that I can end my dependence on my parents.* 3 reliance; trust: *Do not put your dependence in the delivery boy, for he is always late. n.*

de pend en cy (di pen′dən sē), 1 country or territory controlled by another country: *The Virgin Islands is a dependency of the United States.* 2 a trusting or relying on another for support; dependence. *n., pl.* **de pend en cies.**

de pend ent (di pen′dənt), 1 trusting to another for support; relying on another for help: *A child is dependent on its parents.* 2 person who is supported by another. 3 possible if something else takes place; depending: *Good crops are dependent on the right amount of rainfall and sunshine.* 1,3 *adj.,* 2 *n.*

dependent clause, subordinate clause.

de pict (di pikt′), represent by drawing, painting, or describing; portray: *The artist and the poet both tried to depict the splendor of the sunset. v.*

de pic tion (di pik′shən), 1 act of drawing or painting. 2 thing that represents; description. *n.*

de plete (di plēt′), reduce the fullness of; empty; exhaust: *Because the traveler's funds were depleted, he went home. v.,* **de plet ed, de plet ing.**

de ple tion (di plē′shən), an emptying; exhausting: *Years of mining have caused a depletion of coal deposits in the mines. n.*

de plor a ble (di plôr′ə bəl), 1 that is to be deplored; regrettable; lamentable: *a deplorable accident.* 2 wretched; miserable: *Deplorable living conditions exist in slums. adj.*

de plor a bly (di plôr′ə blē), in a deplorable manner; lamentably. *adv.*

de plore (di plôr′), be very sorry about; express great sorrow for; regret deeply: *We deplore the accident. v.,* **de plored, de plor ing.**

de ploy (di ploi′), 1 spread out (troops, etc.) from a column into a long battle line. 2 spread out or extend (anything): *A fleet of ships was deployed over the area in which the astronauts were expected to land. v.*

de pop u late (dē pop′yə lāt), deprive of inhabitants, wholly or in part: *The conquerors depopulated the enemy's capital by driving the inhabitants away. v.,* **de pop u lat ed, de pop u lat ing.**

de pop u la tion (dē pop′yə lā′shən), 1 act of depopulating. 2 condition of being depopulated. *n.*

de port (di pôrt′), 1 force to leave; banish; expel. When an alien is deported, he is sent out of the country, usually back to his native land. 2 behave or conduct (oneself) in a particular manner: *The children deport themselves well when we have guests. v.*

de por ta tion (dē′pôr tā′shən), removal from a country by banishment or expulsion: *Deportation of criminals from England to Australia was once common. n.*

de port ment (di pôrt′mənt), way a person acts; behavior; conduct: *poor deportment. n.*

de pose (di pōz′), 1 put out of office or a position of authority, especially a high one like that of king: *The king was deposed by the revolution.* 2 declare under oath, especially in writing; testify: *The witness deposed that she had seen the prisoner on the day of the murder. v.,* **de posed, de pos ing.**

de pos it (di poz′it), 1 put down; lay down; leave lying: *He deposited his bundles on the table. The flood deposited a layer of mud in the streets.* 2 material laid down or left lying by natural means: *There is often a deposit of mud and sand at the mouth of a river.* 3 put in a place for safekeeping: *Deposit your money in the bank.* 4 something put in a certain place for safekeeping: *Money put in a bank is a deposit.* 5 pay as a pledge to do something or to pay more later: *If you deposit part of the price, a store will keep an article for you until you pay the rest.* 6 money paid as a pledge to do something or to pay more later: *I put down a $25 deposit on the coat, and will pay the balance of $50 on the first of next month.* 7 mass of some mineral in rock or in the ground: *deposits of coal.* 1,3,5 *v.,* 2,4,6,7 *n.*

dep o si tion (dep′ə zish′ən), 1 act of putting out of office or a position of authority; removal from power. 2 the giving of testimony under oath. 3 testimony, especially a sworn statement in writing: *The prisoner made a deposition to use in appealing his case.* 4 a depositing: *the deposition of silt from the floodwaters.* 5 thing deposited; deposit. *n.*

de pos i tor (di poz′ə tər), person who deposits: *Depositors in savings banks may receive interest on the money deposited. n.*

de pos i to ry (di poz′ə tôr′ē), place where anything is stored for safekeeping; storehouse. *n., pl.* **de pos i to ries.**

de pot (dē′pō *for* 1; dep′ō *for* 2,3), 1 a railroad or bus station. 2 storehouse; warehouse. 3 place where military supplies are stored. *n.*

de prave (di prāv′), make bad; injure morally; corrupt: *Drug addiction can* deprave a person's character. *v.*, **de-praved, de·prav·ing.**

de·praved (di prāvd′), having very bad morals; vicious; corrupt: *The murder was committed by a depraved person. adj.*

de·prav·i·ty (di prav′ə tē), 1 a being depraved; wickedness; viciousness; corruption. 2 a corrupt act; bad practice. *n., pl.* **de·prav·i·ties.**

dep·re·cate (dep′rə kāt), express strong disapproval of: *Lovers of peace deprecate war. v.*, **dep·re·cat·ed, dep·re·cat·ing.**

dep·re·ca·tion (dep′rə kā′shən), a strong expression of disapproval; pleading or protesting against something. *n.*

de·pre·ci·ate (di prē′shē āt), 1 lessen in value: *The government has the power to depreciate currency. The longer an automobile is driven the more it depreciates.* 2 speak slightingly of; belittle: *He depreciated the gift I got, saying that his was much nicer. v.*, **de·pre·ci·at·ed, de·pre·ci·at·ing.**

de·pre·ci·a·tion (di prē′shē ā′shən), a lowering or a being lowered in price, value, or estimation. *n.*

dep·re·da·tion (dep′rə dā′shən), act of plundering; robbery; ravaging. *n.*

de·press (di pres′), 1 make sad or gloomy: *Rainy weather always depresses me. She was depressed by the bad news from home.* 2 press down; lower: *When you play the piano, you depress the keys.* 3 make less active; weaken: *Some medicines depress the action of the heart. v.*

de·pres·sant (di pres′nt), drug or other substance that slows or reduces the body's reactions and relaxes muscles: *an appetite depressant. n.*

de·pres·sion (di presh′ən), 1 a pressing down; sinking or lowering: *A rapid depression of the mercury in a barometer usually indicates the approach of a storm.* 2 a depressed condition: *The barometer showed a depression.* 3 a low place; hollow: *Rain formed puddles in the depressions in the ground.* 4 sadness or gloominess; low spirits: *Failure usually brings on a feeling of depression.* 5 reduction of activity; dullness of trade: *Many people lose their jobs during a business depression. n.*

dep·ri·va·tion (dep′rə vā′shən), 1 act of depriving. 2 condition of being deprived; loss; privation. *n.*

de·prive (di prīv′), 1 take away from by force: *The people deprived the cruel king of his power.* 2 keep from having or doing: *Worrying deprived him of sleep. v.*, **de·prived, de·priv·ing.**

dept., department.

depth (depth), 1 distance from top to bottom: *the depth of a hole, the depth of a lake.* 2 distance from front to back: *The depth of our playground is 250 feet.* 3 the deepest or most central part: *the darkest depth of the jungle, the depths of despair.* 4 deep quality; deepness: *The students admired their teacher's depth of understanding.* 5 deep understanding; profoundness: *This story has a good plot but it has no depth at all.* 6 lowness of pitch. *n.*

depth charge, an explosive charge dropped from a ship or airplane and set to explode at a certain depth under water.

dep·u·ta·tion (dep′yə tā′shən), 1 group of persons sent to represent others: *The factory workers appointed a deputation of their fellows to bargain for higher pay.* 2 act of deputing: *The deputation of committee work was the duty of the chairman. n.*

de·pute (di pyüt′), 1 appoint to do one's work or to act in one's place: *The teacher deputed a pupil to take charge of the room while she was gone.* 2 give (one's work, authority, etc.) to another: *The owner deputed the repair of the building to his partner. v.*, **de·put·ed, de·put·ing.**

dep·u·tize (dep′yə tīz), appoint as deputy. *v.*, **dep·u·tized, dep·u·tiz·ing.**

dep·u·ty (dep′yə tē), person appointed to do the work of or take the place of another: *A sheriff's deputies help him enforce the law. n., pl.* **dep·u·ties.**

de·rail (di rāl′), 1 cause (a train, etc.) to run off the rails. 2 run off the rails. *v.*

de·rail·leur (di rā′lər), a spring-driven mechanism on a bicycle that changes gears by causing the chain to move from one sprocket wheel to another. *n.* [from French *dérailleur*]

de·rail·ment (di rāl′mənt), a derailing or a being derailed. *n.*

de·range (di rānj′), 1 disturb the order or arrangement of; throw into confusion: *Sudden illness in the family deranged our plans for the trip.* 2 make insane: *He was temporarily deranged by grief. v.*, **de·ranged, de·rang·ing.**

de·range·ment (di rānj′mənt), 1 disturbance of order or arrangement. 2 mental disorder or insanity. *n.*

Der·by (dèr′bē), 1 a famous horse race run every year since 1780 near London. 2 a horse race of similar importance: *the Kentucky Derby.* 3 **derby,** a stiff hat with a rounded crown and narrow brim.

derby (def. 3)

hat, āge, fär; let, ēqual, tèrm; it, īce; hot, ōpen, ôrder; oil, out; cup, pùt, rüle; ch, child; ng, long; sh, she; th, thin; ŦH, then; zh, measure;

ə represents *a* in about, *e* in taken, *i* in pencil, *o* in lemon, *u* in circus.

n., pl. **Der·bies** or **der·bies.** [from the 12th Earl of *Derby*, died 1834, who founded the race]

der·e·lict (der′ə likt), 1 that has been abandoned; forsaken: *a derelict ship.* 2 ship abandoned at sea. 3 a poor, homeless person who is unwilling or unable to care for himself. 4 failing in one's duty; negligent: *The guard was found derelict in letting the prisoner escape.* 1,4 *adj.*, 2,3 *n.*

der·e·lic·tion (der′ə lik′shən), 1 failure in one's duty; negligence. 2 abandonment; forsaking. *n.*

de·ride (di rīd′), make fun of; laugh at in scorn: *The boys derided him for his fear of the dark. v.*, **de·rid·ed, de·rid·ing.**

de·ri·sion (di rizh′ən), scornful laughter; ridicule: *The derision of his teammates hurt the feelings of the losing pitcher. n.*

de·ri·sive (di rī′siv), that ridicules; mocking. *adj.* —**de·ri′sive·ly,** *adv.* —**de·ri′sive·ness,** *n.*

der·i·va·tion (der′ə vā′shən), 1 act or fact of deriving. 2 origin: *The celebration of Halloween is of Scottish derivation.* 3 system in a language for making new words from old words by adding prefixes and suffixes and by other methods. EXAMPLE: *Quickness = quick + suffix -ness.* 4 statement of how a word was formed; etymology. *n.*

de·riv·a·tive (di riv′ə tiv), 1 not original; derived. 2 something derived: *Many medicines are derivatives of roots and herbs.* 3 word formed by adding a prefix or suffix to another word. *Quickness* and *quickly* are derivatives of *quick.* 1 *adj.*, 2,3 *n.*

de·rive (di rīv′), 1 obtain from a source or origin; get; receive: *She derives much enjoyment from reading adventure stories.* 2 come from a source or origin; originate: *This story derives from an old legend.* 3 trace (a word, custom, etc.) from or to a source or origin: *The word "December" is ultimately derived from the Latin word "decem," which means "ten." v.*, **de·rived, de·riv·ing.**

der·ma (dèr′mə), dermis. *n.*

adj. adjective	*n.* noun
adv. adverb	*prep.* preposition
conj. conjunction	*pron.* pronoun
interj. interjection	*v.* verb
sing. singular	*pl.* plural

der ma tol o gist (dėr/mə tol/ə jist), doctor who treats the skin and its diseases. *n.*

der mis (dėr/mis), the sensitive layer of skin beneath the outer skin; derma. See **epidermis** for diagram. *n.*

de rog a to ry (di rog/ə tôr/ē), lessening the value of; belittling; disparaging; unfavorable: *The stranger's derogatory remarks about the town made him unpopular. adj.*

der rick (der/ik), 1 machine for lifting and moving heavy objects. A derrick has a long arm that swings at an angle from the base of an upright post or frame. 2 a towerlike framework over an oil well that holds the drilling and hoisting machinery. *n.* [earlier meaning "gallows", from *Derrick,* a hangman at London around 1600]

der ring-do (der/ing dü/), daring deeds. *n.*

der vish (dėr/vish), member of a Moslem religious order that practices unusual self-denial and devotion. Some dance and spin about violently. *n., pl.* **der vish es.**

de scend (di send/), 1 go or come down from a higher to a lower place: *The river descends from the mountains to the sea. We descended the stairs to get to the basement.* 2 go or come down from an earlier to a later time: *a superstition descended from the Middle Ages.* 3 go from greater to less numbers; go from higher to lower on any scale: *75-50-25 form a series that descends.* 4 make a sudden attack: *The wolves descended on the sheep and killed them.* 5 be handed down from parent to child: *This land has descended from my grandfather to my mother and now to me.* 6 come down or spring from: *He is descended from pioneers.* 7 lower oneself; stoop: *In order to eat she descended to stealing. v.*

de scend ant (di sen/dənt), 1 person born of a certain family or group: *a descendant of the Pilgrims.* 2 offspring; child, grandchild, great-grandchild, etc. You are a direct descendant of your parents, grandparents, great-grandparents, and earlier ancestors. *n.*

de scent (di sent/), 1 a coming or going down from a higher to a lower place: *the descent of a helicopter.* 2 a downward slope: *We climbed down a steep descent.* 3 a handing down from parent to child: *We can trace the descent of blond hair in this family through five generations.* 4 family line; ancestors: *We trace our descent back to a family in England.* 5 a sinking to a lower condition; decline; fall. 6 a sudden attack: *The descent of the bandits on the village was unexpected. n.*

de scribe (di skrīb/), 1 tell in words how a person looks, feels, or acts, or how a place, a thing, or event looks; tell or write about: *The reporter described the accident in detail.* 2 draw the outline of; trace: *The spinning top described a figure 8. v.,* **de scribed, de scrib ing.**

derrick (def. 1)

de scrip tion (di skrip/shən), 1 a telling in words how a person, place, thing, or event looks or behaves; describing. 2 composition or account that describes or gives a picture in words: *The reporter's vivid description of the hotel fire made me feel as if I were right at the scene.* 3 kind; sort: *I have seen no dog of any description today. n.*

de scrip tive (di skrip/tiv), using description; describing: *A descriptive booklet tells about the places to be seen on the trip. adj.* —**de scrip/tive ly, adv.**

de scry (di skrī/), catch sight of; be able to see; make out; see at a distance; see with difficulty: *We descried the little boat two miles away. v.,* **de scried, de scry ing.**

des e crate (des/ə krāt), treat or use without respect; disregard the sacredness of: *The enemy desecrated the church by using it as a stable. v.,* **des e crat ed, des e crat ing.**

des e cra tion (des/ə krā/shən), 1 act of desecrating: *The Puritans felt that work or amusement on Sunday was a desecration of the Sabbath.* 2 condition of being desecrated. *n.*

de seg re gate (dē seg/rə gāt), abolish racial segregation in: *desegregate a public school. v.,* **de seg re gat ed, de seg re gat ing.**

de seg re ga tion (dē seg/rə gā/shən), a doing away with the practice of racial segregation. *n.*

des ert[1] (dez/ərt), 1 a dry, barren region that is usually sandy and without trees. The Sahara Desert is a great desert in the northern part of Africa. 2 dry and barren: *Arabia is largely desert land.* 3 not inhabited or cultivated; wild: *Robinson Crusoe was shipwrecked on a desert island.* 1 *n.,* 2,3 *adj.* [from Latin *desertum* thing abandoned]

de sert[2] (di zėrt/), go away and leave a person or a place, especially one that should not be left; forsake: *She deserted her old friends when she became famous. A soldier who deserts is punished. The deserted house fell into ruins. v.* [from French *déserter*]

de sert[3] (di zėrt/), what one deserves; suitable reward or punishment: *The reckless driver got his just deserts; he was fined and his driver's license was suspended. n.* [from French of the 1300's *deserte* deserved]

de sert er (di zėr/tər), 1 person who deserts. 2 soldier or sailor who runs away from duty. *n.*

de ser tion (di zėr/shən), 1 act of deserting. 2 condition of being deserted: *Desertion caused the old house to fall into ruin.* 3 a running away from duty, especially from military service. *n.*

de serve (di zėrv/), have a claim or right to; be worthy of: *A hard worker deserves good pay. A naughty child deserves punishment. v.,* **de served, de serv ing.**

de serv ed ly (di zėr/vid lē), according to what is deserved; justly; rightly. *adv.*

de serv ing (di zėr/ving), 1 that deserves; worthy (of something): *Those thieves are deserving of punishment.* 2 worth helping: *The deserving student received a scholarship. adv.*

des ic cate (des/ə kāt), deprive of moisture or water; dry thoroughly: *The soil in a desert is desiccated. v.,* **des ic cat ed, des ic cat ing.**

de sign (di zīn/), 1 a drawing, plan, or sketch made to serve as a pattern from which to work: *The design showed how to build the machine.* 2 arrangement of details, form, and color in painting, weaving, building, etc.: *a wallpaper design in tan and brown.* 3 make a first sketch of; arrange form and color of; draw in outline: *design a dress.* 4 make drawings, sketches, or plans: *He designs for our dress department.* 5 art of making designs, patterns, or sketches: *Architects study and become skilled in design.* 6 scheme of attack; evil plan: *The thief had designs upon the safe.* 7 plan out; form in the mind: *The author of this detective story has designed an exciting plot.* 8 purpose; aim; intention: *Whether by accident or* design, he overturned the lamp. 9 have in mind to do; purpose: *Did you design this result?* 10 set apart; intend: *The nursery was designed for the baby's use.* 1,2,5,6,8 *n.,* 3,4,7,9,10 *v.*

des ig nate (dez′ig nāt), 1 mark out; point out; indicate definitely; show: *Red lines designate main roads on this map.* 2 name: *The ruler of a kingdom is designated king.* 3 select for duty, office, etc.; appoint: *She has been designated by the President as the ambassador to Italy.* *v.,* **des ig nat ed, des ig nat ing.**

des ig na tion (dez′ig nā′shən), 1 act of marking out; pointing out: *The designation of places on a map should be clear.* 2 a descriptive title; name: *"Your Honor" is a designation given to a judge.* 3 appointment to an office or position; selection for a duty: *The designation of cabinet officers is one of the powers of the President.* *n.*

de sign ed ly (di zī′nid lē), on purpose; intentionally. *adv.*

de sign er (di zī′nər), person who designs. A dress designer makes patterns and sketches for women's clothes. *n.*

de sign ing (di zī′ning), 1 scheming; plotting. 2 showing plan or forethought. 3 art of making designs, patterns, sketches, etc. 1,2 *adj.,* 3 *n.*

de sir a bil i ty (di zī′rə bil′ə tē), desirable quality; condition to be wished for: *Nobody doubts the desirability of good health.* *n.*

de sir a ble (di zī′rə bəl), worth wishing for; worth having; pleasing; good: *Main Street is a very desirable location for a large department store.* *adj.*

de sir a bly (di zī′rə blē), in a desirable manner. *adv.*

de sire (di zīr′), 1 a wanting or longing; strong wish: *feel a desire to travel.* 2 wish earnestly for; long for: *The people of the warring nations desire peace.* 3 express a wish for; ask for: *The principal desires your presence in his office.* 4 a wish expressed in words; request. 5 thing wished for: *His greatest desire was a bicycle.* 1,4,5 *n.,* 2,3 *v.,* **de sired, de sir ing.**

de sir ous (di zī′rəs), desiring; wishing; eager: *She is desirous of going to Europe sometime. adj.*

de sist (di zist′), stop doing something; cease. *v.*

desk (desk), 1 piece of furniture with a flat or sloping top on which to write or to rest books for reading. A desk often has drawers. 2 department of work at a certain location or at a desk: *the information desk of a library. n.*

Des Moines (də moin′), capital of Iowa, in the central part.

des o late (des′ə lit *for* 1,2,4,6,7; des′ə lāt *for* 3,5), 1 not producing anything; laid waste; devastated; barren: *desolate land.* 2 not lived in; deserted: *a desolate house.* 3 make unfit to live in; lay waste: *The earthquake desolated the business district.* 4 unhappy; forlorn: *The lost child looked very desolate.* 5 make unhappy: *We are desolated to hear that you are going away.* 6 left alone. 7 dreary; dismal: *a desolate life.* 1,2,4,6,7 *adj.,* 3,5 *v.,* **des o lat ed, des o lat ing.**

des o la tion (des′ə lā′shən), 1 a making desolate: *the desolation of the country by an invading army.* 2 a ruined, lonely, or deserted condition: *After the fire the forest land was in complete desolation.* 3 a desolate place. 4 lonely sorrow; sadness: *desolation at the loss of loved ones. n.*

De So to (di sō′tō), **Hernando,** 1500?-1542, Spanish explorer in North America who discovered the Mississippi River.

de spair (di sper′ *or* di spar′), 1 loss of hope; a being without hope; a dreadful feeling that nothing good can happen to one: *Despair seized us as we felt the boat sinking.* 2 person or thing that causes loss of hope: *Another week without rain was the despair of the farmers.* 3 lose hope; be without hope: *The doctors despaired of saving the sick man's life.* 1,2 *n.,* 3 *v.*

des patch (dis pach′), dispatch. *v., n., pl.* **des patch es.**

des pe ra do (des′pə rä′dō), a bold, reckless criminal; dangerous outlaw. *n., pl.* **des pe ra does** *or* **des pe ra dos.** [from Spanish of the 1600's *desperado* despaired]

des per ate (des′pər it), 1 showing recklessness caused by despair; violent: *Suicide is a desperate act.* 2 ready to run any risk: *a desperate robber.* 3 having little chance for hope or cure; very dangerous: *a desperate illness.* 4 extremely bad: *People in the slums live in desperate circumstances. adj.* —**des′per ate ly,** *adv.* —**des′per ate ness,** *n.*

des pe ra tion (des′pə rā′shən), 1 a hopeless and reckless feeling; readiness to try anything: *He jumped out of the window in desperation when he saw that the stairs were on fire.* 2 despair. *n.*

des pi ca ble (des′pi kə bəl *or* des-pik′ə bəl), to be despised; contemptible: *It is despicable to go away and leave a cat behind to starve. adj.*

des pi ca bly (des′pi kə blē *or* des-pik′ə blē), in a despicable manner; contemptibly. *adv.*

de spise (di spīz′), look down on; feel contempt for; scorn: *They were despised for their trickery. v.,* **de spised, de spis ing.**

hat, āge, fär; let, ēqual, tėrm;
it, īce; hot, ōpen, ôrder;
oil, out; cup, pùt, rüle; ch, child;
ng, long; sh, she; th, thin;
ŦH, then; zh, measure;

ə represents *a* in about,
e in taken, *i* in pencil,
o in lemon, *u* in circus.

de spite (di spīt′), 1 in spite of: *We will go for a walk despite the rain.* 2 insult or injury. 1 *prep.,* 2 *n.*

de spoil (di spoil′), strip of possessions; rob; plunder. *v.* —**de spoil′er,** *n.*

de spond (di spond′), lose heart, courage, or hope: *Do not despond; everything will soon be better. v.*

de spond ence (di spon′dəns), despondency. *n.*

de spond en cy (di spon′dən sē), loss of heart, courage, or hope; discouragement; dejection. *n.*

de spond ent (di spon′dənt), having lost heart, courage, or hope; discouraged; dejected. *adj.* —**de spond′ent ly,** *adv.*

des pot (des′pət), 1 monarch having unlimited power; absolute ruler. 2 person who does just as he likes; tyrant. *n.*

des pot ic (di spot′ik), of a despot; having unlimited power; tyrannical. *adj.*

des pot i cal ly (des pot′ik lē), in a despotic manner; with absolute power. *adv.*

des pot ism (des′pə tiz′əm), 1 government by a monarch having unlimited power. 2 tyranny or oppression. *n.*

des sert (di zėrt′), course of sweets or fruit at the end of a meal. In the United States, pie, cake, and ice cream are desserts. In England, dessert is often fruit and nuts. *n.*

des ti na tion (des′tə nā′shən), place to which a person or thing is going or is being sent. *n.*

des tine (des′tən), 1 set apart for a particular purpose or use; intend: *The prince was destined from birth to be a king.* 2 cause by fate: *My letter was destined never to reach her. v.,* **des tined, des tin ing.**

destined for, intended to go to; bound for: *ships destined for England.*

des ti ny (des′tə nē), 1 what becomes of a person or thing in the end; one's lot or fortune: *It was young Washington's destiny to become the first President of the United States.* 2 what will happen, believed to be determined beforehand

adj.	adjective	*n.*	noun
adv.	adverb	*prep.*	preposition
conj.	conjunction	*pron.*	pronoun
interj.	interjection	*v.*	verb
sing.	singular	*pl.*	plural

in spite of all later efforts to change or prevent it: *She felt that destiny had been unkind to her in making her poor.* n., pl. **des ti nies.**

des ti tute (des′tə tüt *or* des′tə tyüt), lacking necessary things such as food, clothing, and shelter: *A destitute family needs help from charity.* adj.

destitute of, having no; without: *The land was dry and destitute of trees.*

des ti tu tion (des′tə tü′shən *or* des′tə tyü′shən), 1 lack of the means of living; extreme poverty. 2 a being without; lack. *n.*

de stroy (di stroi′), 1 break to pieces; make useless; ruin; spoil: *Drought destroyed the corn crop.* 2 put an end to; do away with: *A heavy rain destroyed all hope of a picnic.* 3 kill: *Fire destroys many trees every year.* v.

de stroy er (di stroi′ər), 1 person or thing that destroys. 2 a small, fast warship with guns, torpedoes, and other weapons. *n.*

de struct i ble (di struk′tə bəl), that can be destroyed. *adj.*

de struc tion (di struk′shən), 1 a destroying: *A bulldozer was used in the destruction of the old barn.* 2 a being destroyed; ruin: *The great fire caused the city's destruction.* 3 thing that destroys. *n.*

de struc tive (di struk′tiv), 1 destroying; causing destruction: *Fires and earthquakes are destructive. Termites are destructive insects.* 2 tearing down; not helpful; not constructive: *Criticism that shows things to be wrong but does not show how to correct them is destructive.* adj. —**de struc′tive ly,** adv. —**de struc′tive ness,** n.

des ul to ry (des′əl tôr′ē), jumping from one thing to another; without aim or method; unconnected: *He read the book in a desultory manner, skipping chapters as he pleased.* adj.

de tach (di tach′), 1 loosen and remove; unfasten; separate: *He detached his watch from the chain.* 2 send away on special duty: *One squad of soldiers was detached to guard the road.* v.

de tach a ble (di tach′ə bəl), that can be detached: *A loose-leaf notebook has detachable pages.* adj.

de tached (di tacht′), 1 separate from others; isolated: *A detached house is separated by land from neighboring houses.* 2 not influenced by others or by one's own interests and prejudices; impartial: *The judge listened to the claims of both sides with a detached air.* adj.

de tach ed ly (di tach′id lē), in a detached manner. *adv.*

de tach ment (di tach′mənt), 1 a taking apart; separation. 2 a standing apart; lack of interest; aloofness: *He watched the dull motion picture with detachment.* 3 freedom from prejudice or bias; impartial attitude. 4 group of soldiers or ships sent on some special duty. *n.*

de tail (di tāl′ *or* dē′tāl), 1 a small or unimportant part: *Her report was complete; it didn't leave out a single detail.* 2 a dealing with small things one by one: *She does not enjoy the details of housekeeping.* 3 tell fully; tell even the small and unimportant parts of: *The new boy detailed to us all the wonders he had seen in his travels.* 4 a small group selected for or sent on some special duty: *A detail of six scouts was sent out to find firewood.* 5 select for or send on special duty: *Policemen were detailed to hold back the crowd watching the parade.* 1,2,4 n., 3,5 v.

in detail, with all the details; part by part.

detailed (def. 1)—The drawing of a rose at the right is a detailed drawing.

de tailed (di tāld′ *or* dē′tāld), 1 full of details: *The witness gave a detailed account of the accident.* 2 minute: *With a microscope a scientist can make a detailed examination of bacteria.* adj.

de tain (di tān′), 1 keep from going ahead; hold back; delay: *The heavy traffic detained us for almost an hour.* 2 keep from going away; hold as a prisoner: *The police detained the suspected thief for further questioning.* v.

de tect (di tekt′), find out; discover; catch: *She was detected hiding the presents in the closet. Can you detect any odor in the room?* v.

de tec tion (di tek′shən), a finding out; discovery. *n.*

de tec tive (di tek′tiv), 1 member of a police force or other person whose work is finding information secretly, discovering who committed a crime, etc. 2 having to do with detectives and their work: *She likes reading detective stories.* 3 used in discovering or finding out: *Scientific detective methods are more accurate than guessing.* 1 n., 2,3 adj.

de tec tor (di tek′tər), 1 person or thing that detects. 2 a vacuum tube or crystal in a radio that helps in the change of radio waves into sound waves. *n.*

de ten tion (di ten′shən), 1 act of detaining; holding back. 2 condition of being detained: *Detention after hours is a common punishment in school.* 3 a keeping in custody; confinement: *A jail is used for the detention of persons who have been arrested.* n.

de ter (di tėr′), keep back; discourage or hinder: *The extreme heat deterred us from going downtown. The barking dog deterred me from crossing the neighbor's yard.* v., **de terred, de ter ring.**

de ter gent (di tėr′jənt), 1 substance used for cleansing. Many detergents are chemical compounds that act like soap. 2 cleansing. 1 n., 2 adj.

de te ri o rate (di tir′ē ə rāt′), 1 become worse; lessen in value: *Machinery deteriorates rapidly if it is not taken care of.* 2 make worse: *A hot, damp climate deteriorates leather.* v., **de te ri o rat ed, de te ri o rat ing.**

de te ri o ra tion (di tir′ē ə rā′shən), a deteriorating; a becoming or making worse: *We had the book rebound because of the deterioration of the cover.* n.

de ter mi nant (di tėr′mə nənt), 1 determining; deciding: *The higher pay offered was the determinant factor in her changing jobs.* 2 thing that determines. 1 adj., 2 n.

de ter mi na tion (di tėr′mə nā′shən), 1 great firmness in carrying out a purpose; fixed purpose: *His determination was not weakened by the difficulties he met.* 2 a finding out the exact amount or kind, by weighing, measuring, or calculating: *the determination of the gold in a sample of rock.* 3 a deciding; settling beforehand: *The determination of textbooks to be used in the coming year was left up to the teachers.* n.

de ter mine (di tėr′mən), 1 make up one's mind very firmly; resolve: *He determined to become the best scout in his troop.* 2 find out exactly: *The captain determined the latitude and longitude of his ship's position.* 3 be the deciding fact in reaching a certain result: *The number of answers you get right determines your mark in this test. Tomorrow's weather will determine whether we go to the beach or stay home.* 4 decide or settle beforehand; fix: *Can we now determine the date for our party?* 5 limit; define: *The meaning* of a word is partly determined by its use in a particular sentence. *v.,* **de ter mined, de ter min ing.**

de ter mined (di tèr′mənd), 1 with one's mind firmly made up; resolved: *He was determined to go in spite of the storm.* 2 firm; resolute: *Her determined look showed that she had made up her mind. adj.* —**de ter′mined ly,** *adv.*

de ter rent (di tèr′ənt), 1 discouraging or hindering; deterring: *A dog in the house is a deterrent influence on burglars.* 2 something that deters: *Fear of sharks is a deterrent to swimming in those waters.* 1 *adj.,* 2 *n.*

de test (di test′), dislike very much; hate: *I detest liars. v.*

de test a ble (di tes′tə bəl), deserving to be detested; hateful: *Murder is a detestable crime. adj.*

de test a bly (di tes′tə blē), in a detestable manner; abominably. *adv.*

de tes ta tion (dē′tes′tā′shən), very strong dislike; hatred: *My cat has a detestation of water. n.*

de throne (di thrōn′), put off a throne or a high position; remove from ruling power; depose: *The rebels dethroned the weak king. v.,* **de throned, de thron ing.**

de throne ment (di thrōn′mənt), removal from a throne or a high position. *n.*

det o nate (det′n āt), explode with a loud noise: *The workmen detonated the dynamite. Suddenly the bomb detonated. v.,* **det o nat ed, det o nat ing.**

det o na tion (det′n ā′shən), explosion with a loud noise. *n.*

det o na tor (det′n ā′tər), fuse, percussion cap, or similar device used to set off an explosive. *n.*

de tour (dē′tùr), 1 road that is used when the main or direct road cannot be traveled. 2 a roundabout way or course: *I took several detours before I got the right answer.* 3 use a detour: *We detoured around the bridge that had been washed out.* 4 cause to use a detour: *The police detoured all traffic on Broadway to keep it open for the parade.* 1,2 *n.,* 3,4 *v.*

de tract (di trakt′), take away a part; remove some of the quality or worth: *The ugly frame detracts from the beauty of the picture. v.*

de trac tion (di trak′shən), a taking away of some quality or worth; a speaking evil of; belittling. *n.*

de trac tor (di trak′tər), person who speaks evil of or belittles another. *n.*

det ri ment (det′rə mənt), 1 loss, damage, or injury: *She worked her way through college without detriment to her studies.* 2 something that causes loss, damage, or injury: *Her poor diet was a detriment to her health. n.*

det ri men tal (det′rə men′tl), harmful; injurious: *Lack of sleep is detrimental to one's health. adj.*

de tri tus (di trī′təs), particles of rock or other material worn away from a mass. *n.*

De troit (di troit′), city in SE Michigan. *n.*

deuce (düs *or* dyüs), 1 a playing card or a side of a die having two spots. 2 (in tennis) a tie score at 40 each in a game, or 5 or more games each in a set. 3 exclamation of annoyance meaning "bad luck" or "the devil." 1,2 *n.,* 3 *interj.*

deu ter i um (dü tir′ē əm *or* dyü-tir′ē əm), an isotope of hydrogen; heavy hydrogen. Its atoms weigh about twice as much as those of ordinary hydrogen. *n.*

Deu te ron o my (dü′tə ron′ə mē *or* dyü′tə ron′ə mē), the fifth book of the Old Testament. *n.*

de Va ler a (dev′ə ler′ə *or* dev′ə-lir′ə), **Eamon,** born 1882, Irish political leader, president of the Republic of Ireland from 1959 to 1973.

de val u ate (dē val′yü āt), devalue. *v.,* **de val u at ed, de val u at ing.**

de val u a tion (dē val′yü ā′shən), a devaluing or a being devalued. *n.*

de val ue (dē val′yü), reduce the value of; fix a lower legal value on; devaluate: *In 1967 Great Britain devalued the pound from $2.80 to $2.40. v.,* **de val-ued, de val u ing.**

dev as tate (dev′ə stāt), make desolate; lay waste; destroy; ravage: *A long war devastated the country. v.,* **dev as-tat ed, dev as tat ing.**

dev as ta tion (dev′ə stā′shən), a devastating or a being devastated; destruction; desolation: *Every year fires cause the devastation of valuable forests. n.*

de vel op (di vel′əp), 1 come into being or activity; grow: *Plants develop from seeds.* 2 bring into being or activity: *Scientists have developed many new drugs to fight disease.* 3 come to have: *She developed an interest in collecting stamps.* 4 make or become bigger, better, more useful, etc.: *Exercise develops the muscles. His business developed very slowly.* 5 work out in greater and greater detail: *Gradually we developed our plans for the club.* 6 treat (a photographic film or plate) with chemicals to bring out the picture: *We shall print all the films we developed.* 7 make or become known: *The detective's investigation did not develop any new facts. v.*

de vel op er (di vel′ə pər), 1 person or thing that develops. 2 chemical used to bring out the picture on a photographic film or plate. *n.*

hat, āge, fär; let, ēqual, tèrm;
it, īce; hot, ōpen, ôrder;
oil, out; cup, pùt, rüle; ch, child;
ng, long; sh, she; th, thin;
ŦH, then; zh, measure;

ə represents *a* in about,
e in taken, *i* in pencil,
o in lemon, *u* in circus.

de vel op ment (di vel′əp mənt), 1 process of developing; growth: *The doctor followed the child's development closely.* 2 outcome; result; new event: *The newspaper described the latest developments in the elections.* 3 a working out in greater and greater detail: *The development of the plans for a rocket flight to the moon took many years.* 4 group of similar houses or apartment buildings built on open land or in place of old buildings. *n.*

de vel op men tal (di vel′əp men′tl), of or having to do with development. *adj.* —**de vel′op men′tal ly,** *adv.*

de vi ate (dē′vē āt), turn aside (from a way, course, rule, truth, etc.): *The mayor deviated from his custom and did not attend the parade. v.,* **de vi at ed, de vi at ing.**

de vi a tion (dē′vē ā′shən), a turning aside from a way, course, rule, truth, etc.: *Running in the halls is a deviation from school rules and will not be allowed. The iron in the ship caused a deviation in the magnetic needle of the compass. n.*

de vice (di vīs′), 1 something invented, devised, or fitted for a particular use or special purpose. A can opener is a device. *Our car has a device to control pollution from exhaust.* 2 a plan, scheme, or trick: *In order to stay outside she used the device of pretending not to hear her mother calling her.* 3 a drawing or figure used in a pattern or as an ornament: *A star and a circle are used as a device in the banner. n.*

leave to one's own devices, leave to do as one thinks best: *The teacher left us to our own devices in choosing the books for our reports.*

dev il (dev′əl), 1 **the Devil,** the evil spirit; the enemy of goodness; Satan. 2 any evil spirit; fiend; demon. 3 a wicked or cruel person. 4 a very clever, energetic, or reckless person: *a mischievous devil.* 5 an unfortunate or wretched person: *That poor devil hasn't eaten a good meal in weeks.* 6 a young helper or errand boy in a printing office. 7 bother or tease: *Her brother deviled her all during the meal.* 1-6 *n.,* 7 *v.*

adj. adjective	*n.* noun
adv. adverb	*prep.* preposition
conj. conjunction	*pron.* pronoun
interj. interjection	*v.* verb
sing. singular	*pl.* plural

dev iled (dev′əld), highly seasoned: *deviled ham, deviled eggs. adj.*

dev il fish (dev′əl fish′), 1 a large ray of warm seas that moves by a flapping motion of its broad fins. 2 octopus. *n., pl.* **dev il fish es** or **dev il fish.**

dev il ish (dev′ə lish), 1 like a devil; worthy of the Devil; very evil: *a devilish temper.* 2 mischievous or daring: *The children played devilish pranks on Halloween. adj.* —**dev′il ish ly,** *adv.* —**dev′il ish ness,** *n.*

dev il-may-care (dev′əl mā ker′ or dev′əl mā kar′), very careless or reckless. *adj.*

dev il ment (dev′əl mənt), devilish action or behavior; deviltry. *n.*

dev il ry (dev′əl rē), deviltry. *n., pl.* **dev il ries.**

dev il try (dev′əl trē), 1 evil action; wicked or cruel behavior. 2 mischievous or daring behavior: *The children were full of deviltry on Halloween. n., pl.* **dev il tries.**

de vi ous (dē′vē əs), 1 out of the direct way; winding; roundabout: *We took a devious route through side streets and alleys to avoid the crowded main streets.* 2 straying from the right course; not straightforward: *a devious scheme for finding out the answers to the test beforehand. adj.* —**de′vi ous ly,** *adv.* —**de′vi ous ness,** *n.*

de vise (di vīz′), 1 think out; plan or contrive; invent: *I devised a way of raising boards up to my tree house by using a pulley.* 2 give or leave (land, buildings, etc.) by a will. *v.,* **de vised, de vis ing.**

de void (di void′), entirely without; empty; lacking: *devoid of sense. A well devoid of water is useless. adj.*

de volve (di volv′), 1 be handed down to someone else; be transferred: *If the president is unable to handle his duties, they devolve upon the vice-president.* 2 transfer (duty, work, etc.) to someone else. *v.,* **de volved, de volv ing.**

Dev on (dev′ən), county in SW England. *n.*

de vote (di vōt′), give up (oneself, one's money, time, or efforts, etc.) to some person, purpose, or service: *She devoted herself to her studies. He is devoting his efforts to improving the environment. That natural history museum devotes two floors to animal exhibits. v.,* **de vot ed, de vot ing.**

de vot ed (di vō′tid), very loyal; faithful: *His dog is a devoted companion. adj.* —**de vot′ed ly,** *adv.*

dev o tee (dev′ə tē′), person who is strongly devoted to something: *Many Americans are devotees of football. n.*

de vo tion (di vō′shən), 1 deep, steady affection; loyalty; faithfulness: *the devotion of a mother to her child.* 2 a giving up or being given up to some person, purpose, or service: *the devotion of much time to study.* 3 **devotions,** *pl.* worship, prayers, or praying. *n.*

de vo tion al (di vō′shə nəl), having to do with religious devotion; used in worship: *devotional hymns. adj.*

de vour (di vour′), 1 eat (usually said of animals): *The lion devoured the sheep.* 2 eat like an animal; eat very hungrily: *The hungry girl devoured her dinner.* 3 consume, waste, or destroy: *The raging fire devoured the forest.* 4 take in with eyes or ears in a hungry, greedy way: *He devoured the new book about airplanes.* 5 absorb wholly: *She was devoured by curiosity about her birthday presents. v.*

de vout (di vout′), 1 active in worship and prayer; religious: *a devout Moslem, a devout Christian.* 2 earnest; sincere; hearty: *You have my devout wishes for a safe trip. adj.* —**de vout′ly,** *adv.* —**de vout′ness,** *n.*

dew (dü or dyü), 1 moisture from the air that condenses in small drops on cool surfaces during the night: *In the morning there was dew on the grass and flowers.* 2 something fresh or refreshing like dew: *the dew of youth, the dew of sleep. n.*

dew ber ry (dü′ber′ē or dyü′ber′ē), 1 the fruit of various blackberry vines that grow along the ground. 2 any of these vines. *n., pl.* **dew ber ries.**

dew drop (dü′drop′ or dyü′drop′), a drop of dew. *n.*

dew lap (dü′lap′ or dyü′lap′), the loose fold of skin under the throat of cattle and some other animals. *n.*

dew point, the temperature of the air at which dew begins to form.

dew y (dü′ē or dyü′ē), 1 wet with dew. 2 fresh or refreshing like dew. *adj.,* **dew i er, dew i est.**

dex ter i ty (dek ster′ə tē), skill in using the hands, body, or mind: *The jeweler's dexterity was shown in the quick, sure way he repaired the watch. Dexterity in questioning witnesses helped the lawyer win many cases. n.*

dex ter ous (dek′stər əs), 1 having skill with the hands: *A typist needs to be dexterous.* 2 quick and skillful in bodily movements: *a dexterous acrobat.* 3 having skill with the mind; clever: *A successful manager must be dexterous in handling people. adj.* Also, **dextrous.** —**dex′ter ous ly,** *adv.* —**dex′ter ous ness,** *n.*

dex trose (dek′strōs), a crystalline sugar less sweet than cane sugar, occurring in many plant and animal tissues and fluids; grape sugar. It is a form of glucose. *n.*

dex trous (dek′strəs), dexterous. *adj.*

di a be tes (dī′ə bē′tis or dī′ə bē′tēz), disease in which a person's system cannot properly absorb normal amounts of sugar and starch because the pancreas fails to secrete enough insulin. *n.*

di a bet ic (dī′ə bet′ik), 1 of or having to do with diabetes. 2 having diabetes. 3 person having diabetes. 1,2 *adj.,* 3 *n.*

di a bol ic (dī′ə bol′ik), very cruel or wicked; devilish; fiendish: *The police discovered a diabolic plot to poison the city's drinking water. adj.* —**di′a bol′i cal ly,** *adv.*

di a bol i cal (dī′ə bol′ə kəl), diabolic. *adj.*

di a crit ic (dī′ə krit′ik), a diacritical mark. *n.*

di a crit i cal mark (dī′ə krit′ə kəl), a small mark like ·· ^ - ′ or ` put on a letter to indicate pronunciation, accent, etc. See the diacritical marks in the short pronunciation key in the upper right corner of the opposite page.

di a dem (dī′ə dem), 1 a crown. 2 an ornamental band of cloth formerly worn as a crown. *n.*

di ag nose (dī′əg nōs′), make a diagnosis of; find out the nature of by examination and careful study: *The doctor diagnosed her illness as measles. v.,* **di ag nosed, di ag nos ing.**

DEWLAP

di ag no sis (dī′əg nō′sis), 1 act or process of finding out what disease a person or animal has by examination and careful study of the symptoms: *The doctor used X rays and blood samples in his diagnosis.* 2 a careful study of the facts about something to find out its essential features, faults, etc.: *We asked the automobile mechanic to make a diagnosis of our car's engine so that we would know what to have repaired.* 3 decision reached after a careful study of symptoms or facts: *The diagnosis blamed the collapse of the bridge on* faulty construction. *n., pl.* **di ag no ses** (dī/əg nō/sēz/).

di ag nos tic (dī/əg nos/tik), 1 of or having to do with diagnosis. 2 helping in diagnosis: *diagnostic tests. adj.*

diagonal (def. 1)
Line AB is
a diagonal.

di ag o nal (dī ag/ə nəl), 1 a line segment connecting two corners that are not next to each other in a four-sided or many-sided figure; line that cuts across in a slanting direction. 2 taking the direction of a diagonal; slanting: *a diagonal stripe in cloth. The ship sailed on a diagonal course across the Atlantic from New York to Cape Town.* 3 any slanting part, course, or arrangement of things. 4 connecting two corners that are not next to each other in a four-sided or many-sided figure: *a diagonal line.* 1,3 *n.,* 2,4 *adj.* —**di ag/o nal ly**, *adv.*

di a gram (dī/ə gram), 1 drawing or sketch showing important parts of something. A diagram may be an outline, a plan, a figure, a chart, or a combination of any of these, made to show clearly what something is, how it works, or the relation between the parts. Diagrams are used in geometry to help in the proof of the problems. 2 put on paper, a blackboard, etc., in the form of a drawing or sketch; make a diagram of: *The architect diagramed the floor plan to show how he would divide the office space.* 1 *n.,* 2 *v.*

di a gram mat ic (dī/ə grə mat/ik), 1 in the form of a diagram. 2 in outline form only; sketchy: *The plot of my story was in a diagrammatic form, with details to be filled in later. adj.*

di al (dī/əl), 1 plate or disk with numbers, letters, or marks on it and a moving pointer that shows amount, time, degree, direction, etc. The face of a clock is a dial around which the hands move to tell time. The moving pointer shows direction on the dial of a compass. In some meters and gauges a pointer moves over a dial to show how much there is of something. 2 plate or disk with numbers or letters on it for tuning in to a radio or television station. 3 tune in by using a radio or television dial: *He dials his favorite station every morning.* 4 part of an automatic telephone, with letters and numbers, used in making telephone calls. 5 call by means of a telephone dial: *She dialed the wrong number.* 6 plate or disk on a lock, with numbers or letters on it, used for opening the lock. 7 turn such a

dial in order to open a lock: *She dialed the combination to open her locker.* 8 sundial. 1,2,4,6,8 *n.,* 3,5,7 *v.*

di a lect (dī/ə lekt), a form of speech spoken in a certain district or by a certain group of people: *The Scottish dialect of English has many words and pronunciations that are not used in standard English. A dialect of French is spoken in southern Louisiana by descendants of French Canadians. n.*

di a lec tal (dī/ə lek/təl), of a dialect; like that of a dialect. *adj.*

di a logue or **di a log** (dī/ə lôg), 1 conversation: *Two actors had a dialogue in the middle of the stage.* 2 conversation written out: *That book has a good plot and much clever dialogue. n.*

di am e ter (dī am/ə tər), 1 a line segment passing from one side to the other through the center of a circle, sphere, etc. 2 the length of such a line segment; measurement from one side to the other through the center; width; thickness: *The diameter of the earth is about 8000 miles. n.*

di a met ric (dī/ə met/rik), 1 of or along a diameter. 2 exactly opposite: *The two candidates have diametric opinions on that issue. adj.*

di a met ri cal (dī/ə met/rə kəl), diametric. *adj.*

di a met ri cal ly (dī/ə met/rik lē), 1 as a diameter. 2 directly; exactly; entirely: *She and I have diametrically opposed views. adv.*

dia mond (dī/mənd *or* dī/ə mənd), 1 a colorless or tinted precious stone, formed of pure carbon in crystals. Diamond is the hardest natural substance known. Inferior diamonds are used to cut glass. 2 figure shaped like this: ◇; lozenge; rhombus. 3 a playing card marked with one or more red, diamond-shaped figures. 4 **diamonds,** *pl.* suit of such playing cards. 5 (in baseball) the area bounded by home plate and the three bases; infield. *n.* —**dia/mond like/,** *adj.*

Di an a (dī an/ə), (in Roman myths) the goddess of the hunt and of the moon. The Greeks called her Artemis. *n.*

di a per (dī/ə pər *or* dī/pər), 1 piece of cloth or other soft material folded and used as underpants for a baby. 2 put a diaper on: *diaper the baby after his bath.* 1 *n.,* 2 *v.*

di aph a nous (dī af/ə nəs), transparent: *Gauze is a diaphanous fabric. adj.*

di a phragm (dī/ə fram), 1 a partition of muscles and tendons separating the cavity of the chest from the cavity of the abdomen; midriff. 2 a thin dividing partition. 3 a thin disk that vibrates rapidly when receiving or producing

hat, āge, fär; let, ēqual, tèrm;
it, īce; hot, ōpen, ôrder;
oil, out; cup, pùt, rüle; ch, child;
ng, long; sh, she; th, thin;
ŦH, then; zh, measure;

ə represents *a* in about,
e in taken, *i* in pencil,
o in lemon, *u* in circus.

sounds, used in telephones, loudspeakers, microphones, and other instruments. 4 disk with a hole in the center for controlling the amount of light entering a camera, microscope, etc. *n.*

di ar rhe a (dī/ə rē/ə), condition of having too many and too loose movements of the bowels. *n.*

di a ry (dī/ər ē), 1 account written down each day of what has happened to one, or what one has done or thought, during that day. 2 book for keeping such a daily account. It has a blank space for each day of the year. *n., pl.* **di a ries.**

Di as or **Di az** (dē/äs), **Bartolomeu,** 1450?-1500, Portuguese navigator who discovered the Cape of Good Hope. *n.*

di as to le (dī as/tl ē), the regular expansion of the heart each time its cavities fill with blood. *n.*

di a tom (dī/ə tom), any of numerous microscopic, one-celled algae that have hard shells. *n.*

di a ton ic (dī/ə ton/ik), of or using only the eight tones of a standard major or minor musical scale. *adj.*

di a tribe (dī/ə trīb), a speech or discussion bitterly and violently denouncing some person or thing. *n.*

dib ble (dib/əl), a pointed tool for making holes in the ground for seeds, bulbs, or young plants. *n.*

dibble

dice (dīs), 1 small cubes with a different number of spots (one to six) on each side. Dice are used in playing some games and in gambling. 2 game played with these. 3 play games or gamble with dice, tossing them to see how many spots there will be on the sides that turn up. 4 cut into small cubes:

237

adj. adjective	*n.* noun
adv. adverb	*prep.* preposition
conj. conjunction	*pron.* pronoun
interj. interjection	*v.* verb
sing. singular	*pl.* plural

Carrots are sometimes diced before they are cooked. 1,2 *n. pl.* of **die**², 3,4 *v.,* **diced, dic ing.**

Dick ens (dik′ənz), **Charles,** 1812-1870, English novelist. *n.*

dick er (dik′ər), 1 trade by barter or by petty bargaining; haggle: *She dickered with the butcher over the price of the steaks.* 2 a petty bargain. 1 *v.,* 2 *n.*

dick ey (dik′ē), 1 a shirt front that can be detached. 2 an insert worn at the neck opening of a blouse, jacket, etc. *n., pl.* **dick eys.**

Dick in son (dik′ən sən), **Emily,** 1830-1886, American poet. *n.*

di cot y le don (dī kot′l ēd′n), a flowering plant that has two cotyledons or seed leaves. Many trees and most cultivated plants are dicotyledons. See **cotyledon** for diagram. *n.*

dic ta (dik′tə), a plural of **dictum.** *n.*

dic tate (dik′tāt), 1 say or read aloud to another person who writes down the words: *The teacher dictated a list of books to the students. She dictates letters to her secretary each morning.* 2 speak with authority; give a direction or order that must be carried out or obeyed: *The country that won the war dictated the terms of peace to the country that lost.* 3 command given with authority; order that must be obeyed: *the dictates of one's conscience, the dictates of a ruler.* 1,2 *v.,* **dic tat ed, dic tat ing;** 3 *n.*

dic ta tion (dik tā′shən), 1 act of saying or reading words aloud to another person who writes them down: *The pupils wrote down the spelling words at the teacher's dictation.* 2 words said or read aloud in this way: *The secretary took the dictation in shorthand and typed it out later.* 3 act of giving orders or making rules: *She was tired of her sister's constant dictation and refused to obey her.* *n.*

dic ta tor (dik′tā tər), 1 person who uses absolute authority: *The dictator seized control of the government and took complete power over the people of the country. French dress designers have long been the dictators in the world of fashion.* 2 person who says or reads something aloud for another to write down: *Who was the dictator of this letter?* *n.*

dic ta to ri al (dik′tə tôr′ē əl), 1 of or like that of a dictator: *That country has a dictatorial government.* 2 fond of commanding and giving orders; domineering; overbearing: *The younger children disliked the dictatorial manner of their older brother.* *adj.* —**dic′ta to′ri al ly,** *adv.*

dic ta tor ship (dik′tā tər ship), 1 position or rank of a dictator. 2 period of time a dictator rules. 3 absolute authority; power to give orders that must be obeyed. *n.*

dic tion (dik′shən), 1 manner of expressing ideas in words; style of speaking or writing. Good diction implies a skillful choice of words accurately used to express clearly the speaker's or writer's ideas. 2 manner of pronouncing words; enunciation: *That radio announcer is easy to understand because he has a very clear diction.* *n.*

dic tion ar y (dik′shə ner′ē), book that explains the words of a language or of some special subject. It is arranged alphabetically. You can use this dictionary to find out the meaning, spelling, or pronunciation of a word. A medical dictionary explains words used in medicine. A German-English dictionary translates German words into English. A dictionary of biography has accounts of people's lives arranged in alphabetical order of their names. *n., pl.* **dic tion ar ies.**

dic tum (dik′təm), 1 a formal comment; authoritative opinion: *The dictum of the critics was that the play was excellent.* 2 maxim; saying: *The old dictum says that love is blind.* *n., pl.* **dic tums** or **dic ta.**

did (did), past tense of **do**¹. *I did my work yesterday.* *v.*

diesel engine—Air entering the cylinder is compressed by the piston and gets very hot. A spray of oil sent into the air burns, causing a forceful expansion of the gas, which forces the piston down.

di dac tic (dī dak′tik), 1 meant to instruct: *Aesop's "Fables" are didactic stories; each one has a moral.* 2 inclined to instruct others; teacherlike: *They called their older brother "Professor" because of his didactic manner.* *adj.* —**di dac′ti cal ly,** *adv.*

did n't (did′nt), did not.

didst (didst), OLD USE. did. "Thou didst" means "You did." *v.*

die¹ (dī), 1 stop living; become dead: *The flowers in the garden died from frost.* 2 lose force or strength; come to an end; stop: *The motor sputtered and died.* 3 INFORMAL. want very much: *The children were dying for ice cream cones.* *v.,* **died, dy ing.** [from a Scandinavian word of the 1200's, such as Icelandic *deyja*]

die away or **die down,** stop or end little by little: *The music died away.*

die off, die one after another until all are dead: *The whole herd of cattle died off in the epidemic.*

die² (def. 1)
for cutting
threads of bolts

die² (dī), 1 tool for shaping, cutting, punching, or stamping things. It is usually a metal block or plate cut in a certain way. Dies are used for coining money and for raising printing up from the surface of paper. 2 one of a set of dice. *n., pl.* **dies** for 1, **dice** for 2. [from French of the 1200's *de*, from Latin *datum* thing given]

the die is cast, the decision is made and cannot be changed.

die-hard (dī′härd′), 1 resisting to the very end; refusing to give in: *The Senator was a die-hard opponent of any changes in the Constitution.* 2 person who refuses to give in: *Grandfather was a die-hard; he refused to use modern machinery on his farm.* 1 *adj.,* 2 *n.*

di er e sis (dī er′ə sis), two dots (¨) placed over the second of two consecutive vowels to indicate that the second vowel is to be pronounced in a separate syllable. EXAMPLES: Noël, naïve. *n., pl.* **di er e ses** (dī er′ə sēz′).

die sel or **Die sel** (dē′zl), 1 a diesel engine. 2 equipped with or run by a diesel engine: *a diesel locomotive, a diesel tractor.* 3 truck, locomotive, train, etc., with a diesel engine. 4 of or for a diesel engine: *diesel fuel.* 1,3 *n.,* 2,4 *adj.* [from Rudolf *Diesel,* 1858-1913, a German engineer, who invented the diesel engine]

diesel engine or **Diesel engine,** an internal-combustion engine that burns oil with heat caused by the compression of air.

di et¹ (dī′ət), 1 the usual kind of food and drink: *My diet is made up of meat, fish, vegetables, fruits, water, and milk. Grass is a large part of a cow's diet.* 2 a special kind of food and drink: *The doctor ordered a diet of liquids for the* sick child. The doctor put my uncle on a diet because he was too fat. 3 have a special kind of food and drink: *Don't give me any cake; I'm dieting to lose weight.* 1,2 *n.,* 3 *v.* [from French of the 1200's *diete,* from Latin *diaeta,* from Greek *diaita* way of life] —**di′et er,** *n.*

di et² (dī′ət), 1 a formal assembly for discussion. 2 the national lawmaking body in certain countries. Switzerland and Japan are governed by diets. *n.* [from Latin *dieta* day's work, meeting of councilors]

di e tar y (dī′ə ter′ē), having to do with diet: *Dietary rules tell what foods to eat for healthy living and how to prepare them. adj.*

di e tet ic (dī′ə tet′ik), of or having to do with diet or dietetics: *Many dietetic foods are without sugar, salt, or fats. adj.*

di e tet ics (dī′ə tet′iks), science that deals with the amount and kinds of food needed by the body. *n.*

di e ti tian or **di e ti cian** (dī′ə tish′-ən), person trained to plan meals that have the right amount of various kinds of food. Many hospitals and schools employ dietitians. *n.*

dif fer (dif′ər), 1 be unlike; be different: *My answer to the arithmetic problem differed from hers.* 2 have or express a different opinion; disagree: *The two of us differ about how we should spend the money. v.*

dif fer ence (dif′ər əns), 1 a being different: *the difference of night and day.* 2 way of being different; point in which people or things are different: *The only difference between the twins is that Jane weighs five pounds more than Sue.* 3 amount by which one quantity is different from another; what is left after subtracting one number from another: *The difference between 6 and 15 is 9.* 4 condition of having a different opinion; disagreement: *The children had a difference over a name for the new puppy.* 5 quarrel; dispute. *n.*

make a difference, have an effect or influence; be important; matter: *Your vote will make a difference in the election.*

dif fer ent (dif′ər ənt), 1 not alike; not like: *We saw different kinds of animals at the zoo. A boat is different from an automobile.* 2 not the same; separate; distinct: *I saw her three different times today.* 3 not like others or most others; unusual: *Our teacher is quite different; she never gives us homework. adj.* —**dif′fer ent ly,** *adv.*

dif fe ren tial (dif′ə ren′shəl), 1 of a difference; showing a difference; depending on a difference: *The differential rates in freight charges are for carrying heavier packages longer distances.*

2 a differential duty, rate, charge, etc. 3 arrangement of gears in an automobile that allows one of the rear wheels to turn faster than the other in going around a corner or curve. 1 *adj.,* 2,3 *n.* —**dif′fe ren′tial ly,** *adv.*

dif fe ren ti ate (dif′ə ren′shē āt), 1 make different; cause to have differences: *Consideration for others differentiates a thoughtful person from a thoughtless one.* 2 tell the difference in or between; find or show to be different: *Almost anyone can differentiate a cow from a horse.* 3 tell the difference; find or show what is different: *A doctor must differentiate between diseases to give the right treatment. v.,* **dif fe ren ti at ed, dif fe ren ti at ing.**

dif fe ren ti a tion (dif′ə ren′shē ā′shən), act or process of differentiating; alteration; modification; distinction. *n.*

dif fi cult (dif′ə kult), 1 hard to do or understand: *Cutting down the tree was difficult. Arithmetic is difficult for some pupils.* 2 hard to deal with or get along with; not easy to please: *That difficult member of the team always wants his own way. adj.*

dif fi cul ty (dif′ə kul′tē), 1 fact or condition of being difficult; degree to which something is difficult: *The difficulty of the job prevented us from finishing it on time.* 2 hard work; much effort: *The lame man walked with difficulty.* 3 something which stands in the way of getting things done; thing that is hard to do or understand: *Lack of time and money were difficulties we had to overcome.* 4 trouble: *Some children have difficulty learning how to spell. She has been in financial difficulty since she lost her job. n., pl.* **dif fi cul ties.**

dif fi dence (dif′ə dəns), lack of self-confidence; shyness: *His diffidence disappeared after he knew us awhile. n.*

dif fi dent (dif′ə dənt), lacking in self-confidence; shy. *adj.* —**dif′fi dent ly,** *adv.*

dif frac tion (di frak′shən), 1 a breaking up of a ray of light into a series of light and dark bands or into colored bands of the spectrum. 2 a similar breaking up of sound waves, electricity, etc. *n.*

dif fuse (di fyüz′ *for 1,3;* di fyüs′ *for 2,4*), 1 spread out so as to cover a large space or surface; scatter widely: *The sun diffuses light and heat. Schools and libraries diffuse knowledge.* 2 not drawn together at a single point; spread out: *a diffuse light.* 3 mix together by spreading into one another: *Alcohol and water will diffuse; oil and water will not.* 4 using many words where a few would do; wordy: *A diffuse book is*

hat, āge, fär; let, ēqual, tėrm; it, īce; hot, ōpen, ôrder; oil, out; cup, pùt, rüle; ch, child; ng, long; sh, she; th, thin; ₮H, then; zh, measure;

ə represents *a* in about, *e* in taken, *i* in pencil, *o* in lemon, *u* in circus.

often tiresome to read. 1,3 *v.,* **dif fused, dif fus ing;** 2,4 *adj.* —**dif fuse′ly,** *adv.*

dif fu sion (di fyü′zhən), 1 a spreading or scattering widely: *The invention of printing greatly increased the diffusion of knowledge.* 2 a being widely spread or scattered. 3 a mixing together by spreading into one another: *the diffusion of gases or liquids.* 4 use of too many words; wordiness. *n.*

dig (dig), 1 use a shovel, spade, hands, claws, or snout to make a hole or to turn over the ground: *Dogs bury bones and dig for them later.* 2 make by digging: *dig a well. The workmen dug a cellar.* 3 make a way by digging: *They dug through the mountain to build a tunnel.* 4 get by digging: *dig potatoes. We dug clams at the beach yesterday.* 5 make a thrust or stab into; prod: *The cat dug its claws into my hand.* 6 a thrust or poke: *The boy gave his friend a dig in the ribs.* 7 a sarcastic remark: *The candidate made a dig at his opponent.* 8 make a careful search or inquiry: *The writer dug into the family records for the story of her pioneer ancestors.* 9 INFORMAL. work or study hard. 10 SLANG. **a** understand: *I dig what you're trying to tell me.* **b** notice; observe: *Did you dig the clothes he was wearing?* **c** like; admire: *I dig that group's music.* 1-5,8-10 *v.,* **dug, dig ging;** 6,7 *n.*

di gest (də jest′ *or* dī jest′ *for 1-3,5;* dī′jest *for 4*), 1 change (food) in the stomach and intestines so that the body can use it: *We digest our food slowly.* 2 be changed in this manner; be digested: *Our food digests.* 3 think over (something) until one understands it clearly, or until it becomes a part of one's thoughts: *It often takes a long time to digest new ideas.* 4 a brief statement of what is in a longer book, article, or statement; summary. 5 make a brief statement of; summarize. 1-3,5 *v.,* 4 *n.*

di gest i ble (də jes′tə bəl *or* dī jes′-tə bəl), that can be digested; easily digested. *adj.*

di ges tion (də jes′chən *or* dī jes′-

239

adj. adjective	*n.* noun
adv. adverb	*prep.* preposition
conj. conjunction	*pron.* pronoun
interj. interjection	*v.* verb
sing. singular	*pl.* plural

chən), 1 the digesting of food: *Proper digestion is necessary for good health.* 2 ability to digest food: *A person's digestion can be affected by illness.* n.

di ges tive (də jes′tiv *or* dī jes′tiv), 1 of or for digestion: *The stomach is an important digestive organ.* 2 helping digestion: *digestive tablets.* adj.

dig ger (dig′ər), 1 person or thing that digs. 2 tool for digging. n.

dig gings (dig′ingz), 1 mine, archaeological site, or other place where digging is being done. 2 material that is dug out. 3 INFORMAL. place to live. n.pl.

dig it (dij′it), 1 any of the figures 0, 1, 2, 3, 4, 5, 6, 7, 8, 9. 2 finger or toe. n.

dig it al (dij′ə təl), of, having to do with, or using digits: *Digital telephone numbers, such as 223-2000, are replacing the old letter and number combinations.* adj.

dig i tal is (dij′ə tal′is), 1 medicine used for stimulating the heart, obtained from the leaves and seeds of some varieties of foxglove. 2 foxglove. n.

dig ni fied (dig′nə fīd), having dignity; noble; stately: *The queen has a dignified manner.* adj.

dig ni fy (dig′nə fī), give dignity to; make noble, worthwhile, or worthy: *The low farmhouse was dignified by the great elms around it.* v., **dig ni fied, dig ni fy ing.**

dig ni tar y (dig′nə ter′ē), person who has a position of honor. A bishop is a dignitary of the church. n., pl. **dig ni tar ies.**

dig ni ty (dig′nə tē), 1 proud and self-respecting character or manner; stateliness: *the dignity of a cathedral. The candidate maintained her dignity during the heated debate.* 2 degree of worth, honor, or importance: *A judge should maintain the dignity of his position.* 3 a high office, rank, or title; position of honor: *He may attain the dignity of the presidency.* 4 worth; nobleness: *Honest work has dignity.* n., pl. **dig ni ties.**

di graph (dī′graf), two letters used together to spell a single sound. EXAMPLES: *ea* in *each, th* in *with.* n.

di gress (də gres′ *or* dī gres′), turn aside from the main subject in talking or writing: *I lost interest in the book be-*

cause the author digressed too much. v.

di gres sion (də gresh′ən *or* dī gresh′ən), a digressing; turning aside from the main subject in talking or writing: *The speaker's many digressions made the lecture longer than usual.* n.

dike (dīk), 1 a bank of earth or a dam built as a defense against flooding by a river or the sea. 2 provide with a dike or dikes. 1 n., 2 v., **diked, dik ing.** Also, **dyke.**

di lap i dat ed (də lap′ə dā′tid), falling to pieces; partly ruined or decayed through neglect: *The ghost town was full of dilapidated houses.* adj.

di lap i da tion (də lap′ə dā′shən), a partial ruin; a falling to pieces. n.

di late (dī lāt′), 1 make or become larger or wider: *When you take a deep breath, you dilate your nostrils. The pupil of the eye dilates when the light gets dim.* 2 speak or write at length: *Most parents enjoy dilating on their children's successes.* v., **di lat ed, di lat ing.**

di la tion (dī lā′shən), a dilating or a being dilated; enlargement; widening: *The dilation of her pupils was the result of applying drops to her eyes. The dilation took twenty minutes.* n.

dil a to ri ly (dil′ə tôr′ə lē), in a dilatory manner. adv.

dil a to ry (dil′ə tôr′ē), 1 tending to delay; not prompt: *People who are dilatory in paying their bills are poor customers.* 2 causing delay: *The carpenter's dilatory work habits held up the completion of the building for weeks.* adj.

di lem ma (də lem′ə), situation requiring a choice between two evils; difficult choice: *She was faced with the dilemma of either telling a lie or betraying a friend.* n., pl. **di lem mas.**

dil et tante (dil′ə tänt *or* dil′ə tan′tē), person who follows some art or science without knowing or learning much about it; dabbler: *He was a dilettante in a dozen fields, an expert in none.* n., pl. **dil et tantes, dil et tan ti** (dil′ə tän′tē *or* dil′ə tan′tē).

dil i gence (dil′ə jəns), a being diligent; careful and steady effort; industry: *The student's diligence was rewarded with high marks.* n.

dil i gent (dil′ə jənt), 1 hard-working; industrious: *The diligent student kept on working until he had finished his homework.* 2 careful and steady: *The detective made a diligent search for clues.* adj. —**dil′i gent ly,** adv.

dill (dil), 1 plant whose spicy seeds or leaves are used to flavor pickles. 2 its seeds or leaves. n.

dill pickle, a cucumber pickle flavored with dill.

dil ly dal ly (dil′ē dal′ē), waste time;

loiter; trifle: *Let's not dillydally over such unimportant matters.* v., **dil ly-dal lied, dil ly dal ly ing.**

dike (def. 1)

di lute (də lüt′ *or* dī lüt′), 1 make weaker or thinner by adding water or some other liquid: *You must dilute the concentrated orange juice with several cups of water. Some thick paints are diluted with turpentine to make them spread easier.* 2 weakened or thinned by the addition of water or some other liquid: *a dilute acid.* 3 weaken; lessen: *The high price of a new car diluted our enthusiasm for buying one.* 1,3 v., **di-lut ed, di lut ing;** 2 adj.

di lu tion (də lü′shən *or* dī lü′shən), 1 a diluting or a being diluted. 2 something diluted. n.

dim (dim), 1 not bright; not clear; not distinct: *the dim light of dusk.* *With the shades drawn, the room was dim.* 2 not clearly seen, heard, or understood; faint: *We could see only the dim outline of the mountain in the distance. That happened so long ago that I have only a dim recollection of it.* 3 not seeing, hearing, or understanding clearly: *Grandfather's eyesight is getting dim.* 4 make or become dim: *She dimmed the car's headlights as the other car approached. The lights in the house dimmed several times during the storm.* 1-3 adj., **dim mer, dim mest;** 4 v., **dimmed, dim ming.** —**dim′ly,** adv. —**dim′ness,** n.

dime (dīm), 1 a copper and nickel coin of the United States, worth 10 cents. 2 a similar coin of Canada, worth 10 cents. n.

di men sion (də men′shən), 1 measurement of length, breadth, or thickness: *I need wallpaper for a room of the following dimensions: 16 ft. long, 12 ft. wide, 9 ft. high.* 2 Also, **dimensions,** pl. size; extent: *Building a park in the slum area was a project of large dimensions.* n.

di min ish (də min′ish), make or become smaller; lessen; reduce; decrease: *Poor crops so diminished the food supply that people were starving. A sound diminishes as you get farther and farther away from it.* v.

di min u en do (də min′yü en′dō), decrescendo. n., pl. **di min u en dos;** adj., adv. [from Italian *diminuendo* diminishing]

dim i nu tion (dim/ə nü/shən or dim/-ə nyü/shən), a diminishing; lessening; reduction; decrease: *The colonists fought to prevent any diminution of their rights by the king.* *n.*

di min u tive (də min/yə tiv), 1 very small; tiny; minute: *The dollhouse contained diminutive furniture.* 2 a small person or thing. 1 *adj.,* 2 *n.* —**di min/u tive ly,** *adv.* —**di min/u tive ness,** *n.*

dim i ty (dim/ə tē), a thin cotton cloth woven with heavy threads in striped or checked arrangement, used for dresses, curtains, etc. *n., pl.* **dim i ties.**

dim mer (dim/ər), 1 person or thing that dims. 2 device that dims an electric light. *n.*

dim ple (dim/pəl), 1 a small hollow place in the skin. A dimple is usually in a person's cheek or chin. 2 any small, hollow place. 3 make or show dimples in: *The shower dimpled the surface of the pond.* 4 form dimples: *She dimples whenever she smiles.* 1,2 *n.,* 3,4 *v.,* **dim pled, dim pling.**

din (din), 1 a loud, confused noise that lasts: *The din of the cheering crowd watching the game was deafening.* 2 make a din. 3 say over and over again; repeat in a tiresome way: *He was always dinning into our ears the importance of hard work.* 1 *n.,* 2,3 *v.,* **dinned, din ning.**

di nar (di när/), unit of money in Yugoslavia, Iraq, Jordan, Kuwait, and Tunisia. *n.*

dine (dīn), 1 eat dinner: *We usually dine at six o'clock.* 2 give dinner to; give a dinner for: *The Chamber of Commerce dined the famous traveler.* *v.,* **dined, din ing.**

din er (dī/nər), 1 person who is eating dinner. 2 a railroad car in which meals are served. 3 restaurant shaped like such a car. *n.*

di nette (dī net/), a small dining room. *n.*

ding (ding), 1 make the sound of a bell; ring continuously. 2 this sound. 1 *v.,* 2 *n.*

ding-dong (ding/dông/), sound made by the continuous ringing of a bell. *n.*

din ghy (ding/ē), 1 a small rowboat. 2 a small boat used as a tender by a large boat. *n., pl.* **din ghies.**

din gi ness (din/jē nis), a being dingy; lack of cleanness and freshness. *n.*

din gle (ding/gəl), a small, deep, shady valley. *n.*

din go (ding/gō), a wolflike wild dog of Australia. *n., pl.* **din goes.**

din gy (din/jē), lacking brightness or freshness; dirty-looking; dull: *Dingy curtains covered the windows of the dusty old room.* *adj.,* **din gi er, din gi est.**

dining room, room in which dinner and other meals are served.

dink y (ding/kē), INFORMAL. small and insignificant. *adj.,* **dink i er, dink i est.**

din ner (din/ər), 1 the main meal of the day: *In the city we have dinner at night, but in the country we have dinner at noon.* 2 a formal meal in honor of some person or occasion: *The city officials gave the mayor a dinner to celebrate his reelection.* *n.*

di no saur (dī/nə sôr), any of a group of extinct reptiles that dominated the earth many millions of years ago. Dinosaurs walked on two or four feet. Some dinosaurs were bigger than elephants; others were smaller than cats. *n.*

dinosaur
brontosaurus, 60 ft. long; 14 ft. tall

dint (dint), force: *By dint of hard work we finished the job on time.* *n.*

di oc e san (dī os/ə sən), 1 of or having to do with a diocese. 2 bishop of a diocese. 1 *adj.,* 2 *n.*

di o cese (dī/ə sis or dī/ə sēs/), church district over which a bishop has authority; bishopric; see. *n.*

Di og e nes (dī oj/ə nēz/), 412?-323 B.C., Greek philosopher who lived in a tub to show his indifference to comfort. *n.*

Di o ny sus (dī/ə nī/səs), (in Greek myths) the god of wine; Bacchus. *n.*

di o ram a (dī/ə ram/ə), scene or exhibit showing a group of lifelike sculptured figures of animals, men, etc., and surrounding objects against a painted or modeled background. *n., pl.* **di o ram as.**

di ox ide (dī ok/sīd), oxide having two atoms of oxygen for each molecule. *n.*

dip (dip), 1 put under water or any liquid and lift quickly out again: *She dipped her hand into the pool to see how cold the water was.* 2 go under water and come quickly out again: *She dipped a few times in the ocean to cool herself off.* 3 a dipping of any kind, especially a quick plunge into and out of a tub of water, the sea, etc.: *She felt refreshed after her dip in the ocean.* 4 liquid in which to dip something for washing or cleaning: *The sheep were driven through a dip to disinfect their coats.* 5 make (a candle) by putting a wick over and over

hat, āge, fär; let, ēqual, tėrm;
it, īce; hot, ōpen, ôrder;
oil, out; cup, pút, rüle; ch, child;
ng, long; sh, she; th, thin;
ᵀH, then; zh, measure;

ə represents *a* in about,
e in taken, *i* in pencil,
o in lemon, *u* in circus.

into hot tallow or wax. 6 take up in the hollow of the hand or with a pail, pan, or other container: *dip water from a bucket, dip up a sample of wheat.* 7 put (one's hand, a spoon, etc.) into to take out something: *He dipped into the jar and snatched a handful of cookies.* 8 a creamy mixture of foods eaten by dipping into with a cracker, piece of bread, etc.: *a cheese dip.* 9 lower and raise again quickly: *The ship's flag was dipped as a salute.* 10 sink or drop down: *The bird dipped low over the water in its flight.* 11 slope downward: *The road dips into the valley.* 12 a sudden drop: *a dip in prices. The dip in the road made the car bounce.* 1,2, 5-7,9-11 *v.,* **dipped, dip ping;** 3,4,8, 12 *n.*

dip into, read or look at for a short time; glance at: *dip into a book on astronomy.*

diph ther i a (dif thir/ē ə or dip thir/ē ə), a dangerous, infectious disease of the throat, usually accompanied by a high fever and formation of a membranous substance that hinders respiration. It is caused by a bacillus. *n.*

diph thong (dif/thông or dip/thông), a vowel sound made up of two vowel sounds pronounced in one syllable, such as *ou* in *house* or *oi* in *noise.* *n.*

di plo ma (də plō/mə), a written or printed paper given by a school, college, or university, which states that a person has completed a certain course of study or has been graduated after a certain amount of work. *n., pl.* **di plo mas.**

di plo ma cy (də plō/mə sē), 1 the management of relations between nations. The making of treaties and international agreements is an important part of diplomacy. 2 skill in managing such relations: *The statesman's great diplomacy prevented an outbreak of war between the two countries.* 3 skill in dealing with people; tact: *My older brother used diplomacy in being very helpful at home the day before he asked to use the car.* *n., pl.* **di plo ma cies.**

dip lo mat (dip/lə mat), 1 person whose work is the management of

adj. adjective	*n.* noun
adv. adverb	*prep.* preposition
conj. conjunction	*pron.* pronoun
interj. interjection	*v.* verb
sing. singular	*pl.* plural

relations between his nation and other nations. 2 person who is skillful in dealing with others; tactful person. *n.*

dip lo mat ic (dip/lə mat/ik), 1 of or having to do with diplomacy: *Ambassadors are the highest-ranking members of the diplomatic service.* 2 having or showing skill in dealing with others; tactful: *He gave a diplomatic answer to avoid hurting his friend's feelings. adj.*

dip lo mat i cal ly (dip/lə mat/ik lē), in a diplomatic manner; with diplomacy. *adv.*

dip per (dip/ər), 1 person or thing that dips. 2 a cup-shaped container with a long handle for dipping water or other liquids. 3 **Dipper,** either of two groups of stars in the northern sky somewhat resembling the shape of a dipper; Big Dipper or Little Dipper. See **constellation** for diagram. *n.*

dipt (dipt), OLD USE. dipped; a past tense and a past participle of **dip**. *He dipt some water from the well. v.*

dire (dīr), causing great fear or suffering; dreadful: *A fire, flood, or earthquake usually has dire results. People in dire poverty have not enough food or clothes. adj.,* **dir er, dir est.** —**dire/ly,** *adv.* —**dire/ness,** *n.*

di rect (də rekt/ *or* dī rekt/), 1 have authority or control over; manage or guide: *The teacher directs the work of the class.* 2 order; command: *The policeman directed the traffic to stop.* 3 tell or show the way: *Can you direct me to the airport? Signposts direct travelers.* 4 point or aim: *Direct the hose at the garden. We should be directing our efforts to the problem at hand.* 5 put the address on (a letter or package). 6 address (words, etc.) to a person: *Direct all your questions to her.* 7 without a stop or turn; straight: *Our house is in a direct line with the school. A bee makes a direct flight to the hive.* 8 in an unbroken line of descent: *That man is a direct descendant of John Adams.* 9 without anyone or anything in between; not through others; immediate: *Selling door to door is direct selling. The new teacher took direct charge of the library.* 10 straightforward; frank; plain; truthful: *I want some direct answers. She made a direct denial of the charge of cheating.*

11 exact; absolute; *the direct opposite.* 12 directly: *This plane flies direct from Chicago to Los Angeles without stopping even once.* 1-6 *v.,* 7-11 *adj.,* 12 *adv.* —**di rect/ness,** *n.*

direct current, a steady electric current that flows in one direction. The current produced by batteries is direct current.

di rec tion (də rek/shən *or* dī rek/shən), 1 a directing; managing or guiding: *the direction of a play or movie. The school is under the direction of the principal.* 2 order; command: *It was her direction that I prepare a report.* 3 Also, **directions,** *pl.* a knowing or telling what to do, how to do something, where to go, etc.; instructions: *Can you give me directions for driving to Chicago?* 4 address on a letter or package. 5 course taken by a moving body, such as a ball or a bullet. 6 any way in which one may face or point. North, south, east, and west are directions. *The school is in one direction from our house and the post office is in another.* 7 course along which something moves; way of moving; tendency: *The town shows improvement in many directions. n.*

di rec tion al (də rek/shə nəl *or* dī rek/shə nəl), 1 of, having to do with, or indicating direction: *the directional signals of an automobile.* 2 sending or receiving radio signals in or from a particular direction: *a directional antenna. adj.*

di rec tive (də rek/tiv *or* dī rek/tiv), order or instruction telling what to do, how to do something, where to go, etc.: *The captain gave a directive to his lieutenants. n.*

di rect ly (də rekt/lē *or* dī rekt/lē), 1 in a direct line or manner; straight: *This road runs directly into the center of town.* 2 exactly; absolutely: *directly opposite.* 3 at once; immediately: *Come home directly! adv.*

direct object, (in grammar) word or words showing the person or thing undergoing the action expressed by the verb. In "The boat struck a rock," *rock* is the direct object of the verb *struck.*

di rec tor (də rek/tər *or* dī rek/tər), 1 person who directs; manager. A person who directs the performance of a play, a motion picture, or a television or radio show is called a director. 2 one of a group of persons who direct the affairs of a company or institution. The owners of a company elect the directors. *n.*

di rec tor y (də rek/tər ē *or* dī rek/tər ē), list of names and addresses, usually in alphabetical order. A telephone book is a directory of people who have telephones. *n., pl.* **di rec tor ies.**

dire ful (dīr/fəl), dire; dreadful; terrible. *adj.* —**dire/ful ly,** *adv.*

dirge (dèrj), a funeral song or tune. *n.*

dir i gi ble (dir/ə jə bəl), airship. *n.*

dirk (dèrk), dagger. *n.*

dirt (dèrt), 1 mud, dust, earth, or anything like them. Dirt soils skin, clothing, houses, or furniture. 2 loose earth or soil. 3 an unclean action, thought, or speech. 4 INFORMAL. scandal; gossip. *n.*

dirt i ness (dèr/tē nis), dirty condition. *n.*

dirt y (dèr/tē), 1 soiled by dirt; not clean: *Children playing in the mud get dirty.* 2 not clean or pure in action, thought, or speech; low; base. 3 stormy or windy; rough: *The hurricane was the dirtiest weather I ever saw.* 4 not clear or pure in color: *a dirty red.* 5 make or become dirty; soil: *You will dirty your new clothes if you play outside on the muddy ground. A white shirt will dirty faster than a dark one.* 1-4 *adj.,* **dirt i er, dirt i est;** 5 *v.,* **dirt ied, dirt y ing.**

dis-, *prefix.* 1 opposite of; lack of; not: *Dishonest = not honest; opposite of honest. Discomfort = lack of comfort.* 2 do the opposite of: *Disentangle = do the opposite of entangle. Disallow = do the opposite of allow.* [from Latin *dis-* apart]

dis a bil i ty (dis/ə bil/ə tē), 1 lack of ability or power: *The player's disability was caused by lameness.* 2 something that disables: *Deafness is a disability for a musician. n., pl.* **dis a bil i ties.**

dis a ble (dis ā/bəl), make unable; make unfit for use, action, etc.; cripple: *A sprained wrist disabled the tennis player for three weeks. He was disabled by polio. v.,* **dis a bled, dis a bling.**

dis a buse (dis/ə byüz/), free from deception or error: *Education should disabuse people of foolish prejudices. v.,* **dis a bused, dis a bus ing.**

dis ad van tage (dis/əd van/tij), 1 lack of advantage; unfavorable condition: *Her shyness was a disadvantage in company.* 2 loss or injury: *The candidate's enemies spread rumors that were to his disadvantage. n.*

dis ad van taged (dis/əd van/tijd), lacking advantages; being in an unfavorable condition: *Many disadvantaged children live in the slums. adj.*

dis ad van ta geous (dis ad/vən tā/jəs), causing disadvantage; unfavorable. *adj.* —**dis ad/van ta/geous ly,** *adv.* —**dis ad/van ta/geous ness,** *n.*

dis af fect ed (dis/ə fek/tid), unfriendly, disloyal, or discontented: *The disaffected crew decided to mutiny. adj.*

dis af fec tion (dis/ə fek/shən), unfriendliness, disloyalty, or discontent:

Lack of food and supplies caused disaffection among the soldiers. n.

dis a gree (dis/ə grē/), 1 fail to agree; be different: *Your account of the accident disagrees with hers.* 2 have unlike opinions; differ: *Doctors sometimes disagree about the proper method of treating a patient.* 3 quarrel; dispute: *The two neighbors never spoke to each other again after they disagreed about their boundary line.* 4 have a bad effect; be harmful: *I can't eat strawberries because they disagree with me. v.,* **dis a greed, dis a gree ing.**

dis a gree a ble (dis/ə grē/ə bəl), 1 not to one's liking; unpleasant: *A headache is disagreeable.* 2 not friendly; bad-tempered; cross: *She is quite disagreeable until she has had her breakfast. adj.* —**dis/a gree/a ble ness,** *n.*

dis a gree a bly (dis/ə grē/ə blē), in a disagreeable manner; unpleasantly. *adv.*

dis a gree ment (dis/ə grē/mənt), 1 failure to agree; difference of opinion: *The disagreement that existed between members of the jury led to a new trial.* 2 quarrel; dispute: *Their disagreement led to blows.* 3 difference; unlikeness: *There is a disagreement between his account of the accident and mine. n.*

dis al low (dis/ə lou/), refuse to allow; deny the truth or value of; reject: *The court disallowed my claim to the property. v.*

dis ap pear (dis/ə pir/), 1 pass from sight; stop being seen: *The dog disappeared around the corner.* 2 pass from existence; stop being: *When spring comes, the snow disappears. v.*

dis ap pear ance (dis/ə pir/əns), act of disappearing: *The disappearance of the airplane brought about a search of the entire area. n.*

dis ap point (dis/ə point/), 1 fail to satisfy or please; leave wanting or expecting something: *The circus disappointed him, for there were no elephants.* 2 fail to keep a promise to: *You said you would help; do not disappoint me. v.*

dis ap point ment (dis/ə point/mənt), 1 a being disappointed; the feeling one has when he does not get what he expected or hoped for: *When she did not get a new bicycle her disappointment was very great.* 2 person or thing that causes disappointment: *The movie was a disappointment to me because the acting was very bad.* 3 act or fact of disappointing: *Finding that we had not saved enough money led to the disappointment of our hopes for a trip to Europe. n.*

dis ap pro ba tion (dis ap/rə bā/shən), disapproval. *n.*

dis ap prov al (dis/ə prü/vəl), opinion or feeling against; expression of an opinion against; dislike: *Hisses from the audience showed its disapproval of the speaker's remarks. n.*

dis ap prove (dis/ə prüv/), 1 have or express an opinion against; show dislike: *Parents often disapprove of rough games in the house.* 2 refuse consent to; reject: *The mayor disapproved the plan. v.,* **dis ap proved, dis ap prov ing.**

dis ap prov ing ly (dis/ə prü/-ving lē), in a disapproving manner; with disapproval: *The librarian looked disapprovingly at the children who were talking. adv.*

dis arm (dis ärm/), 1 take weapons away from: *The sheriff captured the bandits and disarmed them.* 2 stop having an army, navy, etc.; reduce a country's armed forces or their weapons: *The nations agreed to disarm.* 3 remove anger or suspicion from; make friendly: *The little boy's smile could always disarm those who were about to scold or punish him.* 4 make harmless: *The soldiers disarmed the bomb by removing the fuse. v.*

dis ar ma ment (dis är/mə mənt), 1 act of disarming. 2 reduction of a country's armed forces or their weapons. *n.*

dis ar range (dis/ə rānj/), disturb the arrangement of; put out of order: *The wind disarranged her hair. v.,* **dis ar ranged, dis ar rang ing.**

dis ar range ment (dis/ə rānj/mənt), a disarranging or a being disarranged. *n.*

dis ar ray (dis/ə rā/), 1 lack of order; disorder; confusion: *There was disarray on the busy street after the accident.* 2 put into disorder or confusion. 1 *n.,* 2 *v.*

dis as sem ble (dis/ə sem/bəl), take apart: *The mechanic disassembled the motor to repair it. v.,* **dis as sem bled, dis as sem bling.**

dis as ter (də zas/tər), event that causes much suffering or loss; great misfortune. A destructive fire, a flood, a shipwreck, or an earthquake is a disaster. *n.*

dis as trous (də zas/trəs), bringing disaster; causing much suffering or loss: *A disastrous hurricane struck the city, leaving thousands of people without food or homes. adj.* —**dis as/trous ly,** *adv.*

dis a vow (dis/ə vou/), deny that one knows about, approves of, or is responsible for; disclaim: *The driver disavowed any responsibility for the accident. v.*

dis a vow al (dis/ə vou/əl), a disavowing; denial. *n.*

dis band (dis band/), 1 break up; dis-

hat, āge, fär; let, ēqual, tėrm;
it, īce; hot, ōpen, ôrder;
oil, out; cup, pùt, rüle; ch, child;
ng, long; sh, she; th, thin;
ᵺH, then; zh, measure;

ə represents *a* in about,
e in taken, *i* in pencil,
o in lemon, *u* in circus.

miss from service: *When peace was restored, the king disbanded his army.* 2 break ranks; become scattered: *The class disbanded for the summer vacation. v.*

dis bar (dis bär/), take away from (a lawyer) the right to practice law. *v.,* **dis barred, dis bar ring.**

dis bar ment (dis bär/mənt), a disbarring or a being disbarred. *n.*

dis be lief (dis/bi lēf/), lack of belief; refusal to believe: *When she heard the shocking rumor she immediately expressed disbelief. n.*

dis be lieve (dis/bi lēv/), have no belief in; refuse to believe: *His father disbelieved the boy's story that a lion had come into his room in the middle of the night. v.,* **dis be lieved, dis be liev ing.**

dis be liev er (dis/bi lē/vər), person who disbelieves. *n.*

dis bur den (dis bėrd/n), relieve of a burden; unburden: *She disburdened her mind by confessing what she did. v.*

dis burse (dis bėrs/), pay out: *The treasurer is in charge of disbursing money to pay the club's bills. v.,* **dis bursed, dis burs ing.**

dis burse ment (dis bėrs/mənt), 1 a paying out: *Our club treasurer attends to the disbursement of funds.* 2 money paid out: *Disbursements must stay within the budget. n.*

disc (disk), disk. *n.*

dis card (dis kärd/ for 1,4; dis/kärd for 2,3,5), 1 give up as useless or not wanted; throw aside: *I repaired the toy that my sister had discarded. Most people have discarded the belief in witches.* 2 act of throwing aside as useless or not wanted: *The discard of superstition comes with learning.* 3 thing or things thrown aside as useless or not wanted: *That old book is a discard from the library.* 4 get rid of (playing cards not wanted) by throwing them aside or playing them. 5 the cards thrown aside or played as not wanted. 1,4 *v.,* 2,3,5 *n.*

dis cern (də zėrn/ *or* də sėrn/), see clearly; perceive the difference between (two or more things); distinguish or

adj. adjective		*n.* noun
adv. adverb		*prep.* preposition
conj. conjunction		*pron.* pronoun
interj. interjection		*v.* verb
sing. singular		*pl.* plural

recognize: *Through the fog I could discern a person walking toward me. When there are many conflicting opinions, it is hard to discern the truth. v.*

dis cern i ble (də zėr′nə bəl *or* də-sėr′nə bəl), capable of being discerned: *The island was just discernible through the mist. adj.*

dis cern ing (də zėr′ning *or* də-sėr′ning), keen in seeing and understanding; with good judgment; shrewd. *adj.* —**dis cern′ing ly**, *adv.*

dis cern ment (də zėrn′mənt *or* də-sėrn′mənt), 1 keenness in seeing and understanding; good judgment; shrewdness. 2 act of discerning. *n.*

dis charge (dis chärj′ *for 1,3,5,8,11-13,15;* dis chärj′ *or* dis′chärj *for 2,4,6,7,9,10,14,16*), 1 unload cargo or passengers from a ship, train, bus, etc.: *The ship discharged its passengers at the dock.* 2 an unloading: *The discharge of this cargo will not take long.* 3 fire off; shoot: *The policeman discharged his gun at the fleeing robbers. The pistol discharged accidentally.* 4 a firing off of a gun, a blast, etc.: *The discharge of dynamite could be heard for a mile.* 5 release; let go; dismiss: *discharge a patient from a hospital, discharge a lazy employee.* 6 a release; a letting go; a dismissing: *I expect my discharge from the hospital in a few days.* 7 writing that shows a person's release or dismissal; certificate of release: *Many members of the armed services got discharges when the war ended.* 8 give off; let out: *The infection discharged pus.* 9 a giving off; a letting out: *Lightning is a discharge of electricity from the clouds.* 10 thing given off or let out: *a watery discharge from an eye.* 11 come or pour forth: *The river discharged into a bay.* 12 rid of an electric charge; withdraw electricity from. 13 perform: *I have discharged all the errands I was given.* 14 performance: *A public official should be honest in the discharge of his duties.* 15 pay: *You discharge a loan when you return the money.* 16 payment: *Money was set aside for the discharge of the debt.* 1,3,5,8,11-13,15 *v.,* **dis charged, dis charg ing;** 2,4,6, 7,9,10,14,16 *n.*

dis ci ple (də sī′pəl), 1 believer in the thought and teaching of any leader;

follower. 2 (in the Bible) one of the followers of Jesus. *n.*

dis ci pli nar i an (dis′ə plə ner′-ē ən), person who enforces discipline or who believes in strict discipline. *n.*

dis ci pli nar y (dis′ə plə ner′ē), 1 having to do with discipline: *Our teacher has no disciplinary problems, since the children in the class are well behaved.* 2 for discipline; intended to improve discipline: *I will have to take disciplinary measures if you continue to come to work late. adj.*

dis ci pline (dis′ə plin), 1 training, especially training of the mind or character: *Years of discipline have made her an excellent scientist.* 2 a trained condition of order and obedience; order kept among school pupils, soldiers, or members of any group: *When the fire broke out, the students showed good discipline.* 3 bring to a condition of order and obedience; bring under control; train: *An officer should know how to discipline men.* 4 a particular system of rules for conduct: *The discipline of a military school is usually strict.* 5 punishment: *A little discipline would do her a world of good.* 6 punish: *They have never disciplined their children unfairly.* 1,2,4,5 *n.,* 3,6 *v.,* **dis ci plined, dis ci plin ing.**

dis claim (dis klām′), 1 refuse to recognize as one's own; deny connection with: *The motorist disclaimed responsibility for the accident.* 2 give up all claim to: *She disclaimed any share in the inheritance. v.*

dis claim er (dis klā′mər), a disclaiming; denial. *n.*

dis close (dis klōz′), 1 open to view: *The lifting of the curtain disclosed a beautiful painting.* 2 make known: *This letter discloses a secret. v.,* **dis closed, dis clos ing.**

dis clo sure (dis klō′zhər), 1 a disclosing: *disclosure of a secret.* 2 thing disclosed: *The newspaper's disclosures shocked the public. n.*

dis col or (dis kul′ər), 1 change or spoil the color of; stain: *Smoke and grime had discolored the building.* 2 become changed in color: *Many materials fade and discolor if exposed to bright sunshine. v.*

dis col or a tion (dis kul′ə rā′shən), 1 a discoloring or a being discolored. 2 a stain. *n.*

dis com fit (dis kum′fit), 1 defeat completely; rout: *The enemy was discomfited by our sudden attack from ambush.* 2 defeat the plans or hopes of; frustrate: *Our dreams are often discomfited by reality.* 3 embarrass greatly; confuse: *I had come to class unprepared, so I was discomfited by the teacher's question. v.*

dis com fi ture (dis kum′fi chùr), 1 a complete defeat; rout. 2 defeat of plans or hopes; frustration. 3 great embarrassment; confusion: *The crowd laughed at the discomfiture of the fireman who had to ask where the fire was. n.*

dis com fort (dis kum′fərt), 1 lack of comfort; uneasiness: *Embarrassing questions cause discomfort.* 2 thing that causes discomfort: *Mud and cold were the discomforts the campers minded most. n.*

dis com pose (dis′kəm pōz′), disturb the self-possession of; make uneasy; confuse: *The grins of his friends discomposed him when he tried to make his report before the class. v.,* **dis com posed, dis com pos ing.**

dis com po sure (dis′kəm pō′zhər), condition of being discomposed; confusion; uneasiness. *n.*

dis con cert (dis′kən sėrt′), 1 disturb the self-possession of; embarrass greatly; confuse: *He was disconcerted to find that he had come to school wearing one brown sock and one black sock.* 2 upset; disorder: *The chairman's plans were disconcerted when the speaker of the evening did not show up. v.*

dis con nect (dis′kə nekt′), undo or break the connection of; separate; unfasten: *I pulled out the plug to disconnect the toaster. v.*

dis con nect ed (dis′kə nek′tid), 1 not connected; separate: *Our house and the garage are entirely disconnected.* 2 without order or connection; incoherent; broken: *I cannot tell from her disconnected account of the accident what really happened. adj.* —**dis′con nect′ed ly**, *adv.*

dis con so late (dis kon′sə lit), without hope; forlorn; unhappy; cheerless: *She was disconsolate because her kitten died. adj.* —**dis con′so late ly**, *adv.*

dis con tent (dis′kən tent′), 1 a dislike of what one has and a desire for something different; uneasy feeling; dissatisfaction: *Low pay and long hours of work caused discontent among the factory workers.* 2 dissatisfy; displease. 1 *n.,* 2 *v.*

dis con tent ed (dis′kən ten′tid), not contented; not satisfied; displeased and restless: *The discontented workers went on strike. adj.* —**dis′con tent′ed ly**, *adv.*

dis con tin ue (dis′kən tin′yü), 1 put an end or stop to; give up; stop: *After the patient got well, the doctor discontinued his visits.* 2 come to an end or stop: *When the strike began, railroad service discontinued abruptly. v.,* **dis con tin ued, dis con tin u ing.**

dis con tin u ous (dis′kən tin′yü əs),

not continuous; broken; interrupted. *adj.*

dis cord (dis′kôrd), 1 difference of opinion; disagreement; disputing: *Constant argument caused angry discord that spoiled the meeting.* 2 (in music) a lack of harmony in notes sounded at the same time. 3 harsh, clashing sounds. *n.*

dis cord ance (dis kôrd′ns), discord. *n.*

dis cord ant (dis kôrd′nt), 1 not in agreement; differing; disagreeing: *A quarrel started after several discordant opinions had been expressed.* 2 not in harmony: *a discordant note in music.* 3 harsh; clashing: *the discordant sound of automobile horns honking in a traffic jam. adj.* —**dis cord′ant ly**, *adv.*

dis count (dis′kount), 1 take off a certain amount from (a price): *The store discounts 2 per cent on all bills paid when due. Many stores do not discount at all.* 2 the amount taken off from a price: *During the sale the dealer allowed a 10 per cent discount on all cash purchases.* 3 allow for exaggeration in; believe only part of: *You must discount some of what he tells you, for he likes to make up stories.* 4 selling goods at prices below those suggested by manufacturers: *a discount store, a discount house.* 1,3 *v.,* 2 *n.,* 4 *adj.*

dis coun te nance (dis koun′tə nəns), 1 refuse to approve; discourage: *This high school discountenances secret societies.* 2 make ashamed; embarrass greatly; abash; disconcert: *She was discountenanced by her teacher's angry look. v.,* **dis coun te nanced, dis coun te nanc ing.**

dis cour age (dis kėr′ij), 1 take away the courage of; lessen the hope or confidence of; dishearten: *Failing again and again discourages anyone.* 2 try to prevent by disapproving; frown upon: *All their friends discouraged them from sailing their small boat on the ocean.* 3 prevent or hinder: *Fear that it might rain discouraged us from camping out. v.,* **dis cour aged, dis cour ag ing.**

dis cour age ment (dis kėr′ij mənt), 1 condition of being or feeling discouraged. 2 something that discourages. 3 act of discouraging. *n.*

dis course (dis′kôrs for 1,2; dis kôrs′ for 3), 1 a formal speech or writing: *Lectures and sermons are discourses.* 2 talk; conversation. 3 to talk; converse. 1,2 *n.,* 3 *v.,* **dis coursed, dis cours ing.**

dis cour te ous (dis kėr′tē əs), not courteous; rude; impolite. *adj.* —**dis cour′te ous ly**, *adv.*

dis cour te sy (dis kėr′tə sē), 1 lack of courtesy; rudeness; impoliteness. 2 a rude or impolite act: *It is a discour-*

tesy to interrupt another person's remarks. n., pl. **dis cour te sies.**

dis cov er (dis kuv′ər), see or learn of for the first time; find out: *discover a new drug, discover a secret. v.* —**dis cov′er er**, *n.*

dis cov er y (dis kuv′ər ē), 1 act of discovering: *Marie Curie's discovery of the element radium occurred in 1898.* 2 something discovered: *One of Benjamin Franklin's discoveries was that lightning is electricity. n., pl.* **dis cover ies.**

dis cred it (dis kred′it), 1 cast doubt on; destroy belief, faith, or trust in: *The lawyer discredited the witness by proving that he had been bribed.* 2 loss of belief, faith, or trust; doubt: *Columbus's voyage threw discredit on the theory that the earth is flat.* 3 refuse to believe: *We discredit her because she has lied so often.* 4 do harm to the good name or standing of; give a bad reputation to: *His cheating during tests discredited him among his classmates.* 5 loss of good name or standing: *The player who took a bribe brought discredit upon the team.* 6 person or thing that causes loss of good name or standing: *A dishonest politician is a discredit to his party.* 1,3,4 *v.,* 2,5, 6 *n.*

dis cred it a ble (dis kred′ə tə bəl), bringing discredit; disgraceful. *adj.*

dis cred it a bly (dis kred′ə tə blē), in a discreditable manner. *adv.*

dis creet (dis krēt′), very careful in speech and action; having or showing good judgment; wisely cautious: *a discreet person, a discreet answer. adj.* —**dis creet′ly**, *adv.*

discus—man throwing a discus.

dis crep an cy (dis krep′ən sē), lack of consistency; difference: *There was a discrepancy in the two reports of the accident. n., pl.* **dis crep an cies.**

dis crete (dis krēt′), distinct from others; separate; individual: *An apple and a stone are discrete objects. adj.*

dis cre tion (dis kresh′ən), 1 great carefulness in speech or action; good judgment; wise caution: *It requires discretion to criticize someone without hurting his feelings.* 2 freedom to decide or choose: *It is within the principal's discretion to punish a pupil. n.*

dis cre tion ar y (dis kresh′ə ner′ē),

hat, āge, fär; let, ēqual, tėrm; it, īce; hot, ōpen, ôrder; oil, out; cup, pút, rüle; ch, child; ng, long; sh, she; th, thin; ᴛʜ, then; zh, measure;

ə represents *a* in about, *e* in taken, *i* in pencil, *o* in lemon, *u* in circus.

with freedom to decide or choose; left to one's own judgment: *The law gave the mayor certain discretionary powers. adj.*

dis crim i nate (dis krim′ə nāt), 1 make or see a difference; distinguish: *People who are color-blind usually cannot discriminate between red and green. Can you discriminate a good book from a poor one?* 2 show a difference in treatment: *It is wrong to discriminate against people because of their race, religion, or nationality. v.,* **dis crim i nat ed, dis crim i nat ing.**

dis crim i na tion (dis krim′ə nā′shən), 1 a making or recognizing differences and distinctions: *Do not buy clothes without discrimination.* 2 ability to discriminate accurately between things that are very much alike; good judgment: *He lacked discrimination in his choice of friends.* 3 a making or showing a difference in treatment: *Racial or religious discrimination in hiring employees is against the law. n.*

dis cur sive (dis kėr′siv), wandering from one subject to another; rambling: *Her carefully planned speech was not discursive, but stayed right on the subject. adj.* —**dis cur′sive ly**, *adv.*

dis cus (dis′kəs), a heavy, circular plate of wood with a metal rim. It is used in an athletic contest to see who can throw it farthest. *n., pl.* **dis cus es.**

dis cuss (dis kus′), consider from different points of view; talk over: *The class discussed several problems. Congress is discussing tax rates. v.*

dis cus sion (dis kush′ən), a considering from different points of view; discussing things; talk: *After hours of discussion, we came to a decision. n.*

dis dain (dis dān′), 1 look down on; consider beneath oneself; scorn: *The policeman disdained the offer of a bribe. Now that they are rich, they disdain to speak to their old friends.* 2 a looking down on a person or an act as beneath one; scorn: *The older girls treated the younger ones with disdain.* 1 *v.,* 2 *n.*

dis dain ful (dis dān′fəl), feeling or showing disdain; proud and scornful. *adj.* —**dis dain′ful ly**, *adv.*

adj.	adjective	*n.*	noun
adv.	adverb	*prep.*	preposition
conj.	conjunction	*pron.*	pronoun
interj.	interjection	*v.*	verb
sing.	singular	*pl.*	plural

dis ease (də zēz′), 1 condition of poor health; condition in which an organ, system, or part does not function properly; sickness; illness: *People, animals, and plants are all liable to suffer from disease. Cleanliness helps prevent disease.* 2 any particular illness: *Measles and chicken pox are two diseases of children. n.*

dis eased (də zēzd′), having a disease; showing signs of sickness: *a diseased lung, a diseased pet. adj.*

dis em bark (dis′em bärk′), go or put ashore from a ship; land from a ship. *v.*

dis em bod ied (dis′em bod′ēd), separated from the body: *Ghosts are usually thought of as disembodied spirits. adj.*

dis em bow el (dis′em bou′əl), take or rip out the bowels of. *v.*

dis en chant (dis′en chant′), free from enchantment or illusion; disillusion: *I thought that movie would be charming, but I was disenchanted when I saw it. v.*

dis en chant ment (dis′en chant′-mənt), a disenchanting or a being disenchanted. *n.*

dis en cum ber (dis′ən kum′bər), free from a burden, annoyance, or trouble. *v.*

dis en gage (dis′en gāj′), 1 free or release from anything that holds; detach; loosen: *He disengaged his hand from that of the sleeping child. I shifted gears and disengaged the clutch.* 2 free from an engagement, pledge, or obligation. *v.*, **dis en gaged, dis en gag ing.**

dis en tan gle (dis′en tang′gəl), free from tangles or complications; untangle: *The police tried to disentangle the confused victim's story. Nylon rope disentangles more easily than hemp. v.*, **dis en tan gled, dis en tan gling.**

dis en tan gle ment (dis′en tang′-gəl mənt), a disentangling or a being disentangled. *n.*

dis es teem (dis′e stēm′), 1 to scorn or dislike. 2 low esteem; scorn; disfavor. 1 *v.*, 2 *n.*

dis fa vor (dis fā′vər), 1 unfavorable regard; dislike or disapproval: *The workers looked with disfavor on any attempt to lower their wages.* 2 dislike or disapprove. 3 condition of having lost favor or trust: *The government was in disfavor with the people.* 1,3 *n.*, 2 *v.*

dis fig ure (dis fig′yər), spoil the appearance of; hurt the beauty of: *Large billboards disfigure the countryside. A scar disfigured her face. v.*, **dis fig ured, dis fig ur ing.**

dis fig ure ment (dis fig′yər mənt), 1 a disfiguring or a being disfigured. 2 something that disfigures; defect. *n.*

dis fran chise (dis fran′chīz), 1 take the right to vote, hold office, etc., away from. 2 take any right or privilege away from. *v.*, **dis fran chised, dis fran chis ing.**

dis fran chise ment (dis fran′chiz-mənt), a disfranchising or a being disfranchised. *n.*

dis gorge (dis gôrj′), 1 throw up what has been swallowed. 2 pour forth; discharge: *Swollen streams disgorged their waters into the river.* 3 give up unwillingly: *force someone to disgorge secrets. v.*, **dis gorged, dis gorg ing.**

dis grace (dis grās′), 1 loss of honor or respect; shame: *the disgrace of being sent to jail.* 2 loss of favor or trust: *The king's former adviser is now in disgrace.* 3 cause disgrace to; bring shame upon: *The embezzler disgraced his family.* 4 person or thing that causes disgrace: *The slums in our city are a disgrace.* 1, 2,4 *n.*, 3 *v.*, **dis graced, dis grac ing.**

dis grace ful (dis grās′fəl), causing loss of honor or respect; shameful. *adj.* —**dis grace′ful ly**, *adv.*

dis grun tled (dis grunt′ld), in bad humor; discontented. *adj.*

dis guise (dis gīz′), 1 make changes in clothes or appearance to hide who one really is or to look like someone else: *On Halloween I disguised myself as a ghost.* 2 the use of such changes: *Detectives sometimes depend on disguise.* 3 clothes, actions, etc., used in making such changes: *Women's clothes and a wig formed the spy's disguise.* 4 hide what (a thing) really is; make (a thing) seem like something else: *The pirates disguised their ship as a trading vessel. He disguised his handwriting by writing with his left hand.* 5 a false or misleading appearance; deception: *My outward show of indifference was only a disguise for my disappointment.* 1,4 *v.*, **dis guised, dis guis ing;** 2,3,5 *n.*

dis gust (dis gust′), 1 strong dislike; sickening dislike: *We feel disgust for bad odors or tastes.* 2 cause to feel disgust: *The smell of rotten eggs disgusts many people.* 1 *n.*, 2 *v.*

dis gust ed (dis gus′tid), filled with disgust. *adj.* —**dis gust′ed ly**, *adv.*

dis gust ing (dis gus′ting), that disgusts; unpleasant; distasteful. *adj.* —**dis gust′ing ly**, *adv.*

dish (dish), 1 anything to serve food in.

Plates, platters, bowls, cups, and saucers are all dishes. 2 amount of food served in a dish: *I ate two dishes of ice cream.* 3 food served: *Chicken is the dish I like best.* 4 put (food) into a dish for serving at the table: *You may dish up the dinner now.* 1-3 *n.*, 4 *v.*

dis heart en (dis härt′n), cause to lose hope; discourage; depress: *The long drought disheartened the farmer. v.* —**dis heart′en ing ly**, *adv.*

di shev eled (də shev′əld), 1 not neat; rumpled; mussed; untidy: *His disheveled appearance showed that he had slept with his clothes on.* 2 hanging loosely or in disorder: *disheveled hair. adj.*

dis hon est (dis on′ist), 1 not fair play; showing lack of honesty: *Lying, cheating, and stealing are dishonest.* 2 ready to cheat; not upright: *A person who lies or steals is dishonest.* 3 arranged to work in an unfair way: *dishonest scales weighted to cheat the customer. adj.* —**dis hon′est ly**, *adv.*

dis hon es ty (dis on′ə stē), 1 lack of honesty. 2 a dishonest act. *n., pl.* **dis hon es ties.**

dis hon or (dis on′ər), 1 loss of honor or reputation; shame; disgrace: *The robber brought dishonor to his family.* 2 person or thing that causes dishonor: *The team's poor sportsmanship was a dishonor to the school.* 3 bring reproach or shame to; cause dishonor to: *The player who cheated dishonored the entire team.* 1,2 *n.*, 3 *v.*

dis hon or a ble (dis on′ər ə bəl), without honor; disgraceful; shameful. *adj.*

dis hon or a bly (dis on′ər ə blē), in a dishonorable manner. *adv.*

dish tow el (dish′tou′əl), towel to dry dishes with. *n.*

dish wash er (dish′wosh′ər or dish′-wôsh′ər), 1 machine for washing dishes, pots, glasses, etc. 2 person who washes dishes, especially in a restaurant, etc. *n.*

dish wa ter (dish′wô′tər or dish′-wot′ər), water in which dishes have been or are to be washed. *n.*

dis il lu sion (dis′i lü′zhən), 1 to free from illusion: *Children become disillusioned about Santa Claus as they grow older.* 2 freedom from illusion. 1 *v.*, 2 *n.*

dis il lu sion ment (dis′i lü′zhən-mənt), a disillusioning or a being disillusioned. *n.*

dis in cli na tion (dis in′klə nā′shən), unwillingness. *n.*

dis in clined (dis′in klīnd′), unwilling: *I was watching TV and was disinclined to clean up my room. adj.*

dis in fect (dis′in fekt′), destroy the disease germs in or on: *The dentist* *boiled his instruments to disinfect them before examining the next patient.* v.

dis in fect ant (dis′in fek′tənt), 1 substance used to destroy disease germs. Alcohol, iodine, and carbolic acid are disinfectants. 2 used to destroy disease germs: *a disinfectant soap.* 1 n., 2 adj.

dis in her it (dis′in her′it), prevent from inheriting; take away an inheritance from: *She disinherited her son by leaving him out of her will.* v.

dis in te grate (dis in′tə grāt), 1 break up; separate into small parts or bits: *The old papers had disintegrated into a pile of fragments and dust.* 2 change the structure of an atomic nucleus, especially by bombarding it with charged particles. v., **dis in te grat ed, dis in te grat ing.**

dis in te gra tion (dis in′tə grā′shən), 1 a breaking up; separation into small parts or bits: *Rain and frost had caused the gradual disintegration of the rock.* 2 a change in the structure of an atomic nucleus, especially through bombardment by charged particles. n.

dis in ter (dis′in tėr′), take out of a grave or tomb; dig up. v., **dis interred, dis in ter ring.**

dis in ter est (dis in′tər ist), lack of interest; indifference. n.

dis in ter est ed (dis in′tər ə stid), free from selfish motives; impartial; fair: *An umpire makes disinterested decisions.* adj. —**dis in′ter est ed ly,** adv. —**dis in′ter est ed ness,** n.

dis joint (dis joint′), 1 take apart at the joints: *The butcher disjointed the chicken for me.* 2 break up; put out of order: *War disjoints a nation's affairs.* 3 put out of joint; dislocate: *I disjointed my wrist when I fell.* 4 (in mathematics) having no common elements. (0,1,2) and (3,4,5) are disjoint sets. 1,2,3 v., 4 adj.

dis joint ed (dis join′tid), broken up; disconnected; incoherent: *I was so nervous that my speech became rapid and disjointed.* adj. —**dis joint′ed ly,** adv.

disk (disk), 1 a round, flat, thin object shaped like a coin. 2 a round, flat surface that the sun, moon, and other planets seem to have. 3 a round, flat part of a plant or animal: *The yellow center of a daisy is a disk.* 4 a phonograph record. n. Also, **disc.** —**disk′like′,** adj.

disk harrow, harrow with a row of

disk (def. 1)   disk harrow

sharp, revolving disks, used in preparing ground for planting or sowing.

disk jockey, INFORMAL. announcer for a radio program that consists chiefly of recorded popular music.

dis like (dis līk′), 1 not like; object to; have a feeling against: *He dislikes studying and would rather play football.* 2 a feeling of not liking; a feeling against: *Cats have a dislike of snow.* 1 v., **dis liked, dis lik ing;** 2 n.

dis lo cate (dis′lō kāt), 1 put out of joint: *She dislocated her shoulder when she fell down the stairs.* 2 put out of order; disturb; upset: *Our plans for a picnic were dislocated by the rain.* v., **dis lo cat ed, dis lo cat ing.**

dis lo ca tion (dis′lō kā′shən), a dislocating or a being dislocated. n.

dis lodge (dis loj′), drive or force out of a place, position, etc.: *The workman used a crowbar to dislodge a heavy stone from the wall. Heavy gunfire dislodged the enemy from the fort.* v., **dis lodged, dis lodg ing.**

dis loy al (dis loi′əl), not loyal; unfaithful: *a disloyal friend, a disloyal act.* adj. —**dis loy′al ly,** adv.

dis loy al ty (dis loi′əl tē), 1 lack of loyalty; unfaithfulness: *The traitor was imprisoned for disloyalty to his country.* 2 a disloyal act: *Revealing a friend's secret is a disloyalty.* n., pl. **dis loy al ties.**

dis mal (diz′məl), 1 dark and gloomy; dreary: *A damp cave or a rainy day is dismal.* 2 depressed; miserable: *Sickness or bad luck often makes a person feel dismal.* adj. —**dis′mal ly,** adv.

dis man tle (dis man′tl), 1 to strip of covering, equipment, furniture, guns, rigging, etc.: *The ship was dismantled before the hull was sold for scrap iron.* 2 pull down; take apart: *We had to dismantle the bookcases in order to fit them through the doorway.* v., **dis man tled, dis man tling.**

dis may (dis mā′), 1 loss of courage because of dislike or fear of what is about to happen or what has happened: *They were filled with dismay when their son confessed he had robbed a store.* 2 trouble greatly; make afraid: *The thought that she might fail the arithmetic test dismayed her.* 1 n., 2 v.

dis mem ber (dis mem′bər), 1 separate or divide into parts: *After the war the defeated country was dismembered and could no longer be called a united nation.* 2 cut or tear the limbs from; divide limb from limb: *The wolves dismembered the deer's carcass.* v.

dis mem ber ment (dis mem′bər mənt), a dismembering or a being dismembered. n.

dis miss (dis mis′), 1 send away; allow

hat, āge, fär; let, ēqual, tėrm;
it, īce; hot, ōpen, ôrder;
oil, out; cup, pu̇t, rüle; ch, child;
ng, long; sh, she; th, thin;
ᵺH, then; zh, measure;

ə represents *a* in about,
e in taken, *i* in pencil,
o in lemon, *u* in circus.

to go: *At noon the teacher dismissed the class for lunch.* 2 remove from office or service; not allow to keep a job: *We dismissed the painters because their work was so poor.* 3 put out of mind; stop thinking about: *Dismiss your troubles and be happy with what you have.* 4 refuse to consider in a court of law: *The judge dismissed the case because of lack of evidence.* v.

dis miss al (dis mis′l), 1 act of dismissing: *The dismissal of those five workers caused a strike.* 2 condition or fact of being dismissed: *The company refused to announce the reason for the workers' dismissal.* 3 a written or spoken order dismissing someone: *The workers received their dismissal last Friday.* n.

dis mount (dis mount′), 1 get off a horse, bicycle, etc.: *The riders dismounted and led their horses across the stream.* 2 throw or bring down from a horse; unhorse: *The first knight dismounted the second.* 3 take (a thing) from its setting or support: *The cannons were dismounted for shipping to another fort.* 4 take apart; take to pieces: *The repairman dismounted the typewriter to fix the keys.* v.

dis o be di ence (dis′ə bē′dē əns), refusal to obey; failure to obey: *The child was punished for disobedience.* n.

dis o be di ent (dis′ə bē′dē ənt), refusing to obey; failing to obey: *The disobedient child would not do as she was told.* adj. —**dis′o be′ di ent ly,** adv.

dis o bey (dis′ə bā′), refuse to obey; fail to obey: *The student who disobeyed the teacher was punished.* v.

dis o blige (dis′ə blīj′), neglect to oblige; refuse to do a favor for; refuse to oblige: *I am sorry to disoblige you, but I haven't enough money to lend any.* v., **dis o bliged, dis o blig ing.**

dis or der (dis ôr′dər), 1 lack of order; confusion: *Our whole house was in disorder after the birthday party.* 2 put out of order; destroy the order of; throw into confusion: *A series of accidents disordered the shop.* 3 a public

247

adj.	adjective	*n.*	noun
adv.	adverb	*prep.*	preposition
conj.	conjunction	*pron.*	pronoun
interj.	interjection	*v.*	verb
sing.	singular	*pl.*	plural

disturbance; riot: *The National Guard was called to put an end to the disorder in the streets.* **4** sickness; disease: *Eating the wrong food can cause a stomach disorder.* **5** cause sickness in: *Too much chocolate cake may disorder your stomach.* 1,3,4 *n.*, 2,5 *v.*

dis or der li ness (dis ôr′dər lē nis), disorderly condition. *n.*

dis or der ly (dis ôr′dər lē), **1** not orderly; in confusion: *The troops fled in a disorderly retreat. If you hung your clothes in the closet instead of throwing them on the floor, your room would not look so disorderly.* **2** causing disorder; making a disturbance; breaking rules; unruly: *A disorderly mob ran through the streets, shouting and breaking windows. adj.*

dis or gan i za tion (dis ôr′gə nə zā′shən), a disorganizing or a being disorganized; confusion; disorder. *n.*

dis or gan ize (dis ôr′gə nīz), throw into confusion or disorder; upset the order and arrangement of: *Heavy snowstorms delayed all flights and disorganized the airline schedule.* *v.*, **dis or gan ized, dis or gan iz ing.**

dis own (dis ōn′), refuse to recognize as one's own; cast off: *They disowned their daughter. v.*

dis par age (dis par′ij), **1** speak slightingly of; say (something) is of less value or importance than it actually is; belittle: *Perhaps you disparage her accomplishments because you are jealous of them.* **2** lower the reputation of; discredit. *v.*, **dis par aged, dis par ag ing.**

dis par age ment (dis par′ij mənt), **1** act of disparaging. **2** something that lowers a thing or person in value or importance. **3** a lessening in esteem or standing; discredit: *Say nothing that will be to his disparagement with his new employer. n.*

dis par ag ing ly (dis par′ə jing lē), so as to disparage; slightingly. *adv.*

dis par i ty (dis par′ə tē), **1** lack of equality: *The old man ignored the disparity in their ages because he enjoyed the young man's company.* **2** quality of being unlike; difference: *The disparity in the accounts of the two witnesses puzzled the police. n., pl.* **dis par i ties.**

dis pas sion ate (dis pash′ə nit), free from emotion or prejudice; calm and impartial: *To a dispassionate observer, the drivers of both cars seemed equally to blame for the accident. adj.* —**dis pas′sion ate ly,** *adv.*

dis patch (dis pach′), **1** send off to some place or for some purpose: *The captain dispatched a boat to bring a doctor on board ship.* **2** a sending off a letter, a messenger, etc.: *Please hurry the dispatch of this telegram.* **3** a written message or communication: *Our ambassador in France sent a dispatch by a special messenger reporting the possibility of a war in Europe. The correspondent rushed dispatches to his newspaper in New York about the fire in Paris.* **4** get done promptly or speedily: *The teacher dispatched the roll call and began the lesson.* **5** promptness in doing anything; speed: *This boy works with neatness and dispatch.* **6** kill: *He dispatched the deer with his first shot.* **7** INFORMAL. finish off; eat up: *The hungry boy quickly dispatched the meal.* 1,4,6,7 *v.*, 2,3,5 *n., pl.* **dis patch es.** Also, **despatch.**

dis patch er (dis pach′ər), person who dispatches. A train dispatcher is in charge of sending off the trains on schedule. *n.*

dis pel (dis pel′), drive away and scatter; disperse: *The pilot's confidence dispelled my fear of flying. v.*, **dis pelled, dis pel ling.**

dis pen sar y (dis pen′sər ē), place where medicines, medical care, and medical advice are given free or for a very small charge. *n., pl.* **dis pen sar ies.**

dis pen sa tion (dis′pən sā′shən), **1** a giving out; distributing: *the dispensation of food and clothing to the flood victims.* **2** rule; management: *From 1558 to 1603 England was under the dispensation of Elizabeth I.* **3** a religious system: *the Christian dispensation, the Jewish dispensation.* **4** official permission to disregard a rule. *n.*

dis pense (dis pens′), **1** give out; distribute: *The Red Cross dispensed food and clothing to the flood victims.* **2** carry out; put in force; apply: *Judges and courts of law dispense justice.* **3** prepare and give out: *Druggists must dispense medicine with the greatest care. v.*, **dis pensed, dis pens ing.**

dispense with, 1 do away with; make unnecessary: *The electric light has dispensed with the task of cleaning and filling oil lamps.* **2** do without; get along without: *I shall dispense with these crutches as soon as my leg heals.*

dis pens er (dis pen′sər), person or thing that dispenses: *a dispenser of law, a paper-cup dispenser. n.*

dis per sal (dis pèr′səl), a scattering or a being scattered; dispersing: *the dispersal of a crowd. n.*

dis perse (dis pèrs′), spread in different directions; scatter: *The police dispersed the onlookers. The crowd dispersed when it began raining. v.*, **dis persed, dis pers ing.**

dis per sion (dis pèr′zhən), a dispersing or a being dispersed. *n.*

dis pir it (dis pir′it), lower the spirits of; discourage; depress; dishearten: *Three defeats in a row dispirited the team. v.*

dis place (dis plās′), **1** take the place of; replace: *The automobile has displaced the horse and buggy.* **2** remove from a position of authority: *The mayor displaced the police chief.* **3** move from its usual place or position: *Someone has displaced my tools. A floating object displaces its own weight of liquid. v.*, **dis placed, dis plac ing.**

displaced person, person forced out of his own country by war, famine, political disturbance, etc.

dis place ment (dis plās′mənt), **1** a displacing or a being displaced. **2** weight of the volume of water displaced by a ship or other floating object. This weight is equal to that of the floating object. *n.*

displacement (def. 2)
One cubic foot of cork (15.6 pounds), floating in water, displaces its own weight, but not its own volume.

dis play (dis plā′), **1** put on view; show: *Our family always displays the American flag on the Fourth of July. The lecturer displayed her good nature by patiently answering all our questions.* **2** a showing; exhibition: *a child's display of bad temper.* **3** show in a special way, so as to attract attention: *The stores are displaying the new spring clothes in their windows.* **4** a showing off; ostentation: *Their fondness for display led them to buy flashy cars.* **5** a planned showing of a thing, for some special purpose; exhibit: *Grade 6 had two displays of children's drawings.* 1,3 *v.*, 2,4,5 *n.*

dis please (dis plēz′), not please; annoy; offend: *You displease your parents when you disobey them. v.*, **dis pleased, dis pleas ing.**

dis pleas ure (dis plezh′ər), the feeling of being displeased; annoyance; dislike. *n.*

dis port (dis pôrt'), amuse or entertain oneself: *People laughed at the clumsy bears disporting themselves in the water. The baby disported with the new toy in great glee.* v.

dis pos a ble (dis pō'zə bəl), 1 that can be disposed of or thrown away after use: *disposable paper napkins.* 2 at one's disposal; available: *My allowance is my disposable income.* adj.

dis pos al (dis pō'zəl), 1 a getting rid (of something): *The city takes care of the disposal of garbage.* 2 a giving away or selling: *His will provided for the disposal of his property after his death.* 3 a dealing with; settling: *Her disposal of the difficulty satisfied everybody.* 4 a putting in a certain order or position; arrangement: *The disposal of the chairs around the sides of the room left plenty of space in the middle.* n.

at one's disposal, ready for one's use or service at any time; under one's control or management: *I will put my room and my books at your disposal.*

dis pose (dis pōz'), 1 put in a certain order or position; arrange: *The flags were disposed in a straight line for the parade.* 2 make ready or willing; incline: *More pay and shorter hours of work disposed him to take the new job.* 3 make liable or subject: *Getting your feet wet disposes you to catching cold.* v., **dis posed, dis pos ing.**

dispose of, 1 get rid of: *Dispose of that rubbish.* 2 give away: *The Salvation Army will dispose of this clothing among the poor.* 3 sell: *The owner disposed of her house for $35,000.* 4 eat or drink: *They quickly disposed of the picnic lunch.* 5 arrange; settle: *The committee disposed of all its business in an hour.*

dis posed (dis pōzd'), willing; inclined: *Most children are more disposed to play than to work.* adj.

dis po si tion (dis'pə zish'ən), 1 one's habitual ways of acting toward others or of thinking about things; nature: *His cheerful disposition made him popular.* 2 tendency; inclination: *A quarrelsome person has a disposition to start trouble.* 3 a putting in a certain order or position; arrangement: *The general planned the disposition of his soldiers for the battle.* 4 a disposing; settlement: *What disposition did the court make of the case?* 5 disposal: *She had a large sum of money at her disposition.* n.

dis pos sess (dis'pə zes'), 1 force to give up the possession of a house, land, etc.: *The tenant was dispossessed for not paying rent and had to find another place to live.* 2 take away from; deprive: *Fear dispossessed him of his senses.* v.

dis proof (dis prüf'), 1 a disproving; refutation. 2 fact or reason that disproves something. n.

dis pro por tion (dis'prə pôr'shən), lack of proper proportion. n.

dis pro por tion ate (dis'prə pôr'shə nit), out of relation in size, number, etc. (to something else); not well proportioned: *A penny would be disproportionate pay for a day's work.* adj. —**dis'pro por'tion ate ly,** adv.

dis prove (dis prüv'), prove false or incorrect: *She disproved her brother's claim that he had less candy by weighing both boxes.* v., **dis proved, dis prov ing.**

dis put a ble (dis pyü'tə bəl or dis'pyə tə bəl), liable to be disputed; uncertain; questionable: *The existence of flying saucers is disputable.* adj.

dis pu tant (dis'pyə tənt or dis-pyüt'nt), person who takes part in a dispute or debate. n.

dis pu ta tion (dis'pyə tā'shən), 1 debate; controversy. 2 dispute. n.

dis pute (dis pyüt'), 1 give reasons or facts for or against something; argue; debate; discuss: *Congress disputed over the need for new taxes. The lawyers disputed the case before the judge.* 2 argument; debate: *There is a dispute between the taxpayers and the mayor over where to build the new school.* 3 quarrel: *The children disputed over the last piece of cake.* 4 a quarrel: *The dispute between the two neighbors threatened their friendship.* 5 disagree with (a statement); declare to be false or wrong; call in question: *The insurance company disputed his claim for damages to his car.* 6 fight for; fight over; contest: *The soldiers disputed every inch of ground when the enemy attacked.* 7 try to win: *The losing team disputed the victory up to the last minute of play.* 1,3,5-7 v., **dis put ed, dis put ing;** 2,4 n.

dis qual i fi ca tion (dis kwol'ə fə kā'shən), 1 a disqualifying or a being disqualified. 2 something that disqualifies. n.

dis qual i fy (dis kwol'ə fī), 1 make unfit; make unable to do something: *Her broken leg disqualified her from all sports.* 2 declare unfit or unable to do something: *The principal disqualified two members of the school play because they had low marks.* v., **dis qual i fied, dis qual i fy ing.**

dis qui et (dis kwī'ət), 1 make uneasy or anxious; disturb: *The child's strange actions disquieted her parents.* 2 uneasy feelings; anxiety: *Her disquiet made the rest of us uneasy, too.* 1 v., 2 n.

dis qui e tude (dis kwī'ə tüd or dis-kwī'ə tyüd), uneasiness; anxiety. n.

dis qui si tion (dis'kwə zish'ən), a

hat, āge, fär; let, ēqual, tėrm; it, īce; hot, ōpen, ôrder; oil, out; cup, put, rüle; ch, child; ng, long; sh, she; th, thin; ŦH, then; zh, measure;

ə represents *a* in about, *e* in taken, *i* in pencil, *o* in lemon, *u* in circus.

long or formal speech or writing about a subject. n.

dis re gard (dis'ri gärd'), 1 pay no attention to; take no notice of: *Disregarding the child's screams, the doctor cleaned and bandaged the cut.* 2 lack of attention; neglect: *The reckless driver was arrested for his complete disregard of the traffic laws.* 1 v., 2 n.

dis re pair (dis'ri per' or dis'ri par'), bad condition; need of repair: *The house was in disrepair.* n.

dis rep u ta ble (dis rep'yə tə bəl), 1 having a bad reputation: *Police closed the disreputable barroom.* 2 not fit to be used or seen; in poor condition: *The boy was well dressed except for a disreputable old hat.* adj.

dis rep u ta bly (dis rep'yə tə blē), in a disreputable manner. adv.

dis re pute (dis'ri pyüt'), disgrace; discredit; disfavor: *Many old remedies for illness have fallen into disrepute among doctors.* n.

dis re spect (dis'ri spekt'), lack of respect; rudeness; impoliteness: *I am sure he meant no disrespect by his hasty remark.* n.

dis re spect ful (dis'ri spekt'fəl), showing no respect; lacking in courtesy to elders or superiors; rude; impolite: *Making fun of your elders is disrespectful.* adj. —**dis're spect'ful ly,** adv.

dis robe (dis rōb'), undress. v., **dis robed, dis rob ing.**

dis rupt (dis rupt'), break up; split: *A quarrel over money disrupted their friendship. Troublemakers tried to disrupt the assembly.* v.

dis rup tion (dis rup'shən), 1 a breaking up; splitting: *Arguments led to the disruption of their partnership.* 2 a being broken up; a being split: *There was a disruption of telephone service during the storm.* n.

dis rup tive (dis rup'tiv), causing disruption: *Their whispering was a disruptive influence in the library.* adj.

dis sat is fac tion (dis'sat i sfak'-shən), discontent; displeasure: *Poor working conditions caused dissatisfaction among the employees.* n.

249

dissatisfied

dis sat is fied (dis sat′i sfīd), discontented; displeased: *The workers were very dissatisfied with their low wages.* *adj.*

dis sat is fy (dis sat′i sfī), fail to satisfy; make discontented; displease: *My teacher was dissatisfied with the paper I wrote.* *v.,* **dis sat is fied, dis sat is fy ing.**

dis sect (di sekt′ *or* dī sekt′), 1 cut apart (an animal, plant, etc.) in order to examine or study the structure. 2 examine carefully part by part; analyze: *Let us dissect that statement and find out just what it means.* *v.*

dis sec tion (di sek′shən *or* dī sek′shən), 1 act of cutting apart an animal, plant, etc., in order to examine or study the structure. 2 examination of something in detail or point by point; analysis. *n.*

dis sem ble (di sem′bəl), 1 hide (one's real feelings, thoughts, plans, etc.); disguise: *She dissembled her anger with a smile.* 2 put on the appearance of; pretend; feign: *The bored listener dissembled an interest he didn't feel.* *v.,* **dis sem bled, dis sem bling.**

dis sem bler (di sem′blər), person who dissembles. *n.*

dis sem i nate (di sem′ə nāt), scatter widely; spread abroad: *News is disseminated by means of television and radio.* *v.,* **dis sem i nat ed, dis sem i nat ing.**

dis sem i na tion (di sem′ə nā′shən), a scattering or a being scattered widely; spreading abroad; diffusion: *Dissemination of the news is the function of a newspaper.* *n.*

dis sen sion (di sen′shən), violent disagreement; strong difference of opinion; quarreling; disputing: *The club broke up because of dissension among its members.* *n.*

dis sent (di sent′), 1 differ in opinion; disagree: *Two of the judges dissented from the decision of the other three.* 2 difference of opinion; disagreement: *Dissent among the members broke up the club meeting.* 1 *v.,* 2 *n.* —**dis sent′er,** *n.*

dis ser ta tion (dis′ər tā′shən), a formal discussion of a subject. A university student who is working for a doctor's degree is required to write a dissertation. *n.*

dis serv ice (dis ser′vis), bad treatment; harm; injury: *You do a disservice to him when you fail to give him credit for his efforts.* *n.*

dis sev er (di sev′ər), cut into parts; sever; separate. *v.*

dis sim i lar (di sim′ə lər), not similar; unlike; different. *adj.* —**dis sim′i lar ly,** *adv.*

dis sim i lar i ty (di sim′ə lar′ə tē), lack of similarity; unlikeness; difference. *n., pl.* **dis sim i lar i ties.**

dis sim u late (di sim′yə lāt), disguise or hide under a pretense; hide the truth; dissemble: *She dissimulated ignorance by bragging about how much she knew.* *v.,* **dis sim u lat ed, dis sim u lat ing.**

dis sim u la tion (di sim′yə lā′shən), a dissimulating; deceit; pretense; hypocrisy. *n.*

dis si pate (dis′ə pāt), 1 spread in different directions; scatter so as to disappear or cause to disappear; disperse; dispel: *The fog is beginning to dissipate. After a brisk morning wind dissipated the clouds, the sky was clear all day.* 2 spend foolishly; waste on things of little value: *In a very short time I had dissipated my inheritance.* 3 indulge too much in evil or foolish pleasures. *v.,* **dis si pat ed, dis si pat ing.**

dis si pat ed (dis′ə pā′tid), indulging too much in evil or foolish pleasures; dissolute: *a dissipated life spent drinking and gambling. adj.*

dis si pa tion (dis′ə pā′shən), 1 a scattering in different directions. 2 a wasting by misuse. 3 too much indulgence in evil or foolish pleasures; intemperance. *n.*

dis so ci ate (di sō′shē āt), break the connection or association with; separate: *When the lawyer discovered that his client was lying, he immediately dissociated himself from the case.* *v.,* **dis so ci at ed, dis so ci at ing.**

dis so ci a tion (di sō′sē ā′shən *or* di sō′shē ā′shən), a dissociating or a being dissociated. *n.*

dis so lute (dis′ə lüt), living an evil life; very wicked; immoral: *dissolute companions with bad reputations. adj.* —**dis′so lute ly,** *adv.* —**dis′so lute ness,** *n.*

dis so lu tion (dis′ə lü′shən), 1 a breaking up; an ending: *The partners arranged for the dissolution of their partnership.* 2 a making or becoming liquid; dissolving. 3 ruin; destruction. 4 death. *n.*

dis solve (di zolv′), 1 change from a solid or gas to a liquid; form into a solution in a liquid: *Salt or sugar will dissolve in water.* 2 break up; end: *The two partners dissolved their partnership because they could not agree on how to conduct the business.* 3 fade away: *The dream dissolved when she woke up.* *v.,* **dis solved, dis solv ing.**

dis so nance (dis′n əns), 1 harshness and unpleasantness of sound; discord. 2 lack of harmony; disagreement. *n.*

dis so nant (dis′n ənt), 1 harsh and unpleasant in sound; not harmonious; clashing. 2 out of harmony with other conditions, persons, etc.; disagreeing: *The dirty, crowded houses of slums are dissonant with the richness of our country. adj.* —**dis′so nant ly,** *adv.*

dis suade (di swād′), persuade not to do something: *He finally dissuaded his daughter from dropping out of school.* *v.,* **dis suad ed, dis suad ing.**

distaff (def. 1)—Fibers bound to the distaff are drawn out and twisted by the motion and weight of the spindle to make thread.

dis taff (dis′taf), 1 a stick, split at the tip, to hold wool or flax for spinning by hand. 2 staff on a spinning wheel for holding wool or flax. *n.*

distaff side, the mother's side of a family: *My cousin and I are related on the distaff side.*

dis tance (dis′təns), 1 space in between: *The distance from the farm to the town is five miles.* 2 a being far away: *Because of the lake's distance, we will have to stop overnight on the way.* 3 a place far away: *She saw a light in the distance.* 4 leave far behind; do much better than: *The big black horse distanced the others.* 1-3 *n.,* 4 *v.,* **distanced, dis tanc ing.**

at a distance, a long way: *The farm is at a distance from the road.*

keep at a distance, refuse to be friendly or familiar with; treat coldly: *The tutor kept his pupil at a distance.*

keep one's distance, be not too friendly or familiar: *The shy boy kept his distance and did not mingle with his new classmates.*

dis tant (dis′tənt), 1 far away in space: *The sun is distant from the earth.* 2 away: *The town is three miles distant.* 3 far apart in time, relationship, likeness, etc.; not close: *A third cousin is a distant relative. We may take a trip to Europe in the distant future.* 4 not friendly: *She gave him only a distant nod. adj.* —**dis′tant ly,** *adv.*

dis taste (dis tāst′), dislike: *I have always had a distaste for Brussels sprouts.* *n.*

dis taste ful (dis tāst′fəl), unpleasant; disagreeable; offensive: *Cleaning out the garbage cans is a distasteful task.* *adj.* —**dis taste′ful ly,** *adv.* —**dis taste′ful ness,** *n.*

dis tem per (dis tem′pər), an infectious disease of dogs and other animals, accompanied by fever, a short, dry cough, and a loss of strength. *n.*

dis tend (dis tend′), stretch out; swell out; expand: *The balloon was distended almost to the bursting point.* *n.*

dis till or **dis til** (dis til′), 1 heat (a liquid or other substance) and condense the vapor given off. Water obtained by distilling dirty water is clean and pure because the steam given off contains no impurities. A substance is distilled in order to purify it, to separate its liquid parts from its solid parts, or to break it down into separate substances. 2 obtain by distilling: *Gasoline is distilled from crude oil. Alcoholic liquor is distilled from mash made from grain.* 3 get out the essential principle; extract: *A jury must distill the truth from the testimony of witnesses.* 4 give off in drops: *These flowers distill a sweet nectar.* 5 fall in drops; drip: *Tears distilled slowly from his eyes.* *v.,* **dis tilled, dis till ing.**

dis til la tion (dis/tl ā/shən), 1 act of distilling: *the distillation of water to purify it.* 2 process of distilling. 3 something distilled. *n.*

dis till er (dis til/ər), 1 person or thing that distills. 2 person or company that makes whiskey, rum, brandy, etc. *n.*

dis till er y (dis til/ər ē), 1 place where distilling is done. 2 place where whiskey, rum, brandy, etc., are made; still. *n., pl.* **dis till er ies.**

dis tinct (dis tingkt′), 1 not the same; separate: *She asked me about it three distinct times.* 2 different in quality or kind: *Mice are distinct from rats. Reading is distinct from writing.* 3 easily seen, heard, or understood; clear: *Large, distinct print is easy to read.* 4 unmistakable; definite; decided: *A tall player has a distinct advantage in basketball.* *adj.* —**dis tinct′ly,** *adv.* —**dis tinct′ness,** *n.*

dis tinc tion (dis tingk′shən), 1 a distinguishing from others; making a difference: *She treated all her children alike without distinction.* 2 difference: *The distinction between hot and cold is easily noticed.* 3 special quality or feature; point of difference: *He has the distinction of being the tallest boy in his class.* 4 honor: *The senator had served his country with distinction.* 5 mark or sign of honor: *The scientist received*

many awards as distinctions for her achievements. 6 excellence; superiority: *a man of great distinction.* *n.*

dis tinc tive (dis tingk′tiv), distinguishing from others; special; characteristic: *Policemen wear a distinctive uniform.* *adj.* —**dis tinc′tive ly,** *adv.* —**dis tinc′tive ness,** *n.*

distill (def. 1)
Pure water is distilled from salt water by heating until the water turns to vapor. It is changed back to liquid form by cooling in the condenser.

dis tin guish (dis ting′gwish), 1 see or show the differences in; tell apart: *Can you distinguish cotton cloth from wool?* 2 see or show the difference: *You learn to distinguish between right and wrong.* 3 see or hear clearly; make out plainly: *On a clear, bright day you can distinguish things far away.* 4 make different; be a special quality or feature of: *A trunk distinguishes the elephant. The ability to talk distinguishes people from animals.* 5 make famous or well known: *She distinguished herself by winning the Nobel prize.* *v.*

dis tin guish a ble (dis ting′gwish ə bəl), that can be distinguished. *adj.*

dis tin guished (dis ting′gwisht), 1 famous; well-known: *Robert Frost was a distinguished American poet.* 2 looking important or superior: *Your new suit gives you a distinguished look.* *adj.*

dis tort (dis tôrt′), 1 pull or twist out of shape; change the normal appearance of: *Rage distorted his face.* 2 change from the truth: *The driver distorted the facts of the accident to escape blame.* *v.*

dis tor tion (dis tôr′shən), 1 a distorting; twisting out of shape: *Exaggeration is a distortion of the truth.* 2 condition of being distorted. 3 anything distorted: *Their story was full of distortions.* *n.*

dis tract (dis trakt′), 1 draw away (the mind, attention, etc.): *Noise distracts my attention from study.* 2 confuse; disturb: *Several people talking at once distract a listener.* 3 put out of one's mind; make insane: *distracted with fear and anxiety.* *v.*

dis trac tion (dis trak′shən), 1 act of drawing away the mind or attention.

hat, āge, fär; let, ēqual, tėrm;
it, īce; hot, ōpen, ôrder;
oil, out; cup, pùt, rüle; ch, child;
ng, long; sh, she; th, thin;
ᵺ, then; zh, measure;

ə represents *a* in about,
e in taken, *i* in pencil,
o in lemon, *u* in circus.

2 thing that draws away the mind or the attention: *Noise is a distraction when you are trying to study.* 3 confusion of mind; disturbance of thought: *The parents of the lost child scarcely knew what they were doing in their distraction.* 4 relief from continued thought, grief, or effort; amusement: *Movies and television are popular distractions.* *n.*

dis traught (dis trôt′), 1 in a state of mental conflict and confusion; distracted: *The lost child wandered about distraught with fear.* 2 crazed. *adj.*

dis tress (dis tres′), 1 great pain or sorrow; anxiety; trouble: *The child's illness caused her family distress.* 2 cause great pain or sorrow to; make unhappy: *Your tears distress me.* 3 something that causes distress; misfortune: *The failure of his business was a great distress to him.* 4 a dangerous condition; difficult situation: *A burning or sinking ship is in distress.* 1,3,4 *n.,* 2 *v.* —**dis tress′ing ly,** *adv.*

dis tress ful (dis tres′fəl), causing distress; painful. *adj.*

dis trib ute (dis trib′yüt), 1 give some of to each; divide and give out in shares; deal out: *Mother distributed the candy among the children.* 2 spread; scatter: *A painter should distribute the paint evenly over a wall.* 3 divide into parts: *The children were distributed into three groups for the trip to the museum.* 4 arrange; sort out: *A mail clerk distributes mail by putting the letters into the bags of mail for different places.* *v.,* **dis trib ut ed, dis trib ut ing.**

dis tri bu tion (dis/trə byü′shən), 1 act of distributing: *After the contest the distribution of prizes to the winners took place.* 2 way of being distributed: *If some get more than others, there is an uneven distribution.* 3 thing distributed. 4 a distributing to consumers of goods grown or made by producers. *n.*

dis trib u tive (dis trib′yə tiv), 1 having to do with distribution. 2 referring to each individual of a group considered separately. *Each, every,* and *either* are distributive pronouns. 3 of or having to do with a rule that the same product results in multiplication when

distributor

adj. adjective	*n.* noun
adv. adverb	*prep.* preposition
conj. conjunction	*pron.* pronoun
interj. interjection	*v.* verb
sing. singular	*pl.* plural

performed on a set of numbers as when performed on the members of the set individually. EXAMPLE: 3(4+5) = (3×4) + (3×5). *adj.* —**dis trib′u tive ly,** *adv.*

dis trib u tor (dis trib′yə tər), **1** person or thing that distributes. **2** person or company that distributes goods to consumers. **3** part of a gasoline engine that distributes electric current to the spark plugs. *n.*

dis trict (dis′trikt), **1** part of a larger area; region: *The leading farming district of the United States is in the Middle West. They lived in a fashionable district of the city.* **2** part of a country, state, or city marked off for a special purpose. *There are districts for providing schools or courts of law, for electing certain government officials, or for supporting a church.* **3** divide into districts. **1,2** *n.,* **3** *v.*

district attorney, lawyer who handles cases for the government for a certain district of a state or the country.

District of Columbia, district in E United States between Maryland and Virginia, governed by the Federal government. It is entirely occupied by the national capital, Washington.

dis trust (dis trust′), **1** have no confidence in; not trust; be suspicious of: *Some people distrust foreigners. I have distrusted fountain pens ever since one of them splattered me with ink.* **2** lack of trust or confidence; suspicion: *I could not explain my distrust of the stranger.* **1** *v.,* **2** *n.*

dis trust ful (dis trust′fəl), not trusting; suspicious. *adj.* —**dis trust′ful ly,** *adv.* —**dis trust′ful ness,** *n.*

dis turb (dis tėrb′), **1** destroy the peace, quiet, or rest of: *Heavy truck traffic disturbed the neighborhood all day long.* **2** break in upon with noise or change: *Do not disturb the baby; he is asleep.* **3** put out of order: *Someone has disturbed my books; I can't find the one I want.* **4** make uneasy; trouble: *He was disturbed to hear of his friend's illness.* **5** inconvenience: *Don't disturb yourself; I can do it.* *v.* —**dis turb′er,** *n.*

dis turb ance (dis tėr′bəns), **1** a disturbing or a being disturbed. **2** thing that disturbs. **3** confusion; disorder: *The police were called to quiet the dis-*

turbance at the street corner. **4** uneasiness; trouble; worry. *n.*

dis un ion (dis yü′nyən), **1** separation; division. **2** lack of unity; disagreement; unfriendliness. *n.*

dis u nite (dis′yü nīt′), destroy the unity of; cause to disagree or to become unfriendly: *Bad feelings among our relatives disunited the family.* *v.,* **dis u nit ed, dis u nit ing.**

dis use (dis yüs′), lack of use; not being used: *The old tools were rusted from disuse. Many words common in Shakespeare's time have fallen into disuse.* *n.*

ditch (dich), **1** a long, narrow hole dug in the earth. Ditches are usually used to carry off water. **2** dig a ditch in or around. **3** drive or throw into a ditch: *The careless driver skidded off the road and ditched the car.* **4** SLANG. get rid of: *The robber ditched the gun in a sewer.* **1** *n., pl.* **ditch es; 2-4** *v.*

dith er (diŧH′ər), INFORMAL. a confused, excited condition: *She's in a dither about tomorrow's test.* *n.*

dit to (dit′ō), **1** the same; exactly the same as appeared or was said before. **2** ditto mark. **3** INFORMAL. as said before; likewise. **1,2** *n., pl.* **dit tos; 3** *adv.*

ditto mark, a small mark (″) used to avoid repeating something written immediately above. Ditto marks are often used on long lists, bills, tables, etc. EXAMPLE:

6 lb. butter at 75¢ $4.50
4 ″   ″   ″   ″ 3.00

dit ty (dit′ē), a short, simple song or poem. *n., pl.* **dit ties.**

di ur nal (dī ėr′nl), **1** occurring every day; daily: *Sunrise is a diurnal event.* **2** of or belonging to the daytime: *Diurnal temperatures are usually higher than those of the night.* **3** active in the daytime: *Butterflies are diurnal.* *adj.* —**di ur′nal ly,** *adv.*

di van (dī′van or də van′), a long, low, soft couch or sofa. *n.*

dive (dīv), **1** plunge headfirst into water. **2** act of diving: *The crowd applauded the girl's graceful dive.* **3** go down or out of sight suddenly: *The gopher dived into its hole and disappeared.* **4** plunge the hand suddenly into anything: *He dived into his pockets and brought out a dollar.* **5** plunge with the mind; begin with energy and zeal: *She dived into her work with enthusiasm.* **6** plunge downward at a steep angle: *The hawk dived straight at the field mouse.* **7** a downward plunge at a steep angle: *The submarine made a dive toward the bottom.* **8** INFORMAL. a low, cheap tavern or night club. **1,3-6** *v.,* **2,7,8** *n.*

dived or **dove, dived, div ing;**

dive bomber, bomber that releases its load of bombs just before it pulls out of a dive toward the target.

div er (dī′vər), **1** person or thing that dives. **2** person whose occupation is working or diving under water. **3** a diving bird. Loons, penguins, and auks are divers. *n.*

diverge (def. 1)—The lens causes the light rays to diverge.

di verge (də vėrj′ or dī vėrj′), **1** move or lie in different directions from the same point; branch off: *Their paths diverged at the fork in the road; he turned left, and she turned right.* **2** differ; vary; deviate: *Contestants who diverge from the rules will be eliminated from the competition.* *v.,* **di verged, di verg ing.**

di ver gence (də vėr′jəns or dī vėr′jəns), a diverging; difference: *The committee couldn't come to an agreement because of the wide divergence of opinion among its members.* *n.*

di ver gent (də vėr′jənt or dī vėr′jənt), diverging; different. *adj.*

di vers (dī′vərz), more than one; several different; various: *A well-balanced diet is made up of divers foods.* *adj.*

di verse (də vėrs′), not alike; different; varied: *Many diverse opinions were expressed at the meeting. A person of diverse interests can talk on many subjects.* *adj.* —**di verse′ly,** *adv.* —**di verse′ness,** *n.*

di ver si fy (də vėr′sə fī), make diverse; give variety to; vary: *Mountains, plains, trees, and lakes diversify the landscape. Some people diversify their interests by belonging to different clubs and having various hobbies.* *v.,* **di ver si fied, di ver si fy ing.**

di ver sion (də vėr′zhən), **1** a turning aside; a diverting: *A magician's talk creates a diversion of attention so that people do not see how he does his tricks.* **2** distraction from work, care, etc.; amusement; entertainment; pastime: *Golf is my sister's favorite diversion.* *n.*

di ver si ty (də vėr′sə tē), **1** complete difference; unlikeness: *The quiet student and the active athlete were close friends in spite of the diversity of their dispositions.* **2** variety: *The diversity of food on the menu made it hard for her to decide what to order.* *n., pl.* **di ver si ties.**

di vert (də vėrt′), **1** turn aside: *A ditch diverted water from the stream into the* *fields. The siren of the fire engine diverted the audience's attention from the play.* 2 amuse; entertain: *Listening to music diverted him after a hard day's work. v.*

di vest (də vest′), 1 rid or free; strip: *We divested ourselves of our clothes and dived into the water.* 2 force to give up; deprive: *A person in prison is divested of his right to vote. v.*

di vide (də vīd′), 1 separate into parts: *A brook divides the field. The road divides and forms two roads.* 2 separate into equal parts: *When you divide 8 by 2, you get 4.* 3 give some of to each; share: *The children divided the candy.* 4 disagree or cause to disagree; separate in feeling, opinion, etc.: *The school divided on the choice of a new motto. Jealousy divided us.* 5 ridge of land between two regions drained by different river systems: *The Rocky Mountains form part of the Continental Divide.* 1-4 *v.,* **di vid ed, di vid ing;** 5 *n.*

div i dend (div′ə dend), 1 number or quantity to be divided by another: *In 728 ÷ 16, 728 is the dividend.* 2 money earned as profit by a company and divided among the owners or stockholders of the company. 3 share of such money. *n.*

di vid er (də vī′dər), 1 person or thing that divides: *There is a concrete divider in the center of the parkway.* 2 **dividers,** *pl.* compass used for dividing lines, measuring distances, etc. *n.*

div i na tion (div′ə nā′shən), 1 act of foreseeing the future or foretelling the unknown by inspiration, by magic, or by signs and omens. 2 a skillful guess or prediction. *n.*

di vine (də vīn′), 1 of God or a god: *The Bible describes the creation of the world as a divine act.* 2 given by or coming from God: *The queen believed that her power to rule was a divine right.* 3 to or for God; sacred; holy: *divine worship.* 4 like God or a god; heavenly. 5 INFORMAL. excellent or delightful; unusually good or great: *Oh, what a divine vacation we had!* 6 clergyman who knows much about theology; minister; priest. 7 foresee or foretell by inspiration, by magic, or by signs and omens; predict. 8 find out without actually knowing; guess correctly: *She divined who had eaten the cake from the guilty looks on the children's faces.* 1-5 *adj.,* 6 *n.,* 7,8 *v.,* **di vined, di vin ing.** —**di vine′ly,** *adv.*

di vin er (də vī′nər), person who foresees or foretells things; prophet. *n.*

diving bell, a large, hollow container filled with air and open at the bottom. People can work in it under water.

diving suit, a waterproof suit with a

helmet into which air can be pumped through a tube. Diving suits are worn by persons working under water.

di vin i ty (də vin′ə tē), 1 a divine being; god or goddess. 2 **the Divinity,** God. 3 divine nature or quality. 4 study of God, religion, and divine things; theology. *n., pl.* **di vin i ties.**

di vis i ble (də viz′ə bəl), 1 capable of being divided. 2 capable of being divided without leaving a remainder: *12 is divisible by 1, 2, 3, 4, 6, and 12. adj.*

di vi sion (də vizh′ən), 1 a dividing or a being divided. 2 a giving some to each; sharing: *The making of automobiles in large numbers is made possible by a division of labor, in which each worker has a certain part of the work to do.* 3 process of dividing one number by another: *26 ÷ 2 = 13 is a simple division.* 4 thing that divides. A boundary or a partition is a division. 5 one of the parts into which a thing is divided; group; section: *The cat family is a division of the carnivorous animals.* 6 a military unit made up of several brigades or regiments plus supporting troops, usually commanded by a major general. It is smaller than a corps. 7 a difference of opinion, thought, or feeling; disagreement: *There was a division in our class over the date for our spring trip. n.*

di vi sor (də vī′zər), number or quantity by which another is to be divided: *In 728 ÷ 16, 16 is the divisor. n.*

di vorce (də vôrs′), 1 the legal ending of a marriage. 2 end legally a marriage between: *The judge divorced the husband and wife.* 3 separate from by a divorce: *She divorced her husband.* 4 separate: *In America government and religion are divorced.* 5 separation: *In this country there is a complete divorce of government and religion.* 1,5 *n.,* 2-4 *v.,* **di vorced, di vorc ing.**

di vor cée (də vôr sā′), a divorced woman. *n., pl.* **di vor cées.** [from French]

di vulge (də vulj′ or dī vulj′), make known; tell; reveal: *The traitor divulged secret plans to the enemy. v.,* **di vulged, di vulg ing.**

div vy (div′ē), SLANG. share or divide: *We divvied up the money we won between us. v.,* **div vied, div vy ing.**

Dix ie (dik′sē), the southern states of the United States. *n.*

diz zi ly (diz′ə lē), in a dizzy manner. *adv.*

diz zi ness (diz′ē nis), dizzy condition. *n.*

diz zy (diz′ē), 1 likely to fall, stagger, or spin around; not steady: *When you spin round and round, and stop suddenly, you feel dizzy.* 2 confused; bewildered: *The noise and crowds of the city*

hat, āge, fär; let, ēqual, tèrm; it, īce; hot, ōpen, ôrder; oil, out; cup, pùt, rüle; ch, child; ng, long; sh, she; th, thin; ŦH, then; zh, measure;

ə represents *a* in about, *e* in taken, *i* in pencil, *o* in lemon, *u* in circus.

streets made the little boy dizzy. 3 make dizzy: *The ride on the merry-go-round dizzied her.* 4 likely to make dizzy; causing dizziness: *The airplane climbed to a dizzy height.* 1,2,4 *adj.,* **diz zi er, diz zi est;** 3 *v.,* **diz zied, diz zy ing.**

Dja kar ta (jə kär′tə), seaport in NW Java, capital of Indonesia. *n.* Also, **Jakarta.**

DNA, deoxyribonucleic acid.

Dnie per (nē′pər), river flowing from W Soviet Union into the Black Sea. *n.*

Dnies ter (nē′stər), river flowing from SW Soviet Union into the Black Sea. *n.*

do[1] (dü), 1 carry through to an end any action or piece of work; carry out; perform: *He did his work well. She did a book on her travels in Africa.* 2 act; behave: *You have done wisely.* 3 be the cause of; bring about: *Your work does you credit.* 4 deal with; take care of: *do the dishes, do one's hair.* 5 get along; manage; fare: *My sister is doing well in her new job.* 6 be satisfactory: *This hat will do.* 7 **Do** is used: **a** to ask questions: *Do you like milk?* **b** to make what one says stronger: *I do want to go.* **c** to stand for another verb already used: *My dog goes where I do. His son walks just as he does.* **d** in expressions that contain *not: People talk; animals do not. v.,* **did, done, doing.** [Old English *dōn*]

do away with, 1 put an end to; abolish: *do away with a rule.* 2 kill: *The trap did away with the rat.*

do up, 1 wrap up; tie up: *Please do up this package more securely.* 2 arrange: *do up one's hair.*

do[2] (dō), (in music) the first and last tone of the scale. *Do, re, mi, fa, sol, la, ti, do* are the names of the tones of the scale. *n.* [from Italian]

dob bin (dob′ən), a slow, gentle, plodding horse. *n.*

Do ber man pin scher (dō′bər mən pin′shər), a medium-sized, slender, alert dog with short, dark hair.

doc ile (dos′əl), 1 easily managed; obedient: *Persons who are just starting to ride should use a docile horse.* 2 easily taught; willing to learn: *The docile and intelligent pupil was always*

adj.	adjective	*n.*	noun
adv.	adverb	*prep.*	preposition
conj.	conjunction	*pron.*	pronoun
interj.	interjection	*v.*	verb
sing.	singular	*pl.*	plural

ready to study difficult subjects. adj. —**doc′ile ly,** *adv.*

do cil i ty (do sil′ə tē), docile quality. *n.*

dock¹ (dok), **1** platform built on the shore or out from the shore; wharf; pier. Ships load and unload beside a dock. **2** water between two piers, permitting the entrance of ships. **3** place where a ship may be repaired, often built watertight so that the water may be kept high or pumped out. **4** bring (a ship) to a dock: *The crew docked the ship and began to unload it.* **5** come into a dock: *The ship docked during the night.* **1-3** *n.,* **4,5** *v.* [from Dutch of the 1500's *docke*]

dock² (dok), **1** cut down; cut some off of: *The company docks the workers' wages if they come to work late.* **2** cut short; cut off the end of. Horses' and dogs' tails are sometimes docked. **3** the solid, fleshy part of an animal's tail. **1,2** *v.,* **3** *n.* [Old English *-docca,* as in *finger-docca* finger muscle]

dock³ (dok), the place where an accused person stands or sits in a court of law. *n.* [perhaps from Flemish *dok* pen]

dock⁴ (dok), a large weed with sour or bitter leaves and clusters of greenish flowers. *n.* [Old English *docce*]

dock et (dok′it), **1** list of lawsuits to be tried by a court. **2** any list of matters to be considered by some person or group. **3** enter on a docket. **4** label or ticket giving the contents of a package, document, etc. **1,2,4** *n.,* **3** *v.*

dock yard (dok′yärd′), place where ships are built, equipped, and repaired. A dockyard contains docks, workshops, and warehouses for supplies. *n.*

doc tor (dok′tər), **1** person who knows how to treat diseases; physician or surgeon. A doctor must have a license to practice medicine. **2** treat disease in: *My sister doctored me when I had a cold.* **3** dentist. **4** person who has the highest degree given by a university: *a Doctor of Philosophy.* **5** tamper with: *The dishonest cashier doctored the accounts.* **1,3,4** *n.,* **2,5** *v.*

doc tri nal (dok′trə nəl), of or having to do with doctrine. *adj.*

doc trine (dok′trən), **1** what is taught as true by a church, nation, or group of persons; belief: *religious doc-*

trine. **2** what is taught; teachings. *n.*

doc u ment (dok′yə mənt *for* 1; dok′yə ment *for* 2), **1** something written or printed that gives information or proof of some fact; any object used as evidence. Letters, maps, and pictures are documents. **2** prove or support by means of documents or the like: *Can you document your theory with facts?* **1** *n.,* **2** *v.*

doc u men tar y (dok′yə men′tər ē), **1** consisting of documents; in writing, print, etc.: *The photographs were used as documentary evidence at the trial.* **2** presenting or recording factual information in an artistic fashion: *a documentary film about the history of Boston.* **3** a documentary motion picture, book, or radio or television program. **1,2** *adj.,* **3** *n., pl.* **doc u men tar ies.**

doc u men ta tion (dok′yə men tā′shən), preparation and use of documentary evidence. *n.*

dod der (dod′ər), be unsteady; shake; tremble; totter: *The old man doddered from his chair to the door.* *v.*

dodge (doj), **1** move or jump quickly to one side: *As I looked, he dodged behind a bush.* **2** avoid by jumping or moving to one side; get away from by twisting or turning quickly aside: *She dodged the ball as it came flying at her.* **3** a sudden movement to one side. **4** avoid by cleverness; get away from by some trick: *She dodged our question by changing the subject.* **5** a trick to cheat: *a clever dodge.* **1,2,4** *v.,* **3,5** *n.*

dodg er (doj′ər), person who dodges. *n.*

Dodg son (doj′sən), **Charles L.,** the real name of **Lewis Carroll.** *n.*

do do (dō′dō), a large, clumsy bird not able to fly that became extinct in the 1600's. Dodos lived on several islands in the Indian Ocean. *n., pl.* **do dos** or **do does.**

dodo—4 ft. long

doe (dō), the female of a deer, antelope, rabbit, hare, and of most other animals whose male is called a buck. *n.*

do er (dü′ər), person who does something, especially with energy and drive: *He is a dreamer, but his brother is a doer.* *n.*

does (duz), a present tense of **do¹.** *He does all his work. Does she sing well?* *v.*

doe skin (dō′skin′), **1** skin of a doe.

2 leather made from it. **3** a smooth, soft woolen cloth, used for clothing. *n.*

does n't (duz′nt), does not.

doff (dof), take off; remove: *He doffed his hat as the flag passed by.* *v.*

dog (dôg), **1** a four-legged, flesh-eating mammal kept as a pet and used for hunting and for guarding property. Dogs are related to wolves, foxes, and jackals. **2** hunt or follow like a dog: *That bill collector has been dogging me for over a month.* **3** device to hold or grip like a dog's teeth. **1,3** *n.,* **2** *v.,* **dogged, dog ging.** —**dog′like′,** *adj.* **go to the dogs,** be ruined.

dog (def. 3)

DOG

dog cart (dôg′kärt′), **1** a small cart pulled by dogs. **2** a small, open, horse-drawn carriage with two seats that are placed back to back. *n.*

dog catch er (dôg′kach′ər), person whose work is to catch and detain stray dogs. *n.*

dog days, period of very hot and uncomfortable weather during July and August.

doge (dōj), the chief magistrate of Venice or Genoa when they were republics. *n.*

dog-ear (dôg′ir′), **1** a folded-down corner of a page in a book. A dog-ear is often made to mark the page where the reader has stopped. **2** fold down the corner of (a page in a book). **1** *n.,* **2** *v.*

dog fight (dôg′fīt′), **1** combat between individual fighter planes at close quarters. **2** brawl. *n.*

dog fish (dôg′fish′), any of several kinds of small shark. *n., pl.* **dog fish es** or **dog fish.**

dog ged (dô′gid), not giving up; stubborn; persistent: *Her dogged determination helped her to win the prize.* *adj.* —**dog′ged ly,** *adv.* —**dog′ged ness,** *n.*

dog ger el (dô′gər əl), **1** very poor poetry; poetry that is not artistic. **2** crude; poor; not artistic: *doggerel verses.* **1** *n.,* **2** *adj.*

dog house (dôg′hous′), a small house or shelter for a dog. *n., pl.* **dog hous es** (dôg′hou′ziz).

in the doghouse, SLANG. out of favor: *I am in the doghouse with my parents for staying out too late last night.*

do gie (dō′gē), (in the western United States and Canada) a motherless calf on the range or in a range herd. *n.*

dog ma (dôg′mə), 1 belief taught or held as true, especially by authority of a church; doctrine. 2 opinion asserted in a positive manner as if it were of the highest authority. *n., pl.* **dog mas.**

dog mat ic (dôg mat′ik), 1 of or having to do with dogma; doctrinal. 2 positive and emphatic in asserting opinions: *The audience disliked the speaker's dogmatic manner in stating his opinions as if they were facts.* 3 asserted in a positive and emphatic manner: *She gave no evidence to prove her dogmatic statement that the textbook was wrong.* *adj.* —**dog mat′i cal ly,** *adv.*

dog ma tism (dôg′mə tiz′əm), positive and emphatic assertion of opinion: *The team disliked the coach's dogmatism.* *n.*

Dog Star, Sirius.

dog trot (dôg′trot′), a gentle, easy trot. *n.*

dog wood (dôg′wúd′), tree with large white or pinkish flowers in the spring and red berries in the fall. *n.*

doi ly (doi′lē), a small piece of linen, lace, paper, or plastic, used on a table. Doilies are put under plates, bowls, vases, etc. *n., pl.* **doi lies.** [from *Doily,* the name of an English dealer of dry goods in the 1700's]

do ings (dü′ingz), 1 things done; actions. 2 behavior; conduct. *n.pl.*

do-it-your self (dü′it yər self′), designed for use, construction, or assembly by an amateur. *adj.*

dol drums (dol′drəmz *or* dōl′drəmz), 1 gloomy feeling; low spirits: *My brother has been in the doldrums since he failed the history test.* 2 region of the ocean near the equator where the wind is very light or constantly shifting. When a sailing ship gets in the doldrums, it makes little headway. *n.pl.*

dole (dōl), 1 portion of money, food, etc., given in charity. 2 deal out in portions to the poor. 3 a small portion. 4 give in small portions: *The teacher doled out a dab of paste to each student.* 5 relief money given by a government to unemployed workers. 1,3,5 *n.,* 2,4 *v.,* **doled, dol ing.**

dole ful (dōl′fəl), very sad or dreary; mournful; dismal. *adj.* —**dole′ful ly,** *adv.* —**dole′ful ness,** *n.*

doll (dol), 1 a child's toy made to look like a baby, child, or grown person. 2 a pretty child, girl, or woman. 3 INFORMAL. dress in a stylish or showy way: *They were all dolled up in evening dress.* 1,2 *n.,* 3 *v.* —**doll′-like′,** *adj.*

dol lar (dol′ər), 1 unit of money in the United States. 100 cents make one dollar. 2 a similar unit of money in Canada, Australia, and some other countries. 3 a silver coin or piece of paper money equal to 100 cents. *n.*

doll house (dol′hous′), a toy house for children to use in playing with dolls. *n., pl.* **doll hous es** (dol′hou′ziz).

doll y (dol′ē), 1 a child's name for a doll. 2 a small, low frame on wheels, used to move heavy things: *The refrigerator was moved into the house on a dolly.* *n., pl.* **doll ies.**

do lor (dō′lər), sorrow; grief. *n.*

dol or ous (dol′ər əs *or* dō′lər əs), 1 full of or expressing sorrow; mournful. 2 causing or giving rise to sorrow; grievous; painful. *adj.* —**dol′or ous ly,** *adv.* —**dol′or ous ness,** *n.*

dolphin—7 to 12 ft. long

dol phin (dol′fən), a sea mammal related to the whale, but smaller. It has a snout like a beak and remarkable intelligence. *n.*

dolt (dōlt), a dull, stupid person. *n.*

dolt ish (dōl′tish), like a dolt; dull and stupid. *adj.* —**dolt′ish ly,** *adv.* —**dolt′ish ness,** *n.*

-dom, *suffix forming nouns.* 1 (*added to nouns*) position, rank, or realm of a _____: *Kingdom = realm of a king.* 2 (*added to adjectives*) condition of being _____: *Freedom = condition of being free.* 3 (*added to nouns*) all those who are _____: *Heathendom = all those who are heathen.* [Old English *-dōm* state, rank, from *dōm* law, judgment]

do main (dō mān′), 1 territory under the control of one ruler or government. 2 land owned by one person; estate. 3 field of thought or action: *the domain of science, the domain of religion.* *n.*

dome (dōm), 1 a large, rounded roof or ceiling on a circular or many-sided base. 2 something high and rounded: *the dome of a hill.* *n.* —**dome′like′,** *adj.*

do mes tic (də mes′tik), 1 of the home, household, or family affairs: *domestic problems, a domestic scene.* 2 fond of home and family life: *a domestic father who enjoys being with his children.* 3 servant in a household. A butler or a maid is a domestic. 4 not wild; tame. Cats, dogs, cows, horses, and pigs are domestic animals. 5 of or made in one's own country; not foreign: *Most newspapers publish both domestic and foreign news.* 1,2,4,5 *adj.,* 3 *n.* —**do mes′ti cal ly,** *adv.*

hat, āge, fär; let, ēqual, tèrm;
it, īce; hot, ōpen, ôrder;
oil, out; cup, pút, rüle; ch, child;
ng, long; sh, she; th, thin;
ŦH, then; zh, measure;

ə represents *a* in about,
e in taken, *i* in pencil,
o in lemon, *u* in circus.

do mes ti cate (də mes′tə kāt), 1 change from a wild to a tame or cultivated state: *People have domesticated a great many plants and animals.* 2 make fond of home and family life. *v.,* **do mes ti cat ed, do mes ti cat ing.**

do mes ti ca tion (də mes′tə kā′shən), a domesticating or a being domesticated. *n.*

do mes tic i ty (dō′mes tis′ə tē), 1 home and family life. 2 fondness for home and family life. *n., pl.* **do mes tic i ties.**

domestic science, home economics.

dom i cile (dom′ə sīl), 1 a dwelling place; house; home. 2 place of permanent residence. One may have several residences, but only one legal domicile at a time. 3 settle in a domicile. 4 dwell; reside: *They domiciled in Italy part of the year.* 1,2 *n.,* 3,4 *v.,* **dom i ciled, dom i cil ing.**

dom i nance (dom′ə nəns), controlling influence; supreme authority; rule; control. *n.*

dom i nant (dom′ə nənt), 1 most powerful or influential; controlling; ruling; governing: *The principal was the dominant figure at the P.T.A. meeting.* 2 rising high above its surroundings; towering over: *Dominant hills sheltered the bay.* 3 the fifth note in a musical scale. G is the dominant in the key of C. 1,2 *adj.,* 3 *n.* —**dom′i nant ly,** *adv.*

dome (def. 1)
of a cathedral

dom i nate (dom′ə nāt), 1 control or rule by strength or power: *She spoke with the authority needed to dominate the meeting, and we did all she wanted without arguing. Dandelions will dominate over grass if they are not kept out.*

adj.	adjective	*n.*	noun
adv.	adverb	*prep.*	preposition
conj.	conjunction	*pron.*	pronoun
interj.	interjection	*v.*	verb
sing.	singular	*pl.*	plural

2 rise high above; tower over: *The mountain dominates the city and its harbor. v.,* **dom i nat ed, dom i nat ing.**

dom i na tion (dom/ə nā/shən), a dominating; control; rule: *The champion's long domination of archery ended when the challenger defeated her. n.*

dom i neer (dom/ə nir/), rule at one's own will; assert one's authority or opinions in an arrogant way; tyrannize: *The oldest child in a family may sometimes domineer over the younger children. The people finally refused to be domineered by the king. v.*

dom i neer ing (dom/ə nir/ing), inclined to domineer; arrogant; overbearing: *I dislike the domineering attitude of people who always want things done their own way. adj.*

Dom i nic (dom/ə nik), **Saint,** 1170-1221, Spanish priest who founded an order of preaching friars. *n.*

Do min i can (də min/ə kən), 1 of Saint Dominic or the religious order founded by him. 2 friar belonging to the Dominican order. 3 of or having to do with the Dominican Republic. 4 person born or living in the Dominican Republic. *1,3 adj., 2,4 n.*

Dominican Republic, country in the E part of the island of Hispaniola, in the West Indies. *Capital:* Santo Domingo.

dom i nie (dom/ə nē), 1 SCOTTISH. schoolmaster. 2 INFORMAL. clergyman. *n.*

do min ion (də min/yən), 1 power or right of governing and controlling; rule; control: *The ancient Romans had dominion over a large part of the world.* 2 territory under the control of one ruler or government. 3 **Dominion,** name formerly used for a self-governing country within the British Commonwealth. 4 Often, **Dominion.** (in Canada) relating to the country as a whole; national in scope. *1-3 n., 4 adj.*

dom i no (dom/ə nō), 1 **dominoes,** *pl.* game played with 28 flat, oblong pieces of bone, wood, etc., that are either blank or marked with dots. Players try to match pieces having blanks or the same number of dots. 2 one of the pieces used in the game of dominoes. 3 a loose cloak with a small mask covering the upper part of the face. It was formerly worn as a disguise at masquerades. 4 the small mask. *n., pl.* **dom i noes** or **dom i nos.**

don[1] (don), put on (clothing, etc.): *The knight donned his armor. v.,* **donned, don ning.** [contraction of *do on*]

don[2] (don), 1 **Don,** a Spanish title meaning Mr. or Sir: *Don Felipe.* 2 a head, fellow, or tutor of a college at Oxford or Cambridge University in England. *n.* [from Spanish *don,* from Latin *dominum* lord, master]

Don (don), river in SW Soviet Union. *n.*

do nate (dō/nāt), give money or help, especially to a fund or institution; contribute: *She donated $20 to the community chest. v.,* **do nat ed, do nat ing.**

do na tion (dō nā/shən), 1 gift; contribution: *The class decided to make a donation to UNICEF.* 2 a giving; donating. *n.*

done (dun), 1 finished or completed; through: *She is done with her homework.* 2 INFORMAL. worn out; exhausted. 3 cooked: *I want my steak well done.* 4 past participle of **do**[1]. *Have you done all your chores? 1-3 adj., 4 v.*

don jon (dun/jən), a large, strongly fortified tower of a castle. *n.*

Don Juan (don wän/), a legendary Spanish nobleman who led an immoral life.

don key (dong/kē), 1 a small animal somewhat like a horse but with longer ears, a shorter mane, and a tuft of hair at the end of its tail; ass. 2 a stubborn person. 3 a silly fool; stupid person. *n., pl.* **don keys.**

do nor (dō/nər), person who donates; giver; contributor. A blood donor is a person who gives blood for a transfusion. *n.*

Don Qui xo te (don ki hō/tē *or* don kwik/sət), hero of a famous novel of the same name by the Spanish writer Cervantes. Don Quixote is chivalrous and idealistic, but also foolish and impractical.

don't (dōnt), do not.

doo dle (dü/dl), 1 make drawings or marks absent-mindedly while talking or thinking. 2 drawing or mark made absent-mindedly. *1 v.,* **doo dled, doo dling;** *2 n.*

doo dle bug (dü/dl bug/), larva of the ant lion. *n.*

doo dler (düd/lər), person who doodles. *n.*

doom (düm), 1 fate. 2 an unhappy or terrible fate; ruin or death: *As the ship sank, the voyagers faced their doom.* 3 condemn to an unhappy or terrible fate: *The prisoner was doomed to death. Poor health doomed my cousin to an inactive life.* 4 judgment; sentence: *The judge pronounced the prisoner's doom.* 5 make a bad or unwelcome outcome certain: *The weather doomed our hopes for a picnic. 1,2,4 n., 3,5 v.*

dooms day (dümz/dā/), end of the world; Judgment Day. *n.*

door (dôr), 1 a movable slab of wood, stone, or metal to close an opening in a wall of a building. A room has a door through which one may enter or leave; a house or building has several doors. Doors turn on hinges or slide open and shut. 2 doorway: *The salesman had a foot in the door.* 3 room, house, or building to which a door belongs: *Her house is three doors down the street from ours.* 4 way to go in or out; way to get something: *a door to opportunity. The door to knowledge is study. n.*

lay at the door of, blame for.

out of doors, not in a house or building; outside.

door bell (dôr/bel/), bell inside a house to be rung by pressing a button or pulling a handle on the outside of a door as a signal that someone wishes to have the door opened. *n.*

door knob (dôr/nob/), handle on either side of a door, used for opening or closing the door. *n.*

door man (dôr/mən), 1 man whose work is opening the door of a hotel, store, apartment house, etc., for people going in or out. 2 man who guards a door or entrance. *n., pl.* **door men.**

door mat (dôr/mat/), mat placed near a door for wiping off the dirt from the bottom of one's shoes before entering. *n.*

door step (dôr/step/), step leading from an outside door to the ground. *n.*

door way (dôr/wā/), an opening in a wall where a door is. *n.*

door yard (dôr/yärd/), yard near the door of a house; yard around a house. *n.*

dope (dōp), 1 SLANG. a narcotic drug, such as opium or morphine. 2 SLANG. give dope to. 3 SLANG. information. 4 SLANG. a very stupid person. 5 a thick varnish or similar liquid applied to a fabric to strengthen or waterproof it. *1,3-5 n., 2 v.,* **doped, dop ing.**

Doric temple

Do ric (dôr/ik), of or having to do with the oldest and simplest kind of Greek architecture. *adj.*

dor mant (dôr/mənt), 1 sleeping;

seeming to sleep; not moving or feeling: *Bears and other animals that hibernate are dormant during the winter.* 2 without activity; inactive: *Many volcanoes are dormant. The artist's talent for painting was dormant until her teacher discovered it. adj.*

dormer (def. 2) and window

dor mer (dôr′mər), 1 an upright window that projects from a sloping roof. 2 the projecting part of a roof that contains such a window. *n.*

dor mi to ry (dôr′mə tôr′ē), 1 a building with many rooms for sleeping in. Many colleges have dormitories for students whose homes are in other cities. 2 room for sleeping in containing several beds. *n., pl.* **dor mi to ries.**

dor mouse (dôr′mous′), a small rodent that looks somewhat like a squirrel and sleeps all winter. *n., pl.* **dor mice** (dôr′mīs′).

dor sal (dôr′səl), of, on, or near the back: *A shark has a dorsal fin. adj.* —**dor′sal ly,** *adv.*

do ry (dôr′ē), rowboat with a narrow, flat bottom and high sides. It is often used by fishermen. *n., pl.* **do ries.**

dos age (dō′sij), 1 amount of a medicine to be given or taken at one time. 2 the giving of medicine in doses. *n.*

dose (dōs), 1 amount of a medicine to be given or taken at one time: *a dose of cough medicine.* 2 give medicine to in doses; treat with medicine: *The doctor dosed the sick child with penicillin.* 3 amount of anything given or taken at one time; portion: *Our boss always says that a good dose of work never hurt anyone.* 1,3 *n.,* 2 *v.,* **dosed, dos ing.**

dost (dust), OLD USE. do[1]. "Thou dost" means "you do" (singular). *v.*

Dos to ev ski (dos′tə yef′skē), **Feodor,** 1821-1881, Russian novelist. *n.*

dot (dot), 1 a tiny, round mark; point. There is a dot over each *i* in this line. 2 a small spot: *a blue necktie with white dots.* 3 mark with a dot or dots: *Dot your i's and j's.* 4 be here and there in: *Trees and bushes dotted the broad lawn.* 5 a short sound used in sending messages by telegraph or radio. 6 (in music) a tiny, round mark after a note or rest that makes it half again as long. 1,2,5,6 *n.,* 3,4 *v.,* **dot ted, dot ting. on the dot,** INFORMAL. at exactly the

right time: *Our train arrived on the dot.*

dot age (dō′tij), a weak-minded and childish condition that sometimes accompanies old age: *The old man was in his dotage and spent much of his time mumbling to himself. n.*

dot ard (dō′tərd), person who is weak-minded and childish from old age. *n.*

dote (dōt), be weak-minded and childish because of old age. *v.,* **dot ed, dot ing.**
dote on or **dote upon,** be foolishly fond of; be too fond of: *The parents dote on their only son, giving him everything he wants.*

doth (duth), OLD USE. does. "She doth" means "she does." *v.*

dot ing (dō′ting), foolishly fond; too fond: *Doting parents see no fault in their children. adj.* —**dot′ing ly,** *adv.*

dou ble (dub′əl), 1 twice as much, as many, as large, as strong, etc.: *She was given double pay for working on Sunday.* 2 twice; doubly: *I was paid double by mistake. Be double careful when you cross that street.* 3 number or amount that is twice as much: *Four is the double of two.* 4 make twice as much or twice as many: *He doubled his money in ten years by investing it wisely.* 5 become twice as much or twice as many: *Money left in a savings bank will double in about twenty years.* 6 made of two like parts; in a pair: *Double doors open wide.* 7 having two unlike parts; having two meanings, characters, etc. The spelling *b-e-a-r* has a double meaning: *carry* and *a certain animal.* 8 two (of everything) instead of one: *The blow on the head made him see double.* 9 take the place of another; substitute: *The principal is doubling for the teacher today.* 10 person or thing just like another. In a motion picture an actor often has a double to do the dangerous scenes. *Here is the double of your lost glove.* 11 serve two purposes; play two parts: *The chair doubled as a stepladder.* 12 fold; bend: *She doubled her slice of bread to make a sandwich.* 13 a fold; bend. 14 close tightly together; clench: *He doubled his fists in anger.* 15 bend or turn sharply backward: *The fox doubled on its tracks to get away from the dogs.* 16 a sharp backward bend or turn. 17 go around: *The ship doubled Cape Horn.* 18 having more than one set of petals: *Some roses are double; others are single.* 19 hit by which a batter gets to second base in baseball. 20 hit a double in baseball. 21 **doubles,** *pl.* game of tennis, etc., with two players on each side. 1,6,7,18 *adj.,* 2,8 *adv.,* 3,10,13,16,19,21 *n.,* 4,5,9,11,12,14,15,17,20 *v.,* **dou bled, dou bling.**

hat, āge, fär; let, ēqual, tėrm; it, īce; hot, ōpen, ôrder; oil, out; cup, pùt, rüle; ch, child; ng, long; sh, she; th, thin; ᴛʜ, then; zh, measure;

ə represents *a* in about, *e* in taken, *i* in pencil, *o* in lemon, *u* in circus.

double back, 1 fold over: *It ruins a book to double back the pages as a bookmark.* 2 go back the same way that one came: *The fox doubled back to avoid capture.*

double up, 1 fold up; curl up: *She spent the rainy day doubled up on the sofa, reading.* 2 bend over: *He doubled up with laughter.* 3 share room, bed, or quarters with another: *Since there was only one room left at the hotel, the two women doubled up for the night.*

on the double, quickly: *The teacher warned us to stop talking and get to work on the double.*

double bass (bās), a deep-toned stringed instrument shaped like a cello but much larger; bass viol; contrabass.

double bass
The four strings are played with a bow or by plucking with the fingers.

double concave, concave on both sides.

double convex, convex on both sides.

double cross, INFORMAL. act of treachery.

dou ble-cross (dub′əl krôs′), INFORMAL. promise to do one thing and then do another; be treacherous to. *v.* —**dou′ble-cross′er,** *n.*

dou ble-deal er (dub′əl dē′lər), person guilty of double-dealing. *n.*

dou ble-deal ing (dub′əl dē′ling), 1 a pretending to do one thing and then doing another; deceitful action or behavior. 2 ready to deceive; deceitful. 1 *n.,* 2 *adj.*

dou ble head er (dub′əl hed′ər), two games played one after another on the same day. *n.*

dou ble-joint ed (dub′əl join′tid), having joints that let fingers, arms, legs, etc., bend in unusual ways. *adj.*

adj.	adjective	*n.*	noun
adv.	adverb	*prep.*	preposition
conj.	conjunction	*pron.*	pronoun
interj.	interjection	*v.*	verb
sing.	singular	*pl.*	plural

dou ble-park (dub′əl pärk′), park (a car, etc.) beside another car that is occupying the area where parking is allowed. *v.*

double play, a play in baseball in which two base runners are put out.

dou ble-quick (dub′əl kwik′), 1 the next quickest step to a run in marching. 2 very quick. 3 in double-quick time. 1 *n.*, 2 *adj.*, 3 *adv.*

dou blet (dub′lit), a man's close-fitting jacket. Men in Europe wore doublets from the 1400's to the 1600's. *n.*

doublet

dou ble-talk (dub′əl tôk′), speech that is purposely meaningless, but seems meaningful because normal words and intonations are mixed in. *n.*

dou bloon (du blün′), a former Spanish gold coin. Its value varied from about $5 to about $16. *n.*

dou bly (dub′lē), 1 twice as; twice: *Be doubly careful when you swim in the lake alone.* 2 two at a time. *adv.*

doubt (dout), 1 not believe or trust; not be sure of; feel uncertain about: *Do you doubt what I say? He doubted if we would arrive home on time.* 2 difficulty in believing: *Our faith helped overcome our doubt.* 3 an uncertain state of mind: *We were in doubt as to the right road.* 4 an uncertain condition of affairs: *The ship's fate is still in doubt.* 1 *v.*, 2-4 *n.* —**doubt′er,** *n.*

no doubt or **without doubt,** surely; certainly: *No doubt we will win in the end.*

doubt ful (dout′fəl), 1 full of doubt; not sure; uncertain: *We are doubtful about the weather for tomorrow.* 2 causing doubt; open to question or suspicion: *His sly answers made his sincerity doubtful.* *adj.* —**doubt′ful ly,** *adv.*

doubt less (dout′lis), 1 without doubt; surely. 2 probably. 3 having no

doubts; sure; certain. 1,2 *adv.*, 3 *adj.* —**doubt′less ly,** *adv.* —**doubt′lessness,** *n.*

dough (dō), 1 a soft, thick mixture of flour, milk, fat, and other materials for baking. Bread, biscuits, cake, and pie crust are made from dough. 2 INFORMAL. money. *n.* —**dough′like′,** *adj.*

dough nut (dō′nut′), a small cake of sweetened dough cooked in deep fat. A doughnut is usually made in the shape of a ring. *n.*

dough ty (dou′tē), strong and bold; stout; brave; hardy: *King Arthur's doughty knights fought gallantly.* *adj.*, **dough ti er, dough ti est.**

dough y (dō′ē), of or like dough; half-baked; soft and thick; pale and flabby. *adj.*, **dough i er, dough i est.**

Doug lass (dug′ləs), **Frederick,** 1817-1895, American author, orator, and Abolitionist who was himself once a slave.

dour (dûr *or* dour), 1 gloomy or sullen: *They sulked in dour silence.* 2 stern; severe: *Her dour remarks frightened me.* *adj.* —**dour′ly,** *adv.* —**dour′ness,** *n.*

douse (dous), 1 plunge into water or any other liquid. 2 throw water over; drench: *We quickly doused the flames.* 3 INFORMAL. put out; extinguish: *Douse the lights.* *v.*, **doused, dous ing.**

dove[1] (duv), pigeon, especially one of the smaller kinds. The dove is often a symbol of peace. *n.* [Old English *dūfe*]

dove[2] (dōv), dived; a past tense of **dive.** *v.*

dove cot (duv′kot′), dovecote. *n.*

dove cote (duv′kōt′), a small house or shelter for doves or pigeons. *n.*

Do ver (dō′vər), 1 seaport in SE England, the nearest English port to France. 2 narrow channel or strait between N France and SE England. 3 capital of Delaware, in the central part. *n.*

dovetails (def. 1)

dove tail (duv′tāl′), 1 projection at the end of a piece of wood, metal, etc., that can be fitted into a corresponding opening at the end of another piece to form a joint. 2 the joint formed in this way. 3 fasten, join, or fit together with dovetails. 4 fit together exactly: *The various pieces of evidence dovetailed so completely that the mystery was solved at once.* 1,2 *n.*, 3,4 *v.*

dow a ger (dou′ə jər), 1 woman who

holds some title or property from her dead husband: *The queen and her mother-in-law, the queen dowager, were both present.* 2 INFORMAL. a dignified, elderly lady. *n.*

dow di ly (dou′dl ē), in a dowdy manner; shabbily. *adv.*

dow di ness (dou′dē nis), dowdy quality or condition; shabbiness. *n.*

dow dy (dou′dē), 1 poorly dressed; not neat; not stylish; shabby. 2 a poorly dressed woman. 1 *adj.*, **dow di er, dow di est;** 2 *n.*, *pl.* **dow dies.**

dow el (dou′əl), peg on a piece of wood, metal, etc., made to fit into a corresponding hole on another piece, so as to form a joint fastening the two pieces together. *n.*

DOWEL

dow er (dou′ər), 1 a widow's share for life of her dead husband's property. 2 dowry. 3 provide with a dower; endow. 1,2 *n.*, 3 *v.*

down[1] (doun), 1 from a higher to a lower place or condition: *They ran down from the top of the hill. The temperature has gone down.* 2 in a lower place or condition: *Down in the valley the fog still lingers (adv.). The sun is down (adj.).* 3 from an earlier to a later time: *The story has come down through many years.* 4 down along, through, or into: *ride down a hill, walk down a street, sail down a river.* 5 going or pointed down: *the down elevator.* 6 put down; throw down; get down: *She downed the medicine with one swallow. I was downed in a fight. Down, Fido!* 7 sick; ill: *We are both down with colds.* 8 sad; discouraged: *I felt down about my grades.* 9 piece of bad luck: *the ups and downs of life.* 10 actually; really: *Stop talking, and get down to work.* 11 on paper; in writing: *Take down what I say.* 12 in cash when bought: *You can pay $10 down and the rest later (adv.). We made a down payment on a new car (adj.).* 13 (in football) a play from scrimmage. A team has four downs to make at least ten yards. 1-3,10-12 *adv.*, 4 *prep.*, 2,5,7,8,12 *adj.*, 6 *v.*, 9,13 *n.* [Old English *adūne*, from *of dūne* from the hill]

down and out, completely without health, money, friends, etc.; wretched; forsaken.

down on, INFORMAL. angry at; having a grudge against: *The other players were*

down on him for quitting the game.
down with, put down; throw down: *Down with tyranny!*

down² (doun), 1 soft feathers: *the down of a young bird.* 2 soft hair or fluff: *The down on a boy's chin develops into a beard.* n. [from a Scandinavian word of the 1300's, such as Icelandic *dūnn*]

down³ (doun). Usually, **downs,** *pl.* rolling, grassy land. n. [Old English *dūn* hill]

down cast (doun′kast′), 1 directed downward: *They were ashamed and stood before us with downcast eyes.* 2 dejected; sad; discouraged: *After all our plans failed, we felt very downcast.* adj.

down fall (doun′fôl′), 1 a coming to ruin; sudden overthrow: *the downfall of an empire. Pride caused their downfall.* 2 a heavy rain or snow. n.

down grade (doun′grād′), 1 a downward slope. 2 lower in position, importance, reputation, etc.: *downgrade an employee. He downgrades people he does not like, in spite of their merits.* 1 n., 2 v., **down grad ed, down grad ing.**
on the downgrade, growing less in strength, power, value, etc.; declining.

down heart ed (doun′här′tid), in low spirits; discouraged; dejected; depressed. *adj.* —**down′heart′ed ly,** *adv.* —**down′heart′ed ness,** n.

down hill (doun′hil′), 1 down the slope of a hill; downward. 2 going or sloping downward: *a downhill race.* 1 adv., 2 adj.
go downhill, get worse: *Our business has been going downhill since we raised our prices.*

down pour (doun′pôr′), a heavy rain. n.

down right (doun′rīt′), 1 thorough; complete: *a downright fool, a downright lie.* 2 thoroughly; completely: *They were downright rude to me.* 3 plain; positive: *Her downright answer left no doubt as to what she thought.* 1,3 adj., 2 adv.

down stairs (doun′sterz′ or doun′-starz′), 1 down the stairs: *I slipped and fell downstairs.* 2 on or to a lower floor: *Look downstairs for my glasses (adv.). The downstairs rooms are dark (adj.).* 3 the lower floor or floors: *She lived in the downstairs of the house.* 1,2 adv., 2 adj., 3 n.

down stream (doun′strēm′), with the current of a stream; down a stream: *The raft floated downstream (adv.). The downstream current was swift after the flood (adj.). adv., adj.*

down town (doun′toun′), to or in the central or main business section of a town or city: *My parents went down-*

town shopping (adv.). Her office is in downtown Chicago (adj.). adv., adj.

down trod den (doun′trod′n), trampled upon; oppressed. *adj.*

down under, Australia and New Zealand.

down ward (doun′wərd), 1 toward a lower place or condition: *The bird swooped downward on its prey (adv.). The downward trip on the elevator was very slow (adj.).* 2 toward a later time: *There has been great progress in science from the 18th century downward.* 1 adv., adj., 2 adv.

down wards (doun′wərdz), downward. adv.

down wind (doun′wind′), in the same direction as the wind: *a downwind drift (adj.). The boat glided easily downwind (adv.). adj., adv.*

down y (dou′nē), 1 of soft feathers or hair: *a downy pillow.* 2 covered with soft feathers or hair: *a downy chick.* 3 like down; soft and fluffy: *A kitten's fur is downy. adj.,* **down i er, down i est.**

dow ry (dou′rē), 1 money or property that a woman brings to her husband when she marries him. 2 gift of nature; natural talent: *Good health and intelligence are a precious dowry. n., pl.* **dow ries.**

dox ol o gy (dok sol′ə jē), hymn or statement praising God. One familiar doxology begins: "Praise God from whom all blessings flow." *n., pl.* **dox ol o gies.**

Doyle (doil), Sir **Arthur Conan,** 1859-1930, English writer, author of the Sherlock Holmes detective stories. n.

doz., dozen or dozens.

doze (dōz), 1 sleep lightly; be half asleep: *After dinner the old man dozed in his chair.* 2 a light sleep; nap. 1 v., **dozed, doz ing;** 2 n.
doze off, fall into a doze: *The cat dozed off by the fire.*

doz en (duz′n), group of 12; 12: *We had to have dozens of chairs for the party. We will need three dozen eggs and a dozen rolls. n., pl.* **doz ens** or *(after a number)* **doz en.**

DP or **D.P.,** displaced person.

Dr., Doctor.

drab (drab), 1 not attractive; dull; monotonous: *the drab houses of the smoky, dingy mining town.* 2 dull brownish-gray. 3 a dull brownish-gray color. 1,2 adj., **drab ber, drab best;** 3 n. —**drab′ly,** adv. —**drab′ness,** n.

drach ma (drak′mə), 1 unit of money of modern Greece, worth about 3¹/₂ cents. 2 an ancient Greek silver coin. n.

draft (draft), 1 current of air: *I caught cold sitting in a draft.* 2 device for

hat, āge, fär; let, ēqual, tėrm;
it, īce; hot, ōpen, ôrder;
oil, out; cup, pùt, rüle; ch, child;
ng, long; sh, she; th, thin;
₮H, then; zh, measure;

ə represents *a* in about,
e in taken, *i* in pencil,
o in lemon, *u* in circus.

controlling a current of air. Opening the draft of a furnace makes the fire burn faster. 3 a plan; sketch: *Before starting to build, we had the architect make a draft of how the finished house would look.* 4 make a plan or sketch of. 5 a rough copy: *She made two drafts of her book report before she handed in the final form.* 6 write out a rough copy of: *Three members of the club drafted a new set of rules to be discussed and voted on by the membership.* 7 selection of persons for some special purpose. Men needed as soldiers are supplied to the army by draft during periods of war. 8 persons selected for some special purpose. 9 select for some special purpose: *If nobody volunteers to help me, I will draft someone.* 10 a pulling of loads. 11 for pulling loads: *A big, strong horse or ox is a draft animal.* 12 the pulling of a net to catch fish. 13 all the fish caught in a net at one time. 14 a heavy demand or drain on anything: *My long illness was a draft on my resources.* 15 a written order from one person or bank to another, requiring the payment of a stated amount of money. 16 depth of water that a ship needs for floating; depth to which a ship sinks in water. A ship's draft is greater when it is loaded than when it is empty. 17 a single act of drinking: *She emptied the glass at one draft.* 18 amount taken in a single drink. 1-3,5,7,8,10,12-18 n., 4,6,9 v., 11 adj. Also, **draught.** —**draft′er,** n.

draft ee (draf tē′), person who is drafted for military service. n.

draft i ness (draf′tē nis), drafty condition. n.

drafts man (drafts′mən), person who makes plans or sketches. A draftsman draws designs or diagrams from which buildings and machines are made. n., pl. **drafts men.** Also, **draughtsman.**

drafts man ship (drafts′mən ship), work of a draftsman. n.

draft y (draf′tē), 1 in a current of air: *I had a drafty seat near the window.* 2 having many currents of air: *a drafty room. adj.,* **draft i er, draft i est.**

drag (drag), 1 pull or move along

draggle

heavily or slowly; pull or draw along the ground: *A team of horses dragged the big log out of the forest. I dragged along on my sprained ankle.* 2 go too slowly: *Time drags when you have nothing to do.* 3 pull a net, hook, harrow, etc., over or along for some purpose: *The fishermen dragged the lake for fish.* 4 net, hook, harrow, etc., used in dragging. 5 anything that holds back; obstruction; hindrance: *Some old ideas are a drag on progress. If you don't practice, you'll be a drag on the team.* 6 SLANG. take part in a drag race. 1-3,6 *v.*, **dragged, drag ging;** 4,5 *n.*

drag gle (drag′əl), 1 make or become wet or dirty by dragging through mud, water, dust, etc. 2 follow slowly; lag behind; straggle. *v.*, **drag gled, drag gling.**

drag net (drag′net′), 1 net pulled over the bottom of a river, pond, etc., or along the ground. Dragnets are used to catch fish and small birds. 2 set of plans for catching or gathering in: *All kinds of criminals were caught in the police dragnet. n.*

drag on (drag′ən), (in old stories) a huge, fierce animal supposed to look like a snake with wings and claws, which often breathed out fire and smoke. *n.*

drag on fly (drag′ən flī′), a large, harmless insect, with a long, slender body and two pairs of gauzy wings, often found near water. It darts about catching flies, mosquitoes, and other insects. *n., pl.* **drag on flies.**

dra goon (drə gün′), 1 a mounted soldier trained to fight on foot or on horseback. 2 compel by oppression or persecution: *The prisoner was dragooned into signing a false confession.* 1 *n.*, 2 *v.*

drag race, race between cars to determine which can accelerate faster over a given distance.

drain (drān), 1 draw off or flow off slowly: *That ditch drains water from the swamp. The water drains into the river.* 2 draw water or other liquid from; empty or dry by draining: *The farmers drained the swamps to get more land for crops. In one drink he drained the cup. Set the dishes here to drain.* 3 channel or pipe for carrying off water or waste

of any kind. 4 take away from slowly; use up little by little: *The war drained the country of its people and money.* 5 a slow taking away; using up little by little; draining: *Working or playing too hard is a drain on your strength.* 1,2,4 *v.*, 3,5 *n.*

drain age (drā′nij), 1 act or process of draining; drawing off or flowing off of water: *The drainage of swamps improved the park.* 2 system of channels or pipes for carrying off water or waste of any kind. 3 what is drained off. *n.*

drain pipe (drān′pīp′), pipe for carrying off water or other liquid. *n.*

drake (drāk), a male duck. *n.*

Drake (drāk), Sir **Francis,** 1540?-1596, English admiral. He was the first Englishman to sail around the world. *n.*

dram (dram), 1 a small weight. In apothecaries' weight, 8 drams make one ounce; in avoirdupois weight, 16 drams make one ounce. 2 a small drink of intoxicating liquor. *n.*

dra ma (drä′mə *or* dram′ə), 1 a play such as one sees in a theater; story written to be acted out by actors on the stage. 2 the art of writing, acting, or producing plays: *He is studying drama.* 3 series of happenings in real life that seem like those of a play: *The history of America is a great and thrilling drama. n., pl.* **dra mas.**

dra mat ic (drə mat′ik), 1 of drama; having to do with plays: *a dramatic actor.* 2 seeming like a play or story; full of action or feeling; exciting: *a dramatic story, the dramatic reunion of a family separated during wartime. adj.*

dra mat i cal ly (drə mat′ik lē), in a dramatic manner; emotionally. *adv.*

dra mat ics (drə mat′iks), 1 *pl. in form, sing. in use.* art of acting or producing plays: *Dramatics is taught in some colleges.* 2 *pl. in form and use.* plays given by amateurs: *Dramatics are presented in many theaters in the summer.* 3 *pl. in form and use.* INFORMAL. tendency to show off. *n.*

dram a tist (dram′ə tist), writer of plays; playwright. *n.*

dram a ti za tion (dram′ə tə zā′shən), 1 act of dramatizing. 2 what is dramatized: *That play is a dramatization of the life of Joan of Arc. n.*

dram a tize (dram′ə tīz), 1 make a drama of; arrange in the form of a play: *The children dramatized the story of Rip Van Winkle.* 2 show or express in a dramatic way; make seem exciting and thrilling: *The speaker dramatized her story with many actions and gestures. v.*, **dram a tized, dram a tiz ing.**

drank (drangk), past tense of **drink.** *The hungry cat drank its milk rapidly. v.*

drape (drāp), 1 cover or hang with

cloth falling loosely in folds, especially as a decoration: *The buildings were draped with red, white, and blue bunting.* 2 arrange (clothes, hangings, etc.) to hang loosely in folds: *The actors draped the capes around each other's shoulders.* 3 cloth hung in folds: *There were heavy drapes at the windows.* 1,2 *v.*, **draped, drap ing;** 3 *n.*

dra per y (drā′pər ē), 1 hangings or clothing arranged in folds, especially such hangings hung as curtains: *The gay colors of the drapery made the living room bright and cheery.* 2 cloths or fabrics; dry goods. *n., pl.* **dra per ies.**

dras tic (dras′tik), acting with force or violence; extreme: *The police took drastic measures to put a stop to the wave of robberies. adj.* —**dras′ti cal ly,** *adv.*

draught (draft), draft. *n., v., adj.*

draughts (drafts), the game of checkers (a term used in Great Britain). *n.*

draughts man (drafts′mən), draftsman. *n., pl.* **draughts men.**

draw (drô), 1 cause to move by the use of force or effort; pull or drag; haul: *The horses drew the wagon.* 2 pull out; pull up; cause to come out; take out; get: *Draw a pail of water from the well. She drew ten dollars from the bank. Until you hear both sides of the argument, draw no conclusions.* 3 act of drawing: *The cowgirl who was skilled with guns had a quick draw and a fine aim.* 4 come or go; move: *We drew near the fire to get warm.* 5 attract: *A parade draws a crowd.* 6 make a picture or likeness of with pencil, pen, chalk, crayon, etc.: *Draw a circle. He draws very well for a six-year-old.* 7 describe: *The characters in this novel are not fully drawn; they seem unreal.* 8 make a current of air to carry off smoke: *The chimney does not draw well.* 9 breathe in; inhale; take in: *Draw a deep breath.* 10 a tie in a game. If neither side wins, it is a draw. 11 make long or longer; stretch: *draw out a rubber band. His speech was drawn too long. The girls drew the rope taut.* 12 sink to a depth of; need for floating: *A ship draws more water when it is loaded than when it is empty. The big ship draws 28 feet of water.* 13 a small land basin into or through which water drains; kind of valley: *We found the strayed cattle grazing in a draw.* 1,2,4-9,11,12 *v.*, **drew, drawn, draw ing;** 3,10,13 *n.*

draw on, come near; approach: *Evening drew on.*

draw oneself up, stand up straight: *She drew herself up to her full height.*

draw out, persuade to talk: *It is hard to draw out a shy person.*

draw up, 1 arrange in order: *The marchers were drawn up in formation for the parade.* 2 write out in proper form: *The lawyer drew up my mother's will.* 3 stop: *A car drew up in front of the house.*

draw back (drô′bak′), something that makes a situation or experience less complete or satisfying; unfavorable condition; disadvantage: *Our trip was interesting but the rainy weather was a drawback. n.*

draw bridge (drô′brij′), bridge that can be entirely or partly lifted, lowered, or moved to one side. In old castles drawbridges were lifted to keep out enemies. A drawbridge over a river is lifted to let boats pass. *n.*

drawer (drôr *for 1,3;* drô′ər *for 2*), 1 box with handles built to slide in and out of a table, desk, or bureau: *He kept his shirts in the dresser drawer.* 2 person or thing that draws. 3 **drawers,** *pl.* undergarment fitting over the legs and around the waist. *n.*

draw ing (drô′ing), 1 picture, sketch, plan, or design done with pencil, pen, chalk, crayon, etc. 2 the making of such a picture, sketch, plan, or design; representing objects by lines. 3 lottery. *n.*

drawing room, room for receiving or entertaining guests; parlor.

drawl (drôl), 1 talk in a slow way, drawing out the vowels: *He drawled his words in imitation of his favorite movie cowboy.* 2 such a way of talking; speech of someone who drawls: *The old woman sat back in her rocking chair and spoke with a calm, casual drawl.* 1 *v.,* 2 *n.*

drawn (drôn), 1 past participle of **draw.** *That old horse has drawn many loads.* 2 made tense; strained: *a face drawn and stiff with pain.* 1 *v.,* 2 *adj.*

dray (drā), a low, strong cart for carrying heavy loads. *n.*

dray man (drā′mən), person who drives a dray. *n., pl.* **dray men.**

dread (dred), 1 fear greatly (what is to come); feel terror or uneasiness about (what is to happen): *I dreaded my visits to the dentist. My cat dreads water.* 2 great fear of what is to come; feeling of terror or uneasiness about what is to happen. 3 dreaded; fearful; terrible: *The dread day of the trial was approaching.* 4 held in awe; awe-inspiring: *the dread sight of the immense, glowing volcano.* 1 *v.,* 2 *n.,* 3,4 *adj.*

dread ful (dred′fəl), 1 causing dread; fearful; terrible: *a fairy tale about a dreadful dragon.* 2 very bad; very unpleasant: *I have a dreadful cold. adj.* —**dread′ful ness,** *n.*

dread ful ly (dred′fə lē), 1 in a dreadful manner. 2 very; exceedingly. *adv.*

---

dread nought or **dread naught** (dred′nôt′), a big, powerful battleship with heavy armor and large guns. *n.*

dream (drēm), 1 images passing through the mind during sleep: *I had a bad dream last night.* 2 something unreal like a dream; daydream: *Sometimes when I don't want to study, I sit at my desk and have dreams about faraway places.* 3 imagine with the mind during sleep; have a dream or dreams: *I dreamed that I was flying.* 4 have daydreams; form fancies: *For years they dreamed of fame and riches.* 5 think of (something) as possible; imagine: *The day seemed so bright that we never dreamed it would rain.* 6 something having great beauty or charm: *It was a dream of a vacation.* 1,2,6 *n.,* 3-5 *v.,* **dreamed** or **dreamt, dream ing.** —**dream′like′,** *adj.*

dream er (drē′mər), 1 person who dreams. 2 person whose ideas do not fit real conditions. *n.*

dream i ly (drē′mə lē), in a dreamy manner. *adv.*

dream i ness (drē′mē nis), a dreamy condition. *n.*

dream land (drēm′land′), 1 place where a person seems to be when he is dreaming. 2 unreal place. 3 sleep. *n.*

dreamt (dremt), dreamed; a past tense and a past participle of **dream.** *v.*

dream y (drē′mē), 1 full of dreams: *a dreamy sleep.* 2 like a dream; vague; dim: *a dreamy recollection.* 3 fond of daydreaming; fanciful; not practical: *a dreamy person.* 4 causing dreams; soothing: *a dreamy lullaby. adj.,* **dream i er, dream i est.**

drear (drir), OLD USE. dreary. *adj.*

drear i ly (drir′ə lē), in a dreary manner; dismally. *adv.*

drear i ness (drir′ē nis), dreary condition; cheerlessness. *n.*

drear y (drir′ē), without cheer; dull; gloomy; *A cold, rainy day is dreary. adj.,* **drear i er, drear i est.**

dredge¹ (def. 1)

dredge¹ (drej), 1 machine with a scoop or series of buckets for cleaning out or deepening a harbor or channel. 2 clean out or deepen (a channel, harbor, etc.) with a dredge. 3 apparatus

---

hat, āge, fär; let, ēqual, tėrm;
it, īce; hot, ōpen, ôrder;
oil, out; cup, pút, rüle; ch, child;
ng, long; sh, she; th, thin;
ŦH, then; zh, measure;

ə represents *a* in about,
e in taken, *i* in pencil,
o in lemon, *u* in circus.

---

with a net, used for gathering oysters, etc. It is dragged along the bottom of a river or the sea. 4 bring up or gather with a dredge. 1,3 *n.,* 2,4 *v.,* **dredged, dredg ing.** [origin uncertain]

dredge² (drej), sprinkle: *The cook dredged the meat with flour. v.,* **dredged, dredg ing.** [apparently from Middle English *dredge* a grain mixture, from French of the 1300's *dragie* sweetmeats]

dredg er (drej′ər), 1 person who dredges. 2 boat used in dredging. *n.*

dregs (dregz), 1 the solid bits of matter that settle to the bottom of a liquid: *After pouring the coffee I rinsed the dregs out of the coffeepot.* 2 the least desirable part: *the dregs of humanity. n.pl.*

drench (drench), wet thoroughly; soak: *A heavy rain drenched the campers and they had to dry out their wet clothing. v.*

Dres den (drez′dən), city in SE East Germany, on the Elbe River. *n.*

dress (dres), 1 an outer garment worn by women, girls, and babies. 2 clothes; clothing: *I think less about dress than my best friend does.* 3 put clothes on: *Please dress the baby. I dressed quickly because I was late.* 4 wear clothes properly and attractively: *Some people don't know how to dress.* 5 decorate; adorn: *The store windows were dressed for Christmas.* 6 make ready for use; prepare: *The butcher dressed the chicken by pulling out the feathers, cutting off the head and feet, and taking out the insides.* 7 comb, brush, and arrange (hair): *She had her hair dressed for the party.* 8 put medicine, bandages, etc., on (a wound or sore): *The nurse dressed the wound every day.* 9 form in a straight line: *The sergeant ordered the soldiers to dress their ranks.* 10 smooth; finish: *to dress leather.* 1,2 *n., pl.* **dress es;** 3-10 *v.,* **dressed** or **drest, dress ing.**

dress down, 1 scold; rebuke. 2 beat; thrash.

dress up, put on one's best clothes.

dress er¹ (dres′ər), 1 person who dresses (himself, another person, a shop

adj. adjective	*n.* noun
adv. adverb	*prep.* preposition
conj. conjunction	*pron.* pronoun
interj. interjection	*v.* verb
sing. singular	*pl.* plural

window, etc.). 2 tool or machine to prepare things for use. *n.* [*dress* + *-er*[1]]

dress er[2] (dres′ər), 1 piece of furniture with drawers for clothes and usually a mirror; bureau. 2 piece of furniture with shelves for dishes. *n.* [from French of the 1400's *dresseur*, from *dresser* arrange]

dress ing (dres′ing), 1 medicine, bandage, etc., put on a wound or sore. 2 mixture of bread crumbs, seasoning, etc., used to stuff chicken, turkey, etc. 3 sauce for salads, fish, meat, etc. 4 act of one that dresses. *n.*

dressing gown, a loose robe worn while dressing or resting.

dressing table, table with a mirror, at which a person sits to comb the hair, put on make-up, etc.

dress mak er (dres′mā′kər), person whose work is making dresses, etc. *n.*

dress mak ing (dres′mā′king), a making of dresses, etc. *n.*

dress rehearsal, rehearsal of a play with costumes and scenery just as for a regular performance.

dress y (dres′ē), INFORMAL. 1 fond of wearing showy clothes. 2 stylish; fashionable. *adj.,* **dress i er, dress i est.**

drest (drest), dressed; a past tense and a past participle of **dress.** *v.*

drew (drü), past tense of **draw.** *He drew a picture of his mother. v.*

drib ble (drib′əl), 1 flow or let flow in drops or small amounts; trickle: *Gasoline dribbled from the leak in the tank.* 2 let saliva run from the mouth; drool: *Babies dribble on their bibs.* 3 a dropping; dripping; trickle: *There's a dribble of milk running down your chin.* 4 move (a ball) along by bouncing it or giving it short kicks: *dribble a basketball, dribble a soccer ball.* 5 act of dribbling a ball. 1,2,4 *v.,* **drib bled, drib bling;** 3,5 *n.*

drib let (drib′lit), a small amount: *He paid off his big debt in driblets, a dollar or two a week. n.*

dried (drīd), past tense and past participle of **dry.** *I dried my hands. The dishes have already been dried. v.*

dri er (drī′ər), 1 more dry: *This towel is drier than that one.* 2 person or thing that dries. 3 dryer. 1 *adj., comparative of* **dry;** 2,3 *n.*

dries (drīz), a present tense of **dry.**

Dad washes the dishes and Mother dries them. v.

dri est (drī′ist), most dry: *Which is the driest towel? adj., superlative of* **dry.**

drift (drift), 1 carry or be carried along by currents of water or air: *The wind drifted the boat onto the rocks. A raft drifts if it is not steered.* 2 move or appear to move aimlessly: *People drifted in and out of the meeting.* 3 go along without knowing or caring where one is going: *Some people have a purpose in life; others just drift.* 4 a drifting: *the drift of an iceberg.* 5 direction of drifting: *The drift of the Gulf Stream is to the north.* 6 tendency or trend: *Many politicians watch the drift of public opinion to see what to do next.* 7 direction of thought; meaning: *Please explain that again; I did not quite get the drift of your words.* 8 anything carried along by wind, water, or ice. 9 pile or be piled into heaps: *The strong wind drifted the snow. The snow drifted along the fence.* 10 snow, sand, etc., heaped up by the wind: *After the heavy snow there were deep drifts in the yard.* 11 distance that a ship or aircraft is off course because of currents. 1-3,9 *v.,* 4-8,10,11 *n.* —**drift′er,** *n.*

drift wood (drift′wud′), wood carried along by water or washed ashore from the water. *n.*

drill[1] (def. 1) It has two handles so that it may be used vertically or horizontally. The cutting part, or bit, works like an auger.

drill[1] (dril), 1 tool or machine for boring holes. 2 bore a hole in; pierce with a drill. 3 teach by having the learner do a thing over and over: *The sergeant drilled the new soldiers.* 4 teaching or training by having the learners do a thing over and over for practice: *The teacher gave the class plenty of drill in arithmetic. The new band members had drills in marching every day.* 1,4 *n.,* 2,3 *v.* [from Dutch *dril,* from *drillen* to bore] —**drill′er,** *n.*

drill[2] (dril), machine for planting seeds in rows. It makes a small furrow, drops the seed, and then covers the furrow. *n.* [origin uncertain]

dri ly (drī′lē), dryly. *adv.*

drink (dringk), 1 swallow anything liquid: *Cats like to drink milk. We drank from paper cups.* 2 liquid swallowed or

to be swallowed: *Water is a good drink to quench one's thirst.* 3 portion of a liquid: *Please give me a drink of milk.* 4 suck up; absorb: *The dry ground drank up the rain.* 5 alcoholic liquor. 6 drink alcoholic liquor. 1,4,6 *v.,* **drank, drunk, drink ing;** 2,3,5 *n.*

drink in, take in through the senses with eagerness and pleasure: *Our ears drank in the music.*

drink to, drink in honor of; drink with good wishes for: *The guests drank to the happiness of the bride and groom.*

drink er (dring′kər), 1 person who drinks. 2 person who drinks alcoholic liquor often or too much. *n.*

drip (drip), 1 fall or let fall in drops: *Rain drips from an umbrella. The awning dripped water onto her head.* 2 a falling in drops. 3 be so wet that drops fall: *My forehead was dripping with perspiration.* 4 liquid that falls in drops. 1,3 *v.,* **dripped** or **dript, drip ping;** 2,4 *n.*

drip pings (drip′ingz), the melted fat and juice that have dripped down from meat while it was being cooked. *n.pl.*

dript (dript), dripped; a past tense and a past participle of **drip.** *v.*

drive (drīv), 1 make go: *Drive the dog away. Drive the nails into the board. The wind drives the windmill. I have so much homework that it may soon drive me mad.* 2 make go where one wishes; direct the movement of: *drive a team of horses. Can you drive a car?* 3 go or carry in an automobile or carriage; carry in an automobile: *We want to drive through the mountains on the way home. She drove us to the station.* 4 trip in an automobile or carriage: *On Sunday we took a drive in the country.* 5 road to drive on: *He built a drive from the street to his house.* 6 force; urge on: *Hunger drove them to steal.* 7 a driving force; pressure: *Ambition is a drive to action.* 8 carry out with vigor; bring about: *She drove a good bargain at the store.* 9 vigor; energy: *a person with drive.* 10 a special effort of a group for some purpose; campaign: *The town had a drive on to get money for charity.* 11 work hard or compel to work hard: *They said their boss drove them too hard.* 12 dash or rush with force; dash violently: *The ship drove on the rocks.* 13 (in sports) hit very hard and fast: *drive a golf ball.* 14 a very hard, fast hit: *The batter's drive went into deep left field.* 15 act of driving. 16 the thing or things driven: *a drive of cattle.* 17 get or make by drilling, boring, etc.: *drive a well.* 18 part that drives machinery. 19 the means by which power is transmitted to the wheels in a motor vehicle: *rear-wheel drive, four-wheel drive.* 1-

3,6,8,11-13,17 *v.*, **drove, driv en, driv ing;** 4,5,7,9,10,14-16,18,19 *n.*

drive at, mean; intend: *What are you driving at?*

let drive, strike; aim: *The fighter let drive a left to the jaw.*

drive-in (drīv′in′), 1 arranged and equipped so that customers may drive in and be served or entertained while remaining seated in their cars: *a drive-in movie theater, a drive-in bank.* 2 place so arranged and equipped. 1 *adj.,* 2 *n.*

driv el (driv′əl), 1 let saliva run from the mouth. 2 saliva running from the mouth. 3 talk or say in a stupid, foolish manner; talk nonsense. 4 silly talk; nonsense. 1,3 *v.,* 2,4 *n.* —**driv′el er,** *n.*

driv en (driv′ən), past participle of **drive.** *My aunt has often driven me to the zoo. v.*

driv er (drī′vər), 1 person or thing that drives. 2 person who drives an automobile or carriage. 3 person who makes people under him work very hard. 4 a golf club with a wooden head. It is used in hitting the ball off the tee. *n.*

drive way (drīv′wā′), road to drive on. A driveway leads from a house or garage to the road. *n.*

driz zle (driz′əl), 1 rain gently, in very small drops like mist. 2 very small drops of rain like mist: *A steady drizzle made it hard to see across the muddy football field.* 1 *v.,* **driz zled, driz zling;** 2 *n.*

driz zly (driz′lē), drizzling. *adj.,* **driz zli er, driz zli est.**

droll (drōl), odd and amusing; quaint and laughable: *We smiled at the monkey's droll tricks. adj.* —**droll′ness,** *n.*

droll er y (drō′lər ē), 1 something odd and amusing; laughable trick. 2 quaint humor. 3 a jesting; joking. *n., pl.* **droll er ies.**

drom e dar y (drom′ə der′ē), a swift camel with one hump and short hair, found in Arabia and northern Africa and used for riding; Arabian camel. *n., pl.* **drom e dar ies.**

drone (drōn), 1 a male bee, especially a male honey bee. Drones do not sting, gather honey, or help in the upkeep of the hive. 2 make a deep, continuous humming sound: *It was so quiet they could hear the bees drone among the flowers.* 3 a deep continuous humming sound: *the drone of mosquitoes. The hikers heard the drone of a far-off automobile.* 4 talk or say in a monotonous voice: *Several people in the audience fell asleep as the speaker droned on.* 5 person not willing to work; idler; loafer. 6 spend time idly; loaf. 1,3,5 *n.,* 2,4,6 *v.,* **droned, dron ing.**

drool (drül), 1 let saliva run from

the mouth as a teething baby does. 2 SLANG. talk foolishly. 3 SLANG. foolish talk. 1,2 *v.,* 3 *n.*

droop (drüp), 1 hang down; bend down: *These flowers will soon droop if they are not put in water.* 2 a bending position; hanging down: *The droop of the branches brought them within our reach.* 3 become weak; lose strength and energy: *The hikers were drooping by the end of the walk in the hot sun.* 4 become discouraged; be sad and gloomy. 1,3,4 *v.,* 2 *n.*

droop y (drü′pē), 1 hanging down; drooping: *a droopy hat.* 2 discouraged; depressed. *adj.,* **droop i er, droop i est.**

drop (drop), 1 a small amount of liquid in a somewhat round shape: *a drop of rain, a drop of blood.* 2 a very small amount of liquid: *Take a few drops of this medicine.* 3 **drops,** *pl.* liquid medicine given in drops: *eye drops, nose drops.* 4 a very small amount of anything: *Show him a drop of kindness.* 5 fall or let fall in very small amounts. 6 a sudden fall: *a drop in temperature, a drop in prices.* 7 the distance down; length of a fall: *From the top of the cliff to the water is a drop of 200 feet.* 8 fall suddenly; let fall suddenly: *The acrobat dropped from the high rope into the net below. The price of sugar may drop soon.* 9 fall or cause to fall: *It was so quiet you could hear a pin drop.* 10 let fall: *He dropped his package.* 11 fall dead, wounded, or tired out: *After working all day I was ready to drop.* 12 cause to fall dead; kill. 13 go lower; sink: *Her voice dropped to a whisper.* 14 make lower: *Drop your voice.* 15 let go; dismiss: *Members who do not pay their dues will be dropped from the club.* 16 leave out; omit: *Drop the "e" in "drive" before adding "ing."* 17 stop; end: *The matter is not important; let it drop.* 18 send (a letter, etc.): *While you are away on your trip, drop me a card.* 19 come: *Drop in for a chat sometime.* 20 give or express: *I dropped a hint that I would like to be invited to the party.* 21 go with the current or tide: *The raft dropped down the river.* 22 set down from a ship, automobile, carriage, etc.: *He dropped his passengers at Main Street.* 1-4,6,7 *n.,* 5,8-22 *v.,* **dropped** or **dropt, drop ping.** —**drop′like′,** *adj.*

drop out, leave school or college before completing a course or a term.

drop let (drop′lit), a tiny drop. *n.*

drop out (drop′out′), student who leaves school or college before completing a course or a term. *n.*

drop per (drop′ər), a small glass tube with a hollow rubber cap at one end and a small opening at the other end from

which a liquid can be made to fall in drops. *n.*

drop sy (drop′sē), disease in which a watery fluid collects in certain tissues or cavities of the body, often accompanied by swelling; edema. *n.*

dropt (dropt), dropped; a past tense and a past participle of **drop.** *v.*

dross (drôs), 1 waste or scum that comes to the surface of melting metals. 2 waste material; rubbish. *n.*

drought (drout), 1 a long period of dry weather; continued lack of rain: *A drought of three months during the summer caused the brooks and streams to dry up.* 2 lack of moisture; dryness. *n.*

drouth (drouth), drought. *n.*

drove[1] (drōv), past tense of **drive.** *We drove two hundred miles today. v.*

drove[2] (drōv), 1 group of cattle, sheep, hogs, etc., moving or driven along together; flock; herd: *The rancher sent a drove of cattle to market.* 2 many people moving along together; crowd. *n.* [Old English *drāf*]

drov er (drō′vər), 1 person who drives cattle, sheep, hogs, etc., to market. 2 dealer in cattle. *n.*

drown (droun), 1 die under water or other liquid because of lack of air to breathe: *We almost drowned when our sailboat suddenly overturned.* 2 kill by keeping under water or other liquid: *The flood drowned many cattle in the lowlands.* 3 be stronger or louder than; keep from being heard: *The boat's whistle drowned out what she was trying to tell us. v.*

drowse (drouz), 1 be sleepy; be half asleep: *She drowsed, but she did not quite fall asleep.* 2 a being half asleep; sleepiness. 1 *v.,* **drowsed, drows ing;** 2 *n.*

drow si ly (drou′zə lē), in a drowsy manner. *adv.*

drow si ness (drou′zē nis), drowsy condition; sleepiness. *n.*

drow sy (drou′zē), 1 half asleep; sleepy. 2 making one sleepy: *It was a warm, quiet, drowsy afternoon. adj.,* **drow si er, drow si est.**

drub (drub), 1 beat with a stick; whip

hat, āge, fär; let, ēqual, tėrm;
it, īce; hot, ōpen, ôrder;
oil, out; cup, pùt, rüle; ch, child;
ng, long; sh, she; th, thin;
ŦH, then; zh, measure;

ə represents *a* in about,
e in taken, *i* in pencil,
o in lemon, *u* in circus.

adj.	adjective	n.	noun
adv.	adverb	prep.	preposition
conj.	conjunction	pron.	pronoun
interj.	interjection	v.	verb
sing.	singular	pl.	plural

soundly; thrash. **2** defeat by a large margin in a fight, game, contest, etc. *v.*, **drubbed, drub bing.**

drudge (druj), **1** person who does hard, tiresome, or disagreeable work. **2** do hard, tiresome, or disagreeable work. **1** *n.*, **2** *v.*, **drudged, drudg ing.**

drudg er y (druj′ər ē), work that is hard, tiresome, or disagreeable: *My brother thinks that washing dishes every day is drudgery.* *n., pl.* **drudg er ies.**

drug (drug), **1** substance used as a medicine or in preparing medicines. Drugs are obtained from plants, molds, minerals, etc., and are often made from chemicals. Aspirin is a drug. **2** drug that brings drowsiness or sleep, or lessens pain by dulling the nerves; narcotic. Opium is a habit-forming drug. **3** give drugs to, particularly drugs that are harmful or cause sleep: *They drugged the guard and then searched for the secret documents.* **4** mix harmful drugs with (food or drink): *The spy drugged the ambassador's wine.* **5** affect or overcome (the body or the senses) in a way that is not natural: *The wine had drugged her.* **1,2** *n.*, **3-5** *v.*, **drugged, drug ging.**

drug gist (drug′ist), **1** person who sells drugs, medicines, etc. **2** person licensed to fill prescriptions; pharmacist. *n.*

drug store (drug′stôr′), store that sells drugs and other medicines and often also soft drinks, cosmetics, magazines, etc. *n.*

dru id or **Dru id** (drü′id), member of an order of priests among the ancient Celts of Britain, Ireland, and France. The druids were very powerful leaders and judges until the Christian religion was accepted by the Celts. *n.*

drum (drum), **1** a musical instrument that makes a sound when it is beaten. A drum is a hollow cylinder with a covering stretched tightly over the ends. **2** sound made by beating a drum. **3** any sound like this: *the drum of rain on a roof.* **4** beat or play the drum: *I drum in the school band.* **5** beat, tap, or strike again and again: *Stop drumming on the table with your fingers.* **6** teach or drive into one's head by repeating over and over: *Arithmetic had to be drummed into me because I couldn't understand*

it. **7** container or other thing shaped somewhat like a drum: *an oil drum.* **8** a thick bar or cylinder in a machine on which something is wound: *a drum of cable.* **1-3,7,8** *n.*, **4-6** *v.*, **drummed, drum ming. —drum′like′,** *adj.*

drum out of, send away from in disgrace: *The corrupt politician was drummed out of office.*

drum up, 1 call together: *We could not drum up enough players to make a baseball team.* **2** get by asking again and again; obtain: *The company's advertising campaign drummed up more business.*

drum major, leader of a marching band.

drum ma jor ette (mā′jə ret′), a girl or woman who leads parades, twirling a baton.

drum mer (drum′ər), person who plays a drum. *n.*

drum stick (drum′stik′), **1** stick for beating a drum. **2** the lower half of the leg of a cooked chicken, turkey, etc. *n.*

drunk (drungk), **1** overcome by alcoholic liquor; intoxicated: *He was so drunk he could not stand up.* **2** person who is drunk. **3** very much excited or affected: *a person who is drunk with success.* **4** past participle of **drink.** *I have drunk several glasses of milk already.* **5** OLD USE. a past tense of **drink.** **1,3** *adj.*, **2** *n.*, **4,5** *v.*

drunk ard (drung′kərd), person who is often drunk; person who drinks too much alcoholic liquor. *n.*

drunk en (drung′kən), **1** overcome by alcoholic liquor; drunk. **2** caused by being drunk: *a drunken act, drunken words.* **3** OLD USE. a past participle of **drink.** **1,2** *adj.*, **3** *v.* **—drunk′en ly,** *adv.* **—drunk′en ness,** *n.*

dry (drī), **1** not wet; not moist: *Dust is dry.* **2** make or become dry: *She was drying dishes. Clothes dry in the sun.* **3** having little or no rain: *Arizona has a dry climate.* **4** not giving milk: *That cow has been dry for a month.* **5** empty of water or other liquid: *I can't write with a dry pen. The kettle has boiled dry.* **6** wanting a drink; thirsty: *I'm awfully dry after that hike.* **7** not under, in, or on water: *She was glad to be on dry land and away from the swamp.* **8** not shedding tears: *After the sad play there wasn't a dry eye in the theater.* **9** not fresh: *The cook used dry bread to make turkey stuffing.* **10** showing no feeling; cold or restrained: *His dry humor was said without a smile.* **11** not interesting; dull: *A book full of facts and figures is dry.* **12** free from sweetness or fruity flavor: *dry wine.* **13** without butter: *dry toast.* **14** INFORMAL. forbidding the sale of alcoholic drinks: *a dry city, a dry state.* **1,3-14** *adj.*, **dri er, dri est;**

2 *v.*, **dried, dry ing. —dry′ness,** *n.*

dry ad or **Dry ad** (drī′əd), (in Greek myths) a nymph that lives in a tree; wood nymph. *n.*

dry cell, an electric cell in which the chemical producing the current is made into a paste with gelatin, sawdust, etc., so that its contents cannot spill. See **electrode** for diagram.

dry-clean (drī′klēn′), clean (clothes, etc.) with naphtha, benzine, etc., instead of water. *v.*

dry cleaner, person or business that does dry cleaning.

dry cleaning, cleaning of cloth without water, using liquids such as naphtha and benzine.

dry dock, dock built watertight so that the water may be pumped out or kept high. Dry docks are used for building or repairing ships.

dry dock

dry er (drī′ər), **1** device or machine that removes water by heat, air, etc.: *a clothes dryer, a hair dryer.* **2** substance mixed with paint, varnish, ink, etc., to make it dry more quickly. *n.* Also, **drier.**

dry goods, cloth, ribbon, lace, etc., and similar textile fabrics.

Dry Ice, trademark for a very cold, white solid formed when carbon dioxide is greatly compressed and then cooled. It is used for cooling because it changes from a solid back to a gas without becoming liquid.

dry ly (drī′lē), in a dry manner. *adv.* Also, **drily.**

dry measure, system for measuring the volume of such things as grain, vegetables, or fruit. In the United States:

2 pints = 1 quart
8 quarts = 1 peck
4 pecks = 1 bushel

dry run, a practice test or session.

dry-shod (drī′shod′), having dry shoes; without getting the feet wet. *adj.*

D.S.T., daylight-saving time.

du al (dü′əl or dyü′əl), **1** consisting of two parts; double; twofold: *The automobile had dual controls, one set for the learner and one for the teacher.* **2** of two; showing two. *adj.* **—du′al ly,** *adv.*

dub¹ (dub), 1 give a title, name, or nickname to; name; call: *The students dubbed their school "The Thought Factory."* 2 make (a man) a knight by striking his shoulder lightly with a sword. 3 make smooth by cutting, rubbing, or scraping: *We cut the branches off, hewed the log flat, and dubbed it with an adz.* v., **dubbed, dub bing.** [Old English *dubbian*]

dub² (dub), add music, voices, or other sounds to (a motion-picture film, a radio or television broadcast, a recording, etc.): *The Italian film was dubbed with English dialogue.* v., **dubbed, dubbing.** [shortened from *double*]

du bi ous (dü′bē əs *or* dyü′bē əs), 1 filled with or being in doubt; doubtful; uncertain: *a dubious compliment. Many books of the Bible are of dubious authorship. She looked this way and that in a dubious manner.* 2 of questionable character; probably bad: *The police are investigating the swindler's dubious schemes for making money.* adj. —**du′bi ous ly,** adv.

Dub lin (dub′lən), capital of the Republic of Ireland, in the E part. n.

Du Bois (dü bois′), **W(illiam) E(dward) B(urghardt),** 1868-1963, American sociologist and author.

du cal (dü′kəl *or* dyü′kəl), of a duke or dukedom. adj.

duc at (duk′ət), any of various gold or silver coins once used in Europe. n.

duch ess (duch′is), 1 wife or widow of a duke. 2 woman with a rank equal to a duke's. n., pl. **duch ess es.**

duch y (duch′ē), lands ruled by a duke or a duchess. n., pl. **duch ies.**

duck¹ (duk), 1 a wild or tame swimming bird with a short neck, short legs, webbed feet, and a broad, flat bill. Ducks are very often kept to use as food and for their eggs. 2 the female duck. The male is called a drake. 3 flesh of a duck used for food. n. [Old English *düce*]

duck² (duk), 1 dip or plunge suddenly under water and out again. 2 a sudden dip or plunge under water and out again. 3 lower the head or bend the body suddenly to keep from being hit, seen, etc.: *She ducked to avoid a low branch.* 4 a sudden lowering of the head or bending of the body to keep from being hit, seen, etc. 5 INFORMAL. get or keep away from; avoid; dodge: *duck a blow. He ducked my question.* 1,3,5 v., 2,4, n. [Middle English *duken*]

duck³ (duk), 1 a strong cotton or linen cloth with a lighter and finer weave than canvas. Duck is used to make small sails, tarpaulins, tents, and clothes for sailors or people living in hot climates. 2 **ducks,** pl. trousers made of duck. n. [from Dutch *doek* cloth]

duck⁴ (duk), an amphibious truck with a watertight body so that it may move through the water like a boat. n. [spelling for pronunciation of *DUKW,* its code name]

duck bill (duk′bil′), a small water mammal of Australia and Tasmania that lays eggs; platypus. It has webbed feet and a bill somewhat like a duck's. n.

duckbill—about 1½ ft. long

duck ling (duk′ling), a young duck. n.

duck weed (duk′wēd′), a very small plant having no stem, that grows in water and often forms dense, green scum on the surface. n.

duct (dukt), 1 tube, pipe, or channel for carrying liquid, air, etc. 2 a single pipe for electric cables. 3 tube in the body for carrying a bodily fluid: *tear ducts.* n. —**duct′like′,** adj.

duc tile (duk′təl), 1 capable of being hammered out thin or drawn out into a wire: *Gold and copper are ductile metals.* 2 capable of being easily molded or shaped; flexible: *Wax is ductile when it is warm.* 3 easily managed or influenced; docile. adj.

duct less (dukt′lis), having no duct. adj.

ductless gland, endocrine gland.

dud (dud), 1 shell or bomb that fails to explode. 2 SLANG. failure: *The rocket test was a complete dud.* 3 **duds,** pl. INFORMAL. clothes. n.

dude (düd *or* dyüd), 1 man who pays too much attention to his clothes; dandy. 2 (in the western parts of the United States and Canada) person raised in the city, especially an easterner who vacations on a ranch. 3 SLANG. guy; fellow. n.

dude ranch, ranch which is run as a tourist resort.

dudg eon (duj′ən), a feeling of anger or resentment. n.

in high dudgeon, very angry; resentful: *He was in high dudgeon when he found out that we had left without him.*

due (dü *or* dyü), 1 owed as a debt; to be paid as a right; owing: *The money due her for her work was paid today. Respect is due to older people.* 2 what is owed to a person; a person's right: *Courtesy is their due as long as they are your guests.* 3 proper; suitable; rightful: *You will receive a due reward for your good work.* 4 as much as needed; enough: *Use due care in crossing streets.* 5 **dues,** pl. amount of money

hat, āge, fär; let, ēqual, tėrm; it, īce; hot, ōpen, ôrder; oil, out; cup, pùt, rüle; ch, child; ng, long; sh, she; th, thin; ₮H, then; zh, measure;

ə represents *a* in about, *e* in taken, *i* in pencil, *o* in lemon, *u* in circus.

owed or to be paid to a club, etc., by a member; fee or tax for some purpose: *Members who do not pay their dues will be suspended from the club.* 6 promised to come or be ready; looked for; expected: *The train is due at noon. Your report is due tomorrow.* 7 straight; directly: *Columbus sailed due west from Spain until he reached America.* 1,3,4,6 adj., 2,5 n., 7 adv.

due to, 1 caused by: *The accident was due to the driver's carelessness.* 2 INFORMAL. because of: *The game was called off due to rain.*

give a person his due, be fair to a person.

du el (dü′əl *or* dyü′əl), 1 a formal fight between two persons armed with guns or swords. Duels are arranged to settle quarrels, avenge insults, etc., and are fought in the presence of two witnesses called seconds. 2 any fight or contest between two opponents: *The two opposing lawyers fought a duel of wits in the court of law.* 3 fight a duel. 1,2 n., 3 v.

du el ist (dü′ə list *or* dyü′ə list), person who fights a duel or duels. n.

du en na (dü en′ə *or* dyü en′ə), 1 an elderly woman who is the governess and chaperon of young girls in a Spanish or Portuguese family. 2 governess or chaperon. n., pl. **du en nas.** [from Spanish of the 1600's *duenna* married woman, from Latin *domina* mistress]

du et (dü et′ *or* dyü et′), 1 piece of music for two voices or instruments. 2 two singers or players performing together. n.

duf fel (duf′əl), 1 a coarse, woolen cloth with a thick nap. 2 camping equipment. n. [from *Duffel,* a town near Antwerp, Belgium]

duffel bag, a large canvas sack used by soldiers, campers, etc., for carrying clothing and other belongings.

dug (dug), past tense and past participle of **dig.** *The dog dug a hole under the garden fence. The potatoes have all been dug.* v.

dug out (dug′out′), 1 a rough shelter or dwelling formed by digging into the

duke

adj.	adjective	*n.*	noun
adv.	adverb	*prep.*	preposition
conj.	conjunction	*pron.*	pronoun
interj.	interjection	*v.*	verb
sing.	singular	*pl.*	plural

side of a hill, trench, etc. During war, soldiers use dugouts for protection against bullets and bombs. 2 a small shelter at the side of a baseball field. It is used by players who are not at bat or not in the game. 3 boat made by hollowing out a large log. *n.*

duke (dük *or* dyük), 1 nobleman of the highest title, ranking just below a prince. 2 prince who rules a duchy. *n.*

duke dom (dük′dəm *or* dyük′dəm), 1 lands ruled by a duke; duchy. 2 title or rank of a duke. *n.*

dul cet (dul′sit), soothing, especially to the ear; sweet or pleasing: *the dulcet voice of a famous singer. adj.*

dul ci mer (dul′sə mər), a musical instrument with metal strings, played by striking the strings with two hammers. *n.*

dulcimer

dull (dul), 1 not sharp or pointed; blunt: *It is hard to cut with a dull knife.* 2 not bright or clear: *dull, watery eyes, a dull, cloudy day, a dull color.* 3 slow in understanding; stupid: *The child had a dull mind. The dull pupil found schoolwork difficult.* 4 not felt sharply; vague: *The dull pain of a bruise.* 5 not interesting; tiresome; boring: *a long, dull book, a dull joke.* 6 having little life, energy, or spirit; not active: *The fur coat business is usually dull in the summer.* 7 make dull: *Chopping wood dulled the blade of the ax.* 8 become dull: *This cheap knife dulls very easily.* 1-6 *adj.,* 7,8 *v.*

dull ard (dul′ərd), person who is stupid and learns very slowly. *n.*

dull ness (dul′nis), dull condition or quality. *n.*

dul ly (dul′ē), in a dull manner. *adv.*

Du luth (də lüth′), city in E Minnesota, on Lake Superior. *n.*

du ly (dü′lē *or* dyü′lē), 1 according to what is due; as due; rightly; suitably: *The documents were duly signed before*

a lawyer. 2 when due; at the proper time: *The debt will be duly paid. adv.*

Du mas (dü mä′), 1 **Alexandre**, 1802-1870, French novelist and dramatist. 2 his son, **Alexandre**, 1824-1895, French dramatist. *n.*

dumb (dum), 1 not able to speak: *A deaf-mute is a person who is both deaf and dumb. Even intelligent animals are dumb.* 2 silenced for the moment by fear, surprise, shyness, etc.: *She was struck dumb with astonishment.* 3 unwilling to speak; not speaking; silent. 4 INFORMAL. slow in understanding; stupid. *adj.* —**dumb′ly,** *adv.* —**dumb′ness,** *n.*

dumb bell (dum′bel′), 1 a short bar of wood or iron with large, heavy, round ends. Dumbbells are generally used in pairs and are lifted or swung around to exercise the muscles of the arms, back, etc. 2 SLANG. a very stupid person. *n.*

dumb found (dum′found′), dumbfound. *v.*

dumb show, gestures without words; pantomime: *He indicated by dumb show that he wanted to speak to me privately.*

dumb wait er (dum′wā′tər), 1 a box with shelves that can be pulled up or down a shaft. A dumbwaiter is used to send dishes, food, rubbish, etc., from one floor of a building to another. 2 a stand to hold food, dishes, etc., placed near a dining table. *n.*

dum found (dum′found′), amaze and make unable to speak; bewilder; confuse. *v.* Also, **dumbfound.**

dum my (dum′ē), 1 a life-size figure of a person used in place of a real person. Dummies are used to display clothing in store windows, to shoot at in rifle practice, to tackle in football, etc. 2 INFORMAL. a stupid person with no more sense than such a figure; blockhead. 3 person who has nothing to say or who takes no active part in affairs. 4 anything made to resemble a real thing; an imitation. 5 made to resemble the real thing; imitation: *We had a sword fight with dummy swords made of wood.* 6 person who seems to be acting for himself, but is really acting for another. 7 a card player whose cards are laid face up on the table and played by his partner. 1-4,6,7 *n., pl.* **dum-mies;** 5 *adj.*

dump (dump), 1 empty out; throw down in a heap; unload in a mass: *The truck backed up to the hole and dumped the dirt in it.* 2 place for throwing rubbish: *Garbage is taken to the city dump.* 3 heap of rubbish. 4 SLANG. a dirty, shabby, or untidy place. 5 INFORMAL. get rid of; reject: *The party dumped the unpopular candidate.* 6 sell in large quantities at a very low price or

below cost. 7 place for storing military supplies: *an ammunition dump.* 1,5,6 *v.,* 2-4,7 *n.*

dump ling (dump′ling), 1 a rounded piece of dough, boiled or steamed and usually served with meat. 2 a small pudding made by enclosing fruit in a piece of dough and baking or steaming it. *n.*

dumps (dumps), INFORMAL. low spirits; gloomy feelings. *n.pl.*

in the dumps, feeling gloomy or sad: *She was in the dumps because her bike was broken.*

dump truck, truck which can be unloaded of waste, sand, etc., by tipping or by opening downward.

dump y (dump′pē), short and fat. *adj.,* **dump i er, dump i est.**

dun[1] (dun), 1 demand payment of a debt from (someone) again and again: *The store dunned him until his overdue bills were finally paid.* 2 a demand for payment of a debt. 3 person who keeps demanding payment of a debt. 1 *v.,* **dunned, dun ning;** 2,3 *n.* [earlier meaning, "make a din," from a Scandinavian word of the 1600's, such as Icelandic *duna* to thunder]

dun[2] (dun), 1 dull, grayish-brown. 2 a dull, grayish-brown. 1 *adj.,* 2 *n.* [Old English *dunn*]

dunce (duns), 1 child slow at learning his lessons in school. 2 a stupid person. *n.* [from John *Duns* Scotus, 1265?-1308, an English theologian, ridiculed in later centuries by opponents of his ideas]

dune (dün *or* dyün), mound or ridge of loose sand heaped up by the wind. *n.*

dung (dung), waste matter from the intestines of animals, much used as a fertilizer; manure. *n.*

dun ga ree (dung′gə rē′), 1 a coarse cotton cloth, used for work clothes, sails, etc. 2 **dungarees,** *pl.* trousers, work clothes, or overalls made of this cloth. *n.*

dun geon (dun′jən), a dark underground room or cell to keep prisoners in. *n.*

dung hill (dung′hil′), heap of dung or refuse: *a dunghill in the farmyard. n.*

dunk (dungk), INFORMAL. dip (something to eat) into a liquid: *dunk doughnuts in coffee. v.*

Dun kirk (dun′kėrk′), seaport in N France where British forces crossed the English Channel to escape the German forces in 1940. *n.*

du o (dü′ō *or* dyü′ō), 1 duet. 2 INFORMAL. pair. *n., pl.* **du os.**

du o dec i mal (dü′ō des′ə məl *or* dyü′ō des′ə məl), 1 having to do with twelfths or twelve; expressed by twelves. 2 one of a system of numerals,

266

the base of which is twelve instead of ten. 1 *adj.*, 2 *n.*

du o de nal (dü/ō dē/nl *or* dyü/ō dē/nl), of or having to do with the duodenum: *a duodenal ulcer. adj.*

du o de num (dü/ō dē/nəm *or* dyü/ō dē/nəm), the first part of the small intestine, just below the stomach. *n., pl.* **du o de na** (dü/ō dē/nə *or* dyü/ō dē/nə).

dupe (düp *or* dyüp), 1 person easily deceived or tricked. 2 deceive or trick: *They were dishonest and duped their customers.* 1 *n.*, 2 *v.*, **duped, dup ing.**

du plex (dü/pleks *or* dyü/pleks), 1 having two parts; double; twofold. A **duplex apartment** has rooms on two floors. A **duplex house** is a house accommodating two families. 2 a duplex house or apartment. 1 *adj.*, 2 *n.*, *pl.* **du plex es.**

du pli cate (dü/plə kit *or* dyü/plə kit *for* 1,2,4; dü/plə kāt *or* dyü/plə kāt *for* 3), 1 exactly like something else: *We have duplicate keys for the front door.* 2 one of two things exactly alike; an exact copy: *She mailed the letter, but kept a duplicate.* 3 make an exact copy of; repeat exactly: *Duplicate the picture so that we may both have copies of it. Once is enough; don't duplicate the mistake.* 4 having two corresponding parts; twofold; double: *A human being has duplicate lungs but only one heart.* 1,4 *adj.*, 2 *n.*, 3 *v.*, **du pli cat ed, du pli cat ing.**

in duplicate, in two copies exactly alike: *Using carbon paper, he typed the application in duplicate.*

du pli ca tion (dü/plə kā/shən *or* dyü/plə kā/shən), 1 a duplicating or a being duplicated: *Duplication of effort is a waste of time.* 2 a duplicate copy: *Her answers were a duplication of her sister's. n.*

du plic i ty (dü plis/ə tē *or* dyü plis/ə tē), an acting secretly in one way and openly in another in order to deceive; deceitfulness: *I dislike the duplicity of friends who lie about me behind my back. n., pl.* **du plic i ties.**

dur a bil i ty (dùr/ə bil/ə tē *or* dyùr/ə bil/ə tē), lasting quality; ability to withstand wear. *n.*

dur a ble (dùr/ə bəl *or* dyùr/ə bəl), 1 able to withstand wear, decay, etc.: *Work clothes are made of durable fabric.* 2 lasting a long time: *Another war destroyed all hopes of a durable peace between the two nations. adj.*

dur a bly (dùr/ə blē *or* dyùr/ə blē), in a durable manner; lastingly. *adv.*

dur ance (dùr/əns *or* dyùr/əns), imprisonment. *n.*

du ra tion (dù rā/shən *or* dyù rā/shən), length of time; time during which anything continues: *The storm*

was sudden and of short duration. n.

Dü rer (dü/rər), **Albrecht,** 1471-1528, German painter and engraver. *n.*

du ress (dù res/ *or* dyù res/), 1 use of force; compulsion. *The law does not require a person to fulfill a contract signed under duress.* 2 imprisonment; confinement. *n.*

dur ing (dùr/ing *or* dyùr/ing), 1 through the whole time of; throughout: *The children played inside during the storm.* 2 at some time in; in the course of: *Come to see me during my office hours. prep.*

durst (dèrst), OLD USE. dared; a past tense of **dare.** *v.*

dusk (dusk), 1 the darker stage of twilight; time just before dark: *We saw the evening star at dusk.* 2 shade; gloom: *the dusk of a forest.* 3 dark-colored; dusky. 1,2 *n.* 3 *adj.*

dusk i ly (dus/kə lē), in a dusky manner; with partial darkness. *adv.*

dusk i ness (dus/kē nis), dusky condition; partial darkness. *n.*

dusk y (dus/kē), 1 somewhat dark; dark-colored. 2 dim; obscure: *the dusky light of the late afternoon.* 3 sad; gloomy. *adj.*, **dusk i er, dusk i est.**

dust (dust), 1 fine, dry earth: *Dust lay thick on the road.* 2 any fine powder: *The old papers had turned to dust. The bee is covered with yellow dust from the flowers.* 3 brush or wipe the dust from; get dust off: *I try to dust the furniture before vacuuming.* 4 get dust on; soil with dust: *Wipe your shoes or you will dust the carpet.* 5 sprinkle (with dust, powder, etc.): *dust powder over a baby. I dusted the cake with sugar.* 6 earth; ground. 7 cloud of dust floating in the air: *The speeding car on the dirt road raised a great dust.* 8 what is left of a dead body after decay: *The tomb contains the dust of kings.* 9 low or humble condition. 10 a worthless thing. 1,2,6-10 *n.*, 3-5 *v.* —**dust/like/,** *adj.*

bite the dust, 1 fall dead or wounded. 2 be defeated, dismissed, or eliminated: *The other team bit the dust.*

shake the dust off one's feet, go away feeling angry or scornful.

throw dust in one's eyes, deceive or mislead a person.

dust bowl, area, especially in the western plains of the United States and Canada, where dust storms are frequent and violent.

dust er (dus/tər), 1 person or thing that dusts. 2 cloth or brush used to get the dust off things. 3 a long, light garment worn over the clothes to keep dust off them. *n.*

dust i ness (dus/tē nis), dusty condition. *n.*

dust jacket, an outer paper cover for protecting a book; jacket.

hat, āge, fär; let, ēqual, tèrm; it, īce; hot, ōpen, ôrder; oil, out; cup, pùt, rüle; ch, child; ng, long; sh, she; th, thin; ŦH, then; zh, measure;

ə represents *a* in about, *e* in taken, *i* in pencil, *o* in lemon, *u* in circus.

dust pan (dust/pan/), a flat, broad pan with a handle, onto which dust can be swept from the floor. *n.*

dust storm, a strong wind carrying clouds of dust across or from a dry region.

dust y (dus/tē), 1 covered with dust; filled with dust: *She found some dusty old books in the attic.* 2 like dust; dry and powdery: *dusty chalk.* 3 having the color of dust; grayish: *a dusty brown. adj.*, **dust i er, dust i est.**

Dutch (duch), 1 of or having to do with the Netherlands, its people, or their language. 2 the people of the Netherlands. 3 their language. 4 Germans: *The ancestors of the Pennsylvania Dutch came from Germany, not from the Netherlands.* 1 *adj.*, 2,4 *n.pl.*, 3 *n.sing.*

go Dutch, INFORMAL. have each person pay for himself: *Since neither one of us could afford to take the other to the movies we went Dutch.*

in Dutch, SLANG. in trouble or disgrace: *I am in Dutch with my parents for tearing my new jacket.*

Dutch man (duch/mən), 1 person born or living in the Netherlands; Hollander; Netherlander. 2 SLANG. a German. *n., pl.* **Dutch men.**

Dutch treat, INFORMAL. meal or entertainment at which each person pays for himself.

du te ous (dü/tē əs *or* dyü/tē əs), dutiful; obedient. *adj.* —**du/te ous ly,** *adv.*

du ti a ble (dü/tē ə bəl *or* dyü/tē ə bəl), on which a duty or tax must be paid: *Perfumes imported into the United States are dutiable goods. adj.*

du ti ful (dü/tə fəl *or* dyü/tə fəl), doing the duties required of one; obedient: *They are dutiful children, always helping their parents around the house. adj.* —**du/ti ful ly,** *adv.* —**du/ti ful ness,** *n.*

du ty (dü/tē *or* dyü/tē), 1 thing that is right to do; what a person ought to do; obligation: *It is your duty to obey the laws.* 2 the binding force of what is right: *A sense of duty makes a person do what he thinks is right even when he does not want to do it.* 3 thing that a

Dvorák

adj. adjective	*n.* noun
adv. adverb	*prep.* preposition
conj. conjunction	*pron.* pronoun
interj. interjection	*v.* verb
sing. singular	*pl.* plural

person has to do in his work: *One of the duties of a class treasurer is to keep records of the money in the treasury.* 4 proper behavior owed to an older or superior person; obedience and respect. 5 a tax, especially a tax on articles brought into or taken out of a country. *n., pl.* **du ties.**

Dvoř ák (dvôr′zhäk), **Anton**, 1841-1904, Czech composer. *n.*

dwarf (dwôrf), 1 person, animal, or plant much smaller than the usual size for its kind. 2 (in fairy tales) an ugly little man with magic power. 3 much smaller than the usual size for its kind; stopped in growth: *dwarf trees.* 4 keep from growing large; check in growth: *The cold climate dwarfed the trees.* 5 cause to look or seem small: *That tall building dwarfs all those around it.* 1,2 *n., pl.* **dwarfs, dwarves** (dwôrvz); 3 *adj.,* 4,5 *v.*

dwarf ish (dwôr′fish), like a dwarf; much smaller than usual. *adj.* —**dwarf′ish ly,** *adv.*

dwell (dwel), make one's home; live: *They dwell in the country but work in the city.* *v.,* **dwelt** or **dwelled, dwell ing.** —**dwell′er,** *n.*

dwell on or **dwell upon**, 1 think, write, or speak about for a long time: *Her mind dwelt on the pleasant day she had spent in the country.* 2 put stress on: *The speaker dwelt especially on the great need for teachers.*

dwell ing (dwel′ing), place in which one lives; house; residence. *n.*

dwelt (dwelt), a past tense and a past participle of **dwell.** *We dwelt there a long time. We have dwelt in the country for years.* *v.*

dwin dle (dwin′dl), become smaller and smaller; shrink; diminish: *During the blizzard the trapper's supply of food dwindled day by day.* *v.,* **dwin dled, dwin dling.**

dye (dī), 1 a coloring matter used to color cloth, hair, etc. Some dyes are vegetable, others chemical. 2 liquid containing such coloring matter: *We bought a bottle of blue dye.* 3 a color produced by such coloring matter: *A good dye will not fade or run.* 4 color (cloth, hair, etc.) by dipping in a liquid containing coloring matter: *have a shirt dyed.* 5 become colored when treated with a dye: *This material dyes evenly and quickly.* 6 to color or stain: *The spilled grape juice dyed the tablecloth purple.* 1-3 *n.,* 4-6 *v.,* **dyed, dye ing.**

dyed-in-the-wool (dīd′in ᴛнə wúl′), thoroughgoing; complete: *a dyed-in-the-wool conservative in politics.* *adj.*

dye ing (dī′ing), the coloring of fabrics with dye. *n.*

dy er (dī′ər), person whose work or business is dyeing cloth, etc. *n.*

dye stuff (dī′stuf′), substance yielding a dye or used as a dye. Indigo and cochineal are dyestuffs. *n.*

dy ing (dī′ing), 1 about to die: *a dying old man.* 2 coming to an end: *the dying year.* 3 of death; at death: *dying words.* 4 present participle of **die**[1]. *The storm is dying down.* 1-3 *adj.,* 4 *v.*

dyke (dīk), dike. *n., v.,* **dyked, dyk ing.**

dy nam ic (dī nam′ik), 1 having to do with energy or force in motion. 2 having to do with dynamics. 3 active; energetic; forceful: *a dynamic personality, dynamic plans.* *adj.* —**dy nam′i cal ly,** *adv.*

dy nam ics (dī nam′iks), 1 branch of physics dealing with the action of force on bodies either in motion or at rest. 2 the forces at work in any field: *the new dynamics of education.* *n.*

dy na mite (dī′nə mīt), 1 a powerful explosive made of nitroglycerin mixed with an absorbent material and pressed into round sticks. It is used in blasting rock, tree stumps, etc. 2 blow up or destroy, especially with dynamite. 1 *n.,* 2 *v.,* **dy na mit ed, dy na mit ing.**

dy na mit er (dī′nə mī′tər), person who uses dynamite. *n.*

dy na mo (dī′nə mō), generator, especially a generator that produces direct current: *The welders made their own electricity with a small dynamo run by a gasoline engine.* *n., pl.* **dy na mos.**

dy nas tic (dī nas′tik), having to do with a dynasty. *adj.*

dy nas ty (dī′nə stē), 1 succession of rulers who belong to the same family: *The Bourbon dynasty ruled France for more than 200 years.* 2 period of time during which a dynasty rules. *n., pl.* **dy nas ties.**

dyne (dīn), amount of force required to give a mass of one gram an acceleration of one centimeter per second for each second the force is applied. *n.*

dys en ter y (dis′n ter′ē), disease of the intestines, producing diarrhea with blood and mucus. *n.*

dys pep si a (dis pep′sē ə), poor digestion; indigestion. *n.*

dys pep tic (dis pep′tik), 1 having to do with dyspepsia. 2 suffering from dyspepsia. 3 person who has dyspepsia. 4 gloomy; pessimistic. 1,2,4 *adj.,* 3 *n.*

dys pro si um (dis prō′sē əm), a metallic element found in various minerals which forms highly magnetic compounds. *n.*

dz., dozen or dozens.

E e

E or **e** (ē), the fifth letter of the alphabet. *n., pl.* **E's** or **e's.**

E or **E.,** 1 east. 2 eastern.

each (ēch), 1 every one (of two or more persons or things) considered separately or one by one: *Each tool has a name.* 2 every one: *Each went his way.* 3 for each; apiece: *These apples cost ten cents each.* 1 *adj.,* 2 *pron.,* 3 *adv.*

each other, 1 each one the other one: *They struck each other.* 2 one another: *They struck at each other.*

ea ger (ē′gər), wanting very much; desiring very strongly: *The child was eager to have the candy. adj.* —**ea′ger ly,** *adv.* —**ea′ger ness,** *n.*

ea gle (ē′gəl), 1 any of a group of large birds of prey that have keen eyesight and powerful wings. There are many kinds of eagles and they live in every part of the world. The bald eagle is the national emblem of the United States. 2 like that of an eagle: *The eagle eye of the guide saw every move the deer made.* 3 design or picture shaped like an eagle, often used on a flag, coat of arms, coin, stamp, etc. 4 a former gold coin of the United States, worth $10. 1,3,4 *n.,* 2 *adj.*

ea glet (ē′glit), a young eagle. *n.*

ear¹ (ir), 1 part of the body by which people and animals hear. It consists of the external ear, the middle ear, and the inner ear. 2 the outer part of the ear; auricle. 3 thing shaped like the outer part of the ear. The handle of a pitcher is called an ear. 4 Also, **ears,** *pl.* sense of hearing: *There is no need to shout; we have good ears.* 5 ability to hear small differences in sounds: *I have a good ear for music.* 6 attention: *Please give ear to my request. n.* [Old English *ēare*]

be all ears, INFORMAL. listen eagerly; pay careful attention: *The children were all ears while their teacher read them the exciting story.*

ear¹ (def. 1)

play by ear, play (a piece of music or a musical instrument) without using written music: *She can't read notes but she can play any tune on the piano by ear.*

prick up one's ears, 1 point the ears upward: *Her dog pricked up its ears when it heard her walk into the house.* 2 give sudden attention: *I pricked up my ears when I heard my name mentioned.*

ear² (ir), 1 the part of certain plants on which the grain grows. The grains of corn, wheat, oats, barley, and rye come from ears. 2 grow ears; form ears: *Soon the corn will ear.* 1 *n.,* 2 *v.* [Old English *ēar*]

ear ache (ir′āk′), pain in the ear. *n.*

ear drum (ir′drum′), a thin membrane across the middle ear that vibrates when sound waves strike it; tympanic membrane; tympanum. See **ear**¹ for diagram. *n.*

earl (ėrl), a British nobleman ranking below a marquis and above a viscount. *n.*

eagle (def. 1)
3 ft. from head to tail

eagle (def. 3)

earl dom (ėrl′dəm), 1 lands ruled by an earl. 2 title or rank of an earl. *n.*

ear ly (ėr′lē), 1 near the beginning; in the first part: *The sun is not hot early in the day (adv.). In his early years he liked ships (adj.).* 2 before the usual or expected time: *She arrived at work early today (adv.). We had an early dinner (adj.).* 3 before very long; soon: *Spring may come early this year (adv.). We expect an answer at an early date (adj.). adv., adj.,* **ear li er, ear li est.**

early bird, INFORMAL. person who gets up or arrives early.

ear mark (ir′märk′), 1 mark made on the ear of an animal to show who owns it. 2 a special mark, quality, or feature that gives information about a person or thing; sign: *Truthfulness is an earmark of an honest politician.* 3 make an earmark on; identify or give information about: *Careless work earmarks a poor student.* 4 set aside for some special purpose: *A certain amount of*

hat, āge, fär; let, ēqual, tėrm;
it, īce; hot, ōpen, ôrder;
oil, out; cup, pùt, rüle; ch, child;
ng, long; sh, she; th, thin;
ŦH, then; zh, measure;

ə represents *a* in about,
e in taken, *i* in pencil,
o in lemon, *u* in circus.

ear² (def. 1)
ear of corn

money is earmarked to buy books for the library; it cannot be spent for anything else. 1,2 *n.,* 3,4 *v.*

ear muffs (ir′mufs′), pair of coverings to put over the ears to keep them warm. *n.pl.*

earn (ėrn), 1 get for work or service; be paid: *She earns 25 dollars a day.* 2 do enough to get; do good enough work for; deserve: *Considering all the work he does, he is paid less than he earns.* 3 bring or get as deserved: *Her hard work earned her the respect of her teachers.* 4 gain as a profit or return: *Money well invested earns good interest. v.*

ear nest¹ (ėr′nist), strong and firm in purpose; eager and serious: *The earnest pupil tried very hard to do his best. adj.* [Old English *eornost*] —**ear′nest ly,** *adv.* —**ear′nest ness,** *n.*

in earnest, strong and firm in purpose; eager and serious: *The art student is in earnest about her ambition to become a famous painter.*

ear nest² (ėr′nist), part given or done in advance as a pledge for the rest: *Take this money as an earnest of the amount I still owe you. Part of the price he paid to the seller was an earnest that the rest would be paid. n.* [Middle English *ernes*]

earn ings (ėr′ningz), money earned; wages or profits. *n.pl.*

ear phone (ir′fōn′), receiver for a telephone, telegraph, radio, television set, or hearing aid that is fastened or placed over the ear. *n.*

ear ring (ir′ring′), ornament for the ear. *n.*

ear shot (ir′shot′), distance a sound can be heard; range of hearing: *We shouted, but he was already out of ear-*

adj.	adjective	*n.*	noun
adv.	adverb	*prep.*	preposition
conj.	conjunction	*pron.*	pronoun
interj.	interjection	*v.*	verb
sing.	singular	*pl.*	plural

shot and could not hear our voices. *n.*

ear split ting (ir′split′ing), very noisy and loud; deafening: *The bomb exploded with an earsplitting sound. adj.*

earth (ėrth), 1 Also, **Earth.** the planet on which we live; the globe. The earth is the fifth largest planet in the solar system, and the third in distance from the sun. 2 all the people who live on this planet: *People have often wished that the whole earth spoke only one language.* 3 dry land: *the earth, the sea, and the sky.* 4 ground; soil; dirt: *The earth in the garden is soft. n.*

down to earth, seeing things as they really are; practical.

earth en (ėr′thən), 1 made of baked clay: *an earthen jug.* 2 made of earth. *adj.*

earth en ware (ėr′thən wer′ or ėr′thən war′), dishes or containers made of baked clay; crockery. Coarse pottery is earthenware. *n.*

earth ly (ėrth′lē), 1 having to do with the earth, not with heaven. 2 possible: *That rubbish is of no earthly use to us; throw it away. adj.,* **earth li er, earth li est.**

earth quake (ėrth′kwāk′), a shaking or sliding of a portion of the earth's crust. It is caused by the sudden movement of masses of rock along a fault or by changes in the size and shape of masses of rock far beneath the earth's surface. Earthquakes are often associated with the violent activity of volcanoes. *n.*

earth satellite, satellite of the earth made by man.

earth science, any of the sciences dealing with the origin, composition, and physical features of the earth. Geology, geography, meteorology, and oceanography are earth sciences.

earth ward (ėrth′wərd), toward the earth: *The burning airplane hurtled earthward (adv.). The eagle started its earthward descent (adj.). adv., adj.*

earth work (ėrth′wėrk′), bank of earth piled up for a fortification. *n.*

earth worm (ėrth′wėrm′), a reddish-brown or grayish worm that lives in the soil; angleworm. It has minute bristles on each segment that aid in locomotion. *n.*

earth y (ėr′thē), 1 of earth or soil: *Potatoes have an earthy smell.* 2 like earth or soil: *The color of the field was a rich, earthy brown.* 3 down to earth; realistic; practical: *an earthy person.* 4 not refined; coarse: *earthy language. adj.,* **earth i er, earth i est.**

ear wig (ir′wig′), a slender insect somewhat like a beetle. Earwigs were once thought to crawl into people's ears. *n.*

ease (ēz), 1 freedom from pain or trouble; comfort: *When school is out, I am going to live a life of ease for a whole week.* 2 make free from pain or trouble; give comfort to: *Her reassuring words helped ease my worried mind.* 3 freedom from trying hard: *The reporter writes with great ease. You can do this lesson with ease.* 4 freedom from embarrassment; natural or easy manner. 5 lessen; lighten: *Aspirin eased my headache.* 6 loosen: *The belt is too tight; ease it a notch or two.* 7 move slowly and carefully: *We eased the big box through the narrow door.* 1,3,4 *n.,* 2,5-7 *v.,* **eased, eas ing.**

at ease, 1 free from pain or trouble; comfortable: *The doctor soon made the worried patient feel at ease.* 2 with the body relaxed and the feet apart: *Soldiers standing at ease are permitted to talk.*

EASEL

ea sel (ē′zəl), a stand for holding a picture, blackboard, etc. *n.*

eas i ly (ē′zə lē), 1 in an easy manner. 2 without trying hard; with little effort: *Her simple tasks were quickly and easily done.* 3 without pain or trouble; comfortably: *A few hours after the operation, the patient was resting easily.* 4 smoothly or freely: *The cowboy rode his pony easily.* 5 by far; without question: *He is easily the best singer in the choir.* 6 very likely; probably: *She is a good writer who works hard and may easily become famous. adv.*

eas i ness (ē′zē nis), 1 quality or condition of being easy. 2 carelessness or indifference. *n.*

east (ēst), 1 direction of the sunrise. 2 toward the east; farther toward the east: *Walk east to find the road (adv.). Take the east road (adj.).* 3 from the east: *an east wind.* 4 in the east: *the east wing of a house.* 5 Also, **East.** the part of any country toward the east. 6 **the East, a** the eastern part of the United States; region from Maine through Maryland. **b** the countries in Asia; the Orient: *China and Japan are in the East.* 1,5,6 *n.,* 2-4 *adj.,* 2 *adv.*

east of, further east than: *Ohio is east of Indiana.*

East Berlin, capital of East Germany, in the E part.

east bound (ēst′bound′), going east. *adj.*

Eas ter (ē′stər), the yearly celebration of the day on which Christ rose from the grave. Easter comes between March 22 and April 25, on the first Sunday after the first full moon on or after March 21. *n.*

Easter lily, lily with large, white, trumpet-shaped flowers. Easter lilies symbolize purity and are often used at Easter to decorate church altars.

east er ly (ē′stər lē), 1 toward the east. 2 from the east. 3 wind that blows from the east. 1,2 *adj., adv.,* 3 *n., pl.* **east er lies.**

east ern (ē′stərn), 1 toward the east: *an eastern trip.* 2 from the east: *eastern tourists.* 3 of the east; in the east: *eastern schools.* 4 **Eastern, a** of or in the eastern part of the United States. **b** of or in the countries in Asia; Oriental. *adj.*

Eastern Church, group of Christian churches in eastern Europe, western Asia, and Egypt that consider the patriarch of Constantinople as head of the church; Greek Orthodox Church; Orthodox Church; Eastern Orthodox Church.

east ern er (ē′stər nər), 1 person born or living in the east. 2 **Easterner,** person born or living in the eastern part of the United States. *n.*

Eastern Hemisphere, the half of the world that includes Europe, Asia, Africa, and Australia.

east ern most (ē′stərn mōst), farthest east. *adj.*

Eastern Orthodox Church, Eastern Church.

Eastern Standard Time, the standard time in the eastern part of the United States and most of eastern Canada. It is five hours behind Greenwich Time.

Easter Sunday, the Sunday on which Easter is celebrated.

East Germany, country in central Europe, consisting of the part of Germany which came under Soviet control at the end of World War II. *Capital:* East Berlin. See **Germany** for map.

East Indian, 1 of or having to do with the East Indies. 2 person born or living in the East Indies.

East Indies (def. 1)

East Indies, 1 the islands of the Malay Archipelago. 2 these islands, India, and southeastern Asia.

east ward (ēst′wərd), 1 toward the east; east: *She walked eastward (adv.). He sat on the eastward slope of the hill watching the sun rise (adj.).* 2 an eastward part, direction, or point. 1 *adv., adj.,* 2 *n.*

east wards (ēst′wərdz), eastward. *adv.*

eas y (ē′zē), 1 not hard to do or get: *an easy victory, easy work quickly done. Today's arithmetic lesson was easy.* 2 free from pain or trouble; comfortable: *a wealthy person who has an easy life.* 3 giving comfort or rest: *The old cot is an easy bed to lie on.* 4 not strict or harsh: *We bought our new car on easy terms of payment. The new teacher is an easy grader.* 5 smooth and pleasant; not awkward: *Our hosts had easy manners. She has an easy way of speaking to everyone.* 6 slow; not fast: *The old horse moved at an easy pace.* 7 INFORMAL. without much trouble; easily. 1-6 *adj.,* **eas i er, eas i est;** 7 *adv.*

eas y go ing (ē′zē gō′ing), taking matters easily; not worrying: *The new teacher is pleasantly easygoing and relaxed with the class. adj.*

eat (ēt), 1 chew and swallow (food): *Cows eat grass and grain.* 2 have a meal: *Where shall we eat?* 3 gnaw or devour: *Termites have eaten the posts and ruined the fence.* 4 destroy as if by eating; wear away: *The flames ate up the wood. The sea has eaten into the north shore. This acid eats metal.* 5 make by eating: *Moths ate holes in my wool coat.* 6 INFORMAL. bother; annoy: *What's eating him today? v.,* **ate, eat en, eat ing. —eat′er,** *n.*

eat up, use up; waste away: *Extravagant spending ate up our savings.*

eat a ble (ē′tə bəl), 1 fit to eat; edible. 2 eatables, *pl.* things fit to eat; food. 1 *adj.,* 2 *n.*

eat en (ēt′n), past participle of **eat.** *Have you eaten your dinner? v.*

eaves (ēvz), the lower edge of a roof that projects over the side of a building. *n.pl.*

eaves drop (ēvz′drop′), listen to talk one is not supposed to hear; listen secretly to a private conversation. *v.,* **eaves dropped, eaves drop ping.**

eaves drop per (ēvz′drop′ər), person who eavesdrops. *n.*

ebb (eb), 1 a flowing of the tide away from the shore; fall of the tide. 2 flow out; fall: *We waded farther out as the tide ebbed.* 3 a growing less or weaker; decline: *His fortunes were at an ebb because of his long illness and a lack of money.* 4 grow less or weaker; decline: *Her courage began to ebb as she neared the haunted house.* 1,3 *n.,* 2,4 *v.*

ebb tide, a flowing of the tide away from the shore. Ebb tide occurs twice every 24 hours in most parts of the world.

eb on (eb′ən), OLD USE. ebony. *n., adj.*

eb on ite (eb′ə nīt), vulcanite. *n.*

eb on y (eb′ə nē), 1 a hard, black wood, used for the black keys of a piano, for the backs and handles of brushes, and for ornamental woodwork. 2 a tropical tree that yields this wood. 3 made of ebony: *an ebony cane.* 4 like ebony; black; dark. 1,2 *n., pl.* **eb on ies;** 3,4 *adj.*

DIVISIONS OF TROOPS   SHIPS   AIRPLANES

echelon (def. 1)

e bul lient (i bul′yənt), overflowing with excitement or liveliness; very enthusiastic. *adj.*

ec cen tric (ek sen′trik), 1 out of the ordinary; not usual; odd; peculiar: *People stared at the artist's eccentric clothes.* 2 person who behaves in an unusual manner: *The behavior of an eccentric is hard to predict.* 3 not having the same center: *These circles are eccentric.* 4 not perfectly circular: *The planets are in eccentric orbits around the sun.* 5 off center; having its axis set off center: *an eccentric wheel.* 1,3-5 *adj.,* 2 *n.* **—ec cen′tri cal ly,** *adv.*

eccentric (def. 4)
orbit of planet Pluto compared with a perfect circle

ec cen tric i ty (ek′sen tris′ə tē), 1 something out of the ordinary; oddity; peculiarity: *One of my cousin's most noticeable eccentricities was to carry*

around an open umbrella on sunny days. 2 eccentric condition; being unusual or out of the ordinary: *The clock's eccentricity became noticeable when it struck three, whatever the hour. n., pl.* **ec cen tric i ties.**

Ec cle si as tes (i klē′zē as′tēz), book of the Old Testament, supposed to have been written by Solomon. *n.*

ec cle si as tic (i klē′zē as′tik), 1 clergyman. 2 ecclesiastical. 1 *n.,* 2 *adj.*

ec cle si as ti cal (i klē′zē as′tə kəl), of or having to do with the church or the clergy. *adj.* **—ec cle′si as′ti cal ly,** *adv.*

ech e lon (esh′ə lon), 1 arrangement of troops, ships, planes, etc., in a step-like formation. 2 level of command or authority. A unit of an army, such as a company, battalion, division, or corps, is called an echelon. *n.*

e chid na (i kid′nə), a small, egg-laying, ant-eating mammal of Australia with a long, slender snout, no teeth, and a covering of spines. *n., pl.* **e chid nas, e chid nae** (i kid′nē).

echidna—1½ ft. long

e chi no derm (i kī′nə dèrm′), any of a group of small sea animals, including starfish and sea urchins. An echinoderm has a spiny, stony shell and a body whose parts are arranged like the spokes of a wheel. *n.*

ech o (ek′ō), 1 a sounding again; a repeating of a sound. You hear an echo when a sound you make is sent back by a cliff or hill and heard again as if from a distance. 2 sound again; repeat or be repeated in sound: *The gunshot echoed through the valley.* 3 repeat or imitate what another says or does: *The pupils often echoed their teacher's ideas.* 4 **Echo,** (in Greek myths) a nymph who pined away with love for Narcissus

271

until only her voice was left. 1,4 *n., pl.*
ech oes for 1; 2,3 *v.* —**ech′o er,** *n.*

é clair (ā kler′ *or* ā klär′), an oblong
piece of pastry filled with whipped
cream or custard and covered with
icing. *n., pl.* **é clairs.** [from French]

é clat (ā klä′), 1 a brilliant success.
2 fame; glory. *n., pl.* **é clats.** [from
French]

e clipse (i klips′), 1 a complete or partial blocking of light passing from one
heavenly body to another. A **solar
eclipse** occurs when the moon passes
between the sun and the earth. A **lunar
eclipse** occurs when the moon enters
the earth's shadow. 2 cut off or dim the
light from; darken. 3 obscure the importance or reputation of; make dim
by comparison; surpass: *In sports he
eclipsed his older brother.* 4 loss of importance or reputation: *The former
champion has suffered an eclipse.* 1,4
n., 2,3 *v.,* **e clipsed, e clips ing.**

e clip tic (i klip′tik), path that the sun
appears to travel in one year. *n.*

e col o gy (ē kol′ə jē), branch of
biology that deals with the relation of
living things to their environment and to
each other. *n.*

e co nom ic (ē′kə nom′ik *or* ek′ə-
nom′ik), 1 having to do with
economics. Economic problems have to
do with the production, distribution,
and consumption of goods and wealth.
2 having to do with the management of
the income, supplies, and expenses of a
household, community, government,
etc. *adj.*

e co nom i cal (ē′kə nom′ə kəl *or*
ek′ə nom′ə kəl), avoiding waste;
saving; thrifty: *We can finish early if we
are economical in the use of our time.*
adj. —**e′co nom′i cal ly,** *adv.*

e co nom ics (ē′kə nom′iks *or* ek′ə-
nom′iks), science of the production,
distribution, and consumption of goods
and wealth. Economics deals with the
material welfare of mankind and studies
the problems of capital, labor, wages,
prices, taxes, etc. *n.*

e con o mist (i kon′ə mist), an expert
in economics. *n.*

e con o mize (i kon′ə mīz), 1 manage
so as to avoid waste; use to the best
advantage: *If you can economize your
time, you will get more done in less time.*

2 cut down expenses: *We must
economize or we will go into debt.* *v.,*
e con o mized, e con o miz ing.

e con o my (i kon′ə mē), 1 a making
the most of what one has; avoiding
waste in the use of anything; thrift: *By
using economy in buying food and
clothes, we were soon able to save
enough money for the new car we
needed.* 2 management of affairs
and resources so as to avoid waste:
*Under the Roosevelt Administration,
the country's economy improved
greatly.* *n., pl.* **e con o mies.**

ec ru (ek′rü), 1 pale-brown. 2 a pale
brown. 1 *adj.,* 2 *n.*

ec sta sy (ek′stə sē), condition of very
great joy; thrilling or overwhelming
delight; rapture: *The little girl was
speechless with ecstasy over her birthday present.* *n., pl.* **ec sta sies.**

eclipse (def. 1)

ec stat ic (ek stat′ik), 1 very joyful
and thrilling; full of ecstasy: *the ecstatic
faces of two people about to be married.*
2 caused by ecstasy: *He was in an ecstatic mood over the prize he had won.*
adj. —**ec stat′i cal ly,** *adv.*

Ec ua dor (ek′wə dôr), country in NW
South America. *Capital:* Quito. *n.*
—**Ec′ua do′ri an,** *adj., n.*

ec u men i cal (ek′yə men′ə kəl),
1 general; universal. 2 of or representing the whole Christian Church. An
ecumenical council of the Roman
Catholic Church is one that is called by
the pope for a special purpose. *adj.*

ec ze ma (ek′sə mə *or* eg zē′mə), inflammation of the skin with itching and
the formation of patches of scales and
pimples. *n.*

-ed[1], *suffix forming the past tense of
many verbs,* as in *wanted, tried,
dropped.* [Old English -de, -ede]

-ed[2], 1 *suffix forming the past participle
of many verbs,* as in *has echoed.* 2 *suffix
forming adjectives from nouns:* **a** *having*
_____: *Long-legged = having long legs.*
b *having the characteristics of* _____:
*Bigoted = having the characteristics of
a bigot.* [Old English -d, -ed]

ed., 1 edited. 2 edition. 3 editor.

ed dy (ed′ē), 1 water, air, smoke, etc.,
moving against the main current, especially when having a whirling motion;
small whirlpool or whirlwind: *The wind*

moved in an eddy near the sails. 2 move
against the main current in a whirling
motion; whirl: *The water eddied out of
the sink.* 1 *n., pl.* **ed dies;** 2 *v.,*
ed died, ed dy ing.

Ed dy (ed′ē), **Mary Baker,** 1821-
1910, founder of Christian Science. *n.*

e de ma (i dē′mə), dropsy. *n.*

E den (ēd′n), 1 (in the Bible) the
garden where Adam and Eve first lived.
2 a delightful place; paradise. *n.*

edge (ej), 1 line or place where
something ends; part farthest from the
middle; side: *This page has four edges.
We walked to the edge of the water.*
2 brink: *The stag stood on the edge of
the cliff.* 3 the thin side that cuts: *The
knife had a very sharp edge.* 4 put an
edge on; form an edge on: *The gardener edged the path with white stones.*
5 move sideways: *She edged through the
narrow passageway.* 6 move little by
little: *The dog edged nearer to the fire.*
1-3 *n.,* 4-6 *v.,* **edged, edg ing.**

on edge, 1 disturbed; irritated; tense:
*My nerves were on edge from the con-
stant noise.* 2 eager; anxious: *The children were on edge as they awaited the
start of the parade.*

take the edge off, take away the
force, strength, or pleasure of: *The
severe injury suffered by the winning
pitcher took the edge off the team's
victory.*

edge ways (ej′wāz′), with the edge
forward; in the direction of the edge.
adv.

edge wise (ej′wīz′), edgeways. *adv.*

edg ing (ej′ing), thing forming an edge
or put on along an edge; border or
trimming for an edge: *an edging of lace
for a dress.* *n.*

edg y (ej′ē), impatient; irritable: *Father
gets edgy when you ask him too many
questions while he is reading the paper.*
adj., **edg i er, edg i est.**

ed i ble (ed′ə bəl), 1 fit to eat. 2 **ed-
ibles,** *pl.* things fit to eat; food. 1 *adj.,*
2 *n.*

e dict (ē′dikt), a public order or command by some authority; decree: *The
queen issued an edict creating a new
national holiday.* *n.*

ed i fi ca tion (ed′ə fə kā′shən), moral
improvement; spiritual benefit: *The
fable was written to provide for the
edification of the mind.* *n.*

ed i fice (ed′ə fis), a building, especially a large or impressive one. *n.*

ed i fy (ed′ə fī), improve morally;
benefit spiritually; instruct and uplift:
*People go to church to be edified by the
sermon and the religious lessons.* *v.,*
ed i fied, ed i fy ing.

Ed in burgh (ed′n bėr′ō), capital of
Scotland, in the SE part. *n.*

Ed i son (ed′ə sən), **Thomas Alva,**

1847-1931, American inventor. *n.*

ed it (ed′it), 1 prepare (another's writings, etc.) for publication or presentation: *edit a manuscript, edit a film.* 2 have charge of (a newspaper, magazine, etc.) and decide what shall be printed in it: *Two girls were chosen to edit the school paper. v.*

e di tion (i dish′ən), 1 all the copies of a book, newspaper, etc., printed just alike and issued at or near the same time: *The second edition of the book had many corrections for the errors in the first edition.* 2 form in which a book is printed or published: *The reading matter in the cheaper one-volume edition was exactly the same as in the expensive three-volume edition. Some books appear in paperback editions. n.*

ed i tor (ed′ə tər), 1 person who edits: *She is the editor of our school paper.* 2 person who writes editorials. *n.*

ed i to ri al (ed′ə tôr′ē əl), 1 article in a newspaper or magazine giving the editor's or publisher's opinion on some subject. 2 of or having to do with an editor: *editorial work.* 3 of or having to do with an editorial: *an editorial comment.* 1 *n.,* 2,3 *adj.*

ed i to ri al ly (ed′ə tôr′ē ə lē), 1 in an editorial manner, 2 in an editorial. *adv.*

ed i tor ship (ed′ə tər ship), position, duties, or authority of an editor. *n.*

Ed mon ton (ed′mən tən), capital of Alberta, Canada, in the central part. *n.*

ed u cate (ej′ə kāt), 1 develop in knowledge, skill, ability, or character by teaching, training, study, or experience; teach; train: *The job of teachers is to educate the young.* 2 send to school: *My cousin is being educated in England and returns home only for vacations. v.,* **ed u cat ed, ed u cat ing.**

ed u ca tion (ej′ə kā′shən), 1 development in knowledge or skill by teaching, training, or study: *In the United States, public schools offer an education to all children.* 2 knowledge or skill developed by teaching, training, or study: *A person with education knows how to speak, write, and read well.* 3 study of the methods, principles, problems, etc., of teaching and learning. *n.*

ed u ca tion al (ej′ə kā′shə nəl), 1 of or having to do with education: *The teachers in our school belong to the state educational associations.* 2 giving education: *Our science class saw an educational movie about wild animals. adj.* —**ed′u ca′tion al ly,** *adv.*

ed u ca tor (ej′ə kā′tər), 1 person whose profession is education; teacher. 2 leader in education; authority on methods and principles of education. *n.*

e duce (i düs′ *or* i dyüs′), bring out; draw forth: *The science teacher's ques-*

tions educed many facts about gardens and flowers. *v.,* **e duced, e duc ing.**

-ee, suffix added to verbs to form nouns. 1 person who is _____: *Absentee = person who is absent.* 2 person who is _____ed: *Appointee = person who is appointed.* 3 person to whom something is _____ed: *Mortgagee = person to whom something is mortgaged.* [from French before the 1400's -*é,* from Latin -*atum*]

eel (ēl), a long, slippery fish shaped like a snake and lacking ventral fins. *n., pl.* **eels** or **eel.** —**eel′like′,** *adj.*

eel—about 3 ft. long

e'en (ēn), OLD USE. even. *adv.*

e'er (er), OLD USE. ever. *adv.*

eer ie (ir′ē), causing fear because of strangeness or weirdness: *An eerie feeling crept upon us in the dark and eerie old house. adj.,* **eer i er, eer i est.** Also, **eery.**

eer i ly (ir′ə lē), in an eerie manner: *The wind whistled eerily in the chimney. adv.*

eer i ness (ir′ē nis), eerie quality or condition. *n.*

eer y (ir′ē), eerie. *adj.,* **eer i er, eer i est.**

ef face (ə fās′), 1 rub out; blot out; do away with; wipe out; destroy: *The inscriptions on many ancient monuments have been effaced by time. It takes many years to efface the terrible memories of a war.* 2 keep (oneself) from being noticed; make inconspicuous: *The shy boy effaced himself by staying in the background. v.,* **ef faced, ef fac ing.**

ef face ment (ə fās′mənt), an effacing or a being effaced. *n.*

ef fect (ə fekt′), 1 whatever is produced by a cause; something made to happen by a person or thing; result: *The effect of the gale was to overturn several boats.* 2 make happen; bring about: *Florence Nightingale effected many changes in nursing.* 3 power to produce results; force; influence: *The medicine had an immediate effect.* 4 impression produced on the mind or senses: *Sunshine coming through leaves makes a lovely effect.* 5 something which produces such an impression: *The movie used many special effects with sounds and pictures to make its scenes appear real.* 6 **effects,** *pl.* belongings; goods: *We lost all of our personal effects in the fire.* 1,3-6 *n.,* 2 *v.* **for effect,** for show; in order to impress or influence others: *He said that*

hat, āge, fär; let, ēqual, tèrm; it, īce; hot, ōpen, ôrder; oil, out; cup, pùt, rüle; ch, child; ng, long; sh, she; th, thin; ƬH, then; zh, measure;

ə represents *a* in about, *e* in taken, *i* in pencil, *o* in lemon, *u* in circus.

only for effect; he really didn't mean it. **give effect to,** put in operation; make active: *They urged the mayor to give effect to the proposal.*

in effect, 1 almost the same as; practically; virtually: *By constantly looking up at the clock he is saying, in effect, that he wants us to leave.* 2 in force or operation; active: *That law has been in effect for two years.*

take effect, begin to operate; become active: *That pill takes effect as soon as you swallow it.*

ef fec tive (ə fek′tiv), 1 able to produce an effect: *She is a principal who really knows how to make effective rules.* 2 producing the desired effect; getting results: *Penicillin is an effective medicine in the treatment of many diseases.* 3 in operation; active: *The law passed by Congress became effective as soon as the President signed it.* 4 striking; impressive: *Her skillful use of bright colors resulted in a very effective picture. adj.* —**ef fec′tive ly,** *adv.* —**ef fec′tive ness,** *n.*

ef fec tu al (ə fek′chü əl), producing the desired effect; capable of producing the desired effect: *Quinine is an effectual remedy for malaria. adj.* —**ef fec′tu al ly,** *adv.*

ef fem i na cy (ə fem′ə nə sē), effeminate quality or character in a man or boy. *n.*

ef fem i nate (ə fem′ə nit), (of a man or boy) lacking in forceful qualities; showing weakness or softness. *adj.* —**ef fem′i nate ly,** *adv.*

ef fer ent (ef′ər ənt), carrying outward from a central organ or point. Efferent nerves carry impulses from the brain to the muscles. See **afferent** for diagram. *adj.*

ef fer vesce (ef′ər ves′), 1 give off bubbles of gas; bubble: *Ginger ale effervesces.* 2 be lively and gay: *He effervesces at parties but is quiet and serious in private conversation. v.,* **ef fer vesced, ef fer vesc ing.**

ef fer ves cence (ef′ər ves′ns), 1 act or process of giving off bubbles of gas; bubbling. 2 liveliness and gaiety. *n.*

adj.	adjective	*n.*	noun
adv.	adverb	*prep.*	preposition
conj.	conjunction	*pron.*	pronoun
interj.	interjection	*v.*	verb
sing.	singular	*pl.*	plural

ef fer ves cent (ef′ər ves′nt), 1 giving off bubbles of gas; bubbling: *Ginger ale is effervescent.* 2 lively and gay: *Our cheerleader has an effervescent personality. adj.*

ef fete (i fēt′), no longer able to produce; worn out; exhausted: *During the Middle Ages, Greek civilization declined and became effete. adj.*

ef fi ca cious (ef′ə kā′shəs), producing the desired results; effective: *Vaccination is efficacious in preventing smallpox. adj.* —**ef′fi ca′cious ly,** *adv.*

ef fi ca cy (ef′ə kə sē), power to produce the effect wanted: *The efficacy of aspirin in relieving headaches is well known. n., pl.* **ef fi ca cies.**

ef fi cien cy (ə fish′ən sē), 1 ability to produce the effect wanted without waste of time, energy, etc.: *The carpenter worked with great efficiency.* 2 efficient operation: *Friction reduces the efficiency of a machine. n., pl.* **ef fi cien cies.**

ef fi cient (ə fish′ənt), 1 able to produce the effect wanted without waste of time, energy, etc.; capable: *An efficient worker deserves good pay.* 2 actually producing an effect: *Heat is the efficient cause in changing water to steam. adj.* —**ef fi′cient ly,** *adv.*

ef fi gy (ef′ə jē), image or statue, usually of a person: *The dead woman's monument bore her effigy. n., pl.* **ef fi gies.**

burn in effigy or **hang in effigy,** burn or hang an image of a person to show hatred or contempt: *The unpopular ruler was burned in effigy by a mob.*

ef fort (ef′ərt), 1 use of energy and strength to do something; trying hard: *Climbing a steep hill takes effort. With effort the little girl counted to 100.* 2 a hard try; strong attempt: *He did not win, but at least he made an effort.* 3 result of effort; thing done with effort; achievement: *Works of art are artistic efforts. n.*

ef fort less (ef′ərt lis), requiring or showing little or no effort; easy: *The cat pounced on the mouse with an effortless leap. adj.* —**ef′fort less ly,** *adv.* —**ef′fort less ness,** *n.*

ef fron ter y (ə frun′tər ē), shameless boldness; impudence: *My neighbor had*

the effrontery to say that I talk too much. n., pl. **ef fron ter ies.**

ef ful gence (i ful′jəns), brightness; radiance; splendor: *the effulgence of the royal jewels. n.*

ef ful gent (i ful′jənt), shining brightly; radiant. *adj.*

ef fu sion (i fyü′zhən), 1 a pouring out: *There was an effusion of blood from the deep wound.* 2 unrestrained expression of feeling, etc., in talking or writing. *n.*

ef fu sive (i fyü′siv), showing too much feeling; too demonstrative and emotional. *adj.* —**ef fu′sive ly,** *adv.*

eft (eft), a small newt. An eft lives on land until it matures. *n.*

eft soon (eft sün′), OLD USE. soon afterward. *adv.*

e.g., for example; for instance. [abbreviation of Latin *exempli gratia*]

egg¹ (eg), 1 the round or oval body, covered with a shell or membrane, which is laid by the female of birds, many reptiles, amphibians, fishes, insects, and other types of animals. Young animals hatch from these eggs. 2 the contents of an egg, especially a hen's egg, used as food: *She likes two boiled eggs for breakfast.* 3 a female reproductive cell; ovum. *n.* [from a Scandinavian word of the 1300's, such as Icelandic *egg*] —**egg′like′,** *adj.*

egg² (eg), urge or encourage: *We egged the team on to victory. v.* [from a Scandinavian word of the 1200's, such as Icelandic *eggja*]

egg beat er (eg′bē′tər), device with revolving blades for beating eggs, cream, etc. *n.*

egg cell, a female reproductive cell; ovum.

egg nog (eg′nog′), drink made of eggs beaten up with milk and sugar. It often has whiskey, brandy, or wine in it. *n.*

egg plant (eg′plant′), 1 plant with large, purple fruit shaped somewhat like an egg. 2 its fruit, eaten as a vegetable. *n.*

egg shell (eg′shel′), 1 shell covering an egg. 2 like an eggshell; very thin and delicate. 3 a yellowish white. 4 yellowish-white. 1,3 *n.,* 2,4 *adj.*

e gis (ē′jis), aegis. *n.*

eg lan tine (eg′lən tīn), sweetbrier. *n.*

e go (ē′gō), 1 the individual as a whole in his capacity to think, feel, and act. 2 INFORMAL. conceit: *The new boy's display of ego made the other students dislike him. n., pl.* **e gos.** [from Latin *ego* I]

e go ism (ē′gō iz′əm), 1 seeking the welfare of oneself only; selfishness. 2 conceit. *n.*

e go ist (ē′gō ist), 1 person who seeks the welfare of himself only; selfish person. 2 a conceited person. *n.*

e go tism (ē′gə tiz′əm), 1 a thinking, talking, or writing too much of oneself; conceit: *The speaker's egotism showed in his constant use of the words I, my, and me.* 2 selfishness. *n.*

e go tist (ē′gə tist), 1 person who thinks, talks, or writes about himself too much; conceited person. 2 a selfish person. *n.*

e go tis tic (ē′gə tis′tik), 1 characterized by egotism; conceited. 2 selfish. *adj.* —**e′go tis′ti cal ly,** *adv.*

e go tis ti cal (ē′gə tis′tə kəl), egotistic. *adj.*

e gre gious (i grē′jəs), very great: *Their project is so bad that it can be nothing but an egregious waste of time. I once had an egregious need to be successful in everything I did. adj.* —**e gre′gious ly,** *adv.*

e gress (ē′gres), 1 a going out: *The door locked when we closed it, and no egress from the room was possible.* 2 a way out; exit: *The egress was plainly marked on the doors of the theater. n.*

egret (def. 1)
about 3 ft. long

e gret (ē′gret), 1 any of various herons with tufts of beautiful, long plumes. 2 one of its plumes; aigrette. *n.*

E gypt (ē′jipt), country in NE Africa. Its official name is the **United Arab Republic.** *Capital:* Cairo. See **Algeria** for map. *n.*

E gyp tian (i jip′shən), 1 of or having to do with Egypt or its people. 2 person born or living in Egypt. 3 language of the ancient Egyptians. 1 *adj.,* 2,3 *n.*

eh (ā), exclamation expressing doubt, surprise, failure to hear exactly, or suggesting "Yes" for an answer: *Eh? What's that you said? That's a good joke, eh? interj.*

ei der (ī′dər), 1 a large, northern sea duck, usually black and white, with very soft feathers on its breast. 2 eiderdown. *n.*

ei der down (ī′dər doun′), 1 the soft feathers from the breasts of eiders, used to stuff pillows and bed quilts. 2 quilt stuffed with these feathers. *n.*

eight (āt), one more than seven; 8. *n., adj.*

eight een (ā′tēn′), eight more than ten; 18. *n., adj.*

eight eenth (ā′tēnth′), 1 next after the 17th; last in a series of 18. 2 one of 18 equal parts. *adj., n.*

eighth (ātth), 1 next after the seventh;

last in a series of 8. **2** one of 8 equal parts. *adj.*, *n.*

eighth note, (in music) a note played for one eighth as long a time as a whole note. See **note** for diagram.

eight i eth (ā′tē ith), **1** next after the 79th; last in a series of 80. **2** one of 80 equal parts. *adj.*, *n.*

eight y (ā′tē), eight times ten; 80. *n.*, *pl.* **eight ies;** *adj.*

Ein stein (īn′stīn), **Albert,** 1879-1955, American physicist, born in Germany. He developed the theory of relativity. *n.*

ein stein i um (īn stī′nē əm), a rare, radioactive, metallic element produced artificially from plutonium or uranium. *n.* [from Albert *Einstein*]

Eir e (er′ə *or* ar′ə), Republic of Ireland. *n.*

eland—5 to 6 ft. high at the shoulder

Ei sen how er (ī′zn hou′ər), **Dwight D(avid),** 1890-1969, American general, the 34th president of the United States, from 1953 to 1961. *n.*

ei ther (ē′ᵀHər *or* ī′ᵀHər), **1** one or the other of two: *You may read either book* (*adj.*). *Choose either of the candy bars* (*pron.*). *Either come in or go out* (*conj.*). **2** each of two: *There are cornfields on either side of the river.* **3** any more than another: *If you do not go, I shall not go either.* **1** *adj., pron., conj.*, **2** *adj.*, **3** *adv.*

e jac u late (i jak′yə lāt), say suddenly and briefly; exclaim. *v.*, **e jac u lat ed, e jac u lat ing.**

e jac u la tion (i jak′yə lā′shən), something said suddenly and briefly; exclamation. *n.*

e ject (i jekt′), throw out; force out; drive out: *The volcano ejected lava and ashes. The landlady ejected the tenants who did not pay their rent.* *v.*

e jec tion (i jek′shən), **1** an ejecting: *The audience demanded the immediate ejection of all the people who were heckling the speaker.* **2** a being ejected: *The pilot's life was saved by his automatic ejection from the burning plane.* **3** something ejected: *Lava is a volcanic ejection.* *n.*

e jec tor (i jek′tər), person or thing that ejects. *n.*

eke (ēk). **eke out,** **1** add to; increase:

The clerk eked out her regular wages by working evenings. **2** barely manage to make (a living): *He eked out a living doing various odd jobs.* *v.*, **eked, eking.**

el (el), INFORMAL. elevated railroad. *n.*

e lab or ate (i lab′ər it *for 1;* i lab′ə rāt′ *for 2,3*), **1** worked out with great care; having many details: *The scientists made elaborate plans for launching a new satellite.* **2** work out with great care; add details to: *The inventor spent months in elaborating his plans for a new engine.* **3** talk or write in great detail; give added details: *The witness was asked to elaborate on one of his statements.* **1** *adj.*, **2,3** *v.*, **e lab o rat ed, e lab o rat ing. —e lab′or ate ly,** *adv.* **—e lab′or ate ness,** *n.*

e lab o ra tion (i lab′ə rā′shən), **1** an elaborating or a being elaborated. **2** something elaborated. *n.*

e land (ē′lənd), a large, heavy African antelope with twisted horns. *n.*

e lapse (i laps′), slip away; glide by; pass: *Many hours elapsed while I slept.* *v.*, **e lapsed, e laps ing.**

e las tic (i las′tik), **1** that can be stretched, squeezed, bent, etc., and then return to its original size, shape, or position: *Toy balloons, sponges, and steel springs are elastic.* **2** springing back; springy: *He has an elastic step.* **3** recovering quickly from weariness, low spirits, or misfortune: *Her elastic spirits kept her from being discouraged for long.* **4** easily changed to suit conditions; flexible; adaptable: *Mother has an elastic schedule.* **5** tape or cloth woven partly of rubber. **6** a rubber band. **1-4** *adj.*, **5,6** *n.*

e las tic i ty (i las tis′ə tē *or* ē′las tis′ə tē), elastic quality: *Rubber has elasticity. "Good" and "bad" are words having much elasticity of meaning.* *n.*

e late (i lāt′), raise the spirits of; make joyful or proud: *Her success in the writing contest elated both her and her family.* *v.*, **e lat ed, e lat ing.**

e la tion (i lā′shən), high spirits; joy or pride: *He was filled with elation at winning the first prize.* *n.*

El ba (el′bə), Italian island between Italy and Corsica. Napoleon I was in exile there from 1814 to 1815. *n.*

El be (el′bə), river flowing from W Czechoslovakia through East Germany and West Germany into the North Sea. *n.*

el bow (el′bō), **1** joint between the upper and lower arm. **2** anything like a bent arm in shape or position. A bent joint for connecting pipes or a sharp turn in a road or river may be called an elbow. **3** push with the elbow; make one's way by pushing: *Don't elbow me off the sidewalk.* **1,2** *n.*, **3** *v.*

hat, āge, fär; let, ēqual, tèrm;
it, īce; hot, ōpen, ôrder;
oil, out; cup, pùt, rüle; ch, child;
ng, long; sh, she; th, thin;
ᵀH, then; zh, measure;

ə represents *a* in about,
e in taken, *i* in pencil,
o in lemon, *u* in circus.

elbow grease, INFORMAL. hard work.

el bow room (el′bō rüm′ *or* el′bō rüm′), plenty of room; enough room or space to move or work in. *n.*

eld (eld), OLD USE. **1** old age. **2** ancient times. *n.*

eld er[1] (el′dər), **1** older; senior: *my elder sister, an elder statesman.* **2** an older person: *The children finally decided to take the advice of their elders.* **3** one of the older and more influential members of a tribe or community. **4** any of various officers in certain churches. **1** *adj.*, **2-4** *n.* [Old English *eldra,* the comparative of *ald* old]

eld er[2] (el′dər), elderberry. *n.* [Old English *ellærn*]

eld er ber ry (el′dər ber′ē), **1** shrub or tree with flat clusters of white flowers and black or red berries. **2** its berry. Elderberries are sometimes used in making wine. *n., pl.* **eld er ber ries.**

eld er ly (el′dər lē), somewhat old; beyond middle age. *adj.*

eld est (el′dist), oldest. *adj.*

El do ra do (el′də rä′dō), El Dorado. *n., pl.* **El do ra dos.**

El Do ra do (el də rä′dō), **1** an imaginary place supposed to be full of treasure, sought by early Spanish explorers in South America. **2** any wealthy place. *pl.* **El Do ra dos.**

e lect (i lekt′), **1** choose or select for an office by voting: *We elect our class officers every autumn.* **2** elected but not yet in office: *A President-elect of the United States becomes the President after his inauguration.* **3** choose; select: *The children elected to play baseball.* **4 the elect, a** the people selected or chosen by God for salvation and eternal life. **b** people who belong to a group with special rights and privileges. **1,3** *v.*, **2** *adj.*, **4** *n.*

elbow (def. 2) of a pipe

275

election

adj. adjective		*n.* noun
adv. adverb		*prep.* preposition
conj. conjunction		*pron.* pronoun
interj. interjection		*v.* verb
sing. singular		*pl.* plural

e lec tion (i lek′shən), **1** a choosing or selecting for an office by vote: *In our city we have an election for mayor every four years.* **2** a being chosen or selected for an office by vote: *The candidate's excellent and honest campaign resulted in her election.* **3** choice; selection. *n.*

e lec tion eer (i lek′shə nir′), work for the success of a candidate or party in an election. *v.*

e lec tive (i lek′tiv), **1** chosen by an election: *Senators are elective officials.* **2** filled by an election: *The office of President of the United States is elective.* **3** having the right to vote in an election. **4** open to choice; not required: *Spanish is an elective subject in many high schools.* **5** subject or course of study which may be taken, but is not required. 1-4 *adj.*, **5** *n.*

e lec tor (i lek′tər), **1** person who has the right to vote in an election. **2** member of the electoral college. *n.*

e lec tor al (i lek′tər əl), **1** of electors: *electoral votes.* **2** of an election. *adj.*

electoral college, group of people chosen by the voters to elect the President and Vice-President of the United States.

e lec tor ate (i lek′tər it), the persons having the right to vote in an election. *n.*

e lec tric (i lek′trik), **1** of or having to do with electricity: *an electric light, an electric current.* **2** charged with electricity: *an electric battery.* **3** run by electricity: *an electric stove.* **4** exciting; thrilling: *an electric feeling. adj.*

e lec tri cal (i lek′trə kəl), electric. *adj.*

e lec tri cal ly (i lek′trik lē), by electricity. *adv.*

electric eel, a large South American fish resembling an eel, that can give strong electric shocks.

electric eye, photoelectric cell.

e lec tri cian (i lek trish′ən), person whose work is installing or repairing electric wiring, lights, motors, etc. *n.*

e lec tric i ty (i lek tris′ə tē), **1** form of energy which can produce light, heat, and magnetic force. Electricity is produced in generators for people to buy and use, but can be produced in small amounts by running a comb through your hair or by chemical

change in a flashlight battery. **2** electric current: *Most refrigerators are run by electricity. n.*

e lec tri fi ca tion (i lek′trə fə kā′-shən), an electrifying or a being electrified. *n.*

e lec tri fy (i lek′trə fī), **1** charge with electricity. **2** equip for the use of electric power: *Some railroads once run by steam are now electrified.* **3** give an electric shock to. **4** excite; thrill: *The spectators were electrified by the outfielder's diving catch. v.*, **e lec tri fied, e lec tri fy ing.**

e lec tro car di o gram (i lek′trō-kär′dē ə gram), the tracing or record made by an electrocardiograph; cardiogram. *n.*

e lec tro car di o graph (i lek′trō-kär′dē ə graf), instrument that detects and records the electrical impulses produced by the action of the heart with each beat; cardiograph. It is used to diagnose diseases of the heart. *n.*

e lec tro cute (i lek′trə kyüt), kill or execute by electricity: *A live wire electrocuted the man when he touched it. v.*, **e lec tro cut ed, e lec tro cut ing.**

e lec tro cu tion (i lek′trə kyü′shən), a killing or execution by electricity. *n.*

e lec trode (i lek′trōd), either of the two terminals of a battery or any other source of electricity; conductor by which a current is brought into a liquid or a gas. The anode and cathode of an electric cell are electrodes. *n.*

electrodes of a dry cell—The chemical mixture reacts with the zinc, causing positive ions to flow toward the carbon rod and electrons to flow toward the zinc. When the electrodes are connected in a circuit, an electric current leaves the cell at the cathode and returns to it at the anode.

e lec trol y sis (i lek trol′ə sis), decomposition of a chemical compound into its ions by the passage of an electric current through a solution of it. The electrolysis of metallic solutions is useful in putting metal coatings on objects. *n.*

e lec tro lyte (i lek′trə līt), a chemical compound whose water solution will conduct an electric current; chemical compound that ionizes. Acids, bases, and salts are electrolytes. *n.*

e lec tro lyt ic (i lek′trə lit′ik), having to do with electrolysis or with an electrolyte. *adj.*

e lec tro mag net (i lek′trō mag′nit), piece of soft iron that becomes a strong magnet when an electric current is passing through wire coiled around it. *n.*

e lec tro mag net ic (i lek′trō-mag net′ik), of or caused by an electromagnet. *adj.* —**e lec′tro mag net′i cal ly,** *adv.*

electromagnetic wave, wave of energy made up of an electric and a magnetic field. Light waves and radio waves are electromagnetic waves.

e lec tro mag net ism (i lek′trō-mag′nə tiz′əm), **1** magnetism produced by a current of electricity. **2** branch of physics that deals with electricity and magnetism. *n.*

e lec tro mo tive (i lek′trə mō′tiv), **1** producing a flow of electricity. **2** of or having to do with electromotive force. *adj.*

electromotive force, amount of energy derived from an electric source in one second when one unit of current is passing through the source. Electromotive force is produced by differences in electrical charge or potential.

e lec tron (i lek′tron), a tiny particle carrying one unit of negative electricity. All atoms have electrons arranged about a nucleus. *n.*

electron gun, device that produces and guides a flow of electrons. In a television set, an electron gun directs a stream of electrons to the screen.

e lec tron ic (i lek′tron′ik), of or having to do with electrons or electronics. *adj.*

e lec tron i cal ly (i lek′tron′ik lē), by electronic means; in an electronic manner. *adv.*

e lec tron ics (i lek′tron′iks), branch of physics that deals with the flow, motion, and use of electrons in vacuums and gases. Electronics has made possible the development of television, radio, radar, and computers. *n.*

electron microscope, microscope that uses beams of electrons instead of beams of light, and has much higher power than any ordinary microscope.

electron tube, vacuum tube.

electron volt, measure of electrical energy used in nuclear physics. It is equal to the energy gained by an electron when it moves from one point to a point higher in potential by 1 volt. In some particle accelerators, electrons having several billion electron volts of energy are produced.

e lec tro plate (i lek′trə plāt), cover (silverware, printing plates, etc.) with a coating of metal by means of electrolysis *v.*, **e lec tro plat ed, e lec tro plat ing.**

e lec tro scope (i lek′trə skōp), device that indicates the presence of minute charges of electricity and shows whether they are positive or negative. *n.*

POSITIVELY CHARGED ROD

METAL CONDUCTING ROD

STRIPS OF GOLD LEAF

electroscope—When a positively charged rod touches the metal conducting rod, the strips of gold leaf repel each other. When a negative charge is brought into contact with the metal conducting rod, the strips of gold leaf come together again.

e lec tro type (i lek′trə tīp), 1 metal or composition plate used in printing. It is a copy of a page of type, an engraving, or the like, made by electroplating a wax mold of the original. 2 print made from such a plate. 3 make such a plate or plates of. 1,2 *n.*, 3 *v.*, **e lec tro typed, e lec tro typ ing.**

el e gance (el′ə gəns), good taste; refined grace and richness; luxurious beauty: *We admired the elegance of the clothes worn to the formal dinner. n.*

el e gant (el′ə gənt), having or showing good taste; gracefully and richly refined; beautifully luxurious: *The palace had elegant furnishings. adj.* —**el′e gant ly,** *adv.*

el e gy (el′ə jē), a mournful or melancholy poem, usually a lament for the dead. *n., pl.* **el e gies.**

el e ment (el′ə mənt), 1 one of the simple substances from which all other

African elephant 11 ft. high at the shoulder; body 8 ft. long; ears 5 ft. across

Indian elephant 9 ft. high at the shoulder; body 7 ft. long; ears 2 ft. across

things are made up. An element cannot be separated into simpler parts by chemical means. Gold, iron, carbon, sulfur, oxygen, and hydrogen are elements. There are 105 known elements, each composed of atoms that are chemically alike. 2 one of the parts of which anything is made up: *Honesty, industry, and kindness are elements of a good life.* 3 a simple or necessary part to be learned first; first principle: *Most of us learn the elements of arithmetic before the seventh grade.* 4 one of the four substances—earth, water, air, and fire—that were once thought to make up all things. 5 **the elements,** the forces of the atmosphere, especially in bad weather: *The raging storm seemed to be a war of the elements.* 6 natural or suitable surroundings: *A fish's element is water. A person who loves books is in his element in a library.* 7 member of a set in mathematics. 8 the part that does the work in an electrical device. *n.*

el e men tal (el′ə men′tl), 1 of the forces of the atmosphere, especially of the weather: *The storm showed elemental fury in its violence.* 2 natural; simple but powerful: *Hunger is an elemental feeling.* 3 elementary. *adj.*

el e men tar y (el′ə men′tər ē *or* el′ə men′trē), 1 of or dealing with the simple, necessary parts to be learned first; having to do with first principles; introductory: *Addition, subtraction, multiplication, and division are taught in elementary arithmetic.* 2 made up of only one chemical element; not a compound: *Silver is an elementary substance. adj.*

elementary school, 1 school of six grades for pupils from about six to about twelve years of age, followed by junior high school. 2 school of eight grades for pupils from about six to about fourteen years, followed by a four-year high school.

el e phant (el′ə fənt), a huge, heavy mammal, the largest living land animal, with a long, muscular snout called a trunk and ivory tusks. **African elephants** have large ears and both the males and females have tusks. **Asian** or **Indian elephants** have smaller ears and the females often have no tusks. *n., pl.* **el e phants** or **el e phant.**

el e phan tine (el′ə fan′tēn′ *or* el′ə fan′tīn), 1 like an elephant; huge, heavy, and clumsy. 2 of elephants. *adj.*

el e vate (el′ə vāt), lift up; raise: *elevate the stage in a theater, elevate one's mind by studying philosophy. She was elevated to an important position in the company. v.*, **el e vat ed, el e vat ing.**

elevated railroad, railroad raised above the ground on a supporting

hat, āge, fär; let, ēqual, tèrm; it, īce; hot, ōpen, ôrder; oil, out; cup, pùt, rüle; ch, child; ng, long; sh, she; th, thin; ᴛʜ, then; zh, measure;

ə represents *a* in about, *e* in taken, *i* in pencil, *o* in lemon, *u* in circus.

frame; el. It is high enough for cars and buses to pass underneath.

el e va tion (el′ə vā′shən), 1 a raised place; high place: *A hill is an elevation.* 2 height above the earth's surface: *The airplane flew at an elevation of 20,000 feet.* 3 height above sea level: *The elevation of Denver is 5300 feet.* 4 an elevating or a being elevated: *the elevation of Joan of Arc from peasant girl to leader of the French army. n.*

el e va tor (el′ə vā′tər), 1 something which raises or lifts up. 2 a moving platform or cage to carry people and things up and down in a building, mine, etc. 3 grain elevator. 4 an adjustable, flat piece on the tail of an airplane to cause it to go up or down. *n.*

elevator (def. 4) on the tail of an airplane

ELEVATOR

e lev en (i lev′ən), 1 one more than ten; 11. 2 a football or cricket team. 1,2 *n.*, 1 *adj.*

e lev enth (i lev′ənth), 1 next after the 10th; last in a series of 11. 2 one of 11 equal parts. *adj., n.*

eleventh hour, the latest possible moment; time just before it is too late.

elf (elf), a tiny fairy that is full of mischief. *n., pl.* **elves.**

elf in (el′fən), of or suitable for elves; like an elf's: *The child's elfin smile was very charming. adj.*

elf ish (el′fish), like an elf; elfin; mischievous. *adj.* —**elf′ish ly,** *adv.*

El Grec o (el grek′ō), 1541?-1614, Spanish painter born in Crete.

e lic it (i lis′it), draw forth; bring out: *The comedian's joke elicited laughter from the audience. v.*

el i gi bil i ty (el′ə jə bil′ə tē), fitness

277

adj.	adjective	*n.* noun
adv.	adverb	*prep.* preposition
conj.	conjunction	*pron.* pronoun
interj.	interjection	*v.* verb
sing.	singular	*pl.* plural

to be chosen; qualification. *n., pl.* **el i-gi bil i ties.**

el i gi ble (el′ə jə bəl), **1** fit to be chosen; properly qualified: *Pupils had to pass in all subjects to be eligible for the school play.* **2** an eligible person. **1** *adj.,* **2** *n.*

E li jah (i lī′jə), Hebrew prophet who lived in the 800's B.C. *n.*

e lim i nate (i lim′ə nāt), **1** get rid of; remove: *We had to eliminate the losing team from the competition. The new bridge over the railroad tracks eliminated danger in crossing.* **2** leave out; omit: *The architect eliminated the cost of furniture in figuring the cost of the house.* *v.,* **e lim i nat ed, e lim i-nat ing.**

e lim i na tion (i lim′ə nā′shən), an eliminating or a being eliminated. *n.*

El i ot (el′ē ət *or* el′yət), **1 George,** 1819-1880, English woman novelist. **2 T(homas) S(tearns),** 1888-1965, British poet, essayist, and critic, born in the United States. *n.*

E li sha (i lī′shə), Hebrew prophet of the 800's B.C. who was taught by Elijah. *n.*

e lite or **é lite** (i lēt′ *or* ā lēt′), the choice or distinguished part; those thought of as the best people: *Only the elite attended the reception for the visiting queen. n.* [from French *élite*]

e lix ir (i lik′sər), **1** substance supposed to have the power of changing lead, iron, etc., into gold or of lengthening life indefinitely. The alchemists of the Middle Ages sought for it. **2** a universal remedy; cure-all. *n.*

E liz a beth I (i liz′ə bəth), 1533-1603, queen of England from 1558 to 1603, daughter of Henry VIII.

Elizabeth II, born 1926, since 1952 queen of Great Britain and Northern Ireland, and head of the Commonwealth of Nations; daughter of George VI.

E liz a be than (i liz′ə bē′thən *or* i liz′ə beth′ən), **1** of the time when Elizabeth I ruled England (1558-1603): *Elizabethan drama.* **2** Englishman, especially a writer, of the time of Elizabeth I: *Shakespeare is a famous Elizabethan.* **1** *adj.,* **2** *n.*

elk (elk), **1** a large deer of northern Europe and Asia. It has spreading ant-lers like those of a moose. **2** wapiti. *n., pl.* **elks** or **elk.**

ell (el), a former measure of length, equal to 45 inches in England. *n.*

el lipse (i lips′), oval having both ends alike. *n.*

el lip sis (i lip′sis), marks (. . . or * * *) used to show an omission in writing or printing. *n., pl.* **el lip ses** (i lip′sēz′).

el lip tic (i lip′tik), elliptical. *adj.*

el lip ti cal (i lip′tə kəl), shaped like an ellipse. *adj.*

elm (elm), **1** a tall, graceful shade tree. **2** its hard, heavy wood. *n.*

el o cu tion (el′ə kyü′shən), art of speaking or reading clearly and effectively in public. Elocution includes the correct use of the voice and of gestures. *n.*

e lon gate (i lông′gāt), **1** make or become longer; lengthen; extend; stretch: *He elongated the rubber band to fit it around his papers. Bubble gum elongates easily.* **2** long and thin: *Earthworms have elongate bodies.* **1** *v.,* **e lon gat ed, e lon gat ing; 2** *adj.*

e lon ga tion (ē′lông gā′shən), a lengthening; extension. *n.*

e lope (i lōp′), run away to get married. *v.,* **e loped, e lop ing.**

e lope ment (i lōp′mənt), an eloping. *n.*

el o quence (el′ə kwəns), **1** flow of speech that has grace and force: *The eloquence of the lawyer in defending the accused man persuaded the jury to set him free.* **2** power to win by speaking; art of speaking so as to stir the feelings. *n.*

el o quent (el′ə kwənt), **1** having the power of expressing one's feelings or thoughts with grace and force; having eloquence: *an eloquent speaker.* **2** very expressive: *eloquent eyes. adj.* —**el′o-quent ly,** *adv.*

El Pas o (el pas′ō), city in W Texas, on the Rio Grande.

El Sal va dor (el sal′və dôr), country in W Central America. *Capital:* San Salvador.

else (els), **1** other than the person, place, thing, etc., mentioned; different; instead: *Will somebody else speak? What else could I say?* **2** in addition; more; besides: *The Browns are here; do you expect anyone else?* **3** differently: *How else can it be done?* **4** otherwise; if not: *Hurry, else you will be late.* **1,2** *adj.,* **3,4** *adv.*

else where (els′hwer *or* els′hwar), in, at, or to some other place; somewhere else. *adv.*

e lu ci date (i lü′sə dāt), make clear; explain: *The scientist elucidated her theory by performing an experiment.* *v.,* **e lu ci dat ed, e lu ci dat ing.**

e lu ci da tion (i lü′sə dā′shən), a making clear; explanation. *n.*

ellipses

e lude (i lüd′), **1** avoid or escape by cleverness or quickness; slip away from: *The sly fox eluded the dogs.* **2** remain undiscovered or unexplained by; baffle: *A cure for the common cold has eluded all research.* *v.,* **e lud ed, e lud ing.**

e lu sive (i lü′siv), **1** hard to describe or understand; baffling: *I had an idea that was too elusive to put in words.* **2** tending to elude or escape: *The elusive enemy got away. adj.* —**e lu′sive ly,** *adv.* —**e lu′sive ness,** *n.*

elves (elvz), plural of **elf.** *n.*

E ly sian (i lizh′ən), **1** of or having to do with Elysium. **2** happy; delightful. *adj.*

Elysian Fields, Elysium.

E ly sium (i lizh′əm *or* i liz′ē əm), **1** (in Greek myths) a place where heroes and good people lived after death. **2** any place or condition of perfect happiness. *n.*

'em (əm), INFORMAL. them: *pick 'em up. pron.pl.*

e ma ci ate (i mā′shē āt), make unnaturally thin; cause to lose flesh or waste away: *A long illness had emaciated the patient.* *v.,* **e ma ci at-ed, e ma ci at ing.**

e ma ci a tion (i mā′shē ā′shən), an unnatural thinness from loss of flesh; wasting away. *n.*

em a nate (em′ə nāt), come forth; spread out: *Light and heat emanate from the sun. Fragrance emanates from flowers. The rumor emanated from Chicago.* *v.,* **em a nat ed, em a nat-ing.**

em a na tion (em′ə nā′shən), **1** a coming forth; spreading out. **2** anything that comes forth or spreads out from a source: *Light and heat are emanations from the sun. n.*

e man ci pate (i man′sə pāt), set free from slavery or restraint; release: *Lincoln emancipated the slaves. Women have been emancipated from many old restrictions.* *v.,* **e man ci pat ed, e man ci pat ing.**

e man ci pa tion (i man′sə pā′shən), a setting free from slavery or restraint; release: *The emancipation of slaves in the United States was proclaimed in 1863. The discoveries of science have led to man's emancipation from many old superstitions. n.*

e man ci pa tor (i man′sə pā′tər), person who emancipates. *n.*

e mas cu late (i mas′kyə lāt), 1 remove the testicles of; castrate. 2 destroy the force of; weaken: *The editor emasculated the speech by cutting out its strongest passages.* *v.,* **e mas cu lat ed, e mas cu lat ing.**

e mas cu la tion (i mas′kyə lā′shən), an emasculating or a being emasculated. *n.*

em balm (em bäm′ *or* em bälm′), treat (a dead body) with spices, chemicals, drugs, etc., to keep it from decaying. *v.* —**em balm′er,** *n.*

em bank ment (em bangk′mənt), a raised bank of earth, stones, etc., used to hold back water, support a road, etc. *n.*

EMBANKMENT

em bar go (em bär′gō), 1 an order of a government forbidding ships to enter or leave its ports: *During the War of 1812, Congress laid an embargo on commerce with Great Britain.* 2 any restriction put on commerce by law. 3 put under an embargo; forbid to enter or leave port: *The government embargoed all foreign ships.* 1,2 *n., pl.* **em bar goes;** 3 *v.*

em bark (em bärk′), 1 go on board a ship or an aircraft: *Many people embark for Europe at New York harbor.* 2 put on board a ship or an aircraft: *The general embarked his troops.* 3 set out; start: *After leaving college, the young woman embarked upon a business career.* *v.*

em bar ka tion (em′bär kā′shən), an embarking. *n.*

em bar rass (em bar′əs), 1 make uneasy and ashamed; make self-conscious: *She embarrassed me by asking me if I really liked her.* 2 hamper; hinder: *Lack of trucks embarrassed the army's movements.* 3 burden with debt: *The company was financially embarrassed.* *v.*

em bar rass ment (em bar′əs mənt), 1 act of embarrassing. 2 condition of being embarrassed; uneasiness; shame: *She blushed in embarrassment at her son's rudeness to her friends.* 3 thing that embarrasses: *Forgetting the name of an old friend is a great embarrassment.* *n.*

em bas sy (em′bə sē), 1 ambassador and his staff of assistants. An embassy ranks next above a legation. 2 the official residence and offices of an ambassador in a foreign country. 3 position or duties of an ambassador. 4 a special errand; important mission; official message. *n., pl.* **em bas sies.**

em bat tled (em bat′ld), 1 drawn up ready for battle; prepared for battle. 2 fortified. *adj.*

em bed (em bed′), 1 enclose in a surrounding mass; fasten firmly: *Precious stones are often found embedded in rock. Every detail is embedded in my memory.* 2 plant in a bed: *He embedded the bulbs in a box of sand.* *v.,* **em bedded, em bed ding.** Also, **imbed.**

em bel lish (em bel′ish), 1 add beauty to; decorate; adorn; ornament: *She embellished the simple dress with colorful embroidery. He embellished his letters with clever sketches.* 2 make more interesting by adding real or imaginary details: *He embellished the old stories, so that they sounded new.* *v.*

em bel lish ment (em bel′ish mənt), 1 decoration; adornment; ornament. 2 detail, often imaginary, added to make a story or account more interesting. *n.*

em ber (em′bər), 1 piece of wood or coal still glowing in the ashes of a fire. 2 **embers,** *pl.* ashes in which there is still some fire: *She stirred the embers to make them blaze up again.* *n.*

em bez zle (em bez′əl), steal (money entrusted to one's care): *The cashier embezzled $50,000 from the bank and left the country.* *v.,* **em bez zled, em bez zling.**

em bez zle ment (em bez′əl mənt), theft of money entrusted to one's care. *n.*

em bez zler (em bez′lər), person who embezzles. *n.*

em bit ter (em bit′ər), make bitter: *I became embittered by constant failure.* *v.*

em bla zon (em blā′zn), 1 display conspicuously; picture in bright colors: *Posters were emblazoned on the walls of the room.* 2 decorate; adorn: *The knight's shield was emblazoned with his coat of arms.* 3 praise highly; make known the fame of: *King Arthur's exploits were emblazoned in song and story.* *v.*

em blem (em′bləm), sign of an idea; symbol; token: *The dove is an emblem of peace. The Stars and Stripes and the eagle are emblems of the United States.* *n.*

em blem at ic (em′blə mat′ik), used as an emblem; symbolic: *The lion is emblematic of courage.* *adj.*

em bod i ment (em bod′ē mənt), 1 person or thing symbolizing some idea or quality: *They thought their leader was the embodiment of authority.* 2 an embodying or a being embodied. *n.*

em bod y (em bod′ē), 1 put into a form that can be seen; express in definite form: *A building embodies the idea of an architect.* 2 bring together in a single book, law, system, etc.; include: *The Boy Scouts' "Handbook for Boys" embodies the information that a boy needs in order to become a good Scout.* 3 make part of an organized book, law, system, etc.: *The new engineer's suggestions were embodied in the revised plan of the bridge.* *v.,* **em bod ied, em bod y ing.**

em bold en (em bōl′dən), make bold; encourage. *v.*

em bo lism (em′bə liz′əm), a blocking of a blood vessel by a clot, a bit of fat, or some other obstacle carried there by the blood. *n.*

em bos om (em bùz′əm), 1 surround; enclose; envelop. 2 embrace or cherish. *v.*

em boss (em bôs′), 1 decorate with a design or pattern that stands out from the surface: *Our coins are embossed with letters and figures.* 2 cause to stand out from the surface: *He ran his finger over the letters on the book's cover to see if they had been embossed.* *v.*

em bow er (em bou′ər), enclose in a shelter of leafy branches. *v.*

em brace (em brās′), 1 hold in the arms to show love or friendship; hug: *The mother embraced her baby.* 2 take up; take for oneself; accept: *She eagerly embraced the offer of a trip to Europe.* 3 include; contain: *The cat family embraces cats, lions, tigers, and similar animals.* 4 surround; enclose: *Vines embraced the hut.* 5 a clasping in the arms; hug: *The little boy freed himself from his aunt's embrace.* 1-4 *v.,* **embraced, em brac ing;** 5 *n.*

em bra sure (em brā′zhər), an opening in a wall for a gun, with sides that spread outward to permit the gun to swing through a greater arc. *n.*

embrasure

adj.	adjective	*n.*	noun
adv.	adverb	*prep.*	preposition
conj.	conjunction	*pron.*	pronoun
interj.	interjection	*v.*	verb
sing.	singular	*pl.*	plural

em broi der (em broi/dər), 1 ornament (cloth, leather, etc.) with a raised design or pattern of stitches: *She embroidered the shirt with a colorful design.* 2 make (an ornamental design or pattern) on cloth, leather, etc., with stitches: *I embroidered silver stars on my blue jeans.* 3 add imaginary details to; exaggerate: *She often embroiders her stories to make them more interesting. v.*

em broi der y (em broi/dər ē), 1 act or art of embroidering. 2 embroidered work or material; ornamental designs sewn in cloth, leather, etc., with a needle. *n., pl.* **em broi der ies.**

em broil (em broil/), involve in a quarrel: *Even bystanders became embroiled in our argument. v.*

em bry o (em/brē ō), 1 animal in the earlier stages of its development, before birth or hatching. A chicken within an egg is an embryo. A human embryo more than three months old is usually called a fetus. 2 an undeveloped plant within a seed. 3 an undeveloped stage: *a plan in embryo.* 4 undeveloped; embryonic: *an embryo idea.* 1-3 *n., pl.* **em bry os;** 4 *adj.*

em bry ol o gy (em/brē ol/ə jē), branch of biology that deals with the formation and development of embryos. *n.*

em bry on ic (em/brē on/ik), 1 of the embryo. 2 not mature; undeveloped: *an embryonic leaf, an embryonic plan. adj.*

e mend (i mend/), to free from faults or errors; correct: *The scholar emended the faulty text by suggesting changes in it so that it could be read more easily. v.*

e men da tion (ē/men dā/shən), an emending; correction. *n.*

em er ald (em/ər əld), 1 a bright-green precious stone. 2 a bright green. 3 bright-green. 1,2 *n.,* 3 *adj.*

e merge (i mèrj/), 1 come into view; come out; come up: *The sun emerged from behind a cloud.* 2 become known: *New facts emerged as a result of a second investigation. v.,* **e merged, e merg ing.**

e mer gence (i mèr/jəns), act or fact of emerging: *the emergence of a chick from its egg. n.*

e mer gen cy (i mèr/jən sē), 1 a sudden need for immediate action: *I keep a box of tools in my car for use in an emergency.* 2 for a time of sudden need: *When the brakes failed, the driver pulled on the emergency brake and stopped the car. The surgeon performed an emergency operation.* 1 *n., pl.* **e mer gen cies;** 2 *adj.*

e mer gent (i mèr/jənt), emerging. *adj.*

e mer i tus (i mer/ə təs), honorably discharged; retired from active service, but still holding one's rank and title: *At the age of seventy, Professor Arnold became professor emeritus. adj.*

Em er son (em/ər sən), **Ralph Waldo,** 1803-1882, American essayist, poet, and philosopher. *n.*

em er y (em/ər ē), a hard, dark mineral used in powdered form to grind, smooth, and polish metals, stones, etc. *n.*

e met ic (i met/ik), 1 causing vomiting. 2 medicine that causes vomiting. 1 *adj.,* 2 *n.*

em i grant (em/ə grənt), person who leaves his own country to settle in another: *My grandparents were emigrants from Ireland. n.*

←embryo (def. 1)

embryo (def. 2)

EYE

HEART

ENDOSPERM

EMBRYO

em i grate (em/ə grāt), leave one's own country to settle in another: *My grandparents emigrated from Ireland to come to the United States. v.,* **em i grat ed, em i grat ing.**

em i gra tion (em/ə grā/shən), 1 a leaving one's own country to settle in another: *There has been much emigration from Italy to the United States.* 2 body of emigrants: *The largest emigration from Europe came to the United States in 1907. n.*

é mi gré (em/ə grā), 1 emigrant. 2 member of a refugee group. *n., pl.* **é mi grés** (em/ə grāz). [from French]

em i nence (em/ə nəns), 1 rank or position above all or most others; high standing; fame: *The surgeon's eminence was due to his superior skill in operating.* 2 a high place; high point of land: *The lighthouse was built on an eminence rising many feet above the shore.* 3 **Eminence,** title of honor given to a cardinal in the Roman Catholic Church. *n.*

em i nent (em/ə nənt), above all or most others; outstanding; famous; distinguished: *Washington was eminent both as general and as President. adj.*

em i nent ly (em/ə nənt lē), to an eminent degree; so as to be distinguished from others: *Because of her long experience in the state legislature, she was eminently qualified to run for Congress. adv.*

e mir (ə mir/), 1 an Arabian chief, prince, or military leader. 2 title of honor of the descendants of Mohammed. 3 title of certain Turkish officials. *n.* Also, **amir.**

em is sar y (em/ə ser/ē), 1 person sent on a mission or errand. 2 a secret agent; spy. *n., pl.* **em is sar ies.**

e mis sion (i mish/ən), 1 act or fact of emitting: *the emission of light from the sun.* 2 thing emitted. *n.*

e mit (i mit/), give off; send out: *The sun emits light and heat. Volcanoes emit lava. The trapped lion emitted roars of rage. v.,* **e mit ted, e mit ting.**

Em man u el (i man/yü əl), Christ. *n.* Also, **Immanuel.**

e mol lient (i mol/yənt), 1 softening or soothing: *She used an emollient lotion on her hands after washing her car.* 2 something that softens and soothes: *Cold cream is an emollient for the skin.* 1 *adj.,* 2 *n.*

e mol u ment (i mol/yə mənt), profit from a job, office, or position; salary, fees, or wages. *n.*

e mo tion (i mō/shən), a strong feeling of any kind. Joy, grief, fear, hate, love, anger, and excitement are emotions. *n.*

e mo tion al (i mō/shə nəl), 1 of the emotions: *His constant fears show that he is suffering from a serious emotional disorder.* 2 showing emotion: *My reaction to the movie was so emotional that I began to cry.* 3 appealing to the emotions: *The speaker made an emotional plea for money to help crippled children.* 4 easily excited: *Emotional people are likely to cry if they hear sad music or read sad stories. adj.* —**e mo/tion al ly,** *adv.*

e mo tion al ism (i mō/shə nə liz/əm), tendency to show emotion too easily. *n.*

em pan el (em pan/l), impanel. *v.*

em per or (em/pər ər), 1 man who is the ruler of an empire. 2 ruler who has the title of "emperor." Japan has an emperor. *n.*

em pha sis (em/fə sis), 1 special force; stress; importance: *That school puts emphasis on arithmetic and reading.* 2 special force put on particular syllables, words, or phrases: *A speaker puts emphasis on important words by stressing them. A writer sometimes underlines important words for emphasis. n., pl.* **em pha ses** (em/fə sēz/).

em pha size (em/fə sīz), 1 give special force to; make important;

stress: *He emphasized her name by saying it very loudly.* 2 call attention to: *The large number of automobile accidents emphasizes the need for careful driving.* *v.,* **em pha sized, em pha siz ing.**

em phat ic (em fat′ik), 1 said or done with force; strongly expressed: *Her answer was an emphatic "No!"* 2 attracting attention; very noticeable; striking: *The club made an emphatic success of its party.* *adj.*

em phat i cal ly (em fat′ik lē), in an emphatic manner; to an emphatic degree. *adv.*

em phy se ma (em′fə sē′mə), an abnormal swelling in the body tissues due to the presence of air or gas. Emphysema of the lungs makes breathing difficult. *n.*

em pire (em′pīr), 1 group of countries or states under one ruler or government: *The Roman Empire consisted of many separate territories and different peoples.* 2 country that has an emperor or empress: *the Japanese Empire.* 3 absolute power; supreme authority. 4 a large business or group of businesses under the control of a single person, family, syndicate, etc. *n.*

em pir i cal (em pir′ə kəl), based on experiment and observation: *Chemistry is largely an empirical science.* *adj.* —**em pir′i cal ly,** *adv.*

em pir i cism (em pir′ə siz′əm), use of methods based on experiment and observation. *n.*

em place ment (em plās′mənt), space or platform for a heavy gun or guns. *n.*

em ploy (em ploi′), 1 give work and pay to: *That big factory employs many workers.* 2 service for pay; employment: *There are many workers in the employ of that big factory.* 3 use: *You employ a knife, fork, and spoon in eating. She employs her time wisely.* 4 keep busy; occupy: *He employed himself in growing roses after he retired.* 1,3,4 *v.,* 2 *n.*

em ploy ee or **em ploy e** (em ploi′ē or em′ploi ē′), person who works for some person or firm for pay. *n.*

em ploy er (em ploi′ər), person or firm that employs one or more persons. *n.*

em ploy ment (em ploi′mənt), 1 work; job: *He had no difficulty finding employment. His employment was sorting mail.* 2 an employing or a being employed: *A large office requires the employment of many people.* 3 use: *The painter was clever in his employment of brushes and colors.* *n.*

em po ri um (em pôr′ē əm), 1 center of trade; market place. 2 a large store selling many different things. *n.*

em pow er (em pou′ər), 1 give power or authority to; authorize: *The secretary was empowered to sign certain contracts.* 2 enable; permit: *Man's erect position empowers him to use his hands freely.* *v.*

em press (em′pris), 1 wife of an emperor. 2 woman who is the ruler of an empire. *n., pl.* **em press es.**

emp ti ly (emp′tə lē), in an empty manner. *adv.*

emp ti ness (emp′tē nis), a being empty; lack of contents. *n.*

emp ty (emp′tē), 1 with nothing or no one in it: *an empty house. The birds had gone and their nest was empty.* 2 pour out or take out all that is in (a thing); make empty: *She emptied her glass quickly. He emptied the tobacco out of his pipe.* 3 become empty: *The hall emptied as soon as the concert was over.* 4 flow out: *The Mississippi River empties into the Gulf of Mexico.* 5 not real; meaningless: *An empty promise is one that you do not plan to keep. An empty threat has no force behind it.* 1,5 *adj.,* **emp ti er,** **emp ti est;** 2-4 *v.,* **emp tied, emp ty ing.**

empty set, a set that has no elements; null set.

em pyr e al (em pir′ē əl *or* em′pə rē′əl), celestial; heavenly. *adj.*

em py re an (em′pə rē′ən), 1 the highest heaven. 2 the visible heavens; the sky. 3 empyreal. 1,2 *n.,* 3 *adj.*

e mu (ē′myü), a large, three-toed Australian bird like an ostrich, but smaller. Emus cannot fly, but they can run very fast. *n.*

emu—6 ft. tall

em u late (em′yə lāt), try to equal or excel: *The young man wanted to emulate his father's success as a businessman.* *v.,* **em u lat ed, em u lat ing.**

em u la tion (em′yə lā′shən), a trying to equal or excel: *She took dancing lessons in emulation of her aunt, who was a famous ballerina.* *n.*

em u lous (em′yə ləs), wishing to equal or excel: *Members of the team were emulous of the deeds of former athletes.* *adj.* —**em′u lous ly,** *adv.*

e mul si fy (i mul′sə fī), make into an emulsion: *Juice from the pancreas emulsifies fat in the digestion of food.* *v.,* **e mul si fied, e mul si fy ing.**

e mul sion (i mul′shən), mixture of liquids that do not dissolve in each other. In an emulsion one of the liquids contains minute droplets of the other evenly distributed throughout. *n.*

en a ble (en ā′bəl), give ability, power, or means to; make able: *Airplanes enable people to travel great distances rapidly.* *v.,* **en a bled, en a bling.**

en act (en akt′), 1 make into law: *Congress enacted a bill to restrict the sale of guns.* 2 act out; play: *He enacted the part of Long John Silver very well.* *v.*

en act ment (en akt′mənt), 1 an enacting or a being enacted: *After the House and Senate agreed on a compromise the enactment of the bill followed quickly.* 2 a law. *n.*

e nam el (i nam′əl), 1 a glasslike substance melted and then cooled to make a smooth, hard surface. Different colors of enamel are used to cover or decorate metal, pottery, etc. 2 paint or varnish used to make a smooth, hard, glossy surface. 3 the smooth, hard, glossy outer layer of the teeth. 4 cover or decorate with enamel. 1-3 *n.,* 4 *v.*

en am ored (en am′ərd), in love: *The enamored king gave up his throne to marry a commoner. She was enamored of the young man.* *adj.*

en camp (en kamp′), 1 make a camp: *It took the soldiers only an hour to encamp.* 2 live in a camp for a time: *The Scouts encamped all week by the river.* *v.*

en camp ment (en kamp′mənt), 1 an encamping. 2 place where a camp is; camp. *n.*

en case (en kās′), 1 put into a case. 2 cover completely; enclose: *A cocoon encased the caterpillar.* *v.,* **en cased, en cas ing.** Also, **incase.**

-ence, *suffix forming nouns.* 1 (*added to verbs*) act or fact of _____ing: *Abhorrence = act or fact of abhorring. Dependence = act or fact of depending.* 2 (*added to adjectives ending in -ent*) quality or condition of being _____ent: *Prudence = quality of being prudent. Absence = condition of being absent.* [from French before the 1400's *-ence,* from Latin *-entiam* *-ency*]

adj.	adjective	*n.*	noun
adv.	adverb	*prep.*	preposition
conj.	conjunction	*pron.*	pronoun
interj.	interjection	*v.*	verb
sing.	singular	*pl.*	plural

en ceph a li tis (en sef′ə lī′tis), inflammation of the brain caused by injury, infection, poison, etc. Sleeping sickness is one kind of encephalitis. *n.*

en chain (en chān′), 1 fasten with a chain; put in chains; restrain. 2 hold fast: *The speaker's earnestness enchained the attention of his audience. v.*

en chant (en chant′), 1 use magic on; put under a spell: *The witch enchanted the princess so that she slept for a month.* 2 delight greatly; charm: *The music enchanted us all.* *v.* —**en chant′er,** *n.*

en chant ing (en chan′ting), very delightful; charming. *adj.* —**en chant′ing ly,** *adv.*

en chant ment (en chant′mənt), 1 use of magic spells; spell or charm: *In "The Wizard of Oz" Dorothy finds herself at home again by the enchantment of the Good Witch.* 2 delight; rapture. 3 thing that delights or charms: *We felt the enchantment of the moonlight on the lake.* *n.*

en chan tress (en chan′tris), 1 woman who enchants; witch: *Circe was an enchantress who changed Ulysses' men into swine.* 2 a very delightful, charming woman. *n., pl.* **en chan tress es.**

en cir cle (en sėr′kəl), 1 form a circle around; surround: *Trees encircled the pond.* 2 go in a circle around: *The moon encircles the earth.* *v.,* **en cir cled, en cir cling.**

en cir cle ment (en sėr′kəl mənt), an encircling. *n.*

en clave (en′klāv), country or district surrounded by territory of a foreign country: *West Berlin is an enclave in East Germany. n.*

en close (en klōz′), 1 shut in on all sides; surround: *The little park was enclosed by tall apartment buildings.* 2 put a wall or fence around: *We are going to enclose our backyard to keep dogs out.* 3 put in an envelope along with a letter, etc.: *He enclosed a check when he mailed his order.* 4 contain: *a letter enclosing a dollar's worth of stamps.* *v.,* **en closed, en clos ing.** Also, **inclose.**

en clo sure (en klō′zhər), 1 an enclosed place: *A corral is an enclosure for horses.* 2 thing that encloses. A wall or fence is an enclosure. 3 thing enclosed: *The envelope contained a letter and $5 as an enclosure.* 4 an enclosing or a being enclosed. *n.* Also, **inclosure.**

en code (en kōd′), put into code: *The spy encoded his message and gave it to a courier for delivery.* *v.,* **en cod ed, en cod ing.**

en co mi um   (en kō′mē əm), an elaborate expression of praise; high praise. *n., pl.* **en co mi ums, en co mi a** (en kō′mē ə).

en com pass (en kum′pəs),   1 go or reach all the way around; encircle: *The atmosphere encompasses the earth.* 2 include; contain: *Our history book encompasses all the important events in American history since 1607.* *v.*

en core (äng′kôr *or* än′kôr), 1 once more; again: *The audience liked the song so much they shouted, "Encore! Encore!"* 2 a demand by the audience for the repetition of a song, etc., or for another appearance of the performer or performers: *There were only two encores in the whole show.* 3 call for the repetition of (a song, etc.), or the appearance of (a performer, etc.): *The audience encored the singer.* 4 the repetition by the performer. 5 an extra song, appearance, etc., by the performer. 1 *interj.,* 2,4,5 *n.,* 3 *v.,* **en cored, en cor ing.**

en coun ter (en koun′tər),   1 meet unexpectedly: *What if we should encounter a bear?* 2 an unexpected meeting: *A fortunate encounter brought the two friends together after a long separation.* 3 be faced with: *She encountered many difficulties before the job was done.* 4 meet as an enemy; meet in a fight or battle: *He encountered the strange knight in hand-to-hand conflict.* 5 a meeting of enemies; fight; battle: *The two armies had a desperate encounter.* 1,3,4 *v.,* 2,5 *n.*

en cour age (en kėr′ij),   1 give courage; increase the hope or confidence of; urge on: *The cheers of their schoolmates encouraged the players to try to win the game.* 2 be favorable to; help; support: *Sunlight encourages the growth of green plants.* *v.,* **en cour aged, en cour ag ing.**

en cour age ment (en kėr′ij mənt), 1 condition of being or feeling encouraged: *The singer drew his encouragement from his audience.* 2 something that encourages: *The faith of his teacher in his ability to draw was his only encouragement.* 3 act of encouraging: *Her encouragement was a great help to me.* *n.*

en croach (en krōch′),   1 go beyond proper or usual limits: *The sea encroached upon the shore and submerged the beach.* 2 trespass upon the property or rights of another; intrude: *Our neighbor's irrigation system is encroaching on our land.* *v.*

en croach ment (en krōch′mənt), an encroaching: *The cliff is being worn away by the encroachments of the sea.* *n.*

en crust (en krust′), 1 cover with a crust or hard coating: *The inside of the kettle was encrusted with rust.* 2 decorate with a layer of costly material: *The gold crown was encrusted with precious gems.* *v.* Also, **incrust.**

en crus ta tion (en′kru stā′shən), incrustation. *n.*

en cum ber (en kum′bər),   1 hold back; hinder; hamper: *Heavy shoes encumber a runner in a race.* 2 block up; fill: *His yard was encumbered with old boxes and other rubbish.* 3 burden with weight, difficulties, cares, debt, etc.: *The farm was encumbered with a heavy mortgage.* *v.* Also, **incumber.**

en cum brance   (en kum′brəns), something useless or in the way; hindrance; burden: *Shoes would be an encumbrance to a swimmer.* *n.* Also, **incumbrance.**

-ency, suffix forming nouns. 1 (*added to verbs*) act or fact of _____ing: *Dependency = act or fact of depending.* 2 (*added to adjectives ending in -ent*) quality or condition of being _____ent: *Frequency = condition of being frequent.* [from Latin *-entiam*]

en cyc li cal (en sik′lə kəl), letter from the Pope to his bishops, stating the position of the church on important questions. *n.*

en cy clo pae di a (en sī′klə pē′dē ə), encyclopedia. *n., pl.* **en cy clo pae di as.**

en cy clo pae dic   (en sī′klə pē′dik), encyclopedic. *adj.*

en cy clo pe di a (en sī′klə pē′dē ə), 1 book or set of books giving information on all branches of knowledge, with its articles arranged alphabetically. 2 book treating one subject very thoroughly, with its articles arranged alphabetically: *an encyclopedia of art.* *n., pl.* **en cy clo pe di as.** Also, **cyclopedia** or **cyclopaedia.**

en cy clo pe dic   (en sī′klə pē′dik), 1 covering a wide range of subjects; possessing wide and varied information. 2 having to do with an encyclopedia. *adj.* Also, **cyclopedic** or **cyclopaedic.**

en cyst (en sist′), enclose or become enclosed in a cyst or sac. *v.*

end (end), 1 the last part; conclusion: *She read to the end of the book.* 2 the part where a thing begins or stops: *Drive to the end of this road. Every stick has two ends.* 3 bring or come to its last part; stop; finish: *Let us end this fight. The fight ended in a draw.* **4** form the end of; be the end of: *This scene ends the play.* **5** purpose; object: *The end he had in mind was to skip a grade.* **6** result; outcome: *It is hard to tell what the end will be.* **7** part left over; remnant; fragment: *The store had a sale on fabric ends.* **8** death; destruction: *He met his end in the accident.* **9** an offensive or defensive player at either end of the line in football. **1,2,5–9** *n.,* **3,4** *v.*

at loose ends, 1 not settled or established: *The boy was at loose ends until he was put to work cleaning his room.* **2** in confusion or disorder.

end to end, with the ends placed so that they touch; endways.

end up, wind up; come out: *Where will I end up if I take this path?*

in the end, in the long run; ultimately: *In the end, he had to admit his mistake.*

make both ends meet, spend no more than one has; live within one's income: *The poor man had a hard time making both ends meet.*

on end, 1 upright: *Place the log on end. His hair stood on end.* **2** one after another: *It snowed for days on end.*

put an end to, do away with; stop.

en dan ger (en dān′jər), cause danger to: *Fire endangered the hotel's guests, but no lives were lost.* *v.*

en dear (en dir′), make dear: *Her kindness endeared her to all of us.* *v.*

en dear ment (en dir′mənt), **1** an endearing. **2** thing that endears. **3** act or word showing love or affection; caress. *n.*

en deav or (en dev′ər), **1** make an effort; try hard; attempt strongly: *Each time she endeavored to do better than before.* **2** a strong attempt; hard try; effort: *With each endeavor she did better.* **1** *v.,* **2** *n.*

en dem ic (en dem′ik), **1** regularly found among a particular people or in a particular locality: *Cholera is endemic in India.* **2** an endemic disease. **1** *adj.,* **2** *n.*

end ing (en′ding), **1** the last part; end: *The story has a sad ending.* **2** letter or syllable added to a word to change its meaning; suffix: *The common plural ending is "s" or "es."* *n.*

en dive (en′dīv), **1** kind of chicory with broad, smooth leaves, used for salads; escarole. **2** kind of chicory with finely divided, curly leaves, used for salads. **3** kind of chicory which looks like very smooth white celery, used for salads. *n.*

end less (end′lis), **1** having no end; never stopping; lasting or going on forever: *the endless rotation of the earth around the sun.* **2** seeming to have no

end: *an endless scolding.* **3** with the ends joined; without ends: *The chain that turns the rear wheel of a bicycle is an endless chain.* adj. **—end′less ly,** adv. **—end′less ness,** n.

en do crine gland (en′dō krən *or* en′dō krīn), any of various glands that produce secretions that pass directly into the bloodstream or lymph instead of into a duct; ductless gland. The thyroid, the spleen, and the thymus are endocrine glands.

en dorse (en dôrs′), **1** write one's name on the back of (a check, note, or other document): *He had to endorse the check before the bank would cash it.* **2** approve; support: *Parents heartily endorsed the plan for a school playground.* *v.,* **en dorsed, en dors ing.** Also, **indorse.**

en dorse ment (en dôrs′mənt), **1** person's name or other writing on the back of a check, note, bill, or other document. **2** approval; support: *Her idea received endorsement by the entire club.* *n.* Also, **indorsement.**

en dors er (en dôr′sər), person who endorses. *n.* Also, **indorser.**

en do sperm (en′dō spėrm′), food material for the embryo of a plant, enclosed in the seed. See **embryo** for diagram. *n.*

en dow (en dou′), **1** give money or property to provide an income for: *The rich man endowed the college he had attended.* **2** give from birth; provide with some ability, quality, or talent: *Nature endowed him with good looks.* *v.*

en dow ment (en dou′mənt), **1** money or property given a person or institution to provide an income: *This college has a large endowment.* **2** gift from birth; ability; talent: *A good sense of rhythm is a natural endowment.* **3** an endowing. *n.*

end table, a small table suitable for placing beside a couch or chair.

en due (en dü′ *or* en dyü′), **1** provide with a quality or power; furnish; supply. **2** clothe. *v.,* **en dued, en du ing.** Also, **indue.**

en dur a ble (en dur′ə bəl *or* en-dyur′ə bəl), **1** that can be endured; bearable: *The pain was barely endurable.* **2** likely to endure or last. *adj.*

en dur ance (en dur′əns *or* en-dyur′əns), **1** power to last and to with-

endive (A, def. 1; B, def. 2; C, def. 3)

hat, āge, fär; let, ēqual, tèrm; it, īce; hot, ōpen, ôrder; oil, out; cup, pùt, rüle; ch, child; ng, long; sh, she; th, thin; ᴛʜ, then; zh, measure;

ə represents *a* in about, *e* in taken, *i* in pencil, *o* in lemon, *u* in circus.

stand hard wear: *A runner must have great endurance to run 30 miles in a day. Thin, cheap cloth has little endurance.* **2** power to stand something without giving out; holding out; bearing up: *Her endurance of pain is remarkable.* *n.*

en dure (en dur′ *or* en dyur′), **1** keep on; last: *Metal and stone endure for a long time.* **2** put up with; bear; stand: *The pioneers endured many hardships.* *v.,* **en dured, en dur ing.**

en dur ing (en dur′ing *or* en dyur′-ing), lasting; permanent: *Mankind longs for an enduring peace. The works of great writers have enduring value.* *adj.* **—en dur′ing ly,** *adv.*

end ways (end′wāz′), **1** on end; upright. **2** with the end forward; in the direction of the end. **3** lengthwise. **4** with the ends placed so that they touch; end to end. *adv.*

end wise (end′wīz′), endways. *adv.*

en e ma (en′ə mə), injection of liquid into the rectum to flush the bowels. *n., pl.* **en e mas.**

en e my (en′ə mē), **1** person or group that hates and tries to harm another: *He has many friends and few enemies.* **2** a force, nation, army, fleet, or air force that opposes another; person, ship, etc., of a hostile nation. Two countries at war with each other are enemies. **3** anything harmful: *Frost is an enemy of flowers.* *n., pl.* **en e mies.**

en er get ic (en′ər jet′ik), full of energy; eager to work; full of force; active; vigorous: *Cool autumn days make us feel energetic. adj.*

en er get i cal ly (en′ər jet′ik lē), with energy; vigorously. *adv.*

en er gize (en′ər jīz), give energy to; make active: *Ambition energizes people.* *v.,* **en er gized, en er giz ing.**

en er gy (en′ər jē), **1** will to work; vigor: *The boy is so full of energy that he cannot keep still.* **2** power to work or act; force: *All our energies were used in keeping the fire from spreading.* **3** capacity for doing work, such as lifting or moving an object. Light, heat, and electricity are different forms of energy: *A steam engine changes heat*

adj. adjective	*n.* noun
adv. adverb	*prep.* preposition
conj. conjunction	*pron.* pronoun
interj. interjection	*v.* verb
sing. singular	*pl.* plural

into mechanical energy. *n., pl.* **en er gies.**

en er vate (en′ər vāt), lessen the vigor or strength of; weaken: *A hot, damp climate enervates people who are not used to it.* *v.,* **en er vat ed, en er vat ing.**

en er va tion (en′ər vā′shən), an enervating or a being enervated. *n.*

en fee ble (en fē′bəl), make feeble; weaken. *v.,* **en fee bled, en fee bling.**

en fold (en fōld′), 1 fold in; wrap up: *I enfolded myself in a warm blanket.* 2 embrace; clasp: *The little boy enfolded the puppy in his arms.* *v.*

en force (en fôrs′), 1 force obedience to; cause to be carried out: *Monitors help enforce school regulations.* 2 force; compel: *We have laws to enforce the payment of income taxes.* *v.,* **en forced, en forc ing.**

en force a ble (en fôr′sə bəl), that can be enforced. *adj.*

en force ment (en fôrs′mənt), an enforcing; carrying out: *Strict enforcement of the laws against speeding will reduce automobile accidents.* *n.*

en fran chise (en fran′chīz), 1 give the right to vote to: *The 19th amendment to the Constitution enfranchised American women.* 2 set free. *v.,* **en fran chised, en fran chis ing.**

en fran chise ment (en fran′chiz mənt), an enfranchising or a being enfranchised. *n.*

Eng., 1 England. 2 English.

en gage (en gāj′), 1 keep oneself busy; be occupied; be active; take part: *He engages in politics. They engaged in conversation.* 2 keep busy; occupy: *Work engages much of his time.* 3 take for use or work; hire: *We engaged two rooms in the hotel. She engaged a carpenter to repair the porch.* 4 promise or pledge to marry: *He is engaged to my sister. My sister and he are engaged.* 5 catch and hold; attract: *Bright colors engage a baby's attention.* 6 bind by a promise or contract; pledge: *He engaged himself as an apprentice to a printer.* 7 fit into; lock together. 8 start a battle with; attack: *Our soldiers engaged the enemy.* *v.,* **en gaged, en gag ing.**

en gaged (en gājd′), 1 promised or pledged to marry: *The engaged girl wore*

a diamond ring. 2 busy; occupied: *Engaged in conversation, they did not see us.* *adj.*

en gage ment (en gāj′mənt), 1 an engaging or a being engaged. 2 a promise; pledge: *She tries to fulfill all of her engagements.* 3 a promise or pledge to marry: *Their parents announced the young couple's engagement.* 4 a meeting with someone at a certain time; appointment: *He made a point of being punctual in all his engagements.* 5 period of being hired; time of use or work: *The actor had an engagement of three weeks in a play.* 6 a fight; battle. *n.*

en gag ing (en gā′jing), very attractive; pleasing; charming: *an engaging smile.* *adj.* —**en gag′ing ly,** *adv.*

en gen der (en jen′dər), bring into existence; produce; cause: *Filth engenders disease.* *v.*

en gine (en′jən), 1 machine that changes energy from fuel, steam, water pressure, etc., into motion and power. An engine is used to apply power to some work, such as driving other machines. 2 machine that pulls a railroad train; locomotive. 3 anything used to bring about a result; machine; instrument: *Cannons are engines of war.* *n.*

engine block, the main part of an engine, cast as a single unit, containing the cylinders.

en gi neer (en′jə nir′), 1 person who takes care of or runs engines. The man who runs a locomotive is an engineer. 2 person who plans and builds engines, machines, roads, bridges, canals, railroads, forts, and the like; an expert in engineering: *a mining engineer.* 3 member of a military unit trained, equipped, and used for engineering work. 4 plan, build, direct, or work as an engineer. 5 manage cleverly; guide skillfully: *Although most of the members of the club were against her plan, she engineered it through to final approval.* 1-3 *n.,* 4,5 *v.*

en gi neer ing (en′jə nir′ing), science, work, or profession of an engineer: *The Golden Gate bridge is a triumph of engineering.* *n.*

Eng land (ing′glənd), the largest division of Great Britain, in the S part. *Capital:* London. *n.*

GEARS ENGAGED   GEARS DISENGAGED

engage (def. 7)

Eng lish (ing′glish), 1 of or having to do with England, its people, or their language. 2 the people of England. 3 the language of England. English is also spoken in the United States, Canada, Australia, New Zealand, the Republic of South Africa, and many other countries. 4 **english,** a spinning motion given to a ball by hitting, throwing, kicking, etc., on one side of its center. 1 *adj.,* 2 *n.pl.,* 3,4 *n.sing.*

English Channel, strait between England and France.

English horn
about 30 in.
long

English horn, a woodwind instrument resembling an oboe, but larger and having a lower tone.

Eng lish man (ing′glish mən), man born or living in England. *n., pl.* **Eng lish men.**

English sparrow, a small brownish-gray bird, a European finch now very common in America.

Eng lish wom an (ing′glish wùm′ən), woman born or living in England. *n., pl.* **Eng lish wom en.**

en graft (en graft′), graft (a shoot, etc.) from one tree, etc., into another. *v.* Also, **ingraft.**

en grave (en grāv′), 1 cut deeply in; carve in; carve in an artistic way: *The jeweler engraved the boy's initials on the back of the watch.* 2 cut (a picture, design, map, etc.) in lines on a metal plate, block of wood, etc., for printing. 3 print from such a plate, block, etc. 4 fix firmly: *Her face is engraved in my mind.* *v.,* **en graved, en grav ing.**

en grav er (en grā′vər), person who engraves metal plates, blocks of wood, etc., for printing. *n.*

en grav ing (en grā′ving), 1 act or art of an engraver. 2 picture printed from an engraved plate, block, etc.; print. *n.*

en gross (en grōs′), occupy wholly; take up all the attention of: *The artist was so engrossed in his painting that he didn't notice the people watching him.* *v.*

en gulf (en gulf′), swallow up; overwhelm: *A wave engulfed the small boat.* v.

en hance (en hans′), make greater; add to; heighten: *The gardens enhanced the beauty of the house. The growth of a city often enhances the value of land close to it.* v., **en hanced, en hanc ing.**

en hance ment (en hans′mənt), an enhancing or a being enhanced. *n.*

e nig ma (i nig′mə), a baffling or puzzling problem, situation, person, etc.; riddle: *How the magician had been able to get out of the locked trunk was an enigma to the audience.* n., pl. **e nig mas.**

en ig mat ic (en′ig mat′ik), like an enigma or riddle; baffling; puzzling: *an enigmatic smile. We could not understand their enigmatic answers to our questions.* adj. —**en′ig mat′i cal ly,** adv.

en ig mat i cal (en′ig mat′ə kəl), enigmatic. *adj.*

en join (en join′), 1 order, direct, or urge: *The father enjoined his children to always be honest.* 2 forbid; prohibit: *The judge enjoined the contractor from building a factory in an area set aside for homes.* v.

en joy (en joi′), 1 have or use with joy; be happy with; take pleasure in: *The children enjoyed their visit to the museum.* 2 have as an advantage or benefit: *He enjoys good health.* v.

enjoy oneself, have a good time; be happy: *Enjoy yourself at the party.*

en joy a ble (en joi′ə bəl), that can be enjoyed; giving joy; pleasant. *adj.*

en joy ment (en joi′mənt), 1 pleasure; joy; delight. 2 a having as an advantage or benefit; possession or use: *I have the enjoyment of her bicycle while she is away this summer.* n.

en kin dle (en kin′dl), kindle. v., **en kin dled, en kin dling.**

en large (en lärj′), make or become larger; increase in size: *The factory was enlarged to make room for more machinery. The balloon enlarged as we pumped air into it.* v., **en larged, en larg ing.**

enlarge on, talk or write about in more detail: *The principal enlarged on his plans for a new school.*

en large ment (en lärj′mənt), 1 an enlarging or a being enlarged. 2 thing that enlarges something else; addition. 3 photograph or other thing which has been made larger. *n.*

en light en (en līt′n), give truth and knowledge to; free from prejudice, ignorance, etc.; inform; instruct: *His travels enlightened him about many things he had not known before.* v.

en light en ment (en līt′n mənt), an

enlightening or a being enlightened; information; instruction. *n.*

en list (en list′), 1 join the army, navy, or some other branch of the armed forces: *He enlisted in the Air Force when he finished college.* 2 get to join some branch of the armed forces; induct: *Many men were enlisted during the war.* 3 get to join in some cause or undertaking; get the help or support of: *The principal enlisted the students in a drive to keep the playground clean.* 4 join in some cause or undertaking; give help or support: *Many members of our class enlist in the Red Cross drive each year.* v.

enlisted man, man in the armed forces who is not a commissioned officer or warrant officer.

en list ment (en list′mənt), 1 an enlisting or a being enlisted. 2 time for which a person enlists. *n.*

en liv en (en lī′vən), make lively, active, gay, or cheerful: *enliven a speech with humor. Bright curtains enliven a dull room.* v.

en masse (en mas′), in a group; all together. [from French *en masse* in mass]

en mesh (en mesh′), catch in a net; enclose in meshes; entangle. *v.*

en mi ty (en′mə tē), the feeling that enemies have for each other; hostility or hatred. n., pl. **en mi ties.**

en no ble (en nō′bəl), 1 raise in the respect of others; make noble; dignify: *A good deed ennobles the person who does it.* 2 raise to a noble rank; give a title of nobility to: *The king ennobled his general for winning the war.* v., **en no bled, en no bling.**

en nui (än′wē), a feeling of weariness and discontent from having no occupation or interest; boredom. *n.*

e nor mi ty (i nôr′mə tē), 1 extreme wickedness: *The enormity of his crime made it likely that he was not sane.* 2 an extremely wicked crime. n., pl. **e nor mi ties.**

e nor mous (i nôr′məs), extremely large; huge: *Long ago enormous animals lived on the earth. The glutton had an enormous appetite.* adj. —**e nor′mous ness,** n.

e nor mous ly (i nôr′məs lē), in or to an enormous degree; extremely; vastly. *adv.*

e nough (i nuf′), 1 as much or as many as needed or wanted; sufficient: *Buy enough food for the picnic. Are there enough seats for all?* 2 quantity or number needed or wanted; sufficient amount: *I have had enough to eat.* 3 sufficiently; adequately: *Have you played enough?* 4 quite; fully: *He was willing enough to go.* 5 rather; fair-

hat, āge, fär; let, ēqual, tėrm;
it, īce; hot, ōpen, ôrder;
oil, out; cup, pùt, rüle; ch, child;
ng, long; sh, she; th, thin;
ŦH, then; zh, measure;

ə represents *a* in about,
e in taken, *i* in pencil,
o in lemon, *u* in circus.

ly: *She talks well enough for a baby.* 1 adj., 2 n., 3-5 adv.

en quire (en kwīr′), inquire. v., **en quired, en quir ing.**

en quir y (en kwī′rē *or* en′kwər ē), inquiry. n., pl. **en quir ies.**

en rage (en rāj′), make very angry; make furious: *The dog was enraged by the teasing.* v., **en raged, en rag ing.**

en rap ture (en rap′chər), move to rapture; fill with great delight: *The audience was enraptured by the singer's beautiful voice.* v., **en rap tured, en rap tur ing.**

en rich (en rich′), make rich or richer: *An education enriches your mind. Adding vitamins or minerals to food enriches it. Fertilizer enriches the soil.* v.

en rich ment (en rich′mənt), 1 an enriching or a being enriched. 2 thing that enriches. *n.*

en roll or **en rol** (en rōl′), 1 write in a list; register: *The secretary enrolled our names.* 2 have one's name written in a list. 3 make a member: *He enrolled his son in a music school.* 4 become a member: *Her mother enrolled in a sewing class.* 5 enlist: *He enrolled in the navy.* v., **en rolled, en roll ing.**

en roll ment or **en rol ment** (en rōl′mənt), 1 an enrolling: *Enrollment took place in the fall.* 2 number enrolled: *The school has an enrollment of 200 students.* n.

en route (än rüt′), on the way: *We shall stop at Philadelphia en route from New York to Washington.* [from French]

en sconce (en skons′), 1 shelter safely; hide: *The family was ensconced in the cellar when the tornado hit.* 2 settle comfortably and firmly: *The cat ensconced itself in the armchair.* v., **en sconced, en sconc ing.**

en sem ble (än säm′bəl), 1 all the parts of a thing considered together; general effect. 2 group of musicians playing or singing together: *Two violins, a cello, and a harp made up the string ensemble.* 3 a complete, harmonious costume: *Her dress and coat made an attractive ensemble.* n.

en shrine (en shrīn′), 1 enclose in a

adj.	adjective	*n.*	noun
adv.	adverb	*prep.*	preposition
conj.	conjunction	*pron.*	pronoun
interj.	interjection	*v.*	verb
sing.	singular	*pl.*	plural

shrine: *A statue is enshrined in the cathedral.* 2 keep sacred; cherish: *happy memories enshrined in one's heart.* *v.,* **en shrined, en shrin ing.**

en shroud (en shroud´), cover or hide; veil: *Fog enshrouded the ship, but we could hear its whistle.* *v.*

en sign (en´sīn *or* en´sən *for 1,3,4;* en´sən *for 2*), 1 a flag or banner: *The ensign of the United States is the Stars and Stripes.* 2 a navy officer ranking next below a lieutenant, junior grade and next above a warrant officer. An ensign is the lowest commissioned officer in the United States Navy. 3 a former British army officer whose duty was carrying the flag. 4 sign of one's rank, position, or power; symbol of authority: *The ensign of the queen was her crown and scepter.* *n.*

en si lage (en´sə lij), silage. *n.*

en slave (en slāv´), make a slave or slaves of; take away freedom from *v.,* **en slaved, en slav ing.**

en slave ment (en slāv´mənt), an enslaving or a being enslaved. *n.*

en snare (en sner´ *or* en snar´), catch in a snare; trap. *v.,* **en snared, en snar ing.** Also, **insnare.**

en sue (en sü´), 1 come after; follow. The ensuing year means the year following this. 2 happen as a result: *In his anger he pushed the man, and a fight ensued.* *v.,* **en sued, en su ing.**

en sure (en shùr´), 1 make sure or certain: *Careful planning and hard work ensured the success of the party.* 2 make sure of getting; secure: *A letter of introduction will ensure you an interview.* 3 make safe; protect: *Proper clothing ensured us against suffering from the cold.* *v.,* **en sured, en sur ing.**

-ent, suffix added to verbs. 1 *(to form adjectives)* ____ing: *Absorbent = absorbing. Indulgent = indulging.* 2 *(to form nouns)* one that ____s: *Correspondent = one that corresponds. President = one that presides.* 3 *(to form adjectives)* other meanings, as in *competent, confident.* [from Latin *-entem*]

en tail (en tāl´), 1 impose or require: *Owning an automobile entailed greater expense than he had expected.* 2 limit the inheritance of (property) to a specified line of heirs so that it cannot be left to anyone else. An entailed estate usually passes to the eldest son. 3 an entailed inheritance. 4 the order of inheritance settled for an estate: *Though the nobleman quarreled with his heir, he could not break the entail and leave the estate to someone else.* 1,2 *v.,* 3,4 *n.*

en tan gle (en tang´gəl), 1 get twisted up and caught; tangle: *He entangled his feet in the coil of rope and fell down.* 2 get into difficulty; involve: *The villain tried to entangle the hero in an evil scheme.* *v.,* **en tan gled, en tan gling.**

en tan gle ment (en tang´gəl mənt), 1 an entangling or a being entangled: *dishonest business entanglements. The new republic avoided an entanglement with foreign countries.* 2 thing that entangles; snare: *The trenches were protected by barbed wire entanglements.* *n.*

en tente (än tänt´), 1 an understanding; agreement between two or more governments. 2 parties to an understanding; governments that have made an agreement. *n.*

en ter (en´tər), 1 go into; come into: *She entered the house. The bullet entered her heart.* 2 go in; come in: *Let them enter.* 3 become a part or member of; join: *She entered the contest.* 4 cause to join or enter; enroll: *Parents enter their children in school.* 5 begin; start: *After years of training, the doctor entered the practice of medicine.* 6 write or print in a book, list, etc.: *Words are entered alphabetically in a dictionary.* 7 put in regular form; make a record of; record: *The teller entered the deposit in my bankbook. The injured man entered a complaint in court.* *v.*

enter into, take part in; join in: *The two speakers entered into a debate.*

enter on or **enter upon,** begin; start: *He entered on his professional duties as soon as he finished law school.*

en ter prise (en´tər prīz), 1 an important, difficult, or dangerous plan to be tried; great or bold undertaking: *A trip into space is a daring enterprise.* 2 any undertaking; project: *a business enterprise.* 3 readiness to try important, difficult, or dangerous plans; willingness to undertake great or bold projects: *The American pioneers were people of great enterprise.* *n.*

en ter pris ing (en´tər prī´zing), likely to start projects; ready to face difficulties: *an enterprising young businessman.* *adj.*

en ter tain (en´tər tān´), 1 keep pleasantly interested; please or amuse: *The circus entertained the children.* 2 have as a guest: *She entertained ten people at dinner.* 3 have guests; provide entertainment for guests: *She entertains a great deal.* 4 take into the mind; consider: *I refuse to entertain such a foolish idea.* 5 hold in the mind; maintain: *Even after failing twice, we still entertained a hope of success.* *v.*

en ter tain er (en´tər tā´nər), 1 person who entertains. 2 singer, musician, etc., who performs in public. *n.*

en ter tain ing (en´tər tā´ning), interesting; pleasing or amusing. *adj.* —**en´ter tain´ing ly,** *adv.*

en ter tain ment (en´tər tān´mənt), 1 thing that interests, pleases, or amuses. A show or a circus is an entertainment. 2 act of entertaining: *The host and hostess devoted themselves to the entertainment of their guests.* 3 condition of being entertained: *She played the piano for our entertainment.* *n.*

en thrall or **en thral** (en thrôl´), 1 hold captive by beauty or interest; fascinate; charm: *The journalist enthralled the audience with the story of her foreign assignments.* 2 make a slave of; enslave: *The captive peoples were enthralled by their conquerors.* *v.,* **en thralled, en thrall ing.**

en throne (en thrōn´), 1 set on a throne. 2 place highest of all; exalt. *v.,* **en throned, en thron ing.**

en thuse (en thüz´), INFORMAL. 1 show enthusiasm: *She enthused over the idea of going on a picnic.* 2 fill with enthusiasm: *The plan for a trip out West enthused the family.* *v.,* **en thused, en thus ing.**

en thu si asm (en thü´zē az´əm), eager interest; zeal: *The invitation to the birthday party aroused the child's enthusiasm.* *n.*

en thu si ast (en thü´zē ast), person who is filled with enthusiasm: *a football enthusiast.* *n.*

en thu si as tic (en thü´zē as´tik), full of enthusiasm; eagerly interested: *My little brother is very enthusiastic about going to kindergarten.* *adj.*

en thu si as ti cal ly (en thü´zē as´tik lē), with enthusiasm. *adv.*

en tice (en tīs´), attract by arousing hopes or desires; tempt: *The smell of food enticed the hungry children into the house.* *v.,* **en ticed, en tic ing.**

en tice ment (en tīs´mənt), 1 an enticing or a being enticed. 2 thing that entices: *Enticements of milk and meat brought the frightened cat down from the tree.* *n.*

en tire (en tīr´), 1 having all the parts; whole; complete: *The entire class behaved very well on the trip.* 2 not broken; in one piece: *The original property is still entire even though it has had many owners.* *adj.*

en tire ly (en tīr´lē), to the whole

amount or extent; completely; fully: *He is entirely wrong. adv.*

en tire ty (en tīr′tē), the whole; completeness. *n., pl.* **en tire ties.**

in its entirety, wholly; completely: *He gave his farm in its entirety to his son.*

en ti tle (en tī′tl), 1 give a claim or right: *The one who wins is entitled to first prize.* 2 give the title of; call by the name of: *The author entitled his book "Treasure Island." The Queen of England is also entitled "Defender of the Faith." v.,* **en ti tled, en ti tling.**

en ti ty (en′tə tē), 1 something that has a real and separate existence. Persons, mountains, languages, and beliefs are distinct entities. 2 being; existence. *n., pl.* **en ti ties.**

en tomb (en tüm′), place in a tomb; bury. *v.*

en to mo log i cal (en′tə mə loj′ə kəl), of or having to do with entomology. *adj.*

en to mol o gist (en′tə mol′ə jist), an expert in entomology. *n.*

en to mol o gy (en′tə mol′ə jē), branch of zoology that deals with insects. *n.*

en tou rage (än′tü räzh′), group of attendants; people usually accompanying a person: *a queen and her entourage. n.*

en trails (en′trālz *or* en′trəlz), 1 the inner parts of the body of a man or animal: *Before a chicken can be cooked, the entrails are removed.* 2 the intestines; bowels. *n.pl.*

en train (en trān′), 1 get on a train. 2 put on a train: *The soldiers were secretly entrained at night. v.*

en trance[1] (en′trəns), 1 act of entering: *The actor's entrance was greeted with applause.* 2 place by which to enter; door, passageway, etc.: *The entrance to the hotel was blocked with baggage.* 3 freedom or right to enter; permission to enter: *Entrance to the exhibit is on weekdays only. n.* [from French of the 1500's]

en trance[2] (en trans′), 1 fill with joy; delight; charm: *From the first note the singer's voice entranced the audience.* 2 put into a trance. *v.,* **en tranced, en tranc ing.** [*en-* (prefix meaning "put in") + *trance*]

en trant (en′trənt), 1 person who enters. 2 person who takes part in a contest: *There were many entrants in the spelling contest. n.*

en trap (en trap′), 1 catch in a trap. 2 bring into difficulty or danger; trick: *By clever questioning, the lawyer entrapped the witness into contradicting himself. v.,* **en trapped, en trap ping.**

en treat (en trēt′), keep asking earnestly; beg and pray: *She entreated her father to send her to summer camp. The prisoners entreated their captors to*

let them go. *v.* —**en treat′ing ly,** *adv.*

en treat y (en trē′tē), an earnest request; prayer: *Her father gave in to her entreaties. n., pl.* **en treat ies.**

en tree (än′trā), 1 freedom or right to enter; access. 2 the main dish of food at dinner or lunch. *n.* [from French *entrée*]

en trée (än′trā), entree. *n., pl.* **en trées.**

en trench (en trench′), 1 surround with a trench; fortify with trenches: *Our soldiers were entrenched opposite the enemy.* 2 establish firmly: *Exchanging gifts at Christmas is a custom entrenched by long tradition.* 3 trespass; encroach; infringe: *Do not entrench upon the rights of others. v.* Also, **intrench.**

en trench ment (en trench′mənt), 1 an entrenching. 2 an entrenched position. 3 defense consisting of a trench and a rampart of earth or stone. *n.* Also, **intrenchment.**

entrenchment (def. 3) in World War I

en tre pre neur (än′trə prə nėr′), person who organizes and manages a business or industrial undertaking. *n.*

en trust (en trust′), 1 charge with a trust: *We entrusted the class treasurer with all the money for bus fares on our class trip.* 2 give the care of; hand over for safekeeping: *While traveling, they entrusted the child to her grandparents. v.* Also, **intrust.**

en try (en′trē), 1 act of entering: *His sudden entry startled me.* 2 place by which to enter; way to enter: *The entry to the hotel was blocked with luggage so that no one could enter or leave.* 3 thing written or printed in a book, list, etc. Each word explained in a dictionary is an entry or **entry word.** 4 person or thing that takes part in a contest: *The car race had thirty entries. n., pl.* **en tries.**

en twine (en twīn′), 1 twine together: *She entwined two hearts on the valentine she made.* 2 twine around: *Roses entwined the little cottage. v.,* **en twined, en twin ing.**

e nu me rate (i nü′mə rāt′ *or* i nyü′mə rāt′), 1 name one by one; list: *He enumerated the capitals of the 50*

hat, āge, fär; let, ēqual, tėrm;
it, īce; hot, ōpen, ôrder;
oil, out; cup, put, rüle; ch, child;
ng, long; sh, she; th, thin;
ᵀH, then; zh, measure;

ə represents *a* in about,
e in taken, *i* in pencil,
o in lemon, *u* in circus.

states. 2 find out the number of; count. *v.,* **e nu me rat ed, e nu me rat ing.**

e nu me ra tion (i nü′mə rā′shən *or* i nyü′mə rā′shən), 1 an enumerating; listing or counting: *A census is an official enumeration of the people of a country.* 2 a list. *n.*

e nun ci ate (i nun′sē āt), 1 speak or pronounce words: *Radio and television announcers must ennunciate very clearly* 2 state definitely; announce: *After performing many experiments, the scientist enunciated a new theory. v.,* **e nun ci at ed, e nun ci at ing.**

e nun ci a tion (i nun′sē ā′shən), 1 manner of pronouncing words. 2 a definite statement; announcement. *n.*

en vel op (en vel′əp), wrap, cover, or hide: *The baby was so enveloped in blankets that we could hardly see her face. Fog enveloped the village. v.*

en ve lope (en′və lōp *or* än′və lōp), 1 a paper cover in which a letter or anything flat can be mailed. It can usually be folded over and sealed by wetting a gummed edge. 2 a covering; wrapper. *n.*

en vel op ment (en vel′əp mənt), 1 an enveloping or a being enveloped. 2 something that envelops; covering; wrapping. *n.*

en ven om (en ven′əm), 1 make poisonous: *an envenomed arrow.* 2 fill with bitterness, hate, etc.: *The dispute concerning borderlines envenomed the relationship between the nations. v.*

en vi a ble (en′vē ə bəl), to be envied; worth having; desirable: *She has an enviable school record. adj.*

en vi a bly (en′vē ə blē), in an enviable manner. *adv.*

en vi ous (en′vē əs), feeling or showing envy; full of envy: *envious of another's good fortune. adj.* —**en′vi ous ly,** *adv.* —**en′vi ous ness,** *n.*

en vi ron (en vī′rən), hem in; surround; enclose. *v.*

en vi ron ment (en vī′rən mənt), 1 all the surrounding things, conditions, and influences affecting the growth of living things: *A child's character is greatly influenced by his home environment.*

environmental

adj. adjective	*n.* noun
adv. adverb	*prep.* preposition
conj. conjunction	*pron.* pronoun
interj. interjection	*v.* verb
sing. singular	*pl.* plural

Differences in environment often account for differences in the same kind of plant found in different places. 2 surroundings: *an environment of poverty.* **n.**

en vi ron men tal (en vī′rən men′tl), having to do with environment. *adj.*

en vi rons (en vī′rənz), surrounding districts; suburbs: *We visited Boston and its environs.* **n.pl.**

en vis age (en viz′ij), form a mental picture of: *The architect looked at the plans and envisaged the finished house.* **v., en vis aged, en vis ag ing.**

en vi sion (en vizh′ən), envisage. *v.*

en voy (en′voi), 1 messenger or representative. 2 diplomat ranking next below an ambassador and next above a minister. *n.*

en vy (en′vē), 1 feeling of discontent, dislike, or desire because another has what one wants: *The children were filled with envy when they saw her new bicycle.* 2 the object of such feeling; person or thing envied: *She was the envy of the other children in school.* 3 feel envy toward: *Some people envy the rich.* 4 feel envy because of: *He envied his friend's success.* 1,2 *n., pl.* **en vies;** 3,4 *v.,* **en vied, en vy ing.**

en wrap (en rap′), wrap. *v.,* **en wrapped, en wrap ping.**

epidermis (def. 1)

en zyme (en′zīm), substance produced in living cells that influences a chemical reaction within the body without being changed itself. Enzymes help break down food so that it can be digested. Pepsin is an enzyme. *n.*

e o hip pus (ē′ō hip′əs), an extinct horse that was the ancestor of modern horses. It was about 15 inches high and 3½ feet long with toes instead of hoofs. *n., pl.* **e o hip pus es.**

e on (ē′ən), a very long period of time;

many thousands of years: *Eons passed before life existed on the earth.* **n.** Also, **aeon.**

ep au let or **ep au lette** (ep′ə let), ornament on the shoulder of a uniform. Epaulets are now usually worn only as a part of a military uniform. *n.*

e phed rine (i fed′rən), drug used to relieve hay fever, asthma, head colds, etc. *n.*

e phem er al (i fem′ər el), lasting for only a day; lasting for only a very short time; very short-lived. *adj.*

E phe sians (i fē′zhənz), book of the New Testament. It consists of a letter by Saint Paul to the Christians at Ephesus. *n.*

Eph e sus (ef′ə səs), an ancient Greek city in what is now W Turkey. *n.*

eph od (ef′od), vestment worn by the ancient Hebrew high priests. *n.*

ep ic (ep′ik), 1 a long poem that tells the adventures of one or more great heroes. It is written in a dignified, majestic style and often shows the ideals of a nation or race. Homer's *Odyssey* is an epic. 2 any writing having the qualities of an epic. Some very long novels are sometimes called epics. 3 of or like an epic; grand; heroic: *The first flight over the Atlantic was an epic deed.* 1,2 *n.,* 3 *adj.*

ep i cure (ep′ə kyúr), person who enjoys eating and drinking and who is very particular in choosing fine foods, wines, etc. *n.* [from *Epicurus,* 342?-270 B.C., Greek philosopher]

ep i cu re an (ep′ə kyú rē′ən), 1 of or fit for an epicure: *an epicurean banquet.* 2 person who is fond of pleasure and luxury; epicure. 1 *adj.,* 2 *n.*

ep i dem ic (ep′ə dem′ik), 1 the rapid spread of a disease so that many people have it at the same time: *All the schools in the city were closed because of an epidemic of measles.* 2 the rapid spread of an idea, fashion, etc.: *The city suffered from an epidemic of strikes by different labor unions all through the winter.* 3 affecting many people at the same time; widespread: *An outbreak of the flu became epidemic last winter.* 1,2 *n.,* 3 *adj.*

ep i der mis (ep′ə dèr′mis), 1 the outer layer of the skin of vertebrate animals. 2 a skinlike layer of cells in seed plants and ferns. *n.*

ep i glot tis (ep′ə glot′is), a thin, triangular plate of cartilage that covers the entrance to the windpipe during swallowing, so that food and drink do not get into the lungs. *n.*

ep i gram (ep′ə gram), 1 a short, pointed or witty saying. EXAMPLE: "Speech is silver, but silence is golden." 2 a short poem ending in a witty or clever turn of thought. EXAMPLE:

"Here lies our Sovereign Lord the King,
Whose word no man relies on,
Who never said a foolish thing,
Nor ever did a wise one." *n.*

ep i gram mat ic (ep′ə grə mat′ik), 1 like an epigram; short and witty. 2 full of epigrams. *adj.*

ep i lep sy (ep′ə lep′sē), a chronic disorder of the nervous system characterized by complete or partial loss of consciousness and sometimes convulsions. Epilepsy is usually caused by a birth defect or damage to the brain. *n.*

ep i lep tic (ep′ə lep′tik), 1 of epilepsy. 2 having epilepsy. 3 person having epilepsy. 1,2 *adj.,* 3 *n.*

ep i logue or **ep i log** (ep′ə lôg), 1 a concluding part added to a novel, poem, etc. An epilogue may be used to round out or interpret the work. 2 speech or poem at the end of a play. It is addressed to the audience by one of the actors. *n.*

E piph a ny (i pif′ə nē), January 6, the anniversary of the coming of the Three Wise Men to honor the infant Jesus at Bethlehem. *n.*

e pis co pal (i pis′kə pəl), 1 of or having to do with bishops. 2 governed by bishops. 3 **Episcopal,** of or having to do with the Church of England or with the Protestant Episcopal Church. *adj.*

E pis co pa lian (i pis′kə pā′lyən), 1 member of the Protestant Episcopal Church. 2 Episcopal. 1 *n.,* 2 *adj.*

ep i sode (ep′ə sōd), a single happening or group of happenings in real life or in a story: *Being named the best athlete of the year was an important episode in the baseball player's life.* *n.*

e pis tle (i pis′əl), 1 letter. Epistles are usually long, instructive, and written in formal or elegant language. 2 **Epistle,** (in the Bible) any of the letters written by the Apostles to various churches and individuals. The Epistles make up 21 books of the New Testament. *n.*

e pis to lar y (i pis′tl er′ē), 1 carried on by letters. 2 of letters. *adj.*

epiglottis—normal position for breathing. During swallowing, the epiglottis lowers and closes the windpipe.

ep i taph (ep′ə taf), a short statement in memory of a dead person. It is often put on a gravestone or tombstone. *n.*

ep i the li um (ep′ə thē′lē əm), a thin layer of cells forming a tissue that covers surfaces and lines hollow organs. *n., pl.* **ep i the li ums, ep i the li a** (ep/ə thē/lē ə).

ep i thet (ep/ə thet), a descriptive expression; word or phrase expressing some quality or attribute. In "Honest Abe" and "Richard the Lion-Hearted" the epithets are "Honest" and "the Lion-Hearted." *n.*

e pit o me (i pit/ə mē/), 1 a condensed account; summary. An epitome contains only the most important points of a book, essay, article, etc. 2 person or thing that is typical or representative of something: *Solomon is often spoken of as the epitome of wisdom. n.*

e pit o mize (i pit/ə mīz), 1 give a summary of. 2 be typical or representative of: *Helen Keller epitomizes the human ability to overcome handicaps. v.,* **e pit o mized, e pit o miz ing.**

e plu ri bus u num (ē plür/ə bəs yü/nəm), LATIN. out of many, one. It is the motto inscribed on the official seal of the United States. It was once the official motto of the United States, but since 1956 the official motto has been "In God We Trust."

ep och (ep/ək), 1 period of time; era: *There were few peaceful epochs in the history of our country.* 2 period of time in which striking things happened: *The years of the Civil War were an epoch in the United States.* 3 the starting point of such a period: *The invention of the steam engine marked an epoch in the growth of industry. n.*

ep och al (ep/ə kəl), 1 having to do with an epoch. 2 epoch-making: *the epochal discovery of electricity. adj.*

ep och-mak ing (ep/ək mā/king), beginning an epoch; causing important changes: *the epoch-making discovery of America. adj.*

Ep som salts (ep/səm), a bitter, white, crystalline powder taken in water as a laxative. [from *Epsom,* town in England, where it was first obtained from springs]

eq ua ble (ek/wə bəl), changing little; uniform; even; tranquil: *The good-natured traffic policeman had an equable disposition. The Gulf Stream makes England's climate fairly equable. adj.*

eq ua bly (ek/wə blē), uniformly; evenly: *Laws should be equably enforced. adv.*

e qual (ē/kwəl), 1 the same in amount, size, number, value, or rank: *Ten dimes are equal to one dollar. All persons are considered equal before the law.* 2 be the same as: *Four times five equals twenty.* 3 person or thing that is equal: *In spelling she had no equal.* 4 make or do something equal to: *Our team equaled the other team's score, and the game ended in a tie.* 5 the same

throughout; even; uniform: *an equal mixture.* 1,5 *adj.,* 2,4 *v.,* 3 *n.*

equal to, strong enough for: *One horse is not equal to pulling a load of five tons.*

e qual i ty (i kwol/ə tē), sameness in amount, size, number, value, rank, etc.; being equal. *n., pl.* **e qual i ties.**

e qual i za tion (ē/kwə lə zā/shən), an equalizing or a being equalized. *n.*

e qual ize (ē/kwə līz), 1 make equal. 2 make even or uniform. *v.,* **e qual ized, e qual iz ing.**

e qual iz er (ē/kwə lī/zər), 1 person or thing that equalizes. 2 device for equalizing forces, pressures, etc. *n.*

e qual ly (ē/kwə lē), in equal shares; in an equal manner; to an equal degree: *Divide the pie equally. My sister and brother are equally talented. adv.*

e qua nim i ty (ē/kwə nim/ə tē or ek/wə nim/ə tē), evenness of mind or temper; calmness; composure: *The speaker endured the insults of the heckler with equanimity. n.*

e quate (i kwāt/), 1 state to be equal; put into the form of an equation: *I equated 30 inches to 2½ feet.* 2 make equal; treat as equal. *v.,* **e quat ed, e quat ing.**

e qua tion (i kwā/zhən), 1 statement of the equality of two quantities. EXAMPLES: $(4×8) + 12 = 44.$ $C = 2\pi r.$ 2 expression using chemical formulas and symbols to show the substances used and produced in a chemical change. EXAMPLE: $HC1 + NaOH = NaCl + H_2O.$ 3 an equating or a being equated. *n.*

e qua tor (i kwā/tər), an imaginary circle around the middle of the earth, halfway between the North Pole and the South Pole. The United States is north of the equator; Australia is south of it. *n.*

e qua to ri al (ē/kwə tôr/ē əl or ek/wə tôr/ē əl), 1 of, at, or near the equator: *Ecuador is an equatorial country.* 2 like conditions at or near the equator: *The weather was humid and hot enough to be equatorial. adj.*

Equatorial Guinea, country in W Africa consisting of two parts, one on the mainland and the other an island.

eq uer ry (ek/wər ē), 1 officer of a royal or noble household who has charge of the horses or who accompanies his master's carriage. 2 attendant upon a member of the British royal household. *n., pl.* **eq uer ries.**

e ques tri an (i kwes/trē ən), 1 having to do with horseback riding, horses, or horseback riders: *Cowboys have equestrian skill.* 2 on horseback. An equestrian statue shows a person riding a horse. 3 rider or performer on horseback. 1,2 *adj.,* 3 *n.*

e qui dis tant (ē/kwə dis/tənt), equal-

hat, āge, fär; let, ēqual, tèrm;
it, īce; hot, ōpen, ôrder;
oil, out; cup, pùt, rüle; ch, child;
ng, long; sh, she; th, thin;
ŦH, then; zh, measure;

ə represents *a* in about,
e in taken, *i* in pencil,
o in lemon, *u* in circus.

ly distant: *All points of the circumference of a circle are equidistant from the center. adj.*

e qui lat er al (ē/kwə lat/ər əl), having all sides equal. *adj.* —**e/qui-lat/er al ly,** *adv.*

equilateral triangle

e qui lib ri um (ē/kwə lib/rē əm), 1 balance: *The acrobat in the circus maintained equilibrium on a tightrope. Scales are in equilibrium when the weights on each side are equal.* 2 mental poise: *My mother does not let quarrels between my brother and me upset her equilibrium. n.*

e quine (ē/kwīn), 1 of horses. 2 like a horse; like that of a horse. *adj.*

e qui noc tial (ē/kwə nok/shəl), having to do with or occurring at an equinox or at a time when day and night are of equal length: *an equinoctial storm. adj.*

e qui nox (ē/kwə noks), either of the two times in the year when the center of the sun crosses the equator, and day and night are of equal length in all parts of the earth. It occurs about March 21 (**vernal equinox**) and about September 22 (**autumnal equinox**). *n., pl.* **e qui nox es.**

e quip (i kwip/), supply with all that is needed; fit out; provide; furnish: *The scouts equipped themselves with canteens and food for the hike. Is the ship fully equipped for its voyage? v.,* **e quipped, e quip ping.**

eq ui page (ek/wə pij), 1 carriage. 2 carriage with its horses, driver, and servants. 3 equipment; outfit. *n.*

e quip ment (i kwip/mənt), 1 act of equipping; fitting out: *The equipment of the expedition took six months.* 2 what a person or thing is equipped with; outfit; furnishings; supplies: *A soldier must keep his equipment in order. n.*

e qui poise (ē/kwə poiz or ek/wə-poiz), 1 equal distribution of weight or

289

adj. adjective	*n.* noun
adv. adverb	*prep.* preposition
conj. conjunction	*pron.* pronoun
interj. interjection	*v.* verb
sing. singular	*pl.* plural

force; even balance. 2 a balancing force; counterbalance. *n.*

eq ui ta ble (ek′wə tə bəl), fair; just: *It is equitable to pay a person good wages for work well done. adj.*

eq ui ta bly (ek′wə tə blē), in an equitable manner; fairly; justly. *adv.*

eq ui ty (ek′wə tē), fairness; justice: *The judge was noted for the equity of his decisions. n., pl.* **eq ui ties.**

e quiv a lence (i kwiv′ə ləns), condition of being equivalent. *n.*

e quiv a lent (i kwiv′ə lənt), 1 equal; the same in value, force, effect, meaning, etc.: *Nodding your head is equivalent to saying yes.* 2 something equivalent: *Five pennies are the equivalent of a nickel.* 1 *adj.,* 2 *n.* —**e quiv′a lent ly,** *adv.*

e quiv o cal (i kwiv′ə kəl), 1 having two or more meanings; ambiguous: *His equivocal answer was so vague that we could not tell what his real opinion was.* 2 undecided; uncertain: *Nothing was proved because the result of the experiment was equivocal.* 3 questionable; suspicious: *There was something equivocal about her long and secret trips. adj.* —**e quiv′o cal ly,** *adv.*

e quiv o cate (i kwiv′ə kāt), use expressions of double meaning in order to mislead: *When asked if he had finished his arithmetic, he equivocated by saying, "I was working on that an hour ago." v.,* **e quiv o cat ed, e quiv o cat ing.**

e quiv o ca tion (i kwiv′ə kā′shən), 1 the use of expressions with double meaning in order to mislead. 2 an equivocal expression. *n.*

-er[1], *suffix forming nouns.* 1 (*added to verbs*) *person or thing that* _____*s*: *Admirer = a person who admires. Burner = thing that burns.* 2 (*added to nouns*) *person living in* _____: *New Yorker = a person living in New York. Villager = a person living in a village.* 3 (*added to nouns*) *person who makes or works with* _____: *Hatter = a person who makes hats.* [Old English *-ere,* from Latin *-arium* having to do with]

-er[2], *suffix forming the comparative degree of adjectives and adverbs.* more: *Softer = more soft. Slower = more slow.* [Old English *-or, -ra, -re*]

er a (ir′ə), 1 an age in history; historical period: *The years from 1817 to 1824 in United States history are often called the Era of Good Feeling.* 2 period of time starting from an important or significant happening, date, etc.: *We live in the 20th century of the Christian era.* 3 one of the five very large divisions of time in geological history. *n., pl.* **er as.**

e rad i cate (i rad′ə kāt), 1 get rid of entirely; destroy completely: *Yellow fever has been eradicated in the United States.* 2 pull out by the roots: *The gardener eradicated weeds from the garden. v.,* **e rad i cat ed, e rad i cat ing.**

e rad i ca tion (i rad′ə kā′shən), an eradicating; complete destruction; uprooting. *n.*

e rase (i rās′), 1 rub out; remove by rubbing or scraping: *She erased the wrong answer and wrote in the right one.* 2 remove all trace of; blot out: *The blow on his head erased the details of the accident from his memory. v.,* **e rased, e ras ing.**

ermine (def. 1)—11 in. long with tail

e ras er (i rā′sər), something used to erase marks made with pencil, ink, chalk, etc.: *My pencil is equipped with an eraser made of rubber. n.*

E ras mus (i raz′məs), 1466?-1536, Dutch scholar and religious teacher. *n.*

e ra sure (i rā′shər), 1 an erasing: *the erasure of a typing error.* 2 an erased word, letter, etc. 3 place where a word, letter, etc., has been erased. *n.*

er bi um (ėr′bē əm), a soft, lustrous, grayish metallic element which occurs as a minute part of various minerals. *n.* [from (*Ytt*)*erby,* Sweden]

ere (er *or* ar), OLD USE. before. *prep., conj.*

Er e bus (er′ə bəs), (in Greek myths) a dark, gloomy place through which the dead passed on their way to Hades. *n.*

e rect (i rekt′), 1 straight up; not bending; not tipping; upright: *A telephone pole stands erect. The dancer held her body erect.* 2 put straight up; set upright: *They erected a television antenna on the roof. The mast was erected on a firm base.* 3 put up; build: *That house was erected forty years ago.* 1 *adj.,* 2,3 *v.* —**e rect′ly,** *adv.* —**e rect′ness,** *n.*

e rec tion (i rek′shən), 1 a setting up; raising; erecting: *The erection of the tent took only a few minutes.* 2 thing erected; building or other structure. *n.*

er e mite (er′ə mīt), hermit. *n.*

erg (ėrg), unit for measuring work or

energy. It is the amount of work done by one dyne acting through a distance of one centimeter. *n.*

er go (ėr′gō), LATIN. therefore. *adv., conj.*

Er ic son (er′ik sən), **Leif,** Viking chieftain who probably discovered North America about A.D. 1000. *n.*

Er ie (ir′ē), 1 **Lake,** one of the five Great Lakes. 2 city in NW Pennsylvania on Lake Erie. *n.*

Erie Canal, canal in New York State between Buffalo and Albany, connecting Lake Erie with the Hudson River.

Er in (er′ən), Ireland. *n.*

er mine (ėr′mən), 1 weasel of northern regions that is brown in summer but white in winter, except for a black tip on its tail. 2 its soft, white fur, used for women's coats, trimming, etc. The official robes of English judges are trimmed with ermine as a symbol of purity and fairness. 3 position, rank, or duties of a judge. *n., pl.* **er mines** or **er mine.**

e rode (i rōd′), eat or wear away gradually; eat into: *Acid erodes metal. Running water erodes soil and rocks. v.,* **e rod ed, e rod ing.**

Er os (ir′os *or* er′os), (in Greek myths) the god of love, son of Aphrodite. The Romans called him Cupid. *n.*

e ro sion (i rō′zhən), 1 a gradual eating or wearing away by glaciers, running water, waves, or wind: *Trees help prevent the erosion of soil by running water.* 2 a being eaten or worn away: *The face of the cliff had suffered erosion from wind and sea. n.*

err (ėr *or* er), 1 go wrong; make a mistake: *Everyone errs at some time or other.* 2 be wrong; be mistaken or incorrect: *err in an opinion or belief.* 3 do wrong; sin: *To err is human; to forgive, divine. v.*

er rand (er′ənd), 1 a trip to do something: *She has gone on an errand to the store.* 2 what one is sent to do: *She did ten errands in one trip. n.*

er rant (er′ənt), 1 wandering; roving: *an errant knight seeking adventures.* 2 wrong; mistaken. *adj.*

er rat ic (ə rat′ik), 1 uncertain; irregular: *An erratic clock is not dependable.* 2 queer; odd: *erratic behavior. adj.* —**er rat′i cal ly,** *adv.*

er ro ne ous (ə rō/nē əs), not correct; wrong; mistaken: *Years ago many people held the erroneous belief that the earth was flat. adj.* —**er ro/ne ous ly,** *adv.*

er ror (er/ər), 1 something done that is wrong; something that is not the way it ought to be; mistake: *I failed my test because of errors in spelling.* 2 condition of being wrong or mistaken: *You are in error; your answer is wrong.* 3 a faulty play in catching or throwing a baseball that permits a batter who should have been put out to reach base or allows a runner to advance. *n.*

erst while (ėrst/hwīl/), 1 former; past: *an erstwhile companion.* 2 OLD USE. in time past; formerly. 1 *adj.,* 2 *adv.*

er u dite (er/u dīt *or* er/yə dīt), having much knowledge; scholarly; learned: *an erudite teacher, an erudite book. adj.* —**er/u dite/ly,** *adv.*

er u di tion (er/u dish/ən *or* er/yə dish/ən), scholarship; learning: *The professor's erudition came from long years of study. n.*

e rupt (i rupt/), 1 burst forth: *Hot water erupted from the geyser. Headlines erupted around the world.* 2 throw forth: *The volcano erupted lava and ashes.* 3 break out in a rash: *Her skin erupted when she had measles.* 4 break through the gums: *When the baby was seven months old his teeth started to erupt. v.*

e rup tion (i rup/shən), 1 a bursting or throwing forth: *There was an eruption of glowing melted rock from the mountain top.* 2 a breaking out in a rash. 3 red spots on the skin; rash: *Chicken pox causes an eruption on the body. n.*

escapement—In a pendulum clock, the escapement coordinates the movement of the weight with that of the pendulum by preventing the weight from falling too fast. One tooth of the wheel escapes at each swing of the pendulum.

e rup tive (i rup/tiv), 1 bursting forth. 2 causing the skin to break out: *Measles is an eruptive disease. adj.*

-ery, *suffix forming nouns.* 1 (*added to verbs*) place for _____ing: *Cannery = place for canning.* 2 (*added to nouns*) place for _____s: *Nunnery = place for nuns.* 3 (*added to nouns*) art or occupation of a _____: *Cookery = art or occupation of a cook.* 4 (*added to nouns*)

condition of a _____: *Slavery = condition of a slave.* 5 (*added to nouns*) qualities, actions, etc., of a _____: *Knavery = qualities, actions, etc. of a knave.* 6 (*added to nouns*) group of _____s: *Machinery = group of machines.* [from French before the 1400's *-erie*]

er y sip e las (er/ə sip/ə ləs), an acute infectious disease that causes fever and a deep-red inflammation of the skin. *n.*

E sau (ē/sô), (in the Bible) the older son of Isaac and Rebecca, who sold his birthright to his twin brother Jacob. *n.*

es ca late (es/kə lāt), increase or expand by stages: *The commotion in the prison almost escalated into a riot. The general escalated the war by sending in more troops. v.,* **es ca lat ed, es ca lat ing.**

es ca la tion (es/kə lā/shən), an escalating or a being escalated. *n.*

es ca la tor (es/kə lā/tər), a moving stairway: *The big department store had both an elevator and an escalator. n.*

es cal lop (e skol/əp), scallop. *v.*

es ca pade (es/kə pād), a breaking loose from rules or restraint; wild prank. *n.*

es cape (e skāp/), 1 get out and away; get free: *escape from prison. The bird escaped from its cage.* 2 get free from: *He thinks he will never escape hard work.* 3 keep free or safe from; avoid: *We all escaped the measles.* 4 act of escaping: *His escape was aided by the thick fog.* 5 way of escaping: *There was no escape from the trap.* 6 come out or find a way out from a container; leak: *Gas had been escaping from the cylinder all night.* 7 come out of without being intended: *A cry escaped her lips.* 8 fail to be noticed or remembered by: *The pin escaped my eye. I knew his face, but his name escaped me.* 9 relief from boredom, trouble, etc.: *Some people find escape in mystery stories.* 1-3,6-8 *v.,* **es caped, es cap ing;** 4,5,9 *n.*

es cape ment (e skāp/mənt), device that gives a watch or clock its regular movement. *n.*

escape velocity, the velocity that a body such as a rocket must reach to break away permanently from the gravitational pull of the earth or other attracting body. Once a rocket's speed reaches 25,000 miles per hour, it can escape the pull of the earth without further power.

es cap ism (e skā/piz/əm), an avoiding of unpleasant things by daydreaming or by entertainment, such as motion pictures. *n.*

es car ole (es/kə rōl/), endive that has broad, smooth leaves, used for salads. *n.*

hat, āge, fär; let, ēqual, tėrm;
it, īce; hot, ōpen, ôrder;
oil, out; cup, pùt, rüle; ch, child;
ng, long; sh, she; th, thin;
ᴛʜ, then; zh, measure;

ə represents *a* in about,
e in taken, *i* in pencil,
o in lemon, *u* in circus.

es carp ment (e skärp/mənt), 1 a steep slope; cliff. 2 ground made into a steep slope as part of a fortification. *n.*

es chew (es chü/), keep away from; avoid; shun: *The doctor advised me to eschew rich foods. v.*

es cort (es/kôrt *for 1,2;* e skôrt/ *for 3*), 1 one or a group going with another to give protection, show honor, etc.: *An escort of ten policemen accompanied the famous visitor.* 2 man who goes on a date with a woman: *Her escort to the party was a tall young man.* 3 go with as an escort: *Three police cars escorted the governor's limousine in the parade. He enjoyed escorting his cousin to the movies.* 1,2 *n.,* 3 *v.*

escort carrier, an aircraft carrier of the smallest type.

es crow (es/krō *or* e skrō/), deed, bond, or other written agreement held by a third person until certain conditions are met by two other parties. *n.* **in escrow,** held by a third party in accordance with an agreement.

es cutch eon (e skuch/ən), shield on which a coat of arms is put. *n.*

escutcheon
with coat of arms

-ese, *suffix added to nouns.* 1 (*to form adjectives*) of or having to do with _____: *Japanese = of Japan.* 2 (*to form nouns*) person born or living in _____: *Portuguese = person born or living in Portugal.* 3 (*to form nouns*) language of _____: *Chinese = language of China.* [from French before the 1400's *-eis,* from Latin *-ensis* of or from (a place)]

Es ki mo (es/kə mō), 1 member of a people living in the arctic regions of North America and northeastern Asia. 2 language of the Eskimos. 3 of or having to do with the Eskimos or their language. 1,2 *n., pl.* **Es ki mos** *or* **Es ki mo** for 1; 3 *adj.*

adj. adjective	n. noun
adv. adverb	prep. preposition
conj. conjunction	pron. pronoun
interj. interjection	v. verb
sing. singular	pl. plural

Eskimo dog, a strong, broad-chested dog, much used by the Eskimos for pulling sleds; husky. Eskimo dogs have furry outer hair with another coat of fine hair near the skin.

e soph a gus (ē sof′ə gəs), passage for food from the throat to the stomach; gullet. *n.*

es o ter ic (es′ə ter′ik), 1 understood only by a select few; intended for an inner circle of disciples, scholars, etc.: *esoteric literature.* 2 private; secret; confidential. *adj.* —**es′o ter′i cal ly,** *adv.*

esp., especially.

es pe cial (e spesh′əl), more than others; special: *my especial friend, of no especial value. Your birthday is an especial day for you. adj.*

es pe cial ly (e spesh′ə lē), more than others; specially; particularly; principally; chiefly: *This book is designed especially for students. Young people today are especially interested in space travel. adv.*

es pi o nage (es′pē ə nij *or* es′pē- ə näzh), the use of spies; spying. Nations use espionage to find out the military and political secrets of other nations. *n.*

es pla nade (es′plə nād′ *or* es′plə- näd′), any open level space used for public walks or drives, especially along a shore. *n.*

es pous al (e spou′zəl), 1 Also, **es- pousals,** *pl.* ceremony of becoming engaged or married. 2 an espousing; adoption: *The candidate's espousal of the campaign for a new park made her very popular. n.*

es pouse (e spouz′), 1 marry. 2 take up or make one's own; adopt: *Late in life he espoused a new religion.* v., **es poused, es pous ing.**

es prit (e sprē′), FRENCH. lively wit; spirit. *n.*

es prit de corps (e sprē′ də kôr′), FRENCH. group spirit; comradeship: *The club's strong esprit de corps showed itself in the intense loyalty, devotion, and enthusiasm of its members.*

es py (e spī′), see at a distance; catch sight of; spy: *He espied the castle from afar.* v., **es pied, es py ing.**

Esq., Esquire: *Henry Smith, Esq.*

e squire (e skwīr′ *or* es′kwīr), 1 (in

the Middle Ages) a knight's attendant; squire. 2 Englishman ranking next below a knight. 3 **Esquire,** title of respect placed after a man's last name instead of *Mr.* before the name: *John Jones, Esquire = Mr. John Jones. n.*

-ess, *suffix added to nouns to form other nouns.* female _____: *Lioness = a female lion.* [from French *-esse*]

es say (es′ā *for 1;* e sā′ *for 2;* e sā′ *or* e sā′ *for 3*), 1 a short composition written on a certain subject. 2 to try; attempt: *The student essayed her first solo flight.* 3 a try; an attempt. 1,3 *n.,* 2 *v.*

es say ist (es′ā ist), writer of essays. *n.*

es sence (es′ns), 1 that which makes a thing what it is; necessary part or parts: *Being thoughtful of others is the essence of politeness.* 2 a concentrated substance that has the characteristic flavor, fragrance, or effect of the plant or fruit from which it is taken: *Essence of peppermint is a solution of peppermint in alcohol.* 3 perfume. *n.*

es sen tial (ə sen′shəl), 1 needed to make a thing what it is; very important; necessary: *Good food and enough rest are essential to good health.* 2 an absolutely necessary element or quality: *Learn the essentials first; then learn the details.* 3 of or making up the essence of a substance: *The essential oil of a plant or fruit is what gives it its own peculiar flavor or fragrance.* 1,3 *adj.,* 2 *n.*

es sen tial ly (ə sen′shə lē), in essence; in essentials; in an essential manner. *adv.*

-est, *suffix forming the superlative degree of adjectives and adverbs.* most: *Warmest = most warm. Slowest = most slow.* [Old English *-est, -ost*]

E.S.T., Eastern Standard Time.

es tab lish (e stab′lish), 1 set up on a firm or lasting basis: *The early settlers from Europe established colonies in America.* 2 settle in a position; set up in a business: *A new doctor has established himself on our street.* 3 cause to be accepted and used for a long time: *establish a custom.* 4 show beyond dispute; prove: *He established his innocence by showing that he was in another city when the theft was committed.* v.

established church, church that is a national institution recognized and supported by the government. The Church of England is an established church.

es tab lish ment (e stab′lish mənt), 1 an establishing: *The establishment of the business took several years.* 2 a being established: *The custom has already achieved establishment.* 3 some-

thing established. A household, business, church, or army is an establishment. 4 **the Establishment,** group that holds all the positions of influence or authority in a country, society, etc. *n.*

es tan cia (e stän′syä), a large ranch or estate in Latin America. *n., pl.* **es tan- cias.** [from Spanish *estancia* station]

es tate (e stāt′), 1 a large piece of land belonging to a person; landed property: *He has a beautiful estate with a country house and a swimming pool on it.* 2 that which a person owns; property; possessions: *When the rich man died, he left an estate of two million dollars.* 3 condition or stage in life: *A boy reaches man's estate at 21. n.*

es teem (e stēm′), 1 have a very favorable opinion of; think highly of; value: *We esteem courage.* 2 a very favorable opinion; high regard: *Courage is held in esteem.* 3 think; consider: *She esteemed it an honor to be chosen for the task.* 1,3 *v.,* 2 *n.*

es ter (es′tər), compound produced by the reaction of an acid and an alcohol. Animal and vegetable fats and oils are esters. *n.*

Es ther (es′tər), 1 (in the Bible) the Jewish wife of a Persian king, who saved her people from massacre. 2 book of the Old Testament that tells her story. *n.*

es thet ic (es thet′ik), aesthetic. *adj.*

es thet i cal ly (es thet′ik lē), aesthetically. *adv.*

es ti ma ble (es′tə mə bəl), worthy of esteem; deserving high regard: *Unselfishness is an estimable trait. adj.*

es ti mate (es′tə mit *or* es′tə māt *for 1,3;* es′tə māt *for 2*), 1 judgment or opinion about how much, how many, how good, etc.: *My estimate of the length of the room was 15 feet; it actually measured 14 feet, 9 inches.* 2 form a judgment or opinion (about how much, how many, how good, etc.): *We estimated that it would take four hours to weed the garden.* 3 statement of what certain work will cost, made by one willing to do the work: *The painter's estimate for painting the house was $500.* 1,3 *n.,* 2 *v.,* **es ti mat ed, es ti- mat ing.**

es ti ma tion (es′tə mā′shən), 1 judgment or opinion: *In my estimation, your plan will not work.* 2 esteem; respect: *The doctor was held in high estimation by the community.* 3 act or process of estimating. *n.*

Es to ni a (e stō′nē ə), Soviet republic in N Europe, on the Baltic Sea. *n.* —**Es to′ni an,** *adj., n.*

es trange (e strānj′), turn (a person) from affection to indifference, dislike, or hatred; make unfriendly; keep apart;

separate: *A quarrel had estranged him from his family.* v., **es tranged, es trang ing.**

es trange ment (e strānj′mənt), a turning away in feeling; becoming distant or unfriendly: *A misunderstanding had caused the estrangement of the two friends.* n.

es tu ar y (es′chü er′ē), 1 a broad mouth of a river into which the tide flows. 2 inlet of the sea. n., pl. **es tu ar ies.**

etc., et cetera. *Etc.* is usually read "and so forth." The definition of *equality* reads "sameness in amount, size, number, value, rank, etc." *Etc.* in this and similar definitions shows that the definition applies to many similar items in addition to the ones mentioned.

et cet er a (et set′ər ə), and so forth; and others; and the rest; and so on; and the like. [from Latin *et cetera* and other things]

etch (ech), 1 engrave (a drawing or design) on a metal plate, glass, etc., by means of acid that eats away the lines. When filled with ink, the lines of the design will reproduce a copy on paper. 2 make drawings or designs by this method. 3 impress deeply; fix firmly: *Her face was etched in my memory.* v. —**etch′er,** n.

etch ing (ech′ing), 1 picture or design printed from an etched plate. 2 an etched plate; etched drawing or design. 3 art or process of engraving a drawing or design on a metal plate, glass, etc., by means of acid. n.

e ter nal (i tėr′nl), 1 without beginning or ending; lasting throughout all time. 2 always and forever the same: *the eternal truths.* 3 seeming to go on forever; constant: *When will we have an end to this eternal noise?* 4 **the Eternal,** God. 1-3 adj., 4 n.

Eternal City, Rome.

e ter nal ly (i tėr′nl ē), 1 without beginning or ending; throughout all time. 2 always and forever. 3 constantly. adv.

e ter ni ty (i tėr′nə tē), 1 all time; all the past and all the future. 2 the endless period after death. 3 a period of time that seems endless: *The injured man waited an eternity for the ambulance to arrive.* n., pl. **e ter ni ties.**

e ther (ē′thər), 1 a colorless, sweet-smelling liquid that burns and evaporates readily. Its fumes cause unconsciousness when deeply inhaled. Ether is used as an anesthetic and as a solvent for fats and resins. 2 the upper regions of space beyond the earth's atmosphere; clear sky. 3 an invisible, elastic substance formerly supposed to fill all space. n. Also, **aether** for 2,3.

e ther e al (i thir′ē əl), 1 light; airy; delicate: *the ethereal beauty of a butterfly, the ethereal music of a harp.* 2 not of the earth; heavenly: *An angel is an ethereal messenger.* adj. Also, **aethereal.** —**e ther′e al ly,** adv.

eth i cal (eth′ə kəl), 1 having to do with standards of right and wrong; of ethics or morals. 2 morally right: *ethical conduct.* 3 in accordance with formal or professional rules of right and wrong: *It is not considered ethical for a doctor to gossip about a patient.* adj. —**eth′i cal ly,** adv.

eth ics (eth′iks), 1 pl. in form, sing. in use. the study of standards of right and wrong; the part of philosophy dealing with moral conduct, duty, and judgment. 2 pl. in form and use. formal or professional rules of right and wrong: *It is against medical ethics for doctors to advertise.* n.

E thi o pi a (ē′thē ō′pē ə), 1 country in E Africa; Abyssinia. *Capital:* Addis Ababa. 2 ancient region in NE Africa, south of Egypt. n. —**E′thi o′pi an,** adj., n.

eth nic (eth′nik), 1 having to do with the various racial or cultural groups of people and the characteristics, language, and customs of each; of, having to do with, or peculiar to a people. 2 of or having to do with people of foreign birth or descent: *There are many ethnic groups in our large cities.* adj. —**eth′ni cal ly,** adv.

eth no log i cal (eth′nə loj′ə kəl), having to do with ethnology. adj.

eth nol o gy (eth nol′ə jē), science that deals with the various races or cultural groups of people, their origin and distribution, distinctive characteristics, customs, institutions, and culture. n.

eth yl alcohol (eth′əl), ordinary alcohol, made by the fermentation of grain, sugar, etc.

et i quette (et′ə ket), 1 conventional rules for behavior in polite society: *Etiquette requires that we eat peas with a fork, not a spoon.* 2 formal rules for governing behavior in a profession, official ceremony, etc.: *Ambassadors observe diplomatic etiquette.* n.

Et na (et′nə), **Mount,** active volcano in NE Sicily. n. Also, **Aetna.**

E ton (ēt′n), an English school for boys, at Eton, a town near London. n.

E trur i a (i trür′ē ə), ancient country in W Italy. n.

E trus can (i trus′kən), 1 of or having to do with Etruria, its people, their language, art, or customs. 2 person who was born or lived in Etruria. 3 language of Etruria. 1 adj., 2,3 n.

-ette, *suffix often added to nouns to form new nouns.* 1 little _____: *Kitchenette = a little kitchen.* 2 female

_____: *Usherette = a female usher.* 3 substitute for _____: *Leatherette = a substitute for leather.* [from French]

é tude (ā tüd′ or ā tyüd′), piece of music intended to develop skill in technique. n., pl. **é tudes.** [from French *étude* study]

et y mol o gy (et′ə mol′ə jē), 1 the derivation of a word. 2 account or explanation of the origin and history of a word. 3 the study dealing with the origin and history of words. n., pl. **et y mol o gies.**

eu ca lyp tus (yü′kə lip′təs), a very tall evergreen tree that grows mainly in Australia and neighboring islands. It is valued for its timber and for a medicinal oil from its leaves. n., pl. **eu ca lyp tus es.**

Eu char ist (yü′kər ist), 1 sacrament of the Lord's Supper; Holy Communion. 2 the consecrated bread and wine used in this sacrament. n.

Eu cha ris tic (yü′kə ris′tik), having to do with the Eucharist. adj.

Eu clid (yü′klid), Greek mathematician who wrote a famous book on geometry about 300 B.C. n.

eu gen ic (yü jen′ik), having to do with eugenics. adj.

eu gen ics (yü jen′iks), science of improving the human race. Eugenics would apply the same principles of careful selection of parents that have long been applied to animals and plants, and develop healthier and more intelligent children. n. sing. or pl.

eu gle na (yü glē′nə), a microscopic, one-celled organism, usually green, that moves by a whiplike tail. It is easily grown in a culture for study. n., pl. **eu gle nas.**

hat, āge, fär; let, ēqual, tėrm; it, īce; hot, ōpen, ôrder; oil, out; cup, pùt, rüle; ch, child; ng, long; sh, she; th, thin; ᴛʜ, then; zh, measure;

ə represents *a* in about, *e* in taken, *i* in pencil, *o* in lemon, *u* in circus.

ETRURIA

TYRRHENIAN SEA · ADRIATIC SEA · BLACK SEA · MACEDONIA · (GREECE) · AEGEAN SEA · LYDIA · MEDITERRANEAN SEA · Rome

about 700 B.C.

adj.	adjective	*n.*	noun
adv.	adverb	*prep.*	preposition
conj.	conjunction	*pron.*	pronoun
interj.	interjection	*v.*	verb
sing.	singular	*pl.*	plural

eu lo gist (yü′lə jist), person who eulogizes. *n.*

eu lo gis tic (yü′lə jis′tik), of or like a eulogy; praising very highly. *adj.*

eu lo gize (yü′lə jīz), praise very highly. *v.*, **eu lo gized, eu lo giz ing.**

eu lo gy (yü′lə jē), speech or writing in praise of a person or thing; high praise: *She delivered the eulogy at the funeral of her dear friend. n., pl.* **eu lo gies.**

eu nuch (yü′nək), 1 a castrated man. 2 such a man in charge of a harem or the household of an Oriental ruler. *n.*

eu phe mism (yü′fə miz′əm), 1 use of a mild or indirect expression instead of one that is harsh or unpleasantly direct. 2 word or expression used in this way. "Pass away" is a common euphemism for "die"; "not very bright" is a euphemism for "stupid." *n.*

eu phe mis tic (yü′fə mis′tik), using mild or indirect words instead of harsh or unpleasant ones. *adj.*

eu pho ni ous (yü fō′nē əs), pleasing to the ear; sounding agreeable; harmonious: *Our door chimes have a euphonious sound. adj.*

eu pho ny (yü′fə nē), pleasing effect to the ear; agreeable sound. *n., pl.* **eu pho nies.**

eu pho ri a (yü fôr′ē ə), a feeling of happiness and bodily well-being. *n.*

Eu phra tes (yü frā′tēz), river in SW Asia, flowing from E Turkey through Syria and Iraq into the Persian Gulf. It joins the Tigris River in SE Iraq. *n.*

Eur a sia (yùr ā′zhə), Europe and Asia, thought of as a single continent. The Soviet Union is the largest country in Eurasia. *n.*

Eur a sian (yùr ā′zhən), 1 person of mixed European and Asian parentage. 2 of mixed European and Asian parentage. 1 *n.*, 2 *adj.*

eu re ka (yù rē′kə), I have found it! (an exclamation of triumph at any discovery). *interj.*

Eur ope (yùr′əp), continent east of the North Atlantic Ocean and west of Asia. France, Germany, and Spain are countries in Europe. *n.*

Eur o pe an (yùr ə pē′ən), 1 of or having to do with Europe or its people. 2 person born or living in Europe. 1 *adj.*, 2 *n.*

eu ro pi um (yù rō′pē əm), a soft, grayish metallic element which occurs only in combination with other elements. Europium compounds are used in coating color television screens. *n.*

Eus ta chi an tube (yü stā′kē ən *or* yü stā′shən), a slender canal between the pharynx and the middle ear. It equalizes the air pressure on the two sides of the eardrum. See **ear**[1] for diagram. [from Bartolommeo *Eustachio,* an Italian anatomist of the 1500's]

eu tha na sia (yü′thə nā′zhə), a painless killing, especially to end a painful and incurable disease. *n.*

e vac u ate (i vak′yü āt), 1 leave empty; withdraw from: *The tenants evacuated the burning apartment house.* 2 withdraw; remove: *Efforts were made to evacuate all civilians from the war zone.* 3 make empty: *evacuate the stomach. v.*, **e vac u at ed, e vac u at ing.**

e vac u a tion (i vak′yü ā′shən), 1 a leaving empty; withdrawal from. 2 removal; withdrawal: *Volunteers helped in the evacuation of the townspeople from their flooded homes.* 3 a making empty. 4 a discharge. *n.*

e vac u ee (i vak′yü ē′), person who is removed to a place of greater safety: *The evacuees from the flood were housed in the schools and churches. n.*

e vade (i vād′), get away from by trickery; avoid by cleverness: *The thief evaded his pursuers and escaped. When they asked who broke the lamp, I evaded the question by saying, "I wonder who!" v.*, **e vad ed, e vad ing.**

e val u ate (i val′yü āt), find out the value or the amount of; estimate the worth or importance of; appraise: *An expert will evaluate the old furniture you wish to sell. v.*, **e val u at ed, e val u at ing.**

e val u a tion (i val′yü ā′shən), 1 an evaluating: *The jury began its careful evaluation of the evidence.* 2 an estimated value; valuation. *n.*

ev a nes cence (ev′ə nes′ns), a gradual disappearance; fading away; vanishing. *n.*

ev a nes cent (ev′ə nes′nt), gradually disappearing; soon passing away; vanishing: *the evanescent beauty of the sunset. adj.*

e van gel i cal (ē′van jel′ə kəl), 1 of or according to the four Gospels or the New Testament. 2 of or having to do with the Protestant churches that emphasize Christ's atonement and man's salvation by faith as the most important parts of Christianity. Methodists and Baptists are evangelical; Unitarians and Universalists are not. *adj.*

e van gel ism (i van′jə liz′əm), a preaching of the Gospel; earnest effort for the spread of the Gospel. *n.*

e van gel ist (i van′jə list), 1 preacher of the Gospel. 2 a traveling preacher who stirs up religious feeling in revival services. 3 **Evangelist,** writer of one of the four Gospels: Matthew, Mark, Luke, or John. *n.*

e van gel is tic (i van′jə lis′tik), of or by evangelists. *adj.*

e vap o rate (i vap′ə rāt′), 1 change from a liquid or solid into a vapor: *Boiling water evaporates rapidly. Heat evaporates water. Some solids, such as moth balls and Dry Ice, evaporate without melting.* 2 remove water or other liquid from: *Heat is used to evaporate milk.* 3 vanish; disappear: *My good resolutions evaporated soon after New Year. v.*, **e vap o rat ed, e vap o rat ing.**

evaporated milk, a thick, unsweetened, canned milk, prepared by evaporating some of the water from ordinary milk.

e vap o ra tion (i vap′ə rā′shən), act or process of evaporating: *Wet clothes on a line become dry by evaporation of the water in them. n.*

e vap o ra tor (i vap′ə rā′tər), apparatus for removing water or other liquid from a substance: *an evaporator for drying fruits. n.*

e va sion (i vā′zhən), 1 a getting away from something by trickery; avoiding by cleverness: *I had no excuse for the evasion of my responsibilities.* 2 an attempt to escape an argument, a charge, a question, etc.: *The prisoner's evasions of the lawyer's questions convinced the jury that he was guilty. n.*

e va sive (i vā′siv), tending or trying to evade: *"I really haven't given it much thought" is an evasive answer. adj.* —**e va′sive ly,** *adv.* —**e va′sive ness,** *n.*

eve (ēv), 1 the evening or day before a holiday or some other special day: *New Year's Eve, Christmas Eve, the eve of my birthday.* 2 time just before something happens: *The campaign ended on the eve of the election.* 3 OLD USE. evening. *n.*

Eve (ēv), (in the Bible) the first woman, the wife of Adam. *n.*

e ven[1] (ē′vən), 1 having the same height everywhere; level; flat; smooth: *The countryside is even, with no hills or slopes.* 2 at the same level: *The snow was even with the windowsill.* 3 keeping about the same; uniform: *The car travels with an even motion. The boy has an even temper.* 4 no more or less than; equal: *They divided the money in even shares.* 5 make level or equal; make even: *She evened the edges by trimming them.* 6 that can be divided by 2 without a remainder: *2, 4, 6, 8, and 10 are even numbers.* 7 neither more nor less; exact: *Twelve apples make an even dozen.* 8 just: *She left even as you came.* 9 indeed: *He is ready, even eager, to go.* 10 though one would not expect it; as one would not expect: *Even young children can operate this machine. Even the smallest noise disturbs her.* 11 still; yet: *You can read even better if you try.* 1-4, 6, 7 *adj.*, 5 *v.*, 8-11 *adv.* [Old English *efen*] —**e′ven ly,** *adv.* —**e′ven ness,** *n.*

even if, in spite of the fact that; although: *I will come, even if it rains.*

get even, have revenge.

e ven[2] (ē′vən), OLD USE. evening. *n.* [Old English *æfen*]

eve ning (ēv′ning), the last part of day and early part of night; time between sunset and bedtime. *n.*

evening star, a bright planet seen in the western sky after sunset. Venus is often the evening star.

e ven song (ē′vən sông′), vespers. *n.*

e vent (i vent′), 1 a happening, especially an important happening: *Newspapers report all new and unexpected events. The discovery of the polio vaccine was a great event in medicine.* 2 result; outcome: *We made careful plans and awaited the event.* 3 one item in a program of sports: *The 100-yard dash was the last event.* *n.*

in any event, in any case; whatever happens: *In any event, you can always count on my friendship.*

in the event of, if there should be; in case of; if there is: *In the event of rain, the party will be held indoors.*

e vent ful (i vent′fəl), 1 full of events; having many unusual events: *The class spent an eventful day touring the new zoo.* 2 having important results; important: *The discovery of atomic energy began an eventful period in history. adj.* —**e vent′ful ly,** *adv.*

e ven tide (ē′vən tīd′), OLD USE. evening. *n.*

e ven tu al (i ven′chü əl), coming in the end; final: *After several failures, his eventual success surprised us. adj.*

e ven tu al i ty (i ven′chü al′ə tē), a possible occurrence or condition; possibility: *We hope for good weather, but we are ready for the eventuality of rain. n., pl.* **e ven tu al i ties.**

e ven tu al ly (i ven′chü ə lē), in the end; finally: *We waited more than an hour for him but eventually we had to leave without him. adv.*

ev er (ev′ər), 1 at any time: *Is she ever at home?* 2 at all times; always: *She is ever ready to accept a new challenge.* 3 by any chance; in any case; at all: *What did you ever do to make him so angry? adv.*

ever so, INFORMAL. very: *The ocean is ever so deep.*

Ev er est (ev′ər ist), **Mount,** mountain in the Himalayas between Tibet and Nepal. It is the highest mountain in the world. *n.*

ev er glade (ev′ər glād), 1 a large tract of low, wet ground partly covered with tall grass; large swamp or marsh. 2 **the Everglades,** a swampy region in S Florida. *n.*

ev er green (ev′ər grēn′), 1 having green leaves or needles all year round. 2 an evergreen plant. Pine, spruce, cedar, ivy, box, rhododendrons, etc., are evergreens. 3 **evergreens,** *pl.* evergreen twigs or branches used for decoration, especially at Christmas. 1 *adj.*, 2, 3 *n.*

ev er last ing (ev′ər las′ting), 1 lasting forever; never stopping: *the everlasting beauty of nature.* 2 lasting a long time: *We wished them everlasting happiness.* 3 lasting too long; tiresome: *His everlasting complaints annoyed me.* 4 **the Everlasting,** God. 1-3 *adj.*, 4 *n.* —**ev′er last′ing ly,** *adv.*

ev er more (ev′ər môr′), for always; always; forever: *I shall evermore remember this narrow escape from death. adv.*

for evermore, for all time; for eternity: *They swore to love each other for evermore.*

eve ry (ev′rē), 1 each one of the entire number of persons or things: *Read every word on the page. Every student must have a book.* 2 all possible: *We showed him every consideration. adj.*

every now and then, from time to time: *Every now and then we have a frost that ruins the crop.*

every other, every second: *The milkman makes deliveries every other day.*

eve ry bod y (ev′rə bud′ē *or* ev′rē-bod′ē), every person; everyone: *Everybody likes the new principal. pron.*

eve ry day (ev′rē dā′), 1 of every day; daily: *Accidents are everyday occurrences.* 2 for every ordinary day; not for Sundays or holidays: *She wears everyday clothes to work.* 3 not ex-

---

---

citing; usual: *He had only an everyday story to tell. adj.*

eve ry one (ev′rē wun *or* ev′rē wən), each one; everybody: *Everyone took his purchases home. pron.*

eve ry thing (ev′rē thing), 1 every thing; all things: *She did everything she could to help her friend.* 2 something extremely important; very important thing: *This news means everything to us.* 1 *pron.*, 2 *n.*

eve ry where (ev′rē hwer *or* ev′rē-hwar), in every place; in all places: *A smile is understood everywhere. We looked everywhere for our lost dog. adv.*

e vict (i vikt′), expel by law from land, a building, etc.; eject: *The tenant was evicted by the sheriff for not paying her rent. v.*

e vic tion (i vik′shən), an evicting or a being evicted; expulsion: *The tenant who refused to pay his rent was served with a notice of eviction. n.*

ev i dence (ev′ə dəns), 1 anything that shows what is true and what is not; facts; proof: *The jam on his face was evidence that he had been in the kitchen.* 2 facts established and accepted in a court of law: *Before deciding the case, the judge and jury heard all the evidence given by both sides.* 3 indication; sign: *A smile gives evidence of pleasure.* 4 show clearly: *His smile evidenced his pleasure.* 1-3 *n.*, 4 *v.*, **ev i denced, ev i denc ing.**

in evidence, easily seen or noticed: *Poverty is much in evidence in the city slums.*

ev i dent (ev′ə dənt), easy to see or understand; clear; plain: *It was evident that the shattered vase could never be repaired. adj.*

ev i dent ly (ev′ə dənt lē), plainly; clearly: *If he hasn't arrived yet he evidently missed his train. adv.*

e vil (ē′vəl), 1 that causes harm; bad; wrong; wicked: *an evil life, an evil character, an evil plan.* 2 bad or evil quality; wickedness: *There is no evil in that child.* 3 thing that causes harm: *Crime and poverty are some of the evils of society.* 1 *adj.*, 2, 3 *n.* —**e′vil ly,** *adv.* —**e′vil ness,** *n.*

adj.	adjective	*n.*	noun
adv.	adverb	*prep.*	preposition
conj.	conjunction	*pron.*	pronoun
interj.	interjection	*v.*	verb
sing.	singular	*pl.*	plural

e vil do er (ē′vəl dü′ər), person who does evil. *n.*

e vil-mind ed (ē′vəl mīn′did), having an evil mind; wicked; malicious. *adj.*

e vince (i vins′), show clearly: *The dog evinced its dislike of strangers by growling.* *v.,* **e vinced, e vinc ing.**

e vis ce rate (i vis′ə rāt′), remove the bowels from: *The butcher eviscerated a chicken.* *v.,* **e vis ce rat ed, e vis ce-rat ing.**

e voke (i vōk′), call forth; bring out: *The speaker's witty remarks evoked many smiles from the audience.* *v.,* **e voked, e vok ing.**

ev o lu tion (ev′ə lü′shən), 1 a gradual development: *the evolution of the flower from the bud. The evolution of one kind of animal or plant from a simpler kind may take thousands of years.* 2 the theory that all living things developed from a few simple forms of life. 3 movement that is part of a definite plan, design, or series: *the graceful and expressive evolutions of a ballet dancer.* *n.*

ev o lu tion ar y (ev′ə lü′shə ner′ē), 1 having to do with evolution. 2 in accordance with the theory of evolution. *adj.*

ev o lu tion ist (ev′ə lü′shə nist), person who believes in and supports the theory of evolution. *n.*

e volve (i volv′), develop gradually; unfold: *Buds evolve into flowers. The modern automobile evolved from the horse and buggy. The children evolved a plan for earning money during their summer vacation.* *v.,* **e volved, e volv-ing.**

ewe (yü), a female sheep. *n.*

ew er (yü′ər), a wide-mouthed water pitcher. *n.*

ex-, *prefix.* 1 former; formerly: *Ex-president = former president.* 2 out of; from; out: *Express = press out.* 3 thoroughly: *Exterminate = terminate (finish or destroy) thoroughly.* [from Latin *ex* out of, from]

ex act (eg zakt′), 1 without any mistake; correct; accurate; precise: *an exact measurement, the exact amount, an exact thinker.* 2 demand and get: *If you do the work, you can exact payment for it.* 1 *adj.,* 2 *v.*

ex act ing (eg zak′ting), 1 requiring much; hard to please: *An exacting teacher will not permit careless work.* 2 requiring effort, care, or attention: *Flying an airplane is exacting work.* *adj.*

ex ac tion (eg zak′shən), 1 a demanding and getting: *The ruler's repeated exaction of money left the people very poor.* 2 thing exacted. *Taxes, fees, etc., forced to be paid are exactions.* *n.*

ex act i tude (eg zak′tə tüd *or* eg-zak′tə tyüd), exactness. *n.*

ex act ly (eg zakt′lē), 1 accurately; precisely. 2 just so; quite right. *adv.*

ex act ness (eg zakt′nis), a being exact: *He recalled the story with exactness, down to every detail.* *n.*

ex ag ge rate (eg zaj′ə rāt′), 1 make too large; say or think something is greater than it is; go beyond the truth: *The little boy exaggerated when he said there were a million cats in the backyard.* 2 increase or enlarge beyond what is normal: *The artist exaggerated parts of the drawing to make them clearer.* *v.,* **ex ag ge rat ed, ex ag ge-rat ing.**

evolution (def. 1)
of the horse's forefoot from four toes to a single toe (hoof). The toe which became the hoof is shaded.

ex ag ge ra tion (eg zaj′ə rā′shən), 1 an exaggerated statement: *It is an exaggeration to say that you would rather die than touch a snake.* 2 an exaggerating: *His constant exaggeration made people distrust him.* *n.*

ex alt (eg zôlt′), 1 make high in rank, honor, power, character, or quality: *The queen exalted the commoner to the rank of earl.* 2 fill with pride, joy, or noble feeling: *He was exalted by success.* 3 praise; honor; glorify: *The worshipers exalted their god.* *v.*

ex al ta tion (eg′zôl tā′shən), 1 an exalting or a being exalted. 2 lofty emotion; rapture. *n.*

ex am (eg zam′), INFORMAL. examination. *n.*

ex am i na tion (eg zam′ə nā′shən), 1 an examining or a being examined: *The doctor made a thorough examination of my eyes.* 2 test of knowledge or qualifications; list of questions; test: *The teacher gave us an examination in arithmetic.* *n.*

ex am ine (eg zam′ən), 1 look at closely and carefully: *The doctor examined the wound.* 2 test the knowledge or qualifications of; ask questions of; test: *The lawyer examined the witness. The teacher examined the students on the book they read.* *v.,* **ex am ined, ex am in ing.**

ex am in er (eg zam′ə nər), person who examines: *a medical examiner.* *n.*

ex am ple (eg zam′pəl), 1 one thing taken to show what others are like; sample: *New York is an example of a busy city.* 2 person or thing to be imitated; model; pattern: *Children often follow the example set by their parents.* 3 problem in arithmetic, etc.: *She wrote the example on the blackboard.* 4 warning to others: *The principal made an example of the students who were always tardy by making them come to school an hour early for a week.* *n.*

for example, as an example; for instance: *Many flowers are fragrant; lilacs, for example.*

set an example, behave for others to imitate; give, show, or be a model of conduct: *She set an example for the rest of the class by having a perfect record of attendance.*

ex as pe rate (eg zas′pə rāt′), irritate very much; annoy greatly; make angry: *The little girl's constant noise exasperated her parents.* *v.,* **ex as pe rat-ed, ex as pe rat ing.**

ex as pe ra tion (eg zas′pə rā′shən), extreme annoyance; irritation; anger. *n.*

Ex cal i bur (ek skal′ə bər), the magic sword of King Arthur. *n.*

ex ca vate (ek′skə vāt), 1 make hollow; hollow out: *The tunnel was made by excavating the side of a mountain.* 2 make by digging; dig: *The workmen excavated a tunnel for the new subway.* 3 dig out; scoop out: *Steam shovels excavated the dirt and loaded it into trucks.* 4 uncover by digging: *They excavated an ancient buried city.* *v.,* **ex-ca vat ed, ex ca vat ing.**

ex ca va tion (ek′skə vā′shən), 1 an excavating; a digging out: *The excavation for the basement of our new house took three days.* 2 hole made by digging: *The excavation for the new building was fifty feet across.* *n.*

excavator

ex ca va tor (ek′skə vā′tər), person or thing that excavates. A power shovel is an excavator. *n.*

ex ceed (ek sēd′), 1 be more or greater than: *The sum of 5 and 7 exceeds 10.*

Lifting that heavy trunk exceeds my strength. 2 do more than; go beyond: *Drivers are not supposed to exceed the speed limit.* v.

ex ceed ing (ek sē′ding), 1 very great; unusual: *She is a girl of exceeding talent.* 2 exceedingly: *He has done exceeding well.* 1 *adj.,* 2 *adv.*

ex ceed ing ly (ek sē′ding lē), very greatly; to an unusual degree; very: *Yesterday was an exceedingly hot day.* *adv.*

ex cel (ek sel′), 1 be better than; do better than: *He excelled his class in spelling.* 2 be better than others; do better than others: *She excels in arithmetic.* v., **ex celled, ex cel ling.**

ex cel lence (ek′sə ləns), unusually good quality; being better than others; superiority: *His teacher praised him for the excellence of his report.* n.

ex cel len cy (ek′sə lən sē), 1 excellence. 2 **Excellency,** title of honor used in speaking to or of a prime minister, governor, bishop, ambassador, or other high official: *Your Excellency, His Excellency, the British Ambassador.* n., pl. **ex cel len cies.**

ex cel lent (ek′sə lənt), of unusually good quality; better than others; superior: *Excellent work deserves high praise.* adj. —**ex′cel lent ly,** adv.

ex cel si or (ek sel′sē ôr *for 1;* ek-sel′sē ər *for 2*), 1 LATIN. ever upward; higher. "Excelsior" is the motto of New York State. 2 fine, curled shavings of soft wood used for packing dishes, glassware, and other breakable articles. 1 *adj.,* 2 *n.*

ex cept (ek sept′), 1 leaving out; other than: *He works every day except Sunday.* 2 leave out; exclude: *Those who passed the first test were excepted from the second.* 3 only; but: *I would have had a perfect score except I missed the last question.* 1 *prep.,* 2 *v.,* 3 *conj.*

ex cept ing (ek sep′ting), leaving out; other than; except; but: *School is open every day excepting Saturday and Sunday.* prep.

ex cep tion (ek sep′shən), 1 a leaving out; excepting: *I like all my studies, with the exception of arithmetic.* 2 person or thing left out: *She praised the pictures, with two exceptions.* 3 thing that is different from the rule: *He comes on time every day; today is an exception.* 4 objection: *a statement liable to exception.* n.

take exception, 1 object: *Several teachers and students took exception to the plan of having classes on Saturdays.* 2 be offended: *I took exception to their rude remarks.*

ex cep tion a ble (ek sep′shə nə bəl), liable to exception; objectionable. adj.

ex cep tion al (ek sep′shə nəl), out of the ordinary; unusual: *This warm weather is exceptional for January. She is an exceptional student.* adj. —**ex cep′tion al ly,** adv.

ex cerpt (ek′sèrpt′ *for 1;* ek sèrpt′ *for 2*), 1 passage taken out of a book, etc.; quotation; extract: *The English teacher read the class excerpts from several plays by Shakespeare.* 2 take out (passages) from a book, etc.; quote: *In his report on Eleanor Roosevelt, he included some passages excerpted from her speeches.* 1 *n.,* 2 *v.*

ex cess (ek ses′ *for 1,2;* ek′ses *or* ek-ses′ *for 3*), 1 part that is too much; more than enough: *Pour off the excess. We had an excess of snow last month. That movie has an excess of violence.* 2 amount by which one thing is greater than another: *The excess of 7 over 5 is 2.* 3 beyond the usual amount; extra: *Passengers must pay for excess baggage taken on an airplane. I went on a diet to get rid of my excess weight.* 1,2 *n.,* pl. **ex cess es;** 3 *adj.*

in excess of, more than: *The contributions received were in excess of $5000.*

to excess, too much: *He eats candy to excess.*

ex ces sive (ek ses′iv), too much; too great; going beyond what is necessary or right: *Fifty cents is an excessive price for a comic book. Some teen-agers spend an excessive amount of time on the phone.* adj. —**ex ces′sive ly,** adv.

ex change (eks chānj′), 1 give for something else; change: *I will exchange two dimes for twenty pennies. She would not exchange her house for a palace.* 2 give and take (things of the same kind): *We exchanged letters. They exchanged blows.* 3 an exchanging; giving and taking: *Ten pennies for a dime is a fair exchange. During the truce there was an exchange of prisoners.* 4 place where people trade. Stocks are bought, sold, and traded in a stock exchange. 5 a central station or office. A telephone exchange handles telephone calls. 1,2 *v.,* **ex changed, ex chang ing;** 3-5 *n.*

ex change a ble (eks chān′jə bəl), that can be exchanged. adj.

ex cheq uer (eks chek′ər), 1 treasury, especially of a state or nation. 2 **Exchequer,** department of the British government in charge of its finances and the public revenues. 3 INFORMAL. finances; funds. n.

ex cise[1] (ek′sīz *or* ek′sīs), tax on the manufacture, sale, or use of certain articles made, sold, or used within a country: *There is an excise on tobacco.* n. [apparently from Dutch of the 1400's *excijs*]

ex cise[2] (ek sīz′), cut out; remove: *The*

editor excised passages from the book. v., **ex cised, ex cis ing.** [from Latin *excisus* cut out]

ex ci sion (ek sizh′ən), a cutting out; removal. n.

ex cit a bil i ty (ek sī′tə bil′ə tē), quality of being excitable. n.

ex cit a ble (ek sī′tə bəl), easily excited. adj. —**ex cit′a ble ness,** n.

ex cite (ek sīt′), 1 stir up the feelings of: *The news of war excited everybody.* 2 arouse: *Plans for a field trip excited the students' interest.* 3 stir to action: *Do not excite the dog; keep away from him.* v., **ex cit ed, ex cit ing.**

ex cit ed (ek sī′tid), stirred up; aroused: *The excited mob rushed into the mayor's office.* adj. —**ex cit′ed ly,** adv.

ex cite ment (ek sīt′mənt), 1 an excited condition: *The baby's first step caused great excitement in the family.* 2 thing that excites: *The circus was an excitement to every child in town.* n.

ex cit ing (ek sī′ting), causing excitement; arousing; stirring: *We read an exciting story about pirates and buried treasure.* adj. —**ex cit′ing ly,** adv.

ex claim (ek sklām′), speak suddenly in surprise or strong feeling; cry out: *"Here you are at last!" exclaimed his mother.* v.

ex cla ma tion (ek′sklə mā′shən), something said suddenly as the result of surprise or strong feeling. *Oh!, Hurrah!, Well!,* and *Look!* are common exclamations. n.

exclamation mark or **exclamation point,** mark (!) of punctuation used after a word, phrase, or sentence to show that it was exclaimed. EXAMPLE: *Hurrah! We are going to the circus.*

ex clam a to ry (ek sklam′ə tôr′ē), using, containing, or expressing exclamation. adj.

ex clude (ek sklüd′), shut out; keep out: *Curtains exclude light. The government excludes immigrants who have certain diseases.* v., **ex clud ed, ex clud ing.**

ex clu sion (ek sklü′zhən), 1 act of excluding: *We voted for the exclusion of large trucks from residential streets.*

hat, āge, fär; let, ēqual, tèrm;
it, īce; hot, ōpen, ôrder;
oil, out; cup, pùt, rüle; ch, child;
ng, long; sh, she; th, thin;
ŦH, then; zh, measure;

ə represents *a* in about,
e in taken, *i* in pencil,
o in lemon, *u* in circus.

adj.	adjective	*n.*	noun
adv.	adverb	*prep.*	preposition
conj.	conjunction	*pron.*	pronoun
interj.	interjection	*v.*	verb
sing.	singular	*pl.*	plural

2 condition of being excluded: *Her exclusion from the meeting hurt her feelings. n.*

ex clu sive (ek sklü′siv *or* ek-sklü′ziv), 1 each shutting out the other. "Tree" and "animal" are exclusive terms; a thing cannot be both a tree and an animal. 2 shutting out all or most others: *She gave her exclusive attention to the teacher's instructions.* 3 not divided or shared with others; single; sole: *An inventor has an exclusive right for a certain number of years to make what he has invented and patented.* 4 very particular about choosing friends, members, etc.: *It is hard to get admitted to an exclusive club. This school is exclusive; only very bright children can go to it. adj.* **—ex clu′sive ly,** *adv.* **—ex clu′sive ness,** *n.*

exclusive of, excluding; leaving out; not counting: *There are 26 days in that month, exclusive of Sundays.*

ex com mu ni cate (ek′skə myü′nə kāt), cut off from membership in the church; shut out from communion with the church. *v.,* **ex com mu ni cat ed, ex com mu ni cat ing.**

ex com mu ni ca tion (ek′skə myü′nə kā′shən), 1 a cutting off from membership in the church and from any part in its ceremonies. 2 an official statement announcing this. *n.*

ex cre ment (ek′skrə mənt), waste matter that is discharged from the body, especially from the intestines. *n.*

ex cres cence (ek skres′ns), an unnatural growth. A corn or wart is an excrescence. *n.*

ex crete (ek skrēt′), discharge (waste matter) from the body; separate (waste matter) from the blood or tissues: *The sweat glands excrete sweat. v.,* **ex cret ed, ex cret ing.**

ex cre tion (ek skrē′shən), 1 discharge of waste matter from the body; separation of waste matter from the blood or tissues. 2 the waste matter that is separated and discharged: *Sweat is an excretion. n.*

ex cre to ry (ek′skrə tôr′ē), excreting; having the task of excreting: *The kidneys are excretory organs. adj.*

ex cru ci at ing (ek skrü′shē ā′ting),

causing great suffering; very painful. *adj.* **—ex cru′ci at ing ly,** *adv.*

ex cur sion (ek skėr′zhən), 1 a short trip taken for interest or pleasure, often by a number of people together: *Our club went on an excursion to the mountains.* 2 trip on a train, ship, or aircraft, at fares lower than those usually charged. *n.*

ex cus a ble (ek skyü′zə bəl), that can be excused; deserving pardon. *adj.*

ex cuse (ek skyüz′ *for 1,3-5;* ek skyüs′ *for 2,6*), 1 offer an apology for; try to remove the blame of: *She excused her tardiness by blaming traffic.* 2 reason, real or pretended, that is given; explanation: *Sickness was his excuse for being absent from school. He had many excuses for being late.* 3 be a reason or explanation for: *Sickness excuses absence from school.* 4 pardon; forgive: *Excuse me, I have to go now.* 5 free from duty; let off: *Those who passed the first test will be excused from the second one.* 6 act of excusing. 1,3-5 *v.,* **ex cused, ex cus ing;** 2,6 *n.*

excuse oneself, 1 ask to be pardoned: *He excused himself for bumping into me by saying that he was in a hurry.* 2 ask permission to leave: *I excused myself from the table.*

ex e cra ble (ek′sə krə bəl), abominable; detestable. *adj.*

ex e cra bly (ek′sə krə blē), in an execrable manner; abominably. *adv.*

ex e crate (ek′sə krāt), 1 abhor; detest. 2 curse. *v.,* **ex e crat ed, ex e crat ing.**

ex e cra tion (ek′sə krā′shən), 1 act of execrating. 2 a curse: *The mob shouted angry execrations at the assassin.* 3 person or thing execrated. *n.*

ex e cute (ek′sə kyüt), 1 carry out; do: *The nurse executed the doctor's orders.* 2 put into effect; enforce: *Congress makes the laws; the President executes them.* 3 put to death according to law: *The murderer was executed.* 4 make according to a plan or design: *The same artist executed that painting and that statue.* 5 make (a deed, lease, contract, will, etc.) legal by signing, sealing, etc. *v.,* **ex e cut ed, ex e cut ing.**

ex e cu tion (ek′sə kyü′shən), 1 a carrying out; doing: *He was prompt in the execution of his duties.* 2 a putting into effect; enforcing: *the execution of a law.* 3 way of carrying out or doing; skill. 4 a putting to death according to law. 5 a making according to a plan or design. 6 a making legal by signing, sealing, etc.: *the execution of a deed or contract. n.*

ex e cu tion er (ek′sə kyü′shə nər), person who puts criminals to death according to law. *n.*

ex ec u tive (eg zek′yə tiv), 1 having to do with carrying out or managing affairs: *The head of a school has an executive position.* 2 person who carries out or manages affairs: *The president of a business firm is an executive.* 3 having the duty and power of putting the laws into effect: *The President of the United States is the head of the executive branch of the government.* 4 person, group, or branch of government that has the duty and power of putting laws into effect: *The highest executive of a state is the governor.* 1,3 *adj.,* 2,4 *n.*

ex ec u tor (eg zek′yə tər), person chosen to carry out what another person has said shall be done with his money and other belongings after his death. *n.*

ex em plar y (eg zem′plər ē), 1 worth imitating: *exemplary conduct.* 2 serving as a warning to others: *exemplary punishment.* 3 serving as an example; typical: *an exemplary incident. adj.*

ex em pli fi ca tion (eg zem′-plə fə kā′shən), 1 a showing by example; being an example. 2 example. *n.*

ex em pli fy (eg zem′plə fī), show by example; be an example of: *Knights exemplified courage and courtesy. v.,* **ex em pli fied, ex em pli fy ing.**

ex empt (eg zempt′), 1 make free (from a duty, obligation, rule, etc.); release: *Students who get high marks all year will be exempted from the final examinations.* 2 freed from a duty, obligation, rule, etc.; released: *School property is exempt from all taxes.* 1 *v.,* 2 *adj.*

ex emp tion (eg zemp′shən), 1 act of exempting. 2 freedom from a duty, obligation, rule, etc.; release: *exemption from jury duty. n.*

ex er cise (ek′sər sīz), 1 active use; practice: *Exercise of the body is good for the health. Safety requires the exercise of care.* 2 make active use of: *When you vote you exercise your right as a citizen. Exercise caution in crossing streets.* 3 something that gives practice and training or causes improvement: *He performs physical exercises each day to strengthen his body. Study the lesson, and then do the exercises at the end.* 4 give exercise to; train: *She exercises her horse after school every day. Studying books exercises the mind.* 5 take exercise; go through exercises: *I exercise for ten minutes each morning.* 6 carry out in action; perform: *The mayor exercises the duties and powers of his office.* 7 Often, **exercises,** *pl.* ceremony: *She gave the farewell address at the graduation exercises.* 1,3, 7 *n.,* 2,4-6 *v.,* **ex er cised, ex er cis ing.**

ex ert (eg zèrt′), put into use; use fully; use: *A gymnast must exert both strength and skill. A ruler exerts authority.* *v.*

exert oneself, make an effort; try hard; strive: *You will really have to exert yourself to make up the work you missed.*

ex er tion (eg zèr′shən), 1 effort: *The exertions of the firemen kept the fire from spreading.* 2 a putting into action; active use; use: *exertion of the mind, exertion of authority.* *n.*

ex ha la tion (eks′hə lā′shən), 1 an exhaling: *Breathing out is an exhalation of air.* 2 something exhaled; air, vapor, smoke, odor, etc. *n.*

ex hale (eks hāl′), 1 breathe out: *We exhale air from our lungs.* 2 give off (air, vapor, smoke, odor, etc.). *v.,* **ex haled, ex hal ing.**

ex haust (eg zôst′), 1 empty completely: *exhaust an oil well.* 2 use up: *exhaust the supply of water, exhaust one's money, exhaust one's strength.* 3 tire very much: *The long, hard climb up the hill exhausted us.* 4 find out or say everything important about: *Her book about tulips exhausted the subject.* 5 the escape of used steam, spent gases, etc., from an engine. 6 pipe or other means for used steam, spent gases, etc., to escape from an engine. 7 the used steam, spent gases, etc., that escape: *The exhaust from an automobile engine is poisonous.* 1-4 *v.,* 5-7 *n.*

ex haust ed (eg zô′stid), 1 used up: *The teacher's patience was exhausted by the students' constant jabbering.* 2 worn out; very tired: *The exhausted hikers did not have the energy to continue the long walk home.* *adj.*

ex haus tion (eg zôs′chən), 1 act of exhausting. 2 condition of being exhausted. 3 extreme fatigue. *n.*

ex haus tive (eg zô′stiv), tending to exhaust or use up (resources, strength, or a subject); thorough: *The students were given an exhaustive examination covering every point of the year's work.* *adj.* —**ex haus′tive ly,** *adv.*

ex hib it (eg zib′it), 1 show; display: *Both of their children exhibit a talent for music. He exhibits interest whenever you talk about dogs.* 2 show publicly; put on display: *He hopes to exhibit his paintings in New York.* 3 an exhibiting; public showing: *The village art exhibit drew 10,000 visitors.* 4 thing or things shown publicly: *Her exhibit of roses won first prize at the flower show.* 5 thing shown in court as evidence: *The defendant's glove was labeled Exhibit A.* 1,2 *v.,* 3-5 *n.*

ex hib it er (eg zib′ə tər), exhibitor. *n.*

ex hi bi tion (ek′sə bish′ən), 1 a showing; display: *I have never seen such an exhibition of bad manners.* 2 a public show: *The art school holds an exhibition every year.* 3 thing or things shown publicly; exhibit. *n.*

ex hi bi tion ist (ek′sə bish′ə nist), person who tends to show off or behave in an unusual way in order to attract attention. *n.*

ex hib i tor (eg zib′ə tər), person, company, or group that exhibits. *n.*

ex hil a rate (eg zil′ə rāt′), make merry; make lively; cheer: *The joy of the holiday season exhilarates us all.* *v.,* **ex hil a rat ed, ex hil a rat ing.**

ex hil a ra tion (eg zil′ə rā′shən), high spirits; lively joy. *n.*

ex hort (eg zôrt′), urge strongly; advise or warn earnestly: *The preacher exhorted his congregation to live better lives.* *v.*

ex hor ta tion (eg′zôr tā′shən or ek′sôr tā′shən), 1 strong urging; earnest advice or warning. 2 speech, sermon, etc., that exhorts. *n.*

ex hume (eks hyüm′), dig (a dead body) out of a grave or the ground. *v.,* **ex humed, ex hum ing.**

ex i gen cy (ek′sə jən sē), 1 situation demanding prompt action or attention; emergency: *The curtains caught fire, but she proved equal to the exigency and put out the flames with a heavy blanket.* 2 Often, **exigencies,** *pl.* an urgent need; demand for prompt action or attention: *The exigencies of business kept him from taking a vacation.* *n., pl.* **ex i gen cies.**

ex i gent (ek′sə jənt), 1 demanding prompt action or attention; urgent; pressing: *The exigent pangs of hunger sent the bear on a search for food.* 2 demanding a great deal; exacting: *A busy doctor has an exigent occupation.* *adj.*

ex ile (eg′zīl or ek′sīl), 1 force (a person) to leave his country or home, often by law as a punishment; banish: *Napoleon was exiled to Elba.* 2 person who is exiled: *She has been an exile for ten years.* 3 condition of being exiled; banishment: *Napoleon was sent into exile for life.* 1 *v.,* **ex iled, ex il ing;** 2,3 *n.*

ex ist (eg zist′), 1 have being; be: *The world has existed a long time.* 2 be real: *She believes that ghosts exist.* 3 have life; live: *A person cannot exist without air.* 4 be found; occur: *Cases exist of persons who cannot smell anything.* *v.*

ex ist ence (eg zis′təns), 1 being: *When we are born, we come into existence.* 2 a being real: *Most people do not now believe in the existence of ghosts.* 3 life: *Drivers of racing cars lead a dangerous existence.* 4 occurrence: *The newspapers report the*

hat, āge, fär; let, ēqual, tèrm; it, īce; hot, ōpen, ôrder; oil, out; cup, pút, rüle; ch, child; ng, long; sh, she; th, thin; ŦH, then; zh, measure;

ə represents *a* in about, *e* in taken, *i* in pencil, *o* in lemon, *u* in circus.

existence of many new cases of flu in the city. *n.*

ex ist ent (eg zis′tənt), 1 existing. 2 now existing; of the present time. *adj.*

ex it (eg′zit or ek′sit), 1 way out: *The theater had six exits.* 2 a going out; departure: *When the cat came in, the mice made a hasty exit.* 3 act of leaving the stage: *The actor made a graceful exit.* *n.*

ex o dus (ek′sə dəs), 1 a going out; departure: *Every June there is an exodus of students from the colleges.* 2 **the Exodus,** the departure of the Israelites from Egypt under Moses. 3 **Exodus,** the second book of the Old Testament, containing an account of this departure. *n., pl.* **ex o dus es** for 1.

ex of fi ci o (eks ə fish′ē ō), because of one's office: *The Vice-President is, ex officio, the presiding officer of the Senate.* [from Latin]

ex on e rate (eg zon′ə rāt′), free from blame: *Witnesses to the accident completely exonerated the truck driver.* *v.,* **ex on e rat ed, ex on e rat ing.**

ex on e ra tion (eg zon′ə rā′shən), an exonerating or a being exonerated. *n.*

ex or bi tance (eg zôr′bə təns), a being exorbitant. *n.*

ex or bi tant (eg zôr′bə tənt), much too high; unreasonably excessive: *One dollar is an exorbitant price for a pack of bubble gum.* *adj.* —**ex or′bi tant ly,** *adv.*

ex or cise (ek′sôr sīz), 1 drive out (an evil spirit) by prayers, ceremonies, etc. 2 free (a person or place) from an evil spirit. *v.,* **ex or cised, ex or cis ing.** Also, **exorcize.**

ex or cism (ek′sôr siz′əm), 1 an exorcising. 2 the prayers, ceremonies, etc., used in exorcising. *n.*

ex or cize (ek′sôr sīz), exorcise. *v.,* **ex or cized, ex or ciz ing.**

ex o sphere (ek′sō sfir), the outermost region of the atmosphere, beginning about 300 miles above the earth's surface. *n.*

ex ot ic (eg zot′ik), 1 foreign; strange; not native: *We saw many exotic plants at the flower show.* 2 anything exotic. 1 *adj.,* 2 *n.* —**ex ot′i cal ly,** *adv.*

expand

adj.	adjective	*n.*	noun
adv.	adverb	*prep.*	preposition
conj.	conjunction	*pron.*	pronoun
interj.	interjection	*v.*	verb
sing.	singular	*pl.*	plural

ex pand (ek spand′), 1 make or grow larger; increase in size; enlarge: *The balloon expanded as it was filled with air. Our country was expanded by the addition of new territory. Heat expanded the metal.* 2 spread out; open out; unfold: *A bird expands its wings before flying. As the plant grew, its leaves and flowers gradually expanded.* 3 express in fuller form or greater detail: *The writer expanded one sentence into a paragraph.* *v.*

ex pand a ble (ek span′də bəl), that can be expanded. *adj.*

ex panse (ek spans′), open or unbroken stretch; wide, spreading surface: *The Pacific Ocean is an enormous expanse of water.* *n.*

ex pan sion (ek span′shən), 1 an expanding: *Heat causes the expansion of gas.* 2 a being expanded; increase in size, volume, etc.: *The expansion of the factory made room for more machines.* 3 an expanded part or form: *That book is an expansion of a magazine article.* *n.*

ex pan sive (ek span′siv), 1 capable of expanding; tending to expand. 2 wide; spreading. 3 taking in much or many things; broad; extensive. 4 showing one's feelings freely and openly; unrestrained; demonstrative: *Her expansive personality made it easy for her to make friends.* *adj.* —**ex pan′sive ly**, *adv.* —**ex pan′sive ness,** *n.*

ex pa ti ate (ek spā′shē āt), write or talk much: *She expatiated on the thrills of her trip to Hawaii.* *v.,* **ex pa ti at ed, ex pa ti at ing.**

ex pa tri ate (ek spā′trē āt *for 1,2;* ek spā′trē it *or* ek spā′trē āt *for 3*), 1 force to leave one's country; banish. 2 withdraw from one's country or citizenship: *Some Americans expatriate themselves and live in Europe.* 3 an expatriated person. 1,2 *v.,* **ex pa tri at ed, ex pa tri at ing;** 3 *n.*

ex pa tri a tion (ek spā′trē ā′shən), 1 exile. 2 withdrawal from one's country or citizenship. *n.*

ex pect (ek spekt′), 1 think something will probably come or happen; look forward to: *She expects three guests for dinner. He expects to take a vacation in May.* 2 count on as necessary or right: *A nation expects support from its allies.*

3 INFORMAL. think; suppose; guess: *I expect you're right about that.* *v.*

ex pect an cy (ek spek′tən sē), expectation. *n., pl.* **ex pect an cies.**

ex pect ant (ek spek′tənt), thinking something will come or happen; looking for; expecting: *She opened her package with an expectant smile.* *adj.* —**ex pect′ant ly,** *adv.*

ex pec ta tion (ek′spek tā′shən), 1 an expecting or a being expected; anticipation: *the expectation of a good harvest.* 2 something expected. 3 good reason for expecting something; prospect: *She has expectations of money from a rich aunt.* *n.*

ex pec to rate (ek spek′tə rāt′), cough up and spit out (phlegm, etc.); spit. *v.,* **ex pec to rat ed, ex pec to rat ing.**

ex pec to ra tion (ek spek′tə rā′shən), 1 act of expectorating. 2 expectorated matter. *n.*

ex pe di ence (ek spē′dē əns), expediency. *n.*

ex pe di en cy (ek spē′dē ən sē), 1 a helping to bring about a desired result; fitness; usefulness: *There was little doubt about the expediency of postponing our picnic until after the rain stopped.* 2 personal advantage; self-interest: *The salesclerk was influenced more by the expediency of making a sale than by the needs of the buyer.* *n., pl.* **ex pe di en cies.**

ex pe di ent (ek spē′dē ənt), 1 helping to bring about a desired result; useful: *It is expedient to be friendly and pleasant if you want to have friends.* 2 means of bringing about a desired result: *I had no package mix, so I made a cake by the expedient of mixing my own ingredients.* 3 giving or seeking personal advantage; based on self-interest: *No honest judge would make a decision that was expedient rather than fair and just.* 1,3 *adj.,* 2 *n.* —**ex pe′di ent ly,** *adv.*

ex pe dite (ek′spə dīt), make easy and quick; speed up: *Airplanes expedite travel. The telephone expedites business.* *v.,* **ex pe dit ed, ex pe dit ing.**

ex pe di tion (ek′spə dish′ən), 1 journey for some special purpose. A voyage of discovery or a march against the enemy is an expedition. 2 the people, ships, etc., making such a journey. 3 quickness; speed: *He completed his work with expedition.* *n.*

ex pe di tion ar y (ek′spə dish′ə ner′ē), of, having to do with, or making up an expedition: *The United States sent an expeditionary force of soldiers to Europe in World War II.* *adj.*

ex pe di tious (ek′spə dish′əs), efficient and prompt; quick; speedy: *an expeditious method of packing.* *adj.*

ex pel (ek spel′), 1 drive out with much

force; force out; eject: *When we exhale we expel air from our lungs.* 2 put (a person) out; dismiss permanently: *A student caught cheating may be expelled from school.* *v.,* **ex pelled, ex pel ling.**

ex pend (ek spend′), use up; spend: *He expended thought, work, and money on his project.* *v.*

ex pend a ble (ek spen′də bəl), that can be expended or used up. *adj.*

ex pend i ture (ek spen′də chùr *or* ek spen′də chər), 1 a using up; a spending: *To keep such a large house in good repair requires the expenditure of much money, time, and effort.* 2 amount of money, etc., spent; expense: *Her expenditures for Christmas presents were $2 and fourteen hours of work.* *n.*

ex pense (ek spens′), 1 amount of money, etc., spent; cost; charge: *The expense of the trip for the youngest child was slight. He traveled at his uncle's expense.* 2 an expending; a paying out of money; outlay: *Supporting a child at college puts parents to considerable expense.* 3 cause of spending: *Running an automobile is an expense.* 4 **expenses,** *pl.* money to repay a person for what he had to spend to do his job: *In addition to his salary, a traveling salesman often receives expenses.* 5 loss; sacrifice: *The town was captured at great expense to the victors.* *n.*

ex pen sive (ek spen′siv), costly; high-priced: *He had a very expensive knife which cost $10.* *adj.* —**ex pen′sive ly,** *adv.*

ex per i ence (ek spir′ē əns), 1 what happens to a person; what is seen, done, or lived through: *We had several pleasant experiences on our trip. People often learn by experience.* 2 knowledge or skill gained by seeing, doing, or living through things; practice: *Have you any experience in this kind of work? He has had little business experience.* 3 have happen to one; feel: *experience great pain.* 1,2 *n.,* 3 *v.,* **ex per i enced, ex per i enc ing.**

ex per i enced (ek spir′ē ənst), 1 having experience; taught by experience: *The job calls for a person experienced in teaching children.* 2 skillful or wise because of experience: *an experienced teacher, an experienced nurse.* *adj.*

ex per i ment (ek sper′ə ment *for 1;* ek sper′ə mənt *for 2*), 1 try in order to find out; make trials or tests: *The painter is experimenting with different paints to get the color he wants. A baby experiments with his hands.* 2 trial or test to find out something: *a cooking experiment. Scientists test out theories by experiments.* 1 *v.,* 2 *n.* —**ex per′i ment′er,** *n.*

ex per i men tal (ek sper′ə men′tl), 1 based on experiments: *Chemistry is an experimental science.* 2 used for experiments: *A new variety of wheat was developed at the experimental farm.* 3 for testing or trying out: *a young bird's experimental attempts to fly. This trip in the model of the new car will be only experimental.* 4 based on experience, not on theory or authority: *experimental knowledge.* *adj.*

ex per i men tal ly (ek sper′ə men′tl ē), 1 by making experiments. 2 as an experiment. *adv.*

ex per i men ta tion (ek sper′ə men tā′shən), an experimenting: *Cures for diseases are often found by experimentation on animals.* *n.*

ex pert (ek′spėrt′ for 1; ek spėrt′ or ek′spėrt′ for 2,3), 1 a very skillful person; person who knows a great deal about some special thing: *She is an expert at fancy skating.* 2 very skillful; knowing a great deal about some special thing: *He is an expert chemist.* 3 requiring or showing special skill: *expert workmanship, expert testimony.* 1 *n.*, 2,3 *adj.* —**ex pert′ly,** *adv.* —**ex pert′ness,** *n.*

ex pi ate (ek′spē āt), pay the penalty of; atone for: *When she realized how selfish she had been, she expiated her guilt by contributing to charity.* *v.*, **ex pi at ed, ex pi at ing.**

ex pi a tion (ek′spē ā′shən), 1 a making amends for a wrong, sin, etc.; atonement: *He made a public apology in expiation of his error.* 2 means of atonement; amends: *His apology was considered a suitable expiation.* *n.*

ex pi ra tion (ek′spə rā′shən), 1 a coming to an end: *We shall move at the expiration of our lease.* 2 a breathing out; exhalation: *the expiration of air from the lungs.* *n.*

ex pire (ek spīr′), 1 come to an end: *You must obtain a new license for your dog when the old one expires.* 2 die. 3 breathe out; exhale: *Air is expired from the lungs.* *v.*, **ex pired, ex pir ing.**

ex plain (ek splān′), 1 make plain or clear; tell the meaning of: *The teacher explained long division to the class. Will you explain this poem to me?* 2 give reasons for; state the cause of; account for: *Can you explain your friend's absence?* *v.*

ex plain a ble (ek splā′nə bəl), that can be explained. *adj.*

ex pla na tion (ek′splə nā′shən), 1 an explaining; clearing up a difficulty or mistake: *He did not understand the teacher's·explanation of long division.* 2 something that explains: *This diagram is a good explanation of how an automobile engine works.* *n.*

ex plan a to ry (ek splan′ə tôr′ē), that explains; helping to make clear: *Read the explanatory part of the lesson before you try to do the problem.* *adj.*

ex ple tive (ek′splə tiv), 1 word or phrase used for filling out a sentence or a line of verse, without adding to the sense. In the sentence "There is a book on the table," *there* is an expletive. 2 oath or exclamation. "Damn" and "My goodness!" are expletives. *n.*

ex pli ca ble (ek splik′ə bəl *or* ek′splə kə bəl), that can be explained. *adj.*

ex plic it (ek splis′it), clearly expressed; distinctly stated; definite: *She gave such explicit directions that everyone understood them.* *adj.* —**ex plic′it ly,** *adv.* —**ex plic′it ness,** *n.*

ex plode (ek splōd′), 1 burst with a loud noise; blow up: *The building was destroyed when the defective boiler exploded.* 2 cause to explode: *Some people explode firecrackers on the Fourth of July.* 3 burst forth noisily: *The speaker's remark was so funny the audience exploded with laughter.* 4 cause to be rejected; destroy belief in: *Columbus and other navigators helped to explode the theory that the earth is flat.* *v.*, **ex plod ed, ex plod ing.**

ex ploit (ek′sploit *for* 1; ek sploit′ *for* 2,3), 1 a bold, unusual act; daring deed: *This book tells about the exploits of Robin Hood.* 2 make use of: *A mine is exploited for its minerals.* 3 make unfair or selfish use of: *Nations used to exploit their colonies, taking as much wealth out of them as they could.* 1 *n.*, 2,3 *v.* —**ex ploit′er,** *n.*

ex ploi ta tion (ek′sploi tā′shən), 1 use: *the exploitation of the ocean as a source for food.* 2 selfish or unfair use: *There are laws against the exploitation of child labor.* *n.*

ex plo ra tion (ek′splə rā′shən), 1 a traveling in little known lands or seas for the purpose of discovery. 2 a going over carefully; a looking into closely; examining. *n.*

ex plor a to ry (ek splôr′ə tôr′ē), of or having to do with exploration. *adj.*

ex plore (ek splôr′), 1 travel over little known lands or seas for the purpose of discovery: *Admiral Byrd explored the land around the South Pole.* 2 go over carefully; look into closely; examine: *explore a possibility. The children explored the new house from attic to cellar.* *v.*, **ex plored, ex plor ing.**

ex plor er (ek splôr′ər), person who explores. *n.*

ex plo sion (ek splō′zhən), 1 a bursting with a loud noise; a blowing up: *The explosion of the bomb shook the whole neighborhood.* 2 a loud noise caused by this: *People five miles away heard the explosion.* 3 a noisy bursting forth;

outbreak; outburst: *explosions of anger, an explosion of laughter.* 4 a sudden or rapid increase or growth: *The explosion of the world's population has created a shortage of food in many countries.* *n.*

ex plo sive (ek splō′siv), 1 of or for explosion; tending to explode: *Gunpowder is explosive.* 2 an explosive substance: *Explosives are used in making fireworks.* 3 tending to burst forth noisily: *an explosive temper, explosive laughter.* 1,3 *adj.*, 2 *n.* —**ex plo′sive ly,** *adv.* —**ex plo′sive ness,** *n.*

ex po nent (ek spō′nənt), 1 person or thing that explains. 2 person or thing that stands as an example, type, or symbol of something: *Abraham Lincoln is a famous exponent of self-education.* 3 a small number written above and to the right of a symbol or quantity to show how many times the symbol or quantity is to be used as a factor. EXAMPLES: $2^2 = 2 \times 2$. $a^3 = a \times a \times a$. *n.*

ex port (ek spôrt′ *or* ek′spôrt *for* 1; ek′spôrt *for* 2,3), 1 send (goods) out of one country for sale and use in another: *The United States exports many kinds of machinery.* 2 article exported: *Cotton is an important export of the United States.* 3 act or fact of exporting: *the export of wool from Great Britain.* 1 *v.*, 2,3 *n.*

ex por ta tion (ek′spôr tā′shən), 1 an exporting: *the exportation of wheat from Canada to India.* 2 article exported; export: *Machinery and vehicles are among the major exportations of the United States.* *n.*

ex port er (ek spôr′tər *or* ek′spôr tər), person or company whose business is exporting. *n.*

ex pose (ek spōz′), 1 lay open; leave without protection; uncover: *The soldiers in the open field were exposed to the enemy's gunfire. All the children have been exposed to mumps.* 2 show openly; display: *Goods are exposed for sale in a store.* 3 make known; reveal: *He exposed the plot to the police.* 4 put out without shelter; abandon: *The ancient Spartans used to expose babies*

hat, āge, fär; let, ēqual, tėrm;
it, īce; hot, ōpen, ôrder;
oil, out; cup, pùt, rüle; ch, child;
ng, long; sh, she; th, thin;
ŦH, then; zh, measure;

ə represents *a* in about,
e in taken, *i* in pencil,
o in lemon, *u* in circus.

adj. adjective   *n.* noun
adv. adverb   *prep.* preposition
conj. conjunction   *pron.* pronoun
interj. interjection   *v.* verb

sing. singular   *pl.* plural

---

that they did not want. 5 allow light to reach and act on (a photographic film or plate). *v.*, **ex posed, ex pos ing.**

ex po sé (ek′spō zā′), a showing up of crime, dishonesty, fraud, etc.: *a public exposé of graft. n., pl.* **ex po sés.** [from French *exposé* exposed]

ex po si tion (ek′spə zish′ən), 1 a public show or exhibition. A world's fair with exhibits from many countries is an exposition. 2 a detailed explanation. 3 speech or writing explaining a process, thing, or idea. *n.*

ex pos i tor (ek spoz′ə tər), person or thing that explains. *n.*

ex pos i to ry (ek spoz′ə tôr′ē), explanatory. *adj.*

ex pos tu late (ek spos′chə lāt), reason earnestly with a person, protesting against something he means to do or has done; remonstrate in a friendly way: *The teacher expostulated with the student about her poor work. v.,* **expos tu lat ed, ex pos tu lat ing.**

ex pos tu la tion (ek spos′chə lā′shən), earnest protest; friendly remonstrance: *The teacher's expostulations were wasted, for the student made no effort to improve his work. n.*

ex po sure (ek spō′zhər), 1 an exposing; laying open; making known: *The exposure of the real criminal cleared the innocent man. Anyone would dread public exposure of all his faults.* 2 a being exposed: *Exposure to the rain has spoiled this machinery.* 3 position in relation to the sun and wind. A house with a southern exposure is open to sun and wind from the south. 4 time during which light reaches and acts on a photographic film or plate. 5 part of a photographic film for one picture. 6 a putting out without shelter; abandoning. *n.*

ex pound (ek spound′), 1 make clear; explain: *The teacher expounds each new principle in arithmetic to the class.* 2 set forth or state in detail: *The Senator expounded his objections to the bill. v.* —**ex pound′er,** *n.*

ex-pres i dent (eks′prez′ə dənt), a former president; living person who once was president, but no longer is. *n.*

ex press (ek spres′), 1 put into words: *Try to express your ideas clearly.* 2 show by look, voice, or action; reveal:

Your smile expresses joy. 3 clear and definite: *It was his express wish that we should go without him.* 4 for a particular purpose; special: *She came for the express purpose of seeing you.* 5 a quick or direct means of sending things. Packages and money can be sent by express in trains or airplanes. 6 system or company that carries packages, money, etc. 7 things sent by express. 8 send by some quick means: *Express this trunk to Chicago.* 9 by express; directly: *Please send this package express to Boston.* 10 traveling fast and making few stops: *an express train.* 11 train, bus, elevator, etc., traveling fast and making few stops. 12 for fast traveling: *An express highway.* 13 press out; squeeze out: *The juice is expressed from grapes to make wine.* 1,2,8,13 *v.,* 3,4,10,12 *adj.,* 5-7,11 *n., pl.* **ex press es** for 11; 9 *adv.*

express oneself, say what one thinks: *The speaker expressed himself clearly.*

ex press i ble (ek spres′ə bəl), that can be expressed. *adj.*

ex pres sion (ek spresh′ən), 1 a putting into words: *the expression of an idea.* 2 word or group of words used as a unit: *"Wise guy" is a slang expression.* 3 a showing by look, voice, or action: *A sigh is often an expression of sadness.* 4 look that shows feeling: *The baby had a happy expression on his face.* 5 a bringing out of the meaning or beauty of something read, spoken, sung, or played: *Try to read with more expression.* 6 a pressing out: *the expression of oil from plants.* 7 any combination of constants, variables, and symbols expressing some mathematical operation or quantity. *n.*

ex pres sion less (ek spresh′ən lis), without expression: *an expressionless face, an expressionless voice. adj.*

ex pres sive (ek spres′iv), 1 expressing: *"Alas!" is a word expressive of sadness.* 2 full of expression; having much feeling, meaning, etc.: *"His skin hung on his bones" is a more expressive sentence than "He was very thin." adj.* —**ex pres′sive ly,** *adv.* —**ex pres′sive ness,** *n.*

ex press ly (ek spres′lē), 1 plainly; definitely: *The package is not for you; you are expressly forbidden to touch it.* 2 on purpose; specially: *She came expressly to see you. adv.*

ex press way (ek spres′wā′), highway built for motor-vehicle travel at high speeds. *n.*

ex pro pri ate (ek sprō′prē āt), take (land, possessions, etc.) from the owner, especially for public use. A city can expropriate land for a public park. *v.,* **ex pro pri at ed, ex pro pri at ing.**

ex pro pri a tion (ek sprō′prē-

ā′shən), the taking of land, possessions, etc., from the owner, especially for public use. *n.*

ex pul sion (ek spul′shən), 1 a forcing out: *Expulsion of air from the lungs is part of breathing.* 2 a being forced out: *Expulsion from school is a punishment for bad behavior. n.*

ex punge (ek spunj′), remove completely; blot out; erase: *The secretary was directed to expunge certain remarks from the record of the meeting. v.,* **ex punged, ex pung ing.**

ex pur gate (ek′spər gāt), remove objectionable passages or words from (a book, letter, etc.). *v.,* **ex pur gat ed, ex pur gat ing.**

ex qui site (ek′skwi zit *or* ek skwiz′it), 1 very lovely; delicate: *These violets are exquisite.* 2 sharp; intense: *A toothache causes exquisite pain.* 3 of highest excellence; most admirable: *She has exquisite taste and manners. adj.* —**ex′qui site ly,** *adv.* —**ex′qui site ness,** *n.*

ex tant (ek′stənt *or* ek stant′), still existing: *Some of George Washington's letters are extant. adj.*

ex tem po ra ne ous (ek stem′-pə rā′nē əs), spoken or done without preparation; offhand: *an extemporaneous speech. adj.* —**ex tem′po ra′ne ous ly,** *adv.*

ex tem po re (ek stem′pər ē), on the spur of the moment; without preparation; offhand: *Each pupil will be called on to speak extempore. adv.*

ex tem po rize (ek stem′pə riz′), 1 speak, play, sing, or dance, composing as one goes along; improvise: *The pianist was extemporizing instead of following the score.* 2 prepare offhand; make for the occasion: *The campers extemporized a shelter for the night. v.,* **ex tem po rized, ex tem po riz ing.**

ex tend (ek stend′), 1 stretch out: *extend your hand. A road extends to the new bridge.* 2 lengthen: *I am extending my vacation another week.* 3 increase or enlarge: *They plan to extend their research in that field.* 4 offer; give; grant: *This organization extends help to poor people. v.*

ex ten sion (ek sten′shən), 1 an extending: *the extension of one's arm, the extension of a road.* 2 a being extended: *The railroad is in the process of extension.* 3 an extended part; addition: *The new extension to our school will make room for more students.* 4 telephone connected with the main telephone or with a switchboard but in a different location. *n.*

extension cord, length of electric cord fitted with a plug and a socket, used to connect a short cord to an outlet or other source of power.

ex ten sive (ek sten′siv), of great extent; far-reaching; large: *an extensive park, extensive changes. adj.* —**ex ten′sive ly,** *adv.*

ex tent (ek stent′), 1 size, length, amount, or degree to which a thing extends: *Railroads carry people and goods through the whole extent of the country. The extent of a judge's power is limited by law. I agree with your plans, but only to a certain extent.* 2 something extended; extended space: *a vast extent of prairie. n.*

ex ten u ate (ek sten′yü āt), make the seriousness of (guilt, a fault, an offense, etc.) seem less; excuse in part: *His concern over his parents' divorce extenuated his lack of interest in school. v.,* **ex ten u at ed, ex ten u at ing.**

ex ten u a tion (ek sten′yü ā′shən), 1 an extenuating: *The lawyer pleaded her client's youth in extenuation of the crime.* 2 something that lessens the seriousness of guilt, a fault, an offense, etc.; partial excuse. *n.*

ex ter i or (ek stir′ē ər), 1 outer part; outward appearance; outside: *The exterior of the house was made of brick. The gruff man has a harsh exterior but a kind heart.* 2 on the outside; outer: *The skin of an apple is its exterior covering.* 3 coming from without; happening outside: *exterior influences.* 1 *n.,* 2,3 *adj.*

ex ter mi nate (ek stėr′mə nāt), destroy completely: *This poison will exterminate rats. v.,* **ex ter mi nat ed, ex ter mi nat ing.**

ex ter mi na tion (ek stėr′mə nā′shən), complete destruction: *Poison and traps are useful for the extermination of rats. n.*

ex ter mi na tor (ek stėr′mə nā′tər), person or thing that exterminates, especially a person whose business is exterminating fleas, cockroaches, bedbugs, rats, etc. *n.*

ex ter nal (ek stėr′nəl), 1 on the outside; outer: *An ear of corn has an external husk.* 2 an outer surface or part; outside. 3 **externals,** *pl.* clothing, manners, or other outward acts or appearances: *He judges people by mere externals rather than by their characters.* 4 to be used only on the outside of the body: *Liniment and rubbing alcohol are external remedies.* 5 easily seen but not essential: *Going to church is an external act of worship.* 6 having to do with international affairs; foreign: *War affects a nation's external trade.* 1,4-6 *adj.,* 2,3 *n.* —**ex ter′nal ly,** *adv.*

external ear, the outer part of the ear, including the passage leading to the middle ear.

ex tinct (ek stingkt′), 1 no longer existing: *The dinosaur is an extinct animal.* 2 no longer active; extinguished: *an extinct volcano. adj.*

ex tinc tion (ek stingk′shən), 1 an extinguishing: *The sudden extinction of the lights left the room in darkness.* 2 a being extinguished; extinct condition. 3 wiping out; destruction: *Physicians are working toward the extinction of diseases. n.*

ex tin guish (ek sting′gwish), 1 put out: *Water extinguished the fire.* 2 bring to an end; wipe out; destroy: *One failure after another extinguished my hopes. v.*

ex tin guish er (ek sting′gwish ər), person or thing that extinguishes, especially an apparatus for putting out fires. *n.*

ex tir pate (ek′stər pāt), 1 remove completely; destroy totally: *We look forward to the day when disease and poverty will be extirpated.* 2 tear up by the roots. *v.,* **ex tir pat ed, ex tir pat ing.**

ex tir pa tion (ek′stər pā′shən), 1 complete removal; total destruction. 2 a tearing up by the roots. *n.*

ex tol or **ex toll** (ek stōl′), praise highly; commend: *The newspapers extolled the mayor's plan for a new park. v.,* **ex tolled, ex tol ling.**

ex tort (ek stôrt′), obtain (money, a promise, etc.) by threats, force, fraud, or wrong use of authority: *Blackmailers try to extort money from their victims. v.*

ex tor tion (ek stôr′shən), 1 an extorting: *Collecting very high interest on loans is considered extortion and is forbidden by law.* 2 something extorted. *n.*

ex tor tion ate (ek stôr′shə nit), much too great: *Fifty dollars for a softball glove is an extortionate price. adj.*

ex tor tion ist (ek stôr′shə nist), person who is guilty of extortion. *n.*

ex tra (ek′strə), 1 beyond what is usual, expected, or needed; additional: *extra fare, extra pay, extra favors.* 2 something extra; anything beyond what is usual, expected, or needed: *My parents bought a luxurious new car equipped with many extras.* 3 a special edition of a newspaper: *The paper published an extra to announce the end of the war.* 4 person who is employed by the day to play minor parts in motion pictures: *Two hundred extras were hired for the battle scene.* 5 more than usually: *extra fine quality. That store is extra busy on Saturdays.* 1 *adj.,* 2-4 *n., pl.* **ex tras;** 5 *adv.*

ex tract (ek strakt′ *for 1-4;* ek′strakt *for 5,6*), 1 pull out or draw out, usually with some effort: *extract a tooth, extract iron from the earth, extract a confession.* 2 obtain by pressing, squeezing, etc.: *extract oil from olives.*

hat, āge, fär; let, ēqual, tėrm;
it, īce; hot, ōpen, ôrder;
oil, out; cup, pùt, rüle; ch, child;
ng, long; sh, she; th, thin;
ŦH, then; zh, measure;

ə represents *a* in about,
e in taken, *i* in pencil,
o in lemon, *u* in circus.

3 derive; obtain: *extract pleasure from a party.* 4 take out (a passage) from a book, speech, etc.: *He extracted several sections of the article to read at the meeting.* 5 passage taken out of a book, speech, etc.: *He read several extracts from a book of poems.* 6 a concentrated preparation of a substance: *Vanilla extract, made from vanilla beans, is used as flavoring.* 1-4 *v.,* 5,6 *n.*

ex trac tion (ek strak′shən), 1 an extracting or a being extracted: *the extraction of a tooth.* 2 origin; descent: *Miss del Rio is of Spanish extraction; her parents came from Spain. n.*

ex trac tor (ek strak′tər), person or thing that extracts. *n.*

ex tra cur ric u lar (ek′strə kə rik′yə lər), outside the regular course of study: *Football, dramatics, and debating are extracurricular activities in our high school. adj.*

ex tra dite (ek′strə dīt), 1 give up (a fugitive or prisoner) to another state, nation, or authority: *If an escaped prisoner of the state of Ohio is caught in Indiana, he can be extradited by Indiana to Ohio.* 2 obtain the surrender of (such a person). *v.,* **ex tra dit ed, ex tra dit ing.**

ex tra di tion (ek′strə dish′ən), surrender of a fugitive or prisoner by one state, nation, or authority to another. *n.*

ex tra ne ous (ek strā′nē əs), from outside; not belonging: *Sand and some other extraneous matter had got into the butter and ruined it. The speaker made many extraneous remarks. adj.*

ex traor di nar i ly (ek strôr′də ner′ə lē), most unusually. *adv.*

ex traor di nar y (ek strôr′də ner′ē; ek′strə ôr′də ner′ē *especially for 2*), 1 beyond what is ordinary; very unusual; very remarkable: *Eight feet is an extraordinary height for a person.* 2 ranking below the regular class of officials; special. An **envoy extraordinary** is one sent on a special mission. *adj.*

ex trav a gance (ek strav′ə gəns), 1 careless and lavish spending; wastefulness: *Their extravagance kept them always in debt.* 2 a going beyond the

adj.	adjective	n.	noun
adv.	adverb	prep.	preposition
conj.	conjunction	pron.	pronoun
interj.	interjection	v.	verb
sing.	singular	pl.	plural

bounds of reason: *The extravagance of the claims in the advertisement caused me to doubt the worth of the product.* 3 an extravagant action, idea, purchase, etc.: *A mink coat is an extravagance. n.*

ex trav a gant (ek strav′ə gənt), 1 spending carelessly and lavishly; wasteful: *An extravagant person has extravagant tastes and habits.* 2 beyond the bounds of reason: *an extravagant price. To call a poodle "the sweetest thing alive" is extravagant. adj.* —**ex trav′a gant ly,** *adv.*

ex treme (ek strēm′), 1 much more than usual; very great; very strong: *She drove with extreme caution during the snowstorm.* 2 at the very end; farthest possible; last: *The extreme north stops at the North Pole.* 3 something extreme; one of two things as far or as different as possible from each other: *Love and hate are two extremes of feeling.* 4 the highest degree: *Joy is happiness in the extreme. The extreme of coldness is absolute zero.* 1,2 *adj.,* **ex trem er, ex trem est;** 3,4 *n.* —**ex treme′ly,** *adv.*

go to extremes, do or say too much: *Even for an animal lover, owning twenty cats is going to extremes.*

ex trem ist (ek strē′mist), person who goes to extremes; supporter of extreme doctrines or practices. *n.*

ex trem i ty (ek strem′ə tē), 1 the very end; farthest possible place; last part or point: *Alaska is at the western extremity of the American continent.* 2 **extremities,** *pl.* the hands and feet. 3 very great danger or need: *People on a sinking ship are in extremity.* 4 extreme degree: *Joy is the extremity of happiness.* 5 an extreme action or measure: *The government was forced to the extremity of rationing gas during the fuel shortage. n., pl.* **ex trem i ties.**

ex tri cate (ek′strə kāt), free from entanglements, difficulties, embarrassing situations, etc.; release: *He extricated the kitten from the net. v.,* **ex tri cat ed, ex tri cat ing.**

ex tri ca tion (ek′strə kā′shən), an extricating or a being extricated. *n.*

ex trin sic (ek strin′sik), 1 not essential: *extrinsic differences.* 2 outside of a thing; coming from without; external: *extrinsic influences. adj.*

ex tro vert (ek′strə vėrt′), person more interested in what is going on around him than in his own thoughts and feelings; person tending to act rather than think. *n.*

ex trude (ek strüd′), 1 thrust out; push out: *He extruded toothpaste from the tube.* 2 shape (metal, plastics, rubber, or ceramics) by forcing through dies. 3 stick out; protrude. *v.,* **ex trud ed, ex trud ing.**

extrude (def. 2)—Cutaway drawing of cylinder shows the shaping of metal by extruding it. Hot metal is compressed in a cylinder and forced through a die; the extruded metal will have the shape of the die opening.

ex tru sion (ek strü′zhən), an extruding or a being extruded. *n.*

ex u ber ance (eg zü′bər əns), 1 a being exuberant; great abundance. 2 luxuriant growth: *an exuberance of tropical vegetation. n.*

ex u ber ant (eg zü′bər ənt), 1 very abundant; overflowing; lavish: *exuberant health, good nature, or joy. The astronaut received an exuberant welcome when he returned to his home town.* 2 profuse in growth; luxuriant: *the exuberant vegetation of the jungle. adj.* —**ex u′ber ant ly,** *adv.*

ex u da tion (ek′syü dā′shən), 1 an exuding. 2 something exuded. *n.*

ex ude (eg züd′ *or* ek syüd′), 1 come or send out in drops; ooze: *Sweat exudes from the pores in the skin.* 2 give forth: *Some people exude self-confidence. v.,* **ex ud ed, ex ud ing.**

ex ult (eg zult′), be very glad; rejoice greatly: *The winners exulted in their victory. v.* —**ex ult′ing ly,** *adv.*

ex ult ant (eg zul′tənt), rejoicing greatly; exulting; triumphant: *The students gave an exultant shout when the teacher announced that there would be no classes on Monday. adj.* —**ex ult′ant ly,** *adv.*

ex ul ta tion (eg′zul tā′shən *or* ek′sul tā′shən), an exulting; great rejoicing; triumph: *There was exultation over our team's victory. n.*

-ey, *suffix forming adjectives from nouns.* full of; containing; like _____: *Clayey = like or containing clay. Gooey = like goo.* [a different form of *-y¹*]

eye (ī), 1 the organ of the body by which people and animals see. 2 the colored part of the eye; iris: *He has brown eyes.* 3 region surrounding the eye: *The blow gave her a black eye.* 4 Often, **eyes,** *pl.* sense of seeing;

vision; sight: *A jet pilot must have good eyes.* 5 ability to see small differences in things: *A good artist must have an eye for color.* 6 a look; glance: *She cast an eye at the young man.* 7 look at; watch; observe: *The dog eyed the stranger.* 8 Often, **eyes,** *pl.* way of thinking or considering; view; opinion; judgment: *Stealing is a crime in the eyes of the law.* 9 thing shaped like, resembling, or suggesting an eye. The little spots on potatoes, the hole for thread in a needle, and the loop in which a hook fastens are all called eyes. 10 the relatively calm, clear area at the center of a hurricane. 1-6,8-10 *n.,* 7*v.,* **eyed, ey ing** *or* **eye ing.**

an eye for an eye, punishment as severe as the injury.

catch one's eye, attract one's attention: *The bright red sign caught my eye.*

in the public eye, 1 often seen in public. 2 widely known.

keep an eye on, look after; watch carefully: *Keep an eye on the baby while I hang out the wash.*

lay eyes on or **set eyes on,** look at; see: *I never laid eyes on this man until today.*

make eyes at, flirt with: *He was making eyes at the girl across the room.*

open one's eyes, make one see what is really happening.

see eye to eye, agree entirely: *She and her parents do not see eye to eye on her weekly allowance.*

shut one's eyes to, refuse to see or consider; ignore: *He shut his eyes to the faults of his friends.*

eye ball (ī′bôl′), the eye without the surrounding lids and bony socket. It is shaped like a ball. *n.*

eye brow (ī′brou′), 1 arch of hair above the eye. 2 the bony ridge that it grows on. *n.*

eye glass (ī′glas′), 1 a lens to aid poor vision. 2 **eyeglasses,** *pl.* pair of such lenses, mounted in a frame, to correct defective eyesight; glasses; spectacles. *n., pl.* **eye glass es.**

eye hole (ī′hōl′), 1 the bony socket for the eyeball. 2 hole in a mask, fence, etc., to look through. *n.*

eye (def. 1) of a human being

eye lash (ī′lash′), 1 one of the hairs on the edge of the eyelid. 2 fringe of such hairs. *n., pl.* **eye lash es.**

eye less (ī′lis), without eyes. *adj.*

eye let (ī′lit), 1 a small, round hole for a lace or cord to go through. 2 a metal ring around such a hole to strengthen it. 3 a small, round hole with stitches around it, used to make a pattern in embroidery. *n.*

eye lid (ī′lid′), the movable fold of skin, upper or lower, by means of which we can shut and open the eyes. *n.*

EYETEETH

eye piece (ī′pēs′), lens or set of lenses in a telescope, microscope, etc., nearest to the eye of the user. *n.*

eye sight (ī′sīt′), 1 power of seeing; sight: *A hawk has keen eyesight.* 2 range of vision; view: *The water was within eyesight. n.*

eye sore (ī′sôr′), something unpleasant to look at: *That garbage heap is an eyesore. n.*

eye spot (ī′spot′), the simplest kind of organ for seeing in many lower animals. *n.*

eye strain (ī′strān′), a tired or weak condition of the eyes caused by using them too much, reading in a dim light, etc. *n.*

eye tooth (ī′tüth′), an upper canine tooth. *n., pl.* **eye teeth.**

eye wit ness (ī′wit′nis), person who actually sees or has seen some act or happening, and thus can give testimony concerning it. *n., pl.* **eye wit ness es.**

eyr ie or **eyr y** (er′ē, ar′ē, *or* ir′ē), aerie. *n., pl.* **eyr ies.**

hat, āge, fär; let, ēqual, tèrm; it, īce; hot, ōpen, ôrder; oil, out; cup, pùt, rüle; ch, child; ng, long; sh, she; th, thin; ŦH, then; zh, measure;

ə represents *a* in about, *e* in taken, *i* in pencil, *o* in lemon, *u* in circus.

E ze ki el (i zē′kē əl), 1 Hebrew prophet who lived in the 500's B.C. 2 book of the Old Testament containing his prophecies. *n.*

Ez ra (ez′rə), 1 Hebrew scribe who led a revival of Judaism in the 400's or 300's B.C. 2 book of the Old Testament that tells about him. *n.*

F f

F or **f** (ef), the sixth letter of the alphabet. *n., pl.* **F's** or **f's.**

F., Fahrenheit.

fa (fä), the fourth note of the musical scale. *n.* [from Italian]

fa ble (fā′bəl), 1 story which is made up to teach a lesson. Fables are often about animals who can talk, such as *The Hare and the Tortoise* and *The Fox and the Crow.* 2 an untrue story; falsehood. 3 legend; myth. *n.*

fa bled (fā′bəld), 1 told about in fables, legends, or myths. 2 not real; made up. *adj.*

fab ric (fab′rik), 1 woven or knitted material; cloth. Velvet, canvas, linen, and flannel are fabrics. 2 way in which a thing is put together; frame or structure: *The fabric of a person's character may be weak or strong. n.*

fab ri cate (fab′rə kāt), 1 make by putting parts together; build or manufacture: *Automobiles are fabricated from parts made in different factories.* 2 make up; invent (a story, lie, excuse, etc.). *v.,* **fab ri cat ed, fab ri cat ing.**

fab ri ca tion (fab′rə kā′shən), 1 a fabricating; manufacture. 2 something fabricated; false story, lie, excuse, etc. *n.*

fab u lous (fab′yə ləs), 1 not believable; amazing: *Ten dollars is a fabulous price for a pencil.* 2 of or belonging to a fable; imaginary: *The centaur is a fabulous monster.* 3 like a fable. *adj.* —**fab′u lous ly,** *adv.*

facade (def. 1) of a church

fa cade (fə säd′), 1 the front part of a building, especially the part that faces a street or an open space. 2 outward appearance. *n.* [from French *façade*]

fa çade (fə säd′), facade. *n., pl.* **fa-çades.**

face (fās), 1 the front part of the head. The eyes, nose, and mouth are parts of the face. 2 look; expression: *His face was sad.* 3 an ugly or funny look made by twisting the face: *She made a face at me.* 4 the front part; the right side; surface: *The face of a clock or watch has numbers on it.* 5 outward appearance: *His action, on the face of it, looks bad.* 6 have the front toward; be opposite to: *The house faces the street. The picture faces page 60 in my book.* 7 meet bravely or boldly: *face danger, face the enemy.* 8 present itself to: *A crisis faced us.* 9 boldness; impudence: *She had the face to insult our school principal.* 10 dignity; self-respect; personal importance: *lose face. Face is very important to Oriental peoples.* 11 cover with a different material: *A wooden house is sometimes faced with brick.* 12 cover the inside or outside edges of cuffs, a collar, etc., with the same or different material for protection or trimming: *She faced the lapels with velvet.* 13 any of the planes or surfaces that bound a solid figure. A cube has six faces. 1-5,9,10,13 *n.,* 6-8,11,12 *v.,* **faced, fac ing.**

face to face, 1 with faces toward each other: *The enemies stood face to face.* 2 in the actual presence.

in the face of, 1 in the presence of. 2 in spite of: *He insisted he was right in the face of facts that proved he was wrong.*

to one's face, in one's presence; openly; boldly.

face card, king, queen, or jack of playing cards.

facet (def. 1) gem with many facets

fac et (fas′it), 1 one of the small, polished surfaces of a cut gem. 2 any one of several sides or views: *Selfishness was a facet of her character that we seldom saw. n.*

fa ce tious (fə sē′shəs), 1 having the habit of joking; being slyly humorous. 2 said in fun; not to be taken seriously: *facetious remarks. adj.* —**fa ce′tious ly,** *adv.* —**fa ce′tious ness,** *n.*

face value, 1 value stated on a bond, check, note, bill, etc. 2 apparent worth, meaning, etc.

fa cial (fā′shəl), 1 of the face. 2 for the face. 3 massage or treatment of the face. 1,2 *adj.,* 3 *n.* —**fa′cial ly,** *adv.*

fac ile (fas′əl), 1 easily done or used; taking little effort: *Lazy people seek facile tasks. Facile methods speed up work.* 2 moving, acting, or working easily or rapidly: *That gossip has a facile tongue. He writes in a facile style.* 3 easy; easygoing; agreeable; yielding: *Her facile nature adapted itself to any group of people without effort. adj.* —**fac′ile ly,** *adv.*

fa cil i tate (fə sil′ə tāt), make easy; lessen the labor of; help bring about; assist: *A good vacuum cleaner facilitates housework. v.,* **fa cil i tat ed, fa-cil i tat ing.**

fa cil i ty (fə sil′ə tē), 1 absence of difficulty; ease: *Long practice enabled the storekeeper to add up long columns of figures with facility.* 2 power to do anything easily and quickly; skill in using the hands or mind. 3 Usually, **facilities,** *pl.* something that makes an action easy; aid; convenience: *Ropes, swings, and sand piles are facilities for play. n., pl.* **fa cil i ties.**

fac ing (fā′sing), 1 a covering of different material for ornament, protection, etc.: *a wooden house with a brick facing.* 2 material put around the inside or outside edge of cloth to protect or trim it: *a blue coat with red facings on the collar and cuffs. n.*

fac sim i le (fak sim′ə lē), an exact copy or likeness. *n.*

fact (fakt), 1 thing known to be true or to have really happened: *It is a fact that the Pilgrims sailed to America on the Mayflower in 1620.* 2 what is true; truth: *The fact of the matter is, I did want to go to the dance.* 3 thing said or supposed to be true or to have really happened: *We doubted his facts. n.*

as a matter of fact, in fact.

in fact, truly; really.

fac tion (fak′shən), 1 group of persons who stand up for their side or act together for some common purpose against the rest of a larger group: *A faction in our club tried to make the president resign.* 2 strife among the members of a political party, church, club, or neighborhood. *n.*

fac tion al (fak′shə nəl), having to do with factions; partisan. *adj.*

fac tious (fak′shəs), fond of stirring up disputes. *adj.*

fac ti tious (fak tish′əs), developed by effort; not natural; forced; artificial: *Her factitious smile convinced me that she was not sincere. adj.* —**fac ti′-tious ly,** *adv.*

fac tor (fak′tər), 1 any one of the causes that helps bring about a result; one element in a situation: *Ability, industry, and health are factors of his success in business.* 2 any of the numbers or expressions which, when multiplied together, form a product: *5, 3, and 4 are factors of 60.* 3 separate into factors. 4 person who does business for another; agent. 1,2,4 *n.,* 3 *v.*

fac tor y (fak′tər ē), building or group of buildings where things are manufactured. A factory usually has machines in it. *n., pl.* **fac tor ies.**

fac to tum (fak tō′təm), person employed to do all kinds of work. *n.*

fac tu al (fak′chü əl), concerned with fact; consisting of facts: *I kept a detailed factual account of the trip in my diary.* *adj.* —**fac′tu al ly,** *adv.*

fac ul ty (fak′əl tē), 1 power to do some special thing, especially a power of the mind; ability: *the faculty of hearing, the faculty of memory. She has a great faculty for arithmetic. Old people sometimes lose their faculties.* 2 the teachers of a school, college, or university. 3 department of learning in a university: *The faculty of medicine is made up of doctors, surgeons, etc., who teach and do research.* *n., pl.* **fac ul ties.**

fad (fad), something everybody is very much interested in for a short time; fashion or craze: *No one plays that game anymore; it was only a fad.* *n.*

fade (fād), 1 become less bright; lose color: *Daylight fades when the sun sets. My blue dress faded when it was washed.* 2 lose freshness or strength; wither: *The flowers in her garden faded at the end of the summer.* 3 die away; disappear little by little: *The sound of the train faded after it went by.* 4 cause to fade: *Sunlight faded the new curtains.* *v.,* **fad ed, fad ing.**

fade-out (fād′out′), 1 the gradual fading from the screen of a scene in a motion picture or television show. 2 a gradual disappearance. *n.*

fag (fag), tire by work: *After climbing to the top of the mountain he was completely fagged.* *v.,* **fagged, fag ging.**

fag end, 1 the last part or remnant of anything, after the best part has been used: *the fag end of a cigar.* 2 the coarse, unfinished end of a piece of cloth. 3 an untwisted end of rope.

fag ot or **fag got** (fag′ət), bundle of sticks or twigs tied together for fuel: *He built the fire with fagots.* *n.*

Fahr en heit (far′ən hīt), of, based on, or according to a scale for measuring temperature on which 32 degrees marks the freezing point of water and 212 degrees marks the boiling point. The **Fahrenheit thermometer** is marked off according to this scale. *adj.* [from Gabriel D. *Fahrenheit,* 1686-1736, a German physicist, who introduced this scale]

fail (fāl), 1 not succeed; not be able to do or become what is wanted, expected, or attempted; come to nothing: *He tried hard to learn to skate, but he failed. After a long drought, the crops failed.* 2 not do; neglect: *She failed to follow our advice.* 3 be of no use to when needed: *When I wanted her help, she failed me.* 4 be missing; be not enough: *When our supplies failed, we had no food.* 5 lose strength; grow weak; die away: *The sick man's heart was failing.*

6 not be able to pay what one owes; become bankrupt: *The company lost all its money and failed in business.* 7 be unsuccessful in an examination, etc.; receive a mark of failure: *You failed the test because you didn't study.* 8 give the mark of failure to (a student). *v.*

without fail, surely; certainly: *You must do your homework without fail.*

fail ing (fā′ling), 1 failure. 2 fault; weakness; defect: *We all have our failings; none of us is perfect.* 3 in the absence of; lacking; without: *Failing good weather, the tennis match will be played indoors.* 1,2 *n.,* 3 *prep.*

faille (fīl), a soft, ribbed cloth of silk, rayon, or cotton. *n.*

fail ure (fā′lyər), 1 a being unable to do or become what is wanted, expected, or attempted; not succeeding; failing: *failure in one's work.* 2 a not doing; neglecting: *Failure to obey orders on a ship is mutiny.* 3 a being not enough; falling short: *failure of supplies.* 4 a losing strength; becoming weak: *failure of eyesight.* 5 a being unable to pay what one owes. 6 person or thing that has failed: *The picnic was a failure because it rained.* *n.*

fain (fān), OLD USE. 1 gladly; willingly. 2 glad; willing. 1 *adv.,* 2 *adj.*

faint (fānt), 1 not clear or plain; dim: *faint colors, a faint idea.* 2 weak; feeble: *a faint voice, a faint attempt.* 3 a temporary loss of consciousness, often brought on by great hunger, sudden fear, illness, etc. In a faint, a person seems to be asleep and does not know what is going on around him. 4 lose consciousness temporarily. 5 about to lose consciousness; dizzy and weak: *I felt quite faint.* 6 lacking courage; cowardly: *a faint heart.* 1,2,5,6 *adj.,* 3 *n.,* 4 *v.* —**faint′ly,** *adv.* —**faint′ness,** *n.*

faint heart ed (fānt′här′tid), lacking courage; cowardly; timid. *adj.* —**faint′heart′ed ly,** *adv.* —**faint′heart′ed ness,** *n.*

fair[1] (fer *or* far), 1 not favoring one more than others; just; honest: *a fair judge. Every person is entitled to a fair hearing in court.* 2 according to the rules: *fair play.* 3 not good and not bad; average: *a fair student. There is a fair crop of wheat this year.* 4 not dark; light: *A blond person has fair hair and skin.* 5 clear; sunny; not cloudy or stormy: *The weather will be fair today.* 6 pleasing to see; beautiful: *a fair lady.* 7 gentle; civil; courteous: *fair words.* 8 without spots or stains; clean: *She made a fair copy of her letter and threw the dirty one away.* 9 in a fair manner; honestly: *play fair.* 10 easily read; plain: *fair handwriting.* 1-8,10 *adj.,* 9 *adv.* [Old English *fæger*]

bid fair, seem likely; have a good chance.

fair[2] (fer *or* far), 1 a showing of products and manufactured goods for the purpose of helping people see what has been done and urging them to buy: *At the yearly county fair, prizes are given for the best farm products and livestock.* 2 a gathering of people to buy and sell, often held in a certain place at regular times during the year. 3 entertainment and sale of articles; bazaar: *Our church held a fair to raise money for charity.* *n.* [from French of the 1300's *feire,* from Latin *feriae* festival]

fair ball, a batted ball in baseball that is not a foul, permitting the batter to start around the bases.

fair game, 1 animals or birds that it is lawful to hunt. 2 a suitable object of attack: *The playful puppy thought I was fair game.*

fair ground (fer′ground′ *or* far′-ground′), place outdoors where fairs are held. *n.*

fair ly (fer′lē *or* far′lē), 1 in a fair manner; justly; honestly: *That salesman deals fairly with his customers.* 2 moderately; rather: *She is a fairly good pupil, neither bad nor very good.* 3 absolutely; positively: *He was fairly beside himself with anger.* *adv.*

fair ness (fer′nis *or* far′nis), a being fair: *Our teacher is known for his fairness in grading pupils.* *n.*

fair way (fer′wā′ *or* far′wā′), the part of a golf course between the tee and putting green where the grass is kept short. *n.*

fair y (fer′ē *or* far′ē), 1 (in stories) a tiny being with magic powers. Fairies were supposed to help or harm people. 2 of fairies. 3 like a fairy; lovely; delicate. 1 *n., pl.* **fair ies;** 2,3 *adj.*

fair y land (fer′ē land′ *or* far′ē-land′), 1 place where the fairies are supposed to live. 2 a very pleasant or delightful place. *n.*

fairy tale, 1 story about fairies. 2 something said that is not true; falsehood; lie.

faith (fāth), 1 belief without proof; trust: *We have faith in our friends.*

faithful

adj. adjective	*n.* noun
adv. adverb	*prep.* preposition
conj. conjunction	*pron.* pronoun
interj. interjection	*v.* verb
sing. singular	*pl.* plural

2 belief in God or in God's promises. 3 what a person believes. 4 religion: *the Jewish faith, the Christian faith.* 5 a being loyal. 6 truly; indeed. 1-5 *n.,* 6 *interj.*
break faith, break one's promise.
in bad faith, dishonestly.
in good faith, honestly; sincerely.
keep faith, keep one's promise.
faith ful (fāth′fəl), 1 worthy of trust; loyal: *A faithful friend keeps his promises. Several workers were given awards for long and faithful service.* 2 true to fact; accurate: *The witness gave a faithful account of what happened.* 3 **the faithful, a** true believers. **b** loyal followers or supporters. 1,2 *adj.,* 3 *n.* —**faith′ful ly,** *adv.* —**faith′ ful ness,** *n.*
faith less (fāth′lis), 1 failing in one's duty; breaking one's promises; not loyal: *a faithless lover, a faithless traitor.* 2 without faith; unbelieving: *live a faithless life doubting everything and everyone. adj.* —**faith′less ly,** *adv.* —**faith′less ness,** *n.*
fake (fāk), 1 make up to seem satisfactory; hide defects by pretending: *fake illness. The picture was faked by pasting together two photographs.* 2 fraud; deception: *The diamond ring was a fake.* 3 person who fakes: *Anyone who says he can fly like a bird is a fake.* 4 intended to deceive; false: *The salesman showed fake letters approving his product in order to get people to buy.* 1 *v.,* **faked, fak ing;** 2,3 *n.,* 4 *adj.*
fak er (fā′kər), person who fakes. *n.*
fa kir (fə kir′ *or* fā′kər), a Moslem or Hindu holy man who lives by begging. Fakirs sometimes do extraordinary things, such as lying upon sharp knives. *n.*

falchion

fal chion (fôl′chən), a broad, short sword with an edge that curves sharply to the point. *n.*

fal con (fôl′kən, fal′kən, *or* fô′kən), 1 hawk trained to hunt and kill birds and small game. In the Middle Ages, hunting with falcons was a popular sport. 2 a swift-flying hawk having a short, curved bill and long claws and wings. *n.*
fal con er (fôl′kə nər, fal′kə nər, *or* fô′kə nər), 1 person who hunts with falcons. 2 person who breeds and trains falcons. *n.*
fal con ry (fôl′kən rē, fal′kən rē, *or* fô′kən rē), 1 sport of hunting with falcons. 2 the training of falcons to hunt. *n.*
Falk land Islands (fôk′lənd *or* fôlk′lənd), group of British islands in the S Atlantic, east of the Strait of Magellan, claimed also by Argentina. See **Chile** for map.
fall (fôl), 1 drop or come down from a higher place: *The snow falls fast. Leaves fall from the trees.* 2 a dropping from a higher place: *The fall from his horse hurt him.* 3 amount that comes down: *We had a heavy fall of snow last winter.* 4 distance that anything drops or comes down: *The fall of the river here is two feet.* 5 Usually, **falls,** *pl.* fall of water; waterfall: *Niagara Falls.* 6 come down suddenly from a standing position: *My baby sister often falls now that she is learning to walk.* 7 a coming down suddenly from a standing position: *The child had a bad fall.* 8 hang down: *Her curls fell upon her shoulders.* 9 be directed downward: *He blushed, and his eyes fell. She placed the lamp so the light would fall on her book.* 10 do wrong; become bad or worse: *In the Bible Adam was tempted by Eve and he fell.* 11 a becoming bad or worse; downfall: *Adam's fall.* 12 lose position, power, dignity, etc.; be taken by any evil: *The ruler fell from the people's favor. The fort fell to the enemy.* 13 drop wounded or dead; be killed: *Many fell in the battle.* 14 pass into some condition, position, etc.: *She fell sick. The baby fell asleep. The boy and girl fell in love.* 15 come as if by dropping: *When night falls, the stars appear.* 16 come by chance or lot: *Our choice fell on her.* 17 come to pass; happen; occur: *My birthday falls on Sunday this year.* 18 have proper place or position: *The accent of "over" falls on the first syllable.* 19 proper place or position: *The fall of the accent is on the first syllable.* 20 become lower or less: *Prices fell sharply. The water in the river has fallen two feet. Her voice fell.* 21 a becoming lower or less: *a fall in prices, the fall of the tide.* 22 be divided: *The story falls into five parts.* 23 look sad or disappointed: *His face fell at the news.* 24 to slope downward: *The land falls gradually to the beach.* 25 a downward

falcon (def. 2)
17 in. long

slope. 26 season of the year between summer and winter; autumn. 27 way of throwing or being thrown: *falls in wrestling.* 1,6,8-10,12-18,20,22-24 *v.,* **fell, fall en, fall ing;** 2-5,7,11,19,21, 25-27 *n.*
fall back, go toward the rear; retreat: *The enemy fell back as our army advanced.*
fall back on, 1 go back to for safety. 2 turn to for help or support.
fall behind, fail to keep up.
fall in, 1 take a place in line: *"Fall in!" said the officer to the soldiers.* 2 meet: *On our trip, we fell in with some interesting people.* 3 agree: *They fell in with our plans.*
fall off, become less; drop: *The profits of the business fell off last month.*
fall on, attack: *The thieves fell on the man and stole his money.*
fall out, 1 leave a place in line: *"Fall out!" said the officer to the soldiers.* 2 stop being friends; quarrel: *She has fallen out with her friends.*
fall short of, fail to equal: *The sale wasn't a failure, but it did fall short of the success we had expected.*
fall through, fail: *Her plans fell through.*
fall to, 1 begin: *They fell to and worked with a will.* 2 begin to attack, eat, etc.: *When the food was served, they fell to.*
fall under, belong under; be classified as: *Whales fall under the class of mammals.*
fall upon, attack.
fal la cious (fə lā′shəs), 1 deceptive; misleading; false: *a fallacious peace.* 2 not logical: *It is fallacious reasoning to base a general rule on just two or three instances. adj.* —**fal la′cious ly,** *adv.* —**fal la′cious ness,** *n.*
fal la cy (fal′ə sē), 1 a false idea; mistaken belief; error: *It is a fallacy to suppose that riches always bring happiness.* 2 mistake in reasoning; misleading or unsound argument. *n., pl.* **fal la cies.**
fall en (fô′lən), 1 past participle of **fall.** *Much rain has fallen.* 2 dropped: *fallen arches.* 3 face down; down on the ground; down flat: *a fallen tree.* 4 has become bad or worse; degraded. 5 overthrown; destroyed: *a fallen for-*

tress. 6 dead: *fallen heroes.* 1 *v.,* 2-6 *adj.*

fal li bil i ty (fal′ə bil′ə tē), fallible condition or quality. *n.*

fal li ble (fal′ə bəl), liable to be deceived or mistaken; liable to err. *adj.*

falling star, meteor.

fall line, line that marks the end of layers of hard rock of a plateau and the beginning of a softer rock layer of a plain. There are many waterfalls and rapids along this line.

fall out (fôl′out′), the radioactive particles or dust that fall to the earth after a nuclear explosion. *n.*

fal low (fal′ō), 1 plowed and left unseeded for a season or more; uncultivated: *We shall let the north forty acres lie fallow next spring.* 2 land plowed and left unseeded for a season or more. 1 *adj.,* 2 *n.*

fallow deer, a small European deer with a yellowish coat that is spotted with white in the summer.

false (fôls), 1 not true; not correct; wrong: *false statements.* A **false step** is a stumble or mistake. 2 not truthful; lying: *a false witness.* 3 not loyal; not faithful; deceitful: *a false friend, be false to a promise.* 4 used to deceive; deceiving: *false weights, false signals.* A ship sails under **false colors** when she raises the flag of a country other than her own. A **false bottom** in a trunk or drawer is used to form a secret compartment. 5 (in music) not true in pitch: *a false note.* 6 not real; artificial: *false teeth, false diamonds.* 7 based on wrong notions; ill-founded: *False pride kept her from accepting help from her friends when she was out of money.* 8 improperly called or named, usually because of some resemblance: *One name for the locust tree is "false acacia."* 9 in a false manner. 1-8 *adj.,* **fals er, fals est;** 9 *adv.* —**false′ly,** *adv.* —**false′ness,** *n.*

play one false, deceive, cheat, trick, or betray one: *My memory played me false; I called her by the wrong name.*

false hood (fôls′hùd), 1 a false statement; lie. 2 quality of being false. 3 something false. *n.*

fal set to (fôl set′ō), 1 an unnaturally high-pitched voice, especially in a man. 2 person who sings with such a voice. 3 of or for such a voice. 1,2 *n.,* **fal settos;** 3 *adj.*

fal si fi ca tion (fôl′sə fə kā′shən), 1 a falsifying; change made to deceive. 2 a being falsified: *The falsification of the will was not discovered for three months.* *n.*

fal si fy (fôl′sə fī), 1 make false; change to deceive; misrepresent: *falsify tax records.* 2 make false statements; lie. *v.,* **fal si fied, fal si fy ing.**

fal si ty (fôl′sə tē), 1 a being false: *Education often shows the falsity of superstitions.* 2 something false. *n., pl.* **fal si ties.**

Fal staff (fôl′staf), Sir **John,** a fat, jolly, swaggering soldier, brazen and without scruples, in three of Shakespeare's plays. *n.*

fal ter (fôl′tər), 1 not go straight on; draw back or hesitate; waver: *I faltered for a moment before I made my decision.* 2 move unsteadily; stumble; totter: *I faltered up the rocky path in the dark.* 3 speak in hesitating or broken words; stammer: *Greatly embarrassed, he faltered out his thanks.* 4 act of faltering. 1-3 *v.,* 4 *n.*

fame (fām), 1 fact or condition of being very well known; having much said or written about one: *the fame of Benjamin Franklin.* 2 what is said about one; reputation. *n.*

famed (fāmd), famous. *adj.*

fa mil iar (fə mil′yər), 1 well-known; common: *a familiar face. A knife is a familiar tool. French was as familiar to him as English.* 2 well-acquainted: *He is familiar with French and English.* 3 close; personal; intimate: *She spent her vacation visiting old and familiar friends.* 4 a familiar friend or acquaintance. 5 not formal; friendly: *a familiar attitude.* 6 too friendly; presuming; forward: *Her manner is too familiar.* 7 spirit or demon supposed to serve a particular person. A black cat was thought to be a witch's familiar. 1-3,5,6 *adj.,* 4,7 *n.* —**fa mil′iar ly,** *adv.*

fa mil iar i ty (fə mil′yar′ə tē), 1 close acquaintance; knowledge: *The Indian scout's familiarity with the rugged country was a great help to the explorers.* 2 thing done or said in a familiar way: *I dislike such familiarities as the use of my nickname by people that I have just met.* 3 lack of formality or ceremony. *n., pl.* **fa mil iar i ties.**

fa mil iar i za tion (fə mil′yər ə zā′shən), a making or becoming familiar. *n.*

fa mil iar ize (fə mil′yə rīz′), 1 make (a person) well acquainted with something: *Before playing the new game, familiarize yourself with the rules.* 2 make well known: *Exploration in space has familiarized the word "astronaut."* *v.,* **fa mil iar ized, fa mil iar iz ing.**

fam i ly (fam′ə lē), 1 a father, mother, and their children: *Our town has about a thousand families.* 2 children of a father and mother; offspring: *bring up a large family.* 3 group of people living in the same house. 4 all of a person's relatives: *His family holds an annual reunion.* 5 group of related

people; tribe or clan: *The Roosevelt family produced two Presidents, Theodore Roosevelt and Franklin D. Roosevelt.* 6 group of related animals or plants. Lions, tigers, and leopards belong to the cat family. A family ranks below an order and above a genus. 7 any group of related or similar things. *n., pl.* **fam i lies.**

family tree, diagram showing how all the members and ancestors of a family are related.

fam ine (fam′ən), 1 lack of food in a place; a time of starving: *Many people died during the famine in India.* 2 starvation: *Many people died of famine.* 3 a great lack; scarcity; shortage: *a coal famine.* *n.*

fam ish (fam′ish), 1 be very hungry; starve: *She was famished after not eating anything for ten hours.* 2 starve to death. *v.*

fa mous (fā′məs), 1 very well known; much talked about or written about; noted: *The famous singer was greeted by a large crowd.* 2 INFORMAL. very good; excellent. *adj.*

fa mous ly (fā′məs lē), INFORMAL. excellently; very well: *The new neighbors are getting along famously with everyone. adv.*

fan¹ (def. 1)—two kinds of fans

fan¹ (fan), 1 instrument or device with which to stir the air in order to cool or ventilate a room, cool one's face, or blow dust away. One kind of fan can be folded or spread out into part of a circle. Another kind consists of a series of revolving blades turned by an electric motor. 2 stir (the air) with a fan. 3 direct a current of air toward with a fan or anything like a fan: *She fanned*

adj. adjective	*n.* noun
adv. adverb	*prep.* preposition
conj. conjunction	*pron.* pronoun
interj. interjection	*v.* verb
sing. singular	*pl.* plural

herself. Fan the fire to make it burn faster. 4 stir up; arouse: *Bad treatment fanned their dislike into hate.* 5 anything spread out like an open fan. 6 spread out like an open fan: *He fanned the cards.* 7 (in baseball) to strike out. 1,5 *n.*, 2-4,6,7 *v.*, **fanned, fan ning.** [Old English *fann*] —**fan´like´**, *adj.*

fan[2] (fan), INFORMAL. 1 person extremely interested in movies, television, etc. A baseball fan thinks, talks, and reads about baseball besides going to as many games as he can. 2 admirer of an actor, writer, etc. *n.* [shortened from *fanatic*]

fa nat ic (fə nat´ik), 1 person who is carried away beyond reason by his feelings or beliefs: *My friend was such a fanatic about fresh air that she would not stay in any room with the windows closed.* 2 unreasonably enthusiastic; extremely zealous, especially in religion: *a fanatic follower of some leader or belief.* 1 *n.*, 2 *adj.*

fa nat i cal (fə nat´ə kəl), unreasonably enthusiastic; extremely zealous. *adj.* —**fa nat´i cal ly**, *adv.*

fa nat i cism (fə nat´ə siz´əm), unreasonable enthusiasm; extreme zeal. *n.*

fan cied (fan´sēd), imagined. *adj.*

fan ci er (fan´sē ər), person who is especially interested in something: *A dog fancier is interested in breeding and raising dogs. n.*

fan ci ful (fan´sə fəl), 1 showing fancy; quaint; odd; fantastic: *Fanciful decorations are made up, not patterned after something.* 2 led by fancy; using fancies; imaginative: *Hans Christian Andersen was a fanciful writer.* 3 suggested by fancy; imaginary; unreal: *Her story about a trip to a nearby star is fanciful.* *adj.* —**fan´ci ful ly**, *adv.* —**fan´ci ful ness**, *n.*

fan ci ly (fan´sə lē), in a fancy manner. *adv.*

fan cy (fan´sē), 1 picture to oneself; imagine: *Can you fancy yourself on the moon?* 2 power to imagine; imagination: *Dragons, fairies, and giants are creatures of fancy.* 3 something imagined or supposed: *Is it fancy, or do I hear a sound?* 4 have an idea or belief; suppose: *I fancy that is right, but I am not sure.* 5 a liking;

fondness: *He has a fancy for bright ties. They took a great fancy to each other and became close friends.* 6 be fond of; like: *I fancy the idea of having a picnic.* 7 made or arranged especially to please; decorated; ornamental: *a fancy blouse, fancy trimming.* 8 requiring much skill: *fancy skating.* 9 chosen to please the fancy or one's special taste, etc.: *fancy fruit.* 10 much too high: *fancy prices.* 1,4,6 *v.*, **fan cied, fan cy ing;** 2,3,5 *n.*, *pl.* **fan cies;** 7-10 *adj.*, **fan ci er, fan ci est.**

fan cy work (fan´sē werk´), ornamental needlework; embroidery, crocheting, etc. *n.*

fan fare (fan´fer *or* fan´fär), 1 a short tune or call played on trumpets, bugles, or the like. 2 a loud show of activity, talk, etc.: *The new bridge was opened with great fanfare by the mayor and city officials. n.*

fang (def. 1)
fangs of a
poisonous snake

fang (fang), 1 a long, pointed tooth of a dog, wolf, snake, etc. Poisonous snakes have hollow or grooved fangs for injecting venom. 2 something like it. The root of a tooth is called a fang. *n.*

fan tail (fan´tāl´), 1 tail, end, or part spread out like an open fan. 2 pigeon, goldfish, or other animal whose tail spreads out like an open fan. *n.*

fan tas tic (fan tas´tik), 1 very odd or queer; wild and strange in shape or manner; due to fancy: *She saw fantastic things in her dream. The firelight cast weird, fantastic shadows on the walls.* 2 very fanciful; imaginary; unreal: *The idea that machines could be made to fly seemed fantastic a hundred years ago. adj.* —**fan tas´ti cal ly**, *adv.*

fan tas ti cal (fan tas´tə kəl), fantastic. *adj.*

fan ta sy (fan´tə sē), 1 play of the mind; product of the imagination; fancy. Many stories, such as *Gulliver's Travels* and *Alice in Wonderland*, are fantasies. 2 picture existing only in the mind; any strange mental image or illusion. Fantasies seem real to a delirious person. 3 a wild, strange fancy. *n.*, *pl.* **fan ta sies.** Also, **phantasy.**

far (fär), 1 a long way; a long way off: *We searched far and near for the lost dog. He studied far into the night. Far in the past, the Norsemen began sailing westward.* 2 not near; distant: *He lives in a far country. The moon is far from the earth.* 3 more distant: *We live on the far side of the hill.* 4 very much: *It is far better to go by train.* 1,4 *adv.*, **far ther,**

farthest *or* **fur ther, fur thest;** 2,3 *adj.*, **far ther, far thest** *or* **fur ther, fur thest.**

as far as, to the distance, point, or degree that.

by far, very much.

far and away, very much.

far and wide, everywhere; even in distant parts.

how far, to what distance, point, or degree; how much.

in so far as, to the extent that: *In so far as I can tell now, I will be free to go tomorrow.*

Far a day (far´ə dā), **Michael,** 1791-1867, English physicist and chemist. *n.*

far a way (fär´ə wā´), 1 far away; distant; remote: *He read of faraway places in geography books.* 2 dreamy: *A faraway look in her eyes showed that she was thinking of something else. adj.*

farce (färs), 1 a play full of ridiculous happenings, absurd actions, and unreal situations, meant to be very funny. 2 a ridiculous mockery; absurd pretense: *It is obvious that your attempts to find a job were a farce. n.*

far ci cal (fär´sə kəl), of or like a farce; ridiculous; absurd. *adj.*

far cry, a long way.

fantail (def. 2)

fare (fer *or* far), 1 the money that a person pays to ride in a taxi, bus, train, airplane, etc.: *How much is the fare for crossing the river by ferry?* 2 passenger. 3 food: *dainty fare, meager fare.* 4 eat food; be fed: *We fared very well at Thanksgiving dinner.* 5 get along; get on; do: *She is faring well in school.* 6 turn out; happen: *It will fare hard with her if she ignores parking tickets.* 7 OLD USE. go; travel: *fare forth on a journey.* 1-3 *n.*, 4-7 *v.*, **fared, far ing.**

Far East, China, Japan, and other parts of E Asia, including Korea and E Siberia.

fare well (fer´wel´ *or* far´wel´), 1 good luck; good-by. 2 good wishes at parting. 3 departure; leave-taking. 4 of farewell; parting; last: *a farewell kiss. The singer gave a farewell performance.* 1,2,3 *n.*, 1,2 *interj.*, 4 *adj.*

far fetched (fär´fecht´), not closely related to the topic; forced; strained: *His excuse was too farfetched for anyone to believe. adj.*

far-flung (fär´flung´), covering a large area; widely spread: *Many American* banks have far-flung operations in Europe, Asia, and South America. adj.

farm (färm), 1 piece of land which a person uses to raise crops or animals. 2 raise crops or animals either to eat or to sell: *Her parents farm for a living.* 3 cultivate (land): *They farm fifty acres.* 4 anything like a farm. A tract of water for cultivating oysters is an oyster farm. 1,4 n., 2,3 v.

farm out, 1 let for hire: *He farms out the right to pick berries on his land.* 2 assign to a baseball team in a minor league.

farm er (fär′mər), person who owns or works on a farm. n.

farm hand (färm′hand′), person who works on a farm. n.

farm house (färm′hous′), house to live in on a farm. n., pl. **farm hous es** (färm′hou′ziz).

farm ing (fär′ming), business of raising crops or animals on a farm; agriculture. n.

farm stead (färm′sted), farm with its buildings. n.

farm yard (färm′yärd′), yard connected with the farm buildings or enclosed by them. n.

far-off (fär′ôf′), far away; distant. adj.

far-out (fär′out′), SLANG. 1 very unusual; not at all customary: *a far-out idea.* 2 very difficult to understand: *far-out research.* 3 extreme: *far-out political views.* adj.

far-reach ing (fär′rē′ching), having a wide influence or effect: *The use of atomic energy is having far-reaching effects today.* adj.

far row (far′ō), 1 litter of pigs. 2 give birth to a litter of pigs. 1 n., 2 v.

far see ing (fär′sē′ing), 1 able to see far. 2 looking ahead; planning wisely for the future. adj.

far sight ed (fär′sī′tid), 1 seeing distant things more clearly than near ones; not seeing nearby objects clearly. Farsighted people usually wear glasses to correct their vision. 2 looking ahead; planning wisely for the future; shrewd; prudent: *That farsighted man is saving money while his wages are high.* adj. —**far′sight′ed ly,** adv. —**far′sight′ed ness,** n.

far ther (fär′ᴛʜər), 1 more distant: *Three miles is farther than two.* 2 at or to a greater distance: *We walked farther than we meant to.* 3 at or to a more advanced point: *She has investigated the subject farther than anyone else.* 4 in addition; also. 5 more; additional: *Do you need farther help?* 1,5 adj., comparative of **far**; 2-4 adv., comparative of **far.**

far ther most (fär′ᴛʜər mōst), most distant; farthest: *He has traveled to the farthermost points of the earth.* adj.

far thest (fär′ᴛʜist), 1 most distant: *Ours is the house farthest down the road.* 2 to or at the greatest distance: *She hit the ball farthest.* 3 most: *Their ideas were the farthest advanced at that time.* 4 longest: *the farthest journey of Magellan.* 1,4 adj., superlative of **far;** 2,3 adv., superlative of **far.**

far thing (fär′ᴛʜing), a British coin worth a fourth of a British penny. It is no longer used. n.

Far West, the part of the United States between the Rocky Mountains and the Pacific Ocean.

fas ci nate (fas′n āt), 1 attract very strongly; enchant by charming qualities; charm: *She was fascinated by the designs and colors in African art.* 2 hold motionless by strange power or by terror: *Snakes are said to fascinate small birds.* v., **fas ci nat ed, fas ci nat ing.**

fas ci na tion (fas′n ā′shən), 1 a fascinating. 2 very strong attraction; charm; enchantment. n.

fas cism or **Fas cism** (fash′iz′əm), 1 the form of government in Italy from 1922 to 1943, under Benito Mussolini. 2 the principles or methods of this or any similar government, or of a political party favoring such a government. Under fascism, a country is ruled by a dictator, with strong control of industry and labor by the central government, great restrictions upon the freedom of individuals, and extreme nationalism and militarism. n.

fas cist or **Fas cist** (fash′ist), 1 person who favors and supports fascism. 2 of or having to do with fascism or fascists. 1 n., 2 adj.

fash ion (fash′ən), 1 way a thing is made, shaped, or done; manner: *He walks in a peculiar fashion.* 2 current custom in dress, manners, speech, etc.; style: *the latest fashions in shoes.* 3 make, shape, or form: *fashion a whistle out of wood.* 1,2 n., 3 v.

after a fashion or **in a fashion,** in some way or other; not very well: *He played the violin, after a fashion.*

fash ion a ble (fash′ə nə bəl), 1 following the fashion; in fashion; stylish: *fashionable clothes.* 2 of, like, or used by people who set the styles: *They are members of a fashionable club.* adj.

fash ion a bly (fash′ə nə blē), in a fashionable manner. adv.

fast¹ (fast), 1 moving, acting, or doing with speed; quick; rapid; swift: *A fast runner can beat a slow one.* 2 quickly; rapidly; swiftly: *Airplanes go fast.* 3 showing a time ahead of the correct time: *My watch is fast.* 4 too gay or wild: *They led a fast life, drinking and gambling.* 5 firm; secure; tight: *a fast hold on a rope.* 6 firmly; securely;

hat, āge, fär; let, ēqual, tėrm;
it, īce; hot, ōpen, ôrder;
oil, out; cup, pút, rüle; ch, child;
ng, long; sh, she; th, thin;
ᴛʜ, then; zh, measure;

ə represents *a* in about,
e in taken, *i* in pencil,
o in lemon, *u* in circus.

tightly: *He held fast as the sled went on down the hill. The fox was caught fast in the trap.* 7 loyal; faithful: *They have been fast friends for years.* 8 that will not fade easily: *Good cloth is dyed with fast color.* 9 adapted for speed: *a fast track.* 10 thoroughly; soundly: *The baby is fast asleep.* 1,3-5,7-9 adj., 2, 6,10 adv. [Old English *fæst*]

fast² (fast), 1 go without food; eat little or nothing; go without certain kinds of food: *She fasts for religious reasons.* 2 a fasting. 3 day or time of fasting. 1 v., 2,3 n. [Old English *fæstan*]

fas ten (fas′n), 1 tie, lock, or make hold together in any way; fix firmly in place: *fasten a dress, fasten a door.* 2 attach; connect: *try to fasten the blame on others.* 3 direct; fix: *The dog fastened its eyes on the stranger.* v.

fas ten er (fas′n ər), 1 person who fastens. 2 attachment, device, etc., used to fasten a door, garment, etc. A zipper is a fastener. n.

fas ten ing (fas′n ing), thing used to fasten something. Locks, bolts, clasps, hooks, buttons, etc., are all fastenings. n.

fas tid i ous (fa stid′ē əs), hard to please; dainty in taste; easily disgusted: *a fastidious dresser, a fastidious eater.* adj. —**fas tid′i ous ly,** adv. —**fas tid′i ous ness,** n.

fast ness (fast′nis), 1 a strong, safe, place; stronghold: *The bandits hid in their mountain fastness.* 2 a being fast or firm; firmness. 3 a being quick or rapid; swiftness. n., pl. **fast ness es** for 1.

fat (fat), 1 a white or yellow oily substance formed in the bodies of animals. Fat is also found in plants, especially in some seeds. Fats are made up chiefly of carbon, hydrogen, and oxygen. 2 animal tissue composed mainly of such a substance. 3 consisting of or containing fat; oily: *fat meat.* 4 having much flesh; fleshy; plump; well-fed: *a fat boy, a fat pig.* 5 yielding much money; profitable: *That fat job pays well.* 6 full of good things; plentifully supplied; plentiful: *a fat storehouse.* 7 make or become fat: *The farmer is*

adj. adjective	*n.* noun
adv. adverb	*prep.* preposition
conj. conjunction	*pron.* pronoun
interj. interjection	*v.* verb
sing. singular	*pl.* plural

fatting the pigs for market. The pigs *fatted* on corn. **8** too fat; obese. **1,2** *n.*, **3-6,8** *adj.*, **fat ter, fat test; 7** *v.*, **fat ted, fat ting. —fat′ness,** *n.*

live off the fat of the land, have the best of everything.

fa tal (fā′tl), **1** causing death: *Careless drivers cause many fatal accidents.* **2** causing destruction or ruin: *The loss of all our money was fatal to our plans.* **3** important; decisive; fateful: *At last the fatal day for the contest arrived.* *adj.*

fa tal ism (fā′tl iz′əm), **1** belief that fate controls everything that happens. **2** acceptance of everything that happens because of this belief. *n.*

fa tal ist (fā′tl ist), believer in fatalism. *n.*

fa tal is tic (fā′tl is′tik), of or having to do with fatalism or fatalists. *adj.* **—fa′tal is′ti cal ly,** *adv.*

fa tal i ty (fā tal′ə tē), **1** a fatal accident or happening; death: *Careless driving causes thousands of fatalities every year.* **2** a fatal influence or effect: *Doctors are trying to reduce the fatality of diseases.* *n., pl.* **fa tal i ties.**

fa tal ly (fā′tl ē), in a manner leading to death or disaster: *The driver was fatally injured in the accident.* *adv.*

fate (fāt), **1** power supposed to fix beforehand and control what is to happen. Fate is beyond any person's control. **2** one's lot or fortune; what happens to a person, group, etc.: *It seems to be her fate to lose at gambling. History shows the fate of many nations. Death by drowning is a sad fate.* **3** what becomes of a person or thing: *The jury decided the fate of the accused man.* **4 Fates,** *pl.* (in Greek and Roman myths) the three goddesses who controlled human life. One spun the thread of life, one decided how long it should be, and one cut it off. *n.*

fat ed (fā′tid), **1** controlled by fate. **2** destined: *A fortuneteller told me that I was fated to be a great leader.* *adj.*

fate ful (fāt′fəl), **1** controlled by fate. **2** determining what is to happen; important; decisive: *Yorktown was the site of a fateful battle of the Revolutionary War.* **3** showing what will happen according to fate; prophetic: *fateful words.* **4** causing death, destruction,

or ruin; disastrous: *a fateful blow.* *adj.* **—fate′ful ly,** *adv.* **—fate′ful ness,** *n.*

fa ther (fä′ŦHər), **1 a** male parent. **2 Father,** God: *"Our Father in heaven."* **3** be the father of: *He fathered four sons.* **4** take care of; act as father to: *father an orphan.* **5** person who is like a father. **6 a** male ancestor; forefather: *the customs of our fathers.* **7** man who did important work as a maker or leader: *George Washington is often called the father of our country.* **8** be the cause of; make; originate: *Edison fathered many inventions.* **9 Father,** title of respect for a priest: *Father Walker.* **10** priest. **1,2,5-7,9,10** *n.*, **3,4,8** *v.*

faucet—partly cut away to show water flow when the handle is turned to raise the disk-shaped washer. When the washer is screwed down over the circular opening the water flow stops.

fa ther hood (fä′ŦHər hùd), condition of being a father. *n.*

fa ther-in-law (fä′ŦHər in lô′), father of one's husband or wife. *n., pl.* **fathers-in-law.**

fa ther land (fä′ŦHər land′), **1** one's native country. **2** land of one's ancestors. *n.*

fa ther less (fä′ŦHər lis), **1** without a father living. **2** without a known father. *adj.*

fa ther li ness (fä′ŦHər lē nis), fatherly quality. *n.*

fa ther ly (fä′ŦHər lē), **1** of a father. **2** like a father; like a father's: *The old gentleman gave the little boy a fatherly smile. adj.*

Father's Day, the third Sunday in June, set apart in the United States in honor of fathers.

fath om (faŦH′əm), **1** unit of measure equal to 6 feet. It is used mostly in measuring the depth of water and the length of ships' ropes, cables, etc. **2** measure the depth of. **3** get to the bottom of; understand fully: *I can't fathom what you mean.* **1** *n., pl.* **fathoms** or **fath om; 2,3** *v.*

fath om less (faŦH′əm lis), **1** too deep to be measured; bottomless: *The stream disappeared into a fathomless abyss.* **2** impossible to be fully understood: *the fathomless riddle of the origin of the universe. adj.*

fa tigue (fə tēg′), **1** weariness caused by hard work or effort: *Studying for two hours causes me as much fatigue as a game of basketball.* **2** make weary or tired; cause fatigue in. **3 fatigues,** *pl.* work clothes or uniform worn by soldiers for routine work. **1,3** *n.*, **2** *v.*, **fa tigued, fa ti guing.**

fat ten (fat′n), **1** make fat: *The farmer fattened beef cattle for market.* **2** become fat: *The pigs fattened on corn. v.*

fat ty (fat′ē), **1** of fat; containing fat. **2** like fat; oily; greasy. *adj.*, **fat ti er, fat ti est.**

fat u ous (fach′ü əs), stupid but self-satisfied; foolish; silly. *adj.* **—fat′u ous ly,** *adv.*

fau cet (fô′sit), device containing a valve for turning on or off a flow of liquid from a pipe or a container holding it; tap; spigot. *n.*

Faulk ner (fôk′nər), **William,** 1897-1962, American writer of novels and short stories. *n.*

fault (fôlt), **1** something that is not as it should be: *Carelessness is her greatest fault. A fault in the wire started the fire.* **2** mistake; error: *a fault in the answer to an arithmetic problem.* **3** cause for blame; responsibility: *Whose fault was it?* **4** a break in the earth's crust, with the mass of rock on one side of the break pushed up, down, or sideways. **5** failure to serve the ball properly or into the right place in tennis and similar games. *n.*

at fault, deserving blame; wrong.

find fault, find mistakes; complain.

find fault with, object to; criticize.

to a fault, too much; excessively: *She is generous to a fault.*

fault (def. 4)—In the fault shown above in cross section, a mass of rock was pushed upward.

fault find er (fôlt′fin′dər), person who finds fault; person who complains. *n.*

fault find ing (fôlt′fin′ding), **1** act of finding fault. **2** finding fault; complaining. **1** *n.*, **2** *adj.*

fault i ly (fôl′tə lē), in a faulty manner. *adv.*

fault i ness (fôl′tē nis), condition of being faulty; imperfection. *n.*

fault less (fôlt′lis), without a single fault or defect; perfect. *adj.*

—**fault′less ly,** *adv.* —**fault′less-ness,** *n.*

fault y (fôl′tē), having faults; wrong; imperfect; defective: *The leak in the faucet was caused by a faulty valve.* *adj.,* **fault i er, fault i est.**

faun (fôn), (in Roman myths) a minor god that lived in fields and woods. A faun was supposed to look like a man, but to have the pointed ears, small horns, tail, and sometimes the legs, of a goat. *n.*

fau na (fô′nə), animals: *the fauna of Australia, the fauna of the period before the glaciers.* *n.*

Faust (foust), (in German legends) a man who sold his soul to the devil in return for youth, knowledge, and magic powers. *n.*

fa vor (fā′vər), 1 act of kindness: *Will you do me a favor?* 2 show kindness to; oblige: *Favor us with a song.* 3 liking; approval: *They will look with favor on your plan.* 4 like; approve; prefer: *We favor her plan.* 5 more than fair treatment: *He divided the candy among the children without favor to any one.* 6 give more than fair treatment to: *The teacher favors you.* 7 help; aid: *The darkness of the night favored the enemy's approach.* 8 a small token given to every guest at a party, dinner, etc.: *Small hats were used as favors at the birthday party.* 9 look like: *That girl favors her mother rather than her father.* 1,3,5,8 *n.,* 2,4,6,7,9 *v.*

curry favor, seek favor by insincere flattery, constant attentions, etc.: *Most students disliked him because he tried to curry favor with the teacher.*

in favor of, 1 on the side of; supporting. 2 to the advantage of; helping.

in one's favor, for one; to one's benefit.

fa vor a ble (fā′vər ə bəl), 1 favoring; approving: *"Yes" is a favorable answer to a request. The committee gave a favorable report on the secretary's plan.* 2 being to one's advantage; helping; promising: *A favorable wind made the boat go faster. This is a favorable time for a trip.* *adj.* —**fa′vor a ble ness,** *n.*

fa vor a bly (fā′vər ə blē), with consent or approval. *adv.*

fa vor ite (fā′vər it), 1 liked better than others: *What is your favorite flower?* 2 the one liked better than others; person or thing liked very much: *He is a favorite with everybody.* 3 person, horse, etc., expected to win a contest. 1 *adj.,* 2,3 *n.*

fa vor it ism (fā′vər ə tiz′əm), a favoring a certain one or some more than others; having favorites: *He got his job through favoritism, not through ability.* *n.*

fawn¹ (fôn), 1 deer less than a year old.

2 a light, yellowish brown. 3 light yellowish-brown. 1,2 *n.,* 3 *adj.* [from French of the 1300's *faon* young animal]

faun

fawn² (fôn), 1 try to get favor or notice by slavish acts: *Many flattering relatives fawned on the rich old woman.* 2 show fondness by crouching, wagging the tail, licking the hand, etc., as a dog does. *v.* [Old English *fagnian*]

fay (fā), fairy. *n.*

faze (fāz), INFORMAL. disturb; worry; bother: *Nothing we said fazed her; she just did as she pleased.* *v.,* **fazed, faz ing.**

FBI or **F.B.I.,** Federal Bureau of Investigation (a bureau of the United States Department of Justice, established to investigate violations of federal laws and safeguard national security).

F clef, bass clef.

fe al ty (fē′əl tē), 1 loyalty and duty owed by a vassal to his feudal lord: *The nobles swore fealty to the king.* 2 loyalty; faithfulness; allegiance. *n., pl.* **fe al ties.**

fear (fir), 1 a feeling that danger or evil is near; being afraid: *cry out in fear, a fear of heights, shake with fear.* 2 be afraid of: *Our cat fears big dogs. Our baby brother fears loud noises.* 3 feel fear; have an uneasy feeling or idea: *I fear that I won't pass the history test. I fear that I am late.* 4 cause for fear; danger; chance: *There is no fear of our losing.* 5 an uneasy feeling: *a fear for one's life.* 1,4,5 *n.,* 2,3 *v.*

fear ful (fir′fəl), 1 causing fear; terrible; dreadful: *a fearful dragon.* 2 feeling fear; frightened: *fearful of the dark.* 3 showing fear; caused by fear: *fearful cries.* 4 INFORMAL. very bad, unpleasant, ugly, etc.: *I have a fearful cold.* *adj.* —**fear′ful ly,** *adv.* —**fear′ful ness,** *n.*

fear less (fir′lis), without fear;

fawn¹ (def. 1)

hat, āge, fär; let, ēqual, tėrm;
it, īce; hot, ōpen, ôrder;
oil, out; cup, pùt, rüle; ch, child;
ng, long; sh, she; th, thin;
ᵺH, then; zh, measure;

ə represents *a* in about,
e in taken, *i* in pencil,
o in lemon, *u* in circus.

afraid of nothing; brave; daring. *adj.* —**fear′less ly,** *adv.* —**fear′less-ness,** *n.*

fear some (fir′səm), 1 causing fear; frightful: *a fearsome sight.* 2 afraid: *She was fearsome of danger.* *adj.*

fea si bil i ty (fē′zə bil′ə tē), feasible quality. *n.*

fea si ble (fē′zə bəl), 1 that can be done easily; possible without difficulty or damage: *Of the many good plans submitted, the committee selected the plan that seemed most feasible.* 2 likely; probable: *The witness's explanation of the accident sounded feasible.* 3 suitable; convenient: *The road was too rough to be feasible for travel by automobile.* *adj.*

feast (fēst), 1 a rich meal prepared for some special occasion, usually a joyous one; banquet: *We went to the wedding feast.* 2 eat a rich meal; have a feast: *They feasted on goose.* 3 provide a rich meal for: *The king feasted his friends.* 4 give pleasure or joy to; delight: *We feasted our eyes on the sunset.* 5 a religious festival or celebration: *Christmas and Easter are the most important Christian feasts.* 1,5 *n.,* 2-4 *v.*

feat (fēt), a great or unusual deed; act showing great skill, strength, or daring. *n.*

feath er (feᵺH′ər), 1 one of the light, thin growths that cover a bird's skin. Because feathers are soft and light, they are used to fill pillows. 2 something like a feather in shape or lightness. 3 supply or cover with feathers. 4 grow like feathers. 5 turn edgeways: *feather an oar.* 1,2 *n.,* 3-5 *v.* —**feath′er like′,** *adj.*

feather in one's cap, something to be proud of.

feather bed, 1 a very soft, warm mattress filled with feathers. 2 bed with such a mattress.

feath er bed ding (feᵺH′ər bed′ing), the practice on the part of some labor unions of forcing employers to hire more men than are needed for a particular job. *n.*

feath er less (feᵺH′ər lis), without feathers. *adj.*

adj. adjective	*n.* noun
adv. adverb	*prep.* preposition
conj. conjunction	*pron.* pronoun
interj. interjection	*v.* verb
sing. singular	*pl.* plural

feath er weight (feᴛʜ/ər wāt/), boxer who weighs more than 118 and less than 126 pounds. *n.*

feath er y (feᴛʜ/ər ē), 1 having feathers; covered with feathers. 2 like feathers; soft. 3 light; flimsy. *adj.*

fea ture (fē/chər), 1 part of the face. The eyes, nose, mouth, chin, and forehead are features. 2 a distinct part or quality; thing that stands out and attracts attention: *Your plan for the picnic has many good features and some bad ones. The main features of southern California are the climate and the scenery.* 3 a full-length motion picture: *They are showing a good feature this week.* 4 a special article, comic strip, etc., in a newspaper. 5 be or make a feature of: *The local newspapers featured the President's visit.* 1-4 *n.*, 5 *v.*, **fea tured, fea tur ing.**

fea ture less (fē/chər lis), without features; not distinctive. *adj.*

Feb., February.

Feb ru ar y (feb/rü er/ē or feb/yü-er/ē), the second month of the year. It has 28 days except in leap years, when it has 29. *n.*

fe ces (fē/sēz), waste matter discharged from the intestines. *n.pl.*

fe cund (fē/kənd or fek/ənd), able to produce much; fruitful; productive; fertile. *adj.*

fe cun di ty (fi kun/də tē), a being fertile; fruitfulness; productiveness; fertility: *Thomas Edison is remembered for the fecundity of his inventive mind. n.*

fed (fed), past tense and past participle of **feed.** *We fed the birds. Have they been fed today? v.*

fed up, SLANG. bored or disgusted.

fed er al (fed/ər əl), 1 formed by an agreement between states establishing a central government to handle their common affairs while the states keep separate control of local affairs: *Switzerland and the United States both became nations by federal union.* 2 of or having to do with the central government formed in this way: *Congress is the federal lawmaking body of the United States.* 3 Also, **Federal.** of or having to do with the central government of the United States, not of any state or city alone: *Coining money is a federal power. The federal courts are*

managed by the national government. 4 **Federal, a** of or having to do with the Federal Party. **b** supporting the Union during the Civil War. **c** supporter of the Union during the Civil War. 1-3,4a,4b *adj.*, 4c *n.*

fed er al ism (fed/ər ə liz/əm), the federal principle of government. *n.*

fed er al ist (fed/ər ə list), 1 **Federalist,** member of the Federal Party. 2 supporter of the federal principle of government. *n.*

Federal Party or **Federalist Party,** a political party in the United States that favored the adoption of the Constitution and a strong central government. It existed from about 1791 to about 1816.

fed e rate (fed/ə rāt/), form into a union or federation: *a plan to federate the provinces. The provinces federated in order to facilitate trade between them and strengthen their defense. v.*, **fed e-rat ed, fed e rat ing.**

fed e ra tion (fed/ə rā/shən), union by agreement, often a union of states, nations, groups, etc.; league: *Each member of the federation keeps control over its own affairs. n.*

fee (fē), 1 money asked for or paid for some service or privilege; charge: *an admission fee, a license fee. Doctors and lawyers receive fees for their services.* 2 right to keep and use land; fief. 3 an inherited estate in land. 4 ownership. *n.*

fee ble (fē/bəl), lacking strength; weak: *An old or sick person is often feeble. A feeble attempt is liable to fail. adj.*, **fee bler, fee blest. —fee/ble ness,** *n.*

fee ble-mind ed (fē/bəl mīn/did), weak in mind; lacking normal intelligence. *adj.*

fee bly (fē/blē), in a feeble manner; weakly. *adv.*

feed (fēd), 1 give food to: *We feed a baby who cannot feed himself.* 2 give as food: *Feed this grain to the chickens.* 3 eat: *We put cows to feed in the pasture. Cows feed on hay.* 4 food for animals: *Give the chickens their feed.* 5 INFORMAL. meal for a person. 6 supply with material: *feed a machine. Feed the fire.* 1-3,6 *v.*, **fed, feed ing;** 4,5 *n.*

feed back (fēd/bak/), process by which a system, machine, etc., regulates itself by feeding back to itself part of its output. *n.*

feed er (fē/dər), 1 person or thing that feeds. 2 thing that supplies something else with material: *These brooks are feeders of the big river. n.*

feel (fēl), 1 put the hand or some other part of the body on or against; touch: *Feel this cloth.* 2 quality sensed by touch; way something seems to the

touch; feeling: *I like the feel of silk. Wet soap has a greasy feel.* 3 try to find or make (one's way) by touch: *I felt my way across the room when the lights went out.* 4 test or examine by touching: *feel a person's pulse.* 5 try to find by touching: *He felt in his pockets for a dime.* 6 find out by touching: *Feel how cold my hands are.* 7 be aware of: *He felt the cool breeze. She felt the heat.* 8 have the feeling of being; be: *She feels sure. He feels angry. We felt hot.* 9 give the feeling of being; seem: *The air feels cold. Your shirt feels wet.* 10 have in one's mind; experience: *I felt pain. They felt fear of the thunder.* 11 have a feeling: *Try to feel more kindly toward her. He feels for all who suffer. I feel that we shall win.* 1,3-11 *v.*, **felt, feeling;** 2 *n.*

feel like, INFORMAL. have a desire or preference for: *Even though it was raining they felt like going out for a walk.*

feel out, find out from in a cautious way: *Feel them out on this matter.*

feel up to, think one is capable of: *I don't feel up to doing my arithmetic just now.*

feeler (def. 1)—feelers of a beetle

feel er (fē/lər), 1 a special part of an animal's body for touching. A cat's whiskers are its feelers. The long feelers on the heads of insects help them find their way. 2 remark, hint, or question made to find out what others are thinking or planning. *n.*

feel ing (fē/ling), 1 sense of touch. By feeling we tell what is hard from what is soft. 2 a being conscious; awareness; sensation: *I had a feeling that someone was watching me.* 3 emotion. Joy, sorrow, fear, and anger are feelings. *The loss of the ball game stirred up much feeling.* 4 **feelings,** *pl.* tender or sensitive side of one's nature: *You hurt my feelings when you yell at me.* 5 that feels; sensitive: *a feeling heart.* 6 pity; sympathy: *Have you no feeling for that poor, sick creature?* 7 opinion; idea: *I have no feeling about the plan, one way or the other.* 1-4,6,7 *n.*, 5 *adj.*

feel ing ly (fē/ling lē), with emotion: *She spoke feelingly of her years as a teacher. adv.*

feet (fēt), plural of **foot.** *A dog has four feet. n.*

feign (fān), 1 put on a false appearance of; make believe; pretend: *Some animals feign death when in danger. He* isn't sick; he is only feigning. 2 make up to deceive: feign an excuse. v.

feint (fānt), 1 a false appearance; pretense: The girl made a feint of studying hard, though actually she was listening to the radio. 2 movement intended to deceive; sham attack; pretended blow: The fighter made a feint at his opponent with his right hand and struck with his left. 3 make a feint: The fighter feinted with his right hand. 1,2 n., 3 v.

feld spar (feld/spär/), any of a group of white or red crystalline minerals composed of silicate of aluminum. Feldspars are found in igneous rocks and are the most abundant minerals near the surface of the earth. They are used in making glass and pottery. n.

fe lic i tate (fə lis/ə tāt), express good wishes to formally; congratulate: The young woman's friends felicitated her upon her promotion. v., **fe lic i tat ed, fe lic i tat ing.**

fe lic i ta tion (fə lis/ə tā/shən), a formal expression of good wishes; congratulation. n.

fe lic i tous (fə lis/ə təs), well chosen for the occasion; appropriate; well-worded; apt: The poem was full of striking and felicitous phrases. adj.

fe lic i ty (fə lis/ə tē), 1 great happiness; bliss. 2 good fortune; blessing. 3 a pleasing ability in expression; appropriateness or gracefulness: The famous writer phrased his ideas with felicity. 4 an unusually appropriate or graceful expression; well-chosen phrase. n., pl. **fe lic i ties.**

fe line (fē/līn), 1 cat. 2 of a cat: feline eyes. 3 like that of a cat: feline stealth. 4 any animal belonging to a group of meat-eating animals including lions, tigers, leopards, and panthers. 5 belonging to this group. 1,4 n., 2,3,5 adj.

fell¹ (fel), past tense of **fall.** Snow fell last night. v.

fell² (fel), 1 cause to fall; knock down: One blow felled him to the ground. 2 cut down (a tree). 3 turn down and stitch one edge of (a seam) over the other. v. [Old English fellan]

fell³ (fel), 1 extremely bad; cruel; fierce; terrible: a fell blow. 2 deadly; destructive: a fell disease. adj. [from French of the 1300's fel]

fell⁴ (fel), skin or hide of an animal. n. [Old English]

fel loe (fel/ō), the circular rim of a wheel into which the outer ends of the spokes are inserted. n., pl. **fel loes.** Also, **felly.**

fel low (fel/ō), 1 a male person; man or boy. 2 a person; anybody; one: What can a fellow do? 3 dog, horse, etc., addressed in a friendly way. 4 one of the same class; equal; companion; com-

rade: He was cut off from his fellows. 5 the other one of a pair; mate; match; I have the fellow of your glove. 6 being in the same or a like condition, class, etc.: fellow citizens, fellow sufferers. 7 person who has a fellowship from a university or college. 8 member of a learned society. 1-5,7,8 n., 6 adj.

fel low ship (fel/ō ship), 1 companionship; friendliness. 2 a being one of a group; membership: I have enjoyed my fellowship with you in this club. 3 group of people having similar tastes or interests; brotherhood. 4 position or money given by a university or college to a student to enable him to continue his studies. n.

fel ly (fel/ē), felloe. n., pl. **fel lies.**

fel on¹ (fel/ən), person who has committed a felony; criminal. Murderers and thieves are felons. n. [from French of the 1200's]

fel on² (fel/ən), a very painful inflammation of a finger or toe, usually near the nail. n. [perhaps from Latin fel gall]

fe lo ni ous (fə lō/nē əs), having to do with a felony; criminal: break into a house with felonious intent. adj.

fel o ny (fel/ə nē), crime more serious than a misdemeanor. Murder and burglary are felonies. n., pl. **fel o nies.**

felt¹ (felt), past tense and past participle of **feel.** He felt the soft fur of the cat. It was felt that the picnic should be postponed. v.

felt² (felt), 1 cloth made by rolling and pressing together wool, hair, or fur. Felt is used to make hats, slippers, and pads. 2 made of felt: a felt hat. 1 n., 2 adj. [Old English]

fe male (fē/māl), 1 woman or girl. 2 of or having to do with women or girls. 3 belonging to the sex that brings forth young or produces eggs. Mares, cows, and hens are female animals. 4 animal belonging to this sex. 5 (of a plant) having pistils but not stamens. 6 plant bearing only flowers with pistils. 1,4,6 n., 2,3,5 adj.

fem i nine (fem/ə nən), 1 of women or girls. 2 like a woman; womanly. 3 of or belonging to the female sex. 4 (in grammar) of the gender to which nouns and adjectives referring to females belong. Actress and tigress are the feminine nouns for actor and tiger. adj.

fem i nin i ty (fem/ə nin/ə tē), 1 feminine quality or condition. 2 women. n.

fem i nism (fem/ə niz/əm), 1 belief in increased rights and activities for women in their economic, social, political, and private life. 2 movement to obtain these rights. n.

fem i nist (fem/ə nist), 1 person who believes in or favors feminism. 2 believing in or favoring feminism. 1 n., 2 adj.

hat, āge, fär; let, ēqual, tėrm;
it, īce; hot, ōpen, ôrder;
oil, out; cup, pùt, rüle; ch, child;
ng, long; sh, she; th, thin;
ŦH, then; zh, measure;

ə represents a in about,
e in taken, i in pencil,
o in lemon, u in circus.

fe mur (fē/mər), thighbone. n.

fen (fen), low, wet land; marsh. n.

fence (fens), 1 railing, wall, etc., put around a yard, garden, field, farm, etc., to show where it ends or to keep people or animals out or in. Most fences are made of wood, wire, or metal. A fence of growing bushes is a hedge. 2 put a fence around; keep out or in with a fence. 3 fight with long, slender swords or foils. 4 person who buys and sells stolen goods. 1,4 n., 2,3 v., **fenced, fenc ing.**

on the fence, not having made up one's mind which side to take; doubtful.

fenc er (fen/sər), person who knows how to fight with a sword or foil. n.

fencing (def. 1)

fenc ing (fen/sing), 1 art or sport of fighting with swords or foils. 2 material for fences. 3 fences. n.

fend (fend). 1 **fend for oneself,** INFORMAL. provide for oneself; get along by one's own efforts: Most baby fishes have to fend for themselves. 2 **fend off,** ward off; keep off: fend off a blow. v.

fend er (fen/dər), 1 metal frame over the wheel of a car, truck, bicycle, etc., that protects the wheel and reduces splashing in wet weather. 2 cowcatcher. 3 bar, frame, or screen in front of a fireplace to keep hot coals and sparks from the room. 4 rope or log put between a boat and the landing. n.

fen nel (fen/l), 1 a tall, perennial plant with yellow flowers. 2 its fragrant seeds, used in medicine and cooking. n.

Fer di nand V (fėrd/n and), 1452-1516, king of Spain from 1474 to 1516. He and his queen, Isabella I, encouraged Christopher Columbus in his voyages.

fer ment (fər ment/ for 1,5,6; fėr/ment for 2-4), 1 undergo or produce

adj. adjective	*n.* noun
adv. adverb	*prep.* preposition
conj. conjunction	*pron.* pronoun
interj. interjection	*v.* verb
sing. singular	*pl.* plural

a gradual chemical change in which bacteria, yeast, etc., change sugar into alcohol and produce carbon dioxide. Enzymes help ferment animal and vegetable matter. Vinegar is formed when cider ferments. 2 substance that causes others to ferment. Enzymes are ferments. 3 a chemical change caused by a ferment; fermentation. 4 excitement; agitation; unrest: *Rumors of war caused ferment throughout the country.* 5 cause unrest in; excite; agitate. 6 be excited. 1,5,6 *v.*, 2-4 *n.*

fer men ta tion (fèr/men tā/shən), 1 act or process of fermenting: *Fermentation causes milk to sour and bread to rise.* 2 a chemical change caused by a ferment. 3 excitement; ferment. *n.*

Fer mi (fer/mē), **Enrico**, 1901-1954, American physicist, born in Italy. *n.*

fer mi um (fèr/mē əm), a radioactive metallic element produced artificially from plutonium or uranium. *n.* [from Enrico *Fermi*]

fern (fèrn), kind of plant that has roots, stems, and feathery leaves, but does not have flowers or seeds. The plant reproduces by means of spores which grow in little brown clusters on the backs of the leaves. *n.* —**fern/like/**, *adj.*

fe ro cious (fə rō/shəs), 1 very cruel; savage; fierce: *The bear's ferocious growl terrified the hunter.* 2 INFORMAL. intense: *a ferocious headache. adj.* —**fe ro/cious ly**, *adv.* —**fe ro/cious ness**, *n.*

fe roc i ty (fə ros/ə tē), great cruelty; savageness; fierceness: *The wolves fought with bloodthirsty ferocity. n., pl.* **fe roc i ties.**

fer ret (fer/it), 1 a white or yellowish-white weasel used for killing rats, driving rabbits from their holes, etc. 2 hunt with ferrets. 3 hunt; search: *It took the detectives over a year to ferret out the criminal.* 1 *n.*, 2,3 *v.*

Fer ris wheel (fer/is), a large, revolving wheel with seats hanging from its rim, used in carnivals, amusement parks, at fairs, etc. [from George *Ferris*, 1859-1896, American inventor]

fer rule (fer/əl *or* fer/ül), a metal ring or cap put around the end of a cane, wooden handle, umbrella, etc., for strength or protection. *n.* Also, **ferule.**

fer ry (fer/ē), 1 carry (people and goods) in a boat back and forth across a river or narrow stretch of water. 2 the boat that makes the trip; ferryboat. 3 place where boats carry people and goods across a river or narrow stretch of water. 4 go across in a ferryboat. 5 carry back and forth across a wide stretch of water in an airplane. 6 fly an airplane to a destination for delivery. 1,4-6 *v.*, **fer ried, fer ry ing**; 2,3 *n., pl.* **fer ries.**

fer ry boat (fer/ē bōt/), boat used for ferrying. *n.*

fer tile (fèr/tl), 1 able to bear seeds, fruit, young, etc.: *a fertile animal or plant.* 2 able to develop into a new individual; fertilized: *Chicks hatch from fertile eggs.* 3 able to produce much; producing crops easily: *Fertile soil yields good crops.* 4 producing ideas; creative: *a fertile mind. adj.*

fer til i ty (fər til/ə tē), 1 the bearing, or abundant bearing, of seeds, fruits, crops, or young. 2 power to produce: *The fertility of his imagination made him a first-class writer of mystery stories. n.*

fer ti li za tion (fèr/tl ə zā/shən), 1 a fertilizing or a being fertilized. 2 the union of male and female reproductive cells to form a cell that will develop into a new individual. *n.*

fer ti lize (fèr/tl īz), 1 make fertile; make able to produce much. 2 unite with (an egg cell) in fertilization; impregnate. 3 put fertilizer on: *fertilize a lawn. v.*, **fer ti lized, fer ti liz ing.**

fer ti liz er (fèr/tl ī/zər), substance such as manure, chemicals, etc., spread over or put into the soil to make it able to produce more. *n.*

fer ule[1] (fer/əl *or* fer/ül), 1 stick or ruler for punishing children by striking them on the hand. 2 punish with a stick or ruler. 1 *n.*, 2 *v.*, **fer uled, fer ul ing.** [from Latin *ferula*]

fer ule[2] (fer/əl *or* fer/ül), ferrule. *n.* [from French of the 1400's *virelle*]

fer ven cy (fèr/vən sē), fervor. *n.*

fer vent (fèr/vənt), showing great warmth of feeling; very earnest: *She made a fervent plea for more food and medical supplies for the earthquake victims. adj.* —**fer/vent ly**, *adv.*

fer vid (fèr/vid), full of strong feeling; very emotional; ardent; spirited: *The speaker's fervid words stirred the crowd to action. adj.* —**fer/vid ly**, *adv.*

fer vor (fèr/vər), great warmth of feeling; enthusiasm or earnestness: *patriotic fervor. n.*

fes tal (fes/tl), of a feast, festival, or holiday; gay; festive: *A wedding or a birthday is a festal occasion. adj.*

fes ter (fes/tər), 1 form pus: *The neglected wound festered and became very painful.* 2 sore that forms pus; small ulcer. 3 cause pus to form. 4 cause soreness or pain; rankle: *Resentment at the unkind remark festered in his mind.* 1,3,4 *v.*, 2 *n.*

fes ti val (fes/tə vəl), 1 day or special time of rejoicing or feasting, often in memory of some great happening: *Christmas is a Christian festival; Hanukkah is a Jewish festival.* 2 celebration or entertainment: *Every year the city has a music festival during the first week in May. n.*

fes tive (fes/tiv), of or suitable for a feast, festival, or holiday; gay; merry: *A birthday or a wedding is a festive occasion. adj.*

fes tiv i ty (fe stiv/ə tē), 1 festive activity; thing done to celebrate: *The festivities on the Fourth of July included a parade and fireworks.* 2 gaiety; merriment. *n., pl.* **fes tiv i ties.**

festoon (def. 1)

fes toon (fe stün/), 1 a string or chain of flowers, leaves, ribbons, etc., hanging in a curve between two points: *The bunting was draped on the wall in colorful festoons.* 2 decorate with festoons: *The gym was festooned with crepe paper for the dance.* 3 form into festoons; hang in curves: *Draperies were festooned over the window.* 1 *n.*, 2,3 *v.*

fetch (fech), 1 go and get; bring: *Please fetch me my glasses.* 2 cause to come; succeed in bringing: *Her call fetched him at once.* 3 be sold for: *These eggs will fetch a good price. v.*

fetch ing (fech/ing), INFORMAL. attractive; charming: *a fetching new outfit. adj.* —**fetch/ing ly**, *adv.*

fete (fāt), 1 festival or party, especially an elaborate one and often one held outdoors: *A large fete was given for the benefit of the town hospital.* 2 honor with a fete; entertain: *The bride-to-be was feted by her friends.* 1 *n.*, 2 *v.*, **fet ed, fet ing.** [from French *fête* feast]

fête (fāt), fete. *n., pl.* **fêtes**; *v.*, **fêt ed, fêt ing.**

fet id (fet/id), smelling very bad; stinking. *adj.* —**fet/id ly**, *adv.* —**fet/id ness**, *n.*

fe tish (fē/tish *or* fet/ish), 1 thing supposed to have magic powers: *The tribe worshiped a fetish that was a hideous snake carved out of stone.* 2 any object of unreasoning reverence or blind devotion: *Some people make a fetish of stylish clothes. n., pl.* **fe tish es.**

fet lock (fet/lok), 1 tuft of hair above a horse's hoof on the back part of its leg.

2 the part of a horse's leg where this tuft grows. See **horse** for picture. *n.*

fet ter (fet′ər), **1** chain or shackle for the feet: *Fetters prevented the prisoner's escape.* **2** bind with fetters; chain the feet of. **3** anything that shackles or binds; restraint. **4** bind; restrain: *Fetter your temper.* 1,3 *n.,* 2,4 *v.*

fet tle (fet′l), condition; state: *The horse is in fine fettle and should win the race.* *n.*

fe tus (fē′təs), an animal embryo during the later stages of its development in the womb or in the egg, especially a human embryo more than three months old. *n., pl.* **fe tus es.** Also, **foetus.**

feud (fyüd), **1** a long and deadly quarrel between families or tribes. Feuds are often passed down from generation to generation. **2** bitter hatred between two persons or groups. **3** carry on a feud. 1,2 *n.,* 3 *v.*

feu dal (fyü′dl), of or having to do with feudalism: *the feudal system, feudal laws.* *adj.*

feu dal ism (fyü′dl iz′əm), the social, economic, and political system of Europe in the Middle Ages. Under this system vassals gave military and other services to their lord in return for his protection and the use of land. *n.*

feu da to ry (fyü′də tôr′ē), owing feudal services to a lord. *adj.*

fe ver (fē′vər), **1** an unhealthy condition in which the body temperature is higher than normal (98.6 degrees Fahrenheit), often accompanied by rapid pulse and weakness. **2** any sickness that causes or is accompanied by fever: *scarlet fever, typhoid fever.* **3** an excited, restless condition; agitation: *When gold was discovered the miners were in a fever of excitement.* *n.*

fe vered (fē′vərd), **1** having fever. **2** excited; restless. *adj.*

fe ver ish (fē′vər ish), **1** having fever. **2** having a slight degree of fever. **3** caused by fever: *a feverish thirst.* **4** causing fever: *a feverish climate.* **5** infested with fever: *a feverish swamp.* **6** excited; restless: *He packed his bags in feverish haste.* *adj.* —**fe′ver ish ly,** *adv.* —**fe′ver ish ness,** *n.*

few (fyü), **1** not many: *Few people attended the meeting because of the storm.* **2** a small number: *Winter in New England has not many warm days, only a few.* 1 *adj.,* 2 *n.* —**few′ness,** *n.*

quite a few, INFORMAL. a good many: *Quite a few of us went to the game.*

fez (fez), a felt cap, usually red and ornamented with a long, black tassel. *n., pl.* **fez zes.**

ff., and the following pages, sections, etc.; and what follows.

fi an cé (fē′än sā′), man engaged to be married. *n., pl.* **fi an cés.** [from French]

fi an cée (fē′än sā′), woman engaged to be married. *n., pl.* **fi an cées.** [from French]

fi as co (fē as′kō), a complete or ridiculous failure; humiliating breakdown: *The play was a fiasco and closed after only three performances.* *n., pl.* **fi as cos** or **fi as coes.**

fi at (fī′ət *or* fī′at), an authoritative order or command; decree. *n.*

fib (fib), **1** a lie about some small matter. **2** tell such a lie. 1 *n.,* 2 *v.,* **fibbed, fib bing.**

fib ber (fib′ər), person who fibs. *n.*

fi ber (fī′bər), **1** a threadlike part; thread: *A muscle is made up of many fibers.* **2** substance made up of threads or threadlike parts: *Hemp fiber can be spun into rope or woven into a coarse cloth.* **3** texture: *cloth of coarse fiber.* **4** character; nature: *a person of strong moral fiber.* *n.* Also, **fibre.**

fi ber board (fī′bər bôrd′), a building material made by compressing fibers, especially of wood, into flat sheets. *n.*

Fi ber glas (fī′bər glas′), trademark for fiberglass. *n.*

fi ber glass (fī′bər glas′), very fine, flexible filaments of glass; spun glass. It can be used to make textiles, automobile bodies, swimming pools, insulating materials, boats, and fishing rods. *n.*

fi bre (fī′bər), fiber. *n.*

fi brin (fī′brən), a white, tough, elastic substance formed when blood clots. *n.*

fi broid (fī′broid), made up of fibers or fibrous tissue: *a fibroid tumor.* *adj.*

fi brous (fī′brəs), **1** made up of fibers; having fibers. **2** like fiber; stringy. *adj.*

fib u la (fib′yə lə), the outer and thinner of the two bones in the human lower leg. It extends from knee to ankle. *n., pl.* **fib u lae** (fib′yə lē′), **fib u las.**

fick le (fik′əl), likely to change without reason; changing; not constant: *fickle fortune, a fickle friend.* *adj.* —**fick′le ness,** *n.*

fic tion (fik′shən), **1** novels, short stories, and other prose writings that tell about imaginary people and happenings. **2** something imagined or made up: *She exaggerates so much in telling about her experiences that it is impossible to separate fact from fiction.* *n.*

fic tion al (fik′shə nəl), of or having to do with fiction: *Dorothy and Aunt Em in "The Wizard of Oz" are fictional*

fez
worn by men
in North Africa
and Turkey

hat, āge, fär; let, ēqual, tėrm;
it, īce; hot, ōpen, ôrder;
oil, out; cup, pùt, rüle; ch, child;
ng, long; sh, she; th, thin;
ŦH, then; zh, measure;

ə represents *a* in about,
e in taken, *i* in pencil,
o in lemon, *u* in circus.

characters. *adj.* —**fic′tion al ly,** *adv.*

fic ti tious (fik tish′əs), **1** not real; imaginary: *a fictitious story.* **2** used in order to deceive; false: *a fictitious name.* *adj.* —**fic ti′tious ly,** *adv.*

fid dle (fid′l), **1** INFORMAL. violin. **2** INFORMAL. play on a violin. **3** make aimless movements; play nervously; toy: *The embarrassed boy fiddled with his hat.* **4** trifle: *He fiddled away the whole day doing absolutely nothing.* 1 *n.,* 2-4 *v.,* **fid dled, fid dling.**

fid dler (fid′lər), INFORMAL. person who plays a violin. *n.*

fiddler crab
shell width
up to 1⅔ in.

fiddler crab, a small, burrowing crab common along the Atlantic coast of the United States. The male has an enlarged claw.

fid dle stick (fid′l stik′), INFORMAL. **1** the bow with which a violin is played. **2 fiddlesticks,** nonsense! rubbish! 1 *n.,* 2 *interj.*

fi del i ty (fī del′ə tē *or* fə del′ə tē), **1** steadfast faithfulness; loyalty: *a dog's fidelity to its master.* **2** exactness; accuracy: *The reporter wrote her story with absolute fidelity.* **3** the ability of a radio, phonograph, etc., to transmit or reproduce sound accurately. *n., pl.* **fi del i ties.**

fidg et (fij′it), **1** move about restlessly; be uneasy: *My little brother fidgets if he has to sit still a long time.* **2 the fidgets,** a fit of restlessness or uneasiness: *The long speech gave us the fidgets.* 1 *v.,* 2 *n.*

fidg et y (fij′ə tē), restless; uneasy: *That fidgety girl keeps twisting her fingers and moving her feet.* *adj.*

fie (fī), for shame! shame!: *Fie upon you! interj.*

fief (fēf), piece of land held on condition of giving military and other services to the feudal lord owning it, in

adj.	adjective	*n.*	noun
adv.	adverb	*prep.*	preposition
conj.	conjunction	*pron.*	pronoun
interj.	interjection	*v.*	verb
sing.	singular	*pl.*	plural

return for his protection and the use of the land. *n.*

field (fēld), **1** land with few or no trees: *They rode through forest and field.* **2** piece of land used for crops or for pasture. **3** piece of land used for some special purpose: *a baseball field.* **4** battlefield: *the field of Gettysburg.* **5** land yielding some product: *the coal fields of Pennsylvania, the gold fields of South Africa.* **6** a flat space; broad surface: *A field of ice surrounds the North Pole.* **7** surface on which something is pictured or painted; background: *Their flag shows a red circle on a white field.* **8** range of opportunity or interest; sphere of activity: *the field of politics, the field of art, the field of science.* **9** (in physics) the space throughout which a force operates. A magnet has a magnetic field around it. **10** space or area in which things can be seen through a telescope, microscope, etc. **11** area where contests in jumping, throwing, etc., are held. **12** all those in a game, contest, or outdoor sport. **13** (in baseball, cricket, etc.) to stop or catch (a batted ball) and throw it in. **14** send (a player, team, etc.) to the field. **15** of or having to do with a field or fields. 1-12, *n.*, 13,14 *v.*, 15 *adj.*

take the field, begin a battle, campaign, game, etc.

Field (fēld), **Eugene,** 1850-1895, American journalist and poet. *n.*

field day, 1 day for athletic contests and outdoor sports. **2** day when soldiers perform drills, mock fights, etc. **3** day of unusual activity or display.

field er (fēl′dər), (in baseball, cricket, etc.) a player who stops or catches and throws the ball in. A fielder is stationed around or outside the diamond in baseball. *n.*

field glasses or **field glass,** small binoculars for use outdoors.

field goal, goal in football counting three points, made by a place kick.

field house, building near an athletic field, used for storing equipment, for dressing rooms, etc.

field magnet, magnet used to produce or maintain a magnetic field, especially in a dynamo or electric motor.

field marshal, officer ranking next below the commander in chief in the British, French, German, and some other armies.

field mouse, mouse which lives in fields and meadows.

field trip, trip away from school to give students a chance to see important or historic places, things, etc.: *Our class plans to go on a field trip to a nearby cave.*

fiend (fēnd), **1** an evil spirit; devil. **2** a very wicked or cruel person. **3** INFORMAL. person who gives himself up to some habit, practice, game, etc.: *a tennis fiend.* *n.*

fiend ish (fēn′dish), very cruel; wicked; devilish: *fiendish tortures, a fiendish yell.* *adj.* —**fiend′ish ly,** *adv.* —**fiend′ish ness,** *n.*

fierce (firs), **1** savagely cruel; ferocious; wild: *A wounded lion can be fierce.* **2** raging; violent: *fierce anger. A fierce wind blows very hard.* **3** very eager or active: *a fierce determination to win.* *adj.,* **fierc er, fierc est.** —**fierce′ly,** *adv.* —**fierce′ness,** *n.*

fie ry (fī′rē), **1** containing fire; burning; flaming: *a fiery furnace.* **2** like fire; very hot; glowing: *a fiery red, fiery heat.* **3** full of feeling or spirit: *a fiery speech.* **4** easily aroused or excited: *a fiery temper.* *adj.,* **fie ri er, fie ri est.**

fi es ta (fē es′tə), **1** a religious festival; saint's day. **2** holiday or festivity. *n.,* *pl.* **fi es tas.** [from Spanish]

fife (fīf), **1** a small, shrill musical instrument like a flute, played by blowing. Fifes are used with drums to make music for marching. **2** play on a fife. 1 *n.,* 2 *v.,* **fifed, fif ing.**

fife (def. 1)
15½ in. long
with six
finger holes

fif teen (fif′tēn′), five more than ten; 15. *n.,* *adj.*

fif teenth (fif′tēnth′), **1** next after the 14th; last in a series of 15. **2** one of 15 equal parts. *adj.,* *n.*

fifth (fifth), **1** next after the fourth; last in a series of 5. **2** one of 5 equal parts. *adj.,* *n.*

fifth column, persons living within a country who secretly aid its enemies.

fif ti eth (fif′tē ith), **1** next after the 49th; last in a series of 50. **2** one of 50 equal parts. *adj.,* *n.*

fif ty (fif′tē), five times ten; 50. *n.,* *pl.* **fif ties;** *adj.*

fif ty-fif ty (fif′tē fif′tē), INFORMAL. in two equal parts; with two equal shares: *a fifty-fifty chance of winning (adj.), go fifty-fifty on expenses (adv.). adj., adv.*

fig (fig), **1** a small, soft, sweet fruit that grows in warm regions. Figs are sometimes eaten fresh or canned, but usually are dried like dates and raisins. **2** tree that it grows on. **3** a very small amount: *I don't care a fig for his opinion. n.*

fig., figure.

fight (fīt), **1** a violent struggle; combat; contest: *A fight ends when one side gives up.* **2** an angry dispute; quarrel: *Their fights were always over money.* **3** take part in a fight; have a fight: *The boys fought with their fists. Soldiers fight by shooting with guns. Countries fight with armies.* **4** take part in a fight against; struggle against: *fight disease, fight for justice, fight one's fear of the dark.* **5** carry on (a fight, conflict, etc.): *fight a duel.* **6** get or make by fighting: *She had to fight her way through the crowd.* **7** power or will to fight: *There was not much fight in the defeated team.* 1,2,7 *n.,* 3-6 *v.,* **fought, fight ing.**

fight it out, fight until one side wins.

fight shy of, keep away from; avoid.

show fight, be ready to fight; resist.

fight er (fī′tər), **1** one that fights. **2** a professional boxer. *n.*

fig ment (fig′mənt), something imagined; made-up story: *I don't believe it; it's just a figment of your imagination. n.*

fig ur a tive (fig′yər ə tiv), **1** using words out of their literal or ordinary meaning to add beauty or force. **2** having many figures of speech. Much poetry is figurative. **3** representing by a likeness or symbol: *Baptism is a figurative ceremony; it represents cleansing by washing away sin. adj.* —**fig′ur a tive ly,** *adv.*

fig ure (fig′yər), **1** symbol for a number. 1, 2, 3, 4, etc., are figures. **2** use numbers to find out the answer to some problem; calculate: *Please figure out how much I owe you.* **3** **figures,** *pl.* calculations using figures; arithmetic: *She was always very good at figures.* **4** price: *The figure for that house is very high.* **5** form enclosing a surface or space: *Circles, triangles, squares, cubes, and spheres are geometric figures.* **6** form or shape: *In the darkness she saw dim figures moving.* **7** way in which a person looks or appears: *The poor old woman was a figure of distress.* **8** person; character: *That senator may become a well-known figure in American history.* **9** be conspicuous; appear: *The names of great leaders figure in the story of human progress.* **10** picture; drawing; diagram; illustration: *This book has many figures to help explain words.* **11** a design or pattern: *Cloth or* *wallpaper often has figures on it.* **12** outline traced by movements: *figures made by an airplane.* **13** set of movements in dancing or skating. **14** figure of speech. **15** INFORMAL. think; consider: *I figured I should stop where I was.* 1,3-8,10-14 *n.,* 2,9,15 *v.,* **fig ured, fig ur ing.**

figure on, depend on; plan on: *I can figure on my parents' help to pay my way through college.*

figure out, think out; understand: *Even the repairman couldn't figure out what had gone wrong with the washer.*

fig ured (fig′yərd), decorated with a design or pattern; not plain: *figured silk. adj.*

figurehead (def. 2)

fig ure head (fig′yər hed′), **1** person who is the head of a business, government, etc., in name only, without real authority. **2** figure placed for ornament on the bow of a ship. *n.*

figure of speech, expression in which words are used out of their literal meaning or out of their ordinary use to add beauty or force. Similes and metaphors are figures of speech.

fig u rine (fig′yə rēn′), a small, ornamental figure made of stone, pottery, metal, etc.; statuette. *n.*

Fi ji (fē′jē), island country in the S Pacific, consisting of the **Fiji Islands.** It is a member of the Commonwealth of Nations. See **Australasia** for map. *n.*

FILAMENT

filament (def. 1)

fil a ment (fil′ə mənt), **1** a very fine thread; very slender, threadlike part. The wire that gives off light in an electric light bulb is a filament. **2** the heated wire that acts as the negative electrode in a vacuum tube. *n.*

fil bert (fil′bərt), **1** a sweet, thick-

shelled kind of cultivated hazelnut. **2** tree or shrub it grows on. *n.* [from Saint *Philibert,* a Benedictine priest of the A.D. 600's (because the nuts ripen near his feast day, August 20)]

filch (filch), steal in small quantities; pilfer: *She filched cookies from the pantry. v.* —**filch′er,** *n.*

file[1] (fīl), **1** container, drawer, folder, etc., for keeping memorandums, letters, or other papers in order. **2** set of papers kept in order: *a file of receipts.* **3** put away in order: *Please file those letters.* **4** row of persons or things one behind another: *a file of soldiers.* **5** march or move in a file: *The pupils filed out of the room during the fire drill.* **6** place among the records of a court, public office, etc.: *The deed to our house is filed with the county clerk.* 1,2,4 *n.,* 3,5,6 *v.,* **filed, fil ing.** [from French of the 1500's *fil* thread, and *file* row]

in file, one after another; in succession: *ships sailing in file.*

on file, in a file; put away and kept in order: *The principal keeps all our school reports on file.*

file[2] (fīl), **1** a steel tool with many small ridges or teeth on it. Its rough surface is used to smooth rough materials or wear away hard substances. **2** smooth or wear away with a file. 1 *n.,* 2 *v.,* **filed, fil ing.** [Old English *fīl*]

file[2] (def. 1)

fi let (fi lā′ *or* fil′ā), **1** a fillet of fish or meat. **2** net or net lace having a square mesh. *n.*

fil i al (fil′ē əl), due from a son or daughter toward a mother or father: *filial affection. adj.*

fil i bus ter (fil′ə bus′tər), **1** the deliberate hindering of the passage of a bill in a legislature by long speeches or other means of delay. **2** deliberately hinder the passage of a bill by such means. 1 *n.,* 2 *v.* —**fil′i bus′ter er,** *n.*

fil i gree (fil′ə grē), **1** very delicate, lacelike, ornamental work of gold or silver wire. **2** anything very lacy, delicate, or fanciful: *The frost made a beautiful filigree on the windowpane. n.*

fil ings (fī′lingz), small pieces of iron, wood, etc., which have been removed by a file. *n.pl.*

Fil i pi no (fil′ə pē′nō), **1** person born or living in the Philippines. **2** Philippine. 1 *n.,* pl. **Fil i pi nos;** 2 *adj.*

fill (fil), **1** make full; put into until there is room for nothing else: *Fill this bottle*

hat, āge, fär; let, ēqual, tėrm; it, īce; hot, ōpen, ôrder; oil, out; cup, pùt, rüle; ch, child; ng, long; sh, she; th, thin; ∓H, then; zh, measure;

ə represents *a* in about, *e* in taken, *i* in pencil, *o* in lemon, *u* in circus.

with water. Fill this hole with something. **2** become full: *The hall filled rapidly. The well filled with water.* **3** take up all the space in: *The crowd filled the hall.* **4** all that is needed or wanted: *Eat and drink your fill; there is plenty for all of us.* **5** supply with all that is needed or wanted for: *The store filled my mother's order by selling her what she asked for. The druggist filled the doctor's prescription.* **6** stop up or close by putting something in: *After the dentist had taken out the decayed part, he filled my tooth.* **7** hold and do the duties of (a position, office, etc.); occupy: *fill the office of governor.* **8** something that fills. Earth or rock used to make uneven land level is called fill. **9** (of the wind) stretch out (a sail) by blowing fully into it. 1-3,5-7,9 *v.,* 4,8 *n.*

fill in, 1 put in to complete something; insert: *fill in the date of an application.* **2** be a substitute.

fill out, 1 grow larger; swell: *Her cheeks have filled out.* **2** supply what is needed in: *The clerk added a sack of potatoes to fill out the order.*

fill up, fill; fill completely.

fill er (fil′ər), **1** person or thing that fills. **2** thing put in to fill something. A pad of paper for a notebook and a preparation used to fill holes and cracks in wood before painting it are fillers. *n.*

fil let (fi lā′, fil′ā, *or* fil′it for 1,2; fil′it for 3,4), **1** slice of fish or meat without bones or fat; filet. **2** cut (fish or meat) into such slices. **3** a narrow band, ribbon, etc., around the head to hold the hair in place, often ornamental. **4** bind or decorate with a fillet. 1,3 *n.,* 2,4 *v.*

filigree (def. 1)

fill ing (fil′ing), thing put in to fill something: *a filling in a tooth. n.*

filling station, place where gasoline and oil for automobiles, trucks, etc., are sold; gas station; service station.

319

adj.	adjective	*n.*	noun
adv.	adverb	*prep.*	preposition
conj.	conjunction	*pron.*	pronoun
interj.	interjection	*v.*	verb
sing.	singular	*pl.*	plural

fil lip (fil′əp), 1 to strike with the nail of a finger snapped from the end of the thumb. 2 toss or cause to move by striking in this way: *He filliped a speck of lint from the sleeve of his coat.* 3 the quick, slight stroke given in this way. 4 thing that rouses, revives, or excites: *The relishes served as a fillip to my appetite.* 1,2 *v.,* 3,4 *n.*

Fill more (fil′môr), **Millard,** 1800-1874, the 13th president of the United States, from 1850 to 1853. *n.*

fil ly (fil′ē), a young female horse; mare that is less than four or five years old. *n., pl.* **fil lies.**

film (film), 1 a very thin layer, sheet, surface, or coating, often of liquid: *The tanker sank, leaving a film of oil on the water. A film of fog covered the hills.* 2 cover or become covered with a film; dim: *Her eyes filmed over with tears.* 3 roll or sheet of thin, flexible material covered with a coating that is sensitive to light, used in taking photographs. 4 a motion picture. 5 make a motion picture of: *They filmed "Hamlet."* 6 photograph for motion pictures: *They filmed the scene three times.* 1,3,4 *n.,* 2,5,6 *v.*

film strip (film′strip′), series of still pictures printed on a reel of film. *n.*

film y (fil′mē), 1 like a film; very thin. 2 covered with a film. *adj.,* **film i er, film i est.**

fil ter (fil′tər), 1 device for straining out substances from a liquid or a gas by passing it slowly through felt, paper, sand, or charcoal. A filter is used to remove impurities from water. 2 material through which the liquid or gas passes in a filter. 3 device for allowing only certain light rays, frequencies, etc., to pass while blocking all others. A yellow filter placed in front of a camera lens allows less blue light to reach the film. 4 pass or flow very slowly: *Water filters through the sandy soil and into the well.* 5 put through a filter; strain: *We filter this water for drinking.* 6 act as a filter for: *The charcoal filtered the water.* 7 remove by a filter: *Filter out all the dirt before using this water.* 1-3 *n.,* 4-7 *v.*

fil ter a ble (fil′tər ə bəl), 1 that can be filtered. 2 capable of passing through a filter which arrests bacteria: *a filterable virus. adj.*

filth (filth), 1 foul dirt: *The alley was filled with garbage and filth.* 2 dirty words or thoughts. *n.*

filth i ness (fil′thē nis), a filthy condition. *n.*

filth y (fil′thē), very dirty; foul: *a filthy street, a filthy dress. adj.,* **filth i er, filth i est.**

fil trate (fil′trāt), 1 liquid that has been passed through a filter. 2 pass through a filter. 1 *n.,* 2 *v.,* **fil trat ed, fil trat ing.**

fil tra tion (fil trā′shən), a filtering or a being filtered. *n.*

fin (def. 1)—fins of a bass

fin (fin), 1 one of the movable winglike or fanlike parts of a fish's body. By moving its fins a fish can swim and balance itself in the water. 2 thing shaped or used like a fin. Some aircraft have fins to help balance them in flight. See **airplane** for picture. *n.* —**fin′like′,** *adj.*

fi nal (fī′nl), 1 at the end; coming last: *The book was interesting from the first to the final chapter.* 2 deciding completely; settling the question: *The one with the highest authority makes the final decisions.* 3 Often, **finals,** *pl.* the last or deciding set in a series of games or examinations: *If you pass your finals at the end of the term, you will be promoted.* 1,2 *adj.,* 3 *n.*

fi na le (fə nä′lē), 1 the concluding part of a piece of music or a play. 2 the last part; end. *n.* [from Italian]

fi nal ist (fī′nl ist), person who takes part in the last or deciding set in a series of contests. *n.*

fi nal i ty (fī nal′ə tē), condition of being final, finished, or settled: *She refused with finality; we knew that she would not change her mind. n., pl.* **fi nal i ties.**

fi nal ize (fī′nl īz), make final or conclusive. *v.,* **fi nal ized, fi nal iz ing.**

fi nal ly (fī′nl ē), 1 at the end; at last. 2 in such a way as to decide or settle the question. *adv.*

fi nance (fə nans′ or fī′nans), 1 money matters: *A successful banker must have skill in finance.* 2 system by which the income of a nation, state, corporation, etc., is raised and managed. 3 **finances,** *pl.* financial condition; money; funds; revenues: *New taxes were needed to increase the nation's finances.* 4 provide money for: *A part-time job helped finance my college education.* 1-3 *n.,* 4 *v.,* **fi nanced, fi nanc ing.**

fi nan cial (fə nan′shəl *or* fī nan′shəl), 1 having to do with money matters: *His financial affairs are in bad condition.* 2 having to do with the management of large sums of public or private money. *adj.* —**fi nan′cial ly,** *adv.*

fin an cier (fin′ən sir′ *or* fī′nən sir′), 1 person occupied or skilled in finance. Bankers are financiers. 2 person who is active in matters involving large sums of money. *n.*

finch (finch), a small songbird with a bill shaped like a cone. Sparrows, buntings, grosbeaks, canaries, and cardinals are finches. *n., pl.* **finch es.**

find (fīnd), 1 come upon by chance; happen on; meet with: *He found a dime in the road. They find friends everywhere.* 2 look for and get: *Please find my hat for me.* 3 discover; learn: *We found that he could not swim.* 4 get; get the use of: *Can you find time to do this?* 5 arrive at; reach: *Water finds its level. The arrow found its mark.* 6 decide and declare: *The jury found the defendant guilty.* 7 gain or recover the use of: *find one's tongue.* 8 something found. 1-7 *v.,* **found, find ing;** 8 *n.*

find oneself, learn one's abilities and how to make good use of them.

find out, learn about; come to know; discover.

find er (fīn′dər), 1 person or thing that finds. 2 a small, extra lens on the outside of a camera that shows what is being photographed. 3 a small telescope attached to a larger one to help find objects more easily. *n.*

find ing (fīn′ding), 1 discovery. 2 thing found. 3 decision reached after an examination or inquiry. The verdict of a jury is its finding. *n.*

fine[1] (fīn), 1 of very high quality; very good; excellent: *Everybody praised his fine singing. She is a fine scholar.* 2 very small or thin: *Thread is finer than rope. Sand is finer than gravel.* 3 sharp: *a tool with a fine edge.* 4 not coarse or heavy; delicate: *fine linen.* 5 refined; elegant: *fine manners.* 6 subtle: *The law makes fine distinctions.* 7 without impurities. Fine gold is gold not mixed with any other metal. 8 INFORMAL. very well; excellently: *I'm doing fine.* 1-7 *adj.,* **fin er, fin est;** 8 *adv.* [from French of the 1300's *fin* perfected] —**fine′ly,** *adv.* —**fine′ness,** *n.*

fine[2] (fīn), 1 sum of money paid as a punishment for breaking a law or regulation. 2 make pay such a sum: *The judge fined her ten dollars.* 1 *n.,* 2 *v.,* **fined, fin ing.** [from French of the 1300's *fin,* from Latin *finis* end]

fine arts, arts depending upon taste and appealing to the sense of beauty; painting, drawing, sculpture, and architecture. Literature, music, dancing, and acting are also often included in the fine arts.

fin er y (fī′nər ē), showy clothes or ornaments. *n., pl.* **fin er ies.**

fi nesse (fə nes′), 1 delicacy of execution; skill: *That young artist shows wonderful finesse.* 2 the skillful handling of a delicate situation to one's advantage: *A successful diplomat must be a master of finesse.* 3 use finesse. 1,2 *n.,* 3 *v.,* **fi nessed, fi ness ing.**

fin ger (fing′gər), 1 one of the five slender divisions that end the hand, especially the four besides the thumb. 2 part of a glove that covers a finger. 3 anything shaped or used like a finger; thing that reaches out and touches: *a long finger of light.* 4 touch or handle with the fingers; use the fingers on: *finger the keyboard of a piano, finger a gun.* 5 perform or mark (a passage of music) with a certain fingering. 6 width of a finger; 3/4 inch. 1-3,6 *n.,* 4,5 *v.* —**fin′ger like′,** *adj.*

fin ger nail (fing′gər nāl′), a hard layer of horn on the upper side of the end of each finger. *n.*

finger painting, 1 method of painting pictures or designs on large sheets of paper, with fingers or hands instead of brushes. 2 picture or design painted in this way.

fingerprint (def. 1)

fin ger print (fing′gər print′), 1 an impression of the markings on the inner surface of the last joint of a finger or thumb. A person can be identified by his fingerprints because no two fingers have identical markings. 2 take the fingerprints of. 1 *n.,* 2 *v.*

fin i cal (fin′ə kəl), finicky. *adj.*

fin ick i ness (fin′ə kē nis), finicky quality or condition. *n.*

fin ick y (fin′ə kē), too dainty or particular; too precise; fussy. *adj.*

fi nis (fin′is *or* fī′nis), the end. *n.*

fin ish (fin′ish), 1 bring to an end; reach the end of; complete: *finish one's dinner, finish sewing a dress. He started the race but did not finish it.* 2 come to an end: *There was so little wind that the sailing race didn't finish until after dark.* 3 an end: *fight to a finish.* 4 use up

completely: *finish a bottle of milk, finish a spool of thread.* 5 way in which the surface is prepared: *a smooth finish on furniture.* 6 prepare the surface of in some way: *finish metal with a dull surface.* 7 polished condition or quality; perfection: *the finish of a person's manners.* 8 to perfect in detail; polish. 1,2,4,6,8 *v.,* 3,5,7 *n., pl.* **fin ish es.**

finish off, 1 complete. 2 overcome completely; destroy; kill.

finish up, 1 complete: *finish up a job.* 2 use up completely: *I've finished up all the paint.*

finish with, 1 complete. 2 stop being friends with; have nothing to do with.

fin ished (fin′isht), 1 ended or completed. 2 brought to the highest degree of excellence; perfected; polished: *It takes years of study and practice to become a finished musician. adj.*

fi nite (fī′nīt), having limits or bounds; not infinite: *Human understanding is finite. adj.*

fink (fingk), SLANG. 1 informer. 2 an undesirable or inferior person. *n.*

Fin land (fin′lənd), 1 country in N Europe, east of Sweden. *Capital:* Helsinki. 2 **Gulf of,** part of the Baltic Sea, south of Finland. *n.*

Finn (fin), person born or living in Finland. *n.*

fin nan had die (fin′ən had′ē), smoked haddock. [originally *Findon haddock,* from *Findon,* a village in Scotland + *haddock*]

Finn ish (fin′ish), 1 of or having to do with Finland, its people, or their language. 2 the people of Finland. 3 language of Finland. 1 *adj.,* 2 *n.pl.,* 3 *n.sing.*

fin ny (fin′ē), 1 filled with fish. 2 having fins. 3 like a fin. *adj.*

fiord (fyôrd), a long, narrow bay of the sea bordered by steep cliffs. Norway has many fiords. *n.* Also, **fjord.** [from Norwegian *fjord*]

fir (fėr), 1 an evergreen tree that belongs to the same family as the pine. Small firs are often used for Christmas trees. The needles of fir trees have a pleasant smell. 2 its wood. *n.*

fire (fīr), 1 flame, heat, and light caused by something burning. 2 something burning. 3 destruction by burning: *A cigarette thrown into the woods in dry weather may start a fire.* 4 make burn; set on fire. 5 fuel burning or arranged so that it will burn quickly: *A fire was laid in the fireplace.* 6 supply with fuel; tend the fire of: *fire a furnace.* 7 dry with heat; bake: *Bricks are fired to make them hard.* 8 heat of feeling; readiness to act; passion, fervor, enthusiasm, or excitement: *Their hearts were full of patriotic fire.* 9 arouse; excite; inflame: *Stories about adventures fire the*

hat, āge, fär; let, ēqual, tėrm;
it, īce; hot, ōpen, ôrder;
oil, out; cup, pu̇t, rüle; ch, child;
ng, long; sh, she; th, thin;
ŦH, then; zh, measure;

ə represents *a* in about,
e in taken, *i* in pencil,
o in lemon, *u* in circus.

imagination. 10 the shooting or discharge of guns, etc.: *The enemy's fire sent thousands of bullets against us.* 11 discharge (a gun, etc.): *I fired my rifle four times.* 12 shoot: *fire a rocket. The soldiers fired from the fort.* 13 INFORMAL. throw: *fire a stone, fire a ball.* 14 INFORMAL. dismiss from a job, etc. 1-3,5,8,10 *n.,* 4,6,7,9,11-14 *v.,* **fired, fir ing.**

between two fires, attacked from both sides.

catch fire, begin to burn.

fire up, start a fire in a furnace, boiler, etc.

hang fire, be slow in going off or acting; be delayed.

lay a fire, build a fire ready to be lit.

miss fire, 1 fail to go off. 2 fail to do what was attempted.

on fire, 1 burning. 2 full of a feeling or spirit like fire; excited.

open fire, begin shooting.

under fire, 1 exposed to shooting from the enemy's guns. 2 attacked; blamed.

fiord

fire arm (fīr′ärm′), gun, pistol, or other weapon to shoot with. It is usually one that can be carried and used by one person. *n.*

fire ball (fīr′bôl′), the great, luminous cloud of water vapor and dust produced by a nuclear explosion. *n.*

fire boat (fīr′bōt′), boat equipped with apparatus for putting out fires. *n.*

fire box (fīr′boks′), place for the fire in a furnace, boiler, etc. *n., pl.* **fire box es.**

adj. adjective	*n.* noun
adv. adverb	*prep.* preposition
conj. conjunction	*pron.* pronoun
interj. interjection	*v.* verb
sing. singular	*pl.* plural

fire brand (fīr′brand′), 1 piece of burning wood. 2 person who arouses angry feelings in others. *n.*

fire bug (fīr′bug′), INFORMAL. person who purposely sets houses or property on fire; person who commits arson. *n.*

fire company, group of men organized to put out fires.

fire crack er (fīr′krak′ər), a paper roll containing gunpowder and a fuse. Firecrackers explode with a loud noise. *n.*

fire damp (fīr′damp′), gas formed in coal mines, dangerously explosive when mixed with certain proportions of air. *n.*

fire dog (fīr′dôg′), andiron. *n.*

fire engine, truck with a machine for throwing water, chemicals, etc., to put out fires; fire truck.

fire escape, stairway or ladder in or on a building, to use when the building is on fire.

fire extinguisher, container filled with chemicals which, when sprayed upon fire, extinguish it.

fire fly (fīr′flī′), a small beetle that gives off flashes of light which can be seen when it flies at night; lightning bug. *n., pl.* **fire flies.**

fire house (fīr′hous′), building where fire trucks are kept; fire station. *n., pl.* **fire hous es** (fīr′hou′ziz).

fire light (fīr′līt′), light from a fire. *n.*

fire man (fīr′mən), 1 man who belongs to a fire company, trained to put out fires. 2 man whose work is looking after fires in a furnace, boiler, locomotive, etc. *n., pl.* **fire men.**

fire place (fīr′plās′), place built to hold a fire. Indoor fireplaces are usually made of brick or stone, with a chimney leading up from them. *n.*

fire plug (fīr′plug′), hydrant. *n.*

fire proof (fīr′prüf′), 1 that will not burn; almost impossible to burn: *A building made entirely of steel and concrete is fireproof.* 2 make fireproof: *fireproof a theater curtain.* 1 *adj.,* 2 *v.*

fire side (fīr′sīd′), 1 space around a fireplace or hearth. 2 home; hearth: *We were weary of traveling and longed to be back at our own fireside.* 3 home life: *a happy fireside. n.*

fire station, firehouse.

fire tower, tower from which forest rangers can watch for forest fires and give the alarm.

fire trap (fīr′trap′), building that could burn very easily and would be hard to get out of if it were on fire. *n.*

fire truck, fire engine.

fire wa ter (fīr′wô′tər *or* fīr′wot′ər), a strong alcoholic drink. Firewater is a translation of a North American Indian name for whiskey, rum, etc. *n.*

fire wood (fīr′wůd′), wood to make a fire. *n.*

fire work (fīr′wėrk′), 1 a firecracker, bomb, rocket, etc., that makes a loud noise or a beautiful, fiery display at night. 2 **fireworks,** *pl.* a firework display. *n.*

firing pin, the part of the mechanism of a firearm, cannon, etc., that sets off the primer which explodes the charge.

firm[1] (fėrm), 1 not yielding when pressed; solid; hard: *firm flesh, firm ground.* 2 not easily moved or shaken; fixed in place: *a tree firm in the earth.* 3 not easily changed; determined; resolute; positive: *a firm voice, a firm character, a firm belief.* 4 not changing; staying the same; steady: *a firm price. adj.* —**firm′ly,** *adv.* —**firm′ness,** *n.*

firm[2] (fėrm), company of two or more persons in business together. *n.* [from Italian *firma* signature]

fir ma ment (fėr′mə mənt), arch of the heavens; sky. *n.*

first (fėrst), 1 coming before all others: *He is first in his class.* 2 before all others; before anything else: *We eat first and then feed the cat.* 3 person, thing, place, etc., that is first: *We were the first to get here.* 4 the beginning: *At first I did not like school.* 5 for the first time: *When I first met her, she was a child.* 6 rather; sooner: *I'll go to jail first.* 7 (in music) playing or singing the chief part or the part highest in pitch: *first flute, first soprano.* 8 the first day of the month: *I'll see you on the first.* 1,7 *adj.,* 2,5,6 *adv.,* 3,4,8 *n.*

first aid, emergency treatment given to an injured or sick person before a doctor comes.

first-aid (fėrst′ād′), of or for first aid: *a first-aid kit. adj.*

first-born (fėrst′bôrn′), 1 born first; oldest. 2 the first-born child. 1 *adj.,* 2 *n.*

first class, the best and most expensive passenger accommodations offered for travel by ship, airplane, or train.

first-class (fėrst′klas′), 1 of the highest class or best quality; excellent: *a first-class singer.* 2 by the best and most expensive passenger accommodations offered by ship, airplane, or train: *We could not afford to travel first-class.* 1 *adj.,* 2 *adv.*

first hand (fėrst′hand′), from the original source; direct: *This is firsthand information* (adj.). *We got our information firsthand* (adv.). *adj., adv.*

first lady, the official hostess (usually the wife) of the President of the United States or of the governor of a state.

first lieutenant, an army, air force, or marine officer ranking below a captain and above a second lieutenant.

first person, form of a pronoun or verb used to refer to the speaker. *I, me, we,* and *us* are pronouns of the first person.

first quarter, 1 period of time between the new moon and the first half moon. 2 phase of the moon represented by the first half moon after the new moon.

first-rate (fėrst′rāt′), 1 of the highest class; excellent; very good: *a first-rate actor.* 2 INFORMAL. excellently; very well: *He did first-rate on the test.* 1 *adj.,* 2 *adv.*

firth (fėrth), a narrow arm of the sea; estuary of a river. *n.*

fis cal (fis′kəl), 1 financial. 2 having to do with public finance: *Important changes were made in the government's fiscal policy. adj.*

fiscal year, time between one yearly settlement of financial accounts and another. The fiscal year of the United States government begins July 1 and ends June 30.

fish (fish), 1 vertebrate that lives in the water and has gills instead of lungs for breathing. Fish are usually covered with scales and have fins for swimming. Some fishes lay eggs in the water; others produce living young. 2 flesh of fish used for food. 3 catch fish; try to catch fish. 4 try for something as if with a hook: *The boy fished with a stick for his watch which had fallen through a grating.* 5 search: *She fished in her purse for a coin.* 6 find and pull: *She fished an old map out of a box.* 7 try to get by means of cunning: *fish for compliments.* 1,2 *n., pl.* **fish es** or **fish;** 3-7 *v.* —**fish′like′,** *adj.*

fish and chips, fried pieces of fish and French fries.

fish er (fish′ər), 1 person or animal that fishes. 2 kind of marten of North America. 3 its dark-brown fur. *n.*

fisher—about 2 ft. long without the tail

fish er man (fish′ər mən), person who fishes, especially one who makes his living by catching fish. *n., pl.* **fish-er men.**

fish er y (fish′ər ē), 1 occupation of catching fish. 2 place for catching fish. 3 place for breeding fish. *n., pl.* **fish er-ies.**

fish hawk, osprey.

fish hook (fish′huk′), hook with a barb used for catching fish. *n.*

fish ing (fish′ing), the catching of fish for a living or for pleasure. *n.*

fishing rod, a long, light pole with a line and hook attached to it, and often having a reel, used in catching fish.

fishing tackle, rods, lines, hooks, etc., used in catching fish.

fish line (fish′līn′), cord used with a fishhook for catching fish. *n.*

fish mon ger (fish′mung′gər), dealer in fish. *n.*

fish pond (fish′pond′), pond in which fish are stocked to be sold. *n.*

fish wife (fish′wīf′), 1 woman who uses coarse and abusive language. 2 woman who sells fish. *n., pl.* **fish-wives** (fish′wīvz′).

fish y (fish′ē), 1 like a fish in smell, taste, or shape. 2 of fish. 3 full of fish. 4 INFORMAL. not probable; doubtful; unlikely; suspicious: *His excuse sounds fishy; I don't believe it.* 5 without expression or luster; dull: *fishy eyes.* adj., **fish i er, fish i est.**

fis sion (fish′ən), 1 a splitting apart; division into parts. 2 method of reproduction in which the body of the parent divides to form two or more independent individuals. Many animals and plants reproduce by fission. 3 the splitting of an atomic nucleus into two parts, especially when bombarded by a neutron; nuclear fission. Fission releases huge amounts of energy when the nuclei of heavy elements, especially uranium and plutonium, are split. Fission is used to induce the chain reaction in an atomic bomb. *n.*

fis sion a ble (fish′ə nə bəl), capable of nuclear fission. *adj.*

fis sure (fish′ər), a long, narrow opening; split; crack: *Water dripped from a fissure in the rock. n.*

fist (fist), hand closed tightly with the fingers bent against the palm: *He shook his fist at me. n.*

fist i cuffs (fis′tə kufs′), a fight with the fists. *n.pl.*

fis tu la (fis′chə lə), 1 tube or pipe. 2 a deep passage connecting a sore on the skin, etc., with some internal cavity or organ. It is caused by a wound, abscess, disease, etc. *n., pl.* **fis tu las, fis tu lae** (fis′chə lē′).

fit¹ (fit), 1 having the necessary qualities; suitable: *Grass is a fit food for cows; it is not fit for people.* 2 right; proper: *It is fit that we give thanks.* 3 in good physical condition; healthy and strong: *I am now well and fit for work.* 4 be right, proper, or suitable to; be fit: *a punishment that fits the crime.* 5 make right, proper or suitable; suit: *fit the action to the word.* 6 have the right size or shape; have the right size or shape for: *Does this glove fit? The dress fitted her.* 7 try to make fit; adjust: *Father was fitting new seat covers on our car.* 8 way that something fits: *The coat was not a very good fit; it was too tight.* 9 supply with everything needed; equip: *fit a store with counters, fit out a room.* 1-3 adj., **fit ter, fit test;** 4-7,9 *v.,* **fit ted, fit ting;** 8 *n.* [Middle English *fyt*]

see fit or **think fit,** prefer and decide; choose.

fit² (fit), 1 a sudden, sharp attack of disease: *a fit of colic, a fit of epilepsy.* 2 any sudden, sharp attack: *In a fit of anger I broke the dish.* 3 a short period of doing some one thing; spell: *a fit of coughing, a fit of laughter. n.* [Old English *fitt* conflict]

by fits and starts, irregularly; starting, stopping, beginning again, and so on: *He does his homework by fits and starts instead of steadily.*

fitch (fich), 1 polecat of Europe. 2 its fur. *n., pl.* **fitch es.**

fit ful (fit′fəl), going on and then stopping for a while; irregular: *She had a fitful sleep during the storm, waking up every few minutes.* adj. —**fit′ful ly,** adv.

fit ly (fit′lē), in a suitable manner. adv.

fit ness (fit′nis), a being fit. *n.*

fit ter (fit′ər), 1 person whose work is fitting clothes on people. 2 person who supplies and fixes anything necessary for some purpose: *The gas fitter installed our new gas stove. n.*

fit ting (fit′ing), proper and right; suitable. adj. —**fit′ting ly,** adv.

fit tings (fit′ingz), furnishings; fixtures: *Desks, chairs, and files are office fittings. n.pl.*

five (fīv), one more than four; 5. *n., adj.*

five fold (fīv′fōld′), 1 five times as much or as many: *Last year yielded a fivefold increase in profits (adj.). Profits increased fivefold over a three-month period (adv.).* 2 having five parts. 1,2 adj., 1 adv.

Five Nations, a former confederacy of Iroquois Indian tribes consisting of the Mohawk, Oneida, Onondaga, Cayuga, and Seneca tribes.

fix (fiks), 1 make firm; fasten tightly: *We fixed the post in the ground. The boy fixed the spelling lesson in his mind.* 2 settle; set: *I fixed the price at one dollar. Did you fix on a day for the*

hat, āge, fär; let, ēqual, tėrm;
it, īce; hot, ōpen, ôrder;
oil, out; cup, pùt, rüle; ch, child;
ng, long; sh, she; th, thin;
ŦH, then; zh, measure;

ə represents *a* in about,
e in taken, *i* in pencil,
o in lemon, *u* in circus.

picnic? 3 direct or hold steadily (eyes, attention, etc.); be directed or held steadily. 4 make or become stiff or rigid: *eyes fixed in death.* 5 put or place definitely: *She fixed the blame on them.* 6 treat ·to prevent fading or other changes: *fix a dye or a photograph with chemicals.* 7 put in order; set right; arrange: *fix one's hair.* 8 mend; repair: *fix a watch.* 9 prepare (a meal or food): *fix dinner.* 10 put in a condition or position favorable to oneself or unfavorable to one's opponents, especially by bribery: *fix a jury, fix a game.* 11 INFORMAL. **a** get revenge upon; get even with; punish. **b** position hard to get out of; awkward state of affairs: *The boy who cried "Wolf" got himself into a bad fix.* **c** narcotic, or an injection of a narcotic, such as heroin. 1-11a *v.,* 11b-11c *n., pl.* **fix es.**

fix up, INFORMAL. 1 mend; repair. 2 put in order; arrange.

fix a tion (fik sā′shən), 1 a fixing or a being fixed. 2 treatment to prevent something from fading or otherwise changing: *the fixation of a photographic film. n.*

fix a tive (fik′sə tiv), 1 substance used to prevent something from fading or otherwise changing. 2 that prevents fading or change. 1 *n.,* 2 adj.

fixed (fikst), 1 not movable; made firm: *The seats in some modern classrooms are not fixed.* 2 definitely assigned; settled; set: *fixed charges for taxicabs.* 3 steady; not moving: *a fixed gaze. adj.*

fix ed ly (fik′sid lē), in a fixed manner; without change; intently: *She stared fixedly at the ring. adv.*

fixed star, star whose position in relation to other stars appears not to change.

fix ings (fik′singz), INFORMAL. trimmings: *We had turkey and all the fixings for Thanksgiving dinner. n.pl.*

fix ture (fiks′chər), 1 thing put in place to stay: *a bathroom fixture, light fixtures.* 2 person or thing that stays in one place, job, etc.: *He is a fixture in the office. n.*

fizz (fiz), 1 make a hissing sound. 2 a

adj. adjective	*n.* noun
adv. adverb	*prep.* preposition
conj. conjunction	*pron.* pronoun
interj. interjection	*v.* verb
sing. singular	*pl.* plural

hissing sound; bubbling: *the fizz of soda water.* 1 *v.*, 2 *n.*, *pl.* **fizz es.**

fiz zle (fiz′əl), 1 make a hissing sound that dies out weakly: *The firecracker just fizzled instead of exploding with a bang.* 2 a fizzling or hissing. 3 IN-FORMAL. come to a poor end; fail: *The plans for the picnic fizzled out when it began to look like rain.* 4 INFORMAL. failure. 1,3 *v.*, **fiz zled, fiz zling;** 2,4 *n.*

fjord (fyôrd), fiord. *n.*

fl., fluid.

Fla., Florida.

flab ber gast (flab′ər gast), INFOR-MAL. make speechless with surprise; astonish greatly; amaze. *v.*

flab bi ness (flab′ē nis), flabby quality or condition. *n.*

flab by (flab′ē), lacking firmness or force; soft; weak: *flabby cheeks, a flabby nature, a flabby will.* *adj.*, **flab-bi er, flab bi est.**

flac cid (flak′sid), limp; weak: *flaccid muscles, a flaccid will.* *adj.*

flag[1] (flag), 1 piece of cloth with a pattern or picture on it that stands for some country, city, party, club, etc., or which gives some information or signal: *the flag of the United States, the white flag of truce, the red flag showing dan-ger.* Flags are hung on poles over build-ings, ships, army camps, etc. 2 stop or signal (a person, train, etc.) by waving a flag: *The train was flagged at the bridge.* 3 communicate by a flag: *flag a message.* 1 *n.*, 2,3 *v.*, **flagged, flag-ging.** [perhaps from *flag*[3]]

flag[2] (flag), 1 iris with blue, purple, yellow, or white flowers and sword-shaped leaves. 2 its flower. *n.* [perhaps from a Scandinavian word, such as Danish *flæg*]

flag[3] (flag), get tired; grow weak; droop: *My horse was flagging, but I urged him on.* *v.*, **flagged, flag ging.** [perhaps from a Scandinavian word of the 1500's, such as Icelandic *flakka* flutter]

Flag Day, June 14, the anniversary of the day in 1777 when the Second Con-tinental Congress adopted the Stars and Stripes as the flag of the United States.

flag el late (flaj′ə lāt), 1 whip; flog. 2 like a whip; long, thin, and flexible. 1 *v.*, **flag el lat ed, flag el lat ing;** 2 *adj.*

flag el la tion (flaj′ə lā′shən), a whip-ping; flogging. *n.*

fla gel lum (flə jel′əm), 1 a long, whiplike tail or part. Certain bacteria have flagella to enable them to move. 2 whip. *n.*, *pl.* **fla gel la** (flə jel′lə), **fla gel lums.**

flag eo let (flaj′ə let′), a small wind instrument somewhat like a flute, with a mouthpiece at one end, six main holes, and sometimes keys. *n.*

flag man (flag′mən), person who sig-nals with a flag or lantern at a railroad crossing, etc. *n.*, *pl.* **flag men.**

flag on (flag′ən), 1 container for liquids, usually having a handle, a spout, and a cover. 2 a large bottle, holding about two quarts. *n.*

flag pole (flag′pōl′), pole from which a flag is flown; flagstaff. *n.*

fla grant (flā′grənt), 1 notorious; outrageous; scandalous: *a flagrant crime.* 2 glaring: *a flagrant error.* *adj.* —**fla′grant ly,** *adv.*

flag ship (flag′ship′), ship that carries the officer in command of a fleet or squadron and displays his flag. *n.*

flag staff (flag′staf′), flagpole. *n.*

flag stone (flag′stōn′), a large, flat stone, used for paving paths, etc. *n.*

flail (flāl), 1 instrument for threshing grain by hand. A flail consists of a wooden handle with a short, heavy stick fastened at one end by a thong. 2 strike with a flail. 3 beat; thrash. 1 *n.*, 2,3 *v.*

flair (fler *or* flar), 1 natural talent: *The poet had a flair for making clever rhymes.* 2 keen perception: *That trader has a flair for bargains.* *n.*

flake (flāk), 1 a flat, thin piece, usually not very large: *a flake of snow, flakes of rust, corn flakes.* 2 come off in flakes; separate into flakes: *Dirty, gray spots showed where the paint had flaked off.* 1 *n.*, 2 *v.*, **flaked, flak ing.**

flak i ness (flā′kē nis), flaky quality or condition. *n.*

flak y (flā′kē), 1 consisting of flakes. 2 easily broken or separated into flakes. *adj.*, **flak i er, flak i est.**

flam boy ant (flam boi′ənt), 1 gor-geously brilliant; flaming; showily striking: *Some tropical flowers have flamboyant colors.* 2 very ornate; much decorated: *flamboyant architecture.* 3 having wavy lines or flamelike curves: *flamboyant designs.* *adj.* —**flam boy′ant ly,** *adv.*

flame (flām), 1 one of the glowing tongues of light, usually red or yellow, that come when a fire blazes up: *The burning house went up in flames.* 2 a burning gas or vapor. 3 rise up in flames; blaze. 4 a burning with flames; blaze: *The dying fire suddenly burst into flame.* 5 shine brightly; flash: *Her eyes flamed with rage.* 6 burst out quickly

FLAGELLUM

flagellum (def. 1)

and hotly; be or act like a flame. 7 something like flame. 1,2,4,7 *n.*, 3,5,6 *v.*, **flamed, flam ing.** —**flame′like′,** *adj.*

flame throw er (flām′thrō′ər), weapon that throws a stream of burning fuel through the air. *n.*

fla min go (flə ming′gō), a tropical wading bird with very long legs and neck, and feathers that vary from pink to scarlet. *n.*, *pl.* **fla min gos** or **fla-min goes.**

flamingo—4½ ft. tall

flam ma ble (flam′ə bəl), easily set on fire; inflammable. *adj.*

Flan ders (flan′dərz), region in N Europe. It is now a part of Belgium, France, and the Netherlands. *n.*

flange (flanj), a raised edge, collar, or rim on a wheel, pulley, pipe, or other object. It is used to keep an object in place, fasten it to another, strengthen it, etc. Railroad cars have wheels with flanges to keep them on the track. *n.*

flange on railroad car wheel

flank (flangk), 1 side of an animal or person between the ribs and the hip. 2 side of a mountain, building, etc. 3 be at the side of: *A garage flanked the house.* 4 the far right or the far left side of an army, fort, or fleet. 5 get around the far right or the far left side of. 6 attack from or on the side. 1,2,4 *n.*, 3,5,6 *v.*

flan nel (flan′l), 1 a soft, warm, woolen or cotton cloth. 2 **flannels,** *pl.* clothes made of flannel. 3 made of flannel. 1,2 *n.*, 3 *adj.*

flan nel ette (flan′l et′), a soft, warm, cotton cloth with a nap that looks like flannel. *n.*

flap (flap), 1 swing or sway about loosely and with some noise: *The sails flapped in the wind.* 2 move (wings, arms, etc.) up and down: *The goose flapped its wings but could not rise from the ground.* 3 fly by flapping the wings: *The bird flapped away.* 4 a flapping motion; flapping noise: *the flap of banners, the flap of a bird's wing.* 5 strike noisily with something broad and flat: *The clown's big shoes flapped along the ground.* 6 a blow from something broad and flat: *a flap from a beaver's tail.* 7 piece hanging or fastened at one edge only: *His coat had flaps on the pockets.* 1-3,5 *v.*, **flapped, flap ping;** 4,6,7 *n.*

flap jack (flap′jak′), pancake. *n.*

flap per (flap′ər), 1 something that flaps. A broad fin is sometimes called a flapper. 2 a young woman of the 1920's who dressed unconventionally and behaved with considerable freedom. *n.*

flare (fler *or* flar), 1 flame up briefly or unsteadily, sometimes with smoke: *A gust of wind made the torches flare.* 2 a bright, brief, unsteady flame; blaze: *The flare of a match showed us his face.* 3 a dazzling light that burns for a short time, used for signaling, lighting up a battlefield, etc.: *The Coast Guard vessel responded to the flare sent up from the lifeboat.* 4 a sudden outburst. 5 spread out in the shape of a bell: *The sides of a ship flare from the keel to the deck.* 6 a spreading out into a bell shape: *the flare of a skirt.* 1,5 *v.*, **flared, flar ing;** 2-4,6 *n.*

flare up or **flare out,** burst out into open anger, violence, etc.

flash (flash), 1 a sudden, short light or flame: *a flash of lightning.* 2 give out such a light or flame: *Lightning flashed in the sky. The lighthouse flashes signals twice a minute.* 3 come suddenly; pass quickly: *A train flashed by. A thought flashed across his mind.* 4 a sudden, short feeling or display: *a flash of hope, a flash of wit.* 5 a very brief time; instant: *It all happened in a flash.* 6 give out or send out like a flash: *Her eyes flashed defiance.* 7 send by telegraph, radio, etc.: *flash the news across the country.* 8 a news report sent by telegraph, radio, etc. 1,4,5,8 *n.*, *pl.* **flash es;** 2,3,6,7 *v.*

flash back (flash′bak′), a break in the continuous series of events of a novel, motion picture, etc., to introduce some earlier event or scene. *n.*

flash bulb (flash′bulb′), an electric bulb which gives out a brilliant flash of light for a very short time. It is used in taking photographs indoors or at night. *n.*

flash card (flash′kärd′), card bearing a letter, word, number, simple problem, or picture. In drills in elementary reading, arithmetic, etc., the teacher displays a flashcard briefly and the student gives a quick answer. *n.*

flash flood, a very sudden, violent flooding of a river, stream, etc.

flash light (flash′līt′), 1 a portable electric light, operated by batteries. 2 light that flashes, used in a lighthouse or for signaling. *n.*

flash y (flash′ē), 1 brilliant for a short time; flashing. 2 showy; gaudy. *adj.*, **flash i er, flash i est.**

flask (flask), a glass or metal bottle, especially one with a narrow neck. *n.*

flat[1] (flat), 1 smooth and level; even: *flat land. This floor is flat.* 2 at full length; horizontal: *The storm left the trees flat on the ground.* 3 the flat part: *with the flat of the sword. The palm of an open hand is the flat.* 4 land that is flat and level. 5 not very deep or thick: *A plate is flat.* 6 a shallow box or basket: *She started the plants in flats, planning to set them out in the garden in warm weather.* 7 with little air in it: *A nail or sharp stone can cause a flat tire.* 8 INFORMAL. a tire with little air in it. 9 not to be changed; positive: *A flat refusal is complete.* 10 not varied; fixed: *A flat rate has no extra charges.* 11 without much life, interest, flavor, etc.; dull: *a flat voice. Plain food tastes flat.* 12 not shiny or glossy: *a flat yellow.* 13 below the true pitch in music: *sing flat.* 14 one half step or half note below natural pitch in music. 15 such a tone or note: *music written in B flat.* 16 sign (♭) that shows such a tone. 17 in a flat manner; flatly: *I fell flat on the floor.* 18 exactly: *Her time for the race was two minutes flat.* 19 make or become flat. 1,2,5,7, 9-12,14 *adj.*, **flat ter, flat test;** 3, 4,6,8,15,16 *n.*, 13,17,18 *adv.*, 19 *v.*, **flat ted, flat ting.** [from a Scandinavian word of the 1300's, such as Icelandic *flatr*] —**flat′ly,** *adv.* —**flat′ness,** *n.*

fall flat, fail completely: *His attempts at clowning fell flat.*

flat[2] (flat), apartment or set of rooms on one floor. *n.* [Old English *flet*]

flat boat (flat′bōt′), a large boat with a flat bottom, used especially for carrying goods on a river or canal. *n.*

flat car (flat′kär′), a railroad freight car without a roof or sides. *n.*

flat fish (flat′fish′), any of a group of fishes having a flat body, and swimming on its side, with both eyes on the same side of the head; fluke. Halibut, flounder, and sole are flatfishes. *n.*, *pl.* **flat fish es** or **flat fish.**

flat-foot ed (flat′fut′id), having feet with flattened arches. *adj.*

flat i ron (flat′ī′ərn), a household

hat, āge, fär; let, ēqual, tėrm;
it, īce; hot, ōpen, ôrder;
oil, out; cup, pùt, rüle; ch, child;
ng, long; sh, she; th, thin;
ᵮH, then; zh, measure;

ə represents *a* in about,
e in taken, *i* in pencil,
o in lemon, *u* in circus.

appliance with a flat surface which is heated and used for smoothing cloth or pressing clothes; iron. *n.*

flat ten (flat′n), make or become flat: *Use a rolling pin to flatten the pie dough. The silk has been wrinkled, but it will flatten again if you iron it.* *v.*

flat ter (flat′ər), 1 praise too much or beyond the truth; praise insincerely: *Were you only flattering me when you said I sang well, or did you mean it?* 2 show as more beautiful or better looking than is the truth: *This picture flatters me.* 3 try to please or win over by flattering words or actions: *flatter someone with lots of attention and many gifts.* 4 cause to be pleased or feel honored: *You flatter me with your concern for my welfare.* *v.* —**flat′ter er,** *n.*

flat ter y (flat′ər ē), 1 act of flattering. 2 praise that is too much or untrue: *Some people use flattery to get favors.* *n.*, *pl.* **flat ter ies.**

flat top (flat′top′), INFORMAL. an aircraft carrier. *n.*

flat worm (flat′wèrm′), worm with a thin, flat body, that lives in water or as a parasite on some animal. Tapeworms are flatworms. *n.*

flaunt (flônt), 1 show off to impress others: *flaunt expensive new clothing before one's friends.* 2 wave proudly: *Flags and pennants flaunted from the masts of the ship.* *v.*

fla vor (flā′vər), 1 taste, especially a particular taste: *Chocolate and vanilla have different flavors.* 2 give added taste to; season: *The onion flavors the whole stew.* 3 thing used to give a certain taste to food or drink; flavoring. 4 a special quality: *Stories about ships*

flatfish

adj. adjective	*n.* noun
adv. adverb	*prep.* preposition
conj. conjunction	*pron.* pronoun
interj. interjection	*v.* verb
sing. singular	*pl.* plural

and sailors have a flavor of the sea. 1,3,4 *n.,* 2 *v.*

fla vor ing (flā′vər ing), thing used to give a particular taste to food or drink: *chocolate flavoring. n.*

flaw (flô), 1 a slight defect; fault; blemish: *A flaw in the dish caused it to break. Her nasty temper is the only flaw in her character.* 2 make or become defective: *The cut in the diamond showed that it was flawed. This wood flaws and splinters easily.* 1 *n.,* 2 *v.*

flaw less (flô′lis), without a flaw; perfect. *adj.* —**flaw′less ly,** *adv.* —**flaw′less ness,** *n.*

flax (flaks), 1 a slender, upright plant with small, narrow leaves, blue flowers, and slender stems. Linseed oil is made from its seeds. 2 the threadlike parts into which the stems of this plant separate. Flax is spun into thread and woven into linen. *n.*

flax en (flak′sən), 1 made of flax. 2 like the color of flax; pale-yellow: *Flaxen hair is very light. adj.*

flax seed (flaks′sēd′), seed of flax; linseed. Flaxseed is used to make linseed oil and in medicine. *n.*

flay (flā), 1 strip off the skin or outer covering of. 2 scold severely; criticize without pity or mercy. *v.*

flea (flē), a small, jumping insect without wings. Fleas live in the fur of dogs, cats, and other animals and feed on their blood. *n., pl.* **fleas.**

fleck (flek), 1 spot or patch of color or light; speck; mark: *Freckles are brown flecks on the skin.* 2 a small particle; flake: *a fleck of dust.* 3 mark with spots of color or light; speckle: *The bird's breast is flecked with brown.* 1,2 *n.,* 3 *v.*

fled (fled), past tense and past participle of **flee.** *The enemy fled when we attacked. The chicken has fled the coop. v.*

fledge (flej), 1 (of a young bird) grow the feathers needed for flying. 2 provide or cover with feathers: *The Indian fledged his arrows with eagles' feathers. v.,* **fledged, fledg ing.**

fledg ling or **fledge ling** (flej′ling), 1 a young bird just able to fly. 2 a young, inexperienced person. *n.*

flee (flē), 1 run away; get away by running: *The robbers tried to flee, but they were caught.* 2 run away from:

They fled the burning house. 3 go quickly; move swiftly: *The clouds are fleeing before the wind. v.,* **fled, flee ing.**

fleece (flēs), 1 wool that covers a sheep or similar animal. 2 the amount of wool cut off or shorn from a sheep at one time. 3 cut the fleece from. 4 strip of money or belongings; rob; cheat: *The gamblers fleeced him of all his money.* 1,2 *n.,* 3,4 *v.,* **fleeced, fleec ing.**

fleec y (flē′sē), 1 like a fleece; soft and white: *Fleecy clouds floated in the blue sky.* 2 covered with fleece. 3 made of fleece. *adj.,* **fleec i er, fleec i est.**

fleet[1] (flēt), 1 group of ships under one command: *the United States fleet.* 2 group of ships sailing together: *a fleet of fishing boats.* 3 group of airplanes, automobiles, or the like, moving or working together: *A fleet of trucks carried the lumber. n.* [Old English *flēot* ship, from *flēotan* to float]

fleet[2] (flēt), swiftly moving; rapid: *a fleet runner. adj.* [probably from a Scandinavian word of the 1500's, such as Icelandic *fliōtr* swift] —**fleet′ly,** *adv.* —**fleet′ness,** *n.*

fleet admiral, the naval officer of the highest rank in the United States Navy.

fleet ing (flē′ting), passing swiftly; soon gone: *a fleeting smile. adj.*

Flem ing (flem′ing), 1 person born or living in Flanders. 2 a Belgian whose native language is Flemish. 3 Sir **Alexander,** 1881-1955, Scottish bacteriologist who discovered penicillin. *n.*

Flem ish (flem′ish). 1 of or having to do with Flanders, its people, or their language. 2 the people of Flanders. 3 their language. 1 *adj.,* 2 *n.pl.,* 3 *n.sing.*

flesh (flesh), 1 the soft substance of the body that covers the bones and is covered by skin. Flesh consists mostly of muscles and fat. 2 meat. 3 the body, not the soul or spirit. 4 the human race; mankind. 5 all living creatures. 6 the soft part of fruits or vegetables; the part of fruits that can be eaten: *The flesh of a peach is yellow or white. n.*

flesh and blood, family or relatives by birth.

in the flesh, 1 alive. 2 in person.

flesh ly (flesh′lē), 1 of the flesh; bodily. 2 sensual. *adj.,* **flesh li er, flesh li est.**

flesh y (flesh′ē), 1 having much flesh; plump; fat. 2 of flesh; like flesh. *adj.,* **flesh i er, flesh i est.**

fleur-de-lis (flėr′də lē′), 1 design or device used in heraldry to represent an iris. A fleur-de-lis was formerly used

fleur-de-lis (def. 1)

as the coat of arms of the royal family of France. It is also a part of the Boy Scout badge. 2 the iris flower or plant. *n., pl.* **fleurs-de-lis** (flėr′də lēz′). [from French *fleur-de-lis* lily flower]

flew (flü), past tense of **fly**[2]. *The bird flew high in the air. v.*

flex (fleks), bend: *She flexed her stiff arm slowly. v.*

flex i bil i ty (flek′sə bil′ə tē), flexible quality: *The flexibility of rubber bands usually lessens as the rubber becomes old. n.*

flex i ble (flek′sə bəl), 1 easily bent; not stiff; bending without breaking: *Leather, rubber, and wire are flexible.* 2 easily adapted to fit various conditions; easily managed: *The actor's flexible voice accommodated itself to every emotion. adj.*

flex i bly (flek′sə blē), in a flexible manner; with flexibility. *adv.*

flick (flik), 1 a quick, light blow; sudden, snapping stroke: *By a flick of his whip, he drove the fly from the horse's head.* 2 the light, snapping sound of such a blow or stroke: *the flick of an electric light switch.* 3 strike lightly with a quick, snapping blow: *She flicked the dust from her shoes with a handkerchief.* 4 make a sudden, snapping stroke with: *The children flicked wet towels at each other.* 5 move quickly and lightly; flutter. 1,2 *n.,* 3-5 *v.*

flick er[1] (flik′ər), 1 shine or burn with a wavering, unsteady light: *The firelight flickered on the walls.* 2 a wavering, unsteady light or flame: *the flicker of an oil lamp.* 3 move quickly and lightly in and out or back and forth: *We heard the birds flicker among the leaves.* 4 a quick, light movement: *the flicker of an eyelash.* 5 a brief flash; spark: *The speaker failed to arouse the least flicker of enthusiasm in his audience.* 1,3 *v.,* 2,4,5 *n.* [Old English *flicorian*]

flick er[2] (flik′ər), large, common woodpecker of North America, with a brownish back and yellow markings on its wings and tail. *n.* [perhaps an imitation of its call]

flied (flīd), a past tense and past participle of **fly**[2] (def. 12). *The batter flied to center field. v.*

fli er (flī′ər), 1 person or thing that flies: *That eagle is a high flier.* 2 pilot of an airplane; aviator. 3 a very fast train, ship, bus, etc. 4 a small handbill. *n.* Also, **flyer.**

flies[1] (flīz), plural of **fly**[1] and **fly**[2]. *There are many flies on the window. Both batters hit flies to the outfield. n.*

flies[2] (flīz), a present tense of **fly**[2]. *A bird flies. She flies an airplane. v.*

flight[1] (flīt), 1 act or manner of flying: *the flight of a bird across the sky.*

2 distance a bird, bullet, airplane, etc., can fly. **3** group of things flying through the air together: *a flight of pigeons, a flight of arrows, a flight of six airplanes.* **4** trip in an aircraft, especially a scheduled trip on an airline. **5** airplane that makes a scheduled trip: *She took the three o'clock flight to Boston.* **6** a soaring above or beyond the ordinary: *a flight of fancy, a flight of the imagination.* **7** set of stairs or steps from one landing or story of a building to the next. *n.* [Old English *flyht,* related to *fly²*]

flight² (flīt), act of fleeing; running away; escape: *The flight of the prisoners was discovered. n.* [Middle English *fliht,* related to *flee*]

put to flight, force to flee: *Our soldiers put the enemy to flight.*

flight i ness (flī′tē nis), quality or condition of being flighty. *n.*

flight less (flīt′lis), unable to fly: *An ostrich is flightless but it can run with great speed. adj.*

flight y (flī′tē), **1** likely to have sudden fancies; full of whims; frivolous. **2** slightly crazy; light-headed. *adj.,* **flight i er, flight i est.**

flim si ly (flim′zə lē), in a flimsy manner. *adv.*

flim si ness (flim′zē nis), flimsy quality. *n.*

flim sy (flim′zē), **1** light and thin; slight; frail: *The tissue paper she used to wrap my present was flimsy and tore off.* **2** lacking seriousness or sense; feeble; shallow: *Their excuse for being late was so flimsy that no one really believed it. adj.,* **flim si er, flim si est.**

flinch (flinch), **1** draw back from difficulty, danger, or pain; shrink: *The baby flinched when he touched the hot radiator.* **2** act of drawing back. **1** *v.,* **2** *n.*

flippers (left, def. 1; right, def. 2)

fling (fling), **1** throw with force; throw: *fling a stone.* **2** a throw. **3** move hastily or violently; rush; dash: *In a rage the child flung out of the room.* **4** plunge or kick: *The excited horse flung about in its stall.* **5** time of doing as one pleases: *He had his fling when he was young.* **6** a lively Scottish dance. **7** INFORMAL. a try; attempt: *He had a fling at acting, but discovered he had no talent and*

returned to his law studies. **1,3,4** *v.,* **flung, fling ing; 2,5-7** *n.*

flint (flint), **1** a very hard, gray or brown stone which makes a spark when struck against steel. It is a kind of quartz. **2** piece of this used with steel to light fires, explode gunpowder, etc. **3** anything very hard or unyielding: *a heart of flint. n.*

Flint (flint), city in SE Michigan. *n.*

flint lock (flint′lok′), **1** gunlock in which a flint striking against steel makes sparks that explode the gunpowder. **2** an old-fashioned gun with such a gunlock. *n.*

flintlock (def. 1)

flint y (flin′tē), **1** made of flint; containing flint. **2** like flint; very hard; unyielding: *flinty stubbornness. adj.,* **flint i er, flint i est.**

flip (flip), **1** toss or move with a snap of a finger and thumb: *He flipped a coin on the counter.* **2** move with a jerk or toss: *flip the pages of a book. The branch flipped back and scratched her face.* **3** a flipping; snap; smart tap; sudden jerk: *The cat gave the kitten a flip on the ear. Since there was a tie, the winner was picked by the flip of a coin.* **1,2** *v.,* **flipped, flip ping; 3** *n.*

flip pan cy (flip′ən sē), flippant quality or behavior. *n., pl.* **flip pan cies.**

flip pant (flip′ənt), smart or pert in speech or manner; not respectful: *The cocky girl gave a flippant answer to her parents' question. adj.* **—flip′pant ly,** *adv.*

flip per (flip′ər), **1** a broad, flat limb especially adapted for swimming. Seals have flippers. **2** a molded rubber attachment for the human foot, used as an aid to swimming. *n.*

flirt (flėrt), **1** play at making love; make love without meaning it. **2** person who makes love without meaning it. **3** trifle; toy: *He flirted with the idea of going to Europe, even though he couldn't afford it.* **4** move quickly; flutter: *The Spanish dancer flirted her fan. The bird flirted from branch to branch.* **5** a quick movement or flutter: *With a flirt of its tail the squirrel ran off.* **1,3,4** *v.,* **2,5** *n.*

flir ta tion (flėr′tā′shən), **1** act of flirting. **2** a love affair that is not serious. *n.*

flir ta tious (flėr′tā′shəs), **1** inclined to flirt: *a flirtatious girl.* **2** having to do with flirtation: *a flirtatious glance. adj.* **—flir′ta′tious ly,** *adv.*

hat, āge, fär; let, ēqual, tėrm;
it, īce; hot, ōpen, ôrder;
oil, out; cup, pùt, rüle; ch, child;
ng, long; sh, she; th, thin;
ᵗH, then; zh, measure;

ə represents *a* in about,
e in taken, *i* in pencil,
o in lemon, *u* in circus.

flit (flit), **1** fly lightly and quickly; flutter: *Birds flitted from tree to tree.* **2** pass lightly and quickly: *Many idle thoughts flitted through his mind as he lay in the sun.* **3** a light, quick movement; flutter. **1,2** *v.,* **flit ted, flit ting; 3** *n.*

flitch (flich), side of a hog, salted and cured; a side of bacon. *n., pl.* **flitch es.**

float (flōt), **1** stay on top of or be held up by air, water, or other liquid. A cork will float, but a stone sinks. **2** anything that stays up or holds up something else in water. A raft or life preserver is a float. A cork on a fish line is a float. **3** move with a moving liquid; drift: *The boat floated out to sea.* **4** rest or move in a liquid, the air, etc.: *Clouds floated in the sky.* **5** cause to float: *float a ship.* **6** set going (a company, scheme, etc.); launch: *To get money the government floated an issue of bonds.* **7** a hollow, metal ball that regulates the level, supply, or outlet of a liquid. **8** a low, flat car that carries something to be shown in a parade. **1,3-6** *v.,* **2,7,8** *n.* **—float′er,** *n.*

float (def. 7) regulating water level. As water is used, the float drops, opening the valve and permitting more water to enter the tank.

flock (flok), **1** group of animals of one kind keeping, feeding, or moving together: *a flock of geese, a flock of sheep, a flock of birds.* **2** a large group; crowd: *Visitors came in flocks to the zoo to see the new gorilla.* **3** go or gather in a flock; come crowding: *Sheep usually flock together. The children flocked around the ice-cream stand.* **4** people of the same church group. **1,2,4** *n.,* **3** *v.*

floe (flō), field or sheet of floating ice. *n.*

adj. adjective	*n.* noun
adv. adverb	*prep.* preposition
conj. conjunction	*pron.* pronoun
interj. interjection	*v.* verb
sing. singular	*pl.* plural

flog (flog), whip very hard; beat with a whip or stick. *v.*, **flogged, flog ging.**

flood (flud), 1 a great flow of water over what is usually dry land: *The heavy rains caused a serious flood in the riverside district.* 2 **the Flood,** (in the Bible) the water that covered the earth in the time of Noah. 3 flow over: *The river flooded our fields.* 4 fill much fuller than usual; fill to overflowing: *A wave flooded the holes I had dug in the sand.* 5 a great outpouring of anything: *a flood of light, a flood of words.* 6 fill, cover, or overcome like a flood: *The TV star was flooded with requests for autographs. The room was flooded with moonlight.* 7 become covered or filled with water: *During the thunderstorm, our cellar flooded.* 8 rise of the tide; flow. 1,2,5,8 *n.,* 3,4,6,7 *v.*

flood control, control of rivers that tend to overflow by the use of dams, levees, dikes, extra outlets, reforestation, etc.

flood gate (flud´gāt´), 1 gate in a canal, river, stream, etc., to control the flow of water. 2 thing that controls the flow or passage of anything. *n.*

flood light (flud´līt´), 1 lamp that gives a broad beam of light. 2 a broad beam of light from such a lamp. 3 to light with a floodlight: *The baseball field was brightly floodlighted for the night game.* 1,2 *n.,* 3 *v.,* **flood light ed** or **flood lit** (flud´lit´), **flood light ing.**

flood plain (flud´plān´), plain bordering a river and made of soil deposited by floods. *n.*

flood wa ter (flud´wô´tər *or* flud´-wot´ər), water flooding dry land. *n.*

floor (flôr), 1 the part of a room to walk on: *The floor of this room is made of wood.* 2 put a floor in or on: *The carpenter will floor this room with oak.* 3 a flat surface at the bottom: *They dropped their net to the floor of the ocean.* 4 story of a building: *Five families live on the fourth floor.* 5 right to speak: *"You may have the floor," said the chairman.* 6 knock down: *The boxer floored his opponent with one blow.* 7 INFORMAL. confuse; puzzle: *The last question on the examination completely floored us.* 1,3-5 *n.,* 2,6,7 *v.*

floor ing (flôr´ing), 1 floor. 2 floors. 3 material for making or covering

floors, such as wood, linoleum, or tile. *n.*

floor walk er (flôr´wô´kər), person employed in a large store to direct the work of salesclerks and give assistance to customers. *n.*

flop (flop), 1 move loosely or heavily; flap around clumsily: *The fish flopped helplessly on the deck.* 2 fall, drop, throw, or move heavily or clumsily: *The tired boy flopped down into a chair.* 3 a flopping: *Every step caused a flop of the wide brim of her hat.* 4 a dull, heavy sound made by flopping. 5 change or turn suddenly. 6 INFORMAL. failure: *His last book was a flop.* 7 INFORMAL. fail: *Her first business venture flopped completely.* 1,2,5,7 *v.,* **flopped, flopping;** 3,4,6 *n.*

flop py (flop´ē), INFORMAL. tending to flop; flopping: *a floppy hat.* *adj.,* **flop pi er, flop pi est.**

flo ra (flôr´ə), plants: *the flora of the West Indies.* *n.* [from *Flora,* the Roman goddess of flowers]

flo ral (flôr´əl), 1 of or having to do with flowers: *floral decorations.* 2 resembling flowers: *floral patterns.* *adj.*

Flo rence (flôr´əns), city in central Italy. *n.*

Flo ren tine (flôr´ən tēn´), 1 of or having to do with Florence. 2 person born or living in Florence. 1 *adj.,* 2 *n.*

flo ret (flôr´it), a small flower. *n.*

flo rid (flôr´id), 1 highly colored; ruddy: *a florid complexion.* 2 much ornamented; flowery; showy: *florid language, florid architecture.* *adj.* —**flo´rid ly,** *adv.* —**flo´rid ness,** *n.*

Flo ri da (flôr´ə də), one of the southeastern states of the United States. *Capital:* Tallahassee. *n.*

flo rin (flôr´ən), any of various gold or silver coins used in different countries of Europe, especially an English silver and nickel coin worth ten pence. *n.*

flo rist (flôr´ist), person who raises or sells flowers. *n.*

floss (flôs), 1 short, loose, silk fibers. 2 a shiny, untwisted silk thread made from such fibers. It is used for embroidery. Waxed floss is used for cleaning between the teeth. 3 soft, silky fluff or fibers. Milkweed pods contain white floss. *n.*

floss y (flô´sē), 1 of floss. 2 like floss. *adj.,* **floss i er, floss i est.**

flo til la (flō til´ə), 1 a small fleet. 2 fleet of small ships. *n., pl.* **flo til las.**

flot sam (flot´səm), wreckage of a ship or its cargo found floating on the sea. *n.*

flounce¹ (flouns), 1 go with an angry or impatient fling of the body: *flounce out of the room in a rage.* 2 an angry or impatient fling of the body. 1 *v.,* **flounced, flounc ing;** 2 *n.* [perhaps from a Scandinavian word of the

1500's, such as Swedish (dialect) *flunsa* plunge]

flounce² (flouns), 1 a wide strip of cloth, gathered along the top edge and sewed to a dress, skirt, etc., for trimming; a wide ruffle. 2 trim with a flounce or flounces. 1 *n.,* 2 *v.,* **flounced, flounc ing.** [earlier *frounce,* from French of the 1300's *froncir* to fold, wrinkle].

floun der¹ (floun´dər), 1 struggle awkwardly without making much progress; plunge about: *After the storm, horses and cattle were found floundering in the deep snowdrifts.* 2 be clumsy or confused and make mistakes: *Frightened by the audience, the children floundered through their songs and dances.* *v.* [perhaps a blend of *founder¹* and *blunder*]

floun der² (floun´dər), flatfish that has a large mouth. The flounder lives in salt water and is much used for food. *n., pl.* **floun ders** or **floun der.** [from French of the 1400's *flondre*]

flour (flour), 1 the fine meal made by grinding and sifting wheat or other grain. It is used to make bread, rolls, cake, etc. 2 cover or sprinkle with flour. 1 *n.,* 2 *v.*

flour ish (flèr´ish), 1 grow or develop with vigor; do well; thrive: *Your radishes are flourishing. Our newspaper business flourished.* 2 wave in the air: *She flourished the letter when she saw us.* 3 a waving about: *He removed his hat with a flourish.* 4 an extra ornament or curve in handwriting. 5 a showy trill or passage in music: *a flourish of trumpets.* 6 a showy display: *The agent showed us about the house with much flourish.* 1,2 *v.,* 3-6 *n., pl.* **flour ish es.**

flourish (def. 4)
flourishes
in a signature

flour y (flou´rē), 1 of or like flour. 2 covered or white with flour. *adj.*

flout (flout), treat with contempt or scorn; scoff at; mock: *You are foolish to flout such good advice.* *v.*

flow (flō), 1 run like water; move in a current or stream: *Blood flows through our bodies.* 2 current; stream: *There is a constant flow of water from the spring.* 3 pour out; pour along: *The crowd flowed out of the town hall and down the main street.* 4 move easily or smoothly; glide: *a flowing movement in a dance, flowing verse.* 5 any smooth, steady movement: *a rapid flow of speech.* 6 hang loose and waving: *flowing robes, a flowing tie.* 7 act or way of flowing: *a flow of blood.* 8 rate of flowing: *a flow of two feet per second.* 9 the flowing of the tide toward the shore; rise of the tide. 1,3,4,6 *v.*, 2,5,7-9 *n.*

flower
(def. 1)

flow er (flou'ər), 1 part of a plant or tree that produces the seed; blossom. A flower is a shortened branch with modified leaves called petals. Flowers are often beautifully colored or shaped. 2 plant grown for its blossoms. 3 have flowers; produce flowers; bloom. 4 cover or decorate with flowers. 5 the finest part: *the flower of the country's youth.* 6 time when a thing is at its best: *a person in the flower of life.* 7 be at its best. 1,2,5,6 *n.*, 3,4,7 *v.* —**flow'er like', adj.**

flow ered (flou'ərd), 1 having flowers. 2 covered or decorated with flowers: *a flowered bowl, flowered silk. adj.*

flow er et (flou'ər it), a small flower. *n.*

flow er less (flou'ər lis), having no flowers. *adj.*

flow er pot (flou'ər pot'), pot to hold soil for a plant to grow in. *n.*

flow er y (flou'ər ē), 1 having many flowers. 2 full of fine words and fanciful expressions: *a flowery speech. adj.,* **flow er i er, flow er i est.**

flown (flōn), past participle of **fly².** *The bird has flown. The flag is flown on all national holidays. v.*

flu (flü), influenza. *n.*

fluc tu ate (fluk'chü āt), rise and fall; change continually; waver: *Prices fluctuate. The temperature fluctuates from day to day. v.,* **fluc tu at ed, fluc tu at ing.**

fluc tu a tion (fluk'chü ā'shən), a rising and falling; continual change; wavering. *n.*

flue (flü), tube, pipe, or other enclosed passage for smoke or hot air. A chimney often has several flues. *n.*

flu en cy (flü'ən sē), 1 a smooth, easy flow: *The senator had great fluency of speech.* 2 easy, rapid speaking or writing. *n.*

flu ent (flü'ənt), 1 flowing smoothly or easily: *Long practice enabled the American to speak fluent French.* 2 speaking or writing easily and rapidly: *He is a fluent lecturer. adj.* —**flu'ent ly, adv.**

fluff (fluf), 1 soft, light, downy particles: *Woolen blankets often have fluff on them.* 2 a soft, light, downy mass: *The*

little kitten looked like a fluff of fur. 3 shake or puff out (hair, feathers, etc.) into a soft, light, downy mass. 1,2 *n.,* 3 *v.*

fluff i ness (fluf'ē nis), fluffy quality or condition. *n.*

fluff y (fluf'ē), 1 soft and light like fluff: *a fluffy shawl.* 2 covered or filled with fluff; downy: *fluffy baby chicks, a fluffy pillow. adj.,* **fluff i er, fluff i est.**

flu id (flü'id), 1 any liquid or gas; something that will flow. Water, mercury, air, and oxygen are fluids. 2 like a liquid or gas; flowing: *She poured the fluid mass of hot metal into a mold to harden.* 3 changing easily; not fixed: *The situation on the battlefield was fluid.* 1 *n.,* 2,3 *adj.* —**flu'id ly, adv.**

fluke¹
(def. 1)

fluke¹ (flük), 1 the flat, three-cornered piece at the end of each arm of an anchor, which catches in the ground and holds it fast. 2 the barbed head of an arrow or harpoon. 3 either of the two halves of a whale's tail. *n.* [perhaps special use of *fluke³* (because of its shape)]

fluke² (flük), INFORMAL. a lucky stroke in games, business, or life. *n.* [origin uncertain]

fluke³ (flük), 1 flatfish. 2 a parasitic flatworm shaped somewhat like a flatfish; trematode. *n.* [Old English *flōc* flatfish]

flume (flüm), 1 a deep and very narrow valley with a stream running through it. 2 a large, inclined trough or chute for carrying water. Flumes are used to transport logs or to furnish water for power. *n.*

flume (def. 2)

flung (flung), past tense and past participle of **fling.** *I flung my coat on the chair. The paper was flung into the fire. v.*

flunk (flungk), INFORMAL. 1 fail in schoolwork: *She flunked the history examination but passed all the others.* 2 cause to fail: *His answers on the final*

hat, āge, fär; let, ēqual, tėrm;
it, īce; hot, ōpen, ôrder;
oil, out; cup, pùt, rüle; ch, child;
ng, long; sh, she; th, thin;
ᵀH, then; zh, measure;

ə represents *a* in about,
e in taken, *i* in pencil,
o in lemon, *u* in circus.

test flunked him. 3 to mark or grade as having failed. *v.*

flunk out, INFORMAL. dismiss or be dismissed from school or college for failing work.

flunk ey (flung'kē), flunky. *n., pl.* **flunk eys.**

flunk y (flung'kē), 1 a flattering, fawning person. 2 footman, *n., pl.* **flunk ies.**

flu o res cence (flü'ə res'ns), 1 a giving off of light by a substance exposed to X rays, ultraviolet rays, or certain other rays, which continues only as long as exposure to these rays continues. 2 property of a substance that causes this. It is an ability to transform radiation so as to emit rays of a different wavelength or color. 3 light given off in this way. *n.*

flu o res cent (flü'ə res'nt), that gives off light by fluorescence. Fluorescent substances glow in the dark when exposed to X rays. *adj.*

fluorescent lamp, an electric lamp consisting of a tube in which a coating of fluorescent powder exposed to ultraviolet rays gives off a light that is cooler and less glaring than incandescent light.

fluor i date (flür'ə dāt), add small amounts of a fluorine compound to drinking water, especially to decrease tooth decay in children. *v.,* **fluor i dat ed, fluor i dat ing.**

fluor i da tion (flür'ə dā'shən), act or process of fluoridating. *n.*

flu o ride (flü'ə rīd'), compound of fluorine and another element or radical. *n.*

flu o rine (flü'ə rēn'), a pale-yellow, bad-smelling, poisonous gas which occurs only in combination with certain other elements. It is the most active of all the chemical elements and is used in small amounts in water to prevent tooth decay. *n.*

fluor o scope (flür'ə skōp), device for examining the inner parts of a human body, machine, etc., by placing it between a source of radiation, such as an X-ray machine, and a fluorescent screen. The parts of the object under examination cast shadows on the screen

329

flurry

adj.	adjective	*n.*	noun
adv.	adverb	*prep.*	preposition
conj.	conjunction	*pron.*	pronoun
interj.	interjection	*v.*	verb
sing.	singular	*pl.*	plural

in direct proportion to the amount of radiation they absorb. *n.*

flur ry (flėr′ē), **1** a sudden gust: *A flurry of wind upset the small sailboat.* **2** a light fall of rain or snow. **3** a sudden commotion: *a flurry of alarm.* **4** fluster; excite; agitate: *Noise in the audience flurried the actor so that he forgot his lines.* 1-3 *n., pl.* **flur ries;** 4 *v.,* **flurried, flur ry ing.**

flush (flush), **1** become red suddenly; blush; glow: *Her face flushed when they laughed at her.* **2** cause to blush or glow: *Exercise flushed her face.* **3** a rosy glow or blush: *The flush of sunrise was on the clouds.* **4** rush suddenly; flow rapidly: *Embarrassment caused the blood to flush to my cheeks.* **5** a sudden rush; rapid flow. **6** send a sudden flow of water over or through: *The city streets were flushed to make them clean.* **7** make joyful and proud; excite: *The team was flushed with its first victory.* **8** an excited condition or feeling: *the flush of victory.* **9** glowing vigor; freshness: *the first flush of youth.* **10** fly or start up suddenly: *The bird flushed from its cover under the bush.* **11** cause to fly or start up suddenly: *The hunter's dog flushed a partridge in the woods.* **12** even; level: *The edge of the new shelf must be flush with the old one.* **13** so as to be level; evenly: *The two edges met flush.* **14** well supplied; having plenty: *Payday is the only day I am flush with money.* 1,2,4,6,7,10,11 *v.,* 3,5,8,9 *n., pl.* **flush es;** 12,14 *adj.,* 13 *adv.*

flus ter (flus′tər), **1** make nervous and excited; confuse: *The honking of horns flustered the driver, and he stalled his automobile.* **2** nervous excitement; confusion. 1 *v.,* 2 *n.*

flute (flüt), **1** a long, slender, pipelike musical instrument, played by blowing across a hole near one end. Different

flute
(def. 1)

notes are made by opening and closing holes along its side with the fingers or with keys. **2** play on a flute. **3** sing or whistle so as to sound like a flute. **4** a long, round groove. Some columns have flutes. **5** make long, round grooves in. 1,4 *n.,* 2,3,5 *v.,* **flut ed, flut ing.**

flut ed (flü′tid), having long, round grooves: *fluted columns. adj.*

flut ing (flü′ting), decoration made of long, round grooves. *n.*

fluting
on a column

flut ist (flü′tist), person who plays a flute. *n.*

flut ter (flut′ər), **1** wave back and forth quickly and lightly: *The flag fluttered in the breeze.* **2** move or flap the wings rapidly without flying or with short flights: *The chickens fluttered excitedly when they saw the dog.* **3** come or go with a trembling or wavy motion: *The young birds fluttered to the ground.* **4** move restlessly: *They fluttered about making preparations for the party.* **5** move quickly and unevenly; tremble: *My heart fluttered when I rose to give my speech.* **6** a fluttering: *the flutter of curtains in a breeze.* **7** a confused or excited condition: *The appearance of the queen caused a great flutter in the crowd.* 1-5 *v.,* 6,7 *n.*

flux (fluks), **1** a flow; a flowing. **2** continuous change: *New words and meanings keep the English language in a state of flux.* **3** an abnormal discharge of liquid matter from the body. **4** rosin or other substance used in soldering, welding, etc., to clean the surfaces of metals and help them join. *n., pl.* **flux es.**

fly¹ (flī), **1** any of a large group of insects that have two wings, including houseflies, mosquitoes, and gnats. **2** any insect with transparent wings, such as a May fly. **3** fishhook with feathers, silk, tinsel, etc., on it to make it look like an insect. *n., pl.* **flies.** [Old English *flēoge*]

fly² (flī), **1** move through the air with wings: *These birds fly long distances.* **2** float or wave in the air: *Our flag flies every day.* **3** cause to float or wave in the air: *The boys are flying kites.* **4** travel in an aircraft. **5** pilot (an aircraft). **6** carry in an aircraft: *They flew a large number of rare birds from Africa.* **7** move swiftly; go rapidly: *The ship flies before the wind.* **8** run away; flee: *fly from one's enemies.* **9** flap to cover

buttons on clothing. **10** piece of canvas forming an extra, outer top for a tent. **11** baseball batted high in the air. **12** bat a baseball high in the air. 1-8,12 *v.,* **flew, flown, fly ing** for 1-8, **flied, flying** for 12; 9-11 *n., pl.* **flies.** [Old English *flēogan*]

let fly, shoot or throw: *The hunter let fly an arrow.*

on the fly, while still in the air: *He caught the ball on the fly.*

fly catch er (flī′kach′ər), bird that catches flies and other insects while flying. *n.*

fly er (flī′ər), flier. *n.*

flying boat, seaplane with a boatlike hull and floats under its wings.

flying buttress, an arched support or brace built between the wall of a building and a supporting column to bear some of the weight of the roof.

flying colors, success; victory: *The team finished the tournament with flying colors.*

flying disk, flying saucer.

flying fish, a tropical sea fish that has winglike fins and can leap for some distance through the air.

flying jib, a small, triangular sail set in front of the regular jib.

flying saucer, an unidentified disklike object, reported in the sky over many different parts of the world, especially since about 1947.

fly leaf (flī′lēf′), a blank sheet of paper at the beginning or end of a book. *n., pl.* **fly leaves.**

fly pa per (flī′pā′pər), paper covered with a sticky or poisonous substance, used to catch or kill flies. *n.*

fly speck (flī′spek′), **1** a tiny spot left by a fly. **2** any tiny speck. **3** mark with flyspecks. 1,2 *n.,* 3 *v.*

fly way (flī′wā′), route usually followed by migrating birds. *n.*

fly weight (flī′wāt′), boxer who weighs less than 112 pounds. *n.*

fly wheel (flī′hwēl′), a heavy wheel attached to a machine to keep it and its parts moving at an even speed. *n.*

FM or **F.M.,** frequency modulation.

foal (fōl), **1** a young horse, donkey, etc.; colt or filly. **2** give birth to (a foal): *Our mare foaled twin colts last spring. When is she due to foal again?* 1 *n.,* 2 *v.*

foam (fōm), **1** mass of very small bub-

FLYING BUTTRESS

330

bles formed in a liquid by agitation, fermentation, boiling, etc. 2 form or gather foam; froth: *The soda foamed over the glass.* 3 break into foam: *The stream foams over the rocks.* 1 *n.*, 2,3 *v.*

foam i ness (fō′mē nis), foamy quality or condition. *n.*

foam rubber, a soft, spongy rubber used for mattresses, cushions, etc.

foam y (fō′mē), 1 covered with foam; foaming. 2 made of foam. 3 like foam. *adj.,* **foam i er, foam i est.**

fob (fob), 1 a small pocket for holding a watch, etc. 2 a short watch chain, ribbon, etc., that hangs out of such a pocket. 3 ornament worn at the end of such a chain, ribbon, etc. *n.*

f.o.b. or **F.O.B.,** free on board. The price $2500 f.o.b. Detroit, means that the $2500 does not pay for freight or other expenses after the article has been put on board a freight car at Detroit.

fo cal (fō′kəl), of a focus; having to do with a focus. The focal length of a lens is the distance of its focus from the optical center of the lens. *adj.*

fo ci (fō′sī), a plural of **focus.** *n.*

fo cus (fō′kəs), 1 point at which rays of light, heat, etc., meet after being reflected from a mirror or bent by a lens. 2 bring (rays of light, heat, etc.) to a focus: *The lens focused the sun's rays on a piece of paper and burned a hole in it.* 3 distance from a lens or mirror to the point where rays from it meet: *A near-sighted eye has a shorter focus than a normal eye.* 4 the correct adjustment of a lens, the eye, etc., to make a clear image: *If the camera is not brought into focus, the photograph will be blurred.* 5 adjust (a lens, the eye, etc.) to make a clear image: *His eyes were so tired that he had difficulty focusing them. A near-sighted person cannot focus accurately on distant objects.* 6 make (an image, etc.) clear by adjusting a lens, the eye, etc. 7 the central point of attraction, attention, activity. etc.: *The new baby was the focus of attention.* 8 concentrate: *When studying, he focused his mind on his lessons.* 1,3,4,7 *n.,* pl. **fo cus es** or **fo ci;** 2,5,6,8 *v.*

fod der (fod′ər), coarse food for horses, cattle, etc. Hay and cornstalks with their leaves are fodder. *n.*

foe (fō), enemy. *n.*

foe tus (fē′təs), fetus. *n., pl.* **foe-tus es.**

fog (fog), 1 cloud of fine drops of water just above the earth's surface; thick mist. 2 cover with fog. 3 make or become misty or cloudy: *Something fogged six of our photographs. My breath caused the window to fog.* 4 a confused or puzzled condition: *a fog of*

ignorance, *a fog of doubt.* 5 confuse; puzzle. 1,4 *n.*, 2,3,5 *v.*, **fogged, fog-ging.**

fog gi ness (fog′ē nis), foggy or misty condition. *n.*

fog gy (fog′ē), 1 having much fog; misty. 2 not clear; dim; blurred: *Their ideas are confused and rather foggy.* *adj.,* **fog gi er, fog gi est.**

fog horn (fog′hôrn′), horn that warns ships in foggy weather. *n.*

fo gy (fō′gē), old-fashioned person; person who is behind the times. *n., pl.* **fo gies.**

foi ble (foi′bəl), a weak point; weakness: *Talking too much is one of my foibles.* *n.*

foil[1] (foil), prevent from carrying out plans; get the better of; outwit: *Quick thinking by the bank clerk foiled the robbers, and they were captured.* *v.* [from French of the 1300's *fouler* trample]

FOCUS

LENS

focus (def. 1)—Rays of light are brought to a focus by the lens.

foil[2] (foil), 1 metal beaten, hammered, or rolled into a very thin sheet: *Candy is sometimes wrapped in foil to keep it fresh.* 2 anything that makes something else look or seem better by contrast: *The green dress was a foil for her red hair.* *n.* [from French of the 1300's *foille,* from Latin *folia* leaves]

foil[3] (foil), a long, narrow sword with a knob or button on the point to prevent injury, used in fencing. *n.* [origin uncertain.]

foist (foist), palm off as genuine; impose by fraud: *That chain of stores foists inferior goods on its customers.* *v.*

fold[1] (fōld), 1 bend or double over on itself: *You fold a letter or your napkin.* 2 layer of something folded; pleat: *a fold of linen.* 3 mark or line made by folding. 4 bend until close to the body: *You fold your arms. A bird folds its wings.* 5 put the arms around and hold tenderly: *He folded the crying child to him.* 6 wrap: *She folded the pills in a blue paper.* 1,4-6 *v.,* 2,3 *n.* [Old English *faldan, fealdan*]

fold[2] (fōld), 1 pen to keep sheep in. 2 a church group; congregation. *n.* [Old English *falod*]

-fold, *suffix forming adjectives and adverbs.* 1 _____ times as many; _____ times as great: *Tenfold = ten times as many.* 2 formed or divided into _____ parts: *Manifold = formed in many parts.* [Old English *-feald*]

hat, āge, fär; let, ēqual, tėrm; it, īce; hot, ōpen, ôrder; oil, out; cup, pu̇t, rüle; ch, child; ng, long; sh, she; th, thin; ₮H, then; zh, measure;

ə represents *a* in about, *e* in taken, *i* in pencil, *o* in lemon, *u* in circus.

fold er (fōl′dər), 1 holder for papers made by folding a piece of stiff paper once. 2 pamphlet made of one or more folded sheets. 3 person or thing that folds. *n.*

fo li age (fō′lē ij), leaves of a plant. *n.*

fo li o (fō′lē ō), 1 a large sheet of paper folded once to make two leaves, or four pages, of a book. 2 volume consisting of sheets folded once (that is, with four pages to each sheet); volume having pages of the largest size. 3 having to do with or having the form of a folio. 4 the page number of a printed book. 1,2,4 *n., pl.* **fo li os;** 3 *adj.*

folk (fōk), 1 people: *Most city folk know very little about farming.* 2 tribe or nation. 3 **folks,** *pl.* **a** people. **b** INFORMAL. relatives: *How are all your folks?* 4 of or having to do with the common people, their beliefs, legends, customs, etc. 1-3 *n., pl.* **folk** or **folks** for 1,2; 4 *adj.*

folk dance, 1 dance originating and handed down among the common people. 2 music for it.

folk lore (fōk′lôr′), beliefs, legends, customs, etc., of a people or tribe. *n.*

folk singer, person who sings folk songs.

folk song, 1 song originating and handed down among the common people. 2 song imitating a real folk song: *"Oh! Susanna" is a folk song written by Stephen Foster.*

folk sy (fōk′sē), INFORMAL. 1 sociable; friendly. 2 simple; unpretentious. *adj.,* **folk si er, folk si est.**

folk tale, story or legend originating and handed down among the common people.

fol li cle (fol′ə kəl), a small cavity, sac, or gland in the body. Hair grows from follicles. *n.*

fol low (fol′ō), 1 go or come after: *Sheep follow a leader. April follows March. You lead; we'll follow.* 2 result from; result: *Misery follows war. If you eat too much candy, a stomach ache will follow.* 3 go along: *Follow this road to the corner.* 4 pursue: *The dogs followed the fox.* 5 act according to; take as a guide; use; obey: *Follow her ad-*

adj.	adjective	*n.*	noun
adv.	adverb	*prep.*	preposition
conj.	conjunction	*pron.*	pronoun
interj.	interjection	*v.*	verb
sing.	singular	*pl.*	plural

vice. **6** keep the eyes or attention on: *I could not follow that bird's flight.* **7** keep the mind on; keep up with and understand: *Try to follow the President's speech.* **8** take as one's work: *She expects to follow the profession of law. A sailor follows the sea. v.*

follow through, continue a stroke, motion, plan, etc., through to the end.

follow up, **1** follow closely and steadily. **2** carry out to the end. **3** act upon with energy.

fol low er (fol′ō ər), **1** person or thing that follows. **2** person who follows the ideas or beliefs of another: *Christians are followers of Christ.* **3** attendant; servant. *n.*

fol low ing (fol′ō ing), **1** group of followers. **2** that follows; next after: *If that was Sunday, then the following day must have been Monday.* **3 the following,** persons or things now to be named, related, described, etc. **1,3** *n.,* **2** *adj.*

fol ly (fol′ē), **1** a being foolish; lack of sense; unwise conduct: *It was folly to eat too much on the picnic.* **2** a foolish act, practice, or idea; something silly. *n., pl.* **fol lies.**

fo ment (fō ment′), foster (trouble, rebellion, etc.); promote: *Three sailors were fomenting a mutiny on the ship. v.*

fond (fond), **1** loving or liking: *a fond look, fond of children.* **2** loving foolishly or too much. **3** cherished: *fond hopes. adj.* —**fond′ly,** *adv.* —**fond′ness,** *n.*

fon dle (fon′dl), handle or treat with fondness; pet; caress: *They fondled the baby kittens. v.,* **fon dled, fon dling.**

font (font), **1** basin holding water for baptism. **2** basin for holy water. **3** fountain; source. *n.*

food (füd), **1** anything that plants, animals, or people eat, drink, or take in that makes them live and grow: *Milk and green vegetables are valuable foods for young people.* **2** what is eaten: *Give him food and drink.* **3** anything that causes growth: *Books are food for the mind. n.*

food stuff (füd′stuf′), material for food. Grain and meat are foodstuffs. *n.*

fool (fül), **1** person without sense; person who acts unwisely. **2** clown formerly kept by a king or lord to amuse

people; jester. **3** act like a fool for fun; play; joke: *I was only fooling.* **4** make a fool of; deceive; trick: *You can't fool me.* **1,2** *n.,* **3,4** *v.*

fool with, INFORMAL. meddle foolishly with.

fool har di ness (fül′här′dē nis), foolish boldness; rashness. *n.*

fool har dy (fül′här′dē), foolishly bold; rash. *adj.,* **fool har di er, fool har di est.**

fool ish (fü′lish), without sense; unwise; silly: *foolish notions. adj.* —**fool′ish ly,** *adv.* —**fool′ish ness,** *n.*

fool proof (fül′prüf′), INFORMAL. so safe or simple that even a fool can use or do it: *a foolproof device, a foolproof scheme. adj.*

fools cap (fülz′kap′), writing paper in sheets from 12 to 13½ inches wide and 15 to 17 inches long. *n.*

fool's gold, mineral that looks like gold, especially an iron or copper pyrite.

foot (füt), **1** the end part of a leg; part that a person, animal, or thing stands on. **2** part opposite the head of something; end toward which the feet are put: *the foot of a bed.* **3** the lowest part; bottom; base: *the foot of a column, the foot of a hill, the foot of a page.* **4** part of a stocking that covers the foot. **5** walk: *We're footing it instead of riding today. The girls footed the whole ten miles.* **6** measure of length, twelve inches. 3 feet = 1 yard. **7** one of the parts into which a line of poetry is divided. This line has four feet: "The boy│stood on│the burn│ing deck." **8** add: *Foot this column of numbers.* **9** INFORMAL. pay (a bill, etc.): *I'll foot the bill for lunch.* **1-4,6,7** *n., pl.* **feet; 5,8,9** *v.*

on foot, standing or walking.

put one's foot down, make up one's mind and act firmly.

under foot, in the way.

foot ball (füt′bôl′), **1** game played with a large, inflated, leather ball by two teams of eleven players each on a field with a goal at each end. The players try to score by carrying the ball over the goal line by a run or pass, or by kicking it through the goal posts. **2** ball used in this game. *n.*

foot board (füt′bôrd′), **1** board or small platform on which to support the feet. **2** an upright piece across the foot of a bed. *n.*

foot bridge (füt′brij′), bridge for people on foot only. *n.*

foot-can dle (füt′kan′dl), unit for measuring illumination. It is the amount of light produced by a standard candle on a surface at a distance of one foot. *n.*

foot ed (füt′id), having a foot or feet. *adj.*

foot fall (füt′fôl′), sound of steps coming or going. *n.*

foot hill (füt′hil′), a low hill at the base of a mountain or mountain range. *n.*

foot hold (füt′hōld′), **1** place to put a foot; support for the feet: *I climbed the steep cliff by getting footholds in cracks in the rock.* **2** a firm footing or position: *It is hard to break a habit after it has a foothold. n.*

foot ing (füt′ing), **1** a firm placing or position of the feet: *He lost his footing and fell down on the ice.* **2** place to put a foot; support for the feet: *The steep cliff gave us no footing.* **3** a firm position: *The newly rich family struggled for a footing in society.* **4** condition; position; relationship: *The United States and Canada are on a friendly footing. n.*

foot lights (füt′līts′), row of lights at the front of a stage. *n.pl.*

foot man (füt′mən), a male servant who answers the bell, waits on the table, goes with an automobile or carriage to open the door, etc. Footmen usually wear special clothes. *n., pl.* **foot men.**

foot note (füt′nōt′), note at the bottom of a page about something on the page. *n.*

foot pad (füt′pad′), OLD USE. a highway robber who goes on foot. *n.*

foot path (füt′path′), path for people on foot only. *n., pl.* **foot paths** (füt′-paᴛʜz′ *or* füt′paths′).

foot-pound (füt′pound′), unit of work or energy. It is equal to the quantity of energy needed to raise a weight of one pound to a height of one foot. *n.*

foot print (füt′print′), mark made by a foot. *n.*

foot rest (füt′rest′), support to rest the feet on. *n.*

foot soldier, infantryman.

foot sore (füt′sôr′), having sore feet from much walking: *The hike left us footsore and hungry. adj.*

foot step (füt′step′), **1** a person's step. **2** distance covered in one step. **3** sound of steps. **4** footprint.

follow in someone's footsteps, do as someone else has done.

foot stool (füt′stül′), a low stool on which to place the feet when seated. *n.*

foot work (füt′werk′), way of using the feet: *Footwork is important in boxing and dancing. n.*

fop (fop), a vain man who is very fond of fine clothes and has affected manners; dandy. *n.*

fop per y (fop′ər ē), behavior or dress of a fop. *n., pl.* **fop per ies.**

fop pish (fop′ish), **1** of a fop; suitable for a fop: *foppish dress.* **2** vain; affected: *foppish manners. adj.*

for (fôr; *unstressed* fər), **1** in place of: *We used boxes for chairs.* **2** in support of; in favor of: *She is for changing the tax laws.* **3** in consideration of; in return: *These apples are twelve for a dollar. We thanked him for his kindness.* **4** with the object or purpose of: *She went for a walk.* **5** in order to become, have, keep, get to, etc.: *The navy trains men for sailors. He ran for his life. She is hunting for her cat. He has just left for New York.* **6** meant to belong to or be used with; suited to: *a box for gloves, a present for you, books for children.* **7** with a feeling toward: *She has an eye for beauty. We longed for home.* **8** with respect or regard to: *It is warm for April. Eating too much is bad for one's health.* **9** because of; by reason of: *shout for joy. They were punished for stealing. A party was given for her.* **10** because: *We can't go, for it is raining.* **11** as far as: *We walked for a mile.* **12** as long as: *He worked for an hour.* **13** as being: *They know it for a fact.* **14** in spite of: *For all her faults, we still like her.* **15** in proportion to: *For one poisonous snake there are many harmless ones.* **16** to the amount of: *His father gave him a check for $20.* 1-9,11-16 *prep.,* 10 *conj.*

Oh! for, I wish that I might have: *Oh! for a swim.*

fo rage (fôr′ij), **1** hay, grain, or other food for horses, cattle, etc. **2** hunt or search for food: *Rabbits forage in our garden.* **3** get by hunting or searching about. **4** search about; hunt: *The boys foraged for old metal.* **5** plunder: *The soldiers foraged nearby villages.* 1 *n.,* 2-5 *v.,* **fo raged, fo rag ing.**

fo rag er (fôr′i jər), person who forages. *n.*

fo ray (fôr′ā), **1** a raid for plunder: *Armed bandits made forays on the villages and took away cattle.* **2** lay waste; plunder; pillage. 1 *n.,* 2 *v.*

for bade or **for bad** (fər bad′), past tense of **forbid.** *The doctor forbade the sick boy to leave his bed.* *v.*

for bear[1] (fôr ber′ or fôr bar′), **1** hold back; keep from doing, saying, using, etc.: *I forbore telling her the truth because I knew it would upset her.* **2** be patient; control oneself. *v.,* **for bore, for borne, for bear ing.** [Old English *forberan*]

for bear[2] (fôr′ber or fôr′bar), forebear; ancestor. *n.* [*fore* + *be* + *-er*[1]]

for bear ance (fôr ber′əns or fôr-bar′əns), **1** act of forbearing. **2** patience; self-control. *n.*

for bid (fər bid′), not allow; say one must not do; make a rule against; prohibit: *The teacher forbade running in the halls. If my parents had known that I was going, they would have forbidden it.* *v.,* **for bade** or **for bad, for bid den** or **for bid, for bid ding.**

for bid den (fər bid′n), **1** not allowed; against the law or rules: *Eve ate the forbidden fruit.* **2** a past participle of **forbid.** *My parents have forbidden me to swim in that river.* 1 *adj.,* 2 *v.*

for bid ding (fər bid′ing), causing fear or dislike; looking dangerous or unpleasant: *The coast was rocky and forbidding. adj.*

for bore (fôr bôr′), past tense of **forbear**[1]. *She forbore from showing her disappointment.* *v.*

for borne (fôr bôrn′), past participle of **forbear**[1]. *We have forborne from vengeance.* *v.*

force (fôrs), **1** active power; strength: *The speeding car struck the tree with great force.* **2** strength used against a person or thing; violence: *We had to use force to open the locked suitcase.* **3** power to control, influence, persuade, convince, etc.; effectiveness: *She writes with force.* **4** make (a person) act against his will; make do by force: *Give it to me at once, or I will force you to.* **5** get or take by force: *They forced their way in.* **6** break open or through by force: *force a lock, force a door.* **7** make by an unusual or unnatural effort; strain: *The unhappy child forced a smile.* **8** hurry the growth or development of (flowers, fruits, a child's mind, etc.). **9** (in baseball) to cause (a runner) to be put out by requiring him to try to advance to the next base. **10** group of people working or acting together: *our office force, the police force.* **11 forces,** *pl.* army, navy, etc. **12** cause that produces, changes, or stops the motion of a body: *the force of gravitation, magnetic force.* 1-3,10-12 *n.,* 4-9 *v.,* **forced, forc ing.**

by main force, by using full strength: *conquer a country by main force.*

in force, 1 in effect or operation: *The old rules are still in force.* **2** with full strength: *The enemy attacked in force.*

forced (fôrst), **1** made, compelled, or driven by force: *The work of slaves was forced labor.* **2** done by unusual effort: *The soldiers made a forced march of three days.* **3** not natural; strained: *She hid her dislike with a forced smile. adj.*

force ful (fôrs′fəl), having much force; strong; powerful; vigorous; effective: *a forceful manner. adj.* **—force′ful ly,** *adv.* **—force′ful ness,** *n.*

for ceps (fôr′seps), small pincers or tongs used by surgeons, dentists, etc., for seizing and holding. Dentists use forceps for pulling teeth. *n., pl.* **for ceps.**

for ci ble (fôr′sə bəl), **1** made or done by force; using force: *a forcible entrance into a house.* **2** having or showing force; strong; powerful;

hat, āge, fär; let, ēqual, tèrm; it, īce; hot, ōpen, ôrder; oil, out; cup, pùt, rüle; ch, child; ng, long; sh, she; th, thin; ŦH, then; zh, measure;

ə represents *a* in about, *e* in taken, *i* in pencil, *o* in lemon, *u* in circus.

convincing: *a forcible speaker. adj.*

for ci bly (fôr′sə blē), in a forcible manner. *adv.*

ford (fôrd), **1** place where a river, stream, or other body of water is not too deep to cross by walking or driving through the water. **2** cross (a river, etc.) by walking or driving through the water. 1 *n.,* 2 *v.*

Ford (fôrd), **1 Gerald R(udolph),** born 1913, the 38th president of the United States, since 1974, vice-president from 1973 to 1974. **2 Henry,** 1863-1947, American automobile manufacturer. *n.*

fore[1] (fôr), **1** at the front; toward the beginning or front; forward: *The fore wall of a house faces the street.* **2** at or toward the bow or front: *Several of the crew went fore.* **3** the forward part; front. 1 *adj.,* 2 *adv.,* 3 *n.* [Old English]

to the fore, into full view; into a conspicuous place or position: *The question of new taxes will soon come to the fore.*

fore[2] (fôr), (in golf) a shout of warning to persons ahead who are liable to be struck by the ball. *interj.* [perhaps short for *before*]

fore-, *prefix.* **1** front; in front; at or near the front: *Forepaw = a front paw. Foremast = mast near the front of a ship.* **2** before; beforehand: *Foregoing = going before.* [Old English]

fore and aft, 1 at or toward both bow and stern of a ship. **2** lengthwise on a ship; from bow to stern; placed lengthwise.

fore-and-aft (fôr′ən aft′), lengthwise on a ship; from bow to stern. Fore-and-aft sails are set lengthwise. *adj.*

fore arm[1] (fôr′ärm′), the part of the arm between the elbow and the wrist. *n.* [*fore-* + *arm*[1]]

fore arm[2] (fôr ärm′), prepare for trouble ahead of time; arm beforehand. *v.* [*fore-* + *arm*[2], *v.*]

forceps—two kinds used in surgery

adj. adjective		*n.* noun	
adv. adverb		*prep.* preposition	
conj. conjunction		*pron.* pronoun	
interj. interjection		*v.* verb	
sing. singular		*pl.* plural	

fore bear (fôr′ber *or* fôr′bar), ancestor; forefather. *n.* Also, **forbear.**

fore bode (fôr bōd′), 1 give warning of; predict: *Those black clouds forebode a storm.* 2 have a feeling that something bad is going to happen. *v.,* **fore bod ed, fore bod ing.**

fore bod ing (fôr bō′ding), 1 prediction; warning. 2 a feeling that something bad is going to happen. *n.*

fore cast (fôr′kast′), 1 tell what is coming; prophesy; predict: *Cooler weather is forecast for tomorrow.* 2 statement of what is coming; prophecy; prediction: *What is the forecast for the weather today?* 1 *v.,* **fore cast** or **fore cast ed, fore cast ing;** 2 *n.* —**fore′cast′er,** *n.*

fore cas tle (fōk′səl *or* fôr′kas′əl), 1 the upper deck in front of the foremast. 2 the crew's quarters in the forward part of a merchant ship. *n.*

fore close (fôr klōz′), 1 shut out; prevent; exclude: *The club voted to foreclose further discussion of the subject.* 2 take away the right to redeem (a mortgage): *When the conditions of the mortgage were not met, the holder foreclosed and took possession of the house. v.,* **fore closed, fore clos ing.**

fore clo sure (fôr klō′zhər), act of foreclosing a mortgage. *n.*

fore doom (fôr düm′), doom beforehand. *v.*

fore fa ther (fôr′fä′ᵺər), ancestor. *n.*

fore fin ger (fôr′fing′gər), finger next to the thumb; index finger. *n.*

fore foot (fôr′fút′), one of the front feet of an animal having four or more feet. *n., pl.* **fore feet.**

fore front (fôr′frunt′), place of greatest importance, activity, etc.; foremost part; extreme front: *She was at the forefront of the citizens' campaign for cleaner living conditions. n.*

fore gath er (fôr gaᵺ′ər), forgather. *v.*

fore go (fôr gō′), forgo. *v.,* **fore went, fore gone, fore go ing.**

fore go ing (fôr′gō′ing), going before; preceding; previous: *There have been many pictures in the foregoing pages. adj.*

fore gone (fôr′gôn *for 1,2;* fôr gôn′ *for 3*), 1 known or decided beforehand; inevitable: *That the one good student in the class would win the prize was a foregone conclusion.* 2 that has gone before; previous. 3 past participle of **forego.** *He has foregone his vacation to attend summer school.* 1,2 *adj.,* 3 *v.*

fore ground (fôr′ground′), the part of a picture or scene nearest the observer; the part in the front: *The cottage stands in the foreground with the mountains in the background. n.*

fore hand (fôr′hand′), 1 stroke in tennis and other games made with the palm of the hand turned forward. 2 done or made with the palm of the hand turned forward. 1 *n.,* 2 *adj.*

forehand (def. 1)
tennis stroke

fore hand ed (fôr′han′did), providing for the future; prudent; thrifty. *adj.*

fore head (fôr′id *or* fôr′hed′), the part of the face above the eyes. *n.*

POOP   FORECASTLE

forecastle (def. 1)

fo reign (fôr′ən), 1 outside one's own country: *She has traveled much in foreign countries.* 2 coming from outside one's own country: *a foreign ship, a foreign language, foreign money.* 3 having to do with other countries; carried on or dealing with other countries: *foreign trade, foreign affairs.* 4 not belonging; not related: *Sitting still all day is foreign to that healthy girl's nature. adj.*

fo reign er (fôr′ə nər), person from another country; alien; outsider. *n.*

fore know (fôr nō′), know beforehand. *v.,* **fore knew** (fôr nü′ *or* fôr nyü′), **fore known** (fôr nōn′), **fore know ing.**

fore knowl edge (fôr′nol′ij *or* fôr nol′ij), knowledge of a thing before it exists or happens. *n.*

fore leg (fôr′leg′), one of the front legs of an animal having four or more legs. *n.*

fore limb (fôr′lim′), one of the front limbs of an animal having four or more limbs. *n.*

fore lock (fôr′lok′), lock of hair that grows just above the forehead. *n.*

fore man (fôr′mən), 1 person in charge of a group of workers or of some part of a factory. 2 chairman of a jury. *n., pl.* **fore men.**

fore mast (fôr′mast′ *or* fôr′məst), mast nearest the front of a ship.

fore most (fôr′mōst), 1 first: *I am foremost in line (adj.). He stumbled and fell head foremost (adv.).* 2 chief; leading: *Einstein is regarded as one of the foremost scientists of this century.* 1,2 *adj.,* 1 *adv.*

fore noon (fôr′nün′), time between early morning and noon; part of the day from sunrise to noon. *n.*

fo ren sic (fə ren′sik), of or used in a court of law or in public debate: *forensic arguments. adj.*

fore or dain (fôr′ôr dān′), ordain beforehand; determine beforehand; predestine. *v.*

fore part (fôr′pärt′), the front part; early part. *n.*

fore paw (fôr′pô′), a front paw. *n.*

fore quar ter (fôr′kwôr′tər), a front leg, shoulder, and nearby ribs of beef, lamb, pork, etc. *n.*

fore run ner (fôr′run′ər), 1 person who is sent ahead to prepare for and announce another's coming; herald: *John the Baptist was the forerunner of Christ.* 2 sign or warning that something is coming: *Black clouds are forerunners of a storm.* 3 predecessor; ancestor. *n.*

fore sail (fôr′sāl′ *or* fôr′səl), 1 the principal sail on the foremast of a schooner. 2 the lowest sail on the foremast of a square-rigged ship. *n.*

fore saw (fôr sô′), past tense of **foresee.** *She foresaw the huge traffic jams that came about because the city decided not to build a new subway. v.*

fore see (fôr sē′), see or know beforehand: *We didn't take our bathing suits, because we could foresee that the water would be cold. v.,* **fore saw, fore seen, fore see ing.**

fore see a ble (fôr sē′ə bəl), that can be foreseen. *adj.*

fore seen (fôr sēn′), past participle of **foresee.** *Nobody could have foreseen how cold it would be. v.*

fore shad ow (fôr shad′ō), indicate beforehand; be a warning of: *Those dark clouds foreshadow a storm. v.*

foreshorten—All of the broken lines in the cube are foreshortened.

fore short en (fôr shôrt′n), shorten (lines, objects, etc.) in a drawing or painting in order to give the impression of depth and distance to the eye. Foreshortening helps give perspective to a drawing or painting. *v.*

fore sight (fôr′sīt′), 1 power to see or know beforehand what is likely to happen: *No one had enough foresight to predict the winner.* 2 careful thought for the future; prudence: *A spendthrift does not use foresight.* 3 a looking ahead; view into the future. *n.*

fore sight ed (fôr′sī′tid), having or showing foresight. *adj.* —**fore′-sight′ed ly,** *adv.* —**fore′sight′-ed ness,** *n.*

fore skin (fôr′skin′), fold of skin that covers the end of the male sex organ. *n.*

fo rest (fôr′ist), 1 a large piece of land covered with trees; thick woods. 2 the trees themselves. 3 of a forest; in a forest: *Help prevent forest fires.* 4 plant with trees; change into a forest. 1,2 *n.*, 3 *adj.*, 4 *v.*

fore stall (fôr stôl′), 1 prevent by acting first: *The mayor forestalled a strike by starting to negotiate early with the union.* 2 act sooner than and so get the better of; get ahead of: *By settling the deal over the telephone, she had forestalled all her competitors.* *v.*

fo rest a tion (fôr′ə stā′shən), the planting or taking care of forests. *n.*

fo rest ed (fôr′ə stid), covered with trees; thickly wooded. *adj.*

fo rest er (fôr′ə stər), person in charge of a forest to guard against fires, look after timber, etc. *n.*

fo rest ry (fôr′ə strē), science and art of planting and taking care of forests. *n.*

fore taste (fôr′tāst′), a taste beforehand: *The boy got a foretaste of business life by working during his vacation from school.* *n.*

fore tell (fôr tel′), tell or show beforehand; predict; prophesy: *Who can foretell what the future will be?* *v.,* **fore told, fore tell ing.**

fore thought (fôr′thôt′), careful thought or planning for the future; prudence; foresight: *Our children were grateful for our forethought in saving the money to pay for their education. n.*

fore told (fôr tōld′), past tense and past participle of **foretell.** *She foretold the future. The Weather Bureau had foretold the cold wave.* *v.*

fore top (fôr′top′ or fôr′təp), platform at the top of the bottom section of a foremast. *n.*

for ev er (fər ev′ər), 1 without ever coming to an end; for always; for ever: *Nobody lives forever.* 2 all the time; always: *She is forever telling me that I should take more exercise.* *adv.*

for ev er more (fər ev′ər môr′), forever. *adv.*

fore warn (fôr wôrn′), warn beforehand: *We should have been forewarned of his illness when he began to lose weight.* *v.*

fore went (fôr went′), past tense of **forego.** *v.*

fore wing (fôr′wing′), one of the front wings of an insect having four wings. *n.*

fore word (fôr′wèrd′), a brief introduction or preface to a book, speech, etc. *n.*

for feit (fôr′fit), 1 lose or have to give up by one's own act, neglect, or fault: *Careless drivers sometimes forfeit their lives.* 2 thing lost or given up because of some act, neglect, or fault; penalty; fine: *Good health was the forfeit he paid for staying up late every night.* 3 lost or given up as a penalty. 4 loss or giving up of something as a penalty. 1 *v.,* 2,4 *n.,* 3 *adj.*

for fei ture (fôr′fi chər), 1 loss by forfeiting. 2 thing forfeited; penalty; fine. *n.*

for gath er (fôr gaᴛн′ər), 1 gather together; assemble; meet. 2 meet by accident. 3 be friendly; associate. *v.* Also, **foregather.**

for gave (fər gāv′), past tense of **forgive.** *She forgave my mistake.* *v.*

forge[1] (fôrj), 1 place with a furnace or open fire where metal is heated very hot and then hammered into shape. A blacksmith uses a forge. 2 a blacksmith's shop; smithy. 3 heat (metal) very hot and then hammer into shape: *The blacksmith forged a bar of iron into a big, strong hook.* 4 place where iron or other metal is melted and refined. 5 make, shape, or form. 6 make or write (something false) to deceive; sign falsely: *forge a letter of recommendation. He was sent to jail for forging checks.* 1,2,4 *n.,* 3,5,6 *v.,* **forged, forging.** [from French of the 1300's]

forge[2] (fôrj), move forward slowly but steadily: *One runner forged ahead of the others and won the race.* *v.,* **forged, forging.** [origin uncertain]

forg er (fôr′jər), 1 person who forges metals. 2 person who forges another person's name or makes any fraudulent imitation. *n.*

forg er y (fôr′jər ē), 1 act of forging another person's name or making or writing something false. Forgery is a crime and is punishable by law. 2 something made or written falsely to deceive: *The painting was a forgery. The signature on the check was not mine but a forgery.* *n., pl.* **forg er ies.**

for get (fər get′), 1 let go out of the mind; fail to remember: *I forgot the poem which I had memorized.* 2 fail to think of; fail to do, take, notice, etc.: *I forgot to call the dentist. He had forgotten his umbrella.* *v.,* **for got, for got ten** or **for got, for get ting.**

forget oneself, forget what one should do or be; say or do something improper: *The angry man forgot himself and*

hat, āge, fär; let, ēqual, tèrm;
it, īce; hot, ōpen, ôrder;
oil, out; cup, pùt, rüle; ch, child;
ng, long; sh, she; th, thin;
ᴛн, then; zh, measure;

ə represents *a* in about,
e in taken, *i* in pencil,
o in lemon, *u* in circus.

started to shout in front of everybody on the bus.

for get ful (fər get′fəl), 1 apt to forget; having a poor memory: *Old people sometimes become forgetful.* 2 neglecting; heedless: *forgetful of the law.* *adj.* —**for get′ful ly,** *adv.* —**for get′ful ness,** *n.*

for get-me-not (fər get′mē not′), 1 a small plant with hairy stems and clusters of small blue, pink, or white flowers. 2 its flower. *n.*

for giv a ble (fər giv′ə bəl), that can be forgiven; excusable. *adj.*

for give (fər giv′), give up the wish to punish; not have hard feelings at or toward; pardon; excuse: *She forgave me for breaking her tennis racket. Please forgive my mistake.* *v.,* **for gave, for giv en, for giv ing.**

for giv en (fər giv′ən), past participle of **forgive.** *Your mistakes are forgiven, but be more careful.* *v.*

for give ness (fər giv′nis), 1 act of forgiving; pardon. 2 willingness to forgive. *n.*

for giv ing (fər giv′ing), that forgives; willing to forgive. *adj.*

for go (fôr gō′), do without; give up: *She decided to forgo the movies and do her lessons.* *v.,* **for went, for gone, for go ing.** Also, **forego.**

for gone (fôr gôn′), past participle of **forgo.** *I have forgone dessert for a month in an effort to lose weight.* *v.*

for got (fər got′), past tense and a past participle of **forget.** *She was so busy that she forgot to eat her lunch.* *v.*

for got ten (fər got′n), a past participle of **forget.** *He has forgotten much of what he learned.* *v.*

fork (fôrk), 1 instrument with a handle and two or more long, pointed parts at one end. A small fork is used to lift food. A much larger fork, called a pitchfork, is used to lift and throw hay. Another kind is used for digging. 2 lift, throw, or dig with a fork: *fork hay into a wagon.* 3 anything shaped like a fork; any branching. The place where a tree, road, or stream divides into branches is a fork. 4 one of the branches into which anything is divided: *Take the right-hand*

forked

adj. adjective	*n.* noun
adv. adverb	*prep.* preposition
conj. conjunction	*pron.* pronoun
interj. interjection	*v.* verb
sing. singular	*pl.* plural

fork. 5 have a fork or forks; divide into forks: *There is a garage where the road forks.* 1,3,4 *n.*, 2,5 *v.*

fork out, fork over, or **fork up,** SLANG. hand over; pay out: *He forked over the money.*

forked (fôrkt), 1 having a fork or forks; divided into branches: *a forked stick.* 2 zigzag: *forked lightning. adj.*

fork lift, device having horizontal metal prongs that can be inserted under a load and raised or lowered at will. It is used for lifting and putting down loads and is often attached to the front of a truck or other vehicle.

fork lift

for lorn (fôr lôrn′), miserable and hopeless because left alone and neglected: *The lost kitten, a forlorn little animal, was wet and dirty. adj.* —**for lorn′ly,** *adv.*

form (fôrm), 1 appearance apart from color or materials; shape: *Circles and triangles are simple forms.* 2 shape; make: *The cook formed the dough into loaves.* 3 be formed; take shape: *Clouds form in the sky.* 4 become: *Water forms ice when it freezes.* 5 make up; compose: *Parents and children form a family.* 6 organize; establish: *We formed a club.* 7 develop: *She formed the good habit of getting her lessons done each day before looking at television.* 8 kind; sort; variety: *Ice, snow, and steam are forms of water.* 9 way of doing something; manner; method: *He is a fast runner, but his form in running is bad.* 10 a set way of doing something; set way of behaving according to custom or rule; formality; ceremony: *He said "Good morning" as a matter of form, although he hardly noticed me.* 11 document with printing or writing on it and blank spaces to be filled in: *To get a license to drive an automobile you must fill out a form.*

12 arrangement: *Some proverbs are in verse form.* 13 mold; pattern: *Ice cream is often made in forms.* 14 good condition of body or mind: *Athletes exercise to keep in form.* 15 (in grammar) any of the ways in which a word is spelled or pronounced to show its different meanings. *Toys is the plural form of toy. Saw is the past form of see. My and mine are the possessive forms of I.* 16 grade in school: *The girl is now in the fifth form.* 17 a long seat; bench. 1,8-17 *n.*, 2-7 *v.*

for mal (fôr′məl), 1 with strict attention to outward forms and ceremonies; not familar and homelike; stiff: *a formal greeting. A judge has a formal manner in a court of law.* 2 according to set customs or rules: *The ambassador paid a formal call on the prime minister.* 3 done with the proper forms; clear and definite: *A written contract is a formal agreement to do something.* 4 very regular; symmetrical; orderly: *a formal arrangement of furniture, a formal poem.* 5 having to do with the form, not the content of a thing. 6 a formal dance, party, or other affair. 7 gown worn to a formal affair: *The women wore formals to the banquet.* 1-5 *adj.*, 6,7 *n.* —**for′mal ly,** *adv.*

for mal de hyde (fôr mal′də hīd), a colorless gas with a sharp, irritating odor. It is used in a water solution to disinfect and to preserve. *n.*

for mal ism (fôr′mə liz′əm), strict observance of outward forms. *n.*

for mal i ty (fôr mal′ə tē), 1 something required by custom or rule; outward form; ceremony: *At a wedding there are many formalities.* 2 attention to forms and customs: *The queen received her visitors with much formality.* 3 stiffness of manner, behavior, or arrangement: *The formality of the party made me uneasy. n., pl.* **for mal i ties.**

for mal ize (fôr′mə līz), 1 make formal. 2 give a definite form to. *v.,* **for mal ized, for mal iz ing.**

for mat (fôr′mat), shape, size, and general arrangement of a book, magazine, etc. *n.*

for ma tion (fôr mā′shən), 1 the forming, making, or shaping (of something): *Heat causes the formation of steam from water.* 2 way in which something is arranged; arrangement; order: *Football players line up in various formations for their plays. The new band marched in perfect parade formation.* 3 thing formed: *Clouds are formations of tiny drops of water in the sky. n.*

form a tive (fôr′mə tiv), having to do with formation or development; forming; molding: *Home and school are the chief formative influences in a child's life. adj.*

for mer (fôr′mər), 1 the first of two: *When she is offered ice cream or pie, she always chooses the former because she likes ice cream better.* 2 earlier; past; long past: *In former times, cooking was done in fireplaces instead of stoves. adj.*

for mer ly (fôr′mər lē), in the past; some time ago: *Our teacher formerly taught at a different school. adv.*

for mi da ble (fôr′mə də bəl), hard to overcome; hard to deal with; to be dreaded: *a formidable opponent. A long examination is more formidable than a short test. adj.*

for mi da bly (fôr′mə də blē), in a formidable manner. *adv.*

form less (fôrm′lis), without definite or regular form; shapeless. *adj.* —**form′less ly,** *adv.* —**form′less ness,** *n.*

form letter, letter copied from a pattern so that copies may be made easily and sent to many different people.

For mo sa (fôr mō′sə), Taiwan. *n.*

for mu la (fôr′myə lə), 1 a set form of words, especially one which by much use has partly lost its meaning: *"How do you do?" is a polite formula.* 2 recipe or prescription: *a formula for making soap.* 3 expression showing by chemical symbols the composition of a compound: *The formula for water is H_2O.* 4 expression in algebraic symbols of a rule or principle: $(a+b)^2=a^2+2ab+b^2$ *is an algebraic formula. n., pl.* **for mu las** or **for mu lae.**

for mu lae (fôr′myə lē), a plural of **formula.**

for mu late (fôr′myə lāt), state definitely or systematically; express in a formula: *Our country formulates its laws according to its constitution. v.,* **for mu lat ed, for mu lat ing.**

for mu la tion (fôr′myə lā′shən), a definite expression or statement; expression in a formula. *n.*

for sake (fôr sāk′), give up; leave alone; leave; abandon: *He ran away, forsaking his home and friends. v.,* **for sook, for sak en, for sak ing.**

for sak en (fôr sā′kən), 1 past participle of **forsake.** *That girl has forsaken her old friends.* 2 deserted; abandoned: *We found an old, forsaken graveyard out in the country.* 1 *v.,* 2 *adj.*

for sook (fôr sùk′), past tense of **forsake.** *He forsook his family. v.*

for sooth (fôr süth′), OLD USE. in truth; indeed. *adv.*

for swear (fôr swer′ *or* fôr swar′), 1 renounce on oath; swear solemnly to give up: *The coach asked the team to forswear smoking.* 2 be untrue to one's sworn word or promise; perjure (oneself). *v.,* **for swore, for sworn, for swear ing.**

for swore (fôr swôr′), past tense of

forswear. *The team forswore smoking.* *v.*

for sworn (fôr swôrn′), past participle of **forswear**. *He has forsworn his bad habits.* *v.*

for syth i a (fôr sith′ē ə), 1 shrub having many bell-shaped, yellow flowers in early spring before its leaves come out. 2 its flower. *n., pl.* **for syth i as.** [from William *Forsyth*, 1737-1804, a British botanist]

fort (fôrt), a strong building or place that can be defended against an enemy; fortified place; stronghold. *n.*

forte[1] (fôrt), something a person does very well; strong point: *Bowling is her forte.* *n.* [from French *fort* strong]

for te[2] (fôr′tā), (in music) loud. *adj., adv.* [from Italian *forte* strong]

forth (fôrth), 1 forward; onward: *From that day forth he lived alone.* 2 into view; out: *The sun came forth from behind the clouds.* 3 away: *Go forth and seek your fortune.* *adv.*

and so forth, and so on; and the like: *We ate cake, candy, nuts, and so forth.*

forth com ing (fôrth′kum′ing), 1 about to appear; approaching: *The forthcoming week will be busy.* 2 ready when wanted; coming forth: *I needed help, but none was forthcoming.* *adj.*

forth right (fôrth′rīt′), frank and outspoken; straightforward; direct: *The speaker did not like the plan and made forthright objections to it.* *adj.* —**forth′right′ly,** *adv.* —**forth′right′ness,** *n.*

forth with (fôrth′with′ or fôrth′wiŦH′), at once; immediately: *The judge's summons ordered the witness to appear forthwith in court.* *adv.*

for ti eth (fôr′tē ith), 1 next after the 39th; last in a series of 40. 2 one of 40 equal parts. *adj., n.*

for ti fi ca tion (fôr′tə fə kā′shən), 1 a making strong; adding strength to; fortifying: *The general was responsible for the fortification of the town.* 2 wall or fort built to make a place strong. 3 place made strong by building walls and forts. *n.*

for ti fy (fôr′tə fī), 1 build forts, walls, etc.; protect a place against attack; strengthen against attack. 2 give support to; strengthen: *They fortified each other against the coming ordeal.* 3 enrich with vitamins and minerals: *fortify bread.* *v.,* **for ti fied, for ti fy ing.**

for tis si mo (fôr tis′ə mō), (in music) very loud. *adj., adv.* [from Italian *fortissimo,* from *forte* strong]

for ti tude (fôr′tə tüd or fôr′tə tyüd), courage in facing pain, danger, or trouble; firmness of spirit. *n.*

fort night (fôrt′nīt), two weeks. *n.*

fort night ly (fôrt′nīt lē), 1 once in every two weeks. 2 appearing or happening once in every two weeks. 1 *adv.,* 2 *adj.*

for tress (fôr′tris), place built with walls and defenses; large fort or fortification. *n., pl.* **for tress es.**

for tu i tous (fôr tü′ə təs or fôr tyü′ə təs), happening by chance; accidental: *The fortuitous falling of an apple led Newton to formulate the law of gravitation.* *adj.* —**for tu′i tous ly,** *adv.*

for tu nate (fôr′chə nit), 1 having good luck; lucky: *You are fortunate in having such a fine family.* 2 bringing good luck; having favorable results: *a fortunate occurrence.* *adj.* —**for′tu nate ly,** *adv.*

for tune (fôr′chən), 1 a great deal of money or property; riches; wealth: *She made a fortune in oil.* 2 what happens; luck; chance: *Fortune was against us; we lost.* 3 good luck; prosperity; success. 4 what is going to happen to a person; fate: *Gypsies often claim that they can tell people's fortunes.* *n.*

for tune tell er (fôr′chən tel′ər), person who claims to be able to tell what is going to happen to people. *n.*

Fort Wayne (wān), city in NE Indiana.

Fort Worth (wèrth), city in N Texas.

for ty (fôr′tē), four times ten; 40. *n., pl.* **for ties;** *adj.*

for ty-nin er (fôr′tē nī′nər), person who went to California in 1849 to seek gold during the gold rush that had started there in 1848. *n.*

fo rum (fôr′əm), 1 the public square or market place of an ancient Roman city. There business was done and courts and public assemblies were held. 2 assembly for the discussion of questions of public interest: *An open forum is held in the community house once a month.* 3 court of law; tribunal. *n.*

for ward (fôr′wərd), 1 toward the front; onward; ahead: *Forward, march! From this time forward we shall be good friends.* 2 to the front: *come forward (adv.), the forward part of a ship (adj.).* 3 advanced; far ahead: *A child of four years who can read is forward for his age.* 4 into view or consideration; out: *In her talk she brought forward several new ideas.* 5 help along: *She did everything she could to forward her friend's plan.* 6 send on farther: *Please forward my mail to my new address.* 7 ready; eager: *He knew his lesson and was forward with his answers.* 8 impudent; bold: *Don't be so forward as to interrupt the speaker.* 9 player whose position is in the front line in games such as basketball, hockey, or soccer. 1,2,4 *adv.,* 2,3,7,8 *adj.,* 5,6 *v.,* 9 *n.*

for ward ness (fôr′wərd nis), 1 a

hat, āge, fär; let, ēqual, tèrm; it, īce; hot, ōpen, ôrder; oil, out; cup, pùt, rüle; ch, child; ng, long; sh, she; th, thin; ŦH, then; zh, measure;

ə represents *a* in about, *e* in taken, *i* in pencil, *o* in lemon, *u* in circus.

being far ahead. 2 readiness; eagerness. 3 impudence; boldness. *n.*

for wards (fôr′wərdz), forward. *adv.*

for went (fôr went′), past tense of **forgo.** *She forwent the movies in order to do her lessons.* *v.*

fos sil (fos′əl), 1 the hardened remains or traces of an animal or plant of a former age. Fossils of ferns are found in coal. 2 forming a fossil; of the nature of a fossil: *the fossil remains of a dinosaur.* 3 a very old-fashioned person, set in his ways. 4 very old-fashioned; not modern: *fossil ideas.* 1,3 *n.,* 2,4 *adj.*

fos sil ize (fos′ə līz), change into a fossil. *v.,* **fos sil ized, fos sil iz ing.**

fos ter (fô′stər), 1 help the growth or development of; encourage: *a committee to foster better relations between races.* 2 care for fondly; cherish. 3 bring up; help to grow; make grow; rear. 4 in the same family, but not related by birth. A **foster child** is a child brought up by a person or persons who are not his parents. A **foster father, foster mother,** and **foster parent** are persons who bring up the child of another. A **foster brother** or **foster sister** is a boy or girl brought up with another person though not related to him. 1-3 *v.,* 4 *adj.*

Fos ter (fô′stər), Stephen Collins, 1826-1864, American composer. *n.*

fought (fôt), past tense and past participle of **fight.** *We fought for our rights. A battle was fought there.* *v.*

foul (foul), 1 very dirty, nasty, or smelly: *We opened the windows to let out the foul air.* 2 make or become dirty; soil; defile; disgrace: *The oil spilled by the damaged ship fouled the harbor.* 3 very wicked; vile: *Murder is a foul crime.* 4 offending modesty or decency; obscene; profane: *foul language.* 5 done against the rules; unfair. 6 (in football, basketball, etc.) an unfair play; thing done against the rules. 7 make a foul against. 8 foul ball. 9 hit (a foul ball). 10 hit against: *One boat fouled the other.* 11 hitting against: *One boat was foul of the other.* 12 get tangled up with; catch: *The rope they threw fouled our anchor chain.*

foulard

adj. adjective	*n.* noun
adv. adverb	*prep.* preposition
conj. conjunction	*pron.* pronoun
interj. interjection	*v.* verb
sing. singular	*pl.* plural

13 tangled up; caught: *The ship's anchor was foul.* 14 clog up: *Grease fouled the drain.* 15 clogged up: *The fire will not burn because the chimney is foul.* 16 unfavorable; stormy: *Foul weather delayed the ship.* 1,3-5,11,13,15,16 *adj.*, 2,7,9,10,12,14 *v.*, 6,8 *n.* —**foul′ly,** *adv.* —**foul′ness,** *n.*

run foul of, get into trouble or difficulties with: *run foul of the law.*

fou lard (fū lärd′), a soft, thin fabric made of silk, rayon, or cotton, usually with a printed pattern. It is used for neckties, dresses, etc. *n.*

foul ball, (in baseball) a batted ball that lands outside the foul lines.

foul line, (in baseball) either one of two straight lines extending from home plate through first base and third base to the limits of the playing field.

foul play, 1 unfair play; thing or things done against the rules. 2 treachery; violence.

found[1] (found), past tense and past participle of **find.** *We found the treasure. The lost child was found.* *v.*

found[2] (found), 1 set up; establish: *The Pilgrims founded a colony at Plymouth.* 2 rest for support; base: *He founded his claim on facts.* *v.* [from French of the 1200's *fonder,* from Latin *fundare*]

found[3] (found), melt and mold (metal); make of molten metal; cast. *v.* [from French of the 1500's *fondre,* from Latin *fundere*]

foun da tion (foun dā′shən), 1 part on which the other parts rest for support; base: *the foundation of a house.* 2 basis: *This report has no foundation in fact.* 3 a founding or establishing: *The foundation of the United States began in 1776.* 4 a being founded or established. 5 institution founded and endowed. 6 fund given to support an institution. *n.*

foun der[1] (foun′dər), 1 fill with water and sink: *The ship foundered in the storm.* 2 fall down; stumble: *The pony foundered in the swamp.* 3 break down; fail: *Their business has foundered.* *v.* [from French of the 1300's *fondrer,* from *fond* bottom]

found er[2] (foun′dər), person who founds or establishes something. *n.* [*found*[2] + *-er*[1]]

found er[3] (foun′dər), person who casts metals. *n.* [*found*[3] + *-er*[1]]

found ling (found′ling), baby or little child found deserted. *n.*

found ry (foun′drē), 1 place where metal is melted and molded; place where things are made of molten metal. 2 act of melting and molding metal; making things of molten metal. *n., pl.* **found ries.**

fount (fount), 1 fountain. 2 source; origin. *n.*

fox (def. 1)—16 in. high at the shoulder

foun tain (foun′tən), 1 water flowing or rising into the air in a spray. 2 pipes through which the water is forced and the basin built to receive it. 3 spring of water. 4 place to get a drink: *a drinking fountain, a soda fountain.* 5 source; origin: *My friend is a fountain of information about football.* *n.*

foun tain head (foun′tən hed′), 1 source of a stream. 2 an original source. *n.*

fountain pen, pen for writing that gives a steady supply of ink from a rubber or plastic tube.

four (fôr), one more than three; 4. *n., adj.*

on all fours, 1 on all four feet. 2 on hands and knees.

four fold (fôr′fōld′), 1 four times as much or as many: *a fourfold increase in profits (adj.). Profits increased fourfold (adv.).* 2 having four parts. 1,2 *adj.,* 1 *adv.*

four-foot ed (fôr′fut′id), having four feet; quadruped: *A dog is a four-footed animal. adj.*

Four-H clubs or **4-H clubs** (fôr′äch′), a national system of clubs to teach agriculture and home economics to children in rural areas.

four-post er (fôr′pō′stər), bed with four tall corner posts for supporting a canopy. *n.*

four score (fôr′skôr′), four times twenty; 80. *adj., n.*

four some (fôr′səm), 1 group of four people. 2 game played by four people, two on each side. 3 the players. *n.*

four square (fôr′skwer′ or fôr′-skwar′), 1 square. 2 frank; outspoken. 3 firm. *adj.*

four teen (fôr′tēn′), four more than ten; 14. *n., adj.*

four teenth (fôr′tēnth′), 1 next after the 13th; last in a series of 14. 2 one of 14 equal parts. *adj., n.*

fourth (fôrth), 1 next after the third; last in a series of 4. 2 one of 4 equal parts; quarter: *Twenty-five cents is one fourth of a dollar. adj., n.*

Fourth of July, Independence Day. *n.*

fowl (foul), 1 any bird: *a wild fowl.* 2 any of several kinds of large birds used for food. The hen, rooster, and turkey are fowls. 3 flesh of a fowl used for food. *n., pl.* **fowls** or **fowl.**

fowl er (fou′lər), person who hunts or traps wild birds. *n.*

fowling piece, a light gun for shooting wild birds.

fox (foks), 1 a wild animal somewhat like a dog, having a pointed muzzle and bushy tail. In many stories the fox gets the better of other animals by its cunning. 2 its fur. 3 a cunning or crafty person. *n., pl.* **fox es.** —**fox′like′,** *adj.*

fox glove (foks′gluv′), 1 plant with tall stalks having many bell-shaped flowers; digitalis. 2 its flower. *n.*

fountain (defs. 1 and 2)

fox hole (foks′hōl′), hole in the ground, large enough for one or two soldiers, for protection against enemy fire. *n.*

fox hound (foks′hound′), hound with a keen sense of smell, bred and trained to hunt foxes. *n.*

fox i ly (fok′sə lē), in a foxy manner; slyly; craftily. *adv.*

fox i ness (fok′sē nis), foxy quality; slyness; craftiness. *n.*

fox terrier, a small, active dog kept as a pet, once trained to drive foxes from their holes. Fox terriers are white with brown or black spots and may have smooth or rough coats.

fox trot, 1 dance having short, quick steps. 2 music for it.

fox y (fok′sē), like a fox; sly; crafty; cunning. *adj.,* **fox i er, fox i est.**

foy er (foi′ər), 1 a lounging room in a theater, apartment house, or hotel; lobby. 2 an entrance hall. *n.*

fra cas (frā′kəs), a noisy quarrel or fight; disorderly noise; uproar; brawl. *n., pl.* **fra cas es.**

frac tion (frak′shən), 1 division of a number by another number, shown by a line with one quantity above it and another below it: $\frac{1}{2}$, $\frac{2}{3}$, $\frac{3}{4}$, *and* $\frac{5}{6}$ *are fractions; so are* $\frac{4}{3}$ *and* $\frac{10}{6}$. 2 a very small part, amount, etc.; not all of a thing; fragment: *She has done only a fraction of her homework. n.*

frac tion al (frak′shə nəl), 1 having to

do with fractions. **2** forming a fraction: *440 yards is a fractional part of a mile.* **3** small by comparison; insignificant. *adj.* —**frac′tion al ly,** *adv.*

frac tious (frak′shəs), **1** cross; fretful; peevish. **2** hard to manage; unruly. *adj.*

frac ture (frak′chər), **1** a breaking of a bone or cartilage. **2** a breaking or a being broken: *a fracture of the ice, a fracture of friendly relations.* **3** result of breaking; a break; crack: *The fracture in the foundation is widening.* **4** break; crack: *I fell out of the tree and fractured my arm.* **1-3** *n.,* **4** *v.,* **fractured, frac tur ing.**

frag ile (fraj′əl), easily broken, damaged, or destroyed; delicate; frail: *Be careful; that thin glass is fragile.* *adj.*

fra gil i ty (frə jil′ə tē), fragile quality; delicacy; frailness. *n.*

frag ment (frag′mənt), **1** piece of something broken; part broken off: *After I broke the vase, I tried to put the fragments back together.* **2** an incomplete or disconnected part: *Because of the noise he could hear only fragments of the conversation.* *n.*

frag men tar y (frag′mən ter′ē), made up of fragments; incomplete; disconnected: *fragmentary remains of a temple. The patient could give only a fragmentary account of the accident.* *adj.*

fra grance (frā′grəns), a sweet smell; pleasing odor: *the fragrance of flowers or of perfume. n.*

fra grant (frā′grənt), having or giving off a pleasing odor; sweet-smelling: *Fragrant roses perfumed the air. adj.* —**fra′grant ly,** *adv.*

frail (frāl), **1** slender and not very strong; weak: *a frail and sickly child.* **2** easily broken or giving way: *Be careful; those little branches are a very frail support.* **3** morally weak; liable to yield to temptation. *adj.*

frail ty (frāl′tē), **1** a being frail; weakness: *concern about a sick person's physical frailty, frailty of character.* **2** fault caused by weakness: *Nobody is perfect; we all have our frailties. n., pl.* **frail ties.**

frame (def. 1)
part of the frame
of a house

frame (frām), **1** support over which something is stretched or built: *the frame of a house.* **2** body: *a person of*

heavy frame. **3** way in which a thing is put together; structure; system: *the frame of the Constitution.* **4** put together; plan; make: *frame an answer to a difficult question. Thomas Jefferson helped to frame the Constitution.* **5** border in which a thing is set: *a window frame, a picture frame.* **6** put a border around: *frame a picture.* **7** SLANG. make seem guilty by some false arrangement: *frame an innocent person.* **8** one turn at bowling. **1-3,5,8** *n.,* **4,6,7** *v.,* **framed, fram ing.**

frame house, house made of a wooden framework covered with boards.

frame of mind, way one is thinking or feeling; disposition; mood.

frame-up (frām′up′), SLANG. **1** a secret and dishonest arrangement made beforehand. **2** arrangement made to have a person falsely accused. *n.*

frame work (frām′wèrk′), **1** support or skeleton; stiff part which gives shape to a thing: *A bridge often has a steel framework.* **2** way in which a thing is put together; structure; system: *the framework of government. n.*

franc (frangk), **1** unit of money in France, Belgium, Switzerland, and some other countries. The French franc is worth about 24 cents. **2** coin worth one franc. *n.*

France (frans), country in W Europe. *Capital: Paris. n.*

fran chise (fran′chīz), **1** privilege or right granted by a government: *The city granted the company a franchise to operate its buses on the city streets.* **2** right to vote: *The United States gave women the franchise in 1920.* **3** privilege of selling the products of a manufacturer in a given area. *n.*

Fran cis (fran′sis), **Saint,** 1181?-1226, Italian founder of the Franciscan order of friars. *n.*

Fran cis can (fran sis′kən), **1** of Saint Francis or the religious order founded by him in 1209. **2** friar belonging to the Franciscan order. **1** *adj.,* **2** *n.*

fran ci um (fran′sē əm), a radioactive, metallic element produced artificially from actinium or thorium. *n.* [from *France*]

Fran co (frang′kō), **Francisco,** born 1892, Spanish general, ruler of Spain since 1936. *n.*

frank (frangk), **1** free in expressing one's real thoughts, opinions, and feelings; not hiding what is in one's mind; not afraid to say what one thinks; open: *She was frank in telling me that she did not like my new hat.* **2** send (a letter, package, etc.) without charge. **3** mark to show that a letter, package, etc., is to be sent without charge.

hat, āge, fär; let, ēqual, tèrm;
it, īce; hot, ōpen, ôrder;
oil, out; cup, pùt, rüle; ch, child;
ng, long; sh, she; th, thin;
ғн, then; zh, measure;

ə represents *a* in about,
e in taken, *i* in pencil,
o in lemon, *u* in circus.

4 right to send letters, packages, etc., without charge. **1** *adj.,* **2** *v.,* **3,4** *n.* —**frank′ly,** *adv.* —**frank′ness,** *n.*

Frank (frangk), member of the German tribes that conquered Gaul in the A.D. 500's. *n.*

Frank en stein (frang′kən stīn), **1** scientist in a story written in the 1800's who creates a monster that he cannot control. **2** the monster itself. *n.*

Frank fort (frangk′fərt), **1** capital of Kentucky, in the N part. **2** Frankfort on the Main. *n.*

Frankfort on the Main (mān), city in central West Germany. *n.*

frank furt er (frangk′fər tər), a reddish sausage made of beef and pork, or of beef alone; wiener. Frankfurters on buns are called hot dogs. *n.* [from German *Frankfurter* of or from Frankfort]

frank in cense (frang′kən sens), a fragrant resin from certain Asian or African trees. It gives off a sweet, spicy odor when burned. *n.*

Frank ish (frang′kish), of or having to do with the Franks. *adj.*

Frank lin (frang′klən), **Benjamin,** 1706-1790, American statesman, author, scientist, printer, and inventor. *n.*

fran tic (fran′tik), very much excited; wild with rage, fear, pain, or grief: *The trapped animal made frantic efforts to escape. adj.*

fran ti cal ly (fran′tik lē), in a frantic manner; with wild excitement. *adv.*

fra ter nal (frə tèr′nl), **1** of or having to do with brothers or a brother; brotherly. **2** having to do with a group organized for mutual fellowship: *a fraternal association. adj.* —**frater′nal ly,** *adv.*

fraternal twins, twins of the same or opposite sex coming from two separately fertilized egg cells rather than from one egg cell as identical twins do.

fra ter ni ty (frə tèr′nə tē), **1** group of men or boys joined together for fellowship or for some other purpose. There are student fraternities in many American colleges. **2** group having the same interests, kind of work, etc.: *the*

fraternize

musical fraternity, the engineering fraternity. 3 fraternal feeling; brotherhood. *n., pl.* **fra ter ni ties.**

frat er nize (frat′ər nīz), associate in a brotherly way; be friendly. *v.,* **frat ernized, frat er niz ing.**

Frau (frou), GERMAN. 1 Mrs. 2 wife. *n., pl.* **Frau en** (frou′ən).

fraud (frôd), 1 dishonest dealing; trickery; cheating: *obtain a prize by fraud, win an election by fraud.* 2 a dishonest act, statement, etc.; something which is not what it seems to be; trick. 3 INFORMAL. person who is not what he pretends to be. *n.*

fraud u lent (frô′jə lənt), 1 cheating; dishonest: *a fraudulent dealer, a fraudulent schemer.* 2 done by fraud; obtained by trickery: *fraudulent gains. adj.* —**fraud′u lent ly,** *adv.*

fraught (frôt), loaded; filled: *The attempt to climb Mount Everest was fraught with danger. adj.*

Fräu lein (froi′līn), GERMAN. 1 Miss. 2 an unmarried woman; young lady. *n., pl.* **Fräu lein.**

fray¹ (frā), 1 separate into threads; make or become ragged or worn along the edge: *Long wear had frayed the collar and cuffs of his old shirt. His trousers are beginning to fray at the cuffs.* 2 wear away; rub. *v.* [from French *frayer,* from Latin *fricare* rub]

fray² (frā), a noisy quarrel; fight. *n.* [a different form of *affray*]

fraz zle (fraz′əl), 1 wear to shreds; fray; ravel: *The edges of the rug were completely frazzled.* 2 tire out; weary. 3 INFORMAL. a frazzled condition. 1,2 *v.,* **fraz zled, fraz zling;** 3 *n.*

freak (frēk), 1 something very queer or unusual: *A green leaf growing in the middle of a rose would be called a freak of nature.* 2 animal, plant, or person that has developed abnormally: *A circus often has a sideshow of freaks.* 3 very queer or unusual: *a freak storm.* 4 a sudden change of mind without reason; odd notion or fancy. 1,2,4 *n.,* 3 *adj.*

freak ish (frē′kish), full of freaks; very queer or unusual. *adj.*

freck le (frek′əl), 1 a small, light-brown spot on the skin, often caused by exposure to the sun. 2 make freckles on. 3 become marked or spotted with

freckles. 1 *n.,* 2,3 *v.,* **freck led, freckling.**

Fred er ick the Great (fred′ər ik), 1712-1786, king of Prussia from 1740 to 1786.

Fred er ic ton (fred′rik tən), capital of New Brunswick, in SE Canada. *n.*

free (frē), 1 not under another's control; not a captive or slave: *a free man, a free people, a free nation, free speech.* 2 not held back, fastened, or shut up; released; loose: *He set free the bear cub caught in the trap. Let the captives go free.* 3 not hindered; easy: *a free step.* 4 make free; let loose; let go: *We freed the bird from its cage. She freed her foot from the vine that tripped her.* 5 open to all: *a free port.* 6 to clear: *She will have to free herself of this charge of speeding.* 7 without anything to pay: *These tickets are free* (adj.). *Children under 12 attend free* (adv.). 8 having no tax or duty: *free trade.* 9 not following rules, forms, or words exactly; not strict: *a free translation.* 10 not combined with something else: *Oxygen exists free in air.* 11 in a free manner; freely: *The animals ran free around the farm.* 1-3,5,7-10 *adj.,* **fre er, fre est;** 4,6 *v.,* **freed, free ing;** 7,11 *adv.* —**free′ly,** *adv.*

free and easy, paying little attention to rules and customs.

free from or **free of,** without; having no; lacking: *free from fear, air free of dust.*

free boot er (frē′bü′tər), pirate. *n.*

freed man (frēd′mən), man freed from slavery. *n., pl.* **freed men.**

free dom (frē′dəm), 1 condition of being free. 2 power to do, say, or think as one pleases; liberty. 3 free use: *We gave our guest the freedom of the house.* 4 too great liberty; lack of restraint; frankness: *We did not like the freedom of his manner.* 5 ease of movement or action: *A fine athlete performs with freedom. n.*

free enterprise, the right of private business to select and operate undertakings for profit with little control or regulation by the government; private enterprise.

free-for-all (frē′fər ôl′), a fight, race, etc., open to all. *n.*

free hand (frē′hand′), done by hand without using instruments, measurements, etc.: *freehand drawing. adj.*

free hand ed (frē′han′did), generous; liberal. *adj.*

free-lance (frē′lans′), 1 work as an independent writer, artist, etc., who sells his work to anyone who will buy it. 2 of, having to do with, or done by such a writer, artist, etc.: *free-lance journalism.* 1 *v.,* **free-lanced, free-lanc ing;** 2 *adj.*

free man (frē′mən), 1 person who is not a slave or a serf. 2 citizen. *n., pl.* **free men.**

Free ma son (frē′mā′sn), member of a world-wide secret society, whose purpose is mutual aid and fellowship; Mason. *n.*

free press, the publishing of newspapers and magazines without censorship or control by the government.

free stone (frē′stōn′), 1 stone, such as limestone or sandstone, that can easily be cut without splitting. 2 having a fruit stone that is easily separated from the pulp. 3 fruit having such a stone. Certain kinds of peaches and plums are freestones. 1,3 *n.,* 2 *adj.*

free style (frē′stīl′), 1 unrestricted as to style, method, or manner: *A freestyle swimmer is allowed to choose his own stroke.* 2 a freestyle race or figure-skating contest. 1 *adj.,* 2 *n.*

free think er (frē′thing′kər), person who forms his religious opinions independently of authority or tradition. *n.*

free verse, poetry not restricted by the usual conventions of meter, rhyme, etc.

free way (frē′wā′), a high-speed highway on which no tolls are charged. *n.*

free will (frē′wil′), of one's own accord; voluntary: *a freewill offering to the Red Cross. adj.*

free will, will free from outside restraints; voluntary choice; freedom of decision.

freeze (frēz), 1 harden by cold; turn into a solid by removal of heat. Water becomes ice when it freezes. 2 make or become very cold: *The north wind froze the spectators. We will freeze at the football game in this weather.* 3 kill or injure by frost; be killed or injured by frost: *This cold weather will freeze the flowers. The flowers froze last night.* 4 cover or become covered with ice; clog with ice: *The snow and hail will freeze the pond. The pipes froze.* 5 fix or become fixed to something by freezing: *The low temperature has frozen the milk bottles to the porch. His fingers froze to the tray of ice cubes.* 6 a freezing or a being frozen. 7 period during which there is freezing weather. 8 make or become stiff and unfriendly: *The reporter's prying questions froze her and she would not answer. The new boy froze up when I tried to be friendly.* 9 chill or be chilled with fear, etc.: *The howling of the wolves froze him with terror. She froze at the sight of the ghostly hand.* 10 become motionless: *The baby rabbit froze with fear at the strange sound.* 11 fix at a definite amount, usually by governmental decree: *freeze prices, freeze rents.* 1-5,8-11 *v.*, **froze, fro zen, freez ing; 6,7** *n.*

freez er (frē′zər), 1 machine to freeze ice cream. 2 a refrigerator cabinet for freezing foods or storing frozen food. *n.*

freezing point, temperature at which a liquid freezes. The freezing point of water at sea level is 32 degrees Fahrenheit or 0 degrees centigrade.

freight (frāt), 1 goods that a train, truck, ship, or aircraft carries. 2 the carrying of goods on a train, ship, aircraft, or truck: *He sent the box by freight.* 3 price paid for carrying goods. 4 train or ship for carrying goods. 5 load with freight. 6 carry as freight. 7 send as freight. 1-4 *n.*, 5-7 *v.*

freight car, a railroad car for carrying freight.

freight er (frā′tər), ship or aircraft that carries mainly freight. *n.*

freight train, a railroad train of freight cars; freight.

Fré mont (frē′mont), **John Charles,** 1813-1890, American explorer and politician. *n.*

French (french), 1 of or having to do with France, its people, or their language. 2 the people of France. 3 their language. 1 *adj.*, 2 *n.pl.*, 3 *n.sing.*

French and Indian War, war between Great Britain and France, fought in North America from 1754 to 1763. The French were greatly aided by Indian allies.

French Canadian, 1 Canadian whose ancestors came from France. 2 of or having to do with French Canadians.

French Community, association formed in 1958 that includes France, her overseas territories, and many of her former colonies.

French fries, potatoes cut into thin strips and fried in deep fat until crisp on the outside.

French Guiana, French territory in N South America.

French horn—
It has three valves for changing pitch.

French horn, a brass wind instrument that has a mellow tone.

French Indochina, former French territory in SE Asia, south of China, comprising the present countries of Cambodia, Laos, North Vietnam, and South Vietnam.

French man (french′mən), man born

or living in France. *n., pl.* **French men.**

French Revolution, revolution in France from 1789 to 1799 which ousted the monarchy and set up a republic.

French wom an (french′wum′ən), woman born or living in France. *n., pl.* **French wom en.**

fren zied (fren′zēd), very much excited; frantic; wild. *adj.*

fren zy (fren′zē), 1 a state of near madness; frantic condition: *They were in a frenzy when they heard that their child was missing.* 2 a condition of very great excitement: *The crowd was in a frenzy after the home team scored the winning goal. n., pl.* **fren zies.**

fre quen cy (frē′kwən sē), 1 rate of occurrence: *The flashes of light came with a frequency of three per minute.* 2 a frequent occurrence: *The frequency of their visits began to annoy us.* 3 number of complete cycles per second of an alternating current or other electric wave. Different radio and television stations broadcast at different frequencies so that their signals can be received distinctly. *n., pl.* **fre quen cies.**

frequency modulation, a deliberate changing of the frequency of radio waves in order to agree with the changes in the sounds being transmitted. Frequency modulation reduces static.

fre quent (frē′kwənt *for 1;* fri kwent′ *for 2*), 1 happening often, near together, or every little while: *In my part of the country storms are frequent in March.* 2 go to often; be often in: *Frogs frequent ponds, streams, and marshes.* 1 *adj.,* 2 *v.*—**fre quent′er,** *n.*

fre quent ly (frē′kwənt lē), often; repeatedly; every little while. *adv.*

fres co (fres′kō), 1 act or art of painting with water colors on damp, fresh plaster. 2 picture or design so painted: *Beautiful frescoes covered the walls and ceiling of the cathedral.* 3 paint with water colors on damp, fresh plaster. 1,2 *n., pl.* **fres coes** or **fres cos;** 3 *v.*, **fres coed, fres co ing.** [from Italian *fresco* cool, fresh]

fresh[1] (fresh), 1 newly made, grown, or gathered: *fresh footprints. These are fresh vegetables.* 2 not known, seen, or used before; new; recent: *Is there any fresh news from home?* 3 additional; further; another: *After her failure she made a fresh start.* 4 not salty: *Rivers are usually fresh water.* 5 not spoiled; not stale: *Is this milk fresh?* 6 not artificially preserved: *Fresh foods usually have more flavor than canned ones.* 7 not tired out; vigorous; lively: *Put in fresh horses.* 8 not faded or worn; bright: *The party was fresh in her memory.* 9 looking healthy or young: *Grandmother is as hale and fresh in*

appearance as she was ten years ago. 10 pure; cool; refreshing: *a fresh breeze. adj.* —**fresh′ly,** *adv.* —**fresh′ness,** *n.* [Old English *fersc*]

fresh[2] (fresh), INFORMAL. too bold; impudent. *adj.* [from German *frech* impudent]

fresh en (fresh′ən), make or become fresh: *The rest freshened my spirits. The air freshened after the storm. v.*

fresh et (fresh′it), 1 flood caused by heavy rains or melted snow. 2 rush of fresh water flowing into the sea. *n.*

fresh man (fresh′mən), student in the first year of high school or college. *n., pl.* **fresh men.**

fresh wa ter (fresh′wô′tər *or* fresh′wot′ər), of or living in water that is not salty: *a freshwater fish. adj.*

fret[1] (fret), 1 be peevish, unhappy, discontented, or worried: *The baby frets in hot weather. Don't fret over your mistakes.* 2 make peevish, unhappy, discontented, or worried: *His failures fretted him.* 3 condition of worry or discontent: *She is in a fret about her examinations.* 4 eat away; wear; rub. 1,2,4 *v.*, **fret ted, fret ting;** 3 *n.* [Old English *fretan* eat]

fret[2] (fret), any of a series of ridges of wood, ivory, or metal on a guitar, banjo, etc., to show where to put the fingers in order to produce certain tones. *n.* [origin uncertain]

fret ful (fret′fəl), ready to fret; peevish, unhappy, discontented, or worried: *My baby brother is fretful because he is cutting his teeth. adj.* —**fret′ful ly,** *adv.* —**fret′ful ness,** *n.*

fret work (fret′wėrk′), ornamental openwork or carving. *n.*

Freud (froid), **Sigmund,** 1856-1939, Austrian physician who developed a theory and technique of psychoanalysis. *n.*

Fri., Friday.

fri a ble (frī′ə bəl), easily crumbled: *Dry soil is friable. adj.*

fri ar (frī′ər), man who belongs to one of certain religious brotherhoods of the Roman Catholic Church. The Franciscans and Dominicans are two great orders of friars. *n.*

hat, āge, fär; let, ēqual, tėrm;
it, īce; hot, ōpen, ôrder;
oil, out; cup, pùt, rüle; ch, child;
ng, long; sh, she; th, thin;
ŦH, then; zh, measure;

ə represents *a* in about,
e in taken, *i* in pencil,
o in lemon, *u* in circus.

adj.	adjective	*n.*	noun
adv.	adverb	*prep.*	preposition
conj.	conjunction	*pron.*	pronoun
interj.	interjection	*v.*	verb
sing.	singular	*pl.*	plural

fric as see (frik′ə sē′), 1 meat cut up, stewed, and served in a sauce made with its own gravy. 2 prepare (meat) in this way. 1 *n.*, 2 *v.*, **fric as seed, fric as see ing.**

fric tion (frik′shən), 1 a rubbing of one thing against another, such as skates on ice, hand against hand, or a brush on shoes; rubbing: *Matches are lighted by friction.* 2 resistance to motion of surfaces that touch: *Oil reduces friction. A sled moves more easily on smooth ice than on rough ground because there is less friction.* 3 conflict of differing ideas, opinions, etc.; disagreement; clash: *Constant friction between the two families almost created a feud. n.*

Fri day (frī′dē), the sixth day of the week, following Thursday. *n.* [Old English *Frigedæg*, from *Frige* of Fria or Freya (the Germanic goddess of love) + *dæg* day]

fried (frīd), 1 cooked in hot fat. 2 past tense and past participle of **fry.** *I fried the ham. The potatoes had been fried.* 1 *adj.*, 2 *v.*

friend (frend), 1 person who knows and likes another. 2 person who favors and supports: *She was a generous friend to the poor.* 3 person who belongs to the same side or group: *Are you friend or foe?* 4 **Friend,** member of the Society of Friends; Quaker. *n.*
make friends with, become a friend of.

friend less (frend′lis), without friends. *adj.*

friend li ness (frend′lē nis), friendly feeling or behavior. *n.*

friend ly (frend′lē), 1 of a friend; having the attitude of a friend; kind: *a friendly teacher.* 2 like a friend; like a friend's: *a friendly greeting.* 3 on good terms; not hostile: *friendly relations between countries.* 4 wanting to be a friend: *a friendly dog.* 5 favoring and supporting; favorable. *adj.*, **friend li er, friend li est.**

friend ship (frend′ship), 1 condition of being friends. 2 a liking between friends. 3 friendliness. *n.*

frieze (frēz), a horizontal band of decoration around a room, building, or mantel. *n.*

frig ate (frig′it), 1 a fast, three-masted,

sailing warship of medium size. Frigates were much used from 1750 to 1850. 2 a small escort vessel, equipped to destroy submarines. *n.*

frigate (def. 1)

fright (frīt), 1 sudden and extreme fear; sudden terror or alarm: *The howl filled me with fright.* 2 INFORMAL. person or thing that is ugly, shocking, or ridiculous: *You look like a fright in that Halloween costume! n.*

fright en (frīt′n), 1 fill with fright; make or become afraid; scare or terrify: *Thunder frightened the puppy.* 2 drive or force by terrifying: *The sudden noise frightened the deer away. v.* —**fright′en ing ly,** *adv.*

fright ful (frīt′fəl), 1 that would frighten; dreadful; terrible: *a frightful experience.* 2 ugly; shocking: *the frightful destruction caused by a fire.* 3 INFORMAL. very great: *I'm in a frightful hurry. adj.* —**fright′ful ly,** *adv.* —**fright′ful ness,** *n.*

frig id (frij′id), 1 very cold: *Eskimos are used to living in a frigid climate.* 2 cold in feeling or manner; stiff; chilling: *He received a frigid greeting from the man he had insulted. adj.* —**frig′id ly,** *adv.* —**frig′id ness,** *n.*

fri gid i ty (fri jid′ə tē), condition of being frigid. *n.*

Frigid Zone, either of the two polar regions, north of the arctic circle and south of the antarctic circle.

fri jol (frē′hōl), kind of bean much used for food in Mexico and the southwestern United States. *n.*, *pl.* **fri joles** (frē′hōlz *or* fri hō′lēz). [from Spanish]

frill (fril), 1 a ruffle: *Her fancy blouse had frills around the neck and down the front.* 2 put a ruffle on; adorn with ruffles: *frill a curtain.* 3 thing added merely for show; useless ornament. 1,3 *n.*, 2 *v.*

fringe (frinj), 1 border or trimming made of threads, cords, etc., either

frieze

loose or tied together in small bunches. 2 anything like this; border: *A fringe of hair hung over her forehead.* 3 make a fringe for. 4 be a fringe for: *Bushes fringed the road.* 1,2 *n.*, 3,4 *v.*, **fringed, fring ing.**

frisk (frisk), 1 run and jump about playfully; dance and skip joyously: *Our lively puppy frisks all over the house.* 2 SLANG. search (a person) for concealed weapons, stolen goods, etc., by running a hand quickly over his clothes. *v.*

frisk i ly (fris′kə lē), in a frisky manner; briskly. *adv.*

frisk i ness (fris′kē nis), a frisky quality or condition; briskness. *n.*

frisk y (fris′kē), playful; lively. *adj.*, **frisk i er, frisk i est.**

frit ter[1] (frit′ər), waste little by little: *fritter away a day watching television and reading comic books. v.* [from the earlier word *fritters* fragments; origin uncertain]

frit ter[2] (frit′ər), sliced fruit, vegetables, meat, or fish covered with batter and fried. *n.* [from French of the 1400's *friture*, from Latin *frigere* fry]

fri vol i ty (fri vol′ə tē), 1 a being frivolous; silly behavior; trifling. 2 a silly thing; frivolous act. *n.*, *pl.* **fri vol i ties.**

friv o lous (friv′ə ləs), 1 lacking in seriousness or sense; silly: *Frivolous behavior is out of place in a courtroom.* 2 of little worth or importance; trivial: *Don't waste time on frivolous matters. adj.* —**friv′o lous ly,** *adv.*

friz zle[1] (friz′əl), 1 curl (hair) in small, crisp curls. 2 a small, crisp curl. 1 *v.*, **friz zled, friz zling;** 2 *n.* [probably from French *friser* to curl]

friz zle[2] (friz′əl), 1 make a hissing, sputtering noise when cooking; sizzle: *The ham frizzled in the frying pan.* 2 a hissing, sputtering noise; sizzle. 1 *v.*, **friz zled, friz zling;** 2 *n.* [probably blend of *fry* and *sizzle*]

fro (frō). **to and fro,** first one way and then back again; back and forth: *A rocking chair goes to and fro. adv.*

frock (frok), 1 a woman's or girl's dress; gown. 2 robe worn by a clergyman. *n.*

fringe (def. 1) two styles

frog (frog), 1 a small, leaping animal with webbed feet, that lives in or near water. Frogs hatch from eggs as tadpoles and live in the water until they grow legs. Some frogs live in trees. 2 arrangement of a rail where a railroad track crosses or branches from another which guides the flanges of the wheels over the gaps, thus helping the train to stay on its track. 3 an ornamental fastener on a garment, consisting of a loop and a button which passes through it. *n.*

frog (def. 1)
about 3 in. long

frog (def. 2)

frogs (def. 3)

frog man (frog′man′), person trained and equipped with Aqua-Lungs for underwater operations of various kinds. Most of the world's navies now have frogmen. *n., pl.* **frog men.**

frol ic (frol′ik), 1 a joyous game or party; play; fun. 2 play about joyously; have fun together; make merry: *The children frolicked with the puppy.* 1 *n.,* 2 *v.,* **frol icked, frol ick ing.**

frol ic some (frol′ik səm), full of fun; playful; gay; merry. *adj.*

from (from *or* frum; *unstressed* frəm), 1 out of: *a train from New York. Steel is made from iron.* 2 out of the possession of: *Take the book from her.* 3 starting at; beginning with: *from that time forward. Three weeks from today is a holiday.* 4 because of; by reason of: *act from a sense of duty. I am suffering from a cold.* 5 as being unlike; as distinguished from: *Anyone can tell apples from oranges.* 6 off: *He took a book from the table. prep.*

frond
of maidenhair fern

frond (frond), the leaf of a fern or of a palm tree. *n.*

front (frunt), 1 the first part: *the front of a car.* 2 part that faces forward: *the front of a dress.* 3 thing fastened or worn on the front. 4 place where fighting is going on; line of battle. 5 land facing a street, river, etc.: *We*

have a house on the lake front. 6 of, on, in, or at the front: *a front room.* 7 have the front toward; face: *Her house fronts the park.* 8 be in front of. 9 meet face to face; meet as an enemy; defy; oppose. 10 manner of looking or behaving: *a genial front.* 11 INFORMAL. an outward appearance of wealth, importance, etc.: *The newcomer put up an impressive front.* 12 INFORMAL. person or thing that serves as a cover for unlawful activities. 13 the dividing surface between two dissimilar air masses: *A cold front is moving toward this area from Canada.* 1-5, 10-13 *n.,* 6 *adj.,* 7-9 *v.*

front age (frun′tij), 1 front of a building or of a lot. 2 length of this front. 3 land facing a street, river, etc. 4 land between a building and a street, river, etc. *n.*

fron tal (frun′tl), 1 of, on, in, or at the front: *The soldiers charged straight ahead and made a frontal attack on the enemy.* 2 of the forehead: *frontal bones. adj.*

fron tier (frun tir′), 1 the farthest part of a settled country, where the wilds begin. 2 part of a country next to another country; border. 3 an uncertain or undeveloped region: *explore the frontiers of science. n.*

fron tiers man (frun tirz′mən), man who lives on the frontier. *n., pl.* **fron tiers men.**

fron tis piece (frun′tis pēs′), picture facing the title page of a book or of a division of a book. *n.*

front let (frunt′lit), 1 band or ornament worn on the forehead. 2 forehead of an animal. *n.*

frost (frôst), 1 a freezing condition; very cold weather; temperature below the point at which water freezes: *Frost came early last winter.* 2 moisture frozen on or in a surface; feathery crystals of ice formed when water vapor in the air condenses at a temperature below freezing: *On cold fall mornings, there is frost on the grass.* 3 cover with frost. 4 cover with anything that suggests frost: *The cook frosted the cake with a mixture of sugar and beaten whites of egg.* 5 kill or injure by frost or freezing: *A sudden drop in temperature frosted the tomato plants.* 1,2 *n.,* 3-5 *v.*

Frost (frôst), **Robert,** 1875-1963, American poet. *n.*

frost bite (frôst′bīt′), 1 injury to a part of the body caused by exposure to severe cold. 2 injure (a part of the body) by frost; harm by severe cold: *My ears were frostbitten.* 1 *n.,* 2 *v.,* **frost bit** (frôst′bit′), **frost bit ten** (frôst′bit′n), **frost bit ing.**

frost ed (frô′stid), 1 covered with

hat, āge, fär; let, ēqual, tèrm; it, īce; hot, ōpen, ôrder; oil, out; cup, pùt, rüle; ch, child; ng, long; sh, she; th, thin; ŦH, then; zh, measure;

ə represents *a* in about, *e* in taken, *i* in pencil, *o* in lemon, *u* in circus.

frost: *a frosted window.* 2 having a surface like frost: *Frosted glass has a rough surface.* 3 covered with frosting; iced: *a frosted cake.* 4 frozen. *adj.*

frost i ly (frô′stl ē), in a frosty manner. *adv.*

frost i ness (frô′stē nis), condition or quality of being frosty. *n.*

frost ing (frô′sting), 1 mixture of sugar and some liquid, often with the beaten whites of eggs, flavoring, etc., to cover a cake; icing. 2 a dull, rough finish on a glass or metal. *n.*

frost y (frô′stē), 1 cold enough for frost; freezing: *a frosty morning.* 2 covered with frost: *The glass is frosty.* 3 cold and unfriendly; with no warmth of feeling: *a frosty greeting. adj.,* **frost i er, frost i est.**

froth (frôth), 1 mass of very small bubbles formed in liquid; foam: *There was froth on the mad dog's lips.* 2 give out froth; foam. 3 cover with foam. 4 cause to foam by beating, pouring, etc. 5 something light and trifling; unimportant talk. 1,5 *n.,* 2-4 *v.*

froth i ness (frô′thē nis), condition or quality of being frothy. *n.*

froth y (frô′thē), 1 of, like, or having froth; foamy: *frothy soapsuds.* 2 light; trifling; unimportant: *frothy conversation. adj.,* **froth i er, froth i est.**

fro ward (frō′wərd), not easily managed; willful; contrary. *adj.*

frown (froun), 1 a wrinkling of the forehead to show disapproval, anger, etc. 2 wrinkle the forehead to show disapproval, anger, etc.; look displeased or angry: *The teacher frowned when I came in late.* 3 look with disapproval: *The principal frowned on our plan for a picnic just before examinations.* 1 *n.,* 2,3 *v.*

frow zi ness (frou′zē nis), condition or quality of being frowzy. *n.*

frow zy (frou′zē), 1 dirty and untidy; slovenly. 2 smelling bad; musty. *adj.,* **frow zi er, frow zi est.**

froze (frōz), past tense of **freeze.** *The water in the pond froze last week. v.*

fro zen (frō′zn), 1 hardened by cold; turned into ice: *a river frozen over, frozen sherbet.* 2 very cold: *My*

adj. adjective	*n.* noun
adv. adverb	*prep.* preposition
conj. conjunction	*pron.* pronoun
interj. interjection	*v.* verb
sing. singular	*pl.* plural

---

hands are frozen; I need some gloves. 3 preserved by being subjected to low temperatures: *frozen foods.* 4 killed or injured by frost: *frozen flowers.* 5 covered or clogged with ice: *frozen water pipes.* 6 cold and unfeeling: *a frozen heart, a frozen stare.* 7 too frightened or stiff to move: *frozen to the spot in horror.* 8 past participle of **freeze.** *The water has frozen to ice.* 1-7 *adj.,* 8 *v.*

fruc tose (fruk´tōs), sugar present in many fruits and in honey; fruit sugar. It is sweeter than glucose or sucrose. *n.*

fru gal (frü´gəl), 1 without waste; saving; using things well: *My aunt is a frugal housekeeper who buys and uses food carefully.* 2 costing little; barely enough: *He ate a frugal supper of bread and milk. adj.* —**fru´gal ly,** *adv.*

fru gal i ty (frü gal´ə tē), avoidance of waste; tendency to save money. *n., pl.* **fru gal i ties.**

fruit (früt), 1 a juicy or fleshy product of a tree, bush, shrub, or vine which is usually sweet and good to eat. Apples, pears, oranges, bananas, peaches, and plums are fruits. 2 part of a plant which contains the seeds. Pea pods, acorns, cucumbers, and grains of wheat are fruits. 3 the useful product of plants: *The fruits of the earth are used mostly for food.* 4 result of anything; product: *His invention was the fruit of much effort.* 5 have or produce fruit. 1-4 *n.,* 5 *v.*

fruit age (frü´tij), 1 a having or producing fruit. 2 crop of fruit; fruit. 3 product; result. *n.*

fruit cake (früt´kāk´), a rich cake usually containing many fruits and sometimes nuts and spices. *n.*

fruit er er (frü´tər ər), dealer in fruit. *n.*

fruit fly, a small fly whose larvae feed on decaying fruits and vegetables.

fruit ful (früt´fəl), 1 producing much fruit. 2 producing much of anything: *a fruitful mind.* 3 having good results; bringing benefit or profit: *a fruitful plan or idea. adj.* —**fruit´ful ly,** *adv.* —**fruit´ful ness,** *n.*

fru i tion (frü ish´ən), 1 conditon of having results; fulfillment; attainment: *After years of hard work her plans came to fruition.* 2 pleasure that comes from

possession or use. 3 condition of producing fruit. *n.*

fruit less (früt´lis), 1 having no results; useless; unsuccessful: *Our search was fruitless; we could not find the lost book.* 2 producing no fruit; barren: *fruitless soil. adj.* —**fruit´less- ly,** *adv.* —**fruit´less ness,** *n.*

fruit sugar, fructose.

fruit y (frü´tē), tasting or smelling like fruit: *the rich, fruity odor of boiling jam. adj.,* **fruit i er, fruit i est.**

frus trate (frus´trāt), 1 make use- less or worthless; foil; defeat: *Heavy rain frustrated our plans for a picnic.* 2 thwart; oppose: *The struggling artist was often frustrated in her ambition to paint. v.,* **frus trat ed, frus trat ing.**

frus tra tion (fru strā´shən), a frus- trating or a being frustrated. *n.*

fry[1] (frī), 1 cook in hot fat in a deep or shallow pan, often over a flame: *He is frying potatoes.* 2 dish of something fried. 3 an outdoor social gathering at which food is fried and eaten: *a fish fry.* 1 *v.,* **fried, fry ing;** 2,3 *n., pl.* **fries.** [from French of the 1200's *frire*]

fry[2] (frī), young fishes. *n., pl.* **fry.** [from French of the 1300's *frai* spawn]

ft., 1 foot or feet. 2 fort.

fuch sia (fyü´shə), 1 shrub with hand- some pink, red, or purple flowers that droop from the stems. 2 a purplish red. 3 purplish-red. 1,2 *n., pl.* **fuch sias;** 3 *adj.* [from Leonard *Fuchs,* 1501-1566, a German botanist]

fud dle (fud´l), 1 make stupid with drink; intoxicate. 2 confuse; muddle. *v.,* **fud dled, fud dling.**

fudge (fuj), 1 a soft candy made of sugar, milk, chocolate, butter, etc. 2 nonsense. *n.*

Fueh rer (fyür´ər), Führer. *n.*

fu el (fyü´əl), 1 anything that can be burned to produce useful heat or power. Coal, wood, and oil are fuels. 2 any- thing that keeps up or increases a feeling: *His insults were fuel to her hatred.* 3 supply with fuel. 4 get fuel: *The ship will have to fuel at the nearest port.* 1,2 *n.,* 3,4 *v.*

fu gi tive (fyü´jə tiv), 1 person who is running away or who has run away: *The murderer became a fugitive from justice.* 2 running away; having run away: *a fugitive slave.* 3 lasting only a very short time; passing swiftly. 1 *n.,* 2,3 *adj.*

fugue (fyüg), a musical composition based on one or more short themes in which different voices or instruments repeat the same melody with slight variations. *n.*

Füh rer (fyür´ər), a German word meaning leader. It was the title given to Adolf Hitler, the dictator of Nazi Ger- many. *n.* Also, **Fuehrer.**

Fu ji (fü´jē), Fujiyama. *n.*

Fu ji ya ma (fü´jē yä´mə), extinct vol- cano in S Japan, near Tokyo. It is the highest mountain in Japan and has long been considered sacred by many Japanese. *n.*

-ful, *suffix added to nouns to form ad- jectives or other nouns.* 1 full of ___: *Cheerful = full of cheer.* 2 showing ___: *Careful = showing care.* 3 hav- ing a tendency to ___: *Harmful = having a tendency to harm.* 4 enough to fill a ___: *Cupful = enough to fill a cup.* [Old English *-ful,* from adjective *full* full]

LEVER
FULCRUM

ful crum (ful´krəm), support on which a lever turns or rests in moving or lifting something. *n., pl.* **ful crums, ful cra** (ful´krə).

ful fill or **ful fil** (ful fil´), 1 carry out (a promise, prophecy, etc.); cause to happen or take place. 2 perform or do (a duty, command, etc.): *She fulfilled all the teacher's requests.* 3 satisfy (a requirement, condition, etc.): *This diet will fulfill all your needs in food. The new cleanser completely fulfilled its pur- pose.* 4 bring to an end; finish or com- plete (a period of time, work, etc.): *fulfill a contract. v.,* **ful filled, ful fill- ing.**

ful fill ment or **ful fil ment** (ful- fil´mənt), a fulfilling; completion; per- formance; accomplishment. *n.*

full (ful), 1 able to hold no more; with no empty space; filled: *a full cup. My stomach is full.* 2 complete; entire: *a full supply of clothes. I ran a full mile.* 3 completely: *Fill the pail full.* 4 com- pleteness; greatest degree: *He satis- fied his ambition to the full.* 5 more than enough to satisfy; well supplied: *He ate three full meals a day.* 6 well filled out; plump; round: *a full face.* 7 having wide folds or much cloth: *a full skirt.* 8 strong, rich, and distinct: *An orator should have a full voice.* 9 straight; directly: *The ball hit him full in the face.* 1,2,5-8 *adj.,* 3,9 *adv.,* 4 *n.* **full of,** filled with: *The child's room is full of toys.*

in full, 1 to or for the complete amount: *They expect payment in full without delay.* 2 not abbreviated or shortened: *a document reproduced in full.*

full back (ful´bak´), a football player who is a member of the offensive back- field and usually lines up between the halfbacks. *n.*

full-fledged (fùl'flejd'), 1 fully developed. 2 of full rank or standing: *He is now a full-fledged Boy Scout. adj.*

full-grown (fùl'grōn'), fully grown; mature. *adj.*

full-length (fùl'lengkth' or fùl'length'), 1 showing the entire human body: *a full-length portrait.* 2 of considerable length: *I watched a full-length movie on television. adj.*

full moon, the moon seen from the earth as a whole circle.

full ness (fùl'nis), condition of being full: *The bag bulged because of its fullness. n.*

full-rigged (fùl'rigd'), 1 having three or four masts, all completely square-rigged. 2 completely equipped. *adj.*

ful ly (fùl'ē), 1 completely; entirely: *The soldiers were fully armed.* 2 abundantly; plentifully: *The gymnasium was fully equipped with ropes, rings, etc.* 3 quite; exactly: *He could not fully describe what he had seen. adv.*

ful mi nate (fùl'mə nāt), 1 thunder forth censure, threats, decrees, etc.; denounce something violently: *The newspapers fulminated against the crime wave.* 2 explode violently. *v.,* **ful mi nat ed, ful mi nat ing.**

ful mi na tion (fùl'mə nā'shən), 1 a violent denunciation; strong censure. 2 a violent explosion. *n.*

ful some (fùl'səm), so much as to be disgusting: *She was offended by the fulsome flattery of her work. adj.* —**ful'some ly,** *adv.* —**ful'some ness,** *n.*

Ful ton (fùl't'n), **Robert,** 1765-1815, American inventor who built the first successful steamboat in 1803. *n.*

fum ble (fùm'bəl), 1 feel or grope about clumsily; search awkwardly: *He fumbled in the darkness for the doorknob.* 2 handle awkwardly. 3 let (a ball) drop instead of catching and holding it: *The halfback fumbled the ball, and the other team recovered it.* 4 an awkward attempt to find or handle something. 1-3 *v.,* **fum bled, fum bling;** 4 *n.*

fum bler (fùm'blər), person who fumbles. *n.*

fume (fyüm), 1 vapor, gas, or smoke, especially if harmful, strong, or giving out odor: *The fumes from the automobile exhaust nearly choked her. Tobacco fumes filled the air in the room.* 2 give out vapor, gas, or smoke: *The candle fumed, sputtered, and went out.* 3 let off one's rage in angry comments: *She fumed about the slowness of the train.* 4 treat with fumes: *fumed oak.* 1 *n.,* 2-4 *v.,* **fumed, fum ing.**

fu mi gate (fyü'mə gāt), disinfect with fumes; expose to fumes: *fumigate a building to kill the cockroaches. v.,* **fu mi gat ed, fu mi gat ing.**

fu mi ga tion (fyü'mə gā'shən), a

fumigating or a being fumigated. *n.*

fun (fun), merry play; playfulness; amusement; joking: *They had a lot of fun at the party. n.*

for fun or **in fun,** as a joke; playfully.

make fun of or **poke fun at,** laugh at; ridicule.

func tion (fungk'shən), 1 proper work; normal action or use; purpose: *The function of the stomach is to help digest food.* 2 work; act: *One of the older students can function as teacher. This old fountain pen does not function very well.* 3 a formal public or social gathering: *The hotel ballroom is often used for weddings, anniversaries, and other functions.* 4 in mathematics: **a** a quantity whose value depends on the value given to another related quantity: *The area of a circle is a function of its radius.* **b** a relationship between two sets such that each element in the first set is associated with exactly one element in the second set. 1,3,4 *n.,* 2 *v.*

func tion al (fungk'shə nəl), 1 of a function. 2 having a function; working; acting: *The functional wings of an insect are those used for flying. adj.* —**func'tion al ly,** *adv.*

func tion ar y (fungk'shə ner'ē), an official. *n., pl.* **func tion ar ies.**

fund (fund), 1 sum of money set aside for a special purpose: *The school has a fund of $2000 to buy books with.* 2 **funds,** *pl.* **a** money ready to use: *We took $10 from the club's funds to buy a flag.* **b** money: *If you wouldn't use up your entire allowance, you wouldn't always be low in funds.* 3 stock or store ready for use; supply: *There is a fund of information in our new library.* 4 change (a debt) from a short term to a long term. 1-3 *n.,* 4 *v.*

fun da men tal (fun'də men'tl), 1 of or forming a foundation or basis; essential; basic: *Reading is a fundamental skill.* 2 something fundamental; essential part: *the fundamentals of grammar.* 1 *adj.,* 2 *n.* —**fun'da men'tal ly,** *adv.*

Fun dy (fun'dē), **Bay of,** inlet of the Atlantic between Nova Scotia and New Brunswick, Canada. The Bay of Fundy has the highest tides in the world. *n.*

fu ner al (fyü'nər əl), 1 ceremonies performed when a dead person's body is buried or burned. A funeral usually includes a religious service and taking the body to the place where it is buried or burned. 2 of a funeral; suitable for a funeral: *a funeral procession. A funeral march is very slow.* 1 *n.,* 2 *adj.*

fu ner e al (fyü nir'ē əl), of or like a funeral; gloomy; dismal. *adj.*

fun gi (fun'jī), a plural of **fungus.** *n.*

fun gi cide (fun'jə sīd), any substance that destroys harmful fungi. *n.*

hat, āge, fär; let, ēqual, tėrm;
it, īce; hot, ōpen, ôrder;
oil, out; cup, pùt, rüle; ch, child;
ng, long; sh, she; th, thin;
ℱH, then; zh, measure;

ə represents *a* in about,
e in taken, *i* in pencil,
o in lemon, *u* in circus.

fun gous (fung'gəs), 1 of a fungus or fungi; like a fungus. 2 growing or springing up suddenly like a mushroom. 3 caused by a fungus: *Wheat rust is a fungous disease. adj.*

fungus
fungi growing
on a tree

fun gus (fung'gəs), any of a group of plants without flowers, leaves, or green coloring matter. Fungi get their nourishment from dead or living organic matter. Yeasts and many mushrooms are useful fungi and can be eaten as food. Smuts, rusts, and mildews are harmful fungi. Certain fungi, such as molds, are used in medicine. *n., pl.* **fun gi** or **fun gus es.**

funk (fungk), INFORMAL. 1 condition of panic or fear. 2 be afraid of. 1 *n.,* 2 *v.*

funnel (left, def. 1;
right, def. 2—tornado funnel)

fun nel (fun'l), 1 a tapering tube with a wide, cone-shaped mouth. A funnel is used to prevent spilling in pouring liquids, powder, grain, etc., into containers with small openings. 2 anything shaped like a funnel: *a funnel of smoke.* 3 smokestack or chimney on a steamship or steam engine. 4 pass or feed through a funnel: *funnel gasoline into a can. The crowd funneled through the gate.* 1-3 *n.,* 4 *v.*

fun nies (fun'ēz), 1 comic strips;

345

adj.	adjective	*n.*	noun
adv.	adverb	*prep.*	preposition
conj.	conjunction	*pron.*	pronoun
interj.	interjection	*v.*	verb
sing.	singular	*pl.*	plural

comics. 2 section of a newspaper carrying comic strips. *n.pl.*

fun ny (fun′ē), 1 causing laughter; amusing: *The clown's funny jokes and antics kept us laughing.* 2 INFORMAL. strange; queer; odd: *It's funny that he is so late. adj.,* **fun ni er, fun ni est.**

funny bone, place at the bend of the elbow over which a nerve passes. When it is struck, a sharp, tingling sensation is felt in the arm and hand.

fur (fėr), 1 the soft hair covering the skin of many animals. 2 skin with such hair on it. Fur is used to make, cover, trim, or line clothing. 3 Usually, **furs,** *pl.* clothes made of fur: *dressed in furs.* 4 made of fur: *a fur collar.* 5 make, cover, trim, or line with fur. 6 a coating of foul or waste matter like fur. A sick person often has fur on his tongue. 7 coat with foul or waste matter like fur: *My tongue became furred when I had a fever.* 1-3,6 *n.,* 4 *adj.,* 5,7 *v.,* **furred, fur ring. —fur′like′,** *adj.*

fur be low (fėr′bə lō), 1 bit of elaborate trimming: *There were many frills and furbelows on her dress.* 2 trim in a fussy, elaborate way. 1 *n.,* 2 *v.*

fur bish (fėr′bish), 1 brighten by rubbing or scouring; polish: *I furbished the tarnished silver until it shone like new.* 2 restore to good condition; make usable again: *Before going to France, she furbished up her half-forgotten French. v.*

Fur ies (fyùr′ēz), (in Greek and Roman myths) the three spirits of revenge. *n.pl.*

fur i ous (fyùr′ē əs), 1 full of wild, fierce anger: *The owner of the house was furious when she learned of the broken window.* 2 violent; raging: *A hurricane is a furious storm.* 3 of unrestrained energy, speed, etc.: *furious activity, a furious pace or gallop. adj.* **—fur′i ous ly,** *adv.* **—fur′i ous ness,** *n.*

furl (fėrl), roll up; fold up: *The crew began to furl the sails before the anchor was dropped. The birds furled their wings. v.*

fur long (fėr′lông), measure of distance equal to one eighth of a mile; 220 yards. *n.*

fur lough (fėr′lō), 1 leave of absence: *The soldier has two weeks' furlough.*

2 give leave of absence to. 1 *n.,* 2 *v.*

fur nace (fėr′nis), an enclosed chamber or box to make a very hot fire in. Furnaces are used to heat buildings, melt metals, make glass, etc. *n.*

fur nish (fėr′nish), 1 supply with something necessary, useful, or wanted; provide: *furnish an army with blankets. The sun furnishes heat.* 2 supply (a room, house, etc.) with furniture or equipment. *v.*

fur nish ings (fėr′ni shingz), 1 furniture or equipment for a room or a house. 2 articles of clothing: *That store sells men's furnishings. n.pl.*

fur ni ture (fėr′nə chər), 1 movable articles needed in a room or house. Beds, chairs, tables, and desks are furniture. 2 articles needed; equipment. The harness and ornamental coverings for a horse were called furniture in the Middle Ages. *n.*

fur or (fyùr′ôr), 1 wild enthusiasm or excitement: *The news that the first astronauts had orbited the moon caused great furor everywhere.* 2 a craze; mania: *A furor for jogging swept the campus.* 3 a rage; fury. *n.*

fur ri er (fėr′ē ər), 1 dealer in furs. 2 person whose work is preparing furs or making and repairing fur coats, etc. *n.*

fur row (fėr′ō), 1 a long, narrow groove or track cut in the earth by a plow. 2 any long, narrow groove or track: *Heavy trucks made deep furrows in the muddy road.* 3 make furrows in. 4 a wrinkle: *a furrow in one's brow.* 5 make wrinkles in; wrinkle: *The old man's face was furrowed with age.* 1,2,4 *n.,* 3,5 *v.*

furrow (def. 1)—furrows cut by plowshares

fur ry (fėr′ē), 1 of fur; consisting of fur. 2 covered with fur. 3 soft like fur. *adj.,* **fur ri er, fur ri est.**

fur ther (fėr′ŦHər), 1 more distant: *on the further side.* 2 at or to a greater distance: *Go no further than a mile and you will find it.* 3 to a more advanced point: *Inquire further into the matter.* 4 more: *Do you need further help?* 5 help forward; promote: *Let us further the cause of peace.* 6 also; in addition: *My teacher told me to study more and said further that sports were taking too much of my time.* 1,4 *adj.,* comparative *of* **far;** 2,3,6 *adv.,* comparative *of* **far;** 5 *v.*

fur ther ance (fėr′ŦHər əns), act of furthering; helping forward; advancement; promotion. *n.*

fur ther more (fėr′ŦHər môr), in addition; moreover; also; besides. *adv.*

fur ther most (fėr′ŦHər mōst), furthest. *adj.*

fur thest (fėr′ŦHist), 1 most distant. 2 most. 1 *adv.,* superlative *of* **far;** 2 *adj.,* superlative *of* **far.**

fur tive (fėr′tiv), 1 done quickly and with stealth to avoid being noticed; secret: *a furtive snatch at the candy, a furtive glance into the forbidden room.* 2 sly; shifty; stealthy: *She had a furtive manner. adj.* **—fur′tive ly,** *adv.* **—fur′tive ness,** *n.*

fur y (fyùr′ē), 1 wild, fierce anger; rage. 2 violence; fierceness: *the fury of a battle, the fury of a hurricane.* 3 a raging or violent person. *n., pl.* **fur ies.**

furze (fėrz), a low, prickly, evergreen shrub with yellow flowers, common on waste lands in Europe; gorse. *n.*

fuse[1] (def. 1)—This plug fuse screws into an electric circuit. When an overload of current melts the metal strip (as at the right), the fuse must be replaced to restore the circuit.

fuse[1] (fyüz), 1 wire or strip of metal inserted in an electric circuit that melts and breaks the connection when the current becomes dangerously strong. 2 a slow-burning wick or other device used to set off a shell, bomb, a blast of gunpowder, or other explosive charge. *n.* Also, **fuze.** [from Italian *fuso* tube]

fuse[2] (fyüz), 1 join together by melting; melt: *The wax from the two candles fused as they burned. Copper and zinc are fused to make brass.* 2 blend; unite: *The intense heat fused the rocks together. Two political parties fused to form a new third party. v.,* **fused, fus ing.** [from Latin *fusum* poured, melted]

fu see (fyü zē′), 1 a large-headed match that will burn in a wind. 2 flare used by railroads as a signal. A fusee burns with a red light. *n.*

fu se lage (fyü′sə läzh *or* fyü′sə lij), body of an airplane, helicopter, etc., to which the wings, tail, etc., are fastened. The fuselage holds the passengers, cargo, etc. *n.*

fu si bil i ty (fyü′zə bil′ə tē), condition or quality of being fusible. *n.*

fu si ble (fyü′zə bəl), that can be fused or melted. *adj.*

fu sil ier or **fu sil eer** (fyü′zə lir′), 1 (formerly) a soldier armed with a light flintlock musket. 2 soldier belonging to any of several British regiments. *n.*

fu sil lade (fyü′sə lād′), 1 a rapid or continuous discharge of many firearms at the same time. 2 something that resembles a fusillade: *The reporters greeted the mayor with a fusillade of questions. n.*

fu sion (fyü′zhən), 1 a melting together; melting; fusing: *Bronze is made by the fusion of copper and tin.* 2 a blending; union: *A third party was formed by the fusion of independent Republicans and Democrats.* 3 a fused mass. 4 the combining of two atomic nuclei to produce a nucleus of greater mass; nuclear fusion. The fusion of atomic nuclei releases tremendous amounts of energy and is used to produce the reaction in a hydrogen bomb. *n.*

fusion bomb, hydrogen bomb.

fuss (fus), 1 much bother about small matters; useless talk and worry; attention given to something not worth it. 2 make a fuss: *He fussed about his work nervously.* 1 *n., pl.* **fuss es;** 2 *v.*

fuss i ly (fus′ə lē), in a fussy manner. *adv.*

fuss i ness (fus′ē nis), quality or condition of being fussy. *n.*

fuss y (fus′ē), 1 hard to please; never satisfied: *A sick person is likely to be fussy about his food.* 2 elaborately made; much trimmed: *fussy clothes.* 3 full of details; requiring much care: *a fussy job. adj.,* **fuss i er, fuss i est.**

fus tian (fus′chən), 1 a coarse, heavy cloth made of cotton and flax. Fustian was used for clothing in Europe throughout the Middle Ages. 2 a thick cotton cloth like corduroy. 3 made of such cloth. 4 speech or writing made up of pompous, high-sounding words and phrases. 5 pompous and high-sounding. 1,2,4 *n.,* 3,5 *adj.*

fust y (fus′tē), 1 having a stale smell; moldy; stuffy. 2 too old-fashioned; out-of-date. *adj.,* **fusti i er, fust i est.**

fu tile (fyü′tl), 1 not successful; useless: *He fell down after making futile attempts to keep his balance.* 2 not important; trifling: *futile tasks. adj.* —**fu′tile ly,** *adv.*

fu til i ty (fyü til′ə tē), 1 uselessness. 2 unimportance. *n., pl.* **fu til i ties.**

fu ture (fyü′chər), 1 time to come; what is to come; what will be: *You cannot change the past, but you can do better in the future.* 2 that is to come; that will be; coming: *We hope your future years will be happy.* 3 chance of success or prosperity: *She has a job with a future.* 4 the verb form with *shall* or *will* that expresses something taking place in time to come. "I shall go" or "I will go" is the future of "I go." 1,3,4 *n.,* 2 *adj.*

-fy

fu tur i ty (fyü tür′ə tē or fyü tyúr′-ə tē), 1 future. 2 a future state or event. 3 quality of being future. *n., pl.* **fu tur-i ties.**

fuze (fyüz), fuse[1]. *n.*

fuzz (fuz), loose, light fibers or hairs; fine down: *the fuzz on a caterpillar. Peach fuzz washes off easily. n.*

fuzz i ly (fuz′ə lē), in a fuzzy manner. *adv.*

fuzz i ness (fuz′ē nis), quality of being fuzzy. *n.*

fuzz y (fuz′ē), 1 of fuzz. 2 like fuzz. 3 covered with fuzz. 4 blurred; indistinct: *This photograph is too fuzzy for me to identify the people in it. adj.,* **fuzz i er, fuzz i est.**

-fy, *suffix forming verbs chiefly from adjectives.* 1 make _____; cause to be _____: *Simplify = make simple.* 2 become _____: *Solidify = become solid.* [from French *-fier*]

G g

G or **g** (jē), 1 the seventh letter of the alphabet. 2 unit of force exerted on a body by the pull of gravity. The force exerted on a body at rest is 1 G. An accelerating body may experience a force of several G's. *n., pl.* **G's** or **g's.**

g., gram or grams.

Ga., Georgia.

gab (gab), INFORMAL. 1 talk too much; chatter; gabble. 2 idle talk; chatter. 1 *v.,* **gabbed, gab bing;** 2 *n.*

gab ar dine (gab′ər dēn′), 1 a closely woven wool, cotton, or rayon cloth used for raincoats, suits, etc. 2 gaberdine. *n.*

gab ble (gab′əl), 1 talk rapidly and noisily with little or no meaning; jabber. 2 rapid and noisy talk with little or no meaning. 1 *v.,* **gab bled, gab bling;** 2 *n.*

gab er dine (gab′ər dēn′), 1 a man's long, loose outer garment or cloak. Gaberdines were worn in the Middle Ages. 2 gabardine. *n.*

GABLE   GABLE

ga ble (gā′bəl), end of a ridged roof, with the three-cornered piece of wall that it covers. *n.*

ga bled (gā′bəld), built with a gable or gables; having or forming gables. *adj.*

Ga bon (gä bôn′), country in central Africa, on the Atlantic. *n.*

Ga bri el (gā′brē əl), (in the Bible) an archangel who acts as God's messenger. He is the angel of comfort and good news. *n.*

gad (gad), move about restlessly; go about looking for pleasure or excitement: *They were out all day gadding about town. v.,* **gad ded, gad ding.**

gad a bout (gad′ə bout′), person who moves about restlessly or goes about looking for pleasure or excitement. *n.*

gad fly (gad′flī′), 1 fly that bites cattle, horses, and other animals. The horsefly is one kind. 2 person who constantly irritates or annoys, especially to bring about changes in the way things are. *n., pl.* **gad flies.**

gadg et (gaj′it), INFORMAL. a small mechanical device or contrivance; any ingenious device: *Can openers and cookie cutters are kitchen gadgets. n.*

gad o lin i um (gad′l in′ē əm), a highly magnetic metallic element which occurs in combination with certain minerals. *n.* [from Johann *Gadolin,* 1760-1852, a Finnish chemist]

Gael (gāl), 1 a Scottish Highlander. 2 Celt born or living in Scotland, Ireland, or the Isle of Man. *n.*

Gael ic (gā′lik), 1 of or having to do with the Gaels or their language. 2 language of the Gaels. 3 Irish. 1 *adj.,* 2,3 *n.*

GAFF

gaff (def. 3)

gaff (gaf), 1 a strong hook on a handle or barbed spear for pulling large fish out of the water. 2 hook or pull (a fish) out of the water with a gaff. 3 spar or pole used to extend the upper edge of a fore-and-aft sail. 1,3 *n.,* 2 *v.*

stand the gaff, SLANG. hold up well under strain or punishment of any kind.

gag (gag), 1 something put in a person's mouth to keep him from talking or crying out. 2 stop up the mouth of with a gag: *The robbers tied the watchman's arms and gagged him.* 3 choke or strain in an effort to vomit; retch: *Bad-tasting medicines made him gag.* 4 SLANG. joke; amusing remark or trick: *The comedian's gags made the audience laugh.* 1,4 *n.,* 2,3 *v.,* **gagged, gag ging.**

Ga ga rin (gə gär′ən), **Yuri,** 1934-1968, Soviet cosmonaut. He was the first human being to travel in outer space. *n.*

gage[1] (gāj), 1 a pledge to fight; challenge: *The knight threw down his gauntlet as a gage of battle.* 2 glove or other object thrown down as a challenge to combat. 3 pledge; security: *The knight left a diamond as gage for the horse and armor.* 4 OLD USE. to pledge; wager. 1-3 *n.,* 4 *v.,* **gaged, gag ing.** [from French of the 1300's]

gage[2] (gāj), gauge. *n., v.,* **gaged, gag ing.** [from French of the 1300's *gauger* to measure]

Gage (gāj), **Thomas,** 1721-1787, commander-in-chief of the British army at the beginning of the Revolutionary War. *n.*

gai e ty (gā′ə tē), 1 a being gay; cheerful liveliness; joyousness: *Their gaiety helped to make the party a success.* 2 bright appearance: *gaiety of dress. n., pl.* **gai e ties.** Also, **gayety.**

gai ly (gā′lē), 1 in a gay manner; merrily; happily. 2 brightly; showily: *They were gaily dressed in colorful costumes. adv.* Also, **gayly.**

gain (gān), 1 come to have; get; obtain: *The farmer gained possession of more land.* 2 what is gained; increase, addition, or advantage: *a gradual gain in speed, a gain of ten per cent over last year's earnings.* 3 **gains,** *pl.* profits; earnings; winnings. 4 get as an increase, addition, or advantage; profit: *How much did I gain by that?* 5 make progress; improve: *The sick child is gaining and will soon be well.* 6 be the victor in; win: *The stronger army gained the battle.* 7 get to; arrive at; reach: *The swimmer gained the shore.* 1,4-7 *v.,* 2,3 *n.*

gain on, come closer to; catch up with: *One boat is gaining on another.*

gain over, persuade to join one's side.

gain er (gā′nər), 1 person or thing that gains. 2 dive in which the diver turns a back somersault in the air. *n.*

gain ful (gān′fəl), bringing in money or advantage; profitable: *a gainful occupation. adj.* —**gain′ful ly,** *adv.*

gain said (gān′sed′), past tense and past participle of **gainsay.** *Most people gainsaid the contention that the earth is round. Her athletic ability cannot be gainsaid. v.*

gain say (gān′sā′), deny; contradict; dispute: *We could not gainsay his opinion. v.,* **gain said, gain say ing.**

Gains bor ough (gānz′ber′ō), **Thomas,** 1727-1788, English painter. *n.*

gainst or **'gainst** (genst), OLD USE. against. *prep.*

gait (gāt), the kind of steps used in going along; manner of walking or running: *He has a lame gait because of an injured foot. A gallop is one of the gaits of a horse. n.*

gaiters (def. 1)

gai ter (gā′tər), 1 an outer covering for the lower leg or ankle, made of cloth, leather, etc., for outdoor wear. 2 shoe with an elastic strip in each side. *n.*

gal., gallon or gallons.

ga la (gā′lə *or* gal′ə), 1 of festivity; festive: *In our family, Christmas and the Fourth of July are gala days.* 2 a festive occasion; festival. 1 *adj.,* 2 *n., pl.* **ga las.**

ga lac tic (gə lak′tik), of, or having to do with the Milky Way or with other galaxies. *adj.*

Gal a had (gal′ə had), the noblest and purest knight of King Arthur's Round Table, who found the Holy Grail. *n.*

Ga lá pa gos Islands (gə lä′pə gəs *or* gə lä′pə gōs), group of islands in the Pacific, west of and belonging to Ecuador.

Ga la tians (gə lā′shənz), book of the New Testament, written by Saint Paul. *n.*

gal ax y (gal′ək sē), 1 group of billions of stars forming one system. The earth and sun are part of one galaxy. Many galaxies outside our own can be seen with a telescope. 2 **Galaxy,** the Milky Way. 3 a brilliant or splendid group, especially of beautiful, handsome, or distinguished persons. *n., pl.* **gal ax ies.**

gale (gāl), 1 a very strong wind. A gale blows with a velocity of 32 to 63 miles per hour. 2 a noisy outburst: *gales of laughter. n.*

ga le na (gə lē′nə), a metallic, gray mineral containing lead and sulfur. It is the chief source of lead. *n.*

Ga li cia (gə lish′ə), region in central Europe, now divided between Poland and the Soviet Union. *n.*

Gal i le an (gal′ə lē′ən), 1 of or having to do with Galilee or its people. 2 person born or living in Galilee. 3 **the Galilean,** Jesus. 1 *adj.,* 2,3 *n.*

Gal i lee (gal′ə lē′), 1 region in N Israel that was a Roman province in the time of Christ. 2 **Sea of,** a small fresh-water lake in NE Israel. *n.*

Galilee (defs. 1 and 2)

Gal i le o (gal′ə lē′ō), 1564-1642, Italian astronomer and physicist. He was the first to use the telescope to study the heavens. *n.*

gall[1] (gôl), 1 bile of animals. 2 anything very bitter or harsh. 3 bitterness; hate. 4 SLANG. too great boldness; impudence. *n.* [Old English *gealla*]

gall[2] (gôl), 1 make or become sore by rubbing: *The rough strap galled the horse's skin.* 2 annoy; irritate: *It galls me that they are always late for dinner.* 3 a sore spot on the skin caused by rubbing, especially one on a horse's back. 1,2 *v.,* 3 *n.* [from Latin *galla* gall[3]]

gall[3] (gôl), lump or ball that forms on the leaves, stems, or roots of plants

where they have been injured by insects, bacteria, or fungi. The galls of oak trees are used in making ink. *n.* [from French of the 1300's *galle,* from Latin *galla*]

gal lant (gal′ənt *for 1-3;* gal′ənt *or* gə lant′ *for 4,5*), 1 noble in spirit or in conduct; brave: *King Arthur was a gallant knight.* 2 grand; fine; stately: *A ship with all of its sails spread is a gallant sight.* 3 very polite and attentive to women. 4 man who is very polite and attentive to women. 5 man who wears showy, stylish clothes. 1-3 *adj.,* 4,5 *n.* —**gal′lant ly,** *adv.*

gal lant ry (gal′ən trē), 1 noble spirit or conduct; bravery. 2 great politeness and attention to women. 3 a gallant act or speech. *n., pl.* **gal lant ries.**

gall bladder, sac attached to the liver, in which excess bile is stored until needed.

galleon

gal le on (gal′ē ən), a large, high ship with three or four decks, used especially in the 1400's and 1500's. *n.*

gal ler y (gal′ər ē), 1 a hall or long, narrow passage, often with windows along one side. 2 balcony looking down into a large hall or room. 3 the highest balcony of a theater. It contains the cheapest seats. 4 people who sit there. 5 room or building used to show collections of pictures and statues. 6 room or building used for a particular purpose, such as taking photographs or practicing shooting. *n., pl.* **gal ler ies.**

gal ley (gal′ē), 1 a long, narrow ship with oars and sails, used in ancient and medieval times. Galleys were often rowed by slaves or convicts. 2 a large rowboat. 3 kitchen of a ship or airplane. *n., pl.* **gal leys.**

galley slave, person forced or condemned to row a galley.

gall fly (gôl′flī′), insect that deposits its eggs in plants, causing galls to form. *n., pl.* **gall flies.**

Gal lic (gal′ik), 1 of or having to do with Gaul or its people: *Caesar's Gallic Wars.* 2 French: *Gallic wit. adj.*

gall ing (gô′ling), that galls; chafing; irritating. *adj.*

Gal lip o li (gə lip′ə lē), peninsula in NW Turkey, forming the N shore of the Dardanelles. *n.*

gal li um (gal′ē əm), a grayish-white

hat, āge, fär; let, ēqual, tėrm; it, īce; hot, ōpen, ôrder; oil, out; cup, pùt, rüle; ch, child; ng, long; sh, she; th, thin; ∓H, then; zh, measure;

ə represents *a* in about, *e* in taken, *i* in pencil, *o* in lemon, *u* in circus.

metallic element with a low melting point. Gallium occurs as a minute part of bauxite and other minerals. *n.*

gal li vant (gal′ə vant), go about seeking pleasure; gad about. *v.*

gal lon (gal′ən), measure for liquids equal to 4 quarts. *n.*

gal lop (gal′əp), 1 the fastest gait of a horse or other four-footed animal. In a gallop, all four feet are off the ground together at each leap. 2 ride at a gallop: *The hunters galloped after the hounds.* 3 go at a gallop: *The wild horse galloped off when it saw us.* 4 cause to go at a gallop: *She galloped her horse down the road.* 5 go very fast; hurry: *gallop through a speech or book.* 1 *n.,* 2-5 *v.*

gal lows (gal′ōz), 1 a wooden frame made of a crossbar on two upright posts, used for hanging criminals. 2 punishment by hanging: *The judge sentenced the murderer to the gallows. n., pl.* **gal lows es** *or* **gal lows.**

gall stone (gôl′stōn′), a pebblelike mass of cholesterol, mineral salts, etc., that sometimes forms in the gall bladder or its duct. *n.*

ga lore (gə lôr′), in abundance: *Every town we visited had automobiles galore. adv.*

ga losh es (gə losh′iz), rubber or plastic overshoes covering the ankles, worn in wet or snowy weather. *n.pl.*

galley (def. 1)

gal van ic (gal van′ik), 1 of, caused by, or producing an electric current by chemical action. 2 startling. *adj.*

gal van ism (gal′və niz′əm), 1 electricity produced by chemical action. 2 branch of physics dealing with this. 3 use of such electricity for medical purposes. *n.*

gal va nize (gal′və nīz), 1 apply an electric current produced by chemical action to. 2 arouse suddenly; startle: *The ringing of the alarm bell galvanized the dozing firemen into action.* 3 cover

349

adj. adjective	*n.* noun
adv. adverb	*prep.* preposition
conj. conjunction	*pron.* pronoun
interj. interjection	*v.* verb
sing. singular	*pl.* plural

(iron or steel) with a thin coating of zinc to prevent rust. *v.*, **gal va nized, gal va niz ing.** [from Luigi *Galvani*, 1737-1798, an Italian scientist who discovered that electricity can be produced by chemical action]

gal va nom e ter (gal′və nom′ə tər), instrument for detecting an electric current, measuring its strength, and determining its direction. *n.*

Gal ves ton (gal′və stən), seaport in SE Texas. *n.*

Gam bi a (gam′bē ə), country in W Africa, a member of the Commonwealth of Nations. *n.*

gam bit (gam′bit), way of opening a game of chess by purposely sacrificing a pawn or a piece to gain some advantage. *n.*

gam ble (gam′bəl), 1 play games of chance for money: *gamble at cards.* 2 take a risk; take great risks in business or speculation: *Only a rich person can afford to gamble in stocks and bonds.* 3 to risk (money or other things of value): *The daredevil gambled his life on the chance he could leap the deep canyon.* 4 a risky act or undertaking: *Putting money into a new business is often a gamble.* 1-3 *v.*, **gam bled, gam bling;** 4 *n.*

gamble away, lose or squander by gambling: *They recklessly gambled away a fortune in one night.*

gam bler (gam′blər), 1 person who gambles a great deal. 2 person whose occupation is gambling. *n.*

gam bol (gam′bəl), 1 a running and jumping about in play; caper; frolic. 2 run and jump about in play; frolic: *Lambs gamboled in the meadow.* 1 *n.*, 2 *v.*

gambrel roof

gam brel roof (gam′brəl), roof having two slopes on each side. The lower slope is steeper than the upper one.

game[1] (gām), 1 way of playing; pas-

time; amusement: *a game of tag, a game with bat and ball.* 2 things needed to play a game: *This store sells games.* 3 contest with certain rules: *a football game.* One person or side tries to win it. 4 the score in a game: *At the end of the first quarter the game was 14 to 7 in our favor.* 5 plan; scheme: *He tried to trick us, but we saw through his game.* 6 wild animals, birds, or fish hunted or caught for sport or for food. 7 flesh of wild animals or birds used for food. 8 having to do with game, hunting, or fishing: *Game laws protect wildlife.* 9 brave; plucky: *The losing team put up a game fight.* 10 having spirit or will enough: *The children were game for any adventure.* 11 to gamble. 1-7 *n.*, 8-10 *adj.*, **gam er, gam est;** 11 *v.*, **gamed, gam ing.** [Old English *gamen* joy] **—game′ly,** *adv.* **—game′ness,** *n.*

make game of, make fun of; laugh at; ridicule.

play the game, be fair; follow the rules; be a good sport.

the game is up, the plan or scheme has failed.

game[2] (gām), INFORMAL. lame; crippled; injured: *He limps because of a game leg.* *adj.* [origin uncertain]

game cock (gām′kok′), rooster bred and trained for fighting. *n.*

game keep er (gām′kē′pər), person employed to take care of wild animals and birds on an estate or in a certain district and prevent anyone from stealing them or killing them without permission. *n.*

game some (gām′səm), full of play; ready to play. *adj.*

game ster (gām′stər), gambler. *n.*

gam ete (gam′ēt *or* gə mēt′), a mature reproductive cell capable of uniting with another to form a fertilized cell that can develop into a new plant or animal; an egg or sperm cell; germ cell. *n.*

game warden, official whose duty it is to enforce the game laws in a certain district.

gam in (gam′ən), a neglected child left to roam about the streets. *n.*

gam ing (gā′ming), the playing of games of chance for money; gambling. *n.*

gam ma (gam′ə), the third letter of the Greek alphabet (Γ, γ). *n.*

gamma glob u lin (glob′yə lən), part of the human blood. Gamma globulin contains many antibodies which protect against infectious diseases.

gamma ray, electromagnetic radiation of very high frequency given off spontaneously by radium and other radioactive substances. Gamma rays are like X rays but have a shorter wavelength.

gam ut (gam′ət), 1 the whole series of notes on the musical scale. 2 the whole range of anything: *During the day I ran the gamut of feeling from hope to despair.* *n.*

gam y (gā′mē), 1 having a strong taste or smell like the flesh of wild animals or birds. 2 brave; plucky. *adj.*, **gam i er, gam i est.**

gan der (gan′dər), a male goose. *n.*

Gan dhi (gän′dē *or* gan′dē), 1 **Indira,** born 1917, prime minister of India since 1966. 2 **Mohandas K.,** 1869-1948, Hindu political, social, and religious leader. *n.*

gang (gang), 1 group of people acting or going around together, especially a group engaged in wrongdoing: *A gang of toughs robbed me.* 2 group of people working together under one foreman: *A gang of workmen was mending the road.* 3 set of similar tools or machines arranged to work together: *a gang of saws, a gang of plows.* 4 INFORMAL. form a gang: *The boys ganged together to build a raft.* 1-3 *n.*, 4 *v.*

gang up on, oppose as a group.

Gan ges (gan′jēz′), river flowing across N India and Bangladesh into the Bay of Bengal. It is regarded as sacred by the Hindus. *n.*

gan gli a (gan′glē ə), a plural of **ganglion.** *n.*

gan gling (gang′gling), awkwardly tall and slender; lank and loosely built. *adj.*

gan gli on (gang′glē ən), group of nerve cells forming a nerve center, especially outside of the brain or spinal cord. *n.*, *pl.* **gan gli a** or **gan gli ons.**

gang plank (gang′plangk′), a movable bridge used in getting on and off a ship. *n.*

gan grene (gang′grēn′), 1 decay of tissue when the blood supply of a living person or animal is interfered with by injury, infection, or freezing. 2 cause gangrene in. 3 be or become affected with gangrene; decay: *The wounded leg gangrened and had to be amputated.* 1 *n.*, 2,3 *v.*, **gan grened, gan gren ing.**

gan gre nous (gang′grə nəs), of or having gangrene; decaying. *adj.*

gang ster (gang′stər), member of a gang of criminals, roughs, etc. *n.*

gang way (gang′wā′), 1 passageway. 2 passageway on a ship: *This ship has a gangway between the rail and the cabins.* 3 gangplank. 4 INFORMAL. get out of the way! stand aside and make room! 1-3 *n.*, 4 *interj.*

gan net (gan′it), a large, fish-eating sea bird which resembles a goose but has a sharper bill, long, pointed wings, and a shorter tail. *n.*

gant let[1] (gônt′lit), gauntlet[1]. *n.*

gant let[2] (gônt′lit), gauntlet[2]. *n.*

gan try (gan′trē), 1 a movable framework used for servicing vertically mounted rockets or missiles. 2 a bridgelike framework for supporting a kind of suspended crane, light signals over railway tracks, etc. *n., pl.* **gan tries.**

←gantry (def. 1)

gantry (def. 2) supporting a crane

Gan y mede (gan′ə mēd′), (in Greek and Roman myths) a beautiful youth who became cupbearer to the gods of Olympus. *n.*

gaol (jāl), jail (a spelling often used in Great Britain). *n., v.* —**gaol′er,** *n.*

gap (gap), 1 a broken place; opening: *The cows got out of the field through a gap in the fence.* 2 an empty part; unfilled space; blank: *The record is not complete; there are several gaps in it.* 3 a wide difference of opinion, character, etc. 4 a pass through mountains. *n.*

gape (gāp), 1 open wide: *A deep hole in the earth gaped before us.* 2 a wide opening. 3 open the mouth wide; yawn. 4 act of opening the mouth wide; yawning. 5 stare with the mouth open: *The crowd gaped at the daring tricks performed by the tightrope walkers.* 1,3,5 *v.,* **gaped, gap ing;** 2,4 *n.*

ga rage (gə räzh′ *or* gə räj′), 1 place where automobiles are kept. 2 shop for repairing automobiles. 3 put or keep in a garage. 1,2 *n.,* 3 *v.,* **ga raged, ga rag ing.**

garb (gärb), 1 the way one is dressed. 2 clothing: *official garb, military garb, priestly garb.* 3 clothe: *The doctor was garbed in white.* 1,2 *n.,* 3 *v.*

gar bage (gär′bij), scraps of food to be thrown away; waste animal or vegetable matter from a kitchen, store, etc. *n.*

gar ble (gär′bəl), make unfair or misleading selections from (facts, statements, writings, etc.); omit parts of, often in order to misrepresent: *Today's newspaper gave a garbled account of the President's speech.* *v.,* **gar bled, gar bling.**

gar den (gärd′n), 1 piece of ground used for growing vegetables, herbs, flowers, or fruits. 2 take care of a garden; make a garden; work in a garden: *He liked to garden as a hobby.* 3 park or place where people go for amusement or to see things that are displayed: *the botanical garden.* 1,3 *n.,* 2 *v.*

gar den er (gärd′nər), 1 person employed to take care of a garden, lawn, etc. 2 person who makes a garden or works in a garden. *n.*

gar de nia (gär dē′nyə), 1 an evergreen shrub or small tree bearing fragrant, white flowers with smooth, waxy petals. 2 its flower. *n., pl.* **gar de nias.** [from A. *Garden,* 1730-1791, an American botanist]

Gar field (gär′fēld′), **James A.,** 1831-1881, the 20th president of the United States. He was assassinated in 1881, his first year in office. *n.*

gar gle (gär′gəl), 1 wash or rinse the throat with a liquid kept in motion by the outgoing breath: *He gargled with hot salt water to relieve his sore throat.* 2 liquid used for gargling. 1 *v.,* **gar gled, gar gling;** 2 *n.*

gargoyle

gar goyle (gär′goil), spout for carrying off rain water, ending in a grotesque figure of a head that projects from the gutter of a building. *n.*

Gar i bal di (gar′ə bôl′dē), **Giuseppe,** 1807-1882, Italian patriot and general. *n.*

gar ish (ger′ish *or* gar′ish), unpleasantly bright; glaring; showy; gaudy: *The circus performer was dressed in garish colors.* *adj.* —**gar′ish ly,** *adv.* —**gar′ish ness,** *n.*

gar land (gär′lənd), 1 wreath or string of flowers, leaves, etc. 2 decorate with garlands. 1 *n.,* 2 *v.*

gar lic (gär′lik), 1 plant of the same family as the onion, whose strong-smelling bulb is made up of small sections called cloves. 2 its bulb, used to season meats, salads, etc. The flavor of garlic is much stronger than that of the onion. *n.*

gar ment (gär′mənt), any article of clothing. *n.*

gar ner (gär′nər), 1 gather and store away: *Wheat is cut and garnered at harvest time. Squirrels garner nuts in the fall.* 2 storehouse for grain. 1 *v.,* 2 *n.*

gar net (gär′nit), 1 a hard mineral occurring in many varieties. A deep-red, transparent variety is used for jewelry and as an abrasive. 2 a deep red. 3 deep-red. 1,2 *n.,* 3 *adj.*

gar nish (gär′nish), 1 something laid on or around food as a decoration: *The turkey was served with a garnish of* cranberries and parsley. 2 decorate (food). 3 decoration; trimming. 4 decorate; trim: *a gold ring garnished with rubies.* 1,3 *n., pl.* **gar nish es;** 2,4 *v.*

gar nish ee (gär′ni shē′), withhold (a person's money or property) by legal authority in payment of a debt. If a creditor garnishees a debtor's salary, a certain portion of the salary is withheld and paid to the creditor. *v.,* **gar nish eed, gar nish ee ing.**

gar ret (gar′it), space in a house just below a sloping roof; attic. *n.*

gar ri son (gar′ə sən), 1 group of soldiers stationed in a fort, town, etc., to defend it. 2 place that has a garrison. 3 station soldiers in (a fort, town, etc.) to defend it. 4 occupy (a fort, town, etc.) as a garrison. 1,2 *n.,* 3,4 *v.*

gar ru li ty (gə rü′lə tē), 1 talkativeness. 2 wordiness. *n.*

gar ru lous (gar′ə ləs), 1 talking too much; talkative. 2 using too many words; wordy: *garrulous comments.* *adj.* —**gar′ru lous ly,** *adv.* —**gar′ru lous ness,** *n.*

gar ter (gär′tər), 1 band or strap to hold up a stocking or sock. It is usually elastic. 2 fasten with a garter. 1 *n.,* 2 *v.*

Gar ter (gär′tər), 1 **Order of the,** the oldest and most important order of knighthood in Great Britain, established about 1348. 2 badge of this order. *n.*

garter snake, a small, harmless, brownish or greenish snake with light stripes that run along its body.

Gar y (ger′ē *or* gar′ē), city in NW Indiana, on Lake Michigan. It is famous for its steel production. *n.*

gas (gas), 1 substance that is not a solid or a liquid; substance that has no shape or size of its own and can expand without limit. Oxygen and nitrogen are gases at ordinary temperatures. 2 any mixture of gases that can be burned, obtained from coal and other substances. Gas was once much used for lighting, but is now used for cooking and heating. 3 any gas used as an anesthetic. Nitrous oxide is such a gas. 4 substance in the form of a gas that poisons, suffocates, or stupefies. Tear gas is one kind. Poisonous gas has been

hat, āge, fär; let, ēqual, tèrm; it, īce; hot, ōpen, ôrder; oil, out; cup, pút, rüle; ch, child; ng, long; sh, she; th, thin; ₮H, then; zh, measure;

ə represents *a* in about, *e* in taken, *i* in pencil, *o* in lemon, *u* in circus.

adj. adjective	*n.* noun
adv. adverb	*prep.* preposition
conj. conjunction	*pron.* pronoun
interj. interjection	*v.* verb
sing. singular	*pl.* plural

used in warfare. 5 injure or kill by poisonous gas. 6 INFORMAL. gasoline. 7 INFORMAL. supply with gasoline: *gas up the car.* 8 SLANG. talk idly or in a boasting way. 1-4,6 *n., pl.* **gas es;** 5,7,8 *v.,* **gassed, gas sing.**

gas e ous (gas/ē əs), in the form of gas; of or like a gas: *Steam is water in a gaseous condition. adj.*

gash (gash), 1 a long, deep cut or wound. 2 make a long, deep cut or wound in. 1 *n., pl.* **gash es;** 2 *v.*

gas ket (gas/kit), ring or strip of rubber, metal, plaited hemp, etc., packed around a pipe joint, etc., to keep a liquid or a gas from escaping. *n.*

gas light (gas/līt/), 1 light made by burning gas. 2 lamp which burns gas. *n.*

gas mask, helmet or mask that covers the mouth and nose and is supplied with a filter to prevent breathing poisonous gas or smoke.

gas o line or **gas o lene** (gas/ə lēn/ or gas/ə lēn/), a colorless, liquid mixture of hydrocarbons which evaporates and burns very easily. It is made from petroleum or from gas formed in the earth. Gasoline is used chiefly as a fuel to run automobiles, airplanes, and motorboats. *n.*

gasp (gasp), 1 try hard to get one's breath with open mouth. A person gasps when out of breath or surprised. 2 a trying hard to get one's breath with open mouth. 3 utter with gasps: *"Help! Help!" gasped the drowning man.* 1,3 *v.,* 2 *n.*

gas station, filling station.

gas tric (gas/trik), of or near the stomach. *adj.*

gastric juice, the digestive liquid secreted by glands in the lining of the stomach. It contains pepsin and other enzymes and hydrochloric acid.

gas tro pod (gas/trə pod), any of a group of mollusks having eyes and feelers on a distinct head, a muscular belly used for moving, and usually a shell that is spiral or cone-shaped. Snails, slugs, and whelks are gastropods. *n.*

gat (gat), OLD USE. got; a past tense of **get.** *v.*

gate (gāt), 1 a movable frame or door to close an opening in a wall or fence. It turns on hinges or slides open and shut.

2 an opening in a wall or fence where a gate is; gateway. 3 door or valve to stop or control the flow of water in a pipe, dam, canal, lock, etc. 4 number of people who pay to see a contest, exhibition, etc. 5 the total amount of money received from them: *The two teams divided a gate of $3250. n.* —**gate/like/,** *adj.*

gate post (gāt/pōst/), post on either side of a gate. A swinging gate is fastened to one gatepost and closes against the other. *n.*

gate way (gāt/wā/), 1 an opening in a wall or fence where a gate is. 2 way to go in or out; way to get to something: *A college education is one of the gateways to success. n.*

gath er (ga⁊H/ər), 1 bring into one place; collect: *She gathered her books and papers and started to school.* 2 come together; assemble: *A crowd gathered at the scene of the accident.* 3 pick and collect from the place of growth; glean or pluck: *The farmers gathered their crops.* 4 get or gain little by little: *The train gathered speed as it left the station.* 5 put together in the mind; conclude; infer: *I gather from what you say that you are really upset.* 6 pull together in folds: *The dressmaker gathers a skirt at the top. She gathered her brows in a frown.* 7 one of the little folds between stitches when cloth is gathered. 8 come to a head and form pus: *A boil is a painful swelling that gathers under the skin.* 1-6,8 *v.,* 7 *n.* —**gath/er er,** *n.*

gath er ing (ga⁊H/ər ing), 1 a group of people met together; meeting; assembly: *We had a large family gathering at our house on Thanksgiving Day.* 2 swelling that comes to a head and forms pus. *n.*

gauche (gōsh), awkward; clumsy. *adj.*

gau cho (gou/chō), cowboy in the southern plains of South America, usually of mixed Spanish and Indian descent. *n., pl.* **gau chos.** [from American Spanish]

gaud (gôd), a showy ornament; trinket: *The dancer wore many rings, bracelets, beads, and other gauds. n.*

gaud i ly (gô/dl ē), in a gaudy manner. *adv.*

gaud i ness (gô/dē nis), gaudy condition or quality. *n.*

gaud y (gô/dē), too bright and gay to be in good taste; cheap and showy: *gaudy jewelry, a gaudy tie. adj.,* **gaud i er, gaud i est.**

gauge (gāj), 1 a standard measure; scale of standard measurements; measure. There are gauges of the capacity of a barrel, the thickness of sheet iron, the diameter of a shotgun bore or of a wire, etc. 2 instrument for

measuring. A steam gauge measures the pressure of steam. 3 measure accurately; find out the exact measurement of with a gauge. 4 estimate; judge: *It was difficult to gauge the character of the stranger.* 5 distance between the rails of a railroad. Standard gauge between rails is 56¹/₂ inches. 1,2,5 *n.,* 3,4 *v.,* **gauged, gaug ing.** Also, **gage.**

Gau guin (gō gan/), **Paul,** 1848-1903, French painter. *n.*

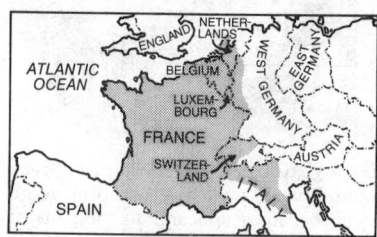

Gaul (def. 1), about 300 B.C., shown by the shaded area on a modern map

Gaul (gôl), 1 ancient region of W Europe. It included what is now France, Belgium, Luxembourg, and parts of Switzerland, Germany, the Netherlands, and N Italy. 2 one of the Celtic inhabitants of ancient Gaul. 3 Frenchman. *n.*

gaunt (gônt), 1 very thin and bony; with hollow eyes and a starved look: *Hunger and suffering had made him gaunt.* 2 looking bare and gloomy; desolate: *the gaunt slopes of a high mountain in winter. adj.* —**gaunt/ly,** *adv.* —**gaunt/ness,** *n.*

gaunt let¹ (gônt/lit), a former punishment or torture in which the offender had to run between two rows of men who struck him with clubs or other weapons as he passed. *n.* Also, **gant let.** [from Swedish *gatlopp* a running through a lane]

run the gauntlet, 1 pass between two rows of men each of whom strikes the runner as he passes. 2 be exposed to unfriendly attacks or severe criticism.

gaunt let² (gônt/lit), 1 a stout, heavy glove with a wide, flaring cuff covering the wrist and lower part of the arm. Gauntlets, usually of leather covered with plates of iron or steel, were part of a knight's armor. 2 a stout, heavy glove with a wide, flaring cuff covering part of the arm. *n.* Also, **gantlet.** [from French of the 1400's *gantelet,* from *gant* glove]

throw down the gauntlet, challenge.

gauze (gôz), a very thin, light cloth, easily seen through. Gauze is often used for bandages. *n.*

gauz i ness (gô/zē nis), gauzy quality. *n.*

gauz y (gô/zē), like gauze; thin and

light as gauze: *a gauzy mist, gauzy wings.* adj., **gauz i er, gauz i est.**

gave (gāv), past tense of **give**. *She gave me some of her candy.* v.

gavel
used by a judge

gav el (gav′əl), a small mallet used by a chairman to signal for attention or order or by an auctioneer to announce that the bidding is over: *The chairman rapped on the table twice with his gavel.* n.

ga votte (gə vot′), 1 an old French dance somewhat like a minuet but much more lively. 2 the music for it. n.

Ga wain (gä′wān *or* gä′win), one of the knights of the Round Table and nephew of King Arthur. n.

gawk (gôk), INFORMAL. 1 stare idly, rudely, or stupidly. 2 an awkward person; clumsy fool. 1 v., 2 n.

gawk i ly (gô′kə lē), in a gawky manner. adv.

gawk i ness (gô′kē nis), gawky condition or quality. n.

gawk y (gô′kē), awkward; clumsy. adj., **gawk i er, gawk i est.**

gay (gā), 1 happy and full of fun; merry: *The gay young people were singing as they decorated the gym for the dance.* 2 bright-colored; showy: *a gay dress.* adj. —**gay′ness**, n.

gay e ty (gā′ə tē), gaiety. n., pl. **gay e ties.**

gay ly (gā′lē), gaily. adv.

gaze (gāz), 1 look long and steadily: *For hours we sat gazing at the stars.* 2 a long, steady look. 1 v., **gazed, gaz ing;** 2 n.

ga zelle (gə zel′), a small, swift, and graceful antelope of Africa and Asia, having soft, lustrous eyes. n., pl. **ga zelles** *or* **ga zelle.**

gaz er (gā′zər), person who gazes: *a star gazer.* n.

ga zette (gə zet′), 1 newspaper: *the "Emporia Gazette."* 2 an official government journal containing lists of appointments, promotions, etc. 3 publish, list, or announce in a gazette. 1,2 n., 3 v., **ga zet ted, ga zet ting.**

gaz et teer (gaz′ə tir′), dictionary of geographical names. Names of places, seas, mountains, etc., are arranged alphabetically. n.

G clef, treble clef.

gear (gir), 1 wheel having teeth that fit into the teeth of another wheel; cog-

wheel; gearwheel. If the wheels are of different sizes they will turn at different speeds. 2 set of such wheels working together to transmit power or change the direction of motion in a machine. In an automobile, power is transmitted from the motor to the wheels by means of gears. In some cars, the driver selects the gear he needs for speed and power by moving the gearshift. 3 connect by gears: *The motor is geared to the rear wheels of the automobile.* 4 any arrangement of gears or moving parts; mechanism; machinery: *The car ran off the road when the steering gear broke.* 5 fit or work together; mesh: *The cogs gear smoothly.* 6 equipment needed for some purpose. Harness, clothes, household goods, tools, tackle, and rigging are various kinds of gear. 7 provide with gear; equip. 8 make fit; adjust; adapt: *The steel industry was geared to the needs of war.* 1,2,4,6 n., 3,5,7,8 v.

in gear, connected to the motor, etc.

out of gear, disconnected from the motor, etc.

shift gears, change from one gear to another; connect a motor, etc., to a different set of gears.

gears (def. 2)
A, to change the speed of axle rotation
B, with angled teeth to run more quietly
C, to transmit motion at right angles

gear ing (gir′ing), set of gears, chains, or parts of machinery for transmitting motion or power; gear. n.

gear shift (gir′shift′), device for connecting a motor, etc., to any of several sets of gears. n.

gear wheel (gir′hwēl′), cogwheel; gear. n.

geck o (gek′ō), a small, harmless, insect-eating lizard with adhesive pads on its feet for walking on ceilings, walls, etc. n., pl. **geck os** *or* **geck oes.**

gee (jē), 1 word of command to horses or oxen directing them to turn to the right. 2 exclamation or mild oath. interj.

geese (gēs), plural of **goose**. n.

Gei ger counter (gī′gər), device which detects and counts ionizing particles. It is used to measure or detect radioactivity, cosmic-ray particles, etc. [from Hans *Geiger*, 1882-1947, a German physicist]

gei sha (gā′shə *or* gē′shə), a Japanese girl trained to be a professional enter-

hat, āge, fär; let, ēqual, tėrm; it, īce; hot, ōpen, ôrder; oil, out; cup, pùt, rüle; ch, child; ng, long; sh, she; th, thin; ₮H, then; zh, measure;

ə represents *a* in about, *e* in taken, *i* in pencil, *o* in lemon, *u* in circus.

tainer and companion for men. n., pl. **gei sha** *or* **gei shas.**

gel a tin *or* **gel a tine** (jel′ə tən), 1 an odorless, tasteless substance like glue or jelly, obtained by boiling the bones, hoofs, and other tissues of animals. It is used in making jellied desserts, glue, camera film, etc. 2 any of various vegetable substances having similar properties. n.

ge lat i nous (jə lat′n əs), 1 of or like jelly. 2 of, like, or containing gelatin. adj.

geld ing (gel′ding), a castrated horse or other animal. n.

gem (jem), 1 a precious stone, especially when cut or polished for ornament; jewel. Diamonds and rubies are gems. 2 person or thing that is very precious, beautiful, etc.: *The gem of her collection was a rare Persian stamp.* 3 set or adorn with gems: *Stars gem the sky.* 4 kind of muffin made of coarse flour. 1,2,4 n., 3 v., **gemmed, gem ming.**

Gen., General.

gen darme (zhän′därm), policeman in France and several other European countries who has had military training. n., pl. **gen darmes** (zhän′därmz). [from French *gendarme*, from *gens d'armes* men of arms]

gen der (jen′dər), 1 the grouping of words into certain classes, such as masculine, feminine, or neuter. In English, except in pronouns (*him—her—it*) and a few nouns with endings such as *-ess* (*actress*), gender is now indicated only by the meaning of the word: *man—*

Geiger counter
The probe detects amount of radiation, which is shown on the dial.

PROBE

adj. adjective	*n.* noun
adv. adverb	*prep.* preposition
conj. conjunction	*pron.* pronoun
interj. interjection	*v.* verb
sing. singular	*pl.* plural

woman, nephew—niece, rooster—hen. 2 one of such classes. 3 sex: *the female gender. n.*

gene (jēn), a minute part of a chromosome that influences the inheritance and development of some character. The genes inherited from its parents determine what kind of plant or animal will develop from a fertilized egg cell. *n.*

ge ne a log i cal (jē′nē ə loj′ə kəl), having to do with genealogy. A genealogical chart is called a family tree. *adj.*

ge ne al o gy (jē′nē al′ə jē *or* jē′nē ol′ə jē), 1 account of the descent of a person or family from an ancestor or ancestors. 2 descent of a person or family from an ancestor; pedigree; lineage. 3 the making or investigation of accounts of descent; study of pedigrees. *n., pl.* **ge ne al o gies.**

gen er a (jen′ər ə), a plural of **genus.** *n.*

gen er al (jen′ər əl), 1 of all; for all; from all: *A government takes care of the general welfare.* 2 common to many or most; not limited to a few; widespread: *In our school there is a general interest in sports.* 3 not detailed: *The teacher gave us only general instructions.* 4 not special: *a general store, a general magazine. A general reader reads different kinds of books.* 5 chief; of highest rank: *The Attorney General is the head of the Justice Department.* 6 a military officer ranking above a colonel, such as a lieutenant general or a major general. 7 (in the United States Army and Air Force) an officer ranking next below a General of the Army or a General of the Air Force and next above lieutenant general. 8 (in the United States Marine Corps) an officer of the highest rank. 1-5 *adj.,* 6-8 *n.*

in general, for the most part; usually; commonly: *He is friendly with me in general, but he was particularly friendly today.*

General Assembly, 1 legislature of certain states of the United States. 2 the main body of the United Nations, made up of delegates from every member nation.

gen er al is si mo (jen′ər ə lis′ə mō), commander in chief of all the military

forces in certain countries: *Generalissimo Chiang Kai-shek. n., pl.* **gen er al is si mos.** [from Italian]

gen e ral i ty (jen′ə ral′ə tē), 1 a general or vague statement; word or phrase not definite enough to have much meaning or value: *The candidates spoke in generalities; not once did they say what they would do if elected.* 2 a general principle or rule: *"Nothing happens without a cause" is a generality.* 3 the greater part; main body; mass: *The generality of people must work for a living.* 4 general quality or condition: *A rule of great generality has very few exceptions. n., pl.* **gen e ral i ties.**

gen er al i za tion (jen′ər ə lə zā′shən), 1 act or process of generalizing: *Don't be hasty in generalization; be sure you have the necessary facts first.* 2 a general idea, statement, principle, or rule: *"Summer is warmer than winter" is a generalization based on long experience. n.*

gen er al ize (jen′ər ə līz), 1 make into one general statement; bring under a common heading, class, or law. 2 infer a general rule from particular facts: *If you have seen cats, lions, leopards, and tigers eat meat, you can generalize and say, "The cat family eats meat."* 3 talk or write indefinitely or vaguely; use generalities: *The commentators generalized because they knew no details.* 4 bring into general use or knowledge; popularize. *v.,* **gen er al ized, gen er al iz ing.**

gen er al ly (jen′ər ə lē), 1 in most cases; usually: *I am generally on time.* 2 for the most part; widely: *It was once generally believed that the earth is flat.* 3 in a general way; without giving details; not specially: *Generally speaking, our coldest weather comes in January. adv.*

General of the Air Force, general of the highest rank in the United States Air Force.

General of the Army, general of the highest rank in the United States Army.

gen er al ship (jen′ər əl ship), 1 ability as a general; skill in commanding an army. 2 skillful management; leadership. 3 rank, commission, authority, or term of office of a general. *n.*

gen e rate (jen′ə rāt′), cause to be; bring into being; produce: *Burning coal can generate steam. The steam can generate electricity by turning an electric generator. v.,* **gen e rat ed, gen e rat ing.**

gen e ra tion (jen′ə rā′shən), 1 all the people born about the same time. Your parents and their friends belong to one generation; you and your friends belong to the next generation. 2 about thirty

years or the time from the birth of one generation to the birth of the next generation. There are three generations in a century. 3 one step or degree in the descent of a family: *The picture showed four generations—great-grandmother, grandmother, mother, and baby.* 4 a bringing into being; generating: *Steam and water power are used for the generation of electricity. n.*

gen e ra tive (jen′ə rā′tiv), 1 having to do with the production of offspring. 2 having the power of producing. *adj.*

gen e ra tor (jen′ə rā′tər), 1 machine that changes mechanical energy into electrical energy and produces either direct or alternating current; dynamo. 2 apparatus for producing gas or steam. 3 person or thing that generates. *n.*

ge ner ic (jə ner′ik), 1 characteristic of a genus, kind, or class: *Cats and lions show generic differences.* 2 general; not specific or special: *"Liquid" is a generic term, but "milk" is a specific term. adj.* —**ge ner′i cal ly,** *adv.*

gen e ros i ty (jen′ə ros′ə tē), 1 a being generous; willingness to share with others; unselfishness: *The millionaire was widely known for his generosity.* 2 nobleness of heart or of mind; willingness to forgive: *She accepted the apology with great generosity.* 3 generous behavior; generous act. *n., pl.* **gen e ros i ties.**

gen er ous (jen′ər əs), 1 willing to share with others; unselfish: *Though she didn't have much to give, she was generous with her money.* 2 noble and forgiving; not mean: *He is generous in accepting the friendship of his former critics.* 3 large; plentiful: *a generous piece of pie. adj.* —**gen′er ous ly,** *adv.* —**gen′er ous ness,** *n.*

gen e sis (jen′ə sis), origin; creation; coming into being: *the genesis of an idea. n., pl.* **gen e ses** (jen′ə sēz′).

Gen e sis (jen′ə sis), the first book of the Old Testament. Genesis gives an account of the creation of the world. *n.*

ge net ic (jə net′ik), 1 having to do with origin and natural growth. 2 of or having to do with genetics. *adj.*

ge net i cal ly (jə net′ik lē), 1 with respect to origin. 2 according to genetics. *adv.*

ge net i cist (jə net′ə sist), an expert in genetics. *n.*

ge net ics (jə net′iks), branch of biology dealing with the principles of heredity and variation in animals and plants of the same or related kinds. *n.*

Ge ne va (jə nē′və), 1 city in SW Switzerland. 2 Lake, long, narrow lake in SW Switzerland and E France. *n.*

Gen ghis Khan (jeng′gis kän),

1162-1227, Mongol conqueror of central Asia.

gen ial (jē′nyəl), 1 smiling and pleasant; cheerful and friendly; kindly: *She was glad to see us again and gave us a genial welcome.* 2 helping growth; pleasantly warming; comforting: *genial sunshine, a genial climate. adj.* —**gen′ial ly,** *adv.*

ge ni al i ty (jē′nē al′ə tē), genial quality or behavior. *n.*

ge nie (jē′nē), spirit or jinni: *When Aladdin rubbed his lamp, the genie came and did what Aladdin asked. n., pl.* **ge nies** or **ge ni i.**

ge ni i (jē′nē ī), 1 a plural of **genius** (def. 5). 2 a plural of **genie.** *n.*

gen i tal (jen′ə təl), having to do with reproduction or the sex organs. *adj.*

gen i tals (jen′ə təlz), the external sex organs. *n.pl.*

gen i tive (jen′ə tiv), 1 showing possession, source, or origin. *Mine, our, his,* and *their* are in the genitive case, or, as usually said for English words, the possessive case. 2 the genitive case. 3 word or construction in the genitive. 1 *adj.,* 2,3 *n.*

gen ius (jē′nyəs), 1 very great natural power of mind: *Important discoveries are usually made by men and women of genius.* 2 person having such power: *Shakespeare was a genius.* 3 great natural ability: *Beethoven played the piano well, but he had a genius for composing music.* 4 the special character or spirit of a person, nation, age, language, etc. 5 a guardian spirit of a person, place, institution, etc. 6 person who powerfully influences another: *An evil genius had them all under his spell. n., pl.* **gen ius es** for 1-4,6, **ge ni i** for 5.

Gen o a (jen′ō ə), seaport in NW Italy. It was the birthplace of Christopher Columbus. *n.*

gen o cide (jen′ə sīd), the extermination of a cultural or racial group. *n.*

Gen o ese (jen′ō ēz′), 1 of Genoa or its people. 2 person born or living in Genoa. 1 *adj.,* 2 *n., pl.* **Gen o ese.**

gen re (zhän′rə), kind; sort; style: *The novel and the drama are two literary genres. n.* [from French]

gen teel (jen tēl′), 1 belonging or suited to polite society. 2 polite; well-bred; fashionable; elegant. 3 artificially polite and courteous. *adj.*

gen tian (jen′shən), plant with usually blue flowers and stemless leaves. *n.*

gen tile or **Gen tile** (jen′tīl), 1 person who is not a Jew. 2 not Jewish. 1 *n.,* 2 *adj.*

gen til i ty (jen til′ə tē), 1 gentle birth; being of good family and social position. 2 good manners. 3 refinement: *The gracious old couple had*

an air of gentility. *n., pl.* **gen til i ties.**

gen tle (jen′tl), 1 not severe, rough, or violent; mild: *a gentle tap.* 2 soft; low: *a gentle sound.* 3 not too much or too fast; not harsh or extreme; moderate: *gentle heat, a gentle slope.* 4 kindly; friendly: *a gentle disposition.* 5 easily handled or managed: *a gentle dog.* 6 of good family and social position; wellborn. 7 having or showing good manners; refined; polite. *adj.,* **gen tler, gen tlest.** —**gen′tle ness,** *n.*

gen tle folk (jen′tl fōk′), people of good family and social position. *n.pl.*

gen tle man (jen′tl mən), 1 man of good family and social position. 2 a well-bred man. 3 a polite term for any man: *"Gentlemen" is often used in speaking or writing to a group of men. n., pl.* **gen tle men.**

gen tle man ly (jen′tl mən lē), like a gentleman; suitable for a gentleman; well-bred; polite. *adj.*

gentleman's agreement, an informal agreement that is not legally binding. The people or countries that make it are bound only by their promise to keep it.

gen tle wom an (jen′tl wùm′ən), 1 woman of good family and social position. 2 a well-bred woman; lady. 3 a woman attendant of a lady of rank. *n., pl.* **gen tle wom en.**

gent ly (jent′lē), 1 in a gentle way; tenderly; softly: *Handle the baby gently.* 2 gradually: *a gently sloping hillside. adv.*

gen try (jen′trē), 1 people of good family and social position. The English gentry are next below the nobility. 2 people of any particular class: *the sporting gentry. n.*

gen u flect (jen′yə flekt), bend the knee as an act of reverence or worship. *v.*

gen u ine (jen′yü ən), 1 actually being what it seems or is claimed to be; real; true: *The table is genuine mahogany, not wood stained to look like it.* 2 without pretense; sincere; frank: *genuine sorrow. adj.* —**gen′u ine ly,** *adv.* —**gen′u ine ness,** *n.*

ge nus (jē′nəs), 1 any group of similar things; kind; sort; class. 2 group of related animals or plants ranking below a family and above a species. *n., pl.* **gen er a** or **ge nus es.**

ge o cen tric (jē′ō sen′trik), 1 viewed or measured from the earth's center. 2 having or representing the earth as a center: *a geocentric universe. adj.*

ge o chem is try (jē′ō kem′ə strē), science dealing with the chemical changes in, and the composition of, the earth's crust. *n.*

ge od e sy (jē od′ə sē), 1 branch of applied mathematics dealing with the

geometric progression

hat, āge, fär; let, ēqual, tėrm;
it, īce; hot, ōpen, ôrder;
oil, out; cup, pùt, rüle; ch, child;
ng, long; sh, she; th, thin;
ŦH, then; zh, measure;

ə represents *a* in about,
e in taken, *i* in pencil,
o in lemon, *u* in circus.

---

measurement of the earth and of large areas on the surface of the earth. 2 branch of surveying dealing with such measurements. *n.*

ge og ra pher (jē og′rə fər), an expert in geography. *n.*

ge o graph ic (jē′ə graf′ik), geographical. *adj.*

ge o graph i cal (jē′ə graf′ə kəl), of or having to do with geography. *adj.* —**ge′o graph′i cal ly,** *adv.*

geographical mile, nautical mile.

ge og ra phy (jē og′rə fē), 1 study of the earth's surface, climate, continents, countries, peoples, industries, and products. 2 the surface features of a place or region: *the geography of New England. n., pl.* **ge og ra phies.**

ge o log ic (jē′ə loj′ik), geological. *adj.*

ge o log i cal (jē′ə loj′ə kəl), of or having to do with geology. *adj.* —**ge′o log′i cal ly,** *adv.*

ge ol o gist (jē ol′ə jist), an expert in geology. *n.*

ge ol o gy (jē ol′ə jē), 1 science that deals with the earth's crust, the layers of which it is composed, and their history. 2 features of the earth's crust in a place or region; rocks, rock formation, etc., of a particular area. *n., pl.* **ge ol o gies.**

geometric (def. 2) designs based on the circle and the square

ge o met ric (jē ə met′rik), 1 of geometry; according to the principles of geometry: *geometric proof.* 2 consisting of straight lines, circles, triangles, etc.; regular and symmetrical: *a geometric design. adj.* —**ge′o met′ri cal ly,** *adv.*

ge o met ri cal (jē′ə met′rə kəl), geometric. *adj.*

geometric progression, sequence of numbers in which each number is

adj. adjective	*n.* noun
adv. adverb	*prep.* preposition
conj. conjunction	*pron.* pronoun
interj. interjection	*v.* verb
sing. singular	*pl.* plural

multiplied by the same factor in order to obtain the following number. 2, 4, 8,16, and 32 form a geometric progression.

ge om e try (jē om′ə trē), branch of mathematics which studies the relationship of points, lines, angles, and surfaces of figures in space; the mathematics of space. Geometry includes the definition, comparison, and measurement of squares, triangles, circles, cubes, cones, spheres, and other plane and solid figures. *n.*

ge o phys i cal (jē′ō fiz′ə kəl), of or having to do with geophysics. *adj.*

ge o phys i cist (jē′ō fiz′ə sist), an expert in geophysics. *n.*

ge o phys ics (jē′ō fiz′iks), study of the relations between the features of the earth and the forces that change or produce them. Geophysics includes geology, meteorology, and similar sciences. *n.*

George (jôrj), **1 Saint,** died A.D. 303?, Christian martyr, the patron saint of England. **2 Lake,** lake in E New York. *n.*

George III, 1738-1820, king of England from 1760 to 1820. America won its independence from England during his reign.

George V, 1865-1936, king of England from 1910 to 1936.

George VI, 1895-1952, king of England from 1936 to 1952.

Geor gia (jôr′jə), **1** one of the southeastern states of the United States. *Capital:* Atlanta. **2** republic in the SW part of the Soviet Union in Europe on the Black Sea. *Capital:* Tiflis. *n.* —**Geor′gian,** *adj., n.*

ge ot ro pism (jē ot′rə piz′əm), response by various parts of plants to the action of gravity. *n.*

ge ra ni um (jə rā′nē əm), **1** plant with fragrant leaves and large clusters of showy flowers, often grown in pots for window plants. **2** a similar wild plant with pink or purple flowers. **3** the flower of either of these plants. *n.*

ger bil (jér′bəl), a small rodent with long hind legs, native to desert regions. Gerbils are used in scientific research and are kept as pets. *n.*

ger i at rics (jer′ē at′riks), branch of medicine dealing with the diseases and treatment of elderly people. *n.*

germ (jérm), **1** a microscopic animal or plant, especially one which causes disease; microbe: *the scarlet fever germ.* **2** the earliest form of a living thing; seed or bud; spore. **3** the beginning of anything; origin: *The germ of the idea for the phonograph came to Edison when he thought of ways of recording telegraph messages automatically. n.*

Ger man (jér′mən), **1** of Germany, its people, or their language. **2** person born or living in Germany. **3** language of Germany. **1** *adj.,* **2,3** *n.*

ger mane (jər mān′), closely connected; to the point; pertinent: *Your statement is not germane to the discussion. adj.*

Ger man ic (jər man′ik), **1** German. **2** of or having to do with the people of northwestern Europe, such as the Germans, Scandinavians, and English, and their languages. English, German, Dutch, and Swedish are Germanic languages. **3** Teutonic. *adj.*

ger ma ni um (jər mā′nē əm), a brittle, silver-white metallic element which occurs in zinc ores. It is used as a semiconductor in transistors. *n.* [from *Germany*]

German measles, a contagious disease resembling measles, but much less serious.

German shepherd, a large, strong, intelligent dog of a breed developed in Germany, often trained to work with soldiers and police or to guide blind persons; police dog.

German silver, nickel silver.

Ger ma ny (jér′mə nē), country in central Europe. Since 1949 Germany has been divided into West Germany and East Germany. *Capital of West Germany:* Bonn. *Capital of East Germany:* East Berlin. *n.*

germ cell, **1** an egg or sperm cell; gamete. **2** a primitive cell from which an egg or sperm cell develops.

ger mi cid al (jér′mə sī′dl), killing germs. *adj.*

ger mi cide (jér′mə sīd), any substance which kills germs, especially disease germs. Disinfectants and fungicides are germicides. *n.*

ger mi nate (jér′mə nāt), **1** begin to grow or develop; sprout: *Seeds ger-*

minate in the spring. **2** cause to grow or develop: *Warmth and moisture germinate seeds. v.,* **ger mi nat ed, ger mi nat ing.**

ger mi na tion (jér′mə nā′shən), a starting to grow or develop; a sprouting. Germination takes place when seeds are warm and moist. *n.*

germ plasm, substance in germ cells that transmits hereditary characteristics to the offspring.

germ warfare, the spreading of germs to produce disease among the enemy in time of war.

Ge ron i mo (jə ron′ə mō), 1829-1909, Apache Indian chief. *n.*

ger ry man der (jér′ē man′dər or ger′ē man′dər), **1** arrange the political divisions of (a state, county, etc.) to give one political party an unfair advantage in elections. **2** act of gerrymandering. **1** *v.,* **2** *n.* [from Elbridge *Gerry,* 1744-1814, whose political party reshaped one district in 1812 so it resembled a *(sala)mander*]

ger und (jer′ənd), a verb form ending in *-ing* and used as a noun. In "Watching him carefully was hard work," *watching* is a gerund used as the subject of *was;* like a verb it takes an object *him* and is modified by an adverb *carefully. n.*

ges ta tion (je stā′shən), **1** a having young developing in the uterus; pregnancy. **2** period of pregnancy. **3** formation and development of a project, idea, plan, etc. *n.*

ges tic u late (je stik′yə lāt), make or use gestures to show ideas or feelings: *The excited speaker gesticulated by raising his arms, pounding the desk, and stamping his foot. v.,* **ges tic u lat ed, ges tic u lat ing.**

ges tic u la tion (je stik′yə lā′shən), **1** a making lively or excited gestures. **2** a lively or excited gesture. *n.*

ges ture (jes′chər), **1** movement of any part of the body to help express an idea or a feeling: *A speaker often makes gestures with his hands or arms to stress something that he is saying.* **2** anything said or done to impress or influence others: *Their refusal was merely a gesture; they really wanted to go.* **3** make gestures; use gestures. **1,2** *n.,* **3** *v.,* **ges tured, ges tur ing.**

get (get), **1** come to have; obtain: *I got a new coat yesterday.* **2** reach: *I got home early last night.* **3** catch; get hold of: *I got the cat by one leg.* **4** cause to be or do: *Get the windows open. They got the fire under control.* **5** be; become: *get sick. Don't get nervous when you take the test.* **6** persuade; influence: *Try to get her to come, too.* **7** make ready; prepare: *Should I help them get dinner?* **8** INFORMAL. possess: *What have* you got in your hand? **9** INFORMAL. to be obliged; need: *We have got to win.* **10** INFORMAL. hit; strike: *The ball got the batter on the arm.* **11** SLANG. understand: *Do you get me? I don't get it.* *v.,* **got,** *got or* **got ten, get ting.**

get around, 1 go from place to place: *The new roads will allow people to get around faster.* **2** become widely known; spread. **3** overcome: *He found the problem hard to get around.* **4** deceive; trick: *You can't get around that child; she's too smart to be fooled.*

get at, 1 reach: *We could not get at the cat on the tree without a ladder.* **2** find out. **3** INFORMAL. tamper with; influence with money or threats.

get away, 1 go away: *Let's get away from here.* **2** escape: *The prisoner got away.*

get away with, INFORMAL. take or do something and escape safely: *get away with lying.*

get back at, SLANG. take revenge on.

get by, INFORMAL. **1** pass: *Let me get by, as I'm in a hurry.* **2** not be noticed or caught. **3** manage: *He has just enough money to get by.*

get in, 1 go in. **2** put in: *They kept talking, and we couldn't get in a word.* **3** arrive: *Our train should get in at 9 p.m.*

get off, 1 come down from or out of: *She got off the horse.* **2** take off. **3** escape punishment. **4** help to escape punishment. **5** start.

get on, 1 go up on or into: *I got on the train.* **2** put on. **3** advance: *get on in years.* **4** manage: *We can't get on without their help.* **5** succeed: *How are you getting on in your new job?* **6** agree: *The roommates got on with each other very well.*

get out, 1 go out. **2** take out. **3** go away. **4** escape. **5** help to escape. **6** become known. **7** publish.

get out of, 1 escape. **2** help to escape.

get over, recover from.

get through, finish.

get together, INFORMAL. **1** bring or come together; meet; assemble. **2** come to an agreement.

get up, 1 arise: *They got up at six o'clock.* **2** stand up. **3** prepare; arrange.

get a way (get′ə wā′), INFORMAL. **1** act of getting away; escape. **2** a start from a complete stop: *a racing car's fast getaway. n.*

Geth sem a ne (geth sem′ə nē), (in the Bible) a garden near Jerusalem, the scene of Jesus's agony, betrayal, and arrest. *n.*

get-to geth er (get′tə geⱦH′ər), INFORMAL. an informal social gathering or party. *n.*

Get tys burg (get′ēz berg′), town in S Pennsylvania. One of the important bat-

tles of the Civil War was fought there July 1, 2, and 3, 1863. *n.*

get-up (get′up′), INFORMAL. **1** way a thing is put together; arrangement or style. **2** dress or costume. *n.*

gew gaw (gyü′gô), **1** a showy trifle; gaudy, useless ornament or toy; bauble. **2** showy but trifling. **1** *n.,* **2** *adj.*

gey ser (gī′zər), a spring that spouts a column of hot water and steam into the air at frequent intervals. There are geysers in Iceland, New Zealand, and Yellowstone National Park. *n.*

Gha na (gä′nə), country in W Africa, a member of the Commonwealth of Nations. *Capital:* Accra. *n.*

ghast li ness (gast′lē nis), ghastly quality or condition. *n.*

ghast ly (gast′lē), **1** causing terror; horrible; shocking: *Murder is a ghastly crime.* **2** like a dead person or ghost; deathly pale: *That very sick man looks ghastly.* **3** INFORMAL. very bad: *a ghastly failure.* **4** in a ghastly manner. **1-3** *adj.,* **ghast li er, ghast li est; 4** *adv.*

Ghent (gent), city in NW Belgium. *n.*

gher kin (ger′kən), a small, prickly cucumber often used for pickles. *n.*

ghet to (get′ō), **1** (formerly) a part of a city where Jews were required to live. **2** part of a city where any racial or other minority group lives. *n., pl.* **ghet tos.**

ghost (gōst), **1** spirit of a dead person. It is supposed to live in another world and appear to living people as a pale, dim, shadowy form. *The ghost of the murdered caretaker was said to haunt the house.* **2** anything pale, dim, or shadowy like a ghost: *Our team didn't have a ghost of a chance to win the basketball game. n.* —**ghost′like′,** *adj.*

give up the ghost, die.

ghost ly (gōst′lē), **1** like a ghost; pale, dim, and shadowy: *A ghostly form walked across the darkened stage.* **2** OLD USE. spiritual. *adj.,* **ghost li er, ghost li est.**

ghost town, a once-flourishing town that has become empty and lifeless.

ghost writ er (gōst′rī′tər), person who writes something for another person who pretends to be the author. *n.*

ghoul (gül), **1** (in Oriental stories) a horrible demon that robs graves and feeds on corpses. **2** person who robs graves or corpses. **3** person who enjoys what is revolting, brutal, and horrible. *n.*

ghoul ish (gü′lish), like a ghoul; revolting, brutal, and horrible. *adj.* —**ghoul′ish ness,** *n.*

GI or **G.I.** (jē′ī′), **1** government issue: *GI shoes, GI socks.* **2** of, having to do with, or for a member of the armed forces: *a GI loan.* **3** INFORMAL. an enlisted soldier in the United States

hat, āge, fär; let, ēqual, tėrm; it, īce; hot, ōpen, ôrder; oil, out; cup, pùt, rüle; ch, child; ng, long; sh, she; th, thin; ⱦH, then; zh, measure;

ə represents *a* in about, *e* in taken, *i* in pencil, *o* in lemon, *u* in circus.

Army; serviceman. **1,2** *adj.,* **3** *n., pl.* **GI's** or **G.I.'s** (jē′īz′).

gi ant (jī′ənt), **1** an imaginary being having human form, but larger and more powerful than a man. **2** person or thing of great size, strength, or importance. **3** like a giant; huge: *a giant potato.* **1,2** *n.,* **3** *adj.*

gi ant ess (jī′ən tis), a female giant. *n.*

giant sequoia, a very large evergreen tree of California; big tree.

gib ber (jib′ər), **1** chatter senselessly; talk in a confused, meaningless way: *The monkeys gibbered angrily at each other.* **2** senseless chattering. **1** *v.,* **2** *n.*

gib ber ish (jib′ər ish), senseless chatter; confused, meaningless talk or writing. *n.*

gib bet (jib′it), **1** an upright post with a projecting arm at the top, from which the bodies of criminals were hung after execution. **2** hang on a gibbet. **3** hold up to public scorn or ridicule. **4** gallows. **5** put to death by hanging. **1,4** *n.,* **2,3,5** *v.*

gibbon
about 3 ft. tall

gib bon (gib′ən), a small ape of southeastern Asia and the East Indies that lives in trees. It has very long arms and no tail. *n.*

gib bous (gib′əs), curved out; humped. A gibbous moon is more than half full but less than full. *adj.*

gibe (jīb), **1** speak sneeringly; jeer; scoff; sneer: *My family gibed at my efforts to paint a picture.* **2** a jeer; taunt; sneer: *Their gibes hurt my feelings.* **1** *v.,* **gibed, gib ing; 2** *n.* Also, **jibe.**

gib let (jib′lit), the heart, liver, or gizzard of a fowl. *n.*

Gi bral tar (jə brôl′tər), **1** seaport and

357

adj. adjective	*n.* noun
adv. adverb	*prep.* preposition
conj. conjunction	*pron.* pronoun
interj. interjection	*v.* verb
sing. singular	*pl.* plural

fortress on a high rock on the Mediterranean Sea, near the S tip of Spain. It is a British colony. **2 Rock of,** the large rock on which this fortress stands. **3 Strait of,** strait between Africa and Europe, connecting the Mediterranean Sea with the Atlantic. *n.*

gid di ly (gid′ə lē), in a giddy manner. *adv.*

gid di ness (gid′ē nis), giddy condition or quality. *n.*

gid dy (gid′ē), **1** having a whirling feeling in one's head; dizzy: *It makes me giddy to go on a merry-go-round.* **2** likely to make dizzy; causing dizziness: *The couples whirled and whirled in their giddy dance.* **3** never serious; frivolous; fickle: *That giddy crowd thinks only of having a gay time.* adj., **gid di er, gid di est.**

gift (gift), **1** something given freely; present: *a birthday gift, the gift of a million dollars to a university.* **2** act of giving freely: *The house came to him by gift from an uncle.* **3** natural ability; special talent: *A great artist must have a gift for painting. n.*

gift ed (gif′tid), having natural ability or special talent; unusually able: *a gifted musician. adj.*

gig[1] (gig), **1** a light, open, two-wheeled carriage drawn by one horse. **2** a long, light ship's boat moved by oars or sails: *The captain's gig was used to take him to and from the ship. n.* [origin uncertain]

gig[2] (gig), **1** a fish spear. **2** spear (fish) with a gig. 1 *n.,* 2 *v.,* **gigged, gig ging.** [origin uncertain]

gi gan tic (jī gan′tik), big like a giant; huge: *The earth is a gigantic ball. adj.*

gig gle (gig′əl), **1** laugh in a silly or undignified way. **2** a silly or undignified laugh. 1 *v.,* **gig gled, gig gling;** 2 *n.*

gig gly (gig′lē), having the habit of giggling. *adj.*

Gi la monster (hē′lə), a large, poisonous lizard of the southwestern United States and northern Mexico, which has a thick tail, a heavy, clumsy body, and is covered with beadlike, orange-and-black scales. [from *Gila,* a river in Arizona and New Mexico]

Gil bert (gil′bərt), Sir **William Schwenck,** 1836-1911, English writer of plays and humorous poems. He

wrote the words for most of the operas for which Sir Arthur Sullivan wrote the music. *n.*

gild[1] (gild), **1** cover with a thin layer of gold or similar material; make golden. **2** make (something) look bright and pleasing. **3** make (something) seem better than it is. *v.,* **gild ed** or **gilt, gild ing.** [Old English *-gyldan,* from *gold* gold]

gild[2] (gild), guild. *n.* [Old English *gield*]

Gil e ad (gil′ē əd), region in ancient Palestine, east of the Jordan River. *n.*

gill[1] (gil), part of the body of a fish, tadpole, or crab by which it breathes in water. Oxygen passes in and carbon dioxide passes out through the thin walls of the gills. *n.* [probably from a Scandinavian word, such as Danish *gjelle*]

gill[2] (jil), a small measure for liquids, equal to one fourth of a pint, or about half a cup. *n.* [from French of the 1200's *gille* a wine measure]

gilt (gilt), **1** gilded. **2** a thin layer of gold or similar material with which a surface is gilded: *The gilt is coming off this frame.* **3** a past tense and a past participle of **gild**[1]. 1 *adj.,* 2 *n.,* 3 *v.*

gim crack (jim′krak′), a showy, useless trifle; knickknack. *n.*

gimlet

gim let (gim′lit), a small tool with a screw point, for boring holes. *n.*

gim mick (gim′ik), SLANG. a clever or tricky idea, stunt, or device. *n.*

gin[1] (jin), a strong alcoholic drink, distilled from grain and usually flavored with juniper berries. *n.* [shortened from *geneva,* from Dutch *genever*]

gin[2] (jin), **1** cotton gin. **2** separate (cotton) from its seeds. 1 *n.,* 2 *v.,* **ginned, gin ning.** [from French of the 1200's *engin* engine]

gin ger (jin′jər), **1** spice made from the root of a tropical plant. It is used for flavoring and in medicine. **2** its root, often preserved in syrup or candied. **3** the plant. **4** INFORMAL. liveliness; energy. *n.*

ginger ale, a bubbling drink flavored with ginger. It contains no alcohol.

ginger beer, drink similar to ginger ale, but made with fermenting ginger.

gin ger bread (jin′jər bred′), **1** cake flavored with ginger and sweetened with molasses. Gingerbread is often made in fancy shapes. **2** something

showy and elaborate; tasteless ornamentation. Cheap carvings glued on furniture are gingerbread. **3** showy; gaudy. Gingerbread work on a house is fussy ornamentation. 1,2 *n.,* 3 *adj.*

gin ger ly (jin′jər lē), **1** with extreme care or caution. **2** extremely cautious or wary. 1 *adv.,* 2 *adj.*

gin ger snap (jin′jər snap′), a thin, crisp cookie flavored with ginger and sweetened with molasses. *n.*

ging ham (ging′əm), a cotton cloth made from colored threads. Its patterns are usually in stripes, plaids, or checks. *n.*

gink go (ging′kō), a large, ornamental tree native to China and Japan, with fan-shaped leaves and nuts that can be eaten. *n., pl.* **gink goes.**

gin rummy, a card game like rummy, usually played by two persons.

gin seng (jin′seng), **1** a low plant of China and North America, with a thick, branched root. **2** this root, much used in medicine by the Chinese. *n.*

Giot to (jot′ō), 1266?-1337, Italian painter and architect whose works mark the beginning of the Renaissance in painting. *n.*

gip sy (jip′sē), gypsy. *n., pl.* **gip sies;** *adj.*

gi raffe (jə raf′), a large African mammal that chews its cud and has a very long neck, long legs, and a spotted skin. Giraffes are the tallest living animals. *n.*

gird (gėrd), **1** put a belt or girdle around. **2** fasten with a belt or girdle: *gird up one's clothes.* **3** surround; enclose. **4** get ready: *She girded herself to face the final examination. v.,* **gird ed** or **girt, gird ing.**

gird er (gėr′dər), a horizontal beam of steel, concrete, or wood, used as a main support. The weight of a floor is usually supported by girders. A tall building or big bridge often has steel girders for its frame. *n.*

GIRDER

gir dle (gėr′dl), **1** belt, sash, cord, etc., worn around the waist. **2** anything that surrounds or encloses: *a girdle of trees around the pond.* **3** a light corset worn about the hips or waist. **4** put a girdle on or around. **5** surround; encircle: *Wide roads girdle the city.* **6** cut away the bark so as to make a ring around (a tree, branch, etc.). 1-3 *n.,* 4-6 *v.,* **gir dled, gir dling.**

girl (gėrl), **1** a female child from birth to about eighteen. **2** a young, unmarried woman. **3** a female servant. **4** IN-

FORMAL. sweetheart. 5 INFORMAL. woman. *n.*

girl friend (gėrl′frend′), INFORMAL. 1 boy's sweetheart or steady female companion. 2 a female friend. *n.*

girl hood (gėrl′hùd), time or condition of being a girl: *The old woman recalled her girlhood with pleasure. n.*

girl ish (gėr′lish), 1 of a girl. 2 like a girl. 3 like a girl's; suitable for a girl. *adj.* —**girl′ish ly,** *adv.* —**girl′ish ness,** *n.*

girl scout, member of the Girl Scouts.

Girl Scouts, organization for girls that seeks to develop health, character, citizenship, usefulness to others, and various skills.

girt (gėrt), girded; a past tense and a past participle of **gird.** *The knight girt himself for battle. v.*

girth (gėrth), 1 the measure around anything: *a man of large girth, the girth of a tree.* 2 strap or band that keeps a saddle, pack, etc., in place on a horse's back. 3 fasten with a strap or band. 4 surround; girdle. 1,2 *n.,* 3,4 *v.*

gist (jist), the essential part; real point; main idea; substance of a longer statement: *The gist of his long talk was that we should build a new school. n.*

give (giv), 1 hand over as a gift; make a present of: *give money to charity. He likes to give books to his friends.* 2 hand over: *Give me that pencil.* 3 hand over in return for something; pay: *She can give as much as $3 for the wagon.* 4 let have; cause to have: *Don't give the teacher any trouble. Give me permission to leave.* 5 deal; administer: *to give medicine, give hard blows.* 6 offer; present: *This newspaper gives a full story of the game.* 7 put forth; utter: *He gave a cry of pain.* 8 yield; furnish; supply: *The cow gives milk. Lamps give light. This farm gives large crops.* 9 yield to force: *The lock gave when they pushed hard against the door.* 10 a yielding to force. 1-9 *v.,* **gave, giv en, giv ing;** 10 *n.*

give away, 1 give as a present: *She gave away her best toy.* 2 present (a bride) to a bridegroom at a wedding. 3 cause to be known; reveal; betray: *The spy gave away secrets to the enemy.*

give back, return: *Give back the book.*

give in, stop fighting and admit defeat; yield: *A stubborn person will not give in easily even when wrong.*

give off, send out; put forth: *This lamp gives off a very bright light.*

give out, 1 send out; put forth. 2 distribute: *The supplies will be given out tomorrow.* 3 make known: *Who has given out this information?* 4 become used up or worn out: *My strength gave out after the long climb.*

give over, 1 hand over; deliver.

2 set aside for a certain purpose.

give up, 1 hand over; deliver; surrender. 2 stop having or doing: *We gave up the search when it got dark.* 3 stop trying: *Don't give up so soon; try again and maybe you will succeed this time.* 4 have no more hope for. 5 devote entirely: *She has given herself up to the study of music.*

give-and-take (giv′ən tāk′), 1 an even or fair exchange. 2 good-natured banter; exchange of talk. *n.*

give a way (giv′ə wā′), INFORMAL. 1 something revealed or made known unintentionally. 2 something given away or sold at a cheap price to promote business or good relations. *n.*

giv en (giv′ən), 1 that has been stated; fixed; specified: *You must finish the test in a given time.* 2 having a fondness or habit; inclined; disposed: *A braggart is given to boasting.* 3 past participle of **give.** *That book was given to me.* 1,2 *adj.,* 3 *v.*

given name, name given to a person in addition to a family name. *Jane is the given name of Jane Smith.*

giv er (giv′ər), person who gives. *n.*

giz zard (giz′ərd), a bird's second stomach, where the food from the first stomach is ground up. The gizzard usually contains bits of sand or gravel. *n.*

gla cial (glā′shəl), 1 of ice or glaciers; having much ice or many glaciers: *a glacial period in geological history.* 2 like ice; very cold; icy. *adj.*

gla cier (glā′shər), a large mass of ice formed over many years from snow on high ground wherever winter snowfall exceeds summer melting. It moves very slowly down a mountain or along a valley, or spreads slowly over a large area of land. *n.*

glad (glad), 1 feeling joy, pleasure, or satisfaction; happy; pleased: *I am glad to be well again.* 2 bringing joy; pleasant: *The glad news made her happy.* 3 bright; gay: *The glad sunshine cheered us.* 4 willing; ready: *I will be glad to go if you need me. adj.,* **glad der, glad dest.** —**glad′ly,** *adv.* —**glad′ness,** *n.*

glad den (glad′n), make or become glad. *v.*

glade (glād), a little open space in a wood or forest. *n.*

glad i a tor (glad′ē ā′tər), slave, captive, or paid fighter who fought at the public shows in the arenas in ancient Rome. *n.*

glad i a to ri al (glad′ē ə tôr′ē əl), of or having to do with gladiators or their combats. *adj.*

glad i o la (glad′ē ō′lə), gladiolus. *n., pl.* **glad i o las.**

glad i o lus (glad′ē ō′ləs), 1 plant that

hat, āge, fär; let, ēqual, tėrm; it, īce; hot, ōpen, ôrder; oil, out; cup, pùt, rüle; ch, child; ng, long; sh, she; th, thin; ∓H, then; zh, measure;

ə represents *a* in about, *e* in taken, *i* in pencil, *o* in lemon, *u* in circus.

grows from bulblike, underground stems and has sword-shaped leaves and spikes of large, handsome flowers in various colors. It is a kind of iris. 2 its flower. *n., pl.* **glad i o li** (glad′ē ō′lē or glad′ē ō′lī), **glad i o lus es.**

glad some (glad′səm), 1 glad; joyful; cheerful. 2 causing gladness; pleasant; delightful. *adj.*

glam or (glam′ər), mysterious fascination; alluring charm; magic attraction: *the glamor of circus life. n.* Also, **glamour.**

glam or ize (glam′ə rīz′), make (someone or something) glamorous. *v.,* **glam or ized, glam or iz ing.**

glam or ous (glam′ər əs), full of glamor; fascinating; charming: *a glamorous job in a foreign city. adj.* —**glam′or ous ly,** *adv.*

glam our (glam′ər), glamor. *n.*

glance (glans), 1 a quick look: *She gave him only a glance.* 2 look quickly: *He glanced out of the window to see if the rain had stopped.* 3 a flash of light; gleam. 4 flash with light; gleam. 5 hit and go off at a slant: *The spear glanced against the wall and missed the target.* 6 a glancing off; slanting movement. 1,3,6 *n.,* 2,4,5 *v.,* **glanced, glanc ing.**

gland (gland), organ in the body which separates materials from the blood and changes them into some secretion for use in the body or into a product to be discharged from the body. The salivary glands make saliva. A cow has glands which make milk. The liver, the kidneys, the pancreas, and the thyroid are glands. *n.* —**gland′like′,** *adj.*

glan du lar (glan′jə lər), of or like a gland; having glands; made up of glands. *adj.*

glare (gler *or* glar), 1 a strong, bright light; light that shines so brightly that it hurts the eyes. 2 give off a strong, bright light; shine so brightly as to hurt the eyes. 3 a bright, smooth surface. 4 bright and smooth. 5 a fierce, angry stare. 6 stare fiercely and angrily. 1,3,5 *n.,* 2,6 *v.,* **glared, glar ing;** 4 *adj.*

glar ing (gler′ing *or* glar′ing), 1 very bright; shining so brightly that it hurts the eyes; dazzling. 2 staring fiercely

adj.	adjective	*n.*	noun
adv.	adverb	*prep.*	preposition
conj.	conjunction	*pron.*	pronoun
interj.	interjection	*v.*	verb
sing.	singular	*pl.*	plural

and angrily. 3 too bright and showy: *a shirt with glaring colors.* 4 very easily seen; conspicuous: *a glaring error in spelling. adj.* —**glar′ing ly**, *adv.*

Glas gow (glas′gō *or* glas′kō), the largest city and chief seaport in Scotland. *n.*

glass (glas), 1 a hard substance that breaks easily and can usually be seen through. It is made by melting sand with soda, potash, lime, or other substances. Windows are made of glass. 2 container to drink from made of glass: *He filled the glass with water.* 3 amount a glass can hold: *drink a glass of water.* 4 mirror: *Look at yourself in the glass.* 5 lens, telescope, thermometer, windowpane, or other thing made of glass. 6 **glasses**, *pl.* eyeglasses. 7 made of glass: *a glass dish.* 8 cover or protect with glass. 1-6 *n., pl.* **glass es**; 7 *adj.,* 8 *v.* —**glass′like′**, *adj.*

glass blowing, art or process of shaping glass objects by blowing air from the mouth through a tube into a blob of molten glass at the other end of the tube.

glass ful (glas′fùl), as much as a glass holds. *n., pl.* **glass fuls.**

glass i ly (glas′ə lē), in a glassy manner. *adv.*

glass i ness (glas′ē nis), glassy appearance or condition. *n.*

glass snake, a limbless, snakelike lizard whose tail breaks off easily.

glass ware (glas′wer′ *or* glas′war′), articles made of glass. *n.*

glass y (glas′ē), 1 like glass; smooth; easily seen through. 2 having a fixed, stupid stare: *The dazed man's eyes were glassy. adj.,* **glass i er, glass i est.**

glau co ma (glô kō′mə), disease of the eye common in old age in which increasing internal pressure causes damage resulting in a gradual loss of sight. *n.*

glaze (glāz), 1 put glass in; cover with glass. Pieces of glass cut to the right size are used to glaze windows and picture frames. 2 a smooth, glossy surface or coating: *the glaze on a china cup. A glaze of ice on the walk is dangerous.* 3 substance used to make such a surface or coating on things. 4 make a glossy or glassy surface on (china, food, etc.). 5 become glossy or

glassy: *eyes glazed with fever.* 1,4,5 *v.,* **glazed, glaz ing;** 2,3 *n.*

gla zier (glā′zhər), person whose work is putting glass in windows, picture frames, etc. *n.*

gleam (glēm), 1 a flash or beam of light: *We saw the gleam of headlights through the rain.* 2 to flash or beam with light: *A candle gleamed in the dark.* 3 a short or faint light: *the gleam of shining metal.* 4 shine with a short or faint light: *gleaming jewelry.* 5 a short appearance; faint show: *The end of the rainfall brought a gleam of hope to the flood victims.* 1,3,5 *n.,* 2,4 *v.*

glean (glēn), 1 gather grain left on a field by reapers. 2 gather little by little: *I was able to glean some information from each book. v.* —**glean′er,** *n.*

glee (glē), 1 a being merry and gay; lively joy; great delight: *The children laughed with glee at the clown's antics.* 2 song for three or more voices singing different parts, usually without accompaniment. *n.*

glee club, group, often of men only, organized for singing songs.

glee ful (glē′fəl), filled with glee; merry and gay; joyous. *adj.* —**glee′ful ly,** *adv.*

glen (glen), a small, narrow valley. *n.*

Glenn (glen), **John,** born 1921, American astronaut. He was the first American to orbit the earth, in 1962. *n.*

glib (glib), speaking or spoken too smoothly and easily: *No one believed their glib excuses. adj.,* **glib ber, glibbest.** —**glib′ly,** *adv.* —**glib′ness,** *n.*

glide (glīd), 1 move along smoothly, evenly, and easily: *Birds, ships, dancers, and skaters glide.* 2 a smooth, even, easy movement. 3 pass gradually, quietly, or without being noticed: *The years glided past.* 4 come down slowly at a slant without using a motor. Under favorable circumstances, an airplane can glide about a mile for every thousand feet that it is above the ground. 5 a coming down in this way. 1,3,4 *v.,* **glid ed, glid ing;** 2,5 *n.*

glid er (glī′dər), 1 airplane without a motor. Rising air currents keep it up in the air. 2 person or thing that glides.

glider (def. 1)

glider (def. 3)

3 a swinging seat suspended on a frame. Gliders are usually placed on porches or outdoors. *n.*

glim mer (glim′ər), 1 a faint, unsteady light. 2 shine with a faint, unsteady light: *The candle glimmered and went out.* 3 a faint idea or feeling: *The doctor's report gave us only a glimmer of hope.* 1,3 *n.,* 2 *v.*

glimpse (glimps), 1 a short, quick view: *I caught a glimpse of the falls as our train went by.* 2 catch a short, quick view of: *I glimpsed the falls as our train went by.* 3 look quickly; glance: *Father glimpsed at the picture I drew and said it was good.* 4 a short, faint appearance: *There were glimpses of truth in what he said.* 1,4 *n.,* 2,3 *v.,* **glimpsed, glimpsing.**

glint (glint), 1 a gleam; flash: *The glint in her eye showed that she was angry.* 2 to gleam; flash. 1 *n.,* 2 *v.*

glis san do (gli sän′dō), in music: 1 performed with a gliding effect. A pianist plays a glissando passage by running one finger rapidly over the white keys or the black keys on a piano. 2 part performed with a gliding effect; glissando passage. 1 *adj.,* 2 *n., pl.* **glis san di** (gli sän′dē), **glis san dos.** [from Italian]

glis ten (glis′n), 1 shine with a twinkling light; glitter; sparkle: *The stars glistened in the sky.* 2 a glitter; sparkle. 1 *v.,* 2 *n.*

glit ter (glit′ər), 1 shine with a bright, sparkling light: *The jewels glittered.* 2 a bright, sparkling light: *the glitter of amusement in her eyes.* 3 be bright and showy. 4 brightness; showiness. 1,3 *v.,* 2,4 *n.*

glit ter y (glit′ər ē), glittering. *adj.*

gloam ing (glō′ming), evening twilight; dusk. *n.*

gloat (glōt), think about or gaze at with great satisfaction: *gloat over a victory. The miser gloated over his gold. v.*

glob (glob), a shapeless mass; blob. *n.*

glob al (glō′bəl), 1 of the earth as a whole; world-wide: *the threat of global war.* 2 shaped like a globe: *a global map. adj.* —**glob′al ly,** *adv.*

globe (glōb), 1 anything round like a ball; sphere. 2 the earth; world. 3 sphere with a map of the earth or sky on it. 4 anything rounded like a globe. An electric light bulb is a globe. *n.*

globe trot ter (glōb′trot′ər), person who travels widely over the world, usually for sightseeing. *n.*

glob u lar (glob′yə lər), 1 shaped like a globe or globule; round; spherical. 2 made up of globules. *adj.*

glob ule (glob′yül), a very small sphere or ball; tiny drop: *Globules of sweat stood out on the worker's forehead. n.*

glockenspiel

glock en spiel (glok′ən spēl′), a percussion instrument made up of a series of tuned metal bells, bars, or tubes mounted in a frame and played by striking with two little hammers. *n.* [from German *Glockenspiel* chimes]

gloom (glüm), 1 deep shadow; darkness; dimness. 2 be or become dark or dim. 3 dark thoughts and feelings; low spirits; sadness. 4 be in low spirits; feel sad. 1,3 *n.*, 2,4 *v.*

gloom i ly (glü′mə lē), in a gloomy manner. *adv.*

gloom i ness (glü′mē nis), a being gloomy; gloom. *n.*

gloom y (glü′mē), 1 dark; dim: *a gloomy winter day.* 2 in low spirits; sad; melancholy: *a gloomy mood.* 3 causing low spirits; discouraging; dismal: *a gloomy scene of poverty. His views about the future are gloomy. adj.,* **gloom i er, gloom i est.**

glo ri a (glôr′ē ə), Gloria. *n., pl.* **glo ri as.**

Glo ri a (glôr′ē ə), 1 song of praise to God. 2 the music for it. *n., pl.* **Glo ri as.** [from Latin *gloria* glory]

glo ri fi ca tion (glôr′ə fə kā′shən), a glorifying or a being glorified. *n.*

glo ri fy (glôr′ə fī), 1 give glory to; make glorious: *glorify a hero or a saint.* 2 to praise; worship: *singing hymns to glorify God.* 3 make more beautiful or splendid than it usually appears: *Sunset glorified the valley. v.,* **glo ri fied, glo ri fy ing.**

glo ri ous (glôr′ē əs), 1 having or deserving glory; illustrious. 2 giving glory: *Our team won a glorious victory.* 3 magnificent; splendid: *The children had a glorious time at the fair. adj.* —**glo′ri ous ly,** *adv.*

glo ry (glôr′ē), 1 great praise and honor given to a person or thing by others; fame: *The heroic act won her glory.* 2 something that brings praise and honor; source of pride and joy: *America's great men and women are her glory.* 3 adoring praise and thanksgiving: *"Glory be to God on high!"* 4 be proud; rejoice: *The teachers gloried in their classes' achievements.* 5 brightness; splendor: *the glory of the royal palace.* 6 condition of greatest magnificence, splendor, or prosperity:

Rome reached its greatest glory during the reign of Augustus. 7 splendor and bliss of heaven; heaven: *the saints in glory.* 1-3,5-7 *n., pl.* **glo ries;** 4 *v.,* **glo ried, glo ry ing.**

go to glory, die.

in one's glory, having one's greatest satisfaction or enjoyment: *He is in his glory when he can sing before an audience.*

gloss (glôs), 1 a smooth, shiny surface; luster: *Varnished furniture has a gloss.* 2 put a smooth, shiny surface on. 3 an outward appearance or surface that covers wrong underneath. 1,3 *n.,* 2 *v.*

gloss over, make (something) seem right even though it is really wrong; smooth over: *They tried to gloss over their mistakes.*

glos sar y (glos′ər ē), list of special, technical, or hard words, usually in alphabetical order, with explanations or comments: *a glossary of terms used in chemistry. Textbooks sometimes have glossaries at the end. n., pl.* **glos sar ies.**

gloss i ly (glô′sə lē), in a glossy manner. *adv.*

gloss i ness (glô′sē nis), glossy condition. *n.*

gloss y (glô′sē), smooth and shiny. *adj.,* **gloss i er, gloss i est.**

glot tis (glot′is), an opening at the upper part of the windpipe, between the vocal cords. *n., pl.* **glot tis es.**

Glouces ter (glos′tər), 1 city in SW England. 2 seaport and fishing center in NE Massachusetts. *n.*

glove (gluv), 1 a covering for the hand, usually with separate places for each of the four fingers and the thumb. Gloves are worn to keep the hands warm or clean. Boxers and baseball players use specially padded gloves for protection. 2 cover with a glove; provide with gloves. 1 *n.,* 2 *v.,* **gloved, glov ing.**

glow (glō), 1 shine because of heat; be red-hot or white-hot: *a glowing ember.* 2 the shine from something that is red-hot or white-hot: *the glow of embers in the fireplace.* 3 a similar shine without heat: *the glow of gold.* 4 give off light without heat: *The cat's eyes glowed in the dark.* 5 a bright, warm color; brightness: *the glow of sunset.* 6 the warm feeling or color of the body: *the glow of health on his cheeks.* 7 show a warm color; look warm; be red or bright: *Her cheeks glowed as she danced.* 8 an eager look on the face: *a glow of interest or excitement.* 9 look or be eager: *Her eyes glowed at the thought of a trip.* 10 warmth of feeling or passion; ardor: *He was filled with the glow of faith in God.* 1,4,7,9 *v.,* 2,3,5,6,8,10 *n.*

glow er (glou′ər), 1 stare angrily; scowl fiercely: *The fighters glowered at*

hat, āge, fär; let, ēqual, tėrm;
it, īce; hot, ōpen, ôrder;
oil, out; cup, půt, rüle; ch, child;
ng, long; sh, she; th, thin;
ŦH, then; zh, measure;

ə represents *a* in about,
e in taken, *i* in pencil,
o in lemon, *u* in circus.

each other. 2 an angry stare; fierce scowl. 1 *v.,* 2 *n.*

glow worm (glō′wėrm′), any insect larva or insect which glows in the dark. Fireflies develop from some glow-worms. *n.*

glu cose (glü′kōs), 1 kind of sugar occurring in plant and animal tissues. Carbohydrate is present in the blood mainly in the form of glucose. Glucose is not as sweet as cane sugar. 2 syrup made from starch. *n.*

glue (glü), 1 substance used to stick things together, made by boiling the hoofs, skins, and bones of animals in water. 2 any similar sticky substance made of casein, rubber, etc.; adhesive. 3 stick together with glue. 4 fasten tightly; attach firmly: *Her hands were glued to the steering wheel as she drove down the dangerous mountain road.* 1,2 *n.,* 3,4 *v.,* **glued, glu ing.** —**glue′like′,** *adj.*

glu ey (glü′ē), 1 like glue; sticky. 2 full of glue; smeared with glue. *adj.,* **glu i er, glu i est.**

glum (glum), gloomy; dismal; sullen: *He felt very glum when his friend moved away. adj.,* **glum mer, glum mest.** —**glum′ly,** *adv.* —**glum′ness,** *n.*

glut (glut), 1 fill full; feed or satisfy fully: *The boys glutted themselves with cake. A year of working aboard ship glutted my appetite for adventure.* 2 a full supply; great quantity. 3 supply more than there is a demand for: *The prices for wheat dropped when the market was glutted with it.* 4 too great a supply. 1,3 *v.,* **glut ted, glut ting;** 2,4 *n.*

glu ten (glüt′n), a tough, sticky substance in the flour of wheat and other grains. *n.*

glu ti nous (glüt′n əs), sticky. *adj.*

glut ton (glut′n), 1 a greedy eater; person who eats too much: *Sometimes I go off my diet and eat like a glutton.* 2 person who never seems to have enough of something: *That boxer is a glutton for punishment. n.*

glut ton ous (glut′n əs), greedy about food; having the habit of eating too much. *adj.* —**glut′ton ous ly,** *adv.*

gluttony

adj. adjective	n. noun
adv. adverb	prep. preposition
conj. conjunction	pron. pronoun
interj. interjection	v. verb
sing. singular	pl. plural

glut ton y (glut′n ē), excess in eating. *n., pl.* **glut ton ies.**

glyc er in or **glyc er ine** (glis′ər ən), a colorless, syrupy, sweet liquid obtained from fats and oils. Glycerin is used in ointments, lotions, antifreeze solutions, and explosives. *n.*

glyc e rol (glis′ə rōl′ or glis′ə rol′), glycerin. *n.*

gly co gen (glī′kə jən), a starchlike carbohydrate stored in the liver and other animal tissues. It is changed into glucose when needed. *n.*

G-man (jē′man′), INFORMAL. a special agent of the United States Department of Justice; agent of the FBI. *n., pl.* **G-men.** [shortened from *Government man*]

gnarl (närl), knot in wood; hard, rough lump: *Wood with gnarls is hard to cut. n.*

gnarled (närld), containing gnarls; knotted; twisted: *The farmer's gnarled hands grasped the plow firmly. adj.*

gnash (nash), strike or grind together: *I gnashed my teeth in rage. v.*

gnat (nat), any of various small, two-winged flies. Most gnats are blood-sucking and give bites that itch. *n.*

gnaw (nô), 1 bite at and wear away: *A mouse has gnawed right through the cover of this box.* 2 make by biting: *A rat can gnaw a hole through wood.* 3 trouble; harass; torment: *The feeling of guilt gnawed at his conscience day and night. v.,* **gnawed, gnawed** or **gnawn, gnaw ing.**

gnawn (nôn), gnawed; a past participle of **gnaw.** *v.*

gneiss (nīs), a very dense rock which occurs in layers and is composed of mica, quartz, feldspar, and hornblende. *n.*

gnome (nōm), (in folklore) a dwarf supposed to live in the earth and guard treasures of precious metals and stones. *n.*

gnu (nü or nyü), a large African antelope with an oxlike head, curved horns, and a long tail. *n., pl.* **gnus** or **gnu.**

go (gō), 1 move along: *Cars go on the road.* 2 move away; leave: *Don't go yet.* 3 be in motion or action; act; work; run: *Make the washing machine go.* 4 get to be; become: *go mad.* 5 be

habitually; be: *go hungry for a week.* 6 proceed; advance: *go to New York.* 7 put oneself: *Don't go to any trouble for me.* 8 extend; reach: *Her memory does not go back that far.* 9 pass: *Summer had gone. Vacation goes quickly.* 10 be given: *First prize goes to you.* 11 be sold: *The painting goes to the highest bidder.* 12 turn out; have a certain result: *How did the game go?* 13 have its place; belong: *This book goes on the top shelf.* 14 make a certain sound: *The cork goes "pop!"* 15 have certain words; be said: *How does that song go?* 16 break down; give way; fail: *My eyesight is going. The engine in the old car finally went.* 17 INFORMAL. try; attempt; chance: *Let's have another go at this problem.* 18 something successful; a success: *She made a go of the new store.* 1-16 *v.,* **went, gone, go ing;** 17,18 *n., pl.* **goes.**

go about, 1 be busy at; work on: *She went about her work with energy.* 2 move from place to place. 3 turn around; change direction.

go along, cooperate: *The club members decided to go along with the president's recommendation.*

go around, satisfy everyone; give some for all: *There were enough apples and nuts to go around.*

go at, 1 attack: *I went at the dog with a stick.* 2 take in hand with energy; work at: *Let's go at this problem in a different way.*

go back on, INFORMAL. not be faithful or loyal to: *She went back on her promise.*

go behind, investigate the real or hidden reasons for.

go by, 1 pass: *We went by that store often. He let the insult go by.* 2 be guided by; follow: *Go by what she says.* 3 be known by: *He goes by the name of Smith.*

go down, 1 descend; decline; sink: *The wrecked ship went down.* 2 be defeated; lose: *Their team went down before our superior playing.*

go for, 1 try to get: *He went for the big prize.* 2 favor; support: *The public goes for her ideas.* 3 INFORMAL. attack: *That dog goes for anyone who gets near it.*

go in for, INFORMAL. take part in; spend time and energy at: *He goes in for football.*

gnu—about 4½ ft. high at the shoulder

go into, 1 enter into a condition or activity: *She went into a rage.* 2 be contained in: *How many pints go into a gallon?* 3 investigate: *The police have gone into the case and made some arrests.*

go in with, join; share with: *go in a partnership with another.*

go it, INFORMAL. go fast.

go off, 1 leave; depart: *My sister has gone off to college.* 2 be fired; explode: *The pistol went off unexpectedly.* 3 take place; happen: *The picnic went off as planned.*

go on, 1 go ahead; continue: *After a pause she went on reading.* 2 happen: *What goes on here?* 3 behave: *He is foolish to go on in this manner.*

go out, 1 go to a party, show, etc.: *We had a very good time when we went out Saturday night.* 2 stop burning: *Don't let the candle go out.*

go over, 1 look at carefully: *go over a problem.* 2 do again; repeat: *I went over the explanation several times.* 3 read again: *Go over the poem till you memorize it.* 4 INFORMAL. succeed: *The play went over on Broadway and became a big hit.*

go through, 1 go to the end of; do all of: *Let's go through the rehearsal without any interruption.* 2 undergo; experience: *I went through a serious operation.* 3 search: *Going through his pockets he found the missing key.* 4 be accepted or approved: *The new schedule did not go through.*

go through with, carry out to the end; complete: *The contractor went through with his bargain to build the house in three months in spite of the rainy weather.*

go together, 1 harmonize; match: *These colors go together.* 2 keep steady company as lovers.

go under, be ruined; fail: *Poor management caused the business to go under.*

go up, 1 rise; ascend: *The barometer is going up.* 2 increase: *The price of milk has gone up.*

go with, 1 go steadily with; accompany: *The girl he had gone with moved out of town.* 2 belong with; go well with: *Cheese goes with salad.*

go without, do without; not have: *You can eat what is on the table or go without.*

let go, 1 allow to escape: *Let me go.* 2 give up one's hold: *Let go of my shirt.*

let oneself go, 1 give way to one's feelings or desires: *He is much too shy to let himself go.* 2 fail to keep oneself in good condition: *The coach warned the boys on the team not to let themselves go during vacation.*

no go, INFORMAL. useless; worthless: *I*

knew that the idea would be no go from the start.

on the go, INFORMAL. busily occupied; active or restless: *She is always on the go.*

goad (gōd), 1 a sharp-pointed stick for driving cattle. 2 anything which drives or urges one on. 3 drive or urge on; act as a goad to: *Hunger goaded him to steal a loaf of bread.* 1,2 *n.,* 3 *v.*

goal (gōl), 1 place where a race ends. 2 place to which players try to advance a ball or puck in certain games in order to make a score. 3 score or points won by reaching this place. 4 something for which an effort is made; something desired: *The goal of her ambition was to be a great doctor. n.*

goal ie (gō′lē), goalkeeper. *n.*

goal keep er (gōl′kē′pər), player who tries to prevent the ball or puck from crossing the goal in certain games. *n.*

goal post, one of a pair of posts with a bar across them, forming a goal in football and soccer.

goat (gōt), 1 a lively, cud-chewing mammal with hollow horns and usually a beard. Goats are closely related to sheep but are stronger, less timid, and more active than sheep. They are raised for their milk and their hides. 2 IN-FORMAL. person made to take the blame or suffer for the mistakes of others; scapegoat. *n., pl.* **goats** or **goat.** —**goat′like′,** *adj.*

get one's goat, INFORMAL. make a person angry or annoyed; tease a person.

goatee

goat ee (gō tē′), a pointed beard on a man's chin. *n.*

goat herd (gōt′hèrd′), person who tends goats. *n.*

goat skin (gōt′skin′), 1 skin of a goat. 2 leather made from it. 3 container made from this leather, used especially for holding wine. *n.*

gob[1] (gob), SLANG. sailor in the United States Navy. *n.* [origin uncertain]

gob[2] (gob), INFORMAL. lump; mass. *n.* [from French of the 1300's *gobe*]

gob ble[1] (gob′əl), eat fast and greedily; swallow quickly in big pieces. *v.,* **gob-bled, gob bling.** [from *gob*[2]]

gob ble[2] (gob′əl), 1 make the throaty sound of a male turkey or a sound like it. 2 the throaty sound that a male turkey makes. 1 *v.,* **gob bled, gob-bling;** 2 *n.* [from an imitation of the sound]

gob ble dy gook (gob′əl dē gùk′), INFORMAL. speech or writing which is hard to understand because it is full of long, involved sentences and big words. *n.*

gob bler (gob′lər), a male turkey. *n.*

go-be tween (gō′bi twēn′), person who goes back and forth between others with messages, proposals, suggestions, etc. *n.*

Go bi (gō′bē), desert in E Asia. Most of it is in Mongolia. *n.*

gob let (gob′lit), a drinking glass with a base and stem. *n.*

goblets

gob lin (gob′lən), (in folklore) a mischievous spirit or elf in the form of an ugly-looking dwarf. *n.*

go cart (gō′kärt′), a low seat on wheels to take a small child around on. *n.*

god (god), 1 a being thought to have supernatural or superhuman powers and considered worthy of worship. 2 likeness or image of a god; idol. 3 person or thing greatly admired and respected. *n.*

God (god), the Supreme Being worshipped in most religions as the maker and ruler of the world. *n.*

god child (god′chīld′), child whom a grown-up person sponsors at its baptism. *n., pl.* **god chil dren** (god′-chil′drən).

god daugh ter (god′dô′tər), a female godchild. *n.*

god dess (god′is), 1 a female god. 2 a very beautiful or charming woman. *n., pl.* **god dess es.**

god fa ther (god′fä′тнər), man who sponsors a child when it is baptized. Often the position of a godfather is mainly one of honor. *n.*

god head (god′hed′), 1 divine nature; divinity. 2 **Godhead,** God. *n.*

god less (god′lis), 1 not believing in God; not religious. 2 ungodly; wicked; evil. *adj.* —**god′less ness,** *n.*

god like (god′līk′), 1 like God or a god; divine. 2 suitable for God or a god. *adj.*

god li ness (god′lē nis), a being religious; obedience to God's laws; piety; righteousness. *n.*

god ly (god′lē), obeying, loving, and fearing God; religious; pious. *adj.,* **god li er, god li est.**

god moth er (god′muтн′ər), woman who sponsors a child when it is baptized. Often the position of a

hat, āge, fär; let, ēqual, tèrm;
it, īce; hot, ōpen, ôrder;
oil, out; cup, pùt, rüle; ch, child;
ng, long; sh, she; th, thin;
тн, then; zh, measure;

ə represents *a* in about,
e in taken, *i* in pencil,
o in lemon, *u* in circus.

godmother is mainly one of honor. *n.*

god par ent (god′per′ənt *or* god′par′-ənt), godfather or godmother. *n.*

god send (god′send′), something unexpected and very welcome, as if sent from God; sudden piece of good luck: *Going to a warm climate was a godsend to the sick man. n.*

god son (god′sun′), a male godchild. *n.*

God speed (god′spēd′), a wish of success to a person starting on a journey or undertaking. *n.*

goes (gōz), a present tense of go. *He goes to school. v.*

Goe the (gèr′tə), **Johann Wolfgang von,** 1749-1832, German poet, prose writer, and dramatist. *n.*

go-get ter (gō′get′ər), SLANG. an energetic person who tries hard for and usually gets what he is after. *n.*

gog gle (gog′əl), 1 roll one's eyes; stare with bulging eyes. 2 roll; bulge: *The children's eyes goggled as the magician pulled a rabbit out of the empty hat.* 3 rolling; bulging: *A frog has goggle eyes.* 4 **goggles,** *pl.* large, close-fitting eyeglasses to protect the eyes from light or dust. 1,2 *v.,* **gog-gled, gog gling;** 3 *adj.,* 4 *n.*

gog gle-eyed (gog′əl īd′), having rolling, bulging, or staring eyes. *adj.*

Gogh (gō). See **Van Gogh.** *n.*

go ing (gō′ing), 1 a going away; leaving: *Her going was very sudden.* 2 moving; acting; working; running: *Set the clock going.* 3 condition of the ground or road for walking or riding: *The going is bad on a muddy road.* 4 that goes well; operating with success: *His business is a going concern.* 1,3 *n.,* 2,4 *adj.*

be going to, will; be about to: *It is going to rain soon.*

go ings-on (gō′ingz on′), actions or events: *the goings-on at the convention. n.pl.*

goi ter *or* **goi tre** (goi′tər), enlargement of the thyroid gland which is often seen as a large swelling in the neck. A goiter is usually caused by a diet with too little iodine. *n.*

gold (gōld), 1 a shiny, bright-yellow,

adj. adjective	*n.* noun
adv. adverb	*prep.* preposition
conj. conjunction	*pron.* pronoun
interj. interjection	*v.* verb
sing. singular	*pl.* plural

precious metallic element which resists rust and other chemical changes and can easily be drawn out into fine wire or hammered into thin sheets. Gold is used chiefly for making coins and jewelry. 2 coins made of gold. 3 money in large sums; wealth; riches. 4 made of gold: *a gold watch.* 5 of or like gold. 6 a bright yellow. 7 bright-yellow. 1-3,6 *n.*, 4,5,7 *adj.*

gold brick (gōld′brik′), INFORMAL. 1 avoid duties by any evasion or excuse, such as pretended illness. 2 person, especially in the armed forces, who avoids duty or shirks work. 1 *v.*, 2 *n.*

Gold Coast, region in W Africa, a former British colony, now largely included in Ghana.

gold en (gōl′dən), 1 made of gold: *a golden medal.* 2 containing or yielding gold: *a golden region or country.* 3 shining like gold; bright-yellow: *golden hair.* 4 very good; excellent; extremely favorable, valuable, or important: *a golden opportunity.* 5 very happy and prosperous; flourishing: *a golden age. adj.*

Golden Fleece, (in Greek legends) a fleece of gold taken from a ram. It was guarded by a dragon until Jason and his companions carried it away with the help of Medea.

Golden Gate, strait forming the entrance to San Francisco Bay from the Pacific.

golden mean, avoidance of extremes; sensible way of doing things.

gold en rod (gōl′dən rod′), plant of the same family as the aster, which blooms in the late summer or early autumn and has many small, yellow flowers on tall, slender stalks. *n.*

golden rule, rule of conduct which states that a person should treat others as he would have them treat him.

gold-filled (gōld′fild′), made of cheap metal covered with a layer of gold. *adj.*

gold finch (gōld′finch′), 1 a small American songbird. The male is yellow marked with black. 2 a European songbird with a patch of yellow on its wings. *n., pl.* **gold finch es.**

gold fish (gōld′fish′), a small, usually reddish-golden fish, often kept in garden pools or in glass bowls indoors. *n., pl.* **gold fish es** or **gold fish.**

gold leaf, gold beaten into very thin sheets, used in gilding.

gold rush, a sudden rush of people to a place where gold has just been found.

gold smith (gōld′smith′), person who makes or sells things made of gold. *n.*

Gold smith (gōld′smith′), **Oliver,** 1730?-1774, British poet, novelist, and dramatist. *n.*

golf (golf), 1 game played on an outdoor course with a small, hard ball and a set of long-handled clubs having wooden or iron heads. The player tries to hit the ball into each of a series of holes with as few strokes as possible. 2 play this game. 1 *n.*, 2 *v.* —**golf′er,** *n.*

Gol go tha (gol′gə thə), (in the Bible) the place of Christ's crucifixion; Calvary. *n.*

Go li ath (gə lī′əth), (in the Bible) a giant whom David killed with a stone from a sling. *n.*

gol ly (gol′ē), exclamation of wonder, pleasure, joy, etc. *interj.*

Go mor rah or **Go mor rha** (gə-môr′ə), (in the Bible) a wicked city destroyed, together with Sodom, by fire from heaven. *n.*

go nad (gō′nad), organ in which reproductive cells develop in the male or female. Ovaries and testes are gonads. *n.*

gondola (def. 1)

gon do la (gon′dl ə), 1 a long, narrow boat with a high peak at each end, used on the canals of Venice. 2 a railroad freight car which has low sides and no top. 3 car which hangs under an airship and holds the passengers, instruments, etc. See **blimp** for picture. *n., pl.* **gon do las.**

gon do lier (gon′dl ir′), person who rows or poles a gondola. *n.*

gone (gôn), 1 moved away; left: *The students are gone on their vacation.* 2 lost: *We had given you up for gone.* 3 dead: *Great-grandmother is gone now.* 4 used up; consumed: *Is all the candy gone?* 5 failed; ruined: *The bankrupt was a gone man.* 6 weak; faint: *a gone feeling.* 7 past participle of **go.** *She has gone far away.* 1-6 *adj.*, 7 *v.*

far gone, much advanced; deeply involved: *The business was far gone in debt and could not be saved.*

gon er (gô′nər), INFORMAL. person or thing that is dead, ruined, or past help. *n.*

gong (gông), a large piece of metal shaped like a bowl or a saucer which

makes a loud noise when struck. A gong is a kind of bell. *n.*

goo (gü), SLANG. thick, sticky matter. *n.*

goo ber (gü′bər), INFORMAL. (in the southern United States) a peanut. *n.*

good (gud), 1 having high quality; superior: *a good piece of work.* 2 as it ought to be; right; proper; satisfactory: *good health, good weather. Do what seems good to you.* 3 that does what is right; well-behaved: *a good girl.* 4 kind; friendly: *Say a good word for me.* 5 desirable: *a good book for children.* 6 honorable; worthy: *my good friend, a good reputation.* 7 reliable; dependable: *good judgment.* 8 real; genuine: *It is hard to tell counterfeit money from good money.* 9 agreeable; pleasant: *Have a good time.* 10 beneficial; advantageous; useful: *drugs good for a fever.* 11 benefit; advantage; use: *work for the common good.* 12 satisfying; enough; full: *a good meal.* 13 skillful; clever: *a good manager, be good at arithmetic.* 14 fairly great; more than a little: *work a good while.* 15 that which is good; *find the good in people.* 16 that is good! 1-10,12-14 *adj.*, **bet ter, best;** 11,15 *n.*, 16 *interj.*

as good as, almost the same as; almost; practically: *The battle was as good as won.*

for good, forever; finally; permanently: *They have moved out for good.*

good and, INFORMAL. very: *Get the water good and hot.*

good for, 1 able to do, live, or last: *Our car is good for another year.* 2 able to pay or contribute: *He is good for about $10.*

make good, 1 make up for; pay for: *The girls made good the damage they had done.* 2 fulfill; carry out: *Will you make good your promise?* 3 succeed in doing: *The soldiers made good their retreat.* 4 succeed: *She made good in business.* 5 prove: *Can you make good your charge against him?*

to the good, on the side of profit or advantage; in one's favor: *By winning the second game our team is now two games to the good in the championship match.*

good afternoon, form of greeting or farewell in the afternoon; hello or good-by.

good-by (gud′bī′), farewell: *We say "Good-by" to friends when they go away. interj., n., pl.* **good-bys.**

good-bye (gud′bī′), good-by. *interj., n., pl.* **good-byes.**

good day, form of greeting or farewell; hello or good-by.

good evening, form of greeting or farewell in the evening; hello or good-by.

good-for-noth ing (gùd/fər nuth/-ing), 1 worthless; useless. 2 person who is worthless or useless. 1 *adj.*, 2 *n.*

Good Friday, the anniversary of Christ's crucifixion, observed on the Friday before Easter.

good-heart ed (gùd/här/tid), kind and generous. *adj.* —**good/-heart/ed-ly,** *adv.* —**good/-heart/ed ness,** *n.*

good-hu mored (gùd/hyü/mərd), having good humor; cheerful; pleasant; amiable. *adj.* —**good/-hu/mored ly,** *adv.* —**good/-hu/mored ness,** *n.*

good li ness (gùd/lē nis), 1 handsomeness. 2 excellence. *n.*

good-look ing (gùd/lùk/ing), having a pleasing appearance; handsome or pretty. *adj.*

good ly (gùd/lē), 1 of good quality; excellent: *a goodly land.* 2 good-looking: *a goodly youth.* 3 considerable; rather large; fairly great: *a goodly quantity. adj.,* **good li er, good li est.**

good man (gùd/mən), OLD USE. 1 master of a household; husband. 2 title of respect for a man ranking below a gentleman: *Goodman Brown. n., pl.* **good men.**

good morning, form of greeting or farewell in the morning; hello or good-by.

good-na tured (gùd/nā/chərd), having a pleasant disposition; kindly; cheerful; obliging. *adj.* —**good/-na/tured ly,** *adv.* —**good/-na/tured-ness,** *n.*

good ness (gùd/nis), 1 a being good; kindness. 2 exclamation of surprise: *My goodness! Goodness me! Goodness gracious!* 1 *n.,* 2 *interj.*

good night, form of farewell said at night.

goods (gùdz), 1 personal property; belongings: *household goods.* 2 thing or things for sale; wares. 3 material for clothing; cloth. *n.pl.*

Good Samaritan, 1 (in the Bible) a traveler who rescued another traveler who had been beaten and robbed by thieves. 2 person who is unselfish in helping others.

Good Shepherd, Jesus Christ.

good-sized (gùd/sīzd/), somewhat large. *adj.*

gopher (def. 1)
about 8 in.
long with tail

good-tem pered (gùd/tem/pərd), easy to get along with; cheerful; agreeable. *adj.*

good turn, a kind or friendly act; favor.

good wife (gùd/wīf/), OLD USE. 1 mistress of a household. 2 title of respect for a woman ranking below a lady: *Goodwife Brown. n., pl.* **good wives.**

good will, 1 kindly or friendly feeling. 2 cheerful consent; willingness. 3 the good reputation that a business has with its customers.

good y (gùd/ē), INFORMAL. 1 something very good to eat; piece of candy or cake. 2 exclamation of pleasure: *Oh, goody!* 1 *n., pl.* **good ies;** 2 *interj.*

goo ey (gü/ē), SLANG. like goo; sticky. *adj.,* **goo i er, goo i est.**

goof (güf), SLANG. 1 make a stupid mistake; blunder. 2 a blunder. 3 waste time or avoid work: *goof off during class.* 4 simpleton; fool. 1,3 *v.,* 2,4 *n.*

goof-off (güf/ôf/), SLANG. person who wastes time or avoids work. *n.*

goof y (gü/fē), SLANG. silly. *adj.,* **goof-i er, goof i est.**

goose (def. 1)
wild goose
of North America
—about 3 ft. long

goose (güs), 1 a wild or tame swimming bird, like a duck but larger and having a longer neck. A goose has webbed feet. 2 a female goose. The male is called a gander. 3 flesh of a goose used for food. 4 a silly person. *n., pl.* **geese.**

cook one's goose, INFORMAL. ruin one's reputation, plan, chances, etc.

goose ber ry (güs/ber/ē), 1 a small, sour berry somewhat like a currant but larger. Gooseberries are used to make pies, tarts, jam, etc. 2 the thorny bush that it grows on. *n., pl.* **goose ber ries.**

goose flesh (güs/flesh/), a rough condition of the skin, like that of a plucked goose, caused by cold or fear; goose pimples. *n.*

goose neck (güs/nek/), something long and curved like a goose's neck, such as a movable support for a lamp or a curved connecting pipe. *n.*

goose pimples, gooseflesh.

goose step, a marching step in which the leg is swung high with straight, stiff knee.

G.O.P., Grand Old Party; the Republican Party in the United States.

go pher (gō/fər), 1 a burrowing rodent of North America with large cheek pouches and long claws, especially on the front feet. 2 a striped ground squirrel of the western plains of the United States. 3 a land tortoise of the southern United States that burrows in the ground. *n.*

Gor di an knot (gôr/dē ən). **cut the**

hat, āge, fär; let, ēqual, tėrm;
it, īce; hot, ōpen, ôrder;
oil, out; cup, pùt, rüle; ch, child;
ng, long; sh, she; th, thin;
ŦH, then; zh, measure;

ə represents *a* in about,
e in taken, *i* in pencil,
o in lemon, *u* in circus.

Gordian knot, find and use a quick, easy way out of a difficulty. [from *Gordius,* an ancient Phrygian king who tied a complicated knot that Alexander the Great cut with a sword]

gore[1] (gôr), blood that is shed; thick blood; clotted blood: *The battlefield was covered with gore. n.* [Old English *gor* dirt, dung]

gore[2] (gôr), wound with a horn or tusk: *The angry bull gored the farmer in the leg. v.,* **gored, gor ing.** [Middle English *goren,* from Old English *gār* spear]

gore[3] (gôr), 1 a long, three-sided piece of cloth put or made in a skirt, sail, etc., to give greater width or change the shape. 2 put or make a gore in. 1 *n.,* 2 *v.,* **gored, gor ing.** [Old English *gāra* angular point]

gorge (gôrj), 1 a deep, narrow valley, usually steep and rocky, especially one with a stream. 2 eat greedily until full; stuff with food: *I gorged myself with cake at the party.* 3 OLD USE. throat. 1,3 *n.,* 2 *v.,* **gorged, gorg ing.**

make one's gorge rise, fill one with great disgust or anger: *Cruelty to animals makes my gorge rise.*

gor geous (gôr/jəs), richly colored; splendid: *The peacock spread its gorgeous tail. The gorgeous sunset thrilled us all. adj.* —**gor/geous ly,** *adv.* —**gor/geous ness,** *n.*

Gor gon (gôr/gən), (in Greek legends) any of three sisters having snakes for hair and faces so horrible that anyone who looked at them turned to stone. *n.*

gorilla
standing height
of male up to 6 ft.

go ril la (gə ril/ə), the largest and most powerful ape. It is found in the forests of central Africa. *n., pl.* **go ril las.**

gor i ness (gôr/ē nis), gory condition. *n.*

gorse

gorse (gôrs), furze. *n.*

gor y (gôr′ē), 1 covered with gore; bloody. 2 with much bloodshed: *a gory accident, a gory tale. adj.,* **gor i er, gor i est.**

gosh (gosh), exclamation or mild oath: *Gosh, it's cold out today! interj.*

gos hawk (gos′hôk′), a powerful, short-winged hawk, formerly much used in falconry. *n.*

Go shen (gō′shən), 1 (in the Bible) a fertile part of Egypt where the Israelites lived before the Exodus. 2 any land of plenty and comfort. *n.*

gos ling (goz′ling), a young goose. *n.*

gos pel (gos′pəl), 1 the teachings of Jesus and the Apostles. 2 **Gospel, a** any one of the first four books of the New Testament, by Matthew, Mark, Luke, and John. They tell about the life and teachings of Christ. **b** part of one of these books read during a religious service. 3 anything earnestly believed or taken as a guide for action: *Drink plenty of water: that is my gospel.* 4 the absolute truth: *They took the doctor's words for gospel. n.*

gos sa mer (gos′ə mər), 1 film or thread of cobweb. 2 any very thin, light cloth or substance. 3 like gossamer; very light and thin; filmy. 1,2 *n.,* 3 *adj.*

gos sip (gos′ip), 1 idle talk, not always true, about other people and their affairs. 2 repeat what one knows or hears about other people and their affairs. 3 person who gossips a good deal. 1,3 *n.,* 2 *v.* **—gos′sip er,** *n.*

gos sip y (gos′ə pē), 1 fond of gossip. 2 full of gossip: *a gossipy letter. adj.*

got (got), past tense and a past participle of **get.** *We got the letter yesterday. We had got tired of waiting for it. v.*

Goth (goth), member of a Germanic people who invaded the Roman Empire in the A.D. 200's, 300's, and 400's. The Goths settled mainly in southern and eastern Europe. *n.*

Goth ic (goth′ik), 1 style of architecture using pointed arches, flying buttresses, and high, steep roofs. It was developed in western Europe during the Middle Ages from about 1150 to 1550. 2 of this kind of architecture. 3 of the Goths or their language. 4 language of the Goths. 1,4 *n.,* 2,3 *adj.*

got ten (got′n), got; a past participle of **get.** *v.*

gouge (gouj), 1 chisel with a curved, hollow blade. Gouges are used for cutting round grooves or holes in wood. 2 cut with a gouge. 3 groove or hole made by gouging. 4 dig out; tear out; force out. 5 INFORMAL. to trick; cheat; swindle. 1,3 *n.,* 2,4,5 *v.,* **gouged, goug ing.**

gou lash (gü′läsh), stew made of beef or veal and vegetables, usually highly seasoned. *n.*

Gou nod (gü′nō), **Charles François,** 1818-1893, French composer. *n.*

gourd (gôrd), 1 any of various fleshy fruits with hard rinds and many flat seeds. Gourds are often dried and hollowed out for use as cups, bottles, bowls, etc. 2 the vine it grows on. 3 cup, bowl, bottle, etc., made from the dried shell of a gourd. *n.* **—gourd′like′,** *adj.*

gour mand (gur′mənd), person who is fond of good eating. A gourmand is not so particular as an epicure nor so greedy as a glutton. *n.*

gour met (gur′mā), person who is expert in judging and choosing fine foods, wines, etc. *n.*

gout (gout), 1 a painful disease of the joints, especially of the big toe. 2 drop, splash, or clot: *There were gouts of blood on the dagger. n.*

gout y (gou′tē), 1 diseased or swollen with gout. 2 of gout; caused by gout. 3 causing gout. *adj.,* **gout i er, gout i est.**

Gov., governor.

gov ern (guv′ərn), 1 direct or manage with authority; rule or control: *The election determined which party would govern the United States for four years.* 2 determine or guide: *What were the motives governing the king's decision to give up his throne?* 3 hold back; restrain: *Govern your temper. v.*

gov ern a ble (guv′ər nə bəl), that can be governed. *adj.*

gov ern ess (guv′ər nis), woman who teaches and trains children in their home. *n.*

gov ern ment (guv′ərn mənt), 1 the ruling of a country, state, district, etc.; direction of the affairs of state; rule, control, or management: *federal government, municipal government, government by the people.* 2 person or persons ruling a country, state, district, etc., at any time: *The government of the United States consists of the President and his cabinet, the Congress, and the Supreme Court.* 3 system of ruling: *The United States has a democratic form of government.* 4 country, state, district, etc., ruled: *Most governments are represented in the United Nations. n.*

gov ern men tal (guv′ərn men′tl), of or having to do with government. *adj.* **—gov′ern men′tal ly,** *adv.*

gov er nor (guv′ər nər), 1 official elected as the executive head of a state of the United States. The governor of a state carries out the laws made by the state legislature. 2 official appointed to govern a province, colony, city, fort, etc. 3 person who manages or directs a club, society, institution, etc. A club often has a board of governors. 4 an automatic device that controls the supply of fuel or power and keeps a machine going at a certain speed. *n.*

gov er nor ship (guv′ər nər ship), position, duties, or term of office of governor. *n.*

govt. or **Govt.,** government.

gown (goun), 1 a woman's dress. 2 a loose outer garment worn by college graduates, judges, clergymen, lawyers, and others to show their position, profession, etc. 3 nightgown or dressing gown. 4 put a gown on; dress in a gown. 1-3 *n.,* 4 *v.*

Go ya (gô′yä), **Francisco,** 1746-1828, Spanish painter and etcher. *n.*

gr., 1 grain or grains. 2 gram or grams.

grab (grab), 1 seize suddenly; snatch: *I grabbed the child before she fell.* 2 snatching; sudden seizing: *He made a grab at the butterfly.* 3 something which is grabbed. 1 *v.,* **grabbed, grab bing;** 2,3 *n.*

grab bag, bag containing various unseen and unknown objects from which a person can take out one.

grace (grās), 1 beauty of form, movement, or manner; pleasing or agreeable quality: *The ballerina danced with much grace.* 2 give or add grace to: *A vase of flowers graced the room.* 3 the favor and love of God: *fall from grace.* 4 a short prayer of thanks given before

gouge (def. 1)

Gothic (def. 1) style of cathedral

or after a meal. **5** favor shown by granting a delay. **6** time of the delay: *Most firms allow a three days' grace after a bill is due.* **7** give grace or honor to: *The queen graced the ball with her presence.* **8** behavior put on to seem attractive: *serve tea with little airs and graces.* **9 Grace,** title of a duke, duchess, or archbishop: *May I assist Your Grace?* **10 Graces,** *pl.* (in Greek myths) three sister goddesses who give beauty, charm, and joy to people and nature. 1,3-6,8-10 *n.,* 2,7 *v.,* **graced, grac ing.**

in one's bad graces, disfavored or disliked by.

in one's good graces, favored or liked by: *I wonder if I am in the teacher's good graces.*

with bad grace, unpleasantly; unwillingly: *The apology was made with bad grace.*

with good grace, pleasantly; willingly: *He obeyed the order with good grace.*

grace ful (grās′fəl), beautiful in form, movement, or manner; pleasing; agreeable: *a graceful dancer, a graceful speech of thanks. adj.* —**grace′ful ly,** *adv.* —**grace′ful ness,** *n.*

grace less (grās′lis), **1** ugly in form, movement, or manner: *awkward, graceless movements.* **2** without any sense of what is right or proper; impolite: *That boy is a graceless rascal. adj.* —**grace′less ly,** *adv.* —**grace′less ness,** *n.*

grace note, (in music) a note or group of notes not essential to the harmony or melody, added for ornament.

gra cious (grā′shəs), **1** pleasant and kindly; courteous: *He welcomed his guests in a gracious manner which made them feel at ease.* **2** pleasant and kindly to people of lower social position: *The queen greeted the crowd with a gracious smile.* **3** exclamation of surprise. 1,2 *adj.,* 3 *interj.* —**gra′cious ly,** *adv.* —**gra′cious ness,** *n.*

grack le (grak′əl), a large blackbird with shiny, black feathers. *n.*

gra da tion (grā dā′shən), **1** a change by steps or stages; gradual change: *Our acts show gradation between right and wrong.* **2** one of the steps in a series: *gradations between poverty and wealth, the gradations of color in a rainbow. n.*

grade (grād), **1** division of elementary school or high school, arranged according to the pupils' progress and covering a year's work: *the seventh grade.* **2 the grades,** elementary school. **3** degree in rank, quality, or value: *Grade A milk is the best milk.* **4** group of persons or things having the same rank, quality, or value. **5** place in classes; arrange in grades; sort: *These apples are graded by size.* **6** number or

letter that shows how well one has done: *Her grade in English is B.* **7** give a grade to: *The teacher graded the papers.* **8** slope of a road or railroad track: *a steep grade.* **9** amount of slope. **10** make more nearly level: *The road up the steep hill was graded.* **11** go through a series of steps or stages; change gradually: *Red and yellow grade into orange.* 1-4,6,8,9 *n.,* 5,7,10,11 *v.,* **grad ed, grad ing.**

make the grade, INFORMAL. be successful: *It takes a lot of hard work to make the grade in business.*

grade crossing, place where a railroad crosses a street or another railroad on the same level.

grad er (grā′dər), **1** person or thing that grades. **2** person who is in a certain grade at school: *a fifth grader. n.*

grade school, elementary school.

gra di ent (grā′dē ənt), **1** rate of upward or downward slope of a road, railroad track, etc.: *steep gradients.* **2** the sloping part of a road, railroad, etc.; grade. **3** rate at which temperature or pressure changes. *n.*

grad u al (graj′ü əl), happening by small steps or degrees; changing step by step; moving little by little: *This low hill has a gradual slope. A child's growth into an adult is gradual. adj.* —**grad′u al ly,** *adv.*

grad u ate (graj′ü āt *for* 1,2,6; graj′ü it *for* 3-5), **1** finish a course of study at a school, college, or university and be given a diploma or paper saying so: *Her brother graduated from the University last year.* **2** give a diploma to for finishing a course of study: *She was graduated with honors.* **3** person who has graduated and has a diploma. **4** that has graduated: *a graduate student.* **5** of or for graduates: *A graduate school is for students continuing their studies after college.* **6** mark out in equal spaces for measuring: *My ruler is graduated in inches.* 1,2,6 *v.,* **grad u at ed, grad u at ing;** 3 *n.,* 4,5 *adj.*

grad u a tion (graj′ü ā′shən), **1** a graduating from a school, college, or university. **2** ceremony of graduating; graduating exercises. **3** division into equal spaces. **4** mark or set of marks to show degrees for measuring. *n.*

graf fi ti (grə fē′tē), drawings or writings scratched or scribbled on a wall or other surface. *n.pl.* of **graf fi to** (grə fē′tō).

graft¹ (graft), **1** put (a shoot, bud, etc. from one tree or plant) into a slit in another tree or plant, so it will grow there permanently; engraft. **2** shoot, bud, etc., used in grafting. A graft from a fine apple tree may be put on a worthless one to improve it. **3** act of grafting. **4** transfer (a piece of skin,

bone, etc.) from one part of the body to another, or to a new body, so that it will grow there permanently. **5** piece of skin, bone, etc., so transferred. 1,4 *v.,* 2,3,5 *n.* [from French of the 1400's *grafe* scion, stylus (the inserted shoot was thought to resemble a writing tool)] —**graft′er,** *n.*

graft² (graft), **1** the taking of money dishonestly in connection with city or government business: *The crooked inspector was guilty of accepting bribes and other forms of graft.* **2** money dishonestly taken. **3** take or get money dishonestly. 1,2 *n.,* 3 *v.* [origin uncertain] —**graft′er,** *n.*

gra ham (grā′əm), made from wholewheat flour that has not been sifted: *graham crackers. adj.* [from Sylvester Graham, 1794-1851, an American reformer of dietetics]

Grail (grāl), (in medieval legends) the cup or dish used by Christ at the Last Supper, and by one of His followers to catch the last drops of Christ's blood at the Cross; Holy Grail. The knights of the Round Table vowed to search for the Grail. *n.*

grain (grān), **1** the seed of wheat, corn, oats, and similar cereal grasses. **2** plants that these seeds grow on. **3** one of the tiny bits of which sand, sugar, salt, etc., are made up. **4** a very small unit of weight. One pound avoirdupois equals 7000 grains; one pound troy equals 5760 grains. **5** the smallest possible amount; tiniest bit: *There isn't a grain of truth in the charge.* **6** the little lines and other markings in wood, marble, etc.; arrangement of the particles of anything: *That mahogany table has a*

graft¹ (defs. 1 and 2)—three types. The pieces are tied or taped together and kept moist until they join.

adj. adjective	*n.* noun
adv. adverb	*prep.* preposition
conj. conjunction	*pron.* pronoun
interj. interjection	*v.* verb
sing. singular	*pl.* plural

fine grain. **7** paint to look like the grain of wood, marble, etc. **8** natural character; disposition: *Laziness went against his grain.* 1-6,8 *n.,* 7 *v.*

grain alcohol, ordinary alcohol, made by the fermentation of grain.

grained (grānd), **1** having little lines and markings. **2** painted to look like the grain in wood, marble, etc. *adj.*

grain elevator, building for storing grain.

grain y (grā′nē), **1** like the grain of wood, marble, etc. **2** granular. *adj.,* **grain i er, grain i est.**

gram (gram), unit of weight or mass in the metric system. Twenty-eight grams weigh about one ounce. *n.* Also, **gramme.**

gra mer cy (grə mėr′sē), OLD USE. many thanks; thank you. *interj.*

gram mar (gram′ər), **1** the study of the forms and uses of words in sentences in a particular language. **2** rules describing the use of words in a language. **3** the use of words according to these rules: *My teacher's grammar is almost always perfect.* *n.*

gram mar i an (grə mer′ē ən), an expert in grammar. *n.*

grammar school, 1 (in the United States) an elementary school. **2** (in England) a secondary school that prepares students for university.

gram mat i cal (grə mat′ə kəl), **1** according to the correct use of words: *Our French teacher speaks grammatical English but has a French accent.* **2** of grammar: *"You should have saw it" is a grammatical mistake.* *adj.*

gram mat i cal ly (grə mat′ik lē), according to the rules of grammar; as regards grammar. *adv.*

gramme (gram), gram. *n.*

gram pus (gram′pəs), **1** a large dolphin with a blunt nose. **2** killer whale. *n., pl.* **gram pus es.**

Gra na da (grə nä′də), city in S Spain, last stronghold of the Moors till they were driven out of Spain in 1492. *n.*

gran ar y (grā′nər ē *or* gran′ər ē), **1** place or building where grain is stored. **2** region producing much grain. *n., pl.* **gran ar ies.**

grand (grand), **1** large and of fine appearance: *grand mountains.* **2** of very high or noble quality; dignified: *a*

very grand palace, grand music, a grand old man. **3** highest or very high in rank; chief: *grand duke.* **4** great; important; main: *the grand staircase.* **5** complete; comprehensive: *grand total.* **6** INFORMAL. very satisfactory: *a grand time, grand weather.* **7** SLANG. a thousand dollars. 1-6 *adj.,* 7 *n.* —**grand′ly,** *adv.* —**grand′ness,** *n.*

gran dam (gran′dam), OLD USE. **1** grandmother. **2** an old woman. *n.*

gran dame (gran′dām), OLD USE. grandam. *n.*

grand aunt (grand′ant′), aunt of one's father or mother; great-aunt. *n.*

Grand Bank or **Grand Banks,** shoal off the SE coast of Newfoundland. It is important for cod fishing

Grand Canyon, deep gorge of the Colorado River, in N Arizona.

grand child (grand′chīld′), child of one's son or daughter. *n., pl.* **grandchil dren.**

grand chil dren (grand′chil′drən), plural of **grandchild.** *n.*

Grand Cou lee (kü′lē), large dam on the Columbia River, in E Washington.

grand daugh ter (gran′dô′tər), daughter of one's son or daughter. *n.*

gran dee (gran dē′), **1** a Spanish or Portuguese nobleman of the highest rank. **2** person of high rank or great importance. *n.*

gran deur (gran′jər), a being grand; majesty; nobility; dignity; splendor: *The grandeur of Niagara Falls is famous.* *n.*

grand fa ther (grand′fä′ƫHər), **1** father of one's father or mother. **2** any forefather. *n.*

grand fa ther ly (grand′fä′ƫHər lē), like or characteristic of a grandfather. *adj.*

grandfather's clock, clock in a tall, wooden case, which stands on the floor.

gran dil o quence (gran dil′ə kwəns), the use of lofty or pompous words. *n.*

gran dil o quent (gran dil′ə kwənt), using lofty or pompous words. *adj.* —**gran dil′o quent ly,** *adv.*

gran di ose (gran′dē ōs), **1** grand in an imposing or impressive way; magnificent. **2** grand in a showy or pompous way; not really magnificent, but trying to seem so. *adj.* —**gran′di ose ly,** *adv.*

grand jury, jury of from 6 to 23 persons chosen to investigate accusations of crime and decide whether there is enough evidence for a trial in court.

grand ma (grand′mä′ *or* gram′ə), INFORMAL. grandmother. *n.*

grand moth er (grand′muƫH′ər), **1** mother of one's father or mother. **2** any ancestress. *n.*

grand moth er ly (grand′muƫH′ər lē), like or characteristic of a grandmother. *adj.*

grand neph ew (grand′nef′yü), son of one's nephew or niece. *n.*

grand niece (grand′nēs′), daughter of one's nephew or niece. *n.*

grand pa (grand′pä′ *or* gram′pə), INFORMAL. grandfather. *n.*

grand par ent (grand′per′ənt *or* grand′par′ənt), grandfather or grandmother. *n.*

grand piano, a large, harp-shaped piano with horizontal strings.

Grand Rapids, city in SW Michigan.

grand sire (grand′sīr′), OLD USE. **1** grandfather. **2** forefather. **3** an old man. *n.*

grand son (grand′sun′), son of one's son or daughter. *n.*

grandstand

grand stand (grand′stand′), the main seating place for people at an athletic field, racetrack, parade, etc. *n.*

grand un cle (grand′ung′kəl), uncle of one's father or mother; great-uncle. *n.*

grange (grānj), **1** farm with its barns and other buildings. **2 Grange,** an association of farmers for the improvement of their welfare. *n.*

gran ite (gran′it), a hard, igneous rock, made of grains of other rocks, chiefly quartz and feldspar. It is much used for buildings and monuments. *n.*

gran ny or **gran nie** (gran′ē), INFORMAL. **1** grandmother. **2** an old woman. **3** a fussy person. *n., pl.* **gran nies.**

granny knot   square knot

granny knot, knot differing from a square knot in having the ends crossed the wrong way.

grant (grant), **1** give what is asked; allow: *grant a request, grant permission.* **2** admit to be true; accept without proof; concede: *I grant that you are right so far.* **3** give or confer (a right, etc.) by formal act. **4** gift, especially land or rights given by the government. **5** act of granting. 1-3 *v.,* 4,5 *n.*

take for granted, 1 assume to be true; regard as proved or agreed to: *We take for granted the existence of atoms.* **2** accept as probable: *We took for* *granted that the sailor could swim.*

Grant (grant), **Ulysses S(impson),** 1822-1885, Union general during the Civil War, and 18th president of the United States, from 1869 to 1877. *n.*

gran u lar (gran′yə lər), 1 consisting of or containing grains or granules; grainy: *granular stone.* 2 like grains or granules. *adj.*

gran u late (gran′yə lāt), 1 make into grains; form grains or granules: *granulated sugar.* 2 roughen the surface of. *v.,* **gran u lat ed, gran u lating.**

gran u la tion (gran′yə lā′shən), formation into grains or granules. *n.*

gran ule (gran′yül), 1 a small grain. 2 a small bit or spot like a grain. *n.*

grape (grāp), 1 a small, round fruit, red, purple, or pale-green, that grows in bunches on a vine. Grapes are eaten raw or made into raisins or wine. 2 grapevine. 3 grapeshot. *n.*

grape fruit (grāp′früt′), 1 a paleyellow, roundish, citrus fruit like an orange, but larger and sourer. 2 tree it grows on. *n.*

grape shot (grāp′shot′), cluster of small iron balls formerly used as a charge for cannon. *n.*

grape sugar, dextrose.

grape vine (grāp′vīn′), 1 vine that grapes grow on. 2 INFORMAL. way in which news or rumors are mysteriously spread. *n.*

graph (def. 1) of the temperature of a winter day for 12 hours

graph (graf), 1 line or diagram showing how one quantity depends on or changes with another. You could draw a graph to show how your weight has changed each year with your change in age. 2 line representing the mathematical relations of the elements in an equation or function. 3 make a graph of. 1,2 *n.,* 3 *v.*

graph ic (graf′ik), 1 producing by words the effect of a picture; lifelike; vivid: *Your graphic description of the English countryside made me feel as though I had been there myself.* 2 of or shown by a graph: *The school board kept a graphic record of school attendance for a month.* 3 of or about drawing, painting, engraving, etching, etc.: *the graphic arts.* 4 of or used in

handwriting: *graphic symbols. adj.*

graph i cal ly (graf′ik lē), in a graphic manner; by a diagram or pictures; vividly. *adv.*

graph ite (graf′īt), a soft, black form of carbon used for lead in pencils and for greasing machinery. *n.*

graph paper, paper ruled in squares, for making graphs, diagrams, etc.

grap nel (grap′nəl), 1 instrument with one or more hooks for seizing and holding something; grapple; grappling iron. Grapnels thrown by ropes were once used to catch on an enemy's ship. 2 a small anchor with three or more hooks. *n.*

grap ple (grap′əl), 1 seize and hold fast; grip or hold firmly. 2 a seizing and holding fast; firm grip or hold. 3 struggle; fight: *The wrestlers grappled in the center of the ring. I grappled with the problem for an hour before I solved it.* 4 grapnel. 1,3 *v.,* **grap pled, grap pling;** 2,4 *n.*

grappling iron, grapnel.

grasp (grasp), 1 seize and hold fast by closing the fingers around: *I grasped the tree limb to keep from falling.* 2 a seizing and holding tightly; clasp of the hand. 3 power of seizing and holding; reach: *Success is within her grasp.* 4 control; possession: *The people regained power from the grasp of the dictator.* 5 understand: *She grasped my meaning at once.* 6 understanding: *He has a good grasp of mathematics.* 1,5 *v.,* 2-4,6 *n.*

grasp at, 1 try to take hold of; try to grasp. 2 accept eagerly: *She grasped at the opportunity.*

grasp ing (gras′ping), eager to get all that one can; greedy. *adj.* —**grasp′ing ly,** *adv.* —**grasp′ing ness,** *n.*

grass (gras), 1 plants with green blades which cover fields, lawns, and pastures. Horses, cows, and sheep eat grass. 2 plant which has jointed stems and long, narrow leaves. Wheat, corn, sugar cane, and bamboo are grasses. 3 land covered with grass; pasture. *n., pl.* **grass es.** —**grass′like′,** *adj.*

grass hop per (gras′hop′ər), a winged insect with strong hind legs for jumping. Locusts and katydids are grasshoppers. *n.*

grass land (gras′land′), land with grass on it, used for pasture. *n.*

grass roots, the ordinary citizens of a region or state taken all together: *The senator is certain to get support from the grass roots.*

grass y (gras′ē), 1 covered with grass; having much grass. 2 of or like grass. *adj.,* **grass i er, grass i est.**

grate¹ (grāt), 1 framework of iron bars to hold burning fuel in a furnace, fireplace, etc. 2 fireplace. 3 framework of

bars over a window or opening; grating. 4 furnish with iron bars: *The windows were strongly grated.* 1-3 *n.,* 4 *v.,* **grated, grat ing.** [from Latin of the 1400's *grata* lattice]

grate² (grāt), 1 have an annoying or unpleasant effect: *Rude manners and loud voices grate on me.* 2 make a harsh, jarring noise by rubbing: *The door grated on its old, rusty hinges.* 3 wear down or grind off in small pieces: *The cook grated the cheese before melting it. v.,* **grated, grat ing.** [from French of the 1400's *grater*]

grate ful (grāt′fəl), 1 feeling kindly because of a favor received; wanting to do a favor in return; thankful: *I am grateful for your help.* 2 pleasing; welcome: *A breeze is grateful on a hot day, a fire on a cold one. adj.* —**grate′ful ly,** *adv.* —**grate′ful ness,** *n.*

grat er (grā′tər), 1 person or thing that grates. 2 instrument with a rough surface for grating: *a nutmeg grater. n.*

grat i fi ca tion (grat′ə fə kā′shən), 1 a gratifying: *The gratification of a person's every wish is not always possible.* 2 a being gratified. 3 something that satisfies or pleases: *Your faith in my ability is a great gratification to me. n.*

grat i fy (grat′ə fī), 1 give pleasure to; please: *Praise gratifies most people.* 2 give satisfaction to; satisfy; indulge: *gratify a craving for sweets. v.,* **gratified, grat i fy ing.** —**grat′i fy′ing ly,** *adv.*

grat ing¹ (grā′ting), framework of parallel or crossed bars; grate. Windows in a prison, bank, or ticket office usually have gratings over them. *n.* [grate¹ + -ing]

grat ing² (grā′ting), 1 not pleasant; annoying; irritating. 2 harsh or jar-

grate¹ (def. 1)

adj.	adjective	*n.*	noun
adv.	adverb	*prep.*	preposition
conj.	conjunction	*pron.*	pronoun
interj.	interjection	*v.*	verb
sing.	singular	*pl.*	plural

ring in sound. *adj.* [**grate**² + *-ing*]

grat is (grat′is *or* grā′tis), for nothing; free of charge: *The club provided the service gratis* (adv.). *The service was gratis to club members* (adj.). *adv., adj.*

grat i tude (grat′ə tüd *or* grat′ə tyüd), kindly feeling because of a favor received; desire to do a favor in return; thankfulness. *n.*

gra tu i tous (grə tü′ə təs *or* grə tyü′ə təs), 1 freely given or obtained; free: *a gratuitous gift.* 2 without reason or cause; unnecessary; uncalled-for: *a gratuitous insult. adj.* —**gra tu′i tous ly,** *adv.*

gra tu i ty (grə tü′ə tē *or* grə tyü′ə tē), present of money in return for service; tip. Gratuities are given to waiters, porters, servants, etc. *n., pl.* **gra tu i ties.**

grave¹ (grāv), 1 hole dug in the ground where a dead body is to be buried. 2 any place of burial: *a watery grave.* 3 death. *n.* [Old English *græf*]

grave² (grāv), 1 important; weighty; momentous: *grave cares, a grave decision.* 2 serious; threatening; critical: *a grave illness, grave news.* 3 sober; dignified; solemn: *a grave face, grave music. adj.,* **grav er, grav est.** [from French of the 1500's *grave,* from Latin *gravis* heavy, serious] —**grave′ly,** *adv.* —**grave′ness,** *n.*

grave³ (grāv), engrave; carve. *v.,* **graved, grav en** *or* **graved, grav ing.** [Old English *grafan*]

grave accent, mark (ˋ) placed over a vowel to show pitch, quality of sound, etc. The phrase *à la mode* has a grave accent. In English poetry a grave accent may be used to indicate that a word is pronounced with one more syllable than usual, as in *wreathèd* (rē′ŦHid).

grav el (grav′əl), 1 pebbles and pieces of rock coarser than sand. Gravel is much used for roads and walks. 2 lay or cover with gravel. 1 *n.,* 2 *v.*

grav el ly (grav′ə lē), 1 having much gravel. 2 of or like gravel. 3 rough; rasping; grating: *a gravelly voice. adj.*

grav en (grā′vən), 1 engraved; carved: *graven images.* 2 a past participle of **grave**³. *Figures had been graven in the rock.* 1 *adj.,* 2 *v.*

grave stone (grāv′stōn′), stone that marks a grave. *n.*

grave yard (grāv′yärd′), cemetery. *n.*

grav i tate (grav′ə tāt′), 1 move or tend to move by the force of gravity: *The planets gravitate toward the sun.* 2 settle down; sink; fall: *The sand and dirt in the water gravitated to the bottom of the bottle.* 3 tend to go; be strongly attracted: *The attention of the audience gravitated to the stage as the lights dimmed. v.,* **grav i tat ed, grav i tat ing.**

grav i ta tion (grav′ə tā′shən), 1 the fact that the earth pulls any object toward it and that the sun, moon, stars, and other such bodies in the universe do the same; the force or pull that makes bodies in the universe tend to move toward one another. 2 a moving or tendency to move caused by this force. 3 a settling down; sinking; falling. 4 a natural tendency toward some point or object of influence: *The gravitation of people to the cities leaves many farms vacant. n.*

grav i ta tion al (grav′ə tā′shə nəl), of or having to do with gravitation. *adj.*

grav i ty (grav′ə tē), 1 the natural force that causes objects to move or tend to move toward the center of the earth. Gravity causes objects to have weight. 2 the natural force that makes objects move or tend to move toward each other; gravitation. 3 heaviness; weight: *He balanced the long pole at its center of gravity.* 4 seriousness; earnestness: *The gravity of the child playing nurse was amusing in one so small.* 5 serious or critical character; importance: *The gravity of the situation was greatly increased by the threats of war. n., pl.* **grav i ties.**

gra vy (grā′vē), 1 juice that comes out of meat in cooking. 2 sauce for meat, potatoes, etc., made from this juice, usually by thickening it with flour. *n., pl.* **gra vies.**

gray (grā), 1 color made by mixing black and white. 2 having a color between black and white: *Ashes, lead, and hair getting white with age are gray.* 3 make or become gray. 4 having gray hair. 5 dark; gloomy; dismal: *a gray day.* 1 *n.,* 2,4,5 *adj.,* 3 *v.* Also, **grey.** —**gray′ly,** *adv.* —**gray′ness,** *n.*

gray beard (grā′bird′), an old man. *n.*

gray ish (grā′ish), somewhat gray. *adj.*

gray ling (grā′ling), a freshwater fish related to the trout and much valued as a food and game fish. *n.*

gray matter, 1 the grayish tissue in the brain and spinal cord that contains nerve cells and some nerve fibers. 2 INFORMAL. intelligence; brains.

graze¹ (grāz), 1 feed on growing grass: *Cattle were grazing in the field.* 2 put (cattle, sheep, etc.) to feed on growing grass or a pasture: *The farmer grazed his sheep. v.,* **grazed, graz ing.** [Old English *grasian,* from *græs* grass]

graze² (grāz), 1 touch lightly in passing; rub lightly against: *The car grazed the garage door.* 2 scrape the skin from: *She grazed her knee when she fell.* 3 a grazing. 4 a slight wound made by grazing. 1,2 *v.,* **grazed, graz ing;** 3,4 *n.* [origin uncertain]

grease (grēs), 1 soft, melted animal fat. 2 any thick, oily substance. 3 rub grease on: *grease a cake pan.* 4 put grease or oil on or in: *Please grease my car.* 1,2 *n.,* 3,4 *v.,* **greased, greas ing.**

grease paint (grēs′pānt′), mixture of tallow or grease and a pigment, used by actors in painting their faces. *n.*

greas i ly (grē′sə lē), in a greasy manner. *adv.*

greas i ness (grē′sē nis), greasy quality or condition. *n.*

greas y (grē′sē), 1 smeared with grease; having grease on it. 2 containing much grease; oily: *Greasy food is hard to digest.* 3 like grease; smooth; slippery. *adj.,* **greas i er, greas i est.**

great (grāt), 1 large in extent, amount, size, or number; big: *a great house, a great crowd.* 2 more than is usual; much: *great pain, great kindness, great ignorance.* 3 high in rank; important; remarkable; famous: *a great composer, a great event, a great achievement.* 4 much in use; favorite: *Her great sport was tennis.* 5 very much of a: *a great talker.* 6 INFORMAL. very good; fine: *We had a great time at the party. adj.*

great-aunt (grāt′ant′), grandaunt. *n.*

Great Barrier Reef, the longest coral reef in the world, in the S Pacific along the NE coast of Australia.

Great Bear, Ursa Major.

Great Britain, England, Scotland, and Wales. Great Britain is the largest island of Europe. See **British Isles** for map.

great circle, any circle on the surface of a sphere having its plane passing through the center of the sphere. The equator is one of the great circles of the earth.

great coat (grāt′kōt′), a heavy overcoat. *n.*

Great Dane, one of a breed of

Great Dane
32 in. high
at shoulder

large, powerful, short-haired dogs.

Great Divide, Continental Divide.

great-grand child (grāt′grand′-chīld′), grandchild of one's son or daughter. *n., pl.* **great-grand children** (grāt′grand′chil′drən).

great-grand daugh ter (grāt′gran′-dô′tər), granddaughter of one's son or daughter. *n.*

great-grand fa ther (grāt′grand′-fä′ᵺ ər), grandfather of one's father or mother. *n.*

great-grand moth er (grāt′grand′-muᵺ ər), grandmother of one's father or mother. *n.*

great-grand par ent (grāt′grand′-per′ənt *or* grāt′grand′par′ənt), great-grandfather or great-grandmother. *n.*

great-grand son (grāt′grand′sun′), grandson of one's son or daughter. *n.*

great-heart ed (grāt′här′tid), 1 no-ble; generous. 2 brave; fearless. *adj.*

Great Lakes, series of five lakes be-tween the United States and Ontario, Canada; Lakes Ontario, Erie, Huron, Michigan, and Superior.

great ly (grāt′lē), 1 in a great man-ner: *Solomon ruled greatly and wisely.* 2 much: *greatly feared. He greatly de-sired to be rich. adv.*

great ness (grāt′nis), 1 a being great; bigness. 2 high place or power. 3 great mind or character. *n.*

Great Plains, semiarid region just east of the Rocky Mountains in the United States and SW Canada. It is mostly pasture land.

Great Salt Lake, shallow lake in NW Utah. Its water is much saltier than ocean water.

Great Spirit, chief god worshiped by certain tribes or groups of American Indians.

great-un cle (grāt′ung′kəl), grandun-cle. *n.*

Great Wall of China, a stone wall about 1500 miles long between China and Mongolia; Chinese Wall. It was begun in the 200's B.C. for the defense of China.

greave (grēv). Often, **greaves,** *pl.* ar-mor for the leg below the knee. *n.*

grebe (grēb), a diving bird like a loon, having feet not completely webbed and a pointed bill. *n.*

Gre cian (grē′shən), 1 Greek. 2 a Greek. 1 *adj.,* 2 *n.*

Greece (grēs), country in SE Europe, on the Mediterranean. *Capital:* Ath-ens. *n.*

greed (grēd), a wanting to get more than one's share; greedy behavior; greedy desire: *a miser's greed for money. n.*

greed i ly (grē′dl ē), in a greedy man-ner. *adv.*

greed i ness (grē′dē nis), greedy

behavior; greedy desire; greed. *n.*

greed y (grē′dē), 1 wanting to get more than one's share. 2 wanting to get a great deal. 3 wanting to eat or drink a great deal in a hurry; piggish. *adj.,* **greed i er, greed i est.**

Greek (grēk), 1 of Greece, its people, or their language. 2 person born or living in Greece. 3 language of Greece. 1 *adj.,* 2,3 *n.*

Greek Orthodox Church, 1 East-ern Church. 2 the part of the Eastern Church forming the established church in Greece.

green (grēn), 1 the color of most growing plants, grass, and the leaves of trees in summer; color in the spectrum between yellow and blue. 2 having this color; of this color: *green paint. An emerald is green.* 3 covered with growing plants, grass, leaves, etc.: *green fields.* 4 not ripe; not fully grown: *Most green fruit is not good to eat.* 5 not dried, cured, seasoned, or otherwise prepared for use: *green tobacco, green wood.* 6 not trained or experienced: *He was green compared with the other ap-prentices in the business.* 7 full of life and strength: *green old age.* 8 ground covered with grass; grassy land: *the village green.* **9 greens,** *pl.* a green leaves and branches used for decoration. b leaves and stems of plants used for food: *beet greens.* 10 a putting green of a golf course. 1,8,9,10 *n.,* 2-7 *adj.* **—green′ness,** *n.*

green back (grēn′bak′), piece of United States paper money having the back printed in green. *n.*

green er y (grē′nər ē), green plants, grass, or leaves. *n., pl.* **green er ies.**

green gage (grēn′gāj′), a large plum having a light-green skin and pulp and a fine flavor. *n.* [*green* + Sir William *Gage,* an English botanist who in-troduced it in England from France about 1725]

green gro cer (grēn′grō′sər), per-son who sells fresh vegetables and fruit. *n.*

green horn (grēn′hôrn′), INFORMAL. 1 person without training or experience. 2 person easy to trick or cheat. *n.*

green house (grēn′hous′), building with a glass roof and glass sides kept warm for growing plants; hothouse. *n., pl.* **green hous es** (grēn′hou′ziz).

green ish (grē′nish), somewhat green. *adj.*

Green land (grēn′lənd), arctic island northeast of North America. It is the largest island in the world and belongs to Denmark. *n.*

green ling (grēn′ling), fish found around rocks and kelp in the northern Pacific, used for food. *n.*

green manure, green, leafy plants,

hat, āge, fär; let, ēqual, tėrm;
it, īce; hot, ōpen, ôrder;
oil, out; cup, pùt, rüle; ch, child;
ng, long; sh, she; th, thin;
ᵺ, then; zh, measure;

ə represents *a* in about,
e in taken, *i* in pencil,
o in lemon, *u* in circus.

such as clover or alfalfa, plowed under to enrich the soil.

Green Mountains, part of the Ap-palachian Mountains extending north and south through Vermont.

green pepper, the unripe fruit of a red pepper plant. It is used as a vegetable, for stuffing, etc.

green sward (grēn′swôrd′), green grass; turf. *n.*

green thumb, a remarkable ability to grow flowers, vegetables, etc.: *When my friend saw our garden she said Mother must certainly have a green thumb.*

Green wich (gren′ich), borough in SE London, England. Longitude is measured east and west of Green-wich. *n.*

Greenwich Time, the standard time used in England and the basis for set-ting standard time elsewhere. It is determined by setting noon as the time at which the sun is directly overhead at the meridian which passes through Greenwich, England.

green wood (grēn′wùd′), forest in spring and summer when the trees are green with leaves. *n.*

greet (grēt), 1 speak or write to in a friendly, polite way; address in wel-come; hail: *They greeted us at the door with a friendly "Hello."* 2 respond to: *His speech was greeted with cheers.* 3 present itself to; meet: *When she opened the door, a strange sight greeted her eyes. v.* **—greet′er,** *n.*

greet ing (grē′ting), 1 act or words of a person who greets another; welcome. 2 **greetings,** *pl.* friendly wishes on a special occasion: *Season's greetings. n.*

gre gar i ous (grə ger′ē əs *or* grə-gar′ē əs), 1 living in flocks, herds, or other groups: *Sheep are gregarious, raccoons are not.* 2 fond of being with others: *Hermits are not gregarious. adj.* **—gre gar′i ous ly,** *adv.* **—gre gar′i-ous ness,** *n.*

Gre go ri an (grə gôr′ē ən), 1 of Pope Gregory I. The **Gregorian chant** is a kind of vocal music introduced by Gregory I and still used in the Roman Catholic Church. 2 of Pope Gregory

adj. adjective	*n.* noun
adv. adverb	*prep.* preposition
conj. conjunction	*pron.* pronoun
interj. interjection	*v.* verb
sing. singular	*pl.* plural

XIII. The **Gregorian calendar**, introduced by Gregory XIII in 1582, is the one we use today. *adj.*

Greg or y I (greg′ər ē), **Saint,** A.D. 540?-604, pope from A.D. 590 to 604. He was called "Gregory the Great."

Gregory XIII, 1502-1585, pope from 1572 to 1585.

grem lin (grem′lən), an imaginary creature that causes trouble in an aircraft, its engines, parts, etc. *n.*

gre nade (grə nād′), 1 a small bomb, which is thrown by hand or fired from a rifle: *The soldiers threw grenades into the enemy's trenches.* 2 a round, glass bottle filled with chemicals which scatter as the glass breaks. Fire grenades are thrown on fires to put them out. *n.*

griffin

gren a dier (gren′ə dir′), 1 (formerly) a soldier who threw grenades. 2 (later) a member of a specially chosen unit of foot soldiers. 3 (now) a member of a special regiment of guards in the British army. *n.*

grew (grü), past tense of **grow.** *It grew colder as the sun went down. v.*

grey (grā), gray. *n., adj., v.*

grey hound (grā′hound′), a tall, slender hunting dog with a long nose. Greyhounds can run very fast. *n.*

grid (grid), 1 framework of parallel iron bars with spaces between them; grating; gridiron. 2 electrode consisting of wires or a screen which controls the

grid (def. 2)
(The anode has been partly cut away to expose the grid and cathode.)
CATHODE
ANODE
GRID

flow of electrons from cathode to anode in a vacuum tube. *n.*

grid dle (grid′l), a heavy, flat plate, usually of metal, on which to cook pancakes, bacon, etc. *n.*

grid dle cake (grid′l kāk′), pancake. *n.*

grid i ron (grid′ī′ərn), 1 grill for broiling. 2 frame or structure like this. A frame for supporting scenery in a theater is a gridiron. 3 a football field. *n.*

grief (grēf), 1 great sadness caused by trouble or loss; heavy sorrow. 2 cause of sadness or sorrow. *n.*

come to grief, have trouble; fail.

Grieg (grēg), **Edvard,** 1843-1907, Norwegian composer. *n.*

griev ance (grē′vəns), a real or imagined wrong; reason for being angry or annoyed: *Report any grievances you may have to your supervisor. n.*

grieve (grēv), 1 feel grief; be very sad: *The little girl grieved over her kitten's death.* 2 cause to feel grief; make very sad: *The news of your illness grieved me. v.,* **grieved, griev ing.**

griev ous (grē′vəs), 1 hard to bear; causing great pain or suffering; severe: *grievous cruelty.* 2 very evil or offensive; outrageous: *Murder is a grievous crime in most societies.* 3 causing grief: *a grievous loss.* 4 full of grief; showing grief: *a grievous cry. adj.* **—griev′ous ly,** *adv.*

grif fin or **grif fon** (grif′ən), an imaginary creature with the head, wings, and forelegs of an eagle, and the body, hind legs, and tail of a lion. *n.*

grill (gril), 1 a cooking utensil with parallel iron bars or wires for broiling meat, fish, etc.; gridiron. 2 cook by holding near the fire; broil. 3 dish of broiled meat, fish, etc. 4 restaurant or dining room that specializes in serving broiled meat, fish, etc. 5 torture with heat. 6 question severely and persistently: *The detectives grilled several suspects concerning the crime.* 1,3,4 *n.,* 2,5,6 *v.*

grill (def. 1)

grille (gril), an openwork, metal structure or screen, used as a gate, door, window, or to cover the opening in front of the radiator of an automobile; grating. *n.*

grill work (gril′wèrk′), pattern of grilles *n.*

grim (grim), 1 without mercy; stern, harsh, or fierce: *grim, stormy weather.* 2 not yielding; not relenting: *The los-*

ing team fought on with grim resolve. 3 looking stern, fierce, or harsh: *My parents were grim when they heard about the broken window.* 4 horrible; frightful; ghastly: *As we walked past the cemetery, she made grim jokes about death and ghosts. adj.,* **grim mer, grim mest. —grim′ly,** *adv.* **—grim′ness,** *n.*

gri mace (grə mās′ *or* grim′is), 1 a twisting of the face; ugly or funny smile: *a grimace caused by pain.* 2 make faces: *The clown grimaced at the children.* 1 *n.,* 2 *v.,* **gri maced, gri mac ing.**

grime (grīm), 1 dirt rubbed deeply and firmly into a surface: *Soap and water removed only a little of the grime on the coal miner's hands.* 2 make very dirty. 1 *n.,* 2 *v.,* **grimed, grim ing.**

grim i ness (grī′mē nis), grimy condition. *n.*

Grimm (grim), **Jakob,** 1785-1863, and his brother, **Wilhelm,** 1786-1859, German philologists and collectors of fairy tales. *n.*

grim y (grī′mē), covered with grime; very dirty: *grimy hands. adj.,* **grim i er, grim i est.**

grin (grin), 1 smile broadly. 2 a broad smile. 3 draw back the lips and show the teeth in anger, pain, scorn, etc.: *The wolf grinned in an ugly way.* 1,3 *v.,* **grinned, grin ning;** 2 *n.*

grind (grind), 1 crush into bits or powder: *That mill grinds corn into meal and wheat into flour. His teeth ground the meat.* 2 crush by harshness or cruelty: *The serfs were ground down by their lords.* 3 sharpen, smooth, or wear by rubbing on something rough: *He ground the ax on the grindstone.* 4 make a harsh sound by rubbing; grate: *grind one's teeth in anger.* 5 force by rubbing or pressing: *grind one's heel in the dirt.* 6 work by turning a handle; produce by turning a crank: *The old man ground out music on the hand organ.* 7 act of grinding. 8 something made by grinding: *a fine grind of coffee.* 9 INFORMAL. long, hard work or study: *To some of the students, mathematics was a grind.* 10 INFORMAL. work or study long and hard. 11 INFORMAL. person who works long and hard at his studies. 1-6,10 *v.,* **ground, grind ing;** 7-9,11 *n.*

grilles
left, on balcony
right, on window

grind er (grīn′dər), 1 person or thing that grinds. 2 person or machine that sharpens tools. 3 molar. *n.*

grindstone

grind stone (grīnd′stōn′), a flat, round stone set in a frame and turned by hand, foot, or a motor. It is used to sharpen tools, such as axes and knives, or to smooth and polish things. *n.*

grip (grip), 1 a firm hold; seizing and holding tight; tight grasp. 2 take a firm hold on; seize and hold tight: *The dog gripped the stick.* 3 power of gripping: *the grip of a bear.* 4 part to take hold of; handle. 5 a certain way of gripping the hand as a sign of belonging to some secret society. 6 a small suitcase or handbag. 7 firm control: *in the grip of poverty.* 8 mental grasp; understanding: *He has a grip of the subject.* 9 get and keep the interest and attention of: *An exciting story grips you.* 10 grippe; influenza. 1,3-8,10 *n.,* 2,9 *v.,* **gripped, grip ping.**

come to grips, 1 fight hand to hand; struggle close together: *come to grips with an enemy.* 2 work hard and seriously; struggle: *come to grips with a problem.*

gripe (grīp), 1 clutch or grasp tightly; pinch. 2 INFORMAL. annoy; irritate. 3 cause pain in the bowels: *Too much unripe fruit can gripe a person.* 4 **gripes,** *pl.* pain in the bowels. 5 INFORMAL. complain: *He was always griping about something.* 6 INFORMAL. complaint. 1-3,5 *v.,* **griped, grip ing;** 4,6 *n.*

grippe (grip), influenza. *n.* Also, **grip.**

gris ly (griz′lē), causing horror; frightful; horrible; ghastly. *adj.,* **gris li er, gris li est.**

grist (grist), 1 grain to be ground: *The farmer took his grist to the mill.* 2 grain that has been ground; meal or flour. *n.*

gris tle (gris′əl), a tough, elastic tissue, such as is found in meat; cartilage. *n.*

gris tly (gris′lē), of, containing, or like gristle. *adj.,* **gris tli er, gris tli est.**

grist mill, mill for grinding grain. *n.*

grit (grit), 1 very fine bits of gravel or sand. 2 a coarse sandstone. 3 courage; pluck; endurance. 4 grate; grind: *The swimmer gritted her teeth and plunged*

into the cold water. 1-3 *n.,* 4 *v.,* **gritted, grit ting.**

grits (grits), corn, oats, wheat, etc., husked and coarsely ground. Grits are eaten boiled. *n.pl.*

grit ti ness (grit′ē nis), condition or quality of being gritty. *n.*

grit ty (grit′ē), 1 of or containing grit; like grit; sandy. 2 INFORMAL. courageous; plucky. *adj.,* **grit ti er, grit ti est.**

griz zled (griz′əld), 1 grayish; gray: *a grizzled beard.* 2 gray-haired. *adj.*

griz zly (griz′lē), 1 grayish; gray. 2 grizzly bear. 1 *adj.,* **griz zli er, griz zli est;** 2 *n., pl.* **griz zlies.**

grizzly bear, a large, fierce, gray or brownish-gray bear of western North America.

groan (grōn), 1 sound made deep in the throat that expresses grief, pain, or disapproval; deep, short moan: *We heard the groans of the injured people.* 2 give a groan or groans: *The movers groaned as they lifted the piano.* 3 be loaded or overburdened: *The table groaned with food.* 4 express by groaning: *He groaned his disapproval.* 1 *n.,* 2-4 *v.*

groat (grōt), an old English silver coin worth fourpence. *n.*

gro cer (grō′sər), person who sells food and household supplies. *n.*

gro cer y (grō′sər ē), 1 store that sells food and household supplies. 2 **groceries,** *pl.* articles of food and household supplies sold by a grocer. *n., pl.* **gro cer ies.**

grog (grog), 1 drink made of rum and water, or whisky and water. 2 any strong, alcoholic drink. *n.*

grog gi ly (grog′ə lē), INFORMAL. in a groggy manner; shakily. *adv.*

grog gi ness (grog′ē nis), INFORMAL. condition of being groggy. *n.*

grog gy (grog′ē), INFORMAL. 1 not steady; shaky: *A blow on the head made me groggy.* 2 drunk; intoxicated. *adj.,* **grog gi er, grog gi est.**

groin (groin), 1 the hollow on either side of the body where the thigh joins the abdomen. 2 the curved edge where two vaults of a roof intersect. 3 form or build with groins: *groined vaults.* 1,2 *n.,* 3 *v.*

groins (def. 2) shown from the inside and outside of the vaults. (The groins are indicated by heavy lines.)

grom met (grom′it), 1 a metal eyelet. 2 ring of rope, used as an oarlock, to hold a sail on its stays, etc. *n.*

groom (grüm *or* grùm), 1 person whose work is taking care of horses. 2 feed, rub down, brush, and generally take care of (horses). 3 take care of the appearance of; make neat and tidy: *He was grooming himself for the party.* 4 prepare (a person) for an office: *The lawyer was being groomed as a candidate for mayor.* 5 bridegroom. 1,5 *n.,* 2-4 *v.*

groove (grüv), 1 a long, narrow channel or furrow, especially one cut by a tool: *My desk has a groove for pencils. The plate rests in a groove on the rack.* 2 any similar channel; rut: *Wheels leave grooves in a dirt road.* 3 make a groove in: *The counter of the sink is grooved so that the water will run off.* 4 a fixed way of doing things: *It is hard to get out of a groove.* 1,2,4 *n.,* 3 *v.,* **grooved, groov ing.**

grope (grōp), 1 feel about with the hands: *I groped for a flashlight when the lights went out.* 2 search blindly and uncertainly: *The detectives groped for some clue to the mysterious crime.* 3 find by feeling about with the hands; feel (one's way) slowly: *She groped her way down the dark, narrow hall.* *v.,* **groped, grop ing.**

gros beak (grōs′bēk′), finch with a large, stout, cone-shaped bill. *n.*

gros grain (grō′grān′), a closely woven silk or rayon cloth with heavy cross threads and a dull finish, used for ribbons, etc. *n.*

gross (grōs), 1 with nothing taken out; total; whole; entire. Gross receipts are all the money taken in before costs are deducted. 2 the whole sum; total amount. 3 make a gross profit of; earn a total of: *gross $20,000 per year.* 4 twelve dozen; 144. 5 very easily seen; glaring; flagrant: *gross misconduct, gross superstition. She makes gross errors in pronouncing words.* 6 coarse; vulgar: *a book with gross language, gross manners.* 7 too big and fat; overfed. 8 thick; heavy; dense: *the gross growth of a jungle.* 1,5-8 *adj.,* 2,4

grotesque

n., pl. **gross es** for 2, **gross** for 4; 3 *v.*
—**gross′ly,** *adv.* —**gross′ness,** *n.*

gro tesque (grō tesk′), 1 odd or un-natural in shape, appearance, manner, etc.; fantastic; queer: *The book had pictures of hideous dragons and other grotesque monsters.* 2 ridiculous; absurd: *The monkey's grotesque antics made us laugh. adj.* —**gro tesque′ly,** *adv.* —**gro tesque′ness,** *n.*

grot to (grot′ō), 1 cave or cavern. 2 an artificial cave made for coolness and pleasure. *n., pl.* **grot toes** or **grot tos.**

grouch (grouch), INFORMAL. 1 a surly, ill-tempered mood; fit of grumbling or complaining. 2 a surly, ill-tempered person; person who tends to grumble or complain. 3 grumble or complain in a surly, ill-tempered way. 1,2 *n., pl.* **grouch es;** 3 *v.*

grouch i ly (grou′chə lē), INFORMAL. in a grouchy manner. *adv.*

grouch i ness (grou′chē nis), INFORMAL. a grouchy manner. *n.*

grouch y (grou′chē), INFORMAL. tending to grumble or complain; surly; ill-tempered. *adj.,* **grouch i er, grouch i est.**

ground¹ (ground), 1 the solid part of the earth's surface; soil: *A blanket of snow covered the ground.* 2 Often, **grounds,** *pl.* any piece of land or region used for some special purpose: *fishing grounds. The school band practices daily on the parade ground.* 3 **grounds,** *pl.* **a** land, lawns, and gardens around a house, school, etc. **b** small bits that sink to the bottom of a drink such as coffee or tea; dregs; sediment. 4 of, on, at, or near the ground: *the ground floor of a building.* 5 put on the ground; cause to touch the ground. 6 run aground; hit the bottom or shore: *The boat grounded in shallow water.* 7 foundation for what is said, thought, claimed, or done; basis; reason: *There is no ground for complaining of his conduct. On what ground do you say that is true?* 8 fix firmly; establish: *Their beliefs are grounded on facts.* 9 instruct in the first principles or elements: *The class is well grounded in arithmetic.* 10 underlying surface; background: *The cloth has a blue pattern on a white ground.* 11 the connection of an electrical conductor with the earth. 12 connect (an electric wire or other conductor) with the earth. 13 keep (a pilot or an aircraft) from flying: *The pilot was grounded by injury.* 14 (in baseball) hit a bouncing or rolling ball. 1-3,7,10,11 *n.,* 4 *adj.,* 5,6,8,9, 12-14 *v.* [Old English *grund* bottom]

break ground, 1 turn up soil with a plow, shovel, etc.; dig; plow. 2 begin building.

cover ground, 1 go over a certain distance or area: *Did you cover much ground on your hike?* 2 do a certain amount of work, etc.: *We covered considerable ground in our history class today.*

gain ground, 1 go forward; advance; progress. 2 become more common or widespread: *His ideas are gaining ground.*

give ground, retreat; yield.

lose ground, 1 go backward; retreat; yield: *We lost ground because of the storm.* 2 become less common or widespread: *Superstition is losing ground as people become more educated.*

ground² (ground), past tense and past participle of **grind.** *The miller ground the corn into meal. The wheat was ground to make flour. v.*

ground cover, low plants, shrubbery, etc., planted for ornament or to enrich the soil and prevent the topsoil from eroding or blowing away.

ground crew, mechanics and other nonflying personnel responsible for conditioning and maintenance of aircraft.

ground er (groun′dər), baseball hit so as to bounce or roll along the ground. *n.*

ground hog (ground′hôg′), woodchuck. *n.*

Groundhog Day, February 2, the day when the groundhog is believed to come out of its hole. If it sees its shadow, it goes back in the hole and winter continues for six more weeks.

ground less (ground′lis), without foundation, basis, or reason: *a groundless rumor. adj.*

ground nut (ground′nut′), 1 plant having underground parts which are used for food, such as the peanut. 2 its tuber, pod, or the like. *n.*

ground pine, kind of club moss used for Christmas decorations, etc.

ground squirrel, 1 a burrowing rodent of western North America related to the squirrels. 2 chipmunk or similar rodent.

ground swell, a broad, deep wave or swell of the ocean caused by a distant storm or earthquake.

ground water, water that flows or seeps downward and saturates the soil. The upper level of this saturated zone is called the water table. Ground water supplies springs and wells.

ground work (ground′wėrk′), foundation; basis. *n.*

group (grüp), 1 number of persons or things together: *A group of children were playing tag.* 2 number of persons or things belonging or classed together: *Wheat, rye, and oats belong to the grain group.* 3 form into a group: *The children grouped themselves at the monkey's cage. Please choose a place for us to group.* 4 put in a group; arrange in groups: *Group the numbers to form three columns.* 5 a military unit made up of two or more battalions of supporting personnel, usually commanded by a colonel. 6 an air-force unit smaller than a wing and composed of two or more squadrons. 1,2,5,6 *n.,* 3,4 *v.*

grouse¹
ruffed grouse
17 in. long

grouse¹ (grous), a reddish-brown game bird with feathered legs. The prairie chicken and ruffed grouse of the United States are two different kinds. *n., pl.* **grouse.** [origin unknown]

grouse² (grous), INFORMAL. grumble; complain. *v.,* **groused, grous ing.** [origin unknown]

grove (grōv), group of trees standing together. An orange grove is an orchard of orange trees. *n.*

grov el (gruv′əl *or* grov′əl), 1 lie face downward; crawl at someone's feet; cringe: *The dog groveled before his master when he saw the whip.* 2 humble oneself: *I will apologize when I am wrong, but I will grovel before no one. v.* —**grov′el er,** *n.*

grow (grō), 1 become bigger by taking in food, as plants and animals do; develop toward full size or age: *Plants grow from seeds.* 2 exist; thrive: *Few trees grow in the desert.* 3 become bigger; increase: *Her fame grew. Their business has grown fast.* 4 cause to grow; produce; raise: *We grow cotton in the southern part of the United States.* 5 come to be; become: *grow rich. It grew cold.* 6 become attached or united by growth: *The vine has grown fast to the wall. v.,* **grew, grown, grow ing.**

grow on, having an increasing effect or influence on: *The habit grew on me.*

grow out of, 1 grow too large for; outgrow: *When I grew out of my jacket, I gave it to my little brother.* 2 result from; develop from: *Several inter-*

esting ideas grew out of the discussion.

grow up, become full-grown; become an adult: *What will you be when you grow up?*

grow er (grō'ər), **1** person who grows something: *a fruit grower.* **2** plant that grows in a certain way: *a quick grower. n.*

growl (groul), **1** make a deep, low, angry sound: *The dog growled at the stranger.* **2** a deep, low, angry sound; deep, warning snarl. **3** complain angrily; grumble: *The sailors growled about the poor food.* **4** an angry complaint; grumble. **5** rumble: *Thunder growled in the distance.* **6** a rumble. **1,3,5** *v.,* **2,4,6** *n.* —**growl'er,** *n.*

grown (grōn), **1** arrived at full growth. A grown person is an adult. **2** past participle of **grow.** *This corn has grown very tall.* **1** *adj.,* **2** *v.*

grown-up (grōn'up'), **1** adult: *a grown-up person, grown-up manners.* **2** an adult: *The boy eats like a grown-up.* **1** *adj.,* **2** *n.*

growth (grōth), **1** process of growing; development. **2** amount grown; increase: *one year's growth.* **3** what has grown or is growing: *A thick growth of bushes covered the ground.* **4** an abnormal mass of tissue formed in or on the body. A tumor is a growth. *n.*

grub (grub), **1** a soft, thick, wormlike larva of an insect, especially that of a beetle. **2** root out of the ground; dig up; dig: *Pigs grub for roots. It took the farmer weeks to grub the stumps on his land.* **3** toil; drudge. **4** SLANG. food. **1,4** *n.,* **2,3** *v.,* **grubbed, grub bing.**

grub bi ly (grub'ə lē), in a grubby manner. *adv.*

grub bi ness (grub'ē nis), grubby condition or quality. *n.*

grub by (grub'ē), dirty; grimy. *adj.,* **grub bi er, grub bi est.**

grub stake (grub'stāk'), INFORMAL. **1** food, equipment, money, etc., supplied to a prospector on the condition of sharing in whatever he finds. **2** supply with a grubstake. **1** *n.,* **2** *v.,* **grubstaked, grub stak ing.**

grudge (gruj), **1** feeling of anger or dislike against because of a real or imaginary wrong; ill will: *She has a grudge against the neighbors who built the fence.* **2** feel anger or dislike toward (a person) because of (something); envy the possession of: *He grudged me my little prize even though he had won a bigger one.* **3** give or let have unwillingly: *grudge an animal even the food that it eats.* **1** *n.,* **2,3** *v.,* **grudged, grudg ing.**

grudg ing ly (gruj'ing lē), unwillingly. *adj.*

gru el (grü'əl), a thin, almost liquid food made by boiling oatmeal, etc., in water or milk. Gruel is often given to those who are sick or old. *n.*

gru el ing (grü'ə ling), INFORMAL. very tiring; exhausting: *Mountain climbing can be grueling. adj.*

grue some (grü'səm), causing fear or horror; horrible; revolting. *adj.* —**grue'some ly,** *adv.* —**grue'someness,** *n.*

gruff (gruf), **1** deep and harsh; hoarse: *a gruff voice.* **2** rough, rude, or unfriendly; bad-tempered: *a gruff manner. adj.* —**gruff'ly,** *adv.* —**gruff'ness.** *n.*

grum ble (grum'bəl), **1** mutter in discontent; complain in a bad-tempered way; find fault: *Everyone was grumbling about the rainy weather.* **2** a mutter of discontent; bad-tempered complaint. **3** make a low, heavy sound like far-off thunder; rumble. **4** a rumble. **1,3** *v.,* **grum bled, grum bling; 2,4** *n.*

grum bler (grum'blər), person who grumbles. *n.*

grump i ly (grum'pə lē), in a grumpy manner. *adv.*

grump i ness (grum'pē nis), grumpy condition, behavior, or quality. *n.*

grump y (grum'pē), surly; ill-humored; gruff: *Grumpy people can find fault with almost anything. adj.,* **grump i er, grump i est.**

grunt (grunt), **1** the deep, hoarse sound that a hog makes. **2** a sound like this: *She picked up the heavy carton with a grunt.* **3** make this sound: *He grunted in discontent.* **4** say with this sound: *The sullen teen-ager grunted an apology.* **1,2** *n.,* **3,4** *v.*

Gua de loupe (gwä'dl üp'), French islands in the West Indies. *n.*

Guam (gwäm), island in the W Pacific, east of the Philippines. Guam belongs to the United States. *n.*

gua no (gwä'nō), waste matter from sea birds, used as a fertilizer. It is found especially on islands near Peru. *n., pl.* **gua nos.**

guar an tee (gar'ən tē'), **1** a promise or pledge to replace or repair a purchased product, return the money paid, etc., if the product is not as represented: *We have a one-year guarantee on our new car.* **2** stand back of; give a guarantee for: *This company guarantees its clocks for a year.* **3** guaranty. **4** person who gives a guarantee; guarantor. **5** undertake to secure for another: *The landlady will guarantee us possession of the house by May.* **6** make secure; protect: *Our home insurance guarantees us against loss in case of fire or theft.* **7** promise (to do something); pledge that (something) has been or will be: *The store guaranteed to deliver my purchase by next Friday. Wealth does*

hat, āge, fär; let, ēqual, tèrm;
it, īce; hot, ōpen, ôrder;
oil, out; cup, pùt, rüle; ch, child;
ng, long; sh, she; th, thin;
ғн, then; zh, measure;

ə represents *a* in about,
e in taken, *i* in pencil,
o in lemon, *u* in circus.

not guarantee happiness. **1,3,4** *n.,* **2,5-7** *v.,* **guar an teed, guar an tee ing.**

guar an tor (gar'ən tôr), person who makes or gives a guarantee. *n.*

guar an ty (gar'ən tē), **1** a pledge or promise by which a person gives security for the payment of a debt or the performance of an obligation by another person; guarantee. **2** property, money, or goods given or taken as security. **3** act or fact of giving security. *n., pl.* **guar an ties.**

guard (gärd), **1** watch over; take care of; keep safe; defend; protect: *The dog guarded the child day and night.* **2** keep from getting out; hold back; check: *Guard the prisoners. Guard your tongue.* **3** person or group that guards. A soldier or group of soldiers guarding a person or place is a guard. **4** take precautions: *guard against errors.* **5** anything that gives protection; arrangement to give safety: *A helmet is a guard against head injuries.* **6** careful watch: *A soldier kept guard over the prisoners.* **7** position in which one is ready to defend in boxing, fencing, or cricket. **8** person who opens and closes the doors or gates on a train. **9** an offensive player at either side of the center in football. **10** either of two players in basketball stationed near the center of the court. **1,2,4** *v.,* **3,5-10** *n.*

on guard, ready to defend or protect; watchful: *A sentry's job is to be on guard at his post.*

guard ed (gär'did), **1** kept safe; carefully watched over; defended; protected. **2** careful; cautious: *"Maybe" was the guarded answer to my question. adj.* —**guard'ed ly,** *adv.*

guard house (gärd'hous'), **1** building used by soldiers on guard. **2** building used as a jail for soldiers. *n., pl.* **guard hous es** (gärd'hou'ziz).

guard i an (gär'dē ən), **1** person who takes care of another or of some special thing. **2** person appointed by law to take care of the affairs of someone who is young or cannot take care of them himself. **3** protecting: *My guardian angel must have looked after me then.* **1,2** *n.,* **3** *adj.*

adj. adjective	*n.* noun
adv. adverb	*prep.* preposition
conj. conjunction	*pron.* pronoun
interj. interjection	*v.* verb
sing. singular	*pl.* plural

guard i an ship (gär′dē ən ship),
position or care of a guardian. *n.*

guard room (gärd′rüm′ or gärd′-
rum′), 1 room used by soldiers on
guard. 2 room used as a jail for soldiers. *n.*

guards man (gärdz′mən), 1 guard.
2 soldier who belongs to the National
Guard. *n., pl.* **guards men.**

Gua te ma la (gwä′tə mä′lə), country
in NW Central America. *Capital:*
Guatemala City. *n.* —**Gua′te ma′lan,**
adj., n.

Guatemala City, capital of Guatemala, in the central part.

gua va (gwä′və), 1 a tropical American tree or shrub with a yellow or red,
round or pear-shaped fruit. 2 its fruit,
used for jelly, jam, etc. *n., pl.* **gua-
vas.**

gu ber na to ri al (gü′bər nə tôr′ē-
əl), of a governor; having to do with a
governor. *adj.*

gudg eon (guj′ən), a small European
freshwater fish that is easy to catch and
is often used for bait. It is related to the
carp. *n.*

guer don (gèrd′n), reward. *n., v.*

gue ril la (gə ril′ə), guerrilla. *n., pl.*
gue ril las; *adj.*

Guern sey (gèrn′zē), 1 one of the
Channel Islands. 2 one of a breed of
tan-and-white dairy cattle which came
from this island. Guernseys give rich,
cream-colored milk. *n., pl.* **Guern seys**
for 2.

guer ril la (gə ril′ə), 1 member of a
band of fighters who harass the enemy
by sudden raids, ambushes, plundering
supply trains, etc. Guerrillas are not
part of a regular army. 2 of or by
guerrillas: *a guerrilla attack.* 1 *n., pl.*
guer ril las; 2 *adj.* Also, **guerilla.**

guess (ges), 1 form an opinion of
something without really knowing: *Do
you know this or are you just guessing?* 2 opinion formed without really
knowing: *My guess is that it will rain
tomorrow.* 3 get right or find out by
guessing: *Can you guess the answer to
that riddle?* 4 think; believe; suppose: *I
guess he was serious after all.* 1,3,4 *v.,* 2
n., pl. **guess es.** —**guess′er,** *n.*

guess work (ges′wèrk′), work, action, or results based on guessing;
guessing. *n.*

guest (gest), 1 person who is received
and entertained at another's home, club,
etc.; visitor. 2 person staying at a hotel,
boarding house, etc. *n.*

guf faw (gu fô′), 1 burst of loud,
coarse laughter. 2 laugh loudly and
coarsely. 1 *n.,* 2 *v.*

Gui a na (gē ä′nə or gē an′ə), region
in N South America. It is divided into
Guyana, Surinam, and French Guiana. *n.*

guid ance (gīd′ns), 1 a guiding;
leadership; direction: *Under her
mother's guidance, she learned how to
swim.* 2 thing that guides: *Common
sense is usually our best guidance.* *n.*

guide (gīd), 1 show the way; lead;
direct: *The scout guided us through the
pass. The counselor guided her in the
choice of a career.* 2 person or thing
that shows the way, leads, or directs:
Tourists sometimes hire guides. 3 part
of a machine for directing or regulating
motion or action. 4 guidebook. 1 *v.,*
guid ed, guid ing; 2-4 *n.*

guide book (gīd′buk′), book of directions and information for travelers,
tourists, etc. *n.*

guided missile, missile that can be
guided in flight to its target by means of
radio signals from the ground or by
automatic devices inside the missile
which direct its course.

guide line (gīd′līn′). Usually, **guidelines,** *pl.* guide, principle, or policy for
determining a future course of action:
guidelines for foreign trade. *n.*

guide post (gīd′pōst′), post with signs
and directions on it. A guidepost where
roads meet tells travelers what places
each road goes to and how far it is to
each place. *n.*

guide word, word put at the top of
a page as a guide to the contents of
the page. The guide words for these
two pages are *guardianship* and
gunshot.

guild (gild), 1 association or society
formed by people having the same interests, work, etc., for some useful or
common purpose: *The author is a
member of the Writers Guild.* 2 (in the
Middle Ages) a union of the men in one
particular trade or craft, formed to keep
its standards high and to protect the
interests of its members. *n.* Also,
gild.

guil der (gil′dər), a silver coin or unit
of money in the Netherlands, worth
about 40½ cents; gulden. *n.*

guild hall (gild′hôl′), 1 hall in which a
guild meets. 2 town hall or city hall (a
term used in Great Britain). *n.*

guile (gīl), crafty deceit; sly tricks; cunning: *By guile the fox got the cheese
from the crow.* *n.*

guile ful (gīl′fəl), crafty and deceitful;

sly and tricky. *adj.* —**guile′ful ly,** *adv.*

guile less (gīl′lis), without guile;
honest; frank; straightforward. *adj.*
—**guile′less ly,** *adv.* —**guile′less-
ness,** *n.*

guillotine (def. 1)

guil lo tine (gil′ə tēn′), 1 machine for
beheading people by means of a heavy
blade that slides down between two
grooved posts. The guillotine was used
during the French Revolution. 2 behead with this machine. 1 *n.,* 2 *v.,*
guil lo tined, guil lo tin ing. [from
Joseph I. *Guillotin,* 1738-1814, a
French doctor who proposed its use]

guilt (gilt), 1 fact or condition of having
done wrong; being guilty; being to
blame: *The evidence proved the accused
man's guilt.* 2 guilty action or conduct;
crime; offense; wrongdoing. 3 a feeling of having done wrong or being to
blame. *n.*

guilt i ly (gil′tə lē), in a guilty manner.
adv.

guilt i ness (gil′tē nis), guilty condition; guilt. *n.*

guilt less (gilt′lis), free from guilt; not
guilty; innocent. *adj.*

guilt y (gil′tē), 1 having done wrong;
deserving to be blamed and punished:
*The jury pronounced the defendant
guilty of theft.* 2 knowing or showing
that one has done wrong: *The one who
committed the crime had a guilty conscience and a guilty look.* *adj.,* **guilt i-
er, guilt i est.**

guimpe (gimp or gamp), blouse worn
under a dress and showing at the neck
or at the neck and arms. A guimpe
is usually worn with a low-necked
dress. *n.*

guin ea (gin′ē), 1 a British gold coin,
not made since 1813, worth 21 shillings.
2 amount equal to 21 shillings, formerly
used in Great Britain in stating prices,
fees, etc. *n.*

Guin ea (gin′ē), country in W Africa
on the Atlantic. *n.*

guinea fowl, a domestic fowl somewhat like a pheasant, having dark-gray

guinea fowl
about 1½ ft. long

feathers with small, white spots. Its flesh and its eggs are eaten.

guinea hen, 1 guinea fowl. 2 a female guinea fowl.

guinea pig (def. 1) about 6 in. long

guinea pig, 1 a small, fat, harmless rodent with short ears and a short tail or no tail. Guinea pigs make good pets and are often used for laboratory experiments. 2 any person or thing serving as a subject for experiment or observation.

Guin e vere (gwin′ə vir), King Arthur's queen, who was loved by Lancelot. *n.*

guise (gīz), 1 style of dress; garb: *The spy went in the guise of a monk and was not recognized by the enemy.* 2 outward appearance: *That theory is nothing but an old idea in a new guise.* 3 assumed appearance; pretense: *Under the guise of friendship he plotted treachery. n.*

gui tar (gə tär′), a musical instrument usually having six strings, played with the fingers or with a pick. *n.*

guitar

gulch (gulch), a very deep, narrow ravine with steep sides, especially one marking the course of a stream or torrent. *n., pl.* **gulch es.**

gul den (gůl′dən), guilder. *n.*

gules (gyülz), red. *n., adj.*

gulf (gulf), 1 a large bay; arm of an ocean or sea extending into the land: *The Gulf of Mexico is between Florida and Mexico.* 2 a very deep break or cut in the earth: *The earthquake made a gulf in the earth.* 3 separation too great to be closed; wide gap: *The quarrel created a gulf between the old friends. n.*

Gulf Stream, current of warm water in the Atlantic. It flows out of the Gulf of Mexico, north along the East coast of the United States, and then northeast across the Atlantic toward the British Isles.

gull[1] (gul), a graceful, gray-and-white bird living on or near large bodies of water. A gull has long wings, webbed feet, and a thick, strong beak. *n.* [probably from a Celtic word, such as Cornish *guilan*]

gull[2] (gul), 1 deceive; cheat. 2 person who is easily deceived or cheated. 1 *v.*, 2 *n.* [origin uncertain]

gul let (gul′it), 1 esophagus. 2 throat. *n.*

gul li bil i ty (gul′ə bil′ə tē), a being gullible; tendency to be easily deceived or cheated. *n.*

gul li ble (gul′ə bəl), easily deceived or cheated. *adj.*

Gul li ver (gul′ə vər), **Lemuel,** hero of voyages to four imaginary regions in Jonathan Swift's satire, *Gulliver's Travels. n.*

gul ly (gul′ē), a narrow gorge; small ravine; ditch made by heavy rains or running water. *n., pl.* **gul lies.**

gulp (gulp), 1 swallow eagerly or greedily: *The hungry girl gulped down the bowl of soup.* 2 act of swallowing: *He ate the cookie in one gulp.* 3 amount swallowed at one time; mouthful: *I took a gulp of the wine.* 4 keep in; choke back: *The disappointed boy gulped down a sob and tried to smile.* 5 to gasp or choke: *The spray of cold water made me gulp.* 1,4,5 *v.*, 2,3 *n.*

gum[1] (gum), 1 a sticky juice given off by certain trees and plants that hardens in the air and dissolves in water. Gum is used for sticking paper and other things together. It is also used to make candy, drugs, etc. 2 gum tree. 3 chewing gum. 4 the sticky substance on the back of a stamp, the flap of an envelope, etc.; mucilage. 5 rubber. 6 smear, stick together, or stiffen with gum. 7 make or become sticky: *My pocket was all gummed with candy.* 1-5 *n.*, 6,7 *v.*, **gummed, gum ming.** [from French of the 1300's *gomme*] —**gum′like′, *adj.***

gum[2] (gum). Often, **gums,** *pl.* the firm flesh around the teeth. *n.* [Old English *gōma* palate]

gum arabic, gum obtained from acacia trees, used in making candy, medicine, and mucilage.

gum bo (gum′bō), 1 the okra plant. 2 its sticky pods. 3 soup usually made of chicken and rice and thickened with these pods. 4 kind of fine soil that becomes very sticky when wet. *n., pl.* **gum bos.**

gum boil (gum′boil′), a small abscess on the gums. *n.*

gum drop (gum′drop′), a stiff, jellylike piece of candy made of gum arabic, gelatin, etc., sweetened and flavored. *n.*

gum my (gum′ē), 1 sticky like gum. 2 covered with gum. 3 giving off gum. *adj.,* **gum mi er, gum mi est.**

gump tion (gump′shən), INFORMAL. 1 initiative; energy. 2 common sense; good judgment. *n.*

gum resin, mixture of gum and resin, obtained from certain plants. Asafetida and myrrh are gum resins.

hat, āge, fär; let, ēqual, tėrm;
it, īce; hot, ōpen, ôrder;
oil, out; cup, půt, rüle; ch, child;
ng, long; sh, she; th, thin;
ᵮH, then; zh, measure;

ə represents *a* in about,
e in taken, *i* in pencil,
o in lemon, *u* in circus.

gum tree, tree that yields gum. The eucalyptus is one kind of gum tree.

gun (gun), 1 weapon with a metal tube for shooting bullets, shot, etc. A rifle or cannon is a gun. Pistols and revolvers are called guns in ordinary speech. 2 anything resembling a gun in use or shape: *a spray gun.* 3 the shooting of a gun as a signal or salute: *The President got a salute of 21 guns.* 4 shoot with a gun; hunt with a gun: *They went gunning for rabbits.* 1-3 *n.*, 4 *v.*, **gunned, gun ning.**

stick to one's guns, keep one's position; refuse to retreat or yield.

gun boat (gun′bōt′), a small warship that can be used in shallow water. *n.*

gun cot ton (gun′kot′n), an explosive made by treating cotton or other cellulose fibers with a mixture of nitric and sulfuric acids. *n.*

gun fire (gun′fīr′), the shooting of a gun or guns. *n.*

gung-ho (gung′hō′), INFORMAL. eager; enthusiastic: *a gung-ho student. adj.*

gun lock (gun′lok′), the part of a gun that controls the hammer and fires the charge. *n.*

gun man (gun′mən), man who uses a gun to rob or kill. *n., pl.* **gun men.**

gun nel (gun′l), gunwale. *n.*

gun ner (gun′ər), 1 man trained to fire artillery; soldier who handles and fires cannon. 2 (in the Navy) a warrant officer in charge of a ship's guns. 3 person who hunts with a gun. *n.*

gun ner y (gun′ər ē), 1 the construction and management of large guns. 2 use of guns; shooting of guns. *n.*

gun ny (gun′ē), 1 a strong, coarse fabric made of jute, used for sacks, bags, etc. 2 gunnysack. *n., pl.* **gun nies.**

gun ny sack (gun′ē sak′), sack, bag, etc., made of gunny. *n.*

gun pow der (gun′pou′dər), powder that explodes when brought into contact with fire, used in guns, blasting, and fireworks. Modern gunpowder is made of saltpeter, sulfur, and charcoal. *n.*

gun shot (gun′shot′), 1 shot fired from a gun. 2 the shooting of a gun: *We heard gunshots.* 3 distance that a gun

377

adj. adjective	*n.* noun
adv. adverb	*prep.* preposition
conj. conjunction	*pron.* pronoun
interj. interjection	*v.* verb
sing. singular	*pl.* plural

will shoot: *The deer was within gunshot.* *n.*

gun smith (gun′smith′), person whose work is making or repairing small guns. *n.*

gun stock (gun′stok′), the wooden support or handle to which the barrel of a gun is fastened. *n.*

GUNWALE

gun wale (gun′l), the upper edge of the side of a ship or boat; gunnel. *n.*

gup py (gup′ē), a very small, brightly colored fish of tropical fresh water, often kept in aquariums. The female bears live young instead of laying eggs. *n., pl.* **gup pies.** [from Robert J. L. *Guppy,* a British scientist who supplied the first specimens for public viewing]

gur gle (gėr′gəl), 1 flow or run with a bubbling sound: *Water gurgles when it is poured out of a bottle or flows over stones.* 2 a bubbling sound. 3 make a bubbling sound: *The baby gurgled happily.* 4 express with a gurgle. 1,3,4 *v.,* **gur gled, gur gling;** 2 *n.*

gush (gush), 1 rush out suddenly; pour out: *Oil gushed from the new well.* 2 rush of water or other liquid from an enclosed space: *If you get a deep cut, there usually is a gush of blood.* 3 INFORMAL. talk in a way that shows too much silly feeling: *All the children gushed about the new puppy.* 4 INFORMAL. talk that shows too much silly feeling. 1,3 *v.,* 2,4 *n.*

gush er (gush′ər), an oil well which gives oil in large quantities without pumping. *n.*

gush y (gush′ē), INFORMAL. showing too much silly feeling. *adj.,* **gush i er, gush i est.**

gus set (gus′it), a triangular piece of material inserted in a garment to give greater strength or more room. *n.*

gust (gust), 1 a sudden, violent rush of wind: *A gust upset the small sailboat.* 2 a sudden burst of rain, smoke, sound, etc. 3 a sudden bursting forth of anger, enthusiasm, or other feeling: *Gusts of laughter greeted the clown.* *n.*

gus to (gus′tō), hearty enjoyment;

keen relish: *The hungry boy ate his dinner with gusto.* *n.*

gust y (gus′tē), coming in gusts; windy; stormy. *adj.,* **gust i er, gust i est.**

gut (gut), 1 the whole alimentary canal or its lower portion; intestine. 2 **guts,** *pl.* **a** entrails; bowels. **b** SLANG. pluck; courage. 3 catgut. 4 remove the entrails of; disembowel. 5 destroy the inside of: *Fire gutted the building and left only the brick walls standing.* 1-3 *n.,* 4,5 *v.,* **gut ted, gut ting.**

Gu ten berg (güt′n bėrg′), **Johann,** 1398?-1468. German printer. He is supposed to have been the first European to print from movable type. *n.*

gut ta-per cha (gut′ə pėr′chə), substance like rubber, made from the thick, milky juice of certain tropical trees. It is used in dentistry, in insulating electric wires, etc. *n.*

gut ter (gut′ər), 1 channel or ditch along the side of a street or road to carry off water; low part of a street beside the sidewalk. 2 channel or trough along the lower edge of a roof to carry off rain water. 3 a channel; groove: *the gutters on either side of a bowling alley.* 4 form gutters in. 5 flow or melt in streams: *Water guttered down the side of the hill. The candle guttered when the melted wax ran down its sides.* 1-3 *n.,* 4,5 *v.*

ROOF — GUTTER
gutter (def. 2)

gut tur al (gut′ər əl), 1 of the throat. 2 formed in the throat; harsh: *The visitor from Germany spoke in a deep, guttural voice.* 3 formed between the back of the tongue and the soft palate. The *g* in *go* is a guttural sound. 4 sound formed between the back of the tongue and the soft palate. The sound *k* is a guttural in the word *cool.* 1-3 *adj.,* 4 *n.*

guy[1] (gī), 1 rope, chain, or wire attached to something to steady or secure it. 2 steady or secure with a guy or guys: *The mast was guyed by four ropes.* 1 *n.,* 2 *v.,* **guyed, guy ing.** [from French of the 1300's *guie* guide]

guy[2] (gī), INFORMAL. 1 fellow. 2 make fun of; tease. 1 *n.,* 2 *v.,* **guyed, guying.** [from *Guy* Fawkes, leader of a plot to blow up the British king and Parliament in 1605]

Guy an a (gī an′ə), country in N South America, a member of the Commonwealth of Nations. *n.*

guz zle (guz′əl), drink greedily; drink

too much: *He's always guzzling soda. Drink slowly; don't guzzle.* *v.,* **guz zled, guz zling.**

gym (jim), INFORMAL. gymnasium. *n.*

gym na si um (jim nā′zē əm), room, building, etc., fitted up for physical exercise or training and for indoor athletic sports. *n., pl.* **gym na si ums, gym na si a** (jim nā′zē ə).

gym nast (jim′nast), an expert in gymnastics. *n.*

gym nas tic (jim nas′tik), having to do with physical exercises or activities. *adj.*

gym nas tics (jim nas′tiks), exercises for developing the muscles and improving physical fitness and health, such as are done in a gymnasium. *n.pl.*

gym no sperm (jim′nə spėrm′), any plant having its seeds exposed, not enclosed in an ovary or fruit. The pine, fir, and spruce are gymnosperms. *n.*

gyp (jip), SLANG. 1 to cheat; swindle. 2 a cheating; swindle. 3 person who cheats; swindler. 1 *v.,* **gypped, gyp ping;** 2,3 *n.*

gyp sum (jip′səm), mineral used to make fertilizer and plaster of Paris. *n.*

gyp sy (jip′sē), 1 Also, **Gypsy.** person belonging to a wandering group of people having dark skin and black hair, who came originally from India. 2 person who looks or lives like a gypsy. 3 of gypsies: *gypsy music.* 1,2 *n., pl.* **gyp sies;** 3 *adj.* Also, **gipsy.** [earlier *gipcyan,* shortened from *Egyptian,* because gypsies were thought to have come from Egypt]

gypsy moth, a brownish or white moth whose larvae damage trees by eating their leaves.

gy rate (jī′rāt), move in a circle or spiral; whirl; rotate: *A spinning top gyrates.* *v.,* **gy rat ed, gy rat ing.**

gy ra tion (jī rā′shən), circular or spiral motion; whirling; rotation. *n.*

gyrfalcon
about 2 ft. long

gyr fal con (jėr′fôl′kən, jėr′fal′kən, *or* jėr′fô′kən), a large falcon of the Arctic, with white, black, or gray feathers. *n.*

gy ro com pass (jī′rō kum′pəs), compass using a gyroscope instead of a magnetic needle. It points to true north instead of to the North Magnetic Pole and is not affected by nearby objects of iron or steel. *n., pl.* **gy ro com pass es.**

gyroscope
The ends of the axis are on bearings. As the base is moved, the rotating axis stays in the same position.

gy ro scope (jī′rə skōp), instrument consisting of a heavy, rotating wheel so mounted that its axis can turn freely in one or more directions. A spinning gyroscope tends to resist any change in the direction of its axis, no matter which way its base is turned. Gyroscopes are used to keep ships and airplanes steady. *n.*

gy ro scop ic (jī′rə skop′ik), having to do with a gyroscope. *adj.*

gyve (jīv), OLD USE. **1** a shackle, especially for the leg; fetter. **2** to fetter; shackle. **1** *n.*, **2** *v.*, **gyved, gyv ing.**

hat, āge, fär; let, ēqual, tėrm;
it, īce; hot, ōpen, ôrder;
oil, out; cup, pùt, rüle; ch, child;
ng, long; sh, she; th, thin;
ŦH, then; zh, measure;

ə represents *a* in about,
e in taken, *i* in pencil,
o in lemon, *u* in circus.

Hh

H or **h** (āch), the eighth letter of the alphabet. *n., pl.* **H's** or **h's.**

ha (hä), 1 exclamation of surprise, joy, or triumph: *"Ha! I've caught you!" cried the giant to Jack.* 2 sound of a laugh: *"Ha! ha! ha!" laughed the boys. interj.* Also, **hah.**

ha be as cor pus (hā'bē əs kôr'pəs), writ or order requiring that a prisoner be brought before a judge or into court to decide whether he is being held lawfully. The right of habeas corpus is a protection against unjust imprisonment. [from Latin *habeas corpus* you may have the person]

hab er dash er (hab'ər dash'ər), dealer in the things men wear, such as hats, ties, shirts, socks, etc. *n.*

hab er dash er y (hab'ər dash'ər ē), 1 store of a haberdasher. 2 articles sold by a haberdasher. *n., pl.* **hab er dash er ies.**

ha bil i ments (hə bil'ə mənts), clothing. *n.pl.*

hab it (hab'it), 1 tendency to act in a certain way; usual way of acting; custom; practice. Doing a thing over and over again makes it a habit. 2 the dress worn by members of a religious order. Monks and nuns often wear habits. 3 a woman's garment for horseback riding: *At the horse show the woman on the bay horse wore a black habit.* 4 condition of body or mind: *The runner was of lean habit.* 5 the usual way that an animal or plant grows: *The honeysuckle has a twining habit. n.*

hab it a ble (hab'ə tə bəl), fit to live in; able to be inhabited: *repair an abandoned house to make it habitable. adj.*

hab i tat (hab'ə tat), 1 place where an animal or plant naturally lives or grows: *The jungle is the habitat of monkeys.* 2 place of living; dwelling place. *n.*

hab i ta tion (hab'ə tā'shən), 1 place or building to live in; home; dwelling. 2 a living in; inhabiting: *A barn is not fit for human habitation. n.*

ha bit u al (hə bich'ü əl), 1 done by habit; caused by habit: *a habitual smile. Habitual courtesy is always being polite to others.* 2 being or doing something by habit; regular; steady: *A habitual reader reads a great deal.* 3 often done, seen, or used; usual; customary: *Ice and snow are a habitual sight in arctic regions. adj.* —**ha bit'u al ly,** *adv.* —**ha bit'u al ness,** *n.*

ha bit u ate (hə bich'ü āt), make used; accustom: *The pioneers were habituated to the hardships of frontier life. v.,* **ha bit u at ed, ha bit u at ing.**

ha ci en da (hä'sē en'də), (in Spanish America) a ranch or country house. *n., pl.* **ha ci en das.** [from Spanish *hacienda,* from Latin *facienda* things to be done]

hack¹ (hak), 1 cut roughly: *He hacked the meat into jagged pieces.* 2 a rough cut. 3 give frequent, short, dry coughs. 4 a short, dry cough. 1,3 *v.,* 2,4 *n.* [Old English *-haccian*]

hack² (hak), 1 carriage for hire: *We rode around the park in a hack.* 2 INFORMAL. taxicab. 3 horse for hire. 4 an old or worn-out horse. 5 horse for ordinary riding. 6 person hired to do routine work; drudge. 7 working just for money; hired; drudging: *a hack writer.* 8 done just for money: *a hack job.* 1-6 *n.,* 7,8 *adj.* [short for *hackney*]

hack le (hak'əl), 1 one of the long, slender feathers on the neck of a rooster, pigeon, peacock, etc. 2 the neck plumage of any of these birds. 3 **hackles,** *pl.* hairs on the back of a dog's neck that can become erect. *n.*
raise the hackles, INFORMAL. arouse anger; make mad.

hack ney (hak'nē), 1 horse for ordinary riding. 2 carriage for hire. 3 hired: *a hackney coach.* 4 use too often; make commonplace. 1,2 *n., pl.* **hack neys;** 3 *adj.,* 4 *v.,* **hack neyed, hack ney ing.** [from *Hackney,* a town near London]

hack neyed (hak'nēd), used too often; commonplace: *"White as snow" is a hackneyed comparison. adj.*

hacksaw

hack saw (hak'sô'), saw for cutting metal, consisting of a narrow, fine-toothed blade fixed in a frame. *n.*

had (had), past tense and past participle of **have.** *She had a party. A fine time was had by all who came. v.*

had dock (had'ək), a food fish of the northern Atlantic, related to the cod, but smaller. *n., pl.* **had docks** or **had dock.**

Ha des (hā'dēz'), 1 (in Greek myths) the home of the dead, a gloomy place below the earth. 2 INFORMAL. hell. *n.*

had n't (had'nt), had not.

Ha dri an (hā'drē ən), A.D.76-138, Roman emperor from A.D. 117 to 138. *n.*

hadst (hadst), OLD USE. had. "Thou hadst" means "you had." *v.*

hae mo glo bin (hē'mə glō'bən *or* hem'ə glō'bən), hemoglobin. *n.*

haf ni um (haf'nē əm), a silvery metallic element which occurs in zirconium ores and is used to make filaments for incandescent lamps. *n.* [from *Hafnia,* the Latin name of Copenhagen, Denmark]

haft (haft), handle of a knife, sword, dagger, etc. *n.*

hag (hag), 1 a very ugly old woman, especially one who is vicious or malicious. 2 witch. *n.*

Hag ga i (hag'ē ī), 1 (in the Bible) a Hebrew prophet. 2 book of the Old Testament. *n.*

hag gard (hag'ərd), looking worn from pain, fatigue, worry, hunger, etc.; careworn: *the haggard faces of the rescued miners. adj.* —**hag'gard ly,** *adv.*

hag gle (hag'əl), 1 to dispute, especially about a price or the terms of a bargain. 2 act of haggling. 1 *v.,* **haggled, hag gling;** 2 *n.*

hag gler (hag'lər), person who haggles. *n.*

Hague (hāg), **The,** unofficial capital of the Netherlands, in the SW part. The official capital is Amsterdam. *n.*

hah (hä), ha. *interj.*

hahn i um (hä'nē əm), name suggested for a radioactive element produced artificially from californium. *n.* [from Otto *Hahn,* 1879-1968, a German chemist]

hai ku (hī'kü), a poem of three lines and containing only 17 syllables. *n., pl.* **hai ku.**

hail¹ (hāl), 1 small, round pieces of ice formed in thunderclouds and falling like rain; hailstones: *Hail fell with such violence that it broke windows.* 2 fall in hail: *Sometimes it hails during a summer thunderstorm.* 3 a shower like hail: *a hail of bullets.* 4 pour down in a shower like hail: *hail blows on an opponent.* 1,3 *n.,* 2,4 *v.* [Old English *hægel*]

hail² (hāl), 1 shout in welcome to; greet; cheer: *The crowd hailed the winner.* 2 a shout of welcome; greeting; cheer. 3 greetings! welcome!: *Hail to the winner!* 4 call loudly to; shout to: *After our car stalled, we hailed passing cars to beg a ride.* 5 a loud call; shout: *Cars passed, not heeding our hails.* 1,4 *v.,* 2,5 *n.,* 3 *interj.* [from a Scandinavian word of the 1200's, such as Icelandic *heill* healthy]
hail from, come from: *The ship hails from Boston.*
within hail, near enough to hear a call or shout: *She came within hail of us.*

Hai le Se las sie (hī'lē sə las'ē), born 1891, emperor of Ethiopia from 1930 to 1936 and since 1941.

hail stone (hāl'stōn'), a ball or pellet of hail. Hailstones are usually very small, but sometimes they are as big as marbles. *n.*

hail storm (hāl/stôrm/), storm with hail. *n.*

hair (her *or* har), 1 a fine, threadlike growth from the skin of people and animals. 2 mass of such growths covering the human head or forming the coat of an animal. 3 a fine, threadlike growth from the outer layer of plants. 4 hair's-breadth: *The ball missed his head by a hair. n.* —**hair/like/,** *adj.*
split hairs, make too fine distinctions.

hair breadth (her/bredth/ *or* har/-bredth/), hair's-breadth. *adj., n.*

hair brush (her/brush/ *or* har/-brush/), a stiff brush for smoothing the hair. *n.*

halberd
held by a soldier

hair cloth (her/klôth/ *or* har/klôth/), a scratchy fabric made of cotton and horsehair or camel's hair. It is used to cover furniture, stiffen garments, etc. *The hermit wore haircloth shirts as a penance. n.*

hair cut (her/kut/ *or* har/kut/), act or manner of cutting the hair. *n.*

hair do (her/dü/ *or* har/dü/), way of arranging the hair. *n., pl.* **hair dos.**

hair dress er (her/dres/ər *or* har/-dres/ər), person whose work is arranging or cutting women's hair. *n.*

hair i ness (her/ē nis *or* har/ē nis), hairy condition. *n.*

hair less (her/lis *or* har/lis), without hair. *adj.*

hair line (her/līn/ *or* har/līn/), 1 a very thin line. 2 the irregular outline where hair growth ends on the head or forehead. *n.*

hair pin (her/pin/ *or* har/pin/), 1 a small, thin piece of metal or plastic, usually shaped like a U, used by women and girls to keep their hair in place. 2 shaped like a hairpin: *a hairpin turn.* 1 *n.,* 2 *adj.*

hair-rais ing (her/rā/zing *or* har/-rā/zing), making the hair stand on end from fright; terrifying: *a hair-raising ghost story. adj.*

hair's-breadth or **hairs breadth** (herz/bredth/ *or* harz/bredth/), 1 very narrow; extremely close: *When the tree fell, we had a hair's-breadth escape.* 2 a very narrow space or distance: *Our team was within a hair's-breadth of winning the game.* 1 *adj.,* 2 *n.* Also, **hairbreadth.**

hair split ting (her/split/ing *or* har/-split/ing), 1 act of making too fine distinctions. 2 making too fine distinctions. 1 *n.,* 2 *adj.*

hair spring (her/spring/ *or* har/-spring/), a fine, hairlike spring which regulates the motion of the balance wheel in a watch or clock. *n.*

hair y (her/ē *or* har/ē), 1 covered with hair; having much hair: *hairy hands, a hairy ape.* 2 of or like hair. *adj.,* **hair i er, hair i est.**

Hai ti (hā/tē), 1 country in the W part of the island of Hispaniola in the West Indies. *Capital:* Port-au-Prince. 2 former name of Hispaniola. *n.* —**Hai ti an** (hā/tē ən *or* hā/shən), *adj., n.*

hake (hāk), a sea fish related to the cod but more slender. *n., pl.* **hakes** or **hake.**

hal berd (hal/bərd), weapon that is both a spear and a battle-ax, used in warfare in the 1400's and 1500's. *n.*

hal bert (hal/bərt), halberd. *n.*

hal cy on (hal/sē ən), calm; peaceful; happy: *The old man remembered the halcyon days of his youth. adj.*

hale[1] (hāl), strong and well; healthy: *His grandfather was still hale and hearty at seventy. adj.,* **hal er, hal est.** [Old English *hāl*]

hale[2] (hāl), 1 force to go: *The company was haled into court for polluting the river with chemicals.* 2 drag by force. *v.,* **haled, hal ing.** [from French of the 1100's *haler*]

Hale (hāl), Nathan, 1755-1776, American patriot hanged as a spy by the British. *n.*

half (haf), 1 one of two equal parts: *A half of 4 is 2. Two halves make a whole.* 2 making half of; needing as much more to make a whole: *a half pound, a half barrel.* 3 to half of the full amount or degree: *half cooked, a glass half full of milk.* 4 one of two nearly equal parts: *He broke his candy bar in two and gave me the bigger half.* 5 one of the two equal periods of active play in certain games. 6 not complete; being only part of: *A half truth is often no better than a lie.* 7 not completely; partly: *She spoke half aloud.* 8 almost; nearly: *She was so tired, she was half asleep.* 1,4,5 *n., pl.* **halves;** 2,6 *adj.,* 3,7,8 *adv.*
not half bad, fairly good.

half back (haf/bak/), (in football) an offensive back who runs with the ball, blocks for another back, or goes downfield as a pass receiver. *n.*

half-baked (haf/bākt/), 1 INFORMAL. not fully worked out; incomplete: *The rebels' half-baked plans resulted in the failure of the revolt.* 2 not cooked enough. 3 INFORMAL. showing poor judgment; inexperienced: *a half-baked*

hat, āge, fär; let, ēqual, tėrm;
it, īce; hot, ōpen, ôrder;
oil, out; cup, pút, rüle; ch, child;
ng, long; sh, she; th, thin;
ŦH, then; zh, measure;

ə represents *a* in about,
e in taken, *i* in pencil,
o in lemon, *u* in circus.

scheme for getting rich quick. adj.

half-breed (haf/brēd/), person whose parents are of different races. *n.*

half brother, brother related through one parent only.

half-caste (haf/kast/), 1 person who has one European parent and one Asian parent. 2 half-breed. *n.*

half crown, a former British coin worth 2 1/2 shillings.

half dollar, a coin of the United States and Canada, worth 50 cents.

half heart ed (haf/här/tid), lacking courage, interest, or enthusiasm; not earnest. *adj.* —**half/heart/ed ly,** *adv.* —**half/heart/ed ness,** *n.*

half hour, 1 thirty minutes. 2 the halfway point in an hour: *The train stops here on the half hour.*

half-hour (haf/our/), of a half hour; lasting a half hour: *a half-hour trip. adj.*

half-life (haf/līf/), length of time it takes for half the atoms of a particular radioactive substance to break down or decay. The half-life of a particular radioactive substance is always the same and it is therefore used to distinguish one radioactive substance from another and to measure radioactivity. *n.*

half-line (haf/līn/), the part of a line on one side of a point on the line; ray. *n.*

half-mast (haf/mast/), position halfway or part way down from the top of a mast, staff, etc. A flag is lowered to half-mast as a mark of respect for someone who has died or as a signal of distress. *n.*

half-moon (haf/mün/), 1 moon when only half of its surface appears bright. 2 something shaped like a half-moon. *n.*

half nelson, hold used in wrestling. It is done by hooking one arm under an opponent's armpit and joining both hands on the back of his neck.

half note, (in music) a note played for one half as long a time as a whole note. See **note** for diagram.

half pen ny (hā/pə nē *or* hāp/nē), a British coin worth half a penny. *n.,*

adj.	adjective	*n.*	noun
adv.	adverb	*prep.*	preposition
conj.	conjunction	*pron.*	pronoun
interj.	interjection	*v.*	verb
sing.	singular	*pl.*	plural

pl. **half pence** (hā′pəns), **half pennies.**

half-plane (haf′plān′), the part of a plane on one side of a line in the plane. *n.*

half sister, sister related through one parent only.

half step, difference in pitch between two keys next to each other on a piano; semitone.

half tone, half step.

half-track

half-track or **half track** (haf′-trak′), a military motor vehicle with wheels in front and short tracks in the rear, used to carry troops and weapons. *n.*

half way (haf′wā′), 1 half the way: *The rope reached only halfway around the tree.* 2 one half: *The lesson is halfway finished.* 3 midway: *a halfway stop in the journey.* 4 not going far enough; incomplete: *Halfway measures often fail.* 1,2 *adv.,* 3,4 *adj.*

meet halfway, do one's share to agree or be friendly with.

half-wit (haf′wit′), 1 a feeble-minded person. 2 a stupid, foolish person. *n.*

half-wit ted (haf′wit′id), 1 feeble-minded. 2 very stupid; foolish. *adj.*

hal i but (hal′ə bət), a large flatfish, much used for food. Halibuts sometimes weigh several hundred pounds. *n., pl.* **hal i buts** or **hal i but.**

Hal i fax (hal′ə faks), seaport in SE Canada, the capital of Nova Scotia. *n.*

hal ite (hal′īt or hā′līt), rock salt. *n.*

hall (hôl), 1 way for going through a building; passageway: *A hall ran the length of the upper floor of the house.* 2 passage or room at the entrance of a building: *Leave your umbrella in the hall.* 3 a large room for holding meetings, parties, banquets, etc.: *No hall in town was large enough for the crowd gathered to hear the famous singer.* 4 building for public business, meetings, etc.: *a village hall.* 5 building

of a school, college, or university in which students live or classes are held. 6 house of an English landowner. *n.*

hal lah (hä′lə), loaf of white bread, usually shaped like a braid, eaten by Jews on the Sabbath and holidays. *n.*

hal le lu jah or **hal le lu iah** (hal′ə-lü′yə), 1 praise ye the Lord! 2 song of praise. 1 *interj.,* 2 *n.* Also, **alleluia.**

Hal ley's comet (hal′ēz), comet seen about every 76 years. It was last seen in 1910. [from Edmund *Halley,* 1656-1742, English astronomer who first predicted the year of its return]

hall mark (hôl′märk′), 1 an official mark indicating standard of purity, put on gold or silver articles. 2 any mark or sign of genuineness or good quality. 3 put a hallmark on. 4 any distinguishing feature: *Self-control is a hallmark of maturity.* 1,2,4 *n.,* 3 *v.*

hal lo (hə lō′), 1 a call or shout to attract attention: *"Hallo!" she called from across the street (interj.). Her hallo stopped me in the middle of the street (n.).* 2 call of greeting or surprise: *Hallo! what's that noise? (interj.). She uttered a startled hallo when she heard the floorboards creak (n.).* 3 a shout; call. 4 to shout; call. 1,2 *interj.,* 1-3 *n., pl.* **hal los;** 4 *v.,* **hal loed, hal lo ing.**

hal loa (hə lō′), hallo. *interj., n., pl.* **hal loas;** *v.,* **hal loaed, hal loa ing.**

hal loo (hə lü′), hallo. *interj., n., pl.* **hal loos;** *v.,* **hal looed, hal loo ing.**

hal low (hal′ō), 1 make holy; make sacred. 2 honor as holy or sacred: *"Hallowed be Thy name."* *v.*

Hal low een or **Hal low e'en** (hal′-ō ēn′), evening of October 31, before All Saints' Day. It is observed especially by children, who masquerade, beg for treats, play pranks, etc. *n.*

hal lu ci na tion (hə lü′sn ā′shən), 1 a seeing or hearing things that exist only in a person's imagination. A person alone in a perfectly quiet room suffers from hallucination if he sees people around him or hears voices. 2 an imaginary thing seen or heard. *n.*

hall way (hôl′wā′), 1 passage in a building; corridor; hall. 2 passageway or room at the entrance of a building. *n.*

halo (def. 2)

ha lo (hā′lō), 1 ring of light around the sun, moon, or other shining body. 2 a golden circle or disk of light rep-

resented about the head of a saint or angel in pictures or statues; nimbus. 3 glory or glamour that surrounds a person or thing: *A halo of romantic adventure surrounds King Arthur and his knights.* *n., pl.* **ha los** or **ha loes.**

hal o gen (hal′ə jən), any of the chemical elements iodine, bromine, chlorine, fluorine, and astatine. A halogen can combine directly with a metal to form a salt. The halogens are highly active elements. *n.*

halt[1] (hôlt), 1 stop for a time: *The hikers halted and rested from their climb. The store halted deliveries during the strike.* 2 a stop for a time: *During a strike work comes to a halt.* 1 *v.,* 2 *n.* [from French *halte*]

call a halt, order a stop.

halt[2] (hôlt), 1 be in doubt; hesitate; waver: *Shyness made her halt as she talked.* 2 lame; crippled; limping. 3 OLD USE. be lame or crippled; limp. 1,3 *v.,* 2 *adj.* [Old English *haltian*] **—halt′ing ly,** *adv.*

halter
(def. 1)

hal ter (hôl′tər), 1 rope or strap with a noose or headstall for leading or tying an animal. 2 rope for hanging a person; noose. 3 a woman's brief blouse which fastens behind the neck and across the back. *n.*

halve (hav), 1 divide into two equal parts; share equally: *He and I agreed to halve expenses on our trip.* 2 cut in half; reduce to half: *The new machine will halve the time and cost of doing the work by hand.* *v.,* **halved, halv ing.**

halves (havz), plural of **half.** *n.* **go halves,** share equally.

hal yard (hal′yərd), rope or tackle used on a ship to raise or lower a sail, yard, or flag. *n.*

ham (ham), 1 meat from the upper part of a hog's hind leg, usually salted and smoked. 2 back of the thigh; thigh and buttock. 3 SLANG. actor or performer who plays poorly and in an exaggerated manner. 4 SLANG. an amateur radio operator. *n.*

Ham burg (ham′berg′), city in N West Germany, on the Elbe River. *n.*

ham burg er (ham′bèr′gər), 1 ground beef, usually shaped into round, flat cakes and fried or broiled. 2 sandwich made with hamburger, usually in a roll or bun. *n.* [from German *Hamburger* of Hamburg]

Ham il ton (ham′əl tən), **Alexander,** 1757-1804, American statesman. He was the first Secretary of the Treasury. *n.*

ham let (ham′lit), a small village; little group of houses in the country. *n.*

Ham let (ham′lit), 1 play by Shakespeare. 2 the principal character in this play, a prince of Denmark, who avenges his father's murder. *n.*

ham mer (ham′ər), 1 tool with a metal head set crosswise on a handle, used to drive nails and to beat metal into shape. 2 something shaped or used like a hammer. The hammer of a gun explodes the charge. 3 drive, hit, or work with a hammer. 4 beat into shape with a hammer: *The silver was hammered into bowls.* 5 fasten by using a hammer. 6 hit again and again: *The visitor hammered against the door with his fists.* 7 force by repeated efforts: *She hammered the formulas into her head until she had memorized them.* 8 work out with much effort. 9 a metal ball attached to a wire with a handle on the other end. It is used by athletes, who twirl it and throw it for distance. 1,2,9 *n.,* 3-8 *v.* —**ham′mer like′,** *adj.*

hammer
(def. 9)

ham mer head (ham′ər hed′), a fierce shark whose wide head looks somewhat like a double-headed hammer. *n.*

ham mer less (ham′ər lis), having no hammer or no visible hammer. A hammerless pistol has its hammer covered. *adj.*

ham mock (ham′ək), a hanging bed or couch made of canvas, netted cord, etc. It has cords or ropes at each end for hanging it between two trees, posts, etc. *n.*

Ham mu ra bi (ham′ə rä′bē), king of Babylon who lived about 1800 B.C. He made a famous code of laws for his people, which bears his name. *n.*

ham per¹ (ham′pər), hold back; hinder: *Poor health and lack of money hampered my efforts to get a college education. v.* [Middle English *hampren*]

ham per² (ham′pər), a large container, often a wicker basket, usually having a cover: *a picnic hamper, a laundry ham-*

per. *n.* [from French before the 1400's *hanapier* kind of case or basket]

ham ster (ham′stər), a small rodent with a short tail and large cheek pouches. Hamsters are used in scientific research and are often kept as pets. *n.*

ham string (ham′string′), 1 one of the tendons at the back of the knee in man. 2 the great tendon at the back of the hock in a four-footed animal. 3 cripple by cutting the hamstring. 4 destroy the activity, efficiency, etc., of; cripple; disable. 1,2 *n.,* 3,4 *v.,* **ham strung, ham string ing.**

ham strung (ham′strung′), past tense and past participle of **hamstring.** *Our building plans have been hamstrung by the bad weather. v.*

Han cock (han′kok), **John,** 1737-1793, American statesman, the first signer of the Declaration of Independence. *n.*

hand (hand), 1 the end part of the arm, below the wrist, which takes and holds objects. Each hand has four fingers and a thumb. 2 end of any limb that grasps, holds, or clings. We call a monkey's feet hands. 3 something like a hand in shape, appearance, or use: *The hands of a clock or watch show the time.* 4 a hired worker who uses his hands: *a factory hand.* 5 give with the hand; pass along: *Please hand me a spoon.* 6 help with the hand: *I handed the old woman into the bus.* 7 **hands,** *pl.* possession; control: *The property is no longer in my hands.* 8 part or share in doing something: *He had no hand in the matter.* 9 side: *At her left hand stood two men.* 10 style of handwriting: *He writes in a clear hand.* 11 skill; ability: *This painting shows the hand of a master.* 12 round of applause or clapping: *The crowd gave the winner a big hand.* 13 promise of marriage. 14 the breadth of a hand; 4 inches: *This horse is 18 hands high.* 15 cards held by a player in one round of a card game. 16 a single round in a card game. 17 player in a card game. 18 of, for, by, or in the hand: *a hand mirror, hand weaving, a hand pump.* 1-4,7-17 *n.,* 5,6 *v.,* 18 *adj.*

at first hand, from direct knowledge or experience.

at hand, 1 within reach; near. 2 ready.

at second hand, from the knowledge or experience of another; not directly: *She heard the story at second hand.*

at the hand of or **at the hands of,** through the act or deed of: *We have received many favors at his hands.*

by hand, by using the hands, not machinery: *embroidered by hand.*

change hands, pass from one person to another: *That building changed hands many times.*

hat, āge, fär; let, ēqual, tėrm; it, īce; hot, ōpen, ôrder; oil, out; cup, pút, rüle; ch, child; ng, long; sh, she; th, thin; ŦH, then; zh, measure;

ə represents *a* in about, *e* in taken, *i* in pencil, *o* in lemon, *u* in circus.

from hand to mouth, without providing for the future: *Many poor people are forced to live from hand to mouth.*

give a hand, help: *Please give me a hand with this trunk.*

hand and glove or **hand in glove,** in close relations; intimate: *I suspect you not only know those gangsters, but are hand and glove with them.*

hand down, pass along: *The story was handed down from father to son.*

hand in, give; deliver: *Notebooks should be handed in at the end of class.*

hand in hand, 1 holding hands. 2 together.

hands down, easily: *She won the contest hands down.*

hand to hand, close together: *The soldiers fought hand to hand.*

have one's hands full, be very busy; be able to do no more; have all one can do: *She has her hands full with her job, her family, and classes in night school.*

in hand, 1 under control. 2 in one's possession; ready: *cash in hand.*

lay hands on, 1 get hold of; seize. 2 arrest: *Sooner or later the law will lay hands on them.* 3 attack; harm.

lend a hand, help: *He asked his brother to lend a hand with the chores.*

off one's hands, out of one's care or charge.

on hand, 1 within reach; near: *Try to be on hand when I need you.* 2 ready: *have cash on hand.* 3 present: *I will be on hand again tomorrow.*

on the one hand, from this point of view: *On the one hand I want to buy this new car, but I feel that it costs too much money.*

on the other hand, from the opposite point of view: *On the other hand, it costs too much money.*

out of hand, 1 out of control: *Your temper is getting out of hand.* 2 at once.

play into the hands of, act so as to give the advantage to.

to hand, 1 within reach; near. 2 in one's possession.

turn one's hand to, work at: *You would not turn your hand to dry a single dish, so I did them alone.*

adj. adjective	*n.* noun
adv. adverb	*prep.* preposition
conj. conjunction	*pron.* pronoun
interj. interjection	*v.* verb
sing. singular	*pl.* plural

wash one's hands of, have no more to do with; refuse to be responsible for: *I washed my hands of those schemers when I discovered what they were up to.*

hand bag (hand′bag′), 1 a woman's small bag for money, keys, cosmetics, etc.; purse. 2 a small traveling bag to hold clothes, etc. *n.*

hand ball (hand′bôl′), 1 game played by hitting a small, hard ball against a wall with the hand. 2 ball used in this game. *n.*

hand bill (hand′bil′), notice or advertisement, usually printed on one page, that is to be handed out to people. *n.*

hand book (hand′bùk′), a small book of directions or reference, especially in some field of study: *a handbook of engineering. n.*

hand car (hand′kär′), a light, open car moved by pumping a handle, used on railroads by workmen. *n.*

hand cart (hand′kärt′), a small cart pulled or pushed by hand; barrow. *n.*

hand clasp (hand′klasp′), the grasp of a person's hand in friendship, agreement, greeting, etc. *n.*

hand craft (hand′kraft′), 1 handicraft. 2 make or work by hand. 1 *n.*, 2 *v.*

hand cuff (hand′kuf′), 1 one of a pair of metal rings joined by a short chain and fastened around the wrists to keep a person from using his hands. 2 put handcuffs on: *handcuff a prisoner.* 1 *n.*, 2 *v.*

Han del (han′dl), **George Frederick,** 1685-1759, English composer, born in Germany. *n.*

hand ful (hand′fùl′), 1 as much or as many as the hand can hold: *a handful of candy.* 2 a small number: *A handful of football fans sat watching the game in the cold rain.* 3 INFORMAL. person or thing that is hard to manage: *That horse is quite a handful. n., pl.* **handfuls.**

hand i cap (han′dē kap), 1 something that puts a person at a disadvantage; hindrance: *A sore throat was a handicap to the singer.* 2 put at a disadvantage; hinder: *A lame arm handicapped our pitcher.* 3 race, contest, or game in which the poorer contestants are given certain advantages and the better ones are given certain disadvantages, so that all have an equal chance to win. 4 the disadvantage or advantage given in such a race, contest, or game: *If a runner has a 5-yard handicap in a 100-yard dash, it means that he has to run either 105 yards or 95 yards.* 5 give a handicap to. 1,3,4 *n.*, 2,5 *v.*, **hand i capped, hand i cap ping.**

hand i craft (han′dē kraft), 1 skill with the hands. 2 trade or art requiring skill with the hands. Weaving baskets from rushes is a handicraft. *n.* Also, **handcraft.**

hand i ly (han′dl ē), in a handy manner. *adv.*

hand i ness (han′dē nis), skill with the hands; being handy. *n.*

hand i work (han′dē wėrk′), 1 work done by a person's hands. 2 work which a person has done himself. *n.*

hand ker chief (hang′kər chif), 1 a soft, usually square piece of cloth used for wiping the nose, face, hands, eyes, etc. 2 kerchief. *n.*

han dle (han′dl), 1 a part of a thing made to be held or grasped by the hand. Spoons, pitchers, hammers, and pails have handles. 2 touch, feel, hold, or use with the hand: *I handled the cat gently, delighting in its softness.* 3 manage; direct: *The captain handles his soldiers well.* 4 behave or act when handled: *This car handles easily.* 5 deal with; treat: *Who handles discipline problems at your school?* 6 deal in; trade in: *That store handles meat and groceries.* 1 *n.*, 2-6 *v.*, **han dled, han dling.**

han dle bar (han′dl bär′). Often, **handlebars,** *pl.* the curved bar on a bicycle, motorcycle, etc., that the rider holds and steers by. *n.*

han dler (han′dlər), 1 person or thing that handles. 2 person who helps train or manage a boxer. *n.*

hand made (hand′mād′), made by hand, not by machine: *handmade Indian pottery. adj.*

hand maid (hand′mād′), 1 a female servant. 2 a female attendant. *n.*

hand maid en (hand′mād′n), handmaid. *n.*

hand-me-down (hand′mē doun′), something handed down from one person to another, such as a used garment. *n.*

hand organ, a large, portable music box which is made to play tunes by turning a crank; barrel organ.

hand organ

hand out (hand′out′), INFORMAL. 1 portion of food, clothing, or money handed out: *The beggar asked for a handout.* 2 a news story or piece of publicity issued to the press by a business organization, government agency, etc. *n.*

hand rail (hand′rāl′), railing used as a guard or as a support to the hand on a stairway, platform, etc. *n.*

hand shake (hand′shāk′), act of clasping and shaking of each other's hands in friendship, agreement, greeting, etc. *n.*

hand some (han′səm), 1 pleasing in appearance; good-looking. We usually say that a man is handsome, but that a woman is pretty or beautiful. 2 fairly large; considerable: *A thousand dollars is a handsome sum of money.* 3 generous: *For the return of his lost dog, he offered a handsome reward of one hundred dollars. adj.,* **hand som er, hand som est. —hand′some ly,** *adv.* **—hand′some ness,** *n.*

hand spike (hand′spīk′), bar used as a lever, especially on a ship. *n.*

handspring

hand spring (hand′spring′), spring or leap in which a person lands on one or both hands and then back on his feet, making a complete turn of the body. *n.*

hand-to-hand (hand′tə hand′), close together; at close quarters: *a hand-to-hand fight. adj.*

hand-to-mouth (hand′tə mouth′), not providing for the future; having nothing to spare; not thrifty: *a hand-to-mouth existence. adj.*

hand work (hand′wėrk′), work done by hand, not by machinery. *n.*

hand writ ing (hand′rī′ting), 1 writing by hand; writing with pen, pencil, etc. 2 manner or style of writing: *He recognized his mother's handwriting on the envelope. n.*

hand y (han′dē), 1 easy to reach or use; saving work; useful; convenient: *a handy device. There were handy shelves near the kitchen sink.* 2 skillful with the hands: *He is handy with tools. adj.,* **hand i er, hand i est.**

Han dy (han′dē), **W(illiam) C.,** 1873-1958, American Negro composer. *n.*

hand y man (han′dē man′), person who can do many kinds of odd jobs. *n., pl.* **hand y men.**

hang (hang), 1 fasten or be fastened to something above: *Hang your hat on the hook. The swing hangs from a tree.* 2 fasten or be fastened so as to swing or turn freely: *hang a door on its hinges.* 3 put to death by hanging with a rope around the neck. 4 die by hanging. 5 bend down; droop: *He hung his head in shame.* 6 cover or decorate with things that are fastened to something above: *hang a window with curtains. The walls were hung with pictures.* 7 attach (paper, etc.) to walls. 8 depend: *His future hangs on your decision.* 9 keep (a jury) from making a decision or reaching a verdict. One member can hang a jury by refusing to agree with the others. 10 way that a thing hangs: *She changed the hang of her skirt.* 11 INFORMAL. way of using or doing: *Riding a bicycle is easy after you get the hang of it.* 12 INFORMAL. idea; meaning: *After studying an hour I finally got the hang of the lesson.* 13 loiter; linger: *hang about a place.* 1-9,13 *v.*, **hung** (or, usually, **hanged** for 3 and 4), **hang ing**; 10-12 *n.*

hang back, be unwilling to go forward; be backward.

hang on, 1 hold tightly: *Hang on to my hand going down these steep stairs.* 2 be unwilling to let go, stop, or leave: *The dying man hung on to life for a few days.*

hang out, 1 lean out: *hang out of a window.* 2 SLANG. live or stay: *This is the corner where that gang hangs out.*

hang over, be about to happen to; threaten: *The prospect of defeat hangs over that political party.*

hang together, 1 stick together; support each other. 2 be coherent or consistent: *The story does not hang together.*

hang up, 1 put on a hook, peg, etc. 2 put a telephone receiver back in place.

hang ar (hang'ər), shed for airplanes or airships. *n.*

hang dog (hang'dôg'), ashamed or sneaking: *a guilty, hangdog look. adj.*

hang er (hang'ər), 1 thing on which something else is hung: *a coat hanger.* 2 person who hangs things. 3 tool or machine that hangs things. *n.*

hang er-on (hang'ər on'), 1 follower or dependent. 2 an undesirable follower. *n., pl.* **hang ers-on.**

hang ing (hang'ing), 1 death by hanging with a rope around the neck. 2 Often, **hangings,** *pl.* thing that hangs from a wall, bed, etc. Curtains and draperies are hangings. 3 that hangs: *a hanging basket of flowers.* 1,2 *n.,* 3 *adj.*

hang man (hang'mən), man who puts condemned criminals to death by hanging them. *n., pl.* **hang men.**

hang nail (hang'nāl'), bit of skin that hangs partly loose near a fingernail. *n.*

hang out (hang'out'), SLANG. place one lives in or goes to often. *n.*

hang o ver (hang'ō'vər), 1 INFORMAL. something that remains from an earlier time or condition. 2 SLANG. headache, nausea, etc., resulting from drinking too much alcoholic liquor. *n.*

hang-up (hang'up'), SLANG. problem, worry, etc., that a person cannot get rid of. *n.*

hank (hangk), 1 coil or loop: *a hank of hair.* 2 bundle of yarn containing a definite number of yards. There are 840 yards in a hank of cotton yarn. *n.*

han ker (hang'kər), have a longing or craving; yearn: *The lonely child hankered for friends. She hankers after things she cannot afford. v.*

Han ni bal (han'ə bəl), 247-183? B.C., general of Carthage who fought the Romans and invaded Italy by crossing the Alps. *n.*

Ha noi (hä noi'), capital of North Vietnam, in the central part. Hanoi was formerly the capital of French Indochina. *n.*

Han o ver (han'ō vər), city in N West Germany. *n.*

hansom

han som (han'səm), a two-wheeled cab for two passengers, drawn by one horse. The driver sits on a seat high up behind the cab, and the reins pass over the roof. *n.* [from Joseph *Hansom,* 1803-1882, a British architect, who designed such cabs]

Ha nuk kah (hä'nə kə), a yearly Jewish festival celebrating the rededication of the temple in Jerusalem after a victory over the Syrians in 165 B.C. Candles are lighted on each of the eight days of Hanukkah. *n.* Also, **Chanukah.**

hap (hap), OLD USE. 1 chance; luck. 2 happen. 1 *n.,* 2 *v.,* **happed, hap ping.**

hap haz ard (hap haz'ərd), 1 not planned; random: *Haphazard answers are often wrong.* 2 by chance; at random: *papers scattered haphazard on the desk.* 3 chance. 1 *adj.,* 2 *adv.,* 3 *n.* **—hap haz'ard ly,** *adv.* **—hap haz'ard ness,** *n.*

hap less (hap'lis), unlucky; unfortunate. *adj.* **—hap'less ly,** *adv.* **—hap'less ness,** *n.*

hap ly (hap'lē), OLD USE. by chance; perhaps. *adv.*

hap pen (hap'ən), 1 come about; take place; occur: *Nothing interesting hap-*

pens here. 2 be or take place by chance: *Accidents will happen.* 3 have the fortune; chance: *I happened to sit beside her at dinner.* 4 be done: *What happened to my book? It's all dirty. v.*

happen on, 1 meet: *The two friends happened on each other by chance.* 2 find: *She happened on a dime while looking for her ball.*

hap pen ing (hap'ə ning), something that happens; event; occurrence: *The evening newscast reviewed the happenings of the day. n.*

hap pen stance (hap'ən stans), a chance occurrence; accident. *n.*

hap pi ly (hap'ə lē), 1 in a happy manner: *I live happily with my family.* 2 by luck; with good fortune: *Happily, I saved you from falling. adv.*

hap pi ness (hap'ē nis), 1 a being happy; gladness. 2 good luck; good fortune. *n.*

hap py (hap'ē), 1 feeling as a person does when he is well and is having a good time; glad; pleased; contented: *She is happy in her new work.* 2 showing that one is glad; showing pleasure and joy: *a happy smile, a happy look.* 3 lucky; fortunate: *By a happy chance, I found my book just where I had left it in the theater.* 4 clever and fitting; successful and suitable: *That writer has a happy way of expressing his ideas. adj.,* **hap pi er, hap pi est.**

hap py-go-luck y (hap'ē gō luk'ē), taking things easily as they come; trusting to luck: *Those people are certainly happy-go-lucky. adj.*

Haps burg (haps'berg'), member of a German princely family, prominent since about 1100. Many rulers of the Holy Roman Empire, Austria, and Spain were Hapsburgs. *n.*

har a-kar i (har'ə kar'ē), hara-kiri. *n.*

har a-kir i (har'ə kir'ē), suicide by ripping open the abdomen with a knife. It was the national form of honorable suicide in Japan for the warrior class. *n.* [from Japanese *hara-kiri*]

ha rangue (hə rang'), 1 a noisy speech. 2 a long, pompous speech. 3 address in a harangue. 4 deliver a

Pronunciation key:

hat, āge, fär; let, ēqual, tèrm; it, īce; hot, ōpen, ôrder; oil, out; cup, pùt, rüle; ch, child; ng, long; sh, she; th, thin; ŦH, then; zh, measure;

ə represents *a* in about, *e* in taken, *i* in pencil, *o* in lemon, *u* in circus.

harangue. 1,2 *n.*, 3,4 *v.*, **ha rangued, ha rangu ing.**

har ass (har′əs *or* hə ras′), 1 trouble by repeated attacks; harry: *Pirates harassed the villages along the coast.* 2 disturb; worry; torment: *The heat and the flies harassed us on the journey.* *v.*

har ass ment (har′əs mənt *or* hə ras′mənt), 1 a harassing or a being harassed; worry. 2 something that harasses. *n.*

har bin ger (här′bən jər), 1 one that goes ahead to announce another's coming; forerunner: *The robin is a harbinger of spring.* 2 announce beforehand; foretell. 1 *n.*, 2 *v.*

har bor (här′bər), 1 area of deep water protected from winds, currents, etc., forming a place of shelter for ships and boats: *Many yachts are in the harbor.* 2 any place of shelter: *The child fled to the harbor of her father's arms.* 3 give shelter to; give a place to hide: *The dog's shaggy hair harbors fleas.* 4 have and keep in the mind: *Don't harbor a grudge against her; she didn't mean to hurt you.* 1,2 *n.*, 3,4 *v.*

hard (härd), 1 like steel, glass, and rock; not yielding to touch; not soft: *a hard nut, hard wood.* 2 so as to be hard, solid, or firm: *The river is frozen hard.* 3 firm; tight: *a hard knot.* 4 firmly; tightly: *He took me by the hand and held me hard.* 5 needing much ability, effort, or time; difficult or troublesome: *a hard problem, a hard job, a hard lesson, a hard man to get on with.* 6 acting or done with energy, persistence, etc.: *a hard worker.* 7 with steady effort or much energy: *Try hard.* 8 vigorous or violent: *a hard storm, a hard run.* 9 with vigor or violence: *It is raining hard.* 10 causing much pain, trouble, care, etc.; bad; severe: *We had a hard winter last year. When my parents were out of work, we had a hard time.* 11 so as to cause trouble, pain, care, etc.; severely; badly: *It will go hard with those kidnappers if they are caught.* 12 not pleasant; harsh; ugly: *a hard face, a hard laugh.* 13 not yielding to influence; stern; unfeeling: *a hard master, a hard heart.* 14 close; near: *The house stands hard by the bridge.* 15 containing mineral salts that keep soap from forming suds: *hard water.*

16 containing much alcohol: *hard liquor.* 17 sounded like the *c* in *corn* or the *g* in *get,* rather than like the soft *c* and *g* in *city* and *gem.* 1,3,5,6,8,10, 12,13,15-17 *adj.*, 2,4,7,9,11,14 *adv.* —**hard′ness,** *n.*

hard and fast, that cannot be changed or broken; strict: *hard and fast rules.*

hard of hearing, somewhat deaf.

hard up, INFORMAL. needing money or anything very badly.

hard-bit ten (härd′bit′n), stubborn; unyielding. *adj.*

hard-boiled (härd′boild′), 1 (of an egg) boiled until the white and yolk are firm. 2 SLANG. not easily moved by the feelings; tough; rough: *a hard-boiled veteran of two wars.* *adj.*

hard coal, anthracite.

hard en (härd′n), make or become hard: *Don't harden your heart to the sufferings of the poor. When the candy cooled, it hardened.* *v.*

hard head ed (härd′hed′id), 1 not easily excited or deceived; practical; shrewd. 2 stubborn; obstinate. *adj.* —**hard′head′ed ly,** *adv.* —**hard′head′ed ness,** *n.*

hard heart ed (härd′här′tid), without pity; cruel; unfeeling. *adj.* —**hard′heart′ed ly,** *adv.* —**hard′heart′ed ness,** *n.*

har di hood (här′dē hüd), boldness; daring. *n.*

har di ly (här′dl ē), in a hardy manner; with hardihood. *adv.*

har di ness (här′dē nis), 1 endurance; strength. 2 hardihood. *n.*

Har ding (här′ding), **Warren Gamaliel,** 1865-1923, the 29th president of the United States, from 1921 to 1923. *n.*

hard ly (härd′lē), 1 only just; barely: *We hardly had time to eat breakfast.* 2 not quite: *He is hardly strong enough to lift that trunk.* 3 probably not: *They will hardly come in all this rain.* 4 with trouble or effort: *a hardly fought game.* 5 in a hard manner; harshly; severely: *Cinderella's sisters treated her hardly.* *adv.*

hard palate, the bony front part of the roof of the mouth.

hard pan (härd′pan′), a hard, firm layer of subsoil through which roots cannot grow; pan. *n.*

hard ship (härd′ship), something hard to bear; hard condition of living: *Hunger, cold, and sickness were among the hardships of pioneer life.* *n.*

hard tack (härd′tak′), a very hard, dry biscuit, eaten by sailors; ship biscuit. *n.*

hard top (härd′top′), a passenger car with a rigid metal or plastic top but with window space comparable to that of a convertible. *n.*

hard ware (härd′wer′ *or* härd′war′), articles made from metal. Locks, hinges, nails, screws, etc., are hardware. *n.*

hard wood (härd′wüd′), 1 any hard, compact wood. 2 tree that has broad leaves, or does not have needles. Oak, cherry, maple, ebony, and mahogany are hardwoods; pine and fir are softwoods. 3 wood of such a tree. 4 having or made of such wood: *a hardwood floor.* 1-3 *n.*, 4 *adj.*

har dy (här′dē), 1 able to bear hard treatment, fatigue, etc.; strong; robust: *Cold weather did not kill the hardy plants.* 2 bold; daring: *a hardy knight.* *adj.*, **har di er, har di est.**

Har dy (här′dē), **Thomas,** 1840-1928, English novelist and poet. *n.*

hare
about 2 ft. long

hare (her *or* har), a gnawing mammal that resembles a rabbit but is larger, has longer ears, and does not live in a burrow. The jack rabbit is a hare; the cottontail is a rabbit. *n., pl.* **hares** *or* **hare.**

hare bell (her′bel′ *or* har′bel′), 1 slender plant with blue, bell-shaped flowers; bluebell. 2 its flower. *n.*

hare brained (her′brānd′ *or* har′brānd′), giddy, heedless, or reckless: *a harebrained scheme.* *adj.*

hare lip (her′lip′ *or* har′lip′), deformity existing from birth, in which the upper lip is divided. It resembles the lip of a hare. *n.*

har em (her′əm *or* har′əm), 1 part of a Moslem house where the women live; seraglio. 2 its occupants; the wives, female relatives, and female servants of a Moslem household. *n.*

hark (härk), listen: *"Hark, hark! the lark at heaven's gate sings."* *v.*

hark back, go back; turn back: *Those ideas hark back twenty years.*

hark en (här′kən), hearken. *v.*

Har lem (här′ləm), part of New York City in the northeastern section of Manhattan. *n.*

har le quin (här′lə kwən *or* här′lə kən), 1 **Harlequin,** character in comedy and pantomime who is usually masked and wears a costume of varied colors. 2 a mischievous person; buffoon. 3 varied in color; many-colored. 1,2 *n.*, 3 *adj.*

har lot (här′lət), prostitute. *n.*

harm (härm), 1 something that causes pain, loss, etc.; injury; damage: *He slipped and fell down but suffered no*

harm. 2 evil; wrong: *It was an accident; she meant no harm.* 3 damage; injure; hurt: *Do not pick or harm the flowers in the park. I hope this failing grade won't harm my chances to go to college.* 1,2 *n.,* 3 *v.*

harm ful (härm′fəl), causing harm; injurious; hurtful: *harmful germs. adj.* —**harm′ful ly,** *adv.* —**harm′ful ness,** *n.*

harm less (härm′lis), causing no harm; not harmful: *harmless gossip. adj.* —**harm′less ly,** *adv.* —**harm′less ness,** *n.*

har mon ic (här mon′ik), 1 having to do with harmony in music. 2 overtone. 3 having to do with such tones. 4 musical. 1,3,4 *adj.,* 2 *n.* —**har mon′i cal ly,** *adv.*

harmonica

har mon i ca (här mon′ə kə), a small musical instrument with metal reeds, played by inhaling and exhaling through a set of openings; mouth organ. *n., pl.* **har mon i cas.**

har mo ni ous (här mō′nē əs), 1 agreeing in feelings, ideas, or actions; getting on well together: *The children played together in a harmonious group.* 2 arranged so that the parts are orderly or pleasing; going well together: *A beautiful picture has harmonious colors.* 3 sweet-sounding; musical: *the harmonious sounds of a choir singing Christmas carols. adj.* —**har mo′ni ous ly,** *adv.*

har mo nize (här′mə nīz), 1 bring into harmony, accord, or agreement; make harmonious: *He harmonized the two plans by using parts of each one.* 2 be in harmony or agreement: *The colors in the room harmonized to give a pleasing effect.* 3 add tones to (a melody) to make chords in music. *v.,* **har mo nized, har mo niz ing.**

har mo niz er (här′mə nī′zər), person who harmonizes. *n.*

har mo ny (här′mə nē), 1 agreement of feeling, ideas, or actions; getting on well together: *The two brothers lived and worked in perfect harmony.* 2 an orderly or pleasing arrangement of parts; going well together: *In a beautiful landscape there is harmony of the different colors.* 3 the sounding together of musical tones in a chord. 4 study of chords in music and of relating them to successive chords. 5 sweet or musical sound; music. *n., pl.* **har mo nies.**

har ness (här′nis), 1 leather straps, bands, and other pieces for a horse,

harness (def. 1)

which connect it to a carriage, wagon, plow, etc. Reins, collar, and bridle are parts of a horse's harness. 2 any similar arrangement of straps, bands, etc., especially a combination of straps by which a parachute is attached to a person. 3 put harness on: *Harness the horse.* 4 cause to produce power: *We have harnessed these streams by building dams and putting in machinery for the water to turn.* 5 OLD USE. armor for a knight or warrior. 6 OLD USE. put armor on. 1,2,5 *n., pl.* **har ness es;** 3,4,6 *v.*

in harness, in one's regular work: *I was glad to get back in harness again after my long vacation.*

harp (def. 1)

harp (härp), 1 a large, stringed musical instrument played by plucking the strings with the fingers. 2 play on the harp. 1 *n.,* 2 *v.* —**harp′er,** *n.*

harp on, talk about very much or too much.

Har pers Ferry (här′pərz), town in NE West Virginia. John Brown's raid on a government arsenal was made there in 1859.

harp ist (här′pist), person who plays the harp. *n.*

har poon (här pün′), 1 a barbed spear with a rope tied to it, used for catching whales and other sea animals. It is thrown by hand or fired from a gun. 2 strike, catch, or kill with a harpoon. 1 *n.,* 2 *v.* —**har poon′er,** *n.*

harp si chord (härp′sə kôrd), a stringed musical instrument like a piano, used especially from about 1550 to 1750. It has a weak and tinkling

hat, āge, fär; let, ēqual, tėrm; it, īce; hot, ōpen, ôrder; oil, out; cup, pùt, rüle; ch, child; ng, long; sh, she; th, thin; ₮H, then; zh, measure;

ə represents *a* in about, *e* in taken, *i* in pencil, *o* in lemon, *u* in circus.

sound because the strings are plucked by leather or quill points instead of being struck by hammers. *n.*

Har py (här′pē), 1 (in Greek and Roman myths) any of various filthy, greedy monsters with women's heads and birds' bodies. 2 **harpy,** a cruel, greedy person; person who preys upon others. *n., pl.* **Har pies.**

har que bus (här′kwə bəs), an old form of portable gun used before muskets were invented. *n., pl.* **har que bus es.** Also, **arquebus.**

har ri er (har′ē ər), 1 a small hound of the kind used to hunt hares. 2 a cross-country runner. *n.*

Har ris burg (har′is bėrg′), capital of Pennsylvania, in the S part. *n.*

Har ri son (har′ə sən), 1 **Benjamin,** 1833-1901, the 23rd president of the United States, from 1889 to 1893. 2 his grandfather, **William Henry,** 1773-1841, American general and ninth president of the United States, in 1841. *n.*

har row (har′ō), 1 a heavy frame with iron teeth or upright disks. Harrows are used by farmers to break up plowed ground into finer pieces or to cover seeds with earth. See **disk harrow** for picture. 2 draw a harrow over (land, etc.). 3 hurt; wound. 4 cause pain or torment to; distress: *She was harrowed with grief and anxiety over the failure of her new business.* 1 *n.,* 2-4 *v.*

har row ing (har′ō ing), that harrows; very painful or distressing: *The hurricane was a harrowing experience. adj.*

har ry (har′ē), 1 raid and rob with violence: *The pirates harried the towns along the coast, burning what they could not carry off.* 2 keep troubling; worry; torment: *Fear of losing her voice harried the ailing opera singer. v.,* **har ried, har ry ing.**

harsh (härsh), 1 rough to the touch, taste, eye, or ear; sharp and unpleasant: *a harsh voice, a harsh climate.* 2 without pity; unfeeling; cruel; severe: *a harsh judge. adj.* —**harsh′ly,** *adv.* —**harsh′ness,** *n.*

hart (härt), a male deer, especially the

adj. adjective	*n.* noun
adv. adverb	*prep.* preposition
conj. conjunction	*pron.* pronoun
interj. interjection	*v.* verb
sing. singular	*pl.* plural

---

male red deer after its fifth year. *n., pl.* **harts** or **hart.**

Hartford (härt′fərd), capital of Connecticut, in the central part. *n.*

harts horn (härts′hôrn′), form of ammonia used as smelling salts. *n.*

har um-scar um (her′əm sker′əm *or* har′əm skär′əm), 1 too hasty; reckless; rash: *What a harum-scarum child you are!* 2 recklessly; rashly: *He rushed harum-scarum down the main street.* 3 a reckless person. 1 *adj.,* 2 *adv.,* 3 *n.*

har vest (här′vist), 1 a reaping and gathering in of grain and other food crops. 2 time or season of the harvest, usually in the late summer or early autumn. 3 gather in and bring home for use: *harvest wheat.* 4 one season's yield of any natural product; crop: *The oyster harvest was small this year.* 5 result; consequences: *She is reaping the harvest of her hard work.* 1,2,4,5 *n.,* 3 *v.*

har vest er (här′və stər), 1 person who works in a harvest field; reaper. 2 machine for harvesting crops, especially grain. *n.*

harvest moon, the full moon at harvest time or about September 23.

Har vey (här′vē), **William,** 1578-1657, English physician who discovered that blood circulates through the body. *n.*

has (haz), a present tense of **have.** *Who has my book? He has been sick.* *v.*

has-been (haz′bin′), INFORMAL. person or thing whose best days are past. *n.*

hash (hash), 1 mixture of cooked meat, potatoes, and other vegetables, chopped into small pieces and fried or baked. 2 chop into small pieces. 3 mixture; jumble. 4 a mess; muddle: *I made such a hash of the job that it had to be done over.* 1,3,4 *n.,* 2 *v.*

hash over, INFORMAL. discuss or review; reminisce about: *hashing over the old days.*

hash ish or **hash eesh** (hash′ēsh′), an extract prepared from the flowering tops of the hemp plant. Hashish is smoked or chewed for its intoxicating effect. *n.*

has n't (haz′nt), has not.

hasp (hasp), clasp or fastening for a door, window, trunk, box, etc., especially a hinged metal clasp that fits

over a staple or into a hole and is fastened by a peg or padlock. *n.*

has sle (has′əl), INFORMAL. a struggle or contest. *n.*

has sock (has′ək), 1 a thick cushion to rest the feet on, sit on, or kneel on. 2 tuft or bunch of coarse grass. *n.*

hast (hast), OLD USE. have. "Thou hast" means "you have." *v.*

haste (hāst), 1 a trying to be quick; hurrying: *All his haste was of no use; he missed the bus anyway.* 2 quickness without thought or care; rashness: *Haste makes waste.* *n.*

make haste, be quick; hurry: *Make haste or you will miss your train.*

has ten (hā′sn), 1 cause to be quick; speed; hurry: *Sunshine and rest hastened his recovery from illness.* 2 be quick; go fast: *She hastened to explain that she had not meant to be rude.* *v.*

hast i ly (hā′stl ē), 1 in a hurried manner. 2 rashly. 3 in a quick-tempered manner. *adv.*

hast i ness (hā′stē nis), 1 quickness of motion. 2 rashness. 3 quick temper. *n.*

Has tings (hā′stingz), town in SE England, where William I defeated the Saxons to become king of England in 1066. *n.*

hast y (hā′stē), 1 done or made in a hurry; quick: *She gave her watch a hasty glance and ran for the train.* 2 not well thought out; rash: *Their hasty decisions caused many mistakes.* 3 easily angered; quick-tempered: *a hasty old gentleman. adj.,* **hast i er, hast i est.**

hasty pudding, mush made of corn meal.

hat (hat), 1 a covering for the head. A hat usually has a crown and a brim and is usually worn outdoors. 2 provide with a hat; put a hat on: *The duchess was beautifully gowned and hatted.* 1 *n.,* 2 *v.,* **hat ted, hat ting.**

pass the hat, ask for contributions; take up a collection.

take off one's hat to, remove the hat, as a salute or sign of respect; honor.

under one's hat, INFORMAL. as a secret; to oneself: *Keep this information under your hat; tell it to no one.*

hat band (hat′band′), band around the crown of a hat, just above the brim. *n.*

hatch[1] (hach), 1 bring forth (young) from an egg or eggs: *A hen hatches chickens.* 2 keep (an egg or eggs) warm until the young come out: *The heat of the sun hatches turtles' eggs.* 3 come

hasp
on a door

out from the egg: *Three of the chickens hatched today.* 4 develop to be young animals; bring forth young: *Not all eggs hatch properly.* 5 the brood hatched: *There are twelve chickens in this hatch.* 6 arrange; plan. 7 plan secretly; plot: *The spies hatched a scheme to steal government secrets.* 1-4,6,7 *v.,* 5 *n., pl.* **hatch es.** [Middle English *hacchen*]

hatch[2] (hach), 1 an opening in a ship's deck or in the floor or roof of a building, etc.; hatchway. A ship's cargo is loaded through the hatch. The escape hatch in an airplane permits passengers to get out in an emergency. 2 a trap door covering such an opening: *The hatches were closed tightly during the storm. n., pl.* **hatch es.** [Old English *hæcc* gate, wicket]

hatch er y (hach′ər ē), place for hatching eggs of fish, hens, etc. *n., pl.* **hatch er ies.**

hatch et (hach′it), a small ax with a short handle and a hammerlike side opposite the blade, for use with one hand. *n.*

bury the hatchet, stop quarreling or fighting; make peace.

dig up the hatchet, make war.

hatch way (hach′wā′), hatch. *n.*

hate (hāt), 1 dislike very much: *Cats usually hate dogs.* 2 a very strong dislike; *feel hate toward an enemy. Her hate of injustice led her to become a lawyer.* 3 object of hatred: *My special hate is bullies.* 1 *v.,* **hat ed, hat ing;** 2,3 *n.*

hate ful (hāt′fəl), 1 causing hate: *hateful behavior.* 2 feeling hate; showing hate: *a hateful comment. adj.* —**hate′ful ly,** *adv.* —**hate′ful ness,** *n.*

hat er (hā′tər), person who hates. *n.*

hath (hath), OLD USE. has. "He hath" means "he has." *v.*

hat pin (hat′pin′), a long pin used by women to fasten a hat to their hair. *n.*

ha tred (hā′trid), very strong dislike; hate. *n.*

hat ter (hat′ər), person who makes or sells hats. *n.*

Hat ter as (hat′ər əs), **Cape,** cape on an island off E North Carolina. *n.*

hau berk (hô′bėrk′), a long coat of mail. *n.*

haugh ti ly (hô′tl ē), in a haughty manner. *adv.*

haugh ti ness (hô′tē nis), a being haughty; disdainful pride; arrogance. *n.*

haugh ty (hô′tē), 1 too proud of oneself and too scornful of others: *A haughty person is often unpopular.* 2 showing too great pride of oneself and scorn for others: *a haughty glance, haughty words. adj.,* **haugh ti er, haugh ti est.**

haul (hôl), 1 pull or drag with force:

The heavy logs were loaded on wagons and hauled to the mill by horses. 2 transport; carry: *Trucks, trains, and ships haul freight.* 3 act of hauling; hard pull. 4 load hauled: *Powerful trucks are used for heavy hauls.* 5 distance that a load is hauled: *Long hauls cost more than short ones.* 6 amount won, taken, etc., at one time; catch: *The fishing boats made a good haul and came back fully loaded.* 7 change the course of (a ship). 1,2,7 *v.*, 3-6 *n.* —**haul′er,** *n.*

haul off, draw back one's arm to give a blow.

haunch (hônch), 1 the fleshy part of the body around the hip; hip. 2 **haunches,** *pl.* the hindquarters of an animal: *The dog sat on his haunches.* 3 the leg and loin of an animal, used for food: *a haunch of venison.* *n., pl.* **haunch es.**

haunt (hônt), 1 go often to; visit frequently: *People say ghosts haunt that old house.* 2 place often gone to or visited: *The swimming pool was the children's favorite haunt on hot summer days.* 3 be often with; come often to: *Memories of his youth haunted the old man.* 1,3 *v.*, 2 *n.* —**haunt′ing ly,** *adv.*

haunt ed (hôn′tid), visited by ghosts: *a haunted house.* *adj.*

haut boy (hō′boi), oboe. *n.*

hau teur (hō tèr′), a being proud and overbearing; haughtiness. *n.* [from French]

Ha van a (hə van′ə), capital of Cuba, on the NW coast. *n.*

have (hav; *unstressed* həv *or* əv), 1 hold in one's hand, in one's keeping, or in one's possession: *I have a stick in my hand. We have a big house and farm. A house has windows. She has no news of her brother. He has a cheerful disposition.* 2 be forced; be compelled: *All animals have to sleep. He will have to go now because his work begins.* 3 cause (somebody to do something or something to be done): *Please have the store send my suit. She will have the car washed for me.* 4 take; get: *You need to have a rest.* 5 experience: *Have a pleasant time. They had trouble with this engine.* 6 engage in; carry on; perform: *Have a talk with him.* 7 allow; permit: *She won't have any noise while she is reading.* 8 know; understand: *She has your idea.* 9 hold in the mind: *have an idea.* 10 *Have* is used with words like *asked, been, broken, done,* or *called* to express completed action. *They have eaten. She had gone before. I have called her. They will have seen her by Sunday.* 11 INFORMAL. person, group, or country that has much property or wealth. 1-10 *v.*, **had, hav ing;** 11 *n.*

have done, be through; stop: *Let's have done with this quarreling.*

have it out, fight or argue until a question is settled: *We have had it out, and now we are friends once more.*

have to do with, relate to; deal with: *Botany has to do with the study of plants.*

ha ven (hā′vən), 1 harbor or port. 2 place of shelter and safety: *To the weary hunters, the cabin was a welcome haven from the storm.* *n.*

have-not (hav′not′), INFORMAL. person, group, or country that has little or no property or wealth. *n.*

have n't (hav′ənt), have not.

haversack

hav er sack (hav′ər sak), bag used by soldiers and hikers for carrying food when on a march or hike. *n.*

hav oc (hav′ək), very great destruction or injury: *Tornadoes, severe earthquakes, and plagues create widespread havoc.* *n.*

play havoc with, injure severely; ruin; destroy.

haw[1] (hô), 1 the red berry of the hawthorn. 2 hawthorn. *n.* [Old English *haga*]

haw[2] (hô), 1 a stammering sound between words: *"I am, haw, hum, very happy to be here," the speaker began* (interj.). *His speech was interrupted with an occasional haw* (n.). 2 make this sound; stammer. 1 *interj., n.*, 2 *v.* [imitation of the sound]

haw[3] (hô), 1 word of command to horses, oxen, etc., directing them to turn to the left: *"Get along! Haw!" the mule driver yelled at the team* (interj.). *You have to make your haws loud enough for the mule to hear* (n.). 2 to turn to the left. 1 *interj., n.*, 2 *v.* [origin uncertain]

Ha wai i (hə wī′ē), 1 state of the United States in the N Pacific, consisting of the Hawaiian Islands. *Capital:* Honolulu. 2 the largest of the Hawaiian Islands. *n.*

Ha wai ian (hə wī′yən), 1 of or having to do with Hawaii, its people, or their language. 2 person born or living in Hawaii. 3 language of Hawaii. 1 *adj.*, 2,3 *n.*

Hawaiian Islands, group of islands in the N Pacific.

hawk[1] (hôk), 1 bird of prey with a strong, hooked beak, long claws, broad wings, and keen sight. Some hawks are trained to hunt and kill other birds and small animals. 2 hunt with trained hawks. 1 *n.*, 2 *v.* [Old English *heafoc*] —**hawk′like′,** *adj.*

hawk[2] (hôk), carry (goods) about and offer them for sale by shouting: *Peddlers hawked their wares in the street.* *v.* [from *hawker*[1]]

hawk[3] (hôk), 1 clear the throat noisily. 2 a noisy clearing of the throat. 1 *v.*, 2 *n.* [probably imitation of the sound]

hawk er[1] (hô′kər), person who carries his wares around and offers them for sale by shouting; peddler. *n.* [probably from earlier German *haker*]

hawk er[2] (hô′kər), person who hunts with trained hawks. *n.* [*hawk*[1] + -*er*[1]]

hawk-eyed (hôk′īd′), having sharp eyes like a hawk. *adj.*

hawse (hôz), 1 part of a ship's bow having holes for hawsers or cables to pass through. 2 one of these holes. *n.*

HAWSE

hawse (defs. 1 and 2)

haw ser (hô′zər), a large rope or small cable, used for mooring or towing ships. *n.*

haw thorn (hô′thôrn), shrub or tree with many thorns and clusters of fragrant white, red, or pink flowers and small, red berries; haw. *n.*

Haw thorne (hô′thôrn), **Nathaniel,** 1804-1864, American writer of novels and short stories. *n.*

hay (hā), 1 grass, alfalfa, clover, etc., cut and dried for use as food for cattle and horses. 2 cut and dry grass, alfalfa, clover, etc., for hay: *The men are haying in the east field.* 3 supply with hay. 1 *n.*, 2,3 *v.*

hay cock (hā′kok′), a small, cone-shaped pile of hay in a field. *n.*

Hay dn (hīd′n), **Franz Joseph,**

hat, āge, fär; let, ēqual, tėrm;
it, īce; hot, ōpen, ôrder;
oil, out; cup, pùt, rüle; ch, child;
ng, long; sh, she; th, thin;
ŦH, then; zh, measure;

ə represents *a* in about,
e in taken, *i* in pencil,
o in lemon, *u* in circus.

adj.	adjective	*n.*	noun
adv.	adverb	*prep.*	preposition
conj.	conjunction	*pron.*	pronoun
interj.	interjection	*v.*	verb
sing.	singular	*pl.*	plural

1732-1809, Austrian composer. *n.*

Hayes (hāz), **Rutherford B.,** 1822-1893, the 19th president of the United States, from 1877 to 1881. *n.*

hay fever, allergy caused by the pollen of ragweed and other plants, characterized by sneezing, a running nose, and itching of the nose, throat, and eyes.

hay field (hā′fēld′), field in which grass, alfalfa, clover, etc., are grown for hay. *n.*

hay fork (hā′fôrk′), 1 pitchfork. 2 a mechanical device equipped with hooks for moving hay into or out of a hayloft. *n.*

hay loft (hā′lôft′), place in a barn or stable where hay is stored. *n.*

hay mow (hā′mou′), 1 hayloft. 2 heap of hay stored in a barn or stable. *n.*

hay rick (hā′rik′), haystack. *n.*

hay ride (hā′rīd′), outing in a wagon partly filled with hay. *n.*

hay stack (hā′stak′), a large pile of hay outdoors. *n.*

hay wire (hā′wīr′), 1 wire used to tie up bales of hay. 2 SLANG. out of order; wrong. 3 SLANG. confused or crazy. 1 *n.,* 2,3 *adj.*

haz ard (haz′ərd), 1 chance of harm; risk; danger; peril: *Mountain climbing is full of hazards.* 2 chance: *take a hazard, games of hazard.* 3 take a chance with; risk; venture: *I would hazard my life on her honesty.* 4 any obstruction on a golf course. 1,2,4 *n.,* 3 *v.*

haz ard ous (haz′ər dəs), full of risk; dangerous; perilous: *Flying across the ocean in a small plane was a hazardous undertaking. adj.* —**haz′ard ous ly,** *adv.* —**haz′ard ous ness,** *n.*

haze[1] (hāz), 1 a small amount of mist, smoke, dust, etc., in the air: *A thin haze veiled the distant hills.* 2 slight confusion; vagueness: *In the haze of passing time, the names of his old friends became jumbled. n.* [origin uncertain]

haze[2] (hāz), (in schools, universities, etc.) force to do humiliating or ridiculous tasks; bully: *The freshmen resented being hazed by the sophomores. v.,* **hazed, haz ing.** [from French of the 1400's *haser* irritate, annoy]

ha zel (hā′zəl), 1 shrub or small tree of the same family as the birch, whose light-brown nuts are good to eat. 2 a light brown. 3 light-brown. 1,2 *n.,* 3 *adj.*

ha zel nut (hā′zəl nut′), nut of a hazel; filbert. *n.*

ha zi ly (hā′zə lē), in a hazy manner. *adv.*

ha zi ness (hā′zē nis), hazy quality or condition. *n.*

ha zy (hā′zē), 1 full of haze; misty; smoky: *a hazy sky.* 2 slightly confused; vague; dim; obscure: *The injured man had only a hazy idea of what had happened. adj.,* **ha zi er, ha zi est.**

H-bomb (āch′bom′), a hydrogen bomb. *n.*

he (hē; *unstressed* ē), 1 boy, man, or male animal spoken about or mentioned before: *He works hard, but his work pays him well.* 2 a male: *Is your dog a he or a she?* 3 anyone: *He who hesitates is lost.* 1,3 *pron., pl.* **they;** 2 *n., pl.* **he's.**

head (hed), 1 the top part of the human body or the front part of an animal where the eyes, nose, ears, and mouth are. Your brain is in your head. 2 the top part of anything: *the head of a pin, the head of a page.* 3 the front part of anything: *the head of a procession, the head of a street.* 4 at the top or front: *the head division of a parade.* 5 be or go at the top or front of: *head a parade.* 6 coming from in front: *a head sea, head tides.* 7 move toward; face toward: *Our ship headed south. It's getting late; we'd better begin to head for home.* 8 chief person; leader: *the head of the school.* 9 chief; leading: *the head clerk in a store.* 10 be the head or chief of; lead: *head a business. Who heads the army?* 11 one or ones; individual or individuals. Ten cows are ten head of cattle. 12 anything rounded like a head: *a head of cabbage or lettuce.* 13 the part of a boil or pimple where pus is about to break through the skin. 14 the striking or cutting part of a tool or implement: *You hit the nail with the head of a hammer. You hit the ball with the head of a golf club.* 15 piece of skin stretched tightly over the end of a drum, etc. 16 mind; understanding; intelligence; intellect: *She has a good head for figures.* 17 topic; point: *She arranged her speech under four main heads.* 18 crisis or conclusion; decisive point: *His sudden refusal brought matters to a head.* 19 pressure of water, gas, etc.: *a full head of steam.* 20 source of a river or stream. 21 put a head on; furnish with a head: *head a letter with a date.* 22 **heads,** *pl.* the top side of a coin. 1-3,8,11-20,22 *n., pl.* **heads** for 1-3,8,12-20,22, **head** for 11; 5,7,10,21 *v.,* 4,6,9 *adj.*

go to one's head, 1 affect one's mind:

The poor man's troubles have gone to his head. 2 make one dizzy: *The wine went to my head.* 3 make one conceited: *I'm afraid all this praise will go to my head.*

head off, get in front of and turn back or aside: *The cowboys tried to head off the stampeding herd.*

keep one's head, stay calm; not get excited.

lose one's head, get excited; lose one's self-control.

out of one's head, INFORMAL. crazy.

over one's head, 1 too hard for one to understand: *Einstein's theory of relativity is way over my head.* 2 passing over a person without giving him a chance to act.

put heads together or **lay heads together,** plan or plot together.

turn one's head, make one conceited.

head ache (hed′āk′), 1 pain in the head. 2 SLANG. something which causes great bother or annoyance. *n.*

head band (hed′band′), band worn around the head. *n.*

headdress
worn about 1400

head dress (hed′dres′), covering or decoration for the head. *n., pl.* **head dress es.**

head er (hed′ər), 1 person, tool, or machine that puts on or takes off heads of grain, barrels, pins, nails, etc. 2 INFORMAL. a plunge, dive, or fall headfirst: *I slipped and took a header over the pool's edge. n.*

head first (hed′fèrst′), 1 with the head first. 2 hastily; rashly. *adv.*

head fore most (hed′fôr′mōst), headfirst. *adv.*

head gear (hed′gir′), 1 covering for the head; hat, cap, helmet, etc. 2 the parts of a harness which fit around an animal's head. *n.*

head ing (hed′ing), 1 something used as a head, top, or front. 2 something written or printed at the top of a page. A letterhead is a heading. 3 title of a page, chapter, topic, etc. 4 direction toward which an aircraft or ship is moving. *n.*

head land (hed′lənd), point of high land jutting out into water; cape; promontory. *n.*

head less (hed′lis), 1 having no head. 2 without a leader. 3 without brains; foolish; stupid. *adj.*

head light (hed′līt′), a bright light at

the front of an automobile, locomotive, etc. *n.*

head line (hed′līn′), 1 words printed in heavy type at the top of a newspaper article telling what it is about. 2 **headlines,** *pl.* publicity: *The invention got headlines.* 3 furnish with a headline. 4 give publicity to: *headline a story.* 5 be or list as the main attraction: *She is headlining in the new show. The last show headlined another performer.* 1,2 *n.,* 3-5 *v.,* **head lined, head lining.**

head long (hed′lông), 1 with the head first: *plunge headlong into the sea (adv.), a headlong plunge or dive (adj.).* 2 with great speed and force: *rush headlong into the crowd (adv.), a headlong course (adj.).* 3 in too great a rush; without stopping to think: *The boy ran headlong across the busy street (adv.). One should not make a headlong decision about something important (adj.).* *adv., adj.*

head man (hed′man′), chief; leader. *n., pl.* **head men.**

head mas ter (hed′mas′tər), man in charge of a school, especially of a private school; principal. *n.*

head-on (hed′on′), with the head or front first: *a head-on collision (adj.), collide head-on (adv.).* *adj., adv.*

head phone (hed′fōn′), a telephone or radio receiver held against the ear by a band over the head. *n.*

head piece (hed′pēs′), 1 helmet worn with a suit of armor. 2 any covering for the head. *n.*

head quar ters (hed′kwôr′tərz), 1 place from which the chief or commanding officer of an army, police force, etc., sends out orders. 2 place from which any organization is controlled and directed; main office: *The headquarters of the American Red Cross is in Washington.* *n. pl. or sing.*

head ship (hed′ship), position of head; chief authority; leadership. *n.*

heads man (hedz′mən), man who cuts off the heads of people condemned to death. *n., pl.* **heads men.**

HEADSTALL

head stall (hed′stôl′), the part of a bridle or halter that fits around a horse's head. *n.*

head stone (hed′stōn′), 1 stone set at the head of a grave; gravestone. 2 cornerstone of a building. *n.*

head strong (hed′strông′), rashly or foolishly determined to have one's own way; hard to control or manage;

obstinate: *a headstrong horse, a headstrong child.* *adj.*

head wait er (hed′wā′tər), man in charge of the waiters in a restaurant, hotel, etc. *n.*

head wa ters (hed′wô′tərz *or* hed′wot′ərz), the sources or upper parts of a river. *n.pl.*

head way (hed′wā′), 1 motion forward; progress: *The ship could make no headway against the strong wind and tide.* 2 progress with work, etc.: *Science has made much headway in fighting disease.* 3 a clear space overhead in a doorway or under an arch, bridge, etc.; clearance. *n.*

head wind, wind blowing from the direction in which a ship, etc., is moving.

head y (hed′ē), 1 hasty; rash; headlong. 2 apt to affect the head and make one dizzy; intoxicating: *a heady wine.* *adj.,* **head i er, head i est.**

heal (hēl), 1 make whole, sound, or well; bring back to health; cure. 2 become whole or sound; get well; return to health; be cured: *My cut finger healed in a few days.* *v.* —**heal′er,** *n.*

health (helth), 1 a being well; freedom from sickness: *Rest, sleep, exercise, and cleanliness are important to your health.* 2 condition of body or mind: *She is in poor health. He is in excellent health.* 3 a drink in honor of a person with a wish that he may be healthy and happy: *We all drank a health to the bride.* *n.*

health ful (helth′fəl), 1 giving health; good for the health: *healthful exercise, a healthful diet.* 2 having good health. *adj.* —**health′ful ly,** *adv.* —**health′ful ness,** *n.*

health i ly (hel′thə lē), in a healthy manner. *adv.*

health i ness (hel′thē nis), healthy condition. *n.*

health y (hel′thē), 1 having good health: *a healthy baby.* 2 showing good health: *a healthy appearance.* 3 giving health; good for the health; healthful: *healthy exercise.* *adj.,* **health i er, health i est.**

heap (hēp), 1 pile of many things thrown or lying together in a confused way: *a heap of stones, a sand heap.* 2 form into a heap; gather in heaps: *I heaped the dirty clothes beside the washing machine. Snow heaped against the fence.* 3 INFORMAL. a large amount: *a heap of trouble.* 4 give generously or in large amounts: *The man heaped praise on his friend.* 5 fill full or more than full: *heap a plate with food.* 1,3 *n.,* 2,4,5 *v.*

hear (hir), 1 take in a sound or sounds through the ear: *He cannot hear well. I can hear my watch tick.* 2 listen: *The town crier shouted "Hear ye!"* 3 listen

hat, āge, fär; let, ēqual, tėrm;
it, īce; hot, ōpen, ôrder;
oil, out; cup, pùt, rüle; ch, child;
ng, long; sh, she; th, thin;
ŦH, then; zh, measure;

ə represents *a* in about,
e in taken, *i* in pencil,
o in lemon, *u* in circus.

to: *You must hear what I have to say.* 4 listen to with favor: *Lord, hear my prayer.* 5 give a formal hearing to: *hear a complaint.* 6 receive news or information: *Have you heard from your friend in Los Angeles?* *v.,* **heard, hear ing.** —**hear′er,** *n.*

will not hear of, will not listen to, think of, agree to, or allow.

heard (hėrd), past tense and past participle of **hear.** *I heard the noise. The gun was heard a mile away.* *v.*

hear ing (hir′ing), 1 sense by which sound is perceived: *Please speak up; my hearing is poor.* 2 act or process of taking in sound, listening, or receiving information: *Hearing the good news made her happy.* 3 a formal or official listening: *The judge gave both sides a hearing in court.* 4 a chance to be heard: *Give us a hearing.* 5 distance that a sound can be heard; earshot: *be within hearing of the baby, talk freely in the hearing of others.* *n.*

hearing aid, a small battery-powered device which amplifies sounds, worn by people who cannot hear well.

heark en (här′kən), pay attention to what is said; listen attentively; listen. *v.* Also, **harken.**

hear say (hir′sā′), common talk; gossip or rumor. *n.*

hearse (hėrs), carriage, automobile, etc., for carrying a coffin to the cemetery. *n.*

heart (härt), 1 a hollow, muscular organ which pumps the blood throughout the body by contracting and relaxing. 2 the part that feels, loves, hates, and desires: *a heavy heart. She has a kind*

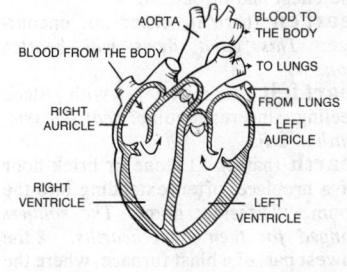

AORTA
BLOOD TO THE BODY
BLOOD FROM THE BODY
TO LUNGS
FROM LUNGS
RIGHT AURICLE
LEFT AURICLE
RIGHT VENTRICLE
LEFT VENTRICLE

heart (def. 1)

adj.	adjective	*n.*	noun
adv.	adverb	*prep.*	preposition
conj.	conjunction	*pron.*	pronoun
interj.	interjection	*v.*	verb
sing.	singular	*pl.*	plural

heart. *He knew in his heart that he was wrong.* 3 love; affection: *give one's heart to someone.* 4 person loved or praised: *group of stout hearts.* 5 kindness; sympathy: *Have you no heart?* 6 spirit; courage; enthusiasm: *The losing team still had plenty of heart.* 7 the innermost part; middle; center: *in the heart of the forest.* 8 the main part; most important part: *the very heart of the matter.* 9 figure shaped like this: ♥ 10 a playing card marked with one or more red, heart-shaped figures. 11 **hearts,** *pl.* suit of such playing cards. *n.*

after one's own heart, just as one likes it; pleasing one perfectly: *Now that's a meal after my own heart!*

at heart, in one's deepest thoughts or feelings: *He is kind at heart, though he appears to be gruff.*

by heart, 1 by memory: *He learned the poem by heart.* 2 from memory: *He can recite the poem by heart.*

take heart, be encouraged.

take to heart, think seriously about; be deeply affected by.

with all one's heart, 1 sincerely: *He said that he loved her with all his heart.* 2 gladly.

heart ache (härt′āk′), great sorrow or grief; deep pain. *n.*

heart beat (härt′bēt′), pulsation of the heart, including one complete contraction and relaxation. *n.*

heart break (härt′brāk′), a crushing sorrow or grief. *n.*

heart break ing (härt′brā′king), crushing with sorrow or grief. *adj.*

heart bro ken (härt′brō′kən), crushed by sorrow or grief. *adj.*

heart burn (härt′bėrn′), a burning feeling in the stomach, often rising to the chest and throat. *n.*

heart en (härt′n), cheer up; encourage: *This good news will hearten you.* *v.*

heart felt (härt′felt′), with deep feeling; sincere; genuine: *heartfelt sympathy.* *adj.*

hearth (härth), 1 stone or brick floor of a fireplace, often extending into the room. 2 fireside; home: *The soldiers longed for their own hearths.* 3 the lowest part of a blast furnace, where the molten metal and slag collects. *n.*

hearth side (härth′sīd′), fireside; home. *n.*

hearth stone (härth′stōn′), 1 stone forming a hearth. 2 fireside; home. *n.*

heart i ly (här′tl ē), 1 in a warm, friendly way; sincerely: *express good wishes very heartily.* 2 with courage, spirit, or enthusiasm; vigorously: *set to work heartily.* 3 with a good appetite: *eat heartily.* 4 very; completely: *I am heartily tired of doing all the work myself.* *adv.*

heart i ness (här′tē nis), hearty quality. *n.*

heart less (härt′lis), without kindness or sympathy; unfeeling; cruel: *heartless words.* *adj.* —**heart′less ly,** *adv.* —**heart′less ness,** *n.*

heart-rend ing (härt′ren′ding), causing mental anguish; very distressing: *The loss of their parents in an accident was a heart-rending experience.* *adj.*

hearts ease (härts′ēz′), peace of mind. *n.*

heart sick (härt′sik′), sick at heart; very depressed; very unhappy. *adj.*

heart strings (härt′stringz′), deepest feelings: *Their sad story tugged at our heartstrings.* *n.pl.*

heart wood (härt′wùd′), the hard, central wood of a tree. *n.*

heart y (här′tē), 1 warm and friendly; full of feeling; sincere: *We gave our old friends a hearty welcome.* 2 strong and well; vigorous: *My grandmother was still hale and hearty at eighty.* 3 full of energy and enthusiasm; not restrained: *He burst out in a loud, hearty laugh.* 4 with plenty to eat; abundant: *A hearty meal satisfied our hunger.* 5 having a good appetite: *People who work outdoors are usually hearty eaters.* *adj.*, **heart i er, heart i est.**

heat (hēt), 1 condition of being hot; hotness; warmth; high temperature. Heat is a form of energy caused by the motion of molecules. Friction, electricity, the sun, and your body all produce heat. 2 make hot or warm: *The stove heats the room.* 3 become hot or warm: *The soup is heating slowly.* 4 warmth or intensity of feeling; violence; excitement: *In the heat of the argument he lost his temper.* 5 fill with strong feeling; excite or become excited: *The stirring speech heated the child's imagination.* 6 section of a race, consisting of a complete running of the course: *I won the first heat, but lost the final race.* 1,4,6 *n.*, 2,3,5 *v.*

heat ed (hē′tid), angry, excited, or violent: *a heated argument.* *adj.* —**heat′ed ly,** *adv.*

heat er (hē′tər), something that gives heat or warmth. A stove, furnace, or radiator is a heater. *n.*

heath (hēth), 1 open, waste land with heather or low bushes growing on it; moor. It has few or no trees. 2 a low bush growing on such land. Heather is a kind of heath. *n.*

hea then (hē′THən), 1 person who does not believe in the God of the Bible; person who is not a Christian, Jew, or Moslem; pagan. 2 people who are heathens. 3 of or having to do with heathens; not Christian, Jewish, or Moslem. 4 person who has no religion or culture. 5 not religious or cultured. 1,2,4 *n., pl.* **hea thens** or **hea then;** 3,5 *adj.*

hea then dom (hē′THən dəm), 1 heathen worship or ways. 2 heathen lands or people. *n.*

hea then ish (hē′THə nish), 1 having to do with heathens. 2 like heathens. *adj.*

heath er (heTH′ər), a low, evergreen shrub with stalks of small, purple or pink, bell-shaped flowers, covering many heaths of Scotland and England. *n.*

heat shield, a coating or covering of special material on the nose cone of a missile or spacecraft to absorb or diffuse heat induced by friction when it reenters the earth's atmosphere.

heat wave, period of very hot weather.

heave (hēv), 1 lift with force or effort: *He heaved the heavy box into the wagon.* 2 lift and throw: *The sailors heaved the anchor overboard.* 3 pull with force or effort; haul: *They heaved on the rope.* 4 give (a sigh, groan, etc.) with a deep, heavy breath. 5 rise and fall alternately: *The waves heaved in the storm.* 6 breathe hard; pant. 7 to vomit. 8 (of a ship) move in some direction. 9 to rise; swell; bulge: *The ground heaved from the earthquake.* 10 act of heaving: *With a mighty heave, we pushed the boat into the water.* 1-9 *v.*, **heaved** or **hove, heav ing;** 10 *n.*

heave ho! sailors' cry when pulling up the anchor, etc.

heave in sight, come into view.

heave to, stop a ship; stop.

heav en (hev′ən), 1 (in Christian and some other religious use) place where God and the angels live and where the blessed go after death. 2 **Heaven,** God; Providence: *It was the will of Heaven.* 3 place or condition of greatest happiness. 4 Usually, **heavens,** *pl.* the upper air; sky: *Millions of stars were shining in the heavens.* *n.*

for heaven's sake! or **good heavens!** exclamation of surprise or protest.

heav en ly (hev′ən lē), 1 of or in heaven; divine: *heavenly angels, heavenly Father.* 2 like heaven; suitable for heaven; very happy, beautiful, or excellent: *a heavenly spot, heavenly peace.*

3 of or in the heavens: *The sun, moon, and stars are heavenly bodies. adj.*

heav en ward (hev′ən wərd), toward heaven: *The rocket soared heavenward (adv.). She cast a heavenward glance (adj.). adv., adj.*

heav i ly (hev′ə lē), in a heavy manner. *adv.*

heav i ness (hev′ē nis), **1** a being heavy; great weight. **2** sadness. *n.*

Heav i side layer (hev′ē sīd), a layer of the ionosphere which reflects low-frequency radio waves. [from Oliver *Heaviside*, 1850-1925, a British physicist]

heav y (hev′ē), **1** hard to lift or carry; of great weight: *a heavy load. Iron is heavy and feathers are light.* **2** of more than usual weight for its kind: *heavy silk, heavy bread.* **3** of great amount, force, or intensity; greater than usual; large: *a heavy rain, a heavy crop, a heavy meal, a heavy sea, a heavy sleep, a heavy vote.* **4** hard to endure: *Her troubles became heavier.* **5** hard to deal with, manage, etc.; trying or difficult in any way: *heavy soil, a difficult trip over heavy roads of mud and sand.* **6** hard to digest: *heavy food.* **7** weighted down; laden: *air heavy with moisture, eyes heavy with sleep.* **8** sorrowful; gloomy: *heavy news.* **9** serious; deep; grave: *a heavy part in a play, a heavy discussion.* **10** cloudy; overcast: *a heavy sky.* **11** broad; thick; coarse: *a heavy line, heavy features.* **12** clumsy; sluggish; slow: *a heavy walk.* **13** uninteresting; dull; ponderous: *heavy reading.* **14** INFORMAL. villain: *the heavy in a play.* **15** in a heavy manner; heavily. 1-13 *adj.*, **heav i er, heav i est;** 14 *n.*, 15 *adv.*

hang heavy, pass slowly and uninterestingly: *Time hung heavy on my hands.*

heavy hydrogen, deuterium.

heavy water, water formed of oxygen and deuterium. Heavy water is much like ordinary water, but is about 1.1 times as heavy and has a higher freezing point. It occurs in very small amounts in ordinary water.

heav y weight (hev′ē wāt′), **1** person or thing of more than average weight. **2** boxer or wrestler who weighs 175 pounds or more. *n.*

He be (hē′bē), (in Greek myths) the goddess of youth. *n.*

He bra ic (hi brā′ik), of or having to do with the Hebrews or their language or culture. *adj.*

He brew (hē′brü), **1** Jew; Israelite. **2** the ancient Semitic language of the Jews, in which the Old Testament was written. Citizens of Israel speak a modern form of Hebrew. **3** Jewish. 1,2 *n.*, 3 *adj.*

He brews (hē′brüz), book of the New Testament. *n.*

Heb ri des (heb′rə dēz′), group of Scottish islands off NW Scotland. *n.pl.*

He bron (hē′brən), town in W Jordan, near Jerusalem. *n.*

Hec a te (hek′ə tē), (in Greek myths) the goddess of the moon, earth, and lower world. She was later associated with magic and witchcraft. *n.*

hec a tomb (hek′ə tōm), **1** (in ancient Greece or Rome) a great public sacrifice of 100 oxen at one time. **2** any great slaughter. *n.*

heck le (hek′əl), interrupt and annoy (a speaker, etc.) by asking bothersome questions, jeering, or making loud remarks. *v.*, **heck led, heck ling.**

heck ler (hek′lər), person who heckles. *n.*

hec tic (hek′tik), very exciting; feverish: *The children had a hectic time getting to school the morning after the big snowstorm. adj.*

hec tor (hek′tər), **1** a bragging, bullying fellow. **2** bluster; bully. **3** to tease. 1 *n.*, 2,3 *v.* [from *Hector*]

Hec tor (hek′tər), (in Greek legends) the bravest of the Trojan warriors. He was killed by Achilles. *n.*

he'd (hēd; *unstressed* ēd), **1** he had. **2** he would.

hedge (hej), **1** a thick row of bushes or small trees, planted as a fence or boundary. **2** any barrier or boundary. **3** put a hedge around: *hedge a garden.* **4** avoid giving a direct answer or taking a definite stand; evade questions. **5** bet on both sides in order to reduce one's possible losses. **6** act of hedging. 1,2,6 *n.*, 3-5 *v.*, **hedged, hedg ing.**

hedge in, hem in; surround on all sides: *The town was hedged in by mountains and a dense forest.*

hedgehog (def. 1)—about 9 in. long

hedge hog (hej′hog′), **1** a small, insect-eating mammal of Europe, Asia, and Africa, with spines on its back.

---

hat, āge, fär; let, ēqual, tėrm;
it, īce; hot, ōpen, ôrder;
oil, out; cup, pùt, rüle; ch, child;
ng, long; sh, she; th, thin;
ŦH, then; zh, measure;

ə represents *a* in about,
e in taken, *i* in pencil,
o in lemon, *u* in circus.

When attacked, hedgehogs roll up into a bristling ball. **2** porcupine. *n.*

hedge hop (hej′hop′), fly an airplane very low. *v.*, **hedge hopped, hedge-hop ping.**

hedge hop per (hej′hop′ər), pilot who hedgehops. *n.*

hedge row (hej′rō′), a thick row of bushes or small trees forming a hedge. *n.*

heed (hēd), **1** give careful attention to; take notice of: *Now heed what I say.* **2** careful attention: *pay heed to one's clothes.* 1 *v.*, 2 *n.*

heed ful (hēd′fəl), careful; attentive. *adj.* **—heed′ful ly,** *adv.*

heed less (hēd′lis), careless; thoughtless. *adj.* **—heed′less ly,** *adv.* **—heed′less ness,** *n.*

hee haw (hē′hô′), **1** the braying sound made by a donkey. **2** make such a sound. **3** a loud, coarse laugh. **4** laugh loudly and coarsely. 1,3 *n.*, 2,4 *v.*

heel[1] (hēl), **1** the back part of a person's foot, below the ankle. **2** the part of a stocking or shoe that covers the heel. **3** the part of a shoe or boot that is under the heel or raises the heel: *a pair of shoes with high heels.* **4** the part of the hind leg of an animal that corresponds to a person's heel: *The horse kicked up his heels trying to throw the rider.* **5** put a heel or heels on: *heel a pair of shoes.* **6** touch the ground with the heel. **7** follow closely. **8** anything shaped, used, or placed at an end like a heel. The end crust of bread, the rind of cheese, the rear end of a ship's keel, or the lower end of a mast are all the heels. **9** INFORMAL. a hateful person. 1-4,8,9 *n.*, 5-7 *v.* [Old English *hēla*]

down at the heel or **down at the heels, 1** with the heel of the shoe worn down. **2** shabby.

take to one's heels, run away.

heel[2] (hēl), **1** lean over to one side; tilt; tip: *The sailboat heeled as it turned.* **2** act of heeling. 1 *v.*, 2 *n.* [Old English *hieldan*]

heft (heft), INFORMAL. **1** weight; heaviness. **2** lift; heave. **3** judge the weight of by lifting. 1 *n.*, 2,3 *v.*

hefty

adj. adjective	n. noun
adv. adverb	prep. preposition
conj. conjunction	pron. pronoun
interj. interjection	v. verb
sing. singular	pl. plural

---

heft y (hef′tē), INFORMAL. 1 weighty; heavy. 2 big and strong. *adj.,* **heft i er, heft i est.**

Hei del berg (hī′dl bėrg′), city in S West Germany. A famous university is located there. *n.*

heif er (hef′ər), a young cow that has not had a calf. *n.*

heigh-ho (hī′hō′ *or* hā′hō′), sound made to express surprise, joy, sadness, or weariness. *interj.*

height (hīt), 1 measurement from top to bottom; how tall a person is; how high a thing is; how far up a thing goes: *the height of a mountain.* 2 a fairly great distance up: *rising at a height above the valley.* 3 a high point or place: *A hill or cliff is a height.* 4 the highest part; top. 5 the highest point; greatest degree: *Fast driving on icy roads is the height of folly. n.*

height en (hīt′n), 1 make or become higher. 2 make or become stronger or greater; increase. *v.*

hei nous (hā′nəs), very wicked; extremely offensive; hateful. *adj.* —**hei′nous ly,** *adv.* —**hei′nous ness,** *n.*

heir (er *or* ar), person who gets or has the right to get someone's property or title after that one dies. *n.*

heir apparent, person who will be heir if he lives longer than the one holding the property or title: *The king's oldest son is heir apparent to the throne. pl.* **heirs apparent.**

heir ess (er′is *or* ar′is), 1 a woman or girl heir. 2 woman or girl inheriting great wealth. *n., pl.* **heir ess es.**

heir loom (er′lüm′ *or* ar′lüm′), possession handed down from generation to generation: *This clock is a family heirloom. n.*

helix
helices in a
Corinthian capital

held (held), past tense and past participle of **hold**[1]. *She held the baby. The swing is held by strong ropes. v.*

Hel e na (hel′ə nə), capital of Montana, in the W part. *n.*

Hel en of Troy (hel′ən), (in Greek legends) a very beautiful Greek woman, the wife of King Menelaus of Sparta. Her kidnaping by Paris caused the Trojan War.

hel i ces (hel′ə sēz′), a plural of **helix.** *n.*

hel i cop ter (hel′ə kop′tər), aircraft lifted from the ground and kept in the air by horizontal propellers. *n.*

he li o cen tric (hē′lē ō sen′trik), 1 viewed or measured from the center of the sun. 2 having or representing the sun as a center. *adj.*

he li o graph (hē′lē ə graf), 1 device for signaling by means of a movable mirror which flashes beams of sunlight to a distance. The flashes of the mirror represent the dots and dashes of the Morse code. 2 to signal by heliograph: *They are heliographing the message to the ship.* 3 apparatus for taking photographs of the sun. 1,3 *n.,* 2 *v.*

heliograph (def. 1)
used by armies
in the late 1800's

He li os (hē′lē os), (in Greek myths) the god of the sun. The Romans called him Sol. *n.*

he li o trope (hē′lē ə trōp), 1 plant with clusters of small, sweet-smelling, purple or white flowers. 2 a pinkish purple. 3 pinkish-purple. 1,2 *n.,* 3 *adj.*

he li ot ro pism (hē′lē ot′rə piz′əm), tendency of plants to turn toward sunlight. *n.*

hel i port (hel′ə pôrt), airport designed for use by helicopters. Heliports may be built on the tops of buildings or other small areas in large cities. *n.*

he li um (hē′lē əm), a very light, colorless, odorless, inert gas that will not burn. It is a chemical element which occurs in small amounts in the air, in natural gas, etc., and which is also produced artificially. Helium is used to inflate balloons and airships and, in the liquid state, as a refrigerant. *n.*

he lix (hē′liks), anything having a spiral, coiled form. A screw thread, a watch spring, or a snail shell is a helix. *n., pl.* **hel i ces** *or* **he lix es.**

hell (hel), 1 (in Christian and some other religious use) place where devils and evil spirits live and where wicked persons are punished after death. 2 home of the dead; Hades. 3 any place or condition of wickedness, torment, or misery. *n.*

he'll (hēl; *unstressed* hil), 1 he will. 2 he shall.

Hel las (hel′əs), Greece. *n.*

helicopter

hell bend er (hel′ben′dər), a large salamander, common in the Ohio River and its tributaries. *n.*

hel le bore (hel′ə bôr), 1 a European plant of the same family as the buttercup, with showy flowers that bloom before spring. 2 its root, which is dried and used in medicine. 3 a tall plant of the same family as the lily, with clusters of purple or white flowers. 4 its root, used in medicine or as a powder to kill insects. *n.*

Hel ene (hel′ēn), a Greek. *n.*

Hel len ic (he len′ik), 1 Greek. 2 of Greek history, language, or culture from 776 B.C. to the death of Alexander the Great in 323 B.C. *adj.*

Hel les pont (hel′i spont), ancient name for the Dardanelles. *n.*

hell ish (hel′ish), fit to have come from hell; devilish; fiendish: *hellish shrieks, a hellish thing to do. adj.* —**hell′ish ly,** *adv.* —**hell′ish ness,** *n.*

hel lo (he lō′ *or* hə lō′), 1 a call or exclamation to attract attention, express greeting, etc. We usually say "hello" when we call or answer a call on the telephone. *"Hello, Mother!" the boy said.* 2 a call or shout: *The girl gave a loud hello to let us know where she was.* 3 say or call "hello"; shout; call: *He asked us to hello until somebody came.* 1 *interj.,* 2 *n., pl.* **hel los;** 3 *v.*

helm[1] (helm), 1 handle or wheel by which a ship is steered. 2 the steering apparatus of a ship, including the wheel, rudder, and connecting parts. 3 position of control or guidance: *Upon the President's death, the Vice-President took the nation's helm. n.* [Old English *helma*]

helm[2] (helm), OLD USE. helmet. *n.* [Old English]

helmets worn by a knight,
a football player, and an astronaut

hel met (hel′mit), covering to protect the head. Knights wore helmets as part of their armor. Soldiers wear steel helmets; firemen often wear leather helmets. *n.*

helms man (helmz'mən), man who steers a ship. *n., pl.* **helms men.**

hel ot (hel'ət *or* hē'lət), 1 slave; serf. 2 **Helot**, member of a class of slaves or serfs in ancient Sparta. *n.*

help (help), 1 give or do what is needed or useful; give aid; assist: *My father helped me with my homework. We could finish the job faster if he would help.* 2 a helping or a being helped; aid; assistance: *I need some help with my work. The dying woman was beyond help.* 3 person or thing that helps; helper: *A sewing machine is a help in making clothes.* 4 a hired helper or group of hired helpers: *The storekeeper treats her help well.* 5 make better; relieve: *This medicine will help your cough.* 6 means of making better; remedy: *The medicine was a help.* 7 prevent; stop: *It can't be helped.* 8 avoid; keep from: *I can't help yawning.* 9 give food to; serve with food: *Help yourselves to some cake.* 1,5,7-9 *v.,* 2-4,6 *n.*

help out, help; help in doing or getting: *The children were asked to help out around the house.*

help er (hel'pər), 1 person who helps. 2 thing that helps. *n.*

help ful (help'fəl), giving help; useful. *adj.* —**help'ful ly,** *adv.* —**help'ful ness,** *n.*

help ing (hel'ping), portion of food served to a person at one time. *n.*

helping verb, auxiliary verb.

help less (help'lis), 1 not able to help oneself: *A little baby is helpless.* 2 without help or protection: *Though he was alone and helpless, he managed to keep the boat from sinking until help arrived.* —**help'less ly,** *adv.* —**help'less ness,** *n.*

help mate (help'māt'), companion and helper; wife or husband. *n.*

help meet (help'mēt'), helpmate. *n.*

Hel sin ki (hel'sing kē), seaport and capital of Finland, in the S part. *n.*

hel ter-skel ter (hel'tər skel'tər), 1 with headlong, disorderly haste: *The children ran helter-skelter when the dog rushed at them.* 2 disorderly; confused: *a helter-skelter way of playing a game.* 1 *adv.,* 2 *adj.*

helve (helv), handle of an ax, hammer, etc. *n.*

hem[1] (hem), 1 border or edge on a garment; edge made on cloth by folding it over and sewing it down. 2 fold over and sew down the edge of (cloth): *She hemmed six napkins.* 1 *n.,* 2 *v.,* **hemmed, hem ming.** [Old English *hemm*]

hem in, hem around, or **hem about,** close in or surround, and not let out.

hem[2] (hem), 1 sound like clearing the throat, used to attract attention or show doubt or hesitation: *Hem! I would like to say something (interj.). We ignored his hems since we didn't want to hear him speak (n.).* 2 make this sound. 1 *interj., n.,* 2 *v.,* **hemmed, hem ming.** [imitation of the sound]

hem and haw, 1 hesitate in speaking. 2 stall or put off.

hem a tite (hem'ə tīt), an important iron ore that is reddish-brown when powdered. *n.*

Hem ing way (hem'ing wā), **Ernest,** 1899-1961, American writer of novels and short stories. *n.*

hem i sphere (hem'ə sfir), 1 half of a sphere or globe. 2 half of the earth's surface. North America and South America are in the Western Hemisphere. Europe, Asia, Africa, and Australia are in the Eastern Hemisphere. All countries north of the equator are in the Northern Hemisphere, and the countries south of it are in the Southern Hemisphere. *n.*

hem i spher ic (hem'ə sfir'ik *or* hem'ə sfer'ik), hemispherical. *adj.*

hem i spher i cal (hem'ə sfir'ə kəl *or* hem'ə sfer'ə kəl), 1 shaped like a hemisphere. 2 of a hemisphere. *adj.*

hem lock (hem'lok), 1 a poisonous plant with spotted stems, finely divided leaves, and small white flowers. It belongs to the same family as the carrot. 2 poison made from it. 3 an evergreen tree of the same family as the pine, with small cones and drooping branches. Bark from hemlocks is used in tanning. 4 its wood. *n.*

he mo glo bin (hē'mə glō'bən *or* hem'ə glō'bən), substance in the red blood cells made up of iron and protein. It carries oxygen from the lungs to the tissues, and carbon dioxide from the tissues to the lungs. Hemoglobin gives blood its red color. *n.* Also, **haemoglobin.**

he mo phil i a (hē'mə fil'ē ə), an inherited disorder of the blood in males in which clotting does not occur normally, making it difficult to stop bleeding even after the slightest injury. *n.*

hem or rhage (hem'ər ij), 1 discharge of blood, especially a heavy discharge from a damaged blood vessel. A nosebleed is a mild hemorrhage. 2 have a hemorrhage; lose much blood. 1 *n.,* 2 *v.,* **hem or rhaged, hem or rhag ing.**

hemp (hemp), 1 a tall plant of Asia whose tough fibers are made into heavy string, rope, and coarse cloth. 2 the tough fibers of this plant. 3 hashish or other narcotic drug obtained from some kinds of hemp. *n.*

hemp en (hem'pən), 1 made of hemp. 2 like hemp. *adj.*

hat, āge, fär; let, ēqual, tėrm;
it, īce; hot, ōpen, ôrder;
oil, out; cup, půt, rüle; ch, child;
ng, long; sh, she; th, thin;
ᴛʜ, then; zh, measure;

ə represents *a* in about,
e in taken, *i* in pencil,
o in lemon, *u* in circus.

hemstitch (def. 1)

hem stitch (hem'stich'), 1 to hem along a line from which threads have been drawn out, gathering the cross threads into a series of little groups. 2 the stitch used. 3 ornamental needlework made by hemstitching. 1 *v.,* 2,3 *n., pl.* **hem stitch es** for 2.

hen (hen), 1 a female domestic fowl: *a hen and her chicks.* 2 female of other birds: *a hen sparrow.* *n.*

hence (hens), 1 as a result of this; therefore: *The king died, and hence his son became king.* 2 from now; from this time onward: *Come back a week hence.* 3 from here: *"Go hence, I pray thee."* 4 go away! *"Hence! foul fiend."* 1-3 *adv.,* 4 *interj.*

hence forth (hens'fôrth'), from this time on; from now on. *adv.*

hence for ward (hens'fôr'wərd), henceforth. *adv.*

hench man (hench'mən), 1 a trusted attendant or follower. 2 an obedient, unscrupulous follower. *n., pl.* **henchmen.**

hen e quen (hen'ə kin), 1 a yellow fiber from leaves of an agave of Yucatán, used for making twine, ropes, coarse fabrics, etc. 2 plant that yields this fiber. *n.*

hen house (hen'hous'), house for poultry. *n., pl.* **hen hous es** (hen'hou'-ziz).

hen na (hen'ə), 1 a reddish-brown dye used on the hair. 2 a small, thorny tree of Asia and Africa from whose leaves this dye is made. 3 a reddish brown. 4 reddish-brown. 5 dye or color with henna. 1-3 *n., pl.* **hen nas;** 4 *adj.,* 5 *v.,* **hen naed, hen na ing.**

hen peck (hen'pek'), domineer over: *He was henpecked by his wife.* *v.*

Hen ry (hen'rē), 1 **O.,** 1862-1910, American writer of short stories. His real name was **William Sydney Porter.** 2 **Patrick,** 1736-1799, American patriot, orator, and statesman. *n.*

adj.	adjective	*n.*	noun
adv.	adverb	*prep.*	preposition
conj.	conjunction	*pron.*	pronoun
interj.	interjection	*v.*	verb
sing.	singular	*pl.*	plural

Henry II, 1133-1189, king of England from 1154 to 1189. His church policies were opposed by Thomas à Becket.

Henry IV, 1553-1610, king of France from 1589 to 1610. He was known as "Henry of Navarre."

Henry VIII, 1491-1547, king of England from 1509 to 1547. He established the Church of England with himself as its head.

he pat i ca (hi pat′ə kə), a low plant with delicate purple, pink, or white flowers that bloom early in the spring; liverwort. *n., pl.* **he pat i cas.**

hep a ti tis (hep′ə tī′tis), inflammation of the liver. *n.*

regular heptagon   irregular heptagon

hep ta gon (hep′tə gon), a plane figure having seven angles and seven sides. *n.*

her (hèr; *unstressed* hər), 1 the girl, woman, or female animal spoken about: *She is not here; have you seen her? Find her.* 2 of her; belonging to her: *her book, her work.* 1 *pron.,* 2 *adj.*

Her a (hir′ə), (in Greek myths) a goddess who was the wife of Zeus. She was the queen of the gods and men and the goddess of marriage. The Romans called her Juno. *n.*

Her a cles (her′ə klēz′), Hercules. *n.*

her ald (her′əld), 1 person who carries messages and makes announcements; messenger. In former times, a herald was an official who made public announcements and carried messages between rulers, etc. *The king sent two heralds to the duke.* 2 bring news of; announce: *The newspapers heralded the arrival of the hero.* 3 person or thing that goes or is sent before and shows something more is coming; harbinger: *Dawn is the herald of day.* 1,3 *n.,* 2 *v.*

he ral dic (he ral′dik), of or having to do with heraldry or heralds. *adj.*

her ald ry (her′əl drē), 1 science or art dealing with coats of arms. Heraldry determines a person's right to use a coat

of arms, traces family descent, designs coats of arms for new countries, etc. 2 coat of arms. 3 ceremony or pomp connected with the life of noble families. *n., pl.* **her ald ries.**

herb (ėrb *or* hèrb), 1 plant whose leaves or stems are used for medicine, seasoning, food, or perfume. Sage, mint, and lavender are herbs. 2 a flowering plant whose stems live only one season. Herbs do not usually form woody tissue as shrubs and trees do. Lilies, corn, and onions are herbs. *n.*

her ba ceous (hèr′bā′shəs), of an herb; like an herb. *adj.*

herb age (ėr′bij *or* hèr′bij), herbs or grass. Cows graze on herbage in a pasture. *n.*

her bi vore (her′bə vôr), any animal that feeds mainly on plants. *n.*

her biv or ous (hèr′biv′ər əs), feeding on grass or other plants. Cattle are herbivorous animals. *adj.*

her cu le an *or* **Her cu le an** (her′-kyü′lē ən *or* hèr′kyə lē′ən), 1 of great strength, courage, or size; very powerful: *a herculean warrior.* 2 requiring great strength, courage, or size; very hard to do: *a herculean task.* 3 Herculean, of or having to do with Hercules. *adj.*

Her cu les (her′kyə lēz′), 1 (in Greek and Roman myths) a hero famous for his great strength and for the twelve great labors he performed. 2 Also, **hercules,** any person of great strength, courage, or size. Also, **Heracles.**

herd (hėrd), 1 group of animals of one kind, especially large animals, keeping, feeding, or moving together: *a herd of cows, a herd of horses, a herd of elephants.* 2 a large number of people. 3 the common people. 4 join together; flock together: *Several people herded under an awning to get out of the rain.* 5 form into a flock, herd, or group: *The farmer herded the cows over to the barn door.* 6 tend or take care of (cattle, sheep, etc.). 1-3 *n.,* 4-6 *v.*

herd er (hèr′dər), herdsman. *n.*

herds man (hèrdz′mən), man who takes care of a herd. *n., pl.* **herds men.**

here (hir), 1 in this place; at this place: *We will stop here. We live here in the summer.* 2 to this place: *Come here.* 3 this place: *Where do we go from here?* 4 at this time; now: *Here the speaker paused.* 5 in this life. 6 this life. 7 an answer showing that one is present when roll is called. 8 exclamation used to call attention to some person or thing: *"Here! take away the dishes."* 1,2,4,5 *adv.,* 3,6 *n.,* 7,8 *interj.*

here and there, in this place and that; at intervals.

here's to you! a wish for health or success.

neither here nor there, not to the point; off the subject; unimportant.

here a bout (hir′ə bout′), about this place; around here; near here. *adv.*

here a bouts (hir′ə bouts′), hereabout. *adv.*

here af ter (hir af′tər), 1 after this; in the future. 2 the future. 3 the life or time after death. 1 *adv.,* 2,3 *n.*

here by (hir bī′), by this; by this means; in this way: *The license said, "You are hereby given the right to hunt and fish in Dover County." adv.*

he red i tar y (hə red′ə ter′ē), 1 coming by inheritance: *"Prince" is a hereditary title.* 2 holding a position by inheritance: *The queen of England is a hereditary ruler.* 3 transmitted or caused by heredity: *Color blindness is hereditary.* 4 taken from one's parents or ancestors: *a hereditary custom or belief.* 5 having to do with inheritance or heredity. *adj.*

he red i ty (hə red′ə tē), 1 the passing on of physical or mental characteristics from parent to offspring by means of genes. 2 qualities of body and mind that have come to offspring from parents. *n., pl.* **he red i ties.**

Here ford (hèr′fərd), one of a breed of reddish-brown beef cattle having a white face and white markings under the body. *n.* [from *Hereford(shire),* a county in England]

here in (hir in′), 1 in this place. 2 in this matter; in this way. *adv.*

here of (hir ov′ *or* hir uv′), of this; about this. *adv.*

here on (hir on′), 1 on this. 2 immediately after this. *adv.*

here's (hirz), here is.

her e sy (her′ə sē), 1 belief different from the accepted belief of a church, school, profession, etc. 2 the holding of such a belief. *n., pl.* **her e sies.**

her e tic (her′ə tik), person who holds a belief that is different from the accepted belief of his church, school, profession, etc. *n.*

he ret i cal (hə ret′ə kəl), 1 of or having to do with heresy or heretics. 2 containing heresy; characterized by heresy. *adj.*

here to (hir tü′), to this place, thing, document, etc. *adv.*

here to fore (hir′tə fôr′), before this time; until now. *adv.*

here un to (hir′un tü′), to this place, thing, document, etc.; hereto. *adv.*

here up on (hir′ə pon′), 1 upon this thing, point, subject, or matter. 2 immediately after this. *adv.*

here with (hir wiŦH′ *or* hir with′), with this: *I am sending ten cents in stamps herewith. adv.*

her it a ble (her′ə tə bəl), 1 capable of being inherited: *heritable diseases,* *heritable tendencies.* 2 capable of inheriting. *adj.*

her it age (her′ə tij), what is handed down from one generation to the next; inheritance: *The heritage of freedom is precious to Americans. n.*

her maph ro dite (hər maf′rə dīt), animal or plant having both male and female reproductive organs. *n.*

Her mes (hėr′mēz), (in Greek myths) a god who was the messenger of Zeus and the other gods. He was the god of travel and commerce, of science and invention, of eloquence, luck, and cunning, and the patron of thieves and gamblers. The Romans called him Mercury. *n.*

her met ic (hər met′ik), closed tightly so that air cannot get in or out; airtight: *The bottle has a hermetic seal. adj.* —**her met′i cal ly,** *adv.*

her met i cal (hər met′ə kəl), hermetic. *adj.*

her mit (hėr′mit), person who goes away from others and lives alone. A hermit often lives a religious life. *n.*

her mit age (hėr′mə tij), home of a hermit. *n.*

hermit crab, crab with a soft body that lives in the empty shells of snails, whelks, etc., as a means of protection.

hermit thrush, a brown thrush of North America, with spotted breast and reddish tail, noted for its song.

her ni a (hėr′nē ə), protrusion of some tissue or organ of the body, especially a part of the intestine, through the wall of the cavity which should hold it in; rupture. *n., pl.* **her ni as.**

her o (hir′ō), 1 person admired for bravery, great deeds, or noble qualities: *Daniel Boone and Clara Barton are American heroes.* 2 the most important male person in a story, play, poem, motion picture, etc. *n., pl.* **her oes.**

Her od (her′əd), 73?-4 B.C., king of Judea from 37? to 4 B.C. Jesus was born during his reign. *n.*

He rod o tus (hə rod′ə təs), 484?-425? B.C., Greek historian. He is called the father of history. *n.*

he ro ic (hi rō′ik), 1 of, like, or suitable for a hero; brave, great, or noble: *the heroic deeds of our firemen.* 2 of or about heroes and their deeds: *The "Iliad" and the "Odyssey" are heroic poems.* 3 unusually daring or bold: *Heroic measures saved the town from the flood. adj.* —**he ro′i cal ly,** *adv.*

he ro i cal (hi rō′ə kəl), heroic. *adj.*

he ro ics (hi rō′iks), words or actions that seem grand or noble, but are only for effect. *n.pl.*

her o in (her′ō ən), a very dangerous, habit-forming drug made from morphine. *n.*

her o ine (her′ō ən), 1 woman or girl admired for her bravery, great deeds, or

noble qualities. 2 the most important female person in a story, play, poem, motion picture, etc. *n.*

her o ism (her′ō iz′əm), 1 actions and qualities of a hero or heroine; great bravery; daring courage. 2 a doing something noble at great cost to oneself; a very brave act. *n.*

her on (her′ən), a wading bird with a long neck, a long bill, and long legs. Herons feed on fish, frogs, etc. *n.*

heron
about 4 ft. tall

her pe tol o gist (hėr′pə tol′ə jist), an expert in herpetology. *n.*

her pe tol o gy (hėr′pə tol′ə jē), branch of zoology dealing with reptiles and amphibians. *n.*

Herr (her), GERMAN. 1 Mr.; Sir. 2 gentleman. *n., pl.* **Her ren** (her′ən).

her ring (her′ing), a small food fish of the northern Atlantic. The grown fish are eaten fresh, salted, or smoked, and the young are canned as sardines. *n., pl.* **her rings** or **her ring.**

her ring bone (her′ing bōn′), 1 having a zigzag pattern or arrangement like the spine of a herring. 2 a zigzag pattern, arrangement, or stitch. 1 *adj.,* 2 *n.*

herringbone
(def. 2)

hers (hėrz), the one or ones belonging to her: *This money is hers. Your answers are wrong; hers are right. pron.*

her self (hər self′), 1 form of *she* or *her* used to make a statement stronger: *She did it herself. She herself bought the book.* 2 form used instead of *she* or *her* in cases like: *She hurt herself. She did it by herself.* 3 her real or true self: *She is so tired that she's not herself. pron.*

hertz (hėrts), unit of frequency equal to one cycle per second. *n.*

he's (hēz; *unstressed* ēz), 1 he is. 2 he has.

hes i tan cy (hez′ə tən sē), hesitation; tendency to hesitate. *n., pl.* **hes i tan cies.**

hes i tant (hez′ə tənt), hesitating; doubtful; undecided: *She was hesitant about accepting the invitation. adj.* —**hes′i tant ly,** *adv.*

hes i tate (hez′ə tāt), 1 fail to act

promptly; hold back because one feels doubtful or undecided; show that one has not yet made up one's mind: *I hesitated about taking his side until I knew the whole story.* 2 feel that perhaps one should not; be unwilling; not want: *I hesitated to ask you; you were so busy.* 3 stop for an instant; pause: *He hesitated before asking the question.* 4 speak with short stops or pauses; stammer. *v.,* **hes i tat ed, hes i tating.** —**hes′i tat′ing ly,** *adv.*

hes i ta tion (hez′ə tā′shən), 1 a hesitating; doubt; indecision; unwillingness; delay. 2 a speaking with short stops or pauses. *n.*

Hes per i des (he sper′ə dēz′), (in Greek myths) the nymphs who guarded the golden apples of Hera. *n.pl.*

Hes per us (hes′pər əs), Venus, when it appears as the evening star. *n.*

Hesse (hes *or* hes′ə), district in central West Germany. *n.*

Hes sian (hesh′ən), 1 of Hesse or its people. 2 person born or living in Hesse. 3 a German soldier hired by England to fight against the Americans during the Revolutionary War. 1 *adj.,* 2,3 *n.*

het er o dox (het′ər ə doks), rejecting generally accepted beliefs or doctrines, especially in a religion; not orthodox. *adj.*

het er o dox y (het′ər ə dok′sē), 1 rejection of generally accepted beliefs or doctrines, especially in a religion; opposite of orthodoxy. 2 belief or doctrine not in agreement with what is generally accepted. *n., pl.* **het er o dox ies.**

het er o ge ne ous (het′ər ə jē′nē əs), 1 different in kind; unlike; varied: *She invited a heterogeneous group of people to her party.* 2 composed of unlike elements or parts; miscellaneous: *Tin cans, old shoes, and papers made a heterogeneous mass of rubbish in the yard. adj.* —**het′er o ge′ne ous ly,** *adv.*

hew (hyü), 1 cut with an ax, sword, etc.; chop: *He hewed down the tree.* 2 cut into shape; form by cutting with an ax, etc.: *hew stone for building, hew*

hat, āge, fär; let, ēqual, tèrm;
it, īce; hot, ōpen, ôrder;
oil, out; cup, pùt, rüle; ch, child;
ng, long; sh, she; th, thin;
ᴛH, then; zh, measure;

ə represents *a* in about,
e in taken, *i* in pencil,
o in lemon, *u* in circus.

adj. adjective	*n.* noun
adv. adverb	*prep.* preposition
conj. conjunction	*pron.* pronoun
interj. interjection	*v.* verb
sing. singular	*pl.* plural

logs into beams. *v.,* **hewed, hewed** or **hewn, hew ing. —hew′er,** *n.*

hewn (hyün), hewed; a past participle of **hew.** *v.*

hex (heks), INFORMAL. **1** practice witchcraft on; bewitch. **2** witch. **3** a magic spell. **1** *v.,* **2,3** *n., pl.* **hex es.**

regular hexagon   irregular hexagon

hex a gon (hek′sə gon), a plane figure having six angles and six sides. *n.*

hex ag o nal (hek sag′ə nəl), having the form of a hexagon. *adj.* —**hex ag′o nal ly,** *adv.*

hex a he dron (hek′sə hē′drən), a solid figure having six faces. *n., pl.* **hex a he drons, hex a he dra** (hek′sə hē′drə).

hexahedrons—A, regular; B, C, irregular

hex am e ter (hek sam′ə tər), line of poetry consisting of six feet or measures. EXAMPLE: "This′ is the| fo′rest pri | me′val. The| mur′mur ing| pines′ and the | hem′locks." *n.*

hey (hā), sound made to attract attention, to express surprise or other feeling, or to ask a question: *"Hey! stop!" "Hey! there's our teacher."* *interj.*

hey day (hā′dā′), period of greatest strength, vigor, spirits, prosperity, etc. *n.*

Hez e ki ah (hez′ə kī′ə), (in the Bible) a king of Judah. *n.*

hi (hī), a call of greeting; hello. *interj.*

H.I., Hawaiian Islands.

hi a tus (hī ā′təs), an empty space; space that needs to be filled; gap: *After the accident there was a hiatus of several hours in his memory of that day's events.* *n., pl.* **hi a tus es** or **hi a tus.**

Hi a wath a (hī′ə woth′ə), the young Indian brave who is the hero of Longfellow's poem *Hiawatha.* *n.*

hi ber nate (hī′bər nāt), spend the winter in sleep or in an inactive condition, as bears, woodchucks, and some other wild animals do. *v.,* **hi ber nat ed, hi ber nat ing.**

hi ber na tion (hī′bər nā′shən), a hibernating. *n.*

hi bis cus (hī bis′kəs), plant, shrub, or tree of the same family as the mallow, with large, red, pink, or white, bell-shaped flowers. *n., pl.* **hi bis cus es.**

hic cough (hik′up), hiccup. *n., v.*

hic cup (hik′up), **1** an involuntary catching of the breath with a sharp, clicking sound, caused by a muscular spasm of the diaphragm. **2 hiccups,** *pl.* condition of having one hiccup after another. **3** have the hiccups. **1,2** *n.,* **3** *v.,* **hic cupped, hic cup ping.**

hick or y (hik′ər ē), **1** any of a group of North American trees of the same family as the walnut, whose hard nuts are good to eat. **2** the tough, hard wood of any of these trees. *n., pl.* **hick or ies.**

hid (hid), past tense and a past participle of **hide¹.** *The dog hid his bone. The money was hid in a safe place.* *v.*

hi dal go (hi dal′gō), a Spanish nobleman ranking below a grandee. *n., pl.* **hi dal gos.**

hid den (hid′n), **1** put or kept out of sight; concealed; secret: *The story is about hidden treasure.* **2** a past participle of **hide¹.** *The moon was hidden behind a dark cloud.* **1** *adj.,* **2** *v.*

hide¹ (hīd), **1** put or keep out of sight; conceal: *Hide it where no one else will ever be able to find it.* **2** cover up; shut off from sight: *Clouds hide the sun.* **3** keep secret: *She hid her disappointment.* **4** hide oneself: *I'll hide, and you find me.* *v.,* **hid, hid den** or **hid, hid ing.** [Old English *hȳdan*]

hide² (hīd), **1** an animal's skin, either raw or tanned. Leather is made from the hides of cattle. **2** INFORMAL. a person's skin: *He tried to save his own hide by putting the blame on us.* **3** INFORMAL. beat; thrash. **1,2** *n.,* **3** *v.,* **hid ed, hid ing.** [Old English *hȳd*]

hide-and-go-seek (hīd′n gō sēk′), hide-and-seek. *n.*

hide-and-seek (hīd′n sēk′), a children's game in which all but one of the players hide and he tries to find them. *n.*

hide a way (hīd′ə wā′), place for hiding or being alone. *n.*

hide bound (hīd′bound′), narrow-minded and stubborn: *Some people are too hidebound to accept new ideas even when they are good.* *adj.*

hid e ous (hid′ē əs), very ugly; frightful; horrible: *a hideous monster, a hideous crime.* *adj.* —**hid′e ous ly,** *adv.* —**hid′e ous ness,** *n.*

hide-out (hīd′out′), place for hiding or being alone. *n.*

hid ing¹ (hī′ding), **1** a being hidden; concealment: *The fox remained in hiding.* **2** place to hide. *n.* [*hide¹* + *-ing¹*]

hid ing² (hī′ding), INFORMAL. a beating; thrashing. *n.* [*hide²* + *-ing¹*]

hie (hī), go quickly; hasten; hurry: *hie oneself to work.* *v.,* **hied, hie ing** or **hy ing.**

hi e rar chy (hī′ə rär′kē), **1** organization of persons or things arranged into higher and lower ranks, classes, or grades. **2** government by priests or church officials. **3** group of church officials of different ranks. The church hierarchy is composed of archbishops, bishops, priests, etc. *n., pl.* **hi e rar chies.**

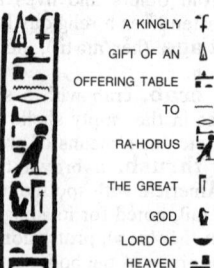

Egyptian hieroglyphics (defs. 1 and 2a)

hi er o glyph ic (hī′ər ə glif′ik), **1** picture, character, or symbol standing for a word, idea, or sound. The ancient Egyptians used hieroglyphics instead of an alphabet like ours. **2 hieroglyphics,** *pl.* **a** writing that uses hieroglyphics. **b** writing that is hard to read. **3** a secret symbol. **4** of or written in hieroglyphics. **1-3** *n.,* **4** *adj.*

hi-fi (hī′fī′), INFORMAL. **1** high fidelity. **2** equipment for high fidelity. **3** of or for high fidelity. **1,2** *n.,* **3** *adj.*

hig gle dy-pig gle dy (hig′əl dē-pig′əl dē), **1** in jumbled confusion. **2** jumbled; confused. **1** *adv.,* **2** *adj.*

high (hī), **1** having height; rising up; tall: *a high building. The mountain is over 20,000 feet high.* **2** above or far above the ground: *an airplane high in the air, a high leap, a high dive.* **3** up above others: *a high official. A general has high rank. Washington was a man of high character.* **4** greater or stronger than others; great: *a high price, high temperature, high winds, high speed.* **5** most important; chief; main: *the high altar.* **6** extreme of its kind; serious; grave: *high treason, high crimes.* **7** not low in pitch; shrill; sharp: *a high voice.* **8** at or to a high point, place, rank, amount, degree, price, pitch, etc.: *The eagle flies high. Strawberries come high in winter.* **9** a high point, level, position, etc.: *Food prices reached a new high last month.* **10** arrangement of gears to give the greatest speed. **1-7** *adj.,* **8** *adv.,* **9,10** *n.*

high and dry, 1 up out of water: *The boat ran ashore, high and dry.* **2** all alone; without help; stranded.

high and low, everywhere: *She searched high and low for her pen.*

on high, 1 high above; up in the air: *On high, clouds were gathering.* **2** in heaven.

high born (hī/bôrn/), of noble birth. *adj.*

high boy (hī/boi/), a tall chest of drawers on legs. *n.*

high brow (hī/brou/), INFORMAL. **1** person who cares or claims to care a great deal about knowledge and culture. **2** of or fit for a highbrow. **1** *n.,* **2** *adj.*

high fa lu tin (hī/fə lüt/n), INFORMAL. high-sounding; pompous. *adj.*

high fidelity, reproduction of sound by a radio or phonograph with as little distortion of the original sound as possible.

high-flown (hī/flōn/), **1** aspiring; extravagant: *high-flown ideas.* **2** attempting to be elegant or eloquent: *high-flown compliments. adj.*

high-grade (hī/grād/), of fine quality; superior: *high-grade oil. adj.*

high-hand ed (hī/han/did), acting or done in a bold, arbitrary way; overbearing: *high-handed methods. adj.* —**high/-hand/ed ly,** *adv.* —**high/-hand/ed ness,** *n.*

high hat, top hat.

high-hat (hī/hat/), SLANG. **1** treat as inferior; snub. **2** snobbish. **1** *v.,* **high-hat ted, high-hat ting; 2** *adj.*

high jump
(def. 2)

high jump, 1 an athletic contest or event to determine how high each contestant can jump over a raised crossbar. **2** the jump itself.

high land (hī/lənd), **1** country or region that is higher and hillier than the neighboring country; land high above sea level. **2 Highlands,** *pl.* a mountainous region in N and W Scotland. *n.*

high land er (hī/lən dər), **1** person born or living in a highland. **2 Highlander,** person born or living in the Highlands of Scotland. *n.*

Highland fling, a lively dance of the Highlands of Scotland.

high light (hī/līt/), **1** cast a bright light on. **2** effect or representation of

bright light. **3** part of a painting, photograph, etc., in which light is represented as falling with greatest intensity. **4** the most prominent or interesting part, event, scene, etc.: *The highlight of the circus was the trained-dog act.* **5** make prominent. **1,5** *v.,* **high light ed, high light ing; 2-4** *n.*

high ly (hī/lē), **1** in a high degree; very much; very: *highly amusing, highly recommended.* **2** very favorably: *He spoke highly of his best friend.* **3** at a high rate or price: *highly paid.* **4** in or to a high position or rank: *a highly placed government official. adv.*

high-mind ed (hī/mīn/did), **1** having or showing high principles and feelings. **2** OLD USE. proud. *adj.*

high ness (hī/nis), **1** a being high; height. **2 Highness,** title of honor given to members of royal families: *The Prince of Wales is addressed as "Your Highness" and spoken of as "His Royal Highness." n.*

high-pitched (hī/picht/), **1** of high tone or sound; shrill: *a high-pitched voice.* **2** having a steep slope: *a high-pitched roof. adj.*

high-pow ered (hī/pou/ərd), having much power: *a high-powered car, a high-powered rifle. adj.*

high-pres sure (hī/presh/ər), **1** having, using, or resisting more than the usual pressure: *a high-pressure boiler.* **2** using strong, vigorous methods: *high-pressure selling.* **3** use strong, vigorous methods on, in selling, etc.: *high-pressure a customer.* **1,2** *adj.,* **3** *v.,* **high-pres sured, high-pres sur ing.**

high road (hī/rōd/), a main road; highway. *n.*

high school, school attended after elementary school or junior high school; secondary school. High school consists of grades 9 through 12 or 10 through 12.

high seas, the open ocean. The high seas are outside the jurisdiction of any country.

high-sound ing (hī/soun/ding), having an imposing or pretentious sound. *adj.*

high-spir it ed (hī/spir/ə tid), **1** proud or courageous: *a high-spirited people.* **2** spirited; fiery: *a high-spirited horse. adj.*

high spirits, happiness; cheerfulness; gaiety: *The team was in high spirits after winning the game.*

high-strung (hī/strung/), very sensitive or nervous; easily excited. *adj.*

hight (hīt), OLD USE. named; called. *adj.*

high-ten sion (hī/ten/shən), having or using a high voltage: *high-tension wires. adj.*

hat, āge, fär; let, ēqual, tèrm;
it, īce; hot, ōpen, ôrder;
oil, out; cup, pùt, rüle; ch, child;
ng, long; sh, she; th, thin;
ᴛʜ, then; zh, measure;

ə represents *a* in about,
e in taken, *i* in pencil,
o in lemon, *u* in circus.

high-test (hī/test/), that passes some test; of good quality: *high-test gasoline. adj.*

high tide, 1 the highest level of the tide. **2** time when the tide is highest.

high time, time just before it is too late: *It is high time for you to begin studying harder.*

high way (hī/wā/), **1** a public road. **2** a main road or route. *n.*

high way man (hī/wā/mən), man who robs travelers on a public road. *n., pl.* **high way men.**

hi jack (hī/jak/), rob or take by force (goods in transit, an airplane in flight, etc.). *v.* —**hi/jack/er,** *n.*

hike (hīk), **1** take a long walk; tramp or march. **2** a long walk; tramp or march: *It was a four-mile hike to the camp.* **3** INFORMAL. raise with a jerk; hitch: *Hike up your socks.* **4** INFORMAL. raise; increase: *The company is going to hike wages.* **1,3,4** *v.,* **hiked, hik ing; 2** *n.*

hik er (hī/kər), person who hikes or goes on a hike. *n.*

hi lar i ous (hə ler/ē əs *or* hə lar/ē əs), very merry; noisily gay: *a hilarious tale, a hilarious party. adj.* —**hi lar/i ous ly,** *adv.* —**hi lar/i ous ness,** *n.*

hi lar i ty (hə lar/ə tē), great merriment; noisy gaiety. *n.*

hill (hil), **1** a raised part of the earth's surface, smaller than a mountain. **2** a little heap or pile: *Ants and moles make hills. The soil put over and around the roots of a plant is a hill.* **3** a plant with a little heap of soil over and around its roots: *a hill of corn. n.*

Hil lar y (hil/ər ē), Sir **Edmund,** born 1919, New Zealand mountain climber who climbed Mount Everest in 1953. *n.*

hill bil ly (hil/bil/ē), INFORMAL. person who lives in the backwoods or a mountain region, especially in the southern United States. *n., pl.* **hill bil lies.**

hill i ness (hil/ē nis), hilly quality or condition. *n.*

hill ock (hil/ək), a little hill. *n.*

hill side (hil/sīd/), side of a hill. *n.*

hill top (hil/top/), top of a hill. *n.*

hill y (hil/ē), **1** having many hills: *hilly country.* **2** like a hill; steep: *a hilly slope. adj.,* **hill i er, hill i est.**

adj. adjective	*n.* noun
adv. adverb	*prep.* preposition
conj. conjunction	*pron.* pronoun
interj. interjection	*v.* verb
sing. singular	*pl.* plural

HILT

hilt (hilt), handle of a sword, dagger, or tool. *n.*

to the hilt, thoroughly; completely: *She was involved to the hilt in politics.*

hi lum (hī′ləm), mark or scar on a seed at the point of attachment to the plant. *n., pl.* **hi la** (hī′lə).

him (him; *unstressed* im), the boy, man, or male animal spoken about: *Take him home. Give him a drink. Go to him.* *pron.*

Him a la yan (him′ə lā′ən *or* hə-mä′lyən), of or having to do with the Himalayas. *adj.*

Him a la yas (him′ə lā′əz *or* hə-mä′lyəz), mountain range along the N borders of India and Pakistan. Mount Everest, the world's highest mountain, is in the Himalayas. *n.pl.*

him self (him self′ *or, except when following a pause,* im self′), 1 form of *he* or *him* used to make a statement stronger: *He himself did it. Did you see John himself?* 2 form used instead of *he* or *him* in cases like: *He cut himself. He cared more for himself than for anybody else.* 3 his real or true self: *He feels like himself again. pron.*

hind[1] (hīnd), back; rear: *hind legs. adj.,* **hind er, hind most** or **hind er most.** [perhaps from *hinder*[2]]

hind[2] (hīnd), a female deer, especially a female red deer in and after its third year. *n., pl.* **hinds** or **hind.** [Old English]

Hin den burg (hin′dən bėrg′), **Paul von,** 1847-1934, German general and field marshal, president of Germany from 1925 to 1934. *n.*

hin der[1] (hin′dər), keep back; hold back; get in the way of; make hard to do; stop: *Deep mud hindered travel. v.* [Old English *hindrian*]

hind er[2] (hīn′dər), hind; back; rear. *adj.* [Old English]

hind er most (hīn′dər mōst), hindmost. *adj.*

Hin di (hin′dē), the official language of India. It is a form of Hindustani. *n.*

hind most (hīnd′mōst), farthest back; nearest the rear; last. *adj.*

hind quar ter (hīnd′kwôr′tər), 1 the rear half of a side of beef, veal, lamb, etc., including the leg, loin, and one or more ribs. 2 **hindquarters,** *pl.* the rear part of an animal's body, including the lower back, buttocks, and thighs; haunches. *n.*

hin drance (hin′drəns), 1 person or thing that hinders; obstacle: *If you won't help, don't be a hindrance. Noise was a hindrance to our studying.* 2 act of hindering. *n.*

hind sight (hīnd′sīt′), ability to see, after the event is over, what should have been done. *n.*

Hin du (hin′dü), 1 native or inhabitant of India. 2 having to do with the Hindus, their language, or their religion. 3 person who believes in Hinduism. 1,3 *n., pl.* **Hin dus;** 2 *adj.*

Hin du ism (hin′dü iz′əm), the religious and social system of the Hindus. The caste system and the worship of many gods are parts of Hinduism. *n.*

Hin du stan (hin′dù stan′), a Persian name for India. *n.*

Hin du stan i (hin′dù stan′ē), 1 of or having to do with India, its people, or their languages. 2 the commonest language of northern India. 1 *adj.,* 2 *n.*

hinge (def. 1)

hinge (hinj), 1 joint on which a door, gate, cover, lid, etc., swings back and forth. 2 furnish with hinges; attach by hinges. 3 hang or turn on a hinge. 4 depend: *The success of the picnic hinges on the kind of weather we will have.* 1 *n.,* 2-4 *v.,* **hinged, hing ing.**

hint (hint), 1 a slight sign; indirect suggestion: *A small black cloud gave a hint of a coming storm.* 2 give a slight sign of; suggest indirectly: *She hinted that she wanted to go to bed by saying, "Do you often stay up this late?"* 1 *n.,* 2 *v.*

hin ter land (hin′tər land′), 1 land or district behind a coast. 2 region far from towns and cities; thinly settled country. *n.*

hip[1] (hip), 1 the fleshy part that sticks out on each side of the body below the waist, where the leg joins the body. 2 a similar part in animals, where the hind leg joins the body. *n.* [Old English *hype*]

hip[2] (hip), seedcase containing the ripe seed of a rose. *n.* [Old English *hēope*]

hip bone (hip′bōn′), either of the two wide, irregular bones which, with the lower backbone, form the pelvis. See **pelvis** for diagram. *n.*

hip pie (hip′ē), person who rejects the usual social customs. Most hippies are young, have long hair, live in groups, and wear unusual clothing. *n.*

Hip poc ra tes (hi pok′rə tēz′), 460?-377? B.C., Greek physician, called "the father of medicine." *n.*

hip po drome (hip′ə drōm), 1 (in ancient Greece and Rome) an oval track for horse races and chariot races, surrounded by tiers of seats for spectators. 2 arena or building for a circus, rodeo, etc. *n.*

hippopotamus—about 13 ft. long

hip po pot a mus (hip′ə pot′ə məs), a huge, hairless mammal with a thick skin, found in and near the rivers of Africa. It often weighs as much as four tons. Hippopotamuses feed on plants and can stay under water for a long time. *n., pl.* **hip po pot a mus es, hip po pot a mi** (hip′ə pot′ə mī).

hire (hīr), 1 pay for the use of (a thing) or the work or services of (a person): *He hired a car and a man to drive it. The storekeeper hired four boys to deliver groceries.* 2 payment for the use of a thing or the work or services of a person: *Do you perform in plays for hire or just for pleasure?* 1 *v.,* **hired, hir ing;** 2 *n.*

hire out, give one's work in return for payment: *hire out as a house painter.*

hire ling (hīr′ling), person who works only for money, without interest or pride in the work. *n.*

Hir o hi to (hir′ō hē′tō), born 1901, emperor of Japan since 1926. *n.*

Hir o shi ma (hir′ō shē′mə), seaport in W Japan, largely destroyed by the first atomic bomb to be used in war, on August 6, 1945. *n.*

hir sute (hėr′süt), hairy. *adj.*

his (hiz; *unstressed* iz), 1 of him; belonging to him: *This is his book.* 2 the one or ones belonging to him: *My books are new; his are old.* 1 *adj.,* 2 *pron.*

His pan ic (hi span′ik), person of Spanish-American descent, who speaks Spanish as a native language. *n.*

His pan io la (his′pə nyō′lə), the second largest island in the West Indies, between Cuba and Puerto Rico. It is divided into the Dominican Republic and Haiti. See **Caribbean Sea** for map. *n.*

hiss (his), 1 make a sound like *ss* or like a drop of water on a hot stove: *Air or steam rushing out of a small opening hisses. Geese and snakes hiss. People sometimes hiss to show disapproval or scorn.* 2 a sound like *ss: Hisses were heard from many who disliked what the speaker was saying.* 3 show disapproval of by hissing: *The audience hissed the dull play.* 4 force or drive by hissing: *They hissed her off the stage.* 1,3,4 *v.,* 2 *n., pl.* **hiss es.**

hist (hist), be still! listen!: *Hist! Did you hear that noise in the distance? interj.*

his to ri an (hi stôr′ē ən), person who writes about history; expert in history. *n.*

his to ric (hi stôr′ik), 1 famous or important in history: *Plymouth Rock and Bunker Hill are historic spots.* 2 historical. *adj.*

his to ri cal (hi stôr′ə kəl), 1 of history; having to do with history: *historical documents.* 2 according to history; based on history: *a historical novel.* 3 known to be real or true; in history, not in legend: *It is a historical fact that in 1920 women in the United States were granted the right to vote.* 4 famous in history; historic: *a historical town. adj.*

his to ri cal ly (hi stôr′ik lē), according to history; as history. *adv.*

his tor y (his′tər ē), 1 story or record of important past events connected with a person or a nation: *the history of the United States.* 2 a known past: *This ship has a history.* 3 all past events considered together; course of human affairs: *the lessons of history.* 4 branch of knowledge or study that deals with past events: *a class in history.* 5 statement of what has happened; account. *n., pl.* **his tor ies.**

his tri on ic (his′trē on′ik), 1 having to do with actors or acting. 2 theatrical; insincere. *adj.*

his tri on ics (his′trē on′iks), 1 dramatic representation; theatricals; dramatics. 2 a theatrical or insincere manner, expression, etc. *n. sing. or pl.*

hit (hit), 1 come against with force; give a blow to; strike; knock: *He hit the ball with the bat. The ball hit against the window. She hit out at the fly buzzing around her head.* 2 a blow; stroke: *The hit on his head knocked him out.* 3 get to (what is aimed at): *Her second arrow hit the bull's-eye.* 4 a getting to what is aimed at. 5 come upon; meet with; reach or find: *We hit the right road in the dark. The boys hit upon a plan for making money.* 6 have a painful effect on; affect severely: *The storekeeper was*

hard hit by the failure of her business. 7 a successful attempt, performance, or production: *The new play is the hit of the season.* 8 a successful hitting of the baseball by a batter so that he gets at least to first base without the help of an error and without forcing out one of his teammates. 1,3,5,6 *v.,* **hit, hit ting;** 2,4,7,8 *n.*

hit it off, get along well together; agree: *The two boys hit it off from the start.*

hit-and-run (hit′n run′), having to do with hitting a person or vehicle and driving away without stopping to see what happened: *a hit-and-run driver, a hit-and-run accident. adj.*

hitch (hich), 1 fasten with a hook, ring, rope, strap, etc.: *She hitched her horse to a post.* 2 become fastened or caught; fasten; catch: *A knot made the rope hitch.* 3 a fastening; catch: *The hitch joining the plow to the tractor is broken.* 4 kind of knot used for temporary fastening. 5 move or pull with a jerk: *He hitched his chair nearer to the fire.* 6 a short, sudden pull or jerk: *The sailor gave his trousers a hitch.* 7 obstacle; hindrance: *A hitch in their plans made them miss the train.* 8 INFORMAL. get (a ride) by hitchhiking. 1,2,5,8 *v.,* 3,4,6,7 *n., pl.* **hitch es.**

hitch hike (hich′hīk′), travel by walking and getting free rides from passing automobiles, trucks, etc. *v.,* **hitch hiked, hitch hik ing.**

hitch hik er (hich′hī′kər), person who hitchhikes. *n.*

hith er (hiŦH′ər), 1 to this place; here: *Come hither, child.* 2 on or toward this side; nearer. 1 *adv.,* 2 *adj.*

hither and thither, here and there.

hith er to (hiŦH′ər tü′), until now: *a fact hitherto unknown. adv.*

hith er ward (hiŦH′ər wərd), toward this place; hither. *adv.*

Hit ler (hit′lər), **Adolf,** 1889-1945, German dictator, born in Austria, ruler of Nazi Germany from 1933 to 1945. *n.*

hit ter (hit′ər), person or thing that hits. *n.*

Hit tite (hit′īt), member of an ancient people in Asia Minor and Syria. Their civilization existed from about 2000 B.C. until about 1200 B.C. They were conquered by the Assyrians. *n.*

hive (def. 1)
two kinds
of hives

hive (hīv), 1 house or box for honeybees to live in; beehive. 2 a large number of bees living in such a place: *The whole hive was busy.* 3 put (bees) in a hive. 4 a busy, swarming place full of

people or animals: *a hive of industry.* 5 live close together as bees do. 1,2,4 *n.,* 3,5 *v.,* **hived, hiv ing.**

hives (hīvz), condition in which the skin itches and shows raised patches of red. It is usually caused by an allergy to some food or drug. *n.*

ho (hō), 1 exclamation of surprise, joy, or scornful laughter. 2 exclamation to get attention: *Ho! Listen to this! interj.*

hoar (hôr), hoary. *adj.*

hoard (hôrd), 1 save and store away: *A squirrel hoards nuts for the winter. The wealthy old woman hoarded her money.* 2 what is saved and stored away; things stored: *She has a hoard of candy.* 1 *v.,* 2 *n.* —**hoard′er,** *n.*

hoar frost (hôr′frôst′), feathery crystals of ice formed when dew freezes; white frost; rime. *n.*

hoar hound (hôr′hound′), horehound. *n.*

hoar i ness (hôr′ē nis), hoary quality or condition. *n.*

hoarse (hôrs), 1 sounding rough and deep: *the hoarse croak of the bullfrog.* 2 having a rough voice: *A bad cold has made her hoarse. adj.,* **hoars er, hoars est.** —**hoarse′ly,** *adv.* —**hoarse′ness,** *n.*

hoar y (hôr′ē), 1 white or gray. 2 white or gray with age: *hoary hair.* 3 old; ancient: *the hoary ruins of a castle. adj.,* **hoar i er, hoar i est.**

hoax (hōks), 1 a mischievous trick, especially a made-up story passed off as true: *The report of an attack on the earth from Mars was a hoax.* 2 play a mischievous trick on; deceive. 1 *n., pl.* **hoax es;** 2 *v.*

hob[1] (hob), shelf at the back or side of a fireplace. Food can be kept warm by placing it on the hob. *n.* [origin uncertain]

hob[2] (hob), hobgoblin; elf. *n.* [from *Hob,* nickname for *Robin* or *Robert*]

play hob or **raise hob,** INFORMAL. cause trouble: *The bad weather played hob with our plans for a picnic.*

Ho bart (hō′bärt), capital of Tasmania, in the S part. *n.*

hob ble (hob′əl), 1 walk awkwardly;

adj.	adjective	*n.*	noun
adv.	adverb	*prep.*	preposition
conj.	conjunction	*pron.*	pronoun
interj.	interjection	*v.*	verb
sing.	singular	*pl.*	plural

hobble (def. 4)

limp: *hobble around with a broken toe.* 2 a limping walk. 3 tie the legs of (a horse, etc.) together: *They hobbled the horses at night so that they would not wander away.* 4 rope or strap used to hobble a horse or other animal. 5 hinder. 1,3,5 *v.*, **hob bled, hobbling;** 2,4 *n.*

hob by (hob′ē), something a person especially likes to work at or study which is not his main business or occupation; favorite pastime: *Growing roses is that lawyer's hobby.* *n.*, *pl.* **hob bies.**

hob by horse (hob′ē hôrs′), 1 stick with a horse's head, used as a toy horse by children. 2 rocking horse. *n.*

hob gob lin (hob′gob′lən), 1 goblin; elf. 2 bogy. *n.*

hob nail (hob′nāl′), a short nail with a large head to protect the soles of heavy boots and shoes. *n.*

hob nob (hob′nob′), be on familiar terms; associate intimately: *They hobnob with some important people.* *v.*, **hob nobbed, hob nob bing.**

ho bo (hō′bō), person who wanders about and lives by begging or doing odd jobs; tramp. *n.*, *pl.* **ho bos** or **ho boes.**

Ho Chi Minh (hō′ chē′ min′), 1890?-1969, Vietnamese political leader, president of North Vietnam from 1954 to 1969.

hock[1] (hok), joint in the hind leg of a horse, cow, etc., corresponding to the ankle of man. *n.* [Old English *hōh*]

hock[2] (hok), SLANG. pawn. *v.*, *n.* [perhaps from Dutch *hok* pen, jail]

hock ey (hok′ē), game played by two teams on ice or on a field. The players hit a puck or ball with curved sticks to drive it across a goal.

ho cus-po cus (hō′kəs pō′kəs), 1 a meaningless form of words used in per-

forming magic tricks. 2 trickery; deception. *n.*

hod (hod), 1 trough or tray on top of a long, straight handle, used for carrying bricks, mortar, etc., on the shoulder. 2 coal scuttle. *n.*

hodge podge (hoj′poj′), a disorderly mixture; mess; jumble. *n.*

hoe (hō), 1 tool with a thin blade set across the end of a long handle, used for loosening soil, cutting weeds, etc. 2 loosen, dig, or cut with a hoe. 3 use a hoe. 1 *n.*, 2,3 *v.*, **hoed, hoe ing.**

hoe cake (hō′kāk′), kind of bread made of corn meal. *n.*

hog (hog), 1 pig. 2 a full-grown pig, raised for its meat. 3 INFORMAL. a selfish, greedy, or dirty person. 4 SLANG. take more than one's share of. 1-3 *n.*, 4 *v.*, **hogged, hog ging.**

ho gan (hō′gän′), dwelling used by the Navaho Indians. Hogans are built with logs and covered with earth. *n.*

Ho garth (hō′gärth), **William,** 1697-1764, English painter and engraver. *n.*

hog gish (hog′ish), 1 very selfish or greedy. 2 dirty; filthy. *adj.* —**hog′gish ly,** *adv.* —**hog′gish ness,** *n.*

hog nose snake (hog′nōz′), a harmless North American snake with an upturned snout; adder.

hogs head (hogz′hed′), 1 a large barrel or cask. In the United States, a hogshead contains from 63 to 140 gallons. 2 a liquid measure equal to 63 gallons. *n.*

Ho hen zol lern (hō′ən zol′ərn), member of a German princely family, prominent since the Middle Ages. The German emperors from 1871 to 1918 were Hohenzollerns. *n.*

hoist (hoist), 1 raise on high; lift up, often with ropes and pulleys: *hoist a flag, hoist sails, hoist blocks of stone in building.* 2 a hoisting; lift; boost: *She gave me a hoist up the wall.* 3 elevator or other apparatus for hoisting heavy loads. 1 *v.*, 2,3 *n.*

Hol bein (hōl′bīn), 1 **Hans,** 1460?-1524, German painter, called "the Elder." 2 his son, **Hans,** 1497-1543, German painter and maker of woodcuts, called "the Younger." *n.*

hock[1]

MAN — ANKLE   CAT — HOCK   HORSE

hold[1] (hōld), 1 grasp and keep: *Please hold my hat. Hold my watch while I play this game.* 2 a grasp or grip: *release one's hold. Take a good hold of this rope.* 3 thing to hold by: *The face of the*

hod (def. 1)
used to carry mortar

cliff had enough holds for a good climber. 4 keep in some position or condition: *Hold the dish level. Hold the paper steady while you draw.* 5 not break, loosen, or give way: *The dike held during the flood.* 6 keep from acting; keep back: *Hold your breath.* 7 keep: *The soldiers held the fort against the enemy.* 8 contain: *How much water will this cup hold? Those two jars hold tea and flour.* 9 have: *Shall we hold a meeting of the club? I hold some property in the city. She has held the office of mayor for ten years. I hold a high opinion of them.* 10 think; consider: *People once held that the world was flat.* 11 be faithful: *He held to his promise.* 12 be true; be in force or effect: *The rule holds in all cases.* 13 keep the same; continue: *The weather held warm.* 14 a controlling force or influence: *A habit has a hold on you.* 15 sign for a pause in music. 16 OLD USE. fort; stronghold. 1,4-13 *v.*, **held, holding;** 2,3,14-16 *n.* [Old English *healdan*]

hold forth, 1 talk or preach. 2 offer.

hold in, 1 keep in; keep back. 2 restrain oneself.

hold off, keep at a distance: *hold off the enemy. The storm may hold off.*

hold on, 1 keep one's hold. 2 keep on; continue. 3 INFORMAL. stop!

hold out, 1 continue; last. 2 keep resisting; not give in.

hold over, 1 keep for future action or consideration; postpone: *The bill has been held over until next year.* 2 stay in office beyond the regular term: *He held over until his successor was appointed.*

hold up, 1 keep from falling; support: *The roof is held up by pillars.* 2 show; display: *She held up the sign so we could all see it.* 3 continue; last; endure: *If this wind holds up, we can go sailing.* 4 stop. 5 INFORMAL. stop by force and rob.

hold with, 1 side with. 2 agree with. 3 approve of.

lay hold of, 1 seize; grasp: *The police laid hold of the thief.* 2 get control of.

hold[2] (hōld), the part inside of a ship or airplane where the cargo is carried. A ship's hold is below the deck. *n.* [a different form of *hole*]

hold back (hōld′bak′), thing that holds back; restraint; hindrance. *n.*

hold er (hōl′dər), 1 person who holds something. An owner or possessor of property is a holder. 2 thing to hold something else with. Pads of cloth are used as holders for lifting hot dishes. *n.*

hold ing (hōl′ding), 1 piece of land or property. 2 Often, **holdings**, *pl.* property in stocks or bonds. *n.*

hold up (hōld′up′), 1 INFORMAL. act of stopping by force and robbing. 2 a stopping. *n.*

hole (hōl), 1 an open place; opening: *a hole in a sock.* 2 a hollow place in something solid: *a hole in the road. Swiss cheese has holes in it.* 3 a hollow place in the earth in which an animal lives; burrow: *a rabbit hole.* 4 make a hole or holes in. 5 a small, dark, dirty place. 6 INFORMAL. flaw; defect: *There's a hole in your argument.* 7 a small, round, hollow place on a green, into which a golf ball is hit. 8 one of the divisions of a golf course. A regular golf course has 18 holes. 9 hit or drive (a golf ball) into a hole. 1-3,5-8 *n.,* 4,9 *v.,* **holed, hol ing.**

hole up, 1 go or put into a hole: *In November the badgers all hole up for the winter.* 2 go or put into hiding for a time: *The robbers holed up in an old cabin.*

hol i day (hol′ə dā), 1 day when one does not work; day of pleasure and enjoyment: *Labor Day and the Fourth of July are holidays in the United States.* 2 Often, **holidays,** *pl.* vacation: *He is spending his holidays in the Bahamas.* 3 of or suited to a holiday; gay: *holiday clothes.* 4 holy day; religious festival. 1,2,4 *n.,* 3 *adj.*

ho li ness (hō′lē nis), 1 a being holy. 2 **Holiness,** title used in speaking to or of the Pope: *The Pope is addressed as "Your Holiness" and spoken of as "His Holiness."* *n.*

Hol land (hol′ənd), Netherlands. *n.*

Hol land er (hol′ən dər), Dutchman. *n.*

hol ler (hol′ər), INFORMAL. 1 cry or shout loudly. 2 a loud cry or shout. 1 *v.,* 2 *n.*

hol lo (hə lō′), hello. *interj., n., pl.* **hol los;** *v.*

hol low (hol′ō), 1 having nothing, or only air, inside; with a hole inside; not solid; empty: *A tube or pipe is hollow. Most rubber balls are hollow.* 2 shaped like a bowl or cup: *a hollow dish for vegetables.* 3 a hollow place; hole: *a hollow in the road.* 4 make by hollowing; bend or dig out to a hollow shape: *She hollowed a whistle out of a piece of wood.* 5 make or become hollow. 6 a low place between hills; valley: *Sleepy Hollow.* 7 as if coming from something

hollow; deep and dull: *the hollow boom of a foghorn. The barrel gave out a hollow sound when I hit it.* 8 deep and sunken: *A starving person has hollow eyes and cheeks.* 9 not real or sincere; false: *You cannot believe hollow promises.* 10 hungry: *By twelve o'clock we felt rather hollow.* 1,2,7-10 *adj.,* 3,6 *n.,* 4,5 *v.* —**hol′low ly,** *adv.* —**hol′low ness,** *n.*

hol ly (hol′ē), 1 an evergreen tree or shrub with shiny, sharp-pointed leaves and bright-red berries. 2 its leaves and berries, often used as Christmas decorations. *n., pl.* **hol lies.**

hol ly hock (hol′ē hok), 1 a tall plant with large showy flowers of various colors that grow along a tall stem. 2 its flower. *n.*

Hol ly wood (hol′ē wud), district of Los Angeles, where many motion pictures are made. *n.*

holm (hōm), 1 an evergreen oak of southern Europe with leaves like those of holly. 2 its hard wood. *n.*

Holmes (hōmz), 1 **Oliver Wendell,** 1809-1894, American author, humorist, and physician. 2 his son, **Oliver Wendell,** 1841-1935, American lawyer, an associate justice of the United States Supreme Court from 1902 to 1932. 3 **Sherlock,** detective with remarkable powers of observation and reasoning in Sir Arthur Conan Doyle's stories. *n.*

hol mi um (hōl′mē əm), a highly magnetic metallic element which occurs in combination with certain minerals. *n.* [from *Holmia,* the Latin name of Stockholm, Sweden, near where it was found]

hol o caust (hol′ə kôst), 1 complete destruction by fire, especially of animals or human beings. 2 great or wholesale destruction. *n.*

Hol stein (hōl′stēn′ or hōl′stīn), one of a breed of large, black-and-white dairy cattle. *n.* [from *Holstein,* a region in northern Germany]

hol ster (hōl′stər), a leather case for a pistol, attached to a person's belt, or for a rifle, attached to a horseman's saddle. *n.*

ho ly (hō′lē), 1 belonging to God; set apart for God's service; coming from God; sacred: *the Holy Bible, holy sacraments.* 2 like a saint; spiritually perfect; very good; pure in heart: *a holy man.* 3 worthy of reverence: *Jerusalem is a holy place to Jews, Christians, and Moslems.* *adj.,* **ho li er, ho li est.**

Holy Communion, 1 a sharing in the Lord's Supper as a part of Christian worship. 2 celebration of the Lord's Supper.

holy day, a religious festival. Good Friday and Ash Wednesday are holy days.

Holy Father, the Pope.

Holy Ghost, spirit of God; third person of the Trinity; Holy Spirit.

Holy Grail, Grail.

Holy Land, Palestine.

holy of holies, 1 the holiest place. 2 the inner shrine of the Jewish Tabernacle and Temple.

Holy Roman Empire, empire in western and central Europe. It began in A.D. 962, or, according to some, in A.D. 800, and ended in 1806.

Holy See, office or jurisdiction of the Pope; the Pope's court.

Holy Sepulcher, tomb at Jerusalem where Christ's body is believed to have lain between his burial and the Resurrection.

Holy Spirit, Holy Ghost.

ho ly stone (hō′lē stōn′), 1 piece of soft sandstone used for scrubbing the decks of ships. 2 scrub with a holystone. 1 *n.,* 2 *v.,* **ho ly stoned, ho ly ston ing.**

holy water, water blessed by a priest.

Holy Week, the week before Easter.

Holy Writ, the Bible.

hom age (hom′ij or om′ij), 1 dutiful respect; reverence; honor: *Everyone paid homage to the great leader.* 2 (in the Middle Ages) a formal acknowledgment by a vassal that he owed loyalty and service to his lord. *n.*

hom bre (ôm′brä), SLANG. man; fellow. *n.* [from Spanish]

home (hōm), 1 place where a person or family lives; one's own house: *Her home is at 25 South Street.* 2 place where a person was born or brought up; one's own town or country: *His home is New York.* 3 place where a thing is very

adj. adjective	*n.* noun
adv. adverb	*prep.* preposition
conj. conjunction	*pron.* pronoun
interj. interjection	*v.* verb
sing. singular	*pl.* plural

common: *Alaska is the home of fur seals.* **4** place where a person can rest and be safe. **5** place where people who are homeless, poor, old, sick, blind, etc., may live: *a nursing home, a home for the aged.* **6** having to do with one's own home or country: *Write me all the home events.* **7** at or to one's own home or country: *I want to go home.* **8** goal in many games. **9** home plate in baseball. **10** to the place where it belongs; to the thing aimed at: *The spear struck home. The criticism struck home.* **11** to the heart or center; deep in: *drive a nail home.* **12** go home. **13** have a home. 1–5,8,9 *n.,* 6 *adj.,* 7,10,11 *adv.,* 12,13 *v.,* **homed, hom ing.**

at home, 1 at ease; comfortable: *to make oneself at home in a friend's house.* **2** ready to receive visitors.

home base, home plate.

home economics, science and art that deals with the management of a household; domestic science. Home economics includes housekeeping, budgeting of finances, preparation of food, child care, etc.

home land (hōm/land/), country that is one's home; one's native land. *n.*

home less (hōm/lis), without a home: *a stray, homeless dog. adj.*

home like (hōm/līk/), familiar or comfortable; like home. *adj.*

home li ness (hōm/lē nis), **1** a being homely; plain looks. **2** familiarity or comfort. *n.*

home ly (hōm/lē), **1** not good-looking; ugly; plain. **2** suited to home life; simple; everyday: *homely pleasures, homely food.* **3** of plain manners; unpretending: *a simple, homely man. adj.,* **home li er, home li est.**

home made (hōm/mād/), made at home: *homemade bread. adj.*

home mak er (hōm/mā/kər), woman who manages a home and its affairs; housewife. *n.*

home plate, block or slab beside which a player stands to bat the ball in baseball, and to which he must return, after getting on base, in order to score.

hom er (hō/mər), INFORMAL. a home run in baseball. *n.*

Ho mer (hō/mər), the great epic poet of ancient Greece. According to legend, Homer lived about the 800's B.C., and was the author of the *Iliad* and the *Odyssey. n.*

Ho mer ic (hō mer/ik), **1** by Homer. The *Iliad* and the *Odyssey* are Homeric poems. **2** of or having to do with Homer. **Homeric laughter** is loud, hearty laughter, such as Homer describes. **3** in the style of Homer. *adj.*

home room (hōm/rüm/ or hōm/rüm/), **1** classroom where members of a class meet to answer roll call, hear announcements, etc. **2** period during which this class meets. *n.*

home run, a hit in baseball which allows the batter to round the bases without a stop and reach home plate to score a run.

home sick (hōm/sik/), overcome by sadness because of being far away from home; ill with longing for home. *adj.* **—home/sick/ness,** *n.*

home spun (hōm/spun/), **1** spun or made at home. **2** cloth made of yarn spun at home. **3** a strong, loosely woven cloth similar to it. **4** made of homespun cloth. **5** not polished; plain; simple: *homespun manners.* 1,4,5 *adj.,* 2,3 *n.*

home stead (hōm/sted/), **1** house with its buildings and grounds; farm with its buildings. **2** public land granted to a settler under certain conditions by the United States government. **3** take up and occupy as a homestead: *He homesteaded 160 acres of land.* 1,2 *n.,* 3 *v.*

home stead er (hōm/sted/ər), **1** person who has a homestead. **2** settler granted a homestead by the United States government. *n.*

home stretch (hōm/strech/), **1** the straight part of a racetrack between the last turn and the finish line. **2** the last part of anything. *n.*

home ward (hōm/wərd), toward home: *We turned homeward (adv.). The ship is on her homeward course (adj.). adv., adj.*

home wards (hōm/wərdz), homeward. *adv.*

home work (hōm/wėrk/), **1** work done at home. **2** lesson to be studied or prepared outside the classroom. *n.*

home y (hō/mē), INFORMAL. homelike. *adj.,* **hom i er, hom i est.**

hom i cid al (hom/ə sī/dl), **1** having to do with homicide. **2** murderous. *adj.*

hom i cide (hom/ə sīd), **1** a killing of one human being by another. Intentional homicide is murder. **2** person who kills another human being. *n.*

hom i ly (hom/ə lē), **1** sermon, usually on some part of the Bible. **2** serious moral talk or writing that warns, urges, or advises. *n., pl.* **hom i lies.**

homing pigeon, pigeon trained to fly home from great distances carrying written messages; carrier pigeon.

hom i ny (hom/ə nē), whole or coarsely ground hulled corn. Hominy is usually eaten boiled. *n.*

ho mo (hō/mō), LATIN. man. *n.*

ho mo ge ne i ty (hō/mə jə nē/ə tē), a being homogeneous. *n.*

ho mo ge ne ous (hō/mə jē/nē əs), **1** of the same kind; similar. **2** made up of similar elements or parts: *The population of the island was homogeneous because there were no foreigners there. adj.* **—ho/mo ge/ne ous ly,** *adv.*

ho mog e nize (hə moj/ə nīz), make homogeneous. In **homogenized milk** the fat is distributed evenly throughout the milk and does not rise to the top in the form of cream. *v.,* **ho mog e nized, ho mog e niz ing.**

hom o graph (hom/ə graf), word having the same spelling as another word, but a different origin and meaning. *Bass* (bas), meaning "a kind of fish," and *bass* (bās), meaning "a male singing voice," are homographs. All homonyms (def. 1) are also homographs. *n.*

hom o nym (hom/ə nim), **1** word having the same pronunciation and spelling as another word, but a different origin and meaning. *Mail,* meaning "letters," and *mail,* meaning "armor," are homonyms. **2** homograph. **3** homophone. *n.*

hom o phone (hom/ə fōn), word having the same pronunciation as another, but a different origin and meaning. *Ate* and *eight* are homophones. All homonyms (def. 1) are also homophones. *n.*

Ho mo sa pi ens (hō/mō sā/pē enz), the species including all existing races of mankind; human beings; man. [from Latin *homo sapiens* intelligent man]

Hon., Honorable.

Hon dur as (hon dur/əs or hon-dyur/əs), country in N Central America. *Capital:* Tegucigalpa. *n.* **—Hon-dur/an,** *adj., n.*

hone (hōn), **1** a fine-grained whetstone on which to sharpen cutting tools, especially razors. **2** sharpen on a hone. 1 *n.,* 2 *v.,* **honed, hon ing.**

hon est (on/ist), **1** fair and upright; truthful; not lying, cheating, or stealing: *Job was an honest man.* **2** without lying, cheating, or stealing: *an honest profit.* **3** not hiding one's real nature; frank; open: *She has an honest face.* **4** not mixed with something of less value; genuine; pure: *Stores should sell honest goods. adj.*

hon est ly (on/ist lē), **1** in an honest way; with honesty: *The salesclerk dealt honestly with her customers.* **2** indeed; really: *Honestly! I never saw such rudeness. adv.*

hon es ty (on/ə stē), honest behavior; honest nature; honest quality. *n.*

hon ey (hun/ē), **1** a thick, sweet, yellow or golden liquid that bees make out of the nectar they collect from flowers. 2 the nectar of flowers, that draws bees to them. 3 something sweet like honey; sweetness. 4 darling; dear. 5 sweeten with honey. 6 talk sweetly to; flatter. 1-4 *n., pl.* **hon eys;** 5,6 *v.,* **hon eyed** or **hon ied, hon ey ing.**

honeybee—life size

hon ey bee (hun′ē bē′), bee that makes honey. *n.*

hon ey comb (hun′ē kōm′), 1 a structure of wax containing rows of six-sided cells made by bees to store honey, pollen, and their eggs. 2 anything like this. 3 like a honeycomb: *a honeycomb weave of cloth, a honeycomb pattern in knitting.* 4 make like a honeycomb; pierce with many holes: *The old castle was honeycombed with passages.* 1,2 *n.,* 3 *adj.,* 4 *v.*

honeycomb (def. 1)

hon ey dew (hun′ē dü′ *or* hun′ē-dyü′), 1 a sweet substance that oozes from the leaves of certain plants in hot weather. 2 a sweet substance on leaves and stems, secreted by aphids or other tiny insects. 3 honeydew melon. *n.*

honeydew melon, variety of muskmelon with sweet, green flesh and a smooth, pale-greenish skin.

hon eyed (hun′ēd), 1 sweetened with honey: *honeyed drinks.* 2 sweet as honey: *honeyed words.* 3 a past tense and a past participle of **honey.** 1,2 *adj.,* 3 *v.* Also, **honied.**

hon ey moon (hun′ē mün′), 1 holiday spent together by a newly married couple. 2 the first month of marriage. 3 a period of good feeling or good relations. 4 spend or have a honeymoon. 1-3 *n.,* 4 *v.* —**hon′ey moon′er,** *n.*

hon ey suck le (hun′ē suk′əl), a climbing shrub with fragrant white, yellow, or red flowers; woodbine. *n.*

Hong Kong (hong′kong′), British colony on the SE coast of China.

hon ied (hun′ēd), 1 honeyed; a past tense and a past participle of **honey.** 2 honeyed. 1 *v.,* 2 *adj.*

honk (hongk), 1 the cry of a wild goose. 2 any similar sound: *the honk of an automobile horn.* 3 make or cause to make such a sound: *We honked as we drove past our friends' house. Stop honking that horn!* 1,2 *n.,* 3 *v.*

Ho no lu lu (hon′ə lü′lü), seaport and capital of Hawaii, in S Oahu. *n.*

hon or (on′ər), 1 credit for acting well; glory, fame, or reputation; good name: *It was greatly to her honor to be given the scholarship.* 2 **honors,** *pl.* special mention given to a student by a school for having done work much above the average. 3 source of credit; person or thing that reflects honor: *to be an honor to one's family, school, country, etc. It is an honor to be chosen class president.* 4 a nice sense of what is right or proper; nobility of mind: *A man of honor always keeps his promises.* 5 great respect; high regard: *I hold honesty and kindness in high honor.* 6 **Honor,** title of respect used in speaking to or of a judge, mayor, etc. 7 act that shows respect or high regard: *funeral honors, military honors.* 8 respect highly; think highly of. 9 show respect to: *We honor our country's dead soldiers on Memorial Day.* 10 give an honor to; favor: *be honored by a royal visit.* 11 accept and pay (a check, note, etc.) when due. 1-7 *n.,* 8-11 *v.*

do the honors, act as host or hostess.

hon or a ble (on′ər ə bəl), 1 having or showing a sense of what is right and proper; honest; upright: *It is not honorable to lie or cheat.* 2 causing honor; bringing honor to the one that has it: *honorable wounds.* 3 worthy of honor; noble: *an honorable name, to perform honorable deeds.* 4 showing honor or respect: *honorable burial.* 5 having a title, rank, or position of honor. 6 **Honorable,** title of respect or distinction before the names of certain officials and others. *adj.* —**hon′-or a ble ness,** *n.*

hon or a bly (on′ər ə blē), in an honorable manner. *adv.*

hon or ar y (on′ə rer′ē), 1 given or done as an honor: *The university awarded honorary degrees to three prominent scientists.* 2 as an honor only; without pay or regular duties: *That association has an honorary secretary as well as a regular paid secretary who does the actual work. adj.*

honor roll, 1 list of students who have achieved the highest grades during the school term or year. 2 a commemorative list of local citizens who served in the armed forces.

honors of war, special favors or courtesies shown to a brave but defeated enemy that allow them to retain their military dignity.

hat, āge, fär; let, ēqual, tėrm; it, īce; hot, ōpen, ôrder; oil, out; cup, pút, rüle; ch, child; ng, long; sh, she; th, thin; ᵺH, then; zh, measure;

ə represents *a* in about, *e* in taken, *i* in pencil, *o* in lemon, *u* in circus.

Hon shu (hon′shü), the largest and most important island of Japan. *n.*

hood (húd), 1 a soft covering for the head and neck, either separate or as part of a coat: *My raincoat has a hood.* 2 anything like a hood in shape or use. 3 a metal covering over the engine of an automobile. 4 cover with a hood; furnish with a hood. 5 fold of cloth, banded with distinguishing colors to show what degrees are held, that hangs down over the gown worn by graduates of universities and colleges. 6 SLANG. hoodlum. 1-3,5,6 *n.,* 4 *v.* —**hood′-like′,** *adj.*

hood (def. 5)

-hood, *suffix added to nouns to form other nouns.* 1 state or condition of being: *Childhood = state of being a child.* 2 character or nature of: *Sainthood = the character of a saint.* 3 group or body of: *Priesthood = the body or group of priests.* [Old English *-hād,* from *hād* condition, position]

hood ed (húd′id), 1 having a hood. 2 shaped like a hood. *adj.*

hood lum (hüd′ləm), INFORMAL. 1 criminal or gangster. 2 a young rowdy; street ruffian. *n.*

hoo doo (hü′dü), 1 INFORMAL. person or thing that brings bad luck. 2 INFORMAL. bad luck. 3 INFORMAL. bring or cause bad luck to. 4 voodoo. 1,2,4 *n., pl.* **hoo doos;** 3 *v.*

hood wink (húd′wingk), 1 mislead by a trick; deceive. 2 blindfold. *v.*

hoof (húf *or* hüf), 1 a hard, horny covering on the feet of horses, cattle, sheep, pigs, and some other animals. 2 the whole foot of such animals. 3 INFORMAL. to walk or dance. 1,2 *n., pl.* **hoofs** or **hooves;** 3 *v.*

on the hoof, not killed and butchered; alive.

hoof beat (húf′bēt′ *or* hüf′bēt′),

adj.	adjective	*n.*	noun
adv.	adverb	*prep.*	preposition
conj.	conjunction	*pron.*	pronoun
interj.	interjection	*v.*	verb
sing.	singular	*pl.*	plural

sound made by an animal's hoof. *n.*

hoofed (hùft *or* hüft), having hoofs. *adj.*

hook (hùk), 1 piece of metal, wood, or other stiff material, curved or having a sharp angle, for catching hold of something or for hanging things on. 2 fasten with a hook or hooks: *Will you hook my dress for me?* 3 catch or take hold of with a hook. 4 a curved piece of wire, usually with a barb at the end, for catching fish. 5 catch (fish) with a hook. 6 anything curved or bent like a hook. A reaping hook is a large, curved knife for cutting down grass or grain. 7 a sharp bend: *a hook in the river.* 8 a curved point of land. 9 be curved or bent like a hook. 10 throw or hit (a ball) so that it curves. 11 a curving throw or hit. 12 (in boxing) a short, swinging blow. 13 hit with such a blow. 1,4,6-8,11,12 *n.*, 2,3,5,9,10,13 *v.* —**hook′like′,** *adj.*

by hook or by crook, in any way at all; by fair means or foul.

hook up, arrange and connect the parts of (a radio set, telephone, etc.).

on one's own hook, INFORMAL. independently.

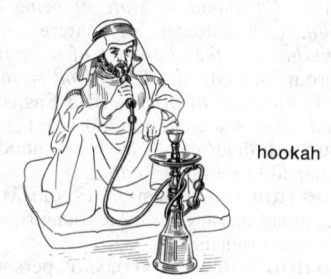

hookah

hook ah (hùk′ə), a tobacco pipe with a long tube by which the smoke is drawn through water and cooled. Hookahs are used in the Orient. *n.*

hooked (hùkt), 1 curved or bent like a hook. 2 having hooks. 3 made with a hook. A **hooked rug** is made by pulling loops of yarn or strips of cloth through a piece of canvas, burlap, etc., with a hook. 4 INFORMAL. slavishly dependent; addicted. *adj.*

hook up (hùk′up′), arrangement and connection of the parts of a radio set, telephone, radio-broadcasting facilities,

etc.: *a nation-wide television hookup. n.*

hook worm (hùk′wèrm′), 1 a small roundworm that enters the body through the skin and fastens itself to the walls of the small intestine. 2 disease caused by this worm, characterized by weakness and apparent laziness. *n.*

hook y (hùk′ē). **play hooky,** INFORMAL. stay away from school without permission. *n.*

hoop (hüp *or* hùp), 1 ring or round, flat band: *a hoop for holding together the staves of a barrel.* 2 bind or fasten together with a hoop or hoops. 3 a large wooden, iron, or plastic ring used as a toy, especially for rolling around the ground. 4 a circular frame formerly used to hold out a woman's skirt. 5 the wicket used in croquet. 6 anything shaped like a hoop. 1,3-6 *n.,* 2 *v.*

hoop skirt, a woman's skirt worn over a frame of flexible hoops to hold out or expand the skirt; crinoline.

hoo ray (hù rā′), hurrah. *interj., n., v.*

hoot (hüt), 1 sound that an owl makes. 2 make this sound or one like it. 3 a shout to show disapproval or scorn. 4 make such a shout. 5 show disapproval of or scorn for by hooting: *The audience hooted the speaker's plan.* 6 force or drive by hooting: *What he said was so foolish that they hooted him off the platform.* 7 INFORMAL. the smallest thought; trifle: *She doesn't give a hoot about what happens to us.* 1,3,7 *n.,* 2,4-6 *v.*

Hoo ver (hü′vər), **Herbert Clark,** 1874-1964, the 31st president of the United States, from 1929 to 1933. *n.*

Hoover Dam, dam on the Colorado River between Arizona and Nevada; Boulder Dam.

hooves (hùvz *or* hüvz), a plural of **hoof.** *n.*

hop[1] (hop), 1 spring, or move by springing, on one foot: *How far can you hop on your right foot?* 2 spring, or move by springing, with both or all feet at once: *Many birds hop.* 3 jump over: *hop a ditch.* 4 INFORMAL. jump on (a train, car, etc.). 5 a hopping; spring. 6 INFORMAL. fly in an airplane. 7 IN-FORMAL. flight in an airplane. 8 IN-FORMAL. a dancing party. 1-4,6 *v.,* **hopped, hop ping;** 5,7,8 *n.* [Old English *hoppian*]

hop[2] (hop), 1 vine having flower clusters that look like small pine cones. 2 **hops,** *pl.* the dried, ripe flower clusters of the hop vine, used to flavor beer and other malt drinks. 3 flavor with hops. 1,2 *n.,* 3 *v.,* **hopped, hop ping.** [from Dutch of the 1400's *hoppe*]

hope (hōp), 1 a feeling that what one desires will happen: *Your encouragement gave me hope.* 2 wish and expect: *I hope to do well in school this year.*

3 thing hoped for. 4 a cause of hope; person or thing that gives hope to others or that others have hope in: *She is the hope of the family.* 1,3,4 *n.,* 2 *v.,* **hoped, hop ing.**

hope ful (hōp′fəl), 1 feeling or showing hope; expecting to receive what one desires: *a hopeful attitude.* 2 giving hope; likely to succeed. 3 boy or girl thought likely to succeed: *a young hopeful.* 1,2 *adj.,* 3 *n.* —**hope′ful ly,** *adv.* —**hope′ful ness,** *n.*

hope less (hōp′lis), 1 feeling no hope: *He was disappointed so often that he became hopeless.* 2 giving no hope: *a hopeless illness. adj.* —**hope′less ly,** *adv.* —**hope′less ness,** *n.*

Ho pi (hō′pē), member of a tribe of Pueblo Indians living in adobe-built villages in northern Arizona. *n., pl.* **Ho pis.**

hopper (def. 3)

hop per (hop′ər), 1 person or thing that hops. 2 grasshopper or other hopping insect. 3 container having a narrow opening at the bottom, used to receive and hold coal, grain, or other material before feeding it into a machine, storage bin, etc.; the receiver in various machines. *n.*

hop scotch (hop′skoch′), a children's game in which the players hop over the lines of a figure drawn on the ground and pick up an object thrown or kicked into one of the numbered squares of the figure. *n.*

Ho race (hôr′is), 65-8 B.C., Roman poet and satirist. *n.*

horde (hôrd), 1 multitude; crowd; swarm: *hordes of grasshoppers.* 2 a wandering tribe or troop: *Hordes of Mongols and Turks invaded Europe in the Middle Ages. n.*

hore hound (hôr′hound′), 1 plant of the same family as the mint, with whitish leaves. 2 candy or cough medicine flavored with a bitter extract made from the leaves of this plant. *n.* Also, **hoarhound.**

ho ri zon (hə rī′zn), 1 line where the

HORIZON

horizon (def. 1)

406

earth and sky seem to meet. You cannot see beyond the horizon. 2 limit of one's thinking, experience, interest, or outlook. *n.*

HORIZONTAL ◄—VERTICAL

horizontal (def. 1)

ho ri zon tal (hôr/ə zon/tl), 1 parallel to the horizon; at right angles to a vertical line. 2 flat; level. 3 a horizontal line, plane, direction, position, etc. 1,2 *adj.,* 3 *n.* —**ho/ri zon/tal ly,** *adv.*

hor mone (hôr/mōn), substance formed in the endocrine glands, which enters the bloodstream and affects or controls the activity of some organ or tissue. Adrenaline and insulin are hormones. *n.*

horn (hôrn), 1 a hard growth, usually curved and pointed, on the heads of cattle, sheep, goats, and some other animals. A deer has a pair of branching horns that fall off and grow back every year. The Devil is often pictured with horns. 2 anything that sticks up on the head of an animal: *a snail's horns, an insect's horns.* 3 the substance or material of horns. Horn is hard and partly transparent. A person's fingernails, the beaks of birds, the hoofs of horses, and tortoise shells are all made of horn. 4 container made by hollowing out a horn. It was used to drink out of or to carry gunpowder in. 5 a musical instrument sounded by blowing into the smaller end. It was once made of horn, but now it is made of brass or other metal. The brass section of an orchestra consists of several kinds of horns. 6 device sounded as a warning signal: *an automobile horn.* 7 anything that sticks out like a horn or is shaped like a horn: *a saddle horn, the horn of a bay.* 8 either pointed tip of a new or old moon, or of a crescent. *n.* —**horn/like/,** *adj.*

horn in, SLANG. meddle or intrude.

Horn (hôrn), **Cape.** See **Cape Horn.** *n.*

horn blende (hôrn/blend/), a common black, dark-green, or brown mineral found in granite and other rocks. *n.*

horn book (hôrn/bùk/), page with the alphabet, etc., on it, covered with a sheet of transparent horn and fastened in a frame with a handle, formerly used in teaching children to read. *n.*

horned (hôrnd), having a horn, horns, or hornlike growths. *adj.*

horned toad, a small lizard with a broad, flat body, short tail, and many hornlike spines.

hor net (hôr/nit), a large wasp that can give a very painful sting. *n.*

horn less (hôrn/lis), without horns. *adj.*

horn of plenty, cornucopia.

horn pipe (hôrn/pīp/), 1 a lively dance done by one person. It was formerly popular among sailors. 2 music for it. *n.*

horn y (hôr/nē), 1 made of horn or a substance like it. 2 hard like a horn; calloused: *A farmer's hands are horny from work.* 3 having a horn or horns; horned. *adj.,* **horn i er, horn i est.**

ho ro scope (hôr/ə skōp), 1 the relative position of the planets at a particular time, especially at the hour of a person's birth, regarded as influencing his life. 2 diagram showing the arrangement of the heavens at a particular time. A horoscope is used in telling fortunes by the planets and the stars. *n.*

hor ren dous (ho ren/dəs), horrible; terrible; frightful. *adj.*

hor ri ble (hôr/ə bəl), 1 causing horror; terrible; dreadful; frightful; shocking: *a horrible crime, a horrible disease.* 2 INFORMAL. extremely unpleasant: *a horrible smell, a horrible noise.* adj.

hor ri bly (hôr/ə blē), in a horrible manner. *adv.*

hor rid (hôr/id), 1 causing great fear; terrible; frightful. 2 INFORMAL. very unpleasant: *a horrid child, a horrid day.* adj. —**hor/rid ly,** adv. —**hor/rid ness,** n.

hor ri fy (hôr/ə fī), 1 cause to feel horror. 2 INFORMAL. shock very much: *We were horrified by his rude behavior.* v., **hor ri fied, hor ri fy ing.**

hor ror (hôr/ər), 1 a shivering, shaking terror. 2 a very strong dislike: *I have a horror of pistols and rifles.* 3 thing that causes horror. *n.*

hors d'oeuvre (ôr/ dėrv/), relish or light food served as an appetizer before the regular courses of a meal. Olives, celery, anchovies, etc., are hors d'oeuvres. *pl.* **hors d'oeuvres** (ôr/ dėrvz/). [from French *hors d'oeuvre* apart from the main work]

horse (hôrs), 1 a large, four-legged mammal with solid hoofs, and a mane and tail of long, coarse hair. Horses are used for riding and for carrying and pulling loads. 2 a full-grown male horse. 3 provide with a horse or horses.

FORELOCK
MANE
WITHERS
BACK LOINS CROUP
MUZZLE
HIP TAIL
GIRTH
FLANK THIGH
BELLY
HEIGHT HAMSTRING
KNEE HOCK
PASTERN
FETLOCK
HOOF

horse (def. 1)

hat, āge, fär; let, ēqual, tėrm; it, īce; hot, ōpen, ôrder; oil, out; cup, pùt, rüle; ch, child; ng, long; sh, she; th, thin; ᵺH, then; zh, measure;

ə represents *a* in about, *e* in taken, *i* in pencil, *o* in lemon, *u* in circus.

horse (def. 5)   horse (def. 6)

4 put on horseback. 5 piece of gymnasium apparatus to jump or vault over. 6 a supporting frame with legs: *Five boards laid on two horses made our picnic table.* 7 soldiers on horses; cavalry: *a troop of horse.* 1,2,5-7 *n., pl.* **hors es** or **horse;** 3,4 *v.,* **horsed, hors ing.**

horse around, SLANG. fool around; get into mischief.

horse back (hôrs/bak/), 1 the back of a horse. 2 on the back of a horse: *ride horseback.* 1 *n.,* 2 *adv.*

horse car (hôrs/kär/), 1 streetcar or railroad car pulled by a horse or horses. 2 car used for carrying horses. *n.*

horse chestnut, 1 a shade tree with spreading branches, large leaves, clusters of showy white flowers, and glossy brown nuts. 2 its nut.

horse fly (hôrs/flī/), a large fly that bites animals, especially horses. *n., pl.* **horse flies.**

horse hair (hôrs/her/ *or* hôrs/har/), 1 hair from the mane or tail of a horse. 2 a stiff fabric made of this hair; haircloth. 3 made of horsehair; stuffed with horsehair: *a horsehair cushion.* 1,2 *n.,* 3 *adj.*

horse hide (hôrs/hīd/), 1 hide of a horse. 2 leather made from this hide. *n.*

horse latitudes, two regions where the winds are usually calm or very light. They extend around the earth at about 30 degrees north and 30 degrees south of the equator.

horse laugh (hôrs/laf/), a loud, boisterous laugh. *n.*

horse less (hôrs/lis), without a horse: *Automobiles used to be called horseless carriages.* adj.

horse man (hôrs/mən), 1 man who rides on horseback. 2 man who is

adj.	adjective	*n.*	noun
adv.	adverb	*prep.*	preposition
conj.	conjunction	*pron.*	pronoun
interj.	interjection	*v.*	verb

sing. singular	*pl.* plural

---

skilled in riding or managing horses. *n.*, *pl.* **horse men.**

horse man ship   (hôrs′mən ship), skill in riding or managing horses: *She is proud of her horsemanship.* *n.*

horse play (hôrs′plā′), rough, boisterous fun. *n.*

horse pow er (hôrs′pou′ər), unit for measuring the power of engines, motors, etc. One horsepower is the power to lift 550 pounds one foot in one second. *n.*

horse rad ish (hôrs′rad′ish), 1 a tall plant with a white, hot-tasting root. 2 its root, which is ground up and used as a relish with meat, fish, salads, etc. 3 relish made of this root. *n.*

horse sense, INFORMAL. plain, practical good sense; common sense.

horse shoe (hôrs′shü′), 1 a metal plate shaped like a U, nailed to a horse's hoof to protect it. 2 put a horseshoe or horseshoes on. 3 thing shaped like a horseshoe. 4 **horseshoes,** *pl.* game in which the players try to throw horseshoes over or near a stake 40 feet away. 1,3,4 *n.*, 2 *v.*, **horse shoed, horse shoe ing.**

horseshoe crab—up to 20 in. long
(left, back view; right, underside)

horseshoe crab, a crablike sea animal related to the spiders, with a horseshoe-shaped shell and a long, spiny tail.

horseshoe magnet, a steel magnet in the shape of a horseshoe.

horse sho er (hôrs′shü′ər), person who puts horseshoes on horses. *n.*

horse whip (hôrs′hwip′), 1 whip for driving or controlling horses. 2 beat with a horsewhip. 1 *n.*, 2 *v.*, **horse whipped, horse whip ping.**

horse wom an   (hôrs′wum′ən), 1 woman who rides on horseback. 2 woman skilled in riding or managing horses. *n.*, *pl.* **horse wom en.**

hors y or **hors ey** (hôr′sē), 1 like a horse or horses. 2 having to do with horses. 3 fond of horses or horse racing. 4 dressing or talking like people who spend much time with horses. *adj.*, **hors i er, hors i est.**

hor ti cul tur al (hôr′tə kul′chər əl), having to do with the growing of flowers, fruits, vegetables, and plants: *Florists sometimes give a horticultural exhibit in the spring or fall.* *adj.*

hor ti cul ture   (hôr′tə kul′chər), 1 science or art of growing flowers, fruits, vegetables, and plants. 2 cultivation of a garden. *n.*

hor ti cul tur ist (hôr′tə kul′chər ist), an expert in horticulture. *n.*

ho san na (hō zan′ə), a shout of praise to God: *The high priest cried, "Hosanna!" interj., n., pl.* **ho san nas.**

hose (hōz), 1 tube of rubber, canvas, plastic, or other material that will bend, for carrying liquid for short distances. A hose is used in pumping gasoline into automobiles. 2 stockings. 3 long, tight breeches formerly worn by men. 4 put water on with a hose. 1-3 *n.*, *pl.* **hos es** for 1, **hose** for 2 and 3; 4 *v.*, **hosed, hos ing.**

Ho se a (hō zē′ə), 1 book of the Old Testament. 2 its author, a Hebrew prophet who lived in the 700's B.C. *n.*

ho sier y (hō′zhər ē), hose; stockings. *n.*

hos pice (hos′pis), house where travelers can stop and rest. It is often kept by monks. *n.*

hos pi ta ble (hos′pi tə bəl *or* hospit′ə bəl), 1 giving or liking to give a welcome, food and shelter, and friendly treatment to guests or strangers: *a hospitable family, a hospitable reception.* 2 with the mind open or receptive: *a person hospitable to new ideas.* *adj.*

hos pi ta bly (hos′pi tə blē *or* hospit′ə blē), in a hospitable manner. *adv.*

hos pi tal (hos′pi təl), place for the care of the sick or injured: *The doctor removed my tonsils at the hospital.* *n.*

hos pi tal i ty (hos′pə tal′ə tē), friendly reception; generous treatment of guests or strangers. *n.*, *pl.* **hos pi tal i ties.**

hos pi tal i za tion (hos′pi tə lə zā′shən), a putting or a being put in a hospital for treatment. *n.*

hos pi tal ize (hos′pi tə līz), put in a hospital for treatment. *v.*, **hos pi tal ized, hos pi tal iz ing.**

host[1] (hōst), 1 person who receives another person as his guest. 2 keeper of an inn or hotel. 3 a living plant or animal in or on which a parasite lives: *The oak tree is the host of the mistletoe that grows on it.* 4 receive or entertain at as a host does: *host a party.* 1-3 *n.*, 4 *v.* [from French of the 1200's *hoste,* from Latin *hospitem* guest, host]

host[2] (hōst), 1 a large number; multitude: *As it grew dark, a few stars* appeared, then a host of them. 2 army. *n.* [from French of the 1200's *host,* from Latin *hostis* (originally) enemy]

Host (hōst), bread or wafer used in the Mass of the Roman Catholic Church. *n.* [from French of the 1300's *hoiste,* from Latin *hostia* animal sacrificed]

hos tage (hos′tij), 1 person given up to another or held by an enemy as a pledge: *The hostage will be kept safe and will be returned when our enemies' promises have been carried out.* 2 pledge; security. *n.*

hos tel (hos′tl), a lodging place, especially a supervised lodging place for young people on bicycle trips, hikes, etc.; inn; hotel. *n.*

hos tel ry (hos′tl rē), inn; hotel. *n.*, *pl.* **hos tel ries.**

host ess (hō′stis), 1 woman who receives another person as her guest. 2 woman who keeps an inn or hotel, or helps her husband to do so. *n.*, *pl.* **host ess es.**

hos tile (hos′tl), 1 of an enemy or enemies: *the hostile army.* 2 opposed; unfriendly; unfavorable: *a hostile look.* *adj.* —**hos′tile ly,** *adv.*

hos til i ty (ho stil′ə tē), 1 the feeling that an enemy has; being an enemy; unfriendliness; opposition: *He showed signs of hostility toward our plan.* 2 state of being at war. 3 **hostilities,** *pl.* acts of war; warfare; fighting: *The peace treaty brought hostilities between the two countries to an end. n., pl.* **hos til i ties.**

hos tler (os′lər *or* hos′lər), person who takes care of horses at an inn or stable. *n.* Also, **ostler.**

hot (hot), 1 having much heat; very warm: *Fire is hot. The sun is hot today. That long run has made me hot.* 2 having a sharp, burning taste: *Pepper and mustard are hot.* 3 fiery: *a hot temper, hot with rage.* 4 very eager: *The children were hot to go camping.* 5 new; fresh: *a hot scent or trail.* 6 following closely: *We were in hot pursuit of the runaway horse.* 7 (in games, treasure hunts, etc.) very near or approaching what one is searching for. 8 radioactive: *the hot debris left by an atomic explosion.* 9 SLANG. obtained illegally; stolen: *hot diamonds.* 10 with much heat: *The sun beats hot upon the sand.* 1-9 *adj.,* **hot ter, hot test;** 10 *adv.* —**hot′ly,** *adv.* —**hot′ness,** *n.*

hot bed (hot′bed′), 1 bed of earth

hotbed
(def. 1)

covered with glass and kept warm for growing plants. **2** place where anything grows and develops rapidly: *Dirty, crowded cities are hotbeds of disease and crime.* *n.*

hot-blood ed (hot′blud′id), **1** easily excited or angered. **2** passionate. *adj.*

hot cake, pancake.

hot dog, INFORMAL. **1** sandwich made with a hot frankfurter enclosed in a bun, often served with mustard, relish, etc. **2** frankfurter.

ho tel (hō tel′), house or large building that supplies rooms and food for pay to travelers and others. *n.*

hot foot (hot′fut′), INFORMAL. go in great haste; hurry. *v.*

hot head ed (hot′hed′id), **1** having a fiery temper; easily angered. **2** impetuous; rash. *adj.* —**hot′head′ed ly,** *adv.* —**hot′head′ed ness,** *n.*

hot house (hot′hous′), greenhouse. *n., pl.* **hot hous es** (hot′hou′ziz).

hot plate, a small, portable electric stove, with one or two burners, for cooking.

hot rod, automobile with a rebuilt motor for faster starts and higher speeds.

Hot ten tot (hot′n tot), **1** member of a people who live mainly in southwestern Africa. The Hottentots are related to the Bushmen. **2** their language. *n.*

hot water, INFORMAL. trouble.

hound (hound), **1** dog of any of various breeds, most of which hunt by scent and have large, drooping ears and short hair. **2** any dog. **3** keep on chasing or driving: *The police hounded the thief until they caught him.* **4** urge on: *The children hounded their parents to buy a swimming pool.* **1,2** *n.,* **3,4** *v.*

hour (our), **1** one of the 12 equal periods of time between noon and midnight, or between midnight and noon; 60 minutes; $\frac{1}{24}$ of a day. **2** the time of day: *This clock strikes the hours and the half hours.* **3** a particular or fixed time: *Our breakfast hour is at seven o'clock.* **4 hours,** *pl.* time for work, study, etc.: *What are the hours in this office? Our school hours are 9 to 12 and 1 to 4.* **5** distance which can be traveled in an hour: *The concert hall is only an hour away.* **6** the present time: *the man of the hour.* *n.*

hourglass—It takes just an hour for sand or mercury to pass through the narrow neck from the top bulb to the bottom bulb.

hour glass (our′glas′), device for measuring one hour. *n., pl.* **hour glass es.**

hour hand, hand on a clock or watch that indicates hours. It moves around the whole dial once in twelve hours.

hour i (húr′ē), one of the young, eternally beautiful girls of the Moslem paradise. *n., pl.* **hour is.**

hour ly (our′lē), **1** done, happening, or counted every hour: *There are hourly reports of the news and weather on this radio station.* **2** every hour; hour by hour: *Give two doses of the medicine hourly.* **3** coming very often; frequent: *hourly messages.* **4** very often; frequently: *Messages were coming from the front hourly.* **1,3** *adj.,* **2,4** *adv.*

house (hous for **1-4,6-8;** houz for **5**), **1** building in which people live. **2** people living in a house; household. **3** family with its ancestors and descendants, especially a noble family: *He was a prince of the house of David.* **4** building for any purpose: *an engine house.* **5** take or put into a house; provide with a house; shelter: *Where can we house all these children? The campers housed their provisions in an abandoned shack.* **6** place of business or a business firm: *a publishing house.* **7** assembly for making laws and considering questions of government; lawmaking body. In the United States, the House of Representatives is the lower house of Congress; the Senate is the upper house. **8** audience: *The singer sang to a large house.* **1-4,6-8** *n., pl.* **hous es** (hou′ziz); **5** *v.,* **housed, hous ing.**

keep house, manage a home and its affairs; do housework.

on the house, paid for by the owner of the business; free.

houseboat

house boat (hous′bōt′), boat fitted out for use as a place to live in. *n.*

house boy (hous′boi′), boy or man employed as a servant in a house. *n.*

house break er (hous′brā′kər), person who breaks into a house to steal or commit some other crime. *n.*

house break ing (hous′brā′king), act of breaking into a house to steal or commit some other crime. *n.*

house bro ken (hous′brō′kən), (of a dog, cat, etc.) trained to have clean habits for living indoors. *adj.*

house coat (hous′kōt′), a loose, flowing garment, worn indoors by women and girls. *n.*

house fly (hous′flī′), a two-winged fly

hat, āge, fär; let, ēqual, tėrm; it, īce; hot, ōpen, ôrder; oil, out; cup, pùt, rüle; ch, child; ng, long; sh, she; th, thin; ŦH, then; zh, measure;

ə represents *a* in about, *e* in taken, *i* in pencil, *o* in lemon, *u* in circus.

that lives around and in houses in all parts of the world, feeding on food, garbage, and filth. Houseflies carry disease germs. *n., pl.* **house flies.**

house hold (hous′hōld), **1** all the people living in a house; family; family and servants. **2** a home and its affairs. **3** of a household; having to do with a household; domestic: *household expenses, household chores.* **1,2** *n.,* **3** *adj.*

house hold er (hous′hōl′dər), **1** person who owns or lives in a house. **2** head of a family. *n.*

house keep er (hous′kē′pər), **1** woman who is hired to manage a home and its affairs and to do housework. **2** woman who is hired to direct the servants that do the housework in a home, hotel, etc. *n.*

house keep ing (hous′kē′ping), management of a home and its affairs; doing the housework. *n.*

house maid (hous′mād′), a woman servant who does housework. *n.*

house moth er (hous′muŦH′ər), woman who supervises and takes care of a group of young people living together like a family. *n.*

House of Commons, the lower house of the Parliament of Great Britain or of Canada, composed of elected representatives; the Commons.

house of correction, place of confinement and reform for persons convicted of minor offenses and not regarded as confirmed criminals.

House of Lords, the upper house of the Parliament of Great Britain, composed of nobles and clergymen of high rank; the Lords.

House of Representatives, the lower house of Congress or of the legislature of certain states of the United States.

house top (hous′top′), top of a house; roof. *n.*

house warm ing (hous′wôr′ming), party given when a family moves into a home for the first time. *n.*

house wife (hous′wīf′), **1** woman who manages a home and its affairs for her family. **2** woman who is the head of

adj. adjective	*n.* noun
adv. adverb	*prep.* preposition
conj. conjunction	*pron.* pronoun
interj. interjection	*v.* verb
sing. singular	*pl.* plural

a household. *n., pl.* **house wives** (hous′wīvz′).

house work (hous′werk′), work to be done in housekeeping, such as washing, ironing, cleaning, and cooking. *n.*

hous ing[1] (hou′zing), 1 act of sheltering; providing shelter. 2 houses: *There is not enough housing in that city for the number of people living there.* 3 shelter; covering. 4 frame or plate to hold part of a machine in place. *n.* [*house* + *-ing*[1]]

hous ing[2] (hou′zing), an ornamental covering on an animal's back, especially a horse: *Under the saddle was a housing of red velvet. n.* [from French of the 1300's *houce* a covering + English *-ing*[1]]

Hous ton (hyü′stən), 1 **Samuel,** 1793-1863, American general and statesman who was twice president of Texas before it became a state in 1845. 2 city in SE Texas. *n.*

hove (hōv), heaved; a past tense and a past participle of **heave.** *The sailors hove at the ropes. v.*

hov el (huv′əl *or* hov′əl), 1 house that is small, crude, and unpleasant to live in. 2 an open shed for sheltering cattle, tools, etc. *n.*

hov er (huv′ər *or* hov′ər), 1 stay in or near one place in the air: *The two birds hovered over their nest.* 2 stay in or near one place; wait nearby: *The dogs hovered around the kitchen door at mealtime.* 3 be in an uncertain condition; waver: *For several days the sick man hovered between life and death. v.*

how (hou), 1 in what way; by what means: *Tell me how to do it. How do you go there? How did it happen?* 2 to what degree or amount: *How tall are you? How hot is it? How much shall I bring you?* 3 in what condition: *How are you today? How is your health? How do I look?* 4 for what reason; why: *How is it you don't like candy? adv.*

how be it (hou bē′it), OLD USE. nevertheless. *adv.*

how dah (hou′də), seat for persons riding on the back of an elephant. *n.*

Howe (hou), **Elias,** 1819-1867, American inventor of the sewing machine. *n.*

how e'er (hou er′ *or* hou ar′), however. *conj., adv.*

how ev er (hou ev′ər), 1 in spite of

that; nevertheless; yet: *We were very late for dinner; however, there was plenty left for us.* 2 to whatever extent, degree, or amount; no matter how: *I'll come however busy I am.* 3 in whatever way; by whatever means: *However did you get so dirty? adv.*

how it zer (hou′it sər), a short cannon for firing shells in a high curve. *n.*

howl (houl), 1 give a long, loud, mournful cry: *Our dog often howls at night. The winter winds howled around our cabin.* 2 a long, loud, mournful cry: *the howl of a wolf.* 3 give a long, loud cry of pain or rage. 4 a loud cry of pain or rage. 5 a yell or shout: *We heard howls of laughter.* 6 yell or shout: *It was so funny that we howled with laughter.* 7 force or drive by howling: *The angry mob howled the speaker off the platform.* 1,3,6,7 *v.,* 2,4,5 *n.*

how so ev er (hou′sō ev′ər), 1 to whatever extent, degree, or amount. 2 in whatever way. *adv.*

hoy den (hoid′n), a boisterous, romping girl; tomboy. *n.*

hoy den ish (hoid′n ish), of or like a hoyden; boisterous; romping. *adj.*

hp., h.p., HP, or **H.P.,** horsepower.

h.q., or **H.Q.,** headquarters.

hr., hour or hours. *pl.,* **hrs.**

H.R.H., 1 Her Royal Highness. 2 His Royal Highness.

ht., height.

WHEEL
AXLE
HUB
TIRE
hub
(def. 1)

hub (hub), 1 the central part of a wheel. 2 center of interest, activity, etc.: *London is the hub of English life. n.*

hub bub (hub′ub), loud, confused noise; uproar: *There was a hubbub in the street as the police tried to break up the crowd mobbing the famous actor. n.*

hub cap (hub′kap′), a removable, dish-shaped metal piece which covers the center of the outer side of a wheel. *n.*

huck le ber ry (huk′əl ber′ē), 1 a small berry like a blueberry, but darker

howdah

in color. 2 shrub that it grows on. *n., pl.* **huck le ber ries.**

huck ster (huk′stər), 1 peddler. 2 person who sells small articles. 3 person willing to profit in a small, mean way. 4 SLANG. person who is in the advertising business. *n.*

hud dle (hud′l), 1 to crowd close: *The sheep huddled together in a corner.* 2 put close together: *We huddled all the children into one bed.* 3 nestle in a heap: *The cat huddled itself on the cushion and went to sleep. She huddled close to the fire on the hearth.* 4 a confused heap, mass, or crowd. 5 IN-FORMAL. a secret consultation: *After the meeting, the lawyer went into a huddle with his partner.* 6 INFORMAL. confer secretly. 7 a grouping of football players behind the line of scrimmage to receive signals, plan the next play, etc. 1-3,6 *v.,* **hud dled, hud dling;** 4,5,7 *n.*

Hud son (hud′sən), 1 **Henry,** died 1611, English navigator and explorer in America. Hudson River and Hudson Bay were named for him. 2 river in E New York State. New York City is at its mouth. *n.*

Hudson Bay, large bay in central Canada. It is an extension of the Atlantic Ocean.

hue (hyü), color, shade, or tint: *all the hues of the rainbow, silk of a pinkish hue. n.*

hue and cry, shouts of alarm or protest.

huff (huf), 1 fit of anger or peevishness: *We had a heated argument about politics, and she left in a huff.* 2 make angry; offend. 3 puff; blow: *"He huffed and he puffed and he blew the house down."* 1 *n.,* 2,3 *v.*

huff i ly (huf′ə lē), in a huffy manner. *adv.*

huff i ness (huf′ē nis), huffy quality. *n.*

huff y (huf′ē), 1 in a huff; offended. 2 easily offended; touchy. *adj.,* **huff i er, huff i est.**

hug (hug), 1 put the arms around and hold close, especially to show love or friendship: *The girl hugged her big dog.* 2 a tight clasp with the arms: *Give Mother a hug.* 3 cling firmly or fondly to: *hug an opinion or belief.* 4 keep close to: *The little boat hugged the shore.* 1,3,4 *v.,* **hugged, hug ging;** 2 *n.*

huge (hyüj), very big; extremely large or great: *A whale or an elephant is a huge animal. He won a huge sum of money in the lottery. adj.,* **hug er, hug est.** —**huge′ly,** *adv.* —**huge′ness,** *n.*

Hu go (hyü′gō), **Victor,** 1802-1885, French writer of poetry, novels, and plays. *n.*

Hu gue not (hyü′gə not), a French Protestant of the 1500's and 1600's. *n.*

huh (hu), sound made to express surprise, contempt, etc., or to ask a question. *interj.*

hu la (hü′lə), a native Hawaiian dance. *n., pl.* **hu las.**

hu la-hu la (hü′lə hü′lə), hula. *n., pl.* **hu la-hu las.**

hulk (hulk), 1 body of an old or worn-out ship. 2 ship used as a prison. 3 a big, clumsy ship. 4 a big, clumsy person or thing: *That hulk of a ladder is hard to manage; we need a smaller and lighter one. n.*

hulk ing (hul′king), big and clumsy: *a large, hulking boy. adj.*

hull (hul), 1 body or frame of a ship. Masts, sails, and rigging are not part of the hull. 2 the main body or frame of a seaplane, airship, etc. 3 the outer covering of a seed. 4 calyx of some fruits. We call the green leaves at the stem of a strawberry its hull. 5 remove the hull or hulls from. 6 any outer covering. 1-4,6 *n.,* 5 *v.* —**hull′er,** *n.*

hul la ba loo (hul′ə bə lü), a loud noise or disturbance; uproar. *n., pl.* **hul la ba loos.**

hum (hum), 1 make a continuous murmuring sound like that of a bee or of a spinning top: *The sewing machine hums busily.* 2 a continuous murmuring sound: *The hum of the bees. There was a hum of activity in the busy shop.* 3 make a low sound like *mm* or *hm* in hesitation, embarrassment, dissatisfaction, etc. 4 a low sound like *mm* or *hm* made in hesitation, embarrassment, etc.: *Hum, I don't know what to do.* 5 sing with closed lips, not sounding words: *She hummed a tune as she worked.* 6 a singing in this way. 7 put or bring by humming: *The father hummed the baby to sleep.* 8 INFORMAL. be busy and active: *The new coach made things hum when he took charge of the team.* 1,3,5,7,8 *v.,* **hummed, hum ming;** 2,6 *n.,* 4 *interj.*

hu man (hyü′mən), 1 of persons; that people have: *Kindness is a human trait. To know all that will happen in the future is beyond human power.* 2 being a person or persons; having the form or qualities of people: *Men, women, and children are human beings. Those monkeys look almost human.* 3 having or showing qualities (good or bad) natural to people: *She is a very human person, warm and understanding and not too perfect.* 4 belonging to mankind: *The history of America has great human interest.* 5 a human being; person. 1-4 *adj.,* 5 *n.* —**hu′man ness,** *n.*

hu mane (hyü mān′), not cruel or brutal; kind; merciful: *We believe in the humane treatment of prisoners. adj.*

—**hu mane′ly,** *adv.* —**hu mane′-ness,** *n.*

hu man ist (hyü′mə nist), 1 student of human nature or affairs. 2 student of the humanities. *n.*

hu man is tic (hyü′mə nis′tik), of humanists. *adj.*

hu man i tar i an (hyü man′ə-ter′ē ən), 1 helpful to humanity; philanthropic. 2 person who is devoted to the welfare of all human beings. 1 *adj.,* 2 *n.*

hu man i ty (hyü man′ə tē), 1 human beings; people; mankind: *Advances in science help all humanity.* 2 a being human; human nature: *Humanity is a mixture of good and bad qualities.* 3 a being humane; humane treatment; kindness; mercy: *Treat animals with humanity.* 4 **the humanities,** *pl.* **a** the Latin and Greek classics. **b** cultural studies as opposed to the sciences, including languages, literature, philosophy, art, etc. *n., pl.* **hu man i ties.**

hu man ize (hyü′mə nīz), 1 make or become human. 2 make or become humane. *v.,* **hu man ized, hu man iz ing.**

hu man kind (hyü′mən kīnd′), human beings; people; mankind. *n.*

hu man ly (hyü′mən lē), 1 by human means: *The doctor did everything humanly possible to save the patient.* 2 according to the feelings, knowledge, or experience of human beings: *Humanly speaking, what he is asking is impossible to achieve.* 3 in a human manner: *Even a judge is humanly liable to make a mistake. adv.*

hum ble (hum′bəl), 1 low in position or condition; not important or grand: *They lived in a humble, one-room cottage. He has a humble job with very low wages.* 2 not proud; modest: *a humble heart, a humble opinion. She is humble in spite of her great success.* 3 make humble; make lower in position, condition, or pride: *The general was humbled by his defeat.* 1,2 *adj.,* **hum bler, hum blest;** 3 *v.,* **hum bled, humbling.** —**hum′ble ness,** *n.*

hum bly (hum′blē), in a humble manner. *adv.*

hum bug (hum′bug′), 1 person who pretends to be what he is not; fraud; cheat; sham. 2 nonsense or pretense: *There's no humbug about her; she speaks her mind straight out.* 3 deceive with a sham; cheat: *I won't be humbugged into buying something I don't want.* 1,2 *n.,* 3 *v.,* **hum bugged, hum bug ging.**

hum drum (hum′drum′), without variety; commonplace; dull: *Reading about travels and adventures helped him forget the humdrum life he was leading. adj.*

hu mer us (hyü′mər əs), the long bone

in the upper part of the arm, from the shoulder to the elbow. *n.*

SCAPULA
HUMERUS
ULNA
RADIUS

hu mid (hyü′mid), slightly wet; moist; damp: *The air is very humid near the sea. adj.*

hu mid i fi er (hyü mid′ə fī′ər), device for keeping air moist. *n.*

hu mid i fy (hyü mid′ə fī), make moist or damp. *v.,* **hu mid i fied, hu mid i-fy ing.**

hu mid i ty (hyü mid′ə tē), 1 a being humid; moistness; dampness: *The humidity today is worse than the heat.* 2 amount of moisture in the air: *On a hot, sultry day the humidity is high. n.*

hu mil i ate (hyü mil′ē āt), lower the pride, dignity, or self-respect of; make ashamed: *We felt humiliated by our failure. The children humiliated their parents by behaving badly in front of the guests. v.,* **hu mil i at ed, hu mil i-at ing.**

hu mil i a tion (hyü mil′ē ā′shən), a lowering of pride, dignity, or self-respect; a making or a being made ashamed. *n.*

hu mil i ty (hyü mil′ə tē), humbleness of mind; lack of pride; meekness. *n., pl.* **hu mil i ties.**

hum ming bird (hum′ing bėrd′), a very small, brightly colored American bird with a long, narrow bill and narrow wings that move so rapidly they make a humming sound. *n.*

hum mock (hum′ək), 1 a very small, rounded hill; knoll; hillock. 2 a bump or ridge in a field of ice. *n.*

hum mock y (hum′ə kē), 1 full of hummocks. 2 like a hummock. *adj.*

411

adj. adjective	*n.* noun
adv. adverb	*prep.* preposition
conj. conjunction	*pron.* pronoun
interj. interjection	*v.* verb
sing. singular	*pl.* plural

hu mor (hyü′mər), 1 funny or amusing quality: *I see no humor in your tricks.* 2 ability to see or show the funny or amusing side of things: *Mark Twain was famous for his humor.* 3 speech, writing, etc., showing this ability. 4 state of mind; mood; disposition; temper: *Is the teacher in a good humor this morning? I feel in the humor for working.* 5 fancy; whim. 6 give in to the fancies or whims of (a person); agree with; indulge: *That sick child has to be humored.* 1-5 *n.,* 6 *v.*

out of humor, in a bad mood; angry; displeased; cross.

hu mor ist (hyü′mər ist), a humorous talker or writer; person who tells or writes jokes and funny stories. *n.*

hu mor ous (hyü′mər əs), full of humor; funny; amusing: *Mark Twain wrote humorous stories. adj.* —**hu′mor ous ly,** *adv.*

hump (hump), 1 a rounded lump that sticks out: *Some camels have two humps on their backs.* 2 raise or bend up into a hump: *The cat humped her back when she saw the dog.* 3 mound. 1,3 *n.,* 2 *v.*

hump back (hump′bak′), 1 hunchback. 2 a back having a hump on it. *n.*

hump backed (hump′bakt′), hunchbacked. *adj.*

humph (humpf), exclamation expressing doubt, disgust, contempt, etc. *interj., n.*

hu mus (hyü′məs), a dark-brown or black part of soil formed from decayed leaves and other vegetable matter. Humus contains valuable plant foods. *n.*

Hun (hun), 1 member of a warlike Asian people who invaded Europe in the 300's and 400's A.D. 2 a barbarous, destructive person. *n.*

hunch (hunch), 1 a hump. 2 to hump: *hunch one's shoulders.* 3 draw, bend, or form into a hump: *She sat hunched up with her chin on her knees.* 4 move, push, or shove by jerks: *He hunched along in the rain.* 5 INFORMAL. a vague feeling or suspicion: *Having had a hunch that it would rain, I took along an umbrella.* 1,5 *n., pl.* **hunch es;** 2-4 *v.*

hunch back (hunch′bak′), person with a hump on his back; humpback. *n.*

hunch backed (hunch′bakt′), having a hump on the back; humpbacked. *adj.*

hun dred (hun′drəd), ten times ten; 100. There are one hundred cents in a dollar. *n., adj.*

hun dred fold (hun′drəd fōld′), a hundred times as much or as many. *adj., adv., n.*

hun dredth (hun′drədth), 1 next after the 99th; last in a series of 100. 2 one of 100 equal parts. *adj., n.*

hun dred weight (hun′drəd wāt′), measure of weight, equal to 100 pounds in the United States and Canada, and 112 pounds in Great Britain. *n., pl.* **hun dred weights** or (*as after a numeral*) **hun dred weight.**

hung (hung), a past tense and a past participle of **hang.** *He hung up his cap. A dress has hung here all day. v.*

Hun gar i an (hung ger′ē ən), 1 of Hungary, its people, or their language. 2 person born or living in Hungary. 3 language of Hungary. 1 *adj.,* 2,3 *n.*

Hun gar y (hung′gər ē), country in central Europe. Hungary was formerly a part of the empire of Austria-Hungary. *Capital:* Budapest. *n.*

hun ger (hung′gər), 1 an uncomfortable or painful feeling in the stomach caused by having had nothing to eat. 2 desire or need for food: *I satisfied my hunger by eating an apple and some cheese.* 3 feel hunger; be hungry. 4 a strong desire; craving; longing: *The badly treated boy had a hunger for kindness and affection.* 5 have a strong desire; crave; long: *The lonely girl hungered for friends.* 1,2,4 *n.,* 3,5 *v.*

hun gri ly (hung′grə lē), in a hungry manner. *adv.*

hun gri ness (hung′grē nis), condition of being hungry. *n.*

hun gry (hung′grē), 1 feeling a desire or need for food: *The boys in our family always seem to be hungry.* 2 showing hunger: *The cook saw a hungry look on the stranger's face.* 3 having a strong desire or craving; eager: *A person who longs to read and study is hungry for knowledge. adj.,* **hun gri er, hun gri est.**

hunk (hungk), INFORMAL. a big lump or piece: *a hunk of cheese. n.*

hunt (hunt), 1 go after (game and other wild animals) to catch or kill them for food or sport. 2 act of hunting. 3 group of persons hunting together. 4 search; seek; look for: *hunt through drawers, hunt for a lost book.* 5 drive; chase: *We hunted the neighbor's chickens out of our yard.* 6 an attempt to find something; search: *The hunt for the lost child continued until she was found.* 1,4,5 *v.,* 2,3,6 *n.*

hunt er (hun′tər), 1 person who hunts. 2 horse or dog trained for hunting. *n.*

hunt ing (hun′ting), act or sport of chasing game. *n.*

hunt ress (hun′tris), woman who hunts. *n., pl.* **hunt ress es.**

hunts man (hunts′mən), 1 hunter. 2 manager of a hunt. *n., pl.* **huntsmen.**

hurdles (def. 1)

hur dle (hėr′dl), 1 barrier for people or horses to jump over in a race. 2 **hurdles,** *pl.* race in which the runners jump over hurdles. 3 jump over: *The horse hurdled both the fence and the ditch.* 4 obstacle, difficulty, etc. 5 overcome (an obstacle, difficulty, etc.). 6 frame made of sticks, used as a temporary fence. 7 enclose with such frames. 1,2,4,6 *n.,* 3,5,7 *v.,* **hur dled, hur dling.**

hur dler (hėrd′lər), person who jumps over hurdles in a race. *n.*

hur dy-gur dy (hėr′dē gėr′dē), hand organ or street piano played by turning a handle. *n., pl.* **hur dy-gur dies.**

hurl (hėrl), 1 throw with much force: *The man hurled his spear at one bear, and the dogs hurled themselves at the other.* 2 a forcible or violent throw. 3 throw forth (words, cries, etc.) violently: *They hurled insults at me.* 1,3 *v.,* 2 *n.* —**hurl′er,** *n.*

hur ly-bur ly (hėr′lē bėr′lē), disorder and noise; commotion; tumult. *n., pl.* **hur ly-bur lies.**

Hur on (hyür′ən), **Lake,** one of the five Great Lakes. *n.*

hur rah (hə rä′ *or* hə rô′), 1 a shout of joy, approval, etc.: "*Hurrah!*" *they shouted as the team scored again* (*interj.*). *Give a hurrah for the hero!* (*n.*). 2 shout hurrahs; cheer: *We hurrahed as the astronauts rode by in the parade.* 1 *interj., n.,* 2 *v.* Also, **hooray.**

hur ray (hə rā′), hurrah. *interj., n., v.*

hur ri cane (hėr′ə kān), 1 storm with violent wind and, usually, very heavy rain. Hurricanes are common in the West Indies. The wind in a hurricane blows with a velocity of above 75 miles per hour. 2 a sudden, violent outburst: *a hurricane of cheers.*

hur ried (hėr′ēd), done or made in a hurry; hasty: *She gave a hurried reply and ran. adj.* —**hur′ried ly,** *adv.*

hur ry (hėr′ē), 1 drive, carry, send, or move quickly: *They hurried the sick child to the doctor.* 2 move or act with more than an easy or natural speed: *If you hurry, your work may be poor. He hurried to get the doctor.* **3** a hurried movement or action: *In her hurry she dropped the eggs.* **4** need to hurry; eagerness to have quickly or do quickly: *She was in a hurry to get to work on time.* **5** urge to act soon or too soon: *The salesman hurried the customer to make a choice.* **6** urge to great speed or to too great speed: *Don't hurry the driver.* **7** make go on or occur more quickly; hasten: *Please hurry dinner.* **1,2,5-7** *v.*, **hur ried, hur ry ing; 3,4** *n.*, *pl.* **hur ries.**

hurt (hėrt), **1** cause pain to; wound; injure: *The stone hurt his foot badly.* **2** a cut, bruise, or fracture; any wound or injury: *A scratch is not a serious hurt.* **3** suffer pain: *My hand hurts.* **4** have a bad effect on; do damage or harm to: *Will it hurt this hat if it gets wet? She hurt her brother's feelings.* **5** a bad effect; damage; harm; wrong: *It would do no hurt to get the house painted this summer.* **1,3,4** *v.*, **hurt, hurt ing; 2,5** *n.*

hurt ful (hėrt′fəl), causing pain, harm, or damage; injurious: *a mean and hurtful remark.* *adj.*

hur tle (hėr′tl), **1** dash or drive violently; rush violently: *The express train hurtled past. The impact of the crash hurtled the driver against the windshield of the car.* **2** act or fact of hurtling; clash. **1** *v.*, **hur tled, hur tling; 2** *n.*

hus band (huz′bənd), **1** man who has a wife; a married man. **2** manage carefully; be saving of: *A sick man must husband his limited strength.* **1** *n.*, **2** *v.*

hus band man (huz′bənd mən), farmer. *n.*, *pl.* **hus band men.**

hus band ry (huz′bən drē), **1** farming. **2** management of one's affairs or resources: *To let a roof leak is bad husbandry.* **3** careful management; thrift. *n.*

hush (hush), **1** stop making a noise; make or become silent or quiet: *The wind has hushed. Hush your dog.* **2** a stopping of noise; silence; quiet; stillness. **3** stop the noise! be silent! keep quiet! **4** soothe; calm. **1,4** *v.*, **2** *n.*, **3** *interj.*

hush up, **1** keep from being told; stop discussion of: *The facts were hushed up to keep them secret.* **2** INFORMAL. hush!

husk (husk), **1** the dry outer covering of certain seeds or fruits. An ear of corn has a husk. **2** the dry or worthless outer covering of anything. **3** remove the husk from: *Husk the corn before cooking it.* **1,2** *n.*, **3** *v.* —**husk′er**, *n.*

husk i ly (hus′kə lē), in a husky voice; hoarsely. *adv.*

husk i ness (hus′kē nis), husky quality or condition. *n.*

husk ing (hus′king), husking bee. *n.*

husking bee, a gathering of neighbors and friends to husk corn.

husk y[1] (hus′kē), **1** big and strong: *a husky young man.* **2** INFORMAL. a big, strong person. **3** dry in the throat; hoarse; rough of voice: *A cold sometimes causes a husky cough.* **4** of, like, or having husks: *a husky covering.* **1,3,4** *adj.*, **husk i er, husk i est; 2** *n.*, *pl.* **husk ies.** [*husk + -y*[1]]

hus ky[2] (hus′kē), **1** any arctic sled dog originating in Siberia. **2** Eskimo dog. *n.*, *pl.* **hus kies** [origin uncertain]

Hus ky (hus′kē), husky[2]. *n.*, *pl.* **Hus kies.**

hus sar (hù zär′), a light-armed cavalry soldier in various European armies. *n.*

hus sy (huz′ē *or* hus′ē), **1** a bad-mannered or pert girl. **2** a woman who flaunts her immorality. *n.*, *pl.* **hus sies.**

hus tle (hus′əl), **1** to hurry: *Mother hustled the baby to bed.* **2** rush roughly; push one's way: *hustle along through the crowd.* **3** push or shove roughly; jostle rudely: *We hustled the intruder right out the door.* **4** INFORMAL. go or work quickly or with energy: *He had to hustle to earn enough money to support his large family.* **5** INFORMAL. tireless energy. **6** a hustling: *It was a hustle to get the dishes washed by seven o'clock.* **1-4** *v.*, **hus tled, hus tling; 5,6** *n.*

hus tler (hus′lər), **1** person who hustles. **2** INFORMAL. a very energetic person. *n.*

hut (hut), a small, roughly made house; small cabin: *The girls and boys built a hut in the woods.* *n.*

hutch (huch), **1** box or pen for small animals. Rabbits are kept in hutches. **2** hut. **3** box; chest; bin. **4** cupboard with open shelves on the upper part for holding dishes, etc. *n.*, *pl.* **hutch es.**

Hux ley (huk′slē), **1** **Aldous**, 1894-1963, English novelist and essayist. **2** his grandfather, **Thomas Henry**, 1825-1895, English biologist. *n.*

huz za (hə zä′), **1** a loud shout of joy, encouragement, or applause; hurrah. **2** shout huzzas; cheer. **1** *interj.*, *n.*, *pl.* **huz zas; 2** *v.*

Hwang ho (hwäng′hō′), Hwang Ho. *n.*

Hwang Ho (hwäng′ hō′), river in China flowing from central China into the Yellow Sea; Yellow River. *n.*

hy a cinth (hī′ə sinth), **1** plant of the same family as the lily, that grows from a bulb and has a spike of small, fragrant, bell-shaped flowers. **2** its flower. *n.*

hy brid (hī′brid), **1** offspring of two animals or plants of different species, varieties, etc. The loganberry is a

hat, āge, fär; let, ēqual, tėrm;
it, īce; hot, ōpen, ôrder;
oil, out; cup, pùt, rüle; ch, child;
ng, long; sh, she; th, thin;
ͲH, then; zh, measure;

ə represents *a* in about,
e in taken, *i* in pencil,
o in lemon, *u* in circus.

hybrid because it is a cross between a red raspberry and a dewberry. **2** bred from two different species, varieties, etc. A mule is a hybrid animal. **3** anything of mixed origin. A word formed of parts from different languages is a hybrid. **4** of mixed origin. **1,3** *n.*, **2,4** *adj.*

hy brid i za tion (hī′brə də zā′shən), production of hybrids; crossing of different species, varieties, etc. *n.*

hy brid ize (hī′brə dīz), **1** cause to produce hybrids: *Botanists hybridize different kinds of plants in order to get new varieties.* **2** produce hybrids. *v.*, **hy brid ized, hy brid iz ing.**

hy dra (hī′drə), **1** kind of freshwater polyp with a tubelike body and stinging tentacles. When its body is cut into pieces, each piece forms a new individual. **2 Hydra,** (in Greek myths) a monster with many snakelike heads. When one head was cut off, two or three grew in its place. Hercules finally killed it. *n.*, *pl.* **hy dras, hy drae** (hī′-drē′).

hy dran gea (hī drān′jə), **1** shrub with large, showy flower clusters, white, pink, or blue in color. **2** its flower. *n.*, *pl.* **hy dran geas.**

hy drant (hī′drənt), a large, upright pipe with a valve for drawing water directly from a water main; hose connection on a street, road, etc.; fireplug. Hydrants are used to get water to put out fires and to wash the streets. *n.*

hy drate (hī′drāt), **1** any chemical compound made when certain substances chemically unite with water. **2** become or cause to become a hydrate; combine with water to form a hydrate. **1** *n.*, **2** *v.*, **hy drat ed, hy drat ing.**

hy drau lic (hī drô′lik), **1** having to do with water or other liquids in motion. **2** operated by the pressure of water or other liquids in motion: *a hydraulic press.* **3** hardening under water: *hydraulic cement.* *adj.* —**hy drau′li cal ly,** *adv.*

hy drau lics (hī drô′liks), science dealing with water and other liquids in motion, their uses in engineering, and the laws of their actions. *n.*

hy dride (hī′drīd), compound of hy-

adj. adjective	*n.* noun
adv. adverb	*prep.* preposition
conj. conjunction	*pron.* pronoun
interj. interjection	*v.* verb
sing. singular	*pl.* plural

drogen with another element or radical. *n.*

hy dro car bon (hī′drō kär′bən), any of a class of chemical compounds containing only hydrogen and carbon. Gasoline is a mixture of hydrocarbons. *n.*

hy dro chlo ric (hī′drə klôr′ik), containing hydrogen and chlorine. *adj.*

hydrochloric acid, a clear, colorless liquid with a strong, sharp odor. Hydrochloric acid is used in cleaning metals.

hy dro cy an ic acid (hī′drō sī-an′ik), a colorless, volatile, poisonous liquid that smells like bitter almonds, used in making plastics, dyes, etc.; prussic acid.

hy dro e lec tric (hī′drō i lek′trik), developing electricity from water power. *adj.*

hydrofoil (defs. 1 and 2)
two types of hydrofoils

hy dro foil (hī′drə foil), 1 fin just below the water line of a boat that raises the hull out of the water at high speeds, decreasing friction and increasing the speed of the boat. 2 boat with hydrofoils. *n.*

hy dro gen (hī′drə jən), a colorless, odorless gas that burns easily. Hydrogen is a chemical element that weighs less than any other known element. It combines with oxygen to form water and is present in most organic compounds. *n.*

hy dro gen ate (hī′drə jə nāt), combine with hydrogen; treat with hydrogen. When vegetable oils are hydrogenated, they become solid fats. *v.,* **hy dro gen at ed, hy dro gen at ing.**

hydrogen bomb, bomb that uses the fusion of atoms to cause an explosion of tremendous force; H-bomb; fusion bomb. It is many times more powerful than the atomic bomb.

hydrogen peroxide, a colorless compound of hydrogen and oxygen; peroxide. It is used in water solution as an antiseptic and to bleach hair.

hy drol y sis (hī drol′ə sis), a chemical process in which a compound is broken down and changed into other compounds by taking up the elements of water. *n., pl.* **hy drol y ses** (hī-drol′ə sēz′).

hy drom e ter (hī drom′ə tər), instrument for finding the specific gravities of liquids. *n.*

hydrometer being used to test an automobile battery. The amount that the weighted inner glass tube sinks in the liquid indicates the concentration of acid in the battery.

hy dro pho bi a (hī′drə fō′bē ə), rabies. *n.*

hy dro plane (hī′drə plān), 1 motorboat that glides on the surface of water. 2 seaplane. *n.*

hy dro pon ics (hī′drə pon′iks), the growing of plants without soil by the use of water containing the necessary nutrients. *n.*

hy dro sphere (hī′drə sfir), 1 water on the surface of the earth. 2 the water vapor in the atmosphere. *n.*

hy drous (hī′drəs), containing water, usually in combination. *adj.*

hy drox ide (hī drok′sīd), a chemical compound that contains a radical made up of an oxygen and a hydrogen atom. Calcium hydroxide is slaked lime. *n.*

hy e na (hī ē′nə), a wild, flesh-eating, wolflike mammal of Africa and Asia which feeds at night, usually on carrion. Hyenas avoid contact with other animals, and are noted for their terrifying yells. *n., pl.* **hy e nas.**

hyena about 2 ft. high at the shoulder

hy giene (hī′jēn′), rules of health; science of keeping well. *n.*

hy gien ic (hī jē′nik *or* hī jen′ik), 1 favorable to health; healthful; sanitary. 2 having to do with health or hygiene. *adj.* —**hy gien′i cal ly,** *adv.*

hy gien ist (hī′jē′nist), an expert in hygiene. *n.*

hy gro graph (hī′grə graf), instrument for recording the amount of moisture in the air. *n.*

hy grom e ter (hī grom′ə tər), instrument for measuring the amount of moisture in the air. *n.*

hy ing (hī′ing), hieing; a present participle of **hie.** *v.*

Hy men (hī′mən), (in Greek myths) the god of marriage. *n.*

hy me ne al (hī′mə nē′əl), having to do with marriage. *adj.*

hymn (him), 1 song in praise or honor of God. 2 any song of praise. *n.* —**hymn′like′,** *adj.*

hym nal (him′nəl), book of hymns. *n.*

hymn book (him′būk′), hymnal. *n.*

hy per bo le (hī pėr′bə lē′), an exaggerated statement used for effect and not meant to be taken literally. EXAMPLE: Waves high as mountains broke over the reef. *n.*

hy per bol ic (hī′pər bol′ik), of, like, or using hyperbole; exaggerated; exaggerating. *adj.*

hy per crit i cal (hī′pər krit′ə kəl), too critical. *adj.* —**hy′per crit′i cal ly,** *adv.*

hy per sen si tive (hī′pər sen′sə tiv), extremely sensitive: *She was hypersensitive to the slightest criticism.* *adj.* —**hy′per sen′si tive ness,** *n.*

hy per sen si tiv i ty (hī′pər sen′-sə tiv′ə tē), extreme sensitiveness. *n.*

hy per son ic (hī′pər son′ik), that moves or is able to move at a speed which is five or more times faster than the speed of sound in air (1087 feet per second): *a hypersonic missile or aircraft. adj.*

hy per ten sion (hī′pər ten′shən), an abnormally high blood pressure. *n.*

hy phen (hī′fən), 1 mark (-) used to join the parts of a compound word, or the parts of a word divided at the end of a line. 2 hyphenate. 1 *n.,* 2 *v.*

hy phen ate (hī′fə nāt), join by a hyphen; write or print with a hyphen. *v.,* **hy phen at ed, hy phen at ing.**

hy phen a tion (hī′fə nā′shən), act of joining by a hyphen; writing or printing with a hyphen. *n.*

hyp no sis (hip nō′sis), condition resembling deep sleep, but more active, in which a person has little will of his own, and acts according to the suggestions of the person who brought about the condition. *n., pl.* **hyp no ses** (hip-nō′sēz′).

hyp not ic (hip not′ik), 1 of hypnosis. 2 causing sleep. 3 drug or other means of causing sleep. 4 person who is hyp-

hair hygrometer—Moisture increases the length of the hairs, allowing the pointer to move to the right.

notized or easily hypnotized. 1,2 *adj.*, 3,4 *n.* —**hyp not′i cal ly,** *adv.*

hyp no tism (hip′nə tiz′əm), 1 a putting into a hypnotic state; a hypnotizing. 2 science dealing with hypnosis. *n.*

hyp no tist (hip′nə tist), person who hypnotizes. *n.*

hyp no tize (hip′nə tīz), 1 put into a hypnotic state; cause hypnosis. 2 dominate or control by suggestion; cast a spell over: *The candidate's eloquence so hypnotized his audience that many of the people present decided to vote for him.* *v.*, **hyp no tized, hypno tiz ing.**

hypodermic syringe and needle

hyp no tiz er (hip′nə tī′zər), hypnotist. *n.*

hy po[1] (hī′pō), a chemical compound used to treat photographic negatives and prints to keep them from fading. *n.*, *pl.* **hy pos.** [shortened from *hyposulfite* salt of a sulfurous acid]

hy po[2] (hī′pō), INFORMAL. hypodermic. *n.*, *pl.* **hy pos.** [shortened from *hypodermic*]

hy po chon dri a (hī′pə kon′drē ə), abnormal anxiety over one's health; imaginary illness. *n.*

hy po chon dri ac (hī′pə kon′drē ak), person who imagines that he is ill when he is not. *n.*

hy poc ri sy (hi pok′rə sē), 1 a pretending to be very good or religious. 2 a pretending to be what one is not; pretense. *n.*, *pl.* **hy poc ri sies.**

hyp o crite (hip′ə krit), 1 person who pretends to be very good or religious. 2 person who pretends to be what he is not; pretender. *n.*

hyp o crit i cal (hip′ə krit′ə kəl), of or like a hypocrite; insincere. *adj.* —**hyp′o crit′i cal ly,** *adv.*

hy po der mic (hī′pə dėr′mik), 1 under the skin. 2 injected or used to inject under the skin: *The doctor used a hypodermic needle.* 3 dose of medicine injected under the skin: *The doctor gave her a hypodermic to make her sleep.* 4 a hypodermic syringe. 1,2 *adj.*, 3,4 *n.*

hypodermic syringe, syringe fitted with a hollow needle, used to inject a dose of medicine under the skin.

hy pot e nuse (hī pot′n üs *or* hīpot′n yüs), the side of a right triangle opposite the right angle. *n.*

hy poth e sis (hī poth′ə sis), 1 something assumed because it seems likely to be a true explanation; theory: *Let us act on the hypothesis that he is honest.* 2 proposition assumed as a basis for reasoning. A theorem in geometry is made up of a hypothesis and a conclusion. *n.*, *pl.* **hy poth e ses** (hī poth′ə sēz′).

hy poth e size (hī poth′ə sīz), 1 make a hypothesis. 2 assume; suppose. *v.*, **hy poth e sized, hy poth e siz ing.**

hy po thet i cal (hī′pə thet′ə kəl), of or based on a hypothesis; assumed; supposed: *a hypothetical case.* *adj.* —**hy′po thet′i cal ly,** *adv.*

hys sop (his′əp), 1 a fragrant, bushy plant, used for medicine, flavoring, etc.

hat, āge, fär; let, ēqual, tėrm; it, īce; hot, ōpen, ôrder; oil, out; cup, pùt, rüle; ch, child; ng, long; sh, she; th, thin; ₮H, then; zh, measure;

ə represents *a* in about, *e* in taken, *i* in pencil, *o* in lemon, *u* in circus.

2 (in the Bible) a plant whose twigs were used in certain religious ceremonies. *n.*

RIGHT ANGLE

hys ter i a (hi stir′ē ə *or* hi ster′ē ə), 1 a mental disorder which is caused by anxiety. The physical symptoms of hysteria may include blindness, paralysis, or stomach upsets. 2 unrestrained excitement or emotion. *n.*

hys ter ic (hi ster′ik), hysterical. *adj.*

hys ter i cal (hi ster′ə kəl), 1 unnaturally excited; emotional: *hysterical weeping.* 2 showing an unnatural lack of self-control; suffering from hysteria: *The hysterical child was unable to stop laughing and crying violently.* 3 of, having to do with, or characteristic of hysteria: *a hysterical fit.* *adj.* —**hyster′i cal ly,** *adv.*

hys ter ics (hi ster′iks), a fit of hysterical laughing and crying. *n.pl.*

I i

I¹ or **i** (ī), 1 the ninth letter of the alphabet. 2 the Roman numeral for 1. *n., pl.* **I's** or **i's.**

I² (ī), the person speaking or writing: *John said, "I am ten years old." I like my dog, and he likes me.* *pron., pl.* **we.**

Ia., Iowa.

i am bic (ī am′bik), 1 a foot or measure in poetry consisting of two syllables, an unaccented followed by an accented. 2 of or containing iambic measures. Much English poetry is iambic. EXAMPLE:

"The sún|that bríef|De cém|ber dáy
Rose chéer|less ó|ver hílls|of gráy."

1 *n.,* 2 *adj.*

-ian, suffix meaning the same as **-an,** as in *mammalian, Italian,* etc. [from Latin *-ianus*]

I ber i a (ī bir′ē ə), peninsula in SW Europe, containing Spain and Portugal. *n.*

ibex
about 2½ ft. high
at the shoulder

i bex (ī′beks), a wild goat of Europe, Asia, and Africa. The male has very large horns which curve backward. *n., pl.* **i bex es** or **i bex.**

i bis (ī′bis), a large, long-legged wading bird of warm regions, related to the heron, and having a long, downward-curving bill. The ancient Egyptians regarded the ibis as sacred. *n., pl.* **i bis es** or **i bis.**

-ible, *suffix added to verbs to form adjectives.* that can be _____ed: *Perfectible = that can be perfected. Reducible = that can be reduced.* [from Latin *-ibilis*]

Ib sen (ib′sən), **Henrik,** 1828-1906, Norwegian dramatist. *n.*

-ic, *suffix added to nouns to form adjectives.* 1 of or having to do with: *Atmos-*

iceberg

pheric = of the atmosphere. 2 having the nature of: *Heroic = having the nature of a hero.* 3 constituting or being: *Bombastic = constituting or being bombast.* 4 containing; made up of: *Alcoholic = containing alcohol.* 5 made by; caused by: *Volcanic = made by a volcano.* 6 like; like that of; characteristic of: *Meteoric = like a meteor.* [from French *-ique* or Latin *-icus* or Greek *-ikos*]

-ical, suffix meaning the same as **-ic,** as in *historical, geometrical, economical.* [from Latin *-icalem,* from Latin *-icus* -ic + -alem -al¹]

Ic ar us (ik′ər əs), (in Greek legends) the son of Daedalus. Icarus and his father escaped from Crete by using wings that Daedalus had made. Icarus flew so high that the sun melted the wax by which his wings were attached, and he drowned in the sea. *n.*

ICBM, Intercontinental Ballistic Missile, missile with a range of over 5000 miles.

ice (īs), 1 water made solid by cold; frozen water. 2 layer or surface of ice. 3 of ice; having to do with ice. 4 something that looks or feels like ice. 5 make cool with ice; put ice in or around: *an iced drink.* 6 cover with ice. 7 turn to ice; freeze. 8 a frozen dessert, usually one made of sweetened fruit juice. 9 a sugary covering for a cake; icing. 10 cover (cake) with icing. 1,2,4,8,9 *n.,* 3 *adj.,* 5-7,10 *v.,* **iced, ic ing.**

break the ice, overcome first difficulties in talking or getting acquainted.

on thin ice, in a dangerous or difficult position.

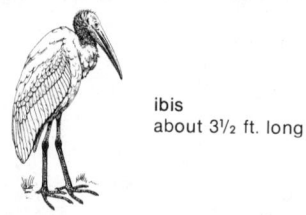

ibis
about 3½ ft. long

ice age, 1 any of the times when much of the earth was covered with glaciers. 2 Usually, **Ice Age.** the most recent such time, when most of the Northern Hemisphere was covered with glaciers.

ice berg (īs′bėrg′), a large mass of ice, detached from a glacier and floating in the sea. About 90 per cent of its mass is below the surface of the water. *n.*

ice boat (īs′bōt′), 1 a triangular frame on runners, fitted with sails or an engine for sailing on ice. 2 icebreaker. *n.*

ice bound (īs′bound′), 1 held fast by ice; frozen in. 2 shut in or obstructed by ice. *adj.*

ice box (īs′boks′), 1 refrigerator. 2 an insulated box in which food is kept cool with ice. *n., pl.* **ice box es.**

ice break er (īs′brā′kər), 1 a strong boat used to break a channel through ice; iceboat. 2 anything that helps overcome first difficulties in talking or getting acquainted. *n.*

ice cap (īs′kap′), a permanent covering of ice over an area, sloping down on all sides from an elevated center. *n.*

ice-cold (īs′kōld′), cold as ice. *adj.*

ice cream, a frozen dessert made of cream or custard sweetened and flavored.

Ice land (īs′lənd), large island in the N Atlantic between Greenland and Norway, formerly a Danish possession. Iceland has been an independent republic since 1944. *Capital:* Reykjavik. *n.*

Ice land er (īs′lan′dər), person born or living in Iceland.

Ice lan dic (īs lan′dik), 1 of or having to do with Iceland, its people, or their language. 2 language of Iceland. 1 *adj.,* 2 *n.*

ice man (īs′man′), man who sells, delivers, or handles ice. *n., pl.* **ice men.**

ice sheet, a broad, thick sheet of ice covering a very large area for a long time.

ice skate, a metal runner attached to a shoe for skating on ice.

ice-skate (īs′skāt′), skate on ice. *v.,* **ice-skat ed, ice-skat ing.**

ice skater, person who ice-skates.

ich neu mon (ik nü′mən or ik-nyü′mən), 1 mongoose of Egypt that looks like a weasel. 2 ichneumon fly. *n.*

ichneumon fly, insect related to bees and wasps that does not sting. Its larvae live as parasites in or on caterpillars and other insect larvae.

i ci cle (ī′si kəl), a pointed, hanging stick of ice formed by the freezing of dripping water. *n.*

i ci ly (ī′sə lē), in an icy manner. *adv.*

i ci ness (ī′sē nis), a being icy. *n.*

ic ing (ī′sing), frosting. *n.*

i con (ī′kon), 1 picture or image of Christ, an angel, or a saint, venerated as sacred in the Eastern Church. 2 picture; image. *n.* Also, **ikon.**

i con o clast (ī kon′ə klast), 1 person

iceboat (def. 1)

who attacks cherished beliefs or institutions which he thinks are wrong or foolish. 2 person opposed to worshiping images. *n.*

i con o clas tic (ī kon′ ə klas′tik), of iconoclasts. *adj.*

i cy (ī′sē), 1 like ice; very cold or slippery. 2 having much ice; covered with ice. 3 of ice. 4 without warm feeling; cold and unfriendly. *adj.*, **i ci er, i ci est.**

I'd (īd), 1 I should. 2 I would. 3 I had.

Id., or **Ida.,** Idaho.

I da ho (ī′də hō), one of the western states of the United States. *Capital:* Boise. *n.* —**I′da ho′an,** *n., adj.*

i de a (ī dē′ə), 1 plan, picture, or belief in the mind: *Swimming is my idea of fun.* 2 thought, fancy, or opinion: *I had no idea that the job would be so difficult.* 3 point or purpose: *The idea of this vacation was to get a rest. n., pl.* **i de as.**

i de al (ī dē′əl), 1 a perfect type; model to be imitated; what one would wish to be: *Her mother is her ideal. Religion holds up high ideals for us to follow.* 2 just as one would wish; perfect: *A warm, sunny day is ideal for a picnic.* 3 existing only in thought; imaginary: *A point without length, breadth, or thickness is an ideal object.* 1 *n.,* 2,3 *adj.*

i de al ism (ī dē′ə liz′əm), 1 an acting according to one's ideals of what ought to be, regardless of what happens or of what other people may think; a cherishing of fine ideals. 2 a neglecting practical matters in following ideals; not being practical. 3 belief that reality is made up of ideas only and not of material objects. *n.*

i de al ist (ī dē′ə list), 1 person who has high ideals and acts according to them. 2 person who neglects practical matters in following ideals. *n.*

i de al is tic (ī′dē ə lis′tik *or* ī dē′-ə lis′tik), 1 having high ideals and acting according to them. 2 forgetting or neglecting practical matters in trying to follow out one's ideals; not practical. 3 of idealism or idealists. *adj.*

i de al i za tion (ī dē′ə lə zā′shən), 1 an idealizing or a being idealized. 2 result of idealizing. *n.*

i de al ize (ī dē′ə līz), make ideal; think of or represent as perfect rather than as is actually true: *She idealized her older sister and thought that everything she did was right. v.,* **i de al ized, i de al iz ing.**

i de al ly (ī dē′ə lē), 1 according to an ideal; perfectly. 2 only as an idea or theory; not really. *adv.*

i den ti cal (ī den′tə kəl), 1 the same: *Both events happened on the identical day.* 2 exactly alike: *identical bicycles. adj.* —**i den′ti cal ly,** *adv.*

identical twins, twins of the same sex and physical appearance coming from a single fertilized egg cell rather than from two egg cells as fraternal twins do.

i den ti fi a ble (ī den′tə fī′ə bəl), that can be identified. *adj.*

i den ti fi ca tion (ī den′tə fə kā′shən), 1 an identifying or a being identified. 2 something used to identify a person or thing: *He offered his driver's license as identification. n.*

i den ti fy (ī den′tə fī), 1 recognize as being, or show to be, a particular person or thing; prove to be the same: *He identified the wallet as his by describing it.* 2 make the same; treat as the same: *The king identified his people's good with his own.* 3 connect closely; associate: *identify with a political party. v.,* **i den ti fied, i den ti fy ing.**

i den ti ty (ī den′tə tē), 1 a being oneself or itself, and not another; who or what one is: *The writer concealed her identity by signing her stories with a pen name.* 2 a being identical; exact likeness; sameness: *The identity of the two crimes led the police to think that the same person committed them.* 3 state or fact of being the same one: *The museum established the identity of the painting with one described in an old document.* 4 identity element. *n., pl.* **i den ti ties.**

identity element, an element of a set that does not change any other element it is combined with under a specific operation; identity. The identity element for addition is 0. EXAMPLE: 28 + 0 = 28. The identity element for multiplication is 1. EXAMPLE: 28 × 1 = 28.

i de o log i cal (ī′dē ə loj′ə kəl *or* id′ē ə loj′ə kəl), having to do with ideology. *adj.*

i de ol o gy (ī′dē ol′ə jē *or* id′ē ol′-ə jē), set of doctrines or body of opinions that a group of people have. A political party or movement usually has an ideology. *n., pl.* **i de ol o gies.**

ides (īdz), (in the ancient Roman calendar) the 15th day of March, May, July, and October, and the 13th day of the other months. *n.pl.*

id i o cy (id′ē ə sē), 1 a being an idiot. 2 great stupidity. 3 a very stupid or foolish action, remark, etc. *n., pl.* **id i o cies.**

id i om (id′ē əm), 1 phrase or expression whose meaning cannot be understood from the ordinary meanings of the words in it. "Give in" is an English idiom meaning "yield." 2 the language or dialect of a particular area or group: *the idiom of the French Canadians. He spoke in the idiom of the New England countryside.* 3 a people's way of expressing themselves: *It is often hard*

hat, āge, fär; let, ēqual, tėrm;
it, īce; hot, ōpen, ôrder;
oil, out; cup, pu̇t, rüle; ch, child;
ng, long; sh, she; th, thin;
ŦH, then; zh, measure;

ə represents *a* in about,
e in taken, *i* in pencil,
o in lemon, *u* in circus.

to translate English into the French idiom. *n.*

id i o mat ic (id′ē ə mat′ik), 1 containing an idiom; having or using idioms. 2 showing the individual character of a language; characteristic of a particular language: *The American spoke excellent idiomatic French. adj.* —**id′i o mat′i cal ly,** *adv.*

id i o syn cra sy (id′ē ō sing′krə sē), a personal peculiarity: *One of his idiosyncrasies was eating a hamburger for breakfast. n., pl.* **id i o syn cra sies.**

id i ot (id′ē ət), 1 person born with such a weak mind that he can never learn to read or count; person who does not develop beyond a mental age of three years. 2 a very stupid or foolish person: *Like an idiot I lost my key. n.*

id i ot ic (id′ē ot′ik), very stupid or foolish. *adj.* —**id′i ot′i cal ly,** *adv.*

i dle (ī′dl), 1 doing nothing; not busy; not working: *the idle hours of a holiday. Give me some help; don't just stand there idle.* 2 fond of doing nothing; not willing to work; lazy: *an idle person.* 3 useless; worthless: *idle pleasures.* 4 without any good reason: *Stop worrying about idle rumors.* 5 be idle; do nothing: *Are you going to spend your whole vacation just idling?* 6 spend or waste (time): *She idled away many hours lying in the hammock.* 7 run slowly without transmitting power. The motor of a car idles when out of gear and running slowly. 1-4 *adj.,* **i dler, i dlest;** 5-7 *v.,* **i dled, i dling.** —**i′dle ness,** *n.*

i dler (ī′dlər), a lazy person. *n.*

i dly (ī′dlē), in an idle manner. *adv.*

i dol (ī′dl), 1 image or other object worshiped as a god. 2 person or thing that is loved or admired very much. *n.*

idol (def. 1)
Mayan idol

417

adj.	adjective	*n.*	noun
adv.	adverb	*prep.*	preposition
conj.	conjunction	*pron.*	pronoun
interj.	interjection	*v.*	verb
sing.	singular	*pl.*	plural

i dol a ter (ī dol′ə tər), person who worships idols. *n.*

i dol a tress (ī dol′ə tris), woman who worships idols. *n., pl.* **i dol a tress es.**

i dol a trous (ī dol′ə trəs), 1 worshiping idols. 2 having to do with idolatry. 3 blindly adoring. *adj.*

i dol a try (ī dol′ə trē), 1 worship of idols. 2 worship of a person or thing; extreme devotion: *The queen was adored to the point of idolatry. n., pl.* **i dol a tries.**

i dol ize (ī′dl īz), 1 love or admire very much; be extremely devoted to: *The boy idolized his older brother.* 2 worship as an idol; make an idol of: *The ancient Hebrews idolized the golden calf. v.,* **i dol ized, i dol iz ing.**

i dyll or **i dyl** (ī′dl), 1 description in poetry or prose of a simple and charming scene or event of country life. 2 a simple and charming scene or event suitable for such a description. *n.*

i dyl lic (ī dil′ik), suitable for an idyll; simple and charming. *adj.* —**i dyl′li cal ly,** *adv.*

i.e., that is; that is to say; namely. [abbreviation of Latin *id est*]

if (if), 1 supposing that; on condition that; in case: *Come if you can. If it rains tomorrow, we shall stay at home.* 2 whether: *I wonder if they will go.* 3 although; even though: *It was a welcome if unexpected holiday. conj.*

ig loo (ig′lü), an Eskimo hut shaped like a dome, often built of blocks of hard snow. *n., pl.* **ig loos.**

igloo

ig ne ous (ig′nē əs), 1 of fire; having to do with fire. 2 formed by the cooling of melted rock material either within or on the surface of the earth. Granite is an igneous rock. *adj.*

ig nite (ig nīt′), 1 set on fire: *He ignited the match by scratching it on the box.* 2 take fire; begin to burn: *Gasoline ignites easily. v.,* **ig nit ed, ig nit ing.**

ig ni tion (ig nish′ən), 1 a setting on fire. 2 a catching on fire. 3 apparatus for igniting the explosive vapor in the

cylinders of an internal-combustion engine. Spark plugs are part of the ignition of most cars. *n.*

ig no ble (ig nō′bəl), 1 without honor; disgraceful; base: *To betray a friend is ignoble.* 2 not of noble birth or position; humble: *Though of ignoble background, she was the queen's favorite. adj.*

ig no bly (ig nō′blē), in an ignoble manner. *adv.*

ig no min i ous (ig′nə min′ē əs), shameful; disgraceful; dishonorable: *After an ignominious defeat the army surrendered. adj.* —**ig′no min′i ous ly,** *adv.*

ig no min y (ig′nə min′ē), public shame and disgrace; dishonor. *n., pl.* **ig no min ies.**

ig no ra mus (ig′nə rā′məs), an ignorant person. *n., pl.* **ig no ra mus es.**

ig nor ance (ig′nər əns), a being ignorant; lack of knowledge. *n.*

ig nor ant (ig′nər ənt), 1 knowing little or nothing; without knowledge. A person who has not had much chance to learn may be ignorant but not stupid. *People who live in the city are often ignorant of farm life.* 2 caused by or showing lack of knowledge: *Saying that the earth is flat is an ignorant remark.* 3 uninformed; unaware: *He was ignorant of the fact that Paris is the capital of France. adj.* —**ig′nor ant ly,** *adv.*

ig nore (ig nôr′), pay no attention to; disregard: *The driver ignored the traffic light and almost hit another car. v.,* **ig nored, ig nor ing.**

iguana
about 5 ft. long

i gua na (i gwä′nə), a large climbing lizard found in tropical America. It has a crest of scales like a fringe along the back. *n., pl.* **i gua nas.**

i kon (ī′kon), icon. *n.*

il-, prefix. form of **in-**[1] before *l,* as in *illegal, illegible,* etc.

Il i ad (il′ē əd), a long Greek epic poem about the siege of Ilium, or Troy. Homer is supposed to be its author. *n.*

Il i um (il′ē əm), ancient Troy. *n.*

ilk (ilk), class; kind; sort: *cattle rustlers, bank robbers, and others of that ilk. n.*

ill (il), 1 in poor health; having some disease; not well; sick: *ill with a fever.* 2 sickness; disease: *All the ills she has had this year have left her very weak.* 3 bad; evil; harmful: *an ill wind, do a person an ill deed.* 4 badly; harmfully:

Her strength was ill used in bullying other children. 5 an evil; harm; trouble: *Poverty is an ill.* 6 something unfavorable or unkind: *I can think no ill of him.* 7 in an unkind manner; harshly; cruelly: *He speaks ill of his former friend.* 8 with trouble or difficulty; scarcely: *You can ill afford to waste your money.* 1,3 *adj.,* **worse, worst;** 2,5,6 *n.,* 4,7,8 *adv.*

ill at ease, uncomfortable.

I'll (īl), 1 I shall. 2 I will.

Ill., Illinois.

ill-ad vised (il′əd vīzd′), acting or done without enough thought; unwise. *adj.*

ill-bred (il′bred′), badly brought up; impolite; rude. *adj.*

il le gal (i lē′gəl), not lawful; against the law; forbidden by law. *adj.* —**il le′gal ly,** *adv.*

il le gal i ty (il′ē gal′ə tē), 1 a being illegal; unlawfulness. 2 an illegal act. *n., pl.* **il le gal i ties.**

il leg i ble (i lej′ə bəl), very hard or impossible to read; not plain enough to read: *The boy's handwriting was so bad that his letter to his mother was illegible. adj.*

il leg i bly (i lej′ə blē), in an illegible manner. *adv.*

il le git i mate (il′i jit′ə mit), 1 not according to the law or the rules. 2 born of parents who are not married. *adj.* —**il′le git′i mate ly,** *adv.*

ill-fat ed (il′fā′tid), 1 sure to have a bad fate or end. 2 bringing bad luck; unlucky. *adj.*

ill-fa vored (il′fā′vərd), 1 not pleasant to look at; ugly. 2 unpleasant; offensive. *adj.*

ill feeling, suspicious dislike; mistrust.

ill-got ten (il′got′n), acquired by evil or unfair means; dishonestly obtained. *adj.*

ill-hu mored (il′hyü′mərd), cross; unpleasant. *adj.* —**ill′-hu′mored ly,** *adv.*

il lib er al (i lib′ər əl), 1 not liberal; narrow-minded; prejudiced. 2 stingy; miserly. *adj.*

il lic it (i lis′it), not permitted by law; forbidden. *adj.* —**il lic′it ly,** *adv.*

il lim it a ble (i lim′ə tə bəl), without limit; boundless; infinite. *adj.*

Il li nois (il′ə noi′ *or* il′ə noiz′), one of the north central states of the United States. *Capital:* Springfield. *n.*

il lit er a cy (i lit′ər ə sē), 1 lack of knowledge of how to read and write. 2 lack of education; lack of knowledge of books and literature. *n., pl.* **il lit er a cies.**

il lit er ate (i lit′ər it), 1 not knowing how to read and write: *People who have never gone to school are usually il-*

literate. **2** person who does not know how to read and write. **3** showing a lack of education: *illiterate writing, an illiterate worker.* **4** an uneducated person. **1,3** *adj.,* **2,4** *n.* —**il lit′er ate ly,** *adv.*

ill-man nered (il/man′ərd), having or showing bad manners; impolite; rude. *adj.*

ill-na tured (il/nā′chərd), cross; disagreeable. *adj.* —**ill′na′tured ly,** *adv.*

ill ness (il/nis), an abnormal, unhealthy condition; disease; sickness: *Scarlet fever is a serious illness.* *n., pl.* **ill ness es.**

il log i cal (i loj′ə kəl), **1** contrary to the principles of sound reasoning; not logical: *Your illogical behavior makes it hard to guess what you will do next.* **2** not reasonable; foolish: *I agree with you that my fear of moths is illogical.* *adj.* —**il log′i cal ly,** *adv.*

ill-starred (il/stärd′), unlucky; unfortunate. *adj.*

ill-tem pered (il/tem′pərd), having or showing a bad temper; often angry or annoyed; cross. *adj.*

ill-timed (il/tīmd′), coming at a bad time; not appropriate. *adj.*

ill-treat (il/trēt′), treat badly or cruelly; do harm to; abuse. *v.*

ill-treat ment (il/trēt′mənt), bad or cruel treatment; harm; abuse. *n.*

il lu mi nate (i lü′mə nāt), **1** light up; make bright: *The room was illuminated by four large lamps. The big searchlight illuminates a spot a mile away.* **2** make clear; explain: *Our teacher could illuminate almost any subject we studied.* **3** decorate with lights: *The streets were illuminated for the celebration.* **4** decorate with gold, colors, pictures, and designs. The letters and pages in some old books and manuscripts were illuminated. *v.,* **il lu mi nat ed, il lu mi nat ing.**

illumination (def. 5)
illuminated letter P from a manuscript of the 1,300's

il lu mi na tion (i lü′mə nā′shən), **1** an illuminating; a lighting up; a making bright. **2** amount of light; light. **3** a making clear; explanation. **4** decoration with many lights. **5** decoration of letters or pages in books with gold, colors, pictures, and designs. *n.*

il lu mine (i lü′mən), make bright; illuminate: *A smile often illumines a*

---

homely face. *v.,* **il lu mined, il lu min ing.**

ill-us age (il/yü′sij), bad, cruel, or unfair treatment. *n.*

ill-use (il/yüz′ *for 1;* il/yüs′ *for 2),* **1** treat badly, cruelly, or unfairly. **2** bad, cruel, or unfair treatment. **1** *v.,* **ill-used, ill-us ing; 2** *n.*

il lu sion (i lü′zhən), **1** appearance or feeling that misleads because it is not real; thing that deceives by giving a false idea. The rails of a railroad track give you an illusion of coming closer and closer together until they meet in the distance. If you put your hand on ice and then in cool water, the water gives you an illusion of being warm. **2** a false notion or belief: *Many people have the illusion that wealth is the chief cause of happiness.* *n.*

illusion (def. 1)—an optical illusion. The parallel vertical lines appear to go apart and come together because of the slanted lines.

il lu sive (i lü′siv), illusory. *adj.*

il lu sor y (i lü′sər ē), due to an illusion; misleading; deceptive. *adj.*

il lus trate (il/ə strāt *or* i lus′trāt), **1** make clear or explain by stories, examples, comparisons, etc.: *The way that a pump works was used by our teacher to illustrate how the heart sends blood around the body.* **2** provide with pictures, diagrams, maps, etc., that explain or decorate: *This book is well illustrated.* *v.,* **il lus trat ed, il lus trat ing.**

il lus tra tion (il/ə strā′shən), **1** picture, diagram, map, etc., used to explain or decorate something. **2** story, example, comparison, etc., used to make clear or explain something: *One portion of an apple cut into four equal pieces is a good illustration of what* 1/4 *means.* **3** act or process of illustrating: *Illustration is used in teaching children.* *n.*

il lus tra tive (i lus′trə tiv *or* il/ə strā′tiv), illustrating; used to illustrate; helping to explain: *A good teacher uses many illustrative examples to explain ideas that are hard to understand.* *adj.*

il lus tra tor (il/ə strā′tər), **1** artist who makes pictures to be used as illustrations. **2** person or thing that illustrates. *n.*

il lus tri ous (i lus′trē əs), very fa-

---

hat, āge, fär; let, ēqual, tėrm;
it, īce; hot, ōpen, ôrder;
oil, out; cup, pùt, rüle; ch, child;
ng, long; sh, she; th, thin;
ᴛʜ, then; zh, measure;

ə represents *a* in about,
e in taken, *i* in pencil,
o in lemon, *u* in circus.

---

mous; great; outstanding: *Washington and Lincoln are illustrious Americans.* *adj.*

ill will, unkind or unfriendly feeling; dislike; spite: *He still bears much ill will toward his old enemy.*

I'm (īm), I am.

im-, *prefix.* form of **in-**[1] before *b, m,* and *p,* as in *imbibe, immoral, impatient.*

im age (im′ij), **1** likeness or copy: *She saw her image in the mirror. She is almost the exact image of her mother.* **2** likeness made of stone, wood, or some other material; statue: *The shelf was full of little images of all sorts of animals. The ancient Greeks and Romans worshiped images of their gods.* **3** picture in the mind; idea. *Your memory or imagination forms images of people and things that you do not actually see.* **4** a comparison, description, or figure of speech that helps the mind to form forceful or beautiful pictures. Poetry often contains images. **5** make or form an image of. **6** reflect as a mirror does: *The clouds were imaged in the still water of the lake.* **7** picture in one's mind; imagine: *While at school, I could image what my family was doing at home.* **1-4** *n.,* **5-7** *v.,* **im aged, im ag ing.**

im age ry (im′ij rē), **1** pictures formed in the mind; things imagined. **2** comparisons, descriptions, and figures of speech that help the mind to form forceful or beautiful pictures. Poetry often contains imagery. **3** images; statues. *n., pl.* **im age ries.**

i mag i na ble (i maj′ə nə bəl), that can be imagined; possible: *We had the best time imaginable at the party.* *adj.*

i mag i nar y (i maj′ə ner′ē), existing only in the imagination; not real: *Elves are imaginary. The equator is an imaginary circle around the earth.* *adj.*

i mag i na tion (i maj′ə nā′shən), **1** power of imagining. Imagination leads people to think they see, hear, or feel things that are not there. A poet, artist, or inventor must have imagination to create new things or ideas or to combine old ones in new forms. **2** thing

---

419

adj.	adjective	*n.* noun
adv.	adverb	*prep.* preposition
conj.	conjunction	*pron.* pronoun
interj.	interjection	*v.* verb
sing.	singular	*pl.* plural

imagined; creation of the mind; fancy. *n.*

i mag i na tive (i maj′ə nə tiv), **1** full of imagination; showing imagination: *Fairy tales are imaginative.* **2** having a good imagination; able to imagine well; fond of imagining: *The imaginative child made up stories about life on other planets.* **3** of imagination. *adj.* —**i mag′i na tive ly,** *adv.*

i mag ine (i maj′ən), **1** picture in one's mind; form an image or idea of: *The girl often likes to imagine herself a doctor.* **2** suppose; guess: *I cannot imagine what you mean.* *v.,* **i mag ined, i mag in ing.**

i ma go (i mā′gō), insect in the final adult, especially winged, stage. *n., pl.* **i ma gos, i mag i nes** (i maj′ə nēz′). [from Latin *imago* image]

im bal ance (im bal′əns), lack of balance. *n.*

im be cile (im′bə səl), **1** person born with such a weak mind that he can be trained to do only very simple tasks and will probably never learn to read; person who does not develop beyond a mental age of three to eight years. **2** weak in the mind; lacking normal intelligence. **3** a very stupid or foolish person. **4** very stupid or foolish. **1,3** *n.,* **2,4** *adj.*

im be cil i ty (im′bə sil′ə tē), **1** a being an imbecile. **2** great stupidity. **3** a very stupid or foolish action, remark, etc. *n., pl.* **im be cil i ties.**

im bed (im bed′), embed. *v.,* **im bed ded, im bed ding.**

im bibe (im bīb′), **1** drink in; drink. **2** absorb: *The roots of a plant imbibe moisture from the earth.* **3** take into one's mind: *A child often imbibes superstitions that last all his life.* *v.,* **im bibed, im bib ing.**

im bro glio (im brō′lyō), **1** a complicated or difficult situation. **2** a complicated misunderstanding or disagreement. *n., pl.* **im bro glios.** [from Italian]

im bue (im byü′), **1** fill the mind of; inspire: *They imbued their child with the ambition to succeed.* **2** fill with moisture or color; saturate or dye. *v.,* **imbued, im bu ing.**

im i tate (im′ə tāt), **1** try to be like or act like; follow the example of: *The little boy imitated his older brother.* **2** make or do something like; copy: *A parrot imitates the sounds it hears.* **3** act like; make fun of by acting like: *She amused the class by imitating a duck, a monkey, and a bear.* **4** be like; look like; resemble: *Wood is sometimes painted to imitate stone.* *v.,* **im i tat ed, im i tat ing.**

im i ta tion (im′ə tā′shən), **1** an imitating: *We learn many things by imitation.* **2** thing that imitates something else; likeness; copy: *Give as good an imitation as you can of a rooster crowing.* **3** made to look like something better; not real: *The imitation diamond was made of glass.* **1,2** *n.,* **3** *adj.*

im i ta tive (im′ə tā′tiv), **1** fond of imitating; likely to imitate others: *Monkeys are imitative.* **2** imitating; showing imitation: *"Bang" and "whiz" are imitative words.* *adj.*

im i ta tor (im′ə tā′tər), person who imitates. *n.*

im mac u late (i mak′yə lit), **1** without a spot or stain; absolutely clean: *The newly washed shirts were immaculate.* **2** without sin; pure. *adj.* —**im mac′u late ly,** *adv.*

Im man u el (i man′yü əl), Christ. *n.* Also, **Emmanuel.**

im ma ter i al (im′ə tir′ē əl), **1** not important; insignificant: *This error is immaterial.* **2** not material; spiritual rather than physical. *adj.*

im ma ture (im′ə chùr′, im′ə tùr′, or im′ə tyùr′), not mature; undeveloped. *adj.* —**im′ma ture′ly,** *adv.*

im ma tur i ty (im′ə chùr′ə tē, im′ə tùr′ə tē, or im′ə tyùr′ə tē), immature condition or quality. *n.*

im meas ur a ble (i mezh′ər ə bəl), too vast to be measured; very great; boundless: *the immeasurable vastness of the universe. She has immeasurable confidence in herself.* *adj.*

im meas ur a bly (i mezh′ər ə blē), beyond measure; to an extent too great to be measured. *adv.*

im me di a cy (i mē′dē ə sē), a being immediate. *n.*

im me di ate (i mē′dē it), **1** coming at once; done without delay: *Please send an immediate reply.* **2** with nothing in between; direct: *Things that are touching are in immediate contact.* **3** closest; nearest; next: *Your immediate neighbors live next door.* **4** close; near: *I expect an answer today, tomorrow, or in the immediate future.* **5** having to do with the present; current: *What are your immediate plans?* *adj.*

im me di ate ly (i mē′dē it lē), **1** at once; without delay: *I answered his letter immediately.* **2** with nothing in between; directly. *adv.*

im me mo ri al (im′ə môr′ē əl), extending back beyond the bounds of memory; extremely old. *adj.* —**im′me mo′ri al ly,** *adv.*

im mense (i mens′), **1** very large; huge; vast: *An ocean is an immense body of water.* **2** SLANG. very good; fine; excellent. *adj.*

im mense ly (i mens′lē), very greatly: *We enjoyed the party immensely.* *adv.*

im men si ty (i men′sə tē), **1** very great size or extent; vastness: *the ocean's immensity.* **2** infinite space or existence; infinity. *n., pl.* **im men si ties.**

im merse (i mèrs′), **1** dip or lower into a liquid until covered by it: *He immersed his aching feet in a bucket of hot water.* **2** baptize by dipping (a person) completely under water. **3** involve deeply; absorb: *The dedicated young musician immersed herself in piano practice seven days a week.* *v.,* **im mersed, im mers ing.**

im mer sion (i mèr′zhən *or* i mèr′shən), **1** an immersing or a being immersed. **2** baptism by dipping a person completely under water. *n.*

im mi grant (im′ə grənt), person who comes into a country or region to live there: *Canada has many immigrants from Europe.* *n.*

im mi grate (im′ə grāt), come into a country or region to live there. *v.,* **im mi grat ed, im mi grat ing.**

im mi gra tion (im′ə grā′shən), **1** a coming into a country or region to live there: *There has been immigration to America from all the countries of Europe.* **2** the persons who immigrate; immigrants: *The immigration of 1956 included many people from Hungary.* *n.*

im mi nence (im′ə nəns), a being imminent. *n.*

im mi nent (im′ə nənt), likely to happen soon; about to occur: *The black clouds, thunder, and lightning show that a storm is imminent.* *adj.* —**im′mi nent ly,** *adv.*

im mo bile (i mō′bəl), **1** not movable; firmly fixed. **2** not moving; not changing; motionless. *adj.*

im mo bil i ty (im′ō bil′ə tē), a being immobile. *n.*

im mo bi li za tion (i mō′bə lə zā′shən), a making immobile. *n.*

im mo bi lize (i mō′bə līz), make immobile. *v.,* **im mo bi lized, im mo bi liz ing.**

im mod er ate (i mod′ər it), not moderate; too much; going too far; extreme; more than is proper: *A fanatic has immoderate ideas.* *adj.* —**im mod′er ate ly,** *adv.*

im mod est (i mod′ist), **1** not modest; bold and rude. **2** indecent; improper. *adj.* —**im mod′est ly,** *adv.*

im mod es ty (i mod′ə stē), 1 lack of modesty; boldness and rudeness. 2 lack of decency; improper behavior. *n.*

im mo late (im′ə lāt), 1 kill as a sacrifice. 2 offer in sacrifice. *v.,* **im mo lat ed, im mo lat ing.**

im mo la tion (im′ə lā′shən), a sacrifice. *n.*

im mo ral (i môr′əl), 1 morally wrong; wicked: *Stealing is immoral.* 2 lewd; unchaste. *adj.* —**im mo′ral ly,** *adv.*

im mo ral i ty (im′ə ral′ə tē), 1 wickedness; wrongdoing; vice. 2 lewdness; lack of chastity. 3 an immoral act or practice. *n., pl.* **im mo ral i ties.**

im mor tal (i môr′tl), 1 living forever; never dying; everlasting: *Most churches believe that a man's body dies, but his soul is immortal.* 2 an immortal being. 3 **immortals,** *pl.* the gods of ancient Greece and Rome. 4 remembered or famous forever: *A great hero is immortal.* 5 person remembered or famous forever: *Shakespeare is one of the immortals.* 1,4 *adj.,* 2,3,5 *n.* —**im mor′tal ly,** *adv.*

im mor tal i ty (im′ôr tal′ə tē), 1 life without death; a living forever. 2 fame that lasts forever. *n.*

im mor tal ize (i môr′tl īz), 1 make immortal. 2 cause to be remembered or famous forever: *Great authors are immortalized by their works.* *v.,* **im mor tal ized, im mor tal iz ing.**

im mov a ble (i mü′və bəl), 1 that cannot be moved; firmly fixed: *immovable mountains.* 2 not moving or changing; motionless. 3 firm; steadfast; unyielding: *She was immovable in her belief in a life after death.* *adj.*

im mov a bly (i mü′və blē), in an immovable manner. *adv.*

im mune (i myün′), 1 protected from disease, poison, etc.; having immunity: *Vaccination makes a person practically immune to polio. Some persons are immune to poison ivy.* 2 free from; exempt: *immune from taxes. Nobody is immune from criticism. adj.*

immune system, system of lymphocytes and antibodies in a person or animal that recognize, attack, and destroy germs and other foreign material that enter the body.

im mu ni ty (i myü′nə tē), 1 resistance to disease, poison, etc.: *One attack of measles usually gives a person immunity to that disease.* 2 freedom; exemption: *The law gives schools and churches immunity from taxation. n., pl.* **im mu ni ties.**

im mu ni za tion (im′yə nə zā′shən), an immunizing or a being immunized. *n.*

im mu nize (im′yə nīz), protect from disease, poison, etc.; give immunity to; make immune: *Vaccination immunizes*

people against smallpox. *v.,* **im mu-nized, im mu niz ing.**

im mure (i myur′), shut up within walls; put in prison; confine. *v.,* **immured, im mur ing.**

im mu ta ble (i myü′tə bəl), never changing; not changeable. *adj.*

im mu ta bly (i myü′tə blē), in an immutable manner. *adv.*

imp (imp), 1 a young or small devil; little demon. 2 a mischievous child. *n.*

im pact (im′pakt), a striking (of one thing against another); collision: *The impact of the heavy stone against the windowpane shattered the glass. n.*

im pact ed (im pak′tid), 1 firmly wedged in place. 2 (of a tooth) wedged between the jawbone and another tooth. *adj.*

im pair (im per′ or im par′), make worse; damage; harm; weaken: *Poor food impaired his health. v.*

im pair ment (im per′mənt or im-par′mənt), 1 an impairing or a being impaired. 2 injury; damage. *n.*

im pale (im pāl′), 1 pierce through with anything pointed; fasten upon anything pointed: *The dead butterflies were impaled on pins stuck in a sheet of cork.* 2 torture or punish by thrusting upon a pointed stake. *v.,* **im paled, im pal-ing.**

im pal pa ble (im pal′pə bəl), 1 that cannot be felt by touching; intangible: *Color is impalpable.* 2 very hard to understand; that cannot be grasped by the mind: *The impalpable distinctions in your argument only confuse me. adj.*

im pal pa bly (im pal′pə blē), in an impalpable manner. *adv.*

im pan el (im pan′l), 1 put on a list for duty on a jury. 2 select (a jury) from the list. *v.* Also, **empanel.**

im part (im pärt′), 1 give a part or share of; give: *The furnishings imparted an air of newness to the old house.* 2 communicate; tell: *I will impart a secret to you. v.*

im par tial (im pär′shəl), showing no more favor to one side than to the other; fair; just: *A judge should be impartial. adj.* —**im par′tial ly,** *adv.*

im par ti al i ty (im′pär shē al′ə tē), fairness; justice. *n.*

im pass a ble (im pas′ə bəl), not passable; so that one cannot go through or across: *Snow and ice made the road impassable. adj.*

im pass a bly (im pas′ə blē), in an impassable manner. *adv.*

im passe (im′pas), position from which there is no escape; deadlock. *n.*

im pas sioned (im pash′ənd), full of strong feeling; stirring; rousing: *The candidate made an impassioned speech to the audience. adj.*

im pas sive (im pas′iv), 1 without

hat, āge, fär; let, ēqual, tėrm;
it, īce; hot, ōpen, ôrder;
oil, out; cup, pút, rüle; ch, child;
ng, long; sh, she; th, thin;
ŦH, then; zh, measure;

ə represents *a* in about,
e in taken, *i* in pencil,
o in lemon, *u* in circus.

feeling or emotion; unmoved: *The Indians trained themselves to endure pain with impassive faces.* 2 not feeling pain or injury; insensible: *The injured man lay as impassive as if he were dead. adj.* —**im pas′sive ly,** *adv.*

im pa tience (im pā′shəns), 1 lack of patience; being impatient. 2 uneasiness and eagerness; restlessness. *n.*

im pa tient (im pā′shənt), 1 not patient; not willing to put up with delay, opposition, pain, bother, etc.: *She is impatient with her little sister.* 2 uneasy and eager; restless: *The horses are impatient to start the race.* 3 showing lack of patience; cross: *an impatient answer. adj.* —**im pa′tient ly,** *adv.*

im peach (im pēch′), 1 accuse (a public official) of wrong conduct during office before a competent tribunal: *The judge was impeached for taking a bribe.* 2 charge with wrongdoing; accuse. 3 cast doubt on; call in question: *impeach the accuracy of a statement. v.*

im peach ment (im pēch′mənt), 1 an impeaching: *The impeachment of the dishonest judge resulted in a verdict of "Guilty."* 2 a being impeached: *The verdict resulting from his impeachment destroyed his political career. n.*

im pec ca ble (im pek′ə bəl), faultless: *impeccable manners, an impeccable appearance. adj.*

im pec ca bly (im pek′ə blē), faultlessly. *adv.*

im pe cu ni ous (im′pi kyü′nē əs), having little or no money; poor. *adj.*

im pede (im pēd′), hinder; obstruct: *Our progress was impeded by the deep snow. v.,* **im ped ed, im ped ing.**

im ped i ment (im ped′ə mənt), 1 hindrance; obstacle. 2 defect in speech: *Stuttering is a speech impediment. n.*

im pel (im pel′), 1 drive or force; cause: *The cold impelled her to go indoors.* 2 cause to move; drive forward; push along: *Wind and tide impelled the boat toward the shore. v.,* **im pelled, im pel ling.**

im pend (im pend′), 1 be likely to happen soon; be about to happen: *Black clouds are signs that a storm impends.* 2 hang threateningly; hang: *Great boul-*

421

adj.	adjective	*n.*	noun
adv.	adverb	*prep.*	preposition
conj.	conjunction	*pron.*	pronoun
interj.	interjection	*v.*	verb
sing.	singular	*pl.*	plural

ders impended over the narrow mountain path. v.

im pend ing (im pen′ding), 1 likely to happen soon; threatening; about to occur: *an impending storm.* 2 overhanging: *Above her were impending cliffs.* adj.

im pen e tra bil i ty (im pen′ə trə bil′ə tē), a being impenetrable. *n.*

im pen e tra ble (im pen′ə trə bəl), 1 that cannot be penetrated; so that one cannot get into or through: *The thorny branches made a thick, impenetrable hedge. A thick sheet of steel is impenetrable by an ordinary bullet.* 2 that cannot be seen into or understood; impossible to explain or understand: *His sudden disappearance was hidden in an impenetrable mystery.* adj.

im pen e tra bly (im pen′ə trə blē), in an impenetrable manner. *adv.*

im pen i tence (im pen′ə təns), lack of any sorrow or regret for doing wrong. *n.*

im pen i tent (im pen′ə tənt), not penitent; feeling no sorrow or regret for having done wrong. *adj.* —**im pen′i tent ly,** *adv.*

im per a tive (im per′ə tiv), 1 not to be avoided; that must be done; urgent: *It is imperative that this very sick child should stay in bed.* 2 command: *The great imperative is "Love thy neighbor as thyself."* 3 (in grammar) having to do with a verb form which expresses a command, request, or advice. 4 form of a verb which expresses this. In "Try to be quiet" and "Make up your mind," *try* and *make* are imperatives. 5 mood of such a verb. 1,3 *adj.*, 2,4,5 *n.*

im per cep ti ble (im′pər sep′tə bəl), that cannot be perceived or felt; very slight; gradual: *There were imperceptible differences between the original painting and the copy.* adj.

im per cep ti bly (im′pər sep′tə blē), in an imperceptible manner. *adv.*

im per fect (im per′fikt), 1 not perfect; having some defect or fault: *A crack in the cup made it imperfect.* 2 not complete; lacking some part. 3 (in grammar) expressing incompleted, continued, or customary action in the past. English has no imperfect tense, but such constructions as *was studying* and *used to study* are like the imperfect

verbs of other languages. *adj.* —**im per′fect ly,** *adv.*

im per fec tion (im′pər fek′shən), 1 lack of perfection; imperfect condition or character. 2 fault; defect. *n.*

im per i al (im pir′ē əl), 1 of or having to do with an empire, emperor, or empress. 2 having to do with the rule or authority of one country over other countries and colonies. 3 having the rank of an emperor. 4 supreme; majestic; magnificent. 5 of larger size or better quality. 6 a small, pointed beard growing beneath the lower lip. 1-5 *adj.*, 6 *n.* —**im per′i al ly,** *adv.*

imperial (def. 6)

im per i al ism (im pir′ē ə liz′əm), 1 policy of extending the rule or authority of one country over other countries and colonies. 2 an imperial system of government. *n.*

im per i al ist (im pir′ē ə list), person who favors imperialism. *n.*

im per i al is tic (im pir′ē ə lis′tik), 1 of imperialism or imperialists. 2 favoring imperialism. *adj.*

im per il (im per′əl), put in danger: *He imperiled their lives by standing up and rocking the rowboat.* v.

im per i ous (im pir′ē əs), 1 haughty or arrogant; domineering; overbearing: *The nobles treated the common people in an imperious way, looking down on them and ordering them around.* 2 not to be avoided; necessary; urgent: *the imperious demands of hunger.* adj. —**im per′i ous ly,** *adv.* —**im per′i ous ness,** *n.*

im per ish a ble (im per′i shə bəl), not perishable; unable to be destroyed; lasting forever; enduring. *adj.*

im per ish a bly (im per′i shə blē), in an imperishable manner. *adv.*

im per ma nent (im per′mə nənt), not permanent; temporary. *adj.*

im per me a ble (im per′mē ə bəl), 1 that cannot be permeated; impassable. 2 not allowing the passage of water, gas, etc.: *Gas masks are only impermeable to certain kinds of gas.* adj.

im per son al (im per′sə nəl), 1 not referring to any one person in particular; not personal: *The teacher's criticism of the class was impersonal. History is usually written from an impersonal point of view.* 2 having no existence as a person: *Electricity is an impersonal force.* 3 (of a verb) not

requiring a subject or having indefinite *it* for a subject. EXAMPLE: *rained* in "It rained yesterday." *adj.* —**im per′son al ly,** *adv.*

im per son ate (im per′sə nāt), 1 play the part of: *He impersonated Long John Silver when we gave "Treasure Island" as a play.* 2 pretend to be; mimic the voice, appearance, and manners of: *She impersonated several of her favorite teachers to amuse us.* 3 represent in personal form; personify; typify: *To many people Daniel Boone impersonates the American pioneer spirit.* v., **im per son at ed, im per son at ing.**

im per son a tion (im per′sə nā′-shən), 1 an impersonating: *The entertainer gave an impersonation of a famous movie actor.* 2 a representation; personification; type. *n.*

im per son a tor (im per′sə nā′tər), 1 person who pretends to be someone else. 2 actor who impersonates particular persons or types; professional mimic. *n.*

im per ti nence (im pert′n əns), 1 a being impertinent; boldness and rudeness; impudence; insolence. 2 an impertinent act or speech. 3 lack of pertinence; irrelevance. *n.*

im per ti nent (im pert′n ənt), 1 rudely bold; impudent; insolent: *Talking back to older people is impertinent.* 2 not pertinent; not to the point; out of place: *His impertinent remarks wasted valuable time.* adj. —**im per′ti nent ly,** *adv.*

im per turb a bil i ty (im′pər ter′bə bil′ə tē), a being imperturbable. *n.*

im per turb a ble (im′pər ter′bə bəl), not easily excited or disturbed; calm. *adj.*

im per turb a bly (im′pər ter′bə blē), in an imperturbable manner. *adv.*

im per vi ous (im per′vē əs), 1 having no way through; allowing no passage: *A coat made of rubber is impervious to rain.* 2 not open to argument, suggestions, etc.: *Because she was impervious to our hints, we finally told her it was time to go.* adj. —**im per′vi ous ness,** *n.*

im pe ti go (im′pə tī′gō), an infectious skin disease characterized by pimples filled with pus. *n.*

im pet u os i ty (im pech′ü os′ə tē), 1 sudden or rash energy; hastiness: *The impetuosity of her temper got her into many arguments.* 2 rushing force or violence: *The impetuosity of the flood destroyed everything in its path.* n.

im pet u ous (im pech′ü əs), 1 acting or done with sudden or rash energy; hasty: *Children are more impetuous than adults.* 2 rushing with force and violence: *The dam broke and an im-*

petuous torrent of water swept away the town. *adj.* —**im pet′u ous ly,** *adv.*

im pe tus (im′pə təs), 1 the force with which a moving body tends to maintain its velocity and overcome resistance: *the impetus of a moving automobile. Anything that you can stop easily has little impetus.* 2 a driving force; cause of action or effort; incentive: *Ambition is an impetus to work for success. n., pl.* **im pe tus es.**

im pi e ty (im pī′ə tē), 1 lack of piety or reverence for God; wickedness. 2 an impious act. *n., pl.* **im pi e ties.**

im pinge (im pinj′), 1 hit; strike: *Rays of light impinge on the eye.* 2 encroach; infringe. *v.,* **im pinged, im ping ing.**

im pinge ment (im pinj′mənt), an impinging. *n.*

im pi ous (im′pē əs *or* im pī′əs), not pious; not having or not showing reverence for God; wicked; profane. *adj.* —**im′pi ous ly,** *adv.*

imp ish (imp′ish), 1 of an imp; like an imp. 2 mischievous. *adj.* —**imp′ish ly,** *adv.* —**imp′ish ness,** *n.*

im pla ca ble (im plā′kə bəl *or* im plak′ə bəl), unable to be appeased; refusing to be reconciled; unyielding: *The new nation was constantly threatened by its implacable enemies. adj.*

im pla ca bly (im plā′kə blē *or* im plak′ə blē), in an implacable manner. *adv.*

im plant (im plant′), 1 instill; fix deeply: *A good teacher implants high ideals in children.* 2 insert: *a steel tube implanted in a socket.* 3 set in the ground; plant. 4 graft or set (a piece of skin, bone, etc.) into the body. *v.*

im plau si ble (im plô′zə bəl), not plausible; not having the appearance of truth or reason. *adj.*

im ple ment (im′plə mənt *for 1;* im′-plə ment *for 2,3*), 1 a useful piece of equipment; tool; instrument; utensil. Plows and threshing machines are farm implements. An ax, a shovel, and a broom are implements. 2 provide with implements or other means. 3 carry out; get done: *Do not undertake a project unless you can implement it.* 1 *n.,* 2,3 *v.*

im ple men ta tion (im′plə men tā′shən), an implementing; a carrying out: *the implementation of a policy or program. n.*

im pli cate (im′plə kāt), 1 show to have a part or to be connected; involve: *She confessed that she had a part in the thefts and implicated two other students.* 2 imply. *v.,* **im pli cat ed, im pli cat ing.**

im pli ca tion (im′plə kā′shən), 1 an implying or a being implied. 2 something implied; indirect suggestion; hint: *She did not actually refuse, but the*

way that she frowned was an implication of her unwillingness. 3 an implicating or a being implicated. *n.*

im plic it (im plis′it), 1 meant, but not clearly expressed; implied: *He gave us implicit consent to take the apples, for he smiled when he saw us do it.* 2 without doubting, hesitating, or asking questions; absolute: *He had implicit confidence in his friend. adj.*

im plic it ly (im plis′it lē), 1 unquestioningly. 2 by implication. *adv.*

im plore (im plôr′), 1 beg earnestly for: *The prisoner implored pardon.* 2 beg (a person) to do something: *She implored her parents to give permission for her to go on the trip. v.,* **im plored, im plor ing.**

im ply (im plī′), mean without saying so; express indirectly; suggest: *Silence often implies consent. The teacher's smile implied that she had forgiven us. v.,* **im plied, im ply ing.**

im po lite (im′pə līt′), not polite; having or showing bad manners; rude; discourteous. *adj.* —**im′po lite′ly,** *adv.* —**im′po lite′ness,** *n.*

im pol i tic (im pol′ə tik), not politic; not expedient; not judicious; unwise: *It is impolitic to offend people who can help you. adj.*

im pon der a ble (im pon′dər ə bəl), 1 without weight that can be felt or measured: *Faith and love are imponderable forces.* 2 something imponderable. 1 *adj.,* 2 *n.*

im port (im pôrt′ *or* im′pôrt *for 1,5,7;* im′pôrt *for 2-4,6*), 1 bring in from a foreign country for sale or use: *The United States imports coffee from Brazil.* 2 article imported: *Rubber is a useful import.* 3 act or fact of importing; importation: *The import of diseased animals was forbidden.* 4 meaning; significance: *Explain your remark; I do not understand its import.* 5 mean; signify: *Tell me what your remark imports.* 6 importance; consequence: *matters of great import.* 7 be important. 1,5,7 *v.,* 2-4,6 *n.*

im por tance (im pôrt′ns), a being important; consequence; value; significance: *Anybody can see the importance of good health. n.*

im por tant (im pôrt′nt), 1 meaning or mattering much; worth noticing or considering; having value or significance: *important business, an important occasion.* 2 having social position or influence: *Our mayor is an important person in our town.* 3 acting as if important; seeming to be important: *He ran around giving orders in an important manner. adj.* —**im por′tant ly,** *adv.*

im por ta tion (im′pôr tā′shən), 1 an importing; bringing in merchandise from foreign countries. 2 thing import-

hat, āge, fär; let, ēqual, tèrm; it, īce; hot, ōpen, ôrder; oil, out; cup, pùt, rüle; ch, child; ng, long; sh, she; th, thin; ŦH, then; zh, measure;

ə represents *a* in about, *e* in taken, *i* in pencil, *o* in lemon, *u* in circus.

ed: *Her shawl is a recent importation from Mexico. n.*

im port er (im pôr′tər *or* im′pôr tər), person or company whose business is importing goods. *n.*

im por tu nate (im pôr′chə nit), asking repeatedly; annoyingly persistent; urgent. *adj.* —**im por′tu nate ly,** *adv.*

im por tune (im′pôr tün′ *or* im′pôr tyün′), ask urgently or repeatedly; annoy with pressing demands: *I importuned the teacher to raise my grade. v.,* **im por tuned, im por tun ing.**

im por tu ni ty (im′pôr tü′nə tē *or* im′pôr tyü′nə tē), urgent or repeated asking; act of demanding again and again. *n., pl.* **im por tu ni ties.**

im pose (im pōz′), 1 put (a burden, tax, or punishment) on: *The judge imposed a fine of $500 on the guilty man.* 2 force or thrust one's authority or influence on another or others. 3 force or thrust (oneself or one's company) on another or others; obtrude; presume. 4 palm off (something upon a person) to deceive. *v.,* **im posed, im pos ing.**

impose on or **impose upon,** 1 take advantage of; use for selfish purposes: *Do not let the children impose on you.* 2 deceive; cheat; trick.

im pos ing (im pō′zing), impressive because of size, appearance, dignity, etc.: *The Capitol at Washington, D.C., is an imposing building. adj.*

im po si tion (im′pə zish′ən), 1 act of putting (a burden, tax, or punishment) on: *protest the imposition of heavy taxes.* 2 a burden, tax, or punishment. 3 an unfair burden, tax, or punishment. 4 an imposing upon a person by taking advantage of his good nature: *Would it be an imposition to ask you to mail this parcel?* 5 deception; fraud; trick. *n.*

im pos si bil i ty (im pos′ə bil′ə tē), 1 a being impossible: *We all realize the impossibility of living long without food.* 2 something impossible. *n., pl.* **im pos si bil i ties.**

im pos si ble (im pos′ə bəl), 1 that cannot be or happen: *It is impossible for two and two to be six.* 2 not possible to use; not to be done: *He proposed an impossible plan.* 3 that cannot be true:

423

adj.	adjective	*n.*	noun
adv.	adverb	*prep.*	preposition
conj.	conjunction	*pron.*	pronoun
interj.	interjection	*v.*	verb
sing.	singular	*pl.*	plural

an impossible story. 4 not possible to endure; very objectionable: *an impossible person. He said a summer without swimming would be impossible. adj.*

im pos si bly (im pos′ə blē), in an impossible manner. *adv.*

im post (im′pōst), a tax or duty, especially on goods brought into a country: *There is an impost on wool imported from other countries. n.*

im pos tor (im pos′tər), 1 person who pretends to be someone else in order to deceive or defraud others. 2 deceiver; fraud. *n.*

im pos ture (im pos′chər), deception; fraud. *n.*

im po tence (im′pə təns), lack of power; helplessness; condition or quality of being impotent: *The government was overthrown because of its impotence when the crisis arose. n.*

im po ten cy (im′pə tən sē), impotence. *n.*

im po tent (im′pə tənt), not having power; helpless: *In an impotent rage she saw the plane take off without her. We were impotent against the force of the tornado. adj.* —**im′po tent ly**, *adv.*

im pound (im pound′), 1 shut up in a pen or pound: *The town impounds stray animals.* 2 enclose or confine within limits: *A dam impounds water.* 3 put in the custody of a court of law: *The court impounded the documents to use as evidence. v.*

im pov er ish (im pov′ər ish), 1 make very poor: *A long war had impoverished the nation's treasury.* 2 exhaust the strength, richness, or resources of: *Careless farming impoverishes the most fertile soil. v.*

im pov er ish ment (im pov′ərish mənt), 1 an impoverishing or a being impoverished. 2 something that impoverishes. *n.*

im prac ti ca bil i ty (im prak′-tə kə bil′ə tē), 1 a being impracticable. 2 something impracticable. *n., pl.* **im prac ti ca bil i ties.**

im prac ti ca ble (im prak′tə kə bəl), 1 that cannot be done without greater difficulty, expense, etc., than is wise or sensible; impossible to put into practice: *impracticable suggestions.* 2 not usable; unfit for use: *an impracticable road. adj.*

im prac ti ca bly (im prak′tə kə blē), in an impracticable manner. *adv.*

im prac ti cal (im prak′tə kəl), 1 not practical; having to do with theory rather than actual practice; not useful. 2 not having good sense. *adj.* —**im prac′ti cal ly,** *adv.*

im pre ca tion (im′prə kā′shən), 1 act of calling down evil on a person; cursing. 2 a curse: *The gardener shouted imprecations at the stray dogs. n.*

im pre cise (im′pri sīs′), not precise; lacking precision; inaccurate. *adj.* —**im′pre cise′ ly,** *adv.*

im preg na bil i ty (im preg′nə-bil′ə tē), a being impregnable. *n.*

im preg na ble (im preg′nə bəl), able to resist attack; not yielding to force, persuasion, etc.: *The lawyer won his case with an impregnable argument. adj.*

im preg nate (im preg′nāt), 1 make pregnant; fertilize. 2 spread through the whole of; fill; saturate: *Seawater is impregnated with salt.* 3 fill the mind of; inspire: *The colonists were impregnated with ideals of freedom and justice. v.,* **im preg nat ed, im preg nat ing.**

im preg na tion (im′preg nā′shən), an impregnating or a being impregnated. *n.*

im pre sa ri o (im′prə sär′ē ō), the organizer, director, or manager of an opera or concert company. *n., pl.* **im pre sa ri os.** [from Italian]

im press[1] (im pres′ *for 1-4;* im′pres *for 5,6),* 1 have a strong effect on the mind or feelings of; influence deeply: *The movie impressed those who saw it.* 2 fix firmly in the mind: *She repeated the words to impress them in her memory.* 3 make marks on by pressing or stamping: *We can impress wax with a seal.* 4 to imprint; stamp. 5 a special mark or quality; impression: *An author leaves the impress of his personality on what he writes.* 6 act of impressing. 1-4 *v.,* 5,6 *n.* [from Latin *impressum* pressed in]

im press[2] (im pres′), 1 seize by force for public use: *The police impressed our car in order to pursue the escaping robbers.* 2 force (men) to serve in the armed forces. *v.* [*in-*[2] + *press*[2]]

im pres sion (im presh′ən), 1 effect produced on a person: *Punishment seemed to make little impression on the stubborn child.* 2 idea; notion: *I have a vague impression that I left the front door unlocked.* 3 mark made by pressing or stamping: *A deer had left impressions of its hoofs in the soft dirt of the garden.* 4 an impressing or a being impressed. *n.*

im pres sion a ble (im presh′ə-nə bəl), sensitive to impressions; easily impressed or influenced: *Children are more impressionable than adults. adj.*

im pres sion ism (im presh′ə-niz′əm), method of painting that conveys the impression of light striking and reflecting from a surface, rather than a photographic reproduction of the surface. *n.*

im pres sion ist (im presh′ə nist), artist who paints in the manner of impressionism. *n.*

im pres sion is tic (im presh′ə nis′-tik), 1 of impressionism or impressionists. 2 giving only a general or hasty impression. *adj.*

im pres sive (im pres′iv), able to impress the mind, feelings, conscience, etc.: *The new minister gave an impressive sermon. adj.* —**im pres′sive-ly,** *adv.* —**im pres′sive ness,** *n.*

im press ment (im pres′mənt), an impressing of property for public use or of men to serve in the armed forces. *n.*

im print (im′print *for 1-3;* im print′ *for 4-6),* 1 mark made by pressure; print: *Your foot made an imprint in the sand.* 2 a special mark or stamp; impression: *Suffering left its imprint on her face.* 3 the printer's or publisher's name, with the place and date of publication, on the title page or at the end of a book. 4 mark by pressing or stamping: *imprint a postmark on an envelope, imprint a letter with a postmark.* 5 put by pressing: *She imprinted a kiss on her father's cheek.* 6 fix firmly in the mind: *His boyhood home was imprinted in his memory.* 1-3 *n.,* 4-6 *v.*

im pris on (im priz′n), 1 put in prison; keep in prison. 2 confine closely; restrain. *v.*

im pris on ment (im priz′n mənt), 1 a putting or keeping in prison: *The imprisonment of their son caused them great sorrow.* 2 a being put or kept in prison: *At the start of her imprisonment she was just 20 years old. n.*

im prob a bil i ty (im prob′ə bil′ə tē), 1 a being improbable; unlikelihood. 2 something improbable. *n., pl.* **im prob a bil i ties.**

im prob a ble (im prob′ə bəl), not probable; not likely to happen; not likely to be true: *They all told an improbable story of seeing a ghost in the haunted house. adj.*

im prob a bly (im prob′ə blē), in an improbable manner. *adv.*

im promp tu (im promp′tü *or* im-promp′tyü), 1 without previous thought or preparation; offhand: *a speech made impromptu.* 2 made or done without previous thought or preparation: *He had not expected to make a speech, but he gave an impromptu talk when he was asked to say a few words.* 3 something so made or done; improvisation. 1 *adv.,* 2 *adj.,* 3 *n.* [from French]

im prop er (im prop′ər), 1 not in accordance with accepted standards; not correct; wrong: *He learned that "You is" is an improper usage.* 2 not suitable: *A bright dress is improper for a funeral.* 3 not decent. *adj.* —**im prop′er ly,** *adv.*

improper fraction, fraction that is equal to or greater than 1. EXAMPLES: $^3/_2$, $^4/_3$, $^{27}/_4$, $^8/_5$, $^{21}/_{12}$, $^4/_4$, $^{12}/_{12}$.

im pro pri e ty (im′prə prī′ə tē), 1 lack of propriety; quality of being improper. 2 an improper act, expression, etc.: *Using "learn" to mean "teach" is an impropriety.* *n., pl.* **im pro pri e ties.**

im prove (im prüv′), 1 make better: *You could improve your handwriting if you tried.* 2 become better: *His health is improving.* 3 increase the value of: *Land is improved by using it for a farm or putting up a building on it.* 4 use well; make good use of: *We had two hours to wait and improved the time by seeing the city.* *v.,* **im proved, im prov ing.**

im prove ment (im prüv′mənt), 1 a making better or becoming better: *Her schoolwork shows much improvement since last term.* 2 an increase in value. 3 a change or addition that increases value: *The improvements in our house cost over a thousand dollars.* 4 better condition; thing that is better than another; a gain; advance: *The new lighting system is an improvement over the previous one.* *n.*

im prov i dence (im prov′ə dəns), lack of foresight; failure to look ahead; carelessness in providing for the future; lack of thrift. *n.*

im prov i dent (im prov′ə dənt), lacking foresight; not looking ahead; not careful in providing for the future; not thrifty: *Improvident people spend their money as fast as they can make it. adj.* —**im prov′i dent ly,** *adv.*

im prov i sa tion (im prov′ə zā′shən), 1 an improvising. 2 something improvised. *n.*

im pro vise (im′prə vīz), 1 make up (music, poetry, etc.) on the spur of the moment; sing, recite, speak, etc., without preparation: *He improvised a new verse for the school song at the football game.* 2 make for the occasion: *The girls improvised a tent out of two blankets and some long poles. v.,* **im pro vised, im pro vis ing.**

im pru dence (im prüd′ns), lack of prudence; imprudent behavior. *n.*

im pru dent (im prüd′nt), not prudent; rash; unwise: *It is imprudent to rush into something without thinking what may happen. adj.* —**im pru′dent ly,** *adv.*

im pu dence (im′pyə dəns), a being impudent; shameless boldness; great rudeness; insolence. *n.*

im pu dent (im′pyə dənt), shamelessly bold; very rude and insolent: *The impudent boy made faces at the teacher. adj.* —**im′pu dent ly,** *adv.*

im pugn (im pyün′), call in question; attack by words or arguments; challenge as false, worthless, etc.: *Do not impugn the umpire's fairness. v.*

im pulse (im′puls), 1 a sudden, driving force or influence; thrust; push: *the impulse of a wave, the impulse of hunger, the impulse of curiosity.* 2 the effect of a sudden, driving force or influence. 3 a sudden inclination or tendency to act: *The angry mob was influenced more by impulse than by reason.* 4 stimulus that is transmitted, especially by nerve cells, and influences action in the muscle, gland, or other nerve cells that it reaches. 5 surge of electrical current in one direction. *n.*

im pul sion (im pul′shən), 1 an impelling; driving force: *The impulsion of hunger drove her to steal food.* 2 impulse. 3 impetus. *n.*

im pul sive (im pul′siv), 1 acting or done upon impulse; with a sudden inclination or tendency to act: *The impulsive girl spent her savings on toys and candy.* 2 driving with sudden force; able to impel; impelling. *adj.* —**im pul′sive ly,** *adv.* —**im pul′sive ness,** *n.*

im pu ni ty (im pyü′nə tē), freedom from punishment, injury, or other bad consequences: *If laws are not enforced, crimes are committed with impunity. n.*

im pure (im pyur′), 1 not pure; dirty; unclean: *The air in cities is often impure.* 2 mixed with something of lower value; adulterated: *The salt we use is slightly impure.* 3 bad; corrupt: *to avoid impure talk, thoughts, acts, and people. adj.* —**im pure′ly,** *adv.*

im pu ri ty (im pyur′ə tē), 1 lack of purity; being impure. 2 impure thing; thing that makes something else impure: *Filtering and boiling the water removed most of the impurities from it. n., pl.* **im pu ri ties.**

im pu ta tion (im′pyə tā′shən), 1 an imputing. 2 a charge or hint of wrongdoing: *No imputation has ever been made against his good name. n.*

im pute (im pyüt′), consider as belonging; attribute; charge (a fault, etc.) to a person; blame: *I impute my failure to laziness. v.,* **im put ed, im put ing.**

in (in). In shows position with reference to space, time, state, circumstances, etc. 1 inside; within: *in the box. We live in the country.* 2 at, during, or after: *in the present time. You can do this in an hour.* 3 into: *Go in the house.* 4 from

among; out of: *one in a hundred.* 5 because of; for: *act in self-defense. The party is in honor of her birthday.* 6 in or into some place, position, condition, etc.; on the inside: *Come in. Lock the dog in. A sheepskin coat has the woolly side in.* 7 present, especially in one's home or office: *The doctor is not in today.* 8 having power or influence: *The in party has won another election.* 9 coming or leading in: *The train is on the in track.* 10 SLANG. in style; fashionable: *That's the in thing to do.* 11 a position of familiarity or influence: *have an in with the company president.* 12 **ins,** *pl.* people in office; political party in power. 1-5 *prep.,* 6,7 *adv.,* 8-10 *adj.,* 11,12 *n.*

in for, unable to avoid; sure to get or have: *We are in for a storm.*

ins and outs, 1 turns and twists; nooks and corners: *He knows the ins and outs of the road because he has traveled it so often.* 2 different parts; details: *The manager knows the ins and outs of the business better than the owner.*

in that, because.

in with, 1 friendly with. 2 partners with: *She was in with him in the robbery.*

in-[1], *prefix.* not; the opposite of; the absence of: *Inexpensive = not expensive. Inattention = the absence of attention.* Also, **il-, im-, ir-.** [from Latin]

in-[2], *prefix.* in; into; on; upon: *Incase = (put) into a case. Intrust = (give) in trust.* [from Latin *in-,* from *in,* prep.]

in-[3], *prefix.* in; within; into; toward: *Indoors = within doors. Inland = toward land.* [Old English]

in., inch or inches.

in a bil i ty (in′ə bil′ə tē), lack of ability, power, or means; being unable. *n.*

in ac ces si bil i ty (in′ak ses′ə bil′ə tē), lack of accessibility; being inaccessible. *n.*

in ac ces si ble (in′ak ses′ə bəl), 1 hard to get at; hard to reach or enter: *The house on top of the steep hill is inaccessible.* 2 not accessible; that cannot be reached or entered at all. *adj.*

inaccessible

hat, āge, fär; let, ēqual, tėrm;
it, īce; hot, ōpen, ôrder;
oil, out; cup, pùt, rüle; ch, child;
ng, long; sh, she; th, thin;
ᴛн, then; zh, measure;

ə represents *a* in about,
e in taken, *i* in pencil,
o in lemon, *u* in circus.

425

adj. adjective	*n.* noun
adv. adverb	*prep.* preposition
conj. conjunction	*pron.* pronoun
interj. interjection	*v.* verb
sing. singular	*pl.* plural

in ac ces si bly (in′ək ses′ə blē), so as to be inaccessible. *adv.*

in ac cu ra cy (in ak′yər ə sē), 1 lack of accuracy; being inaccurate. 2 error; mistake. *n., pl.* **in ac cu ra cies.**

in ac cu rate (in ak′yər it), not accurate; not exact; containing mistakes. *adj.* —**in ac′cur ate ly,** *adv.*

in ac tion (in ak′shən), absence of action; idleness. *n.*

in ac ti vate (in ak′tə vāt), make inactive; destroy the action of: *inactivate a bomb, inactivate a virus. v.,* **in ac ti vat ed, in ac ti vat ing.**

in ac ti va tion (in ak′tə vā′shən), a making or becoming inactive. *n.*

in ac tive (in ak′tiv), not active; idle; slow: *Bears are inactive during the winter. adj.* —**in ac′tive ly,** *adv.*

in ac tiv i ty (in′ak tiv′ə tē), absence of activity; idleness; slowness. *n.*

in ad e qua cy (in ad′ə kwə sē), 1 a being inadequate. 2 something that is inadequate. *n., pl.* **in ad e qua cies.**

in ad e quate (in ad′ə kwit), not adequate; not enough; not as much as is needed: *The amount of food they ordered was inadequate for so many guests. adj.* —**in ad′e quate ly,** *adv.*

in ad mis si ble (in′əd mis′ə bəl), 1 not to be permitted; not allowable. 2 not to be admitted or considered as evidence or proof. *adj.*

in ad vert ence (in′əd vèrt′ns), 1 lack of attention; carelessness. 2 an inadvertent act; oversight; mistake. *n.*

in ad vert ent (in′əd vèrt′nt), 1 not attentive; careless; negligent. 2 not done on purpose; caused by oversight: *His rudeness was inadvertent, and we forgave it. adj.* —**in′ad vert′ent ly,** *adv.*

in ad vis a ble (in′əd vī′zə bəl), not advisable; unwise; not prudent. *adj.*

in al ien a ble (in ā′lyə nə bəl), that cannot be given or taken away: *She felt that her family was interfering with her inalienable right to direct her own life. adj.*

in al ien a bly (in ā′lyə nə blē), in an inalienable manner. *adv.*

in ane (in ān′), silly or foolish; senseless: *The tourists bored the guide with their inane questions. adj.* —**in ane′ly,** *adv.*

in an i mate (in an′ə mit), 1 lifeless: *Stones are inanimate objects.* 2 without liveliness or spirit; dull: *an inanimate face. adj.* —**in an′i mate ly,** *adv.* —**in an′i mate ness,** *n.*

in a ni tion (in′ə nish′ən), 1 weakness from lack of food. 2 emptiness. *n.*

in an i ty (in an′ə tē), 1 silliness; lack of sense. 2 a silly or senseless act, practice, remark, etc. 3 emptiness. *n., pl.* **in an i ties.**

in ap pli ca ble (in ap′lə kə bəl *or* in′ə plik′ə bəl), not applicable; not suitable: *The name Tiny is inapplicable to that big dog. adj.*

in ap pre ci a ble (in′ə prē′shē ə bəl), too small to be noticed or felt; very slight. *adj.*

in ap pro pri ate (in′ə prō′prē it), not appropriate; not suitable; not fitting: *Jokes are inappropriate at a funeral. adj.* —**in′ap pro′pri ate ly,** *adv.* —**in′ap pro′pri ate ness,** *n.*

in apt (in apt′), 1 not apt; not suitable; unfit. 2 unskillful; awkward. *adj.* —**in apt′ly,** *adv.* —**in apt′ness,** *n.*

in ap ti tude (in ap′tə tüd *or* in ap′tə tyüd), 1 unfitness. 2 lack of skill. *n.*

in ar tic u late (in′är tik′yə lit), 1 not distinct; not like regular speech: *When they called to him they heard only an inarticulate mutter.* 2 unable to speak in words; unable to say what one thinks; dumb: *Cats and dogs are inarticulate. Her grief made her inarticulate.* 3 not jointed: *A jellyfish's body is inarticulate. adj.* —**in′ar tic′u late ly,** *adv.* —**in′ar tic′u late ness,** *n.*

in ar tis tic (in′är tis′tik), not artistic; lacking good taste. *adj.* —**in′ar tis′ti cal ly,** *adv.*

in as much as (in′əz much′), because; since: *He was given a head start in the race, inasmuch as he was smaller than the others.*

in at ten tion (in′ə ten′shən), lack of attention; negligence; carelessness: *That girl lost her job through inattention to details. n.*

in at ten tive (in′ə ten′tiv), not attentive; negligent; careless. *adj.* —**in′at ten′tive ly,** *adv.* —**in′at ten′tive ness,** *n.*

in au di ble (in ô′də bəl), that cannot be heard. *adj.*

in au di bly (in ô′də blē), in an inaudible manner; so as not to be heard. *adv.*

in au gur al (in ô′gyər əl), 1 of or for an inauguration: *The President gave an inaugural address when he took office.* 2 the address or speech made by a person when formally admitted to office. 1 *adj.,* 2 *n.*

in au gu rate (in ô′gyə rāt′), 1 install in office with a ceremony: *A President of the United States is inaugurated every four years.* 2 make a formal beginning of; begin: *The invention of the airplane inaugurated a new era in transportation.* 3 open for public use with a ceremony or celebration: *The new city hall was inaugurated with a parade and speeches. v.,* **in au gu rat ed, in au gu rat ing.**

in au gu ra tion (in ô′gyə rā′shən), 1 act or ceremony of installing a person in office. The inauguration of a President of the United States takes place on January 20. 2 a formal beginning; beginning. 3 an opening for public use with a ceremony or celebration. *n.*

in aus pi cious (in′ô spish′əs), with signs of failure; unfavorable; unlucky. *adj.* —**in′aus pi′cious ly,** *adv.*

in board (in′bôrd′), inside the hull of a ship or boat: *an inboard motor. adj.*

in born (in′bôrn′), born in a person; instinctive; natural: *an inborn sense of rhythm. The artist had an inborn talent for drawing. adj.*

in bound (in′bound′), inward bound: *The inbound flights were delayed by the storm. adj.*

in bred (in′bred′), 1 inborn; natural: *Though uneducated, she displayed an inbred courtesy.* 2 produced by breeding between closely related ancestors: *an inbred strain of horses.* 3 past tense and past participle of **inbreed.** 1,2 *adj.,* 3 *v.*

in breed (in′brēd′ *or* in brēd′), breed closely related animals or plants. *v.,* **in bred, in breed ing.**

inc., incorporated.

In ca (ing′kə), 1 member of a highly civilized American Indian people who ruled a large empire in Peru and other parts of South America before its conquest by the Spaniards in the 1500's. 2 ruler of this empire. *n., pl.* **In cas** *or* **In ca.** —**In′can,** *n., adj.*

in cal cu la ble (in kal′kyə lə bəl), 1 too many to be counted; too great to be calculated; innumerable: *The sands of the sea are incalculable in number.* 2 impossible to foretell or reckon beforehand: *A flood in the valley would cause incalculable losses.* 3 that cannot be relied on; uncertain: *He has an incalculable disposition. adj.*

in cal cu la bly (in kal′kyə lə blē), in an incalculable manner. *adv.*

in can des cence (in′kən des′ns), the condition of a body which glows and gives off light when it is heated. *n.*

in can des cent (in′kən des′nt), 1 glowing with heat; red-hot or white-hot: *The embers of the fire were still incandescent even though the flames had disappeared.* 2 shining brightly; brilliant. *adj.*

incandescent lamp, an electric lamp with a filament of very fine wire that becomes white-hot and gives off light when current flows through it.

in can ta tion (in/kan tā/shən), **1** set of words spoken as a magic charm or to cast a magic spell. "Double, double, toil and trouble, Fire burn and caldron bubble," is an incantation. **2** the use of such words. *n.*

in ca pa ble (in kā/pə bəl), having very little ability; not capable; not efficient; not competent: *An employer cannot afford to hire incapable workers. adj.*
incapable of, **1** without the ability, power, or fitness for: *I felt incapable of playing such difficult piano music.* **2** not susceptible to; not open or ready for: *incapable of exact measurement. Gold is incapable of rusting.*

in ca pac i tate (in/kə pas/ə tāt), limit in ability, power, or fitness; disable: *The player's injury incapacitated him for playing football. v.,* **in ca pac i tat ed, in ca pac i tat ing.**

in ca pac i ty (in/kə pas/ə tē), lack of ability, power, or fitness; disability. *n., pl.* **in ca pac i ties.**

in car ce rate (in kär/sə rāt/), imprison. *v.,* **in car ce rat ed, in car ce rat ing.**

in car ce ra tion (in kär/sə rā/shən), imprisonment. *n.*

in car nate (in kär/nit *or* in kär/nāt *for 1;* in kär/nāt *for 2,3),* **1** embodied in flesh, especially in human form: *The villain was evil incarnate.* **2** make or be incarnate; embody: *Lancelot incarnated the spirit of chivalry.* **3** put into an actual form; realize: *The sculptor incarnated his vision in a beautiful statue.* **1** *adj.,* **2,3** *v.,* **in car nat ed, in car nat ing.**

in car na tion (in/kär nā/shən), **1** a taking on of human form by a divine being: *the incarnation of an angel.* **2 the Incarnation,** (in Christian theology) the union of divine nature and human nature in the person of Jesus Christ; assumption of human form by the son of God. **3** person or thing that represents some quality or idea; embodiment: *The miser was an incarnation of greed. n.*

in case (in kās/), encase. *v.,* **in cased, in cas ing.**

in cau tious (in kô/shəs), not cautious; reckless; rash: *In an incautious moment he revealed the secret he had sworn to keep. adj.* **—in cau/tious ly, adv. —in cau/tious ness, n.**

in cen di ar y (in sen/dē er/ē), **1** having to do with the setting of property on fire intentionally. **2** person who intentionally sets fire to property. **3** causing fires; used to start a fire: *The enemy town was set on fire with incendiary bombs.* **4** deliberately stirring up strife or rebellion: *The agitator was arrested*

for making incendiary speeches. 1,3,4 *adj.,* 2 *n., pl.* **in cen di ar ies.**

in cense[1] (in/sens), **1** substance giving off a sweet smell when burned. **2** the perfume or smoke from it. **3** something sweet like incense: *the incense of flowers, the incense of flattery. n.* [from French of the 1200's *encens,* from Latin *incensum*]

in cense[2] (in sens/), make very angry; fill with rage: *Cruelty incenses kind people. v.,* **in censed, in cens ing.** [from Latin *incensum* set on fire, inflamed]

in cen tive (in sen/tiv), thing that urges a person on; cause of action or effort; motive; stimulus: *The fun of playing the game was a greater incentive than the prize. n.*

in cep tion (in sep/shən), beginning: *the inception of a plan. n.*

in ces sant (in ses/nt), never stopping; continual: *The roar of Niagara Falls is incessant. The incessant noise from the factory kept me awake all night. adj.* **—in ces/sant ly, adv.**

in cest (in/sest), an illicit sexual relationship between persons so closely related that their marriage is prohibited by law or custom, as between brother and sister or parent and child. *n.*

inch (inch), **1** measure of length, $1/12$ of a foot. **2** the amount of rainfall or snowfall that would cover a surface to the depth of one inch. **3** the smallest part, amount, or degree; a very little bit. **4** move slowly or little by little: *The worm inched along.* 1-3 *n., pl.* **inch es;** 4 *v.*
by inches, by slow degrees; gradually.
every inch, in every way; completely: *every inch a queen.*
inch by inch, little by little; slowly.
within an inch of, very near; very close to: *The man was within an inch of death.*

inch worm (inch/wėrm/), measuring worm. *n.*

in ci dence (in/sə dəns), **1** the way in which (a tax, disease, etc.) falls or distributes itself; range of occurrence or influence: *In an epidemic the incidence of a disease is widespread. The incidence of a tax is limited if only a few people must pay it.* **2** the falling or striking of a projectile, ray of light, etc., on a surface. *n.*

in ci dent (in/sə dənt), **1** a happening; event: *An exciting story or play is filled with incidents.* **2** a less important happening: *She told us all of the main facts of her trip and a few of the amusing incidents.* **3** liable to happen; belonging: *Hardships are incident to the life of an explorer.* 1,2 *n.,* 3 *adj.*

in ci den tal (in/sə den/tl), **1** happening or likely to happen along with something else more important: *Certain*

hat, āge, fär; let, ēqual, tėrm;
it, īce; hot, ōpen, ôrder;
oil, out; cup, pùt, rüle; ch, child;
ng, long; sh, she; th, thin;
ŦH, then; zh, measure;

ə represents *a* in about,
e in taken, *i* in pencil,
o in lemon, *u* in circus.

discomforts are incidental to camping out.* **2** occurring by chance: *an incidental meeting of an old friend on the street.* **3** Often, **incidentals,** *pl.* something incidental: *On our trip we spent $52 for meals, room, and railroad fare, and $1.50 for incidentals, such as candy, magazines, and stamps.* 1,2 *adj.,* 3 *n.*

in ci den tal ly (in/sə den/tl ē), **1** in an incidental manner; as an incident along with something else: *She mentioned incidentally that she had had no dinner.* **2** by the way: *Incidentally, are you coming to the meeting tonight? adv.*

in cin e rate (in sin/ə rāt/), burn to ashes. *v.,* **in cin e rat ed, in cin e rat ing.**

in cin e ra tion (in sin/ə rā/shən), a burning or a being burned to ashes. *n.*

in cin e ra tor (in sin/ə rā/tər), furnace or other arrangement for burning trash and other things to ashes. *n.*

in cip i ent (in sip/ē ənt), just beginning; in an early stage: *The medicine prevented the boy's incipient cold from becoming worse. adj.* **—in cip/i ent ly, adv.**

in cise (in sīz/), **1** cut into. **2** carve; engrave: *incise a figure or inscription. v.,* **in cised, in cis ing.**

in ci sion (in sizh/ən), **1** cut made in something; gash: *The doctor made a tiny incision to take out the splinter in my hand.* **2** act of incising. *n.*

in ci sive (in sī/siv), that cuts; sharp; penetrating; piercing; keen: *An incisive criticism goes directly to the point and uses plain words. adj.* **—in ci/sive ly, adv. —in ci/sive ness, n.**

in ci sor (in sī/zər), tooth having a sharp edge for cutting; one of the front teeth between the canine teeth in either jaw. Humans have eight incisors. *n.*

INCISORS
CANINE
BICUSPIDS
MOLARS

adj. adjective	*n.* noun
adv. adverb	*prep.* preposition
conj. conjunction	*pron.* pronoun
interj. interjection	*v.* verb
sing. singular	*pl.* plural

in cite (in sīt′), urge on; stir up; rouse: *Agitators incited the workers to strike.* *v.,* **in cit ed, in cit ing.**

in cite ment (in sīt′mənt), 1 thing that urges on, stirs up, or rouses: *Abject poverty can be an incitement to steal.* 2 act of urging on, stirring up, or rousing. *n.*

in ci vil i ty (in′sə vil′ə tē), 1 lack of courtesy; impoliteness; rudeness. 2 a rude or impolite act. *n., pl.* **in ci vil i ties.**

in clem en cy (in klem′ən sē), inclement condition or quality; severity; harshness: *The inclemency of the weather kept us at home during the snowstorm. n., pl.* **in clem en cies.**

in clem ent (in klem′ənt), 1 rough or stormy: *Inclement weather is common in winter.* 2 severe; harsh: *The dictator was an inclement ruler. adj.* —**in clem′ent ly,** *adv.*

in cli na tion (in′klə nā′shən), 1 natural bent; tendency: *My inclination is toward thinness.* 2 preference; liking: *That family has a strong inclination for sports.* 3 a leaning, bending, or bowing: *The inclination of his head showed approval.* 4 a slope; slant: *That high roof has a sharp inclination. n.*

in cline (in klīn′ *for 1-3,6;* in′klīn *for 4,5*), 1 be favorable or willing; tend: *Dogs incline to eat meat as a food.* 2 make favorable or willing; influence: *Incline your hearts to obey God's laws.* 3 to slope; slant. 4 a slope; slant. 5 a sloping surface. The side of a hill is an incline. 6 lean, bend, or bow: *She inclined her head toward the sound.* 1-3,6 *v.,* **in clined, in clin ing;** 4,5 *n.*

in clined (in klīnd′), 1 favorable or willing; tending: *I am inclined to agree with you.* 2 sloping; slanting. *adj.*

RESISTANCE
MOTION
EFFORT
INCLINED PLANE

inclined plane, plank or other plane surface placed at an angle to a horizontal surface and used to move heavy weights to a higher level with little force. It is a simple machine.

in close (in klōz′), enclose. *v.,* **in closed, in clos ing.**

in clo sure (in klō′zhər), enclosure. *n.*

in clude (in klüd′), 1 have within itself; contain; comprise: *Their farm includes 160 acres.* 2 put in a total, a class, or the like; reckon in a count: *The price includes the land, house, and furniture. v.,* **in clud ed, in clud ing.**

in clu sion (in klü′zhən), 1 an including or a being included. 2 thing included. *n.*

in clu sive (in klü′siv), 1 including; taking in; counting in; comprising: *"Read pages 10 to 20 inclusive" means "Begin with page 10 and read through to the very end of page 20."* 2 including much; including everything concerned: *Make an inclusive list of your expenses. adj.* —**in clu′sive ly,** *adv.* —**in clu′sive ness,** *n.*

in cog ni to (in kog′nə tō *or* in′kog nē′tō), 1 with one's real name, character, rank, etc., hidden: *The prince traveled incognito to avoid crowds and ceremonies.* 2 person who is incognito. 3 a disguised condition. 1 *adj., adv.,* 2,3 *n., pl.* **in cog ni tos.** [from Italian]

in co her ence (in′kō hir′əns), 1 disconnected thought or speech: *The drug produced some incoherence.* 2 lack of logical connection. 3 failure to stick together; looseness. *n.*

in co her ent (in′kō hir′ənt), 1 having or showing no logical connection of ideas; not coherent; disconnected; confused. 2 not sticking together. *adj.* —**in′co her′ent ly,** *adv.*

in com bus ti ble (in′kəm bus′tə bəl), that cannot be burned; fireproof. *adj.*

in come (in′kum′), what comes in from property, business, work, etc.; money that comes in; receipts; returns: *A person's yearly income is all the money that he gets in a year. n.*

income tax, tax on a person's or a corporation's income above a certain amount.

in com ing (in′kum′ing), 1 coming in: *The incoming tenant will pay more rent.* 2 a coming in: *the incoming of the tide.* 1 *adj.,* 2 *n.*

in com men su rate (in′kə men′shər it *or* in′kə men′sər it), 1 not in proportion; not adequate: *Her salary is incommensurate to her ability.* 2 having no common measure; that cannot be compared. *adj.* —**in′com men′sur ate ly,** *adv.*

in com mode (in′kə mōd′), cause trouble, difficulty, etc., to; inconvenience: *Will it incommode you if we open the window? v.,* **in com mod ed, in com mod ing.**

in com mu ni ca ble (in′kə myü′-nə kə bəl), that cannot be communicated or told. *adj.*

in com mu ni ca do (in′kə myü′-nə kä′dō), without any way of communicating with others: *After my arrest I was held incommunicado and could not, therefore, call my lawyer or any friends. adj.* [from Spanish]

in com par a ble (in kom′pər ə bəl), 1 without equal; matchless: *incomparable beauty.* 2 not able to be compared; unsuitable for comparison. *adj.*

in com par a bly (in kom′pər ə blē), in an incomparable manner; beyond comparison. *adv.*

in com pat i bil i ty (in′kəm pat′-ə bil′ə tē), quality of being incompatible; lack of harmony. *n., pl.* **in com pat i bil i ties.**

in com pat i ble (in′kəm pat′ə bəl), 1 not able to live or act together peaceably; opposed in character: *My cats and dogs are incompatible.* 2 inconsistent: *Bad eating habits are incompatible with good health. adj.*

in com pat i bly (in′kəm pat′ə blē), in an incompatible manner. *adv.*

in com pe tence (in kom′pə təns), lack of ability, power, or fitness: *The workman was discharged for incompetence. n.*

in com pe tent (in kom′pə tənt), 1 not competent; without ability, power, or fitness. 2 an incompetent person, especially a person suffering from some type of mental deficiency. 1 *adj.,* 2 *n.* —**in com′pe tent ly,** *adv.*

in com plete (in′kəm plēt′), not complete; lacking some part; unfinished. *adj.* —**in′com plete′ly,** *adv.* —**in′com plete′ness,** *n.*

in com pre hen si ble (in′kom pri hen′sə bəl), impossible to understand. *adj.*

in com pre hen si bly (in′kom pri hen′sə blē), in an incomprehensible manner. *adv.*

in com press i ble (in′kəm pres′ə bəl), that cannot be squeezed into a smaller size. *adj.*

in con ceiv a ble (in′kən sē′və bəl), 1 impossible to imagine: *A circle without a center is inconceivable.* 2 hard to believe; incredible: *It is inconceivable that two nations so friendly for centuries should now be at war. adj.*

in con ceiv a bly (in′kən sē′və blē), 1 in an inconceivable manner. 2 to an inconceivable degree. *adv.*

in con clu sive (in′kən klü′siv), not convincing; not settling or deciding something doubtful; not effective: *The result of my blood test was inconclusive, so I'll have to have another test. adj.* —**in′con clu′sive ly,** *adv.* —**in′con clu′sive ness,** *n.*

in con gru i ty (in′kən grü′ə tē), 1 a

being out of place; inappropriateness; unfitness. 2 lack of agreement or harmony; inconsistency. 3 something that is incongruous. *n., pl.* **in con gru i ties.**

in con gru ous (in kong′grü əs), 1 out of keeping; not appropriate; out of place: *A fur coat is incongruous with a bathing suit.* 2 lacking in agreement or harmony; inconsistent. *adj.* —**in con′gru ous ly,** *adv.*

in con se quent (in kon′sə kwent), not logically connected; not to the point; off the subject: *an inconsequent remark, an inconsequent argument. adj.*

in con se quen tial (in′kon sə kwen′shəl), 1 not important; trifling. 2 inconsequent. *adj.* —**in con′se quen′tial ly,** *adv.*

in con sid er a ble (in′kən sid′ər ə bəl), not worth consideration; not important; insignificant. *adj.*

in con sid er ate (in′kən sid′ər it), not thoughtful of others and their feelings; thoughtless. *adj.* —**in′con sid′er ate ly,** *adv.* —**in′con sid′er ate ness,** *n.*

in con sist en cy (in′kən sis′tən sē), 1 lack of agreement or harmony; variance: *There was a great inconsistency between what he said he would do and what he actually did.* 2 failure to keep to the same principles, course of action, etc.; changeableness: *He was accused of inconsistency in upholding what he had previously condemned.* 3 thing, act, etc., that is inconsistent. *n., pl.* **in con sist en cies.**

in con sist ent (in′kən sis′tənt), 1 not consistent; lacking in agreement with itself or something else: *Your failure to arrive on time is inconsistent with your usual promptness.* 2 failing to keep to the same principles, course of action, etc.; changeable: *What an inconsistent person says or does today does not agree with what he said or did yesterday. adj.* —**in′con sist′ent ly,** *adv.*

in con sol a ble (in′kən sō′lə bəl), not to be comforted; broken-hearted: *The girl was inconsolable at the loss of her kitten. adj.*

in con sol a bly (in′kən sō′lə blē), in an inconsolable manner. *adv.*

in con spic u ous (in′kən spik′yü əs), not conspicuous; attracting little or no attention: *The woman's dress was an inconspicuous gray. adj.* —**in′con spic′u ous ly,** *adv.* —**in′con spic′u ous ness,** *n.*

in con stan cy (in kon′stən sē), lack of constancy; changeableness; fickleness. *n.*

in con stant (in kon′stənt), not constant; changeable; fickle. *adj.* —**in con′stant ly,** *adv.*

in con test a ble (in′kən tes′tə bəl), too clear or certain to be denied; beyond dispute or doubt; unquestionable. *adj.*

in con test a bly (in′kən tes′tə blē), so as not to be contested or disputed. *adv.*

in con ti nence (in kon′tə nəns), lack of self-control. *n.*

in con ti nent (in kon′tə nənt), not continent; without self-control. *adj.*

in con tro vert i ble (in′kon trə vér′tə bəl), that cannot be disputed or denied; too clear or certain to be argued about; unquestionable. *adj.*

in con tro vert i bly (in′kon trə vér′tə blē), in an incontrovertible manner. *adv.*

in con ven ience (in′kən vē′nyəns), 1 lack of convenience or ease; trouble; bother. 2 something inconvenient; cause of trouble, difficulty, or bother. 3 cause trouble, difficulty, or bother to: *It will not inconvenience me to wait a few minutes.* 1,2 *n.,* 3 *v.,* **in con ven ienced, in con ven ienc ing.**

in con ven ient (in′kən vē′nyənt), not convenient; causing trouble, difficulty, or bother; troublesome: *Shelves that are too high to reach easily are inconvenient. adj.* —**in′con ven′ient ly,** *adv.*

in cor po rate (in kôr′pə rāt′ *for 1-3;* in kôr′pər it *for 4*), 1 make (something) a part of something else; join or combine (something) with something else: *We will incorporate your suggestion in this new plan.* 2 make into a corporation: *When the business became large, the owners incorporated it.* 3 become a corporation. 4 united; combined; incorporated. 1-3 *v.,* **in cor po rat ed, in cor po rat ing;** 4 *adj.*

in cor po rat ed (in kôr′pə rā′tid), made into a corporation; chartered as a corporation. *adj.*

in cor po ra tion (in kôr′pə rā′shən), 1 an incorporating: *The new design reflected the incorporation of many revisions.* 2 a being incorporated. Incorporation gives a company the power to act as one person. *n.*

in cor po re al (in′kôr pôr′ē əl), not made of any material substance; spiritual. *adj.* —**in′cor po′re al ly,** *adv.*

in cor rect (in′kə rekt′), 1 containing errors or mistakes; not correct; wrong: *The newspaper gave an incorrect account of the accident.* 2 not agreeing with a good standard of taste; improper. *adj.* —**in′cor rect′ly,** *adv.* —**in′cor rect′ness,** *n.*

in cor ri gi ble (in kôr′ə jə bəl), 1 too firmly fixed in bad ways, an annoying habit, etc., to be reformed or changed: *An incorrigible liar will lie in spite of any punishment. Nothing could break her*

hat, āge, fär; let, ēqual, tėrm;
it, īce; hot, ōpen, ôrder;
oil, out; cup, pùt, rüle; ch, child;
ng, long; sh, she; th, thin;
ᴛʜ, then; zh, measure;

ə represents *a* in about,
e in taken, *i* in pencil,
o in lemon, *u* in circus.

---

of her incorrigible habit of interrupting. 2 an incorrigible person. 1 *adj.,* 2 *n.*

in cor ri gi bly (in kôr′ə jə blē), in an incorrigible manner. *adv.*

in cor rupt i ble (in′kə rup′tə bəl), 1 not to be corrupted; honest: *An incorruptible judge cannot be bribed.* 2 not capable of decay; lasting forever: *Diamonds are incorruptible. adj.*

in cor rupt i bly (in′kə rup′tə blē), in an incorruptible manner. *adv.*

in crease (in krēs′ *for 1,2;* in′krēs *for 3,4*), 1 make greater, more numerous, more powerful, etc.; add to: *The driver increased the speed of the car.* 2 become greater; grow in numbers; advance in quality, power, etc.: *His weight has increased by ten pounds. These flowers will increase every year.* 3 a gain in size, numbers, etc.; growth: *an increase in our family. There has been a great increase in student enrollment during the past year.* 4 result of increasing; amount added; addition. 1,2 *v.,* **in creased, in creas ing;** 3,4 *n.*

on the increase, increasing: *The movement of people from the cities to the suburbs is on the increase.*

in creas ing ly (in krē′sing lē), to a greater degree; more and more: *As we traveled south, the weather became increasingly warm. adv.*

in cred i ble (in kred′ə bəl), hard to believe; seeming too extraordinary to be possible; unbelievable: *The racing car took off with incredible speed. Many old superstitions seem incredible to us. adj.*

in cred i bly (in kred′ə blē), so as to be incredible; beyond belief: *an incredibly swift flight. adv.*

in cre du li ty (in′krə dü′lə tē *or* in′krə dyü′lə tē), lack of belief; doubt. *n.*

in cred u lous (in krej′ə ləs), 1 not ready to believe; doubting: *People nowadays are incredulous about ghosts and witches.* 2 showing a lack of belief: *He listened to the neighbor's story with an incredulous smile. adj.* —**in cred′u lous ly,** *adv.*

in cre ment (in′krə mənt), 1 an increase; growth. 2 amount by which something increases: *The wages are*

adj. adjective	*n.* noun
adv. adverb	*prep.* preposition
conj. conjunction	*pron.* pronoun
interj. interjection	*v.* verb
sing. singular	*pl.* plural

$80 a week with an increment of $10 for each year of service. *n.*

in crim i nate (in krim′ə nāt), accuse of a crime; show to be guilty: *The robber's confession incriminated two others who helped to rob the bank.* *v.*, **in crim i nat ed, in crim i nat ing.**

in crim i na tion (in krim′ə nā′shən), an incriminating or a being incriminated. *n.*

in crust (in krust′), encrust. *v.*

in crus ta tion (in′krus tā′shən), 1 an encrusting or a being encrusted. 2 crust or hard coating. 3 a decorative layer of costly material. *n.* Also, **encrustation.**

in cu bate (ing′kyə bāt *or* in′kyə bāt), 1 sit on (eggs) in order to hatch them; brood. 2 keep (eggs, etc.) warm so that they will hatch. *v.*, **in cu bat ed, in cu bat ing.**

in cu ba tion (ing′kyə bā′shən *or* in′kyə bā′shən), 1 an incubating or a being incubated. 2 stage of a disease from the time of infection until the first symptoms appear: *The period of incubation for measles is about ten days. n.*

in cu ba tor (ing′kyə bā′tər *or* in′kyə-bā′tər), 1 box or chamber for hatching eggs by keeping them warm and properly supplied with moisture and oxygen. 2 any similar box or chamber. Very small babies and premature babies are sometimes kept for a time in incubators. *n.*

in cu bus (ing′kyə bəs *or* in′kyə bəs), 1 an evil spirit supposed to descend upon sleeping persons. 2 nightmare. 3 an oppressive or burdensome thing: *This debt will be an incubus until I have paid it. n., pl.* **in cu bi** (ing′kyə bī *or* in′kyə bī), **in cu bus es.** [from Latin]

in cu des (in kyü′dēz), plural of **incus.** *n.*

in cul cate (in kul′kāt), impress by repetition; teach persistently: *Over the years she inculcated a love of books into her pupils. v.*, **in cul cat ed, in cul cat ing.**

in cul ca tion (in′kul kā′shən), act or process of inculcating. *n.*

in cum ben cy (in kum′bən sē), term of office: *During his incumbency as governor the state prospered. n., pl.* **in cum ben cies.**

in cum bent (in kum′bənt), 1 lying, leaning, or pressing on something. 2 resting on a person as a duty: *She felt it incumbent upon her to answer the letter at once.* 3 currently holding an office, position, etc.: *the incumbent governor, the incumbent Republican candidate.* 4 person holding an office, position, etc.: *The former incumbent had been very popular in the district.* 1-3 *adj.*, 4 *n.*

in cum ber (in kum′bər), encumber. *v.*

in cum brance (in kum′brəns), encumbrance. *n.*

in cur (in kėr′), run or fall into (something unpleasant or inconvenient); bring on oneself: *incur many expenses. The pioneers incurred great danger when they tried to cross the mountains. v.*, **in curred, in cur ring.**

in cur a ble (in kyur′ə bəl), 1 not capable of being cured; that cannot be healed or remedied: *an incurable invalid, an incurable disease.* 2 person having an incurable disease: *That building is a home for incurables.* 1 *adj.*, 2 *n.*

in cur a bly (in kyur′ə blē), in an incurable manner; to an incurable degree. *adv.*

in cur sion (in kėr′zhən), a sudden attack; invasion; raid: *The pirates made incursions along the coast. n.*

in cus (ing′kəs), the middle one of a chain of three small bones in the middle ear of man and other animals. It is shaped somewhat like an anvil. *n., pl.* **in cu des.** [from Latin *incus* anvil]

Ind., Indiana.

in debt ed (in det′id), owing money or gratitude; in debt; obliged: *We are indebted to science for many of our comforts. adj.*

in debt ed ness (in det′id nis), 1 condition of being in debt. 2 amount owed; debts. *n.*

in de cen cy (in dē′sn sē), 1 lack of decency; being indecent. 2 an indecent act or word. *n., pl.* **in de cen cies.**

in de cent (in dē′snt), 1 not decent; in very bad taste; improper: *They showed an indecent lack of gratitude to those who had helped them.* 2 not modest; morally bad; disgusting; obscene. *adj.* —**in de′cent ly,** *adv.*

in de ci sion (in′di sizh′ən), lack of decision; tendency to delay or to hesitate. *n.*

in de ci sive (in′di sī′siv), 1 having the habit of hesitating and putting off decisions: *an indecisive person.* 2 not deciding or settling the matter; without a clear result: *Neither side wins in an indecisive battle. "Maybe" is an indecisive answer. adj.* —**in′de ci′sive ly,** *adv.* —**in′de ci′sive ness,** *n.*

in dec o rous (in dek′ər əs), not in accordance with proper behavior; in poor taste; improper. *adj.*

in deed (in dēd′), 1 in fact; in truth; really; surely: *She is hungry; indeed, she is almost starving. War is indeed terrible.* 2 expression of surprise, doubt, contempt, etc.: *Indeed! I never would have thought it.* 1 *adv.*, 2 *interj.*

in de fat i ga ble (in′di fat′ə gə bəl), never getting tired or giving up; tireless: *An indefatigable worker keeps on working until his work is done. adj.*

in de fen si ble (in′di fen′sə bəl), 1 that cannot be defended: *an indefensible island.* 2 not justifiable: *an indefensible lie. adj.*

in de fin a ble (in′di fī′nə bəl), that cannot be defined or described exactly: *indefinable beauty. adj.*

in de fin a bly (in′di fī′nə blē), in an indefinable manner. *adv.*

in def i nite (in def′ə nit), 1 not clearly defined; not exact; vague: *"Maybe" is a very indefinite answer.* 2 not limited: *We have an indefinite time to finish this work. adj.* —**in def′i nite ly,** *adv.* —**in def′i nite ness,** *n.*

indefinite article, the article *a* or *an.* "A dog" or "an animal" means "any dog" or "any animal"; "the dog" means "a certain or particular dog."

in del i ble (in del′ə bəl), 1 that cannot be erased or removed; permanent: *indelible ink. Her experiences in India left an indelible impression on her memory.* 2 making an indelible mark: *The papers were graded with an indelible pencil. adj.*

in del i bly (in del′ə blē), in an indelible manner. *adv.*

in del i ca cy (in del′ə kə sē), lack of delicacy; being indelicate. *n., pl.* **in del i ca cies.**

in del i cate (in del′ə kit), 1 not delicate; coarse; crude: *It is indelicate to boo in a theater.* 2 improper; immodest. *adj.* —**in del′i cate ly,** *adv.*

in dem ni fi ca tion (in dem′nə-fə kā′shən), 1 an indemnifying or a being indemnified. 2 compensation; recompense. *n.*

in dem ni fy (in dem′nə fī), 1 compensate for damage, loss, or hardship; make good; repay: *The railroad indemnified him for his injuries.* 2 secure against damage or loss; insure. *v.*, **in dem ni fied, in dem ni fy ing.**

in dem ni ty (in dem′nə tē), 1 payment for damage, loss, or hardship. Money demanded by a victorious nation at the end of a war as a condition of peace is an indemnity. 2 security against damage or loss; insurance. *n., pl.* **in dem ni ties.**

in dent[1] (in dent′), 1 make notches or jags in (an edge, line, border, etc.): *an*

indent¹ (def. 1)
indented molding

indented coastline. *The mountains indent the horizon.* 2 begin (a line) farther from the left margin than the other lines: *The first line of a paragraph is usually indented.* v. [from French of the 1300's *endenter,* from Latin *indentare* to crunch on with the teeth]

in dent² (in dent′), 1 make a dent in; mark with a dent. 2 press in; stamp. v. [*in-²* + *dent*]

in den ta tion (in′den tā′shən), 1 an indenting or a being indented. 2 a dent, notch, or cut. n.

in den tion (in den′shən), 1 a beginning of a line farther from the left margin than the other lines. 2 the blank space left by doing this. 3 indentation. n.

in den ture (in den′chər), 1 a written agreement. 2 contract by which a person is bound to serve someone else: *An apprentice has an indenture with the master from whom he is learning a trade.* 3 bind by a contract to serve someone else: *Many settlers came to the American colonies indentured for several years.* 1,2 n., 3 v., **in den tured, in den tur ing.**

in de pend ence (in′di pen′dəns), condition of being independent; freedom from the control, influence, support, or help of others: *The American colonies won independence from England.* n.

In de pend ence (in′di pen′dəns), city in W Missouri. n.

Independence Day, holiday in honor of the adoption of the Declaration of Independence on July 4, 1776; Fourth of July.

in de pend ent (in′di pen′dənt), 1 not influenced by others; thinking or acting for oneself: *An independent person votes as he pleases.* 2 not under another's rule or control; ruling, guiding, or governing oneself: *The United States is an independent country.* 3 not connected with others; separate or distinct: *an independent investigation, independent work.* 4 not depending on others for one's support: *Now that I have a better-paying job, I can be completely independent.* 5 enough to live on without working: *an independent income.* 6 person who is independent in thought or behavior. 7 person who votes without regard to party. 1-5 adj., 6,7 n. —**in′de pend′ent ly,** adv.

independent clause, main clause.

in de scrib a ble (in′di skrī′bə bəl), that cannot be described; beyond description: *a scene of indescribable beauty.* adj.

in de scrib a bly (in′di skrī′bə blē), in an indescribable manner. adv.

in de struct i bil i ty (in′di struk′tə bil′ə tē), indestructible quality or condition. n.

in de struct i ble (in′di struk′tə bəl), that cannot be destroyed. adj.

in de struct i bly (in′di struk′tə blē), in an indestructible manner. adv.

in de ter mi nate (in′di tėr′mə nit), not determined; not fixed; indefinite; vague: *As the floodwaters rose, an indeterminate number of people were stranded.* adj. —**in′de ter′mi nate ly,** adv.

in dex (in′deks), 1 list of what is in a book, telling on what pages to find names, topics, etc. An index is usually put at the end of the book and arranged in alphabetical order. 2 provide with an index; make an index of. 3 thing that points out or shows; sign: *A person's face is often an index of his mood.* 4 index finger. 5 pointer. A dial or scale usually has an index. 1,3-5 n., pl. **in dex es** or **in di ces;** 2 v.

index finger, forefinger.

In di a (in′dē ə), 1 country in S Asia, since 1950 an independent republic within the Commonwealth of Nations. *Capital:* New Delhi. 2 region and former country in S Asia. Until August 15, 1947, most of India was under British rule. It is now chiefly divided into the countries of India, Pakistan, and Bangladesh. n.

India
(def. 1, the shaded area; def. 2, the area within the heavy boundary line)

India ink, a black paint or ink.

In di an (in′dē ən), 1 American Indian. 2 of or having to do with American Indians: *an Indian camp, Indian blankets, an Indian language.* 3 any one of the languages of the American Indians. 4 made of Indian corn: *Indian pudding.* 5 of, living in, or belonging to India or the East Indies: *Indian elephants, Indian temples, Indian costumes.* 6 person born or living in India or the East Indies. 1,3,6 n., 2,4,5 adj.

In di an a (in′dē an′ə), one of the north central states of the United States. *Capital:* Indianapolis. n.

In di an ap o lis (in′dē ə nap′ə lis), capital of Indiana, in the central part. n.

Indian club, a bottle-shaped wooden club swung for exercise.

Indian club

Indian corn, 1 kind of cereal grass first raised by American Indians; maize. Various forms of Indian corn have been developed, such as sweet corn, popcorn, and ordinary corn. 2 grain or ears of this plant.

Indian file, single file.

Indian Ocean, ocean south of Asia, east of Africa, and west of Australia.

Indian pipe, a leafless plant with a solitary flower. Each stem, with its flower, looks like a tobacco pipe.

Indian summer, time of mild, dry, hazy weather in late October or early November, after the first frosts of autumn.

India paper, a thin, tough printing paper.

india rubber or **India rubber,** rubber.

in di cate (in′də kāt), 1 point out; make known; show: *The arrow on the sign indicates the right way to go.* 2 be a sign or hint of: *Fever indicates illness.* 3 give a sign or hint of: *People often indicate their feelings by facial expressions.* v., **in di cat ed, in di cat ing.**

in di ca tion (in′də kā′shən), 1 act of indicating: *We use different words for the indication of different meanings.* 2 thing that indicates; sign: *There was no indication that the house was occupied.* n.

in dic a tive (in dik′ə tiv), 1 pointing out; showing; being a sign; suggestive: *A headache is sometimes indicative of eyestrain.* 2 (in grammar) having to do with a verb form which expresses or denotes a state, act, or happening as

adj. adjective	*n.* noun
adv. adverb	*prep.* preposition
conj. conjunction	*pron.* pronoun
interj. interjection	*v.* verb
sing. singular	*pl.* plural

actual, or which asks a simple question of fact. **3** form of a verb which expresses this. In "I go" and "Did you win?" *go* and *did win* are indicatives. **4** mood of such a verb. **1,2** *adj.*, **3,4** *n.*

in di ca tor (in/də kā/tər), **1** person or thing that indicates. **2** pointer on the dial of an instrument that shows the amount of heat, pressure, speed, etc. **3** a measuring or recording instrument. **4** substance which, by changing color, indicates the chemical condition of a solution. Litmus is an indicator. *n.*

in di ces (in/də sēz/), a plural of **index**. *n.*

in dict (in dīt/), **1** charge with an offense or crime; accuse. **2** charge (an accused person) with a crime and hold him for trial on the recommendation of a grand jury which has heard the evidence and considered it sufficient. *v.*

in dict ment (in dīt/mənt), **1** a formal written accusation, especially on the recommendation of a grand jury: *an indictment for murder.* **2** accusation. *n.*

In dies (in/dēz), **1** the East Indies. **2** the West Indies. *n.pl.*

in dif fer ence (in dif/ər əns), **1** lack of interest or attention; not caring: *The boy's indifference to food worried his parents.* **2** lack of importance: *It is a matter of indifference to me whether we play ball or go swimming this afternoon.* *n.*

in dif fer ent (in dif/ər ənt), **1** not caring one way or the other; having or showing no interest: *The girl was indifferent to all admirers. I enjoyed the trip but she was indifferent.* **2** impartial; neutral; without preference: *The Supreme Court makes indifferent decisions.* **3** not mattering much; unimportant: *We can go whenever you please; the time for starting is indifferent to me.* **4** neither good nor bad; just fair: *an indifferent ballplayer. adj.*

in dif fer ent ly (in dif/ər ənt lē), **1** with indifference. **2** without distinction; equally. **3** moderately; tolerably; passably. **4** poorly; badly: *He did his work indifferently. adv.*

in di gence (in/də jəns), poverty. *n.*

in dig e nous (in dij/ə nəs), originating or produced in a particular country; growing or living naturally in a certain region, soil, climate, etc.; native: *Lions are indigenous to Africa. adj.*

in di gent (in/də jənt), poor or needy. *adj.*

in di gest i ble (in/də jes/tə bəl), that cannot be digested; hard to digest. *adj.*

in di ges tion (in/də jes/chən), inability to digest food; difficulty in digesting food: *The rich food we ate gave us indigestion. n.*

in dig nant (in dig/nənt), angry at something unworthy, unjust, or mean: *She was indignant when her sister threw cold water at her. adj.* —**in dig/nant ly,** *adv.*

in dig na tion (in/dig nā/shən), anger at something unworthy, unjust, or mean; anger mixed with scorn; righteous anger: *Cruelty to animals aroused his indignation. n.*

in dig ni ty (in dig/nə tē), an injury to one's dignity; lack of respect or proper treatment; insult: *Bill felt that being called "Willie dear" was an indignity. n., pl.* **in dig ni ties.**

in di go (in/də gō), **1** a blue dye formerly obtained from various plants, but now usually made artificially. **2** plant from which indigo was made. **3** a deep violet-blue. **4** deep violet-blue. **1-3** *n., pl.* **in di gos** or **in di goes;** **4** *adj.* [from Spanish *índigo,* from Latin *indicum*]

in di rect (in/də rekt/), **1** not straightforward and to the point: *She would not say yes or no but gave an indirect answer to my question.* **2** not directly connected; secondary: *Happiness is an indirect result of doing one's work well.* **3** not direct; not straight: *We walk to town by a road that is indirect, but very pleasant. adj.* —**in/di rect/ ly,** *adv.* —**in/di rect/ness,** *n.*

in di rec tion (in/də rek/shən), **1** a roundabout act, course, or method. **2** deceitful or crooked dealing. *n.*

indirect object, (in grammar) a word or group of words that usually comes before the direct object and shows the person or thing to which or for which something is done. In "I gave John a book," *John* is the indirect object and *book* is the direct object.

in dis creet (in/dis krēt/), not discreet; not wise and judicious; imprudent: *You were indiscreet to tell them your secret. adj.* —**in/dis creet/ly,** *adv.*

in dis cre tion (in/dis kresh/ən), **1** a being indiscreet; lack of good judgment; imprudence: *They were embarrassed at his indiscretion in talking about family matters in front of strangers.* **2** an indiscreet act. *n.*

in dis crim i nate (in/dis krim/ə nit), **1** mixed up; confused: *She tipped everything out of her suitcase in an indiscriminate pile.* **2** without discrimination; not distinguishing carefully between persons, things, etc.: *An indiscriminate reader shows no feeling for the differences between good books and bad ones. adj.* —**in/dis crim/i nate ly,** *adv.*

in dis pen sa bil i ty (in/dis pen/sə bil/ə tē), a being indispensable; absolute necessity. *n.*

in dis pen sa ble (in/dis pen/sə bəl), absolutely necessary: *Air is indispensable to life. adj.*

in dis pen sa bly (in/dis pen/sə blē), to an indispensable degree; necessarily. *adv.*

in dis pose (in/dis pōz/), **1** make unwilling; make not inclined: *Hot weather indisposes a person to work hard.* **2** make unfit or unable. **3** make slightly ill. *v.,* **in dis posed, in dis pos ing.**

in dis posed (in/dis pōzd/), **1** slightly ill. **2** unwilling; not inclined. *adj.*

in dis po si tion (in/dis pə zish/ən), **1** a slight illness. **2** unwillingness. *n.*

in dis put a ble (in/dis pyü/tə bəl *or* in dis/pyə tə bəl), too evident to be disputed; undoubted; certain; unquestionable: *an indisputable fact. adj.*

in dis put a bly (in/dis pyü/tə blē *or* in dis/pyə tə blē), in an indisputable manner; unquestionably. *adv.*

in dis sol u ble (in/di sol/yə bəl), that cannot be dissolved, undone, or destroyed; lasting; firm: *Let us make an indissoluble agreement. adj.*

in dis sol u bly (in/di sol/yə blē), in an indissoluble manner. *adv.*

in dis tinct (in/dis tingkt/), not distinct; not clear to the eye, ear, or mind; confused: *an indistinct voice. I had an indistinct memory of the accident. We could hear an indistinct roar from the distant ocean. adj.* —**in/dis tinct/ly,** *adv.* —**in/dis tinct/ness,** *n.*

in dis tin guish a ble (in/dis ting/gwi shə bəl), that cannot be distinguished. *adj.*

in dis tin guish a bly (in/dis ting/gwi shə blē), so as not to be distinguishable. *adv.*

in dite (in dīt/), put in words or writing; compose: *indite a letter. v.,* **in dit ed, in dit ing.**

in di um (in/dē əm), a very soft, silvery metallic element found only in combination with other elements. It is resistant to acids and abrasion and is used as a coating on metal parts. *n.*

in di vid u al (in/də vij/ü əl), **1** person: *He is the tallest individual in his family.* **2** a single person, animal, or thing: *We saw a herd of giraffes containing 30 individuals.* **3** for or by one only; single; particular; separate: *an individual question. Benches are for several people; chairs are individual seats. Washbowls are for general use;*

toothbrushes are for individual use.
4 belonging to or marking off one person or thing specially: *She has an individual style of arranging her hair.* 1,2 *n.,* 3,4 *adj.*

in di vid u al ism (in′də vij′ü ə liz′əm), **1** belief that individual freedom is as important as the welfare of the community or group as a whole. **2** absence of cooperation; wanting a separate existence for oneself. *n.*

in di vid u al ist (in′də vij′ü ə list), **1** person who lives his own life for himself and does not try to cooperate with or follow others. **2** supporter of individualism. *n.*

in di vid u al is tic (in′də vij′ü ə lis′tik), of individualism or individualists. *adj.*

in di vid u al i ty (in′də vij′ü al′ə tē), **1** the character or sum of the qualities which distinguish one person or thing from another. **2** condition of being individual; existence as an individual. *n., pl.* **in di vid u al i ties.**

in di vid u al ize (in′də vij′ü ə līz), **1** make different for each individual: *This school individualizes its course of study.* **2** consider as individuals; list one by one; specify. *v.,* **in di vid u al ized, in di vid u al iz ing.**

in di vid u al ly (in′də vij′ü ə lē), **1** one at a time; as individuals; personally: *Sometimes our teacher helps us individually.* **2** each from the others: *People differ individually. adv.*

in di vis i bil i ty (in′də viz′ə bil′ə tē), indivisible condition or quality. *n.*

in di vis i ble (in′də viz′ə bəl), **1** that cannot be divided: *"One nation under God, indivisible, with liberty and justice for all."* **2** that cannot be divided without a remainder: *Any odd number is indivisible by 2. adj.*

in di vis i bly (in′də viz′ə blē), in an indivisible manner. *adv.*

In do chi na or **In do-Chi na** (in′dō chī′nə), **1** peninsula in SE Asia comprising Burma, Cambodia, Laos, Malaya, Singapore, Thailand,

Indochina
(def. 1, the area within the heavy boundary line; def. 2, the shaded area)

North Vietnam, and South Vietnam. **2** countries in the E part of this peninsula formerly comprising French Indochina; Cambodia, Laos, North Vietnam, and South Vietnam. *n.*

In do chi nese or **In do-Chi nese** (in′dō chī nēz′), of or having to do with Indochina, the peoples living there, or their languages. *adj.*

in doc tri nate (in dok′trə nāt), **1** teach a doctrine, belief, or principle to. **2** teach; instruct. *v.,* **in doc tri nat ed, in doc tri nat ing.**

in doc tri na tion (in dok′trə nā′shən), an indoctrinating or a being indoctrinated. *n.*

in do lence (in′dl əns), dislike of work; laziness; idleness. *n.*

in do lent (in′dl ənt), disliking work; lazy; idle. *adj.* **—in′do lent ly,** *adv.*

in dom i ta ble (in dom′ə tə bəl), that cannot be conquered; unyielding: *The team's indomitable spirit helped them win against overwhelming odds. adj.*

in dom i ta bly (in dom′ə tə blē), in an indomitable manner. *adv.*

Indonesia (def. 1)

In do ne sia (in′dō nē′zhə), **1** country in the East Indies that includes Java, Sumatra, Celebes, parts of Borneo and New Guinea, and over 3000 smaller islands. It formerly belonged to the Netherlands. *Capital:* Djakarta. **2** Malay Archipelago. *n.* **—In′do ne′sian,** *adj., n.*

in door (in′dôr′), done, used, etc., in a house or building: *indoor tennis. adj.*

in doors (in′dôrz′), in or into a house or building: *Go indoors. adv.*

in dorse (in dôrs′), endorse. *v.,* **indorsed, in dors ing.**

in dorse ment (in dôrs′mənt), endorsement. *n.*

in dors er (in dôr′sər), endorser. *n.*

in du bi ta ble (in dü′bə tə bəl or in dyü′bə tə bəl), too evident to be doubted; certain; unquestionable: *It is an indubitable truth that all living matter dies. adj.*

in du bi ta bly (in dü′bə tə blē or in dyü′bə tə blē), in an indubitable manner; without doubt; unquestionably. *adv.*

in duce (in düs′ or in dyüs′), **1** lead on; influence; persuade: *Advertisements induce people to buy.* **2** cause; bring

hat, āge, fär; let, ēqual, tèrm;
it, īce; hot, ōpen, ôrder;
oil, out; cup, pùt, rüle; ch, child;
ng, long; sh, she; th, thin;
ŦH, then; zh, measure;

ə represents *a* in about,
e in taken, *i* in pencil,
o in lemon, *u* in circus.

about: *The doctor says that this medicine will induce sleep.* **3** produce (an electric current, electric charge, or magnetic change) without direct contact. **4** infer by reasoning from particular facts to a general rule or principle. *v.,* **in duced, in duc ing.**

in duce ment (in düs′mənt or in dyüs′mənt), **1** something that influences or persuades; incentive: *A new bicycle for the winner was an inducement to try hard to win the contest.* **2** act of influencing or persuading. *n.*

in duct (in dukt′), **1** put formally in possession (of an office, etc.): *She was inducted into the office of treasurer.* **2** bring in; introduce (into a place, seat, position, etc.). **3** take into the armed forces. *v.*

in duct ance (in duk′təns), property of an electric circuit by which an electromotive force in a nearby circuit is induced. The tuner of a radio varies the inductance of its coils. *n.*

in duc tee (in duk′tē′), person who has been, or soon will be inducted, especially into the armed forces. *n.*

induction (def. 1)
Magnetic induction—the tacks stick to the nail and to each other because of induced magnetism.

in duc tion (in duk′shən), **1** process by which an object having electrical or magnetic properties produces similar properties in a nearby object, without direct contact. **2** a reasoning from particular facts to general truths or principles. **3** a conclusion reached in this way. **4** act of inducting; act or ceremony of installing a person in office. *n.*

in duc tive (in duk′tiv), **1** of or using induction; reasoning by induction. **2** having to do with or caused by elec-

adj.	adjective	*n.*	noun
adv.	adverb	*prep.*	preposition
conj.	conjunction	*pron.*	pronoun
interj.	interjection	*v.*	verb
sing.	singular	*pl.*	plural

tric or magnetic induction. *adj.* —in duc′tive ly, *adv.*

in due (in dü′ or in dyü′), endue. *v.,* in dued, in du ing.

in dulge (in dulj′), 1 give in to one's pleasure; let oneself have, use, or do what one wants: *A smoker indulges in tobacco. An easily angered person often indulges in fits of temper.* 2 give in to; let oneself have, use, or do: *She indulged her fondness for candy by eating a whole box. We cannot indulge all our wants.* 3 give in to the wishes or whims of; humor: *We often indulge a sick person.* *v.,* in dulged, in dulg ing.

in dul gence (in dul′jəns), 1 act of indulging. 2 something indulged in: *Luxuries are indulgences.* 3 favor; privilege: *He was forever seeking indulgence.* 4 (in the Roman Catholic Church) a freeing from the punishment still due for sin after the guilt has been forgiven. *n.*

in dul gent (in dul′jənt), 1 giving in to another's wishes or whims; too kind or agreeable: *His indulgent parents gave him everything he wanted.* 2 making allowances; not critical; lenient: *The indulgent baby-sitter let her stay up late.* *adj.* —in dul′gent ly, *adv.*

In dus (in′dəs), river flowing from W Tibet through Kashmir and Pakistan into the Arabian Sea. *n.*

in dus tri al (in dus′trē əl), 1 of or having to do with industry: *Industrial workers work at trades or in factories. An industrial school teaches trades.* 2 of or having to do with the workers in industries: *industrial insurance.* *adj.* —in dus′tri al ly, *adv.*

in dus tri al ist (in dus′trē ə list), person who manages or owns an industrial enterprise. *n.*

in dus tri al i za tion (in dus′trē ə lə zā′shən), development of large industries in a country or economic system. *n.*

in dus tri al ize (in dus′trē ə līz), make industrial; develop large industries in (a country or economic system). *v.,* in dus tri al ized, in dus tri al iz ing.

Industrial Revolution, the change from an agricultural to an industrial society and from home manufacturing to factory production, especially the one that took place in England from about 1750 to about 1850.

industrial union, a labor union of all persons in the same industry without regard to the various crafts or jobs.

in dus tri ous (in dus′trē əs), working hard and steadily; diligent: *An industrious student usually has good grades.* *adj.* —in dus′tri ous ly, *adv.*

in dus try (in′də strē), 1 any branch of business, trade, or manufacture: *the automobile industry. Industries dealing with steel, copper, coal, and construction employ millions of people.* 2 systematic work or labor; continual employment in some useful work. 3 steady effort; busy application: *She reached her goal with much industry.* *n., pl.* in dus tries.

in e bri ate (in ē′brē āt *for 1;* in ē′brē it *for 2*), 1 make drunk; intoxicate. 2 a drunken person. 1 *v.,* in e bri at ed, in e bri at ing; 2 *n.*

in ed i ble (in ed′ə bəl), not fit to eat: *Poisonous mushrooms are inedible.* *adj.*

in ef fa ble (in ef′ə bəl), not to be expressed in words; too great to be described in words: *the ineffable beauty of a sunset.* *adj.*

in ef fa bly (in ef′ə blē), in an ineffable manner. *adv.*

in ef fec tive (in′ə fek′tiv), 1 not producing the desired effect; of little use: *An ineffective medicine fails to cure a disease or relieve pain.* 2 unfit for work; incapable. *adj.* —in′ef fec′tive ly, *adv.* —in′ef fec′tive ness, *n.*

in ef fec tu al (in′ə fek′chü əl), 1 without effect; failing to have the effect wanted; useless: *The searchlights were ineffectual in the fog.* 2 not able to produce the effect wanted; powerless. *adj.* —in′ef fec′tu al ly, *adv.*

in ef fi cien cy (in′ə fish′ən sē), 1 lack of efficiency; wastefulness. 2 a being incapable; inability to get things done. *n.*

in ef fi cient (in′ə fish′ənt), 1 not efficient; not able to produce an effect without waste of time or energy; wasteful: *A machine that uses too much fuel is inefficient.* 2 not able to get things done; incapable: *The inefficient doctor examined only a few patients.* *adj.* —in′ef fi′cient ly, *adv.*

in e las tic (in′i las′tik), not elastic; stiff; inflexible; unyielding. *adj.*

in el e gant (in el′ə gənt), not elegant; in poor taste; crude; vulgar. *adj.* —in el′e gant ly, *adv.*

in el i gi bil i ty (in el′ə jə bil′ə tē), lack of eligibility; being ineligible. *n.*

in el i gi ble (in el′ə jə bəl), 1 not eligible; not suitable or qualified; unfit to be chosen: *A foreign-born citizen of the United States is ineligible for the* Presidency. 2 person who is not suitable or not qualified. 1 *adj.,* 2 *n.*

in ept (in ept′), 1 not suitable; out of place: *Such a poor player would be an inept choice as captain.* 2 awkward; clumsy: *That was certainly an inept performance.* 3 foolish; absurd. *adj.* —in ept′ly, *adv.* —in ept′ness, *n.*

in e qual i ty (in′i kwol′ə tē), 1 lack of equality; a being unequal in amount, size, value, rank, etc.: *There is a great inequality between the salaries of a bank president and a teller.* 2 lack of evenness, regularity, or uniformity: *There are many inequalities in the New England coastline.* 3 a mathematical expression showing that two quantities are unequal. EXAMPLE: $a > b$ means a is greater than b; $a < b$ means a is less than b; $a \neq b$ means a and b are unequal. *n., pl.* in e qual i ties.

in eq ui ta ble (in ek′wə tə bəl), not equitable; unfair; unjust. *adj.*

in eq ui ta bly (in ek′wə tə blē), not fairly; unjustly. *adv.*

in eq ui ty (in ek′wə tē), lack of equity; unfairness; injustice. *n., pl.* in eq ui ties.

in e rad i ca ble (in′i rad′ə kə bəl), that cannot be rooted out or got rid of. *adj.*

in ert (in ėrt′), 1 having no power to move or act; lifeless: *A stone is an inert mass of matter.* 2 inactive; slow; sluggish: *He was sleepy and inert.* 3 with few or no active properties: *Helium and neon are inert gases; they will rarely combine with other chemical elements.* *adj.* —in ert′ly, *adv.* —in ert′ness, *n.*

in er tia (in ėr′shə), 1 tendency to remain in the state one is in, and not start changes. 2 tendency of all objects and matter in the universe to stay still, or, if moving, to go on moving in the same direction, unless acted on by some outside force. *n.*

in es cap a ble (in′ə skā′pə bəl), that cannot be escaped or avoided; sure to happen. *adj.*

in es cap a bly (in′ə skā′pə blē), in an inescapable manner; inevitably. *adv.*

in es ti ma ble (in es′tə mə bəl), too great to be estimated; priceless; invaluable: *Freedom of speech is an inestimable privilege.* *adj.*

in ev i ta bil i ty (in ev′ə tə bil′ə tē), condition of being inevitable. *n.*

in ev i ta ble (in ev′ə tə bəl), not to be avoided; sure to happen; certain to come: *Death is inevitable.* *adj.*

in ev i ta bly (in ev′ə tə blē), in an inevitable manner. *adv.*

in ex act (in′ig zakt′), not exact; with errors or mistakes; not strictly correct; not just right. *adj.* —in′ex act′ly, *adv.* —in′ex act′ness, *n.*

in ex cus a ble (in′ik skyü′zə bəl),

that ought not to be excused; that cannot be justified; unpardonable: *The winning team's poor sportsmanship was inexcusable. adj.*

in ex cus a bly (in′ik skyü′zə blē), in an inexcusable manner. *adv.*

in ex haust i ble (in′ig zô′stə bəl), 1 that cannot be exhausted; very abundant: *The wealth of our country seems inexhaustible to many people abroad.* 2 tireless: *The new president is a woman of inexhaustible energy. adj.*

in ex haust i bly (in′ig zô′stə blē), in an inexhaustible manner. *adv.*

in ex or a ble (in ek′sər ə bəl), not influenced by prayers or entreaties; relentless; unyielding: *The forces of nature are inexorable. adj.*

in ex or a bly (in ek′sər ə blē), in an inexorable manner. *adv.*

in ex pe di ent (in′ik spē′dē ənt), not expedient; not practicable, suitable, or wise. *adj.* —**in′ex pe′di ent ly,** *adv.*

in ex pen sive (in′ik spen′siv), not expensive; cheap; low-priced. *adj.* —**in′ex pen′sive ly,** *adv.* —**in′ex pen′sive ness,** *n.*

in ex per i ence (in′ik spir′ē əns), lack of experience; lack of practice; lack of skill or wisdom gained from experience. *n.*

in ex per i enced (in′ik spir′ē ənst), not experienced; without practice; lacking the skill and wisdom gained by experience. *adj.*

in ex pert (in′ik spèrt′ *or* in ek′spèrt′), not expert; unskilled. *adj.* —**in′ex pert′ly,** *adv.* —**in′ex pert′ness,** *n.*

in ex pi a ble (in ek′spē ə bəl), that cannot be atoned for: *Murder is an inexpiable crime. adj.*

in ex plic a ble (in′ik splik′ə bəl *or* in ek′splə kə bəl), that cannot be explained; mysterious: *an inexplicable fire. adj.*

in ex plic a bly (in′ik splik′ə blē *or* in ek′splə kə blē), in an inexplicable manner. *adv.*

in ex press i ble (in′ik spres′ə bəl), that cannot be expressed; impossible to express in words; indescribable. *adj.*

in ex press i bly (in′ik spres′ə blē), beyond expression; indescribably. *adv.*

in ex pres sive (in′ik spres′iv), not expressive; lacking in expression. *adj.* —**in′ex pres′sive ly,** *adv.* —**in′ex pres′sive ness,** *n.*

in ex tin guish a ble (in′ik sting′gwi shə bəl), that cannot be put out or stopped: *The scholar had an inextinguishable passion for knowledge. adj.*

in ex tri ca ble (in ek′strə kə bəl), 1 that one cannot get out of: *an inextricable maze, inextricable difficulty.* 2 that cannot be disentangled or solved: *inextricable confusion. adj.*

in fal li bil i ty (in fal′ə bil′ə tē), 1 freedom from error; inability to be mistaken. 2 absolute reliability; sureness. *n.*

in fal li ble (in fal′ə bəl), 1 free from error; that cannot be mistaken: *an infallible rule.* 2 absolutely reliable; sure: *infallible obedience. adj.*

in fal li bly (in fal′ə blē), in an infallible manner; without failure or mistake; certainly; surely. *adv.*

in fa mous (in′fə məs), 1 deserving or causing a very bad reputation; shamefully bad; very wicked: *Benedict Arnold's treason was an infamous betrayal of his country.* 2 having a very bad reputation; in public disgrace: *A traitor's name is infamous. adj.* —**in′fa mous ly,** *adv.*

in fa my (in′fə mē), 1 a very bad reputation; public disgrace: *Traitors are held in infamy.* 2 shameful badness; extreme wickedness. 3 an infamous or disgraceful act. *n., pl.* **in fa mies.**

in fan cy (in′fən sē), 1 condition or time of being an infant; babyhood; early childhood. 2 an early stage; very beginning of development: *Space travel is still in its infancy. n., pl.* **in fan cies.**

in fant (in′fənt), 1 a very young child; baby. 2 of or for an infant: *an infant dress, infant food.* 3 in an early stage; just beginning to develop: *an infant industry.* 4 person under the legal age of responsibility; minor. 1,4 *n.,* 2,3 *adj.*

in fan tile (in′fən tīl), 1 of an infant or infants; having to do with infants: *Measles and chicken pox are infantile diseases.* 2 like an infant; babyish; childish: *I was upset by my friend's infantile show of temper.* 3 in an early stage; just beginning to develop. *adj.*

infantile paralysis, polio.

in fan try (in′fən trē), 1 soldiers trained, equipped, and organized to fight on foot. 2 branch of an army consisting of such troops. *n., pl.* **in fan tries.**

in fan try man (in′fən trē mən), soldier who fights on foot; foot soldier. *n., pl.* **in fan try men.**

in fat u at ed (in fach′ü ā′tid), having an exaggerated fondness or passion; foolishly in love. *adj.*

in fat u a tion (in fach′ü ā′shən), exaggerated fondness or passion; foolish love. *n.*

in fect (in fekt′), 1 cause disease or an unhealthy condition in by introducing germs or viruses: *Dirt infects an open cut. Anyone with a bad cold may infect the people around him.* 2 influence in a bad way: *A noisy pupil may infect the behavior of a whole class.* 3 influence by spreading from one to another: *The artist's good nature infected many of her friends. v.*

in fec tion (in fek′shən), 1 a causing of disease in people, animals, and plants by the introduction of germs or viruses. Air, water, clothing, and insects may all be means of infection. 2 disease caused by the introduction of germs or viruses: *Measles is an infection that spreads from one person to another.* 3 an influence, feeling, or idea spreading from one to another. 4 fact or condition of being infected. *n.*

in fec tious (in fek′shəs), 1 spread by germs or viruses: *Measles is an infectious disease.* 2 causing infection. 3 apt to spread from one to another: *She has a jolly, infectious laugh. adj.* —**in fec′tious ly,** *adv.* —**in fec′tious ness,** *n.*

in fer (in fèr′), 1 find out by reasoning; come to believe after thinking; conclude: *People inferred that so able a governor would make a good President.* 2 be a sign or hint of; suggest indirectly; imply: *Ragged clothing infers poverty. v.,* **in ferred, in fer ring.**

in fer ence (in′fər əns), 1 the process of inferring; finding out by reasoning: *What happened is only a matter of inference; no one saw the accident.* 2 that which is inferred; conclusion: *What inference do you draw from smelling smoke? n.*

in fer i or (in fir′ē ər), 1 below most others; low in quality; below the average: *an inferior mind, an inferior grade of coffee.* 2 not so good or so great; lower in quality; worse: *My grades are inferior this year. This cloth is inferior to real silk.* 3 lower in position, rank, or importance: *A lieutenant is inferior to a captain.* 4 person who is lower in rank or station: *A good leader gets on well with inferiors.* 5 something that is below average. 1-3 *adj.,* 4,5 *n.*

in fer i or i ty (in fir′ē ôr′ə tē), inferior condition or quality. *n.*

in fer nal (in fèr′nl), 1 of the lower world; of hell. 2 fit to have come from hell; hellish; diabolical: *The heartless conqueror showed infernal cruelty. adj.* —**in fer′nal ly,** *adv.*

in fer no (in fèr′nō), 1 hell. 2 place of torment like hell: *Firemen fought their*

adj. adjective	*n.* noun
adv. adverb	*prep.* preposition
conj. conjunction	*pron.* pronoun
interj. interjection	*v.* verb
sing. singular	*pl.* plural

way through a roaring, flaming inferno. *n., pl.* **in fer nos.**

in fer tile (in fėr′tl), not fertile; sterile. *adj.*

in fest (in fest′), trouble or disturb frequently or in large numbers: *Mosquitoes infest swamps. The national park was infested with tourists. v.*

in fi del (in′fə dəl), 1 person who does not believe in religion. 2 not believing in religion. 3 person who does not accept a particular faith. During the Crusades, Moslems called Christians infidels. 4 person who does not accept Christianity. 1,3,4 *n.,* 2 *adj.*

in fi del i ty (in′fə del′ə tē), 1 unbelief in religion, especially in Christianity. 2 lack of faithfulness, especially to husband or wife; disloyalty. *n., pl.* **in fi del i ties.**

in field (in′fēld′), 1 the part of a baseball field roughly bounded by the bases; diamond. 2 first, second, and third basemen and shortstop of a baseball team. *n.*

in field er (in′fēl′dər), player in the infield. *n.*

in fil trate (in fil′trāt), 1 pass into or through by filtering. 2 penetrate or slip through (an enemy's lines) individually or in small groups: *Enemy troops infiltrated the front lines.* 3 penetrate (an organization) for the purposes of spying, sabotage, or the like. 4 filter into or through; permeate. *v.,* **in fil trat ed, in fil trat ing.**

in fil tra tion (in′fil trā′shən), 1 an infiltrating or a being infiltrated. 2 thing that infiltrates. 3 method of attack in which small groups of men penetrate the enemy's lines at various weak points to fire on the enemy from the side or rear. *n.*

in fi nite (in′fə nit), 1 without limits or bounds; endless: *the infinite reaches of outer space.* 2 extremely great: *Teaching little children sometimes takes infinite patience.* 3 that which is infinite. 4 (in mathematics) greater in units than any natural number. 5 **the Infinite,** God. 1,2,4 *adj.,* 3,5 *n.* —**in′fi nite ly,** *adv.* —**in′fi nite ness,** *n.*

in fin i tes i mal (in′fi nə tes′ə məl), so small as to be almost nothing: *Germs are infinitesimal animals or plants. adj.* —**in′fi ni tes′i mal ly,** *adv.*

in fin i tive (in fin′ə tiv), (in grammar) form of a verb not limited by person and number, often preceded by *to.* In "To know her is to like her," *to know* and *to like* are infinitives. In "We must go now," *go* is an infinitive. *n.*

in fin i tude (in fin′ə tüd *or* in fin′ə tyüd), 1 condition of being infinite. 2 an infinite extent, amount, or number. *n.*

in fin i ty (in fin′ə tē), 1 condition of being infinite. 2 an infinite distance, space, time, or quantity. 3 an infinite extent, amount, or number: *the infinity of God's mercy. n., pl.* **in fin i ties.**

in firm (in fėrm′), 1 lacking strength or health; weak; feeble: *The patient was old and infirm.* 2 without a firm purpose; faltering: *infirm judgment. adj.*

in fir mar y (in fėr′mər ē), place for the care of the infirm, sick, or injured; hospital in a school or institution. *n., pl.* **in fir mar ies.**

in fir mi ty (in fėr′mə tē), 1 weakness; feebleness. 2 sickness; illness: *the infirmities of age. n., pl.* **in fir mi ties.**

in flame (in flām′), 1 make more violent; excite: *Her stirring speech inflamed the crowd.* 2 become excited with strong feeling. 3 make or become unnaturally hot, red, sore, or swollen: *The smoke had inflamed the fireman's eyes. v.,* **in flamed, in flam ing.**

in flam ma ble (in flam′ə bəl), 1 flammable: *Paper is very inflammable.* 2 easily excited or aroused; excitable: *an inflammable temper. adj.*

in flam ma tion (in′flə mā′shən), 1 a diseased condition of some part of the body, marked by heat, redness, swelling, and pain: *A boil is an inflammation of the skin.* 2 an inflaming or a being inflamed. *n.*

in flam ma to ry (in flam′ə tôr′ē), 1 tending to excite or arouse: *The leader of the mob made an inflammatory speech attacking the government.* 2 of, causing, or accompanied by inflammation: *An inflammatory condition of the tonsils causes a sore throat. adj.*

in flat a ble (in flā′tə bəl), that can be inflated. *adj.*

in flate (in flāt′), 1 force air or gas into (a balloon, tire, ball, etc.) causing it to swell. 2 swell or puff out: *After his success he was inflated with pride.* 3 increase (prices or amount of currency) beyond the normal amount. *v.,* **in flat ed, in flat ing.**

in fla tion (in flā′shən), 1 a swelling (with air, gas, pride, etc.). 2 a swollen state; too great expansion. 3 increase of the currency of a country by issuing too much paper money. 4 a sharp increase in prices resulting from too great an expansion in paper money or bank credit. *n.*

in fla tion ar y (in flā′shə ner′ē), of or having to do with inflation; tending to inflate. *adj.*

in flect (in flekt′), 1 change the tone or pitch of (the voice). 2 vary the form of (a word) to show case, number, gender, person, tense, mood, voice, or comparison. By inflecting *who* we have *whose* and *whom.* 3 bend; curve. *v.*

in flec tion (in flek′shən), 1 a change in the tone or pitch of the voice: *We usually end questions with a rising inflection.* 2 variation in the form of a word to show case, number, gender, person, tense, mood, voice, or comparison. 3 suffix or ending used for this: *-est* and *-ed* are common inflections in English. 4 a bending; curving. 5 a bend; curve. *n.*

in flec tion al (in flek′shə nəl), of, having to do with, or showing grammatical inflection. *adj.*

in flex i bil i ty (in flek′sə bil′ə tē), lack of flexibility; being inflexible. *n.*

in flex i ble (in flek′sə bəl), 1 not yielding; firm; steadfast: *Neither threats nor promises could change the captain's inflexible stand.* 2 that cannot be changed; unalterable. 3 not easily bent; stiff; rigid: *an inflexible rod. adj.*

in flex i bly (in flek′sə blē), in an inflexible manner; rigidly. *adv.*

in flict (in flikt′), 1 cause to have or suffer; give (a stroke, blow, or wound): *A knife can inflict a bad wound on a person.* 2 cause to be suffered or borne; impose (suffering, punishment, something unwelcome, etc.): *She did not like to inflict pain. The disagreeable woman inflicted herself on her relatives for a long visit. v.*

in flic tion (in flik′shən), 1 act of inflicting: *The cruel emperor delighted in the infliction of pain.* 2 something inflicted; pain; suffering; burden; punishment: *The Bible tells how Job endured many inflictions with patience. n.*

in flo res cence (in′flô res′ns), arrangement of flowers on the stem or axis. *n.*

RACEME   UMBEL   SPIKE
inflorescence—three common types

in flow (in′flō′), 1 a flowing in or into: *The discovery of gold in Alaska caused an inflow of people.* 2 that which flows in. *n.*

in flu ence (in′flü əns), 1 power of acting on others and having an effect without using force: *Use your influence* to persuade your friends to join our club. **2** person or thing that has such power: *His thoughtfulness for others made the captain of our football team a good influence throughout the school.* **3** have an influence on: *The moon influences the tides. What we read influences our thinking.* **4** use influence on: *We tried to influence the teacher by offering him our suggestions.* 1,2 *n.*, 3,4 *v.*, **in flu enced, in flu enc ing.**

in flu en tial (in′flü en′shəl), **1** having much influence: *Influential friends helped her get a good job.* **2** using influence; producing results. *adj.*

in flu en za (in′flü en′zə), an acute, contagious disease caused by a virus, and like a very bad cold in its symptoms, but much more dangerous and exhausting; grippe. *n.*

in flux (in′fluks), a flowing in; steady flow: *An influx of immigrants from Europe greatly increased the population of the United States. n.*

in form (in fôrm′), **1** give knowledge, facts, or news to; tell: *Her letter informed us of how and when she expected to arrive. Please inform your students of the changes in today's schedule.* **2** make an accusation or complaint; accuse: *The thief who was caught informed against the others who had helped him steal. v.*

in for mal (in fôr′məl), **1** not formal; without ceremony: *an informal party.* **2** used in everyday, common talk, but not used in formal talking or writing; colloquial. Such an expression as *kids* for *children* is informal. *adj.* —**in for′mal ly,** *adv.*

in for mal i ty (in′fôr mal′ə tē), **1** a being informal; lack of ceremony. **2** an informal act or behavior. *n., pl.* **in for mal i ties.**

in form ant (in fôr′mənt), person who gives information to another: *I found out what happened from my informant, who saw it happen. n.*

in for ma tion (in′fər mā′shən), **1** knowledge given or received concerning some fact or circumstance; news: *We have just received information of the astronauts' safe landing.* **2** things known; facts; data: *A dictionary contains much information about words.* **3** an informing: *A guidebook is for the information of travelers.* **4** accusation or complaint against a person. *n.*

in for ma tion al (in′fər mā′shə nəl), having to do with or giving information: *A library's reference department provides informational services. adj.*

in form a tive (in fôr′mə tiv), giving information; instructive: *The class trip to see how a newspaper is printed was very informative. adj.*

in formed (in fôrmd′), having information. *adj.*

in form er (in fôr′mər), **1** person who tells authorities of violations of the law; person who informs on another: *An informer told the police that the store was selling stolen goods.* **2** informant. *n.*

in frac tion (in frak′shən), a breaking of a law or obligation; violation: *Reckless driving is an infraction of the law. n.*

in fra red (in′frə red′), of the invisible part of the spectrum whose rays have wavelengths longer than those of the red end of the visible spectrum. Most of the heat from sunlight and incandescent lamps is from infrared rays. *adj.*

in fre quen cy (in frē′kwən sē), a being infrequent; scarcity; rarity. *n.*

in fre quent (in frē′kwənt), occurring seldom or far apart; not frequent; scarce; rare. *adj.* —**in fre′quent ly,** *adv.*

in fringe (in frinj′), **1** act contrary to or violate (a law, obligation, right, etc.): *A confusing label may infringe the food and drug law. The inventor sued the company for infringing her patent.* **2** go beyond the proper or usual limits; trespass; encroach: *Do not infringe upon the rights of others. v.,* **in fringed, in fring ing.**

in fringe ment (in frinj′mənt), **1** violation. **2** a trespassing. *n.*

in fring er (in frin′jər), person who infringes. *n.*

in fur i ate (in fyur′ē āt), fill with wild, fierce anger; make furious; enrage: *Their insults infuriated him. v.,* **in fur i at ed, in fur i at ing.**

in fuse (in fyüz′), **1** pour in; put in; instill: *She infused her excitement into those who listened to her.* **2** inspire: *The crowd was infused with her excitement.* **3** steep or soak (a plant, leaves) in a liquid to get something out: *Tea leaves are infused in hot water to make tea. v.,* **in fused, in fus ing.**

in fu sion (in fyü′zhən), **1** act or process of infusing: *The plan was changed by the infusion of new ideas.* **2** a liquid extract obtained by steeping or soaking: *Tea is an infusion of tea leaves in hot water. n.*

-ing[1], *suffix forming nouns chiefly from verbs.* **1** act of a person or thing that ____s: *Painting = act of one that paints.* **2** product or result of such an act, as *a drawing, a painting.* **3** thing that ____s: *Lining = thing that lines.* [Middle English *-ing*, Old English *-ing, -ung*]

-ing[2], **1** *suffix forming the present participle of verbs,* as in *raining, staying, talking.* **2** *suffix forming adjectives from verbs. that* ____s: *Lasting happiness = happiness that lasts. Growing child = child that grows.* [Middle English *-ing*, variant of *-ind, -end,* Old English *-ende*]

in gen ious (in jē′nyəs), **1** with skill in planning or making; clever: *The ingenious boy made a radio set for himself.* **2** cleverly planned and made: *This mousetrap made of an old tin can and some wire is an ingenious device. adj.* —**in gen′ious ly,** *adv.* —**in gen′ious ness,** *n.*

in ge nue (an′zhə nü), **1** a simple, innocent girl or young woman. **2** actress who plays the part of such a girl or young woman. *n.* [from French *ingénue*]

in gé nue (an′zhə nü), ingenue. *n., pl.* **in gé nues.**

in ge nu i ty (in′jə nü′ə tē *or* in′jə nyü′ə tē), skill in planning or making; cleverness: *The girl showed ingenuity in making toys out of scraps of wood. n.*

in gen u ous (in jen′yü əs), **1** free from restraint or reserve; frank and open; sincere: *He gave an ingenuous account of his acts, concealing nothing.* **2** simple; natural; innocent: *an ingenuous manner. Little children are ingenuous. adj.* —**in gen′u ous ly,** *adv.* —**in gen′u ous ness,** *n.*

in gest (in jest′), take (food, etc.) into the body for digestion: *Higher animals ingest by swallowing. v.*

in ges tion (in jes′chən), act of taking food, etc., into the body for digesting: *Ingestion is the first step in the digestive process. n.*

in gle nook (ing′gəl nùk′), nook or corner beside a fireplace. *n.*

in glo ri ous (in glôr′ē əs), **1** bringing no glory; shameful; disgraceful: *The tennis champion suffered an inglorious defeat at the hands of a mere amateur.* **2** having no glory; not famous; obscure; humble. *adj.* —**in glo′ri ous ly,** *adv.* —**in glo′ri ous ness,** *n.*

in got (ing′gət), mass of metal, such as

ingots
steel ingots
just removed
from molds
by huge tongs
suspended from
a crane

INGOT MOLD

INGOT

adj.	adjective	*n.*	noun
adv.	adverb	*prep.*	preposition
conj.	conjunction	*pron.*	pronoun
interj.	interjection	*v.*	verb
sing.	singular	*pl.*	plural

gold, silver, or steel, cast into a block or bar to be recast, rolled, or forged at a later time. *n.*

in graft (in graft′), engraft. *v.*

in grain (in grān′), dye through the fiber or yarn before manufacture. *v.*

in grained (in grānd′), deeply and firmly fixed in one's very nature or being: *ingrained honesty, an ingrained rebel. adj.*

in grate (in′grāt), an ungrateful person. *n.*

in gra ti ate (in grā′shē āt), bring (oneself) into favor; make (oneself) acceptable: *He tried to ingratiate himself with the teacher by giving her presents. v.*, **in gra ti at ed, in gra ti at ing.** —**in gra′ti at′ing ly,** *adv.*

in grat i tude (in grat′ə tüd *or* in grat′ə tyüd), lack of gratitude or thankfulness; being ungrateful. *n.*

in gre di ent (in grē′dē ənt), one of the parts of a mixture: *The ingredients of a cake usually include eggs, sugar, flour, and flavoring. Honesty is an important ingredient of character. n.*

in gress (in′gres), 1 a going in: *A high fence prevented ingress to the field when the gate was locked.* 2 way of going in; entrance: *A trap door in the floor was the only ingress to the secret room below.* 3 right to go in: *All citizens have free ingress to the public library. n.*

in-group (in′grüp′), group of people united by the same interests. An ingroup often excludes outsiders. *n.*

in grown (in′grōn′), grown into the flesh: *an ingrown toenail. adj.*

in hab it (in hab′it), live in (a place, region, house, cave, tree, etc.): *Fish inhabit the sea. Thoughts inhabit the mind. v.*

in hab it a ble (in hab′ə tə bəl), 1 capable of being inhabited. 2 fit to live in; habitable. *adj.*

in hab it ant (in hab′ə tənt), person or animal that lives in a place; resident; dweller: *Our town has ten thousand inhabitants. n.*

in hab it ed (in hab′ə tid), lived in: *an inhabited house. adj.*

in hal ant (in hā′lənt), medicine to be inhaled. *n.*

in ha la tion (in′hə lā′shən), 1 an inhaling. 2 medicine to be inhaled. *n.*

in hale (in hāl′), draw (air, gas, fra-grance, tobacco smoke, etc.) into the lungs; breathe in. *v.*, **in haled, in hal ing.**

in hal er (in hā′lər), 1 apparatus used in inhaling medicine, oxygen, an anesthetic, etc. 2 person who inhales. *n.*

in har mo ni ous (in′här mō′nē əs), not harmonious; disagreeing; conflicting; discordant. *adj.* —**in′har mo′ni ous ly,** *adv.*

in here (in hir′), belong as a quality or attribute; be inherent; exist: *The need to be loved inheres in human nature. Power inheres in the emperor. v.*, **in hered, in her ing.**

in her ent (in hir′ənt), belonging to a person or thing as a quality or attribute; essential: *Her inherent curiosity about nature led her to study botany. adj.*

in her ent ly (in hir′ənt lē), by its own nature; essentially. *adv.*

in her it (in her′it), 1 get or have after someone dies; receive as an heir: *After Grandfather's death, Mother inherited all of his property.* 2 receive (physical or mental characteristics) from one's parents or ancestors through heredity. 3 receive (anything) by succession from one who came before: *I inherited this old pen from the person who used to have my desk. v.*

in her it ance (in her′ə təns), 1 act or right of inheriting: *He obtained his house by inheritance from an aunt.* 2 anything inherited: *The house was her inheritance. Good health is a fine inheritance from one's parents. n.*

in her i tor (in her′ə tər), person who inherits; heir. *n.*

in hib it (in hib′it), 1 hold back; hinder or restrain; check: *The girl's honesty inhibited her impulse to keep the ring that she found.* 2 prohibit; forbid. *v.*

in hi bi tion (in′hə bish′ən), 1 a holding back; restraint; checking: *Some drugs can cause the inhibition of normal bodily activity.* 2 idea, emotion, attitude, habit, or other inner force holding back or checking one's impulses, desires, etc. 3 prohibition; forbidding. *n.*

in hib i tor (in hib′ə tər), person or thing that inhibits. *n.*

in hib i to ry (in hib′ə tôr′ē), inhibiting; tending to inhibit. *adj.*

in hos pit a ble (in′ho spit′ə bəl *or* in hos′pi tə bəl), 1 not hospitable; not making visitors comfortable: *That inhospitable man never offers visitors any refreshments.* 2 providing no shelter; barren: *a rocky, inhospitable shore. adj.*

in hos pit a bly (in′ho spit′ə blē *or* in hos′pi tə blē), in an inhospitable manner. *adv.*

in hos pi tal i ty (in hos′pə tal′ə tē), lack of hospitality. *n.*

in hu man (in hyü′mən), 1 without kindness, mercy, or tenderness; cruel; brutal: *an inhuman lack of concern for the sufferings of others.* 2 not human; not having the qualities natural to a human being: *Some of the Olympic runners seem to have inhuman powers of endurance. adj.* —**in hu′man ly,** *adv.*

in hu mane (in′hyü mān′), not humane; lacking in kindness, mercy, or tenderness. *adj.* —**in′hu mane′ly,** *adv.*

in hu man i ty (in′hyü man′ə tē), 1 a being inhuman; lack of kindness, mercy, or tenderness; cruelty; brutality. 2 an inhuman, cruel, or brutal act. *n., pl.* **in hu man i ties.**

in im i cal (in im′ə kəl), 1 unfriendly; hostile: *The townspeople were inimical to strangers.* 2 unfavorable; harmful: *Lack of ambition is inimical to success. adj.* —**in im′i cal ly,** *adv.*

in im i ta ble (in im′ə tə bəl), impossible to imitate or copy; matchless. *adj.*

in im i ta bly (in im′ə tə blē), in an inimitable manner. *adv.*

in iq ui tous (in ik′wə təs), very unjust; wicked. *adj.*

in iq ui ty (in ik′wə tē), 1 very great injustice; wickedness. 2 a wicked or unjust act: *Taking children from their parents and selling them was one of the iniquities of slavery. n., pl.* **in iq ui ties.**

i ni tial (i nish′əl), 1 occurring at the beginning; first; earliest: *His initial effort at skating was a failure, but he succeeded the second time that he tried.* 2 the first letter of a word: *The initials U.S. stand for United States.* 3 to mark or sign with initials: *John Allen Smith initialed the note J.A.S.* 4 an extra large letter, often decorated, at the beginning of a chapter or other division of a book. 1 *adj.,* 2,4 *n.,* 3 *v.*

i ni tial ly (i nish′ə lē), at the beginning. *adv.*

i ni ti ate (i nish′ē āt *for 1-3;* i nish′ē it *or* i nish′ē āt *for 4*), 1 be the first one to start; set going; begin: *This year we shall initiate a series of free concerts for the public.* 2 admit (a person) with formal ceremonies into a group or society: *The old members initiated the new members.* 3 help to get a first understanding; introduce into the knowledge of some art or subject: *initiate a person into business methods. The teacher initiated the class into the wonders of science by telling a few interesting things about the earth and stars.* 4 person who is initiated. 1-3 *v.,* **i ni ti at ed, i ni ti at ing;** 4 *n.*

i ni ti a tion (i nish′ē ā′shən), 1 act or process of being the first one to start something; beginning. 2 formal admission into a group or society. 3 ceremonies by which one is admitted to a group or society: *A great many members of the club showed up for the initiation.* *n.*

in i ti a tive (i nish′ē ə tiv), 1 active part in taking the first steps in any undertaking; lead: *She likes to take the initiative in planning class projects.* 2 readiness and ability to be the one to start something: *A good leader must have initiative.* 3 right of citizens outside the legislature to introduce or enact a new law by vote. 4 procedure for doing this. *n.*

—INKHORN

i ni ti a tor (i nish′ē ā′tər), person or thing that initiates. *n.*

in ject (in jekt′), 1 force (liquid, medicine, etc.) into a passage, cavity, or tissue: *Drugs are often injected into the body.* 2 fill (a cavity, etc.) with liquid forced in: *The dentist injected the boy's gums with novocaine.* 3 throw in; insert: *While she and I were talking he injected a remark into the conversation.* *v.*

in jec tion (in jek′shən), 1 act or process of injecting: *Those drugs are given by injection as well as through the mouth.* 2 liquid injected: *A drug is often given as an injection.* *n.*

in jec tor (in jek′tər), person or thing that injects. *n.*

in ju di cious (in′jü dish′əs), showing bad judgment; unwise; not judicious: *An injudicious person says or does things without thinking what their results may be.* *adj.* —**in′ju di′cious ly**, *adv.*

in junc tion (in jungk′shən), 1 command; order: *Injunctions of secrecy did not prevent the news from leaking out.* 2 a formal order from a court of law requiring a person or group to do or not to do something: *The school board got an injunction which prohibited the teachers from striking before the end of the school year.* *n.*

in jure (in′jər), 1 do damage to; harm; hurt: *Do not break or injure the bushes in the park. The misunderstanding injured their friendship.* 2 be unfair or unjust to; do wrong to. *v.,* **in jured, in jur ing.**

in ju ri ous (in jür′ē əs), 1 causing injury; harmful: *Hail is injurious to crops.* 2 unfair; unjust; wrongful. *adj.*

in jur y (in′jər ē), 1 hurt or loss caused to or endured by a person or thing; harm; damage: *She escaped from the train wreck without injury. The accident will be an injury to the reputation of the railroad.* 2 unfairness; injustice; wrong: *You did me an injury when you said I lied.* *n., pl.* **in jur ies.**

in jus tice (in jus′tis), 1 lack of justice; being unjust. 2 an unjust act: *It is an injustice to send an innocent person to jail.* *n.*

ink (ingk), 1 a colored or black liquid used for writing, printing, or drawing. 2 put ink on; mark or stain with ink. 3 a dark liquid thrown out for protection by cuttlefish, squids, etc. 1,3 *n.,* 2 *v.* —**ink′like′**, *adj.*

ink horn (ingk′hôrn′), a small container, often made of horn, formerly used to hold ink. *n.*

ink i ness (ing′kē nis), a being inky; blackness. *n.*

ink ling (ing′kling), vague notion; slight suspicion; hint: *give a person an inkling of what is going on.* *n.*

ink stand (ingk′stand′), 1 stand to hold ink and pens. 2 container used to hold ink. *n.*

ink well (ingk′wel′), container used to hold ink on a desk or table. *n.*

ink y (ing′kē), 1 like ink; dark; black: *inky shadows.* 2 covered with ink; marked or stained with ink. 3 of ink. *adj.,* **ink i er, ink i est.**

in laid (in′lād′ *or* in lād′), 1 set in the surface as a decoration or design: *The top of the desk had an inlaid design of light wood in dark.* 2 decorated with a design or material set in the surface: *The wooden box had an inlaid top of silver.* 3 past tense and past participle of **inlay.** *The workmen inlaid colored tiles in a design in the kitchen floor. The floor was inlaid with colored tiles.* 1,2 *adj.,* 3 *v.*

in land (in′lənd), 1 away from the coast or the border; situated in the interior: *Illinois is an inland state.* 2 interior of a country; land away from the border or the coast. 3 in or toward the interior: *He traveled inland from New York to Chicago.* 4 domestic; not foreign: *Commerce between the states of the United States is inland trade.* 1,4 *adj.,* 2 *n.,* 3 *adv.*

in-law (in′lô′), INFORMAL. person related by marriage. *n.*

in lay (in lā′ *or* in′lā′ *for* 1,2; in′lā′ *for* 3,4), 1 to set in the surface as a decoration or design: *The craftsman inlaid strips of gold in the top of the wooden box.* 2 decorate with a design set in the surface: *inlay a wooden box with gold.* 3 an inlaid decoration, design, or material. 4 a shaped piece of gold, porcelain, etc., cemented in a tooth as a filling. 1,2 *v.,* **in laid, in lay ing;** 3,4 *n.*

hat, āge, fär; let, ēqual, tèrm;
it, īce; hot, ōpen, ôrder;
oil, out; cup, pùt, rüle; ch, child;
ng, long; sh, she; th, thin;
ŦH, then; zh, measure;

ə represents *a* in about,
e in taken, *i* in pencil,
o in lemon, *u* in circus.

in let (in′let), 1 a narrow strip of water running from a larger body of water into the land or between islands: *The fishing village was on a small inlet of the sea.* 2 entrance. *n.*

in mate (in′māt), 1 person confined in a prison, asylum, hospital, etc. 2 person who lives in the same building with another; occupant; inhabitant. *n.*

in me mo ri am (in mə môr′ē əm), LATIN. in memory of; to the memory of.

in most (in′mōst), 1 farthest in; deepest: *We went to the inmost depths of the mine.* 2 most private; most secret: *Her inmost desire was to be a trial lawyer.* *adj.*

inn (in), 1 place where travelers and others can get meals and a room to sleep in. 2 restaurant or tavern. *n.*

in nate (i nāt′ *or* in′āt), born in a person; natural: *A good artist has an innate talent for drawing. A good comedian has an innate wit.* *adj.* —**in nate′ly**, *adv.*

in ner (in′ər), 1 farther in; inside: *The buildings formed a square surrounding an inner courtyard.* 2 more private; more secret: *She kept her inner thoughts to herself.* 3 of the mind or soul: *a person's inner life.* *adj.*

inner ear, innermost part of the ear of man and other mammals, behind the middle ear. It contains the organs of balance and the organs that change sound into nerve messages. See ear[1] for diagram.

in ner most (in′ər mōst), farthest in; inmost: *the innermost parts of a machine.* *adj.*

inner tube, a separate rubber tube

inlay (def. 3)
part of an
inlaid table with
several inlays

adj. adjective	*n.* noun
adv. adverb	*prep.* preposition
conj. conjunction	*pron.* pronoun
interj. interjection	*v.* verb
sing. singular	*pl.* plural

inside the cover of a pneumatic tire that is inflated with air.

in ning (in′ing), 1 division of a baseball game during which each team has a turn at bat. 2 the turn one team or group has to play and score in a game. 3 Usually, **innings,** *pl.* the time a person or party is in power; chance for action: *When our party lost the election, the other side had its innings.* *n.*

inn keep er (in′kē′pər), person who owns, manages, or keeps an inn. *n.*

in no cence (in′ə səns), 1 freedom from sin, wrong, or guilt; being innocent: *The accused woman proved her innocence of the crime.* 2 simplicity; lack of cunning: *the innocence of a little child.* *n.*

in no cent (in′ə sənt), 1 doing no wrong or evil; free from sin or wrong; not guilty: *It is a great injustice to punish an innocent person for another's crime.* 2 without knowledge of evil: *A baby is innocent.* 3 doing no harm; harmless: *innocent amusements.* 4 an innocent person. 1-3 *adj.,* 4 *n.* —**in′no cent ly,** *adv.*

in noc u ous (i nok′yü əs), harmless: *She took my innocuous remark as an insult. adj.* —**in noc′u ous ly,** *adv.*

in no vate (in′ə vāt), make changes; bring in something new or new ways of doing things: *It is difficult to innovate when people feel that the old, familiar way of doing something is better. The scientist innovated new methods of research.* *v.,* **in no vat ed, in no vat ing.**

in no va tion (in′ə vā′shən), 1 change made in the established way of doing things: *The new teacher made many innovations.* 2 a making changes; bringing in new things or new ways of doing things: *Many old people are opposed to innovation. n.*

in no va tor (in′ə vā′tər), person who makes changes or brings in new things or new ways of doing things. *n.*

in nu en do (in′yü en′dō), 1 an indirect hint or reference. 2 an indirect suggestion meant to discredit a person: *She was the victim of a vicious scandal spread by the use of lies and innuendoes. n., pl.* **in nu en does.**

in nu mer a ble (i nü′mər ə bəl *or* i nyü′mər ə bəl), too many to count;

very many; countless: *innumerable stars. adj.*

in nu mer a bly (i nü′mər ə blē *or* i nyü′mər ə blē), in very great numbers; countlessly. *adv.*

in oc u late (in ok′yə lāt), 1 infect (a person or animal) with killed or weakened germs or viruses that will cause a mild form of a disease so that the individual will not get that disease or will suffer only a very mild form of the disease. 2 use disease germs to prevent diseases. Doctors inoculate against smallpox, diphtheria, typhoid fever, and other diseases. 3 put bacteria, serums, etc., into. Farmers inoculate the soil with bacteria that will take nitrogen from the air and change it so it can be used by plants. 4 fill (a person's mind) with ideas, opinions, etc.: *His parents inoculated him with a desire for knowledge.* *v.,* **in oc u lat ed, in oc u lating.**

in oc u la tion (in ok′yə lā′shən), 1 act or process of inoculating: *Inoculation has greatly reduced deaths from polio.* 2 bacteria, serums, etc., used in inoculating. 3 a filling the mind with opinions or ideas: *a thorough inoculation with patriotism. n.*

in of fen sive (in′ə fen′siv), not offensive; not arousing objections; harmless: *"Please try to be more quiet" is an inoffensive way of telling people to stop their noise. adj.* —**in′of fen′sive ly,** *adv.* —**in′of fen′sive ness,** *n.*

in op er a tive (in op′ər ə tiv *or* in op′ə rā′tiv), not operative; not working; without effect. *adj.*

in op por tune (in op′ər tün′ *or* in op′ər tyün′), not opportune; coming at a bad time; unsuitable: *An inopportune telephone call delayed us. adj.*

in or di nate (in ôrd′n it), much too great; excessive: *an inordinate desire for sweets. adj.* —**in or′di nate ly,** *adv.*

in or gan ic (in′ôr gan′ik), 1 not organic; neither animal nor vegetable; not having the organized physical structure characteristic of animals and plants. Water and minerals are inorganic substances. 2 (in chemistry) not containing organic matter. Chemical compounds without hydrocarbons are usually inorganic. *adj.*

in pa tient (in′pā′shənt), patient who is lodged and fed in a hospital while undergoing treatment. *n.*

in put (in′pùt′), 1 what is put in or taken in. 2 power supplied to a machine. 3 coded information fed into a computer. *n.*

in quest (in′kwest), a legal inquiry, especially before a jury: *An inquest was held to determine if his death was the result of a crime. n.*

in quire (in kwīr′), 1 try to find out by questions; ask: *The detective went from house to house, inquiring whether anyone had seen the lost girl.* 2 make a search for information, knowledge, or truth: *The man read many old documents while inquiring into the history of the town.* *v.,* **in quired, in quir ing.** Also, **enquire.** —**in quir′ing ly,** *adv.*

in quir er (in kwī′rər), person who inquires. *n.*

in quir y (in kwī′rē *or* in′kwər ē), 1 act of inquiring; asking. 2 a search for information, knowledge, or truth. 3 question: *The guide answered all our inquiries.* *n., pl.* **in quir ies.** Also, **enquiry.**

in qui si tion (in′kwə zish′ən), 1 a thorough investigation; searching inquiry. 2 an official investigation; judicial inquiry. 3 **the Inquisition,** court established by the Roman Catholic Church in the 1200's to discover and suppress heresy. It was abolished in the 1800's. *n.*

in quis i tive (in kwiz′ə tiv), 1 asking many questions; curious: *Children are usually inquisitive.* 2 prying into other people's affairs; too curious: *Those neighbors are very inquisitive about what our family is doing. adj.* —**in quis′i tive ly,** *adv.* —**in quis′i tive ness,** *n.*

in quis i tor (in kwiz′ə tər), 1 person who makes an inquisition; official investigator. 2 **Inquisitor,** member of the Inquisition. *n.*

in road (in′rōd′), 1 an attack or raid. 2 encroachment by force: *The expenses of her trip made inroads upon the money that she had saved. n.*

in rush (in′rush′), a rushing in; inflow: *The inrush of water soon filled the pool. n.*

in sane (in sān′), 1 not sane; mentally ill; crazy. 2 for insane people: *an insane asylum, an insane ward.* 3 extremely foolish; completely lacking in common sense: *Nobody paid any attention to his insane plan for crossing the ocean in a canoe. adj.* —**in sane′ly,** *adv.*

in san i tar y (in san′ə ter′ē), not sanitary; not healthful. *adj.*

in san i ty (in san′ə tē), 1 a being insane; madness; mental illness: *The accused murderer insisted he had fired the shot during a fit of temporary insanity.* 2 extreme folly; complete lack of common sense: *It is insanity to drive a car without any brakes. n., pl.* **in san i ties.**

in sa tia ble (in sā′shə bəl), that cannot be satisfied; extremely greedy: *The boy had an insatiable appetite for candy. adj.*

in sa tia bly (in sā′shə blē), in an insatiable manner. *adv.*

in sa ti ate (in sā′shē it), never satisfied: *A vain person has an insatiate desire for praise.* *adj.*

in scribe (in skrīb′), 1 write or engrave (words, names, etc.) on stone, metal, paper, etc.: *Her name was inscribed on the ring. Please inscribe my initials on the watch.* 2 mark (stone, metal, paper, etc.) with words, names, etc.: *The ring was inscribed with her name.* 3 address or dedicate (a book, picture, etc.) informally to a person. 4 impress deeply: *My father's words are inscribed in my memory.* 5 put in a list; enroll. *v.*, **in scribed, in scrib ing.**

in scrip tion (in skrip′shən), 1 something inscribed; words, names, etc., written or engraved on stone, metal, paper, etc. A monument or a coin has an inscription on it. 2 an informal dedication in a book, on a picture, etc. 3 act of writing upon or in something. *n.*

in scru ta bil i ty (in skrü′tə bil′ə tē), 1 a being inscrutable. 2 something inscrutable. *n.*

in scru ta ble (in skrü′tə bəl), that cannot be understood; so mysterious or obscure that one cannot make out its meaning; incomprehensible. *adj.*

in scru ta bly (in skrü′tə blē), in an inscrutable manner; mysteriously. *adv.*

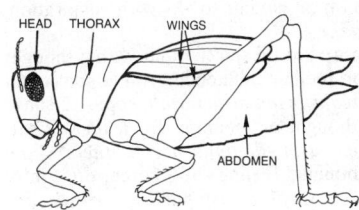

insect (def. 1)—a grasshopper

in sect (in′sekt), 1 any of a group of small animals with no backbone and with the body divided into three parts (head, thorax, and abdomen). Insects have three pairs of legs, and usually two pairs of wings. Flies, mosquitoes, gnats, bees, grasshoppers, and beetles are insects. 2 any similar animal with its body divided into several parts, with several pairs of legs. Spiders, centipedes, mites, and ticks are often called insects. *n.*

in sec ti cide (in sek′tə sīd), substance for killing insects. *n.*

in sec ti vore (in sek′tə vôr), any animal or plant that feeds mainly on insects. Moles and mantises are insectivores. *n.*

in sec tiv or ous (in′sek tiv′ər əs), insect-eating; feeding mainly on insects. *adj.*

in se cure (in′si kyūr′), 1 exposed to danger, loss, attack, etc.; not secure;

unsafe: *a region where life is insecure.* 2 liable to give way; not firm: *an insecure support, an insecure lock, an insecure hold.* *adj.* **—in′se cure′ly,** *adv.*

in se cur i ty (in′si kyūr′ə tē), 1 lack of security; being insecure; unsafe condition. 2 something insecure. *n., pl.* **in se cur i ties.**

in sen sate (in sen′sāt), 1 without sensation; lifeless; inanimate: *insensate stones.* 2 unfeeling; brutal: *insensate cruelty.* 3 senseless; stupid: *insensate folly.* *adj.*

in sen si bil i ty (in sen′sə bil′ə tē), 1 lack of feeling; unawareness. 2 lack of consciousness; senselessness. *n., pl.* **in sen si bil i ties.**

in sen si ble (in sen′sə bəl), 1 not sensitive; not able to feel or notice: *She appeared to be insensible to cold.* 2 not aware; unmoved; indifferent: *I had so many problems of my own that I fear I was insensible to your troubles.* 3 not able to feel anything; unconscious; senseless: *The man hit by the truck was insensible for four hours.* 4 not easily felt; too slow to be noticed: *The room grew cold by insensible degrees as the sun went down.* *adj.*

in sen si bly (in sen′sə blē), by insensible degrees; little by little. *adv.*

in sen si tive (in sen′sə tiv), 1 not sensitive; not able to feel or notice. 2 slow to feel or notice. *adj.* **—in sen′si tive ly,** *adv.* **—in sen′si tive ness,** *n.*

in sen si tiv i ty (in sen′sə tiv′ə tē), insensitive condition or quality. *n.*

in sep ar a bil i ty (in sep′ər ə bil′ə tē), a being inseparable. *n.*

in sep ar a ble (in sep′ər ə bəl), 1 impossible to separate: *Heat is inseparable from fire.* 2 constantly together: *The two friends are inseparable companions.* *adj.*

in sep ar a bly (in sep′ər ə blē), in an inseparable manner. *adv.*

in sert (in sėrt′ *for 1*; in′sėrt′ *for 2*), 1 put in; set in: *He inserted the key into the lock. She inserted a letter into the misspelled word.* 2 something put in or set in: *The newspaper had an insert of several pages of pictures.* 1 *v.*, 2 *n.*

in ser tion (in sėr′shən), 1 act of inserting: *The insertion of one word can change the meaning of a whole sentence.* 2 something inserted. A band of lace or embroidery to be sewed at each edge between parts of other material is an insertion. *n.*

in set (in set′ *for 1*; in′set′ *for 2*), 1 set in; insert. 2 something inserted. 1 *v.,* **in set, in set ting;** 2 *n.*

in shore (in′shôr′), 1 near the shore: *Inshore fishing is not allowed where people swim.* 2 in toward the shore: *The*

hat, āge, fär; let, ēqual, tėrm;
it, īce; hot, ōpen, ôrder;
oil, out; cup, pùt, rüle; ch, child;
ng, long; sh, she; th, thin;
₮H, then; zh, measure;

ə represents *a* in about,
e in taken, *i* in pencil,
o in lemon, *u* in circus.

boat was driven inshore by the winds. 1 *adj.,* 2 *adv.*

in side (in′sīd′ *for 1-3,6;* in′sīd′ *for 4,5*), 1 the part within; the inner surface: *The inside of the box was lined with colored paper.* 2 the contents: *The inside of the book was more interesting than the cover.* 3 being on the inside: *an inside seat.* 4 on or to the inside; within; in the inner part: *Please step inside.* 5 inside of; within the limits of; in: *The nut is inside the shell.* 6 done or known by those inside; secret: *The informer had inside information of the gang's plans.* 1,2 *n.,* 3,6 *adj.,* 4 *adv.,* 5 *prep.*

inside out, 1 so that what should be inside is outside; with the inside showing: *He turned his pockets inside out.* 2 completely; thoroughly: *She learned her lessons inside out.*

in sid er (in′sī′dər), 1 person who belongs to a certain group, club, society, political party, etc. 2 INFORMAL. person who has private or secret information about something not known to most others. *n.*

in sides (in′sīdz′), INFORMAL. parts inside the body. *n.pl.*

in sid i ous (in sid′ē əs), 1 seeking to entrap or ensnare; wily or sly; crafty; tricky. 2 working secretly or subtly; developing without attracting attention: *Tuberculosis is an insidious disease; you can have it without knowing it.* *adj.* **—in sid′i ous ly,** *adv.* **—in sid′i ous ness,** *n.*

insertion (def. 2)

in sight (in′sīt′), 1 a viewing of the inside with understanding: *Take the machine apart and get an insight into how it works.* 2 wisdom and understanding in dealing with people or with

adj.	adjective	*n.*	noun
adv.	adverb	*prep.*	preposition
conj.	conjunction	*pron.*	pronoun
interj.	interjection	*v.*	verb
sing.	singular	*pl.*	plural

facts: *We study science to gain insight into the world we live in.* *n.*

in sig ni a (in sig′nē ə), medals, badges, or other distinguishing marks of a position, honor, military order, etc.: *The crown and the scepter are the insignia of kings.* *n.pl.* of **in sig ne** (in sig′nē).

insignia
of U.S. Army
A, branch of service
B, army or division
C, decorations
D, enlisted man's rank
E, three years service

in sig nif i cance (in/sig nif′ə kəns), 1 unimportance; uselessness. 2 meaninglessness. *n.*

in sig nif i cant (in/sig nif′ə kənt), 1 having little use or importance; trivial: *Don't bother me with such insignificant details! A tenth of a cent is an insignificant amount of money.* 2 having little meaning; meaningless: *insignificant chatter.* *adj.* —**in′sig nif′i cant ly,** *adv.*

in sin cere (in/sin sir′), not sincere; not honest or candid; deceitful. *adj.* —**in′sin cere′ly,** *adv.*

in sin cer i ty (in/sin ser′ə tē), lack of sincerity; being insincere; hypocrisy. *n., pl.* **in sin cer i ties.**

in sin u ate (in sin′yü āt), 1 suggest in an indirect way; hint: *To say "That man can't do it; no coward can" is to insinuate that the man is a coward. Without making any direct charges, she insinuated that the mayor had accepted bribes.* 2 push in or get in by an indirect, subtle way: *The spy insinuated himself into the confidence of important army officers.* *v.,* **in sin u at ed, in sin u at ing.**

in sin u a tion (in sin′yü ā′shən), 1 an insinuating: *the insinuation of oneself into the confidence of others.* 2 an indirect suggestion meant to discredit someone: *The student objected strongly to the insinuation of dishonesty.* 3 hint; suggestion. 4 act or speech to gain favor in an indirect, subtle way. *n.*

in sip id (in sip′id), 1 without any particular flavor; tasteless: *A mixture of milk and water is an insipid drink.*

2 lacking interest or spirit; dull, colorless, or weak: *The insipid conversation bored everyone.* *adj.*

in sist (in sist′), keep firmly to some demand, statement, or position; take a stand and refuse to give in: *The children insisted on playing another game. He insists that he had a right to use his brother's tools. After her arrest she insisted on her innocence.* *v.*

in sist ence (in sis′təns), 1 act of insisting: *We remembered mother's insistence that we comb our hair.* 2 quality of being insistent. *n.*

in sist ent (in sis′tənt), 1 continuing to make a strong, firm demand or statement; insisting: *In spite of the rain she was insistent on going out.* 2 impossible to overlook or disregard; compelling attention or notice; pressing; urgent: *An insistent knocking on the door woke us up.* *adj.* —**in sist′ent ly,** *adv.*

in snare (in sner′ *or* in snar′), ensnare. *v.,* **in snared, in snar ing.**

in so far as (in/sō fär′), to such an extent or degree as: *Insofar as I can tell, the weather should be pleasant tomorrow.*

in sole (in′sōl′), 1 the inner sole of a shoe or boot. 2 layer of warm or waterproof material put on the sole inside a shoe or boot. *n.*

in so lence (in′sə ləns), bold rudeness; insulting behavior or speech; intentional disregard of the feelings of others. *n.*

in so lent (in′sə lənt), boldly rude; intentionally disregarding the feelings of others; insulting: *You were insolent to turn your back on me while I was talking to you.* *adj.* —**in′so lent ly,** *adv.*

in sol u bil i ty (in sol′yə bil′ə tē), insoluble condition or quality. *n.*

in sol u ble (in sol′yə bəl), 1 that cannot be dissolved: *Diamonds are insoluble. Fats are insoluble in water.* 2 that cannot be solved: *The detective finally gave up, declaring the mystery insoluble.* *adj.*

in sol u bly (in sol′yə blē), in an insoluble manner. *adv.*

in sol ven cy (in sol′vən sē), condition of not being able to pay one's debts; bankruptcy. *n., pl.* **in sol ven cies.**

in sol vent (in sol′vənt), unable to pay one's debts; bankrupt. *adj.*

in som ni a (in som′nē ə), inability to sleep; sleeplessness. *n.*

in so much (in/sō much′), in such a way; to such an amount; so. *adv.*

insomuch as, inasmuch as; since.

in sou ci ance (in sü′sē əns), freedom from care or anxiety; carefree feeling. *n.*

in sou ci ant (in sü′sē ənt), free from care or anxiety; carefree. *adj.*

in spect (in spekt′), 1 look over care-

fully; examine: *A dentist inspects my teeth twice a year.* 2 look over officially; examine formally: *Government officials inspect factories and mines to make sure that they are safe for workers.* *v.*

in spec tion (in spek′shən), 1 an inspecting; examination: *An inspection of the roof showed no leaks.* 2 a formal or official examination: *The soldiers lined up for their daily inspection by their officers.* *n.*

in spec tor (in spek′tər), 1 person who inspects. 2 officer or official appointed to inspect: *a milk inspector.* 3 a police officer, usually ranking next below a superintendent. *n.*

in spi ra tion (in/spə rā′shən), 1 influence of thought and strong feelings on actions, especially on good actions: *Some people get inspiration from sermons, some from poetry.* 2 person or thing that puts life or force into others and arouses them to do well: *The teacher was an inspiration to her students.* 3 idea that is inspired; sudden, brilliant idea. 4 God's influence on the minds or souls of people; divine influence. Inspiration helped men to write the Bible. 5 a breathing in; a drawing of air into the lungs. *n.*

in spi ra tion al (in/spə rā′shə nəl), 1 inspiring: *The sermon was both instructive and inspirational.* 2 inspired. 3 of or having to do with inspiration. *adj.*

in spire (in spīr′), 1 fill with a thought or feeling; influence: *A chance to try again inspired her with hope.* 2 cause (thought or feeling): *The leader's courage inspired confidence in others.* 3 put thought, feeling, life, force, etc., into: *The speaker inspired the crowd. The coach inspired the team with a desire to win.* 4 cause to be told or written; suggest: *Helen Keller's life story inspired a movie.* 5 fill with God's influence or with divine force. 6 draw air into the lungs; breathe in. *v.,* **in spired, in spir ing.** —**in spir′ ing ly,** *adv.*

in spir er (in spī′rər), person or thing that inspires. *n.*

in spir it (in spir′it), put spirit into; encourage; hearten; cheer. *v.*

inst., instant (def. 6).

in sta bil i ty (in/stə bil′ə tē), lack of firmness; being unstable; unsteadiness. *n.*

in stall (in stôl′), 1 put (a person) in office with ceremonies: *The new judge was installed without delay.* 2 put in a place or position; settle: *The cat installed itself in a chair near the fireplace.* 3 put in place for use: *The new owner of the house had a telephone installed.* *v.*

in stal la tion (in/stə lā′shən), 1 an installing: *Installation of more electric* lights made the room brighter. 2 a being installed: *I attended my mother's installation as president of the P.T.A.* 3 something installed, especially machinery placed in position for use. 4 a military base or camp, including personnel, equipment, buildings, etc. *n.*

instep (def. 1)

in stall ment[1] or **in stal ment**[1] (in-stôl/mənt), 1 part of a sum of money or of a debt to be paid at certain stated times: *The table cost $100; we paid for it in two installments of $50 each.* 2 one of several parts issued at different times as part of a series: *This magazine has a serial story in six installments.* *n.* [earlier *(e)stallment,* from *stall* agree to the payment of a debt by installments, from French of the 1400's *estaler* fix, place]

in stall ment[2] or **in stal ment**[2] (in-stôl/mənt), 1 an installing: *the installment of electric lights in a house.* 2 a being installed: *our installment in our new home.* *n.* [*install* (from Latin *installare*) + *-ment*]

in stance (in/stəns), 1 person or thing serving as an example; illustration; case: *Lincoln is an instance of a poor boy who became famous.* 2 give as an example; cite: *He instanced the fly as a dirty insect.* 3 stage or step in an action; occasion: *I went in the first instance because I was asked to go.* 4 request, suggestion, or urging: *She came at our instance. At the instance of the losing team we agreed to play them again next week.* 1,3,4 *n.,* 2 *v.,* **in stanced, in stanc ing.**

for instance, as an example: *Her many different hobbies include, for instance, skating and stamp collecting.*

in stant (in/stənt), 1 particular moment: *Stop talking this instant!* 2 moment of time: *He paused for an instant.* 3 coming at once; without delay; immediate: *The medicine gave instant relief from pain.* 4 pressing; urgent: *When there is a fire, there is an instant need for action.* 5 prepared beforehand and requiring little or no cooking, mixing, or additional ingredients: *instant coffee, instant pudding, instant potatoes.* 6 of the present month; present. "The 10th instant" means "the tenth day of the present month." 1,2 *n.,* 3-6 *adj.*

in stan ta ne ous (in/stən tā/nē əs), coming or done in an instant; happening or made in an instant: *A flash of lightning is instantaneous. When the speaker finished talking, the applause was in-*

stantaneous. *adj.* —**in/stan ta/ne ous ly,** *adv.*

in stant ly (in/stənt lē), in an instant; at once; immediately. *adv.*

in stead (in sted/), in another's place; as a substitute: *She stayed home, and her sister went riding instead.* *adv.*

instead of, rather than; in place of; as a substitute for: *Instead of studying, she watched television.*

in step (in/step), 1 the upper surface of the human foot between the toes and the ankle. 2 the part of a shoe, stocking, etc., over the instep. *n.*

in sti gate (in/stə gāt), urge on; stir up: *The older boy instigated a quarrel between his two younger brothers.* *v.,* **in sti gat ed, in sti gat ing.**

in sti ga tion (in/stə gā/shən), an urging on; stirring up. *n.*

in sti ga tor (in/stə gā/tər), person who instigates, especially one who stirs up evil or trouble. *n.*

in still or **in stil** (in stil/), 1 put in little by little; cause to enter the mind, heart, etc., gradually: *Reading good books instills a love for really fine literature.* 2 put in drop by drop. *v.,* **in stilled, in still ing.**

in stinct (in/stingkt for 1,2; in stingkt/ for 3), 1 a natural feeling, knowledge, or power, such as that which guides animals; inborn tendency to act in a certain way: *Birds build their nests by instinct.* 2 a natural tendency or ability; talent: *Even as a child the artist had an instinct for drawing.* 3 charged or filled with something: *The picture is instinct with life and beauty.* 1,2 *n.,* 3 *adj.*

in stinc tive (in stingk/tiv), of or having to do with instinct; caused or done by instinct; born in an animal or person, not learned: *The spinning of webs is instinctive in spiders.* *adj.* —**in stinc/tive ly,** *adv.*

in sti tute (in/stə tüt or in/stə tyüt), 1 organization or society for some special purpose. An art institute teaches or displays art. A technical school or college is often called an institute. 2 building used by such an organization or society: *We spent the afternoon in the Art Institute.* 3 set up; establish; begin; start: *The Pilgrims instituted Thanksgiving. The police instituted an inquiry into the causes of the accident.* 1,2 *n.,* 3 *v.,* **in sti tut ed, in sti tut ing.**

in sti tu tion (in/stə tü/shən or in/stə-tyü/shən), 1 society, club, college, or any organization established for some public or social purpose. A church, school, university, hospital, asylum, or prison is an institution. 2 a building used for the work of an institution. 3 an established law or custom: *Giving presents on Christmas is an institution.*

hat, āge, fär; let, ēqual, tėrm;
it, īce; hot, ōpen, ôrder;
oil, out; cup, pùt, rüle; ch, child;
ng, long; sh, she; th, thin;
ŦH, then; zh, measure;

ə represents *a* in about,
e in taken, *i* in pencil,
o in lemon, *u* in circus.

Marriage is an institution among most peoples of the earth. 4 a setting up; establishing; beginning; starting: *We hope for the institution of hot lunches at school this winter.* *n.*

in sti tu tion al (in/stə tü/shə nəl or in/stə tyü/shə nəl), of or like an institution. *adj.*

in sti tu tion al ize (in/stə tü/shə-nə līz or in/stə tyü/shə nə līz), 1 make into an institution. 2 put into an institution. *v.,* **in sti tu tion al ized, in sti-tu tion al iz ing.**

in struct (in strukt/), 1 give knowledge to; show how to do; teach; train; educate: *We have one teacher who instructs us in reading, English, history, and arithmetic.* 2 give directions to; order: *The doctor instructed him to go to bed and rest. The owner of the house instructed her agent to sell it.* 3 inform; tell: *My lawyer instructs me that the contract will be signed Monday.* *v.*

in struc tion (in struk/shən), 1 a teaching or educating. 2 knowledge or teaching given; lesson. 3 **instructions,** *pl.* directions; orders. *n.*

in struc tion al (in struk/shə nəl), of or for instruction; educational. *adj.*

in struc tive (in struk/tiv), useful for instruction; giving knowledge or information; instructing: *A trip around the world is an instructive experience.* *adj.* —**in struc/tive ly,** *adv.*

in struc tor (in struk/tər), 1 teacher. 2 teacher ranking below professors in American colleges and universities. *n.*

in stru ment (in/strə mənt), 1 thing used to do something; tool or mechanical device: *A forceps and a drill are two instruments used by dentists.* 2 device for producing musical sounds: *wind instruments, stringed instruments. A violin, cello, and piano were the instruments in the trio.* 3 device for measuring, recording, or controlling. A thermometer is an instrument for measuring temperature. 4 thing with or by which something is done; person made use of by another; means: *The master criminal used many men and women as instruments in his crimes.* 5 a formal

adj. adjective	*n.* noun
adv. adverb	*prep.* preposition
conj. conjunction	*pron.* pronoun
interj. interjection	*v.* verb
sing. singular	*pl.* plural

legal document, such as a contract, deed, or grant. *n.*

in stru men tal (in′strə men′tl), 1 acting or serving as a means; useful; helpful: *A friend was instrumental in getting me a job.* 2 played on or written for musical instruments: *The singer was accompanied by instrumental music. adj.* —**in′stru men′tal ly,** *adv.*

in stru men tal ist (in′strə men′tl-ist), person who plays on a musical instrument. *n.*

in stru men tal i ty (in′strə men-tal′ə tē), quality or condition of being instrumental; helpfulness; agency; means. *n., pl.* **in stru men tal i ties.**

in stru men ta tion (in′strə men-tā′shən), 1 arrangement or composition of music for instruments. 2 use of instruments; work done with instruments. *n.*

in sub or di nate (in′sə bôrd′n it), not submitting to authority; refusing to obey; disobedient; rebellious. *adj.*

in sub or di na tion (in′sə bôrd′n ā′-shən), resistance to authority; refusal to obey; disobedience; rebellion. *n.*

in sub stan tial (in′səb stan′shəl), 1 frail; flimsy: *A cobweb is very insubstantial.* 2 unreal; not actual; imaginary: *Dreams and ghosts are insubstantial. adj.* —**in′sub stan′tial ly,** *adv.*

in suf fer a ble (in suf′ər ə bəl), unbearable; intolerable: *The heat of the desert at noon was insufferable. adj.*

in suf fer a bly (in suf′ər ə blē), 1 in an insufferable manner. 2 to an insufferable degree. *adv.*

in suf fi cien cy (in′sə fish′ən sē), too small an amount; lack; deficiency. *n., pl.* **in suf fi cien cies.**

in suf fi cient (in′sə fish′ənt), not enough; less than is needed: *She was tired because she had had insufficient sleep. adj.* —**in′suf fi′cient ly,** *adv.*

in su lar (in′sə lər), 1 of or having to do with islands or islanders. 2 living or situated on an island. 3 standing alone like an island; isolated: *No nation can now keep an insular position in world affairs.* 4 narrow-minded; prejudiced. *adj.*

in su lar i ty (in′sə lar′ə tē), 1 condition of being an island or of living on an island. 2 narrow-mindedness; prejudice. *n.*

in su late (in′sə lāt), 1 keep from losing or transferring electricity, heat, sound, etc., especially by covering, packing, or surrounding with a material that does not conduct electricity, heat, etc.: *Telephone wires are often insulated by a covering of rubber.* 2 set apart; separate from others; isolate: *The English Channel insulates Great Britain from France and Belgium. v.,* **in su lat ed, in su lat ing.**

in su la tion (in′sə lā′shən), 1 an insulating: *The electrician checked the insulation of the wiring.* 2 a being insulated: *The insulation of the outer walls helps keep our house warm in the winter.* 3 material used in insulating: *Asbestos is often used as an insulation against fire. n.*

insulator
glass insulator
for electric wires.
With these, wires can
be fastened to poles
without any loss
of current.

in su la tor (in′sə lā′tər), that which insulates; something that prevents the passage of electricity, heat, or sound; nonconductor: *Glass is an effective insulator. n.*

in su lin (in′sə lən), 1 hormone secreted by the pancreas that enables the body to use sugar and other carbohydrates. 2 drug containing insulin, used in treating diabetes. Insulin is obtained from the pancreas of slaughtered animals. *n.*

in sult (in sult′ *for 1;* in′sult *for 2*), 1 say or do something very scornful, rude, or harsh to: *That girl insulted me by calling me a liar.* 2 an insulting speech or action: *To be called stupid is an insult that hurts one's feelings and makes one angry.* 1 *v.,* 2 *n.* —**in-sult′ing ly,** *adv.*

in su per a ble (in sü′pər ə bəl), that cannot be passed over or overcome: *The deep river was an insuperable barrier to those who could not swim. adj.*

in su per a bly (in sü′pər ə blē), in an insuperable manner. *adv.*

in sup port a ble (in′sə pôr′tə bəl), not endurable; unbearable; intolerable. *adj.*

in sur ance (in shur′əns), 1 an insuring of property, person, or life. Fire insurance, burglary insurance, accident insurance, life insurance, and health insurance are some of the many kinds. 2 the business of insuring property, life, etc. 3 amount of money for which a person or thing is insured: *He has $10,000 insurance, which his wife will* receive if he dies before she does. 4 amount of money paid for insurance; premium: *The fire insurance on our house is $100 a year. n.*

in sure (in shur′), 1 arrange payment of money in case of loss, accident, or death by paying a certain amount of money at intervals. An insurance company will insure your property, person, or life. 2 make safe from financial loss by paying money to an insurance company: *She insured her car against accident, theft, and fire. v.,* **in sured, in sur ing.**

in sured (in shurd′), person who is insured. *n.*

in sur er (in shur′ər), person or company that insures. *n.*

in sur gence (in sėr′jəns), a rising in revolt; rebellion. *n.*

in sur gent (in sėr′jənt), 1 person who rises in revolt; rebel: *The insurgents captured the town.* 2 rising in revolt; rebellious: *The insurgent peasants burned their masters' houses.* 1 *n.,* 2 *adj.*

in sur mount a ble (in′sər moun′-tə bəl), that cannot be overcome. *adj.*

in sur mount a bly (in′sər moun′tə-blē), in an insurmountable manner. *adv.*

in sur rec tion (in′sə rek′shən), a rising against established authority; revolt; rebellion. *n.*

in sur rec tion ist (in′sə rek′shə-nist), person who takes part in or favors an insurrection; rebel. *n.*

in tact (in takt′), with no part missing; whole; untouched; uninjured: *dishes left intact after being dropped. The money was returned intact by the person who found it. adj.*

in take (in′tāk′), 1 place where water, air, gas, etc., enters a channel, pipe, or other narrow opening. 2 act or process of taking in. 3 amount or thing taken in: *The intake through the pipe was 5000 gallons a day. n.*

in tan gi ble (in tan′jə bəl), 1 not capable of being touched or felt: *Sound and light are intangible.* 2 not easily grasped by the mind; vague: *The very attractive man had that intangible quality called charm.* 3 something intangible. 1,2 *adj.,* 3 *n.*

in te ger (in′tə jər), 1 any positive or negative whole number, or zero. 2 thing complete in itself; something whole. *n.*

in te gral (in′tə grəl), 1 necessary to make something complete; essential: *Steel is an integral part of a modern skyscraper.* 2 entire; complete. 3 having to do with an integer; not fractional. *adj.*

in te grate (in′tə grāt), 1 make into a whole; complete. 2 put or bring together (parts) into a whole: *The committee will try to integrate the different ideas into one uniform plan.* 3 make (schools, parks, etc.) available to people of all races on an equal basis: *integrate a neighborhood.* v., **in te grat ed, in te grat ing.**

in te gra tion (in′tə grā′shən), 1 an integrating: *the integration of the activities of all the people who are working on a project.* 2 inclusion of people of all races on an equal basis in schools, parks, neighborhoods, etc. n.

in te gra tion ist (in′tə grā′shə nist), person who believes in the integration of people of all races. n.

in teg ri ty (in teg′rə tē), 1 honesty or sincerity; uprightness: *A man of integrity is respected.* 2 wholeness; completeness: *Soldiers defend the integrity of their country against those who want part of it.* 3 perfect condition; soundness. n.

in teg u ment (in teg′yə mənt), a natural outer covering; skin, shell, rind, etc.; tegument. *The pod of a pea is its integument.* n.

in tel lect (in′tə lekt), 1 power of knowing; understanding; mind. *Our actions are influenced by our intellect, will, and feelings.* 2 great intelligence; high mental ability: *Isaac Newton was a man of intellect.* 3 person of high mental ability: *Einstein was one of the greatest intellects of his time.* n.

in tel lec tu al (in′tə lek′chü əl), 1 needing or using intelligence: *Teaching is an intellectual occupation.* 2 of the intellect: *Thinking is an intellectual process.* 3 having or showing intelligence: *an intellectual person, an intellectual face.* 4 person who is well informed and intelligent. 1-3 adj., 4 n.

in tel lec tu al ly (in′tə lek′chü ə lē), 1 in an intellectual way. 2 so far as intellect is concerned. adv.

in tel li gence (in tel′ə jəns), 1 ability to learn and know; quickness of understanding; mind: *A dog has more intelligence than a worm.* 2 knowledge, news, or information: *The spy gave the general secret intelligence of the plans of the enemy. The intelligence agency, bureau, office, or department of a government collects and studies information that will help its armed forces.* 3 a getting or distributing information, especially secret information. 4 group engaged in obtaining secret information: *Intelligence sent agents to infiltrate the enemy missile bases.* n.

intelligence quotient, number that shows the rating of a person's intelligence. It is found by dividing the mental age shown in tests by the actual age (16 is the largest age used) and multiplying by 100.

intelligence test, any test used to measure mental development.

in tel li gent (in tel′ə jənt), having or showing intelligence; able to learn and know; quick to understand: *Elephants and horses are intelligent animals.* adj. —**in tel′li gent ly,** adv.

in tel li gent si a (in tel′ə jent′sē ə), persons representing, or claiming to represent, the educated class; the intellectuals. n.pl. [from Russian]

in tel li gi ble (in tel′ə jə bəl), capable of being understood; clear. adj.

in tel li gi bly (in tel′ə jə blē), so as to be understood; clearly. adv.

in tem per ance (in tem′pər əns), 1 lack of moderation or self-control; excess: *His intemperance in eating caused him to become very fat.* 2 too much drinking of intoxicating liquor. n.

in tem per ate (in tem′pər it), 1 not moderate; lacking in self-control; excessive: *intemperate anger, an intemperate appetite.* 2 drinking too much intoxicating liquor. 3 not temperate; extreme in temperature; severe: *an intemperate winter.* adj. —**in tem′per ate ly,** adv.

in tend (in tend′), 1 have in mind as a purpose; plan: *I intend to go home soon. We intend that our children shall go to college.* 2 mean for a particular purpose or use: *That gift was intended for you. He is intended for the ministry.* v.

in tend ed (in ten′did), 1 in mind as a purpose; meant; planned: *The medicine had the intended effect and stopped the pain.* 2 going to be; future: *A woman's intended husband is the man she is going to marry.* 3 INFORMAL. an intended husband or wife. 1,2 adj., 3 n.

in tense (in tens′), 1 very much; very great; very strong; extreme: *Intense heat melts iron. A bad burn causes intense pain. Deep, earnest thought is intense.* 2 full of vigorous activity, strong feelings, etc.: *An intense life is crowded with action, interests, etc.* 3 having or showing strong feeling. *An intense person is one who feels things very deeply and is likely to be extreme in action.* adj.

in tense ly (in tens′lē), 1 in an intense manner. 2 exceedingly; extremely. adv.

in ten si fi ca tion (in ten′sə fə kā′shən), a making or becoming more intense. n.

in ten si fi er (in ten′sə fī′ər), (in grammar) an intensive. n.

in ten si fy (in ten′sə fī), make or become intense or more intense; strengthen; increase: *Blowing on a fire intensifies the heat. My first failure only intensified my desire to succeed.* v., **in ten si fied, in ten si fy ing.**

in ten si ty (in ten′sə tē), 1 quality

hat, āge, fär; let, ēqual, tėrm;
it, īce; hot, ōpen, ôrder;
oil, out; cup, pùt, rüle; ch, child;
ng, long; sh, she; th, thin;
ŦH, then; zh, measure;

ə represents *a* in about,
e in taken, *i* in pencil,
o in lemon, *u* in circus.

of being intense; great strength: *the intensity of sunlight.* 2 extreme degree; great vigor; violence: *intensity of thought, intensity of feeling.* 3 amount or degree of strength of electricity, heat, light, sound, etc., per unit of area, volume, etc. n., pl. **in ten si ties.**

in ten sive (in ten′siv), 1 deep and thorough: *An intensive study of a few books is more valuable than much careless reading.* 2 (in grammar) giving force or emphasis; expressing intensity. In "She herself said it," *herself* is an intensive pronoun. 3 word, prefix, etc., that expresses intensity or gives force or emphasis. In "It's terribly late," *terribly* is an intensive. 1,2 adj., 3 n. —**in ten′sive ly,** adv.

in tent (in tent′), 1 that which is intended; purpose; intention: *I'm sorry I hurt you; that wasn't my intent.* 2 meaning; significance: *What is the intent of that remark?* 3 very attentive; having the eyes or thoughts earnestly fixed on something; earnest: *A stare is an intent look. She was intent on her task.* 4 earnestly engaged; much interested: *be intent upon making money. I am intent on doing my best.* 1,2 n., 3,4 adj. —**in tent′ly,** adv. —**in tent′ness,** n.

to all intents and purposes, in almost every way; practically.

in ten tion (in ten′shən), 1 an intending; purpose; design; plan: *If I hurt your feelings, it was without intention. Your intention to help is good, but first you must learn how.* 2 meaning. n.

in ten tion al (in ten′shə nəl), done on purpose; meant; planned; intended: *Her lateness was intentional; she wanted to hear just the last speaker.* adj. —**in ten′tion al ly,** adv.

in ter (in tėr′), put (a dead body) into a grave or tomb; bury. v., **in terred, in ter ring.**

inter-, prefix. 1 one with the other; together: *Intercommunicate = communicate with each other.* 2 between: *Interpose = put between.* 3 between or among a group: *International = between or among nations.* [from Latin *inter* among, between, during]

445

adj. adjective	*n.* noun
adv. adverb	*prep.* preposition
conj. conjunction	*pron.* pronoun
interj. interjection	*v.* verb
sing. singular	*pl.* plural

in ter act (in′tər akt′), act on each other. *v.*

in ter ac tion (in′tər ak′shən), action on each other. *n.*

in ter breed (in′tər brēd′), breed by the mating of different kinds; breed by using different varieties or species of animals or plants. Many of our cultivated plants are hybrids developed by interbreeding various plants to combine their desirable qualities. *v.*, **in ter bred** (in′tər bred′), **in ter breed ing.**

in ter cede (in′tər sēd′), 1 plead for another; ask a favor from one person for another: *The senator interceded with the governor to help us save the state park.* 2 interfere in order to bring about an agreement: *The debate between the lawyers became so heated that the judge had to intercede.* *v.*, **in ter ced ed, in ter ced ing.**

in ter cel lu lar (in′tər sel′yə lər), situated between or among cells: *Intercellular spaces are usually filled with gases or substances secreted by cells.* *adj.*

in ter cept (in′tər sept′), 1 take or seize on the way from one place to another: *intercept a letter, intercept a messenger, intercept a pass in a football game.* 2 cut off (light, water, etc.). 3 check; stop: *The police intercepted the flight of the escaped criminal and put him back in jail.* 4 mark off between two points or lines. *v.*

intercept (def. 4)
Line XY intercepts
arc AB of the circle.

in ter cep tion (in′tər sep′shən), an intercepting or a being intercepted. *n.*

in ter cep tor (in′tər sep′tər), person or thing that intercepts. *n.*

in ter ces sion (in′tər sesh′ən), 1 act or fact of interceding; pleading for another: *The girl's intercession for her brother won their parents' consent to his request. The teacher's timely intercession prevented a quarrel between the two boys.* 2 prayer pleading for others. *n.*

in ter ces sor (in′tər ses′ər), person who intercedes. *n.*

in ter change (in′tər chānj′ *for 1,3;* in′tər chānj′ *for 2,4,5*), 1 put each of

(two or more persons or things) in the other's place: *The two girls interchanged hats.* 2 a putting each of two or more persons or things in the other's place: *The word "team" may be turned into "meat" by the interchange of the first and last letters.* 3 give and take; exchange: *The friends interchanged things when one traded his knife for the other's ball.* 4 a giving and taking; exchanging. 5 a point at which a highway, especially an express highway, connects with another main traffic route. 1,3 *v.,* **in ter changed, in ter chang ing;** 2,4,5 *n.*

interchange (def. 5)

in ter change a ble (in′tər chān′-jə bəl), 1 capable of being used in place of each other. 2 able to change places. *adj.*

in ter change a bly (in′tər chān′-jə blē), in an interchangeable manner. *adv.*

in ter col le giate (in′tər kə lē′jit), between colleges or universities: *intercollegiate football games.* *adj.*

in ter com (in′tər kom′), any apparatus, usually using microphones and loudspeakers, with which members of an office staff, the crew of an airplane, tank, ship, etc., can talk to each other. *n.*

in ter com mu ni cate (in′tər kə-myü′nə kāt), communicate with each other. *v.,* **in ter com mu ni cat ed, in ter com mu ni cat ing.**

in ter com mu ni ca tion (in′tər-kə myü′nə kā′shən), communication with each other. *n.*

in ter con nect (in′tər kə nekt′), connect with each other. *v.*

in ter con nec tion (in′tər kə nek′-shən), connection with each other. *n.*

in ter con ti nen tal (in′tər kon′-tə nen′tl), between continents; from one continent to another: *an intercontinental railroad.* *adj.*

in ter course (in′tər kôrs′), dealings between people; exchange of thoughts, services, and feelings; communication: *Airplanes, good roads, and telephones make intercourse with different parts of the country far easier than it was 50 years ago.* *n.*

in ter de nom i na tion al (in′tər-di nom′ə nā′shə nəl), between or involving different religious denominations. *adj.*

in ter de pend ence (in′tər di-pen′dəns), dependence upon each other. *n.*

in ter de pend ent (in′tər di pen′-dənt), dependent upon each other. *adj.* —**in′ter de pend′ent ly,** *adv.*

in ter dict (in′tər dikt′ *for 1,3a;* in′tər-dikt′ *for 2,3b*), 1 prohibit or forbid; restrain. 2 prohibition based on authority; formal order forbidding something. 3 in the Roman Catholic Church: **a** a cut off from certain church privileges. **b** a cutting off from certain church privileges. 1,3a *v.,* 2,3b *n.*

in ter dic tion (in′tər dik′shən), an interdicting or a being interdicted. *n.*

in ter est (in′tər ist) 1 a feeling of wanting to know, see, do, own, share in, or take part in: *Both my girls have an interest in sports. He has an interest in reading and in collecting stamps.* 2 power of arousing such a feeling: *A dull book lacks interest.* 3 arouse such a feeling in; make curious and hold the attention of: *An exciting story interests us.* 4 a share or part in property and actions: *He bought a half interest in the farm.* 5 cause (a person) to take a share or part in something; arouse the concern, curiosity, or attention of: *The agent tried to interest us in buying a car. We were interested in the results of the election.* 6 thing in which a person has a share or part. Any business, activity, or pastime can be an interest. 7 group of people having the same business, activity, etc.: *the business interests of the town.* 8 advantage; benefit; profit: *Mother and Father look after the interests of the family.* 9 money paid for the use of money, usually a percentage of the amount invested, borrowed, or loaned: *The interest on the loan was 7 per cent a year.* 1,2,4,6-9 *n.,* 3,5 *v.*

in the interest of, for; to help.

in ter est ed (in′tər ə stid *or* in′tə-res′tid), 1 feeling or showing interest; with one's interest and attention aroused: *an interested spectator.* 2 having an interest or share. 3 influenced by personal considerations; prejudiced: *An interested person cannot make a fair decision.* *adj.*

in ter est ing (in′tər ə sting *or* in′tə-res′ting), arousing interest; holding one's attention: *Stories about travel and adventure are interesting.* *adj.* —**in′-ter est ing ly,** *adv.*

in ter faith (in′tər fāth′), 1 for more than one faith or religion: *an interfaith chapel.* 2 of different faiths or religions: *an interfaith conference.* *adj.*

in ter fere (in′tər fir′), 1 get in the

interlace (def. 1) interlaced design used in basket weaving

way of each other; come into opposition; clash: *The two plans interfere; one must be changed. I will come on Saturday if nothing interferes.* 2 mix in the affairs of others; meddle: *That neighbor is always interfering in other people's affairs. Don't interfere with your sister when she's busy.* 3 take part for a purpose: *The teacher interfered to stop the fight.* v., **in ter fered, in ter fer ing.**

in ter fer ence (in′tər fir′əns), 1 act or fact of interfering: *Your interference spoiled our game.* 2 something that interferes. 3 (in radio or television) the interruption of a desired signal by other signals. 4 (in football, hockey, and other sports) the obstruction of an opposing player in a way barred by the rules. *n.*

in ter fuse (in′tər fyüz′), 1 spread through; be diffused through; permeate. 2 fuse together; blend; mix. v., **in ter fused, in ter fus ing.**

in ter im (in′tər im), 1 time between; the meantime. 2 for the meantime; temporary. 1 *n.,* 2 *adj.*

in ter i or (in tir′ē ər), 1 inner surface or part; inside: *The interior of the house was beautifully decorated and furnished.* 2 on the inside; inner. 3 part of a region or country away from the coast or border: *There are deserts in the interior of Asia.* 4 away from the coast or border. 5 affairs within a country, regarded as separate from foreign affairs: *The United States has a Department of the Interior to deal with patents, public lands, Indian affairs, etc.* 6 having to do with such affairs; domestic. 1,3,5 *n.,* 2,4,6 *adj.*

interior decorator, person whose business is planning and arranging the furnishings, decoration, etc., of houses, offices, or public buildings.

interj., interjection (def. 1).

in ter ject (in′tər jekt′), throw in between other things; insert abruptly: *Every now and then the speaker interjected a joke or story to keep us interested.* v.

in ter jec tion (in′tər jek′shən), 1 an exclamation showing emotion. It is regarded as a part of speech. *Oh! ah! alas!* and *hurrah!* are interjections. 2 an interjecting; sudden throwing in; abrupt insertion: *His interjection of amusing stories into his speech made it more interesting.* 3 something interjected; remark thrown in; exclamation. *n.*

in ter lace (in′tər lās′), 1 arrange (threads, strips, or branches) so that they go over and under each other; weave together; intertwine: *Baskets are made by interlacing reeds or fibers.* 2 cross each other over and under; mingle together in an intricate manner: *The branches of the trees interlaced above the path. The pilot looked down upon interlacing roads and streams.* v., **in ter laced, in ter lac ing.**

in ter lard (in′tər lärd′), give variety to; mix; intersperse: *The speaker interlarded his long speech with amusing stories to keep his listeners interested.* v.

in ter line[1] (in′tər līn′), insert an extra lining in (a garment) between the outer cloth and the ordinary lining. v., **in ter lined, in ter lin ing.** [inter- + line[2]]

in ter line[2] (in′tər līn′), write, print, or mark between the lines of (a book, document, etc.): *The teacher interlined the students' themes with her corrections.* v., **in ter lined, in ter lin ing.** [from Latin *interlineare*]

in ter lin ing (in′tər lī′ning), an extra lining inserted between the outer cloth and the ordinary lining of a garment. *n.*

in ter lock (in′tər lok′), join or fit tightly together; lock together: *The two stags were fighting with their horns interlocked. The different pieces of a jigsaw puzzle interlock.* v.

in ter lop er (in′tər lō′pər), person who thrusts himself in where he is not wanted or has no right; intruder. *n.*

in ter lude (in′tər lüd′), 1 anything thought of as filling the time between two things; interval: *There was an interlude of sunshine between the two showers.* 2 piece of music played between the parts of a song, church service, or drama. 3 entertainment between the acts of a play. *n.*

in ter lu nar (in′tər lü′nər), having to do with the time when the moon is not seen at night, between the old moon and the new moon. *adj.*

in ter mar riage (in′tər mar′ij), marriage between members of different families, tribes, religions, or racial groups. *n.*

in ter mar ry (in′tər mar′ē), become connected by marriage (said of families, tribes, religions, or racial groups): *The families of this old town have intermarried for generations.* v., **in ter married, in ter mar ry ing.**

in ter med dle (in′tər med′l), meddle; interfere. v., **in ter med dled, in ter med dling.**

in ter me di ar y (in′tər mē′dē er′ē), 1 person who acts between others to bring about an agreement; person who acts for another; go-between: *The teacher acted as intermediary for the*

students with the principal. 2 acting between others; acting for another. 3 being between; intermediate: *A cocoon is an intermediary stage between caterpillar and butterfly.* 1 *n., pl.* **in ter me di ar ies;** 2,3 *adj.*

in ter me di ate (in′tər mē′dē it), 1 being or occurring between; middle: *The intermediate department of the Sunday School is between the primary and the adult departments. Gray is intermediate between black and white.* 2 something in between. 1 *adj.,* 2 *n.* —**in′ter me′di ate ly,** *adv.*

in ter ment (in tėr′mənt), act of interring; burial. *n.*

in ter mez zo (in′tər met′sō *or* in′tər med′zō), a short musical composition played between the main divisions of an opera, symphony, or other long musical work. *n., pl.* **in ter mez zos, in ter mez zi** (in′tər met′sē *or* in′tər med′zē). [from Italian]

in ter mi na ble (in tėr′mə nə bəl), 1 never stopping; unceasing; endless. 2 so long as to seem endless; very long and tiring. *adj.*

in ter mi na bly (in tėr′mə nə blē), in an interminable manner; endlessly. *adv.*

in ter min gle (in′tər ming′gəl), mix together; mingle: *intermingle several styles of furniture in a room. The hostess encouraged guests with different interests to intermingle at her parties.* v., **in ter min gled, in ter min gling.**

in ter mis sion (in′tər mish′ən), 1 time between periods of activity; pause: *The band played from eight to twelve with a short intermission at ten.* 2 stopping for a time; interruption: *The rain continued all day without intermission.* *n.*

in ter mit tent (in′tər mit′nt), stopping for a time and beginning again; pausing at intervals: *The pilot watched for an intermittent red light, flashing on and off every 15 seconds.* adj. —**in′ter mit′tent ly,** *adv.*

in ter mix (in′tər miks′), mix together; blend: *Oil and water do not intermix.* v.

in ter mix ture (in′tər miks′chər), 1 a mixing together; blending. 2 a mass

hat, āge, fär; let, ēqual, tėrm; it, īce; hot, ōpen, ôrder; oil, out; cup, pút, rüle; ch, child; ng, long; sh, she; th, thin; ₮H, then; zh, measure;

ə represents *a* in about, *e* in taken, *i* in pencil, *o* in lemon, *u* in circus.

adj. adjective	*n.* noun
adv. adverb	*prep.* preposition
conj. conjunction	*pron.* pronoun
interj. interjection	*v.* verb
sing. singular	*pl.* plural

of ingredients mixed together; mixture; blend. *n.*

in tern[1] (in tėrn′), confine within a country or place; force to stay in a certain place. Soldiers who flee to a neutral country in war are interned there until the war is over. *v.* [from French *interner*, from *interne* inner, internal]

in tern[2] (in′tėrn), **1** doctor acting as an assistant and undergoing training in a hospital. After a student graduates from medical school, he is usually an intern for a year before he starts his own practice. **2** be an intern. **1** *n.,* **2** *v.* Also, **interne** for 1. [from French *interne* inner, internal]

in ter nal (in tėr′nl), **1** on the inside; inner: *An accident often causes internal injuries as well as cuts and bruises.* **2** to be taken inside the body: *Pills are internal remedies.* **3** entirely inside; coming from within: *Internal evidence of the date of a book may be obtained from statements made in the book itself.* **4** having to do with affairs within a country; domestic: *internal politics. Internal revenue is money from taxes on business and income in a country.* *adj.*

in ter nal-com bus tion engine (in tėr′nl kəm bus′chən), engine in which power is produced by exploding a mixture of fuel and air inside the engine itself, usually inside cylinders. Gasoline engines are internal-combustion engines; steam engines are not.

in ter nal ly (in tėr′nl ē), **1** inside. **2** inside the body: *This ointment must not be taken internally.* *adv.*

in ter na tion al (in′tər nash′ə nəl), **1** between or among nations: *A treaty is an international agreement.* **2** having to do with the relations between nations: *international law. adj.*

International Date Line, an imaginary line agreed upon as the place where each new calendar day begins. It runs north and south through the Pacific, mostly along the 180th meridian. When it is Sunday just east of the International Date Line, it is Monday just west of it.

in ter na tion al ism (in′tər nash′-ə nə liz′əm), principle of interna-

tional cooperation for the good of all nations. *n.*

in ter na tion al ist (in′tər nash′ə-nə list), person who favors internationalism. *n.*

in ter na tion al ize (in′tər nash′ə-nə līz), make international; bring under the control of several nations. *v.,* **in ter na tion al ized, in ter na tion al iz ing.**

in ter na tion al ly (in′tər nash′ə nə-lē), in an international manner. *adv.*

in terne (in′tėrn′), intern[2] (def. 1). *n.*

in ter ne cine (in′tər nē′sn *or* in′tər-nē′sīn), **1** destructive to both sides. **2** deadly; destructive. *adj.*

in ter nee (in′tėr′nē′), person interned. Prisoners of war, enemy aliens, etc., may be internees. *n.*

in tern ist (in tėr′nist), doctor who treats internal organs or diseases. *n.*

in tern ment (in tėrn′mənt), an interning or a being interned; confinement within the limits of a country or place. *n.*

in ter pen e trate (in′tər pen′ə trāt), penetrate thoroughly or between the parts of; permeate. *v.,* **in ter pen e-trat ed, in ter pen e trat ing.**

in ter plan e tar y (in′tər plan′-ə ter′ē), situated or taking place between the planets; in the region of the planets: *interplanetary gases, interplanetary travel. adj.*

in ter play (in′tər plā′), action or influence on each other: *the interplay of light and shadow, the interplay of events and characters in a story. n.*

in ter po late (in tėr′pə lāt), **1** alter (a book, passage, etc.) by putting in new words or groups of words, especially without authorization or deceptively: *So many later writers had interpolated the old manuscript that it was hard to tell what parts were genuine.* **2** put in (new words, passages, etc.). **3** (in mathematics) find or insert an unknown term between two known terms in a series. *v.,* **in ter po lat ed, in ter-po lat ing.**

in ter po la tion (in tėr′pə lā′shən), **1** an interpolating. **2** something interpolated: *an old manuscript with many interpolations of later date. n.*

in ter pose (in′tər pōz′), **1** put between; insert. **2** come or be between other things. **3** put forward; break in with; interrupt: *He interposed an objection at this point.* **4** interfere in order to help; intervene: *Mother interposed in the dispute between my brothers. v.,* **in ter posed, in ter pos ing.**

in ter po si tion (in′tėr pə zish′ən), **1** an interposing: *the interposition of a remark.* **2** something interposed. *n.*

in ter pret (in tėr′prit), **1** explain the meaning of: *interpret a hard passage in*

a book, interpret a dream. **2** bring out the meaning of (a dramatic work, a character, music, etc.): *The actress interpreted the part of the queen with wonderful skill.* **3** understand: *We interpreted your silence as consent.* **4** serve as an interpreter; translate. *v.*

in ter pre ta tion (in tėr′prə tā′shən), **1** an interpreting; explanation: *People often give different interpretations to the same facts. What is your interpretation of her odd behavior?* **2** a bringing out the meaning: *The newspapers praised the actor's interpretation of Hamlet. A musician usually has his own interpretation of a piece of music. n.*

in ter pre ta tive (in tėr′prə tā′tiv), used for interpreting; explanatory. *adj.*

in ter pret er (in tėr′prə tər), **1** person who interprets. **2** person whose business is translating, especially orally, from a foreign language. *n.*

in ter pre tive (in tėr′prə tiv), interpretative. *adj.*

in ter ra cial (in′tər rā′shəl), between or involving different racial groups. *adj.*

in ter reg num (in′tər reg′nəm), **1** time between the end of one ruler's reign and the beginning of his successor's reign. **2** any time during which a nation is without its usual ruler. **3** period of inactivity; pause. *n.*

in ter re late (in′tər ri lāt′), bring into relation to each other. *v.,* **in ter re lat-ed, in ter re lat ing.**

in ter re lat ed (in′tər ri lā′tid), closely connected with each other; mutually related. *adj.*

in ter re la tion (in′tər ri lā′shən), close connection with each other; mutual relationship. *n.*

in ter re la tion ship (in′tər ri lā′-shən ship), interrelation. *n.*

in ter ro gate (in ter′ə gāt), ask questions of; examine or get information from by asking questions; question thoroughly: *The principal interrogated the girl about the work she had done in her former school. The lawyer took two hours to interrogate the witness. v.,* **in ter ro gat ed, in ter ro gat ing.**

in ter ro ga tion (in ter′ə gā′shən), **1** an interrogating; a questioning. The formal examination of a witness by asking questions is an interrogation. **2** a question. *n.*

interrogation mark or **interrogation point,** question mark; the mark (?).

in ter rog a tive (in′tə rog′ə tiv), **1** asking a question; having the form of a question: *an interrogative sentence, an interrogative look or tone of voice.* **2** (in grammar) a word used in asking a question. *Who, why,* and *what* are interrogatives. **1** *adj.,* **2** *n.*

in ter ro ga tor (in ter′ə gā′tər), person who interrogates; questioner. *n.*

in ter rog a to ry (in′tə rog′ə tôr′ē), questioning. *adj.*

in ter rupt (in′tə rupt′), 1 break in upon (talk, work, rest, a person speaking, etc.); keep from going on; stop for a time; hinder: *A fire drill interrupted the lesson.* 2 cause a break; break in: *It is not polite to interrupt when someone is talking.* 3 make a break in: *A building interrupts the view from our window. v.* —**in′ter rupt′er,** *n.*

in ter rup tion (in′tə rup′shən), 1 an interrupting; breaking in on. 2 a being interrupted; a break; stopping: *The rain continued without interruption all day.* 3 something that interrupts. 4 intermission. *n.*

in ter scho las tic (in′tər skə las′tik), between schools: *Our team won the interscholastic softball competition. adj.*

in ter sect (in′tər sekt′), 1 cut or divide by passing through or crossing: *A path intersects the field.* 2 cross each other: *Streets usually intersect at right angles. v.*

intersection (def. 2)
The line AB intersects the parallel lines at X and Y.

in ter sec tion (in′tər sek′shən), 1 an intersecting: *Bridges are used to avoid the intersection of a railroad and a highway.* 2 point or line where one thing crosses another. 3 (in mathematics) the set that contains only those elements shared by two or more sets. *n.*

intersection (def. 3)
If A has Z and X as members and B has Z and Y as members, then Z is the intersection of A and B.

in ter sperse (in′tər spėrs′), 1 vary with something put here and there: *The grass was interspersed with beds of flowers.* 2 scatter here and there among other things: *Bushes were interspersed among trees. v.,* **in ter spersed, in ter spers ing.**

in ter state (in′tər stāt′), between persons or organizations in different states; between states: *The federal government regulates interstate commerce. adj.*

in ter stel lar (in′tər stel′ər), among the stars: *interstellar space. adj.*

in ter stice (in tėr′stis), a small or narrow space between things or parts; narrow chink, crack, or opening. *n., pl.* **in ter sti ces** (in tėr′stə sēz′).

in ter twine (in′tər twīn′), twine, one with another: *Two vines intertwined on the wall. She intertwined two strips of leather to make a belt.* v., **in ter twined, in ter twin ing.**

in ter ur ban (in′tər ėr′bən), between cities or towns: *Interurban bus lines have replaced many interurban railways. adj.*

in ter val (in′tər vəl), 1 time or space between: *There is an interval of a week between Christmas and New Year's Day. She had one quiet interval in her busy day. An interval of fifty feet separates each tree from the next one.* 2 (in music) the difference in pitch between two tones. *n.*

at intervals, 1 now and then. 2 here and there.

in ter vene (in′tər vēn′), 1 come between; be between: *A week intervenes between Christmas and New Year's Day.* 2 come between persons or groups to help settle a dispute: *The President was asked to intervene in the coal strike. v.,* **in ter vened, in ter ven ing.**

in ter ven tion (in′tər ven′shən), 1 an intervening: *The strike was settled by the intervention of the President.* 2 interference, especially by one nation in the affairs of another. *n.*

in ter view (in′tər vyü′), 1 a meeting, generally of persons face to face, to talk over something special: *My parents had an interview with the teacher about my work.* 2 a meeting between a reporter and a person from whom information is sought for publication or broadcast. 3 newspaper or magazine article, or broadcast containing the information given at such a meeting. 4 have an interview with; meet and talk with, especially to obtain information: *Reporters interviewed the returning explorers.* 1-3 *n.,* 4 *v.* —**in′ter view′er,** *n.*

in ter weave (in′tər wēv′), 1 weave together: *interweave bamboo strips to make a basket. The branches interwove to form an unbroken hedge.* 2 mix together; blend: *interweave truth with fiction in a story. Different impressions of the city interwove in his memory. v.,* **in ter wove** (in′tər wōv′) or **in ter weaved,   in ter woven**   or **in ter wove** or **in ter weaved, in ter weav ing.**

in ter wo ven (in′tər wō′vən), 1 woven together. 2 mixed together; blended.   3 a past participle of **interweave**. *Various strands were interwoven to create a colorful pattern.* 1,2 *adj.,* 3 *v.*

in tes tate (in tes′tāt), having made no will: *to die intestate. adj.*

in tes ti nal (in tes′tə nəl), of or in the intestines. *adj.*

hat, āge, fär; let, ēqual, tėrm;
it, īce; hot, ōpen, ôrder;
oil, out; cup, pùt, rüle; ch, child;
ng, long; sh, she; th, thin;
ŦH, then; zh, measure;

ə represents *a* in about,
e in taken, *i* in pencil,
o in lemon, *u* in circus.

in tes tine (in tes′tən), either of two parts of the alimentary canal, extending from the stomach to the anus. Partially digested food passes from the stomach into the **small intestine**, a winding, narrow tube, where digestion is completed and nutrients are absorbed by the blood. The small intestine empties into the **large intestine**, a wide tube, where water is absorbed and wastes are eliminated. In humans, the small intestine is about twenty feet long and the large intestine is about five feet long. *n.*

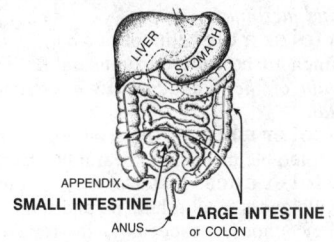

LIVER
STOMACH
APPENDIX
SMALL INTESTINE
ANUS
LARGE INTESTINE
or COLON

in ti ma cy (in′tə mə sē), 1 a being intimate; close acquaintance; closeness. 2 a familiar or intimate act. *n., pl.* **in ti ma cies.**

in ti mate[1] (in′tə mit), 1 very familiar; known very well; closely acquainted: *Although the governor knew many people, he had few intimate friends.* 2 resulting from close familiarity; close: *an intimate connection, intimate knowledge of a matter.* 3 personal; private: *A diary is a very intimate book.* 4 a close friend. 5 far within; deepest; inmost. 1-3,5 *adj.,* 4 *n.* —**in′ti mate ly,** *adv.* [from French of the 1600's *intime,* from Latin *intimus* inmost]

in ti mate[2] (in′tə māt), 1 suggest indirectly; hint: *Her smile intimated that she was pleased.* 2 make known; announce; notify. *v.,* **in ti mat ed, in ti mat ing.** [from Latin *intimare* make known, from *intimus* inmost]

in ti ma tion (in′tə mā′shən), 1 indirect suggestion; hint: *His frown is an intimation of his disapproval.* 2 announcement; notice. *n.*

in tim i date (in tim′ə dāt), 1 make afraid; frighten. 2 influence or force by

intimidation

fear: *The mayor's enemies accused him of trying to use policemen to intimidate voters on election day.* *v.*, **in tim i dat ed, in tim i dat ing.**

in tim i da tion (in tim′ə dā′shən), 1 a making afraid. 2 a being made afraid: *Witnesses were kept from testifying by intimidation.* *n.*

in to (in′tü; *before consonants often* in′tə), 1 to the inside of; toward and inside: *Come into the house. We drove into the city. I will look into the matter.* 2 so as to become; to the form of: *Divide the apple into three parts. Cold weather turns water into ice.* 3 SLANG. involved with; interested in: *They were very much into rock and jazz music.* *prep.*

in tol er a ble (in tol′ər ə bəl), too much to be endured; unbearable: *The pain of the toothache was intolerable.* *adj.*

in tol er a bly (in tol′ər ə blē), in an intolerable manner; unbearably. *adv.*

in tol er ance (in tol′ər əns), 1 unwillingness to let others do and think as they choose, especially in religion: *The Pilgrims came to America because of intolerance and persecution.* 2 inability to tolerate; lack of tolerance: *She developed an intolerance to penicillin.* *n.*

in tol er ant (in tol′ər ənt), not tolerant; not willing to let others do and think as they choose, especially in religion: *Some of the Puritans were strict and intolerant.* *adj.* —**in tol′er ant ly,** *adv.*

intolerant of, not able to endure; unwilling to endure: *intolerant of cold.*

in to na tion (in′tō nā′shən), 1 an intoning. 2 manner of producing musical notes, especially with regard to pitch. 3 manner of sounding words or speaking, especially with regard to the rise and fall of the pitch of the voice. *n.*

in tone (in tōn′), read or recite in a singing voice; chant: *A cantor intones part of the service.* *v.*, **in toned, in ton ing.**

in tox i cant (in tok′sə kənt), 1 alcoholic liquor. 2 anything that intoxicates. *n.*

in tox i cate (in tok′sə kāt), 1 make drunk: *Too much wine intoxicates people.* 2 excite greatly; exhilarate: *The joy*

of winning intoxicated the team. 3 produce changes in perception, behavior, etc.: *Marijuana intoxicates.* *v.*, **in tox i cat ed, in tox i cat ing.**

in tox i cat ed (in tok′sə kā′tid), 1 drunk: *an intoxicated person.* 2 very much excited. *adj.*

in tox i ca tion (in tok′sə kā′shən), 1 an intoxicated condition; drunkenness. 2 great excitement. 3 (in medicine) poisoning. *n.*

in trac ta ble (in trak′tə bəl), hard to handle or manage; stubborn: *The intractable mule refused to budge.* *adj.*

in tra mur al (in′trə myùr′əl), within the walls; inside: *Intramural games are games played between students of the same school.* *adj.*

in tran si tive (in tran′sə tiv), not taking a direct object. The verbs *belong, go,* and *seem* are intransitive. The verb *run* may be transitive or intransitive. In "I run to school" *run* is intransitive. In "I run the machine" *run* is transitive. *adj.* —**in tran′si tive ly,** *adv.*

in tra ve nous (in′trə vē′nəs), 1 within a vein or the veins. 2 into a vein: *When a person is too ill to digest food, glucose is sometimes given by an intravenous injection.* *adj.* —**in′tra ve′nous ly,** *adv.*

in trench (in trench′), entrench. *v.*

in trench ment (in trench′mənt), entrenchment. *n.*

in trep id (in trep′id), very brave; fearless; courageous; dauntless: *an intrepid adventurer.* *adj.* —**in trep′id ly,** *adv.*

in tre pid i ty (in′trə pid′ə tē), great bravery; dauntless courage; fearlessness. *n.*

in tri ca cy (in′trə kə sē), 1 intricate nature or condition; complexity: *The intricacy of the plan made it hard to understand.* 2 an intricate thing or event; complication: *The laws are full of intricacies.* *n., pl.* **in tri ca cies.**

in tri cate (in′trə kit), 1 with many twists and turns; puzzling, entangled, or complicated: *An intricate knot is very hard to tie or untie. A mystery story usually has a very intricate plot.* 2 very hard to understand: *an intricate design, an intricate piece of machinery, intricate directions.* *adj.* —**in′tri cate ly,** *adv.*

in trigue (in trēg′ *or* in′trēg *for 1,2,5;* in trēg′ *for 3,4*), 1 secret scheming and plotting; crafty dealings: *The royal palace was filled with intrigue.* 2 a crafty plot; secret scheme: *The king's younger brother took part in the intrigue to make himself king.* 3 form and carry out plots; plan in a secret or underhand way: *He pretended to be loyal while he intrigued against the king.* 4 excite the curiosity and interest of: *The book's unusual title intrigued me into reading it.*

5 a secret love affair. 1,2,5 *n.,* 3,4 *v.,* **in trigued, in tri guing.**

in tri guing (in trē′ging), exciting the curiosity and interest: *The book's intriguing title caught my attention.* *adj.* —**in tri′guing ly,** *adv.*

in trin sic (in trin′sik), belonging in a thing by its very nature; essential; inherent: *The intrinsic value of a dollar bill is the cost of the paper it's printed on.* *adj.*

in trin si cal ly (in trin′sik lē), by its very nature; essentially. *adv.*

in tro duce (in′trə düs′ *or* in′trə dyüs′), 1 bring in: *She introduced a story into the conversation.* 2 put in; insert: *The doctor introduced a tube into the sick man's throat so he could breathe.* 3 bring into use, notice, knowledge, etc.: *introduce a new food, introduce a reform. Television and space travel are introducing many new words into our language.* 4 bring into acquaintance with; make known: *The principal introduced the speaker to the students. I introduced my visiting cousin to our city by showing her the sights.* 5 bring forward for consideration: *introduce a question for debate.* 6 begin; start: *He introduced his speech by telling a joke.* *v.*, **in tro duced, in tro duc ing.**

in tro duc er (in′trə dü′sər *or* in′trə dyü′sər), one that introduces. *n.*

in tro duc tion (in′trə duk′shən), 1 an introducing: *The introduction of steel made tall buildings easy to build.* 2 a being introduced: *She was confused by her introduction to so many strangers.* 3 thing that introduces; first part of a book, speech, piece of music, etc., leading up to the main part. 4 a first book for beginners. 5 thing introduced; thing brought into use: *Television is a later introduction than radio.* *n.*

in tro duc tor y (in′trə duk′tə rē), used to introduce; serving as an introduction; preliminary: *The speaker began her talk with a few introductory remarks about her subject.* *adj.*

in tro spec tion (in′trə spek′shən), examination of one's own thoughts and feelings. *n.*

in tro spec tive (in′trə spek′tiv), inclined to examine one's own thoughts and feelings. *adj.*

in tro vert (in′trə vèrt′), person more interested in his own thoughts and feelings than in what is going on around him; person tending to think rather than act. *n.*

in tro vert ed (in′trə vèr′tid), characterized by a tendency to be more interested in one's own thoughts and feelings than in what is going on around one. *adj.*

in trude (in trüd′), 1 force oneself in; come unasked and unwanted: *Do not* *intrude upon the privacy of your neighbors.* 2 give unasked and unwanted; force in: *Do not intrude your opinions upon others.* *v.,* **in trud ed, in trud ing.**

in trud er (in trü′dər), one that intrudes. *n.*

in tru sion (in trü′zhən), an intruding; coming unasked and unwanted: *Excuse my intrusion; I didn't know that you were busy.* *n.*

in tru sive (in trü′siv), intruding; coming unasked and unwanted. *adj.*

in trust (in trust′), entrust. *v.*

in tu i tion (in′tü ish′ən *or* in′tyü ish′ən), 1 immediate perception or understanding of truths, facts, etc., without reasoning: *By experience with many kinds of people the doctor had developed great powers of intuition.* 2 truth, fact, etc., perceived or understood immediately and without reasoning. *n.*

in tu i tive (in tü′ə tiv *or* in tyü′ə tiv), 1 perceiving or understanding immediately and without reasoning: *The lawyers had great respect for the judge's intuitive mind.* 2 acquired by intuition; instinctive; natural: *The artist's understanding of color seems to have been intuitive in her.* *adj.* **—in tu′i tive ly,** *adv.*

in un date (in′un dāt), overflow; flood: *Heavy rains caused the river to rise and inundate the valley.* *v.,* **in un dat ed, in un dat ing.**

in un da tion (in′un dā′shən), an overflowing; flood. *n.*

in ure (in yür′), 1 toughen or harden; accustom: *Nurses become inured to the sight of blood.* 2 have effect; be useful: *The agreement inures to the benefit of the employees.* *v.,* **in ured, in ur ing.**

in vade (in vād′), 1 enter with force or as an enemy; attack: *Soldiers invaded the country to conquer it. Grasshoppers invade fields and eat the crops. Disease invades the body.* 2 enter as if to take possession: *Tourists invaded the city. Night invades the sky.* 3 interfere with; break in on; violate: *The law punishes people who invade the rights of others.* *v.,* **in vad ed, in vad ing.**

in vad er (in vā′dər), person or thing that invades. *n.*

in va lid[1] (in′və lid), 1 person who is weak because of sickness or injury. An invalid cannot get around and do things. 2 weak because of sickness or injury; not well; disabled. 3 for the use of invalids: *an invalid chair.* 4 make weak or sick; disable. 5 remove from active service because of sickness or injury: *The wounded soldier was invalided and sent home.* 1 *n.,* 2,3 *adj.,* 4,5 *v.* [from French *invalide,* from Latin *invalidus* not strong]

in val id[2] (in val′id), not valid; without force or effect; without value; worthless: *Unless a check is signed, it is invalid.* *adj.* [from Latin *invalidus* not strong]

in val i date (in val′ə dāt), make not valid; cause to be worthless or not good; deprive of force or effect: *A contract is invalidated if only one party signs it.* *v.,* **in val i dat ed, in val i dat ing.**

in va lid ism (in′və lə diz′əm), prolonged ill health. *n.*

in val u a ble (in val′yü ə bəl *or* in val′yə bəl), valuable beyond measure; very precious; priceless: *Good health is an invaluable blessing.* *adj.*

in var i a bil i ty (in ver′ē ə bil′ə tē *or* in var′ē ə bil′ə tē), lack of variability; being invariable. *n.*

in var i a ble (in ver′ē ə bəl *or* in var′ē ə bəl), always the same; not changing: *After dinner it was his invariable habit to take a walk.* *adj.*

in var i a bly (in ver′ē ə blē *or* in var′ē ə blē), in an invariable manner; without change; without exception: *Spring invariably follows winter.* *adv.*

in va sion (in vā′zhən), an invading; entering by force or as an enemy; attack. *n.*

in vec tive (in vek′tiv), a violent attack in words; abusive speech: *His opponents were overcome by the fury of his invective.* *n.*

in veigh (in vā′), make a violent attack in words: *The agitator inveighed against the government.* *v.*

in vei gle (in vē′gəl *or* in vā′gəl), lead astray by trickery; entice; lure: *The saleswoman inveigled me into buying four magazine subscriptions.* *v.,* **in vei gled, in vei gling.**

in vent (in vent′), 1 make up for the first time; think out (something new): *Alexander Graham Bell invented the telephone.* 2 make up; think up: *Since they had no good reason for being late, they invented an excuse.* *v.*

in ven tion (in ven′shən), 1 a making something new: *the invention of gunpowder.* 2 thing invented: *Television is a modern invention.* 3 power of inventing: *An author must have invention to think up new ideas for stories.* 4 a made-up story; false statement: *The rumor was a gossip's invention.* *n.*

in ven tive (in ven′tiv), 1 good at inventing; quick to invent things: *An inventive person thinks up ways to save time, money, and work.* 2 showing power of inventing. *adj.* **—in ven′tive ly,** *adv.* **—in ven′tive ness,** *n.*

in ven tor (in ven′tər), person who invents: *Edison was a great inventor.* *n.*

in ven to ry (in′vən tôr′ē), 1 a complete and detailed list of articles. An

hat, āge, fär; let, ēqual, tėrm;
it, īce; hot, ōpen, ôrder;
oil, out; cup, pùt, rüle; ch, child;
ng, long; sh, she; th, thin;
ŦH, then; zh, measure;

ə represents *a* in about,
e in taken, *i* in pencil,
o in lemon, *u* in circus.

inventory of property or goods tells how many there are of each article and what they are worth. 2 all the articles listed or to be listed; stock: *The shoe store had a sale to reduce its inventory.* 3 make a complete and detailed list of; enter in a list: *Some stores inventory their stock once a month.* 1,2 *n., pl.* **in ven to ries;** 3 *v.,* **in ven to ried, in ven to ry ing.**

in verse (in vėrs′ *or* in′vėrs′), 1 exactly opposite; reversed in position, direction, or tendency; inverted: *DCBA is the inverse order of ABCD.* 2 something reversed: *Subtraction is the inverse of addition. The inverse of* $^3/_4$ *is* $^4/_3$. 3 direct opposite: *Evil is the inverse of good.* 1 *adj.,* 2,3 *n.* **—in verse′ly,** *adv.*

in ver sion (in vėr′zhən), 1 an inverting or a being inverted. 2 something inverted. *n.*

in vert (in vėrt′), 1 turn upside down: *He inverted the glass and the water ran out.* 2 turn the other way; change to the opposite; reverse in position, direction, order, etc.: *If you invert "I can," you have "Can I?"* *v.*

in ver te brate (in vėr′tə brit *or* in vėr′tə brāt), 1 without a backbone. 2 animal without a backbone. Worms and insects are invertebrates; fishes, amphibians, reptiles, birds, and mammals are vertebrates. 1 *adj.,* 2 *n.*

in vest (in vest′), 1 use (money) to buy something that is expected to produce a profit, or income, or both: *She invested her money in stocks, bonds, and land.* 2 spend or put in (time, energy, etc.) for later benefit: *He has invested his time and energy in the cancer crusade.* 3 clothe; cover; surround: *Darkness invests the earth at night. The castle was invested with mystery and romance.* 4 give power, authority, or right to: *I invested my lawyer with power to act for me.* 5 give a quality or characteristic to: *The author invested the hero with every virtue.* 6 put in office with a ceremony: *A king is invested by being crowned.* 7 surround with soldiers or ships; besiege: *The enemy invested the city and cut it off from our army.* *v.*

adj. adjective	n. noun
adv. adverb	prep. preposition
conj. conjunction	pron. pronoun
interj. interjection	v. verb
sing. singular	pl. plural

in ves ti gate (in ves′tə gāt), look into thoroughly; search into carefully; examine closely: *Detectives investigate crimes to find out who did them. Scientists investigate nature to learn more about it.* v., **in ves ti gat ed, in ves ti gat ing.**

in ves ti ga tion (in ves′tə gā′shən), a careful search; detailed or careful examination: *An investigation of the accident by the police put the blame on the drivers of both cars.* n.

in ves ti ga tor (in ves′tə gā′tər), person who investigates. n.

in ves ti ture (in ves′tə chùr), a formal investing of a person with an office, dignity, power, right, etc. n.

in vest ment (in vest′mənt), 1 an investing; a laying out of money: *Getting an education is a wise investment of time and money.* 2 amount of money invested: *Their investments amount to thousands of dollars.* 3 something that is expected to yield money as income or profit or both: *She has a good income from wise investments. He considers United States bonds a safe investment.* 4 a surrounding with soldiers or ships; siege. n.

in ves tor (in ves′tər), person who invests money. n.

in vet er ate (in vet′ər it), 1 confirmed in a habit, practice, feeling, etc.; habitual: *It is very hard for an inveterate smoker to give up tobacco.* 2 long and firmly established; deeply rooted: *Cats have an inveterate dislike of dogs.* adj.

in vid i ous (in vid′ē əs), likely to cause ill will or resentment; giving offense because unfair or unjust: *Wise teachers avoid invidious rules.* adj.

in vig o rate (in vig′ə rāt′), give vigor to; fill with life and energy: *Exercise invigorates the body. A cool breeze invigorates you on a hot day.* v., **in vig o rat ed, in vig o rat ing.**

in vig o ra tion (in vig′ə rā′shən), an invigorating or a being invigorated. n.

in vin ci bil i ty (in vin′sə bil′ə tē), a being invincible. n.

in vin ci ble (in vin′sə bəl), unable to be conquered; impossible to overcome; unconquerable: *The champion wrestler seemed invincible.* adj.

in vin ci bly (in vin′sə blē), in an invincible manner. adv.

in vi o la bil i ty (in vī′ə lə bil′ə tē), a being inviolable. n.

in vi o la ble (in vī′ə lə bəl), 1 that must not be violated or injured; sacred: *an inviolable vow.* 2 that cannot be violated or injured: *The gods are inviolable.* adj.

in vi o late (in vī′ə lit *or* in vī′ə lāt), not violated; uninjured; unbroken: *An inviolate promise is carried out.* adj.

in vis i bil i ty (in viz′ə bil′ə tē), condition of being invisible. n.

in vis i ble (in viz′ə bəl), not visible; not capable of being seen: *Thought is invisible. The queen kept herself invisible in her palace. Germs are invisible to the naked eye.* adj.

in vis i bly (in viz′ə blē), in an invisible manner; so as not to be seen. adv.

in vi ta tion (in′və tā′shən), 1 a polite request to come to some place or to do something: *The children received invitations to the party.* 2 act of inviting. n.

in vite (in vīt′), 1 ask (someone) politely to come to some place or to do something: *I invited some friends to a party. We invited them to join our club.* 2 make a polite request for: *She invited our opinion of her story.* 3 give a chance for; tend to cause: *New Year's Day invites good resolutions. Carelessness invites trouble.* 4 attract; tempt; encourage: *The cool water invited us to swim.* v., **in vit ed, in vit ing.**

in vit ing (in vī′ting), attractive; tempting: *The cool water looks inviting.* adj. —**in vit′ing ly,** adv.

in vo ca tion (in′və kā′shən), 1 a calling upon in prayer; appealing for help or protection: *A church service often begins with an invocation to God.* 2 a calling forth of spirits with magic words or charms. 3 set of magic words used to call forth spirits. n.

in voice (in′vois), 1 list of goods sent to a purchaser showing prices, amounts, shipping charges, etc. 2 make an invoice of; enter on an invoice. 1 n., 2 v., **in voiced, in voic ing.**

in voke (in vōk′), 1 call on in prayer; appeal to for help or protection: *The Pilgrims invoked God's help in their undertaking.* 2 ask earnestly for; beg for: *The convicted criminal invoked the judge's mercy.* 3 call forth with magic words or charms: *Aladdin invoked the powerful genie of the magic lamp.* v., **in voked, in vok ing.**

in vol un tar i ly (in vol′ən ter′ə lē), in an involuntary manner; without intention; against one's will. adv.

in vol un tar y (in vol′ən ter′ē), 1 not voluntary; not done of one's own free will; unwilling: *He was threatened until he gave involuntary consent to the plan.* 2 not done on purpose; not intended: *An accident is involuntary.* 3 not controlled by the will: *Breathing is mainly involuntary.* adj.

in volve (in volv′), 1 have as a necessary part, condition, or result; take in; include: *Housework involves cooking, washing dishes, sweeping, and cleaning. These changes in the business involve the interests of all the owners.* 2 bring (into difficulty, danger, etc.): *One foolish mistake can involve you in a good deal of trouble.* 3 entangle; complicate: *Long, involved sentences are hard to understand.* 4 take up the attention of; occupy: *She was involved in working out a puzzle.* v., **in volved, in volv ing.**

in volve ment (in volv′mənt), an involving or a being involved. n.

in vul ner a bil i ty (in vul′nər ə bil′ə tē), a being invulnerable. n.

in vul ner a ble (in vul′nər ə bəl), that cannot be wounded or hurt; safe from attack: *Achilles was invulnerable except for his heel.* adj.

in vul ner a bly (in vul′nər ə blē), in an invulnerable manner. adv.

in ward (in′wərd), 1 toward the inside: *a passage leading inward.* 2 placed within; internal: *the inward parts of the body.* 3 directed toward the inside: *an inward slant of the eyes.* 4 into the mind or soul: *Turn your thoughts inward.* 5 in mind or soul: *inward peace.* 1,4 adv., 2,3,5 adj.

in ward ly (in′wərd lē), 1 on the inside; within. 2 toward the inside. 3 in the mind or soul. 4 not aloud or openly. adv.

in wards (in′wərdz for 1; in′wərdz or in′ərdz for 2), 1 inward. 2 parts inside the body; stomach and intestines. 1 adv., 2 n.pl.

in wrought (in rôt′), 1 having a decoration worked in. 2 worked in. adj.

i o dide (ī′ə dīd), a chemical compound of iodine with another element. n.

i o dine (ī′ə dīn), 1 a nonmetallic element in the form of grayish-black crystals which give off a dense, violet vapor with an irritating odor when heated. Iodine occurs naturally only in combination with other elements and is used in medicine, in making dyes, in photography, etc. 2 a brown liquid containing iodine, used as an antiseptic. n.

i o dized salt (ī′ə dīzd), common salt containing iodide as a supplement to the diet, especially of persons with an iodine deficiency.

i on (ī′ən), atom or group of atoms having a negative or positive electric charge as a result of having lost or gained an electron. When an acid, base, or salt dissolves in water, some of its molecules separate into positive and negative ions. Each molecule forms two or more ions whose electric charges neutralize each other when the ions are recombined into a molecule. Cations are positive ions formed by the loss of electrons; anions are negative ions formed by the gain of electrons. *n.*

-ion, *suffix added to verbs to form nouns.* **1** act of _____ing: *Attraction = act of attracting. Calculation = act of calculating.* **2** condition of being _____ed: *Adoption = condition of being adopted. Fascination = condition of being fascinated.* **3** result of _____ing: *Abbreviation = result of abbreviating. Collection = result of collecting.* [from French before the 1400's *-ion,* from Latin *-ionem*]

I o ni a (ī ō′nē ə), ancient region on the W coast of Asia Minor, with the islands near it. The Greeks colonized Ionia in very early times. *n.*

i on ic (ī on′ik), having to do with ions. *adj.*

Ionic (def. 1)
Ionic temple

I on ic (ī on′ik), **1** of or having to do with the order of Greek architecture having scrolls in the capitals of the columns. **2** of Ionia or its people. *adj.*

i o ni um (ī ō′nē əm), a radioactive isotope of thorium. *n.*

i on i za tion (ī′ə nə zā′shən), separation into ions; formation of ions. *n.*

i on ize (ī′ə nīz), separate into ions; produce ions in. Acids, bases, and salts ionize when dissolved in a solution. The gas in a neon light must be ionized before it can conduct an electric current. *v.,* **i on ized, i on iz ing.**

i on o sphere (ī on′ə sfir), region of ionized layers of air beyond the stratosphere, which extends from about 50 to 400 miles above the earth's surface. The ionosphere reflects certain radio waves, making transmission over long distances on earth possible. See **Heaviside layer** for diagram. *n.*

i o ta (ī ō′tə), **1** a very small part or quantity; bit: *There is not an iota of truth in the story.* **2** the ninth letter of the Greek alphabet (I or ι). *n., pl.* **i o tas.**

I O U or **I.O.U.** (ī′ō′yü′), **1** I owe you. **2** an informal note showing a debt: *Write me your IOU for ten dollars.*

I o wa (ī′ə wə), one of the midwestern states of the United States. *Capital:* Des Moines. *n.* **—I′o wan,** *adj., n.*

IQ or **I.Q.,** intelligence quotient.

ir-, *prefix.* form of **in-¹** before *r,* as in *irrational, irregular,* etc.

I ran (i ran′ *or* i rän′), country in SW Asia, south of the Caspian Sea. *Capital:* Teheran. Formerly called **Persia.** *n.*

I ra ni an (i rā′nē ən), **1** of or having to do with Iran, its people, or their language. **2** person born or living in Iran. **3** language of Iran. **1** *adj.,* **2,3** *n.*

I raq (i rak′ *or* i räk′), country in SW Asia, west of Iran. *Capital:* Baghdad. *n.*

I raq i (i rak′ē *or* i rä′kē), **1** of or having to do with Iraq, its people, or their language. **2** person born or living in Iraq. **3** Arabic as spoken in Iraq. **1** *adj.,* **2,3** *n.*

i ras ci ble (i ras′ə bəl), easily made angry; with a quick temper; irritable. *adj.*

i rate (ī′rāt *or* ī rāt′), angry. *adj.* **—i′rate ly,** *adv.*

IRBM, Intermediate Range Ballistic Missile, a missile with a range of up to 1500 nautical miles.

ire (īr), anger; wrath. *n.*

ire ful (īr′fəl), angry; wrathful. *adj.*

Ire land (īr′lənd), **1** one of the British Isles, divided into the Republic of Ireland and Northern Ireland. **2 Republic of,** country in NW, central, and S Ireland; Irish Republic; Eire. *Capital:* Dublin. *n.*

ir i des cence (ir′ə des′ns), display of changing colors; change of color when moved or turned: *the iridescence of mother-of-pearl, opals, a peacock's feather, or the rainbow. n.*

ir i des cent (ir′ə des′nt), displaying changing colors; changing color when moved or turned: *Soap bubbles are iridescent. adj.* **—ir′i des′cent ly,** *adv.*

i rid i um (i rid′ē əm), a silver-white, hard metallic element which occurs in platinum ores and is used as an alloy with platinum for jewelry and the points of fountain pens. *n.*

i ris (ī′ris), **1** plant with sword-shaped leaves and large flowers with three upright parts and three drooping parts; fleur-de-lis. **2** its flower. **3** the colored part of the eye around the pupil. **4** rainbow. *n., pl.* **i ris es.**

I rish (ī′rish), **1** of or having to do with Ireland, its people, or their language. **2** the people of Ireland. **3** the Celtic language spoken by some of the Irish; Gaelic. **4** English as spoken by the Irish. **1** *adj.,* **2** *n.pl.,* **3,4** *n.sing.*

I rish man (ī′rish mən), man born or living in Ireland. *n., pl.* **I rish men.**

Irish potato, another name for the potato.

Irish Republic, Republic of Ireland.

Irish Sea, part of the Atlantic between Ireland and England.

Irish terrier, a small dog with reddish-brown, wiry hair. It is somewhat like a small Airedale.

hat, āge, fär; let, ēqual, tėrm; it, īce; hot, ōpen, ôrder; oil, out; cup, pút, rüle; ch, child; ng, long; sh, she; th, thin; ᵺ, then; zh, measure;

ə represents *a* in about, *e* in taken, *i* in pencil, *o* in lemon, *u* in circus.

I rish wom an (ī′rish wúm′ən), woman born or living in Ireland. *n., pl.* **I rish wom en.**

irk (ėrk), cause to feel disgusted, annoyed, or troubled; weary by being tedious or disagreeable; bore: *It irks us to wait for people who are late. v.*

irk some (ėrk′səm), tiresome; tedious: *Washing dishes all day would be an irksome task. adj.* **—irk′some ness,** *n.*

i ron (ī′ərn), **1** a silver-gray, malleable, heavy metallic element. Iron is the most useful metal and is used to make steel. Iron occurs in the hemoglobin of the red blood cells where it serves to carry oxygen to all parts of the body. Iron deficiency in a person's diet is a cause of anemia. **2** made of iron: *an iron fence.* **3** something made of iron. **4** like iron; hard and strong; unyielding: *an iron will.* **5** great hardness and strength; firmness: *men of iron.* **6 irons,** *pl.* chains or bands of iron; handcuffs; shackles. **7** flatiron. **8** smooth or press (cloth, etc.) with a heated flatiron. **1,3,5-7** *n.,* **2,4** *adj.,* **8** *v.*

iron out, smooth away or overcome (difficulties, differences, inconsistencies, etc.): *The dispute between the two players was ironed out by the coach.*

Iron Age, period after the Bronze Age, when people used iron tools, weapons, etc.

i ron clad (ī′ərn klad′), **1** warship protected with iron plates. **2** very hard to change or get out of: *An ironclad agreement must be kept.* **1** *n.,* **2** *adj.*

Iron Curtain, 1 an imaginary wall or dividing line separating the Soviet Union and the countries under Soviet control or influence from the non-Communist nations. Behind it strict censorship and secrecy are enforced. **2 iron curtain,** any similar imaginary wall or dividing line.

i ron ic (ī ron′ik), ironical. *adj.*

i ron i cal (ī ron′ə kəl), **1** expressing one thing and meaning the opposite: *"Speedy" was the ironical name of our turtle. Her ironical laugh showed that she wasn't the least bit amused.* **2** contrary to what would naturally be expected: *It was ironical that the man was*

adj. adjective	*n.* noun	
adv. adverb	*prep.* preposition	
conj. conjunction	*pron.* pronoun	
interj. interjection	*v.* verb	
sing. singular	*pl.* plural	

run over by his own automobile. *adj.*
—**i ron/i cal ly,** *adv.*

ironing board, a padded flat surface covered with a smooth cloth, on which clothes are ironed. Most ironing boards include folding legs.

iron lung, device which applies periodic pressure on the chest wall in order to force air in and out of the lungs. It is used to enable people to breathe whose chest muscles are paralyzed.

iron lung

iron oxide, compound of iron and oxygen, used especially as a pigment.

i ron wood (ī/ərn wùd/), 1 any of various trees with hard, heavy wood. 2 the wood itself. *n.*

i ron work (ī/ərn wėrk/), things made of iron; work in iron. *n.*

i ron work er (ī/ərn wėr/kər), 1 person whose work is making iron or iron articles. 2 person whose work is building the steel framework of bridges, skyscrapers, etc. *n.*

i ron works (ī/ərn wėrks/), place where iron is made or worked into iron articles. *n.pl. or sing.*

i ro ny (ī/rə nē), 1 way of speaking or writing in which the ordinary meaning of the words is the opposite of the thought in the speaker's mind: *The tallest person was called "Shorty" in irony.* 2 event or outcome which is the opposite of what would naturally be expected: *By the irony of fate the farmers had rain when they needed sun, and sun when they needed rain. n., pl.* **i ro nies.**

Ir o quois (ir/ə kwoi), member of a powerful confederacy of American Indian tribes called the Five Nations, formerly living mostly in what is now New York State. *n., pl.* **Ir o quois.**

ir ra di ate (i rā/dē āt), 1 shine upon;

light up; make bright; illuminate. 2 shine. 3 radiate; give out. 4 treat with electromagnetic rays. *v.,* **ir ra di at ed, ir ra di at ing.**

ir ra di a tion (i rā/dē ā/shən), an irradiating or a being irradiated. *n.*

ir ra tion al (i rash/ə nəl), 1 not rational; contrary to reason; unreasonable: *It is irrational to be afraid of the number 13.* 2 unable to think and reason clearly. *adj.* —**ir ra/tion al ly,** *adv.*

irrational number, any real number that cannot be expressed as an integer or as a ratio between two integers. √2̄ and π are irrational numbers.

Ir ra wad dy (ir/ə wod/ē), river flowing from E Tibet through Burma into the Bay of Bengal. *n.*

ir re claim a ble (ir/i klā/mə bəl), that cannot be reclaimed. *adj.*

ir rec on cil a ble (i rek/ən sī/lə bəl), that cannot be reconciled; that cannot be made to agree; opposed: *irreconcilable enemies. Good and evil are irreconcilable. adj.*

ir re cov er a ble (ir/i kuv/ər ə bəl), that cannot be got back, regained, or remedied: *Wasted time is irrecoverable. adj.*

ir re deem a ble (ir/i dē/mə bəl), 1 that cannot be redeemed or bought back. 2 that cannot be exchanged for coin: *irredeemable paper money.* 3 impossible to change; beyond remedy; hopeless: *The auditor's mistake was serious, but not irredeemable. adj.*

ir re duc i ble (ir/i dü/sə bəl or ir/i dyü/sə bəl), 1 impossible to make less, smaller, simpler, etc. 2 unable to be changed or brought into a wanted condition. 3 impossible to conquer or overcome. *adj.*

ir ref u ta ble (i ref/yə tə bəl or ir/i fyü/tə bəl), that cannot be refuted or disproved; undeniable; unanswerable: *irrefutable arguments. adj.*

ir reg u lar (i reg/yə lər), 1 not regular; not according to rule; out of the usual order or natural way: *It would be quite irregular for a child of ten to drive a car.* 2 not even; not smooth or straight; broken and rough: *New England has a very irregular coastline.* 3 not according to law or morals: *irregular behavior.* 4 (of a word) not inflected in the usual way. *Be* is an irregular verb. *adj.* —**ir reg/u lar ly,** *adv.*

ir reg u lar i ty (i reg/yə lar/ə tē), 1 lack of regularity; being irregular. 2 something irregular. *n., pl.* **ir reg u lar i ties.**

ir rel e vance (i rel/ə vəns), 1 a being irrelevant. 2 something irrelevant. *n.*

ir rel e vant (i rel/ə vənt), not to the point; off the subject: *A question about arithmetic is irrelevant in a French lesson. adj.* —**ir rel/e vant ly,** *adv.*

ir re li gious (ir/i lij/əs), 1 not religious; indifferent to religion. 2 contrary to religious principles; impious. *adj.* —**ir/re li/gious ly,** *adv.*

ir re me di a ble (ir/i mē/dē ə bəl), that cannot be corrected or remedied; incurable. *adj.*

ir rep ar a ble (i rep/ər ə bəl), that cannot be repaired or put right: *Our car suffered irreparable damage in the accident. adj.*

ir rep ar a bly (i rep/ər ə blē), in an irreparable manner. *adv.*

ir re place a ble (ir/i plā/sə bəl), not replaceable; impossible to replace with another. *adj.*

ir re press i ble (ir/i pres/ə bəl), that cannot be repressed or restrained; uncontrollable: *irrepressible laughter. adj.*

ir re press i bly (ir/i pres/ə blē), in an irrepressible manner; uncontrollably. *adv.*

ir re proach a ble (ir/i prō/chə bəl), free from blame; faultless: *The Frenchman spoke excellent, irreproachable English. adj.*

ir re sist i ble (ir/i zis/tə bəl), that cannot be resisted; too great to be withstood; overwhelming: *She had an irresistible desire for some ice cream. adj.*

ir re sist i bly (ir/i zis/tə blē), in an irresistible manner; overwhelmingly. *adv.*

ir res o lute (i rez/ə lüt), not resolute; unable to make up one's mind; not sure of what one wants; hesitating: *Irresolute persons make poor leaders. adj.* —**ir res/o lute ly,** *adv.* —**ir res/o lute ness,** *n.*

ir res o lu tion (i rez/ə lü/shən), a being irresolute; lack of firm decision; hesitation. *n.*

ir re spec tive (ir/i spek/tiv), regardless: *All pupils, irrespective of age, may join the club. adj.*

ir re spon si bil i ty (ir/i spon/sə bil/ə tē), lack of responsibility; being irresponsible. *n.*

ir re spon si ble (ir/i spon/sə bəl), 1 not responsible; that cannot be called to account: *A dictator is an irresponsible ruler.* 2 without a sense of responsibility; untrustworthy; unreliable. *adj.*

ir re spon si bly (ir/i spon/sə blē), in an irresponsible manner. *adv.*

ir re triev a ble (ir/i trē/və bəl), that cannot be retrieved or recovered; impossible to recall or restore to its former condition. *adj.*

ir re triev a bly (ir/i trē/və blē), in an irretrievable manner. *adv.*

ir rev er ence (i rev/ər əns), 1 lack of reverence; disrespect. 2 an act showing irreverence. *n.*

ir rev er ent (i rev/ər ənt), not reverent; disrespectful. *adj.* —**ir rev′er ent ly,** *adv.*

ir re vers i ble (ir/i vėr′sə bəl), 1 not capable of being turned the other way. 2 unable to be changed or repealed; unalterable. *adj.*

ir re vers i bly (ir/i vėr′sə blē), in an irreversible manner. *adv.*

ir rev o ca ble (i rev′ə bəl), 1 not able to be revoked; final: *Nothing could change his irrevocable decision to leave.* 2 impossible to call or bring back: *Yesterday belongs to the irrevocable past. adj.*

ir rev o ca bly (i rev′ə kə blē), in an irrevocable manner. *adv.*

ir ri gate (ir′ə gāt), 1 supply (land) with water by using ditches, by sprinkling, etc.: *After a desert is irrigated, crops will grow there.* 2 supply some part of the body with a continuous flow of some liquid: *The doctor showed her how to irrigate her nose and throat with warm water. v.,* **ir ri gat ed, ir ri gating.**

ir ri ga tion (ir′ə gā′shən), a supplying of land with water from ditches, sprinklers, etc.; irrigating: *Irrigation is needed to make crops grow in dry regions. n.*

ir ri ta bil i ty (ir′ə tə bil′ə tē), 1 a being irritable; impatience. 2 (in biology) the property that living plant or animal tissue has of responding to a stimulus. *n., pl.* **ir ri ta bil i ties.**

ir ri ta ble (ir′ə tə bəl), 1 easily made angry; impatient: *When the rain spoiled her plans, she was irritable for the rest of the day.* 2 more sensitive than is natural or normal: *A baby's skin is often quite irritable.* 3 (in biology) able to respond to stimuli. *adj.* —**ir′ri ta bleness,** *n.*

ir ri ta bly (ir′ə tə blē), in an irritable manner. *adv.*

ir ri tant (ir′ə tənt), 1 thing that causes irritation: *Chlorine in swimming pools can be an irritant to the eyes.* 2 causing irritation. 1 *n.,* 2 *adj.*

ir ri tate (ir′ə tāt), 1 make impatient or angry; annoy; provoke; vex: *It irritates me that you are always borrowing things. Flies irritate horses.* 2 make unnaturally sensitive or sore: *Sunburn irritates the skin.* 3 (in biology) stimulate (an organ, muscle, tissue, etc.) to perform its characteristic action or function: *A muscle contracts when it is irritated by an electric shock. v.,* **ir ri tat ed, ir ri tat ing.**

ir ri ta tion (ir′ə tā′shən), 1 act or process of irritating; annoyance; vexation. 2 irritated condition: *Irritation of his nose made him sneeze. n.*

ir rup tion (i rup′shən), a breaking or bursting in; violent invasion: *The irruption of barbarians was one*

cause of the downfall of the Roman Empire. *n.*

Ir ving (ėr′ving), **Washington,** 1783-1859, American writer, author of *Rip Van Winkle. n.*

is (iz), form of the verb **be** used with *he, she, it* or any singular noun to indicate the present tense. *The earth is round. He is at school. Flour is sold by the pound. v.*

as is, as it is now; in its present condition.

I saac (ī′zək), (in the Bible) the son of Abraham and Sarah, and father of Jacob and Esau. *n.*

Is a bel la I (iz′ə bel′ə), 1451-1504, queen of Castile. She and her husband Ferdinand V were patrons of Columbus.

I sai ah (ī zā′ə), 1 Hebrew prophet of the late 700's B.C. 2 book of the Old Testament containing his prophecies. *n.*

Is car i ot (i skar′ē ət), 1 surname of Judas, the disciple who betrayed Jesus for money. 2 a traitor. *n.*

-ish, *suffix added to adjectives or nouns to form adjectives.* 1 somewhat ____: *Sweetish = somewhat sweet.* 2 like a ____: *Childish = like a child.* 3 like that of a ____: *Girlish = like that of a girl.* 4 of or having to do with ____: *English = of or having to do with England.* [Old English *-isc*]

Ish ma el (ish′mē əl), 1 (in the Bible) the son of Abraham and Sarah's maid, driven into the desert by Sarah. 2 an outcast. *n.*

i sin glass (ī′zn glas′), 1 kind of gelatin obtained from certain fishes, used for making glue, clearing liquors, etc. 2 mica. *n.*

I sis (ī′sis), the chief goddess of ancient Egypt, sister and wife of Osiris. She represented fertility. *n.*

Is lam (is′ləm *or* i släm′), 1 the Moslem religion, based on the teachings of Mohammed as they appear in the Koran. 2 Moslems as a group. 3 the countries under Moslem rule. *n.*

Is lam a bad (iz lä′mə bad), capital of Pakistan, in the northeast part. *n.*

Is lam ic (i slam′ik *or* i släm′ik), Moslem. *adj.*

is land (ī′lənd), 1 body of land smaller than a continent and completely surrounded by water: *Cuba is a large island. To reach the island you go by boat.* 2 something that suggests a body of land surrounded by water. Platforms in the middle of busy streets are called **safety islands.** *n.* —**is′land like′,** *adj.*

is land er (ī′lən dər), person born or living on an island. *n.*

isle (īl), 1 a small island. 2 island. *n.*

Isle of Man, small island in the Irish

isolationist

hat, āge, fär; let, ēqual, tėrm;
it, īce; hot, ōpen, ôrder;
oil, out; cup, pùt, rüle; ch, child;
ng, long; sh, she; th, thin;
ŦH, then; zh, measure;

ə represents *a* in about,
e in taken, *i* in pencil,
o in lemon, *u* in circus.

Sea, west of N England; one of the British Isles.

is let (ī′lit), a small island. *n.*

-ism, *suffix forming nouns.* 1 *(added to verbs)* act or practice of ____ing: *Baptism = act or practice of baptizing.* 2 *(added to nouns or adjectives)* quality or condition of being a ____: *Heroism = quality of being a hero. Paganism = condition of being a pagan.* 3 *(added to nouns or adjectives)* illustration or instance of being ____: *Witticism = instance of being witty.* 4 *(added to nouns)* an unhealthy condition caused by ____: *Alcoholism = an unhealthy condition caused by alcohol.* [from Greek *-ismos*]

is n't (iz′nt), is not.

isobars—with pressure given in inches at the bottom and millibars at the top

i so bar (ī′sə bär), line on a weather map connecting places having the same average atmospheric pressure. Isobars show the distribution of atmospheric pressure at a particular time, and are used in making forecasts of the weather. *n.*

i so late (ī′sə lāt), set apart; separate from others; keep alone: *People with contagious diseases should be isolated. v.,* **i so lat ed, i so lat ing.**

i so la tion (ī′sə lā′shən), an isolating or a being isolated. *n.*

i so la tion ism (ī′sə lā′shə niz′əm), principles or policy of avoiding political and economic relations with other nations. *n.*

i so la tion ist (ī′sə lā′shə nist), person who believes in the principles or policy of isolationism. *n.*

adj. adjective	*n.* noun
adv. adverb	*prep.* preposition
conj. conjunction	*pron.* pronoun
interj. interjection	*v.* verb
sing. singular	*pl.* plural

isosceles triangles

i sos ce les (ī sos′ə lēz′), (of a triangle) having two sides equal. *adj.*

i so therm (ī′sə thėrm′), line on a weather map connecting places having the same average temperature. *n.*

isotherms

i so tope (ī′sə tōp), any of two or more forms of a chemical element that have the same chemical properties and the same atomic number (number of protons), but different atomic weights (number of neutrons). Chlorine, whose atomic weight is 35.5, is a formation of two isotopes, one having an atomic weight of 37, the other, 35. Hydrogen and heavy hydrogen are isotopes. *n.*

Is ra el (iz′rē əl), 1 country in SW Asia, on the Mediterranean, including the major part of Palestine. It was declared a Jewish state May 14, 1948. *Capital:* Jerusalem. 2 ancient Jewish kingdom in N Palestine. See **Judah** for map. 3 (in the Bible) a name given to Jacob after he had wrestled with the angel. 4 name given to his descendants; the Jews; the Hebrews. *n.*

Is rae li (iz rā′lē), 1 person born or living in Israel. 2 of or having to do with Israel. 1 *n., pl.* **Is rae lis;** 2 *adj.*

Is ra el ite (iz′rē ə līt), Jew; Hebrew; descendant of Israel. *n.*

is su ance (ish′ü əns), an issuing; issue. *n.*

is sue (ish′ü), 1 send out; put forth: *This magazine is issued every week. The government issues money and stamps.* 2 something sent out: *The last issue of our weekly paper consisted of 1000 copies.* 3 a sending out; a putting forth: *The government controls the issue of stamps.* 4 come out; go out; pro-

ceed: *Smoke issues from the chimney.* 5 a coming forth; a flowing out; a discharge: *the issue of blood from a deep flesh wound.* 6 way out; outlet; exit. 7 result; outcome: *The issue of the battle was in doubt.* 8 point to be debated; problem: *Peace is one of the main issues of this political campaign.* 9 child or children; offspring. 1,4 *v.,* **is sued, is su ing;** 2,3,5-9 *n.*

at issue, 1 in question; to be considered or decided. 2 in disagreement: *The children were at issue as to who would captain the team.*

take issue, disagree: *I must take issue with you on that point.*

-ist, *suffix forming nouns chiefly from other nouns.* 1 person who does or makes: *Tourist = a person who tours. Theorist = a person who deals with theories.* 2 an expert in a science: *Botanist = an expert in botany.* 3 person who plays a musical instrument: *Organist = a person who plays the organ.* 4 person engaged in or working with: *Journalist = a person engaged in journalism. Machinist = a person working with machines.* 5 person who believes in: *Socialist = a person who believes in socialism.* [from Greek *-istes*]

Is tan bul (is′tän bül′), city in European Turkey, on the Bosporus. Formerly called **Constantinople.** *n.*

isth mus (is′məs), a narrow strip of land with water on both sides, connecting two larger bodies of land: *The Isthmus of Panama connects North America and South America. n., pl.* **isth mus es.**

isthmus
Isthmus
of Panama

it (it), 1 the thing, part, animal, or person spoken about: *Here is your paper; read it. Look at it carefully. He said, "It is I. What is it you want?" It snows in winter. It is now my turn.* 2 (in games) the player who must catch, find, guess, etc. 1 *pron., pl.* **they;** 2 *n.*

I tal ian (i tal′yən), 1 of Italy, its people, or their language. 2 person born or living in Italy. 3 language of Italy. 1 *adj.,* 2,3 *n.*

i tal ic (i tal′ik *or* ī tal′ik), 1 of or in type whose letters slant to the right: *These words are in italic type.* 2 **italics,** *pl.* type whose letters slant to the right. 1 *adj.,* 2 *n.* [from its introduction by an *Italian* printer]

i tal i cize (i tal′ə sīz), 1 print in type in which the letters slant to the right: *This*

sentence is italicized. 2 underline with a single line to indicate italics. We italicize expressions which we wish to distinguish or emphasize. 3 use italics. *v.,* **i tal i cized, i tal i ciz ing.**

It a ly (it′l ē), country in S Europe on the Mediterranean. Sicily and Sardinia are parts of Italy. *Capital:* Rome. *n.*

itch (ich), 1 a ticklish, prickling feeling in the skin that makes one want to scratch. 2 disease causing this feeling. 3 cause this feeling: *Mosquito bites itch.* 4 feel this way in the skin: *My nose itches.* 5 a restless, uneasy feeling, longing, or desire for anything: *Don't you ever have an itch to get away and explore?* 6 have an uneasy desire: *I itched to find out their secret.* 1,2,5 *n., pl.* **itch es;** 3,4,6 *v.*

itch i ness (ich′ē nis), a being itchy. *n.*

itch y (ich′ē), itching; like the itch. *adj.,* **itch i er, itch i est.**

i tem (ī′təm), 1 a separate thing or article: *The list had twelve items on it.* 2 piece of news; bit of information: *There were several interesting items in today's paper. n.*

i tem ize (ī′tə mīz), give each item of; list by items: *The storekeeper itemized the bill to show each article and its cost. v.,* **i tem ized, i tem iz ing.**

it e rate (it′ə rāt′), say again or repeatedly; repeat. *v.,* **it e rat ed, it e rat ing.**

it e ra tion (it′ə rā′shən), repetition. *n.*

Ith a ca (ith′ə kə), small island west of Greece, the legendary home of Ulysses. *n.*

i tin er ant (ī tin′ər ənt), 1 traveling from place to place. 2 person who travels from place to place. 1 *adj.,* 2 *n.*

i tin er ar y (ī tin′ə rer′ē), 1 route of travel; plan of travel. 2 record of travel. 3 guidebook for travelers. *n., pl.* **i tin er ar ies.**

it'll (it′l), 1 it will. 2 it shall.

its (its), of it; belonging to it: *The dog wagged its tail. adj.*

it's (its), 1 it is: *It's my turn.* 2 it has: *It's been a beautiful day.*

it self (it self′), 1 form of *it* used to make a statement stronger: *The land itself is worth the money, without the house.* 2 form used instead of *it* in cases like: *The horse tripped and hurt itself. The dog saw itself in the mirror.* 3 its normal or usual self: *After a few minor repairs my car was itself again. pron.*

-ity, *suffix added to adjectives to form nouns.* quality, condition, or fact of being _____: *Sincerity = quality or condition of being sincere.* Also, **-ty.** [from French before 1400 *-ité,* from Latin *-itatem*]

I've (īv), I have.

i vied (ī′vēd), covered or overgrown with ivy. *adj.*

i vor y (ī′vər ē), **1** a hard, white substance making up the tusks of elephants, walruses, etc. Ivory is used for piano keys, billiard balls, combs, ornaments, etc. **2** substance like ivory. **3** made of ivory. **4** of or like ivory. **5** a creamy white. **6** creamy-white. **1,2,5** *n., pl.* **i vor ies; 3,4,6** *adj.*

Ivory Coast, country in W Africa, on the Atlantic. *Capital:* Abidjan.

i vy (ī′vē), **1** a climbing plant with smooth, shiny, evergreen leaves, also called **English ivy. 2** any of various other climbing plants, such as poison ivy. *n., pl.* **i vies.**

-ize, *suffix added to adjectives and nouns to form verbs.* **1** make _____: *Legalize = make legal. Apologize = make an apology.* **2** become _____: *Crystallize = become crystal.* **3** engage in or use _____: *Criticize = engage in criticism.* **4** treat or combine with _____: *Oxidize = combine with oxygen.* [from French *-iser* or Latin *-izare* or Greek *-izein*]

Iz mir (iz′mir *or* iz mir′), seaport in W Turkey, on the Aegean Sea. Formerly called **Smyrna.** *n.*

hat, āge, fär; let, ēqual, tėrm;
it, īce; hot, ōpen, ôrder;
oil, out; cup, pùt, rüle; ch, child;
ng, long; sh, she; th, thin;
ŦH, then; zh, measure;

ə represents *a* in about,
e in taken, *i* in pencil,
o in lemon, *u* in circus.

J j

J or **j** (jā), the tenth letter of the alphabet. *n., pl.* **J's** or **j's.**

jab (jab), **1** thrust with something pointed; poke: *He jabbed his fork into the potato.* **2** a thrust with something pointed; poke: *She gave him a jab with her elbow.* **3** in boxing: **a** a blow in which the arm is extended straight from the shoulder. **b** to hit with a jab. **1,3b** *v.*, **jabbed, jab bing; 2,3a** *n.*

jab ber (jab′ər), **1** talk very fast in a confused, senseless way; chatter. **2** very fast, confused, or senseless talk; chatter. **1** *v.*, **2** *n.*

ja bot (zha bō′ *or* zhab′ō), ruffle or frill of lace, worn at the throat or down the front of a shirt, dress, or blouse. *n.* [from French]

jack (def. 1) for automobile

jack (jak), **1** a portable tool or machine for lifting or pushing up heavy weights a short distance: *He raised the car off the ground with a jack to change the flat tire.* **2** lift or push up with a jack: *jack up a car.* **3** a playing card with a picture of a servant or soldier on it; knave. **4** pebble or small six-pointed metal piece used in the game of jacks; jackstone. **5 jacks**, *pl.* a children's game played with jacks; jackstones. Each player bounces the ball and picks up the jacks in between bounces. **6** a small flag used on a ship to show nationality or as a signal. **7** device for turning a spit in roasting meat. **8** a male donkey. **9** man or fellow. **10** an electrical device which can receive a plug to make a connection in a circuit. **1,3-10** *n.*, **2** *v.*

jack up, INFORMAL. raise (prices, wages, etc.): *Supermarkets have jacked up prices in recent months.*

jack al (jak′əl *or* jak′ôl), a wild dog of Asia, Africa, and eastern Europe, about as big as a fox. Jackals hunt in packs at

jackal
about 15 in. high at the shoulder

night and feed on small animals and carrion left by large animals. They were formerly supposed to hunt prey for the lion and eat what the lion left. *n.*

jack a napes (jak′ə nāps), an impertinent, forward person. *n.*

jack ass (jak′as′), **1** a male donkey. **2** a very stupid or foolish person. *n., pl.* **jack ass es.**

jack boot (jak′büt′), a heavy military boot reaching above the knee. *n.*

jack daw (jak′dô′), a small crow of Europe and North Africa; daw. *n.*

jack et (jak′it), **1** a short coat. **2** an outer covering. The paper cover for a book, the casing around a steam pipe, and the skin of a potato are jackets. *n.*

Jack Frost, frost or freezing weather thought of as a person.

jack-in-the-box (jak′in ฮฮə boks′), toy consisting of a figure that springs up from a box when the lid is opened. *n., pl.* **jack-in-the-box es.**

jack-in-the-pul pit (jak′in ฮฮə pul′pit), plant with a greenish, petallike sheath arched over the flower stalk. It is a kind of arum. *n., pl.* **jack-in-the-pul pits.**

jack knife (jak′nīf′), **1** a large, strong pocketknife. **2** kind of dive in which the diver touches his feet with his hands in midair, and straightens out before entering the water. **3** double up like a jackknife. **1,2** *n., pl.* **jack knives** (jak′nīvz′); **3** *v.*, **jack knifed, jack knif ing.**

jack of all trades, person who can do many different kinds of work fairly well.

jack-o'-lan tern (jak′ə lan′tərn), pumpkin hollowed out and cut to look like a face, used as a lantern at Halloween. *n.*

jack pot (jak′pot′), stakes that accumulate in a game until some player wins. *n.*

hit the jackpot, 1 get the big prize. **2** have a stroke of very good luck.

jack rabbit, a large hare of western North America, having very long hind legs and long ears.

jack screw (jak′skrü′), tool or machine for lifting heavy weights, operated by a screw. *n.*

Jack son (jak′sən), **1 Andrew,** 1767-1845, the seventh president of the United States, from 1829 to 1837. He was also a general in the War of 1812. **2 Thomas Jonathan,** 1824-1863, Confederate general. He was called "Stonewall" Jackson. **3** capital of Mississippi, in the central part. *n.*

Jack son ville (jak′sən vil), city in NE Florida. *n.*

jack stone (jak′stōn′), **1** piece used in the game of jacks; jack. **2 jack stones,** *pl.* the game of jacks. *n.*

jack straw (jak′strô′), **1** straw, strip of wood, bone, etc., used in the game of jackstraws. **2 jackstraws,** *pl.* a children's game played with these. A set of jackstraws is thrown down in a pile and each player tries to pick them up one at a time without moving any of the others. *n.*

Ja cob (jā′kəb), (in the Bible) the son of Isaac, and younger twin brother of Esau. The 12 tribes of Israel traced their descent from Jacob's 12 sons. *n.*

jade (jād), **1** a hard stone used for jewelry and ornaments. Most jade is green, but some is whitish. **2** a light green. **3** light-green. **1,2** *n.*, **3** *adj.*

jad ed (jā′did), worn out; tired; weary. *adj.*

jag (jag), **1** a sharp point sticking out: *a jag of rock.* **2** cut or tear unevenly: *jag cloth.* **3** make notches in. **1** *n.*, **2,3** *v.*, **jagged, jag ging.**

jag ged (jag′id), with sharp points sticking out: *We cut our bare feet on the jagged rocks.* *adj.* —**jag′ged ly,** *adv.*

jaguar—6 to 8 ft. long including tail

jag uar (jag′wär), a fierce animal much like a leopard, but more heavily built. It lives in forests in tropical America. *n.*

jail (jāl), **1** prison, especially one for persons awaiting trial or being punished for some small offense. **2** put in jail; keep in jail. **1** *n.*, **2** *v.*

jail break (jāl′brāk′), an escape from jail or prison. *n.*

jail er or **jail or** (jā′lər), keeper of a jail. *n.*

Ja kar ta (jə kär′tə), Djakarta. *n.*

ja lop y (jə lop′ē), INFORMAL. an old automobile or airplane in bad condition. *n., pl.* **ja lop ies.**

jal ou sie (jal′ə sē), shade or shutter made of horizontal slats which may be tilted to let in light and air but keep out sun and rain. *n.*

jam¹ (jam), **1** press or squeeze tightly between two surfaces: *The ship was jammed between two rocks.* **2** crush by squeezing; bruise: *I jammed my fingers in the door.* **3** press or squeeze (things or persons) tightly together: *A crowd jammed into the bus. They jammed us all into one bus.* **4** mass of people or things crowded together so that they cannot move freely: *She was delayed by the traffic jam.* **5** fill or block up (the way, etc.) by crowding: *The river was jammed with logs.* **6** stick or catch so that it cannot be worked: *The window has jammed; I can't open it.* **7** cause to stick or catch so that it cannot be worked: *The key broke off and jammed the lock.* **8** push or thrust (a thing) hard (into a place); shove: *jam one more book into the bookcase.* **9** INFORMAL. a difficulty or tight spot: *She was in a jam.* **10** make (radio signals, etc.) unintelligible by sending out others of approximately the same frequency. 1-3,5-8,10 *v.,* **jammed, jam ming;** 4,9 *n.* [perhaps an imitation of the sound of squeezing]

jam² (jam), preserve made by boiling fruit with sugar until thick: *raspberry jam. n.* [perhaps special use of *jam¹*]

Ja mai ca (jə mā′kə), island country in the West Indies, south of Cuba, a member of the Commonwealth of Nations. *Capital:* Kingston. *n.* —**Ja mai′can,** *adj., n.*

jamb (jam), an upright piece forming the side of a doorway, window, or fireplace. *n.*

jam bo ree (jam′bə rē′), **1** a large rally or gathering of Boy Scouts. **2** INFORMAL. a noisy party. *n.*

James (jāmz), **1** in the Bible: **a** one of the apostles of Christ, sometimes called **James the Greater. b** another of the twelve apostles, sometimes called **James the Less. 2** book of the New Testament. **3 Henry,** 1843-1916, American novelist who lived in England. **4 William,** 1842-1910, American psychologist and philosopher, brother of Henry James. *n.*

James I, 1566-1625, the first Stuart king of England, from 1603 to 1625. The King James version of the Bible was written during his reign.

James town (jāmz′toun), restored village in SE Virginia. The first successful English settlement in North America was made there in 1607. *n.*

Jan., January.

jan gle (jang′gəl), **1** sound harshly; make a loud, clashing noise: *The pots and pans jangled in the kitchen.* **2** cause to make a harsh, clashing sound: *The boys jangled cowbells.* **3** a harsh sound; clashing noise or ring: *the jangle of the telephone.* **4** a quarrel; dispute. **5** talk

or argue in an angry or quarrelsome manner. 1,2,5 *v.,* **jan gled, jan gling;** 3,4 *n.*

jan i tor (jan′ə tər), person hired to take care of a building or offices; caretaker. *n.*

Jan u ar y (jan′yü er′ē), the first month of the year. It has 31 days. *n.* [from *Janus*]

Ja nus (jā′nəs), (in Roman myths) the god of gates and doors, and of beginnings and endings, represented with two faces, one looking forward and the other looking backward. *n.*

ja pan (jə pan′), **1** a hard, glossy varnish. Black japan is used on wood or metal. **2** put japan on. **3** articles varnished and ornamented in the Japanese manner. 1,3 *n.,* 2 *v.,* **ja panned, japan ning.** [from *Japan*]

Ja pan (jə pan′), **1** country made up of four large islands and many smaller ones in the W Pacific, east of the Asian mainland. The Japanese name for Japan is **Nippon.** *Capital:* Tokyo. **2 Sea of,** sea between Japan and the Asian mainland. *n.*

Jap a nese (jap′ə nēz′), **1** of Japan, its people, or their language: *Japanese art, Japanese writings, Japanese customs.* **2** person born or living in Japan. **3** language of Japan. 1 *adj.,* 2,3 *n., pl.* **Jap a nese.** Also, **Nipponese.**

Japanese beetle, a small, green-and-brown beetle that eats fruits, leaves, and grasses. It causes much damage to crops in the United States.

jar¹ (jär), **1** a deep container made of glass, earthenware, or stone, with a wide mouth. **2** amount that it holds. *n.* [from French of the 1500's *jarre* earthen vessel, from Arabic *jarrah*]

jar² (jär), **1** cause to shake or rattle; vibrate: *Your heavy footsteps jar my table.* **2** a shake; rattle. **3** make a harsh, grating noise. **4** a harsh, grating noise. **5** have a harsh, unpleasant effect on; send a shock through (the ears, nerves, feelings, etc.): *The children's screams jarred my nerves.* **6** a slight shock to the ears, nerves, feelings, etc. **7** clash; quarrel: *We did not get on well together; our opinions always jarred.* **8** a clash; quarrel. 1,3,5,7 *v.,* **jarred, jar ring;** 2,4,6,8 *n.* [probably an imitation of the sound of rattling]

jar gon (jär′gən), **1** confused, meaningless talk or writing. **2** language that is not understood: *the jargon of foreigners.* **3** talk containing a mixture of languages. **4** language of a special group, profession, etc. Doctors, actors, and sailors have jargons. *n.*

jas mine (jas′mən), shrub or vine with clusters of fragrant flowers. There are yellow, white, and red jasmines. *n.* Also, **jessamine.**

hat, āge, fär; let, ēqual, tèrm;
it, īce; hot, ōpen, ôrder;
oil, out; cup, pùt, rüle; ch, child;
ng, long; sh, she; th, thin;
ŦH, then; zh, measure;

ə represents *a* in about,
e in taken, *i* in pencil,
o in lemon, *u* in circus.

Ja son (jā′sn), (in Greek legends) the Greek hero who led the expedition of the Argonauts and secured the Golden Fleece. *n.*

jas per (jas′pər), an opaque, colored quartz, usually red, yellow, or brown. *n.*

jaun dice (jôn′dis), **1** disease that causes yellowness of the skin, eyes, and body fluids. It is caused by too much bile pigment in the blood. **2** cause jaundice in. **3** a disturbed or unnaturally sour mental outlook due to envy, discontent, jealousy, etc. **4** prejudice the mind and judgment of, by envy, discontent, jealousy, etc.; sour the temper of. 1,3 *n.,* 2,4 *v.,* **jaun diced, jaun dicing.**

jaunt (jônt), **1** a short journey or excursion, especially for pleasure: *a jaunt to the seashore.* **2** take such a trip. 1 *n.,* 2 *v.*

jaun ti ly (jôn′tl ē), in an easy, lively manner; smartly. *adv.*

jaun ti ness (jôn′tē nis), quality of being jaunty; airiness; sprightliness. *n.*

jaun ty (jôn′tē), **1** easy and lively; sprightly: *The happy children walked with jaunty steps.* **2** smart; stylish: *She wore a jaunty little hat. adj.,* **jaun ti er, jaun ti est.**

Ja va (jä′və *or* jav′ə), **1** large island southeast of Sumatra. It is the most important island of Indonesia. **2** kind of coffee obtained from Java and nearby islands. **3** SLANG. coffee. *n.*

Java man, a very early form of man, known from fossil remains found in Java.

Jav a nese (jav′ə nēz′), **1** of Java, its people, or their language. **2** person born or living in Java. **3** language of Java. 1 *adj.,* 2,3 *n., pl.* **Jav a nese.**

jave lin (jav′lən), **1** a light spear thrown by hand. **2** a wooden or metal spear, thrown for distance in track and field contests. *n.*

jaw (jô), **1** the lower part of the face. **2** the upper or lower bone or set of bones, that together form the framework of the mouth. The lower jaw is movable. **3** Usually, **jaws,** *pl.* mouth with its jawbones and teeth. **4 jaws,** *pl.*

adj. adjective	*n.* noun
adv. adverb	*prep.* preposition
conj. conjunction	*pron.* pronoun
interj. interjection	*v.* verb
sing. singular	*pl.* plural

a a narrow entrance to a valley, mountain pass, channel, etc. **b** the parts in a tool or machine that grip and hold. A vise has jaws. **5** SLANG. go on talking at great length, in a boring way. **6** SLANG. find fault; scold. 1-4 *n.*, 5,6 *v.*

jaw bone (jô′bōn′), one of the bones in which the teeth are set, especially the lower jaw. *n.*

jay (jā), any of various crested birds of Europe and North America which are related to the crow. The blue jay is one kind of jay. *n.*

Jay (jā), **John,** 1745-1829, first chief justice of the United States Supreme Court, from 1789 to 1795. *n.*

jay walk (jā′wôk′), INFORMAL. walk across a street without paying attention to traffic rules. *v.* —**jay′walk′er,** *n.*

jazz (jaz), **1** a popular kind of music in which the accents fall at unusual places. The musicians slide from tone to tone, introduce dissonances, independent tones, long-drawn wavering or wailing sounds, etc. Jazz is native to the United States. **2** of or like jazz: *a jazz band, jazz records.* **3** play jazz music or dance to jazz music. 1 *n.*, 2 *adj.*, 3 *v.*

jeal ous (jel′əs), **1** fearful that a person one loves may love or prefer someone else: *When my brother sees mother holding the new baby, he becomes jealous.* **2** full of envy; envious: *She is jealous of her sister's good grades.* **3** requiring complete loyalty or faithfulness: *"The Lord thy God is a jealous God."* **4** watchful in keeping or guarding something; careful: *Our city is jealous of its rights within the State.* **5** close; watchful; suspicious: *The dog was such a jealous guardian of the little girl that he would not let her cross the street.* *adj.* —**jeal′ous ly,** *adv.* —**jeal′ous ness,** *n.*

jeal ous y (jel′ə sē), dislike or fear of rivals; jealous condition or feeling; envy. *n.*, *pl.* **jeal ous ies.**

jean (jēn), **1** a strong, twilled cotton cloth, used for overalls, etc. **2** **jeans,** *pl.* overalls or trousers made of this cloth: *The cowboy wore faded jeans.* *n.*

Jeanne d'Arc (zhän′ därk′), FRENCH. Joan of Arc.

jeep (jēp), a small but powerful automobile in which power is transmitted to all four wheels, used for many purposes

by soldiers, farmers, builders, etc. It was originally designed for use by the United States Army. *n.*

jeer (jir), **1** make fun rudely or unkindly; mock; scoff: *Do not jeer at the mistakes or misfortunes of others.* **2** a mocking or insulting remark. 1 *v.*, 2 *n.* —**jeer′ing ly,** *adv.*

Jef fer son (jef′ər sən), **Thomas,** 1743-1826, American statesman, third president of the United States, from 1801 to 1809. He drafted the Declaration of Independence. *n.*

Jefferson City, capital of Missouri, in the central part.

Je ho vah (ji hō′və), one of the names of God in the Old Testament. *n.*

jell (jel), **1** become jelly; thicken or congeal. **2** INFORMAL. take definite form; become fixed: *Her hunch soon jelled into a plan.* **3** jelly. 1,2 *v.*, 3 *n.*

jel lied (jel′ēd), **1** turned into jelly. **2** spread with jelly. *adj.*

jel ly (jel′ē), **1** a food, liquid when hot, but somewhat firm and partly transparent when cold. Jelly can be made by boiling fruit juice and sugar together, or by cooking bones and meat in water, or by using some thickening agent like gelatin. **2** a jellylike substance. **3** become jelly or like jelly; thicken; congeal: *The strong soup jellied when it was chilled in the refrigerator.* 1,2 *n.*, *pl.* **jel lies;** 3 *v.*, **jel lied, jel ly ing.** —**jel′ly like′,** *adj.*

jel ly bean (jel′ē bēn′), a small candy made of jellied sugar, often shaped like a bean. *n.*

jel ly fish (jel′ē fish′), any of a group of invertebrate sea animals with a body formed of a mass of almost transparent jellylike tissue; medusa. Most jellyfish have long, trailing tentacles that bear stinging cells. *n.*, *pl.* **jel ly fish es** or **jel ly fish.**

Jen ner (jen′ər), **Edward,** 1749-1823, English physician who discovered vaccination. *n.*

jen net (jen′it), **1** a small Spanish horse. **2** a female donkey. *n.*

jen ny (jen′ē), **1** spinning jenny. **2** female of certain animals: *jenny wren.* *n.*, *pl.* **jen nies.**

jeop ar dize (jep′ər dīz), put in danger; risk; endanger; imperil: *The raging forest fire jeopardized many lives.* *v.*, **jeop ar dized, jeop ar diz ing.**

jeop ar dy (jep′ər dē), risk; danger; peril: *The woodman's life was in*

jeep

jeopardy as the tree suddenly fell. *n.*

jer bo a (jər bō′ə), a small, jumping, mouselike mammal of Asia and northern Africa. *n.*, *pl.* **jer bo as.**

jerboa
15 in. long
including tail

Jer e mi ah (jer′ə mī′ə), **1** born 650 B.C.?, Hebrew prophet. **2** book of the Old Testament containing his prophecies. *n.*

Jer i cho (jer′ə kō), city in ancient Palestine. According to the Bible, its walls fell down at the noise made by the trumpets of Joshua's attacking army. *n.*

jerk[1] (jėrk), **1** a sudden, sharp pull, twist, or start: *The old car started with a jerk.* **2** a pull or twist of the muscles that one cannot control; twitch. **3** pull or twist suddenly: *If the water is unexpectedly hot, you jerk your hand out.* **4** move with a jerk: *The old wagon jerked along.* **5** SLANG. a stupid or simple-minded person. 1,2,5 *n.*, 3,4 *v.* [probably an imitation of the sound of jerking]

jerk[2] (jėrk), preserve (meat) by cutting into long thin slices and drying in the sun. The early settlers in America used to jerk beef. *v.* [from American Spanish *charquear,* from *charqui* jerked meat]

jerk i ly (jėr′kə lē), in a jerky manner; by fits and starts. *adv.*

jerkin
leather jerkin worn
by men in the 1500's
and 1600's

jer kin (jėr′kən), a short, close-fitting coat or jacket without sleeves. *n.*

jerk i ness (jėr′kē nis), quality or condition of being jerky. *n.*

jerk y[1] (jėr′kē), with sudden starts and stops; with jerks. *adj.*, **jerk i er, jerk i est.** [*jerk*[1] + *-y*[1]]

jerk y[2] (jėr′kē), strips of dried meat, usually beef. *n.* [from American Spanish *charqui* jerked meat]

Je rome (jə rōm′), **Saint,** A.D. 340?-420, monk and scholar, author of the Latin translation of the Bible known as the Vulgate. *n.*

jer sey (jėr′zē), **1** a machine-knitted cloth with a tight weave. **2** a close-fitting, pullover sweater made of this cloth. *n., pl.* **jer seys.** [from the island of *Jersey*]

Jer sey (jėr′zē), **1** one of the Channel Islands. **2** one of a breed of small, usually fawn-colored cattle that came from this island. Jerseys give very rich milk. *n., pl.* **Jer seys** for 2.

Jersey City, seaport in NE New Jersey, across the Hudson River from New York City.

Je ru sa lem (jə rü′sə ləm), capital of Israel, in the E part. It is a holy city to Jews, Christians, and Moslems. *n.*

jes sa mine (jes′ə mən), jasmine. *n.*

jest (jest), **1** a joke. **2** to joke. **3** poke fun; make fun: *He jested at other people's ideas.* **4** act of poking fun at; mockery. **5** thing to be laughed at. 1,4,5 *n.,* 2,3 *v.*

in jest, in fun; not seriously: *His words were spoken in jest.*

jest er (jes′tər), person who jests. In the Middle Ages, kings and lords often had jesters to amuse them. *n.*

Jes u it (jezh′ü it *or* jez′yü it), member of the Society of Jesus, a Roman Catholic religious order of men founded by Saint Ignatius of Loyola in 1534. Some of the first explorers of North America were Jesuits. *n.*

Je sus (jē′zəs), 6 B.C.?-A.D. 29?, founder of the Christian religion. The name means "God is salvation." *n.*

Jesus Christ, Jesus.

jet¹ (jet), **1** stream of water, steam, gas, or any liquid, sent with force, especially from a small opening: *A fountain sends up a jet of water.* **2** spout or nozzle for sending out a jet. **3** shoot forth in a jet or forceful stream; gush out: *Water jetted from the broken pipe.* **4** jet plane. 1,2,4 *n.,* 3 *v.,* **jet ted, jet ting.** [from French of the 1400's *giet* a throwing, from Latin *jectus*]

jet² (jet), **1** a hard, black kind of coal, glossy when polished, used for making beads, buttons, and ornaments. **2** made of jet. **3** a deep, glossy black. **4** deep, glossy black: *jet hair.* 1,3 *n.,* 2,4 *adj.* [from French of the 1300's *jaiet,* from Greek *gagates* of Gagas, a town in Asia Minor]

jet engine, engine using jet propulsion.

jet pilot, person who operates a jet plane.

jet plane, airplane that is driven by jet propulsion; jet. See **airplane** for picture.

jet port (jet′pôrt′), airport designed for use by jet planes. *n.*

jet-pro pelled (jet′prə peld′), driven by jet propulsion. *adj.*

jet propulsion, propulsion in one direction caused by a jet of air, gas, etc., forced in the opposite direction.

jet sam (jet′səm), goods which are

thrown overboard to lighten a ship in distress and often afterwards washed ashore. *n.*

jet stream, 1 current of air traveling at very high speed from west to east at altitudes of six to eight miles. The jet stream is often used by airplane pilots to gain extra speed when traveling in an eastward direction. **2** the exhaust from a jet engine.

jet ti son (jet′ə sən), **1** throw (goods) overboard to lighten a ship in distress. **2** act of throwing goods overboard to lighten a ship in distress. **3** throw away; discard. 1,3 *v.,* 2 *n.*

jet ty (jet′ē), **1** structure of stones or wooden piles projecting out from the shore to break the force of a current or waves; breakwater. **2** a landing place; pier. *n., pl.* **jet ties.**

Jew (jü), **1** person descended from the Semitic people led by Moses, who settled in Palestine and now live in Israel and many other countries; Hebrew; Israelite. **2** person whose religion is Judaism. *n.*

jew el (jü′əl), **1** a precious stone; gem. **2** a valuable ornament to be worn, set with precious stones. **3** person or thing that is very precious. **4** gem or other hard material used as a bearing in a watch. **5** set or adorn with jewels or with things like jewels: *a jeweled comb, a sky jeweled with stars.* 1-4 *n.,* 5 *v.* —**jew′el like′,** *adj.*

jew el er (jü′ə lər), person who makes, sells, or repairs jewelry and watches. *n.*

jew el ry (jü′əl rē), **1** jewels and ornaments set with gems: *She keeps her jewelry in a small, locked box.* **2** ring, bracelet, necklace, or other ornament to be worn, usually set with imitation gems or made of silver, gold-colored metal, etc. *n.*

Jew ish (jü′ish), of the Jews; belonging to the Jews; characteristic of the Jews: *Jewish religious beliefs. adj.*

jet engine—Air is sucked in the front of the engine, compressed, and mixed with fuel. This mixture is burned in the burners, giving off gas which passes out in a powerful jet through the rear of the engine, producing thrust.

jews'-harp or **jew's-harp** (jüz′härp′), a simple musical instrument, held between the teeth and played by striking the free end of a flexible piece of metal with a finger. *n.*

Jez e bel (jez′ə bəl), **1** (in the Bible) the wicked wife of Ahab, king of Israel.

2 a shameless, immoral woman. *n.*

jib (jib), a triangular sail in front of the foremast. *n.*

jibe¹ (jīb), gibe. *v.,* **jibed, jib ing;** *n.* [a different form of *gibe*]

jibe² (jīb), INFORMAL. be in harmony; agree: *Our opinions jibe; we both have the same idea.* *v.,* **jibed, jib ing.** [origin uncertain]

jibe³ (jīb), **1** shift (a sail) from one side to the other when sailing before the wind. **2** shift itself in this way: *Be careful or your mainsail will jibe.* **3** change the course of a ship so that the sails shift in this way. *v.,* **jibed, jib ing.** [perhaps from Dutch *gijben*]

jif fy (jif′ē), INFORMAL. a very short time; moment: *He was on his bike in a jiffy, pedaling down the drive.* *n., pl.* **jif fies.**

jig¹ (jig), **1** a lively dance, often in triple time. **2** music for it. **3** dance a jig. 1,2 *n.,* 3 *v.,* **jigged, jig ging.** [from French of the 1500's *giguer* to dance]

the jig is up, it's all over; there is no more chance.

jig² (jig), **1** a fishing lure consisting of a fishhook or a set of fishhooks weighted with a piece of bright metal. It is bobbed up and down or pulled through the water. **2** any of various devices used to hold a piece of work and guide a drill, file, saw, etc., toward it. *n.* [origin uncertain]

jig gle (jig′əl), **1** shake or jerk slightly: *Stand still and don't jiggle the camera. Don't jiggle the desk when I'm trying to write.* **2** a slight shake; light jerk. 1 *v.,* **jig gled, jig gling;** 2 *n.*

jig saw (jig′sô′), saw with a narrow blade mounted in a frame and worked

adj.	adjective	n.	noun
adv.	adverb	prep.	preposition
conj.	conjunction	pron.	pronoun
interj.	interjection	v.	verb
sing.	singular	pl.	plural

jigsaw

with an up-and-down motion. It is used to cut curves or irregular lines. *n.*

jigsaw puzzle, picture sawed into irregular pieces that can be fitted together again.

jilt (jilt), cast off (a lover or sweetheart) after giving encouragement. *v.*

Jim Crow (jim′ krō′), discrimination against Negroes.

jim my (jim′ē), 1 a short crowbar used especially by burglars to force open windows, doors, or other things. 2 force open with a jimmy. 1 *n., pl.* **jim mies;** 2 *v.,* **jim mied, jim my ing.**

jim son weed (jim′sən wēd′), a tall, coarse, bad-smelling weed with white flowers and poisonous, narcotic leaves. *n.* [a different form of *Jamestown,* where it was first found]

jin gle (jing′gəl), 1 a sound like that of little bells, or of coins or keys striking together. 2 make a sound like bells, coins, or keys striking together: *The sleigh bells jingle as we ride.* 3 cause to jingle: *jingle one's money.* 4 verse or song that has repetition of similar sounds, or a catchy rhyme. "Higgledy, piggledy, my black hen" is a jingle. 5 be full of simple repetitions or catchy rhymes: *a jingling nursery rhyme.* 1,4 *n.,* 2,3,5 *v.,* **jin gled, jin gling.**

jin gly (jing′glē), like a jingle. *adj.*

jin go (jing′gō), person who favors an aggressive foreign policy that might lead to war with other nations. *n., pl.* **jin goes.**

jinn (jin), (in Moslem myths) spirits or spirit that can appear in human or animal form. Jinn do both good and evil. *The good jinn helped Aladdin when he rubbed a magic lamp. n. pl. or sing.*

jin ni (ji nē′), one of the jinn; genie. *n., pl.* **jinn.**

jin rick sha (jin rik′shə *or* jin-rik′shô), jinrikisha. *n., pl.* **jin rick-shas.**

jin rik i sha (jin rik′shə *or* jin-

rik′shô), a small, two-wheeled, hooded carriage pulled by one man, formerly used in the Orient. *n., pl.* **jin rik i-shas.** Also, **rickshaw** or **ricksha.**

jinx (jingks), INFORMAL. 1 person or thing that brings bad luck. 2 bring bad luck to. 1 *n., pl.* **jinx es;** 2 *v.*

jit ney (jit′nē), SLANG. automobile that carries passengers for a small fare. It usually travels along a regular route. *n., pl.* **jit neys.**

jit ter bug (jit′ər bug′), 1 a lively dance for couples, with rapid twirling movements and acrobatics. It was especially popular in the 1940's. 2 dance the jitterbug. 1 *n.,* 2 *v.,* **jit ter bugged, jit ter bug ging.**

jit ters (jit′ərz), INFORMAL. extreme nervousness. *n.pl.*

jit ter y (jit′ər ē), INFORMAL. nervous. *adj.*

jiu jit su (jü jit′sü), jujitsu. *n.*

Joan of Arc (jōn′ əv ärk′), 1412-1431, French heroine who led armies against the invading English and saved the city of Orléans. She was condemned as a witch and burned to death in 1431. In 1920 she was made a saint. Also FRENCH, **Jeanne d'Arc.**

job (job), 1 piece of work: *We had the job of painting the boat.* 2 a definite piece of work undertaken for a fixed price: *If you want your house painted, they will do the job for $500.* 3 done by the job; hired for a particular piece of work. 4 INFORMAL. work done for pay; employment: *My sister is hunting for a job. What kind of job does your father have?* 5 anything a person has to do: *I'm not going to wash the dishes; that's your job.* 1,2,4,5 *n.,* 3 *adj.*

Job (jōb), 1 (in the Bible) a very patient man who kept his faith in God in spite of many troubles. 2 book of the Old Testament that tells about him. *n.*

job ber (job′ər), person who buys goods from manufacturers in large quantities and sells them to retail dealers in small quantities. *n.*

job less (job′lis), having no job; unemployed. *adj.*

jock ey (jok′ē), 1 person whose occupation is riding horses in races. 2 ride (a horse) in a race. 3 trick; cheat: *Swindlers jockeyed him into buying some worthless land.* 4 maneuver so as to get advantage: *The crews were jockeying their boats to get into the best position for the race.* 1 *n., pl.* **jock eys;** 2-4 *v.*

jo cose (jō kōs′), jesting; humorous; joking. *adj.* —**jo cose′ly,** *adv.*

jo cos i ty (jō kos′ə tē), jocose quality. *n.*

joc u lar (jok′yə lər), funny; joking. *adj.* —**joc′u lar ly,** *adv.*

joc u lar i ty (jok′yə lar′ə tē), 1 jocu-

jinrikisha

lar quality. 2 jocular talk or behavior. 3 a jocular remark or act. *n., pl.* **joc u-lar i ties.**

joc und (jok′ənd), cheerful; merry; gay. *adj.*

jodh purs (jod′pərz), breeches for horseback riding, loose above the knees and close-fitting below the knees. *n.pl.*

jodhpurs

Jo el (jō′əl), 1 Hebrew prophet of the 400's B.C. 2 book of the Old Testament containing his prophecies. *n.*

jog[1] (jog), 1 shake with a push or jerk: *She jogged my elbow to get my attention.* 2 a shake, push, or nudge. 3 stir up with a hint or reminder: *He tied a string around his finger to jog his memory.* 4 a hint or reminder: *give one's memory a jog.* 5 move up or down with a jerk or a shaking motion: *The old horse jogged along, and jogged me on its back.* 6 walk or trot slowly: *I try to go jogging every day for exercise.* 7 a slow walk or trot. 1,3,5,6 *v.,* **jogged, jog-ging;** 2,4,7 *n.* [Middle English *joggen* to prick or spur]

jog[2] (jog), part that sticks out or in; unevenness in a line or surface: *We hid behind a jog in the wall. n.* [a different form of *jag*]

jog ger (jog′ər), one that jogs. *n.*

jog gle (jog′əl), 1 shake slightly. 2 a slight shake. 1 *v.,* **jog gled, jog gling;** 2 *n.*

Jo han nes burg (jō han′is bėrg′), city in NE South Africa, noted for its gold mines. *n.*

John (jon), 1 (in the Bible) one of Christ's twelve apostles. According to tradition, he wrote the Gospel of Saint John, the three epistles of John, and Revelation. 2 the fourth book of the New Testament. 3 John the Baptist. 4 **King John,** 1167?-1216, king of England from 1199 to 1216. He signed the Magna Charta in 1215. *n.*

John XXIII, 1881-1963, pope from 1958 to 1963.

John Bull, 1 a typical Englishman. 2 the English nation; Englishmen.

John Doe, a made-up name used in legal forms or proceedings for the name of an unknown person.

John Hancock, a person's signature. [from the signature of *John Hancock*, first signer of the Declaration of Independence]

john ny cake (jon′ē kāk′), corn bread in the form of a flat cake. *n.*

John son (jon′sən), 1 **Andrew,** 1808-1875, the 17th president of the United States, from 1865 to 1869. 2 **Lyndon Baines,** 1908-1973, the 36th president of the United States, from 1963 to 1969. 3 **Samuel,** 1709-1784, English author, dictionary maker, and literary leader. *n.*

John the Baptist, died A.D. 29?, Hebrew prophet who foretold the coming of Christ and baptized Him.

join (join), 1 bring or put together; connect, fasten, or clasp together: *join hands, join an island to the mainland by a bridge.* 2 come together; meet: *The two roads join here. The brook joins the river just below the mill.* 3 make or become one; combine; unite: *join in marriage. The two clubs joined forces during the campaign.* 4 take part with others: *join in a song.* 5 become a member of: *She joined a tennis club. My uncle has joined the army.* 6 come into the company of: *Go now, and I'll join you later.* 7 take or return to one's place in: *After a few days on shore the sailor joined his ship.* 8 be next to; adjoin: *Our farm joins theirs.* 9 point or line where things are joined. 1-8 *v.,* 9 *n.*

join er (joi′nər), 1 person or thing that joins. 2 carpenter who makes doors, windows, molding, and other inside woodwork. *n.*

joints (def. 3, above; def. 4, below)

joint (joint), 1 the place at which two things or parts are joined together. A pocket knife has a joint to fold the blade inside the handle. 2 connect by a joint or joints. 3 part in an animal where two bones join, allowing motion, and the way those bones are fitted together. 4 one of the parts of which a jointed thing is made up: *the middle joint of the finger.* 5 part of the stem of a plant from which a leaf or branch grows. 6 a large piece of meat for roasting, usually with a bone in it. 7 divide at the joints: *Please ask the butcher to joint the chicken.* 8 shared or done by two or more persons: *By our joint efforts we managed to push the car back on the road.* 9 joined together; sharing: *My sister and I are joint owners of this boat.* 10 INFORMAL. a cheap, low restaurant, bar, hotel, etc. 1,3-6,10 *n.,* 2,7 *v.,* 8,9 *adj.*

out of joint, 1 out of place at the joint: *The fall put my shoulder out of joint.* 2 out of order; in bad condition.

joint ly (joint′lē), together; as partners: *The two girls owned the boat jointly. adv.*

JOIST
STUD
FLOOR
JOIST

joist (joist), one of the parallel beams of timber or steel which support the boards of a floor or ceiling. *n.*

joke (jōk), 1 something said or done to make somebody laugh; remark that is clever and funny; something funny; jest: *Looking for the hat that was on my head was a good joke on me.* 2 make jokes; say or do something as a joke; jest. 3 person or thing laughed at. 4 laugh at; make fun of; tease. 1,3 *n.,* 2,4 *v.,* **joked, jok ing.**

no joke, a serious matter: *The loss of my bicycle was no joke.*

jok er (jō′kər), 1 person who jokes. 2 an extra playing card used in some games. 3 phrase or sentence hidden away in a legislative bill or contract to defeat its apparent purpose. *n.*

jok ing ly (jō′king lē), in a joking manner. *adv.*

Jo li et (jō′lē et), **Louis,** 1645-1700, French explorer of the Mississippi River, born in Canada. *n.*

jol li ness (jol′ē nis), jolly condition or quality. *n.*

jol li ty (jol′ə tē), fun; merriment. *n.*

jol ly (jol′ē), 1 full of fun; very cheerful; merry. 2 INFORMAL. pleasant or delightful. 3 INFORMAL. extremely; very: *a jolly good time.* 4 INFORMAL. flatter (a person) to make him feel good or agreeable: *Jolly him up a bit.* 1,2 *adj.,* **jol li er, jol li est;** 3 *adv.,* 4 *v.,* **jol lied, jol ly ing.**

Jolly Rog er (roj′ər), a pirates' black flag with a white skull and crossbones on it.

hat, āge, fär; let, ēqual, tėrm;
it, īce; hot, ōpen, ôrder;
oil, out; cup, pút, rüle; ch, child;
ng, long; sh, she; th, thin;
ᴛʜ, then; zh, measure;

ə represents *a* in about,
e in taken, *i* in pencil,
o in lemon, *u* in circus.

jolt (jōlt), 1 shake up; jar: *The wagon jolted us when the wheel went over a rock.* 2 a jar, shock, or jerk: *I put the brakes on suddenly and the car stopped with a jolt.* 3 move with a shock or jerk: *The car jolted across the rough ground.* 1,3 *v.,* 2 *n.*

Jo nah (jō′nə), 1 (in the Bible) a Hebrew prophet who was thrown overboard during a storm because he disobeyed God. He was swallowed by a large fish and later cast up on land. 2 book of the Old Testament that tells about him. 3 person whose presence is supposed to bring bad luck. *n.*

Jon a than (jon′ə thən), (in the Bible) a son of Saul, and devoted friend of David. *n.*

Jones (jōnz), **John Paul,** 1747-1792, American naval commander in the Revolutionary War. *n.*

jon gleur (jong′glər), a wandering minstrel or entertainer in the Middle Ages. *n.* [from French]

jon quil (jong′kwəl), 1 plant with yellow or white flowers and long slender leaves. It is a kind of narcissus that is much like a daffodil. 2 its flower. *n.*

Jor dan (jôrd′n), 1 river flowing from SW Syria through Israel and Jordan into the Dead Sea. 2 country in SW Asia, east of Israel. Part of Palestine was added to it in 1950. *Capital:* Amman. *n.*

Jo seph (jō′zəf), in the Bible: 1 the favorite son of Jacob. His jealous brothers sold him into slavery in Egypt, where he finally became governor. 2 the husband of Mary, mother of Jesus. *n.*

josh (josh), INFORMAL. make good-natured fun of; tease playfully; banter. *v.*

Josh u a (josh′ü ə), 1 (in the Bible) the successor of Moses, who led the Israelites into the Promised Land. 2 book of the Old Testament. *n.*

joss (jos), image of a Chinese god; Chinese idol. *n., pl.* **joss es.**

joss stick, a slender stick of dried, fragrant paste, burned as incense.

jos tle (jos′əl), 1 shove, push, or crowd against; elbow roughly: *We were jostled by the big crowd at the entrance to the*

jot

adj. adjective	*n.* noun
adv. adverb	*prep.* preposition
conj. conjunction	*pron.* pronoun
interj. interjection	*v.* verb
sing. singular	*pl.* plural

circus. 2 a jostling; push; knock. 1 *v.*, **jos tled, jos tling;** 2 *n.* Also, **justle.**

jot (jot), 1 write briefly or in haste: *The clerk jotted down the order.* 2 a little bit; very small amount: *I do not care a jot.* 1 *v.*, **jot ted, jot ting;** 2 *n.*

joule (joul), measure of the amount of work done. It is equal to ten million ergs. *n.* [from James P. *Joule*, 1818-1889, a British physicist]

jounce (jouns), 1 shake up and down; bounce; bump; jolt: *At every step of the camel, the rider was jounced around. The car jounced along on the rough road.* 2 a bump or jolt: *She sat down on the bench with a jounce.* 1 *v.*, **jounced, jounc ing;** 2 *n.*

jour nal (jėr´nl), 1 a daily record. A diary is a journal of what a person thinks, feels, or notices. A ship's log is a journal of what happens on a ship. A lawmaking body or a society keeps a journal of its daily business. 2 newspaper or magazine. 3 (in bookkeeping) a book in which every item of business is written down, so that the item can be entered under the proper account. 4 the part of a shaft or axle that turns in a bearing. *n.*

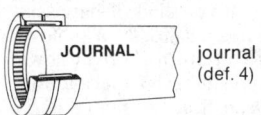

JOURNAL

journal (def. 4)

jour nal ism (jėr´nl iz´əm), work of writing for, editing, managing, or publishing a newspaper or magazine. *n.*

jour nal ist (jėr´nl ist), person whose work is writing for, editing, managing, or publishing a newspaper or magazine. Editors and reporters are journalists. *n.*

jour nal is tic (jėr´nl is´tik), of or like journalism or journalists. *adj.*

jour ney (jėr´nē), 1 a traveling from one place to another; trip: *a journey around the world.* 2 distance traveled: *a week's journey.* 3 take a trip; travel: *to journey to Europe.* 1,2 *n.*, *pl.* **jour neys;** 3 *v.*

jour ney man (jėr´nē mən), 1 workman who knows a trade. 2 workman who has served an apprenticeship and is qualified to practice a trade. *n.*, *pl.* **jour ney men.**

joust (joust *or* just), 1 combat between

---

two knights on horseback, armed with lances. 2 fight with lances on horseback. Knights used to joust with each other for sport. 1 *n.*, 2 *v.* Also, **just.** —**joust´er,** *n.*

Jove (jōv), (in Roman myths) Jupiter. *n.*

by Jove, exclamation of surprise, pleasure, etc.

jo vi al (jō´vē əl), good-hearted and full of fun; good-humored and merry: *Santa Claus is pictured as a jovial fellow. adj.* [from Latin *Jovis* Jove] —**jo´vi al ly,** *adv.*

jo vi al i ty (jō´vē al´ə tē), jollity; merriment. *n.*

Jo vi an (jō´vē ən), of or like the god Jove. *adj.*

jowl[1] (joul), 1 jaw, especially the part under the jaw. 2 cheek. *n.* [Old English *ceafl*]

jowl[2] (joul), fold of flesh hanging from the jaw. *n.* [perhaps related to Old English *ceole* throat]

joy (joi), 1 a strong feeling of pleasure; gladness; happiness: *He jumped for joy when he saw the circus.* 2 something that causes gladness or happiness: *On a hot day, a cool swim is a joy. n.*

Joyce (jois), **James,** 1882-1941, Irish poet, novelist, and short-story writer. *n.*

joy ful (joi´fəl), 1 glad; happy: *a joyful heart.* 2 causing joy: *joyful news.* 3 showing joy: *a joyful look. adj.* —**joy´ful ly,** *adv.* —**joy´ful ness,** *n.*

joy less (joi´lis), without joy; sad; dismal. *adj.*

joy ous (joi´əs), joyful; glad; gay: *a joyous song, a joyous person. adj.* —**joy´ous ly,** *adv.* —**joy´ous ness,** *n.*

joy ride, INFORMAL. a ride in an automobile for pleasure, especially when the car is driven recklessly or without the owner's permission.

jr. or **Jr.,** Junior.

ju bi lant (jü´bə lənt), expressing or showing joy; rejoicing: *People were jubilant when the war was over. adj.* —**ju´bi lant ly,** *adv.*

ju bi la tion (jü´bə lā´shən), a rejoicing. *n.*

ju bi lee (jü´bə lē), 1 an anniversary thought of as a time of rejoicing: *a twenty-fifth or fiftieth wedding jubilee.* 2 time of rejoicing or great joy: *have a jubilee in celebration of a victory.* 3 a rejoicing; great joy: *a day of jubilee. n.*

Ju dae a (jü dē´ə), Judea. *n.*

Ju dah (jü´də), 1 in the Bible: **a** a son of Jacob and ancestor of the tribe of Judah. **b** the most powerful of the twelve tribes of Israel. 2 ancient Hebrew kingdom in S Palestine, made up of the tribes of Judah and Benjamin. *n.*

Ju da ic (jü dā´ik), of or having to do with the Jews or Judaism. *adj.*

Ju da ism (jü´dē iz´əm), religion of the Jews, based on the teachings of Moses and the prophets as found in the Old Testament. Judaism believes in the same God as Christianity, but holds that the Messiah is still to come. *n.*

Ju das (jü´dəs), 1 (in the Bible) Judas Iscariot, the disciple who betrayed Jesus for money. 2 an utter traitor; person treacherous enough to betray a friend. *n.*

Jude (jüd), 1 (in the Bible) one of Christ's twelve apostles. 2 book of the New Testament. *n.*

Ju de a (jü dē´ə), the S part of Palestine when it was a province of the Roman Empire. See **Galilee** for map. *n.* Also, **Judaea.**

judge (juj), 1 a public official appointed or elected to hear and decide cases in a court of law. 2 hear and decide (a case) in a court of law; act as a judge. 3 person chosen to settle a dispute or decide who wins a race, contest, etc. 4 settle a dispute; decide who wins a race, contest, etc. 5 person who can decide how good a thing is: *a good judge of dogs, a poor judge of poetry, a judge of character.* 6 form an opinion or estimate about: *judge the merits of a book.* 7 think; suppose; conclude: *I judged that you had forgotten to come.* 8 consider and blame; criticize; condemn: *You had little cause to judge him so harshly.* 1,3,5 *n.*, 2,4,6-8 *v.*, **judged, judg ing.**

judge ment (juj´mənt), judgment. *n.*

Judg es (juj´iz), book of the Old Testament dealing with the period in Jewish history between the death of Joshua and Saul's accession to the throne. *n.*

judge ship (juj´ship), position, duties, or term of office of a judge. *n.*

judg ment (juj´mənt), 1 result of judging; opinion or estimate: *In my judgment dogs make better pets than cats.* 2 ability to form sound opinions; power to judge well; good sense: *Solomon was a man of judgment. Since she has judgment in such matters, we will ask her.* 3 act of judging, especially a decision, decree, or sentence given by a judge in a court of law. 4 decision made by anybody who judges. 5 criticism; condemnation: *pass judgment on one's*

Judah (def. 2)

---

neighbors. 6 misfortune thought of as a punishment from God. *n.* Also, **judgement.**

Judgment Day, day of God's final judgment of mankind at the end of the world; doomsday.

ju di cial (jü dish′əl), 1 of or by judges; having to do with courts or the administration of justice: *a judicial decision.* 2 of or suitable for a judge; impartial; fair: *A judicial mind considers both sides of a dispute fairly before making a decision. adj.* —**ju di′cial ly,** *adv.*

ju di ci ar y (jü dish′ē er′ē), 1 branch of government that administers justice; system of courts of law of a country. 2 judges of a country, state, or city. 3 of or having to do with courts, judges, or the administration of justice. 1,2 *n., pl.* **ju di ci ar ies;** 3 *adj.*

ju di cious (jü dish′əs), having, using, or showing good judgment; wise; sensible: *Judicious parents encourage their children to make their own decisions. A judicious historian selects and weighs facts carefully and critically. adj.* —**ju di′cious ly,** *adv.*

Ju dith (jü′dith), (in the Apocrypha) a Jewish widow who saved her countrymen by killing a Babylonian general. *n.*

ju do (jü′dō), jujitsu. *n.* [from Japanese]

Ju dy (jü′dē), wife of Punch in the puppet show *Punch and Judy. n.*

jug (jug), container for holding liquids. A jug usually has a short, narrow neck and a handle. *n.*

jug ger naut (jug′ər nôt), something to which a person blindly devotes himself or is cruelly sacrificed. *n.*

jug gle (jug′əl), 1 do tricks that require skill of hand and eye: *He juggled with knives by balancing them on his nose.* 2 do such tricks with: *She can juggle three balls, keeping them all in the air at one time.* 3 change by trickery: *The dishonest cashier juggled the store's accounts to hide his thefts.* 4 deceive; cheat: *She juggled her brother out of his share of the money. v.,* **jug gled, jug gling.**

jug gler (jug′lər), 1 person who can do juggling tricks. 2 person who uses tricks, deception, or fraud. *n.*

jug gler y (jug′lər ē), 1 skill or tricks of a juggler; sleight of hand. 2 trickery; deception; fraud. *n., pl.* **jug gler ies.**

Ju go slav (yü′gō släv′), Yugoslav. *n., adj.*

Ju go sla vi a (yü′gō slä′vē ə), Yugoslavia. *n.*

jug u lar (jug′yə lər), 1 of the neck or throat. 2 of the jugular vein. *adj.*

jugular vein, one of the two large veins in each side of the neck and head that return blood from the head and neck to the heart.

juice (jüs), 1 the liquid part of fruits, vegetables, and meats: *the juice of a lemon, meat juice.* 2 fluid in the body. The juices of the stomach help to digest food. 3 SLANG. electricity. *n.*

juic i ly (jü′sə lē), in a juicy manner. *adv.*

juic i ness (jü′sē nis), juicy quality or condition. *n.*

juic y (jü′sē), 1 full of juice; having much juice: *a juicy orange.* 2 INFORMAL. full of interest; lively. *adj.,* **juic i er, juic i est.**

ju jit su (jü jit′sü), a Japanese way of wrestling or of fighting without weapons that uses the strength and weight of an opponent to his disadvantage; judo. *n.* Also, **jiujitsu.**

juke box (jük′boks′), an automatic phonograph that plays records for money deposited in the coin slot. *n., pl.* **juke box es.**

Jul ian (jül′yən), of Julius Caesar. In the **Julian calendar,** which was introduced by Julius Caesar in 46 B.C., the average length of a year was 365¼ days. *adj.*

Ju li et (jü′lē et), heroine of Shakespeare's play *Romeo and Juliet. n.*

Jul ius Caesar (jül′yəs). See **Caesar.**

Ju ly (jù lī′), the seventh month of the year. It has 31 days. *n.*

jum ble (jum′bəl), 1 mix or confuse: *She jumbled up everything in the drawer while hunting for a roll of tape.* 2 a mixed-up mess; state of confusion; muddle. 1 *v.,* **jum bled, jum bling;** 2 *n.*

jum bo (jum′bō), INFORMAL. 1 a big, clumsy person, animal, or thing; something unusually large of its kind. 2 very big: *a jumbo ice-cream cone.* 1 *n., pl.* **jum bos;** 2 *adj.*

jump (jump), 1 spring from the ground; leap; bound: *How high can you jump? How far can you jump? Jump across the puddle.* 2 a spring from the ground; leap; bound: *The horse made a fine jump.* 3 leap over: *jump a stream. The speeding car jumped the curb and crashed.* 4 cause to jump: *jump a horse over a fence.* 5 thing to be jumped over: *The horse cleared the jump.* 6 distance jumped: *a ten-foot jump.* 7 contest in jumping for height or distance. 8 give a sudden start or jerk: *He jumped when the sudden noise startled him.* 9 a sudden nervous start or jerk: *She gave a jump at the crash of thunder.* 10 rise suddenly: *Prices jumped.* 11 a sudden rise: *a jump in the cost of living.* 12 pounce upon; attack. 1,3,4,8,10,12 *v.,* 2,5-7,9,11 *n.*

get the jump on or **have the jump**

hat, āge, fär; let, ēqual, tėrm;
it, īce; hot, ōpen, ôrder;
oil, out; cup, pùt, rüle; ch, child;
ng, long; sh, she; th, thin;
ŦH, then; zh, measure;

ə represents *a* in about,
e in taken, *i* in pencil,
o in lemon, *u* in circus.

on, SLANG. get or have an advantage over.

jump at, accept eagerly and quickly: *jump at a chance, jump at an offer of help.*

jump er[1] (jum′pər), person or thing that jumps. *n.* [*jump* + *-er*[1]]

jump er[2] (jum′pər), 1 a sleeveless dress to wear over a blouse. 2 a loose jacket. Jumpers are worn by workers to protect their clothes. 3 **jumpers,** *pl.* rompers. *n.* [from French of the 1500's *juppe* skirt]

jump i ness (jum′pē nis), jumpy condition or quality. *n.*

jumping jack, a toy man or animal that can be made to jump by pulling a string.

jump y (jum′pē), 1 moving by jumps; making sudden, sharp jerks. 2 easily excited or frightened; nervous. *adj.,* **jump i er, jump i est.**

jun co (jung′kō), any of several small North American finches; snowbird. One kind is often seen in flocks during the winter. *n., pl.* **jun cos** or **jun coes.**

junc tion (jungk′shən), 1 a joining or a being joined: *The junction of the two rivers results in a large flow of water downstream.* 2 place of joining or meeting. A railroad junction is a place where railroad lines meet or cross. *n.*

junc ture (jungk′chər), 1 point or line where two things join; joint. 2 point of time. 3 state of affairs. 4 a joining or a being joined. *n.*

at this juncture, when affairs are in this state; at this moment.

June (jün), the sixth month of the year. It has 30 days. *n.*

Ju neau (jü′nō), capital of Alaska, in the SE part. *n.*

June bug, 1 a large brown beetle of North America that appears in June. 2 a large green beetle of the southern United States, very destructive to fruit.

Jung frau (yùng′frou′), mountain in the Alps of S Switzerland. *n.*

jun gle (jung′gəl), wild land thickly overgrown with bushes, vines, trees, etc. Jungles are hot and humid regions with many kinds of plants and wild animals. *n.*

adj. adjective	*n.* noun	
adv. adverb	*prep.* preposition	
conj. conjunction	*pron.* pronoun	
interj. interjection	*v.* verb	
sing. singular	*pl.* plural	

jungle gym, framework of steel bars for children to climb or swing on as a pastime.

jun ior (jü′nyər), 1 the younger (used of a son having the same name as his father): *John Parker, Junior, is the son of John Parker, Senior.* 2 a younger person: *She is her sister's junior by two years.* 3 of or for younger people: *a junior choir.* 4 of lower rank or shorter service; of less standing than some others: *a junior officer, a junior partner.* 5 person of lower rank or shorter service. 6 student in the third year of high school or college. 7 of or having to do with these students: *the junior class. Are you going to the Junior Prom?* 1,3,4,7 *adj.,* 2,5,6 *n.*

junior college, school giving only the first two years of a regular four-year college course.

junior high school, school consisting of grades 7, 8, and sometimes 9, attended after elementary school and followed by high school.

ju ni per (jü′nə pər), an evergreen shrub or tree with small berrylike cones. The cones of one kind of juniper contain an oil used in flavoring gin and in medicines. *n.*

junk[1] (jungk), 1 old metal, paper, rags, etc. 2 INFORMAL. rubbish; trash. 3 INFORMAL. throw away or discard as junk. 1,2 *n.,* 3 *v.* [Middle English *jonk* old cable]

junk[2]

junk[2] (jungk), a Chinese sailing ship. *n.* [from Portuguese *junco,* from Javanese *jong*]

jun ket (jung′kit), 1 curdled milk, sweetened and flavored. 2 a feast or picnic. 3 hold a feast; join in a picnic. 4 a pleasure trip. 5 go on a pleasure trip. 1,2,4 *n.,* 3,5 *v.*

junk man (jungk′man′), man who buys and sells old metal, paper, rags, etc. *n., pl.* **junk men.**

Ju no (jü′nō), (in Roman myths) the wife of Jupiter and queen of the gods. She was the goddess of women and marriage. The Greeks called her Hera. *n.*

jun ta (jun′tə *or* hùn′tə), 1 a political or military group holding power after a revolution. 2 an assembly or council for deliberation or administration, especially in Spain and Latin America. 3 junto. *n., pl.* **jun tas.** [from Spanish]

jun to (jun′tō), group of plotters, partisans, etc.; faction; clique. *n., pl.* **jun tos.** [a different form of *junta*]

Ju pi ter (jü′pə tər), 1 (in Roman myths) the chief god, ruler of gods and men; Jove. The Greeks called him Zeus. 2 the largest planet in the solar system. It is the fifth in distance from the sun. *n.*

ju rid i cal (jù rid′ə kəl), 1 having to do with the administration of justice. 2 of law; legal. *adj.* —**ju rid′i cal ly,** *adv.*

jur is dic tion (jùr′is dik′shən), 1 right or power to give out justice; the giving out of justice. 2 authority; power; control: *The principal has jurisdiction over the teachers in a school.* 3 the things over which authority extends: *A school is the principal's jurisdiction.* 4 territory over which authority extends. *n.*

jur is pru dence (jùr′i sprüd′ns), 1 science or philosophy of law. 2 system of laws. 3 branch of law. Medical jurisprudence deals with the use of medical knowledge in certain questions of law. *n.*

jur ist (jùr′ist), 1 an expert in law. 2 a learned writer on law. *n.*

jur or (jùr′ər), member of a jury. *n.*

jur y (jùr′ē), 1 group of persons chosen to hear evidence in a court of law and sworn to give a decision in accordance with the evidence presented to them. A petit jury is made up of 12 jurors; a grand jury is made up of from 6 to 23 jurors. *The question put before the jury was, "Is this person guilty or not?"* 2 group of persons chosen to give a judgment or to decide who is the winner in a contest: *The jury gave her poem the first prize. n., pl.* **jur ies.**

jur y man (jùr′ē mən), member of a jury; juror. *n., pl.* **jur y men.**

just[1] (just), 1 no more than; only; merely: *He is just an ordinary man.* 2 barely: *The shot just missed the mark.* 3 INFORMAL. quite; truly; positively: *The weather is just glorious.* 4 exactly: *That is just a pound.* 5 almost exactly: *See the picture just above.* 6 a very little while ago: *She has just gone.* 7 right; fair: *a just price.* 8 deserved; merited: *a*

just reward. 9 having good grounds; well-founded: *just anger.* 10 true; correct; exact: *just weights, a just description.* 11 righteous: *a just life.* 1-6 *adv.,* 7-11 *adj.* [from French of the 1300's *juste,* from Latin *justus* upright, from *jus, juris* right, law] —**just′ness,** *n.*

just now, only a very short time ago: *I saw him just now.*

just[2] (just), joust. *n., v.* [from French of the 1200's *jouster* to joust]

jus tice (jus′tis), 1 just conduct; fair dealing: *Judges should have a sense of justice.* 2 a being just; fairness; rightness: *the justice of a claim, uphold the justice of our cause.* 3 well-founded reason; rightfulness; lawfulness: *They complained with justice of the bad treatment they had received.* 4 just treatment; deserved reward or punishment. 5 administration of law; trial and judgment by process of law: *a court of justice.* 6 a judge. The Supreme Court of the United States consists of nine justices. *n.*

do justice to, 1 treat fairly. 2 see the good points of; show proper appreciation for.

do oneself justice, do as well as one really can do: *He did not do himself justice on the test.*

justice of the peace, a local magistrate who tries minor cases, administers oaths, performs civil marriages, etc.

jus ti fi a ble (jus′tə fī′ə bəl), capable of being justified; proper: *An act is justifiable if it can be shown to be just or right. adj.*

jus ti fi a bly (jus′tə fī′ə blē), in a justifiable manner. *adv.*

jus ti fi ca tion (jus′tə fə kā′shən), 1 a justifying or a being justified. 2 fact or circumstance that justifies; good reason or excuse: *What is your justification for being so late? n.*

jus ti fy (jus′tə fī), 1 give a good reason for: *The fine quality of the cloth justifies its high price.* 2 show to be just or right: *Can you justify your act?* 3 clear of blame or guilt: *The court ruled that he was justified in hitting the man in self-defense. v.,* **jus ti fied, jus ti fy ing.**

jus tle (jus′əl), jostle. *v.,* **jus tled, jus tling;** *n.*

just ly (just′lē), 1 in a just manner: *deal justly with others.* 2 rightly: *You argue justly. adv.*

jut (jut), 1 stick out; stand out; project: *The pier juts out from the shore into the water.* 2 part that sticks out; projection. 1 *v.,* **jut ted, jut ting;** 2 *n.*

jute (jüt), 1 a strong fiber used for making coarse fabrics, rope, etc. Jute is obtained from two tropical plants. 2 either of these plants. *n.*

Jute (jüt), member of a Germanic tribe that, with the Angles and Saxons, conquered England in the A.D. 400's and 500's. *n.*

Jut land (jut/lənd), peninsula on which most of Denmark and part of West Germany are located. The British and German navies fought near there in 1916. *n.*

ju ve nile (jü/və nəl *or* jü/və nīl), 1 young; youthful. 2 a young person. 3 of or for boys and girls: *juvenile books.* 4 book for boys and girls. 5 actor who plays youthful parts. 1,3 *adj.*, 2,4,5 *n.*

juvenile delinquent, boy or girl under 18 years of age who has committed a legal offense.

jux ta pose (juk/stə pōz/), put close together; place side by side. *v.,* **jux ta posed, jux ta pos ing.**

jux ta po si tion (juk/stə pə zish/ən), 1 a putting close together; a placing side by side. 2 position close together or side by side. *n.*

hat, āge, fär; let, ēqual, tėrm; it, īce; hot, ōpen, ôrder; oil, out; cup, pùt, rüle; ch, child; ng, long; sh, she; th, thin; ŦH, then; zh, measure;

ə represents *a* in about, *e* in taken, *i* in pencil, *o* in lemon, *u* in circus.

K k

K or **k** (kā), the 11th letter of the alphabet. *n., pl.* **K's** or **k's**.

Kaa ba (kä′bə), the most sacred shrine of the Moslems. The Kaaba is a small structure, containing a black stone, in the courtyard of the great mosque at Mecca. *n.*

Ka bul (kä′bul), capital of Afghanistan, in the E part. *n.*

kai ak (kī′ak), kayak. *n.*

kai ser (kī′zər), 1 title of the rulers of Germany and Austria before 1918. 2 title of the emperors of the Holy Roman Empire. *n.*

kale (kāl), 1 kind of cabbage that has loose, curled leaves instead of a compact head. 2 its leaves, which are eaten as a vegetable. *n.*

ka lei do scope (kə lī′də skōp′), 1 tube containing bits of colored glass and two mirrors. As it is turned, it reflects continually changing patterns. 2 a continually changing pattern. *n.*

ka lei do scop ic (kə lī′də skop′ik), of or like a kaleidoscope; continually changing. *adj.*

ka mi ka ze (kä′mē kä′zē), a Japanese suicide pilot in World War II, trained to dive an airplane loaded with explosives into a selected target, usually a naval vessel. *n.* [from Japanese *kamikaze* divine wind]

kan ga roo (kang′gə rü′), mammal of Australia and New Guinea having small forelegs and very strong hind legs, which give it great leaping power. The female kangaroo has a pouch in front in which she carries her young. *n., pl.* **kan ga roos** or **kan ga roo.**

kangaroo
about 8 ft. long, including the tail

kangaroo rat, a small, burrowing rodent of dry areas of the western United States. Kangaroo rats have cheek pouches and long hind legs and tails.

Kans., Kansas.

Kan san (kan′zən), 1 of or having to do with Kansas. 2 person born or living in Kansas. 1 *adj.*, 2 *n.*

Kan sas (kan′zəs), one of the midwestern states of the United States. *Capital:* Topeka. *n.*

Kansas City, 1 city in W Missouri, on the Missouri River. 2 city in NE Kansas adjoining it.

ka o lin (kā′ə lən), a fine white clay, used in making porcelain. *n.*

ka pok (kā′pok), the silky fibers around the seeds of a tropical tree, used for stuffing pillows and mattresses. *n.*

Ka ra chi (kə rä′chē), city in S Pakistan, a former capital. *n.*

kar a kul (kar′ə kəl), caracul. *n.*

kar at (kar′ət), 1/24 part of gold by weight in an alloy. A gold ring of 18 carats is 18 parts pure gold and six parts alloy. *n.* Also, **carat.**

ka ra te (kä rä′tē), a Japanese method of fighting without weapons, striking with the hands, elbows, knees, and feet at certain vulnerable parts of the opponent's body. *n.*

Kash mir (kash mir′), area north of India, claimed by both India and Pakistan. *n.*

Kat man du (kät′män dü′), capital of Nepal, in the central part. *n.*

ka ty did (kā′tē did′), a large, green grasshopper. The male makes a shrill noise sounding like its name. *n.*

Kau ai (kou ī′ or kou′ī), the fourth largest island of Hawaii. *n.*

kayak (def. 1)

kay ak (kī′ak), 1 an Eskimo canoe made of skins stretched over a light frame of wood or bone with an opening in the middle for a person. 2 a similar craft of other material. *n.* Also, **kaiak.**

kc., kilocycle or kilocycles.

ke a (kē′ə), a large, green parrot of New Zealand with a powerful, hooked bill which it uses to dig out insects. It will attack sheep when very hungry. *n., pl.* **ke as.**

Keats (kēts), **John,** 1795-1821, English poet. *n.*

keel (kēl), 1 the main timber or steel piece that extends the whole length of the bottom of a ship or boat. The whole ship is built up on the keel. 2 OLD USE. ship. 3 part in an aircraft resembling a ship's keel. 4 turn upside down; upset. 1-3 *n.*, 4 *v.*

keel over, 1 turn upside down; upset: *The sailboat keeled over in the storm.* 2 fall over suddenly: *keel over in a faint.*

on an even keel, horizontal: *The boat sailed on an even keel in good weather.*

keel son (kel′sən or kēl′sən), beam or line of timbers or iron plates fastened along the top of a ship's keel to strengthen it. *n.*

keen[1] (kēn), 1 so shaped as to cut well: *a keen blade.* 2 sharp; cutting: *a keen wind, keen hunger, keen pain, keen wit.* 3 strong; vivid: *keen competition.* 4 able to do its work quickly and accurately: *a keen mind, a keen sense of smell.* 5 full of enthusiasm; eager: *He is keen about sailing. adj.* [Old English *cēne*] —**keen′ly,** *adv.* —**keen′ness,** *n.*

keen[2] (kēn), IRISH. 1 a wailing lament for the dead. 2 wail; lament. 1 *n.*, 2 *v.* [from Irish *caoine*] —**keen′er,** *n.*

keep (def. 14)

KEEP

keep (kēp), 1 have for a long time or forever: *You may keep this book.* 2 have and not let go: *Can you keep a secret?* 3 have and take care of: *She keeps chickens. My aunt keeps two boarders.* 4 take care of and protect; guard: *The bank keeps money for people.* 5 have; hold: *Keep this in mind.* 6 hold back; prevent: *Keep the baby from crying. What is keeping her?* 7 maintain in good condition; preserve: *A refrigerator keeps food fresh.* 8 stay in good condition: *Milk does not keep long in hot weather.* 9 stay the same; continue: *Keep along this road for two miles.* 10 cause to continue; cause to stay the same: *The blanket keeps the baby warm. Keep the fire burning.* 11 do the right thing with; celebrate; observe: *keep Thanksgiving as a holiday.* 12 be faithful to: *keep a promise.* 13 food and a place to sleep: *He works for his keep.* 14 the strongest part of a castle or fort. 1-12 *v.*, **kept, keep ing;** 13,14 *n.*

for keeps, 1 for the winner to keep his winnings. 2 INFORMAL. forever.

keep in with, INFORMAL. keep acquaintance or friendship with.

keep on, continue; go on: *The boys kept on swimming in spite of the rain.*

keep to oneself, 1 avoid associating with others: *That man always keeps to himself.* 2 keep a secret.

keep up, 1 continue; prevent from ending: *We kept up a small fire.*

2 maintain in good condition. **3** not fall behind.

keep up with, not fall behind; go or move as fast as: *You walk so fast that I cannot keep up with you.*

keep er (kē′pər), one that watches, guards, or takes care of persons or things: *the keeper of an inn. n.*

keep ing (kē′ping), **1** care; charge: *The two older children were left in their grandfather's keeping.* **2** celebration; observance: *The keeping of Thanksgiving Day is an old American custom.* **3** agreement; harmony: *Don't trust him; his actions are not in keeping with his promises. n.*

keep sake (kēp′sāk′), thing kept in memory of the giver: *Before my friend went away, she gave me her picture as a keepsake. n.*

keg (keg), a small barrel, usually holding less than 10 gallons. *n.*

Kel ler (kel′ər), **Helen (Adams),** 1880-1968, American writer and lecturer who was both deaf and blind. *n.*

kelp (kelp), **1** a large, tough, brown seaweed. **2** ashes of seaweed, used as a source of iodine. *n.*

Kel vin (kel′vən), of, based on, or according to a scale for measuring temperature on which 273 degrees marks the freezing point of water, 373 degrees marks the boiling point, and 0 degrees marks absolute zero. *adj.* [from Lord *Kelvin,* 1824-1907, a British physicist]

ken (ken), **1** range of sight. **2** range of knowledge: *What happens on Mars is no longer beyond our ken.* **3** SCOTTISH. know. **1,2** *n.,* **3** *v.,* **kenned** or **kent** (kent), **ken ning.**

Ken ne dy (ken′ə dē), **1 Cape,** former name of **Cape Canaveral. 2 John F(itzgerald),** 1917-1963, the 35th president of the United States, 1961-1963. *n.*

Kennedy International Airport, a major international and domestic airport, in the Borough of Queens in New York City.

ken nel (ken′l), **1** house for a dog or dogs. **2** Often, **kennels,** *pl.* place where dogs are bred or boarded. **3** put into or keep in a kennel. **1,2** *n.,* **3** *v.*

Kent (kent), county in SE England. *n.*

Ken tuck i an (kən tuk′ē ən), **1** of Kentucky or its people. **2** person born or living in Kentucky. **1** *adj.,* **2** *n.*

Ken tuck y (kən tuk′ē), one of the south central states of the United States. *Capital:* Frankfort. *n.*

Ken ya (ken′yə *or* kē′nyə), country in E Africa, a member of the Commonwealth of Nations. *Capital:* Nairobi. *n.*

Kep ler (kep′lər), **Johann,** 1571-1630, German astronomer. *n.*

kept (kept), past tense and past participle of **keep.** *I gave him the book and he kept it. The milk was kept in bottles. v.*

ker chief (kėr′chif), **1** piece of cloth worn over the head or around the neck. **2** handkerchief. *n.*

ker nel (kėr′nl), **1** the softer part inside the hard shell of a nut or inside the stone of a fruit. **2** a grain or seed like that of wheat or corn. **3** the central or most important part of anything, around which it is formed or built up. *n.*

ker o sene or **ker o sine** (ker′ə sēn′), a thin, oily mixture of hydrocarbons distilled from petroleum; coal oil. It is used as fuel in lamps and stoves. *n.*

ketch (kech), a small sailing ship with a large mainmast toward the bow and a smaller mast toward the stern. *n., pl.* **ketch es.**

ketch up (kech′əp), catsup. *n.*

ket tle (ket′l), **1** any metal container for boiling liquids, cooking fruit, etc. **2** teakettle. *n.*

kettle of fish, awkward state of affairs; mess; muddle.

kettledrums

ket tle drum (ket′l drum′), drum consisting of a hollow brass or copper hemisphere and a parchment top. *n.*

key[1] (kē), **1 a** small metal instrument for locking and unlocking the lock of a door, a padlock, or any other thing. **2** anything shaped like it: *the key of a clock.* **3** the answer to a puzzle or a problem: *The key to this puzzle will be published next week.* **4** sheet or book of answers: *a key to a test.* **5** a systematic explanation of abbreviations, symbols, etc., used in a dictionary, map, etc. The pronunciation key in this dictionary lists all the symbols of the sounds in English that are used in the pronunciations in this book, and also gives examples of words that contain these sounds. **6** place that commands or gives control of a sea, a district, etc., because of its position: *Gibraltar is the key to the Mediterranean.* **7** controlling; very important: *the key industries of a nation.* **8** an important or essential person, thing, etc. **9** pin, bolt, wedge, or other piece put in a hole or space to hold parts together. **10** fasten or adjust with a key. **11** one of a set of levers pressed down by the fingers in playing a piano, and in operating a typewriter or other instruments: *Don't hit the keys so hard.* **12** scale or system of related tones in

hat, āge, fär; let, ēqual, tėrm;
it, īce; hot, ōpen, ôrder;
oil, out; cup, pùt, rüle; ch, child;
ng, long; sh, she; th, thin;
ŦH, then; zh, measure;

ə represents *a* in about,
e in taken, *i* in pencil,
o in lemon, *u* in circus.

music which are based on a keynote: *a song written in the key of C.* **13** tone of voice; style of thought or expression: *The poet wrote in a melancholy key.* **14** regulate the pitch of; tune: *key a musical instrument in preparation for a concert.* **1-6,8,9,11-13** *n., pl.* **keys; 7** *adj.,* **10,14** *v.* [Old English *cæg*]

key up, raise the courage or nerve of: *The coach keyed up the team for the big game. I keyed myself up to ask for a higher salary.*

key[2] (kē), a low island; reef. There are keys south of Florida. *n., pl.* **keys.** [from Spanish *cayo*]

Key (kē), **Francis Scott,** 1779-1843, American author who wrote the words to "The Star-Spangled Banner." *n.*

key board (kē′bôrd′), the set of keys in a piano, organ, typewriter, etc. *n.*

key hole (kē′hōl′), opening in a lock through which a key is inserted. *n.*

key note (kē′nōt′), **1** tone on which a scale or system of tones in music is based; tonic. **2** main idea; guiding principle: *World peace was the keynote of the speech. n.*

keynote address, speech, usually at a political gathering, that presents the principal issues in which those present are interested.

key punch, machine having a keyboard similar to that of a typewriter, used to record and code information by punching patterns of holes in cards.

KEYSTONE — keystone (def. 1)

key stone (kē′stōn′), **1** the middle stone at the top of an arch, holding the other stones or pieces in place. **2** part on which other related parts depend; essential principle. *n.*

kg., **1** keg or kegs. **2** kilogram or kilograms.

khak i (kak′ē *or* kä′kē), **1** a dull yellowish brown. **2** dull yellowish-brown. **3** a heavy twilled cloth of this color, much used for soldiers' uniforms. **4 khakis,** *pl.* uniform made of this

khan

cloth: *Khakis will be worn in the parade.* 1,3,4 *n.*, *pl.* **khak is**; 2 *adj.*

khan (kän), 1 (formerly) a title of a ruler among Tartar or Mongol tribes. 2 title of respect in Iran, Afghanistan, India, etc. *n.*

Khar kov (kär′kôf), city in SW Soviet Union. *n.*

Khar toum (kär tüm′), capital of Sudan, on the Nile. *n.*

khe dive (kə dēv′), title of the Turkish viceroys who ruled Egypt between 1867 and 1914. *n.*

Khmer Republic (kmer), official name of Cambodia.

Khru shchev (krüsh chôf′), **Nikita S.**, 1894-1971, premier of the Soviet Union from 1958 to 1964. *n.*

Khy ber Pass (kī′bər), important mountain pass between N Pakistan and E Afghanistan.

kib itz er (kib′it sər), INFORMAL. person who gives unwanted advice; meddler. *n.*

kick (kik), 1 strike out with the foot: *That horse kicks when anyone comes near him.* 2 strike with the foot: *The horse kicked the boy.* 3 drive, force, or move by kicking: *kick a ball along the ground, kick off one's shoes, kick up dust.* 4 a blow with the foot: *The horse's kick knocked the boy down.* 5 the recoil or backward motion of a gun when it is fired. 6 spring back when fired; recoil: *This shotgun kicks.* 7 INFORMAL. find fault; complain; grumble. 8 INFORMAL. complaint; objection. 9 excitement; thrill: *She got a kick out of winning the game.* 1-3,6,7 *v.*, 4,5,8,9 *n.* —**kick′er**, *n.*

kick back, 1 INFORMAL. spring back suddenly and unexpectedly: *The gun kicked back with great force.* 2 SLANG. return (a stolen item) to its owner: *The thief kicked back the wallet but kept the money.* 3 SLANG. return a portion of money received as a fee.

kick off, put a football in play with a kick at the beginning of each half and after a score has been made: *The visiting team kicked off.*

kick out, expel or turn out in a humiliating or disgraceful way: *be kicked out of school.*

kick back (kik′bak′), SLANG. 1 portion or amount of a fee returned, especially as a bribe for having received a contract: *The dishonest builder offered to pay a kickback to the mayor if the city would award business to his firm.* 2 a returning of stolen goods. *n.*

kick off (kik′ôf′), kick that puts a football in play at the beginning of each half and after a score has been made. *n.*

kid[1] (kid), 1 a young goat. 2 leather made from the skin of young goats, used for gloves and shoes. 3 INFORMAL. child. *n.* [from a Scandinavian word of the 1200's, such as Icelandic *kith*]

kid[2] (kid), SLANG. 1 tease playfully; talk in a joking way; banter. 2 humbug; fool. *v.*, **kid ded, kid ding.** [perhaps from *kid*[1] in the sense of "treat as a child"]

Kidd (kid), **William**, 1645?-1701, Scottish privateer and pirate, known as "Captain Kidd." *n.*

kid der (kid′ər), SLANG. person who kids. *n.*

kid nap (kid′nap), steal (a child); carry off (a person) by force: *Four men kidnaped the boy, but the police soon caught them and rescued him.* *v.*, **kid naped, kid nap ing** or **kid napped, kid nap ping.** —**kid′nap er** or **kid′nap per**, *n.*

kidney (def. 1)—kidneys of a human being

kid ney (kid′nē), 1 one of the pair of organs in the body that separates waste matter from the blood and passes it off through the bladder as urine. 2 kidney or kidneys of an animal, cooked for food. 3 nature; disposition. *n.*, *pl.* **kid neys.** —**kid′ney like′**, *adj.*

kidney bean, 1 a large, red bean, shaped like a kidney and used as a vegetable. 2 the plant it grows on.

Kiel (kēl), seaport in N West Germany, on the Baltic Sea. *n.*

Kiel Canal, a ship canal in N West Germany from the North Sea to the Baltic Sea.

Ki ev (kē′ef), capital of the Ukraine, in SW Soviet Union. *n.*

Kil i man ja ro (kil′ə mən jär′ō), **Mount**, the highest mountain in Africa, in NE Tanzania. *n.*

kill[1] (kil), 1 put to death; cause the death of: *A bolt of lightning killed the tree.* 2 cause death: *"Thou shalt not kill."* 3 act of killing. 4 animal killed. 5 put an end to; get rid of; destroy: *kill odors, kill faith.* 6 cancel (a word, paragraph, item, etc.); delete. 7 defeat or veto (a legislative bill). 8 spoil the effect of: *One color may kill another near it.* 9 use up (time): *We killed an hour at the zoo.* 10 INFORMAL. overcome completely: *My sore foot is killing me. Her jokes really kill me.* 1,2,5-10 *v.*, 3,4 *n.* [Middle English *kyllen*]

kill[2] (kil), DIALECT. stream; creek; river. *n.* [from Dutch *kil*]

kill deer (kil′dir′), a North American plover which has two black bands across its breast. It has a loud, shrill cry. *n.*, *pl.* **kill deers** or **kill deer.**

kill er (kil′ər), person, animal, or thing that kills. *n.*

killer whale, dolphin that travels in schools and kills and eats large fish, seals, and even other whales; grampus.

kill joy (kil′joi′), person who spoils other people's fun. *n.*

kiln (kil *or* kiln), furnace or oven for burning, baking, or drying something. Limestone is burned in a kiln to make lime. Bricks are baked in a kiln. *n.*

ki lo (kē′lō *or* kil′ō), 1 kilogram. 2 kilometer. *n.*, *pl.* **ki los.**

kil o cy cle (kil′ə sī′kəl), 1 1000 cycles. 2 1000 cycles per second, used formerly to express the frequency of radio waves, which are now expressed in kilohertz. *n.*

kil o gram (kil′ə gram), measure of mass or weight equal to 1000 grams, or 2.2046 pounds avoirdupois. *n.*

kil o hertz (kil′ə herts′), 1000 hertz, used to express the frequency of radio waves. *n.*, *pl.* **kil o hertz.**

kil o li ter (kil′ə lē′tər), measure of volume equal to 1000 liters, or one cubic meter; 264.17 United States gallons, or 1.308 cubic yards. *n.*

kil om e ter (kə lom′ə tər *or* kil′ə-mē′tər), measure of length equal to 1000 meters, or 3280.8 feet. *n.*

kil o ton (kil′ə tun′), 1 measure of weight equal to 1000 tons. 2 measure of atomic power equivalent to the energy released by one thousand tons of high explosive, specifically TNT. *n.*

kil o watt (kil′ə wot′), measure of electrical power equal to 1000 watts. *n.*

kil o watt-hour (kil′ə wot′ our′), measure of electrical energy equal to the work done by one kilowatt acting for one hour. *n.*

kilt (kilt), a pleated skirt reaching to the knees, worn especially by men in the Scottish Highlands. *n.*

kil ter (kil′tər). **out of kilter**, INFORMAL. out of working order; not in good condition: *Our radio is so out of kilter* *that we cannot tune in most stations. n.*

ki mo no (kə mō′nə), 1 a loose outer garment held in place by a sash, worn by Japanese men and women. 2 a woman's loose dressing gown. *n., pl.* **ki mo nos.**

kin (kin), 1 a person's family or relatives; kindred: *All our kin came to the family reunion.* 2 family relationship; connection by birth or marriage: *What kin is she to you?* 3 related: *Your cousin is also kin to me.* 1,2 *n.,* 3 *adj.*
next of kin, nearest living relative.

kind[1] (kīnd), 1 doing good rather than harm; friendly: *Kind people try to help others and make them happy. Sharing your book was a kind thing to do.* 2 gentle: *Be kind to animals. adj.* [Old English *gecynde* natural, from *gecynd* nature]

kind[2] (kīnd), 1 group of individuals or objects having characteristics in common; class; sort: *He likes many kinds of candy. A kilt is a kind of skirt.* 2 natural group; race: *Snakes belong to the serpent kind. n.* [Old English *gecynd*]
in kind, 1 in goods or produce, not in money: *make payments in kind.* 2 in something of the same sort: *I returned their insults in kind by insulting them.* 3 in characteristic quality: *difference in kind, not merely in degree.*
kind of, INFORMAL. nearly; almost; somewhat; rather: *The room was kind of dark.*
of a kind, 1 of the same sort; alike: *The cakes were all of a kind — chocolate.* 2 of a poor or mediocre quality: *Two boxes and a plank make a table of a kind.*

kin der gar ten (kin′dər gärt′n), school or class for children from about 4 to 6 years old that educates them by games, toys, and pleasant occupations. *n.*

kin der gart ner (kin′dər gärt′nər), child who goes to kindergarten. *n.*

kind heart ed (kīnd′här′tid), having or showing a kind heart; kindly; sympathetic. *adj.* —**kind′heart′ed ly,** *adv.* —**kind′heart′ed ness,** *n.*

kin dle (kin′dl), 1 set on fire; light: *Use a burning torch to kindle the bonfire.* 2 catch fire; begin to burn: *This damp wood will never kindle.* 3 stir up; arouse: *kindle anger, kindle enthusiasm.* 4 light up; brighten: *The girl's face kindled as she told about the circus. Pleasure kindled the boy's face. v.,* **kin dled, kin dling.**

kind li ness (kīnd′lē nis), 1 kindly feeling or quality. 2 a kindly act. *n., pl.* **kind li ness es.**

kin dling (kind′ling), small pieces of wood for starting a fire. *n.*

kind ly (kīnd′lē), 1 kind; friendly: *kindly faces, kindly people.* 2 in a kind or

friendly way: *We thank you kindly for your help.* 3 pleasant; agreeable: *a kindly shower.* 4 pleasantly; agreeably: *He does not take kindly to criticism.* 1,3 *adj.,* **kind li er, kind li est;** 2,4 *adv.*

kind ness (kīnd′nis), 1 kind nature; being kind: *We admire his kindness.* 2 kind treatment: *Thank you for your kindness.* 3 a kind act: *They showed me many kindnesses. n., pl.* **kind ness es.**

kin dred (kin′drid), 1 like; similar: *We are studying about dew, frost, and kindred facts of nature.* 2 related: *kindred tribes.* 3 a person's family or relatives. 4 family relationship: *Does she claim kindred with you?* 5 a being alike; resemblance: *There is kindred among the words "receive," "receipt," and "reception."* 1,2 *adj.,* 3-5 *n.*

kine (kīn), OLD USE. cows or cattle. *n.pl.*

kin es thet ic (kin′əs thet′ik), having to do with sensations of motion from the muscles and joints. *adj.* —**kin′es thet′i cal ly,** *adv.*

ki net ic (ki net′ik), 1 of motion. 2 caused by motion. *adj.*

kinetic energy, energy which a body has because it is in motion.

kin folk (kin′fōk′), kinsfolk. *n.pl.*

king (king), 1 the male ruler of a nation; male sovereign, usually with a hereditary position and with either absolute or limited power: *Richard the Lion-Hearted was king of England. The kings of England really do not rule England now.* 2 INFORMAL. man supreme in a certain sphere: *a baseball king, a steel king.* 3 something best in its class: *The lion is the king of the beasts.* 4 the chief piece in chess. 5 piece that has moved entirely across the board in checkers. 6 a playing card bearing a picture of a king. *n.* —**king′like′,** *adj.*

King (king), **Martin Luther, Jr.,** 1929-1968, American minister who led a nonviolent movement to end racial discrimination in the United States. *n.*

king bird (king′bėrd′), any of several American flycatchers, especially a bold, black-and-white flycatcher of the eastern United States. *n.*

king dom (king′dəm), 1 nation that is governed by a king or a queen; land or territory ruled by one king. 2 a realm, domain, or province: *The mind is the kingdom of thought.* 3 one of the three divisions of the natural world; the animal kingdom, the vegetable kingdom, or the mineral kingdom. *n.*

king fish er (king′fish′ər), a bright-colored bird with a large head and a strong beak. Kingfishers eat fish and insects. *n.*

king li ness (king′lē nis), kingly quality; majesty. *n.*

king ly (king′lē), 1 of a king or kings;

hat, āge, fär; let, ēqual, tėrm;
it, īce; hot, ōpen, ôrder;
oil, out; cup, pùt, rüle; ch, child;
ng, long; sh, she; th, thin;
ŦH, then; zh, measure;

ə represents *a* in about,
e in taken, *i* in pencil,
o in lemon, *u* in circus.

of royal rank. 2 fit for a king: *a kingly crown.* 3 like a king; royal; noble: *kingly pride.* 4 as a king does. 1-3 *adj.,* **king li er, king li est;** 4 *adv.*

Kings (kingz), 1 (in the Protestant Old Testament) either of two books (I Kings or II Kings) containing the history of the reigns of the Hebrew kings after David. 2 (in the Roman Catholic Old Testament) one of four books that include I and II Samuel and I and II Kings. *n.*

king ship (king′ship), 1 position, rank, or dignity of a king. 2 rule of a king; government by a king. *n.*

king-size (king′sīz′), INFORMAL. large or long for its kind: *a king-size cigarette. adj.*

king-sized (king′sīzd′), INFORMAL. king-size. *adj.*

Kings ton (king′stən), capital and chief seaport of Jamaica, in the SE part. *n.*

kink (kingk), 1 a twist or curl in thread, rope, hair, etc. 2 form a kink or kinks: *The rope kinked as she rolled it up.* 3 make kinks in: *Don't kink the clothesline.* 4 pain or stiffness in the muscles of the neck, back, etc.; crick. 5 INFORMAL. a mental twist; queer idea. 1,4,5 *n.,* 2,3 *v.*

kink y (king′kē), 1 full of kinks; twisted; curly. 2 INFORMAL. quite unusual; odd; extreme: *kinky styles in clothing. adj.,* **kink i er, kink i est.**

kins folk (kinz′fōk′), a person's family or relatives; kin. *n.pl.* Also, **kinfolk.**

Kin sha sa (kēn shä′sä), capital of Zaïre, in the W part. Formerly called **Léopoldville.** *n.*

kin ship (kin′ship), 1 a being kin; family relationship: *His kinship with the owner of the factory helped him to get a job.* 2 relationship. 3 resemblance. *n.*

kins man (kinz′mən), a male relative. One's brothers and uncles are one's kinsmen. *n., pl.* **kins men.**

kins wom an (kinz′wùm′ən), a female relative. *n., pl.* **kins wom en.**

ki osk (kē osk′ *or* kī′osk), a small building with one or more sides open, used

471

adj. adjective *n.* noun
adv. adverb *prep.* preposition
conj. conjunction *pron.* pronoun
interj. interjection *v.* verb

sing. singular *pl.* plural

---

as a newsstand, a bandstand, or an opening to a subway. *n.*

Kip ling (kip′ling), **Rudyard,** 1865-1936, English writer of stories, novels, and poems. He was born in India. *n.*

kip per (kip′ər), 1 salt and dry or smoke (herring, salmon, etc.). 2 herring, salmon, etc., that has been kippered. 1 *v.*, 2 *n.*

kirk (kėrk), SCOTTISH. church. *n.*

kir tle (kėr′tl), OLD USE. skirt. *n.*

kiss (kis), 1 touch with the lips as a sign of love, greeting, or respect: *The two sisters kissed. He kissed his mother good-by.* 2 a touch with the lips as a sign of love, greeting, or respect. 3 touch gently: *A soft wind kissed the treetops.* 4 a gentle touch. 5 put, bring, take, etc., by kissing: *kiss away tears.* 6 piece of candy containing coconut, nuts, or the like. 7 a small, fancy cake made of white of egg and powdered sugar. 1,3,5 *v.*, 2,4,6,7 *n.*, *pl.* **kiss es.**

kit (kit), 1 the parts of anything to be put together by the buyer: *a radio kit, a model airplane kit.* 2 a person's equipment packed for traveling: *a soldier's kit.* 3 outfit of tools or supplies: *a plumber's kit, a first-aid kit. n.*

kitch en (kich′ən), 1 room where food is cooked. 2 the cooking department. 3 outfit for cooking. *n.*

kitch en ette (kich′ə net′), 1 a very small, compactly arranged kitchen. 2 part of a room fitted up as a kitchen. *n.*

kitchen police, a military duty of helping the cook prepare and serve food, wash dishes, and clean up the kitchen.

kitch en ware (kich′ən wer′ or kich′ən war′), kitchen utensils. Pots, kettles, and pans are kitchenware. *n.*

kite (kīt), 1 a light wooden frame covered with paper, cloth, or plastic. Kites are flown in the air on the end of a long string. 2 hawk with long, pointed wings and usually a notched or forked tail. *n.*

kith (kith), friends; acquaintances. *n.*
kith and kin, friends and relatives.

kit ten (kit′n), a young cat. *n.*

kit ten ish (kit′n ish), 1 like a kitten. 2 coquettish. *adj.* —**kit′ten ish ly,** *adv.* —**kit′ten ish ness,** *n.*

kit ty (kit′ē), 1 kitten. 2 a pet name for a cat. *n.*, *pl.* **kit ties.**

Kitty Hawk, village in NE North Carolina. Wilbur and Orville Wright made the first successful airplane flight there in 1903.

ki wi (kē′wē), bird of New Zealand that cannot fly. *n.*, *pl.* **ki wis.**

KKK or **K.K.K.,** Ku Klux Klan.

Klee nex (klē′neks), trademark for a disposable paper tissue used as a handkerchief, etc. *n.*

Klon dike (klon′dīk), region in NW Canada, along the Yukon River, famous for its gold fields. *n.*

km., kilometer or kilometers.

knack (nak), special skill; power to do something easily: *That clown has the knack of making very funny faces. n.*

knap sack (nap′sak′), a canvas or leather bag with two shoulder straps, used for carrying clothes, equipment, etc., on the back; rucksack. *n.*

knapsack

knave (nāv), 1 a tricky, dishonest person; rogue; rascal. 2 the jack, a playing card with a picture of a servant or soldier on it. 3 OLD USE. a male servant; man of humble birth or position. *n.*

knav er y (nā′vər ē), 1 behavior of a knave or rascal; trickery; dishonesty. 2 a tricky, dishonest act. *n.*, *pl.* **knav er ies.**

knav ish (nā′vish), tricky; dishonest. *adj.* —**knav′ish ly,** *adv.* —**knav′ish ness,** *n.*

knead (nēd), 1 work over or work up (moist flour or clay) usually by pressing with the hands into dough or paste: *A baker kneads dough.* 2 make or shape by kneading. 3 press and squeeze with the hands; massage: *Kneading the muscles in a stiff shoulder will take away the stiffness. v.*

knee (nē), 1 the joint between the thigh and the lower leg. 2 any joint in a four-footed animal corresponding to the human knee or elbow. 3 anything like a bent knee in shape or position. 4 part of a garment covering the knee. *n.*
bring to one's knees, force to yield.

knee cap (nē′kap′), the flat, movable bone at the front of the knee; patella. *n.*

kneel (nēl), 1 go down on one's knee or knees: *She knelt down to pull a weed from the flower bed.* 2 remain in this position: *They knelt in prayer for half an hour. v.*, **knelt** or **kneeled, kneel ing.**

knell (nel), 1 sound of a bell rung slowly after a death or at a funeral.

kiwi—up to 24 in. long

2 ring slowly. 3 a warning sign of death, failure, etc.: *Their refusal rang the knell of our hopes.* 4 give such a warning sign. 5 a mournful sound. 6 make a mournful sound. 1,3,5 *n.*, 2,4,6 *v.*

knelt (nelt), a past tense and a past participle of **kneel.** *She knelt and prayed. v.*

knew (nü or nyü), past tense of **know.** *She knew the right answer. v.*

Knick er bock er (nik′ər bok′ər), 1 person descended from the early Dutch settlers of New York. 2 person living in New York. *n.*

knick er bock ers (nik′ər bok′ərz), knickers. *n.pl.*

knick ers (nik′ərz), short, loose-fitting trousers gathered in at, or just below, the knee. *n.pl.*

knick knack (nik′nak′), a pleasing trifle; ornament; trinket. *n.* Also, **nick-nack.**

knife (nīf), 1 a thin, flat metal blade fastened in a handle so that it can be used to cut or spread. 2 a sharp blade forming part of a tool or machine: *the knives of a lawn mower.* 3 cut or stab with a knife. 1,2 *n.*, *pl.* **knives;** 3 *v.*, **knifed, knif ing.** —**knife′like′,** *adj.*

knight (nīt), 1 (in the Middle Ages) a man raised to an honorable military rank and pledged to do good deeds. After serving as a page and squire, a man was made a knight by the king or a lord. 2 (in modern times) a man raised to an honorable rank because of great achievement or service. A British knight ranks just below a baronet and uses the title *Sir* before his name. EXAMPLE: Sir John Smith or Sir John. 3 raise to the rank of knight: *He was knighted by the queen.* 4 one of the pieces in the game of chess. 1,2,4 *n.*, 3 *v.*

knight-er rant (nīt′er′ənt), knight traveling in search of adventure. *n.*, *pl.* **knights-er rant.**

knight-er rant ry (nīt′er′ən trē), 1 conduct or action characteristic of a knight-errant. 2 quixotic conduct or action. *n.*, *pl.* **knight-er rant ries.**

knight hood (nīt′hud), 1 rank of a knight. 2 profession or occupation of a knight. 3 character or qualities of a knight. 4 knights as a group or class: *the knighthood of France. n.*

knight ly (nīt′lē), 1 of a knight; brave, generous, and courteous; chivalrous. 2 as a knight should do; bravely, generously, courteously. 1 *adj.,* 2 *adv.*

Knights Templars, a religious and military order of the Middle Ages. Its members were called Templars.

knit (nit), 1 make (cloth or an article of clothing) by looping yarn or thread together with long needles, or by machinery which forms loops instead of weaving: *She is knitting a sweater. She knits rapidly. Jersey is knitted cloth.* 2 join closely and firmly together: *David and Jonathan were knit in friendship.* 3 grow together: *A broken bone knits.* 4 draw (the brows) together in wrinkles: *She knits her brows when she frowns.* *v.,* **knit ted** or **knit, knit ting.**

knit ter (nit′ər), person or thing that knits. *n.*

knit ting (nit′ing), knitted work: *Her knitting was on the table. n.*

knives (nīvz), plural of **knife.** *n.*

knob (nob), 1 a rounded lump. 2 handle on a door, drawer, etc. 3 a rounded hill or mountain. *n.*

knob by (nob′ē), 1 covered with knobs. 2 rounded like a knob. *adj.,* **knob bi er, knob bi est.**

knock (nok), 1 give a hard blow or blows to with the fist, knuckles, or anything hard; hit: *She knocked him on the head.* 2 a hit: *The hard knock made him angry.* 3 hit and cause to fall: *The speeding car knocked down several signs.* 4 hit with a noise: *She knocked on the door.* 5 a hit with a noise. 6 make a noise, especially a rattling or pounding noise: *The engine is knocking.* 7 act of knocking. 8 sound of knocking: *She did not hear the knock at the door.* 9 sound in an internal-combustion engine caused by loose parts or improper burning of fuel: *a knock in the engine.* 10 INFORMAL. find fault with; criticize: *The critics knocked the new book.* 1,3, 4,6,10 *v.,* 2,5,7-9 *n.*

knock about, INFORMAL. wander from place to place.

knock down, take apart: *We knocked down the bookcases and packed them in the car.*

knock off, INFORMAL. 1 take off; deduct: *He will knock off a dollar from the price if you pay cash.* 2 stop work: *We knock off at noon for lunch.*

knock out, hit so hard as to make helpless or unconscious.

knock together, make or put together hastily: *The boys knocked together a sort of raft out of old boards.*

knock a bout (nok′ə bout′), 1 a small, easily handled sailboat having one mast, a mainsail, and a jib, but no bowsprit. 2 suitable for rough use. 1 *n.,* 2 *adj.*

knock er (nok′ər), 1 person or thing that knocks. 2 a hinged knob, ring, or the like, usually of iron or brass, fas-

knit (def. 1)

tened on a door for use in knocking. *n.*

knock-kneed (nok′nēd′), having legs bent inward at the knees. *adj.*

knock out (nok′out′), 1 act of knocking out: *The boxer won the fight by a knockout.* 2 condition of being knocked out. 3 blow that knocks out. *n.*

knoll (nōl), a small, rounded hill; mound. *n.*

knot (not), 1 a fastening made by tying or twining together pieces of one or more ropes, cords, strings, etc.: *a square knot, a slip knot.* 2 tie or twine together in a knot: *He knotted two ropes together.* 3 tangle in knots: *My thread has knotted.* 4 bow or interlacing of ribbon, cord, braid, etc., worn as an ornament or badge of rank: *a shoulder knot.* 5 group; cluster: *A knot of students stood talking outside the classroom.* 6 the hard mass of wood formed in a tree where a branch grows out, which shows as a roundish, cross-grained piece in a board. 7 a hard lump. A knot sometimes forms in a tired muscle. 8 form into a hard lump. 9 joint where the leaves grow out on the stem of a plant. 10 measure of speed used on ships, equal to one nautical mile per hour: *The ship averaged 12 knots.* 11 nautical mile; 6076.11549 feet. 12 difficulty or problem. 13 unite closely in a way that is hard to undo. 14 thing that unites closely or intricately. 1,4-7,9-12,14 *n.,* 2,3,8,13 *v.,* **knot ted, knot ting.**

knot hole (not′hōl′), hole in a board where a knot has fallen out. *n.*

knot ty (not′ē), 1 full of knots: *knotty wood.* 2 difficult; puzzling: *a knotty problem. adj.,* **knot ti er, knot ti est.**

know (nō), 1 have the facts of; be skilled in: *She knows arithmetic. A carpenter must know his trade.* 2 have the facts and be sure that they are true: *We know that 2 and 2 are 4. She was there at the time; she will know.* 3 have knowledge: *I know from experience how to drive on icy roads.* 4 be acquainted with: *I know her very well, but I don't know her sister.* 5 tell apart from others; distinguish: *You will know his house by the red roof.* *v.,* **knew, known, know ing. —know′er,** *n.*

knocker (def. 2)

OVERHAND   FIGURE EIGHT

SQUARE   SLIP

knot (def. 1)—four common types of knots

in the know, INFORMAL. having inside information.

know what's what, INFORMAL. be well-informed.

let know, tell; inform.

know a ble (nō′ə bəl), capable of being known. *adj.*

know-how (nō′hou′), INFORMAL. ability to do something. *n.*

know ing (nō′ing), 1 having knowledge; well-informed. 2 clever; shrewd. 3 suggesting shrewd or secret understanding of matters: *His only answer was a knowing look. adj.*

know ing ly (nō′ing lē), 1 in a knowing way. 2 on purpose: *I would not knowingly hurt anyone. adv.*

knowl edge (nol′ij), 1 what one knows: *a hunter's knowledge of guns.* 2 all that is known or can be learned: *Science is a part of knowledge.* 3 fact of knowing: *The knowledge of our victory caused great joy.* 4 act of knowing: *a knowledge of the surrounding countryside. n.*

to one's knowledge, as far as one knows: *I have never met him to the best of my knowledge.*

knowl edge a ble (nol′i jə bəl), IN-FORMAL. well-informed, especially about a particular subject. *adj.*

known (nōn), past participle of **know.** *George Washington is known as the father of his country. v.*

Knox ville (noks′vil), city in E Tennessee, on the Tennessee River. *n.*

knuck le (nuk′əl), 1 a joint in a finger, especially one of the joints between a finger and the rest of the hand. 2 put the knuckles on the ground in playing marbles. 3 knee or hock joint of an animal used as food: *boiled pigs' knuckles.* 1,3 *n.,* 2 *v.,* **knuck led, knuck ling.**

knuckle down, 1 INFORMAL. work hard. 2 submit; yield: *He would not*

K.O.

knuckle *down under their attacks.*
knuckle under, submit; yield.
K.O. or **k.o.,** knockout.
ko a la (kō ä/lə), a gray, furry mammal of Australia that lives in trees. The female koala carries her young in a pouch. *n., pl.* **ko a las.**

koala
about 2 ft. long

Koch (kôk), **Robert,** 1843-1910, German bacteriologist and physician. *n.*
Ko dak (kō/dak), trademark for a small camera with rolls of film on which photographs are taken. *n.*
kohl ra bi (kōl/rä/bē), 1 plant related to the cabbage and having a turnip-shaped stem. 2 its stem, which is eaten as a vegetable. *n., pl.* **kohl ra bies.**
Ko hou tek (kə hō/tek), comet discovered in 1973. It will come within sight of earth again in about 75 thousand years. *n.* [from Luboš *Kohoutek,* born 1935, Czechoslovakian astronomer who discovered it]
koo doo (kü/dü), kudu. *n., pl.* **koo-doos.**
kook a bur ra (kůk/ə bėr/ə), a large kingfisher of Australia that has a harsh cackling voice; laughing jackass. *n., pl.* **kook a bur ras.**
ko peck or **ko pek** (kō/pek), a coin of the Soviet Union. 100 kopecks make one ruble. *n.*
Ko ran (kô rän/ *or* kô ran/), the sacred book of the Moslems. It consists of revelations to the prophet Mohammed and is the standard by which Moslems regulate their lives. *n.*
Ko re a (kô rē/ə), former country on a peninsula in E Asia, divided into two countries, North Korea and South Korea, after World War II. The Japanese name for Korea is **Chosen.** *Capital of North Korea:* Pyongyang. *Capital of South Korea:* Seoul. See **China** for map. *n.*
Ko re an (kô rē/ən), 1 of Korea, its people, or their language. 2 person born or living in Korea. 3 language of Korea. 1 *adj.,* 2,3 *n.*
Korean War, war between South Korea, aided by the United Nations, and North Korea, aided by communist China. The war lasted from June 1950 to July 1953.
Kos ci us ko (kos/ē us/kō), **Thaddeus,** 1746-1817, Polish general who served in the American army during the Revolutionary War. *n.*
ko sher (kō/shər), 1 right or clean according to Jewish law: *kosher meat.* 2 prepare (food) according to the Jewish law. 3 SLANG. all right; fine: *It's not kosher to change the rules while you are playing the game.* 1,3 *adj.,* 2 *v.* [from Hebrew *kasher* proper]
Ko sy gin (kə sē/gin), **Aleksei N.,** born 1904, premier of the Soviet Union since 1964. *n.*

kohlrabi
(defs. 1 and 2)

kow tow (kou/tou/), 1 kneel and touch the ground with the forehead to show deep respect, submission, or worship. 2 show slavish respect or obedience. 3 act of kowtowing. 1,2 *v.,* 3 *n.*
K.P., kitchen police.
kraal (kräl), 1 village of South African natives, protected by a fence or stockade. 2 pen for cattle or sheep in South Africa. *n.* [from Afrikaans]
Krem lin (krem/lən), citadel of Moscow. The chief offices of the Soviet government are in the Kremlin. *n.*
Kriss Krin gle (kris/ kring/gəl), Santa Claus.

kryp ton (krip/ton), a colorless, inert gas that forms a very small part of the air. It is a chemical element. Krypton is used to fill some fluorescent lamps. *n.*
Kua la Lum pur (kwä/lə lùm/pùr/), capital of the Federation of Malaysia, in W Malaya.

kudu
about 4½ ft. high
at the shoulder

ku du (kü/dü), a large, grayish-brown African antelope with white stripes. *n.* Also, **koodoo.**
Ku Klux Klan (kü/ kluks/ klan/ *or* kyü/ kluks/ klan/), 1 a secret society of white people in the southern United States formed after the Civil War to suppress certain minority groups and maintain white supremacy. 2 a secret society founded in 1915 in the United States, violently opposed to certain minority groups, radicals, and foreigners.
kum quat (kum/kwot), 1 a yellow or orange fruit somewhat like a small orange. It has a sour pulp and a sweet rind, and is used in preserves and candy. 2 tree that it grows on. *n.* Also, **cumquat.**
kung fu (kùng/ fü/), any of various styles of Chinese boxing, most of which use punches, kicks, and blocking actions similar to those of karate.
Ku rile Islands or **Ku ril Islands** (kür/əl *or* kü rēl/), chain of more than 30 large islands and several smaller ones N of Japan.
Ku wait (kü wāt/), 1 country in E Arabia, on the Persian Gulf. 2 its capital. *n.*
kw., kilowatt.
kwhr., kilowatt-hour or kilowatt-hours.
Ky., Kentucky.
Kyo to (kyō/tō), city in central Japan. It was formerly the capital. *n.*
Kyu shu (kyü/shü), large island at the SW end of Japan. *n.*

L l

L or **l** (el), 1 the 12th letter of the alphabet. 2 the Roman numeral for 50. *n., pl.* **L's** or **l's.**

L (el), anything shaped like the letter L. *n., pl.* **L's.**

la (lä), the sixth tone of the musical scale. *n.*

La., Louisiana.

lab (lab), INFORMAL. laboratory. *n.*

la bel (lā′bəl), 1 slip of paper or other material attached to anything and marked to show what or whose it is, or where it is to go: *Can you read the label on the bottle?* 2 put or write a label on: *The bottle is labeled "Poison."* 3 a word or phrase used to describe some person, thing, or idea: *In winter, Chicago deserves its label of "the Windy City."* 4 describe as; call; name: *label someone a liar.* 1,3 *n.,* 2,4 *v.* —**la′bel er,** *n.*

la bi al (lā′bē əl), 1 of the lips. 2 pronounced with the lips closed, nearly closed, or rounded. 3 sound made in this way. *B, p,* and *m* are labials. 1,2 *adj.,* 3 *n.*

la bor (lā′bər), 1 effort in doing or making something; work; toil: *The carpenter was well paid for his labor.* 2 piece of work to be done; task: *The king gave Hercules twelve labors to perform.* 3 work, especially manual work, done by skilled and unskilled workers for wages: *Digging ditches is labor.* 4 such workers as a group: *Labor favors safe working conditions.* 5 do work; work hard; toil: *I labored all day at the factory.* 6 move slowly and heavily: *The ship labored in the heavy seas. The old car labored as it climbed the steep hill.* 7 childbirth. 8 be in childbirth. 1-4,7 *n.,* 5,6,8 *v.* Also, **labour.**

lab o ra to ry (lab′rə tôr′ē), 1 place where scientific work is done; room or building fitted with apparatus for conducting scientific experiments, investigations, tests, etc.: *a chemical laboratory.* 2 place for manufacturing drugs, medicines, explosives, etc. *n., pl.* **lab o ra to ries.**

Labor Day, the first Monday in September, a legal holiday throughout the United States in honor of labor and laborers.

la bored (lā′bərd), done with much effort; forced: *labored breathing, a labored attempt at humor. adj.*

la bor er (lā′bər ər), 1 person who does work that requires strength rather than skill or training. 2 worker. *n.*

la bo ri ous (lə bôr′ē əs), 1 needing or taking much effort; requiring hard work: *Climbing a mountain is laborious.* 2 showing signs of effort; labored: *The student who was always late made up laborious excuses.* 3 willing to work hard; industrious: *a careful and laborious watchmaker. adj.* —**la bo′ri ous ly,** *adv.*

la bor-sav ing (lā′bər sā′ving), that takes the place of or lessens labor: *A washing machine is a labor-saving device. adj.*

labor union, group of workers joined together to protect and promote their interests by dealing as a group with their employers; union.

la bour (lā′bər), labor. *n., v.*

Lab ra dor (lab′rə dôr), 1 peninsula in NE North America, between Hudson Bay and the Atlantic Ocean. 2 the E part of this peninsula, part of the Canadian province of Newfoundland. *n.*

la bur num (lə bėr′nəm), a small, poisonous tree or shrub with hanging clusters of bright-yellow flowers. *n.*

lab y rinth (lab′ə rinth′), 1 number of connecting passages so arranged that it is hard to find one's way from point to point; maze. 2 **Labyrinth,** (in Greek myths) the maze built by Daedalus for King Minos of Crete to imprison the Minotaur. 3 any confusing, complicated arrangement: *We could not find our way out of the labyrinth of dark and narrow streets. n.*

lab y rin thine (lab′ə rin′thən), confusing and complicated; intricate. *adj.*

lac (lak), a sticky substance deposited on various trees by scale insects. Lac is used in making sealing wax, varnish, etc. *n.*

lace (lās), 1 an open weaving or net of fine thread in an ornamental pattern. 2 trim with lace: *a velvet cloak laced with gold.* 3 cord, string, or leather strip passed through holes to pull or hold together the opposite edges of a shoe, garment, etc.: *These shoes need new laces.* 4 put laces through; pull or hold together with a lace or laces: *Lace up your shoes.* 5 interlace; intertwine: *She sat with her fingers laced together.* 6 beat; thrash. 1,3 *n.,* 2,4-6 *v.,* **laced, lac ing.** —**lace′like′,** *adj.*

lace into, 1 strike again and again; lash: *The two angry children laced into each other until the teacher separated them.* 2 criticize severely: *The coach laced into the team for not trying hard enough to win.*

lac e rate (las′ə rāt′), 1 tear roughly; mangle: *The hawk's talons lacerated the field mouse.* 2 cause pain or suffering to; distress: *The coach's sharp words*

hat, āge, fär; let, ēqual, tėrm;
it, īce; hot, ōpen, ôrder;
oil, out; cup, pùt, rüle; ch, child;
ng, long; sh, she; th, thin;
ŦH, then; zh, measure;

ə represents *a* in about,
e in taken, *i* in pencil,
o in lemon, *u* in circus.

lacerated my feelings. v., **lac e rat ed, lac e rat ing.**

lac e ra tion (las′ə rā′shən), 1 a rough tearing or mangling. 2 a rough tear; mangled place. A torn, jagged wound is a laceration. *n.*

lach ry mal gland (lak′rə məl), either of the two glands above the eyes that produce tears.

lac i ness (lā′sē nis), lacy condition or quality. *n.*

lack (lak), 1 have no; be without: *Some guinea pigs lack tails.* 2 a being without: *Lack of a fire made us cold.* 3 have not enough: *This book lacks excitement.* 4 not having enough: *Lack of rest made her tired.* 5 thing needed: *The campers' main lack was fuel for a fire.* 1,3 *v.,* 2,4,5 *n.*

lack a dai si cal (lak′ə dā′zə kəl), lacking interest or enthusiasm; languid; listless. *adj.* —**lack′a dai′si cal ly,** *adv.*

lack ey (lak′ē), 1 a male servant; footman. 2 follower who obeys orders as if he were a servant; toady. *n., pl.* **lackeys.**

lack ing (lak′ing), 1 not having enough; deficient: *A weak person is lacking in strength.* 2 without; not having: *Lacking butter, we ate jam on our bread.* 3 absent; not here: *Water is lacking because the pipe is broken.* 1,3 *adj.,* 2 *prep.*

lack lus ter (lak′lus′tər), lacking brightness; dull and drab. *adj.*

la con ic (lə kon′ik), using few words; brief in speech or expression; concise. *adj.* —**la con′i cal ly,** *adv.*

lac quer (lak′ər), 1 varnish used to give a protective coating or a shiny appearance to metals, wood, paper, etc. Lacquers are made in all colors that are commonly found in paints. 2 coat with lacquer. 3 articles coated with lacquer. 1,3 *n.,* 2 *v.*

la crosse (lə krôs′), game played on a field with a ball and long-handled sticks with webbed baskets by two teams, usually of 10 players each. The players carry the ball and pass it to each other in an attempt to send it into the other team's goal. *n.*

adj.	adjective	*n.*	noun
adv.	adverb	*prep.*	preposition
conj.	conjunction	*pron.*	pronoun
interj.	interjection	*v.*	verb
sing.	singular	*pl.*	plural

lac te al (lak′tē əl), of milk; milky. *adj.*

lac tic acid (lak′tik), a colorless, odorless acid formed when milk sours, vegetable juices ferment, etc.

lac tose (lak′tōs), a crystalline sugar present in milk; milk sugar. *n.*

la cu na (lə kyü′nə), an empty space; gap; blank: *There was a lacuna in the old letter where the ink had faded. n., pl.* **la cu nae** (lə kyü′nē), **la cu nas.**

lac y (lā′sē), 1 of lace. 2 like lace: *the lacy leaves of a fern. adj.,* **lac i er, lac i est.**

lad (lad), boy; youth. *n.*

lad der (lad′ər), 1 set of rungs or steps fastened to two sidepieces for use in climbing up or down. 2 means of climbing higher: *Hard work is often a ladder to success. n.*

lad die (lad′ē), SCOTTISH. lad. *n.*

lade (lād), put a burden on; load. *v.,* **lad ed, lad en** or **lad ed, lad ing.**

lad en (lād′n), 1 loaded; burdened: *a ship laden with goods.* 2 a past participle of **lade.** *The camels were laden with bundles of silk.* 1 *adj.,* 2 *v.*

ladle
(def. 1)

la dle (lā′dl), 1 a large cup-shaped spoon with a long handle, for dipping out liquids. 2 dip: *The cook ladled out the soup into large bowls.* 1 *n.,* 2 *v.,* **la dled, la dling.**

la dy (lā′dē), 1 woman of good family and high social position: *a lady by birth.* 2 a well-bred woman. 3 a polite term for any woman: *"Ladies" is often used in speaking or writing to a group of women.* 4 woman who has the rights and authority of a lord. 5 woman whom a man loves or is devoted to. 6 **Lady,** title used in speaking to or of women of certain ranks in Great Britain: *Lord Grey and his wife, Lady Grey, attended the Queen's reception.* 7 **Our Lady,** a title of the Virgin Mary. *n., pl.* **la dies.**

la dy bird (lā′dē bėrd′), ladybug. *n.*

la dy bug (lā′dē bug′), a small beetle that has a rounded back and is often bright red or yellow with black spots. Ladybugs eat harmful insects. *n.*

la dy-in-wait ing (lā′dē in wā′ting), lady who accompanies or serves a queen or princess. *n., pl.* **la dies-in-wait ing.**

la dy like (lā′dē līk′), like a lady; suitable for a lady; well-bred; polite. *adj.*

la dy ship (lā′dē ship), 1 rank or position of a lady. 2 **Ladyship,** title used in speaking to or of a woman having the rank of Lady in Great Britain: *your Ladyship, her Ladyship. n.*

la dy-slip per (lā′dē slip′ər), lady's-slipper. *n.*

la dy's-slip per (lā′dēz slip′ər), a wild orchid whose flower looks somewhat like a slipper. *n.*

La fa yette (lä′fē et′ *or* laf′ē et′), **Marquis de,** 1757-1834, French general and statesman who served in the American army during the Revolutionary War. *n.*

lag (lag), 1 move too slowly; fall behind: *The child lagged because he was tired.* 2 a falling behind; lagging: *There was a long lag in forwarding mail to us while we were on vacation.* 3 amount by which a person or thing falls behind: *There was a month's lag between the order for our car and its delivery.* 4 become weaker; flag: *Our interest lagged as we watched the dull program.* 1,4 *v.,* **lagged, lag ging;** 2,3 *n.*

lag gard (lag′ərd), 1 person who moves too slowly or falls behind; loiterer. 2 falling behind; slow; backward. 1 *n.,* 2 *adj.*

la goon (lə gün′), 1 pond or small lake connected with a larger body of water. 2 shallow water separated from the sea by low ridges of sand. 3 water within a ring-shaped coral island. *n.*

La gos (lä′gōs *or* lā′gos), capital of Nigeria, in the SW part. *n.*

La hore (lə hôr′), city in E Pakistan. *n.*

laid (lād), past tense and past participle of **lay**[1]. *She laid down the heavy bundle. Those eggs were laid this morning. v.*

lain (lān), past participle of **lie**[2]. *The snow has lain on the ground a week. v.*

lair (ler *or* lar), den or resting place of a wild animal. *n.*

laird (lerd *or* lard), SCOTTISH. owner of land. *n.*

lais sez faire (les′ā fer′ *or* les′ā far′), 1 principle that trade, business, industry, etc., should operate with a minimum of regulation and interference by government. 2 principle that people should do as they please. [from French *laissez faire* allow to do (as one pleases)]

la i ty (lā′ə tē), persons who are not members of the clergy or of a particular profession; laymen: *Doctors use many words that the laity do not know. n.*

lake (lāk), 1 body of water entirely or nearly surrounded by land. A lake usually consists of fresh water and is larger than a pond. 2 pool of liquid. *n.*

lake dweller, person who lived in a house built on piles over a lake in prehistoric times.

lake shore lāk′shôr′), lakeside. *n.*

lake side (lāk′sīd′), the edge or shore of a lake. *n.*

lake trout, a large, dark trout of the lakes of North America.

la ma (lä′mə), a Buddhist priest or monk in Tibet and Mongolia. *n., pl.* **la mas.**

la ma ser y (lä′mə ser′ē), a monastery of lamas in Tibet and Mongolia. *n., pl.* **la ma ser ies.**

lamb (lam), 1 a young sheep. 2 meat from a lamb: *roast lamb.* 3 lambskin. 4 give birth to a lamb or lambs. 5 a young, innocent, or dear person. 1-3,5 *n.,* 4 *v.*—**lamb′like′,** *adj.*

Lamb (lam), **Charles,** 1775-1834, English writer of essays. *n.*

lam baste (lam bāst′), INFORMAL. 1 strike again and again; beat severely; thrash. 2 scold roughly. *v.,* **lam bast ed, lam bast ing.**

lam bent (lam′bənt), 1 moving lightly over a surface: *a lambent flame.* 2 playing lightly and brilliantly over a subject: *lambent wit.* 3 shining with a soft, clear light: *Moonlight is lambent. adj.*

lamb kin (lam′kən), a little lamb. *n.*

lamb skin (lam′skin′), 1 skin of a lamb, especially with the wool on it. 2 leather made from the skin of a lamb. 3 parchment. *n.*

lame (lām), 1 not able to walk properly; having an injured leg or foot; crippled: *He limps because he has been lame since birth.* 2 stiff and sore: *My arm is lame from playing ball.* 3 make lame; cripple: *The accident lamed me for life.* 4 not very good; unsatisfactory: *Oversleeping is a lame excuse for being late.* 1,2,4 *adj.,* **lam er, lam est;** 3 *v.,* **lamed, lam ing.**—**lame′ly,** *adv.* —**lame′ness,** *n.*

la mé (la mā′), a rich fabric made with gold or silver threads. *n.*

lame duck, 1 a public official who has been defeated for reelection and is serving the last part of his term. 2 a disabled or helpless person.

la ment (lə ment′), 1 feel or show grief for; mourn aloud for: *We lament the dead.* 2 feel or show grief; mourn aloud; weep: *Why do they lament so?* 3 expression of grief or sorrow; wail. 4 poem, song, or tune that expresses grief. 5 feel sorry about; regret: *We lamented his absence.* 1,2,5 *v.,* 3,4 *n.*

lam en ta ble (lam′ən tə bəl *or* lə-men/tə bəl), 1 to be regretted or pitied; giving cause for sorrow: *It was a lamentable day when our dog was run over.* 2 not so good; inferior; pitiful: *The singer gave a lamentable performance.* *adj.*

lam en ta bly (lam/ən tə blē), to a lamentable degree; regrettably; deplorably: *They are lamentably ignorant about everything except sports.* *adv.*

lance (def. 1)

lam en ta tion (lam/ən tā/shən), loud grief; cries of sorrow; mourning; wailing. *n.*

Lam en ta tions (lam/ən tā/shənz), book of the Old Testament. According to tradition it was written by Jeremiah. *n.*

lam i na (lam/ə nə), a thin plate, scale, or layer. *n., pl.* **lam i nae** (lam/ə nē/), **lam i nas.**

lam i nate (lam/ə nāt), 1 make (plywood, plastics, glass, etc.) by fastening together layer on layer of one or more materials. 2 beat or roll (metal) into a thin plate. 3 split into thin layers. *v.,* **lam i nat ed, lam i nat ing.**

lam i na tion (lam/ə nā/shən), 1 a laminating or a being laminated. 2 a laminated structure; arrangement in thin layers. 3 a thin layer. *n.*

lamp (lamp), 1 device that gives artificial light. Oil lamps hold oil and a wick by which the oil is burned. A gas or electric light, especially when covered by a glass globe or other shade, is called a lamp. 2 a similar device that gives heat or radiant energy: *an ultraviolet lamp.* 3 anything that gives light. *n.*

lamp black (lamp/blak/), a fine black soot that is deposited when oil, gas, etc., burn incompletely. Lampblack is used as a coloring matter in paint and ink. *n.*

lamp light (lamp/līt/), light from a lamp. *n.*

lamp light er (lamp/lī/tər), 1 person who lights street lamps. 2 torch, twisted paper, etc., used to light lamps. *n.*

lam poon (lam pün/), 1 piece of writing that attacks and makes fun of a person in a malicious or abusive way. 2 attack and make fun of in a lampoon. 1 *n.,* 2 *v.*

lamp post (lamp/pōst/), post used to support a street lamp. *n.*

lam prey (lam/prē), a water animal having a body like an eel, gill slits like a fish, no jaws, and a large, round mouth. Lampreys attach themselves to fishes

with their mouths, sucking the body fluids. *n., pl.* **lam preys.**

La nai (lä nī/), island in the central part of the Hawaiian Islands. *n.*

Lan ca shire (lang/kə shər), county in NW England. *n.*

Lan cas ter (lang/kə stər), 1 the English royal house from 1399 to 1461. Its emblem was a red rose. 2 Lancashire. *n.*

lance (lans), 1 a long, wooden spear with a sharp iron or steel head: *The knights carried lances as they rode into battle.* 2 lancer. 3 any instrument like a soldier's lance. A spear for harpooning a whale is called a lance. 4 pierce with a lance: *lance a fish.* 5 cut open with a lancet: *The dentist lanced the gum where a new tooth had difficulty coming through.* 1-3 *n.,* 4,5 *v.,* **lanced, lancing.**

Lan ce lot (lan/sə lot), the bravest of King Arthur's knights of the Round Table. *n.*

lanc er (lan/sər), a mounted soldier armed with a lance; lance. *n.*

lan cet (lan/sit), a small, pointed knife with two sharp edges, used by doctors and surgeons in opening boils, abscesses, etc. *n.*

land (land), 1 the solid part of the earth's surface: *After months at sea, the voyagers sighted land.* 2 come to land: *The ship landed at the pier. The disabled plane landed in a field.* 3 bring to land: *The pilot landed the airplane in Seattle.* 4 put on land; set ashore: *The ship landed its passengers.* 5 go on shore from a ship or boat: *The passengers landed.* 6 ground; soil: *This is good land for a garden.* 7 ground or soil used as property: *The farmer invested in land and machinery.* 8 country; region: *The explorers traveled north until they reached the land of the midnight sun. Switzerland is a mountainous land.* 9 people of a country; nation: *She collected folk songs from all the land.* 10 come to a stop; arrive: *The burglar landed in jail. The car landed in the ditch.* 11 cause to arrive: *This boat will land you in London.* 12 INFORMAL. get; catch: *land a job, land a fish.* 13 SLANG. strike; hit: *I landed a blow on his chin.* 1,6-9 *n.,* 2-5,10-13 *v.*

lan dau (lan/dou *or* lan/dô), a four-wheeled carriage with two seats and a top made in two parts that can be folded back. *n.* [from *Landau,* a German town, where it was first made]

landau

hat, āge, fär; let, ēqual, tėrm;
it, īce; hot, ōpen, ôrder;
oil, out; cup, pùt, rüle; ch, child;
ng, long; sh, she; th, thin;
ᴛʜ, then; zh, measure;

ə represents *a* in about,
e in taken, *i* in pencil,
o in lemon, *u* in circus.

land breeze, breeze blowing from the land toward the sea.

land ed (lan/did), 1 owning land: *landed nobles.* 2 consisting of land. Landed property is called real estate. *adj.*

land fall (land/fôl/), 1 a sighting of land. 2 the land sighted or reached. *n.*

land hold er (land/hōl/dər), person who owns or occupies land. *n.*

land ing (lan/ding), 1 a coming to land or something solid like land: *the landing of the Pilgrims at Plymouth. There are many millions of take-offs and landings at the nation's airports each year.* 2 place where persons or goods are landed from a ship, helicopter, etc. A wharf, dock, or pier is a landing for boats. 3 platform between flights of stairs. *n.*

landing field, field large enough and smooth enough for airplanes to land on and take off from safely.

landing gear, wheels, pontoons, etc., under an aircraft. When on land or water an aircraft rests on its landing gear.

landing strip, airstrip.

land la dy (land/lā/dē), 1 woman who owns buildings or land that she rents to others. 2 woman who runs an inn or rooming house. *n., pl.* **land la dies.**

land less (land/lis), without land; owning no land. *adj.*

land locked (land/lokt/), 1 shut in, or nearly shut in, by land: *The landlocked harbor was protected from the full force of the wind and waves.* 2 living in waters shut off from the sea: *Landlocked salmon have to spend their lives in fresh water instead of making the migration to salt water.* *adj.*

land lord (land/lôrd/), 1 person who owns buildings or land that he rents to others. 2 person who runs an inn or rooming house. *n.*

land lub ber (land/lub/ər), person not used to being on ships; person who is awkward on board ship because of lack of experience: *The ship's crew laughed at the landlubbers.* *n.*

land mark (land/märk/), 1 something familiar or easily seen, used as a guide: *The traveler did not lose her way in the*

adj. adjective	*n.* noun
adv. adverb	*prep.* preposition
conj. conjunction	*pron.* pronoun
interj. interjection	*v.* verb
sing. singular	*pl.* plural

forest because the rangers' high tower served as a landmark. 2 any important fact or event; any happening that stands out above others: *The inventions of the printing press, telephone, telegraph, radio, and television are landmarks in the history of communication.* 3 stone or other object that marks the boundary of a piece of land. *n.*

land own er (land′ō′nər), person who owns land. *n.*

land scape (land′skāp), 1 view of scenery on land that can be taken in at a glance from one point of view: *From the church tower the two hills with the valley formed a beautiful landscape.* 2 painting, etching, etc., showing such a view. 3 make (land) more pleasant to look at by arranging trees, shrubs, flowers, etc.: *This park is landscaped.* 1,2 *n.,* 3 *v.,* **land scaped, land scap ing.**

Land's End, the SW tip of England.

land slide (land′slīd′), 1 a sliding down of a mass of earth or rock on a steep slope. 2 the mass that slides down. 3 an overwhelming majority of votes for one candidate or political party in an election. *n.*

lands man (landz′mən), man who lives or works on land; person who is not a seaman. *n., pl.* **lands men.**

land ward (land′wərd), toward the land or shore. *adv., adj.*

land wards (land′wərdz), landward. *adv.*

lane (lān), 1 path between hedges, walls, or fences. 2 a narrow country road or city street. 3 any narrow way: *The bride and groom walked down a lane formed by two lines of wedding guests.* 4 course or route used by cars, ships, or aircraft going in the same direction. 5 bowling alley. *n.*

lan guage (lang′gwij), 1 human speech, spoken or written: *Civilization would be impossible without language.* 2 the speech used by one nation, tribe, or other similar large group of people: *the French language, the Navaho language.* 3 form, style, or kind of language; manner of expression: *bad language, strong language, Shakespeare's language.* 4 wording or words: *The lawyer explained to us very carefully the language of the contract.* 5 the special terms used by a science, art, or profession, or

by a class of persons: *the language of chemistry, builders' language.* 6 the expression of thoughts and feelings otherwise than by words: *sign language. Our dog's language is made up of barks, whines, growls, and tail-waggings.* 7 the study of language or languages; linguistics. *n.*

language arts, course of study in elementary schools and high schools that includes reading, spelling, speech, composition, and other subjects that develop skill in using language.

lan guid (lang′gwid), 1 feeling weak; without energy; drooping: *A hot, sticky day makes a person languid.* 2 without interest or enthusiasm; indifferent: *The lazy child felt too languid to do anything.* *adj.* —**lan′guid ly,** *adv.* —**lan′guid ness,** *n.*

lan guish (lang′gwish), 1 grow weak; become weary; lose energy; droop: *The flowers languished from lack of water.* 2 become weak or wasted through pain, hunger, etc.; suffer under any unfavorable conditions: *Wild animals often languish in captivity.* 3 droop with longing; pine with love or grief: *The refugees languished for the homeland they had been forced to leave.* *v.*

lan guish ing (lang′gwi shing), 1 drooping; pining; longing. 2 tender; sentimental; loving. 3 lasting; lingering. *adj.* —**lan′guish ing ly,** *adv.*

lan guor (lang′gər), 1 lack of energy; weakness; weariness: *A long illness caused my languor.* 2 lack of interest or enthusiasm; indifference. 3 softness or tenderness of mood. 4 quietness; stillness: *the languor of a summer afternoon.* 5 lack of activity; sluggishness. *n.*

lan guor ous (lang′gər əs), languid; listless. *adj.* —**lan′guor ous ly,** *adv.*

lank (langk), 1 long and thin; slender: *a lank boy, lank grasses.* 2 straight and flat; not curly or wavy: *lank locks of hair.* *adj.* —**lank′ly,** *adv.* —**lank′ness,** *n.*

lank i ly (lang′kə lē), in a lanky condition or form. *adv.*

lank i ness (lang′kē nis), condition of being lanky. *n.*

lank y (lang′kē), awkwardly long and thin; tall and ungraceful: *a lanky teenager.* *adj.,* **lank i er, lank i est.**

lan o lin (lan′l ən), fatty substance obtained from the natural coating on wool fibers, used in cosmetics, ointments, shoe polish, etc. *n.*

Lan sing (lan′sing), capital of Michigan, in the S part. *n.*

lan tern (lan′tərn), case to protect a light from wind, rain, etc. A lantern has sides of glass, paper, or some other material through which the light can shine. *n.*

lan tern-jawed (lan′tərn jôd′), hav-

ing long thin jaws and hollow cheeks. *adj.*

lan tha num (lan′thə nəm), a malleable metallic element which occurs in various minerals. It is used in making alloys. *n.*

lan yard (lan′yərd), 1 a short rope or cord used on ships to fasten rigging. 2 a loose cord around the neck on which to hang a knife, whistle, etc. 3 a short cord with a hook at one end, used in firing certain kinds of cannon. *n.*

La oc o ön (lā ok′ō on), (in Greek legends) a priest of Apollo at Troy who warned the Trojans against the wooden horse. He and his two sons were killed by two serpents sent by Athena. *n.*

La os (lä′os *or* lä′ōs), country in SE Asia, west of Vietnam. *Capitals:* Vientiane and Luang Prabang. *n.*

La o tian (lā ō′shən), 1 of Laos, its people, or their language. 2 person born or living in Laos. 1 *adj.,* 2 *n.*

lap[1] (lap), 1 the front part from the waist to the knees of a person sitting down, with the clothing that covers it: *I held the baby on my lap.* 2 a loosely hanging edge of clothing; flap. *n.* [Old English *læppa* edge of a garment]

in the lap of fortune, fortunate.

in the lap of luxury, in luxurious circumstances.

lap[2] (lap), 1 lay or lie together, one partly over or beside another; overlap: *We lapped shingles on the roof.* 2 the part that laps over. 3 amount that a part laps over. 4 extend out beyond a limit: *The reign of Elizabeth I (queen of England from 1558 to 1603) lapped over into the 1600's.* 5 to wind or wrap; fold: *She lapped the blanket around her. Lap this edge over that.* 6 one time around a racetrack: *Who won the first lap of the race?* 7 part of any course traveled: *The last lap of our all-day hike was the toughest.* 1,4,5 *v.,* **lapped, lap ping;** 2,3,6,7 *n.* [from *lap*[1]]

lap[3] (lap), 1 drink by lifting up with the tongue: *Cats and dogs lap water.* 2 move or beat gently with a lapping sound; splash gently: *Little waves lapped against the boat.* 3 act of lapping: *With one lap of the tongue the bear finished the honey.* 4 sound of lapping: *The lap of the waves against a boat put me to sleep.* 1,2 *v.,* **lapped, lapping;** 3,4 *n.* [Old English *lapian* to lick]

lap up, take in eagerly or greedily;

lantern of the type which burns gasoline and has a single mantle

MANTLE

devour: *The scouts were so hungry after the long hike that they lapped up their dinners. The children lapped up the tales about frontier adventures.*

La Paz (lä päs′), one of the two capitals of Bolivia, in the W part. Sucre is the other capital.

lap board (lap′bôrd′), a thin, flat board held on the lap and used as a table. *n.*

lap dog, a small pet dog.

LAPEL

la pel (lə pel′), either of the two front parts of a coat folded back just below the collar. *n.*

lap ful (lap′fül), as much as a lap can hold. *n., pl.* **lap fuls** or **laps ful.**

lap i dar y (lap′ə der′ē), person who cuts, polishes, or engraves precious stones. *n., pl.* **lap i dar ies.**

lap is laz u li (lap′is laz′yə lī), 1 a deep-blue, opaque, semiprecious stone used for an ornament. 2 deep blue.

Lap land (lap′land′), region in N Norway, N Sweden, N Finland, and NW Soviet Union. *n.*

Lap land er (lap′lan′dər), person born or living in Lapland. *n.*

La Pla ta (lä plä′tə), seaport in E Argentina, near Buenos Aires.

Lapp (lap), 1 one of a group of people that live in Lapland. The Lapps are small in stature with short, broad heads. 2 language of the Lapps. *n.*

lap pet (lap′it), a small flap or fold: *a lappet on a dress. n.*

lapse (laps), 1 a slight mistake or error: *a lapse of the tongue because of carelessness, a lapse of memory.* 2 make a slight mistake or error. 3 a slipping by; a passing away: *A minute is a short lapse of time.* 4 slip by; pass away: *Our interest in the dull story soon lapsed.* 5 a slipping back; sinking down; slipping into a lower condition: *a lapse into savage ways.* 6 slip back; sink down: *The abandoned house lapsed into disrepair.* 7 a falling or passing into any

state: *a lapse into silence.* 8 fall or pass into any state: *Our discussion lapsed into silence.* 9 the ending of a right or privilege because not renewed, not used, or otherwise neglected: *the lapse of a lease.* 10 end in this way: *My driver's license lapsed when I failed to renew it.* 1,3,5,7,9 *n.,* 2,4,6,8,10 *v.,* **lapsed, laps ing.**

lap wing (lap′wing′), a crested plover of Europe, Asia, and northern Africa that has a slow, irregular flight and a peculiar, wailing cry. *n.*

Lar a mie (lar′ə mē), city in SE Wyoming. *n.*

lar board (lär′bərd), 1 side of a ship to the left of a person looking from the stern toward the bow; port. 2 on the left side of a ship. 1 *n.,* 2 *adj.*

lar ce nous (lär′sə nəs), 1 characterized by larceny; guilty of larceny: *Burglary is a larcenous offense.* 2 thievish: *Blue jays are known for their larcenous habits. adj.*

lar ce ny (lär′sə nē), 1 the unlawful taking and using of the personal property of another person without his consent. 2 theft. *n., pl.* **lar ce nies.**

larch (lärch), 1 tree belonging to the same family as the pine, with small woody cones and needles that fall off in autumn. 2 the strong, tough wood of this tree. *n., pl.* **larch es.**

lard (lärd), 1 the fat of pigs or hogs, melted down and made clear: *The cook uses lard in making pies.* 2 put strips of bacon or pork in (meat) before cooking. 3 put lard on or in; grease: *Lard the pan well.* 4 give variety to; enrich: *The speaker larded his speech with jokes and stories.* 1 *n.,* 2-4 *v.*

lar der (lär′dər), 1 place where food is kept; pantry. 2 supply of food: *The hunter's larder included deer meat, flour, salt, and bacon. n.*

La re do (lə rā′dō), city in S Texas. *n.*

large (lärj), 1 of more than the usual size, amount, or number; big: *America is a large country. A hundred thousand dollars is a large sum of money.* 2 having much scope or range; broad: *a person of large experience. adj.,* **larg er, larg est. —large′ness,** *n.*

at large, 1 at liberty; free: *Is the escaped prisoner still at large?* 2 as a whole; altogether: *The people at large want peace.* 3 representing the whole of a state or district, not merely one division of it: *a congresswoman at large.*

large-heart ed (lärj′här′tid), generous; liberal. *adj.*

large intestine, the lower part of the intestines into which the small intestine discharges food that has been digested. It is a wide tube in which water is absorbed and wastes are eliminated. See **intestine** for diagram.

hat, āge, fär; let, ēqual, tėrm;
it, īce; hot, ōpen, ôrder;
oil, out; cup, pút, rüle; ch, child;
ng, long; sh, she; th, thin;
ŦH, then; zh, measure;

ə represents *a* in about,
e in taken, *i* in pencil,
o in lemon, *u* in circus.

large ly (lärj′lē), to a great extent; mainly: *This region consists largely of desert. adv.*

large-scale (lärj′skāl′), 1 involving many persons or things; great; extensive: *The great Chicago fire of 1871 was a large-scale disaster.* 2 made or drawn to a large scale: *This large-scale map shows many details. adj.*

lar gess or **lar gesse** (lär′jis), 1 generous giving. 2 a generous gift or gifts. *n.*

larg ish (lär′jish), rather large. *adj.*

lar go (lär′gō), in music: 1 slow and dignified; stately. 2 in a slow and dignified manner. 3 a slow, stately passage or piece of music. 1 *adj.,* 2 *adv.,* 3 *n., pl.* **lar gos.** [from Italian]

lar i at (lar′ē ət), 1 rope for fastening horses, mules, etc., to a stake while they are grazing. 2 lasso. *n.*

lark[1] (lärk), 1 a small songbird of Europe, Asia, America, and northern Africa with brown feathers and long hind claws. The skylark is one kind. Larks often sing while soaring in the air. 2 any of several similar songbirds in America, such as the meadowlark. *n.* [Old English *lāwerce*]

lark[2] (lärk), 1 something that is good fun; a merry or gay time; frolic: *What a lark we had at the circus!* 2 have fun; play; frolic. 1 *n.,* 2 *v.* [origin uncertain]

lark spur (lärk′spėr′), plant with clusters of blue, pink, or white flowers on tall stalks. *n.*

lar va (lär′və), 1 the early form of an insect from the time it leaves the egg until it becomes a pupa. A caterpillar is the larva of a butterfly or moth. A grub is the larva of a beetle. Maggots are the larvae of flies. The silkworm is a larva. 2 an immature form of certain animals that is different in structure from the adult form and must undergo a change or metamorphosis to become like the parent. A tadpole is the larva of a frog or toad. *n., pl.* **lar vae** (lär′vē).

lar val (lär′vəl), 1 of or having to do with larvae. 2 in the form of a larva. *adj.*

lar yn gi tis (lar′ən jī′tis), inflam-

larynx

mation of the larynx, usually accompanied by hoarseness. *n.*

lar ynx (lar′ingks), the upper end of the windpipe, where the vocal cords are; voice box. *n., pl.* **la ryn ges** (lə rin′jēz), **lar ynx es.**

LARYNX
WINDPIPE

la sa gna (lə zä′nyə), dish consisting of chopped meat, cheese, and tomato sauce, baked with layers of wide noodles. *n.* [from Italian]

La Salle (lə sal′), **Robert Cavelier, Sieur de,** 1643-1687, Frenchman who explored the Mississippi and Ohio rivers.

las car (las′kər), a native sailor of the East Indies. *n.*

las civ i ous (lə siv′ē əs), 1 feeling lust. 2 showing lust. 3 causing lust. *adj.* —**las civ′i ous ly,** *adv.* —**las civ′i ous ness,** *n.*

la ser (lā′zər), device that produces a very narrow and intense beam of light of only one wavelength going in only one direction. Laser beams are used to cut or melt hard materials, remove diseased body tissues, transmit television signals, etc. *n.* [formed from *l(ight) a(mplification by) s(timulated) e(mission of) r(adiation)*]

lash¹ (lash), 1 the part of a whip that is not the handle: *The leather lash cut the side of the horse.* 2 a stroke or blow with a whip: *The driver gave his horse a lash.* 3 strike with a whip; flog: *The driver of the team lashed her horses on.* 4 beat back and forth: *The lion lashed its tail. The wind lashes the sails.* 5 a sudden, swift movement: *the lash of an animal's tail.* 6 strike violently; hit: *The wild horse lashed out at the Indian with its hoofs. The rain lashed against the windows.* 7 attack severely in words; scold sharply: *In her speech she lashed out at corrupt politicians.* 8 eyelash. 1,2,5,8 *n., pl.* **lash es;** 3,4,6,7 *v.* [Middle English *lasshe*] —**lash′er,** *n.*

lash² (lash), tie or fasten with a rope or cord: *We lashed logs together to make a raft.* *v.* [from French of the 1400's *lachier, lacier,* from *lache* a lace]

lash ing (lash′ing), rope or cord, used in tying or fastening. *n.*

lass (las), a girl or young woman. *n., pl.* **lass es.**

las sie (las′ē), girl; lass. *n.*

las si tude (las′ə tüd *or* las′ə tyüd), lack of energy; a feeling of weakness; weariness: *a period of renewed excitement after an interval of lassitude.*

las so (las′ō *or* la sü′), 1 a long rope with a running noose at one end; lariat: *The cowboy threw the lasso at the calves to catch them and brand them.* 2 catch with a lasso. 1 *n., pl.* **las sos** or **las soes;** 2 *v.*

last¹ (last), 1 coming after all others; being at the end; final: *the last page of the book. Z is the last letter of the alphabet; A is the first.* 2 after all others; at the end; finally: *He came last in the line.* 3 latest: *When did you see her last?* 4 most unlikely: *Fighting is the last thing I would do.* 5 person or thing that comes after all others: *She was the last in the line.* 6 end: *You have not heard the last of this.* 1,4 *adj.,* 2,3 *adv.,* 5,6 *n.* [Old English *latost,* superlative of *lǣt* late]

at last, at the end; after a long time; finally: *At last the baby fell asleep.*

last² (last), 1 go on; hold out; continue to be; endure: *The storm lasted three days. Can you last through the race? How long will our money last?* 2 continue in good condition, force, etc.: *I hope these shoes last a year.* *v.* [Old English *lǣstan*]

last³ (last), block shaped like a person's foot, on which shoes and boots are formed or repaired. *n.* [Old English *lǣste* footprint]

last ing (las′ting), that lasts; that will last; that will last a long time; permanent: *The powerful experience had a lasting effect on her.* *adj.* —**last′ing ly,** *adv.* —**last′ing ness,** *n.*

last ly (last′lē), in conclusion; finally: *Lastly, I want to thank all of you for your help.* *adv.*

last quarter, 1 period of time between the second half moon and the new moon. 2 phase of the moon represented by the half moon after the full moon.

last straw, last of a series of troublesome things that finally causes a collapse, outburst, etc.

Last Supper, supper of Jesus and His disciples on the evening before He was crucified; Lord's Supper.

Las Ve gas (läs vā′gəs), city in SE Nevada.

lat., latitude.

Lat., Latin.

latch (lach), 1 a catch for fastening a

latch (def. 1)

door, gate, or window, often one not needing a key. A latch consists of a movable piece of metal or wood that fits into a notch or opening. 2 fasten with a latch: *Latch and bar the door.* 1 *n., pl.* **latch es;** 2 *v.*

latch key (lach′kē′), key used to draw back or unfasten the latch on a door. *n., pl.* **latch keys.**

latch string (lach′string′), string passed through a hole in a door for the purpose of unfastening the latch from the outside. *n.*

late (lāt), 1 after the usual or proper time: *We had a late dinner last night* (*adj.*). *He worked late* (*adv.*). 2 near the end: *She reached success late in life* (*adj.*). *It rained late in the afternoon* (*adv.*). 3 not long past; recent: *How much damage was done by the late storm?* 4 recently dead: *The late Mr. Lee was a good neighbor.* 5 gone out of or retired from office: *The late president is still working actively.* 6 recently but no longer: *Jane Smith, late of Boston.* 1-5 *adj.,* **lat er** or **lat ter, lat est** or **last;** 1,2,6 *adv.,* **lat er, lat est** or **last.** —**late′ness,** *n.*

of late, a short time ago; lately; recently: *I haven't seen them of late.*

late com er (lāt′kum′ər), person or group that has arrived late or recently: *The latecomers to the play missed part of the first act.* *n.*

la teen-rigged (la tēn′rigd′), having a lateen sail. *adj.*

lateen sails

la teen sail (la tēn′), a triangular sail held up by a long yard on a short mast.

late ly (lāt′lē), a little while ago; not long ago; recently: *He has not been looking well lately.* *adv.*

la tent (lā′nt), present but not active; hidden: *The power of a seed to grow into a plant remains latent if it is not planted.* *adj.* —**la′tent ly,** *adv.*

lat er al (lat'ər əl), of the side; at the side; from the side; toward the side: *A lateral fin of a fish grows from its side. A lateral pass in football is thrown toward the side of the field. adj.*

lat er al ly (lat'ər ə lē), in a lateral direction; at the side; sideways. *adv.*

la tex (lā'teks), a milky liquid found in milkweed, poppies, and plants yielding rubber. It hardens in the air, and is used to make chicle, rubber, and other products. *n.*

latitude (def. 1)—circles of latitude

lath (lath), 1 a thin, narrow strip of wood used with others like it to form a support for the plaster of a wall, ceiling, etc., or to make a lattice. 2 a wire cloth or sheet metal with holes in it, used in place of laths. 3 cover or line with laths. 1,2 *n., pl.* **laths** (laᴛHz *or* laths); 3 *v.*

lathe (lāᴛH), machine for holding pieces of wood, metal, etc., and turning them rapidly against a cutting tool which shapes them. *n.*

ELECTRIC MOTOR

PIECE OF WOOD

lathe

lath er (laᴛH'ər), 1 foam made from soap and water. 2 put lather on: *He lathers his face before shaving.* 3 form a lather: *This soap lathers well.* 4 foam formed in sweating: *the lather on a horse after a race.* 5 become covered with such foam: *The horse lathered from its hard gallop.* 1,4 *n.,* 2,3,5 *v.*

Lat in (lat'n), 1 language of the ancient Romans, used in written form by scholars through the Middle Ages. It is still used in official documents of the Roman Catholic Church. 2 of Latin; in Latin: *Latin poetry, Latin grammar, a Latin scholar.* 3 member of any of the peoples whose languages came from Latin. The Italians, French, Spanish, Portuguese, and Romanians are Latins.

4 of these peoples or their languages. 1,3 *n.,* 2,4 *adj.*

Latin America, South America, Central America, Mexico, and most of the West Indies. The languages spoken in Latin America are Spanish, Portuguese, and French, all of which came from Latin.

Lat in-A mer i can (lat'n ə mer'ə-kən), of or having to do with Latin America. *adj.*

Latin American, person born or living in Latin America.

lat ish (lā'tish), rather late. *adj., adv.*

lat i tude (lat'ə tüd *or* lat'ə tyüd), 1 distance north or south of the equator, measured in degrees. A degree of latitude is about 69 miles. 2 place or region having a certain latitude: *Polar bears live in the cold latitudes.* 3 room to act or think; freedom from narrow rules; scope: *We were allowed much latitude in choosing our bedtimes. n.*

lat ter (lat'ər), 1 the second of two: *Canada and the United States are in North America; the former lies north of the latter.* 2 more recent; nearer the end; later: *Friday comes in the latter part of the week. adj.,* one of the comparative forms of **late.**

Lat ter-day Saint (lat'ər dā'), Mormon.

lat ter ly (lat'ər lē), at a recent time; lately. *adv.*

lat tice (lat'is), 1 structure of crossed wooden or metal strips with open spaces between them. 2 furnish with a lattice: *The windows are latticed with iron bars.* 3 window, gate, etc., having a lattice. 4 form into a lattice: *The cook latticed strips of dough across the pie.* 1,3 *n.,* 2,4 *v.,* **lat ticed, lat tic ing.**

lat tice work (lat'is wėrk'), 1 a lattice. 2 lattices: *Many old New Orleans houses are decorated with latticework of wrought iron. n.*

Lat vi a (lat'vē ə), Soviet republic in N Europe, on the Baltic Sea. *Capital:* Riga. *n.* —**Lat'vi an,** *adj., n.*

laud (lôd), 1 praise highly; extol: *Our teacher lauded our efforts to raise money for the new library.* 2 song or hymn of praise. 1 *v.,* 2 *n.*

laud a ble (lô'də bəl), deserving praise; commendable: *Her desire to help her mother in the store is laudable. adj.*

laud a bly (lô'də blē), in a laudable manner. *adv.*

lau da num (lôd'n əm), solution of opium in alcohol, used to lessen pain. *n.*

laud a to ry (lô'də tôr'ē), expressing praise; extolling. *adj.*

laugh (laf), 1 make the sounds and movements of the face and body that show one is happy or amused: *We all laughed at the joke.* 2 act or sound of laughing: *a hearty laugh.* 3 drive,

hat, āge, fär; let, ēqual, tėrm;
it, īce; hot, ōpen, ôrder;
oil, out; cup, pùt, rüle; ch, child;
ng, long; sh, she; th, thin;
ᴛH, then; zh, measure;

ə represents *a* in about,
e in taken, *i* in pencil,
o in lemon, *u* in circus.

put, bring, etc., by or with laughing: *The children laughed their tears away.* 1,3 *v.,* 2 *n.* —**laugh'er,** *n.*

have the last laugh, get the better of (someone) after appearing to lose: *In the race between the hare and the tortoise, the tortoise had the last laugh.*

laugh at, make fun of; ridicule: *They laughed at me for believing in ghosts.*

laugh off, pass off or dismiss with a laugh: *I laughed off my friend's warning that the ice was not safe and walked out to the middle of the pond.*

lattice
(def. 1)

laugh a ble (laf'ə bəl), causing laughter; amusing; funny: *a laughable mistake. adj.* —**laugh'a ble ness,** *n.*

laugh a bly (laf'ə blē), in a laughable manner. *adv.*

laugh ing (laf'ing), that laughs or seems to laugh: *a laughing brook. adj.*

no laughing matter, matter that is serious.

laughing jackass, kookaburra.

laugh ing stock (laf'ing stok'), person or thing that is made fun of. *n.*

laugh ter (laf'tər), 1 sound of laughing: *Laughter filled the room.* 2 action of laughing: *The clown's antics brought forth laughter from the children. n.*

launch[1] (lônch), 1 cause to slide into the water; set afloat: *The new ship was launched from the supports on which it was built.* 2 push out or put forth into the air: *launch a plane from an aircraft carrier. The satellite was launched in a rocket.* 3 act of launching a rocket, missile, aircraft, ship, etc.: *The launch of the first space vehicle was a historic event.* 4 set going; set out; start: *Our friends launched us in business by lending us money. We used the money to launch into a new business. The traveler launched into a long description* launch

of her voyage. 5 send out; throw; hurl: *We used a slingshot to launch pebbles into the air. I launched a wild challenge at my opponent.* 6 burst; plunge: *The rebels launched into a violent attack on their government.* 1,2,4-6 *v.,* 3 *n., pl.* **launch es.** [from French of the 1300's *lanchier* throw a lance] —**launch′er,** *n.*

launch² (lônch), 1 an open motorboat used for pleasure trips, for ferrying passengers, etc. 2 the largest boat carried by a warship. *n., pl.* **launch es.** [from Spanish and Portuguese *lancha* kind of long boat]

launching pad, surface or platform on which a rocket or missile is prepared for launching and from which it is launched.

laun der (lôn′dər), 1 wash and iron (clothes, tablecloths, towels, etc.). 2 be able to be washed; stand washing: *Cotton materials usually launder well.* *v.*

laun dress (lôn′dris), woman whose work is washing and ironing clothes, tablecloths, towels, etc. *n., pl.* **laundress es.**

Laun dro mat (lôn′drə mat), trademark for a self-service laundry consisting of coin-operated washing machines and dryers. *n.*

laun dry (lôn′drē), 1 room or building where clothes, tablecloths, towels, etc., are washed and ironed. 2 clothes, tablecloths, towels, etc., washed or to be washed. *n., pl.* **laun dries.**

laun dry man (lôn′drē mən), man who works in or for a laundry: *Our laundryman collects and delivers our laundry every Monday.* *n., pl.* **laun dry men.**

lau re ate (lôr′ē it), 1 crowned with a laurel wreath as a mark of honor. 2 honored; distinguished. 3 poet laureate. 1,2 *adj.,* 3 *n.*

lau rel (lôr′əl), 1 a small evergreen tree of southern Europe, with smooth, shiny leaves; bay. The ancient Greeks and Romans made wreaths of laurel to put on the heads of persons they wished to honor. 2 any tree or shrub of the same family as the laurel. 3 mountain laurel. 4 **laurels,** *pl.* **a** high honor; fame. **b** victory. *n.*

look to one's laurels, guard one's reputation or record from rivals: *You will have to look to your laurels unless you study harder.*

rest on one's laurels, be satisfied with the honors that one has already won or the achievements one has already attained: *Instead of resting on her laurels, she went on to further success.*

Lau ren tian Mountains (lô ren′shən), range of low mountains or high hills in E Canada, between Hudson Bay and the St. Lawrence River.

la va (lä′və *or* lav′ə), 1 hot, melted rock flowing from a volcano. 2 rock formed by the cooling of this melted rock. Some lavas are hard and glassy; others are light and porous. *n.*

lav a to ry (lav′ə tôr′ē), 1 room where a person can wash his hands and face. 2 bowl or basin to wash in. 3 bathroom; toilet. *n., pl.* **lav a to ries.**

lave (lāv), OLD USE. 1 wash; bathe. 2 wash or flow against. *v.,* **laved, laving.**

lav en der (lav′ən dər), 1 pale-purple. 2 a pale purple. 3 a small shrub with spikes of fragrant, pale-purple flowers, yielding an oil much used in perfumes. 4 its dried flowers, leaves, and stalks, used to perfume or preserve linens or clothes. 1 *adj.,* 2-4 *n.*

la ver (lā′vər), OLD USE. bowl to wash in. *n.*

lav ish (lav′ish), 1 too free in giving or spending; extravagant: *A very rich person can be lavish with money.* 2 very abundant; more than is needed: *a lavish helping of dessert.* 3 give or spend very freely or too freely: *We lavished kindness on our sick friend.* 1,2 *adj.,* 3 *v.* —**lav′ish er,** *n.* —**lav′ish ly,** *adv.* —**lav′ish ness,** *n.*

law (lô), 1 rule or regulation made by a country, state, etc., for all the people who live there: *a law against kidnaping, a traffic law.* 2 system of such rules formed to protect society: *English law is different from French law.* 3 the study of such a system of rules; the profession of a lawyer: *My cousin is planning a career in law.* 4 controlling influence of these rules: *The police maintain law and order.* 5 law as a system: *courts of law.* 6 all the rules concerned with a particular subject: *commercial law, criminal law.* 7 any rule that must be obeyed: *the laws of hospitality. The laws of a game must be obeyed by all players.* 8 statement of what always occurs under certain conditions: *the law of gravitation. Scientists study the laws of nature.* 9 one of God's rules or commandments. 10 **the Law,** the first five books of the Old Testament, containing the Mosaic law. *n.*

go to law, appeal to courts of law; contest in a lawsuit: *The two neighbors could not agree on their property line and had to go to law to settle the matter.*

lay down the law, 1 give orders that must be obeyed: *There is no official to lay down the law on this question.* 2 give a scolding: *The teacher laid down the law to the noisy class.*

take the law into one's own hands, protect one's rights or punish a crime without appealing to courts of law: *The mob took the law into its own hands.*

law-a bid ing (lô′ə bī′ding), obeying the law; peaceful and orderly: *As a law-abiding citizen, I don't litter.* *adj.*

law break er (lô′brā′kər), person who breaks the law. *n.*

law court, court of law.

law ful (lô′fəl), 1 according to law; done as the law directs: *lawful arrest.* 2 allowed by law; rightful: *lawful demands.* *adj.* —**law′ful ly,** *adv.* —**law′ful ness,** *n.*

law giv er (lô′giv′ər), person who prepares and puts into effect a system of laws for a people. *n.*

law less (lô′lis), 1 paying no attention to the law; breaking the law: *A thief leads a lawless life.* 2 having no laws: *In pioneer days much of the American West was lawless.* 3 hard to control; disorderly; unruly: *a wild and lawless sea.* *adj.* —**law′less ly,** *adv.* —**law′less ness,** *n.*

law mak er (lô′mā′kər), person who helps make the laws of a country; member of a legislature, congress, or parliament; legislator. *n.*

law mak ing (lô′mā′king), 1 having the duty and power of making laws; legislative: *Congress is a lawmaking body.* 2 the making of laws; legislation. 1 *adj.,* 2 *n.*

lawn¹ (lôn), piece of land covered with grass kept closely cut, especially near or around a house. *n.* [from French of the 1300's *launde* wooded ground]

lawn² (lôn), a kind of thin, sheer linen or cotton cloth. *n.* [probably from *Laon,* a town in France, an important center of linen manufacture]

lawn mower, machine with revolving blades for cutting the grass on a lawn.

lawn tennis, tennis, especially when played on a grass court.

law ren ci um (lô ren′sē əm), a radioactive metallic element produced artificially from californium. *n.* [from Ernest O. *Lawrence,* 1901-1958, an American physicist]

law suit (lô′süt′), case in a court of law started by one person to claim something from another; application to a court started by one person to compel another to do him justice. *n.*

law yer (lô′yər), person whose profession is giving advice about the laws or acting for others in a court of law. *n.*

lax (laks), **1** not tight or firm; slack: *The package was tied so loosely that the cord was lax.* **2** not strict; careless: *Don't let yourself become lax about the schedule you have set for doing your homework.* **3** not exact; vague. *adj.* —**lax′ly,** *adv.* —**lax′ness,** *n.*

lax a tive (lak′sə tiv), **1** a medicine that makes the bowels move. **2** making the bowels move. **1** *n.,* **2** *adj.*

lax i ty (lak′sə tē), lax condition or quality; slackness. *n.*

lay¹ (lā), **1** place in a certain position; put down: *Lay your hat on the table.* **2** bring down; beat down: *A storm laid the crops low. A shower has laid the dust.* **3** place in a lying-down position: *Lay the baby down gently.* **4** place or set: *Lay your hand on your heart. The British laid a tax on tea. I always lay great emphasis on quick thinking. The scene of this story is laid in New York.* **5** put: *Lay aside that book for me. The horse laid its ears back.* **6** put in place: *lay bricks. They laid the carpet on the floor.* **7** put into a certain state or condition: *lay a wound open.* **8** put down as a bet; offer as a bet; wager: *I lay five dollars that she won't come.* **9** make quiet or make disappear: *lay a ghost.* **10** blame; attribute: *I laid my failure on my lack of effort.* **11** give forth; produce (an egg or eggs): *Birds, fish, and reptiles lay eggs. All the hens were laying well.* **12** apply oneself vigorously: *The rowers laid to their oars.* *v.,* **laid, lay ing.** [Old English *lecgan* to cause to lie]

lay about, hit out on all sides: *Attacked by thieves, the merchant laid about with his walking stick.*

lay aside, lay away, or **lay by,** put away for future use; save: *I laid away a dollar a week toward purchasing a new bicycle.*

lay down, 1 declare; state: *The umpire laid down the conditions for settling the dispute.* **2** give; sacrifice: *lay down one's life for the cause of liberty.*

lay for, stay hidden ready to attack: *We laid for our classmates with snowballs.*

lay in, put aside for the future; provide: *The trapper laid in enough supplies for the winter.*

lay into, 1 beat; thrash: *She laid into the vicious dog with a stick.* **2** INFORMAL. scold: *My parents laid into me for not doing my homework.*

lay off, 1 put aside: *He laid off his coat as he approached the fire.* **2** put out of work for a time: *During the slack season many workers were laid off.* **3** mark off: *The coach laid off the boundaries of the tennis court.* **4** INFORMAL.

stop teasing or interfering with: *Let's lay off the new boy and give him a chance.*

lay of the land, the nature of the place; the position of hills, water, woods, etc.: *She learned the lay of the land while on a nature hike.*

lay oneself out, make a big effort; take great pains: *He laid himself out to be agreeable.*

lay open, 1 make bare; expose: *The captured spy laid open to us the whole scheme of the attack.* **2** make an opening in; wound.

lay out, 1 spread out: *Supper was laid out on the table.* **2** arrange; plan: *The road was laid out but not yet paved.* **3** pay out; spend: *I had to lay out a lot of money for my new bicycle.* **4** prepare (a dead body) for burial.

lay over, stop for a time in a place: *It was raining so hard one day on our trip that we laid over until the rain stopped.*

lay to, head into the wind and stand still: *The ship lay to until the fog lifted.*

lay up, 1 put away for future use: *After the sailing season was over we laid our boat up for the winter.* **2** cause to stay in bed or indoors because of illness: *I was laid up with a bad cold last week.*

lay² (lā), past tense of **lie².** *I took a long walk and then lay down for a rest.* *v.*

lay³ (lā), **1** of the people of a church not belonging to the clergy. A lay sermon is one given by a person who is not a clergyman. **2** of the people who do not belong to a particular profession: *I am not a doctor, but my lay opinion is that you have the flu.* *adj.* [from French of the 1300's *lai*]

lay⁴ (lā), **1** poem to be sung: *Scott's poem, "The Lay of the Last Minstrel," tells the story of a feud between two Scottish border families.* **2** song; tune. *n.* [from French of the 1200's *lai* song]

lay er (lā′ər), **1** one thickness or fold: *the layer of clothing next to the skin, a layer of clay between two layers of sand.* **2** one that lays: *That hen is a champion layer.* **3** branch of a plant bent down and partly covered by earth so that it will take root. **4** spread by layers. **5** form (new plants) by layers. **1-3** *n.,* **4,5** *v.*

layer cake, cake made in layers put together with frosting or filling.

lay ette (lā et′), set of clothes and bedding for a newborn baby. *n.*

lay man (lā′mən), **1** member of a church who is not a clergyman: *The priest and several laymen planned the church budget.* **2** person who is not a member of a particular profession: *It is hard for most laymen to understand doctors' prescriptions. n., pl.* **lay men.**

hat, āge, fär; let, ēqual, tėrm; it, īce; hot, ōpen, ôrder; oil, out; cup, pùt, rüle; ch, child; ng, long; sh, she; th, thin; ₮H, then; zh, measure;

ə represents *a* in about, *e* in taken, *i* in pencil, *o* in lemon, *u* in circus.

lay off (lā′ôf′), **1** a dismissing of workmen temporarily. **2** time during which the workmen are out of work. *n.*

lay out (lā′out′), **1** arrangement; plan: *This map shows the layout of the camp.* **2** a plan or design for an advertisement, book, etc. **3** thing laid or spread out; display. **4** act of laying out. *n.*

lay o ver (lā′ō′vər), a stopping for a time in a place: *After a twenty-minute layover in Chicago we flew on to Los Angeles. n.*

Laz ar us (laz′ər əs), (in the Bible) the brother of Mary and Martha, whom Jesus raised from the dead. *n.*

laze (lāz), be lazy or idle. *v.,* **lazed, laz ing.**

la zi ly (lā′zə lē), in a lazy manner. *adv.*

la zi ness (lā′zē nis), dislike of work; unwillingness to work or be active; being lazy. *n.*

la zy (lā′zē), **1** not willing to work or be active: *Most bees are workers but the drones are lazy.* **2** moving slowly; not very active: *A lazy stream winds through the meadow. adj.,* **la zi er, la zi est.**

la zy bones (lā′zē bōnz′), INFORMAL. a very lazy person. *n.*

lb., pound. *pl.* **lb.** or **lbs.** [abbreviation of Latin *libra* pound]

lea (lē), a grassy field; meadow; pasture. *n., pl.* **leas.**

layer (def. 3)

leach (lēch), **1** run water through slowly; filter. **2** dissolve out by running water through slowly: *Potash is leached from wood ashes and used to make soap.* **3** lose soluble parts when water passes through. *v.*

lead¹ (lēd), **1** show the way by going along with or in front of: *She led the horses to water.* **2** be first among: *She leads the class in spelling.* **3** guidance or direction; leadership: *Many countries in*

lead

adj. adjective	*n.* noun
adv. adverb	*prep.* preposition
conj. conjunction	*pron.* pronoun
interj. interjection	*v.* verb
sing. singular	*pl.* plural

the western world followed the lead of the United States after World War II. 4 guide or direct in action, policy, opinion, etc.; influence; persuade: *Such actions lead us to distrust them.* 5 be a way or road: *Hard work leads to success.* 6 pass or spend (time) in some special way: *He leads a quiet life in the country.* 7 go first; begin a game or other activity: *You may lead this time.* 8 be chief of; command; direct: *A general leads an army. She leads the community orchestra. A woman led the singing.* 9 place of leader; place in front: *He always takes the lead when we plan to do anything.* 10 right to go or begin first: *It is your lead this time.* 11 the principal part in a play. 12 person who plays this part. 13 amount that one is ahead: *I had a lead of 3 yards in the race.* 14 a guiding indication: *He was not sure where to look for the information, but the librarian gave him several good leads.* 15 the opening paragraph in a newspaper or magazine article. A lead usually summarizes the information in the body of the article. 1,2,4-8 *v.,* **led, lead ing;** 3,9-15 *n.* [Old English *lǣdan*]
lead off, begin; start.
lead up to, prepare the way for.
lead² (led), 1 a soft, heavy, bluish-gray metallic element which occurs in galena and is used to make pipe, radiation shields, etc. 2 made of lead: *a lead pipe.* 3 something made of lead. 4 bullets; shot: *a hail of lead.* 5 a long, thin piece of graphite used in pencils. 6 weight on a line used to find out the depth of water; plumb. 7 to cover, frame, or weight with lead. 1,3-6 *n.,* 2 *adj.,* 7 *v.* [Old English *lēad*]
lead en (led′n), 1 made of lead: *a leaden coffin.* 2 hard to lift or move; heavy: *leaden arms tired from working.* 3 dull; gloomy. 4 bluish-gray: *Do you suppose those leaden clouds may mean snow? adj.* **—lead′en ly,** *adv.* **—lead′en ness,** *n.*
lead er (lē′dər), person who leads, or is well fitted to lead: *an orchestra leader. That girl is a born leader. n.*
lead er ship (lē′dər ship), 1 condition of being a leader. 2 ability to lead: *Leadership is a great asset to an officer.* 3 guidance or direction:

Our group needs some leadership. n.
lead ing (lē′ding), 1 showing the way; guiding; directing: *to ask someone a leading question.* 2 most important; chief; principal: *She has the leading role in the play. adj.*
leaf (lēf), 1 one of the thin, usually flat, green parts of a tree or other plant that grow on the stem or grow up from the roots. 2 put forth leaves: *The trees along the river leaf earlier than those on the hill.* 3 petal of a flower: *a rose leaf.* 4 sheet of paper. Each side of a leaf is called a page. 5 turn the pages: *to leaf through a book or magazine.* 6 a very thin sheet of metal, etc.: *gold leaf.* 7 a flat, movable piece in the top of a table: *We put two extra leaves in the table to make it larger for the party.* 1,3,4,6,7 *n., pl.* **leaves;** 2,5 *v.* **—leaf′like′,** *adj.*
turn over a new leaf, start all over again; try to do or be better in the future: *I promised to turn over a new leaf and study harder.*
leaf less (lēf′lis), having no leaves. *adj.*
leaf let (lēf′lit), 1 a small, flat or folded sheet of printed matter: *Pass out these advertising leaflets at the store entrance.* 2 a small or young leaf. 3 one of the separate blades or divisions of a compound leaf. *n.*
leaf y (lē′fē), 1 having many leaves; covered with leaves. 2 resembling a leaf. *adj.,* **leaf i er, leaf i est.**
league¹ (lēg), 1 a union of persons, parties, or nations formed to help one another. 2 unite in a league; form a union. 3 association of sports clubs or teams: *a baseball league.* 1,3 *n.,* 2 *v.,* **leagued, lea guing.** [from French of the 1400's *ligue,* ultimately from Latin *ligare* to bind]
in league, associated by agreement; allied.
league² (lēg), measure of distance equal to about 3 miles. *n.* [from Latin *leuga*]

League of Nations, organization
intended to promote cooperation among nations and to maintain peace. It was established in 1920 and disbanded in 1946.
lea guer (lē′gər), member of a league. *n.*
Le ah (lē′ə), (in the Bible) the older sister of Rachel, and the first wife of Jacob. *n.*
leak (lēk), 1 hole or crack not meant to be there that lets something in or out: *a leak in a paper bag that lets the sugar run out, a leak in the roof.* 2 go in or out through a hole or crack, or in ways suggesting a hole or crack: *Spies leaked into the city. The gas leaked out.* 3 let something in or out which is meant to

stay where it is: *My boat leaks and lets water in. That pipe leaks gas.* 4 leakage: *a leak of water, a leak of information.* 5 means of escape. 6 become known gradually: *The secret leaked out.* 1,4,5 *n.,* 2,3,6 *v.*

leaf (def. 1)—several types of leaves

SIMPLE   PALMATE   PINNATE
          COMPOUND

leak age (lē′kij), 1 a leaking; entrance or escape by a leak. 2 that which leaks in or out. 3 amount of leaking: *a leakage of a pailful an hour. n.*
leak i ness (lē′kē nis), leaky condition. *n.*
leak y (lē′kē), having a leak or leaks; leaking. *adj.,* **leak i er, leak i est.**
lean¹ (lēn), 1 to stand slanting, not upright; bend: *The small tree leans over in the wind.* 2 to rest sloping or slanting: *Lean against me.* 3 set or put in a leaning position: *Lean the ladder against the wall.* 4 act of leaning; inclination. 5 depend; rely: *lean on a friend's advice.* 6 bend or turn a little: *lean toward mercy.* 1-3,5,6 *v.,* **leaned** or **leant, lean ing;** 4 *n.* [Old English *hleonian*]
lean² (lēn), 1 not fat; thin: *a lean and hungry stray dog.* 2 meat having little fat. 3 producing little; scant: *a lean harvest, a lean year for business.* 1,3 *adj.,* 2 *n.* [Old English *hlǣne*] **—lean′ness,** *n.*
lean ing (lē′ning), tendency; inclination. *n.*
leant (lent), leaned; a past tense and a past participle of **lean¹.** *v.*

lean-to (def. 1)

lean-to (lēn′tü′), 1 a small building attached to another, with a roof sloping downward from the side of the larger building. 2 having supports or a roof so arranged: *a lean-to shed.* 3 a crude shelter built against a tree or post. It is usually open on one side. 1,3 *n., pl.* **lean-tos;** 2 *adj.*
leap (lēp), 1 a jump or spring. 2 thing to be jumped. 3 distance covered by a jump. 4 to jump: *That frog leaps very high.* 5 to jump over: *He leaped the wall.* 6 cause to leap: *She leaped her*

horse over many hurdles as she raced through the forest. **7** pass, come, rise, etc., as if with a leap or bound: *An idea leaped to her mind.* **1-3** n., **4-7** v., **leaped** or **leapt, leap ing. —leap'-er,** n.

leap frog (lēp'frog'), game in which players take turns jumping over another player who is bending over. n.

leapt (lept or lēpt), leaped; a past tense and a past participle of **leap.** v.

leap year, year having 366 days. The extra day is February 29. A year is a leap year if its number can be divided exactly by four, except years at the end of a century, which must be exactly divisible by 400. The years 1968 and 2000 are leap years; 1967 and 1900 are not.

Lear (lir), a king in Shakespeare's play *King Lear,* who had one loving daughter and two very ungrateful ones. n.

learn (lèrn), **1** gain knowledge or skill: *Some children learn slowly.* **2** memorize: *learn a poem by heart.* **3** find out; come to know: *He learned that* $1/4 + 1/4 = 1/2.$ **4** find out about; gain knowledge of: *She is learning history and geography.* **5** become able by study or practice: *In school we learn to read.* v., **learned** or **learnt, learn ing.**

learn ed (lèr'nid), having, showing, or requiring much knowledge; scholarly: *a learned professor.* adj.

learn er (lèr'nər), **1** person who is learning. **2** beginner. n.

learn ing (lèr'ning), **1** the gaining of knowledge or skill. **2** possession of knowledge gained by study; scholarship: *men and women of great learning.* **3** knowledge. n.

learnt (lèrnt), learned; a past tense and a past participle of **learn.** v.

lease (lēs), **1** the right to use property for a certain length of time by paying rent for it. **2** a written statement saying for how long a certain property is rented and how much money shall be paid for it. **3** the property held by a lease. **4** length of time for which a lease is made. **5** give a lease on. **6** to rent: *We have leased an apartment for one year.* **1-4** n., **5,6** v., **leased, leas ing.**

leash (lēsh), **1** a strap or chain for holding an animal in check: *The girl leads the dog on a leash.* **2** fasten or hold in with a leash; control: *He leashed his anger and did not say a harsh word.* **1** n., pl. **leash es; 2** v.

hold in leash, control.

least (lēst), **1** less than any other; smallest; slightest: *Ten cents is a little money; five cents is less; one cent is least.* **2** smallest amount; smallest thing: *The least you can do is to thank her.* **3** to the smallest extent, amount,

or degree: *She liked that book least of all.* **1** adj., **2** n., **3** adv.

at least, 1 at the lowest estimate: *The temperature was at least 95 degrees yesterday.* **2** at any rate; in any case: *He may have been late, but at least he came.*

least wise (lēst'wīz'), INFORMAL. at least; at any rate. adv.

leath er (leᴛʜ'ər), **1** material made from the skins of animals by removing the hair and then tanning them: *Shoes are made of leather.* **2** article made of leather. **3** made of leather: *leather gloves.* **4** furnish or cover with leather. **1,2** n., **3** adj., **4** v.

Leath er ette (leᴛʜ'ə ret'), trademark for imitation leather, made of paper or cloth. n.

leath ern (leᴛʜ'ərn), made of leather. adj.

leath er y (leᴛʜ'ər ē), like leather; tough: *a face made leathery from exposure to harsh weather.* adj.

leave[1] (lēv), **1** go away: *We leave tonight.* **2** go away from: *They left the room. He has left his home and friends and gone to sea.* **3** stop living in, belonging to, or working at or for: *leave the country, leave the Boy Scouts, leave one's job.* **4** go without taking; let stay behind: *I left a book on the table.* **5** let stay (in a certain condition): *leave unsaid or undone. I was left alone as before. The story left him unmoved.* **6** let alone: *The potatoes must be left to boil for half an hour.* **7** give (to family, friends, charity) when one dies: *She left a fortune to her children.* **8** give or hand over (to someone else) to do: *I left the driving to my sister.* **9** not attend to: *I shall leave my homework until tomorrow.* v., **left, leav ing.** [Old English *lǣfan*]

leave off, stop: *Continue the story from where I left off.*

leave out, not do, say, or put in; omit: *She left out two words when she read the sentence.*

leave[2] (lēv), **1** permission; consent: *They gave him leave to go.* **2** permission to be absent from duty. A **leave of absence** is an official permission to be absent from one's work, school, or military duty. **3** length of time that this lasts: *Our annual leave is thirty days.* n. [Old English *lēaf*]

take leave of, say good-by to.

leave[3] (lēv), put forth leaves; leaf: *Trees leave in the spring.* v., **leaved, leav ing.** [Middle English *levien*]

leav en (lev'ən), **1** any substance, such as yeast, that will cause fermentation and raise dough. **2** raise with a leaven; make (dough) light or lighter. **3** an influence which, spreading silently and strongly, changes conditions or opin-

ions. **4** spread through and transform. **1,3** n., **2,4** v.

leav en ing (lev'ə ning), thing that leavens. n.

leaves (lēvz), plural of **leaf.** n.

leave-tak ing (lēv'tā'king), act of taking leave; saying good-by. n.

leav ings (lē'vingz), things left; leftovers; remnants. n.pl.

Leb a nese (leb'ə nēz'), **1** of or having to do with Lebanon or its people. **2** person born or living in Lebanon. **1** adj., **2** n., pl. **Leb a nese.**

Leb a non (leb'ə nən), country in the Middle East, at the E end of the Mediterranean. *Capital:* Beirut. n.

lech er ous (lech'ər əs), lewd. adj.

lech er y (lech'ər ē), lewdness. n.

lec i thin (les'ə thən), a fatty substance found in plant and animal tissues. Lecithin is extracted from egg yolk, soybeans, and corn. It is used in candy, drugs, paints, etc. n.

lectern
(def. 1)

lec tern (lek'tərn), **1** a reading desk in a church, especially the desk from which the lessons are read at daily prayer. **2** a reading desk or stand. n.

lec ture (lek'chər), **1** a planned talk on a chosen subject; such a talk written down or printed; speech. **2** give a lecture: *The explorer lectured on life in the Arctic.* **3** a scolding: *My parents give me a lecture when I come home late.* **4** scold; reprove. **1,3** n., **2,4** v., **lectured, lec tur ing.**

lec tur er (lek'chər ər), person who lectures. n.

led (led), past tense and past participle of **lead**[1]. *The policeman led the child across the street. We were led through the cave by an experienced guide.* v.

hat, āge, fär; let, ēqual, tèrm;
it, īce; hot, ōpen, ôrder;
oil, out; cup, pùt, rüle; ch, child;
ng, long; sh, she; th, thin;
ᴛʜ, then; zh, measure;

ə represents *a* in about,
e in taken, *i* in pencil,
o in lemon, *u* in circus.

ledge

adj. adjective		*n.* noun
adv. adverb		*prep.* preposition
conj. conjunction		*pron.* pronoun
interj. interjection		*v.* verb
sing. singular		*pl.* plural

ledge (lej), 1 a narrow shelf: *a window ledge.* 2 shelf or ridge of rock. *n.*

ledg er (lej/ər), book of accounts in which a business keeps a record of all money transactions. *n.*

lee (lē), 1 a shelter. 2 side or part sheltered or away from the wind: *The wind was so fierce that we ran to the lee of the house.* 3 sheltered from the wind: *the lee side of a ship.* 1,2 *n.,* 3 *adj.*

Lee (lē), **Robert E.,** 1807-1870, Confederate general in the Civil War. Lee surrendered to Grant at Appomattox on April 9, 1865. *n.*

leech (lēch), 1 worm living especially in fresh-water ponds and streams, that sucks the blood of animals. Doctors used to use leeches to suck blood from sick people. 2 person who tries persistently to get what he can out of others, without doing anything to earn it. 3 OLD USE. doctor. *n., pl.* **leech es.**

leek (lēk), vegetable somewhat like an onion, but with larger leaves, a smaller bulb shaped like a cylinder, and a milder flavor. *n.*

leer (lir), 1 a sly, nasty look to the side; evil glance. 2 give a sly, evil glance. 1 *n.,* 2 *v.*

leer y (lir/ē), INFORMAL. suspicious; wary: *We are leery of his advice. adj.*

lees (lēz), dregs; sediment. *n.pl.*

lee shore, shore toward which the wind is blowing.

Leeu wen hoek (lā/vən hůk), **Anton van,** 1632-1723, Dutch scientist who was the first to study blood cells and tiny organisms through magnifying lenses. *n.*

lee ward (lē/wərd *or* lü/ərd), 1 on the side away from the wind. 2 the side away from the wind; lee. 3 in the direction toward which the wind is blowing. 1,3 *adj., adv.,* 2 *n.*

Lee ward Islands (lē/wərd), the N part of the Lesser Antilles in the West Indies.

lee way (lē/wā/), 1 the sideways movement of a ship to leeward, out of its course. 2 extra space at the side; time, money, etc., more than needed; margin of safety: *If you take $30 on a trip that should cost $20, you are allowing yourself a leeway of $10. n.*

left[1] (left), 1 belonging to the side of the less used hand (in most people); of the side that is turned west when the main side is turned north: *the left hand. I sprained my left ankle.* 2 on this side when viewed from in front: *Take a left turn at the next light.* 3 on or to the left side: *Turn left.* 4 the left side or hand: *I sat at her left.* 5 part of a lawmaking body consisting of the more liberal or radical groups. 6 having liberal or radical ideas in politics. 1,2,6 *adj.,* 3 *adv.,* 4,5 *n.* [Old English *lyft* weak]

left[2] (left), past tense and past participle of **leave**[1]. *I left my hat in the hall. Milk is left at our door. She left at four o'clock. v.*

left field, (in baseball) the section of the outfield behind third base.

left-hand (left/hand/), 1 on or to the left. 2 of, for, or with the left hand. *adj.*

left-hand ed (left/han/did), 1 using the left hand more easily and readily than the right. 2 done with the left hand. 3 made to be used with the left hand. 4 turning from right to left: *a left-handed screw.* 5 doubtful or insincere: *a left-handed compliment.* 6 toward the left; with the left hand. 1-5 *adj.,* 6 *adv.*

left ist (lef/tist), 1 person who has liberal or radical ideas in politics. 2 member of a liberal or radical political organization. 3 having liberal or radical ideas. 1,2 *n.,* 3 *adj.*

left o ver (left/ō/vər), 1 thing that is left. Scraps of food from a meal are leftovers. 2 that is left; remaining: *I made some sandwiches with the leftover meat.* 1 *n.,* 2 *adj.*

left wing, the liberal or radical members, especially of a political party.

left y (lef/tē), SLANG. a left-handed person. *n., pl.* **left ies.**

leg (leg), 1 one of the limbs on which people and animals stand and walk: *I ran as fast and as far as my legs would carry me.* 2 part of a garment that covers a leg: *I fell and tore my pants' leg.* 3 anything shaped or used like a leg; any support that is much longer than it is wide: *a table leg.* 4 one of the parts or stages of any course: *the last leg of a trip.* 5 INFORMAL. walk or run: *We could not get a ride, so we had to leg it.* 6 either of the two sides of a right triangle that is not the hypotenuse. 1-4,6 *n.,* 5 *v.,* **legged, leg ging.**

on one's last legs, about to fail, collapse, or die.

pull one's leg, INFORMAL. fool, trick, or make fun of one.

leg a cy (leg/ə sē), 1 money or other property left to a person by the will of someone who has died. 2 something that has been handed down from an ancestor or predecessor. *n., pl.* **leg a cies.**

le gal (lē/gəl), 1 of law: *legal knowledge.* 2 of lawyers: *legal advice.* 3 according to law; lawful: *Hunting is legal only during certain seasons. adj.*

le gal i ty (li gal/ə tē), accordance with law; lawfulness. *n., pl.* **le gal i ties.**

le gal i za tion (lē/gə lə zā/shən), act of legalizing. *n.*

le gal ize (lē/gə līz), make legal; authorize by law; sanction. *v.,* **le gal ized, le gal iz ing.**

le gal ly (lē/gə lē), 1 in a legal manner. 2 according to law: *They are legally responsible for their child's debts. adv.*

legal tender, money that must, by law, be accepted in payment of debts.

leg ate (leg/it), ambassador or representative, especially a representative of the Pope. *n.*

leg a tee (leg/ə tē/), person to whom a legacy is left. *n.*

le ga tion (li gā/shən), 1 the diplomatic representative of a country and his staff of assistants. A legation ranks next below an embassy. 2 the official residence, offices, etc., of such a representative in a foreign country. 3 office, position, or dignity of a legate. *n.*

le ga to (li gä/tō), (in music) smooth and connected; without breaks between successive tones. *adj., adv.* [from Italian *legato* bound]

leg end (lej/ənd), 1 story coming down from the past, which may be based on actual people and events but is not regarded as historically true: *The stories about King Arthur and his knights of the Round Table are legends.* 2 such stories as a group. 3 what is written on a coin or medal: *Read the legend on a five-cent piece.* 4 words accompanying a picture or diagram: *The legend underneath the picture identified the woman as Queen Elizabeth I. n.*

leg end ar y (lej/ən der/ē), of a legend or legends; like a legend; not historical: *Robin Hood is a legendary person. adj.*

legs (def. 6)

leg er de main (lej/ər də mān/), 1 sleight of hand; conjuring tricks; jugglery: *A common trick of legerdemain is to take rabbits from an apparently empty hat.* 2 trickery. *n.*

leg gings (leg/ingz), extra outer coverings of cloth or leather for the legs, for use out of doors. *n.pl.*

leg gy (leg/ē), 1 having long legs. 2 having awkwardly long legs. *adj.,* **leg gi er, leg gi est.**

leg horn (leg′hôrn *or* leg′ərn), 1 hat made of fine, smooth, plaited straw. 2 **Leghorn,** a rather small, domestic fowl which produces large numbers of eggs. *n.*

leg i bil i ty (lej′ə bil′ə tē), legible condition or quality; clearness of print or writing. *n.*

leg i ble (lej′ə bəl), 1 that can be read. 2 easy to read; plain and clear: *Her handwriting is quite large and legible.* *adj.*

leg i bly (lej′ə blē), clearly. *adv.*

le gion (lē′jən), 1 a division in the ancient Roman army containing several thousand foot soldiers and several hundred horsemen. 2 a large body of soldiers; army. 3 a great many; very large number: *Legions of grasshoppers destroyed the crops.* *n.*

lei of flowers

le gion ar y (lē′jə ner′ē), 1 of or belonging to a legion. 2 member of a legion. 1 *adj.,* 2 *n., pl.* **le gion ar ies.**

leg is late (lej′ə slāt), 1 make laws: *Congress legislates for the United States.* 2 force by legislation: *The council legislated him out of office.* *v.,* **leg is lat ed, leg is lat ing.**

leg is la tion (lej′ə slā′shən), 1 the making of laws: *Congress has the power of legislation.* 2 the laws made: *Important legislation is reported in today's newspaper.* *n.*

leg is la tive (lej′ə slā′tiv), 1 having to do with making laws: *legislative reforms.* 2 having the duty and power of making laws: *The British Parliament is a legislative body.* 3 ordered by law; made to be as it is by law: *a legislative decree.* *adj.* —**leg′is la′tive ly,** *adv.*

leg is la tor (lej′ə slā′tər), member of a legislative body; lawmaker. Senators and Representatives are legislators. *n.*

leg is la ture (lej′ə slā′chər), group of persons that has the duty and power of making laws for a state or country. Each state of the United States has a legislature. *n.*

le git i ma cy (lə jit′ə mə sē), a being legitimate or lawful; being recognized as lawful or proper. *n.*

le git i mate (lə jit′ə mit), 1 allowed or admitted by law; rightful; lawful: *a legitimate title or right, a legitimate ruler.* 2 valid; logical; acceptable: *a legitimate conclusion. Sickness is a legitimate rea-*

son for a child's absence from school. 3 born of parents who are married: *a legitimate child. adj.* —**le git′i mate ly,** *adv.*

le git i mize (lə jit′ə mīz), make or declare to be legitimate. *v.,* **le git i mized, le git i miz ing.**

leg less (leg′lis), having no legs; without legs. *adj.*

leg ume (leg′yüm *or* li gyüm′), 1 plant which bears pods containing a number of seeds. Beans and peas are legumes. Many legumes can absorb nitrogen from the air. 2 the pod of such a plant. A peanut is really a legume, not a nut. *n.*

le gu mi nous (li gyü′mə nəs), 1 of or bearing legumes. 2 of or belonging to the same group of plants as beans and peas. *adj.*

Le Ha vre (lə hä′vrə), seaport in N France.

lei (lā), wreath of flowers, leaves, etc., worn as an ornament around the neck or on the head. *n., pl.* **leis.** [from Hawaiian]

Leip zig (līp′sig), city in S East Germany. *n.*

lei sure (lē′zhər), 1 time free from required work in which a person may rest, amuse himself, and do the things he likes to do: *She's been too busy to have much leisure. I spend part of my leisure in reading.* 2 free; not busy: *leisure hours.* 1 *n.,* 2 *adj.*

at one's leisure, when one has leisure; at one's convenience: *Let me hear from you at your leisure.*

lei sure ly (lē′zhər lē), without hurry; taking plenty of time: *a leisurely person, a leisurely stroll through the park (adj.). He walked leisurely across the street (adv.). adj., adv.*

lemming—about 6 in. long

lem ming (lem′ing), a small, mouselike, arctic rodent, having a short tail and furry feet. At certain times some species of lemmings migrate in great masses to the sea, where they swim a short distance and drown. *n.*

lem on (lem′ən), 1 a sour, light-yellow citrus fruit that grows in warm climates. 2 the thorny tree it grows on. 3 pale-yellow. 4 a pale yellow. 5 flavored with lemon. 6 SLANG. something or someone that is worthless or unpleasant. 1,2,4,6 *n.,* 3,5 *adj.*

lem on ade (lem′ə nād′), a drink made of lemon juice, sugar, and water. *n.*

hat, āge, fär; let, ēqual, tėrm;
it, īce; hot, ōpen, ôrder;
oil, out; cup, pùt, rüle; ch, child;
ng, long; sh, she; th, thin;
ŦH, then; zh, measure;

ə represents *a* in about,
e in taken, *i* in pencil,
o in lemon, *u* in circus.

le mur (lē′mər), a small mammal somewhat like a monkey, but having a fox-like face and woolly fur. Lemurs are found mainly in Madagascar. They live in trees and are active chiefly at night. *n.*

lemur—about 3 ft. long with tail

lend (lend), 1 let another have or use for a time: *Will you lend me your bicycle for an hour?* 2 give the use of (money) for a fixed or specified amount of payment: *Banks lend money and charge interest.* 3 make a loan or loans: *A person who borrows should be willing to lend.* 4 give for a time; add; contribute: *A lace curtain lends charm to a window. The Red Cross is quick to lend aid in time of disaster.* *v.,* **lent, lend ing.** —**lend′er,** *n.*

lend oneself to, help or be suitable for.

length (lengkth *or* length), 1 how long a thing is; what a thing measures from end to end; the longest way a thing can be measured: *the length of your arm, the length of a room, eight inches in length.* 2 how long something lasts or goes on: *the length of a visit, a speech, or a book.* 3 distance: *The length of this race is one mile.* 4 a long stretch or extent: *Quite a length of hair hung down in a braid.* 5 piece of cloth, etc., of a given length: *a length of rope, a dress length of silk.* 6 (in poetry) the force with which a syllable or vowel is spoken, or the way it is pronounced. *n.*

at full length, with the body stretched out flat: *The snake lay at full length on the rock, sunning itself.*

at length, 1 at last; finally: *At length,*

adj. adjective	*n.* noun
adv. adverb	*prep.* preposition
conj. conjunction	*pron.* pronoun
interj. interjection	*v.* verb
sing. singular	*pl.* plural

after many delays, the meeting started. 2 with all the details; in full: *She told of her adventures at length.*

go to any length, do everything possible: *I will go to any length to help you.*

keep at arm's length, discourage from becoming friendly.

length en (lengk′thən *or* leng′thən), 1 make longer: *A tailor can lengthen your trousers.* 2 become or grow longer: *Your legs have lengthened a great deal since you were 5 years old.* *v.*

length i ly (lengk′thə lē *or* leng′thə lē), in a lengthy manner. *adv.*

length i ness (lengk′thē nis *or* leng′-thē nis), lengthy condition or quality. *n.*

length ways (lengkth′wāz′ *or* length′-wāz′), lengthwise. *adv., adj.*

length wise (lengkth′wīz′ *or* length′-wīz′), in the direction of the length: *He cut the cloth lengthwise* (*adv.*). *The tailor made a lengthwise cut* (*adj.*). *adv., adj.*

length y (lengk′thē *or* leng′thē), long; too long: *His directions were so lengthy that everybody lost interest.* *adj.,* **length i er, length i est.**

len ience (lē′nyəns), leniency. *n.*

len ien cy (lē′nyən sē), lenient quality; mildness; gentleness; mercy. *n.*

len ient (lē′nyənt), mild or gentle; not harsh or stern; merciful: *a lenient judge, a lenient punishment.* *adj.* **—len′ient-ly,** *adv.*

Len in (len′ən), **Nikolai,** 1870-1924, Russian Communist leader, the founder of the Soviet government and its first premier, from 1918 to 1924. *n.*

Len in grad (len′ən grad), seaport in NW Soviet Union, on the Gulf of Finland. It was formerly called **St. Petersburg** and later **Petrograd.** *n.*

len i ty (len′ə tē), leniency. *n.*

lens (lenz), 1 a curved piece of glass or other transparent material which brings closer together or sends wider apart the rays of light passing through it. The lens of a camera forms images on film. The lenses of a telescope make distant objects look larger and nearer. Also see **concave** and **convex** for diagrams of types of lenses. 2 the part of the eye that directs light rays upon the retina. See **eye** for diagram. *n., pl.* **lens es.**

lent (lent), past tense and past participle of **lend.** *I lent you my pencil. He had lent me his eraser.* *v.*

Lent (lent), the forty weekdays between Ash Wednesday and Easter, observed in many Christian churches as a time for fasting and repenting of sins. *n.*

lent en or **Lent en** (len′tən), of Lent; during Lent; suitable for Lent. *adj.*

len til (len′tl), 1 plant of the pea family having pods which contain small, flat seeds. 2 its seed, which is used as a vegetable. Lentils are cooked like peas and are often eaten in soup. *n.*

Le o nar do da Vin ci (lā′ə när/-dō də vin′chē). See **da Vinci.**

le o nine (lē′ə nīn), of or like a lion. *adj.*

leop ard (lep′ərd), a large, fierce mammal of Africa and Asia, having a dull-yellowish fur spotted with black. It belongs to the cat family. *n.*

leopards
about 8 ft. long with tail

Lé o pold ville (lē′ə pōld vil′), former name of **Kinshasa.** *n.*

lep er (lep′ər), person who has leprosy. *n.*

lep re chaun (lep′rə kôn), (in Irish legends) an elf resembling a little old man, believed to possess hidden gold. *n.*

lep ro sy (lep′rə sē), disease caused by certain rod-shaped bacteria that attack the skin and nerves, causing lumps or spots which may become ulcers. If not treated, the injury to the nerves results in numbness, paralysis, and deformity. *n.*

lep rous (lep′rəs), 1 having leprosy: *a leprous person.* 2 of or like leprosy: *white, leprous scabs.* *adj.*

lens (def. 1) The double convex lens shown above bends light rays to produce a magnified image.

lese maj es ty (lēz′ maj′ə stē), crime or offense against the sovereign power in a state; treason. [from French of the 1400's *lèse-majesté* insulted majesty]

le sion (lē′zhən), 1 an injury; hurt. 2 an abnormal change in the structure of an organ or body tissue, caused by disease or injury. *n.*

Le so tho (lə sō′tō), country in S Africa, a member of the Commonwealth of Nations. It is entirely surrounded by the Republic of South Africa. See **South Africa** for map. *n.*

less (les), 1 smaller: *of less width, less importance.* 2 not so much; not so much of: *to have less rain, to put on less butter, to eat less meat.* 3 lower in age, rank, or importance: *no less a person than the President.* 4 a smaller amount or quantity: *could do no less, weigh less than before. She refused to take less than $5.* 5 to a smaller extent or degree; not so; not so well: *less bright, less talked of, less known, less important.* 6 with (something) taken away; without; minus: *five less two, a coat less one sleeve.* 1-3 *adj.,* 4 *n.,* 5 *adv.,* 6 *prep.*

-less, suffix forming adjectives. 1 (added to nouns) without a ____; that has no ____: *Homeless = without a home.* 2 (added to verbs) that does not ____: *Ceaseless = that does not cease.* 3 (added to verbs) that cannot be ____ed: *Countless = that cannot be counted.* [Old English *-lēas,* from *lēas* without]

les see (le sē′), person to whom a lease is granted. *n.*

less en (les′n), 1 grow less: *The fever lessened during the night.* 2 make less; decrease. *v.*

less er (les′ər), 1 less; smaller. 2 the less important of two. *adj.*

les son (les′n), 1 something to be learned or taught; something that has been learned or taught: *Children study many different lessons in school.* 2 unit of learning or teaching; what is to be studied or taught at one time: *Tomorrow we take the tenth lesson.* 3 an instructive experience, serving to encourage or warn: *The accident taught me a lesson: always look before you leap.* 4 a selection from the Bible, read as part of a church service. *n.*

les sor (les′ôr), person who grants a lease. *n.*

lest (lest), 1 for fear that: *Be careful lest you fall from that tree.* 2 that (after words meaning fear, danger, etc.): *I was afraid lest they should come too late to save us.* *conj.*

let[1] (let), 1 not stop from doing or having something; allow; permit: *Let the dog have a bone.* 2 allow to pass, go, or come: *They let the visitor on board the ship.* 3 allow to run out: *Doctors used to let some of the blood of their fever patients.* 4 hire out; rent: *That woman lets rooms to students.* 5 be rented: *This room lets for $80 a month.*

6 *Let* is used in giving suggestions and commands: *"Let's go home" means "I suggest that we go home."* *Let every one do his duty.* **7** suppose; assume: *Let the two lines be parallel.* *v.*, **let, letting.** [Old English *lǣtan*]

let down, 1 lower: *He let the box down from the roof.* **2** slow up: *As her interest in the work wore off, she began to let down.* **3** disappoint: *Don't let us down today; we're counting on you to win.*

let in, permit to enter; admit: *Let in some fresh air.*

let off, allow to go free; excuse from punishment, etc.: *I was let off with a warning to do better in the future.*

let on, INFORMAL. **1** allow to be known; reveal one's knowledge of: *He didn't let on his surprise at the news.* **2** make believe; pretend: *She let on that she didn't see me.*

let out, 1 permit to go out. **2** make larger: *Let out the hem on this skirt.* **3** rent: *Has the room been let out yet?*

let up, INFORMAL. stop; pause: *They refused to let up in the fight.*

let² (let), **1** OLD USE. prevention; hindrance; obstruction. **2** interference with the ball in tennis and similar games. The ball or point must be played over again. *n.* [Old English *lettan* hinder, from *lǣt* late]

without let or hindrance, with nothing to prevent, hinder, or obstruct.

-let, suffix added to nouns to form other nouns. **1** little ____: *Booklet = a little book.* **2** band worn around the ____: *Anklet = band worn around the ankle.* [from French before the 1400's *-elet*]

let down (let/doun/), **1** a slowing up. **2** INFORMAL. disappointment: *Losing the contest was a big letdown for her.* *n.*

le thal (lē/thəl), causing death; deadly: *lethal weapons, a lethal dose of a drug.* *adj.*

le thar gic (lə thär/jik), **1** unnaturally drowsy; sluggish; dull: *A hot, humid day makes most people feel lethargic.* **2** producing lethargy. *adj.*

leth ar gy (leth/ər jē), **1** drowsy dullness; lack of energy; sluggish inactivity. **2** an unnatural sleep. *n., pl.* **leth ar gies.**

Le the (lē/thē), **1** (in Greek myths) a river in Hades. Drinking its water caused forgetfulness of the past. **2** forgetfulness; oblivion. *n.*

let's (lets), let us.

let ter (let/ər), **1** a mark or sign that stands for any one of the sounds that make up words. There are 26 letters in our alphabet. **2** mark with letters: *Please letter a new sign.* **3** a written or printed message: *He told me about his vacation in a letter.* **4** exact wording; actual terms: *She kept the letter of the*

law but not the spirit. **5** a block of type bearing a letter, used in printing. **6** the initial of a school, college, or other institution, given as an award or trophy to members of a sports team, etc. It is usually made of cloth and sewn to a garment. **7 letters,** *pl.* literature: *men of letters.* **1,3-7** *n.,* **2** *v.*

to the letter, very exactly; just as one has been told: *I carried out your orders to the letter.*

let ter head (let/ər hed/), **1** words printed at the top of a sheet of paper, usually a name and address. **2** a sheet of paper so printed. *n.*

let ter ing (let/ər ing), **1** letters drawn, painted, or stamped. **2** act of making letters. *n.*

let ter-per fect (let/ər pėr/fikt), **1** knowing one's part or lesson perfectly. **2** correct in every detail: *letter-perfect copies.* *adj.*

let tuce (let/is), **1** a garden plant having large, crisp, green leaves. **2** its leaves, much used in salad. *n.*

let up (let/up/), INFORMAL. a stop or pause. *n.*

leu co cyte (lü/kə sīt), white blood cell. *n.*

leu ke mi a (lü kē/mē ə), a rare, and usually fatal, disease characterized by a large excess of white blood cells in the blood. *n.*

Le vant (lə vant/), the region about the E Mediterranean from Greece to Egypt, especially Syria, Lebanon, and Israel. *n.*

Le van tine (lə van/tən), **1** of the Levant. **2** person or ship of the Levant. **1** *adj.,* **2** *n.*

lev ee¹ (lev/ē), **1** a bank built to keep a river from overflowing: *There are levees in many places along the lower Mississippi River.* **2** a landing place for boats. *n.* [from French *levée*, from *lever* to raise]

lev ee² (lev/ē), reception. French kings used to hold levees in the morning while they were getting up and dressing. *n.* [from French *levé*, from *lever* to raise]

lev el (lev/əl), **1** having the same height everywhere; flat; even: *a level floor.* **2** of equal height, importance, etc.: *The table is level with the sill of the window.* **3** something that is level; level or flat surface, tract of land, etc. **4** an in-

first class lever—
fulcrum between effort and resistance; motion in direction opposite effort

second class lever—
resistance between effort and fulcrum; motion in same direction as effort

third class lever—
effort between resistance and fulcrum; motion in same direction as effort

hat, āge, fär; let, ēqual, tėrm;
it, īce; hot, ōpen, ôrder;
oil, out; cup, pùt, rüle; ch, child;
ng, long; sh, she; th, thin;
ŦH, then; zh, measure;

ə represents *a* in about,
e in taken, *i* in pencil,
o in lemon, *u* in circus.

level (def. 4) If the surface is level, an air bubble stays at the center of a glass tube containing liquid (as in middle tube above). If the surface is not level, the bubble moves to one side.

strument for showing whether a surface is level. **5** a level position or condition. **6** make level; put on the same level: *The contractor leveled the ground with a bulldozer.* **7** lay low; bring to the level of the ground: *The tornado leveled every house in the valley.* **8** raise and hold level for shooting; aim: *The soldier leveled his rifle at the target.* **9** height: *The flood rose to a level of 60 feet.* **10** stage of learning, achievement, etc.; position; rank: *They told me that my work is not up to a professional level.* **11** remove or reduce (differences, etc.). **12** INFORMAL. well-balanced; sensible: *a level head.* **1,2,12** *adj.,* **3-5,9,10** *n.,* **6-8,11** *v.* —**lev/el er,** *n.* —**lev/el ly,** *adv.* —**lev/el ness,** *n.*

level off, 1 come to an equilibrium; even off; steady. **2** return (an aircraft) to a horizontal position in landing, or after a climb or dive.

on the level, INFORMAL. fair and straightforward; honest; legitimate.

lev el head ed (lev/əl hed/id), having good common sense or good judgment; sensible. *adj.*

lev er (lev/ər *or* lē/vər), **1** bar which turns on a fixed support called the fulcrum and is used to transmit effort and motion. It is a simple machine. **2** any

levers (def. 1)

adj.	adjective	*n.*	noun
adv.	adverb	*prep.*	preposition
conj.	conjunction	*pron.*	pronoun
interj.	interjection	*v.*	verb
sing.	singular	*pl.*	plural

bar working on an axis or support: *the gearshift lever of an automobile.* 3 move, lift, push, etc., with a lever. 1,2 *n.*, 3 *v.*

lev er age (lev′ər ij *or* lē′vər ij), 1 action of a lever. 2 advantage or power gained by using a lever. 3 increased power of action. *n.*

Le vi (lē′vī), (in the Bible) a son of Jacob and ancestor of the Levites. *n.*

le vi a than (lə vī′ə thən), 1 (in the Bible) a huge sea animal. 2 any great and powerful person or thing. *n.*

Le vi's (lē′vīz), trademark for tight-fitting, heavy blue denim trousers reinforced at strain points with copper rivets or extra stitching. *n.pl.*

Le vite (lē′vīt), member of the tribe descended from Levi, from which assistants to the Jewish priests were chosen. *n.*

Le vit i cus (lə vit′ə kəs), the third book of the Old Testament, containing the laws for the priests and Levites and the ritual for Jewish ceremonies. *n.*

lev i ty (lev′ə tē), lightness of mind, character, or behavior; lack of proper seriousness or earnestness: *Giggling in class shows levity.* *n., pl.* **lev i ties.**

lev y (lev′ē), 1 order to be paid: *The government levies taxes to pay its expenses.* 2 money collected by authority or force. 3 draft or enlist (men) for an army: *Troops are levied in time of war.* 4 undertake or begin; wage: *to levy war against the enemy.* 5 men drafted or enlisted for an army. 6 seize by law for unpaid debts: *They levied on his property for unpaid rent.* 7 act of levying. 1,3,4,6 *v.*, **lev ied, lev y ing;** 2,5,7 *n., pl.* **lev ies.**

lewd (lüd), not decent; lustful. *adj.* —**lewd′ly,** *adv.* —**lewd′ness,** *n.*

Lew is (lü′is), 1 **Meriwether,** 1774-1809, American explorer of the American northwest together with William Clark. 2 **Sinclair,** 1885-1951, American novelist. *n.*

lex i cog ra pher (lek′sə kog′rə fər), writer or maker of a dictionary. *n.*

lex i cog ra phy (lek′sə kog′rə fē), the writing or making of dictionaries. *n.*

lex i con (lek′sə kən), 1 dictionary, especially of Greek, Latin, or Hebrew. 2 the vocabulary belonging to a certain subject, group, or activity. *n.*

Lex ing ton (lek′sing tən), 1 town in E Massachusetts where the first battle of the Revolutionary War was fought on April 19, 1775. 2 city in N Kentucky. *n.*

Ley den jar (līd′n), device for storing an electric charge, consisting essentially of a glass jar lined inside and outside with tin or aluminum foil and sealed with a stopper containing a metal rod. [from *Leyden*, city in the Netherlands, where it was first used]

Lha sa (lä′sə), capital of Tibet, in the S part. *n.*

li a bil i ty (lī′ə bil′ə tē), 1 state of being liable: *liability to disease, liability for a debt.* 2 debt. 3 something that is to one's disadvantage: *My poor handwriting was a liability in spelling classes.* *n., pl.* **li a bil i ties.**

li a ble (lī′ə bəl), 1 likely; unpleasantly likely: *That glass is liable to break. You are liable to slip on ice.* 2 in danger of having, doing, etc.: *We are all liable to diseases.* 3 responsible; under obligation; bound by law to pay: *The Postal Service is not liable for damage to an uninsured package.* *adj.*

li ai son (lē′ā zon′ *or* lē ā′zon), connection between parts of an army to secure proper cooperation. *n.*

li ar (lī′ər), person who tells lies; person who says what is not true. *n.*

li ba tion (lī bā′shən), 1 a pouring out of wine, water, etc., as an offering to a god. 2 the wine, water, etc., offered in this way. *n.*

li bel (lī′bəl), 1 a written or published statement that is likely to harm the reputation of the person about whom it is made; false or damaging statement. 2 write or publish such a statement about. 3 act or crime of writing or publishing such a statement. 1,3 *n.*, 2 *v.*

li bel er (lī′bə lər), person who libels another. *n.*

li bel ous (lī′bə ləs), 1 containing a libel. 2 spreading libels: *a libelous tongue.* *adj.*

lib er al (lib′ər əl), 1 giving or given freely; generous: *a liberal giver, a liberal donation.* 2 plentiful; abundant: *We put in a liberal supply of coal for the winter.* 3 not narrow in one's ideas; broad-minded; tolerant: *a liberal thinker.* 4 not limited; broad. A liberal education develops the mind broadly by including courses in the liberal arts. 5 favoring progress and reforms. 6 person favorable to progress and reforms. 7 Often, **Liberal.** of or belonging to a political party that favors progress and reforms. 1-5,7 *adj.*, 6 *n.* —**lib′er al ly,** *adv.* —**lib′er al ness,** *n.*

liberal arts, subjects studied for culture rather than for immediate practical use. Literature, languages, history, and philosophy are some of the liberal arts.

lib er al ism (lib′ər ə liz′əm), liberal views or opinions; belief in progress and reforms. *n.*

lib e ral i ty (lib′ə ral′ə tē), 1 generous act or behavior; generosity. 2 tolerant and progressive nature; broad-mindedness. *n., pl.* **lib e ral i ties.**

lib er al i za tion (lib′ər ə lə zā′shən), a making or becoming liberal. *n.*

lib er al ize (lib′ər ə līz), make or become liberal. *v.*, **lib er al ized, lib er al iz ing.**

lib e rate (lib′ə rāt′), set free: *Lincoln liberated the slaves.* *v.*, **lib e rat ed, lib e rat ing.**

lib e ra tion (lib′ə rā′shən), a setting or a being set free. *n.*

lib e ra tor (lib′ə rā′tər), person who sets free; deliverer. *n.*

Li be ri a (lī bir′ē ə), country in W Africa, first settled by freed American Negro slaves in 1822. *Capital:* Monrovia. *n.* —**Li ber′i an,** *adj., n.*

lib er tar i an (lib′ər ter′ē ən), person who advocates liberty, especially in thought or conduct. *n.*

lib er tine (lib′ər tēn′), person without moral restraints; immoral or licentious person. *n.*

lib er ty (lib′ər tē), 1 condition of being free; freedom; independence: *Lincoln granted liberty to slaves. The American colonies won their liberty.* 2 right or power to do as one pleases; power or opportunity to do something: *liberty of speech or action.* 3 leave granted to a sailor to go ashore. 4 right of being in, using, etc.: *We give our dog the liberty of the yard.* 5 too great freedom: *The author took liberties with the facts to make the story more interesting.* *n., pl.* **lib er ties.**

at liberty, 1 free: *The escaped lion is still at liberty.* 2 allowed; permitted: *You are at liberty to make any choice you please.* 3 not busy: *The doctor will see us as soon as she is at liberty.*

Liberty Bell, bell that was rung at Philadelphia on July 8, 1776, when the Continental Congress passed the Declaration of Independence. It is regarded as a symbol of liberty.

li brar i an (lī brer′ē ən), 1 person in charge of a library. 2 person trained for work in a library. *n.*

li brar y (lī′brer′ē), 1 a collection of books: *Our neighbor has a library of travel books.* 2 room or building where a collection of books, magazines, etc., is kept for public reading and borrowing. *n., pl.* **li brar ies.**

li bret tist (lə bret′ist), writer of a libretto. *n.*

li bret to (lə bret′ō), 1 the words of an opera or other long musical composition. 2 book containing the words.

n., pl. **li bret tos, li bret ti** (lə bret′ē). [from Italian]

Lib y a (lib′ē ə), country in N Africa, west of Egypt. *Capitals:* Tripoli and Benghazi. *n.* —**Lib′y an,** *adj., n.*

lice (līs), plural of **louse.** *n.*

li cence (lī′sns), license. *n., v.,* **li cenced, li cenc ing.**

li cense (lī′sns), 1 permission given by law to do something: *A license to drive an automobile is issued by the state.* 2 paper, card, plate, etc., showing such permission: *The policeman asked the reckless driver for her license.* 3 give a license to; permit by law: *A doctor is licensed to practice medicine.* 4 fact or condition of being allowed to do something. 5 freedom of action, speech, thought, etc., that is permitted or conceded. Poetic license is the freedom from rules that is permitted in poetry and other arts. 6 too much liberty of action; lack of proper control; abuse of liberty. 1,2,4-6 *n.,* 3 *v.,* **li censed, li cens ing.**

li cen tious (lī sen′shəs), not restrained by morality; loose in sexual activities; immoral. *adj.* —**li cen′tious ly,** *adv.* —**li cen′tious ness,** *n.*

li chen (lī′kən), a flowerless plant that looks somewhat like moss and consists of a fungus and an alga growing together as one plant. Lichens grow in patches on rocks, trees, and other surfaces. They are gray, yellow, brown, black, or greenish in color. *n.*

lick (lik), 1 pass the tongue over: *lick a stamp.* 2 lap up with the tongue: *The cat licked the milk.* 3 make or bring by using the tongue: *The cat licked the plate clean.* 4 a stroke of the tongue over something: *He gave the ice-cream cone a big lick.* 5 pass about or play over like a tongue: *The flames were licking the roof of the burning house.* 6 place where natural salt is found and where animals go to lick it up. 7 INFORMAL. a blow: *Though I lost the fight, I got in a few good licks.* 8 INFORMAL. to beat or thrash. 9 INFORMAL. to defeat in a fight, etc.; conquer: *She licked him at chess.* 10 a small quantity: *She didn't do a lick of work.* 1-3,5,8,9 *v.,* 4,6,7,10 *n.*

lick e ty-split (lik′ə tē split′), INFORMAL. at full speed; headlong; rapidly: *A frightened rabbit ran lickety-split into the bushes.* *adv.*

lic or ice (lik′ər is *or* lik′ər ish), 1 the sweet-tasting, dried root of a European plant. 2 the plant. 3 a black substance obtained from the root, used in medicine and candy. 4 candy flavored with this substance. *n.*

lid (lid), 1 a movable cover; top: *a jar lid.* 2 eyelid. 3 SLANG. hat or cap. *n.*

lid ded (lid′id), having a lid; covered with a lid. *adj.*

lid less (lid′lis), having no lid or lids. *adj.*

lie[1] (lī), 1 something said that is not true; something that is not true said to deceive: *Saying his friend stole it was a lie.* 2 speak falsely; tell a lie: *He says that he has never lied, but I think he is lying when he says it.* 3 give a false impression; mislead: *That clock must be lying; it isn't noon yet.* 1 *n.,* 2,3 *v.,* **lied, ly ing.** [Old English *lyge*]

give the lie to, 1 call a liar; accuse of lying. 2 show to be false: *Her actions gave the lie to her statement.*

lie[2] (lī), 1 have one's body in a flat position along the ground or other surface: *lie on the grass, lie in bed.* 2 assume such a position: *lie down on the couch.* 3 rest (on a surface): *The book was lying on the table.* 4 be kept or stay in a given state: *lie idle, lie hidden, lie unused.* 5 be; be placed: *land that lies high, a road that lies among trees, a ship lying offshore at anchor. The lake lies to the south of us.* 6 exist; be found to be: *The cure for ignorance lies in education.* 7 be in the grave; be buried: *His body lies in Plymouth.* 8 manner, position, or direction in which something lies: *the lie of the land.* 1-7 *v.,* **lay, lain, ly ing;** 8 *n.* [Old English *licgan*]

lie over, be left waiting until a later time.

lie to, (of a ship, etc.) come almost to a stop, facing the wind: *During the storm, the sailing ship lay to.*

take (something) lying down, yield to (something); not stand up to (something).

Liech ten stein (lik′tən stīn), small country between W Austria and E Switzerland. *n.*

lied (līd), past tense and past participle of **lie**[1]. *That girl lied about her work. She has lied before.* *v.*

lief (lēf), willingly: *I would as lief go hungry as eat that nasty mess.* *adv.*

liege (lēj), in the Middle Ages: 1 lord having a right to the homage and loyal service of his vassals. 2 having a right to the homage and loyal service of vassals. 3 vassal obliged to give homage and loyal service to his lord. 4 obliged to give homage and loyal service to a lord. 1,3 *n.,* 2,4 *adj.*

liege man (lēj′mən), 1 vassal. 2 a faithful follower. *n., pl.* **liege men.**

lien (lēn), (in law) a claim on the property of another for payment of a debt: *The garage owner has a lien upon my automobile until I pay his bill.* *n.*

lieu (lü). **in lieu of,** in place of; instead of. *n.*

Lieut., Lieutenant.

lieu ten an cy (lü ten′ən sē), rank,

hat, āge, fär; let, ēqual, tèrm;
it, īce; hot, ōpen, ôrder;
oil, out; cup, pùt, rüle; ch, child;
ng, long; sh, she; th, thin;
ᴛʜ, then; zh, measure;

ə represents *a* in about,
e in taken, *i* in pencil,
o in lemon, *u* in circus.

commission, or authority of a lieutenant. *n., pl.* **lieu ten an cies.**

lieu ten ant (lü ten′ənt), 1 person who acts in the place of someone above him in authority: *The scoutmaster used the two boys as his lieutenants.* 2 (in the army, air force, or Marine Corps) a first lieutenant or a second lieutenant. 3 (in the navy) an officer ranking next below a lieutenant commander and next above a lieutenant junior grade. 4 a police officer, usually ranking next below a captain and next above a sergeant. *n.*

lieutenant colonel, (in the army, air force, or Marine Corps) an officer ranking next below a colonel and next above a major.

lieutenant commander, (in the navy) an officer ranking next below a commander and next above a lieutenant.

lieutenant general, (in the army, air force, or Marine Corps) an officer ranking next below a general and next above a major general.

lieutenant governor, (in the United States) a public official next in rank to the governor of a state. In case of the governor's absence or death, the lieutenant governor takes his place.

lieutenant junior grade, (in the navy) an officer ranking next below a lieutenant and next above an ensign.

life (līf), 1 a living or being alive; quality which people, animals, and plants have but which rocks and minerals do not. Life is shown by growing and reproducing. 2 time of being alive. Each person has his own life or existence. *During his life he was an outstanding doctor.* 3 time of existence or action of inanimate things: *a machine's life, a lease's life.* 4 a living being; person: *Five lives were lost.* 5 living beings: *The desert island had almost no animal or vegetable life.* 6 way of living: *a dull life, a country life.* 7 account of a person's life: *Several lives of Lincoln have been written.* 8 spirit; vigor: *Put more life into your work.* *n., pl.* **lives.**

life belt, a life preserver made like a belt.

life blood (līf′blud′), 1 blood neces-

adj.	adjective	*n.*	noun
adv.	adverb	*prep.*	preposition
conj.	conjunction	*pron.*	pronoun
interj.	interjection	*v.*	verb
sing.	singular	*pl.*	plural

sary to life. 2 source of strength and energy. *n.*

life boat (līf′bōt′), a strong boat specially built for saving lives at sea or along the coast. *n.*

life buoy, a cork or plastic ring, belt, or jacket used as a life preserver; buoy.

life guard (līf′gärd′), person employed on a bathing beach or at a swimming pool to help in case of accident or danger to bathers. *n.*

life insurance, 1 system by which a person pays a small sum regularly to have a large sum paid to his family or heirs at his death. 2 sum paid by the insurance company at death.

life jacket, a sleeveless, canvas jacket filled with cork or air, worn as a life preserver.

life less (līf′lis), 1 without life: *a lifeless planet.* 2 dead: *a lifeless body.* 3 dull: *a lifeless party. adj.* —**life′less·ly,** *adv.* —**life′less·ness,** *n.*

life like (līf′līk′), like life; looking as if alive; like the real thing: *a lifelike portrait. adj.*

life line (līf′līn′), 1 rope for saving life, such as one thrown to a person in the water. 2 a diver's signaling line. 3 anything that maintains or helps to maintain something that cannot exist by itself, as a remote military position, etc. *n.*

life long (līf′lông′), lasting all one's life: *a lifelong friendship. adj.*

life preserver, a wide belt, jacket, circular tube, etc., usually made of cloth and cork, to keep a person afloat in the water until he is rescued.

life raft

life raft, raft for saving lives in a shipwreck or the wreck of an aircraft at sea.

life sav er (līf′sā′vər), 1 person who saves people from drowning. 2 any lifesaving person or thing. *n.*

life sav ing (līf′sā′ving), 1 a saving of people's lives; keeping people from

drowning. 2 designed or used to save people's lives. 1 *n.,* 2 *adj.*

life-size (līf′sīz′), as big as the living person, animal, etc.: *a life-size statue. adj.*

life-sized (līf′sīzd′), life-size. *adj.*

life-style (līf′stīl′), a person's or group's characteristic manner of living; one's style of life. *n.*

life time (līf′tīm′), time of being alive; period during which a life lasts: *Grandfather has seen many changes during his lifetime. n.*

lifeboat

life work (līf′wėrk′), work that takes or lasts a whole lifetime; main work in life. *n.*

lift (lift), 1 raise into the air; raise up higher; take up; pick up: *Please help me lift this box of books.* 2 raise in rank, condition, estimation, etc.; elevate; exalt. 3 an elevating influence or effect: *The promotion gave him a lift.* 4 rise and go; go away: *The fog lifted at dawn.* 5 go up; be raised: *This window will not lift.* 6 act of lifting: *the lift of a helping hand.* 7 distance through which a thing is lifted. 8 a helping hand: *Give me a lift with this job.* 9 a ride in a vehicle given to a traveler on foot; free ride: *Can you give the children a lift to school?* 10 INFORMAL. pick or take up; steal: *lift things from a store.* 11 elevator. 12 one of the layers of leather in the heel of a shoe. 13 the quantity or weight that can be lifted at one time: *A lift of fifty pounds is all I can manage.* 1,2,4,5,10 *v.,* 3,6-9,11-13 *n.* —**lift′er,** *n.*

lift off (lift′ôf′), the firing or launching of a rocket. *n.*

lig a ment (lig′ə mənt), band of strong tissue which connects bones or holds organs of the body in place. *n.*

lig a ture (lig′ə chùr *or* lig′ə chər), 1 anything used to bind or tie up; band, bandage, cord, etc. 2 thread, wire, etc., used by surgeons to tie up a bleeding artery or vein. 3 two or three letters joined in printing. Æ and ffl are ligatures. *n.*

light¹ (līt), 1 that by which we see; form of radiant energy that acts on the retina of the eye. Light consists of electromagnetic waves that travel at about 186,282 miles per second. 2 having light. 3 thing that gives light. The sun, a lamp, or a lighthouse is

called a light. 4 supply of light: *A tall building cuts off our light.* 5 cause to give light: *She lighted the lamp.* 6 give light to; provide with light: *The room is lighted by six windows.* 7 bright; clear: *It is as light as day.* 8 brightness; clearness; illumination; particular case of this: *a strong or dim light.* 9 a bright part: *light and shade in a painting.* 10 make bright or clear: *Her face was lighted by a smile.* 11 show the way by means of a light: *Here is a candle to light you to bed.* 12 become light: *The sky lights up at dawn.* 13 daytime: *The workman gets up before light.* 14 dawn. 15 pale in color; approaching white: *light hair, light blue.* 16 window or other means of letting in light. 17 thing with which to start something burning: *He wanted a light for his cigar.* 18 set fire to: *She lighted the candles.* 19 take fire: *Matches light when you strike them.* 20 knowledge; information: *We need more light on this subject.* 21 public knowledge; open view: *The reporter brought to light graft in the city government.* 22 aspect in which a thing is viewed: *The principal put the matter in the right light.* 23 shining model or example: *Louis Pasteur is one of the leading lights of science because of his work on the causes of disease.* 1,3,4,8,9, 13,14,16,17,20-23 *n.,* 2,7,15 *adj.,* 5,6, 10-12,18,19 *v.,* **light ed** or **lit, lighting.** [Old English *lēoht*]

in the light of, because of; considering: *In the light of all these facts, what you did was completely right.*

see the light or **see the light of day,** 1 be born. 2 be made public. 3 get the right idea.

shed light on or **throw light on,** make clear; explain.

light² (līt), 1 easy to carry; not heavy: *a light load.* 2 having little weight for its size: *Feathers are light.* 3 having less than usual weight: *light summer clothing.* 4 less than usual in amount, force, etc.: *a light sleep, a light rain, a light meal, a light wine.* 5 easy to do or bear; not hard or severe: *light punishment, a light task.* 6 not looking heavy; graceful; delicate: *a light bridge, light carving.* 7 moving easily; nimble: *a light step.* 8 cheerfully careless; gay: *a light laugh.* 9 not serious enough; fickle: *a light mind, light of purpose.* 10 aiming to entertain; not serious: *light reading.* 11 not important: *light losses.* 12 porous; sandy: *a light soil.* 13 that has risen properly; not soggy: *light dough.* 14 lightly armed or equipped: *light cavalry, in light marching order.* 15 lightly. 1-14 *adj.,* 15 *adv.* [Old English *lēoht, līht*]

light in the head, 1 dizzy. 2 silly; foolish.

make light of, treat as of little importance.

light[3] (līt), 1 come down to the ground: *He lighted from his horse.* 2 come down from flight: *A bird lighted on the branch.* 3 come by chance: *Her eye lighted upon a coin in the road.* 4 fall suddenly: *The blow lighted on his head.* *v.,* **light ed** or **lit, light ing.** [Old English *līhtan*]

light out, SLANG. leave suddenly; go away quickly.

light en[1] (līt′n), 1 make or become brighter; brighten: *Dawn lightens the sky. Her face lightened.* 2 flash with lightning: *It thundered and lightened outside.* v. [Middle English, from *light*[1]] —**light′en er,** *n.*

light en[2] (līt′n), 1 reduce the load of; make or become lighter: *lighten the burden of his work.* 2 make or become more cheerful: *The good news lightened our hearts.* v. [Middle English, from *light*[2]] —**light′en er,** *n.*

light er[1] (līt′ər), thing or person that starts something burning. *n.* [*light*[1] + *-er*[1]]

light er[2] (līt′ər), 1 a flat-bottomed barge used for loading and unloading ships. 2 carry (goods) in such a barge. 1 *n.,* 2 *v.* [*light*[3] + *-er*[1]]

light face (līt′fās′), printing type that has thin, light lines. This sentence is in lightface. *n.*

light-foot ed (līt′fut′id), stepping lightly. *adj.*

light-head ed (līt′hed′id), 1 dizzy; giddy; out of one's head: *The sick man was light-headed from fever.* 2 empty-headed; silly; thoughtless: *That frivolous, light-headed crowd thinks of nothing but parties and games. adj.*

light heart ed (līt′här′tid), without worry; carefree; cheerful; gay. *adj.* —**light′heart′ed ly,** *adv.* —**light′heart′ed ness,** *n.*

light heavyweight, boxer who weighs more than 160 and less than 175 pounds.

lighthouse

light house (līt′hous′), tower or framework with a bright light that shines far over the water. It is often located at a dangerous place to warn and guide ships. *n., pl.* **light hous es** (līt′hou′ziz).

light ing (līt′ing), 1 a giving of light;

providing with light. 2 way in which lights are arranged. *n.*

light ly (līt′lē), 1 with little weight or force: *Cares rested lightly on her.* 2 to a small degree or extent; not much: *lightly clad.* 3 in an airy way: *flags floating lightly.* 4 quickly; easily: *She jumped lightly aside.* 5 cheerfully: *take bad news lightly.* 6 indifferently; in a slighting way: *speak lightly of a person.* 7 thoughtlessly; carelessly; frivolously: *behave lightly. adv.*

light-mind ed (līt′mīn′did), empty-headed; thoughtless; frivolous. *adj.*

light ness[1] (līt′nis), 1 brightness; clearness. 2 paleness; whitishness. 3 amount of light: *The lightness of the sky showed that the rain was really over. n.* [Old English *līhtnes,* from *lēoht* *light*[1]]

light ness[2] (līt′nis), 1 a being light; not being heavy: *The lightness of this load is a relief after the heavy one I was carrying.* 2 a being gay or cheerful: *lightness of spirits.* 3 lack of proper seriousness: *Such lightness of conduct is out of place in a courtroom. n.* [*light*[2] + *-ness*]

light ning (līt′ning), flash of light in the sky caused by a discharge of electricity between clouds, or between a cloud and the earth's surface. The sound that it makes is thunder. *n.*

lightning bug, firefly.

—LIGHTNING ROD
←WIRE
GROUND ROD→

lightning rod
Lightning which strikes the rod is conducted down a heavy wire and grounded through a metal rod.

lightning rod, a metal rod fixed on a building or ship to conduct lightning into the earth or water.

light ship (līt′ship′), ship with a bright light, anchored at a dangerous place to warn ships away. *n.*

light some (līt′səm), 1 nimble; lively: *lightsome feet.* 2 happy; gay; cheerful: *a lightsome heart.* 3 frivolous. *adj.*

light weight (līt′wāt′), 1 person or thing of less than average weight. 2 light in weight. 3 boxer who weighs more than 126 and less than 135 pounds. 1,3 *n.,* 2 *adj.*

light-year (līt′yir′), distance that light travels in one year, about six trillion (6,000,000,000,000) miles. It is used to measure astronomical distances. *n.*

lig nite (lig′nīt), a dark-brown coal, often having a woody texture. *n.*

lik a ble (lī′kə bəl), having qualities

hat, āge, fär; let, ēqual, tėrm;
it, īce; hot, ōpen, ôrder;
oil, out; cup, put, rüle; ch, child;
ng, long; sh, she; th, thin;
ͯH, then; zh, measure;

ə represents *a* in about,
e in taken, *i* in pencil,
o in lemon, *u* in circus.

that win good will or friendship; popular; pleasing: *the most likable boy in school. adj.* Also, **likeable.** —**lik′a ble ness,** *n.*

like[1] (līk), 1 resembling something or each other; similar to: *Our house is like theirs. I never saw anything like it.* 2 in the same way as; as well as: *sing like a bird, work like a beaver.* 3 of the same form, kind, amount, etc.; the same or almost the same; similar: *drawing, painting, or like arts. Her aunt promised her $10 if she could earn a like sum.* 4 such as one would expect of; characteristic of: *Isn't it just like him to be late?* 5 in the right condition for: *I feel like working.* 6 giving promise of: *It looks like rain.* 7 person or thing like another; counterpart or equal: *We shall not see her like again.* 8 INFORMAL. as if: *He acted like he was afraid.* 9 INFORMAL. as: *It was like she said it was.* 10 INFORMAL. probably: *Like enough it will rain.* 11 OLD USE. likely. 1,2,4-6 *prep.,* 3,11 *adj.,* 10 *adv.,* 7 *n.,* 8,9 *conj.* [Old English *(ge)līc*]

and the like, 1 and so forth: *He studied music, painting, and the like.* 2 and other like things: *At the zoo we saw lions, tigers, bears, and the like.*

like[2] (līk), 1 be pleased with; be satisfied with: *My cat likes milk.* 2 have a kindly or friendly feeling for: *to like a person.* 3 wish for; wish: *I'd like more time to finish this. Come whenever you like.* 4 **likes,** *pl.* liking; preference: *You know all my likes and dislikes.* 1-3 *v.,* **liked, lik ing;** 4 *n.* [Old English *līcian* to please]

-like, *suffix added to nouns to form adjectives.* 1 like: *Wolflike = like a wolf.* 2 like that of; characteristic of: *Childlike = like that of a child.* 3 suited to; fit or proper for: *Businesslike = suited to business.* [from *like*[1]]

like a ble (lī′kə bəl), likable. *adj.* —**like′a ble ness,** *n.*

like li hood (līk′lē hud), probability: *Is there any likelihood of rain today? n.*

like ly (līk′lē), 1 probable: *One likely result of this heavy rain is the rising of the river.* 2 probably: *I shall very likely be home all day.* 3 to be expected: *It is

adj.	adjective	*n.*	noun
adv.	adverb	*prep.*	preposition
conj.	conjunction	*pron.*	pronoun
interj.	interjection	*v.*	verb
sing.	singular	*pl.*	plural

likely to be hot in August. 4 suitable: *Is this a likely place to fish?* 5 promising: *a likely boy.* 1,3-5 *adj.*, **like li er, like li est;** 2 *adv.*

lik en (lī′kən), represent as like; compare. *v.*

like ness (līk′nis), 1 a resembling; being alike: *The girl's likeness to her aunt was striking.* 2 something that is like; copy; picture: *The stamp has a good likeness of Lincoln on it.* 3 appearance; shape: *I watched a large cloud assume the likeness of a sailing ship. n., pl.* **like ness es.**

like wise (līk′wīz′), 1 the same: *See what I do. Now you do likewise.* 2 also; moreover; too: *I must go home now, and she likewise. adv.*

lik ing (lī′king), kindly feeling; preference; fondness: *a liking for apples, a liking for children. n.*

li lac (lī′lək), 1 shrub with clusters of tiny, fragrant, pale pinkish-purple or white blossoms. 2 a cluster of these blossoms. 3 a pale pinkish-purple. 4 pale pinkish-purple. 1-3 *n.,* 4 *adj.*

lilt (lilt), 1 sing or play (a tune) in a light, tripping manner. 2 a lively song or tune with a swing. 3 a lively, springing movement: *She walks with a lilt.* 1 *v.,* 2,3 *n.*

lil y (lil′ē), 1 plant that grows from a bulb. Its flowers are usually large, bell-shaped, and beautiful, and are often divided into six parts. 2 its flower. The white lily is a symbol of purity. 3 like a white lily; pure and lovely. 4 any of various related or similar plants, such as the calla lily or water lily. 1,2,4 *n., pl.* **lil ies;** 3 *adj.* —**lil′y like′,** *adj.*

lily of the valley, 1 plant having tiny, sweet-smelling, bell-shaped, white flowers arranged up and down a single flower stem. 2 its flowers. *pl.* **lilies of the valley.**

Li ma (lē′mə), capital of Peru, in the W part. *n.*

li ma bean (lī′mə), 1 a broad, flat, pale-green bean, used as a vegetable. 2 the plant it grows on. [from *Lima*]

limb (lim), 1 leg, arm, or wing. 2 a large branch: *They sawed the dead limb off the tree. n.*

lim ber (lim′bər), 1 bending easily; flexible: *A piano player should have limber fingers. Willow is a limber wood.* 2 make or become limber: *He is stiff*

when he begins to skate, but limbers up quickly. 1 *adj.,* 2 *v.* —**lim′ber ly,** *adv.* —**lim′ber ness,** *n.*

limb less (lim′lis), having no limbs. *adj.*

lim bo (lim′bō), 1 Often, **Limbo.** (in the belief of Roman Catholics) a region for souls of people who die unbaptized but who do not deserve the punishment of sinners. The souls of righteous people who died before the coming of Christ were kept in Limbo until after the Resurrection. 2 place for persons and things forgotten, cast aside, or out of date: *The belief that the earth is flat belongs to the limbo of outworn ideas. n., pl.* **lim bos.**

Lim burg er (lim′bėr′gər), a soft cheese having a strong smell. *n.* [from *Limburg,* a province in Belgium]

lime[1] (līm), 1 a solid white compound of calcium and oxygen obtained by burning limestone, shells, bone, etc.; quicklime; calcium oxide. Lime is used in making mortar and on fields to improve the soil. 2 put lime on. 1 *n., 2 v.,* **limed, lim ing.** [Old English *līm*]

lime[2] (līm), 1 a juicy, greenish-yellow citrus fruit which is smaller and sourer than a lemon. Its juice is used for flavoring and in medicine. 2 tree that it grows on. *n.* [from French *lime,* from Spanish *lima,* from Arabic *limun*]

lime[3] (līm), the linden tree. *n.* [earlier *line,* Old English *lind*]

lime light (līm′līt′), 1 a strong light thrown upon the stage of a theater to light up certain persons or objects and draw attention to them. 2 the glare of public observation: *Some people are never happy unless they are in the limelight. n.*

lim er ick (lim′ər ik), kind of humorous verse of five lines. EXAMPLE:

"There was a young lady from Lynn
Who was so exceedingly thin
    That when she essayed
    To drink lemonade
She slid down the straw and fell in."

n. [apparently from a song about *Limerick,* a county and city in Ireland]

lime stone (līm′stōn′), rock made mostly of calcium carbonate, used for building and for making lime. Marble is a kind of limestone. *n.*

lime wa ter (līm′wô′tər *or* līm′wot′- ər), solution of slaked lime in water. It is used to counteract an acid condition of the digestive tract. *n.*

lim it (lim′it), 1 farthest point or edge; where something ends or must end: *the limit of one's vision, the limit of a person's authority. I have reached the limit of my patience.* 2 **limits,** *pl.* boundary; bounds: *Keep within the limits of the school grounds.* 3 set a limit to; restrict: *We must limit the expense to $10. Her*

diet was limited to milk and soft foods. 1,2 *n.,* 3 *v.*

lim i ta tion (lim′ə tā′shən), 1 a limiting or a being limited. 2 that which limits; limiting rule or circumstance; restriction; boundary. *n.*

lim it ed (lim′ə tid), 1 kept within limits; restricted: *a limited space, a limited number.* 2 traveling fast and making only a few stops: *a limited train or bus.* 3 train or bus that travels fast and makes only a few stops. 1,2 *adj.,* 3 *n.*

lim it less (lim′it lis), without limits; boundless; infinite. *adj.*

limn (lim), 1 paint (a picture). 2 portray in words. *v.*

lim ou sine (lim′ə zēn′ *or* lim′ə zēn′), a closed automobile, seating from three to five passengers inside, with a driver's seat separated from the passengers by a partition. *n.* [from *Limousin,* a former French province]

limp[1] (limp), 1 a lame step or walk. 2 walk with a limp: *After falling down the stairs, he limped for several days.* 1 *n.,* 2 *v.* [perhaps related to Old English *lemphealt* lame] —**limp′er,** *n.*

limp[2] (limp), lacking stiffness or firmness; ready to bend or droop: *The lettuce in our garden gets limp in hot weather. I am so tired I feel as limp as a rag. adj.* [perhaps related to Icelandic *lempinn* pliable, gentle] —**limp′ly,** *adv.* —**limp′ness,** *n.*

SIDE VIEW

limpet   UNDERSIDE

lim pet (lim′pit), a small shellfish that clings to rocks and other objects, used for bait and sometimes for food. *n.*

lim pid (lim′pid), clear or transparent: *a spring of limpid water, limpid eyes. adj.* —**lim′pid ly,** *adv.*

lim pid i ty (lim pid′ə tē), limpid quality or condition. *n.*

lim y (lī′mē), of, containing, or resembling lime. *adj.,* **lim i er, lim i est.**

linch pin (linch′pin′), pin inserted through a hole in the end of an axle to keep the wheel on. *n.*

Lin coln (ling′kən), 1 **Abraham,** 1809-1865, the 16th president of the United States, from 1861 to 1865. 2 capital of Nebraska, in the SE part. *n.*

Lind bergh (lind′bėrg′), **Charles Augustus,** born 1902, American aviator who made the first solo flight across the Atlantic, in 1927. *n.*

lin den (lin′dən), tree with heart-shaped leaves and clusters of small, sweet-smelling, yellowish flowers; lime. It is often used for shade and ornament. *n.*

line[1] (līn), **1** piece of rope, cord, or wire: *a telegraph line.* Reins are sometimes called lines. **2** a cord for measuring, making level, etc. A plumb line is used to see if a wall is vertical or to find the depth of water. **3** a long narrow mark: *Draw two lines along the margin.* **4** anything that is like a long narrow mark: *the lines in your face.* **5** mark with lines: *Please line your paper with a pencil and ruler.* **6** cover with lines: *a face lined with age.* **7** a straight line: *The lower edges of the two pictures are about on a line.* **8** **the line,** the equator. **9** (in mathematics) the path traced by a moving point. It has length, but no thickness. **10** the use of lines in drawing: *a picture in line, clearness of line in an artist's work.* **11** **lines,** *pl.* outline; contour: *a ship of fine lines.* **12** an edge or boundary: *the line between Texas and Mexico.* **13** row of persons or things: *a line of trees.* **14** arrange in line: *Line your shoes along the edge of the shelf.* **15** arrange a line along; form a line along: *Cars lined the road for a mile.* **16** a row of words on a page or in a column: *a column of 40 lines.* **17** a short letter; note: *Drop me a line.* **18** a connected series of persons or things following one another in time: *The Stuarts were a line of English kings.* **19** family or lineage: *of noble line.* **20** a course, track, or direction: *a railroad line, the line of march of an army.* **21** a certain way of doing: *Please proceed on these lines till further notice.* **22** (in warfare) a front row of trenches or other defenses. **23** formation of soldiers or ships placed side by side. **24** wire or system of wires connecting points or stations in a telegraph or telephone system. **25** any rope, wire, pipe, hose, etc., running from one point to another. **26** a single track of railroad. **27** one branch of a system of transportation: *the main line of a railroad.* **28** a whole system of transportation or conveyance: *the Grand Trunk Line.* **29** a branch of business; kind of activity: *the dry-goods line. This is not my line.* **30** a kind or branch of goods: *He carries the best line of shoes in town.* **31** a single verse of poetry. **32** **lines,** *pl.* words that an actor speaks in a play: *forget one's lines.* **33** in football: **a** line of scrimmage. **b** players along the line of scrimmage at the start of a play. Usually the offensive team has seven men in the line, and the defensive team has four. **34** one of the horizontal lines that make a staff in music. 1-4,7-13,16-34 *n.,* 5,6, 14,15 *v.,* **lined, lin ing.** [fusion of Old English *līne* line, rope, and French before 1400's *ligne* line, both from Latin *linea* line, linen thread, from *linum* flax]

all along the line, at every point; everywhere: *This car has given us trouble all along the line.*

bring into line, cause to agree or conform.

come into line, agree; conform.

draw a line, set a limit.

get a line on, INFORMAL. get or have information about.

in line, 1 in alignment: *The children are all in line.* **2** in agreement: *This plan is in line with their thinking.*

line up, form a line; form into a line: *Cars were lined up along the road.*

on a line, even; level.

out of line, in disagreement.

read between the lines, get more from the words than they say; find a hidden meaning.

toe the line, conform to a certain standard of duty, conduct, etc.

line[2] (līn), **1** put a layer of paper, cloth, felt, etc., inside of (a dress, hat, box, bag, etc.). **2** fill: *line one's pockets with money.* **3** serve as a lining for: *This piece of silk would line your coat very nicely.* *v.,* **lined, lin ing.** [Old English *līn* flax, linen thread or cloth]

lin e age (lin/ē ij), **1** descent in a direct line from an ancestor. **2** family or race. *n.*

lin e al (lin/ē əl), **1** in the direct line of descent: *She is a lineal descendant of her grandmother.* **2** of or like a line. *adj.*

lin e al ly (lin/ē ə lē), in the direct line of descent: *He is descended lineally from his grandfather. adv.*

lin e a ment (lin/ē ə mənt), part or feature, especially a part or feature of a face with attention to its outline. *n.*

lin e ar (lin/ē ər), **1** of a line or lines; in a line or lines: *The royal crown is passed from father to son in a linear succession.* **2** made of lines; making use of lines: *linear designs.* **3** of length: *An inch is a linear measure.* **4** like a line; long and narrow: *A pine tree has linear leaves. adj.* **—lin/e ar ly,** *adv.*

line back er (līn/bak/ər), (in football) a defensive player whose position is directly behind the line. *n.*

line drive, baseball hit so that it goes in almost a straight line, usually close to the ground; liner.

line man (līn/mən), **1** person who sets up or repairs telegraph, telephone, or electric wires; linesman. **2** (in football) a player in the line; a center, guard, tackle, or end. **3** person who inspects railroad tracks. **4** person who carries the line in surveying. *n., pl.* **line men.**

lin en (lin/ən), **1** cloth or thread made from flax. **2** articles made of linen or some substitute. Tablecloths, napkins, sheets, towels, and shirts are all called

hat, āge, fär; let, ēqual, tėrm; it, īce; hot, ōpen, ôrder; oil, out; cup, pùt, rüle; ch, child; ng, long; sh, she; th, thin; ᴛʜ, then; zh, measure;

ə represents *a* in about, *e* in taken, *i* in pencil, *o* in lemon, *u* in circus.

linen. **3** made of linen. 1,2 *n.,* 3 *adj.*

line of duty, performance of duty or service, especially military duty: *The guard was injured in the line of duty.*

line of scrimmage, (in football) an imaginary line running across the field at any point where the ball is placed; scrimmage line.

lin er[1] (lī/nər), **1** ship or airplane belonging to a transportation system. **2** person or thing that makes lines. **3** line drive. *n.* [*line*[1] + *-er*[1]]

lin er[2] (lī/nər), **1** person who lines or fits a lining to anything. **2** something that serves as a lining. *n.* [*line*[2] + *-er*[1]]

line segment, segment (def. 2c).

lines man (līnz/mən), **1** lineman. **2** (in certain games) person who watches the lines which mark out the field, court, etc., and assists the umpire. *n., pl.* **lines men.**

line-up or **line up** (līn/up/), **1** formation of persons or things into a line. A police line-up is an arrangement of a group of persons for identification. **2** list of the players who will take part or are taking part in a game of football, baseball, etc. *n.*

lin ger (ling/gər), stay on; go slowly, as if unwilling to leave: *Daylight lingers long in the summertime. She lingered after the others had left. v.*

lin ge rie (lan/zhə rē/ or län/zhə rā/), women's underwear, nightgowns, etc. *n.* [from French]

lin go (ling/gō), INFORMAL. language or talk that sounds strange or is not understood: *baseball lingo. She speaks a foreign lingo. n., pl.* **lin goes.**

lin guist (ling/gwist), **1** an expert in languages or linguistics. **2** person skilled in a number of languages. *n.*

lin guis tic (ling gwis/tik), having to do with language or the study of languages. *adj.* **—lin guis/ti cal ly,** *adv.*

lin guis tics (ling gwis/tiks), science of language; comparative study of languages. *n.*

lin i ment (lin/ə mənt), a soothing liquid which is rubbed on the skin to relieve the pain of sore muscles, sprains, bruises, etc. *n.*

lin ing (lī/ning), layer of material cov-

link

adj. adjective	*n.* noun
adv. adverb	*prep.* preposition
conj. conjunction	*pron.* pronoun
interj. interjection	*v.* verb
sing. singular	*pl.* plural

lions (def. 1)
about 3 ft. high at the shoulder;
male lion above, lioness below

ering the inner surface of something: *the lining of a coat. n.*

link (lingk), **1** any ring or loop of a chain. **2** anything that joins as a link joins: *a cuff link.* **3** a fact or thought that connects others: *a link in a chain of evidence.* **4** join as a link does; unite or connect: *Your story links up with what she told us.* **1-3** *n.,* **4** *v.*

link age (ling′kij), **1** a linking or a being linked. **2** arrangement or system of links. *n.*

linking verb, verb with little or no meaning of its own, used to connect a subject with a predicate adjective or a predicate noun. In "The trees are maples," *are* is a linking verb. *Am, are, is,* and *seem* are common linking verbs.

links (lingks), a golf course. *n.pl.*

lin net (lin′it), a small songbird of Europe, Asia, and Africa. *n.*

li no le um (lə nō′lē əm), **1** a floor covering made by putting a hard surface of ground cork mixed with linseed oil on a canvas or burlap back. **2** any similar floor covering. *n.*

lin seed (lin′sēd′), the seed of flax. *n.*

linseed oil, a yellowish oil obtained by pressing linseed. It is used in making paints, printing inks, and linoleum.

lin sey-wool sey (lin′zē wůl′zē), a strong, coarse fabric made of linen and wool or of cotton and wool. *n., pl.* **lin sey-wool seys.**

lint (lint), **1** the soft down or fleecy material obtained by scraping linen. Formerly, lint was put on wounds to keep out air and dirt. **2** tiny bits of thread: *Lint collects on the carpet. n.*

LINTEL →

← SILL

lin tel (lin′tl), a horizontal beam or stone above a door or window to support the structure above it. *n.*

lint y (lin′tē), **1** full of or marked with lint. **2** like lint. *adj.,* **lint i er, lint i est.**

li on (lī′ən), **1** a large, strong, flesh-eating mammal of the cat family, with a dull-yellowish coat, found in Africa and southern Asia. The male has a full, flowing mane of coarse hair. **2** a very brave or strong person. **3** a famous person. *n.*

li on ess (lī′ə nis), a female lion. *n., pl.* **li on ess es.**

li on ize (lī′ə nīz), treat as very important. *v.,* **li on ized, li on iz ing.**

lip (lip), **1** either of the two fleshy, movable edges of the mouth. **2** the folding or bent-out edge of any opening: *the lip of a pitcher.* **3** not heartfelt or deep, but just on the surface: *give lip service to an idea, but never practice it.* **1,2** *n.,* **3** *adj.* —**lip′like′,** *adj.*

keep a stiff upper lip, be brave and firm; show no fear or discouragement.

lip-read (lip′rēd′), understand speech by watching the movements of the speaker's lips. *v.,* **lip-read** (lip′red′), **lip-read ing.** —**lip′-read′er,** *n.*

lip reading, understanding of speech by watching the movements of the speaker's lips.

lip stick (lip′stik′), a small stick of a waxlike cosmetic, used for coloring the lips. *n.*

liq ue fac tion (lik′wə fak′shən), **1** process of changing into a liquid. **2** liquefied condition. *n.*

liq ue fy (lik′wə fī), change into a liquid; make or become liquid: *Liquefied air is extremely cold. v.,* **liq ue fied, liq ue fy ing.**

li queur (li kėr′), a strong, sweet, highly flavored alcoholic liquor. *n.*

liq uid (lik′wid), **1** substance that is not a solid or a gas; substance that flows freely like water. Mercury is a liquid at room temperature. **2** in the form of a liquid; melted: *liquid soap, butter heated until it is liquid.* **3** clear and bright like water. **4** clear and smooth-flowing in sound: *the liquid notes of a bird.* **5** the sound of *l* or *r.* **6** easily turned into cash: *United States bonds are a liquid investment.* **1,5** *n.,* **2-4,6** *adj.* —**liq′uid ly,** *adv.* —**liq′uid ness,** *n.*

liquid air, an intensely cold liquid formed by putting air under very great pressure and then cooling it. It is used as a refrigerant.

liq ui date (lik′wə dāt), **1** pay (a debt). **2** settle the accounts of (a business, etc.); clear up the affairs of (a bankrupt). **3** get rid of (an undesirable person or thing): *The Russian Revolution liquidated the nobility.* **4** kill ruthlessly; exterminate. *v.,* **liq ui dat ed, liq ui dat ing.**

liq ui da tion (lik′wə dā′shən), a liquidating or a being liquidated. *n.*

li quid i ty (li kwid′ə tē), liquid condition or quality. *n.*

liquid measure, system for measuring liquids. In the United States:

4 gills	=	1 pint
2 pints	=	1 quart
4 quarts	=	1 gallon
31½ gallons	=	1 barrel
2 barrels (63 gallons)	=	1 hogshead.

liquid oxygen, an intensely cold liquid formed by putting oxygen under very great pressure and then cooling it; lox. It is used as a rocket fuel.

liq uor (lik′ər), **1** an alcoholic drink, especially brandy, gin, rum, or whiskey. **2** any liquid, especially a liquid in which food is packaged, canned, or cooked: *Pickles are put up in a salty liquor. n.*

lir a (lir′ə), **1** the unit of money in Italy. Five lire are worth about one cent. **2** coin worth a lira. *n., pl.* **lir e** (lir′ā), **lir as.**

Lis bon (liz′bən), capital of Portugal, in the SW part. *n.*

lisle (līl), **1** a fine, strong, linen or cotton thread, used for making stockings, gloves, etc. **2** made of lisle: *lisle stockings.* **1** *n.,* **2** *adj.* [from *Lisle,* a town in France]

lisp (lisp), **1** use the sound of *th* in *thin* and *then,* instead of the sound of *s* or the sound of *z* in speaking: *A person who lisps might say, "Thing a thong" for "Sing a song."* **2** act, habit, or sound of saying a *th* sound for *s* and *z: He spoke with a lisp.* **3** speak imperfectly: *Young children sometimes lisp when they are learning to talk.* **1,3** *v.,* **2** *n.*

lis some or **lis som** (lis′əm), bending easily; lithe; limber; supple. *adj.*

list¹ (list), **1** series of names, numbers, words, or phrases: *a shopping list.* **2** make a list of; enter in a list: *A dictionary lists words in alphabetical order.* **1** *n.,* **2** *v.* [from French *liste*]

list² (list), the edge of cloth, where the material is a little different. *n.* [Old English *līste*]

list³ (list), **1** a tipping to one side; tilt: *the list of a ship.* **2** tip to one side: *The sinking ship was listing so that water lapped its decks.* **1** *n.,* **2** *v.* [perhaps extended use of *list⁴* in the sense of "being inclined to"]

list⁴ (list), OLD USE. please; choose; like. *v.* [Old English *lystan*]

496

list⁵ (list), OLD USE. listen; listen to. *v.* [Old English *hlystan*]

lis ten (lis′n), 1 try to hear; attend with the ears so as to hear: *She listened for the sound of a car. I like to listen to music.* 2 give heed (to advice, temptation, etc.); pay attention. *v.* —**lis′ten er,** *n.*

listen in, 1 listen to others talking on a telephone: *If you want to hear what he says, listen in on the extension.* 2 listen to the radio: *Listen in next week for the exciting conclusion of our story.*

Lis ter (lis′tər), **Joseph,** 1827-1912, English surgeon. He was the first to use antiseptic methods in performing operations. *n.*

list less (list′lis), seeming too tired to care about anything; not interested in things; not caring to be active: *a dull and listless mood. adj.* —**list′less ly,** *adv.* —**list′less ness,** *n.*

lists (lists), place where knights fought in tournaments. *n.pl.*

enter the lists, join in a contest; take part in a fight, argument, etc.

Liszt (list), **Franz,** 1811-1886, Hungarian composer and pianist. *n.*

lit¹ (lit), lighted; a past tense and a past participle of **light¹.** *v.*

lit² (lit), lighted; a past tense and a past participle of **light³.** *v.*

lit., 1 liter. 2 literature.

lit a ny (lit′n ē), 1 prayer consisting of a series of supplications said by the minister and responses said by the people. 2 any similar series. *n., pl.* **lit a nies.**

li ter (lē′tər), the basic measure of volume in the metric system; 1.0567 quarts liquid measure, or .908 quart dry measure. A liter is the volume of one kilogram of water. *n.* Also, **litre.**

lit er a cy (lit′ər ə sē), ability to read and write. *n.*

lit er al (lit′ər əl), 1 following the exact words of the original: *a literal translation.* 2 taking words in their usual meaning, without exaggeration or imagination; matter-of-fact: *the literal meaning of a phrase, a literal type of mind.* 3 true to fact: *a literal account. adj.* —**lit′er al ness,** *n.*

lit er al ly (lit′ər ə lē), 1 word for word; without exaggeration or imagination: *Write the story literally as it happened.* 2 actually: *He is literally without fear. adv.*

lit er ar y (lit′ə rer′ē), 1 having to do with literature. 2 knowing much about literature. 3 engaged in literature as a profession. *adj.*

lit er ate (lit′ər it), 1 able to read and write. 2 person who can read and write. 3 acquainted with literature; educated. 4 an educated person. 1,3 *adj.,* 2,4 *n.*

lit er a ture (lit′ər ə chùr *or* lit′ər

chər), 1 writings of a period or of a country, especially those kept alive by their beauty of style or thought: *Shakespeare is a great name in English literature.* 2 all the books and articles on a subject: *the literature of stamp collecting.* 3 writing books as a profession. 4 the study of literature: *I shall take literature and mathematics this spring.* 5 INFORMAL. printed matter of any kind: *election campaign literature. n.*

lithe (līᴛʜ), bending easily; supple: *lithe of body, a lithe willow. adj.* —**lithe′ly,** *adv.* —**lithe′ness,** *n.*

lith i um (lith′ē əm), a soft, silver-white, metallic element which occurs in various minerals. Lithium is the lightest of all metals. *n.*

lith o graph (lith′ə graf), 1 print made from a flat, specially prepared, stone or metal plate. 2 to print from such a stone or plate. 1 *n.,* 2 *v.*

li thog ra pher (li thog′rə fər), person who makes lithographs. *n.*

li thog ra phy (li thog′rə fē), art or process of making lithographs. *n.*

lith o sphere (lith′ə sfir), crust of the earth. *n.*

Lith u a ni a (lith′ü ā′nē ə), Soviet republic in N Europe, on the Baltic Sea. *n.* —**Lith′u a′ni an,** *adj., n.*

lit i gant (lit′ə gənt), person engaged in a lawsuit. *n.*

lit i ga tion (lit′ə gā′shən), 1 a carrying on a lawsuit. 2 a going to law. 3 a lawsuit or legal proceeding. *n.*

lit mus (lit′məs), a blue dye obtained from lichens, used in litmus paper as a chemical indicator. *n.*

litmus paper, paper treated with litmus. Blue litmus paper turns red when put into acid; red litmus paper turns blue when put into alkali.

li tre (lē′tər), liter. *n.*

lit ter (lit′ər), 1 little bits left around in disorder; things scattered about: *Everyone should pick up his own litter.* 2 leave odds and ends lying around; scatter things about; make untidy: *You have littered the room with your papers.* 3 the young animals produced at one time: *a litter of puppies.* 4 give birth to (young animals). 5 straw, hay, etc., used as bedding for animals. 6 make a bed for (an animal) with straw, hay, etc. 7 stretcher for carrying a sick or wounded person. 8 framework to be carried on men's shoulders or by beasts of burden, with a couch usually enclosed by curtains. 1,3,5,7,8 *n.,* 2,4,6 *v.*

lit tle (lit′l), 1 not big or large; small. A grain of sand or the head of a pin is little. 2 not long in time or in distance; short: *Wait a little while and I'll go a little way with you.* 3 not much; small in number, amount, degree, or importance: *A sick child has very little*

hat, āge, fär; let, ēqual, tėrm; it, īce; hot, ōpen, ôrder; oil, out; cup, pùt, rüle; ch, child; ng, long; sh, she; th, thin; ᴛʜ, then; zh, measure;

ə represents *a* in about, *e* in taken, *i* in pencil, *o* in lemon, *u* in circus.

strength and can eat only a little food. 4 small in mind, feeling, nature, or power: *It was little of them to make such a big fuss over a scratch on an old car.* 5 a small amount: *She had a big box of candy but gave her sister only a little.* 6 a short time or distance: *move a little to the left. After a little you will feel better.* 7 to a small extent: *The teacher read from an interesting book that was little known to us.* 8 not at all: *A coward is little liked.* 1-4 *adj.,* **less** or **less er, least;** or **lit tler, lit tlest;** 5,6 *n.,* 7,8 *adv.,* **less, least.** —**lit′tle ness,** *n.*

little by little, by a small amount at a time; slowly; gradually.

make little of, treat or represent as of little importance.

not a little, much; very: *We were not a little upset by the accident.*

think little of, not value much; consider as unimportant or worthless.

Little America, camp near the South Pole established by Admiral Richard E. Byrd in 1929. See **Antarctica** for map.

Little Bear, Ursa Minor.

Little Dipper, group of seven bright stars in the constellation Ursa Minor. See **constellation** for diagram.

Little Rock, capital of Arkansas, in the central part.

li tur gi cal (lə tėr′jə kəl), 1 of liturgies. 2 used in liturgies. *adj.*

lit ur gy (lit′ər jē), a form of public worship. Different churches use different liturgies. *n., pl.* **lit ur gies.**

litter (def. 8)

liv a ble (liv′ə bəl), 1 fit to live in: *a livable house.* 2 easy to live with: *a livable person.* 3 worth living; endurable. *adj.*

live¹ (liv), 1 have life; be alive; exist: *All creatures have an equal right to live.* 2 remain alive: *if I live till May.* 3 last;

adj.	adjective	*n.*	noun
adv.	adverb	*prep.*	preposition
conj.	conjunction	*pron.*	pronoun
interj.	interjection	*v.*	verb
sing.	singular	*pl.*	plural

endure: *His good name will live forever.* 4 keep up life: *Most of us live by working.* 5 feed or subsist: *Lions live upon other animals.* 6 dwell: *live in the country. Who lives in this house?* 7 pass (life): *live a life of ease, live well.* 8 carry out or show in life: *live one's ideals.* 9 have a rich and full life. *v.*, **lived, living.** [Old English *lifian, libban*]

live down, live so worthily that (some fault or sin of the past) is overlooked or forgotten.

live up to, act according to; do (what is expected or promised).

live² (līv), 1 having life; alive: *a live dog.* 2 burning or glowing: *live coals.* 3 full of energy or activity: *a live person.* 4 of present interest; up-to-date: *a live question.* 5 still in use or to be used: *live steam.* 6 carrying an electric current: *a live wire.* 7 loaded: *a live cartridge.* 8 not recorded on tape or film: *a live television show. adj.* [a different form of *alive*]

live li hood (līv′lē hůd), means of keeping alive; what is needed to support life; a living: *write for a livelihood. He earned his livelihood by working for a farmer. n.*

live li ness (līv′lē nis), lively quality or condition. *n.*

live long (liv′lông′), whole length of; whole; entire: *She is busy the livelong day. adj.*

live ly (līv′lē), 1 full of life and spirit; active; vigorous: *A good night's sleep made us all lively again.* 2 exciting: *We had a lively time during the hurricane.* 3 bright; vivid: *lively colors.* 4 cheerful; gay: *a lively conversation.* 5 bouncing well and quickly: *a lively baseball.* 6 in a lively manner. 1-5 *adj.,* **live li er, live li est;** 6 *adv.*

liv en (lī′vən), 1 put life into; cheer up. 2 become more lively; brighten: *As he grew well, his spirits began to liven again. v.*

live oak (līv), an evergreen oak of the southern United States.

liv er¹ (liv′ər), 1 the large, reddish-brown organ in vertebrate animals that makes bile and aids in the absorption of food. The liver frees the blood of its waste matter and changes sugar into glycogen. 2 the liver of an animal used as food. *n.* [Old English *lifer*]

liv er² (liv′ər), person who lives. *n.* [*live¹* + *-er¹*]

liv er ied (liv′ər ēd), clothed in livery. *adj.*

Liv er pool (liv′ər půl), seaport city in W England. *n.*

liv er wort (liv′ər wėrt′), 1 plant that grows mostly on damp ground, the trunks of trees, etc. Liverworts are somewhat like mosses. 2 hepatica. *n.*

liv er wurst (liv′ər wėrst′), sausage consisting largely of liver. *n.*

liv er y (liv′ər ē), 1 any uniform provided for servants, or adopted by any group or profession: *a chauffeur in green livery.* 2 any characteristic dress, garb, or outward appearance. 3 the feeding, stabling, and care of horses for pay. 4 the hiring out of horses and carriages. 5 the keeping of cars, boats, bicycles, etc., for hire. 6 livery stable. *n., pl.* **liv er ies.**

livery stable, stable where horses are cared for for pay or hired out.

lives (līvz), plural of **life.** *n.*

live stock (līv′stok′), farm animals. Cows, horses, sheep, and pigs are livestock. *n.*

live wire (līv), INFORMAL. an energetic, wide-awake person.

liv id (liv′id), 1 having a dull-bluish or grayish color, as from a bruise: *livid marks on an arm.* 2 very pale: *livid with shock.* 3 flushed; reddish: *livid with rage.* 4 INFORMAL. very angry: *Their insults made me livid. adj.* —**liv′id ly,** *adv.* —**liv′id ness,** *n.*

liv ing (liv′ing), 1 having life; being alive: *a living plant.* 2 condition of being alive: *The old man is tired of living.* 3 means of keeping alive; livelihood: *work for a living.* 4 manner of life: *healthful living.* 5 full of life; vigorous; strong; active: *a living faith.* 6 in actual existence; still in use; alive: *a living language.* 7 true to life; vivid; lifelike: *a picture which is the living image of a person.* 8 of life; for living in: *the poor living conditions in the slums.* 9 sufficient to live on: *a living wage.* 10 of or having to do with human beings: *within living memory.* 11 (in Great Britain) a benefice. 1,5-10 *adj.,* 2-4,11 *n.*

living room, room for general family use; sitting room.

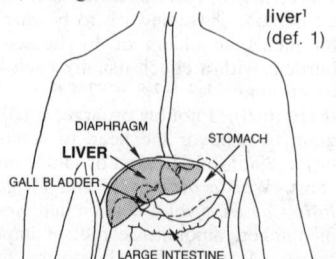

liver¹
(def. 1)

DIAPHRAGM
LIVER
GALL BLADDER
STOMACH
LARGE INTESTINE

Liv ing stone (liv′ing stən), **David,** 1813-1873, Scottish missionary and explorer in Africa. *n.*

Liv y (liv′ē), 59 B.C.-A.D. 17, Roman historian. *n.*

liz ard (liz′ərd), reptile with a long body, long tail, movable eyelids, and usually four legs. Some lizards have no legs and look much like snakes. The iguana, chameleon, and horned toad are lizards. *n.* —**liz′ard like′,** *adj.*

lla ma (lä′mə), a South American mammal that chews the cud and has woolly hair. It is somewhat like a camel, but smaller and without a hump. Llamas are used as beasts of burden. *n., pl.* **lla mas** or **lla ma.** [from Spanish]

llamas
about 4 ft. high at the shoulder

lla no (lä′nō), (in Spanish America) a broad, treeless, grassy plain. *n., pl.* **lla nos.** [from Spanish]

lo (lō), look! see! behold! *interj.*

load (lōd), 1 what one is carrying; burden: *The cart has a load of hay. That's a load off my mind.* 2 amount that usually is carried: *Send us four loads of sand.* 3 place on or in something for conveyance; heap or pile on: *load grain.* 4 put in or put on whatever is to be carried: *load a car, ship, horse, basket, etc. She loaded the camera with film.* 5 take on a load: *The ship loaded in five days.* 6 burden; oppress: *load the mind with worries.* 7 supply amply or in excess: *They loaded her with compliments on her singing.* 8 **loads,** *pl.* INFORMAL. a great quantity or number. 9 the weight supported by a structure or part. 10 the total amount of power supplied by a dynamo, generator, or other source of electricity in a given time. 11 one charge of powder and shot for a gun. 12 put a charge in (a gun): *The frontiersman loaded his musket with powder and shot.* 1,2,8-11 *n.,* 3-7,12 *v.* —**load′er,** *n.*

load ed (lō′did), INFORMAL. full of meaning and implications: *a loaded question. adj.*

load star (lōd′stär′), lodestar. *n.*

load stone (lōd′stōn′), 1 piece of magnetite that attracts iron and steel. It is a natural magnet. 2 something that attracts: *Gold was the loadstone that drew people to Alaska. n.* Also, **lodestone.**

loaf¹ (lōf), 1 bread shaped and baked as one piece: *The loaf came apart easily from the loaves it was baked with.* 2 anything like a loaf in shape. Meat loaf is meat chopped and mixed with other things and then baked. 3 a cone-shaped mass of sugar. *n., pl.* **loaves.** [Old English *hlāf* loaf, bread]

loaf² (lōf), spend time idly; do nothing: *Now that vacation has come, I shall loaf for a few days. v.* [origin uncertain]

loaf er (lō′fər), 1 person who loafs; lazy idler. 2 **Loafer,** trademark for a shoe resembling a moccasin, but with sole and heel stitched to the upper. *n.*

loam (lōm), rich, fertile earth in which decaying leaves, etc., are mixed with clay and sand. *n.*

lobster (def. 1)—about 1 to 2 ft. long

loam y (lō′mē), of or like loam. *adj.*

loan (lōn), 1 a lending: *She asked for a loan of his pen.* 2 anything that is lent, especially money: *He asked his brother for a small loan.* 3 make a loan; lend: *His brother loaned him the money.* 1,2 *n.,* 3 *v.*

loath (lōth), unwilling or reluctant: *The little girl was loath to admit that she had lied. adj.* Also, **loth.**

loathe (lōฐH), feel strong dislike and disgust for; abhor; hate: *We loathe rotten food or a nasty smell. v.,* **loathed, loath ing.**

loath ing (lō′ฐHing), strong dislike and disgust; intense aversion. *n.*

loath some (lōฐH′səm), making one feel sick; disgusting: *a loathsome odor.* —**loath′some ly,** *adv.* —**loath′some ness,** *n.*

loaves (lōvz), plural of **loaf¹.** *n.*

lob (lob), 1 a tennis ball hit in a high arc, usually to the back of the opponent's court. 2 hit (a tennis ball) in a high arc, usually to the back of an opponent's court. 3 throw (a cricket ball) with a slow underhand movement. 1 *n.,* 2,3 *v.,* **lobbed, lob bing.**

lob by (lob′ē), 1 entrance hall; passageway: *the lobby of a theater. A hotel lobby usually has chairs and couches to sit on.* 2 person or persons that try to influence members of a lawmaking body. 3 try to influence the members of a lawmaking body: *The cotton farmers of the South lobbied against a law to allow importing cotton from Egypt.* 1,2 *n., pl.* **lob bies;** 3 *v.,* **lob bied, lob by ing.**

lob by ist (lob′ē ist), person who tries to influence members of a lawmaking body. *n.*

lobe (lōb), a rounded projecting part. The lobe of the ear is the lower rounded end. *n.*

lobed (lōbd), having a lobe or lobes. *adj.*

lo bel ia (lō bē′lyə), plant with blue, red, yellow, or white flowers. *n., pl.* **lo bel ias.** [from Matthias de *Lobel,* 1538-1616, a Flemish botanist]

lob lol ly (lob′lol′ē), 1 a pine tree of the southern United States that has a thick bark, long needles, and cones with spiny tips. 2 its coarse wood. *n., pl.* **lob lol lies.**

lob ster (lob′stər), 1 a large crustacean having five pairs of legs, with large claws on the front pair. Its shell turns a bright red when boiled. 2 its flesh, used as food. *n.*

lo cal (lō′kəl), 1 of a place; having to do with a certain place or places: *the local doctor, local self-government, local news.* 2 of just one part of the body: *a local pain, local disease, local application of a remedy.* 3 making all, or almost all, stops: *a local train.* 4 train, bus, etc., that stops at all of the stations on its route. 5 branch or chapter of a labor union, fraternity, etc. 1-3 *adj.,* 4,5 *n.*

lo cale (lō kal′), a place, especially with reference to events or circumstances connected with it: *The locale of "Don Quixote" is Spain in the 1600's. n.*

lo cal ism (lō′kə liz′əm), a local expression, custom, etc. *n.*

lo cal i ty (lō kal′ə tē), one place and the places near it; region, district, or neighborhood: *He knows many people in the locality of Boston. n., pl.* **lo cal i ties.**

lo cal i za tion (lō′kə lə zā′shən), a localizing or a being localized. *n.*

lo cal ize (lō′kə līz), make local; fix in, assign, or limit to a particular place or locality: *The infection seemed to be localized in the foot. v.,* **lo cal ized, lo cal iz ing.**

lo cal ly (lō′kə lē), in a local manner; with regard to place; in one place; in a number of places, but not widely: *Outbreaks of the disease occurred locally. adv.*

lo cate (lō′kāt), 1 establish in a place: *They located their store on Main Street.* 2 establish oneself in a place: *Early settlers located where there was water.* 3 find out the exact position of: *We followed the stream for a long way until we located its source.* 4 to state or show

hat, āge, fär; let, ēqual, tėrm;
it, īce; hot, ōpen, ôrder;
oil, out; cup, pút, rüle; ch, child;
ng, long; sh, she; th, thin;
ฐH, then; zh, measure;

ə represents *a* in about,
e in taken, *i* in pencil,
o in lemon, *u* in circus.

the position of: *Can you locate Paris and Berlin on the map?* 5 establish the boundaries or rights of: *locate a claim. v.,* **lo cat ed, lo cat ing.**

be located, be situated; lie: *Albany is located on the Hudson.*

lo ca tion (lō kā′shən), 1 a locating or a being located: *The scouts argued about the location of the camp.* 2 position or place: *The camp was in a bad location as there was no water near it.* 3 plot of ground marked out by boundaries; lot: *a mining location. n.*

loch (lok), SCOTTISH. 1 lake: *Loch Lomond.* 2 arm of the sea partly shut in by land. *n.*

Loch Lomond. See **Lomond.**

lo ci (lō′sī), plural of **locus.** *n.*

lock¹ (lok), 1 a means of fastening doors, boxes, etc., consisting of a bolt and usually needing a key of special shape to open it: *The front door of most houses has a lock.* 2 fasten with a lock: *Lock and bar the door.* 3 shut (something in or out or up): *We lock up jewels in a safe.* 4 hold fast: *The ship was locked in ice. The secret was locked in her heart.* 5 an enclosed section of a canal or dock in which the level of the water can be changed by letting water in or out, to raise or lower ships. 6 the part of a gun by means of which it is

lock¹ (def. 5)
Locks in a canal enable ships to go where there were formerly waterfalls or to go around a dam. If the ship enters at the lower level, the gates are closed, the water level is raised (by means of pipes) to equal the level above the lock, then the upper gates are opened. If the ship is coming downstream, the process is reversed.

adj. adjective	*n.* noun
adv. adverb	*prep.* preposition
conj. conjunction	*pron.* pronoun
interj. interjection	*v.* verb
sing. singular	*pl.* plural

---

fired. **7** device to keep a wheel from turning. A lock is used when a vehicle is going downhill. **8** join, fit, jam, or link together: *The girls locked arms and walked down the street together.* **9** a kind of hold in wrestling. 1,5-7,9 *n.,* 2-4,8 *v.* [Old English *loc*]

lock out, refuse to give work to employees until they accept the employer's terms.

lock² (lok), **1** curl of hair. **2** portion of hair, wool, flax, etc. **3 locks,** *pl.* the hair of the head: *The child has curly locks. n.* [Old English *locc*]

lock er (lok′ər), **1** a chest, small closet, cupboard, or other compartment that can be locked. **2** a refrigerated compartment for storing frozen foods. *n.*

lock et (lok′it), a small, ornamental case of gold, silver, etc., for holding a picture of someone or a lock of hair. A locket is usually worn around the neck on a chain. *n.*

lock jaw (lok′jô′), a form of tetanus in which the jaws become firmly closed. *n.*

lock out (lok′out′), the refusal of an employer to furnish work to employees, used as a means of making them accept his terms. *n.*

lock smith (lok′smith′), person who makes or repairs locks. *n.*

lock up (lok′up′), jail. *n.*

lo co mo tion (lō′kə mō′shən), act or power of moving from place to place. Walking, swimming, and flying are common forms of locomotion. *n.*

lo co mo tive (lō′kə mō′tiv), **1** engine that moves from place to place on its own power, used to pull railroad trains. **2** moving from place to place: *locomotive bacteria.* **3** having to do with the power to move from place to place. 1 *n.,* 2,3 *adj.*

lo cus (lō′kəs), **1** place or locality. **2** (in mathematics) a figure that contains all the points, and only those points, that satisfy a given condition. The locus of all the points which are equidistant from a given point is the surface of a sphere. *n., pl.* **lo ci.**

lo cust (lō′kəst), **1** any of various kinds of grasshoppers which migrate in great swarms, often destroying the crops along their way. **2** cicada. **3** tree with small rounded leaflets and clusters of sweet-smelling, white or rose-colored flowers. *n.*

lo cu tion (lō kyü′shən), **1** style of speech. **2** form of expression. *n.*

lode (lōd), a vein of metal ore: *The miners struck a rich lode of copper. n.*

lode star (lōd′stär′), **1** star that shows the way. **2** the North Star. **3** a guide. *n.* Also, **loadstar.**

lode stone (lōd′stōn′), loadstone. *n.*

lodge (loj), **1** live in a place for a time: *We lodged in motels on our trip.* **2** supply with a place to live in or sleep in for a time: *Can you lodge us for the weekend?* **3** a place to live in; a house, especially a small or temporary house: *My uncle rents a lodge in the mountains for the summer.* **4** live in a rented room in another's house: *We are merely lodging at present.* **5** get caught or stay in a place without falling or going further: *My kite lodged in the branches of a big tree.* **6** put or send into a particular place: *The hunter lodged a bullet in the lion's heart.* **7** put for safekeeping. **8** put before some authority: *We lodged a complaint with the police.* **9** branch of a secret society. **10** the place where it meets. **11** the den of an animal, such as a beaver or an otter. 1,2,4-8 *v.,* **lodged, lodg ing;** 3,9-11 *n.*

lodg er (loj′ər), person who lives in a rented room in another's house. *n.*

lodg ing (loj′ing), **1** place where one is living only for a time: *a lodging for the night.* **2 lodgings,** *pl.* a rented room or rooms in a house, not in a hotel. *n.*

lodg ment (loj′mənt), **1** act of lodging. **2** condition of being lodged: *the lodgment of a claim against a company.* **3** something lodged or deposited: *a lodgment of earth on a ledge of rock. n.*

lo ess (lō′is), a yellowish-brown loam, usually deposited by the wind. *n.*

loft (lôft), **1** space just below the roof in a cabin; attic. **2** room under the roof of a barn: *This loft is full of hay.* **3** gallery in a church or hall: *a choir loft.* **4** an upper floor of a business building or warehouse. **5** hit (a golf ball) high up. 1-4 *n.,* 5 *v.*

loft i ly (lôf′tə lē), in a lofty manner. *adv.*

loft i ness (lôf′tē nis), lofty quality or condition. *n.*

loft y (lôf′tē), **1** very high: *lofty mountains.* **2** exalted; dignified; grand: *lofty aims.* **3** proud; haughty: *He had a lofty contempt for others. adj.,* **loft i er, loft i est.**

log (lôg), **1** a length of wood just as it comes from the tree. **2** made of logs: *a log house.* **3** to cut down trees, cut them into logs, and get them out of the forest. **4** cut (trees) into logs. **5** the daily record of a ship's voyage. **6** enter in a ship's log. **7** record of an airplane trip,

log (def. 8) A sailor throws the log into the water behind the ship. By noting the length of line which runs off the reel in a given time he obtains a rough estimate of the ship's speed.

performance of an engine, etc. **8** a float for measuring the speed of a ship. 1,5,7,8 *n.,* 2 *adj.,* 3,4,6 *v.,* **logged, log ging. —log′like′,** *adj.*

lo gan ber ry (lō′gən ber′ē), **1** a large, purplish-red fruit of a plant which is a cross between a blackberry and a red raspberry. **2** the plant it grows on. *n., pl.* **lo gan ber ries.** [from J. H. Logan, 1841-1928, an American horticulturist, who developed it]

lo ga rithm (lô′gə riŦH′əm), **1** the power to which a fixed number or base (usually 10) must be raised in order to produce a given number. If the fixed number or base is 10, the logarithm of 1000 is 3; the logarithm of 10,000 is 4; the logarithm of 100,000 is 5. **2** one of a system of such numbers used to shorten calculations in mathematics. *n.*

log book (lôg′bùk′), **1** book in which a daily record of a ship's voyage is kept. **2** a book for records of an airplane's trip. **3** journal of travel. *n.*

log ger (lô′gər), **1** person whose work is logging. **2** machine for loading or hauling logs. *n.*

log ger head (lô′gər hed′), **1** a stupid person. **2** a large sea turtle of the Atlantic. *n.*

log gia (loj′ə), gallery or arcade open to the air on at least one side. *n., pl.* **log gias.**

log ging (lô′ging), work of cutting down trees, sawing them into logs, and moving the logs out of the forest. *n.*

log ic (loj′ik), **1** science of proof and of reasoning. **2** use of argument; reasoning. **3** sound sense; reason: *There is much logic in what you say. n.*

log i cal (loj′ə kəl), **1** having to do with logic; according to the principles of logic: *logical reasoning.* **2** reasonable; reasonably expected: *A failing grade is the logical result of her frequent absences from school.* **3** reasoning correctly: *a logical person, a clear and logical mind. adj.* **—log′i cal ly,** *adv.* **—log′i cal ness,** *n.*

lo gi cian (lō jish′ən), an expert in logic. *n.*

lo gis tic (lō jis′tik), of or having to do with logistics. *adj.*

lo gis tics (lō jis′tiks), the planning and carrying out of any complex or large-scale operation, especially one of military movement, evacuation, and supply. *n.*

log roll ing (lôg′rō′ling), **1** a giving of political aid in return for a like favor. **2** act of rolling logs, especially by treading on them. *n.*

log wood (lôg′wu̇d′), **1** the heavy, brownish-red wood of a tropical American tree, used in dyeing. **2** the tree. *n.*

lo gy (lō′gē), heavy, sluggish, or dull. *adj.,* **lo gi er, lo gi est.**

loin (loin), **1** Usually, **loins,** *pl.* the part of the body of an animal or man between the ribs and the hipbones. The loins are on both sides of the backbone and nearer to it than the flanks. **2** a piece of meat from this part of an animal: *a loin of pork. n.*

gird up one's loins, get ready for action.

loin
(def. 2)

loin cloth (loin′klôth′), piece of cloth worn around the hips and between the thighs by natives of warm countries. *n., pl.* **loin cloths** (loin′klô͟ᴛʜz′ or loin′-klôths′).

Loire (lwär), river flowing from S France into the Bay of Biscay. It is the longest river in France. *n.*

loi ter (loi′tər), **1** linger idly; stop and play along the way: *She loitered along the street, looking into all the store windows.* **2** spend (time) idly: *loiter the hours away. v.* —**loi′ter er,** *n.*

Lo ki (lō′kē), (in Norse myths) the god of destruction. *n.*

loll (lol), **1** recline or lean in a lazy manner: *loll on a sofa.* **2** hang loosely or droop: *A dog's tongue lolls out in hot weather.* **3** allow to hang or droop: *A dog lolls out his tongue. v.*

lol li pop or **lol ly pop** (lol′ē pop), piece of hard candy, usually on the end of a small stick. *n.*

Lom bard y (lom′bər dē), region in N Italy. *n.*

Lo mond (lō′mənd), **Loch,** lake in S central Scotland. *n.*

Lon don (lun′dən), **1** capital of the United Kingdom of Great Britain and Northern Ireland, in SE England, on the Thames. London is one of the largest cities in the world. **2 Jack,** 1876-1916, American writer of novels and short stories. *n.*

lone (lōn), **1** without others; alone; solitary; single: *The lone traveler was glad to reach home.* **2** lonesome; lonely: *They lived a lone life after their children grew up and moved away.*

3 standing apart; isolated: *a lone house. adj.*

lone li ness (lōn′lē nis), a being lonely; solitude. *n.*

lone ly (lōn′lē), **1** feeling oneself alone and longing for company or friends: *He was lonely while his brother was away.* **2** without many people: *a lonely road.* **3** alone; isolated: *a lonely tree. adj.,* **lone li er, lone li est.**

lone some (lōn′səm), **1** feeling lonely. **2** making one feel lonely: *a lonesome journey.* **3** unfrequented; desolate: *a lonesome road.* **4** solitary: *One lonesome pine stood in the yard. adj.,* **lone som er, lone som est.** —**lone′some ly,** *adv.* —**lone′some ness,** *n.*

long¹ (lông), **1** that measures much from end to end: *An inch is short; a mile is long. A year is a long time. He told a long story.* **2** in length: *My table is three feet long.* **3** having a long narrow shape: *a long board.* **4** a long time: *Summer will come before long.* **5** for a long time: *I can't stay long.* **6** for its whole length: *all summer long, all day long.* **7** at a point of time far distant from the time indicated: *long before, long since.* **8** (of vowels or syllables) taking a comparatively long time to speak. A vowel like *a* in *late, e* in *be,* or *o* in *note* is a long vowel. 1-3,8 *adj.,* **long er** (lông′-gər), **long est** (lông′gist); 4 *n.,* 5-7 *adv.* [Old English *lang*]

as long as or **so long as,** provided that.

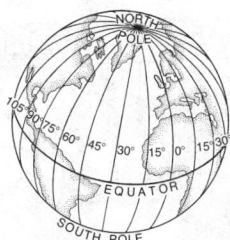

circles of longitude

long² (lông), wish very much; desire greatly: *long for one's family, long to see a good friend. v.* [Old English *langian,* from *lang* long¹]

long., longitude.

long boat (lông′bōt′), the largest boat carried by a sailing ship. *n.*

long bow (lông′bō′), a large bow drawn by hand, for shooting a long, feathered arrow. *n.*

long distance, operator or exchange that takes care of long-distance calls.

long-dis tance (lông′dis′təns), of or having to do with telephone service between distant places. *adj.*

lon gev i ty (lon jev′ə tē), long life: *A good diet promotes longevity. n.*

Long fel low (lông′fel′ō), **Henry Wadsworth,** 1807-1882, American poet. *n.*

long hand (lông′hand′), ordinary writing, not shorthand or typewriting. *n.*

long horn (lông′hôrn′), one of a breed of cattle with very long horns, formerly common in the southwestern United States. *n.*

long house, a large, rectangular dwelling of certain North American Indian tribes, especially the Iroquois. Many families lived together in one long house.

long ing (lông′ing), **1** earnest desire: *a longing for home.* **2** having or showing earnest desire: *a child's longing look at a window full of toys.* 1 *n.,* 2 *adj.* —**long′ing ly,** *adv.*

long ish (lông′ish), somewhat long. *adj.*

Long Island, large island south of Connecticut. It is part of New York State.

Long Island Sound, long, narrow strip of water between Connecticut and Long Island. It is an inlet of the Atlantic.

lon gi tude (lon′jə tüd or lon′jə tyüd), distance east or west on the earth's surface, measured in degrees from a certain meridian, usually the one through Greenwich, England. *n.*

lon gi tu di nal (lon′jə tüd′n əl or lon′jə tyüd′n əl), **1** of length; in length: *longitudinal measurements.* **2** running lengthwise: *The flag of the United States has longitudinal stripes.* **3** of longitude: *The longitudinal difference between New York and Seattle is about 50 degrees. adj.*

lon gi tu di nal ly (lon′jə tüd′n ə lē or lon′jə tyüd′n ə lē), **1** lengthwise. **2** according to longitude. *adv.*

long jump, broad jump.

long-lived (lông′līvd′ or lông′livd′), living or lasting a long time. *adj.*

long-play ing record (lông′-plā′ing), a phonograph record playing at 33-1/3 revolutions per minute. A long-playing record 12 inches in diameter provides about 25 minutes of sound on each side.

adj. adjective	*n.* noun
adv. adverb	*prep.* preposition
conj. conjunction	*pron.* pronoun
interj. interjection	*v.* verb
sing. singular	*pl.* plural

long-range (lông'rānj'), 1 looking ahead; future: *long-range plans.* 2 having a long range; covering a great distance: *a long-range ballistic missile. adj.*

long shore man (lông'shôr'mən), man whose work is loading and unloading ships. *n., pl.* **long shore men.**

long shot, an attempt at something difficult.

not by a long shot, not at all.

long-sight ed (lông'sī'tid), 1 far-sighted. 2 having foresight; wise. *adj.* —**long'-sight'ed ness,** *n.*

long stand ing (lông'stan'ding), having lasted for a long time: *a long-standing feud. adj.*

long-suf fer ing (lông'suf'ər ing), 1 enduring trouble, pain, or injury long and patiently. 2 a long and patient endurance of trouble, pain, or injury. 1 *adj.,* 2 *n.*

long ways (lông'wāz'), longwise. *adv.*

long-wind ed (lông'win'did), talking or writing at great length; tiresome: *a long-winded speaker, a long-winded magazine article. adj.*

long wise (lông'wīz'), in the direction of the length; lengthwise. *adv.*

look (lùk), 1 turn the eyes; see; try to see: *Look at the pictures.* 2 look hard; stare: *look questioningly.* 3 search: *I looked through the drawer to see if I could find my keys.* 4 a glance; seeing: *He took a quick look at the magazine.* 5 examine; pay attention: *You must look at all the facts.* 6 have a view; face: *Our house looks upon a garden.* 7 expect; anticipate: *I have been looking to hear from you.* 8 seem; appear: *She looks pale.* 9 appearance; aspect: *A deserted house has a desolate look.* 10 show how one feels by one's appearance: *He said nothing but looked his disappointment.* 11 **looks,** *pl.* personal appearance: *She has her mother's good looks.* 1-3,5-8,10 *v.,* 4,9,11 *n.* —**look'er,** *n.*

look after, attend to; take care of: *She looked after her little brother.*

look back, think about the past; recollect.

look down on, despise; scorn.

look for, expect: *We'll look for you tonight.*

look forward to, expect with pleasure; be eager for.

look in, make a short visit.

look into, examine; inspect.

look on, 1 watch without taking part: *The teacher conducted the experiment while we looked on.* 2 regard; consider: *I look on her as a very able person.*

look oneself, seem like oneself; seem well.

look out, be careful; watch out: *Look out for cars as you cross the street.*

look over, examine; inspect: *The policeman looked over my license.*

look to, 1 attend to; take care of. 2 turn to for help. 3 look forward to; expect.

look up, 1 refer to; find: *She looked up the unfamiliar word in a dictionary.* 2 INFORMAL. call on; visit: *Look me up when you come to town.* 3 INFORMAL. get better; improve: *Things are looking up for me since I got the new job.*

look up to, respect; admire.

look er-on (lùk'ər on'), onlooker. *n., pl.* **look ers-on.**

looking glass, mirror.

look out (lùk'out'), 1 a sharp watch for someone to come or for something to happen: *Keep a lookout for Mother.* 2 place from which to watch. A crow's-nest is a lookout. 3 the person who has the duty of watching: *The lookout cried, "Land ho!"* 4 what one sees ahead; outlook: *See those clouds! A poor lookout for our picnic.* 5 INFORMAL. thing to be cared for or worried about. *n.*

loom[1]—To make cloth the weaver passes the shuttle carrying the thread of the woof through the threads of the warp. Foot pedals raise and lower alternate warp threads.

loom[1] (lüm), frame or machine for weaving cloth. *n.* [Old English *(ge)lōma* implement]

loom[2] (lüm), appear dimly or vaguely as a large, threatening shape: *A large iceberg loomed through the thick, gray fog. War loomed ahead. v.* [origin uncertain]

loon[1] (lün), a large, web-footed diving bird. Loons have a loud, wild cry. *n.* [earlier *loom,* from a Scandinavian word of the 1200's, such as Icelandic *lōmr*]

loon[2] (lün), a worthless, stupid person. *n.* [origin uncertain]

loon y (lü'nē), SLANG. crazy, foolish, or silly. *adj.,* **loon i er, loon i est.**

l g b p **loop** (def. 2)—some letters with loops

loop (lüp), 1 the part of a curved string, ribbon, bent wire, etc., that crosses itself. 2 thing, bend, course, or motion shaped like this. In writing, *b* and *g* and *h* and *l* have loops. *The road makes a wide loop around the lake.* 3 a fastening or ornament formed of cord, etc., bent and crossed. 4 make a loop of. 5 make loops in. 6 fasten with a loop: *She looped the sail to the mast with a rope.* 7 encircle with a loop. 8 form a loop or loops. 9 a turn like the letter *l,* especially one made by an airplane. 1-3,9 *n.,* 4-8 *v.*

loop hole (lüp'hōl'), 1 a small opening in a wall for looking through, for letting in air, or for firing through at an enemy outside. 2 a means of escape: *The clever lawyer found a loophole in the law that may save me from having to pay a large tax. n.*

loose (lüs), 1 not fastened: *a loose thread.* 2 not tight: *loose clothing.* 3 not firmly set or fastened in: *a loose tooth.* 4 not bound together: *loose papers.* 5 not put up in a box, can, etc.: *loose coffee.* 6 not shut in or up; free: *The dog has been loose all night.* 7 not pressed close together: *loose earth, cloth with a loose weave.* 8 not strict, close, or exact: *a loose translation from another language, a loose account of the accident.* 9 careless about morals or conduct: *a loose character.* 10 set free; let go: *With an effort I loosed my arm from her grip. The archers loosed a volley of arrows at the targets.* 11 make loose; untie; unfasten: *loose a knot.* 12 in a loose manner. 1-9 *adj.,* **loos er, loosest;** 10,11 *v.,* **loosed, loos ing;** 12 *adv.* —**loose'ly,** *adv.* —**loose'ness,** *n.*

break loose, run away; free oneself.

cast loose, unfasten; separate.

let loose, set loose, or **turn loose,** set free; let go; release.

loose-joint ed (lüs'join'tid), able to move very freely. *adj.*

loose-leaf (lüs'lēf'), having pages or sheets that can be taken out and replaced: *a loose-leaf notebook. adj.*

loos en (lü'sn), 1 make loose or looser; untie; unfasten: *The doctor loosened the stricken man's collar.* 2 become loose or looser: *The collar loosened around his neck. v.* —**loos'en er,** *n.*

loot (lüt), 1 things taken in plundering; spoils; booty: *loot taken by soldiers from a captured town, burglar's loot.* 2 plunder; rob: *The burglar looted the*

jewelry store. 1 *n.*, 2 *v.* —**loot′er,** *n.*

lop[1] (lop), 1 cut; cut off. 2 cut branches or twigs from. *v.*, **lopped, lop ping.** [Middle English *loppe* smaller branches and twigs]

lop[2] (lop), 1 hang loosely; droop. 2 flop. 3 hanging loosely; drooping. 1,2 *v.*, **lopped, lop ping;** 3 *adj.* [origin uncertain]

lope (lōp), 1 to run with a long, easy stride: *The horse loped along the trail in an easy gallop.* 2 a long, easy stride. 1 *v.*, **loped, lop ing;** 2 *n.*

lorry (def. 2)

lop sid ed (lop′sī′did), larger or heavier on one side than the other; unevenly balanced; leaning to one side. *adj.* —**lop′sid′ed ly,** *adv.* —**lop′sid′ed ness,** *n.*

lo qua cious (lō kwā′shəs), talking much; fond of talking. *adj.* —**lo qua′cious ly,** *adv.*

lo quac i ty (lō kwas′ə tē), inclination to talk a great deal; talkativeness. *n.*

lo quat (lō′kwot), 1 a small evergreen tree with small, yellow, plumlike fruit, native to China and Japan. 2 its fruit, which is good to eat. *n.*

lo ran (lôr′an), device that helps the navigator of an aircraft or ship find his geographical position quickly in any kind of weather by means of signals sent out from two or more fixed radio stations. *n.* [from *lo(ng) ra(nge) n(avigation)*]

lord (lôrd), 1 ruler, master, or chief; person who has the power. 2 rule proudly or absolutely. 3 a feudal superior. 4 **Lord, a** God. **b** Christ: *the year of our Lord.* 5 (in Great Britain) a man of any of certain high ranks. 6 **Lord, a** title used in writing or speaking about noblemen of certain high ranks in Great Britain: *Lord Tennyson.* **b** title given by courtesy to men of certain ranks in Great Britain: *the Lord Chief Justice, the Lord Mayor of London.* 7 **the Lords, a** House of Lords. **b** members of the House of Lords. 1,3-7 *n.*, 2 *v.* **lord it over,** domineer over: *She was the oldest and lorded it over the rest of us.*

lord ly (lôrd′lē), 1 like a lord; suitable for a lord; grand; magnificent. 2 haughty; insolent; scornful: *lordly airs, a lordly indifference to making money. adj.,* **lord li er, lord li est.**

lord ship (lôrd′ship), 1 rank or posi-

tion of a lord. 2 **Lordship,** title used in speaking to or of a man having the rank of Lord: *your Lordship, his Lordship. n.*

Lord's Prayer, (in the Bible) the prayer given by Jesus to His disciples which begins with the words "Our Father Who art in Heaven."

Lord's Supper, 1 Last Supper. 2 Holy Communion.

lore (lôr), 1 facts and stories about a certain subject: *fairy lore, bird lore, Irish lore.* 2 learning; knowledge. *n.*

lor gnette (lôr nyet′), eyeglasses or opera glasses mounted on a handle. *n.*

lorn (lôrn), forsaken; forlorn. *adj.*

Lor raine (lə rān′), region in NE France, formerly part of Alsace-Lorraine. *n.*

lor ry (lôr′ē), 1 a motor truck (a term used in Great Britain). 2 a long, flat wagon without sides. *n., pl.* **lor ries.**

Los An ge les (lôs an′jə ləs *or* lôs an′jə lēz′), the principal city in S California and the third largest city in the United States.

lose (lüz), 1 not have any longer; have taken away from one by accident, carelessness, parting, death, etc.: *lose a dollar, lose one's life, lose a limb, lose a father.* 2 be unable to find: *lose a book.* 3 fail to keep, preserve, or maintain; cease to have: *lose patience, lose all fear.* 4 fail to follow with eye, hearing, mind, etc.: *lose a few words of what was said.* 5 fail to have, get, catch, etc.: *lose a train, lose a sale.* 6 fail to win: *lose the prize.* 7 be defeated: *Our team lost.* 8 bring to destruction; ruin: *The ship and its crew were lost.* 9 spend or let go by without any result; waste: *lose an opportunity, lose time waiting. The hint was not lost on me.* 10 be or become worse off in money, in numbers, etc.: *lose at poker, lose heavily in a battle.* 11 cause the loss of: *Delay lost the battle.* 12 cause to lose: *That one act of misconduct lost me my job. v.,* **lost, los ing.**

lose oneself, 1 let oneself go astray; become bewildered. 2 become absorbed.

los er (lü′zər), 1 person who loses something. 2 person who is beaten in a game or battle. *n.*

los ing (lü′zing), 1 that cannot win or be won: *You are playing a losing game if you are not careful crossing streets.* 2 **losings,** *pl.* losses. 1 *adj.*, 2 *n.*

loss (lôs), 1 a losing or a being lost: *Loss of one's health is serious but the loss of a pencil is not.* 2 person or thing lost: *Her house was a complete loss to the fire.* 3 harm or disadvantage caused by losing something; value of the thing lost: *The loss from the fire was $10,000.* 4 a defeat: *Our team had two losses and*

Lot

hat, āge, fär; let, ēqual, tėrm;
it, īce; hot, ōpen, ôrder;
oil, out; cup, pùt, rüle; ch, child;
ng, long; sh, she; th, thin;
ᴛʜ, then; zh, measure;

ə represents *a* in about,
e in taken, *i* in pencil,
o in lemon, *u* in circus.

one tie out of ten games played. *n., pl.* **loss es.**

at a loss, not sure; puzzled; uncertain; in difficulty: *He was embarrassed and at a loss as to how to act.*

lost (lôst), 1 past tense and past participle of **lose.** *I lost my new pen. I had already lost my ruler.* 2 no longer possessed or retained: *lost friends.* 3 no longer to be found; missing: *lost articles.* 4 met with defeat; not won: *a lost battle.* 5 hopeless: *a lost cause.* 6 not used to good purpose; wasted: *lost time.* 7 having gone astray: *a lost child.* 8 destroyed or ruined: *a lost soul.* 9 bewildered: *a lost expression.* 1 *v.,* 2-9 *adj.*

be lost on, have no effect on; fail to influence.

lost in, completely absorbed or interested in: *He was lost in a book and failed to hear us come in.*

lost to, insensible to: *She was enjoying herself so much, she was lost to all sense of responsibility.*

lot (lot), 1 one of a set of objects, such as straws, bits of paper, wood, etc., used to decide something by chance. 2 such a method of deciding: *It was settled by lot.* 3 choice made in this way: *The lot fell to me.* 4 what one gets by lot; one's share or portion. 5 one's fate or fortune: *It was his lot later to become president.* 6 a plot of ground: *Her house is between two empty lots.* 7 a portion or part: *I divided the fruit into ten lots.* 8 a number of persons or things considered as a group; collection: *This lot of oranges is not so good as the last.* 9 Often, **lots,** *pl.* INFORMAL. a great many; a great deal: *a lot of books, lots of money. I have a lot of marbles. You have lots of time.* 10 a great deal; much: *I feel a lot better.* 1-9 *n.,* 10 *adv.*

cast in one's lot with or **throw in one's lot with,** share the fate of; become a partner with.

cast lots or **draw lots,** use lots to decide something.

Lot (lot), (in the Bible) Abraham's nephew, who was allowed to escape from Sodom before God destroyed it. His

adj.	adjective	*n.*	noun
adv.	adverb	*prep.*	preposition
conj.	conjunction	*pron.*	pronoun
interj.	interjection	*v.*	verb
sing.	singular	*pl.*	plural

wife looked back and was changed into a pillar of salt. *n.*

loth (lōth), loath. *adj.*

lo tion (lō′shən), a liquid medicine or cosmetic which is applied to the skin. Lotions are used to relieve pain, to heal, to cleanse, or to beautify the skin. *n.*

lot ter y (lot′ər ē), a scheme for distributing prizes by lot or chance. In a lottery a large number of tickets are sold, some of which draw prizes. *n., pl.* **lot ter ies.**

lo tus (lō′təs), 1 kind of water lily that grows in Egypt and Asia. 2 a shrubby plant with red, pink, or white flowers. 3 (in Greek legends) a plant supposed to cause a dreamy mental state in which one forgets real life. *n., pl.* **lo tus es.**

loud (loud), 1 making a great sound; not quiet or soft: *a loud voice. The door slammed with a loud noise.* 2 resounding; noisy: *loud music, a loud place to study.* 3 in a loud manner: *The hunter called long and loud.* 4 clamorous; insistent: *be loud in demands.* 5 INFORMAL. showy in dress or manner: *loud clothes.* 6 INFORMAL. obtrusive; somewhat vulgar: *a loud person.* 1,2,4-6 *adj.,* 3 *adv.* —**loud′ly,** *adv.* —**loud′ness,** *n.*

loud speak er (loud′spē′kər), device for making sounds louder, especially in a radio or phonograph. With a loudspeaker, speech or music received by radio can be heard throughout a large room and farther. *n.*

Lou is XIV (lü′ē), 1638-1715, king of France from 1643 to 1715. He was called "Louis the Great."

Louis XVI, 1754-1793, king of France from 1774 to 1792. He was beheaded during the French Revolution.

Lou i si an a (lü ē′zē an′ə), one of the south central states of the United States. *Capital:* Baton Rouge. *n.*

Louisiana Purchase, large region that the United States bought from France in 1803. It extended from the Mississippi River to the Rocky Mountains and from Canada to the Gulf of Mexico.

Lou is ville (lü′ē vil), city in N Kentucky, on the Ohio River. *n.*

lounge (lounj), 1 stand, stroll, sit, or lie at ease in a lazy way: *He lounged in an old chair.* 2 pass time lazily or at one's ease. 3 a comfortable and informal room in which one can lounge and be at ease: *a theater lounge.* 4 a couch or sofa. 1,2 *v.,* **lounged, loung ing;** 3,4 *n.*

lour (lour), lower². *v., n.*

louse (lous), 1 a small, wingless insect that infests the hair or skin of people and animals, causing great irritation. 2 any of various other insects that infest animals or plants, such as the aphid: *We spray plants to kill the lice. n., pl.* **lice.**

lous y (lou′zē), 1 infested with lice. 2 INFORMAL. bad; poor; of low quality. *adj.,* **lous i er, lous i est.**

lout (lout), an awkward, stupid fellow; boor. *n.*

lout ish (lou′tish), awkward and stupid; boorish. *adj.*

louvers (def. 1, left; def. 2, right)

lou ver (lü′vər), 1 any of several overlapping horizontal boards or strips of wood set slanting in a window or other opening, so as to keep out rain, but provide ventilation and light. 2 window or other opening covered with these boards. *n.*

Lou vre (lü′vrə), a famous museum in Paris, formerly a palace of the kings of France. *n.*

lov a ble (luv′ə bəl), worthy of being loved; endearing: *She was a most lovable person, always kind and thoughtful. adj.* Also, **loveable.** —**lov′a ble ness,** *n.*

lov a bly (luv′ə blē), in a lovable manner. *adj.*

love (luv), 1 a warm and tender liking; deep feeling of fondness and friendship; great affection or devotion: *love of one's family, love for a sweetheart.* 2 have such a warm liking or deep feeling for: *She loves her mother. We love our parents. I love my country.* 3 person who is loved; sweetheart. 4 a strong liking: *a love of books.* 5 like very much; take great pleasure in: *He loves music. Most children love ice cream.* 6 a score of zero in tennis and certain other games. 1,3,4,6 *n.,* 2,5 *v.,* **loved, loving.**

fall in love, begin to love; come to feel love.

for the love of, for the sake of; because of.

in love, feeling love.

make love, caress, kiss, etc., as lovers do; pay loving attention; woo.

love a ble (luv′ə bəl), lovable. *adj.*

love bird (luv′bėrd′), a small parrot that shows great affection for its mate. They are often kept in cages as pets. *n.*

love knot, knot or bow of ribbons as a symbol or token of love.

love less (luv′lis), without love; not loved. *adj.*

love li ness (luv′lē nis), beauty. *n.*

love lorn (luv′lôrn′), suffering because of love; forsaken by the person whom one loves. *adj.*

love ly (luv′lē), 1 beautiful or endearing in appearance or character; lovable: *They are the loveliest children we know.* 2 INFORMAL. very pleasing; delightful: *We had a lovely holiday. adj.,* **love li er, love li est.**

lov er (luv′ər), 1 person who is in love with another. 2 person having a strong liking: *a lover of books. n.*

love seat, seat or small sofa for two persons.

love sick (luv′sik′), languishing because of love. *adj.*

lov ing (luv′ing), feeling or showing love; affectionate; fond. *adj.* —**lov′ing ly,** *adv.*

loving cup, a large cup with handles, awarded as a trophy.

lov ing-kind ness (luv′ing kīnd′nis), kindness coming from love: *the loving-kindness of one's parents. n.*

low¹ (lō), 1 not high or tall; short: *low walls. This footstool is very low.* 2 near the ground; close to the earth: *a low shelf, a low jump.* 3 of humble rank; lowly: *He rose rapidly from a low position to president of the company.* 4 less than usual in amount, degree, force, value, etc.; small: *a low price, low temperature, low speed.* 5 nearly used up: *Our supply of coal is very low.* 6 unfavorable; poor: *I have a low opinion of their work.* 7 mean; coarse; vulgar: *low company.* 8 feeble; weak: *a low state of health.* 9 deep in pitch: *a low note.* 10 not loud; soft: *a low whisper.* 11 at or to a low point, place, rank, amount, degree, price, pitch, etc.: *The sun sank low. Supplies are running low.* 12 arrangement of gears to give the

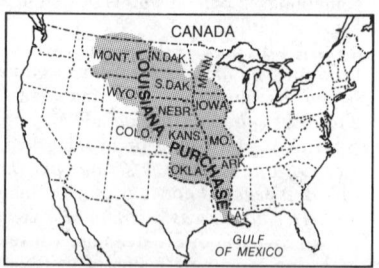

Louisiana Purchase
shown by shaded area on a modern map

lowest speed and the greatest power. **13 a** low point, level, position, etc.: *Many stocks fell to new lows after the bad news was received.* **1-10** *adj.*, **11** *adv.*, **12,13** *n.* [from a Scandinavian word of the 1200's, such as Icelandic *lāgr*] —**low′ness,** *n.*

lay low, 1 knock down: *The boxer laid low his opponent.* **2** kill.

lie low, INFORMAL. stay hidden; keep still: *The robbers lay low for a time.*

low² (lō), **1** make the sound of a cow; moo. **2** the sound a cow makes; mooing. **1** *v.*, **2** *n.* [Old English *hlōwan*]

low brow (lō′brou′), INFORMAL. **1** person who is not cultured or intellectual. **2** of or suitable for a lowbrow. **1** *n.*, **2** *adj.*

Low Countries, the Netherlands, Belgium, and Luxembourg.

low down (lō′doun′), SLANG. actual facts or truth: *She gave me the lowdown on several rumors that I had heard.* *n.*

low-down (lō′doun′), INFORMAL. low; mean; contemptible: *Selling me a broken radio was a low-down trick.* *adj.*

Low ell (lō′əl), **1 James Russell,** 1819-1891, American poet, essayist, and diplomat. **2** city in NE Massachusetts. *n.*

low er¹ (lō′ər), **1** let down or haul down: *We lower the flag at night.* **2** make lower: *lower the volume of a radio.* **3** sink; become lower: *The sun lowered slowly.* **4** bring down in rank, station, or estimation; degrade; dishonor. **5** more low: *Prices were lower last year than this.* **1-4** *v.*, **5** *adj.*, *adv.* [*low¹* + *-er²*]

low er² (lou′ər), **1** (of the sky, weather, etc.) look dark and threatening. **2** (of the sky, weather, etc.) a dark and threatening look. **3** frown; scowl. **4** a frown; scowl. **1,3** *v.*, **2,4** *n.* Also, **lour.** [Middle English *louren*]

Low er California (lō′ər), a narrow peninsula in NW Mexico, south of California.

lower house or **Lower House,** the larger and more representative branch of a lawmaking body that has two branches, made up of members usually elected by popular vote. The House of Representatives is the lower house of Congress.

low er most (lō′ər mōst), lowest. *adj.*

lower world, 1 hell; Hades. **2** earth.

low land (lō′lənd), **1** country or region that is lower and flatter than the neighboring country. **2 Lowlands,** *pl.* a low, flat region in S and E Scotland. *n.*

low land er (lō′lən dər), **1** person born or living in a lowland. **2 Lowlander,** person born or living in the Lowlands of Scotland. *n.*

low li ness (lō′lē nis), humbleness of

feeling or behavior; humble station in life. *n.*

low ly (lō′lē), **1** low in rank, station, position, or development: *a lowly corporal, a lowly occupation.* **2** modest in feeling, behavior, or condition; humble; meek: *He held a lowly opinion of himself.* **3** humbly; meekly. **1,2** *adj.*, **low li er, low li est; 3** *adv.*

low-pitched (lō′picht′), **1** of low tone or sound; deep. **2** having little slope. *adj.*

low-spir it ed (lō′spir′ə tid), sad; depressed. *adj.*

low spirits, sadness; depression.

low tide, 1 the lowest level of the tide. **2** time when the tide is lowest. *n.*

lox¹ (loks), a kind of smoked salmon. *n.* [from Yiddish *laks*]

lox² (loks), liquid oxygen. *n.* [formed from *l(iquid) ox(ygen)*]

loy al (loi′əl), **1** true and faithful to love, promise, or duty. **2** faithful to one's king, government, or country. *adj.* —**loy′al ly,** *adv.*

loy al ist (loi′ə list), person who supports his king or the existing government, especially in time of revolt. *n.*

loy al ty (loi′əl tē), loyal feeling or behavior; faithfulness. *n.*, *pl.* **loy al ties.**

Loy o la (loi ō′lə), **Ignatius of,** 1491-1556, Spanish soldier, priest, and saint, founder of the Jesuit order. *n.*

loz enge (loz′inj), **1** design or figure shaped like this:◇; diamond; rhombus. **2** a small tablet of any shape used as medicine or candy. Cough drops are sometimes called lozenges. *n.*

LSD, an extremely powerful drug which produces hallucinations and distorted perceptions.

Lt., Lieutenant.

Ltd. or **ltd.,** limited.

Lu an da (lü än′də), capital of Angola, on the Atlantic. *n.*

Lu ang Pra bang (lü äng′ prä bäng′), royal capital of Laos, in the N part.

lub ber (lub′ər), **1** a big, clumsy, stupid fellow. **2** a clumsy sailor. *n.*

lu bri cant (lü′brə kənt), oil, grease, etc., for putting on parts of machines that slide or move against one another, to make them smooth and slippery so that they will work easily. *n.*

lu bri cate (lü′brə kāt), **1** make machinery smooth, slippery, and easy to work by putting on oil, grease, etc. **2** make slippery or smooth. *v.*, **lu bri cat ed, lu bri cat ing.**

lu bri ca tion (lü′brə kā′shən), a lubricating or a being lubricated. *n.*

lu bri ca tor (lü′brə kā′tər), **1** person or thing that lubricates. **2** device for lubricating machinery. *n.*

lu cent (lü′snt), **1** bright or shining;

hat, āge, fär; let, ēqual, tėrm;
it, īce; hot, ōpen, ôrder;
oil, out; cup, pùt, rüle; ch, child;
ng, long; sh, she; th, thin;
ᴛʜ, then; zh, measure;

ə represents *a* in about,
e in taken, *i* in pencil,
o in lemon, *u* in circus.

luminous. **2** letting the light through; clear. *adj.*

lu cid (lü′sid), **1** easy to follow or understand: *A good explanation is lucid.* **2** sane: *An insane person sometimes has lucid intervals.* **3** clear; transparent: *a lucid stream.* **4** shining; bright. *adj.* —**lu′cid ly,** *adv.* —**lu′cid ness,** *n.*

lu cid i ty (lü sid′ə tē), lucid quality or condition. *n.*

Lu ci fer (lü′sə fər), the chief rebel angel who was cast out of heaven; Satan; the Devil. *n.*

luck (luk), **1** that which seems to happen or come to one by chance; fortune; chance: *Luck favored me, and I won.* **2** good luck: *She gave me a penny for luck.* *n.*

in luck, having good luck; lucky: *I am in luck today; I found a quarter.*

out of luck, having bad luck; unlucky.

luck i ly (luk′ə lē), by good luck; fortunately. *adv.*

luck i ness (luk′ē nis), quality or condition of being lucky. *n.*

luck less (luk′lis), having or bringing bad luck; unlucky. *adj.* —**luck′less ly,** *adv.*

luck y (luk′ē), having or bringing good luck: *a lucky day, a lucky meeting.* *adj.*, **luck i er, luck i est.**

lu cra tive (lü′krə tiv), bringing in money; profitable. *adj.*

lu cre (lü′kər), money considered as bad or degrading. *n.*

Lu cre tius (lü krē′shəs), 99?-55 B.C., Roman poet and philosopher. *n.*

lu di crous (lü′də krəs), amusingly absurd; ridiculous: *the ludicrous acts of a clown.* *adj.* —**lu′di crous ly,** *adv.* —**lu′di crous ness,** *n.*

luff (luf), **1** turn the bow of a ship toward the wind. **2** act of turning the bow of a ship toward the wind. **3** the forward edge of a fore-and-aft sail. **1** *v.*, **2,3** *n.*

lug¹ (lug), pull along or carry with effort; drag: *We lugged the rug to the yard to clean it.* *v.*, **lugged, lug ging.** [perhaps from a Scandinavian word, such as Swedish *lugga* pull by the hair]

lug² (lug), a projecting part used to hold

adj.	adjective	*n.*	noun
adv.	adverb	*prep.*	preposition
conj.	conjunction	*pron.*	pronoun
interj.	interjection	*v.*	verb
sing.	singular	*pl.*	plural

or grip something. *n.* [origin uncertain]

lug gage (lug/ij), baggage. *n.*

lug ger (lug/ər), boat with lugsails. *n.*

lug sail (lug/sāl/ *or* lug/səl), a four-cornered sail held by a yard that slants across the mast. *n.*

lu gu bri ous (lü gü/brē əs *or* lü gyü/brē əs), too sad; overly mournful: *the lugubrious howl of a dog. adj.* —**lu gu/bri ous ly,** *adv.*

lug worm (lug/wėrm/), kind of worm that burrows in sand along the seashore. *n.*

Luke (lük), 1 (in the Bible) a physician who was the companion of the apostle Paul. 2 the third book of the New Testament. It tells the story of the life of Christ. *n.*

luke warm (lük/wôrm/), 1 neither hot nor cold; moderately warm. 2 showing little enthusiasm; half-hearted: *a lukewarm greeting. adj.*

lull (lul), 1 soothe with sounds or caresses; hush to sleep: *The mother lulled the crying baby.* 2 make or become calm or more nearly calm; quiet: *Their confidence lulled my fears. The wind lulled.* 3 period of less noise or violence; brief calm: *a lull in a storm.* 1,2 *v.,* 3 *n.*

lul la by (lul/ə bī), song for singing to a child in a cradle; soft song to lull a baby to sleep. *n., pl.* **lul la bies.**

lum ba go (lum bā/gō), pain in the muscles of the small of the back and in the loins. *n.*

lum bar (lum/bər), of the loin or loins: *the lumbar region. adj.*

lum ber[1] (lum/bər), 1 timber that has been roughly cut into boards, planks, etc., and prepared for use. 2 cut and prepare lumber. 3 household articles no longer in use that take up room. 1,3 *n.,* 2 *v.* [original meaning, "useless goods," perhaps from an early form of *lombard* pawnshop]

lum ber[2] (lum/bər), move along heavily and noisily; roll along with difficulty: *The old truck lumbered down the road. v.* [Middle English *lomeren*]

lum ber ing (lum/bər ing), business of cutting and preparing timber for use. *n.*

lum ber jack (lum/bər jak/), person whose work is cutting down trees and sending the logs to the sawmill; woodsman; logger. *n.*

lum ber man (lum/bər mən), 1 lumberjack. 2 man who prepares lumber or buys and sells lumber. *n., pl.* **lum ber men.**

lum ber yard (lum/bər yärd/), place where lumber is stored and sold. *n.*

lu mi nar y (lü/mə ner/ē), 1 a heavenly body that gives or reflects light. 2 a famous person. *n., pl.* **lu mi nar ies.**

lugger

lu mi nes cence (lü/mə nes/ns), emission of light occurring at a temperature below that of incandescent bodies. Luminescence includes phosphorescence and fluorescence. *n.*

lu mi nes cent (lü/mə nes/nt), giving out light without much heat. *adj.*

lu mi nos i ty (lü/mə nos/ə tē), 1 luminous quality or condition. 2 something luminous. *n., pl.* **lu mi nos i ties.**

lu mi nous (lü/mə nəs), 1 shining by its own light: *The sun and stars are luminous bodies.* 2 full of light; bright: *a luminous sunset.* 3 easily understood; clear; enlightening. *adj.* —**lu/mi nous ly,** *adv.*

lump[1] (lump), 1 a small, solid mass of no particular shape: *a lump of coal.* 2 a swelling; bump: *a lump on the head.* 3 form into a lump or lumps: *The cornstarch lumped because we cooked it too fast.* 4 in lumps; in a lump: *lump coal, lump sugar.* 5 put together; deal with in a mass or as a whole: *We will lump all our expenses.* 6 including a number of items: *I was given a lump sum of money for all of my living expenses.* 1,2 *n.,* 3,5 *v.,* 4,6 *adj.* [Middle English *lumpe,* perhaps from Dutch of the 1200's *lompe* mass, chunk]

a lump in the throat, feeling of inability to swallow, caused by pity, sorrow, or other strong emotion.

lump[2] (lump), INFORMAL. put up with; endure: *If you don't like it, you can lump it. v.* [origin uncertain]

lump i ness (lum/pē nis), a being lumpy or full of lumps. *n.*

lump ish (lum/pish), 1 like a lump; heavy and clumsy. 2 dull; stupid. *adj.*

lump y (lum/pē), 1 full of lumps: *lumpy gravy.* 2 covered with lumps: *lumpy ground. adj.,* **lump i er, lump i est.**

Lu na (lü/nə), (in Roman myths) the goddess of the moon. The Greeks called her Selene. *n.*

lu na cy (lü/nə sē), 1 insanity. 2 extreme folly. *n., pl.* **lu na cies.**

lu nar (lü/nər), 1 of the moon. 2 like the moon. *adj.*

lunar module, an independent part of a spacecraft, which carries astronauts from the moon-orbiting craft to the surface of the moon and back.

lunar month, the period of one complete revolution of the moon around the earth; the interval between one new moon and the next; about 29½ days.

lu na tic (lü/nə tik), 1 an insane person. 2 insane. 3 for insane people: *a lunatic asylum.* 4 extremely foolish; idiotic: *a lunatic search for buried treasure.* 1 *n.,* 2-4 *adj.*

lunch (lunch), 1 a light meal between breakfast and dinner: *We usually have lunch at noon.* 2 a light meal. 3 food for a lunch. 4 eat lunch. 1-3 *n., pl.* **lunch es;** 4 *v.*

lunch eon (lun/chən), 1 lunch. 2 a formal lunch. 3 eat lunch. 1,2 *n.,* 3 *v.*

lunch eon ette (lun/chə net/), restaurant in which light meals are served. *n.*

lunch room (lunch/rüm/ *or* lunch/-rùm/), 1 restaurant in which light meals are served. 2 room in a school, factory, etc., where light meals are served. *n.*

lunch time (lunch/tīm/), time at which lunch is eaten or served. *n.*

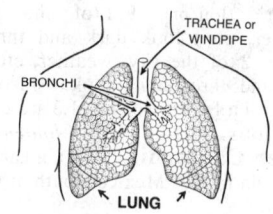
TRACHEA or WINDPIPE
BRONCHI
LUNG

lung (lung), either one of a pair of saclike, spongy organs found in the chest of vertebrates that breathe air. The lungs absorb oxygen from the air, give the blood the oxygen it needs, and relieve it of carbon dioxide. *n.*

lunge (lunj), 1 any sudden forward movement, such as a thrust with a sword or other weapon. 2 move suddenly forward; thrust: *The dog lunged at the stranger.* 1 *n.,* 2 *v.,* **lunged, lung ing.**

lung fish (lung/fish/), fish having a lunglike sac in addition to gills, enabling it to obtain oxygen both in and out of the water. Lungfishes are found in Australia, Africa, and South America. *n., pl.* **lung fish es** or **lung fish.**

lu pine (lü'pən), plant of the same family as peas and beans, with long spikes of flowers, clusters of hairy leaflets, and flat pods with bean-shaped seeds. *n.*

lurch[1] (lèrch), 1 a sudden leaning or roll to one side, like that of a ship, a car, or a staggering person: *The car gave a lurch and upset.* 2 make a lurch; stagger: *The wounded deer lurched forward.* 1 *n., pl.* **lurch es;** 2 *v.* [origin uncertain]

lurch[2] (lèrch). **leave in the lurch,** leave in a helpless condition or difficult situation. *n.* [from French *lourche,* name of a game]

lute

lure (lür), 1 power of attracting or fascinating; charm; allure; attraction: *Many people feel the lure of the sea.* 2 lead away or into something by arousing desire; attract; tempt: *Bees are lured by the scent of flowers.* 3 a decoy or bait, especially an artificial bait used in fishing. 4 attract with a bait: *We lured the fox into a trap.* 1,3 *n.,* 2,4 *v.,* **lured, lur ing.**

lur id (lür'id), 1 lighted up with a red or fiery glare: *The sky was lurid with the flames of the burning city.* 2 glaring in brightness or color: *a lurid red.* 3 terrible; sensational; startling: *lurid crimes.* 4 pale and dismal in color; wan and sallow. *adj.* —**lur'id ly,** *adv.* —**lur'id ness,** *n.*

lurk (lèrk), 1 stay about without arousing attention; wait out of sight; be hidden: *A tiger was lurking in the jungle.* 2 move about in a secret and sly manner: *Several people were seen lurking near the house before it was robbed.* *v.*

lus cious (lush'əs), 1 delicious; richly sweet: *a luscious peach.* 2 very pleasing to taste, smell, hear, see, or feel: *a luscious garden.* *adj.* —**lus'cious ly,** *adv.* —**lus'cious ness,** *n.*

lush (lush), 1 tender and juicy; growing thick and green: *Lush grass grows along the river banks.* 2 characterized by abundant growth; producing abundantly. 3 rich in ornament; flowery: *lush description.* *adj.* —**lush'ly,** *adv.* —**lush'ness,** *n.*

lust (lust), 1 strong desire. 2 strong sexual desire. 3 have a strong desire: *lust after money and power.* 1,2 *n.,* 3 *v.*

lus ter (lus'tər), 1 a bright shine on the surface: *the luster of pearls.* 2 brightness: *Her eyes lost their luster.* 3 fame; glory; brilliance: *Many prizes added luster to the artist's reputation.* 4 a shiny, metallic, often iridescent surface on pottery or china. *n.* Also, **lustre.**

lust ful (lust'fəl), full of lust or desire; sensual; lewd. *adj.*

lust i ly (lus'tə lē), in a lusty manner; vigorously; heartily. *adv.*

lust i ness (lus'tē nis), a being lusty; vigor. *n.*

lus tre (lus'tər), luster. *n.*

lus trous (lus'trəs), having luster; shining; glossy: *lustrous satin.* *adj.*

lust y (lus'tē), strong and healthy; full of vigor: *a lusty athlete.* *adj.,* **lust i er, lust i est.**

lute (lüt), a musical instrument, much used in the 1500's and 1600's, having a pear-shaped body and usually six pairs of strings. It is played by plucking the strings. *n.*

lu te ti um (lü tē'shē əm), a metallic element which usually occurs in nature with ytterbium. *n.* [from Latin *Lutetia,* ancient name for Paris, because a French scientist discovered it]

Lu ther (lü'thər), **Martin,** 1483-1546, leader of the Protestant Reformation in Germany. *n.*

Lu ther an (lü'thər ən), 1 having to do with Luther or the church that was named for him. 2 member of the Lutheran Church. 1 *adj.,* 2 *n.*

Lux em bourg or **Lux em burg** (luk'səm bèrg'), 1 small country surrounded by Germany, France, and Belgium. 2 its capital. *n.*

lux ur i ance (lug zhur'ē əns or luk-shùr'ē əns), luxuriant growth or productiveness; rich abundance. *n.*

lux ur i ant (lug zhur'ē ənt or luk-shùr'ē ənt), 1 growing thick and green. 2 producing abundantly. 3 rich in ornament. *adj.* —**lux ur'i ant ly,** *adv.*

lux ur i ate (lug zhur'ē āt or luk-shùr'ē āt), 1 indulge in luxury. 2 take great delight: *The campers planned to luxuriate in hot baths and clean clothes when they came home.* 3 grow very abundantly. *v.,* **lux ur i at ed, lux ur i at ing.**

lux ur i ous (lug zhur'ē əs or luk-shùr'ē əs), 1 fond of luxury; tending toward luxury; self-indulgent: *a luxurious taste for fine food.* 2 giving luxury; very comfortable and beautiful: *Some theaters are luxurious.* *adj.* —**lux ur'i ous ly,** *adv.* —**lux ur'i ous ness,** *n.*

lux ur y (luk'shər ē or lug'zhər ē), 1 comforts and beauties of life beyond what is really necessary: *Even very poor people today live in what would have*

hat, āge, fär; let, ēqual, tèrm;
it, īce; hot, ōpen, ôrder;
oil, out; cup, pùt, rüle; ch, child;
ng, long; sh, she; th, thin;
₮H, then; zh, measure;

ə represents *a* in about,
e in taken, *i* in pencil,
o in lemon, *u* in circus.

been considered luxury 1000 years ago. 2 use of the best and most costly food, clothes, houses, furniture, and amusements: *The movie star was accustomed to luxury.* 3 thing that one enjoys, usually something choice and costly: *He saves money for luxuries such as fine paintings.* 4 thing pleasant but not necessary: *Candy is a luxury.* 5 providing lavish comfort and enjoyment; luxurious: *a luxury hotel.* 1-4 *n., pl.* **lux ur ies;** 5 *adj.*

Lu zon (lü zon'), chief island of the Philippines. *n.*

-ly[1], suffix added to adjectives to form adverbs. 1 in a ____ manner. *Cheerfully = in a cheerful manner.* 2 in ____ ways or respects: *Financially = in financial respects.* 3 to a ____ degree or extent: *Greatly = to a great degree.* 4 in, to, or from a ____ direction: *Northerly = to or from the north.* 5 in a ____ place: *Thirdly = in the third place.* 6 at a ____ time: *Recently = at a recent time.* [Old English *-līce,* from *-līc* **-ly**[2]]

-ly[2], suffix added to nouns to form adjectives. 1 like a ____: *Ghostly = like a ghost.* 2 like that of a ____; characteristic of a ____: *Brotherly = like that of a brother.* 3 suited to a ____; fit or proper for a ____: *Womanly = suited to a woman.* 4 of each or every ____; occurring once per ____: *Daily = of every day.* 5 being a ____; that is a ____: *Heavenly = that is a heaven.* [Old English *-līc,* from *līc* body, form]

ly cée (lē sā'), a French secondary school maintained by the government. *n., pl.* **ly cées.**

ly ce um (lī sē'əm), 1 lecture hall; place where lectures are given. 2 an association for instruction and entertainment through lectures, debates, and concerts. *n.*

Lyd i a (lid'ē ə), ancient country in W Asia Minor, famous for its wealth and luxury. See **Persia** for map. *n.*

lye (lī), any strong alkaline solution. Lye is used in making soap and in cleaning. *n.*

ly ing[1] (lī'ing), 1 a telling a lie; habit of

adj.	adjective	n.	noun
adv.	adverb	prep.	preposition
conj.	conjunction	pron.	pronoun
interj.	interjection	v.	verb
sing.	singular	pl.	plural

telling lies. **2** false; untruthful. **3** present participle of **lie**[1]. *I was not lying; I told the truth.* **1** *n.,* **2** *adj.,* **3** *v.*

ly ing[2] (lī′ing), present participle of **lie**[2]. *I was lying on the ground.* *v.*

lymph (limf), a nearly colorless liquid in the tissues of the body, somewhat like blood without the red corpuscles. Lymph bathes and nourishes the tissues. *n.*

lym phat ic (lim fat′ik), **1** of lymph; carrying lymph. **2** sluggish; pale; lacking energy. A lymphatic appearance or temperament was formerly thought to be due to having too much lymph in the body. *adj.*

lymphatic vessel, tube or canal through which lymph is carried from different parts of the body.

lymph node or **lymph gland,** any of the small oval bodies occurring along the paths of the lymphatic vessels. Lymph nodes filter out bacteria and other harmful microorganisms from the lymph.

lymph o cyte (lim′fə sīt), a type of white blood cell, produced by lymph tissues. *n.*

lymph oid (lim′foid), of or having to do with lymph, lymphocytes, or lymph tissue. *adj.*

lynch (linch), put (an accused person) to death, usually by hanging, without a lawful trial: *The angry mob lynched an innocent man.* *v.* [apparently from Charles *Lynch,* a planter of Virginia who lived in the 1700's and was said to have organized a body of neighbors to judge and pass sentence on offenders without a lawful trial]

lynx (lingks), any of various wildcats with short tails, rather long legs, and tufts of hair at the ends of their ears. *n.,* *pl.* **lynx es** or **lynx.**

lynx—about 3 ft. long with the tail

lynx-eyed (lingks′īd′), having sharp eyes or keen sight. *adj.*

ly on naise (lī′ə nāz′), fried with pieces of onions: *lyonnaise potatoes.* *adj.* [from French *lyonnaise* of Lyons]

Ly ons (lī′ənz *or* lē ôn′), large city in E France, on the Rhone River. *n.*

Ly ra (lī′rə), a small northern constellation that was thought of as arranged in the shape of a lyre. It contains the star Vega. *n.*

lyre

lyre (līr), an ancient stringed musical instrument somewhat like a small harp. It was used by the ancient Greeks as accompaniment for singing and reciting. *n.*

lyre bird (līr′bėrd′), an Australian bird. The male has a long tail that is lyre-shaped when spread. *n.*

lyr ic (lir′ik), **1** a short poem expressing personal emotion. A love poem, a patriotic song, a lament, and a hymn might all be lyrics. **2** having to do with such poems: *a lyric poet.* **3** characterized by a spontaneous expression of feeling. **4** of, expressed in, or suitable for song. **5** Usually, **lyrics,** *pl.* the words for a song. **1,5** *n.,* **2-4** *adj.*

lyr i cal (lir′ə kəl), **1** emotional; poetic: *She became almost lyrical when she described the scenery.* **2** lyric. *adj.* —**lyr′i cal ly,** *adv.*

lyr i cism (lir′ə siz′əm), lyric character, form, or expression. *n.*

lyr i cist (lir′ə sist), **1** person who writes the words for a song; writer of lyrics. **2** a lyric poet. *n.*

ly sin (lī′sn), antibody that can dissolve bacteria, red cells, and other cellular elements. *n.*

M m

M or **m** (em), 1 the 13th letter of the alphabet. 2 the Roman numeral for 1000. *n., pl.* **M's** or **m's.**

ma (mä), INFORMAL. mamma; mother. *n., pl.* **mas.**

ma'am (mam), madam. *n.*

ma ca bre (mə kä′brə *or* mə kä′bər), gruesome; horrible; ghastly. *adj.*

ma cad am (mə kad′əm), 1 small, broken stones. Layers of macadam are rolled until solid and smooth to make roads. 2 road or pavement made of this. *n.* [from John L. *McAdam*, 1756-1836, a Scottish engineer who invented this kind of road]

ma cad am ize (mə kad′ə mīz), make or cover (a road) with macadam. *v.,* **ma cad am ized, ma cad am iz ing.**

Ma cao (mə kou′), 1 seaport on a peninsula on the S coast of China. 2 Portuguese colony that includes this peninsula and two small islands nearby. *n.*

macaques—about 2 ft. long with tail

ma caque (mə käk′), any of a group of short-tailed monkeys of Asia, the East Indies, and North Africa. *n.*

mac a ro ni (mak′ə rō′nē), flour paste that has been dried, usually in the form of hollow tubes, to be cooked for food. *n., pl.* **mac a ro nis** or **mac a ro nies.**

mac a roon (mak′ə rün′), a very sweet cookie made of whites of eggs, sugar, and ground almonds or coconut. *n.*

Mac Ar thur (mək är′thər), Douglas, 1880-1964, American general in World War II and the Korean War. *n.*

Ma cau lay (mə kô′lē), **Thomas Babington**, Baron, 1800-1859, English essayist, historian, poet, and statesman. *n.*

ma caw (mə kô′), a large parrot of South and Central America, with a long tail, brilliant feathers, and a harsh voice. *n.*

Mac beth (mək beth′), 1 play by Shakespeare. 2 the principal character in this play, who murders his king and becomes king himself. His wife, Lady Macbeth, helps him do this. *n.*

mace[1] (mās), 1 a club with a heavy metal head, often spiked, used as a weapon in the Middle Ages. 2 staff carried by or before an official as a symbol of his authority. *n.* [from French of the 1200's *mace*, from Latin *matteola* a digging tool]

mace[1]
(def. 1, left;
def. 2, right)

mace[2] (mās), spice made from the dried outer covering of nutmegs. *n.* [from French of the 1300's *macis*, from Latin *macir* a fragrant resin, from Greek *makir*]

Mac e don (mas′ə don), Macedonia. *n.*

Mac e do ni a (mas′ə dō′nē ə), ancient country in SE Europe, north of Greece. Macedonia now forms parts of Yugoslavia, Bulgaria, and Greece. *n.* —**Mac′e do′ni an,** *adj., n.*

mac e rate (mas′ə rāt′), 1 soften or separate the parts of a substance by soaking for some time. Flowers are macerated to extract their perfume. 2 become or cause to become thin. *v.,* **mac e rat ed, mac e rat ing.**

ma chet e (mə shet′ē *or* mə chet′ē), a large, heavy knife, used as a tool and weapon in South America, Central America, and the West Indies. *n.*

Mach i a vel li (mak′ē ə vel′ē), 1469-1527, Italian statesman and writer who placed advantage above fairness in politics. He advised rulers to use craft and deceit to maintain their authority. *n.*

Mach i a vel li an (mak′ē ə vel′ē ən), 1 of Machiavelli or his political theory. 2 characterized by subtle or unscrupulous cunning; crafty. *adj.*

mach i nate (mak′ə nāt), contrive or devise artfully or with evil purpose; plot; intrigue. *v.* **mach i nat ed, mach i nat ing.**

mach i na tion (mak′ə nā′shən), 1 evil or artful plotting; scheming against authority. 2 an evil plot; secret or cunning scheme: *The election of our candidate was almost prevented by the machinations of the opponent. n.*

mach i na tor (mak′ə nā′tər), person who machinates; one who schemes with evil designs. *n.*

ma chine (mə shēn′), 1 arrangement of fixed and moving parts for doing work, each part having some special function: *Sewing machines and washing ma-*

chines make housework easier. 2 of or having to do with a machine or machines: *the machine age, machine action.* 3 make or finish with a machine: *The steel was machined to exact specifications.* 4 by or with a machine, not by hand: *machine printing.* 5 device for applying force or changing its direction. Levers and pulleys are simple machines. 6 automobile. 7 airplane. 8 person or group that acts without thinking. 9 group of people controlling an organization: *a political machine.* 1,5-9 *n.,* 2,4 *adj.,* 3 *v.,* **ma chined, ma chin ing.**

machine gun

machine gun, gun that fires ammunition automatically and can keep up a rapid fire of bullets.

ma chine-gun (mə shēn′gun′), fire at with a machine gun. *v.,* **ma chine-gunned, ma chine-gun ning.**

ma chin er y (mə shē′nər ē), 1 machines: *A factory contains much machinery.* 2 the parts or works of a machine: *The machinery of a typewriter should be kept clean.* 3 any combination of persons or things by which something is kept going or something is done: *Policemen, judges, courts, and prisons are legal machinery. n., pl.* **ma chin er ies.**

machine shop, workshop where machines or parts of machines are made or repaired.

machine tool, a power-driven tool or machine used to form metal into desired shapes by cutting, hammering, squeezing, etc.

ma chin ist (mə shē′nist), 1 a skilled worker with machine tools. 2 person who runs a machine. 3 person who makes and repairs machinery. *n.*

Mach number (mäk), number expressing the ratio of the speed of an object to the speed of sound in the same medium. An aircraft traveling at the speed of sound has a Mach number of

hat, āge, fär; let, ēqual, tèrm; it, īce; hot, ōpen, ôrder; oil, out; cup, pùt, rüle; ch, child; ng, long; sh, she; th, thin; ₮H, then; zh, measure;

ə represents *a* in about, *e* in taken, *i* in pencil, *o* in lemon, *u* in circus.

adj.	adjective	*n.* noun
adv.	adverb	*prep.* preposition
conj.	conjunction	*pron.* pronoun
interj.	interjection	*v.* verb
sing.	singular	*pl.* plural

1; at twice the speed of sound its Mach number is 2. [from Ernst *Mach*, 1838-1916, an Austrian physicist who studied the action of bodies moving through gases]

Mac ken zie (mə ken′zē), river in NW Canada flowing into the Arctic Ocean. *n.*

mack er el (mak′ər əl), a saltwater fish of the northern Atlantic, much used for food. *n., pl.* **mack er el** or **mack- er els.**

mackerel sky, sky spotted with small, white, fleecy clouds.

Mack i nac (mak′ə nô), **Straits of,** strait connecting Lake Michigan and Lake Huron. *n.*

mack i naw (mak′ə nô), 1 kind of short coat made of heavy woolen cloth. 2 kind of thick woolen blanket, often with bars of color, used in northern and western United States by Indians, lumbermen, etc. *n.* [from *Mackinaw* City, town in Michigan]

mack in tosh (mak′ən tosh), 1 a waterproof coat; raincoat. 2 waterproof cloth. *n., pl.* **mack in tosh es.** [from Charles *Macintosh,* 1766-1843, the inventor]

mac ro cosm (mak′rə koz′əm), the universe. *n.*

ma cron (mā′kron), a straight, horizontal line (¯) placed over a vowel to show that it is pronounced as a long vowel. EXAMPLES: cāme, bē. *n.*

mad (mad), 1 out of one's mind; crazy; insane: *Her wild ravings made me wonder if she were mad.* 2 very angry; furious: *The insult made me mad.* 3 much excited; wild: *The dog made mad efforts to catch up with the automobile.* 4 foolish; unwise: *a mad undertaking.* 5 blindly and unreasonably fond: *My friend is mad about playing badminton.* 6 wildly gay or merry: *Tomorrow will be the maddest, merriest day of the year.* 7 having rabies. A mad dog often foams at the mouth and may bite people. *adj.,* **mad der, mad dest.**

like mad, INFORMAL. furiously; very hard, fast, etc.: *I ran like mad to catch the train.*

Mad a gas car (mad′ə gas′kər), large island country in the Indian Ocean, east of S Africa. Its official name is **Malagasy Republic.** *n.*

mad am (mad′əm), a polite title used in writing or speaking to any woman: *Good day, madam. n., pl.* **mad ams** or **mes dames.**

mad ame (mad′əm *or* mä däm′), FRENCH. title for a married woman; Mrs. *n., pl.* **mes dames.**

mad cap (mad′kap′), 1 person who goes ahead and carries out wild ideas without stopping to think first. 2 wild; hasty. 1 *n.,* 2 *adj.*

mad den (mad′n), make or become mad: *The crowd was maddened by the umpire's decision. v.*

made (mād), 1 past tense and past participle of **make.** *The cook made the cake. It was made of flour, milk, butter, eggs, and sugar.* 2 built; formed: *a strongly made swing.* 3 specially prepared: *made gravy, a made dish.* 1 *v.,* 2,3 *adj.*

Ma deir a (mə dir′ə), 1 group of Portuguese islands in the Atlantic, west of N Africa. 2 the most important island of this group. 3 kind of wine made there. *n.*

mad e moi selle (mad′ə mə zel′), FRENCH. title for an unmarried woman; Miss. *n., pl.* **mes de moi selles.**

made-to-or der (mād′tü ôr′dər), made according to the buyer's wishes. *adj.*

made-up (mād′up′), 1 not real; invented; imaginary: *a made-up story.* 2 painted, powdered, etc., with cosmetics: *made-up lips. adj.*

mad house (mad′hous′), 1 asylum for insane people. 2 place of uproar and confusion: *The arena was a madhouse after the home team won the championship game. n., pl.* **mad hous es** (mad′hou′ziz).

Mad i son (mad′ə sən), 1 **James,** 1751-1836, the fourth president of the United States, from 1809 to 1817. He had an important part in drawing up the Constitution of the United States. 2 capital of Wisconsin, in the S part. *n.*

mad ly (mad′lē), 1 insanely. 2 furiously. 3 foolishly. *adv.*

mad man (mad′man′), an insane man; crazy person: *The explosion was probably caused by a madman. n., pl.* **mad men.**

mad ness (mad′nis), 1 a being crazy; insane condition; loss of one's mind. 2 great anger; rage; fury: *In his madness he kicked the fence post.* 3 folly: *It would be madness to try to sail a boat in this storm. n.*

Ma don na (mə don′ə), 1 Mary, the mother of Jesus. 2 picture or statue of her. *n., pl.* **Ma don nas** for 2.

mad ras (mad′rəs *or* mə dras′), a closely woven cotton cloth, used for shirts, dresses, etc. *n.* [from *Madras*]

Ma dras (mə dras′), seaport in SE India. *n.*

Ma drid (mə drid′), capital of Spain, in the central part. *n.*

mad ri gal (mad′rə gəl), 1 a short poem, often about love, that can be set to music. 2 song with parts for several voices, usually sung without instrumental accompaniment. *n.*

mael strom (māl′strəm), 1 a great or turbulent whirlpool. 2 **Maelstrom,** a dangerous whirlpool off the NW coast of Norway. 3 a violent confusion of feelings, ideas, or conditions. *n.*

maes tro (mī′strō), 1 a great composer, teacher, or conductor of music. 2 master of any art. *n., pl.* **maes tros.** [from Italian *maestro,* from Latin *magister* a master]

mag a zine (mag′ə zēn′ *or* mag′ə zēn′), 1 a publication issued at regular intervals, especially weekly or monthly, which contains stories, articles, photographs, etc., by various contributors. 2 room in a fort or warship for storing gunpowder and other explosives. 3 a building for storing gunpowder, guns, food, or other military supplies. 4 place in a repeating or automatic gun from which cartridges are fed into the firing chamber. 5 place for holding a roll or reel of film in a camera or projector. *n.*

Ma gel lan (mə jel′ən), 1 **Ferdinand,** 1480?-1521, Portuguese navigator. His ship was the first to sail around the world, though he himself was killed soon after he had discovered the Philippine Islands. 2 **Strait of,** strait at the S tip of South America. *n.*

ma gen ta (mə jen′tə), 1 a purplish-red dye. 2 purplish-red. 3 a purplish red. 1,3 *n.,* 2 *adj.*

mag got (mag′ət), the legless larva of any of various kinds of flies. Maggots usually live in decaying matter. *n.*

Ma gi (mā′jī), (in the Bible) the Three Wise Men who followed the star to Bethlehem and brought gifts to the infant Jesus. *n.pl.*

mag ic (maj′ik), 1 the pretended art of using secret charms, spirits, etc., to make unnatural things happen: *The fairy's magic changed the brothers into swans.* 2 done by magic or as if by magic: *A magic palace stood in place of their hut.* 3 something that produces results as if by magic; mysterious influence; unexplained power: *the magic of music.* 4 art or skill of creating illusions, especially by sleight of hand. 1,3,4 *n.,* 2 *adj.*

mag i cal (maj′ə kəl), done by magic or as if by magic: *The waving of the fairy's wand produced a magical effect. adj.* —**mag′i cal ly,** *adv.*

ma gi cian (mə jish′ən), 1 person

skilled in the use of magic: *The wicked magician cast a spell over the princess.* 2 person who entertains by magic tricks: *The magician pulled — not one, but three rabbits out of his hat! n.*

magic lantern, an early type of projector for showing photographic slides on a screen.

mag is ter i al (maj/ə stir/ē əl), 1 of a magistrate; suited to a magistrate: *A judge has magisterial rank.* 2 showing authority: *The principal spoke with a magisterial voice.* 3 imperious; domineering; overbearing: *He paced up and down with a magisterial stride. adj.*

mag is tra cy (maj/ə strə sē), 1 position, rank, or duties of a magistrate. 2 magistrates as a group. *n., pl.* **mag is tra cies.**

mag is trate (maj/ə strāt), 1 a government official who has power to apply the law and put it in force. The President is the chief magistrate of the United States. 2 judge in a minor court. A justice of the peace is a magistrate. *n.*

mag ma (mag/mə), the molten material beneath the earth's crust from which igneous rock is formed. *n.*

Mag na Char ta or **Mag na Car ta** (mag/nə kär/tə), 1 the great charter which the English barons forcibly secured from King John at Runnymede on June 15, 1215. The Magna Charta provided a basis for guaranteeing the personal and political liberties of the people of England, and placed the king under the rule of the law. 2 any fundamental constitution guaranteeing civil and political rights. [from Latin *magna carta* great charter]

mag na nim i ty (mag/nə nim/ə tē), magnanimous nature or quality; nobility of soul or mind: *show magnanimity by forgiving someone who harmed you. n.*

mag nan i mous (mag nan/ə məs), noble in soul or mind; generous in forgiving; free from mean or petty feelings or acts: *He has a magnanimous attitude toward his children when they misbehave. adj.* —**mag nan/i mous ly,** *adv.*

mag nate (mag/nāt), an important, powerful, or prominent person: *a railroad magnate. n.*

mag ne sia (mag nē/zhə), a white, tasteless powder, used in medicine as an antacid and a laxative, and in industry in making fertilizers and heat-resistant building materials. *n.*

mag ne si um (mag nē/zhē əm), a light, silver-white metallic element that burns with a dazzling white light. Magnesium is used in photography, fireworks, and metal alloys. *n.*

mag net (mag/nit), 1 stone or piece of metal that has the property, either natural or induced, of attracting iron or steel. A loadstone is a natural magnet.

Bar magnets and horseshoe magnets are steel magnets which retain their magnetism for a long time. 2 anything that attracts: *The rabbits in our backyard were a magnet that attracted all the children in the neighborhood. n.*

mag net ic (mag net/ik), 1 having the properties of a magnet: *the magnetic needle of a compass.* 2 of or having to do with magnetism; producing magnetism: *a magnetic circuit.* 3 of or having to do with the earth's magnetism: *the magnetic meridian.* 4 capable of being magnetized or of being attracted by a magnet: *magnetic nickel.* 5 very attractive: *a magnetic personality. adj.* —**mag net/i cal ly,** *adv.*

magnetic field, space around a magnet or electric current in which the magnetic force of the magnet or current is felt.

magnetic needle, a slender bar of magnetized steel used as a compass. When mounted so that it turns easily, it points approximately north and south toward the earth's Magnetic Poles.

Magnetic Pole (def. 2)

magnetic pole, 1 one of the two poles of a magnet. 2 **Magnetic Pole,** one of the two points on the earth's surface toward which a compass needle points. The **North Magnetic Pole** is in the Arctic; the **South Magnetic Pole** is in Antarctica.

magnetic tape, plastic or paper tape, coated with iron oxide, on which sounds or images can be recorded.

mag net ism (mag/nə tiz/əm), 1 properties or qualities of a magnet; the showing of magnetic properties: *the magnetism of iron and steel.* 2 branch of physics dealing with magnets and magnetic properties. 3 power to attract or charm: *A person with magnetism has many friends and admirers. n.*

mag net ite (mag/nə tīt), an important iron ore that is strongly attracted by a magnet. *n.*

mag net ize (mag/nə tīz), 1 give the properties or qualities of a magnet to: *You can magnetize a needle by rubbing it with a magnet.* 2 attract or influence (a person): *Her stirring speech magnetized the audience. v.,* **mag net ized, mag net iz ing.**

mag ne to (mag nē/tō), a small machine which uses a magnetic field to

hat, āge, fär; let, ēqual, tėrm;
it, īce; hot, ōpen, ôrder;
oil, out; cup, půt, rüle; ch, child;
ng, long; sh, she; th, thin;
ŦH, then; zh, measure;

ə represents *a* in about,
e in taken, *i* in pencil,
o in lemon, *u* in circus.

produce an electric current. In some internal-combustion engines, a magneto supplies an electric spark to explode the gasoline vapor. *n., pl.* **mag ne tos.**

Mag nif i cat (mag nif/ə kat), 1 hymn of the Virgin Mary beginning "My soul doth magnify the Lord." 2 music for this hymn. *n.*

mag ni fi ca tion (mag/nə fə kā/shən), act of magnifying. *n.*

mag nif i cence (mag nif/ə səns), richness of material, color, and ornament; grand beauty; splendor: *We were dazzled by the magnificence of the mountain scenery. n.*

mag nif i cent (mag nif/ə sənt), richly colored or decorated; splendid; grand; stately: *a magnificent royal palace, magnificent diamonds and emeralds, a magnificent view of the mountains. adj.* —**mag nif/i cent ly,** *adv.*

mag ni fi er (mag/nə fī/ər), 1 one that magnifies. 2 magnifying glass. *n.*

mag ni fy (mag/nə fī), 1 cause to look larger than the real size; increase the apparent size of an object: *A microscope magnifies bacteria so that they can be seen and studied.* 2 make too much of; go beyond the truth in telling: *In describing the fish that I almost caught, I magnified its size. v.,* **mag nified, mag ni fy ing.**

magnifying glass, lens or combination of lenses that causes things to look larger than they really are.

mag nil o quence (mag nil/ə kwəns), 1 use of big and unusual words, elaborate phrases, etc.; high-flown, lofty style of speaking or writing. 2 boastfulness. *n.*

magneto
The coil is turned rapidly by means of the crank. Electricity is produced in the coil as it moves through the magnetic field of a series of magnets.

511

adj. adjective	*n.* noun
adv. adverb	*prep.* preposition
conj. conjunction	*pron.* pronoun
interj. interjection	*v.* verb
sing. singular	*pl.* plural

mag nil o quent (mag nil′ə kwənt), 1 using big and unusual words; expressed in high-flown language. 2 boastful. *adj.* —**mag nil′o quent ly,** *adv.*

mag ni tude (mag′nə tüd *or* mag′nə tyüd), 1 greatness of size: *the height, strength, and magnitude of a building.* 2 great importance, effect, or consequence: *The war brought problems of very great magnitude to many nations.* 3 measure of brightness of a star. Stars of the first magnitude are the brightest. *n.*

mag nol ia (mag nō′lyə), 1 any of several trees or shrubs of North America and Asia, having large white, yellow, pink, or purplish flowers. 2 its flower. *n., pl.* **mag nol ias.** [from Pierre *Magnol,* 1638-1715, a French botanist]

mag pie (mag′pī), 1 a black-and-white bird that chatters a great deal. It has a long tail and short wings and is related to the jays. 2 person who chatters. *n.*

Mag yar (mag′yär), 1 member of the chief group of people living in Hungary. 2 their language; Hungarian. 3 of the Magyars or their language. 1,2 *n.,* 3 *adj.*

ma ha ra ja (mä′hə rä′jə), a ruling prince in India, especially one who rules a state. *n., pl.* **ma ha ra jas.**

ma ha ra jah (mä′hə rä′jə), maharaja. *n.*

ma ha ra nee (mä′hə rä′nē), 1 wife of a maharaja. 2 a ruling princess in India, especially one who rules a state. *n.*

ma ha ra ni (mä′hə rä′nē), maharanee. *n., pl.* **ma ha ra nis.**

ma hat ma (mə hät′mə), a wise and holy person, especially in India. *n., pl.* **ma hat mas.**

mail²—mail of the 1000's made of leather with small metal scales sewn to it

mah-jongg *or* **mah-jong** (mä′jong′), game of Chinese origin played by four people with many small tiles resembling dominoes. Each player tries to form winning combinations by drawing or discarding. *n.*

ma hog a ny (mə hog′ə nē), 1 any of several large tropical American trees which yield a hard, reddish-brown wood. 2 its wood, used in making furniture. 3 made of mahogany: *a mahogany chest of drawers.* 4 dark reddish-brown. 5 a dark reddish brown. 1,2,5 *n., pl.* **ma hog a nies;** 3,4 *adj.*

Ma hom et (mə hom′it), Mohammed. *n.*

Ma hom et an (mə hom′ə tən), Mohammedan. *adj., n.*

ma hout (mə hout′), (in the East Indies) the keeper and driver of an elephant. *n.*

maid (mād), 1 a young unmarried woman; girl. 2 an unmarried woman. 3 a woman servant. *n.*

maid en (mād′n), 1 a young unmarried woman; maid; girl. 2 of a maiden: *maiden grace.* 3 unmarried: *a maiden aunt.* 4 first: *a ship's maiden voyage, the senator's maiden speech in the Senate.* 1 *n.,* 2-4 *adj.*

maid en hair (mād′n her′ *or* mād′n har′), fern with very slender stalks and delicate, finely divided fronds. *n.*

maid en hood (mād′n hůd), condition or time of being a maiden. *n.*

maid en ly (mād′n lē), 1 of a maiden. 2 like a maiden; gentle; modest. 3 suited to a maiden: *maidenly reserve.* *adj.*

maiden name, a woman's surname before her marriage.

maid of honor, 1 an unmarried woman who is the chief attendant of the bride at a wedding. 2 an unmarried noble lady who attends a queen or princess.

maid serv ant (mād′sėr′vənt), a woman servant. *n.*

mail¹ (māl), 1 letters, postcards, papers, parcels, etc., to be sent by post. 2 system by which such mail is sent, managed by the Post Office Department: *You can pay most bills by mail.* 3 all that comes by one post or delivery: *The morning mail is full of advertisements.* 4 train, boat, etc., that carries mail. 5 send by mail; put in a mailbox. 6 of or for mail. 1-4 *n.,* 5 *v.,* 6 *adj.* [from French of the 1200's *male* wallet, bag]

mail² (māl), a flexible armor made of metal rings or small loops of chain linked together, or of overlapping plates, for protecting the body against arrows, spears, etc. *n.* [from French of the 1300's *maille*]

mail box (māl′boks′), 1 a public box

from which mail is collected. 2 a private box to which mail is delivered. *n., pl.* **mail box es.**

mail carrier, mailman.

mail man (māl′man′), person who carries or delivers mail; postman. *n., pl.* **mail men.**

mail order, order for goods sent by mail.

maim (mām), cut off or make useless an arm, leg, ear, etc., of; cripple; disable: *His foot was maimed in the accident.* *v.*

main (mān), 1 most important; largest: *the main dish at dinner, the main street of town.* 2 a large pipe or conductor which carries water, gas, sewage, or electricity to or from smaller branches: *When the water main broke, our cellar was flooded.* 3 the open sea; ocean: *Our fleet shall sail the main.* 4 exerted to the utmost; full; sheer: *I moved the dresser by main strength.* 1,4 *adj.,* 2,3 *n.*

in the main, for the most part; chiefly; mostly: *Her grades are excellent in the main.*

with might and main, with all one's force: *They argued with might and main.*

main clause, (in grammar) a clause in a complex sentence that can act by itself as a sentence; independent clause.

Maine (mān), one of the northeastern states of the United States. *Capital:* Augusta. *n.*

main land (mān′land′ *or* mān′lənd), the main part of a continent or land mass, apart from outlying islands and peninsulas. *n.*

main ly (mān′lē), for the most part; chiefly; mostly: *He is interested mainly in art. Our garden is mainly vegetables.* *adv.*

main mast (mān′mast′ *or* mān′məst), the principal mast of a ship. *n.*

main sail (mān′sāl′ *or* mān′səl), the largest sail of a ship on the mainmast. *n.*

main sheet (mān′shēt′), rope or tackle that controls the angle at which the mainsail is set. *n.*

main spring (mān′spring′), 1 the principal spring in a clock, watch, etc. 2 the main cause, motive, or influence. *n.*

main stay (mān′stā′), 1 rope or wire

supporting the mainmast. **2** main support: *Loyal friends are a person's mainstay in time of trouble.* *n.*

main stream (mān′strēm′), a main course or direction in the development of an idea, institution, country, etc. *n.*

main tain (mān tān′), **1** keep; keep up; carry on: *One must maintain a footing in tug of war.* **2** support; uphold: *maintain an opinion. He maintains his family.* **3** declare to be true: *She maintains that she is innocent.* **4** affirm; assert against opposition: *He maintains his innocence.* *v.*

main te nance (mān′tə nəns), **1** a maintaining: *Maintenance of quiet is necessary in a hospital.* **2** a being maintained; support: *A government collects taxes to pay for its maintenance.* **3** a keeping in good repair: *A state devotes much time to the maintenance of roads.* **4** enough to support life; means of living: *Her small farm provides a maintenance, but not much more.* *n.*

main top (mān′top′), platform on the mainmast. *n.*

maize (māz), **1** corn; Indian corn. **2** the color of ripe corn; yellow. *n.*

Maj., Major.

ma jes tic (mə jes′tik), of or having majesty; grand; noble; dignified; stately. *adj.* —**ma jes′ti cal ly,** *adv.*

ma jes ti cal (mə jes′tə kəl), majestic. *adj.*

maj es ty (maj′ə stē), **1** royal dignity; stately appearance; nobility: *the majesty of the starry heavens, the great majesty of the Grand Canyon.* **2** supreme power or authority: *Policemen and judges uphold the majesty of the law.* **3 Majesty,** title used in speaking to or of a king, queen, emperor, empress, etc.: *Your Majesty, His Majesty, Her Majesty.* *n., pl.* **maj es ties.**

ma jor (mā′jər), **1** more important; larger; greater: *Take the major share of the profits.* **2** officer in the army, air force, or marines ranking next below a lieutenant colonel and next above a captain. **3** in music: **a** greater by a half step than the corresponding minor interval: *a major chord.* **b** noting a scale or key having half steps after the third and seventh tones: *the C major scale or key.* **c** a major scale, key, chord, interval, etc. **4** subject or course of study to which a student gives most of his time and attention: *Her major is mathematics.* **5** have or take as a major subject of study: *He will major in mathematics.* **1,3a,b** *adj.,* **2,3c,4** *n.,* **5** *v.*

ma jor-do mo (mā′jər dō′mō), **1** man in charge of a royal or noble household. **2** butler; steward. *n., pl.* **ma jor-do mos.**

major general, officer in the army, air force, or marines ranking next below

a lieutenant general and next above a brigadier general.

ma jor i ty (mə jôr′ə tē), **1** the larger number or part; more than half: *A majority of the children chose red covers for the books they had made.* **2** the number by which the votes on one side are more than those on the other: *He had 18 votes, and she had 12; so he had a majority of 6.* **3** the legal age of responsibility. Under the varying laws of the states of the United States, a person reaches his majority at the age of 18 or 21. *n., pl.* **ma jor i ties.**

major league, either of the two chief leagues in American professional baseball.

make (māk), **1** bring into being; put together; build; form; shape: *make a new dress, make a fire, make a will, make jelly.* **2** way in which a thing is made; style; build; character: *Do you like the make of that coat?* **3** kind; brand: *What make of car is this?* **4** have the qualities needed for: *Wood makes a good fire.* **5** cause; bring about: *make trouble, make a noise, make peace.* **6** cause to; force to: *He made me go.* **7** cause to be or become; cause oneself to be: *make a room warm, make a fool of oneself.* **8** turn out to be; become: *He will make a good legislator.* **9** get ready for use; arrange: *I make my own bed.* **10** get; obtain; acquire; earn: *make a fortune, make one's living.* **11** do; perform: *make a speech, make an attempt, make a mistake.* **12** amount to; add up to; count as: *Two and two make four.* **13** think of as; figure to be: *I make the distance across the room 15 feet.* **14** reach; arrive at: *The ship made port.* **15** go; travel: *Some airplanes can make 600 miles an hour.* **16** cause the success of: *One big deal made the young businessman.* **17** INFORMAL. get on; get a place on: *She made the tennis team.* **1,4-17** *v.,* **made, mak ing; 2,3** *n.*

make after, follow; chase; pursue.

make away with, 1 get rid of. **2** kill. **3** steal: *The treasurer made away with the club's funds.*

make believe, pretend: *She liked to make believe she was an airplane pilot.*

make fast, attach firmly.

make for, 1 go toward: *Make for the hills!* **2** help bring about; favor: *The new facts made for the prisoner's acquittal.*

make it, INFORMAL. succeed.

make off with, steal: *He made off with his neighbor's car.*

make out, 1 write out: *She made out a marketing list.* **2** show to be; try to prove: *That makes me out most selfish.* **3** understand: *The boy had a hard time making out the problem.* **4** see with difficulty: *I can barely make out three*

hat, āge, fär; let, ēqual, tèrm; it, īce; hot, ōpen, ôrder; oil, out; cup, pùt, rüle; ch, child; ng, long; sh, she; th, thin; ŦH, then; zh, measure;

ə represents *a* in about, *e* in taken, *i* in pencil, *o* in lemon, *u* in circus.

ships near the horizon. **5** INFORMAL. get along; manage: *We must try to make out with what we have.*

make over, 1 alter; make different: *She had to make over her dress because it was too big.* **2** hand over; transfer ownership of: *Grandfather made over his farm to father.*

make up, 1 put together: *make up cloth into a dress.* **2** invent: *make up a story.* **3** settle (a dispute, etc.); reconcile: *make up one's differences.* **4** give or do in place of: *make up for lost time.* **5** become friends again after a quarrel: *There we were, quarreling and making up by turns.* **6** put rouge, lipstick, powder, etc., on the face. **7** arrange (type, pictures, etc.) in the pages of a book, paper, or magazine: *make up a page of type.* **8** decide: *make up one's mind.* **9** compose; constitute: *Children made up the audience.*

make up to, try to get the friendship of; flatter: *We all made up to the new boy the first day.*

make-be lieve (māk′bi lēv′), **1** pretense: *Fairies live in the land of make-believe.* **2** pretended: *Some children have make-believe playmates.* **1** *n.,* **2** *adj.*

mak er (mā′kər), person or thing that makes. *n.*

make shift (māk′shift′), **1** something used for a time instead of the right thing; temporary substitute: *When the fuse for the lights blew, we used candles as a makeshift.* **2** used for a time instead of the right thing: *makeshift awnings.* **1** *n.,* **2** *adj.*

make-up (māk′up′), **1** way of being put together. **2** nature; disposition: *a nervous make-up.* **3** way in which an actor is dressed and painted to look his part. **4** rouge, lipstick, powder, etc., put on the face; cosmetics. **5** arrangement of type, pictures, etc., in a book, paper, or magazine. *n.*

Mal a chi (mal′ə kī), **1** Hebrew prophet who lived about 450 B.C. **2** the last book of the Old Testament. *n.*

mal a chite (mal′ə kīt), a green mineral that is an ore of copper and is used for ornamental articles. *n.*

mal ad just ed (mal′ə jus′tid), badly

adj.	adjective	*n.*	noun
adv.	adverb	*prep.*	preposition
conj.	conjunction	*pron.*	pronoun
interj.	interjection	*v.*	verb
sing.	singular	*pl.*	plural

adjusted; not in a healthy relation with one's environment. *adj.*

mal ad just ment (mal/ə just/mənt), a bad adjustment. *n.*

mal a droit (mal/ə droit/), unskillful; awkward; clumsy. *adj.* —**mal/- a droit/ly,** *adv.* —**mal/a droit/- ness,** *n.*

mal a dy (mal/ə dē), 1 any bodily disorder or disease, especially one that is chronic or deep-seated: *Cancer and malaria are serious maladies.* 2 any unwholesome or disordered condition: *Poverty and slums are social maladies.* *n., pl.* **mal a dies.**

Mál a ga (mal/ə gə), province in S Spain. *n.*

Mal a gas y Republic (mal/ə- gas/ē), official name of Madagascar. It is a member of the French Community. See **South Africa** for map. *n.*

ma laise (ma lāz/), an uneasy, disturbed, or disordered condition. *n.*

ma lar i a (mə ler/ē ə *or* mə lar/ē ə), disease characterized by periodic chills, fever, and sweating. Malaria is caused by minute parasitic animals in the blood and is transmitted by the bite of mosquitoes which have bitten infected persons. *n.*

ma lar i al (mə ler/ē əl *or* mə lar/ē əl), 1 having malaria. 2 of or like malaria. *adj.*

Ma la wi (mə lä/wē), country in SE Africa, a member of the Commonwealth of Nations. It was formerly called **Nyasaland.** See **South Africa** for map. *n.*

Ma lay (mā/lā), 1 member of the native people of the Malay Peninsula and nearby islands. 2 their language. 3 of the Malays, their country, or their language. 1,2 *n.,* 3 *adj.*

Ma lay a (mə lā/ə), 1 Malay Peninsula. 2 former country on the Malay Peninsula, now part of the Federation of Malaysia. *n.* —**Ma lay/an,** *adj., n.*

Malay Archipelago, group of islands between SE Asia and Australia; East Indies; Indonesia. See **East Indies** for map.

Malay Peninsula, peninsula in SE Asia, north of Sumatra; Malaya.

Ma lay sia (mə lā/zhə), **Federation of,** federation consisting of Sabah, Sarawak, Malaya, and many small islands

of the Malay Archipelago, a member of the Commonwealth of Nations. *Capital:* Kuala Lumpur. *n.* —**Ma lay/sian,** *adj., n.*

mal con tent (mal/kən tent/), 1 discontented; rebellious. 2 a discontented person; rebellious person. 1 *adj.,* 2 *n.*

Mal dive Islands (mal/dīv), group of islands in the Indian Ocean.

Mal dives (mal/dīvz), country in the Indian Ocean southwest of Ceylon, consisting of the Maldive Islands. *n.*

male (māl), 1 man or boy. 2 of or having to do with men or boys. 3 belonging to the sex that can father young. Bucks, bulls, and roosters are male animals. 4 animal belonging to this sex. 5 (of a plant) having stamens but not pistils. 6 plant bearing only flowers with stamens. 1,4,6 *n.,* 2,3,5 *adj.* —**male/ness,** *n.*

mal e dic tion (mal/ə dik/shən), a curse. *n.*

mal e fac tor (mal/ə fak/tər), a criminal; evildoer. *n.*

ma lev o lence (mə lev/ə ləns), the wish that evil may happen to others; ill will; spite. *n.*

ma lev o lent (mə lev/ə lənt), wishing evil to happen to others; showing ill will; spiteful. *adj.* —**ma lev/o lent ly,** *adv.*

mal fea sance (mal fē/zns), official misconduct; violation of a public trust or duty: *A judge is guilty of malfeasance if he accepts a bribe.* *n.*

mal for ma tion (mal/fôr mā/shən), bad shape; faulty structure: *A hunchback has a spine malformation.* *n.*

mal formed (mal fôrmd/), badly shaped; having a faulty structure. *adj.*

mal func tion (mal/fungk/shən), 1 an improper functioning; failure to work or perform: *a malfunction of the body or in a machine.* 2 function badly; work or perform improperly. 1 *n.,* 2 *v.*

Ma li (mä/lē), country in W Africa, south of Algeria. *Capital:* Bamako. See **Algeria** for map. *n.*

mal ice (mal/is), active ill will; wish to hurt or make suffer; spite: *Lincoln asked the people to act "with malice toward none, with charity for all."* *n.*

ma li cious (mə lish/əs), showing ill will; wishing to hurt or make suffer; spiteful: *That story is malicious gossip.* *adj.* —**ma li/cious ly,** *adv.*

ma lign (mə līn/), 1 speak evil of; slander: *You malign a generous person when you call him stingy.* 2 evil; injurious: *Gambling can have a malign influence.* 3 hateful; malicious. 1 *v.,* 2,3 *adj.* —**ma lign/er,** *n.*

ma lig nan cy (mə lig/nən sē), malignant quality or tendency. *n., pl.* **ma lig nan cies.**

ma lig nant (mə lig/nənt), 1 very evil,

hateful, or malicious. 2 very harmful or dangerous; deadly: *A cancer is a malignant growth.* *adj.* —**ma lig/nant ly,** *adv.*

ma lig ni ty (mə lig/nə tē), 1 great malice; extreme hate or ill will. 2 great harmfulness; dangerous quality; deadliness. *n., pl.* **ma lig ni ties.**

ma lin ger (mə ling/gər), pretend to be sick in order to escape work or duty; shirk. *v.* —**ma lin/ger er,** *n.*

mall (môl), a shaded walk; public walk or promenade. *n.*

mal lard (mal/ərd), kind of wild duck. The male has a green head and a white band around his neck. *n., pl.* **mal lards** or **mal lard.**

mal le a bil i ty (mal/ē ə bil/ə tē), malleable quality or condition: *Manganese increases the malleability of steel.* *n.*

mal le a ble (mal/ē ə bəl), 1 that can be hammered, rolled, or extended into various shapes without being broken. Gold, silver, copper, and tin are malleable; they can be beaten into thin sheets. 2 adaptable; yielding: *A malleable person can adjust to changed plans.* *adj.*

mallet with a rubber head used to pound out a dent in an automobile fender

mal let (mal/it), a hammer, usually with a wooden head. Specially shaped mallets are used to play croquet and polo. *n.*

mal low (mal/ō), plant with purple, pink, or white five-petaled flowers, and hairy leaves and stems. *n.*

malm sey (mäm/zē), kind of strong, sweet wine. *n.*

mal nu tri tion (mal/nü trish/ən *or* mal/nyü trish/ən), a poorly nourished condition. People suffer from malnutrition because of eating wrong kinds of food as well as from lack of food. *n.*

mal o dor ous (mal ō/dər əs), smelling bad. *adj.* —**mal o/dor ous ly,** *adv.*

mal prac tice (mal prak/tis), 1 criminal neglect or wrong treatment of a patient by a doctor. 2 wrong practice or conduct in any official or professional position; misconduct. *n.*

malt (môlt), 1 barley or other grain soaked in water until it sprouts, and then dried and aged. Malt has a sweet taste and is used in making beer and ale. 2 make or change into malt. 3 prepare with malt: *malted milk.* 1 *n.,* 2,3 *v.*

Mal ta (môl′tə), 1 island in the Mediterranean, south of Sicily. 2 country including Malta and smaller islands nearby, a member of the Commonwealth of Nations. *n.*

Mal tese (môl tēz′), 1 person born or living in Malta. 2 language of Malta. 3 of Malta, its people, or their language. 1,2 *n., pl.* **Mal tese;** 3 *adj.*

Maltese cat, a short-haired, bluish-gray cat.

Maltese cross

Maltese cross, a cross with four equal arms resembling arrowheads pointed toward the center.

mal tose (môl′tōs), a white, crystalline sugar made by the action of various enzymes on starch. It is formed in the body during digestion. *n.*

mal treat (mal trēt′), treat roughly or cruelly; abuse: *maltreat animals, maltreat a fine automobile. v.*

mal treat ment (mal trēt′mənt), rough or cruel treatment; abuse. *n.*

ma ma (mä′mə), mother. *n., pl.* **ma mas.**

mam ma (mä′mə), mother. *n., pl.* **mam mas.**

mam mal (mam′əl), any of a class of warm-blooded vertebrate animals, the females of which have glands that produce milk to feed their young. Human beings, horses, dogs, lions, bats, and whales are all mammals. *n.*

mam ma li an (ma mā′lē ən), of or belonging to the mammals. *adj.*

mam mar y gland (mam′ər ē), the milk-producing gland of female mammals.

mam mon (mam′ən), riches thought of as an evil; greed for wealth. *n.*

mam moth (mam′əth), 1 a very large, extinct kind of elephant with a hairy skin and long, curved tusks. 2 huge; gigantic: *Digging the Panama Canal was a mammoth undertaking.* 1 *n.,* 2 *adj.*

mam my (mam′ē), mamma; mother. *n., pl.* **mam mies.**

man (man), 1 an adult male person. When a boy grows up, he becomes a man. 2 human being; person. 3 the human race: *Man has existed for thousands of years.* 4 a male follower, serv-

manatee
8 to 13 ft. long

ant, or employee: *Robin Hood and his merry men.* 5 husband: *man and wife.* 6 one of the pieces used in games such as chess and checkers. 7 supply with men: *Sailors man a ship.* 8 serve or operate; get ready to operate: *Man the guns.* 9 make strong; brace: *I manned myself to endure the Arctic winter.* 1-6 *n., pl.* **men;** 7-9 *v.,* **manned, manning.**

be one's own man, 1 be free to do as one pleases. 2 have complete control of oneself.

to a man, without an exception; all: *We accepted his idea to a man.*

Man., Manitoba.

man a cle (man′ə kəl), 1 fetter for the hands; handcuff. 2 put manacles on: *The pirates manacled their prisoners.* 3 restrain; hamper. 1 *n.,* 2,3 *v.,* **man a cled, man a cling.**

man age (man′ij), 1 to guide or handle with skill or authority; control; direct: *manage a business, manage a horse.* 2 succeed in accomplishing; contrive: *I shall manage to keep warm.* 3 get along: *manage on one's allowance. v.,* **man aged, man ag ing.**

man age a ble (man′ə jə bəl), that can be managed. *adj.*

man age ment (man′ij mənt), 1 a managing or handling; control; direction: *Bad management caused the bank's failure.* 2 persons that manage a business or an institution: *a dispute between labor and management. The management of the store decided to increase the size of the parking lot. n.*

mammoth (def. 1)
about 10 ft. high at the shoulder

man ag er (man′ə jər), person who manages, especially one who manages a business: *a store manager. n.*

man a ger i al (man′ə jir′ē əl), of a manager; having to do with management: *Executives are given training in managerial methods. adj.*

Ma na gua (mə nä′gwə), capital of Nicaragua, in the W part. *n.*

man-at-arms (man′ət ärmz′), 1 soldier. 2 a heavily armed soldier on horseback. *n., pl.* **men-at-arms.**

man a tee (man′ə tē′), a large sea mammal with two flippers and a flat, oval tail; sea cow. Manatees live in warm, shallow water near coasts. *n.*

hat, āge, fär; let, ēqual, tėrm; it, īce; hot, ōpen, ôrder; oil, out; cup, pùt, rüle; ch, child; ng, long; sh, she; th, thin; ŦH, then; zh, measure;

ə represents *a* in about, *e* in taken, *i* in pencil, *o* in lemon, *u* in circus.

Man ches ter (man′ches′tər), a city in W England, important in textile manufacturing. *n.*

Man chu (man′chü), 1 member of a Mongoloid people living in Manchuria, who conquered China in 1644 and ruled it until 1912. 2 their language. 3 of the Manchus, their country, or their language. 1,2 *n.,* 3 *adj.*

Man chu kuo or **Man chou kuo** (man′chü′kwō′), former Japanese state (1931-1945) in E Asia, north of China, now a part of China. *n.*

Man chur i a (man chùr′ē ə), region in NE China, including several provinces of China. *n.* —**Man chur′i an,** *adj., n.*

Man da lay (man′də lā′), city in central Burma. *n.*

man dar in (man′dər ən), 1 an official of high rank under the Chinese empire. 2 **Mandarin,** the main dialect of the Chinese language, spoken by officials and educated people. 3 a small, sweet, spicy citrus fruit with a thin, orange-colored, very loose peel and segments that separate easily. 4 tree it grows on. *n.*

man date (man′dāt), 1 an order or command, especially a legal order from a higher court or official to a lower one. 2 the expressed will of voters to their representative. 3 commission given to one nation by a group of nations to administer the government and affairs of a territory, etc. The system of mandates established after World War I was administered by the League of Nations. 4 put (a territory, etc.) under the administration of another nation. 5 a mandated territory. 1-3,5 *n.,* 4 *v.,* **man dat ed, man dat ing.**

man da to ry (man′də tôr′ē), commanded; of or containing a command. *adj.*

man di ble (man′də bəl), 1 organ in

MANDIBLE
MAXILLA
mandible
(def. 1)

adj. adjective	*n.* noun
adv. adverb	*prep.* preposition
conj. conjunction	*pron.* pronoun
interj. interjection	*v.* verb
sing. singular	*pl.* plural

insects for seizing and biting: *The ant grasped the dead fly with its mandibles.* 2 either part of a bird's beak. 3 a jaw, especially the lower jaw. *n.*

man do lin (man′də lin′ *or* man′dl-ən), a musical instrument with a pear-shaped body and four or five pairs of metal strings. It is played with a pick. *n.*

mandolin

man drake (man′drāk), herb of the same family as the nightshade. It has a very short stem and a thick, often forked root thought to resemble the human form. Mandrake roots were formerly used in medicine. *n.*

man drill (man′drəl), a large, fierce baboon of western Africa. The face of the male mandrill is marked with blue and scarlet. *n.*

mane (mān), the long, heavy hair growing on the back of or around the neck of a horse, lion, etc. *n.*

Ma net (mä nā′), Édouard, 1832-1883, French painter. *n.*

ma neu ver (mə nü′vər), 1 a planned movement of troops or warships: *Every year the army and navy hold maneuvers for practice.* 2 perform or cause troops to perform maneuvers. 3 a skillful plan or movement; clever trick: *When we refused to use his idea, he tried to force it on us by a series of maneuvers.* 4 plan skillfully; use clever tricks; scheme: *A scheming person is always maneuvering for some advantage.* 5 to force by skillful plans; get by clever tricks: *She maneuvered her lazy sister out of bed.* 6 move or manipulate skillfully: *I maneuvered the car through the heavy traffic with ease.* 1,3 *n.*, 2,4-6 *v.* Also, **manoeuvre.**

ma neu ver a bil i ty (mə nü′vər-ə bil′ə tē), quality or power of being maneuverable. *n.*

ma neu ver a ble (mə nü′vər ə bəl), that can be maneuvered. *adj.*

man ful (man′fəl), manly; brave; resolute. *adj.* —**man′ful ly,** *adv.* —**man′ful ness,** *n.*

man ga nese (mang′gə nēz′), a hard, brittle, grayish metallic element. Manganese is used chiefly in making alloys of steel. Compounds of manganese are used in fertilizers, paints, insecticides, and industrial chemicals. *n.*

mange (mānj), a skin disease of animals, marked by scabs and loss of hair. It is caused by parasitic mites. *n.*

man ger (mān′jər), box or trough in which hay or other food can be placed for horses or cows to eat. *n.*

man gi ness (mān′jē nis), mangy quality or condition. *n.*

man gle[1] (mang′gəl), 1 cut or tear roughly: *The two cats bit and clawed until both were much mangled.* 2 spoil; ruin: *The song was too difficult for the children and they mangled it badly.* *v.*, **man gled, man gling.** [from French of the 1300's *mahaignier* to maim]

man gle[2] (mang′gəl), 1 machine with rollers for pressing and smoothing sheets, towels, and other flat things after washing. 2 press or smooth in a mangle. 1 *n.*, 2 *v.*, **man gled, man gling.** [from Dutch *mangel,* from Latin *manganum,* from Greek *manganon* contrivance]

mandrill
3 ft. long

man go (mang′gō), 1 a slightly sour, juicy, oval fruit with a thick, yellowish-red rind. Mangoes are eaten ripe or are pickled for eating when green. 2 the tropical tree that it grows on. *n., pl.* **man goes** or **man gos.**

man grove (mang′grōv), a tropical tree or shrub having branches that send down many roots which look like additional trunks. Mangroves grow in swamps and along the banks of rivers. *n.*

mang y (mān′jē), 1 having the mange; caused by the mange; with the hair falling out. 2 shabby and dirty: *a mangy dog.* *adj.*, **mang i er, mang i est.**

man han dle (man′han′dl), treat roughly; pull or push about. *v.*, **man han dled, man han dling.**

Man hat tan (man hat′n), island on which the chief business section of New York City is located. It is a borough of New York City. *n.*

man hole (man′hōl′), hole through which a workman can enter a sewer, steam boiler, etc., to inspect or repair it. *n.*

man hood (man′hùd), 1 condition or time of being a man: *The boy was about to enter manhood.* 2 character or qualities of a man. 3 men as a group: *the manhood of the United States.* *n.*

man-hour (man′our′), hour of work by one man, used as a time unit in industry. *n.*

MANGER

ma ni a (mā′nē ə), 1 kind of mental disorder characterized by great excitement and sometimes violence. 2 unusual or unreasonable fondness; craze: *a mania for dancing.* *n., pl.* **ma ni as.**

ma ni ac (mā′nē ak), 1 an insane person; raving lunatic. 2 insane; raving. 1 *n.*, 2 *adj.*

ma ni a cal (mə nī′ə kəl), insane; raving. *adj.* —**ma ni′a cal ly,** *adv.*

man ic (man′ik *or* mā′nik), 1 of or like mania. 2 suffering from mania. *adj.*

man i cure (man′ə kyùr), 1 to care for (the fingernails and hands); trim, clean, and polish (the fingernails). 2 the care of the hands; trimming, cleaning, and polishing of fingernails. 3 manicurist. 1 *v.*, **man i cured, man i cur ing;** 2,3 *n.*

man i cur ist (man′ə kyùr′ist), person whose work is manicuring. *n.*

man i fest (man′ə fest), 1 apparent to the eye or to the mind; plain; clear: *His guilt was manifest.* 2 show plainly; reveal; display. 3 a list of cargo of a ship or aircraft. 4 prove; put beyond doubt. 1 *adj.*, 2,4 *v.*, 3 *n.* —**man′i fest′ly,** *adv.*

mangrove

man i fes ta tion (man′ə fə stā′shən), a showing; a making manifest; an act that shows or proves: *Entering the burning building was a manifestation of courage.* *n.*

man i fes to (man′ə fes′tō), a public declaration of intentions, purposes, or motives by an important person or group; proclamation. *n., pl.* **man i fes toes** or **man i fes tos.**

man i fold (man′ə fōld), **1** of many kinds; many and various: *manifold duties.* **2** having many parts or forms: *a music strange and manifold.* **3** doing many things at the same time. **4** pipe with several openings for connection with other pipes. The exhaust manifold on a car connects the cylinders in the engine with the exhaust pipe. **5** make many copies. **1-3** *adj.,* **4** *n.,* **5** *v.*

manifold (def. 4) of automobile engine

man i kin (man′ə kən), **1** a little man; dwarf. **2** mannequin. *n.* Also, **mannikin.**
ma nil a (mə nil′ə), **1** Manila hemp. **2** Manila paper. *n.*
Ma nil a (mə nil′ə), largest city and former capital of the Philippines. *n.*
Manila hemp, abaca.
Manila paper, a strong, brown or brownish-yellow wrapping paper.
man i oc (man′ē ok), cassava. *n.*
ma nip u late (mə nip′yə lāt), **1** handle or treat, especially with skill: *manipulate the controls of an airplane.* **2** manage by clever use of personal influence, especially unfair influence: *He manipulated other people by offering them large sums of money in return for their favors.* **3** to change for one's own purpose or advantage; treat unfairly or dishonestly: *The bookkeeper manipulated the company's accounts to conceal his theft.* *v.,* **ma nip u lat ed, ma nip u lat ing.**
ma nip u la tion (mə nip′yə lā′shən), **1** skillful handling or treatment. **2** clever use of influence. **3** a change made for one's own purpose or advantage. *n.*
ma nip u la tor (mə nip′yə lā′tər), person who manipulates. *n.*
man i to (man′ə tō), spirit worshiped by Algonquian Indians as a force of nature with supernatural powers. *n., pl.* **man i tos.** Also, **manitou.**
Man i to ba (man′ə tō′bə), **1** province in S Canada. *Capital:* Winnipeg. **2 Lake,** lake in S Manitoba. *n.*
man i tou (man′ə tü), manito. *n.*
man kind (man′kīnd′ *for 1;* man′kīnd′ *for 2),* **1** the human race; all human beings. **2** men as a group. *n.*
man like (man′līk′), **1** like a man. **2** suitable for a man. *adj.*
man li ness (man′lē nis), manly quality or behavior. *n.*
man ly (man′lē), **1** having qualities traditionally admired in a man: *a man-*

ly show of strength. **2** suitable for a man; masculine: *Boxing is a manly sport.* *adj.,* **man li er, man li est.**
man-made (man′mād′), made by man; not natural; artificial: *a man-made satellite. adj.*
Mann (man *for 1;* män *for 2),* **1 Horace,** 1796-1859, American educator. He established the first school for training teachers in the United States. **2 Thomas,** 1875-1955, German novelist. *n.*
man na (man′ə), **1** (in the Bible) the food miraculously supplied to the Israelites in the wilderness. **2** food for the soul or mind. **3** a much needed thing that is unexpectedly supplied: *Her inheritance came as manna from heaven. n.*
man ne quin (man′ə kən), **1** woman whose work is wearing new clothes to show them to customers. **2** a model or figure of a person used by tailors, artists, stores, etc. *n.* Also, **manikin, mannikin.**
man ner (man′ər), **1** way of doing, being done, or happening: *The trouble arose in this manner.* **2** way of acting or behaving: *She has a kind manner.* **3 manners,** *pl.* polite ways of behaving: *That child has poor table manners.* **4** kind or kinds: *We saw all manner of birds in the forest. n.*
by all manner of means, most certainly.
by no manner of means, not at all; under no circumstances.
in a manner of speaking, as one might say; so to speak.
man nered (man′ərd), affected; artificial; having many mannerisms: *a mannered style of writing. adj.*
man ner ism (man′ə riz′əm), **1** too much use of some manner in speaking, writing, or behaving. **2** an odd little trick; queer habit; peculiar way of acting. *n.*
man ner ly (man′ər lē), **1** having or showing good manners; polite. **2** politely. **1** *adj.,* **2** *adv.*
man ni kin (man′ə kən), **1** manikin. **2** mannequin. *n.*
man nish (man′ish), **1** characteristic of a man: *a mannish way of walking.* **2** like a man, not a woman; imitating a man: *a mannish style of dress. adj.*
ma noeu vre (mə nü′vər), maneuver. *n., v.,* **ma noeu vred, ma noeu vring.**
man-of-war (man′əv wôr′), warship of a type used in former times. *n., pl.* **men-of-war.**
ma nom e ter (mə nom′ə tər), instrument for measuring the pressure of gases or vapors. *n.*
man or (man′ər), **1** (in the Middle Ages) a feudal estate, part of which was set aside for the lord and the rest di-

hat, āge, fär; let, ēqual, tèrm;
it, īce; hot, ōpen, ôrder;
oil, out; cup, pùt, rüle; ch, child;
ng, long; sh, she; th, thin;
ŦH, then; zh, measure;

ə represents *a* in about,
e in taken, *i* in pencil,
o in lemon, *u* in circus.

vided among his peasants, who paid the owner rent in goods, services, or money. If the lord sold his manor, the peasants or serfs were sold with it. **2** a large estate. **3** the main house or mansion of an estate. *n.*
ma no ri al (mə nôr′ē əl), **1** of a manor. **2** forming a manor. *adj.*
man pow er (man′pou′ər), **1** power supplied by human physical labor. **2** strength thought of in terms of the number of men needed or available: *a country's military manpower. n.*

mansard (def. 1)

man sard (man′särd), **1** roof with two slopes on each side. **2** the story under such a roof. *n.* [from F. *Mansard,* 1598-1666, French architect]
manse (mans), a minister's house; parsonage. *n.*
man serv ant (man′sèr′vənt), a male servant. *n., pl.* **men serv ants.**
man sion (man′shən), a large house; stately residence. *n.*
man slaugh ter (man′slô′tər), **1** the killing of a human being. **2** (in law) the killing of a person unlawfully but without deliberate intent: *The charge against the prisoner was changed from murder to manslaughter. n.*
man tel (man′tl), **1** shelf above a fireplace. **2** the decorative framework around a fireplace: *a mantel of tile. n.*

manometer—Gas enters tube at left. Its pressure on liquid L is measured by height of column AB.

adj.	adjective	n.	noun
adv.	adverb	prep.	preposition
conj.	conjunction	pron.	pronoun
interj.	interjection	v.	verb
sing.	singular	pl.	plural

man tel piece (man′tl pēs′), mantel (def. 1). *n.*

man til la (man til′ə), 1 a veil or scarf, often of lace, covering the hair and falling over the shoulders. Spanish and Latin-American women sometimes wear mantillas. 2 a short mantle or cape. *n., pl.* **man til las.** [from Spanish]

mantis
2½ in. long

man tis (man′tis), insect that holds its forelegs doubled up as if praying; praying mantis. It eats other insects. *n., pl.* **man tis es, man tes** (man′tēz′).

man tle (man′tl), 1 a loose cloak without sleeves. 2 anything that covers like a mantle: *The ground had a mantle of snow.* 3 to cover with a mantle. 4 redden: *Her cheeks mantled with embarrassment.* 5 a lacelike tube around a flame that gets so hot it glows and gives light. See **lantern** for picture. 6 fold of the body wall of a mollusk that lines the shell and secretes the material which forms the shell. 7 the part of the earth beneath the crust and above the outer core. 1,2,5-7 *n.,* 3,4 *v.,* **man tled, man tling.**

Man tu a (man′chü ə), city in N Italy. Vergil was born there. *n.*

man u al (man′yü əl), 1 of the hands; done with the hands: *manual labor.* 2 a small book that helps its readers to understand and use something; handbook. A cookbook is a manual. 1 *adj.,* 2 *n.* —**man′u al ly,** *adv.*

manual training, training in work done with the hands; practice in various arts and crafts, especially in making things out of wood or metal.

man u fac ture (man′yə fak′chər), 1 make by hand or by machine. A big factory manufactures goods in large quantities by using machines and dividing the work up among many people. 2 a making of articles by hand or by machine, especially in large quantities. 3 thing manufactured. 4 make into something useful: *manufacture steel into rails.* 5 make up; invent: *The dis-*

honest lawyer manufactured evidence. 1,4,5 *v.,* **man u fac tured, man u fac tur ing;** 2,3 *n.*

man u fac tur er (man′yə fak′chər ər), person or company whose business is manufacturing; owner of a factory. *n.*

ma nure (mə nùr′ *or* mə nyùr′), 1 substance put in or on the soil to make it rich. Dung or refuse from stables is manure. 2 put manure in or on. 1 *n.,* 2 *v.,* **ma nured, ma nur ing.**

man u script (man′yə skript), book or paper written by hand or with a typewriter. Before printing was invented, all books and papers were handwritten manuscripts. *n.*

Manx (mangks), 1 of the Isle of Man, its people, or their language. 2 people of the Isle of Man. 3 their Celtic language. 1 *adj.,* 2,3 *n.*

Manx cat, kind of domestic cat with short hair and no tail.

man y (men′ē), 1 consisting of a great number; numerous: *many years ago. There are many children in the city.* 2 a great number: *Do you know many of them?* 3 many people or things: *There were many at the dance.* 1 *adj.,* **more, most;** 2,3 *n., pron.*

a good many, a fairly large number.

how many, what number of: *How many days until summer vacation?*

mantle (def. 1)

man y-sid ed (men′ē sī′did), 1 having many sides. 2 having many interests or abilities. *adj.*

Ma o ri (mä′ōr ē), 1 member of the native Polynesian people of New Zealand. 2 their language. 3 of the Maoris or their language. 1,2 *n., pl.* **Ma o ris;** 3 *adj.*

Ma o Tse-tung (mä′ō dzu′dùng′ *or* mou′ tse′tùng′), born 1893, Chinese Communist leader, chairman of the Chinese Communist Party since 1945.

map (map), 1 a drawing representing the earth's surface or part of it, usually showing countries, cities, rivers, seas, lakes, and mountains. 2 a drawing of the sky or a part of it, showing the position of the stars, etc. 3 make a map of; show on a map. 4 plan; arrange in detail: *Each Monday we map out the week's work.* 1,2 *n.,* 3,4 *v.,* **mapped, map ping.**

ma ple (mā′pəl), 1 tree grown for shade, ornament, its wood, or its sap. There are many kinds of maples, but all have dry fruits with two wings and opposite leaves without stipules. 2 its hard, light-colored wood. 3 flavor of maple sugar or maple syrup. *n.*

maple leaf, 1 leaf of the maple tree. 2 this leaf as a popular Canadian emblem.

maple sugar, sugar made from the sap of one variety of maple.

maple syrup, syrup made from the sap of one variety of maple.

mar (mär), spoil the beauty of; damage; injure; ruin: *The nails in my shoes marred the floor. Weeds mar a garden.* *v.,* **marred, mar ring.**

Mar., March.

ma ra ca (mə rä′kə), instrument consisting of seeds, pebbles, etc., enclosed in a dry gourd and shaken like a rattle. Maracas are usually played in pairs. *n., pl.* **ma ra cas.** [from Portuguese]

Mar a cai bo (mar′ə kī′bō), 1 seaport in NW Venezuela. 2 **Lake,** lake in NW Venezuela. *n.*

mar a schi no cherry (mar′ə skē′nō), cherry preserved in a sweet syrup. It is used to decorate and add flavor to drinks, desserts, etc.

Ma rat (mä rä′), **Jean Paul,** 1743-1793, leader in the French Revolution. *n.*

mar a thon (mar′ə thon), 1 a foot race of 26 miles, 385 yards, named after Marathon. 2 any long race or contest. 3 **Marathon,** plain in Greece about 25 miles northeast of Athens. After the Athenians defeated the Persians there in 490 B.C., a runner ran all the way to Athens with the news of the victory. *n.*

ma raud (mə rôd′), go about in search of plunder; make raids for booty: *The marauding pirates blocked the harbor and attacked the city.* *v.* —**ma raud′er,** *n.*

mar ble (mär′bəl), 1 a hard rock formed from limestone by heat and pressure. It may be white or colored and can be polished to a smooth gloss. Marble is used for statues and in buildings. 2 made of marble. 3 like marble; hard, cold, or unfeeling: *a marble heart.* 4 to color in imitation of the patterns in marble: *Binders marble the edges of some books.* 5 a small, usually colored ball of clay, glass, marble, etc., used in games. 6 **marbles,** *pl.* a children's game played with small, usually colored balls. Each player uses a larger marble to knock the smaller marbles out of a ring. 1,5,6 *n.,* 2,3 *adj.,* 4 *v.,* **mar bled, mar bling.**

mar cel (mär sel′), 1 series of regular waves put in the hair. 2 to wave (the hair) in a series of regular waves. 1 *n.,*

2 v., **mar celled, mar cel ling**. [from *Marcel,* a French hairdresser of the 1800's, who originated it]

march[1] (märch), 1 walk as soldiers do, in time and with steps of the same length: *The members of the band marched in the parade to the beat of the drums.* 2 act or fact of marching: *The news of the enemy's march made whole villages flee.* 3 music meant for marching. 4 distance marched: *The camp is a day's march away.* 5 a long, hard walk. 6 walk or go on steadily: *He marched to the front of the room and began his speech.* 7 cause to march or go: *The teacher marched the children out to the playground.* 8 an advance; progress: *History records the march of events.* 1,6,7 *v.,* 2-5,8 *n., pl.* **march es.** [from French of the 1500's *marcher* to march, trample, ultimately from Latin *marcus* a hammer] —**march′er,** *n.*

steal a march, gain an advantage without being noticed.

march[2] (märch), the land along the border of a country; frontier; border: *Troops guarded the far marches of the Roman Empire. n., pl.* **march es.** [from French of the 1200's *marche,* from a Germanic word]

March (märch), the third month of the year. It has 31 days. *n.*

mar chio ness (mär′shə nis), marquise. *n., pl.* **mar chio ness es.**

marimba—The pipes underneath give a rich quality to the tones.

Mar co ni (mär kō′nē), **Guglielmo,** 1874-1937, Italian inventor who perfected the wireless telegraph. *n.*

Mar co Po lo (mär′kō pō′lō), 1254?-1324?, Italian merchant who wrote about his travels in Asia.

Mar di gras (mär′dē grä′), the last day before Lent; Shrove Tuesday. It is celebrated in New Orleans and other cities with parades and festivities. [from French *mardi gras* fat (that is, meat-eating) Tuesday]

mare[1] (mer *or* mar), a female horse, donkey, etc. *n.* [Old English *mere*]

ma re[2] (mär′ē), 1 any of certain dark regions on the surface of the moon. 2 a similar dark region on any planet. *n., pl.* **ma ri a** (mär′ē ə). [from Latin *mare* sea]

mar gar in (mär′jər ən), margarine. *n.*

mar gar ine (mär′jər ən *or* mär′jə rēn′), a substitute for butter, usually made from cottonseed oil, soybean oil, or other vegetable oils; oleomargarine: *We like margarine on bread. n.*

mar gin (mär′jən), 1 an edge or border: *the margin of a lake.* 2 the blank space around the writing or printing on a page: *Do not write in the margin.* 3 an extra amount; amount beyond what is necessary; difference: *We allow a margin of 15 minutes in catching a train. n.*

mar gin al (mär′jə nəl), 1 written or printed in a margin. 2 of, in, or on a margin. 3 barely capable of producing goods, crops, etc., at a profitable rate: *marginal land, a marginal farmer. adj.* —**mar′gin al ly,** *adv.*

mar gue rite (mär′gə rēt′), 1 kind of daisy with white petals and a yellow center. 2 any of several chrysanthemums with daisylike flowers. *n.*

Mar i an a Islands (mar′ē an′ə), group of 15 small islands in the Pacific, east of the Philippines. The largest island, Guam, belongs to the United States.

Ma rie An toi nette (mə rē′ an′twə net′), 1755-1793, wife of King Louis XVI of France. She was beheaded during the French Revolution.

mar i gold (mar′ə gōld), 1 plant of the same family as the aster, with yellow, orange, brownish, or red flowers. 2 its flower. *n.*

mar i jua na *or* **mar i hua na** (mar′ə wä′nə), 1 kind of hemp. 2 its dried leaves and flowers, used for their intoxicating effect. *n.* [from Mexican Spanish *marihuana*]

ma rim ba (mə rim′bə), a musical instrument somewhat like a xylophone. *n., pl.* **ma rim bas.**

ma ri na (mə rē′nə), a dock where moorings and supplies are available for small boats. *n., pl.* **ma ri nas.**

mar i nade (mar′ə nād′), a spiced vinegar or wine used to pickle meat or fish. *n.*

mar i nate (mar′ə nāt), 1 soak in brine or marinade. 2 soak in oil and vinegar. *v.,* **mar i nat ed, mar i nat ing.**

ma rine (mə rēn′), 1 of the sea; found in the sea; produced by the sea: *Seals and whales are marine animals.* 2 of shipping; of the navy; for use at sea: *marine law, marine power, marine supplies.* 3 shipping; fleet: *our merchant marine.* 4 soldier formerly serving only at sea, now also participating in action on land and in the air. 5 Also, **Marine.** person serving in the Marine Corps. 1,2 *adj.,* 3-5 *n.*

Marine Corps, a branch of the armed forces of the United States. Its members are trained especially for

hat, āge, fär; let, ēqual, tėrm;
it, īce; hot, ōpen, ôrder;
oil, out; cup, pùt, rüle; ch, child;
ng, long; sh, she; th, thin;
ŦH, then; zh, measure;

ə represents *a* in about,
e in taken, *i* in pencil,
o in lemon, *u* in circus.

landing operations. The Marine Corps has its own sea, air, and land units.

mar i ner (mar′ə nər), one who navigates a ship; sailor; seaman. *n.*

mar i o nette (mar′ē ə net′), doll or puppet moved by strings or by the hands, often on a little stage. *n.*

marionette

mar i tal (mar′ə təl), of marriage; having to do with marriage: *A man and woman take marital vows when they marry. adj.* —**mar′i tal ly,** *adv.*

mar i time (mar′ə tīm), 1 of the sea; having to do with shipping and sailing: *Ships and sailors are governed by maritime law.* 2 on or near the sea: *Boston is a maritime city.* 3 living near the sea: *Many maritime peoples are fishermen. adj.*

Maritime Provinces, provinces of Canada along the Atlantic coast; New Brunswick, Newfoundland, Nova Scotia, and Prince Edward Island.

mar jor am (mär′jər əm), a fragrant herb of the same family as mint, used as flavoring in cooking. *n.*

mark[1] (märk), 1 trace or impression made by some object on another. A line, dot, spot, stain, or scar is a mark. 2 line or dot to show position: *This mark shows how far you jumped.* 3 the line where a race starts: *On the mark; get set; go.* 4 something that shows what or whose a thing is; sign; indication: *Courtesy is a mark of good breeding.* 5 a written or printed stroke or sign: *punctuation marks. She took up her pen and made a few marks on the paper.* 6 letter or number to show how well one has done; grade or rating: *My mark in arithmetic was B.* 7 give grades to; rate: *The teacher marked our exami-*

adj. adjective	*n.* noun
adv. adverb	*prep.* preposition
conj. conjunction	*pron.* pronoun
interj. interjection	*v.* verb
sing. singular	*pl.* plural

nation papers. **8** a cross or other sign made by a person who cannot write, instead of signing his name: *Make your mark here.* **9** make a mark on or put one's name on to show whose a thing is. **10** make a mark on by stamping, cutting, writing, etc.: *Be careful not to mark the table.* **11** put in a pin, make a line, etc., to show where a place is: *Mark all the large cities on this map.* **12** show clearly; manifest: *A tall pine marks the beginning of the trail. A frown marked her displeasure.* **13** something to be aimed at; target; goal: *Standing there, the lion was an easy mark.* **14** what is usual, proper, or expected; standard: *A tired person does not feel up to the mark.* **15** influence; impression: *The Industrial Revolution left its mark on society.* **16** distinguish; set off: *Many important inventions mark the last 150 years.* **17** give attention to; notice; observe; see: *Mark how carefully he moves. Mark my words; their plan will fail.* **18** record (the score of a game). **19** a tag with a mark on it: *Remove the price mark from your new suit.* **20** put a price mark on; tag. 1-6,8,13-15,19 *n.*, 7,9-12,16-18,20 *v.* [Old English *mearc* boundary, limit]

beside the mark, **1** not hitting the thing aimed at. **2** not to the point; not relevant.

hit the mark, **1** succeed in doing what one tried to do. **2** be exactly right.

make one's mark, become well known; succeed.

mark down, **1** write down; note down. **2** mark for sale at a lower price.

mark off or **mark out,** make lines, etc., to show the position of or to separate: *We marked out a tennis court. The hedge marks off one yard from another.*

mark out for, set aside for; select for: *She seemed marked out for success.*

mark up, **1** deface or disfigure: *Don't mark up the desks.* **2** mark for sale at a higher price.

miss the mark, **1** fail to do what one tried to do. **2** be not exactly right.

of mark, important or famous: *That doctor is a man of mark.*

mark² (märk), a German unit of money. The mark of West Germany is worth about 42 cents. *n.* [from German *Mark*]

Mark (märk), **1** (in the Bible) one of Christ's twelve apostles. He was one of the four Evangelists and a fellow worker with Paul and Peter. **2** the second book of the New Testament. It tells the story of the life of Christ. *n.*

Mark An to ny (märk′ an′tə nē). See **Antony.**

mark down (märk′doun′), **1** a decrease in the price of an article. **2** the amount of this decrease. *n.*

marked (märkt), **1** having a mark or marks. **2** very noticeable; very plain; easily recognized: *There are marked differences between apples and oranges.* **3** distinguished or singled out as if by a mark: *Even as a youth he was marked for success. adj.*

mark ed ly (mär′kid lē), in a marked manner or degree; noticeably; plainly. *adv.*

mark er (mär′kər), **1** person or thing that marks, especially one who keeps the score in a game. **2** bookmark. *n.*

mar ket (mär′kit), **1** a meeting of people for buying and selling. **2** the people at such a meeting: *Excitement stirred the market.* **3** an open space or covered building where food, cattle, etc., are shown for sale. **4** buy or sell in a market. **5** sell: *The farmers can't market all of their corn.* **6** a store for the sale of food: *a meat market.* **7** chance to sell or buy: *There is always a market for wheat.* **8** the demand (for something); price offered: *a rising market for automobiles. The drought created a high market for corn.* **9** center of trade; region in which goods may be sold: *South America is a market for American automobiles.* 1-3,6-9 *n.*, 4,5 *v.* —**mar′ket er,** *n.*

be in the market for, be a possible buyer of.

marmoset
about 16 in. long
with tail

mar ket a bil i ty (mär′kə tə bil′ə tē), quality of being marketable. *n.*

mar ket a ble (mär′kə tə bəl), that can be sold; salable. *adj.*

mar ket place (mär′kət plās′), place where a market is held. *n.*

mark ing (mär′king), **1** mark or marks. **2** arrangement of marks. *n.*

marks man (märks′mən), **1** person who shoots well: *He is noted as a marksman.* **2** person who shoots: *a poor marksman. n., pl.* **marks men.**

marks man ship (märks′mən ship), skill in shooting. *n.*

Mark Twain (märk′ twān′). See **Twain.**

mark up (märk′up′), **1** an increase in the price of an article. **2** the amount of this increase. **3** percentage or amount added to the cost of an article to determine the selling price. *n.*

marl (märl), a loose, crumbly soil containing clay and calcium carbonate, used as a fertilizer. *n.*

Marl bor ough (märl′bėr′ō), **Duke of,** 1650-1722, John Churchill, English general who defeated the French in 1704. *n.*

mar lin (mär′lən), a large sea fish related to the swordfish and the sailfish. *n.*

mar line (mär′lən), a small cord which sailors wind around the ends of a rope to keep it from fraying. *n.*

MARLINESPIKE

mar line spike or **mar lin spike** (mär′lən spīk′), a pointed iron implement used by sailors to separate strands of rope in splicing, etc. *n.*

Mar lowe (mär′lō), **Christopher,** 1564-1593, English dramatist and poet. *n.*

mar ma lade (mär′mə lād), a preserve similar to jam, made of oranges or of other fruit. The peel is usually sliced up and boiled with the fruit. *n.*

Mar mar a (mär′mər ə), **Sea of,** a small sea between Europe and Asia Minor. It is connected with the Aegean Sea by the Dardanelles and with the Black Sea by the Bosporus. See **Dardanelles** for map. *n.*

mar mo set (mär′mə set), a very small monkey with soft, thick fur, that lives in South and Central America. *n.*

mar mot (mär′mət), rodent related to the squirrels, having a thick body and a bushy tail. Woodchucks are marmots. *n.*

Marne (märn), river flowing from NE France into the Seine. *n.*

ma roon¹ (mə rün′), **1** very dark brownish-red. **2** a very dark brownish red. 1 *adj.*, 2 *n.* [from French of the 1500's *marron*, from Italian *marrone* chestnut]

ma roon² (mə rün′), **1** put (a person) ashore in a desolate place and leave him: *Pirates used to maroon people on desert islands.* **2** leave in a lonely, helpless position: *During the storm we were marooned in a cabin miles from town.* v. [from French *marron* an escaped slave, perhaps from American Spanish *cimarrón* wild, hiding in the bushes]

marque (märk), official permission from a government to capture enemy merchant ships. Governments used to issue letters of marque to individuals authorizing them to plunder an enemy's shipping. *n.*

mar quee (mär kē′), a rooflike shelter over an entrance, especially of a theater or hotel. Theater marquees usually display the names of shows being featured. *n.*

Mar que sas Islands (mär kā′səs), group of eleven islands in the S Pacific.

mar quess (mär′kwis), marquis (a term used in Great Britain). *n., pl.* **mar quess es.**

Mar quette (mär ket′), **Father,** 1637-1675, French Jesuit missionary who explored part of the Mississippi River and its valley. *n.*

mar quis (mär′kwis *or* mär kē′), nobleman ranking below a duke and above an earl or count. *n., pl.* **mar quis es, mar quis** (mär kē′). Also, **marquess.**

mar quise (mär kēz′), 1 wife or widow of a marquis. 2 woman equal in rank to a marquis. *n.*

mar qui sette (mär′kə zet′), a very thin silk, cotton, or synthetic fabric, often used for window draperies. *n.*

mar riage (mar′ij), 1 a living together as husband and wife; married life: *We wished the bride and groom a happy marriage.* 2 the ceremony of being married; a marriage; wedding. 3 a close union: *The marriage of words and melody in that song was unusually effective. n.*

mar riage a ble (mar′i jə bəl), fit for marriage; old enough to marry: *of marriageable age. adj.*

mar ried (mar′ēd), 1 living together as husband and wife: *a married couple.* 2 having a husband or wife: *a married man.* 3 of marriage; of husbands and wives: *Married life has many duties. adj.*

mar row (mar′ō), 1 the soft tissue that fills the hollow central part of most bones. 2 the inmost or important part: *The icy wind chilled me to the marrow. n.*

mar row bone (mar′ō bōn′), bone containing marrow which can be eaten. *n.*

mar ry[1] (mar′ē), 1 join as husband and wife: *The minister married them.* 2 take as husband or wife: *She plans to marry him.* 3 become married; take a husband or wife: *She married late in life.* 4 give in marriage: *They have married off all of their children.* 5 bring together

in any close union. *v.,* **mar ried, mar ry ing.** [from French of the 1200's *marier,* from Latin *maritare,* from *maritus* husband]

mar ry[2] (mar′ē), OLD USE. exclamation showing surprise, indignation, etc. *interj.* [from (the Virgin) *Mary*]

marquee of a theater

Mars (märz), 1 (in Roman myths) the god of war. The Greeks called him Ares. 2 the planet next beyond the earth. It is the seventh largest planet in the solar system and the fourth in distance from the sun. *n.*

Mar seil laise (mär′sə lāz′), the French national anthem, written in 1792 during the French Revolution. *n.*

Mar seilles (mär sā′ *or* mär sālz′), seaport city in SE France, on the Mediterranean. *n.*

marsh (märsh), low land covered at times by water; soft, wet land; swamp; fen. *n., pl.* **marsh es.**

mar shal (mär′shəl), 1 officer of various kinds, especially a police officer. A United States marshal is an officer of a federal court whose duties are like those of a sheriff. 2 chief of police or head of the fire department in some cities. 3 a high officer in an army. A Marshal of France is a general of the highest rank in the French Army. 4 person who arranges the order of march in a parade. 5 arrange in proper order: *He took great care in marshaling his facts for the debate.* 6 person in charge of events or ceremonies. 7 conduct with ceremony: *The foreign visitor was marshaled into the presence of the king.* 1-4,6 *n.,* 5,7 *v.*

Mar shall (mär′shəl), 1 **George Catlett,** 1880-1959, American general and statesman, chief of staff of the United States Army in World War II. 2 **John,** 1755-1835, chief justice of the United States Supreme Court from 1801 to 1835. *n.*

Marshall Islands, group of islands in the N Pacific, near the equator, administered by the United States.

marsh gas, methane.

marsh land (märsh′land′), marshy land. *n.*

marsh mal low (märsh′mal′ō *or* märsh′mel′ō), a soft, white, spongy candy, covered with powdered sugar. *n.*

marsh mallow, kind of mallow with

hat, āge, fär; let, ēqual, tėrm; it, īce; hot, ōpen, ôrder; oil, out; cup, pùt, rüle; ch, child; ng, long; sh, she; th, thin; ŦH, then; zh, measure;

ə represents *a* in about, *e* in taken, *i* in pencil, *o* in lemon, *u* in circus.

pink flowers that grows in marshy places.

marsh marigold, plant with bright yellow flowers that grows in moist meadows and swamps; cowslip.

marsh y (mär′shē), soft and wet like a marsh: *a marshy field. adj.,* **marsh i er, marsh i est.**

mar su pi al (mär sü′pē əl), 1 mammal that carries its young in a pouch. Kangaroos and opossums are marsupials. 2 having a pouch for carrying the young. 1 *n.,* 2 *adj.*

mart (märt), center of trade; market: *New York and London are two great marts of the world. n.*

marten (def. 1)—2½ ft. long with tail

mar ten (märt′n), 1 a slender, carnivorous mammal like a weasel, but larger, valued for its fur. 2 its fur. *n., pl.* **mar tens** *or* **mar ten.**

Mar tha (mär′thə), (in the Bible) the sister of Lazarus and Mary. *n.*

Martha's Vineyard, island south of Cape Cod. It is part of Massachusetts.

mar tial (mär′shəl), 1 of war; suitable for war: *martial music.* 2 given to fighting; warlike: *a martial nation. adj.* —**mar′tial ly,** *adv.*

martial law, rule by the army in a time of trouble or of war instead of by the ordinary civil authorities.

Mar tian (mär′shən), 1 of the planet Mars. 2 a supposed inhabitant of the planet Mars. 1 *adj.,* 2 *n.*

mar tin (märt′n), any of several swallows with long, pointed wings and a forked tail. The **purple martin** is a large, blue and black martin of North America. *n.*

mar ti net (märt′n et′), person who upholds and enforces very strict discipline on those under him. *n.* [from General J. *Martinet,* French general of the 1600's]

mar tin gale (märt′n gāl), strap of a horse's harness that prevents the horse

adj.	adjective	*n.*	noun
adv.	adverb	*prep.*	preposition
conj.	conjunction	*pron.*	pronoun
interj.	interjection	*v.*	verb
sing.	singular	*pl.*	plural

GIRTH MARTINGALE

from rising on its hind legs or throwing back its head. *n.*

Mar ti nique (märt/n ēk/), French island in the West Indies. *n.*

mar tyr (mär/tər), 1 person who is put to death or made to suffer greatly because of his religion or other beliefs. Many of the early Christians were martyrs. 2 put (a person) to death or torture because of his religion or other beliefs. 3 person who suffers greatly. 4 cause to suffer greatly; torture. 1,3 *n.*, 2,4 *v.*

mar tyr dom (mär/tər dəm), 1 death or suffering of a martyr. 2 great suffering; torment. *n.*

mar vel (mär/vəl), 1 something wonderful; astonishing thing: *The airplane is one of the marvels of science.* 2 be filled with wonder; be astonished: *I marvel at your boldness. She marveled at the beautiful sunset.* 1 *n.*, 2 *v.*

mar vel ous or **mar vel lous** (mär/və ləs), 1 causing wonder; extraordinary. 2 improbable: *Children like tales of marvelous things, like that of Aladdin and his lamp.* 3 INFORMAL. excellent; splendid; fine: *a marvelous time. adj.* —**mar/vel ous ly, mar/vel lous ly,** *adv.* —**mar/vel ous ness, mar/vel lous ness,** *n.*

Marx (märks), **Karl,** 1818-1883, German writer on economics and advocate of socialism. *n.*

Marx ism (märk/siz/əm), theories of Karl Marx. *n.*

Marx ist (märk/sist), 1 of Marx or his theories. 2 follower of Marx; believer in his theories. 1 *adj.*, 2 *n.*

Mar y (mer/ē or mar/ē), in the Bible: 1 the mother of Jesus. 2 the sister of Lazarus and Martha. *n.*

Mar y land (mer/ə lənd), one of the southeastern states of the United States. *Capital:* Annapolis. *n.*

Mary Mag da lene (mag/də lēn/), (in the Bible) a woman from whom Jesus cast out seven devils. She is com-

monly supposed to be the repentant sinner forgiven by Jesus.

Mary, Queen of Scots, 1542-1587, queen of Scotland from 1542 to 1567. She was beheaded by order of her cousin, Queen Elizabeth I.

mas car a (ma skar/ə), preparation used for coloring the eyelashes. *n.*

mas cot (mas/kot), animal, person, or thing supposed to bring good luck. *n.*

mas cu line (mas/kyə lin), 1 of men or boys. 2 like a man; manly. 3 of or belonging to the male sex. 4 (in grammar) of the gender to which nouns and adjectives referring to males belong. *Actor* and *tiger* are the masculine nouns for *actress* and *tigress. adj.*

mas cu lin i ty (mas/kyə lin/ə tē), masculine quality or condition. *n.*

ma ser (mā/zər), device which amplifies or generates electromagnetic waves, especially microwaves, with great stability and accuracy. Masers are used in long-distance radar and radio astronomy. *n.* [formed from *m(icrowave) a(mplification by) s(timulated) e(mission of) r(adiation)*]

mash (mash), 1 a soft mixture; soft mass. 2 beat into a soft mass; crush to a uniform mass: *I'll mash the potatoes.* 3 a warm mixture of bran or meal and water for horses and other animals. 4 crushed malt or meal soaked in hot water for making beer. 5 mix (crushed malt or meal) with hot water in brewing. 1,3,4 *n., pl.* **mash es;** 2,5 *v.* —**mash/er,** *n.*

mask (mask), 1 a covering to hide or protect the face: *The burglar wore a mask.* 2 cover (the face) with a mask. 3 a false face worn for amusement. 4 a masked person. 5 a clay, wax, or plaster likeness of a person's face. 6 a disguise: *She hid her dislike under a mask of friendship.* 7 hide or disguise: *A smile masked his disappointment.* 1,3-6 *n.,* 2,7 *v.* —**mask/er,** *n.*

masked ball, dance at which masks are worn.

masking tape, a gummed tape used to hold things in place or protect surfaces not to be painted, sprayed, treated, etc.

ma son (mā/sn), 1 man whose work is building with stone, brick, or similar materials. 2 **Mason,** Freemason. *n.*

Ma son-Dix on line (mā/sn dik/sən), boundary between Pennsylvania and Maryland, formerly thought of as separating the North and the South of the United States.

ma son ic or **Ma son ic** (mə son/ik), of Masons, or the society of Freemasons. *adj.*

ma son ry (mā/sn rē), 1 wall, foundation, or part of a building built by a mason; stonework or brickwork. 2 the

trade or skill of a mason. *n., pl.* **ma son ries.**

masque (mask), 1 an amateur dramatic entertainment in which fine costumes, scenery, music, and dancing are more important than the story. Masques were much given in England in the 1500's and 1600's, at court and at the homes of nobles. 2 masked ball; masquerade. *n.*

mas que rade (mas/kə rād/), 1 disguise oneself; go about under false pretenses: *The king masqueraded as a beggar to find out if his people really liked him.* 2 party or dance at which masks and fancy costumes are worn. 3 the costume and mask worn at such a party or dance. 4 take part in a masquerade. 5 false pretense; disguise. 1,4 *v.*, **mas que rad ed, mas que rad ing;** 2,3,5 *n.* **mas que rad er** (mas/kə rā/dər), person who masquerades. *n.*

mass[1] (mas), 1 a lump: *a mass of dough.* 2 a large quantity together: *a mass of treasure.* 3 form or collect into a mass; assemble: *It would look better to mass the peonies behind the roses than to mix them.* 4 majority; greater part: *The great mass of the population wanted peace.* 5 **the masses,** the common people; the working classes; the lower classes of society. 6 of or by many people: *a mass protest.* 7 on a large scale: *mass buying.* 8 bulk or size: *the sheer mass of an iceberg.* 9 the quantity of matter a body contains; the property of a physical body which gives it inertia: *The mass of a piece of lead is not changed by melting it.* 1,2,4,5,8,9 *n., pl.* **mass es;** 3 *v.,* 6,7 *adj.* [from French of the 1300's *masse,* from Latin *massa* kneaded dough, lump, from Greek *maza* barley bread]

in the mass, as a whole; without distinguishing parts or individuals.

Mass or **mass**[2] (mas), 1 the central service of worship in the Roman Catholic Church and in some other churches; Holy Eucharist as a sacrifice. The ritual of the Mass consists of various prayers and ceremonies. 2 music written for certain parts of it. *n., pl.* **Mass es** or **mass es.** [Old English *mæsse,* from Latin *missa,* from *mittere* send away]

Mass., Massachusetts.

Mas sa chu setts (mas/ə chü/sits), one of the northeastern states of the United States. *Capital:* Boston. *n.*

mas sa cre (mas/ə kər), 1 a wholesale, pitiless slaughter of people or animals. 2 kill (many people or animals) needlessly or cruelly; slaughter in large numbers. 1 *n.,* 2 *v.,* **mas sa cred, mas sa cring.**

mas sage (mə säzh/), 1 a rubbing and kneading of the muscles and joints to make them work better and to increase the circulation of blood: *A thorough massage feels good when you are tired.* 2 give a massage to: *Let me massage your back for you.* 1 *n.,* 2 *v.,* **mas saged, mas sag ing.**

Mas sa soit (mas′ə soit), 1580?-1661, American Indian chief who was friendly to the Pilgrims. *n.*

mas seur (mə sėr′), man whose work is massaging people. *n.*

mas sive (mas′iv), 1 big and heavy; large and solid; bulky: *a massive wrestler.* 2 giving the impression of being large and broad: *a massive forehead.* *adj.* —**mas′sive ly,** *adv.* —**mas′sive ness,** *n.*

mass meeting, a large assembly to hear or discuss some matter of common interest: *The school held a mass meeting to plan for a field day.*

mass production, the making of goods in large quantities, especially by machinery.

mass y (mas′ē), massive. *adj.,* **mass i er, mass i est.**

mast
(def. 1)

mast (mast), 1 a long pole of wood or metal set upright on a ship to support the sails and rigging. 2 any tall, upright pole: *the mast of a derrick.* *n.*

before the mast, serving as a common sailor. Such sailors used to sleep in the forward part of the ship.

mas ter (mas′tər), 1 person who has power or authority over others, such as the head of a household, a school, a ship, etc.; the one in control; the owner, employer, or director. 2 a male teacher, especially in private schools: *The master taught his pupils how to read.* 3 title of respect for a boy: *First prize goes to Master Henry Adams.* 4 an expert, such as a great artist or skilled workman; person who knows all there is to know about a subject. 5 picture or painting by a great artist: *an old master.* 6 being master of; of a master; by a master. 7 main; controlling: *a master plan, a master switch.* 8 become master of; conquer; control: *Learn to master your temper.* 9 become expert in; become skillful at; learn: *She has mastered algebra.* 10 person who has taken a degree above bachelor and below

doctor at a college or university. 1-5,10 *n.,* 6,7 *adj.,* 8,9 *v.*

mas ter ful (mas′tər fəl), 1 fond of power or authority; domineering. 2 expert or skillful; masterly: *a masterful performance.* *adj.* —**mas′ter ful ly,** *adv.*

mas ter ly (mas′tər lē), 1 very skillful; expert: *a masterly argument, a masterly painter.* 2 in an expert or skillful way. 1 *adj.,* 2 *adv.*

mas ter mind (mas′tər mīnd′), 1 person who plans and supervises a scheme or operation, usually behind the scenes. 2 devise and conduct (a plan of action), usually behind the scenes. 1 *n.,* 2 *v.*

master of ceremonies, person in charge of a ceremony or entertainment. He usually welcomes guests and introduces speakers or performers.

mas ter piece (mas′tər pēs′), 1 anything done or made with wonderful skill; perfect piece of art or workmanship. 2 a person's greatest piece of work. *n.*

mas ter work (mas′tər wėrk′), masterpiece. *n.*

mas ter y (mas′tər ē), 1 power such as a master has; rule; control. 2 the upper hand; victory: *The two teams vied for mastery.* 3 a very great skill or knowledge: *The teacher had a mastery of the subject.* *n., pl.* **mas ter ies.**

mast head (mast′hed′), 1 top of a ship's mast. A crow's-nest near the masthead of the lower mast is used as a lookout. 2 the part of a newspaper or magazine that gives the title, owner, address, rates, etc. *n.*

mas tic (mas′tik), 1 a yellowish resin obtained from the bark of a small Mediterranean evergreen tree. It is used in making varnish, chewing gum, and incense, and as an astringent. 2 the tree it comes from. *n.*

mas ti cate (mas′tə kāt), chew. *v.,* **mas ti cat ed, mas ti cat ing.**

mas ti ca tion (mas′tə kā′shən), act of chewing. *n.*

mas tiff (mas′tif), a large, strong dog with a short, thick coat and drooping ears. *n.*

mas to don (mas′tə don), any of a large group of extinct animals much like mammoths and present-day elephants. *n.*

mas toid (mas′toid), projection of bone behind the ear. *n.*

mat[1] (mat), 1 piece of coarse fabric made of woven rushes, fiber, straw, rope, etc., used for floor covering, for wiping mud from the shoes, etc. A mat is like a small rug. 2 piece of material to put under a dish, vase, lamp, etc. A mat is put under a hot dish when it is brought to the table. 3 cover with mats. 4 anything growing thickly packed or

hat, āge, fär; let, ēqual, tėrm;
it, īce; hot, ōpen, ôrder;
oil, out; cup, pùt, rüle; ch, child;
ng, long; sh, she; th, thin;
ᵺ, then; zh, measure;

ə represents *a* in about,
e in taken, *i* in pencil,
o in lemon, *u* in circus.

tangled together: *a mat of weeds.* 5 pack or tangle together like a mat: *The swimmer's wet hair was matted. The fur collar mats when it gets wet.* 6 a large, thick pad covering part of a floor to protect wrestlers or gymnasts. 1,2,4,6 *n.,* 3,5 *v.,* **mat ted, mat ting.** [Old English *matt, meatt,* from Latin *matta*]

mat[2] (mat), border or background for a picture; used as a frame or placed between the picture and its frame. *n.* [from French *mat* (originally) dull, dead]

mastheads (def. 1)

mat a dor (mat′ə dôr), the chief performer in a bullfight. He kills the bull with his sword. *n.* [from Spanish *matador* killer]

matador

match[1] (mach), 1 a short, slender piece of wood, pasteboard, etc., tipped with a mixture that takes fire when rubbed on a rough or specially prepared surface. 2 a wick or cord prepared to burn at a uniform rate, for firing guns and cannon. *n., pl.* **match es.** [from French of the 1500's *meiche,* probably ultimately from Greek *myxa* lamp wick]

match[2] (mach), 1 person or thing equal

523

adj. adjective	*n.* noun
adv. adverb	*prep.* preposition
conj. conjunction	*pron.* pronoun
interj. interjection	*v.* verb
sing. singular	*pl.* plural

to another or much like another; an equal: *A boy is not a match for a man.* 2 be equal to in a contest: *No one could match the skill of the unknown archer.* 3 two persons or things that are alike or go well together: *Those two horses make a good match.* 4 be alike; go well together: *The rugs and the wallpaper match.* 5 find the equal of or one exactly like: *match a vase so as to have a pair.* 6 make like; fit together. 7 game; contest: *a tennis match.* 8 try (one's skill, strength, etc.) against; oppose: *He matched his strength against his brother's.* 9 marriage. 10 arrange a match for; marry. 11 person considered as a possible husband or wife. 1,3,7,9,11 *n.,* *pl.* **match es;** 2,4-6,8,10 *v.* [Old English *mæcca,* from *(ge)mæcca* companion] —**match′er,** *n.*

match book (mach′bŭk′), a folder of safety matches, especially a folder of two rows of safety matches, with a surface for striking at the bottom. *n.*

match less (mach′lis), so great or wonderful that it cannot be equaled: *Daniel Boone had matchless courage.* *adj.* —**match′less ly,** *adv.*

match lock (mach′lok′), 1 an old form of musket fired by lighting the charge of powder with a wick or cord. 2 gunlock on such a gun. *n.*

match mak er (mach′mā′kər), 1 person who arranges, or tries to arrange, marriages for others. 2 person who arranges contests, prize fights, races, etc. *n.*

mate (māt), 1 one of a pair: *Where is the mate to this glove?* 2 join in a pair: *Birds mate in the spring.* 3 husband or wife. 4 marry. 5 officer of a ship ranking next below the captain. 6 assistant: *cook's mate.* 7 a petty officer who assists a warrant officer in the United States Navy. 8 companion or fellow worker: *Hand me a hammer, mate.* 1,3,5-8 *n.,* 2,4 *v.,* **mat ed, mat ing.**

ma té (mä′tā), kind of tea made from the dried leaves and twigs of a South American holly. Maté is a popular drink in Argentina and Uruguay. *n.* [from American Spanish *mate*]

ma ter i al (mə tir′ē əl), 1 what a thing is made from or done with: *dress material, building materials, writing materi-*

als, *the material of which history is made.* 2 of matter or things; physical: *the material world.* 3 of the body: *Food and shelter are material comforts.* 4 leaving out or forgetting the spiritual side of things; worldly: *a material point of view.* 5 that matters; important: *Hard work was a material factor in his success.* 1 *n.,* 2-5 *adj.*

ma ter i al ism (mə tir′ē ə liz′əm), 1 belief that reality is made up of material things only and not of ideas. 2 tendency to care too much for the things of this world and neglect spiritual needs. *n.*

ma ter i al ist (mə tir′ē ə list), 1 believer in materialism. 2 person who cares too much for the things of this world and neglects spiritual needs. *n.*

ma ter i al is tic (mə tir′ē ə lis′tik), of materialism or materialists. *adj.* —**ma ter′i al is′ti cal ly,** *adv.*

ma ter i al i za tion (mə tir′ē ə lə zā′shən), a materializing or a being materialized. *n.*

ma ter i al ize (mə tir′ē ə līz), 1 become an actual fact; be realized: *Our plans for the party did not materialize.* 2 give material form to: *The inventor materialized his ideas by building a model.* 3 appear or cause to appear in material or bodily form: *A spirit materialized from the smoke of the magician's fire.* *v.,* **ma ter i al ized, ma ter i al iz ing.**

ma ter i al ly (mə tir′ē ə lē), 1 with regard to material things; physically: *He improved materially and spiritually.* 2 considerably; greatly: *The tide helped the progress of the boat materially.* *adv.*

ma ter i el or **ma tér i el** (mə tir′ē el′), everything used by an army, business, undertaking, etc.; equipment. *n.* [from French *matériel* material]

ma ter nal (mə tèr′nl), 1 of or like a mother; motherly: *maternal kindness.* 2 related on the mother's side of the family: *Everyone has two maternal grandparents and two paternal grandparents.* 3 received or inherited from one's mother: *His blue eyes were a maternal inheritance.* *adj.* —**ma ter′nal ly,** *adv.*

ma ter ni ty (mə tèr′nə tē), 1 motherhood; being a mother. 2 motherliness; qualities of a mother. 3 for a woman soon to have a baby: *maternity clothes.* 1,2 *n.,* 3 *adj.*

math (math), INFORMAL. mathematics. *n.*

math e mat i cal (math′ə mat′ə kəl), 1 of mathematics; having to do with mathematics: *Mathematical problems are not always easy.* 2 exact; accurate: *mathematical measurements.* *adj.*

math e mat i cal ly (math′ə mat′ik lē), 1 according to mathematics. 2 exactly; accurately. *adv.*

math e ma ti cian (math′ə mə tish′ən), an expert in mathematics. *n.*

math e mat ics (math′ə mat′iks), science dealing with the measurement, properties, and relationships of quantities, as expressed in numbers or symbols. Mathematics includes arithmetic, algebra, geometry, calculus, etc. *n.*

mat i nee (mat′n ā′), a dramatic or musical performance held in the afternoon. *n.*

mat i née (mat′n ā′), matinee. *n., pl.* **mat i nées.** [from French *matinée,* from French before 1400 *matin* morning (that is, daytime)]

mat ins (mat′nz), 1 a church service held at dawn or in the morning. 2 a morning song. *n.pl.*

Ma tisse (mä tēs′), **Henri,** 1869-1954, French painter. *n.*

ma tri arch (mā′trē ärk), 1 mother who is the ruler of a family or tribe. 2 a venerable old woman. *n.*

ma tri ar chal (mā′trē är′kəl), 1 of a matriarch. 2 suitable for a matriarch. *adj.*

ma tri ces (mā′trə sēz′ or mat′rə sēz′), a plural of **matrix.** *n.*

ma tric u late (mə trik′yə lāt), enroll as a student; admit to membership and privileges in a college or university by enrolling. *v.,* **ma tric u lat ed, ma tric u lat ing.**

ma tric u la tion (mə trik′yə lā′shən), a matriculating; enrollment as a student or candidate for a degree. *n.*

mat ri mo ni al (mat′rə mō′nē əl), of or having to do with marriage. *adj.*

mat ri mo ny (mat′rə mō′nē), marriage. *n., pl.* **mat ri mo nies.**

ma trix (mā′triks or mat′riks), that which gives origin or form to something enclosed within it. A mold for a casting or the rock in which gems are embedded is called a matrix. *n., pl.* **ma tri ces** or **ma trix es.**

ma tron (mā′trən), 1 wife or widow, especially an older married woman. 2 woman who manages the household matters of a school, hospital, dormitory, or other institution. A police matron has charge of the women in a jail. *n.*

ma tron ly (mā′trən lē), like a matron; suitable for a matron; dignified. *adj.*

mat ted (mat′id), 1 formed into a mat; roughly tangled: *a dog's matted hair.* 2 covered with mats or matting. *adj.*

mat ter (mat′ər), 1 what things are made of; material; substance. Matter occupies space, has weight, and can exist as a solid, liquid, or gas. Animals and plants are organic matter; minerals and water are inorganic matter. 2 the substance of the material world; the opposite of mind or spirit. 3 affair:

business matters, *a matter of life and death.* 4 what is said or written, thought of apart from the way in which it appears: *There was very little matter of interest in his speech.* 5 reason or cause; grounds; basis: *The accident was your fault; you have no matter for complaint.* 6 an instance or case; thing or things: *a matter of fact, a matter of record, a matter of accident.* 7 things written or printed: *reading matter. Second-class matter requires less postage than first-class matter.* 8 amount; quantity: *a matter of 20 miles, a matter of two days.* 9 importance; significance: *Let it go since it is of no matter.* 10 be important: *Nothing seems to matter when you are very sick.* 11 pus. 12 form or discharge pus. 1-9,11 *n.,* 10,12 *v.*

as a matter of course, as something that is to be expected.

as a matter of fact, in truth; in reality; actually.

for that matter, so far as that is concerned.

no matter, 1 it is not important; let it go. 2 regardless of.

What is the matter? What is wrong?

Mat ter horn (mat′ər hôrn), mountain peak in the Alps, between Switzerland and Italy. *n.*

mat ter-of-fact (mat′ər əv fakt′), sticking to facts; not imaginative or fanciful. *adj.*

Mat thew (math′yü), 1 (in the Bible) one of Christ's twelve apostles. He was a tax collector who became one of the four Evangelists. 2 the first book of the New Testament. It tells the story of the life of Christ. *n.*

mat ting (mat′ing), fabric of grass, straw, hemp, or other fiber, for mats, floor covering, wrapping material, etc. *n.*

mattock

mat tock (mat′ək), a large tool with a steel head like a pickax, but having a flat blade on one side or flat blades on both sides, used for loosening soil and cutting roots. *n.*

mat tress (mat′ris), a covering of strong cloth stuffed with hair, cotton, straw, or some other material. It is used on a bed or as a bed. A spring mattress contains wire springs. *n., pl.* **mattress es.**

mat u ra tion (mach′ù rā′shən), a ripening or maturing. *n.*

ma ture (mə chùr′, mə tùr′, *or* mə tyùr′), 1 ripe or full-grown: *Fifty is a mature age. Grain is harvested when it is mature.* 2 ripen; come to full growth: *These apples are maturing fast.* 3 bring to full growth. 4 characteristic of full development: *a mature appearance, mature wisdom.* 5 fully worked out; carefully thought out; fully developed: *mature plans.* 6 work out carefully: *She matured her plans for the long trip.* 7 due; payable. 8 fall due: *This note to the bank matured yesterday.* 1,4,5,7 *adj.,* 2,3,6,8 *v.,* **ma tured, ma tur ing.** —**ma ture′ly,** *adv.*

ma tur i ty (mə chùr′ə tē, mə tùr′ə tē, *or* mə tyùr′ə tē), 1 full development; ripeness: *He reached maturity at twenty years.* 2 condition of being completed or ready: *Our plans have reached maturity.* 3 a falling due; time a note or debt is payable. *n.*

mat zo (mät′sə), a thin piece of unleavened bread, eaten especially during the Jewish holiday of Passover. *n., pl.* **mat zoth** (mät′sōt′), **mat zos.** [from Hebrew]

maud lin (môd′lən), 1 sentimental in a weak, silly way: *We saw a maudlin movie about a boy who lost his dog.* 2 tearfully silly because of drunkenness or excitement. *adj.*

Maugham (môm), **Somerset,** 1874-1965, English writer of novels, plays, and short stories. *n.*

Mau i (mou′ē), the second largest island of Hawaii. *n.*

maul (môl), 1 a very heavy hammer or mallet. 2 beat and pull about; handle roughly: *The lion mauled its keeper badly.* 1 *n.,* 2 *v.* —**maul′er,** *n.*

Mau na Lo a (mou′nə lō′ə), an active volcano on the island of Hawaii.

maun der (môn′dər), 1 talk in a rambling, foolish way: *People who maunder talk much but say little.* 2 move or act in an aimless, confused manner: *The injured man maundered about in a daze.* *v.*

Mau pas sant (mō′pə sänt), **Guy de,** 1850-1893, French writer of novels and short stories. *n.*

Mau ri ta ni a (môr′ə tā′nē ə *or* môr′ə tā′nyə), country in W Africa, on the Atlantic. *n.*

Mau ri tius (mô rish′əs), island country in the Indian Ocean, east of Madagascar. It is a member of the Commonwealth of Nations. *n.*

mau so le um (mô′sə lē′əm), a large, magnificent tomb. *n., pl.* **mau so le ums, mau so le a** (mô′sə lē′ə).

mauve (mōv), 1 delicate, pale purple. 2 a delicate, pale purple. 1 *adj.,* 2 *n.*

mav er ick (mav′ər ik), 1 calf or other animal not marked with an owner's

hat, āge, fär; let, ēqual, tėrm;
it, īce; hot, ōpen, ôrder;
oil, out; cup, pùt, rüle; ch, child;
ng, long; sh, she; th, thin;
ŦH, then; zh, measure;

ə represents *a* in about,
e in taken, *i* in pencil,
o in lemon, *u* in circus.

brand. 2 INFORMAL. one who refuses to affiliate with a regular political party. *n.* [from Samuel *Maverick,* 1803-1870, a cattle owner of Texas who did not brand the calves of one of his herds]

ma vis (mā′vis), the European song thrush. *n., pl.* **ma vis es.**

maw (mô), 1 mouth, throat, or gullet, especially of a meat-eating animal. 2 stomach. *n.*

mawk ish (mô′kish), 1 sickening. 2 sickly sentimental; weakly emotional. *adj.* —**mawk′ish ly,** *adv.* —**mawk′ish ness,** *n.*

max il la (mak sil′ə), 1 jaw or jawbone, especially the upper jawbone. 2 either of a pair of appendages just behind the mandibles of insects, crabs, etc. *n., pl.* **max il lae** (mak sil′ē).

max il lar y (mak′sə ler′ē), 1 of or having to do with the jaw or jawbone, especially the upper jawbone. 2 maxilla. 1 *adj.,* 2 *n., pl.* **max il lar ies.**

maul (def. 1)

max im (mak′səm), a short rule of conduct; proverb: *"A stitch in time saves nine"* and *"Look before you leap"* are *maxims. n.*

Max i mil ian (mak′sə mil′yən), 1832-1867, archduke of Austria, emperor of Mexico from 1864 to 1867. *n.*

max i mize (mak′sə mīz), to increase or magnify to the highest possible amount or degree: *to maximize sales or profits. v.,* **max i mized, max i miz ing.**

max i mum (mak′sə məm), 1 the largest or highest amount; greatest possible amount: *Sixteen miles in a day was the maximum that any of our club walked last summer.* 2 largest; highest; greatest possible: *The maximum score on this test is 100.* 1 *n., pl.* **max i-**

adj. adjective	*n.* noun
adv. adverb	*prep.* preposition
conj. conjunction	*pron.* pronoun
interj. interjection	*v.* verb
sing. singular	*pl.* plural

mums, max i ma (mak′sə mə); 2 *adj.*

may (mā), 1 be permitted or allowed to: *May I have an apple?* 2 be possible that it will: *It may rain tomorrow.* 3 it is hoped that: *May you have a pleasant trip. v., past tense* **might.**

May (mā), the fifth month of the year. It has 31 days. *n.*

Ma ya (mī′ə), 1 one of an ancient Indian people who lived in Central America and Mexico. The Mayas had a high degree of civilization from about A.D. 350 to about A.D. 800, long before they were discovered by the Spaniards. 2 their language. *n., pl.* **Ma yas.** —**Ma′yan,** *adj., n.*

may be (mā′bē), it may be; possibly; perhaps: *Maybe you'll have better luck next time. adv.*

May Day, the first day of May, often celebrated by crowning a girl honored as the queen of May, dancing around the maypole, etc. In some parts of the world, labor parades and meetings are held on May Day.

may flow er (mā′flou′ər), any of several plants whose flowers blossom in May, as the trailing arbutus (in the United States), and the hawthorn or cowslip (in England). *n.*

May flow er (mā′flou′ər), ship on which the Pilgrims came to America in 1620. *n.*

may fly (mā′flī), a slender insect, having lacy front wings which are much larger than the hind wings. It dies soon after reaching the adult stage. *n., pl.* **may flies.**

may hap (mā′hap), OLD USE. perhaps. *adv.*

may hem (mā′hem), crime of intentionally maiming a person or injuring him so that he is less able to defend himself. *n.*

may n't (mā′ənt), may not.

may on naise (mā′ə nāz′), a salad dressing made of egg yolks, vegetable oil, vinegar or lemon juice, and seasoning, beaten together until thick. *n.*

may or (mā′ər), person at the head of a city or town government; chief official of a city or town. *n.*

may or al ty (mā′ər əl tē *or* mer′əl tē), 1 position of mayor. 2 mayor's term of office. *n., pl.* **may or al ties.**

may pole or **May pole** (mā′pōl′), a high pole decorated with flowers or ribbons, around which merrymakers dance on May Day. *n.*

mayst (māst), OLD USE. may. "Thou mayst" means "you may." *v.*

maze (māz), 1 network of paths through which it is hard to find one's way: *A guide led us through a maze of caves.* 2 state of confusion; muddled condition: *He was in such a maze he couldn't speak. n.*

ma zur ka (mə zėr′kə *or* mə zur′kə), 1 a lively Polish dance. 2 music for it. *n., pl.* **ma zur kas.**

ma zour ka (mə zėr′kə *or* mə-zur′kə), mazurka. *n., pl.* **ma zour kas.**

maz y (mā′zē), like a maze; intricate. *adj.,* **maz i er, maz i est.**

M.C., Master of Ceremonies.

Mc Clel lan (mə klel′ən), **George B.,** 1826-1885, Union general in the Civil War. *n.*

Mc Cor mick (mə kôr′mik), **Cyrus Hall,** 1809-1884, American inventor of harvesting machinery. *n.*

Mc Kin ley (mə kin′lē), 1 **William,** 1843-1901, the 25th president of the United States, from 1897 to 1901. 2 **Mount,** mountain in central Alaska, the highest peak in North America. *n.*

Md., Maryland.

M.D., Doctor of Medicine.

me (mē). *I* and *me* mean the person speaking. *She said, "Give the dog to me. I like it and it likes me." pron.*

Me., Maine.

mead[1] (mēd), meadow. *n.* [Old English *mæd*]

mead[2] (mēd), an alcoholic drink made from fermented honey and water. *n.* [Old English *medu*]

Meade (mēd), **George Gordon,** 1815-1872, Union general in the Civil War. *n.*

mead ow (med′ō), piece of grassy land, especially one used for growing hay or as a pasture for grazing animals. *n.*

mead ow lark (med′ō lärk′), an American songbird about as big as a robin, having a thick body, short tail, and a yellow breast marked with black. *n.*

mea ger or **mea gre** (mē′gər), 1 poor or scanty: *a meager meal.* 2 thin; lean: *a meager face. adj.* —**mea′ger ness, mea′gre ness,** *n.*

meal[1] (mēl), 1 breakfast, lunch, dinner, supper, or tea. 2 food served or eaten at any one time: *We enjoyed each meal at the hotel. n.* [Old English *mæl* appointed time, meal]

meal[2] (mēl), 1 coarsely ground grain: *corn meal.* 2 anything ground to a powder. *n.* [Old English *melu*]

meal i ness (mē′lē nis), mealy condition or quality. *n.*

maze (def. 1)

meal time (mēl′tīm′), the usual time for eating a meal. *n.*

meal y (mē′lē), 1 like meal; dry and powdery: *mealy potatoes.* 2 of meal. 3 covered with meal: *the miller's mealy hands.* 4 pale: *a mealy complexion. adj.,* **meal i er, meal i est.**

meal y-mouthed (mē′lē mouᴛʜd′ *or* mē′lē moutht′), unwilling to tell the straight truth in plain words; using soft words insincerely. *adj.*

mean[1] (mēn), 1 have as its thought; signify; import; denote: *What does this word mean?* 2 intend to say or indicate: *"Keep out; that means you."* 3 have as a purpose; have in mind; intend: *Do you think they mean to fight us? Do you mean to use the chops for dinner?* 4 set aside for a definite purpose; destine: *Fate meant us for each other. He was meant to be a priest. v.,* **meant, meaning.** [Old English *mǣnan* mean, tell, say]

mean well by, have kindly feelings toward.

mean[2] (mēn), 1 not noble; petty; unkind; small-minded: *It is mean to spread gossip about your friends.* 2 low in quality or grade; poor: *"He is no mean scholar"* means *"he is a good scholar."* 3 low in social position or rank; humble: *A peasant is of mean birth; a king is of noble birth.* 4 of poor appearance; shabby: *The poor widow lived in a mean hut.* 5 stingy or selfish: *A miser is mean about money.* 6 INFORMAL. hard to manage; troublesome; bad-tempered: *a mean horse. adj.* [Old English *(ge)mǣne* common] —**mean′ly,** *adv.*

mean[3] (mēn), 1 halfway between two extremes; average: *Six is the mean number between three and nine.* 2 condition, quality, or course of action halfway between two extremes: *Eight hours is a happy mean between too much sleep and too little.* 3 (in mathematics) quantity having a value intermediate between the values of other quantities, especially the average obtained by dividing the sum of several quantities by the total number of quantities: *Six is the mean of three, seven, and eight.* 4 **means,** *pl.* **a** what something is done by or the way something is brought about: *We won the game by fair*

means. *Her quick thinking was the means of saving his life.* **b** wealth: *a man of means.* 1 *adj.*, 2-4 *n.* [from French of the 1300's *meien,* from Latin *medianus* of the middle, from *medius* middle of]

by all means, without fail; certainly: *By all means I must visit my sick friend.*

by any means, at all; in any possible way; at any cost.

by means of, by the use of; through; with: *I found my dog by means of a notice in the paper.*

by no means, certainly not; not at all; in no way.

me an der (mē an′dər), 1 follow a winding course: *A brook meanders through the meadow.* 2 a winding course. 3 wander aimlessly: *We meandered through the park.* 4 an aimless wandering. 1,3 *v.*, 2,4 *n.* [from Latin *Maeander,* a winding river in Asia Minor]

mean ing (mē′ning), 1 that which is meant or intended; significance: *The meaning of the sentence is clear.* 2 that means something; expressive: *a meaning look.* 3 OLD USE. intention or purpose. 1,3 *n.*, 2 *adj.* —**mean′ing ly,** *adv.*

mean ing ful (mē′ning fəl), full of meaning; having much meaning; significant. *adj.* —**mean′ing ful ly,** *adv.* —**mean′ing ful ness,** *n.*

mean ing less (mē′ning lis), without meaning; not making sense; not significant. *adj.* —**mean′ing less ly,** *adv.* —**mean′ing less ness,** *n.*

mean ness (mēn′nis), 1 a being mean in grade or quality; poorness. 2 a being selfish in small things; stinginess. 3 a mean act. *n., pl.* **mean ness es.**

meant (ment), past tense and past participle of **mean**[1]. *He explained what he meant. That sign was meant as a warning. v.*

mean time (mēn′tīm′), 1 time between. 2 in the time between. 3 at the same time. 1 *n.*, 2,3 *adv.*

mean while (mēn′hwīl′), meantime. *n., adv.*

mea sles (mē′zəlz), 1 a contagious disease caused by a virus, characterized by the symptoms of a bad cold, fever, and a breaking out of small, red spots on the skin. Measles is more common in children than in grown-ups. 2 a less severe disease with a similar breaking out; German measles. *n. sing. or pl.*

mea sly (mē′zlē), 1 of or like measles. 2 having measles. 3 SLANG. scanty; meager. *adj.*, **mea sli er, mea sli est.**

meas ur a ble (mezh′ər ə bəl), that can be measured. *adj.*

meas ur a bly (mezh′ər ə blē), to an amount or degree that can be measured; perceptibly: *Your work has improved measurably this semester. adv.*

meas ure (mezh′ər), 1 find the size or amount of anything; find out how long, wide, deep, large, much, etc., (a thing) is: *We measured the room and found it was 20 feet long and 15 feet wide. We measured the pail by finding out how many quarts of water it would hold.* 2 mark off or out (in inches, feet, quarts, etc.): *Measure off 2 yards of silk. Measure out a bushel of potatoes.* 3 compare with a standard or with some other person or thing by estimating, judging, or acting: *I measured my swimming ability with hers by racing her across the pool.* 4 be of a certain size or amount: *Buy some paper that measures 8 by 10 inches.* 5 take measurements; find out size or amount: *Can he measure accurately?* 6 serve as a measure of: *A clock measures time.* 7 size or amount: *His waist measure is 30 inches.* **Short measure** means less than it should be; **full measure** means all it should be. 8 something with which to measure. A foot rule, a yardstick, and a quart dipper are common measures. 9 a unit or standard of measure, such as an inch, mile, acre, peck, quart, gallon, etc. 10 any standard of comparison, estimation, or judgment. 11 system of measuring: *square measure.* 12 limit; bound: *"Her joy knew no measure"* means it was very great. 13 quantity, degree, or proportion: *Carelessness is in large measure responsible for many automobile accidents.* 14 rhythmical movement or arrangement in poetry or music: *the measure in which a poem or song is written.* 15 a bar of music. 16 a dance, especially a slow, stately dance. 17 action meant as means to an end: *What measures shall we take to solve the mystery?* 18 a proposed law; a law: *This measure has passed the Senate.* 1-6 *v.*, meas ured, meas ur ing; 7-18 *n.*

beyond measure, very greatly; exceedingly.

measure up to, meet the standard of: *The movie did not measure up to my expectations.*

meas ured (mezh′ərd), 1 regular; uniform: *measured portions of food.* 2 rhythmical; metrical: *measured lines of poetry.* 3 deliberate and restrained: *measured speech. adj.*

meas ure less (mezh′ər lis), without measure; unlimited; vast: *the measureless ocean. adj.*

meas ure ment (mezh′ər mənt), 1 way of measuring; way of finding the size or amount: *Clocks give us a measurement of time.* 2 act or fact of measuring; finding the size or amount: *The measurement of length by a yardstick is easy.* 3 size or amount found by measuring: *The measurements of the room*

are 10 by 15 feet. 4 system of measuring or of measures: *Metric measurement is used in most European countries. n.*

measuring worm, the larva of certain moths; inchworm. It moves by bringing the rear end of its body forward, forming a loop, and then advancing the front end.

meat (mēt), 1 animal flesh used for food. Fish and poultry are not usually called meat. 2 food of any kind: *meat and drink.* 3 part of anything that can be eaten: *The meat of the walnut is tasty.* 4 the essential part or parts: *the meat of an argument, the meat of a book. n.*

meat less (mēt′lis), without meat. *adj.*

measures (def. 15)

meat y (mē′tē), 1 of meat; having the flavor of meat. 2 like meat. 3 full of meat. 4 full of substance; solid and nourishing: *It was a meaty lesson containing many valuable ideas. adj.*, **meat i er, meat i est.**

Mec ca (mek′ə), 1 the religious capital of Saudi Arabia, in the W part. Because Mohammed was born there, Moslems turn toward Mecca when praying and go there on pilgrimages. 2 Also, **mec ca.** **a** place that many people visit. **b** place that a person longs to visit. **c** goal of one's desires or ambitions. *n.*

me chan ic (mə kan′ik), workman skilled with tools, especially one who makes, repairs, or uses machines: *an airplane mechanic, an automobile mechanic. n.*

me chan i cal (mə kan′ə kəl), 1 having to do with a machine, mechanism, or machinery: *mechanical problems, mechanical ability.* 2 made or worked by machinery. 3 like a machine; like that of a machine; automatic; without expression: *Her reading is very me-*

adj.	adjective	*n.*	noun
adv.	adverb	*prep.*	preposition
conj.	conjunction	*pron.*	pronoun
interj.	interjection	*v.*	verb
sing.	singular	*pl.*	plural

medal
of U.S. Army

medallion (def. 2)
of lace

chanical. **4** having to do with or in accordance with the science of mechanics. *adj.*

mechanical drawing, drawing of machines, tools, etc., done to exact scale with rulers, squares, compasses, etc.

me chan i cal ly (mə kan′ik lē), **1** in a mechanical manner: *He greeted us mechanically.* **2** in mechanical respects: *That new engine is mechanically perfect.* **3** toward mechanics: *She is mechanically inclined. adv.*

me chan ics (mə kan′iks), **1** *pl. in form, sing. in use.* branch of physics dealing with the action of forces on solids, liquids, and gases at rest or in motion. **2** *pl. in form, sing. in use.* knowledge dealing with machinery. **3** *pl. in form and use.* mechanical part; technique: *The mechanics of playing the piano are easy for some people to acquire. n.*

mech a nism (mek′ə niz′əm), **1** means or way by which something is done; machinery. **2** a machine or its working parts: *Father said something must be wrong with the mechanism of our refrigerator.* **3** system of parts working together as the parts of a machine do: *The bones and muscles are parts of the mechanism of the body.* **4** mechanical part; technique. *n.*

mech a nis tic (mek′ə nis′tik), **1** of or having to do with mechanics or mechanical theories. **2** of or having to do with the belief that everything in the universe is produced by and can be explained by mechanical or material forces. *adj.*

mech a ni za tion (mek′ə nə zā′shən), a mechanizing or a being mechanized. *n.*

mech a nize (mek′ə nīz), **1** make mechanical. **2** do by machinery, rather than by hand: *Much housework can be mechanized.* **3** replace men or animals by machinery in (a business, etc.). **4** equip (a military unit) with armored vehicles, tanks, and other machines. *v.,* **mech a nized, mech a niz ing.**

med al (med′l), piece of metal like a coin, with a figure or inscription stamped on it: *The captain won a medal for bravery. She won the gold medal for figure skating at the Olympic games.*

A medal was struck to commemorate the coronation. n.

me dal lion (mə dal′yən), **1** a large medal. **2** design, ornament, etc., shaped like a medal. A design on a book or a pattern in lace may be called a medallion. *n.*

med dle (med′l), busy oneself with or in other people's things or affairs without being asked or needed: *Don't meddle with my books or my toys. That busybody has been meddling in my business. v.,* **med dled, med dling.**

med dler (med′lər), person who interferes or meddles. *n.*

med dle some (med′l səm), likely to meddle in other people's affairs; meddling; interfering. *adj.*

Mede (mēd), person who was born or lived in Media. *n.*

Me de a (mi dē′ə), (in Greek legends) an enchantress who helped Jason win the Golden Fleece and returned to Greece with him. Later he deserted her. *n.*

me di a (mē′dē ə), a plural of **medium** (defs. 3 and 4). *Newspapers, magazines, billboards, TV, and radio are important media for advertising. n.*

Me di a (mē′dē ə), ancient country in SW Asia, south of the Caspian Sea. *n.*

me di ae val (mē′dē ē′vəl or med′ē ē′vəl), medieval. *adj.*

me di al (mē′dē əl), **1** in the middle. **2** average; ordinary. *adj.*

me di an (mē′dē ən), **1** in the middle: *the median vein of a leaf.* **2** the middle number of a series: *The median of 1,3,4,8,9 is 4.* **1** *adj.,* **2** *n.*

me di ate (mē′dē āt), **1** come in to help settle a dispute; be a go-between; act in order to bring about an agreement between persons or sides: *The mayor tried to mediate between the bus company and its employees.* **2** effect by intervening; settle by intervening: *mediate an agreement, mediate a strike.* **3** be a connecting link between. *v.,* **me di at ed, me di at ing.**

me di a tion (mē′dē ā′shən), a mediating; effecting an agreement; friendly intervention. *n.*

me di a tor (mē′dē ā′tər), person who mediates: *Mother acts as a mediator when the children quarrel. n.*

med ic (med′ik), INFORMAL. **1** phy-

sician. **2** a medical student. **3** soldier or sailor in the medical corps who is trained to perform medical services, especially giving first aid in combat. *n.*

Med i caid (med′ə kād′), program that provides medical benefits for needy or disabled persons not covered by social security. It is sponsored by the federal, state, and local governments. *n.*

med i cal (med′ə kəl), of or having to do with healing or with the science and art of medicine: *medical advice, medical schools, medical treatment. adj.* —**med′i cal ly,** *adv.*

med ic a ment (mə dik′ə mənt), substance used to cure or heal; medicine. *n.*

Med i care (med′ə ker′ or med′ə kar′), a government-sponsored program of medical care and hospital services for elderly people covered by social security. *n.*

med i cate (med′ə kāt), **1** treat with medicine: *medicate an infection.* **2** put medicine on or in: *medicated gauze. v.,* **med i cat ed, med i cat ing.**

med i ca tion (med′ə kā′shən), **1** treatment with medicine. **2** a putting medicine on or in. **3** medicine. *n.*

Med i ci (med′ə chē′), member of a rich, famous, and powerful family of Florence, Italy, during the 1400's and 1500's. The Medicis were patrons of many painters, sculptors, and writers. *n., pl.* **Med i cis.**

me dic i nal (mə dis′n əl), having value as medicine; healing; helping; relieving. *adj.*

me dic i nal ly (mə dis′n ə lē), as medicine. *adv.*

med i cine (med′ə sən), **1** substance, such as a drug, used to treat, prevent, or cure disease: *The sick boy has to take his medicine three times a day.* **2** science of treating, preventing, or curing disease; study or practice of maintaining and improving health: *The young doctor had studied medicine for a number of years.* **3** any object or ceremony that certain primitive peoples believe has magic power over disease, evil spirits, etc. **4** this power. *n.*

medicine man, man supposed by North American Indians and certain primitive peoples to have magic power over diseases, evil spirits, and other things.

me di e val (mē′dē ē′vəl or med′ē ē′vəl), belonging to or having to do with the Middle Ages (the years from about A.D. 500 to about 1450). *adj.* Also, **mediaeval.**

Me di na (mə dē′nə), city in W Saudi Arabia. Mohammed's tomb is there. *n.*

me di o cre (mē′dē ō′kər or mē′dē ō′kər), neither good nor bad; of average or lower than average quality; ordinary: *a mediocre book, a mediocre poet.* *adj.*

me di oc ri ty (mē′dē ok′rə tē), 1 quality that is neither good nor bad; mediocre quality. 2 mediocre ability or accomplishment. 3 a mediocre person. *n., pl.* **me di oc ri ties.**

med i tate (med′ə tāt), 1 think quietly; reflect, especially on sacred or solemn objects. 2 think about; consider; plan; intend: *She meditated a subject for her report.* *v.,* **med i tat ed, med i tat ing.**

med i ta tion (med′ə tā′shən), quiet thought; reflection, especially on sacred or solemn subjects. *n.*

med i ta tive (med′ə tā′tiv), fond of meditating; thoughtful. *adj.* **—med′- i ta′tive ly,** *adv.*

Med i ter ra ne an Sea (med′ə- tə rā′nē ən), large sea bordered by Europe, Asia, and Africa.

me di um (mē′dē əm), 1 having a middle position, quality, or condition; moderate: *He is of medium height. Cook my eggs medium, not soft.* 2 that which is in the middle; neither one extreme nor the other; middle condition: *a happy medium between city and country life.* 3 substance or agent through which anything acts or through which an effect is produced; a means: *Television and radio are media of communication. Money is a medium of exchange. Copper wire is a medium of electric transmission.* 4 substance in which something can live; environment: *Water is the medium in which fish live.* 5 person through whom messages from the spirits of the dead are supposedly sent to the living. 1 *adj.,* 2-5 *n., pl.* **me di- ums** or also for 3,4 **me di a.**

med ley (med′lē), 1 mixture of things that ordinarily do not belong together. 2 piece of music made up of parts from other pieces. *n., pl.* **med leys.**

me dul la (mi dul′ə), 1 medulla oblongata. 2 the inner substance of an organ or structure. 3 the pith of plants. *n., pl.* **me dul lae** (mi dul′ē′).

medulla ob lon ga ta (ob′long- gä′tə), the lowest part of the brain, at the top end of the spinal cord, containing nerve centers which control breathing and other involuntary functions. See **brain** for diagram. [from

Latin after 1500, prolonged medulla]

me du sa (mə dü′sə *or* mə dyü′sə), jellyfish. *n., pl.* **me du sas, me du sae** (mə dü′sē′ *or* mə dyü′sē′). [from *Medusa*]

Me du sa (mə dü′sə *or* mə dyü′sə), (in Greek legends) one of the three Gorgons or horrible monsters with snakes for hair. *n., pl.* **Me du sas.**

meed (mēd), OLD USE. what one deserves or has earned; reward. *n.*

meek (mēk), 1 not easily angered; mild; patient. 2 submitting tamely when ordered about or injured by others; yielding: *The boy was meek as a lamb after he was punished.* *adj.* **—meek′ly,** *adv.* **—meek′ness,** *n.*

meer schaum (mir′shəm), 1 a soft, white, clayey mineral used to make tobacco pipes. 2 a tobacco pipe made of this material. *n.* [from German *Meerschaum* sea foam]

meet[1] (mēt), 1 come face to face (with something or someone coming from the other direction): *Their cars met on the narrow road. Our car met another car on a narrow bridge.* 2 come together; come into contact or connection with; join: *Two roads meet near the church. Sword met sword in battle.* 3 keep an appointment with: *Meet me at one o'clock.* 4 be introduced to; become acquainted: *Have you met my sister?* 5 receive and welcome on arrival: *I must go to the station to meet my mother.* 6 be perceived by; be seen or heard by: *There is more to this matter than meets the eye.* 7 fulfill; put an end to; satisfy: *The campers took along enough food to meet their needs for a week.* 8 pay (one's debts, etc.) when due: *He did not have enough money to meet his bills.* 9 fight with; oppose; deal with: *meet an enemy in battle.* 10 face directly: *He met her glance with a smile.* 11 experience: *He met open scorn before he won fame.* 12 assemble: *Congress will meet next month.* 13 a meeting; a gathering: *an athletic meet.* 1-12 *v.,* **met, meet ing;** 13 *n.* [Old English *mētan,* from *mōt* meeting]

meet with, 1 come across; light upon: *We met with bad weather.* 2 have; get: *The plan met with approval.*

meet[2] (mēt), suitable; proper; fitting: *It is meet that you should help your friends.* *adj.* [Old English *(ge)mǣte*] **—meet′ly,** *adv.*

meet ing (mē′ting), 1 a coming together. 2 a coming together or assembly of people for worship: *a Quaker meeting, a prayer meeting.* 3 any coming together or assembly of people: *The club held a meeting.* 4 place where things meet; junction: *a meeting of roads.* *n.*

meet ing house (mē′ting hous′), a building used for worship; church. *n.,*

hat, āge, fär; let, ēqual, tèrm;
it, īce; hot, ōpen, ôrder;
oil, out; cup, pùt, rüle; ch, child;
ng, long; sh, she; th, thin;
ᴛʜ, then; zh, measure;

ə represents *a* in about,
e in taken, *i* in pencil,
o in lemon, *u* in circus.

pl. **meet ing hous es** (mē′ting- hou′ziz).

meg a cy cle (meg′ə sī′kəl), one million cycles. *n.*

megaliths at Stonehenge

meg a lith (meg′ə lith), stone of great size, especially in monuments left by people of prehistoric times. *n.*

meg a lo ma ni a (meg′ə lō mā′nē ə), insanity marked by delusions of greatness, wealth, etc. *n.*

meg a phone (meg′ə fōn), a large, funnel-shaped horn used to increase the loudness of the voice or the distance at which it can be heard. *n.*

megaphone
cheerleader using
a megaphone

meg a ton (meg′ə tun′), 1 measure of weight equal to one million tons. 2 measure of atomic power equivalent to the energy released by one million tons of the explosive TNT. *n.*

Me ir (me ir′), **Golda,** born 1898, prime minister of Israel from 1969 to 1974. *n.*

Me kong (mā′kong′), river flowing from E Tibet through Indochina. *n.*

mel an chol ic (mel′ən kol′ik), melancholy; gloomy. *adj.*

mel an chol y (mel′ən kol′ē), 1 low spirits; sadness; tendency to be sad. 2 sad; gloomy: *a melancholy person.* 3 causing sadness; depressing: *a melancholy scene.* 1 *n.,* 2,3 *adj.*

adj. adjective	*n.* noun
adv. adverb	*prep.* preposition
conj. conjunction	*pron.* pronoun
interj. interjection	*v.* verb
sing. singular	*pl.* plural

Mel a ne sia (mel′ə nē′zhə), group of islands in the Pacific, northeast of Australia. *n.* —**Mel′a ne′sian,** *adj., n.*

mé lange (mā länzh′), mixture; medley. *n., pl.* **mé langes.** [from French]

Mel bourne (mel′bərn), seaport in SE Australia. *n.*

meld (meld), 1 announce and show (cards for a score) in pinochle, etc. 2 act of melding. 3 cards which can be melded. 1 *v.,* 2,3 *n.*

me lee (mā′lā), a confused fight; hand-to-hand fight among a number of fighters. *n.* [from French *mêlée*]

mê lée (mā′lā), melee. *n., pl.* **mê lées.**

mel lif lu ous (mə lif′lü əs), sweetly or smoothly flowing: *We enjoyed the mellifluous speech of the orator. adj.*

mel low (mel′ō), 1 soft and full-flavored from ripeness; sweet and juicy: *a mellow apple.* 2 fully matured: *mellow wine.* 3 soft and rich: *a violin with a mellow tone, a mellow light in a picture, a mellow color.* 4 softened and made wise by age and experience. 5 make or become mellow: *The apples mellowed after we picked them. Time had mellowed his youthful temper.* 1-4 *adj.,* 5 *v.* —**mel′low ly,** *adv.* —**mel′low ness,** *n.*

me lod ic (mə lod′ik), 1 having to do with melody. 2 melodious. *adj.* —**me lod′i cal ly,** *adv.*

me lo di ous (mə lō′dē əs), 1 sweet-sounding; pleasing to the ear; musical: *a melodious voice.* 2 producing melody.

adj. —**me lo′di ous ly,** *adv.* —**me lo′di ous ness,** *n.*

mel o dra ma (mel′ə drä′mə *or* mel′ə dram′ə), 1 a sensational drama with exaggerated appeal to the emotions and, usually, a happy ending: *Most mystery shows are melodramas.* 2 any sensational writing, speech, or action with exaggerated appeal to the emotions. *n., pl.* **mel o dra mas.**

mel o dra mat ic (mel′ə drə mat′ik), of, like, or suitable for melodrama; sensational and exaggerated. *adj.* —**mel′o dra mat′i cal ly,** *adv.*

mel o dy (mel′ə dē), 1 sweet music; any sweet sound. 2 succession of single tones in music; tune. Most music has melody, harmony, and rhythm. 3 the main tune in music with harmony; the air. *n., pl.* **mel o dies.**

mel on (mel′ən), a large, juicy fruit of a vine much like the pumpkin, squash, and cucumber. Watermelons, cantaloupes, and honeydew melons are different kinds. *n.* —**mel′on like′,** *adj.*

Mel pom e ne (mel pom′ə nē), (in Greek myths) the Muse of tragedy. *n.*

melt (melt), 1 turn into a liquid by applying heat. Ice becomes water when it melts. *Great heat melts iron.* 2 dissolve: *Sugar melts in water.* 3 disappear or cause to disappear gradually: *The clouds melted away, and the sun came out.* 4 change very gradually; blend; merge: *In the rainbow, the green melts into blue, the blue into violet. Dusk melted the colors of the hills into a soft gray.* 5 soften: *Their kindness melted her heart. v.,* **melt ed, melt ed** *or* **mol ten, melt ing.** —**melt′er,** *n.*

melting point, temperature at which a solid substance melts. Different substances have different melting points. Tungsten has the highest melting point of all metallic elements.

Mel ville (mel′vil), **Herman,** 1819-1891, American novelist. *n.*

mem ber (mem′bər), 1 person, animal, or thing belonging to a group: *Every member of the family was home for Mother's Day. The lion is a member of the cat family. The senator is a member of Congress.* 2 a constituent part of a whole: *a member of an equation, the members of a set.* 3 part or organ of an animal, human body, or plant, especially a leg, arm, or wing. *n.*

mem ber ship (mem′bər ship), 1 fact or state of being a member: *Do you enjoy your membership in the Girl Scouts?* 2 members as a group: *The whole membership of the class was present.* 3 number of members: *We have a large membership in our club this year. n.*

mem brane (mem′brān), 1 a thin, soft sheet or layer of animal tissue, lining or covering some part of the body. 2 a similar layer of vegetable tissue. *n.*

mem bra nous (mem′brə nəs), 1 of or like membrane. 2 characterized by the formation of a membrane or a lining like a membrane. In membranous croup, a deposit similar to a membrane forms in the throat and hinders breathing. *adj.*

me men to (mə men′tō), something serving as a reminder, warning, or remembrance: *These post cards are mementos of our trip abroad. n., pl.* **me men tos** *or* **me men toes.**

mem o (mem′ō), INFORMAL. memorandum. *n., pl.* **mem os.**

mem oir (mem′wär), 1 biography. 2 memoirs, *pl.* a record of facts and events written from personal knowledge or special information: *The retired general wrote his memoirs of army life.* b record of a person's own life and experiences; autobiography. *n.*

mem o ra bil i a (mem′ər ə bil′ē ə), things or events worth remembering. *n.pl.*

mem o ra ble (mem′ər ə bəl), worth remembering; not to be forgotten; notable: *The play "Peter Pan" has many memorable scenes. adj.*

mem o ra bly (mem′ər ə blē), in a memorable manner; so as to be remembered. *adv.*

mem o ran da (mem′ə ran′də), a plural of **memorandum.** *n.*

mem o ran dum (mem′ə ran′dəm), 1 a short written statement for future use; note to aid one's memory: *Make a memorandum of the things we'll need for the trip.* 2 an informal letter, note, or report. *n., pl.* **mem o ran dums** *or* **mem o ran da.**

me mo ri al (mə môr′ē əl), 1 something that is a reminder of some event or person, such as a statue, an arch or column, a book, or a holiday. 2 helping people to remember some person, thing, or event: *memorial services.* 1 *n.,* 2 *adj.*

Memorial Day, day for honoring the American servicemen who have died for their country, observed by decorating their graves and memorials; Decoration Day. It is a legal holiday, observed in most states on the last Monday in May.

me mo ri al ize (mə môr′ē ə līz), preserve the memory of; commemorate. *v.,* **me mo ri al ized, me mo ri al izing.**

mem or i za tion (mem′ər ə zā′shən), act of memorizing. *n.*

mem o rize (mem′ə rīz′), commit to memory; learn by heart: *memorize the alphabet.* *v.,* **mem o rized, mem o rizing.**

mem or y (mem′ər ē), 1 ability to remember or keep in the mind: *She will recall when that happened, for she has a good memory.* 2 act of remembering; remembrance: *My memory of the trip is still fresh.* 3 person, thing, or event that is remembered: *His childhood is now only a vague memory.* 4 all that a person remembers. 5 length of past time that is remembered: *This has been the hottest summer within my memory.* *n., pl.* **mem or ies.**

in memory of, to help in remembering; as a reminder of: *I sent this card in memory of our summer together.*

Mem phis (mem′fis), 1 city in SW Tennessee, on the Mississippi. 2 city in ancient Egypt, near the mouth of the Nile. *n.*

men (men), 1 plural of **man.** 2 human beings; people in general: *"All men are created equal." Men and animals have some things in common.* *n.pl.*

men ace (men′is), 1 threat: *In dry weather forest fires are a great menace.* 2 threaten: *Floods menaced the valley with destruction.* 1 *n.,* 2 *v.,* **men aced, men ac ing. —men′ac ing ly,** *adv.*

me nag er ie (mə naj′ər ē), 1 a collection of wild animals kept in cages for exhibition. 2 place where such animals are kept. *n.*

mend (mend), 1 put in good condition again; make whole; repair: *mend a road, mend a broken doll, mend stockings.* 2 correct faults in; set right; improve: *He should mend his manners.* 3 place that has been mended: *The mend in your shirt scarcely shows.* 4 get back one's health; recover from illness or injury: *My sprained ankle has mended.* 1,2,4 *v.,* 3 *n.* **—mend′er,** *n.*

on the mend, getting better; improving.

men da cious (men dā′shəs), 1 lying; untruthful. 2 false; untrue. *adj.*

men dac i ty (men das′ə tē), 1 habit of telling lies; untruthfulness. 2 a lie. *n., pl.* **men dac i ties.**

Men del (men′dl), **Gregor,** 1822-1884, Austrian monk and biologist. His investigations of heredity laid the foundations for the science of genetics. *n.*

men de le vi um (men′dl ē′vē əm), a radioactive metallic element, produced artificially from einsteinium. *n.* [from D. I. *Mendeleev,* 1834-1907, a Russian chemist]

Men dels sohn (men′dl sən *or* men′dl sōn), **Felix,** 1809-1847, German composer. *n.*

men di cant (men′də kənt), 1 begging: *Mendicant friars ask alms for charity.* 2 a beggar: *We were surrounded by mendicants asking for money.* 1 *adj.,* 2 *n.*

Men e la us (men′ə lā′əs), (in Greek legends) a king of Sparta, husband of Helen, and brother of Agamemnon. *n.*

men folk (men′fōk′), 1 men. 2 the male members of a family or other group. *n.pl.*

men folks (men′fōks′), menfolk. *n.pl.*

men ha den (men hād′n), a sea fish common along the eastern coast of the United States, used for making oil and fertilizer. *n., pl.* **men ha den.**

me ni al (mē′nē əl), 1 belonging to or suited to a servant; low; mean: *Cinderella had to do menial tasks.* 2 servant who does the humblest and most unpleasant tasks. 1 *adj.,* 2 *n.* **—me′ni al ly,** *adv.*

men in gi tis (men′in jī′tis), a very serious disease in which the membranes surrounding the brain or spinal cord become inflamed. *n.*

Men non ite (men′ə nīt), member of a Christian church opposed to infant baptism, taking oaths, holding public office, and military service. The Mennonites often wear very plain clothes and live simply. *n.* [from *Menno* Simons, 1492-1559, a leader of the group in the Netherlands and Germany]

men-of-war (men′əv wôr′), plural of **man-of-war.** *n.*

menorah—The center candle is used to light one candle on each of the eight days of Hanukkah.

me no rah (mə nôr′ə), candlestick with eight branches used during the Jewish festival of Hanukkah. *n.* [from Hebrew]

men stru ate (men′strü āt), have a

discharge of blood from the uterus, normally at intervals of about four weeks. *v.,* **men stru at ed, men stru at ing.**

men stru a tion (men′strü ā′shən), act or period of menstruating. *n.*

men su ra tion (men′shə rā′shən), 1 act, art, or process of measuring. 2 branch of mathematics that deals with finding lengths, areas, and volumes. *n.*

-ment, suffix added to verbs to form nouns. 1 act of _____ing: *Enjoyment = act of enjoying. Measurement = act of measuring.* 2 condition of being _____ed: *Amazement = condition of being amazed.* 3 product or result of _____ing: *Pavement = product of paving. Measurement = result of measuring.* 4 means of or instrument for _____ing: *Inducement = means of inducing.* [from French before the 1400's *-ment,* from Latin *-mentum* result of]

men tal (men′tl), 1 of the mind: *a mental test, a mental disease.* 2 for the mind; done by the mind: *mental arithmetic.* 3 having a mental disease or weakness: *a mental patient.* 4 for people having mental disease: *a mental hospital. adj.*

mental age, the level of a person's mental development as compared to that of the average person of his own age. A ten-year-old child with a mental age of thirteen has a higher-than-average intelligence.

men tal i ty (men tal′ə tē), 1 mental capacity; mind: *a student with a high mentality.* 2 attitude or outlook: *a mature mentality.* *n., pl.* **men tal i ties.**

men tal ly (men′tl ē), in the mind; with the mind: *Grandmother is still strong physically and mentally. adv.*

men thol (men′thôl), a white, crystalline substance obtained from oil of peppermint, used in medicine. *n.*

men tion (men′shən), 1 speak about; refer to: *I mentioned your idea to the planning committee.* 2 a short statement; a mentioning; reference: *There was mention of our school party in the newspaper.* 1 *v.,* 2 *n.*

make mention of, speak of; refer to:

adj.	adjective	*n.*	noun
adv.	adverb	*prep.*	preposition
conj.	conjunction	*pron.*	pronoun
interj.	interjection	*v.*	verb
sing.	singular	*pl.*	plural

He made mention of a book he had read recently.

men tor (men′tər), a wise and trusted adviser. *n.* [from *Mentor*]

Men tor (men′tər), (in Greek legends) a faithful friend of Ulysses. When Ulysses went to fight the Trojans, he left his son with Mentor to be taught and advised. *n.*

men u (men′yü), 1 list of the food served at a meal; bill of fare. 2 the food served: *Everybody enjoyed the fine menu.* *n.*

me ow (mē ou′), 1 sound made by a cat or kitten. 2 make this sound. 1 *n.*, 2 *v.*

Meph i stoph e les (mef′ə stof′-ə lēz′), 1 the devil of the Faust legend. 2 a powerful evil spirit; crafty devil. *n.*

mer can tile (mėr′kən til), of merchants or trade; commercial: *a mercantile firm, mercantile law.* *adj.*

Mer ca tor (mər kā′tər), Gerhardus, 1512-1594, Flemish map maker. *n.*

mer ce nar y (mėr′sə ner′ē), 1 working for money only; acting with money as the motive. 2 done for money or gain. 3 soldier serving for pay in a foreign army. 1,2 *adj.*, 3 *n.*, *pl.* **mer ce nar ies.**

mer cer (mėr′sər), dealer in cloth. *n.*

mer cer ize (mėr′sə rīz′), treat (cotton thread or cloth) with a chemical solution that strengthens the cotton, makes it hold dyes better, and gives it a silky luster. *v.*, **mer cer ized, mer cer iz ing.** [from John *Mercer*, 1791-1866, English inventor]

mer chan dise (mėr′chən dīz′), 1 goods for sale; wares; articles bought and sold. 2 buy and sell; trade. 3 to further the sales of (goods and services) by advertising and other methods. 1 *n.*, 2,3 *v.*, **mer chan dised, mer chan dis ing.**

mer chant (mėr′chənt), 1 person who buys and sells for profit; trader: *Some merchants do most of their business with foreign countries.* 2 storekeeper. 3 trading; having to do with trade; commercial: *merchant ships.* 1,2 *n.*, 3 *adj.*

mer chant man (mėr′chənt mən), ship used in commerce. *n.*, *pl.* **mer chant men.**

merchant marine, 1 the trading ships of a nation; ships used in commerce. 2 the body of officers and sailors who serve on such ships: *His brother is in the merchant marine.*

mer ci ful (mėr′si fəl), having mercy; showing or feeling mercy; full of mercy. *adj.* —**mer′ci ful ly,** *adv.*

mer ci less (mėr′si lis), without mercy; having no mercy; showing no mercy. *adj.* —**mer′ci less ly,** *adv.* —**mer′ci less ness,** *n.*

mer cur i al (mər kyur′ē əl), 1 sprightly and animated; quick. 2 changeable; fickle. 3 caused by the use of mercury: *mercurial poisoning.* 4 containing mercury: *a mercurial ointment.* *adj.*

mer cur ic (mər kyur′ik), (of compounds) containing mercury. *adj.*

Mer cur o chrome (mər kyur′ə-krōm′), trademark for a red liquid used as an antiseptic. *n.*

mer cur y (mėr′kyər ē), 1 a heavy, silver-white, metallic element that is liquid at ordinary temperatures; quicksilver. It occurs naturally in the mineral cinnabar. Mercury combines with most other metals to form amalgams. 2 the column of mercury in a thermometer or barometer. *n.*, *pl.* **mer cur ies.** [from Latin *Mercurius* Mercury]

Mer cur y (mėr′kyər ē), 1 (in Roman myths) the messenger of the gods. He was the god of commerce, skill of hands, quickness of wit, and eloquence. The Greeks called him Hermes. 2 the smallest planet in the solar system and the one nearest to the sun. *n.*

mer cy (mėr′sē), 1 more kindness than justice requires; kindness beyond what can be claimed or expected: *The judge showed mercy to the young offender.* 2 kindly treatment; pity. 3 something to be thankful for; blessing: *It's a mercy that you weren't injured in the accident.* *n.*, *pl.* **mer cies.**

at the mercy of, in the power of.

merino (def. 1)
about 2 ft. high at the shoulder

mere[1] (mir), nothing else than; only; simple: *The cut was the merest scratch. The mere sight of a dog makes me afraid.* *adj., superlative* **mer est.** [from Latin *merus* pure, unmixed]

mere[2] (mir), OLD USE. lake or pond. *n.* [Old English *mere* body of water]

Mer e dith (mer′ə dith), George, 1828-1909, English novelist and poet. *n.*

mere ly (mir′lē), simply; only; and nothing more; and that is all. *adv.*

mer e tri cious (mer′ə trish′əs), attractive in a showy way; alluring by false charms: *A wooden building painted to look like marble is meretricious.* *adj.* —**mer′e tri′cious ly,** *adv.* —**mer′e tri′cious ness,** *n.*

mer gan ser (mər gan′sər), any of several kinds of large, fish-eating ducks with long, slender bills which are hooked at the tip; sheldrake. They often have crested heads. *n.*, *pl.* **mer gan sers** or **mer gan ser.**

merge (mėrj), 1 cause to be swallowed up or absorbed so as to lose its own character or identity; combine or consolidate: *The big company merged various small businesses.* 2 become swallowed up or absorbed in something else: *The twilight merges into darkness. The two railroads merged into one.* *v.*, **merged, merg ing.**

merg er (mėr′jər), act of merging; combination; consolidation: *One big company was formed by the merger of four small ones.* *n.*

NORTH POLE
SOUTH POLE
meridians (def. 2)
of longitude

me rid i an (mə rid′ē ən), 1 an imaginary circle passing through any place on the earth's surface and through the North and South Poles. 2 the half of such a circle from pole to pole. All the places on the same meridian have the same longitude. 3 the zenith of the sun or any star. 4 the highest point: *The meridian of life is the prime of life.* *n.*

me ringue (mə rang′), 1 a mixture of white of egg and sugar, beaten stiff. Meringue is often spread on pies, puddings, etc., and lightly browned in the oven. 2 a shell made of this mixture and filled with fruit, whipped cream, etc. *n.*

me ri no (mə rē′nō), 1 Often, **Merino.** kind of sheep with long, fine wool. 2 wool of this sheep. 3 a soft, woolen yarn made from it. 4 a thin, soft, woolen cloth made from this yarn or some substitute. *n.*, *pl.* **me ri nos.** [from Spanish *merino*]

mer it (mer′it), 1 worth or value; goodness: *Each child will get a mark according to the merit of his work.* 2 something that deserves praise or reward. 3 deserve: *Your excellent work merits praise.* 4 Usually, **merits,** *pl.* actual facts or qualities, whether good or bad: *The judge will consider the case on its merits.* 1,2,4 *n.*, 3 *v.*

mer i to ri ous (mer′ə tôr′ē əs), deserving reward or praise; having merit; worthy: *His work at school was meritorious, but not brilliant.* *adj.* —**mer′i to′ri ous ly,** *adv.* —**mer′i to′ri ous ness,** *n.*

merle or **merl** (mèrl), the common European blackbird. *n.*

Mer lin (mèr′lən), magician who helped King Arthur. *n.*

mer maid (mėr′mād′), an imaginary sea maiden having the form of a fish from the waist down. *n.*

mer man (mėr′man′), an imaginary man of the sea having the form of a fish from the waist down. *n., pl.* **mer men.**

mer ri ly (mer′ə lē), in a merry manner; laughing and gay. *adv.*

Mer ri mac (mer′ə mak), a United States frigate rebuilt with iron armor by the Confederates during the Civil War and renamed the **Virginia.** The Merrimac was the first armored warship. *n.*

Mer ri mack (mer′ə mak), river flowing from central New Hampshire through NE Massachusetts into the Atlantic. *n.*

mer ri ment (mer′ē mənt), laughter and gaiety; fun; mirth; merry enjoyment. *n.*

mer ri ness (mer′ē nis), a being merry. *n.*

mer ry (mer′ē), 1 laughing and gay; full of fun: *merry talk.* 2 gay; joyful: *a merry holiday.* *adj.,* **mer ri er, mer ri est.**

make merry, laugh and be gay; have fun.

mer ry-an drew (mer′ē an′drü), clown or buffoon. *n.*

mer ry-go-round (mer′ē gō round′), 1 set of animal figures and seats on a circular platform that is driven round and round by machinery and that children ride for fun; carrousel. 2 any whirl or rapid round: *The holidays were a merry-go-round of parties.* *n.*

mer ry mak er (mer′ē mā′kər), person who is being merry; person engaged in merrymaking. *n.*

mer ry mak ing (mer′ē mā′king), 1 laughter and gaiety; fun. 2 gay festival; merry entertainment. 3 gay and full of fun; having a merry time. 1,2 *n.,* 3 *adj.*

mesa

me sa (mā′sə), a small, high plateau with a flat top and steep sides, common in dry regions of the western and southwestern United States. *n., pl.* **me sas.** [from Spanish *mesa* table, from Latin *mensa*]

mes dames (mā däm′), 1 a plural of

madam. 2 FRENCH. plural of **madame.** *n.*

mes de moi selles (mād mwä zel′), FRENCH. plural of **mademoiselle.** *n.*

mesh (mesh), 1 an open space of a net, sieve, or screen: *This net has half-inch meshes.* 2 cord, wire, etc., used in a net or screen: *We found an old fly swatter made of wire mesh.* 3 **meshes,** *pl.* **a** network: *Seaweed was caught in the meshes of the net.* **b** snares: *The spy was entangled in the meshes of his own plot to steal defense secrets.* 4 catch or be caught in a net. 5 engage or become engaged. The teeth of a small gear mesh with the teeth of a larger one. 1-3 *n., pl.* **mesh es;** 4,5 *v.*

in mesh, in gear; fitted together.

mes mer ic (mez mer′ik or mesmer′ik), hypnotic. *adj.*

mes mer ism (mez′mə riz′əm or mes′mə riz′əm), hypnotism. *n.*

mes mer ize (mez′mə rīz′ or mes′mə rīz′), hypnotize. *v.,* **mes mer ized, mes mer iz ing.** [from Franz *Mesmer,* 1734-1815, an Austrian doctor who made hypnotism popular]

mes on (mes′on), a highly unstable particle found in the nucleus of an atom, having a mass greater than that of an electron and less than that of a proton. A meson may have a positive, negative, or neutral charge. *n.*

Mes o po ta mi a (mes′ə pə tā′mē ə), ancient country in SW Asia, between the Tigris and Euphrates rivers. *n.*

mes o sphere (mes′ə sfir), region of the atmosphere between the stratosphere and the ionosphere, which extends from about 20 to 50 miles above the earth's surface. Most of the ozone in the atmosphere is created in the mesosphere and there is almost no variation in the temperature. *n.*

Mes o zo ic (mes′ə zō′ik), 1 the geological era before the present era; the age of reptiles. 2 of this era or its rocks. 1 *n.,* 2 *adj.*

me squite (me skēt′), tree or shrub, common in the southwestern United States and Mexico, that often grows in dense clumps or thickets. Its pods furnish a valuable food for cattle. *n.* [from Mexican Spanish *mezquite*]

mess (mes), 1 a dirty or untidy mass or group of things; dirty or untidy condition: *The children have been told to clean up the mess in their room.* 2 make dirty or untidy: *She messed up her book by scribbling in it.* 3 confusion or difficulty: *His business affairs are in a mess.* 4 make a failure of; spoil: *He messed up his chances of winning the race.* 5 an unpleasant or unsuccessful affair or state of affairs: *She made a mess of her final examinations.* 6 group of people who take meals together reg-

hat, āge, fär; let, ēqual, tėrm; it, īce; hot, ōpen, ôrder; oil, out; cup, put, rüle; ch, child; ng, long; sh, she; th, thin; ₮H, then; zh, measure;

ə represents *a* in about, *e* in taken, *i* in pencil, *o* in lemon, *u* in circus.

ularly, especially such a group in the army or navy. 7 meal of such a group: *The officers are at mess now.* 8 take one's meals (with). 9 portion of food, especially soft food: *a mess of oatmeal, a mess of fish.* 1,3,5-7,9 *n., pl.* **mess es;** 2,4,8 *v.*

mess about or **mess around,** be busy without really accomplishing anything; putter around.

mes sage (mes′ij), 1 words sent from one person to another: *a radio message, a message of welcome.* 2 an offical speech or writing: *the President's message to Congress.* 3 lesson or moral contained in a story, play, speech, etc. *n.*

mes sen ger (mes′n jər), 1 person who carries a message or goes on an errand. 2 anything thought of as carrying a message: *Each bullet was a messenger of death.* 3 a sign that something is coming; forerunner; herald: *Dawn is the messenger of day.* *n.*

Mes si ah (mə sī′ə), 1 the expected deliverer of the Jewish people. 2 (in Christian use) Jesus. 3 Often, **messiah.** any person hailed as or thought of as a savior. *n.*

Mes si an ic (mes′ē an′ik), 1 of the Messiah. 2 Often, **messianic.** of or characteristic of a messiah or savior. *adj.*

mes sieurs (mes′ərz; *French* mā syü′), plural of **monsieur.** *n.*

mess i ly (mes′ə lē), in a messy manner. *adv.*

mess i ness (mes′ē nis), messy condition. *n.*

mess kit, a shallow, metal container that includes a fork, spoon, knife, and metal cup, for use by a soldier in the field, a camper, etc.

mess mate (mes′māt′), one of a group of people who eat together regularly. *n.*

Messrs., messieurs, used before names as the plural of **Mr.:** *Messrs. Smith and Jones.*

mess y (mes′ē), in a mess; like a mess; untidy; in disorder; dirty. *adj.,* **mess i er, mess i est.**

mes ti zo (me stē′zō), person of mixed blood, especially the child of a Spaniard

met

adj. adjective	*n.* noun
adv. adverb	*prep.* preposition
conj. conjunction	*pron.* pronoun
interj. interjection	*v.* verb
sing. singular	*pl.* plural

and an American Indian. *n., pl.* **mes ti zos** or **mes ti zoes.** [from Spanish *mestizo,* from Latin *mixtus* mixed]

met (met), past tense and past participle of **meet**[1]. *My father met us this morning at ten. We were met at the gate by our dog. v.*

met a bol ic (met′ə bol′ik), having to do with metabolism. *adj.* —**met′a bol′i cal ly,** *adv.*

me tab o lism (mə tab′ə liz′əm), process by which all living things turn food into energy and living tissue. In metabolism food is broken down to produce energy, which is then used by the body to build up new cells and tissues, provide heat, and engage in physical activity. Growth and action depend on metabolism. *n.*

met al (met′l), 1 any of a group of chemical elements which have usually a shiny surface, are good conductors of heat and electricity, and can be melted or fused, hammered into thin sheets, or drawn out into wires. Iron, gold, silver, copper, lead, tin, and aluminum are metals. 2 any alloy or fused mixture of these, such as steel, bronze, and brass. 3 any chemical element or mixture of chemical elements which lose electrons from their atoms in most chemical reactions and react with certain acids to form salts. 4 made of metal: *a metal container, a metal coin.* 5 anything made out of metal: *a piece of metal.* 6 broken stone, cinders, etc., used for roads and roadbeds. 7 mettle. 1-3,5-7 *n.,* 4 *adj.*

me tal lic (mə tal′ik), 1 of, containing, or consisting of metal: *a metallic substance.* 2 like metal; characteristic of metal; that suggests metal: *a metallic luster, a metallic voice. adj.*

met al lur gi cal (met′l ėr′jə kəl), of or having to do with metallurgy. *adj.*

met al lur gist (met′l ėr′jist), an expert in metallurgy. *n.*

met al lur gy (met′l ėr′jē), science or art of metals, including the study of their properties and structure, the separation and refining of metals from their ores, and the production of alloys. *n.*

met al work (met′l wėrk′), 1 things made out of metal. 2 a making things out of metal. *n.*

met al work er (met′l wėr′kər), person who makes things out of metal. *n.*

met al work ing (met′l wėr′king), act or process of making things out of metal. *n.*

met a mor phic (met′ə môr′fik), 1 characterized by change of form; having to do with change of form. 2 changed in structure by heat and pressure. Slate is a metamorphic rock that is formed from shale, a sedimentary rock. *adj.*

met a mor phose (met′ə môr′fōz), change in form; transform: *The witch metamorphosed people into animals. v.,* **met a mor phosed, met a mor phos ing.**

metamorphosis (def. 1) of a butterfly
1 Caterpillar prepares to change form.
2 It sheds skin, exposing chrysalis.
3 Chrysalis is entirely exposed.
4 Adult emerges from the chrysalis.

met a mor pho sis (met′ə môr′fə sis), 1 change of form. Tadpoles become frogs by metamorphosis; they lose their tails and grow legs. 2 the changed form. 3 a noticeable or complete change of character, appearance, or condition. *n., pl.* **met a mor pho ses** (met′ə môr′fə sēz′).

met a phor (met′ə fôr), an implied comparison between two different things; a figure of speech in which a word or phrase that ordinarily means one thing is applied to another thing in order to suggest a likeness between the two. "A copper sky" and "a heart of stone" are metaphors. *n.*

met a phor i cal (met′ə fôr′ə kəl), using metaphors; figurative. *adj.* —**met′a phor′i cal ly,** *adv.*

met a phys i cal (met′ə fiz′ə kəl), 1 of metaphysics; about the real nature of things. 2 highly abstract; hard to understand. *adj.*

met a phys ics (met′ə fiz′iks), branch of philosophy that tries to explain reality and knowledge; the study of the real nature of things. *n.*

mete (mēt), give to each his share or what is due him; distribute; allot: *mete out punishment, mete out praise. v.,* **met ed, met ing.**

me te or (mē′tē ər), mass of stone or metal that enters the earth's atmosphere from outer space with enormous speed; shooting star. Meteors become so hot from rushing through the air that they glow and often burn up. *n.*

me te or ic (mē′tē ôr′ik), 1 of meteors: *meteoric dust, a meteoric shower.* 2 flashing like a meteor; brilliant and soon ended; swift: *a meteoric rise to fame.* 3 of the atmosphere: *Wind and rain are meteoric phenomena. adj.*

meteorite

me te o rite (mē′tē ə rīt′), mass of stone or metal that has fallen to the earth from outer space; a fallen meteor. *n.*

me te or o log i cal (mē′tē ər ə loj′ə kəl), having to do with the atmosphere and weather; having to do with meteorology. *adj.*

me te o rol o gist (mē′tē ə rol′ə jist), an expert in meteorology. *n.*

me te o rol o gy (mē′tē ə rol′ə jē), science dealing with the atmosphere and weather. The study of atmospheric conditions, such as winds, moisture, temperature, etc., and forecasts of the weather are part of meteorology. *n.*

me ter[1] (mē′tər), 1 the basic measure of length in the metric system. A meter is equal to 39.37 inches. 2 any kind of poetic rhythm; the arrangement of beats or accents in a line of poetry: *The meter of "Jack and Jill went up the hill" is not the meter of "One, two, buckle my shoe."* 3 musical rhythm; the arrangement of beats in music: *Three-fourths meter is waltz time. n.* Also, **metre.** [from French *mètre,* from Latin *metrum* measure, from Greek *metron*]

me ter[2] (mē′tər), device that measures, or measures and records, the amount of gas, water, electricity, etc., used: *an electric meter. n.* [*mete* (Old English *metan* to measure) + *-er*[1]]

meter maid, woman who issues tickets for violating parking regulations.

meth ane (meth′ān), a colorless, odorless, flammable gas, the simplest of the hydrocarbons; marsh gas. Methane occurs in marshes, petroleum wells, volcanoes, and coal mines. It is obtained commercially from natural gas. *n.*

me thinks (mi thingks′), OLD USE. it seems to me. *v., past tense* **me thought.**

meth od (meth′əd), 1 way of doing something: *a method of teaching music. Roasting is one method of cooking meat.* 2 order or system in getting things done or in thinking: *If you used more method, you wouldn't waste so much time. n.*

me thod ic (mə thod′ik), methodical. *adj.*

me thod i cal (mə thod′ə kəl), 1 done according to a method; systematic; orderly: *a methodical check of one's work.* 2 acting according to a method: *A scientist is usually a methodical person. adj.* —**me thod′i cal ly,** *adv.*

Meth od ism (meth′ə diz′əm), the doctrine, organization, and manner of worship of the Methodist Church. *n.*

Meth od ist (meth′ə dist), 1 member of a church that had its origin in the teachings and work of John Wesley; Wesleyan. 2 of the Methodists or Methodism. 1 *n.,* 2 *adj.*

meth od ol o gy (meth′ə dol′ə jē), system of methods or procedures used in any field. *n.*

me thought (mi thôt′), OLD USE. past tense of **methinks.** *v.*

Me thu se lah (mə thü′zə lə), 1 (in the Bible) a man who lived 969 years. 2 a very old man. *n.*

meth yl alcohol (meth′əl), wood alcohol.

me tic u lous (mə tik′yə ləs), extremely or excessively careful about small details. *adj.* —**me tic′u lous ly,** *adv.*

me tre (mē′tər), meter[1] (the spelling generally used in Great Britain and Canada). *n.*

met ric (met′rik), 1 of the meter or the metric system. 2 metrical. *adj.*

met ri cal (met′rə kəl), 1 of or written in meter, not in prose; having a regular arrangement of accents: *metrical verse as opposed to free verse.* 2 of, having to do with, or used in measurement. *adj.* —**met′ri cal ly,** *adv.*

metric system, a decimal system of weights and measures, or one which counts by tens. It is based on the meter as its unit of length, the gram as its unit of mass or weight, and the liter as its unit of volume.

metronome
Moving the weight up or down changes the speed of the ticking. If weight is near top, it ticks more slowly. Moving it down increases the speed.
WEIGHT

met ro nome (met′rə nōm), a device that can be adjusted to make loud ticking sounds at different speeds. Metronomes are used especially to mark time for persons practicing on musical instruments. *n.*

me trop o lis (mə trop′ə lis), 1 the most important city of a country or region: *New York is the metropolis of the United States.* 2 a large city; important center: *London is a busy metropolis. n., pl.* **me trop o lis es.**

met ro pol i tan (met′rə pol′ə tən), 1 of a large city; belonging to large cities: *metropolitan newspapers.* 2 person who lives in a large city and knows its ways. 3 archbishop presiding over a church province. 1 *adj.,* 2,3 *n.*

metropolitan area, the area or region including a large city and its suburbs.

Met ter nich (met′ər nik), **Prince von,** 1773-1859, Austrian diplomat and statesman. *n.*

met tle (met′l), disposition or temperament; spirit; courage. *n.*

on one's mettle, ready to do one's best.

met tle some (met′l səm), full of mettle; spirited; courageous. *adj.*

mev or **MeV** (mev), a million electron volts, used as a measure of energy in nuclear physics. *n.*

mew[1] (myü), 1 sound made by a cat or kitten. 2 make this sound: *Our kitten mews when it gets hungry.* 1 *n.,* 2 *v.* [probably an imitation of the sound]

mew[2] (myü), a sea gull; a gull. *n.* [Old English *mæw*]

mew[3] (myü), 1 a cage. 2 shut up in a cage; conceal; confine. 1 *n.,* 2 *v.* [from French of the 1300's *müe*]

mewl (myül), 1 cry like a baby; whimper. 2 the cry of a baby. 1 *v.,* 2 *n.*

mews (myüz), stables built around a court or alley. *n. sing. or pl.*

Mex., 1 Mexican. 2 Mexico.

Mex i can (mek′sə kən), 1 of Mexico or its people. 2 person born or living in Mexico. 1 *adj.,* 2 *n.*

Mexican War, war between the United States and Mexico from 1846 to 1848.

Mex i co (mek′sə kō), 1 country in North America, just south of W United States. *Capital:* Mexico City. 2 **Gulf of,** gulf of the Atlantic, south of the United States and east of Mexico. *n.*

Mexico City, capital of Mexico, in the central part.

mez za nine (mez′n ēn′), a low story, usually extending above a part of the main floor to form a balcony. In a theater the lowest balcony is often called a mezzanine. In a hotel the upper part of the lobby is often surrounded by a mezzanine. *n.*

mez zo-so pran o (met′sō sə pran′ō), 1 a voice between soprano and contralto. 2 singer having such a voice. *n., pl.* **mez zo-so pran os.** [from Italian *mezzo-soprano* middle soprano]

mg., milligram or milligrams.

Mgr., Manager.

mi (mē), the third note of the musical scale. *n.*

hat, āge, fär; let, ēqual, tėrm;
it, īce; hot, ōpen, ôrder;
oil, out; cup, put, rüle; ch, child;
ng, long; sh, she; th, thin;
ⱦH, then; zh, measure;

ə represents *a* in about,
e in taken, *i* in pencil,
o in lemon, *u* in circus.

mi., mile or miles.

Mi am i (mī am′ē), city in SE Florida, famous as a winter resort. *n.*

mi as ma (mī az′mə), a bad-smelling vapor rising from decaying matter on the earth. The miasma of swamps was formerly supposed to cause disease. *n., pl.* **mi as mas, mi as ma ta** (mī az′mə tə).

mi ca (mī′kə), mineral containing silicon that divides into thin, partly transparent layers; isinglass. Mica is highly resistant to heat and is used in electric fuses, lanterns, and stove doors. *n.*

Mi cah (mī′kə), 1 Hebrew prophet of the 700's B.C. 2 book of the Old Testament. *n.*

mice (mīs), plural of **mouse.** *n.*

Mich., Michigan.

Mi chael (mī′kəl), **Saint,** the archangel who led the loyal angels in defeating the revolt of Lucifer. *n.*

Mich ael mas (mik′əl məs), September 29, a church festival in honor of the archangel Michael. *n.*

Mi chel an ge lo (mī′kə lan′jə lō), 1475-1564, Italian sculptor, painter, architect, and poet. *n.*

Mich i gan (mish′ə gən), 1 one of the north central states of the United States. *Capital:* Lansing. 2 **Lake,** one of the five Great Lakes. It is entirely in the United States. *n.*

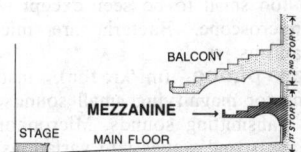
BALCONY
MEZZANINE
STAGE   MAIN FLOOR

mick le (mik′əl), DIALECT. much. *adj., adv., n.*

mi crobe (mī′krōb), germ. *n.*

mi cro bi ol o gist (mī′krō bī ol′ə jist), an expert in microbiology. *n.*

mi cro bi ol o gy (mī′krō bī ol′ə jē), science dealing with microorganisms. *n.*

mi cro cosm (mī′krō koz′əm), 1 a little world; universe in miniature. 2 man thought of as a miniature representation of the universe. *n.*

mi cro film (mī′krō film′), 1 film for

adj. adjective		*n.* noun	
adv. adverb		*prep.* preposition	
conj. conjunction		*pron.* pronoun	
interj. interjection		*v.* verb	
sing. singular		*pl.* plural	

making very small photographs of pages of a book, newspapers, records, etc., to preserve them in a very small space. 2 photograph on microfilm. 1 *n.,* 2 *v.*

mi cro me te o rite (mī′krō mē′- tē ə rīt′), a tiny particle of meteoric dust, so small that it does not burn as it falls to the earth from outer space. *n.*

mi crom e ter (mī krom′ə tər), 1 instrument for measuring very small distances, angles, objects, etc. Certain kinds are used with a microscope or telescope. 2 a micrometer caliper. *n.*

micrometer caliper

micrometer caliper, a caliper having a screw with a very fine thread, used for very accurate measurement.

mi cron (mī′kron), one millionth of a meter. *n., pl.* **mi crons, mi cra** (mī′- krə).

Mi cro ne sia (mī′krō nē′zhə), group of small islands in the Pacific, east of the Philippines. See **Melanesia** for map. *n.*

mi cro or gan ism (mī′krō ôr′gə- niz′əm), an animal or vegetable organism too small to be seen except with a microscope. Bacteria are microorganisms. *n.*

mi cro phone (mī′krə fōn), instrument for magnifying small sounds or for transmitting sounds. Microphones change sound waves into variations of an electric current. Radio and television stations use microphones for broadcasting. *n.*

mi cro scope (mī′krə skōp), instrument with a lens or combination of lenses for making small things look larger. Bacteria, blood cells, and other objects not visible to the naked eye are clearly visible through a microscope. *n.*

mi cro scop ic (mī′krə skop′ik), 1 that cannot be seen without using a microscope; tiny: *microscopic germs.* 2 like a microscope; suggesting a micro-

scope: *a microscopic eye for mistakes.* 3 of a microscope; with a microscope: *She made a microscopic examination of a fly's wing. adj.*

mi cro scop i cal ly (mī′krə skop′- ik lē), 1 by the use of a microscope. 2 as if with a microscope; in great detail. *adv.*

mi cros co py (mī kros′kə pē), the use of a microscope; microscopic investigation. *n.*

mi cro sec ond (mī′krō sek′ənd), one millionth of a second. *n.*

mi cro wave (mī′krō wāv′), an electromagnetic wave, usually having a wavelength of less than one meter. *n.*

mid[1] (mid), in the middle of; middle. *adj.* [Old English *midd*]

mid[2] or **'mid** (mid), OLD USE. amid. *prep.* [a different form of *amid*]

mid-, *prefix.* 1 the middle point or part of: *Midcontinent = the middle part of a continent.* 2 of, in, or near the middle of: *Midsummer = in the middle of summer.* [from *mid*[1]]

mid air (mid′er′ or mid′ar′), the middle of the air; the air above the ground: *The acrobat made a somersault in midair. n.*

Mi das (mī′dəs), (in Greek myths) a king of Phrygia who had the power to turn everything he touched into gold. *n.*

mid day (mid′dā′), 1 the middle of the day; noon. 2 of midday: *a midday meal.* 1 *n.,* 2 *adj.*

mid dle (mid′l), 1 the point or part that is the same distance from each end or side; the center: *the middle of the road.* 2 halfway between; in the center; at the same distance from either end or side: *the middle house in the row.* 3 in between; medium: *a man of middle size.* 4 the middle part of a person's body; waist. 1,4 *n.,* 2,3 *adj.*

middle age, time of life between youth and old age.

mid dle-aged (mid′l ājd′), between

microscope
There are magnifying lenses in the eyepiece and objective. The mirror reflects light up through the platform, which has an opening in it or is made of glass.

EYEPIECE

FOCUS ADJUSTER

OBJECTIVE

PLATFORM

MIRROR

youth and old age; being of middle age. *adj.*

Middle Ages, period of history between ancient and modern times; period from about A.D. 500 to about 1450.

Middle America, the area between the United States and South America. It includes Mexico, Central America, and usually the islands of the West Indies.

middle C, the musical note on the first added line below the treble staff and the first above the bass staff. See **clef** for diagram.

middle class, class of people who are socially and economically between the very wealthy class and the class of unskilled laborers and unemployed people. The middle class includes businessmen, professional people, office workers, and many skilled workers.

mid dle-class (mid′l klas′), of, having to do with, or characteristic of the middle class. *adj.*

middle ear, a hollow space between the eardrum and the inner ear; tympanum. In human beings it contains three small bones which pass on sound waves from the eardrum to the inner ear. See **ear** for diagram.

Middle East, region extending from Sudan, Egypt, and Turkey in the west to Iran in the east, and including the countries of SW Asia. Iraq, Israel, Jordan, Syria, and Saudi Arabia are countries in the Middle East.

Middle English, 1 period in the development of the English language between Old English and Modern English, lasting from about 1100 to about 1500. 2 language of this period. Chaucer wrote in Middle English.

mid dle man (mid′l man′), 1 trader or merchant who buys goods from the producer and sells them to a retailer or directly to the consumer. 2 person who acts as a go-between for two persons or groups concerned in some matter of business. *n., pl.* **mid dle men.**

Mid dle sex (mid′l seks), county in SE England. *n.*

mid dle weight (mid′l wāt′), 1 person of average weight. 2 boxer who weighs more than 147 pounds and less than 160 pounds. *n.*

Middle West, part of the United States west of the Appalachian Mountains, east of the Rocky Mountains, and north of the Ohio River and the S boundaries of Missouri and Kansas. Also, **Midwest.**

Middle Western, of or having to do with the Middle West. Also, **Midwestern.**

mid dling (mid′ling), 1 medium in size, quality, grade, etc.; ordinary; average. 2 **middlings,** *pl.* **a** products of medium size, quality, grade, or price.

b coarse particles of ground wheat mixed with bran. 1 *adj.*, 2 *n.*

mid dy (mid'ē), 1 INFORMAL. midshipman. 2 middy blouse. *n., pl.* **mid dies.**

middy blouse, a loose blouse like a sailor's, having a collar with a broad flap at the back, worn by children and young girls.

midge (mij), kind of very small insect; gnat. *n.*

midg et (mij'it), 1 person very much smaller than normal; a tiny person. 2 anything much smaller than the usual size for its type or kind. 3 very small; miniature; diminutive. 1,2 *n.*, 3 *adj.*

mid land (mid'lənd), 1 the middle part of a country; the interior. 2 **Midlands,** *pl.* the central part of England. 3 in or of the midland. 1,2 *n.*, 3 *adj.*

mid most (mid'mōst'), in the exact middle; nearest the middle. *adj.*

mid night (mid'nīt'), 1 twelve o'clock at night; the middle of the night. 2 of or at midnight. 3 dark as midnight. 1 *n.*, 2,3 *adj.*

midnight sun, sun seen throughout the day and night in the arctic and antarctic regions during their summers.

mid rib (mid'rib'), the central vein of a leaf. *n.*

MIDRIB   PETIOLE

mid riff (mid'rif), 1 the diaphragm separating the chest cavity from the abdomen. 2 the middle portion of the human body. *n.*

mid ship (mid'ship'), in, of, or belonging to the middle part of a ship. *adj.*

mid ship man (mid'ship'mən), 1 student at the United States Naval Academy at Annapolis. 2 a graduate of the British naval schools or an officer of the same rank as such a graduate. 3 (in former times) a boy or young man who assisted the officers of a ship. *n., pl.* **mid ship men.**

midst[1] (midst), middle. *n.* [perhaps from phrase *amidst of*]

in our midst, among us: *a traitor in our midst.*

in the midst of, 1 in the middle of; among; surrounded by: *in the midst of a forest.* 2 during.

midst[2] or **'midst** (midst), amidst; amid. *prep.* [short for *amidst*]

mid stream (mid'strēm'), the middle of a stream. *n.*

mid sum mer (mid'sum'ər), 1 the middle of summer. 2 the time around June 21. 3 in the middle of summer. 1,2 *n.*, 3 *adj.*

mid way (mid'wā'), 1 in the middle; halfway: *midway between the hill and*

---

middy blouse

the city (adv.), a midway position (adj.). 2 place for games, rides, and other amusements at a fair. 1 *adv., adj.*, 2 *n.*

Midway Islands, group of small islands in the Pacific, belonging to the United States. They are about halfway between the United States and the Philippines.

mid week (mid'wēk'), 1 the middle of the week. 2 in the middle of the week. 1 *n.*, 2 *adj.*

Mid west (mid'west'), Middle West. *n.*

Mid west ern (mid'wes'tərn), Middle Western. *adj.*

mid wife (mid'wīf'), woman who helps women in childbirth. *n., pl.* **mid wives.**

mid win ter (mid'win'tər), 1 the middle of winter. 2 the time around December 21. 3 in the middle of winter. 1,2 *n.*, 3 *adj.*

mid year (mid'yir'), happening in the middle of the year: *a midyear examination. adj.*

mien (mēn), manner of holding the head and body; way of acting and looking: *have the mien of a judge. n.*

miff (mif), INFORMAL. 1 a peevish fit; petty quarrel. 2 be offended; have a petty quarrel. 1 *n.*, 2 *v.*

might[1] (mīt), past tense of **may.** *Mother said that we might play in the barn. He might have done it when you were not looking. v.* [Old English *mihte, meahte*]

might[2] (mīt), great power; strength: *Work with all your might. n.* [Old English *miht*]

with might and main, with all one's strength.

might i ly (mī'tə lē), 1 in a mighty manner; powerfully; vigorously: *Samson strove mightily and pulled the pillars down.* 2 very much; greatly: *We were mightily pleased at winning. adv.*

might i ness (mī'tē nis), power; strength. *n.*

might y (mī'tē), 1 showing strength or power; powerful; strong: *a mighty ruler, mighty force.* 2 very great: *a mighty famine.* 3 INFORMAL. very: *a mighty long time.* 1,2 *adj.*, **might i er, might i est;** 3 *adv.*

mi gnon ette (min'yə net'), a plant with long, pointed clusters of small, fragrant, greenish-white flowers. *n.*

mi graine (mī'grān), a severe headache, usually on one side only. *n.*

mi grant (mī'grənt), 1 migrating; roving: *a migrant worker.* 2 person, animal,

---

mileage

hat, āge, fär; let, ēqual, tėrm;
it, īce; hot, ōpen, ôrder;
oil, out; cup, pùt, rüle; ch, child;
ng, long; sh, she; th, thin;
ŦH, then; zh, measure;

ə represents *a* in about,
e in taken, *i* in pencil,
o in lemon, *u* in circus.

bird, or plant that migrates. 1 *adj.*, 2 *n.*

mi grate (mī'grāt), 1 move from one place to settle in another: *Pioneers from New England migrated to all parts of the United States.* 2 go from one region to another with the change in the seasons: *Most birds migrate to warmer countries in the winter. v.*, **mi grat ed, mi grat ing.**

mi gra tion (mī grā'shən), 1 a migrating. 2 number of people or animals migrating together. *n.*

mi gra to ry (mī'grə tôr'ē), 1 moving from one place to another; migrating: *migratory laborers, migratory birds.* 2 of or having to do with migration: *the migratory pattern of elephants. adj.*

mi ka do or **Mi ka do** (mə kä'dō), a former title of the emperor of Japan. It is seldom used now except in poetry. *n., pl.* **mi ka dos** or **Mi ka dos.**

mike (mīk), SLANG. microphone. *n.*

mil (mil), measure of length equal to .001 of an inch. It is used in measuring the diameter of wires. *n.*

mi la dy or **mi la di** (mi lā'dē), 1 my lady. 2 an English lady. *n., pl.* **mi la dies.**

Mi lan (mi lan'), city in N Italy. *n.*

milch (milch), giving milk; kept for the milk it gives: *a milch cow. adj.*

mild (mīld), 1 gentle or kind: *a mild disposition.* 2 calm; warm; temperate; not harsh or severe: *a mild climate, a mild winter.* 3 soft or sweet to the senses; not sharp, sour, bitter, or strong in taste: *mild cheese, a mild cigar. adj.* —**mild'ly,** *adv.* —**mild'ness,** *n.*

mil dew (mil'dü or mil'dyü), 1 kind of fungus that appears on plants or on paper, clothes, leather, etc., during damp weather: *Mildew killed the rosebuds in our garden.* 2 the coating or discoloration, or the diseased condition, produced by such a fungus: *Damp clothes left in a pile will show mildew in a few days.* 3 cover or become covered with mildew: *A pile of damp clothes in the closet mildewed.* 1,2 *n.*, 3 *v.*

mile (mīl) 1 measure of distance equal to 5280 feet; statute mile. 2 nautical mile. *n.*

mile age (mī'lij), 1 miles covered or

---

adj.	adjective	*n.*	noun
adv.	adverb	*prep.*	preposition
conj.	conjunction	*pron.*	pronoun
interj.	interjection	*v.*	verb
sing.	singular	*pl.*	plural

traveled: *Our car's mileage last year was 10,000 miles.* 2 miles traveled per gallon of gasoline: *Do you get good mileage with your car?* 3 length, extent, or distance in miles: *The mileage of a railroad is its total number of miles of roadbed.* 4 an allowance for traveling expenses at so much a mile: *Congressmen are given mileage between their homes and Washington, D.C. n.*

mile post (mīl/pōst/), post set up to show the distance in miles to a certain place: *A milepost showed that we were 38 miles from Chicago. n.*

mile stone (mīl/stōn/), 1 stone set up to show the distance in miles to a certain place. 2 an important event: *The invention of printing was a milestone in progress. n.*

mi lieu (mē lyü/), surroundings, environment. *n.* [from French]

mil i tan cy (mil/ə tən sē), warlike behavior or tendency; militant spirit or policy. *n.*

mil i tant (mil/ə tənt), 1 aggressive; fighting; warlike: *a militant nature, a militant nation.* 2 active in serving a cause or in spreading a belief: *a militant churchman.* 3 a militant person. 1,2 *adj.*, 3 *n.* —**mil/i tant ly,** *adv.*

mil i tar i ly (mil/ə ter/ə lē), in a military manner. *adv.*

mil i ta rism (mil/ə tə riz/əm), 1 policy of making military organization and power very strong. 2 military spirit and ideals. *n.*

mil i tar ist (mil/ə tər ist), 1 person who believes in a very powerful military organization. 2 an expert in warfare and military matters. *n.*

mil i ta ris tic (mil/ə tə ris/tik), of or having to do with militarists or militarism. *adj.*

mil i tar i za tion (mil/ə tər ə zā/shən), a militarizing or a being militarized. *n.*

mil i ta rize (mil/ə tə rīz/), 1 make the military organization of (a country) very powerful. 2 fill with military spirit and ideals. *v.*, **mil i ta rized, mil i ta riz ing.**

mil i tar y (mil/ə ter/ē), 1 of soldiers or war: *military training, military history.* 2 done by soldiers: *military maneuvers.* 3 fit for soldiers: *military discipline.* 4 suitable for war; warlike:

military valor. **5 the military,** the armed forces: *an officer of the military.* 1-4 *adj.*, 5 *n.*

mil i tate (mil/ə tāt), have or exert force; act; work; operate (against or in favor of): *Bad weather militated against the success of the picnic. v.*, **mil i tat ed, mil i tat ing.**

mi li tia (mə lish/ə), a military force; army of citizens who are not regular soldiers but who undergo training for emergency duty or national defense. Every state of the United States has a militia called the National Guard. *n., pl.* **mi li tias.**

mi li tia man (mə lish/ə mən), soldier in the militia. *n., pl.* **mi li tia men.**

milk (milk), 1 the white liquid secreted by female mammals for the nourishment of their young, especially that from cows, which we drink and use in cooking. 2 any kind of liquid resembling this, such as the white juice of a plant, tree, or nut: *the milk of a coconut.* 3 draw milk from (a cow, goat, etc.). 4 drain contents, strength, information, wealth, etc., from; exploit: *The dishonest treasurer milked the club treasury.* 1,2 *n.*, 3,4 *v.*

milk er (mil/kər), 1 person who milks. 2 machine that milks. 3 cow, goat, etc., that gives milk. *n.*

milk i ness (milk/kē nis), condition of being milky or of resembling milk in appearance or quality. *n.*

milk maid (milk/mād/), 1 woman who milks cows. 2 woman who works in a dairy. *n.*

milk man (milk/man/), man who sells milk or delivers it to customers. *n., pl.* **milk men.**

milk of magnesia, a milk-white medicine in water, used as a laxative and to counteract acidity.

milk shake, a drink consisting of milk, flavoring, and often ice cream, shaken or beaten until frothy.

milk sop (milk/sop/), an unmanly fellow; coward. *n.*

milk sugar, lactose.

milk tooth, one of the first set of teeth; temporary tooth of a young child or animal.

milk weed (milk/wēd/), weed with white juice that looks like milk. *n.*

milk-white (milk/hwīt/), white as milk. *adj.*

milk y (mil/kē), 1 like milk; white as milk; whitish. 2 of milk; containing milk. *adj.*, **milk i er, milk i est.**

Milky Way, 1 a broad band of faint light that stretches across the sky at night. It is made up of countless stars too far away to be seen separately without a telescope. 2 the galaxy in which these countless stars are found; Galaxy. The earth, sun, and all the

planets around the sun are part of the Milky Way.

mill[1] (mil), 1 machine for grinding grain into flour or meal. 2 a building containing such a machine. 3 grind (grain) into flour or meal. 4 any machine for crushing or grinding: *a coffee mill, a pepper mill.* 5 grind into powder or pulp; grind very fine. 6 a building where manufacturing is done: *Cotton cloth is made in a cotton mill.* 7 cut a series of fine notches or ridges on the edge of (a coin): *A dime is milled.* 8 move around in a confused way: *The frightened cattle began to mill.* 1,2,4,6 *n.*, 3,5,7,8 *v.* [Old English *mylen*]

mill[2] (mil), \$.001, or $^1/_{10}$ of a cent. Mills are used in figuring, but not as coins. *n.* [short for Latin *millesimus* one thousandth, from *mille* thousand]

Mill (mil), **John Stuart,** 1806-1873, English economist and philosopher. *n.*

Mil lay (mə lā/), **Edna St. Vincent,** 1892-1950, American poet. *n.*

mil len ni al (mə len/ē əl), 1 of a thousand years. 2 like that of a millennium; fit for the millennium. *adj.*

mil len ni um (mə len/ē əm), 1 period of a thousand years: *The world is many millenniums old.* 2 (in the Bible) the period of a thousand years during which Christ is expected to reign on earth. 3 period of righteousness and happiness. *n., pl.* **mil len ni ums, mil len ni a** (mə len/ē ə).

mil le pede (mil/ə pēd/), millipede. *n.*

mill er (mil/ər), 1 person who owns or runs a mill, especially a flour mill. 2 moth whose wings look as if they were powdered with flour. *n.*

mil let (mil/it), 1 a very small grain used for food in Europe, Asia, and Africa. 2 the plant that it grows on. In the United States and Europe, millet is used for hay. *n.*

Mil let (mə lā/), **Jean François,** 1814-1875, French painter. *n.*

mil li bar (mil/ə bär), measure of atmospheric pressure equal to 1000 dynes per square centimeter. Standard atmospheric pressure at sea level is about 1013 millibars or 14.69 pounds per square inch. *n.*

mil li gram or **mil li gramme** (mil/ə gram), $^1/_{1000}$ of a gram, equal to .0154 of a grain, or about two millionths of a pound. *n.*

Mil li kan (mil/ə kən), **Robert A.,** 1868-1953, American physicist. *n.*

mil li li ter or **mil li li tre** (mil/ə lē/tər), $^1/_{1000}$ of a liter, equal to 1.000027 cubic centimeters or .061 cubic inch. *n.*

mil li me ter or **mil li me tre** (mil/ə mē/tər), $^1/_{1000}$ of a meter, or .03937 inch. *n.*

mil li ner (mil/ə nər), person who

mil li ner y (mil′ə ner′ē), 1 women's hats. 2 business of making, trimming, or selling women's hats. *n.*

mil lion (mil′yən), 1 one thousand thousand; 1,000,000. 2 a very large number; very many: *She can always think of a million reasons for not helping with the dishes.* 1 *n.,* 1,2 *adj.*

mil lion aire (mil′yə ner′ or mil′yə-när′), 1 person whose wealth amounts to a million or more dollars, pounds, francs, etc. 2 a very wealthy person. *n.*

mil lionth (mil′yənth), 1 last in a series of a million. 2 one of a million equal parts. *adj., n.*

millipede—about 1 in. long

mil li pede (mil′ə pēd′), a small, wormlike arthropod that has two pairs of legs apiece for most of its segments. *n.* Also, **millepede.**

mill pond (mil′pond′), pond supplying water to drive a mill wheel. *n.*

mill race (mil′rās′), 1 current of water that drives a mill wheel. 2 channel in which it flows to the mill. *n.*

mill stone (mil′stōn′), 1 either of a pair of round, flat stones for grinding corn, wheat, etc. 2 a heavy burden. 3 anything that grinds or crushes. *n.*

mill wheel, wheel that is turned by water and supplies power for a mill.

Milne (miln), **A. A.,** 1882-1956, English writer of children's verses, stories, and plays. *n.*

mi lord (mi lôrd′), 1 my lord. 2 an English gentleman. *n.*

milque toast (milk′tōst′), an extremely timid person. *n.*

milt (milt), 1 the sperm cells of male fishes with the milky fluid containing them. 2 the reproductive gland in male fishes. *n.*

Mil ton (milt′n), **John,** 1608-1674, English poet who wrote *Paradise Lost. n.*

Mil wau kee (mil wôk′ē), city in SE Wisconsin, on Lake Michigan. *n.*

mime (mīm), 1 a mimic, jester, or clown. 2 imitate; mimic. 3 pantomime. 4 actor, especially in a pantomime. 5 act in a pantomime; act without using words. 1,3,4 *n.,* 2,5 *v.,* **mimed, miming.**

mim e o graph (mim′ē ə graf), 1 machine for making copies of written or typewritten materials by means of stencils. 2 make (copies) with a mimeograph. 1 *n.,* 2 *v.*

mim ic (mim′ik), 1 make fun of by imitating: *We like to get him to mimic all his old teachers.* 2 person or thing that imitates. 3 copy closely; imitate: *A parrot can mimic a person's voice.* 4 resemble closely in form, color, etc.: *Some insects mimic leaves.* 5 not real, but imitated or pretended for some purpose: *We staged a mimic rescue of a drowning victim in our first-aid class.* 6 imitative: *mimic gestures.* 1,3,4 *v.,* **mim icked, mim ick ing;** 2 *n.,* 5,6 *adj.*

mim ic ry (mim′ik rē), 1 a mimicking. 2 the close outward resemblance of an animal to its surroundings or to some different animal, especially for protection or concealment. *n., pl.* **mim ic ries.**

mi mo sa (mi mō′sə), tree, shrub, or herb growing in warm regions, and usually having fernlike leaves and heads of small pink, yellow, or white flowers. *n., pl.* **mi mo sas.**

min., 1 minimum. 2 minute or minutes.

min a ret (min′ə ret′), a slender, high tower attached to a Moslem mosque with one or more projecting balconies, from which a crier calls the people to prayer. *n.*

millstones (def. 1) Grain is dropped into the center hole in the top stone. When the top stone is turned around the spindle, the grain is ground between it and the larger hollowed-out bottom stone.

mince (mins), 1 chop up into very small pieces. 2 meat cut up into very small pieces. 3 mincemeat. 4 put on fine airs in speaking or walking. 5 walk with little short steps. 1,4,5 *v.,* **minced, minc ing;** 2,3 *n.*

not to mince matters or **not to mince words,** to speak plainly and frankly.

mince meat (mins′mēt′), mixture of chopped apples, suet, raisins, currants, spices, etc., and sometimes meat, used as a filling for pies. *n.*

mince pie, pie filled with mincemeat.

minc ing (min′sing), 1 putting on a dainty and refined manner: *a mincing voice.* 2 walking with little short steps. *adj.* —**minc′ing ly,** *adv.*

mind (mīnd), 1 the part of a person that knows, remembers, thinks, feels, wish-

hat, āge, fär; let, ēqual, tėrm; it, īce; hot, ōpen, ôrder; oil, out; cup, pút, rüle; ch, child; ng, long; sh, she; th, thin; ŦH, then; zh, measure;

ə represents *a* in about, *e* in taken, *i* in pencil, *o* in lemon, *u* in circus.

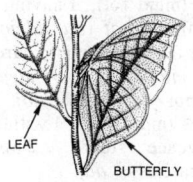

LEAF   BUTTERFLY

mimicry (def. 2)

es, wills, etc. 2 mental ability; intelligence; intellect: *have a good mind.* 3 person who has intelligence: *the greatest minds of the period.* 4 reason; sanity: *be out of one's mind.* 5 what one thinks or feels: *change one's mind.* 6 remembrance or recollection; memory: *Keep the rules in mind.* 7 bear in mind; give heed to: *Mind my words!* 8 take notice; observe. 9 be careful concerning: *Mind the step.* 10 take care: *Mind that you come on time.* 11 look after; take care of; tend: *Mind the baby.* 12 obey: *Mind your father and mother.* 13 feel bad about; object to: *Do you mind closing the door for me? Some people don't mind cold weather.* 14 DIALECT. remember. 1-6 *n.,* 7-14 *v.*

bear in mind or **keep in mind,** remember.

be of one mind, have the same opinion; agree.

cross one's mind, occur to one; come into one's thoughts suddenly.

have a mind to, intend to; think of doing.

have in mind, 1 remember. 2 think of; consider.

make up one's mind, decide: *I made up my mind to study harder and get better grades.*

never mind, INFORMAL. don't let it trouble you; it does not matter.

on one's mind, in one's mind; in one's thoughts.

put in mind, remind: *Your joke puts me in mind of a joke I heard yesterday.*

set one's mind on, want very much.

to one's mind, in one's opinion; to one's way of thinking.

Min da na o (min′də nä′ō), the second largest island in the Philippines. *n.*

mind ed (mīn′did), inclined; disposed:

mindful

adj.	adjective	*n.*	noun
adv.	adverb	*prep.*	preposition
conj.	conjunction	*pron.*	pronoun
interj.	interjection	*v.*	verb
sing.	singular	*pl.*	plural

Come a little early, if you are so minded. *adj.*

mind ful (mīnd′fəl), 1 having in mind; heedful: *Mindful of your advice, I went slowly.* 2 taking thought; careful: *We had to be mindful of every step we took on the slippery sidewalk.* *adj.*

mind less (mīnd′lis), 1 without mind or intelligence; stupid. 2 not taking thought; careless. *adj.*

mind's eye, mental view or vision; imagination.

mine¹ (mīn), 1 the one or ones belonging to me: *This book is mine. Your shoes are black; mine are brown.* 2 OLD USE. my (used only before a vowel or *h*): *mine eyes.* 1 *pron.,* 2 *adj.* [Old English *mīn*]

mine² (mīn), 1 a large hole or space dug in the earth to get out ores, precious stones, coal, salt, etc.: *a coal mine, a gold mine.* 2 dig a mine; make a hole or space underground. 3 dig in for coal, gold, etc.: *to mine the earth.* 4 get from a mine: *to mine coal, to mine gold.* 5 to work in a mine. 6 a rich or plentiful source: *The book proved to be a mine of information about radio.* 7 an underground passage in which an explosive is placed to blow up an enemy's forts, etc. 8 make underground passages below. 9 bomb put under water, laid on the ground, or shallowly buried to blow up enemy troops or equipment. 10 lay mines under: *to mine the mouth of a harbor.* 1,6,7,9 *n.,* 2-5,8,10 *v.,* **mined, min ing.** [from French of the 1200's]

min er (mī′nər), man who works in a mine: *a coal miner.* *n.*

min er al (min′ər əl), 1 substance obtained by mining or digging in the earth. Coal, gold, and mica are minerals. 2 any substance that is neither plant nor animal. Salt and sand are minerals. 3 of minerals. 4 like a mineral. 5 containing minerals. 1,2 *n.,* 3-5 *adj.*

min er a log i cal (min′ər ə loj′ə kəl), of mineralogy. *adj.*

min e ral o gist (min′ə rol′ə jist), an expert in mineralogy. *n.*

min e ral o gy (min′ə rol′ə jē), science of minerals. *n.*

mineral water, water containing mineral salts or gases. People drink various mineral waters for their health.

Mi ner va (mə nèr′və), (in Roman myths) the goddess of wisdom, the arts, and war. The Greeks called her Athena. *n.*

min gle (ming′gəl), 1 combine in a mixture; mix; blend: *Two rivers that join mingle their waters.* 2 associate: *mingle with important people, mingle with everyone at a party.* *v.,* **min gled, min gling.**

min i a ture (min′ē ə chủr *or* min′ə chər), 1 anything represented on a small scale: *In the museum there is a miniature of the ship "Mayflower."* 2 done or made on a very small scale; tiny: *miniature cars, miniature furniture for a dollhouse.* 3 a very small painting, usually a portrait on ivory or vellum. 1,3 *n.,* 2 *adj.*

min i a tur ize (min′ē ə chə rīz′ *or* min′ə chə rīz′), reduce to a very small size: *miniaturized electronic devices.* *v.,* **min i a tur ized, min i a tur iz ing.**

min i mal (min′ə məl), least possible; very small; having to do with a minimum: *minimal damage, a minimal cost.* *adj.* —**min′i mal ly,** *adv.*

min i mize (min′ə mīz), 1 reduce to the least possible amount or degree: *The polar explorers took every precaution to minimize the dangers of their trip.* 2 to state at the lowest possible estimate; make the least of: *She minimized the work involved in the job in order to get me to do it.* *v.,* **min i mized, min i miz ing.**

min i mum (min′ə məm), 1 the least possible amount; lowest amount: *Each of the children had to drink some milk at breakfast; half a glass was the minimum.* 2 least possible; lowest: *Eighteen is the minimum age for voting in most states. The workers wanted a minimum wage of two dollars and a half an hour.* 1 *n., pl.* **min i mums, min i ma** (min′ə mə); 2 *adj.*

min ing (mī′ning), 1 the working of mines for ores, coal, etc. 2 business of digging coal or ores from mines. 3 the laying of explosive mines. *n.*

min ion (min′yən), 1 servant or follower willing to do whatever he is ordered to do by his master. 2 a darling; a favorite. *n.*

min is ter (min′ə stər), 1 clergyman serving a church; spiritual guide; pastor. 2 act as a servant or nurse; be of service or aid; be helpful: *minister to a sick person's wants.* 3 person who is given charge of a department of the government: *the Minister of Labor.* 4 person sent to a foreign country to represent his own government: *the United States Minister to Switzerland.* 1,3,4 *n.,* 2 *v.*

min is ter i al (min′ə stir′ē əl), 1 of a minister; having to do with a minister. 2 suited to a clergyman: *a ministerial manner.* *adj.*

min is trant (min′ə strənt), 1 that ministers; ministering. 2 person who ministers. 1 *adj.,* 2 *n.*

min is tra tion (min′ə strā′shən), 1 service as a minister of a church. 2 help; aid; give ministration to the poor. *n.*

min is try (min′ə strē), 1 office, duties, or time of service of a minister. 2 ministers of a church; clergy. 3 ministers of a government. 4 a government department under a minister. 5 a ministering or serving. *n., pl.* **min is tries.**

mink (def. 1)—2 ft. long with tail

mink (mingk), 1 a small mammal of North America that resembles a weasel and lives in water part of the time. 2 its valuable brown fur. *n.*

Minn., Minnesota.

Min ne ap o lis (min′ē ap′ə lis), city in SE Minnesota, on the Mississippi. *n.*

Min ne so ta (min′ə sō′tə), one of the midwestern states of the United States. *Capital:* St. Paul. *n.* —**Min′ne so′tan,** *adj., n.*

min now (min′ō), 1 any of various very small fresh-water fish, especially those belonging to the same family as the carp. 2 any very tiny fish. *n.*

mi nor (mī′nər), 1 less important; smaller; lesser: *a minor fault. Your paper is good; it contains only a few minor errors.* 2 of a lower rank or order: *a minor poet, a minor political party.* 3 person under the legal age of responsibility (18 or 21 years). 4 in music: **a** less by a half step than the corresponding major interval: *a minor chord.* **b** noting a scale or key whose third tone is minor in relation to the main tone: *the C minor scale or key.* **c** a minor scale, key, chord, interval, etc. 5 subject or course of study to which a student gives much time and attention, but less than to his major subject: *His minor is French.* 6 have or take as a minor subject of study: *He will minor in French.* 1,2,4a,4b *adj.,* 3,4c,5 *n.,* 6 *v.*

mi nor i ty (mə nôr′ə tē *or* mī nôr′ə tē), 1 the smaller number or part; less than half: *A minority of the children wanted a party, but the majority chose a picnic.* 2 a group within a country, state, etc., that differs in race, religion, or national origin from the larger part of the population. 3 condition or time of being under the legal age of responsibility. *n., pl.* **mi nor i ties.**

minor league, any professional baseball league or association other than the major leagues.

Mi nos (mī′nəs), in Greek legends: 1 a king and lawgiver of Crete, the son of Zeus, who became a judge in Hades. 2 his grandson, who built the Labyrinth at Crete and kept the Minotaur in it. *n.*

Min o taur (min′ə tôr), (in Greek legends) a monster with a bull's head and a man's body, kept in the Labyrinth at Crete and fed with human flesh. Theseus killed the Minotaur. *n.*

Minsk (minsk), city in W Soviet Union, capital of Byelorussia. *n.*

min ster (min′stər), 1 church of a monastery. 2 a large or important church; cathedral. *n.*

min strel (min′strəl), 1 singer or musician in the Middle Ages who entertained in the household of a lord or went about singing or reciting poems, often of his own making. 2 member of a minstrel show. *n.*

minstrel show, show or entertainment in which the performers blackened their faces and hands with burnt cork and played music, sang songs, and told jokes. Minstrel shows were very popular until the end of the 1800's.

min strel sy (min′strəl sē), 1 art or practice of a minstrel. 2 collection of songs and ballads. 3 company of minstrels. *n., pl.* **min strel sies.**

mint¹ (mint), 1 a sweet-smelling plant used for flavoring. Peppermint and spearmint are kinds of mint. 2 piece of candy flavored with mint. *n.* [Old English *minte,* from Latin *menta*]

mint² (mint), 1 place where money is coined by government authority. 2 to coin (money). 3 a large amount: *A million dollars is a mint of money.* 4 without a blemish; as good as new: *a car in mint condition.* 1,3 *n.,* 2 *v.,* 4 *adj.* [Old English *mynet* a coin, from Latin *moneta* mint]

min u end (min′yü end), number or quantity from which another is to be subtracted: *In 100 − 23 = 77, the minuend is 100. n.*

min u et (min′yü et′), 1 a slow, stately dance, fashionable in the 1700's. 2 music for it. *n.*

minuet (def. 1)

mi nus (mī′nəs), 1 decreased by; less: *5 minus 2 leaves 3.* 2 INFORMAL. without; lacking: *a book minus its cover.* 3 less than: *A mark of B minus is not so high as a mark of B.* 4 minus sign. 5 less than zero: *If you have no money, and owe someone 10 cents, you have minus 10 cents.* 1,2 *prep.,* 3,5 *adj.,* 4 *n., pl.* **mi nus es.**

minus sign, the sign (−), indicating that the number or quantity following it is to be subtracted, or is a negative number or quantity.

min ute¹ (min′it), 1 one of the 60 equal periods of time that make up an hour; sixty seconds. 2 a short time; instant: *I'll be there in a minute.* 3 an exact point of time: *The minute you see her coming, please tell me.* 4 one sixtieth of a degree. 10°10 means ten degrees and ten minutes. 5 **minutes,** *pl.* a written summary of what happened at a meeting, kept by the secretary. *n.* [from French of the 1300's *minute,* from Latin *minuta* minute, small part]

mi nute² (mī nüt′ *or* mī nyüt′), 1 very small; tiny: *a minute speck of dust.* 2 going into or concerned with small details: *a minute observer. He gave me minute instructions about my work. adj.* [from Latin *minutum* made small, from *minus* less] —**mi nute′ly,** *adv.* —**mi nute′ness,** *n.*

min ute hand (min′it), hand on a clock or watch that indicates minutes. It moves around the whole dial once in an hour.

min ute man (min′it man′), member of the American militia just before and during the Revolutionary War. The minutemen kept themselves ready for military service at a minute's notice. *n., pl.* **min ute men.**

mi nu ti ae (mi nü′shē ē *or* mi nyü′shē ē), very small matters; trifling details. *n.pl.*

minx (mingks), a pert girl. *n., pl.* **minxes.**

mir a cle (mir′ə kəl), 1 a wonderful happening that is contrary to, or independent of, the known laws of nature: *It would be a miracle if we should see the sun stand still in the heavens for an hour.* 2 something marvelous; a wonder: *It was a miracle you weren't hurt in that accident.* 3 a remarkable example: *an engineering miracle. The children's nursery school teacher is a miracle of patience. n.*

mi rac u lous (mə rak′yə ləs), 1 contrary to, or independent of, the known laws of nature: *Alchemists tried to find a miraculous liquid that could change lead into gold.* 2 marvelous; wonderful: *miraculous good fortune. adj.* —**mi rac′u lous ly,** *adv.*

hat, āge, fär; let, ēqual, tėrm; it, īce; hot, ōpen, ôrder; oil, out; cup, pùt, rüle; ch, child; ng, long; sh, she; th, thin; ₮H, then; zh, measure;

ə represents *a* in about, *e* in taken, *i* in pencil, *o* in lemon, *u* in circus.

mi rage (mə räzh′), an optical illusion, usually in the desert, at sea, or on a paved road, in which some distant scene appears to be much closer than it actually is. It is caused by the refraction of light rays from the distant scene by air layers of different temperatures. Often what is reflected is seen upside down or as something other than it is. Travelers on the desert may see a mirage of palm trees and water. *n.*

mire (mīr), 1 soft, deep mud; slush. 2 wet, swampy ground; bog; swamp. 3 get stuck in mire: *He mired his car and had to go for help.* 4 to soil with mud or mire. 1,2 *n.,* 3,4 *v.,* **mired, mir ing.**

mir ror (mir′ər), 1 a piece of glass that reflects images; looking glass. It is coated on one side with silver or aluminum. 2 reflect as a mirror does: *The still water mirrored the trees along the bank.* 3 whatever reflects or gives a true description: *This book is a mirror of the life of the pioneers.* 1,3 *n.,* 2 *v.*

mirth (mėrth), merry fun; being joyous or gay; laughter. *n.*

mirth ful (mėrth′fəl), merry; joyous; gay; laughing. *adj.* —**mirth′ful ly,** *adv.*

mirth less (mėrth′lis), without mirth; joyless; gloomy. *adj.* —**mirth′less ly,** *adv.*

mir y (mī′rē), 1 muddy; swampy. 2 dirty; filthy. *adj.,* **mir i er, mir i est.**

mis-, *prefix.* 1 bad: *Misgovernment = bad government.* 2 badly: *Misbehave = behave badly.* 3 wrong: *Mispronunciation = wrong pronunciation.* 4 wrongly: *Misapply = apply wrongly.* [Old English *mis-* or (in borrowed words) from French before the 1400's *mes-*]

mis ad ven ture (mis′əd ven′chər), an unfortunate accident; bad luck; mishap. *n.*

mis an thrope (mis′ən thrōp), person who dislikes or distrusts people in general; hater of mankind. *n.*

mis an throp ic (mis′ən throp′ik), of or like a misanthrope. *adj.*

mis an thro py (mis an′thrə pē), hatred, dislike, or distrust of people in general. *n.*

541

adj.	adjective	*n.*	noun
adv.	adverb	*prep.*	preposition
conj.	conjunction	*pron.*	pronoun
interj.	interjection	*v.*	verb
sing.	singular	*pl.*	plural

mis ap pli ca tion (mis′ap/lə kā′shən), a misapplying or a being misapplied; wrong application. *n.*

mis ap ply (mis′ə plī′), apply wrongly: *to misapply a fact, knowledge, wealth, etc. v.,* **mis ap plied, mis ap ply ing.**

mis ap pre hend (mis′ap/ri hend′), misunderstand. *v.*

mis ap pre hen sion (mis′ap/ri hen/shən), wrong idea; misunderstanding. *n.*

mis ap pro pri ate (mis′ə prō/prē at), 1 use dishonestly as one's own: *The treasurer had misappropriated the club funds.* 2 put to a wrong use. *v.,* **mis ap pro pri at ed, mis ap pro pri at ing.**

mis ap pro pri a tion (mis′ə prō/prē ā/shən), 1 dishonest use as one's own. 2 any act of putting to a wrong use. *n.*

mis be have (mis′bi hāv′), behave badly. *v.,* **mis be haved, mis be hav ing.**

mis be hav ior (mis′bi hā/vyər), bad behavior. *n.*

misc., miscellaneous.

mis cal cu late (mis kal/kyə lāt), calculate wrongly or incorrectly. *v.,* **mis cal cu lat ed, mis cal cu lat ing.**

mis cal cu la tion (mis′kal/kyə lā/shən), a wrong or incorrect calculation. *n.*

mis call (mis kôl′), call by a wrong name. *v.*

mis car riage (mis kar/ij), 1 failure: *Because the judge was unfair, that trial resulted in a miscarriage of justice.* 2 birth of a baby before it is able to live. *n.*

mis car ry (mis kar/ē), 1 go wrong; be unsuccessful: *Our plans miscarried, and we could not come.* 2 give birth to a baby before it is able to live. *v.,* **mis car ried, mis car ry ing.**

mis cel la ne ous (mis′ə lā/nē əs), not all of one kind or nature: *He had a miscellaneous collection of stones, butterflies, stamps, and many other things. adj.* **—mis′cel la/ne ous ly,** *adv.*

mis cel la ny (mis′ə lā/nē), 1 a miscellaneous collection; mixture. 2 Also, **miscellanies,** *pl.,* a collection of miscellaneous articles in one book. *n., pl.* **mis cel la nies.**

mis chance (mis chans′), 1 bad luck; misfortune: *By some mischance she didn't receive my telegram.* 2 piece of bad luck; an unlucky accident. *n.*

mis chief (mis′chif), 1 conduct that causes harm or trouble, often unintentionally: *The children were playing with matches, and their mischief resulted in a serious fire.* 2 harm or injury, usually done by some person: *Why are you angry? He did you no mischief.* 3 person who does harm or causes annoyance, often just in fun: *You little mischief! You have hidden my glasses.* 4 merry teasing: *Her eyes were full of mischief. n.*

mis chie vous (mis′chə vəs), 1 causing mischief; naughty: *mischievous behavior.* 2 harmful: *mischievous gossip.* 3 full of pranks and teasing fun: *mischievous children. adj.* **—mis′chie vous ly,** *adv.* **—mis′chie vous ness,** *n.*

mis con ceive (mis′kən sēv′), have wrong ideas about; misunderstand. *v.,* **mis con ceived, mis con ceiv ing.**

mis con cep tion (mis′kən sep/shən), a mistaken idea or notion; wrong conception. *n.*

mis con duct (mis kon/dukt *for 1,3;* mis′kən dukt′ *for 2,4*), 1 bad behavior: *The misconduct of the children resulted in their being punished.* 2 behave badly. 3 bad management: *The misconduct of that business nearly ruined it.* 4 manage badly. 1,3 *n.,* 2,4 *v.*

mis con struc tion (mis′kən struk/shən), wrong or mistaken meaning; misunderstanding: *What you said was open to misconstruction. n.*

mis con strue (mis′kən strü′), take in a wrong or mistaken sense; misunderstand: *Shyness is sometimes misconstrued as unfriendliness. v.,* **mis con strued, mis con stru ing.**

mis count (mis kount′ *for 1;* mis′kount′ *for 2*), 1 count wrongly or incorrectly. 2 a wrong or incorrect count. 1 *v.,* 2 *n.*

mis cre ant (mis′krē ənt), 1 having very bad morals; wicked; base. 2 a base or wicked person; villain. 1 *adj.,* 2 *n.*

mis deal (mis dēl′ *for 1;* mis′dēl′ *for 2*), 1 deal wrongly at cards. 2 a wrong deal at cards. 1 *v.,* **mis dealt** (mis delt′), **mis deal ing;** 2 *n.*

mis deed (mis dēd′), a bad act; wicked deed. *n.*

mis de mean or (mis′di mē/nər), 1 a breaking of the law, not so serious as a felony. Disturbing the peace and breaking traffic laws are misdemeanors. 2 a wrong deed. *n.*

mis di rect (mis′də rekt′ *or* mis′dī rekt′), direct wrongly; give wrong directions to. *v.*

mis do ing (mis dü′ing), wrongdoing. *n.*

mi ser (mī′zər), person who loves money for its own sake; one who lives poorly in order to save money and keep it. A miser dislikes to spend money for anything, except to gain more money. *n.*

mis er a ble (miz′ər ə bəl), 1 very unhappy or unfortunate; wretched: *A sick child is often miserable.* 2 causing trouble or unhappiness: *a miserable cold.* 3 poor; pitiful: *a miserable failure. They live in miserable surroundings. adj.*

mis er a bly (miz′ər ə blē), in a miserable manner. *adv.*

mi ser li ness (mī′zər lē nis), condition or quality of being miserly. *n.*

mi ser ly (mī′zər lē), of, like, or suited to a miser; stingy. *adj.*

mis er y (miz′ər ē), 1 a miserable, unhappy state of mind: *Think of the misery of having no home or friends.* 2 poor, mean, miserable circumstances: *They lived in the misery of the slums. n., pl.* **mis er ies.**

mis fire (mis fīr′), 1 fail to fire or explode properly: *The pistol misfired.* 2 failure to discharge or start. 3 go wrong; fail: *I tried to sneak into the movie without paying, but my plan misfired.* 1,3 *v.,* **mis fired, mis fir ing;** 2 *n.*

mis fit (mis′fit′ *for 1,2;* mis fit′ *for 3*), 1 person who does not fit in a job, a group, etc.; maladjusted person. 2 a bad fit: *Do not buy shoes that are misfits.* 3 fit badly: *His clothes misfit; they were too big and baggy.* 1,2 *n.,* 3 *v.,* **mis fit ted, mis fit ting.**

mis for tune (mis fôr/chən), 1 bad luck: *She had the misfortune to break her arm.* 2 piece of bad luck; unlucky accident. *n.*

mis give (mis giv′), cause to feel doubt, suspicion, or anxiety. *v.,* **mis gave** (mis gāv′), **mis giv en** (mis giv′ən), **mis giv ing.**

mis giv ing (mis giv′ing), a feeling of doubt, suspicion, or anxiety: *We started off through the storm with some misgivings. n.*

mis gov ern (mis guv′ərn), govern or manage badly. *v.*

mis gov ern ment (mis guv′ərn mənt), bad government or management. *n.*

mis guid ed (mis gī′did), led into mistakes or wrongdoing; misled: *a misguided person, misguided plans. adj.*

mis han dle (mis han/dl), handle badly; maltreat. *v.,* **mis han dled, mis han dling.**

mis hap (mis′hap), an unlucky accident: *By some mishap the letter went astray. n.*

mish mash (mish′mash′), a confused mixture; hodgepodge; jumble. *n.*

mis in form (mis′in fôrm′), give wrong or misleading information to. *v.*

mis in for ma tion (mis′in fər mā′-shən), wrong or misleading information. *n.*

mis in ter pret (mis′in tèr′prit), interpret wrongly; explain wrongly; misunderstand. *v.*

mis in ter pre ta tion (mis′in tèr′prə tā′shən), wrong interpretation; wrong explanation; misunderstanding. *n.*

mis judge (mis juj′), judge wrongly or unjustly: *The archer misjudged the distance to the target, and his arrow fell short. The teacher soon discovered that she had misjudged the girl's character. v.*, **mis judged, mis judg ing.**

mis judg ment or **mis judge ment** (mis juj′mənt), wrong or unjust judgment. *n.*

mis laid (mis lād′), past tense and past participle of **mislay**. *The boy mislaid his books. I have mislaid my pen. v.*

mis lay (mis lā′), 1 put in a place and then forget where it is; lose temporarily: *Mother is always mislaying her glasses.* 2 put in an incorrect place. *v.*, **mis laid, mis lay ing.**

mis lead (mis lēd′), 1 cause to go in the wrong direction; lead astray: *Our guide misled us in the woods, and we got lost.* 2 cause to do wrong; lead into wrongdoing: *a person who has been misled by bad companions.* 3 lead to think what is not so; deceive: *Sometimes advertisements are so exaggerated that they mislead people. v.*, **mis led, mis lead ing.**

mis lead ing (mis lē′ding), 1 leading to wrong conclusions; deceiving: *The detectives found that the clue was false and misleading.* 2 causing error or wrongdoing: *Bad advice can be misleading. adj.*

mis led (mis led′), past tense and past participle of **mislead**. *We were misled on our long hike by a careless guide. v.*

mis man age (mis man′ij), manage badly: *If you mismanage the business, you will lose money. v.*, **mis man aged, mis man ag ing.**

mis man age ment (mis man′ij-mənt), bad management. *n.*

mis match (mis mach′), 1 match badly or unsuitably. 2 a bad or unsuitable match. 1 *v.*, 2 *n., pl.* **mis match es.**

mis name (mis nām′), call by a wrong name. *v.*, **mis named, mis nam ing.**

mis no mer (mis nō′mər), 1 a name that describes wrongly: *"Lightning" is a misnomer for that slow, old horse.* 2 error in naming. *n.*

mis place (mis plās′), 1 put in the wrong place. 2 INFORMAL. put in a place and then forget where it is; mislay: *I have misplaced my pencil.* 3 give

(one's love or trust) to the wrong person: *misplace one's confidence in an untrustworthy friend. v.*, **mis placed, mis plac ing.**

mis place ment (mis plās′mənt), a misplacing or a being misplaced. *n.*

mis play (mis plā′), 1 a wrong play. 2 play wrongly: *She misplayed her hand in cards.* 1 *n.*, 2 *v.*

mis print (mis′print′ *for 1;* mis print′ *for 2*), 1 a mistake in printing. 2 to print wrongly. 1 *n.*, 2 *v.*

mis pro nounce (mis′prə nouns′), pronounce incorrectly. *v.*, **mis pronounced, mis pro nounc ing.**

mis pro nun ci a tion (mis′prə-nun′sē ā′shən), an incorrect pronunciation. *n.*

mis quo ta tion (mis′kwō tā′shən), an incorrect quotation. *n.*

mis quote (mis kwōt′), quote incorrectly. *v.*, **mis quot ed, mis quoting.**

mis read (mis rēd′), 1 read wrongly. 2 interpret wrongly; misunderstand: *I misread the recipe and spoiled the cake. v.*, **mis read** (mis red′), **mis read ing.**

mis rep re sent (mis′rep′ri zent′), represent falsely; give a wrong idea of: *He misrepresented the value of the automobile when he said it was in good condition. v.*

mis rep re sen ta tion (mis′rep ri-zen tā′shən), 1 a false representation: *Tell the truth; do not resort to misrepresentation.* 2 an incorrect story or explanation: *The report is a misrepresentation of the facts in the case. n.*

mis rule (mis rül′), 1 bad or unwise rule; misgovernment. 2 rule badly. 3 condition of disorder. 1,3 *n.*, 2 *v.*, **mis ruled, mis rul ing.**

miss (mis), 1 fail to hit: *He hammers away, but half the time he misses the nail. He fired twice, but both shots missed.* 2 failure to hit or reach: *make more misses than hits.* 3 fail to find, get, or meet: *I set out to meet my father, but in the dark I missed him.* 4 let slip by; not seize: *I missed the chance of a ride to town.* 5 fail to catch: *miss the train.* 6 leave out: *miss a word in reading.* 7 fail to hear or understand: *miss the point of a remark. What did you say? I missed a word or two.* 8 fail to keep, do, or be present at: *I missed my music lesson today.* 9 escape or avoid: *barely miss being hit, miss death by a hair.* 10 notice the absence of; feel keenly the absence of: *I did not miss my purse till I got home. I miss my mother when she goes away.* 1,3-10 *v.*, 2 *n., pl.* **miss es.**

A miss is as good as a mile. A close miss has the same effect as a wide miss.

Miss (mis), 1 title put before a girl's or

hat, āge, fär; let, ēqual, tèrm;
it, īce; hot, ōpen, ôrder;
oil, out; cup, pùt, rüle; ch, child;
ng, long; sh, she; th, thin;
ℱH, then; zh, measure;

ə represents *a* in about,
e in taken, *i* in pencil,
o in lemon, *u* in circus.

---

unmarried woman's name: *Miss Brown, the Misses Brown, the Miss Browns.* 2 **miss**, a young unmarried woman; girl. *n., pl.* **Miss es.**

Miss., Mississippi.

mis sal (mis′əl), book containing the prayers, etc., for celebrating Mass throughout the year. *n.*

mis shap en (mis shā′pən), badly shaped; deformed. *adj.*

missile (def. 2)
of the type guided by radar to destroy enemy aircraft or missiles in midair

mis sile (mis′əl), 1 object that is thrown or shot, such as a stone, an arrow, a bullet, or a lance. 2 a self-propelled projectile, especially a rocket containing explosives. There are ballistic missiles and guided missiles. Missiles can be launched from land, air, or sea. *n.*

mis sile man (mis′əl mən), person who works with missiles, either in construction or in use and maintenance. *n., pl.* **mis sile men.**

miss ing (mis′ing), not found when looked for; lacking; wanting; absent; gone: *One book is missing from the set. adj.*

mis sion (mish′ən), 1 a sending or being sent on some special work; errand. An operation by one or more aircraft against the enemy is called a mission. 2 group sent on some special business: *She was one of a mission sent by our government to France.* 3 group of persons sent by a religious organization into other parts of the world to spread its beliefs. 4 **missions**, *pl.* an organized effort by a religious group to set up churches, schools, hospitals, etc.: *foreign missions.* 5 business on which a mission is sent. 6 station or headquarters of a religious mission. 7 business or purpose in life; calling: *It seemed to*

adj. adjective	*n.* noun
adv. adverb	*prep.* preposition
conj. conjunction	*pron.* pronoun
interj. interjection	*v.* verb
sing. singular	*pl.* plural

be her mission to help improve living conditions in the city. n.

mis sion ar y (mish′ə ner′ē), 1 person sent on a religious mission: *Missionaries helped start churches, schools, and hospitals in many places.* 2 person who works to advance some cause or idea. 3 of religious missions or missionaries. 1,2 *n., pl.* **mis sion ar ies**; 3 *adj.*

Mis sis sip pi (mis′ə sip′ē), one of the south central states of the United States. *Capital:* Jackson. *n.*

Mississippi River, large river in North America. It flows south through the United States from N Minnesota to the Gulf of Mexico.

mis sive (mis′iv), a written message; letter. *n.*

Mis sour i (mə zúr′ē *or* mə zúr′ə), one of the midwestern states of the United States. *Capital:* Jefferson City. *n.*

Missouri River, large river in the N part of the United States, flowing from SW Montana into the Mississippi. *n.*

mis spell (mis spel′), spell incorrectly. *v.,* **mis spelled** or **mis spelt** (misspelt′), **mis spell ing.**

mis spell ing (mis spel′ing), an incorrect spelling. *n.*

mis spent (mis spent′), spent foolishly or wrongly; wasted: *a misspent fortune, a misspent life. adj.*

mis state (mis stāt′), state wrongly or incorrectly. *v.,* **mis stat ed, mis stat ing.**

mis state ment (mis stāt′mənt), a wrong or incorrect statement. *n.*

mis step (mis step′), 1 a wrong step. 2 error or slip in conduct. *n.*

mist (mist), 1 cloud of very fine drops of water suspended in the air; haze. Mist can be seen through more easily

than fog. 2 come down in mist; rain in very fine drops. 3 anything that dims, blurs, or obscures: *She did not cry, but a mist came over her eyes. A mist of prejudice spoiled his judgment.* 4 become covered with a mist; become dim: *The windows are misting.* 5 cover with a mist; put a mist before; make dim: *Tears misted his eyes.* 1,3 *n.,* 2,4, 5 *v.*

mis take (mə stāk′), 1 misunderstanding of a thing's use or meaning; error; blunder: *It was a mistake to leave before the snow stopped. I used your towel by mistake.* 2 misunderstand (what is seen or heard). 3 take wrongly; take (to be some other person or thing): *I mistook that stick for a snake.* 1 *n.,* 2,3 *v.,* **mis took, mis tak en, mis tak ing.**

mis tak en (mə stā′kən), 1 wrong in opinion; having made a mistake: *I saw I was mistaken and admitted my error.* 2 wrongly judged; wrong; misplaced: *It was a mistaken kindness to give that boy more candy; it will make him sick.* 3 past participle of **mistake.** *She was mistaken for the queen.* 1,2 *adj.,* 3 *v.* **—mis tak′en ly,** *adv.*

Mis ter (mis′tər), 1 Mr., a title put before a man's name or the name of his office: *Mr. Smith, Mr. President.* 2 **mister,** INFORMAL. sir. *n.*

mist i ly (mis′tə lē), in a misty manner. *adv.*

mist i ness (mis′tē nis), misty condition. *n.*

mis tle toe (mis′əl tō), plant with small, waxy, white berries and yellow flowers, that grows as a parasite on trees. It is used as a Christmas decoration. *n.*

mis took (mə stúk′), past tense of **mistake.** *I mistook you for your sister yesterday. v.*

mis treat (mis trēt′), treat badly. *v.*

mis treat ment (mis trēt′mənt), bad treatment. *n.*

mis tress (mis′tris), 1 woman who is at the head of a household. 2 woman or country that is in control or can rule: *England was sometimes called mistress of the seas.* 3 woman who has a thorough knowledge or mastery: *She is a complete mistress of the art of cookery.* 4 woman teaching in a school, or at the head of a school, or giving lessons in a special subject: *the dancing mistress.* 5 OLD USE. woman loved and courted

miter (def. 1, left; def. 2, below)

MITER

by a man. 6 woman who lives as a wife with a man without being married to him. 7 **Mistress,** OLD USE. Mrs., Madam, or Miss. *n., pl.* **mis tress es.**

mis tri al (mis trī′əl), 1 trial in which the jury fails to come to a decision. 2 trial of no effect in law because of some error in the proceedings. *n.*

mis trust (mis trust′), 1 feel no trust or confidence in; distrust; doubt: *I mistrusted my ability to learn to swim.* 2 lack of trust or confidence; suspicion: *He looked with mistrust at the stranger.* 1 *v.,* 2 *n.*

mis trust ful (mis trust′fəl), lacking confidence; distrustful; doubting; suspicious. *adj.* **—mis trust′ful ly,** *adv.*

mist y (mis′tē), 1 of mist. 2 characterized by mist; full of or covered with mist: *misty hills, misty air.* 3 not clearly seen or outlined. 4 as if seen through a mist; vague; indistinct: *a misty notion. adj.,* **mist i er, mist i est.**

mis un der stand (mis′un dər stand′), 1 understand wrongly. 2 take in a wrong sense; give the wrong meaning to. *v.,* **mis un der stood, mis un der stand ing.**

mis un der stand ing (mis′un dər stan′ding), 1 wrong understanding; failure to understand; mistake as to meaning. 2 disagreement: *After their misunderstanding they scarcely spoke to each other for months. n.*

mis un der stood (mis′un dər stúd′), past tense and past participle of **misunderstand.** *She misunderstood what the teacher said and so did the wrong homework. v.*

mis use (mis yüz′ for 1,2; mis yüs′ for 3), 1 use for the wrong purpose: *He misuses his knife at the table by lifting food with it.* 2 treat badly; mistreat; abuse: *The children misused their dog by trying to ride on its back.* 3 a wrong use: *I notice a misuse of the word "who" in your letter.* 1,2 *v.,* **mis used, mis us ing;** 3 *n.*

mite[1]
about 1/16 in. long

mite[1] (mīt), a very tiny animal related to the spider. It lives in foods, on plants, or on other animals. *n.* [Old English *mīte*]

mite[2] (mīt), 1 anything very small; little bit: *I can't eat even a mite of supper.* 2 coin of slight value. 3 a very small child: *What a mite your baby nephew is! n.* [from Dutch of the 1300's]

mi ter (mī′tər), 1 a tall, pointed, folded cap worn by bishops during sacred ceremonies. 2 kind of joint or corner where two pieces of wood are fitted together at right angles with the ends cut slanting. 3 join thus; prepare (ends of wood) for such joining. The corners of a picture frame are mitered. 1,2 *n.*, 3 *v.* Also, **mitre.**

Mith ri da tes (mith′rə dā′tēz), 131?-63 B.C., king of an ancient country in Asia Minor. He apparently took gradually increasing doses of poison to make himself immune to it, but eventually poisoned himself. *n.*

mit i gate (mit′ə gāt), make or become mild or milder; make or become less harsh; soften. Anger, grief, pain, punishments, heat, cold, and many other conditions may be mitigated. *v.*, **mit i gat ed, mit i gat ing.**

mit i ga tion (mit′ə gā′shən), 1 a mitigating or a being mitigated. 2 something that mitigates: *The breeze was a welcome mitigation of the heat.* *n.*

mi to sis (mī tō′sis), process by which a cell of a plant or animal divides to form two new cells, each containing the same number of chromosomes as the original cell. *n.*

mi tre (mī′tər), miter. *n.*, *v.*, **mi tred, mi tring.**

mitt (mit), 1 kind of long glove without fingers, or with very short fingers. 2 glove with a big pad over the palm and fingers, used by baseball players: *a catcher's mitt.* 3 mitten. *n.*

mit ten (mit′n), kind of winter glove covering the four fingers together and the thumb separately. *n.*

mix (miks), 1 put together; stir well together: *We mix butter, sugar, milk, and flour to make a cake.* 2 prepare by putting different things together: *mix a cake.* 3 join: *mix business and pleasure.* 4 be mixed: *Oil and water do not mix.* 5 associate together; get along together: *She likes people and mixes well in almost any group.* 6 preparation that is already mixed: *a cake mix.* 1-5 *v.*, **mixed** or **mixt** (mikst), **mix ing;** 6 *n.*, pl. **mix es.**

mix up, 1 confuse: *I was so mixed up that I did very badly on the examination.* 2 involve; concern: *They were mixed up in a plot to overthrow the monarchy.*

mixed (mikst), 1 formed of different kinds: *mixed candies, mixed emotions.* 2 of or for persons of both sexes: *a mixed chorus.* *adj.*

mixed number, number consisting of a positive or negative integer and a fraction. EXAMPLES: $1^1/_2$, $16^2/_3$, $-25^9/_{10}$.

mix er (mik′sər), 1 thing that mixes: *a bread mixer, an electric mixer.* 2 one who mixes. A person who gets along well with others is called a good mixer. *n.*

mix ture (miks′chər), 1 a mixing: *The mixture of the paints took two hours.*

2 mixed condition: *The audience felt a mixture of relief and disappointment.* 3 something that has been mixed; a product of mixing: *Orange is a mixture of yellow and red.* *n.*

mix-up (miks′up′), INFORMAL. 1 confusion; mess. 2 a confused fight. *n.*

miz zen (miz′n), 1 a fore-and-aft sail on a mizzenmast. See **mainmast** for picture. 2 mizzenmast. *n.*

miz zen mast (miz′n mast′ or miz′n-məst), mast nearest the stern in a two-masted or three-masted ship. See **mainmast** for picture. *n.*

Mlle., Mademoiselle. *pl.* **Mlles.**

mm., millimeter or millimeters.

Mme., Madame. pl. **Mmes.**

mo., month. *pl.* **mo.** or **mos.**

Mo., Missouri.

Mo ab (mō′ab), ancient kingdom in the region east of the Dead Sea and the lower Jordan River. See **Judah** for map. *n.*

moan (mōn), 1 a long, low sound of suffering. 2 any similar sound: *the moan of the winter wind.* 3 make moans. 4 utter with a moan: *"I'm so stiff I can't move," she moaned.* 5 complain; grieve: *He was always moaning about his bad luck.* 6 complain about; grieve for: *to moan one's fate.* 1,2 *n.*, 3-6 *v.*

moat (mōt), a deep, wide ditch dug around a castle or town as a protection against enemies. Moats were usually kept filled with water. *n.*

mob (mob), 1 a lawless crowd, easily moved to act without thinking. 2 a large number of people; crowd. 3 to crowd around in curiosity, anger, etc.: *We eagerly mobbed the ice cream truck the moment it appeared.* 4 attack with violence, as a mob does. 5 the common mass of people. 6 SLANG. group of criminals who work together; gang. 1,2,5,6 *n.*, 3,4 *v.*, **mobbed, mob bing.**

mo bile (mō′bəl for 1,2; mō′bēl′ for 3), 1 easy to move; movable: *The arms and legs are mobile.* 2 moving easily; changing easily: *a face with mobile features, a mobile mind.* 3 pieces of metal, wood, paper, etc., suspended on wires or threads and so balanced as to move in a slight breeze, used for decoration. 1,2 *adj.*, 3 *n.*

Mo bile (mō bēl′), seaport in SW Alabama, on the Gulf of Mexico. *n.*

mobile home, a house trailer.

mo bil i ty (mō bil′ə tē), a being mobile; ability or readiness to move or be moved. *n.*

mo bi li za tion (mō′bə lə zā′shən), 1 act of mobilizing; calling troops or ships into active military service. 2 condition of being mobilized. *n.*

mo bi lize (mō′bə līz), 1 call (troops or ships) into active military service; organize for war. 2 assemble and prepare

hat, āge, fär; let, ēqual, tėrm;
it, īce; hot, ōpen, ôrder;
oil, out; cup, pùt, rüle; ch, child;
ng, long; sh, she; th, thin;
ᴛʜ, then; zh, measure;

ə represents *a* in about,
e in taken, *i* in pencil,
o in lemon, *u* in circus.

for war: *The troops mobilized quickly.* 3 put into motion or active use: *mobilize the wealth of a country.* *v.*, **mo bi lized, mo bi liz ing.**

mob ster (mob′stər), SLANG. a criminal; gangster. *n.*

moccasin (def. 1)

moc ca sin (mok′ə sən), 1 a soft leather shoe or sandal. Moccasins were originally worn by American Indians. 2 water moccasin. *n.*

moccasin flower, a pink or white North American lady's-slipper.

mo cha (mō′kə), 1 a choice variety of coffee originally coming from Arabia. 2 flavored with coffee, or with chocolate and coffee. 1 *n.*, 2 *adj.* [from *Mocha*, a seaport in Yemen, where it was shipped from]

mock (mok), 1 laugh at; make fun of. 2 make fun of by copying or imitating: *My friends mocked the way I hobbled around on my sore foot.* 3 imitate; copy. 4 not real; pretended; copying; imitation: *a mock battle, mock modesty.* 5 an action or speech that mocks; mockery. 6 deceive or disappoint. 1-3,6 *v.*, 4 *adj.*, 5 *n.* —**mock′er,** *n.* —**mock′ing ly,** *adv.*

mock er y (mok′ər ē), 1 a making fun; ridicule: *Their mockery of my new hat hurt my feelings.* 2 person or thing to be made fun of: *The foolish jester became a mockery in the royal court.* 3 a bad copy or imitation: *Their pretended sorrow was but a mockery of real grief.* 4 a wasted or useless thing; naught: *The unfair trial made a mockery of justice.* *n.*, pl. **mock er ies.**

mock ing bird (mok′ing bėrd′), a grayish songbird of the southern United States that imitates the calls of other birds. *n.*

mock orange, syringa.

mo dal (mō′dəl), 1 of or having to do with mode, manner, or form. 2 (in grammar) having to do with the mood of a verb. *adj.*

mode[1] (mōd), 1 manner or way in

mode

which a thing is done: *Riding on a donkey is a slow mode of travel.* 2 (in grammar) mood. *n.* [from Latin *modus* measure, manner]

mode² (mōd), style, fashion, or custom that prevails; the way most people are behaving, talking, dressing, etc. *n.* [from French *mode*, from Latin *modus* measure, manner]

mod el (mod′l), 1 a small copy: *a model of a ship or an engine.* 2 figure in clay or wax that is to be copied in marble, bronze, etc.: *a model for a statue.* 3 make, shape, or fashion; design; plan: *to model a horse in clay.* 4 way in which a thing is made; design; style: *Our television set is a new model.* 5 thing or person to be copied or imitated: *Your mother is a fine person; make her your model.* 6 to form on a particular model: *Model yourself on your father.* 7 just right or perfect, especially in conduct: *a model child.* 8 serving as a model: *a model house.* 9 person who poses for artists, photographers, etc. 10 person employed by a clothing store to wear or be photographed in garments so that customers can see how the garments look. 11 be a model: *I modeled for an illustrator.* 1,2,4,5,9,10 *n.*, 3,6,11 *v.*, 7,8 *adj.*

mod er ate (mod′ər it *for 1-4;* mod′ə-rāt′ *for 5,6*), 1 kept or keeping within proper bounds; not extreme: *moderate expenses, moderate styles.* 2 not violent; calm: *moderate in speech or opinion.* 3 not very large or good; fair; medium: *make a moderate profit.* 4 person who holds moderate opinions. 5 make or become less extreme or violent: *The wind is moderating.* 6 act as moderator; preside (over). 1-3 *adj.*, 4 *n.*, 5,6 *v.*, **mod er at ed,** **mod er at ing.** —**mod′er ate ly,** *adv.*

mod e ra tion (mod′ə rā′shən), 1 act of moderating. 2 freedom from excess; proper restraint; temperance: *It is all right to eat candy in moderation.* *n.*

mod e ra tor (mod′ə rā′tər), a presiding officer; chairman: *the moderator of a town meeting, the moderator of a panel discussion.* *n.*

mod ern (mod′ərn), 1 of the present time; of times not long past: *Color television is a modern invention.* 2 person of modern times. 3 up-to-date; not

old-fashioned: *modern views.* 4 person who has modern ideas and tastes. 1,3 *adj.*, 2,4 *n.*

Modern English, 1 period in the development of the English language from about 1500 through the present. 2 the English language of this period.

modern history, history from about 1450 to the present time.

mod ern is tic (mod′ər nis′tik), 1 modern. 2 having modern attitudes, methods, or style. *adj.*

mod ern i za tion (mod′ər nə zā′-shən), a modernizing or a being modernized; bringing up to present ways or standards. *n.*

mod ern ize (mod′ər nīz), 1 make modern; bring up to present ways or standards. 2 become modern. *v.*, **mod ern ized, mod ern iz ing.**

mod est (mod′ist), 1 not thinking too highly of oneself; not vain; humble: *In spite of many honors, the scientist remained a modest person.* 2 held back by a sense of what is fit and proper; not bold or forward; bashful; shy: *a modest child.* 3 having or showing decency of actions, thoughts, clothing, etc. 4 not too great; not asking too much: *a modest request.* 5 not gaudy; humble in appearance; quiet: *a modest little house.* *adj.* —**mod′est ly,** *adv.*

mod est y (mod′ə stē), 1 freedom from vanity; being modest or humble. 2 shyness; bashfulness. 3 decency of actions, thoughts, clothing, etc. *n., pl.* **mod est ies.**

mod i cum (mod′ə kəm), a small or moderate quantity: *She is so bright that even with a modicum of effort she gets high marks.* *n.*

mod i fi ca tion (mod′ə fə kā′shən), 1 partial alteration or change: *With these modifications your composition will do for the school paper.* 2 a making less severe or strong; a toning down: *A modification of the workers' demands helped settle the long strike.* 3 limitation of meaning; qualification. 4 a modified form; variety. *n.*

mod i fi er (mod′ə fī′ər), 1 word or group of words that limits the meaning of another word or group of words. In "a very tight coat," the adjective *tight* is a modifier of *coat,* and the adverb *very* is a modifier of *tight.* 2 person or thing that modifies. *n.*

mod i fy (mod′ə fī), 1 change somewhat: *modify the design of an automobile, modify the terms of a lease.* 2 make less; tone down; make less severe or strong: *He has modified his demands.* 3 limit the meaning of; qualify. Adverbs modify verbs, adjectives, and other adverbs. *v.,* **mod i fied, mod i fy ing.**

mod ish (mō′dish), fashionable;

stylish. *adj.* —**mod′ish ly,** *adv.* —**mod′ish ness,** *n.*

mod u late (moj′ə lāt), 1 regulate or adjust; soften; tone down. 2 alter (the voice) in pitch, tone, or volume for expression. 3 change from one musical key to another. 4 change (a radio wave) by adding sound waves to it. *v.,* **mod u lat ed, mod u lat ing.**

mod u la tion (moj′ə lā′shən), 1 a modulating or a being modulated. 2 the change from one key to another in the course of a piece of music. *n.*

Mo gul (mō′gul), 1 a Mongol or Mongolian. 2 one of the Mongol conquerors of India in the 1500's or one of their descendants. 3 **mogul,** an important person: *a mogul in the automobile industry.* *n.*

mo hair (mō′her *or* mō′har), 1 cloth made from the long, silky hair of the Angora goat; angora. 2 a similar cloth made of wool and cotton. *n.*

Mo ham med (mō ham′id), A.D 570?-632, Arab prophet, founder of Islam, a religion widely accepted in Asia and Africa. *n.* Also, **Mahomet, Muhammad.**

Mo ham med an (mō ham′ə dən), 1 of Mohammed. 2 Moslem. 3 a Moslem. 1,2 *adj.*, 3 *n.* Also, **Mahometan.**

Mo ham med an ism (mō ham′ə-də niz′əm), Islam, the religion of the Moslems. *n.*

Mo hawk (mō′hôk), member of a tribe of Iroquois Indians formerly living in central New York State. *n., pl.* **Mohawks** *or* **Mo hawk.**

Mo he gan (mō hē′gən), member of a tribe of American Indians related to the Mohicans, formerly living in western Connecticut. *n., pl.* **Mo he gans** *or* **Mo he gan.**

Mo hi can (mō hē′kən), member of a tribe of American Indians formerly living along the Hudson River in New York State. *n., pl.* **Mo hi cans** *or* **Mo hi can.**

moi e ty (moi′ə tē), 1 half. 2 part: *Only a small moiety of college students win scholarships.* *n., pl.* **moi e ties.**

moist (moist), slightly wet; damp. *adj.* —**moist′ly,** *adv.* —**moist′ness,** *n.*

mois ten (moi′sn), make or become moist: *His eyes moistened with tears.* *v.*

mois ture (mois′chər), slight wetness; water or other liquid suspended in very small drops in the air or spread on a surface. Dew is moisture that collects at night on the grass. *n.*

Mo ja ve (mō hä′vē), large desert in S California. *n.*

mo lar (mō′lər), tooth with a broad surface for grinding; grinder. A person's back teeth are molars. See **incisor** for diagram. *n.*

mo las ses (mə las′iz), a sweet syrup

obtained in the process of making sugar from sugar cane; treacle. *n.*

mold[1] (mōld), 1 a hollow shape in which anything is formed, cast, or solidified, such as the mold into which melted metal is poured to harden into shape, or the mold in which gelatin is left to stiffen. 2 the shape or form which is given by a mold: *The molds of ice cream were turkeys and pumpkins.* 3 the model according to which anything is shaped: *The son is formed in his father's mold.* 4 form; shape: *Children mold figures out of clay.* 5 something shaped in a mold: *a mold of pudding.* 6 make or form into shape: *We mold wax into candles. Her character was molded by the trials she went through.* 7 nature; character: *a man of base mold.* 1-3,5,7 *n.,* 4,6 *v.* Also, **mould.** [from French of the 1200's *modle,* from Latin *modulus* small measure, from *modus* measure]

mold[2] (mōld), 1 a woolly or furry fungous growth, often greenish in color, that appears on food and other animal or vegetable substances when they are left too long in a warm, moist place. 2 become covered with mold. 1 *n.,* 2 *v.* Also, **mould.** [Middle English *moul;* probably influenced by *mold*[3]]

mold[3] (mōld), loose earth; fine, soft, rich soil: *Many wild flowers grow in the forest mold. n.* Also, **mould.** [Old English *molde*]

Mol da vi a (mol dā′vē ə), Soviet republic in SW Soviet Union. *n.*

mold board (mōld′bôrd′), a curved metal plate in a plow, that turns over the earth from the furrow. See **plowshare** for picture. *n.*

mold er (mōl′dər), turn into dust by natural decay; waste away; crumble. *v.* Also, **moulder.**

mold i ness (mōl′dē nis), state of being moldy. *n.*

mold ing (mōl′ding), 1 act of shaping: *the molding of dishes from clay.* 2 something molded; a decorative outline used in architecture. 3 a strip, usually of wood, around the upper walls of a room, used to support pictures, to cover electric wires, for decoration, etc. *n.* Also, **moulding.**

mold y (mōl′dē), 1 covered with mold: *a moldy crust of bread, moldy cheese.* 2 musty; stale: *a moldy smell. adj.,* **mold i er, mold i est.** Also, **mouldy.**

mole[1] (mōl), a spot on the skin, usually brown, that was there at birth. *n.* [Old English *māl*]

mole[2] (mōl), a small mammal that lives underground most of the time. Moles have dark, velvety fur and very small eyes that cannot see well. *n.* [Middle English *molle*]

mole[3] (mōl), barrier built of stone to break the force of the waves; breakwater. *n.* [from Latin *moles* mass]

mo lec u lar (mə lek′yə lər), having to do with, caused by, or consisting of molecules. *adj.*

mol e cule (mol′ə kyül), 1 the smallest particle into which an element or compound can be divided without changing its chemical properties. A molecule of an element consists of one or more atoms. A molecule of a compound consists of two or more atoms. 2 a very small particle. *n.*

mole hill (mōl′hil′), 1 a small mound or ridge of earth raised up by moles burrowing under the ground. 2 something insignificant. *n.*

mo lest (mə lest′), meddle with and injure; interfere with and trouble; disturb: *It is cruel to molest animals. v.*

mo les ta tion (mō′les′tā′shən), a molesting or a being molested; annoying or hostile interference. *n.*

Mol ière (mō lyer′), 1622-1673, French writer of comedies. *n.*

moll (mol), SLANG. the female companion of a gangster, gunman, or other criminal. *n.*

mol li fy (mol′ə fī), soften, especially in temper; appease; mitigate: *I tried to mollify my parents' anger by apologizing. v.,* **mol li fied, mol li fy ing.**

mol lusk or **mol lusc** (mol′əsk), any of a large group of animals having soft bodies not composed of segments, and usually covered with a hard shell. Snails, mussels, oysters, clams, and octopuses are mollusks. *n.*

mol ly cod dle (mol′ē kod′l), 1 boy or man accustomed to being fussed over and pampered; milksop. 2 coddle; pamper. 1 *n.,* 2 *v.,* **mol ly cod dled, mol ly cod dling.**

Mo loch (mō′lok), 1 a fire god of ancient times. Parents sacrificed their children to Moloch. 2 anything requiring frightful sacrifice: *War is a Moloch. n.*

Mo lo kai (mō′lō kī′), the fifth largest island of Hawaii. *n.*

molt (mōlt), 1 shed the feathers, skin, etc., before a new growth. Birds and snakes molt. 2 shed (feathers, skin, etc.): *We saw the snake molt its skin.* 3 act or process of molting. 1,2 *v.,* 3 *n.* Also, **moult.**

mol ten (mōlt′n), 1 made liquid by heat; melted: *molten steel.* 2 made by melting and casting: *a molten image.* 3 melted; a past participle of **melt.** 1,2 *adj.,* 3 *v.*

mole[2]—about 7 in. long with the tail

hat, āge, fär; let, ēqual, tèrm;
it, īce; hot, ōpen, ôrder;
oil, out; cup, pút, rüle; ch, child;
ng, long; sh, she; th, thin;
ℍH, then; zh, measure;

ə represents *a* in about,
e in taken, *i* in pencil,
o in lemon, *u* in circus.

Mo luc cas (mə luk′əz), group of islands in Indonesia between Celebes and New Guinea; Spice Islands. *n.pl.*

mo lyb de num (mə lib′də nəm), a heavy, hard, grayish metallic element. Molybdenum is much used to strengthen and harden steel. *n.*

mom (mom), INFORMAL. mother. *n.*

mo ment (mō′mənt), 1 a very short space of time; instant: *In a moment the house was in flames. Won't you stay for a moment?* 2 a particular point of time: *We both arrived at the same moment. I can't recall her name at the moment.* 3 importance: *The Congress is busy on a matter of moment. n.*

mo men tar i ly (mō′mən ter′ə lē), 1 for a moment: *She hesitated momentarily and then made her decision.* 2 at any moment: *We were expecting our visitors momentarily. adv.*

mo men tar y (mō′mən ter′ē), lasting only a moment: *a momentary silence. After a momentary hesitation I started across the shaky bridge. adj.*

mo men tous (mō men′təs), very important: *Choosing between peace and war is a momentous decision. adj.* —**mo men′tous ness,** *n.*

mo men tum (mō men′təm), 1 the force with which a body moves, equal to the product of its mass and its velocity: *A falling object gains momentum as it falls.* 2 impetus resulting from movement: *The runner's momentum carried him far beyond the finish line. n.*

mom my (mom′ē), INFORMAL. mother. *n., pl.* **mom mies.**

Mon., Monday.

Mon a co (mon′ə kō *or* mə nä′kō), very small country on the SE coast of France, on the Mediterranean. *n.*

mon arch (mon′ərk), 1 king, queen, emperor, etc.; ruler. 2 person or thing like a monarch: *The tall, solitary pine was monarch of the forest.* 3 a very large, orange-and-black butterfly. *n.*

mo nar chi cal (mə när′kə kəl), 1 of a monarch or monarchy. 2 favoring a monarchy. *adj.*

mon ar chist (mon′ər kist), person who supports or favors government by a monarch. *n.*

547

monarchy

adj. adjective	*n.* noun
adv. adverb	*prep.* preposition
conj. conjunction	*pron.* pronoun
interj. interjection	*v.* verb
sing. singular	*pl.* plural

mon ar chy (mon'ər kē), 1 government by a monarch. 2 nation governed by a monarch. *n., pl.* **mon ar chies.**

mon as ter y (mon'ə ster'ē), building or buildings where monks live together according to fixed rules and under religious vows. *n., pl.* **mon as ter ies.**

mo nas tic (mə nas'tik), 1 of monks or nuns: *the monastic vows of chastity, poverty, and obedience.* 2 of monasteries: *monastic architecture.* 3 like that of monks or nuns. 4 monk. 1-3 *adj.,* 4 *n.*

mo nas ti cism (mə nas'tə siz'əm), system or condition of living a monastic life. *n.*

Mon day (mun'dē), the second day of the week; day after Sunday. *n.*

Mo net (mō nā'), **Claude,** 1840-1926, French painter of landscapes. *n.*

mon e tar y (mon'ə ter'ē), 1 of the money of a country: *The monetary unit in the United States is the dollar.* 2 of money: *a monetary reward. adj.*

mon ey (mun'ē), 1 coins of gold, silver, or other metal, or paper notes which represent these metals, issued by a government for use in buying and selling: *He has five dollars in Canadian money. The treasurer was responsible for the moneys entrusted to him.* 2 any object or material used for buying and selling, such as checks drawn on a bank, or nuggets or the dust of a precious metal. 3 wealth: *He is a man of money. n., pl.* **mon eys** or **mon ies.**

make money, 1 get money: *He made money in the stock market.* 2 become rich: *His ambition is to make money and retire young.*

mon eyed (mun'ēd), 1 having money; wealthy. 2 consisting of or representing money: *moneyed resources. adj.*

mon ey lend er (mun'ē len'dər), person whose business is lending money at interest. *n.*

money order, order for the payment of money. You can buy a money order at the post office or a bank and send it to a person in another city, who can get the money at the post office or a bank there.

Mon gol (mong'gəl), 1 member of an Asian people now inhabiting Mongolia

and nearby parts of China and Siberia. 2 of this people. 3 a Mongoloid. 1,3 *n.,* 2 *adj.*

Mongol Empire, former empire of the Mongols, which encompassed most of Asia and part of E Europe during the late 1200's.

Mon go li a (mong gō'lē ə), vast region in Asia, south of Siberia. Mongolia includes part of N China and the Mongolian People's Republic. *n.*

Mon go li an (mong gō'lē ən), 1 of Mongolia, the Mongols, or their languages. 2 language or languages of the Mongols or Mongolia. 3 person born or living in Mongolia; Mongol. 4 Mongoloid. 1,4 *adj.,* 2-4 *n.*

Mongolian People's Republic, country in central Asia, north of China and south of the Soviet Union.

monkey (defs. 1 and 2)
about 4 ft. long, including the tail

Mon gol oid (mong'gə loid), 1 of, belonging to, or resembling the Mongols. The Chinese, Japanese, Tartars, and Eskimos are Mongoloid peoples. 2 member of the Mongoloid race. 1 *adj.,* 2 *n.*

mongoose—about 2 ft. long with tail

mon goose or **mon goos** (mong'-güs), a slender, flesh-eating mammal of Asia and Africa that resembles a ferret. It is often kept as a pet for destroying rats and is noted for its ability to kill poisonous snakes. *n., pl.* **mon goos es.**

mon grel (mung'grəl *or* mong'grəl), 1 animal or plant of mixed breed, especially a dog. 2 of mixed breed, race, origin, or nature: *a mongrel speech that is half Spanish and half Indian.* 1 *n.,* 2 *adj.*

mon ies (mun'ēz), a plural of **money.** *n.*

mon i tor (mon'ə tər), 1 pupil in school with special duties, such as helping to keep order and taking attendance. 2 person who gives advice or warning. 3 a low, armored warship having one

Mongol Empire—Shaded area shows the Empire at its greatest extent in 1294.

or more turrets for guns. It was used in the 1800's. 4 **Monitor,** a low, armored warship of the Union, having a big gun in a revolving turret. It fought the Merrimac during the Civil War. 5 receiver used for checking and listening to radio or television transmissions, telephone messages, etc., as they are being recorded or broadcast. 6 check and listen to (radio or television transmissions, telephone messages, etc.) by using a receiver. 1-5 *n.,* 6 *v.*

mon i to ry (mon'ə tôr'ē), admonishing; warning: *the monitory growl of a dog. adj.*

monk (mungk), man who gives up all worldly things and enters a monastery to live a life devoted to religion. *n.*

mon key (mung'kē), 1 mammal of the group most closely resembling man. 2 one of the smaller mammals in this group, not a chimpanzee, gorilla, or other large ape. It usually has a long tail. 3 person, especially a child, who is full of mischief. 4 INFORMAL. play in a mischievous way; fool; trifle: *Don't monkey with the television.* 1-3 *n., pl.* **mon keys;** 4 *v.* **—mon'key like',** *adj.*

mon key shine (mung'kē shīn'), SLANG. a mischievous trick; clownish joke. *n.*

monkey wrench, a wrench with a movable jaw that can be adjusted to fit different sizes of nuts.

monkey wrench

monk ish (mung'kish), of a monk or monks; like a monk. *adj.*

monks hood (mungks'hùd'), kind of aconite grown for its purple or white hooded flowers. It is the source of the drug aconite. *n.*

mon o chrome (mon'ə krōm), a painting, drawing, print, etc., in a single color or shades of a single color. *n.*

548

monocle (left)
monogram (below)

mon o cle (mon′ə kəl), eyeglass for one eye. *n.*

mon o cot y le don (mon′ə kot′-l ēd′n), plant with only one cotyledon. *n.*

mo nog a my (mə nog′ə mē), practice or condition of being married to only one person at a time. –*n.*

mon o gram (mon′ə gram), a person's initials combined in one design. Monograms are used on note paper, table linen, clothing, jewelry, etc. *n.*

mon o graph (mon′ə graf), book or article, especially a scholarly one, about a particular subject. *n.*

mon o lith (mon′l ith), 1 a single large block of stone. 2 monument, column, statue, etc., formed of a single large block of stone. *n.*

mon o lith ic (mon′l ith′ik), of a monolith; being a monolith. *adj.*

mon o logue or **mon o log** (mon′l-ôg), 1 a long speech by one person in a group. 2 entertainment by a single speaker. 3 a play for a single actor. 4 part of a play in which a single actor speaks alone. *n.*

mon o ma ni a (mon′ə mā′nē ə), 1 a mental disorder in which a person is obsessed by a single idea or subject. 2 an interest or tendency so strong as to seem almost insane. *n., pl.* **mon o ma ni as.**

Mo non ga he la (mə non′gə hē′lə), river flowing from N West Virginia which, with the Allegheny River, forms the Ohio River at Pittsburgh. *n.*

mon o plane (mon′ə plān), airplane with only one pair of wings. Most modern airplanes are monoplanes. *n.*

mo nop o list (mə nop′ə list), 1 person who has a monopoly. 2 person who favors monopoly. *n.*

mo nop o lis tic (mə nop′ə lis′tik), 1 that monopolizes. 2 having to do with monopolies or monopolists. *adj.*

mo nop o lize (mə nop′ə līz), 1 have or get exclusive possession or control of: *This firm practically monopolizes the production of linen thread.* 2 occupy wholly; keep entirely to oneself. *v.*, **mo nop o lized, mo nop o liz ing.**

mo nop o ly (mə nop′ə lē), 1 the exclusive control of a commodity or service: *The only milk company in town has a monopoly on milk delivery.* 2 such control granted by a government: *An inventor has a monopoly on his invention for a certain number of years.* 3 control that, though not exclusive, enables the person or company to fix prices. 4 a commercial product or service that is exclusively controlled or nearly so. 5 person or company that has a monopoly on some commodity or service. 6 the exclusive possession or control of something: *a monopoly on another person's time. n., pl.* **mo nop o lies.**

mon o rail (mon′ə rāl), 1 a single rail serving as a complete track. 2 railway in which cars run on a single rail, either balanced on it or suspended from it. *n.*

mon o syl lab ic (mon′ə sə lab′ik), 1 having only one syllable. 2 consisting of a word or words of one syllable: *"No, not now," is a monosyllabic reply. adj.*

mon o syl la ble (mon′ə sil′ə bəl), word of one syllable. *Yes, no,* and *grand* are monosyllables. *n.*

mon o the ism (mon′ə thē iz′əm), belief that there is only one God. *n.*

mon o the ist (mon′ə thē′ist), believer in only one God. *n.*

mon o the is tic (mon′ə thē is′tik), 1 believing in only one God. 2 having to do with belief in only one God. *adj.*

mon o tone (mon′ə tōn), sameness of tone, style of writing, color, etc.: *Don't read in a monotone; use expression. n.*

mo not o nous (mə not′n əs), 1 continuing in the same tone: *She spoke in a monotonous voice.* 2 not varying; without change: *monotonous food.* 3 wearying because of its sameness: *monotonous work. adj.* —**mo not′o nous ly,** *adv.*

mo not o ny (mə not′n ē), 1 sameness of tone or pitch: *The monotony of the man's voice was irritating.* 2 lack of variety. 3 wearisome sameness. *n., pl.* **mo not o nies.**

mon ox ide (mo nok′sīd), oxide containing one oxygen atom in each molecule. *n.*

Mon roe (mən rō′), **James,** 1758-1831, the fifth president of the United States, from 1817 to 1825. *n.*

Monroe Doctrine, doctrine that European nations should not interfere with American nations or try to acquire more territory in the Western Hemisphere. The Monroe Doctrine was derived from President Monroe's message to Congress on December 2, 1823.

Mon ro vi a (mon rō′vē ə), capital of Liberia, on the Atlantic. It was named after President James Monroe. *n.*

mon sei gneur or **Mon sei gneur** (môn se nyèr′), FRENCH. title of honor meaning my lord. It is given to princes, bishops, and other persons of importance. *n.*

mon sieur (mə syèr′), FRENCH. Mr.; sir. *n., pl.* **mes sieurs.**

mon si gnor or **Mon si gnor** (mon-sē′nyər), 1 title given to certain dignitaries in the Roman Catholic Church. 2 person having this title. *n.*

mon soon (mon sün′), 1 a seasonal wind of the Indian Ocean and southern Asia. It blows from the southwest from April to October and from the northeast during the rest of the year. 2 the rainy season during which this wind blows from the southwest. *n.*

mon ster (mon′stər), 1 any animal or plant that is very unlike those usually found in nature. A cow with two heads is a monster. Imaginary animals having parts of different animals, such as centaurs, sphinxes, and griffins, are monsters. 2 person too wicked to be considered human: *a ghastly crime committed by a monster of cruelty.* 3 a huge creature or thing. 1-3 *n.,* 4 *adj.*

mon stros i ty (mon stros′ə tē), 1 monster. 2 condition or character of being monstrous. *n., pl.* **mon stros i ties.**

mon strous (mon′strəs), 1 huge; enormous. 2 wrongly formed or shaped; like a monster. 3 so wrong or absurd as to be almost unheard of. 4 shocking; horrible; dreadful. *adj.* —**mon′strous ly,** *adv.*

Mont., Montana.

Mon taigne (mon tān′), **Michel de,** 1533-1592, French essayist. *n.*

Mon tan a (mon tan′ə), one of the western states of the United States. *Capital:* Helena. *n.*

Mont Blanc (môn blän′), the highest mountain in the Alps, between France and Italy.

Mont calm (mont käm′), **Marquis de,** 1712-1759, French general defeated by the English at Quebec. *n.*

Mon te Car lo (mon′tə kär′lō), town in Monaco, noted as a gambling resort.

Mon te ne gro (mon′tə nē′grō), former country in S Europe, on the Adriatic Sea. It is now a part of Yugoslavia. *n.*

Mon te vi de o (mon′tə vi dā′ō), capital of Uruguay, in the S part. *n.*

Mon te zu ma II (mon′tə zü′mə), 1480?-1520, Aztec emperor of Mexico, from 1502 to 1520, defeated by Cortés.

Mont gom er y (mont gum′ər ē), cap-

hat, āge, fär; let, ēqual, tėrm; it, īce; hot, ōpen, ôrder; oil, out; cup, pùt, rüle; ch, child; ng, long; sh, she; th, thin; ₮H, then; zh, measure;

ə represents *a* in about, *e* in taken, *i* in pencil, *o* in lemon, *u* in circus.

adj.	adjective	*n.*	noun
adv.	adverb	*prep.*	preposition
conj.	conjunction	*pron.*	pronoun
interj.	interjection	*v.*	verb
sing.	singular	*pl.*	plural

ital of Alabama, in the central part. *n.*

month (munth), **1** one of the 12 parts into which the year is divided. September, April, June, and November have 30 days; February has 28 days except in leap years, when it has 29; all the other months have 31 days. **2** time from any day of one month to the corresponding day of the next month. **3** lunar month. *n.*

month ly (munth/lē), **1** of a month; for a month; lasting a month: *a monthly supply, a monthly salary.* **2** done, happening, payable, etc., once a month: *a monthly meeting, a monthly examination.* **3** once a month; every month: *Some magazines come monthly.* **4** magazine published once a month. **1,2** *adj.,* **3** *adv.,* **4** *n., pl.* **month lies.**

Mon ti cel lo (mon/tə sel/ō *or* mon/tə chel/ō), home of Thomas Jefferson, in central Virginia. *n.*

Mont pel ier (mont pē/lyər), capital of Vermont, in the central part. *n.*

Mon tre al (mon/trē ôl/), large seaport in Quebec, Canada, on the St. Lawrence River. *n.*

mon u ment (mon/yə mənt), **1** something set up to keep a person or an event from being forgotten. A monument may be a building, pillar, arch, statue, tomb, or stone. **2** an enduring or prominent instance: *The Hoover Dam is a monument of engineering. n.*

mon u men tal (mon/yə men/tl), **1** of a monument. **2** serving as a monument. **3** like a monument. **4** weighty and lasting; important: *A great encyclopedia is a monumental production.* **5** very great: *monumental ignorance. adj.* —**mon/u men/tal ly,** *adv.*

moo (mü), **1** sound made by a cow. **2** make this sound. **1** *n., pl.* **moos; 2** *v.*

mooch (müch), SLANG. get from another by begging or sponging. *v.*

mood[1] (müd), state of mind or feeling: *I am in the mood to play now; I don't want to study. n.* [Old English *mōd* mind, heart, courage]

mood[2] (müd), form of a verb which shows whether the act or state it expresses is thought of as a fact, condition, command, etc. In "I am hungry," *am* is in the indicative mood. In "I demand that she answer," *answer* is in the subjunctive mood. In "Open the window," *open* is in the imperative mood. *n.* Also, **mode.** [a different form of *mode*[1]; influenced by *mood*[1]]

mood i ly (mü/də lē), in a moody manner. *adv.*

mood i ness (mü/dē nis), moody condition. *n.*

mood y (mü/dē), **1** likely to have changes of mood. **2** often having gloomy moods: *She has been moody ever since she lost her job.* **3** sunk in sadness; gloomy; sullen: *She sat in moody silence. adj.,* **mood i er, mood i est.**

moon (def. 1)

moon (mün), **1** a heavenly body that revolves around the earth once in about 29$\frac{1}{2}$ days. It is a natural satellite of the earth and is held in orbit by the earth's gravity. The force of the moon's gravity on the earth causes tides in the oceans. **2** the moon at a certain period of time. The moon looks bright when it is in such a position that it reflects the sun's light from the surface turned toward the earth. **3** one lunar month; about 29$\frac{1}{2}$ days. The Indians counted time by moons. **4** moonlight. **5** something shaped like the moon in any of its appearances. **6** satellite of any planet: *the moons of Jupiter.* **7** an artificial earth satellite. **8** wander about idly or gaze dreamily: *Don't moon when you have work to do.* **1-7** *n.,* **8** *v.* —**moon/like/,** *adj.*

moon beam (mün/bēm/), ray of moonlight. *n.*

moon less (mün/lis), without a moon or moonlight: *a moonless night. adj.*

moon light (mün/līt/), **1** light of the moon. **2** having the light of the moon: *a moonlight night.* **3** while the moon is shining; by night: *a moonlight swim.* **1** *n.,* **2,3** *adj.*

moon lit (mün/lit/), lighted by the moon. *adj.*

moon shine (mün/shīn/), **1** moonlight. **2** empty talk; foolish talk or ideas; nonsense. **3** INFORMAL. intoxicating liquor made unlawfully or smuggled into the country. *n.*

moon stone (mün/stōn/), a whitish, translucent gem with a pearly luster. Moonstone is a variety of feldspar. *n.*

moon struck (mün/struk/), dazed, crazed, or confused. *adj.*

moor[1] (mür), **1** put or keep (a ship, etc.) in place by means of ropes or chains fastened to the shore or to anchors. **2** fix firmly; secure. **3** moor a ship. **4** be made secure by ropes, anchors, etc. *v.* [Middle English *moren*]

moor[2] (mür), open waste land, especially if heather grows on it. *n.* [Old English *mōr*]

Moor (mür), member of a Moslem people of mixed Arab and Berber ancestry, living in northwestern Africa. In the A.D. 700's the Moors invaded and conquered Spain. They were finally driven out in 1492. *n.*

Moore (mür *or* môr), **1** Marianne, 1887-1972, American poet. **2** Thomas, 1779-1852, Irish poet. *n.*

moor ings (mür/ingz), **1** ropes, cables, or anchors by which a ship is fastened. **2** place where a ship is moored. *n.pl.*

Moor ish (mür/ish), of the Moors. *adj.*

moor land (mür/lənd), land covered with heather; moor. *n.*

moose (müs), a large mammal of the same family as the deer, found in Canada and the northern United States. The male has a large head and broad antlers. *n., pl.* **moose.**

moose—about 6 ft. high at the shoulder

moot (müt), **1** that is doubtful or debatable: *a moot point.* **2** bring forward (a point, subject, case, etc.) for discussion. **1** *adj.,* **2** *v.*

mop (mop), **1** bundle of coarse yarn, rags, or cloth, etc., or a sponge fastened at the end of a stick or handle, for cleaning floors, dishes, etc. **2** wash or wipe up; clean with a mop: *to mop up the floor.* **3** wipe tears or sweat from: *mop one's brow with one's handkerchief.* **4** a thick head of hair like a mop. **1,4** *n.,* **2,3** *v.,* **mopped, mop ping.**

mope (mōp), **1** be dull, silent, and sad. **2** person who allows himself to be dull, silent, and sad. **1** *v.,* **moped, mop ing; 2** *n.*

mop pet (mop/it), a little child. *n.*

mo raine (mə rān/), mass or ridge of rocks, dirt, etc., deposited at the sides or end of a glacier. The material is scraped up by the glacier as it moves along. *n.*

mo ral (môr′əl), 1 good in character or conduct; virtuous according to civilized standards of right and wrong; right; just: *a moral act, a moral man.* 2 **morals,** *pl.* principles in regard to conduct; character or behavior in matters of right and wrong. 3 capable of understanding right and wrong: *A little baby is not a moral being.* 4 having to do with character or with the difference between right and wrong: *Whether finding should be keeping is a moral question.* 5 lesson, inner meaning, or teaching of a fable, a story, or an event: *The moral of the story was "Look before you leap."* 6 teaching a good lesson; having a good influence. 7 that raises one's morale; inspiring confidence: *We gave moral support to the team by cheering them enthusiastically.* 8 practical: *a moral certainty.* 1,3,4,6-8 *adj.,* 2,5 *n.*

mo rale (mə ral′), moral or mental condition as regards courage, confidence, enthusiasm, etc.: *The morale of the team was low after its defeat. n.*

mo ral ist (môr′ə list), 1 person who thinks much about moral duties, sees the moral side of things, and leads a moral life. 2 person who teaches, studies, or writes about morals. *n.*

mo ral is tic (môr′ə lis′tik), 1 moralizing; teaching the difference between right and wrong. 2 of or having to do with a moralist or moral teaching. *adj.*

mo ral i ty (mə ral′ə tē), 1 the right or wrong of an action: *They spent the evening arguing about the morality of war.* 2 doing right; virtue: *She has high standards of morality.* 3 system of morals; set of rules or principles of conduct. *n., pl.* **mo ral i ties.**

mo ral ize (môr′ə līz), 1 think, talk, or write about questions of right and wrong. 2 point out the lesson or inner meaning of. 3 improve the morals of. *v.,* **mo ral ized, mo ral iz ing.**

mo ral ly (môr′ə lē), 1 in a moral manner: *He tried to behave morally.* 2 in morals; as to morals: *The king was a good man morally but too easily swayed by his crafty advisers.* 3 from a moral point of view; ethically: *What you did was morally wrong.* 4 practically: *I am morally sure that I locked the door. adv.*

moral victory, defeat that has the effect on the mind that a victory would have.

mo rass (mə ras′), piece of low, soft, wet ground; swamp. *n., pl.* **mo rass es.**

mo ra to ri um (môr′ə tôr′ē əm), 1 a legal authorization to delay payments of money due. 2 period during which such authorization is in effect. *n., pl.* **mo ra to ri ums, mo ra to ri a** (môr′ə tôr′ē ə).

Mo ra vi a (mô rā′vē ə), region in central Czechoslovakia. *n.* —**Mo ra′vi an,** *adj., n.*

mor bid (môr′bid), 1 not wholesome; unhealthy; sickly: *morbid fancies, a morbid book. A liking for horrors is morbid.* 2 caused by disease; characteristic of disease; diseased: *Cancer is a morbid growth.* 3 horrible; gruesome; grisly: *the morbid details of a murder. adj.* —**mor′bid ly,** *adv.*

mor bid i ty (môr bid′ə tē), 1 morbid condition or quality. 2 proportion of sickness. *n.*

mor dant (môrd′nt), 1 biting; cutting; sarcastic: *The mordant criticism hurt my feelings.* 2 substance that fixes colors in dyeing. 3 acid that eats into metal, used in etching. 1 *adj.,* 2,3 *n.*

more (môr), 1 greater in amount, degree, or number: *more men, more help. A foot is more than an inch.* 2 a greater or additional amount, degree, or number: *Tell me more about your camping trip. We will need more than two people in order to play this game.* 3 in a higher degree; to a greater extent: *A burn hurts more than a scratch does.* 4 in addition; farther: *Take one step more. Sing once more.* 5 further; additional: *This plant needs more sun.* 6 *More* helps to make the comparative form of most adverbs, and of most adjectives longer than one syllable: *more easily, more truly, more careful, more common. "More common" means "commoner."* 1,5 *adj., comparative of* **much** *and* **many;** 2 *n.,* 3,4,6 *adv., comparative of* **much.**

more or less, 1 somewhat: *Most people are more or less selfish.* 2 about; approximately: *The distance is fifty miles more or less.*

More (môr), Sir **Thomas,** 1478-1535, English statesman and author, canonized in 1935. *n.*

more o ver (môr ō′vər), in addition to that; also; besides: *Our field trip was informative; moreover, it was fun. adv.*

mo res (môr′āz), traditional rules and customs of a group of people or a society. They are accepted as right and morally binding. *n.pl.*

Mor gan (môr′gən), 1 Sir **Henry,** 1635?-1688, British buccaneer. 2 **John Pierpont,** 1837-1913, American financier and art collector. *n.*

mor ga nat ic (môr′gə nat′ik), having to do with a form of marriage in which a man of high rank, such as a king or duke, marries a woman of lower rank with an agreement that neither she nor her children shall have any claim to his rank or property. *adj.*

Mor gan le Fay (môr′gən lə fā′), King Arthur's half sister, a fairy, usually represented as harming him whenever she could.

morphine

hat, āge, fär; let, ēqual, tèrm;
it, īce; hot, ōpen, ôrder;
oil, out; cup, pùt, rüle; ch, child;
ng, long; sh, she; th, thin;
ᴛʜ, then; zh, measure;

ə represents *a* in about,
e in taken, *i* in pencil,
o in lemon, *u* in circus.

morgue (môrg), 1 place in which the bodies of unknown persons found dead are kept until they can be identified and taken away by their family or friends. 2 the reference library in a newspaper office. *n.*

mo ri bund (môr′ə bund), dying. *adj.*

Mor mon (môr′mən), 1 member of the Church of Jesus Christ of Latter-day Saints, founded in 1830 by Joseph Smith. 2 of or having to do with the Mormons or their religion. 1 *n.,* 2 *adj.*

morn (môrn), OLD USE. morning. *n.*

morn ing (môr′ning), 1 the early part of the day, ending at noon. 2 of or in the morning. 1 *n.,* 2 *adj.*

morn ing-glo ry (môr′ning glôr′ē), 1 a climbing vine that has heart-shaped leaves and funnel-shaped flowers of blue, lavender, pink, or white. 2 its flower, which blooms early in the day. *n., pl.* **morn ing-glo ries.**

morning star, a bright planet, especially Venus, seen in the eastern sky before sunrise.

mo roc co (mə rok′ō), a fine leather made from goatskin, used in binding books. *n., pl.* **mo roc cos.** [from *Morocco,* where it was first made]

Mo roc co (mə rok′ō), country in NW Africa, most of which was formerly under French and Spanish control. *n.* —**Mo roc′can,** *adj., n.*

mo ron (môr′on), 1 person born with such a weak mind that he can be trained to do only routine tasks, but probably can learn to read; person who does not develop beyond a mental age of eight to twelve years. 2 INFORMAL. a very stupid or foolish person. *n.*

mo ron ic (mə ron′ik), of or like a moron. *adj.*

mo rose (mə rōs′), gloomy; sullen; illhumored. *adj.* —**mo rose′ly,** *adv.*

mor pheme (môr′fēm), the smallest part of a word that has meaning of its own. Morphemes may be words, prefixes, suffixes, or endings that show inflection. In the word *carelessness,* the morphemes are *care, -less,* and *-ness. n.*

Mor phe us (môr′fē əs *or* môr′fyüs), (in Greek myths) the god of dreams. *n.*

mor phine (môr′fēn′), drug made

adj.	adjective	n.	noun
adv.	adverb	prep.	preposition
conj.	conjunction	pron.	pronoun
interj.	interjection	v.	verb
sing.	singular	pl.	plural

from opium, used to dull pain and to cause sleep. *n.* [from French *morphine,* from *Morpheus*]

mor phol o gy (môr fol′ə jē), 1 branch of biology that deals with the forms and structure of animals and plants. 2 branch of the science of language that deals with the form of words, including inflection and derivation. *n.*

mor ris chair (môr′is), armchair with an adjustable back. [from William *Morris,* 1834-1896, English poet and craftsman, who designed it]

morris dance, an old English dance performed by people in fancy costumes.

mor row (môr′ō), 1 the following day or time. 2 OLD USE. morning. *n.*

Morse (môrs), **Samuel F. B.,** 1791-1872, American painter and inventor who made the first telegraph instrument. The Morse code is named after him. *n.*

Morse code, system by which letters, numbers, etc., are represented by dots, dashes, and spaces or by long and short sounds or flashes of light. Morse code is now used mainly in signaling, and in some telegraphy.

mor sel (môr′səl), 1 a small portion of food. 2 piece; fragment. *n.*

mor tal (môr′tl), 1 sure to die sometime. 2 a being that is sure to die sometime. All living creatures are mortals. 3 of man; of mortals: *Mortal flesh has many pains and diseases.* 4 man; human being: *"Lord, what fools these mortals be!"* 5 of death. 6 causing death: *a mortal wound, a mortal illness.* 7 to the death: *a mortal enemy, a mortal battle.* 8 very great; deadly: *mortal terror.* 9 (in the Roman Catholic Church) causing death of the soul: *Stealing is considered a mortal sin.* 1,3,5-9 *adj.,* 2,4 *n.*

mor tal i ty (môr tal′ə tē), 1 mortal nature; being sure to die sometime. 2 loss of life on a large scale: *The mortality from automobile accidents is dreadful.* 3 death rate; number of deaths in proportion to population or to a specified part of a population: *The mortality from typhoid fever is decreasing. n., pl.* **mor tal i ties.**

mor tal ly (môr′tl ē), 1 fatally; so as to cause death: *mortally wounded.* 2 very greatly; bitterly; grievously: *mortally offended. adv.*

mor tar[1] (môr′tər), mixture of lime, cement, sand, and water, for holding bricks or stones together. *n.* [from French of the 1200's *mortier,* from Latin *mortarium* mortar[2]]

mor tar[2] (môr′tər), 1 bowl of porcelain, glass, or other very hard material, in which substances may be pounded to a powder with a pestle. 2 a very short cannon for shooting shells or fireworks high into the air. *n.* [Old English *mortere,* from Latin *mortarium*]

PESTLE

mortar[2] (def. 1)

MORTAR

mor tar board (môr′tər bôrd′), 1 a flat, square board used by masons to hold mortar while working with it. 2 cap with a close-fitting crown topped by a stiff, flat, cloth-covered square piece from which usually a tassel hangs, worn at graduation exercises and other academic occasions. *n.*

mort gage (môr′gij), 1 a claim on property, given to a person, bank, or firm that has loaned money in case the money is not repaid when due. 2 document that gives such a claim. 3 give a lender a claim to (one's property) in case a debt is not paid when due. 4 put under some obligation; pledge: *Faust mortgaged his soul to the Devil.* 1,2 *n.,* 3,4 *v.,* **mort gaged, mort gag ing.**

mort gag ee (môr′gi jē′), person to whom property is mortgaged. *n.*

mort ga gor or **mort gag er** (môr′gi jər), person who mortgages his property. *n.*

mor tice (môr′tis), mortise. *n., v.,* **mor ticed, mor tic ing.**

mor ti cian (môr tish′ən), undertaker. *n.*

mor ti fi ca tion (môr′tə fə kā′shən), 1 a feeling of shame; humiliation: *mortification at having spilled food on the table.* 2 a cause of shame or humiliation. 3 a mortifying or a being mortified: *the mortification of the body by fasting.* 4 death of one part of the body while the rest is alive: *His leg had to be amputated because mortification had set in. n.*

mor ti fy (môr′tə fī), 1 wound the feelings of; make feel humbled and ashamed; humiliate: *He mortified his parents with his bad behavior.* 2 overcome (bodily desires and feelings) by pain and going without things: *The saint mortified her body.* 3 die; decay: *The injured foot has mortified and must be cut off. v.,* **mor ti fied, mor ti fy ing.**

mortise (def. 1)

TENON

MORTISE

mor tise (môr′tis), 1 hole in one piece of wood cut to receive the tenon on another piece so as to form a joint. 2 fasten by a mortise: *Good furniture is mortised together, not nailed.* 1 *n.,* 2 *v.,* **mor tised, mor tis ing.** Also, **mor tice.**

mor tu ar y (môr′chü er/ē), 1 a building where dead bodies are kept until burial or cremation. 2 having to do with death or burial. 1 *n., pl.* **mor tu ar ies,** 2 *adj.*

mos., months.

mo sa ic (mō zā′ik), 1 decoration made of small pieces of stone, glass, wood, etc., of different colors inlaid to form a picture or design. 2 such a picture or design. Mosaics are used in the floors, walls, or ceilings of some fine buildings. 3 formed by, having to do with, or resembling a mosaic. 4 anything like a mosaic: *Her music is a mosaic of folk tunes.* 1,2,4 *n.,* 3 *adj.*

mosaic (def. 2)

Mo sa ic (mō zā′ik), of Moses: *the Mosaic law. adj.*

Mos cow (mos′kou or mos′kō), capital of the Soviet Union, in the W part. *n.*

Mo ses (mō′ziz), (in the Bible) the great leader and lawgiver of the Israelites, who led them out of Egypt. *n.*

Mos lem (moz′ləm), 1 follower of Mohammed; believer in the religion founded by him; a Mohammedan; Mussulman. 2 of Mohammed, his followers, or the religion founded by him; Mohammedan. 1 *n., pl.* **Mos lems** or **Mos lem;** 2 *adj.* Also, **Muslim, Muslem.**

mosque

mosque (mosk), a Moslem place of worship. *n.*

mo squi to (mə skē′tō), any of various small, slender insects with two wings. The female can pierce the skin of people and animals and draw blood, causing itching. One kind of mosquito transmits malaria; another transmits yellow fever. *n., pl.* **mo squi toes** or **mo squi tos.**

moss (môs), very small, soft, green or brown plants that grow close together like a carpet on the ground, on rocks, on trees, etc. *n., pl.* **moss es.**

moss y (mô′sē), 1 covered with moss: *a mossy bank.* 2 like moss: *mossy green. adj.,* **moss i er, moss i est.**

most (mōst), 1 greatest in amount, degree, or number: *The winner gets the most money.* 2 the greatest amount, degree, or number: *He did most of the work. Who gave the most?* 3 in the highest degree; to the greatest extent: *This tooth hurts most. She was most kind to the lonely boy.* 4 almost all: *Most children like candy.* 5 *Most* helps to make the superlative form of most adverbs, and of most adjectives longer than one syllable: *most easily, most truly, most careful, most common. "Most common" means "commonest."* 1,4 *adj., superlative of* **much** *and* **many;** 2 *n.,* 3,5 *adv., superlative of* **much.**

at most or **at the most,** not more than.
for the most part, mainly; usually.
make the most of, make the best use of.

-most, *suffix forming superlatives of adjectives and adverbs.* greatest in amount, degree, or number, as in *foremost, inmost, topmost, uttermost.* [Old English *-mest;* influenced by *most*]

most ly (mōst′lē), almost all; for the most part; mainly; chiefly. *adv.*

mote (mōt), speck of dust. *n.*

mo tel (mō tel′), roadside hotel or group of furnished cottages or cabins providing overnight lodging for motorists. Most motels have parking next to or near the units. *n.*

moth (môth), a broad-winged insect very much like a butterfly, but flying mostly at night. Moths are destructive only in the larval stage. One kind, the clothes moth, lays eggs in cloth, fur, etc., and its larvae eat holes in the material. Some larvae, such as the silkworm, are useful to man. *n., pl.* **moths** (môᴛʜz *or* môths).

moth ball (môth′bôl′), a small ball of camphor, used to keep moths away from wool, silk, fur, etc. *n.*

moth-eat en (môth′ēt′n), 1 eaten by moths; having holes made by moths. 2 worn-out. *adj.*

moth er[1] (muᴛʜ′ər), 1 a female parent. 2 take care of; act as mother to: *She mothers her baby sister.* 3 the cause or source of anything. 4 mother superior. 5 that is a mother: *the mother church.* 6 like a mother. 7 of a mother. 8 native: *our mother tongue, one's mother country.* 1,3,4 *n.,* 2 *v.,* 5-8 *adj.* [Old English *mōdor*]

moth er[2] (muᴛʜ′ər), a stringy, sticky substance formed in vinegar or on the surface of liquids that are turning to vinegar. Mother consists of bacteria. *n.* [special use of *mother*[1]]

Mother Goose, the imaginary author of certain old fairy tales and nursery rhymes.

moth er hood (muᴛʜ′ər hủd), condition of being a mother. *n.*

moth er-in-law (muᴛʜ′ər in lô′), mother of one's husband or wife. *n., pl.* **moth ers-in-law.**

moth er land (muᴛʜ′ər land′), 1 one's native country. 2 land of one's ancestors. *n.*

moth er less (muᴛʜ′ər lis), having no mother: *a motherless child. adj.*

moth er li ness (muᴛʜ′ər lē nis), motherly quality. *n.*

moth er ly (muᴛʜ′ər lē), 1 of a mother. 2 like a mother; like a mother's; kindly: *a motherly old lady, motherly love. adj.*

moth er-of-pearl (muᴛʜ′ər əv-pėrl′), the hard, smooth, glossy lining of the shell of the pearl oyster and certain other shells; nacre. It changes colors as the light changes. It is used to make buttons and ornaments. *n.*

Mother's Day, the second Sunday of May, set apart in the United States and Canada in honor of mothers.

mother superior, woman who is the head of a convent of nuns; mother.

mo tif (mō tēf′), 1 a subject for development or treatment in art, literature, or music; a principal idea or feature: *This opera contains a love motif.* 2 a distinctive figure in a design. *n.*

mo tile (mō′tl), (in biology) moving or able to move by itself. *adj.*

mo tion (mō′shən), 1 change of position or place; movement; moving. Anything is in motion which is not at rest. *Can you feel the motion of the ship? Avoid unnecessary motion of your hand while you are writing.* 2 make a movement, as of the hand or head, to show

hat, āge, fär; let, ēqual, tėrm;
it, īce; hot, ōpen, ôrder;
oil, out; cup, pùt, rüle; ch, child;
ng, long; sh, she; th, thin;
ᴛʜ, then; zh, measure;

ə represents *a* in about,
e in taken, *i* in pencil,
o in lemon, *u* in circus.

one's meaning: *He motioned to show us the way.* 3 show (a person) what to do by such a motion: *He motioned me out.* 4 a formal suggestion made in a meeting or court of law, to be voted on: *The motion to adjourn was carried.* 1,4 *n.,* 2,3 *v.*

mo tion less (mō′shən lis), not moving. *adj.* —**mo′tion less ly,** *adv.* —**mo′tion less ness,** *n.*

motion picture, 1 series of pictures projected on a screen in such rapid succession that the viewer gets the impression that the persons and things pictured are moving; moving picture; movie. 2 story or drama told by means of this.

mo ti vate (mō′tə vāt), provide with a motive or incentive; induce to act. *v.,* **mo ti vat ed, mo ti vat ing.**

mo ti va tion (mō′tə vā′shən), a furnishing with an incentive or inducement to action. *n.*

mo tive (mō′tiv), 1 thought or feeling that makes one act: *My motive in going away was a wish to travel.* 2 that makes something move: *motive power of steam or electricity.* 3 motif. 1,3 *n.,* 2 *adj.*

mot ley (mot′lē), 1 made up of different things: *a motley collection of butterflies, shells, and stamps.* 2 mixture of things that are different. 3 of different colors like a clown's suit. 4 suit of more than one color worn by clowns: *At the costume party he wore motley.* 1,3 *adj.,* 2,4 *n., pl.* **mot leys.**

mo tor (mō′tər), 1 engine that makes a machine go: *an electric motor, a gasoline motor.* 2 an internal-combustion engine. 3 run by a motor: *a motor vehicle.* 4 automobile. 5 having to do with or by means of automobiles: *a motor tour.* 6 to travel by automobile. 7 causing or having to do with motion. Motor nerves arouse muscles to action. 1,2,4 *n.,* 3,5,7 *adj.,* 6 *v.*

mo tor boat (mō′tər bōt′), boat that is propelled by a motor. *n.*

mo tor cade (mō′tər kād), procession or long line of automobiles. *n.*

mo tor car (mō′tər kär′), automobile. *n.*

adj. adjective	*n.* noun
adv. adverb	*prep.* preposition
conj. conjunction	*pron.* pronoun
interj. interjection	*v.* verb
sing. singular	*pl.* plural

motorcycle
(def. 1)

mo tor cy cle (mō′tər sī′kəl), 1 vehicle like a bicycle run by a motor. 2 travel by motorcycle. 1 *n.,* 2 *v.,* **mo tor cy cled, mo tor cy cling.**

mo tor cy clist (mō′tər sī′klist), person who rides a motorcycle. *n.*

mo tor ist (mō′tər ist), person who drives or travels in an automobile. *n.*

mo tor ize (mō′tə rīz′), 1 furnish with a motor. 2 supply with motor-driven vehicles in place of horses and horse-drawn vehicles. *v.,* **mo tor ized, mo tor iz ing.**

mo tor man (mō′tər mən), 1 man who runs an electric subway train or streetcar. 2 man who runs a motor. *n., pl.* **mo tor men.**

motor scooter

motor scooter, vehicle like a child's scooter, except that the driver is seated. It is propelled by a motor.

motor truck, truck with the engine, frame, and wheels made for carrying heavy loads.

mot tle (mot′l), 1 mark with spots or streaks of different colors. 2 a mottled coloring or pattern. 1 *v.,* **mot tled, mot tling;** 2 *n.*

mot to (mot′ō), 1 a brief sentence adopted as a rule of conduct: *"Think before you speak" is a good motto.* 2 sentence, word, or phrase written or engraved on some object. *n., pl.* **mot toes** or **mot tos.**

mould (mōld), mold. *n., v.*

mould er (mōl′dər), molder. *v.*

mould ing (mōl′ding), molding. *n.*

mould y (mōl′dē), moldy. *adj.,* **mould i er, mould i est.**

moult (mōlt), molt. *v., n.*

mound (mound), 1 a bank or heap of earth or stones. 2 heap up. 3 a small hill. 4 the slightly elevated ground from which a baseball pitcher pitches. 1,3,4 *n.,* 2 *v.*

mount[1] (mount), 1 go up; ascend: *mount stairs.* 2 get up on: *mount a horse, mount a platform.* 3 get on a horse: *Paul Revere mounted in haste.* 4 put on a horse; furnish with a horse: *Many policemen in this city are mounted.* 5 horse provided for riding: *The riding instructor had an excellent mount.* 6 rise; increase; rise in amount: *The cost of living mounts steadily.* 7 put in proper position or order for use: *mount specimens on slides.* 8 have or carry (guns) as a fortress or ship does: *The ship mounts eight guns.* 9 fix in a setting, backing, support, etc.: *mount a picture on cardboard.* 10 a setting; backing; support: *the mount for a picture.* 11 provide (a play) with scenery and costumes. 1-4,6-9,11 *v.,* 5,10 *n.* [from French of the 1500's *monter,* from Latin *mons, montis* mountain]

mount[2] (mount), mountain; high hill. *Mount* is often used before the names of mountains. *Mount Rainier. n.* [Old English *munt,* from Latin *mons, montis* mountain]

moun tain (moun′tən), 1 a very high hill. 2 of or having to do with mountains: *mountain air, mountain plants.* 3 a very large heap or pile of anything: *a mountain of rubbish.* 4 a huge amount: *She overcame a mountain of difficulties.* 1,3,4 *n.,* 2 *adj.*

make a mountain out of a molehill, give great importance to something which is really insignificant.

moun tain eer (moun′tə nir′), 1 person who lives in the mountains. 2 person skilled in mountain climbing. 3 climb mountains. 1,2 *n.,* 3 *v.*

mountain goat, the white, goatlike antelope of the Rocky Mountains.

mountain laurel, an evergreen shrub with glossy leaves and pale-pink or white flowers.

mountain lion, puma.

moun tain ous (moun′tə nəs), 1 covered with mountain ranges: *mountainous country.* 2 huge: *a mountainous wave. adj.*

mountain range, row of connected mountains; large group of mountains.

moun tain side (moun′tən sīd′), the slope of a mountain below the summit. *n.*

Mountain Standard Time, the standard time in the Rocky Mountain regions of the United States and Canada. It is seven hours behind Greenwich Time.

moun tain top (moun′tən top′), top or summit of a mountain. *n.*

moun te bank (moun′tə bangk), 1 person who sells quack medicines in public, appealing to his audience by tricks, stories, jokes, etc. 2 anybody who tries to deceive people by tricks, stories, etc. *n.*

Mount ie (moun′tē), INFORMAL. member of the Royal Canadian Mounted Police, a force maintained by the government of Canada. *n.*

mount ing (moun′ting), support, setting, etc. The mounting of a photograph is the paper or cardboard on which it is pasted. *n.*

Mount Ver non (vėr′nən), 1 home of George Washington in Virginia, on the Potomac River near Washington, D.C. 2 city in SE New York State.

mourn (môrn), 1 grieve. 2 feel or show grief over: *She mourned her lost dog. v.*

mourn er (môr′nər), person who mourns, especially at a funeral. *n.*

mourn ful (môrn′fəl), 1 full of grief; sad; sorrowful: *a mournful voice.* 2 causing sorrow or mourning. *adj.* **—mourn′ful ly,** *adv.* **—mourn′ful ness,** *n.*

mourn ing (môr′ning), 1 the wearing of black or some other color to show sorrow for a person's death. 2 a draping of buildings, flying flags at half-mast, etc., as an outward sign of sorrow for death. 3 clothes or decorations to show sorrow for death. 4 of mourning; used in mourning. 1-3 *n.,* 4 *adj.*

mourning dove, a wild dove of North America that has a mournful call.

mountain goat
3 ft. high
at the shoulder

mouse (mous *for 1,4;* mouz *or* mous *for 2,3*), 1 a small, gnawing rodent. The gray mouse usually found in houses is between three and four inches long. Field mice live in fields and meadows. 2 to hunt for mice; catch mice for food: *Cats and owls go mousing at night.* 3 search as a cat does; move about as if searching. 4 a shy, timid person. 1,4 *n., pl.* **mice;** 2,3 *v.,* **moused, mous ing.** **—mouse′like′,** *adj.*

mous er (mou′zər), animal that catches mice. *n.*

mouse trap (mous′trap′), trap for catching mice. *n.*

mous ey (mou′sē), mousy. *adj.*, **mous i er, mous i est.**

mousse (müs), a fancy food made with whipped cream, either frozen or stiffened with gelatin: *chocolate mousse, tomato mousse. n.*

mous tache (mus′tash *or* mə stash′), mustache. *n.*

mous y (mou′sē), 1 resembling or suggesting a mouse in color, odor, behavior, etc.: *mousy hair.* 2 quiet as a mouse. 3 infested with mice. *adj.*, **mous i er, mous i est.** Also, **mousey.**

mouth (mouth *for 1-3,6;* mouŦH *for 4,5*), 1 the opening through which a person or animal takes in food; space containing the tongue and teeth. 2 an opening suggesting a mouth: *the mouth of a cave, the mouth of a bottle.* 3 a part of a river or the like where its waters are emptied into some other body of water: *the mouth of the Ohio River.* 4 utter (words) in an affected, pompous way: *I dislike actors who mouth their speeches.* 5 seize or rub with the mouth. 6 a grimace: *She made mouths at the cold, greasy food.* 1-3,6 *n., pl.* **mouths** (mouŦHz); 4,5 *v.*

mouth ful (mouth′fúl), 1 the amount the mouth can easily hold. 2 what is taken into the mouth at one time. 3 a small amount. *n., pl.* **mouth fuls.**

mouth organ, harmonica.

mouth piece (mouth′pēs′), 1 the part of a pipe, horn, etc., that is placed in or against a person's mouth. 2 person, newspaper, etc., that speaks for others. *n.*

mov a ble (mü′və bəl), 1 that can be moved: *Our fingers are movable.* 2 that can be carried from place to place as personal belongings can. 3 changing from one date to another in different years: *Thanksgiving is a movable holiday.* 4 piece of furniture that is not a fixture but can be moved to another house. 1-3 *adj.*, 4 *n.* Also, **moveable.**

move (müv), 1 change the place or position of: *Do not move your hand. Move your chair to the other side of the table.* 2 change place or position: *The child moved in her sleep.* 3 change one's place of living: *We move to the country next week. They will move into their new home as soon as the present tenants move out.* 4 put or keep in motion; shake; stir: *The wind moves the leaves.* 5 make progress; go: *The train moved slowly.* 6 act of moving; movement. 7 cause to act: *Castor oil moves the bowels.* 8 to act: *God moves in a mysterious way.* 9 action taken to bring about some result: *a move to disconcert an opponent.* 10 impel; rouse; excite:

What moved you to do this? 11 affect with emotion; excite to tender feeling: *The sad story moved me to tears.* 12 make a move in a game; be moved in a game: *move a pawn in chess.* 13 the moving of a piece in a game: *That was a good move.* 14 a player's turn to move in a game: *It's your move now.* 15 make a formal request, application, or proposal; propose: *Madam Chairman, I move that we adjourn.* 16 be active: *move in the best society.* 1-5,7,8,10-12,15, 16 *v.*, **moved, mov ing;** 6,9,13,14 *n.*

move in, move oneself, one's family, one's belongings, etc., into a new place to live.

on the move, moving about: *He's been on the move from job to job for years.*

move a ble (mü′və bəl), movable. *adj., n.*

move ment (müv′mənt), 1 act or fact of moving: *We run by movements of the legs.* 2 a change in the placing of troops or ships. 3 the moving parts of a machine; special group of parts that move on each other. The movement of a watch consists of many little wheels. 4 in music: **a** the kind of rhythm and tempo a piece has: *The movement of a waltz is very different from the movement of a march.* **b** one division of a symphony, sonata, or other long selection: *the second movement of Beethoven's Fifth Symphony.* 5 the efforts and results of a group of people working together to bring about some one thing: *the movement for a safe and sane Fourth of July.* 6 an emptying of the bowels. 7 the waste matter emptied from the bowels. *n.*

mov er (mü′vər), 1 person or thing that moves. 2 person whose occupation is moving furniture, etc., from one house or place to another. *n.*

mov ie (mü′vē), 1 motion picture. 2 theater showing motion pictures: *a neighborhood movie.* 3 **the movies,** a showing of motion pictures: *go to the movies. n.*

mov ing (mü′ving), 1 that moves: *a moving car.* 2 causing action: *He was the moving spirit in planning for the party.* 3 touching; pathetic: *a moving story. adj.* —**mov′ing ly,** *adv.*

moving picture, motion picture.

mow[1] (mō), 1 cut down with a machine or a scythe: *mow grass.* 2 cut down the grass or grain from: *mow a field.* 3 cut down grass, etc.: *The men are mowing today.* 4 destroy at a sweep or in large numbers, as if by mowing: *The enemy fire mowed down a platoon of soldiers. v.*, **mowed, mowed** *or* **mown, mowing.** [Old English *māwan*]

mow[2] (mou), 1 the place in a barn where hay, grain, or the like is piled or stored. 2 a pile or stack of hay, grain,

etc., in a barn. *n.* [Old English *mūga, mūwa*]

mow er (mō′ər), person or thing that mows. *n.*

mown (mōn), mowed; a past participle of **mow**[1]. *v.*

Mo zam bique (mō′zam bēk′), Portuguese colony in SE Africa. *n.*

Mo zart (mōt′särt), **Wolfgang Amadeus,** 1756-1791, Austrian composer. *n.*

MP or **M.P.,** 1 Member of Parliament. 2 Military Police.

mph or **m.p.h.,** miles per hour.

Mr. or **Mr** (mis′tər), Mister, a title put in front of a man's name or the name of his position: *Mr. Jackson, Mr. President. pl.* **Messrs.**

Mrs. or **Mrs** (mis′iz), a title put in front of a married woman's name: *Mrs. Jackson. pl.* **Mmes.**

ms., Ms., or **MS.** manuscript. *pl.* **mss., Mss.,** or **MSS.**

Ms. (miz), a title put in front of a woman's name: *Ms. Jane Smith. pl.* **Mses.**

Msgr., Monsignor.

M.S.T., Mountain Standard Time.

mt., mountain, *pl.* **mts.**

Mt., Mount: *Mt. Everest. pl.* **Mts.**

mtn., mountain.

much (much), 1 in great amount or degree: *much money, not much time.* 2 a great amount: *Don't eat too much of this cake. Much of this is true.* 3 to a high degree; greatly: *I was much pleased.* 4 nearly; about: *This is much the same as the other.* 1 *adj.*, **more, most;** 3,4 *adv.*, **more, most;** 2 *n.*

make much of, pay much attention to or do much for.

not much of a, not a very good: *Thirty dollars a week is not much of a wage.*

too much for, more than a match for.

mu ci lage (myü′sə lij), a sticky, gummy substance used to make things stick together. *n.*

muck (muk), 1 dirt; filth. 2 moist farmyard manure, used as a fertilizer. 3 a heavy, moist, dark soil made up chiefly of decayed plants. *n.*

muck rake (muk′rāk′), hunt for and

hat, āge, fär; let, ēqual, tèrm; it, īce; hot, ōpen, ôrder; oil, out; cup, pùt, rüle; ch, child; ng, long; sh, she; th, thin; ŦH, then; zh, measure;

ə represents *a* in about, *e* in taken, *i* in pencil, *o* in lemon, *u* in circus.

adj. adjective	*n.* noun
adv. adverb	*prep.* preposition
conj. conjunction	*pron.* pronoun
interj. interjection	*v.* verb
sing. singular	*pl.* plural

expose corruption. *v.*, **muck raked, muck rak ing.**

muck rak er (muk′rā′kər), person, especially a journalist, who muck-rakes. *n.*

mu cous (myü′kəs), 1 of or like mu-cus. 2 containing or secreting mucus. *adj.*

mucous membrane, the lining of the nose, throat, and other cavities of the body that open to the air.

mu cus (myü′kəs), a slimy substance that is secreted by and moistens the mucous membranes. Excess mucus is discharged from the nose when one has a cold. *n.*

mud (mud), earth so wet that it is soft and sticky: *The bare earth turned quick-ly to mud during the rain. Thick mud covered the bottom of the pond. n.*

mud di ly (mud′l ē), in a muddy man-ner. *adv.*

mud dle (mud′l), 1 mix up; bring (things) into a mess: *to muddle a piece of work.* 2 think or act in a confused, blundering way: *muddle over a problem, muddle through a difficulty.* 3 make confused or stupid: *The more you talk, the more you muddle me.* 4 mess; disor-der; confusion: *The family that rented our summer cottage left it in a muddle.* 1-3 *v.*, **mud dled, mud dling;** 4 *n.*

mud dle head ed (mud′l hed′id), stupid; confused. *adj.*

mud dy (mud′ē), 1 of or like mud: *muddy footprints on the floor.* 2 having much mud; covered with mud: *a muddy road, muddy shoes.* 3 clouded with mud; dull; not pure: *muddy water, a muddy color.* 4 confused; not clear: *muddy thinking.* 5 make muddy; be-come muddy. 1-4 *adj.*, **mud di er, mud di est;** 5 *v.*, **mud died, mud dy-ing.**

mu ez zin (myü ez′n), crier who, at cer-tain hours, calls Moslems to prayer. *n.*

muff (muf), 1 a covering of fur or other material for keeping both hands warm. One hand is put in at each end. 2 fail to catch (a ball) when it comes into one's hands. 3 a clumsy failure to catch a ball that comes into one's hands: *The catch-er's muff allowed the runner to score.* 4 handle awkwardly; bungle. 5 an awkward handling; bungling. 1,3,5 *n.*, 2,4 *v.*

muf fin (muf′ən), a small, round cake made of wheat flour, corn meal, or the like, often without sugar. Muffins are eaten with butter and usually served hot. *n.*

muf fle (muf′əl), 1 wrap or cover up in order to keep warm and dry: *She muffled her throat in a warm scarf.* 2 wrap in something in order to soften or stop the sound: *A bell can be muffled with cloth.* 3 dull or deaden (a sound). 4 a muffled sound. 1-3 *v.*, **muf fled, muf fling;** 4 *n.*

muf fler (muf′lər), 1 wrap or scarf worn around the neck for warmth. 2 anything used to deaden sound. An automobile muffler, attached to the end of the exhaust pipe, deadens the sound of the engine's exhaust. *n.*

muf ti (muf′tē), ordinary clothes, not a uniform: *The retired general appeared in mufti. n.*

mug (mug), 1 a heavy china or metal drinking cup with a handle. 2 amount a mug holds: *to drink a mug of milk.* 3 SLANG. face or mouth. 4 SLANG. at-tack (a person) from behind, usually to rob. 1-3 *n.*, 4 *v.*, **mugged, mug ging.**

mug ger (mug′ər), SLANG. person who mugs. *n.*

mug gi ness (mug′ē nis), muggy con-dition. *n.*

mug gy (mug′ē), warm and humid; damp and close: *The weather was mug-gy. adj.*, **mug gi er, mug gi est.**

mug wump (mug′wump′), person who is independent in politics. *n.*

Mu ham mad (mù ham′əd), Moham-med. *n.*

mu lat to (mə lat′ō *or* myü lat′ō), per-son having one white parent and one Negro parent. *n.*, *pl.* **mu lat toes.**

mul ber ry (mul′ber′ē), 1 any of var-ious trees with small, berrylike fruit that can be eaten. The leaves of one kind are used for feeding silkworms. 2 its sweet, usually dark purple fruit. 3 a dark pur-plish red. *n.*, *pl.* **mul ber ries.**

mulch (mulch), 1 straw, leaves, loose earth, etc., spread on the ground around trees or plants. Mulch is used to protect the roots from cold or heat, to prevent evaporation of moisture from the soil, or to keep the fruit clean. 2 to cover with straw, leaves, etc. 1 *n.*, *pl.* **mulch-es;** 2 *v.*

mulct (mulkt), 1 deprive of something by cunning or deceit; defraud: *He was mulcted of his money by a shrewd trick.*

muff (def. 1)

2 punish (a person) by a fine. 3 a fine; penalty. 1,2 *v.*, 3 *n.*

mule[1] (myül), 1 offspring of a donkey and a horse. It has the form and size of a horse and the large ears, small hoofs, and tufted tail of a donkey. 2 IN-FORMAL. a stubborn person. 3 kind of spinning machine which twists cotton fibers into yarn and winds it on spindles. *n.* [partly Old English *mūl*, partly from French of the 1200's *mule*; both from Latin *mulus*]

mule[1] (def. 1)
4 to 5 ft. high at the shoulder

mule[2] (myül), kind of slipper that leaves the heel uncovered. *n.* [from French of the 1500's *mule*, from Dutch *muil*, from Latin *mulleus* red leather (shoe)]

mu le teer (myü′lə tir′), driver of mules. *n.*

mul ish (myü′lish), like a mule; stub-born; obstinate. *adj.* —**mul′ish ly,** *adv.* —**mul′ish ness,** *n.*

mull[1] (mul), INFORMAL. think about without making much progress; ponder. *v.* [origin uncertain]

mull[2] (mul), make (wine, beer, cider, etc.) into a warm drink, adding sugar and spices. *v.* [origin uncertain]

mul lein *or* **mul len** (mul′ən), a weed with coarse, woolly leaves and spikes of yellow flowers. *n.*

mul let (mul′it), kind of fish that lives close to the shore in warm waters. It is good to eat. There are red mullets and gray mullets. *n.*, *pl.* **mul lets** *or* **mul-let.**

mul ti col ored (mul′ti kul′ərd), hav-ing many colors. *adj.*

mul ti far i ous (mul′tə fer′ē əs *or* mul′tə far′ē əs), 1 having many differ-ent parts, elements, forms, etc. 2 many and varied. *adj.*

mul ti form (mul′tə fôrm), having many different shapes, forms, or kinds. *adj.*

mul ti lat er al (mul′ti lat′ər əl), 1 having many sides. 2 involving three or more nations. *adj.*

mul ti mil lion aire (mul′ti mil′-yə ner′ *or* mul′ti mil′yə nar′), person who owns property worth several millions (of dollars, pounds, francs, etc.); millionaire many times over. *n.*

mul ti ple (mul′tə pəl), 1 of, having, or involving many parts, elements, relations, etc.: *a man of multiple interests.* 2 number that contains another number a certain number of times without a remainder: *12 is a multiple of 3.* 1 *adj.,* 2 *n.*

mul ti pli cand (mul′tə plə kand′), number to be multiplied by another: *In 497 multiplied by 5, the multiplicand is 497. n.*

mummy—Egyptian mummy and coffin. The body was treated with chemicals and wrapped in linen.

mul ti pli ca tion (mul′tə plə kā′shən), 1 a multiplying or a being multiplied. 2 operation of multiplying one number by another. *n.*

mul ti plic i ty (mul′tə plis′ə tē), a manifold variety; a great many: *a multiplicity of interests. n., pl.* **mul ti plic i ties.**

mul ti pli er (mul′tə plī′ər), 1 number by which another number is to be multiplied: *In 83 multiplied by 5, the multiplier is 5.* 2 person or thing that multiplies. *n.*

mul ti ply (mul′tə plī), 1 add (a number) a given number of times: *To multiply 16 by 3 means to add 16 three times, making 48.* 2 increase in number or amount: *My problems multiplied rapidly. v.,* **mul ti plied, mul ti ply ing.**

mul ti ra cial (mul′ti rā′shəl), having a number of races: *a multiracial community. adj.*

mul ti tude (mul′tə tüd *or* mul′tə tyüd), a great many; crowd: *a multitude of difficulties, a multitude of enemies. n.*

mul ti tu di nous (mul′tə tüd′n əs *or* mul′tə tyüd′n əs), forming a multitude; very numerous. *adj.* —**mul′ti tu′di nous ly, adv.**

mum (mum), 1 saying nothing; silent: *Keep mum about this; tell no one.* 2 be silent! say nothing! 1 *adj.,* 2 *interj.*

mum's the word, be silent; say nothing.

mum ble (mum′bəl), 1 speak indistinctly, as a person does when his lips are partly closed. 2 a mumbling: *There was a mumble of protest from the team against the umpire's decision.* 3 chew as a person does who has no teeth: *The old dog mumbled the crust of bread.*

1,3 *v.,* **mum bled, mum bling;** 2 *n.*

mum ble ty-peg (mum′bəl tē peg′), game in which the players in turn flip a knife from various positions, trying to make it stick in the ground. *n.*

mum mer (mum′ər), 1 person who wears a mask, fancy costume, or disguise for fun: *Six mummers acted in a play at Christmas.* 2 actor. *n.*

mum mer y (mum′ər ē), 1 performance of mummers. 2 a useless or silly show or ceremony. *n., pl.* **mum mer ies.**

mum mi fi ca tion (mum′ə fə kā′shən), act or process of mummifying. *n.*

mum mi fy (mum′ə fī), 1 make into a mummy; make like a mummy. 2 shrivel; dry up. *v.,* **mum mi fied, mum mi fy ing.**

mum my (mum′ē), a dead body preserved from decay. Egyptian mummies have lasted more than 3000 years. *n., pl.* **mum mies.**

mumps (mumps), a contagious disease caused by a virus, characterized by swelling of the glands in the neck and difficulty in swallowing. *n.*

munch (munch), chew vigorously and steadily; chew noisily: *The horse munched his oats. v.* —**munch′er, n.**

mun dane (mun′dān), 1 of this world, not of heaven; earthly. 2 of the universe; of the world. *adj.*

Mu nich (myü′nik), large city in S West Germany. *n.*

mu nic i pal (myü nis′ə pəl), 1 of or having to do with the affairs of a city, town, or other municipality: *The state police assisted the municipal police.* 2 run by a city, town, or other municipality. *adj.* —**mu nic′i pal ly, adv.**

mu nic i pal i ty (myü nis′ə pal′ə tē), city, town, or other district having local self-government. *n., pl.* **mu nic i pal i ties.**

mu nif i cence (myü nif′ə səns), very great generosity. *n.*

mu nif i cent (myü nif′ə sənt), extremely generous. *adj.* —**mu nif′i cent ly, adv.**

mu ni tion (myü nish′ən), 1 Usually, **munitions,** *pl.* material used in war. Munitions are military supplies, such as guns, powder, or bombs. 2 having to do with military supplies: *A munition plant is a factory for making munitions.* 3 provide with military supplies: *munition a fort.* 1 *n.,* 2 *adj.,* 3 *v.*

mur al (myúr′əl), 1 on a wall: *A mural painting is painted on a wall of a building.* 2 picture painted on a wall. 3 of a wall; having to do with walls; like a wall. 1,3 *adj.,* 2 *n.*

mur der (mèr′dər), 1 the unlawful killing of a human being when it is planned beforehand. 2 an instance of such a

hat, āge, fär; let, ēqual, tèrm;
it, īce; hot, ōpen, ôrder;
oil, out; cup, pùt, rüle; ch, child;
ng, long; sh, she; th, thin;
ŦH, then; zh, measure;

ə represents *a* in about,
e in taken, *i* in pencil,
o in lemon, *u* in circus.

crime: *The detective solved the murder.* 3 kill a human being intentionally: *Cain murdered his brother Abel.* 4 do very badly; spoil or ruin: *I really murdered my recital piece.* 1,2 *n.,* 3,4 *v.*

mur der er (mèr′dər ər), person who murders somebody. *n.*

mur der ous (mèr′dər əs), 1 able to kill: *a murderous blow.* 2 ready to murder: *a murderous villain.* 3 causing murder: *a murderous hate. adj.* —**mur′der ous ly, adv.**

murk (mèrk), darkness; gloom: *A light flashed through the murk of the night. n.*

murk i ly (mèr′kə lē), in a murky manner. *adv.*

murk i ness (mèr′kē nis), murky condition. *n.*

murk y (mèr′kē), 1 dark; gloomy: *a murky prison.* 2 very thick and dark; misty; hazy: *murky smoke. adj.,* **murk i er, murk i est.**

mur mur (mèr′mər), 1 a soft, low, indistinct sound that rises and falls a little and goes on without breaks: *the murmur of a stream, the murmur of little waves, the murmur of voices in another room.* 2 make a soft, low, indistinct sound. 3 a sound in the heart or lungs, especially an abnormal sound due to a leaky valve in the heart. 4 a softly spoken word or speech. 5 say in a murmur: *The shy child murmured his thanks.* 6 complaint made under the breath, not aloud. 7 complain under the breath; grumble. 1,3,4,6 *n.,* 2,5,7 *v.*

mur rain (mèr′ən), an infectious disease of cattle. *n.*

mus cle (mus′əl), 1 the tissue in the bodies of people and animals which can be tightened or loosened to make the body move. 2 a special bundle of such tissue which moves some particular bone or part. See **biceps** for diagram. 3 strength. *n.*

mus cle-bound (mus′əl bound′), having some of the muscles enlarged or tight, and lacking normal elasticity, usually as a result of too much exercise. *adj.*

Mus co vite (mus′kə vīt), Russian. *n., adj.*

557

adj. adjective	*n.* noun
adv. adverb	*prep.* preposition
conj. conjunction	*pron.* pronoun
interj. interjection	*v.* verb
sing. singular	*pl.* plural

Mus co vy (mus′kə vē), OLD USE. Russia. *n.*

mus cu lar (mus′kyə lər), 1 of the muscles; influencing the muscles: *a muscular strain.* 2 having well-developed muscles; strong: *a muscular arm.* 3 consisting of muscle. *adj.*

muscular dys tro phy (dis′trə fē), a disease in which the muscles gradually weaken and waste away.

mus cu la ture (mus′kyə lə chùr), system or arrangement of muscles. *n.*

muse (myüz), 1 think in a dreamy way; think; meditate: *The boy spent the whole afternoon in musing.* 2 look thoughtfully. *v.,* **mused, mus ing.**

Muse (myüz), 1 (in Greek myths) one of the nine goddesses of the fine arts and sciences. 2 Sometimes, **muse.** spirit that inspires a poet or composer. *n.*

mu se um (myü zē′əm), a building or rooms where a collection of objects illustrating science, art, history, or other subjects is kept and displayed. *n.* [from Latin *museum* place or seat of the Muses]

mush[1] (mush), 1 corn meal boiled in water. 2 a soft, thick mass: *After the heavy rain the dirt road turned to mush.* *n., pl.* **mush es.** [a different form of *mash* (Old English *māsc-*)]

mush[2] (mush), 1 a journey on foot through snow, driving a dog sled. 2 to travel in this way. 3 a shout to a team of sled dogs to start or to speed up. 1 *n., pl.* **mush es;** 2 *v.,* 3 *interj.* [perhaps used for *mush on,* altered from French *marchons* let us advance] —**mush′-er,** *n.*

mush room (mush′rüm *or* mush′-rùm), 1 a small fungus, shaped like an umbrella, that grows very fast. Some mushrooms are good to eat; some are poisonous. 2 of or like a mushroom. 3 of very rapid growth: *a mushroom town.* 4 grow rapidly: *Their business mushroomed when they opened the new store.* 1 *n.,* 2,3 *adj.,* 4 *v.*

mushrooms
(def. 1)
stalk
2 to 5 in. high

mush y (mush′ē), 1 like mush; pulpy. 2 INFORMAL. weakly sentimental. *adj.,* **mush i er, mush i est.**

mu sic (myü′zik), 1 art of putting sounds together in beautiful, pleasing, or interesting arrangements. 2 beautiful, pleasing, or interesting arrangements of sounds. 3 written or printed signs for tones: *Can you read music?* 4 any pleasant sound: *the music of a bubbling brook, the music of the wind. n.*

face the music, INFORMAL. meet trouble boldly or bravely.

set to music, provide (the words of a song, etc.) with music.

mu si cal (myü′zə kəl), 1 of music: *a musical composer.* 2 sounding beautiful or pleasing; like music: *a musical voice.* 3 set to music; accompanied by music: *a musical performance.* 4 fond of music. 5 skilled in music. 6 musical comedy. 1-5 *adj.,* 6 *n.*

musical comedy, play or motion picture with songs, choruses, and dances.

musk ox—to 5 ft. high at shoulder

mu si cale (myü′zə kal′), a social gathering to enjoy music. *n.*

musical instrument, piano, violin, or other instrument for producing music.

mu si cal ly (myü′zik lē), 1 in a musical manner. 2 in music: *She is well educated musically. adv.*

music box, box or case containing apparatus for producing music mechanically.

mu si cian (myü zish′ən), 1 person skilled in music. 2 person who sings or who plays on a musical instrument, especially as a profession or business: *An orchestra is composed of many musicians.* 3 composer of music. *n.*

mu si cian ship (myü zish′ən ship), skill in playing, conducting, or composing music; musical ability. *n.*

mu si col o gy (myü′zə kol′ə jē), the systematic study of music, especially its history, forms, and principles. *n.*

musk (musk), 1 substance with a strong and lasting odor, used in making perfumes. Musk is found in a special gland in the male musk deer. 2 a similar substance found in the glands of other animals, such as the mink and muskrat. 3 odor of musk. 4 any plant whose leaves or flowers smell like musk. *n.*

musk deer, a small, hornless deer of central Asia, the male of which has a gland containing musk.

mus kel lunge (mus′kə lunj), a very large North American pike. The muskellunge is valued as a food and game fish. It is a very hard fish to catch. *n., pl.* **mus kel lunge.**

mus ket (mus′kit), kind of old gun used before rifles were invented. *n.*

musket

mus ket eer (mus′kə tir′), soldier armed with a musket. *n.*

mus ket ry (mus′kə trē), 1 muskets. 2 art of shooting with muskets or rifles. 3 the fire of muskets: *a sudden crackle of musketry. n.*

musk i ness (mus′kē nis), musky quality or conditon. *n.*

musk mel on (musk′mel′ən), kind of small, sweet melon with a hard rind and a smell like that of musk. The cantaloupe and honeydew melon are muskmelons. *n.*

musk ox, an arctic mammal having a shaggy coat and a strong, musky smell. It looks like a sheep in some ways and like an ox in others.

musk rat (musk′rat′), 1 a water rodent of North America somewhat like a rat but larger; water rat. 2 its valuable, dark-brown fur. *n., pl.* **musk rats** or **musk rat.**

muskrat (def. 1)
to 22 in. long with tail

musk y (mus′kē), of or like musk; like that of musk: *a musky odor. adj.,* **musk i er, musk i est.**

Mus lim or **Mus lem** (muz′ləm), Moslem. *n., adj.*

mus lin (muz′lən), 1 a thin, fine cotton cloth, used for dresses, curtains, etc. 2 a heavier cotton cloth, used for sheets, undergarments, etc. 3 made of muslin: *white muslin curtains.* 1,2 *n.,* 3 *adj.*

muss (mus), put into disorder; rumple: *The child's new outfit was mussed. v.*

mus sel (mus/əl), any of several mollusks having two hinged parts to their shells. Mussels resemble clams and are found in both fresh and salt water. Sea mussels have dark-blue shells and can be eaten. The shells of fresh-water mussels are used to make buttons. *n.*

Mus so li ni (mús/ə lē/nē *or* mü/sə-lē/nē), Benito, 1883-1945, leader of the Italian Fascists and prime minister of Italy from 1922 to 1943. *n.*

Mus sul man (mus/əl mən), a Moslem. *n., pl.* **Mus sul mans.**

muss y (mus/ē), INFORMAL. untidy; messy; rumpled. *adj.,* **muss i er, muss i est.**

must (must; *unstressed* məst), 1 be obliged to; be forced to: *You must eat to live.* 2 ought to; should: *I must go home soon. You really must read this story.* 3 be certain or likely to be, do, etc.: *This man must be crazy to talk so. I must seem very rude.* 4 *Must* is sometimes used with its verb omitted. *We must away.* 5 something necessary; obligation: *This rule is a must.* 6 INFORMAL. demanding attention or doing; necessary: *a must item, must legislation.* 1-4 *v., past tense* **must;** 5 *n.,* 6 *adj.*

mus tache (mus/tash *or* mə stash/), 1 hair growing on a man's upper lip. 2 hairs or bristles growing near the mouth of an animal. *n.* Also, **moustache.**

mus ta chio (mə stä/shō), mustache. *n., pl.* **mus ta chios.**

mus tang (mus/tang), a small, wild or half-wild horse of the North American plains. *n.*

mus tard (mus/tərd), 1 plant whose seeds have a sharp, hot taste. 2 a yellow powder or paste made from its seeds. It is used as seasoning to give a pungent taste to meats, etc. *n.*

mustard plaster, mixture of mustard and water, or of mustard, flour, and water, spread on cloth and applied to the body as medicine.

mus ter (mus/tər), 1 gather together; assemble; collect. 2 assembly; collection. 3 summon: *muster up courage.* 4 a bringing together of men or troops for review or service: *There was a muster of all the guards.* 5 list of those assembled. 6 the number assembled. 1,3 *v.,* 2,4-6 *n.*

muster out, to discharge.

pass muster, be inspected and approved; come up to the required standards.

mus ti ness (mus/tē nis), musty condition or quality. *n.*

must n't (mus/nt), must not.

mus ty (mus/tē), 1 having a smell or taste suggesting mold or damp; moldy: *a musty room, musty crackers.* 2 stale;

out-of-date: *musty laws about witches. adj.,* **mus ti er, mus ti est.**

mu ta bil i ty (myü/tə bil/ə tē), 1 tendency to change. 2 fickleness. *n.*

mu ta ble (myü/tə bəl), 1 liable to change: *mutable customs.* 2 fickle: *a mutable person. adj.*

mu tant (myüt/nt), a new variety of plant or animal resulting from mutation. *n.*

mu tate (myü/tāt), 1 to change. 2 undergo or produce mutation. *v.,* **mu-tat ed, mu tat ing.**

mu ta tion (myü tā/shən), 1 a change; alteration. 2 a change within a gene or chromosome resulting in a new feature or character that appears suddenly in animals or plants and can be inherited. 3 such a new feature or character. 4 mutant. *n.*

mute (myüt), 1 not making any sound; silent: *The little girl stood mute with astonishment.* 2 dumb; unable to speak. 3 person who cannot speak. 4 clip, pad, or other device put on a musical instrument to muffle the sound. 5 put such a device on; muffle the sound of with a mute: *She muted the strings of her violin.* 6 not pronounced. The *e* in *mute* is mute. 1,2,6 *adj.,* 3,4 *n.,* 5 *v.,* **mut ed, mut ing. —mute/ly,** *adv.* **—mute/ness,** *n.*

mu ti late (myü/tl āt), 1 cut, tear, or break off a part of; injure seriously by cutting, tearing, or breaking off some part: *The book was badly mutilated by someone who had torn some pages and written on others.* 2 make (a story, song, etc.) imperfect by removing parts. *v.,* **mu ti lat ed, mu ti lat ing.**

mu ti la tion (myü/tl ā/shən), a mutilating or a being mutilated. *n.*

mu ti neer (myüt/n ir/), person who takes part in a mutiny. *n.*

mu ti nous (myüt/n əs), rebellious: *a mutinous crew. adj.* **—mu/ti nous ly,** *adv.*

mu ti ny (myüt/n ē), 1 open rebellion against lawful authority, especially by sailors or soldiers against their officers. 2 take part in a mutiny; rebel. 1 *n., pl.* **mu ti nies;** 2 *v.,* **mu ti nied, mu ti ny-ing.**

mutt (mut), SLANG. dog, especially a mongrel. *n.*

mut ter (mut/ər), 1 speak or utter (words) low and indistinctly, with lips partly closed. 2 complain; grumble. 3 a muttering. 4 muttered words: *We heard a mutter of discontent.* 1,2 *v.,* 3,4 *n.*

mut ton (mut/n), meat from a sheep: *We had roast mutton for dinner. n.*

mu tu al (myü/chü əl), 1 done, said, felt, etc., by each toward the other; given and received: *mutual promises, mutual dislike. They had mutual affection for each other; each liked the others*

hat, āge, fär; let, ēqual, tèrm; it, īce; hot, ōpen, ôrder; oil, out; cup, pùt, rüle; ch, child; ng, long; sh, she; th, thin; ŦH, then; zh, measure;

ə represents *a* in about, *e* in taken, *i* in pencil, *o* in lemon, *u* in circus.

and was liked by them. 2 each to the other: *mutual enemies.* 3 belonging to each of several: *We are happy to have him as our mutual friend. adj.* **—mu/tu al ly,** *adv.*

mutual fund, a financial organization that pools the money of its members to invest it in a variety of securities.

muzzle (def. 2)

muz zle (muz/əl), 1 the nose, mouth, and jaws of a four-footed animal. 2 a cover or cage of straps or wires to put over the head and mouth of an animal to keep it from biting or eating. 3 put such a muzzle on. 4 compel (a person) to keep silent about something: *Fear that they might betray friends muzzled them.* 5 the open front part of the barrel of a gun, pistol, etc. 1,2,5 *n.,* 3,4 *v.,* **muz-zled, muz zling.**

my (mī), 1 of me; belonging to me: *My house is around the corner. I learned my lesson.* 2 INFORMAL. exclamation of surprise. 1 *pron.,* 2 *interj.*

my ce li um (mī sē/lē əm), the main part of a fungus, consisting of interwoven fibers. *n., pl.* **my ce li a** (mī-sē/lē ə).

My ce nae (mī sē/nē), very ancient city in S Greece. *n.*

my col o gy (mī kol/ə jē), branch of botany that deals with fungi. *n.*

my na (mī/nə), any of several starlings that can imitate human speech, found in India and neighboring countries. *n., pl.* **my nas.**

my nah (mī/nə), myna. *n.*

Myn heer (mīn her/ *or* mīn hir/), DUTCH. Sir; Mr. *n.*

my o pi a (mī ō/pē ə), near-sightedness. *n.*

my op ic (mī op/ik), near-sighted. *adj.*

myr i ad (mir/ē əd), 1 ten thousand. 2 a very great number: *There are myriads of stars.* 3 countless. 1,2 *n.,* 1,3 *adj.*

adj. adjective	*n.* noun
adv. adverb	*prep.* preposition
conj. conjunction	*pron.* pronoun
interj. interjection	*v.* verb
sing. singular	*pl.* plural

Myr mi don (mėr′mə don), 1 (in Greek legends) a member of a warlike people of ancient Thessaly who accompanied Achilles, their king, to the Trojan War. 2 **myrmidon,** an obedient and unquestioning follower. *n.*

myrrh (mėr), a fragrant, gummy substance with a bitter taste used in medicines, perfumes, and incense. It is obtained from a shrub that grows in Arabia and eastern Africa. *n.*

myr tle (mėr′tl), 1 an evergreen shrub of southern Europe, with shiny leaves, fragrant white flowers, and black berries. 2 periwinkle. *n.*

my self (mī self′), 1 form of *me* or *I* used to make a statement stronger: *I myself will go.* 2 form used instead of *me* or *I* in cases like: *I can cook for myself. I hurt myself.* 3 my real or true self: *I am not myself today.* *pron., pl.* **our selves.**

mys ter i ous (mi stir′ē əs), 1 full of mystery; hard to explain or understand; secret; hidden: *Electricity is mysterious.* 2 suggesting mystery: *a mysterious look.* *adj.* —**mys ter′i ous ly,** *adv.* —**mys ter′i ous ness,** *n.*

mys ter y (mis′tər ē), 1 something that is hidden or unknown; secret. 2 secrecy; obscurity. 3 something that is not explained or understood: *the mystery of the migration of birds.* 4 novel, story, etc., about a mysterious event or events which are not explained until the end, so as to keep the reader in suspense. 5 a sacramental rite of the Christian religion. 6 a secret religious rite to which only initiated persons are admitted. 7 a medieval religious play based on the Bible. *n., pl.* **mys ter ies.**

mys tic (mis′tik), 1 mystical. 2 person who believes that truth or God can be known through spiritual insight, independent of the mind. 1 *adj.*, 2 *n.*

mys ti cal (mis′tə kəl), 1 having some secret meaning; beyond human understanding; mysterious. 2 spiritually symbolic: *The lamb, the dove, and the wheel are mystical religious symbols.* 3 of or concerned with mystics or mysticism. 4 of or having to do with secret rites open only to the initiated. *adj.* —**mys′ti cal ly,** *adv.*

mys ti cism (mis′tə siz′əm), 1 beliefs or mode of thought of mystics. 2 vague or fuzzy thinking; dreamy speculation. *n.*

mys ti fi ca tion (mis′tə fə kā′shən), 1 a mystifying or a being mystified; bewilderment; perplexity. 2 something that mystifies or is designed to mystify. *n.*

mys ti fy (mis′tə fī), 1 bewilder purposely; puzzle; perplex: *The magician's tricks mystified the audience.* 2 make mysterious. *v.,* **mys ti fied, mys ti fy ing.**

myth (mith), 1 legend or story, usually one that attempts to account for something in nature: *The myth of Proserpina is the ancient Roman explanation of summer and winter.* 2 any invented story. 3 an imaginary person or thing: *Her trip to Europe was a myth invented to impress others.* *n.*

myth i cal (mith′ə kəl), 1 of a myth; like a myth; in myths: *a mythical interpretation of nature, mythical monsters, mythical places.* 2 not real; made-up; imaginary: *His great wealth is merely mythical.* *adj.* —**myth′i cal ly,** *adv.*

myth o log i cal (mith′ə loj′ə kəl), of mythology: *The phoenix is a mythological bird.* *adj.* —**myth′o log′i cal ly,** *adv.*

my thol o gy (mi thol′ə jē), 1 a group of myths relating to a particular country or person: *Greek mythology.* 2 study of myths. *n., pl.* **my thol o gies.**

N n

N or **n** (en), the 14th letter of the alphabet. *n., pl.* **N's** or **n's**.

n, (in algebra) an indefinite number.

N or **N.,** 1 North. 2 Northern.

n., 1 north. 2 northern. 3 noun.

N.A.A.C.P., National Association for the Advancement of Colored People.

nab (nab), SLANG. 1 catch or seize suddenly; grab. 2 arrest: *The police soon nabbed the thief.* *v.,* **nabbed, nab bing.**

na bob (nā′bob), a very rich man. *n.*

na cre (nā′kər), mother-of-pearl. *n.*

na dir (nā′dər), 1 the point in the heavens directly beneath the place where one stands; the point opposite the zenith. 2 the lowest point. *n.*

nadir (def. 1)
The nadir, the center of the earth, and the zenith are in a straight line.

nag[1] (nag), find fault with (a person) all the time; irritate or annoy by peevish complaints; scold: *I will clean up in a minute; please don't nag me. When I am upset I nag at everybody.* *v.,* **nagged, nag ging.** [probably from a Scandinavian word, such as Icelandic *nagga* grumble]

nag[2] (nag), 1 INFORMAL. a horse. 2 an old or inferior horse. *n.* [Middle English *nagge* pony]

Na ga sa ki (nä′gə sä′kē), seaport in SW Japan, target of the second atomic bomb to be used in war, on August 9, 1945. *n.*

Na hua tl (nä′wä təl), language of the Aztecs, Toltecs, and other American Indian tribes of central Mexico and parts of Central America. *n.*

Na hum (nā′əm), 1 (in the Bible) a Hebrew prophet. 2 book of the Old Testament containing his prophecies. *n.*

nai ad (nā′ad), 1 Also, **Naiad.** (in Greek and Roman myths) a nymph guarding a stream or spring. 2 a girl

swimmer. *n., pl.* **nai ads, nai a des** (nā′ə dēz′).

nail (nāl), 1 a slender piece of metal having a point at one end and usually a flat or rounded head at the other end. Nails are hammered into or through pieces of wood to hold them together. 2 fasten with a nail or nails. 3 hold or keep fixed: *nailed to a promise, nail one's eyes on a picture.* 4 INFORMAL. catch; seize. 5 the thin, hard, horny layer on the upper side of the end of a finger or toe. 1,5 *n.,* 2-4 *v.*

hit the nail on the head, guess or understand correctly; say or do something just right.

nail down, find out definitely; make certain; settle finally: *The buyer nailed down the terms of the sale.*

nail set (nāl′set′), tool for driving nails beneath the surface. *n.*

nain sook (nān′sùk), a very soft, fine cotton cloth. *n.*

Nai ro bi (nī rō′bē), capital of Kenya, in the S part. *n.*

na ïve or **na ive** (nä ēv′), simple in nature; like a child; artless; not sophisticated. *adj.* **—na ïve′ly, na ive′ly,** *adv.*

na i ve te (nä ē′və tā′), naïveté. *n.*

na ï ve té (nä ē′və tā′), 1 quality of being naïve; unspoiled freshness; artlessness. 2 a naïve action, remark, etc. *n., pl.* **na ï ve tés.**

na ked (nā′kid), 1 with no clothes on; nude; bare. 2 not covered; stripped: *naked fields.* 3 not protected; exposed: *a naked sword.* 4 without addition of anything else; plain. The **naked truth** is the plain truth without ornament. The **naked eye** is the eye unaided by any glass, telescope, or microscope. *adj.* **—na′ked ly,** *adv.* **—na′ked ness,** *n.*

nam by-pam by (nam′bē pam′bē), 1 weakly simple, silly, or sentimental; lacking strength or firmness. 2 a namby-pamby person. 1 *adj.,* 2 *n., pl.* **nam by-pam bies.**

name (nām), 1 word or words by which a person, animal, place, or thing is spoken of or to: *Our dog's name is Butch. She knows all her chickens by name. "The Corn State" is a name for Iowa.* 2 give a name to: *name a newborn baby.* 3 call by name; mention by name: *Three persons were named in the report.* 4 give the right name for: *Can you name these flowers?* 5 reputation; fame: *get a bad name, make a name for oneself.* 6 mention; speak of; state: *name several reasons.* 7 specify or fix; settle on: *name a price. The class named the day for its party.* 8 choose for some duty or office; nominate; appoint: *He was named for class president.* 9 well-known: *Is this coffee a name brand?*

NAILSET

1,5 *n.,* 2-4,6-8 *v.,* **named, nam ing;** 9 *adj.*

call names, call bad names; swear at; curse.

in the name of, 1 for the sake of. 2 acting for: *I ordered the supplies in the name of my supervisor.*

know only by name, know only by hearing about.

to one's name, belonging to one: *not a dollar to his name.*

name less (nām′lis), 1 having no name: *a nameless stranger.* 2 not marked with a name: *a nameless grave.* 3 that cannot be named or described: *a strange, nameless longing.* 4 not fit to be mentioned: *nameless crimes.* 5 not named; unknown; obscure: *a book by a nameless writer.* *adj.* **—name′less ness,** *n.*

name ly (nām′lē), that is to say: *The railroad connects two cities—namely, New York and Chicago.* *adv.*

name sake (nām′sāk′), one having the same name as another, especially one named after another: *My sister, Florence, is the namesake of Florence Nightingale.* *n.*

nan keen or **nan kin** (nan kēn′) a firm yellow or buff cloth. *n.* [from *Nanking,* where it was first made]

Nan king (nan′king′), city in E China, on the Yangtze River. It was the capital of China from 1928 to 1937 and from 1946 to 1949. *n.*

nan ny goat (nan′ē), a female goat.

Nantes (nants *or* nänt), port in W France, on the Loire River. *n.*

Nan tuck et (nan tuk′it), island south of Cape Cod. It is part of Massachusetts. *n.*

adj.	adjective	*n.*	noun
adv.	adverb	*prep.*	preposition
conj.	conjunction	*pron.*	pronoun
interj.	interjection	*v.*	verb
sing.	singular	*pl.*	plural

Na o mi (nā ō′mē), (in the Bible) the mother-in-law of Ruth. *n.*

nap[1] (nap), 1 a short sleep: *The baby takes a nap after lunch.* 2 take a short sleep: *Grandfather naps in his armchair.* 3 be off guard; be unprepared: *The test caught me napping.* 1 *n.,* 2,3 *v.,* **napped, nap ping.** [Old English *hnappian* to doze]

nap[2] (nap), the soft, short, woolly threads or hairs on the surface of cloth: *the nap on velvet or flannelette. n.* [from Dutch of the 1400's *noppe*]

na palm (nā′päm′ *or* nā′pälm′), 1 a chemical substance used to thicken gasoline. 2 the thickened or jellied gasoline, used for making incendiary bombs and in flamethrowers. *n.*

nape (nāp *or* nap), the back of the neck. *n.*

na per y (nā′pər ē), tablecloths, napkins, and doilies. *n.*

naph tha (naf′thə *or* nap′thə), any of several highly volatile liquids made from petroleum, coal tar, etc., used as fuel and to take spots from clothing. *n.,* *pl.* **naph thas.**

naph tha lene (naf′thə lēn′ *or* nap′thə lēn′), a white, crystalline compound made from coal tar or petroleum, used in making mothballs, dyes, lubricants, etc. *n.*

nap kin (nap′kin), 1 piece of cloth or paper used at meals for protecting the clothing or for wiping the lips or fingers. 2 any similar piece, such as a baby's diaper or a small towel. *n.*

Na ples (nā′pəlz), seaport on the SW coast of Italy, famous for its beautiful bay. *n.*

Na po le on I (nə pō′lē ən), 1769-1821, Napoleon Bonaparte, general of the French army who made himself emperor of the French in 1804. He conquered a large part of Europe, but was defeated at Waterloo in 1815 and exiled to the island of St. Helena.

Napoleon III, 1808-1873, Louis Napoleon, nephew of Napoleon I, president of France from 1848 to 1852 and emperor of France from 1852 to 1870.

Na po le on ic (nə pō′lē on′ik), of, having to do with, or resembling Napoleon I. *adj.*

nar cis sus (när sis′əs), 1 a spring plant with yellow or white flowers and long, slender leaves. It grows from a bulb. Jonquils and daffodils are narcissuses. 2 its flower. *n., pl.* **nar cis sus es, nar cis si** (när sis′ī).

Nar cis sus (när sis′əs), (in Greek myths) a beautiful youth who fell in love with his reflection in a spring. He pined away and was changed into the flower narcissus. *n.*

nar cot ic (när kot′ik), 1 any drug that produces drowsiness, sleep, dullness, or an insensible condition, and lessens pain by dulling the nerves. Opium is a powerful narcotic. 2 having the properties and effects of a narcotic. 3 of or having to do with narcotics or their use. 1 *n.,* 2,3 *adj.*

Nar ra gan sett Bay (nar′ə gan′sit), bay of the Atlantic, in E Rhode Island.

nar rate (nar′āt *or* na rāt′), tell (a story, etc.); relate. *v.,* **nar rat ed, nar rat ing.**

nar ra tion (na rā′shən), 1 act of telling. 2 the form of composition that relates an event or a story. Novels, short stories, histories, and biographies are forms of narration. 3 story or account. *n.*

nar ra tive (nar′ə tiv), 1 story; tale: *Her trip through the Near East made an interesting narrative.* 2 narration; story-telling. 3 that narrates: *"Hiawatha" is a narrative poem.* 1,2 *n.,* 3 *adj.*

nar ra tor (nar′ā tər *or* na rā′tər), person who tells a story. *n.*

nar row (nar′ō), 1 not wide; having little width; less wide than usual for its kind: *narrow cloth. A path a foot wide is narrow.* 2 **narrows,** *pl.* the narrow part of a river, strait, sound, valley, pass, etc. 3 limited or small in extent, space, amount, range, scope, opportunity, etc.: *He had only a narrow circle of friends.* 4 make or become narrower; decrease in breadth, extent, etc.; limit: *The doctor narrowed his interest to diseases of the throat. The road narrows above the bend.* 5 with little margin; close: *a narrow escape.* 6 lacking breadth of view or sympathy; prejudiced: *a narrow mind.* 7 with barely enough to live on: *live in narrow circumstances.* 1,3,5-7 *adj.,* 2 *n.,* 4 *v.* —**nar′row ly,** *adv.* —**nar′row ness,** *n.*

nar row-mind ed (nar′ō mīn′did), lacking breadth of view or sympathy; prejudiced. *adj.* —**nar′row-mind′ed ly,** *adv.* —**nar′row-mind′ed ness,** *n.*

nar whal (när′hwəl), a toothed whale of the arctic seas. The male has a long tusk extending forward from a tooth in the upper jaw. *n.*

nar y (ner′ē *or* nar′ē), DIALECT. not: *nary a one. adj.*

na sal (nā′zəl), 1 of, in, or from the nose: *nasal bones, a nasal discharge.* 2 spoken with the nose passage open. *M, n,* and *ng* represent nasal sounds. 3 a nasal sound. 1,2 *adj.,* 3 *n.* —**na′sal ly,** *adv.*

nas cent (nas′nt *or* nā′snt), in the process of coming into existence; just beginning to exist, grow, or develop. *adj.*

Nash ville (nash′vil), capital of Tennessee, in the central part. *n.*

Nas sau (nas′ô), capital of the Bahama Islands. *n.*

Nas ser (nä′sər), **Gamal Abdel,** 1918-1970, chief executive of the Egyptian republic from 1954 to 1970, and president of the United Arab Republic from 1958 to 1970. *n.*

nas ti ly (nas′tl ē), in a nasty manner. *adv.*

nas ti ness (nas′tē nis), 1 disgusting dirtiness; filth. 2 moral filth; vileness. 3 extreme unpleasantness. *n.*

na stur tium (nə stėr′shəm), 1 a garden plant with yellow, orange, or red flowers, and sharp-tasting seeds and leaves. 2 its flower. *n.*

nas ty (nas′tē), 1 disgustingly dirty; filthy: *a nasty room.* 2 morally filthy; vile: *a nasty mind.* 3 very unpleasant: *nasty weather, a nasty temper. adj.,* **nas ti er, nas ti est.**

na tal (nā′tl), of one's birth: *Her natal day is September 3. adj.*

Na tal (nə tal′), province of the Republic of South Africa, on the E coast. *n.*

na tion (nā′shən), 1 people occupying the same country, united under the same government, and usually speaking the same language: *The President appealed to the nation for support of his policies.* 2 a sovereign state; country: *the nations of the West.* 3 a people, race, or tribe; those having the same descent, language, and history: *The Armenian nation.* 4 a North American Indian tribe, especially one belonging to a confederacy: *the Sioux nation. n.*

na tion al (nash′ə nəl), 1 of a nation; belonging to a whole nation: *national laws, a national disaster.* 2 citizen of a nation: *Many nationals of Canada visit our country.* 1 *adj.,* 2 *n.*

National Guard, the reserve militia of each state of the United States, sup-

narwhal—up to 16 ft. long without tusk

ported in part by the Federal government. The National Guard may be called upon to serve either the state or the Federal government in time of emergency.

na tion al ism (nash′ə nə liz′əm), 1 patriotic feelings or efforts. 2 desire and plans for national independence. *n.*

na tion al ist (nash′ə nə list), 1 upholder of nationalism; person who believes in nationalism. 2 nationalistic. 1 *n.*, 2 *adj.*

Nationalist China, the Republic of China.

na tion al is tic (nash′ə nə lis′tik), of nationalism or nationalists. *adj.* —**na′tion al is′ti cal ly,** *adv.*

na tion al i ty (nash′ə nal′ə tē), 1 nation. 2 condition of belonging to a nation. Citizens of the same country have the same nationality. 3 condition of being an independent nation: *After the Revolutionary War the colonies attained nationality.* *n., pl.* **na tion al i ties.**

na tion al i za tion (nash′ə nə lə zā′shən), a nationalizing or a being nationalized. *n.*

na tion al ize (nash′ə nə līz), 1 make national. 2 bring (land, industries, railroads, etc.) under the control or ownership of a nation. 3 make into a nation. *v.,* **na tion al ized,** **na tion al iz ing.**

na tion al ly (nash′ə nə lē), 1 in a national manner; as a nation. 2 throughout the nation: *The President's speech was broadcast nationally.* *adv.*

national park, land kept by the national government for people to enjoy because of its beautiful scenery, historical interest, etc.

National Socialist Party, the fascist party, led by Adolf Hitler, which ruled Germany from 1933 to 1945.

na tion wide (nā′shən wīd′), extending throughout the nation: *a nationwide election.* *adj.*

na tive (nā′tiv), 1 person born in a certain place or country. The natives are the people living in a place, not visitors or foreigners. 2 born in a certain place or country: *People born in New York are native sons and daughters of New York.* 3 belonging to one because of his birth: *The United States is my native land.* 4 belonging to one because of his country or the nation to which he belongs: *French is his native language.* 5 born in a person; natural: *native ability, native courtesy.* 6 one of the people found in a place or country by its conquerors, settlers, or visitors, especially a member of a less civilized people. 7 of or having to do with the natives, especially those of a less civi-

lized people: *native customs, native huts.* 8 animal or plant that originated in a place. 9 originating, grown, or produced in a certain place: *Tobacco is native to America.* 10 found pure in nature; not produced artificially: *native copper. Native salt is refined for use.* 1,6,8 *n.*, 2-5,7,9,10 *adj.*

na tive-born (nā′tiv bôrn′), born in the place or country indicated: *a native-born American. adj.*

na tiv i ty (nə tiv′ə tē), 1 birth. **2 the Nativity,** a birth of Christ. b Christmas. *n., pl.* **na tiv i ties.**

natl., national.

NA TO (nā′tō), North Atlantic Treaty Organization (an alliance of fourteen non-Communist European and North American nations providing for joint military cooperation). *n.*

nat ti ly (nat′l ē), in a natty manner; with neatness: *nattily dressed. adv.*

nat ti ness (nat′ē nis), natty condition or quality. *n.*

nat ty (nat′ē), trim and tidy; neatly smart in dress or appearance: *a natty uniform, a natty young officer. adj.,* **nat ti er, nat ti est.**

nat ur al (nach′ər əl), 1 produced by nature; coming or occurring in the ordinary course of events: *natural feelings and actions, a natural complexion, a natural death, a natural result.* 2 not man-made or artificial: *Coal and oil are natural products.* 3 belonging to the nature one is born with; instinctive; inborn: *natural ability. It is natural for ducks to swim.* 4 in accordance with the nature of things or the circumstances of the case: *a natural conclusion.* 5 instinctively felt to be right and fair: *natural law, natural rights.* 6 like nature; true to nature: *The picture looked natural.* 7 free from affectation or restraint: *a natural manner.* 8 (in music) neither sharp nor flat; not changed in pitch by a sharp or a flat: *C natural.* 9 a natural tone or note. 10 sign (♮) used to cancel the effect of a preceding sharp or flat. 11 INFORMAL. person who is especially suited for something because of inborn talent or ability: *He is a natural on the saxophone.* 1-8 *adj.,* 9-11 *n.* —**nat′ur al ness,** *n.*

natural gas, a combustible gas formed naturally in the earth, consisting primarily of methane. It is used as a fuel.

natural history, the study of animals, plants, minerals, and other things in nature.

nat ur al ist (nach′ər ə list), person who makes a study of animals and plants. *n.*

nat ur al is tic (nach′ər ə lis′tik), 1 of natural history or naturalists. 2 of or in accordance with nature. *adj.*

hat, āge, fär; let, ēqual, tėrm;
it, īce; hot, ōpen, ôrder;
oil, out; cup, put, rüle; ch, child;
ng, long; sh, she; th, thin;
ᵺ, then; zh, measure;

ə represents *a* in about,
e in taken, *i* in pencil,
o in lemon, *u* in circus.

nat ur al i za tion (nach′ər ə lə zā′shən), a naturalizing or a being naturalized. *n.*

nat ur al ize (nach′ər ə līz), 1 admit (a foreigner) to citizenship. After living in the United States for a certain number of years, an immigrant can be naturalized if he passes a test. 2 adopt (a foreign word or custom): *"Chauffeur" is a French word that has been naturalized in English.* 3 introduce and make at home in another country: *The English oak has become naturalized in parts of Massachusetts.* 4 become like a native. *v.,* **nat ur al ized, nat ur al iz ing.**

nat ur al ly (nach′ər ə lē), 1 in a natural way: *Speak naturally; don't try to imitate someone else.* 2 by nature: *a naturally obedient child.* 3 as might be expected; of course: *She offered me some candy; naturally, I took it. adv.*

natural number, a positive integer. The natural numbers are 1,2,3,4, etc.

natural resources, materials supplied by nature that are useful or necessary for life. Minerals, forests, and water power are natural resources.

natural science, any science dealing with the facts of nature or the physical world. Biology, geology, physics, and chemistry are natural sciences.

na ture (nā′chər), 1 the world; all things except those made by man: *the wonders of nature.* 2 Also, **Nature.** all the forces at work throughout the world: *the laws of nature.* 3 the instincts or inborn tendencies that direct behavior: *It is the nature of birds to fly.* 4 life without artificial things: *Wild animals live in a state of nature.* 5 what a thing really is; quality; character: *It is against her nature to be petty.* 6 sort; kind: *She loves to read books of a scientific nature.* 7 physical being; vital powers: *food sufficient to sustain nature. n.*

nature study, study of animals, plants, and other things and events in nature.

naught (nôt), 1 nothing. 2 zero; 0. *n.* Also, **nought.**

naugh ti ly (nô′tə lē), in a naughty manner. *adv.*

adj.	adjective	*n.*	noun
adv.	adverb	*prep.*	preposition
conj.	conjunction	*pron.*	pronoun
interj.	interjection	*v.*	verb
sing.	singular	*pl.*	plural

naugh ti ness (nô′tē nis), bad behavior; disobedience; mischief. *n.*

naugh ty (nô′tē), 1 bad; not obedient: *The naughty child hit his baby sister.* 2 somewhat improper: *a naughty joke.* *adj.*, **naugh ti er, naugh ti est.**

Na u ru (nä ü′rü), small island country in the S Pacific, northeast of the Solomon Islands. It is a member of the Commonwealth of Nations. *n.*

nau se a (nô′zē ə *or* nô′shə), 1 the feeling that one has when about to vomit. 2 extreme disgust; loathing. *n.*

nau se ate (nô′zē āt *or* nô′shē āt), 1 cause nausea in; make sick. 2 feel nausea; become sick. 3 cause to feel loathing. *v.*, **nau se at ed, nau se at ing.**

nau seous (nô′shəs *or* nô′zē əs), 1 causing nausea; sickening. 2 disgusting; loathsome: *The garbage dump was nauseous.* 3 feeling nausea; nauseated. *adj.*

nau ti cal (nô′tə kəl), of or having to do with ships, sailors, or navigation. *adj.* —**nau′ti cal ly,** *adv.*

nautical mile, measure of distance equal to 6076.11549 feet; geographical mile.

GAS-FILLED CHAMBER

MOUTH

TENTACLES (RETRACTED)

pearly (or chambered) nautilus shell to 6 in. in diameter

nau ti lus (nô′tl əs), either of two small mollusks. The **pearly nautilus** or **chambered nautilus** has a spiral shell divided into many compartments which have a pearly lining. The **paper nautilus** resembles the octopus and has a thin shell. *n., pl.* **nau ti lus es, nau ti li** (nô′tl ī).

Nav a ho (nav′ə hō), member of a tribe of American Indians living mainly in New Mexico, Arizona, and Utah. *n., pl.* **Nav a hos** or **Nav a hoes.**

Nav a jo (nav′ə hō), Navaho. *n., pl.* **Nav a jos** or **Nav a joes.**

na val (nā′vəl), 1 of or for warships or the navy: *a naval officer, naval supplies.* 2 having a navy: *a naval power.* *adj.*

Na varre (nə vär′), former kingdom including parts of SW France and N Spain. *n.*

nave (nāv), the main part of a church or cathedral between the side aisles. The nave extends from the main entrance to the transepts. See **apse** for diagram. *n.*

na vel (nā′vəl), the mark or scar in the middle of the surface of the abdomen, where the umbilical cord was attached before birth. *n.*

navel orange, a seedless orange with a small growth at one end shaped somewhat like a navel.

nav i ga bil i ty (nav′ə gə bil′ə tē), condition of being navigable. *n.*

nav i ga ble (nav′ə gə bəl), 1 that ships can travel on: *The Mississippi River is deep enough to be navigable.* 2 that can be sailed; seaworthy. 3 that can be steered: *Without a rudder the ship was not navigable.* *adj.*

nav i gate (nav′ə gāt), 1 sail, manage, or steer (a ship, aircraft, etc.). 2 sail on or over (a sea or river). 3 travel by water; sail the seas. 4 manage a ship or aircraft. *v.*, **nav i gat ed, nav i gat ing.**

nav i ga tion (nav′ə gā′shən), 1 act or process of navigating. 2 art or science of finding a ship's or an aircraft's position and course. *n.*

nav i ga tor (nav′ə gā′tər), 1 person who sails the seas. 2 person who has charge of the navigating of a ship or aircraft or who is skilled in navigating. 3 explorer of the seas. *n.*

na vy (nā′vē), 1 Often, **Navy.** the branch of a nation's armed forces which includes its ships of war, the officers and personnel who run them, and the department that manages them. 2 OLD USE. fleet of ships. 3 a dark blue; navy blue. *n., pl.* **na vies.**

navy bean, a small, common, white bean, dried for use.

navy blue, a dark blue.

nay (nā), 1 OLD USE. no. 2 not only that, but also: *We are willing, nay, eager to go.* 3 no; a denial or refusal. 4 a negative vote or voter. 1,2 *adv.*, 3,4 *n.*

Naz a rene (naz′ə rēn′ *or* naz′ə rēn′), 1 person born or living in Nazareth. 2 **the Nazarene,** Jesus Christ. 3 an early Christian. *n.*

Naz a reth (naz′ər əth), town in N Israel. It was the home of Jesus Christ during His early youth. *n.*

Naz a rite (naz′ə rīt′), (among the ancient Hebrews) a Jew who had taken certain strict religious vows. *n.*

Na zi (nä′tsē *or* nat′sē), 1 member or supporter of the National Socialist Party, a fascist political party in Germany, led by Adolf Hitler. 2 of or having to do with the Nazis. 1 *n., pl.* **Na zis;** 2 *adj.*

Na zi ism (nä′tsē iz′əm *or* nat′sē iz′əm), Nazism. *n.*

Na zism (nä′tsiz′əm *or* nat′siz′əm), the doctrines and practices of the Nazis, including totalitarian government, state control of industry, anti-Semitism, and opposition to communism. *n.*

N.B., New Brunswick.

N.B. or **n.b.,** note well; observe carefully. [abbreviation of Latin *nota bene*]

N.C., North Carolina.

N. Dak. or **N.D.,** North Dakota.

NE or **N.E.,** 1 northeast. 2 northeastern.

Ne an der thal (nē an′dər täl *or* nē-an′dər thôl), belonging to a group of prehistoric people who lived in caves in Europe, North Africa, and parts of Asia in the early Stone Age. The Neanderthal man of Europe had a large, heavy skull and low forehead, a broad, flat nose, and a heavy lower jaw. *adj.* [from the *Neanderthal* Gorge in Germany, where its fossils were first found]

neap (nēp), 1 of or having to do with those tides which attain the least height. 2 neap tide. 1 *adj.*, 2 *n.*

Ne a pol i tan (nē′ə pol′ə tən), 1 of or having to do with Naples. 2 person born or living in Naples. 1 *adj.*, 2 *n.*

neap tide, tide that occurs when the difference in height between high and low tide is least; the lowest level of high tide. Neap tide comes twice a month.

near (nir), 1 to or at a short distance; not far; close: *They searched far and near. The holiday season is drawing near.* 2 close by; not distant; less distant: *The post office is quite near.* 3 close to in space, time, condition, etc.: *Our house is near the river.* 4 come or draw near to; approach: *The ship neared the land.* 5 close in feeling; intimate; familiar: *a near friend.* 6 closely related: *a near relative.* 7 INFORMAL. all but; almost: *The war lasted near a year.* 8 on the left-hand side; left: *The near horse and the off horse make a team.* 9 short; direct: *Go by the nearest route.* 10 by a close margin: *a near escape.* 11 stingy. 1,7 *adv.*, 2,5,6,8-11 *adj.*, 3 *prep.*, 4 *v.* —**near′ness,** *n.*

come near doing, almost do: *I came near forgetting my glasses.*

near at hand, 1 within easy reach. 2 not far in the future.

near by (nir′bī′), near; close at hand: *a nearby house (adj.). They went nearby to visit (adv.).* *adj., adv.*

Near East, the countries of SW Asia, sometimes including the Balkan States and Egypt.

near ly (nir′lē), 1 almost: *I nearly missed the train.* 2 closely: *It will cost more than we can afford, as nearly as I can figure it.* *adv.*

near sight ed (nir′sī′tid), not able to

see far; seeing distinctly at a short distance only: *Nearsighted people usually wear glasses.* *adj.* —**near'-sight'ed ly,** *adv.* —**near'sight'ed-ness,** *n.*

neat (nēt), 1 clean and in order: *a neat desk, a neat room, a neat suit.* 2 able and willing to keep things in order: *a neat child.* 3 well-formed; in proportion: *a neat design.* 4 skillful; clever: *a neat trick.* 5 without anything mixed in it: *He drinks his brandy neat.* *adj.* —**neat'ly,** *adv.* —**neat'ness,** *n.*

neath or **'neath** (nēth), OLD USE. beneath. *prep.*

Ne bo (nē'bō), **Mount,** (in the Bible) the mountain from which Moses looked down upon Canaan, the Promised Land. *n.*

Nebr. or **Neb.,** Nebraska.

Ne bras ka (nə bras'kə), one of the midwestern states of the United States. *Capital:* Lincoln. *n.* —**Ne bras'kan,** *adj., n.*

Neb u chad nez zar (neb'yə-kəd nez'ər), died 562 B.C., king of Babylon from 605 to 562 B.C. He twice captured Jerusalem and destroyed it in 586 B.C. *n.*

neb u la (neb'yə lə), a cloudlike cluster of stars or a mass of dust particles and gases which occurs in interstellar space. A nebula may be either luminous or dark in appearance. *n., pl.* **neb u lae** (neb'yə lē'), **neb u las.**

neb u lar (neb'yə lər), of or having to do with a nebula or nebulae. *adj.*

neb u lous (neb'yə ləs), 1 hazy; vague; indistinct; confused. 2 cloud-like. 3 of or like a nebula or nebulae. *adj.* —**neb'u lous ly,** *adv.* —**neb'u-lous ness,** *n.*

nec es sar i ly (nes'ə ser'ə lē), 1 because of necessity: *Leaves are not necessarily green.* 2 as a necessary result: *War necessarily causes misery and waste.* *adv.*

nec es sar y (nes'ə ser'ē), 1 that must be, be had, or be done; inevitable; required; indispensable: *Death is a necessary end. Work is a necessary part of life.* 2 thing impossible to do without: *Food, clothing, and shelter are necessaries of life.* 1 *adj.,* 2 *n., pl.* **nec es sar-ies.**

ne ces si tate (nə ses'ə tāt), 1 make necessary: *Her broken leg necessitated an operation.* 2 compel; force. *v.,* **ne ces si tat ed, ne ces si tat ing.**

ne ces si ty (nə ses'ə tē), 1 fact of being necessary; extreme need: *We understand the necessity of eating.* 2 that which cannot be done without; a necessary thing: *Water is a necessity.* 3 that which forces one to act in a certain way: *Necessity often drives people to do disagreeable things.* 4 need; poverty:

a family in great necessity. *n., pl.* **ne-ces si ties.**

of necessity, because it must be.

neck (nek), 1 the part of the body that connects the head with the shoulders. 2 the part of a garment that fits the neck: *the neck of a shirt.* 3 any narrow part like a neck: *a neck of land.* *n.*

neck and neck, 1 abreast. 2 running equal or even in a race or contest.

risk one's neck, put oneself in a dangerous position.

neck er chief (nek'ər chif), cloth worn around the neck. *n.*

neck lace (nek'lis), string of jewels, gold, silver, beads, etc., worn around the neck as an ornament. *n.*

neck line (nek'līn'), the line around the neck where a garment ends. *n.*

neck tie (nek'tī'), a narrow band or a tie worn around the neck, under the collar of a shirt, and tied in front. *n.*

neck wear (nek'wer' or nek'war'), collars, ties, and other articles that are worn around the neck. *n.*

needles
for: A, sewing (def. 1); B, knitting (def. 2); C, crocheting (def. 3)

nec ro man cer (nek'rə man'sər), 1 person who is supposed to foretell the future by communicating with the dead. 2 magician; sorcerer. *n.*

nec ro man cy (nek'rə man'sē), 1 a foretelling of the future by communicating with the dead. 2 magic; sorcery. *n.*

nec tar (nek'tər), 1 (in Greek myths) the drink of the gods. 2 any delicious drink. 3 a sweet liquid found in many flowers. Bees gather nectar and make it into honey. *n.*

nec ta rine (nek'tə rēn'), 1 kind of peach having no down on its skin. 2 tree it grows on. *n.*

nee or **née** (nā), born. *Nee* is placed after the name of a married woman to show her maiden name: *Pam Smith, nee Adams. adj.* [from French]

need (nēd), 1 be in want of; be unable to do without; lack: *We need money. I need a new hat. Plants need water.* 2 thing wanted or lacking; that for which a want is felt: *In the jungle their need was fresh water.* 3 lack of a useful or desired thing; want: *His writing showed need of a knowledge of grammar.* 4 situation or time of difficulty: *When I lacked money, my uncle was a friend in need.* 5 lack of money; extreme poverty: *This family's need was so great the children did not have shoes.*

hat, āge, fär; let, ēqual, tėrm;
it, īce; hot, ōpen, ôrder;
oil, out; cup, pùt, rüle; ch, child;
ng, long; sh, she; th, thin;
ŦH, then; zh, measure;

ə represents *a* in about,
e in taken, *i* in pencil,
o in lemon, *u* in circus.

6 must; should; have to; ought to: *He need not go. Need she go?* 7 something that has to be; necessity: *There is no need to hurry.* 1,6 *v.,* 2-5,7 *n.*

have need to, must; should; have to; ought to: *I have need to go to town.*

if need be, if it has to be.

need ful (nēd'fəl), needed; necessary: *a needful change. adj.* —**need'ful ly,** *adv.* —**need'ful ness,** *n.*

need i ness (nē'dē nis), condition of being needy; poverty; want. *n.*

nee dle (nē'dl), 1 a very slender tool, pointed at one end and with a hole or eye to pass a thread through, used in sewing. 2 a slender rod used in knitting. 3 rod with a hook at one end used in crocheting, etc. 4 a thin steel pointer on a compass or on electrical machinery. 5 a very slender steel tube with a sharp point at one end. It is used at the end of a hypodermic syringe for injecting a liquid below the skin, or at the end of a rubber tube for extracting a liquid from the body. 6 the small, pointed piece of metal in a phonograph which picks up and transmits the vibrations from the record. The pointed tip is usually a diamond, sapphire, or some other material. 7 the needle-shaped leaf of a fir tree or pine tree. 8 any of various small objects resembling a needle in sharpness: *needles of broken glass, ice, etc.* 9 INFORMAL. vex by repeated sharp prods, gibes, etc.; goad or incite. 1-8 *n.,* 9 *v.,* **nee dled, nee dling.** —**nee'dle-like',** *adj.*

nee dle point (nē'dl point'), embroidery made on a canvas cloth, usually with woolen yarn. *n.*

need less (nēd'lis), not needed; unnecessary: *It is silly to take a needless risk. adj.* —**need'less ly,** *adv.* —**need'less ness,** *n.*

nee dle wom an (nē'dl wùm'ən), 1 woman who is a skillful sewer. 2 woman who earns her living by sewing. *n., pl.* **nee dle wom en.**

nee dle work (nē'dl werk'), work done with a needle; sewing; embroidery. *n.*

need n't (nēd'nt), need not.

needs (nēdz), because of necessity;

needy

adj. adjective	*n.* noun
adv. adverb	*prep.* preposition
conj. conjunction	*pron.* pronoun
interj. interjection	*v.* verb
sing. singular	*pl.* plural

---

necessarily: *A soldier needs must go where duty calls. adv.*

need y (nē′dē), very poor; not having enough to live on: *a needy family. adj.,* **need i er, need i est.**

ne'er (ner), OLD USE. never. *adv.*

ne'er-do-well (ner′dü wel′), a worthless fellow; good-for-nothing person. *n.*

ne far i ous (ni fer′ē əs *or* ni fär′ē əs), very wicked; villainous. *adj.* —**ne far′i ous ness,** *n.*

ne gate (ni gāt′), 1 destroy, nullify, or make ineffective. 2 declare not to exist; deny. *v.,* **ne gat ed, ne gat ing.**

ne ga tion (ni gā′shən), 1 a denying; denial: *Shaking the head is a sign of negation.* 2 absence or opposite of some positive thing or quality: *Darkness is the negation of light. n.*

neg a tive (neg′ə tiv), 1 stating that something is not so; saying no: *His answer was negative.* 2 word or statement that says no or denies: *"I won't" is a negative.* 3 the side that says no or argues against a question being debated; side opposing the affirmative. 4 not positive: *Her negative suggestions are not helpful.* 5 less than zero; minus: *−5 is a negative number.* 6 a negative number or quantity. 7 of the kind of electrical charge produced on resin when it is rubbed with silk. 8 showing the lights and shadows reversed: *the negative image on a photographic plate.* 9 a photographic image in which the lights and shadows are reversed. Prints are made from it. 10 showing the absence of a particular disease, condition, germ, etc. 1,4,5,7,8,10 *adj.,* 2,3,6,9 *n.* —**neg′a tive ly,** *adv.*

in the negative, expressing disagreement by saying no; denying.

neg a tiv ism (neg′ə tə viz′əm), tendency to say or do the opposite of what is suggested. *n.*

neg a tiv i ty (neg′ə tiv′ə tē), negative quality or condition. *n.*

ne glect (ni glekt′), 1 give too little care or attention to: *neglect one's health.* 2 leave undone; not attend to: *neglect one's work.* 3 omit; fail: *Don't neglect to water the plants before you leave.* 4 act or fact of neglecting; disregard: *a persistent neglect of duty.* 5 want of attention to what should be done: *That car has been ruined by ne-*

---

glect. 6 a being neglected: *The children suffered from neglect.* 1-3 *v.,* 4-6 *n.*

ne glect ful (ni glekt′fəl), careless; negligent: *Someone who does not vote is neglectful of his duty. adj.* —**ne glect′ful ly,** *adv.* —**ne glect′ful ness,** *n.*

neg li gee (neg′lə zhā′), 1 a woman's loose dressing gown. 2 easy, informal dress or attire. *n.*

neg li gence (neg′lə jəns), 1 lack of proper care or attention; neglect: *Negligence was the cause of the accident.* 2 careless conduct; indifference. *n.*

neg li gent (neg′lə jənt), 1 given to neglect; showing neglect; neglectful. 2 careless; indifferent. *adj.* —**neg′li gent ly,** *adv.*

neg li gi ble (neg′lə jə bəl), that can be disregarded: *In buying a shirt, a difference of ten cents in prices is negligible. adj.*

neg li gi bly (neg′lə jə blē), in a quantity or to a degree that can be disregarded. *adv.*

ne go tia bil i ty (ni gō′shə bil′ə tē), condition of being negotiable. *n.*

ne go tia ble (ni gō′shə bəl), 1 that can be negotiated or sold; whose ownership can be transferred: *negotiable securities.* 2 that can be got past or over: *a negotiable path. adj.*

ne go ti ate (ni gō′shē āt), 1 talk over and arrange terms; confer; consult: *The colonists negotiated for peace with the Indians.* 2 arrange for: *They finally negotiated a peace treaty.* 3 INFORMAL. get past or over: *The car negotiated the sharp curve by slowing down.* 4 sell. *v.,* **ne go ti at ed, ne go ti at ing.**

ne go ti a tion (ni gō′shē ā′shən), a negotiating; arrangement: *Negotiations for the new school are finished. n.*

ne go ti a tor (ni gō′shē ā′tər), person who negotiates. *n.*

Ne gro (nē′grō), 1 member of the so-called black race. The chief peoples of Africa south of the Sahara are Negroes. 2 any person having black ancestry. 3 of, having to do with, or resembling Negroes. 1,2 *n., pl.* **Negroes;** 3 *adj.*

Ne groid (nē′groid), 1 of, resembling, or related to the Negro race. 2 person belonging to a Negroid people. 1 *adj.,* 2 *n.*

Ne he mi ah (nē′ə mī′ə), 1 Hebrew leader of the 400's B.C. He rebuilt the walls of Jerusalem about 444 B.C. 2 book of the Old Testament describing his achievements. *n.*

Neh ru (nā′rü), **Jawaharlal,** 1889-1964, prime minister of India from 1947 to 1964. *n.*

neigh (nā), 1 sound that a horse makes. 2 make this sound. 1 *n.,* 2 *v.*

---

neigh bor (nā′bər), 1 someone who lives in the next house or nearby. 2 person or thing that is near another: *The big tree brought down several of its smaller neighbors as it fell.* 3 be near or next to; adjoin: *The United States neighbors Canada to the North and Mexico to the south.* 4 a fellow human being. 1,2,4 *n.,* 3 *v.*

neigh bor hood (nā′bər hud), 1 region near some place or thing: *She lives in the neighborhood of the mill.* 2 place or district: *Is North Street a good neighborhood?* 3 people living near one another; people of a place: *The whole neighborhood came to the big party.* 4 neighborly feeling or conduct. 5 of or having to do with a neighborhood: *a neighborhood newspaper.* 1-4 *n.,* 5 *adj.*

in the neighborhood of, INFORMAL. somewhere near; about: *The car cost in the neighborhood of $3500.*

neigh bor ing (nā′bər ing), living or being near; bordering; adjoining; near: *We heard the bird calls from the neighboring woods. adj.*

neigh bor li ness (nā′bər lē nis), neighborly disposition or quality. *n.*

neigh bor ly (nā′bər lē), like or befitting a good neighbor; kindly, friendly, or sociable. *adj.*

nei ther (nē′ŦHər *or* nī′ŦHər), 1 not either: *Neither you nor I will go (conj.). Neither statement is true (adj.). Neither of the statements is true (pron.).* 2 nor yet; nor: *"They toil not, neither do they spin."* 1,2 *conj.,* 1 *adj.,* 1 *pron.*

Nel son (nel′sən), Viscount **Horatio,** 1758-1805, British admiral, noted for victories over Napoleon I. *n.*

Nem e sis (nem′ə sis), 1 (in Greek myths) the goddess of vengeance. 2 nemesis, a just punishment for evil deeds. b person who punishes another for evil deeds: *Sherlock Holmes was the nemesis of many criminals. n., pl.* **nem e ses** (nem′ə sēz′).

ne o dym i um (nē′ō dim′ē əm), a yellowish metallic element found in combination with various minerals. The rose-colored salts of neodymium are used to color glass. *n.*

Ne o lith ic (nē′ə lith′ik), of the later Stone Age, marked by the beginning of agriculture and the use of polished stone tools: *Neolithic man. adj.*

ne on (nē′on), a colorless, odorless, inert gas, forming a very small part of the air. It is a chemical element. Tubes containing neon are used in electric signs, lamps, etc., giving off a fiery red glow. *n.*

ne o phyte (nē′ə fīt), 1 a new convert; one recently admitted to a religious body. 2 beginner; novice. *n.*

Ne pal (nə pôl′), country between

India and Tibet. *Capital:* Katmandu. *n.*

neph ew (nef′yü), son of one's brother or sister; son of one's brother-in-law or sister-in-law. *n.*

ne phri tis (ni frī′tis), inflammation of the kidneys. *n.*

nep o tism (nep′ə tiz′əm), the showing of too much favor by one in power to his relatives, especially by giving them desirable appointments. *n.*

Nep tune (nep′tün *or* nep′tyün), 1 (in Roman myths) the god of the sea. The Greeks called him Poseidon. 2 the fourth largest planet in the solar system and the eighth in distance from the sun. It is visible only through a telescope. *n.*

nep tu ni um (nep tü′nē əm *or* nep tyü′nē əm), a radioactive metallic element which occurs in minute amounts in uranium ore and is produced artificially from an isotope of uranium. *n.* [from *Neptune,* planet whose orbit lies beyond Uranus]

Ner e id (nir′ē id), (in Greek myths) any of the fifty daughters of a sea god. The Nereids were sea nymphs who attended Poseidon. *n.*

Ner o (nir′ō), A.D. 37-68, Roman emperor from A.D. 54 to A.D. 68. He was noted for his vices, cruelty, and tyranny. *n.*

nest (def. 1)

nest (def. 2) of a colony of wasps

nerve (nėrv), 1 fiber or bundle of fibers through which impulses pass between the brain or spinal cord and the eyes, ears, muscles, glands, etc. 2 mental strength; courage: *It takes nerve to pilot an airplane.* 3 arouse strength or courage in: *The players nerved themselves for the championship game.* 4 SLANG. rude boldness; impudence. 5 vein of a leaf. 6 pulp of a tooth. 7 **nerves,** *pl.* a nervousness. b attack of nervousness. 1,2,4-7 *n.,* 3 *v.,* **nerved, nerving.**

get on one's nerves, annoy or irritate one.

strain every nerve, exert oneself to the utmost.

nerve cell, 1 neuron. 2 the cell body of a neuron, excluding its fibers.

nerve fiber, any of the threadlike processes or fibers of a neuron; an axon or a dendrite.

nerve less (nėrv′lis), 1 without strength or vigor; feeble; weak: *The cup dropped from his nerveless hand.* 2 without nervousness; controlled; calm: *be nerveless before an examination. adj.*

nerve-rack ing or **nerve-wrack ing** (nėrv′rak′ing), extremely irritating; causing great annoyance; very trying: *a nerve-racking day at the office. adj.*

nerv ous (nėr′vəs), 1 of the nerves: *a nervous disorder, nervous energy.* 2 having easily excited nerves; jumpy: *a nervous, impatient person.* 3 easily excited or upset; restless, uneasy, or timid: *She is nervous about staying alone at night.* 4 strong; vigorous: *paint with quick, nervous strokes. adj.* —**nerv′ous ly,** *adv.* —**nerv′ous ness,** *n.*

nervous system, the system of nerve fibers, nerve cells, and other nervous tissue in a person or animal by means of which impulses are received and interpreted. The nervous system of vertebrates includes the brain and spinal cord.

nerv y (nėr′vē), 1 SLANG. rude and bold. 2 requiring courage or firmness. 3 nervous. *adj.,* **nerv i er, nerv i est.**

-ness, *suffix added to adjectives to form nouns.* 1 quality or condition of being _____: *Preparedness = the condition of being prepared.* 2 _____ action; _____ behavior: *Carefulness = careful action; careful behavior.* [Old English *-ness, -niss*]

nest (nest), 1 structure or place shaped something like a bowl, built by birds out of twigs, straw, etc., as a place in which to lay their eggs and protect their young ones: *a robin's nest.* 2 structure or place used by insects, fishes, turtles, rabbits, or the like, for a similar purpose. 3 a snug abode, retreat, or resting place: *The little boy cuddled down in a nest among the sofa cushions.* 4 a place that swarms (usually with something bad): *a nest of thieves.* 5 the birds, animals, etc., living in a nest. 6 make and use a nest: *The bluebirds are nesting here now.* 7 settle or place in, or as if in, a nest. 8 set or series (often from large to small) such that each fits within another: *a nest of drinking cups.* 1-5,8 *n.,* 6,7 *v.*

nest egg, 1 a natural or artificial egg left in a nest to induce a hen to continue laying eggs there. 2 something, usually a sum of money, saved up as the beginning of a fund or as a reserve.

hat, āge, fär; let, ēqual, tėrm; it, īce; hot, ōpen, ôrder; oil, out; cup, pùt, rüle; ch, child; ng, long; sh, she; th, thin; ₮H, then; zh, measure;

ə represents *a* in about, *e* in taken, *i* in pencil, *o* in lemon, *u* in circus.

nes tle (nes′əl), 1 settle oneself comfortably or cozily: *She nestled down into the big chair.* 2 be settled comfortably or cozily; be sheltered: *The little house nestled among the trees.* 3 press close in affection or for comfort: *nestle up to one's mother, nestle a baby in one's arms. v.,* **nes tled, nes tling.**

nest ling (nest′ling), bird too young to leave the nest. *n.*

Nes tor (nes′tər), 1 (in Greek legends) the oldest and wisest of the Greeks at the siege of Troy. 2 a wise old man. *n.*

nets[1] (def. 1)—top, tennis net; left, fish net; right, mosquito net

net¹ (net), 1 an open fabric made of string, cord, thread, or hair, knotted together in such a way as to leave holes regularly arranged. A fish net is used for catching fish. A mosquito net keeps off mosquitoes. A hair net holds the hair in place. 2 anything like a net; set of things that cross each other. 3 a lacelike cloth. 4 a trap or snare: *The conspirator was caught in the net of his own lies.* 5 catch in a net: *net a fish.* 6 cover, confine, or protect with a net. 7 make into net: *to net cord.* 1-4 *n.,* 5-7 *v.,* **net ted, net ting.** [Old English *nett*]

net² (net), 1 remaining after deductions; free from deductions. A net gain or profit is the actual gain after all working expenses have been paid. The net weight of a glass jar of candy is the weight of the candy itself. The net price of a book is the real price, from which no discount can be made. 2 the net

adj. adjective	*n.* noun
adv. adverb	*prep.* preposition
conj. conjunction	*pron.* pronoun
interj. interjection	*v.* verb
sing. singular	*pl.* plural

weight, profit, price, etc. 3 to gain: *The sale netted me a good profit.* 1 *adj.*, 2 *n.*, 3 *v.*, **net ted, net ting.** [from French of the 1500's]

neth er (neᴛʜ/ər), lower. *adj.*

Neth er land er (neᴛʜ/ər lan/dər), Dutchman. *n.*

Neth er lands (neᴛʜ/ər ləndz), small country in Europe, west of Germany and north of Belgium; Holland. *Capitals:* The Hague and Amsterdam. *n.*

Netherlands Antilles, territory of the Netherlands consisting of six islands in the S Caribbean.

neth er most (neᴛʜ/ər mōst), lowest. *adj.*

net ting (net/ing), 1 a netted or meshed material: *wire netting for window screens.* 2 process of making a net. *n.*

net tle (net/l), 1 kind of plant having sharp hairs on the leaves and stems that sting the skin when touched. 2 sting the mind of; make angry; irritate; provoke; vex: *Their refusal to help nettled me.* 1 *n.*, 2 *v.*, **net tled, net tling.**

net work (net/wėrk/), 1 a netting; net. 2 any system of lines that cross: *a network of vines, a network of railroads.* 3 group of radio or television stations, so connected that the same program may be broadcast by all. *n.*

neur al (nur/əl *or* nyur/əl), of or having to do with a nerve, neuron, or nervous system. *adj.*

neur al gia (nu ral/jə *or* nyu ral/jə), a pain, usually sharp, along the course of a nerve. *n.*

neu ri tis (nu rī/tis *or* nyu rī/tis), inflammation of a nerve or nerves. *n.*

neu rol o gist (nu rol/ə jist *or* nyu rol/ə jist), an expert in neurology. *n.*

neu rol o gy (nu rol/ə jē *or* nyu rol/ə jē), study of the nervous system and its diseases. *n.*

neur on (nur/on *or* nyur/on), one of the cells of which the brain, spinal cord, and nerves are composed; nerve cell. Neurons conduct impulses. A neuron consists of a cell body containing the nucleus, and usually several branching processes called dendrites and a single longer process called an axon. *n.*

neur one (nur/ōn *or* nyur/ōn), neuron. *n.*

neu ro sis (nu rō/sis *or* nyu rō/sis), any of various mental or emotional dis-

orders, characterized by depression, anxiety, abnormal fears, compulsive behavior, etc. *n., pl.* **neu ro ses** (nu rō/sēz *or* nyu rō/sēz/).

neu rot ic (nu rot/ik *or* nyu rot/ik), 1 having or suffering from a neurosis. 2 too nervous. 3 person having or suffering from a neurosis. 1,2 *adj.*, 3 *n.* —**neu rot/i cal ly,** *adv.*

neu ter (nü/tər *or* nyü/tər), 1 (in grammar) neither masculine nor feminine. *It is a neuter pronoun.* 2 a neuter word or form. 3 the neuter gender. 4 without sex organs or with sex organs that are not fully developed. Worker bees are neuter. 5 an animal, plant, or insect that is neuter. 6 being on neither side; neutral. 1,4,6 *adj.*, 2,3,5 *n.*

neu tral (nü/trəl *or* nyü/trəl), 1 on neither side in a quarrel or war. 2 a neutral person or country; one not taking part in a war. 3 of or belonging to a neutral country or neutral zone: *a neutral port.* 4 neither one thing nor the other; indefinite. 5 having little or no color; grayish. 6 neither acid nor alkaline. 7 (of electricity) neither positive nor negative. 8 position of gears when they do not transmit motion from the engine to the wheels or other working parts. 1,3-7 *adj.*, 2,8 *n.*

neu tral ist (nü/trə list *or* nyü/trə list), 1 person who practices or advocates neutrality, especially in international affairs. 2 practicing or advocating neutrality. 1 *n.*, 2 *adj.*

neu tral i ty (nü tral/ə tē *or* nyü tral/ə tē), condition of being neutral; the attitude or policy of a nation that does not take part directly or indirectly in a war between other nations; neutral character or status. *n.*

neu tral i za tion (nü/trə lə zā/shən *or* nyü/trə lə zā/shən), act of neutralizing. *n.*

neu tral ize (nü/trə līz *or* nyü/trə līz), 1 make neutral; keep war out of: *The city was neutralized so that peace talks could be held there.* 2 make of no effect by some opposite force; counterbalance: *Bases neutralize acids. She neutralized the bright colors in her room by using a tan rug.* *v.,* **neu tral ized, neu tral iz ing.**

neuron

neu tral iz er (nü/trə lī/zər *or* nyü/trə lī/zər), person or thing that neutralizes. *n.*

neutral vowel, schwa.

neu tri no (nü trē/nō *or* nyü trē/nō), a stable atomic particle having no electric

charge and a mass close to zero. *n., pl.* **neu tri nos.**

neu tron (nü/tron *or* nyü/tron), an atomic particle that is neutral electrically and has about the same mass as a proton. *n.*

Nev., Nevada.

Ne vad a (nə vad/ə *or* nə vä/də), one of the western states of the United States. *Capital:* Carson City. *n.* —**Ne vad/an,** *adj., n.*

nev er (nev/ər), 1 not ever; at no time: *I have never been to New York.* 2 in no case; not at all; to no extent or degree: *never the wiser.* *adv.*

nev er more (nev/ər môr/), never again. *adv.*

nev er the less (nev/ər ᴛʜə les/), however; nonetheless; for all that; in spite of it: *She was very tired; nevertheless she kept on working.* *adv.*

new (nü *or* nyü), 1 never having existed before; now first made, thought out, known or heard of, felt, or discovered: *a new invention, a new idea.* 2 lately grown, come, or made; not old: *a new bud.* 3 now first used; not worn or used up: *a new path.* 4 beginning again: *Sunrise marks a new day.* 5 changed or renewed: *to go on with new courage. He is a new man now.* 6 not familiar; not yet used: *a new country to me, new to the work.* 7 later; modern; recent: *new dances.* 8 just come; having just reached the position: *a new arrival, a new president.* 9 further; additional; more: *He sought new information on the subject.* 10 newly; recently or lately; freshly: *new-fallen snow, a new-found friend.* 11 again; anew. 1-9 *adj.*, 10,11 *adv.* —**new/ness,** *n.*

New Amsterdam, name of New York City when it was a Dutch colonial town.

New ark (nü/ərk *or* nyü/ərk), city in NE New Jersey, near New York City. *n.*

New Bed ford (bed/fərd), seaport in SE Massachusetts, formerly an important whaling port.

new born (nü/bôrn/ *or* nyü/bôrn/), 1 recently or only just born: *a newborn baby.* 2 ready to start a new life; born again. *adj.*

New Bruns wick (brunz/wik), province in SE Canada. *Capital:* Fredericton.

new com er (nü/kum/ər *or* nyü/kum/ər), person who has just come or who came not long ago. *n.*

New Deal, the policies and measures advocated by President Franklin D. Roosevelt as a means of improving the economic and social welfare of the United States.

New Del hi (del/ē), capital of India, in the N part.

newel

new el (nü′əl *or* nyü′əl), the post at the top or bottom of a stairway that supports the railing. *n.*

New England, the NE part of the United States. Maine, New Hampshire, Vermont, Massachusetts, Rhode Island, and Connecticut are the New England states.

New Eng land er (ing′glən dər), person born or living in New England.

new fan gled (nü′fang′gəld *or* nyü′fang′gəld), lately come into fashion; of a new kind. *adj.*

New found land (nü′fənd lənd *or* nü found′lənd; nyü′fənd lənd *or* nyü-found′lənd), 1 large island northeast of Nova Scotia. It is part of Canada. 2 province in E Canada that includes Newfoundland and Labrador. *Capital:* St. John′s. 3 a shaggy, intelligent dog like a spaniel, but much larger, usually having a black coat. *n.*

Newfoundland (def. 3)
26 to 28 in. high at the shoulder

New Guinea, large island north of Australia; Papua. The W part of New Guinea belongs to Indonesia, the E part to Australia.

New Hamp shire (hamp′shər), one of the northeastern states of the United States. *Capital:* Concord.

New Haven, city in S Connecticut.

New Jersey, one of the northeastern states of the United States. *Capital:* Trenton.

new ly (nü′lē *or* nyü′lē), 1 lately; recently: *newly wedded, newly discovered.* 2 once again; freshly: *a newly revived scandal. adv.*

New man (nü′mən *or* nyü′mən), **John Henry,** 1801-1890, English theologian and author who became a Roman Catholic and was made a cardinal. *n.*

New Mexico, one of the southwestern states of the United States. *Capital:* Santa Fe.

new moon, 1 moon when seen as a thin crescent with the hollow side on the left. 2 the moon when its dark side is towards the earth, appearing almost invisible.

New Netherland, former Dutch colony in America, from 1613 to 1664. England captured it in 1664 and divided it into the colonies of New York and New Jersey.

New Or le ans (ôr′lē ənz, ôr lēnz′, *or* ôr′lənz), city in SE Louisiana, near the mouth of the Mississippi River.

news (nüz *or* nyüz), 1 something told as having just happened; information about something that has just happened or will soon happen: *The news that our teacher was leaving made us sad.* 2 a report of a current happening or happenings in a newspaper, on television, radio, etc. *n.*

news boy (nüz′boi′ *or* nyüz′boi′), person who sells or delivers newspapers; paperboy. *n.*

news cast (nüz′kast′ *or* nyüz′kast′), a radio or television broadcast devoted to news. *n.*

news cast er (nüz′kas′tər *or* nyüz′kas′tər), 1 person who gives the news on a newscast. 2 commentator on the news. *n.*

news let ter (nüz′let′ər *or* nyüz′let′ər), letter or report giving informal or confidential news. Organizations often issue newsletters to members or subscribers. *n.*

news man (nüz′man′ *or* nyüz′man′), 1 man who sells or delivers newspapers. 2 newspaperman. *n., pl.* **news men.**

New South Wales, state in SE Australia. *Capital:* Sydney.

news pa per (nüz′pā′pər *or* nyüz′-pā′pər), a daily or weekly publication printed on large sheets of paper folded together, telling the news, carrying advertisements, and having stories, pictures, articles, and useful information. *n.*

news pa per man (nüz′pā′pər man′ *or* nyüz′pā′pər man′), a reporter, editor, or other person who works for a newspaper. *n., pl.* **news pa per men.**

news print (nüz′print′ *or* nyüz′print′), a soft, cheap paper made from wood pulp, on which newspapers are usually printed. *n.*

news reel (nüz′rēl′ *or* nyüz′rēl′), a motion picture showing current events. *n.*

news stand (nüz′stand′ *or* nyüz′stand′), place where newspapers and magazines are sold. *n.*

news y (nü′zē *or* nyü′zē), INFORMAL. full of news: *a newsy letter. adj.,* **news i er, news i est.**

newt (nüt *or* nyüt), any of various small salamanders that live in water part of the time. *n.*

New Testament, the later part of the Bible, which contains the life and teachings of Christ recorded by His followers, together with their own experiences and teachings.

New ton (nüt′n *or* nyüt′n), Sir **Isaac,** 1642-1727, English scientist and mathematician who discovered the law of gravitation. *n.*

New to ni an (nü tō′nē ən *or* nyü-tō′nē ən), of or by Sir Isaac Newton. *adj.*

New World, the Western Hemisphere; North America and South America.

new-world *or* **New-World** (nü′-wėrld′ *or* nyü′wėrld′), of or having to do with the Western Hemisphere; not of the Old World: *new-world monkeys. adj.*

New Year *or* **New Year′s,** the first day or days of the year.

New Year′s Day, January 1, usually observed as a legal holiday.

New York, 1 Often, **New York State.** one of the northeastern states of the United States. *Capital:* Albany. 2 Often, **New York City.** seaport in SE New York State, at the mouth of the Hudson River. It is the largest city in the United States.

New York Bay, bay south of Manhattan island, at the mouth of the Hudson River.

New York er (yôr′kər), person born or living in New York City or New York State.

New Zea land (zē′lənd), country in the S Pacific, consisting of two main islands and various small ones. It is a member of the Commonwealth of Nations. *Capital:* Wellington.

next (nekst), 1 following at once; nearest: *the next train, the next room.* 2 the first time after this: *When you next*

newt—3 to 4 in. long

adj.	adjective	*n.*	noun
adv.	adverb	*prep.*	preposition
conj.	conjunction	*pron.*	pronoun
interj.	interjection	*v.*	verb
sing.	singular	*pl.*	plural

come, bring it. **3** in the place or time or position that is nearest: *I am going to do my arithmetic problems next. Your name comes next.* **4** nearest to: *the house next the church.* **1** *adj.,* **2,3** *adv.,* **4** *prep.*

next to, 1 nearest to. **2** almost; nearly.

next door, 1 in or at the next house, apartment, etc.: *They live next door.* **2** very close: *Her requests are next door to commands.*

next-door (nekst'dôr'), in or at the next house: *my next-door neighbor.* *adj.*

Nfld., Newfoundland.

N.H., New Hampshire.

ni a cin (nī'ə sən), nicotinic acid. *n.*

Ni ag ar a (nī ag'rə), **1** short river flowing from Lake Erie into Lake Ontario over Niagara Falls. **2** Niagara Falls. *n.*

Niagara Falls, great waterfall of the Niagara River, on the boundary between the United States and Canada.

nib (nib), **1** point of a pen. **2** point or tip of anything. **3** beak or bill of a bird. *n.*

nib ble (nib'əl), **1** eat away with quick, small bites, as a rabbit or mouse does. **2** bite gently or lightly: *A fish nibbles at the bait.* **3** a nibbling; small bite. **1,2** *v.,* **nib bled, nib bling; 3** *n.*

nib bler (nib'lər), person or animal that nibbles. *n.*

Nic a ra gua (nik'ə rä'gwə), country in Central America, north of Costa Rica. *Capital:* Managua. *n.* —**Nic'a ra'-guan,** *adj., n.*

nice (nīs), **1** that is good or pleasing; agreeable; satisfactory: *a nice face, a nice ride, a nice day.* **2** thoughtful or kind: *He was nice to us.* **3** very fine; minute; subtle: *a nice distinction, a nice shade of meaning.* **4** making very fine distinctions; exact; precise: *a nice ear for music.* **5** delicately skillful; requiring care, skill, or tact: *a nice problem.* **6** exacting; particular; hard to please; fastidious; dainty: *nice in one's habits or dress.* **7** refined; cultured: *a nice accent. adj.,* **nic er, nic est.** —**nice'-ly,** *adv.* —**nice'ness,** *n.*

Nice (nēs), seaside resort in SE France. *n.*

ni ce ty (nī'sə tē), **1** exactness; accuracy; delicacy: *Television sets require nicety of adjustment.* **2** a fine point; small distinction; detail: *I play tennis* but have not mastered its niceties. **3** quality of being particular; daintiness; refinement. **4** something dainty or refined. *n., pl.* **ni ce ties.**

to a nicety, just right: *cakes browned to a nicety.*

niche (nich), **1** a recess or hollow in a wall for a statue, vase, etc. **2** a suitable place or position; place for which a person is suited: *I have yet to find my niche in the world. n.*

Nich o las (nik'ə ləs), **Saint, 1** the patron saint of Russia, and of young people, sailors, travelers, and merchants. He was a bishop in Asia Minor in the A.D. 300's. **2** Santa Claus. *n.*

Nicholas II, 1868-1918, the last czar of Russia, from 1894 to 1917, executed during the Russian Revolution.

nick (nik), **1** place where a small bit has been cut or broken out; notch; groove: *She cut nicks in a stick to keep score.* **2** make a nick or nicks in. **1** *n.,* **2** *v.*

in the nick of time, just at the right moment.

nick el (nik'əl), **1** a hard, silvery-white metallic element found in igneous rocks. It is used as an alloy and in electroplating. **2** cover or coat with nickel. **3** coin containing a mixture of nickel and copper; a United States or Canadian five-cent piece. **1,3** *n.,* **2** *v.*

nickel silver, a white alloy of copper, zinc, and nickel, used for ornaments, utensils, wire, etc.; German silver.

nick nack (nik'nak'), knickknack. *n.*

nick name (nik'nām'), **1** name added to a person's real name or used instead of it. *"Ed" is a nickname for "Edward." Roy's nickname was "Buzz."* **2** give a nickname to: *They nicknamed the short girl "Shorty."* **1** *n.,* **2** *v.,* **nick named, nick nam ing.**

nic o tine (nik'ə tēn'), poison contained in the leaves, roots, and seeds of tobacco. *n.* [from French *nicotine,* from Jacques *Nicot,* about 1530-1600, French diplomat who introduced tobacco to France]

nic o tin ic acid (nik'ə tin'ik), one of a group of vitamins of the vitamin B complex, found especially in lean meat, yeast, liver, and wheat germ; niacin. It is used to treat and prevent pellagra.

niece (nēs), daughter of one's brother or sister; daughter of one's brother-in-law or sister-in-law. *n.*

Nie tzsche (nē'chə), **Friedrich Wilhelm,** 1844-1900, German philosopher and writer. *n.*

nif ty (nif'tē), INFORMAL. attractive or stylish. *adj.,* **nif ti er, nif ti est.**

Ni ger (nī'jər), **1** country in W Africa north of Nigeria. **2** long river in W Africa. See **Algeria** for map. *n.*

Ni ger i a (nī jir'ē ə), country in W Africa, a member of the Commonwealth of Nations. *Capital:* Lagos. See **Upper Volta** for map. *n.* —**Ni ger'i an,** *adj., n.*

nig gard (nig'ərd), **1** a stingy person. **2** stingy. **1** *n.,* **2** *adj.*

niche (def. 1) for a vase

nig gard li ness (nig'ərd lē nis), niggardly quality; stinginess. *n.*

nig gard ly (nig'ərd lē), **1** stingy. **2** stingily. **3** meanly small or scanty: *a niggardly gift.* **1,3** *adj.,* **2** *adv.*

nig gling (nig'ling), trifling; mean; petty. *adj.*

nigh (nī), **1** near. **2** nearly. **1,2** *adv.,* **1** *adj.,* **1** *prep.*

night (nīt), **1** the time between evening and morning; the time from sunset to sunrise, especially when it is dark. **2** the darkness of night; the dark. **3** the darkness of ignorance, sin, sorrow, old age, death, etc. **4** evening; nightfall. **5** of night. **1-4** *n.,* **5** *adj.*

night cap (nīt'kap'), **1** a cap to be worn in bed. **2** INFORMAL. drink taken just before going to bed. *n.*

night club (nīt'klub'), place for dancing, eating, and entertainment, open only at night. *n.*

night fall (nīt'fôl'), the coming of night; dusk. *n.*

night gown (nīt'goun'), a long, loose garment worn by a woman or child in bed. *n.*

night hawk (nīt'hôk'), **1** bird related to the whippoorwill that flies about at dusk in search of insects. **2** INFORMAL. person who stays up late at night. *n.*

night ie (nī'tē), INFORMAL. nightgown or nightshirt. *n.* Also, **nighty.**

nightingale 6 to 7 in. long

night in gale (nīt'n gāl), a small, reddish-brown bird of Europe. The male sings sweetly at night as well as in the daytime. *n.*

Night in gale (nīt'n gāl), **Florence,** 1820-1910, English nurse who brought about great improvements in nursing. *n.*

night light, a small light to be kept burning all night.

night long (nīt/lông/),   1 lasting all night. 2 through the whole night. 1 *adj.*, 2 *adv.*

night ly (nīt/lē),   1 done, happening, or appearing every night. 2 every night: *Performances are given nightly except on Sunday.* 3 done, happening, or appearing at night: *nightly dew.* 4 at night; by night: *Many animals come out only nightly.* 1,3 *adj.*, 2,4 *adv.*

night mare (nīt/mer/ *or* nīt/mar/),   1 a very distressing dream. 2 a very distressing experience: *The dust storm was a nightmare. n.*

night mar ish (nīt/mer/ish *or* nīt/-mar/ish),   like a nightmare; causing fear or anxiety; very distressing: *a nightmarish experience. adj.*

night owl, INFORMAL. person who often stays up late.

night school, school held in the evening for persons who work during the day.

night shade (nīt/shād/),   any of various plants somewhat like the potato and the tomato. The black nightshade has white flowers and black berries. Belladonna, or the deadly nightshade, has red flowers and black berries. *n.*

night shirt (nīt/shėrt/),   a long, loose shirt worn by a man or boy in bed. *n.*

night stick (nīt/stik/),   a policeman's club. *n.*

night time (nīt/tīm/),   time between evening and morning. *n.*

night watch,   1 watch or guard kept during the night. 2 person or persons keeping such a watch.

night y (nī/tē),   nightie. *n., pl.* **nighties.**

ni hil ism (nī/ə liz/əm),   1 entire rejection of the established religion, morals, government, laws, etc. 2 use of violent methods against a government. *n.*

ni hil ist (nī/ə list),   1 person who believes in some form of nihilism. 2 terrorist. *n.*

ni hil is tic (nī/ə lis/tik),   of nihilists or nihilism. *adj.*

Ni jin sky (nə jin/skē),   Vaslav, 1890-1950, great Russian ballet dancer. *n.*

Ni ke (nī/kē),   (in Greek myths) the goddess of victory, usually represented with wings. *n.*

nil (nil),   nothing. *n.*

Nile (nīl),   river in E Africa flowing north from Lake Victoria through Uganda, Sudan, and Egypt into the Mediterranean Sea. The Nile is the longest river in the world. *n.*

nim ble (nim/bəl),   1 active and surefooted; light and quick; agile: *Goats are nimble in climbing among the rocks.* 2 quick to understand and to reply; clever: *The student had a nimble mind that could quickly come up with solutions to most problems the teacher gave her.*

adj., **nim bler, nim blest. —nim/bleness,** *n.*

nim bly (nim/blē),   quickly and lightly. *adv.*

nim bus (nim/bəs),   1 halo. 2 a bright cloud surrounding a god, person, or thing. 3 a low, dark-gray layer of rain or snow clouds. *n., pl.* **nim bus es, nimbi** (nim/bī).

Nim rod (nim/rod),   1 (in the Bible) a great hunter. 2 hunter. *n.*

nin com poop (nin/kəm püp),   fool; simpleton. *n.*

nine (nīn),   1 one more than eight; 9. 2 set of nine persons or things: *a baseball nine.* 1,2 *n.,* 1 *adj.*

nine fold (nīn/fōld/),   nine times as much or as great. *adj., adv.*

nine pins (nīn/pinz/),   game in which nine large wooden pins are set up to be bowled over with a ball. *n.*

nine teen (nīn/tēn/),   nine more than ten; 19. *n., adj.*

nine teenth (nīn/tēnth/),   1 next after the 18th; last in a series of 19. 2 one of 19 equal parts. 1 *adj.,* 1,2 *n.*

nine ti eth (nīn/tē ith),   1 next after the 89th; last in a series of 90. 2 one of 90 equal parts. 1 *adj.,* 1,2 *n.*

nine ty (nīn/tē),   nine times ten; 90. *n., pl.* **nine ties;** *adj.*

Nin e veh (nin/ə və),   ancient capital of Assyria. Its ruins are on the Tigris River. *n.*

nin ny (nin/ē),   fool. *n., pl.* **nin nies.**

ninth (nīnth),   1 next after the eighth; last in a series of nine. 2 one of nine equal parts. 1 *adj.,* 1,2 *n.*

Ni o be (nī/ō bē/),   (in Greek myths) the daughter of Tantalus whose fourteen beautiful children were slain because she boasted about them. Turned by Zeus into a stone fountain, she weeps forever for her children. *n.*

ni o bi um (nī ō/bē əm),   a soft, steel-gray metallic element that is found in nature with tantalum. It is used in making stainless steel and in alloys. *n.* [from *Niobe* (because she was the daughter of Tantalus, for whom tantalum was named)]

nip[1] (nip),   1 squeeze tight and sud-

denly; pinch; bite: *The crab nipped my toe.* 2 a tight squeeze; pinch; sudden bite. 3 take off by biting, pinching, or snipping. 4 hurt at the tips; spoil; injure: *Some of our tomato plants were nipped by frost.* 5 injury caused by frost. 6 have a sharp, biting effect on: *Cold winds nip your ears and nose.* 7 sharp cold; chill: *There is a nip in the air on a frosty morning.* 8 a small bit. 1,3,4,6 *v.,* **nipped, nip ping;** 2,5,7,8 *n.* [Middle English *nyppen*]

nip and tuck, INFORMAL. even in a race or contest.

nip[2] (nip),   a small drink. *n.* [origin uncertain]

nip per (nip/ər),   1 person or thing that nips. 2 a big claw of a lobster or crab. 3 **nippers,** *pl.* pincers, forceps, pliers, or any tool that nips. *n.*

nip ple (nip/əl),   1 the small projection on a breast or udder through which an infant or a baby animal gets its mother's milk; teat. 2 the rubber cap or mouthpiece of a baby's bottle, through which the baby gets milk and other liquids. 3 anything shaped or used like a nipple. *n.* **—nip/ple like/,** *adj.*

Nip pon (ni pon/),   Japanese name for **Japan.** *n.*

Nip pon ese (nip/ə nēz/),   Japanese. *adj., n., pl.* **Nip pon ese.**

nip py (nip/ē),   biting; sharp: *a nippy wind, nippy cheese. adj.,* **nip pi er, nip pi est.**

nir va na *or* **Nir va na**   (nir vä/nə),   1 the Buddhist idea of heavenly peace; condition in which the soul is free from all desire and pain. 2 any condition like this; blessed oblivion. *n.*

Ni sei (nē/sā/),   a native-born United States or Canadian citizen whose parents were Japanese immigrants. *n., pl.* **Ni sei.**

nit (nit),   1 the egg of a louse or similar insect. 2 a very young louse or similar insect. *n.*

ni ter (nī/tər),   1 potassium nitrate, especially when it occurs naturally as a white salt in the soil and encrusted on rocks; saltpeter. It is used in making gunpowder. 2 sodium nitrate, especially as it occurs in natural deposits.

hat, āge, fär; let, ēqual, tėrm; it, īce; hot, ōpen, ôrder; oil, out; cup, put, rüle; ch, child; ng, long; sh, she; th, thin; ŦH, then; zh, measure;

ə represents *a* in about, *e* in taken, *i* in pencil, *o* in lemon, *u* in circus.

adj.	adjective	*n.* noun
adv.	adverb	*prep.* preposition
conj.	conjunction	*pron.* pronoun
interj.	interjection	*v.* verb
sing.	singular	*pl.* plural

It is used as a fertilizer. *n.* Also, **nitre**.

ni trate (nī′trāt), 1 a salt or ester of nitric acid. 2 potassium nitrate or sodium nitrate when used as fertilizers. *n.*

ni tre (nī′tər), niter. *n.*

ni tric (nī′trik), of or containing nitrogen. *adj.*

nitric acid, a clear, colorless liquid that eats into flesh, clothing, metal, and other substances. It is used in etching and metallurgy and in making dyes and explosives.

ni tro gen (nī′trə jən), a colorless, odorless, tasteless gas which forms about four fifths of the atmosphere. Nitrogen is one of the most important chemical elements and is a necessary part of all animal and vegetable tissues. *n.*

nitrogen cycle, the circulation of nitrogen and its compounds by living organisms in nature. Nitrogen in the air passes into the soil where it is changed to nitrate by bacteria and used by green plants and then in turn by animals. Decaying plants and animals, and animal waste products, are in turn acted on by bacteria and the nitrogen in them is again made available for circulation.

ni trog e nous (nī troj′ə nəs), containing nitrogen. *adj.*

ni tro glyc er in or **ni tro glyc er ine** (nī′trə glis′ər ən), an oily, explosive liquid made by treating glycerine with nitric and sulfuric acids. Nitroglycerine is used in making dynamite and as a heart stimulant. *n*

ni trous (nī′trəs), 1 of nitrogen; containing nitrogen. 2 of niter. *adj.*

nitrous oxide, a colorless gas that causes laughing and dulls pain. It is sometimes used as an anesthetic by dentists.

nit wit (nit′wit′), SLANG. a very stupid person. *n.*

Nix on (nik′sən), **Richard Milhous,** born 1913, the 37th president of the United States, from 1969 to 1974, vice-president from 1953 to 1961. *n.*

N.J., New Jersey.

N.M. or **N. Mex.,** New Mexico.

no (nō), 1 word used to indicate that one can't or won't, or that something is wrong; word used to deny, refuse, or disagree. *No* means the same as shaking your head from side to side. *Will you*

come? No. Can a cow fly? No. 2 not in any degree; not at all: *He is no better.* 3 not any; not a: *They have no friends. Dogs have no wings.* 4 denial; refusal. 5 a vote against; person voting against: *The noes won.* 1,2 *adv.*, 3 *adj.*, 4,5 *n.*, *pl.* **noes.**

no. or **No.,** number. [abbreviation of Latin *numero*]

No ah (nō′ə), (in the Bible) a man whom God told to make an ark to save himself, his family, and a pair of each kind of animal from the Flood. *n.*

No bel (nō bel′), **Alfred Bernhard,** 1833-1896, Swedish inventor of dynamite and manufacturer of explosives, founder of the Nobel prizes. *n.*

no be li um (nō bē′lē əm), a radioactive chemical element produced artificially by bombarding curium with carbon ions. *n.* [from Alfred B. *Nobel*]

Nobel prize, any of five money prizes established by Alfred B. Nobel to be given annually to those persons or organizations who have done outstanding work in physics, chemistry, medicine or physiology, literature, and the promotion of peace. A sixth category, economics, was added in 1969.

no bil i ty (nō bil′ə tē), 1 people of noble rank, title, or birth. Earls, counts, countesses, and marquises belong to the nobility. 2 noble birth; noble rank. 3 noble character. *n., pl.* **no bil i ties.**

no ble (nō′bəl), 1 high and great by birth, rank, or title: *a noble family.* 2 person high and great by birth, rank, or title. 3 high and great in character; showing greatness of mind; good: *a noble person, a noble deed.* 4 excellent; fine; splendid; magnificent: *Niagara Falls is a noble sight.* 1,3,4 *adj.*, nobler, no blest; 2 *n.* —**no′ble ness,** *n.*

no ble man (nō′bəl mən), man of noble rank, title, or birth. *n., pl.* **no ble men.**

no ble wom an (nō′bəl wum′ən), woman of noble rank, title, or birth. *n., pl.* **no ble wom en.**

no bly (nō′blē), in a noble manner; splendidly; as a noble person would do. *adv.*

no bod y (nō′bod′ē), 1 no one; no person. 2 person of no importance. 1 *pron.*, 2 *n., pl.* **no bod ies.**

noc tur nal (nok tèr′nl), 1 of the night: *Stars are a nocturnal sight.* 2 in the night: *a nocturnal visitor.* 3 active in the night: *The owl is a nocturnal bird. The bat is a nocturnal animal.* 4 closed by day, open by night: *a nocturnal flower. adj.*

noc tur nal ly (nok tèr′nl ē), 1 at night. 2 every night. *adv.*

noc turne (nok′tèrn′), 1 a dreamy or pensive musical piece. 2 a painting of a night scene. *n.*

nod (nod), 1 bow (the head) slightly and raise it again quickly. 2 express by nodding: *I quietly nodded my approval.* 3 a nodding of the head: *She gave us a nod as she passed.* 4 let the head fall forward and bob about when sleepy or falling asleep. 5 be sleepy; become careless and dull. 6 droop, bend, or sway back and forth: *Trees nod in the wind.* 1,2,4-6 *v.*, **nod ded, nod ding;** 3 *n.*

nod al (nō′dl), having to do with nodes; like a node. *adj.*

node (nōd), 1 a knot, knob, or swelling. 2 a joint on a stem where leaves grow out. *n.*

nodes (def. 2)

nod u lar (noj′ə lər), having nodules. *adj.*

nod ule (noj′ül), 1 a small knot, knob, or swelling. 2 a small rounded mass or lump: *nodules of pure gold. n.*

No el or **No ël** (nō el′), 1 Christmas. 2 noel or **noël,** a Christmas song; carol. *n., pl.* **no els** or **no ëls** for 2. [from French *Noël*]

nog gin (nog′ən), 1 a small cup or mug. 2 a small drink; ¼ pint. 3 INFORMAL. a person's head. *n.*

no how (nō′hou′), INFORMAL. in no way; not at all. *adv.*

noise (noiz), 1 a sound that is not musical or pleasant; loud or harsh sound: *the noise of dishes breaking, the noise of machinery. The noise kept me awake.* 2 any sound: *the noise of rain on the roof.* 3 din of voices and movements; loud shouting; outcry; clamor: *The children made so much noise that they were asked to leave the theater.* 4 spread the news of; tell: *It was noised abroad that the prime minister was ill.* 1-3 *n.*, 4 *v.*, **noised, nois ing.**

noise less (noiz′lis), making no noise; making little noise. *adj.* —**noise′less ly,** *adv.* —**noise′less ness,** *n.*

noise mak er (noiz′mā′kər), 1 person who makes too much noise. 2 thing that makes noise, especially a horn, rattle, etc., used to make noise at a party. *n.*

nois i ly (noi′zə lē), in a noisy manner. *adv.*

nois i ness (noi′zē nis), a being noisy; making a noise. *n.*

noi some (noi′səm), 1 that disgusts; offensive; smelling bad: *a noisome slum, a noisome sewer.* 2 harmful; injurious: *a noisome pestilence.* *adj.*

nois y (noi′zē), 1 making much noise: *a noisy child, a noisy crowd, a noisy machine.* 2 full of noise: *a noisy street, the noisy city.* 3 having much noise with it: *a noisy quarrel, a noisy game.* *adj.,* **nois i er, nois i est.**

no mad (nō′mad), 1 member of a tribe which moves from place to place to have food or pasture for its cattle: *Many Arabs are nomads.* 2 wandering from place to place to find pasture. 3 wanderer. 4 wandering. 1,3 *n.,* 2,4 *adj.*

regular nonagon   irregular nonagon

no mad ic (nō mad′ik), of nomads or their life; wandering; roving: *Most of the Indians of the American plains were nomadic. adj.*

nom de plume (nom′ də plüm′), a pen name. [formed in English from the French words *nom* name, *de* of, *plume* pen]

Nome (nōm), seaport and mining town in W Alaska, on the Bering Sea. *n.*

no men cla ture (nō′mən klā′chər), set or system of names or terms: *the nomenclature of music. n.*

nom i nal (nom′ə nəl), 1 existing in name only; not real: *The president is the nominal head of the club, but the secretary is the one who really runs its affairs.* 2 too small to be considered: *We paid our friend a merely nominal rent for the cottage each summer—$5 a month. adj.*

nom i nal ly (nom′ə nə lē), in name; as a matter of form; in a nominal way only. *adv.*

nom i nate (nom′ə nāt), 1 name as candidate for an office; designate: *William Jennings Bryan was nominated three times for President, but he was never elected.* 2 appoint to an office or duty: *In 1933 Roosevelt nominated the first woman cabinet member in U.S. history. v.,* **nom i nat ed, nom i nat ing.**

nom i na tion (nom′ə nā′shən), 1 a naming as a candidate for office: *The nominations for president of the club were written on the blackboard.* 2 selection for office or duty; appointment to office or duty. 3 a being nominated: *Her friends were pleased by her nomination. n.*

nom i na tive (nom′ə nə tiv), 1 showing the subject of a verb or the words agreeing with the subject. *I, he, she, we,*

and *they* are in the nominative case. 2 the nominative case. 3 a word in that case. *Who* and *I* are nominatives. 1 *adj.,* 2,3 *n.*

nom i na tor (nom′ə nā′tər), person who nominates. *n.*

nom i nee (nom′ə nē′), person nominated for an office or to be a candidate for election to an office. *n.*

non-, *prefix.* not; not a; opposite of; lack of: *Nonessential = not essential. Nonresident = not a resident. Nonconformity = lack of conformity.* [from Latin *non,* from *non* not]

non ag gres sion (non′ə gresh′ən), a refraining from aggression: *A pact of nonaggression was signed by the two nations. n.*

non a gon (non′ə gon), a plane figure having nine angles and nine sides. *n.*

non al co hol ic (non′al kə hô′lik), containing no alcohol: *a nonalcoholic drink. adj.*

non break a ble (non brā′kə bəl), not breakable. *adj.*

nonce (nons), the one or particular occasion or purpose. *n.*

for the nonce, for the present time or occasion.

non cha lance (non′shə ləns *or* non′-shə läns′), cool unconcern; indifference: *She received the prize with pretended nonchalance. n.*

non cha lant (non′shə lənt *or* non′-shə länt′), without enthusiasm; coolly unconcerned; indifferent: *It was hard to remain nonchalant during all the excitement. adj.* **—non′cha lant ly,** *adv.*

non com bat ant (non′kəm bat′nt *or* non kom′bə tənt), 1 person in the armed forces who takes no part in combat. Surgeons, nurses, chaplains, etc., are noncombatants. 2 not fighting; having civilian status in wartime. 1 *n.,* 2 *adj.*

non com mer cial (non′kə mėr′-shəl), not commercial: *a noncommercial airline. adj.*

non com mis sioned (non′kə mish′-ənd), without a commission; not commissioned. *adj.*

noncommissioned officer, officer in the armed forces who does not hold a commission or a warrant, especially one with the rank of corporal, sergeant, or petty officer.

non com mit tal (non′kə mit′l), not committing oneself; not saying yes or no: *"I will think it over" is a noncommittal answer. adj.* **—non′com mit′-tal ly,** *adv.*

non con duc tor (non′kən duk′tər), substance which does not readily conduct heat, electricity, or sound. Rubber is a nonconductor of electricity. *n.*

non con form ist (non′kən fôr′mist), 1 person who refuses to conform to an

hat, āge, fär; let, ēqual, tėrm; it, īce; hot, ōpen, ôrder; oil, out; cup, půt, rüle; ch, child; ng, long; sh, she; th, thin; ₮H, then; zh, measure;

ə represents *a* in about, *e* in taken, *i* in pencil, *o* in lemon, *u* in circus.

established church or social group. 2 **Nonconformist,** Protestant who is not a member of the Church of England. *n.*

non con form i ty (non′kən fôr′-mə tē), lack of conformity; refusal to conform. *n.*

non con ta gious (non′kən tā′jəs), not contagious: *noncontagious diseases. adj.*

non de script (non′də skript), 1 not easily classified; not of any one particular kind: *He had nondescript eyes, neither brown, blue, nor gray.* 2 a nondescript person or thing. 1 *adj.,* 2 *n.*

none (nun), 1 not any: *We have none of that paper left.* 2 no one; not one: *None of these is a typical case.* 3 no persons or things: *None have arrived.* 4 to no extent; in no way; not at all: *Our supply is none too great.* 1-3 *pron.,* 4 *adv.*

non en ti ty (non en′tə tē), person or thing of little or no importance. *n., pl.* **non en ti ties.**

non es sen tial (non′ə sen′shəl), 1 not essential; not necessary. 2 person or thing not essential. 1 *adj.,* 2 *n.*

none the less (nun′₮Hə les′), nevertheless. *adv.*

non ex ist ence (non′ig zis′təns), 1 condition of not existing. 2 thing that has no existence. *n.*

non ex ist ent (non′ig zis′tənt), having no existence. *adj.*

non fic tion (non fik′shən), writing that is not fiction; form of writing that deals with real people and events rather than imaginary ones. Biographies and histories are nonfiction. *n.*

non fic tion al (non fik′shə nəl), not fictional. *adj.*

non flam ma ble (non flam′ə bəl), that will not catch fire: *a nonflammable paint remover. adj.*

non liv ing (non liv′ing), not living. *adj.*

non mag net ic (non′mag net′ik), not having the properties of a magnet; that cannot be attracted by a magnet. *adj.*

non met al (non met′l), a chemical element lacking the physical properties of a metal. *n.*

non me tal lic (non′mə tal′ik), not

adj.	adjective	*n.*	noun
adv.	adverb	*prep.*	preposition
conj.	conjunction	*pron.*	pronoun
interj.	interjection	*v.*	verb
sing.	singular	*pl.*	plural

like a metal. Carbon, oxygen, sulfur, and nitrogen are nonmetallic chemical elements. *adj.*

non pa reil (non′pə rel′), 1 having no equal. 2 person or thing having no equal. 3 a beautifully colored finch of the southern United States. 1 *adj.*, 2,3 *n.*

non par ti san or **non par ti zan** (non pär′tə zən), not partisan; not supporting, or controlled by, any of the regular political parties: *a nonpartisan voter. adj.*

non pay ment (non pā′mənt), failure to pay or condition of not being paid. *n.*

non plus (non plus′ or non′plus), puzzle completely; make unable to say or do anything: *We were nonplused to see two roads leading off to the left where we had expected only one. v.,* **non plused, non plus ing** or **non plussed, non plus sing.**

non poi son ous (non poi′zn əs), containing no poison. *adj.*

non pro duc tive (non′prə duk′tiv), 1 not productive. 2 not directly connected with production. *adj.*

non prof it (non prof′it), not for profit; without profit: *The Salvation Army is a nonprofit organization. adj.*

noose (def. 1)

non res i dent (non rez′ə dənt), 1 living elsewhere; not living in a particular place. 2 not living where official duties require one to live. 3 a nonresident person. 1,2 *adj.*, 3 *n.*

non re stric tive (non′ri strik′tiv), not restricting or limiting. *adj.*

nonrestrictive clause, (in grammar) any clause which adds descriptive detail but is not an essential part of the sentence in which it appears. EXAMPLE: My bicycle, *which had a flat tire,* was stolen today.

non sched uled (non skej′ůld), not operating according to regular schedule: *a nonscheduled airline, a nonscheduled flight. adj.*

non sec tar i an (non′sek ter′ē ən), not connected with any religious denomination. *adj.*

non sense (non′sens), 1 words, ideas, or acts without meaning; foolish talk or

doings; a plan or suggestion that is foolish: *That tale about the ghost that haunts the old mansion is nonsense.* 2 worthless stuff; junk: *a drawer full of useless gadgets and other nonsense. n.*

non sen si cal (non sen′sə kəl), foolish or absurd. *adj.*

non stop (non′stop′ for *adj.;* non′-stop′ for *adv.*), without stopping: *We took a nonstop flight from New York to Paris (adj.). He flew nonstop from New York to Los Angeles (adv.). adj., adv.*

non un ion (non yü′nyən), 1 not belonging to a trade union. 2 not following trade-union rules. 3 not recognizing or favoring trade unions. *adj.*

non vi o lence (non vī′ə ləns), belief in the use of peaceful methods to achieve any goal; opposition to any form of violence. *n.*

non vi o lent (non vī′ə lənt), not violent; opposing violence: *nonviolent protest. adj.*

non vot er (non vō′tər), person who does not vote or is not eligible to vote. *n.*

noo dle[1] (nü′dl), a mixture of flour and water, or flour and eggs, like macaroni, but made in flat strips. *n.* [from German *Nudel*]

noo dle[2] (nü′dl), 1 a very stupid person; fool. 2 SLANG. head. *n.* [origin uncertain]

nook (nůk), 1 a cozy little corner: *a nook facing the fire.* 2 a hidden spot; sheltered place: *My sister and I have found a wonderful nook in the woods behind our house. n.*

noon (nün), 12 o'clock in the daytime; middle of the day. *n.*

noon day (nün′dā′), noon. *n.*

no one, no person; nobody.

no-one (nō′wun), no one. *pron.*

noon tide (nün′tīd′), noon. *n.*

noon time (nün′tīm′), noon. *n.*

noose (nüs), 1 a loop with a slip knot that tightens as the string or rope is pulled. Nooses are used especially in lassos and snares. 2 a snare or bond. 3 catch with a noose; snare. 4 **the noose,** death by hanging. 1,2,4 *n.*, 3 *v.*, **noosed, noos ing.**

nor (nôr), 1 and no: *There was neither river nor stream in that desert. He had neither food nor drink left.* 2 neither: *Nor silver nor gold can buy it.* 3 and not: *I have not gone there, nor will I ever go. conj.*

Nor dic (nôr′dik), 1 belonging to or characteristic of the people of northern Europe. 2 a northern European. Scandinavians are Nordics. 1 *adj.*, 2 *n.*

Nor folk (nôr′fək), seaport in SE Virginia, near the mouth of Chesapeake Bay. *n.*

norm (nôrm), standard for a certain

group; type, model, or pattern: *In arithmetic this class is above the norm for the eighth grade. n.*

nor mal (nôr′məl), 1 of the usual standard; regular; usual: *The normal temperature of the human body is 98.6 degrees.* 2 the usual state or level: *He is ten pounds above normal for his age.* 3 not diseased, defective, or insane. 1,3 *adj.*, 2 *n.*

nor mal cy (nôr′məl sē), normal condition. *n.*

nor mal i ty (nôr mal′ə tē), normal condition. *n.*

nor mal ize (nôr′mə līz), make normal: *normalize the relations between two countries. v.,* **nor mal ized, nor mal iz ing.**

nor mal ly (nôr′mə lē), in the normal way; regularly; if things are normal: *Children normally begin to lose their baby teeth when they are six years old. adv.*

normal school, school where people are trained to be teachers.

Nor man (nôr′mən), 1 person born or living in Normandy. 2 member of the people descended from the Scandinavians who settled in Normandy in the A.D 800's and the French who lived there. 3 of the Normans or Normandy. 1,2 *n.*, 3 *adj.*

Norman Conquest, conquest of England by the Normans in 1066, under the leadership of William I.

Nor man dy (nôr′mən dē), region and former province in NW France. The invasion of Europe in World War II began when the Allies landed on the beaches of Normandy on June 6, 1944. *n.*

Norse (nôrs), 1 of or having to do with ancient Scandinavia, its people, or their language. 2 people of ancient Scandinavia; Norsemen; Northmen. 3 language of these people. 4 of or having to do with Norway or its people. 5 Norwegians. 6 language of Norway. 1,4 *adj.*, 2,5 *n.pl.*, 3,6 *n.sing.*

Norse man (nôrs′mən), one of the Nordic people of ancient Scandinavia. The Norsemen were great sailors and sea fighters. The Vikings were Norsemen. *n., pl.* **Norse men.**

north (nôrth), 1 direction to which a compass needle points; direction to the right as one faces the setting sun. 2 toward the north; farther toward the north: *Drive north for the next mile* (adv.). *We live on the north side of town* (adj.). 3 from the north: *a north wind.* 4 in the north: *the north window of a house.* 5 Also, **North.** the part of any country toward the north. 6 **North,** the northern part of the United States; the states north of Maryland, the Ohio River, and Missouri, making up most of the states that formed the Union side in the Civil War. 1,5,6 *n.,* 2 *adv.,* 2-4 *adj.*

north of, further north than: *Canada is north of the United States.*

North America, the northern continent of the Western Hemisphere. The United States, Mexico, and Canada are the three largest countries in North America.

North American, 1 of or having to do with North America or its people. 2 person born or living in North America.

north bound (nôrth′bound′), going north. *adj.*

North Carolina, one of the southeastern states of the United States. *Capital:* Raleigh.

North Dakota, one of the midwestern states of the United States. *Capital:* Bismarck.

north east (nôrth′ēst′), 1 halfway between north and east. 2 a northeast direction. 3 a place that is in the northeast part or direction. 4 toward the northeast. 5 from the northeast: *a northeast wind.* 6 in the northeast: *the northeast district.* 1,5,6 *adj.,* 2,3 *n.,* 4 *adv.*

north east er (nôrth′ē′stər), wind or storm from the northeast. *n.*

north east er ly (nôrth′ē′stər lē), 1 toward the northeast. 2 from the northeast. *adj., adv.*

north east ern (nôrth′ē′stərn), 1 toward the northeast. 2 from the northeast. 3 of or in the northeast. *adj.*

north er ly (nôr′ŦHər lē), 1 toward the north: *The windows face northerly.* 2 from the north: *a northerly wind. adj., adv.*

north ern (nôr′ŦHərn), 1 toward the north: *a northern view.* 2 from the north: *a northern breeze.* 3 of or in the north: *northern countries.* 4 **Northern,** of or in the northern part of the United States. *adj.*

north ern er (nôr′ŦHər nər), 1 person born or living in the north. 2 **Northerner,** person born or living in the northern part of the United States. *n.*

Northern Hemisphere, the half of the earth that is north of the equator.

Northern Ireland, self-governing district in NE Ireland that voted not to join the Republic of Ireland and is a part of the United Kingdom of Great Britain and Northern Ireland. *Capital:* Belfast. See **United Kingdom** for map.

northern lights, the aurora borealis.

north ern most (nôr′ŦHərn mōst), farthest north. *adj.*

North Island, the northernmost main island of New Zealand.

North Korea, country on the Korean peninsula, north of the 38th parallel. *Capital:* Pyongyang.

north land (nôrth′lənd), 1 land in the north; the northern part of a country. 2 **Northland,** the northern regions of the world. *n.*

North man (nôrth′mən), Norseman. *n., pl.* **North men.**

North Pole, the northern end of the earth's axis. See **arctic circle** for map.

Northwest Territory—the shaded area

North Sea, sea that is part of the Atlantic Ocean, east of Great Britain, west of Denmark, and south of Norway.

North Star, the bright star almost directly above the North Pole, formerly much used as a guide by sailors; Polaris; polestar; lodestar.

North um bri a (nôr thum′brē ə), ancient kingdom in N England. *n.*

North Vietnam, country in SE Asia, north of the 17th parallel. *Capital:* Hanoi.

north ward (nôrth′wərd), 1 toward the north; north: *Rocks lay northward of the ship's course* (adv.). *The orchard is on the northward slope of the hill* (adj.). 2 a northward part, direction, or point. 1 *adv., adj.,* 2 *n.*

north wards (nôrth′wərdz), northward. *adv.*

north west (nôrth′west′), 1 halfway between north and west. 2 a northwest direction. 3 a place that is in the northwest part or direction. 4 toward the northwest. 5 from the northwest: *a northwest wind.* 6 in the northwest: *The northwest climate is good for wheat.* 1,5,6 *adj.,* 2,3 *n.,* 4 *adv.*

north west er (nôrth′wes′tər), wind or storm from the northwest. *n.*

hat, āge, fär; let, ēqual, tėrm;
it, īce; hot, ōpen, ôrder;
oil, out; cup, pút, rüle; ch, child;
ng, long; sh, she; th, thin;
ŦH, then; zh, measure;

ə represents *a* in about,
e in taken, *i* in pencil,
o in lemon, *u* in circus.

north west er ly (nôrth′wes′tər lē), 1 toward the northwest. 2 from the northwest. *adj., adv.*

north west ern (nôrth′wes′tərn), 1 toward the northwest. 2 from the northwest. 3 of or in the northwest. 4 **Northwestern,** of or in the northwestern part of the United States. *adj.*

Northwest Passage, passage for ships from the Atlantic to the Pacific along the N coast of North America.

Northwest Territories, division of N Canada, east of the Yukon territory.

Northwest Territory, former name for lands north of the Ohio River and east of the Mississippi River, now forming Ohio, Indiana, Illinois, Michigan, Wisconsin, and part of Minnesota.

Nor way (nôr′wā), mountainous country in N Europe, west and north of Sweden. *Capital:* Oslo. *n.*

Nor we gian (nôr wē′jən), 1 of Norway, its people, or their language: *Norwegian villages, a Norwegian costume.* 2 person born or living in Norway. 3 language of Norway. 1 *adj.,* 2,3 *n.*

nose (nōz), 1 the part of the face or head just above the mouth. The nose has openings for breathing and smelling. 2 sense of smell: *Most dogs have a good nose. A mouse has a good nose for cheese.* 3 discover by smell; smell out. 4 to smell; sniff (at). 5 faculty for perceiving or detecting: *A reporter must have a nose for news.* 6 rub with the nose: *The cat nosed its kittens.* 7 part that stands out, especially the bow of a ship, boat, or airplane: *We saw the little steamer's nose poking around the cliff.* 8 push (its way) with the nose: *The boat nosed along.* 9 search (for); pry (into). 1,2,5,7 *n.,* 3,4,6,8,9 *v.,* nosed, nos ing.

follow one's nose, go straight ahead.

look down one's nose at or **turn up one's nose at,** treat with contempt or scorn.

pay through the nose, pay a great deal too much.

poke one's nose into, pry or meddle in a nosy way: *Our gossipy neighbors were always poking their noses into other people's business.*

adj.	adjective	*n.*	noun
adv.	adverb	*prep.*	preposition
conj.	conjunction	*pron.*	pronoun
interj.	interjection	*v.*	verb
sing.	singular	*pl.*	plural

nose bleed (nōz′blēd′), flow of blood from the nose. *n.*

nose cone, the cone-shaped front section of a missile or rocket, made to carry a bomb to a target or instruments or passengers into space. The nose cone is made to withstand high temperatures from friction with air molecules. It usually separates from the rest of the missile or rocket after the fuel runs out.

←— NOSE CONE

nose dive, 1 a swift plunge straight downward by an aircraft. 2 a sudden, sharp drop: *The thermometer took a nose dive the first day of winter.*

nose-dive (nōz′dīv′), take a nose dive. *v.,* **nose-dived, nose-div ing.**

nose gay (nōz′gā′), a bunch of flowers; bouquet. *n.*

nos tal gia (no stal′jə), a painful or wistful yearning for one's home, country, city, or for anything far removed in space or time. *n.*

nos tal gic (no stal′jik), feeling or showing nostalgia. *adj.* —**nos tal′gi cal ly,** *adv.*

nos tril (nos′trəl), either of the two openings in the nose. Air is breathed into the lungs, and smells come into the sensitive parts of the nose, through the nostrils. *n.*

nos trum (nos′trəm), 1 medicine made by the person who is selling it; quack remedy; patent medicine. 2 a pet scheme for producing wonderful results; cure-all. *n.*

nos y or **nos ey** (nō′zē), INFORMAL. prying or inquisitive. *adj.,* **nos i er, nos i est.**

not (not), word that says no; a negative: *not in any way, not to any extent. Six and two are not ten. adv.*

no ta bil i ty (nō′tə bil′ə tē), 1 quality of being notable; distinction. 2 a prominent person. *n., pl.* **no ta bil i ties.**

no ta ble (nō′tə bəl), 1 worthy of notice; striking; remarkable; important: *a notable event, a notable man, a notable book, a notable painter.* 2 person who is notable: *Many notables came to the President's reception.* 1 *adj.,* 2 *n.*

no ta bly (nō′tə blē), in a notable manner; to a notable degree. *adv.*

no ta rize (nō′tə rīz), certify (a contract, deed, will, etc.). *v.,* **no ta rized, no ta riz ing.**

no tar y (nō′tər ē), notary public. *n., pl.* **no tar ies.**

notary public, a public officer authorized to certify deeds and contracts, to record the fact that a certain person swears that something is true, and to attend to other legal matters. *pl.* **notaries public** or **notary publics.**

no ta tion (nō tā′shən), 1 a set of signs or symbols used to represent numbers, quantities, or other values: *In arithmetic we use the Arabic notation (1, 2, 3, 4, etc.) and sometimes the Roman notation (I, II, III, IV, etc.).* 2 the representing of numbers, quantities, or other values by symbols or signs: *Music has a special system of notation, and so has chemistry.* 3 a note to assist memory; record; jotting: *He made a notation on the margin of the paper.* 4 act of noting. *n.*

notch (noch), 1 a V-shaped nick or cut made in an edge or on a curving surface: *The Indians cut notches on a stick to keep count of numbers.* 2 make a notch or notches in. 3 a deep, narrow pass or gap between mountains. 4 INFORMAL. grade; step; degree: *In this hot weather many people set their air conditioners several notches higher.* 1,3,4 *n., pl.* **notch es;** 2 *v.*

note (nōt), 1 a short sentence, phrase, or single word written down to remind one of what was in a book, a speech, an agreement, etc.: *Her notes helped her remember what the speaker said. I must make a note of that.* 2 write down as a thing to be remembered: *Our class notes the weather daily on a chart.* 3 a comment, remark, or piece of information added concerning a word or a passage in a book, often to help pupils in studying the book: *There are many helpful notes at the back of our chemistry textbook.* 4 a very short letter: *a note of thanks.* 5 a formal letter from one government to another: *England sent a note of protest to France.* 6 promissory note. 7 certificate of a government or bank used as money. 8 greatness; fame: *a person of note.* 9 observe carefully; give attention to; take notice of: *Now, please note what I do next.* 10 notice; heed; observation.

○ WHOLE	♪ EIGHTH
♩ HALF	♬ SIXTEENTH
♩ QUARTER	♬ THIRTY-SECOND

notes (def. 12a)

11 mention specially. 12 in music: **a** a written sign to show the pitch and length of a sound. **b** a single sound of definite pitch made by an instrument or voice: *Sing this note for me.* **c** any one of the black or white keys of a piano: *to strike the wrong note.* 13 a song or call of a bird. 14 a significant sound or way of expression: *There was a note of anxiety in her voice.* 1,3-8,10,12-14 *n.,* 2,9,11 *v.,* **not ed, not ing.**

compare notes, exchange ideas or opinions.

take note of, take notice of; give attention to; observe.

take notes, write down things to be remembered.

note book (nōt′bük′), book in which to write notes of things to be learned or remembered. *n.*

not ed (nō′tid), especially noticed; conspicuous; well-known; celebrated; famous: *Samson was noted for his strength. "Little Women" was written by the noted American author Louisa May Alcott. adj.*

notches (def. 1)

note wor thi ness (nōt′wėr′FHē nis), condition or fact of being noteworthy. *n.*

note wor thy (nōt′wėr′FHē), worthy of notice; remarkable: *The first flight across the Atlantic was a noteworthy achievement. adj.*

noth ing (nuth′ing), 1 not anything; no thing: *Nothing arrived by mail.* 2 thing that does not exist: *create a world out of nothing.* 3 thing of no importance or value; person of no importance: *Don't worry, it's nothing.* 4 zero; naught. 5 not at all: *She is nothing like her sister in looks.* 1-4 *n.,* 5 *adv.*

noth ing ness (nuth′ing nis), 1 being nothing; condition of not existing. 2 a being of no value; worthlessness. *n.*

no tice (nō′tis), 1 attention or heed; observation; awareness: *escape one's notice. A sudden movement caught his notice.* 2 give attention to; observe; perceive: *I noticed a hole in my stocking.* 3 announcement or warning: *The whistle blew to give notice that the boat was about to leave.* 4 a written or printed sign; paper posted in a public place; a large sheet of paper giving information or directions: *We saw a notice of today's motion picture outside* *the theater.* **5** a telling that one is leaving or must leave rented quarters or a job, at a given time: *A month's notice is required from whichever person wishes to end this agreement.* **6** a written or printed account in a newspaper: *There is a notice in the paper describing the wedding.* **7** mention; refer to; speak of. 1,3-6 *n.*, 2,7 *v.*, **no ticed, no tic ing.**

serve notice, give warning; announce: *The landlord served notice that the noisy tenants would have to move out within one month.*

take notice of, give attention to; observe: *Take no notice of them.*

no tice a ble (nō′ti sə bəl), **1** easily seen or noticed; discernible: *The class has made a noticeable improvement in spelling.* **2** worth noticing. *adj.*

no tice a bly (nō′ti sə blē), to a noticeable degree: *It is noticeably cooler in the shade. Oranges are noticeably less sour than lemons. adv.*

no ti fi ca tion (nō′tə fə kā′shən), **1** a notifying. **2** notice: *He received a notification of the meeting. n.*

no ti fy (nō′tə fī), give notice to; let know; inform; announce to: *Our teacher notified us that there would be a test on Monday. We have a letter notifying us that he will visit us soon. v.*, **no ti fied, no ti fy ing.**

no tion (nō′shən), **1** idea or understanding: *I have no notion of what you mean.* **2** opinion, view, or belief: *One common notion is that red hair means a quick temper.* **3** intention: *He has no notion of risking his money.* **4** inclination or desire; fancy; whim: *She had a sudden notion to take a short vacation.* **5** a foolish notion or opinion: *Grow oranges in Alaska? What a notion!* **6 notions,** *pl.* small, useful articles, such as pins, needles, thread, tape, etc. *n.*

no tion al (nō′shə nəl), **1** in one's imagination or thought only; not real. **2** full of notions; having strange notions. *adj.*

no to chord (nō′tə kôrd), **1** a flexible, rodlike structure of cells running lengthwise in the back of the lowest vertebrates. It forms the main supporting structure of the body. **2** a similar structure in the embryos of higher vertebrates. *n.*

no to ri e ty (nō′tə rī′ə tē), **1** a being famous for something bad; ill fame: *A crime or scandal brings much notoriety to those involved in it.* **2** a being widely known. *n.*, *pl.* **no to ri e ties.**

no to ri ous (nō tôr′ē əs), well-known or commonly known, especially because of something bad: *a notorious underworld figure. Our neighbors are notorious for giving wild parties. adj.* —**no to′ri ous ly,** *adv.* —**no to′ri ous ness,** *n.*

Not ting ham (not′ing əm), **1** county

in central England. **2** city in this county. Many of Robin Hood's adventures took place in Nottingham. *n.*

not with stand ing (not′wiŦH-stan′ding *or* not′with stan′ding), **1** in spite of: *I bought it notwithstanding the high price.* **2** in spite of the fact that: *Notwithstanding there was need for haste, he still delayed.* **3** in spite of it; nevertheless: *It is raining; but I shall go, notwithstanding.* 1 *prep.*, 2 *conj.*, 3 *adv.*

nou gat (nü′gət), a kind of soft candy containing nuts. *n.*

nought (nôt), naught. *n.*

noun (noun), **1** word used as the name of a person, place, thing, quality, or event. Words like *Lisa, table, school, bookcase, kindness, skill,* and *party* are nouns. **2** used as a noun. 1 *n.*, 2 *adj.*

nour ish (nėr′ish), **1** make grow, or keep alive and well, with food; feed; nurture: *Milk is all we need to nourish our small baby.* **2** maintain; foster; support; encourage: *nourish a hope. v.*

nour ish ment (nėr′ish mənt), **1** food. **2** a nourishing or a being nourished. *n.*

Nov., November.

no va (nō′və), star that suddenly becomes brighter and then gradually fades back to its normal brightness. *n.*, *pl.* **no vae** (nō′vē′), **no vas.**

No va Sco tia (nō′və skō′shə), province in SE Canada consisting chiefly of a peninsula that extends into the Atlantic. *Capital:* Halifax.

nov el (nov′əl), **1** of a new kind or nature; strange; new; unfamiliar: *a novel idea, a novel sensation.* **2** story with characters and a plot, long enough to fill one or more volumes. Novels are usually about people, scenes, and happenings such as might be met in real life. 1 *adj.*, 2 *n.*

nov el ette (nov′ə let′), a short novel. *n.*

nov el ist (nov′ə list), writer of novels. *n.*

nov el ty (nov′əl tē), **1** novel character; newness: *After the novelty of washing dishes wore off, we did not want to do it any more.* **2** a new or unusual thing: *Staying up late was a novelty to the children, and they enjoyed it.* **3 novelties,** *pl.* small, unusual articles, such as toys, cheap jewelry, etc. *n.*, *pl.* **nov el ties.**

No vem ber (nō vem′bər), the 11th month of the year; month just before December. It has 30 days. *n.*

nov ice (nov′is), **1** one who is new to what he is doing; beginner: *Novices are likely to make some mistakes.* **2** person in the period of trial and preparation before becoming a monk or a nun. *n.*

no vi ti ate *or* **no vi ci ate** (nō-vish′ē it), **1** the period of trial and preparation in a religious order. **2** house or rooms occupied by religious novices. **3** the state or period of being a beginner in anything. *n.*

now (nou), **1** at this time: *She is here now. Most people do not believe in ghosts now.* **2** by this time: *She must have reached the city now.* **3** the present; this time: *by now, until now, from now on.* **4** at once: *Do it now!* **5** inasmuch as; now that; since: *Now you mention it, I do remember. Now I am older, I can stay up longer.* **6** as things are; as it is: *I would believe almost anything now.* **7** then; next: *Now you see it; now you don't.* **8** at the time referred to: *The clock now struck three.* **9** a little while ago: *I just now saw him.* **10** *Now* is also used to introduce or emphasize. *Now what do you mean? Oh, come now! Now you knew that was wrong.* 1,2,4,6-10 *adv.*, 3 *n.*, 5 *conj.*

now and then *or* **now and again,** from time to time; once in a while.

now a days (nou′ə dāz′), **1** at the present day; in these times: *Nowadays people travel in automobiles rather than carriages.* **2** the present day; these times. 1 *adv.*, 2 *n.*

no way (nō′wā), nowise. *adv.*

no where (nō′hwer *or* nō′hwar), **1** in no place; at no place; to no place. **2** a nonexistent place. 1 *adv.*, 2 *n.*

nowhere near, INFORMAL. not nearly; not by a long way.

no wise (nō′wīz), in no way; not at all. *adv.*

nox ious (nok′shəs), very harmful; poisonous: *Poison ivy is a noxious plant; avoid touching its leaves. adj.* —**nox′ious ly,** *adv.* —**nox′ious ness,** *n.*

noz zle (noz′əl), a tip put on a hose, pipe, etc., forming an outlet: *He adjusted the nozzle so that the water came out in a fine spray. n.*

NOZZLE HOSE

adj. adjective	*n.* noun
adv. adverb	*prep.* preposition
conj. conjunction	*pron.* pronoun
interj. interjection	*v.* verb
sing. singular	*pl.* plural

N.S., Nova Scotia.

N.T., New Testament.

nth (enth), last in the series 1, 2, 3, 4. . . *n;* being of the indefinitely large or small amount denoted by *n. adj.*

to the nth degree, to the utmost: *He was dressed to the nth degree.*

nu ance (nü äns′, nü′äns, nyü äns′, *or* nyü′äns), 1 shade of expression, meaning, feeling, etc. 2 shade of color or tone. *n.*

nub (nub), 1 knob or protuberance. 2 lump or small piece. 3 INFORMAL. point or gist of anything. *n.*

nub bin (nub′ən), 1 a small or imperfect ear of corn. 2 an undeveloped fruit. *n.*

nub by (nub′ē), knobby or lumpy. *adj.,* **nub bi er, nub bi est.**

Nu bi a (nü′bē ə *or* nyü′bē ə), region in NE Africa between the Red Sea and the Nile River, including parts of SE Egypt and NE Sudan. *n.* —**Nu′bi an,** *adj., n.*

nu cle ar (nü′klē ər *or* nyü′klē ər), 1 of or having to do with nuclei or a nucleus, especially the nucleus of an atom: *nuclear particles.* 2 of or having to do with atoms or atomic energy; atomic: *a nuclear reactor. adj.*

nuclear energy, atomic energy.

nuclear fission, fission (def. 3).

nuclear fusion, fusion (def. 4).

nuclear physics, branch of physics dealing with the structure of atomic nuclei and the behavior of nuclear particles.

nu cle ic acid (nü klē′ik *or* nyü klē′ik), a complex chemical compound found in all living cells. It occurs chiefly in combination with proteins. One form of nucleic acid, deoxyribonucleic acid or DNA, is responsible for the transmission of inherited characteristics.

nu cle o lus (nü klē′ə ləs *or* nyü klē′ə ləs), a small, usually round structure found within the nucleus of a cell. *n., pl.* **nu cle o li** (nü klē′ə lī *or* nyü klē′ə lī).

nu cle on (nü′klē on *or* nyü′klē on), a proton or a neutron. *n.*

nu cle us (nü′klē əs *or* nyü′klē əs), 1 a central part or thing around which other parts or things are collected. 2 a beginning to which additions are to be made: *His five-dollar bill became the nucleus of a flourishing bank account.* 3 the central part of an atom, consisting of protons, neutrons, and some other particles. The nucleus carries a positive charge and forms a core around which electrons orbit. It contains most of the mass of the whole atom. See **atom** for diagram. 4 mass of specialized protoplasm found in most plant and animal cells, without which the cell cannot grow and divide. See **cell** for diagram. 5 the dense, central part of a comet's head. *n., pl.* **nu cle i** (nü′klē ī *or* nyü′klē ī), **nu cle us es.**

nude (nüd *or* nyüd), 1 naked. 2 a naked figure in painting, sculpture, or photography. 1 *adj.,* 2 *n.* —**nude′ness,** *n.*

in the nude, in a naked condition.

nudge (nuj), 1 push slightly; jog with the elbow to attract attention, etc. 2 a slight push or jog. 1 *v.,* **nudged, nudg ing;** 2 *n.*

nu di ty (nü′də tē *or* nyü′də tē), a naked condition; nakedness. *n., pl.* **nu di ties.**

nug get (nug′it), 1 valuable lump; lump: *nuggets of gold.* 2 anything valuable: *nuggets of wisdom. n.*

nui sance (nü′sns *or* nyü′sns), thing or person that annoys, troubles, offends, or is disagreeable; annoyance: *Flies are a nuisance. n.*

null (nul), 1 not binding; of no effect; as if not existing: *A promise obtained by force is legally null.* 2 unimportant; useless; meaningless; empty; valueless. 3 not any; zero. *adj.*

null and void, without legal force or effect; worthless.

nul li fi ca tion (nul′ə fə kā′shən), a nullifying or a being nullified: *the nullification of a treaty. n.*

nul li fy (nul′ə fī), 1 make not binding or not the law; render void: *nullify a law.* 2 make of no effect; destroy; cancel; wipe out: *The difficulties of the plan nullify its advantages. v.,* **nul lified, nul li fy ing.**

nul li ty (nul′ə tē), 1 condition of being null; nothingness. 2 a mere nothing: *The power of certain European monarchs is practically a nullity.* 3 something that is null, such as a nullified law or agreement. *n., pl.* **nul li ties.**

null set, empty set.

numb (num), 1 having lost the power of feeling or moving: *My fingers are numb with cold.* 2 make numb. 3 dull the feelings of: *numbed with grief.* 1 *adj.,* 2,3 *v.* —**numb′ly,** *adv.* —**numb′ness,** *n.*

num ber (num′bər), 1 the count or sum of a group of things or persons; amount: *The number of students in our class is twenty.* 2 word that tells exactly how many. Two, fourteen, twenty-six, second, fourteenth, and twenty-sixth are numbers. 3 find out the number of; count. 4 figure or mark that stands for a number; numeral. 2, 7, and 9 are numbers. 5 mark with a number; give a number to; distinguish with a number: *The pages of this book are numbered.* 6 be or amount to a given number: *The states in the Union number 50. This city numbers a million inhabitants.* 7 quantity, especially a rather large quantity: *We saw a number of birds.* 8 **numbers,** *pl.* a arithmetic. b many: *There were numbers who stayed out of school that day.* 9 reckon as one of a class or collection: *I number you among my best friends.* 10 a being more: *win a battle by force of numbers.* 11 a single issue of a magazine: *The May number has an unusually good story.* 12 one of a numbered series, often a particular numeral identifying a person or thing: *a telephone number, a house number.* 13 a single part of a program, etc.: *The program consisted of four musical numbers.* 14 fix the number of; limit: *Our old dog's days are numbered.* 15 (in grammar) a word form or ending which shows whether one or more is meant. *Boy, ox,* and *this* are in the singular number; *boys, oxen,* and *these* are in the plural number. 1,2,4,7,8,10-13,15 *n.,* 3,5,6,9,14 *v.*

beyond number, too many to count.

number one, INFORMAL. oneself: *He said it pays to look out for number one.*

without number, too many to be counted: *stars without number.*

num ber less (num′bər lis), very numerous; too many to count: *There are numberless fish in the sea. adj.*

number line, line divided into equal segments by points corresponding to integers. The points to the right of 0 are positive; those to the left are negative. The set of all the points on the line corresponds to the set of real numbers.

Num bers (num′bərz), the fourth book of the Old Testament. It tells about the counting of the Israelites after they left Egypt. *n.*

nu mer al (nü′mər əl *or* nyü′mər əl), 1 a word, figure, or group of figures standing for a number. One, five, and ten are numerals. 7, 25, and 463 are Arabic numerals. III, VI, and XIX are Roman numerals for 3, 6, and 19. 2 of numbers; standing for a number. 3 **numerals,** *pl.* big cloth numbers given by a school for excellence in some sport. They state the year in which the person who wins them will graduate. 1,3 *n.,* 2 *adj.*

nu me rate (nü′mə rāt′ *or* nyü′mə rāt′), to number, count, or enumerate. *v.,* **nu me rat ed, nu me rat ing.**

nu me ra tion (nü′mə rā′shən *or*

nyü′mə rā′shən), 1 a numbering, counting, or enumerating. 2 the reading of numbers expressed in figures. *n.*

nu me ra tor (nü′mə rā′tər *or* nyü′mə rā′tər), number above the line in a fraction, which shows how many parts are taken: *In* ³/₈, *3 is the numerator and 8 is the denominator. n.*

nu mer i cal (nü mer′ə kəl *or* nyü-mer′ə kəl), 1 of a number; having to do with numbers; in numbers; by numbers. 2 shown by numbers, not by letters: *10 is a numerical quantity; bx is an algebraic quantity. adj.*

nu mer i cal ly (nü mer′ik lē *or* nyü-mer′ik lē), by numbers; in a numerical manner; in numerical respects; so far as numbers are concerned: *The size of our school is numerically larger than theirs. adv.*

nu mer ous (nü′mər əs *or* nyü′mər-əs), 1 very many; several: *The child asked numerous questions.* 2 in great numbers: *He has a numerous acquaintance among politicians. adj.* —**nu′-mer ous ly,** *adv.* —**nu′mer ous-ness,** *n.*

nu mis mat ics (nü′miz mat′iks *or* nyü′miz mat′iks), the study or collecting of coins and medals. *n.*

nu mis ma tist (nü miz′mə tist *or* nyü miz′mə tist), an expert in numismatics. *n.*

num skull (num′skul′), INFORMAL. a stupid person; blockhead. *n.*

nun (nun), woman who gives up all worldly things and enters a convent to live a life devoted to religion. Some nuns teach; some care for the poor and sick. *n.*

nun ci o (nun′shē ō), an official representative or ambassador from the Pope to a government. *n., pl.* **nun-ci os.**

nun ner y (nun′ər ē), building or buildings where nuns live; convent. *n., pl.* **nun ner ies.**

nup tial (nup′shəl), 1 of marriage or weddings. 2 **nuptials,** *pl.* a wedding or the wedding ceremony. 1 *adj.,* 2 *n.*

nutcracker (def. 1)

Nur em berg (nur′əm bèrg′ *or* nyür′-əm bèrg′), city in SE West Germany, noted for the manufacture of toys. *n.*

nurse (nèrs), 1 person who is trained to take care of the sick, the injured, or the old, especially under a doctor's supervision. 2 be or act as a nurse for sick people; wait on or take care of the sick. 3 cure or try to cure by care: *She nursed a bad cold by going to bed.*

4 woman who cares for and brings up the young children or babies of another person. 5 act as a nurse; have charge of or bring up (another's baby or young child). 6 one who feeds and protects. 7 make grow; nourish; protect: *nurse a plant, nurse a fire, nurse a grudge.* 8 use or treat with special care: *He nursed his sore arm by using it very little.* 9 hold closely; clasp fondly. 10 feed milk to (a baby) at the breast. 11 suck milk from the breast of a mother or nurse. 1,4,6 *n.,* 2,3,5,7-11 *v.,* **nursed, nurs ing.**

nurse maid (nèrs′mād′), girl or woman employed to care for children. *n.*

nurs er y (nèr′sər ē), 1 room set apart for the use of the children of the household. 2 piece of ground or place where young trees and plants are raised for transplanting or sale. 3 nursery school. *n., pl.* **nurs er ies.**

nurs er y man (nèr′sər ē mən), man who grows or sells young trees and plants. *n., pl.* **nurs er y men.**

nursery rhyme, a short poem for children. "Sing a Song of Sixpence" is a famous nursery rhyme.

nursery school, school for children not old enough to go to kindergarten.

nurs ling (nèrs′ling), 1 a baby that is being nursed. 2 any person or thing that is receiving tender care. *n.*

nur ture (nèr′chər), 1 bring up; care for; foster; rear; train: *They nurtured the child as if she were their own.* 2 a bringing up; rearing; training; education: *The two sisters had received very different nurture, one at home and the other at a convent.* 3 nourish. 4 nourishment. 1,3 *v.,* **nur tured, nur-tur ing;** 2,4 *n.*

nut (nut), 1 a dry fruit or seed with a hard, woody, or leathery shell and a kernel inside which is good to eat. 2 kernel of a nut. 3 gather nuts. 4 a small, usually metal block having a threaded hole, which screws on to a bolt to hold the bolt in place. 5 SLANG. a queer or crazy person. 1,2,4,5 *n.,* 3 *v.,* **nut ted, nut ting.** —**nut′like,** *adj.*

nut crack er (nut′krak′ər), 1 instrument for cracking the shells of nuts. 2 bird related to the crow which feeds especially on pine seeds. *n.*

nut hatch (nut′hach′), a small, sharp-beaked bird that feeds on small nuts, seeds, and insects. *n., pl.* **nut-hatch es.**

nut let (nut′lit), a small nut or nutlike fruit. *n.*

nut meat (nut′mēt′), kernel of a nut. *n.*

nut meg (nut′meg), 1 a hard, spicy seed about as big as a marble, obtained from the fruit of a tree of the East

Indies. The seed is grated and used for flavoring food. 2 the tree it grows on. *n.*

nu tri a (nü′trē ə *or* nyü′trē ə), 1 coypu. 2 its valuable beaverlike fur. *n., pl.* **nu tri as.**

nu tri ent (nü′trē ənt *or* nyü′trē ənt), 1 nourishing. 2 a nourishing substance; food. 1 *adj.,* 2 *n.*

nu tri ment (nü′trə mənt *or* nyü′trə-mənt), nourishment; food. *n.*

nu tri tion (nü trish′ən *or* nyü-trish′ən), 1 food; nourishment: *A balanced diet provides nutrition for your body.* 2 series of processes by which food is used by animals and plants for growth, energy, etc. *n.*

nu tri tion al (nü trish′ə nəl *or* nyü-trish′ə nəl), having to do with nutrition. *adj.* —**nu tri′tion al ly,** *adv.*

nu tri tious (nü trish′əs *or* nyü-trish′əs), valuable as food; nourishing: *Oranges and bread are nutritious. adj.* —**nu tri′tious ly,** *adv.* —**nu tri′-tious ness,** *n.*

nu tri tive (nü′trə tiv *or* nyü′trə tiv), 1 having to do with foods and the use of foods. Digestion is part of the nutritive process. 2 nutritious. *adj.*

nuts (def. 4)
above, five kinds
left, nut on a bolt

nut shell (nut′shel′), shell of a nut. *n.* **in a nutshell,** in very brief form; in a few words.

nut ting (nut′ing), a looking for nuts; gathering nuts. *n.*

nut ty (nut′ē), 1 containing many nuts: *nutty cake.* 2 like nuts; tasting like nuts. 3 SLANG. queer; crazy. 4 SLANG. very interested or enthusiastic. *adj.,* **nut ti-er, nut ti est.**

nuz zle (nuz′əl), 1 poke or rub with the nose; press the nose against: *The calf nuzzled its mother.* 2 nestle; snuggle; cuddle. *v.,* **nuz zled, nuz zling.**

NW or **N.W.,** 1 northwest. 2 northwestern.

N.W.T., Northwest Territories.

N.Y., New York State.

Nyasaland

adj.	adjective	*n.*	noun
adv.	adverb	*prep.*	preposition
conj.	conjunction	*pron.*	pronoun
interj.	interjection	*v.*	verb
sing.	singular	*pl.*	plural

Ny as a land (nī as′ə land′), former British protectorate in SE Africa, now Malawi. *n.*

N.Y.C., New York City.

ny lon (nī′lon), 1 an extremely strong, elastic, and durable synthetic substance, used to make clothing, stockings, bristles, etc. **2 nylons,** *pl.* stockings made of nylon. 3 made of nylon: *Many toothbrushes have nylon bristles. Nylon rollers are often used to make drawers slide in and out smoothly.* 1,2 *n.,* 3 *adj.*

nymph (nimf), 1 (in Greek and Roman myths) a lesser goddess of nature, found in seas, rivers, fountains, hills, woods, or trees. 2 a beautiful or graceful young woman. 3 any of certain insects in the stage of development between the egg and the adult form. It resembles the adult but has no wings. *n.* —**nymph′like′,** *adj.*

N.Z., New Zealand.

O o

O¹ or **o** (ō), 1 the 15th letter of the alphabet. 2 zero. *n., pl.* **O's** or **o's.**

O² (ō), oh! *interj.*

o' (ə *or* ō), of: *man-o'-war, will-o'-the-wisp. prep.*

O., Ohio.

oaf (ōf), 1 a very stupid person. 2 a clumsy person. *n.*

oaf ish (ō′fish), very stupid; clumsy. *adj.*

O a hu (ō ä′hü), the third largest island of Hawaii. Honolulu, the capital of Hawaii, is on Oahu. *n.*

oak (ōk), 1 any of a group of trees or shrubs found in most parts of the world, with strong, hard, durable wood and nuts called acorns. 2 its wood, used in building, for flooring, etc. 3 of an oak: *oak leaves.* 4 made of oak wood; oaken: *an oak table.* 1,2 *n.,* 3,4 *adj.*

oak en (ō′kən), made of oak wood: *the old oaken bucket. adj.*

Oak land (ōk′lənd), city in W California, just east of San Francisco. *n.*

Oak Ridge, city in E Tennessee. Oak Ridge is a research center for studying atomic energy.

oa kum (ō′kəm), a loose fiber obtained by untwisting and picking apart old ropes, used for stopping up the seams or cracks in ships. *n.*

oar (ôr), 1 a long pole with a flat blade at one end, used in rowing. Sometimes an oar is used to steer a boat. 2 use an oar; row. 3 person who rows: *She is the best oar in our crew.* 1,3 *n.,* 2 *v.*

put one's oar in, meddle; interfere.

rest on one's oars, stop working or trying and take a rest.

oar lock (ôr′lok′), a notch or U-shaped support for holding the oar in place while rowing; rowlock. *n.*

oars man (ôrz′mən), 1 person who rows. 2 person who rows well. *n., pl.* **oars men.**

o a sis (ō ä′sis), 1 a fertile spot in the desert where there is water and some vegetation. 2 any fertile spot in a barren land; any pleasant place in a deso-

oasis (def. 1)

late region. *n., pl.* **o a ses** (ō ä′sēz′).

oat (ōt), 1 a tall cereal grass whose seed is used in making oatmeal and as a food for horses. 2 **oats,** *pl.* seeds of the oat plant. *n.*

feel one's oats, SLANG. 1 be lively or frisky. 2 feel pleased or important and show it.

oat en (ōt′n), 1 made of oats or oatmeal. 2 made of oat straw. *adj.*

oath (ōth), 1 a solemn promise or statement that something is true, which God or some holy person or thing is called on to witness: *He made an oath that he would tell the whole truth and nothing but the truth.* 2 name of God or some holy person or thing used as an exclamation to add force or to express anger. 3 a curse; word used in swearing. *n., pl.* **oaths** (ōᵀHz *or* ōths).

take oath, make an oath; promise or state solemnly.

under oath, bound by an oath.

oat meal (ōt′mēl′), 1 oats made into meal; ground or rolled oats. 2 a cooked cereal made from oatmeal. *n.*

O ba di ah (ō′bə dī′ə), 1 (in the Bible) a Hebrew prophet. 2 book of the Old Testament containing his prophecies. *n.*

ob du ra cy (ob′dər ə sē *or* ob′dyər-ə sē), hardness of heart; stubbornness. *n.*

ob du rate (ob′dər it *or* ob′dyər it), 1 stubborn or unyielding; obstinate: *an obdurate refusal.* 2 hardened in feelings or heart; not repentant: *an obdurate criminal. adj.* —**ob′dur ate ly,** *adv.*

o be di ence (ō bē′dē əns), an obeying; doing what one is told to do; submission to authority or law: *Parents desire obedience from their children. Both sides in the dispute were told that they must act in obedience to the judge's ruling. n.*

oarlock

o be di ent (ō bē′dē ənt), doing what one is told; willing to obey: *The obedient dog came at its owner's whistle. adj.* —**o be′di ent ly,** *adv.*

o bei sance (ō bā′sns *or* ō bē′sns), 1 movement of the body expressing deep respect; deep bow: *The villagers made obeisance to the queen.* 2 deference; homage: *acts of obeisance. n.*

ob e lisk (ob′ə lisk), a tapering, four-sided shaft of stone with a top shaped like a pyramid. *n.*

O be ron (ō′bə ron′), (in Shakespeare's *A Midsummer Night's Dream*)

hat, āge, fär; let, ēqual, tėrm; it, īce; hot, ōpen, ôrder; oil, out; cup, put, rüle; ch, child; ng, long; sh, she; th, thin; ᵀH, then; zh, measure;

ə represents *a* in about, *e* in taken, *i* in pencil, *o* in lemon, *u* in circus.

the king of the fairies. He was the husband of Titania. *n.*

o bese (ō bēs′), extremely fat. *adj.*

o bes i ty (ō bē′sə tē), extreme fatness. *n.*

o bey (ō bā′), 1 do what one is told to do: *The dog obeyed and went home.* 2 follow the orders of: *Obey your parents.* 3 act in accordance with; comply with: *A good citizen obeys the laws.* 4 yield to the control of: *A horse obeys the rein. v.*

o bi (ō′bē), a long, broad sash worn by Japanese around the waist of a kimono. *n., pl.* **o bis.**

o bit u ar y (ō bich′ü er′ē), 1 a notice of death, often with a brief account of the person's life. 2 of a death; recording a death: *the obituary notices in the newspaper.* 1 *n., pl.* **o bit u ar ies;** 2 *adj.*

ob ject (ob′jikt *for* 1-4; əb jekt′ *for* 5,6), 1 something that can be seen or touched; thing: *What is that object by the fence? A dark object moved between me and the door.* 2 person or thing toward which feeling, thought, or action is directed: *an object of charity, an object of study, an object of someone's affection.* 3 thing aimed at; end; purpose; goal: *Her object in examining a number of new cars was to determine which make was best.* 4 (in grammar) a word or group of words toward which the action of the verb is directed or to which a preposition expresses some relation. In "He threw the ball to his brother," *ball* is the object of *threw,* and *brother* is the object of *to.* 5 make objections; be opposed; feel dislike: *Many people object to loud noise.*

obelisk
from
ancient Egypt

objection

adj. adjective	n. noun
adv. adverb	prep. preposition
conj. conjunction	pron. pronoun
interj. interjection	v. verb
sing. singular	pl. plural

6 give as a reason against something; bring forward in opposition; oppose: *I objected that we did not have enough money to go on a trip.* 1-4 *n.*, 5,6 *v.*

ob jec tion (əb jek′shən), 1 something said in objecting; reason or argument against something: *One of his objections to the plan was that it would cost too much.* 2 feeling of disapproval or dislike: *an energetic person with no objection to hard work.* *n.*

ob jec tion a ble (əb jek′shə nə bəl), 1 likely to be objected to. 2 unpleasant; disagreeable. *adj.*

ob jec tive (əb jek′tiv), 1 something aimed at: *My objective this summer will be learning to play tennis better.* 2 existing outside the mind as an actual object and not merely in the mind as an idea; real. Buildings are objective; ideas are subjective. 3 about outward things, not about the thoughts and feelings of the speaker, writer, painter, etc.; giving facts as they are without a bias toward either side; impersonal: *an objective analysis of a poem or novel. Scientists must be objective in their experiments.* 4 showing the direct object of a verb or the object of a preposition. In "She saw me," *me* is in the objective case. 5 the objective case. 6 word in that case. *Whom* and *me* are objectives. 7 lens or lenses nearest to the thing seen through a telescope, microscope, etc. 1,5-7 *n.*, 2-4 *adj.* —**ob jec′tive ly**, *adv.*

ob jec tiv i ty (ob′jek tiv′ə tē), condition or quality of being objective; intentness on objects external to the mind; external reality. *n.*

object lesson, a practical illustration of a principle: *Many accidents are object lessons in the dangers of carelessness.*

ob jec tor (əb jek′tər), person who objects. *n.*

o bla tion (o blā′shən), 1 act of offering to God or a god. 2 the offering of bread and wine in the Communion service. 3 something offered to a god; sacrifice. 4 gift for religious uses. *n.*

ob li gate (ob′lə gāt), bind morally or legally; pledge: *A witness in court is obligated to tell the truth.* *v.*, **ob li gat ed, ob li gat ing.**

ob li ga tion (ob′lə gā′shən), 1 duty under the law; duty due to a promise or contract; duty on account of social relationship or kindness received: *We all have an obligation to our friends. Paying taxes is an obligation which may fall on everybody.* 2 binding power (of a law, promise, sense of duty, etc.): *The one who did the damage is under obligation to pay for it.* 3 a binding legal agreement; bond; contract: *The firm was not able to meet its obligations.* 4 a binding oneself or being bound by oath, promise, etc., to do something: *It was his obligation to return her favor.* *n.*

o blig a to ry (ə blig′ə tôr′ē), binding morally or legally; required: *Attendance in school is obligatory.* *adj.*

o blige (ə blīj′), 1 bind by a promise, contract, duty, etc.; compel; force: *The law obliges parents to send their children to school.* 2 put under a debt of thanks for some favor or service: *We are very much obliged for your kind offer.* 3 do a favor: *Kindly oblige me by closing the door.* *v.*, **o bliged, o blig ing.**

o blig ing (ə blī′jing), willing to do favors; helpful: *Her obliging good nature wins her friends everywhere she goes.* *adj.* —**o blig′ing ly**, *adv.*

oblique (def. 1)
AB, CD, EF, and GH are oblique lines.

o blique (ə blēk′), 1 not straight up and down; not straight across; slanting. 2 not straightforward; indirect: *She made an oblique reference to her book, but did not mention it directly.* *adj.* —**o blique′ly**, *adv.*

oblique angle, any angle that is not a right angle. Acute angles and obtuse angles are oblique angles.

o bliq ui ty (ə blik′wə tē), 1 indirectness or crookedness of thought or behavior, especially conduct that is not upright and moral. 2 a being oblique. *n.*, *pl.* **o bliq ui ties.**

o blit er ate (ə blit′ə rāt′), remove all traces of; wipe or blot out; efface: *The heavy rain obliterated the footprints.* *v.*, **o blit er at ed, o blit er at ing.**

o blit er a tion (ə blit′ə rā′shən), an obliterating or a being obliterated; effacement. *n.*

o bliv i on (ə bliv′ē ən), 1 condition of being entirely forgotten: *Many ancient cities have long since passed into oblivion.* 2 forgetfulness: *The magic drink caused oblivion of all sorrows.* *n.*

o bliv i ous (ə bliv′ē əs), 1 forgetful; not mindful: *The book was so interesting that I was oblivious of my surroundings.* 2 bringing or causing forgetfulness: *an oblivious slumber.* *adj.*

oblong (def. 2)

ob long (ob′lông), 1 longer than broad: *an oblong loaf of bread.* 2 rectangle that is not a square. 1 *adj.*, 2 *n.*

ob lo quy (ob′lə kwē), 1 public reproach; abuse; blame. 2 disgrace; shame. *n.*, *pl.* **ob lo quies.**

ob nox ious (əb nok′shəs), very disagreeable; offensive; hateful: *Their rudeness and bad manners made them obnoxious to me.* *adj.* —**ob nox′ious ly**, *adv.*

oboe

o boe (ō′bō), a woodwind instrument in which a thin, high-pitched tone is produced by a double reed. *n.*

ob scene (əb sēn′), offending modesty or decency; impure; filthy; vile. *adj.* —**ob scene′ly**, *adv.*

ob scen i ty (əb sen′ə tē), 1 obscene quality. 2 obscene language or behavior; an obscene word or act. *n.*, *pl.* **ob scen i ties.**

ob scure (əb skyúr′), 1 not clearly expressed; hard to understand; vague: *an obscure passage in a book, an obscure style of writing.* 2 not well known; attracting no notice: *an obscure little village, an obscure poet, an obscure position in the government.* 3 not easily discovered; hidden: *an obscure path, an obscure meaning.* 4 not distinct; not clear: *an obscure form, obscure sounds, an obscure view.* 5 dark; dim: *an obscure corner.* 6 make obscure; hide from view; dim; darken: *Clouds obscure the sun. His difficult style obscures his meaning.* 1-5 *adj.*, 6 *v.*, **ob scured, ob scur ing.** —**ob scure′ly**, *adv.*

ob scur i ty (əb skyúr′ə tē), 1 lack of clearness; difficulty in being understood: *The obscurity of the passage makes several interpretations possible.* 2 something obscure; thing hard to understand; point or passage not clearly expressed; doubtful or vague meaning. 3 condition of being unknown: *Lincoln rose from obscurity to fame.* 4 lack of light; dimness: *The dog hid in the obscurity of the thick bushes.* *n.*, *pl.* **ob scur i ties.**

ob se quies (ob′sə kwēz), funeral rites or ceremonies; a stately funeral. *n.pl.*

ob se qui ous (əb sē′kwē əs), polite or obedient from hope of gain or from fear; servile; fawning: *Obsequious courtiers greeted the king. adj.* —**ob se′qui ous ly**, *adv.* —**ob se′qui ous ness**, *n.*

ob serv a ble (əb zėr′və bəl), 1 that can be noticed; noticeable; easily seen: *That distant star is observable on a dark night.* 2 that can be followed or practiced: *This rule may not be observable. adj.*

ob serv a bly (əb zėr′və blē), so as to be observed; to an observable degree. *adv.*

ob serv ance (əb zėr′vəns), 1 act of observing or keeping laws or customs: *the observance of the Sabbath.* 2 act performed as a sign of worship or respect; religious ceremony. 3 observation. *n.*

ob serv ant (əb zėr′vənt), 1 quick to notice; watchful; observing: *If you are observant in the fields and woods, you will find many flowers that others fail to notice.* 2 careful in observing a law, rule, custom, etc.: *A good driver is observant of the traffic rules. adj.* —**ob serv′ant ly**, *adv.*

ob ser va tion (ob′zėr vā′shən), 1 act, habit, or power of seeing and noting: *She is an artist much admired for her close observation of people and places.* 2 fact or condition of being seen; notice: *The spy avoided observation.* 3 something seen and noted: *The student of bird life kept a record of her observations.* 4 act of watching for some special purpose; study: *The observation of nature is important in science.* 5 a remark; comment: *"Haste makes waste," was Father's observation when I spilled the ice cream. n.*

ob ser va tion al (ob′zėr vā′shə nəl), of or based on observation: *observational evidence. adj.*

observatory (def. 1)

ob serv a to ry (əb zėr′və tôr′ē), 1 place or building with a telescope for observing the stars and other heavenly bodies. 2 place or building for observing facts or happenings of nature. 3 a high place or building giving a wide view. *n., pl.* **ob serv a to ries.**

ob serve (əb zėrv′), 1 see and note; notice: *I observed nothing strange in her behavior.* 2 examine for some special purpose; study: *An astronomer observes the stars.* 3 to remark; comment: *"Bad weather," the copilot observed.* 4 keep; follow in practice: *observe silence, observe a rule.* 5 show regard for; celebrate: *observe a holiday. v.,* **observed, ob serv ing.**

ob serv er (əb zėr′vər), person who observes. *n.*

ob serv ing (əb zėr′ving), observant; quick to notice. *adj.*

ob sess (əb ses′), fill the mind of; keep the attention of: *I studied hard because I was obsessed with the fear that I might fail the final exam. v.*

ob ses sion (əb sesh′ən), 1 an obsessing or a being obsessed; influence of a feeling, idea, or impulse that a person cannot escape. 2 the feeling, idea, or impulse itself. *n.*

ob ses sive (əb ses′iv), having to do with or causing obsession: *an obsessive feeling or idea. adj.*

ob sid i an (ob sid′ē ən), a hard, dark, glassy rock that is formed when lava cools. *n.*

ob so les cence (ob′sə les′ns), a passing out of use; getting out of date; becoming obsolete. *n.*

ob so les cent (ob′sə les′nt), passing out of use; tending to become out of date: *Horse carriages are obsolescent. adj.*

ob so lete (ob′sə lēt′ or ob′sə lēt′), 1 no longer in use; disused: *"Eft" (meaning again) is an obsolete word. Wooden warships are obsolete.* 2 not commonly used in the present; out of date; old-fashioned: *We still use this machine though it is obsolete. adj.*

ob sta cle (ob′stə kəl), something that stands in the way or stops progress; hindrance: *A fallen tree was an obstacle to traffic. Lack of money was an obstacle to the success of our plans. n.*

ob stet ric (ob stet′rik), having to do with the care of women before, in, and after childbirth. *adj.*

ob stet ri cal (ob stet′rə kəl), obstetric. *adj.*

ob ste tri cian (ob′stə trish′ən), a doctor who specializes in obstetrics. *n.*

ob stet rics (ob stet′riks), branch of medicine concerned with treating women before, in, and after childbirth. *n.*

ob sti na cy (ob′stə nə sē), 1 a being obstinate; stubbornness: *Obstinacy drove the boy to repeat his statement even after he knew it was wrong.* 2 an obstinate act. *n., pl.* **ob sti na cies.**

ob sti nate (ob′stə nit), 1 not giving in; stubborn: *They were obstinate and wanted to do everything their own way.* 2 hard to control or treat: *an obstinate cough. adj.* —**ob′sti nate ly**, *adv.*

ob strep er ous (əb strep′ər əs),

hat, āge, fär; let, ēqual, tėrm; it, īce; hot, ōpen, ôrder; oil, out; cup, pùt, rüle; ch, child; ng, long; sh, she; th, thin; ŦH, then; zh, measure;

ə represents *a* in about, *e* in taken, *i* in pencil, *o* in lemon, *u* in circus.

1 loud or noisy; boisterous: *Most children are naturally obstreperous when playing games.* 2 unruly; disorderly. *adj.*

ob struct (əb strukt′), 1 make hard to pass through; block up: *Fallen trees obstruct the road.* 2 be in the way of; hinder: *Trees obstruct our view of the ocean. A shortage of materials obstructed the work of the factory. v.*

ob struc tion (əb struk′shən), 1 thing that obstructs; something in the way; obstacle: *The old path was blocked by such obstructions as boulders and fallen trees. Lying and deception are obstructions to justice.* 2 a blocking or hindering: *the obstruction of justice by lies and deception. n.*

ob struc tion ism (əb struk′shə niz′əm), act or practice of hindering the progress of business in a meeting, legislature, etc. *n.*

ob struc tion ist (əb struk′shə nist), person who hinders (progress, legislation, reform, etc.). *n.*

ob struc tive (əb struk′tiv), tending or serving to obstruct; blocking or hindering. *adj.*

ob tain (əb tān′), 1 get through effort; come to have: *obtain a prize, obtain possession of a house one has rented, obtain knowledge through study.* 2 be in use; be customary; prevail: *Different rules obtain in different schools. v.*

ob tain a ble (əb tā′nə bəl), that can be obtained. *adj.*

ob trude (əb trüd′), 1 put forward unasked and unwanted; force: *Don't obtrude your opinions on others.* 2 come unasked and unwanted; force oneself; intrude. 3 push out; thrust forward: *A turtle obtrudes its head from its shell. v.,* **ob trud ed, ob trud ing.**

ob tru sion (əb trü′zhən), 1 an obtruding. 2 something obtruded. *n.*

ob tru sive (əb trü′siv), inclined to obtrude; putting oneself forward; intrusive. *adj.* —**ob tru′sive ly**, *adv.* —**ob tru′sive ness**, *n.*

ob tuse (əb tüs′ or əb tyüs′), 1 not sharp or acute; blunt. 2 slow in understanding; stupid: *They were too obtuse to take the hint.* 3 not sensitive; dull;

adj.	adjective	*n.*	noun
adv.	adverb	*prep.*	preposition
conj.	conjunction	*pron.*	pronoun
interj.	interjection	*v.*	verb
sing.	singular	*pl.*	plural

One's hearing often becomes obtuse in old age. *adj.* —**ob tuse′ness,** *n.*

obtuse angle, angle larger than a right angle but less than 180 degrees.

ob verse (ob′vėrs′), 1 side of a coin, medal, etc., that has the principal design on it. 2 the face of anything that is meant to be turned toward the observer; front. *n.*

ob vi ate (ob′vē āt), meet and dispose of; clear out of the way; remove: *obviate a difficulty, obviate danger, obviate objections. v.,* **ob vi at ed, ob vi at ing.**

ob vi ous (ob′vē əs), easily seen or understood; clear to the eye or mind; not to be doubted; plain: *It is obvious that two plus two does not equal five. The frail and sickly child was in obvious need of food and sunshine. adj.* —**ob′vi ous ly,** *adv.* —**ob′vi ous ness,** *n.*

ocarina

oc a ri na (ok′ə rē′nə), a small wind instrument with holes as in a flute and a mouthpiece like a whistle. It produces a soft sound. *n., pl.* **oc a ri nas.**

oc ca sion (ə kā′zhən), 1 a particular time: *We have met her on several occasions.* 2 a special event: *A royal wedding or a coronation is a splendid occasion.* 3 a good chance; opportunity: *The trip gave us an occasion to get better acquainted.* 4 a cause; reason: *The dog that was the occasion of the quarrel had run away.* 5 to cause; bring about: *His strange behavior occasioned talk.* 1-4 *n.,* 5 *v.*

on occasion, now and then; once in a while.

oc ca sion al (ə kā′zhə nəl), 1 happening or coming now and then, or once in a while: *We had fine weather all through July except for an occasional thunderstorm.* 2 caused by or used for some special time or event: *He composed a piece of occasional music to be played at the inauguration.* 3 for use once in a while: *occasional chairs. adj.*

oc ca sion al ly (ə kā′zhə nə lē), at times; now and then; once in a while. *adv.*

Oc ci dent (ok′sə dənt), 1 countries in Europe and America; the West. The Occident and the Orient have different ideals and customs. 2 **occident,** the west. *n.*

Oc ci den tal (ok′sə den′tl), 1 Western; of the Occident. 2 a native of the West. Europeans are Occidentals. 3 **occidental,** western. 1,3 *adj.,* 2 *n.*

OBTUSE ANGLE   RIGHT ANGLE

oc cip i tal (ok sip′ə təl), of or having to do with the back part of the head or skull. *adj.*

oc clude (o klüd′), 1 stop up (a passage, pores, etc.); close. 2 shut in, out, or off. 3 meet closely. The teeth in the upper jaw and those in the lower jaw should occlude. *v.,* **oc clud ed, oc clud ing.**

oc clu sion (ə klü′zhən), an occluding or a being occluded. *n.*

oc cult (ə kult′ *or* ok′ult), 1 beyond the bounds of ordinary knowledge; mysterious. 2 outside the laws of the natural world; magical: *Astrology and alchemy are occult sciences. adj.*

oc cu pan cy (ok′yə pən sē), act or fact of occupying; holding (land, houses, a pew, etc.) by being in possession: *After five years of occupancy the homesteaders received a title to the land they lived on. n.*

oc cu pant (ok′yə pənt), 1 one that occupies: *The occupant of the shack stepped out as I approached.* 2 person in actual possession of a house, estate, office, etc. *n.*

oc cu pa tion (ok′yə pā′shən), 1 work a person does regularly or to earn his living; business; employment; trade: *Caring for the sick is a nurse's occupation.* 2 an occupying or a being occupied; possession: *the occupation of a house by a family, the occupation of a town by the enemy. n.*

oc cu pa tion al (ok′yə pā′shə nəl), of or having to do with a person's occupation. An occupational hazard or disease is one that results from a person's particular work or occupation. *adj.* —**oc′cu pa′tion al ly,** *adv.*

oc cu pi er (ok′yə pī′ər), one that occupies; occupant. *n.*

oc cu py (ok′yə pī), 1 take up; fill: *The building occupies an entire block. The lessons occupy the morning.* 2 keep busy; engage; employ: *Composing music occupied her attention.* 3 take possession of: *The enemy occupied our*

fort. 4 keep possession of; have; hold: *A judge occupies an important position.* 5 live in: *Two families occupy the house next door. v.,* **oc cu pied, oc cu py ing.**

oc cur (ə kėr′), 1 take place; happen: *Storms often occur in winter.* 2 be found; exist: *"E" occurs in print more than any other letter.* 3 come to mind; suggest itself: *Did it occur to you to close the window? v.,* **oc curred, oc cur ring.**

oc cur rence (ə kėr′əns), 1 an occurring: *The occurrence of storms delayed our trip.* 2 event; happening: *an unexpected occurrence. n.*

o cean (ō′shən), 1 the great body of salt water that covers almost three fourths of the earth's surface; the sea. 2 any of its four main divisions; the Atlantic, Pacific, Indian, and Arctic oceans. The waters around the Antarctic continent are considered by some to form a separate ocean. *n.*

O ce an i a (ō′shē an′ē ə), 1 islands of the central and south Pacific, north, northeast, and east of Australia. 2 these islands, together with Australasia and the Malay Archipelago. *n.*

o ce an ic (ō′shē an′ik), 1 of the ocean: *oceanic islands.* 2 living in the ocean: *oceanic fish.* 3 like the ocean; wide; vast. *adj.*

o cean og ra pher (ō′shə nog′rə fər), an expert in oceanography. *n.*

o cean og ra phy (ō′shə nog′rə fē), branch of physical geography dealing with the ocean. *n.*

o ce lot (ō′sə lot *or* os′ə lot), a spotted wildcat somewhat like a leopard, found from Texas south through Mexico and into parts of South America. *n.*

o cher or **o chre** (ō′kər), 1 any of various earthy mixtures containing clay and iron oxide, ranging in coloring from pale yellow to yellowish brown, used as pigments. 2 a pale brownish yellow. *n.*

o'clock (ə klok′), of the clock; by the clock: *What o'clock is it? It is one o'clock.*

Oct., October.

regular octagon   irregular octagon

oc ta gon (ok′tə gon), a plane figure having eight angles and eight sides. *n.*

oc tag o nal (ok tag′ə nəl), having eight angles and eight sides. *adj.*

oc tane (ok′tān), a colorless, liquid hydrocarbon that occurs in petroleum.

High quality gasoline contains more octane than the lower grades. *n.*

oc tave (ok'tiv *or* ok'tāv), 1 interval between a musical tone and another tone having twice or half as many vibrations. From middle C to the C above it is an octave. 2 the eighth tone above or below a given tone, having twice or half as many vibrations per second. 3 series of tones or of keys of an instrument, filling the interval between a tone and its octave. 4 the sounding together of a tone and its octave. 5 group of eight. *n.*

oc ta vo (ok tā'vō), 1 the page size of a book in which each leaf is one eighth of a whole sheet of paper. 2 having this size. 3 book having this size, usually about 6 by 9 inches. 1,3 *n.*, *pl.* **oc ta vos;** 2 *adj.*

oc tet (ok tet'), 1 piece of music for eight voices or instruments. 2 group of eight singers or players performing together. 3 any group of eight. *n.*

Oc to ber (ok tō'bər), the tenth month of the year. It has 31 days. *n.*

oc to ge nar i an (ok'tə jə ner'ē ən), 1 person who is 80 years old or between 80 and 90 years old. 2 80 years old or between 80 and 90 years old. 1 *n.*, 2 *adj.*

oc to pus (ok'tə pəs), 1 a sea mollusk having a soft body and eight arms with suckers on them; devilfish. 2 anything like an octopus. A powerful, grasping organization with far-reaching influence is often called an octopus. *n.*, *pl.* **oc to pus es, oc to pi** (ok'tə pī).

oc u lar (ok'yə lər), 1 of or having to do with the eye: *an ocular muscle.* 2 received by actual sight; seen: *ocular proof. adj.*

oc u list (ok'yə list), doctor who examines and treats defects and diseases of the eye; ophthalmologist. *n.*

odd (od), 1 left over; extra: *Pay the bill with this money and keep the odd change.* 2 being one of a pair or set of which the rest is missing: *an odd stocking.* 3 occasional: *odd jobs, odd moments, odd numbers or volumes of a magazine.* 4 with some extra: *six hundred-odd children in school, thirty-odd dollars.* 5 leaving a remainder of 1 when divided by 2: *Three, five, and seven are odd numbers.* 6 having an odd number: *the odd symphonies of Beethoven.* 7 strange; peculiar; unusual: *It's odd that I can't remember her name, because her face is surely familiar. adj.* **—odd'ness,** *n.*

odd ball (od'bôl'), SLANG. a very eccentric person. *n.*

odd i ty (od'ə tē), 1 strangeness; peculiarity: *the oddity of wearing a fur coat over a bathing suit.* 2 a strange, unusual, or peculiar person or thing. *n.*, *pl.* **odd i ties.**

odd ly (od'lē), in an odd manner; queerly; strangely. *adv.*

odds (odz), 1 difference in favor of one and against another; advantage. In betting, odds of 3 to 1 mean that the person giving odds will pay 3 if the bet is lost or receive 1 if the bet is won. *The odds are in our favor and we should win.* 2 (in games) an extra allowance given to the weaker side. *n. pl. or sing.*

at odds, quarreling; disagreeing: *My sister and brother were often at odds.*

odds and ends, things left over; extra bits; scraps; remnants: *I went about the house picking up the odds and ends.*

the odds are, the chances are; the probability is: *Since we are a better team, the odds are we will win.*

odds-on (odz'ôn'), having the odds in one's favor; having a good chance to win in a contest. *adj.*

ode (ōd), a lyric poem full of noble feeling expressed with dignity. It is often addressed to some person or thing. *n.*

O der (ō'dər), river flowing from Czechoslovakia through W Poland into the Baltic Sea. In its lower course it is now the boundary between Poland and East Germany. *n.*

octopus (def. 1) from 6 in. to 20 ft. across

O des sa (ō des'ə), seaport in SW Soviet Union, on the Black Sea. *n.*

O din (ō'n), (in Scandinavian myths) the chief god. Odin was the god of wisdom, culture, war, and the dead. The Anglo-Saxons called him Woden. *n.*

o di ous (ō'dē əs), very displeasing; hateful; offensive: *an odious smell, odious lies. adj.* **—o'di ous ly,** *adv.* **—o'di ous ness,** *n.*

o di um (ō'dē əm), 1 hatred; great dislike. 2 reproach; blame: *to bear the odium of having betrayed one's friend. n.*

o dom e ter (ō dom'ə tər), device for measuring distance traveled by a vehicle, by recording the number of revolutions of a wheel. *n.*

o dor (ō'dər), 1 smell or scent: *the odor of roses, the odor of garbage.* 2 reputation: *Three of the students were in bad odor because they were suspected of cheating on the final examination. n.*

o dor if er ous (ō'də rif'ər əs), giving forth an odor, especially a pleasant

hat, āge, fär; let, ēqual, tėrm;
it, īce; hot, ōpen, ôrder;
oil, out; cup, pùt, rüle; ch, child;
ng, long; sh, she; th, thin;
ŦH, then; zh, measure;

ə represents *a* in about,
e in taken, *i* in pencil,
o in lemon, *u* in circus.

odor; fragrant: *The rose is an odoriferous flower. adj.*

o dor less (ō'dər lis), without any odor: *Water is odorless. adj.*

o dor ous (ō'dər əs), giving forth or having an odor, especially a pleasant odor; sweet-smelling; fragrant: *Spices are odorous. adj.*

O dys se us (ō dis'ē əs *or* ō dis'yüs), Ulysses. *n.*

Od ys sey (od'ə sē), 1 a long Greek epic poem describing the ten years of wandering of Ulysses after the Trojan War and his final return home. Homer is supposed to be its author. 2 Also, **odyssey,** any long series of wanderings and adventures. *n., pl.* **Od ys seys.**

Oed i pus (ed'ə pəs *or* ē'də pəs), (in Greek legends) a Greek king who unknowingly killed his father and married his mother. When he learned this, he blinded himself and passed the rest of his life wandering miserably. *n.*

o'er (ôr), OLD USE. over. *prep., adv.*

of (ov *or* uv; *unstressed* əv), 1 belonging to: *the children of a family, a friend of my childhood, the news of the day, the driver of the car, the cause of the quarrel.* 2 made from: *a house of bricks, castles of sand.* 3 that has; containing; with: *a house of six rooms.* 4 that has as a quality: *a look of pity, a word of encouragement, a woman of good judgment.* 5 that is; named: *the city of Chicago.* 6 away from; from: *north of Boston, ten minutes of six, shoot wide of the mark, take leave of a friend.* 7 having to do with; in regard to; concerning; about: *think well of someone, be fond of, be hard of heart, be fifteen years of age.* 8 as a result of having or using; out of; owing to: *expect much of a new medicine, die of grief. She came of a noble family.* 9 among: *a mind of the finest, a friend of mine.* 10 *Of* connects nouns and adjectives having the meaning of a verb with the noun which would be the object of the verb: *the eating of fruit, his drinking of milk, the love of truth, in search of a ball, a hall smelling of onions. prep.*

off (ôf), 1 from the usual or correct position, condition, etc.: *He took off his*

adj.	adjective	*n.*	noun
adv.	adverb	*prep.*	preposition
conj.	conjunction	*pron.*	pronoun
interj.	interjection	*v.*	verb
sing.	singular	*pl.*	plural

hat. 2 from; away from: *I jumped off the step. We are miles off the main road.* 3 away; at or to a distance: *go off on a journey. Christmas is only five weeks off.* 4 so as to stop or lessen: *Turn the water off. The game was called off.* 5 not on; not connected: *A button is off his coat* (prep.). *The electricity is off* (adj.). 6 without work: *an afternoon off* (adv.). *He pursues his hobby during off hours* (adj.). 7 in full; wholly: *She cleared off her desk.* 8 in a specified condition in regard to money, property, etc.: *How well off are the Smiths?* 9 not very good; not up to average: *Bad weather made last summer an off season for fruit.* 10 possible but not likely: *I came on the off chance that I would find you.* 11 on one's way: *The train started and we were off on our trip.* 12 in error; wrong: *Your figures are way off.* 13 on the right-hand side; right: *The near horse and the off horse make a team.* 14 seaward from: *The ship anchored off Maine.* 1,3,4,6,7,11 *adv.*, 2,5,14 *prep.*, 5,6,8-10,12,13 *adj.*

be off, go away; leave quickly.

off and on, at some times and not at others; now and then: *She has lived in Europe off and on for ten years.*

off with, 1 take off. 2 away with!

of fal (ô/fəl), 1 the waste parts of an animal killed for food. 2 garbage; refuse. *n.*

off beat (ôf/bēt/), 1 a musical beat with little or no accent. 2 out of the ordinary; unusual; unconventional: *an offbeat display, offbeat drama.* 1 *n.*, 2 *adj.*

Of fen bach (ô/fən bäk), **Jacques,** 1819-1880, French composer of light operas. *n.*

of fence (ə fens/), offense (the spelling generally used in Great Britain and Canada). *n.*

of fend (ə fend/), 1 hurt the feelings of; make angry; displease; pain: *My friend was offended by my laughter.* 2 affect in an unpleasant or disagreeable way. 3 to sin or do wrong: *In what way have I offended? v.*

of fend er (ə fen/dər), 1 person who offends. 2 person who does wrong or breaks a law: *No trespassing; offenders will be prosecuted. n.*

of fense (ə fens/), 1 a breaking of the

law; crime or sin. Offenses against the law are punished by fines or imprisonment. *Lying and cruelty are offenses.* 2 condition of being offended; hurt feelings; anger: *He tried not to cause offense.* 3 act of offending; hurting someone's feelings: *No offense was meant.* 4 something that offends or causes displeasure. 5 act of attacking; attack: *A gun is a weapon of offense.* 6 an attacking team or force. *n.*

give offense, offend.

take offense, be offended.

of fen sive (ə fen/siv), 1 giving offense; irritating; annoying: *"Shut up" is an offensive remark.* 2 unpleasant; disagreeable; disgusting: *Bad eggs have an offensive odor.* 3 used for attack; having to do with attack: *offensive weapons, an offensive war for conquest.* 4 position or attitude of attack: *The army took the offensive.* 5 an attack: *An all-out offensive against polio was begun when the proper vaccine was developed.* 1-3 *adj.*, 4,5 *n.* —**of fen/sive ly,** *adv.* —**of fen/sive ness,** *n.*

of fer (ô/fər), 1 hold out to be taken or refused; present; proffer: *offer one's hand, offer a gift. She offered us her help.* 2 be willing if another approves: *They offered to help us.* 3 propose; advance; suggest: *offer a price. She offered a few ideas to improve the plan.* 4 to present in worship: *offer prayers.* 5 give or show intention; attempt; try: *The thieves offered no resistance to the policemen. I did not offer to hit back.* 6 present itself; occur: *I will come if the opportunity offers.* 7 act of offering: *an offer of money, an offer to sing, an offer of marriage, an offer of $20,000 for a house.* 1-6 *v.*, 7 *n.*

of fer ing (ô/fər ing), 1 the giving of something as an act of worship. 2 contribution; gift. 3 act of one that offers. *n.*

of fer to ry (ô/fər tôr/ē), 1 collection at a religious service. 2 verses said or the music sung or played while the offering is received. *n., pl.* **of fer to ries.**

off hand (ôf/hand/ *for 1;* ôf/hand/ *for 2-4*), 1 without previous thought or preparation; at once: *The carpenter could not tell offhand how much the work would cost.* 2 done or made offhand: *His offhand remarks were sometimes very wise.* 3 casual; informal. 4 without due courtesy; impolite: *The child's offhand ways angered her parents.* 1 *adv.*, 2-4 *adj.*

of fice (ô/fis), 1 place in which the work of a business or profession is done; room or rooms in which to work: *The doctor's office is on the second floor. The insurance company's office is on Main Street.* 2 position, especially in

the public service: *The President holds the highest office in the United States.* 3 duty of one's position; task; job; work: *A teacher's office is teaching. Her office is to decide on applications for aid.* 4 staff of persons carrying on work in an office: *Half the office is on vacation.* 5 act of kindness or unkindness; attention; service; injury: *Through the good offices of a friend, he was able to get a job.* 6 a religious ceremony or prayer: *There are seven daily offices in the Catholic Church. n.*

of fice hold er (ô/fis hōl/dər), person who holds a public office; government official. *n.*

of fi cer (ô/fə sər), 1 (in the armed forces) person who commands others, especially a person who holds a commission, such as a major, a general, a captain, or an admiral. 2 person who holds a public, church, or government office: *a health officer, a police officer.* 3 the president, vice-president, secretary, treasurer, etc., of a club, society, or similar organization. 4 provide with officers. 5 direct; conduct; manage: *The army was officered by able individuals.* 1-3 *n.*, 4,5 *v.*

of fi cial (ə fish/əl), 1 person who holds a public position or who is in charge of some public work or duty: *The mayor is a government official.* 2 person holding office; officer: *bank officials.* 3 of or having to do with an office or officers: *official duties. Policemen wear an official uniform.* 4 having authority: *an official representative. An official record is kept of the proceedings of Congress.* 5 suitable for a person in office: *the official dignity of a judge.* 1,2 *n.*, 3-5 *adj.* —**of fi/cial ly,** *adv.*

of fi ci ate (ə fish/ē āt), 1 perform the duties of any office or position: *The president officiates as chairman at all club meetings.* 2 perform the duties of a priest, minister, or rabbi: *The rabbi officiated at the bar mitzvah. v.,* **of fi ci at ed, of fi ci at ing.**

of fi cious (ə fish/əs), too ready to offer services or advice; minding other people's business; fond of meddling. *adj.* —**of fi/cious ly,** *adv.* —**of fi/cious ness,** *n.*

off ing (ô/fing), 1 the more distant part of the sea as seen from the shore. 2 position at a distance from the shore. *n.*

in the offing, 1 just visible from the shore. 2 within sight. 3 not far off: *trouble in the offing.*

off ish (ô/fish), INFORMAL. inclined to keep aloof; distant and reserved in manner. *adj.*

off set (ôf/set/ *for 1,2;* ôf/set/ *for 3-6*), 1 make up for; compensate for: *The better roads offset the greater distance.*

2 set off or balance: *offset a trip to the mountains against a summer job.* 3 something which makes up for something else; compensation: *In football, his weight and strength were an offset to his slowness.* 4 a short side shoot from a main stem or root that starts a new plant. 5 any offshoot. 6 process of printing in which the inked impression is first made on a rubber roller and then on the paper, instead of directly on the paper. 1,2 *v.*, **off set, off set ting;** 3-6 *n.*

off shoot (ôf/shüt/), 1 shoot or branch growing out from the main stem of a plant, tree, etc. 2 anything coming, or thought of as coming, from a main part, stock, race, etc.: *an offshoot of a mountain range. n.*

off shore (ôf/shôr/), off or away from the shore: *offshore fisheries (adj.). A wind blowing offshore hindered our sailing near the beach (adv.). adj., adv.*

off side (ôf/sīd/), (in sports) not on the side allowed by the rules: *According to an official, two linemen were offside before the play began. adj.*

off spring (ôf/spring/), the young of a person, animal, or plant; descendant: *Every one of their offspring had red hair. n., pl.* **off spring** or **off springs.**

off stage (ôf/stāj/), away from the part of the stage that the audience can see. *adj.*

off-the-rec ord (ôf/ŦHə rek/ərd), not intended for publication; not to be repeated publicly or issued as news: *an off-the-record opinion. adj.*

oft (ôft), OLD USE. often. *adv.*

of ten (ô/fən), in many cases; many times; frequently: *Blame is often misdirected. We come here often. adv.,* **of ten er, of ten est.**

of ten times (ô/fən tīmz/), often. *adv.*

oft times (ôft/tīmz/), often. *adv.*

o gle (ō/gəl), 1 look at with desire; make eyes at. 2 an ogling look. 1 *v.,* **o gled, o gling;** 2 *n.*

o gler (ō/glər), person who ogles. *n.*

o gre (ō/gər), 1 (in fairy tales) giant or monster that supposedly eats people. 2 a man like such a monster in appearance or character. *n.*

oh or **Oh** (ō), 1 word used before names in addressing persons: *Oh Mary, look!* 2 expression of surprise, joy, grief, pain, and other feelings: *Oh, dear me! interj.* Also, **O.**

O'Hare Airport (ō her/ or ō har/), major international and domestic airport in Chicago, Illinois; world's busiest commercial airport.

O. Henry. See Henry, O.

O hi o (ō hī/ō), one of the north central states of the United States. *Capital:* Columbus. *n.* **—O hi/o an,** *adj., n.*

Ohio River, river in the United States, flowing SW from Pittsburgh into the Mississippi River.

ohm (ōm), measure of electrical resistance. A wire in which one volt produces a current of one ampere has a resistance of one ohm. *n.* [from Georg Ohm, 1787-1854, a German physicist]

oil (oil), 1 any of several kinds of thick, fatty or greasy liquids that are lighter than water, burn easily, and are soluble in alcohol, but not in water. Mineral oils, such as kerosene, are used for fuel; animal and vegetable oils, such as olive oil, are used in cooking, medicine, and in many other ways. Essential oils, such as oil of peppermint, are distilled from plants, leaves, flowers, etc., and are thin and evaporate very quickly. 2 petroleum. 3 put oil on or in: *oil the squeaky hinges of a door.* 4 become oil: *Butter oils when heated.* 5 oil color. 6 an oil painting. 1,2,5,6 *n.*, 3,4 *v.*

strike oil, 1 find oil by boring a hole in the earth. 2 find something very profitable.

oil burner, furnace, ship, etc., that uses oil for fuel.

oil cloth (oil/klôth/), 1 cloth made waterproof by coating it with paint or oil. It is used to cover floors, shelves, tables, etc. 2 piece of this cloth; oilskin: *an oilcloth on a kitchen table. n., pl.* **oil cloths** (oil/klôŦHz/ *or* oil/klôths/).

oil color, 1 paint made by mixing pigment with oil; oil. 2 painting done in such colors.

oil er (oi/lər), 1 person or thing that oils. 2 can with a long spout used in oiling machinery. *n.*

oil i ness (oi/lē nis), oily quality or state. *n.*

oil of vitriol, sulfuric acid.

oil painting, 1 picture painted with oil colors. 2 art of painting with oil colors.

oil skin (oil/skin/), 1 cloth treated with oil to make it waterproof. 2 Usually, **oilskins,** *pl.* coat and trousers made of this cloth. *n.*

oil stone (oil/stōn/), any fine-grained stone which is oiled and used for sharpening tools. *n.*

oil well, well drilled in the earth to get oil.

oil y (oi/lē), 1 of oil: *an oily smell.* 2 containing oil: *oily salad dressing.* 3 covered or soaked with oil: *oily rags.* 4 like oil; smooth; slippery. 5 too smooth; suspiciously or disagreeably smooth: *an oily smile. adj.,* **oil i er, oil i est.**

oint ment (oint/mənt), substance made from oil or fat, often containing medicine, used on the skin to heal, soothe, or beautify it. Cold cream and salve are ointments. *n.*

hat, āge, fär; let, ēqual, tėrm;
it, īce; hot, ōpen, ôrder;
oil, out; cup, pùt, rüle; ch, child;
ng, long; sh, she; th, thin;
ŦH, then; zh, measure;

ə represents *a* in about,
e in taken, *i* in pencil,
o in lemon, *u* in circus.

O jib wa (ō jib/wä), member of a large tribe of American Indians formerly living around Lake Superior; Chippewa. *n., pl.* **O jib wa** or **O jib was.**

O jib way (ō jib/wä), Ojibwa. *n., pl.* **O jib way** or **O jib ways.**

OK (ō/kā/), INFORMAL. 1 all right; correct; approved: *The new schedule was OK (adj.). He's doing OK at work (adv.). "OK, OK!" he yelled (interj.).* 2 endorse; approve. 3 approval. 1 *adj., adv., interj.,* 2 *v.,* **OK'd, OK'ing;** 3 *n., pl.* **OK's.**

O.K. (ō/kā/), OK. *adj., adv. interj., v.,* **O.K.'d, O.K.'ing;** *n., pl.* **O.K.'s.**

okapi
about 5 ft. high
at the shoulder

o ka pi (ō kä/pē), an African mammal related to the giraffe, but smaller, without spots, and with a much shorter neck. *n., pl.* **o ka pis** or **o ka pi.**

o kay (ō/kā/), INFORMAL. OK. *adj., adv., v., interj., n.*

O khotsk (ō kotsk/), **Sea of,** sea east of Siberia and north of Japan. *n.*

O ki na wa (ō/kə nä/wə), largest of the Ryukyu Islands, belonging to Japan. It was administered by the United States from 1945 to 1972. *n.*

Okla., Oklahoma.

O kla ho ma (ō/klə hō/mə), one of the southwestern states of the United States. *Capital:* Oklahoma City. *n.*

Oklahoma City, capital of Oklahoma, in the central part.

o kra (ō/krə), 1 plant cultivated for its sticky pods, which are used in soups and as a vegetable; gumbo. 2 the pods. *n.*

old (ōld), 1 not young; having existed long; aged: *an old wall. We are old friends.* 2 of age; in age: *The baby is ten months old.* 3 not new; not recent;

adj. adjective	*n.* noun
adv. adverb	*prep.* preposition
conj. conjunction	*pron.* pronoun
interj. interjection	*v.* verb
sing. singular	*pl.* plural

made long ago; ancient: *an old excuse, an old tomb, an old debt, an old family.* 4 much worn by age or use: *old clothes.* 5 looking or seeming old; like an old person in wisdom, feebleness, etc.; mature: *That child is old for her years.* 6 having much experience: *be old in wrongdoing.* 7 former: *An old student returned to visit her teacher.* 8 familiar; dear: *good old fellow.* 9 time long ago; the past: *the heroes of old.* 10 the old, old people: *a home for the old.* 1-8 *adj.,* **old er, old est** or **eld er, eld est**; 9,10 *n.* —**old′ness,** *n.*

old age, years of life from about 65 on.

old country, country an emigrant comes from.

old en (ōl′dən), of old; old; ancient: *King Arthur lived in olden times. adj.*

Old English, 1 period in the history of the English language before 1100. 2 language of this period; Anglo-Saxon.

old-fash ioned (ōld′fash′ənd), 1 of an old fashion; out of date in style, construction, etc.: *an old-fashioned dress.* 2 keeping to old ways, ideas, etc.: *an old-fashioned housekeeper. adj.*

Old Glory, flag of the United States; the Stars and Stripes.

old hand, a very skilled or experienced person; expert: *an old hand at marbles.*

old ish (ōl′dish), somewhat old. *adj.*

old-line (ōld′līn′), 1 keeping to old ideas and ways; conservative. 2 having a long history; established. *adj.*

old maid, 1 woman who has not married and seems unlikely to. 2 a prim, fussy person. 3 a simple card game in which players draw cards from each other's hands to make pairs. The player holding the extra queen at the end of the game loses.

old-maid ish (ōld′mā′dish), like, suggesting, or befitting an old maid; prim; fussy. *adj.*

old ster (ōld′stər), INFORMAL. an old or older person. *n.*

Old Testament, the earlier part of the Bible, which contains the religious and social laws of the Hebrews, a record of their history, their important literature, and writings of their prophets.

old-time (ōld′tīm′), of former times; like old times. *adj.*

old-tim er (ōld′tī′mər), INFORMAL.

person who has long been a resident, member, worker, etc. *n.*

Old World, the Eastern Hemisphere; Europe, Asia, and Africa.

old-world (ōld′wėrld′), 1 Also, **Old-World.** of or having to do with the Eastern Hemisphere; not of the New World: *old-world monkeys.* 2 belonging to or characteristic of a former period: *old-world courtesy.* 3 of or having to do with the ancient world: *The mammoth was an old-world elephant. adj.*

o le an der (ō′lē an′dər), a poisonous evergreen shrub with fragrant red, pink, or white flowers. *n.*

o le o (ō′lē ō), oleomargarine. *n.*

o le o mar gar ine (ō′lē ō mär′jər ən or ō′lē ō mär′jə rēn′), a substitute for butter made from vegetable oils; margarine. *n.*

ol fac tor y (ol fak′tər ē), 1 having to do with smelling; of smell. The nose is an olfactory organ. 2 an olfactory organ. 1 *adj.,* 2 *n., pl.* **ol fac tor ies.**

ol i garch (ol′ə gärk), one of the rulers in an oligarchy. *n.*

ol i gar chic (ol′ə gär′kik), of an oligarchy or oligarchs; having to do with rule by a few. *adj.*

ol i gar chi cal (ol′ə gär′kə kəl), oligarchic. *adj.*

ol i gar chy (ol′ə gär′kē), 1 form of government in which a few people have the ruling power. 2 country or state having such a government. Ancient Sparta was really an oligarchy, though it had two kings. 3 the ruling few. *n., pl.* **ol i gar chies.**

ol ive (ol′iv), 1 kind of evergreen tree with gray-green leaves that grows in southern Europe and other warm regions. 2 fruit of this tree, with a hard stone and bitter pulp. Olives are eaten green or ripe as a relish and are used to make olive oil. 3 wood of the olive tree. 4 olive branch. 5 a yellowish green. 6 a yellowish brown. 7 yellowish-green. 8 yellowish-brown. 1-6 *n.,* 7-8 *adj.*

olive branch (defs. 1 and 2)
left, olive branch in bloom
right, olive branches as symbol of peace

olive branch, 1 branch of the olive tree. 2 one or more such branches, used as an emblem or symbol of peace. 3 anything offered as a sign of peace.

olive oil, oil pressed from olives, used in cooking, in medicine, etc.

Ol ives (ol′ivz), **Mount of,** a small

ridge of hills, just east of Jerusalem, where Jesus talked with his disciples. *n.*

O lym pi a (ō lim′pē ə), 1 plain in ancient Greece where the Olympic games were held. 2 capital of Washington, in the W part. *n.*

O lym pi an (ō lim′pē ən), 1 having to do with Olympia in Greece or with Mount Olympus. 2 like a god; heavenly; magnificent; superior: *Olympian calm, Olympian manners.* 3 one of the major Greek gods. 4 contender in the Olympic games. 1,2 *adj.,* 3,4 *n.*

O lym pic (ō lim′pik), 1 of or having to do with Olympia in ancient Greece. 2 of or having to do with Mount Olympus. 3 of or having to do with the Olympic games. 4 **Olympics,** *pl.* Olympic games. 1-3 *adj.,* 4 *n.*

Olympic games, 1 contests in athletics, poetry, and music, held every four years by the ancient Greeks in honor of Zeus. 2 modern athletic contests imitating the athletic contests of these games. They are held once every four years in a different country, and athletes from many nations compete in them.

O lym pus (ō lim′pəs), **Mount,** mountain in NE Greece, where the major Greek gods were supposed to live. *n.*

O ma ha (ō′mə hô or ō′mə hä), city in E Nebraska, on the Missouri River. *n.*

O man (ō män′), country in SE Arabia. *n.*

O mar Khay yám (ō′mär kī yäm′), 1050?-1123?, Persian poet, astronomer, and mathematician who wrote the famous poem *The Rubáiyát.*

om buds man (om′budz mən′), a government official appointed to receive and investigate grievances of citizens against the government. *n., pl.* **ombuds men.**

o meg a (ō meg′ə or ō mē′gə), 1 the last letter of the Greek alphabet (Ω or ω). 2 the last of a series; end. *n.*

om e let or **om e lette** (om′lit), eggs beaten up with milk or water, fried or baked, and then folded over. *n.*

o men (ō′mən), sign of what is to happen; object or event that is believed to mean good or bad fortune: *Spilling salt is said to be an omen of misfortune. n.*

om i nous (om′ə nəs), of bad omen; unfavorable; threatening: *Those black clouds look ominous.* —**om′i nous ly,** *adv.* —**om′i nous ness,** *n.*

o mis sion (ō mish′ən), 1 an omitting or a being omitted: *the omission of a paragraph in copying a story.* 2 thing omitted: *His song was the only omission from the program. n.*

o mit (ō mit′), 1 leave out: *omit a letter in a word.* 2 fail to do; neglect: *omit cleaning up. v.,* **o mit ted, o mit ting.**

om ni bus (om′nə bus), 1 bus. 2 volume of works by a single author or of similar works by several authors: *an omnibus of detective stories.* 3 covering many things at once: *an omnibus law.* 1,2 *n., pl.* **om ni bus es;** 3 *adj.*

om nip o tence (om nip′ə təns), complete power; unlimited power: *the omnipotence of God.* *n.*

om nip o tent (om nip′ə tənt), 1 having all power; almighty. 2 **the Omnipotent,** God. 1 *adj.,* 2 *n.*

om ni pres ence (om′nə prez′ns), presence everywhere at the same time: *God's omnipresence.* *n.*

om ni pres ent (om′nə prez′nt), present everywhere at the same time. *adj.*

om nis cience (om nish′əns), knowledge of everything; complete or infinite knowledge. *n.*

om nis cient (om nish′ənt), knowing everything; having complete or infinite knowledge. *adj.* —**om nis′cient ly,** *adv.*

om niv or ous (om niv′ər əs), 1 eating every kind of food. 2 eating both animal and vegetable food: *Man is an omnivorous animal.* 3 taking in everything; fond of all kinds: *An omnivorous reader reads all kinds of books.* *adj.* —**om niv′or ous ly,** *adv.*

on (ôn *or* on), 1 above and supported by: *The book is on the table.* 2 touching so as to cover, be around, etc.: *a ring on one's finger.* 3 close to: *a house on the shore.* 4 in the direction of; toward: *The workers marched on the Capitol.* 5 against; upon: *The picture is on the wall.* 6 on something: *The walls are up, and the roof is on.* 7 to something: *Hold on, or you may fall.* 8 toward something: *Some played; the others looked on.* 9 farther: *March on.* 10 by means of; by the use of: *This news is on good authority.* 11 in the condition of; in the process of; in the way of: *on half pay, on purpose, on duty.* 12 in or into a condition, process, manner, action, etc.: *Turn the gas on.* 13 taking place: *The race is on.* 14 at the time of; during: *They greeted us on our arrival.* 15 from a time; forward: *later on, from that day on.* 16 concerning; in relation to; in connection with: *a book on animals.* 17 for the purpose of: *I went on an errand.* 18 in addition to: *Defeat on defeat discouraged them.* 19 among: *Who are on the committee?* 1-5,10, 11,14,16-19 *prep.,* 6-9,12,15 *adv.,* 13 *adj.*

and so on, and more of the same.

on and off, at some times and not at others; now and then.

on and on, without stopping: *The music played on and on through the entire evening.*

once (wuns), 1 one time: *He comes once a day.* 2 a single occasion: *Once is*

enough. 3 at some one time in the past; formerly: *a once powerful nation.* 4 even a single time; ever: *if the facts once become known.* 5 if ever; whenever: *Once you cross the river you are safe.* 6 former: *a once friend.* 1,3,4 *adv.,* 2 *n.,* 5 *conj.,* 6 *adj.*

all at once, suddenly: *All at once the lights went out.*

at once, 1 immediately: *Come at once.* 2 at one and the same time: *Everyone started shouting at once.*

for once, for one time at least.

once and again, repeatedly.

once and for all or **once for all,** finally or decisively.

once in a while, at one time or another; now and then: *We see our neighbors on the next farm once in a while.*

once or twice, a few times.

once upon a time, long ago; once.

once-o ver (wuns′ō′vər), SLANG. a short, quick look. *n.*

on com ing (ôn′kum′ing *or* on′kum′ing), 1 approaching or advancing: *oncoming winter.* 2 approach or advance: *the oncoming of the storm.* 1 *adj.,* 2 *n.*

one (wun), 1 the first and lowest whole number; the number 1. 2 being a single unit or individual: *one apple, one dozen.* 3 a single person or thing: *I gave her the one she wanted.* 4 some: *One day you'll be sorry.* 5 some person or thing: *One of Longfellow's poems was selected for the new reader.* 6 any person or thing: *One must work hard to achieve success.* 7 the same: *They held one opinion.* 8 the same person or thing: *In Robert Louis Stevenson's story, the kind Dr. Jekyll and the evil Mr. Hyde were one.* 9 joined together; united: *They replied in one voice.* 10 a certain: *One Lynn Smith was elected.* 1,3 *n.,* 2,4,7,9,10 *adj.,* 5,6,8 *pron.*

all one, 1 exactly the same. 2 making no difference; of no consequence.

at one, in agreement or harmony.

make one, 1 form or be one of a number, assembly, or party. 2 join together; unite in marriage.

one and all, everyone.

one by one, one after another.

one or two, a few.

one another, one the other; each other: *They looked at one another. They were in one another's way.*

O nei da (ō nī′də), member of a tribe of Iroquois Indians formerly living in New York State. *n., pl.* **O nei da** or **O nei das.**

O'Neill (ō nēl′), **Eugene,** 1888-1953, American playwright. *n.*

one ness (wun′nis), 1 quality of being one in number or the only one of its kind; singleness. 2 quality of being the same in kind; sameness. 3 fact of forming one whole; unity. 4 agreement in

mind, feeling, or purpose; harmony. *n.*

on er ous (on′ər əs), hard to take or carry; burdensome; oppressive: *Overtime work is well paid, but it is often onerous.* *adj.*

one self (wun self′), one's own self: *One should not praise oneself.* *pron.*

be oneself, 1 have full control of one's mind or body. 2 act naturally.

one-sid ed (wun′sī′did), 1 seeing only one side of a question; partial; unfair; prejudiced: *The umpire seemed one-sided in his decisions.* 2 uneven; unequal: *If one team is much better than the other, a game is one-sided.* 3 having but one side. 4 on only one side. 5 having one side larger or more developed than the other. *adj.*

one-time (wun′tīm′), of the past; former. *adj.*

one-track (wun′trak′), 1 having only one track. 2 INFORMAL. understanding or doing only one thing at a time; narrow: *a one-track mind.* *adj.*

one-way (wun′wā′), moving or allowing movement in only one direction: *a one-way street, a one-way ticket.* *adj.*

on go ing (ôn′gō′ing *or* on′gō′ing), continuous; uninterrupted. *adj.*

on ion (un′yən), 1 a bulb with a sharp, strong smell and taste, eaten raw and used in cooking. 2 the plant it grows on. *n.*

on look er (ôn′lùk′ər *or* on′lùk′ər), person who watches without taking part; spectator. *n.*

on look ing (ôn′lùk′ing *or* on′lùk′ing), watching; seeing; noticing. *adj.*

on ly (ōn′lē), 1 by itself or themselves; one and no more; sole or single: *an only child. Water is my only drink. This is the only road to the cabin.* 2 merely; just: *She sold only two.* 3 and no one else; and nothing more; and that is all: *Only he remained. I did it only through friendship.* 4 except that; but: *I would have gone, only you objected.* 5 in a class by itself; best; finest: *He is the only writer for my taste.* 6 but then; it must be added that: *We had camped right beside a stream, only the water was not fit to drink.* 1,5 *adj.,* 2,3 *adv.,* 4,6 *conj.*

adj.	adjective	n.	noun
adv.	adverb	prep.	preposition
conj.	conjunction	pron.	pronoun
interj.	interjection	v.	verb
sing.	singular	pl.	plural

if only, I wish: *If only the sun would shine!*

only too, very: *She was only too glad to help us.*

On on da ga (on′ən dô′gə), member of a tribe of Iroquois Indians formerly living in central New York State. *n., pl.* **On on da ga** or **On on da gas.**

on rush (ôn′rush′ *or* on′rush′), a violent forward rush: *He was knocked down by the onrush of water. n., pl.* **on rush es.**

on set (ôn′set′ *or* on′set′), 1 the beginning or start: *The onset of this disease is gradual.* 2 an attack: *The onset of the enemy took us by surprise. n.*

on shore (ôn′shôr′ *or* on′shôr′), toward or on the shore. *adv., adj.*

on side (ôn′sīd′ *or* on′sīd′), (in sports) on the side allowed by the rules; not offside. *adj.*

on slaught (ôn′slôt′ *or* on′slôt′), a vigorous attack: *The pirates made an onslaught on the ship. n.*

Ont., Ontario.

On tar i o (on ter′ē ō), 1 province in Canada, north of the Great Lakes. *Capital:* Toronto. 2 **Lake,** the smallest of the five Great Lakes. *n.*

on to (ôn′tü *or* on′tü), 1 on to; to a position on: *throw a ball onto the roof, get onto a horse.* 2 SLANG. familiar with; aware of: *Before very long, I was onto their tricks. prep.*

o nus (ō′nəs), burden; responsibility: *The onus of housekeeping fell upon the daughters. n., pl.* **o nus es.**

on ward (ôn′wərd *or* on′wərd), toward the front; further on; on; forward: *The crowd around the store window began to move onward* (adv.). *An onward movement began* (adj.). *adv., adj.*

on wards (ôn′wərdz *or* on′wərdz), onward. *adv.*

onyx
before cutting
and polishing

on yx (on′iks), variety of quartz having straight bands of different colors and shades. It is a semiprecious stone used in making cameos. *n.*

oo dles (ü′dlz), INFORMAL. large or unlimited quantities; heaps; loads: *oodles of money. n.pl.*

ooze¹ (üz), 1 pass out slowly through small openings; leak out slowly and quietly: *Blood still oozed from the cut. My courage oozed away as I waited.* 2 a slow flow. 3 something that oozes. 1 *v.,* **oozed, ooz ing;** 2,3 *n.* [Old English *wōs* juice]

ooze² (üz), a soft mud or slime, especially at the bottom of a pond or river or on the ocean bottom. *n.* [Old English *wāse* mud]

oo zy (ü′zē), muddy and soft; slimy: *an oozy meadow. adj.,* **oo zi er, oo zi est.**

o pal (ō′pəl), any of various forms of silica which show beautiful changes of color. Opals are valued as gems. Black opals show brilliant colored lights against a black background; milk opals are milky white with rather pale lights. *n.*

o pal es cence (ō′pə les′ns), a play of colors like that of an opal. *n.*

o pal es cent (ō′pə les′nt), having a play of colors like that of an opal. *adj.*

o paque (ō pāk′), 1 not letting light through; not transparent: *Muddy water is opaque.* 2 not shining; dark; dull: *an opaque star, an opaque light.* 3 obscure; hard to understand. 4 stupid. *adj.* —**o paque′ly,** *adv.* —**o paque′ness,** *n.*

ope (ōp), OLD USE. open. *v.,* **oped, op ing;** *adj.*

o pen (ō′pən), 1 not shut; not closed; letting (anyone or anything) in or out: *Open windows let in the fresh air.* 2 not having its door, gate, lid, etc., closed; not shut up: *an open drawer, an open box, an open house.* 3 not closed in: *an open field, the open sea, an open car.* 4 **the open, a** the open country, air, sea, etc.: *sleep out in the open.* **b** public view or knowledge: *The secret is now out in the open.* 5 having spaces or holes: *open ranks, cloth of open texture.* 6 unfilled; not taken: *a position still open, have an hour open.* 7 that may be entered, used, shared, competed for, etc., by all, or by a person or persons mentioned: *an open meeting, an open market. The race is open to anyone under 15.* 8 not covered or protected; exposed: *an open fire, an open jar, open to temptation.* 9 exposed to general view, knowledge, etc.; not secret: *open war, open disregard of rules.* 10 frank and sincere: *an open heart. Please be open with me.* 11 generous; liberal: *give with an open hand.* 12 make or become open: *open a path through the woods.* 13 have an opening or passage: *This door opens into the dining room.* 14 spread out or unfold: *open a fan, a book, or a letter.* 15 come apart or burst open: *a crack where the earth had*

opened. *The clouds opened and the sun shone through.* 16 start or set up; establish: *She opened a new store.* 17 begin: *open a debate. School opens today.* 18 free from frost: *an open winter.* 19 free from hindrance, especially from ice: *open water on the lake, a river or harbor now open.* 1-3,5-11,18,19 *adj.,* 4 *n.,* 12-17 *v.* —**o′pen ly,** *adv.*

open to, ready to take; willing to consider.

open up, make or become open.

open air, outdoors: *Children like to play in the open air.*

o pen-air (ō′pən er′ *or* ō′pən ar′), outdoor; *an open-air concert. adj.*

o pen-and-shut (ō′pən ən shut′), INFORMAL. simple and direct; obvious; straightforward: *The prosecutor was sure he had an open-and-shut case against the suspect. adj.*

o pen er (ō′pə nər), 1 person or thing that opens. 2 INFORMAL. the first game of a scheduled series. *n.*

o pen-eyed (ō′pən īd′), 1 having eyes wide open as in wonder. 2 having the eyes open; watchful or vigilant; observant. *adj.*

o pen-faced (ō′pən fāst′), 1 having the face uncovered. 2 having a frank face. *adj.*

o pen hand ed (ō′pən han′did), generous; liberal. *adj.* —**o′pen hand′ed ly,** *adv.* —**o′pen hand′ed ness,** *n.*

o pen heart ed (ō′pən här′tid), free in expressing one's real thoughts, opinions, and feelings; candid; frank; unreserved. *adj.* —**o′pen heart′ed ly,** *adv.* —**o′pen heart′ed ness,** *n.*

o pen-hearth process (ō′pən-härth′), process of making steel in a furnace that reflects the heat from the roof onto the raw material.

open house, 1 party or other social event that is open to all who wish to come. 2 an occasion on which an open house is held: *The High School open house is every other Friday evening.*

o pen ing (ō′pə ning), 1 an open or clear space; gap; hole: *an opening in a wall, an opening in the forest.* 2 the first part; the beginning: *the opening of a lecture.* 3 first; beginning: *the opening words of his speech.* 4 a formal beginning: *The opening will be at three o'clock tomorrow afternoon.* 5 place or position that is open or vacant: *an opening for a teller in a bank, an opening for a teacher in a school.* 6 a favorable chance or opportunity: *In talking with your mother, I made an opening to ask her about sending you to camp. As soon as I saw an opening, I got up quickly and left the room.* 7 act of making open or fact of becoming open. 1,2,4-7 *n.,* 3 *adj.*

open letter, letter of protest, criticism, or appeal addressed to a person but published in a newspaper, magazine, etc.

o pen-mind ed (ō/pən mīn/did), having or showing a mind open to new arguments or ideas. *adj.* —**o/pen-mind/ed ly,** *adv.* —**o/pen-mind/ed ness,** *n.*

o pen-mouthed (ō/pən mouŦHd/ or ō/pən moutht/), 1 having the mouth open. 2 gaping with surprise or astonishment. 3 having a wide mouth: *an open-mouthed pitcher. adj.*

o pen ness (ō/pən nis), 1 condition of being open. 2 lack of secrecy. 3 frankness. 4 willingness to consider new ideas or arguments. *n.*

open ses a me (ses/ə mē), 1 the magic command that made the door of the robbers' cave fly open in the story of Ali Baba. 2 anything which removes the barriers to entering a restricted place or to reaching a certain goal.

open shop, factory or business that employs both members of labor unions and nonunion workers on equal terms.

o pen work (ō/pən wėrk/), 1 ornamental work that shows openings. 2 resembling such ornamental work. 1 *n.,* 2 *adj.*

op er a[1] (op/ər ə), a play in which music is an essential and prominent part, featuring arias, choruses, etc., with orchestral accompaniment. *Faust, Lohengrin,* and *Carmen* are well-known operas. *n., pl.* **op er as.** [from Italian *opera,* from Latin *opera* effort, (originally) plural of *opus* work]

op er a[2] (op/ər ə), a plural of **opus.** *n.*

opera glasses

opera glasses, small binoculars for use at the opera and in theaters.

op e rate (op/ə rāt/), 1 be at work; run: *The machinery operates night and day.* 2 keep at work; control or manage: *The company operates three factories. Who operates this elevator?* 3 produce an effect; work; act: *Several causes operated to bring on the war.* 4 produce a desired effect: *The medicine operated quickly.* 5 do something to the body, usually with instruments, to improve or restore health; perform surgery: *The doctor operated on the patient, removing the damaged spleen.* *v.,* **op e rat ed, op e rat ing.**

op e rat ic (op/ə rat/ik), of or like the opera: *operatic music, an operatic so-*

prano. *adj.* —**op/e rat/i cal ly,** *adv.*

op e ra tion (op/ə rā/shən), 1 a working: *The operation of a railroad requires many people.* 2 the way a thing works: *The operation of this machine is simple.* 3 a doing; action; activity: *the operation of brushing one's teeth.* 4 something done to the body, usually with instruments, to improve or restore health: *Taking out the tonsils is a common operation.* 5 movements of soldiers, ships, supplies, etc.: *military and naval operations.* 6 something done to a number or quantity in mathematics. Addition, subtraction, multiplication, and division are the four commonest operations in arithmetic. *n.*

in operation, in action or in use.

op e ra tion al (op/ə rā/shə nəl), 1 of or having to do with operations of any kind. 2 in condition to operate effectively. *adj.*

op er a tive (op/ər ə tiv or op/ə-rā/tiv), 1 in operation; effective: *the laws operative in a community.* 2 worker; laborer: *The company hired a skilled machine operative.* 3 having to do with work or productiveness: *operative sections of a factory.* 4 detective. 1,3 *adj.,* 2,4 *n.*

op er a tor (op/ə rā/tər), 1 person who operates. 2 a skilled worker who runs a machine, telephone, telegraph, etc. 3 person who runs a factory, mine, etc. *n.*

op e ret ta (op/ə ret/ə), a short, amusing opera with some spoken dialogue. *n., pl.* **op e ret tas.**

oph thal mi a (of thal/mē ə), an acute inflammation of the eye or the membrane around the eye, caused by infection or injury and sometimes causing blindness. *n.*

oph thal mol o gist (of/thal mol/ə-jist), doctor who specializes in ophthalmology; oculist. *n.*

oph thal mol o gy (of/thal mol/ə jē), branch of medicine dealing with the structure, functions, and diseases of the eye. *n.*

o pi ate (ō/pē it or ō/pē āt), 1 drug that contains opium and so dulls pain or brings sleep. 2 containing opium. 3 anything that quiets. 4 bringing sleep or ease. 1,3 *n.,* 2,4 *adj.*

o pine (ō pīn/), hold or express an opinion; think: *She opined that the book was exciting.* *v.,* **o pined, o pin ing.**

o pin ion (ə pin/yən), 1 what one thinks; belief not so strong as knowledge; judgment: *I try to learn the facts and form my own opinions.* 2 impression; estimate: *What is your opinion of her as a candidate?* 3 a formal judgment by an expert; professional advice: *He wanted the doctor's opinion about the cause of his headache. n.*

hat, āge, fär; let, ēqual, tėrm;
it, īce; hot, ōpen, ôrder;
oil, out; cup, pùt, rüle; ch, child;
ng, long; sh, she; th, thin;
ŦH, then; zh, measure;

ə represents *a* in about,
e in taken, *i* in pencil,
o in lemon, *u* in circus.

o pin ion at ed (ə pin/yə nā/tid), obstinate or conceited with regard to one's opinions; dogmatic: *He is too opinionated to listen to anybody else. adj.*

o pi um (ō/pē əm), a powerful drug that causes sleep and eases pain. Opium is made from a kind of poppy. *n.*

o pos sum (ə pos/əm), a small mammal that carries its young in a pouch; possum. When it is caught or frightened, it becomes unconscious and appears to be dead. The opossum is common in the southern and eastern United States. *n., pl.* **o pos sums** or **o possum.**

opossum—about 33 in. long with tail

Op pen hei mer (op/ən hī/mər), J. Robert, 1904-1967, American physicist. He directed the building of the first atomic bomb. *n.*

op po nent (ə pō/nənt), 1 person who is on the other side in a fight, game, or discussion; person fighting, struggling, or speaking against another: *He defeated his opponent in the election.* 2 opposing. 1 *n.,* 2 *adj.*

op por tune (op/ər tün/ or op/ər-tyün/), fortunate or well-chosen; suitable; favorable: *You have come at a most opportune moment, for I need your advice. adj.* —**op/por tune/ly,** *adv.* —**op/por tune/ness,** *n.*

op por tun ism (op/ər tü/niz/əm or op/ər tyü/niz/əm), policy or practice of using every opportunity to one's advantage without considering whether such an action is right or wrong in each particular circumstance. *n.*

op por tun ist (op/ər tü/nist or op/ər-tyü/nist), person who uses every opportunity to his advantage, regardless of right or wrong. *n.*

op por tun is tic (op/ər tù nis/tik or

adj. adjective	*n.* noun
adv. adverb	*prep.* preposition
conj. conjunction	*pron.* pronoun
interj. interjection	*v.* verb
sing. singular	*pl.* plural

op′ər tyü nis′tik), of or given to opportunism. *adj.*

op por tu ni ty (op′ər tü′nə tē *or* op′-ər tyü′nə tē), a good chance; favorable time; convenient occasion: *I had an opportunity to earn some money picking blueberries. I have had no opportunity to give him your message, because I have not seen him. n., pl.* **op por tu ni ties.**

op pose (ə pōz′), 1 be against; be in the way of; act, fight, or struggle against; try to hinder; resist: *A cliff opposed our way up the mountain. Many people opposed building a new highway because of the cost.* 2 set up against; place in the way of: *Let us oppose good nature to anger, and smiles to cross words.* 3 put in contrast: *Love is opposed to hate. Night is opposed to day. v.,* **op posed, op pos ing.**

op po site (op′ə zit), 1 placed against; as different in direction as can be; face to face; back to back: *The house straight across the street is opposite to ours.* 2 as different as can be; just contrary: *North and south are opposite directions. Sour is opposite to sweet.* 3 person or thing as different as can be: *Night is the opposite of day. A hero is the opposite of a villain.* 4 opposite to: *opposite the church.* 1,2 *adj.,* 3 *n.,* 4 *prep.* **—op′po site ly,** *adv.* **—op′po site ness,** *n.*

op po si tion (op′ə zish′ən), 1 action against; resistance: *There was some opposition to the workers' request for higher wages.* 2 contrast: *His views are in opposition to mine.* 3 Also, **Opposition. a** a political party opposed to the party which is in power. **b** any party or body of opponents. 4 a placing opposite. *n.*

op press (ə pres′), 1 govern harshly; keep down unjustly or by cruelty: *Governments should not oppress the poor.* 2 weigh down; lie heavily on; burden: *A sense of trouble ahead oppressed my spirits. v.*

op pres sion (ə presh′ən), 1 cruel or unjust treatment; tyranny; persecution; despotism: *Oppression of the poor often leads to revolution. Our camp rules were so strict that we considered them unnecessary oppression.* 2 a heavy, weary feeling. *n.*

op pres sive (ə pres′iv), 1 hard to bear; burdensome: *The great heat was oppressive.* 2 harsh; severe; unjust: *Oppressive measures were taken to crush the rebellion. adj.* **—op pres′sive ly,** *adv.* **—op pres′sive ness,** *n.*

op pres sor (ə pres′ər), person who is cruel or unjust to people under him. *n.*

op pro bri ous (ə prō′brē əs), 1 expressing scorn, reproach, or abuse: *Liar and thief are opprobrious names.* 2 disgraceful; shameful; infamous. *adj.* **—op pro′bri ous ly,** *adv.*

op pro bri um (ə prō′brē əm), disgrace or reproach caused by shameful conduct; infamy; scorn; abuse. *n.*

opt (opt), choose or favor: *The class opted to go on a field trip. v.*

op tic (op′tik), of the eye; of the sense of sight. The **optic nerve** goes from the eye to the brain. *adj.*

op ti cal (op′tə kəl), 1 of the eye or the sense of sight; visual: *an optical illusion. Nearsightedness is an optical defect.* 2 made to assist sight: *Telescopes and microscopes are optical instruments.* 3 of vision and light in relation to each other. *adj.* **—op′ti cal ly,** *adv.*

op ti cian (op tish′ən), maker or seller of eyeglasses and other optical instruments. *n.*

op tics (op′tiks), science that deals with light and vision. *n.*

op ti mal (op′tə məl), most favorable. *adj.*

op ti mism (op′tə miz′əm), 1 tendency to look on the bright side of things. 2 belief that everything will turn out for the best. 3 doctrine that the existing world is the best of all possible worlds. *n.*

op ti mist (op′tə mist), 1 person who looks on the bright side of things. 2 person who believes that everything in life will turn out for the best. *n.*

op ti mis tic (op′tə mis′tik), 1 inclined to look on the bright side of things. 2 hoping for the best: *I am optimistic about the chance of continued good weather.* 3 having to do with optimism. *adj.* **—op′ti mis′ti cal ly,** *adv.*

op ti mum (op′tə məm), the best or most favorable point, degree, amount, etc., for the purpose. *n., pl.* **op ti mums,** *or* **op ti ma** (op′tə mə).

op tion (op′shən), 1 right or freedom of choice: *Pupils in our school have the option of taking Spanish, French, or German.* 2 act of choosing: *Where to travel should be left to each person's option.* 3 right to buy or sell something at a certain price within a certain time: *She paid $500 for an option on the land. n.*

op tion al (op′shə nəl), left to one's choice; not required: *Attendance at graduation is optional. adj.* **—op′tion al ly,** *adv.*

op tom e trist (op tom′ə trist), person skilled in examining the eyes and prescribing eyeglasses. An optometrist is not an M.D. but is legally authorized to do such work. *n.*

op tom e try (op tom′ə trē), measurement of the powers of sight; practice or occupation of testing eyes in order to fit them with glasses. *n.*

op u lence (op′yə ləns), 1 much money or property; wealth; riches. 2 abundance; plenty. *n.*

op u lent (op′yə lənt), 1 having wealth; rich. 2 abundant; plentiful. *adj.*

o pus (ō′pəs), a work or composition: *The violinist played her own opus, No. 16. n., pl.* **op er a** *or* **o pus es.**

or (ôr), 1 word used to express a choice, or a difference, or to connect words or groups of words of equal importance in the sentence: *You can go or stay. Is it sweet or sour?* 2 and if not; otherwise: *Either eat this or go hungry. Hurry, or you will be late.* 3 that is; being the same as: *an igloo or Eskimo snowhouse. This is the end or last part. conj.*

-or, *suffix added to verbs to form nouns.* person or thing that _____s: *Actor = person who acts. Accelerator = thing that accelerates.* [from French before the 1400's *-our,* from Latin *-or*]

o ra cle (ôr′ə kəl), 1 (in ancient times) an answer believed to be given by a god through a priest or priestess to some question. It often had a hidden meaning that was hard to understand. 2 place where the god was believed to give such answers. A famous oracle was at Delphi. 3 the priest, priestess, or other means by which the god's answer was believed to be given. 4 a very wise person. 5 something regarded as a reliable and sure guide. *n.*

o rac u lar (ô rak′yə lər), 1 of or like an oracle. 2 with a hidden meaning that is difficult to make out. 3 very wise. *adj.* **—o rac′u lar ly,** *adv.*

o ral (ôr′əl), 1 using speech; spoken: *An oral agreement is not enough; we must have a written promise.* 2 of the mouth: *The oral opening in an earthworm is small. adj.*

o ral ly (ôr′ə lē), 1 by spoken words. 2 by the mouth. *adv.*

o range (ôr′inj), 1 a round, reddish-yellow, juicy citrus fruit that is good to eat. Oranges grow in warm climates. 2 the tree it grows on. The orange is an evergreen with fragrant white blossoms. 3 reddish-yellow. 4 a reddish yellow. 1,2,4 *n.,* 3 *adj.*

o range ade (ôr′inj ād′), a drink made of orange juice, sugar, and water. *n.*

orange pekoe, a black tea that

comes from Ceylon or India. **o rang-ou tang** (ô rang′ù tang′), orangutan. *n.*

o rang u tan (ô rang′ù tan′), a large ape of the forests of Borneo and Sumatra, that has very long arms and long, reddish-brown hair. It lives mostly in trees and eats fruits and leaves. *n.*

orangutan
about 4 1/2 ft. tall

o rate (ô rāt′), make an oration; talk in a grand manner. *v.,* **o rat ed, o rat ing.**

o ra tion (ô rā′shən), a formal public speech delivered on a special occasion: *the orations of Cicero. n.*

o ra tor (ôr′ə tər), 1 person who makes an oration. 2 person who can speak very well in public. *n.*

o ra tor i cal (ôr′ə tôr′ə kəl), 1 of oratory; having to do with orators or oratory: *an oratorical contest.* 2 characteristic of orators or oratory: *She often talks in an oratorical manner. adj.* —**o′ra tor′i cal ly,** *adv.*

o ra to ri o (ôr′ə tôr′ē ō), a musical composition, usually based on a religious theme, for solo voices, chorus, and orchestra, dramatic in character but performed without action, costumes, or scenery. *n., pl.* **o ra to ri os.**

o ra to ry[1] (ôr′ə tôr′ē), 1 skill in public speaking; fine speaking. 2 the art of public speaking. *n.* [from Latin *(ars) oratoria* oratorical (art), from *orare* plead, speak formally]

o ra to ry[2] (ôr′ə tôr′ē), a small chapel; room set apart for prayer. *n., pl.* **o ra to ries.** [from Latin *oratorium,* from *orare* plead, pray]

orb (ôrb), 1 anything round like a ball; sphere; globe. 2 sun, moon, planet, or star. 3 the eyeball or eye. 4 form into a circle or sphere. 1-3 *n.,* 4 *v.*

or bit (ôr′bit), 1 the curved, usually elliptical, path of a heavenly body, planet, or satellite about another body in space: *the earth's orbit about the sun, the moon's orbit about the earth, the*

orbits
(def. 1)

orbit of a weather satellite about the earth. 2 the curved path of an electron about the nucleus of an atom. 3 travel in an orbit or go into an orbit: *Some artificial satellites can orbit the earth in less than an hour.* 4 put into an orbit. 5 the socket in which the eyeball is set. 1,2,5 *n.,* 3,4 *v.*

or bit al (ôr′bə təl), of an orbit. *adj.*

or chard (ôr′chərd), 1 piece of ground on which fruit trees are grown. 2 the trees in an orchard: *The orchard should bear a good crop this year. n.*

or ches tra (ôr′kə strə), 1 group of musicians playing together on various stringed, wind, and percussion instruments. Orchestras usually play at concerts, operas, or plays. 2 the violins, cellos, clarinets, and other instruments played together by such a group. 3 the part of a theater just in front of the stage, where the musicians sit to play. 4 the main floor of a theater, especially the part near the front: *Buy two seats in the orchestra. n., pl.* **or ches tras.**

or ches tral (ôr kes′trəl), of an orchestra; composed for or performed by an orchestra. *adj.*

or ches trate (ôr′kə strāt), compose or arrange (music) for performance by an orchestra. *v.,* **or ches trat ed, or ches trat ing.**

or ches tra tion (ôr′kə strā′shən), arrangement of music for an orchestra. *n.*

or chid (ôr′kid), 1 any of a group of plants with beautiful flowers that often have strange shapes and colors. 2 its flower. An orchid has three petals. 3 light-purple. 4 a light purple. 1,2,4 *n.,* 3 *adj.*

or dain (ôr dān′), 1 pass as a law; order; fix; decide; appoint: *The law ordains that all citizens shall have equal rights.* 2 appoint or consecrate officially as a clergyman. *v.*

or deal (ôr dēl′), 1 a severe test or experience: *I dreaded the ordeal of a visit to the dentist.* 2 (in early times) an effort to decide the guilt or innocence of an accused person by making him do something dangerous like holding fire or taking poison. The idea was that God would not let an innocent person be harmed by such danger. *n.*

or der (ôr′dər), 1 the way one thing follows another: *in order of size, in alphabetical order, to copy them in order.* 2 condition in which every part or piece is in its right place: *put a room in order.* 3 put in proper condition; arrange: *order one's affairs.* 4 condition; state: *My affairs are in good order.* 5 the way the world works; way things happen: *the order of nature.* 6 state or condition of things in which the law is obeyed and there is no trouble: *keep*

order

hat, āge, fär; let, ēqual, tėrm;
it, īce; hot, ōpen, ôrder;
oil, out; cup, pùt, rüle; ch, child;
ng, long; sh, she; th, thin;
ŦH, then; zh, measure;

ə represents *a* in about,
e in taken, *i* in pencil,
o in lemon, *u* in circus.

order. Order was established. Perfect order reigned throughout the country after the revolution. 7 principles and rules by which a meeting is run. 8 a command; telling what to do: *Our parents expect us to obey their orders.* 9 tell what to do; command; bid; give an order: *The teacher ordered the noisy students to be quiet.* 10 give orders or directions: *Please order for me.* 11 a paper saying that money is to be given or paid, or something handed over: *a postal money order.* 12 a spoken or written request for goods that one wants to buy or receive: *Mother gave the grocer an order for two dozen eggs, a loaf of bread, and two cans of tomatoes.* 13 goods so requested: *Mother asked when they would deliver our order.* 14 give (a store, etc.) an order for: *Father ordered milk, eggs, and bread from the grocer.* 15 decide; will: *The gods ordered it otherwise.* 16 kind or sort: *have ability of a high order.* 17 group of related animals or plants ranking below a class and above a family. The rose family, the pea family, and several others belong to one order. 18 a social rank, grade, or class: *all orders of society.* 19 rank or position in the church: *the order of bishops.* 20 a society of monks, friars, or nuns: *the Franciscan order.* 21 society to which one is admitted as an honor: *the Order of the Golden Fleece.* 22 a modern fraternal organization: *the Order of Masons.* 23 the badge worn by those belonging to an honorary order. 24 any of several styles of columns and architecture: *the Doric, Ionic, and Corinthian orders of Greek architecture.* 25 a regular form of worship for a given occasion. 26 portion or serving of food

DORIC   IONIC   CORINTHIAN

order (def. 24)
portions of columns illustrating
three orders of Greek architecture

adj.	adjective	*n.*	noun
adv.	adverb	*prep.*	preposition
conj.	conjunction	*pron.*	pronoun
interj.	interjection	*v.*	verb
sing.	singular	*pl.*	plural

served in a restaurant, etc. 1,2,4-8,11-13,16-26 *n.*, 3,9,10,14,15 *v.*

by order, according to an order given by the proper person: *The bank was closed by order of the governor.*

call to order, ask to be quiet and start work: *The chairman called the meeting to order.*

in order, 1 in the right arrangement or condition. 2 working right. 3 allowed by the rules of a meeting, etc.

in order that, so that; with the aim that.

in order to, as a means to; with a view to; for the purpose of: *She worked hard in order to win the prize.*

in short order, quickly: *They got the broken window replaced in short order.*

on order, having been ordered but not yet received.

on the order of, somewhat like; similar to.

order about or **order around,** send here and there; tell to do this and that.

out of order, 1 in the wrong arrangement or condition. 2 not working right. 3 against the rules of a meeting, etc.

take (holy) orders, become ordained as a Christian minister or priest.

to order, according to the buyer's wishes.

ordered pair, a set of two numbers in which one number is considered as the first and the other as the second.

or der li ness (ôr′dər lē nis), orderly condition or behavior. *n.*

or der ly (ôr′dər lē), 1 in order; with regular arrangement, method, or system: *an orderly arrangement of dishes on shelves, an orderly mind.* 2 keeping order; well-behaved or regulated: *an orderly class.* 3 soldier who attends a superior officer to carry orders, etc.: *The general's orderly delivered the message.* 4 a hospital attendant who keep things clean and in order. 1,2 *adj.*, 3,4 *n., pl.* **or der lies.**

or di nal number (ôrd′n əl), number that shows order or position in a series. First, second, third, etc., are ordinal numbers; one, two, three, etc., are cardinal numbers.

or di nance (ôrd′n əns), rule of law made by authority; decree: *a city ordinance that outlaws firecrackers. n.*

or di nar i ly (ôrd′n er′ə lē), 1 usually; regularly; normally: *We ordinarily go to the movies on Saturday.* 2 to the usual extent. *adv.*

or di nar i ness (ôrd′n er′ē nis), ordinary quality or condition; commonness: *the ordinariness of these stories. n.*

or di nar y (ôrd′n er′ē), 1 according to habit or custom; usual; regular; normal: *an ordinary day's work. My ordinary lunch is a sandwich.* 2 not special; common; everyday; average: *an ordinary person, an ordinary situation.* 3 somewhat below the average: *The speaker was ordinary and tiresome. adj.*

out of the ordinary, not regular or customary; unusual; extraordinary.

or di na tion (ôrd′n ā′shən), 1 act or ceremony of ordaining a person to the ministry of a church. 2 a being ordained as a clergyman: *An ordination gives a person the right to conduct a marriage or a funeral. n.*

ord nance (ôrd′nəns), 1 cannon or artillery. 2 military weapons of all kinds. *n.*

ore (ôr), mineral or rock containing enough of a metal or metals to make mining it profitable. The ore may be found in its natural state or chemically combined with other substances. *n.*

Ore. or **Oreg.,** Oregon.

O re gon (ôr′ə gən *or* ôr′ə gon), one of the Pacific states of the United States. *Capital:* Salem. *n.* **—O re go ni an** (ôr′ə gō′nē ən), *adj., n.*

Oregon Trail, trail from Missouri northwest into Oregon, much used by early pioneers and settlers in the 1800's.

O res tes (ô res′tēz), (in Greek legends) the son of Agamemnon and Clytemnestra, who killed his mother because she had murdered his father. He was pursued by the Furies for this crime. *n.*

or gan (ôr′gən), 1 a musical instrument made of pipes of different lengths, which are sounded by air blown by a bellows and played by keys. Organs are used especially in church. 2 any of certain smaller instruments somewhat like the pipe organ but sounded by electronic devices. 3 any of various other musical instruments, such as a hand organ, a reed organ, or a mouth organ. 4 any part of an animal or plant that is composed of various tissues organized to perform some particular function. The eyes, stomach, heart, and lungs are organs of the body. Stamens and pistils are organs of flowers. 5 means of action; instrument: *A court is an organ of government.* 6 a newspaper or magazine that speaks for and gives the views of a political party or some other organization. *n.*

or gan dy or **or gan die** (ôr′gən dē′), a fine, thin, stiff muslin, used for dresses, curtains, etc. *n., pl.* **or gan dies.**

organ grinder, person who plays a hand organ by turning a crank.

or gan ic (ôr gan′ik), 1 of the bodily organs; vital; affecting the structure of an organ: *an organic disease.* 2 of, having to do with, or obtained from plants or animals: *organic fertilizer.* 3 (in chemistry) of or having to do with organic compounds containing carbon. Starch is an organic compound. Organic chemistry deals with carbon compounds found in food, fuels, etc. 4 made up of related parts, but being a unit; coordinated: *The United States is an organic whole made up of 50 states.* 5 that is part of the structure or constitution of a person or thing; fundamental: *The Constitution is the organic law of the United States. adj.* **—or gan′i cal ly,** *adv.*

or gan ism (ôr′gə niz′əm), 1 a living body made up of separate parts, such as cells, tissues, and organs, which work together to carry on the various processes of life; an individual animal or plant. 2 a whole made up of related parts that work together. Human society, or any community, may be spoken of as a social organism. *n.*

or gan ist (ôr′gə nist), person who plays an organ: *a church organist. n.*

or gan i za tion (ôr′gə nə zā′shən), 1 group of persons united for some purpose. Churches, clubs, and political parties are organizations. 2 an organizing; grouping and arranging parts to form a whole: *The organization of a big picnic takes time and thought.* 3 the way in which a thing's parts are arranged to work together: *The organization of the human body is very complicated.* 4 thing made up of related parts, each having a special duty: *A tree is an organization of roots, trunk, branches, leaves, and fruit. n.*

or gan ize (ôr′gə nīz), 1 put into working order; get together and arrange: *We helped our teacher organize a trip to the city zoo.* 2 combine in a company, political party, labor union, etc. *v.,* **or gan ized, or gan iz ing.**

or gan iz er (ôr'gə nī'zər), person who organizes or brings elements or parts together. *n.*

or gy (ôr'jē), 1 a wild, drunken revel. 2 **orgies,** *pl.* secret rites or ceremonies in the worship of certain Greek and Roman gods, especially the god of wine, celebrated with drinking, wild dancing, and singing. *n., pl.* **or gies.**

o ri el (ôr'ē əl), a bay window projecting from the outer face of a wall. *n.*

oriel

o ri ent (ôr'ē ənt *for 1-3,7,8;* ôr'ē ent *for 4-6*), 1 the east. 2 **Orient,** the East; eastern countries. China and Japan are important nations of the Orient. The Orient usually includes Asia and countries east and southeast of the Mediterranean. 3 eastern. 4 to place so as to face the east. 5 to place so as to face any indicated direction: *The building is oriented north and south.* 6 to place in the right position. 7 bright; shining: *an orient pearl.* 8 rising: *the orient sun.* 1,2 *n.,* 3,7,8 *adj.,* 4-6 *v.*

orient oneself, get in the right relations to the things or persons about one: *orient oneself on coming to a new city, orient oneself in the group of people one is to work with.*

O ri en tal (ôr'ē en'tl), 1 Eastern; of the Orient: *The Oriental way of life is quite different from ours.* 2 a native of the East. Turks, Arabs, Iranians, Indians, and Chinese are Orientals. 3 **oriental,** eastern. 1,3 *adj.,* 2 *n.*

o ri en tal ist or **O ri en tal ist** (ôr'ē en'tl ist), person skilled in Oriental languages, literature, history, etc. *n.*

o ri en tate (ôr'ē en tāt), orient. *v.,* **o ri en tat ed, o ri en tat ing.**

o ri en ta tion (ôr'ē en tā'shən), 1 an orienting or a being oriented. 2 a finding out of the actual facts or conditions and putting oneself in the right relation to them. *n.*

o ri fice (ôr'ə fis), an opening or hole; mouth: *the orifice of a tube or pipe. n.*

o ri ga mi (ôr'ə gä'mē), the Japanese art of folding paper to make decorative objects, such as birds and flowers. *n.*

o ri gin (ôr'ə jin), 1 thing from which anything comes; starting point; source:

beginning: *the origin of a quarrel, the origin of a disease.* 2 parentage, ancestry, or birth: *Joan of Arc was a woman of humble origin.* 3 the point where the horizontal and vertical axes cross in a system of coordinates. *n.*

o rig i nal (ə rij'ə nəl), 1 belonging to the beginning; first; earliest: *The Dutch were the original settlers of New York. The hat has been marked down from its original price.* 2 new; fresh; novel: *It is hard to plan original games for a party.* 3 able to do, make, or think something new; inventive: *a very original writer.* 4 not copied, imitated, or translated from something else: *She wrote an original poem.* 5 thing from which another is copied, imitated, or translated: *The original of this picture is in Rome.* 6 the language in which a book was first written: *Our teacher can read the Greek poets in the original.* 7 an unusual or peculiar person. 8 origin; source. 1-4 *adj.,* 5-8 *n.*

o rig i nal i ty (ə rij'ə nal'ə tē), 1 ability to do, make, or think up something new. 2 freshness; novelty. 3 a being original. *n.*

o rig i nal ly (ə rij'ə nə lē), 1 by origin: *a plant originally African.* 2 at first; in the first place: *a house originally small.* 3 in an original manner: *We want this room decorated originally. adv.*

o rig i nate (ə rij'ə nāt), 1 cause to be; invent: *originate a new style of painting.* 2 come into being; begin; arise: *Where did that story originate? v.,* **o rig i nat ed, o rig i nat ing.**

o rig i na tion (ə rij'ə nā'shən), an originating; origin. *n.*

o rig i na tor (ə rij'ə nā'tər), person who originates; inventor. *n.*

O ri no co (ôr'ə nō'kō), large river in South America, flowing through Venezuela into the Atlantic. *n.*

o ri ole (ôr'ē ōl), 1 any of several American songbirds having yellow-and-black or orange-and-black feathers. 2 any of several European birds having yellow-and-black feathers. *n.*

O ri on (ō rī'ən), constellation near the equator of the celestial sphere that contains the extremely bright star Betelgeuse. To the ancients it suggested a man wearing a belt and a sword and holding a shield and a club. *n.*

o ri son (ôr'ə zən), OLD USE. prayer. *n.*

Ork ney Islands (ôrk'nē), group of islands northeast of, and belonging to, Scotland.

Or lé ans (ôr'lē ənz), city in central France. Joan of Arc was called the **Maid of Orléans** after she led the French against the English there in 1429. *n.*

Or lon (ôr'lon), trademark for a lightweight synthetic fiber that resists sun,

hat, āge, fär; let, ēqual, tėrm; it, īce; hot, ōpen, ôrder; oil, out; cup, pùt, rüle; ch, child; ng, long; sh, she; th, thin; ŦH, then; zh, measure;

ə represents *a* in about, *e* in taken, *i* in pencil, *o* in lemon, *u* in circus.

rain, and acids. It is used for clothing, sails, awnings, etc. *n.*

Or ly (ôr'lē), small town near Paris, site of a major international airport. *n.*

or na ment (ôr'nə mənt *for 1-3;* ôr'nə ment *for 4*), 1 something pretty or decorative; something to add beauty; adornment; decoration: *Lace, jewels, vases, and statues are ornaments.* 2 use of ornaments. 3 person or act that adds beauty, grace, or honor: *The famous painter was an ornament to the age he lived in.* 4 add beauty to; make more pleasing or attractive; adorn; decorate. 1-3 *n.,* 4 *v.*

or na men tal (ôr'nə men'tl), 1 of or having to do with ornament. 2 for ornament; used as an ornament: *ornamental plants.* 3 decorative: *ornamental designs in wallpaper. adj.* —**or'na men'tal ly,** *adv.*

or na men ta tion (ôr'nə men tā'shən), 1 an ornamenting or a being ornamented. 2 decorations; ornaments: *The pilgrim was dressed simply, with no ornamentation. n.*

or nate (ôr nāt'), much adorned; much ornamented: *an ornate vase. adj.* —**or nate'ly,** *adv.* —**or nate'ness,** *n.*

or ner y (ôr'nər ē), INFORMAL. mean in disposition: *an ornery horse. adj.,* **or ner i er, or ner i est.**

or ni thol o gist (ôr'nə thol'ə jist), an expert in ornithology. *n.*

or ni thol o gy (ôr'nə thol'ə jē), branch of zoology dealing with the study of birds. *n.*

o ro tund (ôr'ə tund), 1 strong, full, rich, and clear in voice or speech. 2 pompous; bombastic. *adj.*

or phan (ôr'fən), 1 child whose parents are dead; child whose father or mother is dead. 2 of or for such a child or children: *an orphan asylum.* 3 without a father or mother or both. 4 make an orphan of: *The war orphaned him at an early age.* 1 *n.,* 2,3 *adj.,* 4 *v.*

or phan age (ôr'fə nij), 1 home for orphans. 2 a being an orphan. *n.*

Or phe us (ôr'fē əs *or* ôr'fyüs), (in Greek myths) a musician who played his lyre so sweetly that animals and even trees and rocks followed him. *n.*

oryx
about 5 ft. high
at the shoulder

adj.	adjective	*n.*	noun
adv.	adverb	*prep.*	preposition
conj.	conjunction	*pron.*	pronoun
interj.	interjection	*v.*	verb
sing.	singular	*pl.*	plural

or ris (ôr′is), 1 orrisroot. 2 plant that it grows on; kind of iris. *n.*

or ris root (ôr′is rüt′ *or* ôr′is rüt′), a fragrant rootstock of a variety of iris, used in making perfume, toothpowder, etc. *n.*

or tho don tia (ôr′thə don′chə), orthodontics. *n.*

or tho don tics (ôr′thə don′tiks), branch of dentistry that deals with straightening and adjusting teeth. *n.*

or tho don tist (ôr′thə don′tist), dentist who specializes in orthodontics. *n.*

or tho dox (ôr′thə doks), 1 generally accepted, especially in religion. 2 having generally accepted views or opinions, especially in religion; adhering to established customs and traditions: *an orthodox Methodist, an orthodox Jew.* 3 approved by convention; usual; customary: *the orthodox Thanksgiving dinner of turkey. adj.*

Orthodox Church, Eastern Church.

or tho dox y (ôr′thə dok′sē), the holding of correct or generally accepted beliefs; orthodox practice, especially in religion; being orthodox. *n., pl.* **or tho dox ies.**

or tho graph ic (ôr′thə graf′ik), 1 having to do with orthography. 2 correct in spelling. *adj.* —**or′tho graph′i cal ly,** *adv.*

or thog ra phy (ôr thog′rə fē), 1 correct spelling; spelling considered as right or wrong. 2 art of spelling; study of spelling. 3 any system of spelling. *n., pl.* **or thog ra phies.**

or tho pe dics (ôr′thə pē′diks), branch of surgery that deals with the deformities and diseases of bones and joints, especially in children. *n.*

or tho pe dist (ôr′thə pē′dist), surgeon who specializes in orthopedics. *n.*

Or well (ôr′wel), **George,** 1903-1950, English novelist and essayist. *n.*

-ory, *suffix forming adjectives and nouns.* 1 _____*ing: Contradictory = contradicting.* 2 of or having to do with _____*ion; characterized by* _____*ion: Illusory = of or having to do with illusion. Compulsory = characterized by compulsion.* 3 *serving to* _____*: Preparatory = serving to prepare.* 4 *tending to* _____*; inclined to* _____*: Conciliatory = inclined to conciliate.* 5 *place or establishment for*

_____*ing: Depository = place for depositing.* [from French before the 1400's *-oir, -oire,* from Latin *-orius, -oria, -orium*]

o ryx (ôr′iks), an African antelope with long, nearly straight horns. *n., pl.* **o ryx es** or **o ryx.**

O sa ka (ō sä′kə), large city and seaport in S Japan. *n.*

os cil late (os′l āt), 1 swing to and fro like a pendulum; move to and fro between two points. 2 vary between opinions, purposes, etc. 3 cause an electric current to alternate at a high frequency. *v.,* **os cil lat ed, os cil lat ing.**

os cil la tion (os′l ā′shən), 1 a swinging to and fro like a pendulum. 2 a single swing of a vibrating body: *Each oscillation of the pendulum takes one second.* 3 a single backward and forward surge of a charge of electricity. *n.*

os cil la tor (os′l ā′tər), 1 person or thing that oscillates. 2 device which converts direct current into an alternating current of a particular frequency. The oscillator in a radio transmitting apparatus is a vacuum tube which produces the carrier wave for a radio signal. *n.*

os cu late (os′kyə lāt), to kiss. *v.,* **os cu lat ed, os cu lat ing.**

os cu la tion (os′kyə lā′shən), 1 act of kissing. 2 a kiss. *n.*

o sier (ō′zhər), kind of willow whose branches are used in making baskets or other wickerwork. *n.*

O si ris (ō sī′ris), one of the chief gods of ancient Egypt, ruler of the lower world and judge of the dead. He represented good and productivity and is identified with the Nile. *n.*

Os lo (oz′lō), capital of Norway, in the SE part. *n.*

os mi um (oz′mē əm), a hard, heavy, bluish-white, metallic element which occurs with platinum and iridium. Osmium is the heaviest or densest known element and is used for electric-light filaments and phonograph needles. *n.*

os mo sis (oz mō′sis), 1 the tendency of two fluids of different strengths that are separated by something porous to go through it and become mixed. Osmosis is the chief means by which the body absorbs food. Fluid in the tissues moves into the blood vessels by osmosis. 2 (in chemistry) the diffusion or spreading of fluids through a membrane or partition till they are mixed. 3 a gradual, often unconscious, absorbing of facts, theories, ideas, etc.: *to learn by osmosis. n.*

os mot ic (oz mot′ik), of or having to do with osmosis. *adj.*

os prey (os′prē), a large hawk that feeds on fish; fish hawk. *n., pl.* **os preys.**

Os sa (os′ə), **Mount,** mountain in NE Greece. *n.*

os se ous (os′ē əs), 1 bony. 2 containing bones. *adj.*

os si fi ca tion (os′ə fə kā′shən), 1 process of changing into bone. 2 being changed into bone. 3 a part that is ossified. *n.*

os si fy (os′ə fī), 1 change into bone; become bone: *The soft parts of a baby's skull ossify as he grows older.* 2 harden like bone; make or become fixed, hardhearted, or very conservative. *v.,* **os si fied, os si fy ing.**

os ten si ble (o sten′sə bəl), according to appearances; apparent; pretended; professed: *My ostensible purpose for going to the library was to study, but I was really reading magazines. adj.*

os ten si bly (o sten′sə blē), on the face of it; as openly stated or shown; apparently: *Though ostensibly studying his history, he was really drawing pictures behind the big book. adv.*

os ten ta tion (os′ten tā′shən), a showing off; display intended to impress others: *the ostentation of a newly rich family. n.*

os ten ta tious (os′ten tā′shəs), 1 done for display; intended to attract notice: *They drove their new car up and down in front of our house in an ostentatious way.* 2 showing off; liking to attract notice. *adj.* —**os′ten ta′tious ly,** *adv.*

os te o path (os′tē ə path), person who specializes in osteopathy. *n.*

os te op a thy (os′tē op′ə thē), treatment of diseases by manipulating the bones and muscles. Osteopathy also includes other types of medical and physical therapy. *n.*

ost ler (os′lər), hostler. *n.*

os tra cism (os′trə siz′əm), 1 banishment from one's native country. 2 a being shut out from society, from favor, from privileges, or from association with one's fellows. *n.*

os tra cize (os′trə sīz), 1 condemn to leave a country; banish. The ancient Greeks ostracized an unpopular citizen by public vote. 2 shut out from society, from favor, from privileges, etc.: *A person who constantly interrupts and* says rude things may be ostracized until he learns how to be more considerate of others. *v.*, **os tra cized, os tra ciz ing.**

os trich (ôs′trich), a large African and Arabian bird that can run swiftly but cannot fly. Ostriches have two toes and are the largest of existing birds. They have large feathers or plumes which were much used as ornaments. *n., pl.* **os trich es.**

O.T., Old Testament.

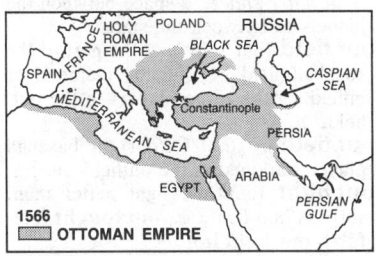

1566
■ OTTOMAN EMPIRE

O thel lo (ə thel′ō), 1 play by Shakespeare. 2 the principal character in this play, a brave but jealous Moor who kills his wife after being falsely persuaded that she is not true to him. *n.*

oth er (uᴛʜ′ər), 1 remaining: *He is here, but the other boys are at school.* 2 additional or further: *I have no other place to go.* 3 not the same as one or more already mentioned: *Come some other day.* 4 different: *I would not have you other than you are.* 5 the other one; not the same ones: *Each praises the other.* 6 other person or thing: *There are others to be considered.* 7 in any different way; otherwise: *I could not do other than I did.* 1-4 *adj.*, 5,6 *pron.*, 7 *adv.*

every other, every second; alternate: *We buy milk every other day.*

of all others, more than all others.

the other day (night, etc.), recently.

oth er wise (uᴛʜ′ər wīz′), 1 in a different way; differently: *I could not do otherwise.* 2 different: *It might have been otherwise.* 3 in other ways: *It is windy, but otherwise a very nice day.* 4 under other circumstances; in a different condition: *She reminded me of what I would otherwise have forgotten.* 5 or else; if not: *Come at once; otherwise you will be too late.* 1,3,4 *adv.*, 2 *adj.*, 5 *conj.*

other world, the life to come; life after death.

Ot ta wa (ot′ə wə), capital of Canada, in SE Ontario. *n.*

ot ter (ot′ər), 1 a water mammal, related to the weasels, that eats fish. The otter is a good swimmer and has webbed toes with claws. 2 its fur. Otter is thick and glossy, somewhat like seal or beaver. *n., pl.* **ot ters** or **ot ter.**

ostrich
up to 8 ft. tall

ot to man (ot′ə mən), 1 a low, cushioned seat without back or arms. 2 a cushioned footstool. *n., pl.* **ot to mans.** [from *Ottoman*]

Ot to man (ot′ə mən), 1 Turk. 2 Turkish. 1 *n., pl.* **Ot to mans;** 2 *adj.*

Ottoman Empire, a former Turkish empire which occupied Asia Minor and parts of northern Africa, southeastern Europe, and southwestern Asia in the middle 1500's.

ouch (ouch), exclamation of sudden pain. *interj.*

ought[1] (ôt), 1 have a duty; be obliged: *You ought to obey your parents.* 2 be right or suitable: *Cruelty and bullying ought not to be allowed.* 3 be wise: *I ought to go before it rains.* 4 be expected: *At your age you ought to know better.* 5 be very likely: *It ought to be a fine day tomorrow.* *v.* [Old English *āhte,* past tense of *āgan* owe, own]

ought[2] (ôt), aught; anything. *n.* [a different form of *aught*[1]]

ounce (ouns), 1 measure of weight, $1/16$ of a pound in avoirdupois, and $1/12$ of a pound in troy weight. 2 measure of capacity for liquids. 16 ounces = 1 pint. 3 a little bit; very small amount: *"An ounce of prevention is worth a pound of cure."* *n.*

our (our), of us; belonging to us: *We need our coats now.* *adj.*

ours (ourz), the one or ones belonging to us: *This garden is ours. Ours is a large house. I like ours better than theirs.* *pron.*

our self (our self′), myself. *Ourself* is used by an author, king, judge, etc. *"We will ourself reward the victor,"* said the queen. *pron.*

our selves (our selvz′), 1 form of *we* or *us* used to make a statement stronger: *We ourselves will do the work.* 2 form used instead of *we* or *us* in cases

otter (def. 1)— up to 4 ft. long with tail

hat, āge, fär; let, ēqual, tėrm; it, īce; hot, ōpen, ôrder; oil, out; cup, pùt, rüle; ch, child; ng, long; sh, she; th, thin; ᴛʜ, then; zh, measure;

ə represents *a* in about, *e* in taken, *i* in pencil, *o* in lemon, *u* in circus.

like: *We cook for ourselves. We cannot see ourselves as others see us.* 3 our real or true selves: *We weren't ourselves when we said that.* *pron.pl.*

-ous, suffix added to nouns to form adjectives. 1 having; having much; full of: *Famous = having much fame. Joyous = full of joy.* 2 characterized by: *Zealous = characterized by zeal.* 3 having the nature of: *Villainous = having the nature of a villain.* 4 like: *Thunderous = like thunder.* [from French before the 1400's *-os, -us,* from Latin *-osum*]

oust (oust), force out; drive out: *The sparrows have ousted the bluebirds from their nest.* *v.*

oust er (ou′stər), an ousting, especially an illegal forcing of a person out of his property. *n.*

out (out), 1 away; forth: *The water will rush out. Spread the rug out.* 2 not in or at a place, position, or state: *That tie is out of fashion. The miners are going out on strike.* 3 not at home; away from one's office, work, etc.: *My mother is out just now.* 4 not in possession or control; not having power: *The Democrats are in, the Republicans out.* 5 **outs,** *pl.* people not in office; political party not in power. 6 (in baseball) not successful in reaching base or advancing from one base to another: *The outfielder caught the fly and the batter was out.* 7 a being out or putting out in baseball: *An inning lasts until three outs are made.* 8 not in use, action, fashion, etc.: *The fire is out. Full skirts are out this season.* 9 from the usual place, condition, position, etc.: *Put the light out. I turned all my pockets out.* 10 not correct: *He was out in his figuring.* 11 from a state of composure, satisfaction, or harmony: *feel put out.* 12 at a money loss: *be out ten dollars.* 13 from out; forth from: *He went out the door.* 14 into the open; made public; made known; into being; so as to be seen: *The secret is out now. Her new book is out. Many flowers were coming out.* 15 to or at an end: *Work it out!* 16 ɪɴ-ꜰᴏʀᴍᴀʟ. out along: *Drive out Second Street.* 17 go or come out; be dis-

adj.	adjective	*n.* noun
adv.	adverb	*prep.* preposition
conj.	conjunction	*pron.* pronoun
interj.	interjection	*v.* verb
sing.	singular	*pl.* plural

closed: *The truth will out.* 18 aloud; plainly: *Speak out so that all can hear.* 19 completely; effectively: *fit out a boat.* 20 so as to project or extend: *stand out.* 21 to others: *let out rooms. Give out the books.* 22 from among others: *Pick out an apple for me.* 23 from a number, stock, store, source, cause, material, etc.: *She picked out a new coat.* 24 a defense or excuse: *have an out for stealing.* 25 OLD USE. exclamation of indignation, reproach, etc. 26 external; exterior; outer; outlying: *an out island.* 1-3,9-12,14,15,18-23 *adv.,* 4,6,8,26 *adj.,* 5,7,24 *n.,* 13,16 *prep.,* 17 *v.,* 25 *interj.*

at outs or **on the outs,** quarreling; disagreeing.

out and away, by far: *This is out and away the warmest day we have had this summer.*

out for, looking for; trying to get: *He is out for the best deal he can get.*

out of, 1 from within: *He came out of the house.* 2 not within: *He is out of town.* 3 away from: *forty miles out of San Francisco.* 4 beyond the reach of: *She was out of sight.* 5 not having; without: *She is out of work. We are out of coffee.* 6 so as to take away: *I was cheated out of my money.* 7 from: *His hat was made out of silk.* 8 from among: *We picked our puppy out of that litter.* 9 because of: *I went only out of curiosity.*

out to, eagerly trying to.

out-, *prefix.* 1 outward; forth; away: *Outbound = outward bound. Outburst = a bursting forth.* 2 outside; at a distance: *Outlying = lying outside.* 3 more than or longer than: *Outlive = live longer than.* 4 better than: *Outdo = do better than.* [from *out*]

out-and-out (out′n out′), thorough; complete: *an out-and-out defeat. adj.*

out bid (out bid′), bid higher than (someone else). *v.,* **out bid, out bid** or **out bid den, out bid ding.**

out board (out′bôrd′), 1 outside the hull of a ship or boat. 2 away from the center line of a ship, boat, or aircraft. *adj., adv.*

outboard motor, a gasoline motor, often portable, attached to the outside of the stern of a boat or canoe.

out bound (out′bound′), outward

bound: *an outbound ship, outbound flights. adj.*

out break (out′brāk′), 1 a breaking out: *outbreaks of anger.* 2 a riot; public disturbance. *n.*

out build ing (out′bil′ding), a shed or building built against or near a main building: *Barns are outbuildings on a farm. n.*

out burst (out′bèrst′), a bursting forth: *an outburst of laughter, an outburst of smoke. n.*

out cast (out′kast′), 1 person or animal cast out from home and friends: *Criminals are outcasts of society. That kitten was just a little outcast when he found it.* 2 being an outcast; homeless; friendless. 1 *n.,* 2 *adj.*

out class (out klas′), be of higher class than; be much better than. *v.*

out come (out′kum′), a result; consequence: *the outcome of a race. n.*

OUTCROP

EARTH'S SURFACE

outcrop (def. 2)

out crop (out′krop′ for 1,2; out krop′ for 3), 1 a coming to the surface of the earth: *the outcrop of a vein of coal.* 2 part that comes to the surface: *The outcrop that we found proved to be very rich in gold.* 3 come to the surface; appear. 1,2 *n.,* 3 *v.,* **out cropped, out crop ping.**

out cry (out′krī′), 1 a crying out; sudden cry or scream. 2 a great noise or clamor. *n., pl.* **out cries.**

out dat ed (out dā′tid), out-of-date; old-fashioned. *adj.*

out did (out did′), past tense of **outdo.** *The girls outdid the boys in diving. v.*

out dis tance (out dis′tans), leave behind; outstrip: *The winner outdistanced all the other runners in the race. v.,* **out dis tanced, out dis tanc ing.**

out do (out dü′), do more or better than; surpass: *Men will outdo boys in most things. v.,* **out did, out done, out doing.**

out done (out dun′), past participle of **outdo.** *The girls were outdone by the boys in softball. v.*

out door (out′dôr′), done, used, or living outdoors: *outdoor games, an outdoor meal. adj.*

out doors (out′dôrz′), 1 out in the open air; not indoors or in the house:

outboard motor

I don't want to go outdoors until it stops raining. 2 the world outside of houses; the open air: *We must protect the wildlife of the great outdoors.* 1 *adv.,* 2 *n.*

out er (ou′tər), on the outside; farther out: *Shingles are used as an outer covering for many roofs. adj.*

out er most (ou′tər mōst), farthest out. *adj.*

outer space, 1 space immediately beyond the earth's atmosphere: *The moon is in outer space.* 2 space between the planets or between the stars.

out field (out′fēld′), 1 the part of the baseball field beyond the diamond or infield. 2 the three players in the outfield. *n.*

out field er (out′fēl′dər), a baseball player stationed in the outfield. *n.*

out fight (out fit′), fight better than; surpass in a fight. *v.,* **out fought** (out-fôt′), **out fight ing.**

out fit (out′fit), 1 all the articles necessary for any undertaking or purpose: *a sailor's outfit, an outfit for a camping trip, a skiing outfit.* 2 furnish with everything necessary for any purpose; equip: *She outfitted herself for camp.* 3 group working together, such as a military unit: *Her father and mine were in the same outfit during the war.* 1,3 *n.,* 2 *v.,* **out fit ted, out fit ting.**

out fit ter (out′fit′ər), person who outfits, especially a dealer in outfits for traveling, athletic sports, etc. *n.*

out flank (out flangk′), 1 go or extend beyond the flank of (an opposing army, etc.); turn the flank of. 2 get the better of; circumvent. *v.*

out flow (out′flō′), 1 a flowing out: *the outflow from a waterpipe, an outflow of sympathy.* 2 that which flows out. *n.*

out gen er al (out jen′ər əl), be a better general than; get the better of by superior strategy. *v.*

out go (out′gō′), what goes out; what is paid out; amount that is spent. *n., pl.* **out goes.**

out go ing (out′gō′ing), 1 a going out. 2 that which goes out. 3 outward bound; departing: *outgoing steamships.* 4 friendly and helpful to others; sociable: *a very outgoing person.* 1,2 *n.,* 3,4 *adj.*

out grow (out grō′), 1 grow too large for: *outgrow one's clothes.* 2 grow beyond or away from; get rid of by growing older: *outgrow early friends, outgrow a babyish habit.* 3 grow faster or taller than: *This variety of tomato will outgrow most other kinds. By the time he was ten, he had outgrown his older brother. v.,* **out grew** (out-grü′), **out grown** (out grōn′), **out growing.**

out growth (out′grōth′), 1 a natural

development, product, or result: *This big store is an outgrowth of a little shop they started ten years ago.* 2 offshoot; something that has grown out: *A corn is an outgrowth on a toe.* 3 a growing out or forth: *the outgrowth of new leaves in the spring.* n.

out guess (out ges′), be too clever for; get the better of. v.

out house (out′hous′), 1 a separate building used in connection with a main building: *Near the farmhouse were sheds and other outhouses.* 2 an outdoor toilet. n., pl. **out hous es** (out′hou′ziz).

out ing (ou′ting), a short pleasure trip; walk or airing; holiday spent outdoors away from home: *On Sunday the family went on an outing to the beach.* n.

out land ish (out lan′dish), not familiar; queer; strange or ridiculous: *an outlandish hat.* adj.

out last (out last′), last longer than. v.

out law (out′lô′), 1 a lawless person; criminal. 2 person outside the protection of the law; exile; outcast. 3 make or declare illegal: *A group of nations agreed to outlaw war.* 4 make or declare (a person) an outlaw. 5 deprive of legal force. An outlawed debt is one that cannot be collected because it has been due too long. 1,2 n., 3-5 v.

out law ry (out′lôr′ē), 1 a being condemned as an outlaw; being outlawed. Outlawry was formerly used as a punishment in England. 2 condition of being an outlaw. n., pl. **out law ries.**

out lay (out′lā for 1,2; out lā′ for 3), 1 a laying out money; spending; expense: *a large outlay for clothing.* 2 the amount spent: *an outlay of eleven dollars.* 3 expend: *outlay money in improvements.* 1,2 n., 3 v., **out laid, out lay ing.**

out let (out′let), 1 means or place of letting out or getting out; way out; vent; opening; exit: *the outlet of a lake, an outlet for one's energies.* 2 market for a product. 3 point in an electric circuit where an electric plug may be inserted to receive power. An outlet is usually set in a wall. n.

outlet (def. 3)

out line (out′līn′), 1 line that shows the shape of an object; line that bounds a figure: *We saw the outlines of the mountains against the evening sky. The outline of Italy suggests a boot.* 2 a drawing or style of drawing that gives only outer lines: *Make an outline of the scene*

before you paint it. 3 draw the outer line of: *Outline a map of America.* 4 a general plan; rough draft: *Make an outline before trying to write a composition. The teacher gave a brief outline of the work planned for the term.* 5 give a plan of; sketch: *She outlined their trip abroad.* 1,2,4 n., 3,5 v., **out lined, out lin ing.**

in outline, 1 with only the outline shown. 2 with only the main features.

out live (out liv′), live or last longer than; survive; outlast: *She outlived her older sister. The idea was good once, but it has outlived its usefulness.* v., **out lived, out liv ing.**

out look (out′lúk′), 1 what one sees on looking out; view: *The room has a pleasant outlook.* 2 what seems likely to happen; prospect: *The outlook for our picnic is not very good; it looks as if it will rain.* 3 way of thinking about things; attitude of mind; point of view: *a cheerful outlook on life.* 4 lookout; tower to watch from. n.

out ly ing (out′lī′ing), lying outside the boundary; far from the center; remote: *We live in an outlying suburb of the city.* adj.

out ma neu ver (out′mə nü′vər), outdo in maneuvering; get the better of by maneuvering. v.

out mod ed (out mō′did), out-of-date. adj.

out most (out′mōst), farthest out. adj.

out num ber (out num′bər), be more than; exceed in number: *They outnumbered us three to one.* v.

out-of-bounds (out′əv boundz′), outside the boundary line; out of play: *an out-of-bounds ball* (adj.). *He kicked the ball out-of-bounds* (adv.). adj., adv.

out-of-date (out′əv dāt′), not in present use; old-fashioned: *A horse and buggy is an out-of-date method of transportation.* adj.

out-of-door (out′əv dôr′), outdoor. adj.

out-of-doors (out′əv dôrz′), 1 outdoor. 2 outdoors. 1 adj., 2 n., adv.

out-of-the-way (out′əv ᵺə wā′), 1 seldom visited; remote; unfrequented; secluded: *an out-of-the-way cottage.* 2 seldom met with; unusual: *out-of-the-way bits of information.* adj.

out pa tient (out′pā′shənt), patient receiving treatment at a hospital but not staying there. n.

out play (out plā′), play better than. v.

out post (out′pōst′), 1 a guard, or small number of soldiers, placed at some distance from an army or camp to prevent surprise attacks. 2 place where they are stationed. 3 a settlement or village in an outlying place: *a frontier outpost, a distant outpost of civilization.* n.

hat, āge, fär; let, ēqual, tèrm; it, īce; hot, ōpen, ôrder; oil, out; cup, pùt, rüle; ch, child; ng, long; sh, she; th, thin; ᵺ, then; zh, measure;

ə represents *a* in about, *e* in taken, *i* in pencil, *o* in lemon, *u* in circus.

out pour (out′pôr′ *for 1,2;* out pôr′ *for 3*), 1 a pouring out. 2 that which is poured out. 3 pour out. 1,2 n., 3 v.

out put (out′pùt′), 1 what is put out; amount produced; product or yield: *the daily output of automobiles.* 2 a putting forth: *With a sudden output of effort he moved the rock.* 3 information produced from the storage unit of a computer. n.

out rage (out′rāj), 1 an act showing no regard for the rights or feelings of others; overturning of the rights of others by force; act of violence; offense; insult: *The tyrant was guilty of many outrages.* 2 offend greatly; do violence to; insult: *The cattlemen outraged the farmers by setting fire to their crops.* 3 break (the law, a rule of morality, etc.) openly; treat as nothing at all: *She outraged all rules of politeness by throwing tomatoes at her parents' guests.* 1 n., 2,3 v., **out raged, out rag ing.**

out ra geous (out rā′jəs), very bad or insulting; shocking: *outrageous language.* adj. **—out ra′geous ly,** adv. **—out ra′geous ness,** n.

out ran (out ran′), past tense of **out-run.** *She outran me easily.* v.

out rank (out rangk′), rank higher than: *A captain outranks a lieutenant.* v.

outrigger
(def. 1)

out rig ger (out′rig′ər), 1 framework extending outward from the side of a light boat or canoe and ending in a float. It keeps the boat from turning over. 2 boat equipped with brackets extending outward from either side to hold oarlocks. n.

out right (out′rīt′), 1 not gradually;

adj. adjective		*n.* noun
adv. adverb		*prep.* preposition
conj. conjunction		*pron.* pronoun
interj. interjection		*v.* verb
sing. singular		*pl.* plural

altogether; entirely: *We paid for our car outright.* **2** without restraint; openly: *I laughed outright.* **3** complete; thorough: *an outright criminal, an outright lie.* **4** downright; straightforward; direct: *an outright refusal.* **5** entire; total. **6** at once. *1,2,6 adv., 3-5 adj.*

out run (out run′), **1** run faster than: *She can outrun her older sister.* **2** leave behind; run beyond; pass the limits of: *Your story completely outruns the facts.* *v.,* **out ran, out run, out run ning.**

out sell (out sel′), **1** outdo in selling; sell more than: *He outsold every salesman in the company last year.* **2** be sold in greater quantity than: *This brand outsells the other brands on the market.* *v.,* **out sold** (out sōld′), **out sell ing.**

out set (out′set′), a setting out; start; beginning: *At the outset, it looked like a nice day.* *n.*

out shine (out shīn′), **1** shine more brightly than. **2** be more brilliant or excellent than; surpass. *v.,* **out shone** (out shōn′), **out shin ing.**

out side (out′sīd′; *for 5,6 also* out′-sīd′), **1** the side or surface that is out; outer part: *polish the outside of a car, the outside of a house.* **2** on the outside; of or nearer the outside: *the outside leaves.* **3** on or to the outside; outdoors: *Run outside and play.* **4** space that is beyond or not inside. **5** INFORMAL. with the exception (of): *Outside of him, none of us liked the play.* **6** out of; beyond the limits of: *Stay outside the house. That is outside my plans.* **7** not belonging to a certain group, set, district, etc.: *Outside people tried to get control of the business.* **8** INFORMAL. highest; largest; reaching the utmost limit: *an outside estimate of the cost.* **9** INFORMAL. barely possible; very slight: *The team has an outside chance to win.* *1,4 n., 2,7-9 adj., 3 adv., 5,6 prep.*

at the outside, INFORMAL. at the utmost limit: *I can do it in a week, at the outside.*

out sid er (out′sī′dər), person not belonging to a particular group, set, company, party, district, etc. *n.*

out size (out′sīz′), larger than the usual size. *adj.*

out skirts (out′skèrts′), the outer parts or edges of a town, district, etc.,

or of a subject of discussion; outlying parts: *We have a farm on the outskirts of town. n.pl.*

out smart (out smärt′), INFORMAL. outdo in cleverness. *v.*

out spo ken (out′spō′kən), not reserved; frank: *an outspoken person, outspoken criticism. Your own family is likely to be outspoken in its remarks about you.* *adj.* —**out′spo′ken ly,** *adv.* —**out′spo′ken ness,** *n.*

out spread (out′spred′ *for 1;* out-spred′ *for 2*), **1** spread out; extended: *an eagle with outspread wings.* **2** to spread out; extend. *1 adj., 2 v.,* **out spread, out spread ing.**

oval (def. 1)   ovals (def. 2)

out stand ing (out stan′ding), **1** standing out from others; well-known; important: *He is an outstanding baseball pitcher because of his control.* **2** unpaid: *outstanding debts.* **3** standing out; projecting. *adj.* —**out stand′ing ly,** *adv.*

out stay (out stā′), stay longer than. *v.*

out stretched (out′strecht′), stretched out; extended: *He welcomed his old friend with outstretched arms. adj.*

out strip (out strip′), **1** go faster than; leave behind in a race: *A horse can outstrip a man.* **2** do better than; excel: *She can outstrip most of her classmates in mathematics.* *v.,* **out stripped, out strip ping.**

out ward (out′wərd), **1** going toward the outside; turned toward the outside: *an outward motion. She gave one outward glance.* **2** toward the outside; away: *A porch extends outward from the house.* **3** outer: *to all outward appearances.* **4** on the outside: *He turned the coat with the lining outward.* **5** that can be seen; plain to see: *the outward man, outward behavior. 1,3,5 adj., 2,4 adv.*

out ward ly (out′wərd lē), **1** on the outside or outer surface. **2** in appearance: *Though frightened, she remained outwardly calm. adv.*

out wards (out′wərdz), outward. *adv.*

out wear (out wer′ *or* out war′), **1** wear longer than. **2** wear out: *outwear someone's patience.* **3** outgrow. *v.,* **out wore** (out wôr′), **out worn, out wear ing.**

out weigh (out wā′), **1** weigh more than. **2** exceed in value, importance, influence, etc.: *The advantages of the plan outweigh its disadvantages. v.*

out wit (out wit′), get the better of by being more intelligent; be too clever

for: *The prisoner outwitted the guards and escaped.* *v.,* **out wit ted, out wit ting.**

out work (out′wèrk′ *for 1;* out wèrk′ *for 2*), **1** a part of the fortifications of a place lying outside the main ones; a less important defense: *the outworks of a castle.* **2** surpass in working; work harder or faster than. *1 n., 2 v.*

out worn (out′wôrn′ *for 1,2;* out-wôrn′ *for 3*), **1** worn out: *outworn clothes.* **2** out-of-date; outgrown: *outworn opinions, outworn habits.* **3** past participle of **outwear.** *I have outworn the coat I bought last year. 1,2 adj., 3 v.*

o val (ō′vəl), **1** shaped like an egg. **2** shaped like an ellipse. **3** something having an oval shape. *1,2 adj., 3 n.*

o var y (ō′vər ē), **1** the organ of a female animal in which eggs are produced. **2** the enlarged lower part of the pistil of a flowering plant, enclosing the young seeds. *n., pl.* **o var ies.**

ovary (def. 2)

o vate (ō′vāt), egg-shaped: *an ovate leaf. adj.*

o va tion (ō vā′shən), an enthusiastic public welcome; burst of loud clapping or cheering: *The President received a great ovation. n.*

ov en (uv′ən), **1** an enclosed space usually in a stove or near a fireplace, for baking food. **2** a small furnace for heating or drying pottery; kiln. *n.*

ov en bird (uv′ən bèrd′), any of various birds that build nests with dome-shaped roofs. *n.*

o ver (ō′vər), **1** above in place or position: *the roof over one's head* (*prep.*), *the cliff hung over* (*adv.*). **2** above in authority, power, etc.: *We have a captain over us.* **3** above and to the other side of; across: *leap over a wall. Can you climb over that hill?* **4** from one side to another; to the other side; across any intervening space: *Go over to the store for me. Hand the money over.* **5** down; out and down (from an edge or from an upright position): *The ball went too near the edge and rolled over.* **6** out and down from; down from the edge of: *It fell over the edge of the cliff.* **7** so as to cover the surface, or affect the whole surface: *Cover the tar over with sand until it has hardened.* **8** at all or various places on; on; upon: *a blanket lying over a bed. A blush came over his face. Farms were scattered over the valley.* **9** here and there on or in; round about; all through: *We shall travel over Europe.* **10** from end to end of; along: *We drove over the new thruway.* **11** from beginning to end; again; in repetition: *ten times over, read a newspaper over.* **12** during: *over many years.* **13** at an end: *The play is over.* **14** about; concerning; in connection with: *He is worried over his health. Don't go to sleep over your work.* **15** more than; beyond: *It costs over ten dollars.* **16** by means of: *They spoke over the telephone.* **17** in excess or addition; too; more; besides: *to be over careful, receive the full sum and something over.* **18** so as to bring the upper side or end down or under: *turn over a page.* **19** higher up; surplus; extra: *an over drapery.* **20** on the other side; at some distance: *over in Europe, over by the hill.* 1-3,6,8-10,12,14-16 *prep.,* 1,4,5,7,11,17,18,20 *adv.,* 13,19 *adj.*

over again, once more: *Let's do that over again.*

over against, **1** opposite to; in front of: *a house over against the park.* **2** so as to bring out a difference: *consider one book over against another.*

over and above, besides; in addition to: *over and above what it had cost him.*

over and over, again and again: *Play the piece over and over until you do it right.*

over-, *prefix.* **1** above: *Overhead = above the head.* **2** higher in rank; superior: *Overlord = superior lord.* **3** across: *Overseas = across the seas.* **4** too; too much; too long, etc.: *Overcrowded = too crowded. Overburden = burden too much.* **5** above normal; extra: *Oversize = above normal size. Overtime = extra time.* **6** being above; worn as an outer covering: *Overcoat = coat that is worn as an outer covering.* [from *over*]

o ver act (ō′vər akt′), act to excess; overdo in acting; act (a part) in an exaggerated manner. *v.*

o ver all (ō′vər ôl′), **1** from one end to the other: *an overall measurement.* **2** including everything: *an overall estimate. adj.*

o ver alls (ō′vər ôlz′), loose trousers worn over clothes to keep them clean. Overalls usually have a part that covers the chest. *n.pl.*

o ver anx ious (ō′vər angk′shəs), too anxious. *adj.*

o ver arch (ō′vər ärch′), **1** arch over; span with or like an arch: *The street was overarched by elm trees.* **2** to curve like an arch. *v.*

o ver arm (ō′vər ärm′), with the arm

raised above the shoulder; overhand. *adj.*

o ver ate (ō′vər āt′), past tense of **overeat.** *I have a stomach ache because I overate.* *v.*

o ver awe (ō′vər ô′), overcome or restrain with awe: *Eclipses of the sun overawed primitive peoples.* *v.,* **o ver awed, o ver aw ing.**

o ver bal ance (ō′vər bal′əns), **1** be greater than in weight, importance, value, etc.: *The gains overbalanced the losses.* **2** cause to lose balance: *As he leaned over the side, his weight overbalanced the canoe and it upset.* *v.,* **o ver bal anced, o ver bal anc ing.**

o ver bear (ō′vər ber′ *or* ō′vər bar′), **1** overcome by weight or force; oppress; master: *My friends overbore all my objections.* **2** bear down by weight or force; overthrow; upset. *v.,* **o ver bore, o ver borne, o ver bear ing.**

o ver bear ing (ō′vər ber′ing *or* ō′vər bar′ing), inclined to dictate; forcing others to one's own will; masterful; domineering: *We found it hard to like our new neighbors because of their overbearing ways.* *adj.* —**o′ver bear′ing ly,** *adv.*

o ver board (ō′vər bôrd′), from a ship or boat into the water: *to fall overboard.* *adv.*

go overboard, go too far in an effort because of extreme enthusiasm.

throw overboard, **1** throw into the water. **2** INFORMAL. get rid of; give up; abandon; discard.

o ver bold (ō′vər bōld′), too bold. *adj.*

o ver bore (ō′vər bôr′), past tense of **overbear.** *v.*

o ver borne (ō′vər bôrn′), past participle of **overbear.** *v.*

o ver bur den (ō′vər bėrd′n), load with too great a burden. *v.*

o ver came (ō′vər kām′), past tense of **overcome.** *I finally overcame my shyness.* *v.*

overcast (def. 3)

o ver cast (ō′vər kast′), **1** cloudy or dark; gloomy: *The sky was overcast before the storm.* **2** cover or be covered with clouds or darkness. **3** sew over and through (the edges of a seam) with long stitches to prevent raveling. 1 *adj.,* 2,3 *v.,* **o ver cast, o ver cast ing.**

o ver charge (ō′vər chärj′ *for 1,3;* ō′vər chärj′ *for 2),* **1** charge too high a price: *The grocer overcharged you for the eggs.* **2** a charge that is too great.

hat, āge, fär; let, ēqual, tėrm;
it, īce; hot, ōpen, ôrder;
oil, out; cup, pùt, rüle; ch, child;
ng, long; sh, she; th, thin;
ᵭH, then; zh, measure;

ə represents *a* in about,
e in taken, *i* in pencil,
o in lemon, *u* in circus.

3 load too heavily; fill too full: *The overcharged old musket burst.* 1,3 *v.,* **o ver charged, o ver charg ing;** 2 *n.*

o ver cloud (ō′vər kloud′), **1** cloud over or become clouded over; darken. **2** make or become gloomy. *v.*

o ver coat (ō′vər kōt′), an outer coat worn over the regular clothing for warmth in cold weather. *n.*

o ver come (ō′vər kum′), **1** get the better of; win the victory over; conquer; defeat: *overcome an enemy, overcome one's faults, overcome all difficulties.* **2** make weak or helpless: *Weariness overcame her and she fell asleep.* *v.,* **o ver came, o ver come, o ver com ing.**

o ver con fi dent (ō′vər kon′fə dənt), too confident. *adj.*

o ver cooked (ō′vər kùkt′), cooked too much or too long. *adj.*

o ver crowd (ō′vər kroud′), crowd too much; put in too much or too many. *v.*

o ver de vel op (ō′vər di vel′əp), develop too much or too long. If a photograph is overdeveloped, it is too dark. *v.*

o ver did (ō′vər did′), past tense of **overdo.** *v.*

o ver do (ō′vər dü′), **1** do or attempt to do too much: *She overdoes exercise. She overdid and became tired.* **2** exaggerate: *The funny scenes in the play were overdone.* **3** cook too much: *The vegetables were overdone.* **4** exhaust; tire. *v.,* **o ver did, o ver done, o ver do ing.**

o ver done (ō′vər dun′), past participle of **overdo.** *v.*

o ver dose (ō′vər dōs′ *for 1;* ō′vər dōs′ *for 2),* **1** too big a dose. **2** give too large a dose to. 1 *n.,* 2 *v.,* **o ver dosed, o ver dos ing.**

o ver draft (ō′vər draft′), **1** an overdrawing of an account, especially a bank account. **2** amount of the excess. *n.*

o ver draw (ō′vər drô′), **1** draw from (a bank account, allowance, etc.) more than the amount one has to his credit or at his disposal. **2** exaggerate: *The characters in the book were greatly over-*

601

overdress

adj. adjective   **n.** noun
adv. adverb   **prep.** preposition
conj. conjunction   **pron.** pronoun
interj. interjection   **v.** verb

sing. singular   **pl.** plural

---

drawn. *v.,* **o ver drew** (ō′vər drü′),
o ver drawn (ō′vər drôn′), **o ver-
draw ing.**

o ver dress (ō′vər dres′ *for 1;* ō′vər-
dres′ *for 2*), 1 to dress too elaborately.
2 a dress worn over the main dress.
1 *v.,* 2 *n.*

o ver drive (ō′vər drīv′), an arrangement of gears in an automobile that
produces greater speed while using less
power than when the car is in high. *n.*

o ver due (ō′vər dü′ *or* ō′vər dyü′),
more than due; due some time ago but
not yet arrived, paid, etc.: *The train is
overdue. This bill is overdue. adj.*

o ver eat (ō′vər ēt′), eat too much. *v.,*
o ver ate, o ver eat en, o ver eat ing.

o ver eat en (ō′vər ēt′n), past participle of **overeat.** *Nearly everyone has
overeaten at the picnic. v.*

o ver em pha size (ō′vər em′fə sīz),
give too much force or emphasis to;
stress too much. *v.,* **o ver em pha-
sized, o ver em pha siz ing.**

o ver es ti mate (ō′vər es′tə māt *for
1;* ō′vər es′tə mit *for 2*), 1 to estimate
at too high a value, amount, rate, etc.
2 an estimate that is too high. 1 *v.,*
**o ver es ti mat ed, o ver es ti mat-
ing;** 2 *n.*

o ver ex po sure (ō′vər ek spō′zhər),
too much or too long an exposure. *n.*

o ver feed (ō′vər fēd′), feed too much.
v., **o ver fed** (ō′vər fed′), **o ver feeding.**

o ver flow (ō′vər flō′ *for 1-6;* ō′vər-
flō′ *for 7,8*), 1 to flow over the bounds:
Rivers often overflow in the spring. 2 to
cover or flood: *The river overflowed my
garden.* 3 have the contents flowing
over: *My cup is overflowing.* 4 flow
over the top of: *The milk is overflowing
the cup.* 5 extend out beyond; be too
many for: *The crowd overflowed the
little parlor and filled the hall.* 6 be very
abundant: *an overflowing harvest, overflowing kindness.* 7 an overflowing; excess. 8 outlet or container for overflowing liquid. 1-6 *v.,* **o ver flowed,
o ver flown** (ō′vər flōn′), **o ver flowing;** 7,8 *n.*

o ver grew (ō′vər grü′), past tense of
overgrow. *Vines overgrew the wall. v.*

o ver grow (ō′vər grō′), 1 grow
over: *The wall is overgrown with vines.*
2 grow too fast; become too big. *v.,*

**o ver grew, o ver grown, o ver-
grow ing.**

o ver grown (ō′vər grōn′), 1 grown
too big: *an overgrown boy.* 2 past participle of **overgrow.** *The vines have
overgrown the wall.* 1 *adj.,* 2 *v.*

o ver growth (ō′vər grōth′), 1 too
great or too rapid growth. 2 growth
overspreading or covering something. *n.*

o ver hand (ō′vər hand′), 1 with the
hand raised above the shoulder: *an overhand throw* (adj.), *pitch overhand*
(adv.). 2 with the knuckles upward.
adj., adv.

o ver hang (ō′vər hang′ *for 1;* ō′vər-
hang′ *for 2,3*), 1 hang over; project
over: *Trees overhang the street to form
an arch of branches.* 2 a hanging over.
3 something that projects: *The overhang of the roof shaded the flower bed
beneath.* 1 *v.,* **o ver hung, o ver-
hang ing;** 2,3 *n.*

o ver haul (ō′vər hôl′ *for 1,2;* ō′vər-
hôl′ *for 3*), 1 examine thoroughly so as
to make any repairs or changes that are
needed: *Once a year we overhaul our
boat.* 2 gain upon; overtake: *The pirate's ship was overhauling ours.* 3 an
overhauling. 1,2 *v.,* 3 *n.*

o ver head (ō′vər hed′ *for 1;* ō′vər-
hed′ *for 2,3*), 1 over the head; on high;
above: *the stars overhead, the family
overhead, the flag overhead.* 2 placed
above; placed high up: *overhead wires.*
3 general expenses of running a business, such as rent, lighting, heating,
taxes, repairs. 1 *adv.,* 2 *adj.,* 3 *n.*

o ver hear (ō′vər hir′), hear when one
is not meant to hear: *They spoke so loud
that I could not help overhearing what
they said.* *v.,* **o ver heard, o ver-
hear ing.**

o ver heard (ō′vər hėrd′), past tense
and past participle of **overhear.** *I overheard what you told him. v.*

o ver heat (ō′vər hēt′), heat too
much. *v.*

o ver hung (ō′vər hung′ *for 1;* ō′vər-
hung′ *for 2*), 1 hung from above: *an
overhung door.* 2 past tense and past
participle of **overhang.** *A big awning
overhung the sidewalk.* 1 *adj.,* 2 *v.*

o ver in dulge (ō′vər in dulj′), indulge too much. *v.,* **o ver in dulged,
o ver in dulg ing.**

o ver joy (ō′vər joi′), make very joyful. *v.*

o ver joyed (ō′vər joid′), very joyful;
filled with joy; delighted. *adj.*

o ver laid (ō′vər lād′), past tense and
past participle of **overlay¹.** *The workmen overlaid the dome with gold. The
iron had become overlaid with rust. v.*

o ver lain (ō′vər lān′), past participle
of **overlie.** *v.*

o ver land (ō′vər land′), on land; by

land: *travel overland from New York to
Florida* (adv.), *an overland route* (adj.).
adv., adj.

o ver lap (ō′vər lap′ *for 1;* ō′vər lap′
for 2,3), 1 lap over; cover and extend
beyond: *Shingles are laid to overlap
each other.* 2 a lapping over. 3 part that
overlaps. 1 *v.,* **o ver lapped, o ver-
lap ping;** 2,3 *n.*

overlap (def. 1)—overlapping shingles

o ver lay¹ (ō′vər lā′ *for 1,2;* ō′vər lā′
for 3), 1 lay or place (one thing) over or
upon another. 2 cover, overspread, or
surmount with something; finish with a
layer or applied decoration of something: *wood overlaid with gold.*
3 something laid over something else;
layer or decoration; covering. 1,2 *v.,*
o ver laid, o ver lay ing; 3 *n.* [*over- +
lay¹*]

o ver lay² (ō′vər lā′), past tense of
overlie. *v.*

o ver leap (ō′vər lēp′), leap over; pass
beyond: *Her joy overleaped all bounds.*
v., **o ver leaped** or **o ver leapt** (ō′vər-
lept′), **o ver leap ing.**

o ver lie (ō′vər lī′), lie over; lie upon.
v., **o ver lay, o ver lain, o ver ly ing.**

o ver load (ō′vər lōd′ *for 1;* ō′vər lōd′
for 2), 1 load too heavily: *overload a
boat.* 2 too great a load: *The overload
of electric current blew the fuse.* 1 *v.,*
2 *n.*

o ver look (ō′vər lùk′ *for 1-3;* ō′vər-
lùk′ *for 4*), 1 fail to see: *overlook a bill.*
2 pay no attention to; excuse: *I will
overlook your bad behavior this time.*
3 have a view of from above; be higher
than: *This high window overlooks half
the city.* 4 a high place from which
scenery or points of interest may be
viewed. 1-3 *v.,* 4 *n.*

o ver lord (ō′vər lôrd′), person who is
lord over another lord or other lords:
*The duke was the overlord of barons
and knights who held land from him. n.*

o ver ly (ō′vər lē), overmuch; excessively; too. *adv.*

o ver mas ter (ō′vər mas′tər), overcome; overpower. *v.*

o ver match (ō′vər mach′), be more
than a match for; surpass. *v.*

o ver much (ō′vər much′), too much.
adj., adv., n.

o ver night (ō′vər nīt′ *for 1,4,5;*
ō′vər nīt′ *for 2,3*), 1 during the night:
stay overnight. 2 done, occurring, etc.,
during the night: *an overnight stop.*
3 for the night: *overnight guests. An
overnight bag contains articles needed for*

one night's stay. **4** on the night before: *Preparations were made overnight for an early start.* **5** at once; immediately; in a very short time: *Change will not come overnight.* 1,4,5 *adv.,* 2,3 *adj.*

o ver pass (ō′vər pas′ *for 1;* ō′vər pas′ *for 2-4*), **1** bridge over a road, railroad, canal, etc. **2** pass over (a region, bounds, etc.). **3** go beyond; exceed; surpass. **4** pass without notice; overlook; disregard. 1 *n., pl.* **o ver pass es;** 2-4 *v.,* **o ver passed** or **o ver past** (ō′vər past′), **o ver pass ing.**

o ver pay (ō′vər pā′), **1** pay too much. **2** pay more than (an amount due). *v.,* **o ver paid** (ō′vər pād′), **o ver pay ing.**

o ver play (ō′vər plā′), **1** play (a part, etc.) in an exaggerated manner. **2** play better than; surpass. *v.*

o ver pow er (ō′vər pou′ər), **1** overcome or conquer; master; overwhelm: *overpower one's enemies. I was overpowered by the heat.* **2** be much greater or stronger than: *The wind brought a terrible smell which overpowered all others. Sudden anger overpowered every other feeling. v.*

o ver pro duc tion (ō′vər prə duk′shən), production of more than is needed or more than can be sold. *n.*

o ver ran (ō′vər ran′), past tense of **overrun.** *v.*

o ver rate (ō′vər rāt′), rate or estimate too highly: *He overrated his strength and soon had to ask for help. v.,* **o ver rat ed, o ver rat ing.**

o ver reach (ō′vər rēch′), **1** reach over or beyond. **2** reach too far. **3** get the better of by cunning: *overreach someone in a bargain. v.*
overreach oneself, 1 fail or miss by trying for too much. **2** fail by being too crafty or tricky.

o ver ride (ō′vər rīd′), **1** act in spite of: *override advice or objections.* **2** prevail over: *The new rule overrides all previous ones.* **3** ride over; trample on. **4** ride over (a region, place, etc.). **5** tire out by riding; ride too much: *override a horse. v.,* **o ver rode** (ō′vər rōd′), **o ver rid den** (ō′vər rid′n), **o ver rid ing.**

o ver ripe (ō′vər rīp′), too ripe; more than ripe. *adj.*

o ver rule (ō′vər rül′), **1** rule or decide against (a plea, argument, objection, etc.); set aside: *The president overruled my plan.* **2** prevail over; be stronger than: *I was overruled by the majority. v.,* **o ver ruled, o ver rul ing.**

o ver run (ō′vər run′), **1** spread over and spoil or harm in some way, as weeds, insects, disease, or invading troops do. **2** spread over: *Vines overran the wall.* **3** run or go beyond; exceed: *The TV show overran its time limit. v.,*

o ver ran, o ver run, o ver run ning.

o ver saw (ō′vər sô′), past tense of **oversee.** *v.*

o ver sea (ō′vər sē′ *for adv.;* ō′vər sē′ *for adj.*), overseas. *adv., adj.*

o ver seas (ō′vər sēz′ *for 1;* ō′vər sēz′ *for 2,3*), **1** across the sea; beyond the sea; abroad: *travel overseas.* **2** done, used, or serving overseas: *overseas service, overseas equipment.* **3** of countries across the sea; foreign: *overseas trade.* 1 *adv.,* 2,3 *adj.*

o ver see (ō′vər sē′), look after and direct (work or workers); supervise; manage: *oversee a factory. v.,* **o ver saw, o ver seen** (ō′vər sēn′), **o ver see ing.**

o ver se er (ō′vər sē′ər), person who oversees others or their work. *n.*

o ver set (ō′vər set′ *for 1;* ō′vər set′ *for 2*), **1** to upset; overturn. **2** an upset. 1 *v.,* **o ver set, o ver set ting;** 2 *n.*

o ver shad ow (ō′vər shad′ō), **1** be more important than: *That older girl overshadows her sister in school.* **2** cast a shadow over; make dark or gloomy. *v.*

overshoes

o ver shoe (ō′vər shü′), a waterproof shoe or boot, often made of rubber, worn over another shoe to keep the foot dry and warm. *n.*

o ver shoot (ō′vər shüt′), **1** shoot over, higher than, or beyond. **2** go over, higher than, or beyond. **3** go too far. *v.,* **o ver shot, o ver shoot ing.**

o ver shot (ō′vər shot′ *for 1,2;* ō′vər shot′ *for 3*), **1** having the upper jaw projecting beyond the lower. **2** driven by water flowing over from above. **3** past tense and past participle of **overshoot.** 1,2 *adj.,* 3 *v.*

o ver sight (ō′vər sīt′), **1** failure to notice or think of something: *Through an oversight, the kitten got no supper last night.* **2** watchful care: *While children are at school they are under their teacher's oversight and direction. n.*

o ver size (ō′vər sīz′), too big; larger than the proper or usual size. *adj.*

o ver sized (ō′vər sīzd′), oversize. *adj.*

o ver sleep (ō′vər slēp′), sleep beyond (a certain hour); sleep too long. *v.,* **o ver slept, o ver sleep ing.**

o ver slept (ō′vər slept′), past tense and past participle of **oversleep.** *I overslept and missed the bus. I have overslept three days in a row. v.*

o ver spread (ō′vər spred′), spread

hat, āge, fär; let, ēqual, tėrm;
it, īce; hot, ōpen, ôrder;
oil, out; cup, put, rüle; ch, child;
ng, long; sh, she; th, thin;
ͰH, then; zh, measure;

ə represents *a* in about,
e in taken, *i* in pencil,
o in lemon, *u* in circus.

over: *Ivy overspread the old cabin. v.,* **o ver spread, o ver spread ing.**

o ver state (ō′vər stāt′), state too strongly; exaggerate. *v.,* **o ver stat ed, o ver stat ing.**

o ver state ment (ō′vər stāt′mənt), too strong a statement; exaggeration. *n.*

o ver stay (ō′vər stā′), stay beyond the time of. *v.*

o ver step (ō′vər step′), go beyond; exceed. *v.,* **o ver stepped, o ver step ping.**

o ver stock (ō′vər stok′ *for 1;* ō′vər stok′ *for 2*), **1** supply with more than is needed. **2** too great a stock or supply. 1 *v.,* 2 *n.*

o ver sup ply (ō′vər sə plī′ *for 1;* ō′vər sə plī′ *for 2*), **1** supply with more than is needed. **2** too great a supply. 1 *v.,* **o ver sup plied, o ver sup ply ing;** 2 *n., pl.* **o ver sup plies.**

o vert (ō′vėrt′ *or* ō vėrt′), open or public; evident; not hidden: *Hitting someone is an overt act. adj.* **—o′vert ly,** *adv.*

overshot (def. 2)—overshot water wheel

o ver take (ō′vər tāk′), **1** come up with; catch up to: *I ran and overtook my friends.* **2** come upon suddenly: *A storm overtook the children. v.,* **o ver took, o ver tak en, o ver tak ing.**

o ver tak en (ō′vər tā′kən), past participle of **overtake.** *v.*

o ver tax (ō′vər taks′), **1** tax too heavily. **2** put too heavy a burden on. *v.*

o ver threw (ō′vər thrü′), past tense of **overthrow.** *v.*

o ver throw (ō′vər thrō′ *for 1-4;* ō′vər thrō′ *for 5*), **1** take away the power of; defeat: *overthrow a king.* **2** put an end to; destroy: *overthrow slavery.* **3** to overturn; upset; knock down. **4** throw (a ball) past the place for which it is

adj.	adjective	*n.*	noun
adv.	adverb	*prep.*	preposition
conj.	conjunction	*pron.*	pronoun
interj.	interjection	*v.*	verb
sing.	singular	*pl.*	plural

intended. **5** a defeat; upset: *The overthrow of his plans left him much discouraged.* 1-4 *v.*, **o ver threw, o ver thrown, o ver throw ing;** 5 *n.*

o ver thrown (ō′vər thrōn′), past participle of **overthrow.** *v.*

o ver time (ō′vər tīm′), **1** extra time; time beyond the regular hours. **2** wages for this period. **3** beyond the regular hours: *to work overtime.* **4** of or for overtime: *overtime work.* 1,2 *n.*, 3 *adv.*, 4 *adj.*

o ver tone (ō′vər tōn′), a fainter and higher musical tone heard along with the main or fundamental tone; harmonic. *n.*

o ver took (ō′vər tůk′), past tense of **overtake.** *v.*

o ver top (ō′vər top′), **1** rise above; be higher than: *The new building will overtop all the others.* **2** surpass; excel. *v.*, **o ver topped, o ver top ping.**

o ver ture (ō′vər chùr), **1** proposal or offer: *The enemy is making overtures for peace.* **2** a musical composition played by the orchestra as an introduction to an opera, oratorio, or other long musical composition. *n.*

o ver turn (ō′vər tèrn′ *for 1-3;* ō′vər tèrn′ *for 4*), **1** turn upside down. **2** upset; fall down; fall over: *The boat overturned.* **3** make fall down; overthrow; defeat; destroy the power of: *The rebels overturned the government.* **4** an overturning. 1-3 *v.*, 4 *n.*

o ver ween ing (ō′vər wē′ning). thinking too much of oneself; conceited; self-confident; presumptuous. *adj.*

o ver weight (ō′vər wāt′ *for 1-3;* ō′vər wāt′ *for 4*), **1** having too much weight: *a boy overweight for his age.* **2** too much weight. **3** extra weight: *The butcher gave us overweight on this roast.* **4** overburden: *a small child overweighted with heavy schoolbooks.* 1 *adj.*, 2,3 *n.*, 4 *v.*

o ver whelm (ō′vər hwelm′), **1** overcome completely; crush: *overwhelm with grief.* **2** cover completely as a flood would: *A great wave overwhelmed the boat.* *v.*

o ver whelm ing (ō′vər hwel′ming), too many, too great, or too much to be resisted; overpowering: *an overwhelming majority of votes.* *adj.* —**o′ver whelm′ing ly,** *adv.*

o ver work (ō′vər wèrk′ *for 1,3;* ō′vər wèrk′ *for 2,4*), **1** too much or too hard work: *exhausted from overwork.* **2** work too hard or too long. **3** extra work. **4** to use to excess. 1,3 *n.*, 2,4 *v.*, **o ver worked** or **o ver wrought, o ver work ing.**

o ver wrought (ō′vər rôt′), **1** wearied or exhausted by too much work or excitement; greatly excited: *overwrought nerves.* **2** too elaborate. **3** overworked; a past tense and past participle of **overwork.** 1,2 *adj.*, 3 *v.*

Ov id (ov′id), 43 B.C.-A.D. 17?, Roman poet. *n.*

o vi duct (ō′və dukt), tube through which the ovum or egg passes from the ovary. *n.*

o vip ar ous (ō vip′ər əs), producing eggs that are hatched after leaving the body. Birds are oviparous. *adj.*

o vi pos i tor (ō′və poz′ə tər), (in certain female insects) an organ at the end of the abdomen, by which eggs are deposited. *n.*

o void (ō′void), **1** egg-shaped. **2** an egg-shaped object. 1 *adj.*, 2 *n.*

o vule (ō′vyül), **1** a small ovum, especially when immature or unfertilized. **2** part of a plant that develops into a seed. See **ovary** for diagram. *n.*

o vum (ō′vəm), the germ cell produced by the female in the ovary; egg. After the ovum is fertilized, a new organism or embryo develops. *n.*, *pl.* **o va** (ō′və).

owe (ō), **1** have to pay; be in debt for: *I owe the grocer $10.* **2** be in debt: *I am always owing for something.* **3** be obliged or indebted for: *We owe a great deal to our parents.* *v.*, **owed, ow ing.**

ow ing (ō′ing), due; owed: *pay what is owing.* *adj.*

owing to, on account of; because of; as a result of: *Owing to a serious illness, she was absent from school for over a month.*

oxford (def. 1)

owl (oul), bird with a big head, big eyes, and a short, hooked beak. Owls hunt small animals and birds at night. Some kinds have tufts of feathers on their heads, called "horns" or "ears." *n.*

owl et (ou′lit), **1** a young owl. **2** a small owl. *n.*

owl ish (ou′lish), like an owl; like an owl's: *owlish eyes, an owlish look of wisdom.* *adj.*

own (ōn), **1** have or possess: *They own much land. I own many books.* **2** of oneself or itself; belonging to oneself or itself: *We have our own troubles. The house is her own.* **3** acknowledge; admit; confess: *He owned his guilt. She owns to many faults.* **4** acknowledge as belonging to: *Her family will not own her.* 1,3,4 *v.*, 2 *adj.*

come into one's own, 1 get what belongs to one. **2** get the success or credit that one deserves.

hold one's own, keep one's position; not be forced back.

of one's own, belonging to oneself.

on one's own, not ruled or directed by someone else.

own up, confess fully: *own up to a crime.*

own er (ō′nər), one who owns: *Who is the owner of this dog?* *n.*

own er ship (ō′nər ship), condition of being an owner; the possessing (of something); right of possession: *He claimed ownership of the abandoned car.* *n.*

ox (oks), **1** the full-grown male of domestic cattle, that has been castrated and is used for farm work or for beef. The ox is slow-moving but very strong. **2** any of the group of mammals with horns and cloven hoofs to which domestic cattle, buffaloes, and bison belong. *n.*, *pl.* **ox en.** —**ox′like′,** *adj.*

oxbows
(def. 1)

YOKE

OXBOW

ox bow (oks′bō′), **1** a U-shaped piece of wood placed under and around the neck of an ox, with the upper ends inserted in the bar of the yoke. **2** a U-shaped bend in a river. *n.*

ox cart (oks′kärt′), cart drawn by oxen. *n.*

ox en (ok′sən), plural of **ox.** *n.*

ox ford (ok′sfərd), **1** kind of low shoe, laced over the instep. **2** kind of cotton or rayon cloth used for shirts, blouses, and other garments. *n.* [from *Oxford,* the city]

Ox ford (ok′sfərd), **1** city in S England. **2** the very old and famous English university located there. *n.*

ox i da tion (ok′sə dā′shən), **1** an oxi-

owl
about 2 ft. tall

dizing; the combining of oxygen with another element to form one or more new substances. Burning is one kind of oxidation. 2 a being oxidized. *n.*

ox ide (ok′sīd), compound of oxygen with another element or radical. *n.*

ox i dize (ok′sə dīz), combine or cause to combine with oxygen: *Fuel oxidizes rapidly, producing heat. Water oxidizes some metals, producing rust. v.,* **ox i dized, ox i diz ing.**

ox y a cet y lene (ok′sē ə set′l ēn′), of, having to do with, or using a mixture of oxygen and acetylene. An oxyacetylene torch is used for welding or cutting metals. *adj.*

ox y gen (ok′sə jən), a colorless, odorless gas that forms about one fifth of the atmosphere. Oxygen is a chemical element present in combined form in water, carbon dioxide, iron ore, and many other substances. Animals and plants cannot live, and fire will not burn, without oxygen. *n.*

ox y gen ate (ok′sə jə nāt), treat or combine with oxygen. *v.,* **ox y gen at ed, ox y gen at ing.**

ox y gen a tion (ok′sə jə nā′shən), act or process of oxygenating. *n.*

oxygen mask, device worn over the nose and mouth through which oxygen is supplied from an attached container. Oxygen masks are used by aviators at high altitudes, by firemen, by submarine crews, etc.

oxygen tent, a small, usually transparent tent which is supplied with a constant, regulated flow of oxygen and placed over the head and shoulders of a patient who has difficulty breathing.

o yez (ō′yes), hear! attend! a cry uttered, usually three times, by a public or court crier to command silence and attention before a proclamation is made. *interj., n.*

oys ter (oi′stər), kind of mollusk much used as food, having a rough, irregular shell in two halves. Oysters are found in shallow water along seacoasts. Some kinds yield pearls. *n.*

oyster bed, a place where oysters breed or are cultivated.

oz., ounce. *pl.* **oz.** or **ozs.**

hat, āge, fär; let, ēqual, tėrm;
it, īce; hot, ōpen, ôrder;
oil, out; cup, pùt, rüle; ch, child;
ng, long; sh, she; th, thin;
ŦH, then; zh, measure;

ə represents *a* in about,
e in taken, *i* in pencil,
o in lemon, *u* in circus.

O zark Mountains (ō′zärk), a low mountain range in S Missouri, N Arkansas, and E Oklahoma.

O zarks (ō′zärks), the Ozark Mountains. *n.pl.*

o zone (ō′zōn), 1 form of oxygen with a sharp, pungent odor, produced by electricity and present in the air, especially after a thunderstorm. It is a strong oxidizing agent and is produced commercially for use in bleaching, in sterilizing water, etc. 2 INFORMAL. pure air that is refreshing. *n.*

Pp

P or **p** (pē), the 16th letter of the alphabet. *n., pl.* **P's** or **p's.**

mind one's P's and Q's, be careful about what one says or does.

p., 1 page. 2 participle.

pa (pä), INFORMAL. papa; father. *n.*

Pa., Pennsylvania.

pace (pās), 1 a step. 2 walk with regular steps: *The tiger paced up and down his cage.* 3 walk over with regular steps: *pace the floor.* 4 the length of a step in walking; about 2½ feet: *There were perhaps ten paces between me and the bear.* 5 measure by paces: *We paced off the distance and found it to be 69 paces.* 6 way of stepping. The walk, trot, and canter are some of the paces of the horse. 7 a particular pace of some horses in which the feet on the same side are lifted and put down together. 8 move at a pace: *Some horses are trained to pace.* 9 rate or speed: *a fast pace in walking.* 10 set the pace for: *A motorboat will pace the crew training for the rowing match.* 1,4,6,7,9 *n.,* 2,3,5,8,10 *v.,* **paced, pac ing.**

keep pace with, keep up with; go as fast as.

put one through his paces, try one out; find out what one can do.

set the pace, 1 set an example of speed for others to keep up with. 2 be an example or model for others to follow.

pac er (pā′sər), 1 person or thing that paces. 2 horse that lifts and puts down the feet on the same side together. *n.*

pach y derm (pak′ə dėrm′), a thick-skinned mammal with hoofs. The elephant, hippopotamus, and rhinoceros are pachyderms. *n.*

pa cif ic (pə sif′ik), 1 tending to make peace; making peace: *The traders made pacific advances toward the natives.* 2 loving peace; not warlike: *The Quakers are a pacific people.* 3 peaceful; calm; quiet: *pacific weather. adj.* —**pa-cif′i cal ly,** *adv.*

Pa cif ic (pə sif′ik), 1 ocean west of North and South America. It extends to Asia and Australia. 2 of the Pacific Ocean. 3 on, in, over, or near the Pacific Ocean: *Pacific air routes.* 4 of or on the Pacific coast of the United States: *California is one of the Pacific states.* 1 *n.,* 2-4 *adj.*

pac i fi ca tion (pas′ə fə kā′shən), a pacifying; making peaceful; being in a state of peace. *n.*

Pacific Standard Time, the stan-dard time in the westernmost parts of the continental United States and Canada, excluding most of Alaska. It is eight hours behind Greenwich Time.

pac i fi er (pas′ə fī′ər), 1 person or thing that pacifies. 2 a rubber or plastic nipple or ring given to a baby to suck. *n.*

pac i fism (pas′ə fiz′əm), the principle or policy of universal peace; settlement of all differences between nations by peaceful means; opposition to war. *n.*

pac i fist (pas′ə fist), person who is opposed to war and favors settling all disputes between nations by peaceful means. *n.*

pac i fy (pas′ə fī), 1 make peaceful; quiet down: *pacify angry demonstrators, pacify a crying baby.* 2 bring under control; subdue: *pacify a rebellious region.* *v.,* **pac i fied, pac i fy ing.**

pack[1] (pak), 1 bundle of things wrapped up or tied together for carrying: *The hiker carried a pack on her back.* 2 put things together in a bundle, box, bale, etc.: *Pack your clothes in this bag. Are you ready to pack?* 3 put into a container to be sold or stored: *Meat, fish, and vegetables are often packed in cans.* 4 fill with things; put one's things into: *Pack your trunk.* 5 press or crowd closely together: *A hundred men were packed into one small room.* 6 fill (a space) with all that it will hold: *pack a small theater with a large audience.* 7 a set; lot; a number together: *a pack of thieves, a pack of nonsense, a pack of lies.* 8 a number of animals of the same kind hunting together: *Wolves hunt in packs; lions hunt alone.* 9 group of dogs kept together for hunting. 10 a complete set of playing cards, usually 52. 11 a large area of floating pieces of ice pushed together: *A ship forced its way through the pack.* 12 make tight with something that water, steam, air, etc., cannot leak through: *The plumber packed the joint in the two sections of pipe with string and a special compound.* 13 INFORMAL. carry: *pack a gun.* 1,7-11 *n.,* 2-6,12,13 *v.* [probably from Dutch of the 1200's *pac*]

pack off, send away: *The child was packed off to bed.*

send packing, send away in a hurry.

pack[2] (pak), arrange unfairly. To pack a jury is to fill it with those who will favor one side. *v.* [perhaps special use of *pack*[1]]

pack age (pak′ij), 1 bundle of things packed or wrapped together; box with things packed in it; parcel. 2 put in a package. 1 *n.,* 2 *v.,* **pack aged, pack-ag ing.**

pack animal, animal used for carrying loads or packs.

pack er (pak′ər), person or thing that packs, especially a person or company that packs meat, fruit, vegetables, etc., to be sold to wholesalers. *n.*

pack et (pak′it), 1 a small package; parcel: *a packet of letters.* 2 packet boat. *n.*

packet boat, boat that carries mail, passengers, and goods regularly on a fixed route.

pack horse (pak′hôrs′), horse used to carry packs of goods. *n.*

pack ing (pak′ing), 1 material used to keep water, steam, etc., from leaking through: *the packing around the valves of a radiator.* 2 material placed around goods to protect them from damage in shipment, storage, etc. 3 business of preparing and packing meat, fish, fruit, vegetables, etc., to be sold. *n.*

packing house, place where foods are prepared and packed to be sold.

pack rat, a large North American rat with a bushy tail, that carries away bits of food, clothing, small tools, etc., and hides them in its nest.

pact (pakt), agreement; compact: *The three nations signed a peace pact.* *n.*

pad[1] (pad), 1 a soft mass used for comfort, protection, or stuffing; cushion: *The baby's carriage has a pad made to fit it.* 2 fill with something soft; stuff: *pad a chair, pad a suit for football.* 3 one of the cushionlike parts on the bottom side of the feet of dogs, foxes, and some other animals. 4 foot of a dog, fox, etc. 5 the large floating leaf of the water lily. 6 number of sheets of paper fastened along one edge; tablet. 7 cloth soaked with ink to use with a rubber stamp. 8 use words just to fill space: *pad a short story with anecdotes.* 9 launching pad: *The huge rocket rose from the pad at sunrise.* 10 SLANG. room, house, or apartment: *My pad is on the third floor.* 1,3-7,9,10 *n.,* 2,8 *v.,* **pad ded, pad ding.** [origin uncertain]

pad[2] (pad), 1 go on foot; walk; tramp; trudge. 2 walk or trot softly: *a wolf padding through the forest.* 3 a dull sound, as of footsteps on the ground. 1,2 *v.,* **pad ded, pad ding;** 3 *n.* [probably from earlier Dutch *pad* path]

pad ding (pad′ing), 1 material used to pad with, such as hair, cotton, or straw. 2 words used just to fill space in making a speech or a written paper longer. *n.*

pad dle[1] (pad′l), 1 a short, lightweight oar with a broad blade at one end or both ends, usually held with both hands

paddle[1]
(def. 1)

in rowing a boat or canoe. 2 row (a boat or canoe) with a paddle or paddles. 3 act of paddling; a turn at the paddle. 4 one of the broad boards fixed around a water wheel or a paddle wheel to push, or be pushed by, the water. 5 a paddle-shaped piece of wood used for stirring, for beating clothes, etc. 6 a small, flat wooden racket used to hit the ball in table tennis. 7 beat with a paddle; spank. 1,3-6 *n.*, 2,7 *v.*, **pad dled, pad dling.** [origin uncertain]

pad dle[2] (pad/l), move the hands or feet about in water: *Children love to paddle at the beach.* *v.*, **pad dled, pad dling.** [apparently related to *pad*[2]]

pad dler (pad/lər), person who paddles a canoe or boat. *n.*

PADDLE WHEEL

paddle wheel, wheel with paddles fixed around it for propelling a ship over the water.

pad dock (pad/ək), 1 a small, enclosed field near a stable or house, used for exercising animals or as a pasture. 2 pen at a race track where horses are saddled before a race. *n.*

pad dy (pad/ē), 1 rice in the husk, uncut or gathered. 2 field of rice. *n., pl.* **pad dies.**

Pad e rew ski (pad/ə ref/skē), Ignace Jan, 1860-1941, Polish pianist, composer, and statesman. *n.*

padlock (def. 1)

pad lock (pad/lok/), 1 a lock that can be put on and removed. It hangs by a curved bar, hinged at one end and snapped shut at the other. 2 fasten with a padlock. 1 *n.*, 2 *v.*

pa dre (pä/drā), 1 father. It is used as a name for a priest, especially in regions where Spanish, Portuguese, or Italian is spoken. 2 INFORMAL. chaplain in the armed forces. *n.*

pae an (pē/ən), song of praise, joy, or triumph. *n.*

pa gan (pā/gən), 1 person who is not a Christian, Jew, or Moslem; one who worships many gods or no god; a heathen. The ancient Greeks and Romans were pagans. 2 of or having to do with pagans; heathen: *pagan customs.* 3 person who has no religion. 1,3 *n.*, 2 *adj.*

Pa ga ni ni (pag/ə nē/nē), **Nicolò,** 1782-1840, Italian violinist. *n.*

pa gan ism (pā/gə niz/əm), 1 a pagan attitude toward religion or morality. 2 the beliefs and practices of pagans. 3 condition of being a pagan. *n.*

page[1] (pāj), 1 one side of a leaf or sheet of paper: *a page in this book.* 2 the print or writing on one side of a leaf. 3 a record: *the pages of history.* 4 a happening or time considered as part of history: *The settling of the West is an exciting page in American history.* 5 number the pages of. 1-4 *n.*, 5 *v.*, **paged, pag ing.** [from French of the 1400's *page,* from Latin *pagina*]

page[2] (pāj), 1 person who runs errands or delivers messages. Pages at hotels usually wear uniforms. 2 try to find (a person) at a hotel, club, etc., by having his name called out. 3 a youth who attends a person of rank. 4 a youth who was preparing to be a knight. 1,3,4 *n.*, 2 *v.*, **paged, pag ing.** [from French of the 1200's *page,* perhaps from Latin *pagius* country person]

pag eant (paj/ənt), 1 an elaborate spectacle; procession in costume; pomp; display; show: *The coronation of a new ruler is always a splendid pageant.* 2 a public entertainment that represents scenes from history, legend, or the like: *Our school gave a pageant of the coming of the Pilgrims to America.* *n.*

pag eant ry (paj/ən trē), 1 a splendid show; gorgeous display; pomp. 2 mere show; empty display. *n., pl.* **pag eantries.**

pa go da (pə gō/də), temple having many stories, with a roof curving upward from each story. There are pagodas in India, China, Japan, and other Asian countries. *n., pl.* **pa go das.**

paid (pād), 1 receiving money; hired: *a paid worker, a paid informer.* 2 past tense and past participle of **pay.** *I paid my bills. These bills have been paid.* 1 *adj.*, 2 *v.*

pail (pāl), 1 a round container for carrying liquids, etc.; bucket: *a milk pail.* 2 the amount a pail holds; pailful. *n.*

pail ful (pāl/ful), amount that fills a pail. *n., pl.* **pail fuls.**

pain (pān), 1 a feeling of being hurt; suffering: *A cut gives pain. The death of one we love causes pain.* 2 cause to suffer; give pain: *Does your tooth pain you?* 1 *n.*, 2 *v.*

on pain of or **under pain of,** with the punishment or penalty of unless a certain thing is done: *The traitor was ordered to leave the country on pain of death.*

hat, āge, fär; let, ēqual, tėrm; it, īce; hot, ōpen, ôrder; oil, out; cup, pùt, rüle; ch, child; ng, long; sh, she; th, thin; ᵮH, then; zh, measure;

ə represents *a* in about, *e* in taken, *i* in pencil, *o* in lemon, *u* in circus.

take pains, be careful: *I took pains to be neat with my book report.*

Paine (pān), **Thomas,** 1737-1809, American writer on politics and religion, born in England. *n.*

pained (pānd), 1 hurt, distressed, grieved, etc.: *I am greatly pained to learn of your refusal.* 2 expressing or showing pain: *a pained look.* *adj.*

pain ful (pān/fəl), 1 causing pain; unpleasant; hurting: *a painful illness, a painful duty.* 2 difficult. *adj.* —**pain/ful ly,** *adv.* —**pain/ful ness,** *n.*

pain less (pān/lis), without pain; causing no pain. *adj.* —**pain/less ly,** *adv.*

pains tak ing (pānz/tā/king), very careful; particular; scrupulous: *a painstaking painter.* *adj.* —**pains/tak/ing ly,** *adv.*

pagoda in the Chinese style of architecture

paint (pānt), 1 substance consisting of solid coloring matter or pigment mixed with a liquid, that can be spread on a surface to make a layer or film of white, black, or colored matter. 2 cover or decorate with paint: *paint a house.* 3 use paint. 4 represent (an object) in colors: *The artist painted fairies and angels.* 5 make pictures. 6 picture vividly in words. 7 coloring matter put on the face or body. 8 put on like paint: *The doctor painted iodine on the cut.* 1,7 *n.*, 2-6,8 *v.*

paint brush (pānt/brush/), brush for putting on paint. *n., pl.* **paint brushes.**

paint er[1] (pān/tər), 1 person who paints pictures; artist. 2 person who paints houses, woodwork, etc. *n.* [from French of the 1300's *peinteur,* from Latin *pictorem,* from *pingere* to paint]

painter

adj. adjective	*n.* noun
adv. adverb	*prep.* preposition
conj. conjunction	*pron.* pronoun
interj. interjection	*v.* verb
sing. singular	*pl.* plural

SOFT PALATE
HARD PALATE

palate (def. 1)

paint er² (pān′tər), a rope, usually fastened to the bow of a boat, for tying it to a ship, pier, etc. *n.* [probably from French of the 1400's *pentoir* cordage for hanging, from Latin *pendere* to hang]

paint er³ (pān′tər), puma. *n.* [a different form of earlier English *panter* panther]

paint ing (pān′ting), 1 something painted; picture. 2 act of one who paints. *n.*

pair (per *or* par), 1 a set of two; two that go together: *a pair of shoes, a pair of horses.* 2 arrange or be arranged in pairs: *The gloves were neatly paired in a drawer.* 3 a single thing consisting of two parts that cannot be used separately: *a pair of scissors, a pair of trousers.* 4 two people who are married or are engaged to be married. 5 join in love and marriage. 6 two animals that are mated. 7 to mate. 8 two members on opposite sides in a legislative body who agree not to vote on a certain question. 9 the arrangement thus made. 1,3,4, 6,8,9 *n., pl.* **pairs** or **pair**; 2,5,7 *v.*
pair off, arrange in pairs; form into pairs.

pais ley (pāz′lē), having a detailed and colorful pattern: *a paisley shirt.* *adj.*

pa ja mas (pə jä′məz *or* pə jam′əz), garments to sleep in, etc., consisting of a coat and loose trousers fastened at the waist. *n.pl.* Also, **pyjamas.**

Pak i stan (pak′ə stan), country in S Asia, west of India. *Capital:* Islamabad. *n.*

Pak i stan i (pak′ə stan′ē), 1 person born or living in Pakistan. 2 of or having to do with Pakistan. 1 *n., pl.* **Pak i stan is** or **Pak i stan i**; 2 *adj.*

pal (pal), 1 a close friend; playmate; comrade. 2 to associate as pals. 1 *n.,* 2 *v.,* **palled, pal ling.**

pal ace (pal′is), 1 the official home of a king, queen, bishop, or some other exalt-ed personage. 2 a very fine house or building. *n.*

pal an quin or **pal an keen** (pal′-ən kēn′), a covered couch carried by poles resting on men's shoulders, formerly used in the Orient. *n.*

pal at a bil i ty (pal′ə tə bil′ə tē), palatable quality or condition. *n.*

pal at a ble (pal′ə tə bəl), agreeable to the taste; pleasing: *That was a most palatable lunch. I find your suggestion extremely palatable. adj.*

pal at a bly (pal′ə tə blē), in a palatable manner; agreeably. *adv.*

pal ate (pal′it), 1 the roof of the mouth. The bony part in front is the hard palate, and the fleshy part in back is the soft palate. 2 sense of taste: *The new flavor pleased my palate.* 3 a liking: *She loves sports but has little palate for card games. n.*

pa la tial (pə lā′shəl), like a palace; fit for a palace; magnificent: *a palatial apartment. adj.* **—pa la′tial ly,** *adv.*

pal a tine (pal′ə tīn), having royal rights in one's own territory. A count palatine was subject only to the emperor or king. *adj.*

pa lav er (pə lav′ər), 1 a parley or conference, especially between travelers and uncivilized natives. 2 smooth, persuading talk; flowing talk; flattery. 3 talk fluently and flatteringly. 1,2 *n.,* 3 *v.*

pale¹ (pāl), 1 without much color; whitish: *When you have been ill, your face is sometimes pale.* 2 not bright; dim: *pale blue. The bright stars are surrounded by hundreds of pale ones.* 3 turn pale: *His face paled at the bad news.* 1,2 *adj.,* **pal er, pal est;** 3 *v.,* **paled, pal ing.** [from French of the 1200's *pale,* from Latin *pallidum*] **—pale′ly,** *adv.*

pale² (pāl), 1 a long, narrow board, pointed at the top, used for fences. 2 boundary: *Criminals are outside the pale of civilized society.* 3 enclose with pales. 1,2 *n.,* 3 *v.,* **paled, pal ing.** [from French of the 1300's *pal,* from Latin *palum* stake]

palisades (def. 4)

pale face (pāl′fās′), a white person. The American Indians are said to have called white people palefaces. *n.*

pale ness (pāl′nis), condition of being pale. *n.*

palanquin

Pa le o lith ic (pā′lē ə lith′ik), of or having to do with the earlier part of the Stone Age. Paleolithic tools were crudely chipped out of stone. *adj.*

pa le on tol o gist (pā′lē on tol′-ə jist), an expert in paleontology. *n.*

pa le on tol o gy (pā′lē on tol′ə jē), science of the forms of life existing in prehistoric time, as represented by fossil animals and plants. *n.*

Pa le o zo ic (pā′lē ə zō′ik), 1 the geological era whose fossils represent early forms of life. Fishes, insects, and reptiles developed during the Paleozoic. 2 of this era or its rocks. 1 *n.,* 2 *adj.*

Pa ler mo (pə ler′mō), seaport and capital of Sicily, in the NW part. *n.*

Pal es tine (pal′ə stīn), region or country in SW Asia between the Mediterranean Sea and the Jordan River. The name has been applied since ancient times to the land of the Jews. Palestine is often called the Holy Land and in the Bible is called Canaan. It is now divided chiefly between Israel and Jordan. *n.*

palette (def. 1)

pal ette (pal′it), 1 a thin board, usually oval or oblong, with a thumb hole at one end, used by painters to lay and mix colors on. 2 set of colors on this board. *n.*

pal frey (pôl′frē), OLD USE. a gentle riding horse, especially one used by women. *n., pl.* **pal freys.**

pal ing (pā′ling), 1 fence of pales. 2 pale in a fence. *n.*

pal i sade (pal′ə sād′), 1 a long, strong, wooden stake pointed at the top end. 2 a fence of stakes set firmly in the ground to enclose or defend. 3 furnish or surround with a palisade. 4 **pal i sades,** *pl.* a line of high, steep cliffs. 1,2,4 *n.,* 3 *v.,* **pal i sad ed, pal i sad ing.**

pall¹ (pôl), 1 a heavy, dark cloth, often made of velvet, spread over a coffin, a hearse, or a tomb. 2 a dark, gloomy covering: *A thick pall of smoke shut out the sun from the city. n.* [Old English *pæll*, from Latin *pallium* cloak]

pall[2] (pôl), become distasteful or very tiresome because there has been too much of it: *Even the most tasty food palls if it is served day after day without variety. v.* [a different form of *appall*, which came from French of the 1300's *apallir* become pale]

pal la di um (pə lā′dē əm), a soft, light, silver-white metallic element which occurs in nature with platinum. Palladium is used in making scientific instruments, in alloys with precious metals such as gold and silver, and as a catalyst. *n.*

Pal las (pal′əs), (in Greek myths) a name of Athena. *n.*

pall bear er (pôl′ber′ər *or* pôl′bar′-ər), one of the men who walk with or carry the coffin at a funeral. *n.*

pal let (pal′it), bed of straw; poor bed. *n.*

pal li ate (pal′ē āt), 1 lessen without curing; mitigate: *palliate a disease.* 2 make appear less serious; excuse: *palliate a fault. v.*, **pal li at ed, pal li at ing.**

pal li a tive (pal′ē ā′tiv), 1 useful to lessen or soften; mitigating; excusing. 2 something that lessens, softens, mitigates, or excuses. 1 *adj.*, 2 *n.*

pal lid (pal′id), lacking color; pale: *a pallid face. adj.*

pal lor (pal′ər), lack of color from fear, illness, death, etc.; paleness. *n.*

palm[1] (päm), 1 the inside of the hand between the wrist and the fingers. 2 the width of a hand; 3 to 4 inches. 3 the part of a glove covering the palm. 4 conceal in the hand: *The magician palmed the nickel.* 5 pass or get accepted (something not good). 1-3 *n.*, 4,5 *v.* [from French of the 1300's *paume*, from Latin *palma*]

palm off, pass off or get accepted by tricks, fraud, or false representation.

palm[2] (päm), 1 any of a group of trees or shrubs which grow in warm climates. Most palms have tall trunks, no branches, and many large leaves at the top. 2 leaf or stalk of leaves of a palm tree, used as a symbol of victory or triumph. 3 victory; triumph. *n.* [Old English *pælm*, from Latin *palma* palm tree, palm[1] (perhaps because the shape of the leaves is somewhat like a hand)] —**palm′like′, adj.**

bear off the palm or **carry off the palm,** be the victor; win: *She bore off the palm both in tennis and swimming.*

pal mate (pal′māt), shaped like a hand with the fingers spread out: *a palmate leaf.* See **leaf** for picture. *adj.*

Palm Beach, winter resort in SE Florida.

palm er (pä′mər), 1 pilgrim returning from the Holy Land bringing a palm branch as a token. 2 pilgrim. *n.*

pal met to (pal met′ō), kind of palm with fan-shaped leaves, abundant on the southeastern coast of the United States. *n., pl.* **pal met tos** or **pal met toes.**

palm ist (pä′mist), person who claims to be able to tell fortunes by examining the palm of the hand. *n.*

palm is try (pä′mə strē), the supposed art of telling a person's fortune from lines and marks in the palm of his hand. *n.*

Palm Sunday, the Sunday before Easter Sunday.

palm y (pä′mē), 1 abounding in palms; shaded by palms. 2 flourishing; prosperous; glorious: *palmy days of peace. adj.*, **palm i er, palm i est.**

pal o mi no (pal′ə mē′nō), a cream-colored or golden-tan horse of Arabian stock. Its mane and tail are usually lighter colored. *n., pl.* **pal o mi nos.**

pal pa ble (pal′pə bəl), 1 readily seen or heard and recognized; obvious: *a palpable error.* 2 that can be felt by touching; tangible. *adj.*

pal pa bly (pal′pə blē), 1 plainly; obviously. 2 to the touch. *adv.*

pal pi tate (pal′pə tāt), 1 beat very rapidly; throb: *Your heart palpitates when you are excited.* 2 quiver; tremble: *They palpitated with terror. v.*, **pal pi tat ed, pal pi tat ing.**

pal pi ta tion (pal′pə tā′shən), 1 a very rapid beating of the heart; throb. 2 a quivering; trembling. *n.*

pal sied (pôl′zēd), 1 having palsy; paralyzed. 2 shaking; trembling. *adj.*

pal sy (pôl′zē), 1 paralysis, especially a form of paralysis occurring late in life, characterized by trembling and muscular weakness. 2 afflict with palsy; paralyze. 1 *n., pl.* **pal sies;** 2 *v.*, **pal sied, pal sy ing.**

pal ter (pôl′tər), 1 talk or act insincerely; trifle deceitfully: *Do not palter with the truth.* 2 act carelessly; trifle: *Do not palter with a decision involving life and death.* 3 deal crookedly; use tricks and dodges in bargaining. *v.*

pal tri ness (pôl′trē nis), very slight value; meanness. *n.*

pal try (pôl′trē), almost worthless; trifling; petty; mean: *Pay no attention to paltry gossip. We sold our old, broken-down car for a paltry sum of money. adj.*, **pal tri er, pal tri est.**

pam pas (pam′pəz), the vast, grassy, treeless plains of South America, especially in Argentina. *n.pl.*

pam per (pam′pər), indulge too much; allow too many privileges: *pamper a child, pamper a sick person, pamper one's appetite. v.* —**pam′per er, n.**

hat, āge, fär; let, ēqual, tėrm;
it, īce; hot, ōpen, ôrder;
oil, out; cup, pùt, rüle; ch, child;
ng, long; sh, she; th, thin;
ŦH, then; zh, measure;

ə represents *a* in about,
e in taken, *i* in pencil,
o in lemon, *u* in circus.

pam phlet (pam′flit), booklet in paper covers. It often deals with a question of current interest. *n.*

pam phlet eer (pam′flə tir′), 1 writer of pamphlets. 2 write and issue pamphlets. 1 *n.*, 2 *v.*

pan (pan), 1 dish for cooking and other household uses, usually broad, shallow, and with no cover: *pots and pans.* 2 anything like this. Gold and other metals are sometimes obtained by washing ore in pans. The dishes on a pair of scales are called pans. 3 cook in a pan. 4 wash (gravel, sand, etc.) in a pan to separate the gold. 5 (in old-fashioned guns) the hollow part of the lock that held a little gunpowder to set the gun off. 6 hardpan. 7 INFORMAL. criticize severely: *The drama critic panned the new play.* 1,2,5,6 *n.*, 3,4,7 *v.*, **panned, pan ning.**

pan out, INFORMAL. turn out; work out: *His scheme panned out well.*

Pan (pan), (in Greek myths) the god of forests, pastures, flocks, and shepherds. Pan is described as a man with the legs, horns, and ears of a goat and as playing on musical pipes. *n.*

pan a ce a (pan′ə sē′ə), a remedy for all diseases or ills; cure-all. *n., pl.* **pan a ce as.**

Pan a ma (pan′ə mä), 1 Isthmus of, a narrow neck of land which connects North America with South America. 2 country on the Isthmus of Panama, on either side of the Canal Zone. 3 its capital, a seaport on the Bay of Panama. 4 **Bay of,** bay of the Pacific on the S coast of the Isthmus of Panama. 5 **panama,** a fine hat woven from the young leaves of a palmlike plant of Central and South America. *n., pl.* **pan a mas** for 5.

Panama Canal, canal cut across the Isthmus of Panama to connect the Atlantic and Pacific oceans. It was built and is owned by the United States.

Panama Canal Zone. See **Canal Zone.**

Pan a ma ni an (pan′ə mä′nē ən), 1 of or having to do with Panama. 2 person born or living in Panama. 1 *adj.*, 2 *n.*

Pan-American

adj.	adjective	n.	noun
adv.	adverb	prep.	preposition
conj.	conjunction	pron.	pronoun
interj.	interjection	v.	verb
sing.	singular	pl.	plural

Pan-A mer i can (pan/ə mer/ə kən), of all the people or countries of North, Central, and South America. *adj.*

pan cake (pan/kāk/), a thin, flat cake made of batter and fried or baked in a pan or on a griddle. *n.*

pan chro mat ic (pan/krō mat/ik), sensitive to light of all colors: *a panchromatic photographic film. adj.*

pan cre as (pan/krē əs), gland near the stomach that helps digestion. The pancreas secretes insulin into the blood and pancreatic juice, a digestive juice which contains various enzymes, into the small intestine. The pancreas of animals when used for food is called sweetbread. *n.*

pan cre at ic (pan/krē at/ik), of the pancreas: *pancreatic secretions. adj.*

panda (def. 1)—about 5 ft. long

pan da (pan/də), 1 a bearlike mammal of Tibet and parts of southern and southwestern China, mostly white with black legs, often called the **giant panda.** 2 a reddish-brown mammal somewhat like a raccoon, that lives in the Himalayas, often called the **lesser panda.** *n., pl.* **pan das.**

pan de mo ni um (pan/də mō/nē əm), 1 place of wild disorder or lawless confusion. 2 wild uproar or lawlessness. *n.*

pan der (pan/dər), 1 person who helps other people indulge low desires, passions, or vices. 2 act as a pander; supply material or opportunity for vices: *The newspaper pandered to people's liking for sensational stories.* 1 *n.,* 2 *v.* [shortened from *Pandarus,* a go-between in love affairs portrayed by Chaucer and Shakespeare]

Pan do ra (pan dôr/ə), (in Greek myths) the first woman, created by the gods to punish mankind for having learned the use of fire. Curiosity led her to open a box (**Pandora's box**) and thus let out all sorts of ills into the world. Only Hope remained at the bottom. *n.*

pane (pān), a single sheet of glass in a division of a window, a door, or a sash: *Hailstones as big as eggs broke several panes of glass. n.*

pan e gyr ic (pan/ə jir/ik), 1 speech or writing in praise of a person or thing. 2 enthusiastic or extravagant praise. *n.*

pan el (pan/l), 1 a strip or surface that is different in some way from what is around it. A panel is often sunk below or raised above the rest, and used for a decoration. Panels may be in a door or other woodwork, on large pieces of furniture, or made as parts of a dress. 2 arrange in panels; furnish or decorate with panels: *The room was paneled with oak.* 3 picture, photograph, or design much longer than wide. 4 list of persons called as jurors; the members of a jury. 5 a group formed for discussion: *A panel of experts gave its opinion on ways to solve the traffic problem.* 6 board containing the instruments, controls, or indicators used in operating an automobile, aircraft, computer, or other mechanism. 1,3-6 *n.,* 2 *v.*

panel discussion, the discussion of a particular issue by a selected group of people.

pan el ing (pan/l ing), panels collectively. *n.*

pan el ist (pan/l ist), person who takes part in a panel discussion. *n.*

pang (pang), a sudden, short, sharp pain or feeling: *the pangs of a toothache. A pang of pity moved my heart. n.*

pan han dle (pan/han/dl), 1 handle of a pan. 2 a narrow strip of land projecting like a handle: *the Texas panhandle. n.*

pan ic (pan/ik), 1 a fear spreading through a multitude of people so that they lose control of themselves; unreasoning fear: *When the theater caught fire, there was a panic. When four banks failed in one day, there was a panic among merchants.* 2 caused by panic; showing panic; unreasoning: *panic terror, panic haste.* 3 affect or be affected with panic: *The audience panicked when the fire broke out.* 1 *n.,* 2 *adj.,* 3 *v.,* **pan icked, pan ick ing.** [from Greek *Panikos* of the god *Pan,* because of his frightening effect upon people]

pan ick y (pan/ə kē), 1 caused by panic: *panicky haste.* 2 showing panic: *panicky actions.* 3 like panic: *panicky feelings.* 4 liable to lose self-control and have a panic. *adj.*

pan ic-strick en (pan/ik strik/ən), frightened out of one's wits; demoralized by fear. *adj.*

pan ni er (pan/ē ər), basket, especially one of a pair of considerable size to be slung across the shoulders or across the back of a beast of burden. *n.*

pan o plied (pan/ə plēd), completely armed, equipped, covered, or arrayed. *adj.*

pan o ply (pan/ə plē), 1 a complete suit of armor. 2 complete equipment or covering: *an Indian in panoply of paint and feathers. n., pl.* **pan o plies.**

panels (def. 1) in a wall

pan o ram a (pan/ə ram/ə), 1 a wide, unbroken view of a surrounding region: *a panorama of beach and sea.* 2 a complete survey of some subject: *a panorama of history.* 3 picture of a landscape or other scene, often shown as if seen from a central point; picture unrolled a part at a time and made to pass continuously before the spectators. 4 a continuously passing or changing scene: *the panorama of city life. n., pl.* **pan o ram as.**

pan o ram ic (pan/ə ram/ik), of or like a panorama: *a panoramic view. adj.*

panpipe

pan pipe (pan/pīp/), an early musical instrument made of reeds or tubes of different lengths, fastened together side by side, in order of their length. The reeds or tubes were closed at one end and the player blew across their open tops. *n.*

pan sy (pan/zē), 1 a flower somewhat like a violet but much larger and having flat, velvety petals, usually of several

panniers

610

colors. 2 the plant it grows on. *n., pl.* **pan sies.**

pant (pant), 1 breathe hard and quickly: *She is panting from playing tennis.* 2 a short, quick breath. 3 speak with short, quick breaths: *"Hurry, hurry,"* he *panted.* 4 long eagerly: *I am just panting for my turn.* 5 a puff of an engine. 6 emit steam or the like in loud puffs. 7 a throb. 1,3,4,6 *v.,* 2,5,7 *n.*

pan ta lets or **pan ta lettes** (pan′tl ets′), long drawers extending to the ankles, formerly worn by women and girls. *n.pl.*

pan ta loon (pan′tl ün′), 1 clown. 2 **Pantaloon,** a lean, foolish, old man wearing tight-fitting trousers who is a comic character in old Italian comedies. 3 **pantaloons,** *pl.* trousers. *n.*

pan the ism (pan′thē iz′əm), belief that God and the universe are the same; doctrine that God is an expression of the physical forces of nature. *n.*

pan the ist (pan′thē ist), believer in pantheism. *n.*

pan the is tic (pan′thē is′tik), of or having to do with pantheism or pantheists. *adj.*

Pan the on (pan′thē on), temple for all the gods, built at Rome about 27 B.C. and later used as a Christian church. *n.*

pan ther (pan′thər), 1 leopard, especially a black leopard. 2 puma. 3 jaguar. *n., pl.* **pan thers** or **pan ther.**

pan tie (pan′tē). Usually, **panties,** *pl.* undergarment with short legs worn by women and children. *n.* Also, **panty.**

pan to mime (pan′tə mīm), 1 a play without words, in which the actors express themselves by gestures. 2 gestures without words; dumb show. 3 express by gestures. 1,2 *n.,* 3 *v.,* **pan to mimed, pan to mim ing.**

pan try (pan′trē), a small room in which food, dishes, silverware, or table linen are kept. *n., pl.* **pan tries.**

pants (pants), 1 trousers. 2 underpants. *n.pl.*

pant suit (pant′süt′), a woman's or girl's suit consisting of a jacket and trousers. *n.*

pan ty (pan′tē), pantie. *n., pl.* **panties.**

pap (pap), soft food for infants or invalids. *n.*

pa pa (pä′pə), father; daddy. *n.*

pa pa cy (pā′pə sē), 1 position, rank, or authority of the pope. 2 time during which a pope rules. 3 all the popes. 4 government by a pope. *n., pl.* **pa pa cies.**

pa pal (pā′pəl), 1 of or having to do with the pope: *a papal letter.* 2 of the papacy. 3 of the Roman Catholic Church: *papal ritual. adj.*

pa paw (pô′pô), 1 a small North American tree having oblong, yellowish fruit.

---

2 its fruit, which is good to eat. 3 papaya. *n.* Also, **pawpaw.**

pa pa ya (pə pä′yə), 1 a tropical American tree that looks like the palm tree and bears a fruit with yellowish pulp that looks like a melon. 2 its fruit, which is good to eat. *n., pl.* **pa pa yas.**

pa per (pā′pər), 1 a material used for writing, printing, drawing, wrapping packages, and covering walls. Paper is made in thin sheets from wood pulp, rags, etc. 2 piece or sheet of paper. 3 piece or sheet of paper with writing or printing on it; document: *Important papers were stolen.* 4 **papers,** *pl.* documents telling who or what one is. 5 wrapper, container, or sheet of paper containing something: *a paper of pins.* 6 newspaper. 7 article; essay: *The professor read a paper on the teaching of English.* 8 a written promise to pay money; note. 9 made of paper: *paper dolls, paper money.* 10 like paper; thin: *almonds with paper shells.* 11 wallpaper. 12 cover with wallpaper: *paper a room.* 1-8,11 *n.,* 9,10 *adj.,* 12 *v.* —**pa′per er,** *n.*

on paper, 1 in writing or print. 2 in theory.

pa per back (pā′pər bak′), book with a paper binding or cover, usually sold at a low price. *n.*

pa per boy (pā′pər boi′), person who delivers or sells newspapers; newsboy. *n.*

pa per hang er (pā′pər hang′ər), person whose business is to cover walls with wallpaper. *n.*

paper money, money made of paper, not metal. A dollar bill is paper money.

pa per weight (pā′pər wāt′), a small, heavy object put on papers to keep them from being scattered. *n.*

pa pier-mâ ché (pā′per mə shā′), 1 a paper pulp mixed with some stiffener and molded when moist. It becomes hard and strong when dry. 2 made of papier-mâché. 1 *n.,* 2 *adj.* [from French *papier mâché* chewed paper]

pa pil la (pə pil′ə), a small, nipple-like projection having to do with the senses of touch, taste, or smell: *the papillae on the tongue. n., pl.* **pa pil lae** (pə pil′ē).

pa poose or **pap poose** (pa püs′), an American Indian baby. *n.*

pa pri ka (pa prē′kə *or* pap′rə kə), the ground, dried fruit of certain mild red peppers, used as a seasoning in food. *n., pl.* **pa pri kas.**

Pap u a (pap′yü ə), New Guinea. *n.*

pa py rus (pə pī′rəs), 1 a tall water plant from which the ancient Egyptians, Greeks, and Romans made a kind of paper to write on. 2 a writing material made from the pith of papyrus plants. 3 an ancient record written on papyrus. *n., pl.* **pa py ri** (pə pī′rī).

---

hat, āge, fär; let, ēqual, tèrm;
it, īce; hot, ōpen, ôrder;
oil, out; cup, pùt, rüle; ch, child;
ng, long; sh, she; th, thin;
ŦH, then; zh, measure;

ə represents *a* in about,
e in taken, *i* in pencil,
o in lemon, *u* in circus.

---

par (pär), 1 an equal level; equality: *The gains and losses are about on a par. He is quite on a par with his sister in intelligence.* 2 an average or normal amount, degree, or condition: *A sick person feels below par.* 3 average; normal. 4 the value of a bond, a note, a share of stock, etc., that is printed on it; face value: *That stock is selling above par.* 5 of or at par. 6 (in golf) a score which is used as a standard for a particular hole or course and which represents the number of strokes that will be taken if the hole or course is played well. Par is based on the length and difficulty of the hole or course. 1,2,4,6 *n.,* 3,5 *adj.*

par., 1 paragraph. 2 parallel.

par a ble (par′ə bəl), a brief story used to teach some truth or moral lesson: *The teacher explained the parable. n.*

parabola
The parabola
is curve ABC.

par ab o la (pə rab′ə lə), a plane curve formed by the intersection of a cone with a plane parallel to a side of the cone. *n., pl.* **par ab o las.**

par a chute (par′ə shüt), 1 apparatus shaped like an umbrella and made of nylon or silk, used in descending gradually through the air from a great height. 2 come down by, or as if by, a parachute: *The pilot of the burning plane*

parachute (def. 1)

611

adj.	adjective	*n.*	noun
adv.	adverb	*prep.*	preposition
conj.	conjunction	*pron.*	pronoun
interj.	interjection	*v.*	verb
sing.	singular	*pl.*	plural

parachuted safely to the ground. 3 convey by a parachute. 1 *n.,* 2,3 *v.,* **par a chut ed, par a chut ing.**

par a chut ist (par′ə shü′tist), person who uses a parachute or is skilled in making descents with a parachute. *n.*

pa rade (pə rād′), 1 a march for display; procession: *The circus had a parade.* 2 to march through with display: *The performers and animals paraded the streets.* 3 to march in procession; walk proudly as if in a parade. 4 group of people walking for display or pleasure. 5 place where people walk for display or pleasure. 6 a great show or display: *The modest man did not make a parade of his wealth.* 7 make a great show of: *parade one's wealth.* 8 a military display or review of troops. 9 come together in military order for review or inspection. 10 assemble (troops) for review. 11 the place used for the regular parade of troops. 1,4-6,8,11 *n.,* 2,3,7,9,10 *v.,* **pa rad ed, pa rad ing.**

pa rad er (pə rā′dər), person who parades. *n.*

par a digm (par′ə dim *or* par′ə dīm), 1 pattern; example. 2 example of a noun, verb, pronoun, etc., in all its inflections. *n.*

par a dise (par′ə dīs), 1 heaven. 2 place or condition of great happiness: *The summer camp was a paradise for her.* 3 place of great beauty. 4 Also, **Paradise.** the garden of Eden. *n.*

par a dox (par′ə doks), 1 statement that may be true but seems to say two opposite things: *"More haste, less speed"* and *"The child is father to the man"* are *paradoxes.* 2 statement that is false because it says two opposite things. 3 person or thing that seems to be full of contradictions. *n., pl.* **par a dox es.**

par a dox i cal (par′ə dok′sə kəl), of paradoxes; having to do with a paradox. *adj.* —**par′a dox′i cal ly,** *adv.*

par af fin (par′ə fin), 1 a white, tasteless, waxy substance, used for making candles and for sealing jars of jelly or jam. It is obtained chiefly from crude petroleum. 2 treat with paraffin. 1 *n.,* 2 *v.*

par a gon (par′ə gon), model of excellence or perfection. *n.*

par a graph (par′ə graf), 1 group of sentences relating to the same idea or topic and forming a distinct part of a chapter, letter, or other piece of writing. Paragraphs usually begin on a new line and are indented. 2 divide into paragraphs. 3 a separate note or item of news in a newspaper. 4 write paragraphs about. 5 sign (¶) used to show where a paragraph begins or should begin. It is used mostly in correcting written work. 1,3,5 *n.,* 2,4 *v.*

Par a guay (par′ə gwā *or* par′ə gwī), 1 country in central South America, between Bolivia, Brazil, and Argentina. *Capital:* Asunción. 2 river in South America. *n.* —**Par′a guay′an,** *adj., n.*

par a keet (par′ə kēt), any of various small parrots, most of which have slender bodies and long tails. *n.* Also, **parrakeet.**

parallax—Viewed from A, C appears to be the middle tree in a group of three trees. From B, C appears to be a single tree in front of the cabin.

par al lax (par′ə laks), the apparent change in the position of an object when it is seen from two different points which are not on a direct line with the object. Parallax is used in surveying, astronomy, etc., to determine distances of objects. *n.*

par al lel (par′ə lel), 1 at or being the same distance apart everywhere, like the two rails of a railroad track. 2 be at the same distance from throughout the length: *The street parallels the railroad.* 3 a parallel line or surface. 4 any of the imaginary circles around the earth parallel to the equator, marking degrees of latitude: *The 49th parallel marks much of the boundary between Canada and the United States.* 5 comparison to show likeness: *draw a parallel between this winter and last winter.* 6 compare in order to show likeness. 7 find a case which is similar or parallel to: *Can you parallel that for friendliness?* 8 similar; corresponding: *parallel customs in different countries.* 9 thing like or similar to another: *Her experience was an interesting parallel to ours.* 10 be like; be similar to: *Your story closely parallels his.* 1,8 *adj.,* 2,6,7,10 *v.,* 3-5,9 *n.*

parallel bars, a pair of raised bars horizontal to the ground, used in gymnastics to develop the muscles of the arms, chest, etc.

par al lel ism (par′ə lel′iz′əm), 1 a being parallel. 2 likeness; similarity; correspondence; agreement. *n.*

par al lel o gram (par′ə lel′ə gram), a four-sided plane figure whose opposite sides are parallel and equal. *n.*

parallelograms

par a lyse (par′ə līz), paralyze. *v.,* **par a lysed, par a lys ing.**

pa ral y sis (pə ral′ə sis), 1 a lessening or loss of the power of motion or sensation in any part of the body: *The accident left him with paralysis of the legs.* 2 condition of powerlessness or helpless inactivity; crippling: *The war caused a paralysis of trade. n., pl.* **pa ral y ses** (pə ral′ə sēz′).

par a lyt ic (par′ə lit′ik), 1 of paralysis; having paralysis. 2 person who has paralysis. 1 *adj.,* 2 *n.*

par a lyze (par′ə līz), 1 affect with a lessening or loss of the power of motion or feeling: *Her left arm was paralyzed.* 2 make powerless or helplessly inactive; cripple; stun; deaden: *Fear paralyzed my mind. v.,* **par a lyzed, par a lyz ing.** Also, **paralyse.**

par a me ci um (par′ə mē′shē əm), an extremely small one-celled animal shaped like a slender slipper, covered with cilia, and having a groove along one side leading into an open mouth. Paramecia live in almost all fresh water. *n., pl.* **par a me ci a** (par′ə mē′shē ə).

parallel (def. 1)
parallel lines

par a med ic (par′ə med′ik), person who assists a doctor. *n.*

par a mount (par′ə mount), chief in importance; above others; supreme: *Truth is of paramount importance. adj.*

par a noi a (par′ə noi′ə), 1 a mental disorder in which a person imagines that he is being persecuted or that he is very great or important. 2 an irrational distrust of others. *n.*

par a pet (par′ə pet), 1 a low wall or mound of stone, earth, etc., to protect soldiers. 2 a low wall at the edge of a balcony, roof, bridge, etc. *n.*

PARAPET

parapet (def. 1)

par a pher nal ia (par′ə fər nā′-lyə), 1 personal belongings: *My paraphernalia are ready to be shipped.* 2 equipment; outfit: *A photographer's paraphernalia includes cameras, film, lenses, lights, tripods, etc. n.pl.*

par a phrase (par′ə frāz), 1 state the meaning of (a passage) in other words. 2 an expression of the meaning of a passage in other words. 1 *v.,* **par a phrased, par a phras ing;** 2 *n.*

par a site (par′ə sīt), 1 animal or plant that lives on or in another from which it gets its food. Lice and tapeworms are parasites on animals. Mistletoe is a parasite on oak trees. 2 person who lives on others without making any useful and fitting return; hanger-on: *The lazy man was a parasite on his family. n.*

par a sit ic (par′ə sit′ik), of or like a parasite; living on others. *adj.* —**par′a sit′i cal ly,** *adv.*

par a sol (par′ə sôl), a light umbrella used as a protection from the sun. *n.*

par a thy roid glands (par′ə thī′-roid), small glands in or near the thyroid gland. Their secretion, which enables the body to use calcium, is necessary for life.

par a troop er (par′ə trü′pər), soldier trained to use a parachute for descent from an aircraft into a battle area. *n.*

par a troops (par′ə trüps′), troops trained to use parachutes for descent from an aircraft into a battle area. *n.pl.*

par boil (pär′boil′), boil till partly cooked: *parboil beans before baking them. v.*

par cel (pär′səl), 1 bundle of things wrapped or packed together; package: *She had her arms filled with parcels of gifts.* 2 container with things packed in it: *Put your shirts in this parcel.* 3 piece: *a parcel of land.* 4 lot; pack: *The peddler had a whole parcel of odds and ends in his sack.* 5 make into a parcel; put up in parcels. 1-4 *n.,* 5 *v.*
parcel out, divide into, or distribute in, portions.

parcel post, branch of the postal service which carries parcels.

parch (pärch), 1 dry by heating; roast slightly: *The Indians parched corn.* 2 make or become hot and dry or thirsty: *The fever parched him. I am parched with the heat. v.*

parch ment (pärch′mənt), 1 the skin of sheep or goats, prepared for use as a writing material. 2 manuscript or document written on parchment. 3 paper that looks like parchment. *n.*

par don (pärd′n), 1 a passing over an offense without punishment; forgiveness. 2 forgive: *Grandmother pardoned the mischievous children.* 3 excuse or toleration: *I beg your pardon,* but *I missed your last remark.* 4 set free from punishment: *The governor pardoned the prisoner.* 5 a setting free from punishment. 6 a legal document setting a person free from punishment. 1,3,5,6 *n.,* 2,4 *v.* —**par′don er,** *n.*

par don a ble (pärd′n ə bəl), that can be pardoned; excusable. *adj.*

pare (per *or* par), 1 cut, trim, or shave off the outer part of; peel: *pare an apple, pare one's toenails.* 2 cut away little by little: *pare down expenses. v.,* **pared, par ing.**

par e gor ic (par′ə gôr′ik), a soothing medicine containing camphor and a very little opium. *n.*

par ent (per′ənt *or* par′ənt), 1 father or mother. 2 any animal or plant that produces offspring. 3 source; cause: *Too much leisure can be the parent of mischief. n.*

par ent age (per′ən tij *or* par′ən tij), descent from parents; family line; ancestry. *n.*

pa ren tal (pə ren′tl), of or having to do with a parent or parents; like a parent's: *parental advice. adj.* —**paren′tal ly,** *adv.*

pa ren the sis (pə ren′thə sis), 1 word, phrase, sentence, etc., inserted within a sentence to explain or qualify something. 2 either or both of two curved lines ( ) used to set off such an expression. *n., pl.* **pa ren the ses** (pə-ren′thə sēz′).

par en thet ic (par′ən thet′ik), 1 serving or helping to explain; qualifying. 2 enclosed in parentheses. 3 using parentheses. *adj.* —**par′en thet′i cal ly,** *adv.*

par en thet i cal (par′ən thet′ə kəl), parenthetic. *adj.*

par ent hood (per′ənt hůd *or* par′-ənt hůd), condition of being a parent. *n.*

par fait (pär fā′), 1 ice cream with syrup or crushed fruit and whipped cream, served in a tall glass. 2 a rich ice cream containing eggs and whipped cream. *n.*

pa ri ah (pə rī′ə), outcast. *n.*

par ing (per′ing *or* par′ing), the part pared off; skin; rind: *apple parings. n.*

Par is (par′is), 1 capital and largest city of France, in the N part. Paris is on the Seine River. 2 (in Greek legends) a son of Priam, king of Troy. The kidnaping of Helen by Paris was the cause of the Trojan War. *n.*

par ish (par′ish), 1 district that has its own church and clergyman. 2 people of a parish. 3 members of the congregation of a particular church. 4 (in Louisiana) a county. *n.*

pa rish ion er (pə rish′ə nər), member of a parish. *n.*

Pa ri sian (pə rizh′ən), 1 of or having

hat, āge, fär; let, ēqual, tėrm; it, īce; hot, ōpen, ôrder; oil, out; cup, půt, rüle; ch, child; ng, long; sh, she; th, thin; ₮H, then; zh, measure;

ə represents *a* in about, *e* in taken, *i* in pencil, *o* in lemon, *u* in circus.

to do with Paris or its people. 2 person born or living in Paris. 1 *adj.,* 2 *n.*

par i ty (par′ə tē), similarity or close correspondence with regard to state, position, condition, value, quality, degree, etc.; equality. *n.*

park (pärk), 1 land set apart for the pleasure of the public: *Many cities have beautiful parks.* 2 land set apart for wild animals: *a game park.* 3 grounds around a fine house. 4 leave (an automobile, etc.) for a time in a certain place: *Park your car here. She parked near the library.* 1-3 *n.,* 4 *v.*

par ka (pär′kə), 1 a fur jacket with a hood, worn in Alaska and northeastern Asia. 2 jacket with a hood. *n., pl.* **par kas.**

parka (def. 1)

park way (pärk′wā′), a broad road with spaces planted with grass, trees, etc. *n.*

par lance (pär′ləns), way of speaking; talk; language: *legal parlance. n.*

par ley (pär′lē), 1 conference or informal talk to discuss terms or matters in dispute: *The general held a parley with the enemy about exchanging prisoners.* 2 discuss matters, especially with an enemy. 1 *n., pl.* **par leys;** 2 *v.*

par lia ment (pär′lə mənt), 1 council or congress that is the highest lawmaking body in some countries. 2 **Parliament, a** the national lawmaking body of Great Britain, consisting of the House of Lords and the House of Commons. **b** the national lawmaking body of Canada, consisting of the Senate and the House of Commons. **c** the lawmaking body of a country or colony having the British system of government. *n.*

par lia men tar i an (pär′lə men-

613

adj.	adjective	*n.*	noun
adv.	adverb	*prep.*	preposition
conj.	conjunction	*pron.*	pronoun
interj.	interjection	*v.*	verb
sing.	singular	*pl.*	plural

tar′ē ən), person skilled in parliamentary procedure or debate. *n.*

par li a men tar y (pär′lə men′tər ē), 1 of a parliament: *parliamentary authority.* 2 done by a parliament: *parliamentary statutes.* 3 according to the rules and customs of a parliament or other lawmaking body: *The United States Congress functions in accordance with the rules of parliamentary procedure.* 4 having a parliament: *a parliamentary form of government. adj.*

par lor (pär′lər), 1 room for receiving or entertaining guests; sitting room. 2 room or suite of rooms used for various commercial purposes, requiring special or elaborate decoration, fittings, etc.: *a funeral parlor, a beauty parlor. n.*

parlor car, a railroad passenger car for day travel, with more comfortable seats than a coach.

par lous (pär′ləs), OLD USE. 1 full of peril; dangerous. 2 very clever; shrewd. 3 extremely. 1,2 *adj.,* 3 *adv.*

Par nas sus (pär nas′əs), **Mount,** mountain in central Greece. In ancient Greek times it was sacred to Apollo and the Muses. *n.*

pa ro chi al (pə rō′kē əl), 1 of or in a parish: *parochial calls, a parochial church.* 2 narrow; limited: *His viewpoint was too parochial. adj.*

parochial school, school maintained by a church or a religious organization.

par o dy (par′ə dē), 1 a humorous imitation of a serious writing. A parody follows the form of the original, but changes its sense to nonsense, thus making fun of the writer's characteristics. 2 make fun of by imitating; make a parody on. 1 *n., pl.* **par o dies;** 2 *v.,* **par o died, par o dy ing.**

pa role (pə rōl′), 1 conditional release from prison or jail before the full term is served. 2 conditional freedom allowed in place of imprisonment. 3 word of honor: *The prisoner of war gave his parole not to try to escape.* 4 give a conditional release from jail or prison before the full term is served: *The prisoner was paroled after serving two years of his three-year sentence.* 1-3 *n.,* 4 *v.,* **pa roled, pa rol ing.**

par ox ysm (par′ək siz′əm), 1 a sudden, severe attack of the symptoms of a disease, usually recurring periodically: *a paroxysm of coughing.* 2 a sudden outburst of emotion or activity: *a paroxysm of rage. n.*

par quet (pär kā′ *or* pär ket′), 1 an inlaid wooden flooring. 2 the main floor of a theater; orchestra. 3 part of the main floor of a theater from the orchestra to the part under the balcony. *n.*

par quet ry (pär′kə trē), mosaic of wood used for floors, wainscoting, etc. *n., pl.* **par quet ries.**

parquetry
The design, covering about one square foot, is repeated to form a parquet floor.

par ra keet (par′ə kēt), parakeet. *n.*

par ri cide (par′ə sīd), 1 the crime of killing one's parent or parents. 2 person who kills his parent or parents. *n.*

par rot (par′ət), 1 bird with a stout, hooked bill and often with bright-colored feathers. Some parrots can imitate sounds and repeat words and sentences. 2 person who repeats words or acts without understanding them. 3 repeat without understanding. 1,2 *n.,* 3 *v.* —**par′rot like′,** *adj.*

parrot (def. 1)
about 1 ft. tall

par ry (par′ē), 1 ward off; turn aside; evade (a thrust, stroke, weapon, question, etc.): *He parried the sword with his dagger. She parried our question by asking us one.* 2 act of parrying; avoiding. 1 *v.,* **par ried, par ry ing;** 2 *n., pl.* **par ries.**

parse (pärs), 1 analyze (a sentence) grammatically, telling its parts of speech and their uses in the sentence. 2 describe (a word) grammatically, telling what part of speech it is, its form, and its use in a sentence. *v.,* **parsed, pars ing.**

Par see *or* **Par si** (pär′sē), member of a Zoroastrian sect in India, descended from Persians who settled there in the A.D. 700's. *n.*

par si mo ni ous (pär′sə mō′nē əs), too economical; stingy. *adj.* —**par′si mo′ni ous ly,** *adv.*

par si mo ny (pär′sə mō′nē), extreme economy; stinginess. *n.*

par sley (pär′slē), a garden plant with finely divided, fragrant leaves. Parsley is used to flavor food and to trim platters of meat, fish, etc. *n., pl.* **par sleys.**

par snip (pär′snip), 1 plant having a long, tapering, whitish root. It belongs to the same family as the carrot. 2 its root, which is eaten as a vegetable. *n.*

par son (pär′sən), 1 minister in charge of a parish. 2 any clergyman; minister. *n.*

par son age (pär′sə nij), house provided for a minister by a church. *n.*

part (pärt), 1 something less than the whole; not all: *He ate part of an apple. What part of the chicken do you like best?* 2 each of several equal quantities into which a whole may be divided; fraction: *A dime is a tenth part of a dollar.* 3 thing that helps to make up a whole: *A radio has many parts.* 4 share: *I had no part in the mischief.* 5 side in a dispute or contest: *He always takes his brother's part.* 6 character in a play, motion picture, etc.; role: *He played the part of Hamlet.* 7 the words spoken by a character: *She spoke the part of the heroine in our play.* 8 divide into two or more pieces. 9 force apart; divide: *The policeman on horseback parted the crowd.* 10 go apart; separate: *The friends parted in anger.* 11 a dividing line left in combing one's hair. 12 comb (the hair) away from a dividing line. 13 one of the voices or instruments in a piece of music: *the tenor part, the violin part.* 14 the music for it. 15 less than the whole: *part Irish.* 16 in some measure or degree; partly. 17 **parts,** *pl.* **a** ability; talent: *a man of parts.* **b** regions; districts; places: *She has traveled much in foreign parts.* 1-7,11,13,14,17 *n.,* 8-10,12 *v.,* 15 *adj.,* 16 *adv.*

for one's part, as far as one is concerned.

for the most part, mostly: *The attempts were for the most part unsuccessful.*

in good part, in a friendly or gracious way.

in part, in some measure or degree; to some extent; partly.

on the part of one *or* **on one's part,** 1 as far as one is concerned. 2 by one.

part and parcel, a necessary part.

part from, go away from; leave.

part with, give up; let go.

take part, take or have a share.

par take (pär tāk′), 1 eat or drink some; take some: *We are eating lunch. Will you partake?* 2 take or have a share. *v.,* **par took, par tak en, par tak ing.**

partake of, 1 take some; have a share in: *Will you partake of this cake?* 2 have to some extent the nature or character of: *Her graciousness partakes of condescension.*

par tak en (pär tā′kən), past participle of **partake**. *v.*

par tak er (pär tā′kər), person who partakes. *n.*

part ed (pär′tid), divided into parts; severed; cloven. *adj.*

Par the non (pär′thə non), temple of Athena on the Acropolis in Athens, regarded as the finest example of Doric architecture. *n.*

par tial (pär′shəl), 1 not complete; not total: *My parents made a partial payment on our new car.* 2 inclined to favor one side more than another; favoring unfairly: *Parents should not be partial to any one of their children.* 3 having a liking for; favorably inclined: *I am partial to sports. adj.*

par ti al i ty (pär′shē al′ə tē), 1 the favoring of one more than another or others; favorable prejudice; being partial. 2 a particular liking; fondness; preference; bent: *Children often have a partiality for candy. n., pl.* **par ti al i ties.**

par tial ly (pär′shə lē), 1 in part; not generally or totally; partly. 2 in a partial manner; with undue bias. *adv.*

par tic i pant (pär tis′ə pənt), person who shares or participates. *n.*

par tic i pate (pär tis′ə pāt), have a share; take part: *The teacher participated in the children's games. v.,* **par tic i pat ed, par tic i pat ing.**

par tic i pa tion (pär tis′ə pā′shən), a participating; taking part. *n.*

par tic i pa tor (pär tis′ə pā′tər), person who participates. *n.*

par ti cip i al (pär′tə sip′ē əl), of or having to do with a participle. We often use participial adjectives (a *masked* man, a *becoming* dress) and participial nouns (in *cutting* ice, the fatigue of *marching*). *adj.*

par ti ci ple (pär′tə sip′əl), a verb form that retains all the attributes of a verb, such as tense, voice, power to take an object, and modification by adverbs, but may be used as an adjective. EXAMPLES: the girl *writing* sentences at the blackboard, the man *waiting* for a train, the *stolen* silver, the boy *having missed* the boat. In these phrases, *writing* and *waiting* are present participles; *stolen* and *having missed* are past participles. *n.*

par ti cle (pär′tə kəl), 1 a very little bit: *I got a particle of dust in my eye.* 2 any of the extremely small units of matter of which all atoms are composed, such as the electron, proton, and neutron. 3 prefix or suffix. *Un-* and *-ment* are particles. 4 preposition, conjunction, article, or interjection. *In, if, an,* and *ah* are particles. *n.*

particle accelerator, any of several machines, such as the betatron and cyclotron, that greatly increase the speed and energy of protons, electrons, and other atomic particles and direct them in a steady stream at a target; accelerator. The accelerated particles are used to bombard the nuclei of atoms, causing the nuclei to release new particles.

par ti-col ored (pär′tē kul′ərd), colored differently in different parts: *a parti-colored shirt. adj.*

par tic u lar (pər tik′yə lər), 1 apart from others; considered separately; single: *That particular chair is already sold.* 2 belonging to some one person, thing, group, occasion, etc.: *His particular task is to care for the dog. A particular characteristic of a skunk is its smell.* 3 different from others; unusual; special: *This vacation was of particular importance to her, for she was going to Brazil. He is a particular friend of mine.* 4 hard to please; wanting everything to be just right; very careful: *She is very particular; nothing but the best will do.* 5 an individual part; item; point: *The work is complete in every particular. All the particulars of the accident are now known.* 1-4 *adj.,* 5 *n.*

in particular, especially: *We strolled around, going nowhere in particular.*

par tic u lar i ty (pər tik′yə lar′ə tē), 1 detailed quality; minuteness. 2 special carefulness. 3 attentiveness to details. 4 a particular feature or trait. *n., pl.* **par tic u lar i ties.**

par tic u lar i za tion (pər tik′yə lər ə zā′shən), act of particularizing. *n.*

par tic u lar ize (pər tik′yə lə rīz′), 1 mention particularly; treat in detail. 2 mention individually; state or discuss in detail. *v.,* **par tic u lar ized, par tic u lar iz ing.**

par tic u lar ly (pər tik′yə lər lē), 1 in a high degree; especially: *The teacher praised her particularly. I am particularly fond of her. She mentioned that point particularly.* 2 in a particular manner; in detail; in all its parts; minutely: *The inspector examined the machine particularly. adv.*

part ing (pär′ting), 1 a going away; taking leave; departure: *The friends were sad at parting.* 2 given, taken, done, etc., at parting: *a parting request, a parting shot.* 3 departing. 4 dividing; separating. 5 division; separation. 6 place of division or separation: *hair arranged with a side parting.* 1,5,6 *n.,* 2-4 *adj.*

par ti san (pär′tə zən), 1 a strong supporter of a person, party, or cause; one whose support is based on feeling rather than on reasoning. 2 member of light, irregular troops; guerrilla. 3 of or like a partisan: *There are often partisan*

hat, āge, fär; let, ēqual, tėrm;
it, īce; hot, ōpen, ôrder;
oil, out; cup, pùt, rüle; ch, child;
ng, long; sh, she; th, thin;
ᴛʜ, then; zh, measure;

ə represents *a* in about,
e in taken, *i* in pencil,
o in lemon, *u* in circus.

favors in politics. 1,2 *n.,* 3 *adj.* Also, **partizan.**

par ti san ship (pär′tə zən ship), 1 strong loyalty to a party or cause. 2 a taking sides. *n.* Also, **partizanship.**

par ti tion (pär tish′ən), 1 division into parts: *the partition of a man's wealth when he dies.* 2 divide into parts: *partition an empire among three brothers, partition a house into rooms.* 3 wall between rooms, etc. 4 separate by a partition. 1,3 *n.,* 2,4 *v.*

par ti zan (pär′tə zən), partisan. *n., adj.*

par ti zan ship (pär′tə zən ship), partisanship. *n.*

part ly (pärt′lē), in part; in some measure or degree: *You are partly to blame. adv.*

part ner (pärt′nər), 1 one who shares: *My sister was the partner of my walks.* 2 member of a company or firm who shares the risk and profits of the business. 3 wife or husband. 4 companion in a dance. 5 player on the same team or side in a game. *n.*

part ner ship (pärt′nər ship), 1 a being a partner; joint interest; association: *a business partnership, the partnership of marriage.* 2 company or firm with two or more members who share in the risk and profits of the business: *a law partnership.* 3 the contract that creates such a relation. *n.*

part of speech, any of the classes into which words are divided according to their use or function in sentences. The traditional parts of speech are the noun, pronoun, adjective, verb, adverb, preposition, conjunction, and interjection.

par took (pär tùk′), past tense of **partake**. *We partook of food and drink. v.*

par tridge (pär′trij), 1 any of several

partridge (def. 1)
10 to 12 in. long

adj.	adjective	*n.*	noun
adv.	adverb	*prep.*	preposition
conj.	conjunction	*pron.*	pronoun
interj.	interjection	*v.*	verb
sing.	singular	*pl.*	plural

game birds of Europe, Asia, and Africa belonging to the same family as the quail and pheasant. 2 any of several similar birds of the United States, such as the ruffed grouse and the quail or bobwhite. *n., pl.* **par tridg es** or **par tridge.**

part song, song with parts in simple harmony for two or more voices, especially one meant to be sung without an accompaniment.

part-time (pärt′tīm′), for part of the usual time: *a part-time job. adj.*

par tu ri tion (pär′tù rish′ən *or* pär′tyù rish′ən), childbirth. *n.*

par ty (pär′tē), 1 a gathering of a group of people to have a good time together: *On her birthday she had a party and invited her friends.* 2 group of people doing something together: *a sewing party, a dinner party, a scouting party of three soldiers.* 3 group of people organized to gain political influence and control: *The Whig party and the Tory party were important political parties in British history.* 4 of or having to do with a party: *a party mood.* 5 one who takes part in, aids, or knows about: *He was a party to our secret.* 6 each of the persons or sides in a contract, lawsuit, etc. 7 INFORMAL. person: *The party you were calling is on the telephone now.* 1-3,5-7 *n., pl.* **par ties;** 4 *adj.*

par ve nu (pär′və nü *or* pär′və nyü), 1 person who has risen above his class. 2 person who has risen to a higher place than he is fit for; upstart. *n.*

Pas a de na (pas′ə dē′nə), city in SW California, near Los Angeles. *n.*

Pas cal (pa skal′), **Blaise,** 1623-1662, French philosopher, mathematician, and physicist. *n.*

pa sha (pə shä′), a former title used after the name of Turkish civil or military officials of high rank. *n., pl.* **pa shas.**

pass (pas), 1 go by; move past: *The parade passed. We passed the big truck. Many people pass our house every day.* 2 move on; go: *The days pass quickly. The salesman passed from house to house.* 3 go from one to another: *The property passed from the father to the daughter. Hot words passed dur-*

ing their quarrel. 4 hand from one to another; hand around: *Please pass the butter.* 5 get through or by: *The ship passed the channel.* 6 go across or over: *The horse passed the stream.* 7 to move: *Pass your hand over the velvet and feel how soft it is. He passed a rope around his waist for support.* 8 go away; depart. 9 be successful in (an examination, a course, etc.): *I passed Latin.* 10 success in an examination, etc.; passing an examination but without honors. 11 act of passing; passage. 12 cause or allow to go through something; sanction or approve: *The inspector passed the item after examining it.* 13 ratify or enact: *pass a bill or law.* 14 be approved by (a lawmaking body, etc.): *The new law passed the city council.* 15 come to an end; die: *The king passed in peace.* 16 go beyond; exceed; surpass: *His strange story passes belief.* 17 use or spend: *We passed the days pleasantly.* 18 to change: *Water passes from a liquid to a solid state when it freezes.* 19 take place; happen: *Tell me all that passed.* 20 be accepted for or as: *Use silk or a material that will pass for silk. She could pass for twenty.* 21 express; pronounce: *A judge passes sentence on guilty persons.* 22 give a judgment or opinion: *The judges passed on each contestant. Please pass upon this question.* 23 go without notice: *He was rude, but I let it pass.* 24 a note, license, etc., permitting one to do something: *He needed a pass to enter the fort.* 25 free ticket: *a pass to the circus.* 26 state; condition: *Things have come to a strange pass when children give orders to their parents.* 27 motion of the hand or hands. 28 a narrow road, path, way, channel, etc.: *A pass crosses the mountains.* 29 throw (the ball) to another player in basketball, football, etc. 30 a throw of the ball to another player in basketball, football, etc. 31 (in card playing) refrain from bidding or playing a hand. 32 a thrust in fencing. 1-9,12-23,29,31 *v.,* **passed, passed** or **past, pass ing;** 10,11,24-28,30,32 *n., pl.* **pass es.** —**pass′er,** *n.*

bring to pass, to cause to be; accomplish.

come to pass, take place; happen.

pass away, come to an end; die.

pass by, fail to notice; overlook; disregard.

pass off, 1 go away. 2 take place; be done. 3 get accepted; pretend to be.

pass out, 1 give out; distribute. 2 SLANG. faint; lose consciousness.

pass over, fail to notice; overlook; disregard.

pass up, give up; renounce: *pass up a chance to go to college.*

pass a ble (pas′ə bəl), 1 fairly good;

moderate: *a passable knowledge of geography.* 2 that can be passed: *a passable road, a passable river. adj.*

pass a bly (pas′ə blē), fairly; moderately. *adv.*

pas sage (pas′ij), 1 hall or way through a building; passageway. 2 means of passing; way through: *open a passage through a crowd.* 3 right, liberty, or leave to pass: *The guard refused us passage.* 4 a passing: *the passage of time.* 5 piece from a speech, writing, or musical composition: *a passage from the Bible.* 6 a going across; voyage: *We had a stormy passage across the Atlantic.* 7 ticket that entitles the holder to transportation, especially by boat: *obtain passage for Europe.* 8 a making into law by a favoring vote of a legislature: *the passage of a bill.* 9 what passes between persons. *n.*

pas sage way (pas′ij wā′), way along which one can pass. Halls and alleys are passageways. *n.*

pas sé (pa sā′), out of date. *adj.* [from French]

pas sen ger (pas′n jər), traveler in an aircraft, bus, ship, train, etc., usually one that pays a fare. *n.*

passenger pigeon, kind of wild pigeon of North America, now extinct, that flew in very large flocks.

pass er-by (pas′ər bī′), one that passes by. *n., pl.* **pass ers-by.**

pass ing (pas′ing), 1 that passes. 2 act of one that passes; a going by; a departure. 3 done or given in passing: *a passing smile.* 4 not lasting; fleeting: *a passing fancy.* 5 allowing one to pass an examination or test: *75 will be a passing mark.* 6 means or place of passing. 7 death: *the passing of a great leader.* 8 OLD USE. surpassingly; very. 1,3-5 *adj.,* 2,6,7 *n.,* 8 *adv.*

in passing, in that connection; incidentally.

pas sion (pash′ən), 1 very strong feeling: *Hate and fear are passions.* 2 violent anger; rage: *He flew into a passion.* 3 love between a man and a woman. 4 very strong liking: *She has a passion for music.* 5 object of a passion: *Music is her passion.* 6 OLD USE. suffering. 7 **the Passion,** a the sufferings of Jesus on the Cross or after the Last Supper. b story of these sufferings in the Bible. *n.*

pas sion ate (pash′ə nit), 1 having or showing strong feelings: *She has always been a passionate believer in human rights.* 2 easily moved to a fit or mood of some emotion, especially to anger. 3 resulting from strong feeling: *He made a passionate speech against capital punishment. adj.* —**pas′sion ate ly,** *adv.*

pas sion less (pash′ən lis), without passion; calm. *adj.*

passion play or **Passion Play,** play representing the sufferings and death of Christ.

pas sive (pas′iv), 1 being acted on without itself acting; not acting in return: *a passive mind or disposition.* 2 not resisting; yielding or submitting to the will of another: *The children gave passive obedience to their strict parents.* 3 (in grammar) showing the subject as acted on. In "The race was won by her," *was won* is in the passive voice. 4 a verb form in the passive voice. 1-3 *adj.,* 4 *n.* —**pas′sive ly,** *adv.* —**pas′sive ness,** *n.*

pas siv i ty (pa siv′ə tē), a being passive; lack of action or resistance. *n.*

pass key (pas′kē′), 1 key for opening several locks. 2 a private key. *n., pl.* **pass keys.**

Pass o ver (pas′ō′vər), an annual Jewish holiday in memory of the escape of the Hebrews from Egypt, where they had been slaves. It is so called because according to the Bible a destroying angel "passed over" the houses of the Hebrews when it killed the first-born child in every Egyptian home. *n.*

pass port (pas′pôrt), 1 paper or book giving official permission to travel abroad, under the protection of one's own government. 2 anything that gives one admission or acceptance: *A sense of curiosity can be a passport to knowledge. n.*

pass word (pas′werd′), a secret word that allows a person who says it to pass a guard. *n.*

past (past), 1 gone by; ended: *Summer is past. Our troubles are past.* 2 just gone by: *The past year was full of trouble. For some time past I have been ill.* 3 time gone by; time before; what has happened: *Life began far back in the past. History is a study of the past.* 4 a past life or history: *Our country has a glorious past. He cannot change his past.* 5 beyond; farther on than: *The arrow went past the mark.* 6 after; later than: *It is past noon.* 7 so as to pass by or beyond: *The cars go past once an hour.* 8 beyond in number, amount, or degree. 9 beyond the ability, range, scope, etc., of: *absurd fancies that are past belief.* 10 having served a term in office: *a past president.* 11 the past tense or a verb form in it. 12 passed; a past participle of **pass.** 1,2,10 *adj.,* 3,4,11 *n.,* 5,6,8,9 *prep.,* 7 *adv.,* 12 *v.*

paste (pāst), 1 mixture, such as flour and water boiled together, that will stick paper together. 2 to stick with paste. 3 dough for pastry. 4 a soft, doughlike

mixture. Fish paste is pounded fish, highly seasoned. Pottery is made from a paste of clay and water. 5 a hard, glassy material used in making imitations of precious stones. 6 SLANG. hit with a hard, sharp blow. 1,3-5 *n.,* 2,6 *v.,* **past ed, past ing.**

paste board (pāst′bôrd′), a stiff material made of sheets of paper pasted together or of paper pulp pressed and dried. *n.*

pas tel (pa stel′), 1 kind of chalklike crayon used in drawing. 2 a drawing made with such crayons. 3 a soft, pale shade of some color. 4 soft and pale: *pastel pink, pastel shades.* 1-3 *n.,* 4 *adj.*

past er (pā′stər), 1 a slip to paste on or over something. 2 person or thing that pastes. *n.*

pas tern (pas′tərn), the part of a horse's foot between the fetlock and the hoof. See **horse** for picture. *n.*

Pas teur (pa stėr′), **Louis,** 1822-1895, French chemist who invented a way of preventing rabies and of keeping milk from spoiling. *n.*

pas teur i za tion (pas′chər ə zā′shən), 1 process of pasteurizing. 2 fact or condition of being pasteurized. *n.*

pas teur ize (pas′chə rīz′), heat (milk, wine, beer, etc.) to a high temperature, and then chill it quickly to destroy harmful bacteria. When milk is pasteurized, it is heated to about 140 degrees Fahrenheit for 30 minutes. *v.,* **pas teur ized, pas teur iz ing.** [from Louis *Pasteur*]

pas teur iz er (pas′chə rī′zər), apparatus for pasteurizing milk, wine, beer, etc. *n.*

pas time (pas′tīm′), a pleasant way of passing time; amusement; recreation. Games and sports are pastimes. *Baseball is often called the American national pastime. n.*

past i ness (pā′stē nis), pasty quality, condition, or consistency. *n.*

pas tor (pas′tər), minister in charge of a church; spiritual guide. *n.*

pas tor al (pas′tər əl), 1 of shepherds or country life: *The pastoral tribes of the mountains graze their sheep on the hillsides.* 2 play, poem, or picture dealing with shepherds or country life. 3 simple or naturally beautiful like the country: *a pastoral landscape.* 4 of a pastor or his duties: *a pastoral letter.* 1,3,4 *adj.,* 2 *n.*

pas tor ate (pas′tər it), 1 position or duties of a pastor. 2 term of service of a pastor. 3 pastors as a group. *n.*

past participle, participle that indicates time gone by, or a former action or condition. *Played* and *thrown* are past participles in "She has played all day," "The ball should have been thrown to me."

hat, āge, fär; let, ēqual, tėrm;
it, īce; hot, ōpen, ôrder;
oil, out; cup, pùt, rüle; ch, child;
ng, long; sh, she; th, thin;
ᵺH, then; zh, measure;

ə represents *a* in about,
e in taken, *i* in pencil,
o in lemon, *u* in circus.

pas tra mi (pə strä′mē), a smoked and well-seasoned cut of beef, especially a shoulder cut. *n.*

pas try (pā′strē), 1 pies, tarts, and other baked goods wholly or partly made of rich flour paste. 2 any food made of baked flour paste, made rich with lard, butter, or vegetable shortening. *n., pl.* **pas tries.**

past tense, 1 tense expressing time gone by, or a former action or condition. 2 a verb form in the past tense.

pas tur age (pas′chər ij), 1 the growing grass and other plants for cattle, sheep, or horses to feed on. 2 pasture land. 3 a pasturing. *n.*

pas ture (pas′chər), 1 a grassy field or hillside; grasslands on which cattle, sheep, or horses can feed. 2 grass and other growing plants: *These lands afford good pasture.* 3 put (cattle, sheep, etc.) out to pasture. 4 feed on (growing grass, etc.). 1,2 *n.,* 3,4 *v.,* **pas tured, pas tur ing.**

past y[1] (pā′stē), 1 like paste. 2 pale. 3 flabby. *adj.,* **past i er, past i est.** [*paste* + -*y*[1]]

pas ty[2] (pas′tē), pie filled with meat, fish, etc.: *a venison pasty. n., pl.* **pas ties.** [from French of the 1200's *paste* paste, dough, from Latin *pasta*]

pat (pat), 1 strike or tap lightly with something flat: *He patted the dough into a flat cake.* 2 to tap with the hand as a sign of sympathy, approval, or affection: *pat a dog.* 3 a light stroke or tap with the hand or with something flat. 4 sound made by patting. 5 a small mass, especially of butter. 6 apt; suitable; to the point: *a pat reply.* 7 aptly; exactly; suitably. 1,2 *v.,* **pat ted, pat ting;** 3-5 *n.,* 6 *adj.,* **pat ter, pat test;** 7 *adv.*

have pat or **know pat,** INFORMAL. have perfectly; know thoroughly.

pat on the back, praise; compliment.

stand pat, INFORMAL. hold to things as they are and refuse to change.

Pat a go ni a (pat′ə gō′nē ə), region in the extreme south of South America. The larger part of Patagonia is in Argen-

patch

tina; the rest is in Chile. *n.* —**Pat′a-go′ni an,** *adj., n.*

patch (pach), **1** piece put on to mend a hole or a tear. **2** piece of cloth, etc., put over a wound or a sore. **3** a pad over a hurt eye to protect it. **4** a small bit of black cloth women used to wear on their faces to show off their fair skin. **5** put patches on; mend; protect or adorn with a patch or patches. **6** a small, uneven spot: *a patch of brown on the skin.* **7** piece of ground: *a garden patch.* **8** scrap or bit of cloth left over. **9** make by joining patches or pieces together: *patch a quilt.* **10** piece together; make hastily. 1-4,6-8 *n., pl.* **patch es;** 5,9,10 *v.*

patch up, 1 put an end to; settle: *patch up a quarrel.* **2** make right hastily or for a time: *patch up a leaking faucet.* **3** put together hastily or poorly: *patch up a costume for a play.*

patch work (pach′wėrk′), **1** pieces of cloth of various colors or shapes sewed together: *I made a cover of patchwork for the old cushion.* **2** anything like this: *From the airplane, we saw a patchwork of fields and woods. n.*

patch y (pach′ē), **1** abounding in or characterized by patches. **2** occurring in, forming, or resembling patches. *adj.,* **patch i er, patch i est.**

pate (pāt), top of the head; head: *a bald pate. n.*

pa tel la (pə tel′ə), kneecap. *n., pl.* **pa tel las, pa tel lae** (pə tel′ē).

pat ent (pat′nt *for 1-5;* pāt′nt *or* pat′nt *for 6*), **1** a government grant which gives a person or company sole rights to make, use, or sell a new invention for a certain number of years. **2** given or protected by a patent. **3** get a patent for: *She patented her new invention.* **4** invention that is patented. **5** an offi-

cial document from a government giving a right or privilege. **6** open to view or knowledge; evident; plain: *It is patent that cats dislike dogs.* 1,4,5 *n.,* 2,6 *adj.,* 3 *v.*

pat ent ee (pat′n tē′), person to whom a patent is granted. *n.*

pat ent leather (pat′nt), leather with a very glossy, smooth surface, usually black. Some shoes are made of patent leather.

pa tent ly (pāt′nt lē *or* pat′nt lē), plainly or openly; clearly; obviously. *adv.*

pat ent medicine (pat′nt), **1** any medicine that may be purchased without a doctor's prescription. **2** medicine sold by a company which has a patent on its manufacture and trade name.

pa ter nal (pə tėr′nl), **1** of or like a father; fatherly. **2** related on the father's side of the family: *Everyone has two paternal grandparents and two maternal grandparents.* **3** derived or inherited from one's father: *Her blue eyes were a paternal inheritance. adj.* —**pa-ter′nal ly,** *adv.*

pa ter nal ism (pə tėr′nl iz′əm), principle or practice of managing the affairs of a country or group of people as a father manages the affairs of his children. *n.*

pa ter nal is tic (pə tėr′nl is′tik), having to do with or characterized by paternalism. *adj.*

pa ter ni ty (pə tėr′nə tē), **1** a being a father; fatherhood. **2** paternal origin: *King Arthur's paternity was unknown. n.*

pat er nos ter (pat′ər nos′tər *or* pā′-tər nos′tər), the Lord's Prayer, especially in Latin. *n.* [from Latin *pater noster* our Father (the first two words of the prayer)]

path (path), **1** way made by people or animals walking. It is usually too narrow for automobiles or wagons. **2** way made to walk upon: *a garden path.* **3** line along which a person or thing moves; route; track: *The moon has a regular path through the sky.* **4** way of acting or behaving; way of life: *Some choose paths of glory; some choose paths of ease. n., pl.* **paths** (paᵗʜz *or* paths).

pa thet ic (pə thet′ik), arousing pity; pitiful: *The stray dog was a pathetic sight. adj.* —**pa thet′i cal ly,** *adv.*

path find er (path′fīn′dər), one who finds a path or way, as through a wilderness. *n.*

path less (path′lis), having no path through or across it: *a pathless mountain. adj.*

path o gen ic (path′ə jen′ik), producing disease. *adj.*

path o log ic (path′ə loj′ik), pathological. *adj.*

path o log i cal (path′ə loj′ə kəl), **1** of pathology; dealing with diseases or concerned with diseases: *pathological studies.* **2** due to disease or accompanying disease: *a pathological condition of the blood cells. adj.* —**path′o-log′i cal ly,** *adv.*

pa thol o gist (pa thol′ə jist), an expert in pathology. *n.*

pa thol o gy (pa thol′ə jē), **1** study of the causes and nature of diseases. **2** unhealthy conditions and processes caused by a disease. *n., pl.* **pa thol o-gies.**

pa thos (pā′thos), quality in speech, writing, music, events, or a scene that arouses a feeling of pity or sadness. *n.*

path way (path′wā′), path. *n.*

pa tience (pā′shəns), **1** willingness to put up with waiting, pain, trouble, etc.; calm endurance of anything that annoys, troubles, or hurts: *People need to have patience while the dentist fills their teeth. The cat watched the mouse hole with patience.* **2** long, hard work; steady effort. **3** card game played by one person; solitaire. *n.*

pa tient (pā′shənt), **1** having or showing patience. **2** person who is being treated by a doctor. 1 *adj.,* 2 *n.* —**pa′-tient ly,** *adv.*

pat i o (pat′ē ō), **1** an inner court or yard open to the sky. Houses in Spanish-speaking countries are often built around patios. **2** terrace for outdoor eating, lounging, etc. *n., pl.* **pat i-os.**

pat ois (pat′wä), dialect spoken by the common people of a district: *the patois of the French Canadians. n., pl.* **pat ois** (pat′wäz). [from French]

pa tri arch (pā′trē ärk), **1** father and ruler of a family or tribe. In the Bible, Abraham, Isaac, and Jacob are patriarchs. **2** a venerable old man. **3** bishop of the highest rank in the Eastern Church and the Roman Catholic Church. *n.*

pa tri ar chal (pā′trē är′kəl), **1** suitable for a patriarch; having to do with a patriarch. **2** under the rule of a patriarch: *patriarchal life, a patriarchal church. adj.*

pa tri cian (pə trish′ən), **1** member of the nobility of ancient Rome. **2** a noble; aristocrat. **3** of high social rank; aristocratic. **4** suitable for an aristocrat. 1,2 *n.,* 3,4 *adj.*

Pat rick (pat′rik), **Saint,** A.D. 389?-461?, British missionary and bishop who converted Ireland to Christianity. He is the patron saint of Ireland. *n.*

pat ri mo ni al (pat′rə mō′nē əl), having to do with a patrimony; inherited from one's father or ancestors. *adj.*

pat ri mo ny (pat′rə mō′nē), **1** property inherited from one's father or ancestors. **2** property belonging to a church, monastery, or convent. **3** any heritage. *n., pl.* **pat ri mo nies.**

pa tri ot (pā'trē ət), person who loves and loyally supports his country. *n.*

pa tri ot ic (pā'trē ot'ik), **1** loving one's country. **2** showing love and loyal support of one's own country. *adj.* —**pa'tri ot'i cal ly,** *adv.*

pa tri ot ism (pā'trē ə tiz'əm), love and loyal support of one's country. *n.*

pa trol (pə trōl'), **1** go around in an area watching and guarding in order to protect life and property: *The police patrolled once every hour.* **2** go around (a town, camp, etc.) to watch or guard. **3** a going of the rounds to watch or guard. **4** persons who patrol: *The patrol was changed at midnight.* **5** group of soldiers, ships, or airplanes, sent to find out all they can about the enemy. **6** unit of eight boy or girl scouts. **1,2** *v.,* **pa trolled, pa trolling; 3-6** *n.*

patrol car, automobile used by the police to patrol an area.

pa trol man (pə trōl'mən), **1** person who patrols. **2** policeman who patrols a certain district. *n., pl.* **pa trol men.**

patrol wagon, a closed wagon or truck used by the police for carrying prisoners.

pa tron (pā'trən), **1** one who buys regularly at a given store or goes regularly to a given restaurant, hotel, etc. **2** person who gives his approval and support to some person, art, cause, or undertaking: *a patron of artists.* **3** a guardian saint or god; protector. **4** guarding; protecting: *a patron saint.* **1-3** *n.,* **4** *adj.*

pa tron age (pā'trə nij *or* pat'rə nij), **1** regular business given to a store, hotel, etc., by customers. **2** favor, encouragement, or support given by a patron. **3** condescending favor: *an air of patronage.* **4** power to give jobs or favors: *the patronage of a governor, a mayor, or a member of Congress.* **5** political jobs or favors. *n.*

pa tron ess (pā'trə nis *or* pat'rə nis), a woman patron. *n., pl.* **pa tron ess es.**

pa tron ize (pā'trə nīz *or* pat'rə nīz), **1** be a regular customer of; give regular business to: *We patronize our neighborhood stores.* **2** act as a patron toward; support or protect: *patronize the ballet.* **3** treat in a condescending way: *We dislike to have anyone patronize us.* *v.,* **pa tron ized, pa tron iz ing.** —**pa'tron iz'ing ly,** *adv.*

pa troon (pə trün'), landowner who had certain privileges under the old Dutch governments of New York and New Jersey. A patroon usually owned a large amount of land. *n.*

pat sy (pat'sē), SLANG. an easy victim or scapegoat. *n., pl.* **pat sies.**

pat ter[1] (pat'ər), **1** make rapid taps: *The rain patters on a windowpane. Bare feet patter along the hard floor.* **2** series of quick taps or the sound they make: *the patter of rain, the patter of little feet.* **1** *v.,* **2** *n.* [from *pat*]

pat ter[2] (pat'ər), **1** rapid and easy talk: *a magician's patter.* **2** talk or say rapidly and easily, without much thought: *patter a prayer.* **1** *n.,* **2** *v.* [a different form of *pater* in *paternoster* (because the prayer was said very rapidly)]

pat tern (pat'ərn), **1** arrangement of forms and colors; design: *the patterns of wallpaper, rugs, cloth, and jewelry.* **2** a model or guide for something to be made: *I used a paper pattern in cutting the cloth for my coat.* **3** a fine example; model to be followed: *He was a pattern of generosity.* **4** make according to a pattern: *Pattern yourself after your mother.* **5** any arrangement: *behavior pattern, a speech pattern.* **1-3,5** *n.,* **4** *v.*

pavilion (def. 1)

pat ty (pat'ē), **1** a hollow form of pastry filled with chicken, oysters, etc. **2** a small, round, flat piece of food or candy. *n., pl.* **pat ties.**

pau ci ty (pô'sə tē), **1** a small number; fewness. **2** a small amount; scarcity; lack. *n.*

Paul (pôl), **Saint,** died A.D. 67?, apostle who started Christian groups in many countries and wrote many of the books in the New Testament. *n.*

Paul VI, born 1897, pope since 1963.

paunch (pônch), **1** belly; stomach. **2** a large, protruding belly. *n.*

paunch y (pôn'chē), having a big paunch. *adj.,* **paunch i er, paunch i est.**

pau per (pô'pər), a very poor person; person supported by charity. *n.*

pau per ism (pô'pə riz'əm), a being very poor; poverty. *n.*

pau per ize (pô'pə rīz'), make a pauper of. *v.,* **pau per ized, pau per izing.**

pause (pôz), **1** stop for a time; wait: *The dog paused when it heard me.* **2** a brief stop or rest: *After a pause for lunch the employees returned to work. After a short pause I went on reading.* **3** dwell; linger: *pause upon a word.* **4** a sign (⌣ or ⌒) above or below a musical note or rest, meaning that it is to be held

hat, āge, fär; let, ēqual, tėrm; it, īce; hot, ōpen, ôrder; oil, out; cup, půt, rüle; ch, child; ng, long; sh, she; th, thin; ŦH, then; zh, measure;

ə represents *a* in about, *e* in taken, *i* in pencil, *o* in lemon, *u* in circus.

for a longer time. **1,3** *v.,* **paused, paus ing; 2,4** *n.*

pave (pāv), **1** cover (a street, sidewalk, etc.) with a pavement: *pave a road with concrete.* **2** make smooth or easy; prepare: *The invention paved the way for new discoveries.* *v.,* **paved, pav ing.**

pave ment (pāv'mənt), **1** a covering or surface for streets, sidewalks, etc., made of asphalt, concrete, gravel, stones, etc. **2** a paved road. *n.*

pa vil ion (pə vil'yən), **1** a light building, usually somewhat open, used for shelter, pleasure, etc.: *a bathing pavilion.* **2** a large tent with a floor raised on posts. **3** part of a building higher and more decorated than the rest. **4** one of a group of buildings forming a hospital. **5** any building that houses an exhibition at a fair. *n.*

pav ing (pā'ving), **1** material for pavement. **2** pavement. *n.*

Pav lov (pav'lov *or* päv'lôf), **Ivan,** 1849-1936, Russian physiologist famous for his studies of the digestive glands and of the reflexes. *n.*

paw (pô), **1** foot of a four-footed animal having claws. **2** strike or scrape with the paws or feet: *The cat pawed the mouse. The horse pawed the ground, eager to be going again.* **3** IN-FORMAL. handle awkwardly, roughly, or in too familiar a manner: *The young child pawed the delicate glass swan.* **1** *n.,* **2,3** *v.*

pawl—The ratchet wheel is moved in the direction of the arrow by pawl A when the lever is moved up, and by pawl B when the lever is moved down.

pawl (pôl), a pivoted bar arranged to catch in the teeth of a ratchet or the like so as to prevent movement backward or to impart motion. *n.*

pawn[1] (pôn), **1** leave (something) with

pawn

another person as security that borrowed money will be repaid; pledge: *I pawned my watch to buy food until I could get work.* 2 something left as security. 1 *v.,* 2 *n.* [from French of the 1400's *pan*]

in pawn, in another's possession as security: *His watch is in pawn.*

pawn² (pôn), 1 (in chess) one of the 16 pieces of lowest value. 2 an unimportant person or thing used by someone to gain some advantage. *n.* [from French of the 1300's *peon* (originally) foot soldier, from Latin *pedonem,* from *pedem* foot]

pawn bro ker (pôn′brō′kər), person who lends money at interest on articles that are left with him as security for the loan. *n.*

Paw nee (pô nē′), member of an American Indian tribe that once lived in Nebraska and Kansas, and now lives in Oklahoma. *n., pl.* **Paw nees** or **Paw nee.**

pawn shop (pôn′shop′), pawnbroker's shop. *n.*

paw paw (pô′pô), papaw. *n.*

pay (pā), 1 give money to for things, work, etc.: *He paid the doctor.* 2 money given for things or work: *She gets her pay every Saturday.* 3 give money for: *Pay your fare. Pay your debts.* 4 give what is due: *She owes it and must pay.* 5 to return for favors or hurts; reward or punish: *He paid them for their insults by causing them trouble.* 6 a return for favors or hurts: *Dislike is the pay for being mean.* 7 give; offer; make: *pay attention, pay compliments, pay a visit.* 8 be worthwhile: *It pays me to keep that stock. It pays to be polite.* 9 yield as a return: *That stock pays me four per cent.* 10 let out (a rope, etc.). 11 containing a device for receiving money for use: *a pay telephone.* 1,3-5,7-10 *v.,* **paid** (or **payed** for 10), **pay ing;** 2,6 *n.,* 11 *adj.*

in the pay of, paid by and working for: *The police are in the pay of the city.*

pay back, 1 return borrowed money. 2 give the same treatment as received: *I hope to be able to pay back her help.*

pay off, 1 give all the money that is owed; pay in full. 2 get even with; get revenge on.

pay up, pay; pay in full.

pay a ble (pā′ə bəl), 1 required to be paid; due: *I must spend $100 soon on bills payable.* 2 that may be paid. *adj.*

pay check (pā′chek′), check given in payment of wages or salary. *n.*

pay day (pā′dā′), day on which wages are paid. *n.*

pay ee (pā ē′), person to whom money is paid or is to be paid. *n.*

pay er (pā′ər), person who pays or is to pay. *n.*

pay load (pā′lōd′), load carried by a vehicle. Passengers are the payload of a bus, train, or airplane. The payload of a rocket is contained in the nose cone, and may be instruments, cargo, or astronauts. The payload of a missile is the warhead. *n.*

pay mas ter (pā′mas′tər), person whose job is to pay wages. *n.*

pay ment (pā′mənt), 1 a paying. 2 amount paid: *a monthly payment of $10.* 3 pay: *The pleasure of being able to help you is payment enough for me.* 4 reward or punishment. *n.*

pay off (pā′ôf′), 1 a paying of wages. 2 time of such payment. 3 returns from an enterprise, action, etc. 4 SLANG. climax (of a story, situation, etc.). *n.*

pay roll (pā′rōl′), 1 list of persons to be paid and the amount that each one is to receive. 2 the total amount to be paid to them. *n.*

pd., paid.

pea (pē), 1 the round seed in the pod of a leguminous plant, used as a vegetable. 2 the plant itself. *n., pl.* **peas** or **pease.**

as like as two peas, exactly alike.

peace (pēs), 1 freedom from strife of any kind; condition of quiet, order, and security: *peace in the family.* 2 freedom from war: *work for world peace.* 3 agreement between enemies to end war: *to sign the peace.* 4 quiet; calm; stillness: *peace of mind. We enjoy the peace of the country.* *n.*

at peace, 1 not in a state of war. 2 not quarreling. 3 in a state of quietness; quiet; peaceful.

hold one's peace, be silent; keep still.

peace a ble (pē′sə bəl), 1 liking peace; keeping peace: *Peaceable people keep out of quarrels.* 2 peaceful. *adj.*

peace a bly (pē′sə blē), in a peaceable manner. *adv.*

Peace Corps, agency of the United States government, established in 1961, which sends trained volunteers to help improve conditions in underdeveloped countries.

peace ful (pēs′fəl), 1 full of peace; quiet; calm: *It was peaceful in the mountains.* 2 liking peace; keeping peace: *peaceful neighbors.* 3 of or having to do with peace: *settle a dispute by peaceful means.* *adj.* —**peace′ful ly,** *adv.* —**peace′ful ness,** *n.*

peace mak er (pēs′mā′kər), person who makes peace. *n.*

peace pipe, pipe smoked by American Indians as a token or pledge of peace.

peace time (pēs′tīm′), 1 a time of peace. 2 of or having to do with a time of peace. 1 *n.,* 2 *adj.*

peach (pēch), 1 a juicy, nearly round fruit having downy skin and a rough stone or pit. It is good to eat. Peaches are grown in temperate climates. 2 tree it grows on. 3 a yellowish pink. 4 yellowish-pink. 1-3 *n., pl.* **peach es;** 4 *adj.* —**peach′like′,** *adj.*

peach y (pē′chē), SLANG. fine; wonderful. *adj.,* **peach i er, peach i est.**

peacock—body without tail 20 in. long

pea cock (pē′kok′), a large male bird of Asia and Africa, related to the pheasant. It has beautiful green, blue, and gold feathers and a splendid tail. The tail feathers have spots like eyes on them and may be spread out and held upright like a fan. *n., pl.* **pea cocks** or **pea cock.**

pea hen (pē′hen′), the female of the peacock. It is smaller and less showy than the peacock. *n.*

pea jacket, a short coat of thick woolen cloth, worn by sailors.

peak (pēk), 1 the pointed top of a mountain or hill: *snowy peaks.* 2 mountain that stands alone: *Pikes Peak.* 3 any pointed end or top: *the peak of a beard, the peak of a roof.* 4 the highest point: *reach the peak of one's profession.* 5 the front part or the brim of a cap, which stands out. 6 the narrow part of a ship's hold, at either end. *n.*

peaked¹ (pēkt), having a peak; pointed: *a peaked hat. adj.* [peak + -ed²]

peak ed² (pē′kid), sickly in appearance; wan; thin. *adj.* [from earlier *peak* look sick; origin uncertain]

peal (pēl), 1 a loud, long sound: *a peal of thunder, peals of laughter.* 2 the loud ringing of bells. 3 set of bells; chimes. 4 sound out in a peal; ring: *The bells pealed forth their message of Christmas joy.* 1-3 *n.,* 4 *v.*

pea nut (pē′nut′), 1 the large, nutlike seed of a plant of the same family as the pea. Peanuts, when roasted, are used for food and are pressed to obtain their oil for use in cooking. 2 pod of this plant, ripening underground, and usually consisting of two of the seeds. 3 the plant itself. *n.*

peanut butter, food made of roasted peanuts ground until soft and smooth. It is spread on bread, crackers, etc.

peanut oil, oil pressed from peanuts, used especially in cooking and in margarine.

peccary—about 3 ft. long

pear (per *or* par), 1 a sweet, juicy fruit rounded at one end and smaller toward the stem end. It is good to eat. 2 tree it grows on. *n.*

pearl (pėrl), 1 a white or nearly white gem that has a soft shine like satin. Pearls are formed inside the shell of a kind of oyster, or other similar shellfish. 2 thing that looks like a pearl, such as a dewdrop or a tear. 3 a very fine one of its kind: *He is a pearl of courtesy.* 4 a very pale, clear, bluish gray. 5 very pale, clear bluish-gray. 6 mother-of-pearl: *pearl buttons.* 1-4,6 *n.*, 5 *adj.*

pearl gray, a soft, pale, bluish gray.

Pearl Harbor, United States naval base near Honolulu, on the S coast of Oahu. An attack on it by Japanese bombers on December 7, 1941, was the immediate cause of American entry into World War II.

pearl y (pėr′lē), like a pearl in color or luster: *pearly teeth. adj.,* **pearl i er, pearl i est.**

Pear y (pir′ē), Robert Edwin, 1856-1920, American naval officer and arctic explorer, discoverer of the North Pole in 1909. *n.*

peas ant (pez′nt), 1 farmer of the working class in Europe. 2 of peasants: *peasant labor.* 1 *n.,* 2 *adj.*

peas ant ry (pez′n trē), peasants. *n.*

pease (pēz), a plural of **pea.** *n.*

peat (pēt), kind of turf made of partly rotted moss and plants found in bogs. It is dried and used as fuel in Ireland and Great Britain. *n.* —**peat′like′, adj.**

peat moss, kind of moss from which peat has formed or may form. It is dried and used as fertilizer.

peb ble (peb′əl), 1 a small stone, usually worn and rounded by being rolled about by water. 2 pave with pebbles: *pebble a walk.* 1 *n.,* 2 *v.,* **peb bled, peb bling.** —**peb′ble like′, adj.**

peb bly (peb′lē), having many pebbles; covered with pebbles: *The pebbly beach*

hurt our bare feet. adj., **peb bli er, peb bli est.**

pe can (pi kän′ *or* pi kan′), 1 an olive-shaped nut with a smooth, thin shell, that grows on a kind of hickory tree common in the southern United States. It is good to eat. 2 tree it grows on. *n.*

pec ca dil lo (pek′ə dil′ō), a slight sin or fault. *n., pl.* **pec ca dil loes** or **pec ca dil los.**

pec car y (pek′ər ē), kind of wild pig found in South America and as far north as Texas. *n., pl.* **pec car ies** or **pec car y.**

peck[1] (pek), 1 strike and pick with the beak or a pointed tool. 2 stroke made with the beak or a pointed tool: *The hen gave me a peck.* 3 make by striking with the beak or a pointed tool: *Woodpeckers peck holes in trees.* 4 hole or mark made by pecking. 5 make a pecking motion. 6 strike at and pick up with the beak: *A hen pecks corn.* 7 INFORMAL. eat only a little, bit by bit. 8 INFORMAL. a stiff, unwilling kiss. 1,3,5-7 *v.,* 2,4,8 *n.* [apparently a different form of *pick*[1]]

peck at, 1 try to peck. 2 INFORMAL. eat only a little, bit by bit: *Because she is not feeling well, she just pecks at her food.* 3 keep criticizing.

peck[2] (pek), 1 measure of capacity for grain, fruit, vegetables, and other dry things, equal to 8 quarts or ¼ of a bushel: *a peck of beans, a peck of potatoes.* 2 container holding just a peck, to measure with. 3 a great deal: *a peck of trouble. n.* [Middle English *pek*]

pec tin (pek′tən), substance that occurs in ripe fruits and makes fruit jelly stiff. *n.*

pec tor al (pek′tər əl), of, in, or on the breast or chest. *adj.*

pec u late (pek′yə lāt), steal (money or goods entrusted to one); embezzle. *v.,* **pec u lat ed, pec u lat ing.**

pec u la tion (pek′yə lā′shən), a peculating; embezzlement. *n.*

pe cul iar (pi kyü′lyər), 1 strange; odd; unusual: *It was peculiar that the fish market had no fish last Friday. A clock without any hands looks rather peculiar.* 2 belonging to one person or thing and not to another; special: *This old watch has a peculiar value. The Quakers wore a dress peculiar to themselves. adj.* —**pe cul′iar ly, adv.**

pe cu li ar i ty (pi kyü′lē ar′ə tē), 1 a being peculiar; strangeness; oddness; unusualness: *We noticed the peculiarity of her manner at once.* 2 some little thing that is strange or odd: *One of his peculiarities is that his two eyes are not the same color.* 3 a peculiar or characteristic quality. *n., pl.* **pe cu li ar i ties.**

pe cu ni ar y (pi kyü′nē er′ē), of or having to do with money; in the form of money. *adj.*

hat, āge, fär; let, ēqual, tėrm;
it, īce; hot, ōpen, ôrder;
oil, out; cup, pùt, rüle; ch, child;
ng, long; sh, she; th, thin;
ŦH, then; zh, measure;

ə represents *a* in about,
e in taken, *i* in pencil,
o in lemon, *u* in circus.

ped a gog ic (ped′ə goj′ik), of teachers or teaching; of pedagogy. *adj.* —**ped′a gog′i cal ly, adv.**

ped a gog i cal (ped′ə goj′ə kəl), pedagogic. *adj.*

ped a gogue or **ped a gog** (ped′ə-gog), 1 teacher of children. 2 a dull, narrow-minded teacher; pedant. *n.*

ped a go gy (ped′ə gō′jē), 1 a teaching. 2 science or art of teaching. *n.*

ped al (ped′l), 1 lever worked by the foot; the part on which the foot is placed to move any kind of machinery. Organs and pianos have pedals for changing the tone. The two pedals of a bicycle, pushed down one after the other, make it go. 2 work or use the pedals; move by pedals: *I pedaled my bicycle slowly up the hill.* 3 of or having to do with the foot or feet. 4 of or having to do with a pedal or pedals. 1 *n.,* 2 *v.,* 3,4 *adj.*

ped ant (ped′nt), 1 person who displays his knowledge in an unnecessary or tiresome way. A pedant may make a show of knowledge without knowing how to use it well. 2 a dull, narrow-minded teacher or scholar. *n.*

pe dan tic (pi dan′tik), 1 displaying one's knowledge more than is necessary. 2 tediously learned; scholarly in a dull and narrow way. *adj.*

ped ant ry (ped′n trē), 1 an unnecessary or tiresome display of knowledge. 2 overemphasis on rules, details, etc., especially in learning. *n., pl.* **ped ant ries.**

ped dle (ped′l), 1 carry from place to place and sell: *The fruit seller peddled fruit from house to house.* 2 sell or deal out in small quantities: *peddle candy, peddle gossip.* 3 travel about with things to sell. *v.,* **ped dled, ped dling.**

ped dler (ped′lər), person who travels about selling things that he carries in a pack or in a cart. *n.* Also, **pedlar.**

ped es tal (ped′i stəl), 1 base on which a column or a statue stands. 2 base of a tall vase, lamp, etc. 3 any base; support; foundation. *n.*

place on a pedestal, accord a very high place to; idolize.

pe des tri an (pə des′trē ən), 1 person

adj.	adjective	*n.*	noun
adv.	adverb	*prep.*	preposition
conj.	conjunction	*pron.*	pronoun
interj.	interjection	*v.*	verb
sing.	singular	*pl.*	plural

who goes on foot; walker: *Pedestrians have to watch for automobiles turning corners.* 2 going on foot; walking. 3 without imagination; dull; slow: *a pedestrian style of writing.* 1 *n.*, 2,3 *adj.*

pe di at ric (pē′dē at′rik), of or having to do with pediatrics. *adj.*

pe di a tri cian (pē′dē ə trish′ən), doctor who specializes in pediatrics. *n.*

pe di at rics (pē′dē at′riks), branch of medicine dealing with children's diseases and the care of babies and children. *n.*

PEDICEL

PEDUNCLE

ped i cel (ped′ə səl), a small stalk or stalklike part. *n.*

ped i gree (ped′ə grē′), 1 list of ancestors of a person or animal; family tree. 2 ancestry; line of descent. *n.* [from French of the 1400's *pie de grue* foot of the crane (because the symbol /|\ was used in showing descent)]

ped i greed (ped′ə grēd′), having a known pedigree: *Her dog is pedigreed. Horses, cows, dogs, and other animals of known and recorded ancestry are called pedigreed stock.* *adj.*

PEDIMENT

pediment (def. 1)

ped i ment (ped′ə mənt), 1 the low triangular part on the front of buildings in the Greek style. A pediment is like a gable. 2 any similar decorative part on a building, door, bookcase, etc. *n.*

ped lar (ped′lər), peddler. *n.*

pe dom e ter (pi dom′ə tər), instrument for recording the number of steps taken and thus measuring the distance traveled. *n.*

pe dun cle (pi dung′kəl), stalk; stem; stalklike part. See **pedicel** for picture. *n.*

peek (pēk), 1 look quickly and slyly; peep: *You must not peek while you are*

counting in such games as hide-and-seek. 2 a quick, sly look. 1 *v.*, 2 *n.*

peel (pēl), 1 the rind or outer covering of fruit, etc. 2 to strip the skin, rind, or bark from: *to peel an orange, to peel a potato.* 3 strip: *The Indians peeled the bark from trees to make canoes.* 4 come off: *When I was sunburned, my skin peeled. The paint on the shed is peeling.* 1 *n.*, 2-4 *v.*

keep one's eyes peeled, INFORMAL. be on the alert.

peel ing (pē′ling), part peeled off or pared off. *n.*

peep[1] (pēp), 1 look through a small or narrow hole or crack. 2 a look through a hole or crack; little look: *take a peep into the pantry.* 3 look when no one knows it. 4 a secret look: *take a peep at the presents.* 5 look out, as if peeping; come partly out: *Violets peeped among the leaves.* 6 the first looking or coming out: *at the peep of day.* 1,3,5, *v.*, 2,4,6 *n.* [perhaps a different form of *peek*]

peep[2] (pēp), 1 the cry of a young bird or chicken; a sound like a chirp or squeak. 2 make such a sound; chirp. 1 *n.*, 2 *v.* [probably an imitation of the sound]

peep er[1] (pē′pər), INFORMAL. eye. [from *peep*[1]]

peep er[2] (pē′pər), 1 person or thing that peeps. 2 any of certain frogs that make peeping noises. *n.* [from *peep*[2]]

peep hole (pēp′hōl′), hole through which one may peep. *n.*

peer[1] (pir), 1 person of the same rank, ability, etc., as another; equal: *He is so fine a man that it would be hard to find his peer.* 2 man who has a title; man who is high and great by birth or rank; nobleman. A duke, marquis, earl, count, viscount, or baron is a peer. *n.* [from French of the 1200's *per,* from Latin *par* equal]

peer[2] (pir), 1 look closely to see clearly, as a near-sighted person does: *She peered at the tag to read the price.* 2 come out slightly; peep out: *The sun was peering from behind a cloud.* *v.* [perhaps a different form of *appear*]

peer age (pir′ij), 1 rank or dignity of a peer. 2 peers of a country. 3 book giving a list of peers of a country and their family histories. *n.*

peer ess (pir′is), 1 wife or widow of a peer. 2 woman having the rank of peer in her own right. *n., pl.* **peer ess es.**

peer less (pir′lis), without an equal; matchless: *His peerless performance won him a prize. adj.*

peeve (pēv), INFORMAL. 1 make peevish. 2 an annoyance. 1 *v.,* peeved, peev ing; 2 *n.*

pee vish (pē′vish), feeling cross; fretful; complaining: *A peevish child is unhappy and makes others unhappy. adj.*

—**pee′vish ly,** *adv.* —**pee′vish ness,** *n.*

pee wee (pē′wē), a very small person or thing. *n.*

peg (peg), 1 pin or small bolt of wood, metal, etc., used to fasten parts together, to hang things on, to stop a hole, to make fast a rope or string, to mark the score in a game, etc. 2 fasten or hold with pegs: *peg down a tent.* 3 mark with pegs. 4 work hard: *I pegged away at my studies so that I would get high marks.* 5 step; degree: *Her work is several pegs above yours.* 6 INFORMAL. a hard throw of a ball, especially in baseball. 7 INFORMAL. throw hard: *peg the ball to the shortstop.* 1,5,6 *n.,* 2-4,7 *v.,* pegged, peg ging.

take down a peg, lower the pride of; humble.

Pegasus (def. 1)

Peg a sus (peg′ə səs), (in Greek myths) a horse with wings, the steed of the Muses. *n.*

peg board (peg′bôrd′), board with evenly spaced holes in which pegs or hooks are inserted to hold tools, displays, etc. *n.*

P.E.I., Prince Edward Island.

Pei ping (pā′ping′ *or* bā′ping′), former name of **Peking,** from 1928 to 1949. *n.*

Pe kin ese (pē′kə nēz′), Pekingese. *n., pl.* **Pe kin ese.**

Pe king (pē′king′), capital of China, in the NE part. *n.* Formerly, **Peiping.**

Pekingese—6 to 9 in. high at shoulder

Pe king ese (pē′kə nēz′ *or* pē′king-ēz′), a small dog with long hair and a broad, flat face. *n., pl.* **Pe king ese.** Also, **Pekinese.**

pe koe (pē′kō), kind of black tea from Ceylon or India. *n.*

pelf (pelf), money or riches, thought of as bad or degrading. *n.*

pel i can (pel′ə kən), a very large,

pelican
about 4 ft. long;
wingspread 6½ ft.

fish-eating water bird with a huge bill
and a pouch on the underside of the bill
for scooping up fish. *n.*

Pe li on (pē′lē ən), **Mount,** mountain
in NE Greece. According to Greek
myths, when the giants made war on the
gods, they piled Mount Pelion upon
Mount Ossa in an attempt to reach their
foes on Mount Olympus. *n.*

pe lisse (pə lēs′), 1 coat lined or
trimmed with fur. 2 woman's long
cloak. *n.*

pel lag ra (pə lag′rə), disease marked
by inflammation and scaling of the skin,
nervousness, and sometimes mental
disorders. It is caused by a lack of
nicotinic acid in the diet. *n.*

pel let (pel′it), 1 a little ball of
mud, paper, food, medicine, etc.; pill.
2 bullet. *n.*

pell-mell or **pell mell** (pel′mel′),
1 in a rushing, tumbling mass or crowd:
*The children dashed pell-mell down the
beach and into the waves.* 2 in headlong
haste. 3 headlong; tumultuous. 1,2
adv., 3 *adj.*

pel lu cid (pə lü′sid), 1 transparent;
clear: *a pellucid stream.* 2 clearly expressed; easy to understand: *pellucid
language. adj.*

Pel o pon ne sian (pel′ə pə nē′shən),
1 of or having to do with the Peloponnesus or its people. 2 person born or
living in the Peloponnesus. 1 *adj.,* 2 *n.*

Pel o pon ne sus (pel′ə pə nē′səs),
peninsula that constitutes the S part of
Greece. *n.*

pelt¹ (pelt), 1 throw things at; attack;
assail: *Children were pelting each other
with snowballs.* 2 beat heavily: *The rain
came pelting down.* 3 to throw: *The
clouds pelted rain upon us.* 4 a blow
from something thrown. 5 speed: *The
horse is coming at full pelt.* 1-3 *v.,* 4,5 *n.*
[origin uncertain]

pelt² (pelt), skin of a sheep, goat, or
small fur-bearing animal, before it is
tanned. *n.* [probably from earlier *pelt-
ry,* from French of the 1400's *peleterie*
pelts, furs, from *pel* skin, from Latin
pellem]

pel vic (pel′vik), of or having to do
with the pelvis. *adj.*

pel vis (pel′vis), 1 the basin-shaped
cavity formed by the hipbones and the
end of the backbone. 2 bones forming
this cavity. *n.*

Pem ba (pem′bə), island off E Africa.
It is part of Tanzania. *n.*

pem mi can or **pem i can** (pem′ə-
kən), dried meat pounded into a paste
with melted fat. *n.*

pen¹ (pen), 1 instrument used for writing or drawing with ink. Most pens are
either ball-point pens or fountain pens.
2 style of writing; writing. 3 write: *I
penned a brief note.* 1,2 *n.,* 3 *v.,*
penned, pen ning. [from French of
the 1300's *penne,* from Latin *penna*
feather]

pen² (pen), 1 a small, closed yard for
cows, sheep, pigs, chickens, etc. 2 enclosure for keeping a baby, a dog, etc.,
confined. 3 shut in a pen. 4 shut in;
confine closely: *They had me penned in
a corner where I could not escape.* 1,2
n., 3,4 *v.,* **penned** or **pent, pen ning.**
[Old English *penn*]

pen³ (pen), SLANG. penitentiary. *n.*
[shortened from *penitentiary*]

pe nal (pē′nl), 1 of, having to do with,
or given as punishment: *penal laws,
penal labor.* 2 liable to be punished:
Robbery is a penal offense. adj.

pe nal ize (pē′nl īz), 1 declare punishable by law or by rule; set a penalty
for: *Speeding on city streets is penalized. Fouls are penalized in many
games.* 2 inflict a penalty on; punish:
*Our football team was penalized five
yards. v.,* **pe nal ized, pe nal iz ing.**

pen al ty (pen′l tē), 1 punishment imposed by law: *The penalty for speeding is usually a fine.* 2 disadvantage
imposed on a side or player for breaking
the rules of some game or contest.
3 disadvantage attached to some act or
condition: *the penalties of old age. n.,*
pl. **pen al ties.**

pen ance (pen′əns), 1 punishment
borne to show sorrow for sin, to make
up for a wrong done, and to obtain
pardon for sin. 2 any act done to show
that one is sorry or repents. *n.*

pence (pens), a plural of **penny** (def.
2). *n.*

pen chant (pen′chənt), a strong taste
or liking; inclination: *a penchant for
taking long walks. n.*

pen cil (pen′səl), 1 instrument used
for writing or drawing, made of a slender rod of graphite encased in wood or
in a metal tube. 2 mark or write with a
pencil. 3 stick of coloring matter. 1,3
n., 2 *v.*

pend ant (pen′dənt), 1 a hanging or-

pelvis (def. 2)

hat, āge, fär; let, ēqual, tėrm;
it, īce; hot, ōpen, ôrder;
oil, out; cup, pu̇t, rüle; ch, child;
ng, long; sh, she; th, thin;
ᵬн, then; zh, measure;

ə represents *a* in about,
e in taken, *i* in pencil,
o in lemon, *u* in circus.

nament, such as a locket. 2 pendent.
1 *n.,* 2 *adj.*

pend ent (pen′dənt), 1 hanging: *the
pendent branches of a willow.* 2 overhanging. 3 pending. 4 pendant. 1-3
adj., 4 *n.*

pend ing (pen′ding), 1 waiting to be
decided or settled: *while the agreement
was pending.* 2 while waiting for; until:
*Pending your return, we'll get everything
ready.* 3 during; *pending the investigation.* 4 likely to happen soon; threatening; about to occur. 1,4 *adj.,* 2,3
prep.

pen du lous (pen′jə ləs), 1 hanging
loosely: *The oriole builds a pendulous
nest.* 2 swinging. *adj.*

PENDULUM

pen du lum (pen′jə ləm), weight so
hung from a fixed point that it is free to
swing to and fro. The movement of the
works of a tall clock is often timed by a
pendulum. *n.*

Pe nel o pe (pə nel′ə pē), (in Greek
legends) the faithful wife of Ulysses.
She waited twenty years for his return
in spite of the entreaties of her many
suitors. *n.*

pen e tra bil i ty (pen′ə trə bil′ə tē),
capability of being penetrated. *n.*

pen e tra ble (pen′ə trə bəl), that can
be penetrated. *adj.*

pen e trate (pen′ə trāt), 1 get into or
through: *The bullet penetrated this wall,
and two inches into the one beyond.*
2 pierce through; make a way: *Our eyes
could not penetrate the darkness. Even
where the trees were thickest, the sunshine penetrated.* 3 soak through;
spread through: *The rain penetrated our
clothes. The odor penetrated the whole
house.* 4 see into; understand: *I could

623

adj.	adjective	*n.*	noun
adv.	adverb	*prep.*	preposition
conj.	conjunction	*pron.*	pronoun
interj.	interjection	*v.*	verb
sing.	singular	*pl.*	plural

not penetrate the mystery. 5 affect or impress very much. *v.,* **pen e trat ed, pen e trat ing.**

pen e trat ing (pen′ə trā′ting), 1 sharp; piercing. 2 having an acute mind; understanding thoroughly. *adj.* —**pen′e trat′ing ly,** *adv.*

pen e tra tion (pen′ə trā′shən), 1 act or power of penetrating. 2 sharpness of intellect; insight. *n.*

pen e tra tive (pen′ə trā′tiv), penetrating; piercing; acute; keen. *adj.*

penguin
about 3 ft. tall

pen guin (pen′gwin), a web-footed sea bird that has black and white plumage and wings like flippers, which it uses for diving and swimming, not for flying. Penguins live in Antarctica and other cold areas of the Southern Hemisphere. *n.*

pen i cil lin (pen′ə sil′ən), antibiotic made from a penicillium mold, used to treat diseases caused by certain bacteria. *n.*

pen i cil li um (pen′ə sil′ē əm), any of a certain kind of fungi. The mold on cheese is a penicillium. *n., pl.* **pen i cil li ums, pen i cil li a** (pen′ə sil′ē ə).

pe nin su la (pə nin′sə lə *or* pə-nin′syə lə), piece of land almost surrounded by water, or extending far out into the water. Florida is a peninsula. *n., pl.* **pe nin su las.**

pe nin su lar (pə nin′sə lər *or* pə-nin′syə lər), 1 like a peninsula. 2 in or of a peninsula. *adj.*

pe nis (pē′nis), the sex organ of a male animal. Urine leaves the body of male mammals through the penis. *n., pl.* **pe nis es.**

pen i tence (pen′ə təns), sorrow for sinning or doing wrong; repentance. *n.*

pen i tent (pen′ə tənt), 1 sorry for sinning or doing wrong; repenting: *The penitent child promised never to cheat*

again. 2 person who is sorry for sin, especially one who confesses and does penance for his sins under the direction of a church. 1 *adj.,* 2 *n.* —**pen′i tent-ly,** *adv.*

pen i ten tial (pen′ə ten′shəl), 1 of, showing, or having to do with penitence: *The penitential psalms express remorse for sin.* 2 of or having to do with penance. *adj.*

pen i ten tiar y (pen′ə ten′shər ē), 1 prison for criminals, especially a state or federal prison. 2 making one liable to punishment in a prison: *a penitentiary offense.* 3 used for punishment, discipline, and reformation: *penitentiary measures.* 4 of penance; penitential. 1 *n., pl.* **pen i ten tiar ies;** 2-4 *adj.*

pen knife (pen′nīf′), a small pocketknife. *n., pl.* **pen knives** (pen′nīvz′).

pen man (pen′mən), 1 writer. 2 person whose handwriting is good. *n., pl.* **pen men.**

pen man ship (pen′mən ship), 1 writing with pen, pencil, etc.; handwriting. 2 manner or style of composing a written work. *n.*

Penn (pen), **William,** 1644-1718, English Quaker who founded the first settlement in Pennsylvania, at Philadelphia. *n.*

Penn. or **Penna.,** Pennsylvania.

pen name, name used by a writer instead of his real name; nom de plume.

pen nant (pen′ənt), 1 flag, usually long and tapering, used on ships, in signaling, as a school banner, etc. 2 flag taken as an emblem of superiority or success, especially in an athletic contest. *n.*

pennant (def. 1)

pen ni less (pen′ē lis), without a cent of money; very poor: *I spent my allowance the day I got it and was penniless the rest of the week.* *adj.*

pen non (pen′ən), 1 a long, usually triangular flag, originally carried on the lance of a knight. 2 any flag or banner. *n.*

Penn syl van ia (pen′səl vā′nyə), one of the northeastern states of the United States. *Capital:* Harrisburg. *n.* —**Penn′syl van′ian,** *adj., n.*

Pennsylvania Dutch, 1 the descendants of immigrants of the 1600's and 1700's to southeastern Pennsylvania from southern Germany and Switzerland. 2 dialect of German with English intermixed, spoken by them.

pen ny (pen′ē), 1 cent. 100 pennies = 1 dollar. 2 British coin equal to ¹/₁₀₀ of a pound since February 1971. Formerly, equal to ¹/₂₄₀ of a pound and to ¹/₁₂ of a

shilling. *n., pl.* **pen nies** (or **pence** for 2).

a pretty penny, INFORMAL. a large sum of money.

pen ny weight (pen′ē wāt′), 24 grains or ¹/₂₀ of an ounce in troy weight. *n.*

pen ny-wise (pen′ē wīz′), saving in regard to small sums. *adj.*

penny-wise and pound-foolish, saving in small expenses and wasteful in big ones.

pen ny worth (pen′ē wėrth′), 1 as much as can be bought for a penny. 2 a small amount: *Give me a pennyworth of advice.* *n.*

Pe nob scot (pə nob′skot), 1 river flowing from NW Maine into the Atlantic. 2 member of an American Indian tribe formerly living near this river. *n.*

pen sion (pen′shən), 1 a regular payment to a person which is not wages. Pensions are often paid because of long service, special merit, or injuries received. 2 give a pension to: *The company pensioned several employees who were sixty-five years old.* 1 *n.,* 2 *v.*

pen sion er (pen′shə nər), person who receives a pension. *n.*

pen sive (pen′siv), thoughtful in a serious or sad way: *She was in a pensive mood, and sat staring out the window.* *adj.* —**pen′sive ly,** *adv.* —**pen′sive ness,** *n.*

pen stock (pen′stok′), channel or pipe for carrying water to a water wheel or turbine. *n.*

pent (pent), 1 closely confined; penned; shut: *pent in the house all winter.* 2 penned; a past tense and a past participle of **pen².** 1 *adj.,* 2 *v.*

pen ta gon (pen′tə gon), 1 a plane figure having five sides and five angles. 2 **the Pentagon,** a five-sided building that is the headquarters of the Department of Defense of the United States. It is in Arlington, Virginia. *n.*

pentagon (def. 1)
left, regular; right, irregular

pen tag o nal (pen tag′ə nəl), having five sides and five angles. *adj.*

Pen ta teuch (pen′tə tük *or* pen′tə-tyük), the first five books of the Old Testament. Genesis, Exodus, Leviticus, Numbers, and Deuteronomy are the Pentateuch. *n.*

pen tath lon (pen tath′lən), an athletic contest consisting of five different events. The person having the highest total score wins. *n.*

Pen te cost (pen′tə kôst), 1 the seventh Sunday after Easter; Whitsunday. Pentecost is a Christian festival in memory of the descent of the Holy Ghost upon the apostles. 2 a Jewish festival, observed about seven weeks after Passover, celebrating the harvest and the giving of the law to Moses. *n.*

pent house (pent′hous′), apartment or house built on the top of a building. *n., pl.* **pent hous es** (pent′hou′ziz).

pent-up (pent′up′), shut up; closely confined: *Her pent-up anger could no longer be restrained, and she walked out, slamming the door. adj.*

pe num bra (pi num′brə), 1 the partial shadow outside of the complete shadow formed by the sun, moon, etc., during an eclipse. See **eclipse** for diagram. 2 the grayish outer part of a sunspot. *n., pl.* **pe num brae** (pi-num′brē), **pe num bras.**

pe nur i ous (pi núr′ē əs *or* pi-nyür′ē əs), mean about spending or giving money; stingy. *adj.,* **—pe nur′i-ous ly,** *adv.*

pen ur y (pen′yər ē), very great poverty. *n.*

pe on (pē′on), 1 (in Spanish America) a person doing work that requires little skill. 2 (in the southwestern United States and Mexico) a worker held for service to work off a debt. *n.*

pe on age (pē′ə nij), 1 condition or service of a peon. 2 practice of holding persons to work off debts. *n.*

pe o ny (pē′ə nē), 1 a garden plant with large, showy red, pink, or white flowers. 2 its flower. *n., pl.* **pe o nies.**

peo ple (pē′pəl), 1 men, women, and children; persons: *There were ten people present.* 2 race; nation: *the peoples of Asia, the American people.* 3 body of citizens of a state; the public. 4 persons of a place, class, or group: *city people, Southern people.* 5 the common people; lower classes: *The French nobles oppressed the people.* 6 persons in relation to a superior: *a queen and her people.* 7 family; relatives: *Both of them prefer to remain at home with their own people.* 8 fill with people; populate: *Immigrants from many nations peopled the New World.* 1-7 *n., pl.* **peo ple** (or **peo ples** for 2); 8 *v.,* **peo pled, peo pling.**

Pe o ri a (pē ôr′ē ə), city in central Illinois. *n.*

pep (pep), INFORMAL. 1 spirit; energy; vim. 2 **pep up,** fill or inspire with energy, etc.; put new life into. 1 *n.,* 2 *v.,* **pepped, pep ping.**

pep per (pep′ər), 1 a seasoning with a hot, spicy taste, made from the berries of a tropical plant and used for soups, meats, vegetables, etc. **Black pepper** is made from whole berries; **white**

pepper is made from husked berries. 2 plant bearing these berries. 3 any of several hollow, mild or hot, red or green vegetables with many seeds. They are eaten raw, cooked, pickled, or dried and ground for use as seasoning in food. 4 plant bearing any such vegetable. 5 season or sprinkle with pepper. 6 sprinkle thickly: *His face is peppered with freckles.* 7 hit with small objects sent thick and fast: *We peppered the enemy's lines with our shot.* 1-4 *n.,* 5-7 *v.*

pep per corn (pep′ər kôrn′), one of the dried berries that are ground up to make pepper. *n.*

pep per mint (pep′ər mint), 1 herb grown for its oil, used in medicine and in candy. 2 this oil. 3 candy flavored with peppermint oil. *n.*

pep per y (pep′ər ē), 1 full of pepper; like pepper. 2 hot; sharp. 3 having a hot temper; easily made angry. 4 angry and sharp: *peppery words. adj.*

pep py (pep′ē), INFORMAL. full of pep; energetic; lively: *Scotch terriers are peppy dogs. adj.,* **pep pi er, pep pi est.**

pep sin (pep′sən), 1 enzyme in the gastric juice of the stomach that helps to digest meat, eggs, cheese, and other proteins. 2 medicine to help digestion, containing this enzyme. *n.*

per (pər; *stressed* pèr), 1 for each; for every: *a pint of milk per child, ten cents per pound.* 2 by means of; by; through: *I send this per my son. prep.*

per ad ven ture (pèr′əd ven′chər), OLD USE. maybe; perhaps. *adv.*

per am bu late (pə ram′byə lāt), 1 walk through. 2 walk or travel about; stroll. 3 walk through and examine. *v.,* **per am bu lat ed, per am bu lat ing.**

per am bu la tion (pə ram′byə-lā′shən), a perambulating. *n.*

perambulator

per am bu la tor (pə ram′byə lā′tər), a small carriage in which a baby is pushed about. *n.*

per an num (pər an′əm), per year; for each year; yearly: *Her salary was $10,000 per annum.* [from Latin]

per cale (pər kāl′), a closely woven cotton cloth with a smooth finish. *n.*

per cap i ta (pər kap′ə tə), for each

person: *a poor country with a low per capita income.* [from Latin]

per ceive (pər sēv′), 1 be aware of through the senses; see, hear, taste, smell, or feel: *Did you perceive the colors of that bird?* 2 take in with the mind; observe: *I soon perceived that I could not make him change his mind. v.,* **per ceived, per ceiv ing.**

per cent (pər sent′), per cent. *n.*

per cent, 1 parts in each hundred; hundredths. 5 per cent is 5 of each 100, or $5/100$ of the whole. 2 percentage: *A large per cent of the state's apple crop was ruined.*

per cent age (pər sen′tij), 1 rate or proportion of each hundred; part of each hundred; per cent: *What percentage of children were absent?* 2 part or proportion: *A large percentage of schoolbooks now have pictures.* 3 allowance, commission, discount, rate of interest, etc., figured by per cent. *n.*

per cep ti ble (pər sep′tə bəl), that can be perceived: *The other ship was barely perceptible in the fog. adj.*

per cep ti bly (pər sep′tə blē), in a perceptible way or amount; to a perceptible degree. *adv.*

per cep tion (pər sep′shən), 1 act of perceiving: *His perception of the change came in a flash.* 2 power of perceiving: *a keen perception.* 3 the understanding that is the result of perceiving: *She had a clear perception of the problem, and soon solved it. n.*

per cep tive (pər sep′tiv), 1 having to do with perception. 2 having the power of perceiving; intelligent: *a perceptive reader of poetry, a perceptive audience. adj.*

perch[1] (pèrch), 1 a bar, branch, or anything else on which a bird can come to rest. 2 alight and rest; sit: *A robin perched on our porch railing.* 3 a rather high seat or position. 4 sit rather high: *He perched on a stool.* 5 to place high up: *a village perched high among the hills.* 6 measure of length equal to $5\frac{1}{2}$ yards; rod. 1,3,6 *n., pl.* **perch es;** 2,4,5 *v.* [from French of the 1200's *perche,* from Latin *pertica* pole]

perch[2] (pèrch), 1 a small fresh-water

adj.	adjective	*n.*	noun
adv.	adverb	*prep.*	preposition
conj.	conjunction	*pron.*	pronoun
interj.	interjection	*v.*	verb
sing.	singular	*pl.*	plural

fish, used for food. 2 a similar saltwater fish. *n., pl.* **perch es** or **perch.** [from French of the 1200's *perche,* from Latin *perca,* from Greek *perke*]

per chance (pər chans′), perhaps. *adv.*

per co late (pėr′kə lāt), 1 drip or drain through small holes or spaces: *Let the coffee percolate for seven minutes.* 2 filter through; permeate: *Water percolates sand. v.,* **per co lat ed, per co lat ing.**

per co la tion (pėr′kə lā′shən), act or process of percolating. *n.*

per co la tor (pėr′kə lā′tər), kind of coffeepot in which boiling water drains over and over again through ground coffee. *n.*

per cus sion (pər kush′ən), 1 the striking of one body against another with force; stroke; blow. 2 shock made by the striking of one body against another with force; impact. 3 the striking of sound upon the ear. *n.*

percussion cap, a small cap containing powder. When struck, it explodes and sets off a larger charge.

percussion instrument, a musical instrument played by striking it, such as a drum or cymbal.

per di em (pər dē′əm), per day; for each day: *Rental of the boat per diem was $10.* [from Latin]

per di tion (pər dish′ən), 1 loss of one's soul and the joys of heaven. 2 hell. 3 utter loss or destruction; complete ruin. *n.*

per e gri na tion (per′ə grə nā′shən), a journey; travel. *n.*

per e grine (per′ə grən), a large, swift, powerful falcon, the kind preferred for falconry. *n.*

pe remp tor i ly (pə remp′tər ə lē), in a peremptory manner. *adv.*

pe remp tor y (pə remp′tər ē), 1 leaving no choice; decisive; final; absolute: *a peremptory decree.* 2 allowing no denial or refusal: *a peremptory command.* 3 imperious; dictatorial: *a peremptory teacher. adj.*

pe ren ni al (pə ren′ē əl), 1 lasting through the whole year: *a perennial stream.* 2 lasting for a very long time; enduring: *the perennial beauty of the hills.* 3 living more than two years: *perennial garden plants.* 4 a perennial plant. Roses are perennials. 1-3 *adj.,* 4 *n.* —**per en′ni al ly,** *adv.*

per fect (pėr′fikt *for 1,3-5,7,8;* pər fekt′ *for 2,6*), 1 without defect; not spoiled at any point; faultless: *a perfect spelling paper, a perfect apple, a perfect life. Perfect work shows great care.* 2 remove all faults from; make perfect; add the finishing touches to: *perfect an invention. The artist was perfecting his picture.* 3 completely skilled; expert: *a perfect golfer.* 4 having all its parts; whole; complete: *The set was perfect; nothing was missing or broken.* 5 exact: *a perfect copy, a perfect circle.* 6 carry through; complete: *perfect a plan.* 7 entire; utter; absolute: *He was a perfect stranger to us.* 8 (in grammar) showing an action or event completed at the time of speaking or at the time spoken of. Three perfect tenses in English are: **present perfect,** *I have eaten;* **past perfect,** *I had eaten;* and **future perfect,** *I will have eaten.* 1-3,5-7,8 *adj.,* 2,6 *v.* —**per′fect ness,** *n.*

per fect i bil i ty (pər fek′tə bil′ə tē), capability of becoming, or being made, perfect. *n.*

per fect i ble (pər fek′tə bəl), capable of becoming, or being made, perfect. *adj.*

per fec tion (pər fek′shən), 1 perfect condition; highest excellence; faultlessness. 2 a perfect person or thing. 3 a making complete or perfect: *Perfection of our plans will take another week. n.* **to perfection,** perfectly: *She played the difficult violin concerto to perfection.*

per fec tion ist (pər fek′shə nist), person who is not content with anything that is not perfect or nearly perfect. *n.*

per fect ly (pėr′fikt lē), in a perfect manner; fully or faultlessly. *adv.*

per fid i ous (pər fid′ē əs), deliberately faithless; treacherous. *adj.* —**per fid′i ous ly,** *adv.*

per fi dy (pėr′fə dē), a breaking faith; base treachery; being false to a trust. *n., pl.* **per fi dies.**

per fo rate (pėr′fə rāt′), 1 make a hole or holes through: *Bullets perforated the target.* 2 make a row or rows of holes through: *Sheets of postage stamps are perforated. v.,* **per fo rat ed, per fo rat ing.**

per fo ra tion (pėr′fə rā′shən), 1 hole bored or punched through something: *the perforations in the top of a salt shaker.* 2 a perforating or a being perforated. *n.*

per force (pər fôrs′), by necessity; necessarily. *adv.*

per form (pər fôrm′), 1 do: *Perform your duties well.* 2 put into effect; carry out: *Perform your promise. The surgeon performed an operation.* 3 go through; render: *perform a piece of music.* 4 act, play, sing, or do tricks in public: *The performing dog danced on its hind legs. v.*

per form ance (pər fôr′məns), 1 carrying out; doing; performing: *in the performance of one's regular duties, the efficient performance of an automobile.* 2 thing performed; act; deed: *The child's kicks and screams made a disgraceful performance.* 3 the giving of a play, concert, circus, or other show: *The performance is at 8 o'clock. n.*

per form er (pər fôr′mər), person who performs, especially one who performs for the entertainment of others. *n.*

per fume (pėr′fyüm *or* pər fyüm′ *for 1,3;* pər fyüm′ *for 2,4*), 1 liquid having a sweet smell. 2 put a sweet-smelling liquid on. 3 a sweet smell; fragrance: *the perfume of flowers.* 4 give a sweet smell to; fill with sweet odor: *Flowers perfumed the air.* 1,3 *n.,* 2,4 *v.,* **per fumed, per fum ing.**

per fum er y (pər fyü′mər ē), 1 perfume or perfumes. 2 business of making or selling perfumes. *n., pl.* **per fum er ies.**

per func tor i ly (pər fungk′tər ə lē), in a perfunctory manner. *adv.*

per func tor y (pər fungk′tər ē), 1 done merely for the sake of getting rid of the duty; done from force of habit; mechanical; indifferent: *The little boy gave his face a perfunctory washing.* 2 acting in a perfunctory way: *The new nurse was perfunctory; she did not really care about her work. adj.*

per haps (pər haps′), it may be; maybe; possibly: *Perhaps a letter will come to you today. adv.*

Per i cles (per′ə klēz′), 490?-429 B.C., Athenian statesman, orator, and military commander. *n.*

perigee—the moon in orbit around the earth shown at perigee and apogee

per i gee (per′ə jē), point closest to the earth in the orbit of the moon or any other earth satellite. *n.*

perihelion—a planet in orbit around the sun at perihelion and aphelion

per i he li on (per′ə hē′lē ən), point closest to the sun in the orbit of a planet or comet. *n., pl.* **per i he li a** (per′ə hē′lē ə).

per il (per′əl), 1 chance of harm; danger: *This bridge is not safe; cross it at your peril.* 2 put in danger. 1 *n.,* 2 *v.*

per il ous (per′ə ləs), full of peril;

dangerous: *a perilous journey. adj.*
—per′il ous ly, *adv.* **—per′il ous-
ness,** *n.*

pe rim e ter (pə rim′ə tər), 1 the outer
boundary of a figure or area: *the perimeter of a circle, the perimeter of a garden.* 2 distance around such a boundary. The perimeter of a square equals
four times the length of one side. *n.*

per i od (pir′ē əd), 1 portion of time:
He visited us for a short period. 2 portion of time marked off by events
that happen again and again; time after
which the same things begin to happen
again: *A month, from new moon to new
moon, is a period.* 3 a certain series of
years: *the period of World War II.*
4 portion of a game during which there
is actual play. 5 one of the portions of
time into which a school day is divided.
6 an end; termination. 7 dot (.) marking
the end of a declarative sentence or
showing an abbreviation. EXAMPLES:
Mr., Dec. 8 the pause at the end of
a sentence. 9 one of the divisions of
time into which a geological era is
divided. 10 the time of menstruating;
menstruation. *n.*

per i od ic (pir′ē od′ik), 1 occurring,
appearing, or done again and again at
regular intervals: *periodic attacks of
malaria. The coming of the new moon is
a periodic event.* 2 happening every
now and then: *a periodic fit of clearing
up one's desk. adj.*

per i od i cal (pir′ē od′ə kəl), 1 magazine that appears regularly. 2 of
or having to do with periodicals. 3 published at regular intervals, less often than daily. 4 periodic. 1 *n.*, 2-4
adj.

per i od i cal ly (pir′ē od′ik lē), 1 at
regular intervals. 2 every now and then.
adv.

per i o dic i ty (pir′ē ə dis′ə tē), periodic character; tendency to happen at
regular intervals. *n., pl.* **per i o dic i-
ties.**

periodic table, table in which the
chemical elements, arranged in the order of their atomic numbers, are shown
in related groups.

per i pa tet ic (per′ə pə tet′ik), walking about; traveling from place to
place. *adj.*

pe riph er al (pə rif′ər əl), having to
do with, situated in, or forming an outside boundary: *the peripheral areas of
the city. adj.* **—pe riph′er al ly,** *adv.*

pe riph er y (pə rif′ər ē), an outside
boundary. The periphery of a circle is
called the circumference. *n., pl.* **pe-
riph er ies.**

per i scope (per′ə skōp), instrument
that allows those in a submarine or
trench to obtain a view of the surface. It
is a tube with an arrangement of prisms

or mirrors that reflect light rays down
the tube. *n.*

per ish (per′ish), be destroyed; die:
*Soldiers perish in battle. Flowers perish
when frost comes. v.*

per ish a ble (per′i shə bəl), 1 liable
to spoil or decay: *Fruit is perishable.*
2 Usually, **perishables,** *pl.* something
perishable. 1 *adj.*, 2 *n.*

per i stal sis (per′ə stal′sis), the wavelike contractions of the alimentary
canal or other tubular organ by which
its contents are moved onward. *n., pl.*
per i stal ses (per′ə stal′sēz).

per i to ne um (per′ə tə nē′əm),
membrane that lines the walls of the
abdomen and covers the organs in it. *n.,
pl.* **per i to ne a** (per′ə tə nē′ə).

per i to ni tis (per′ə tə nī′tis), inflammation of the peritoneum. *n.*

per i wig (per′ə wig), wig. *n.*

per i win kle[1] (per′ē wing′kəl), a low,
trailing evergreen plant with blue flowers; myrtle. *n.* [Old English *pervince,*
from Latin *pervinca;* influenced by *periwinkle*[2]]

per i win kle[2] (per′ē wing′kəl), a sea
snail with a thick shell, used for food
in Europe. *n.* [Old English *pīnewin-
cle*]

per jure (per′jər), make (oneself)
guilty of perjury. *v.,* **per jured, per-
jur ing.**

perjure oneself, swear falsely; lie under oath: *The witness perjured himself
by lying about what he did on the night
of the crime.*

per jur er (per′jər ər), person who
commits perjury. *n.*

per jur y (per′jər ē), act of swearing
that something is true which one knows
to be false. *n., pl.* **per jur ies.**

perk (perk), 1 raise smartly or briskly:
*The dog perked its ears when it heard its
master.* 2 make trim or smart: *They are
perked out in their best clothes. v.*

perk up, brighten up; become lively
and vigorous: *The birds perked up as the
sun rose over the hill.*

perk y (per′kē), smart; brisk; saucy;
pert: *a perky squirrel. adj.,* **perk i er,
perk i est.**

per ma nence (per′mə nəns), a being
permanent; lasting quality or condition. *n.*

per ma nen cy (per′mə nən sē),
1 permanence. 2 a permanent person,

MIRROR

MIRROR

periscope
on a submarine.
It can be turned
in any direction,
and also be raised
and lowered.

thing, or position. *n., pl.* **per ma nen-
cies.**

per ma nent (per′mə nənt), 1 intended to last; not for a short time
only; lasting: *a permanent filling in a
tooth. After doing odd jobs for a week, I
got a permanent position as salesclerk.*
2 INFORMAL. permanent wave. 1 *adj.*, 2
n. **—per′ma nent ly,** *adv.*

permanent wave, wave put in the
hair by a special process so as to last
several months; permanent.

per me a bil i ty (per′mē ə bil′ə tē), a
being permeable. *n.*

per me a ble (per′mē ə bəl), that can
be permeated: *A sponge is permeable by
water. adj.*

per me ate (per′mē āt), 1 spread
through the whole of; pass through:
Smoke permeated the house. 2 penetrate: *Water will easily permeate cotton
cloth. v.,* **per me at ed, per me at-
ing.**

per me a tion (per′mē ā′shən), a per-
meating. *n.*

per mis si ble (pər mis′ə bəl), that can
be permitted; allowable. *adj.*

per mis sion (pər mish′ən), consent;
leave: *I asked the teacher's permission
to go early. My sister gave me her permission to use her camera. n.*

per mis sive (pər mis′iv), not forbidding; tending to permit; allowing: *a
permissive attitude, permissive parents.
adj.*

per mit (pər mit′ *for 1,2;* per′mit *or
pər mit′ for 3),* 1 let; allow: *My parents
will not permit me to stay up late. The
law does not permit smoking in this
store.* 2 give leave or opportunity: *I will
go on Monday, if the weather permits.*
3 a formal written order giving permission to do something: *Have you a
permit to fish in this lake?* 1,2 *v.,*
per mit ted, per mit ting; 3 *n.*

per ni cious (pər nish′əs), that will
destroy or ruin; causing great harm or
damage; injurious: *Taking drugs is a
pernicious habit. adj.* **—per ni′cious-
ly,** *adv.*

per o ra tion (per′ə rā′shən), the last
part of an oration or discussion. It sums
up what has been said. *n.*

adj.	adjective	*n.*	noun
adv.	adverb	*prep.*	preposition
conj.	conjunction	*pron.*	pronoun
interj.	interjection	*v.*	verb
sing.	singular	*pl.*	plural

pe rox ide (pə rok′sīd), 1 oxide of an element or radical that contains the greatest possible proportion of oxygen. 2 hydrogen peroxide. *n.*

per pen dic u lar (per′pən dik′-yə lər), 1 standing straight up; vertical; upright: *a perpendicular cliff.* 2 at right angles. One line is perpendicular to another when it makes a square corner with another. The floor of a room is perpendicular to the side walls and parallel to the ceiling. 3 a perpendicular line or plane. 1,2 *adj.,* 3 *n.* —**per′pen dic′u lar ly,** *adv.*

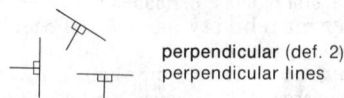

perpendicular (def. 2)
perpendicular lines

per pe trate (per′pə trāt), do or commit (a crime, fraud, trick, or anything bad or foolish): *The two thieves perpetrated the robbery of the jewelry store.* *v.,* **per pe trat ed, per pe trat ing.**

per pe tra tion (per′pə trā′shən), 1 act of perpetrating. 2 something perpetrated. *n.*

per pe tra tor (per′pə trā′tər), person who perpetrates or does something bad or foolish. *n.*

per pet u al (pər pech′ü əl), 1 lasting forever; eternal: *the perpetual hills.* 2 lasting throughout life: *a perpetual income.* 3 never ceasing; continuous: *a perpetual stream of visitors.* *adj.*

per pet u al ly (pər pech′ü ə lē), forever. *adv.*

per pet u ate (pər pech′ü āt), make perpetual; keep from being forgotten: *The monument was built to perpetuate the memory of George Washington.* *v.,* **per pet u at ed, per pet u at ing.**

per pet u a tion (pər pech′ü ā′shən), a perpetuating or a being perpetuated. *n.*

per pe tu i ty (per′pə tü′ə tē *or* per′-pə tyü′ə tē), a being perpetual; existence forever. *n., pl.* **per pe tu i ties. in perpetuity,** forever.

per plex (pər pleks′), trouble with doubt; puzzle; confuse; bewilder: *This problem is hard enough to perplex even the teacher.* *v.*

per plex i ty (pər plek′sə tē), 1 perplexed condition; being puzzled; a not

knowing what to do or how to act; confusion: *His perplexity was so great that he had to ask many persons for advice.* 2 something that perplexes: *There are many perplexities in such a complicated job.* *n., pl.* **per plex i ties.**

per qui site (per′kwə zit), anything received for work besides the regular pay: *The minister had a parsonage as a perquisite.* *n.*

Per ry (per′ē), **Matthew C.,** 1794-1858, American naval officer. He arranged a treaty between the United States and Japan which opened Japan to American trade. *n.*

per se cute (per′sə kyüt), 1 treat badly; do harm to again and again; oppress: *The gang persecuted the new boy by constantly attacking him on his way home.* 2 treat badly because of one's principles or beliefs: *Christians were persecuted in ancient Rome.* 3 annoy; harass: *persecuted by silly questions.* *v.,* **per se cut ed, per se cut ing.**

per se cu tion (per′sə kyü′shən), 1 a persecuting: *the children's persecution of the kitten.* 2 a being persecuted: *The kitten's persecution by the children made it run away.* *n.*

per se cu tor (per′sə kyü′tər), person who persecutes. *n.*

Per seph o ne (pər sef′ə nē), (in Greek myths) the daughter of Zeus and Demeter, made queen of the lower world by Pluto. The Romans called her Proserpina. *n.*

Per se us (per′sē əs), 1 (in Greek legends) a hero who slew Medusa and rescued Andromeda from a sea monster. 2 a northern constellation near Cassiopeia. *n.*

per se ver ance (per′sə vir′əns), a sticking to a purpose or an aim; never giving up what one has set out to do: *By perseverance she finally learned to swim.* *n.*

per se vere (per′sə vir′), continue steadily in doing something hard; persist. *v.,* **per se vered, per se ver ing.**

Per shing (per′shing), **John Joseph,** 1860-1948, general in command of the United States Army in World War I. *n.*

Per sia (per′zhə), 1 former country in SW Asia south of the Caspian Sea. Its name was officially changed to Iran in 1935. 2 ancient empire in W and SW Asia. *n.*

Per sian (per′zhən), 1 of or having to do with Persia, its people, or their language. 2 person born or living in Persia. 3 language of Persia. 1 *adj.,* 2,3 *n.*

Persian Gulf, gulf of the Arabian Sea, between Iran and Saudi Arabia.

per si flage (per′sə fläzh), light, joking talk or writing. *n.*

per sim mon (pər sim′ən), 1 a North American tree with a plumlike fruit.

2 fruit of this tree, very bitter when green, but sweet and good to eat when very ripe. *n.*

per sist (pər sist′), 1 continue firmly; refuse to stop or be changed: *She persists in reading at the dinner table.* 2 remain in existence; last; stay: *On the tops of very high mountains snow persists throughout the year.* 3 say again and again; maintain: *He persisted that he was innocent of the crime.* *v.*

per sist ence (pər sis′təns), 1 a being persistent: *the persistence of a fly buzzing around one's head.* 2 a continuing existence: *the stubborn persistence of a cough.* *n.*

per sist en cy (pər sis′tən sē), persistence. *n.*

per sist ent (pər sis′tənt), 1 not giving up, especially in the face of dislike, disapproval, or difficulties; persisting: *a persistent worker, a persistent salesman.* 2 going on; continuing; lasting: *a persistent headache that lasted for days.* *adj.* —**per sist′ent ly,** *adv.*

per son (per′sən), 1 man, woman, or child; human being: *Any person who wishes may come to the fair.* 2 the human body: *The person of the king was well guarded.* 3 bodily appearance: *He kept his person neat and trim.* 4 (in grammar) a form of pronouns or verbs used to show the person speaking, the person spoken to, or the person or thing spoken of. *I* and *we* are used for the first person; *you,* for the second person; *he, she, it,* and *they,* for the third person. *n.*

in person, with or by one's own action or presence; personally: *appear in person. Come in person; do not write or phone.*

per son a ble (per′sə nə bəl), having a pleasing appearance; good-looking; attractive. *adj.*

per son age (per′sə nij), 1 person of importance. 2 person. 3 character in a book or play. *n.*

per son al (per′sə nəl), 1 belonging to a person; individual; private: *a personal letter, a personal matter.* 2 done in person; directly by oneself, not through others or by letter: *a personal visit.* 3 of the body or bodily appearance: *person-*

Persia (def. 2)—Shaded area indicates the empire at its greatest extent.

al beauty, personal charm. 4 about or against a person or persons: *personal remarks, personal abuse.* 5 (in grammar) showing person. *I, we, you, he, she, it,* and *they* are personal pronouns. 6 (in law) of or having to do with property that can be moved, such as furniture and clothing, as contrasted with real property, such as land and buildings. 7 a short paragraph in a newspaper about a particular person or persons. 1-6 *adj.,* 7 *n.*

per son al i ty (pėr′sə nal′ə tē), 1 the personal or individual quality that makes one person be different or act differently from another: *A baby two weeks old does not have much personality.* 2 pleasing or attractive qualities of a person: *That boy may be smart, but he has no personality.* 3 **personalities,** *pl.* remarks made about or against some particular person: *Please refrain from personalities and stick to the issues.* 4 person; personage: *personalities of stage and screen. n., pl.* **per son al i ties.**

per son al ly (pėr′sə nə lē), 1 in person; not by the aid of others: *The hostess saw to the comforts of her guests personally.* 2 as far as oneself is concerned: *Personally, I like apples better than oranges.* 3 as a person: *We like him personally, but dislike his way of earning a living.* 4 as being meant for oneself: *I intended no insult to you; do not take what I said personally. adv.*

per son ate (pėr′sə nāt), 1 act the part of (a character in a play, etc.). 2 pretend to be. *v.,* **per son at ed, per son at ing.**

per son i fi ca tion (pər son′ə fə kā′shən), 1 a striking example; embodiment; type: *A miser is the personification of greed.* 2 a representing as a person. Mother Nature, Father Time, and Uncle Sam are personifications. 3 figure of speech in which a lifeless thing or quality is spoken of as if alive. EXAMPLES: The music sobbed. Duty calls us. *n.*

per son i fy (pər son′ə fī), 1 be a type of; embody: *Satan personifies evil.* 2 regard or represent as a person. We often personify the sun and moon, referring to the sun as *he* and the moon as *she. v.,* **per son i fied, per son i fy ing.**

per son nel (pėr′sə nel′), persons employed in any work, business, or service. *n.*

per spec tive (pər spek′tiv), 1 art of picturing objects on a flat surface so as to give the appearance of distance. 2 drawn so as to show the proper perspective: *a perspective drawing.* 3 effect of distance on the appearance of ob-

perspective (def. 1) illustrated by the convergence of the parallel lines of the road, the diminishing distance between the equally-spaced poles, and the decreasing size of the poles

jects: *Railroad tracks seem to meet at the horizon because of perspective.* 4 effect of the distance of events upon the mind: *Perspective makes many happenings of last year seem less important.* 5 a view of things or facts in which they are in the right relations. 6 a view in front; distant view: *a perspective of lakes and hills.* 1,3-6 *n.,* 2 *adj.*

per spi ca cious (pėr′spə kā′shəs), keen in observing and understanding; discerning. *adj.* —**per′spi ca′cious ly,** *adv.*

per spi cac i ty (pėr′spə kas′ə tē), keen perception; wisdom and understanding in dealing with people or with facts; discernment. *n.*

per spi cu i ty (pėr′spə kyü′ə tē), ease in being understood; clearness in expression. *n.*

per spic u ous (pər spik′yü əs), easily understood; clear: *a perspicuous argument. adj.*

per spi ra tion (pėr′spə rā′shən), 1 sweat: *The runner's forehead was damp with perspiration.* 2 sweating. *n.*

per spire (pər spīr′), to sweat: *The lumberjack perspired as he cut the tree down in the hot sun. v.,* **per spired, per spir ing.**

per suade (pər swād′), win over to do or believe; make willing or sure by urging or arguing: *I knew I should study, but he persuaded me to go to the movies. We persuaded her that she was wrong. v.,* **per suad ed, per suad ing.**

per sua sion (pər swā′zhən), 1 a persuading: *All our attempts at persuasion were of no use; she would not come with us.* 2 power of persuading. 3 firm belief; conviction: *The two brothers had different political persuasions.* 4 religious belief or denomination: *All Christians are not of the same persuasion. n.*

per sua sive (pər swā′siv), able, intended, or fitted to persuade: *The salesman had a very persuasive way of talking. adj.* —**per sua′sive ly,** *adv.* —**per sua′sive ness,** *n.*

pert (pėrt), 1 too forward or free in

speech or action; saucy; bold: *a pert reply.* 2 stylish; jaunty: *a pert outfit. adj.* —**pert′ly,** *adv.*

per tain (pər tān′), 1 belong or be connected as a part or possession: *We own the house and the land pertaining to it.* 2 be related; refer: *"Pertaining to school" means "having to do with school."* 3 be appropriate: *We had turkey and everything else that pertains to Thanksgiving. v.*

Perth (pėrth), city in SW Australia. *n.*

per ti na cious (pėrt′n ā′shəs), holding firmly to a purpose, action, or opinion; very persistent: *A bulldog is a pertinacious fighter. adj.*

per ti nac i ty (pėrt′n as′ə tē), great persistence; holding firmly to a purpose, action, or opinion. *n.*

per ti nence (pėrt′n əns), a being to the point; fitness; relevance: *The pertinence of the girl's replies showed that she was alert and intelligent. n.*

per ti nent (pėrt′n ənt), having to do with what is being considered; relating to the matter in hand; to the point; relevant: *If your question is pertinent, I will answer it. adj.*

per turb (pər tėrb′), disturb greatly; make uneasy or troubled: *Mother and Dad were perturbed by my illness. v.*

per tur ba tion (pėr′tər bā′shən), 1 a perturbing. 2 a perturbed condition. 3 thing, act, or event that causes disturbance or agitation. *n.*

Pe ru (pə rü′), mountainous country on the W coast of South America. *Capital:* Lima. *n.*

peruke

pe ruke (pə rük′), wig. Men wore perukes in the 1600's and 1700's. *n.*

pe rus al (pə rü′zəl), a perusing; reading: *I have just finished the perusal of your letter. n.*

pe ruse (pə rüz′), read, especially thor-

adj. adjective	*n.* noun
adv. adverb	*prep.* preposition
conj. conjunction	*pron.* pronoun
interj. interjection	*v.* verb
sing. singular	*pl.* plural

oughly and carefully: *peruse the newspaper at breakfast.* *v.*, **pe rused, pe rus ing.**

Pe ru vi an (pə rü′vē ən), 1 of or having to do with Peru or its people. 2 person born or living in Peru. 1 *adj.*, 2 *n.*

Peruvian bark, cinchona.

per vade (pər vād′), go or spread throughout; be throughout: *The odor of pines pervades the air. She worked so hard that weariness pervaded her whole body.* *v.*, **per vad ed, per vad ing.**

per va sive (pər vā′siv), 1 tending to pervade. 2 having power to pervade. *adj.* —**per va′sive ly,** *adv.*

per verse (pər vėrs′), 1 contrary and willful; stubborn: *The perverse child did just what we told him not to do.* 2 persistent in wrong. 3 wicked. 4 not correct; wrong: *perverse reasoning. adj.* —**per verse′ly,** *adv.* —**per verse′ness,** *n.*

per ver sion (pər vėr′zhən), a turning or being turned to what is wrong; a change to what is unnatural, abnormal, or wrong: *A tendency to eat sand is a perversion of appetite.* *n.*

per ver si ty (pər vėr′sə tē), 1 quality of being perverse. 2 perverse character or conduct. *n., pl.* **per ver si ties.**

per vert (pər vėrt′ *for 1-3;* pėr′vėrt′ *for 4*), 1 lead or turn from what is true, desirable, good, or morally right; corrupt: *pervert the cause of justice.* 2 give a wrong meaning to: *His enemies perverted his friendly remark and made it into an insult.* 3 use for wrong purposes or in a wrong way: *A clever criminal perverts his talents.* 4 a perverted person. 1-3 *v.,* 4 *n.*

pes ky (pes′kē), INFORMAL. troublesome; annoying: *a pesky cold, pesky mosquitoes. adj.*, **pes ki er, pes ki est.**

pe so (pā′sō), 1 unit of money in various countries of Latin America and in the Philippines. 100 centavos make a peso. 2 coin or piece of paper money equal to 100 centavos. *n., pl.* **pe sos.**

pes si mism (pes′ə miz′əm), 1 tendency to look on the dark side of things or to see all the difficulties and disadvantages. 2 belief that things naturally tend to evil. 3 doctrine that the evil in life outweighs the good. *n.*

pes si mist (pes′ə mist), 1 person in-

clined to look on the dark side of things or to see all the difficulties and disadvantages. 2 person who believes that things naturally tend to evil, or that the evil in life outweighs the good. *n.*

pes si mis tic (pes′ə mis′tik), 1 inclined to look on the dark side of things or to see all the difficulties and disadvantages. 2 expecting the worst: *The poor student was pessimistic about her chances of passing the test.* 3 having to do with or characterized by pessimism. *adj.* —**pes′si mis′ti cal ly,** *adv.*

pest (pest), 1 thing or person that causes trouble, injuries, or destruction; nuisance: *Flies and mosquitoes are pests. Whining children are pests.* 2 OLD USE. pestilence. *n.*

pes ter (pes′tər), annoy; trouble; vex: *Flies pester us. Don't pester me with foolish questions.* *v.*

PETIOLE → ← STEM

pest house (pest′hous′), hospital for persons ill with very contagious diseases. *n., pl.* **pest hous es** (pest′hou′ziz).

pes tif er ous (pe stif′ər əs), 1 bringing disease or infection: *Rats are pestiferous.* 2 bringing moral evil: *the pestiferous influence of a bad example.* 3 INFORMAL. troublesome; annoying. *adj.*

pes ti lence (pes′tl əns), any disease that spreads rapidly, causing many deaths. Smallpox, yellow fever, and plague are pestilences. *n.*

pes ti lent (pes′tl ənt), 1 often causing death: *Smallpox is a pestilent disease.* 2 harmful to morals; destroying peace: *a pestilent den of vice, the pestilent effects of war.* 3 troublesome; annoying. *adj.*

pes ti len tial (pes′tl en′shəl), 1 like a pestilence; having to do with pestilences. 2 causing or likely to cause pestilence. *adj.*

pes tle (pes′əl), 1 tool for pounding or crushing substances into powder in a mortar. See **mortar** for picture. 2 pound or crush with a pestle. 1 *n.,* 2 *v.,* **pes tled, pes tling.**

pet[1] (pet), 1 animal kept as a favorite and treated with affection. 2 treated as a pet: *a pet rabbit.* 3 treat as a pet; touch lovingly and gently; stroke or pat: *She is petting the kitten.* 4 a darling or favorite: *teacher's pet.* 5 favorite: *a pet chair, a pet theory.* 6 showing affection: *a pet name.* 1,4 *n.,* 2,5,6 *adj.,* 3 *v.,* **pet ted, pet ting.** [perhaps shortened

from *petty,* from French of the 1300's *petit* small]

pet[2] (pet), fit of being cross or peevish: *When he didn't get his way, he jumped on his bicycle and rode off in a pet.* *n.* [origin uncertain]

pet al (pet′l), one of the parts of a flower that are usually colored; one of the leaves of a corolla. A daisy has many petals. *n.* —**pet′al like′,** *adj.*

pet aled or **pet alled** (pet′ld), having petals: *six-petaled. adj.*

pet cock (pet′kok′), a small faucet or valve in a pipe or cylinder, for reducing pressure or draining liquids. *n.*

Pe ter (pē′tər), 1 **Saint,** died A.D. 67?, one of Christ's twelve apostles. He was also called Simon or Simon Peter. 2 either of two books in the New Testament that bear his name. *n.*

Peter I, 1672-1725, czar of Russia from 1682 to 1725. He was called "Peter the Great."

pet i ole (pet′ē ōl), the slender stalk by which a leaf is attached to the stem. *n.*

pe tite (pə tēt′), of small size; little; tiny: *a petite woman or girl. adj.*

pe ti tion (pə tish′ən), 1 a formal request to someone in authority for some privilege, right, or benefit: *The people on our street signed a petition asking the city council for a new sidewalk.* 2 ask earnestly; make a formal request to: *They petitioned the mayor to use his influence with the city council.* 3 prayer. 4 pray. 1,3 *n.,* 2,4 *v.* —**pe ti′tion er,** *n.*

pet it jury (pet′ē), group of 12 persons chosen to decide a case in court.

Pe trarch (pē′trärk), 1304-1374, Italian poet, famous for his sonnets. *n.*

petrel—storm petrel; about 5½ in. long

pet rel (pet′rəl), a small, black-and-white sea bird with long, pointed wings. *n.*

pet ri fy (pet′rə fī), 1 turn into stone: *There is a petrified forest in Arizona.* 2 paralyze with fear, horror, or surprise: *The bird was petrified as the snake came near.* *v.,* **pet ri fied, pet ri fy ing.**

Pet ro grad (pet′rə grad), former capital of Russia, now called **Leningrad.** *n.*

pet rol (pet′rəl), gasoline (the term

generally used in Great Britain and sometimes elsewhere). *n.*

pe tro le um (pə trō′lē əm), a dark, oily, flammable liquid found in the earth's crust, consisting mainly of a mixture of various hydrocarbons. Gasoline, kerosene, and paraffin are made from petroleum. *n.*

pet ti coat (pet′ē kōt), 1 skirt worn beneath a dress or outer skirt by women and girls. 2 skirt, trimmed and sometimes stiffened. 3 female or feminine: *petticoat government.* 1,2 *n.,* 3 *adj.*

pet ti ness (pet′ē nis), smallness; meanness; petty nature or behavior. *n.*

pet tish (pet′ish), peevish; cross: *a pettish reply, a pettish child. adj.* —**pet′tish ly,** *adv.*

pet ty (pet′ē), 1 having little importance or value; small: *Don't let petty disturbances upset you.* 2 mean; narrow-minded: *A gossip is a petty person.* 3 lower in rank or importance; subordinate: *a petty official. adj.,* **pet ti er, pet ti est.**

petty officer, a noncommissioned officer in the navy.

pet u lance (pech′ə ləns), a being peevish; bad humor; being irritated by trifles. *n.*

pet u lant (pech′ə lənt), likely to have little fits of bad temper; irritable over trifles; peevish. *adj.* —**pet′u lant ly,** *adv.*

pe tun ia (pə tü′nyə *or* pə tyü′nyə), a common garden plant that has white, pink, red, or purple flowers shaped like funnels. *n., pl.* **pe tun ias.**

pew (pyü), bench in a church for people to sit on, fastened to the floor and with a back. In some churches the pews are separated by partitions and are set apart for the use of a certain family or group of people. *n.*

pe wee (pē′wē), any of several small American birds with an olive-colored or gray back. A pewee's call sounds somewhat like its name. *n.*

pew ter (pyü′tər), 1 alloy of tin with lead, copper, or other metals. 2 dishes or other utensils made of this alloy. 3 made of pewter: *a pewter mug.* 1,2 *n.,* 3 *adj.*

phaeton

pha e ton (fā′ə tən), a light, four-wheeled carriage with or without a top. *n.*

phag o cyte (fag′ə sīt), a cell, such as a white blood cell, capable of ab-

sorbing and destroying waste or harmful material, such as bacteria that produce disease. *n.*

pha lanx (fā′langks), 1 (in ancient Greece) a special battle formation of infantry fighting in close ranks with their shields joined and long spears overlapping each other. 2 a compact or closely massed body of persons, animals, or things: *A phalanx of sheep blocked the road.* 3 number of persons united for a common purpose. *n., pl.* **pha lanx es, pha lan ges** (fə lan′jēz).

phan tasm (fan′taz əm), 1 thing seen only in one's imagination; unreal fancy: *the phantasms of a dream.* 2 a deceiving likeness (of something). *n.*

phan ta sy (fan′tə sē), fantasy. *n., pl.* **phan ta sies.**

phan tom (fan′təm), 1 image in the mind which seems to be real: *phantoms of a dream.* 2 a vague, dim, or shadowy appearance; ghost. 3 like a ghost; unreal: *a phantom ship.* 4 mere show; appearance with no substance: *a phantom of a government.* 1,2,4 *n.,* 3 *adj.*

phar aoh *or* **Phar aoh** (fer′ō), any of the kings of ancient Egypt. *n.*

Phar i see (far′ə sē), 1 member of a Jewish sect at the time of Christ that was very strict in keeping to tradition and the laws of its religion. 2 **pharisee,** person who makes a show of religion rather than following its spirit, and thinks he is better than others. *n.*

phar ma ceu tic (fär′mə sü′tik), pharmaceutical. *adj., n.*

phar ma ceu ti cal (fär′mə sü′tə kəl), 1 having to do with pharmacy. 2 a medicinal drug. 1 *adj.,* 2 *n.*

phar ma cist (fär′mə sist), person licensed to fill prescriptions; druggist. *n.*

phar ma col o gy (fär′mə kol′ə jē), science of drugs, their preparation, uses, and effects. *n.*

phar ma cy (fär′mə sē), 1 place where drugs and medicines are prepared or sold; drugstore. 2 preparation and dispensing of drugs and medicines; occupation of a druggist. *n., pl.* **phar ma cies.**

phar ynx (far′ingks), cavity at the back of the mouth where the passages to the nose, lungs, and stomach begin. *n., pl.* **phar ynx es, pha ryn ges** (fə rin′jēz).

phase (fāz), 1 one of the changing states or stages of development of a person or thing: *At present his voice is changing; that is a phase all boys go through.* 2 one side, part, or view (of a subject): *What phase of arithmetic are*

CRESCENT   FIRST QUARTER   GIBBOUS   FULL MOON

phase (def. 3)—four phases of the moon

hat, āge, fär; let, ēqual, tèrm; it, īce; hot, ōpen, ôrder; oil, out; cup, pùt, rüle; ch, child; ng, long; sh, she; th, thin; ϮH, then; zh, measure;

ə represents *a* in about, *e* in taken, *i* in pencil, *o* in lemon, *u* in circus.

you studying now? 3 the shape of the moon or of a planet as it is seen from the earth at a particular time. *n.*

pheas ant (fez′nt), any of a group of large game birds related to the domestic fowl and the peacock with brightly colored feathers in the male, and long, pointed tail feathers. Pheasants are native to Asia but now live in many parts of Europe and America. *n., pl.* **pheasants** or **pheas ant.**

pheasant
about 3½ ft. long
including the tail

phe nix (fē′niks), phoenix. *n.*

phe nol (fē′nol *or* fē′nōl), carbolic acid. *n.*

phe nom e na (fə nom′ə nə), a plural of **phenomenon.** *n.*

phe nom e nal (fə nom′ə nəl), 1 of or having to do with a phenomenon or phenomena. 2 having the nature of a phenomenon. 3 extraordinary: *a phenomenal memory. adj.* —**phe nom′e nal ly,** *adv.*

EPIGLOTTIS
LARYNX
PHARYNX
ESOPHAGUS

phe nom e non (fə nom′ə non), 1 fact, event, or circumstance that can be observed: *Lightning is an electrical phenomenon.* 2 any sign or symptom: *Fever and inflammation are phenomena of disease.* 3 something or someone extraordinary or remarkable: *The*

631

adj.	adjective	*n.*	noun
adv.	adverb	*prep.*	preposition
conj.	conjunction	*pron.*	pronoun
interj.	interjection	*v.*	verb
sing.	singular	*pl.*	plural

Grand Canyon is a phenomenon of nature. The fond parents think their child is a phenomenon. **n., pl. phe nom e na** (or **phe nom e nons** for 3).

phi al (fī′əl), vial. *n.*

Phid i as (fid′ē əs), 500?-432? B.C., Greek sculptor. *n.*

Phil a del phi a (fil′ə del′fē ə), city in SE Pennsylvania, on the Delaware River. *n.*

phil an throp ic (fil′ən throp′ik), 1 having to do with or characterized by philanthropy. 2 charitable; benevolent; kindly: *a philanthropic nature. adj.* —**phil′an throp′i cal ly,** *adv.*

phil an throp i cal (fil′ən throp′ə kəl), philanthropic. *adj.*

phi lan thro pist (fə lan′thrə pist), person who practices philanthropy, especially by giving sizable donations of money to worthy causes. *n.*

phi lan thro py (fə lan′thrə pē), 1 love of mankind shown by practical kindness and helpfulness to humanity: *The charity appealed to philanthropy.* 2 thing that benefits humanity; a philanthropic agency, enterprise, gift, act, etc.: *A hospital is a useful philanthropy.* **n., pl. phi lan thro pies.**

phi lat e list (fə lat′l ist), collector of postage stamps, postmarks, etc. *n.*

phi lat e ly (fə lat′l ē), the collecting, arranging, and study of postage stamps, stamped envelopes, post cards, etc. *n.*

Phi le mon (fə lē′mən), book of the New Testament written by Paul. *n.*

phil har mon ic (fil′här mon′ik), 1 devoted to music; loving music: *A musical club is often called a philharmonic society.* 2 given by a philharmonic society: *a philharmonic concert.* 3 a philharmonic society or concert. 1,2 *adj.,* 3 *n.*

Phil ip (fil′əp), (in the Bible) one of Christ's twelve apostles. *n.*

Phil ip pine (fil′ə pēn′), of or having to do with the Philippines or its inhabitants; Filipino. *adj.*

Philippine Islands, Philippines.

Phil ip pines (fil′ə pēnz′), country in the W Pacific, southeast of China and northeast of Borneo, consisting of over 7000 islands. The Philippines were governed by the United States from 1898 until 1946. *Capital:* Quezon City. *n.pl.*

Phil is tine (fil′ə stēn′ or fə lis′tən), 1 (in the Bible) one of the warlike people in southwestern Palestine who fought the Israelites many times. 2 of the Philistines. 3 Also, **philistine. a** person who is commonplace in ideas and tastes. **b** lacking culture; commonplace. 1,3a *n.,* 2,3b *adj.*

phil o den dron (fil′ə den′drən), a climbing, evergreen plant with smooth, shiny leaves, often grown as a house plant. *n.*

phil o log i cal (fil′ə loj′ə kəl), having to do with philology. *adj.*

phi lol o gist (fə lol′ə jist), an expert in philology. *n.*

phi lol o gy (fə lol′ə jē), 1 an older name for linguistics; the science of language. 2 the study of literary and other records. *n.*

phi los o pher (fə los′ə fər), 1 person who studies philosophy a great deal. 2 person who has a system of philosophy. 3 person who is calm and reasonable under hard conditions, accepting life and making the best of it. *n.*

phil o soph ic (fil′ə sof′ik), philosophical. *adj.*

phil o soph i cal (fil′ə sof′ə kəl), 1 of philosophy or philosophers. 2 knowing much about philosophy. 3 devoted to philosophy. 4 wise; calm; reasonable. *adj.* —**phil′o soph′i cal ly,** *adv.*

phi los o phize (fə los′ə fīz), think or reason as a philosopher does; try to understand and explain things: *The old woman philosophized about life and death.* *v.,* **phi los o phized, phi los o phiz ing.**

phi los o phy (fə los′ə fē), 1 the study of the truth or principles underlying all real knowledge; study of the most general causes and principles of the universe. 2 explanation or theory of the universe, especially the particular explanation or system of a philosopher: *the philosophy of Plato.* 3 system for guiding life. 4 the general principles of a particular subject or field of activity: *the philosophy of history, the army's military philosophy.* 5 a calm and reasonable attitude; accepting things as they are and making the best of them. *n., pl.* **phi los o phies.**

phil ter or **phil tre** (fil′tər), drug or magic potion which is supposed to make a person fall in love. *n.*

phlegm (flem), 1 the thick mucus discharged into the mouth and throat during a cold or other respiratory disease. 2 sluggish disposition or temperament; indifference. 3 coolness; calmness. *n.*

phleg mat ic (fleg mat′ik), 1 sluggish; indifferent. 2 cool; calm: *My parents are phlegmatic; they never seem to get excited about anything. adj.*

phlo em (flō′em), tissue in a plant or tree through which the sap containing dissolved food materials passes downward to the stems and roots. *n.*

phlox (floks), a common garden plant with clusters of showy flowers in various colors. *n., pl.* **phlox es.**

Phnom Penh (pə nôm′ pen′), capital of Cambodia, in the S part.

pho bi a (fō′bē ə), a morbid or insane fear of a certain thing or group of things: *a phobia of water, a phobia about snakes. n., pl.* **pho bi as.**

phoe be (fē′bē), a small American bird with a grayish-brown back, a yellowish-white breast, and a low crest on the head. *n.*

Phoe be (fē′bē), 1 (in Greek myths) the goddess of the moon. Phoebe was also called Artemis by the Greeks and Diana by the Romans. 2 the moon. *n.*

Phoe bus (fē′bəs), 1 (in Greek myths) Apollo, the god of the sun. 2 the sun. *n.*

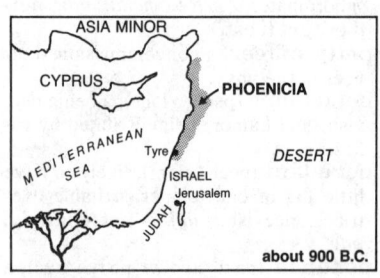

Phoe ni cia (fə nish′ə), ancient country on the Mediterranean Sea, in the region of Lebanon, W Syria, and N Israel. It was famous for its traders. *n.*

Phoe ni cian (fə nish′ən), 1 of or having to do with Phoenicia, its people, or their language. 2 one of the people of Phoenicia. 3 language of Phoenicia. 1 *adj.,* 2,3 *n.*

phoe nix (fē′niks), a mythical bird, the only one of its kind, said to live 500 or 600 years, to burn itself on a funeral pile, and to rise again from the ashes, fresh and beautiful, for another long life. *n., pl.* **phoe nix es.** Also, **phenix.**

Phoe nix (fē′niks), capital of Arizona, in the central part. *n.*

phone (fōn), INFORMAL. telephone. *n., v.,* **phoned, phon ing.**

pho net ic (fə net′ik), 1 of or having to do with sounds made with the voice. Phonetic exercises are drills in pronunciation. 2 representing sounds made with the voice. Systems of phonetic spelling spell words as they are pronounced and represent the same sound by the same letter. Phonetic symbols are marks used to show pronunciation. We use TH as the phonetic symbol for the sound of *th* in *the* or *then.* 3 of or having to do with phonetics. *adj.*

pho net i cal ly (fə net′ik lē), in a phonetic manner; as regards the sound and not the spelling of words. *adv.*

pho net ics (fə net′iks), science dealing with sounds made in speech and the art of pronunciation. *n.*

phon ic (fon′ik), 1 of or having to do with sound. 2 of sounds made in speech; phonetic. *adj.*

phon ics (fon′iks), 1 simplified phonetics for teaching reading. 2 science of sound. *n.*

pho no graph (fō′nə graf), instrument that reproduces sounds from phonograph records; record player. *n.*

pho no graph ic (fō′nə graf′ik), of a phonograph. *adj.*

phonograph needle, needle (def. 6).

phonograph record, record (def. 5).

pho ny (fō′nē), SLANG. 1 not genuine; counterfeit; fake. 2 a fake; pretender. 1 *adj.,* **pho ni er, pho ni est;** 2 *n., pl.* **pho nies.**

phos phate (fos′fāt), 1 salt or ester of phosphoric acid. Bread contains phosphates. 2 fertilizer containing such salts. 3 a drink of carbonated water flavored with fruit syrup, and containing a little phosphoric acid. *n.*

phos phor (fos′fər), substance which gives off light when exposed to certain types of energy, such as ultraviolet rays or X rays. Phosphor is widely used in fluorescent lamps and television tubes. *n.*

phos pho res cence (fos′fə res′ns), 1 act or process of giving out light without burning or by very slow burning that seems not to give out heat: *the phosphorescence of fireflies.* 2 light given out in this way. *n.*

phos pho res cent (fos′fə res′nt), showing phosphorescence. *adj.*

phos phor ic (fo sfôr′ik), having to do with or containing phosphorus. *adj.*

phosphoric acid, a colorless, odorless acid containing phosphorus, used in making fertilizers.

phos phor ous (fos′fər əs), having to do with or containing phosphorus. *adj.*

phos phor us (fos′fər əs), a nonmetallic element which exists in several forms. The most common form is a yellow, poisonous, waxy substance which burns slowly at ordinary temperatures and glows in the dark. *n.*

pho to (fō′tō), INFORMAL. a photograph. *n., pl.* **pho tos.**

pho to e lec tric cell (fō′tō i lek′trik), vacuum tube that varies the flow of current according to the amount of light reaching its sensitive element; electric eye. Variations or interruptions of the light can start machines to work that open doors, set off alarms, etc.

pho to gen ic (fō′tə jen′ik), having characteristics that photograph very well: *a photogenic face. adj.*

pho to graph (fō′tə graf), 1 picture made with a camera. A photograph is made by the action of light rays from the thing pictured coming through the lens of the camera onto a piece of film. 2 take a photograph of. 3 look (clear, unnatural, etc.) in a photograph: *I do not photograph well.* 1 *n.,* 2-3 *v.*

pho tog ra pher (fə tog′rə fər), 1 person who takes photographs. 2 person whose business is taking photographs. *n.*

pho to graph ic (fō′tə graf′ik), 1 of or like photography: *photographic accuracy.* 2 used in or produced by photography: *photographic plates, a photographic record of a trip. adj.* —**pho′to graph′i cal ly,** *adv.*

pho tog ra phy (fə tog′rə fē), the taking of photographs. *n.*

pho to play (fō′tə plā′), a motion-picture story or scenario. *n.*

pho to syn the sis (fō′tō sin′thə sis), process by which plant cells make carbohydrates from carbon dioxide and water in the presence of chlorophyll and light. *n.*

pho tot ro pism (fō to′trə piz′əm), tendency of plants to turn in response to light. *n.*

phrase (frāz), 1 combination of words: *Would you please speak in simple phrases so that we can understand you?* 2 expression often used: *"Run out" is a common phrase for "come to an end."* 3 a short, striking expression. EXAMPLES: A Fair Deal. A war to end wars. Liberty or death. 4 express in a particular way: *I tried to phrase my excuse politely.* 5 group of words not containing a subject and predicate and used as a single word within a sentence. EXAMPLES: in the house; coming by the church; to eat too fast. 6 division of a piece of music, usually several measures in length. 1-3,5,6 *n.,* 4 *v.,* **phrased, phras ing.**

phra se ol o gy (frā′zē ol′ə jē), selection and arrangement of words; the

photoelectric cell in a burglar alarm. When light strikes the cathode of the photoelectric cell, it emits electrons which flow to the anode. Interrupting the light beam causes an interruption of this flow which triggers the alarm.

hat, āge, fär; let, ēqual, tėrm;
it, īce; hot, ōpen, ôrder;
oil, out; cup, pùt, rüle; ch, child;
ng, long; sh, she; th, thin;
ŦH, then; zh, measure;

ə represents *a* in about,
e in taken, *i* in pencil,
o in lemon, *u* in circus.

particular way in which thoughts are expressed in language: *scientific phraseology, the phraseology of the Bible, the phraseology of the sports page in a newspaper. n., pl.* **phra se ol o gies.**

phre nol o gy (fri nol′ə jē), 1 theory that the shape of the skull shows what sort of mind and character a person has. 2 practice of reading character from the shape of the skull. *n.*

Phryg i a (frij′ē ə), ancient country in the central and NW part of Asia Minor. *n.* —**Phryg′i an,** *adj., n.*

phthi sis (thī′sis), a wasting disease of the body or of some part of the body, especially tuberculosis of the lungs. *n.*

phy lum (fī′ləm), a primary division of the animal or vegetable kingdom, consisting of one or more classes. The animals or plants in a phylum are thought to be related by descent from a common ancestral form. *n., pl.* **phy la** (fī′lə).

phys ic (fiz′ik), 1 medicine, especially one that acts as a laxative. 2 OLD USE. art of healing; science and practice of medicine. *n.*

phys i cal (fiz′ə kəl), 1 of the body: *physical exercise, physical strength, a physical disability.* 2 of matter; material: *The tide is a physical force.* 3 according to the laws of nature: *It is a physical impossibility for the sun to rise in the west.* 4 of the science of physics. *adj.* —**phys′i cal ly,** *adv.*

physical education, instruction in how to exercise and take care of the body, especially as a course at a school or college.

physical geography, branch of geography that deals with the natural features of the earth's surface, such as land forms, climate, winds, and ocean currents.

physical therapy, treatment of diseases and defects by physical remedies, such as exercise and massage, rather than by drugs; physiotherapy.

phy si cian (fə zish′ən), doctor of medicine. *n.*

phys i cist (fiz′ə sist), an expert in physics. *n.*

phys ics (fiz′iks), science that deals with matter and energy and the relation-

physiognomy

adj.	adjective	*n.*	noun
adv.	adverb	*prep.*	preposition
conj.	conjunction	*pron.*	pronoun
interj.	interjection	*v.*	verb
sing.	singular	*pl.*	plural

ships between them. Physics includes the study of force, motion, mechanics, heat, light, sound, electricity, and atomic energy. *n.*

phys i og no my (fiz′ē og′nə mē), 1 kind of features or type of face one has; one's face: *a ruddy physiognomy, a kindly physiognomy.* 2 art of estimating character from the features of the face or the form of the body. 3 the general aspect or looks of a countryside, a situation, etc.: *the rugged physiognomy of northern Scotland. n., pl.* **phys i og no mies.**

phys i o log i cal (fiz′ē ə loj′ə kəl), having to do with physiology: *Digestion is a physiological process. adj.* —**phys′i o log′i cal ly,** *adv.*

phys i ol o gist (fiz′ē ol′ə jist), an expert in physiology. *n.*

phys i ol o gy (fiz′ē ol′ə jē), 1 science dealing with the normal functions of living things or their parts: *animal physiology, plant physiology, the physiology of the blood.* 2 all the functions and activities of a living thing or of one of its parts. *n.*

phys i o ther a py (fiz′ē ō ther′ə pē), physical therapy. *n.*

phy sique (fə zēk′), bodily structure, organization, or development: *The swimmer had a strong physique. n.*

pi (pī), the Greek letter π, used as the symbol for the ratio of the circumference of any circle to its diameter. $\pi = 3.141592 +$. *n., pl.* **pis.**

P.I., Philippine Islands.

pi a nis si mo (pē′ə nis′ə mō), in music: 1 very soft. 2 very softly. 1 *adj.,* 2 *adv.* [from Italian, from *piano* soft]

pi an ist (pē an′ist *or* pē′ə nist), person who plays the piano. *n.*

pi an o[1] (pē an′ō), a large musical instrument whose tones come from many wires. The wires are sounded by hammers that are worked by striking keys on a keyboard. *n., pl.* **pi an os.** [shortened from *pianoforte*]

pi an o[2] (pē an′ō), in music: 1 soft. 2 softly. 1 *adj.,* 2 *adv.* [from Italian *piano,* from Latin *planus* plain, flat]

pi an o for te (pē an′ə fôr′tē), piano[1]. *n.* [from Italian, from *piano* soft + *forte* loud]

pi az za (pē az′ə *for 1;* pē ät′sə *or* pē-az′ə *for 2*), 1 a large porch along one or more sides of a house. 2 an open public square in Italian towns. *n., pl.* **pi az zas.**

pi broch (pē′brok), kind of musical piece performed on the bagpipe. It is usually warlike or sad. *n.*

pi ca (pī′kə), 1 size of type, 12 point.

This sentence is in pica.

2 this size used as a measure; about ⅙ inch. *n., pl.* **pi cas.**

Pic ar dy (pik′ər dē), region in N France. See **Normandy** for map. *n.*

Pi cas so (pi kä′sō), **Pablo,** 1881-1973, Spanish painter and sculptor. *n.*

pic a yune (pik′ə yün′), 1 small; petty; mean: *picayune criticism.* 2 an insignificant person or thing; trifle. 3 any coin of small value. 1 *adj.,* 2,3 *n.*

Pic ca dil ly (pik′ə dil′ē), one of the main business streets of London. *n.*

pic ca lil li (pik′ə lil′ē), relish made of chopped pickles, onions, tomatoes, etc., with hot spices. *n.*

pic co lo (pik′ə lō), a small, shrill flute, sounding an octave higher than an ordinary flute. *n., pl.* **pic co los.**

pick[1] (pik), 1 choose out of a number or quantity; select: *I picked a winning horse at the races.* 2 choice; selection: *This red rose is my pick.* 3 the best or most desirable part: *We got a high price for the pick of our peaches.* 4 pull away with the fingers; gather: *We pick fruit and flowers.* 5 amount of a crop gathered at one time. 6 pierce, dig into, or break up with something pointed: *pick ground, pick rocks.* 7 use something pointed to remove things from: *pick one's teeth, pick a bone.* 8 open with a pointed instrument, wire, etc.: *The burglar picked the lock on the garage.* 9 steal the contents of: *In the crowded waiting room I didn't feel the hand that picked my pocket.* 10 prepare for use by removing feathers, waste parts, etc.: *pick a chicken.* 11 pull apart: *The hair in the pillow needs to be picked, as it has matted.* 12 pluck at with the fingers or a plectrum: *play a banjo by picking its strings.* 13 thing held in the fingers and used to pull on the strings of a musical instrument; plectrum. 14 seek and find occasion for; seek and find: *pick a quarrel, pick flaws.* 1,4,6-12,14 *v.,* 2,3,5,13 *n.* [Middle English *picken,* perhaps from a Scandinavian word of the 1200's, such as Icelandic *pikka*]

pick at, 1 pull on with the fingers, etc.: *She picked at the scab on her finger.* 2 eat only a little at a time: *The bird picks at the bread.*

pick off, shoot one at a time.

pick on, INFORMAL. 1 find fault with: *The teacher picked on him for always*

piazza (def. 1)

being late. 2 annoy; tease: *My older brother and sister are always picking on me.*

pick out, 1 choose with care; select: *Pick out a coat you will like to wear.* 2 distinguish (a thing) from surroundings: *Can you pick me out in this group picture?*

pick over, look over carefully: *pick over vegetables before buying.*

pick up, 1 take up: *She picked up the hammer.* 2 get by chance: *pick up a bargain.* 3 learn without being taught: *He picks up games easily.* 4 take up into a vehicle or ship: *The bus picked up passengers at every other corner.* 5 INFORMAL. recover; improve: *He seemed to pick up quickly after his fever went down.* 6 go faster; increase in speed. 7 succeed in seeing, hearing, etc.: *She picked up a radio broadcast from Paris.* 8 INFORMAL. become acquainted with without being introduced. 9 tidy up; put in order: *pick up a room, pick up one's desk.*

pick[2] (pik), 1 pickax. 2 a sharp-pointed tool. Ice is broken into pieces with a pick. *n.* [Middle English *pik,* a different form of *pike* pike[2]]

pick a back (pik′ə bak′), piggyback. *adv.*

pickax

pick ax or **pick axe** (pik′aks′), tool with a heavy metal bar, pointed at one or both ends, attached through the center to a wooden handle; pick. It is used for breaking up dirt, rocks, etc. *n., pl.* **pick ax es.**

pick er (pik′ər), 1 person who gathers, picks, or collects. 2 tool for picking anything. *n.*

pick er el (pik′ər əl), a fresh-water fish with a long, narrow pointed head, used for food. It is a kind of pike. *n., pl.* **pick er els** or **pick er el.**

pick et (pik′it), 1 a pointed stake or peg placed upright to make a fence, to tie a horse to, etc. 2 enclose with pickets; fence. 3 tie to a picket: *picket a horse.* 4 a small body of troops, or a single soldier, posted at some place to watch for the enemy and guard against surprise attacks. **5** person stationed by a labor union near a factory, store, etc., where there is a strike. Pickets try to prevent employees from working or customers from buying. **6** person who takes part in a public demonstration or boycott to support a cause. **7** station as pickets. **8** station pickets at or near: *picket a factory.* **9** act as a picket. 1,4-6 *n.,* 2,3,7-9 *v.*

picket fence

picket fence, fence made of pickets.
pick ings (pik′ingz), **1** amount picked. **2** things left over; scraps. *n.pl.*
pick le (pik′əl), **1** salt water, vinegar, or other liquid in which meat and vegetables can be preserved. **2** cucumber preserved in pickle. **3** any other vegetable preserved in pickle. **4** preserve in pickle: *We pickled several quarts of beets yesterday.* **5** INFORMAL. trouble; difficulty: *I got in a bad pickle today.* 1-3,5 *n.,* 4 *v.,* **pick led, pick ling.**
pick pock et (pik′pok′it), person who steals from people's pockets. *n.*
pick up (pik′up′), **1** a picking up: *the daily pickup of mail.* **2** INFORMAL. a getting better; improvement: *a pickup in business, a pickup in one's health.* **3** acceleration; going faster; increase in speed. **4** device that transforms into electrical current the vibrations set up in a phonograph needle by variations in the grooves of a record. **5** reception of sounds or images in radio or television and their conversion into electric waves for broadcasting. **6** apparatus for such reception or the place where it occurs. **7** a small, light truck with an open back, used for light hauling. *n.*
pic nic (pik′nik), **1** a pleasure trip with a meal in the open air. **2** go on such a trip: *Our family often picnics at the beach.* **3** eat in picnic style. 1 *n.,* 2,3 *v.,* **pic nicked, pic nick ing.**
pic nick er (pik′ni kər), person who picnics. *n.*
pi cot (pē′kō), one of a number of fancy loops in embroidery, tatting, etc., or along the edge of lace, ribbon, etc. *n.*
Pict (pikt), member of an ancient people formerly living in Scotland, especially northern Scotland, between A.D. 200's and 900's. *n.*
pic to graph (pik′tə graf), picture used as a sign or symbol. *n.*
pic to ri al (pik tôr′ē əl), **1** having to do with pictures; expressed in pictures.

2 making a picture for the mind; vivid. **3** illustrated by pictures: *a pictorial history, a pictorial magazine.* **4** having to do with painters or painting: *pictorial skill. adj.* —**pic to′ri al ly,** *adv.*
pic ture (pik′chər), **1** a drawing, painting, portrait, or photograph; a print of any of these: *The book contains a good picture of a tiger.* **2** scene: *The trees and brook make a lovely picture.* **3** something beautiful: *The old castle was a picture in the bright sunlight.* **4** draw, paint, etc.; make into a picture: *The artist pictured life in the old Indian tribes.* **5** image; likeness: *He is the picture of his father. She was the picture of happiness.* **6** form a picture of in the mind; imagine: *It is hard to picture life a hundred years ago.* **7** a mental image; idea: *have a clear picture of the problem.* **8** a vivid description. **9** show by words; describe vividly: *The speaker pictured the suffering of the poor.* **10** a motion picture. **11** image on a television set. **12** INFORMAL. state of affairs; condition; situation: *the employment picture.* 1-3,5,7,8,10-12 *n.,* 4,6,9 *v.,* **pic tured, pic tur ing.**
pic tur esque (pik′chə resk′), **1** quaint or interesting enough to be used as the subject of a picture: *a picturesque old mill.* **2** making a picture for the mind; vivid: *picturesque language. adj.* —**pic′tur esque′ness,** *n.*
pidg in English (pij′ən), one of several forms of English, with simplified grammatical structure and often a mixed vocabulary, used in western Africa, Australia, Melanesia, and China, largely as a language of trade between natives and foreigners.
pie[1] (pī), fruit, meat, etc., enclosed in pastry and baked: *apple pie, chicken pie. n.* [Middle English *pye*]
pie[2] (pī), magpie. *n.* [from French of the 1200's *pie,* from Latin *pica*]
pie bald (pī′bôld′), **1** spotted in two colors, especially black and white. **2** a piebald animal, especially a horse. 1 *adj.,* 2 *n.*
piece (pēs), **1** one of the parts into which a thing is divided or broken; bit: *The cup broke in pieces.* **2** portion; limited part; small quantity: *a piece of land containing two acres, a piece of bread.* **3** a single thing of a set or class: *This set of china has 144 pieces.* **4** a single composition in an art: *a piece of music.* **5** coin: *A nickel is a five-cent piece.* **6** example; instance: *That silly story is a piece of nonsense.* **7** quantity in which goods are made: *cloth sold*

only by the piece. **8** the amount of work done: *paid by the piece.* **9** gun; cannon. **10** make or repair by adding or joining pieces: *piece a quilt.* **11** join the pieces of. 1-9 *n.,* 10,11 *v.,* **pieced, piec ing.**
go to pieces, **1** fall apart; break up: *Another ship had gone to pieces on the rocks.* **2** break down; collapse: *When her business failed, she went completely to pieces.*
of a piece, of the same kind; in keeping: *That plan is of a piece with the rest of their silly suggestions.*
piece of one's mind, a scolding: *He gave the boy a piece of his mind for coming late again.*
piece meal (pēs′mēl′), **1** piece by piece; a little at a time: *work done piecemeal.* **2** piece from piece; to pieces; into fragments: *The lamb was torn piecemeal by the wolves.* **3** done piece by piece. 1,2 *adv.,* 3 *adj.*
piece of eight, an old Spanish peso, used during the Spanish colonization of America. It corresponded to the United States dollar.
piece work (pēs′wėrk′), work paid for by the amount done, not by the time it takes. *n.*
piece work er (pēs′wėr′kər), person who does piecework. *n.*
pie crust (pī′krust′), pastry used for the bottom or top of a pie. *n.*
pied (pīd), having patches of two or more colors; many-colored. *adj.*
Pied mont (pēd′mont), **1** plateau in the United States between the Appalachian Mountains and the low land along the Atlantic coast. The Piedmont extends over parts of New Jersey, Pennsylvania, Delaware, New York, Maryland, Virginia, North Carolina, South Carolina, Georgia, and Alabama. **2** region in NW Italy. *n.*
pier (pir), **1** structure supported on columns extending into the water, used as a walk or a landing place for ships. **2** breakwater. **3** one of the solid supports on which the arches of a bridge rest; pillar. **4** the solid part of a wall between windows, doors, etc. *n.*
pierce (pirs), **1** make a hole in; bore into or through: *A nail pierced the tire of*

hat, āge, fär; let, ēqual, tėrm;
it, īce; hot, ōpen, ôrder;
oil, out; cup, pùt, rüle; ch, child;
ng, long; sh, she; th, thin;
ŦH, then; zh, measure;

ə represents *a* in about,
e in taken, *i* in pencil,
o in lemon, *u* in circus.

OX   WINDOW   WEAPONS   FENCE   POST   EYE

pictographs

adj. adjective	*n.* noun
adv. adverb	*prep.* preposition
conj. conjunction	*pron.* pronoun
interj. interjection	*v.* verb
sing. singular	*pl.* plural

our car. 2 go into; go through: *A tunnel pierces the mountain.* 3 force a way; force a way through or into: *A sharp cry pierced the air.* 4 make a way through with the eye or mind: *pierce a disguise, pierce a mystery.* 5 affect sharply with some feeling: *a heart pierced with grief.* *v.,* **pierced, pierc ing.**

Pierce (pirs), **Franklin,** 1804–1869, the 14th president of the United States, from 1853 to 1857. *n.*

pierc ing (pir′sing), that pierces; penetrating; sharp; keen: *piercing cold, a piercing look. adj.* —**pierc′ing ly,** *adv.*

Pierre (pir), capital of South Dakota, in the central part. *n.*

pi e ty (pī′ə tē), 1 a being pious; reverence for God; devotion to religion; holiness; goodness. 2 dutiful regard for one's parents. 3 a pious act, remark, belief, etc. *n., pl.* **pi e ties.**

pif fle (pif′əl), INFORMAL. silly talk; nonsense. *n.*

pig (pig), 1 a four-footed mammal with a stout, heavy body, cloven hoofs, and a broad snout; hog; swine. Domesticated pigs are raised for their meat. 2 a young pig. 3 pork. 4 INFORMAL. person who seems or acts like a pig; one who is greedy, dirty, dull, sullen, or stubborn. 5 an oblong mass of metal that has been poured into a mold while molten. *n.* —**pig′like′,** *adj.*

pigeon
15 in. long

pig eon (pij′ən), any of a group of birds with thick bodies and short tails, especially one of the larger kinds. The smaller kinds are usually called doves. *n.*

pig eon hole (pij′ən hōl′), 1 a small place built, usually as one of a series, for a pigeon to nest in. 2 one of a set of boxlike compartments for holding papers and other articles in a desk, a cabinet, etc. 3 put in a pigeonhole; put away. 4 classify and lay aside in memory where one can refer to it. 5 put aside with the idea of dismissing, forgetting, or neglecting: *The city council pigeon-*

holed the people's request for a new park. 1,2 *n.,* 3-5 *v.,* **pig eon holed, pig eon hol ing.**

pig eon-toed (pij′ən tōd′), having the toes or feet turned inward. *adj.*

pig gish (pig′ish), 1 very selfish; greedy. 2 dirty; filthy. *adj.* —**pig′-gish ly,** *adv.* —**pig′gish ness,** *n.*

pig gy (pig′ē), a little pig. *n., pl.* **pig-gies.**

pig gy back (pig′ē bak′), on the back: *a parent carrying a baby piggyback. Flatcars often take trucks piggyback from one place to another. adv.* Also, **pickaback.**

piggy bank, 1 a small container in the shape of a pig, with a slot in the top for coins. 2 any coin bank.

pig-head ed (pig′hed′id), stupidly obstinate or stubborn. *adj.*

pig iron, crude iron as it first comes from the blast furnace or smelter, usually cast into oblong masses called pigs.

pilaster

pig ment (pig′mənt), 1 a coloring matter, especially a powdered dry substance. Paint and dyes are made by mixing pigments with liquid. 2 substance that occurs in and colors the tissues of an animal or plant. The color of a person's hair, skin, and eyes is due to pigment. *n.*

pig men ta tion (pig′mən tā′shən), deposit of pigment in the tissue of a living animal or plant, causing coloration or discoloration. *n.*

pig my (pig′mē), pygmy. *n., pl.* **pig-mies;** *adj.*

pig pen (pig′pen′), 1 pen where pigs are kept. 2 a filthy place. *n.*

pig skin (pig′skin′), 1 the skin of a pig. 2 leather made from it. 3 INFORMAL. a football. 4 INFORMAL. saddle. *n.*

pig sty (pig′stī′), pigpen. *n., pl.* **pig-sties.**

pig tail (pig′tāl′), braid of hair hanging from the back of the head. *n.*

pike¹ (pīk), a long, wooden shaft with a sharp-pointed metal head; spear. Foot soldiers used to carry pikes. *n.* [from French of the 1500's *pique,* from *piquer* pierce]

pike² (pīk), a sharp point; spike. *n.* [Old English *pīc*]

pike³ (pīk), any of a group of large,

slender, fresh-water fish of the Northern Hemisphere, having a long, pointed head. The muskellunge and pickerel are pikes. *n., pl.* **pikes** or **pike.** [apparently shortened from *pikefish,* from *pike²* + *fish* (because of the shape of its head)]

piggyback—trailer carried piggyback

pike⁴ (pīk), turnpike. *n.* [shortened from *turnpike,* from *turn* + *pike²*]

pik er (pī′kər), SLANG. person who does things in a small or cheap way. *n.*

Pikes Peak (pīks), mountain of the Rocky Mountains in central Colorado.

pike staff (pīk′staf′), staff or shaft of a pike or spear. *n., pl.* **pike staves** (pīk′stāvz′).

pi las ter (pə las′tər), a rectangular pillar, especially when not standing alone, but supporting a part of a wall from which it projects somewhat. *n.*

Pi late (pī′lət), **Pontius,** Roman governor who, from A.D. 26 to 36?, ruled over Judea in Palestine. During his rule Christ was crucified. *n.*

pile¹ (pīl), 1 many things lying one upon another in a more or less orderly way: *a pile of wood.* 2 a mass like a hill or mound: *a pile of dirt.* 3 make into a pile; heap up; stack: *The campers piled the extra wood in a corner.* 4 gather or rise in piles: *Snow piled against the fences.* 5 a large structure or mass of buildings. 6 INFORMAL. a large amount: *I have a pile of work to do.* 7 cover with large amounts: *pile a plate with food.* 8 go in a confused, rushing crowd: *pile out into the street.* 9 heap of wood on which a dead body or sacrifice is burned. 10 reactor. 1,2,5,6,9,10 *n.,* 3,4,7,8 *v.,* **piled, pil ing.** [from French of the 1400's *pile,* from Latin *pila* pillar]

pile² (pīl), a heavy beam driven upright into the earth, often under water, to help support a bridge, wharf, building, etc. *n.* [Old English *pīl* stake, from Latin *pilum* javelin]

pile³ (pīl), 1 a soft, thick nap on velvet, plush, and many carpets: *The pile of that Chinese rug is almost half an inch long.* 2 a soft, fine hair or down. *n.* [from Latin *pilus* hair]

pile driver, machine for driving down piles or stakes, usually a tall framework in which a heavy weight is raised and then allowed to fall upon the pile.

pil fer (pil′fər), steal in small quantities; steal: *The children pilfered apples from the neighbor's orchard. v.*

pil grim (pil′grəm), **1** person who goes on a journey to a sacred or holy place as an act of religious devotion. In the Middle Ages, many people went as pilgrims to Jerusalem and to holy places in Europe. **2** traveler; wanderer. **3 Pilgrim,** one of the Puritan settlers of Plymouth Colony in 1620. *n.*

pil grim age (pil′grə mij), **1** a pilgrim's journey; a journey to some sacred place as an act of religious devotion. **2** a long journey. *n.*

pil ing (pī′ling), **1** piles or heavy beams driven into the ground, etc. **2** structure made of piles. *n.*

pill (pil), **1** medicine made up into a small pellet, tablet, or capsule to be swallowed whole. **2** a very small ball or mass of anything; pellet. *n.*

pil lage (pil′ij), **1** rob with violence; plunder: *Pirates pillaged the towns along the coast.* **2** plunder; robbery. **1** *v.,* **pil laged, pil lag ing; 2** *n.*

pil lar (pil′ər), **1** a slender, upright structure; column. Pillars are usually made of stone, wood, or metal and used as supports or ornaments for a building. Sometimes a pillar stands alone as a monument. **2** anything slender and upright like a pillar. **3** an important support or supporter: *a pillar of society, a pillar of the church. n.*

from pillar to post, from one thing or place to another without any definite purpose.

pil lared (pil′ərd), **1** having pillars. **2** formed into pillars. *adj.*

pill box (pil′boks′), **1** box, usually shallow and often round, for holding pills. **2** a small, low fortress with thick, concrete walls and roof, equipped with machine guns and other weapons. *n., pl.* **pill box es.**

pil lion (pil′yən), pad attached behind a saddle for a person to sit on. *n.*

pillory (def. 1)

pil lor y (pil′ər ē), **1** frame of wood with holes through which a person's head and hands were put. The pillory was formerly used as a punishment, being set up in a public place where the crowd could make fun of the offender. **2** put in the pillory. **3** expose to public ridicule, contempt, or abuse: *The news-*

papers pilloried the unpopular mayor. **1** *n., pl.* **pil lor ies; 2,3** *v.,* **pil lor ied, pil lor y ing.**

pil low (pil′ō), **1** bag or case filled with feathers, down, or other soft material, usually used to support the head when resting or sleeping. **2** rest on a pillow. **3** be a pillow for: *He lay with his arm pillowing his head.* **1** *n.,* **2,3** *v.*

pil low case (pil′ō kās′), a cotton or linen cover pulled over a pillow. *n.*

pil low slip (pil′ō slip′), pillowcase. *n.*

pi lot (pī′lət), **1** person who steers a ship or boat. **2** person trained to steer ships in or out of a harbor or through dangerous waters. A ship takes on a pilot before coming into a strange harbor. **3** person who operates the controls of an aircraft in flight. **4** act as the pilot of; steer: *An aviator pilots an airplane.* **5** a guide; leader. **6** to guide; lead: *The manager piloted us through the big factory.* **7** device in a machine, motor, etc., that controls or activates a larger and more complex part. **1-3,5,7** *n.,* **4,6** *v.*

pi lot house (pī′lət hous′), an enclosed place on the deck of a ship, sheltering the steering wheel and pilot; wheelhouse. *n., pl.* **pi lot hous es** (pī′lət hou′ziz).

pilot light, a small flame kept burning all the time and used to light a main burner whenever desired. Gas stoves and gas water heaters have pilot lights.

pi men to (pə men′tō), **1** kind of sweet pepper, used as a vegetable, relish, and stuffing for green olives. **2** allspice. **3** tree which bears berries from which allspice is made. *n., pl.* **pi men tos.**

pi mien to (pi myen′tō), pimento (def. 1). *n., pl.* **pi mien tos.**

pim per nel (pim′pər nel), plant having small scarlet, purple, or white flowers that close in bad weather. *n.*

pim ple (pim′pəl), a small, inflamed swelling of the skin. *n.* **—pim′ple like′,** *adj.*

pim pled (pim′pəld), having pimples. *adj.*

pim ply (pim′plē), pimpled. *adj.,* **pim pli er, pim pli est.**

pin (pin), **1** a short, slender piece of wire with a point at one end and a head at the other, for fastening things together. **2** badge with a pin or clasp to fasten it to the clothing: *She wore her class pin.* **3** brooch. **4** peg made of wood, metal, or plastic, used to fasten things together, hold something, hang things on, etc. **5** any of various fastenings, such as a hairpin or safety pin. **6** fasten with a pin or pins; put a pin through. **7** fasten or attach firmly to or on; tack; fasten as if with pins. **8** hold fast in one position: *When the tree fell, it pinned his shoulder to the ground.* **9** a

hat, āge, fär; let, ēqual, tėrm; it, īce; hot, ōpen, ôrder; oil, out; cup, pùt, rüle; ch, child; ng, long; sh, she; th, thin; ᵺH, then; zh, measure;

ə represents *a* in about, *e* in taken, *i* in pencil, *o* in lemon, *u* in circus.

bottle-shaped piece of wood used in the game of ninepins, tenpins, etc. **1-5,9** *n.,* **6-8** *v.,* **pinned, pin ning. —pin′like′,** *adj.*

on pins and needles, very anxious or uneasy.

pin down, hold or bind to an undertaking or pledge.

pin on, fix (blame, responsibility, etc.) on: *You're not going to pin the blame on me!*

pin a fore (pin′ə fôr′), **1** a child's apron that covers most of the dress. **2** a light dress without sleeves. *n.*

pince-nez (pans′nā′ *or* pins′nā′), eyeglasses kept in place by a spring that clips onto the bridge of the nose. *n., pl.* **pince-nez** (pans′nāz′ *or* pins′nāz′). [from French *pince-nez* "pinch-nose"]

pincers (def. 1)

pin cers (pin′sərz), **1** tool for gripping and holding tight, made like scissors but with jaws instead of blades. **2** the large claw or pair of claws of crabs, lobsters, etc., which are used to grip and hold the prey. *n. pl. or sing.* Also, **pinchers.**

pinch (pinch), **1** squeeze between two hard edges; squeeze with thumb and forefinger: *pinch a child's cheek playfully.* **2** act of pinching; a squeeze between two hard edges. **3** press so as to hurt; squeeze: *These new shoes pinch my feet.* **4** sharp pressure that hurts; squeeze: *the pinch of tight shoes.* **5** sharp discomfort or distress: *the pinch of cold.* **6** cause to shrink or become thin: *a face pinched by hunger.* **7** time of special need; emergency: *I will help you in a pinch.* **8** as much as can be taken up with the tips of finger and thumb: *a pinch of salt.* **9** be stingy; be stingy with: *He was so miserly that he even pinched nickels and pennies.* **10** SLANG. to arrest. **11** SLANG. an arrest. **12** SLANG. to steal: *The grocer caught*

adj. adjective	*n.* noun
adv. adverb	*prep.* preposition
conj. conjunction	*pron.* pronoun
interj. interjection	*v.* verb
sing. singular	*pl.* plural

them pinching apples. **13** SLANG. a stealing. 1,3,6,9,10,12 *v.*, 2,4,5,7, 8,11,13 *n.*, *pl.* **pinch es.**

pinch ers (pin/chərz), pincers. *n. pl. or sing.*

pinch-hit (pinch/hit/), **1** (in baseball) to bat for another player, especially when a hit is badly needed. **2** take another's place in an emergency. *v.*, **pinch-hit, pinch-hit ting.**

pinch hitter, one who pinch-hits for another.

pin cush ion (pin/kush/ən), a small cushion to stick pins in until they are needed. *n.*

pine[1] (pīn), **1** any of a group of evergreen trees that have cones, and clusters of needle-shaped leaves that grow out from temporary scalelike leaves. Pines are valuable for timber, turpentine, resin, tar, etc. **2** the wood of any of these trees. *n.* [Old English *pīn,* from Latin *pinus*]

pine[2] (pīn), **1** long eagerly; yearn: *The homesick child pined to see his parents.* **2** waste away with pain, hunger, grief, or desire. *v.,* **pined, pin ing.** [Old English *pīnian* suffer, from *pīn* torture, punishment, from Latin *poena* penalty]

pineapple
(def. 1)

pine ap ple (pī/nap/əl), **1** a large, juicy fruit growing in hot climates, that looks somewhat like a large pine cone and is good to eat. **2** plant with slender, stiff leaves that it grows on. *n.*

pine needle, the very slender leaf of a pine tree.

pine y (pī/nē), piny. *adj.,* **pin i er, pin i est.**

pin feath er (pin/feŦH/ər), an undeveloped feather, especially one just breaking through the skin, that looks like a small stub. *n.*

Ping-Pong (ping/pong/), trademark for table tennis. *n.*

pin head (pin/hed/), **1** the head of a pin. **2** something very small or worthless. *n.*

pin hole (pin/hōl/), **1** hole made by a pin. **2** hole for a pin or peg to go in. *n.*

pin ion[1] (pin/yən), **1** the last joint of a bird's wing. **2** a wing. **3** any one of the stiff flying feathers of the wing. **4** cut off or tie the pinions of (a bird) to prevent flying. **5** bind; bind the arms of; bind (to something): *pinion a person's arms.* 1-3 *n.,* 4,5 *v.* [from French of the 1400's *pignon,* from Latin *pinnionem,* from *penna* feather and *pinna* wing]

pin ion[2] (pin/yən), a small gear with teeth that fit into those of a larger gear or rack. *n.* [from French *pignon*]

pink[1] (pingk), **1** the color obtained by mixing red with white; light or pale red. **2** having this color; pale-red. **3** the highest degree or condition: *The athlete was in the pink of health.* **4** a garden plant with spicy-smelling flowers of various colors, mostly white, pink, and red. A carnation is a variety of pink. **5** this plant's flower. 1,3-5 *n.,* 2 *adj.* [origin uncertain]

pink[2] (pingk), **1** prick or pierce with a sword, spear, or dagger. **2** cut the edge of (cloth) in small scallops or notches. **3** ornament with small, round holes. *v.* [Middle English *pynken*]

pink eye (pingk/ī/), a contagious disease characterized by inflammation and soreness of the membrane that lines the eyelids and covers the eyeball. *n.*

pink ie (ping/kē), the smallest finger. *n.* Also, **pinky.**

pinking shears, shears for pinking cloth.

pink ish (ping/kish), somewhat pink. *adj.*

pink y (ping/kē), pinkie. *n., pl.* **pink ies.**

pin money, **1** allowance of money made by a man to his wife or daughter for her own use. **2** a small amount of money used to buy extra things for one's own use.

pin nace (pin/is), **1** a ship's boat. **2** a very small schooner. *n.*

pin na cle (pin/ə kəl), **1** a high peak or point of rock. **2** the highest point: *at the pinnacle of one's fame.* **3** a slender turret or spire. *n.*

pin nate (pin/āt), **1** like a feather. **2** (of a leaf) having leaflets on each side of a stalk. See **leaf** for picture. *adj.*

pi noch le (pē/nuk/əl), **1** game played with 48 cards, in which points are scored according to the value of certain combinations of cards. **2** combination of the jack of diamonds and the queen of spades in this game. *n.*

piñ on (pin/yən *or* pē/nyōn), **1** pine, especially of the Rocky Mountain region, producing large, nutlike seeds which are good to eat. **2** its seed. *n., pl.* **piñ ons.** [from Spanish]

pin point (pin/point/), **1** the point of a pin. **2** aim at accurately; determine precisely. **3** extremely accurate or precise: *pinpoint bombing.* 1 *n.,* 2 *v.,* 3 *adj.*

pint (pint), measure of capacity for liquids and dry things, equal to 1/2 quart; 2 cups; 16 ounces. *n.*

pin to (pin/tō), **1** spotted in two or more colors; pied. **2** a pinto horse. 1 *adj.,* 2 *n., pl.* **pin tos.**

pin wheel (pin/hwēl/), **1** toy made of a wheel fastened to a stick by a pin so that it revolves in the wind. **2** kind of firework that revolves when lighted. *n.*

pin y (pī/nē), **1** abounding in or covered with pine trees: *piny mountains.* **2** having to do with or suggesting pine trees: *a piny odor. adj.,* **pin i er, pin i est.** Also, **piney.**

pi o neer (pī/ə nir/), **1** person who settles in a part of a country, preparing it for others: *The pioneers of the American West included trappers, woodsmen, farmers, and explorers.* **2** person who goes first, or does something first, and so prepares a way for others: *a pioneer in medical science.* **3** prepare or open up for others; take the lead in doing: *Astronauts are pioneering in exploring outer space.* 1,2 *n.,* 3 *v.*

pi ous (pī/əs), **1** having or showing reverence for God; religious. **2** done under pretense of religion or of serving a good cause: *a pious fraud. adj.* **—pi/ous ly,** *adv.*

pinking shears

pip[1] (pip), seed of an apple, orange, etc. *n.* [apparently shortened from *pippin,* from French of the 1200's *pepin*]

pip[2] (pip), a contagious disease of birds, characterized by the secretion of thick mucus in the mouth and throat. *n.* [apparently from Dutch of the 1400's *pippe,* from Latin *pippita,* from *pituita* phlegm]

pip[3] (pip), one of the spots on playing cards, dominoes, or dice. *n.* [origin uncertain]

pipe (pīp), **1** tube through which a liquid or gas flows. **2** carry by means of a pipe or pipes. **3** supply with pipes: *Our street is being piped for gas.* **4** tube with a bowl of clay, wood, or other material at one end, for smoking. **5** a musical instrument with a single tube into which the player blows. **6** pipes, *pl.* **a** set of musical tubes: *the pipes of Pan.* **b** bagpipe. **7** play on a pipe. **8** any one of the tubes in an organ. **9** make a shrill noise; sing in a shrill voice. **10** a shrill sound, voice, or song: *the pipe of the lark.* 1,4-6,8,10 *n.,* 2,3,7,9 *v.,* **piped, pip ing. —pipe′like′,** *adj.*

pipe down, SLANG. be quiet; shut up.

pipe line (pīp′līn′), **1** line of pipes for carrying oil or other liquids. **2** source of information, usually secret. *n.*

pip er (pī′pər), person who plays on a pipe or bagpipe. *n.*

pay the piper, pay for one's pleasure; bear the consequences.

pipette
Uncovering the top of the tube allows the liquid to flow from the other end.

pi pette (pī pet′ *or* pi pet′), a slender pipe or tube for transferring or measuring small quantities of liquids. *n.*

pip ing (pī′ping), **1** a shrill sound: *the piping of frogs in the spring.* **2** shrill. **3** so as to hiss; boiling: *The tea is piping hot.* **4** pipes: *lead piping.* **5** material for pipes. **6** music of pipes. **7** a narrow band of material, sometimes containing a cord, used for trimming along edges and seams. 1,4-7 *n.,* 2,3 *adj.*

pip it (pip′it), a small bird somewhat like a lark, that sings while flying; tit-lark. *n.*

pip pin (pip′ən), any of several kinds of apple: *a yellow pippin.* *n.*

pi quan cy (pē′kən sē), **1** quality of exciting the mind pleasantly. **2** quality of exciting the appetite, being odd to the taste, or pleasantly sharp. *n.*

pi quant (pē′kənt), **1** stimulating to the mind, interest, etc.: *a piquant bit of news, a piquant face.* **2** pleasantly sharp; stimulating to the taste: *a piquant sauce. adj.*

pique (pēk), **1** a feeling of anger at being slighted; wounded pride: *In a pique, he left the party.* **2** cause a feeling of anger in; wound the pride of: *It piqued her that they should have a secret she did not share.* **3** arouse; stir up: *The children's curiosity was piqued by the locked trunk.* 1 *n.,* 2,3 *v.,* **piqued, pi quing.**

pique oneself on, feel proud about: *She piqued herself on her carpentry skills.*

pi qué (pi kā′), fabric of cotton, rayon, or silk, with narrow ribs or raised stripes. *n.* [from French]

pi ra cy (pī′rə sē), **1** robbery on the sea. **2** act of publishing or using a book, play, invention, etc., without permission. *n., pl.* **pi ra cies.**

pi rate (pī′rit), **1** person who attacks and robs ships unlawfully; robber on the sea; buccaneer; freebooter. **2** be a pirate; plunder; rob. **3** ship used by pirates. **4** publish or use without the author's, inventor's, or owner's permission. 1,3 *n.,* 2,4 *v.,* **pi rat ed, pi rat ing.**

pi rat i cal (pī rat′ə kəl), of pirates; like pirates; like piracy. *adj.*

pi rogue (pə rōg′), **1** canoe hollowed from the trunk of a tree; dugout. **2** any canoe. *n.*

pir ou ette (pir′ü et′), **1** a whirling about on one foot or on the toes, as in dancing. **2** whirl in this way. 1 *n.,* 2 *v.,* **pir ou et ted, pir ou et ting.**

Pi sa (pē′zə), city in NW Italy, famous for its leaning tower. *n.*

pis ta chi o (pi stä′shē ō *or* pi-stash′ē ō), **1** a greenish nut having a flavor that suggests almond. **2** a small tree that it grows on. **3** the flavor of this nut. **4** a light green. **5** light-green. 1-4 *n., pl.* **pis ta chi os;** 5 *adj.*

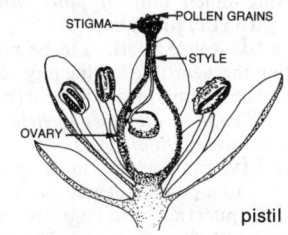

STIGMA — POLLEN GRAINS

— STYLE

OVARY —

pistil

pis til (pis′tl), the part of a flower that produces seeds. It consists, when complete, of an ovary, a style, and a stigma. *n.*

pis til late (pis′tl āt), **1** having a pistil or pistils. **2** having a pistil or pistils but no stamens. *adj.*

pis tol (pis′tl), a small, short gun held and fired with one hand. *n.*

CYLINDER

PISTON RING

PISTON ROD **PISTON**

pis ton (pis′tən), a short cylinder, or a flat, round piece of wood or metal, fitting closely inside a tube or hollow cylinder in which it is moved back and forth by the force of exploding vapor or steam. A piston receives or transmits motion by means of a piston rod that is

hat, āge, fär; let, ēqual, tėrm;
it, īce; hot, ōpen, ôrder;
oil, out; cup, pùt, rüle; ch, child;
ng, long; sh, she; th, thin;
ŦH, then; zh, measure;

ə represents *a* in about,
e in taken, *i* in pencil,
o in lemon, *u* in circus.

attached to it. Pistons are used in pumps, engines, compressors, etc. *n.*

piston ring, a metal ring fitted in a groove around a piston to ensure a tight fit against the cylinder wall.

piston rod, a rod by which a piston imparts motion, or by which motion is imparted to it.

pit[1] (pit), **1** a natural hole in the ground. **2** hole dug deep into the earth. A mine or the shaft of a mine is a pit. **3** hollow on the surface of anything. The pit of the stomach is the place just below the breastbone where in most people there is a slight hollow or depression. **4** a little hole or scar, such as is left by smallpox. **5** to mark with small pits or scars. **6** a covered hole used as a trap for wild animals. **7** place where dogs or cocks are made to fight. **8** set to fight or compete; match: *She was pitted against her friend in the finals of the tennis ma ch.* **9** hell. 1-4,6,7,9 *n.,* 5,8 *v.,* **pit ted, pit ting.** [Old English *pytt,* from Latin *puteus* pit, well]

pit[2] (pit), **1** the hard seed of a cherry, peach, plum, date, etc.; stone. **2** remove pits from (fruit). 1 *n.,* 2 *v.,* **pit ted, pit ting.** [from Dutch *pit* kernel]

pit a pat (pit′ə pat′), pitter-patter. *n.*

pitch[1] (pich), **1** throw or fling; hurl; toss: *They were pitching horseshoes.* **2** throw (a baseball, etc.) for the batter to hit. **3** fix firmly in the ground; set up: *pitch a tent.* **4** fall or plunge forward: *The man lost his balance and pitched down the cliff.* **5** plunge with the bow rising and then falling: *The ship pitched about in the storm.* **6** set at a certain point, degree, or level. **7** determine the key of (a tune, etc.). **8** point; position; degree: *That family has reached the lowest pitch of bad fortune.* **9** degree of highness or lowness of a sound. Notes in music with a low pitch have a slower rate of vibration than those with a high pitch. **10** height: *the pitch of an arch.* **11** act or manner of pitching. **12** that which is pitched. **13** slope downward; incline; dip. **14** amount of slope: *Some roads in the Rocky Mountains have a very steep pitch.* 1-7,13 *v.,* 8-12,14 *n.,*

pitch

pl. **pitch es.** [Middle English *picchen*]
pitch in, INFORMAL. work vigorously: *All the neighbors pitched in to build the new barn.*

pitch into, INFORMAL. attack.

pitch² (pich), 1 a thick, black, sticky substance made from tar or turpentine, used to fill the seams of wooden ships, to cover roofs, to make pavements, etc. 2 cover with pitch. 3 resin from certain evergreen trees. 1,3 *n., pl.* **pitch es;** 2 *v.* [Old English *pic,* from Latin *picem*] —**pitch/like/ , *adj.***

pitch-black (pich/blak/), very black or dark. *adj.*

pitch blende (pich/blend/), mineral consisting largely of an oxide of uranium, occurring in black, pitchlike masses. It is a source of radium, uranium, and actinium. *n.*

pitch-dark (pich/därk/), pitch-black. *adj.*

pitched battle, battle with troops properly arranged.

pitch er¹ (pich/ər), 1 container for holding and pouring liquids, with a lip on one side and a handle on the other. 2 amount that a pitcher holds. *n.* [from French of the 1200's *pichier*]

pitch er² (pich/ər), the player on a baseball team who throws the ball for the batter to hit. *n.* [*pitch¹* + *-er¹*]

pitch er ful (pich/ər fùl), quantity sufficient to fill a pitcher. *n., pl.* **pitch er fuls.**

pitcher plant, plant with leaves shaped somewhat like a pitcher. These leaves often contain a liquid secretion in which insects are captured and digested by the plant.

pitch fork (pich/fôrk/), a large fork with a long handle, for lifting and throwing hay, etc.; hayfork. *n.*

pitchfork

pitch pipe, a small musical pipe having one or more notes, used to give the pitch for singing or for tuning an instrument.

pitch y (pich/ē), 1 full of pitch. 2 like pitch; sticky. 3 black. *adj.,* **pitch i er, pitch i est.**

pit e ous (pit/ē əs), to be pitied; moving the heart; deserving pity: *The child's sad face was piteous. adj.* —**pit/e ous ly,** *adv.* —**pit/e ous ness,** *n.*

pit fall (pit/fôl/), 1 a hidden pit to catch animals in. 2 any trap or hidden danger. *n.*

pith (pith), 1 the central, spongy tissue in the stems of certain plants. 2 a similar tissue occurring in other parts of plants, as that lining the skin of an orange. 3 the soft inner substance of a bone, feather, etc. 4 the important or essential part: *the pith of a speech.* 5 strength; energy. *n.*

pith i ly (pith/ə lē), in a pithy manner; forcibly; concisely. *adv.*

pith y (pith/ē), 1 full of substance, meaning, force, or vigor: *pithy phrases, a pithy speaker.* 2 of or like pith. 3 having much pith: *a pithy orange. adj.,* **pith i er, pith i est.**

pit i a ble (pit/ē ə bəl), 1 to be pitied; moving the heart; deserving pity. 2 deserving contempt; mean; to be scorned: *His half-hearted attempts to help with the work were pitiable. adj.*

pit i a bly (pit/ē ə blē), in a pitiable manner; to a pitiable degree. *adv.*

pit i ful (pit/i fəl), 1 to be pitied; moving the heart; deserving pity: *The deserted children were pitiful.* 2 feeling or showing pity; feeling sorrow for the trouble of others. 3 deserving contempt; mean; to be scorned: *Driving away after hitting a dog is a pitiful act. adj.* —**pit/i ful ly,** *adv.*

pit i less (pit/ē lis), without pity or mercy. *adj.* —**pit/i less ly,** *adv.*

Pitt (pit), 1 **William,** 1708-1778, the first Earl of Chatham, English statesman. 2 his son, **William,** 1759-1806, prime minister of England from 1783 to 1801 and from 1804 to 1806. *n.*

pit tance (pit/ns), 1 a small allowance of money. 2 a small amount or share. *n.*

pit ter-pat ter (pit/ər pat/ər), a quick succession of light beats or taps; pitapat: *the pitter-patter of rain, the pitter-patter of a child's steps. n.*

Pitts burgh (pits/bėrg/), city in SW Pennsylvania, a center of the iron and steel industry. *n.*

pi tu i tar y (pə tü/ə ter/ē *or* pə tyü/ə ter/ē), 1 the pituitary gland. 2 having to do with the pituitary gland. 1 *n.,* 2 *adj.*

pituitary gland, a small, oval endocrine gland situated at the base of the brain. It secretes hormones that promote growth, stimulate other glands, and regulate many bodily functions.

pit y (pit/ē), 1 sorrow for another's suffering or distress; feeling for the sorrows of others; sympathy. 2 feel pity for: *I pitied the sobbing child.* 3 cause for pity or regret; thing to be sorry for: *It is a pity to be kept in the house in good weather.* 1,3 *n., pl.* **pit ies;** 2 *v.,* **pit ied, pit y ing.** —**pit/y ing ly,** *adv.*

have pity on or **take pity on,** show pity for.

Pi us XII (pī/əs), 1876-1958, pope from 1939 to 1958.

piv ot (piv/ət), 1 shaft, pin, or point on which something turns. 2 mount on, attach by, or provide with a pivot. 3 turn on a pivot: *pivot on one's heel.* 4 a turn on a pivot. 5 that on which something turns, hinges, or depends; central point: *His pitching was the pivot of our hopes.* 1,4,5 *n.,* 2,3 *v.*

piv ot al (piv/ə təl), 1 of, having to do with, or serving as a pivot. 2 being that on which something turns, hinges, or depends; very important. *adj.*

pix y or **pix ie** (pik/sē), fairy or elf. *n., pl.* **pix ies.**

Pi zar ro (pi zär/ō), **Francisco,** 1471?-1541, Spanish conqueror of Peru. *n.*

piz za (pēt/sə), a spicy Italian dish made by baking a large flat layer of bread dough covered with cheese, tomato sauce, herbs, etc. *n., pl.* **piz zas.**

piz ze ri a (pēt/sə rē/ə), restaurant or bakery where pizzas are baked and sold. *n., pl.* **piz ze ri as.**

pk., 1 park. 2 peak. 3 peck.

pkg., package.

pl., 1 place. 2 plural.

pla ca ble (plā/kə bəl), that may be placated. *adj.*

plac ard (plak/ärd), 1 notice to be posted in a public place; poster. 2 put placards on or in: *The circus placarded the city with advertisements.* 1 *n.,* 2 *v.*

pla cate (plā/kāt *or* plak/āt), soothe or satisfy the anger of; make peaceful; appease: *placate a person one has offended. v.,* **pla cat ed, pla cat ing.**

place (plās), 1 the part of space occupied by a person or thing. 2 city, town, village, district, etc.: *What place do you come from?* 3 building or spot used for a certain purpose: *A school is a place of learning. A store or office is a place of business.* 4 house; house and grounds; dwelling: *Her parents have a beautiful place in the country.* 5 part or spot in something: *a sore place on one's foot. The dentist filled the decayed place in the tooth.* 6 the proper or natural position: *books in place on shelves.*

There is a time and place for everything.
7 rank; position; way of life: *She won first place in the essay contest. They have a high place in society.* **8** position in time; part of time occupied by an event: *The performance went too slowly in several places.* **9** (in arithmetic) position of a figure in a number or series: *in the third decimal place.* **10** space or seat for a person: *Keep a place for me if you reach the boat first.* **11** put (in a spot, position, condition, or relation): *The orphan was placed in a good home. The people placed confidence in their leader.* **12** give the place, position, or condition of; identify: *I remember his name, but I cannot place him.* **13** finish among the leaders in a race or competition: *I failed to place in the first race and was eliminated.* **14** situation; post or office; official employment or position: *get a place in a store.* **15** appoint (a person) to a post or office; find a situation, etc., for. **16** duty; business: *It is not my place to find fault.* **17** a step or point in order of proceeding: *In the first place, the room is too small; in the second place, it is too dirty.* **18** a short street or court: *Waverley Place.* 1-10,14,16-18 *n.,* 11-13,15 *v.,* **placed, plac ing.**

give place, 1 make room. **2** yield; give in: *My anger gave place to remorse.*

in place, 1 in the proper or usual place; in the original place. **2** fitting, appropriate, or timely.

in place of, instead of: *Use water in place of milk in that recipe.*

know one's place, act according to one's position in life.

out of place, 1 not in the proper or usual place. **2** inappropriate or ill-timed.

take place, happen; occur.

place kick, the kicking of a ball placed or held on the ground in football, soccer, etc.

plaid (def. 1)

place-kick (plās′kik′), make a place kick. *v.*

place mat, a mat of linen, plastic, paper, etc., put under a person's plate or table setting.

place ment (plās′mənt), **1** a placing or a being placed; location; arrange-

ment. **2** the finding of work or a job for a person. **3** a placing of a football on the ground for an attempt to kick a goal by a place kick. *n.*

pla cen ta (plə sen′tə), organ by which the fetus is attached to the wall of the uterus and nourished. *n., pl.* **pla cen tas.**

plac er (plas′ər), deposit of sand, gravel, or earth in the bed of a stream, containing particles of gold or other valuable minerals. *n.*

plac id (plas′id), pleasantly calm or peaceful; quiet: *a placid lake, a placid temper. adj.* —**plac′id ly,** *adv.*

pla cid i ty (plə sid′ə tē), calmness; peace; tranquility. *n.*

plack et (plak′it), an opening or slit in a garment, especially at the top of a skirt, to make it easy to put on. *n.*

pla gia rism (plā′jə riz′əm), act of plagiarizing. *n.*

pla giar ist (plā′jər ist), person who plagiarizes. *n.*

pla gia rize (plā′jə rīz′), take and use as one's own (the thoughts, writings, etc., of another), especially to take and use (a passage, plot, etc.) from the work of another writer. *v.,* **pla gia rized, pla gia riz ing.**

plague (plāg), **1** a very dangerous disease that spreads rapidly and often causes death. It occurs in several forms, one of which is bubonic plague. The plague is common in Asia and has several times swept through Europe. **2** any epidemic disease; pestilence. **3** punishment thought to be sent from God. **4** cause to suffer from a plague. **5** thing or person that torments, vexes, annoys, troubles, offends, or is disagreeable. **6** vex; annoy; bother: *The people of the colony were plagued with high taxes.* 1-3,5 *n.,* 4,6 *v.,* **plagued, pla guing.**

plaice (plās), **1** a European flatfish that is important for food. It sometimes weighs more than ten pounds. **2** any of various American flatfishes or flounders. *n., pl.* **plaice** or **plaic es.**

plaid (plad), **1** a long piece of woolen cloth, usually having a pattern of checks or stripes in many colors, worn over one shoulder by the Scottish Highlanders. **2** any cloth with a pattern of checks or crisscross stripes. **3** a pattern of this kind. **4** having a pattern of checks or crisscross stripes: *a plaid dress.* 1-3 *n.,* 4 *adj.*

plain (plān), **1** easy to understand; easily seen or heard; clear: *The meaning is plain.* **2** in a plain manner; clearly. **3** without ornament or decoration; simple: *a plain dress.* **4** without figured pattern, varied weave, or variegated color: *a plain blue fabric.* **5** not rich or highly seasoned: *plain food.* **6** com-

---

plane

hat, āge, fär; let, ēqual, tèrm;
it, īce; hot, ōpen, ôrder;
oil, out; cup, pùt, rüle; ch, child;
ng, long; sh, she; th, thin;
ŦH, then; zh, measure;

ə represents *a* in about,
e in taken, *i* in pencil,
o in lemon, *u* in circus.

---

mon; ordinary; simple in manner: *a plain man of the people.* **7** not beautiful or handsome. **8** not very hard; easy. **9** frank; honest; sincere: *plain speech.* **10** flat; level; smooth. **11** a flat stretch of land; prairie: *Cattle and horses wandered over the plains.* 1,3-10 *adj.,* 2 *adv.,* 11 *n.* —**plain′ly,** *adv.* —**plain′ness,** *n.*

plains man (plānz′mən), man who lives on the plains. *n., pl.* **plains men.**

plain-spo ken (plān′spō′kən), plain or frank in speech. *adj.*

plaint (plānt), **1** complaint. **2** OLD USE. lament. *n.*

plain tiff (plān′tif), person who begins a lawsuit: *The plaintiff accused the defendant of fraud. n.*

plain tive (plān′tiv), mournful; sad: *a plaintive song. adj.* —**plain′tive ly,** *adv.*

plait (plāt *or* plat), **1** a braid of hair, ribbon, etc.: *She wore her hair in a plait.* **2** to braid: *She plaits her hair.* **3** a flat, usually narrow, fold made in cloth by doubling it on itself; a pleat. **4** fold or arrange in plaits; pleat: *a plaited skirt.* 1,3 *n.,* 2,4 *v.*

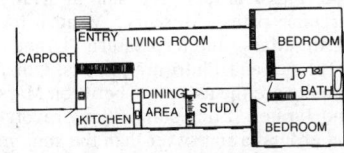

plan (def. 4) of a house

plan (plan), **1** way of making or doing something that has been worked out beforehand; scheme of action: *Our summer plans were upset by mother's illness.* **2** think out beforehand how (something) is to be made or done; design, scheme, or devise: *plan a trip.* **3** have in mind as a purpose; intend. **4** a drawing or diagram to show how a garden, a floor of a house, a park, etc., is arranged. **5** make a drawing or diagram of. 1,4 *n.,* 2,3,5 *v.,* **planned, planning.**

plane[1] (plān), **1** any flat or level surface. **2** flat; level. **3** level; grade: *Try to keep your work on a high plane.* **4** a

641

plane

adj.	adjective	*n.*	noun
adv.	adverb	*prep.*	preposition
conj.	conjunction	*pron.*	pronoun
interj.	interjection	*v.*	verb
sing.	singular	*pl.*	plural

thin, flat or curved supporting surface of an airplane. 5 airplane. 6 surface such that if any two points on it are joined by a straight line, the line will be contained wholly in the surface. 7 of or having to do with figures wholly in a plane: *plane geometry.* 1,3-6 *n.,* 2,7 *adj.* [from Latin *planum* level place]

plane² (def. 1)

plane² (plān), 1 a carpenter's tool with a blade for smoothing or shaping wood. 2 smooth (wood) with a plane. 3 remove with a plane. 1 *n.,* 2,3 *v.,* **planed, plan ing.** [from French of the 1300's *plane,* from Latin *plana,* from *planare* make level]

plan er (plā′nər), person or thing that planes, especially a machine for planing wood or for finishing flat surfaces on metal. *n.*

plan et (plan′it), 1 one of the heavenly bodies (except comets and meteors) that move around the sun in nearly circular paths. Mercury, Venus, the earth, Mars, Jupiter, Saturn, Uranus, Neptune, and Pluto are planets. Other planets are the asteroids between Mars and Jupiter. 2 any similar body revolving around a star other than the sun. *n.*

plan e tar i um (plan′ə ter′ē əm *or* plan′ə tar′ē əm), 1 apparatus that shows the movements of the sun, moon, planets, and stars by projecting lights on the inside of a dome. 2 room or building with such an apparatus. *n., pl.* **plan e tar i a** (plan′ə ter′ē ə *or* plan′-ə tar′ē ə), **plan e tar i ums.**

plan e tar y (plan′ə ter′ē), of a planet; having to do with planets. *adj.*

plan et oid (plan′ə toid), asteroid. *n.*

plane tree, the sycamore tree of America.

plank (plangk), 1 a long, flat piece of sawed timber thicker than a board. 2 cover or furnish with planks. 3 cook on a board: *Steak is sometimes planked.* 4 article or feature of the platform of a political party or other organization. 1,4 *n.,* 2,3 *v.*

plank down, INFORMAL. put down or pay down and there: *He planked down the package. She planked down her money.*

walk the plank, be put to death by being forced to walk off a plank extending from a ship's side over the water. Pirates used to make their prisoners do this.

plank ing (plang′king), 1 act of laying or covering with planks. 2 planks collectively. *n.*

plank ton (plangk′tən), the small animal and plant organisms that float or drift in water, especially at or near the surface. *n.*

plan ner (plan′ər), person who plans. *n.*

plant (plant), 1 any living thing that is not an animal. Plants lack a nervous system and sense organs, and are unable to move about by themselves. Plants containing chlorophyll manufacture their own food. Trees, shrubs, herbs, fungi, algae, etc., are plants. 2 a living thing that has leaves, roots, and a soft stem, and is small in contrast with a tree or shrub: *a tomato plant, a house plant.* 3 a young growth ready to be set out in another place: *The farmer set out 100 cabbage plants.* 4 put or set in the ground to grow: *Farmers plant seeds.* 5 furnish; stock; put seed in: *He planted his garden with beans.* 6 set firmly; put; place: *The boy planted his feet far apart.* 7 establish or set up (a colony, city, etc.). 8 put in or instill (principles, doctrines, ideas, etc.): *Parents try to plant ideals in their children.* 9 the buildings, machinery, etc., used in manufacturing some article. 1-3,9 *n.,* 4-8 *v.*

Plan tag e net (plan taj′ə nit), member of the royal family that ruled England from 1154 to 1485. *n.*

plan tain¹ (plan′tən), 1 kind of large banana. 2 plant that it grows on. *n.* [from Spanish *plátano*]

plan tain² (plan′tən), a common weed with large, spreading leaves close to the ground and long, slender spikes carrying flowers and seeds. *n.* [from French of the 1300's *plantain,* from Latin *plantanus*]

plan ta tion (plan tā′shən), 1 a large farm or estate, especially in a tropical or semitropical country, on which cotton, tobacco, sugar cane, rubber trees, etc., are grown. The work on a plantation is done by laborers who live there. 2 a large group of trees or other plants that have been planted: *a rubber plantation.* 3 colony; settlement. *n.*

plant er (plan′tər), 1 person who owns or runs a plantation: *a cotton planter.* 2 machine for planting: *a corn planter.* 3 person who plants. 4 an early settler; colonist. 5 a box, stand, or other holder, usually decorative, for plants. *n.*

plant louse, aphid.

plaque (plak), 1 an ornamental tablet of metal, porcelain, etc. 2 a platelike ornament or badge. 3 a thin film of saliva and food particles which forms on the surface of the teeth. *n.*

plasm (plaz′əm), plasma. *n.*

plas ma (plaz′mə), 1 the clear, almost colorless, liquid part of blood or lymph, in which the corpuscles or blood cells float. Plasma consists of water, salts, proteins, and other substances, and it makes up the largest part of the blood. 2 the watery part of milk, as distinguished from the globules of fat. *n.*

plas ter (plas′tər), 1 a soft mixture of lime, sand, and water that hardens in drying, used for covering walls or ceilings. 2 cover (walls, ceilings, etc.) with plaster. 3 spread with anything thickly: *Her shoes were plastered with mud.* 4 make smooth and flat: *He plastered his hair down.* 5 a medical preparation consisting of some substance spread on cloth, that will stick to the body and protect cuts, relieve pain, etc. 6 apply a plaster to. 7 apply like a plaster. 1,5 *n.,* 2-4,6,7 *v.*

plas ter board (plas′tər bôrd′), a large, flat board made of a layer of plaster between two layers of heavy paper and used to cover walls and partitions. *n.*

plas ter er (plas′tər ər), person who plasters walls, etc. *n.*

plas ter ing (plas′tər ing), covering of plaster on walls, etc. *n.*

plaster of Paris, mixture of powdered gypsum and water, which hardens quickly. It is used for making molds, cheap statuary, casts, etc.

plas tic (plas′tik), 1 any of a large group of substances made chemically from materials such as coal, water, and limestone, and molded by heat, pressure, etc., into various forms, such as sheets, fibers, and bottles. Nylon, vinyl, and many cellulose products are plastics. 2 made of plastic: *a plastic bottle, a plastic dish or toy.* 3 easily molded or shaped: *Clay, wax, and plaster are plastic substances.* 4 molding or giving shape to material: *Sculpture is a plastic art.* 1 *n.,* 2-4 *adj.*

plas tic i ty (pla stis′ə tē), plastic quality. *n.*

plas ti cize (plas′tə sīz), make or become plastic. *v.,* **plas ti cized, plas ti-ciz ing.**

plastic surgery, surgery that restores or improves the outer appearance of the body.

plat (plat), 1 a map, chart, or plan. 2 map out in detail; chart; plan. 3 a small piece of ground; plot. 1,3 *n.*, 2 *v.*, **plat ted, plat ting.**

plate (plāt), 1 dish, usually round, that is almost flat. Our food is served on plates. 2 contents of such a dish: *a small plate of stew.* 3 something having the shape of a plate: *A plate is passed in church to receive the collection.* 4 dishes and food served to one person at a meal. 5 dishes or utensils of silver or gold: *The family plate included a silver pitcher, candlesticks, and the usual knives, forks, and spoons.* 6 dishes and utensils covered with a thin layer of silver or gold. 7 cover with a thin layer of silver, gold, or other metal. 8 a thin, flat sheet or piece of metal: *The warship was covered with steel plates.* 9 cover with metal plates for protection. 10 a thin, flat piece of metal on which something is engraved. Plates are used for printing pictures. 11 something printed from such a piece of metal, especially a full-page illustration printed on special paper. 12 a metal copy of a page of type. 13 a thin sheet of glass coated with chemicals that are sensitive to light. Plates are sometimes used in taking photographs. 14 piece of metal or other firm material with false teeth set into it. 15 home plate. 16 a thin cut of beef from the lower end of the ribs. 17 the positive electrode in a vacuum tube. 1-6,8,10-17 *n.*, 7,9 *v.*, **plat ed, plat ing. —plate′like′,** *adj.*

plateau (def. 1)

pla teau (pla tō′), 1 plain in the mountains or at a height above the sea; large, high plain; tableland. 2 a level, especially the level at which something is stabilized for a period. *n., pl.* **plateaus, pla teaux** (pla tōz′).

plate ful (plāt′fùl), as much as a plate will hold. *n., pl.* **plate fuls.**

plate glass, thick and very clear glass made in smooth, polished sheets, used for large windowpanes, mirrors, etc.

plate let (plāt′lit), one of many small disks which float in the blood plasma and are involved in blood clotting. *n.*

plat form (plat′fôrm), 1 a raised level surface. There usually is a platform beside the track at a railroad station. A hall usually has a platform for speakers. 2 plan of action or statement of principles of a group. A political party has a platform made up of planks. *n.*

plat ing (plā′ting), 1 a thin layer of silver, gold, or other metal. 2 a covering of metal plates. *n.*

plat i num (plat′n əm), a heavy, silver-white, metallic element with a very high melting point. Platinum is a precious metal which is resistant to acid and does not tarnish easily. It is used in chemical and industrial equipment and in jewelry. *n.*

plat i tude (plat′ə tüd *or* plat′ə tyüd), 1 a dull or commonplace remark, especially one given out solemnly as if it were fresh and important: *"Better late than never" is a platitude.* 2 flatness; triteness; dullness. *n.*

Pla to (plā′tō), 427?-347? B.C., Greek philosopher who was the pupil of Socrates and the teacher of Aristotle. *n.*

Pla ton ic (plə ton′ik), 1 of or having to do with Plato or his philosophy. 2 Also, **platonic.** friendly but not like a lover. 3 idealistic; not practical: *The League of Nations seemed a Platonic scheme to many people.* *adj.*

pla toon (plə tün′), 1 a military unit made up of two or more squads, usually commanded by a lieutenant. It is smaller than a company. 2 a small group. *n.*

Platte (plat), river flowing from central Nebraska into the Missouri River. *n.*

plat ter (plat′ər), a large, shallow dish for holding or serving food, especially meat and fish. *n.*

plat y pus (plat′ə pəs), duckbill. *n., pl.* **plat y pus es, plat y pi** (plat′ə pī).

plau dit (plô′dit). Usually, **plaudits,** *pl.* round of applause; enthusiastic expression of approval or praise: *The actress bowed in response to the plaudits of the audience.* *n.*

plau si bil i ty (plô′zə bil′ə tē), appearance of being true or reasonable; plausible quality. *n.*

plau si ble (plô′zə bəl), 1 appearing true, reasonable, or fair. 2 apparently worthy of confidence but often not really so: *a plausible liar.* *adj.*

plau si bly (plô′zə blē), with an appearance of truth or trustworthiness; in a way that seems true or right: *The story was plausibly told—whether it was true or not remains to be seen.* *adv.*

play (plā), 1 something done to amuse oneself; fun; sport; recreation: *The children are happy at play.* 2 have fun; do something in sport: *The kitten plays with its tail. He played a joke on his sister.* 3 take part in (a game): *Children play tag and ball.* 4 take part in a game against: *Our team played the sixth-grade team.* 5 cause to play. 6 a turn, move, or act in a game: *It is your play next.* 7 act of carrying on a game: *Play was slow in the first half of the game.* 8 a story written for or presented as a dramatic performance; drama: *"Peter Pan" is a charming play.* 9 act a part; act the part of (a character in a play, etc.). 10 act in a specified way: *play sick, play*

hat, āge, fär; let, ēqual, tèrm;
it, īce; hot, ōpen, ôrder;
oil, out; cup, pùt, rüle; ch, child;
ng, long; sh, she; th, thin;
ŦH, then; zh, measure;

ə represents *a* in about,
e in taken, *i* in pencil,
o in lemon, *u* in circus.

fair, play the fool. 11 action; operation; working: *foul play, fair play. They brought all their strength into play to move the rock.* 12 make believe; pretend in fun: *Let's play the hammock is a boat.* 13 make music; produce (music) on an instrument. 14 perform on (a musical instrument): *play a piano.* 15 move lightly or quickly: *A breeze played on the water.* 16 a light, quick movement: *the play of sunlight on leaves, the play of color in an opal.* 17 freedom for action, movement, etc.: *The children gave their fancies full play in telling what they could do with a million dollars.* 18 cause to act, move, or work; direct (on, over, along): *play a hose on a burning building. The ship played its light along the coast.* 19 put into action in a game: *Play your ten of hearts.* 20 act carelessly; do foolish things: *Don't play with matches.* 21 gambling. 22 gamble or bet on: *He plays the horses.* 1,6-8,11,16,17,21 *n.*, 2-5,9, 10,12-15,18-20,22 *v.*

play down, make light of; understate.

played out, 1 exhausted. 2 finished; done with.

play off, 1 play an additional game or match in order to decide (a draw or tie). 2 pit (one person or thing against another), especially for one's own advantage.

play on or **play upon,** take advantage of; make use of: *We played on our friend's good nature, too often making her the victim of our jokes.*

play out, play to the end; bring to an end.

play up, make the most of; exploit.

play up to, SLANG. try to get the favor of; flatter: *play up to a celebrity.*

play bill (plā′bil′), 1 a handbill or placard announcing a play. 2 program of a play. *n.*

play boy (plā′boi′), man whose chief interest is in having a good time. *n.*

play er (plā′ər), 1 person who plays. 2 actor in a theater. 3 musician. 4 thing or device that plays. *n.*

play fel low (plā′fel′ō), playmate. *n.*

play ful (plā′fəl), 1 full of fun; fond of playing: *a playful puppy.* 2 joking;

adj. adjective	*n.* noun
adv. adverb	*prep.* preposition
conj. conjunction	*pron.* pronoun
interj. interjection	*v.* verb
sing. singular	*pl.* plural

not serious: *a playful remark. adj.*
—**play'ful ly,** *adv.* —**play'ful-
ness,** *n.*

play go er (plā′gō′ər), person who goes often to the theater. *n.*

play ground (plā′ground′), place for outdoor play. *n.*

play house (plā′hous′), 1 a small house for a child to play in. 2 doll-house. 3 theater. *n., pl.* **play hous es** (plā′hou′ziz).

playing card, card used in playing games like bridge, poker, and pinochle, usually being one of a set of 52 cards including 4 suits (spades, hearts, diamonds, and clubs) of 13 cards each.

play mate (plā′māt′), person who plays with another. *n.*

play-off (plā′ôf′), an extra game or round played to settle a tie. *n.*

play on words, pun.

play pen (plā′pen′), a small folding pen for a baby or young child to play in. *n.*

play room (plā′rüm′ *or* plā′rüm′), room for children to play in. *n.*

play thing (plā′thing′), thing to play with; toy. *n.*

play wright (plā′rīt′), writer of plays; dramatist. *n.*

plaz a (plaz′ə *or* plä′zə), a public square in a city or town. *n., pl.* **plaz as.**

plea (plē), 1 request or appeal; an asking: *a plea for pity.* 2 an excuse or defense: *The man's plea was that he did not see the signal.* 3 answer made by a defendant to a charge against him in a court of law. *n.*

plead (plēd), 1 offer reasons for or against; argue. 2 ask earnestly; make an earnest appeal: *When the rent was due, the young couple pleaded for more time.* 3 offer as an excuse: *The woman who stole pleaded poverty.* 4 speak for or against in a court of law: *He had a good lawyer to plead his case.* 5 answer to a charge in a court of law: *The defendant pleaded guilty. v.,* **plead ed** *or* **pled, plead ing.** —**plead′ing ly,** *adv.*

plead er (plē′dər), person who pleads, especially in a court of law. *n.*

pleas ant (plez′nt), 1 that pleases; giving pleasure; agreeable: *a pleasant swim on a hot day.* 2 easy to get along with; friendly. 3 fair; not stormy. *adj.*

—**pleas′ant ly,** *adv.* —**pleas′ant-
ness,** *n.*

pleas ant ry (plez′n trē), 1 a good-natured joke; witty remark. 2 joking. *n., pl.* **pleas ant ries.**

please (plēz), 1 be agreeable to: *Toys please children.* 2 be agreeable: *Such a fine meal cannot fail to please.* 3 wish; think fit: *Do what you please.* 4 be the will of: *May it please the court to show mercy.* 5 may it please you (now used merely as a polite addition to requests or commands): *Come here, please. v.,* **pleased, pleas ing.**

be pleased, 1 be moved to pleasure. 2 be disposed; like; choose.

if you please, if you like; with your permission.

pleas ing (plē′zing), giving pleasure; pleasant: *a pleasing smile, a very well-mannered and pleasing young person. adj.* —**pleas′ing ly,** *adv.*

pleas ur a ble (plezh′ər ə bəl), pleasant; agreeable. *adj.*

pleas ure (plezh′ər), 1 a feeling of being pleased; enjoyment; delight; joy: *The child's pleasure in the gift was good to see.* 2 something that pleases; cause of joy or delight: *It would be a pleasure to see you again.* 3 anything that amuses; sport; play: *She takes her pleasure in riding and hunting.* 4 one's will, desire, or choice: *What is your pleasure in this matter? n.*

pleat (def. 1)
pleats in a skirt

pleat (plēt), 1 a flat, usually narrow, fold made in cloth by doubling it on itself. 2 fold or arrange in pleats: *a pleated skirt.* 1 *n.,* 2 *v.*

ple be ian (pli bē′ən), 1 belonging or having to do with the common people; common; vulgar. 2 one of the common people. 3 belonging or having to do with the lower class of citizens in ancient Rome. 4 member of this class. 1,3 *adj.,* 2,4 *n.*

pleb i scite (pleb′ə sīt), a direct vote by the qualified voters of a state on some important question. *n.*

plec trum (plek′trəm), a small piece of ivory, horn, metal, etc., used for plucking the strings of a mandolin, lyre, zith-er, etc.; pick. *n., pl.* **plec trums, plec tra** (plek′trə).

pled (pled), INFORMAL. pleaded; a past tense and past participle of **plead.** *v.*

pledge (plej), 1 a solemn promise: *He made a pledge to give money to charity.* 2 promise solemnly: *We pledge allegiance to the flag.* 3 cause to promise solemnly; bind by a promise: *pledge*

hearers to secrecy. 4 something that secures or makes safe; security: *The knight left a jewel as pledge for the borrowed horse.* 5 give as security. 6 condition of being held as security. 7 drink a health to; drink in honor of (someone) and wish (him) well: *The nobles rose from the banquet table to pledge the queen.* 8 the drinking of a health or toast. 9 something given to show favor or love as a promise of something to come; sign; token. 1, 4,6,8,9 *n.,* 2,3,5,7 *v.,* **pledged, pledg-
ing.**

Ple ia des (plē′ə dēz′), 1 cluster of several hundred stars in the constellation Taurus. Six of these stars can normally be seen with the naked eye. 2 (in Greek myths) seven of the daughters of Atlas, who were transformed by the gods into this group of stars. *n.pl.*

ple nar y (plē′nər ē *or* plen′ər ē), 1 not lacking in any way; full; complete; absolute: *an ambassador with plenary power.* 2 attended by all of its qualified members: *a plenary session of a committee. adj.*

plen i po ten ti ar y (plen′ə pə ten′-
shē er′ē), 1 a diplomatic agent having full power or authority. 2 having or giving full power and authority. The United States has either an ambassador or a minister plenipotentiary in every important foreign country. 1 *n.,* **plen i-
po ten ti ar ies;** 2 *adj.*

plen i tude (plen′ə tüd *or* plen′ə-
tyüd), fullness; completeness; abundance. *n.*

plen te ous (plen′tē əs), plentiful. *adj.*

plen ti ful (plen′ti fəl), more than enough; ample; abundant: *We took along a plentiful supply of food on our camping trip. adj.* —**plen′ti ful ly,** *adv.*

plen ty (plen′tē), 1 a full supply; all that one needs; a large enough number or quantity: *You have plenty of time to catch the train.* 2 quality or condition of being plentiful; abundance: *years of peace and plenty. n.*

pleth or a (pleth′ər ə), excessive full-ness; too much; superabundance: *a plethora of words, a plethora of food. n.*

ple thor ic (ple thôr′ik *or* pleth′ər ik), too full; inflated: *a plethoric style of writing. adj.*

pleur a (plür′ə), a thin membrane covering each lung and folded back to make a lining for the thorax or chest cavity. *n., pl.* **pleur ae** (plür′ē).

pleur i sy (plür′ə sē), inflammation of the pleura, often marked by fever, chest pains, and difficulty in breathing. *n.*

plex us (plek′səs), network of nerve fibers or blood vessels. The solar plexus is a collection of nerves behind the stomach. *n., pl.* **plex us es** *or* **plex us.**

pli a bil i ty (plī′ə bil′ə tē), pliable condition or quality. *n.*

pli a ble (plī′ə bəl), 1 easily bent; flexible; supple: *Willow twigs are pliable.* 2 easily influenced; yielding: *He is too pliable to be a good leader. adj.*

pli an cy (plī′ən sē), pliant condition or quality. *n.*

pli ant (plī′ənt), 1 bending easily; flexible; supple: *pliant leather.* 2 easily influenced; yielding: *a pliant nature.* 3 changing easily to fit different conditions; adaptable. *adj.*

pliers

pli ers (plī′ərz), small pincers with long jaws for bending or cutting wire, holding small objects, etc. *n. pl. or sing.*

plight[1] (plīt), condition or situation, usually bad: *He was in a sad plight when he became ill and had no money. n.* [Middle English *plite* condition, (originally) manner of folding, from French of the 1300's *pleit,* from Latin *plicare* to fold]

plight[2] (plīt), 1 promise solemnly; pledge: *plight one's loyalty.* 2 a solemn promise; pledge. 1 *v.,* 2 *n.* [Old English *plihtan,* from *pliht* (originally) danger, risk]

plinth (plinth), 1 the lower, square part of the base of a column. 2 a square base of a pedestal. *n.*

plod (plod), 1 walk heavily: trudge: *The hikers plodded wearily along the road.* 2 proceed in a slow or dull way; work patiently with effort: *I plodded away at the lessons until I learned them. v.,* **plod ded, plod ding.**

plod der (plod′ər), 1 person who plods. 2 person who works hard but slowly. *n.*

plop (plop), 1 sound like that of a flat object striking water without a splash. 2 make such a sound. 1 *n.,* 2 *v.,* **plopped, plop ping.**

plot (plot), 1 secret plan, especially to do something wrong: *They formed a plot to rob the bank.* 2 plan secretly with others; plan: *The rebels plotted against the government.* 3 plan or main story of a play, novel, poem, etc.: *I like plots filled with action and adventure.* 4 a small piece of ground: *a garden plot.* 5 divide (land) into plots: *The farm was plotted out into house lots.* 6 map; diagram. 7 make a map or diagram of: *The nurse plotted a chart to show the patient's temperature over several days.* 8 mark the position of (something) on a map or diagram: *The nurse*

plotted the patient's temperature over several days. 1,3,4,6 *n.,* 2,5,7,8 *v.,* **plot ted, plot ting.**

plot ter (plot′ər), person who plots. *n.*

plough (plou), plow. *n., v.*

plough boy (plou′boi′), plowboy. *n.*

plough man (plou′mən), plowman. *n., pl.* **plough men.**

plough share (plou′sher′ or plou′-shar′), plowshare. *n.*

plov er (pluv′ər or plō′vər), a shore bird with a short tail and bill, and long, pointed wings. *n.*

plow (plou), 1 a farm implement used for cutting the soil and turning it over. 2 turn up the soil of with a plow; furrow: *plow a field.* 3 snowplow. 4 use a plow. 5 move through anything as a plow does; advance slowly and with effort: *The ship plowed through the waves.* 1,3 *n.,* 2,4,5 *v.* Also, **plough.**

plow boy (plou′boi′), boy who guides a plow or the horses drawing a plow. *n.* Also, **ploughboy.**

plow man (plou′mən), 1 person who guides a plow. 2 a farm worker. *n., pl.* **plowmen.** Also, **ploughman.**

MOLDBOARD   **PLOWSHARE**

plow share (plou′sher′ or plou′-shar′), blade of a plow; the part that cuts the soil. *n.* Also, **ploughshare.**

pluck (pluk), 1 pull off; pick: *She plucked flowers in the garden.* 2 pull at; pull; tug; jerk: *She plucked at the loose threads of her coat.* 3 act of picking or pulling. 4 pull on (the strings of a musical instrument). 5 pull off the feathers or hair from: *pluck a chicken.* 6 SLANG. rob; swindle. 7 courage: *The cat showed pluck in fighting the dog.* 1,2,4-6 *v.,* 3,7 *n.*

pluck up, get new courage; cheer up: *Pluck up! You aren't hurt badly.*

pluck i ly (pluk′ə lē), in a plucky manner; with courage or spirit. *adv.*

pluck i ness (pluk′ē nis), character of being plucky; pluck; courage. *n.*

pluck y (pluk′ē), having or showing courage: *a plucky dog. adj.,* **pluck i er, pluck i est.**

plug (plug), 1 piece of wood, etc., used to stop up a hole. 2 stop up or fill with a plug. 3 device to make an electrical connection. Some plugs screw into sockets; others have prongs. 4 hydrant. 5 cake of pressed tobacco; piece of this cut off for chewing. 6 SLANG. hit; shoot. 7 INFORMAL. work steadily; plod: *We plugged away at our typewriters.*

hat, āge, fär; let, ēqual, tėrm;
it, īce; hot, ōpen, ôrder;
oil, out; cup, pùt, rüle; ch, child;
ng, long; sh, she; th, thin;
ᵺ, then; zh, measure;

ə represents *a* in about,
e in taken, *i* in pencil,
o in lemon, *u* in circus.

8 INFORMAL. recommend or advertise, especially on a radio or television program: *plug a new product.* 9 INFORMAL. advertisement or recommendation, especially on a radio or television program. 10 INFORMAL. a worn-out or inferior horse. 1,3-5,9,10 *n.,* 2,6-8 *v.,* **plugged, plug ging.**

plug in, make an electrical connection by inserting a plug.

plum (plum), 1 a roundish, juicy fruit with a smooth skin and a stone or pit. There are purple, red, green, and yellow plums. 2 tree that it grows on. 3 raisin in a pudding, cake, etc. 4 something very good or desirable: *His new job is a fine plum.* 5 a dark, bluish purple. 6 dark bluish-purple. 1-5 *n.,* 6 *adj.* —**plum′like′,** *adj.*

plum age (plü′mij), feathers of a bird: *A parrot has bright plumage. n.*

plumb (plum), 1 a small weight used on the end of a line to find the depth of water or to see if a wall is vertical; plummet; lead. 2 to test or adjust by a plumb line; sound: *Our line was not long enough to plumb the depths of the lake.* 3 vertical. 4 get to the bottom of: *No one could plumb the deep mystery.* 5 INFORMAL. completely; thoroughly: *That horse is plumb worn out.* 1 *n.,* 2,4 *v.,* 3 *adj.,* 5 *adv.*

out of plumb or **off plumb,** not vertical.

plumb (def. 1) used to test vertical line of a wall

plumb er (plum′ər), person whose work is putting in and repairing water pipes and fixtures in buildings: *When the water pipe froze, we sent for a plumber. n.*

plumb ing (plum′ing), 1 work or trade of a plumber. 2 the water pipes and fixtures in a building: *bathroom plumbing. n.*

adj.	adjective	*n.*	noun
adv.	adverb	*prep.*	preposition
conj.	conjunction	*pron.*	pronoun
interj.	interjection	*v.*	verb
sing.	singular	*pl.*	plural

plumb line, line with a plumb at the end, used to find the depth of water or to see if a wall is vertical.

plume (plüm), 1 a large, long feather; feather. 2 a feather, bunch of feathers, or tuft of hair worn as an ornament on a hat, helmet, etc. 3 furnish with plumes. 4 smooth or arrange the feathers of: *The eagle plumed its wing.* 5 show pride in (oneself): *She plumed herself on her skill in tennis.* 1,2 *n.,* 3-5 *v.,* **plumed, plum ing.**

plum met (plum′it), 1 plumb. 2 plunge; drop: *to plummet into the sea.* 1 *n.,* 2 *v.*

plump[1] (plump), 1 rounded out; attractively fat: *A healthy baby has plump cheeks.* 2 make plump; become plump: *Plump the pillows on your bed.* 1 *adj.,* 2 *v.* [origin uncertain] —**plump′ness,** *n.*

plump[2] (plump), 1 fall or drop heavily or suddenly: *All out of breath, she plumped down on a chair.* 2 INFORMAL. a sudden plunge; heavy fall. 3 INFORMAL. sound made by a plunge or fall. 4 heavily or suddenly: *He ran plump into me.* 5 direct; downright; blunt: *a plump denial.* 1 *v.,* 2,3 *n.,* 4 *adv.,* 5 *adj.* [imitation of a heavy fall or drop]

plump for, give one's complete support to; champion vigorously: *plump for lower taxes.*

plum pudding, a rich, boiled or steamed pudding containing raisins, currants, spices, etc.

plum y (plü′mē), 1 having plumes or feathers. 2 adorned with a plume or plumes. 3 like a plume; feathery. *adj.*

plun der (plun′dər), 1 rob by force; rob: *The pirates entered the harbor and began to plunder the town.* 2 things taken in plundering; booty; loot: *They carried off the plunder in their ships.* 3 act of robbing by force: *In olden times soldiers gained great wealth by plunder of a conquered city.* 1 *v.,* 2,3 *n.* —**plun′der er,** *n.*

plunge (plunj), 1 throw or thrust with force into a liquid, place, or condition: *plunge one's hand into water, plunge the world into war.* 2 throw oneself (into water, danger, a fight, etc.): *He plunged into the river and saved the boy.* 3 rush; dash: *The fullback plunged forward five*

yards. 4 a jump or thrust; a dive: *Her plunge won the race.* 5 pitch suddenly and violently: *The ship plunged about in the storm.* 6 SLANG. gamble heavily. 1-3,5,6 *v.,* plunged, plung ing; 4 *n.*

plung er (plun′jər), 1 person or thing that plunges. 2 part of a machine, such as a piston in a pump, that acts with a plunging motion. 3 a rubber suction cup on a long stick, used for unplugging stopped-up drains, toilets, etc. *n.*

plunk (plungk), 1 pluck (a banjo, guitar, etc.). 2 make a sudden twanging sound like the plucking of a stringed musical instrument; twang. 3 put, drop, etc., heavily or suddenly. 4 INFORMAL. act or sound of plunking. 1-3 *v.,* 4 *n.*

plur al (plür′əl), 1 more than one in number: *"Girl" is singular; "girls" is plural.* 2 showing more than one in number: *the plural ending -s, the plural noun "fishes."* 3 the plural number in grammar. *Books* is the plural of *book; men,* of *man; are,* of *is; we,* of *I; these,* of *this.* 4 a word in the plural number. 1,2 *adj.,* 3,4 *n.*

plu ral i ty (plü ral′ə tē), 1 difference between the number of votes received by the winner of an election and the number received by the next highest candidate. 2 the greater number; the majority. 3 a large number; multitude. 4 state or fact of being plural. *n., pl.* **plu ral i ties.**

plur al ize (plür′ə līz), make plural; express in the plural form. *v.,* **plur al ized, plur al iz ing.**

plur al ly (plür′ə lē), in the plural number; so as to express or imply more than one. *adv.*

plus (plus), 1 added to: *3 plus 2 equals 5.* 2 and also: *The work of an engineer requires intelligence plus experience.* 3 and more: *a grade average of B plus.* 4 plus sign. 5 INFORMAL. additional; extra: *a plus value.* 1,2 *prep.,* 3,5 *adj.,* 4 *n.*

plush (plush), fabric like velvet but thicker and softer. *n.*

plus sign, the sign (+), indicating that the number or quantity following is to be added, or is a positive number or quantity.

Plu tarch (plü′tärk), A.D. 46?-120?, Greek who wrote biographies of famous Greeks and Romans. *n.*

Plu to (plü′tō), 1 (in Greek and Roman myths) the god of the region of the dead. 2 the eighth largest planet in the solar system and the farthest from the sun. *n.*

plu toc ra cy (plü tok′rə sē), 1 government in which the rich rule. 2 a ruling class of wealthy people. *n., pl.* **plu toc ra cies.**

plu to crat (plü′tə krat), 1 person who has power or influence because of

his wealth. 2 a wealthy person. *n.*

plu to ni um (plü tō′nē əm), a radioactive metallic element produced artificially from uranium and found in minute quantities in pitchblende and other uranium ores. It is used as a source of energy in nuclear reactors and bombs. *n.* [from *Pluto,* the planet]

plu vi al (plü′vē əl), 1 of or having to do with rain. 2 caused by rain. *adj.*

ply[1] (plī), 1 work with; use: *The dressmaker plies her needle.* 2 keep up work on; work away at or on: *to ply one's trade. We plied the water with our oars.* 3 urge again and again: *She plied me with questions to make me tell her what was in the package.* 4 supply with in a pressing manner: *ply a person with food or drink.* 5 go back and forth regularly between certain places: *A bus plies between the station and the hotel.* *v.,* **plied, ply ing.** [a different form of *apply,* from French of the 1300's *aplier,* from Latin *applicare*]

ply[2] (plī), thickness, fold, or twist. *n., pl.* **plies.** [from French of the 1400's *plier* to fold, from Latin *plicare*]

Plym outh (plim′əth), 1 seaport in SW England, on the English Channel. 2 town in SE Massachusetts. *n.*

Plymouth Colony, settlement established by the Pilgrims in 1620, on the site of Plymouth, Massachusetts.

Plymouth Rock, 1 rock at Plymouth, Massachusetts, on which the Pilgrims are said to have landed in 1620. 2 one of an American breed of medium-sized fowls kept for the production of meat and eggs.

ply wood (plī′wud′), board or boards made of several thin layers of wood glued together. *n.*

p.m. or **P.M.,** the time from noon to midnight: *School ends at 3 p.m.* [abbreviation of Latin *post meridiem* after noon]

pneu mat ic (nü mat′ik or nyü-mat′ik), 1 filled with air; containing air: *a pneumatic tire.* 2 worked by air: *a pneumatic drill.* 3 having to do with air and other gases. *adj.*

pneu mo nia (nü mō′nyə or nyü-mō′nyə), an infectious disease in which the lung becomes inflamed, often following a bad cold or other disease. Pneumonia in both lungs is called double pneumonia. *n.*

Po (pō), river flowing from NW Italy into the Adriatic Sea. *n.*

p.o. or **P.O.,** post office.

poach[1] (pōch), 1 trespass on (another's land), especially to hunt or fish. 2 take (game or fish) without any right. *v.* [from French of the 1500's *pocher* poke out]

poach[2] (pōch), cook (an egg) by breaking it into boiling water. *v.* [from

French of the 1400's *pochier*, from *poche* cooking spoon]

poach er (pō′chər), person who hunts or fishes on another's land without any right. *n.*

Po ca hon tas (pō′kə hon′təs), 1595?-1617, American Indian who in her childhood is said to have saved the life of Captain John Smith. *n.*

pock (pok), pimple, mark, or pit on the skin, caused by smallpox and certain other diseases. *n.*

pock et (pok′it), 1 a small bag sewed into clothing for carrying money or other small articles. 2 put in one's pocket. 3 meant to be carried in a pocket: *a pocket handkerchief.* 4 small enough to go in a pocket: *a pocket camera.* 5 a hollow place; enclosed place. 6 a small bag or pouch. 7 bag at the corner or side of a pool or billiard table. 8 hole in the earth containing gold or other ore; single lump of ore: *The miner struck a pocket of silver.* 9 shut in; hem in. 10 hold back; suppress; hide: *I pocketed my pride and said nothing.* 11 take and endure, without doing anything about it: *pocket an insult.* 12 take secretly or dishonestly: *Our partner pocketed the profits.* 13 air pocket. 1,5-8,13 *n.,* 2,9-12 *v.,* 3,4 *adj.*
be out of pocket, spend or lose money.

pock et book (pok′it bùk′), 1 a woman's purse. 2 a small, flat or folded case for carrying money, papers, etc., in a pocket; wallet. 3 a person's supply of money; income: *This coat is too expensive for my pocketbook. n.*

pock et ful (pok′it fùl), as much as a pocket will hold. *n., pl.* **pock et fuls.**

pock et knife (pok′it nīf′), a small knife with one or more blades that fold into the handle. *n., pl.* **pock et knives** (pok′it nīvz′).

pock et-size (pok′it sīz′), 1 small enough to go in a pocket: *a pocket-size radio, camera, etc.* 2 INFORMAL. small for its kind: *a pocket-size field. adj.*

pocket veto, method of vetoing a bill that can be used by the President of the United States on a bill presented to him within ten days of the end of a session of Congress. If the President does not sign the bill before Congress adjourns, it does not become a law.

pock mark (pok′märk′), mark or pit on the skin; pock. *n.*

pock marked (pok′märkt′), marked with pocks. *adj.*

pod (pod), 1 the shell or case in which plants like beans and peas grow their seeds. 2 produce pods. 1 *n.,* 2 *v.,* **pod ded, pod ding.**

po di um (pō′dē əm), a raised platform. The conductor of an orchestra or a speaker before an audience often stands on a podium. *n., pl.* **po di ums, po di a** (pō′dē ə).

Poe (pō), Edgar Allan, 1809-1849, American poet, critic, and writer of tales. *n.*

po em (pō′əm), 1 arrangement of words in lines having rhythm or a regularly repeated accent and, often, rhyme; composition in verse. 2 any composition showing great beauty or nobility of language or thought. *n.*

po e sy (pō′ə sē), OLD USE. poetry. *n.*

po et (pō′it), person who writes poetry. Dickinson and Scott were poets. *n.*

po et ess (pō′i tis), a woman poet. *n., pl.* **po et ess es.**

po et ic (pō et′ik), 1 having to do with poems or poets. 2 suitable for poems or poets. *Alas, o'er, plenteous,* and *blithe* are poetic words. 3 showing beautiful or noble language, imagery, or thought: *poetic fancies. adj.* —**po et′i cal ly,** *adv.*

po et i cal (pō et′ə kəl), poetic. *adj.*

poetic justice, ideal justice, with virtue being suitably rewarded and wickedness properly punished, as shown often in poems, plays, and stories.

poet laureate, 1 (in Great Britain) a poet appointed by the king or queen to write poems in celebration of court and national events. 2 any poet regarded as the best or most typical of his country or region. *pl.* **poets laureate.**

po et ry (pō′i trē), 1 poems: *a collection of poetry.* 2 art of writing poems: *Our class is studying the masters of English poetry.* 3 poetic quality; poetic spirit or feeling. *n.*

po go stick (pō′gō), toy consisting of a stick that contains a spring, and has footrests near the bottom and a handle at the top. One can hop from place to place by jumping up and down on the footrests, while holding the handle.

poign an cy (poi′nyən sē), a being poignant; sharpness; piercing quality: *poignancy of flavor, poignancy of delight. n.*

poign ant (poi′nyənt), 1 very painful; piercing: *poignant suffering.* 2 keen; intense: *a subject of poignant interest, a poignant delight.* 3 sharp to the taste or smell: *poignant sauces, poignant perfumes. adj.* —**poign′ant ly,** *adv.*

poin set ti a (poin set′ē ə), plant having a small flower surrounded by large, scarlet leaves that look like petals. Poinsettias are much used as Christmas decorations. *n., pl.* **poin set ti as.** [from Joel R. *Poinsett,* 1779-1851,

pod (def. 1)
opened to show peas

hat, āge, fär; let, ēqual, tėrm; it, īce; hot, ōpen, ôrder; oil, out; cup, pùt, rüle; ch, child; ng, long; sh, she; th, thin; ŦH, then; zh, measure;

ə represents *a* in about, *e* in taken, *i* in pencil, *o* in lemon, *u* in circus.

American diplomat who discovered the plant]

point (point), 1 a sharp end; something having a sharp end: *the point of a needle.* 2 sharpen: *point a pencil.* 3 a tiny round mark; a punctuation mark; dot: *A period is a point. Use a point to set off decimals.* 4 mark with dots; punctuate. 5 (in mathematics) something that has position without length or width. Two lines meet or cross at a point. 6 place; spot: *Stop at this point.* 7 any particular or definite position, condition, or time; degree; stage: *boiling point, freezing point.* 8 item; detail: *He answered my questions point by point.* 9 a distinguishing mark or quality: *Courage and endurance were her good points.* 10 the main idea or purpose; important or essential thing: *I missed the point of your talk.* 11 give force to (speech, action, etc.): *The teacher told a story to point her advice.* 12 direct a finger, weapon, etc.; aim; tend: *Don't point your gun at me.* 13 indicate position or direction, or direct attention with, or as if with, the finger: *He pointed the way to the village over the hills.* 14 (of a dog) show the presence of game by standing rigid and looking toward it. 15 have a specified direction: *The signboard points north.* 16 any of the 32 positions indicating direction marked at the circumference of the card of a compass. North, south, east, and west are the four main, or cardinal, points of the compass. 17 piece of land with a sharp end sticking out into the water; cape. 18 unit of scoring or measuring: *We won by three points. The price of my stock has gone up a point. The university accredited her with five points for the semester's work.* 1,3,5-10,16-18 *n.,* 2,4,11-15 *v.*

at the point of, in the act of; very near to: *at the point of leaving.*

beside the point, having nothing to do with the subject; not appropriate.

in point, pertinent: *a case in point.*

make a point of, insist upon: *He made a point of arriving on time.*

on the point of, just about; on the verge of: *She was on the point of*

647

adj.	adjective	*n.*	noun
adv.	adverb	*prep.*	preposition
conj.	conjunction	*pron.*	pronoun
interj.	interjection	*v.*	verb
sing.	singular	*pl.*	plural

going out when a neighbor came in.
point off, mark off with points or dots.
point out, show or call attention to: *Please point out my mistakes.*
stretch a point, 1 exceed the reasonable limit. **2** make a special exception.
to the point, appropriate to the subject at hand; apt: *His speech was brief and to the point.*
point-blank (point′blangk′ *for 1,2,4;* point′blangk′ *for 3,5),* **1** aimed straight at the mark. **2** close enough for aim to be taken in this way: *I fired the gun from point-blank range.* **3** straight at the mark: *to fire point-blank.* **4** plain and blunt; direct: *a point-blank question.* **5** plainly and bluntly; directly: *She gave excuses, but her friend refused point-blank.* *1,2,4 adj., 3,5 adv.*
point ed (poin′tid), **1** having a point or points: *a pointed roof.* **2** sharp; piercing: *a pointed wit.* **3** directed; aimed: *a pointed remark.* **4** emphatic: *She showed me pointed attention.* *adj.* —**point′ed ly,** *adv.*
point er (poin′tər), **1** person or thing that points. **2** a long, tapering stick used in pointing things out on a map, blackboard, etc. **3** hand of a clock, meter, etc. **4** a short-haired hunting dog trained to show where game is by standing rigid and looking toward it. **5** INFORMAL. hint; suggestion: *She gave him some pointers on improving his tennis.* **6** Also, **Pointers,** *pl.* the two stars in the Big Dipper which point to the North Star in the Little Dipper. *n.*
point less (point′lis), **1** without a point: *a pointless sword, a pointless pencil.* **2** without meaning or purpose: *a pointless question.* *adj.* —**point′less ly,** *adv.*
point of view, **1** position from which one looks at something. **2** attitude of mind: *Happy and sad people have different points of view toward life.*
poise (poiz), **1** mental balance, com-

poke³

posure, or self-possession: *He has perfect poise and never seems embarrassed.* **2** the way in which the body, head, etc., are held; carriage. **3** balance: *Poise yourself on your toes.* **4** hang supported or suspended. **5** hold or carry evenly or steadily: *The waiter poised the tray on his hand.* *1,2 n., 3-5 v.,* **poised, poising.**
poi son (poi′zn), **1** drug or other substance very dangerous to life and health. Strychnine and arsenic are both poisons. **2** kill or harm by poison. **3** put poison in or on. **4** poisonous. **5** anything dangerous or deadly: *the poison of hate.* **6** have a dangerous or harmful effect on: *poison the mind with lies.* *1,5 n., 2,3,6 v., 4 adj.* —**poi′son er,** *n.*
poison ivy, a shrub or climbing plant that looks like ivy, with glossy green compound leaves of three leaflets each, that causes a painful rash on most people if they touch it.
poison oak, **1** kind of poison ivy that grows as a shrub. **2** poison sumac.
poi son ous (poi′zn əs), **1** containing poison; very harmful to life and health: *The rattlesnake's bite is poisonous.* **2** having a dangerous or harmful effect: *a poisonous lie.* *adj.* —**poi′son ous ly,** *adv.*
poison sumac, shrub growing in swamps that has leaves composed of seven to thirteen leaflets and white berrylike fruit. It causes a severe rash on most people if they touch it.

pointer (def. 4)
about 26 in. high at the shoulder

poke[1] (pōk), **1** push against with something pointed; prod: *She poked me in the ribs with her elbow.* **2** thrust; push: *He poked his head in the kitchen window.* **3** a poking; thrust; push. **4** search; grope; pry. **5** make by poking: *She poked a hole in the paper.* **6** go lazily; loiter. **7** a slow, lazy person. **8** INFORMAL. hit with the fist; punch: *poke someone in the nose.* **9** INFORMAL. a blow with the fist; a punch. *1,2,4-6,8 v.,* **poked, poking;** *3,7,9 n.* [Middle English *poken*]
poke[2] (pōk), DIALECT. bag; sack. *n.* [Middle English]
poke[3] (pōk), bonnet or hat with a large brim in front. *n.* [perhaps special use of *poke*[1]]
pok er[1] (pō′kər), **1** person or thing that pokes. **2** a metal rod for stirring a fire. *n.* [*poke*[1] + *-er*[1]]

pok er[2] (pō′kər), a card game in which the players bet on the value of the cards that they hold in their hands. *n.* [origin uncertain]
pok y or **pok ey** (pō′kē), **1** moving or acting slowly; puttering; slow; dull: *a poky old man.* **2** small and cramped; confined; mean. *adj.,* **pok i er, pok i est.**
Po land (pō′lənd), country in central Europe between East Germany and the Soviet Union. *Capital:* Warsaw. *n.*
po lar (pō′lər), **1** of or near the North or South Pole: *It is very cold in the polar regions.* **2** having to do with a pole or poles. **3** of the poles of a magnet, electric battery, etc. **4** opposite in character, like the poles of a magnet: *Love and hatred are polar feelings or attitudes.* *adj.*
polar bear, a large, white bear of the arctic regions.
Po lar is (pō ler′is *or* pō lar′is), the North Star. *n.*
po lar i ty (pō lar′ə tē), **1** the possession of two opposed poles. A magnet or battery has polarity. **2** a positive or negative polar condition, as in electricity. **3** possession of two opposite or contrasted principles or tendencies. *n., pl.* **po lar i ties.**
po lar i za tion (pō′lər ə zā′shən), production or acquisition of polarity. *n.*
po lar ize (pō′lə rīz′), give polarity to; cause polarization in. *v.,* **po lar ized, po lar iz ing.**
pol der (pōl′dər), tract of lowland reclaimed from the sea or other body of water and protected by dikes. *n.*
pole[1] (pōl), **1** a long, slender piece of wood, etc.: *a telephone pole.* **2** make (a boat) go with a pole. *1 n., 2 v.,* **poled, pol ing.** [Old English *pāl,* from Latin *palus* stake]
pole[2] (pōl), **1** either end of the earth's axis. The North Pole and the South Pole are opposite each other. **2** either of two parts where opposite forces are strongest. A magnet or battery has both a positive pole and a negative pole. **3** either end of the axis of any sphere. *n.* [from Latin *polus,* from Greek *polos*]
Pole (pōl), person born or living in Poland. *n.*
pole cat (pōl′kat′), **1** a small, dark-brown, carnivorous European mammal related to the weasel, that can emit a

polecat (def. 1)—2½ ft. long with tail

very disagreeable odor; fitch. 2 the North American skunk. *n.*

po lem ic (pə lem′ik), 1 a disputing discussion; controversy; argument. 2 of controversy or disagreement; of dispute. 1 *n.,* 2 *adj.*

po lem i cal (pə lem′ə kəl), polemic. *adj.*

pole star (pōl′stär′), 1 the North Star. 2 a guiding principle; guide. 3 center of attraction, interest, or attention. *n.*

pole vault

pole vault, a jump or leap over a high, horizontal bar by using a long pole.

po lice (pə lēs′), 1 persons whose duty is keeping order and arresting people who break the law. 2 department of government that keeps order and arrests persons who break the law. 3 keep order in: *police the streets.* 4 the cleaning and keeping in order of a military camp, area, etc., or those who do it. 5 keep (a military camp, area, etc.) clean and in order: *police an army camp.* 1,2,4 *n.,* 3,5 *v.,* **po liced, po lic ing.**

police dog, 1 German shepherd. 2 any dog trained to work with policemen.

po lice man (pə lēs′mən), member of the police. *n., pl.* **po lice men.**

po lice wom an (pə lēs′wüm′ən), woman who is a member of the police. *n., pl.* **po lice wom en.**

pol i cy[1] (pol′ə sē), 1 plan of action; way of management: *It is a poor policy to promise more than you can do. The candidates explained their policies.* 2 practical wisdom; prudence. *n., pl.* **pol i cies.** [from French of the 1300's *policie,* from Latin *politia* citizenship, from Greek *politeia,* from *polis* city]

pol i cy[2] (pol′ə sē), a written agreement about insurance: *My fire insurance policy states that I shall receive $10,000 if my house burns down. n., pl.* **pol i cies.** [from French of the 1500's *police,* from Italian *polizza,* from Latin *apodixis* proof, from Greek *apodeixis*]

po li o (pō′lē ō), an acute, infectious, virus disease that destroys nervous tissue in the spinal cord, causing fever, paralysis of various muscles, and sometimes death; infantile paralysis; poliomyelitis. Before a vaccine was developed to control it, it attacked children

especially, often leaving them crippled. *n.*

po li o my e li tis (pō′lē ō mī′ə lī′tis), polio. *n.*

pol ish (pol′ish), 1 make smooth and shiny: *polish shoes.* 2 become smooth and shiny; take on a polish. 3 substance used to give smoothness or shine: *silver polish.* 4 put into a better condition; improve; refine: *polish one's French.* 5 polished condition; smoothness; refinement: *The polish of the furniture reflected our faces like a mirror. Travel with polite people gave polish to his manners.* 1,2,4 *v.,* 3,5 *n., pl.* **pol ish es.** —**pol′ish er,** *n.*

Pol ish (pō′lish), 1 of or having to do with Poland, its people, or their language. 2 language of Poland. 1 *adj.,* 2 *n.*

po lite (pə līt′), 1 having or showing good manners; behaving properly: *The polite girl gave the old woman her seat on the bus.* 2 refined; elegant: *I tried to learn all the customs of polite society. adj.,* **po lit er, po lit est.** —**po lite′ly,** *adv.* —**po lite′ness,** *n.*

pol i tic (pol′ə tik), 1 wise in looking out for one's own interests; prudent: *A politic person tries not to offend people.* 2 scheming; crafty. 3 political: *The state is a body politic. adj.*

po lit i cal (pə lit′ə kəl), 1 of or concerned with politics. 2 having to do with citizens or government: *Treason is a political offense.* 3 of politicians or their methods. *adj.* —**po lit′i cal ly,** *adv.*

political science, science of the principles and conduct of government.

pol i ti cian (pol′ə tish′ən), 1 person who gives much time to political affairs; person who is experienced in politics. 2 person active in politics chiefly for his own profit or that of his party. 3 person holding a political office. *n.*

pol i tics (pol′ə tiks), 1 management of political affairs; the science and art of government: *Our senior senator has been engaged in politics for many years.* 2 political principles or opinions: *My parents' politics are strongly against rule by any one person.* 3 political methods or maneuvers. *n. sing. or pl.*

pol i ty (pol′ə tē), 1 government. 2 a particular form or system of government. 3 community with a government; state. *n., pl.* **pol i ties.**

Polk (pōk), **James Knox,** 1795-1849, the 11th president of the United States, from 1845 to 1849. *n.*

pol ka (pōl′kə *or* pō′kə), 1 a kind of lively dance. 2 music for it. *n., pl.* **pol kas.**

pol ka dot (pō′kə), 1 dot or round spot repeated to form a pattern on

cloth. 2 pattern or fabric with such dots.

poll (pōl), 1 a voting; collection of votes: *The class had a poll to decide where it would have its picnic.* 2 number of votes cast: *If it rains on election day, there is usually a light poll.* 3 **polls,** *pl.* place where votes are cast and counted: *The polls will be open all day.* 4 list of persons, especially a list of voters. 5 receive at an election: *The mayor polled a record vote.* 6 vote; cast (a vote). 7 take or register the votes of: *to poll a village.* 8 a survey of public opinion concerning a particular subject. 9 the head, especially the part of it on which the hair grows. 10 cut off or cut short the hair, wool, horns, branches, etc., of. 1-4,8,9 *n.,* 5-7,10 *v.*

pol len (pol′ən), a fine, yellowish powder formed on the anthers of flowers. Grains of pollen carried to the stigmas of flowers fertilize them. *n.*

pollen count, a count of the number of grains of pollen to be found at a specified time and place in a cubic yard of air.

pol li nate (pol′ə nāt), carry pollen from anthers to stigmas of; shed pollen on. Many flowers are pollinated by bees. *v.,* **pol li nat ed, pol li nat ing.**

pol li na tion (pol′ə nā′shən), a carrying pollen to the stigmas of flowers. *n.*

pol li wog (pol′ē wog), tadpole. *n.* Also, **pollywog.**

poll tax, a tax on every adult citizen, especially as a prerequisite to the right to vote in public elections.

pol lute (pə lüt′), make dirty; defile: *The water at the bathing beach was polluted by refuse from the factory. v.,* **pol lut ed, pol lut ing.**

pol lu tion (pə lü′shən), a polluting; defiling; uncleanness. *n.*

Pol lux (pol′əks), (in Greek and Roman myths) one of the twin sons of Zeus. Pollux was immortal; his brother, Castor, was mortal. *n.*

pol ly wog (pol′ē wog), polliwog. *n.*

po lo (pō′lō), game like hockey, played on horseback with long-handled mallets and a wooden ball. *n.*

Polo

adj.	adjective	*n.*	noun
adv.	adverb	*prep.*	preposition
conj.	conjunction	*pron.*	pronoun
interj.	interjection	*v.*	verb
sing.	singular	*pl.*	plural

Po lo (pō′lō), **Marco.** See **Marco Polo.** *n.*

pol o naise (pol′ə nāz′ *or* pō′lə nāz′), 1 a slow, stately dance in three-quarter time. 2 music for it. *n.* [from French *(danse) Polonaise* Polish (dance), from *Polonia,* Latin name of Poland]

po lo ni um (pə lō′nē əm), a radioactive metallic element found in pitchblende. *n.* [from *Polonia,* Latin name of Poland, the homeland of Marie Curie, who discovered this element]

pol troon (pol trün′), a wretched coward. *n.*

po lyg a mous (pə lig′ə məs), having more than one wife or more than one husband at the same time. *adj.*

po lyg a my (pə lig′ə mē), practice or condition of being married to more than one person at the same time. *n.*

pol y glot (pol′ē glot), 1 knowing several languages. 2 person who knows several languages. 3 written in several languages. 4 book written in several languages. 1,3 *adj.,* 2,4 *n.*

polygons

pol y gon (pol′ē gon), a closed plane figure having three or more angles and straight sides. *n.*

po lyg o nal (pə lig′ə nəl), of or having to do with a polygon. *adj.*

pol y he dron (pol′ē hē′drən), a solid figure having four or more faces. *n., pl.* **pol y he drons** *or* **pol y he dra** (pol′ē hē′drə).

polyhedron

pol y mer (pol′ə mər), a chemical compound in which each molecule is made up of two or more simpler molecules strung together. Nylon and cellulose are polymers. *n.*

Pol y ne sia (pol′ə nē′zhə), group of many small islands in the Pacific, east of Micronesia and Melanesia. See **Melanesia** for map. *n.*

Pol y ne sian (pol′ə nē′zhən), 1 member of any of the brown peoples that live in Polynesia. 2 the languages of Polynesia, including Maori, Hawaiian, etc. 3 of or having to do with Polynesia, its people, or their languages. 1,2 *n.,* 3 *adj.*

pol yp (pol′ip), a small water animal with a tubular body and a mouth at one end surrounded by fingerlike tentacles to gather in food. Polyps often grow in colonies, with their bases connected. Corals and sea anemones are polyps. *n.*

pol y syl lab ic (pol′ē sə lab′ik), of more than three syllables. *adj.*

pol y syl la ble (pol′ē sil′ə bəl), word of more than three syllables. *Politician* is a polysyllable, and so is *possibility. n.*

pol y tech nic (pol′ē tek′nik), having to do with or dealing with many crafts or sciences: *a polytechnic school. adj.*

pol y the ism (pol′ē thē iz′əm), belief in more than one god. The religion of the ancient Greeks was polytheism. *n.*

po made (pə mād′), a perfumed ointment for the scalp and hair. *n.*

pome gran ate (pom′gran′it), 1 a reddish-yellow fruit with a thick skin and many seeds, each enveloped in a juicy red pulp which has a pleasant, slightly sour taste. 2 tree it grows on. *n.*

pom mel (pum′əl *or* pom′əl), 1 part of a saddle that sticks up at the front. 2 a rounded knob on the hilt of a sword, dagger, etc. 3 pummel. 1,2 *n.,* 3 *v.*

pomp (pomp), stately or showy display; splendor; magnificence: *The graduation ceremony had great pomp. n.*

pom pa dour (pom′pə dôr), arrangement of hair in which it is puffed high over the forehead or brushed straight up and back from the forehead. *n.* [from the Marquise de *Pompadour,* 1721-1764, mistress of Louis XV of France]

Pom pei an (pom pā′ən), of or having to do with Pompeii or its people. *adj.*

Pom peii (pom pā′), city in ancient Italy, which was buried by an eruption of Mount Vesuvius in A.D. 79. Its ruins have been partly laid bare by excavation. *n.*

Pom pey (pom′pē), 106-48 B.C., Roman general and statesman. *n.*

Pom pi dou (pom′pē dü), **Georges,** 1911-1974, president of France from 1969 to 1974. *n.*

pom pon (pom′pon), 1 an ornamental tuft or ball of feathers, silk, etc., worn on a hat, dress, or on shoes. 2 kind of chrysanthemum or dahlia with very small, rounded flowers. *n.*

pom pos i ty (pom pos′ə tē), 1 pompous quality. 2 pompous show of self-importance. *n., pl.* **pom pos i ties.**

pom pous (pom′pəs), 1 trying to seem magnificent; fond of display; acting proudly; self-important: *The leader of the band bowed in a pompous manner.* 2 characterized by pomp; splendid; magnificent; stately. *adj.* —**pom′pous ly,** *adv.* —**pom′pous ness,** *n.*

Ponce de Le ón (pons′ də lē′ən), **Juan,** 1460?-1521, Spanish soldier who discovered Florida. He sought the fabled fountain of youth, believed to restore youth to the old.

pon cho (pon′chō), a large piece of cloth, often waterproof, with a slit in the middle for the head to go through. Ponchos are worn in South America as cloaks. Waterproof ponchos are used in the armed forces and by hikers and campers. *n., pl.* **pon chos.**

pond (pond), body of still water, smaller than a lake. *n.*

pon der (pon′dər), consider carefully; think over: *ponder a problem. v.*

POMMEL →

pommel
(def. 1)

pon der ous (pon′dər əs), 1 very heavy. 2 heavy and clumsy: *A hippopotamus is ponderous.* 3 dull; tiresome: *The speaker talked in a ponderous way. adj.* —**pon′der ous ly,** *adv.*

POMPADOUR →

pone (pōn), 1 bread made of corn meal, popular in the southern United States. 2 loaf or cake of this bread. *n.*

pon gee (pon jē′), kind of soft silk, usually left in natural brownish-yellow color. *n.*

pon iard (pon′yərd), dagger. *n.*

pon tiff (pon′tif), 1 the pope. 2 bishop. 3 a high priest; chief priest. *n.*

pon tif i cal (pon tif′ə kəl), 1 of or having to do with the pope; papal. 2 of or having to do with a bishop. 3 characteristic of a pontiff; stately; pompous. *adj.*

pon tif i cate (pon tif′ə kit *or* pon tif′ə kāt *for 1;* pon tif′ə kāt *for 2,3*), 1 office or term of office of a pontiff. 2 officiate as a pontiff. 3 behave or

speak pompously. 1 *n.*, 2,3 *v.*, **pon tif-
i cat ed, pon tif i cat ing.**

pon toon (pon tün′), 1 a low, flat-
bottomed boat. 2 such a boat, or some
other floating structure, used as one of
the supports of a temporary bridge.
3 either of two boat-shaped parts of an
airplane, for landing on or taking off
from water. *n.*

pontoon bridge, a temporary bridge
supported by low, flat-bottomed boats
or other floating structures.

po ny (pō′nē), horse of a small breed.
Ponies are usually less than 5 feet tall at
the shoulder. *n., pl.* **po nies.**

pony express, system of carrying
letters and small packages in the western United States in 1860 and 1861 by
relays of men riding fast ponies or
horses.

pooch (püch), SLANG. dog. *n., pl.*
pooch es.

poo dle (pü′dl), one of a breed of intelligent dogs with thick, curly hair that is
often clipped and shaved in an elaborate manner. *n.*

poodle—9 to 23 in. high at the shoulder

pooh (pü), exclamation of contempt:
Pooh! You don't dare jump. interj.

pooh-pooh (pü′pü′ *or* pü′pü′), express contempt for; make light of. *v.*

pool¹ (pül), 1 tank of water to swim or
bathe in: *a swimming pool.* 2 a small
body of still water; small pond. 3 a still,
deep place in a stream. 4 puddle: *a pool
of grease under a car. n.* [Old English
pōl]

pool² (pül), 1 game like billiards played
on a special table with six pockets. The
players try to drive numbered balls into
the pockets with long sticks called cues.
2 put (things or money) together for
common advantage: *We plan to pool
our savings for a year so that we can
buy a boat.* 3 things or money put
together by different persons for
common advantage. 4 group of people,
usually having the same skills, who are
drawn upon as needed: *the labor pool.*
5 persons who form a pool. 6 stake
played for in some games. 1,3-6 *n.*, 2 *v.*
[from French *poule* booty, (originally)
hen, from Latin *pulla* chick]

pool room (pül′rüm′ *or* pül′rūm′),

pontoons
(def. 2)

room or place in which the game of pool
is played. *n.*

poop (püp), 1 deck at the stern above
the ordinary deck, often forming the
roof of a cabin. 2 stern of a ship. *n.*

POOP

poop
(def. 1)

poor (pùr), 1 having few things or
nothing; lacking money or property;
needy: *He was so poor that he could not
afford to buy a warm coat.* 2 **the poor,**
persons who are needy. 3 not good in
quality; lacking something needed: *poor
soil, a poor crop, a poor cook, poor
health.* 4 needing pity; unfortunate:
a poor stray dog. 1,3,4 *adj.*, 2 *n.*
—poor′ness, *n.*

poor house (pùr′hous′), house in
which paupers live at public expense.
n., pl. **poor hous es** (pùr′hou′ziz).

poor ly (pùr′lē), in a poor manner; not
enough; badly; meanly: *A desert is poorly supplied with water. The student did
poorly on the test. adv.*

pop¹ (pop), 1 make a short, quick,
explosive sound: *The firecrackers
popped in bunches.* 2 a short, quick,
explosive sound: *the pop of a cork.*
3 burst open or cause to burst open with
such a sound: *The chestnuts were popping in the fire. He popped the balloon.*
4 move, go, or come suddenly or unexpectedly: *Our neighbor popped in for a
short call.* 5 thrust or put suddenly: *She
popped her head out through the window.* 6 INFORMAL. fire a gun or pistol;
shoot. 7 a shot from a gun, etc. 8 bulge:
The surprise made her eyes pop out.
9 (in baseball) hit a short, high ball over
the infield. 10 a nonalcoholic carbonated drink: *strawberry pop.* 1,3-
6,8,9 *v.*, **popped, pop ping;** 2,7,10 *n.*
[imitation of the sound]

pop² (pop), INFORMAL. papa; father. *n.*
[a different form of *papa*]

pop corn (pop′kôrn′), 1 kind of Indian corn, the kernels of which burst
open and puff out when heated. 2 the
white, puffed-out kernels. *n.*

pope or **Pope** (pōp), the supreme
head of the Roman Catholic Church:
the last three popes, the Pope. n.

pop gun (pop′gun′), a toy gun that
shoots with a popping sound. *n.*

hat, āge, fär; let, ēqual, tèrm;
it, īce; hot, ōpen, ôrder;
oil, out; cup, pùt, rüle; ch, child;
ng, long; sh, she; th, thin;
ᵀH, then; zh, measure;

ə represents *a* in about,
e in taken, *i* in pencil,
o in lemon, *u* in circus.

pop in jay (pop′in jā), a vain, overly
talkative person; conceited, silly person. *n.*

pop lar (pop′lər), 1 any of several
trees that grow very rapidly and produce light, soft wood. The cottonwood
and the aspen are two kinds of poplars.
2 wood of such a tree. *n.*

pop lin (pop′lən), a ribbed fabric,
made of silk, wool, cotton, or rayon,
and used for making dresses, curtains,
etc. *n.*

pop o ver (pop′ō′vər), a very light and
hollow muffin. *n.*

pop py (pop′ē), 1 kind of plant with
showy red, yellow, or white flowers.
Opium is made from one kind of poppy.
2 its flower. *n., pl.* **pop pies.**

pop py cock (pop′ē kok′), INFOR-
MAL. nonsense; bosh. *n., interj.*

poppy seed, seed of the poppy, used
in baking to flavor rolls, bread, cookies,
etc.

pop u lace (pop′yə lis), the common
people. *n.*

pop u lar (pop′yə lər), 1 liked by most
people: *a popular song.* 2 liked by
acquaintances or associates: *Her ability
and good nature make her the most
popular girl in the class.* 3 of the people; by the people; representing the
people: *a popular election. The United
States has a popular government.* 4 widespread among many people; common:
*It is a popular belief that black cats
bring bad luck.* 5 suited to or intended
for ordinary people: *popular science.
adj.*

pop u lar i ty (pop′yə lar′ə tē), fact or
condition of being liked by most people. *n.*

pop u lar i za tion (pop′yə lər ə zā′-
shən), a making or a being made popular. *n.*

pop u lar ize (pop′yə lə rīz′), make
popular. *v.*, **pop u lar ized, pop u lar-
iz ing.**

pop u lar ly (pop′yə lər lē), 1 in a
popular manner. 2 by the people; in
general. *adv.*

pop u late (pop′yə lāt), 1 live in; inhabit: *This city is densely populated.*
2 furnish with inhabitants: *Europe pop-*

adj.	adjective	*n.*	noun
adv.	adverb	*prep.*	preposition
conj.	conjunction	*pron.*	pronoun
interj.	interjection	*v.*	verb
sing.	singular	*pl.*	plural

ulated much of America. v., **pop u lat-
ed, pop u lat ing.**

pop u la tion   (pop′yə lā′shən),
1 people of a city, country, or district.
2 the number of people. 3 part of the
inhabitants distinguished in any way
from the rest: *the urban population.*
4 act or process of furnishing with inhabitants. *n.*

pop u lous (pop′yə ləs), full of people;
having many people per square mile.
adj.

por ce lain (pôr′sə lin), very fine
earthenware; china: *Teacups are often
made of porcelain.* n.

porch (pôrch), 1 a covered entrance to
a building: *Our house has a big sleeping porch at the back.* 2 veranda. *n., pl.*
porch es.

porcupine—about 2½ ft. long with tail

por cu pine (pôr′kyə pin),   rodent
covered with spines or quills. *n.*

pore[1] (pôr), 1 gaze earnestly or steadily. 2 study long and steadily: *He would
rather pore over a book than play.*
3 meditate or ponder intently: *We pored
over the problem until we solved it.* v.,
pored, por ing.   [Middle English
pouren]

pore[2] (pôr), a very small opening.
Sweat comes through the pores in the
skin. *n.* [from French of the 1300's
pore, from Latin *porus,* from Greek
poros passage]

por gy (pôr′gē), any of various saltwater food fishes of Mediterranean and
Atlantic waters. *n., pl.* **por gies** or
por gy.

pork (pôrk), meat of a pig or hog used
for food. *n.*

pork er (pôr′kər), pig, especially one
fattened to eat. *n.*

po ros i ty (pô ros′ə tē), porous quality
or condition. *n.*

po rous (pôr′əs), full of pores or tiny

holes; permeable by water, air, etc.:
*Cloth, blotting paper, and ordinary
flowerpots are porous. Aluminum and
steel are not porous. adj.*

por phyr y (pôr′fər ē), 1 a hard red or
purplish Egyptian rock which contains
crystals of feldspar. 2 any igneous rock
in which coarse crystals are scattered
through a mass of finer-grained minerals. *n., pl.* **por phyr ies.**

por poise (pôr′pəs), 1 a sea mammal
with a blunt, rounded snout. Porpoises
are related to the whale, and live in
groups in the northern Atlantic and
Pacific. 2 any of several other small sea
mammals, especially the dolphin. *n., pl.*
por pois es or **por poise.**

por ridge (pôr′ij), food made of oatmeal or other cereal boiled in water or
milk until it thickens. *n.*

por rin ger (pôr′ən jər), a small dish
from which soup, porridge, bread and
milk, etc., can be eaten. *n.*

port[1] (pôrt), 1 place where ships and
boats can be sheltered from storms;
harbor. 2 place where ships and boats
can load and unload; city or town by a
harbor: *New York, Baltimore, and San
Francisco are important American
ports.* n. [Old English *port,* from Latin
portus]

port[2] (pôrt), 1 porthole. 2 cover for a
porthole. 3 opening in a cylinder or
pipe for steam, air, water, etc., to pass
through. *n.* [from French of the 1200's
porte, from Latin *porta* gate]

port[3] (pôrt), 1 the left side of a ship or
aircraft when facing the bow or front.
2 on the left side of a ship or aircraft.
3 turn or shift to the left side.   1 *n.*
2 *adj.,* 3 *v.* [origin uncertain]

port[4] (pôrt), way of holding one's head
and body; bearing. *n.* [from French of
the 1300's *port,* from *porter* carry, from
Latin *portare*]

port[5] (pôrt), a strong, sweet wine that is
dark red or tawny. *n.* [shortened from
Oporto, city in Portugal from which it
was shipped]

port a ble (pôr′tə bəl),   capable of
being carried; easily carried: *a portable
typewriter, a portable phonograph.*
adj.

por tage (pôr′tij),   1 a carrying of
boats, provisions, etc., overland from
one river, lake, etc., to another. 2 place
over which this is done.   3 cost of
carrying. *n.*

por tal (pôr′tl), door, gate, or entrance,
usually an imposing one. *n.*

Port-au-Prince (pôrt′ō prins′), seaport and capital of Haiti, in the S
part. *n.*

port cul lis   (pôrt kul′is),   a strong
gate or grating of iron sliding up and
down in grooves, used to close the
gateway of an ancient castle or

fortress.   *n., pl.*   **port cul lis es.**

por tend (pôr tend′), indicate beforehand; give warning of: *Black clouds por-
tend a storm.* v.

porpoise (def. 1)—4 to 8 ft. long

por tent (pôr′tent), a warning, usually
of coming evil; sign; omen: *The black
clouds were a portent of bad weather.* n.

por ten tous (pôr ten′təs),   1 indicating evil to come; ominous; threatening. 2 amazing; extraordinary. *adj.*
—por ten′tous ly, *adv.*

por ter[1] (pôr′tər), 1 person employed
to carry loads or baggage: *Give your
bags to the porter.* 2 attendant in a
parlor car or sleeping car of a railway
train. *n.* [from French of the 1300's
porteur, from Latin *portator,* from
portare carry]

por ter[2] (pôr′tər), 1 doorman. 2 janitor. *n.* [from French of the 1200's
portier, from Latin *portarius,* from
porta gate]

por ter[3] (pôr′tər), a heavy, dark-brown
beer. *n.* [shortened from *porter's ale,*
apparently from *porter*[2] (who perhaps
originally drank it)]

Por ter (pôr′tər), **William Sydney,**
the real name of **O. Henry.** *n.*

por ter house   (pôr′tər hous′),   a
choice beefsteak containing the tender-
loin. *n.*

port fo li o (pôrt fō′lē ō), 1 a portable
case for loose papers, drawings, etc.;
briefcase.   2 position and duties of a
cabinet member or a minister of state:
*The Secretary of Defense resigned
his portfolio.* 3 holdings in the form
of stocks, bonds, etc. *n., pl.* **port fo-
li os.**

port hole (pôrt′hōl′),   1 opening in
a ship's side to let in light and air.
2 opening in a ship, wall, etc., through
which to shoot. *n.*

Por tia (pôr′shə), heroine in Shakespeare's *Merchant of Venice,* who acts
as a lawyer. *n.*

portcullis

portico

por ti co (pôr′tə kō), roof supported by columns, forming a porch or a covered walk. *n., pl.* **por ti coes** or **por ti cos.**

por tiere (pôr tyer′), curtain hung at a doorway. *n.* [from French *portière*]

por tière (pôr tyer′), portiere. *n., pl.* **por tières.**

por tion (pôr′shən), 1 a part or share: *A portion of each school day is devoted to arithmetic.* 2 quantity of food served for one person: *Each child ate his portion.* 3 divide into parts or shares: *The money was portioned out among the children.* 4 dowry. 1,2,4 *n.,* 3 *v.*

Port land (pôrt′lənd), 1 seaport in SW Maine. 2 seaport in NW Oregon. *n.*

port li ness (pôrt′lē nis), portly condition. *n.*

port ly (pôrt′lē), 1 having a large body; stout. 2 stately; dignified. *adj.,* **port li er, port li est.**

port man teau (pôrt man′tō), a stiff, oblong traveling bag with two compartments opening like a book. *n., pl.* **port man teaus** or **port man teaux** (pôrt man′tōz).

Port-of-Spain (pôrt′əv spān′), capital of Trinidad and Tobago, a seaport in NW Trinidad. *n.*

Por to Ri co (pôr′tō rē′kō), former name of **Puerto Rico.**

por trait (pôr′trit *or* pôr′trāt), 1 picture of a person, especially of the face. 2 picture in words; description. *n.*

por trait ist (pôr′trā tist), person who paints portraits. *n.*

por trai ture (pôr′trə chùr′), 1 act of portraying. 2 portrait. *n.*

por tray (pôr trā′), 1 make a likeness of in a drawing or painting; make a picture of: *portray a historical scene.* 2 picture in words; describe: *The book "Black Beauty" portrays the life of a horse.* 3 represent in a play or motion picture; impersonate; act. *v.*

por tray al (pôr trā′əl), 1 a portraying by drawing or in words. 2 a picture or description. *n.*

Por tu gal (pôr′chə gəl), country in SW Europe, west of Spain. *Capital:* Lisbon. *n.*

Por tu guese (pôr′chə gēz′), 1 person born or living in Portugal. 2 language of Portugal. Portuguese is also the chief language of Brazil. 3 of or having to do with Portugal, its people, or their language. 1,2 *n., pl.* **Por tu guese;** 3 *adj.*

pose (pōz), 1 position of the body; way of holding the body: *a natural pose, a pose taken in exercising.* 2 hold a position: *He posed an hour for his portrait.* 3 put in a certain position: *The artist posed him before painting his picture.* 4 attitude assumed for effect; pretense; affectation: *Her interest in other people is quite real; it is not just a pose.* 5 put on an attitude for effect; make a false pretense: *He posed as a rich man though he owed more than he owned.* 6 put forward for discussion; state: *pose a question.* 1,4 *n.,* 2,3,5,6 *v.,* **posed, pos ing.**

Po sei don (pə sīd′n), (in Greek myths) the god of the sea. The Romans called him Neptune. *n.*

pos er (pō′zər), person who poses. *n.*

po si tion (pə zish′ən), 1 place where a thing or person is: *The flowers grew in a sheltered position behind the house.* 2 way of being placed: *Sit in a more comfortable position.* 3 proper place: *The band got into position to march in the parade.* 4 condition with reference to place or circumstances: *I maneuvered for position before shooting the basketball. Your careless remark put me in an awkward position.* 5 job: *He has a position in a bank.* 6 rank or standing, especially high standing: *She was raised to the position of manager.* 7 way of thinking; set of opinions: *What is your position on this question?* 8 to place in a certain position: *The photographer positioned us so that the tall students stood behind the shorter ones.* 1-7 *n.,* 8 *v.*

pos i tive (poz′ə tiv), 1 permitting no question; without doubt; sure: *We have positive knowledge that the earth moves around the sun.* 2 too sure; too confident: *Her positive manner annoys people.* 3 definite; emphatic: *"No. I will not," was his positive refusal.* 4 the simple form of an adjective or adverb, as distinct from the comparative and superlative. *Fast* is the positive; *faster* is the comparative; *fastest* is the superlative. 5 of the simple form of an adjective or adverb. 6 that can be thought of as real and present: *Light is a positive thing; darkness is only the absence of light.* 7 showing that a particular disease, condition, germ, etc., is present. 8 that definitely does something or adds something; practical: *Don't just make criticisms; give us some positive help.* 9 of the kind of electrical charge produced by rubbing glass with silk. 10 greater than zero; plus: *Five above zero is a positive quantity.* 11 a positive degree or quantity. 12 (in photography) having the lines and shadows in the same position as in the original. 13 print made from a photographic film

hat, āge, fär; let, ēqual, tèrm; it, īce; hot, ōpen, ôrder; oil, out; cup, pùt, rüle; ch, child; ng, long; sh, she; th, thin; ᴛʜ, then; zh, measure;

ə represents *a* in about, *e* in taken, *i* in pencil, *o* in lemon, *u* in circus.

or plate. 1-3,5-10,12 *adj.,* 4,11,13 *n.*
—**pos′i tive ness,** *n.*

pos i tive ly (poz′ə tiv lē), 1 in a positive way: *He knew positively that he disliked camping out.* 2 to a great extreme; absolutely: *The player was positively furious when the umpire called him out.* *adv.*

pos se (pos′ē), group of men summoned by a sheriff to help him: *The posse pursued the bandit.* *n.*

pos sess (pə zes′), 1 have as belonging to one; own: *My aunt possessed great intelligence and determination.* 2 hold as property; hold; occupy. 3 control; influence strongly: *She was possessed by the desire to be rich.* 4 control by an evil spirit: *He fought like one possessed.* *v.*

pos ses sion (pə zesh′ən), 1 a possessing; holding: *I have in my possession the books you thought you'd lost.* 2 ownership: *On her 21st birthday she came into possession of 50 thousand dollars.* 3 thing possessed; property: *Please move your possessions from my room.* 4 territory under the rule of a country: *Guam is a possession of the United States.* 5 domination by a particular feeling, idea, evil spirit, etc. 6 self-control. *n.*

pos ses sive (pə zes′iv), 1 of possession. 2 showing possession. *My, your, his,* and *our* are in the possessive case because they indicate who possesses or owns. 3 the possessive case. 4 word in this case. In "the boy's books," *boy's* is a possessive. 5 desirous of ownership: *a possessive nature.* 1,2,5 *adj.,* 3,4 *n.*
—**pos ses′sive ly,** *adv.* —**pos ses′sive ness,** *n.*

pos ses sor (pə zes′ər), person who possesses; owner; holder. *n.*

pos si bil i ty (pos′ə bil′ə tē), 1 a being possible: *There is a possibility that the train may be late.* 2 a possible thing, person, or event: *A whole week of rain is a possibility.* *n., pl.* **pos si bil i ties.**

pos si ble (pos′ə bəl), 1 that can be; that can be done; that can happen: *Come if possible. It is possible to cure tuberculosis.* 2 that can be true or a fact: *It is possible that he went.* 3 that

653

possibly

can be done, chosen, etc., properly: *the only possible action, the only possible candidate. adj.*

pos si bly (pos′ə blē), 1 by any possibility; no matter what happens: *I cannot possibly go.* 2 perhaps: *Possibly you are right. adv.*

pos sum (pos′əm), opossum. *n., pl.* **pos sums** or **pos sum.**

play possum, put on a false appearance; pretend.

post¹ (pōst), 1 piece of timber, iron, etc., firmly set up, usually to support something else: *the posts of a door, a hitching post.* 2 fasten (a notice) up in a place where it can easily be seen: *The list of winners will be posted soon.* 3 make known by, or as if by, a posted notice; make public: *post a reward.* 4 put (a name) in a list that is published or posted up: *Her train is posted as on time.* 5 put up notices warning people to keep out of: *That farmer posts his land.* 1 *n.,* 2-5 *v.* [Old English *post,* from Latin *postis*]

post² (pōst), 1 the place where a soldier, policeman, etc., is stationed; place where one is supposed to be when on duty: *When the fire alarm sounds, each man rushes to his post.* 2 a place where soldiers are stationed; military station; fort. 3 to station at a post: *They posted guards at the door.* 4 job or position: *the post of secretary, a diplomatic post.* 5 trading post. 1,2,4,5 *n.,* 3 *v.* [from French of the 1500's *poste,* from Italian *posto,* from Latin *positum* stationed, placed]

post³ (pōst), 1 an established system for carrying letters, papers, packages, etc.; the mail: *I shall send the package by post.* 2 a single delivery of mail: *this morning's post.* 3 send by post; mail: *post a letter.* 4 one of a series of fixed stations along a route that furnished relays of men and horses for carrying the mail. 5 travel with haste; hurry. 6 supply with up-to-date information; inform: *to be well posted on current events. Baseball fans always keep themselves posted as to the standing of the teams.* 1,2,4 *n.,* 3,5,6 *v.* [from French of the 1500's *poste,* from Italian *posta,* from Latin *posita* placed]

post age (pō′stij), amount paid on anything sent by mail. *n.*

postage stamp, stamp (def. 1).

post al (pō′stəl), having to do with mail and post offices: *postal rules. adj.*

postal card, post card.

Postal Service, an independent agency of the United States government that provides mail services, sells postage stamps, etc. It replaced the U.S. Post Office Department in 1971.

post card (pōst′kärd′), post card. *n.*

post card, card, usually about 3½ by 5½ inches, for sending a message by mail. Some post cards have a government postage stamp printed on them. Others have pictures on one side.

post chaise, a hired carriage that was used for traveling before there were railroads.

post er (pō′stər), 1 a large printed sheet or notice put up in some public place. 2 person who posts notices, etc. *n.*

pos ter i or (po stir′ē ər), 1 situated behind; back; rear; hind. 2 coming after; later. *adj.*

pos ter i ty (po ster′ə tē), 1 generations of the future: *Posterity may travel to distant planets.* 2 anyone's children, and their children, and their children, and so on and on; all of a person's descendants. *n.*

pos tern (pō′stərn or pos′tərn), 1 a back door or gate. 2 any small door or gate. 3 rear; lesser: *The castle had a postern door.* 1,2 *n.,* 3 *adj.*

post grad u ate (pōst graj′ü it), 1 student who continues studying in college or at school after graduation. 2 taking a course of study after graduation. 3 of or for postgraduates: *postgraduate courses.* 1 *n.,* 2,3 *adj.*

post haste (pōst′hāst′), very speedily; in great haste. *adv.*

post hu mous (pos′chə məs), 1 happening after death: *posthumous fame.* 2 published after the death of the author: *a posthumous book.* 3 born after the death of the father: *a posthumous child. adj.* —**post′hu mous ly,** *adv.*

pos til ion or **pos til lion** (pō-stil′yən or po stil′yən), person who guides a team of horses drawing a carriage by riding the left-hand horse. *n.*

post man (pōst′mən), mailman. *n., pl.* **post men.**

post mark (pōst′märk′), 1 an official mark stamped on mail to cancel the postage stamp and record the place and date of mailing. 2 to stamp with a postmark. 1 *n.,* 2 *v.*

post mas ter (pōst′mas′tər), person in charge of a post office. *n.*

postmaster general, 1 person at the head of the postal system of a country. 2 **Postmaster General,** the chief executive officer of the Postal Service. *pl.* **postmasters general.**

post mis tress (pōst′mis′tris), woman in charge of a post office. *n., pl.* **post mis tress es.**

post-mor tem (pōst′môr′təm), 1 after death: *A post-mortem examination showed that the man had been poisoned.* 2 autopsy. 1 *adj.,* 2 *n.*

post office, 1 place where mail is handled and postage stamps are sold. 2 Often, **Post Office.** the former government department in charge of mail, replaced by the Postal Service in 1971.

post paid (pōst′pād′), with the postage paid for. *adj.*

post pone (pōst pōn′), put off till later; put off to a later time; delay: *The picnic was postponed because of rain. v.,* **post poned, post pon ing.**

post pone ment (pōst pōn′mənt), a putting off till later; a putting off to a later time; delay: *The postponement of the picnic disappointed the children. n.*

post road, 1 road or route over which mail is or was carried. 2 road with stations which furnished horses.

post script (pōst′skript), 1 addition to a letter, written after the writer's name has been signed. 2 a supplementary part added to any composition or literary work. *n.*

pos tu late (pos′chə lit for *1;* pos′chə-lāt for *2,3*), 1 something taken for granted or assumed as a basis for reasoning; fundamental principle; necessary condition: *One postulate of plane geometry is that a straight line is the shortest distance between any two points.* 2 assume without proof; take for granted: *Geometry postulates certain things as a basis for its reasoning.* 3 require; demand; claim. 1 *n.,* 2,3 *v.,* **pos tu lat ed, pos tu lat ing.**

pos ture (pos′chər), 1 position of the body; way of holding the body: *Good posture is important to health.* 2 take a certain position: *The dancer postured before the mirror, bending and twisting her body.* 3 put in a certain posture. 4 condition; situation; state: *In the present posture of public affairs it is difficult to predict what will happen.* 1,4 *n.,* 2,3 *v.,* **pos tured, pos tur ing.**

post war (pōst′wôr′), after the war. *adj.*

po sy (pō′zē), 1 flower. 2 bunch of flowers; bouquet. 3 motto or line of poetry engraved within a ring. *n., pl.* **po sies.**

pot (pot), 1 kind of vessel or dish. There are many different kinds and shapes of pots. They are made of iron, tin, earthenware, and other substances. A pot may hold food or drink or contain earth for flowers to grow in. 2 amount a pot can hold: *He ate a small pot of beans.* 3 put into a pot: *pot young tomato plants.* 4 cook and preserve in a

pot. 5 take a pot shot at; shoot. 1,2 *n.*, 3-5 *v.*, **pot ted, pot ting.**

go to pot, go to ruin.

pot ash (pot′ash′), any of several compounds of potassium made from various minerals, wood ashes, etc., and used in making soap, fertilizers, and glass. *n.*

po tas si um (pə tas′ē əm), a soft, silver-white, metallic element, occurring in nature only in compounds. Potassium is one of the most abundant elements in the earth's crust, and is essential for the growth of plants. Its compounds are used in making soap and as fertilizers. *n.*

potassium hydroxide, a white, solid substance which releases great heat when it dissolves in water; caustic potash. It is used in bleaching, in making liquid soaps, and in medicine.

potassium nitrate, a white or colorless crystalline compound with a salty taste, produced from sodium nitrate and another potassium compound; niter; saltpeter. It is used in explosives, fertilizers, medicine, and meat preservatives.

po ta tion (pō tā′shən), 1 act of drinking. 2 a drink, especially of alcoholic liquor. *n.*

po ta to (pə tā′tō), 1 plant with a starchy tuber used as a vegetable. 2 this vegetable, which is round or oval, hard, and has a very thin skin; Irish potato; white potato. The potato is one of the most widely used vegetables in Europe and America. 3 sweet potato. *n., pl.* **po ta toes.**

potato chip, a thin slice of potato fried in deep fat.

pot bel lied (pot′bel′ēd), 1 having a potbelly. 2 shaped like a potbelly: *a potbellied stove. adj.*

pot bel ly (pot′bel′ē), a bulging or protuberant belly. *n., pl.* **pot bel lies.**

po ten cy (pōt′n sē), power; strength: *the potency of an argument, the potency of a drug. n., pl.* **po ten cies.**

po tent (pōt′nt), having great power; powerful; strong: *a potent remedy for a disease, potent reasons. adj.*

po ten tate (pōt′n tāt), 1 person having great power. 2 ruler. Kings, queens, and emperors are potentates. *n.*

po ten tial (pə ten′shəl), 1 possible as opposed to actual; capable of coming into being or action: *There is a potential danger of being bitten when playing with a strange dog.* 2 something potential; possibility. 3 (in grammar) expressing possibility by the use of *may, might, can, could,* etc.: *the potential mood of a verb.* 4 amount of electrification of a point with reference to some standard. A current of high potential is used in transmitting electric power over long

distances. 1,3 *adj.*, 2,4 *n.*, —**po ten′tial ly,** *adv.*

potential energy, energy which a body has because of its position. A coiled spring or a raised weight has potential energy.

po ten ti al i ty (pə ten′shē al′ə tē), 1 potential condition or quality; possible power. 2 something potential; possibility. *n., pl.* **po ten ti al i ties.**

pot ful (pot′fùl), as much as a pot can hold. *n., pl.* **pot fuls.**

poth er (poŦH′ər), 1 confusion;disturbance; fuss: *The children are making a great pother about the picnic.* 2 to bother; fuss. 1 *n.*, 2 *v.*

pot herb (pot′èrb′ *or* pot′hèrb′), 1 any plant whose leaves and stems are boiled for use as a vegetable, such as spinach. 2 plant used as seasoning in cooking, such as sage. *n.*

pot hold er (pot′hōl′dər), a thick pad of cloth or other material for handling hot pots, lids, etc. *n.*

pot hole (pot′hōl′), 1 a deep, round hole, especially one made in the rocky bed of a river by stones and gravel being spun around in the current. 2 depression or hollow part forming a defect in the surface of a street or road. *n.*

pot hook (pot′hùk′), 1 hook for hanging a pot or kettle over an open fire. 2 rod with a hook for lifting hot pots. 3 an S-shaped stroke in writing, especially one made by children in learning to write. *n.*

po tion (pō′shən), a drink, especially one that is used as a medicine or poison, or in magic. *n.*

pot luck (pot′luk′), whatever food happens to be ready or on hand for a meal: *Come and take potluck with me. n.*

Po to mac (pə tō′mək), river flowing from E West Virginia between Maryland and Virginia, into Chesapeake Bay. Washington, D.C., is on the Potomac River. *n.*

pot pie (pot′pī′), 1 a baked meat pie. 2 a stew with dumplings. *n.*

pot pour ri (pō′pù rē′), 1 medley or mixture: *a potpourri of Italian, French, and Austrian folk songs.* 2 a fragrant mixture of dried flower petals and spices. *n.*

pot roast, beef browned in a pot and cooked slowly with only a little water.

pot shot (pot′shot′), 1 shot fired at game to get food, with little regard to skill or the rules of sport. 2 a quick shot at something from close range without careful aim. 3 Often, **potshots,** *pl.* criticism, usually made in a careless manner: *She disregarded their potshots at her invention. n.*

pot tage (pot′ij), a thick soup. *n.*

pot ter[1] (pot′ər), person who makes

hat, āge, fär; let, ēqual, tèrm;
it, īce; hot, ōpen, ôrder;
oil, out; cup, pùt, rüle; ch, child;
ng, long; sh, she; th, thin;
ŦH, then; zh, measure;

ə represents *a* in about,
e in taken, *i* in pencil,
o in lemon, *u* in circus.

pottery. *n.* [Old English *pottere*, from *pott* pot + *-ere* -er[1]]

pot ter[2] (pot′ər), to putter. *v.* [apparently from earlier *pote* to poke, Old English *potian* to push]

potter's field, piece of public ground set aside for the burial of people who die without friends or money.

potter's wheel operated by means of a treadle. The momentum of the heavy wheel at the bottom helps keep the upper wheel in motion. Some kinds are operated by electricity.

potter's wheel, a rotating horizontal disk upon which clay is molded into dishes, etc.

pot ter y (pot′ər ē), 1 pots, dishes, vases, etc., made from clay and hardened by heat. 2 art or business of making them. 3 place where such pots, dishes, vases, etc., are made. *n., pl.* **pot ter ies.**

pouch (pouch), 1 bag or sack: *a tobacco pouch.* 2 a baglike fold of skin. A kangaroo carries its young in a pouch. *The old man had pouches under his eyes.* 3 put into a pouch. 4 form a pouch. 1,2 *n., pl.* **pouch es;** 3,4 *v.*

poul tice (pōl′tis), 1 a soft, moist mass of mustard, herbs, etc., applied to the body as a medicine. 2 put a poultice on. 1 *n.*, 2 *v.*, **poul ticed, poul tic ing.**

poul try (pōl′trē), birds raised for their meat or eggs, such as chickens, turkeys, geese, ducks, etc. *n.*

pounce (pouns), 1 come down with a rush and seize something: *The cat pounced upon the mouse.* 2 dash, come, or jump suddenly: *The actor pounced onto the stage.* 3 a sudden swoop or pouncing. 1,2 *v.*, **pounced, pounc-ing;** 3 *n.*

pound

adj.	adjective	*n.*	noun
adv.	adverb	*prep.*	preposition
conj.	conjunction	*pron.*	pronoun
interj.	interjection	*v.*	verb
sing.	singular	*pl.*	plural

pound[1] (pound), 1 measure of weight, 16 ounces in avoirdupois, and 12 ounces in troy weight. 2 pound sterling. 3 unit of money of Nigeria, Egypt, and certain other countries. *n., pl.* **pounds** or **pound.** [Old English *pund,* from Latin *pondo* by weight]

pound[2] (pound), 1 hit hard again and again; hit heavily: *He pounded the door with his fist.* 2 beat hard; throb: *After running fast you can feel your heart pound.* 3 make into a powder or pulp by pounding: *to pound drugs with a pestle in a mortar.* 4 move with a pounding sound: *He pounded down the hill to catch the bus.* 5 a heavy blow, or its sound. 1-4 *v.,* 5 *n.* [Old English *pūnian*]

pound[3] (pound), 1 an enclosed place in which to keep stray animals: *a dog or cat pound.* 2 enclosure for keeping, confining, or trapping animals. *n.* [Old English *pund-*]

pound-fool ish (pound/fü/lish), foolish or careless in regard to large sums of money. *adj.*

pound sterling, unit of money of Great Britain. Since February 1971, 1 pound = 100 pence. Formerly, 1 pound = 240 pence. The gold in one pound sterling is worth about $2.40.

pour (pôr), 1 flow or cause to flow in a steady stream: *I poured the milk from the bottle. The crowd poured out of the church.* 2 make known freely or without reserve: *The melancholy poet poured forth his sorrow in a song.* 3 rain heavily. 4 a heavy rain; downpour. 1-3 *v.,* 4 *n.*

pout (pout), 1 thrust or push out the lips, as a displeased or sulky child does. 2 a pushing out of the lips when displeased or sulky. 1 *v.,* 2 *n.*

pout er (pou/tər), 1 person who pouts. 2 one of a breed of domestic pigeons that puff out their crops. *n.*

pov er ty (pov/ər tē), 1 condition of being poor: *Their tattered clothing and broken furniture indicated their poverty.* 2 lack of what is needed; poor quality: *The poverty of the soil makes the crops small.* 3 a small amount; fewness: *A dull person's talk shows poverty of ideas. n.*

pov er ty-strick en (pov/ər tē-strik/ən), extremely poor. *adj.*

POW, prisoner of war.

pow der (pou/dər), 1 a solid reduced to dust by pounding, crushing, or grinding. 2 make into powder; become powder: *The soil powdered in the heat.* 3 some special kind of powder: *face powder, talcum powder, powders taken as medicine.* 4 sprinkle or cover with powder. 5 sprinkle: *The ground was powdered with snow.* 6 put powder on (the face, etc.): *powder one's nose.* 7 gunpowder. 1,3,7 *n.,* 2,4-6 *v.*

powder flask, flask or case of horn, metal, or leather for carrying gunpowder.

powder horn, powder flask made of an animal's horn.

powder horn

powder puff, a soft puff or pad for applying powder to the skin.

powder room, lavatory for women, especially one with a dressing table.

pow der y (pou/dər ē), 1 of powder. 2 like powder; in the form of powder. 3 easily made into powder. 4 sprinkled or covered with powder. *adj.*

pow er (pou/ər), 1 strength or force; might: *Penicillin is a medicine of great power.* 2 ability to do or act: *I will give you all the help in my power.* 3 particular ability: *He has great powers of concentration.* 4 authority; influence; control; right: *Congress has power to declare war.* 5 person, thing, body, or nation having authority or influence: *Five powers held a peace conference.* 6 energy or force that can do work: *Running water produces power to run mills.* 7 provide with power or energy: *a boat powered by an outboard motor.* 8 operated by a motor; equipped with its own motor: *a power drill.* 9 product of a number multiplied by itself one or more times: *16 is the 4th power of 2 (2×2×2×2= 16).* 10 capacity of an instrument to magnify. An object seen through a microscope with a power of ten looks ten times its actual size. 1-6,9,10 *n.,* 7 *v.,* 8 *adj.*

in power, having control or authority.
the powers that be, those who have control or authority.

pow er boat (pou/ər bōt/), boat propelled by an engine on board; motorboat. *n.*

pow er ful (pou/ər fəl), having great power or force; mighty; strong: *a powerful person, a powerful medicine, a powerful argument, a powerful nation. adj.* —**pow/er ful ly,** *adv.*

pow er house (pou/ər hous/), 1 a building containing boilers, engines, dynamos, etc., for generating electric power. 2 INFORMAL. a powerful, energetic, or highly effective person or group. *n., pl.* **pow er hous es** (pou/ər hou/ziz).

pow er less (pou/ər lis), without power; helpless: *The mouse was powerless in the cat's claws. adj.* —**pow/er less ly,** *adv.*

power loom, loom worked by steam, electricity, water power, etc., not by hand.

power of attorney, a written statement giving one person legal power to act for another.

power saw, saw worked by a motor, not by hand.

power shovel, machine for digging operated by an engine, especially a diesel or gasoline engine.

Pow ha tan (pou/ə tan/), 1550?-1618, Indian chief in Virginia. *n.*

pow wow (pou/wou/), 1 an American Indian ceremony, usually accompanied by magic, feasting, and dancing, performed for the cure of disease, success in hunting, etc. 2 council or conference of or with American Indians. 3 INFORMAL. any conference or meeting. 4 an American Indian priest or medicine man. 5 hold a powwow; confer. 1-4 *n.,* 5 *v.*

pox (poks), any disease that covers the body or parts of the body with sores, such as chicken pox or smallpox. *n.*

pp., 1 pages. 2 past participle.
p.p., past participle.
ppr., present participle.
pr., 1 pair. 2 price.
P.R., Puerto Rico.

prac ti ca bil i ty (prak/tə kə bil/ə tē), quality of being practicable. *n.*

prac ti ca ble (prak/tə kə bəl), 1 that can be done; capable of being put into practice: *a practicable idea.* 2 that can be used: *a practicable road. adj.*

prac ti ca bly (prak/tə kə blē), in a practicable manner. *adv.*

prac ti cal (prak/tə kəl), 1 having to do with action or practice rather than thought or theory: *Earning a living is a practical matter.* 2 fit for actual practice: *a practical plan.* 3 useful: *An outdoor swimming pool is more practical in Florida than in Minnesota.* 4 having good sense: *A practical person does not spend time and money foolishly.* 5 engaged in actual practice or work: *A practical farmer works a farm.* 6 being such in effect; virtual: *So many of our players were injured that our victory was a practical defeat. adj.*

prac ti cal i ty (prak/tə kal/ə tē), 1 quality of being practical; practical usefulness; practical habit of mind. 2 a practical matter. *n., pl.* **prac ti cal i ties.**

practical joke, trick played on a person to have a laugh at him.

prac ti cal ly (prak′tik lē), **1** so far as the results will be; in effect; really. **2** INFORMAL. almost; nearly: *Our house is around the corner, so we are practically home.* **3** in a practical way; in a useful way. **4** by actual practice: *I learned the game practically, not just by watching others play. adv.*

prairie chicken
about 16 in. long

practical nurse, person whose occupation is to care for the sick, but who does not have the hospital training or diploma of a trained nurse.

prac tice (prak′tis), **1** action done many times over for skill: *Practice makes perfect.* **2** skill gained by experience or exercise: *They were out of practice at batting.* **3** do (some act) again and again to learn to do it well: *I practiced pitching the ball. She practices on the piano every day.* **4** action or process of doing or being something: *His plan is good in theory, but not in actual practice.* **5** do usually; make a custom of: *Practice what you preach.* **6** follow, observe, or use day after day: *People who are too fat must learn to practice moderation in what they eat.* **7** the usual way; custom: *It is the practice at the factory to blow a whistle at noon.* **8** work at or follow as a profession: *practice medicine.* **9** practice a profession: *That young lawyer is just beginning to practice.* **10** the working at or following of a profession: *She is engaged in the practice of law.* **11** business of a doctor or lawyer: *The old doctor sold his practice.* 1,2,4,7,10,11 *n.,* 3,5,6,8,9 *v.,* **prac ticed, prac tic ing.** Also, **practise.**

prac ticed or **prac tised** (prak′tist), experienced; skilled; expert: *Years of study have made him a practiced musician. adj.*

prac tise (prak′tis), practice. *v.,* **prac tised, prac tis ing.**

prac ti tion er (prak tish′ə nər), person engaged in the practice of a profession: *She was a medical practitioner for ten years; later she taught medicine. n.*

prae tor (prē′tər), magistrate or judge in ancient Rome. A praetor ranked next below a consul. *n.*

prae to ri an (prē tôr′ē ən), **1** of or having to do with a praetor. **2** Often, **Praetorian.** having to do with the bodyguard of a Roman commander or em-

peror. **3** Often, **Praetorian.** soldier of the bodyguard of a Roman commander or emperor. 1,2 *adj.,* 3 *n.*

prag mat ic (prag mat′ik), concerned with practical results or values; having to do with pragmatism. *adj.*

prag ma tism (prag′mə tiz′əm), philosophy that tests the value and truth of ideas by their practical consequences. *n.*

Prague (präg), capital and largest city of Czechoslovakia, in the W part. *n.*

prair ie (prer′ē), a large area of level or rolling land with grass but no trees. *n.*

prairie chicken, any of several grouse that live on the prairies of North America.

prairie dog, a burrowing animal like a woodchuck but smaller, found on the Great Plains and in the Rocky Mountain region. Prairie dogs bark.

prairie dog
about 15 in. long
with the tail

prairie schooner, a large covered wagon used in crossing the plains of North America before the railroads were built.

prairie schooner

praise (prāz), **1** a saying that a thing or person is good; words that tell the worth or value of a thing or person. **2** express approval or admiration of: *Everyone praised the winning team for its fine play.* **3** to worship in words or song: *praise God.* **4** words or song worshiping God. 1,4 *n.,* 2,3 *v.,* **praised, prais ing.**

sing the praises of, praise with enthusiasm.

praise wor thy (prāz′wer′ᵀHē), worthy of praise; deserving approval. *adj.*

prance (prans), **1** spring about on the hind legs: *Horses prance when they feel lively.* **2** ride on a horse doing this. **3** move gaily or proudly: *The children pranced about in their new Halloween costumes.* **4** a prancing. 1-3 *v.,* **pranced, pranc ing;** 4 *n.*

hat, āge, fär; let, ēqual, tėrm;
it, īce; hot, ōpen, ôrder;
oil, out; cup, pùt, rüle; ch, child;
ng, long; sh, she; th, thin;
ᵀH, then; zh, measure;

ə represents *a* in about,
e in taken, *i* in pencil,
o in lemon, *u* in circus.

prank (prangk), piece of mischief; playful trick: *On April Fools' Day people often play pranks on others. n.*

prank ish (prang′kish), **1** full of pranks; fond of pranks. **2** like a prank. *adj.*

prank ster (prangk′stər), person who plays pranks. *n.*

pra se o dym i um (prā′zē ō dim′ē-əm), a yellowish-white metallic element which occurs with neodymium. Its green salts are used to tint ceramics. *n.*

prate (prāt), talk a great deal in a foolish way. *v.,* **prat ed, prat ing.**

prat tle (prat′l), **1** tell freely and carelessly, as some children do. **2** talk in a foolish way. **3** childish or foolish talk. **4** sounds like baby talk; babble: *the prattle of a brook.* 1,2 *v.,* **prat tled, prat tling;** 3,4 *n.*

prawn (prôn), any of several shellfish used for food. Prawns are much like shrimps but larger. *n.*

pray (prā), **1** ask from God; speak to God in worship: *They prayed that there be an end to the famine.* **2** ask earnestly for: *pray one's forgiveness.* **3** bring or get by praying. **4** please: *Pray come with me. v.*

prayer (prer *or* prar), **1** act of praying. **2** thing prayed for: *Our prayers were granted.* **3** form of words to be used in praying: *the Lord's Prayer.* **4** form of worship. **5** an earnest or humble request. *n.*

prayer book, book of prayers.

prayer ful (prer′fəl *or* prar′fəl), having the habit of praying often; devout. *adj.* —**prayer′ful ly,** *adv.*

praying mantis, mantis.

pre-, *prefix.* **1** before: *Prewar = before the war.* **2** beforehand: *Preview = view beforehand.* [from Latin *prae-*]

preach (prēch), **1** speak on a religious subject; deliver (a sermon). **2** make known by preaching; proclaim: *preach the gospel.* **3** recommend strongly; urge: *The coach was always preaching exercise and fresh air. Practice what you preach.* **4** give earnest advice: *preach about good table manners. v.*

preach er (prē′chər), person who preaches; clergyman; minister. *n.*

adj.	adjective	*n.*	noun
adv.	adverb	*prep.*	preposition
conj.	conjunction	*pron.*	pronoun
interj.	interjection	*v.*	verb
sing.	singular	*pl.*	plural

preach ing (prē′ching), what is preached; sermon. *n.*

pre am ble (prē′am′bəl), introduction to a speech or a writing. The reasons for a law and its general purpose are often stated in a preamble. *n.*

pre ar range (prē′ə ranj′), arrange beforehand. *v.*, **pre ar ranged, pre ar rang ing.**

pre car i ous (pri ker′ē əs *or* pri kar′ē əs), not safe or secure; uncertain; dangerous; risky: *A racing-car driver leads a precarious life. His hold on the branch was precarious. adj.* —**pre car′i ous ly,** *adv.* —**pre car′i ous ness,** *n.*

pre cau tion (pri kô′shən), 1 care taken beforehand; thing done beforehand to ward off evil or secure good results: *Locking doors is a precaution against thieves.* 2 a taking care beforehand: *Proper precaution is prudent. n.*

pre cau tion ar y (pri kô′shə ner′ē), of or using precaution: *She wore warm clothing as a precautionary measure against catching a cold. adj.*

pre cede (prē sēd′), 1 go or come before: *A precedes B in the alphabet. The band preceded the floats in the parade.* 2 be higher than in rank or importance: *A major precedes a captain. v.,* **pre ced ed, pre ced ing.**

prec e dence (pres′ə dəns *or* pri sēd′ns), 1 act or fact of preceding; a going or coming before in time or order. 2 higher position or rank; greater importance: *This work takes precedence over all other work.* 3 right to precede others in ceremonies or social affairs; social superiority: *A Senator takes precedence over a Representative. n.*

prec e dent (pres′ə dənt *for* 1; pri sēd′nt *or* pres′ə dənt *for* 2), 1 action that may serve as an example or reason for a later action: *A decision of a court often serves as a precedent in other courts. Last year's school picnic set a precedent for having one this year.* 2 preceding. 1 *n.,* 2 *adj.*

pre ced ing (prē sē′ding), going before; coming before; previous: *Turn back and look for the answer on the preceding page. adj.*

pre cept (prē′sept), rule of action or behavior; maxim: *"If at first you don't*

succeed, try, try again" is a familiar precept. n.

pre cep tor (pri sep′tər), instructor; teacher. *n.*

pre cinct (prē′singkt), 1 a part or district of a city: *an election precinct, a police precinct.* 2 space within a boundary: *Do not leave the school precincts during school hours.* 3 boundary; limit: *The parade will be held within the precincts of the town. n.*

pre cious (presh′əs), 1 having great value; worth much; valuable. Gold, platinum, and silver are often called the precious metals. Diamonds, rubies, and sapphires are precious stones. 2 much loved; dear: *a precious child.* 3 too nice; overrefined: *precious language.* 4 INFORMAL. very great: *He's put things in a precious mess!* 5 INFORMAL. very: *precious little money.* 1-4 *adj.,* 5 *adv.* —**pre′cious ly,** *adv.* —**pre′cious ness,** *n.*

prec i pice (pres′ə pis), a very steep or almost vertical face of a rock, etc.; cliff, crag, or steep mountainside. *n.*

pre cip i tant (pri sip′ə tənt), 1 falling or rushing headlong; acting in a hasty or rash manner; very sudden or abrupt: *Rain put the picnickers to precipitant flight.* 2 substance that causes another substance to be separated out of a solution as a solid. 1 *adj.,* 2 *n.*

pre cip i tate (pri sip′ə tāt *for* 1,3,4,6; pri sip′ə tit *or* pri sip′ə tāt *for* 2,5), 1 hasten the beginning of; bring about suddenly: *precipitate an argument.* 2 with great haste and force; plunging or rushing; hasty; rash: *a precipitate action.* 3 throw headlong; hurl: *precipitate a rock down a cliff; precipitate oneself into a struggle.* 4 separate (a substance) out from a solution as a solid. 5 substance separated out from a solution as a solid. 6 condense (water vapor) from the air in the form of rain, dew, snow, etc. 1,3,4,6 *v.,* **pre cip i tat ed, pre cip i tat ing;** 2 *adj.,* 5 *n.* —**pre cip′i tate ly,** *adv.*

pre cip i ta tion (pri sip′ə tā′shən), 1 act or condition of precipitating; a throwing down or falling headlong. 2 a hastening or hurrying. 3 a sudden bringing on: *the precipitation of a quarrel, the precipitation of a war without warning.* 4 unwise or rash rapidity; sudden haste. 5 the separating out of a substance from a solution as a solid. 6 the depositing of moisture in the form of rain, dew, snow, etc. 7 something that is precipitated, such as rain, dew, or snow. *n.*

pre cip i tous (pri sip′ə təs), 1 like a precipice; very steep: *precipitous cliffs.* 2 hasty; rash. *adj.*

pre cise (pri sīs′), 1 very definite or correct; exact; accurate: *The directions*

they gave were so precise that we found our way easily. The precise sum was 34 cents. 2 very careful: *precise handwriting. She is precise in her work.* 3 strict: *We had precise orders to come home by nine o'clock. adj.* —**pre cise′ly,** *adv.* —**pre cise′ness,** *n.*

pre ci sion (pri sizh′ən), a being exact; accuracy: *the precision of a machine, to speak with precision. n.*

pre clude (pri klüd′), shut out; make impossible; prevent: *The heavy thunderstorm precluded our going to the beach. v.,* **pre clud ed, pre clud ing.**

pre co cious (pri kō′shəs), developed earlier than usual in knowledge, skill, etc.: *This very precocious child could read well at the age of four. adj.* —**pre co′cious ly,** *adv.* —**pre co′cious ness,** *n.*

pre coc i ty (pri kos′ə tē), precocious development; early maturity: *Mozart's precocity was extraordinary, for when he was only five years old, he began to compose music. n.*

pre con ceive (prē′kən sēv′), form an idea or opinion of beforehand: *The beauty of the scenery surpassed all our preconceived notions. v.,* **pre con ceived, pre con ceiv ing.**

pre con cep tion (prē′kən sep′shən), idea or opinion formed beforehand. *n.*

pre con cert (prē′kən sèrt′), arrange beforehand: *At a preconcerted signal we sang "Happy Birthday." v.*

pre cur sor (pri kèr′sər), forerunner: *A severe cold may be the precursor of pneumonia. n.*

pred a tor (pred′ə tər), animal or person that is predatory. *n.*

pred a to ry (pred′ə tôr′ē), 1 living by preying upon other animals. Lions and tigers are predatory animals. Hawks and owls are predatory birds. 2 inclined to plundering or robbery: *Predatory pirates infested the seas. adj.*

pred e ces sor (pred′ə ses′ər), person holding a position or office before another: *John Adams was Jefferson's predecessor as President. n.*

pre des ti na tion (prē des′tə nā′shən), 1 an ordaining beforehand; destiny; fate. 2 action of God in deciding beforehand what shall happen; doctrine that by God's decree certain souls will be saved and others lost. *n.*

pre des tine (prē des′tən), determine or settle beforehand; foreordain. *v.,* **pre des tined, pre des tin ing.**

pre de ter mine (prē′di tèr′mən), determine or decide beforehand: *We met at the predetermined time. v.,* **pre de ter mined, pre de ter min ing.**

pre dic a ment (pri dik′ə mənt), an unpleasant, difficult, or dangerous situation: *She was in a predicament when she missed the last train home. n.*

pred i cate (pred′ə kit *for 1,2;* pred′- ə kāt *for 3-5*), 1 (in grammar) the word or words expressing what is said about the subject. EXAMPLES: Dogs *bark.* The dogs *dug holes.* The dogs *are beagles.* 2 (in grammar) belonging to the predicate. In "Horses are strong," *strong* is a **predicate adjective.** In "The dogs are beagles," *beagles* is a **predicate noun.** 3 found or base (a statement, action, etc.) on something. 4 declare, assert, or affirm to be real or true: *Most religions predicate life after death.* 5 declare to be an attribute or quality (of some person or thing): *We predicate trustworthiness of friends.* 1 *n.,* 2 *adj.,* 3-5 *v.,* **pred i cat ed, pred i cat ing.**

pre dict (pri dikt′), tell beforehand; prophesy: *The Weather Bureau predicts rain for tomorrow.* *v.*

pre dict a bil i ty (pri dik′tə bil′ə tē), quality of being predictable. *n.*

pre dict a ble (pri dik′tə bəl), that can be predicted. *adj.*

pre dict a bly (pri dik′tə blē), in a predictable manner. *adv.*

pre dic tion (pri dik′shən), 1 act of predicting. 2 thing predicted; prophecy: *The official predictions about the weather often come true.* *n.*

pre di gest (prē′də jest′ *or* prē′dī- jest′), treat (food) by an artificial process similar to digestion, in order to make it more easily digestible. *v.*

pre di lec tion (prē′də lek′shən *or* pred′ə lek′shən), a liking; preference. *n.*

pre dis pose (prē′dis pōz′), give an inclination or tendency to; make liable or susceptible: *A cold predisposes a person to other diseases.* *v.,* **pre dis- posed, pre dis pos ing.**

pre dis po si tion (prē′dis′pə- zish′ən), a being predisposed; inclination or tendency: *a predisposition to look on the dark side of things.* *n.*

pre dom i nance (pri dom′ə nəns), a being predominant: *the predominance of weeds in a deserted garden.* *n.*

pre dom i nant (pri dom′ə nənt), 1 having more power, authority, or influence than others; superior: *The United States is probably the predominant nation in the Western Hemisphere today.* 2 most noticeable; prevailing: *Red was the predominant color in the fabric.* *adj.* **—pre dom′i nant ly,** *adv.*

pre dom i nate (pri dom′ə nāt), be greater in power, strength, influence, or numbers: *Sunny days predominate over rainy days in desert regions.* *v.,* **pre- dom i nat ed, pre dom i nat ing.**

pre dom i na tion (pri dom′ə- nā′shən), act of predominating; superior power or influence; prevalence. *n.*

pre em i nence or **pre-em i nence** (prē em′ə nəns), a being outstanding or

preeminent; superiority: *the preeminence of an Olympic skier.* *n.*

pre em i nent or **pre-em i nent** (prē em′ə nənt), standing out above all others; superior to others. *adj.* **—pre em′i nent ly, pre-em′i nent ly,** *adv.*

pre empt or **pre-empt** (prē empt′), 1 secure before someone else can; acquire beforehand: *preempt the most comfortable chair.* 2 take over; replace: *A special preempted regular TV programing.* 3 settle on (land) with the right to buy it before others. *v.*

pre emp tion or **pre-emp tion** (prē emp′shən), act or right of purchasing before others or in preference to others. *n.*

preen (prēn), 1 smooth or arrange (the feathers) with the beak, as a bird does. 2 dress (oneself) carefully. *v.*

pre ex ist or **pre-ex ist** (prē′ig- zist′), exist beforehand, or before something else. *v.*

pre ex ist ence or **pre-ex ist ence** (prē′ig zis′təns), previous existence. *n.*

pre ex ist ent or **pre-ex ist ent** (prē′ig zis′tənt), existing previously. *adj.*

pre fab ri cate (prē fab′rə kāt), make all standardized parts of (a building, etc.). The erection of a prefabricated house requires merely the assembling of the various sections. *v.,* **pre fab ri- cat ed, pre fab ri cat ing.**

pref ace (pref′is), 1 introduction to a book, writing, or speech: *This book has a preface written by the author.* 2 introduce by written or spoken remarks; give a preface to. 3 be a preface to; begin. 1 *n.,* 2,3 *v.,* **pref aced, pref ac- ing.**

pref a to ry (pref′ə tôr′ē), of or like a preface; made as a preface; introductory; preliminary. *adj.*

pre fect (prē′fekt), 1 (in ancient Rome) the title of various military and civil officers. 2 the chief administrative official of a department of France. *n.*

pre fec ture (prē′fek chər), office, jurisdiction, territory, or official residence of a prefect. *n.*

pre fer (pri fėr′), 1 like better; choose rather: *I will come later, if you prefer. She prefers reading to playing.* 2 put forward; present: *prefer a claim to property. The policeman preferred charges of speeding against the driver.* 3 promote; advance: *He was preferred to the rank of major.* *v.,* **pre ferred, pre fer ring.**

pref er a ble (pref′ər ə bəl), to be preferred; more desirable. *adj.*

pref er a bly (pref′ər ə blē), by choice: *She needs an assistant, preferably one who is a college graduate.* *adv.*

pref er ence (pref′ər əns), 1 act or

hat, āge, fär; let, ēqual, tėrm; it, īce; hot, ōpen, ôrder; oil, out; cup, pùt, rüle; ch, child; ng, long; sh, she; th, thin; ŦH, then; zh, measure;

ə represents *a* in about, *e* in taken, *i* in pencil, *o* in lemon, *u* in circus.

attitude of preferring; liking better: *My preference is for beef rather than lamb.* 2 thing preferred; first choice: *My preference in reading is a mystery story.* 3 the favoring of one above another: *A teacher should not show preference for any student.* *n.*

pref e ren tial (pref′ə ren′shəl), of, giving, or receiving preference: *preferential treatment.* *adj.* **—pref′e- ren′tial ly,** *adv.*

pre fer ment (pri fėr′mənt), advancement; promotion: *seek preferment in one's job.* *n.*

pre fig ure (prē fig′yər), 1 represent beforehand by a figure or type: *In one painting of Christ, His shadow is that of a cross, prefiguring the Crucifixion.* 2 imagine to oneself beforehand. *v.,* **pre fig ured, pre fig ur ing.**

pre fix (prē′fiks *for 1;* prē fiks′ *for 2*), 1 syllable, syllables, or word put at the beginning of a word to change its meaning or to make another word, as *pre-* in *prepaid, under-* in *underline, dis-* in *disappear, un-* in *unlike,* and *re-* in *redo.* 2 put before: *We prefix "Mr." to a man's name.* 1 *n., pl.* **pre fix es;** 2 *v.*

preg nan cy (preg′nən sē), pregnant quality or condition. *n., pl.* **preg nan- cies.**

preg nant (preg′nənt), 1 having one or more offspring developing in the womb; soon to have a baby. 2 filled; loaded. 3 fertile; rich; abounding: *a mind pregnant with ideas.* 4 filled with meaning; very significant: *proverbs and other pregnant sayings.* *adj.*

pre hen sile (pri hen′səl), adapted for

prehensile monkey with a prehensile tail

659

adj.	adjective	*n.*	noun
adv.	adverb	*prep.*	preposition
conj.	conjunction	*pron.*	pronoun
interj.	interjection	*v.*	verb
sing.	singular	*pl.*	plural

seizing, grasping, or holding on. Many monkeys have prehensile tails. *adj.*

pre his to ric (prē′hi stôr′ik), of or belonging to times before histories were written: *We find stone tools made by prehistoric peoples. adj.* —**pre′his to′-ri cal ly,** *adv.*

pre his to ri cal (prē′hi stôr′ə kəl), prehistoric. *adj.*

pre judge (prē juj′), judge beforehand; judge without knowing all the facts. *v.*, **pre judged, pre judg ing.**

prej u dice (prej′ə dis), 1 opinion formed without taking time and care to judge fairly: *a prejudice against doctors, a prejudice toward foreigners.* 2 cause a prejudice in; fill with prejudice: *One unfortunate experience prejudiced them against all lawyers.* 3 harm or injury: *I will do nothing to the prejudice of my cousin in this matter.* 4 to harm or injure. 1,3 *n.,* 2,4 *v.,* **prej u diced, prej u dic ing.**

prej u di cial (prej′ə dish′əl), causing prejudice or disadvantage; hurtful: *acting in a manner prejudicial to others. adj.* —**prej′u di′cial ly,** *adv.*

prel a cy (prel′ə sē), 1 position or rank of a prelate. 2 prelates. 3 church government by prelates. *n., pl.* **prel a cies.**

prel ate (prel′it), clergyman of high rank, such as a bishop. *n.*

pre lim i nar y (pri lim′ə ner′ē), 1 coming before the main business; leading to something more important: *After the preliminary exercises of prayer and song, the speaker of the day gave an address.* 2 a preliminary step; something preparatory: *An examination is a preliminary to entering that school.* 1 *adj.,* 2 *n., pl.* **pre lim i nar ies.**

prel ude (prel′yüd *or* prē′lüd), 1 anything serving as an introduction: *The German invasion of Poland was a prelude to World War II.* 2 be a prelude or introduction to. 3 in music: **a** a composition, or part of it, that introduces another composition or part. **b** an independent instrumental composition, usually short. 4 introduce with a prelude. 1,3 *n.,* 2,4 *v.,* **prel ud ed, prel ud ing.**

pre ma ture (prē′mə chùr′, prē′mə-tür′, *or* prē′mə tyùr′), before the proper time; too soon: *Their arrival an hour before the party began was pre-*mature. *adj.* —**pre′ma ture′ly,** *adv.*

pre med i cal (prē med′ə kəl), preparing for the study of medicine: *a premedical student, a premedical course. adj.*

pre med i tate (prē med′ə tāt), consider or plan beforehand: *premeditate a move in chess. The murder was premeditated. v.,* **pre med i tat ed, pre-med i tat ing.**

pre med i ta tion (prē′med ə tā′-shən), previous deliberation or planning. *n.*

pre mier (pri mir′ *for 1;* prē′mē ər *for 2,3*), 1 prime minister. 2 first in rank; chief. 3 first in time; earliest. 1 *n.,* 2,3 *adj.*

pre miere (pri mir′ *or* prə myer′), 1 a first public performance: *the premiere of a new play.* 2 premier; first. 1 *n., pl.* **pre mieres;** 2 *adj.* [from French]

prem ise (prem′is *for 1,2;* pri mīz′ *for 3*), 1 (in logic) a statement assumed to be true and used to draw a conclusion. EXAMPLE: Major premise: Children should go to school. Minor premise: He is a child. Conclusion: He should go to school. 2 **premises,** *pl.* **a** house or building with its grounds. **b** (in law) things mentioned previously, such as the names of the parties concerned, a description of the property, the price, grounds for complaint, etc. **c** (in law) the property forming the subject of a document. 3 set forth as an introduction. 1,2 *n.,* 3 *v.,* **pre mised, pre mis ing.**

pre mi um (prē′mē əm), 1 a reward, especially one given as an incentive to buy; prize: *Some magazines give premiums for obtaining new subscriptions.* 2 something more than the ordinary price or wages: *Tickets for the concert were scarce and selling at a premium.* 3 money paid for insurance: *I pay premiums on my life insurance four times a year.* 4 unusual or unfair value: *put too high a premium on neatness. n.*

at a premium, 1 at more than the usual value or price. 2 very valuable; much wanted.

pre mo lar (prē mō′lər), bicuspid. *n.*

pre mo ni tion (prē′mə nish′ən), a forewarning: *a vague premonition of disaster. n.*

pre mon i to ry (pri mon′ə tôr′ē), giving warning beforehand. *adj.*

pre na tal (prē nā′tl), previous to birth: *A woman soon to have a baby requires prenatal care. adj.*

pre oc cu pa tion (prē ok′yə pā′-shən), 1 act of preoccupying. 2 condition of being preoccupied; absorption. *n.*

pre oc cu pied (prē ok′yə pīd), absorbed; engrossed. *adj.*

pre oc cu py (prē ok′yə pī), 1 take up all the attention of; absorb: *The prob-*lem of getting to New York preoccupied her mind. 2 occupy beforehand; take possession of before others: *Our favorite seats had been preoccupied. v.,* **pre oc cu pied, pre oc cu py ing.**

pre or dain (prē′ôr dān′), decide or settle beforehand; foreordain. *v.*

prep (prep), INFORMAL. preparatory: *a prep school. adj.*

prep., preposition.

pre paid (prē pād′), past tense and past participle of **prepay.** *Send this shipment prepaid. v.*

prep a ra tion (prep′ə rā′shən), 1 a preparing; making ready: *I sharpened the knife in preparation for carving the meat.* 2 a being ready. 3 thing done to get ready: *He made thorough preparations for his trip by carefully planning which routes to take.* 4 a specially made medicine or food or mixture of any kind. *n.*

pre par a to ry (pri par′ə tôr′ē), 1 of or for preparation; making ready; preparing. Preparatory schools fit pupils for college. 2 as an introduction; preliminary: *preparatory remarks. adj.*

pre pare (pri per′ *or* pri par′), 1 make ready; get ready: *prepare lessons, prepare dinner.* 2 make by a special process: *prepare aluminum from bauxite. v.,* **pre pared, pre par ing.**

pre par ed ness (pri per′id nis *or* pri-par′id nis), 1 a being prepared; readiness. 2 having adequate military forces and defenses to meet threats or outbreaks of war. *n.*

pre pay (prē pā′), 1 pay in advance. 2 pay for in advance. *v.,* **pre paid, pre pay ing.**

pre pay ment (prē pā′mənt), payment in advance. *n.*

pre pon der ance (pri pon′dər-əns), 1 greater number; greater weight; greater power or influence: *In July the hot days have the preponderance.* 2 a being the chief or most important element: *the preponderance of oaks in these woods. n.*

pre pon der ant (pri pon′dər ənt), 1 weighing more; being stronger or more numerous; having more power or influence. 2 most important; chief: *Lush vegetation is the preponderant characteristic of the jungle. adj.* —**pre-pon′der ant ly,** *adv.*

pre pon der ate (pri pon′də rāt′), 1 be greater than something else in weight, power, force, influence, number, amount, etc. 2 be chief; be most important. *v.,* **pre pon der at ed, pre-pon de rat ing.**

prep o si tion (prep′ə zish′ən), word that expresses some relation to a noun, pronoun, phrase, or clause which follows it. *With, for, by,* and *in* are prepositions in the sentence "A man *with* rugs for sale walked *by* our house *in* the morning." *n.*

prep o si tion al (prep/ə zish/ə nəl), 1 having to do with a preposition: *a prepositional phrase.* 2 having the nature or function of a preposition. *adj.*

pre pos sess (prē/pə zes/), 1 fill with a favorable feeling or opinion: *We were prepossessed by the actor's modest behavior.* 2 fill with a feeling or opinion. *v.*

pre pos sess ing (prē/pə zes/ing), making a favorable impression; attractive; pleasing: *In my old, ragged work clothes, my appearance was not very prepossessing. adj.*

pre pos ses sion (prē/pə zesh/ən), a favorable feeling or opinion formed beforehand: *A well-written letter applying for a position will create a prepossession toward the writer. n.*

pre pos ter ous (pri pos/tər əs), contrary to nature, reason, or common sense; absurd; senseless; foolish: *It would be preposterous to shovel snow with a teaspoon. That the moon is made of green cheese is a preposterous notion. adj.* —**pre pos/ter ous ly,** *adv.*

pre req ui site (prē rek/wə zit), 1 something required beforehand: *The completion of a high-school course is the usual prerequisite to college work.* 2 required beforehand. 1 *n.,* 2 *adj.*

pre rog a tive (pri rog/ə tiv), right or privilege that nobody else has: *The government has the prerogative of coining money. n.*

pres age (pres/ij *for 1,3;* pres/ij *or* pri sāj/ *for 2,4*), 1 a sign felt as a warning; omen. 2 give warning of; predict: *Some people think that a circle around the moon presages a storm.* 3 a feeling that something is about to happen. 4 have or give a prophetic impression of. 1,3 *n.,* 2,4 *v.,* **pre saged, pre sag ing.**

pres by ter (prez/bə tər), 1 an elder in the early Christian church. 2 a minister or a lay elder in the Presbyterian Church. 3 a minister or a priest in the Episcopal Church. *n.*

Pres by ter i an (prez/bə tir/ē ən), 1 of or belonging to a Protestant denomination or church governed by elected presbyters or elders all of equal rank. 2 member of a Presbyterian church. 1 *adj.,* 2 *n.*

Pres by ter i an ism (prez/bə tir/ē ə niz/əm), 1 system of church government by elders all (including ministers) of equal rank. 2 beliefs of Presbyterian churches. *n.*

pres by ter y (prez/bə ter/ē), 1 (in the Presbyterian Church) a meeting or court of all the ministers and certain of the elders within a district. 2 district under the jurisdiction of such a meeting

or court. 3 the part of a church set aside for the clergy. *n., pl.* **pres by ter ies.**

pre school (prē/skül/), before the age of going to regular school: *preschool training, preschool children. adj.*

pre sci ence (prē/shē əns), knowledge of things before they exist or happen; foreknowledge; foresight: *Some people believe that animals have an instinctive prescience of the approach of danger. n.*

pre sci ent (prē/shē ənt), knowing beforehand; foreseeing. *adj.*

pre scribe (pri skrīb/), 1 lay down as a rule to be followed; order; direct: *Good citizens do what the laws prescribe.* 2 order as a medicine or treatment: *The doctor prescribed penicillin.* 3 give medical advice; issue a prescription. *v.,* **pre scribed, pre scrib ing.**

pre scrip tion (pri skrip/shən), 1 order; direction. 2 a written direction or order for preparing and using a medicine: *a prescription for a cough.* 3 the medicine. *n.*

pre scrip tive (pri skrip/tiv), 1 prescribing. 2 established by law or custom. *adj.*

pres ence (prez/ns), 1 a being present in a place: *I just learned of her presence in the city.* 2 a place where a person is: *The messenger was admitted to the king's presence.* 3 appearance; bearing: *The queen is a person of noble presence.* 4 something present, especially a ghost, spirit, or the like. *n.*

in the presence of, in the sight or company of: *I signed my name in the presence of two witnesses.*

presence of mind, ability to think calmly and quickly under stress.

pres ent¹ (prez/nt), 1 being in the place or thing in question; at hand, not absent: *Every member of the class was present. Oxygen is present in the air.* 2 at this time; being or occurring now: *the present ruler, present prices.* 3 the time being; this time; now: *That is enough for the present. At present people need courage.* 4 the present tense or a verb form in that tense. 1,2 *adj.,* 3,4 *n.* [from Latin *praesentem,* from *prae-* *before* + *esse* be]

pre sent² (pri zent/ *for 1,3-8;* prez/nt *for 2*), 1 give: *They presented flowers to their teacher.* 2 thing given; gift: *a birthday present.* 3 offer formally; offer: *The servant presented the sandwiches to each guest.* 4 make acquaint-

ed; bring (a person) before somebody; introduce: *She was presented at court. Miss Smith, may I present Mr. Brown?* 5 offer to view or notice: *The new library presents a fine appearance.* 6 bring before the public: *Our school presented a play.* 7 set forth in words; offer: *The speaker presented arguments for his side.* 8 hand in; send in: *The grocer presented his bill.* 1,3-8 *v.,* 2 *n.* [from French of the 1200's *presenter,* from Latin *praesentare,* from *praesentem* present¹]

present with, give to: *Our class presented the school with a picture.*

pre sent a ble (pri zen/tə bəl), 1 fit to be seen: *to make a house presentable for company.* 2 suitable in appearance, dress, manners, etc., for being introduced into society or company. 3 suitable to be offered or given. *adj.*

pres en ta tion (prez/n tā/shən *or* prē/zen tā/shən), 1 act of giving; delivering: *the presentation of a gift.* 2 the gift that is presented. 3 a bringing forward; offering: to be considered: *the presentation of a plan.* 4 an offering to be seen; showing; exhibition: *the presentation of a play or a motion picture.* 5 a formal introduction: *the presentation of a lady to the queen. n.*

pres ent-day (prez/nt dā/), of the present time. *adj.*

pre sen ti ment (pri zen/tə mənt), a feeling or impression that something is about to happen; vague sense of approaching misfortune; foreboding. *n.*

pres ent ly (prez/nt lē), 1 before long; soon: *The clock will strike presently.* 2 at the present time; at this time; now: *Most eleven-year-old children are presently in sixth grade. adv.*

pre sent ment (pri zent/mənt), 1 a bringing forward; offering to be considered. 2 a showing; offering to be seen. 3 something brought forward or shown. *n.*

present participle, participle that indicates time that is now. In "Singing merrily, we turn our steps toward home," *singing* is a present participle.

present tense, 1 tense that ex-

presbytery (def. 3)

preservation

adj. adjective	n. noun
adv. adverb	prep. preposition
conj. conjunction	pron. pronoun
interj. interjection	v. verb
sing. singular	pl. plural

presses time that is now. 2 a verb form in the present tense.

pres er va tion (prez/ər vā/shən), 1 a preserving; keeping safe: *Doctors work for the preservation of our health.* 2 a being preserved; being kept safe: *Egyptian mummies have been in a state of preservation for thousands of years.* n.

pre serv a tive (pri zėr/və tiv), 1 any substance that will prevent decay or injury: *Paint is a preservative for wood surfaces. Salt is a preservative for meat.* 2 that preserves. 1 n., 2 adj.

press¹ (def. 6) for making cider

pre serve (pri zėrv/), 1 keep from harm or change; keep safe; protect. 2 keep up; maintain. 3 keep from spoiling: *Ice helps to preserve food.* 4 prepare (food) to keep it from spoiling. Boiling with sugar, salting, smoking, and pickling are different ways of preserving food. 5 **preserves,** pl. fruit cooked with sugar and sealed from the air: *Try our homemade plum preserves.* 6 a place where wild animals, fish, or trees and plants are protected: *People are not allowed to hunt in that preserve.* 1-4 v., **pre served, pre serv ing;** 5,6 n.

pre serv er (pri zėr/vər), person or thing that saves and protects from danger. Life preservers help to save people from drowning. n.

pre set (prē set/), set in advance: *The course of the missile was preset before it was launched.* v., **pre set, pre set ting.**

pre side (pri zīd/), 1 hold the place of authority; have charge of a meeting: *Our principal will preside at our election of school officers.* 2 have authority; have control: *The manager presides over the business of this store.* v., **pre sid ed, pre sid ing.**

pres i den cy (prez/ə dən sē), 1 office of president: *She was elected to the presidency of the Junior Club.* 2 time in which a president is in office: *The United States entered World War II during the presidency of Franklin D. Roosevelt.* n., pl. **pres i den cies.**

pres i dent (prez/ə dənt), 1 the chief officer of a company, college, society, club, etc. 2 Often, **President.** the highest executive officer of a republic. n.

pres i dent-e lect (prez/ə dənt i-lekt/), president who has been elected but not yet inaugurated. n.

pres i den tial (prez/ə den/shəl), of or having to do with a president or presidency: *a presidential election, a presidential candidate.* adj.

press¹ (pres), 1 use force or weight steadily against; push with steady force: *Press the button to ring the bell.* 2 squeeze out; squeeze: *press apples for cider. Press all the juice from the oranges.* 3 make smooth; flatten: *Press clothes with an iron.* 4 clasp; hug: *I pressed the puppy to me.* 5 a pressing; pressure; push: *The press of many duties keeps the principal very busy.* 6 machine for pressing: *an ironing press.* 7 establishment for printing books, etc. 8 the business of printing newspapers and magazines: *Many editors, writers, and printers work for the press.* 9 newspapers and magazines and the people who write for them: *Our school picnic was reported by the press.* 10 push forward; keep pushing: *I pressed on in spite of the strong wind.* 11 urge onward; cause to hurry. 12 a crowd; throng: *The little boy was lost in the press.* 13 to crowd; throng: *The people pressed about the famous actor.* 14 keep asking (somebody) earnestly; urge: *Because it was so stormy, we pressed our guest to stay all night.* 15 compel; force. 16 harass; oppress; trouble. 17 cupboard or closet for clothes, books, etc. 1-4,10,11,13-16 v., 5-9,12,17 n., pl. **press es.** [from French of the 1200's *presser,* from Latin *pressare*] —**press/er,** n.

go to press, begin to be printed: *The newspaper goes to press at midnight.*

press² (pres), force into service, usually naval or military. Naval officers used to visit towns and merchant ships to press men for the fleet. v. [earlier *prest,* from French of the 1400's *prester* furnish, from Latin *praestare*]

press agent, agent in charge of publicity for a person, organization, etc.; publicist.

press ing (pres/ing), requiring immediate action or attention; urgent: *A person with a broken leg is in pressing need of a doctor's help. She left town quickly on some pressing business.* adj.

pres sure (presh/ər), 1 the continued action of a weight or force: *The small box was flattened by the pressure of the heavy book on it. The pressure of the wind filled the sails of the boat.* 2 force per unit of area: *There is a pressure of 27 pounds to the square inch in this tire.* 3 a state of trouble or strain: *the pressure of poverty, working under pressure.* 4 a compelling force or influence: *I was under pressure from the others to change my mind.* 5 force or urge by exerting pressure: *The car dealer tried to pressure my parents into buying a car.* 6 need for prompt or decisive action; urgency: *the pressure of business.* 1-4,6 n., 5 v., **pres sured, pres sur ing.**

pressure cooker, an airtight container for cooking with steam under pressure.

pres sur ize (presh/ə rīz/), keep the atmospheric pressure inside (the cabin of an aircraft) at a normal level in spite of the altitude. v., **pres sur ized, pres sur iz ing.**

pres tige (pre stēzh/), reputation, influence, or distinction based on what is known about one's abilities, achievements, opportunities, associations, etc.: *Her prestige rose when her classmates learned that she knew how to ski.* n.

pres to (pres/tō), in music: 1 very quickly. 2 very quick. 3 a very quick part in a piece of music. 1 adv., 2 adj., 3 n., pl. **pres tos.**

pre sum a ble (pri zü/mə bəl), that can be presumed or taken for granted; probable; likely: *Unless they lose their way, noon is the presumable time of their arrival.* adj.

pre sum a bly (pri zü/mə blē), as may be reasonably supposed; probably. adv.

press¹ (def. 17)

pre sume (pri züm/), 1 take for granted without proving; suppose: *You'll play out of doors, I presume, if there is sunshine. The law presumes innocence until guilt is proved.* 2 take upon oneself; venture; dare: *May I presume to tell you you are wrong?* 3 take an unfair advantage: *Don't presume on his good nature by borrowing from him every week.* 4 act with improper boldness; take liberties: *It would be presuming to* camp in a farmer's field without permission. *v.*, **pre sumed, pre sum ing.**

pre sum ed ly (pri zü′mid lē), presumably. *adv.*

pre sump tion (pri zump′shən), 1 unpleasant boldness: *It is presumption to go to a party when one has not been invited.* 2 thing taken for granted: *Since she had left the room last, the presumption was that she turned out the lights.* 3 cause or reason for presuming; probability. 4 act of presuming. *n.*

pre sump tive (pri zump′tiv), 1 based on likelihood; presumed: *a presumptive title to an estate.* 2 giving ground for presumption or belief: *Their running away was regarded as presumptive evidence of their guilt. adj.* —**presump′tive ly,** *adv.*

pre sump tu ous (pri zump′chü əs), acting without permission or right; too bold; forward. *adj.* —**pre sump′tuous ly,** *adv.* —**pre sump′tu ous ness,** *n.*

pre sup pose (prē′sə pōz′), 1 take for granted in advance; assume beforehand: *Let's presuppose that we will be going and make some plans for the trip.* 2 require as a condition; imply: *A debate presupposes debaters. v.,* **presup posed, pre sup pos ing.**

pre sup po si tion (prē′sup ə zish′ən), 1 a presupposing. 2 thing presupposed: *The detective acted upon the presupposition that the thief knew the value of the jewels. n.*

pre tence (prē′tens *or* pri tens′), pretense. *n.*

pre tend (pri tend′), 1 make believe: *Let's pretend that we are grown-ups.* 2 claim falsely: *I pretended to like the meal so that my host would be pleased.* 3 claim falsely to have: *I pretended illness.* 4 claim: *I don't pretend to be a musician.* 5 lay claim: *The Scottish king pretended to the English throne. v.*

pre tend ed (pri ten′did), claimed falsely; asserted falsely. *adj.*

pre tend er (pri ten′dər), 1 person who pretends. 2 person who lays claim, especially falsely, to a title or throne. *n.*

pre tense (prē′tens *or* pri tens′), 1 make-believe; pretending: *My anger was all pretense.* 2 a false appearance: *Under pretense of dropping a pencil, the student looked at a classmate's test.* 3 a false claim: *She made a pretense of being surprised but knew of the party all along.* 4 a claim: *He makes no pretense to a knowledge of electronics.* 5 a showing off; display: *Her manner is free from pretense. n.* Also, **pretence.**

pre ten sion (pri ten′shən), 1 a claim: *The young prince has pretensions to the throne.* 2 a putting forward of a claim; laying claim to. 3 a doing things for show or to make a fine appearance;

showy display: *We were annoyed by the pretensions of our wealthy neighbor. n.*

pre ten tious (pri ten′shəs), 1 making claims to excellence or importance: *a pretentious person, a pretentious book, a pretentious speech.* 2 doing things for show or to make a fine appearance: *a pretentious style of entertaining guests. adj.* —**pre ten′tious ly,** *adv.* —**pre ten′tious ness,** *n.*

pret er it *or* **pret er ite** (pret′ər it), in grammar: 1 a verb form that expresses occurrence in the past; past tense. EXAMPLES: *Obeyed* is the preterit of *obey; spoke,* of *speak;* and *saw,* of *see.* 2 expressing past time. 1 *n.,* 2 *adj.*

pre ter nat ur al (prē′tər nach′ər əl), 1 out of the ordinary course of nature; abnormal. 2 due to something above or beyond nature; supernatural. *adj.*

pre text (prē′tekst), a false reason concealing the real reason; misleading excuse; pretense: *He did not go, on the pretext of being too tired. n.*

Pre to ri a (pri tôr′ē ə), administrative capital of the Republic of South Africa, in the NE part. *n.*

pret ti ly (prit′ə lē), in a pretty manner; pleasingly. *adv.*

pret ti ness (prit′ē nis), state or quality of being pretty; pleasing appearance. *n.*

pret ty (prit′ē), 1 pleasing to the eye, ear, etc.: *a pretty face, a pretty dress, a pretty tune.* 2 not at all pleasing: *This is a pretty mess, indeed.* 3 a pretty person or thing. 4 fairly; rather: *It is pretty late.* 1,2 *adj.,* **pret ti er, pret ti est;** 3 *n., pl.* **pret ties;** 4 *adv.*

sitting pretty, in an advantageous position: *They certainly are sitting pretty since they made all that money.*

pret zel (pret′səl), a crisp cracker, usually in the form of a knot or stick, salted on the outside. *n.*

pre vail (pri vāl′), 1 exist in many places; be in general use: *The custom of exchanging gifts at Christmas still prevails.* 2 be the most usual or strongest: *Sadness prevailed in our minds.* 3 be the stronger; gain the victory; succeed: *prevail against an enemy. Reason prevailed over emotion. v.*

prevail on *or* **prevail upon,** persuade: *Can't I prevail upon you to stay for dinner?*

pre vail ing (pri vā′ling), 1 in general use; common: *a prevailing style. The prevailing summer winds here are from the west.* 2 that prevails; having superior force or influence; victorious. *adj.*

prev a lence (prev′ə ləns), widespread occurrence; general use: *the prevalence of complaints about the weather, the prevalence of automobiles. n.*

prev a lent (prev′ə lənt), in general

hat, āge, fär; let, ēqual, tėrm; it, īce; hot, ōpen, ôrder; oil, out; cup, pùt, rüle; ch, child; ng, long; sh, she; th, thin; ₮H, then; zh, measure;

ə represents *a* in about, *e* in taken, *i* in pencil, *o* in lemon, *u* in circus.

use; widespread; common: *Colds are prevalent in the winter. adj.*

pre var i cate (pri var′ə kāt), turn aside from the truth in speech or action; lie. *v.,* **pre var i cat ed, pre var i cat ing.**

pre var i ca tion (pri var′ə kā′shən), a prevaricating; turning aside from the truth. *n.*

pre var i ca tor (pri var′ə kā′tər), person who turns aside from the truth in speech or action. *n.*

pre vent (pri vent′), 1 keep (from): *Illness prevented him from doing his work.* 2 keep from happening: *Rain prevented the game.* 3 hinder: *I'll meet you at six if nothing prevents. v.*

pre vent a ble *or* **pre vent i ble** (pri ven′tə bəl), that can be prevented. *adj.*

pre ven tion (pri ven′shən), 1 a preventing: *the prevention of fire.* 2 something that prevents. *n.*

pre ven tive (pri ven′tiv), 1 that prevents: *preventive measures against disease.* 2 something that prevents: *Vaccination is a preventive against smallpox.* 1 *adj.,* 2 *n.*

pre view (prē′vyü′), 1 a previous view, inspection, survey, etc.: *a preview of things to come.* 2 to view beforehand. 3 an advance showing of scenes from a motion picture, play, television program, etc. 1,3 *n.,* 2 *v.*

pre vi ous (prē′vē əs), 1 coming or going before; that came before; earlier: *She did better in the previous lesson.* 2 INFORMAL. quick; hasty: *Don't be too previous about refusing. adj.* —**pre′vi ous ly,** *adv.*

previous to, before: *Previous to her departure she gave a party.*

pre vi sion (prē vizh′ən), 1 foresight; foreknowledge. 2 prophetic vision or perception: *Some prevision warned the plane's pilot of trouble. n.*

pre war (prē′wôr′), before the war. *adj.*

prey (prā), 1 animal hunted and killed for food by another animal: *Mice and birds are the prey of cats.* 2 habit of hunting and killing other animals for food: *Hawks are birds of prey.* 3 per-

663

adj.	adjective	n.	noun
adv.	adverb	prep.	preposition
conj.	conjunction	pron.	pronoun
interj.	interjection	v.	verb
sing.	singular	pl.	plural

son or thing injured; victim: *to be a prey to fear, to be a prey to disease.* 4 **prey on** or **prey upon, a** hunt or kill for food: *Cats prey upon mice.* **b** be a strain upon; injure; irritate: *Worry about debts preys on her mind.* **c** rob; plunder. 1-3 *n.,* 4 *v.*

Pri am (prī′əm), (in Greek legends) the king of Troy at the time of the Trojan War. *n.*

price (prīs), 1 the amount for which a thing is sold or can be bought; the cost to the buyer: *The price of this hat is $10.* 2 put a price on; set the price of: *The hat was priced at $10.* 3 IN-FORMAL. ask the price of; find out the price of: *Mother is pricing cars.* 4 reward offered for the capture of a person alive or dead: *Every member of the gang has a price on his head.* 5 what must be given, done, undergone, etc., to obtain a thing; amount paid for any result: *The Pilgrims paid a heavy price for staying in America, for half of them died during the first winter.* 6 value; worth: *a diamond of great price.* 1,4-6 *n.,* 2,3 *v.,* **priced, pric ing.**

at any price, at any cost, no matter how great: *We wanted to win at any price.*

beyond price or **without price,** so valuable that it cannot be bought, or be given a value in money.

price less (prīs′lis), beyond price; extremely valuable: *Many museums have collections of priceless paintings by famous artists.* *adj.* —**price′less-ness,** *n.*

prick (prik), 1 a sharp point. 2 a little hole or mark made by a sharp point. 3 make a little hole or mark on with a sharp point: *I pricked the map with a pin to show our route.* 4 a pain like that made by a sharp point: *the prick of conscience.* 5 cause sharp pain to: *The cat pricked me with its claws. Thorns prick.* 6 act of pricking. 7 cause or feel a sharp pain. 8 to point upwards; raise or erect: *The dog pricked up its ears at the noise.* 9 OLD USE. ride fast; spur. 1,2,4,6 *n.,* 3,5,7-9 *v.* —**prick′er,** *n.*

prick le (prik′əl), 1 a small, sharp point; thorn; spine. 2 feel a prickly or smarting sensation: *My skin prickled as I listened to the scary story.* 3 such a sensation. 4 cause such a sensation in.

1,3 *n.,* 2,4 *v.,* **prick led, prick ling.**

prick li ness (prik′lē nis), prickly condition or quality. *n.*

prick ly (prik′lē), 1 having many sharp points or thorns: *a prickly rose-bush, the prickly porcupine.* 2 sharp and stinging; itching; smarting: *Heat sometimes causes a prickly rash on the skin.* *adj.,* **prick li er, prick li est.**

prickly pear, 1 a pear-shaped fruit of a certain kind of cactus. It is good to eat. 2 plant that it grows on. •

pride (prīd), 1 a high opinion of one's own worth or possessions: *Pride in our city should make us help to keep it clean.* 2 pleasure or satisfaction in something concerned with oneself: *to take pride in a hard job well done.* 3 something that one is proud of: *Their oldest child is their great pride.* 4 too high an opinion of oneself; scorn of others; haughtiness: *Pride goes before a fall.* 5 **pride oneself on,** be proud of: *We pride ourselves on our clean streets.* 1-4 *n.,* 5 *v.,* **prid ed, prid ing.**

priest (prēst), 1 clergyman or minister of a Christian church. 2 a special servant of a god, who performs certain public religious acts: *priests of Apollo.* *n.*

priest ess (prē′stis), woman who serves at an altar or in sacred rites: *a priestess of Diana.* *n., pl.* **priest ess es.**

priest hood (prēst′hud), 1 position or rank of priest: *He was admitted to the priesthood.* 2 priests as a group: *the priesthood of Spain.* *n.*

priest ly (prēst′lē), 1 of or having to do with a priest. 2 like a priest; suitable for a priest. *adj.,* **priest li er, priest li est.**

prig (prig), person who is too particular about speech and manners, and prides himself on being better than others. *n.*

prig gish (prig′ish), too particular about doing right in things that show outwardly; priding oneself on being better than others. *adj.* —**prig′gish-ness,** *n.*

prim (prim), stiffly precise, neat, proper, or formal. *adj.,* **prim mer, prim mest.** —**prim′ly,** *adv.* —**prim′-ness,** *n.*

pri ma cy (prī′mə sē), 1 a being first in order, rank, importance, etc. 2 the position of a bishop of highest rank. 3 (in the Roman Catholic Church) the supreme power of the pope. *n., pl.* **pri ma-cies.**

pri ma don na (prē′mə don′ə), 1 the principal woman singer in an opera. 2 a temperamental person. *pl.* **pri ma don nas.** [from Italian *prima donna* first lady]

pri mal (prī′məl), 1 of early times; first; primeval. 2 chief; fundamental. *adj.* —**pri′mal ly,** *adv.*

pri mar i ly (prī′mer′ə lē or prī′mar-ə lē), 1 above all; chiefly; principally: *The scientist was primarily interested in physics.* 2 at first; originally. *adv.*

pri mar y (prī′mer′ē), 1 first in time or order; original; fundamental: *the primary causes of unemployment.* 2 first in importance; chief: *A balanced diet is primary to good health.* 3 anything that is first in order, rank, or importance. 4 an election in which members of a political party choose candidates for office. Primaries are held before the regular election. 1,2 *adj.,* 3,4 *n., pl.* **pri mar ies.**

primary accent, 1 the strongest accent in the pronunciation of a word. 2 mark (′) used to show this.

primary color, any of a group of pigments or colors which, when mixed together, yield all other colors. Red, yellow, and blue are the primary colors in pigments. In light they are red, green, and blue.

primary school, the first three or four grades of elementary school.

pri mate (prī′mit or prī′māt), 1 archbishop or bishop ranking above all other bishops in a country or church province. 2 any of the highest order of mammals, including human beings, apes, monkeys, and lemurs. *n.*

prime[1] (prīm), 1 first in rank; chief: *The town's prime need is a new school.* 2 first in time or order; primary: *the prime causes of pollution.* 3 first in quality; first-rate; excellent: *prime ribs of beef.* 4 prime number. 1-3 *adj.,* 4 *n.* [from Latin *primus* first] —**prime′-ness,** *n.*

prime[2] (prīm), 1 the best part; best time; best condition: *My parents are in the prime of life.* 2 the first part; beginning. 3 springtime. *n.* [Old English *prīm* the first period of the day, from Latin *prima (hora)* first (hour)]

prime[3] (prīm), 1 prepare by putting something in or on. 2 supply (a gun) with powder. 3 cover (a surface) with a first coat of paint or oil so that the finishing coat of paint will not soak in. 4 equip (a person) with information, words, etc.: *prime a person with a speech.* 5 pour water into (a pump) to start action. *v.,* **primed, prim ing.** [origin uncertain]

prime meridian, meridian from which the longitude east and west is measured. It passes through Greenwich, England, and its longitude is 0 degrees.

prime minister, the chief minister in certain governments; premier. The prime minister is the head of the cabinet.

prime number, number not exactly divisible by some counting number other than itself and 1; prime. 2, 3, 5, 7, and 11 are prime numbers; 4, 6, and 9 are composite numbers.

prim er[1] (prim′ər), 1 a first book in reading. 2 a first book; beginner's book: *a primer of statistics.* n. [from Latin *primarius* first in rank]

prim er[2] (prī′mər), 1 person or thing that primes. 2 cap or cylinder containing a little gunpowder, used for firing a charge. n. [*prime*[3] + *-er*[1]]

pri me val (prī mē′vəl), 1 of or having to do with the first age or ages, especially of the world: *In its primeval state the earth was without any forms of life.* 2 ancient: *primeval forests untouched by the ax.* adj. —**pri me′val ly,** adv.

prim ing (prī′ming), 1 powder or other material used to set fire to an explosive. 2 a first coat of paint, oil, etc. n.

prim i tive (prim′ə tiv), 1 of early times; of long ago: *Primitive people often lived in caves.* 2 first of the kind: *primitive Christians.* 3 very simple; such as people had early in human history: *A primitive way of making fire is by rubbing two sticks together.* 4 artist belonging to an early period. 5 work of art by such an artist. 6 person living in a primitive society or in primitive times. 1-3 adj., 4-6 n. —**prim′i tive ly,** adv.

pri mo gen i ture (prī′mə jen′ə chŭr or prī′mə jen′ə chər), 1 fact of being the first-born among the children of the same parents. 2 the right or rule by which the eldest son inherits his father's land and buildings; inheritance by the first-born. n.

pri mor di al (prī môr′dē əl), 1 existing at the very beginning; primitive. 2 original; elementary. adj.

primp (primp), 1 dress (oneself) for show. 2 dress carefully. v.

prim rose (prim′rōz′), 1 any of a large group of plants with flowers of various colors. The common primrose of Europe is pale yellow. 2 its flower. 3 pale-yellow. 4 a pale yellow. 1,2,4 n., 3 adj.

primrose path, a pleasant way; path of pleasure.

prince (prins), 1 son of a king or queen; son of a king's or queen's son. 2 sovereign. 3 ruler of a small state or country. 4 the English equivalent of certain titles of nobility of varying importance or rank in other countries. 5 the greatest or best of a group; chief: *a merchant prince, a prince of artists.* n.

prince dom (prins′dəm), 1 lands ruled by a prince. 2 title or rank of a prince. n.

Prince Edward Island, province in E Canada consisting of an island in the Gulf of St. Lawrence, just north of Nova Scotia. *Capital:* Charlottetown.

prince ly (prins′lē), 1 of a prince or his rank; royal. 2 like a prince; noble. 3 fit for a prince; magnificent: *Some presidents of businesses earn princely salaries.* adj., **prince li er, prince li est.**

Prince of Wales, title given to the eldest son, or heir apparent, of the British sovereign.

prin cess (prin′ses or prin′sis), 1 daughter of a king or queen; daughter of a king's or queen's son. 2 wife or widow of a prince. 3 woman having the rank of a prince. n., pl. **prin cess es.**

princess royal, the oldest daughter of a king or queen.

prin ci pal (prin′sə pəl), 1 most important; main; chief: *Chicago is the principal city of Illinois.* 2 a chief person; one who gives orders. 3 the head, or one of the heads, of an elementary or secondary school. 4 sum of money on which interest is paid. 5 money or property from which income or interest is received. 6 person who hires another person to act for him: *My mother does the business of renting the houses for the owner, her principal.* 1 adj., 2-6 n.

prin ci pal i ty (prin′sə pal′ə tē), 1 a small state or country ruled by a prince. 2 the country from which a prince gets his title. 3 supreme power. n., pl. **prin ci pal i ties.**

prin ci pal ly (prin′sə pə lē), for the most part; above all; chiefly; mainly. adv.

principal parts, the main parts of a verb, from which the rest can be derived. In English the principal parts are the present infinitive, past tense, and past participle. These parts, plus the present participle, are shown for many verbs in this dictionary. EXAMPLES: go, went, gone; do, did, done; drive, drove, driven; push, pushed, pushed.

prin ci ple (prin′sə pəl), 1 a truth that is a foundation for other truths: *the principles of democratic government.* 2 a fundamental belief: *religious principles.* 3 a rule of action or conduct: *I make it a principle to save some money each week.* 4 uprightness; honor: *The Pilgrims were men and women of principle.* 5 a rule of science explaining how things act: *the principle by which a machine works.* n.

on principle, 1 according to a certain principle. 2 for reasons of right conduct.

print (print), 1 use type, plates, etc., to stamp in ink or dye (letters, words, pictures, etc.) on paper or the like. 2 stamp letters, words, etc., on (paper or the like) with type, etc., and ink or dye. 3 cause to be printed; publish:

hat, āge, fär; let, ēqual, tėrm;
it, īce; hot, ōpen, ôrder;
oil, out; cup, pùt, rüle; ch, child;
ng, long; sh, she; th, thin;
ŦH, then; zh, measure;

ə represents *a* in about,
e in taken, *i* in pencil,
o in lemon, *u* in circus.

print books. Most newspapers are printed daily. 4 printed words, letters, etc.: *This book has clear print.* 5 a printed publication; newspaper or magazine. 6 make words or letters the way they look in print instead of in writing: *Print your name clearly. Most children learn to print before learning to write.* 7 mark (cloth, paper, etc.) with patterns or designs: *This machine prints wallpaper.* 8 cloth with a pattern printed on it: *This print will make a nice shirt.* 9 a picture or design printed from an engraved plate, block, etc. 10 produce (marks or figures) by pressure; stamp; impress. 11 a mark made by pressing or stamping: *the print of a foot.* 12 something that prints; stamp; die. 13 something that has been marked or shaped by pressing or stamping: *a print of butter.* 14 photograph produced from a negative. 15 produce a photograph by transmission of light through a negative. 1-3,6,7,10,15 v., 4,5,8,9,11-14 n.

in print, 1 in printed form. 2 (of books, etc.) still available for purchase from the publisher.

out of print, no longer sold by the publisher.

print a ble (prin′tə bəl), 1 capable of being printed. 2 fit to be printed. adj.

print er (prin′tər), person whose business or work is printing or setting type. n.

print ing (prin′ting), 1 the producing of books, newspapers, etc., by stamping in ink or dye from movable type, plates, etc. 2 printed words, letters, etc. 3 all the copies printed at one time. 4 letters made like those in print. n.

printing press, machine for printing from movable type, plates, etc.

pri or[1] (prī′ər), coming before; earlier: *I can't go with you because I have a prior engagement.* adj. [from Latin]

prior to, coming before in time, order, or importance; earlier than; before.

pri or[2] (prī′ər), head of a priory or monastery for men. Priors usually rank below abbots. n. [Old English, from Latin *prior*, noun use of *prior* prior[1]]

pri or ess (prī′ər is), woman at the head of a convent or priory for women.

adj.	adjective	*n.*	noun
adv.	adverb	*prep.*	preposition
conj.	conjunction	*pron.*	pronoun
interj.	interjection	*v.*	verb
sing.	singular	*pl.*	plural

Prioresses usually rank below abbesses. *n., pl.* **pri or ess es.**

pri or i ty (prī ôr/ə tē), **1** a coming before in order or importance: *Fire engines and ambulances have priority over other traffic.* **2** a being earlier in time: *Their claim to the land has priority over the other claims because they were the first to live on it.* **3** a governmental rating giving preference to persons or things in order of their importance to national defense or other essential affairs of state. *n., pl.* **pri or i ties.**

pri or y (prī/ər ē), a religious house governed by a prior or prioress. A priory is often, but not necessarily, dependent on an abbey. *n., pl.* **pri or ies.**

 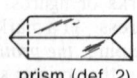

prism (def. 1)   prism (def. 2)

prism (priz/əm), **1** a solid whose bases or ends have the same size and shape and are parallel to one another, and each of whose sides has two pairs of parallel edges. A six-sided pencil before it is sharpened has the shape of one kind of prism. **2** a transparent solid, often of glass, having the shape of a prism, usually with three-sided ends. A prism separates white light passing through it into the colors of the spectrum. *n.*

pris mat ic (priz mat/ik), **1** of or like a prism. **2** formed by a transparent prism. **3** varied in color; brilliant. *adj.* —**pris mat/i cal ly**, *adv.*

prismatic colors, colors formed when white light is passed through a prism; red, orange, yellow, green, blue, indigo, and violet. These are the colors of the spectrum.

pris on (priz/n), **1** a public building in which criminals are confined: *Burglars are put in prison.* **2** any place where a person or animal is shut up against his will: *The small apartment was a prison to the big dog from the farm.* *n.*

pris on er (priz/n ər), **1** person who is under arrest or held in a jail or prison. **2** any person who is confined against his will, or who is not free to move. **3** person taken by the enemy in war. *n.*

pris tine (pris/tēn/), as it was in its earliest time or state; original; primi-tive: *The colors of the paintings inside the pyramid had kept their pristine freshness in spite of their age. adj.*

prith ee (priᴛн/ē), OLD USE. I pray thee; I ask you. *interj.*

pri va cy (prī/və sē), **1** condition of being private; being away from others: *in the privacy of one's home.* **2** absence of publicity; secrecy: *He told me his reasons in strict privacy. n., pl.* **pri va cies.**

pri vate (prī/vit), **1** not for the public; for just a few special people or for one: *a private road, a private house, a private letter.* **2** not public; individual; personal: *the private life of a famous person, my private opinion.* **3** confidential; secret: *News reached her through private channels. I hid it in a private safe.* **4** secluded: *some private corner.* **5** having no public office: *a private citizen.* **6** soldier or marine of the lowest rank: *The private was promoted to corporal last week.* 1-5 *adj.*, 6 *n.* —**pri/vate ly**, *adv.* —**pri/vate ness**, *n.*

in private, 1 not publicly: *My parents spoke to the principal in private.* **2** secretly: *We met in private to plan his surprise birthday party.*

private enterprise, free enterprise.

pri va teer (prī/və tir/), **1** an armed ship owned by private persons and holding a government commission to attack and capture enemy ships. **2** commander or one of the crew of a privateer. **3** cruise as a privateer. 1,2 *n.*, 3 *v.*

private first class, soldier or marine ranking next below a corporal and next above a private.

pri va tion (prī vā/shən), **1** lack of the comforts or of the necessities of life: *Many people were hungry and homeless because of privation during the war.* **2** a being deprived; loss; absence: *Hermits sometimes suffer from the privation of love and companionship. n.*

priv et (priv/it), any of several shrubs much used for hedges. Some are evergreen. *n.*

priv i lege (priv/ə lij), **1** a special right, advantage, or favor: *My sister has the privilege of driving the family car.* **2** give a privilege to: *The nobility in Europe was a privileged class.* 1 *n.*, 2 *v.*, **priv i leged, priv i leg ing.**

priv i ly (priv/ə lē), in a private manner; secretly. *adv.*

priv y (priv/ē), **1** private. **2** OLD USE. secret; hidden. **3** a small outhouse used as a toilet. 1,2 *adj.*, 3 *n., pl.* **priv ies.**

privy to, having secret or private knowledge of.

privy council, group of personal advisers to a ruler.

prize[1] (prīz), **1** a reward won after trying against other people: *Prizes will be given for the three best stories.* **2** given as a prize. **3** that has won a prize. **4** worthy of a prize: *prize vegetables.* **5** a reward worth working for. 1,5 *n.*, 2-4 *adj.* [from French of the 1200's *pris,* from Latin *pretium,* price, reward]

prize[2] (prīz), thing or person captured in war, especially an enemy's ship and its cargo taken at sea. *n.* [from French of the 1300's *prise* seizure, from Latin *prensum* seized]

prize[3] (prīz), **1** value highly: *She prizes her new bicycle.* **2** estimate the value of. *v.*, **prized, priz ing.** [from French of the 1300's *prisier,* from Latin *pretiare,* from *pretium* prize[1]]

prize fight (prīz/fīt/), a boxing match between prizefighters. *n.*

prize fight er (prīz/fī/tər), man who fights or boxes for money. *n.*

prize fight ing (prīz/fī/ting), boxing for money. *n.*

pro[1] (prō), **1** in favor of; for. **2** a reason in favor of. The pros and cons of a question are the arguments for and against it. 1 *adv.*, 2 *n., pl.* **pros.** [from Latin]

pro[2] (prō), INFORMAL. professional. *n., pl.* **pros;** *adj.* [shortened from *professional*]

prob a bil i ty (prob/ə bil/ə tē), **1** quality or fact of being likely or probable; good chance: *There is a probability that school will close a week earlier than usual.* **2** something likely to happen: *A storm is a probability for tomorrow. n., pl.* **prob a bil i ties.**

in all probability, probably.

prob a ble (prob/ə bəl), **1** likely to happen: *Cooler weather is probable after this shower.* **2** likely to be true: *Something I ate is the probable cause of my upset stomach. adj.*

prob a bly (prob/ə blē), more likely than not. *adv.*

pro bate (prō/bāt), **1** the official proving of the will of a person who has died as genuine. **2** of or concerned with the probating of wills: *a probate court.* **3** prove by legal process the genuineness of (a will). **4** a true copy of a will with a certificate that it has been proved genuine. 1,4 *n.*, 2 *adj.*, 3 *v.*, **pro bat ed, pro bat ing.**

pro ba tion (prō bā/shən), **1** trial or testing of conduct, character, qualifications, etc.: *He was admitted to the sixth grade on probation. After a period of probation a novice becomes a nun.* **2** the system of letting young offenders against the law, or first offenders, go free under supervision without receiving the punishment which they are sentenced to unless there is a further offense. *n.*

pro ba tion er (prō bā′shə nər), person who is on probation. *n.*

probation officer, officer appointed to supervise offenders who have been placed on probation.

probe (prōb), 1 search into; examine thoroughly; investigate: *probe one's thoughts or feelings to find out why one acted as one did.* 2 search; penetrate: *probe into the causes of crime.* 3 a thorough examination; investigation: *a probe into juvenile delinquency.* 4 investigation, usually by a lawmaking body, in an effort to discover evidences of law violation. 5 a slender instrument for exploring something. A doctor or dentist uses a probe to explore the depth or direction of a wound or cavity. A Geiger counter uses a probe to detect the amount of radiation in radioactive matter, such as a rock. 6 spacecraft carrying scientific instruments to record or report back information about planets, etc.: *a lunar probe.* 7 the launching of such a spacecraft. 8 examine with a probe. 1,2,8 *v.,* **probed, prob ing;** 3-7 *n.*

pro bi ty (prō′bə tē), high principle; uprightness; honesty. *n.*

prob lem (prob′ləm), 1 a question, especially a difficult question: *How to do away with poverty is a problem that concerns the government.* 2 a matter of doubt or difficulty: *The president of a large company has to deal with many problems.* 3 something to be worked out: *a problem in arithmetic.* 4 that causes difficulty: *a problem child.* 1-3 *n.,* 4 *adj.*

prob lem at ic (prob′lə mat′ik), having the nature of a problem; doubtful; uncertain; questionable: *What the weather will be is often problematic.* *adj.* —**prob′lem at′i cal ly,** *adv.*

prob lem at i cal (prob′lə mat′ə kəl), problematic. *adj.*

proboscis (def. 2)
monkey
with a proboscis

pro bos cis (prō bos′is), 1 an elephant's trunk. 2 a long, flexible snout, like that of the tapir. 3 the tubelike mouth parts of some insects, such as flies or mosquitoes, developed for piercing or sucking. *n., pl.* **pro bos cises.**

pro ce dur al (prə sē′jər əl), of or having to do with procedure. *adj.*

pro ce dure (prə sē′jər), 1 way of proceeding; method of doing things: *What is your procedure in making bread?* 2 the customary manners or ways of conducting business: *parliamentary procedure, legal procedure.* *n.*

pro ceed (prə sēd′), 1 go on after having stopped; move forward: *Please proceed with your story. The train proceeded at the same speed as before.* 2 carry on any activity: *I proceeded to light the fire.* 3 come forth; issue; go out; emanate: *Heat proceeds from fire.* *v.*

pro ceed ing (prə sē′ding), 1 what is done; action; conduct. 2 **proceedings,** *pl.* **a** action in a case in a court of law. **b** record of what was done at the meetings of a society, club, etc. *n.*

pro ceeds (prō′sēdz′), money obtained from a sale, etc.: *The proceeds from the school play will be used to buy a new curtain for the stage. n.pl.*

proc ess (pros′es *or* prō′ses), 1 set of actions or changes in a special order: *By what process is cloth made from wool?* 2 treat or prepare by some special method: *This cloth has been processed to make it waterproof.* 3 part that grows out or sticks out: *the process of a bone.* 4 a written command or summons to appear in a court of law. 1,3,4 *n., pl.* **proc ess es;** 2 *v.*

in process, 1 in the course or condition: *In process of time the house will be finished.* 2 in the course or condition of being done: *The author has just finished one book and has another in process.*

pro ces sion (prə sesh′ən), 1 something that moves forward; persons marching or riding: *A funeral procession filled the street.* 2 an orderly moving forward: *We formed lines to march in procession onto the platform.* *n.*

pro ces sion al (prə sesh′ə nəl), 1 of a procession. 2 used or sung in a procession: *a processional hymn.* 3 processional music: *The choir and clergy marched into the church singing the processional.* 4 book containing hymns, etc., for use in religious processions. 1,2 *adj.,* 3,4 *n.*

proc es sor (pros′ə sər), person who processes. *n.*

process server, person who serves summonses, subpoenas, etc.

pro claim (prə klām′), make known publicly and officially; declare publicly: *proclaim a holiday. The congresswoman proclaimed that she would run for reelection.* *v.*

proc la ma tion (prok′lə mā′shən), an official announcement; public declaration: *the President's annual Thanksgiving proclamation.* *n.*

pro cliv i ty (prō kliv′ə tē), tendency; inclination. *n., pl.* **pro cliv i ties.**

pro con sul (prō kon′səl), governor or military commander of an ancient Roman province with duties and powers like a consul's. *n.*

pro cras ti nate (prō kras′tə nāt), put

hat, āge, fär; let, ēqual, tèrm;
it, īce; hot, ōpen, ôrder;
oil, out; cup, pùt, rüle; ch, child;
ng, long; sh, she; th, thin;
ŦH, then; zh, measure;

ə represents *a* in about,
e in taken, *i* in pencil,
o in lemon, *u* in circus.

things off until later; delay. *v.,* **pro cras ti nat ed, pro cras ti nat ing.**

pro cras ti na tion (prō kras′tə nā′shən), act or habit of putting things off till later; delay. *n.*

pro cras ti na tor (prō kras′tə nā′tər), person who procrastinates. *n.*

pro cre a tion (prō′krē ā′shən), the producing of offspring; reproduction; begetting. *n.*

proc tor (prok′tər), 1 officer in a university or school who keeps good order. 2 serve as a proctor at (an examination). 1 *n.,* 2 *v.*

pro cur a ble (prə kyùr′ə bəl), that may be procured; obtainable. *adj.*

proc u ra tor (prok′yə rā′tər), 1 person employed to manage the affairs of another or to act for another; agent. 2 a financial agent or administrator in an ancient Roman province. *n,*

pro cure (prə kyùr′), 1 get by care or effort; obtain; secure: *procure a job in a bank. It is hard to procure water in a desert.* 2 bring about; cause: *The lawyer procured the prisoner's release.* *v.,* **procured, pro cur ing.**

pro cure ment (prə kyùr′mənt), act of procuring. *n.*

prod (prod), 1 poke or jab with something pointed: *prod an animal with a stick.* 2 stir up; urge on: *The lateness of the hour prodded me to finish quickly.* 3 a poke; thrust: *That prod in the ribs hurt.* 4 a sharp-pointed stick; goad. 5 words, actions, or feelings that prod. 1,2 *v.,* **prod ded, prod ding;** 3-5 *n.*

prod i gal (prod′ə gəl), 1 spending too much; wasting money or other resources; wasteful: *America has been prodigal of its forests.* 2 abundant; lavish. 3 person who is wasteful or extravagant; spendthrift: *The father welcomed the repentant prodigal back home.* 1,2 *adj.,* 3 *n.* —**prod′i gal ly,** *adv.*

prod i gal i ty (prod′ə gal′ə tē), 1 wasteful or reckless extravagance. 2 rich abundance; profuseness. *n., pl.* **prod i gal i ties.**

pro di gious (prə dij′əs), 1 very great; huge; vast: *The ocean contains a prodigious amount of water.* 2 won-

adj. adjective	*n.* noun
adv. adverb	*prep.* preposition
conj. conjunction	*pron.* pronoun
interj. interjection	*v.* verb
sing. singular	*pl.* plural

derful; marvelous. *adj.* **—pro di′- gious ly,** *adv.* **—pro di′gious ness,** *n.*

prod i gy (prod′ə jē), 1 a marvel; wonder. An infant prodigy is a child remarkably brilliant in some respect. 2 a wonderful sign or omen: *An eclipse of the sun seemed a prodigy to early man. n., pl.* **prod i gies.**

pro duce (prə düs′ *or* prə dyüs′ *for 1-6;* prod′üs, prod′yüs, prō′düs, *or* prō′dyüs *for* 7), 1 bring into existence; make: *This factory produces stoves.* 2 bring about; cause: *Hard work produces success.* 3 bring forth or yield offspring, crops, products, dividends, interest, etc. 4 bring forth; supply; create; yield: *Hens produce eggs.* 5 bring forward; show: *Produce your proof.* 6 bring (a play, motion picture, etc.) before the public: *Our class produced a play.* 7 what is produced; yield: *Vegetables are a garden's produce.* 1-6 *v.,* **pro duced, pro duc ing;** 7 *n.*

pro duc er (prə dü′sər *or* prə dyü′sər), 1 person or thing that produces, especially a person who grows or manufactures things that are used by others. 2 person in charge of presenting a play, a motion picture, or a television or radio show. *n.*

prod uct (prod′əkt), 1 that which is produced; result of work or of growth: *factory products, farm products.* 2 number or quantity resulting from multiplying two or more numbers together: *40 is the product of 8 and 5. n.*

pro duc tion (prə duk′shən), 1 act of producing; creation; manufacture: *the production of automobiles.* 2 something produced: *the yearly production of a farm.* 3 amount produced: *a decline in production. n.*

pro duc tive (prə duk′tiv), 1 producing abundantly; fertile: *a productive farm, a productive writer.* 2 producing food or other articles of commerce: *Farming is productive labor.* 3 bringing forth; producing: *That field is productive only of weeds. Hasty words are productive of quarrels. adj.* **—pro duc′tive ly,** *adv.* **—pro duc′tive ness,** *n.*

pro duc tiv i ty (prō′duk tiv′ə tē), power to produce; productiveness. *n.*

pro em (prō′em), introduction; preface. *n.*

prof. or **Prof.,** professor.

prof a na tion (prof′ə nā′shən), act of showing contempt or disregard toward something holy; treatment of something sacred as it should not be treated. *n.*

pro fane (prə fān′), 1 with contempt or disregard for God or holy things: *a profane person, profane language.* 2 treat (holy things) with contempt or disregard: *Soldiers profaned the church when they stabled their horses in it.* 3 put to wrong or unworthy use. 4 not sacred; worldly: *profane literature.* 1,4 *adj.,* 2,3 *v.,* **pro faned, pro fan ing.** **—pro fane′ly,** *adv.* **—pro fane′- ness,** *n.*

pro fan i ty (prə fan′ə tē), 1 use of profane language; swearing. 2 a being profane; lack of reverence. *n., pl.* **pro- fan i ties.**

pro fess (prə fes′), 1 lay claim to; claim: *I don't profess to be an expert in chemistry.* 2 declare one's belief in: *Christians profess Christ and the Christian religion.* 3 declare openly: *He professed his loyalty to the United States.* 4 have as one's business or profession: *profess law. v.*

pro fessed (prə fest′), 1 avowed or acknowledged; openly declared; *a professed Christian, a professed candidate for office.* 2 alleged or pretended: *accused by their professed friends.* 3 having taken the vows of, or been received into, a religious order. *adj.*

pro fes sion (prə fesh′ən), 1 an occupation requiring special education, such as law, medicine, teaching, or the ministry. 2 the people engaged in such an occupation: *The medical profession favors this law.* 3 act of professing; open declaration: *I don't believe her profession of friendship for us.* 4 declaration of belief in a religion. *n.*

pro fes sion al (prə fesh′ə nəl), 1 of or having to do with a profession; appropriate to a profession: *Our doctor has a professional seriousness unlike his ordinary joking manner.* 2 engaged in a profession: *A lawyer or a doctor is a professional person.* 3 making a business or trade of something which others do for pleasure: *a professional ballplayer, professional musicians.* 4 person who does this. 5 undertaken or engaged in by professionals rather than amateurs: *a professional ball game.* 1-3,5 *adj.,* 4 *n.* **—pro fes′sion- al ly,** *adv.*

pro fes sion al ism (prə fesh′ə nə- liz′ əm), 1 professional character, spirit, or methods. 2 the standing, practice, or methods of a professional, as distinguished from those of an amateur. *n.*

pro fes sor (prə fes′ər), 1 teacher of the highest rank in a college or university. 2 INFORMAL. teacher. 3 person who professes. *n.*

pro fes so ri al (prō′fə sôr′ē əl *or* prof′ə sôr′ē əl), of, having to do with, or characteristic of a professor. *adj.* **—pro′fes so′ri al ly,** *adv.*

pro fes sor ship (prə fes′ər ship), position or rank of a professor. *n.*

prof fer (prof′ər), 1 offer for acceptance; present; tender: *We proffered our regrets at having to leave so early.* 2 an offer made: *Her proffer of advice was accepted.* 1 *v.,* 2 *n.*

pro fi cien cy (prə fish′ən sē), a being proficient; knowledge; skill; advanced state of expertness. *n., pl.* **pro fi cien- cies.**

pro fi cient (prə fish′ənt), advanced in any art, science, or subject; skilled; expert: *She was very proficient in mathematics. adj.* **—pro fi′cient ly,** *adv.*

profile (def. 1)
of Queen Victoria

pro file (prō′fīl), 1 a side view, especially of the human face. 2 outline. 3 a concise description of a person's abilities, personality, or career. *n.*

prof it (prof′it), 1 the gain from a business; what is left when the cost of carrying on the business is subtracted from the amount of money taken in: *The profits in this business are not large.* 2 make a gain from business; make a profit. 3 advantage; benefit: *What profit is there in worrying?* 4 get advantage; gain; benefit: *A wise person profits from his mistakes.* 5 be an advantage or benefit (to). 1,3 *n.,* 2,4,5 *v.*

prof it a ble (prof′ə tə bəl), 1 yielding a financial profit: *The sale held by the Girl Scouts was very profitable.* 2 giving a gain or benefit; useful: *We spent a profitable afternoon in the library. adj.* **—prof′it a ble ness,** *n.*

prof it a bly (prof′ə tə blē), with profit. *adv.*

prof it eer (prof′ə tir′), 1 person who makes an unfair profit by charging excessive prices for scarce goods. 2 seek or make such unfair profits. 1 *n.,* 2 *v.*

prof it less (prof′it lis), without profit. *adj.*

profit sharing, the sharing of profits between employer and employees.

prof li ga cy (prof′lə gə sē), 1 great wickedness; vice. 2 reckless extravagance. *n.*

prof li gate (prof/lə git), 1 very wicked; shamelessly bad. 2 recklessly extravagant. 3 person who is very wicked or extravagant. 1,2 *adj.,* 3 *n.*

pro found (prə found/), 1 very deep: *a profound sigh, a profound sleep.* 2 deeply felt; very great: *profound despair, profound sympathy.* 3 going far deeper than what is easily understood; having or showing great knowledge or understanding: *a profound book, a profound thinker, a profound thought. adj.* —**pro found/ly,** *adv.* —**pro found/ ness,** *n.*

pro fun di ty (prə fun/də tē), 1 a being profound; great depth. 2 a very deep thing or place. *n., pl.* **pro fun di ties.**

pro fuse (prə fyüs/), 1 very abundant: *profuse thanks.* 2 spending or giving freely; lavish; extravagant: *He was so profuse with his money that he is now poor. adj.* —**pro fuse/ly,** *adv.* —**pro fuse/ness,** *n.*

pro fu sion (prə fyü/zhən), 1 great abundance. 2 extravagance; lavishness. *n.*

pro gen i tor (prō jen/ə tər), ancestor in the direct line; forefather. *n.*

prog e ny (proj/ə nē), children or offspring; descendants: *Kittens are a cat's progeny. n., pl.* **prog e nies.**

prog nos tic (prog nos/tik), 1 indicating something in the future. 2 indication; sign. 3 a forecast; prediction. 1 *adj.,* 2,3 *n.*

prog nos ti cate (prog nos/tə kāt), predict from facts; forecast. *v.,* **prog nos ti cat ed,** **prog nos ti cat ing.**

prog nos ti ca tion (prog nos/tə kā/ shən), a forecast; prediction. *n.*

prog nos ti ca tor (prog nos/tə kā/tər), person or thing that prognosticates. *n.*

pro gram (prō/gram), 1 list of items or events; list of performers, etc. There are concert programs, theater programs, and programs of a meeting. 2 items making up an entertainment: *The entire program was delightful.* 3 plan of what is to be done: *a school program, a business program, a government program.* 4 set of instructions for an electronic computer or other automatic machine outlining the steps to be performed by the machine in a specific operation. 5 arrange or enter in a program. 6 draw up a program or plan for. 7 prepare a set of instructions for (a computer or other automatic machine). 8 series of statements and questions to each of which a student is required to respond before he can go on to the next and usually more difficult level. 9 arrange a series of statements and questions in such a sequence: *programmed*

instruction. 1-4,8 *n.,* 5-7,9 *v.,* **pro grammed** or **pro gramed, pro gram ming** or **pro gram ing.**

pro gramme (prō/gram), program. *n., v.,* **pro grammed, pro gram ming.**

pro gram mer (prō/gram/ər), person who prepares a program or programs. *n.*

prog ress (prog/res for *1,3;* prə gres/ for *2,4*), 1 an advance or growth; development; improvement: *the progress of science. He is showing rapid progress in his studies.* 2 get better; advance; develop: *We progress in learning step by step.* 3 a moving forward; going ahead: *make rapid progress on a journey.* 4 move forward; go ahead: *The building of the new school progressed quickly during the summer.* 1,3 *n.,* 2,4 *v.*

pro gres sion (prə gresh/ən), 1 a progressing; a moving forward; going ahead: *Creeping is a slow method of progression.* 2 (in mathematics) series of numbers in which there is always the same relation between a number and the one after it. 2, 4, 6, 8, 10 are in arithmetical progression. 2, 4, 8, 16, 32 are in geometric progression. *n.*

pro gres sive (prə gres/iv), 1 making progress; advancing to something better; improving: *a progressive nation.* 2 favoring progress; wanting improvement or reform in government, business, etc. 3 person who favors improvement and reform in government, religion, or business. 4 moving forward; developing: *a progressive disease.* 1,2,4 *adj.,* 3 *n.* —**pro gres/sive ly,** *adv.* —**pro gres/sive ness,** *n.*

pro hib it (prō hib/it), 1 forbid by law or authority: *Picking flowers in this park is prohibited.* 2 prevent: *Rainy weather and fog prohibited flying. v.*

pro hi bi tion (prō/ə bish/ən), 1 act of prohibiting: *The prohibition of swimming in the city's reservoirs is sensible.* 2 law or order that prohibits. 3 law or laws against making or selling alcoholic liquors. National prohibition existed in the United States between 1920 and 1933. *n.*

pro hi bi tion ist (prō/ə bish/ə nist), person who favors laws against the manufacture and sale of alcoholic liquors. *n.*

pro hib i tive (prō hib/ə tiv), that prohibits; preventing: *Gold would make excellent roofs, if the price were not prohibitive. adj.*

pro hib i to ry (prō hib/ə tôr/ē), prohibitive. *adj.*

proj ect (proj/ekt for *1,3,7,8;* prə jekt/ for *2,4-6*), 1 a plan; scheme: *Flying in a heavy machine was once thought an impossible project.* 2 to plan; scheme: *project a tax decrease.* 3 an under-

hat, āge, fär; let, ēqual, tėrm;
it, īce; hot, ōpen, ôrder;
oil, out; cup, pùt, rüle; ch, child;
ng, long; sh, she; th, thin;
ŦH, then; zh, measure;

ə represents *a* in about,
e in taken, *i* in pencil,
o in lemon, *u* in circus.

taking; enterprise. 4 throw or cast forward: *A cannon projects shells.* 5 cause to fall on a surface: *Motion pictures are projected on the screen. The tree projects a shadow on the grass.* 6 stick out: *The rocky point projects far into the water.* 7 a special assignment planned and carried out by a student, a group of students, or an entire class. 8 group of apartment buildings built and run as a unit. 1,3,7,8 *n.,* 2,4-6 *v.*

pro jec tile (prə jek/təl), 1 any object that is thrown, hurled, or shot, such as a stone or bullet. 2 capable of being thrown, hurled, or shot: *Bullets and arrows are projectile weapons.* 3 forcing forward; impelling: *a projectile force.* 1 *n.,* 2,3 *adj.*

pro jec tion (prə jek/shən), 1 part that projects or sticks out: *rocky projections on the face of a cliff.* 2 a sticking out. 3 a throwing or casting forward: *the projection of a shell from a cannon, the projection of a photographic image on a screen.* 4 representation on a flat surface of all or part of the surface of the earth. *n.*

pro jec tor (prə jek/tər), 1 apparatus for projecting an image on a screen. 2 person who forms projects; schemer. *n.*

Pro kof iev (prō kô/fyef), **Sergei Sergeyevich,** 1891-1953, Russian composer. *n.*

pro le tar i an (prō/lə ter/ē ən *or* prō/lə tar/ē ən), 1 of or belonging to the proletariat. 2 person belonging to the proletariat. 1 *adj.,* 2 *n.*

pro le tar i at (prō/lə ter/ē ət *or* prō/ lə tar/ē ət), the lowest class in economic and social status, especially industrial workers working for wages; the working or laboring class. *n.*

pro lif ic (prə lif/ik), 1 producing offspring abundantly: *Rabbits are prolific.* 2 producing much: *a prolific garden, a prolific imagination, a prolific writer. adj.* —**pro lif/i cal ly,** *adv.*

pro lix (prō liks/ *or* prō/liks), using too many words; too long; tedious. *adj.*

pro lix i ty (prō lik/sə tē), too great length; tedious length of speech or writing. *n.*

prologue

adj.	adjective	*n.*	noun
adv.	adverb	*prep.*	preposition
conj.	conjunction	*pron.*	pronoun
interj.	interjection	*v.*	verb
sing.	singular	*pl.*	plural

pro logue or **pro log** (prō′lôg),
1 introduction to a novel, poem, or other literary work. 2 speech or poem addressed to the audience by one of the actors at the beginning of a play. 3 any introductory act or event. *n.*

pro long (prə lông′), make longer; extend; stretch; protract: *Good care may prolong a sick person's life. The dog uttered prolonged howls whenever the family left the house. v.*

pro lon ga tion (prō′lông gā′shən),
1 lengthening in time or space; extension: *the prolongation of one's school days by a year of graduate study.* 2 added part: *The summer kitchen was a prolongation of the shed. n.*

prom (prom), INFORMAL. dance or ball given by a college or high-school class. *n.*

prom e nade (prom′ə nād′ or prom′-ə näd′), 1 a walk for pleasure or for show: *The Easter promenade is well known as a fashion show.* 2 walk about or up and down for pleasure or for show: *We promenaded back and forth on the ship's deck.* 3 a public place for such a walk: *Atlantic City has a famous promenade along the beach.* 4 a dance or ball. 5 a march of all the guests at the opening of a formal dance. 1,3-5 *n.,* 2 *v.,* **prom e nad ed, prom e nad ing.**

Pro me the us (prə mē′thē əs or prə-mē′thūs), (in Greek myths) one of the Titans. He stole fire from heaven and taught men its use. Zeus punished him by chaining him to a rock. *n.*

pro me thi um (prə mē′thē əm), a radioactive metallic element which is a product of the fission of uranium, thorium, and plutonium. *n.* [from *Prometheus*]

prom i nence (prom′ə nəns), 1 a being prominent: *the prominence of athletics in some schools, the prominence of Jefferson as a statesman.* 2 something that juts out or projects, especially upward. A hill is a prominence. 3 cloud of gas which erupts from the sun and is seen as either a projection from, or a dark spot on, the surface of the sun. *n.*

prom i nent (prom′ə nənt), 1 well-known or important; distinguished: *a prominent citizen.* 2 easy to see: *A single tree in a field is prominent.*
3 standing out; projecting: *Some insects have prominent eyes. adj.* —**prom′i-nent ly,** *adv.*

prom is cu i ty (prom′i skyü′ə tē), fact or condition of being promiscuous. *n.*

pro mis cu ous (prə mis′kyü əs), 1 mixed and in disorder: *a promiscuous heap of clothing on your closet floor.* 2 making no distinctions; not discriminating: *promiscuous friendships. adj.* —**pro mis′cu ous ly,** *adv.*

prom ise (prom′is), 1 words said or written, binding a person to do or not to do something: *You can count on her to keep her promise.* 2 give one's word; make a promise: *They promised to stay till we came.* 3 make a promise of: *to promise help.* 4 indication of what may be expected: *The clouds give promise of rain.* 5 that which gives hope of success: *a young scholar who shows promise.* 6 give hope; give hope of: *The rainbow promises fair weather.* 1,4,5 *n.,* 2,3,6 *v.,* **prom ised, prom is ing.**

Promised Land, 1 (in the Bible) the country promised by God to Abraham and his descendants; Canaan. 2 **promised land,** a place or condition of expected happiness: *America is a promised land for many immigrants.* 3 heaven.

prom is ing (prom′ə sing), likely to turn out well; hopeful: *a promising beginning, a bright, promising student. The young pianist has a great deal of talent and is very promising. adj.* —**prom′is-ing ly,** *adv.*

prom is so ry (prom′ə sôr′ē), containing a promise. *adj.*

promissory note, a written promise to pay a stated sum of money to a certain person at a certain time.

prom on to ry (prom′ən tôr′ē), a high point of land extending from the coast into the water; headland. *n., pl.* **prom-on to ries.**

pro mote (prə mōt′), 1 raise in rank, condition, or importance: *Pupils who pass the test will be promoted to the next higher grade.* 2 help to grow or develop; help to success: *A kindly feeling toward other countries will promote peace.* 3 help to organize; start: *Several bankers promoted the new company.* 4 further the sale of (an article) by advertising. *v.,* **pro mot ed, pro mot ing.**

pro mot er (prə mō′tər), 1 person or thing that encourages or furthers some-
thing: *a promoter of friendship.* 2 person who organizes new companies and secures capital for them. *n.*

pro mo tion (prə mō′shən), 1 an advance in rank or importance: *The clerk was given a promotion and an increase in salary.* 2 helping to grow or develop; a helping along to success: *The doctors were busy in the promotion of a health campaign.* 3 a helping to organize; starting: *It took much time and money for the promotion of the new company. n.*

pro mo tion al (prə mō′shə nəl), having to do with or used in the promotion of a person, product, or enterprise: *promotional pamphlets. adj.*

prompt (prompt), 1 ready and willing; on time; quick: *Be prompt to obey.* 2 done at once; made without delay: *I expect a prompt answer.* 3 cause (someone) to do something: *Her curiosity prompted her to ask questions.* 4 give rise to; suggest; inspire: *A kind thought prompted the gift.* 5 remind (a learner, speaker, actor, etc.) of the words or actions needed: *Do you know your part in the play or shall I prompt you?* 1,2 *adj.,* 3-5 *v.* —**prompt′ly,** *adv.* —**prompt′ness,** *n.*

prompt er (promp′tər), person who tells actors, speakers, etc., what to say when they forget. *n.*

promp ti tude (promp′tə tüd or promp′tə tyüd), readiness in acting or deciding; promptness. *n.*

prom ul gate (prom′əl gāt or prō-mul′gāt), 1 proclaim formally; announce officially: *The king promulgated a decree.* 2 spread far and wide: *Schools try to promulgate knowledge and good habits. v.,* **prom ul gat ed, prom ul gat ing.**

promontory

prom ul ga tion (prom′əl gā′shən or prō′mul gā′shən), a promulgating or a being promulgated. *n.*

prom ul ga tor (prom′əl gā′tər or prō mul′gā tər), person who promulgates. *n.*

pron., 1 pronoun. 2 pronunciation.

prone (prōn), 1 inclined or disposed; liable: *We are prone to think evil of people we dislike.* 2 lying face down: *be prone on the bed.* 3 lying flat: *fall prone on the ground. adj.*

prone ness (prōn′nis), 1 inclination; tendency; preference. 2 prone position. *n.*

prominences (def. 3)

670

prong (prông), one of the pointed ends of a fork, antler, etc. *n.*

pronged (prôngd), having prongs. *adj.*

prong horn (prông′hôrn′), mammal like an antelope, found on the plains of western North America. *n., pl.* **prong-horns** or **prong horn.**

pro noun (prō′noun), word used to indicate without naming; word used instead of a noun. EXAMPLES: I, we, you, he, it, they, who, whose, which, this, mine, whatever. In "John did not like to go because he was sick," *he* is a pronoun used in the second part of the sentence to avoid repeating *John. n.*

pro nounce (prə nouns′), 1 make the sounds of; speak: *Pronounce your words clearly.* 2 declare (a person or thing) to be: *The doctor pronounced her cured.* 3 declare solemnly or positively: *The judge pronounced sentence on the criminal. v.,* **pro nounced, pro-nounc ing.**

pro nounce a ble (prə noun′sə bəl), that can be pronounced. *adj.*

pro nounced (prə nounst′), strongly marked; emphatic; decided: *She held pronounced opinions on gambling. adj.*

pro nounce ment (prə nouns′mənt), 1 a formal statement; declaration. 2 opinion; decision. *n.*

pro nun ci a tion (prə nun′sē ā′-shən), 1 way of pronouncing. This book gives the pronunciation of each main word. 2 a making the sounds of words; speaking. *n.*

proof (prüf), 1 way or means of showing beyond doubt the truth of something: *Is what you say a guess or have you proof?* 2 establishment of the truth of anything. 3 act of testing; trial: *That box looks big enough; but let us put it to the proof.* 4 a trial impression from type. A book is first printed in proof so that errors can be corrected. *Did the author correct the page proofs?* 5 a trial print of an etching, photographic negative, etc. 6 of tested value against something; capable of resisting or withstanding: *proof against being taken by surprise.* 1-5 *n.,* 6 *adj.*

proof read (prüf′rēd′), read and mark errors to be corrected. *v.,* **proof-read** (prüf′red′), **proof read ing.** —**proof′read′er,** *n.*

prop[1] (prop), 1 hold up by placing a support under or against: *Prop the clothesline with a stick. He was propped up in bed with pillows.* 2 support; sustain: *prop a failing cause.* 3 thing or person used to support another: *Their son was a prop to them in their old age.* 1,2 *v.,* **propped, prop ping;** 3 *n.* [from Dutch of the 1400's *proppe*]

prop[2] (prop), property (def. 5). *n.* [shortened from *property*]

prop a gan da (prop′ə gan′də),

pronghorn—3 ft. high at the shoulder

1 systematic efforts to spread opinions or beliefs; any plan or method for spreading opinions or beliefs: *The life insurance companies engaged in health propaganda. Clever propaganda misled the enemy into believing that it could not win the war.* 2 the opinions or beliefs thus spread: *The enemy spread false propaganda about us. n.*

prop a gan dist (prop′ə gan′dist), 1 person who gives time or effort to the spreading of some opinion or belief. 2 of propaganda or propagandists. 1 *n.,* 2 *adj.*

prop a gan dize (prop′ə gan′dīz), 1 propagate or spread (opinions or beliefs) by propaganda. 2 carry on propaganda. *v.,* **prop a gan dized, prop-a gan diz ing.**

prop a gate (prop′ə gāt), 1 produce offspring; reproduce: *Trees propagate themselves by seeds.* 2 cause to increase in number by the production of young: *Cows and sheep are propagated on farms.* 3 spread (news or knowledge): *Don't propagate unkind reports.* 4 pass on; send further: *Sound is propagated by vibrations. v.,* **prop a gat ed, prop a gat ing.**

prop a ga tion (prop′ə gā′shən), 1 the breeding of plants or animals: *Our propagation of poppies is by seed, and of roses by cuttings.* 2 spreading; getting more widely believed; making more widely known: *the propagation of the principles of science.* 3 passing on; sending further; spreading or extending: *the propagation of the shock of an earthquake. n.*

pro pane (prō′pān), a heavy, colorless, flammable gas, a hydrocarbon. Propane occurs in crude petroleum and is used as a fuel, refrigerant, or solvent. *n.*

pro pel (prə pel′), drive forward; force ahead: *propel a boat by oars, a person propelled by ambition. v.,* **pro pelled, pro pel ling.**

pro pel lant (prə pel′ənt), substance that propels, especially the fuel of a rocket. *n.*

pro pel lent (prə pel′ənt), 1 propelling; driving forward. 2 thing or person that propels. 1 *adj.,* 2 *n.*

pro pel ler (prə pel′ər), 1 device consisting of a revolving hub with blades,

hat, āge, fär; let, ēqual, tėrm;
it, īce; hot, ōpen, ôrder;
oil, out; cup, pùt, rüle; ch, child;
ng, long; sh, she; th, thin;
ŦH, then; zh, measure;

ə represents *a* in about,
e in taken, *i* in pencil,
o in lemon, *u* in circus.

for propelling boats and aircraft. 2 person or thing that propels. *n.*

pro pen si ty (prə pen′sə tē), a natural inclination or bent; leaning: *Most children have a propensity for playing games. n., pl.* **pro pen si ties.**

prop er (prop′ər), 1 right for the occasion; fitting: *Night is the proper time to sleep, and bed is the proper place.* 2 strictly so called; in the strict sense of the word: *Puerto Rico is not part of the United States proper.* 3 decent; respectable: *proper conduct.* 4 belonging to one or a few; not common to all. *John Adams is a proper name. adj.*

proper fraction, fraction less than 1. EXAMPLES: $2/3$, $1/8$, $3/4$, and $199/200$.

prop er ly (prop′ər lē), 1 in a proper, correct, or fitting manner: *Eat properly.* 2 rightly; justly: *An honest person is properly indignant at the offer of a bribe.* 3 strictly: *Properly speaking, a whale is not a fish. adv.*

proper noun, noun naming a particular person, place, or thing. *Jane, Chicago,* and *Monday* are proper nouns. *Girl, city,* and *day* are common nouns.

prop er ty (prop′ər tē), 1 thing or things owned; possession or possessions: *This house is that man's property. That book is my property; please return it to me.* 2 ownership. 3 piece of land or real estate: *She owns property out West.* 4 quality or power belonging specially to something: *Soap has the property of removing dirt. Copper has several important properties.* 5 any piece of furniture or small article (everything except scenery and clothes) used in staging a play or a motion-picture or television scene; prop. *n., pl.* **prop er ties.**

proph e cy (prof′ə sē), 1 a telling what will happen; foretelling future

propellers (def. 1)

adj. adjective	*n.* noun
adv. adverb	*prep.* preposition
conj. conjunction	*pron.* pronoun
interj. interjection	*v.* verb
sing. singular	*pl.* plural

events. 2 thing told about the future. 3 a divinely inspired utterance, revelation, writing, etc. *n., pl.* **proph e cies.**

proph e sy (prof′ə sī), 1 tell what will happen; foretell; predict: *The fortuneteller prophesied my future.* 2 speak when or as if inspired by God. *v.,* **proph e sied, proph e sy ing.**

proph et (prof′it), 1 person who tells what will happen: *Don't be a bad-luck prophet.* 2 person who preaches what he thinks has been revealed to him: *Every religion has its prophets. n.*

proph et ess (prof′i tis), a woman prophet. *n., pl.* **proph et ess es.**

pro phet ic (prə fet′ik), 1 belonging to a prophet; such as a prophet has: *prophetic power.* 2 containing prophecy: *a prophetic saying.* 3 giving warning of what is to happen; foretelling: *Thunder is prophetic of showers. adj.* —**pro phet′i cal ly,** *adv.*

pro phy lac tic (prō′fə lak′tik), 1 protecting from disease. 2 medicine or measure that protects against disease: *He took vitamins as a prophylactic against colds.* 1 *adj.,* 2 *n.*

pro pin qui ty (prō ping′kwə tē), 1 nearness in place, especially personal nearness. 2 nearness of blood; kinship. *n.*

pro pi ti ate (prə pish′ē āt), prevent or reduce the anger of; win the favor of; appease or conciliate. *v.,* **pro pi ti at ed, pro pi ti at ing.**

pro pi ti a tion (prə pish′ē ā′shən), act of propitiating. *n.*

pro pi ti a to ry (prə pish′ē ə tôr′ē), intended to propitiate; making propitiation; conciliatory: *a propitiatory offering, a propitiatory prayer. adj.*

pro pi tious (prə pish′əs), 1 holding well; favorable: *propitious weather for our trip.* 2 favorably inclined; gracious. *adj.* —**pro pi′tious ly,** *adv.* —**pro pi′tious ness,** *n.*

pro po nent (prə pō′nənt), 1 person who makes a proposal or proposition. 2 favorer; supporter. *n.*

pro por tion (prə pôr′shən), 1 relation of two things in magnitude; size, number, amount, or degree compared to another: *Each girl's pay will be in proportion to the work she does. Mix water and orange juice in the proportions of three to one by adding three* measures of water to every measure of orange juice. 2 a proper relation between parts: *His short legs were not in proportion to his long body.* 3 fit (one thing to another) so that they go together: *The designs in that rug are well proportioned.* 4 adjust in proper proportion or relation: *The punishment was proportioned to the crime.* 5 part; share: *A large proportion of Nevada is desert.* 6 statement of equality between two ratios. EXAMPLE: 4 is to 2 as 10 is to 5. **7 proportions,** *pl.* **a** size; extent. **b** dimensions. 1,2,5-7 *n.,* 3,4 *v.*

pro por tion al (prə pôr′shə nəl), 1 in the proper proportion; corresponding: *The increase in price is proportional to the improvement in the car. The pay will be proportional to the amount of time put in.* 2 one of the terms of a proportion in mathematics. 1 *adj.,* 2 *n.*

pro por tion al ly (prə pôr′shə nə lē), in proportion. *adv.*

pro por tion ate (prə pôr′shə nit), in the proper proportion; proportioned; proportional: *The money obtained by the fair was really not proportionate to the effort we put into it. adj.*

pro por tion ate ly (prə pôr′shə nit lē), in proportion: *The money the children earned was divided proportionately to the time each worked. adv.*

pro pos al (prə pō′zəl), 1 what is proposed; plan, scheme, or suggestion: *The club will now hear this member's proposal.* 2 an offer of marriage. 3 act of proposing: *Proposal is easier than performance. n.*

pro pose (prə pōz′), 1 put forward; suggest: *I propose that we take turns at the swing.* 2 present (the name of someone) for an office: *I am proposing Jack for president.* 3 intend; plan: *She proposes to save half of all she earns.* 4 make an offer of marriage. *v.,* **proposed, pro pos ing.**

prop o si tion (prop′ə zish′ən), 1 what is offered to be considered; proposal: *The tailor made a proposition to buy out his rival's business.* 2 statement. EXAMPLE: "All men are created equal." 3 statement that is to be proved true. EXAMPLE: Resolved: that our school should have a bank. 4 problem to be solved: *a proposition in geometry. n.*

pro pound (prə pound′), put forward; propose: *propound a theory, propound a riddle. v.* —**pro pound′er,** *n.*

pro pri e tar y (prə prī′ə ter′ē), 1 belonging to a proprietor. 2 holding property. 3 owned by a private person or company; belonging to or controlled by a private person as property. A proprietary medicine is a patent medicine. 4 owner or group of owners of a grant from the king of England. William Penn was a proprietary. 1-3 *adj.,* 4 *n., pl.* **pro pri e tar ies.**

pro pri e tor (prə prī′ə tər), owner. *n.*

pro pri e tor ship (prə prī′ə tər ship), ownership. *n.*

pro pri e tress (prə prī′ə tris), a woman owner. *n., pl.* **pro pri e tress es.**

pro pri e ty (prə prī′ə tē), 1 quality of being proper; fitness. 2 proper behavior: *She acted with propriety.* 3 **proprieties,** *pl.* the customs and rules of proper behavior: *The proprieties require that we use good table manners. n., pl.* **pro pri e ties.**

pro pul sion (prə pul′shən), 1 a driving forward or onward. 2 a propelling force or impulse: *Most large aircraft are powered by propulsion of jet engines. n.*

pro rate (prō rāt′ or prō′rāt′), divide proportionally: *I prorated the money according to the number of days each had worked. v.,* **pro rat ed, pro rat ing.**

pro sa ic (prō zā′ik), like prose; matter-of-fact; ordinary; not exciting. *adj.* —**pro sa′i cal ly,** *adv.*

pro sce ni um (prō sē′nē əm), 1 the part of the stage in front of the curtain. 2 curtain and the framework that holds it. 3 stage of an ancient theater. *n.*

pro scribe (prō skrīb′), 1 prohibit as wrong or dangerous; talk against; condemn: *Some religions proscribe dancing, drinking, and card playing.* 2 put outside the protection of the law; outlaw. In ancient Rome, a proscribed person's property belonged to the state and anyone might kill him. 3 forbid to come into a certain place; banish. *v.,* **proscribed, pro scrib ing.**

pro scrip tion (prō skrip′shən), a proscribing or a being proscribed; banishment; outlawry. *n.*

prose (prōz), 1 the ordinary form of spoken or written language; plain language; plain language not arranged in verses. 2 of prose; in prose. 3 lacking imagination; matter-of-fact; commonplace. 1 *n.,* 2,3 *adj.*

pros e cute (pros′ə kyüt), 1 bring before a court of law: *Reckless drivers will be prosecuted.* 2 bring a case before a court of law. 3 carry out; follow up: *We started an inquiry into the cause of the fire, and prosecuted it for several weeks.* 4 carry on (a business or occupation). *v.,* **pros e cut ed, pros e cut ing.**

pros e cu tion (pros′ə kyü′shən), 1 the carrying on of a lawsuit: *The prosecution will be abandoned if the stolen money is returned.* 2 side that starts action against another in a court of law. The prosecution makes certain charges against the defense. 3 a carrying out; following up: *the prosecution of a plan. n.*

pros e cu tor (pros′ə kyü′tər), 1 the lawyer who takes charge of the government's side of a case against an accused person. 2 person who starts legal proceedings against another person: *Who is the prosecutor in this case? n.*

pros e lyte (pros′ə līt), 1 person who has changed from one opinion, religious belief, etc., to another. 2 to convert from one opinion, religious belief, etc., to another. 1 *n.*, 2 *v.*, **pros e lyt ed, pros e lyt ing.**

pros e lyt ize (pros′ə lə tīz), make converts; proselyte. *v.*, **pros e lyt ized, pros e lyt iz ing.**

Pro ser pi na (prō sėr′pə nə), (in Roman myths) the daughter of Jupiter and Ceres. The Greeks called her Persephone. She was carried off by Pluto and made queen of the lower world, but she was allowed to spend part of the year on earth with her mother. At that time the earth blooms, but while Proserpina is in the lower world there is winter. *n.*

Pro ser pi ne (prō sėr′pə nē′), Proserpina. *n.*

pros o dy (pros′ə dē), the science of poetic meters and versification. *n.*

pros pect (pros′pekt), 1 thing expected or looked forward to: *The prospects from our gardens are good this year.* 2 act of looking forward; expectation: *The prospect of a vacation is pleasant.* 3 outlook for the future. 4 view; scene: *The prospect from the mountain was grand.* 5 to search or look: *prospect for gold, prospect a region for silver.* 6 person who may become a customer, candidate, etc.: *The salesman called on several prospects.* 1-4,6 *n.*, 5 *v.*

in prospect, looked forward to; expected.

pro spec tive (prə spek′tiv), 1 likely to happen; probable; expected: *a prospective client.* 2 looking forward in time; future. *adj.*

pro spec tive ly (prə spek′tiv lē), in prospect or expectation; in the future. *adv.*

pros pec tor (pros′pek tər), person who explores or examines a region, searching for gold, silver, oil, uranium, etc., or estimating the value of some product of the region. *n.*

pro spec tus (prə spek′təs), a printed statement describing and advertising something: *the prospectus of a new company or issue of stock. n., pl.* **pro spec tus es.**

pros per (pros′pər), 1 be successful; have good fortune; flourish: *Our business prospered.* 2 make successful. *v.*

pros per i ty (pro sper′ə tē), prosperous condition; good fortune; suc-

cess: *Peace brings prosperity. n., pl.* **pros per i ties.**

Pros per o (pros′pər ō), an exiled duke living on an enchanted island in Shakespeare's play *The Tempest. n.*

pros per ous (pros′pər əs), 1 doing well; successful; thriving; fortunate: *a prosperous merchant.* 2 favorable; helpful: *prosperous weather for growing wheat. adj.* —**pros′per ous ly,** *adv.* —**pros′per ous ness,** *n.*

pros the sis (pros′thə sis), 1 the addition of a false tooth, artificial leg, etc., to the body. 2 the part itself. *n., pl.* **pros the ses** (pros′thə sēz′).

pros ti tute (pros′tə tüt or pros′tə-tyüt), 1 woman who has sexual relations with men for money. 2 person who does base things for money. 3 put to an unworthy or base use: *to prostitute artistic skills.* 1,2 *n.*, 3 *v.*, **pros ti tut ed, pros ti tut ing.**

pros ti tu tion (pros′tə tü′shən or pros′tə tyü′shən), the use of one's body, honor, talents, etc., in a base way. *n.*

pros trate (pros′trāt), 1 lay down flat; cast down: *The captives prostrated themselves before the conqueror.* 2 lying with face downward: *They were humbly prostrate in prayer.* 3 lying flat: *He stumbled and fell prostrate on the floor.* 4 make very weak or helpless; exhaust: *Sickness often prostrates people.* 5 helpless; overcome: *They were prostrate with grief.* 1,4 *v.*, **pros trat ed, pros trat ing;** 2,3,5 *adj.*

pros tra tion (pro strā′shən), 1 act of prostrating; bowing down low or lying face down before a king, before idols, or before God. Prostration is an act of submission, of respect, or of worship. 2 a being very much worn out or used up in body or mind; exhaustion; dejection. *n.*

pros y (prō′zē), like prose; commonplace; dull; tiresome. *adj.*, **pros i er, pros i est.**

pro tac tin i um (prō′tak tin′ē əm), a very rare, heavy, radioactive metallic element which occurs in pitchblende. It disintegrates to form actinium. *n.*

pro tag o nist (prō tag′ə nist), 1 the main character in a play, story, or novel. 2 person who takes a leading part; active supporter. *n.*

pro te an (prō′tē ən), readily assuming different forms or characters; exceedingly variable. *adj.* [from *Proteus*]

pro tect (prə tekt′), shield from harm or danger; shelter; defend; guard: *Protect yourself from danger. Protect the baby's eyes from the sun. v.*

pro tec tion (prə tek′shən), 1 act of protecting; condition of being kept from harm; defense: *We have a large dog for protection.* 2 thing or person that

hat, āge, fär; let, ēqual, tėrm;
it, īce; hot, ōpen, ôrder;
oil, out; cup, pùt, rüle; ch, child;
ng, long; sh, she; th, thin;
ᴛʜ, then; zh, measure;

ə represents *a* in about,
e in taken, *i* in pencil,
o in lemon, *u* in circus.

prevents damage: *A hat is protection from the sun.* 3 system of taxing foreign goods so that people are more likely to buy goods made in their own country; the opposite of free trade. *n.*

pro tec tive (prə tek′tiv), 1 being a defense; protecting: *the hard protective covering of a turtle.* 2 preventing injury to those around: *a protective device on a machine.* 3 guarding against foreign-made goods by putting a high tax or duty on them: *a protective tariff. adj.* —**pro tec′tive ly,** *adv.* —**pro tec′tive ness,** *n.*

protective coloring, a coloring some animals have that makes them hard to distinguish from the things they live among, or that makes them resemble a harmful or distasteful animal, and so protects them from their enemies.

pro tec tor (prə tek′tər), person or thing that protects; defender. *n.*

pro tec tor ate (prə tek′tər it), 1 a weak country under the protection and partial control of a strong country. 2 such protection and control. *n.*

pro té gé (prō′tə zhā), person who has been taken under the protection or kindly care of a friend or patron. *n., pl.* **pro té gés.** [from French]

pro tein (prō′tēn), one of the substances containing nitrogen which are a necessary part of the cells of animals and plants. Meat, milk, cheese, eggs, and beans contain protein. Protein is built up of amino acids. *n.*

pro test (prō′test for 1,4,6; prə test′ for 2,3,5), 1 statement that denies or objects strongly: *They yielded only after protest.* 2 make objections; object: *We protested against staying after school.* 3 object to: *protest an umpire's decision.* 4 expressing objection against some condition: *a protest movement.* 5 declare solemnly; assert: *protest one's innocence.* 6 a statement that a bill, note, check, etc., has not been paid. 1,6 *n.*, 2,3,5 *v.*, 4 *adj.*

under protest, unwillingly; objecting.

Prot es tant (prot′ə stənt), 1 member of any of certain Christian churches which split off from the Roman Catholic Church during the Reformation of the

adj. adjective		*n.* noun
adv. adverb		*prep.* preposition
conj. conjunction		*pron.* pronoun
interj. interjection		*v.* verb
sing. singular		*pl.* plural

1500's or developed thereafter. Lutherans, Baptists, Presbyterians, Methodists, Quakers, and many others are Protestants. 2 of Protestants or their religion. 1 *n.,* 2 *adj.*

Protestant Episcopal Church, a church in the United States that has about the same principles and beliefs as the Church of England.

Prot es tant ism (prot′ə stən tiz′əm), 1 the religion of Protestants. 2 their principles and beliefs. 3 Protestants or Protestant churches as a group. *n.*

prot es ta tion (prot′ə stā′shən), 1 a solemn declaration; protesting: *make a protestation of one's innocence.* 2 a protest. *n.*

Pro te us (prō′tē əs *or* prō′tyüs), (in Greek myths) a sea god who could assume different forms. *n.*

pro to col (prō′tə kol), rules of etiquette of the diplomatic corps. *n.*

pro ton (prō′ton), a tiny particle carrying one unit of positive electricity. All atoms are composed of electrons and protons. The number of protons in an atom is the atomic number of an element. *n.*

pro to plasm (prō′tə plaz′əm), the mixture of proteins, fats, and many other complex substances suspended in water which forms the living matter of all plant and animal cells; the substance that is the physical basis of life. *n.*

pro to plas mic (prō′tə plaz′mik), of or having to do with protoplasm. *adj.*

pro to type (prō′tə tīp), the first or primary type of anything; the original or model; archetype: *A modern ship has its prototype in the hollowed log used by primitive peoples. n.*

pro to zo an (prō′tə zō′ən), any of a group of microscopic, one-celled animals. Amoebas and paramecia are protozoans. *n.*

pro tract (prō trakt′), 1 draw out; lengthen in time: *protract a visit.* 2 slide out; thrust out; extend. *v.*

pro trac tion (prō trak′shən), act of drawing out; extension. *n.*

pro trac tor (prō trak′tər), 1 instrument for drawing or measuring angles. 2 person or thing that protracts. *n.*

pro trude (prō trüd′), 1 thrust forth; stick out: *The saucy child protruded his tongue.* 2 be thrust forth; project: *Her*

teeth protrude too far. *v.,* **pro trud ed, pro trud ing.**

pro tru sion (prō trü′zhən), 1 a sticking out: *Starvation caused the protrusion of the poor cat's bones.* 2 something that sticks out; projection: *A protrusion of rock gave us shelter from the storm. n.*

pro tu ber ance (prō tü′bər əns *or* prō tyü′bər əns), part that sticks out; bulge; swelling: *From the protuberance in their father's coat pocket, the children guessed that he had bought them candy. n.*

pro tu ber ant (prō tü′bər ənt *or* prō tyü′bər ənt), bulging out; sticking out; prominent. *adj.* **—pro tu′ber ant ly,** *adv.*

proud (proud), 1 thinking well of oneself. 2 feeling or showing pleasure or satisfaction: *I am proud to call him my friend.* 3 having a becoming sense of what is due oneself, one's position, or one's character: *The family was too proud to ask for charity.* 4 thinking too well of oneself; haughty; arrogant. 5 very pleasing to one's feelings or one's pride: *It was a proud moment for her when she was awarded the scholarship.* 6 grand; magnificent: *The big ship was a proud sight. adj.* **—proud′ly,** *adv.*

proud of, thinking well of; being well satisfied with: *to be proud of oneself, to be proud of one's family.*

prove (prüv), 1 show that (a thing) is true and right: *Prove your statement.* 2 turn out; be found to be: *This book proved interesting.* 3 try out; test: *prove a new product. v.,* **proved, proved** or **prov en, prov ing.**

prov en (prü′vən), proved; a past participle of **prove.** *v.*

Pro ven çal (prō′vən säl′), 1 of or having to do with Provence, its people, or their language. 2 person born or living in Provence. 3 language of Provence. In its medieval form, it was widely known in Europe as one of the principal languages of the troubadours. 1 *adj.,* 2,3 *n.*

Pro vence (prô väns′), part of SE France, ancient Rome's first province, famous during the Middle Ages for chivalry and poetry. *n.*

prov en der (prov′ən dər), 1 dry food for animals, such as hay or corn. 2 INFORMAL. food. *n.*

prov erb (prov′ėrb′), a short, wise

protractor
(def. 1)

saying used for a long time by many people. "Haste makes waste" is a proverb. *n.*

pro ver bi al (prə vėr′bē əl), 1 of proverbs; expressed in a proverb; like a proverb: *proverbial brevity, proverbial wisdom, a proverbial saying.* 2 that has become a proverb: *the proverbial stitch in time.* 3 well-known: *the proverbial loyalty of dogs. adj.* **—pro ver′bi al ly,** *adv.*

Prov erbs (prov′ėrbz′), book of the Old Testament made up of sayings of the wise men of Israel. *n.*

pro vide (prə vīd′), 1 give what is needed or wanted; supply; furnish: *Sheep provide us with wool. Parents provide for their children.* 2 take care of for the future: *provide against accident, provide for old age.* 3 arrange in advance; state as a condition beforehand: *Our club's rules provide that dues must be paid monthly.* 4 get ready; prepare beforehand: *They provided a good dinner. v.,* **pro vid ed, pro vid ing.**

pro vid ed (prə vī′did), on the condition that; if: *She will go provided her friends can go also. conj.*

prov i dence (prov′ə dəns), 1 God's care and help: *Trusting in providence, the Pilgrims sailed for the unknown world.* 2 **Providence,** God. 3 instance of God's care and help. 4 care for the future; good management: *Greater providence on my part would have kept me out of debt. n.*

Prov i dence (prov′ə dəns), capital of Rhode Island, in the NE part. *n.*

prov i dent (prov′ə dənt), having or showing foresight; careful in providing for the future: *Provident people lay aside a little money each month. adj.*

Provence—Smaller area of shading shows Provence in 1225. Larger area of shading to left and above shows the additional territory it occupied while a Roman province in 50 B.C.

prov i den tial (prov′ə den′shəl), 1 fortunate: *Our delay seemed providential, for the train we had planned to take was wrecked.* 2 of or proceeding from God's care: *providential help. adj.* **—prov′i den′tial ly,** *adv.*

pro vid er (prə vī′dər), person or thing that provides. *n.*

pro vid ing (prə vī′ding), on the condition that; if: *I shall go providing it doesn't rain.* conj.

prov ince (prov′əns), 1 one of the main divisions of a country. Canada is made up of provinces instead of states. 2 **the provinces,** part of a country outside the capital or the largest cities: *I was accustomed to city life and did not like living in the provinces.* 3 proper work or activity: *Teaching spelling is not within the province of a college.* 4 division; department: *the province of science, the province of literature.* 5 an ancient Roman territory outside Italy, ruled by a Roman governor. n.

pro vin cial (prə vin′shəl), 1 of a province: *provincial government.* 2 person born or living in a province. 3 belonging or peculiar to some particular province or provinces rather than to the whole country; local: *provincial English, provincial customs.* 4 having the manners, speech, dress, point of view, etc., of people living in a province. 5 lacking refinement or polish; narrow: *a provincial point of view.* 6 a provincial person. 1,3-5 adj., 2,6 n. —**pro vin′cial ly,** adv.

pro vin cial ism (prə vin′shə liz′əm), 1 provincial manners, habit of thought, etc. 2 narrow-mindedness. 3 word, expression, or way of pronunciation peculiar to a district of a country. *Reckon* for *think* and *br'er* for *brother* are provincialisms. n.

pro vi sion (prə vizh′ən), 1 statement making a condition: *A provision of the lease is that the rent must be paid promptly.* 2 act of providing; preparation: *They made provision for their children's education.* 3 care taken for the future; arrangement made beforehand: *There is a provision for making the building larger if necessary.* 4 that which is made ready; supply; stock, especially of food; food. 5 **provisions,** pl. a supply of food and drink: *They took plenty of provisions on their trip.* 6 to supply with provisions: *The cave was well provisioned; they had bread, oil, figs, cheese, and wine.* 1-5 n., 6 v.

pro vi sion al (prə vizh′ə nəl), for the time being; temporary: *a provisional agreement, a provisional governor.* adj.

pro vi sion al ly (prə vizh′ə nə lē), 1 for the time being; temporarily. 2 conditionally. adv.

pro vi so (prə vī′zō), statement making a condition; requirement; provision: *He was admitted to the eighth grade with the proviso that he was to be put back if he failed any subject.* n., pl. **pro vi sos** or **pro vi soes.**

prov o ca tion (prov′ə kā′shən), 1 a provoking. 2 something that stirs one up; cause of anger: *Their insult-*

ing remarks were a provocation. n.

pro voc a tive (prə vok′ə tiv), 1 irritating; vexing. 2 tending or serving to call forth action, thought, laughter, anger, etc.: *a provocative remark.* adj. —**pro voc′a tive ly,** adv.

pro voke (prə vōk′), 1 make angry; vex: *She provoked him by her teasing.* 2 stir up; excite: *An insult provokes a person to anger.* 3 call forth; bring about; start into action; cause: *The President's speech provoked much discussion.* v., **pro voked, pro vok ing.**

pro vok ing (prə vō′king), that provokes; irritating. adj. —**pro vok′ing ly,** adv.

prov ost (prō′vōst), 1 a high-ranking administrative officer in some colleges and universities. 2 head or dean of the clergymen assigned to a cathedral. 3 the chief magistrate in a Scottish town. n.

pro vost marshal (prō′vō), 1 (in the army) an officer acting as head of police in a camp or district, and charged with the maintenance of order, etc. 2 (in the navy) an officer charged with the safekeeping of prisoners until their trial by court-martial.

prow (def. 1)

—PROW

prow (prou), 1 the front part of a ship or boat; bow. 2 the projecting front part of anything: *the prow of an aircraft.* n.

prow ess (prou′is), 1 bravery; daring. 2 brave or daring acts. 3 unusual skill or ability: *She is famous for her prowess at figure skating.* n.

prowl (proul), 1 go about slowly and secretly hunting for something to eat or steal: *Many wild animals prowl at night.* 2 wander: *He got up and prowled about his room.* 3 a prowling: *It was only a wild animal on its nightly prowl.* 1,2 v., 3 n. —**prowl′er,** n.
on the prowl, prowling about.

prox i mate (prok′sə mit), 1 next; nearest. 2 near the exact amount; approximate. adj.

prox im i ty (prok sim′ə tē), nearness; closeness: *She and her cat enjoy proximity to the fire.* n.

prox y (prok′sē), 1 action of a deputy or substitute. In marriage by proxy, someone is substituted for the absent bride or bridegroom at the marriage service. 2 agent; deputy; substitute. 3 a

writing authorizing a proxy to act or vote for a person. n., pl. **prox ies.**

prude (prüd), person who is too proper or too modest; person who puts on extremely proper or modest airs. n.

pru dence (prüd′ns), 1 wise thought before acting; good judgment. 2 good management; economy. n.

pru dent (prüd′nt), planning carefully ahead of time; sensible; discreet: *My prudent friend saves part of her wages.* adj. —**pru′dent ly,** adv.

pru den tial (prü den′shəl), of, marked by, or showing prudence. adj. —**pru den′tial ly,** adv.

prud er y (prü′dər ē), 1 extreme modesty or propriety, especially when not genuine. 2 a prudish act or remark. n., pl. **prud er ies.**

prud ish (prü′dish), like a prude; extremely proper or modest; too modest. adj. —**prud′ish ly,** adv. —**prud′ish ness,** n.

prune[1] (prün), kind of sweet plum that is dried: *We had stewed prunes for breakfast.* n. [from French of the 1300's *prune,* from Latin *prunum,* from Greek *prounon* plum]

prune[2] (prün), 1 cut out useless or undesirable parts from: *The editor pruned the writer's manuscript.* 2 cut superfluous or undesirable twigs or branches from (a bush, tree, etc.): *prune fruit trees or grape vines.* 3 cut off or out: *Prune all the dead branches.* v., **pruned, prun ing.** [from French of the 1400's *proignier*]

Prus sia (prush′ə), former duchy and kingdom in N Europe which became the

Prussia—Shading to right shows the duchy of Prussia in 1648. Shading to left shows the additional territory in the kingdom of Prussia in 1871.

adj. adjective	*n.* noun
adv. adverb	*prep.* preposition
conj. conjunction	*pron.* pronoun
interj. interjection	*v.* verb
sing. singular	*pl.* plural

most important state in the confederation of German states united by Bismarck in 1871. *n.* —**Prus′sian,** *adj., n.*

prus sic acid (prus′ik), hydrocyanic acid.

pry[1] (prī), 1 look with curiosity; peep: *pry into another's private affairs.* 2 an inquisitive person. 1 *v.,* **pried, prying;** 2 *n., pl.* **pries.** [Middle English *prien*]

pry[2] (prī), 1 raise or move by force: *Pry up that stone with your pickax.* 2 lever for prying. 3 get with much effort: *We finally pried the secret out of him.* 1,3 *v.,* **pried, pry ing;** 2 *n., pl.* **pries.** [from earlier *prize* a lever, taken as a plural, from French of the 1300's *prise*]

pry ing (prī′ing), looking or searching curiously; inquisitive. *adj.*

P.S., 1 postscript. 2 Public School.

psalm (säm), 1 a sacred song or poem. 2 **Psalm,** any of the 150 sacred songs or hymns that together form a book of the Old Testament. *n.*

psalm ist (sä′mist), 1 author of a psalm or psalms. 2 **the Psalmist,** King David, to whom many of the Psalms were traditionally ascribed. *n.*

Psalms (sämz), book of the Old Testament consisting of 150 psalms. *n.*

Psal ter (sôl′tər), 1 the book of Psalms. 2 version of the Psalms for liturgical or devotional use. 3 a prayer book containing such a version. *n.*

psaltery

psal ter y (sôl′tər ē), an ancient musical instrument played by plucking the strings. *n., pl.* **psal ter ies.**

pseu do (sü′dō), false; sham; pretended: *a pseudo religion, pseudo anger.* *adj.*

pseu do nym (süd′n im), name used by an author instead of his real name; pen name. Mark Twain is a pseudonym for Samuel Langhorne Clemens. *n.*

pshaw (shô), exclamation expressing impatience, contempt, or dislike. *interj., n.*

PST, Pacific Standard Time.

psy che (sī′kē), 1 the human soul or spirit. 2 the mind. 3 **Psyche,** (in Greek and Roman myths) the human soul or spirit pictured as a beautiful young girl, usually with butterfly wings. Psyche was loved by Cupid (Eros) and was made immortal. *n.*

psy chi at ric (sī kē at′rik), of or having to do with the treatment of mental disorders. *adj.*

psy chi a trist (sī kī′ə trist), doctor who treats mental disorders. *n.*

psy chi a try (sī kī′ə trē), study and treatment of mental disorders. *n.*

psy chic (sī′kik), 1 of the soul or mind; mental: *illness due to psychic causes.* 2 outside the known laws of physics; supernatural. A psychic force or influence is believed by spiritualists to explain telepathy, table moving and tappings, etc. 3 especially susceptible to psychic influences. *adj.* —**psy′chi cal ly,** *adv.*

psy chi cal (sī′kə kəl), psychic. *adj.*

psy cho a nal y sis (sī′kō ə nal′ə sis), 1 examination of a person's mind to discover the unconscious desires, fears, anxieties, etc., which produce certain mental and emotional disorders. 2 method of psychotherapy based on such examination. *n.*

psy cho an a lyst (sī′kō an′l ist), person who practices psychoanalysis. *n.*

psy cho an a lyze (sī′kō an′l īz), examine by psychoanalysis. *v.,* **psy cho an a lyzed, psy cho an a lyz ing.**

psy cho log i cal (sī′kə loj′ə kəl), 1 of the mind. Memories and dreams are psychological processes. 2 of psychology or psychologists: *a psychological problem, a psychological explanation.* *adj.*

psy cho log i cal ly (sī′kə loj′ik lē), 1 in a psychological manner. 2 in psychological respects. *adv.*

psychological moment, 1 the very moment to get the desired effect in the mind. 2 the critical moment.

psy chol o gist (sī kol′ə jist), an expert in psychology. *n.*

psy chol o gy (sī kol′ə jē), 1 science of the mind. Psychology tries to explain why people act, think, and feel as they do. 2 the mental states and processes of a person or persons; mental nature and behavior: *The long illness had a bad effect on the patient's psychology.* *n., pl.* **psy chol o gies.**

psy cho path (sī′kə path), person having a mental disorder. *n.*

psy cho path ic (sī′kə path′ik), 1 of or having to do with mental disorders. 2 having a mental disorder. *adj.*

psy cho sis (sī kō′sis), any severe form of mental disorder which seriously disrupts behavior and social functioning. *n., pl.* **psy cho ses** (sī kō′sēz′).

psy cho ther a py (sī′kō ther′ə pē), treatment of mental or emotional disorders by psychological means. *n.*

psy chot ic (sī kot′ik), 1 having a psychosis. 2 a psychotic person. 1 *adj.,* 2 *n.* —**psy chot′i cal ly,** *adv.*

pt., 1 past tense. 2 pint or pints.

P.T.A., Parent-Teacher Association.

ptar mi gan (tär′mə gən), any of several kinds of grouse that have feathered feet and are found in mountainous and cold regions. *n., pl.* **ptar mi gans** or **ptar mi gan.**

pterodactyl wingspread about 20 ft.

pter o dac tyl (ter′ə dak′təl), an extinct flying reptile that had wings somewhat like a bat's. *n.*

Ptol e ma ic (tol′ə mā′ik), of or having to do with the astronomer Ptolemy. The **Ptolemaic system** of astronomy taught that the earth was the fixed center of the universe and that the sun, moon, and other heavenly bodies moved around it. *adj.*

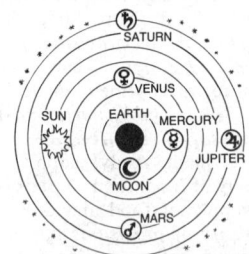
Ptolemaic system of astronomy

Ptol e my (tol′ə mē), Claudius, Greek mathematician, astronomer, and geographer at Alexandria. He lived in the A.D. 100's. *n.*

pto maine (tō′mān), any of several chemical compounds produced by bacteria in decaying matter. Improperly canned foods may contain ptomaines. Some ptomaines are poisonous. *n.*

pub (pub), saloon; tavern (a term used in Great Britain). *n.*

pu ber ty (pyü′bər tē), age at which a person is first able to produce offspring; the physical beginning of manhood and womanhood. Puberty comes at about

14 in boys and about 12 in girls. *n.*

pub lic (pub′lik), 1 of, belonging to, or concerning the people as a whole: *public affairs, public buildings.* 2 the people in general; all the people: *inform the public.* 3 done, made, acting, etc., for the people as a whole: *public relief.* 4 open to all the people; serving all the people: *a public park, public meetings.* 5 of or engaged in the affairs or service of the people: *a public official.* 6 known to many or all; not private: *The fact became public.* 7 a particular section of the people: *A popular actor has a large public.* 1,3-6 *adj.*, 2,7 *n.*

in public, not in private or secretly; publicly; openly: *to stand up in public for what you believe.*

pub li can (pub′lə kən), 1 keeper of a pub (a meaning common in Great Britain). 2 a tax collector of ancient Rome. *n.*

pub li ca tion (pub′lə kā′shən), 1 book, newspaper, or magazine; anything that is published. 2 the printing and selling of books, newspapers, magazines, etc.: *She helped in the publication of a new book.* 3 a making known; a being made known; public announcement: *There is prompt publication of any important news over the radio. n.*

public house, saloon; tavern (a term used in Great Britain).

pub li cist (pub′lə sist), 1 person skilled or trained in law or in public affairs. 2 writer on law, politics, or public affairs. 3 press agent. *n.*

pub lic i ty (pub lis′ə tē), 1 public notice: *the publicity that actors desire.* 2 measures used for getting, or the process of getting, public notice: *a campaign of publicity for a new automobile.* 3 articles, announcements, etc., used to get public notice: *She was hired to write publicity. n.*

pub li cize (pub′lə sīz), give publicity to. *v.*, **pub li cized, pub li ciz ing.**

pub lic ly (pub′lik lē), 1 in a public manner; openly. 2 by the public. *adv.*

public opinion, opinion of the people in a country, community, etc.: *make a survey of public opinion.*

public school, 1 (in the United States) a free school maintained by taxes. 2 (in Great Britain) a private boarding school.

pub lic-spir it ed (pub′lik spir′ə tid), having or showing an unselfish desire for the public good. *adj.*

public utility, company formed or chartered to render essential services to the public, such as a company furnishing electricity, gas, or water, or an airline, a railroad, a bus line, etc.

public works, things built by the government at public expense and for public use, such as roads, docks, canals, and waterworks.

pub lish (pub′lish), 1 prepare and offer (a book, paper, map, piece of music, etc.) for sale or distribution. 2 make publicly or generally known: *Don't publish the faults of your friends. v.*

pub lish er (pub′li shər), person or company whose business is to publish books, newspapers, magazines, etc.: *Look at the bottom of the title page of this book for the publisher's name. n.*

Puc ci ni (pü chē′nē), **Giacomo,** 1858-1924, Italian composer of operas. *n.*

puck¹ (puk), 1 a mischievous spirit; elf. 2 **Puck,** a mischievous fairy in English folklore, who appears in Shakespeare's play *A Midsummer Night's Dream. n.* [Old English *pūca*]

puck² (puk), a rubber disk used in the game of ice hockey. *n.* [a different form of *poke¹*]

puck er (puk′ər), 1 draw into wrinkles or irregular folds: *pucker one's brow, pucker cloth in sewing. My lips puckered as I tasted the sour grapefruit.* 2 an irregular fold; wrinkle: *There are puckers at the shoulders of this ill-fitting coat.* 1 *v.*, 2 *n.*

puck ish (puk′ish), mischievous; impish: *a puckish twinkling of the eyes. adj.*

pud ding (pùd′ing), a soft cooked food, usually sweet: *Rice pudding is nourishing. n.*

pud dle (pud′l), 1 a small pool of water, especially dirty water: *a puddle of rain water.* 2 a small pool of any liquid: *a puddle of ink.* 3 wet clay and sand stirred into a paste, used as a watertight lining for embankments, canals, etc. 4 use such a mixture to stop water from running through: *Puddle up that hole.* 5 stir (molten pig iron) along with an oxidizing agent to make wrought iron. 1-3 *n.*, 4,5 *v.*, **pud dled, pud dling.**

pudg i ness (puj′ē nis), condition of being short and fat. *n.*

pudg y (puj′ē), short and fat or thick: *a child's pudgy hand, a pudgy little man. adj.*, **pudg i er, pudg i est.**

pueb lo (pweb′lō), 1 an Indian village built of adobe and stone. There were once many pueblos in the southwestern United States. 2 **Pueblo,** member of

puffin
about 14 in. long

puffy

hat, āge, fär; let, ēqual, tėrm;
it, īce; hot, ōpen, ôrder;
oil, out; cup, pùt, rüle; ch, child;
ng, long; sh, she; th, thin;
ŦH, then; zh, measure;

ə represents *a* in about,
e in taken, *i* in pencil,
o in lemon, *u* in circus.

any of a group of Indian tribes in the southwestern United States and northern Mexico living in such villages. *n.*, *pl.* **pueb los.**

pu er ile (pyü′ər əl), foolish for a grown person to say or do; childish. *adj.*

Puer to Ri co (pwer′tō rē′kō), island in the E part of the West Indies. Puerto Rico is a self-governing commonwealth under the protection of the United States. *Capital:* San Juan. Formerly, **Porto Rico. —Puer′to Ri′can.**

puff (puf), 1 to blow with short, quick blasts: *The bellows puffed on the fire.* 2 a short, quick blast: *A puff of wind blew away the letter.* 3 breathe quick and hard: *We puffed as we climbed the stairs.* 4 give out puffs; move with puffs: *The engine puffed out of the station.* 5 smoke: *puff a cigar.* 6 swell with air or pride: *puff out one's cheeks. He puffed out his chest when the teacher praised his work.* 7 act or process of swelling. 8 a slightly swollen part; swelling. 9 arrange in soft, round masses; arrange softly and loosely. 10 a soft, round mass: *a puff of hair, a puff of cotton.* 11 a small pad for putting powder on the skin. 12 a light pastry filled with whipped cream, jam, etc.: *a cream puff.* 13 praise in exaggerated language: *puff someone to the skies.* 14 extravagant praise. 15 a quilted bed coverlet filled with cotton, wool, down, or similar material. 1,3-6, 9,13 *v.*, 2,7,8,10-12,14,15 *n.*

puff adder, a large and very poisonous African snake that puffs up its body when excited.

puff ball (puf′bôl′), a ball-shaped fungus somewhat like a mushroom. A ripe puffball gives off a cloud of tiny spores when suddenly broken. *n.*

puff er (puf′ər), 1 person or thing that puffs. 2 any of various fishes capable of inflating the body. *n.*

puf fin (puf′ən), a sea bird of northern waters that has a high, narrow, furrowed bill of several colors. *n.*

puff i ness (puf′ē nis), puffy condition or quality. *n.*

puff y (puf′ē), 1 puffed out; swollen:

adj.	adjective	*n.*	noun
adv.	adverb	*prep.*	preposition
conj.	conjunction	*pron.*	pronoun
interj.	interjection	*v.*	verb
sing.	singular	*pl.*	plural

My eyes were puffy from crying. 2 puffed up; vain. 3 coming in puffs. *adj.,* **puff i er, puff i est.**

pug (pug), 1 a small, heavy-bodied dog with a curly tail and a short nose on a wide, wrinkled face. 2 pug nose. *n.*

pug (def. 1)
11 in. high
at the shoulder

Pu get Sound (pyü′jit), a long narrow bay of the Pacific in NW Washington.

pu gi lism (pyü′jə liz′əm), art or sport of boxing. *n.*

pu gi list (pyü′jə list), boxer. *n.*

pu gi lis tic (pyü′jə lis′tik), of or having to do with boxing. *adj.*

pug na cious (pug nā′shəs), having the habit of fighting; fond of fighting; quarrelsome. *adj.* —**pug na′cious ly,** *adv.* —**pug na′cious ness,** *n.*

pug nac i ty (pug nas′ə tē), fondness for fighting; quarrelsomeness. *n.*

pug nose, a short, turned-up nose.

pu is sance (pyü′ə səns *or* pwis/ns), power; might; strength. *n.*

pu is sant (pyü′ə sənt *or* pwis/nt), powerful; mighty; strong. *adj.* —**pu′is sant ly,** *adv.*

puke (pyük), INFORMAL. vomit. *n., v.,* **puked, puk ing.**

Pu las ki (pù las′kē), Count **Casimir,** 1748-1779, Polish nobleman who was a general in the American Revolutionary army. *n.*

pule (pyül), cry in a thin voice, as a sick child does; whimper; whine. *v.,* **puled, pul ing.**

Pu litz er (pyü′lit sər *or* pùl′it sər), **Joseph,** 1847-1911, American journalist and newspaper publisher. *n.*

pull (pùl), 1 move (something) by grasping it and drawing toward oneself: *Pull the door open; don't push it.* 2 move, usually with effort or force: *pull a sled uphill.* 3 take hold of and tug: *pull a person's hair. She pulled at my sleeve to get my attention.* 4 take hold of and draw out with the fingers or a clutching

tool held with the fingers: *She used the claw of a hammer to pull nails. The dentist decided to pull my bad tooth.* 5 move; go: *When our tire started going flat we had to pull over to the side of the road and stop.* 6 pick; pluck: *pull flowers.* 7 tear; rip: *The baby pulled the toy to pieces.* 8 stretch too far; strain: *I pulled a muscle in my leg while skiing.* 9 row: *Pull for the shore as fast as you can.* 10 act of pulling; tug: *The boy gave a pull at the rope.* 11 effort of pulling: *It was a hard pull to get up the hill.* 12 handle, rope, ring, or other thing to pull by: *a bell pull, a curtain pull.* 13 force that attracts: *magnetic pull.* 14 SLANG. perform; carry through: *Don't pull any tricks.* 15 SLANG. influence; advantage: *use political pull to get a job.* 1-9,14 *v.,* 10-13,15 *n.* —**pull′er,** *n.*

pull down, demolish; destroy: *pull down an old building.*

pull for, SLANG. give help to.

pull in, arrive: *He pulled in this morning.*

pull off, SLANG. do successfully; succeed in.

pull oneself together, gather one's faculties, energy, etc.

pull out, leave: *The train pulled out of the station.*

pull through, get through a difficult or dangerous situation.

pull up, bring or come to a halt; stop.

pul let (pùl′it), a young hen, usually less than a year old. *n.*

pul ley (pùl′ē), 1 wheel with a grooved rim in which a rope can run and so change the direction of pull. It is a simple machine and is used to raise heavy weights. 2 set of such wheels used to increase the power applied. *n., pl.* **pul leys.**

Pull man (pùl′mən), 1 sleeping car. 2 parlor car. *n.* [from George M. Pullman, 1831-1897, an American inventor, who designed railroad cars]

Pullman car, Pullman.

pull o ver (pùl′ō′vər), sweater put on by pulling it over the head. *n.*

pul mo nar y (pùl′mə ner′ē), of or having to do with the lungs. Pneumonia is a pulmonary disease. *adj.*

pulp (pulp), 1 the soft, fleshy part of any fruit or vegetable. 2 the soft inner part of a tooth, containing blood vessels

puma
8 ft. long
with tail

and nerves. 3 any soft, wet mass. Paper is made from wood ground to a pulp. 4 reduce to pulp. 1-3 *n.,* 4 *v.*

pul pit (pùl′pit), 1 platform or raised structure in a church from which the minister preaches. 2 preachers or preachings: *the influence of the pulpit. n.*

pulp wood (pulp′wùd′), any soft wood suitable for reducing to pulp to make paper. *n.*

pulp y (pùl′pē), of pulp; like pulp; fleshy; soft. *adj.,* **pulp i er, pulp i est.**

pul sate (pùl′sāt), 1 beat; throb: *The patient's heart was pulsating rapidly.* 2 vibrate; quiver. *v.,* **pul sat ed, pul sat ing.**

pul sa tion (pùl sā′shən), 1 a beating; throbbing. 2 a beat; throb. 3 vibration; quiver. *n.*

pulse¹ (puls), 1 the regular beating of the arteries caused by the rush of blood into them after each contraction of the heart. By feeling a person's pulse in the artery of the wrist, one can count the number of times his heart beats each minute. 2 any regular, measured beat: *the pulse in music, the pulse of an engine.* 3 beat; throb; vibrate: *My heart pulsed with excitement.* 4 feeling; sentiment: *the pulse of the nation.* 1,2,4 *n.,* 3 *v.,* **pulsed, puls ing.** [from Latin *pulsus,* from *pellere* to beat]

pulley (def. 1)—two types of pulleys

pulse² (puls), 1 the seeds of a group of plants, such as peas, beans, and lentils, used as food. 2 plant that yields such seeds. *n.* [from French of the 1200's *pols,* from Latin *puls* porridge]

pul ve rize (pùl′və rīz′), 1 grind to powder or dust. 2 become dust. 3 break to pieces; demolish: *pulverize an enemy force by bombardment, pulverize the hopes of the people. v.,* **pul ve rized, pul ve riz ing.**

pu ma (pyü′mə), a large, tawny wildcat found in many parts of North and South America; cougar; mountain lion. *n., pl.* **pu mas.**

pum ice (pum′is), a light, porous stone thrown up from volcanoes, used for cleaning, smoothing, and polishing: *Rub your hands with pumice to remove the ink. n.*

pum mel (pum′əl), strike or beat; beat with the fists. *v.* Also, **pommel.**

pump¹ (pump), 1 machine for forcing liquids or gases into or out of things: *a water pump, an oil pump.* 2 move (liquids, air, etc.) by a pump: *Pump water from the well into a pail.* 3 blow air into: *Pump up the car's tires.* 4 remove water, etc., from by a pump: *Pump the well dry.* 5 work as a pump does. 6 move by, or as if by, a pump handle: *He pumped my hand.* 7 get information out of; try to get information out of: *Don't let them pump you.* 1 *n.*, 2-7 *v.* [Middle English *pompe*] —**pump′er,** *n.*

pump¹ (def. 1)
As handle is raised, plunger moves downward forcing water through valve A and out spout. As handle is pushed down, plunger is raised, pulling water upward through valve B from shaft.

pump² (pump), a low shoe with a thin sole and no fasteners. *n.* [origin uncertain]

pum per nick el (pum′pər nik′əl), a heavy, dark, slightly sour bread made from whole, coarse rye. *n.*

pump kin (pump′kin *or* pung′kin), 1 a large, roundish, orange-yellow fruit of a trailing vine, used for making pies, as a vegetable, as food for livestock, and for jack-o'-lanterns. 2 vine it grows on. *n.*

pun (pun), 1 a humorous use of a word where it can have different meanings; play on words: *"We must all hang together, or we shall all hang separately"* is a pun by Benjamin Franklin. 2 make puns. 1 *n.*, 2 *v.*, **punned, pun ning.**

punch¹ (punch), 1 hit with the fist: *punch someone on the arm. They began punching each other madly.* 2 a quick thrust or blow with the fist. 3 tool for making holes. 4 tool or apparatus for piercing or stamping materials, impressing a design, etc. 5 pierce, cut, stamp, or make with a punch: *to punch metal. The train conductor punched our tickets.* 6 to herd or drive cattle: *Cowboys punch cows for a living.* 1,5,6 *v.*, 2-4 *n.*, *pl.* **punch es.** [apparently shortened from earlier *puncheon* a stamping tool used by goldsmiths, from French of the 1300's *poinchon*, from Latin *punctionem* a pricking, from *pungere* pierce] —**punch′er,** *n.*

punch² (punch), drink made of different liquids, often fruit juices or carbonated beverages, mixed together. *n.*, *pl.* **punch es.** [probably from Hindustani *panch* five, from Sanskrit *panca* (because of the number of ingredients in the drink)]

Punch (punch), a hook-nosed, hunchbacked doll who quarrels violently with his wife Judy in the puppet show *Punch and Judy. n.*

pleased as Punch, very much pleased.

punch card, card on which information is recorded by means of holes punched according to a code, for use in processing data by machine, electronic computer, etc.

punch line, the line or sentence in a story play, or drama which makes or enforces the point.

punc til i o (pungk til′ē ō), 1 a little point or detail of honor, conduct, ceremony, etc.: *I did not neglect the least punctilio.* 2 care in attending to such little points. *n.*, *pl.* **punc til i os.**

punc til i ous (pungk til′ē əs), 1 very careful and exact: *punctilious in obeying orders, a punctilious concern about neatness.* 2 paying strict attention to details of conduct and ceremony. *adj.* —**punc til′i ous ly,** *adv.*

punc tu al (pungk′chü əl), on time; prompt: *She is punctual to the minute. adj.* —**punc′tu al ly,** *adv.*

punc tu al i ty (pungk′chü al′ə tē), a being on time; promptness. *n.*

punc tu ate (pungk′chü āt), 1 use periods, commas, and other marks in writing or printing to help make the meaning clear. 2 put punctuation marks in. 3 interrupt now and then: *a speech punctuated with cheers.* 4 give point or emphasis to: *She punctuated her remarks with gestures. v.*, **punc tu at ed, punc tu at ing.**

punc tu a tion (pungk′chü ā′shən), 1 use of periods, commas, and other marks to help make the meaning of a sentence clear. Punctuation does for writing and printing what pauses and changes of voice do for speech. 2 punctuation marks. *n.*

punch¹ (def. 3)

punctuation mark, mark used in writing or printing to help make the meaning clear. Periods, commas, question marks, colons, etc., are punctuation marks.

punc ture (pungk′chər), 1 hole made

hat, āge, fär; let, ēqual, tėrm; it, īce; hot, ōpen, ôrder; oil, out; cup, pùt, rüle; ch, child; ng, long; sh, she; th, thin; ŦH, then; zh, measure;

ə represents *a* in about, *e* in taken, *i* in pencil, *o* in lemon, *u* in circus.

by something pointed. 2 make such a hole in. 3 have or get a puncture. 4 act or process of puncturing. 5 reduce, spoil, or destroy as if by a puncture. 1,4 *n.*, 2,3,5 *v.*, **punc tured, punc tur ing.**

pun dit (pun′dit), a very learned person; expert; authority. *n.*

pun gen cy (pun′jən sē), sharpness (of taste, smell, feeling, etc.): *the pungency of pepper, the pungency of wit. n.*

pun gent (pun′jənt), 1 sharply affecting the organs of taste and smell: *a pungent pickle, the pungent smell of burning leaves.* 2 sharp; biting: *pungent criticism.* 3 stimulating to the mind; keen; lively: *a pungent wit. adj.* —**pun′gent ly,** *adv.*

pu ni ness (pyü′nē nis), puny condition. *n.*

pun ish (pun′ish), 1 cause pain, loss, or discomfort to for some fault or offense: *punish criminals for wrongdoing.* 2 cause pain, loss, or discomfort for: *The law punishes crimes.* 3 INFORMAL. deal with severely, roughly, or greedily: *punish a car by very fast driving. v.*

pun ish a ble (pun′i shə bəl), 1 liable to punishment. 2 deserving punishment. *adj.*

pun ish ment (pun′ish mənt), 1 a punishing or a being punished. 2 pain, suffering, or loss: *Her punishment for stealing was a year in prison.* 3 INFORMAL. severe or rough treatment. *n.*

pu ni tive (pyü′nə tiv), 1 concerned with punishment: *punitive laws.* 2 inflicting punishment: *The judge imposed a punitive sentence on the prisoner. adj.*

Pun jab (pun jäb′ *or* pun′jäb), former province in N India, now divided between the countries of India and Pakistan. *n.*

punk¹ (pungk), 1 a preparation that burns very slowly. A stick of punk is used to light fireworks. 2 decayed wood used as tinder. *n.* [perhaps from Algonquian *ponk* ashes]

punk² (pungk), SLANG. 1 poor or bad in quality. 2 a young hoodlum. 3 a young, inexperienced person. 1 *adj.*, 2,3 *n.* [origin unknown]

679

punster

adj. adjective	*n.* noun
adv. adverb	*prep.* preposition
conj. conjunction	*pron.* pronoun
interj. interjection	*v.* verb
sing. singular	*pl.* plural

pun ster (pun′stər), person fond of making puns. *n.*

punt (punt), 1 a shallow, flat-bottomed boat with square ends, usually moved by pushing with a pole against the bottom of a river, etc. 2 propel (a boat) by pushing with a pole against the bottom of a river, pond, etc. 3 use a punt; travel by punt. 4 kick (a football) before it touches the ground after dropping it from the hands. 5 such a kick. 1,5 *n.*, 2-4 *v.* —**punt′er,** *n.*

pu ny (pyü′nē), 1 of less than usual size and strength; small and weak. 2 petty; not important. *adj.,* **pu ni er, pu ni est.**

pup (pup), 1 a young dog; puppy. 2 a young fox, wolf, seal, etc. *n.*

PUPA 3

ADULT 4

2 LARVA

1 EGGS

pupa (def. 2)
four stages in the life of a beetle

pu pa (pyü′pə), 1 stage between the larva and the adult in the development of many insects. 2 insect in this stage. Most pupae are inactive and some, such as those of many moths, are enclosed in a tough case or cocoon. *n., pl.* **pu pae** (pyü′pē), **pu pas.**

pu pal (pyü′pəl), of, having to do with, or in the form of a pupa. *adj.*

pu pate (pyü′pāt), become a pupa. *v.,* **pu pat ed, pu pat ing.**

pu pil[1] (pyü′pəl), person who is learning in school or being taught by someone: *The music teacher takes private pupils. n.* [from French of the 1300's *pupille,* from Latin *pupillus, pupilla* ward, from *pupus* boy, *pupa* girl]

pu pil[2] (pyü′pəl), the opening in the center of the iris of the eye which looks like a black spot. The pupil, which is the only place where light can enter the eye, expands and contracts, thus controlling the amount of light that strikes the retina. *n.* [from Latin *pupilla* (originally) little doll, from *pupa* girl, doll

(because of the tiny reflection of oneself that may be seen in the eye of another person)]

pup pet (pup′it), 1 a small doll. 2 figure made to look like a person or animal and moved by wires, strings, or the hands. 3 anybody who is not independent, waits to be told how to act, and does what somebody else says. *n.* —**pup′pet like′,** *adj.*

puppet show, play performed with puppets on a small stage.

pup py (pup′ē), 1 a young dog. 2 a silly, conceited, young man. *n., pl.* **pup pies.**

pup tent, a small, low tent, usually for one or two persons.

pur (pėr), purr. *n., v.,* **purred, pur ring.**

pur blind (pėr′blīnd), 1 nearly blind. 2 slow to understand. *adj.* —**pur′-blind′ness,** *n.*

pur chas a ble (pėr′chə sə bəl), that can be bought. *adj.*

pur chase (pėr′chəs), 1 get by paying a price; buy: *We purchased a new car.* 2 a buying: *the purchase of a new car.* 3 thing bought: *That hat was a good purchase.* 4 get in return for something: *purchase safety at the cost of happiness.* 5 a firm hold to help move something or to keep from slipping: *Wind the rope twice around the tree to get a better purchase.* 1,4 *v.,* **pur chased, pur chas ing;** 2,3,5 *n.*

pur chas er (pėr′chə sər), buyer. *n.*

pure (pyur), 1 not mixed with anything else; unadulterated; genuine: *pure gold.* 2 perfectly clean; spotless: *pure hands.* 3 perfect; correct; without defects: *speak pure French.* 4 nothing else than; mere; sheer: *pure accident.* 5 with no evil; without sin; chaste: *a pure mind.* 6 concerned with theory rather than practical use; not applied; abstract: *pure mathematics. adj.,* **pur er, pur est.** —**pure′ness,** *n.*

pure bred (pyur′bred′), of pure breed or stock; having ancestors known to have all belonged to one breed: *pure-bred Holstein cows. adj.*

pu rée (pyu rā′ *or* pyur′ā), 1 food boiled to a pulp and pushed through a sieve. 2 a thick soup. 3 make into a purée. 1,2 *n., pl.* **pu rées;** 3 *v.,* **pu réed, pu rée ing.** [from French *purée* strained]

pure ly (pyur′lē), 1 in a pure manner. 2 exclusively; entirely. 3 merely. 4 innocently; chastely. *adv.*

pur ga tive (pėr′gə tiv), 1 medicine that causes emptying of the bowels. Castor oil is a purgative. 2 purging; cleansing. 1 *n.,* 2 *adj.*

pur ga to ri al (pėr′gə tôr′ē əl), of, like, or having to do with purgatory. *adj.*

pur ga to ry (pėr′gə tôr′ē), 1 (in Roman Catholic belief) a temporary condition or place in which the souls of those who have died penitent are purified from sin by punishment. 2 any condition or place of temporary suffering or punishment. *n., pl.* **pur ga to ries.**

purge (pėrj), 1 wash away all that is not clean; make clean. 2 a purging. 3 clear of any undesired thing or person, such as air in a water pipe or opponents in a nation. 4 elimination of undesired persons from a nation or party. 5 empty (the bowels). 6 medicine that purges. 1,3,5 *v.,* **purged, purging;** 2,4,6 *n.*

pur i fi ca tion (pyur′ə fə kā′shən), a purifying or a being purified. *n.*

pur i fi er (pyur′ə fī′ər), person or thing that purifies. *n.*

pur i fy (pyur′ə fī), 1 make pure: *Filters are used to purify water.* 2 become pure. *v.,* **pur i fied, pur i fy ing.**

pur ist (pyur′ist), person who is very careful or too careful about purity in language. A purist dislikes slang and all expressions that are not formally correct. *n.*

Pur i tan (pyur′ə tən), 1 member of a group in the Church of England during the 1500's and 1600's who wanted simpler forms of worship and stricter morals. Many Puritans settled in New England. 2 of the Puritans. 3 **puritan,** person who is very strict in morals and religion. 1,3 *n.,* 2 *adj.*

pur i tan ic (pyur′ə tan′ik), puritanical. *adj.*

Pur i tan i cal (pyur′ə tan′ə kəl), 1 having to do with or like the Puritans. 2 **puritanical,** of or like a puritan; very strict or too strict in morals or religion. *adj.*

Pur i tan ism (pyur′ə tə niz′əm), 1 the principles and practices of the Puritans. 2 **puritanism,** puritanical behavior or principles. *n.*

pur i ty (pyur′ə tē), 1 freedom from dirt or mixture; clearness; cleanness: *the purity of drinking water.* 2 freedom from evil; innocence: *a soul full of goodness and purity.* 3 careful correctness: *purity of style. n., pl.* **pur i ties.**

purl[1] (pėrl), 1 flow with rippling motions and a murmuring sound: *A shallow brook purls.* 2 a purling motion or sound. 1 *v.,* 2 *n.* [perhaps from a Scandinavian word, such as Norwegian *purla* to ripple]

purl[2] (pėrl), knit with inverted stitches. *v.* [origin uncertain]

pur lieu (pėr′lü), 1 piece of land on the border of a forest. 2 any bordering, neighboring, or outlying region or district. *n.*

pur loin (pər loin′), steal. *v.*

pur ple (pėr′pəl), 1 a dark color made by mixing red and blue. 2 of this color. 3 crimson. This was the ancient meaning of purple. 4 purple cloth or clothing, especially as worn by emperors, kings, etc., to indicate high rank. 5 imperial, royal, or high rank. A prince is born to the purple. 6 imperial; royal. 1,3-5 *n.*, 2,3,6 *adj.*

Purple Heart, medal awarded to members of the armed forces of the United States for wounds received in action against an enemy or as a result of enemy action.

pur plish (pėr′plish), somewhat purple. *adj.*

pur port (pər pôrt′ *for 1,2;* pėr′pôrt *for 3*), 1 to claim or profess: *The document purported to be official.* 2 have as its main idea; mean: *a statement purporting certain facts.* 3 meaning; main idea: *The purport of her letter was that she could not come.* 1,2 *v.*, 3 *n.*

pur pose (pėr′pəs), 1 something one has in mind to get or do; plan; aim; intention. 2 object or end for which a thing is made, done, used, etc. 3 to plan; aim; intend. 1,2 *n.*, 3 *v.*, **purposed, pur pos ing.**

on purpose, with a purpose; not by accident: *He tripped me on purpose.*

to good purpose, with good results.

to little purpose or **to no purpose,** with few or no results.

pur pose ful (pėr′pəs fəl), having a purpose. *adj.* —**pur′pose ful ly,** *adv.* —**pur′pose ful ness,** *n.*

pur pose less (pėr′pəs lis), lacking a purpose. *adj.* —**pur′pose less ly,** *adv.* —**pur′pose less ness,** *n.*

pur pose ly (pėr′pəs lē), on purpose; intentionally: *Did you leave the door open purposely? adv.*

purr (pėr), 1 a low, murmuring sound, such as a cat makes when pleased. 2 make this sound. 1 *n.*, 2 *v.* Also, **pur.**

purse (pėrs), 1 a small bag or container to hold small change, usually carried in a handbag or pocket. 2 handbag. 3 money; resources; treasury. 4 sum of money: *A purse was made up for the victims of the fire.* 5 draw together; press into folds or wrinkles: *She pursed her lips and frowned.* 1-4 *n.*, 5 *v.*, **pursed, purs ing.**

purs er (pėr′sər), a ship's officer who keeps accounts, pays wages, and attends to other matters of business. The purser is responsible for the welfare of passengers. *n.*

pur slane (pėr′slān), a common plant that has small, yellow flowers and small, thick leaves. It is sometimes used for salad or for flavoring. *n.*

pur su ance (pər sü′əns), a following; carrying out; pursuit: *In pursuance of*

her duty, the lifeguard risked her life. *n.*

pur su ant (pər sü′ənt), following; carrying out; according. *adj.*

pursuant to, following; acting according to; in accordance with.

pur sue (pər sü′), 1 follow to catch or kill; chase: *The dogs pursued the rabbit.* 2 proceed along; follow in action; follow: *He pursued a wise course by taking no chances.* 3 strive for; try to get; seek: *pursue pleasure.* 4 carry on; keep on with: *She pursued the study of French for four years.* 5 continue to annoy or trouble: *pursue a teacher with questions. v.*, **pur sued, pur su ing.**

pur su er (pər sü′ər), person who pursues. *n.*

pur suit (pər süt′), 1 a pursuing; chase: *The dog is in pursuit of the cat.* 2 that which one does, as a profession, business, recreation, etc.; occupation: *Fishing is her favorite pursuit; reading is mine. n.*

pur vey (pər vā′), supply (food or provisions); provide; furnish: *purvey meat for an army, purvey for a royal household. v.*

pur vey ance (pər vā′əns), 1 a purveying. 2 provisions; supplies. *n.*

pur vey or (pər vā′ər), 1 person who supplies provisions: *a purveyor of fine foods and meats.* 2 person who supplies anything: *a purveyor of gossip. n.*

pus (pus), a thick, yellowish-white fluid formed in sores, abscesses, and other infected tissues in the body. It consists of white blood cells, bacteria, etc. *n.*

push (push), 1 move (something) away by pressing against it: *Push the door; don't pull it.* 2 press hard: *We pushed with all our might.* 3 thrust: *Trees push their roots down into the ground.* 4 go forward by force: *push on at a rapid pace. We pushed through the crowd.* 5 make go forward; urge: *He pushed his plans cleverly. Please push this job and get it done this week.* 6 extend: *The railroad pushed its tracks across the prairie.* 7 urge the use, sale, etc., of. 8 INFORMAL. force; energy; power to succeed: *She has plenty of push.* 9 a pushing: *Give the door a push.* 10 hard effort; determined advance. 1-7 *v.*, 8-10 *n., pl.* **push es. —push′er,** *n.*

push around, INFORMAL. treat roughly or with contempt; bully.

push off, move from shore: *We pushed off in the boat.*

push cart (pùsh′kärt′), a light cart pushed by hand: *The peddler's pushcart was filled with fruit and vegetables. n.*

Push kin (pùsh′kən), **Alexander,** 1799-1837, Russian poet and writer of short stories and novels. *n.*

push o ver (pùsh′ō′vər), SLANG. 1 something very easy to do. 2 person very easy to beat in a contest. *n.*

hat, āge, fär; let, ēqual, tėrm;
it, īce; hot, ōpen, ôrder;
oil, out; cup, pùt, rüle; ch, child;
ng, long; sh, she; th, thin;
ŦH, then; zh, measure;

ə represents *a* in about,
e in taken, *i* in pencil,
o in lemon, *u* in circus.

push up (pùsh′up′), exercise done by lying face down and raising the body with the arms while keeping the back straight and the toes on the ground. *n.*

push y (pùsh′ē), forward; aggressive. *adj.*, **push i er, push i est.**

pu sil la nim i ty (pyü′sə lə nim′ə tē), cowardliness; timidity. *n.*

pu sil lan i mous (pyü′sə lan′ə məs), cowardly; fainthearted; timid: *a pusillanimous man, pusillanimous conduct. n.*

puss (pùs), cat. *n., pl.* **puss es.**

puss y (pùs′ē), 1 cat. 2 catkin. *n., pl.* **puss ies.**

puss y foot (pùs′ē fùt′), SLANG. 1 move softly and cautiously to avoid being seen. 2 be cautious and timid about revealing one's opinions or committing oneself. *v.*

pussy willow, a small American willow with silky catkins.

pus tule (pus′chùl), a small, pus-filled bump on the skin. *n.*

put (pùt), 1 cause to be in some place or position; place; lay: *I put sugar in my tea. Put away your toys. Put on your hat.* 2 cause to be in some state, condition, position, relation, etc.: *The murderer was put to death. Put your room in order. Put the question in writing.* 3 express: *The teacher puts things clearly.* 4 set at a particular place, point, amount, etc., in a scale of estimation; appraise: *He puts the distance at five miles.* 5 apply: *I put my writing skill to good use.* 6 impose: *put a tax on gasoline.* 7 throw or cast (a 12-lb. or 16-lb. ball) from the hand placed close to the shoulder. 8 such a throw or cast. 1-7 *v.*, **put, put ting;** 8 *n.*

put about, (of a ship) change direction.

put across, SLANG. 1 carry out successfully. 2 get accepted or understood: *He could not put across his point of view to the audience.*

put by, save for future use.

put down, 1 put an end to; suppress: *The rebellion was quickly put down.*

pushup

adj. adjective	n. noun
adv. adverb	prep. preposition
conj. conjunction	pron. pronoun
interj. interjection	v. verb
sing. singular	pl. plural

2 write down. 3 slight or belittle; snub.

put forth, 1 grow; sprout; issue: *put forth buds.* 2 use fully; exert: *put forth effort.*

put forward, propose or submit for consideration, deliberation, etc.

put in, 1 spend (time) as specified: *put in a full day of work.* 2 enter a place for safety, supplies, etc.: *The ship put in at Singapore.* 3 make a claim, plea, or offer: *put in for a loan.*

put off, 1 lay aside; postpone: *Don't put off going to the dentist or your teeth will suffer from neglect.* 2 go away; start out: *The Mayflower put off for America in 1620.*

put on, 1 present on a stage; produce: *The class put on a play.* 2 take on or add to oneself: *put on weight.* 3 assume or take on, especially as a pretense: *I put on an air of innocence.* 4 apply or exert: *put on pressure.*

put out, 1 extinguish; make an end to; destroy: *put out a fire, put out one's eye.* 2 go; turn; proceed: *The ship put out to sea.* 3 offend; provoke. 4 cause to be out in a game. 5 publish.

put over, SLANG. 1 carry out successfully. 2 do or carry out by trickery: *put over a fraud.*

put through, carry out successfully.

put to it, force to a course; put in difficulty: *I was put to it to keep up with her fast pace.*

put up, 1 offer: *put up a house for sale.* 2 give or show: *put up a brave front.* 3 build: *put up a monument.* 4 lay aside (work). 5 propose for election or adoption: *His name was put up for president of the club.* 6 pack up or preserve (fruit, etc.). 7 give lodging or food to. 8 INFORMAL. get (a person) to do: *put someone up to mischief.*

put upon, impose upon; take advantage of; victimize.

put up with, bear with patience; tolerate.

pu tre fac tion (pyü′trə fak′shən), a putrefying; decay; rotting. *n.*

pu tre fy (pyü′trə fī), break down by the action of bacteria and fungi, producing bad-smelling gases; rot; decay: *The meat putrefied because it was not refrigerated.* *v.,* **pu tre fied, pu tre fy ing.**

pu trid (pyü′trid), 1 decaying; rotten:

putrid meat. 2 characteristic of putrefying matter; foul: *a putrid odor.* *adj.*

putt (put), 1 strike (a golf ball) gently and carefully in an effort to make it roll into the hole. 2 the stroke itself. 1 *v.,* 2 *n.*

put tee (put′ē *or* pu tē′), 1 a long, narrow strip of cloth wound around the leg from ankle to knee, worn by sportsmen, soldiers, etc. 2 gaiter of cloth or leather reaching from ankle to knee, worn by soldiers, riders, etc. *n.*

puttees
(def. 1, left)
(def. 2, right)

put ter¹ (put′ər), keep busy in an aimless or useless way: *I like to spend the afternoon puttering in the garden.* *v.* Also, **potter.** [a different form of *potter²*] —**put′ter er,** *n.*

putt er² (put′ər), 1 person who putts. 2 a golf club used in putting. *n.* [*putt* + *-er¹*]

putt ing green (put′ing), the very smooth turf around the hole into which a player putts a golf ball.

put ty (put′ē), 1 a soft mixture of powdered chalk and linseed oil, used for fastening panes of glass in window frames, etc. 2 stop up or cover with putty: *We puttied up the holes in the woodwork before painting it.* 1 *n., pl.* **put ties;** 2 *v.,* **put tied, put ty ing.**

puz zle (puz′əl), 1 a hard problem: *How to get all my things into one trunk is a puzzle.* 2 problem or task to be done for fun: *A famous Chinese puzzle has seven pieces of wood to fit together.* 3 make unable to answer, solve, or understand something; perplex: *How the cat got out puzzled us.* 4 be perplexed. 5 exercise one's mind on something hard: *They puzzled over their arithmetic.* 1,2 *n.,* 3-5 *v.,* **puz zled, puz zling.**

puzzle out, find out by thinking or trying hard: *puzzle out the meaning of a sentence.*

puz zle ment (puz′əl mənt), puzzled condition. *n.*

puz zler (puz′lər), person or thing that puzzles. *n.*

Pvt., Private.

pyg my (pig′mē), 1 Pygmy, one of a group of people of equatorial Africa who are less than five feet tall. 2 of or having to do with the Pygmies. 3 a very small person; dwarf. 4 very small: *a*

pygmy marmoset. 1,3 *n., pl.* **pyg mies;** 2,4 *adj.* Also, **pigmy.**

py ja mas (pə jä′məz *or* pə jam′əz), pajamas (the spelling generally used in Great Britain and Canada). *n.pl.*

py lon (pī′lon), 1 post or tower for guiding aviators. 2 a tall steel framework used to carry high-tension wires across country. 3 one of a pair of high supporting structures that marks an entrance at either end of a bridge. 4 gateway, particularly to an ancient Egyptian temple, usually consisting of two huge towers. *n.*

py lo rus (pī lôr′əs), the opening that leads from the stomach into the intestine. *n.*

Pyong yang (pyong′yäng′), capital of North Korea, in the SW part. *n.*

py or rhe a *or* **py or rhoe a** (pī′ə rē′ə), disease of the gums in which pockets of pus form about the teeth, the gums shrink, and the teeth become loose. *n.*

pyramid (def. 1)
two types
of pyramids

pyr a mid (pir′ə mid), 1 a solid having a polygon for a base and triangular sides which meet in a point. 2 anything having the form of a pyramid: *a pyramid of stones.* 3 be or put in the form of a pyramid. 4 raise or increase (costs, wages, etc.) gradually. 5 **Pyramids,** *pl.* the huge, massive stone pyramids, serving as royal tombs, built by the ancient Egyptians. 1,2,5 *n.,* 3,4 *v.*

Pyramids (def. 5)

pyre (pīr), pile of wood for burning a dead body. *n.*

Pyr e nees (pir′ə nēz′), mountain range between France and Spain. *n.pl.*

Py rex (pī′reks), trademark for a kind of glassware that will not break when heated. *n.*

py rite (pī′rīt), 1 a yellow mineral, a compound of iron and sulfur, which looks like and is often mistaken for gold; fool's gold. It is used to make sulfuric acid. 2 **pyrites,** *pl.* any of various compounds of sulfur and a metal, such as tin pyrites, an ore of tin. *n.*

py ro ma ni a (pī′rə mā′nē ə), an uncontrollable desire to set things on fire. *n.*

py ro ma ni ac (pī′rə mā′nē ak), person with an uncontrollable desire to set things on fire. *n.*

py ro tech nic (pī′rə tek′nik), 1 of or having to do with fireworks: *a pyrotechnic display.* 2 resembling fireworks; brilliant; sensational: *pyrotechnic eloquence. adj.*

py ro tech ni cal (pī′rə tek′nə kəl), pyrotechnic. *adj.*

py ro tech nics (pī′rə tek′niks), 1 the making of fireworks. 2 use of fireworks. 3 display of fireworks. 4 a brilliant or sensational display. *n.*

Pyr rhic victory (pir′ik), victory won at too great cost. [from *Pyrrhus,* who won a battle against the Ro-mans with an enormous loss of life]

Pyr rhus (pir′əs), 318?-272 B.C., a king in Greece from about 300 to 272 B.C. *n.*

Py thag or as (pə thag′ər əs), 582?-500? B.C., Greek philosopher, religious teacher, and mathematician. *n.*

Py thag o re an (pə thag′ə rē′ən), 1 of or having to do with Pythagoras, his teachings, or his followers. 2 a follower of Pythagoras. 1 *adj.,* 2 *n.*

Pyth i as (pith′ē əs), (in Roman legends) a man famous for his devoted friendship with Damon. *n.*

py thon (pī′thon), any of several large snakes of Asia, Africa, and Australia that are related to the boas and kill their prey by squeezing. *n.*

hat, āge, fär; let, ēqual, tėrm;
it, īce; hot, ōpen, ôrder;
oil, out; cup, pùt, rüle; ch, child;
ng, long; sh, she; th, thin;
ŦH, then; zh, measure;

ə represents *a* in about,
e in taken, *i* in pencil,
o in lemon, *u* in circus.

Q q

Q or **q** (kyü), the 17th letter of the alphabet. *Q* is followed by *u* in most English words. *n., pl.* **Q's** or **q's.**

Qa tar (kä′tär), country in E Arabia. *n.*

Q.E.D., which was to be proved. [abbreviation of Latin *quod erat demonstrandum*]

qt., quart. *pl.* **qt.** or **qts.**

quack[1] (kwak), 1 the sound a duck makes. 2 make such a sound. 1 *n.,* 2 *v.* [probably imitation of the sound]

quack[2] (kwak), 1 a dishonest person who pretends to be a doctor. 2 an ignorant pretender to knowledge or skill of any sort. 3 used by quacks: *quack medicine.* 4 not genuine: *a quack doctor.* 1,2 *n.,* 3,4 *adj.* [short for *quacksalver* hawker of salves, from Dutch]

quack er y (kwak′ər ē), practices or methods of a quack. *n., pl.* **quack er ies.**

quad ran gle (kwod′rang′gəl), 1 a four-sided space or court wholly or nearly surrounded by buildings: *the quadrangle of a palace, a college quadrangle.* 2 buildings around a quadrangle. 3 a plane figure with four angles and four sides; quadrilateral. *n.*

qua dran gu lar (kwo drang′gyə lər), like a quadrangle; having four corners or angles: *a spacious, quadrangular house. adj.*

quad rant (kwod′rənt), 1 quarter of the circumference of a circle; arc of 90 degrees. 2 the area contained by such an arc and two radii drawn perpendicular to each other. 3 instrument with a scale of 90 degrees, used in astronomy, navigation, and surveying for measuring altitudes. *n.*

quadrant (def. 1)
left, quadrant of a circle
right, quadrant of a circumference

qua drat ic (kwo drat′ik), 1 of or like a square. 2 of or having to do with an equation in which one or more of the terms is squared. $x^2 + 3x + 2 = 12$ is a quadratic equation. *adj.*

qua dren ni al (kwo dren′ē əl), 1 occurring every four years: *The United States has a quadrennial presidential election.* 2 of or for four years. *adj.* —**qua dren′ni al ly,** *adv.*

quad ri lat er al (kwod′rə lat′ər əl), 1 having four sides and four angles. 2 a plane figure having four sides and four angles. 1 *adj.,* 2 *n.*

qua drille (kwo dril′), 1 a square dance for four couples that usually has five parts or movements. 2 music for such a dance. *n.*

quad ru ped (kwod′rə ped), 1 animal that has four feet. 2 having four feet. 1 *n.,* 2 *adj.*

qua dru ple (kwo drü′pəl), 1 consisting of four parts; including four parts or parties; fourfold: *a quadruple agreement.* 2 four times; four times as great. 3 number, amount, etc., four times as great as another: *80 is the quadruple of 20.* 4 make or become four times as great. 1,2 *adj.,* 2 *adv.,* 3 *n.,* 4 *v.,* **qua dru pled, qua dru pling.**

qua dru plet (kwo drü′plit), 1 one of four children born at the same time from the same mother. 2 any group or combination of four. *n.*

quaff (kwäf *or* kwaf), drink in large swallows; drink freely. *v.*

quag mire (kwag′mīr′), 1 soft, muddy ground; boggy or miry place. 2 a difficult situation. *n.*

quail[1] or bobwhite
about 10 in. long

quail[1] (kwāl), any of various plump game birds belonging to the same family as the pheasant, especially the bobwhite. *n., pl.* **quails** or **quail.** [from French of the 1300's *quaille*]

quail[2] (kwāl), be afraid; lose courage; shrink back in fear: *quail at the sight of a rattlesnake. v.* [apparently from French of the 1400's *coaillier* coagulate, from Latin *coagulare*]

quaint (kwānt), strange or odd in an interesting, pleasing, or amusing way: *Old photographs seem quaint to us today. adj.* —**quaint′ly,** *adv.* —**quaint′ness,** *n.*

quake (kwāk), 1 shake; tremble: *I quaked with fear.* 2 a shaking; trembling. 3 earthquake. 1 *v.,* **quaked, quak ing;** 2,3 *n.*

Quak er (kwā′kər), member of a Christian group called the Society of Friends. Quakers favor simple religious services and are opposed to war and to taking oaths. *n.*

qual i fi ca tion (kwol′ə fə kā′shən), 1 that which makes a person fit for a job, task, office, etc.: *A knowledge of trails is one qualification for a guide.*

quadrilateral (def. 2)
several kinds of quadrilaterals

2 that which limits, changes, or makes less free and full: *His enjoyment of the trip had one qualification; his friends could not enjoy it, too.* 3 modification; limitation; restriction: *The statement was made without any qualification. n.*

qual i fied (kwol′ə fīd), 1 having the desirable or required qualifications; fitted; competent: *A qualified airplane pilot must have good eyesight and hold a license to fly.* 2 modified; limited: *His qualified answer was, "I will go, but only if you will come with me." adj.*

qual i fi er (kwol′ə fī′ər), 1 person or thing that qualifies. 2 word that limits or modifies the meaning of another word. Adjectives and adverbs are qualifiers. *n.*

qual i fy (kwol′ə fī), 1 make fit or competent: *qualify oneself for a job.* 2 become fit; show oneself fit: *qualify for a driver's license.* 3 make less strong; change somewhat; limit; modify: *Qualify your statement that dogs are loyal by adding "usually."* 4 limit or modify the meaning of: *Adverbs qualify verbs. v.,* **qual i fied, qual i fy ing.**

qual i ta tive (kwol′ə tā′tiv), concerned with quality or qualities: *The qualitative facts about food have to do with its vitamin content and its nutritional value. adj.* —**qual′i ta′tive ly,** *adv.*

qualitative analysis, a testing of a substance or mixture to find out what its chemical constituents are.

qual i ty (kwol′ə tē), 1 something special about a person or object that makes it what it is; characteristic; attribute: *One quality of iron is hardness; one quality of sugar is sweetness. She has many fine qualities.* 2 nature, kind, or character of something: *the quality of a sound, the refreshing quality of a drink.* 3 grade of excellence; degree of worth: *food of poor quality. That is the finest quality of cloth.* 4 fineness; merit; excellence: *Look for quality rather than quantity.* 5 high rank; good or high social position: *people of quality. n., pl.* **qual i ties.**

qualm (kwäm *or* kwälm), 1 a sudden disturbing feeling in the mind; uneasiness; misgiving; doubt: *I tried the test with some qualms.* 2 disturbance or scruple of conscience: *I had no qualms about neglecting my work on such a sunny day.* 3 a feeling of faintness or sickness, especially of nausea, that lasts for just a moment. *n.*

qualm ish (kwä′mish *or* kwäl′mish),

1 inclined to have qualms. 2 having qualms. *adj.*

quan dar y (kwon′dər ē), state of perplexity or uncertainty; dilemma. *n., pl.* **quan dar ies.**

quan ti ta tive (kwon′tə tā′tiv), 1 concerned with quantity or quantities. 2 that can be measured. *adj.* —**quan′ti ta′tive ly,** *adv.*

quantitative analysis, a testing of a substance or mixture to find out the amounts and proportions of its chemical constituents.

quan ti ty (kwon′tə tē), 1 number; amount: *Use equal quantities of nuts and raisins in the cake.* 2 a large amount; large number: *The baker buys flour in quantity. She owns quantities of books.* 3 length of a note in music. 4 length of a sound or syllable in speech or poetry. *n., pl.* **quan ti ties.**

quarter (def. 1)
One quarter of this circle is shaded.

quan tum (kwon′təm), (in physics) the basic unit of radiant energy; the smallest amount of energy capable of existing independently. Light and heat are given off and absorbed in quanta. *n., pl.* **quan ta** (kwon′tə).

quantum theory, theory that whenever radiant energy is transferred, the transfer occurs in pulsations rather than continuously, and that the amount transferred during each pulsation is a definite amount or quantum.

quar an tine (kwôr′ən tēn′), 1 keep (a person, animal, plant, ship, etc.) away from others for a time to prevent the spread of an infectious disease: *People with smallpox are quarantined.* 2 condition of being quarantined: *The house was in quarantine for three weeks when the child had scarlet fever.* 3 detention, isolation, and other measures taken to prevent the spread of an infectious disease. 4 place or time in which people, animals, plants, ships, etc., are held until it is sure that they have no infectious diseases, insect pests, etc. 1 *v.,* **quar an tined, quar an tin ing;** 2-4 *n.*

quar rel (kwôr′əl), 1 an angry dispute; a fight with words: *The children had a quarrel over the division of the candy.* 2 fight with words; dispute or disagree angrily: *The two friends quarreled and now they don't speak to each other.* 3 cause for a dispute or disagreement; reason for breaking off friendly relations: *I have no quarrel with your plan; I think it is a good one. That bully likes to pick quarrels.* 4 find fault: *It is useless to quarrel with fate,*

because one does not have control over it. 1,3 *n.,* 2,4 *v.*

quar rel some (kwôr′əl səm), too ready to quarrel; fond of fighting and disputing: *A quarrelsome child has few friends. adj.* —**quar′rel some ness,** *n.*

quar ri er (kwôr′ē ər), worker who quarries stone, slate, etc. *n.*

quar ry[1] (kwôr′ē), 1 place where stone is dug, cut, or blasted out for use in building. 2 obtain from a quarry: *We watched the workmen quarry out a huge block of stone.* 1 *n., pl.* **quar ries;** 2 *v.,* **quar ried, quar ry ing.** [from Latin *quadraria,* from *quadrus* a square]

quar ry[2] (kwôr′ē), animal chased in a hunt; game; prey. *n., pl.* **quar ries.** [from French of the 1400's *cuiree,* from *cuir* skin, from Latin *corium*]

quart (kwôrt), 1 measure of capacity for liquids, equal to one fourth of a gallon: *a quart of milk.* 2 measure of capacity for dry things, equal to one eighth of a peck: *a quart of berries. n.*

quar ter (kwôr′tər), 1 one fourth; half of a half; one of four equal or corresponding parts: *a quarter of an apple, a quarter of lamb. A quarter of an hour is 15 minutes.* 2 divide into fourths: *She quartered the apple.* 3 one fourth of a dollar; 25 cents: *These peaches are one pound for a quarter.* 4 a copper and nickel coin of the United States, worth 25 cents: *Do you have change for a quarter?* 5 a similar coin of Canada, worth 25 cents. 6 one of four equal periods of play in football, basketball, soccer, etc. 7 one fourth of a year; 3 months: *Many savings banks pay interest every quarter.* 8 one of the four periods of the moon, lasting about 7 days each. 9 being one of four equal parts; being equal to only about one fourth of full measure. 10 point of the compass; direction: *From what quarter did the wind blow?* 11 region; place; section: *the French quarter, visit a distant quarter of the globe.* 12 **quarters,** *pl.* place to live or stay: *The circus has its winter quarters in the South. The servants have quarters in a cottage.* 13 give a place to live in: *Soldiers were quartered in all the houses of the town.* 14 mercy shown a defeated enemy in sparing his life: *The pirates gave no quarter to their victims.* 15 one of the four legs of an animal, with its adjoining parts. 1,3-8,10-12,14,15 *n.,* 2,13 *v.,* 9 *adj.*

at close quarters, very close together; almost touching: *The cars had to pass at close quarters on the narrow mountain road.*

quar ter back (kwôr′tər bak′), an offensive back who stands directly behind the center in football. He calls the plays, and usually hands the ball off to a

hat, āge, fär; let, ēqual, tèrm;
it, īce; hot, ōpen, ôrder;
oil, out; cup, pùt, rüle; ch, child;
ng, long; sh, she; th, thin;
ŦH, then; zh, measure;

ə represents *a* in about,
e in taken, *i* in pencil,
o in lemon, *u* in circus.

running back, or passes it to one of his receivers. *n.*

quar ter deck (kwôr′tər dek′), part of the upper deck between the mainmast and the stern, used especially by the officers of a ship. *n.*

quar tered (kwôr′tərd), 1 divided into quarters. 2 furnished with rooms or lodging. *adj.*

quartered (def. 1)
quartered arms

quarter horse, a strong horse originally bred for racing on quarter-mile tracks, now used by cowboys for sorting out cattle, in playing polo, and for riding.

quar ter ly (kwôr′tər lē), 1 happening, done, etc., four times a year: *to make quarterly payments on one's insurance.* 2 once each quarter of a year: *to pay one's insurance premiums quarterly.* 3 magazine published every three months. 1 *adj.,* 2 *adv.,* 3 *n., pl.* **quar ter lies.**

quar ter mas ter (kwôr′tər mas′tər), 1 (in the army) an officer who has charge of providing quarters, clothing, fuel, transportation, etc., for troops. 2 (in the navy) a petty officer who has charge of the steering, the compasses, signals, etc., on a ship. *n.*

quarter note, (in music) a note played for one fourth as long a time as a whole note. See **note** for diagram.

quar ter staff (kwôr′tər staf′), an old English weapon consisting of a stout pole 6 to 8 feet long, tipped with iron. *n., pl.* **quar ter staves** (kwôr′tər stāvz′).

quar tet or **quar tette** (kwôr tet′), 1 group of four singers or players performing together. 2 piece of music for four voices or instruments. 3 any group of four. *n.*

quar to (kwôr′tō), 1 the page size (usually about 9 by 12 inches) of a book in which each leaf is one fourth of a whole sheet of paper. 2 having this size.

adj.	adjective	*n.*	noun
adv.	adverb	*prep.*	preposition
conj.	conjunction	*pron.*	pronoun
interj.	interjection	*v.*	verb
sing.	singular	*pl.*	plural

3 book having this size. 1,3 *n., pl.* **quar tos;** 2 *adj.*

quartz (kwôrts), a very hard mineral composed of silica and found in many different types of rocks, such as sandstone and granite. Crystals of pure quartz are colorless and transparent. Colored varieties of quartz include flint, agate, and amethyst. *n.*

quartz ite (kwôrt′sīt), a granular rock consisting of compressed sandstone. *n.*

qua sar (kwā′sär), a heavenly object which emits powerful light and radio waves. It is larger than a star and smaller than a galaxy. *n.* [from *quas(i) (stell)ar*]

quash[1] (kwosh), put down completely; crush: *quash a revolt.* *v.* [from French of the 1300's *quasser,* from Latin *quassare* shatter, from *quatere* shake]

quash[2] (kwosh), make void; annul: *The judge quashed the charges against the defendant.* *v.* [from French of the 1300's *quasser,* from Latin *cassare,* from *cassus* null]

qua si (kwā′zī, kwā′sī, *or* kwä′sē), 1 seeming; not real; halfway: *quasi humor.* 2 seemingly; not really; partly; almost: *a quasi-humorous remark, a quasi-official statement.* 1 *adj.,* 2 *adv.*

quat rain (kwot′rān), stanza or poem of four lines. *n.*

qua ver (kwā′vər), 1 shake tremulously; tremble: *The old man's voice quavered.* 2 sing or say in trembling tones. 3 a shaking or trembling, especially of the voice. 4 trill in singing or in playing on a musical instrument. 1,2,4 *v.,* 3 *n.*

quay (kē), a solid landing place for ships, often built of stone. *n.*

quay

Que., Quebec.

quea si ly (kwē′zə lē), in a queasy manner. *adv.*

quea si ness (kwē′zē nis), 1 nausea. 2 uneasiness. 3 squeamishness. *n.*

quea sy (kwē′zē), 1 inclined to nausea; easily upset: *a queasy stomach.*

2 tending to unsettle the stomach. 3 uneasy; uncomfortable. 4 squeamish. *adj.,* **quea si er, quea si est.**

Que bec (kwi bek′), 1 province in E Canada. 2 its capital, on the St. Lawrence River. *n.*

que bra cho (kā brä′chō), any of several South American trees with very hard wood. The wood and sometimes the bark are used in tanning and dyeing. The bark of some kinds is used in medicine. *n., pl.* **que bra chos.**

queen (kwēn), 1 wife of a king. 2 the female ruler of a nation. 3 woman who is very important, stately, or beautiful: *the queen of society.* 4 a fully developed female in a colony of bees, ants, etc., that lays eggs. There is usually only one queen in a hive of bees. 5 a playing card bearing a picture of a queen. 6 the most valuable piece in chess. It can move in any straight or diagonal row. *n.* —**queen′like′,** *adj.*

queen it, act like a queen: *She queens it over everyone.*

Queen Anne's lace, a wild variety of the carrot, having lacy clusters of small, white flowers. [from *Queen Anne,* 1665-1714, queen of Great Britain and Ireland]

queen ly (kwēn′lē), 1 of a queen; fit for a queen: *queenly rank or majesty.* 2 like a queen; like a queen's: *queenly dignity.* 3 in a queenly manner; as a queen does. 1,2 *adj.,* **queen li er, queen li est;** 3 *adv.*

queen mother, widow of a former king and mother of a reigning king or queen.

Queens (kwēnz), borough of New York City, on Long Island, east of Brooklyn. *n.*

Queens land (kwēnz′lənd), state in E Australia. *n.*

queer (kwir), 1 not usual or normal; strange; odd; peculiar: *That was a queer remark for her to make.* 2 not well; faint; giddy: *The motion of the ship made him feel queer.* 3 SLANG. spoil; ruin. 1,2 *adj.,* 3 *v.* —**queer′ly,** *adv.*

quell (kwel), put down; overcome; subdue: *quell a riot, quell one's fears.* *v.*

quench (kwench), 1 put an end to; stop: *quench one's thirst.* 2 drown out; put out: *Water quenched the fire.* *v.*

quer u lous (kwer′ə ləs), complaining; fretful; peevish: *He is very querulous when he is sick.* *adj.* —**quer′u lous ly,** *adv.*

quer y (kwir′ē), 1 a question; inquiry. 2 ask; ask about; inquire into. 3 express doubt about. 4 the sign (?) put after a question or used to express doubt about something written or printed. 1,4 *n., pl.* **quer ies;** 2,3 *v.,* **quer ied, quer y ing.**

quest (kwest), 1 a search or hunt: *She*

went to the library in quest of something to read. 2 search or seek for; hunt. 3 expedition of knights: *There are many stories about the quests of King Arthur's knights.* 1,3 *n.,* 2 *v.*

ques tion (kwes′chən), 1 thing asked; sentence in interrogative form, addressed to someone to get information; inquiry: *The teacher answered the children's questions about the story he had been reading to them.* 2 ask in order to find out; seek information from: *Then the teacher questioned the children about what happened in the story.* 3 matter of doubt or dispute; controversy: *A question arose about the ownership of the property.* 4 to doubt; dispute: *question the truth of a story.* 5 matter to be talked over, investigated, considered, etc.; problem: *What is the question you have raised?* 6 proposal to be voted on: *The president asked if the club members were ready for the question.* 7 an asking: *to examine by question and answer.* 1,3,5-7 *n.,* 2,4 *v.* —**ques′tion er,** *n.*

beg the question, take for granted the very thing being argued about.

beside the question, off the subject.

beyond question, without a doubt; not to be disputed: *The statements in that book are true beyond question.*

call in question, dispute; challenge: *My honesty was called in question when they suggested I had cheated on the test.*

in question, 1 under consideration or discussion. 2 in dispute.

out of the question, not to be considered; impossible.

without question, without a doubt; not to be disputed: *That is without question the most beautiful sunset I've ever seen.*

ques tion a ble (kwes′chə nə bəl), 1 open to question or dispute; doubtful; uncertain: *a questionable statement.* 2 of doubtful propriety or morality: *questionable behavior.* *adj.*

ques tion a bly (kwes′chə nə blē), in a questionable manner; doubtfully. *adv.*

ques tion ing ly (kwes′chə ning lē), as one who questions; in a questioning manner. *adv.*

question mark, mark (?) put after a question in writing or printing; interrogation mark.

ques tion naire (kwes′chə ner′ *or* kwes′chə nar′), a written or printed list of questions used to gather information, to obtain a sampling of opinion, etc. *n.*

quet zal (ket säl′), a Central American bird having brilliant golden-green and scarlet plumage. The male has long, flowing tail feathers. *n.*

queue (kyü), 1 braid of hair hanging

queue (def. 1)

down from the back of the head. **2** a line of people, automobiles, etc.: *There was a long queue in front of the theater.* **3** form or stand in a long line. 1,2 *n.,* 3 *v.,* **queued, queu ing.** Also, **cue.**

Que zon (kā/sôn), **Manuel Luis,** 1878-1944, Philippine statesman and patriot. *n.*

Quezon City, capital of the Philippines, just northeast of Manila.

quib ble (kwib/əl), **1** an unfair and petty evasion of the point or truth by using words with a double meaning: *a legal quibble.* **2** evade the point or the truth by twisting the meaning of words. 1 *n.,* 2 *v.,* **quib bled, quib bling.**

quib bler (kwib/lər), person who quibbles. *n.*

quick (kwik), **1** fast and sudden; swift: *The cat made a quick jump. Many weeds have a quick growth.* **2** coming soon; prompt: *a quick reply.* **3** not patient; hasty: *a quick temper.* **4** acting quickly; ready; lively: *a quick wit.* **5** understanding or learning fast: *a child who is quick in school.* **6** quickly. **7** tender, sensitive flesh, especially the flesh under a fingernail or toenail: *bite one's nails down to the quick.* **8** the tender, sensitive part of one's feelings: *Their insults cut me to the quick.* **9** living persons: *the quick and the dead.* 1-5 *adj.,* 6 *adv.,* 7-9 *n.* **—quick/ness,** *n.*

quick en (kwik/ən), **1** move more quickly; hasten: *Quicken your pace.* **2** stir up; make alive: *quicken hot ashes into flames. Reading adventure stories quickens my imagination.* **3** become more active or alive: *His pulse quickened.* *v.*

quick-freeze (kwik/frēz/), subject (food) to rapid freezing to prepare it for storing at freezing temperatures. *v.,* **quick-froze** (kwik/frōz/), **quick-fro zen** (kwik/frō/zn), **quick-freez ing.**

quick lime (kwik/līm/), lime[1]. *n.*

quick ly (kwik/lē), rapidly; with haste; very soon. *adv.*

quick sand (kwik/sand/), a very deep, soft, wet sand that will not hold up a person's weight. Quicksand may engulf people and animals. *n.*

quick sil ver (kwik/sil/vər), mercury. *n.*

quick step (kwik/step/), **1** step used in marching in quick time. **2** a lively

dance step. **3** music in a brisk march rhythm. *n.*

quick-tem pered (kwik/tem/pərd), easily angered. *adj.*

quick-wit ted (kwik/wit/id), having a quick mind; mentally alert. *adj.*

quid[1] (kwid), **1** piece to be chewed. **2** bite of chewing tobacco. *n.* [Old English *cwidu* cud]

quid[2] (kwid), one pound, or 20 shillings (a slang term used in Great Britain). *n., pl.* **quid.** [origin uncertain]

qui es cence (kwī es/ns), absence of activity; quietness; stillness; motionlessness. *n.*

qui es cent (kwī es/nt), inactive; quiet; still; motionless. *adj.* **—qui es/cent ly,** *adv.*

qui et (kwī/ət), **1** making no sound; with little or no noise: *quiet footsteps, a quiet room.* **2** moving very little; still: *a quiet river.* **3** at rest; not busy: *a quiet evening at home.* **4** peaceful; gentle: *quiet manners, a quiet person.* **5** state of rest; stillness; absence of motion or noise. **6** freedom from disturbance; peace: *to read in quiet.* **7** make quiet: *Soft words quieted the frightened child.* **8** become quiet: *The wind quieted down.* **9** not showy or bright: *Gray is a quiet color.* 1-4,9 *adj.,* 5,6 *n.,* 7,8 *v.* **—qui/et ly,** *adv.* **—qui/et ness,** *n.*

qui e tude (kwī/ə tüd *or* kwī/ə tyüd), quietness; stillness; calmness. *n.*

qui e tus (kwī ē/təs), a final getting rid of anything; finishing stroke; anything that ends or settles: *The arrival of the militia gave the riot its quietus.* *n.*

quill (kwil), **1** a large, stiff feather. **2** the hollow stem of a feather. **3** anything made from the hollow stem of a feather, such as a pen, a toothpick, or an instrument for plucking the strings of a musical instrument. **4** a stiff, sharp hair or spine like the end of a feather. A porcupine has quills on its back. *n.*

quill (def. 3)

quilt (kwilt), **1** a bed cover made of two pieces of cloth with a soft pad between, held in place by lines of stitching. **2** make quilts. **3** stitch together with a soft lining: *quilt a bathrobe.* 1 *n.,* 2, 3 *v.*

quilt ing (kwil/ting), **1** quilted work. **2** material for making quilts; a stout fabric so woven as to appear quilted. *n.*

quince (kwins), **1** a hard, yellowish, acid, pear-shaped fruit, used for preserves and jelly. **2** tree it grows on. *n.*

hat, āge, fär; let, ēqual, tėrm;
it, īce; hot, ōpen, ôrder;
oil, out; cup, pút, rüle; ch, child;
ng, long; sh, she; th, thin;
ŦH, then; zh, measure;

ə represents *a* in about,
e in taken, *i* in pencil,
o in lemon, *u* in circus.

qui nine (kwī/nīn), a bitter drug made from the bark of a cinchona tree, used in treating malaria and fevers. *n.*

quin sy (kwin/zē), tonsillitis with pus; a very sore throat with an abscess in the tonsils. *n.*

quint (kwint), INFORMAL. quintuplet. *n.*

quin tes sence (kwin tes/ns), **1** the purest form of some quality; pure essence. **2** the most perfect example of something: *The ballerina's dancing was the quintessence of grace and agility. n.*

quin tet or **quin tette** (kwin tet/), **1** group of five singers or players performing together. **2** piece of music for five voices or instruments. **3** any group of five. *n.*

quin tu plet (kwin tü/plit, kwin tyü/plit, *or* kwin/tə plit), **1** one of five children born at the same time from the same mother: *The birth of quintuplets is so rare that it is reported on television and in the newspapers.* **2** any group or combination of five. *n.*

quip (kwip), **1** a clever or witty saying. **2** make quips. 1 *n.,* 2 *v.,* **quipped, quip ping.**

qui pu (kē/pü *or* kwip/ü), cord with knotted strings or threads of various colors, used by the ancient Peruvians to record events, keep accounts, and send messages. *n.*

quire (kwīr), 24 or 25 sheets of paper of the same sort and size. *n.*

quirk (kwėrk), **1** a peculiar way of acting: *Each person has his own quirks.* **2** a clever or witty saying. **3** a quibble. **4** a sudden twist or turn: *a quirk of fate, a mental quirk.* **5** a flourish in writing. *n.*

quirt (kwėrt), a riding whip with a short, stout handle and a lash of braided leather. *n.*

quis ling (kwiz/ling), person who treacherously helps to prepare the way for enemy occupation of his own country. *n.* [from Vidkun *Quisling,* 1887-1945, a Norwegian who became a traitor by helping the Nazis occupy Norway in World War II]

quit (kwit), **1** stop: *They quit work at five.* **2** leave: *quit one's job. He quit his*

quitclaim

room in anger. *If they don't pay their rent, they will receive notice to quit.* 3 pay back; pay off (a debt). 4 free; clear; rid: *I gave them money to be quit of them.* 5 OLD USE. behave or conduct (oneself). 1-3,5 *v.,* **quit** or **quit ted, quit ting;** 4 *adj.*

quit claim (kwit′klām′), 1 the giving up of a claim. 2 document stating that somebody gives up a claim. 3 give up claim to (a possession, etc.). 1,2 *n.,* 3 *v.*

quite (kwīt), 1 completely; entirely: *a hat quite out of fashion. I am quite alone.* 2 actually; really; positively: *quite the thing.* 3 INFORMAL. to a considerable extent or degree: *quite pretty. It is quite hot. adv.*

Qui to (kē′tō), capital of Ecuador, in the N part. *n.*

quit rent (kwit′rent′), rent paid in money, instead of services rendered under a feudal system. *n.*

quits (kwits), even or on equal terms by having given or paid back something: *We each won a game, so we are quits. After the argument I gave back the gift, and we were quits. adj.*

call it quits, abandon an attempt to do something: *Since we could not manage to set up camp in the rain, we finally called it quits and hiked home.*

quit tance (kwit′ns), 1 a release from debt or obligation. 2 the paper certifying this; a receipt. 3 a getting back at somebody. *n.*

quit ter (kwit′ər), INFORMAL. one who shirks or gives up easily. *n.*

quiv er[1] (kwiv′ər), 1 to shake; shiver; tremble: *The dog quivered with excitement.* 2 a quivering; shaking or trembling: *A quiver of his mouth showed that he was about to cry.* 1 *v.,* 2 *n.* [Old English *cwifer* nimble]

quiv er[2] (kwiv′ər), case to hold ar-

rows. *n.* [from French of the 1200's *quivre*]

Qui xo te (kē hō′tē *or* kwik′sət), **Don.** See **Don Quixote.** *n.*

quix ot ic (kwik sot′ik), 1 resembling Don Quixote; extravagantly chivalrous or romantic. 2 visionary; not practical. *adj.* —**quix ot′i cal ly,** *adv.*

quiz (kwiz), 1 a short or informal test: *Each week the teacher gives us a quiz in geography.* 2 give such a test to: *quiz a class in history.* 3 to question; interrogate: *The lawyer quizzed the witness.* 4 a questioning. 1,4 *n., pl.* **quiz zes;** 2,3 *v.,* **quizzed, quiz zing.**

quiz show, a radio or television program in which contestants are asked questions and win prizes if they answer correctly.

quiz zi cal (kwiz′ə kəl), 1 that suggests making fun of others; teasing: *a quizzical smile.* 2 questioning; baffled: *a quizzical expression on one's face.* 3 odd; queer; comical. *adj.* —**quiz′zi cal ly,** *adv.*

quoin (koin *or* kwoin), 1 an outside angle or corner of a wall or building. 2 a stone forming an outside angle of a wall; cornerstone. *n.*

quoit (def. 1)

quoit (kwoit), 1 a heavy, flattish iron or rope ring thrown to encircle a peg stuck in the ground or to come as close to it as possible. 2 **quoits,** *pl.* game so played. *n.*

quon dam (kwon′dəm), that once was; former: *The quondam servant is now master. adj.*

Quon set hut (kwon′sit), a prefabricated metal building shaped like a half cylinder. [from *Quonset* Point, a naval air station in Rhode Island where the hut was first built in 1941]

Quonset hut

quiver[2]

quo rum (kwôr′əm), number of members of any society or assembly that must be present if the business done is to be legal or binding. *n.*

quo ta (kwō′tə), the share of a total due from or to a particular district, state, person, etc.: *Each member of the club was given his quota of tickets to sell for the party. n., pl.* **quo tas.**

quot a ble (kwō′tə bəl), 1 that can be quoted. 2 suitable for quoting. *adj.*

quo ta tion (kwō tā′shən), 1 somebody's words repeated exactly by another person; passage quoted from a book, speech, etc.: *From what author does this quotation come?* 2 a quoting: *Quotation is a habit of some teachers.* 3 the current price of a stock, commodity, etc.: *today's market quotation on wheat. n.*

quotation mark, one of a pair of marks used to indicate the beginning and end of a quotation. For an ordinary quotation use these marks (" "). For a quotation within another quotation use these (' ').

quote (kwōt), 1 repeat the exact words of; give words or passages from: *Our teacher often quotes Shakespeare.* 2 repeat exactly the words of another or a passage from a book: *The commentator quoted from the senator's speech.* 3 bring forward as an example or authority: *Judges quote various cases in support of their opinions.* 4 give (a price): *quote a price on a house up for sale.* 5 quotation. 6 a quotation mark. 1-4 *v.,* **quot ed, quot ing;** 5,6 *n.*

quoth (kwōth), OLD USE. said. *v.*

quo tient (kwō′shənt), number obtained by dividing one number by another. In $26 \div 2 = 13$, 13 is the quotient. *n.*

q.v., which see. [abbreviation of Latin *quod vide*]

R r

R or **r** (är), the 18th letter of the alphabet. *n., pl.* **R's** or **r's.**

the three R's, reading, writing, and arithmetic.

Ra (rä), the Egyptian sun god and supreme deity, typically represented as a man with the head of a hawk bearing the sun on his head. *n.*

rab bi (rab′ī), teacher of the Jewish law and religion; leader of a Jewish congregation; Jewish clergyman. *n., pl.* **rab bis.**

rab bin i cal (rə bin′ə kəl), of or having to do with rabbis, their learning, teachings, etc. *adj.*

rab bit (rab′it), **1** a small burrowing mammal with soft fur, long ears, long hind legs, and a short, fluffy tail. Rabbits are similar to hares, but smaller. **2** its fur. *n.* —**rab′bit like′,** *adj.*

rab ble (rab′əl), **1** a disorderly crowd; mob. **2 the rabble,** the lower classes: *The nobles scorned the rabble. n.*

Rab e lais (rab′ə lā), **François,** 1495?-1553, French writer of satires. *n.*

rab id (rab′id), **1** unreasonably extreme; fanatical; violent: *The rebels are rabid idealists.* **2** furious; raging: *rabid with anger.* **3** having rabies; mad: *a rabid dog. adj.* —**rab′id ly,** *adv.* —**rab′id ness,** *n.*

ra bies (rā′bēz), a virus disease that attacks the central nervous system of warm-blooded animals, causing mental disturbance, muscular spasms, and paralysis; hydrophobia. The disease is usually transmitted by the bite of a rabid animal, and is fatal unless treated with serum. *n.*

raccoon (def. 1)—32 in. long with tail

rac coon (ra kün′), **1** a small, grayish, flesh-eating mammal with a bushy, ringed tail, that lives mostly in wooded areas near water, and is active at night. **2** its fur. *n.* Also, **racoon.**

race[1] (rās), **1** contest of speed, as in running, driving, riding, sailing, etc.: *a dog race, a car race.* **2** engage in a contest of speed. **3** run or cause to run in a race with: *I'll race you to the corner.* **4** any contest that suggests a race: *a political race.* **5** run, move, or go swiftly. **6** cause to run, move, or go swiftly. **7** cause (a motor, wheel, etc.) to run faster than necessary when load or resistance is lessened, or when the transmission is not engaged. **8** a strong or fast current of water. **9** channel leading water to or from a place where its energy is utilized. 1,4,8,9 *n.,* 2,3,5-7 *v.,* **raced, rac ing.** [Middle English *ras,* from a Scandinavian word of the 1200's, such as Icelandic *rās*]

race[2] (rās), **1** any of the major divisions of mankind, each having certain distinctive physical characteristics and a common ancestry: *the Mongoloid race, the Caucasian race, the Negro race.* **2** group of persons, animals, or plants having similar characteristics or ancestry: *the Nordic race, the canine race, the human race.* **3** group, class, or kind (especially of people): *the brave race of seamen. n.* [from French of the 1500's *rasse,* from Italian *razza*]

race course (rās′kôrs′), racetrack. *n.*

race horse (rās′hôrs′), horse for racing. *n.*

raceme
of
lily of the valley

ra ceme (rā sēm′ *or* rə sēm′), a simple flower cluster having its flowers on nearly equal stalks along a stem, the lower flowers blooming first. The lily of the valley, currant, and chokecherry have racemes. *n.*

rac er (rā′sər), **1** person, animal, boat, automobile, etc., that takes part in races. **2** any of various North American snakes that can move very rapidly. The blacksnake is a racer. *n.*

race track (rās′trak′), ground laid out for racing, usually circular or oval. *n.*

Ra chel (rā′chəl), (in the Bible) the favorite wife of Jacob, and the mother of Joseph and Benjamin. *n.*

Rach ma ni noff (räk mä′ni nôf), **Sergei,** 1873-1943, Russian pianist and composer. *n.*

ra cial (rā′shəl), **1** having to do with a race; characteristic of a race: *racial traits.* **2** of or involving races: *racial discrimination. adj.* —**ra′cial ly,** *adv.*

Ra cine (ra sēn′), **Jean Baptiste,** 1639-1699, French poet and dramatist. *n.*

rac i ness (rā′sē nis), vigor; liveliness. *n.*

rac ism (rā′siz′əm), **1** belief that a particular race, especially one's own, is superior to other races. **2** discrimination or prejudice against a race or races based on this belief. *n.*

rac ist (rā′sist), **1** a person who believes in, supports, or practices racism. **2** of or having to do with racism. 1 *n.,* 2 *adj.*

hat, āge, fär; let, ēqual, tèrm;
it, īce; hot, ōpen, ôrder;
oil, out; cup, pùt, rüle; ch, child;
ng, long; sh, she; th, thin;
₮H, then; zh, measure;

ə represents *a* in about,
e in taken, *i* in pencil,
o in lemon, *u* in circus.

rack[1] (def. 1)—three types of racks

rack[1] (rak), **1** a frame with bars, shelves, or pegs to hold, arrange, or keep things on: *a hat rack, a tool rack, a baggage rack.* **2** framework set on a wagon for carrying hay, straw, etc. **3** instrument once used for torturing people by stretching them. **4** hurt very much: *racked with grief. A toothache racked my jaw.* **5** stretch; strain. **6** bar with pegs or teeth on one edge, into which teeth on the rim of a wheel or pinion can fit. Many kinds of machines use a rack. 1-3,6 *n.,* 4,5 *v.* [Middle English *rakke*]

on the rack, in great pain; suffering very much.

rack up, INFORMAL. accumulate: *rack up three runs in the ninth inning.*

rack[2] (rak). **go to rack and ruin,** wreck; destruction: *Over the years, the vacant house went to rack and ruin. n.* [a different form of *wrack,* from German of the 1300's *wrak* wreck]

rack et[1] (rak′it), **1** loud noise; loud talk; din. **2** INFORMAL. scheme for getting money from people through bribery, threats of violence, and other illegal means. *n.* [probably from earlier British slang term *racket* kind of fraud]

rack et[2] (rak′it), **1** an oval wooden or metal frame strung with netting and having a long handle, used to hit the ball in tennis, squash, badminton, etc. **2** a paddle-shaped wooden implement with a short handle, used to hit the ball in table tennis. *n.* Also, **racquet.** [from French of the 1500's *raquette,* from Arabic *rāha* palm of the hand]

adj.	adjective	*n.*	noun
adv.	adverb	*prep.*	preposition
conj.	conjunction	*pron.*	pronoun
interj.	interjection	*v.*	verb
sing.	singular	*pl.*	plural

rack et eer (rak/ə tir/), INFORMAL. 1 person who gets money from people through bribery, threats of violence, and other illegal means. 2 get money in this way. 1 *n.*, 2 *v.*

ra coon (ra kün/), raccoon. *n.*

rac quet (rak/it), racket². *n.*

rac y (rā/sē), 1 vigorous; lively: *a racy discussion.* 2 having an agreeably peculiar taste or flavor: *a racy food.* 3 suggestive of indecency; somewhat improper: *a racy story. adj.,* **rac i er, rac i est.**

ra dar (rā/där), instrument for determining the distance, direction, speed, etc., of unseen objects by the reflection of radio waves. *n.* [formed from *ra-(dio) d(etecting) a(nd) r(anging)*]

radial (def. 1)
radial pattern

ra di al (rā/dē əl), 1 of or like radii or rays. 2 arranged like or in radii or rays. *adj.* —**ra/di al ly,** *adv.*

ra di ance (rā/dē əns), vivid brightness: *the radiance of the sun, the radiance of a smile. n.*

ra di an cy (rā/dē ən sē), radiance. *n.*

ra di ant (rā/dē ənt), 1 shining; bright; beaming: *a radiant smile.* 2 sending out rays of light or heat: *The sun is a radiant body.* 3 sent off in rays from some source; radiated: *radiant heat. adj.* —**ra/di ant ly,** *adv.*

radiant energy, energy in the form of rays or waves, especially electromagnetic waves. X rays, radio waves, and visible light are forms of radiant energy.

ra di ate (rā/dē āt), 1 give out rays of: *The sun radiates light and heat.* 2 issue in rays: *Heat radiates from those hot steam pipes.* 3 give out; send forth: *Her face radiates joy.* 4 spread out from a center: *Roads radiate from the city in every direction.* 5 having rays: *A daisy is a radiate flower.* 6 radiating from a center. 1-4 *v.,* **ra di at ed, ra di at ing;** 5,6 *adj.*

ra di a tion (rā/dē ā/shən), 1 act or process of giving out light, heat, or other radiant energy. 2 energy radiated: *That radiator does not provide enough radiation for so large a room.* 3 radioactive ray or rays emitted by the atoms and molecules of a radioactive substance as a result of the disintegration of atomic nuclei. Some radiations from nuclei are alpha particles, beta particles, and neutrons. Radiation is harmful to living tissue. *n.*

ra di a tor (rā/dē ā/tər), 1 a heating device consisting of a set of pipes through which steam or hot water circulates. 2 device for cooling water. The radiator of an automobile gives off heat very fast and so cools the water circulating inside it. *n.*

rad i cal (rad/ə kəl), 1 going to the root; fundamental: *To lose weight, I had to make radical changes in my eating habits.* 2 favoring extreme changes or reforms; extreme. 3 person who favors extreme changes or reforms, especially in politics; person with extreme opinions. 4 atom or group of atoms acting as a unit in chemical reactions. A carbonate molecule (CO_3) is a radical in sodium carbonate (Na_2CO_3), becoming part of that compound without undergoing change, as if it were a single element instead of two. 5 having to do with or forming the root of a number or quantity. 6 radical sign. 1,2,5 *adj.,* 3,4,6 *n.* —**rad/i cal ly,** *adv.*

rad i cal ism (rad/ə kə liz/əm), principles or practices of radicals; support or advocacy of extreme changes or reforms, especially in politics. *n.*

radical sign, a mathematical sign ($\sqrt{\ }$) put before a number or expression to show that a root of it is to be found by calculation. $\sqrt{16}$ = the square root of 16 = 4. $\sqrt[3]{27}$ = the cube root of 27 = 3.

ra di i (rā/dē ī), a plural of **radius.** *n.*

ra di o (rā/dē ō), 1 the sending and receiving of sound or television signals by means of electromagnetic waves without the use of connecting wires between sender and receiver. 2 apparatus for sending or receiving and making audible the sound signals sent in this way. 3 of, having to do with, used in, or sent by radio: *a radio set, radio programs.* 4 transmit or send out by radio: *The ship radioed a call for help.* 5 business of broadcasting by radio: *He left acting and got a job in radio.* 1,2,5 *n., pl.* **ra di os** for 2; 3 *adj.,* 4 *v.*

ra di o ac tive (rā/dē ō ak/tiv), of, having, or caused by radioactivity. Radium, uranium, and thorium are radioactive metallic elements. *adj.*

ra di o ac tiv i ty (rā/dē ō ak tiv/ə tē), 1 the property, exhibited by certain elements, of giving off radiant energy in the form of alpha particles, beta particles, or gamma rays as the result of spontaneous disintegration of the nuclei of atoms. 2 the radiation given off. *n.*

radio astronomy, branch of astronomy dealing with the detection of objects in space by means of radio waves that these objects give off. It enables observers to study heavenly bodies beyond the range of ordinary telescopes.

ra di o car bon (rā/dē ō kär/bən), a radioactive isotope of carbon, especially carbon 14. *n.*

radio frequency, any electromagnetic wave frequency suitable for radio broadcasting, usually above 10,000 cycles per second.

ra di o gram (rā/dē ō gram/), 1 message transmitted by radio. 2 radiograph. *n.*

ra di o graph (rā/dē ō graf/), picture produced by X rays or other rays on a photographic plate, commonly called an X-ray picture. *n.*

ra di ol o gist (rā/dē ol/ə jist), an expert in radiology. *n.*

ra di ol o gy (rā/dē ol/ə jē), science dealing with X rays or the rays from radioactive substances, especially for medical diagnosis or treatment. *n.*

ra di o sonde (rā/dē ō sond), instrument carried into the atmosphere by a balloon from which it descends by parachute, automatically reporting data on atmospheric conditions to observers on the ground by means of a small radio transmitter. *n.*

radio telescope, device consisting of a radio receiver and a very large, bowl-shaped antenna for detecting and recording radio waves coming from stars and other objects that are beyond the range of optical telescopes.

radio telescope with 250 ft. wide reflector

radio wave, an electromagnetic wave within the radio frequencies.

rad ish (rad/ish), 1 the small, crisp root of a plant related to the mustard, with a red or white skin, used as a relish and in salads. 2 the plant. *n.*

ra di um (rā/dē əm), a radioactive metallic element found in very small amounts in uranium ores such as pitchblende. Radium is very unstable and gives off alpha particles and gamma rays in breaking down in successive forms into radon, polonium, and, finally, lead. Radium is used in treating cancer and in making luminous paint. *n.*

radius (def. 1)
Each line from C (center) is a radius.

ra di us (rā′dē əs), 1 a line segment going straight from the center to the outside of a circle or a sphere. Any spoke in a wheel is a radius. 2 a circular area measured by the length of its radius: *The explosion could be heard within a radius of ten miles.* 3 that one of the two bones of the forearm which is on the thumb side. *n., pl.* **ra di i** or **ra di us es.**

ra don (rā′don), a heavy, inert, radioactive gas formed by the decay of radium. It is a chemical element. *n.*

raf fi a (raf′ē ə), 1 fiber from the leaf stalks of a kind of palm tree growing on Madagascar, used in making baskets, mats, etc. 2 tree from which this fiber is obtained. *n.*

raf fle (raf′əl), 1 sale in which many people each pay a small sum for a chance to win a prize. 2 sell (an article) by a raffle. 1 *n.,* 2 *v.,* **raf fled, raf fling.**

raft[1] (raft), logs or boards fastened together to make a floating platform: *Having no boat, we had to cross the stream on a raft. n.* [from a Scandinavian word of the 1200's, such as Icelandic *raptr* log]

raft[2] (raft), INFORMAL. a large number; abundance: *a raft of troubles. n.* [a different form of Middle English *raff* heap]

RAFTER   RAFTER

raft er (raf′tər), a slanting beam of a roof. *n.*

rag[1] (rag), 1 a torn or waste piece of cloth: *Use clean rags to rub this mirror bright.* 2 **rags,** *pl.* clothing that is torn and in tatters. 3 a small piece of cloth. 4 made from rags: *a rag doll, a rag rug.* 1-3 *n.,* 4 *adj.* [perhaps from a Scandinavian word of the 1200's, such as Icelandic *rögg* shaggy tuft]

rag[2] (rag), SLANG. 1 scold. 2 tease; play jokes on. *v.,* **ragged, rag ging.** [origin uncertain]

rag a muf fin (rag′ə muf′ən), 1 a ragged, disreputable fellow. 2 a ragged child. *n.*

rage (rāj), 1 violent anger: *a voice quivering with rage.* 2 be furious with anger. 3 violence: *the rage of a savage tiger.* 4 talk or act violently; move, proceed, or continue with great violence: *A storm is raging. Keep your temper; don't rage.* 5 what everybody wants for a short time; the fashion: *Red*

ties were all the rage last season. 1,3,5 *n.,* 2,4 *v.,* **raged, rag ing.**

rag ged (rag′id), 1 worn or torn into rags. 2 wearing torn or badly worn-out clothing: *a ragged beggar.* 3 not straight and tidy; rough: *an Airedale's ragged coat, a ragged garden.* 4 having loose shreds or bits: *a ragged wound.* 5 having rough or sharp points; uneven; jagged: *ragged rocks. adj.* —**rag′ged ly,** *adv.* —**rag′ged ness,** *n.*

rag lan (rag′lən), having sleeves cut so as to continue up to the collar: *a raglan topcoat. adj.* [from Baron *Raglan,* 1788-1855, a British field marshal]

raglan sleeve

rag man (rag′man′), man who gathers, buys, or sells rags, old newspapers, etc. *n., pl.* **rag men.**

ra gout (ra gü′), a highly seasoned stew of meat and vegetables. *n.*

rag time (rag′tīm′), 1 musical rhythm with accents falling at unusual places. 2 form of jazz using this rhythm. *n.*

rag weed (rag′wēd′), any of several coarse weeds of the same family as the aster, whose pollen is one of the most common causes of hay fever. *n.*

raid (rād), 1 a sudden attack: *The pirates planned a raid on the harbor.* 2 attack suddenly: *The enemy raided our camp.* 3 an entering and seizing what is inside: *The hungry girls made a raid on the pantry.* 4 force a way into; enter and seize what is in: *The police raided the gambling house.* 1,3 *n.,* 2,4 *v.* —**raid′er,** *n.*

rail[1] (rāl), 1 bar of wood or of metal. There are stair rails, fence rails, rails protecting monuments, etc. Bars laid along the ground for a railroad track are called rails. 2 railroad: *ship by rail.* 3 enclose with bars: *They railed off a space for the horses.* 1,2 *n.,* 3 *v.* [from French of the 1200's *reille,* from Latin *regula* straight rod]

rail[2] (rāl), complain bitterly; use violent and reproachful language: *rail at one's hard luck. v.* [from French of the 1400's *railler,* from Latin *ragere* to bray, brawl]

rail[3] (rāl), a small bird with short wings and tail, narrow body, long toes, and a harsh cry. It lives in marshes and swamps. *n., pl.* **rails** or **rail.** [from French of the 1400's *raale*]

rail ing (rā′ling), 1 fence made of rails.

2 material for rails. 3 rails collectively. *n.*

rail ler y (rā′lər ē), good-humored ridicule; joking; teasing. *n., pl.* **rail ler ies.**

rail road (rāl′rōd′), 1 road or track with parallel steel rails on which the wheels of the cars go. Engines pull trains on railroads. 2 tracks, stations, trains, and other property of a system of transportation that uses rails, together with the people who manage them. 3 to work on a railroad. 4 INFORMAL. send along quickly or too quickly to be fair: *His enemies tried to railroad him to prison without a fair trial.* 1,2 *n.,* 3,4 *v.*

rail way (rāl′wā′), 1 railroad. 2 track made of rails. *n.*

rai ment (rā′mənt), clothing; garments. *n.*

rain (rān), 1 water falling in drops from the clouds. Rain is formed from moisture condensed from water vapor in the atmosphere. *The rain spattered the windows.* 2 the fall of such drops: *a hard rain.* 3 to fall in drops of water: *It rained all day.* 4 a thick, fast fall of anything: *a rain of bullets.* 5 fall like rain: *Sparks rained down from the burning roof.* 6 send like rain: *The crowd rained confetti on the parade.* 1,2,4 *n.,* 3,5,6 *v.*

rain bow (rān′bō′), 1 bow or arch of colored light seen sometimes in the sky, or in mist or spray, when the sun shines on it from behind the observer. A rainbow shows all the colors of the spectrum: red, orange, yellow, green, blue, indigo, and violet. 2 having many colors like a rainbow. 1 *n.,* 2 *adj.*

rain coat (rān′kōt′), a waterproof coat worn for protection from rain. *n.*

rain drop (rān′drop′), drop of rain. *n.*

rain fall (rān′fôl′), 1 shower of rain. 2 amount of water in the form of rain, snow, etc., falling within a given time and area: *The yearly rainfall in New York is much greater than that in Arizona. n.*

rain forest, a very dense forest in a region where rain is very heavy throughout the year. Rain forests are usually in tropical areas.

Rainier

Rai ni er (rə nir′), **Mount,** mountain in W Washington. *n.*

rain i ness (rā′nē nis), a rainy condition. *n.*

rain proof (rān′prüf′), that will not let rain through; waterproof. *adj.*

rain storm (rān′stôrm′), storm with much rain. *n.*

rain y (rā′nē), 1 having rain; having much rain: *The weather was gloomy, dark, and rainy.* 2 bringing rain: *The sky is filled with dark, rainy clouds.* 3 wet with rain: *rainy streets. adj.,* **rain i er, rain i est.**

rainy day, a possible time of greater need in the future: *to save money for a rainy day.*

raise (rāz), 1 lift up; put up: *Each morning we raise the flag. Children in school raise their hands to answer a question.* 2 cause to rise: *The automobile raised a cloud of dust. Dough for bread is raised by yeast.* 3 put or take into a higher position; make higher or nobler: *raise a salesman to manager.* 4 increase in degree, amount, price, pay, etc.: *raise the rent, raise one's courage.* 5 an increase in amount, price, pay, etc.: *a raise in pay.* 6 gather together; collect; manage to get: *raise funds for a hospital.* 7 breed; grow: *The farmer raises crops and cattle.* 8 bring about; cause: *A funny remark raises a laugh.* 9 build; create; produce; start; set up: *raise a monument to a famous person, raise a skyscraper.* 10 rouse; stir up: *The dog raised a rabbit from the underbrush.* 11 bring up; rear: *Parents raise their children.* 12 bring back to life: *raise the dead.* 13 put an end to: *Our soldiers raised the siege of the fort by driving away the enemy.* 1-4,6-13 *v.,* **raised, rais ing;** 5 *n.*

rais er (rā′zər), person who grows or raises things: *a cattle raiser. n.*

rai sin (rā′zn), a sweet, dried grape. *n.*

ra ja (rä′jə), rajah. *n., pl.* **ra jas.**

ra jah (rä′jə), ruler or chief in India, Java, Borneo, etc. *n.*

rake[1] (rāk), 1 a long-handled tool having a bar at one end with teeth in it. A rake is used for smoothing the soil or gathering together loose leaves, hay, straw, etc. 2 move with a rake: *Rake the leaves off the grass.* 3 make clear,

clean, smooth, etc., with a rake, or as if with a rake: *Rake the yard.* 4 search carefully: *I raked the want ads, hoping to find a bicycle for sale.* 5 fire guns along the length of (a ship, line of soldiers, etc.). 1 *n.,* 2-5 *v.,* **raked, rak ing.** [Old English *raca*]

rake[2] (rāk), person who shamelessly indulges in vice; immoral or dissolute person. *n.* [shortened from *rakehell,* perhaps from *rake*[1] and *hell*]

rak ish (rā′kish), 1 smart; jaunty; dashing: *a hat set at a rakish angle.* 2 suggesting dash and speed: *They own a rakish boat.* 3 like a rake; immoral; dissolute. *adj.* —**rak′ish ly,** *adv.*

Ra leigh (rô′lē), 1 Sir **Walter,** 1552?-1618, English soldier, explorer, statesman, and author. 2 capital of North Carolina, in the central part. *n.*

RAMP

ral ly[1] (ral′ē), 1 bring together, especially to get in order again: *The commander was able to rally the fleeing troops.* 2 come or bring together in a body for a common purpose or action: *The people rallied to rebuild the dike before the river flooded their homes.* 3 come to help a person, party, or cause: *He rallied to the side of his injured friend.* 4 recover health and strength: *The sick man may rally now.* 5 a rallying; recovery. 6 a mass meeting or assembly for a common purpose or action: *a political rally.* 1-4 *v.,* **ral lied, ral ly ing;** 5,6 *n., pl.* **ral lies.** [from French of the 1500's *rallier,* from *re-* again + *allier* to ally]

ral ly[2] (ral′ē), make fun of good-naturedly; tease: *We rallied our professor on his forgetfulness. v.,* **ral lied, ral ly ing.** [from French *railler* rail[2]]

ram (ram), 1 a male sheep. 2 butt against; strike head on; strike violently: *One ship rammed the other ship.* 3 push hard; drive down or in by heavy blows. 4 machine or part of a machine that strikes heavy blows. The ram on a pile driver is the weight that drives the piles into the ground. 5 battering ram. 1,4,5 *n.,* 2,3 *v.,* **rammed, ram ming.**

ram ble (ram′bəl), 1 wander about: *We rambled here and there through the woods.* 2 a walk for pleasure, not to go to any special place. 3 talk or write about first one thing and then another with no useful connections. 4 spread irregularly in various directions: *Vines rambled over the wall.* 1,3,4 *v.,* **rambled, ram bling;** 2 *n.*

ram bler (ram′blər), 1 person or thing that rambles. 2 any of various climbing roses having clusters of small red, yellow, or white flowers. *n.*

ram bling (ram′bling), 1 that rambles; wandering about. 2 going from one thing to another with no useful connections: *a rambling speech.* 3 extending irregularly in various directions; not planned in an orderly way: *a rambling old farmhouse. adj.*

ram bunc tious (ram bungk′shəs), INFORMAL. 1 wild and uncontrollable; unruly. 2 noisy and violent; boisterous. *adj.* —**ram bunc′tious ly,** *adv.* —**ram bunc′tious ness,** *n.*

Ram e ses (ram′ə sēz), Ramses. *n.*

ram i fi ca tion (ram′ə fə kā′shən), 1 a dividing or spreading out into branches or parts. 2 manner or result of branching; branch; part; subdivision. *n.*

ram i fy (ram′ə fī), divide or spread out into branches or parts resembling branches. *v.,* **ram i fied, ram i fy ing.**

ramp (ramp), a sloping way connecting two different levels of a building, road, etc.; slope. *n.*

ram page (ram′pāj *for 1;* ram pāj′ *for 2*), 1 fit of rushing wildly about; spell of violent behavior; wild outbreak: *The mad elephant went on a rampage and killed its keeper.* 2 rush wildly about; behave violently; rage. 1 *n.,* 2 *v.,* **rampaged, ram pag ing.**

ram pant (ram′pənt), 1 growing without any check: *The vines ran rampant over the fence.* 2 passing beyond restraint or usual limits; unchecked: *Looting was rampant during the riot.* 3 angry; excited; violent. 4 (in heraldry) standing up on the hind legs. *adj.* —**ram′pant ly,** *adv.*

rampant (def. 4)
lion rampant

ram part (ram′pärt), 1 a wide bank of earth, often with a wall on top, built around a fort to help defend it. 2 anything that defends; defense; protection. *n.*

PARAPET
RAMPART
PARADE GROUND INSIDE FORT
DITCH

rampart (def. 1)

ram rod (ram′rod′), 1 rod for ramming down the charge in a gun that is loaded from the muzzle. 2 rod for cleaning the barrel of a gun. *n.*

Ram ses (ram′sēz), the name of several kings of ancient Egypt. *n.* Also, **Rameses.**

ram shack le (ram′shak′əl), loose and shaky; likely to come apart: *The buildings on this farm are old and ramshackle. adj.*

ran (ran), past tense of **run.** *The dog ran after the cat. v.*

ranch (ranch), **1** a large farm with grazing land, used for raising cattle, sheep, or horses. **2** any farm, especially one used to raise one kind of animal or crop: *a chicken ranch, a fruit ranch.* **3** to work on a ranch; manage a ranch. **1,2** *n.,* **3** *v.*

ranch er (ran′chər), person who owns, manages, or works on a ranch. *n.*

ranch man (ranch′mən), rancher. *n.,* *pl.* **ranch men.**

ran cid (ran′sid), **1** stale; spoiled: *rancid butter.* **2** tasting or smelling like stale fat or butter: *a rancid odor. adj.* —**ran′cid ly,** *adv.* —**ran′cid ness,** *n.*

ran cid i ty (ran sid′ə tē), rancid quality or condition. *n.*

ran cor (rang′kər), bitter resentment or ill will; extreme hatred or spite. *n.*

ran cor ous (rang′kər əs), spiteful; bitterly malicious. *adj.* —**ran′cor ous ly,** *adv.*

ran dom (ran′dəm), by chance; with no plan; haphazard: *a random guess, random questions, pick a random number. adj.* —**ran′dom ly,** *adv.*

at random, by chance; with no plan or purpose: *The librarian took a book at random from the shelf.*

rang (rang), past tense of **ring². ²** *The telephone rang. v.*

range (rānj), **1** distance between certain limits; extent: *a range of prices from $5 to $25, the range of colors, the range of hearing.* **2** vary within certain limits: *prices ranging from $5 to $10.* **3** distance a gun can shoot. **4** a place to practice shooting. **5** land for grazing. **6** wander; rove; roam: *Dinosaurs once ranged the earth. Our talk ranged over all that had happened on vacation.* **7** row or line of mountains: *Mount Rainier is in the Cascade Range.* **8** row; line: *ranges of books in perfect order.* **9** put in a row or rows: *Range the books by size.* **10** put in groups or classes. **11** put in line on someone's side: *Loyal citizens ranged themselves with the king.* **12** district in which certain plants or animals live. **13** run in a line; extend: *a boundary ranging east and west.* **14** be found; occur: *a plant ranging from Canada to Mexico.* **15** a stove for cooking. **1,3–5,7,8,12,15** *n.,* **2,6,9–11,13,14** *v.,* **ranged, rang ing.**

rang er (rān′jər), **1** person employed to guard a tract of forest. **2** one of a body of armed men employed in ranging over a region to police it. **3** soldier

in the United States Army trained for raids and surprise attacks. **4** person or thing that ranges; rover. *n.*

Ran goon (rang gün′), capital and chief port of Burma, in the S part. *n.*

rang y (rān′jē), slender and long-limbed: *a rangy horse. adj.,* **rang i er, rang i est.**

rank¹ (rangk), **1** row or line, especially of soldiers, placed side by side. **2 ranks,** *pl.* **a** army; soldiers. **b** rank and file. **c** formation: *open ranks, close ranks.* **3** arrange in a row or line. **4** position; grade; class: *the rank of colonel.* **5** high position: *A duke is a man of rank.* **6** have a certain rank: *rank high in a spelling test.* **7** put in some special order in a list: *Rank the states in the order of size.* **8** be more important than; outrank: *A major ranks a captain.* **1,2,4,5** *n.,* **3,6–8** *v.* [from French of the 1500's *rang*]

rank² (rangk), **1** large and coarse: *rank grass.* **2** growing thickly in a coarse way: *a rank growth of weeds.* **3** producing a dense and coarse growth: *rank swampland.* **4** having a strong, bad smell or taste: *rank meat, rank tobacco.* **5** strongly marked; extreme: *rank ingratitude, rank nonsense. adj.* [Old English *ranc* proud] —**rank′ly,** *adv.* —**rank′ness,** *n.*

rank and file, 1 common soldiers, especially those with the rank of corporal or below; ranks. **2** common people.

ran kle (rang′kəl), be sore; cause soreness; continue to give pain: *The memory of the insult rankled in his mind. v.,* **ran kled, ran kling.**

ran sack (ran′sak), **1** search thoroughly through: *A thief ransacked the house for jewelry.* **2** rob; plunder: *The invading army ransacked the city and carried off its treasure. v.*

ran som (ran′səm), **1** price paid or demanded before a captive is set free: *The robbers held the travelers prisoners for ransom.* **2** obtain the release of (a captive) by paying a price: *They ransomed the kidnaped child with a great sum of money.* **3** a ransoming. **1,3** *n.,* **2** *v.* —**ran′som er,** *n.*

rant (rant), **1** speak wildly, extravagantly, violently, or noisily. **2** extravagant, violent, or noisy speech. **1** *v.,* **2** *n.*

rap¹ (rap), **1** a quick, light blow; a light, sharp knock: *a rap at the door.* **2** knock sharply; tap: *The chairman rapped on the table for order.* **3** say sharply: *rap out an answer.* **1** *n.,* **2,3** *v.,* **rapped, rap ping.** [probably imitation of the sound]

take the rap, SLANG. pay the penalty; take the blame.

rap² (rap), INFORMAL. the least bit: *I don't care a rap. n.* [origin uncertain]

hat, āge, fär; let, ēqual, tėrm;
it, īce; hot, ōpen, ôrder;
oil, out; cup, pùt, rüle; ch, child;
ng, long; sh, she; th, thin;
ŦH, then; zh, measure;

ə represents *a* in about,
e in taken, *i* in pencil,
o in lemon, *u* in circus.

rap³ (rap), INFORMAL. **1** conversation; talk. **2** talk together in an informal way. **1** *n.,* **2** *v.,* **rapped, rap ping,** [perhaps short for *rapport*]

ra pa cious (rə pā′shəs), **1** seizing by force; plundering: *rapacious pirates.* **2** grasping; greedy: *a rapacious miser.* **3** living by the capture of prey; predatory: *rapacious birds. adj.* —**ra pa′cious ly,** *adv.* —**ra pa′cious ness,** *n.*

ra pac i ty (rə pas′ə tē), rapacious spirit, action, or practice; greed. *n.*

rape¹ (rāp), **1** a seizing and carrying off by force. **2** crime of using force against a woman or girl for a sexual purpose. **3** commit rape on. **1,2** *n.,* **3** *v.,* **raped, rap ing.** [from Latin *rapere* seize, lift]

rape² (rāp), plant whose leaves are used as food for sheep and hogs. Rape seeds yield an oil that is used as a lubricant. *n.* [from Latin *rapa* and *rapum* turnip]

Raph a el (raf′ē əl *or* rā′fē əl), 1483–1520, Italian painter. *n.*

rap id (rap′id), **1** moving, acting, or doing with speed; very quick; swift: *a rapid worker, rapid growth.* **2 rapids,** *pl.* part of a river's course where the water rushes quickly, often over rocks near the surface: *The boat overturned in the rapids.* **1** *adj.,* **2** *n.* —**rap′id ly,** *adv.*

rap id-fire (rap′id fīr′), **1** firing shots in quick succession. **2** ready and quick; occurring in quick succession: *rapid-fire commands. adj.*

ra pid i ty (rə pid′ə tē), swiftness; speed. *n.*

ra pi er (rā′pē ər), a long and light sword used for thrusting. *n.*

rap ine (rap′ən), a robbing by force and carrying off; plundering: *The invading army got their food by rapine. n.*

rap port (ra pôr′ *or* ra pôrt′), **1** relation; connection. **2** agreement; harmony. *n.*

rap proche ment (rä prôsh män′), establishment or renewal of friendly relations. *n.* [from French]

rap scal lion (rap skal′yən), rascal; rogue; scamp. *n.*

rapt (rapt), **1** lost in delight. **2** so busy thinking of or enjoying one thing that

adj. adjective   *n.* noun
adv. adverb   *prep.* preposition
conj. conjunction   *pron.* pronoun
interj. interjection   *v.* verb

sing. singular   *pl.* plural

one does not know what else is happening: *Rapt in my work, I did not hear the footsteps coming closer.* 3 showing a rapt condition; caused by a rapt condition: *a rapt smile, in rapt attention. adj.*

rap ture (rap/chər), a strong feeling that absorbs the mind; very great joy: *In rapture the child gazed at the toys in the shop window. n.*

rap tur ous (rap/chər əs), full of rapture; expressing or feeling rapture. *adj.* —**rap/tur ous ly,** *adv.*

rare[1] (rer *or* rar), 1 seldom seen or found: *Storks and peacocks are rare birds in the United States.* 2 not happening often; unusual: *Snow is rare in Florida.* 3 unusually good or great: *Edison had rare powers as an inventor.* 4 thin; not dense: *The higher we go above the earth, the rarer the air is. adj.,* **rar er, rar est.** [from Latin *rarus*] —**rare/ness,** *n.*

rare[2] (rer *or* rar), not cooked much: *a rare steak. adj.,* **rar er, rar est.** [Old English *hrēr* lightly cooked] —**rare/ness,** *n.*

rare bit (rer/bit *or* rar/bit), Welsh rabbit. *n.*

rar e fy (rer/ə fī *or* rar/ə fī), 1 make or become less dense: *The air on high mountains is rarefied.* 2 refine; purify. *v.,* **rar e fied, rar e fy ing.**

rare ly (rer/lē *or* rar/lē), 1 seldom; not often. 2 unusually; unusually well. *adv.*

rar ing (rer/ing *or* rar/ing), INFORMAL. very eager: *raring to go, raring for a fight. adj.*

rar i ty (rer/ə te *or* rar/ə te), 1 something rare: *A person over a hundred years old is a rarity.* 2 fewness; scarcity: *The rarity of diamonds makes them valuable.* 3 lack of density; thinness: *The rarity of the air in the mountains is bad for people with weak hearts. n., pl.* **rar i ties.**

ras cal (ras/kəl), 1 a bad, dishonest person. 2 a mischievous person, child, or animal. *n.*

ras cal i ty (ra skal/ə tē), rascally character, conduct, or act. *n., pl.* **ras cal i ties.**

ras cal ly (ras/kə lē), mean; dishonest; bad: *a rascally trick. adj.*

rash[1] (rash), too hasty; careless; reckless; taking too much risk: *It is rash to cross the street without looking both ways. adj.* [Middle English *rasch* quick] —**rash/ly,** *adv.* —**rash/ness,** *n.*

rash[2] (rash), a breaking out with many small red spots on the skin. Scarlet fever causes a rash. *n., pl.* **rash es.** [from French *rasche, rasque* scurvy]

rash er (rash/ər), a thin slice of bacon or ham for frying or broiling. *n.*

rasp (rasp), 1 make a harsh, grating sound: *The file rasped as I worked.* 2 a harsh, grating sound: *the rasp of crickets, a rasp in a person's voice.* 3 utter with a grating sound: *rasp out a command.* 4 affect harshly; irritate; grate on: *Their constant squabbling began to rasp my nerves.* 5 scrape with a rough instrument. 6 a coarse file with pointed teeth. 1,3-5 *v.,* 2,6 *n.*

rasp (def. 6)

rasp ber ry (raz/ber/ē), 1 a small fruit that grows on bushes. It is usually red or black, but some kinds are white or yellow. 2 bush that it grows on. 3 SLANG. sound of disapproval or derision made with the tongue and lips. *n., pl.* **rasp ber ries.**

rat (rat), 1 a long-tailed rodent like a mouse but larger. Rats are gray, black, brown, or white. 2 hunt for rats; catch rats. 3 SLANG. a low, mean, disloyal person. 4 INFORMAL. behave in a low, mean, disloyal way. 5 SLANG. turn informer against one's associates; squeal. 1,3 *n.,* 2,4,5 *v.,* **rat ted, rat ting.**

smell a rat, suspect a trick or scheme.

ra tan (ra tan/), rattan. *n.*

ratch et (rach/it), 1 wheel or bar with teeth that come against a catch so that motion is permitted in one direction but not in the other. 2 the catch. 3 the entire device, wheel and catch or bar and catch. *n.*

rate[1] (rāt), 1 quantity, amount, or degree measured in proportion to something else: *The rate of interest is 6 cents on the dollar. The car was going at the rate of 40 miles an hour.* 2 price: *We pay the regular rate.* 3 put a value on: *We rated the house as worth $20,000.* 4 consider; regard: *He was rated as one of the richest men in town.* 5 class; grade; rating: *first rate, second rate.* 6 put in a certain class or grade: *rate a baseball player.* 7 be regarded; be classed; rank: *She rates high as a musi-cian.* 8 INFORMAL. be worthy of: *She rates the best seat in the house.* 1,2,5 *n.,* 3,4,6-8 *v.,* **rat ed, rat ing.** [from French of the 1400's *rate,* from Latin *rata (pars)* fixed (amount), from *reri* reckon]

at any rate, in any case; under any circumstances; anyway.

rate[2] (rāt), scold. *v.,* **rat ed, rat ing.** [Middle English *rāten*]

rath er (raтн/ər), 1 more readily; more willingly: *I would rather go today than tomorrow.* 2 more properly or justly; with better reason: *This is rather for your parents to decide than for you.* 3 more truly: *It was late Monday night or, rather, early Tuesday morning.* 4 to some extent; somewhat; more than a little: *After working so long he was rather tired.* 5 on the contrary: *The lesson wasn't difficult to do; rather, it was easy.* 6 INFORMAL. yes, indeed! certainly! very much so! 1-5 *adv.,* 6 *interj.*

had rather, would more willingly; prefer to: *She had rather play than rest.*

rat i fi ca tion (rat/ə fə kā/shən), confirmation; approval: *the ratification of a treaty by the Senate. n.*

rat i fy (rat/ə fī), confirm; approve; sanction; authorize: *The two countries will ratify the agreement made by their representatives. v.,* **rat i fied, rat i fy ing.**

rat ing (rā/ting), 1 class; grade. 2 position in a class or grade: *the rating of a seaman, the rating of a ship according to tonnage. n.*

ra ti o (rā/shē ō), 1 relation of one number or quantity to another, expressed as a quotient. "He has sheep and cows in the ratio of 10 to 3" means that he has ten sheep for every three cows. 2 quotient expressing this relation. The ratio between two quantities is the number of times one contains the other. The ratio of 10 to 3 is written as 10:3, 10/3, 10÷3, or $\frac{10}{3}$. The ratios of 3 to 5 and 6 to 10 are the same. *n., pl.* **ra ti os.**

RATCHET

ratchet
(def. 1)

CATCH

ra tion (rash/ən *or* rā/shən), 1 a fixed allowance of food; the daily allowance of food for a person or animal. 2 portion of anything dealt out; share; allotment: *rations of sugar.* 3 allow only certain amounts to: *ration citizens when supplies are scarce.* 4 distribute in limited amounts: *Food was rationed to the public during the war.* 5 supply with rations: *ration an army.* 1,2 *n.,* 3-5 *v.*

ra tion al (rash′ə nəl), 1 reasoned out; sensible; reasonable: *When very angry, people seldom act in a rational way.* 2 able to think and reason clearly: *As children grow older, they become more rational.* 3 of reason; based on reasoning: *There is a rational explanation for thunder and lightning. adj.* —**ra′tion al ly,** *adv.*

ra tion ale (rash′ə nal′), the fundamental reason. *n.*

ra tion al ism (rash′ə nə liz′əm), principle or habit of accepting reason as the supreme authority in matters of opinion, belief, or conduct. *n.*

rattlesnake

RATTLE

ra tion al ist (rash′ə nə list), person who accepts reason as the supreme authority in matters of opinion, belief, or conduct. *n.*

ra tion al is tic (rash′ə nə lis′tik), of rationalism or rationalists. *adj.*

ra tion al i ty (rash′ə nal′ə tē), the possession of reason; reasonableness: *That man is odd in some ways, but no one doubts his rationality. n.*

ra tion al i za tion (rash′ə nə lə zā′shən), a rationalizing or a being rationalized. *n.*

ra tion al ize (rash′ə nə līz), 1 make rational or conformable to reason. 2 treat or explain in a rational manner. 3 find (often unconsciously) an explanation or excuse for: *I rationalized drinking two sodas by thinking "I must eat enough to keep up my strength."* 4 find excuses for one's desires. *v.,* **ra tion al ized, ra tion al iz ing.**

rational number, any number that can be expressed as an integer or as a ratio between two integers, excluding zero as a denominator. 2, 5, and ¹/₂ are rational numbers.

rat line or **rat lin** (rat′lən), one of the small ropes that cross the shrouds of a ship, used as steps for going aloft. *n.*

rat tan (ra tan′), 1 kind of palm with a very long stem. 2 stems of such palm trees, used for wickerwork, canes, etc. 3 cane or switch made from a piece of such a stem. *n.* Also, **ratan.**

rat ter (rat′ər), 1 one that catches rats: *Our terrier is a good ratter.* 2 one who deserts his associates. *n.*

rat tle (rat′l), 1 make or cause to make a number of short, sharp sounds: *The window rattled in the wind. He rattled*

the dishes. 2 a number of short, sharp sounds: *the rattle of empty bottles.* 3 move with short, sharp sounds: *The old cart rattled down the street.* 4 toy, instrument, etc., that makes a noise when it is shaken: *The baby shakes his rattle.* 5 series of horny pieces at the end of a rattlesnake's tail. See **rattlesnake** for picture. 6 talk or say quickly, on and on. 7 INFORMAL. confuse; upset: *I was so rattled that I forgot my speech.* 1,3,6,7 *v.,* **rat tled, rat tling;** 2,4,5 *n.*

rat tler (rat′lər), INFORMAL. 1 rattlesnake. 2 machine or vehicle that rattles. *n.*

rat tle snake (rat′l snāk′), a poisonous American snake with a thick body and a broad, triangular head, that makes a rattling noise with its tail. *n.*

rat tle trap (rat′l trap′), 1 a rattling, rickety wagon or other vehicle. 2 any shaky, rattling object. *n.*

rau cous (rô′kəs), hoarse; harsh-sounding: *the raucous caw of a crow. adj.* —**rau′cous ly,** *adv.* —**rau′cous ness,** *n.*

rav age (rav′ij), 1 damage greatly; lay waste; destroy: *The forest fire ravaged many miles of country.* 2 violence; destruction; great damage: *War causes ravage.* 1 *v.,* **rav aged, rav ag ing;** 2 *n.*

rave (rāv), 1 talk wildly. An excited, angry person raves; so does a madman. 2 talk with too much enthusiasm: *They raved about the food.* 3 howl; roar; rage: *The wind raved about the lighthouse.* 4 a raving; frenzy or great excitement. 1-3 *v.,* **raved, rav ing;** 4 *n.*

rav el (rav′əl), 1 fray out; separate into threads: *The sweater has raveled at the elbow.* 2 to tangle; involve; confuse. *v.*

SHROUD

MAST

RATLINE

Ra vel (rə vel′), **Maurice,** 1875-1937, French composer. *n.*

rav el ing or **rav el ling** (rav′ə ling), a thread drawn from a woven or knitted fabric. *n.*

ra ven (rā′vən), 1 a large, black bird like a crow, but larger. 2 deep, glossy black: *She has raven hair.* 1 *n.,* 2 *adj.*

rav en ing (rav′ə ning), ravenous. *adj.*

rav en ous (rav′ə nəs), 1 very hungry. 2 greedy. *adj.* —**rav′en ous ly,** *adv.*

hat, āge, fär; let, ēqual, tėrm; it, īce; hot, ōpen, ôrder; oil, out; cup, pùt, rüle; ch, child; ng, long; sh, she; th, thin; ŦH, then; zh, measure;

ə represents *a* in about, *e* in taken, *i* in pencil, *o* in lemon, *u* in circus.

ra vine (rə vēn′), a long, deep, narrow valley eroded by running water. *n.*

rav ing (rā′ving), 1 that raves; delirious; frenzied; raging. 2 INFORMAL. remarkable; extraordinary: *a raving beauty. adj.*

rav i o li (rav′ē ō′lē), small, thin pieces of dough filled with chopped meat, cheese, etc. Ravioli is cooked by boiling in water, and is usually served with a highly seasoned tomato sauce. *n. sing. or pl.*

rav ish (rav′ish), 1 fill with great delight; enrapture. 2 carry off by force. 3 rape. *v.*

rav ish ing (rav′i shing), very delightful; enchanting: *jewels of ravishing beauty. adj.*

raw (rô), 1 not cooked: *raw oysters, raw meat.* 2 in the natural state; not manufactured, treated, or prepared: *raw materials. Raw milk has not been pasteurized.* 3 not experienced; not trained: *a raw recruit.* 4 with the skin off; sore: *a raw spot on a horse where the harness rubbed.* 5 damp and cold: *raw weather.* 6 SLANG. harsh; unfair: *a raw deal. adj.* —**raw′ness,** *n.*

Ra wal pin di (rä wəl pin′dē), former capital of Pakistan, a city in the NE part. *n.*

raw boned (rô′bōnd′), having little flesh on the bones; gaunt. *adj.*

raw hide (rô′hīd′), 1 the untanned skin of cattle. 2 rope or whip made of this. *n.*

raw material, substance in its natural state; anything that can be manufactured, treated, or prepared to make it more useful or increase its value. Coal, iron ore, petroleum, cotton, and animal hides are raw materials.

ray[1] (rā), 1 a line or beam of light: *rays of the sun.* 2 a line or stream of radiant

raven (def. 1) about 2 ft. long

ray

energy in the form of heat, electricity, light, etc.: *the invisible rays of the spectrum.* 3 a thin line like a ray, coming out from a center. 4 part like a ray. The petals of a daisy and the arms of a starfish are rays. 5 a slight trace; faint gleam: *Not a ray of hope pierced our gloom.* 6 half-line. *n.* [from French of the 1300's *rai*, from Latin *radius*]

ray² (rā), any of various fishes, related to the sharks, that have broad, flat bodies with very broad fins. See **stingray** for picture. *n.* [from French of the 1300's *raie*, from Latin *raia*]

ray on (rā′on), 1 fiber or fabric made from cellulose treated with chemicals. Rayon is used to make lightweight clothing, automobile tires, etc. 2 made of rayon: *a rayon sweater.* 1 *n.*, 2 *adj.*

raze (rāz), tear down; destroy completely: *The old school was razed to the ground, and a new one was built.* *v.*, **razed, raz ing.**

ra zor (rā′zər), tool with a sharp blade to shave with. *n.*

razz (raz), SLANG. 1 laugh at; make fun of. 2 strong disapproval; derision. 3 express disapproval of; boo: *The angry crowd razzed the umpire.* 1,3 *v.*, 2 *n.*

R.C., 1 Red Cross. 2 Roman Catholic.

rd., 1 road. 2 rod or rods.

Rd., Road.

R.D., Rural Delivery.

re¹ (rā), the second tone of the musical scale. *n.* [from Latin]

re² (rē), with reference to; in the matter or case of; about; concerning: *re your letter of the 7th.* *prep.* [from Latin (*in*) *re* (in) the matter of]

re-, *prefix.* 1 again; anew; once more: *Reappear = appear again.* 2 back: *Repay = pay back.* [from Latin]

reach (rēch), 1 get to; come to; arrive at: *reach the top of a hill, reach the end of a book, reach an agreement.* 2 hold out; stretch out: *A hand reached from the dark and seized him.* 3 extend in space, time, influence, etc.: *The power of Rome reached to the ends of the known world. The radio reaches millions.* 4 touch: *The anchor reached bottom. I can reach to the top of the wall.* 5 move to touch or seize something; try to get: *I reached for the rope.* 6 get at; influence: *Some people are reached by flattery. The speaker reached*

the hearts of the audience. 7 take or pass with the hand: *Please reach me the newspaper.* 8 get in touch with (someone): *I could not reach you by telephone.* 9 a stretching out; reaching: *By a long reach, the drowning man grasped the rope.* 10 extent or distance of reaching: *Food and water were left within reach of the sick dog.* 11 range; power; capacity: *Philosophy is not beyond a child's reach; he can understand it.* 12 a continuous stretch or extent: *vast reaches of snow in the Antarctic.* 1-8 *v.*, 9-12 *n.*, *pl.* **reach es.**

re act (rē akt′), 1 act back; have an effect on the one that is acting: *Unkindness often reacts on the unkind person.* 2 act in response: *Dogs react to kindness by showing affection.* 3 act chemically. Acids react on metals. *v.*

react against, act unfavorably toward or take an unfavorable attitude toward: *Some individuals react against fads.*

re ac tion (rē ak′shən), 1 action in response to some influence or force: *Our reaction to a joke is to laugh. The doctor observed carefully the patient's reactions to certain tests.* 2 action in the opposite direction: *Fever is a common reaction from a chill.* 3 the chemical action of two substances on each other which results in the formation of one or more additional substances. The reaction between nitrogen and hydrogen produces ammonia. 4 a political tendency toward a previous state of affairs. *n.*

re ac tion ar y (rē ak′shə ner′ē), 1 having to do with or favoring a return to a previous state of affairs: *The bad results of the revolution brought about a reactionary feeling.* 2 person who favors a return to a previous state of affairs, especially in politics. 1 *adj.*, 2 *n.*, *pl.* **re ac tion ar ies.**

re ac ti vate (rē ak′tə vāt), make active again; restore to active service. *v.*, **re ac ti vat ed, re ac ti vat ing.**

re ac tor (rē ak′tər), apparatus for the release of atomic energy by a controlled chain reaction; pile. Reactors consist of layers of fissionable material, such as uranium, spaced with moderators, such as graphite and heavy water, which reduce the speed and number of the neutrons intended for splitting the atomic nuclei. *n.*

read¹ (rēd), 1 get the meaning of (writing or print): *read a book. The blind read by touching special raised print with their fingertips.* 2 learn from writing or print: *I read of the event in the paper.* 3 speak (printed or written words); say aloud the words one sees or touches: *Read this story to me.* 4 show by letters, figures, signs, etc.: *The thermometer reads 70 degrees.* 5 be

worded in a certain way: *This line reads differently in the first edition.* 6 study: *read law.* 7 get the meaning of; understand: *God reads men's hearts.* 8 give the meaning of; interpret: *A prophet reads the future.* 9 introduce (something not expressed or directly indicated) by one's manner of understanding or interpreting: *read a hostile intent in a friendly letter.* *v.*, **read** (red), **read ing.** [Old English *rǣdan* to guess, read, counsel]

read into, interpret in a certain way, often attributing more than intended: *He read into the statement a deep insult.*

read² (red), 1 having knowledge gained by reading; informed: *She is widely read in history.* 2 past tense and past participle of **read¹**. *I read that book last year. He has read it too.* 1 *adj.*, 2 *v.* [(originally) past participle of *read¹*]

read a bil i ty (rē′də bil′ə tē), readable quality. *n.*

read a ble (rē′də bəl), 1 easy to read; interesting. 2 capable of being read. *adj.*

read er (rē′dər), 1 person who reads. 2 book for learning and practicing reading. *n.*

read i ly (red′l ē), 1 quickly; promptly; without delay: *A bright student answers readily.* 2 easily; without difficulty: *readily accessible.* 3 willingly. *adv.*

read i ness (red′ē nis), 1 a being ready; preparedness. 2 quickness; promptness. 3 ease; facility. 4 willingness. *n.*

read ing (rē′ding), 1 act or process of getting the meaning of writing or printing. 2 a speaking out loud of written or printed words; public recital. 3 written or printed matter read or to be read. 4 amount shown by letters, figures, or signs on the scale of an instrument: *The reading of the thermometer was 96 degrees.* 5 the form of a given word or passage in a particular edition of a book: *No two editions have the same reading for that passage.* 6 interpretation: *Each actor gave the lines a different reading.* 7 used in or for reading: *reading glasses.* 1-6 *n.*, 7 *adj.*

re ad just (rē′ə just′), adjust again; arrange again. *v.*

re ad just ment (rē′ə just′mənt), a readjusting. *n.*

read y (red′ē), 1 prepared for action or use at once; prepared: *Dinner is ready. We are ready for the test.* 2 willing: *I am ready to forget our disagreement.* 3 quick; prompt: *a ready welcome, a ready wit.* 4 apt; likely; liable: *She is too ready to find fault.* 5 easy to get at; immediately available: *ready money.* 6 make ready; prepare: *The expedition readied itself during the summer.*

7 condition or position of being prepared for action: *The soldiers walked down the road with their guns at the ready.* 1-5 *adj.,* **read i er, read i est;** 6 *v.,* **read ied, read y ing;** 7 *n.*

read y-made (red′ē mād′), ready for immediate use; made for anybody who will buy; not made to order: *Department stores sell ready-made clothes. adj.*

re af firm (rē′ə fėrm′), affirm again or anew. *v.*

re a gent (rē ā′jənt), substance used to detect the presence of other substances by the chemical reactions it causes. *n.*

re al[1] (rē′əl), 1 existing as a fact; not imagined or made up; actual; true: *a real experience, the real reason.* 2 genuine: *a real diamond.* 3 (in law) of or having to do with immovable property. Lands and houses are called real property. 4 INFORMAL. very; extremely: *real soon. It was real kind of you to come.* 1-3 *adj.,* 4 *adv.* [from Latin *realis,* from *res, rei* matter, thing]

re al[2] (rē′əl *or* rā äl′), a former small silver coin of Spain and Spanish America, worth about 12½ cents. *n., pl.* **re als, re a les** (rā ä′lās). [from Spanish *real (de plata)* royal (coin of silver), from Latin *regalis* regal, from *rex, regis* king]

real estate, land together with the buildings, fences, trees, water, minerals, etc., that belong with it.

re al ism (rē′ə liz′əm), 1 thought and action based on realities: *His realism caused him to dislike fanciful schemes.* 2 (in art and literature) the picturing of life as it actually is. *n.*

re al ist (rē′ə list), 1 person interested in what is real and practical rather than what is imaginary or theoretical. 2 artist or writer who represents things as they are in real life. *n.*

re al is tic (rē′ə lis′tik), 1 like the real thing; lifelike. 2 (in art and literature) representing life as it actually is. 3 seeing things as they really are; practical. 4 having to do with realists or realism. *adj.* —**re′al is′ti cal ly,** *adv.*

re al i ty (rē al′ə tē), 1 actual existence; true state of affairs: *Ghosts have no place in reality.* 2 a real thing; actual fact: *Slaughter and destruction are terrible realities of war. n., pl.* **re al i ties. in reality,** really; actually; in fact; truly: *They thought I was serious, but in reality I was joking.*

re al i za tion (rē′ə lə zā′shən), 1 a realizing or a being realized: *the realization of your hopes.* 2 clear understanding; full awareness; perception: *The explorers had a realization of the dangers that they must face. n.*

re al ize (rē′ə līz), 1 understand clearly; be fully aware of: *I realize how*

hard you worked. 2 make real; bring into actual existence: *Her uncle's present made it possible for her to realize her dream of going to college.* 3 change (property) into money: *Before going to England to live, he realized all his American property.* 4 obtain as a return or profit: *I realized $50 from mowing lawns. v.,* **re al ized, re al iz ing.**

re al ly (rē′ə lē), 1 actually; truly; in fact: *We should learn to accept things as they really are.* 2 indeed: *Oh, really? adv.*

realm (relm), 1 kingdom. 2 region; range; extent: *The President's realm of influence is very wide.* 3 a particular field of something: *the realm of biology, the realm of poetry. n.*

real number, any rational or irrational number.

Re al tor (rē′əl tər), trademark for a person in the real estate business who is a member of the National Association of Real Estate Boards. *n.*

re al ty (rē′əl tē), real estate. *n., pl.* **re al ties.**

ream[1] (rēm), 1 480, 500, or 516 sheets of paper of the same size and quality. 2 a very large quantity: *ream upon ream of nonsense. n.* [from French of the 1300's *raime,* from Arabic *razma* bundle]

ream[2] (rēm), 1 enlarge or shape (a hole). 2 remove with a reamer. *v.* [Middle English *reamen*]

reamer (def. 1)

ream er (rē′mər), 1 tool for enlarging or shaping a hole. 2 utensil for squeezing the juice out of oranges, lemons, etc. *n.*

re an i mate (rē an′ə māt), restore to life; give fresh spirit, vigor, activity, etc., to: *Winning a game reanimated the discouraged team. v.,* **re an i mat ed, re an i mat ing.**

reap (rēp), 1 cut (grain). 2 gather (a crop). 3 cut grain or gather a crop from: *reap fields.* 4 get as a return or reward: *Kind acts often reap happy smiles. v.*

reap er (rē′pər), person or machine that cuts grain or gathers a crop. *n.*

re ap pear (rē′ə pir′), appear again. *v.*

re ap pear ance (rē′ə pir′əns), a reappearing. *n.*

rear[1] (rir), 1 the back part; back: *the rear of the house.* 2 at the back; in the back: *Leave by the rear door of the bus.* 3 the last part of an army, fleet, etc. 1,3 *n.,* 2 *adj.* [probably shortened from *rearguard,* from French of the 1400's

hat, āge, fär; let, ēqual, tėrm;
it, īce; hot, ōpen, ôrder;
oil, out; cup, pùt, rüle; ch, child;
ng, long; sh, she; th, thin;
ᴛʜ, then; zh, measure;

ə represents *a* in about,
e in taken, *i* in pencil,
o in lemon, *u* in circus.

rereguarde, from *rer* back + *guarde* guard]

bring up the rear, move onward as the rear part; come last in order.

rear[2] (rir), 1 make grow; help to grow; bring up: *They reared their children to respect other people.* 2 to breed (livestock). 3 set up; build: *The Romans reared temples to their gods.* 4 raise; lift up: *The snake reared its head.* 5 (of an animal) rise on the hind legs; rise: *The horse reared and threw its rider. v.* [Old English *rǣran* to raise]

rear admiral, a naval officer ranking next above a captain and next below a vice-admiral.

re arm (rē ärm′), 1 arm again; arm oneself again. 2 supply with new or better weapons. *v.*

re ar ma ment (rē är′mə mənt), rearming. *n.*

re ar range (rē′ə rānj′), 1 arrange in a new or different way: *They rearranged the living room furniture for the party.* 2 arrange again: *I had to rearrange my papers after the wind blew them on the floor. v.,* **re ar ranged, re ar rang ing.**

re ar range ment (rē′ə rānj′mənt), a new or different arrangement. *n.*

rear ward (rir′wərd), toward or in the rear. *adv., adj.*

rear wards (rir′wərdz), rearward. *adv.*

re as cend (rē′ə send′), go up again. *v.*

rea son (rē′zn), 1 cause or motive for an action, feeling, etc.: *I have my own reasons for doing this.* 2 justification; explanation: *What is your reason for doing such poor work?* 3 ability or power to think: *The poor old man has lost his reason.* 4 think logically; think things out: *Most animals can't reason.* 5 draw conclusions or inferences from facts or premises. 6 right thinking; common sense. 7 consider; discuss; argue: *Reason with her and try to make her change her mind.* 1-3,6 *n.,* 4,5,7 *v.*

bring to reason, cause to be reasonable: *The stubborn child was at last brought to reason.*

adj. adjective	*n.* noun
adv. adverb	*prep.* preposition
conj. conjunction	*pron.* pronoun
interj. interjection	*v.* verb
sing. singular	*pl.* plural

by reason of, on account of; because of: *School was dismissed by reason of the teachers' conference.*

in reason or **within reason,** within reasonable and sensible limits: *I will do anything in reason.*

stand to reason, be reasonable and sensible: *It stands to reason that he would resent your insults.*

rea son a ble (rē′zn ə bəl), **1** according to reason; sensible; not foolish. **2** not asking too much; fair; just. **3** not high in price; inexpensive: *a reasonable price.* **4** able to reason. *adj.* —**rea′son a ble ness,** *n.*

rea son a bly (rē′zn ə blē), in a reasonable manner; with reason. *adv.*

rea son ing (rē′zn ing), **1** process of drawing conclusions from facts or premises. **2** reasons; arguments. *n.*

re as sem ble (rē′ə sem′bəl), come or bring together again. *v.,* **re as sem bled, re as sem bling.**

re as sert (rē′ə sèrt′), assert again. *v.*

re as sume (rē′ə süm′), assume again or anew; resume. *v.,* **re as sumed, re as sum ing.**

re as sur ance (rē′ə shùr′əns), **1** new or fresh assurance. **2** restoration of courage or confidence. *n.*

re as sure (rē′ə shùr′), **1** restore to confidence: *The crew's calmness during the storm reassured the passengers.* **2** assure again or anew. **3** insure again. *v.,* **re as sured, re as sur ing.**

re a wak en (rē′ə wā′kən), awaken again or anew. *v.*

re bate (rē′bāt), **1** return of part of money paid; partial refund; discount. **2** to return part of money paid. **1** *n.,* **2** *v.,* **re bat ed, re bat ing.**

Re bec ca (ri bek′ə), (in the Bible) the wife of Isaac, and the mother of Esau and Jacob. *n.*

reb el (reb′əl *for 1,2;* ri bel′ *for 3,4*), **1** person who resists or fights against authority instead of obeying: *The rebels armed themselves against the government.* **2** defying law or authority: *a rebel army.* **3** resist or fight against law or authority: *Unfair taxes made the colonists rebel.* **4** feel a great dislike or opposition: *We rebelled at having to stay in on so fine a day.* **1** *n.,* **2** *adj.,* **3,4** *v.,* **re belled, re bel ling.**

re bel lion (ri bel′yən), **1** armed resist-

ance or fight against one's government. **2** resistance or fight against any power or restriction. **3** act or condition of rebelling; revolt. *n.*

re bel lious (ri bel′yəs), **1** defying authority; acting like a rebel; mutinous: *a rebellious army.* **2** hard to manage; hard to treat; disobedient: *a rebellious child.* *adj.* —**re bel′lious ly,** *adv.* —**re bel′lious ness,** *n.*

re bind (rē bīnd′), bind again or anew: *This book with the broken back needs rebinding.* *v.,* **re bound, re bind ing.**

re birth (rē′bèrth′ *or* rē bèrth′), a new birth; being born again: *a rebirth of confidence, a rebirth of national pride.* *n.*

re born (rē bôrn′), born again. *adj.*

re bound (ri bound′ *for 1,3;* rē′bound′ *or* ri bound′ *for 2*), **1** to spring back. **2** a springing back: *In handball, you hit the ball on the rebound.* **3** the past tense and past participle of **re bind.** *Send this book to be rebound.* **1,3** *v.,* **2** *n.*

re buff (ri buf′), **1** a blunt or sudden check to a person who makes advances, offers help, makes a request, etc.: *Her offer to help him met with the rebuff, "Let me alone."* **2** give a rebuff to: *The friendly dog was rebuffed by a kick.* **1** *n.,* **2** *v.*

re build (rē bild′), build again or anew. *v.,* **re built, re build ing.**

re built (rē bilt′), past tense and past participle of **rebuild.** *v.*

re buke (ri byük′), **1** express disapproval of; reprove. **2** expression of disapproval; scolding: *The child feared the teacher's rebuke.* **1** *v.,* **re buked, re buk ing; 2** *n.*

re bus (rē′bəs), representation of a word or phrase by pictures suggesting the syllables or words. A picture of a cat on a log is a rebus for catalog. *n., pl.* **re bus es.**

re but (ri but′), oppose by evidence on the other side or by argument; try to disprove: *rebut the argument of the other team in a debate.* *v.,* **re but ted, re but ting.**

re but tal (ri but′l), a rebutting. *n.*

re cal ci trance (ri kal′sə trəns), refusal to submit, conform, or comply. *n.*

re cal ci trant (ri kal′sə trənt), resisting authority or control; disobedient: *The recalcitrant patient would not take the medicine.* *adj.*

re call (ri kôl′ *for 1,3,5;* ri kôl′ *or* rē′kôl′ *for 2,4,6,7*), **1** call back to mind; remember: *I can recall stories told to me when I was a small child.* **2** a recalling to mind. **3** call back; order back: *The ambassador was recalled.* **4** a calling back; ordering back. **5** take back; withdraw: *The order has been given and cannot be recalled.* **6** a taking

back; revocation; annulment. **7** procedure by which a public official can be removed from office before his term has expired by vote of the people. **1,3,5** *v.,* **2,4,6,7** *n.*

re cant (ri kant′), **1** take back formally or publicly; withdraw or renounce (a statement, opinion, purpose, etc.): *The reporter recanted the story when evidence proved it was false.* **2** renounce an opinion or allegiance: *The rebellious colonists knew there would be war with England, yet they would not recant.* *v.*

re can ta tion (rē′kan tā′shən), a recanting; a public or formal renouncing. *n.*

re ca pit u late (rē′kə pich′ə lāt), repeat or recite the main points of; tell briefly; sum up. *v.,* **re ca pit u lat ed, re ca pit u lat ing.**

re ca pit u la tion (rē′kə pich′ə lā′shən), a brief statement of the main points; summary. *n.*

re cap ture (rē kap′chər), **1** capture again; have again. **2** to recall: *The picture album recaptured the days of the horse and buggy.* *v.,* **re cap tured, re cap tur ing.**

re cast (rē kast′), **1** cast again or anew: *recast a bell.* **2** make over; remodel: *recast a sentence.* *v.,* **re cast, re cast ing.**

re cede (ri sēd′), **1** go backward; move backward; withdraw: *Houses and trees seem to recede as you ride past in a train.* **2** slope backward: *a chin that recedes.* *v.,* **re ced ed, re ced ing.**

re ceipt (ri sēt′), **1** a written statement that money, a package, a letter, etc., has been received. **2** write on (a bill, etc.) that something has been received or paid for: *Pay the bill and ask the grocer to receipt it.* **3 receipts,** *pl.* money received; amount or quantity received: *Our expenses were less than our receipts.* **4** a receiving or a being received: *On receipt of the news he went home.* **5** recipe. **1,3,4,5** *n.,* **2** *v.*

re ceiv a ble (ri sē′və bəl), **1** fit for acceptance: *Gold is receivable all over the world.* **2** on which payment is to be received. Bills receivable is the opposite of bills payable. **3** which is to be received. *adj.*

re ceive (ri sēv′), **1** take (something offered or sent); take into one's hands or possession: *receive gifts.* **2** be given; get: *receive a letter from home.* **3** take; support; bear; hold: *The boat received a heavy load.* **4** take or let into the mind; accept: *receive new ideas.* **5** experience; suffer; endure: *receive a blow.* **6** let into one's house, society, etc.: *The people of the neighborhood were glad to receive the new couple.* **7** be at home to friends and visitors: *She receives on Tuesdays.* **8** change electromagnetic waves into

sound or picture signals: *Our television receives well since we had a new antenna put on.* v., **re ceived, re ceiv ing.**

re ceiv er (ri sē′vər), 1 person who receives. 2 thing that receives: *Public telephones have coin receivers for nickels, dimes, and quarters.* 3 the part of a telephone held to the ear. 4 device that changes electromagnetic waves into sound or picture signals: *a radio or television receiver.* 5 one appointed by law to take charge of the property of others: *He will act as receiver for the firm that has failed in business.* n.

re ceiv er ship (ri sē′vər ship), 1 position of a receiver in charge of the property of others. 2 condition of being in the control of a receiver. n.

re cent (rē′snt), 1 done or made not long ago: *recent events.* 2 not long past; modern: *a recent period in history.* adj. —**re′cent ly,** adv. —**re′cent ness,** n.

re cep ta cle (ri sep′tə kəl), any container or place used to put things in to keep them conveniently. Bags, baskets, and vaults are all receptacles. n.

re cep tion (ri sep′shən), 1 a receiving or a being received: *calm reception of bad news. Her reception as a club member pleased her.* 2 manner of receiving: *a warm reception.* 3 a gathering to receive and welcome people: *Our school gave a reception for our new principal.* 4 quality of the sound reproduced in a radio or of the sound and picture in a television receiver: *Reception was poor because we were so far from the transmitter.* n.

re cep tion ist (ri sep′shə nist), person employed to receive callers: *She is a receptionist in a doctor's office.* n.

re cep tive (ri sep′tiv), able, quick, or willing to receive ideas, suggestions, impressions, etc. adj. —**re cep′tive ly,** adv. —**re cep′tive ness,** n.

re cep tiv i ty (rē′sep tiv′ə tē), ability or readiness to receive. n.

re cep tor (ri sep′tər), cell or group of cells sensitive to stimuli; sense organ. n.

re cess (rē′ses or ri ses′ for 1,3,5; ri ses′ for 2,4), 1 time during which work stops: *There will be a short recess before the next meeting.* 2 take a recess: *The convention recessed until afternoon.* 3 part in a wall set back from the rest; alcove; niche. 4 put in a recess; set back. 5 an inner place or part; quiet, secluded place: *the recesses of a cave, the recesses of one's secret thoughts.* 1,3,5 n., 2,4 v.

re ces sion (ri sesh′ən), 1 a going backward; moving or sloping backward; withdrawal. 2 period of temporary business reduction, shorter and less extreme than a depression. n.

re ces sion al (ri sesh′ə nəl), hymn or piece of music sung or played while the clergy and the choir retire from the church at the end of a service. n.

re ces sive (ri ses′iv), likely to go back; receding. adj.

re charge (rē chärj′), 1 to charge again or anew: *recharge a battery.* 2 a second or additional charge. 1 v., **recharged, re charg ing;** 2 n.

rec i pe (res′ə pē), 1 set of directions for preparing something to eat: *Give me your recipe for cookies.* 2 set of directions for doing or preparing anything: *a recipe for happiness.* n.

re cip i ent (ri sip′ē ənt), person or thing that receives something: *The recipients of the prizes had their names printed in the paper.* n.

re cip ro cal (ri sip′rə kəl), 1 in return: *Although she gave me a present, she expected no reciprocal gift from me.* 2 existing on both sides; mutual: *reciprocal liking, reciprocal distrust.* 3 (in grammar) expressing mutual action or relation. In "The two children like each other," *each other* is a reciprocal pronoun. 4 number so related to another that when multiplied together they give 1: *3 is the reciprocal of* $1/3$, *and* $1/3$ *is the reciprocal of 3.* 1-3 adj.. 4 n. —**re cip′ro cal ly,** adv.

re cip ro cate (ri sip′rə kāt), 1 give, do, feel, or show in return: *She likes me, and I reciprocate her liking.* 2 interchange: *to reciprocate favors.* 3 move or cause to move with an alternating backward and forward motion. v., **re cip ro cat ed, re cip ro cat ing.**

re cip ro ca tion (ri sip′rə kā′shən), a reciprocating; return: *a reciprocation of a favor received.* n.

rec i proc i ty (res′ə pros′ə tē), 1 reciprocal state; mutual action. 2 a mutual exchange, especially an exchange of special privileges in regard to trade between two countries. n., pl. **rec i proc i ties.**

re cit al (ri sī′tl), 1 a reciting; telling facts in detail: *I hope that my lengthy recital of my problems hasn't bored you.* 2 story; account. 3 a musical entertainment, given usually by a single performer: *My music teacher will give a piano recital Tuesday afternoon.* n.

rec i ta tion (res′ə tā′shən), 1 a reciting; a telling of facts in detail. 2 a reciting of a prepared lesson by pupils before a teacher. 3 a repeating of something from memory. 4 piece repeated from memory. n.

rec i ta tive (res′ə tə tēv′), 1 passage, part, or piece of music which is sung with the rhythm and phrasing of ordinary speech. Operas often contain long recitatives. 2 this style of singing. n.

hat, āge, fär; let, ēqual, tėrm;
it, īce; hot, ōpen, ôrder;
oil, out; cup, pùt, rüle; ch, child;
ng, long; sh, she; th, thin;
ŦH, then; zh, measure;

ə represents *a* in about,
e in taken, *i* in pencil,
o in lemon, *u* in circus.

re cite (ri sīt′), 1 say over; repeat: *He can recite that poem from memory.* 2 say part of a lesson; answer a teacher's questions. 3 give an account of in detail: *She recited the day's adventures.* v., **re cit ed, re cit ing.**

re cit er (ri sī′tər), person who recites. n.

reck (rek), OLD USE. 1 care; heed. 2 be important or interesting; matter. v.

reck less (rek′lis), rash; heedless; careless: *a reckless act. Reckless driving causes many automobile accidents.* adj. —**reck′less ly,** adv. —**reck′less ness,** n.

reck on (rek′ən), 1 find the number or value of; count: *Reckon the cost before you decide.* 2 consider; judge; account: *He is reckoned the best speller in the class.* 3 INFORMAL. think; suppose. 4 depend; rely: *You can reckon on our help.* 5 settle; settle accounts. v.

reckon with, take into consideration.

reck on ing (rek′ə ning), 1 method of computing; count; calculation: *By my reckoning we are miles from home.* 2 settlement of an account: *a day of reckoning.* 3 bill, especially at an inn or tavern. 4 calculation of the position of a ship. n.

re claim (ri klām′), 1 bring back to or put into a useful, good condition: *The farmer reclaimed the swamp by draining it.* 2 get from discarded things: *to reclaim metal from old tin cans, to reclaim rubber.* 3 demand or ask for the return of: *We reclaimed our luggage at the end of the trip.* v.

rec la ma tion (rek′lə mā′shən), a reclaiming or a being reclaimed; restoration to a useful, good condition: *the reclamation of deserts by irrigation.* n.

re cline (ri klīn′), lean back; lie or lay down: *recline on a couch.* v., **re clined, re clin ing.**

re cluse (rek′lüs or ri klüs′), person who lives shut up or withdrawn from the world. n.

rec og ni tion (rek′əg nish′ən), 1 a knowing again; recognizing. 2 a being recognized: *By a good disguise he escaped recognition.* 3 acknowledgment: *We insisted on complete recognition of*

adj.	adjective	*n.*	noun
adv.	adverb	*prep.*	preposition
conj.	conjunction	*pron.*	pronoun
interj.	interjection	*v.*	verb
sing.	singular	*pl.*	plural

our rights. **4** favorable notice; acceptance: *The author soon won recognition from the public. n.*

rec og niz a ble (rek′əg nī′zə bəl), that can be recognized. *adj.*

re cog ni zance (ri kog′nə zəns), in law: **1** a bond binding a person to do some particular act. **2** the sum of money to be forfeited if the act is not performed. *n.*

rec og nize (rek′əg nīz), **1** know again: *You have grown so much that I scarcely recognized you.* **2** identify: *recognize a person from a description.* **3** acknowledge acquaintance with; greet: *recognize a person on the street.* **4** acknowledge; accept; admit: *recognize and do one's duty.* **5** take notice of: *The delegate waited till the chairman recognized her.* **6** show appreciation of. **7** acknowledge and agree to deal with: *For some years other nations did not recognize the new government.* *v.,* **rec og nized, rec og niz ing.**

re coil (ri koil′ *for 1,2;* ri koil′ *or* rē′-koil *for 3*), **1** draw back; shrink back: *Most people would recoil at seeing a snake in the path.* **2** spring back: *The gun recoiled after I fired.* **3** a drawing or springing back. *1,2 v., 3 n.*

rec ol lect (rek′ə lekt′), call back to mind; remember. *v.*

re-col lect (rē′kə lekt′), **1** collect again. **2** recover control of (oneself). *v.*

rec ol lec tion (rek′ə lek′shən), **1** act or power of calling back to mind. **2** memory; remembrance: *This has been the hottest summer within my recollection.* **3** thing remembered. *n.*

re com bine (rē′kəm bīn′), to combine again or anew. *v.,* **re com bined, re com bin ing.**

re com mence (rē′kə mens′), begin again or anew. *v.,* **re com menced, re com menc ing.**

rec om mend (rek′ə mend′), **1** speak in favor of; suggest favorably: *We recommended him for the job. Can you recommend a good adventure story? The waiter recommended fried chicken as the best dish on the menu.* **2** advise: *The doctor recommended that the patient stay in bed.* **3** make pleasing or attractive: *The location of the camp recommends it as a summer home. v.*

rec om men da tion (rek′ə men dā′-

shən), **1** act of recommending. **2** anything that recommends a person or thing. **3** words of advice or praise. **4** thing recommended. *n.*

rec om pense (rek′əm pens), **1** pay (a person); pay back; reward: *The travelers recompensed the man who so carefully directed them.* **2** make a fair return for (an action, anything lost, damage done, or hurt received): *The insurance company recompensed her for the loss of her car.* **3** payment; reward. **4** return; amends: *She received $2000 in recompense for the loss of her car.* *1,2 v.,* **rec om pensed, rec om pens ing;** *3,4 n.*

rec on cile (rek′ən sīl), **1** make friends again: *The children had quarreled but were soon reconciled.* **2** settle (a quarrel or difference): *The teacher reconciled the dispute between the two pupils.* **3** make agree; bring into harmony: *It is impossible to reconcile his story with the facts.* **4** make satisfied; make no longer opposed: *It is hard to reconcile oneself to being sick a long time. v.,* **rec on ciled, rec on cil ing.**

rec on cile ment (rek′ən sīl′mənt), reconciliation. *n.*

rec on cil i a tion (rek′ən sil′ē ā′-shən), **1** a reconciling; bringing together again in friendship. **2** a being reconciled; settlement or adjustment of disagreements or differences: *a reconciliation of opposite points of view. n.*

rec on dite (rek′ən dīt), **1** hard to understand; profound. **2** little known; obscure. *adj.*

re con di tion (rē′kən dish′ən), restore to a good or satisfactory condition; put in good condition by repairing, making over, etc. *v.*

re con firm (rē′kən ferm′), confirm anew. *v.*

re con nais sance (ri kon′ə səns), examination or survey, especially for military purposes. *n.*

rec on noi ter (rek′ə noi′tər *or* rē′kə-noi′tər), **1** approach and examine or observe in order to learn something: *Our scouts will reconnoiter the enemy's position before we attack.* **2** approach a place and make a first survey of it: *It seemed wise to reconnoiter before entering the town. v.*

rec on noi tre (rek′ə noi′tər *or* rē′kə-noi′tər), reconnoiter. *v.,* **rec on noi-tred, rec on noi tring.**

re con sid er (rē′kən sid′ər), consider again: *The assembly voted to reconsider a bill. v.*

re con sid er a tion (rē′kən sid′ə-rā′shən), a reconsidering or a being reconsidered. *n.*

re con struct (rē′kən strukt′), construct again; rebuild; make over. *v.*

re con struc tion (rē′kən struk′-

shən), **1** act of reconstructing. **2** thing reconstructed. **3 Reconstruction, a** process by which the southern states after the Civil War were reorganized and their relations with the national government were reestablished. **b** period when this was done, from 1865 to 1877. *n.*

re cord (ri kôrd′ *for 1,2,6;* rek′ərd *for 3-5,7-10*), **1** set down in writing so as to keep for future use: *Listen to the speaker and record what he says.* **2** put in some permanent form; keep for remembrance: *We record history in books.* **3** the thing written or kept. **4** an official written account: *The secretary kept a record of what was done at the meeting.* **5** a thin, flat disk, usually of vinyl or other plastic, with narrow grooves on its surface, used on a phonograph. Variations in the grooves of the record are picked up by the needle of a phonograph and transformed into audible sound. **6** put (music, words, or sounds) on such a disk or on specially treated wire or tape. **7** the known facts about what a person, group, etc., has done: *She has a fine record at school.* **8** the best yet done; best amount, rate, speed, etc., yet attained: *Who holds the record for the high jump?* **9** making or affording a record: *a record wheat crop.* **10** a recording or a being recorded: *What happened is a matter of record.* *1,2,6 v., 3-5,7,8,10 n., 9 adj.*

break a record, make a better record. **off the record,** not to be recorded or quoted.

on record, recorded.

re cord er (ri kôr′dər), **1** person whose business is to make and keep records. **2** machine or part of a machine that records. The recorder of a cash register adds up and prints the amount of sales made. **3** tape recorder. **4** title given to certain judges in some cities. **5** a wooden musical instrument with a tone somewhat like a flute. *n.*

recorder
(def. 5)

re cord ing (ri kôr′ding), **1** a phonograph record. **2** the original transcription of any sound or combination of sounds. *n.*

record player, phonograph.

re count[1] (ri kount′), tell in detail; give an account of: *He recounted all the* happenings of the day. v. [from French of the 1400's *reconter,* from *re-* again + *conter* relate, count[1]]

re count[2] or **re-count** (rē kount′ for 1; rē′kount′ for 2), 1 count again: *The miser counted and recounted his money.* 2 a second count: *to make a recount of the votes.* 1 v., 2 n. [*re-* + *count*[1]]

re coup (ri küp′), 1 make up for: *recoup one's losses.* 2 repay: *I will recoup you for any money you spend.* v.

re course (rē′kôrs or ri kôrs′), 1 an appealing; turning for help or protection: *Our recourse in illness is to a doctor.* 2 person or thing appealed to or turned to for help or protection: *His only recourse in trouble was his family.* n.

have recourse to, appeal to; turn to for help: *When we do not know what a word means, we have recourse to a dictionary.*

re cov er (ri kuv′ər), 1 get back (something lost, taken away, or stolen): *recover one's temper or health, recover a lost purse.* 2 make up for (something lost or damaged): *recover lost time.* 3 get well; get back to a normal condition: *She is recovering from a cold.* 4 get back to the proper position or condition: *He started to fall but recovered himself.* 5 regain in usable form; reclaim. *Many useful substances are now recovered from materials that used to be thrown away.* v.

re-cov er (rē kuv′ər), put a new cover on: *We had our couch re-covered.* v.

re cov er y (ri kuv′ər ē), 1 act of recovering. 2 a coming back to health or normal condition: *recovery from a fever.* 3 a getting back something that was lost, taken away, stolen, or sent out: *the recovery of a space capsule.* 4 a getting back to a proper position or condition: *She started to fall, but made a quick recovery.* n., pl. **re cov er ies.**

rec re ant (rek′rē ənt), 1 lacking courage; cowardly. 2 coward. 3 unfaithful; false; disloyal; traitorous. 4 traitor. 1,3 adj., 2,4 n.

re-cre ate (rē′krē āt′), create anew. v., **re-cre at ed, re-cre at ing.**

rec re a tion (rek′rē ā′shən), play or amusement. *Walking, gardening, and reading are quiet forms of recreation.* n.

rec re a tion al (rek′rē ā′shə nəl), of or having to do with recreation. adj.

re crim i nate (ri krim′ə nāt), accuse (someone) in return: *He said she had lied, and she recriminated by saying he had lied too.* v., **re crim i nat ed, re crim i nat ing.**

re crim i na tion (ri krim′ə nā′shən), an accusing in return; counter accusation: *The quarreling children indulged in many recriminations.* n.

re cross (rē krôs′), cross again. v.

re cru des cence (rē′krü des′ns), a breaking out afresh; renewed activity: *the recrudescence of an influenza epidemic.* n.

re cru des cent (rē′krü des′nt), breaking out anew. adj.

re cruit (ri krüt′), 1 a newly enlisted soldier, sailor, etc. 2 get (men) to join an army, navy, etc. 3 a new member of any group or class: *The Nature Club needs recruits.* 4 get by enrolling, hiring, etc.: *recruit new members, recruit volunteers.* 5 renew; get a sufficient number or amount of; replenish: *Before sailing, we recruited our provisions.* 1,3 n., 2,4,5 v. —**re cruit′er,** n.

re cruit ment (ri krüt′mənt), 1 act or business of recruiting. 2 condition of being recruited. n.

rec tal (rek′təl), of or having to do with the rectum. adj.

rec tan gle (rek′tang′gəl), a four-sided plane figure with four right angles. n.

rectangles

rec tan gu lar (rek tang′gyə lər), shaped like a rectangle. adj. —**rec tan′gu lar ly,** adv.

rec ti fi ca tion (rek′tə fə kā′shən), act of rectifying. n.

rec ti fi er (rek′tə fī′ər), 1 person or thing that makes right, corrects, adjusts, etc. 2 device for changing alternating current into direct current. n.

rec ti fy (rek′tə fī), 1 make right; put right; adjust; remedy: *The storekeeper admitted his mistake and was willing to rectify it.* 2 change (an alternating current) into a direct current. 3 purify or refine: *rectify a liquor by distilling it several times.* v., **rec ti fied, rec ti fy ing.**

rec ti lin e ar (rek′tə lin′ē ər), 1 in a straight line; moving in a straight line. 2 bounded or formed by straight lines. adj.

rec ti tude (rek′tə tüd or rek′tə tyüd), upright conduct or character; honesty; righteousness. n.

rec tor (rek′tər), 1 clergyman in the Protestant Episcopal Church or the Church of England who has charge of a parish. 2 priest in the Roman Catholic Church who has charge of a congregation or religious house. 3 the head of some schools, colleges, and universities. n.

rec tor y (rek′tər ē), 1 a rector's house. 2 the church living with all its rights, tithes, and lands held by a rector. n., pl. **rec tor ies.**

hat, āge, fär; let, ēqual, tėrm;
it, īce; hot, ōpen, ôrder;
oil, out; cup, pùt, rüle; ch, child;
ng, long; sh, she; th, thin;
ᵺH, then; zh, measure;

ə represents *a* in about,
e in taken, *i* in pencil,
o in lemon, *u* in circus.

rec tum (rek′təm), the lowest part of the large intestine. n.

re cum bent (ri kum′bənt), lying down; reclining; leaning. adj. —**re cum′bent ly,** adv.

re cu pe rate (ri kyü′pə rāt′ or ri kü′pə rāt′), 1 recover from sickness, exhaustion, loss, etc.: *It took us a few days to recuperate after the long trip.* 2 get back; regain: *She recuperated gradually everything she had lost.* v., **re cu pe rat ed, re cu pe rat ing.**

re cu pe ra tion (ri kyü′pə rā′shən or ri kü′pə rā′shən), recovery from sickness, exhaustion, loss, etc. n.

re cur (ri kėr′), 1 come up again; occur again; be repeated: *Leap year recurs every four years.* 2 return in thought or speech: *Old memories often recurred to her. He recurred to the matter of cost.* v., **re curred, re cur ring.**

re cur rence (ri kėr′əns), occurrence again; repetition; return: *prevent the recurrence of a mistake.* n.

re cur rent (ri kėr′ənt), occurring again; repeated; recurring: *recurrent attacks of hay fever.* adj. —**re cur′rent ly,** adv.

re cy cle (re sī′kəl), to process or treat (something) in order that it may be used again. *Paper, aluminum, and glass products are commonly recycled.* v., **re cy cled, re cy cling.**

red (red), 1 the color of blood or of a ruby. 2 having the color of blood or of a ruby: *red paint, a red light, red ink.* 3 being like or suggesting the color of blood: *red hair, a red fox.* 4 a red pigment or dye. 5 a red or reddish person, animal, or thing. 6 **Red, a** a Communist or, sometimes, any extreme radical. *Revolutionaries, socialists, and anarchists are often called Reds.* **b** Communist or extremely radical. 1,4-6a n., 2,3,6b adj.

in the red, INFORMAL. in debt; losing money.

see red, INFORMAL. become very angry.

red bird (red′bėrd′), any of several birds with red feathers, such as the cardinal and the scarlet tanager. n.

red blood cell, cell in the blood,

adj.	adjective	*n.*	noun
adv.	adverb	*prep.*	preposition
conj.	conjunction	*pron.*	pronoun
interj.	interjection	*v.*	verb
sing.	singular	*pl.*	plural

formed in bone marrow and containing hemoglobin, that carries oxygen from the lungs to various parts of the body.

red breast (red′brest′), robin. *n.*

red cap (red′kap′), porter at a railroad or bus station who usually wears a red cap as part of his uniform. *n.*

red cell, red blood cell.

red coat (red′kōt′), (in former times) a British soldier. *n.*

red corpuscle, red blood cell.

Red Cross, 1 an international organization to care for the sick and wounded in war, and to relieve suffering caused by floods, fire, diseases, and other calamities. Its badge is a red cross on a white background. 2 a national society that is a branch of this organization.

red deer, 1 deer native to the forests of Europe and Asia, and formerly very abundant in England. 2 the common deer of America in its summer coat.

red den (red′n), 1 make or become red. 2 blush. *v.*

red dish (red′ish), somewhat red. *adj.*

re dec o rate (rē dek′ə rāt′), decorate again or anew, especially by painting or papering a room, etc. *v.*, **re dec o rat ed, re dec o rat ing.**

re ded i ca tion (rē′ded ə kā′shən), act of dedicating anew. *n.*

re deem (ri dēm′), 1 buy back: *I redeemed my watch from the pawnbroker's shop.* 2 pay off: *We redeemed the mortgage.* 3 make up for; balance: *A very good feature will sometimes redeem several bad ones.* 4 carry out; make good; fulfill: *We redeem a promise by doing what we said we would.* 5 set free; rescue; save; liberate; deliver; release: *redeemed from sin. v.*

re deem a ble (ri dē′mə bəl), 1 that can be redeemed. 2 that will be redeemed or paid: *bonds redeemable in 1978. adj.*

re deem er (ri dē′mər), 1 person who redeems. 2 **Redeemer,** Jesus Christ. *n.*

re demp tion (ri demp′shən), 1 a buying back; paying off. 2 a ransom. 3 deliverance; rescue. 4 deliverance from sin; salvation. *n.*

red-hand ed (red′han′did), in the very act of crime, mischief, etc.: *be caught red-handed in a robbery. adj.*

red head (red′hed′), person having red hair. *n.*

red head ed (red′hed′id), having red hair. *adj.*

red herring, something used to draw attention away from the real issue.

red-hot (red′hot′), 1 red with heat; very hot: *a red-hot iron.* 2 very enthusiastic; excited; violent: *a red-hot fanatic.* 3 fresh from the source: *red-hot rumors. adj.*

re di rect (rē′də rekt′ *or* rē′dī rekt′), direct again or anew. *v.*

re dis cov er (rē′dis kuv′ər), discover again or anew. *v.*

red-let ter (red′let′ər), memorable; especially happy: *Graduation is a red-letter day in one's life. adj.*

red ness (red′nis), quality of being red; red color. *n.*

re do (rē dü′), do again; do over. *v.*, **re did** (rē did′), **re done** (rē dun′), **re do ing.**

red o lence (red′l əns), redolent condition or quality. *n.*

red o lent (red′l ənt), 1 having a pleasant smell; fragrant. 2 smelling strongly; giving off an odor: *a house redolent of fresh paint.* 3 suggesting thoughts or feelings: *Rome is a city redolent of history. adj.* —**red′o-lent ly,** *adv.*

re dou ble (rē dub′əl), 1 double again. 2 increase greatly; double: *As she neared the finish line, the skater redoubled her speed and won the race.* 3 double back: *The fox redoubled on its trail to escape the hunters. v.*, **re dou-bled, re dou bling.**

re doubt (ri dout′), a small fort standing alone. *n.*

re doubt a ble (ri dou′tə bəl), that should be feared or dreaded: *a redoubtable warrior, a redoubtable debater. adj.*

re dound (ri dound′), come back as a result; contribute: *The courage of the pioneers redounds to the glory of the nation. v.*

red pepper, 1 cayenne. 2 any of several varieties of pepper that have hollow, sweet or mild fruits which are red when ripe. 3 the fruit of any of these plants.

re dress (ri dres′ *for 1*; rē′dres *or* ri dres′ *for 2*), 1 set right; repair; remedy: *King Arthur tried to redress wrongs in his kingdom.* 2 a setting right; reparation; relief: *Anyone who has been injured unfairly deserves redress.* 1 *v.*, 2 *n.*

Red Sea, narrow sea between the Arabian peninsula and Africa. It is part of the Indian Ocean and is connected with the Mediterranean Sea by the Suez Canal.

red skin (red′skin′), a North American Indian (a term often considered offensive). *n.*

red start (red′stärt′), 1 a fly-catching warbler of America. 2 a small European bird with a reddish tail. *n.*

red tape, too much attention to details and forms.

re duce (ri düs′ *or* ri dyüs′), 1 make less; make smaller; decrease: *We have reduced expenses this year. She is trying to reduce her weight.* 2 become less in weight: *His doctor advised him to reduce.* 3 bring down; lower: *The family's misfortunes reduced them to poverty. The major was reduced to the rank of captain.* 4 change to another form: *The chalk was reduced to powder. Reduce that statement to writing. If you reduce 3 lbs. 7 oz. to ounces, you have 55 ounces.* 5 bring to a certain state, form, or condition: *The teacher soon reduced the noisy class to order. I was reduced to tears by the cruel words.* 6 conquer; subdue: *The army reduced the fort by a sudden attack.* 7 remove oxygen from. *v.*, **re duced, re duc ing.**

re duc er (ri dü′sər *or* ri dyü′sər), person or thing that reduces. *n.*

re duc i ble (ri dü′sə bəl *or* ri dyü′sə bəl), that can be reduced: *⁴/₈ is reducible to ½. adj.*

re duc tion (ri duk′shən), 1 a reducing or a being reduced: *a reduction of ten pounds in weight. Failure to obey orders caused the corporal's reduction to the rank of private.* 2 amount by which a thing is reduced: *The reduction in cost was $5.* 3 form of something produced by reducing; copy of something on a smaller scale. 4 any chemical reaction in which oxygen is removed from a compound. *n.*

re dun dance (ri dun′dəns), redundancy. *n.*

re dun dan cy (ri dun′dən sē), 1 more than is needed. 2 a redundant thing, part, or amount. 3 the use of too many words for the same idea. *n., pl.* **re dun dan cies.**

re dun dant (ri dun′dənt), 1 not needed; extra: *a redundant word.* 2 using too many words for the same idea; wordy: *The use of "two" in the phrase "the two twins" is redundant. adj.* —**re dun′dant ly,** *adv.*

re du pli cate (ri dü′plə kāt *or* ri dyü′plə kāt), to double; repeat. *v.*, **re du pli cat ed, re du pli cat ing.**

re du pli ca tion (ri dü′plə kā′shən *or* ri dyü′plə kā′shən), 1 a reduplicating or a being reduplicated; doubling; repetition. 2 something resulting from repeating; duplicate; copy: *To the prisoner each day seemed a reduplication of the preceding day. n.*

red wing (red′wing′), 1 blackbird of North America. The male has a scarlet patch on each wing. **2** a European thrush with a reddish color on the underside of the wings. *n.*

red-winged blackbird (red′-wingd′), redwing (def. 1).

red wood (red′wủd′), **1** a very large evergreen tree of California and Oregon; sequoia; big tree. It grows to a height of over 300 feet. **2** its brownish-red wood.

re ech o (rē ek′ō), **1** to echo back: *The house reechoes children's laughter. The thunder reechoed far behind.* **2** an echo of an echo. **1** *v.,* **2** *n., pl.* **re ech oes.**

re-ech o (rē ek′ō), reecho. *v., n., pl.* **re-ech oes.**

reed (rēd), **1** a kind of tall grass with a hollow, jointed stalk that grows in wet places. **2** such a stalk. **3** anything made from the stalk of a reed, such as a pipe to blow on or an arrow. **4** a thin piece of wood, metal, or plastic in a musical instrument that produces sound when a current of air moves it. *n.*

reed instrument, a musical instrument that produces sound by means of a vibrating reed or reeds. Oboes, clarinets, and saxophones are reed instruments.

reed organ, a musical instrument producing tones by means of small metal reeds and played by keys.

reed y (rē′dē), **1** full of reeds: *a reedy pond.* **2** made of a reed or reeds. **3** like a reed or reeds: *reedy grass.* **4** sounding like a reed instrument: *a thin, reedy voice. adj.,* **reed i er, reed i est.**

reef[1] (rēf), a narrow ridge of rocks, sand, or coral at or near the surface of the water: *The ship was wrecked on a hidden reef. n.* [probably from earlier Dutch *riffe* or *rif*]

reef[2] (def. 2)
reefed sail

REEFED SAIL

reef[2] (rēf), **1** the part of a sail that can be rolled or folded up to reduce the area exposed to the wind. **2** reduce the area of (a sail) by rolling or folding up a part of it. **1** *n.,* **2** *v.* [from a Scandinavian word of the 1200's, such as Icelandic *rif* rib, reef, ridge]

reef er (rē′fər), **1** person who reefs. **2** a short coat of thick cloth, worn especially by sailors and fishermen. *n.*

reek (rēk), **1** a strong, unpleasant smell: *the reek of a cesspool.* **2** send out a strong, unpleasant smell: *The beach reeks of dead fish.* **1** *n.,* **2** *v.*

reel[1] (rēl), **1** a frame turning on an axis, for winding thread, yarn, a fish line, rope, wire, etc. **2** spool; roller. **3** something wound on a reel: *two reels of*

motion-picture film. **4** to wind on a reel. **5** draw with a reel or by winding: *She reeled in a fish.* **1-3** *n.,* **4,5** *v.* [Old English *hrēol*]

reel off, say, write, or make in a quick, easy way: *He can reel off stories by the hour.*

reel[2] (rēl), **1** sway, swing, or rock under a blow or shock: *She reeled when the ball struck her.* **2** sway in standing or walking: *The dazed boy reeled down the street.* **3** be in a whirl; be dizzy: *My head was reeling after the fast dance.* **4** a reeling or staggering movement. **5** become unsteady; waver: *The platoon reeled when the enemy attacked.* **1-3,5** *v.,* **4** *n.* [Middle English *relen,* probably from *reel*[1]]

reel[3] (rēl), **1** a lively dance. One kind is the Virginia reel. **2** music for it. *n.* [apparently from *reel*[2]]

re e lect or **re-e lect** (rē′i lekt′), elect again. *v.*

re e lec tion or **re-e lec tion** (rē′i lek′shən), election again; election for a second time. *n.*

re en force (rē′en fôrs′), reinforce. *v.,* **re en forced, re en forc ing.**

re-en force (rē′en fôrs′), reinforce. *v.,* **re-en forced, re-en forc ing.**

re en force ment or **re-en force-ment** (rē′en fôrs′mənt), reinforcement. *n.*

re en list or **re-en list** (rē′en list′), enlist again or for an additional term. *v.*

re en list ment or **re-en list ment** (rē′en list′mənt), act or fact of reenlisting. *n.*

re en ter or **re-en ter** (rē en′tər), enter again; go in again: *reenter a room, reenter public life. v.*

re en try (rē en′trē), an entering again or returning, especially of a rocket or spacecraft into the earth's atmosphere after flight into outer space. *n., pl.* **re en tries.**

re-en try (rē en′trē), reentry. *n., pl.* **re-en tries.**

re es tab lish or **re-es tab lish** (rē′ə stab′lish), establish again; restore. *v.*

re es tab lish ment or **re-es tab-lish ment** (rē′ə stab′lish mənt), an establishing again; restoration. *n.*

re ex am i na tion or **re-ex am i-na tion** (rē′eg zam′ə nā′shən), a second or renewed examination. *n.*

re ex am ine (rē′eg zam′ən), examine

REEL

reel[1] (def. 1)
reels for winding film on a movie projector

hat, āge, fär; let, ēqual, tėrm;
it, īce; hot, ōpen, ôrder;
oil, out; cup, pút, rüle; ch, child;
ng, long; sh, she; th, thin;
ŦH, then; zh, measure;

ə represents *a* in about,
e in taken, *i* in pencil,
o in lemon, *u* in circus.

again. *v.,* **re ex am ined, re ex am in-ing.**

re-ex am ine (rē′eg zam′ən), reexamine. *v.,* **re-ex am ined, re-ex am-in ing.**

re fec tor y (ri fek′tər ē), a room for meals, especially in a monastery, convent, or school. *n., pl.* **re fec tor ies.**

re fer (ri fėr′), **1** to direct attention: *refer to a passage in the Bible. In her speech she referred to newspaper accounts of the election campaign.* **2** relate; apply: *The rule refers only to special cases.* **3** send or direct for information, help, or action: *They referred me to another department.* **4** turn for information or help: *A person refers to a dictionary to find the meaning of words.* **5** hand over; submit: *Let's refer the dispute to the umpire.* **6** think of as belonging or due; assign: *They referred their failure to bad luck. v.,* **re ferred, re fer ring.**

ref e ree (ref′ə rē′), **1** a judge of play in certain games and sports: *a football referee.* **2** person to whom something is referred for decision or settlement. **3** act as referee; act as referee in. **1,2** *n.,* **3** *v.,* **ref e reed, ref e ree ing.**

ref er ence (ref′ər əns), **1** a referring or a being referred. **2** direction of the attention: *Our history book contains many references to larger histories.* **3** statement referred to: *You will find that reference on page 16.* **4** something used for information or help: *A dictionary is a book of reference.* **5** used for information or help: *a reference library.* **6** person who can give information about another person's character or ability: *He gave his principal as a reference.* **7** statement about someone's character or ability: *When she left the company, she received an excellent reference from her boss.* **8** relation; respect; regard: *This test is to be taken by all pupils without reference to age or grade.* **1-4,6-8** *n.,* **5** *adj.*

in reference to or **with reference to,** about; concerning.

make reference to, mention: *Don't make any reference to his black eye.*

ref e ren dum (ref′ə ren′dəm),

adj.	adjective	n.	noun
adv.	adverb	prep.	preposition
conj.	conjunction	pron.	pronoun
interj.	interjection	v.	verb
sing.	singular	pl.	plural

1 process of submitting a bill already passed by the lawmaking body to the direct vote of the citizens for approval or rejection. **2** the submitting of any matter to a direct vote. *n., pl.* **ref e ren dums, ref e ren da** (ref′ə ren′də).

re fer ral (ri fėr′əl), **1** a referring. **2** person who is referred. *n.*

re fill (rē fil′ *for 1;* rē′fil′ *for 2*), **1** fill again. **2** something to refill with: *Refills can be bought for some kinds of pens and pencils.* **1** *v.,* **2** *n.*

reflector (def. 1) for flash bulb on a camera

re fine (ri fīn′), **1** make or become pure: *Sugar, oil, and metals are refined before being used.* **2** make or become fine, polished, or cultivated: *Reading good books and discussing them helped to refine her speech.* **3** make very fine, subtle, or exact. *v.,* **re fined, re fin ing.**

refine on or **refine upon, 1** improve. **2** excel.

re fined (ri fīnd′), **1** freed from impurities; made pure: *refined sugar.* **2** free from grossness, coarseness, crudeness, or vulgarity: *refined tastes, a refined voice.* **3** having or showing nice feeling, taste, manners, etc.; well-bred: *refined manners. adj.*

re fine ment (ri fīn′mənt), **1** fineness of feeling, taste, manners, or language: *Good manners and correct speech are marks of refinement.* **2** act or result of refining: *Gasoline is produced by the refinement of petroleum.* **3** improvement. *n.*

re fin er (ri fī′nər), person or thing that refines. *n.*

re fin er y (ri fī′nər ē), a building and machinery for purifying metal, sugar, petroleum, or other things. *n., pl.* **re fin er ies.**

re fin ish (rē fin′ish), give (wood, metal, etc.) a new finish. *v.*

re fit (rē fit′), **1** fit, prepare, or equip for use again: *The old ship was refitted for*

the voyage. **2** a refitting. **1** *v.,* **re fit ted, re fit ting; 2** *n.*

re flect (ri flekt′), **1** turn back or throw back (light, heat, sound, etc.): *The sidewalks reflect heat on a hot day.* **2** give back a likeness or image of: *The sky was reflected in the still pond.* **3** reproduce or show like a mirror: *The newspaper reflected the owner's opinions.* **4** think carefully: *Take time to reflect before doing important things.* **5** cast blame, reproach, or discredit: *The children's spoiled behavior reflected on their parents.* **6** serve to cast or bring: *A kind act reflects credit on the person who does it. v.*

re flec tion (ri flek′shən), **1** a reflecting or a being reflected. **2** something reflected. **3** likeness; image: *You can see your reflection in a mirror.* **4** careful thinking: *On reflection, the plan seemed too dangerous.* **5** idea or remark resulting from careful thinking. **6** remark or action that casts blame or discredit. **7** blame; discredit. *n.*

re flec tive (ri flek′tiv), **1** that reflects; reflecting: *the reflective surface of polished metal.* **2** thoughtful: *The judge had a reflective look. adj.*

re flec tor (ri flek′tər), **1** any thing, surface, or device that reflects light, heat, sound, etc., especially a piece of glass or metal, usually concave, for reflecting light in a required direction. **2** a telescope with a concave mirror which reflects and focuses light. *n.*

re flex (rē′fleks), **1** an involuntary action in direct response to a stimulation of some nerve cells. Sneezing, vomiting, and shivering are reflexes. **2** not voluntary; not controlled by the will; coming as a direct response to a stimulation of some sensory nerve cells. Yawning is a reflex action. **1** *n., pl.* **re flex es; 2** *adj.*

re flex ive (ri flek′siv), **1** (in grammar) expressing an action that refers back to the subject. **2** a reflexive verb or pronoun. In "The boy hurt himself," *hurt* and *himself* are reflexives. **1** *adj.,* **2** *n.* —**re flex′ive ly,** *adv.*

re fo rest (rē fôr′ist), replant with trees. *v.*

re fo rest a tion (rē′fôr ə stā′shən), a replanting or a being replanted with trees. *n.*

re form (ri fôrm′), **1** make better; improve by removing faults: *Some prisons try to reform criminals instead of just punishing them.* **2** become better: *They promised to reform if given another chance.* **3** a change intended to improve conditions; improvement: *The new government made many reforms.* **1,2** *v.,* **3** *n.*

re-form (rē fôrm′), **1** form again. **2** take a new shape. *v.*

ref or ma tion (ref′ər mā′shən), **1** a reforming or a being reformed; change for the better; improvement. **2 Reformation,** the great religious movement in Europe in the 1500's that aimed at reform within the Roman Catholic Church but led to the establishment of Protestant churches. *n.*

re form a to ry (ri fôr′mə tôr′ē), **1** an institution for reforming young offenders against the laws; prison for young criminals. **2** serving to reform; intended to reform. **1** *n., pl.* **re form a to ries; 2** *adj.*

re form er (ri fôr′mər), person who reforms, or tries to reform, some state of affairs, custom, etc.; supporter of reforms. *n.*

re fract (ri frakt′), bend (a ray, waves, etc.) from a straight course. Water refracts light. *v.*

refraction
In the diagram, the ray of light SP in passing into the water is refracted from its original direction SPL to SPR.

re frac tion (ri frak′shən), the turning or bending of a ray of light, sound waves, a stream of electrons, etc., when passing from one medium into another of different density. *n.*

re frac tive (ri frak′tiv), refracting; having power to refract. *adj.*

re frac tor i ly (ri frak′tər ə lē), stubbornly; obstinately. *adv.*

re frac tor i ness (ri frak′tər ē nis), refractory quality or condition. *n.*

re frac tor y (ri frak′tər ē), **1** hard to manage; stubborn; obstinate: *Mules are refractory.* **2** not yielding readily to treatment: *She had a refractory cough.* **3** hard to melt, reduce, or work: *Some ores are more refractory than others. adj.*

re frain¹ (ri frān′), hold oneself back: *Refrain from wrongdoing. v.* [from French of the 1300's *refrener,* from Latin *refrenare* furnish with a bridle]

re frain² (ri frān′), phrase or verse repeated regularly in a song or poem. In "The Star-Spangled Banner" the refrain is "O'er the land of the free and the home of the brave." *n.* [from French of the 1300's *refrain,* from *refraindre* break off, from Latin *refringere*]

re fresh (ri fresh′), make fresh again; freshen up; renew: *His bath refreshed him. He refreshed his memory by a glance at the book. She refreshed herself with a cup of tea. v.*

re fresh er (ri fresh′ər), **1** helping to renew knowledge or abilities, or to bring a person new needed knowledge:

to take a refresher course in typing.
2 person or thing that refreshes. 1 *adj.*,
2 *n.*

re fresh ing (ri fresh′ing), 1 that refreshes: *Cool drinks are refreshing on
a warm day.* 2 welcome as a pleasing change. *adj.* —**re fresh′ing ly,**
adv.

re fresh ment (ri fresh′mənt), 1 a
refreshing or a being refreshed. 2 thing
that refreshes. 3 **refreshments,** *pl.*
food or drink: *Cake and lemonade were
the refreshments at our party. n.*

re frig er ant (ri frij′ər ənt), something that cools. Ice is a refrigerant. *n.*

re frig e rate (ri frij′ə rāt′), make or
keep (food, etc.) cold or cool: *Milk,
meat, and ice cream must be refrigerated to prevent spoiling. v.,* **re-
frig e rat ed, re frig e rat ing.**

re frig e ra tion (ri frij′ə rā′shən),
act or process of cooling or keeping
cold. *n.*

re frig e ra tor (ri frij′ə rā′tər), something that keeps things cool. An electric refrigerator keeps food cool without ice. *n.*

re fu el (rē fyü′əl), 1 supply with fuel
again. 2 take on a fresh supply of
fuel. *v.*

ref uge (ref′yüj), shelter or protection
from danger or trouble; safety; security: *The cat took refuge in a tree. n.*

ref u gee (ref′yə jē′ *or* ref′yə jē′),
person who flees for refuge or safety,
especially to a foreign country, in time
of persecution, war, or disaster: *The
homeless refugees from the flooded town
were helped by the Red Cross. Many
refugees came from Europe to America. n.*

re ful gence (ri ful′jəns), a shining
brightly; radiance. *n.*

re ful gent (ri ful′jənt), shining brightly; radiant; splendid: *a refulgent sunrise.
adj.*

re fund (ri fund′ *for 1;* rē′fund *for 2,
3*), 1 pay back: *If these shoes do not
wear well, the shop will refund your
money.* 2 a return of money paid. 3 the
money paid back. 1 *v.,* 2,3 *n.*

re fur bish (rē fèr′bish), polish up
again; do up anew; brighten; renovate:
refurbish an old house. v.

re fus al (ri fyü′zəl), 1 act of refusing:
*His refusal to play the game provoked
the other boys.* 2 the right to refuse or
take a thing before it is offered to
others: *Please give me first refusal of
your car if you decide to sell it. n.*

re fuse¹ (ri fyüz′), 1 say no to; decline to accept; reject: *He refuses the
offer. They refused to go with me, so
I went by myself.* 2 say no: *She is free
to refuse.* 3 say one will not do it, give
it, etc.: *refuse to obey. v.,* **re fused,
re fus ing.** [from French of the 1300's

refuser, from Latin *refundere* pour
back]

ref use² (ref′yüs), useless stuff; waste;
rubbish: *The street-cleaning department
took away all refuse from the streets. n.*
[from French of the 1400's *refus,* from
refuser refuse¹]

ref u ta tion (ref′yə tā′shən), disproof
of a claim, opinion, or argument. *n.*

re fute (ri fyüt′), show (a claim, opinion, or argument) to be false or incorrect; prove wrong; disprove: *How
would you refute the statement that the
cow jumped over the moon? v.,* **re fut-
ed, re fut ing.**

re fut er (ri fyü′tər), person or thing
that refutes. *n.*

re gain (ri gān′), 1 get again; recover:
regain health. 2 get back to; reach
again: *You can regain the main road by
turning left two miles ahead. v.*

re gal (rē′gəl), 1 belonging to a king
or queen; royal: *regal power.* 2 fit
for a king or queen; stately; splendid;
magnificent: *It was a regal banquet.
adj.*

re gale (ri gāl′), 1 entertain agreeably;
delight with something pleasing: *Grandmother regaled us with stories about her
childhood.* 2 entertain with a choice
repast; feast: *The children regaled
themselves with ice cream and candy.
v.,* **re galed, re gal ing.**

re ga li a (ri gā′lē ə), 1 the emblems of
royalty. Crowns and scepters are regalia. 2 the emblems or decorations of
any society or order. 3 clothes, especially fine clothes: *in party regalia.
n.pl.*

re gard (ri gärd′), 1 think of; consider:
*Our school band is regarded as the best
in the state.* 2 show thought or
consideration for; care for; respect: *regard the rights of others.* 3 take notice
of; heed: *regard all traffic laws.*
4 consideration; thought; care: *Have
regard for the feelings of others.* 5 look
at; look closely at; watch: *The cat regarded me anxiously when I picked up
her kittens.* 6 a steady look; gaze: *The
man's regard seemed fixed upon some
distant object.* 7 esteem; favor; good
opinion: *The teacher has high regard for
your ability.* 8 **regards,** *pl.* good wishes; an expression of esteem: *She sends
her regards.* 9 point; particular matter.
1-3,5 *v.,* 4,6-9 *n.*

as regards, with respect to; concerning: *As regards money, I have enough.*

in regard to or **with regard to,** relating to; concerning; about; regarding:
*The teacher spoke to me in regard to
being late.*

re gard ful (ri gärd′fəl), heedful or
observant; mindful. *adj.*

re gard ing (ri gär′ding), with regard
to; concerning; about: *A letter regarding*

hat, āge, fär; let, ēqual, tèrm;
it, īce; hot, ōpen, ôrder;
oil, out; cup, pùt, rüle; ch, child;
ng, long; sh, she; th, thin;
ŦH, then; zh, measure;

ə represents *a* in about,
e in taken, *i* in pencil,
o in lemon, *u* in circus.

*the field trip to the museum was sent to
my parents. prep.*

re gard less (ri gärd′lis), 1 with no
heed; careless: *Regardless of grammar,
he said, "Him and I have went."* 2 IN-
FORMAL. in spite of what happens:
*We plan to leave on Monday, and we
will leave then, regardless.* 1 *adj.,* 2 *adv.*
—**re gard′less ly,** *adv.* —**re gard′-
less ness,** *n.*

re gat ta (ri gat′ə), a boat race or a
series of boat races: *the annual regatta
of the yacht club. n.*

re gen cy (rē′jən sē), 1 the position,
office, or function of a regent or group
of regents: *The Queen Mother held the
regency till the young king became of
age.* 2 a body of regents. 3 a government consisting of regents. 4 the time
during which there is a regency. *n., pl.*
re gen cies.

re gen e rate (ri jen′ə rāt′ *for 1-4;* ri-
jen′ər it *for 5,6*), 1 give a new and
better spiritual life to: *Being converted
regenerated the man.* 2 improve the
moral condition of; put new life and
spirit into. 3 reform. 4 grow again;
bring or come into new existence: *If a
young crab loses a claw, it will often
regenerate a new one.* 5 born again
spiritually. 6 made over in better form;
formed anew morally. 1-4 *v.,* **re gen e-
rat ed, re gen e rat ing;** 5,6 *adj.*

re gen e ra tion (ri jen′ə rā′shən), a
regenerating or a being regenerated. *n.*

re gen e ra tive (ri jen′ə rā′tiv), tending to regenerate; regenerating. *adj.*

re gent (rē′jənt), 1 person who rules
when the regular ruler is absent, disabled, or too young: *The Queen will be
the regent till her son grows up.* 2 member of a governing board. Many universities have boards of regents. *n.*

reg i cide (rej′ə sīd), 1 crime of killing
a king. 2 person who kills a king. *n.*

re gime (ri zhēm′ *or* rā zhēm′), 1 system of government or rule: *the Communist regime in China.* 2 regimen. *n.*
[from French *régime*]

ré gime (ri zhēm′ *or* rā zhēm′), regime. *n., pl.* **ré gimes.**

reg i men (rej′ə men), a set of rules or
habits of diet, exercise, or manner of

regiment

living, intended to improve health, reduce weight, etc.: *The baby's regimen includes two naps a day.* *n.*

reg i ment (rej′ə mənt *for 1,2;* rej′ə ment *for 3,4*), 1 a military unit made up of several battalions or squadrons, usually commanded by a colonel. It is smaller than a brigade. 2 a large number. 3 form into a regiment or organized group. 4 treat in a strict or uniform manner: *A totalitarian state regiments its citizens.* 1,2 *n.,* 3,4 *v.*

reg i men tal (rej′ə men′tl), 1 of or having to do with a regiment. 2 **regimentals,** *pl.* a military uniform. 1 *adj.,* 2 *n.*

reg i men ta tion (rej′ə men tā′shən), 1 formation into organized or uniform groups. 2 a making uniform. 3 subjection to control. *n.*

Re gi na (ri jī′nə), city in S Canada, capital of the province of Saskatchewan. *n.*

re gion (rē′jən), 1 a large part of the earth's surface: *the region of the equator.* 2 any place, space, or area: *an unhealthful region, a mountainous region.* 3 a part of the body: *the region of the heart.* 4 a field of thought or action; sphere: *the region of the imagination.* *n.*

re gion al (rē′jə nəl), of or in a particular region: *a regional storm.* *adj.*
—**re′gion al ly,** *adv.*

reg is ter (rej′ə stər), 1 write in a list or record: *Register the names of the new members.* 2 have one's name written in a list or record: *A person must register before he can vote.* 3 a list or record: *A register of attendance is kept in our school.* 4 book in which a list or record is kept: *Look up his record in the register.* 5 have (a letter, parcel, etc.) recorded in a post office, paying extra postage for special care in delivery: *She registered the letter containing the check.* 6 thing that records. A cash register shows the amount of money taken in. 7 indicate; record: *The thermometer registers 90 degrees.* 8 show (surprise, joy, anger, etc.) by the expression on one's face or by actions. 9 the range of a voice or an instrument. 10 an opening in a wall or floor with a device to regulate the amount of heated or cooled air that passes through. 1, 2,5,7,8 *v.,* 3,4,6,9,10 *n.*

registered nurse, a graduate nurse licensed by state authority to practice nursing.

reg is trant (rej′ə strənt), person who registers. *n.*

reg is trar (rej′ə strär), official who keeps a register; official recorder. *n.*

reg is tra tion (rej′ə strā′shən), 1 act of registering. 2 an entry in a register. 3 number of people registered: *Registration for camp is higher than last year.* *n.*

reg is try (rej′ə strē), 1 a registering; registration. 2 place where a register is kept; office of registration. 3 book in which a list or record is kept; register. *n., pl.* **reg is tries.**

re gress (ri gres′), go back; move in a backward direction. *v.*

re gres sion (ri gresh′ən), act of going back; backward movement. *n.*

re gret (ri gret′), 1 feel sorry for or about: *We regretted his absence.* 2 feel sorry; mourn: *He wrote regretting that he could not visit us.* 3 the feeling of being sorry; sense of loss; sorrow: *It is a matter of regret that I could not see my mother before leaving.* 4 **regrets,** *pl.* a polite reply declining an invitation: *She could not come to the party, but she sent regrets.* 1,2 *v.,* **re gret ted, re gret ting;** 3,4 *n.*

re gret ful (ri gret′fəl), feeling or expressing regret; sorrowful; sorry. *adj.*
—**re gret′ful ly,** *adv.*

re gret ta ble (ri gret′ə bəl), that should be or is regretted. *adj.*

re gret ta bly (ri gret′ə blē), with regret; regretfully. *adv.*

reg u lar (reg′yə lər), 1 fixed by custom or rule; usual; normal: *Six o'clock was her regular hour of rising.* 2 following some rule or principle; according to rule: *A period is the regular ending for a sentence.* 3 coming, acting, or done again and again at the same time: *Saturday is a regular holiday.* 4 steady; habitual: *A regular customer trades often at the same store.* 5 even in size, spacing, or speed; well-balanced: *regular features, regular teeth, regular breathing.* 6 symmetrical. 7 orderly; methodical: *He leads a regular life.* 8 properly fitted or trained: *The regular cook in our school cafeteria is sick.* 9 (of a word) having the usual endings; inflected in the usual way. "Ask" is a regular verb. 10 INFORMAL. thorough; complete: *a regular bore.* 11 INFORMAL. fine; agreeable: *He's a regular fellow.* 12 member of a regularly paid group of any kind: *The fire department was made up of regulars and volunteers.* 13 of or belonging to the permanent army of a country. 14 person belonging to a religious order bound by certain rules. 15 (in sports) a

player who plays in all or most of a team's games. 1-11,13 *adj.,* 12,14,15 *n.*

reg u lar i ty (reg′yə lar′ə tē), a being regular; order; system; steadiness. *n.*

reg u lar ly (reg′yə lər lē), 1 in a regular manner. 2 at regular times. *adv.*

reg u late (reg′yə lāt), 1 control by rule, principle, or system: *Private schools regulate the behavior of students.* 2 put in condition to work properly: *My watch is losing time; I will have to have it regulated.* 3 keep at some standard: *This instrument regulates the temperature of the room.* *v.,* **reg u lat ed, reg u lat ing.**

reg u la tion (reg′yə lā′shən), 1 control by rule, principle, or system. 2 rule; law: *traffic regulations.* 3 according to or required by some rule; regular; standard: *Soldiers wear a regulation uniform.* 4 usual; ordinary. 1,2 *n.,* 3,4 *adj.*

reg u la tive (reg′yə lā′tiv), regulating. *adj.*

reg u la tor (reg′yə lā′tər), 1 person or thing that regulates. 2 device in a clock or watch for causing it to go faster or slower. *n.*

reg u la to ry (reg′yə lə tôr′ē), regulating. *adj.*

re gur gi tate (rē gėr′jə tāt), 1 (of liquids, gases, undigested foods, etc.) rush, surge, or flow back. 2 throw up: *The baby regurgitated food from his stomach.* *v.,* **re gur gi tat ed, re gur gi tat ing.**

re gur gi ta tion (rē gėr′jə tā′shən), act of regurgitating. *n.*

re ha bil i tate (rē′hə bil′ə tāt), 1 restore to a good condition; make over in a new form: *The old neighborhood is to be rehabilitated.* 2 restore to former standing, rank, rights, privileges, reputation, etc.: *The former criminal rehabilitated himself and again became a trusted and respected citizen.* *v.,* **re ha bil i tat ed, re ha bil i tat ing.**

re ha bil i ta tion (rē′hə bil′ə tā′shən), restoration to a good condition or to a former standing. *n.*

re hash (rē hash′ *for 1;* rē′hash *for 2*), 1 deal with again; work up (old material) in a new or different form: *The question had been rehashed again and again.* 2 a rehashing; a putting something old into a new or different form: *That composition is simply a rehash of an article in the encyclopedia.* 1 *v.,* 2 *n.*

re hears al (ri hėr′səl), a rehearsing; performance beforehand for practice or drill. *n.*

re hearse (ri hėrs′), 1 practice (a play, part, etc.) for a public performance: *We rehearsed our parts for the school play.* 2 drill or train (a person, etc.) by repetition. 3 tell in detail; repeat: *She rehearsed all the happenings of the day* *from beginning to end. v.,* **re hearsed, re hears ing.**

Reich (rīk), Germany as a state; the German nation. *n.* [from German *Reich* empire]

reign (rān), 1 period of power of a ruler: *Queen Victoria's reign lasted sixty-four years.* 2 to rule: *A king reigns over his kingdom.* 3 act of ruling; royal power; rule: *The reign of a wise ruler benefits his country.* 4 exist everywhere; prevail: *On a still night silence reigns.* 5 existence everywhere; prevalence. 1,3,5 *n.,* 2,4 *v.*

re im burse (rē′im bėrs′), pay back. You reimburse a person for expenses made for you. *v.,* **re im bursed, re im burs ing.**

re im burse ment (rē′im bėrs′mənt), a paying back; repayment (for expenses, loss, etc.). *n.*

Reims (rēmz), city in NE France. Nearly all the French kings were crowned in its cathedral. *n.* Also, **Rheims.**

rein (rān), 1 a long, narrow strap or line fastened to the bit of a bridle, by which to guide and control an animal. A driver or rider of a horse holds the reins in his hands. 2 check or pull with reins. 3 a means of control and direction: *seize the reins of government.* 4 guide and control: *Rein your tongue. She reined her horse well.* 1,3 *n.,* 2,4 *v.*

draw rein, 1 tighten the reins. 2 slow down; stop.

give rein to, let move or act freely, without guidance or control: *give rein to one's feelings.*

take the reins, assume control: *When the President was ill, the Vice-President took the reins of government.*

re in car nate (rē′in kär′nāt), give a new body to (a soul). *v.,* **re in car nat ed, re in car nat ing.**

re in car na tion (rē′in kär nā′shən), 1 rebirth of the soul in a new body. 2 a new incarnation or embodiment. *n.*

reindeer
about 4 ft. high at the shoulder

rein deer (rān′dir′), a kind of large deer with branching antlers, living in northern regions. It is used to pull sleighs and also for meat, milk, and hides. *n., pl.* **rein deer.**

re in force (rē′in fôrs′), 1 strengthen with new force or materials: *reinforce*

an army, reinforce a bridge. 2 strengthen: *reinforce an argument, reinforce a plea, reinforce a supply.* *v.,* **re in forced, re in forc ing.** Also, **reen force** or **re-enforce.**

re in force ment (rē′in fôrs′mənt), 1 a reinforcing or a being reinforced. 2 something that reinforces. 3 **reinforcements,** *pl.* extra soldiers, warships, planes, etc.: *Reinforcements were sent to the battlefront. n.* Also, **reenforcement** or **re-enforcement.**

re in state (rē′in stāt′), put back in a former position or condition; establish again. *v.,* **re in stat ed, re in stat ing.**

re in state ment (rē′in stāt′mənt), a putting back in a former position or condition; establishing again. *n.*

re in ter pret (rē′in tėr′prit), interpret anew. *v.*

re it e rate (rē it′ə rāt′), say or do several times; repeat again and again: *The boy did not move though the teacher reiterated her command.* *v.,* **re it e rat ed, re it e rat ing.**

re it e ra tion (rē it′ə rā′shən), a reiterating; repetition. *n.*

re ject (ri jekt′ *for 1,2*; rē′jekt *for 3*), 1 refuse to take: *She rejected our help. He tried to join the army but was rejected because of poor health.* 2 throw away as useless or unsatisfactory: *Reject all apples with soft spots.* 3 a rejected person or thing. 1,2 *v.,* 3 *n.*

re jec tion (ri jek′shən), 1 a rejecting or a being rejected: *The inspector ordered the rejection of the faulty parts.* 2 thing rejected: *All rejections by the inspector were destroyed at once. n.*

re joice (ri jois′), 1 be glad; be filled with joy: *She rejoiced at our success.* 2 make glad; fill with joy. *v.,* **re joiced, re joic ing.**

re joic ing (ri jois′ing), the feeling or expression of joy. *n.*

re join[1] (rē join′), 1 join again; unite again: *The members of our family will rejoin at Thanksgiving.* 2 join the company of again: *The sailor will rejoin his comrades. v.* [re- + join]

re join[2] (ri join′), answer; reply: *"Come with me!" "Not on your life,"* he rejoined. *v.* [from French of the 1400's *rejoindre,* from *re-* back + *joindre* join]

re join der (ri join′dər), an answer to a reply; response: *a debater's rejoinder. n.*

re ju ve nate (ri jü′və nāt), make young or vigorous again; give youthful qualities to: *The long vacation rejuvenated her.* *v.,* **re ju ve nat ed, re ju ve nat ing.**

re ju ve na tion (ri jü′və nā′shən), restoration to youth, youthful appearance, vigor, etc. *n.*

re kin dle (rē kin′dl), set on fire again;

hat, āge, fär; let, ēqual, tėrm;
it, īce; hot, ōpen, ôrder;
oil, out; cup, pùt, rüle; ch, child;
ng, long; sh, she; th, thin;
ᵺ, then; zh, measure;

ə represents *a* in about,
e in taken, *i* in pencil,
o in lemon, *u* in circus.

kindle anew. *v.,* **re kin dled, re kin dling.**

re-laid (rē lād′), past tense and past participle of **re-lay.** *The pavement on our street has just been re-laid. v.*

re lapse (ri laps′), 1 fall or slip back into a former state or way of acting: *After one cry of surprise she relapsed into silence.* 2 a falling or slipping back into a former state or way of acting: *He seemed to be getting over his illness but had a relapse.* 1 *v.,* **re lapsed, re laps ing;** 2 *n.*

re late (ri lāt′), 1 give an account of; tell: *The traveler related her adventures.* 2 connect in thought or meaning: *"Better" and "best" are related to "good."* 3 be connected in any way: *We are interested in what relates to ourselves.* *v.,* **re lat ed, re lat ing.**

re lat ed (ri lā′tid), 1 connected in any way. 2 belonging to the same family; connected by a common origin: *Cousins are related. adj.* —**re lat′ed ness,** *n.*

re la tion (ri lā′shən), 1 act of telling; account: *We were interested by the hunter's relation of his adventures.* 2 connection in thought or meaning: *Your answer has no relation to the question.* 3 connection by family ties of blood or marriage; relationship: *the close relation of mother and child.* 4 person who belongs to the same family as another; relative. 5 **relations,** *pl.* dealings between persons, groups, countries, etc.: *international relations. Our firm has business relations with their firm. n.*

in relation to or **with relation to,** in reference to; in regard to; about; concerning: *We must plan in relation to the future.*

re la tion ship (ri lā′shən ship), 1 connection: *What is the relationship of clouds to rain?* 2 condition of belonging to the same family. *n.*

rel a tive (rel′ə tiv), 1 person who belongs to the same family as another, such as father, brother, aunt, nephew, or cousin. 2 related or compared to each other: *Before ordering our dinner we considered the relative merits of chicken and roast beef.* 3 depending for

707

adj. adjective	*n.* noun
adv. adverb	*prep.* preposition
conj. conjunction	*pron.* pronoun
interj. interjection	*v.* verb
sing. singular	*pl.* plural

meaning on a relation to something else: *East is a relative term; for example, Chicago is east of California but west of New York.* 4 referring to a person or thing mentioned. In "The man who wanted it is gone," *who* is a relative pronoun, and *who wanted it* is a relative clause. 5 a relative pronoun. *Who, which, what,* and *that* are relatives. 1,5 *n.,* 2-4 *adj.*

relative to, 1 about; concerning: *The teacher asked me some questions relative to my plans for the summer.* 2 in proportion to; in comparison with; for: *She is strong relative to her size.*

rel a tive ly (rel′ə tiv lē), 1 in relation to something else; comparatively: *One inch is a relatively small difference in a person's height.* 2 in relation or with reference: *the value of one thing relatively to that of other things.* 3 in proportion: *He is strong relatively to his size. adv.*

rel a tiv i ty (rel′ə tiv′ə tē), 1 a being relative. 2 theory dealing with the physical laws which govern time, space, mass, motion, and gravitation, expressed in certain equations by Albert Einstein. According to it, the only velocity we can measure is velocity relative to some body. *n.*

re lax (ri laks′), 1 loosen up; make or become less stiff or firm: *Relax your muscles to rest them. Relax when you dance.* 2 make or become less strict or severe; lessen in force: *Discipline is relaxed on the last day of school.* 3 relieve or be relieved from work or effort; give or take recreation or amusement: *Take a vacation and relax. Relax your mind.* 4 weaken: *Don't relax your efforts because the examinations are over. v.*

re lax a tion (rē′lak sā′shən), 1 a loosening: *the relaxation of the muscles.* 2 a lessening of strictness, severity, force, etc.: *the relaxation of discipline over the holidays.* 3 relief from work or effort; recreation; amusement: *Walking and reading are relaxations.* 4 condition of being relaxed. *n.*

re lay (rē′lā *for 1,3-5;* rē′lā *or* ri lā′ *for 2*), 1 a fresh supply: *New relays of men were sent to the battlefront.* 2 take and carry farther: *relay a message.* 3 a relay race. 4 one part of a relay race. 5 an electromagnetic device with a weak current which acts as a switch for a circuit with a stronger current. Relays are used in equipment for transmitting telegraph and telephone messages. 1,3-5 *n.,* 2 *v.*

re-lay (rē lā′), lay again: *That floor must be re-laid. v.,* **re-laid, re-lay ing.**

re lay race (rē′lā), race in which each member of a team runs, swims, etc., only a certain part of the distance.

re lease (ri lēs′), 1 let go: *Release the catch and the box will open.* 2 let loose; set free: *She released him from his promise.* 3 relieve: *The nurse is released from duty at seven o'clock.* 4 a letting go; setting free: *announce the release of the prisoners of war.* 5 freedom; relief: *This medicine will give you release from pain.* 6 part of a machine that sets other parts free to move. 7 the legal surrender of right, estate, etc., to another. 8 give up (legal right, claim, etc.); make over to another (property, etc.). 9 document that does this. 10 permit to be published, shown, sold, etc. 11 permission for publication, exhibition, sale, etc. 12 article, statement, etc., distributed for publication. 1-3, 8,10 *v.,* **re leased, re leas ing;** 4-7, 9,11,12 *n.*

rel e gate (rel′ə gāt), 1 put away, usually to a lower position or condition: *relegate a dress to the rag bag.* 2 send into exile; banish. 3 hand over (a matter, task, etc.). *v.,* **rel e gat ed, rel e gat ing.**

relief (def. 8)
left, bas-relief; right, high relief

re lent (ri lent′), become less harsh; be more tender and merciful: *After I pleaded for hours, my parents relented and let me go on the trip. v.*

re lent less (ri lent′lis), without pity; not relenting; unyielding; harsh: *The storm raged with relentless fury. adj.* —**re lent′less ly,** *adv.* —**re lent′less ness,** *n.*

rel e vance (rel′ə vəns), a being relevant. *n.*

rel e van cy (rel′ə vən sē), relevance. *n.*

rel e vant (rel′ə vənt), bearing upon or connected with the matter in hand; to the point: *relevant questions. adj.*

re li a bil i ty (ri lī′ə bil′ə tē), quality of being reliable; trustworthiness; dependability: *We bought our washing machine from that store because it has a reputation for reliability. n.*

re li a ble (ri lī′ə bəl), worthy of trust; that can be depended on: *a reliable brand of canned goods. A teller in a bank must be reliable. adj.*

re li a bly (ri lī′ə blē), in a reliable manner; to a reliable extent or degree. *adv.*

re li ance (ri lī′əns), 1 trust or dependence: *A child has reliance on his parents.* 2 confidence. 3 thing on which one depends. *n.*

re li ant (ri lī′ənt), 1 trusting or depending; relying. 2 confident. 3 relying on oneself. *adj.*

rel ic (rel′ik), 1 thing left from the past: *This ruined bridge is a relic of the Civil War.* 2 something belonging to a holy person, kept as a sacred memorial. 3 object having interest because of its age or its associations with the past; keepsake; souvenir. *n.*

re lief (ri lēf′), 1 the lessening of, or freeing from, a pain, burden, difficulty, etc.: *His relief from pain came as the medicine began to work.* 2 something that lessens or frees from pain, burden, difficulty, etc.; aid; help: *Relief was sent to the people made homeless by the tornado.* 3 help given to poor people. 4 something that makes a pleasing change or lessens strain. 5 freedom from a post of duty: *This nurse is on duty from seven in the morning until seven at night, with only two hours' relief.* 6 change of persons on duty. 7 persons who relieve others from duty; person who does this: *The nurse's relief arrives at seven.* 8 projection of figures or designs from a surface in sculpture, drawing, or painting. 9 figure or design standing out from the surface from which it is cut, shaped, or stamped. 10 the appearance of standing out from a surface, given to a drawing or painting by the use of shading, color, etc. 11 differences in height between the summits and lowlands of a region. *n.*

in relief, standing out from a surface.
on relief, receiving money to live on from public funds.

relief map, map that shows the different heights of a surface by using shading, colors, etc., or solid materials such as clay.

re lieve (ri lēv′), 1 make less; make easier; reduce the pain or trouble of: *Aspirin will relieve a headache. We telephoned to relieve our parent's uneasiness.* 2 set free: *Your coming relieves me of the bother of writing a long letter.* 3 free (a person on duty) by taking his place. 4 bring aid to; help: *Soldiers were sent to relieve the fort.* 5 give variety or a pleasing change to: *The black dress was relieved by red trimming.* 6 make stand out more clearly. *v.,* **re lieved, re liev ing.**

re liev er (ri lē′vər), person or thing that relieves. *n.*

re li gion (ri lij′ən), 1 belief in and worship of God or gods. 2 a particular system of faith and worship: *the Christian religion, the Moslem religion. n.*

re li gi os i ty (ri lij′ē os′ə tē), 1 religious feeling or sentiment; piety. 2 affectation of religious feeling. *n.*

re li gious (ri lij′əs), 1 of religion; connected with religion: *religious meetings, religious books, religious differences.* 2 much interested in religion; devoted to religion: *He is very religious and goes to church every day.* 3 monk, nun, friar, etc.; member of a religious order: *There are sixty religious teaching in this school.* 4 very careful; strict; scrupulous: *Mother gave religious attention to the doctor's orders.* 1,2,4 *adj.,* 3 *n., pl.* **re li gious. —re li′gious ly,** *adv.* **—re li′gious ness,** *n.*

re lin quish (ri ling′kwish), give up; let go: *The small dog relinquished his bone to the big dog. She has relinquished all hope of going to Europe this year. v.*

re lin quish ment (ri ling′kwish mənt), a giving up; abandonment; surrender. *n.*

rel ish (rel′ish), 1 a pleasant taste; good flavor: *Hunger gives relish to simple food.* 2 something to add flavor to food. Olives and pickles are relishes. 3 liking; appetite; enjoyment: *The hungry girl ate with great relish. The teacher has no relish for jokes.* 4 like the taste of; like; enjoy: *A cat relishes cream. We did not relish the prospect of staying after school.* 1-3 *n.,* 4 *v.*

re live (rē liv′), live over or through again. *v.,* **re lived, re liv ing.**

re load (rē lōd′), load again. *v.*

re lo cate (rē lō′kāt), locate or settle anew; move to a new location. *v.,* **re lo cat ed, re lo cat ing.**

re luc tance (ri luk′təns), 1 a reluctant feeling or action; unwillingness: *She agreed with reluctance to take part in the game.* 2 slowness in action because of unwillingness. *n.*

re luc tant (ri luk′tənt), 1 unwilling; showing unwillingness: *The teacher led the reluctant boy to the principal.* 2 slow to act because unwilling: *I am reluctant to go out in very cold weather. adj.* **—re luc′tant ly,** *adv.*

re ly (ri lī′), depend or trust: *Rely on your own efforts. I relied upon your promise. v.,* **re lied, re ly ing.**

re main (ri mān′), 1 continue in a place; stay: *We shall remain at the seashore till October.* 2 continue; last;

keep on: *The town remains the same year after year.* 3 be left: *A few apples remain on the trees. If you take 2 from 5, 3 remains.* 4 **remains,** *pl.* **a** what is left: *The remains of the meal were fed to the dog.* **b** a dead body: *Washington's remains are buried at Mount Vernon.* 1-3 *v.,* 4 *n.*

re main der (ri mān′dər), 1 the part left over; the rest: *After studying an hour, she spent the remainder of the afternoon in play.* 2 in arithmetic: **a** a number left over after subtracting one number from another. In 9 − 2, the remainder is 7. **b** number left over after dividing one number by another. In 14 ÷ 3, the quotient is 4 with a remainder of 2. *n.*

re make (rē māk′), make anew; make over. *v.,* **re made** (rē mād′), **re mak ing.**

re mand (ri mand′), 1 send back. 2 send back (a prisoner or an accused person) into custody. 3 a remanding. 1,2 *v.,* 3 *n.*

re mark (ri märk′), 1 say in a few words; state; comment: *She remarked that soon it would be warm enough to go swimming.* 2 something said in a few words; short statement: *The president made a few remarks.* 3 notice; observe: *Did you remark that queer cloud?* 4 act of noticing; observation. 1,3 *v.,* 2, 4 *n.*

re mark a ble (ri mär′kə bəl), worthy of notice; unusual: *He has a remarkable memory. adj.* **—re mark′a ble ness,** *n.*

re mark a bly (ri mär′kə blē), notably; unusually: *The day of the blizzard was remarkably cold. adv.*

re mar riage (rē mar′ij), any marriage after one's first marriage. *n.*

re mar ry (rē mar′ē), marry again. *v.,* **re mar ried, re mar ry ing.**

Rem brandt (rem′brant), 1606–1669, Dutch painter and etcher. *n.*

re me di a ble (ri mē′dē ə bəl), that can be remedied or cured. *adj.*

re me di al (ri mē′dē əl), remedying; curing; helping; relieving. *adj.* **—re me′di al ly,** *adv.*

rem e dy (rem′ə dē), 1 a means of removing or relieving diseases or any bad condition; cure: *Aspirin and a mustard plaster are two old cold remedies.* 2 put right; make right; cure: *A thorough cleaning of the carburetor remedied the trouble.* 1 *n., pl.* **rem e dies;** 2 *v.,* **rem e died, rem e dy ing.**

re mem ber (ri mem′bər), 1 call back to mind: *I can't remember that man's name.* 2 have (something) return to the mind: *Then I remembered where I was.* 3 keep in mind; take care not to forget: *Remember me when I am gone.* 4 keep in mind as deserving a reward, gift, etc.: *Uncle remembered us in his will.*

5 mention (a person) as sending friendly greetings: *She asked to be remembered to you. v.*

re mem brance (ri mem′brəns), 1 power to remember; act of remembering; memory: *America holds its heroes in grateful remembrance.* 2 anything or action that makes one remember a person; souvenir; keepsake. 3 **remembrances,** *pl.* greetings: *Give my remembrances to your sister when you write to her. n.*

re mind (ri mīnd′), make (one) think of something; cause to remember: *This picture reminds me of a story I heard. v.*

re mind er (ri mīn′dər), something to help one remember. *n.*

rem i nisce (rem′ə nis′), talk or think about past experiences or events. *v.,* **rem i nisced, rem i nisc ing.**

rem i nis cence (rem′ə nis′ns), 1 a remembering; recalling past persons, events, etc. 2 Often, **reminiscences,** *pl.* account of something remembered; recollection: *reminiscences of college, an old man's reminiscences. n.*

rem i nis cent (rem′ə nis′nt), 1 recalling past persons, events, etc.: *reminiscent talk.* 2 awakening memories of something else; suggestive: *a manner reminiscent of a statelier age. adj.* **—rem′i nis′cent ly,** *adv.*

re miss (ri mis′), careless or slack in doing what one has to do; negligent: *A policeman who lets a thief escape is remiss in his duties. adj.* **—re miss′ly,** *adv.* **—re miss′ness,** *n.*

re mis sion (ri mish′ən), 1 a letting off (from debt, punishment, etc.): *The bankrupt sought remission of his debts.* 2 pardon; forgiveness: *remission of sins.* 3 a lessening (of pain, force, labor, etc.): *The storm continued without remission. n.*

re mit (ri mit′), 1 send money to a person or place: *Enclosed is our bill; please remit.* 2 send (money due). 3 refrain from carrying out; cancel: *The governor is remitting the prisoner's punishment.* 4 pardon; forgive: *the power to remit sins.* 5 make less; decrease: *After we had rowed the boat into calm water, we remitted our*

adj.	adjective	*n.*	noun
adv.	adverb	*prep.*	preposition
conj.	conjunction	*pron.*	pronoun
interj.	interjection	*v.*	verb
sing.	singular	*pl.*	plural

efforts. *v.*, **re mit ted, re mit ting.**

re mit tance (ri mit′ns), **1** a sending money to someone at a distance. **2** the money that is sent. *n.*

re mit ter (ri mit′ər), person or thing that remits. *n.*

rem nant (rem′nənt), **1** a small part left: *This town has only a remnant of its former population.* **2** piece of cloth, ribbon, lace, etc., left after the rest has been used or sold. *n.*

re mod el (rē mod′l), make over; change or alter: *The old barn was remodeled into a house.* *v.*

re mon strance (ri mon′strəns), act of remonstrating; protest; complaint. *n.*

re mon strate (ri mon′strāt), speak, reason, or plead in complaint or protest: *The teacher remonstrated with us about our unruly behavior.* *v.*, **re mon strated, re mon strat ing.**

re morse (ri môrs′), deep, painful regret for having done wrong: *The thief felt remorse for his crime and confessed.* *n.*

re morse ful (ri môrs′fəl), feeling or expressing remorse. *adj.* —**re morse′ful ly,** *adv.*

re morse less (ri môrs′lis), **1** without remorse. **2** pitiless; cruel: *a remorseless slaughter.* *adj.* —**re morse′less ly,** *adv.*

re mote (ri mōt′), **1** far away; far off: *The North Pole is a remote part of the world. Dinosaurs lived in remote ages.* **2** out of the way; secluded: *Mail comes to this remote village only once a week.* **3** distant: *He is a remote relative.* **4** slight; faint: *I haven't the remotest idea what you mean.* *adj.*, **re mot er, re mot est.** —**re mote′ly,** *adv.* —**re mote′ness,** *n.*

remote control, control from a distance of a machine, operation, etc., usually by electrical impulses or radio signals: *Some model airplanes can be flown by remote control.*

re mount (rē mount′ *for 1,2;* rē′mount′ *for 3*), **1** mount again: *remount a picture, remount a horse.* **2** furnish with fresh horses. **3** a fresh horse, or a supply of fresh horses, for use. **1,2** *v.*, **3** *n.*

re mov a ble (ri mü′və bəl), that can be removed. *adj.*

re mov al (ri mü′vəl), **1** a removing; taking away: *After the removal of the soup, fish was served.* **2** a change of

place: *The store announced its removal to larger quarters.* **3** dismissal from an office or position. *n.*

re move (ri müv′), **1** move from a place or position; take off; take away: *Remove your hat.* **2** get rid of; put an end to: *An experiment removed all our doubt about the fact that water is made up of two gases.* **3** dismiss from an office or position: *The mayor removed the chief of police for failing to do his duty.* **4** go away; move away. **5** a moving away. **6** step or degree of distance: *At every remove the mountain seemed smaller.* **1-4** *v.*, **re moved, re mov ing; 5,6** *n.*

re mov er (ri mü′vər), person or thing that removes: *a bottle of ink remover.* *n.*

re mu ne rate (ri myü′nə rāt′), pay for work, services, trouble, etc.; reward: *The club remunerated the speaker.* *v.*, **re mu ne rat ed, re mu ne rat ing.**

re mu ne ra tion (ri myü′nə rā′shən), a reward; pay; payment. *n.*

re mu ne ra tive (ri myü′nə rā′tiv), paying; profitable. *adj.*

Re mus (rē′məs), (in Roman legends) the twin brother of Romulus. *n.*

ren ais sance (ren′ə säns′ *or* ren′ə-säns), **1** a new birth; revival. **2 the Renaissance, a** the great revival of art and learning in Europe during the 1300's, 1400's and 1500's. **b** the period of time when this revival occurred. **c** the style of art, architecture, etc., of this period. *n.*

Renaissance (def. 2c)
an Italian church built in the 1400's

re nal (rē′nl), of, having to do with, or located near the kidneys. *adj.*

re name (rē nām′), give a new name to; name again. *v.*, **re named, re nam ing.**

re nas cence (ri nas′ns *or* ri nā′sns), **1** a new birth; revival; renewal: *a renascence of religion.* **2 Renascence,** the Renaissance. *n.*

re nas cent (ri nas′nt *or* ri nā′snt), being born again; reviving; springing again into being or vigor. *adj.*

rend (rend), **1** pull apart violently; tear: *Wolves will rend a lamb in pieces.* **2** split: *Lightning rent the tree.* **3** disturb violently: *She was rent by a wish to*

keep the money she found and the knowledge that she ought to return it. **4** remove with force or violence. *v.*, **rent, rend ing.**

ren der (ren′dər), **1** cause to become; make: *Fright rendered me speechless.* **2** give; do: *render judgment. She rendered us a great service by her help.* **3** hand in; report: *The treasurer rendered an account of all the money spent.* **4** give in return: *Render thanks for your blessings.* **5** pay as due: *The conquered rendered tribute to the conqueror.* **6** bring out the meaning of; represent: *The actor rendered the part of Hamlet well.* **7** play or sing (music). **8** change from one language to another; translate: *She rendered a French poem into English.* **9** give up; surrender: *The knights rendered their swords to the victors.* **10** melt (fat, etc.); clarify or extract by melting. *Fat from hogs is rendered for lard.* *v.*

ren dez vous (rän′də vü), **1** an appointment or engagement to meet at a fixed place or time; meeting by agreement. **2** a meeting place; gathering place: *The family's favorite rendezvous was the garden.* **3** place agreed on for a meeting at a certain time, especially of troops or ships. **4** a meeting at a fixed place or time: *the rendezvous of a lunar module and the command ship.* **5** meet at a rendezvous. **1-4** *n., pl.* **ren dez vous** (rän′də vüz); **5** *v.*, **ren dez voused** (rän′də vüd), **ren dez vous ing** (rän′də vü′ing).

ren di tion (ren dish′ən), **1** act of rendering. **2** the rendering of a dramatic part, music, etc., so as to bring out the meaning. **3** translation. *n.*

ren e gade (ren′ə gād), **1** deserter from a religious faith, a political party, etc.; traitor. **2** like a traitor; deserting; disloyal. **1** *n.*, **2** *adj.*

re nege (ri nig′), **1** fail to play a card of the same suit as that first played, although one is able to do so. It is against the rules of card games to renege. **2** INFORMAL. back out; fail to follow up: *renege on a promise or responsibility.* *v.*, **re neged, re neg ing.**

re new (ri nü′ *or* ri nyü′), **1** make new again; make like new; restore: *Rain renews the greenness of the fields.* **2** begin again; get again; say, do, or give again: *He renewed his efforts to open the window.* **3** replace by new material or a new thing of the same sort; fill again: *The well renews itself no matter how much water is taken away.* **4** give or get for a new period: *We renewed our lease for another year.* *v.*

re new a ble (ri nü′ə bəl *or* ri nyü′-bəl), that can be renewed: *a renewable contract.* *adj.*

re new al (ri nü′əl *or* ri nyü′əl), a renewing or a being renewed: *When hot weather comes there will be a renewal of interest in swimming. n.*

ren net (ren′it), substance containing rennin, obtained from the stomach lining of a calf or other ruminant, used for making cheese and junket. *n.*

ren nin (ren′ən), enzyme in the gastric juice that coagulates or curdles milk. *n.*

Re no (rē′nō), city in W Nevada. *n.*

Ren oir (ren′wär), **Pierre Auguste,** 1841-1919, French painter. *n.*

re nounce (ri nouns′), **1** declare that one gives up; give up entirely; give up: *He renounces his claim to the money.* **2** cast off; refuse to recognize as one's own: *The people renounced the dictator.* *v.,* **re nounced, re nounc ing.**

re nounce ment (ri nouns′mənt), a giving up; renunciation. *n.*

ren o vate (ren′ə vāt), make new again; make like new; restore to good condition: *renovate a garment or a house.* *v.,* **ren o vat ed, ren o vat ing.**

ren o va tion (ren′ə vā′shən), restoration to good condition; renewal. *n.*

ren o va tor (ren′ə vā′tər), person or thing that renovates. *n.*

re nown (ri noun′), fame: *A doctor who finds a cure for a disease wins renown. n.*

re nowned (ri nound′), famous. *adj.*

rent[1] (rent), **1** a regular payment for the use of property. **2** pay at regular times for the use of (property): *We rent a house from them.* **3** receive regular pay for the use of (property): *They rent several other houses.* **4** be leased or let for rent: *This farm rents for $1500 a year.* **1** *n.,* **2-4** *v.* [from French of the 1100's *rente,* from assumed Latin *rendita,* from *rendere* render] —**rent′er,** *n.*

for rent, available in return for rent paid: *That vacant apartment is for rent.*

rent[2] (rent), **1** a torn place; tear; split. **2** torn; split. **3** past tense and past participle of **rend.** *The tree was rent by the wind.* **1** *n.,* **2** *adj.,* **3** *v.*

rent al (ren′tl), **1** amount received or paid as rent: *The yearly rental of her house is $1800.* **2** something rented. **3** having to do with or collecting rent: *a rental agent.* **1,2** *n.,* **3** *adj.*

re nun ci a tion (ri nun′sē ā′shən), a giving up of a right, title, possession, etc.; a renouncing. *n.*

re o pen (rē ō′pən), **1** open again: *He reopened the window when it grew warmer outside. School will reopen in September.* **2** discuss again: *The matter is settled and cannot be reopened. v.*

re or gan i za tion (rē ôr′gə nə-zā′shən), a reorganizing or a being reorganized. *n.*

re or gan ize (rē ôr′gə nīz), organize anew; form again; arrange in a new way: *Classes will be reorganized after*

the first four weeks. *v.,* **re or gan ized, re or gan iz ing.**

Rep., 1 Republic. **2** Republican.

re paid (ri pād′), past tense and past participle of **repay.** *She repaid the money she had borrowed. All debts should be repaid. v.*

re pair[1] (ri per′ *or* ri par′), **1** put in good condition again; mend: *He repairs shoes.* **2** act or work of repairing: *Repairs on the school building are made during the summer.* **3** instance or piece of repairing. **4** condition fit to be used: *The state keeps the roads in repair.* **5** condition with respect to repairing: *The house was in bad repair.* **6** make up for: *How can I repair the harm done?* **1,6** *v.,* **2-5** *n.* [from Latin *reparare,* from *re-* again + *parare* prepare] —**re pair′er,** *n.*

re pair[2] (ri per′ *or* ri par′), go (to a place): *After dinner we repaired to the porch. v.* [from French of the 1300's *repairier,* from Latin *repatriare* repatriate, from *re-* back + *patria* native land]

re pair a ble (ri per′ə bəl *or* ri par′ə-bəl), that can be repaired. *adj.*

re pair man (ri per′man′ *or* ri-par′man′), man whose work is repairing. *n., pl.* **re pair men.**

rep ar a ble (rep′ər ə bəl), that can be repaired or remedied. *adj.*

rep a ra tion (rep′ə rā′shən), **1** a giving of satisfaction or compensation for wrong or injury done. **2** **reparations,** *pl.* compensation for wrong or injury, especially payments made by a defeated country for the devastation of territory during war: *England and France demanded reparations from Germany after World War I.* **3** a repairing or a being repaired; restoration to good condition. *n.*

rep ar tee (rep′ər tē′), **1** a witty reply or replies. **2** cleverness and wit in making replies. *n.*

re past (ri past′), meal; food: *Breakfast at our house is a light repast. n.*

re pa tri ate (rē pā′trē āt), send back or restore to one's own country: *After peace was declared, refugees and prisoners of war were repatriated. v.,* **re pa-tri at ed, re pa tri at ing.**

re pa tri a tion (rē pā′trē ā′shən), restoration to one's own country. *n.*

re pay (ri pā′), **1** pay back; give back: *He tried to repay the money he had borrowed.* **2** make return for: *No thanks can repay such kindness.* **3** make return to: *Think nothing of it; your happiness more than repays me. v.,* **re paid, re pay ing.**

re pay ment (ri pā′mənt), payment in return for something. *n.*

re peal (ri pēl′), **1** take back; withdraw; do away with: *The 18th amend-*

hat, āge, fär; let, ēqual, tėrm; it, īce; hot, ōpen, ôrder; oil, out; cup, pùt, rüle; ch, child; ng, long; sh, she; th, thin; ᵺ, then; zh, measure;

ə represents *a* in about, *e* in taken, *i* in pencil, *o* in lemon, *u* in circus.

ment of the U.S. Constitution was repealed by the 21st. **2** act of repealing; withdrawal; abolition: *She voted for the repeal of that law.* **1** *v.,* **2** *n.*

re peat (ri pēt′), **1** do or make again: *repeat an error.* **2** say again: *repeat a word for emphasis.* **3** say over; recite: *repeat a poem from memory.* **4** say after another says: *Repeat the oath after me.* **5** tell to another or others: *I promised not to repeat the secret.* **6** a repeating. **7** thing repeated. **8** passage in music to be repeated. **1-5** *v.,* **6-8** *n.* —**re peat′er,** *n.*

repeat oneself, say what one has already said.

re peat ed (ri pē′tid), said, done, or made more than once: *Her repeated efforts at last won success. adj.* —**re peat′ed ly,** *adv.*

re pel (ri pel′), **1** force back; drive back; drive away: *They repelled the enemy. We can repel bad thoughts.* **2** keep off or out; fail to mix with: *Oil and water repel each other. This tent repels moisture.* **3** force apart or away by some inherent force: *Particles with similar electric charges repel each other.* **4** be displeasing to; cause disgust in: *Spiders and worms repel me.* **5** reject: *repel a proposition. v.,* **re pelled, re-pel ling.**

re pel lent (ri pel′ənt), **1** disagreeable or distasteful; unattractive: *a person with a cold, repellent manner. Cheating and lying are repellent to most people.* **2** repelling; driving back. **3** anything that repels: *We sprayed insect repellent on our arms and legs before we went on the picnic.* **1,2** *adj.,* **3** *n.*

re pent (ri pent′), **1** feel sorry for having done wrong and seek forgiveness: *The sinner repented.* **2** feel sorry for; regret: *They bought a white rug and repented their choice. v.*

re pent ance (ri pen′təns), sorrow for having done wrong; regret. *n.*

re pent ant (ri pen′tənt), repenting; feeling regret; sorry for wrongdoing: *a repentant criminal. adj.* —**re pent′ant ly,** *adv.*

re per cus sion (rē′pər kush′ən), **1** an indirect influence or reaction from an

711

adj. adjective	*n.* noun
adv. adverb	*prep.* preposition
conj. conjunction	*pron.* pronoun
interj. interjection	*v.* verb
sing. singular	*pl.* plural

event: *repercussions of war.* 2 sound flung back; echo. 3 a springing back; rebound; recoil: *the repercussion of a cannon. n.*

rep er toire (rep′ər twär), the list of plays, operas, parts, pieces, etc., that a company, an actor, a musician, or a singer is prepared to perform. *n.*

rep er to ry (rep′ər tôr′ē), 1 repertoire. 2 store or stock of things ready for use. *n., pl.* **rep er to ries.**

rep e ti tion (rep′ə tish′ən), 1 a repeating; doing again; saying again: *Repetition helps learning.* 2 thing repeated; repeated occurrence. *n.*

rep e ti tious (rep′ə tish′əs), full of repetitions; repeating in a tiresome way. *adj.* —**rep′e ti′tious ly,** *adv.* —**rep′e ti′tious ness,** *n.*

re pet i tive (ri pet′ə tiv), of or characterized by repetition. *adj.*

re place (ri plās′), 1 fill or take the place of: *A substitute replaced our teacher.* 2 get another in place of: *I will replace the cup I broke.* 3 put back; put in place again: *Replace the books on the shelf. v.,* **re placed, re plac ing.**

re place ment (ri plās′mənt), 1 a replacing or a being replaced: *the replacement of steam locomotives by diesel engines.* 2 something or someone that replaces. *n.*

re play (rē plā′ *for 1;* rē′plā′ *for 2,3*), 1 play (a match, game, etc.) again. 2 a match or game played again. 3 a rerun of the videotape of a play, or portion of a game that is being televised: *We saw the touchdown again on the replay.* 1 *v.,* 2,3 *n.*

re plen ish (ri plen′ish), fill again; provide a new supply for: *Once our natural resources are used up we cannot replenish them. v.* —**re plen′ish er,** *n.*

re plen ish ment (ri plen′ish mənt), 1 a replenishing or a being replenished. 2 a fresh supply. *n.*

re plete (ri plēt′), abundantly supplied; filled: *The tour of London was replete with unexpected thrills. adj.*

re ple tion (ri plē′shən), a being replete; fullness. *n.*

rep li ca (rep′lə kə), copy; reproduction: *There is a replica of the Mayflower in Plymouth, Massachusetts. n., pl.* **rep li cas.**

re ply (ri plī′), 1 answer by words or

action; respond: *She replied with a shout. The enemy replied to the attack with heavy gunfire.* 2 act of replying; response: *I didn't hear your reply to the question.* 1 *v.,* **re plied, re ply ing;** 2 *n., pl.* **re plies.**

re port (ri pôrt′), 1 an account of something seen, heard, read, done, or considered. 2 an account officially or formally expressed, generally in writing: *a school report, a committee report to the President.* 3 make a report; give an account of something; announce or state: *Our treasurer reports that all dues are paid up. The rules committee will report after lunch.* 4 repeat (what one has heard, seen, etc.); bring back an account of; describe; tell: *The radio reports the news and weather. The divers reported the treasures they had found in the sunken ship.* 5 present oneself; appear: *Report for duty at 9 a.m.* 6 announce as a wrongdoer; denounce: *report someone to the police.* 7 the sound of a shot or an explosion: *the report of a gun.* 8 common talk; rumor: *Report has it that our neighbors are leaving town.* 9 reputation: *a just man of good report.* 1,2,7-9 *n.,* 3-6 *v.*

re port a ble (ri pôr′tə bəl), capable of being reported; worth reporting. *adj.*

report card, a report sent regularly by a school to parents or guardians, indicating the quality of a student's work.

re port ed ly (ri pôr′tid lē), according to reports: *A new school is reportedly going to be built next year. adv.*

re port er (ri pôr′tər), 1 person who reports. 2 person who gathers news for a newspaper, magazine, radio or television station, etc. *n.*

re pose[1] (ri pōz′), 1 rest or sleep: *Do not disturb her repose.* 2 lie at rest: *The cat reposed upon the cushion.* 3 lay to rest: *Repose yourself in the hammock.* 4 quietness; ease: *She has repose of manner.* 5 peace; calmness: *the repose of the country.* 1,4,5 *n.,* 2,3 *v.,* **re posed, re pos ing.** [from French of the 1400's *repos,* from *reposer* to repose, from Latin *repausare,* from *re-* again + *pausare* to pause]

re pose[2] (ri pōz′), put; place: *We repose complete confidence in his honesty. v.,* **re posed, re pos ing.** [from Latin *repositum* placed back, from *re-* back + *ponere* to place]

re pos i to ry (ri poz′ə tôr′ē), place or container where things are stored or kept: *The box was a repository for old magazines. n., pl.* **re pos i to ries.**

re pos sess (rē′pə zes′), possess again; get possession of again. *v.*

rep re hend (rep′ri hend′), reprove or blame. *v.*

rep re hen si ble (rep′ri hen′sə bəl), deserving reproof or blame: *Cheating is a reprehensible act. adj.*

rep re hen si bly (rep′ri hen′sə blē), in a reprehensible manner. *adv.*

rep re sent (rep′ri zent′), 1 stand for; be a sign or symbol of: *The 50 stars in our flag represent the 50 states.* 2 act in place of; speak and act for: *We chose a committee to represent us.* 3 act the part of: *Each child will represent an animal at the party.* 4 show in a picture, statue, carving, etc.; give a likeness of; portray: *This painting by Leonardo da Vinci represents the Last Supper.* 5 be a type of; be an example of: *A log represents a very simple kind of boat.* 6 describe; set forth: *He represented the plan as safe, but it was not.* 7 bring before the mind; make one think of: *His fears represented the undertaking as impossible. v.*

rep re sen ta tion (rep′ri zen tā′shən), 1 act of representing. 2 condition or fact of being represented: *"Taxation without representation is tyranny."* 3 representatives considered as a group. 4 likeness; picture; model. 5 performance of a play; presentation: *A representation of the story of Rip Van Winkle will be given in the school assembly today.* 6 account; statement: *They deceived us by false representations.* 7 protest; complaint: *make representations to the police about a nuisance. n.*

rep re sen ta tion al (rep′ri zentā′shə nəl), of or having to do with representation. *adj.*

rep re sent a tive (rep′ri zen′tə tiv), 1 person appointed or elected to act or speak for others: *He is the club's representative at the convention.* 2 **Representative,** member of the House of Representatives. 3 having its citizens represented by chosen persons: *a representative government.* 4 representing: *Images representative of animals were made by the children.* 5 a typical example; type: *The tiger is a representative of the cat family.* 6 serving as an example of; typical: *Oak and maple are representative American hardwoods.* 1,2,5 *n.,* 3,4,6 *adj.*

re press (ri pres′), 1 prevent from acting; check: *She repressed an impulse to cough.* 2 keep down; put down; suppress: *repress a revolt. v.*

re pres sion (ri presh′ən), 1 act of repressing: *The repression of a laugh made him choke.* 2 condition of being repressed: *Repression made the people revolt against the government. n.*

re pres sive (ri pres′iv), tending to repress; having power to repress. *adj.*

re prieve (ri prēv′), 1 postpone the punishment of (a person), especially the execution of (a person condemned to death. 2 a delay in carrying out a punishment, especially of the death penalty. 3 the order giving authority for such delay. 4 temporary relief from any evil or trouble. 5 give such relief to. 1,5 *v.*, **re prieved, re priev ing**; 2-4 *n.*

rep ri mand (rep'rə mand), 1 a severe or formal reproof. 2 reprove severely or formally: *The careless captain was reprimanded and demoted.* 1 *n.*, 2 *v.*

re print (rē print' *for 1*; rē'print' *for 2*), 1 print again; print a new impression of. 2 a reprinting; a new impression of printed work. 1 *v.*, 2 *n.*

re pris al (ri prī'zəl), injury done in return for injury, especially by one nation to another. *n.*

re proach (ri prōch'), 1 blame or censure: *Their conduct is above reproach.* 2 to blame; censure: *They reproached me for being late.* 3 a cause of blame or disgrace: *bring reproach on one's family.* 4 to disgrace; shame: *reproach one's life.* 5 object of blame, censure, or disapproval. 6 expression of blame, censure, or disapproval. 1,3,5,6 *n., pl.* **re proach es**; 2,4 *v.*

re proach ful (ri prōch'fəl), full of reproach; expressing reproach. *adj.* —**re proach'ful ly**, *adv.*

rep ro bate (rep'rə bāt), 1 a very wicked or unprincipled person; scoundrel. 2 very wicked; unprincipled. 1 *n.*, 2 *adj.*

rep ro ba tion (rep'rə bā'shən), disapproval; condemnation; censure. *n.*

re pro duce (rē'prə düs' *or* rē'prə dyüs'), 1 produce again; make or create anew: *Some animals are able to reproduce lost parts or organs of their bodies. The exact conditions that existed ten years ago cannot be reproduced today.* 2 make a copy of: *Can you reproduce my handwriting?* 3 produce offspring: *Most plants reproduce by seeds.* *v.*, **re pro duced, re pro duc ing**.

re pro duc er (rē'prə dü'sər *or* rē'prə dyü'sər), person or thing that reproduces. *n.*

re pro duc i ble (rē'prə dü'sə bəl *or* rē'prə dyü'sə bəl), that can be reproduced. *adj.*

re pro duc tion (rē'prə duk'shən), 1 a reproducing or a being reproduced: *the reproduction of sounds.* 2 a copy. 3 process by which animals and plants produce offspring. *n.*

re pro duc tive (rē'prə duk'tiv), 1 that reproduces. 2 for or concerned with reproduction. *adj.* —**re'pro duc'tive ly**, *adv.*

re proof (ri prüf'), words of blame or disapproval; rebuke. *n.*

re prove (ri prüv'), show disapproval

of; find fault with; scold: *Reprove the children for teasing the cat.* *v.*, **re proved, re prov ing**.

rep tile (rep'təl), 1 any of a group of cold-blooded vertebrates which usually have skin covered with horny plates or scales. Reptiles creep or crawl. Snakes, lizards, turtles, alligators, and crocodiles are reptiles. 2 of or like a reptile; crawling; creeping. 3 a low, mean person. 1,3 *n.*, 2 *adj.*

rep til i an (rep til'ē ən), 1 of or having to do with reptiles. 2 like a reptile; base; mean. 3 a reptile. 1,2 *adj.*, 3 *n.*

re pub lic (ri pub'lik), nation or state in which the citizens elect representatives to manage the government, which is usually headed by a president. The United States and Mexico are republics. *n.*

re pub li can (ri pub'lə kən), 1 of a republic; like that of a republic: *Many countries have a republican form of government.* 2 person who favors a republic: *The republicans fought with the king's supporters.* 3 **Republican**, **a** of the Republican Party. **b** member of the Republican Party. 1,3a *adj.*, 2,3b *n.*

Republican Party, one of the two main political parties in the United States. The other is the Democratic Party.

re pu di ate (ri pyü'dē āt), 1 refuse to accept; reject: *repudiate a doctrine.* 2 refuse to acknowledge or pay: *repudiate a debt.* 3 cast off; disown: *repudiate a son.* *v.*, **re pu di at ed, re pu di at ing**.

re pu di a tion (ri pyü'dē ā'shən), a repudiating or a being repudiated. *n.*

re pug nance (ri pug'nəns), strong dislike, distaste, or aversion: *Some people feel a repugnance for snakes.* *n.*

re pug nant (ri pug'nənt), 1 disagreeable or offensive; distasteful: *Work is repugnant to lazy people.* 2 objecting; averse; opposed: *We are repugnant to every sort of dishonesty.* *adj.* —**re pug'nant ly**, *adv.*

re pulse (ri puls'), 1 drive back; repel: *Our soldiers repulsed the enemy.* 2 a driving or a being driven back: *After the second repulse, the enemy surrendered.* 3 refuse to accept; reject: *She coldly repulsed him.* 4 refusal; rejection: *Her repulse was quite unexpected.* 1,3 *v.*, **re pulsed, re puls ing**; 2,4 *n.*

re pul sion (ri pul'shən), 1 strong dislike or aversion. 2 a repelling or a being repelled; repulse. *n.*

re pul sive (ri pul'siv), 1 causing strong dislike or aversion: *Snakes are repulsive to some people.* 2 tending to drive back or repel. *adj.* —**re pul'sive ly**, *adv.* —**re pul'sive ness**, *n.*

rep u ta ble (rep'yə tə bəl), having a

good reputation; well thought of; respectable: *a reputable citizen, a reputable newspaper.* *adj.*

rep u ta bly (rep'yə tə blē), in a reputable manner; respectably: *They conduct their business reputably.* *adv.*

rep u ta tion (rep'yə tā'shən), 1 what people think and say the character of a person or thing is; character in the opinion of others; name; repute: *This store has an excellent reputation for fair dealing. She has the reputation of being very bright.* 2 good name; good reputation: *Cheating at the game ruined that player's reputation.* 3 fame: *an international reputation.* *n.*

re pute (ri pyüt'), 1 reputation: *This is a district of bad repute on account of many robberies.* 2 suppose to be; consider; suppose: *He is reputed the richest man in the state.* 1 *n.*, 2 *v.*, **re put ed, re put ing**.

re put ed (ri pyü'tid), accounted or supposed to be such: *the reputed author of a book.* *adj.* —**re put'ed ly**, *adv.*

re quest (ri kwest'), 1 ask for; ask as a favor: *She requested a loan from the bank.* 2 ask: *He requested her to go with him.* 3 act of asking: *She did it at our request.* 4 what is asked for: *He granted my request.* 5 state of being asked for or sought after: *She is such a good speaker that she is in great request.* 1,2 *v.*, 3-5 *n.*

by request, in response to a request.

req ui em or **Req ui em** (rek'wē əm), 1 Mass for the dead; musical church service for the dead. 2 music for it. *n.*

re quire (ri kwīr'), 1 have need for; need; want: *We shall require more help.* 2 to command; order; demand: *The rules require us all to be present.* *v.*, **re quired, re quir ing**.

re quire ment (ri kwīr'mənt), 1 a need; thing needed: *Patience is a requirement in teaching.* 2 a demand; thing demanded: *fulfill the requirements for graduation.* *n.*

req ui site (rek'wə zit), 1 required by circumstances; needed; necessary; essential; indispensable: *the qualities requisite for a leader, the number of votes*

adj.	adjective	*n.*	noun
adv.	adverb	*prep.*	preposition
conj.	conjunction	*pron.*	pronoun
interj.	interjection	*v.*	verb
sing.	singular	*pl.*	plural

requisite for election. 2 thing needed; requirement: *Food and air are requisites for life.* 1 *adj.*, 2 *n.*

req ui si tion (rek/wə zish/ən), 1 act of requiring. 2 a demand made, especially a formal, written demand: *the requisition of supplies for troops.* 3 to demand or take by authority: *requisition supplies.* 4 make demands upon: *The hospital requisitioned the city for more funds.* 5 state of being required for use or called into service: *The car was in constant requisition for errands.* 1,2,5 *n.*, 3,4 *v.*

re quit al (ri kwī/tl), repayment; return: *What requital can we make for all their kindness to us? n.*

re quite (ri kwīt/), 1 pay back; make return for: *requite kindness with love.* 2 make return to; reward: *The knight requited the boy for his warning. v.,* **re quit ed, re quit ing.**

re read (rē rēd/), read again or anew: *reread a good book. v.,* **re read** (rē-red/), **re read ing.**

re route (rē rüt/ *or* rē rout/), send by a new or different route. *v.,* **re rout ed, re rout ing.**

re run (rē run/ *for 1;* rē/run/ *for 2,3*), 1 run again. 2 a running again. 3 a television program or motion-picture film that is shown again. 1 *v.,* **re ran, re run ning;** 2,3 *n.*

re sale (rē/sāl/), act of selling again: *the resale of a house. n.*

re scind (ri sind/), deprive of force; repeal; cancel: *rescind a law. v.*

res cue (res/kyü), 1 save from danger, capture, harm, etc.; free; deliver: *rescue someone from drowning.* 2 a saving or freeing from danger, capture, harm, etc.: *The fireman was praised for his brave rescue of the children. A dog was chasing our cat when your sister came to the rescue.* 1 *v.,* **res cued, res cu ing;** 2 *n.*

res cu er (res/kyü ər), one that rescues. *n.*

re search (ri sėrch/ *or* rē/sėrch/), 1 a careful hunting for facts or truth; inquiry; investigation: *cancer research, the researches of historians.* 2 make researches. 1 *n., pl.* **re search es;** 2 *v.*

re search er (ri sėr/chər *or* rē/-sėr/chər), person who makes researches; investigator. *n.*

re sem blance (ri zem/bləns), similar appearance; likeness: *Twins often show great resemblance. n.*

re sem ble (ri zem/bəl), be like; be similar to; have likeness to in form, figure, or qualities: *An orange resembles a grapefruit. v.,* **re sem bled, re sem bling.**

re sent (ri zent/), feel injured and angry at; feel indignation at: *Our cat seems to resent having anyone sit in its chair. v.*

re sent ful (ri zent/fəl), feeling resentment; injured and angry; showing resentment. *adj.* **—re sent/ful ly,** *adv.*

re sent ment (ri zent/mənt), the feeling that one has at being injured or insulted; indignation: *Everyone feels resentment at being treated unfairly. n.*

res er va tion (rez/ər vā/shən), 1 a keeping back; hiding in part; something not expressed: *She outwardly approved of the plan with the mental reservation that she would change it to suit herself.* 2 a limiting condition: *We accepted the plan with reservations plainly stated.* 3 land set aside for a special purpose. *The government has set apart Indian reservations.* 4 arrangement to keep a thing for a person; securing of accommodations, etc., in advance: *Please make reservations for rooms at a hotel and seats at the theater that night. n.*

re serve (ri zėrv/), 1 keep back; hold back: *Mother reserved judgment until she had heard both sides of the argument.* 2 set apart: *He reserves his evenings to spend them with his family.* 3 save for use later: *Reserve enough money for your fare home.* 4 the actual cash in a bank or assets that can be turned into cash quickly. Banks must keep a reserve of money. 5 body of soldiers kept ready to help the main army in battle. 6 **reserves,** *pl.* soldiers or sailors not in active service but ready to serve when needed. 7 public land set apart for a special purpose: *a forest reserve.* 8 anything kept back for future use; store: *a reserve of food or energy.* 9 act of keeping back or holding back; a setting apart: *You may speak before her without reserve.* 10 fact, state, or condition of being kept, set apart, or saved for use later: *keep money in reserve.* 11 to set aside for the use of a particular person or persons: *reserve a table at a restaurant.* 12 kept in reserve; forming a reserve: *a reserve stock, a reserve force.* 13 a keeping one's thoughts, feelings, and affairs to oneself; self-restraint in action or speech; lack of friendliness. 14 a silent manner that keeps people from making friends easily. 1-3,11 *v.,* **re served, re serv ing;** 4-10,13,14 *n.,* 12 *adj.*

re served (ri zėrvd/), 1 kept in reserve; kept by special arrangement: *a reserved seat.* 2 set apart. 3 self-restrained in action or speech. 4 disposed to keep to oneself: *A reserved person does not make friends easily. adj.*

re serv ed ly (ri zėr/vid lē), in a reserved manner; with reserve. *adv.*

re serv ist (ri zėr/vist), member of the reserves; soldier or sailor not in active service but available if needed. *n.*

RESERVOIR

WATER UNDER PRESSURE

reservoir (def. 1)—tank type cut away to show pipes inside

res er voir (rez/ər vwär), 1 place where water is collected and stored for use: *This reservoir supplies the entire city.* 2 anything to hold a liquid: *A fountain pen has an ink reservoir.* 3 place where anything is collected and stored: *Her mind was a reservoir of facts.* 4 a great supply: *a reservoir of weapons. n.*

re set (rē set/), set again: *The diamonds were reset in platinum. My broken arm had to be reset. v.,* **re set, re set ting.**

re ship ment (rē ship/mənt), 1 a shipping again. 2 that which is shipped again. *n.*

re side (ri zīd/), 1 live in or at (a place) for a long time; dwell: *This family has resided in our town for 100 years.* 2 be; exist: *The power to declare war resides in Congress. v.,* **re sid ed, re sid ing.**

res i dence (rez/ə dəns), 1 the place where a person lives; house; home; abode: *The President's residence is the White House in Washington, D.C.* 2 a residing; living; dwelling: *Long residence in France made them very fond of the French.* 3 period of residing in a place: *They spent a residence of ten years in France. n.*

res i dent (rez/ə dənt), 1 person living in a place permanently; dweller: *The residents of the town are proud of their new library.* 2 staying; dwelling in a place: *A resident owner lives on his property.* 3 living in a place while on duty or doing active work: *She is a resident physician at the hospital.* 1 *n.,* 2,3 *adj.*

res i den tial (rez/ə den/shəl), 1 of, having to do with, or fitted for homes or residences: *They live in a large residential district outside the city.* 2 having to do with residence: *The city is considering the adoption of a residential requirement for all city employees to live within the city limits. adj.*

re sid u al (ri zij′ü əl), of or forming a residue; remaining; left over. *adj.*

res i due (rez′ə dü *or* rez′ə dyü), what remains after a part is taken; remainder: *His will directed that after the payment of all debts and $10,000 to his brother the residue of his property should go to his son. The syrup had dried up, leaving a sticky residue.* n.

re sign (ri zīn′), give up a job, position, etc.; renounce: *I resigned my position on the school paper.* v.

resign oneself, submit quietly; adapt oneself without complaint; yield: *He had to resign himself to a week in bed when he hurt his back.*

res ig na tion (rez′ig nā′shən), 1 act of resigning: *There have been so many resignations from the committee that a new one must be formed.* 2 a written statement giving notice that one resigns. 3 patient acceptance; quiet submission: *bear pain with resignation.* n.

re signed (ri zīnd′), accepting what comes without complaint. *adj.*

re sign ed ly (ri zī′nid lē), in a resigned manner; with resignation. *adv.*

re sil i ence (ri zil′ē əns), 1 power of springing back; elasticity; resilient quality or nature: *Rubber has resilience.* 2 buoyancy; cheerfulness. n.

re sil i en cy (ri zil′ē ən sē), resilience. n.

re sil i ent (ri zil′ē ənt), 1 springing back; returning to the original form or position after being bent, compressed, or stretched: *resilient steel, resilient turf.* 2 buoyant; cheerful: *a resilient nature that throws off trouble. adj.* —**re sil′i ent ly,** *adv.*

res in (rez′n), a sticky, yellow or brown substance that flows from certain plants and trees, especially the pine and fir. It is also derived chemically and is used in medicine and varnish. When pine resin is heated it yields turpentine; the hard yellow substance that remains after heating is called rosin. n.

res in ous (rez′n əs), 1 of resin. 2 like resin. 3 containing resin; full of resin. *adj.*

re sist (ri zist′), 1 act against; strive against; oppose: *The window resisted all efforts to open it.* 2 strive successfully against; keep from: *I could not resist laughing.* 3 withstand the action or effect of (an acid, storm, etc.): *A healthy body resists disease.* v.

re sist ance (ri zis′təns), 1 act of resisting: *The bank clerk made no resistance to the robbers.* 2 power to resist: *Some people have very little resistance to colds.* 3 thing or act that resists; opposing force; opposition: *An airplane can overcome the resistance of the air and go in the desired direction, while a balloon just drifts.* 4 people who se-

cretly organize and fight for their freedom in a country occupied and controlled by a foreign power: *the French resistance in World War II.* 5 property of a conductor that opposes the passage of an electric current and changes electric energy into heat. Copper has a low resistance. n.

re sist ant (ri zis′tənt), resisting. *adj.*

re sist less (ri zist′lis), that cannot be resisted: *We were helpless against the resistless force of the hurricane. adj.*

re sis tor (ri zis′tər), conductor used to control voltage in an electric circuit, etc., because of its resistance. n.

res o lute (rez′ə lüt), having a fixed resolve; determined; firm: *be resolute against all opposition. She was resolute in her attempt to climb to the top of the mountain. adj.* —**res′o lute′ly,** *adv.* —**res′o lute′ness,** *n.*

res o lu tion (rez′ə lü′shən), 1 thing decided on; thing determined: *We made a resolution to get up early.* 2 act of resolving or determining. 3 power of holding firmly to a purpose; determination: *Lincoln's resolution overcame his poverty and lack of schooling.* 4 a formal expression of opinion: *The club passed a resolution thanking the teacher for his help throughout the year.* 5 a breaking into parts. 6 act or result of solving; solution: *resolution of a problem.* n.

re solve (ri zolv′), 1 make up one's mind; determine; decide: *I resolved to do better work in the future.* 2 thing determined on; thing decided: *He kept his resolve to do better.* 3 firmness in carrying out a purpose; determination: *Helen Keller was a woman of resolve.* 4 decide by vote: *It was resolved that our class should have a picnic.* 5 answer and explain; solve: *His letter resolved all our doubts.* 6 break into parts; break up: *Some chemical compounds can be resolved by heat.* 7 change: *The assembly resolved itself into a committee.* 1,4-7 v., re solved, re solv ing; 2,3 n.

re solved (ri zolvd′), determined; firm; resolute. *adj.*

res o nance (rez′n əns), 1 resounding quality; a being resonant: *the resonance of an organ.* 2 a reinforcing and prolonging of sound by reflection or by vibration of other objects. The hollow body of a guitar gives it resonance. n.

res o nant (rez′n ənt), 1 resounding; continuing to sound; echoing. 2 tending to increase or prolong sounds. *adj.* —**res′o nant ly,** *adv.*

re sort (ri zôrt′), 1 go often; go: *Many people resort to the beaches in hot weather.* 2 place people go to, usually for recreation: *There are many summer resorts in the mountains.* 3 turn for

hat, āge, fär; let, ēqual, tėrm;
it, īce; hot, ōpen, ôrder;
oil, out; cup, pùt, rüle; ch, child;
ng, long; sh, she; th, thin;
ŦH, then; zh, measure;

ə represents *a* in about,
e in taken, *i* in pencil,
o in lemon, *u* in circus.

help: *The parents resorted to punishment to make the child obey.* 4 act of turning for help: *The resort to force is forbidden in this school.* 5 person or thing turned to for help: *Books are her resort when she is lonely. Friends are the best resort in trouble.* 1,3 v., 2,4,5 n.

re sound (ri zound′), 1 give back sound; echo: *The hills resounded when we shouted. The buildings resounded the siren's warning.* 2 sound loudly: *Radios resound from every house.* 3 be filled with sound: *The room resounded with the children's shouts.* 4 be much talked about: *The fame of the first flight across the Atlantic resounded all over the world.* v. —**re sound′ing ly,** *adv.*

re source (ri sôrs′ *or* rē′sôrs), 1 any supply that will meet a need. We have resources of money, of knowledge, of quick wit, of strength, etc. 2 **resources,** pl. the actual and potential wealth of a country: *natural resources, human resources.* 3 any means of getting success or getting out of trouble: *Climbing a tree is a cat's resource when chased by a dog.* 4 skill in meeting difficulties, getting out of trouble, etc. n.

re source ful (ri sôrs′fəl), good at thinking of ways to do things; quickwitted: *That resourceful girl mowed lawns all summer to earn enough money to buy a new bicycle. adj.* —**re source′ful ly,** *adv.* —**re source′ful ness,** *n.*

re spect (ri spekt′), 1 high regard; honor; esteem: *The children always showed great respect for their grandparents.* 2 feel or show honor or esteem for: *We respect an honest person.* 3 consideration; care; regard: *Show respect for other people's property.* 4 show consideration for; care for: *Respect the ideas and feelings of others.* 5 **respects,** pl. expressions of respect; regards: *We must pay our respects to the governor.* 6 feature; point; matter; detail: *The plan is unwise in many respects.* 7 relation; reference: *We must plan with respect to the future.* 8 relate to; refer to; be connected with. 1,3,5-7 n., 2,4,8 v. —**re spect′er,** *n.*

adj.	adjective	n.	noun
adv.	adverb	prep.	preposition
conj.	conjunction	pron.	pronoun
interj.	interjection	v.	verb
sing.	singular	pl.	plural

re spect a bil i ty (ri spek′tə bil′ə tē), 1 quality or condition of being respectable. 2 respectable social standing. *n., pl.* **re spect a bil i ties.**

re spect a ble (ri spek′tə bəl), 1 worthy of respect; having a good reputation; honest and decent: *He is a kindly and respectable old gentleman. They are very respectable people.* 2 fairly good; moderate in size or quality: *His record in school was respectable but not brilliant.* 3 good enough to use; fit to be seen: *respectable clothes. adj.*

re spect a bly (ri spek′tə blē), in a respectable manner. *adv.*

re spect ful (ri spekt′fəl), showing respect; considerate and polite. *adj.* —**re spect′ful ly,** *adv.* —**re spect′-ful ness,** *n.*

re spect ing (ri spek′ting), regarding; about; concerning: *A discussion arose respecting the merits of different automobiles. prep.*

re spec tive (ri spek′tiv), belonging to each; particular; individual: *The classes went to their respective rooms. adj.*

re spec tive ly (ri spek′tiv lē), as regards each of several persons or things in turn or in the order mentioned: *Pat, José, and Kathy are 16, 18, and 20 years old, respectively. adv.*

re spell (rē spel′), spell over again, especially in a phonetic alphabet. *v.*

res pi ra tion (res′pə rā′shən), 1 act of inhaling and exhaling; breathing: *A bad cold hinders respiration.* 2 the processes by which an animal or plant secures oxygen from the air or water, distributes it, combines it with substances in the tissues, and gives off carbon dioxide. *n.*

res pi ra tor (res′pə rā′tər), 1 a device, usually of gauze, worn over the nose and mouth to prevent inhaling harmful substances. 2 device used to help a person to breathe. Respirators are used by underwater swimmers and in giving artificial respiration. *n.*

res pir a to ry (res′pər ə tôr′ē), having to do with or used for respiration. The lungs are respiratory organs. *adj.*

re spire (ri spīr′), inhale and exhale; breathe. *v.,* **re spired, re spir ing.**

res pite (res′pit), 1 time of relief and rest; lull: *A thick cloud brought a respite from the glare of the sun.* 2 a putting off; delay, especially in carrying out a sentence of death; reprieve. *n.*

re splend ence (ri splen′dəns), great brightness; gorgeous appearance; splendor. *n.*

re splend ent (ri splen′dənt), very bright; shining; splendid: *a gown resplendent with jewels, a face resplendent with joy. adj.* —**re splend′ent ly,** *adv.*

re spond (ri spond′), 1 answer; reply: *He responded briefly to the question.* 2 act in answer; react: *A dog responds to kind treatment by loving its master. She responded quickly to the medicine and was well in a few days. v.*

re sponse (ri spons′), 1 an answer by word or act: *Her response to my letter was prompt. She laughed in response to his joke.* 2 words said or sung by the congregation or choir in answer to the minister. 3 the reaction of body or mind to a stimulus. *n.*

rest¹ (def. 16b)—different types of rests

re spon si bil i ty (ri spon′sə bil′ə tē), 1 a being responsible; obligation: *A little child does not feel much responsibility.* 2 thing for which one is responsible: *Keeping my room clean and feeding the cat are my responsibilities. n., pl.* **re spon si bil i ties.**

re spon si ble (ri spon′sə bəl), 1 obliged or expected to account for; accountable; answerable: *Each pupil is responsible for the care of the books given him.* 2 deserving credit or blame: *The bad weather is responsible for the small attendance.* 3 trustworthy; reliable: *A responsible person should take care of the money.* 4 involving obligation or duties: *The presidency is a very responsible position. adj.*

re spon si bly (ri spon′sə blē), in a responsible manner. *adv.*

re spon sive (ri spon′siv), 1 making answer; responding: *a responsive glance.* 2 easily moved; responding readily: *have a responsive nature, be responsive to kindness.* 3 using or containing responses: *responsive reading in church in which minister and congregation read in turn. adj.* —**re spon′sive ly,** *adv.* —**re spon′sive ness,** *n.*

rest¹ (rest), 1 state of quiet and ease; sleep; repose: *a good night's rest.* 2 be still or quiet; sleep: *Lie down and rest.* 3 ease after work or effort: *All the swimmers left the pool for a short rest.* 4 freedom from anything that tires, troubles, disturbs, or pains; peace: *The medicine gave the sick man some rest from pain.* 5 be free from work, effort, care, trouble, etc.: *Teachers rest in the* summer. 6 absence of motion; stillness: *The driver brought the car to rest.* 7 give rest to; refresh by rest: *Stop and rest your horse.* 8 to place or be placed for support; lie; lay; lean: *He rested his rake against the fence. The roof of the porch rests on columns. He spent the whole day resting in a chair.* 9 a support; something to lean on: *a rest for a billiard cue.* 10 be fixed; look: *Our eyes rested on the open book.* 11 be at ease: *Don't let her rest until she promises to visit us.* 12 be or become inactive; let remain inactive: *Let the matter rest. Rest the matter there.* 13 base or be based; rely; trust; depend: *Our hope rests on you. We rest our hope on you.* 14 be found; be present; lie: *In a democracy, government rests with the people. The blame rested on all of us.* 15 place for resting: *a travelers' rest.* 16 in music: **a** a silence of definite length between notes. **b** a mark to show such a silence. 17 (in reading) a pause. 18 death; the grave. 19 be dead; lie in the grave: *The old man rests with his ancestors.* 1,3,4,6,9,15-18 *n.,* 2,5,7,8, 10-14,19 *v.* [Old English *reste*]

lay to rest, bury: *Lay a body to rest.*

rest² (rest), 1 what is left; those that are left: *The sun was out in the morning but it rained for the rest of the day. One horse was running ahead of the rest.* 2 continue to be; remain: *You may rest assured that I will keep my promise. The final decision rests with you.* 1 *n.,* 2 *v.* [from French of the 1400's *reste,* from *rester* remain, from Latin *restare,* from *re-* back + *stare* stand]

re state (rē stāt′), 1 state again or anew. 2 state in a new way. *v.,* **re stat ed, re stat ing.**

re state ment (rē stāt′mənt), 1 act of stating again. 2 statement made again. 3 a new statement. *n.*

res taur ant (res′tər ənt), place to buy and eat a meal. *n.*

rest ful (rest′fəl), 1 full of rest; giving rest: *She had a restful nap.* 2 quiet; peaceful. *adj.* —**rest′ful ly,** *adv.* —**rest′ful ness,** *n.*

res ti tu tion (res′tə tü′shən or res′tə tyü′shən), 1 the giving back of what has been lost or taken away. 2 act of making good any loss, damage, or injury: *It is only fair that those who do the damage should make restitution. n.*

res tive (res′tiv), 1 restless; uneasy: *a restive audience.* 2 hard to manage: *a restive child.* 3 refusing to go ahead; balky: *a restive mule. adj.* —**res′tive ly,** *adv.* —**res′tive ness,** *n.*

rest less (rest′lis), 1 unable to rest; uneasy: *The dog seemed restless as if he sensed some danger.* 2 without rest or sleep; not restful: *The sick child passed a restless night.* 3 rarely or never still or quiet; always moving: *The nervous child was very restless.* adj. —**rest′less ly,** adv. —**rest′less ness,** n.

res to ra tion (res′tə rā′shən),   1 a restoring or a being restored; bringing back to a former condition: *the restoration of health, the restoration of a king.* 2 something restored: *The house we slept in was a restoration of a colonial mansion.* n.

re stor a tive (ri stôr′ə tiv),   1 capable of restoring; tending to restore health or strength: *a restorative medicine.* 2 something that restores health, strength, or consciousness: *Ammonia is used as a restorative when a person has fainted.* 1 adj., 2 n.

re store (ri stôr′),   1 bring back; establish again: *The police restored order.* 2 bring back to a former condition or to a normal condition: *The old house has been restored.* 3 give back; put back: *The boy restored the money he had found to its owner.* v., **re stored, re stor ing.**

re stor er (ri stôr′ər), person or thing that restores. n.

re strain (ri strān′), hold back; keep down; keep in check; keep within limits: *I could not restrain my curiosity to see what was in the box. We restrained the excited dog when guests came.* v. —**re strain′er,** n.

re straint (ri strānt′),   1 a restraining or a being restrained: *Noisy children sometimes need restraint.* 2 means of restraining. 3 tendency to restrain natural feeling; reserve: *He was very angry, but he spoke with restraint.* n.

re strict (ri strikt′), keep within limits; confine: *Our club membership is restricted to twelve.* v.

re strict ed (ri strik′tid),   1 limited; kept within limits: *She is on a very restricted diet, and can have no sweets.* 2 having restrictions or limiting rules: *Factories may not be built in this restricted residential section.* adj.

re stric tion (ri strik′shən),   1 something that restricts; limiting condition or rule: *The restrictions on the use of the playground are: No fighting; no damaging property.* 2 a restricting or a being restricted: *This park is open to the public without restriction.* n.

re stric tive (ri strik′tiv), restricting;

limiting: *Some laws are prohibitive; some are only restrictive.* adj. —**re stric′tive ly,** adv. —**re stric′tive ness,** n.

restrictive clause, a subordinate clause that qualifies the noun it modifies so definitely that it cannot be left out without changing the meaning of the sentence. EXAMPLE: *All employees who have been with this firm for five years will receive bonuses.*

rest room, lavatory in a public building.

re sult (ri zult′),   1 that which happens because of something; what is caused; outcome: *The result of the fall was a broken leg.* 2 good or useful effect: *The new medicine got results.* 3 be a result; follow as a consequence: *Sickness often results from eating too much.* 4 have as a result; end: *Eating too much often results in sickness.* 5 quantity, value, etc., obtained by calculation. 1,2,5 n., 3,4 v.

re sult ant (ri zult′nt),   1 resulting. 2 a result. 1 adj., 2 n.

re sume (ri züm′),   1 begin again; go on: *Resume reading where we left off.* 2 get or take again: *Those standing may resume their seats.* v., **re sumed, re sum ing.**

rés u mé (rez′ə mā′), summary: *résumé of a person's education, résumé of a book.* n., pl. **rés u més.** [from French]

re sump tion (ri zump′shən), a resuming: *the resumption of duties after absence.* n.

re sur gence (ri sèr′jəns), a rising again: *resurgence of interest.* n.

res ur rect (rez′ə rekt′),   1 raise from the dead; bring back to life. 2 bring back to sight, use, etc.: *resurrect an old custom.* v.

res ur rec tion (rez′ə rek′shən),   1 a coming to life again; rising from the dead. 2 **Resurrection,** the rising again of Christ after His death and burial. 3 a being alive again after death. 4 restoration from decay, disuse, etc.; revival. n.

re sus ci tate (ri sus′ə tāt), bring or come back to life or consciousness; revive: *The doctor resuscitated the man who was overcome by gas.* v., **re sus ci tat ed, re sus ci tat ing.**

re sus ci ta tion (ri sus′ə tā′shən), restoration to life or consciousness. n.

re sus ci ta tor (ri sus′ə tā′tər), device used to revive persons overcome by gas, water in the lungs, etc. It produces artificial respiration by forcing oxygen into the lungs through a tight-fitting mask or cup attached to the victim's face. n.

re tail (rē′tāl *for 1-4;* ri tāl′ *or* rē′tāl *for 5),* 1 sale of goods in small quan-

resuscitator

hat, āge, fär; let, ēqual, tèrm;
it, īce; hot, ōpen, ôrder;
oil, out; cup, pùt, rüle; ch, child;
ng, long; sh, she; th, thin;
ŦH, then; zh, measure;

ə represents *a* in about,
e in taken, *i* in pencil,
o in lemon, *u* in circus.

tities directly to the consumer: *Our grocer buys at wholesale and sells at retail.* 2 in small quantities: *The wholesale price of this coat is $20; the retail price is $30.* 3 selling in small quantities: *the retail trade, a retail merchant.* 4 sell or be sold in small quantities. 5 tell over again: *My little brother retails to the neighbors everything he hears our family discuss during dinner.* 1 n., 2,3 adj., 4,5 v.

re tail er (rē′tā lər), a retail merchant or dealer. n.

re tain (ri tān′),   1 continue to have or hold; keep: *Our china teapot retains heat for quite a long time. Our baseball team retained a lead throughout the game.* 2 keep in mind; remember: *She retained the tune but not the words of the song.* 3 employ by payment of a fee: *I retained the best lawyer in the state.* v.

re tain er¹ (ri tā′nər), person who serves a person of rank; vassal; attendant; follower: *The queen had many retainers.* n. [retain + -er¹]

re tain er² (ri tā′nər), fee paid to secure services: *This lawyer receives a retainer before he begins work on a case.* n. [noun use of French of the 1400's *retenir* retain, from Latin *retinere,* from *re-* back + *tenere* hold]

re take (rē tāk′ *for 1,2;* rē′tāk′ *for 3),* 1 take again. 2 take back. 3 a retaking: *a retake of a scene in a motion picture.* 1,2 v., **re took, re tak en** (rē tā′kən), **re tak ing;** 3 n.

re tal i ate (ri tal′ē āt), pay back wrong, injury, etc.; return like for like, usually to return evil for evil: *If we insult them, they will retaliate.* v., **re tal i at ed, re tal i at ing.**

re tal i a tion (ri tal′ē ā′shən), paying back a wrong, injury, etc.; return of evil for evil. n.

re tal i a to ry (ri tal′ē ə tôr′ē), returning like for like, especially evil for evil. adj.

re tard (ri tärd′), make slow; delay the progress of; keep back; hinder: *Lack of education retards progress. Bad roads retarded the car.* v. —**re tard′er,** n.

re tar da tion (rē′tär dā′shən),   1 act

retarded

adj. adjective	*n.* noun
adv. adverb	*prep.* preposition
conj. conjunction	*pron.* pronoun
interj. interjection	*v.* verb
sing. singular	*pl.* plural

of retarding. **2** that which retards; hindrance. *n.*

re tard ed (ri tär′did), slow in mental development; backward. *adj.*

retch (rech), make efforts to vomit; make movements like those of vomiting. *v.*

re tell (rē tel′), tell again. *v.*, **re told, re tell ing.**

re ten tion (ri ten′shən), **1** a retaining or a being retained. **2** power to retain. **3** ability to remember. *n.*

re ten tive (ri ten′tiv), **1** able to hold or keep: *a material retentive of moisture.* **2** able to remember easily: *a retentive memory. adj.* —**re ten′tive ly,** *adv.* —**re ten′tive ness,** *n.*

ret i cence (ret′ə səns), tendency to be silent or say little; reserve in speech. *n.*

ret i cent (ret′ə sənt), disposed to keep silent or say little; not speaking freely; reserved in speech. *adj.* —**ret′i cent ly,** *adv.*

reticulate wings   reticulate leaf

re tic u late (ri tik′yə lit *or* ri tik′yə-lāt), covered with a network. Reticulate leaves have the veins arranged like the threads of a net. *adj.*

ret i na (ret′n ə), layer of cells at the back of the eyeball that is sensitive to light and receives the images of things looked at. See **eye** for diagram. *n., pl.* **ret i nas, ret i nae** (ret′n ē′).

ret i nal (ret′n əl), of or on the retina. *adj.*

ret i nue (ret′n ü *or* ret′n yü), group of attendants or retainers; a following: *The king's retinue accompanied him on the journey. n.*

re tire (ri tīr′), **1** give up an office, occupation, etc., especially because of old age: *Our teachers retire at 65.* **2** remove from an office, occupation, etc. **3** go away, especially to a place which is more quiet or private: *They retired to the country.* **4** withdraw; draw back; send back: *The government retires worn or torn dollar bills from use.* **5** go back; retreat: *The enemy retired*

before the advance of our troops. **6** go to bed: *We retire early.* **7** withdraw from circulation and pay off (bonds, loans, etc.). **8** put out (a batter, side, etc.) in baseball and cricket. *v.*, **re tired, re tir ing.**

re tired (ri tīrd′), **1** withdrawn from one's occupation: *a retired accountant.* **2** reserved; retiring: *a shy, retired nature.* **3** secluded; shut off; hidden: *a retired spot. adj.*

re tire ment (ri tīr′mənt), **1** a retiring or a being retired; withdrawal: *The teacher's retirement from service was regretted by the school.* **2** a quiet way or place of living: *The artist lives in retirement, away from city life. n.*

re tir ing (ri tī′ring), shrinking from society or publicity; reserved; shy: *a retiring nature. adj.*

re told (rē tōld′), past tense and past participle of **retell.** *He then retold the story for the newcomers. v.*

re took (rē tuk′), past tense of **retake.** *The photographer retook my picture. v.*

re tool (rē tül′), change the tools, machinery, designs, etc., in a plant to make new models or products. *v.*

re tort[1] (ri tôrt′), **1** reply quickly or sharply: *"It's none of your business," he retorted.* **2** a sharp or witty reply: *"Why are your teeth so sharp?" asked Red Ridinghood. "The better to eat you with," was the wolf's retort.* **3** return in kind; turn back on: *retort insult for insult or blow for blow.* **1,3** *v.*, **2** *n.* [from Latin *retortum* turned back, from *re-* back + *torquere* to twist]

re tort[2] (ri tôrt′), container used for distilling or decomposing substances by heat. *n.* [from Latin *retorta* (originally) feminine of *retortum* turned back]

re touch (rē tuch′), improve (a photographic negative, painting, etc.) by new touches or slight changes. *v.*

re trace (rē trās′), go back over: *We retraced our steps to where we started. v.*, **re traced, re trac ing.**

re tract (ri trakt′), **1** draw back or in: *The kitten retracted her claws and purred when I petted her.* **2** withdraw; take back: *retract an offer, retract an opinion. v.*

re trac tion (ri trak′shən), **1** a drawing or a being drawn back or in. **2** a taking back; withdrawal of a promise, statement, etc.: *The newspaper pub-*

retriever—2 ft. high at the shoulder

lished a retraction of the inaccurate report about the senator. *n.*

re tread (rē tred′ *for* 1; rē′tred′ *for* 2), **1** put a new tread on. **2** a tire that has been retreaded. **1** *v.*, **2** *n.*

re treat (ri trēt′), **1** go back; move back; withdraw: *The enemy retreated before the advance of our soldiers.* **2** act of going back or withdrawing: *The army's retreat was orderly.* **3** a signal for retreat: *The drums beat a retreat.* **4** a signal on a bugle or drum, given at sunset during the lowering of the flag. **5** a safe, quiet place; place of rest or refuge. **6** a retirement, or period of retirement, by a group of people for religious exercises, meditation, etc.: *The monks conducted a retreat.* **1** *v.*, **2-6** *n.*

beat a retreat, run away; retreat: *We dropped the apples and beat a hasty retreat when the farmer chased us.*

re trench (ri trench′), cut down or reduce expenses, etc.: *In hard times, we must retrench to keep out of debt. v.*

re trench ment (ri trench′mənt), a cutting down or reduction of expenses, etc. *n.*

re tri al (rē trī′əl), a second trial; new trial. *n.*

RETORT   RECEIVER

retort[2]

re tri bu tion (ret′rə byü′shən), a deserved punishment; return for evil done. *n.*

re trib u tive (ri trib′yə tiv), paying back; bringing or inflicting punishment in return for some evil, wrong, etc. *adj.*

re triev al (ri trē′vəl), act of retrieving; recovery. *n.*

re trieve (ri trēv′), **1** get again; recover: *retrieve a lost pocketbook.* **2** bring back to a former or better condition; restore: *retrieve one's fortunes.* **3** make good; make amends for; repair: *retrieve a mistake, retrieve a loss or defeat.* **4** find and bring to a person: *A dog can be trained to retrieve game. v.*, **re trieved, re triev ing.**

re triev er (ri trē′vər), dog trained to find killed or wounded game and bring it to a hunter. *n.*

ret ro ac tive (ret′rō ak′tiv), acting back; having an effect on what is past. *A retroactive law applies to events that*

718

occurred before the law was passed. *adj.*

ret ro grade (ret′rə grād), 1 moving backward; retreating. 2 move or go backward. 3 becoming worse. 4 fall back toward a worse condition; grow worse; decline. 1,3 *adj.,* 2,4 *v.,* **ret rograd ed, ret ro grad ing.**

ret ro gress (ret′rə gres *or* ret′rə gres′), 1 move backward; go back. 2 become worse. *v.*

ret ro gres sion (ret′rə gresh′ən), 1 a backward movement. 2 a becoming worse; falling off; decline. *n.*

ret ro rock et (ret′rō rok′it), a small rocket at the front of a rocket or spacecraft. It produces thrust opposite to the motion of the spacecraft in order to reduce speed for landing or for reentry. *n.*

ret ro spect (ret′rə spekt), survey of past time, events, etc.; thinking about the past. *n.*

in retrospect, when looking back: *He saw, in retrospect, that the accident could have been avoided.*

ret ro spec tion (ret′rə spek′shən), act of looking back on things past; survey of past events or experiences: *Old people often enjoy retrospection. n.*

ret ro spec tive (ret′rə spek′tiv), 1 looking back on things past; surveying past events or experiences. 2 applying to the past; retroactive. *adj.* —**ret′ro spec′tive ly,** *adv.*

re turn (ri tėrn′), 1 go back; come back: *Return home for your report card. My brother will return this summer.* 2 a going or coming back; happening again: *We look forward all winter to our return to the country. We wish you many happy returns of your birthday.* 3 bring, give, send, put, or pay back: *Return that book to the library. I left a message for her to return my telephone call.* 4 a bringing back; giving back; sending back; hitting back; putting back: *Such bad behavior was a poor return for kindness.* 5 thing returned. 6 Often, **returns,** *pl.* profit; amount received: *The returns from the sale were more than a hundred dollars.* 7 yield: *The concert returned about $50 over expenses.* 8 report; account: *election returns. I must make out my income-tax return.* 9 report or announce officially: *The jury returned a verdict of guilty.* 10 to reply; answer: *"No!" he returned crossly.* 11 of or having to do with a return: *a return ticket to the point of starting.* 12 sent, given, done, etc., in return: *a return game.* 1,3,7,9,10 *v.,* 2,4-6,8 *n.,* 11,12 *adj.*

in return, as a return; to return something: *If you will loan me your skates now, I'll loan you my tennis racket next summer in return.*

re turn a ble (ri tėr′nə bəl), 1 that can be returned. 2 meant or required to be returned. *adj.*

re turn ee (ri tėr′nē′), person who has returned, especially one who has returned to his own country after capture in a war or from service abroad. *n.*

re un ion (rē yü′nyən), 1 a coming together again: *the reunion of parted friends.* 2 a social gathering of persons who have been separated or who have interests in common: *We have a family reunion every summer. n.*

re u nite (rē′yü nīt′), bring together again; come together again: *The two friends were reunited after a long separation. v.,* **re u nit ed, re u nit ing.**

rev (rev), INFORMAL. 1 a revolution of an engine or motor. 2 increase the speed of (an engine or motor). 1 *n.,* 2 *v.,* **revved, rev ving.**

Rev., Reverend.

re vamp (rē vamp′), patch up; repair: *revamp an old car, revamp plans. v.*

re veal (ri vēl′), 1 make known: *Never reveal my secret.* 2 display; show: *Her smile revealed her even teeth. v.*

rev eil le (rev′ə lē), a signal on a bugle or drum to waken soldiers or sailors in the morning. *n.*

rev el (rev′əl), 1 take great pleasure: *The children revel in country life.* 2 a noisy good time; merrymaking: *Christmas revels with feasting and dancing were common in England.* 3 make merry. 1,3 *v.,* 2 *n.* —**rev′el er,** *n.*

rev e la tion (rev′ə lā′shən), 1 act of making known: *The revelation of the fact that I had won first prize in the essay contest left me speechless.* 2 the thing made known: *Her true nature was a revelation to me.* 3 **Revelation,** the last book of the New Testament, supposed to have been written by the apostle John. *n.*

rev el ry (rev′əl rē), boisterous reveling or festivity; wild merrymaking. *n., pl.* **rev el ries.**

re venge (ri venj′), 1 harm done in return for a wrong; vengeance; returning evil for evil: *a blow struck in revenge.* 2 desire for vengeance. 3 do harm in return for. 4 a chance to win in a return game after losing a game. 1,2,4 *n.,* 3 *v.,* **re venged, re veng ing.**

be revenged or **revenge oneself,** get revenge.

re venge ful (ri venj′fəl), feeling or showing a strong desire for revenge. *adj.* —**re venge′ful ly,** *adv.*

rev e nue (rev′ə nü *or* rev′ə nyü), money coming in; income. The government gets revenue from taxes. *n.*

re ver be rate (ri vėr′bə rāt′), 1 echo back: *His deep, rumbling voice reverberates from the high ceiling.* 2 cast or be cast back; reflect (light or heat). *v.,*

hat, āge, fär; let, ēqual, tėrm;
it, īce; hot, ōpen, ôrder;
oil, out; cup, pút, rüle; ch, child;
ng, long; sh, she; th, thin;
ŦH, then; zh, measure;

ə represents *a* in about,
e in taken, *i* in pencil,
o in lemon, *u* in circus.

re ver be rat ed, re ver be rat ing.

re ver be ra tion (ri vėr′bə rā′shən), 1 an echoing back of sound; echo. 2 reflection of light or heat. *n.*

re vere (ri vir′), love and respect deeply; honor greatly; show reverence for: *We revere sacred things. People revered the great saint. v.,* **re vered, re ver ing.**

Re vere (ri vir′), **Paul,** 1735-1818, American patriot. He is famous for his night ride through eastern Massachusetts to warn colonists of the approach of British troops in 1775. *n.*

rev er ence (rev′ər əns), 1 a feeling of deep respect, mixed with wonder, awe, and love. 2 regard with reverence; revere: *reverence those who live nobly.* 3 a deep bow. 4 **Reverence,** title used in speaking of or to a clergyman. 1,3,4 *n.,* 2 *v.,* **rev er enced, rev er enc ing.**

rev er end (rev′ər ənd), 1 worthy of great respect. 2 **Reverend,** title for clergymen: *the Reverend Thomas A. Johnson.* 1 *adj.,* 2 *n.*

rev er ent (rev′ər ənt), feeling reverence; showing reverence: *He gave reverent attention to the sermon. adj.* —**rev′er ent ly,** *adv.*

rev e ren tial (rev′ə ren′shəl), reverent. *adj.*

rev er ie (rev′ər ē), dreamy thoughts; dreamy thinking of pleasant things: *He loved to indulge in reveries about the future. n.* Also, **revery.**

re ver sal (ri vėr′səl), change to the opposite; a reversing or a being reversed. *n.*

re verse (ri vėrs′), 1 the opposite or contrary: *She did the reverse of what I suggested.* 2 turned backward; opposite or contrary in position or direction: *the reverse side of a phonograph record.* 3 the back: *His name is on the reverse of the medal.* 4 acting in a manner opposite or contrary to that which is usual. 5 causing an opposite or backward movement. 6 turn the other way; turn inside out; turn upside down: *Reverse that hose; don't point it at me.* 7 an opposite or contrary motion or direction: *a reverse in dancing.* 8 arrangement of gears that reverses the

adj.	adjective	*n.*	noun
adv.	adverb	*prep.*	preposition
conj.	conjunction	*pron.*	pronoun
interj.	interjection	*v.*	verb
sing.	singular	*pl.*	plural

movement of machinery: *Drive the automobile in reverse until you get out of the garage.* **9** change to the opposite; repeal: *The court reversed its decree of imprisonment and the man went free.* **10** a change to bad fortune; check; defeat: *He used to be rich, but he met with reverses.* 1,3,7,8,10 *n.,* 2,4,5 *adj.,* 6,9 *v.,* **re versed, re vers ing. —reverse′ly,** *adv.*

re vers i ble (ri vėr′sə bəl), **1** that can be reversed; that can reverse. **2** (of a fabric, etc.) finished on both sides so that it can be worn with either side showing. *adj.*

re ver sion (ri vėr′zhən), **1** return to a former condition, practice, belief, etc.; return. **2** the return of an estate to the person who makes the grant or to his heirs after the grant expires. **3** right to future possession of a property, title, etc. *n.*

re vert (ri vėrt′), **1** go back; return: *My thoughts reverted to the last time that I had seen her.* **2** go back to a former possessor or to his heirs: *Property reverts to the state if a person dies without heirs.* *v.*

rev er y (rev′ər ē), reverie. *n., pl.* **rever ies.**

re view (ri vyü′), **1** study again; look at again: *Review today's lesson for tomorrow. He reviewed the scene of the crime.* **2** a studying again: *Before the examinations we have a review of the term's work.* **3** look back on: *Before falling asleep, she reviewed the day's happenings.* **4** a looking back on; survey: *A review of the trip was pleasant.* **5** examine again; look at with care; examine: *A superior court may review decisions of a lower court.* **6** examination; inspection: *A review of the troops will be held during the general's visit to the camp.* **7** inspect formally: *The admiral reviewed the fleet.* **8** an account of a book, play, etc., giving its merits and faults: *Have the reviews of that movie made you decide to see it?* **9** examine to give an account of: *She reviews books for a living.* 1,3,5,7,9 *v.,* 2,4,6,8 *n.*

re view er (ri vyü′ər), **1** person who reviews. **2** person who writes articles discussing books, plays, etc. *n.*

re vile (ri vīl′), call bad names; abuse with words: *The pedestrian reviled the reckless driver.* *v.,* **re viled, re viling.**

re vil er (ri vī′lər), a person who acts or speaks abusively. *n.*

re vise (ri vīz′), **1** read carefully in order to correct; look over and change; examine and improve: *She has revised the long story she wrote to make it shorter.* **2** change; alter: *revise one's opinion.* *v.,* **re vised, re vis ing.**

re vis er (ri vī′zər), person who revises a manuscript, book, etc. *n.*

re vi sion (ri vizh′ən), **1** act or work of revising. **2** a revised form: *a revision of a book.* *n.*

re viv al (ri vī′vəl), **1** a bringing or coming back to life or consciousness. **2** restoration to vigor or health. **3** a bringing or coming back to style, use, activity, etc.: *the revival of an old musical.* **4** an awakening or increase of interest in religion. **5** special services or efforts made to awaken or increase interest in religion. *n.*

re vive (ri vīv′), **1** bring back or come back to life or consciousness: *revive a half-drowned person. The half-drowned swimmer revived.* **2** bring or come back to a fresh, lively condition: *Flowers revive in water.* **3** make or become fresh; restore: *Hot coffee revived the cold, tired man.* **4** bring back or come back to notice, use, fashion, memory, activity, etc.: *revive an old song. An old play is sometimes revived on the stage.* *v.,* **re vived, re viv ing.**

rev o ca ble (rev′ə kə bəl), that can be repealed, canceled, or withdrawn. *adj.*

rev o ca tion (rev′ə kā′shən), a repeal; a canceling; withdrawal: *the revocation of a law.* *n.*

re voke (ri vōk′), take back; repeal; cancel; withdraw: *revoke a driver's license.* *v.,* **re voked, re vok ing.**

re volt (ri vōlt′), **1** act or state of rebelling: *The town is in revolt.* **2** turn away from and fight against a leader; rise against the government's authority: *The people revolted against the dictator.* **3** turn away with disgust: *revolt at a bad smell.* **4** cause to feel disgust: *Senseless cruelty revolts me.* 1 *n.,* 2-4 *v.*

re volt ing (ri vōl′ting), disgusting; repulsive: *a revolting odor.* *adj.*

rev o lu tion (rev′ə lü′shən), **1** a complete overthrow of an established government or political system: *The era of the American Revolution, from 1763 to 1783, ended with the war which gave independence to the colonies.* **2** a complete change: *The automobile caused a revolution in ways of traveling.* **3** movement in a circle or curve around some point: *One revolution of the earth around the sun takes a year.* **4** act or fact of turning round a center or axis; rotation: *The wheel of the motor turns at* a rate of more then one thousand revolutions per minute. **5** time or distance of one revolution. **6** a complete cycle or series of events: *The revolution of the four seasons fills a year.* *n.*

rev o lu tion ar y (rev′ə lü′shə ner′ē), **1** of a revolution; connected with a revolution. **2** bringing or causing great changes: *Radio and television were two revolutionary inventions of this century.* **3** revolutionist. 1,2 *adj.,* 3 *n., pl.* **rev o lu tion ar ies.**

Revolutionary War, the war from 1775 to 1783 by which the thirteen American colonies won independence from England; American Revolution.

rev o lu tion ist (rev′ə lü′shə nist), person who advocates, or takes part in, a revolution. *n.*

rev o lu tion ize (rev′ə lü′shə nīz), change completely; produce a very great change in: *The automobile, radio, and television have revolutionized country life. The new chief of police says he will revolutionize that department.* *v.,* **rev o lu tion ized, rev o lu tion izing.**

re volve (ri volv′), **1** move in a circle; move in a curve round a point: *The moon revolves around the earth.* **2** turn round a center or axis; rotate: *The wheels of a moving car revolve.* **3** cause to move round. **4** move in a complete cycle or series of events: *The seasons revolve.* **5** turn over in the mind; consider from many points of view: *I'd like to revolve the problem before giving an answer.* *v.,* **re volved, re volv ing.**

revolver

re volv er (ri vol′vər), pistol that can be fired several times without being loaded again. It has a revolving cylinder in which the cartridges are contained. *n.*

re vue (ri vyü′), a theatrical entertainment with singing, dancing, parodies of recent plays, humorous treatments of happenings and fads of the year, etc. *n.*

re vul sion (ri vul′shən), a sudden, violent change or reaction, especially of disgust: *My feeling of friendship turned to revulsion when I realized his dishonesty.* *n.*

re ward (ri wôrd′), **1** return made for something done. **2** a money payment given or offered for capture of criminals, the return of lost property, etc. **3** give a reward to. **4** give a reward for. 1,2 *n.,* 3,4 *v.*

re word (rē wėrd′), put into other words. *v.*

re write (rē rīt′), write again; write in a different form; revise. *v.*, **re wrote** (rē rōt′), **re writ ten** (rē rit′n), **re writ ing.**

Rey kja vik (rā′kyə vēk′), capital of Iceland, in the SW part. *n.*

Reyn ard (ren′ərd *or* rā′närd), name for the fox in stories and poems. Reynard the Fox is the main character in a group of medieval fables about animals. *n.*

Reyn olds (ren′ldz), Sir **Joshua,** 1723-1792, English portrait painter. *n.*

R.F.D., Rural Free Delivery.

rhap sod ic (rap sod′ik), rhapsodical. *adj.*

rhap sod i cal (rap sod′ə kəl), of, having to do with, or characteristic of rhapsody; extravagantly enthusiastic; ecstatic. *adj.*

rhap so dy (rap′sə dē), 1 utterance or writing marked by extravagant enthusiasm: *go into rhapsodies over a present.* 2 (in music) an instrumental composition irregular in form: *Liszt's Hungarian rhapsodies. n., pl.* **rhap so dies.**

rhe a (rē′ə), any of several large birds of South America that are much like the ostrich, but are smaller and have three toes instead of two. *n., pl.* **rhe as.**

Rheims (rēmz), Reims. *n.*

Rhen ish (ren′ish), of the Rhine River or the regions near it. *adj.*

rhe ni um (rē′nē əm), a rare, hard, grayish metallic element which occurs in molybdenum ore. It has a very high melting point and is used in making alloys. *n.* [from Latin *Rhenus* Rhine River]

rhizome—three forms of rhizomes

rhe o stat (rē′ə stat), instrument for regulating the strength of an electric current by introducing different amounts of resistance into the circuit. *n.*

rhe sus (rē′səs), a small, yellowish-brown monkey with a short tail, found in India. It is often used in medical research. *n.*

rhet or ic (ret′ər ik), 1 art of using words effectively in speaking or writing. 2 book about this art. 3 mere display in language. *n.*

rhe to ri cal (ri tôr′ə kəl), 1 of or having to do with rhetoric. 2 using rhetoric. 3 intended especially for display; artificial. 4 oratorical. *adj.* —**rhe to′ri cal ly,** *adv.*

rhetorical question, question asked only for effect, not for information. EXAMPLE: "Who can tell whether or not life exists on other planets?"

rhet o ri cian (ret′ə rish′ən), 1 person skilled in rhetoric. 2 person given to display in language. *n.*

rheum (rüm), 1 a watery discharge, such as mucus, tears, or saliva. 2 catarrh; cold. *n.*

rheu mat ic (rü mat′ik), 1 of rheumatism. 2 having rheumatism; liable to have rheumatism. 3 caused by rheumatism. 4 person who has rheumatism. 1-3 *adj.,* 4 *n.* —**rheu mat′i cal ly,** *adv.*

rhea—3 ft. tall

rheumatic fever, disease more common among children than among grown-ups, characterized by fever, pains in the joints, and often damage to the heart.

rheu ma tism (rü′mə tiz′əm), 1 disease with inflammation, swelling, and stiffness of the joints. 2 rheumatic fever. *n.*

rheum y (rü′mē), 1 full of rheum. 2 causing rheum; damp and cold. *adj.*

Rhine (rīn), river flowing from central Switzerland through West Germany and the Netherlands into the North Sea. *n.*

Rhine land (rīn′land′), 1 the region along the Rhine. 2 the part of West Germany west of the Rhine. *n.*

rhine stone (rīn′stōn′), an imitation diamond, made of glass or paste. *n.*

rhi no (rī′nō), rhinoceros. *n., pl.* **rhi nos.**

rhi noc er os (rī nos′ər əs), a large, thick-skinned mammal of Africa and Asia with one or two upright horns on the snout. Rhinoceroses eat grass and other plants. *n., pl.* **rhi noc er os es** or **rhi noc er os.**

rhi zome (rī′zōm), a rootlike stem, lying on or underneath the ground, which sends out roots below and leafy shoots above; rootstock. *n.*

hat, āge, fär; let, ēqual, tėrm;
it, īce; hot, ōpen, ôrder;
oil, out; cup, pu̇t, rüle; ch, child;
ng, long; sh, she; th, thin;
ŦH, then; zh, measure;

ə represents *a* in about,
e in taken, *i* in pencil,
o in lemon, *u* in circus.

Rhode Island (rōd), one of the northeastern states of the United States. Rhode Island is the smallest state. *Capital:* Providence.

Rhodes (rōdz), 1 island in the Aegean Sea. The Colossus of Rhodes stood over the harbor entrance. 2 **Cecil John,** 1853-1902, British colonial statesman and administrator in South Africa. *n.*

Rho de sia (rō dē′zhə), country in SE Africa, a former self-governing British colony. *Capital:* Salisbury. See **South Africa** for map. *n.* —**Rho de′sian,** *adj., n.*

rho di um (rō′dē əm), a silver-white metallic element found chiefly in platinum ores. It is resistant to acids, and is used for plating silverware, jewelry, etc. *n.*

rho do den dron (rō′də den′drən), 1 an evergreen shrub with beautiful pink, purple, or white flowers. 2 its flower. *n.*

rhombuses

rhom bus (rom′bəs), parallelogram with equal sides, usually having two obtuse angles and two acute angles. *n., pl.* **rhom bus es, rhom bi** (rom′bī).

Rhone or **Rhône** (rōn), river flowing from S Switzerland through SE France into the Mediterranean Sea. See **Rhine** for map. *n.*

rhu barb (rü′bärb), 1 a garden plant with very large leaves, whose sour stalks are used for making sauce, pies, etc. 2 its stalks. 3 SLANG. a violent argument or protest. *n.*

rhyme (rīm), 1 sound alike in the last

rhinoceros—5½ ft. high at the shoulder

rhymer

adj.	adjective	n.	noun
adv.	adverb	prep.	preposition
conj.	conjunction	pron.	pronoun
interj.	interjection	v.	verb
sing.	singular	pl.	plural

part: *"Long" and "song" rhyme. "Go to bed" rhymes with "sleepyhead."* 2 word or line having the same last sound as another: *"Cat" is a rhyme for "mat." "Hey! diddle, diddle" and "The cat and the fiddle" are rhymes.* 3 verses or poetry with some of the lines ending in similar sounds. 4 agreement in the final sounds of words or lines. 5 put or make into rhyme: *rhyme a translation.* 6 make rhymes. 7 use (a word) with another that rhymes with it: *rhyme "love" and "dove."* 1,5-7 *v.,* **rhymed, rhym ing;** 2-4 *n.* Also, **rime.**
without rhyme or reason, having no system or sense.
rhym er (rī′mər), person who makes rhymes. *n.*
rhythm (riŦH′əm), 1 movement with a regular repetition of a beat, accent, rise and fall, or the like: *the rhythm of dancing, the rhythm of the tides, the rhythm of one's heartbeats.* 2 repetition of an accent; arrangement of beats in a line of poetry: *The rhythms of "The Lord's Prayer," "The Night Before Christmas," and "America" are different.* 3 a grouping by accents or beats: *triple rhythm. n.*
rhyth mic (riŦH′mik), rhythmical: *the rhythmic beat of the heart. adj.*
rhyth mi cal (riŦH′mə kəl), having rhythm; of or having to do with rhythm: *the rhythmical sound of the music. adj.* —**rhyth′mi cal ly,** *adv.*
R.I., Rhode Island.

rib (def. 1)
ribs of a
human being

rib (rib), 1 one of the curved bones extending round the chest from the backbone to the front of the body. 2 something like a rib. The curved timbers in a ship's frame are called ribs. The thick vein of a leaf is also called a rib. An umbrella has ribs. 3 furnish or strengthen with ribs. 4 ridge in cloth, knitting, etc. 5 a cut of meat containing a rib: *a rib of beef.* 6 mark with riblike ridges. 7 SLANG. to tease. 1,2,4,5 *n.,* 3,6,7 *v.,* **ribbed, rib bing.** —**rib′like′,** *adj.*
rib ald (rib′əld), offensive in speech; coarsely mocking; irreverent; indecent; obscene. *adj.*
rib ald ry (rib′əl drē), ribald language. *n., pl.* **rib ald ries.**
ribbed (ribd), having ribs or ridges: *ribbed cloth. adj.*
rib bon (rib′ən), 1 a strip or band of silk, satin, velvet, etc. Bows for the hair, belts, and badges are often made of ribbon. 2 anything like such a strip: *a typewriter ribbon. Her dress was torn to ribbons by the thorns and briers she had come through. n.* —**rib′bon like′,** *adj.*
rib boned (rib′ənd), decorated with ribbons; tied with a ribbon. *adj.*
ri bo fla vin (rī′bō flā′vən), a constituent of the vitamin B complex, present in liver, eggs, milk, spinach, etc. It is sometimes called vitamin G or B₂. Persons who lack riboflavin are retarded in growth. *n.*
ri bo nu cle ic acid (rī′bō nü klē′ik *or* rī′bō nyü klē′ik), a complex chemical compound found in the cytoplasm and sometimes in the nuclei of all living cells. It plays an important part in making proteins.
rice (rīs), 1 the starchy seeds or grain of a plant grown in warm climates. Rice is an important food in India, China, and Japan. 2 the plant itself. Rice is a kind of grass. 3 reduce to a form like rice: *to rice potatoes.* 1,2 *n.,* 3 *v.,* **riced, ricing.**
rice bird (rīs′bėrd′), (in the southern United States) a bobolink. *n.*
rich (rich), 1 having much money, land, goods, etc.: *Henry Ford and John D. Rockefeller were rich men.* 2 **the rich,** rich people. 3 well supplied; abounding: *The United States is rich in oil and coal.* 4 producing much; fertile: *rich soil, a rich mine.* 5 having great worth; valuable: *a rich harvest, rich advice.* 6 costly; elegant: *rich dress, rich jewels, rich carpets.* 7 containing plenty of butter, eggs, flavoring, etc.: *a rich fruit cake.* 8 (of colors, sounds, smells, etc.) deep; full; vivid: *a rich red, a rich tone.* 9 INFORMAL. very amusing; ridiculous. 1,3-9 *adj.,* 2 *n.* —**rich′ly,** *adv.* —**rich′ness,** *n.*
Rich ard I (rich′ərd), 1157-1199, king of England from 1189 to 1199. He was called "Richard the Lion-Hearted."
Rich e lieu (rish′ə lü), 1585-1642, French cardinal and statesman who virtually controlled France from 1624 to 1642. *n.*
rich es (rich′iz), much money, land, goods, etc.; abundance of property; wealth. *n.pl.*

Rich mond (rich′mənd), 1 capital of Virginia, in the E part. 2 borough of New York City consisting of Staten Island. *n.*
rick (rik), an outdoor stack of hay, straw, etc., especially one which is covered to protect it from rain. *n.*
rick ets (rik′its), disease of childhood, caused by lack of vitamin D and calcium. It results in softening, and sometimes bending, of the bones. *n.*
rick et y (rik′ə tē), 1 liable to fall or break down; shaky; weak: *a rickety old chair.* 2 having rickets; suffering from rickets. 3 feeble in the joints. *adj.*
rick sha (rik′shô), jinrikisha. *n., pl.* **rick shas.**
rick shaw (rik′shô), jinrikisha. *n.*
ric o chet (rik′ə shā′), 1 the skipping or jumping motion of an object as it goes along a flat surface: *the ricochet of a stone thrown along the surface of water.* 2 move with a skipping or jumping motion: *The bullets struck the ground and ricocheted through the grass.* 1 *n.,* 2 *v.,* **ric o cheted** (rik′ə shād′), **ric o chet ing** (rik′ə shā′ing).
rid¹ (rid), make free: *What will rid a house of mice? v.,* **rid** *or* **rid ded, rid ding.** [Middle English *ridden* to clear land, from a Scandinavian word of the 1200's, such as Icelandic *rythja*]
be rid of, be freed from.
get rid of, 1 get free from: *I can't get rid of this cold.* 2 do away with: *Poison will get rid of the rats in the barn.*
rid² (rid), OLD USE. a past tense and a past participle of **ride.** *v.*
rid dance (rid′ns), a clearing away or out; removal. *n.*
good riddance, exclamation expressing relief that something or somebody has been removed.
rid den (rid′n), past participle of **ride.** *I had ridden my horse all day. v.*
rid dle¹ (rid′l), 1 a puzzling question, statement, problem, etc. EXAMPLE: When is a door not a door? ANSWER: When it is ajar. 2 person or thing that is hard to understand, explain, etc. 3 speak in riddles. 4 solve a riddle or question. 1,2 *n.,* 3,4 *v.,* **rid dled, rid dling.** [Middle English *redel,* from earlier *redels* (taken as a plural), Old English *rædels,* from *rædan* to guess, explain]
rid dle² (rid′l), 1 pierce with holes: *Insects had riddled the old tree stump.* 2 a coarse sieve. 3 sift: *riddle gravel.* 1,3 *v.,* 2 *n.* [Old English *hriddel* sieve]
ride (rīd), 1 sit on a horse and make it go. 2 sit on something and make it go: *ride a camel, ride a bicycle.* 3 be carried along by anything: *ride on a train, ride in a car.* 4 ride over, along, or through. 5 be carried on: *The eagle rides the*

winds. 6 a trip on horseback, in an automobile, on a train, etc.: *On Sundays we take a ride into the country. My brother enjoyed his ride on the merry-go-round.* 7 move or float on the water: *The ship rides at anchor.* 8 INFORMAL. make fun of; tease. 9 cause to ride; carry: *She rode her little brother piggyback.* 10 control, dominate, or tyrannize over: *be ridden by foolish fears.* 1-5,7-10 *v.,* **rode, rid den, rid ing;** 6 *n.*

let ride, leave undisturbed or inactive: *Let the matter ride until the next meeting.*

ride down, 1 knock down. 2 overcome. 3 overtake by riding.

ride out, endure successfully: *The small boat rode out the storm without damage.*

rid er (rī′dər), 1 person who rides: *a horseback rider.* 2 anything added to a record, document, legislative bill, or statement after it was supposed to be complete. *n.*

rid er less (rī′dər lis), without a rider. *adj.*

ridge (rij), 1 the long and narrow upper part of something: *the ridge of an animal's back.* 2 the line where two sloping surfaces meet: *the ridge of a roof.* 3 a long, narrow chain of hills or mountains: *the Blue Ridge of the Appalachian Mountains.* 4 any raised narrow strip: *the ridges on corduroy cloth, the ridges in plowed ground.* 5 to form or make into ridges. 6 to cover with ridges; mark with ridges. 1-4 *n.,* 5,6 *v.,* **ridged, ridg ing.**

RIDGE

RIDGEPOLE

ridge pole (rij′pōl′), the horizontal timber along the top of a roof or tent; rooftree. *n.*

rid i cule (rid′ə kyül), 1 laugh at; make fun of: *People once ridiculed the Wright brothers' invention.* 2 laughter in mockery; words or actions that make fun of somebody or something: *I was very hurt by the ridicule of my classmates.* 1 *v.,* **rid i culed, rid i cul ing;** 2 *n.*

ri dic u lous (ri dik′yə ləs), deserving ridicule; absurd; laughable: *It would be ridiculous to walk backward all the time. adj.* —**ri dic′u lous ly,** *adv.* —**ri dic′u lous ness,** *n.*

rife (rīf), 1 happening often; common; numerous; widespread: *Sudden noises,* so rife in the big city, bothered the visitor from the country. 2 well supplied; full; abounding: *Our town was rife with rumors that the bank had no funds. adj.*

riff raff (rif′raf′), 1 disreputable people. 2 trash. *n.*

ri fle (rī′fəl), 1 gun with spiral grooves in its long barrel which spin or rotate the bullet as it is shot. A rifle is usually fired from the shoulder. 2 cut such grooves in (a gun). 3 search and rob; ransack and rob. 4 take away; steal. 5 strip bare: *The boys rifled the apple tree.* 1 *n.,* 2-5 *v.,* **ri fled, ri fling.**

ri fle man (rī′fəl mən), 1 soldier armed with a rifle. 2 man skilled in the use of a rifle. *n., pl.* **ri fle men.**

ri fler (rī′flər), person who rifles; robber. *n.*

ri fling (rī′fling), 1 act or process of cutting spiral grooves in a gun barrel. 2 system of spiral grooves in a rifle. *n.*

rift (rift), 1 a split; break; crack: *The sun shone through a rift in the clouds.* 2 to split; cleave. 1 *n.,* 2 *v.*

rig (def. 2) on a ketch

rig (rig), 1 fit out (a ship) with masts, sails, and ropes: *My sister and brother rigged a toy boat for me.* 2 the arrangement of masts, sails, ropes, etc., on a ship. A schooner has a fore-and-aft rig; that is, the sails are set lengthwise on the ship. 3 outfit; equipment: *a camper's rig, an oil-drilling rig.* 4 equip; fit out: *rig out a football team with uniforms.* 5 INFORMAL. to dress: *On Halloween the children rig themselves up in funny clothes.* 6 INFORMAL. set of clothes; costume: *His rig consisted of a silk hat and overalls.* 7 get ready for use. 8 put together in a hurry or by using odds and ends: *The girls rigged up a tent with a rope and a blanket.* 9 arrange in an unfair way: *The race was rigged.* 10 INFORMAL. carriage, with its horse or horses. 1,4,5,7-9 *v.,* **rigged, rig ging;** 2,3,6,10 *n.*

Ri ga (rē′gə), 1 seaport on the Baltic Sea and capital of Latvia. 2 **Gulf of,** gulf on the Baltic Sea. *n.*

rig ger (rig′ər), person who rigs. *n.*

rig ging (rig′ing), 1 ropes, chains, and cables, used to support and work the masts, yards, sails, etc., on a ship. 2 tackle; equipment: *Do you need all that rigging for a trip of only two days? n.*

right (rīt), 1 that is as it ought to be; good; just; lawful: *She did the right thing when she told the truth.* 2 in a way that is good, just, or lawful: *He acted right when he told the truth.* 3 that which is right, just, good, or true: *Do right, not wrong.* 4 a just claim; something that is due to a person: *Each member of the club has a right to vote. I demand my rights.* 5 correct; true: *the right answer.* 6 correctly; truly: *She guessed right.* 7 proper; suitable; fitting: *Learn to say the right thing at the right time.* 8 properly; well: *It's faster to do a job right the first time.* 9 in good condition; well; healthy: *He was thin and pale, and said he didn't feel quite right.* 10 meant to be seen; most important: *the right side of cloth.* 11 make correct; set right: *right a wrong.* 12 do justice to: *right the oppressed.* 13 fair treatment; justice. 14 get or put into proper position: *The ship righted as the wave passed. We righted the sailboat.* 15 opposite of left; belonging to the side that is turned east when the main side is turned north. Most people eat, write, and work with their right hands. 16 on this side when viewed from the front: *Make a right turn at the corner.* 17 on or to the right side: *Turn right.* 18 the right side or hand: *Please sit on my right.* 19 exactly; just; precisely: *Your cap is right where you left it.* 20 at once; immediately: *Stop playing right now.* 21 very: *the Right Honorable Lord Mayor.* 22 DIALECT. extremely: *I am right glad to see you.* 23 in a straight line; directly: *Look me right in the eye.* 24 straight: *a right line.* 25 completely: *My hat was knocked right off.* 26 part of a lawmaking body consisting of the conservative or reactionary political groups. 27 having conservative or reactionary ideas in politics. 28 OLD USE. rightful; real. 1,5,7,9,10,15,16,24,27, 28 *adj.,* 2,6,8,17,19-23,25 *adv.,* 3,4,13, 18,26 *n.,* 11,12,14 *v.* —**right′ness,** *n.*

by rights or **by right,** properly; rightly; correctly.

in the right, right.

right about! turn in the opposite direction.

adj.	adjective	*n.*	noun
adv.	adverb	*prep.*	preposition
conj.	conjunction	*pron.*	pronoun
interj.	interjection	*v.*	verb
sing.	singular	*pl.*	plural

right away or **right off**, at once; immediately: *He promised to do it right away.*

to rights, INFORMAL. in or into proper condition, order, etc.

right angle, an angle that is formed by a line perpendicular to another line; angle of 90 degrees. The angles in a square or in the capital letters F, L, and T are right angles.

right angles—five right angles

right-an gled (rīt′ang′gəld), containing a right angle or right angles; rectangular. *adj.*

right eous (rī′chəs), 1 doing right; virtuous; behaving justly: *a righteous person.* 2 proper; just; right: *righteous indignation. adj.* —**right′eous ly,** *adv.*

right eous ness (rī′chəs nis), upright conduct; virtue; being righteous. *n.*

right field, (in baseball) the section of the outfield behind first base.

right ful (rīt′fəl), 1 according to law; by rights: *the rightful owner of this dog.* 2 just and right; proper. *adj.* —**right′ful ness,** *n.*

right ful ly (rīt′fə lē), 1 according to right, law, or justice. 2 properly; fittingly. *adv.*

right-hand (rīt′hand′), 1 on or to the right. 2 of, for, or with the right hand. 3 most helpful or useful: *He is the scoutmaster's right-hand man. adj.*

right-hand ed (rīt′han′did), 1 using the right hand more easily and readily than the left. 2 done with the right hand. 3 made to be used with the right hand. 4 turning from left to right: *a right-handed screw.* 5 toward the right; with the right hand. 1-4 *adj.,* 5 *adv.*

right ist (rī′tist), 1 person who has conservative or reactionary ideas in politics. 2 member of a conservative or reactionary political organization. 3 having conservative or reactionary ideas. 1,2 *n.,* 3 *adj.*

right ly (rīt′lē), 1 in a just manner; fairly. 2 correctly: *She guessed rightly that it would rain.* 3 properly; suitably. *adv.*

right of way, 1 the right to go first, especially the right of a vehicle to cross in front of another. 2 the right to pass over another's property.

right triangle, triangle with one right angle.

right wing, the conservative or reactionary members, especially of a political party.

rig id (rij′id), 1 not bending; stiff; firm: *Hold your arm rigid.* 2 not changing; strict: *In our home, it is a rigid rule to wash one's hands before eating. adj.* —**rig′id ly,** *adv.* —**rig′id ness,** *n.*

ri gid i ty (ri jid′ə tē), 1 stiffness; firmness. 2 strictness; severity. *n.*

rig ma role (rig′mə rōl′), foolish talk or activity; words or action without meaning; nonsense. *n.*

rig or (rig′ər), 1 strictness; severity: *The new recruits were trained with great rigor.* 2 harshness: *endure the rigors of a long, cold winter.* 3 logical exactness: *the rigor of scientific method. n.*

rig or ous (rig′ər əs), 1 severe; strict: *the rigorous discipline in the army.* 2 harsh: *a rigorous climate.* 3 thoroughly logical and scientific; exact: *the rigorous methods of science. adj.* —**rig′or ous ly,** *adv.* —**rig′or ous ness,** *n.*

rile (rīl), INFORMAL. roil. *v.,* **riled, ril ing.**

Ri ley (rī′lē), **James Whitcomb,** 1849-1916, American poet. *n.*

rill (ril), a tiny stream; little brook. *n.*

rim (rim), 1 an edge, border, or margin on or around anything: *the rim of a wheel, the rim of a cup.* 2 form a rim around; put a rim around: *Wild flowers and grasses rimmed the little pool.* 1 *n.,* 2 *v.,* **rimmed, rim ming.**

rime[1] (rīm), rhyme. *v.,* **rimed, rim ing;** *n.* [from French of the 1200's *rime,* from Latin *rhythmus* rhythm]

rime[2] (rīm), 1 white frost; hoarfrost. 2 cover with rime. 1 *n.,* 2 *v.,* **rimed, rim ing.** [Old English *hrīm*]

Rim sky-Kor sa kov (rim′skē kôr′-sə kôf), **Nikolay,** 1844-1908, Russian composer. *n.*

rind (rīnd), 1 the firm outer covering of oranges, melons, cheeses, etc. 2 the bark of a tree or plant. *n.*

ring[1] (ring), 1 a circle: *You can tell the age of a tree by counting the number of rings in its wood; one ring grows every year. The elves danced in a ring.* 2 a thin circle of metal or other material: *a napkin ring, a wedding ring, a key ring.* 3 persons or things arranged in a circle. 4 the outer edge or border of a coin, plate, wheel, or anything round. 5 put a ring around; enclose; form a circle around. 6 toss a horseshoe, ring, etc., over: *He ringed the post.* 7 provide with a ring. 8 put a ring in the nose of (an animal). 9 form a ring or rings.

10 an enclosed space (for races, or games): *a circus ring, a ring for a fight.* 11 prizefighting. 12 group of people combined for a selfish or bad purpose: *A ring of corrupt politicians controlled the city.* 1-4,10-12 *n.,* 5-9 *v.,* **ringed, ring ing.** [Old English *hring*] —**ring′like′,** *adj.*

run rings around, INFORMAL. surpass with great ease; beat easily.

ring[2] (ring), 1 give forth a clear sound, as a bell does: *Did the telephone ring?* 2 cause to give forth a clear ringing sound: *Ring the bell.* 3 cause a bell to sound: *Did you ring?* 4 make (a sound) by ringing: *The bells rang a joyous peal.* 5 a sound of a bell: *Did you hear a ring?* 6 a sound like that of a bell: *On a cold night we can hear the ring of skates on ice.* 7 announce or proclaim by bells; usher; conduct: *Ring out the old year; ring in the new.* 8 proclaim or repeat loudly everywhere: *ring a person's praises.* 9 resound; sound loudly: *The room rang with shouts of laughter.* 10 to echo; give back sound: *The mountains rang with the roll of thunder.* 11 be filled with report or talk. 12 sound: *His words rang true.* 13 have a sensation as of sounds of bells; hear inner sounds: *My ears ring.* 14 a characteristic sound or quality: *a ring of sincerity.* 15 call up on a telephone: *I'll ring you tomorrow.* 16 a call on the telephone. 1-4,7-13,15 *v.,* **rang, rung, ring ing;** 5,6,14,16 *n.* [Old English *hringan*]

ring for, summon by a bell.

ring in, INFORMAL. bring in dishonestly or trickily.

ring off, end a telephone call.

ring up, record (a specific amount) on a cash register.

ringed (ringd), 1 having or wearing a ring or rings. 2 marked or decorated with a ring or rings. 3 surrounded by a ring or rings. 4 formed of or with rings; ringlike. *adj.*

ring er[1] (ring′ər), person or thing that encircles, surrounds with a ring, etc. *n.* [*ring*[1] + *-er*[1]]

ring er[2] (ring′ər), 1 person or thing that rings; device for ringing a bell. 2 SLANG. person or thing very much like another. *n.* [*ring*[2] + *-er*[1]]

ring lead er (ring′lē′dər), person who leads others in opposition to authority or law: *the ringleaders of the mutiny. n.*

ring let (ring′lit), 1 curl: *The baby's hair was in ringlets.* 2 a little ring: *Drops of rain made ringlets in the pond. n.*

ring side (ring′sīd′), 1 a place just outside the ring at a circus, prizefight, etc. 2 a place affording a close view. *n.*

ring worm (ring′wėrm′), any of several contagious skin diseases caused by fungi. One kind appears in the form of ring-shaped patches. Athlete's foot is a common type of ringworm.

rink (ringk), 1 sheet of ice for skating. 2 a smooth floor for roller-skating. *n.*

rinse (rins), 1 wash with clean water: *Rinse all the soap out of your hair after you wash it.* 2 wash lightly: *Rinse your mouth with water and soda.* 3 a rinsing: *Give the plate a final rinse in cold water.* 4 a preparation used in water to add color or luster to the hair. 1,2 *v.*, **rinsed, rins ing;** 3,4 *n.*

Ri o de Ja nei ro (rē′ō dā zhə-ner′ō), seaport on the SE coast of Brazil.

Rio Grande (rē′ō grand′ or rē′ō grän′dē), river forming part of the boundary between the United States and Mexico.

ri ot (rī′ət), 1 a wild, violent public disturbance; disorder caused by an unruly crowd or mob: *The guards stopped several riots in the prison.* 2 behave in a wild, disorderly way. 3 to revel. 4 a bright display: *The garden was a riot of color.* 5 INFORMAL. a very amusing person or performance: *He was a riot at the party.* 1,4,5 *n.,* 2,3 *v.* —**ri′ot er,** *n.*

read the riot act, give orders for disturbance to cease.

run riot, 1 act without restraint. 2 grow wildly or luxuriantly. 3 run wild.

ri ot ous (rī′ə təs), 1 taking part in a riot. 2 boisterous; disorderly: *Sounds of riotous glee came from the playhouse.* *adj.* —**ri′ot ous ly,** *adv.*

rip[1] (rip), 1 cut roughly; tear apart; tear off: *Rip the cover off this box.* 2 become torn apart. 3 cut or pull out (the threads in the seams of a garment). 4 a torn place, especially a seam burst in a garment: *Please sew up this rip in my sleeve.* 5 saw (wood) along the grain, not across the grain. 6 INFORMAL. move fast or violently. 7 INFORMAL. speak or say with violence: *He ripped out an angry oath.* 1-3,5-7 *v.,* **ripped, rip ping;** 4 *n.* [Middle English *rippen*] **rip off,** SLANG. steal: *rip off an expensive camera.*

rip[2] (rip), 1 a stretch of rough water made by opposing currents meeting. 2 a swift current made by the tide. *n.* [perhaps special use of *rip*[1]]

rip current, a strong, narrow surface current which flows rapidly away from the shore; riptide.

ripe (rīp), 1 full-grown and ready to be gathered and eaten: *ripe fruit.* 2 fully developed; mature: *a ripe cheese, ripe in knowledge.* 3 ready: *That country is ripe for revolt.* 4 advanced in years: *the ripe age of 75. adj.,* **rip er, rip est.** —**ripe′ness,** *n.*

rip en (rī′pən), become or make ripe. *v.*

rip-off (rip′ôf′), SLANG. 1 theft. 2 something that exploits a popular trend or interest. *n.*

rip per (rip′ər), 1 person who rips. 2 tool for ripping. *n.*

rip ple (rip′əl), 1 a very little wave: *Throw a stone into still water and watch the ripples spread in rings.* 2 anything that seems like a tiny wave: *ripples in hair.* 3 a sound that reminds one of little waves: *a ripple of laughter in the crowd.* 4 make a sound like rippling water. 5 form or have ripples. 6 make ripples on: *A breeze rippled the quiet waters.* 1-3 *n.,* 4-6 *v.,* **rip pled, rip pling.**

rip saw (rip′sô′), saw for cutting wood along the grain, not across the grain. *n.*

rip tide (rip′tīd′), rip current. *n.*

Rip Van Win kle (rip′ van wing′kəl), hero of a story by Washington Irving who falls asleep and wakes twenty years later to find everything changed.

rise (rīz), 1 get up from a lying, sitting, or kneeling position; stand up: *Please rise from your seat when you recite.* 2 get up from sleep or rest: *The farmer's wife rises at 6 every morning.* 3 go up; come up; move up; ascend: *The curtain rose on the first act of the play. Mercury rises in a thermometer on a hot day.* 4 go higher; increase: *Prices are rising. My anger rose at that remark. The wind rose rapidly.* 5 a going up; a going higher: *We watched the rise of the balloon. There has been a great rise in prices since the war.* 6 an advance in rank, power, etc. 7 to advance in importance, rank, etc.: *He rose from errand boy to president of the company.* 8 to slope upward: *Hills rise in the distance.* 9 an upward slope: *The rise of that hill is gradual.* 10 piece of rising or high ground; hill: *The house is situated on a rise.* 11 the vertical height of a step, slope, arch, etc. 12 come above the horizon: *The sun rises in the morning.* 13 start; begin: *The river rises from a spring. Quarrels often rise from trifles.* 14 come into being or action: *The wind rose rapidly.* 15 origin; beginning; start: *the rise of industrialism, the rise of a river, the rise of a storm, the rise of a new problem.* 16 become more cheerful; improve: *Our spirits rose at the good news.* 17 to revolt; rebel: *The people rose against their leaders.* 18 grow larger and lighter: *Yeast makes dough rise.* 19 come to life again: *Christ is risen.* 20 end a meeting or session. 1-4,7,8,12-14,16-20 *v.,* **rose, ris en, ris ing;** 5,6,9-11,15 *n.*

get a rise out of, INFORMAL. get an emotional reaction from: *get a rise out of a person by teasing him.*

give rise to, bring about; start; begin;

hat, āge, fär; let, ēqual, tėrm; it, īce; hot, ōpen, ôrder; oil, out; cup, pùt, rüle; ch, child; ng, long; sh, she; th, thin; ŦH, then; zh, measure;

ə represents *a* in about, *e* in taken, *i* in pencil, *o* in lemon, *u* in circus.

cause: *The circumstances of her disappearance gave rise to a suspicion that she may have been kidnaped.*

rise to, be equal to; be able to deal with: *They rose to the occasion.*

ris en (riz′n), past participle of **rise.** *They had risen before dawn. v.*

ris er (rī′zər), 1 person or thing that rises: *an early riser.* 2 the vertical part of a step.

risk (risk), 1 chance of harm or loss; danger: *If you drive carefully, there is no risk of being fined.* 2 expose to the chance of harm or loss: *You risk your neck trying to climb that tree.* 3 take the risk of: *They risked defeat in fighting the larger army.* 1 *n.,* 2,3 *v.*

run a risk or **take a risk,** expose oneself to the chance of harm or loss.

risk y (ris′kē), full of risk; dangerous. *adj.,* **risk i er, risk i est.**

rite (rīt), 1 a solemn ceremony. Most churches have rites for baptism, marriage, and burial. Secret societies have their special rites. 2 a particular form or system of ceremonies. The Roman Catholic Church uses a Latin rite. *n.*

rit u al (rich′ü əl), 1 a form or system of rites. The rites of baptism, marriage, and burial are parts of the ritual of most churches. Secret societies have a ritual for initiating new members. 2 book containing rites or ceremonies. 3 of or having to do with rites; done as a rite: *a ritual dance, ritual laws.* 4 the carrying out of rites. 1,2,4 *n.,* 3 *adj.* —**rit′u al ly,** *adv.*

rit u al ism (rich′ü ə liz′əm), 1 fondness for ritual; insistence upon ritual. 2 study of ritual practices or religious rites. *n.*

ri val (rī′vəl), 1 person who wants and tries to get the same thing as another or who tries to equal or do better than another; competitor: *The two girls were rivals for the same class office. They were also rivals in sports.* 2 wanting the same thing as another; trying to equal or outdo another; competing: *The rival store tried to get our grocer's trade.* 3 try to equal or outdo; compete with: *The stores rival each other in beautiful window displays.* 4 equal; match: *The*

adj. adjective	*n.* noun	
adv. adverb	*prep.* preposition	
conj. conjunction	*pron.* pronoun	
interj. interjection	*v.* verb	
sing. singular	*pl.* plural	

sunset *rivaled the sunrise in beauty.* 5 thing that will bear comparison with something else; equal; match. 1,5 *n.,* 2 *adj.,* 3,4 *v.*

ri val ry (rī′vəl rē), effort to obtain something another person wants; competition: *There is rivalry among business firms for trade. n., pl.* **ri val ries.**

riv en (riv′ən), torn apart; split. *adj.*

riv er (riv′ər), 1 a large, natural stream of water that flows into a lake, ocean, etc. The Nile is the longest river in the world. 2 any abundant stream or flow: *rivers of blood. n.*

riv er bank (riv′ər bangk′), the ground bordering a river. *n.*

river basin, land that is drained by a river and its tributaries.

riv er side (riv′ər sīd′), 1 the bank of a river: *We walked along the riverside.* 2 beside a river: *The riverside path is much used.* 1 *n.,* 2 *adj.*

rivet (def. 1)

riv et (riv′it), 1 a metal bolt with a head at one end, the other end being hammered into a head after insertion. Rivets fasten heavy steel beams together. 2 fasten with a rivet or rivets. 3 fasten firmly; fix firmly: *Their eyes were riveted on the speaker.* 1 *n.,* 2,3 *v.* —**riv′et er,** *n.*

Riv i er a (riv′ē er′ə), section of SE France and NW Italy along the Mediterranean Sea, famous as a resort. *n.*

riv u let (riv′yə lit), a very small stream. *n.*

Ri yadh (ri yäd′), capital of Saudi Arabia, in the central part. Mecca is the religious capital. *n.*

rm., 1 ream. 2 room. *pl.* **rms.**

RNA, ribonucleic acid.

roach¹ (rōch), cockroach. *n., pl.* **roach es.** [shortened from *cockroach,* from Spanish *cucaracha*]

roach² (rōch), a silvery European freshwater fish related to the carp. *n., pl.* **roach es** or **roach.** [from French of the 1300's *roche*]

road (rōd), 1 a way between places; way made for automobiles, trucks, etc., to travel on: *the road from New York to*

Boston. 2 a way or course: *the road to ruin, a road to peace.* 3 railroad. 4 Also, **roads,** *pl.* roadstead. *n.*

on the road, traveling, especially as a salesman.

road bed (rōd′bed′), foundation for a road or for railroad tracks. *n.*

road block (rōd′blok′), an obstacle. *n.*

road hog, INFORMAL. person who uses more of the road than is necessary, especially by driving in the center of the road.

road map, map for automobile travel, showing the roads in a region and the distances between cities and towns.

road run ner (rōd′run′ər), a long-tailed bird of the deserts of the southwestern United States that is related to the cuckoo. It usually runs instead of flying. *n.*

road side (rōd′sīd′), 1 the side of a road: *Flowers grew along the roadside.* 2 beside a road: *a roadside inn.* 1 *n.,* 2 *adj.*

road stead (rōd′sted), a place near the shore where ships may anchor; road. *n.*

road ster (rōd′stər), an open automobile with a single wide seat. *n.*

road way (rōd′wā′), 1 road. 2 the part of a road used by wheeled vehicles: *Walk on the path, not in the roadway. n.*

roam (rōm), 1 go about with no special plan or aim; wander: *roam through the fields.* 2 wander over. *v.* —**roam′er,** *n.*

roan (rōn), 1 yellowish- or reddish-brown sprinkled with gray or white. 2 horse or other animal of a roan color. 3 a roan color. 1 *adj.,* 2,3 *n.*

roar (rôr), 1 make a loud, deep sound; make a loud noise: *The lion roared. The wind roared at the windows.* 2 a loud, deep sound; loud noise: *the roar of the cannon, a roar of laughter.* 3 utter loudly: *roar out an order.* 4 laugh loudly: *The audience roared at the clown.* 1,3,4 *v.,* 2 *n.* —**roar′er,** *n.*

roast (rōst), 1 cook by dry heat; cook before a fire; bake: *We roasted meat and potatoes.* 2 piece of baked meat; piece of meat to be roasted. 3 an informal outdoor meal, at which some food is cooked over an open fire: *a wiener roast.* 4 roasted: *roast beef, roast pork.* 5 prepare by heating: *roast coffee, roast a metal ore.* 6 make or become very hot. 7 INFORMAL. make fun of; ridicule. 1,5-7 *v.,* 2,3 *n.,* 4 *adj.*

roast er (rō′stər), 1 pan used in roasting. 2 something fit to be roasted. 3 one that roasts. *n.*

rob (rob), 1 take away from by force or threats; steal from; plunder; pillage: *Bandits robbed the bank of thousands of dollars.* 2 steal: *Some girls robbed fruit from the orchard. They said they*

would not rob again. 3 take away some characteristic; keep from having or doing: *The disease has robbed him of his strength. v.,* **robbed, rob bing.**

rob ber (rob′ər), person who robs; thief. *n.*

rob ber y (rob′ər ē), act of robbing; theft; stealing: *a bank robbery. n., pl.* **rob ber ies.**

robe (rōb), 1 a long, loose outer garment: *The priests wore robes.* 2 garment that shows rank, office, etc.: *a judge's robe, the king's robes of state.* 3 a covering or wrap: *Put a robe over you when you go for a ride on a cold day.* 4 put a robe on; dress. 5 bathrobe or dressing gown. 1-3,5 *n.,* 4 *v.,* **robed, rob ing.**

rob in (rob′ən), 1 a large American thrush with a reddish breast. 2 a small European bird with a yellowish-red breast. *n.*

roadster—1924 model, with folding top

Robin Hood, (in English legends) an outlaw who robbed the rich but gave money to the poor.

Rob in son Crusoe (rob′ən sən). See Crusoe.

ro bot (rō′bət), 1 machine made in imitation of a human being; a mechanical device that does routine work in response to commands. 2 person who acts or works in a dull, mechanical way. *n.*

ro bust (rō bust′ or rō′bust), 1 strong and healthy; sturdy: *a robust person, a robust mind.* 2 rough; rude. *adj.* —**robust′ly,** *adv.* —**ro bust′ness,** *n.*

roc (rok), a bird having enormous size and strength, famous in Arabian tales. *n.*

Ro cham beau (rō shäm bō′), **Count de,** 1725-1807, commander of the French forces sent to help the American army in the Revolutionary War. *n.*

Roch es ter (roch′es′tər), city in W New York State. *n.*

rock¹ (rok), 1 a large mass of stone: *The ship was wrecked on the rocks.* 2 any piece of stone; a stone: *I threw a rock in the lake.* 3 the mass of mineral matter of which the earth's crust is made up. 4 a particular layer or kind of such matter. Granite, sandstone, and gneiss are rocks. 5 something firm like a rock; support; defense: *The Lord is my rock. n.* [from French of the 1300's *roque,* from Latin *rocca*] —**rock′like′,** *adj.*

on the rocks, 1 wrecked; ruined. 2 INFORMAL. bankrupt.

rock² (rok), 1 move backward or forward, or from side to side; sway: *My chair rocks. The waves rocked the ship. The earthquake rocked the houses.* 2 put (to sleep, rest, etc.) with swaying movements: *Mother rocked the baby to sleep.* 3 a rocking movement. 4 INFORMAL. rock'n'roll. 1,2 *v.,* 3,4 *n.* [Old English *roccian*]

rock bottom, the very bottom; lowest level.

rock-bound (rok′bound′), surrounded by rocks; rocky: *a rock-bound harbor. adj.*

rock candy, sugar in the form of large, hard crystals.

Rock e fel ler (rok′ə fel′ər), 1 **John D(avison),** 1839-1937, American capitalist and philanthropist. 2 his son, **John D(avison),** 1874-1960, American capitalist and philanthropist. *n.*

rock er (rok′ər), 1 one of the curved pieces on which a cradle, rocking chair, etc., rocks. 2 rocking chair. *n.*

rocket (def. 1) which uses liquid fuel

rock et (rok′it), 1 projectile consisting of a tube open at one end and filled with some substance that burns rapidly, and the oxygen required for the combustion of this fuel, creating expanding gases which escape at very high velocities from the open end, propelling the tube and whatever is attached to it rapidly upward or forward. Some rockets, used for fireworks and signaling, shoot up high in the air and explode into showers of sparks or stars. Other rockets carry exploding warheads and are used as weapons. Large rockets are used for carrying capsules and satellites into outer space. 2 spacecraft, missile, etc., propelled by such a projectile. 3 go like a rocket; rise very fast; skyrocket: *rocket across the finish line in a race. The author rocketed to fame when her book was published.* 1,2 *n.,* 3 *v.*

rocket launcher, device consisting of a tube or cluster of tubes from which rockets are launched.

rocket launcher

rock et ry (rok′ə trē), the science of building, using, and firing rockets. *n.*

Rock ies (rok′ēz), Rocky Mountains. *n.pl.*

rock i ness (rok′ē nis), a being shaky; weakness. *n.*

rocking chair, chair mounted on rockers, or on springs, so that it can rock back and forth; rocker.

rocking horse, a toy horse on rockers for children to ride; hobbyhorse.

rock 'n' roll (rok′ən rōl′), 1 kind of popular music with a strong beat and simple melody. 2 a vigorous dance done to this music. *n.*

rock salt, common salt as it occurs in the earth in large crystals; halite. Rock salt is often used to melt ice on roads and sidewalks.

rock wool, woollike fibers made from rock or slag and used for insulation and soundproofing.

rock y¹ (rok′ē), 1 full of rocks: *a rocky shore.* 2 made of rock. 3 like rock; hard; firm: *rocky determination. adj.,* **rock i er, rock i est.** [*rock¹* + *-y¹*]

rock y² (rok′ē), 1 likely to rock; shaky: *That table is a bit rocky; put a piece of wood under the short leg.* 2 SLANG. sickish; weak; dizzy. *adj.,* **rock i er, rock i est.** [*rock²* + *-y¹*]

Rocky Mountains, chief group of mountain ranges in W North America; the Rockies. They extend from Alaska to New Mexico.

rococo (def. 2)
rococo mirror frame

ro co co (rə kō′kō), 1 style of architecture and decoration with elaborate ornamentation, combining shellwork, scrolls, foliage, etc., much used in the 1700's. 2 of or having to do with this style. 1 *n.,* 2 *adj.*

rod (rod), 1 a thin, straight bar of metal or wood. An atomic reactor is made to operate by rods of some radioactive substance. 2 a thin, straight stick, either growing or cut off. 3 a stick used to beat or punish. 4 punishment. 5 fishing rod. 6 measure of length equal to 5½ yards or 16½ feet; perch. A square rod is 30¼ square yards or 272¼ square feet. 7 staff or wand carried as a symbol of one's position. *n.* —**rod′like′,** *adj.*

spare the rod, fail to punish.

rode (rōd), past tense of **ride.** *We rode ten miles yesterday. v.*

hat, āge, fär; let, ēqual, tėrm;
it, īce; hot, ōpen, ôrder;
oil, out; cup, pu̇t, rüle; ch, child;
ng, long; sh, she; th, thin;
ᵀH, then; zh, measure;

ə represents *a* in about,
e in taken, *i* in pencil,
o in lemon, *u* in circus.

ro dent (rōd′nt), 1 any of a group of mammals having teeth especially adapted for gnawing wood and similar material. Rats, mice, and squirrels are rodents. 2 gnawing. 1 *n.,* 2 *adj.*

ro de o (rō′dē ō *or* rō dā′ō), 1 a contest or exhibition of skill in roping cattle, riding horses and steers, etc. 2 (in the western United States) the driving of cattle together. *n., pl.* **ro de os.**

Ro din (rō dan′), **Auguste,** 1840-1917, French sculptor. *n.*

roe¹ (rō), a small deer of Europe and Asia, with forked antlers. *n., pl.* **roes** or **roe.** [Old English *rā*]

roe² (rō), fish eggs. *n.* [Middle English *rowe,* perhaps from *rown* (taken as a plural), from a Scandinavian word of the 1200's, such as Icelandic *hrogn*]

roe buck (rō′buk′), a male roe deer. *n.*

roent gen (rent′gən), measure of radiation intensity in X rays and gamma rays. *n.* [from Wilhelm K. *Roentgen*]

Roent gen (rent′gən), **Wilhelm Konrad,** 1845-1923, German physicist who discovered X rays. *n.*

Roentgen ray, X ray.

rog er (roj′ər), SLANG. O.K.; message received and understood. *interj.*

rogue (rōg), 1 dishonest or unprincipled person; rascal. 2 a mischievous person: *The little rogue has his grandpa's glasses on.* 3 animal with a savage nature that lives apart from the herd: *An elephant that is a rogue is very dangerous. n.*

ro guer y (rō′gər ē), 1 conduct of rogues. 2 playful mischief. *n., pl.* **ro guer ies.**

rogues' gallery, collection of photographs of known criminals.

ro guish (rō′gish), 1 having to do with or like rogues; dishonest; rascally. 2 playfully mischievous: *with a roguish twinkle in his eyes. adj.* —**ro′guish ly,** *adv.* —**ro′guish ness,** *n.*

roil (roil), 1 make (water, etc.) muddy by stirring up sediment. 2 disturb; irritate; vex. *v.*

rois ter (roi′stər), be boisterous; revel noisily; swagger. *v.* —**rois′ter er,** *n.*

727

Roland

Ro land (rō′lənd), the most famous of Charlemagne's knights. *n.*

role or **rôle** (rōl), 1 an actor's part in a play, motion picture, etc.: *She played the leading role in the school play.* 2 a part played in real life: *A judge's role is to be fair in his decisions. n.* [from French *rôle* the roll (of paper, etc.) on which a part was written]

roll (rōl), 1 move along by turning over and over: *A ball rolls. Wheels roll. The child rolls a hoop.* 2 turn round and round on itself or on something else; wrap; be wrapped round: *The boy rolled himself up in a blanket. Roll the string into a ball.* 3 something rolled up: *rolls of paper, a roll of carpet.* 4 a rounded or rolled-up mass: *a roll of butter.* 5 move or be moved on wheels or rollers: *roll a bicycle. The car rolled along.* 6 move smoothly; sweep along: *Waves roll in on the beach. The years roll on.* 7 move with a side-to-side motion: *roll one's eyes. The ocean liner rolled in the waves.* 8 act of rolling; motion from side to side: *The ship's roll made many people sick.* 9 rise and fall again and again: *rolling country, rolling waves.* 10 make flat or smooth with a roller; spread out with a rolling pin, etc.: *Rolling the grass makes a smooth lawn. Roll the dough thin for these cookies.* 11 make deep, loud sounds: *Thunder rolls.* 12 a deep, loud sound: *the roll of thunder.* 13 beat (a drum) with rapid, continuous strokes. 14 a rapid, continuous beating on a drum. 15 trill: *roll one's r's.* 16 a list of names; record; list: *I will call the roll to find out who are absent.* 17 roller. 18 a kind of bread or cake: *a sweet roll.* 1,2,5-7,9-11,13,15 *v.,* 3,4,8,12,14, 16-18 *n.*

roll up, pile up or become piled up; increase: *Bills roll up fast.*

roll call, the calling of a list of names, as of soldiers, pupils, etc., to find out who are present.

roll er (rō′lər), 1 thing that rolls; cylinder on which something is rolled along or rolled up. The shades for many windows are raised and lowered on rollers. 2 cylinder of metal, stone, wood, etc., used for smoothing, pressing, crushing, etc.: *A heavy roller was used to smooth the tennis court.* 3 a long, swelling wave: *Huge rollers broke on the sandy beach.* 4 person who rolls something. 5 kind of canary that has a trilling voice. *n.*

roller bearing, a bearing in which the shaft turns on rollers to lessen friction.

roller coaster, railway for amusement, consisting of inclined tracks along which small cars roll, abruptly dip, turn, etc.

roller skate, a skate with small wheels instead of a runner, for use on a floor or sidewalk; skate.

roll er-skate (rō′lər skāt′), move on roller skates: *The children roller-skated to the park. v.,* **roll er-skat ed, roll er-skat ing.**

rol lick (rol′ik), enjoy oneself in a free, hearty way; be merry; frolic. *v.*

rol lick ing (rol′ə king), frolicking; jolly; lively: *I had a rollicking good time at the picnic. adj.*

rolling mill, 1 factory where metal is rolled into sheets and bars. 2 machine for doing this.

rolling pin, cylinder of wood or glass about a foot long for rolling out dough.

rolling stock, the locomotives and cars of a railroad.

ro ly-po ly (rō′lē pō′lē), 1 short and plump: *a roly-poly child.* 2 a short, plump person or animal. 1 *adj.,* 2 *n., pl.* **ro ly-po lies.**

Ro man (rō′mən), 1 of or having to do with ancient or modern Rome or its people. 2 person born or living in Rome. 3 citizen of ancient Rome. 4 of or having to do with the Roman Catholic Church. 5 **roman, a** the style of type most used in printing and typewriting. This sentence is in roman. **b** of or in roman type. 1,4,5b *adj.,* 2,3,5a *n.*

Romanesque
(def. 1)

Roman Catholic, 1 of, having to do with, or belonging to the Christian church that recognizes the pope as the supreme head. 2 member of this church.

ro mance (rō mans′ or rō′mans *for 1-6;* rō mans′ *for 7-9*), 1 a love story. 2 story of adventure: *"The Arabian Nights"* and *"Treasure Island"* are *romances.* 3 story or poem telling of heroes: *Have you read the romances about King Arthur and his knights?* 4 real happenings that are like stories of heroes and are full of love, excitement, or noble deeds: *The boy dreamed of traveling in search of romance. The explorer's life was filled with romance.* 5 a love affair: *"Cinderella"* is the story of the romance between a beautiful girl and a prince. 6 a made-up story: *Nobody believes her romances about the wonderful things that have happened to her.* 7 make up romances: *Some children romance because of their lively imaginations.* 8 think or talk in a romantic way. 9 exaggerate; lie. 1-6 *n.,* 7-9 *v.,* **ro manced, ro manc ing.**

roller bearing cut away to show rollers

Romance languages, French, Italian, Spanish, Portuguese, Romanian, Provençal, and other languages that came from Latin, the language of the Romans.

Roman Empire
The shaded area shows the Empire at its greatest extent in A.D. 117.

Roman Empire, empire of ancient Rome lasting from 27 B.C. to A.D. 395. It was divided into the **Eastern Roman Empire** (A.D. 395-1453) and the **Western Roman Empire** (A.D. 395-476).

Ro man esque (rō′mə nesk′), 1 style of architecture developed in Europe during the early Middle Ages before the Gothic period. Romanesque used round arches and vaults. 2 of, in, or having to do with this style of architecture. 1 *n.,* 2 *adj.*

Ro ma ni a (rō mā′nē ə), country in SE Europe. *Capital:* Bucharest. Also, **Rumania** or **Roumania.** *n.* —**Ro ma′ni an,** *n., adj.*

Roman nose, nose that has a prominent bridge.

Roman nose

728

Roman numerals, numerals like XXIII, LVI, and MDCCLX, used by the ancient Romans in numbering. In this system I = 1, V = 5, X = 10, L = 50, C = 100, D = 500, and M = 1000.

Ro mans (rō′mənz), book of the New Testament, an epistle by Saint Paul to the Christians of Rome. *n.*

ro man tic (rō man′tik), 1 characteristic of romances or romance; appealing to fancy and the imagination: *romantic tales of love and adventure, a romantic life in exotic lands.* 2 interested in adventure and love; having ideas or feelings suited to romance: *The old couple reminisced about the days of their courtship, when they were young and romantic.* 3 suited to a romance: *The orchestra played soft, romantic music.* 4 of or having to do with romanticism in literature, art, and music. 5 not based on fact; fanciful; imaginary; unreal. 6 not customary or practical; fantastic; extravagant; quixotic: *romantic illusion.* 7 a romanticist. 8 a romantic person. 1-6 *adj.,* 7,8 *n.* —**ro man′ti cal ly,** *adv.*

ro man ti cism (rō man′tə siz′əm), a style of literature, art, and music especially widespread in the 1800's. Romanticism allows freedom of form and stresses strong feeling, imagination, love of nature, and often the unusual and supernatural. *n.*

ro man ti cist (rō man′tə sist), follower of romanticism in literature, art, or music. Wordsworth and Schubert were romanticists. *n.*

ro man ti cize (rō man′tə sīz), make romantic; give a romantic character to. *v.,* **ro man ti cized, ro man ti ciz ing.**

Rome (rōm), 1 capital of Italy, on the Tiber River. The headquarters of the pope and the Roman Catholic Church are in Vatican City, an independent state within Rome. 2 an ancient city in the same place, the capital of the Roman Empire. It was captured by the barbarians in A.D. 410. 3 the ancient Roman republic or the ancient Roman Empire. *n.*

Ro me o (rō′mē ō), hero of Shakespeare's play *Romeo and Juliet. n.*

romp (romp), 1 play in a rough, boisterous way; rush, tumble, and punch in play. 2 a rough, lively play or frolic: *A pillow fight is a romp.* 3 girl or boy who likes to romp. 1 *v.,* 2,3 *n.* —**romp′er,** *n.*

romp ers (rom′pərz), a loose outer garment, worn by young children at play; jumpers. *n.pl.*

Rom u lus (rom′yə ləs), (in Roman legends) the founder and first king of Rome. He and his twin brother, Remus, abandoned as infants, were nourished by a wolf. *n.*

rood (rüd), 1 40 square rods; one fourth of an acre. 2 OLD USE. the cross on which Christ died. 3 a representation of it; crucifix. *n.*

roof (rüf *or* rùf), 1 the top covering of a building. 2 something like it: *the roof of a cave, the roof of a car, the roof of the mouth.* 3 cover with a roof; form a roof over: *The trees roofed the glade where we camped.* 1,2 *n., pl.* **roofs;** 3 *v.* —**roof′like′,** *adj.*

raise the roof, INFORMAL. make a disturbance; create an uproar or confusion.

roof er (rü′fər *or* rùf′ər), person who makes or repairs roofs. *n.*

roof ing (rü′fing *or* rùf′ing), material used for roofs. Shingles are a common roofing for houses. *n.*

roof less (rüf′lis *or* rùf′lis), 1 having no roof. 2 having no shelter. *adj.*

roof tree (rüf′trē′ *or* rùf′trē′), ridgepole. *n.*

rook[1] (rùk), 1 a European crow that often nests in trees near buildings. 2 person who cheats at cards, dice, etc. 3 to cheat. 1,2 *n.,* 3 *v.* [Old English *hrōc*]

rook[2] (rùk), piece in the game of chess; castle. A rook can move in a straight line across any number of unoccupied squares. *n.* [from French of the 1300's *roc,* from Arabic *rukhkh*]

rook er y (rùk′ər ē), 1 a breeding place of rooks; colony of rooks. 2 a breeding place or colony where other birds or animals are crowded together: *a rookery of seals.* 3 a crowded, mean, and poor tenement house or group of such houses. *n., pl.* **rook er ies.**

rook ie (rùk′ē), SLANG. 1 an inexperienced recruit. 2 beginner; novice. 3 a new player on an athletic team, especially a professional baseball player in his first season. *n.*

room (rüm *or* rùm), 1 a part of a house, or other building, with walls of its own. 2 people in a room: *The whole room laughed.* 3 space occupied by, or available for, something: *The street was so crowded that the cars did not have room to move. There is room for one more in the automobile.* 4 opportunity: *There is room for improvement in his work.* 5 occupy a room; live in a room: *He rooms in the gray house. Three girls from our town roomed together at college.* 6 provide with a room. 7 **rooms,** *pl.* lodgings. 1-4,7 *n.,* 5,6 *v.*

room er (rü′mər *or* rùm′ər), person who lives in a rented room or rooms in another's house; lodger. *n.*

room ful (rüm′fùl *or* rùm′fùl), 1 enough to fill a room. 2 people or things in a room. *n., pl.* **room fuls.**

room i ness (rü′mē nis *or* rùm′ē nis), ample space; abundance of room. *n.*

hat, āge, fär; let, ēqual, tèrm; it, īce; hot, ōpen, ôrder; oil, out; cup, pùt, rüle; ch, child; ng, long; sh, she; th, thin; ᴛʜ, then; zh, measure;

ə represents *a* in about, *e* in taken, *i* in pencil, *o* in lemon, *u* in circus.

rooming house, house with rooms to rent.

room mate (rüm′māt′ *or* rùm′māt′), person who shares a room with another or others. *n.*

room y (rü′mē *or* rùm′ē), having plenty of room; large; spacious. *adj.,* **room i er, room i est.**

Roo se velt (rō′zə velt), 1 (**Anna**) **Eleanor,** 1884-1962, American author and stateswoman, wife of Franklin Delano Roosevelt. 2 **Franklin Delano,** 1882-1945, the 32nd president of the United States, from 1933 to 1945. 3 **Theodore,** 1858-1919, the 26th president of the United States, from 1901 to 1909. *n.*

roost (rüst), 1 bar, pole, or perch on which birds rest or sleep. 2 sit as birds do on a roost; settle for the night. 3 place for birds to roost in. 4 place to rest or stay in: *a robber's roost in the mountains.* 1,3,4 *n.,* 2 *v.*

come home to roost, come back so as to harm the doer or user; backfire; boomerang.

rule the roost, INFORMAL. be master.

roost er (rü′stər), a male domestic fowl. *n.*

root[1] (def. 1)—the four main types: A. taproot; B. fibrous roots; C. storage roots; D. aerial roots

root[1] (rüt *or* rùt), 1 the part of a plant that grows downward, usually into the ground, to hold the plant in place, absorb water and mineral foods from the soil, and often to store food material. 2 any underground part of a plant. 3 something like a root in shape, position, use, etc.: *root of a tooth, the roots of the hair.* 4 a part from which other things grow and develop; cause; source: *"The love of money is the root of all evil."*

adj.	adjective	n.	noun
adv.	adverb	prep.	preposition
conj.	conjunction	pron.	pronoun
interj.	interjection	v.	verb
sing.	singular	pl.	plural

5 send out roots and begin to grow; become fixed in the ground: *Some plants root more quickly than others.* 6 fix firmly: *He was rooted to the spot by surprise.* 7 become firmly fixed. 8 pull, tear, or dig (up, out, etc.) by the roots; get completely rid of. 9 the essential part; base. 10 quantity that produces another quantity when multiplied by itself a certain number of times. 2 is the square root of 4 and the cube root of 8 ($2 \times 2 = 4$, $2 \times 2 \times 2 = 8$). 11 word from which others are derived. *Room* is the root of *roominess, roomer, roommate,* and *roomy.* 1-4,9-11 *n.,* 5-8 *v.* [Old English *rōt*] —**root'like',** *adj.*

take root, 1 send out roots and begin to grow. 2 become firmly fixed.

root² (rüt *or* rùt), 1 dig with the snout: *The pigs rooted up the garden.* 2 rummage: *She rooted through the closet looking for her old shoes.* *v.* [Old English *wrōtan*]

root³ (rüt *or* rùt), SLANG. cheer or support a team, contestant, candidate, etc., enthusiastically. *v.* [probably from an earlier sense meaning "work hard" of *root²*] —**root'er,** *n.*

root beer, a soft drink flavored with the juice of the roots of certain plants, such as sarsaparilla, sassafras, etc.

root ed (rü'tid *or* rùt'id), 1 having roots. 2 having taken root; firmly fixed: *a deeply rooted belief.* *adj.*

root hair, a hairlike outgrowth from the root of a plant. Root hairs absorb water and dissolved minerals from the soil.

root less (rüt'lis *or* rùt'lis), without a root or roots; not rooted. *adj.*

root let (rüt'lit *or* rùt'lit), a little root; small branch of a root. *n.*

root stock (rüt'stok' *or* rùt'stok'), rhizome. *n.*

rope (rōp), 1 a strong, thick line or cord made by twisting smaller cords together. 2 tie, bind, or fasten with a rope. 3 enclose or mark off with a rope. 4 a lasso. 5 catch (a horse, calf, etc.) with a lasso. 6 a number of things twisted or strung together: *a rope of pearls, a rope of onions.* 7 cord or noose for hanging a person. 8 a sticky, stringy mass: *Molasses candy forms a rope.* 9 form a sticky, stringy mass; become ropy: *Cook the syrup until it ropes when you*

lift it with a spoon. 1,4,6-8 *n.,* 2,3,5,9 *v.,* **roped, rop ing.**

give one rope, INFORMAL. let one act freely.

know the ropes, 1 know the various ropes of a ship. 2 SLANG. know about a business or activity.

rope in, SLANG. get or lead in by tricking.

the end of one's rope, the end of one's resources, activities, etc.

rop er (rō'pər), 1 person who makes ropes. 2 person who uses a lasso. *n.*

rop y (rō'pē), 1 forming sticky threads; stringy: *a ropy syrup.* 2 like a rope or ropes. *adj.,* **rop i er, rop i est.**

ro sar y (rō'zər ē), 1 string of beads for keeping count in saying a series of prayers. 2 a series of prayers. 3 a garden of roses; bed of roses. *n., pl.* **ro sar ies.**

rose¹ (rōz), 1 flower that grows on a bush with thorny stems. Roses are red, pink, white, or yellow and usually smell very sweet. 2 the bush it grows on. 3 any of various related or similar plants or flowers. 4 pinkish-red. 5 a pinkish red. 6 something shaped like a rose or suggesting a rose, such as a rosette. 1-3,5,6 *n.,* 4 *adj.* [Old English, from Latin *rosa*] —**rose'like',** *adj.*

rose² (rōz), past tense of **rise.** *The cat rose and stretched itself.* *v.*

ro se ate (rō'zē it *or* rō'zē āt), 1 rose-colored; rosy. 2 cheerful; optimistic. *adj.*

rose bud (rōz'bud'), the bud of a rose. *n.*

rose bush (rōz'bùsh'), shrub or vine bearing roses. *n., pl.* **rose bush es.**

rose mar y (rōz'mer'ē *or* rōz'mar'ē), a fragrant evergreen shrub whose leaves are used in making perfume and in seasoning food. Rosemary is a symbol or emblem of remembrance. *n., pl.* **rose-mar ies.**

rosettes used in architecture

ro sette (rō zet'), an ornament shaped like a rose. Rosettes are often made of ribbon. Carved or molded rosettes are used in architecture. *n.*

rose water, water made fragrant with oil of roses.

rose wood (rōz'wùd'), 1 a beautiful reddish wood used in fine furniture. 2 any of the tropical trees that it comes from. *n.*

Rosh Ha sha nah (rosh' hə shä'-nə), the Jewish New Year. It usually occurs in September.

ros i ly (rō'zə lē), 1 with a rosy tinge or color. 2 brightly; cheerfully. *adv.*

ros in (roz'n), 1 a hard, yellow substance that remains when turpentine is evaporated from pine resin. Rosin is rubbed on violin bows and on the shoes of acrobats to keep them from slipping. 2 to cover or rub with rosin. 1 *n.,* 2 *v.*

ros i ness (rō'zē nis), rosy color. *n.*

Ross (rôs), Betsy, 1752-1836, American woman who is said to have made the first American flag. *n.*

Ros si ni (rō sē'nē), **Gioacchino Antonio,** 1792-1868, Italian composer of operas. *n.*

ros ter (ros'tər), 1 list giving each person's name and duties. 2 any list. *n.*

ros trum (ros'trəm), platform for public speaking. *n., pl.* **ros trums, ros tra** (ros'trə).

ros y (rō'zē), 1 like a rose; rose-red; pinkish-red. 2 bright; cheerful: *a rosy future.* *adj.,* **ros i er, ros i est.**

rot (rot), 1 become rotten; decay; spoil: *So much rain will make the fruit rot.* 2 cause to decay. 3 process of rotting; decay. 4 a disease of plants and animals, especially sheep. 5 lose vigor; degenerate. 6 SLANG. nonsense; rubbish. 1,2,5 *v.,* **rot ted, rot ting;** 3,4,6 *n.*

ro tar y (rō'tər ē), 1 turning like a top or a wheel; rotating. 2 having parts that rotate. 3 traffic circle. 1,2 *adj.,* 3 *n., pl.* **ro tar ies.**

rotary engine, Wankel engine.

ro tate (rō'tāt), 1 move around a center or axis; turn in a circle; revolve. Wheels, tops, and the earth rotate. 2 change in a regular order; take turns or cause to take turns: *The officials will rotate in office. Farmers rotate crops.* *v.,* **ro tat ed, ro tat ing.**

ro ta tion (rō tā'shən), 1 a turning round a center or axis; turning in a circle; revolving: *the rotation of a top. The earth's rotation causes night and day.* 2 a change in a regular order. *n.*

in rotation, in turn; in regular succession.

rotation of crops, the varying from year to year of crops grown in the same field to keep the soil from losing its fertility.

ro ta tor (rō'tā tər), person or thing that rotates. *n.*

ro ta to ry (rō'tə tôr'ē), 1 turning like a top or wheel; rotating. 2 causing rotation: *a rotatory muscle.* 3 passing or following from one to another in succession: *a rotatory office in a club.* *adj.*

R.O.T.C., Reserve Officers' Training Corps.

rote (rōt), a set, mechanical way of doing things. *n.*

by rote, by memory without thought of the meaning: *to learn a lesson by rote.*

ro tis ser ie (rō tis'ər ē), an electric appliance with a spit for roasting food, rotated by an electric motor. *n.*

ro to gra vure (rō′tə grə vyůr′), 1 process of printing from an engraved copper cylinder on which the pictures, letters, etc., have been depressed instead of raised. 2 a print or section of a newspaper made by this process. *n.*

ro tor (rō′tər), 1 the rotating part of a machine or apparatus. 2 system of rotating blades by which a helicopter is able to fly. *n.*

rot ten (rot′n), 1 decayed or spoiled: *a rotten egg.* 2 foul; disgusting: *a rotten smell.* 3 unsound; weak: *rotten ice, rotten beams.* 4 corrupt; dishonest: *rotten government.* 5 bad; nasty: *rotten luck, to feel rotten. adj.* —**rot′ten ly,** *adv.* —**rot′ten ness,** *n.*

Rot ter dam (rot′ər dam′), seaport in SW Netherlands. *n.*

ro tund (rō tund′), 1 round or plump: *a rotund face.* 2 sounding rich and full; full-toned: *a rotund voice. adj.* —**ro tund′ly,** *adv.* —**ro tund′ness,** *n.*

rotunda

ro tun da (rō tun′də), a round building or room, especially one with a dome: *The Capitol at Washington has a large rotunda. n., pl.* **ro tun das.**

ro tun di ty (rō tun′də tē), 1 roundness or plumpness. 2 something round. 3 rounded fullness of tone. *n., pl.* **ro tun di ties.**

rou ble (rü′bəl), ruble. *n.*

Rou en (rü än′), city in N France, on the Seine River, famous for its cathedral. Joan of Arc was burned at the stake in Rouen in 1431. *n.*

rouge (rüzh), 1 a red powder, paste, or liquid for coloring the cheeks or lips. 2 to color with rouge. 3 a red powder, chiefly an oxide of iron, used for polishing metal, jewels, etc. 1,3 *n.,* 2 *v.,* **rouged, roug ing.**

rough (ruf), 1 not smooth; not level; not even: *rough boards, the rough bark of an oak tree, a rough, rocky hill.* 2 stormy: *rough weather, a rough sea.* 3 likely to hurt others; not gentle; harsh; rude: *rough manners.* 4 without luxury and ease: *rough life in*

camp. 5 without polish or fine finish: *rough diamonds.* 6 not completed or perfected; done as a first try; without details: *a rough drawing, a rough idea.* 7 coarse and tangled: *rough fur, a dog with a rough coat of hair.* 8 a coarse, violent person. 9 INFORMAL. unpleasant; hard; severe: *I was in for a rough time.* 10 make rough; roughen. 11 treat roughly: *The angry mob roughed up the suspected traitor.* 12 shape or sketch roughly: *rough out a plan, rough in the outlines of a face.* 13 in a rough manner; roughly: *Those older boys play too rough for me.* 14 ground where there is long grass, etc., on a golf course. 1-7,9 *adj.,* 8,14 *n.,* 10-12 *v.,* 13 *adv.* —**rough′ness,** *n.*

in the rough, not polished or refined; coarse; crude.

rough it, live without comforts and conveniences.

rough age (ruf′ij), 1 rough or coarse material. 2 the coarser parts or kinds of food which stimulate the movement of food and waste products through the intestines. Bran, fruit skins, and certain fruits are roughage. *n.*

rough en (ruf′ən), make or become rough. *v.*

rough-hew (ruf′hyü′), hew (timber, stone, etc.) roughly; shape roughly without smoothing or finishing. *v.,* **rough-hewed, rough-hewed** or **rough-hewn, rough-hew ing.**

rough ly (ruf′lē), 1 in a rough manner. 2 approximately: *From New York to Los Angeles is roughly three thousand miles. adv.*

rough neck (ruf′nek′), SLANG. a rough, coarse fellow. *n.*

rough rid er (ruf′rī′dər), 1 man used to rough, hard riding. 2 person who rides rough, wild horses. *n.*

rough shod (ruf′shod′), having horseshoes with sharp calks to prevent slipping. *adj.*

ride roughshod over, domineer over; show no consideration for; treat roughly.

roulette (def. 1)—roulette wheel

rou lette (rü let′), 1 a gambling game in which the players bet on which numbered section of a revolving wheel a small ball will come to rest in. 2 a small wheel with sharp teeth for making lines of marks, dots, or perforations: *a rou-*

hat, āge, fär; let, ēqual, tėrm; it, īce; hot, ōpen, ôrder; oil, out; cup, půt, rüle; ch, child; ng, long; sh, she; th, thin; ₮H, then; zh, measure;

ə represents *a* in about, *e* in taken, *i* in pencil, *o* in lemon, *u* in circus.

lette for perforating sheets of postage stamps. n.

Rou ma ni a (rü mā′nē ə), Romania. *n.* —**Rou ma′ni an,** *adj., n.*

round (round), 1 shaped like a ball, a ring, or the trunk of a tree; having a circular or curved outline. A hoop or a wheel is round; so is a candle or a roller. 2 anything shaped like this; thing that is circular, curved, cylindrical, etc. The rungs of a ladder are sometimes called rounds. 3 plump: *Her figure was short and round.* 4 make or become round: *The carpenter rounded the corners of the table. The girl's lips rounded when she whistled.* 5 in a circle; with a whirling motion: *Wheels go round.* 6 on all sides; in every direction: *The travelers were compassed round by dangers.* 7 on all sides of: *Bullets fell round him, but he was not hit.* 8 in circumference; in distance around: *The pumpkin measures 50 inches round.* 9 go around; make a turn to the other side of: *The ship rounded Cape Horn. The car rounded the corner at high speed.* 10 so as to make a turn to the other side of: *She walked round the corner.* 11 so as to encircle or surround: *They built a fence round the yard.* 12 by a longer road or way: *We went round by the candy store on our way home.* 13 to all or various parts of: *We took our cousins round the town.* 14 Often, **rounds,** *pl.* a fixed course ending where it begins: *The watchman makes his rounds of the building every hour.* 15 movement in a circle or about an axis: *the earth's yearly round.* 16 from one to another: *A report is going round that the schools will close early.* 17 through a round of time: *Summer will soon come round again.* 18 about; around: *He doesn't look fit to be round* (*adv.*). *She stood still and looked round her* (*prep.*). 19 for all: *There is just enough cake to go round.* 20 series (of duties, events, etc.); routine: *a round of pleasures.* 21 distance between any limits; range; circuit: *the round of human knowledge.* 22 section of a game or sport: *a round in a boxing match.* 23 a complete game or unit: *a*

adj. adjective	*n.* noun
adv. adverb	*prep.* preposition
conj. conjunction	*pron.* pronoun
interj. interjection	*v.* verb
sing. singular	*pl.* plural

round of golf. 24 discharge of firearms by a group of soldiers at the same time. 25 bullets, powder, etc., for one such discharge, or for a single shot: *The sergeant had three rounds of ammunition left in his rifle.* 26 an act that a number of people do together: *a round of applause, a round of cheers.* 27 round dance. 28 a short song sung by several persons or groups beginning one after the other; catch. "Row, Row, Row Your Boat" is a round. 29 full; complete; large: *a round dozen, a good round sum of money.* 30 plainly expressed; plain-spoken; frank: *I was scolded in good round terms for being so late.* 31 with a full tone: *a mellow, round voice.* 32 vigorous; brisk; quick: *a round trot.* 33 spoken with the lips rounded: *O is a round vowel.* 34 utter (a vowel) with a small circular opening of the lips. 35 a cut of beef just above the hind leg and below the rump. See **loin** for diagram. 1,3,29-33 *adj.,* 2,14,15, 20-28,35 *n.,* 4,9,34 *v.,* 5,6,8,12,16-19 *adv.,* 7,10,11,13,18 *prep.* —**round′ness,** *n.*

in the round, 1 in a form of sculpture in which the figures are apart from any background. 2 having seats all around a central stage: *theater in the round.*

round off or **round out,** 1 make or become round. 2 finish; complete.

round up, drive or bring together: *The cowboys rounded up the cattle.*

round a bout (round′ə bout′), not straight; indirect: *a roundabout route, speak in a roundabout way. adj.*

round dance, 1 a ballroom dance in which couples dance with circular or revolving movements. 2 a dance with dancers in a circle.

roun de lay (roun′dl ā), 1 song in which a phrase or a line is repeated again and again. 2 round dance. *n.*

round house (round′hous′), 1 a circular building for storing or repairing locomotives. It is built about a platform that turns around. 2 cabin on the after part of a ship's quarterdeck. *n., pl.* **round hous es** (round′hou′ziz).

round ish (roun′dish), somewhat round. *adj.*

round ly (round′lē), 1 in a round manner; in a circle, curve, globe, etc. 2 plainly; bluntly; severely: *scold*

roundly. 3 fully; completely. *adv.*

round number, a number in even tens, hundreds, thousands, etc. 3874 in round numbers would be 3900 or 4000.

round-shoul dered (round′shōl′dərd), having the shoulders bent forward. *adj.*

round table, 1 group of persons assembled for an informal discussion, etc. 2 **Round Table, a** table around which King Arthur and his knights sat. **b** King Arthur and his knights.

round trip, trip to a place and back again.

round up (round′up′), 1 act of driving or bringing cattle together from long distances. 2 the men and horses that do this. 3 any similar gathering: *a roundup of old friends. n.*

round worm (round′wėrm′), any of a group of worms that have long, round bodies and live in soil or water, or are parasites in animals and plants. The hookworm is a roundworm. *n.*

rouse (rouz), wake up; stir up; arouse: *I was roused by the ring of the telephone. The dogs roused a deer from the bushes. She was roused to anger by the insult. v.,* **roused, rous ing.**

rous ing (rou′zing), stirring; vigorous; brisk: *a rousing speech. adj.*

Rous seau (rü sō′), **Jean Jacques,** 1712-1778, French philosopher who wrote about government and education. *n.*

roust a bout (roust′ə bout′), an unskilled laborer on wharves, ships, ranches, etc. *n.*

rout[1] (rout), 1 flight of a defeated army in disorder: *The enemy's retreat soon became a rout.* 2 put to flight in disorder: *Our soldiers routed the enemy.* 3 a complete defeat. 4 defeat completely: *The baseball team routed its opponents by a score of ten to one.* 1,3 *n.,* 2,4 *v.* [from French of the 1500's *route,* from Latin *rupta* dispersed soldiers, from *rumpere* to break]

rout[2] (rout), 1 dig (out); get by searching. 2 put (out); force (out): *The farmer routed his sons out of bed at five o'clock.* 3 dig with the snout: *The pigs were routing for nuts under the trees.* 4 hollow out; scoop out; gouge. *v.* [a different form of *root*[2]]

route (rüt *or* rout), 1 way to go; road: *Will you go to the coast by the northern route?* 2 arrange the route for: *The automobile club routed us on our vacation to Canada.* 3 send by a certain route: *The signs routed us around the construction work and over a side road.* 4 a fixed, regular course or area assigned to a person making deliveries, sales, etc.: *a newspaper route, a milk route.* 1,4 *n.,* 2,3 *v.,* **rout ed, rout ing.**

rou tine (rü tēn′), 1 a fixed, regular

method of doing things; habitual doing of the same things in the same way: *Getting up and going to bed are parts of your daily routine.* 2 using routine: *routine methods, a routine operation.* 3 average or ordinary; run-of-the-mill: *a routine show with routine performances.* 1 *n.,* 2,3 *adj.* —**rou tine′ly,** *adv.*

rove (rōv), wander about; wander; roam; ramble; range: *She loved to rove through the fields and woods. v.,* **roved, rov ing.**

rov er[1] (rō′vər), person who roves; wanderer. *n.* [*rove* + *-er*[1]]

ro ver[2] (rō′vər), 1 pirate. 2 a pirate ship. *n.* [from Dutch of the 1300's *rover,* from *roven* to rob]

row[1] (rō), 1 line of people or things: *The children stood in a row in front of the row of chairs. Corn is planted in rows.* 2 street with a line of buildings on either side. *n.* [Old English *rāw*]

hard row to hoe, a difficult thing to do.

row[2] (rō), 1 use oars to move a boat: *We rowed across the lake.* 2 cause (a boat) to move by the use of oars. 3 carry in a rowboat: *I rowed them to shore.* 4 trip in a rowboat: *It's only a short row to the island.* 1-3 *v.,* 4 *n.* [Old English *rōwan*] —**row′er,** *n.*

row[3] (rou), a noisy quarrel or disturbance; squabble: *The three children had a row over the bicycle. What's all this row about? n.* [origin unknown]

row boat (rō′bōt′), boat moved by oars. *n.*

row di ness (rou′dē nis), a being rowdy; disorderliness. *n.*

row dy (rou′dē), 1 a rough, disorderly, quarrelsome person. 2 rough; disorderly; quarrelsome. 1 *n., pl.* **row dies;** 2 *adj.,* **row di er, row di est.**

row dy ish (rou′dē ish), like a rowdy; rough and disorderly; quarrelsome. *adj.*

row dy ism (rou′dē iz′əm), disorderly, quarrelsome conduct; rough, noisy behavior. *n.*

ROWEL

row el (rou′əl), a small wheel with sharp points, attached to the end of a spur. *n.*

row lock (rō′lok′), oarlock. *n.*

roy al (roi′əl), 1 of kings and queens: *the royal family.* 2 belonging to a king or queen: *royal power, a royal palace.* 3 from or by a king or queen: *a royal command.* 4 of a kingdom: *a royal* army or navy. **5** appropriate for a king; splendid: *a royal welcome, a royal feast.* **6** like a king; noble; majestic: *The lion is a royal beast.* **7** a small mast or sail set above the topgallant. 1-6 *adj.*, 7 *n.* —**roy′al ly,** *adv.*

roy al ist (roi′ə list), **1** supporter of a king or of a royal government. The royalists supported the British king during the Revolutionary War. **2** of or having to do with royalists: *royalist principles, a royalist party.* 1 *n.*, 2 *adj.*

roy al ty (roi′əl tē), **1** a royal person or royal persons. Kings, queens, princes, and princesses are royalty. **2** rank or dignity of a king or queen; royal power: *The crown is the symbol of royalty.* **3** kingly nature; royal quality; nobility. **4** a share of the receipts or profits paid to an owner of a patent or copyright; payment for the use of any of various rights. An author receives royalties from the publishers of his books. *n., pl.* **roy al ties.**

rpm or **r.p.m.,** revolutions per minute.

R.R., railroad.

R.S.V.P. or **r.s.v.p.,** please answer. [abbreviation of French *répondez s'il vous plaît*]

rub (rub), **1** move one thing back and forth against another: *Rub your hands to warm them. He rubbed soap on his hands.* **2** push and press along the surface of: *The nurse rubbed my lame back. That door rubs on the floor.* **3** make or bring by rubbing: *rub silver bright.* **4** clean, smooth, or polish by moving one thing firmly against another: *Rub the silver with a soft cloth.* **5** act of rubbing: *Give the silver a rub with the polish.* **6** thing that hurts the feelings: *He didn't like her mean rub at his slowness.* **7** irritate or make sore by rubbing: *The new shoe rubbed his heel, causing a blister.* **8** difficulty: *The rub is that all the children want to sit in the front seat.* 1-4,7 *v.*, **rubbed, rub bing;** 5,6,8 *n.*

rub down, rub (the body); massage. **rub it in,** SLANG. keep on mentioning something unpleasant.
rub off, remove or be removed by rubbing: *Rub off the dust on your sleeve. Ink rubs off easily with this eraser.*
rub the wrong way, annoy; irritate.

rub ber[1] (rub′ər), **1** an elastic substance obtained from the milky juice of certain tropical plants, or produced artificially by a chemical process; india rubber. Rubber will not let air or water through. **2** something made from this substance. We wear rubbers on our feet when it rains. Pencils often have rubbers for erasing pencil marks. **3** made of rubber: *a rubber tire.* **4** person or

thing that rubs. 1,2,4 *n.*, 3 *adj.* [rub + -er[1]] —**rub′ber like′,** *adj.*

rub ber[2] (rub′ər), **1** series of two games out of three or three games out of five won by the same side. **2** the deciding game in such a series: *If each side has won two games, the fifth game will be the rubber. n.* [origin uncertain]

rubber band, a circular strip of rubber, used to hold things together.

rub ber ize (rub′ə rīz′), cover or treat with rubber: *rubberized cloth. v.*, **rubber ized, rub ber iz ing.**

rubber stamp, **1** stamp made of rubber, used with ink for printing dates, signatures, etc. **2** INFORMAL. person or group that approves or endorses something without thought or without power to refuse.

rub ber y (rub′ər ē), like rubber; elastic; tough. *adj.*

rudder (def. 1, left; def. 2, right)

rub bish (rub′ish), **1** worthless or useless stuff; waste; trash: *Pick up the rubbish and burn it.* **2** silly words and thoughts; nonsense: *Gossip is often a lot of rubbish. n.*

rub ble (rub′əl), **1** rough broken stones, bricks, etc.: *the rubble left by an explosion or an earthquake.* **2** masonry made of this: *The house was built of rubble and plaster. n.*

rub down (rub′doun′), a massage. *n.*

Ru bens (rü′bənz), **Peter Paul,** 1577-1640, Flemish painter. *n.*

Ru bi con (rü′bə kon), small river forming the N boundary of ancient Italy. By crossing the Rubicon in 49 B.C., Julius Caesar started the civil war that made him master of Rome. *n.*
cross the Rubicon, make an important decision from which one cannot turn back.

ru bi cund (rü′bə kund), reddish; ruddy: *The jolly captain had a rubicund face. adj.*

ru bid i um (rü bid′ē əm), a soft, silver-white, metallic element which reacts violently in water and burns spontaneously in air. *n.*

ru ble (rü′bəl), **1** unit of money in the Soviet Union. 100 kopecks make one ruble. **2** silver coin or piece of paper money worth one ruble. *n.* Also, **rouble.**

ru bric (rü′brik), **1** title or heading of a chapter, a law, etc., written or printed in red or in special lettering. **2** direction for the conducting of religious services

hat, āge, fär; let, ēqual, tėrm; it, īce; hot, ōpen, ôrder; oil, out; cup, pút, rüle; ch, child; ng, long; sh, she; th, thin; ₮H, then; zh, measure;

ə represents *a* in about, *e* in taken, *i* in pencil, *o* in lemon, *u* in circus.

inserted in a prayer book, ritual, etc. *n.*

ru by (rü′bē), **1** a clear, hard, deep-red variety of corundum. Rubies are valued as precious stones. **2** deep, glowing red: *ruby lips, ruby wine.* **3** a deep, glowing red. 1,3 *n., pl.* **ru bies;** 2 *adj.*

ruck sack (ruk′sak′), knapsack. *n.*

ruck us (ruk′əs), SLANG. a noisy disturbance or uproar; row. *n., pl.* **ruck us es.**

rud der (rud′ər), **1** a flat piece of wood or metal hinged vertically to the rear end of a boat or ship and used to steer it. **2** a similar piece on an aircraft. *n.*

rud der less (rud′ər lis), without a rudder. *adj.*

rud di ness (rud′ē nis), quality or state of being ruddy; redness. *n.*

rud dy (rud′ē), **1** red or reddish: *the ruddy glow of a fire.* **2** having a fresh, healthy, red look: *ruddy cheeks. adj.*, **rud di er, rud di est.**

rude (rüd), **1** not courteous; impolite: *It is rude to stare at people.* **2** roughly made or done; without finish or polish; coarse: *rude tools, a rude sketch. We made a rude bed from the branches of evergreen trees.* **3** rough in manner or behavior; violent; harsh: *The rude hands of the dogcatcher seized the dog. I had a rude shock when I discovered that my bicycle was gone.* **4** not having learned much; rather wild; barbarous: *a rude, primitive culture. Life is rude in tribes that have few tools. adj.*, **rud er, rud est.** —**rude′ly,** *adv.* —**rude′-ness,** *n.*

ru di ment (rü′də mənt), **1** part to be learned first; beginning: *the rudiments of grammar.* **2** something in an early stage: *the rudiments of wings on a baby chick. n.*

ru di men tar y (rü′də men′tər ē), **1** to be learned or studied first; elementary: *It is almost impossible to learn multiplication without knowing the rudimentary steps of addition.* **2** in an early stage of development; undeveloped: *rudimentary wings. adj.*

rue[1] (rü), **1** be sorry for; regret: *She will rue the day she dropped out of school.* **2** sorrow; regret. 1 *v.*, **rued, ru ing;** 2 *n.* [Old English *hrēowan*]

rue

adj.	adjective	*n.*	noun
adv.	adverb	*prep.*	preposition
conj.	conjunction	*pron.*	pronoun
interj.	interjection	*v.*	verb
sing.	singular	*pl.*	plural

rue² (rü), plant with yellow flowers, and leaves that have a strong smell and bitter taste. *n.* [from French of the 1300's *rue*, from Latin *ruta*]

rue ful (rü′fəl), 1 sorrowful; unhappy; mournful: *a rueful expression.* 2 causing sorrow or pity: *a rueful sight.* *adj.* —**rue′ful ly**, *adv.* —**rue′fulness**, *n.*

ruff (ruf), 1 a deep frill, stiff enough to stand out, worn around the neck by men and women in the 1500's and 1600's. 2 a collarlike growth of long or specially marked feathers or hairs on the neck of a bird or other animal. *n.*

ruffed (ruft), having a ruff. *adj.*

ruffed grouse, a North American game bird with a tuft of feathers on each side of the neck. It is in some places called a partridge and in others a pheasant.

ruf fi an (ruf′ē ən), 1 a rough, brutal, or cruel person; bully; hoodlum. 2 rough; brutal; cruel. 1 *n.*, 2 *adj.*

ruffle (def. 2)
ruffles on a skirt

ruf fle (ruf′əl), 1 destroy the smoothness of; make rough or uneven: *A breeze ruffled the lake. The hen ruffled her feathers at the sight of the dog.* 2 a strip of cloth, ribbon, or lace gathered along one edge and used for trimming. Women's dresses often have ruffles; some men's shirts for evening wear have ruffles. 3 gather into a ruffle. 4 trim with ruffles. 5 become ruffled: *The flag ruffled in the breeze.* 6 disturb; annoy: *Nothing can ruffle her calm temper.* 7 disturbance; annoyance. 1,3-6 *v.*, **ruf fled, ruf fling;** 2,7 *n.*

rug (rug), 1 a piece of thick, heavy fabric, used as a floor covering: *a rag rug, a fur rug.* Rugs usually cover only part of a room's floor. 2 a thick, warm cloth used as covering: *The Indian*
wrapped his woolen rug around him. n.

Rug by (rug′bē), 1 a famous English school for boys. 2 an English form of the game of football. *n.* [from *Rugby,* a town in central England, where the school is located]

rug ged (rug′id), 1 covered with rough edges; rough and uneven: *rugged ground, rugged rocks.* 2 able to do and endure much; sturdy; hardy: *Pioneers were rugged people.* 3 strong and irregular: *rugged features.* 4 harsh; stern; severe: *rugged times.* 5 rude; unpolished; unrefined: *rugged manners.* 6 stormy: *rugged weather. adj.* —**rug′ged ly**, *adv.* —**rug′ged ness**, *n.*

ruff (def. 1)

Ruhr (rür), 1 river in West Germany flowing into the Rhine. 2 a rich mining and industrial region along this river. *n.*

ru in (rü′ən), 1 Often, **ruins,** *pl.* that which is left after destruction, decay, or downfall, especially a building, wall, etc., that has fallen to pieces: *the ruins of an ancient city. That ruin was once a famous castle.* 2 very great damage; destruction; overthrow; decay: *The ruin of property caused by the earthquake was enormous. His enemies planned the duke's ruin.* 3 condition of destruction, decay, or downfall: *The house had gone to ruin from neglect.* 4 cause of destruction, decay, or downfall: *Reckless spending will be your ruin.* 5 bring to ruin; destroy; spoil: *Rain ruined our picnic.* 6 make bankrupt. 1-4 *n.*, 5,6 *v.*

ru in a tion (rü′ə nā′shən), ruin; destruction; downfall. *n.*

ru in ous (rü′ə nəs), 1 bringing ruin; causing destruction: *ruinous expense, a ruinous war.* 2 fallen into ruins; ruined: *a building in a ruinous condition. adj.* —**ru′in ous ly**, *adv.*

rule (rül), 1 statement of what to do and not to do; a principle governing conduct, action, arrangement, etc.; law: *the rules of a club, to obey the rules of the game, the rules of the road.* 2 set of rules; code: *Different kinds of monks live under different rules.* 3 make a rule; decide. 4 make a formal decision: *The judge ruled against them.* 5 to control, govern, or manage: *She tries to rule her family as a dictator rules a nation.* 6 control; government: *In a democracy the people have the rule.* 7 period of power of a ruler; reign: *The Revolutionary War took place during the rule of George III.* 8 a regular method; thing
that usually happens or is done; what is usually true: *Fair weather is the rule in Arizona.* 9 prevail; dominate: *Wit rules all her poems.* 10 ruler (def. 2). 11 mark with lines: *I used a ruler to rule the paper.* 1,2,6-8,10 *n.*, 3-5,9,11 *v.*, **ruled, rul ing.**

as a rule, normally; generally.

rule out, decide against; exclude.

rule of thumb, 1 rule based on experience or practice rather than on scientific knowledge. 2 a rough, practical method of procedure.

rul er (rü′lər), 1 person who rules or governs. A king is a ruler. 2 a straight strip of wood, metal, etc., often marked in inches or centimeters, used in drawing lines or in measuring. *n.*

rul ing (rü′ling), 1 decision of a judge or court: *a ruling on a point of law.* 2 that rules; governing; controlling. 3 predominating; prevalent; chief. 1 *n.*, 2,3 *adj.*

rum¹ (rum), 1 an alcoholic liquor made from sugar cane, molasses, etc. 2 any alcoholic liquor. *n.* [apparently shortened from the old word *rumbullion,* of unknown origin]

rum² (rum), SLANG. odd; queer. *adj.* [origin uncertain]

Ru ma ni a (rü mā′nē ə), Romania. *n.* —**Ru ma′ni an,** *adj., n.*

rum ba (rum′bə), 1 a lively ballroom dance that originated in Cuba. 2 music for this dance. *n., pl.* **rum bas.**

rum ble (rum′bəl), 1 make a deep, heavy, continuous sound. 2 a deep, heavy, continuous sound: *We heard the far-off rumble of thunder.* 3 move with such a sound: *The train rumbled through the station.* 1,3 *v.*, **rum bled, rum bling;** 2 *n.*

rumble seat, an extra, outside seat for two in the back of some coupes and roadsters.

ru mi nant (rü′mə nənt), 1 animal that chews the cud. Cows, sheep, and camels are ruminants. 2 belonging to the group of ruminants. 3 meditative; reflective. 1 *n.*, 2,3 *adj.*

ru mi nate (rü′mə nāt), 1 chew the cud. 2 chew again: *A cow ruminates its food.* 3 think or ponder; meditate; reflect: *She ruminated on the strange events of the past week. v.*, **ru mi nat ed, ru mi nat ing.**

ru mi na tion (rü′mə nā′shən), 1 a chewing of the cud. 2 meditation; reflection. *n.*

rum mage (rum′ij), 1 search thoroughly by moving things about: *I rummaged three drawers before I found my gloves.* 2 search in a disorderly way: *He rummaged in the drawer for a sheet of paper.* 3 pull from among other things; bring to light: *She rummaged change from the bottom of* her purse. **4** a thorough search in which things are moved about. 1-3 *v.*, **rum maged, rum mag ing;** 4 *n.*

rummage sale, sale of odds and ends, old clothing, etc., usually held to raise money for charity.

rum my (rum′ē), a kind of card game in which points are scored by forming sets of three or four cards of the same rank or sequences of three or more cards of the same suit. *n.*

ru mor (rü′mər), **1** story or statement talked of as news without any proof that it is true: *The rumor spread that a new school would be built here.* **2** vague, general talk: *Rumor has it that the new girl went to school in France.* **3** tell or spread by rumor: *It was rumored that the government was going to increase taxes.* 1,2 *n.*, 3 *v.*

rump (rump), **1** the hind part of the body of an animal, where the legs join the back. **2** a cut of beef from this part. See **loin** for diagram. *n.*

rum ple (rum′pəl), **1** crumple; crush; wrinkle: *a rumpled sheet of paper.* **2** tousle; disorder: *The wind rumpled my hair.* **3** a wrinkle; crease. 1,2 *v.*, **rum pled, rum pling;** 3 *n.*

rum pus (rum′pəs), INFORMAL. a noisy disturbance or uproar; row. *n., pl.* **rum pus es.**

run (run), **1** go by moving the legs quickly; go faster than walking: *A horse can run faster than a man.* **2** go in a hurry; hasten: *Run for help.* **3** make a quick trip: *Let's run over to the lake for the weekend.* **4** escape; flee: *Run for your life.* **5** cause to run; cause to move: *run a horse up and down a track.* **6** do by running: *run a race, run errands.* **7** keep going; go; move: *This train runs from Kansas City to St. Louis. Does your watch run well?* **8** go on; proceed: *Prices of hats run as high as $50.* **9** creep; trail; climb: *Vines run up the sides of the chimney.* **10** pass or cause to pass quickly: *The thought ran through my mind that I might forget my speech. She ran her eyes over the old notes before discarding them.* **11** stretch; extend: *Shelves run along the walls. A fence runs around the yard. The road runs from New York to Atlanta.* **12** drive; force; thrust: *He ran a splinter into his hand.* **13** flow with; flow: *Blood runs from a cut. The streets ran oil after an oil truck overturned.* **14** discharge fluid, mucus, or pus: *My nose runs whenever I have a cold.* **15** get; become: *Never run into debt. The well ran dry.* **16** have a specified character, quality, form, size, etc.: *These potatoes run large.* **17** spread: *The color ran when the dress was washed.* **18** continue; last: *a lease to run two years. The play ran for a whole season.*

19 have currency or be current; occur: *The story runs that school will close early.* **20** take part in a race or contest. **21** be a candidate for election: *run for class president.* **22** expose oneself to: *run the risk of catching cold.* **23** move easily, freely, or smoothly; keep operating: *A rope runs in a pulley. The engine ran all day without overheating.* **24** cause to move easily, freely, or smoothly; cause to keep operating: *run a machine.* **25** be worded or expressed: *How does the first verse run?* **26** act of running: *When the bell rang we set out at a run.* **27** spell or period of causing (a machine, etc.) to operate; amount of anything produced in such a period: *During a run of eight hours the factory produced a run of 100 cars.* **28** a trip: *The train makes a run of one hundred miles in two hours. We took a run up to the country for the day.* **29** to conduct; manage: *run a business.* **30** unit of score in baseball or cricket. **31** time; period; spell: *a run of wet weather, a run of bad luck.* **32** succession of performances: *This play has had a run of two years.* **33** onward movement; progress; course; trend: *the run of events.* **34** a sudden demand or series of demands: *a run on the bank to draw out money.* **35** (in music) a rapid succession of tones. **36** kind or class: *the common run of mankind.* **37** free use: *The guests were given the run of the house.* **38** go without restraint: *The children were allowed to run about the streets.* **39** flow or rush of water; small stream. **40** number of fish moving together: *a run of salmon.* **41** stretch or enclosed space for animals: *a dog run, a chicken run.* **42** drop stitches; ravel: *Nylon stockings often run.* **43** a place where stitches have slipped out or become undone: *a run in a stocking.* **44** sew by pushing a needle in and out with even stitches in a line. **45** get past or through: *Enemy ships tried to run the blockade.* **46** publish (an advertisement, story, etc.) in a newspaper, magazine, etc.: *She ran an ad in the evening paper.* **47** shape by melting: *run bullets in a mold.* 1-25,29,38,42,44-47 *v.*, **ran, run, run ning;** 26-28,30-37,39-41,43 *n.*

a run for one's money, 1 strong competition. **2** satisfaction for one's expenditures, efforts, etc.: *The travel agent promised to give the tourists a run for their money.*

in the long run, on the whole; in the end.

on the run, 1 hurrying. **2** in retreat or rout; fleeing.

run away with, win easily over others: *He ran away with every prize in the tournament.*

run down, 1 stop working or going:

hat, āge, fär; let, ēqual, tėrm; it, īce; hot, ōpen, ôrder; oil, out; cup, půt, rüle; ch, child; ng, long; sh, she; th, thin; ᴛʜ, then; zh, measure;

ə represents *a* in about, *e* in taken, *i* in pencil, *o* in lemon, *u* in circus.

The clock has run down. **2** to chase till caught: *The fox ran down the hare.* **3** knock down by running against. **4** speak evil against. **5** fall into poor physical condition: *Her health has run down because of overwork.*

run for it, run for safety.

run in, 1 SLANG. arrest and put in jail. **2** pay a short visit.

run into, 1 meet by chance. **2** crash into; collide with.

run off, 1 cause to be run or played. **2** to print: *to run off 1000 copies for a first edition.*

run out, come to an end: *After three minutes his time ran out on the telephone call.*

run out of, use up; have no more.

run out on, 1 leave suddenly; desert: *My friends didn't run out on me when I was having a difficult time.* **2** back out of; not be faithful to: *They ran out on their promise to help me.*

run over, 1 ride or drive over: *The car ran over some glass.* **2** overflow. **3** go through quickly.

run through, 1 use up, spend, or consume rapidly or recklessly. **2** pierce. **3** to review or rehearse: *The teacher ran through the homework assignment a second time.*

run up, INFORMAL. **1** make quickly: *The team ran up a big lead in the first quarter.* **2** collect; accumulate: *Don't run up a big bill.*

run a bout (run′ə bout′), **1** a light, open automobile or carriage with a single seat. **2** a small motorboat. **3** person who runs about from place to place, such as a vagabond or peddler. *n.*

run a way (run′ə wā′), **1** person, horse, etc., that runs away. **2** a running away. **3** running with nobody to guide or stop it; out of control: *a runaway horse, a runaway car.* **4** done by runaways: *a runaway marriage.* **5** easily won: *a runaway victory.* 1,2 *n.*, 3-5 *adj.*

run down (run′doun′), an account; summary: *The reporter gave a brief rundown of the week's news. n.*

run-down (run′doun′), **1** tired; sick. **2** falling to pieces; partly ruined: *a run-*

735

adj.	adjective	*n.*	noun
adv.	adverb	*prep.*	preposition
conj.	conjunction	*pron.*	pronoun
interj.	interjection	*v.*	verb
sing.	singular	*pl.*	plural

down old building. 3 that has stopped going or working. *adj.*

rune[1] (rün), 1 any letter of an ancient Germanic alphabet. 2 a mark, verse, or saying which is believed to have some mysterious, magic meaning. *n.* [Old English *rūn,* from a Scandinavian word of the 1000's, such as Icelandic *rūn* secret, rune]

rune[2] (rün), an old Scandinavian poem or song. *n.* [from Finnish *runo,* from a Scandinavian word of the 1000's, such as Icelandic *rūn*]

rung[1] (rung), past participle of **ring**[2]. *The bell has rung. v.*

rung[2] (def. 1, left; def. 2, right)

rung[2] (rung), 1 a round rod or bar used as a step of a ladder. 2 crosspiece set between the legs of a chair or as part of the back or arm of a chair. 3 spoke of a wheel. 4 bar of wood having a similar shape and use. *n.* [Old English *hrung*]

ru nic (rü′nik), consisting of runes; written in runes; marked with runes. *adj.*

run-in (run′in′), INFORMAL. a sharp disagreement; argument; quarrel. *n.*

run let (run′lit), runnel. *n.*

run nel (run′l), a small stream or brook. *n.*

run ner (run′ər), 1 person, animal, or thing that runs; racer. 2 messenger: *a runner for a bank.* 3 either of the narrow pieces on which a sleigh or sled slides. 4 blade of a skate. 5 a long, narrow strip: *We have a runner of carpet in our hall, and runners of linen and lace on our bureaus.* 6 person or ship that tries to evade somebody; smuggler: *a blockade runner.* 7 a slender stem that takes root along the ground, thus producing new plants. Strawberry plants spread by runners. *n.*

run ner-up (run′ər up′), player or team that takes second place in a contest. *n.*

run ning (run′ing), 1 act of a person, animal, or thing that runs. 2 that runs: *A running sore discharges pus. Running handwriting joins all letters of a word together. For three nights running is for three nights in succession. A running leap is one made with a run first.* 1 *n.,* 2 *adj.*

be in the running, have a chance to win.

be out of the running, have no chance to win.

running board, a metal step or footboard attached below the door on some cars and trucks.

running knot, slipknot.

running mate, candidate running on the same ticket with another, but for a less important office, such as a candidate for vice-president.

Run ny mede (run′ē mēd′), meadow near London where King John granted the Magna Charta in 1215. *n.*

run off (run′ôf′), 1 something that runs off, such as rain that flows from the land in streams. 2 a final, deciding race or contest. *n.*

run-of-the-mill (run′əv ғнə mil′), average or commonplace; ordinary. *adj.*

run-on entry (run′ôn′ or run′on′), a dictionary entry which is not defined. It is formed by adding a common suffix to a defined entry and appears in heavy type at the end of that entry. The run-on entry **rusher** appears at the end of the entry **rush**[1].

runt (runt), animal, person, or plant which is smaller than the usual size. *n.*

run way (run′wā′), 1 a paved strip at an airport on which aircraft land and take off. 2 way, track, groove, trough, etc., along which something moves, slides, etc. 3 the beaten track of deer or other animals. 4 an enclosed place for animals to run in. *n.*

ru pee (rü pē′), unit of money in India, Pakistan, and Ceylon. *n.*

rup ture (rup′chər), 1 a breaking or a being broken: *the rupture of a blood vessel.* 2 a breaking off of friendly relations. 3 break off; burst; break. 4 hernia. 5 affect with or suffer hernia. 1,2,4 *n.,* 3,5 *v.,* **rup tured, rup tur ing.**

rur al (rür′əl), in the country; belonging to the country; like that of the country: *Rural life is quiet. adj.*

rural free delivery, free delivery of mail in country districts by regular carriers.

ruse (rüz *or* rüs), trick; stratagem. *n.*

rush[1] (rush), 1 move with speed or force: *The river rushed past. We rushed to the station.* 2 send, push, or force with speed or haste: *Rush this order, please.* 3 go or act with speed or haste: *He rushes into things without knowing anything about them.* 4 to attack with much speed and force: *The soldiers rushed the enemy.* 5 act of rushing; dash: *The rush of the flood swept everything before it.* 6 busy haste; hurry: *the rush of city life.* 7 a great or sudden effort of many people to go somewhere or get something: *a gold rush. The Christmas rush is hard on clerks.* 8 eager demand; pressure: *a rush for tickets to a play. A sudden rush of business kept everyone working hard.* 9 requiring haste: *A rush order must be filled at once.* 1-4 *v.,* 5-8 *n., pl.* **rush es;** 9 *adj.* [Middle English *ruschen* force out of place by violent impact, probably from French of the 1300's *russher, ruser* get out of the way, dodge] —**rush′-er,** *n.*

rush[2] (rush), 1 any of various grasslike plants with pithy or hollow stems, that grow in wet soil or marshy places. 2 stem of such a plant, used for making chair seats, baskets, floor mats, etc. *n., pl.* **rush es.** [Old English *rysc*]

rush hour, time of day when traffic is heaviest or when trains, buses, etc., are most crowded.

Rush more (rush′môr′), **Mount,** mountain in the Black Hills of South Dakota. Huge heads of Washington, Jefferson, Lincoln, and Theodore Roosevelt are carved on the side of the peak. *n.*

rusk (rusk), 1 piece of bread or cake toasted in the oven. 2 kind of light, soft, sweet biscuit. *n.*

Rus kin (rus′kin), **John,** 1819-1900, English author, art critic, and social reformer. *n.*

Rus sell (rus′əl), **Bertrand,** 1872-1970, British philosopher, mathematician, and writer. *n.*

rus set (rus′it), 1 yellowish-brown or reddish-brown. 2 a yellowish brown or a reddish brown. 3 a coarse, russet-colored cloth. The English peasants used to make and wear russet. 4 kind of winter apple with a rough, brownish skin. 1 *adj.,* 2-4 *n.*

Rus sia (rush′ə), 1 the Soviet Union. 2 former country in E Europe and N Asia. It now forms most of the Soviet Union. Before 1917 it was part of an empire ruled by a czar. *n.*

Rus sian (rush′ən), 1 of or having to do with Russia, its people, or their language. 2 person born or living in Rus-

runner (def. 7) of a strawberry plant

sia. 3 the chief language of Russia. 1 *adj.*, 2,3 *n.*

Russian Revolution, revolution which overthrew the government of Nicholas II in 1917, and later that year established the Bolshevik government under Lenin.

Russian Soviet Federated Socialist Republic, the largest republic in the Soviet Union, occupying three fourths of the country's area.

rust (rust), 1 the reddish-brown or orange coating that forms on iron or steel which is exposed to air or moisture. 2 cover or become covered with rust: *Don't let the tools rust by leaving them out in the rain. The rain rusted the tools.* 3 spoil by not using. 4 become spoiled by not being used: *Don't let your mind rust during vacation.* 5 a plant disease that spots leaves and stems. 6 any of various fungi that produce this disease: *wheat rust.* 7 reddish-brown or orange. 8 a reddish brown or orange. 1,5,6,8 *n.*, 2-4 *v.*, 7 *adj.*

rus tic (rus′tik), 1 belonging to the country; suitable for the country; rural. 2 simple; plain: *His rustic speech and ways made him feel out of place in the royal palace.* 3 rough; awkward. 4 a country person: *The rustics had gathered at the country fair.* 5 made of branches with the bark still on them: *rustic furniture, a rustic fence.* 1-3,5 *adj.*, 4 *n.* —**rus′ti cal ly,** *adv.*

rus tic i ty (rus′tis′ə tē), 1 rustic quality, characteristic, or peculiarity. 2 rural life. 3 awkwardness; ignorance. *n., pl.* **rus tic i ties.**

rust i ly (rus′tl ē), in a rusty manner. *adv.*

rust i ness (rus′tē nis), rusty condition. *n.*

rus tle (rus′əl), 1 a light, soft sound of things gently rubbing together. 2 make

or cause to make this sound: *The leaves rustled in the breeze. The wind rustled the papers.* 3 INFORMAL. steal (cattle, horses, etc.). 1 *n.*, 2,3 *v.*, **rus tled, rus tling.**

rustle up, 1 gather; find. 2 get ready; prepare: *The cook rustled up some food.*

rus tler (rus′lər), 1 INFORMAL. a cattle thief. 2 SLANG. an active, energetic person. *n.*

rust proof (rust′prüf′), resisting rust. *adj.*

rust y (rus′tē), 1 covered with rust; rusted: *a rusty knife.* 2 made by rust: *a rusty stain, a rusty spot.* 3 colored like rust. 4 faded: *a rusty black, a rusty old coat.* 5 no longer good or effective from lack of use or practice: *I hadn't played tennis for months, so my game was rusty.* *adj.*, **rust i er, rust i est.**

rut (rut), 1 a track made in the ground by wheels. 2 make ruts in. 3 a fixed or established way of acting: *The old man was so set in his ways that everyone said he was in a rut.* 1,3 *n.*, 2 *v.*, **rut ted, rut ting.**

ru ta ba ga (rü′tə bā′gə), kind of large, yellow or white turnip. *n., pl.* **ru ta ba gas.**

Ruth (rüth), 1 (in the Bible) a widow who was very devoted to her mother-in-law, Naomi. Ruth left her native land of Moab to go with Naomi to Bethlehem. 2 book of the Old Testament about her. 3 **George Herman,** 1895-1948, American baseball player. He was better known as Babe Ruth. *n.*

ru the ni um (rü thē′nē əm), a brittle, white, metallic element which is found in platinum ores. *n.* [from Latin *Ruthenia* Russia (because of its discovery in the Ural Mountains)]

Ruth er ford (ruᴛн′ər fərd), **Ernest,** 1871-1937, British physicist, born in New Zealand, who developed the basic theories of nuclear physics. *n.*

hat, āge, fär; let, ēqual, tėrm;
it, īce; hot, ōpen, ôrder;
oil, out; cup, pu̇t, rüle; ch, child;
ng, long; sh, she; th, thin;
ᴛн, then; zh, measure;

ə represents *a* in about,
e in taken, *i* in pencil,
o in lemon, *u* in circus.

ruth er for di um (ruᴛн′ər fôr′dē əm), name suggested for a radioactive element produced artificially from californium. *n.* [from Ernest *Rutherford*]

ruth less (rüth′lis), having no pity; showing no mercy; cruel. *adj.* —**ruth′less ly,** *adv.* —**ruth′less ness,** *n.*

Rwan da (rü än′də), country in central Africa, north of Burundi. See **Congo** for map. *n.*

Ry., railway.

-ry, *suffix forming nouns from other nouns.* 1 occupation or work of a ____: *Dentistry = occupation or work of a dentist.* 2 act of a ____: *Mimicry = act of a mimic.* 3 condition of a ____: *Rivalry = condition of a rival.* 4 group or collection of ____s: *Jewelry = collection of jewels.* [shortened from -*ery*]

rye (rī), 1 a hardy annual plant widely grown in cold regions. Rye is a grass. 2 its seeds or grain, used for making flour, as food for livestock, and in making whiskey. 3 made from rye grain or flour: *rye bread.* 4 whiskey made from rye. 1,2,4 *n.*, 3 *adj.*

Ry u kyu Islands (rē ü′kyü′), chain of about 100 Japanese islands extending from Japan to Taiwan. Okinawa is the largest island.

S s

S or s (es), 1 the 19th letter of the alphabet. 2 anything shaped like an S: *The road curved in a big S. n., pl.* **S's** or **s's.**

S or S., 1 south. 2 southern.

Saar (sär *or* zär), 1 river flowing from NE France into West Germany. 2 state in West Germany, along the Saar River. *n.*

Sa bah (sä'bə), state in N Borneo, a member of the Federation of Malaysia. *n.*

Sab bath (sab'əth), day of the week used for rest and worship. Sunday is the Sabbath for most Christians; Saturday is the Jewish Sabbath. *n.*

sab bat i cal (sə bat'ə kəl), 1 of or suitable for the Sabbath. 2 of or for a rest from work. Once in seven years some teachers obtain a sabbatical leave for rest, study, or travel. *adj.*

sa ber (sā'bər), a heavy sword, usually slightly curved, having a single cutting edge. *n.* Also, **sabre.**

sa ber-toothed tiger (sā'bər tütht'), an extinct, tigerlike mammal whose upper canine teeth were very long and curved.

Sa bin (sā'bən), **Albert Bruce,** born 1906, American scientist who developed a vaccine against polio that can be taken by mouth. *n.*

sa ble (sā'bəl), 1 a small, flesh-eating mammal valued for its dark-brown, glossy fur. 2 its fur. Sable is one of the most costly furs. 3 OLD USE. black; dark. 4 **sables,** *pl.* mourning garments. 1,2,4 *n.,* 3 *adj.*

sabot (def. 1)

sab ot (sab'ō *or* sa bō'), 1 shoe hollowed out of a single piece of wood, worn by peasants in France, Belgium, etc. 2 a coarse leather shoe with a thick wooden sole. *n.*

sab o tage (sab'ə täzh), 1 damage done to work, tools, machinery, etc., by workmen as an attack or threat against an employer. 2 such damage done by enemy agents or sympathizers, by civilians of a conquered nation, etc. 3 damage or destroy deliberately: *to sabotage an ammunition plant.* 1,2 *n.,* 3 *v.,* **sab o taged, sab o tag ing.**

sab o teur (sab'ə tėr'), person who sabotages. *n.*

sa bre (sā'bər), saber. *n.*

sac (sak), a part like a bag in an animal or plant, often one containing liquids. The human bladder is a sac. *n.* —**sac'like',** *adj.*

Sac a ja we a or **Sac a ga we a** (sak'ə jə wē'ə), 1787?-1812, American Indian guide and interpreter. She accompanied the Lewis and Clark expedition to the American northwest. *n.*

sac char in (sak'ər ən), a very sweet substance obtained from coal tar, used as a substitute for sugar. *n.*

sac char ine (sak'ər ən), 1 overly sweet; sugary: *a saccharine smile.* 2 of or like sugar. 3 saccharin. 1,2 *adj.,* 3 *n.*

sac er do tal (sas'ər dō'tl), of priests or the priesthood; priestly. *adj.*

sa chem (sā'chəm), (among some North American Indians) the chief of a tribe or confederation. *n.*

sa chet (sa shā' *or* sash'ā), a small bag or pad containing perfumed powder, placed among articles of clothing. *n.*

sack[1] (sak), 1 a large bag made of coarse cloth. Sacks are used for holding grain, flour, potatoes, and coal. 2 such a bag with what is in it: *He bought two sacks of corn.* 3 amount that a sack will hold: *We burned two sacks of coal.* 4 any bag with what is in it: *a sack of candy.* 5 put into a sack or sacks: *to sack grain or salt.* 6 a loose coat: *a knitted sack for a baby.* 1-4,6 *n.,* 5 *v.* [Old English *sacc,* from Latin *saccus,* from Greek *sakkos*]

saber-toothed tiger
about 7 ft. long including the tail

sack[2] (sak), 1 plunder (a captured city). 2 a plundering of a captured city: *the sack of Rome by the barbarians.* 1 *v.,* 2 *n.* [from French of the 1500's (*mettre à) sac* (put to the) sack, from Italian *sacco* sack[1], from Latin *saccus*]

sack[3] (sak), sherry or other strong, light-colored wine. *n.* [from French of the 1500's (*vin) sec* dry (wine), from Latin *siccus*]

sack cloth (sak'klôth'), 1 coarse cloth for making sacks. 2 coarse cloth worn as a sign of mourning or penance. *n.*

sack ful (sak'fùl), enough to fill a sack. *n., pl.* **sack fuls.**

sack ing (sak'ing), coarse cloth for making sacks. *n.*

sac ra ment (sak'rə mənt), 1 (in Christian churches) any of certain religious ceremonies considered especially sacred. Baptism and the Eucharist are sacraments. 2 Often, **Sacrament.** the Eucharist; Holy Communion. 3 something especially sacred. *n.*

sac ra men tal (sak'rə men'tl), 1 of or having to do with a sacrament; used in a sacrament: *sacramental wine.* 2 especially sacred. *adj.*

Sac ra men to (sak'rə men'tō), capital of California, in the central part. *n.*

sa cred (sā'krid), 1 belonging to or dedicated to God; holy: *the sacred altar, a sacred building.* 2 connected with religion; religious: *sacred writings, sacred music.* 3 worthy of reverence: *the sacred memory of a dead hero.* 4 that must not be violated or disregarded: *a sacred promise. adj.* —**sa'cred ness,** *n.*

sac ri fice (sak'rə fīs), 1 act of offering to a god. 2 the thing offered: *The ancient Hebrews killed animals on the altars as sacrifices to God.* 3 give or offer to a god: *They sacrificed oxen, sheep, and doves.* 4 a giving up of one thing for another: *Our teacher does not approve of any sacrifice of studies to sports.* 5 give up: *sacrifice one's life for another, sacrifice business for pleasure.* 6 loss from selling something below its value: *They sold their house at a sacrifice because they needed the money.* 7 sell at a loss. 8 (in baseball) a bunt that helps a base runner to advance, or a fly that allows a base runner to score, although the batter is put out. 1,2,4,6,8 *n.,* 3,5,7 *v.,* **sac ri ficed, sac ri fic ing.**

sac ri fi cial (sak'rə fish'əl), having to do with or used in a sacrifice: *sacrificial rites. adj.*

sac ri lege (sak'rə lij), an intentional injury to anything sacred; disrespectful treatment of anyone or anything sacred: *Robbing the church was a sacrilege. n.*

sac ri le gious (sak'rə lij'əs), injurious or insulting to sacred persons or things. *adj.*

sac ris tan (sak'ri stən), person in charge of the sacred vessels, robes, etc., of a church. *n.*

sac ris ty (sak'ri stē), place where the sacred vessels, robes, etc., of a church are kept. *n., pl.* **sac ris ties.**

sac ro sanct (sak'rō sangkt), very holy; very sacred. *adj.*

sad (sad), 1 not happy; full of sorrow: *You feel sad if your best friend goes away.* 2 causing sorrow: *a sad accident.* 3 extremely bad: *a sad state of affairs. adj.,* **sad der, sad dest.** —**sad'ly,** *adv.* —**sad'ness,** *n.*

sad den (sad'n), make or become sad: *Her face saddened at the news. v.*

sad dle (sad'l), 1 seat for a rider on a horse's back, on a bicycle, etc. 2 part of a harness that holds the shafts, or to which a checkrein is attached. 3 thing shaped like a saddle. A ridge between two mountain peaks is called a saddle. **4** put a saddle on. **5** to burden: *He is saddled with too many jobs.* **6** a cut of mutton, venison, lamb, etc., consisting of both loins and the back portion between them. 1-3,6 *n.*, 4,5 *v.*, **sad dled, sad dling.**

in the saddle, in a position of control.

sad dle bag (sad′l bag′), one of a pair of bags laid over an animal's back behind the saddle. *n.*

saddle horse, horse for riding.

sad dler (sad′lər), person who makes or sells saddles and harnesses. *n.*

saddle shoe, a low shoe, usually white, with the instep crossed by a band of leather of a different color. Saddle shoes are used for casual wear.

sa dism (sā′diz əm *or* sad′iz əm), **1** practice of a person who gets pleasure from hurting someone else. **2** an unnatural love of cruelty. *n.* [from French *sadisme,* from Marquis de *Sade,* 1740-1814, who wrote about it]

sa dist (sā′dist *or* sad′ist), **1** person who gets pleasure from hurting someone else. **2** person having an unnatural love of cruelty. *n.*

sa dis tic (sə dis′tik), of sadism or sadists. *adj.*

sae ter (sē′tər), in Norway: **1** a mountain pasture. **2** a mountain dairy farm. *n.*

sa fa ri (sə fär′ē), **1** journey or hunting expedition in eastern Africa. **2** any long trip or expedition. *n., pl.* **sa fa ris.**

safe (sāf), **1** free from harm or danger: *Keep money in a safe place.* **2** not harmed: *He returned from war safe and sound.* **3** out of danger; secure: *We feel safe with the dog in the house.* **4** put beyond power of doing harm: *a criminal safe in prison.* **5** careful: *a safe guess, a safe move.* **6** that can be depended on: *a safe guide.* **7** a steel or iron box for money, jewels, papers, etc. **8** (in baseball) reaching a base without being out. 1-6,8 *adj.,* **saf er, saf est;** 7 *n.* —**safe′ly,** *adv.* —**safe′ness,** *n.*

safe-con duct (sāf′kon′dukt), **1** privilege of passing safely through a region, especially in time of war: *At the start of the war, neutrals were given safe-conduct out of the country.* **2** paper granting this privilege. *n.*

safe guard (sāf′gärd′), **1** keep safe; guard against hurt or danger; protect: *Pure food laws safeguard our health.* **2** protection; defense: *Keeping clean is a safeguard against disease.* 1 *v.,* 2 *n.*

safe keep ing (sāf′kē′ping), protection; keeping safe; care. *n.*

safe ty (sāf′tē), **1** a being safe; freedom from harm or danger: *A bank assures safety for your money. You can cross the street in safety when the police-*

man holds up his hand to stop the cars. **2** device to prevent injury or accident. A gun cannot be fired if the safety is on. **3** giving safety; making harm unlikely: *a safety match, a safety belt.* 1,2 *n., pl.* **safe ties;** 3 *adj.*

safety glass, glass that resists shattering, made of two or more layers of glass joined together by a layer of transparent plastic.

safety pin, pin bent back on itself to form a spring and having a guard that covers the point and prevents accidental unfastening.

safety valve, 1 valve in a steam boiler, etc., that opens and lets steam or fluid escape when the pressure becomes too great. Pressure cookers have a safety valve. **2** something that helps a person get rid of anger, nervousness, etc., in a harmless way.

saf flow er (saf′lou′ər), herb like a thistle, with large flower heads. Its seeds yield an oil used for cooking. Its dried petals are used in making certain red dyes. *n.*

saf fron (saf′rən), **1** an autumn crocus with purple flowers having orange-yellow stigmas. **2** an orange-yellow coloring matter obtained from the dried stigmas of this crocus. Saffron is used to color and flavor candy, drinks, etc. **3** an orange yellow. **4** orange-yellow. 1-3 *n.,* 4 *adj.*

sag (sag), **1** to sink under weight or pressure; bend down in the middle, as a rope, beam, cable, plank, etc. **2** hang down unevenly: *Your dress sags in the back.* **3** become less firm or elastic; yield through weakness, weariness, or lack of effort; droop; sink: *Our courage sagged.* **4** act, state, or degree of sagging. **5** place where anything sags. 1-3 *v.,* **sagged, sag ging;** 4,5 *n.*

sa ga (sä′gə), **1** a medieval Norse or Icelandic story of heroic deeds. **2** any story of heroic deeds. *n., pl.* **sa gas.**

sa ga cious (sə gā′shəs), wise in a keen, practical way; shrewd. *adj.* —**sa ga′cious ly,** *adv.* —**sa ga′cious ness,** *n.*

sa gac i ty (sə gas′ə tē), keen, sound judgment; mental acuteness; shrewdness: *The lawyer displayed sagacity in questioning the witnesses. n.*

sag a more (sag′ə môr), (among some North American Indians) a chief or great man, sometimes below a sachem. *n.*

sage[1] (sāj), **1** showing wisdom or good judgment: *a sage reply.* **2** wise: *The queen surrounded herself with sage advisers.* **3** wise-looking; grave; solemn: *Owls are sage birds.* **4** a very wise man: *The sage gave advice to his king.* 1-3 *adj.,* **sag er, sag est;** 4 *n.* [from French of the 1200's *sage,*

hat, āge, fär; let, ēqual, tėrm;
it, īce; hot, ōpen, ôrder;
oil, out; cup, pùt, rüle; ch, child;
ng, long; sh, she; th, thin;
ⱦH, then; zh, measure;

ə represents *a* in about,
e in taken, *i* in pencil,
o in lemon, *u* in circus.

from Latin *sapius,* from *sapere* be wise]
—**sage′ly,** *adv.* —**sage′ness,** *n.*

sage[2] (sāj), **1** plant related to mint whose gray-green leaves are used as seasoning and in medicine: *The turkey dressing was seasoned with sage.* **2** sagebrush. *n.* [from French of the 1300's *sauge,* from Latin *salvia* "the healing plant," from *salvus* safe]

sage brush (sāj′brush′), a grayish shrub that smells like sage, common on the dry plains of western North America. *n.*

sa go (sā′gō), **1** a starchy food used in making puddings, etc. **2** an East Indian palm tree from whose pith this starchy food is made. *n., pl.* **sa gos.**

sa gua ro (sə gwär′ō), a very tall, branching cactus of Arizona and neighboring regions. *n., pl.* **sa gua ros.**

Sa har a (sə her′ə *or* sə har′ə), the world's largest desert, in N Africa. *n.*

sa hib (sä′ib), sir; master. Natives in colonial India called a European "sahib" when speaking to or of him. *n.* [from Hindi, from Arabic]

said (sed), **1** past tense and past participle of **say.** *He said he would come. She had said "No" every time.* **2** named or mentioned before: *the said witness, the said sum of money.* 1 *v.,* 2 *adj.*

Sai gon (sī gon′), capital of South Vietnam, in the S part. *n.*

sail (sāl), **1** piece of cloth attached to the rigging of a ship to catch the wind and make the ship move through the water. **2** something like a sail, such as the part of an arm of a windmill that catches the wind. **3** ship or ships: *a fleet of thirty sail.* **4** trip on a boat with sails or on any other vessel: *Let's go for a sail.* **5** to travel on water by the action of wind on sails. **6** to travel on a steamboat, etc. **7** move smoothly like a ship with sails: *The eagle sailed by. The duchess sailed into the room.* **8** sail upon, over, or through: *sail the seas.* **9** manage a ship or boat: *The girls are learning to sail.* **10** begin a trip by water: *We sail at 2 p.m.* 1-4 *n.,* 5-10 *v.*

make sail, 1 spread out the sails of a ship. **2** begin a trip by water.

adj.	adjective	*n.*	noun
adv.	adverb	*prep.*	preposition
conj.	conjunction	*pron.*	pronoun
interj.	interjection	*v.*	verb
sing.	singular	*pl.*	plural

sail into, SLANG. 1 attack; beat. 2 criticize; scold.

set sail, begin a trip by water.

under sail, with the sails spread out.

sail boat (sāl′bōt′), boat that is moved by a sail or sails. Schooners and sloops are kinds of sailboats. *n.*

sail cloth (sāl′klôth′), canvas or other material used for making sails. *n., pl.* **sail cloths** (sāl′klôŦHz′ or sāl′-klôths′).

sail fish (sāl′fish′), a large, saltwater fish that has a long, high fin on its back. It is related to the swordfish. *n., pl.* **sail fish es** or **sail fish.**

sail or (sā′lər), 1 person whose work is handling a sailboat or other vessel. In these days most sailors are on steamships. 2 member of a ship's crew. The men in our navy are called sailors if they are not officers. 3 like that of a sailor: *My blouse has a sailor collar.* 4 a flat-brimmed straw hat modeled after the kind of hat sailors used to wear long ago. 1,2,4 *n.*, 3 *adj.*

sail or ly (sā′lər lē), like a sailor; suitable for a sailor. *adj.*

saint (sānt), 1 a very holy person. 2 person who has gone to heaven. 3 person declared a saint by the Roman Catholic Church. 4 person who is very humble, patient, etc., like a saint. 5 make a saint of; canonize. 1-4 *n.*, 5 *v.*

Saint. For names of saints look under the Christian name, and for places beginning with "Saint" look under the **St.** words.

Saint Ber nard (bər närd′), one of a breed of big, red-and-white dogs with large heads. These intelligent dogs were first bred by the monks at the hospice of Grand St. Bernard, a pass in the Swiss Alps, to rescue travelers lost in the snow.

Saint Bernard
25½ to 29 in. high at the shoulder

saint ed (sān′tid), 1 declared to be a saint. 2 thought of as a saint; gone to heaven. 3 sacred; very holy; saintly. *adj.*

saint hood (sānt′hu̇d), character or status of a saint. *n.*

saint li ness (sānt′lē nis), piety; holiness. *n.*

saint ly (sānt′lē), like a saint; very holy; very good. *adj.*, **saint li er, saint li est.**

Saint Patrick's Day, March 17. It is an Irish national holiday.

Saint Valentine's Day, February 14, day on which valentines are exchanged.

Saint Vitus's dance. See **St. Vitus's dance.**

saith (seth), OLD USE. says. *v.*

sake (sāk), 1 cause; account; interest: *Put yourself to no trouble for our sakes.* 2 purpose; end: *We moved to the country for the sake of peace and quiet. n.*

sa laam (sə läm′), 1 a greeting that means "Peace," used especially in Moslem countries. 2 a very low bow, with the palm of the right hand placed on the forehead. 3 greet with a salaam. 4 make a salaam. 1,2 *n.*, 3,4 *v.* [from Arabic *salam*]

sal a bil i ty (sā′lə bil′ə tē), salable condition or quality. *n.*

sal a ble (sā′lə bəl), that can be sold; fit to be sold; easily sold. *adj.* Also, **saleable.**

sa la cious (sə lā′shəs), 1 obscene; indecent. 2 lustful; lewd. *adj.* —**sa la′cious ly,** *adv.* —**sa la′cious ness,** *n.*

sal ad (sal′əd), raw green vegetables, such as lettuce, cabbage, and celery, served with a dressing. Often cold meat, fish, eggs, cooked vegetables, or fruits are used along with, or instead of, the raw green vegetables. *n.*

Sal a din (sal′ə dən), 1137?-1193, sultan of Egypt and Syria from about 1175 to 1193. He captured Jerusalem and defeated the Crusaders led by Richard I of England. *n.*

sal a man der (sal′ə man′dər), 1 animal shaped like a lizard, but belonging to the same group as frogs and toads. Salamanders have moist, smooth skin and live in water or in damp places. 2 (in old myths) a lizard or reptile supposed to live in or be able to endure fire. *n.*

sa la mi (sə lä′mē), kind of thick sausage, often flavored with garlic. It is usually sliced and eaten cold. *n., pl.* **sa la mis.**

sal ar ied (sal′ər ēd), receiving or bringing in a salary: *a salaried employee, a salaried position. adj.*

sal ar y (sal′ər ē), fixed pay for regular work. Teachers, government officials,

and business executives receive salaries. *n., pl.* **sal ar ies.**

sale (sāl), 1 act of selling; exchange of goods or property for money: *no sale yet this morning, the sale of a house.* 2 **sales,** *pl.* amount sold: *Today's sales were larger than yesterday's.* 3 chance to sell; demand; market: *There is almost no sale for washboards in these days.* 4 a selling at lower prices than usual: *This store is having a sale on suits.* 5 an auction. 6 **sales,** *pl.* business of selling: *His first job was in sales. n.*

for sale, to be sold: *There are several houses in the neighborhood for sale, but none for rent.*

on sale, for sale at lower prices than usual: *The grocer has coffee on sale.*

sale a ble (sā′lə bəl), salable. *adj.*

Sa lem (sā′ləm), 1 seaport in NE Massachusetts, settled in 1626. 2 capital of Oregon, in the NW part. *n.*

sales clerk (sālz′klėrk′), person whose work is selling in a store. *n.*

sales girl (sālz′gėrl′), girl whose work is selling in a store. *n.*

sales la dy (sālz′lā′dē), saleswoman. *n., pl.* **sales la dies.**

sales man (sālz′mən), man whose work is selling. *n., pl.* **sales men.**

sales man ship (sālz′mən ship), 1 work of a salesman. 2 ability at selling. *n.*

sales per son (sālz′pėr′sən), person whose work is selling, especially in a store. *n.*

sales tax, tax based on the amount received for articles sold.

sales wom an (sālz′wu̇m′ən), woman whose work is selling, especially in a store. *n., pl.* **sales wom en.**

sal i cyl ic acid (sal′ə sil′ik), a white, crystalline powder used as a mild antiseptic and preservative, and in making aspirin.

sa li ent (sā′lē ənt), 1 standing out; easily seen or noticed; prominent; striking: *the salient features in a landscape, the salient points in a speech.* 2 part of a fortification or line of trenches that projects toward the enemy. 1 *adj.*, 2 *n.*

sa line (sā′lēn′), 1 of salt; like salt; salty. 2 containing common salt or any other salts: *a saline solution.* 3 solution with a high concentration of salt, used in medical examinations and treatment. 1,2 *adj.*, 3 *n.*

sa lin i ty (sə lin′ə tē), saline condition or quality; saltiness. *n.*

Salis bur y (sôlz′ber′ē), 1 city in S England. A famous cathedral is located there. 2 capital of Rhodesia, in the NE part. *n.*

sa li va (sə lī′və), liquid produced by glands in the mouth to keep it moist, help in chewing, and start digestion. *n.*

sal i var y (sal′ə ver′ē), of or producing saliva: *the salivary glands.* *adj.*

sal i vate (sal′ə vāt), secrete saliva. *v.*, **sal i vat ed, sal i vat ing.**

Salk (sôlk), **Jonas Edward,** born 1914, American scientist who developed the Salk vaccine. *n.*

Salk vaccine, vaccine containing dead polio viruses which cause the body to produce antibodies. It protects against infection from live polio viruses.

sal low (sal′ō), having a sickly, yellowish color or complexion. *adj.*

sal ly (sal′ē), 1 rush forth suddenly; go out; set out briskly: *We sallied forth at dawn.* 2 a sudden rushing forth: *The men in the fort made a brave sally and returned with many prisoners.* 3 a going forth; trip; excursion. 4 a witty remark: *She continued her story undisturbed by the merry sallies of her hearers.* 1 *v.*, **sal lied, sal ly ing;** 2-4 *n., pl.* **sal lies.**

salm on (sam′ən), 1 a large marine and freshwater fish with silvery scales and yellowish-pink flesh. It is common in the northern Atlantic and northern Pacific near the mouths of large rivers which it swims up in order to spawn. The salmon is one of the chief food fishes. 2 a yellowish pink. 3 yellowish-pink. 1,2 *n., pl.* **salm ons** or **salm on;** 3 *adj.*

sa lon (sə lon′), 1 a large room for receiving or entertaining guests. 2 a gathering of distinguished persons in such a room. 3 place used to exhibit works of art. 4 a fashionable or stylish shop. *n.*

sa loon (sə lün′), 1 place where alcoholic drinks are sold and drunk; tavern. 2 a large room for general or public use: *The ship's passengers ate in the dining saloon. n.*

salsify
stem to 4 ft. high; root to 1 ft. long

sal si fy (sal′sə fī), plant with purple flowers and a long root like a parsnip whose flavor is thought to be like that of an oyster. *n., pl.* **sal si fies.**

sal soda (sal), sodium carbonate.

salt (sôlt), 1 a white substance found in the earth and in sea water; sodium chloride. Salt is used to season and preserve food. 2 containing salt: *salt water.* 3 tasting like salt; salty: *food that is too salt.* 4 mix or sprinkle with salt. 5 cure or preserve with salt. 6 cured or preserved with salt. 7 provide with salt: *to salt cattle.* 8 flooded with or growing in salt water: *salt marshes, salt grass.* 9 season; make pungent: *conversation salted with wit.* 10 that which gives liveliness, piquancy, or pungency to anything. 11 **salts,** *pl.* **a** a medicine that causes movement of the bowels. **b** smelling salts. 12 a chemical compound derived from an acid by replacing the hydrogen in the acid wholly or partly by a metal or a radical. A salt is formed when an acid and a base neutralize each other. Sodium bicarbonate is a salt. 13 INFORMAL. sailor. 1, 10-13 *n.*, 2,3,6,8 *adj.*, 4,5,7,9 *v.* —**salt′er,** *n.*

salt away or **salt down,** 1 pack with salt to preserve: *The fish were salted down in a barrel.* 2 SLANG. store away: *She salted away money for her old age.*

salt of the earth, the best people.

with a grain of salt, with some reservation or allowance: *Her story must be taken with a grain of salt.*

worth one's salt, worth one's support, wages, etc.

salt cel lar (sôlt′sel′ər), shaker or dish for holding salt, used on the table. *n.*

salt ine (sôl tēn′), a thin, crisp, salted cracker. *n.*

salt i ness (sôl′tē nis), salty condition or quality. *n.*

Salt Lake City, capital of Utah, in the N part.

salt lick, place where natural salt is found on the surface of the ground and where animals go to lick it up.

salt pe ter or **salt pe tre** (sôlt′pē′-tər), 1 naturally occurring potassium nitrate; niter. 2 sodium nitrate. **Chile saltpeter** is a naturally occurring form of sodium nitrate and is used as a fertilizer. *n.*

salt shak er (sôlt′shā′kər), container for salt, with a perforated top through which the salt is sprinkled. *n.*

salt wa ter (sôlt′wô′tər or sôlt′wot′-ər), 1 consisting of or containing salt water: *a saltwater solution.* 2 living in the sea or in water like sea water: *saltwater fish.* 3 working on the sea: *a saltwater fisherman. adj.*

salt y (sôl′tē), 1 containing salt; tasting of salt. Sweat and tears are salty. 2 to the point; witty and a bit improper: *a salty remark. adj.,* **salt i er, salt i est.**

sa lu bri ous (sə lü′brē əs), healthful: *a salubrious diet. adj.*

sal u tar y (sal′yə ter′ē), 1 beneficial: *The teacher gave the boy salutary advice.* 2 good for the health; wholesome: *Walking is a salutary exercise. adj.*

sal u ta tion (sal′yə tā′shən), 1 a

hat, āge, fär; let, ēqual, tėrm;
it, īce; hot, ōpen, ôrder;
oil, out; cup, pùt, rüle; ch, child;
ng, long; sh, she; th, thin;
ŦH, then; zh, measure;

ə represents *a* in about,
e in taken, *i* in pencil,
o in lemon, *u* in circus.

greeting; saluting: *The man raised his hat in salutation.* 2 something uttered, written, or done to salute. You begin a letter with a salutation, such as "Dear Sir" or "My Dear Mrs. Jones." *A formal bow was her parting salutation. n.*

sa lu ta to ri an (sə lü′tə tôr′ē ən), student who delivers the address of welcome at the graduation of a class. The salutatorian is often the student who ranks second in his class. *n.*

sa lu ta to ry (sə lü′tə tôr′ē), 1 expressing greeting; welcoming. 2 an opening address welcoming guests at the graduation of a class. 1 *adj.,* 2 *n., pl.* **sa lu ta to ries.**

sa lute (sə lüt′), 1 to honor in a formal manner by raising the hand to the head, by firing guns, by dipping flags, etc.: *We salute the flag every day at school. The soldier saluted the officer.* 2 meet with kind words, a bow, a kiss, etc.; greet: *The old gentleman walked along the avenue saluting his friends.* 3 act of saluting; sign of welcome, farewell, or honor: *The queen gracefully acknowledged the salutes of the crowd.* 4 make a salute. 5 position of the hand, gun, etc., in saluting. 1,2,4 *v.,* **sa lut ed, sa lut ing;** 3,5 *n.*

Sal va dor (sal′və dôr). See **El Salvador.** *n.*

sal vage (sal′vij), 1 act of saving a ship or its cargo from wreck, capture, etc. 2 payment for saving it. 3 rescue of property from fire, flood, shipwreck, etc. 4 save from fire, flood, shipwreck, etc. 5 property salvaged: *the salvage from a shipwreck or a fire.* 1-3,5 *n.,* 4 *v.,* **sal vaged, sal vag ing.**

sal va tion (sal vā′shən), 1 a saving or a being saved. 2 person or thing that saves. Christians believe that Christ is the salvation of the world. 3 a saving of the soul; deliverance from sin and from punishment for sin. *n.*

Salvation Army, organization to spread religion and help the poor, founded in England in 1865 by William Booth.

salve (sav), 1 a soft, greasy ointment put on wounds and sores to soothe or

salver

adj. adjective	*n.* noun
adv. adverb	*prep.* preposition
conj. conjunction	*pron.* pronoun
interj. interjection	*v.* verb
sing. singular	*pl.* plural

heal them. **2** put salve on. **3** something soothing; balm: *The kind words were a salve to his hurt feelings.* **4** soothe; smooth over: *She salved her conscience by the thought that her lie harmed no one.* 1,3 *n.,* 2,4 *v.,* **salved, salv ing.**

sal ver (sal′vər), tray. *n.*

sal vo (sal′vō), **1** the discharge of several guns at the same time as a broadside or as a salute. **2** round of cheers or applause. *n., pl.* **sal vos** or **sal voes.**

Salz burg (sôlz′bėrg′), city in W Austria. Annual music festivals are held there. *n.*

Sa mar i a (sə mer′ē ə), **1** district in the N part of ancient Palestine, now in Jordan. **2** chief city of this district. *n.*

Sa mar i tan (sə mar′ə tən), **1** person born or living in Samaria. **2** of or having to do with Samaria or its people. **3** person who helps another in trouble or distress; Good Samaritan. 1,3 *n.,* 2 *adj.*

sa mar i um (sə mer′ē əm *or* sə-mar′ē əm), a hard, brittle, grayish-white, metallic element occurring with cerium. *n.* [from Colonel *Samarski,* a Russian officer and mine inspector of the 1800's]

same (sām), **1** not another; identical: *We came back the same way we went.* **2** just alike; not different: *Her name and mine are the same.* **3** unchanged: *He is the same kind old man.* **4** just spoken of: *They were talking about a strange man. This same man always dressed in white.* **5** the same person or thing. **6 the same,** in the same manner: *"Sea" and "see" are pronounced the same.* 1-4 *adj.,* 5 *pron.,* 6 *adv.*

all the same, notwithstanding; nevertheless.

just the same, 1 in the same manner. **2** nevertheless.

same ness (sām′nis), **1** state of being the same; exact likeness. **2** lack of variety; tiresomeness. *n.*

sam i sen (sam′ə sen), a Japanese instrument like a guitar, having three strings and played by plucking the strings. *n.*

Sa mo a (sə mō′ə), group of islands in the S Pacific. Several of these islands (**American Samoa**) belong to the United States and the rest make up the independent country of **Western**

Samoa. See **Melanesia** for map. *n.* —**Sa mo′an,** *adj., n.*

sam o var (sam′ə vär), a metal urn used for heating water for tea. *n.*

sam pan (sam′pan), any of various small boats of China, etc. A sampan is sculled by one or more oars at the stern; it usually has a single sail and a cabin made of mats. *n.*

sampan

sam ple (sam′pəl), **1** part to show what the rest is like; one thing to show what the others are like: *Pushing people aside to get on a bus is a sample of her bad manners.* **2** serving as a sample: *a sample copy.* **3** take a part of; test a part of: *We sampled the cake and found it very good.* 1 *n.,* 2 *adj.,* 3 *v.,* **sampled, sam pling.**

sam pler¹ (sam′plər), person who samples. *n.* [*sample* + *-er¹*]

sam pler² (sam′plər), piece of cloth embroidered to show skill in needlework. *n.* [from French of the 1200's *essamplaire,* from Latin *exemplarium* a model pattern]

sam pling (sam′pling), **1** act or process of taking samples. **2** something taken or serving as a sample. *n.*

Sam son (sam′sən), **1** (in the Bible) a man who had very great strength. He was one of the judges of Israel. **2** any very strong man. *n.*

Sam u el (sam′yü əl), **1** a Hebrew leader, judge, and prophet of the 1000's B.C. He anointed Saul and David kings of Israel. **2** either of two books in the Old Testament named after Samuel. *n.*

sam u rai (sam′ù rī′), **1** the military class in feudal Japan, consisting of the retainers of the great nobles. **2** member of this class. *n., pl.* **sam u rai.**

San An to ni o (san an tō′nē ō), city in S Texas. The Alamo is there. *n.*

san a to ri um (san′ə tôr′ē əm), place for treatment of the sick or those recovering from illness. People who are suffering from a sickness that takes a long time to cure, like tuberculosis, often go to sanatoriums. *n., pl.* **san a to ri ums, san a to ri a** (san′ə tôr′ē ə). Also, **sanitarium.**

sanc ti fi ca tion (sangk′tə fə kā′-shən), a sanctifying or a being sanctified; consecration; purification from sin. *n.*

sanc ti fy (sangk′tə fī), **1** make holy; make free from sin. **2** set apart as sa-

cred; observe as holy: *"Lord, sanctify this our offering to Thy use."* **3** make right; justify or sanction: *a custom sanctified by law.* *v.,* **sanc ti fied, sanc ti fy ing.**

sanc ti mo ni ous (sangk′tə mō′nē-əs), making a show of holiness; putting on airs of sanctity. *adj.* —**sanc′ti-mo′ni ous ly,** *adv.*

sanc tion (sangk′shən), **1** permission with authority; support; approval: *We have the sanction of the law to play ball in this park.* **2** authorize; approve; allow: *Her conscience does not sanction stealing.* **3** action by several nations toward another, such as a blockade, economic restrictions, etc., intended to force it to obey international law: *to apply economic sanctions instead of military ones.* 1,3 *n.,* 2 *v.*

sanc ti ty (sangk′tə tē), **1** holiness; saintliness; godliness. **2** sacredness; holy character: *the sanctity of a church, the sanctity of the home.* *n.*

sanc tu ar y (sangk′chü er′ē), **1** a sacred place. A church is a sanctuary. **2** part of a church around the altar. **3** place of refuge or protection: *a wild-life sanctuary.* **4** refuge or protection: *The cabin provided sanctuary from the rain.* *n., pl.* **sanc tu ar ies.**

sanc tum (sangk′təm), **1** a sacred place. **2** a private room or office where a person can be undisturbed. *n.*

sand (sand), **1** tiny grains of worn-down or disintegrated rock: *the sands of the desert, the sands of the seashore.* **2** spread sand over: *The highway department sanded the icy road.* **3** fill up with sand. **4** add sand to: *to sand sugar.* **5** clean, smooth, or polish with sand, sandpaper, etc.: *to sand the edges of a piece of wood.* 1 *n.,* 2-5 *v.*

san dal (san′dl), **1** kind of shoe made of a sole fastened to the foot by straps. **2** any of various kinds of low-cut shoes, slippers, etc. *n.*

san dal wood (san′dl wùd′), **1** the fragrant heartwood of certain trees of Asia, used for making boxes, fans, etc., and burned as incense. **2** any of the trees it comes from. *n.*

sand bag (sand′bag′), **1** bag filled with sand. Sandbags are used to protect trenches and as ballast on balloons. **2** furnish with sandbags. **3** a small bag of sand used as a club. **4** hit or stun

samovar

with or as if with a sandbag. 1,3 *n.*, 2,4 *v.*, **sand bagged, sand bag ging.**

sand bank (sand′bangk′), ridge of sand forming a shoal or hillside. *n.*

sand bar (sand′bär′), ridge of sand in a river or along a shore, formed by the action of tides or currents. *n.*

sand blast (sand′blast′), 1 blast of air or steam containing sand, used to clean, grind, cut, or decorate hard surfaces, such as glass, stone, or metal. 2 use a sandblast on; clean, grind, cut, or decorate by a sandblast. 1 *n.*, 2 *v.*

sand box (sand′boks′), box for holding sand, especially for children to play in. *n.*, *pl.* **sand box es.**

Sand burg (sand′berg′), **Carl**, 1878-1967, American poet and biographer. *n.*

sand dollar, a small, flat, round sea urchin that lives on sandy bottoms of the ocean.

sand er (san′dər), person or apparatus that sands or sandpapers. *n.*

sand glass (sand′glas′), hourglass. *n.*, *pl.* **sand glass es.**

San Di e go (san dē ā′gō), seaport in SW California.

sand lot (sand′lot′), of or having to do with games, especially baseball, played on vacant city lots, small fields, etc. *adj.*

sand man (sand′man′), a fabled man said to make children sleepy by sprinkling sand on their eyes. *n.*

sand pa per (sand′pā′pər), 1 a strong paper with a layer of sand or similar substance glued on it, used for smoothing, cleaning, or polishing. 2 smooth, clean, or polish with sandpaper. 1 *n.*, 2 *v.*

sand pip er (sand′pī′pər), a small bird with a long bill, living on sandy shores. *n.*

sand stone (sand′stōn′), kind of sedimentary rock formed mostly of sand held together by silica, calcite, or iron oxide. Sandstone is used in building. *n.*

sand storm (sand′stôrm′), windstorm that carries along clouds of sand. *n.*

sand wich (sand′wich), 1 two or more slices of bread with meat, jelly, cheese, or some other filling between them. 2 put or squeeze in (between): *He was sandwiched between two fat women.* 1 *n.*, *pl.* **sand wich es;** 2 *v.* [from John Montagu, the fourth Earl of Sandwich, 1718-1792, who supposedly invented it]

Sandwich Islands, former name of the Hawaiian Islands.

sand y (san′dē), 1 containing sand; consisting of sand: *sandy soil.* 2 covered with sand: *Most of the shore is rocky, but there is a sandy beach.* 3 yellowish-red: *She has sandy hair.* *adj.*, **sand i er, sand i est.**

sane (sān), 1 having a healthy mind; normal; sound; rational. 2 having or showing good sense; sensible: *She has a sane attitude toward driving and never takes unnecessary chances.* *adj.*, **san er, san est.** —**sane′ly,** *adv.*

San Fran cis co (san frən sis′kō), large seaport in W California.

San Francisco Bay, bay of the Pacific on which San Francisco and Oakland, California, are located.

sang (sang), a past tense of **sing.** *The bird sang.* *v.*

san gui nar y (sang′gwə ner′ē), 1 with much blood or bloodshed; bloody: *a sanguinary battle.* 2 delighting in bloodshed; bloodthirsty: *a sanguinary rebel.* *adj.*

san guine (sang′gwən), 1 naturally cheerful and hopeful: *a sanguine disposition.* 2 confident; hopeful: *sanguine of success.* 3 having a healthy red color; ruddy: *a sanguine complexion.* *adj.*

san i tar i um (san′ə ter′ē əm), sanatorium. *n.*, *pl.* **san i tar i ums, san i tar i a** (san′ə ter′ē ə).

san i tar y (san′ə ter′ē), 1 of or having to do with health; favorable to health; preventing disease: *sanitary regulations in a hospital.* 2 free from dirt and filth: *Food should be kept in a sanitary place.* *adj.*

san i ta tion (san′ə tā′shən), the working out and practical application of sanitary measures. Disposal of sewage and government inspection of milk, meat, and other foods are important parts of sanitation. *n.*

san i ty (san′ə tē), 1 soundness of mind; mental health. 2 soundness of judgment; sensibleness. *n.*

San Jo sé (san hō zā′), capital of Costa Rica, in the central part.

San Juan (san wän′), seaport and capital of Puerto Rico, in the NE part.

sank (sangk), a past tense of **sink.** *The ship sank before help reached it.* *v.*

San Ma ri no (san mə rē′nō), 1 tiny country in N Italy. 2 its capital.

sans (sanz), without. *prep.*

San Sal va dor (san sal′və dôr), 1 island of the central Bahamas, the first land seen by Columbus. 2 capital of El Salvador, in the central part.

San skrit or **San scrit** (san′skrit), the ancient literary language of India. *n.*

San ta (san′tə *for 1;* san′tə *or* sän′tä *for 2*), 1 Santa Claus. 2 a Spanish or an Italian word meaning *holy* or *saint,* used in combinations, as in *Santa Maria.* 1 *n.*, 2 *adj.*

San ta An na (san′tə an′ə *or* sän′tä ä′nä), **Antonio López de,** 1795-1876, Mexican general and politician. His army defeated the Texans at the Alamo.

hat, āge, fär; let, ēqual, tėrm;
it, īce; hot, ōpen, ôrder;
oil, out; cup, pùt, rüle; ch, child;
ng, long; sh, she; th, thin;
ŦH, then; zh, measure;

ə represents *a* in about,
e in taken, *i* in pencil,
o in lemon, *u* in circus.

San ta Claus (san′tə klôz′), the spirit or saint of Christmas giving; Saint Nicholas. He is pictured as a fat, jolly, old man with a white beard, dressed in a fur-trimmed red suit.

San ta Fe (san′tə fā′), capital of New Mexico, in the N part.

Santa Fe Trail, an early trade route between Independence, Missouri, and Santa Fe, New Mexico. See **Oregon Trail** for map.

San ta Ma ri a (san′tə mə rē′ə), flagship of Columbus in his voyage of 1492.

San ti a go (san′tē ä′gō), capital of Chile, in the central part. *n.*

San to Do min go (san′tō də ming′-gō), capital of the Dominican Republic, in the S part. It was established in 1496 and was the first town founded by Europeans in the Western Hemisphere. Formerly called **Ciudad Trujillo.**

São Pau lo (sou pou′lù), large city in S Brazil.

sap[1] (sap), liquid that circulates through a plant, carrying water, food, etc., as blood does in animals. Rising sap carries water and salt from the roots; sap traveling downward carries sugar, gums, resins, etc. Maple sugar is made from the sap of some maple trees. *n.* [Old English *sæp*]

sap[2] (sap), 1 dig under or wear away the foundation of: *The walls of the boathouse had been sapped by the waves.* 2 weaken; use up: *The extreme heat sapped our strength.* *v.*, **sapped, sap ping.** [from French of the 1500's *sapper,* from *sappe* spade, from Italian *zappa*]

sa pi ence (sā′pē əns), wisdom. *n.*

sa pi ent (sā′pē ənt), wise; sage. *adj.*

sap less (sap′lis), 1 without sap; withered. 2 without energy or vigor. *adj.*

sap ling (sap′ling), a young tree. *n.*

sap o dil la (sap′ə dil′ə), 1 a large evergreen tree of tropical America that yields chicle and bears large berries tasting like pears. 2 its fruit. *n.*, *pl.* **sap o dil las.**

sa pon i fi ca tion (sə pon′ə fə kā′-shən), 1 process of saponifying. 2 condition of being saponified. *n.*

sa pon i fy (sə pon′ə fī), 1 make (a fat

adj.	adjective	*n.*	noun
adv.	adverb	*prep.*	preposition
conj.	conjunction	*pron.*	pronoun
interj.	interjection	*v.*	verb
sing.	singular	*pl.*	plural

or oil) into soap by treating with an alkali. 2 become soap. *v.*, **sa pon i fied, sa pon i fy ing.**

sap phire (saf′ir), 1 a clear, hard, bright-blue variety of corundum. Sapphires are valued as precious stones. 2 bright-blue. 3 a bright blue. 1,3 *n.*, 2 *adj.*

sap py (sap′ē), 1 full of sap; juicy. 2 SLANG. silly; foolish. *adj.*, **sap pi er, sap pi est.**

sap ro phyte (sap′rō fīt), any plant that lives on decaying organic matter. Certain fungi are saprophytes. *n.*

sap suck er (sap′suk′ər), a small American woodpecker that feeds on the sap of trees. *n.*

sap wood (sap′wúd′), the soft, new, living wood between the bark and the hard inner wood of most trees. *n.*

Sar a cen (sar′ə sən), 1 an Arab. 2 a Moslem at the time of the Crusades. 3 of or having to do with the Saracens. 1,2 *n.*, 3 *adj.*

Sar ah (ser′ə), (in the Bible) the wife of Abraham and the mother of Isaac. *n.*

Sa ra je vo (sär′ə yä′vō), city in central Yugoslavia. The assassination of the Austrian archduke in 1914 which brought on World War I took place there. *n.*

sa ran (sə ran′), a plastic resin produced as a fiber, film, or molded form and highly resistant to damage and soiling. It is used especially to package food. *n.*

sa ra pe (sə rä′pē), serape. *n.*

Sa ra wak (sə rä′wäk), state in N Borneo, a member of the Federation of Malaysia. *n.*

sar casm (sär′kaz əm), 1 a sneering or cutting remark; ironical taunt. 2 act of making fun of a person to hurt his feelings; harsh or bitter irony: *"How unselfish you are!" said the little girl in sarcasm as her brother took the biggest piece of cake. n.*

sar cas tic (sär kas′tik), using sarcasm; sneering; cutting: *"Don't hurry!" was her father's sarcastic comment as she began to dress at her usual slow rate. adj.* —**sar cas′ti cal ly,** *adv.*

sar coph a gus (sär kof′ə gəs), a stone coffin, especially an ornamental one. *n.*, *pl.* **sar coph a gi** (sär kof′ə jī), **sar coph a gus es.**

sar dine (sär dēn′), a young or small herring or related fish, often preserved in oil for food. *n.*, *pl.* **sar dines** or **sar dine.**

packed like sardines, very much crowded.

Sar din i a (sär din′ē ə), large Italian island in the Mediterranean Sea, west of Italy. *n.* —**Sar din′i an,** *adj.*, *n.*

sar don ic (sär don′ik), bitterly sarcastic, scornful, or mocking: *a sardonic laugh. adj.* —**sar don′i cal ly,** *adv.*

sar gas so (sär gas′ō), any of a group of brown seaweeds that have berrylike air bladders and float in large masses. *n.*, *pl.* **sar gas sos.**

Sar gas so Sea (sär gas′ō), part of the Atlantic extending from the West Indies northeast to the Azores. *n.*

Sar gent (sär′jənt), **John Singer,** 1856-1925, American portrait painter. *n.*

sa ri (sär′ē), a long piece of cotton or silk worn wound around the body with one end thrown over the head or shoulder. It is the outer garment of Hindu women. *n.*, *pl.* **sa ris.**

sari   sarong

sa rong (sə rông′), a rectangular piece of cloth, usually a brightly colored, printed material, worn as a skirt by men and women in the East Indies. *n.*

sar sa pa ril la (sas′pə ril′ə or sär′sə pə ril′ə), 1 a tropical American climbing or trailing plant. 2 its dried root, used for flavoring. 3 a cooling drink flavored with this root. *n.*, *pl.* **sar sa pa ril las.**

sar to ri al (sär tôr′ē əl), of tailors or their work: *His clothes were a sartorial triumph. adj.*

sash[1] (sash), a long, broad strip of cloth or ribbon, worn as an ornament round the waist or over one shoulder. *n.*, *pl.* **sash es.** [from Arabic *shash* muslin cloth]

sash[2] (sash), frame which holds the glass in a window or door. *n.*, *pl.* **sash es.** [earlier *shashes* (taken as plural) from French *châssis*, from *châsse* frame or sash]

sa shay (sa shā′), INFORMAL. glide, move, or go about. *v.*

Sask., Saskatchewan.

Sa skatch e wan (sa skach′ə won), province in S Canada. *Capital:* Regina. *n.*

sass (sas), INFORMAL. 1 rudeness; back talk; impudence. 2 be saucy to: *The little girl sassed her mother.* 1 *n.*, 2 *v.*

sas sa fras (sas′ə fras), 1 a slender American tree that has fragrant, yellow flowers and bluish-black fruit. 2 the aromatic dried bark of its root, used in medicine and to flavor candy, soft drinks, etc. *n.*

sas sy (sas′ē), saucy. *adj.*, **sas si er, sas si est.**

sat (sat), past tense and past participle of **sit.** *Yesterday I sat in a train all day. The cat has sat at that mouse hole for hours. v.*

Sat., Saturday.

Sa tan (sāt′n), the evil spirit; the enemy of goodness; the Devil. *n.*

sa tan ic (sā tan′ik), of Satan; like Satan; like that of Satan; very wicked. *adj.*

satch el (sach′əl), a small bag for carrying clothes, books, etc.; handbag. *n.*

sate (sāt), 1 satisfy fully (any appetite or desire): *A long drink sated his thirst.* 2 supply with more than enough, so as to weary or disgust. *v.*, **sat ed, sat ing.**

sa teen (sa tēn′), a cotton cloth made to imitate satin. It is often used for lining sleeves. *n.*

sat el lite (sat′l īt), 1 a heavenly body that revolves around a planet, especially around one of the nine major planets of the solar system. The moon is a satellite of the earth. 2 a man-made object launched by rocket into an orbit around the earth or other heavenly body. 3 follower or attendant upon a person of importance. 4 country that is supposedly independent but actually under the control of a more powerful country, especially a country under the control of the Soviet Union. *n.*

satellites (def. 2)
left, Tiros I, used to photograph storm centers;
right, Explorer IV, used to obtain radiation and temperature data in space

sa ti ate (sā′shē āt), 1 feed fully; satisfy fully. 2 supply with too much; weary or disgust with too much: *She was so satiated with bananas that she would not even look at one. v.*, **sa ti ated, sa ti at ing.**

sa ti e ty (sə tī′ə tē), the feeling of having had too much; disgust or weariness caused by excess; satiated condition. *n.*

sat in (sat′n), 1 a silk, rayon, nylon, or cotton cloth with one very smooth, glossy side. 2 of or like satin; smooth and glossy. 1 *n.*, 2 *adj.*

sat in wood (sat′n wud′), 1 the smooth wood of an East Indian tree, used to ornament furniture, etc. 2 the tree itself. *n.*

sat in y (sat′n ē), like satin in smoothness and gloss. *adj.*

sat ire (sat′ir), 1 the use of sarcasm, irony, or wit, to attack or ridicule a habit, idea, custom, etc. 2 poem, essay, story, etc., that attacks or ridicules in this way. *n.*

sa tir ic (sə tir′ik), satirical. *adj.*

sa tir i cal (sə tir′ə kəl), of satire; containing satire; fond of using satire. *adj.* —**sa tir′i cal ly,** *adv.*

sat i rist (sat′ə rist), writer of satires; person who uses satire. The follies and vices of their own times are the chief subjects of satirists. *n.*

sat i rize (sat′ə rīz′), attack with satire; criticize with mockery; seek to improve by ridicule. *v.*, **sat i rized, sat i rizing.**

sat is fac tion (sat′i sfak′shən), 1 a satisfying; fulfillment: *The satisfaction of hunger requires food.* 2 condition of being satisfied, or pleased and contented: *She felt satisfaction at winning a prize.* 3 anything that makes us feel pleased or contented: *It is a great satisfaction to have things turn out just the way you want.* 4 payment of debt; discharge of an obligation; making up for wrong or injury done. *n.*

give satisfaction, 1 satisfy. 2 fight a duel because of an insult.

sat is fac tor i ly (sat′i sfak′tər ə lē), in a satisfactory manner. *adv.*

sat is fac tor y (sat′i sfak′tər ē), satisfying; good enough to satisfy; pleasing or adequate. *adj.*

sat is fy (sat′i sfī), 1 give enough to; fulfill (desires, hopes, demands, etc.); put an end to (needs, wants, etc.): *He satisfied his hunger with a sandwich and milk.* 2 make contented; please: *Are you satisfied now?* 3 pay; make right: *After the accident he satisfied all claims for the damage he had caused.* 4 set free from doubt; convince: *He was satisfied that it was an accident.* *v.*, **sat is fied, sat is fy ing.** —**sat′is fy′ing ly,** *adv.*

sa trap (sā′trap), 1 ruler, often a tyrant, who is subordinate to a higher ruler. 2 governor of a province under the ancient Persian monarchy. *n.*

sat u rate (sach′ə rāt′), 1 soak thoroughly; fill full: *During the fog, the air was saturated with moisture. The rain had saturated us by the time we had*

walked all the way home. 2 cause (a substance) to unite with the greatest possible amount of another substance. A saturated solution of sugar or salt is one that cannot dissolve any more sugar or salt. *v.*, **sat u rat ed, sat u rat ing.**

sat u ra tion (sach′ə rā′shən), 1 act or process of saturating. 2 fact of being saturated; saturated condition. The saturation of a color increases as the amount of white in it is decreased. *n.*

Sat ur day (sat′ər dē), the seventh day of the week, following Friday. *n.* [Old English *Sæternesdæg,* from *Sætern* Saturn + *dæg* day]

Sat urn (sat′ərn), 1 (in Roman myths) the god of agriculture. Saturn ruled during a golden age. 2 the second largest planet in the solar system and the sixth in distance from the sun. Saturn is encircled by three rings made up of tiny particles of matter. *n.*

sat ur na li a (sat′ər nā′lē ə), 1 period of unrestrained revelry and license. 2 **Saturnalia,** the ancient Roman festival of Saturn, celebrated in December with much feasting and merrymaking. *n. pl. or sing.*

sat ur nine (sat′ər nīn), gloomy; grave; taciturn. *adj.*

sa tyr (sā′tər or sat′ər), (in Greek myths) a deity of the woods, part man and part goat or horse. The satyrs were merry followers of Bacchus, the god of wine. *n.*

satyr

sauce (sôs), 1 something, usually a liquid, served with food to make it taste better. We eat cranberry sauce with turkey, mint sauce with lamb, egg sauce with fish, and many different sauces with puddings. 2 stewed fruit. 3 prepare with sauce; season. 4 give interest or flavor to. 5 INFORMAL. sauciness: *I don't like her sauce.* 6 INFORMAL. be saucy to. 1,2,5 *n.*, 3,4,6 *v.*, **sauced, sauc ing.**

sauce pan (sôs′pan′), a metal dish with a handle, used for stewing, boiling, etc. *n.*

sau cer (sô′sər), 1 a shallow dish to set a cup on. 2 a small, round dish with its edge curved up. 3 something round and shallow like a saucer. *n.* —**sau′cer like′,** *adj.*

sau ci ly (sô′sə lē), in a saucy manner. *adv.*

hat, āge, fär; let, ēqual, tėrm; it, īce; hot, ōpen, ôrder; oil, out; cup, pùt, rüle; ch, child; ng, long; sh, she; th, thin; ᵺ, then; zh, measure;

ə represents *a* in about, *e* in taken, *i* in pencil, *o* in lemon, *u* in circus.

sau ci ness (sô′sē nis), pertness; impudence. *n.*

sau cy (sô′sē), 1 showing lack of respect; rude: *saucy language or conduct.* 2 pert; smart: *She wore a saucy hat.* *adj.*, **sau ci er, sau ci est.**

Sa u di Arabia (sä ü′dē), country in central Arabia. *Capitals:* Riyadh and Mecca.

sauer kraut (sour′krout′), cabbage cut fine, salted, and allowed to sour. *n.*

Sauk (sôk), member of a tribe of American Indians formerly living in Michigan and Wisconsin. *n.*

Saul (sôl), in the Bible: 1 the first king of Israel. 2 the original name of the apostle Paul. *n.*

saun ter (sôn′tər), 1 walk along slowly and happily; stroll: *People sauntered through the park on summer evenings.* 2 a stroll. 1 *v.*, 2 *n.* —**saun′ter er,** *n.*

sau ri an (sôr′ē ən), 1 a lizard. 2 any similar reptile, such as a crocodile or dinosaur. *n.*

sau sage (sô′sij), chopped pork, beef, or other meats, seasoned and usually stuffed into a very thin casing. *n.*

sau té (sō tā′ or sô tā′), 1 cooked or browned in a little fat. 2 dish of food cooked or browned in a little fat. 3 fry quickly in a little fat. 1 *adj.*, 2 *n.*, 3 *v.*, **sau téed, sau té ing.** [from French]

sav age (sav′ij), 1 member of a primitive, uncivilized people. 2 not civilized; barbarous: *savage customs.* 3 fierce; cruel; ready to fight; brutal: *a savage dog.* 4 a fierce, brutal, or cruel person. 5 wild or rugged: *savage mountain scenery.* 1,4 *n.*, 2,3,5 *adj.* —**sav′age ly,** *adv.* —**sav′age ness,** *n.*

sav age ry (sav′ij rē), 1 a being fierce; cruelty; brutality. 2 wildness. 3 an uncivilized condition. *n., pl.* **sav age ries.**

sa van na (sə van′ə), a grassy plain with few or no trees, especially one in the southern United States or near the tropics. *n., pl.* **sa van nas.**

sa van nah (sə van′ə), savanna. *n.*

Sa van nah (sə van′ə), 1 seaport in E Georgia. 2 river between South Carolina and Georgia. *n.*

adj.	adjective	n.	noun
adv.	adverb	prep.	preposition
conj.	conjunction	pron.	pronoun
interj.	interjection	v.	verb
sing.	singular	pl.	plural

sa vant (sə vänt′ or sav′ənt), man of learning. *n.*

save[1] (sāv), 1 make safe from harm, danger, loss, etc.; rescue: *The dog saved the boy's life. She saved her jewels from the fire.* 2 keep safe from harm, danger, hurt, loss, etc.; protect: *save one's honor.* 3 lay aside; store up: *save money. She saves pieces of string.* 4 keep from spending or wasting: *Save your strength.* 5 avoid expense or waste: *She saves in every way she can.* prevent: *save work, save trouble,* 7 treat carefully to lessen wear, weariness, etc.: *Large print saves one's eyes.* 8 prevent the loss of: *Another goal will save the game.* 9 set free from sin and its results. *v.,* **saved, sav ing.** [from French of the 1200's *sauver,* from Latin *salvare,* from *salvus* safe]

save[2] (sāv), except; but: *He works every day save Sundays.* prep. [a different form of *safe,* in sense of "not being involved"]

sav er (sā′vər), person or thing that saves: *A washing machine is a saver of time and strength. n.*

sav ing (sā′ving), 1 that saves. 2 tending to save up money; avoiding waste; economical. 3 way of saving money, time, etc.: *It will be a saving to take this shortcut.* 4 act of preserving, rescuing, etc. 5 that which is saved. 6 **savings,** *pl.* money saved. 7 with the exception of; save; except: *Saving a few crusts, we had eaten nothing all day.* 8 with all due respect to or for. 9 compensating; redeeming. 1,2,9 *adj.,* 3-6 *n.,* 7,8 *prep.,* 7 *conj.*

savings account, account in a savings bank.

savings bank, bank which accepts money only for savings and investment and which pays interest on all deposits.

savings bond, bond issued by the United States government to help pay its expenses. Savings bonds can be cashed with interest after a certain time.

sav ior or **sav iour** (sā′vyər), person who saves or rescues. *n.*

Sav iour or **Sav ior** (sā′vyər), Jesus Christ. *n.*

sa vor (sā′vər), 1 a taste or smell; flavor: *The soup has a savor of onion.* 2 enjoy the taste or smell of: *He sa-*

vored the soup with pleasure. 3 to taste or smell (of): *That sauce savors of lemon.* 4 give flavor to; season. 5 a distinctive quality; noticeable trace: *There is a savor of conceit in everything she says.* 6 have the quality or nature (of): *The plot savored of treason.* 1,5 *n.,* 2-4,6 *v.* —**sa′vor er,** *n.*

sa vor y[1] (sā′vər ē), 1 pleasing in taste or smell: *the savory smell of roasting turkey.* 2 morally pleasing; agreeable. *adj.,* **sa vor i er, sa vor i est.** [from French of the 1200's *savoure,* from *savourer* to taste, from *savour* taste, savor, from Latin *sapor*]

sa vor y[2] (sā′vər ē), any of several fragrant herbs related to the mint, used for seasoning food. *n., pl.* **sa vor ies.** [from French of the 1300's *savoreie,* from Latin *satureia*]

Sa voy (sə voi′), region in SE France. *n.*

saw[1] (sô), 1 tool for cutting, made of a thin blade with sharp teeth on the edge. 2 a machine with such a tool for cutting. 3 cut with a saw: *The man saws wood.* 4 make with a saw: *Boards are sawed from logs.* 5 use a saw: *Can you saw straight?* 6 be sawed: *Pine saws more easily than oak.* 1,2 *n.,* 3-6 *v.,* **sawed, sawed** or **sawn, saw ing.** [Old English *sagu, saga*]

saw[2] (sô), past tense of **see**[1]. *I saw a robin yesterday. v.*

saw[3] (sô), a wise saying; proverb: *"A stitch in time saves nine" is a familiar saw. n.* [Old English *sagu,* related to *secgan* say]

saw buck (sô′buk′), 1 sawhorse. 2 SLANG. a ten-dollar bill. *n.*

saw dust (sô′dust′), particles of wood made by sawing. *n.*

sawed-off (sôd′ôf′), 1 having one end sawed or cut off: *a sawed-off shotgun.* 2 SLANG. small in size; short. *adj.*

saw horse (sô′hôrs′), frame for holding wood that is being sawed. *n.*

saw mill (sô′mil′), 1 a building where machines saw timber into planks, boards, etc. 2 a machine for such sawing. *n.*

sawn (sôn), sawed; a past participle of **saw**[1]. *v.*

saw yer (sô′yər), man whose work is sawing timber. *n.*

sax (saks), INFORMAL. saxophone. *n., pl.* **sax es.**

sax i frage (sak′sə frij), 1 plant with white, yellow, or red flowers. Saxifrages are often grown in rock gardens. 2 its flower. *n.*

Sax on (sak′sən), 1 member of a Germanic tribe that, with the Angles and Jutes, conquered England in the A.D. 400's and 500's. 2 language of the Saxons. 3 having to do with the Saxons or their language. 4 Anglo-Saxon. 5 a

native of Saxony in modern Germany. 1,2,4,5 *n.,* 3 *adj.*

Sax o ny (sak′sə nē), region and former state in E Germany. *n.*

sax o phone (sak′sə fōn), a woodwind instrument having a curved metal body with keys for the fingers and a mouthpiece with a single reed. *n.* [from Adolphe *Sax,* 1814-1894, a Belgian inventor and Greek *phone* sound]

saxophone

sax o phon ist (sak′sə fō′nist), a saxophone player. *n.*

say (sā), 1 speak; utter: *What did you say? "Thank you," he said.* 2 put into words; express; declare: *Say what you think.* 3 recite; repeat: *Say your prayers.* 4 let us suppose or guess: *You can learn to dance in, say, ten lessons.* 5 express an opinion: *It is hard to say which dress is prettier.* 6 what a person says or has to say: *She said her say and sat down.* 7 chance to say something: *Has everyone had his say? If so, let's vote on the matter.* 8 power; authority: *Who has the final say in this matter?* 1-5 *v.,* **said, say ing;** 6-8 *n.* —**say′er,** *n.*

that is to say, that is; in other words.

say est (sā′ist), OLD USE. say. "Thou sayest" means "you say." *v.*

sawhorse

say ing (sā′ing), 1 something said; statement. 2 proverb: *"Haste makes waste" is a saying. n.*

go without saying, be too obvious to need mention.

says (sez), a present tense of **say.** *He says "No" to everything. v.*

say-so (sā′sō′), INFORMAL. 1 one's mere word: *Do you believe that, just on his say-so?* 2 authority or power to decide. *n., pl.* **say-sos.**

sayst (sāst), OLD USE. sayest; say. "Thou sayst" means "You say." *v.*

S.C., South Carolina.

scab (skab), 1 the crust that forms over

a sore or wound as it heals: *A scab formed on the spot where he was vaccinated.* 2 a skin disease in animals, especially sheep; scabies or mange. 3 any of several fungous or bacterial diseases of plants, usually producing dark, crustlike spots. 4 become covered with a scab. 5 INFORMAL. workman who will not join a labor union or who takes a striker's job. 6 INFORMAL. act or work as a scab. 1-3,5 *n.*, 4,6 *v.*, **scabbed, scab bing.**

scab bard (skab/ərd), a sheath or case for the blade of a sword, dagger, etc. *n.*

scab by (skab/ē), 1 covered with scabs. 2 having the skin disease scab. *adj.*, **scab bi er, scab bi est.**

sca bies (skā/bēz), disease of the skin caused by mites that live as parasites under the skin and cause itching. *n.*

scads (skadz), INFORMAL. a large quantity. *n.pl.*

scaf fold (skaf/əld), 1 a temporary structure for holding workmen and materials. 2 a raised platform on which criminals are put to death. 3 any raised framework. *n.*

scaffold
(def. 1)

scaf fold ing (skaf/əl ding), 1 scaffold. 2 materials for scaffolds. *n.*

scal a wag (skal/ə wag), INFORMAL. a dishonorable person; scamp; rascal. *n.*

scald (skôld), 1 to burn with hot liquid or steam: *I scalded myself with hot grease.* 2 a burn caused by hot liquid or steam: *The scald on his hand came from lifting a pot cover carelessly.* 3 pour boiling liquid over; use boiling liquid on: *Scald the dishes before drying them.* 4 heat almost to boiling, but not quite: *Scald the milk.* 5 to burn as if with boiling water. 1,3-5 *v.*, 2 *n.*

scale¹ (skāl), 1 the dish or pan of a balance. 2 Usually, **scales**, *pl.* balance; instrument for weighing: *She weighed some meat on the scales.* 3 weigh: *He scales 180 pounds.* 4 weigh in scales; measure; compare. 1,2 *n.*, 3,4 *v.*, **scaled, scal ing.** [from a Scandinavian word of the 1200's, such as Icelandic *skāl*]

tip the scales, 1 have as one's weight. 2 overbalance one for another.

turn the scales, decide.

scale² (skāl), 1 one of the thin, flat, hard plates forming the outer covering of some fishes, snakes, and lizards. 2 a thin layer like a scale: *Scales of skin peeled off after she had scarlet fever.* 3 remove scales from: *He scaled the fish with a sharp knife.* 4 come off in scales: *The paint is scaling off the house.* 5 one of the parts that cover a bud or other plant part. 6 scale insect. 1,2,5,6 *n.*, 3,4 *v.*, **scaled, scal ing.** [from French of the 1300's *escale*, from a Germanic word] —**scale/like/**, *adj.*

scale³ (skāl), 1 series of steps or degrees; scheme of graded amounts: *The scale of wages in this factory ranges from ten dollars to twenty-five dollars a day.* 2 series of marks made along a line at regular distances to use in measuring: *A thermometer has a scale.* 3 an instrument marked in this way, used for measuring. 4 the size of a plan, map, drawing, or model compared with what it represents: *This map is drawn to the scale of one inch for each 100 miles.* 5 relative size or extent: *That rich family entertains on a large scale.* 6 system of numbering: *The decimal scale counts by tens, as in cents, dimes, dollars.* 7 reduce by a certain amount in relation to other amounts: *To draw this map, mileage was scaled down to one inch for each 100 miles.* 8 (in music) a series of tones ascending or descending in pitch according to fixed intervals: *She practices scales on the piano.* 9 climb: *They scaled the wall by ladders.* 10 make according to a scale. 1-6,8 *n.*, 7,9,10 *v.*, **scaled, scal ing.** [from Latin *scalae* ladder, steps, from *scandere* to climb]

scale insect, any of various small insects that feed on and often destroy plants by piercing them and sucking the sap. The females have the body and eggs covered by a scale or shield formed by a secretion from the body.

scale less (skāl/lis), without scales. *adj.*

scal i ness (skā/lē nis), scaly quality or condition. *n.*

scal lion (skal/yən), 1 kind of onion that has no large, distinct bulb. 2 leek. *n.*

scal lop (skol/əp *or* skal/əp), 1 shellfish somewhat like a clam, with a rounded, fan-shaped shell. In some kinds the large muscle that opens and closes the shell is good to eat. 2 bake with sauce and bread crumbs in a dish; escallop: *scalloped oysters, scalloped tomatoes.* 3 one of a series of curves on the edge of anything: *This cuff has scallops.* 4 make such curves on: *She scalloped the edge of the quilt.* 1,3 *n.*, 2,4 *v.* Also, **scollop.**

scalp (skalp), 1 the skin on the top and

hat, āge, fär; let, ēqual, tėrm;
it, īce; hot, ōpen, ôrder;
oil, out; cup, pùt, rüle; ch, child;
ng, long; sh, she; th, thin;
ᴛʜ, then; zh, measure;

ə represents *a* in about,
e in taken, *i* in pencil,
o in lemon, *u* in circus.

back of the head, usually covered with hair. 2 part of this skin, formerly kept as a token of victory by certain American Indians. 3 cut or tear the scalp from. 1,2 *n.*, 3 *v.*

scal pel (skal/pəl), a small, straight knife used by surgeons. *n.*

scalpel
with
interchangeable
blades

scal y (skā/lē), 1 covered with scales; having scales like a fish: *This iron pipe is scaly with rust.* 2 suggesting scales. *adj.*, **scal i er, scal i est.**

scamp (skamp), 1 a dishonorable person; rascal; rogue. 2 do (work, etc.) in a hasty, careless manner. 1 *n.*, 2 *v.*

scam per (skam/pər), 1 run quickly: *The mice scampered when the cat came.* 2 a quick run: *Let the dog out for a scamper.* 1 *v.*, 2 *n.*

scan (skan), 1 look at closely; examine with care: *You should scan every word in the contract before you sign it.* 2 INFORMAL. glance at; look over hastily. 3 mark off (lines of poetry) into feet. EXAMPLE: Sing/ a | song/ of | six/pence. 4 read or recite (poetry), marking off the lines into feet. 5 (in television) expose bits of a surface in rapid succession to beams of electrons in order to transmit a picture. *v.*, **scanned, scan ning.**

scan dal (skan/dl), 1 a shameful action, condition, or event that brings disgrace or shocks public opinion: *It was a scandal for the city treasurer to take tax money for personal use.* 2 damage to reputation; disgrace. 3 public talk about a person that will hurt his reputation; evil gossip; slander; defamation. *n.*

scan dal ize (skan/dl īz), offend by doing something thought to be wrong or improper; shock: *Her short skirt scandalized her grandfather.* *v.*, **scan dal ized, scan dal iz ing.**

adj. adjective	*n.* noun
adv. adverb	*prep.* preposition
conj. conjunction	*pron.* pronoun
interj. interjection	*v.* verb
sing. singular	*pl.* plural

scan dal mon ger (skan′dl mung′-gər), person who spreads scandal and evil gossip. *n.*

scan dal ous (skan′dl əs), 1 bringing disgrace; shameful; shocking: *scandalous behavior.* 2 spreading scandal or slander: *a scandalous piece of gossip. adj.* —**scan′dal ous ly,** *adv.*

Scan di na vi a (skan′də nā′vē ə), 1 region of NW Europe that includes Norway, Sweden, Denmark, and sometimes Finland and Iceland. 2 peninsula on which Norway and Sweden are located. *n.*

Scan di na vi an (skan′də nā′vē ən), 1 of or having to do with Scandinavia, its people, or their languages. 2 person born or living in Scandinavia. 3 languages of Scandinavia, both modern and historical. Scandinavian includes Danish, Icelandic, Norwegian, and Swedish. 1 *adj.,* 2,3 *n.*

scan di um (skan′dē əm), a gray, metallic element found in many minerals in Scandinavia. *n.* [from Latin *Scandia* Scandinavia]

scan sion (skan′shən), the marking off of lines of poetry into feet; scanning. In the oral scansion of poetry, a reader stresses the accented syllables heavily. *n.*

scant (skant), 1 not enough in size or quantity: *Her coat was short and scant.* 2 barely enough; barely full; bare: *Use a scant cup of butter in the cake. You have a scant hour in which to pack.* 3 make scant; cut down; limit; stint: *Don't scant the butter if you want a rich cake.* 1,2 *adj.,* 3 *v.*

scant of, having not enough: *She was scant of breath.*

scant i ly (skan′tl ē), in a scanty manner; insufficiently. *adv.*

scant i ness (skan′tē nis), too small an amount; scanty quality or condition. *n.*

scant y (skan′tē), 1 not enough: *His scanty clothing did not keep out the cold.* 2 barely enough; meager: *Drought caused a scanty harvest. adj.,* **scant i er, scant i est.**

scape goat (skāp′gōt′), person made to bear the blame for the mistakes or sins of others. *n.*

scape grace (skāp′grās′), a reckless, dishonorable person; scamp. *n.*

scap u la (skap′yə lə), shoulder blade. *n., pl.* **scap u lae** (skap′yə lē′), **scap u las.**

scar (skär), 1 the mark left by a healed cut, wound, burn, or sore: *My vaccination scar is small.* 2 any mark like this: *See the scars your shoes have made on the chair. War leaves many deep scars on the minds of those who endure it. A fallen leaf leaves a scar where it joined the stem.* 3 mark with a scar: *He scarred the door with a hammer.* 4 form a scar; heal: *His wound is scarring well.* 1,2 *n.,* 3,4 *v.,* **scarred, scar ring.**

scar ab (skar′əb), 1 a beetle, especially the sacred beetle of the ancient Egyptians. 2 an image of this beetle. Scarabs were much used in ancient Egypt as charms or ornaments. *n.*

scarab (def. 2)—A, top; B, bottom

scarce (skers *or* skars), 1 hard to get; rare: *Water is becoming scarce in some parts of the country.* 2 scarcely. 1 *adj.,* **scarc er, scarc est;** 2 *adv.* —**scarce′ness,** *n.*

make oneself scarce, INFORMAL. 1 go away. 2 stay away.

scarce ly (skers′lē *or* skars′lē), 1 not quite; barely: *We could scarcely see the ship through the fog.* 2 decidedly not: *She can scarcely have said that. adv.*

scar ci ty (sker′sə tē *or* skar′sə tē), too small a supply; lack; rarity: *There is a scarcity of nurses. n., pl.* **scar ci ties.**

scare (sker *or* skar), 1 make or become afraid; frighten: *We were scared and ran away. Courageous people don't scare easily.* 2 a fright. 3 frightened condition. 4 frighten (away); drive off: *The watchdog scared away the robber by barking.* 1,4 *v.,* **scared, scar ing;** 2,3 *n.*

scare up, INFORMAL. get; raise: *scare up a few extra blankets on a cold night.*

scare crow (sker′krō′ *or* skar′krō′), 1 figure of a man dressed in old clothes, set in a field to frighten birds away from crops. 2 person, usually skinny, dressed in ragged clothes. 3 anything that fools people into being frightened. *n.*

scarf (skärf), 1 a long, broad strip of silk, lace, etc., worn about the neck, shoulders, head, or waist. 2 necktie with hanging ends. 3 a long strip of linen, etc., used as a cover for a bureau, table, piano, etc. *n., pl.* **scarfs** *or* **scarves.**

scar i ly (sker′ə lē *or* skar′ə lē), INFORMAL. in a scary manner. *adv.*

scar i ness (sker′ē nis *or* skar′ē nis),

INFORMAL. scary feeling or condition. *n.*

scar la ti na (skär′lə tē′nə), 1 scarlet fever. 2 a mild form of scarlet fever. *n.*

scar let (skär′lit), 1 a very bright red. Scarlet is much lighter than crimson. 2 very bright red. 3 cloth or clothing having this color. 1,3 *n.,* 2 *adj.*

scarlet fever, a very contagious disease that affects chiefly children, causing a scarlet rash, sore throat, and fever; scarlatina.

scarlet tanager, the common tanager of eastern North America; redbird. The male has black wings and tail and a scarlet body.

scarp (skärp), 1 a steep slope. 2 the inner slope or side of a ditch surrounding a fortification. 3 make into a steep slope; slope steeply. 1,2 *n.,* 3 *v.*

scarves (skärvz), a plural of **scarf.** *n.*

scar y (sker′ē *or* skar′ē), INFORMAL. 1 causing fright or alarm. 2 easily frightened. *adj.,* **scar i er, scar i est.**

scat (skat), INFORMAL. 1 exclamation used to drive away an animal. 2 go away, especially in a hurry. 1 *interj.,* 2 *v.,* **scat ted, scat ting.**

scath ing (skā′ᴛʜing), bitterly severe: *scathing criticism. adj.* —**scath′ing ly,** *adv.*

scat ter (skat′ər), 1 throw here and there; sprinkle: *I scattered ashes on the icy sidewalk.* 2 separate and drive off in different directions: *The police scattered the disorderly crowd.* 3 separate and go in different directions: *The chickens scattered in fright when the truck honked at them.* 4 act or fact of scattering. 1-3 *v.,* 4 *n.* —**scat′ter er,** *n.*

scat ter brain (skat′ər brān′), a thoughtless, flighty person. *n.*

scat ter brained (skat′ər brānd′), not able to think steadily; flighty; thoughtless. *adj.*

scat ter ing (skat′ər ing), 1 widely separated; occurring here and there. 2 a small amount or number scattered. 1 *adj.,* 2 *n.*

scarecrow (def. 1) made of two sticks and clothes stuffed with straw

scatter rug, a small rug.

scav en ger (skav′ən jər), 1 animal that feeds on decaying matter. Vultures and jackals are scavengers. 2 person who searches through discarded objects for something of value. 3 person who cleans streets, etc., of dirt and filth. *n.*

sce nar i o (si ner′ē ō *or* si när′ē ō),
1 the outline of a motion picture, giving
the main facts about the scenes, persons, and acting. 2 the outline of any
play, opera, etc. *n., pl.* **sce nar i os.**
sce nar ist (si ner′ist *or* si när′ist),
person who writes scenarios. *n.*

scepter

scene (sēn), 1 the time, place, circumstances, etc., of a play or story: *The
scene of the novel is laid in Virginia
during the Civil War.* 2 the painted
screens, hangings, etc., used in a theater
to represent places: *The scene represents a city street.* 3 part of an act of a
play: *The king comes to the castle in Act
I, Scene 2.* 4 a particular incident of a
play: *The trial scene is the most exciting
one in "The Merchant of Venice."*
5 action, incident, situation, etc., occurring in reality or represented in literature or art: *He has painted a series of
pictures called "Scenes of My Boyhood."* 6 view; picture: *The white sailboats in the blue water made a pretty
scene.* 7 show of strong feeling in front
of others; exhibition; display: *The child
kicked, screamed, and made a dreadful
scene. n.*
behind the scenes, 1 out of sight of
the audience. 2 not publicly; privately;
secretly.
scen er y (sē′nər ē), 1 the general appearance of a place; the natural features
of a landscape: *She enjoys mountain
scenery very much.* 2 the painted hangings, screens, etc., used in a theater to
represent places: *The scenery pictures a
garden in the moonlight. n., pl.* **scen-
er ies.**
scen ic (sē′nik *or* sen′ik), 1 of or
having to do with natural scenery: *The
scenic splendors of Yellowstone Park
are famous.* 2 having much fine scenery: *a scenic highway.* 3 of or having to
do with stage scenery or stage effects:
*The production of the musical comedy
was a scenic triumph. adj.*
scent (sent), 1 a smell: *The scent of
roses filled the air.* 2 to smell: *The dog
scented a rabbit and ran off after it.*
3 sense of smell: *Bloodhounds have a
keen scent.* 4 hunt by using the sense of
smell: *The dog scented about till he
found the trail.* 5 smell left in passing:
The dogs followed the fox by the scent.
6 means by which a thing or a person

can be traced: *The police are on the
scent of the thieves.* 7 have a suspicion
of; be aware of: *I scent a trick in their
offer.* 8 a perfume: *She used too much
scent.* 9 fill with odor; perfume: *I
scented the room to rid it of the fish
smell.* 1,3,5,6,8 *n.,* 2,4,7,9 *v.*
scent less (sent′lis), having no smell.
adj.
scep ter (sep′tər), the rod or staff carried by a ruler as a symbol of royal
power or authority. *n.* Also, **sceptre.**
scep tic (skep′tik), skeptic. *n.*
scep ti cal (skep′tə kəl), skeptical.
adj.
scep ti cism (skep′tə siz′əm), skep-
ticism. *n.*
scep tre (sep′tər), scepter. *n.*
sched ule (skej′ül), 1 a written or
printed statement of details; list: *A timetable is a schedule of the coming and
going of trains. The teacher posted the
schedule of classes.* 2 make a schedule
of; enter in a schedule. 3 to plan or
arrange (something) for a definite time
or date: *Schedule the convention for the
fall.* 4 the time fixed for doing something, arrival at a place, etc.: *The bus
was an hour behind schedule.* 1,4 *n.,*
2,3 *v.,* **sched uled, sched ul ing.**
sche mat ic (skē mat′ik), having the
nature of a diagram, plan, or scheme.
adj. —**sche mat′i cal ly,** *adv.*
scheme (skēm), 1 program of action;
plan: *He has a scheme for extracting
salt from sea water.* 2 a plot: *a scheme
to cheat the government.* 3 devise plans,
especially underhanded or evil ones;
plot: *They schemed to bring the jewels
into the country without paying duty.*
4 system of connected things, parts,
thoughts, etc.: *The color scheme of the
room is blue and gold.* 1,2,4 *n.,* 3 *v.,*
schemed, schem ing.
schem er (skē′mər), person who plans
or plots. *n.*
schem ing (skē′ming), making tricky
schemes; crafty. *adj.*
Sche nec ta dy (skə nek′tə dē), city
in E New York State. *n.*
scher zo (sker′tsō), a light or playful
movement of a sonata or symphony. *n.,
pl.* **scher zos, scher zi** (sker′tsē).
Schick test (shik), a test to determine
if a person is immune to diphtheria,
made by injecting a very small amount
of diphtheria toxin under the skin.
[from Béla *Schick,* 1877-1967, American pediatrician born in Hungary who
developed the test]
Schil ler (shil′ər), **Johann Friedrich
von,** 1759-1805, German poet and
dramatist. *n.*
schism (siz′əm), 1 division into hostile
groups, especially division because of
some difference of opinion about religion. 2 offense of causing or trying to

hat, āge, fär; let, ēqual, tėrm;
it, īce; hot, ōpen, ôrder;
oil, out; cup, pùt, rüle; ch, child;
ng, long; sh, she; th, thin;
ᵺH, then; zh, measure;

ə represents *a* in about,
e in taken, *i* in pencil,
o in lemon, *u* in circus.

cause a religious schism. 3 sect or
group formed by a schism within a
church. *n.*
schis mat ic (siz mat′ik), 1 causing or
likely to cause schism. 2 inclined toward, or guilty of, schism. 3 person who
tries to cause a schism or takes part in a
schism. 1,2 *adj.,* 3 *n.*
schist (shist), kind of crystalline rock
that splits easily into layers. *n.*
Schles wig-Hol stein (shles′wig-
hōl′stīn), state in N West Germany, just
south of Denmark. *n.*
Schlie mann (shlē′män), **Heinrich,**
1822-1890, German archaeologist who
discovered and excavated the site of
ancient Troy. *n.*
schol ar (skol′ər), 1 a learned person;
person having much knowledge: *The
professor was a famous Latin scholar.*
2 pupil at school; learner. 3 student
who is given a scholarship. *n.*
schol ar ly (skol′ər lē), 1 of a scholar;
like that of a scholar: *scholarly habits.*
2 fit for a scholar. 3 having much
knowledge; learned. 4 fond of learning; studious. 5 thorough and orderly
in methods of study: *a scholarly book.*
6 in a scholarly manner. 1-5 *adj.,* 6 *adv.*
schol ar ship (skol′ər ship), 1 possession of knowledge gained by study;
quality of learning and knowledge.
2 money or other aid given to help a
student continue his studies: *The college offered her a scholarship of one
thousand dollars. n.*
scho las tic (skə las′tik), of schools,
scholars, or education; academic: *scholastic methods, scholastic life. adj.*
—**scho las′ti cal ly,** *adv.*
school[1] (skül), 1 place for teaching and
learning: *Children go to school to study.*
2 learning in school; instruction: *Most
children start school when they are
about five years old.* 3 regular meetings
of teachers and pupils for teaching and
learning: *We attend school every day.*
4 the time or period of such meetings:
to stay after school. 5 pupils who are
taught and their teachers: *The entire
school was present.* 6 any place, situation, experience, etc., as a source of
instruction or training: *the school of*

adj.	adjective	*n.*	noun
adv.	adverb	*prep.*	preposition
conj.	conjunction	*pron.*	pronoun
interj.	interjection	*v.*	verb
sing.	singular	*pl.*	plural

adversity. 7 group of people holding the same beliefs or opinions: *the Dutch school of painting, a gentleman of the old school.* 8 a particular department or group in a university: *a medical school, a law school.* 9 teach; train; discipline: *School yourself to control your temper.* 10 of or having to do with a school or schools. 1-8 *n.,* 9 *v.,* 10 *adj.* [Old English *scōl,* from Latin *schola,* from Greek *schole* discussion]

school² (skül), 1 a large number of the same kind of fish or water animals swimming together: *a school of mackerel.* 2 swim together in a school. 1 *n.,* 2 *v.* [from Dutch of the 1300's]

school age, 1 age at which a child begins to go to school. 2 years during which going to school is compulsory or customary.

school bag (skül/bag/), briefcase or other bag used to carry books, papers, pencils, etc., to and from school. *n.*

school board, a local board or committee managing the public schools.

school book (skül/bük/), book for study in schools. *n.*

school boy (skül/boi/), boy attending school. *n.*

school bus, bus that carries children to and from school.

school child (skül/chīld/), schoolboy or schoolgirl. *n., pl.* **school chil dren** (skül/chil/drən).

school girl (skül/gèrl/), girl attending school. *n.*

school house (skül/hous/), building used as a school. *n., pl.* **school hous es** (skül/hou/ziz).

school ing (skül/ling), instruction in school; education received at school. *n.*

school mas ter (skül/mas/tər), man who teaches in a school, or is its principal. *n.*

school mate (skül/māt/), companion at school. *n.*

school mis tress (skül/mis/tris), woman who teaches in a school, or is its principal. *n., pl.* **school mis tress es.**

school room (skül/rüm *or* skül/rúm/), room in which pupils are taught. *n.*

school teach er (skül/tē/chər), person who teaches in a school. *n.*

school work (skül/wèrk/), a student's work in school. *n.*

school yard (skül/yärd/), piece of ground around or near a school, used for play, games, etc. *n.*

school year, part of the year during which a school is in session. *n.*

schoon er (skü/nər), 1 ship with two or more masts and fore-and-aft sails. 2 prairie schooner. *n.*

schot tische (shot/ish), 1 a dance somewhat like the polka but slower, popular in the 1800's. 2 music for it. *n.* [from German *Schottische* Scottish]

Schu bert (shü/bərt), **Franz,** 1797-1828, Austrian composer. *n.*

scimitar

Schu mann (shü/män), **Robert,** 1810-1856, German composer. *n.*

schwa (shwä), an unstressed vowel sound such as *a* in *about* or *u* in *circus,* represented by the symbol ə. *n., pl.* **schwas.**

Schwei tzer (shwī/tsər), **Albert,** 1875-1965, Alsatian physician, philosopher, musician, and missionary in Africa. *n.*

sci at i ca (sī at/ə kə), pain in a sciatic nerve and its branches. *n.*

sci at ic nerve (sī at/ik), a large nerve which extends from the lower back down the back part of the thigh and leg.

sci ence (sī/əns), 1 knowledge based on observed facts and tested truths arranged in an orderly system: *the laws of science.* 2 branch of such knowledge. Chemistry and physics are physical sciences. Zoology and botany are biological sciences. Economics and sociology are social sciences. 3 skill based on training and practice; technique: *the science of judo, the science of sailing. n.*

science fair, group of school exhibits, each demonstrating a scientific principle, process, development, etc.

science fiction, story or novel that combines science and fantasy. Science fiction deals with life in the future, on other galaxies, etc., but makes much use of the latest discoveries of science and technology.

sci en tif ic (sī/ən tif/ik), 1 using the facts and laws of science: *a scientific method, a scientific farmer.* 2 of or having to do with science; used in science: *scientific books. adj.*

sci en tif i cal ly (sī/ən tif/ik lē), 1 in a scientific manner: *Einstein and Edison thought scientifically.* 2 according to the facts and laws of science: *A perpetual motion machine is scientifically impossible. adv.*

sci en tist (sī/ən tist), 1 person who

schooner
(def. 1)

has expert knowledge of some branch of science. Persons specially trained in and familiar with the facts and laws of such fields of knowledge as biology, chemistry, mathematics, physics, geology, and astronomy are scientists. 2 **Scientist,** Christian Scientist. *n.*

scim i tar *or* **scim i ter** (sim/ə tər), a short, curved sword used by Turks, Persians, and other Oriental peoples. *n.*

scin til la (sin til/ə), a spark; particle; trace: *not a scintilla of truth. n.*

scin til late (sin/tl āt), to sparkle; flash: *The snow scintillates in the sun like diamonds. Brilliant wit scintillates. v.,* **scin til lat ed, scin til lat ing.**

scin til la tion (sin/tl ā/shən), 1 a sparkling; flashing. 2 a spark; flash. *n.*

sci on (sī/ən), 1 bud or branch cut for grafting or planting. 2 descendant; heir: *the scion of a wealthy family. n.*

Scip i o (sip/ē ō), 1 237?-183? B.C., Roman general who defeated Hannibal in 202 B.C. He is called "Scipio the Elder." 2 185?-129 B.C., Roman general who destroyed Carthage in 146 B.C. He is called "Scipio the Younger." *n.*

scis sors (siz/ərz), tool or instrument for cutting that has two sharp blades so fastened that their edges slide against each other. *n. pl. or sing.*

scler a (sklir/ə), the tough, white outer membrane of the eyeball. *n.*

scle rot ic coat (sklə rot/ik), sclera.

scoff (skôf), 1 make fun to show one does not believe something; mock: *We scoffed at the idea of swimming in three inches of water.* 2 mocking words or acts. 3 something ridiculed or mocked. 1 *v.,* 2,3 *n.* —**scoff/er,** *n.* —**scoff/ing ly,** *adv.*

scold (skōld), 1 find fault with; blame with angry words: *I scolded them for tracking in mud on the clean floor.* 2 find fault; talk angrily: *Don't scold so much.* 3 person who scolds, especially a noisy, scolding woman. 1,2 *v.,* 3 *n.* —**scold/er,** *n.*

scol lop (skol/əp), scallop. *n., v.*

sconce (skons), a bracket projecting

sconce

from a wall, used to hold a candle or other light. *n.*

scone (skōn), a thick, flat, round cake cooked on a griddle or in an oven. Some scones taste much like bread; some are like buns. *n.*

scoop (def. 1)   scoop (def. 2)

scoop (sküp), 1 tool like a small shovel, having a short handle and a deep, hollow part for dipping out or shoveling up things. A kitchen utensil to take out flour, sugar, etc., is a scoop. A large ladle is a scoop. A cuplike scoop is used to dish up ice cream. 2 the part of a dredge, power shovel, etc., that takes up or holds coal, sand, etc. 3 amount taken up at one time by a scoop: *She used two scoops of flour and one of sugar.* 4 act of taking up. 5 place hollowed out: *The rabbit hid in the scoop it had made in the earth.* 6 take up or out with a scoop, or as a scoop does: *Scoop out a quart of grain. The children scooped up the snow with their hands to make snowballs.* 7 hollow out; dig out; make by scooping: *The children scooped holes in the sand.* 8 INFORMAL. the publishing of a piece of news before a rival newspaper does. 9 INFORMAL. the piece of news. 10 INFORMAL. publish a piece of news before (a rival newspaper). 1-5,8,9 *n.*, 6,7,10 *v.*

scoop ful (sküp′fúl), enough to fill a scoop. *n., pl.* **scoop fuls.**

scoot (süt), INFORMAL. 1 go quickly; dart: *He scooted out the door.* 2 act of scooting. 1 *v.*, 2 *n.*

scoot er (skü′tər), 1 a child's vehicle consisting of a footboard between two wheels, one in front of the other, steered by a long, upright handle bar and pushed by one foot against the ground. 2 motor scooter. 3 sailboat with runners, for use on either water or ice. *n.*

scope (skōp), 1 distance the mind can reach; extent of view: *Very hard words are not within the scope of a child's understanding.* 2 the area over which any activity extends: *This subject is not within the scope of our investigation.* 3 space; opportunity: *Football gives scope for courage and quick thinking. n.*

scorch (skôrch), 1 burn slightly; burn on the outside: *The cake tastes scorched.*

He scorched his shirt while he was ironing it. 2 a slight burn. 3 dry up; wither: *The grass is scorched by so much hot sunshine.* 1,3 *v.*, 2 *n.*

scorch er (skôr′chər), 1 person or thing that scorches. 2 INFORMAL. a very hot day. *n.*

score (skôr), 1 the record of points made in a game, contest, or test: *The score was 9 to 2 in favor of our school. He had nearly a perfect score on the history exam.* 2 make as points in a game, contest, or test: *score two runs in the second inning. She scored 85 per cent on the final exam.* 3 make points; succeed. 4 keep a record of the number of points made in a game, contest, or test: *The teacher will appoint some pupil to score for both sides.* 5 make as an addition to the score; gain; win: *She scored five points for our team.* 6 amount owed; debt; account: *He paid his score at the inn.* 7 to record; mark; set down: *The innkeeper scored on a slate the number of meals each person had.* 8 group or set of twenty; twenty: *A score or more came to the meeting.* 9 **scores,** *pl.* a large number: *Scores died in the epidemic.* 10 a written or printed piece of music arranged for different instruments or voices: *She was studying the score of the symphony she was learning to conduct.* 11 arrange (a piece of music) for different instruments or voices: *score a sonata for piano and strings.* 12 a cut; scratch; stroke; mark; line: *The carpenter used a nail to make a score on the board.* 13 to cut; scratch; mark; line: *Mistakes are scored in red ink. Moving the furniture across the floor scores the polish.* 14 an account; reason; ground: *Don't worry on that score.* 15 **the score,** INFORMAL. the truth about anything or things in general; the facts: *The new man doesn't know the score yet.* 1,6,8-10,12,14,15 *n.*, 2-5,7,11,13 *v.*, **scored, scor ing.**

pay off a score or **settle a score,** get even for an injury or wrong: *She had an old score to settle with them.*

score board (skôr′bôrd′), a large board on which the scores of a sporting event are posted. *n.*

score keep er (skôr′kē′pər), person who keeps score. *n.*

score less (skôr′lis), having no score: *The game ended in a scoreless tie. adj.*

scor er (skôr′ər), 1 scorekeeper. 2 person who makes a score in a game, contest, or test. *n.*

scorn (skôrn), 1 look down upon; think of as mean or low; despise: *Most children scorn a tattletale.* 2 reject or refuse as low or wrong: *The judge scorned to take a bribe.* 3 a feeling that a person, animal, or act is mean or low; contempt: *She attacked their plans in*

hat, āge, fär; let, ēqual, tėrm;
it, īce; hot, ōpen, ôrder;
oil, out; cup, půt, rüle; ch, child;
ng, long; sh, she; th, thin;
ŦH, then; zh, measure;

ə represents *a* in about,
e in taken, *i* in pencil,
o in lemon, *u* in circus.

words of bitter scorn. 4 person, animal, or thing that is scorned or despised: *That tattler is the scorn of the school.* 5 OLD USE. an expression of contempt; taunt; insult. 1,2 *v.*, 3-5 *n.* —**scorn′er,** *n.*

scorn ful (skôrn′fəl), showing contempt; mocking; full of scorn: *He spoke of our old car in a scornful voice. adj.* —**scorn′ful ly,** *adv.* —**scorn′fulness,** *n.*

scorpion (def. 1)
1 to 8 in. long

scor pi on (skôr′pē ən), 1 a small animal belonging to the same group as the spider and having a poisonous sting at the end of its tail. 2 a whip or scourge. *n.*

Scot (skot), person born or living in Scotland. *n.*

scotch (skoch), 1 stamp on; make harmless. 2 to cut or gash. *v.*

Scotch (skoch), 1 whiskey made in Scotland. 2 of Scotland; Scottish. 3 the people of Scotland. 4 English as it is spoken by the people of Scotland. 1,4 *n.sing.*, 3 *n.pl.*, 2 *adj.*

Scotch man (skoch′mən), Scotsman. *n., pl.* **Scotch men.**

Scotch tape, trademark for a very thin, transparent or opaque adhesive tape used for mending, sealing, etc.

Scotch terrier
about 10 in. high
at the shoulder

Scotch terrier, one of a breed of short-legged terriers with rough, wiry hair and pointed, standing ears.

scot-free (skot′frē′), free from punishment, loss, or injury: *One of the two*

Scotland

adj.	adjective	*n.*	noun
adv.	adverb	*prep.*	preposition
conj.	conjunction	*pron.*	pronoun
interj.	interjection	*v.*	verb
sing.	singular	*pl.*	plural

speeding drivers was fined, but the other got off scot-free. adj.*

Scot land (skot′lənd), division of Great Britain north of England; the land of the Scottish people. *Capital:* Edinburgh. *n.*

Scotland Yard, 1 headquarters of the London police. 2 the London police, especially the department that does detective work.

Scots (skots), 1 of Scotland; Scottish. 2 the people of Scotland. 1 *adj.*, 2 *n.pl.*

Scots man (skots′mən), man born or living in Scotland; Scotchman. *n., pl.* **Scots men.**

Scott (skot), Sir **Walter,** 1771-1832, Scottish novelist and poet. *n.*

Scot tish (skot′ish), 1 of or having to do with Scotland, its people, or their language: *Scottish lakes. "Laird" is a Scottish word.* 2 the people of Scotland. 3 English as it is spoken by the people of Scotland. 1 *adj.*, 2 *n.pl.*, 3 *n.sing.*

scoun drel (skoun′drəl), person without honor or good principles; villain; rascal: *The scoundrels who set fire to the barn have been caught. n.*

scoun drel ly (skoun′drə lē), 1 having the character of a scoundrel. 2 having to do with or characteristic of a scoundrel. *adj.*

scour[1] (skour), 1 clean or polish by hard rubbing: *Mother scours the frying pan with cleanser and the floor with a mop and soap.* 2 remove dirt and grease from (anything) by rubbing. 3 make clear by flowing through or over: *The stream had scoured a channel.* 4 clean; cleanse. 5 act of scouring. 1-4 *v.*, 5 *n.* [from Dutch of the 1200's *schuren*] —**scour′er,** *n.*

scour[2] (skour), 1 move quickly over: *They scoured the country round about for the lost child.* 2 go rapidly in search or pursuit. *v.* [probably from a Scandinavian word of the 1200's, such as Icelandic *skura* rush violently]

scourge (skėrj), 1 a whip. 2 any means of punishment. 3 to whip; punish. 4 some thing or person that causes great trouble or misfortune. Formerly, an outbreak of disease was called a scourge. 5 trouble very much; afflict. 1,2,4 *n.*, 3,5 *v.*, **scourged, scourging.**

scout[1] (skout), 1 person sent to find out what the enemy is doing. A scout usually wears a uniform; a spy does not. 2 thing that acts as a scout. Some ships and airplanes are scouts. 3 act as a scout; hunt around to find something: *Go and scout for firewood for the picnic.* 4 person who is sent out to get information. 5 observe or examine to get information. 6 act of scouting. 7 person belonging to the Boy Scouts or Girl Scouts. 8 SLANG. fellow; person: *He's a good scout.* 1,2,4,6-8 *n.*, 3,5 *v.* [from French of the 1300's *escoute* listener, from *escouter* listen, from Latin *auscultare*] —**scout′er,** *n.*

scout[2] (skout), refuse to believe in; reject with scorn: *She scouted the idea of a dog with two tails. v.* [from a Scandinavian word of the 1200's, such as Icelandic *skūta* to taunt]

scout ing (skou′ting), activities of scouts. *n.*

scout mas ter (skout′mas′tər), man in charge of a troop or band of Boy Scouts. *n.*

scow (skou), a large, flat-bottomed boat used to carry freight, sand, etc. *n.*

scowl (skoul), 1 look angry or sullen by lowering the eyebrows; frown: *The angry girl scowled at her father.* 2 an angry, sullen look; frown. 1 *v.*, 2 *n.* —**scowl′er,** *n.*

scrab ble (skrab′əl), 1 scratch or scrape about with hands, claws, etc.; scramble. 2 to scrawl; scribble. 3 a scraping; scramble. 1,2 *v.*, **scrab bled, scrab bling;** 3 *n.*

scrag (skrag), 1 a lean, skinny person or animal. An old bony horse is a scrag. 2 the lean, bony end of a neck of veal or mutton. 3 SLANG. neck. 4 SLANG. wring the neck of; hang. 1-3 *n.*, 4 *v.*, **scragged, scrag ging.**

scrag gly (skrag′lē), rough or irregular; ragged. *adj.*, **scrag gli er, scrag gli est.**

scrag gy (skrag′ē), 1 having little flesh; lean; thin. 2 scraggly. *adj.*, **scrag gi er, scrag gi est.**

scram (skram), SLANG. go at once. *v.*, **scrammed, scram ming.**

scram ble (skram′bəl), 1 make one's way by climbing, crawling, etc.: *The girls scrambled up the steep, rocky hill.* 2 a climb or walk over rough ground: *It was a long scramble through bushes and over rocks to the top of the hill.* 3 struggle with others for something: *The children scrambled to get the ball.* 4 a struggle to possess: *the scramble for wealth and power.* 5 any disorderly struggle or activity; scrambling: *The pile of boys on the football seemed a wild scramble of arms and legs.* 6 mix together in a confused way. 7 cook (eggs) with the whites and yolks mixed

together. 8 (in the U.S. Air Force) put aircraft into the air quickly to intercept enemy aircraft. 1,3,6-8 *v.*, **scrambled, scram bling;** 2,4,5 *n.*

Scran ton (skran′tən), city in NE Pennsylvania. *n.*

scrap[1] (skrap), 1 a small piece; little bit; small part left over: *The cook gave some scraps of meat to the dog. Put the scraps of paper in the wastebasket.* 2 old metal fit only to be melted and used again. 3 make into scraps; break up: *The army scrapped the old tanks.* 4 throw aside as useless or worn out. 5 in the form of scraps: *scrap metal.* 1,2 *n.*, 3,4 *v.*, **scrapped, scrap ping;** 5 *adj.* [from a Scandinavian word of the 1200's, such as Icelandic *skrap*]

scrap[2] (skrap), SLANG. 1 a fight, quarrel, or struggle. 2 to fight, quarrel, or struggle: *Those two dogs are always scrapping.* 1 *n.*, 2 *v.*, **scrapped, scrap ping.** [probably a different form of *scrape*]

scrap book (skrap′bůk′), book in which pictures or clippings are pasted and kept. *n.*

scrape (skrāp), 1 rub with something sharp or rough; make smooth or clean by doing this: *Scrape your muddy shoes with this old knife.* 2 remove by rubbing with something sharp or rough: *The man scraped some paint off the table when he pushed it through the doorway.* 3 scratch or graze by rubbing against something rough: *She fell and scraped her knee on the sidewalk.* 4 act of scraping. 5 a scraped place. 6 rub with a harsh sound; rub harshly: *Don't scrape your feet on the floor. The branch of the tree scraped against the window.* 7 give a harsh sound; grate. 8 a harsh, grating sound: *the scrape of the bow of a violin.* 9 dig: *The child scraped a hole in the sand.* 10 collect by scraping or with difficulty: *The hungry boy scraped up the last crumbs from his plate. I have scraped together enough money to buy a bicycle.* 11 position hard to get out of; difficulty: *Children often get into scrapes.* 12 to bow with a drawing back of the foot. 1-3,6,7,9, 10,12 *v.*, **scraped, scrap ing;** 4,5,8, 11 *n.*

scrape through, get through with difficulty: *I barely scraped through the examination.*

scrap er (skrā′pər), instrument or tool for scraping: *We removed the loose paint with a scraper. n.*

scrap iron, broken or waste pieces of old iron to be melted and used again.

scrap per (skrap′ər), SLANG. person who scraps or fights. *n.*

scratch (skrach), 1 break, mark, or cut slightly with something sharp or rough: *Your feet have scratched the chair.*

2 mark made by scratching: *There are deep scratches on this desk.* 3 tear or dig with the nails or claws: *The cat scratched me.* 4 a very slight cut: *That scratch on your hand will soon be well.* 5 rub or scrape to relieve itching: *Don't scratch your mosquito bites.* 6 rub with a harsh noise; rub: *He scratched a match on the wall.* 7 sound of scratching: *the scratch of a pen.* 8 write in a hurry or carelessly. 9 any act of scratching. 10 scrape out; strike out; draw a line through. 11 withdraw (a horse, candidate, etc.) from a race or contest. 12 the starting place of a race or contest. 13 for quick notes, a first draft, etc.: *scratch paper.* 14 collected by chance: *a scratch football team.* 1,3,5,6,8,10,11 *v.*, 2,4,7,9,12 *n.*, pl. **scratch es**; 13,14 *adj.*

from scratch, with no advantages; without help.

up to scratch, up to standard; in good condition.

scratch y (skrach′ē), 1 that scratches, scrapes, or grates: *a scratchy pen.* 2 consisting of mere scratches: *It was only a quick, scratchy drawing. adj.,* **scratch i er, scratch i est.**

scrawl (skrôl), 1 write or draw poorly or carelessly. 2 poor, careless handwriting. 3 something scrawled, such as a hastily or badly written letter or note. 1 *v.*, 2,3 *n.* —**scrawl′er,** *n.*

scraw ny (skrô′nē), INFORMAL. having little flesh; lean; thin; skinny: *Turkeys have scrawny necks. adj.,* **scraw ni er, scraw ni est.**

screw (def. 2)

scream (skrēm), 1 make a loud, sharp, piercing cry. People scream in fright, in anger, and in sudden pain. 2 a loud, sharp, piercing cry. 3 utter loudly. 4 something extremely funny. 1,3 *v.*, 2,4 *n.* —**scream′er,** *n.*

scream ing (skrē′ming), 1 that screams. 2 evoking screams of laughter: *a screaming farce.* 3 startling: *screaming headlines, screaming colors. adj.*

screech (skrēch), 1 cry out sharply in a high voice; shriek. 2 a shrill, harsh scream. 1 *v.*, 2 *n.*, pl. **screech es.** —**screech′er,** *n.*

screech owl, a small owl with hornlike tufts of feathers and a wavering cry.

screen (skrēn), 1 a covered frame that hides, protects, or separates: *She keeps her trunk behind a screen.* 2 wire woven together with small openings in between: *We have screens at our windows to keep out flies.* 3 an ornamental partition. 4 anything like a screen: *A screen of trees hides our house from the road.* 5 shelter, protect, or hide with, or as with, a screen: *screen a porch. She screened her eyes from the sun with her hand. The lawyer tried to screen his client from the reporters.* 6 surface on which motion pictures, television or radar images, or slides appear or are shown. 7 show (a motion picture) on a screen. 8 to photograph with a motion-picture camera. 9 motion pictures; films. 10 sieve for sifting sand, gravel, coal, seed, etc. 11 sift with a screen or as with a screen: *screen sand. Many government agencies screen their employees for loyalty.* 1-4,6,9,10 *n.*, 5,7,8,11 *v.* —**screen′like′,** *adj.*

screen play (skrēn′plā′), a motion-picture story in manuscript form, including the dialogue, descriptions of scenes, action, camera directions, etc. *n.*

screw (def. 1)—two types of screws

screw (skrü), 1 device for holding or fastening objects, consisting of a metal cylinder with a ridge twisted evenly round its length and often a groove across the head. 2 cylinder with an inclined plane wound around it and fitting into a threaded, cylindrical hole. It is a simple machine. Screws are used in jacks to lift heavy loads. 3 anything that turns like a screw or looks like one. 4 a turn of a screw; screwing motion. 5 to turn as one turns a screw; twist: *Screw the lid on the jar.* 6 wind; twist: *His face was screwed up with fear.* 7 fasten or tighten with a screw or screws: *The carpenter screwed the hinges to the door.* 8 to force, press, or stretch tight by using screws. 9 get by force or pressure to tell, give up, etc.: *screw money out of someone.* 10 gather for an effort: *She finally screwed up enough courage to dive.* 11 a very stingy person; miser. 12 propeller that moves a boat or ship. 1-4,11,12 *n.*, 5-10 *v.*

have a screw loose, SLANG. be crazy.

put the screws on, use pressure or force to get something.

screw ball (skrü′bôl′), 1 SLANG. an eccentric person. 2 SLANG. eccentric; erratic: *a screwball idea.* 3 (in baseball) a pitch thrown with a spin opposite to that of a curve. 1,3 *n.*, 2 *adj.*

screw driv er (skrü′drī′vər), tool for

putting in or taking out screws by turning them. *n.*

screw propeller, a revolving hub with radiating blades for propelling a steamship, aircraft, etc.

screw propeller on an ocean liner

scrib ble (skrib′əl), 1 write or draw carelessly or hastily. 2 make marks that do not mean anything. 3 something scribbled. 1,2 *v.*, **scrib bled, scrib bling;** 3 *n.*

scrib bler (skrib′lər), 1 person who scribbles. 2 author who has little or no importance. *n.*

scribe (skrīb), 1 person who copies manuscripts. Before printing was invented, there were many scribes. 2 (in ancient times) a teacher of the Jewish law. 3 writer; author. 4 a public clerk or secretary. *n.*

scrim (skrim), a loosely woven cotton or linen material, much used for window curtains. *n.*

scrim mage (skrim′ij), 1 a rough fight or struggle. 2 take part in a rough fight or struggle. 3 the play in football that takes place when the two teams are lined up and the ball is snapped back. 4 take part in such a play. 5 football playing for practice: *an hour of scrimmage between the first and second teams.* 1,3,5 *n.*, 2,4 *v.*, **scrim maged, scrim mag ing.**

scrimmage line, line of scrimmage.

scrimp (skrimp), 1 be sparing of; be very economical; stint; skimp: *Many parents have to scrimp to keep their children in school.* 2 treat stingily or very economically. *v.*

scrip (skrip), 1 a writing. 2 receipt showing a right to something. 3 paper money in denominations of less than a dollar, formerly issued in the United States. *n.*

adj.	adjective	*n.*	noun
adv.	adverb	*prep.*	preposition
conj.	conjunction	*pron.*	pronoun
interj.	interjection	*v.*	verb
sing.	singular	*pl.*	plural

script (skript), 1 written letters, figures, signs, etc.; handwriting: *German script.* 2 a style of printing that looks like handwriting. 3 manuscript of a play, motion picture, radio or television broadcast, etc. *n.*

scrip tur al or **Scrip tur al** (skrip′chər əl), of the Scriptures; according to the Scriptures; based on the Scriptures. *adj.* —**scrip′tur al ly,** *adv.*

Scrip ture (skrip′chər), 1 the Bible. 2 **the Scriptures** or **the Holy Scriptures,** the Bible. 3 **scripture,** any sacred writing. *n.*

scrive ner (skriv′nər), OLD USE. a public writer of letters or documents for others; clerk; notary. *n.*

scrod (skrod), a young cod, especially one split for cooking. *n.*

scrof u la (skrof′yə lə), a form of tuberculosis that causes a swelling of the lymphatic glands, inflammation of the joints, etc. *n.*

scrof u lous (skrof′yə ləs), 1 of or having to do with scrofula. 2 having scrofula. *adj.*

scroll (def. 1)

scroll (skrōl), 1 roll of parchment or paper, especially one with writing on it. 2 ornament resembling a partly unrolled sheet of paper, or having a spiral or coiled form. *n.* —**scroll′-like′,** *adj.*

scroll saw, a very narrow saw for cutting thin wood in curved or ornamental patterns.

Scrooge (skrüj), the old miser in Dickens's story *A Christmas Carol. n.*

scro tum (skrō′təm), pouch that contains the testicles. *n.*

scrounge (skrounj), SLANG. 1 search about for what one can find. 2 beg; get by begging. 3 pilfer. *v.,* **scrounged, scroung ing.**

scrub[1] (skrub), 1 rub hard; wash or clean by rubbing: *I scrubbed the floor with a brush and soap.* 2 a scrubbing: *Give your hands a good scrub.* 3 cancel;

reject: *scrub a rocket launch.* 1,3 *v.,* **scrubbed, scrub bing;** 2 *n.* [perhaps from Dutch of the 1300's *schrubben*]

scrub[2] (skrub), 1 low, stunted trees or shrubs. 2 anything small, or below the usual size: *He is a little scrub of a man.* 3 small; poor; inferior: *scrub pine.* A scrub ball team is made up of inferior, substitute, or untrained players. 4 player not on the regular or varsity team. 5 of or for players not on the regular or varsity team. 1,2,4 *n.,* 3,5 *adj.* [from a Scandinavian word of the 1300's, such as Danish *skrubbe*]

scrub by (skrub′ē), 1 below the usual size; low; stunted; small: *scrubby trees.* 2 covered with scrub: *scrubby land.* 3 shabby; mean. *adj.,* **scrub bi er, scrub bi est.**

scruff (skruf), the skin at the back of the neck; back of the neck. *n.*

scrump tious (skrump′shəs), SLANG. elegant; splendid; first-rate. *adj.*

scrunch (skrunch), 1 crunch; crush; crumple; squeeze. 2 the noise made by scrunching. 1 *v.,* 2 *n.*

scru ple (skrü′pəl), 1 a feeling of doubt about what one ought to do: *No scruple ever holds her back from prompt action.* 2 a feeling of uneasiness that keeps a person from doing something: *She has scruples about playing cards for money.* 3 hesitate or be unwilling (to do something): *A dishonest person does not scruple to deceive others.* 4 have scruples. 5 measure of apothecaries' weight equal to 20 grains. 3 scruples make 1 dram. 1,2,5 *n.,* 3,4 *v.,* **scru pled, scru pling.**

scru pu lous (skrü′pyə ləs), 1 very careful to do what is right. 2 attending thoroughly to details; very careful: *We tried to pay scrupulous attention to our orders.* *adj.* —**scru′pu lous ly,** *adv.* —**scru′pu lous ness,** *n.*

scru ti nize (skrüt′n īz), examine closely; inspect carefully: *The jeweler scrutinized the diamond for flaws.* *v.,* **scru ti nized, scru ti niz ing.**

scru ti ny (skrüt′n ē), close examination; careful inspection: *His work will not bear scrutiny. n., pl.* **scru ti nies.**

scroll (def. 2) on carved molding

scu ba (skü′bə), portable breathing equipment, including one or more tanks of compressed air, used by underwater swimmers and divers. See **skin diver** for picture. *n.* [formed from *s(elf)-c(ontained) u(nderwater) b(reathing) a(pparatus)*]

scud (skud), 1 run or move swiftly: *Clouds scud across the sky when there is a high wind.* 2 a scudding.

3 clouds or spray driven by the wind. 1 *v.,* **scud ded, scud ding;** 2,3 *n.*

scuff (skuf), 1 walk without lifting the feet; shuffle. 2 wear or injure the surface of by hard use: *scuff one's shoes.* 3 act of scuffing. 1,2 *v.,* 3 *n.*

scuf fle (skuf′əl), 1 to struggle or fight in a rough, confused manner: *The two children scuffled and fell down.* 2 a confused, rough struggle or fight: *I lost my hat in the scuffle.* 3 to shuffle. 4 a shuffling. 1,3 *v.,* **scuf fled, scuf fling;** 2,4 *n.*

scull (skul), 1 oar worked with a side twist over the end of a boat to make it go. 2 one of a pair of oars used, one on each side, by a single rower. 3 propel (a boat) by a scull or by sculls. 4 act of propelling by sculls. 5 a light racing boat for one or more rowers. 1,2,4,5 *n.,* 3 *v.*

scull (def. 3)

scull er (skul′ər), 1 person who sculls. 2 boat propelled by sculling. *n.*

scull er y (skul′ər ē), a small room where the dirty, rough work of a kitchen is done. *n., pl.* **scull er ies.**

scul lion (skul′yən), OLD USE. servant who does the dirty, rough work in a kitchen. *n.*

sculp tor (skulp′tər), person who makes figures by carving, modeling, casting, etc.; artist in sculpture. Sculptors work in marble, wood, bronze, etc. *n.*

sculp tress (skulp′tris), a woman sculptor. *n., pl.* **sculp tress es.**

sculp tur al (skulp′chər əl), of or having to do with sculpture; like sculpture. *adj.*

sculp ture (skulp′chər), 1 the art of making figures by carving, modeling, casting, etc. Sculpture includes the cutting of statues from blocks of marble, stone, or wood, casting in bronze, and modeling in clay or wax. 2 make figures this way. 3 sculptured work; piece of such work: *There are many famous sculptures in Italy.* 4 cover or ornament with sculpture. 1,3 *n.,* 2,4 *v.,* **sculptured, sculp tur ing.**

sculp tured (skulp′chərd), covered or ornamented with sculpture. *adj.*

scum (skum), 1 a thin layer that rises to the top of a liquid: *Green scum floated on the top of the pond. When the cook*

makes jelly, she skims off the scum.
2 form scum; become covered with
scum. 3 disreputable people: *The
saloon is filled with the scum of the
town.* 4 skim. 1,3 *n.*, 2,4 *v.*, **scummed,
scum ming.**

scum my (skum′ē), 1 consisting of or
containing scum. 2 low; worthless.
adj., **scum mi er, scum mi est.**

scup per (skup′ər), an opening in the
side of a ship to let water run off the
deck. *n.*

scup per nong (skup′ər nông), a
large, yellowish-green grape grown in
the southern United States. *n.* [from
the *Scuppernong,* a river in North Caro-
lina]

scurf (skėrf), 1 small scales of dead
skin. Dandruff is a kind of scurf. 2 any
scaly matter on a surface. *n.*

scur ril i ty (skə ril′ə tē), 1 coarse
joking. 2 indecent abuse. 3 an indecent
or coarse remark. *n., pl.* **scur ril i ties.**

scur ri lous (skėr′ə ləs), 1 coarsely
joking. 2 abusive in an indecent way.
adj. —**scur′ri lous ly,** *adv.* —**scur′ri-
lous ness,** *n.*

scur ry (skėr′ē), 1 run quickly; scamper; hurry: *We could hear the mice
scurry about in the walls.* 2 a hasty
running; hurrying: *With much fuss and
scurry, they at last got started.* 1 *v.*,
scur ried, scur ry ing; 2 *n., pl.* **scur-
ries.**

scur vi ly (skėr′və lē), in a manner
deserving contempt; meanly. *adv.*

scur vy (skėr′vē), 1 disease caused by
a lack of vitamin C in the diet. It causes
swollen and bleeding gums, extreme
weakness, and livid spots on the skin.
Scurvy used to be common among sailors when they had little to eat except
bread and salt meat. 2 mean; contemptible; base: *a scurvy fellow, a scurvy
trick.* 1 *n.,* 2 *adj.,* **scur vi er, scur vi-
est.**

scut tle[1] (skut′l), kind of bucket for
holding or carrying coal. *n.* [Old English *scutel,* from Latin *scutella* platter]

scut tle[2] (skut′l), scamper; scurry: *The
dogs scuttled off into the woods.* *v.*,
scut tled, scut tling. [a different form
of earlier *scuddle,* from *scud*]

scut tle[3] (skut′l), 1 an opening in the
deck or side of a ship, with a lid or
cover. 2 an opening in a wall or roof,
with a lid or cover. 3 the lid or cover for
any such opening. 4 cut a hole or holes
through the bottom or sides of (a ship)
to sink it: *The crew scuttled the old ship
after its last voyage.* 1-3 *n.,* 4 *v.,*
scut tled, scut tling. [perhaps from
French of the 1400's *escoutille,* from
Spanish *escotilla* hatchway]

Scyl la (sil′ə), 1 a dangerous rock supposedly located opposite the whirlpool
Charybdis, off the southwestern tip of

Italy. 2 (in Greek myths) a monster
with six heads and twelve feet that lived
on this rock and snatched sailors from
ships. *n.*

between Scylla and Charybdis,
between two dangers, one of which
must be met.

scythe (sīⱦ), a long, slightly curved
blade on a long handle, for cutting
grass, etc. *n.*

S.Dak. or **S.D.,** South Dakota.

SE or **S.E.,** 1 southeast. 2 southeastern.

sea (sē), 1 the great body of salt water
that covers almost three fourths of the
earth's surface; the ocean. 2 any large
body of salt water, smaller than an
ocean, partly or wholly enclosed by
land: *the North Sea, the Mediterranean
Sea.* 3 a large lake of fresh water: *the
Sea of Galilee.* 4 a large, heavy wave: *A
high sea swept away the ship's masts.*
5 the swell of the ocean: *a heavy sea.*
6 an overwhelming amount or number:
a sea of trouble. 7 a broad expanse: *a
sea of faces.* 8 of, on, or from the sea;
marine: *a sea animal, a sea route, a sea
breeze.* 1-7 *n., pl.* **seas;** 8 *adj.*

at sea, 1 out on the sea: *We were at sea
out of sight of land for ten days.*
2 puzzled; confused: *I can't understand
this problem; I'm all at sea.*

follow the sea, be a sailor.

go to sea, 1 become a sailor. 2 begin a
voyage.

put to sea, begin a voyage.

sea anemone, a flowerlike polyp
with a fleshy, cylindrical body and a
mouth surrounded by many brightly
colored tentacles.

sea bird, any bird that lives on or near
the sea. The petrel is a sea bird.

sea board (sē′bôrd′), land bordering
on the sea; seacoast: *New York City is
on the Atlantic seaboard.* *n.*

sea breeze, breeze blowing from the
sea toward the land.

sea coast (sē′kōst′), land along the
sea; coast: *the seacoast of Maine.* *n.*

sea cow, any of several large, fishlike,
plant-eating mammals living in the sea.
The manatee is one kind of sea cow.

sea cucumber—about 10 in. long

sea cucumber, any of a group of
small, spiny sea animals related to the
starfishes, most of which have flexible
bodies that look somewhat like cucumbers.

sea dog, sailor, especially one with
long experience.

hat, āge, fär; let, ēqual, tėrm;
it, īce; hot, ōpen, ôrder;
oil, out; cup, pu̇t, rüle; ch, child;
ng, long; sh, she; th, thin;
ⱦн, then; zh, measure;

ə represents *a* in about,
e in taken, *i* in pencil,
o in lemon, *u* in circus.

sea far er (sē′fer′ər *or* sē′far′ər),
1 sailor. 2 traveler on the sea. *n.*

sea far ing (sē′fer′ing *or* sē′far′ing),
1 going, traveling, or working on the
sea: *a hardy seafaring people.* 2 business or calling of a sailor. 3 act or fact
of traveling by sea. 1 *adj.,* 2,3 *n.*

sea food (sē′füd′), saltwater fish and
shellfish that are good to eat. *n.*

sea girt (sē′gėrt′), surrounded by the
sea. *adj.*

sea go ing (sē′gō′ing), 1 going by sea;
seafaring. 2 fit for going to sea: *a
seagoing merchant ship.* adj.

sea green, light bluish green.

sea gull, any gull, especially one living
on or near the sea.

sea horse (def. 1)
4 to 12 in. long

sea horse, 1 kind of small fish with a
prehensile tail and a head suggesting
that of a horse. 2 walrus. 3 (in old
stories) a sea animal supposed to be half
horse and half fish.

seal[1] (sēl), 1 design stamped on a piece
of wax or other soft material to show
ownership or authenticity. The seal of
the United States is attached to important government papers. 2 stamp for
marking things with such a design: *a
seal with one's initials on it.* 3 piece of
wax, paper, metal, etc., on which the
design is stamped. 4 mark (a document)
with a seal to certify it or make it
binding: *The treaty was signed and
sealed by both governments.* 5 close
tightly; shut; fasten: *Seal the letter before mailing it. We sealed the jars of
fruit. Her promise sealed her lips.*
6 thing that fastens or closes something tightly. 7 something that secures;
pledge: *under seal of secrecy.* 8 something that settles or determines: *the seal
of authority.* 9 settle; determine: *The
outcome of the elections sealed his
fate.* 10 give a sign that (a thing) is true:

755

seal

adj.	adjective	*n.*	noun
adv.	adverb	*prep.*	preposition
conj.	conjunction	*pron.*	pronoun
interj.	interjection	*v.*	verb
sing.	singular	*pl.*	plural

seal a promise with a kiss. *They sealed their bargain by shaking hands.* 11 a mark; sign. 12 a special kind of stamp: *Christmas seals, Easter seals.* 1-3,6-8, 11,12 *n.*, 4,5,9,10 *v.* [from French of the 1200's *seel,* from Latin *sigillum,* from *signum* a sign]

set one's seal to, approve.

seal² (sēl), 1 a flesh-eating sea mammal with limbs developed into large flippers for swimming, living usually in cold regions. Some kinds are hunted for their valuable fur. 2 its skin or fur; sealskin. 3 leather made from the skin of a seal. 4 hunt seals. 1-3 *n.*, *pl.* **seals** or **seal;** 4 *v.* [Old English *seolh*]

seal² (def. 1)—up to 6 ft. long

sea legs, INFORMAL. legs accustomed to walking steadily on a rolling or pitching ship.

seal er¹ (sē′lər), person or thing that seals. *n.* [*seal¹* + *-er¹*]

seal er² (sē′lər), 1 person who hunts seals. 2 ship used for hunting seals. *n.* [*seal²* + *-er¹*]

sea level, level of the surface of the sea, especially when halfway between mean high and low water. Mountains, plains, ocean beds, etc., are measured as so many feet above or below sea level.

sealing wax, a hard, brittle substance made of resin and shellac, which becomes soft when heated, used for sealing letters, packages, etc.

sea lion, a large seal of the Pacific coast.

seal skin (sēl′skin), 1 skin or fur of the seal, prepared for use. 2 garment made of this fur. *n.*

seam (sēm), 1 line formed by sewing two pieces of cloth, canvas, leather, etc., together: *the seams of a coat, the seams of a sail.* 2 any line where edges join: *The seams of the boat must be*

filled in if they leak. 3 sew the seam of; join with a seam. 4 any mark or line like a seam: *The old sword cut had left a seam in his face.* 5 mark (the face, etc.) with wrinkles, scars, etc. 6 layer; stratum: *a seam of coal.* 1,2,4,6 *n.*, 3,5 *v.*

sea man (sē′mən), 1 sailor. 2 (in the navy) any sailor ranking below a petty officer. *n.*, *pl.* **sea men.**

sea man like (sē′mən līk′), like a seaman; having the skill of a good seaman. *adj.*

sea man ship (sē′mən ship), skill in managing a ship. *n.*

sea mew, sea gull.

seam less (sēm′lis), without a seam or seams: *seamless stockings, seamless shoes. adj.*

seam stress (sēm′stris), woman whose work is sewing. *n.*, *pl.* **seamstress es.**

seam y (sē′mē), 1 having or showing seams. 2 worst; least pleasant: *A policeman sees much of the seamy side of life. adj.*, **seam i er, seam i est.**

sé ance (sā′äns), a meeting of people trying to communicate with spirits of the dead by the help of a medium. *n.*, *pl.* **sé anc es.** [from French]

sea plane (sē′plān′), airplane that takes off from and lands on water, especially one which has floats instead of wheels; hydroplane. *n.*

sea port (sē′pôrt′), port or harbor on the seacoast; city or town with a harbor that ships can reach from the sea: *San Francisco and New Orleans are seaports. n.*

sea power, 1 a nation having a strong navy. 2 naval strength.

sear (sir), 1 burn or char the surface of: *The cook seared the roast to seal in its juice. The hot iron seared my hand.* 2 dry up; wither: *The hot sun seared the grain.* 3 OLD USE. dried up; withered; sere. 1,2 *v.*, 3 *adj.*

search (sèrch), 1 try to find by looking; seek; look for (something): *We searched all day for the lost cat.* 2 look through; go over carefully; examine, especially for something concealed: *The police searched the prisoner to see if he had a gun.* 3 act of searching; examination: *She found her book after a long search.* 1,2 *v.*, 3 *n.*, *pl.* **search es.** —**search′er,** *n.*

in search of, trying to find; looking for: *The children went in search of their lost dog.*

search out, find by searching: *She searched out all the facts in the case.*

search ing (sèr′ching), 1 examining carefully; thorough: *a searching gaze or look, a searching examination.* 2 piercing; sharp: *a searching wind. adj.* —**search′ing ly,** *adv.*

search light (sèrch′līt′), 1 device that can throw a very bright beam of light in any direction desired. 2 the beam of light thrown by this device. *n.*

search warrant, a written court order authorizing the search of a house or building for stolen goods, criminals, illegal narcotics, etc.

sea rover, 1 pirate. 2 a pirate ship.

sea shell (sē′shel′), shell of any sea animal, especially a mollusk such as an oyster, a conch, etc. *n.*

sea shore (sē′shôr′), land at the edge of a sea; shore. *n.*

sea sick (sē′sik′), sick because of a ship's motion. *adj.*

sea sick ness (sē′sik′nis), sickness caused by a ship's motion. *n.*

sea side (sē′sīd′), 1 seashore. 2 of or at the seaside: *a seaside inn.* 1 *n.*, 2 *adj.*

sea son (sē′zn), 1 one of the four periods of the year; spring, summer, autumn, or winter. 2 any period of time marked by something special: *a holiday season, the harvest season.* 3 a suitable or fit time. 4 improve the flavor of: *season soup with salt.* 5 give interest or character to: *season conversation with wit.* 6 make or become fit for use by a period of keeping or treatment: *Wood is seasoned for building by drying and hardening it.* 7 accustom; make used: *Soldiers are seasoned to battle by experience in war.* 8 make less severe; soften: *Season justice with mercy.* 1-3 *n.*, 4-8 *v.*

for a season, for a time.

in good season, early enough.

in season, 1 at the right or proper time. 2 in the time or condition for eating, hunting, etc.: *Cherries are in season in June.* 3 early enough.

in season and out of season, at all times.

out of season, not in season.

sea son a ble (sē′zn ə bəl), 1 suitable to the season: *Hot weather is seasonable in July.* 2 coming at the right or proper time: *Our business would have failed without your seasonable advice. adj.* —**sea′son a ble ness,** *n.*

sea son a bly (sē′zn ə blē), in due time or season; at the right moment; early enough: *to sow or plant seasonably. adv.*

sea son al (sē′zn əl), having to do with the seasons; depending on a

sea lion—up to 11½ ft. long

season; happening at regular intervals: *seasonal variations in the weather, a seasonal business, a seasonal worker.* *adj.* —**sea′son al ly**, *adv.*

sea son ing (sē′zn ing), 1 something that gives a better flavor. Salt, pepper, and herbs are seasonings. 2 something that gives interest or character: *We like conversation with a seasoning of humor.* *n.*

seat (sēt), 1 thing to sit on. Chairs, benches, and stools are seats. 2 place to sit. 3 place in which one has the right to sit. If a man has a seat in Congress or a seat in the stock exchange, it means that he is a member. 4 that part of a chair, bench, stool, etc., on which one sits: *This bench has a broken seat.* 5 that part of the body on which one sits, or the clothing covering it: *The seat of her jeans was patched.* 6 manner of sitting on horseback: *That rider has a good seat.* 7 to set or place on a seat: *seat a person on a chair, seat oneself at the piano.* 8 have or provide seats for (a specified number): *Our school assembly seats one thousand pupils.* 9 put a seat on (a chair, trousers, etc.). 10 an established place or center: *A university is a seat of learning. The seat of our government is ˋin Washington, D.C.* 11 residence; home: *The family seat of the Howards is in Kent.* 1-6,10,11 *n.*, 7-9 *v.*

be seated, 1 sit down. 2 be sitting. 3 be situated.

seat belt, belt attached to the seat of an automobile or airplane, used to hold its occupant in the seat in the event of a crash, jolt, bump, etc.

Se at tle (sē at′l), seaport in W Washington, on Puget Sound. *n.*

sea urchin, any of a group of small, round sea animals with spiny shells.

sea urchin diameter about 3 in.

sea wall, a strong wall or embankment made to prevent the waves from wearing away the shore, to act as a breakwater, etc.

sea ward (sē′wərd), 1 toward the sea: *a seaward breeze (adj.). Our house faces seaward (adv.).* 2 direction toward the sea: *The island lies a mile to seaward.* 1 *adj., adv.,* 2 *n.*

sea wards (sē′wərdz), seaward. *adv.*

sea wa ter (sē′wô′tər *or* sē′wot′ər), the salt water of the sea or ocean. *n.*

sea way (sē′wā′), 1 an inland waterway that is deep enough to permit ocean shipping: *Ocean-going freighters reach Detroit by passing through the St. Law-*

rence Seaway. 2 a way over the sea. *n.*

sea weed (sē′wēd′), any plant or plants growing in the sea. *n.*

sea wor thy (sē′wėr′ᴛʜē), fit for sailing on the sea; able to stand storms at sea: *a seaworthy ship.* *adj.*

se ba ceous (si bā′shəs), 1 having to do with fat; fatty; greasy. 2 secreting a fatty or oily substance. *adj.*

sebaceous gland, gland in an inner layer of the skin that supplies oil to the skin and hair.

sec., 1 second or seconds. 2 secretary. 3 section or sections.

se cant (sē′kənt), in geometry: 1 a line that intersects a curve at two or more points. 2 intersecting: *a secant plane.* 1 *n.*, 2 *adj.*

secants (def. 1)—AB and CD are secants.

se cede (si sēd′), withdraw formally from an organization. *v.*, **se ced ed, se ced ing.**

se ces sion (si sesh′ən), 1 a formal withdrawing from an organization. 2 Also, **Secession.** the seceding of the eleven Southern states from the Union in 1860-1861, which resulted in the Civil War. *n.*

se ces sion ist (si sesh′ə nist), 1 person who favors secession. 2 person who secedes. *n.*

se clude (si klüd′), keep apart from company; shut off from others: *He secludes himself and sees only his close friends.* *v.*, **se clud ed, se clud ing.**

se clud ed (si klü′did), shut off from others; undisturbed: *a secluded cottage in the woods.* *adj.*

se clu sion (si klü′zhən), 1 a secluding or a being secluded; retirement: *She lives in seclusion apart from her friends.* 2 a secluded place. *n.*

sec ond[1] (sek′ənd), 1 next after the first: *the second seat from the front, the second prize.* 2 below the first; inferior: *the second officer on a ship, cloth of second quality.* 3 another; other: *Napoleon has been called a second Caesar.* 4 in the second group, division, rank, etc.; secondly: *to speak second.* 5 person or thing that is second. 6 **seconds,** *pl.* goods below first quality: *These stockings are seconds and have some slight defects.* 7 person who supports or aids another; backer: *The prizefighter had a second.* 8 express approval of; back up; support: *second another person's idea. One member made a motion to adjourn the meeting, and another seconded it.* 9 rendering a part lower in pitch: *second soprano.* 1-3,9 *adj.,* 4 *adv.,* 5-7 *n.,* 8 *v.* [from

hat, āge, fär; let, ēqual, tėrm;
it, īce; hot, ōpen, ôrder;
oil, out; cup, pùt, rüle; ch, child;
ng, long; sh, she; th, thin;
ᴛʜ, then; zh, measure;

ə represents *a* in about,
e in taken, *i* in pencil,
o in lemon, *u* in circus.

French of the 1200's *seconde,* from Latin *secundus* following, from *sequi* follow]

sec ond[2] (sek′ənd), 1 one of the 60 very short equal periods of time that make up a minute; $1/60$ of a minute; $1/3600$ of an hour. The time between the ticks of some clocks is a second. 2 a very short time; instant; moment. 3 $1/3600$ of a degree of an angle. 12° 10′ 30″ means 12 degrees, 10 minutes, 30 seconds. *n.* [from French of the 1300's *seconde,* from Latin *secunda (minuta)* second (minute)]

sec ond ar i ly (sek′ən der′ə lē), in a secondary manner. *adv.*

sec ond ar y (sek′ən der′ē), 1 next after the first in order, place, time, or importance: *A secondary industry uses products produced by other industries as its raw materials.* 2 not main or chief; having less importance: *Reading fast is secondary to reading well.* 3 not original; derived: *a secondary source of the report.* *adj.*

secondary accent, 1 an accent that is weaker than the strongest accent in the pronunciation of a word but stronger than no accent. The second syllable of *ab bre′vi a′tion* has a secondary accent. 2 mark (′) used to show this.

secondary school, high school.

sec ond-class (sek′ənd klas′), 1 of or belonging to the class next after the first: *second-class mail.* 2 on a second-class ship, train, etc.: *We could afford only to travel second-class.* 3 of inferior grade or quality. 1,3 *adj.,* 2 *adv.*

second hand, hand on a clock or watch, pointing to the seconds. It moves around the whole dial once in a minute.

sec ond-hand (sek′ənd hand′), 1 not original; obtained from another: *second-hand information.* 2 not new; used already by someone else: *second-hand clothes.* 3 dealing in used goods: *a second-hand bookshop.* 4 from other than the original source; not firsthand: *The information came to us second-hand.* 1-3 *adj.,* 4 *adv.*

second lieutenant, a commissioned officer in the army, air force, or marines

adj.	adjective	*n.*	noun
adv.	adverb	*prep.*	preposition
conj.	conjunction	*pron.*	pronoun
interj.	interjection	*v.*	verb
sing.	singular	*pl.*	plural

having the lowest rank, next below a first lieutenant.

sec ond ly (sek′ənd lē), in the second place. *adv.*

second nature, habit, quality, knowledge, etc., that a person has acquired and had for so long that it seems to be almost a part of his nature.

second person, form of a pronoun or verb used to refer to the person spoken to. *You* and *yours* are pronouns of the second person.

sec ond-rate (sek′ənd rāt′), 1 rated as second-class. 2 inferior: *a second-rate performance. adj.*

se cre cy (sē′krə sē), 1 condition of being secret or of being kept secret. 2 ability to keep things secret. 3 tendency to conceal; lack of frankness: *maintain secrecy as to one's plans. n., pl.* **se cre cies.**

se cret (sē′krit), 1 kept from the knowledge of others: *a secret errand, a secret formula, a secret weapon.* 2 keeping to oneself what one knows: *Be as secret as the grave.* 3 known only to a few: *a secret society, a secret sign.* 4 kept from sight; hidden: *a secret drawer.* 5 working or acting in secret: *secret police.* 6 something secret or hidden: *Can you keep a secret?* 7 a hidden cause or reason: *the secret of her success, the secret of his charm.* 1-5 *adj.,* 6,7 *n.* —**se′cret ly,** *adv.*

in secret, in private; not openly; secretly.

secret agent, agent of a government secret service.

sec re tar i al (sek′rə ter′ē əl), of a secretary; having to do with a secretary: *I learned to do stenography, typewriting, and other secretarial work. adj.*

sec re tar i at (sek′rə ter′ē it), 1 office or position of secretary or secretary-general. 2 the department or administrative unit controlled by a secretary or secretary-general: *the secretariat of the United Nations.* 3 group of secretaries. 4 place where a secretary transacts business. *n.*

sec re tar y (sek′rə ter′ē), 1 person who writes letters, keeps records, etc., for a person, company, club, etc.: *Our club has a secretary who keeps the minutes of the meeting.* 2 person who

has charge of a department of the government or similar organization. The Secretary of the Treasury is the head of the Treasury Department. 3 a writing desk with a set of drawers and often with shelves for books. *n., pl.* **sec re tar ies.**

sec re tar y-gen er al (sek′rə ter′ē jen′ər əl), the chief secretary; the administrative head of a secretariat: *the secretary-general of the United Nations. n., pl.* **sec re tar ies-gen er al.**

se crete (si krēt′), 1 keep secret; hide. 2 produce and discharge: *Glands in the mouth secrete saliva. v.,* **se cret ed, se cret ing.**

se cre tion (si krē′shən), 1 substance that is secreted by some part of an animal or plant: *Bile is the secretion of the liver.* 2 a producing and discharging of such a substance. 3 a concealing; hiding. *n.*

se cre tive (sē′krə tiv *or* si krē′tiv *for 1;* si krē′tiv *for 2).* 1 having the habit of secrecy; not frank and open. 2 causing or aiding secretion. *adj.* —**se′cre tive ly,** *adv.* —**se′cre tive ness,** *n.*

secret service, 1 branch of a government that makes secret investigations. 2 **Secret Service,** branch of the United States Treasury Department concerned with discovering and preventing counterfeiting, with protecting the President, etc.

sect (sekt), group of people having the same principles, beliefs, or opinions: *a philosophical sect. Each religious sect in the town had its own church. n.*

sec tar i an (sek ter′ē ən), 1 of or having to do with a sect; denominational. 2 characteristic of one sect only; strongly prejudiced in favor of a certain sect. 3 a devoted member of a sect, especially a narrow-minded or strongly prejudiced member. 1,2 *adj.,* 3 *n.*

sec tion (sek′shən), 1 a part separated or cut off; part; division; slice: *Divide the cake into sections. Her section of the family estate was larger than her brother's.* 2 division of a book: *Study sections 10 to 16 of Chapter V of your grammar for tomorrow's lesson.* 3 part of a country, city, etc.; region or district: *The city has a business section and a residential section.* 4 act of cutting. 5 cut or divide into sections: *section an orange.* 6 a representation of a thing as it would appear if cut straight through. 7 area of land one mile square; 640 acres. A township usually contains 36 sections. 1-4,6,7 *n.,* 5 *v.*

sec tion al (sek′shə nəl), 1 having to do with a particular section; regional or local: *sectional interests, sectional prejudices.* 2 made of sections: *a sectional bookcase. adj.* —**sec′tion al ly,** *adv.*

sec tion al ism (sek′shə nə liz′əm),

too great regard for sectional interests; sectional prejudice or hatred. *n.*

sec tor (sek′tər), 1 the part of a circle between two radii and the included arc. 2 a clearly defined military area which a given military unit protects or covers with fire; part of a front held by a unit. 3 any section, zone, or quarter. 4 divide into sectors; provide with sectors. 1-3 *n.,* 4 *v.*

sector (def. 1) of a circle (shaded area)

sec u lar (sek′yə lər), 1 not religious or sacred; worldly: *secular music, a secular education.* 2 living in the world; not belonging to a religious order: *the secular clergy, a secular priest. adj.*

sec u lar ize (sek′yə lə rīz′), make secular or worldly; separate from religious connection or influence. *v.,* **sec u lar ized, sec u lar iz ing.**

se cure (si kyùr′), 1 safe against loss, attack, escape, etc.: *keep a vicious dog secure on a chain. This is a secure hiding place. Land in a growing city is a secure investment.* 2 make safe; protect: *Every loan was secured by bonds or mortgages. We must secure against the dangers of the coming storm.* 3 sure; certain; that can be counted on: *We know in advance that our victory is secure.* 4 make (something) sure or certain; ensure. 5 free from care or fear: *He hoped for a secure old age.* 6 firmly fastened; not liable to give way: *Are the prisoner's bonds secure? The boards of this bridge do not look secure.* 7 make firm or fast: *Secure the locks on the windows.* 8 get; obtain: *Secure your tickets early.* 1,3,5,6 *adj.,* 2,4,7,8 *v.,* **se cured, se cur ing.** —**se cure′ly,** *adv.* —**se cure′ness,** *n.*

se cur i ty (si kyùr′ə tē), 1 freedom from danger, care, or fear; feeling or condition of being safe: *We swam with a sense of security because we knew the lifeguard was nearby.* 2 something that secures or makes safe: *Rubber soles on shoes are a security against slipping. My watchdog is a security against burglars.* 3 something given as a pledge that a person will fulfill some duty, promise, etc.: *A life-insurance policy may serve as security for a loan.* 4 Usually, **securities,** *pl.* bond or stock certificates: *These railroad securities can be sold for $5000.* 5 person who agrees to be responsible for another. *n., pl.* **se cur i ties.**

secy. or **sec'y.,** secretary.

se dan (si dan′), 1 a closed automobile with a front and back seat, seating four or more persons. 2 sedan chair. *n.*

Se dan (si dan′), town in NE France. Prussia defeated France there in 1870. *n.*

sedan chair, a covered chair carried on poles by two men. Sedan chairs were much used during the 1600's and 1700's.

se date (si dāt′), quiet; calm; serious: *I was very sedate as a child and often preferred reading to playing. adj.* —**se date′ly,** *adv.* —**se date′ness,** *n.*

sed a tive (sed′ə tiv), 1 medicine that lessens pain or excitement. 2 lessening pain or excitement. 3 soothing; calming. 1 *n.,* 2,3 *adj.*

sed en tar y (sed′n ter′ē), 1 used to sitting still much of the time: *Sedentary people get little physical exercise.* 2 that keeps one sitting still much of the time: *Bookkeeping is a sedentary occupation. adj.*

sedge (sej), a grasslike plant that grows chiefly in wet places. *n.*

sedg y (sej′ē), 1 abounding in or covered with sedge; bordered with sedge: *a sedgy brook.* 2 like sedge. *adj.,* **sedg i er, sedg i est.**

sed i ment (sed′ə mənt), 1 matter that settles to the bottom of a liquid; dregs. 2 (in geology) earth, stones, etc., deposited by water, wind, or ice: *Each year the Nile overflows and deposits sediment on the land. n.*

sed i men tar y (sed′ə men′tər ē), 1 of sediment; having to do with sediment. 2 (in geology) formed by the depositing of sediment. Shale is a sedimentary rock. *adj.*

sed i men ta tion (sed′ə men tā′shən), a depositing of sediment. *n.*

se di tion (si dish′ən), speech or action causing discontent or rebellion against the government; incitement to discontent or rebellion. *n.*

se di tious (si dish′əs), 1 stirring up discontent or rebellion. 2 taking part in sedition; guilty of sedition. 3 having to do with sedition. *adj.*

se duce (si düs′ or si dyüs′), 1 tempt to wrongdoing; persuade to do wrong: *Benedict Arnold, seduced by the offer of great wealth, betrayed his country to the enemy.* 2 lead away from virtue; lead astray; beguile. *v.,* **se duced, se duc ing.**

se duc er (si dü′sər or si dyü′sər), person who seduces. *n.*

se duc tion (si duk′shən), 1 a seducing or a being seduced. 2 something that seduces; temptation; attraction. *n.*

se duc tive (si duk′tiv), 1 that tempts or entices; alluring: *a very seductive offer.* 2 captivating; charming: *a seductive smile. adj.* —**se duc′tive ly,** *adv.* —**se duc′tive ness,** *n.*

sed u lous (sej′ə ləs), hard-working; diligent; painstaking. *adj.* —**sed′u lous ly,** *adv.*

sedan chair

see[1] (sē), 1 be aware of by using the eyes; look at: *See that black cloud.* 2 have the power of sight: *The blind do not see.* 3 be aware of with the mind; understand: *I see what you mean.* 4 find out; learn: *I will see what needs to be done.* 5 take care; make sure: *See that the work is done properly. See that you lock the back door.* 6 think; consider: *You may go if you see fit to do so.* 7 have knowledge or experience of: *That coat has seen hard wear.* 8 attend; escort; go with: *See a girl home.* 9 have a talk with; call on; meet: *He wishes to see you alone. I went to see a friend.* 10 receive a visit from: *She is too ill to see anyone.* 11 visit; attend: *We saw the World's Fair. v.,* **saw, seen, see ing.** [Old English *sēon*]

see into, understand the real character or hidden purpose of.

see off, go with to the starting place of a journey.

see out, go through with; finish.

see through, 1 understand the real character or hidden purpose of. 2 go through with; finish. 3 watch over or help through: *Friends saw her through her time of illness.*

see to, look after; take care of.

see[2] (sē), 1 position or authority of a bishop. 2 district under a bishop's authority; diocese; bishopric. *n.* [from French of the 1200's *sie, sied,* from Latin *sedes* seat, from *sedere* sit]

seed (sēd), 1 the part of a plant from which another plant like it can grow. A seed consists of a protective outer skin or coat which encloses the embryo that will become the new plant and a supply of food for its growth. Farmers often save part of a crop for the seeds. 2 bulb, sprout, or any part of a plant from which a new plant will grow. 3 of or containing seeds; used for seeds. 4 sow with seeds; scatter seeds over: *The farmer seeded his field with corn. Dandelions seed themselves.* 5 produce seeds; shed seeds. 6 remove the seeds from: *seed raisins.* 7 source or beginning of anything: *seeds of trouble.* 8 children; descendants: *The Jews are the seed of Abraham.* 1,2,7,8 *n., pl.* **seeds** or **seed;** 3 *adj.,* 4-6 *v.* —**seed′like′,** *adj.*

hat, āge, fär; let, ēqual, tėrm; it, īce; hot, ōpen, ôrder; oil, out; cup, pùt, rüle; ch, child; ng, long; sh, she; th, thin; ₮H, then; zh, measure;

ə represents *a* in about, *e* in taken, *i* in pencil, *o* in lemon, *u* in circus.

go to seed, 1 come to the time of yielding seeds: *Dandelions go to seed when their heads turn white.* 2 come to the end of vigor, usefulness, prosperity, etc.: *After the mines closed, the miners left and the town went to seed.*

seed case (sēd′kās′), any pod, capsule, or other dry, hollow fruit that contains seeds. *n.*

seed er (sē′dər), 1 person who seeds. 2 machine or device for planting seeds. 3 machine or device for removing seeds. *n.*

seed i ly (sē′də lē), shabbily. *adv.*

seed i ness (sē′dē nis), seedy condition. *n.*

seed less (sēd′lis), without seeds: *seedless grapes. adj.*

seed ling (sēd′ling), 1 a young plant grown from a seed. 2 a young tree less than three feet high. *n.*

seed pearl, a very small pearl.

seed plant, any plant that bears seeds. Most seed plants have flowers and produce seeds in fruits; some, such as the pines, form seeds on cones.

seeds man (sēdz′mən), 1 sower of seed. 2 dealer in seed. *n., pl.* **seeds men.**

seed y (sē′dē), 1 full of seed. 2 gone to seed. 3 shabby; no longer fresh or new: *seedy clothes. adj.,* **seed i er, seed i est.**

see ing (sē′ing), 1 in view of the fact; considering: *Seeing that it is 10 o'clock, we will wait no longer.* 2 ability to see; sight. 3 that sees. 1 *conj.,* 2 *n.,* 3 *adj.*

seek (sēk), 1 try to find; look for; hunt; search: *seek for something lost. We are seeking a new home.* 2 try to get: *Friends sought her advice. Some people seek wealth.* 3 try; attempt: *We seek to make peace with our enemies. v.,* **sought, seek ing.** —**seek′er,** *n.*

seem (sēm), 1 look like; appear to be: *This apple seemed good but was rotten inside. He seemed a very old man. Does this room seem hot to you?* 2 appear to oneself: *I still seem to hear the music.* 3 appear to exist: *There seems no need to wait longer.* 4 appear to be true or to be the case: *It seems likely to rain.*

seeming

This, it seems, is your idea of cleaning a room. *v.*

seem ing (sē′ming), 1 apparent; that appears to be: *a seeming advantage.* 2 appearance: *It was worse in its seeming than in reality.* 1 *adj.*, 2 *n.* —**seem′ing ly,** *adv.*

seem li ness (sēm′lē nis), fitness; suitability; propriety; decorum. *n.*

seem ly (sēm′lē), 1 suitable; proper: *Some old people do not consider modern dances seemly.* 2 properly; becomingly; fittingly: *Try to behave seemly.* 1 *adj.*, **seem li er, seem li est;** 2 *adv.*

seen (sēn), past participle of **see**[1]. *Have you seen Father?* *v.*

seep (sēp), to ooze, trickle, or leak: *Water seeps through sand.* *v.*

seep age (sē′pij), 1 a seeping; slow leakage. 2 moisture or liquid that seeps: *two feet of seepage in the cellar.* *n.*

seer (sir), person who foresees or foretells future events; prophet. *n.*

seer suck er (sir′suk′ər), cloth with alternate stripes of plain and crinkled material. *n.*

see saw (sē′sô′), 1 plank resting on a support near its middle so the ends can move up and down; teeter-totter. 2 a children's game in which the children sit at opposite ends of such a plank and move alternately up and down. 3 move up and down on such a plank: *The two boys seesawed in the playground for some time.* 4 to move up and down or back and forth. 5 moving up and down or back and forth. 6 movement up and down or back and forth: *the seesaw of a storm-tossed ship.* 1,2,6 *n.*, 3,4 *v.*, 5 *adj.*

seethe (sēṮH), 1 be excited; be disturbed: *The pirate crew was seething with discontent and ready for open rebellion.* 2 bubble and foam: *Water seethed under the falls.* 3 boil: *The cook seethed the mutton.* *v.*, **seethed, seeth ing.**

seg ment (seg′mənt), 1 piece or part cut, marked, or broken off; division; section: *A tangerine is easily pulled apart into its segments.* 2 in geometry: **a** part of a circle cut off by a line, especially a part bounded by an arc and its chord. **b** part of a sphere cut off by two parallel planes. **c** any finite section between two points on a line; line segment. 3 divide into segments. 1,2 *n.*, 3 *v.*

seg men tal (seg men′tl), 1 composed of segments. 2 of or having to do with segments. 3 having the form of a segment of a circle. *adj.*

seg men ta tion (seg′mən tā′shən), 1 division into segments. 2 growth and division of a cell into two, four, eight cells, and so on. *n.*

seg re gate (seg′rə gāt), 1 to separate from others; set apart; isolate: *The doctor segregated the child sick with mumps to protect the other patients.* 2 to separate from the rest and collect in one place. 3 to separate or keep apart one racial group from another or from the rest of society by maintaining separate schools, separate public facilities, etc. *v.*, **seg re gat ed, seg re gat ing.**

seg re ga tion (seg′rə gā′shən), 1 separation from others; a setting apart; isolation: *the segregation of lepers.* 2 separation of one racial group from another or from the rest of society, especially in schools, theaters, etc. The United States Supreme Court ruled in 1954 that segregation in public schools is unconstitutional. *n.*

seg re ga tion ist (seg′rə gā′shə nist), person who believes in or practices racial segregation. *n.*

sei gneur (sē nyėr′), a feudal lord or landowner. A **grand seigneur** was a person of high rank or one who behaved as a person of high rank should. *n.*

seine (def. 1)

seine (sān), 1 a fishing net that hangs straight down in the water. It has floats at the upper edge and sinkers at the lower. 2 fish or catch fish with a seine. 1 *n.*, 2 *v.*, **seined, sein ing.**

Seine (sān *or* sen), river flowing from E France into the English Channel. Paris is on the Seine. See **Rhine** for map. *n.*

seis mic (sīz′mik), 1 of earthquakes; having to do with an earthquake. 2 caused by an earthquake. *adj.*

seis mo graph (sīz′mə graf), instrument for recording the direction, intensity, and duration of earthquakes. *n.*

seize (sēz), 1 take hold of suddenly; clutch; grasp: *In fright I seized her arm.* 2 take possession of by force: *The rebels seized the palace.* 3 take prisoner; arrest; catch: *seize someone wanted for murder.* 4 take possession of or come upon suddenly: *A fever seized him.* 5 take possession of by legal authority: *seize smuggled goods.* 6 grasp with the mind: *seize an idea.* *v.*, **seized, seizing.**

seize on or **seize upon,** 1 take hold of suddenly. 2 take possession of.

sei zure (sē′zhər), 1 act of seizing. 2 condition of being seized. 3 a sudden attack of disease: *an epileptic seizure.* 4 a sudden onset of some emotion. *n.*

sel dom (sel′dəm), not often; rarely: *I am seldom ill.* *adv.*

se lect (si lekt′), 1 pick out; choose: *Select the book you want.* 2 picked as best; chosen specially: *She was one of a select group of skiers going to the Olympics.* 3 choice; superior: *That store carries a very select line of merchandise.* 4 careful in choosing; particular as to friends, company, etc.: *She belongs to a very select club.* 1 *v.*, 2-4 *adj.*

se lec tion (si lek′shən), 1 act of selecting; choice: *His selection of a hat took a long time. The shop offered a very good selection of hats.* 2 person, thing, or group chosen: *The plain blue hat was her selection.* *n.*

se lec tive (si lek′tiv), 1 having the power to select; selecting. 2 having to do with selection. *adj.* —**se lec′tive ly,** *adv.*

selective service, compulsory military service of persons selected from the general population according to age, physical fitness, etc.

se lec tiv i ty (si lek′tiv′ə tē), quality of being selective. *n.*

se lect man (si lekt′mən), member of a board of town officers in New England, chosen each year to manage the town's public affairs. *n., pl.* **se lect men.**

se lec tor (si lek′tər), 1 person who selects. 2 a mechanical or electrical device that selects. *n.*

Se le ne (sə lē′nē), (in Greek myths) the goddess of the moon. The Romans called her Luna. *n.*

se le ni um (sə lē′nē əm), a nonmetallic element found with sulfur in various ores. Because its electrical conductivity increases with the intensity of light striking it, it is used in photoelectric cells. *n.*

self (self), 1 one's own person: *his very self.* 2 one's own welfare or interests: *A selfish person puts self first.* 3 nature or character of a person or thing: *She does not seem like her former self.* 4 myself; himself; herself; yourself: *a check made payable to self.* 1-3 *n.*, 4 *pron.*, *pl.* **selves.**

self-, *prefix.* 1 of or over oneself: *Self-conscious = conscious of oneself. Self-control = control over oneself.* 2 by or

segment (def. 2a, left; def. 2b, right)

in oneself: *Self-inflicted = inflicted by oneself. Self-evident = evident in oneself.* 3 to or for oneself: *Self-addressed = addressed to oneself. Self-respect = respect for oneself.* 4 automatic; automatically: *Self-winding = winding automatically.* [from *self*]

self-act ing (self'ak'ting), working of itself: *a self-acting machine. adj.*

self-ad dressed (self'ə drest'), addressed to oneself: *a self-addressed envelope. adj.*

self-ap point ed (self'ə poin'tid), appointed by oneself, not by anyone else: *a self-appointed arbiter in a dispute. adj.*

self-as ser tion (self'ə sėr'shən), insistence on one's own wishes, opinions, claims, etc. *n.*

self-as ser tive (self'ə sėr'tiv), putting oneself forward; insisting on one's own wishes, opinions, etc. *adj.*

self-as sur ance (self'ə shùr'əns), self-confidence. *n.*

self-as sured (self'ə shùrd'), self-confident; sure of oneself. *adj.*

self-cen tered (self'sen'tərd), 1 occupied with one's own interests and affairs. 2 selfish. *adj.* —**self'-cen'tered ness,** *n.*

self-com mand (self'kə mand'), control of oneself. *n.*

self-com pla cent (self'kəm plā'snt), pleased with oneself; self-satisfied. *adj.*

self-con ceit (self'kən sēt'), conceit; too much pride in oneself or one's ability. *n.*

self-con fi dence (self'kon'fə dəns), belief in one's own ability, power, judgment, etc.; confidence in oneself. *n.*

self-con fi dent (self'kon'fə dənt), believing in one's own ability, power, judgment, etc. *adj.* —**self'-con'fi dent ly,** *adv.*

self-con scious (self'kon'shəs), made conscious of how one is appearing to others; embarrassed, especially by the presence or the thought of other people and their attitude toward one; shy. *adj.* —**self'-con'scious ly,** *adv.* —**self'-con'scious ness,** *n.*

self-con tained (self'kən tānd'), 1 saying little; reserved. 2 containing in oneself or itself all that is necessary; independent of what is external. *adj.*

self-con trol (self'kən trōl'), control of one's actions, feelings, etc. *n.*

self-de feat ing (self'di fē'ting), defeating oneself or itself; contrary to one's own purpose or interests. *adj.*

self-de fense (self'di fens'), defense of one's own person, property, reputation, etc. *n.*

self-de ni al (self'di nī'əl), sacrifice of one's own desires and interests; going without things one wants; austerity. *n.*

self-de ny ing (self'di nī'ing), unselfish; sacrificing one's own wishes and interests. *adj.*

self-de ter mi na tion (self'di-tėr'mə nā'shən), 1 direction from within only, without influence or force from without. 2 the deciding by the people of a nation what form of government they shall have, without reference to the wishes of any other nation. *n.*

self-dis ci pline (self'dis'ə plin), careful control and training of oneself. *n.*

self-ed u cat ed (self'ej'ə kā'tid), self-taught; educated by one's own efforts. *adj.*

self-em ployed (self'em ploid'), not employed by others; working for oneself. Doctors, lawyers, and farmers are usually self-employed. *adj.*

self-es teem (self'e stēm'), 1 thinking well of oneself; self-respect. 2 thinking too well of oneself; conceit. *n.*

self-ev i dent (self'ev'ə dənt), evident by itself; needing no proof. *adj.*

self-ex plan a to ry (self'ek splan'ə-tôr'ē), explaining itself; that needs no explanation; obvious. *adj.*

self-ex pres sion (self'ek spresh'ən), expression of one's personality. *n.*

self-gov ern ing (self'guv'ər ning), that governs itself: *a self-governing territory. adj.*

self-gov ern ment (self'guv'ərn-mənt), 1 government of a group by its own members: *self-government through elected representatives.* 2 self-control. *n.*

self-help (self'help'), a helping oneself; getting along without assistance from others. *n.*

self-im por tance (self'im pôrt'ns), a having or showing too high an opinion of one's own importance; conceit; behavior showing conceit. *n.*

self-im por tant (self'im pôrt'nt), having or showing too high an opinion of one's own importance. *adj.*

self-im posed (self'im pōzd'), imposed on oneself by oneself: *a self-imposed task. adj.*

self-im prove ment (self'im-prüv'mənt), improvement of one's character, mind, etc., by one's own efforts. *n.*

self-in dul gence (self'in dul'jəns), gratification of one's own desires, passions, etc., with too little regard for the welfare of others. *n.*

self-in dul gent (self'in dul'jənt), characterized by self-indulgence. *adj.*

self-in flict ed (self'in flik'tid), inflicted on oneself by oneself: *a self-inflicted wound. adj.*

self-in ter est (self'in'tər ist), 1 interest in one's own welfare with too

hat, āge, fär; let, ēqual, tėrm;
it, īce; hot, ōpen, ôrder;
oil, out; cup, pùt, rüle; ch, child;
ng, long; sh, she; th, thin;
ᴛʜ, then; zh, measure;

ə represents *a* in about,
e in taken, *i* in pencil,
o in lemon, *u* in circus.

little care for the welfare of others; selfishness. 2 personal advantage. *n.*

self ish (sel'fish), 1 caring too much for oneself; caring too little for others. A selfish person puts his own interests first. 2 showing care solely or chiefly for oneself: *selfish motives. adj.* —**self'ish ly,** *adv.* —**self'ish ness,** *n.*

self less (self'lis), having no regard or thought for self; unselfish. *adj.* —**self'less ly,** *adv.* —**self'less-ness,** *n.*

self-love (self'luv'), 1 love of oneself; selfishness. 2 conceit. *n.*

self-made (self'mād'), 1 made by oneself. 2 successful through one's own efforts. A self-made man is one who succeeds in business, etc., without help from others. *adj.*

self-pit y (self'pit'ē), pity for oneself. *n.*

self-por trait (self'pôr'trit), portrait made by a person of himself. *n.*

self-pos sessed (self'pə zest'), having or showing control of one's feelings and actions; not excited, embarrassed, or confused; calm. *adj.*

self-pos ses sion (self'pə zesh'ən), control of one's feelings and actions; composure; calmness. *n.*

self-pres er va tion (self'prez'ər-vā'shən), preservation of oneself from harm or destruction. *n.*

self-pro pelled (self'prə peld'), propelled by an engine, motor, etc., within itself: *a self-propelled missile. adj.*

self-reg is ter ing (self'rej'ə star-ing), registering automatically. *adj.*

self-reg u lat ing (self'reg'yə-lā'ting), regulating oneself or itself. Automatic devices are self-regulating. *adj.*

self-re li ance (self'ri lī'əns), reliance on one's own acts, abilities, etc. *n.*

self-re li ant (self'ri lī'ənt), having or showing self-reliance. *adj.*

self-re proach (self'ri prōch'), blame by one's own conscience. *n.*

self-re spect (self'ri spekt'), respect for oneself; proper pride. *n.*

self-re spect ing (self'ri spek'ting), having self-respect; properly proud. *adj.*

adj.	adjective	*n.*	noun
adv.	adverb	*prep.*	preposition
conj.	conjunction	*pron.*	pronoun
interj.	interjection	*v.*	verb
sing.	singular	*pl.*	plural

self-re strained (self/ri straīnd/), showing self-control. *adj.*

self-re straint (self/ri straīnt/), self-control. *n.*

self-right eous (self/rī/chəs), thinking that one is more moral than others; thinking that one is very good and pleasing to God. *adj.* —**self/-right/eous ly,** *adv.* —**self/-right/eous ness,** *n.*

self-rule (self/rül/), self-government. *n.*

self-sac ri fice (self/sak/rə fīs), sacrifice of one's own interests and desires, for one's duty, another's welfare, etc. *n.*

self-sac ri fic ing (self/sak/rə fī/sing), unselfish; giving up things for someone else. *adj.*

self same (self/sām/), very same: *We study the selfsame books that you do. adj.*

self-sat is fac tion (self/sat/is-fak/shən), satisfaction with oneself; complacency. *n.*

self-sat is fied (self/sat/i sfīd), pleased with oneself; complacent. *adj.*

self-seek er (self/sē/kər), person who seeks his own interests too much. *n.*

self-seek ing (self/sē/king), 1 selfish. 2 selfishness. 1 *adj.,* 2 *n.*

self-serv ice (self/sèr/vis), act or process of serving oneself in a restaurant, store, etc. *n.*

self-styled (self/stīld/), called by oneself: *a self-styled leader whom no one follows. adj.*

self-suf fi cien cy (self/sə fish/-ən sē), 1 ability to supply one's own needs. 2 conceit; self-assurance. *n.*

self-suf fi cient (self/sə fish/ənt), 1 asking no help; independent. 2 having too much confidence in one's own resources, power, etc.; conceited. *adj.*

self-sup port ing (self/sə pôr/ting), earning one's expenses; getting along without help. *adj.*

self-sus tain ing (self/sə stā/ning), self-supporting. *adj.*

self-taught (self/tôt/), taught by oneself without aid from others. *adj.*

self-will (self/wil/), insistence on having one's own way. *n.*

self-willed (self/wild/), insisting on having one's own way; objecting to doing what others ask or command. *adj.*

self-wind ing (self/wīn/ding), that is wound automatically. A self-winding watch winds itself by the movements of the person wearing it. *adj.*

sell (sel), 1 to exchange for money or other payment: *sell a house.* 2 deal in; keep for sale: *The butcher sells meat.* 3 be given in exchange; be on sale; be sold: *Strawberries sell at a high price in January.* 4 give up; betray: *The traitor sold his country for money.* 5 cause to be accepted, approved, or adopted by representations and methods characteristic of salesmanship: *sell an idea to the public.* 6 INFORMAL. win acceptance, approval, or adoption: *an idea that will sell.* *v.,* **sold, sell ing.**

sell out, 1 sell all that one has of; get rid of by selling. 2 SLANG. betray by a secret bargain.

sell er (sel/ər), 1 person who sells: *The stock exchange was filled with buyers and sellers of stocks.* 2 thing considered with reference to its sale: *This book is a good seller. n.*

sel vage or **sel vedge** (sel/vij), the edge of a woven fabric finished off to prevent raveling. *n.*

selves (selvz), plural of **self.** *She had two selves—one that liked to save money and one that liked to spend it. n., pron.*

se man tic (sə man/tik), 1 having to do with the meanings of words. 2 having to do with semantics. *adj.* —**se man/ti cal ly,** *adv.*

se man tics (sə man/tiks), the scientific study of the meanings, and the development of meanings, of words. *n.*

sem a phore (sem/ə fôr), 1 an upright post or structure with movable arms, or an arrangement of colored lights, lanterns, flags, etc., used in railroad signaling. 2 system of signals for sending messages by using different positions of the arms or flags, or by using lanterns or other mechanical devices. 3 to signal by semaphore. 1,2 *n.,* 3 *v.,* **sem a phored, sem a phor ing.**

sem blance (sem/bləns), 1 outward appearance: *Their story had the semblance of truth but was really false.* 2 likeness: *These clouds have the semblance of a huge head. n.*

se men (sē/mən), fluid containing the male reproductive cells. *n.*

se mes ter (sə mes/tər), a division, often one half, of a school year. *n.*

semi-, *prefix.* 1 half: *Semicircle = half a circle.* 2 partly; incompletely: *Semiskilled = partly skilled.* 3 twice. *Semi____ly* means in each half of a ____, or twice in a ____: *Semiannually = every half year, or twice a year.* [from Latin]

sem i an nu al (sem/ē an/yü əl), 1 occurring every half year. 2 lasting a half year. *adj.* —**sem/i an/nu al ly,** *adv.*

sem i ar id (sem/ē ar/id), having little rainfall. *adj.*

sem i au to mat ic (sem/ē ô/tə-mat/ik), 1 partly automatic; self-acting in some part of its operation. 2 gun like an automatic but requiring a press of the trigger to fire each shot. 1 *adj.,* 2 *n.*

semicircle

sem i cir cle (sem/i sèr/kəl), half a circle: *We sat in a semicircle around the fire. n.*

sem i cir cu lar (sem/i sèr/kyə lər), having the form of half a circle. *adj.*

semicircular canal, any of three curved, tubelike canals in the inner ear that help to maintain balance.

sem i co lon (sem/i kō/lən), mark of punctuation (;) that shows a separation not so complete as that shown by a period but more so than that shown by a comma. EXAMPLE: We arrived much later than we had intended; consequently there was almost no time left for swimming. *n.*

sem i con duc tor (sem/i kən duk/-tər), a mineral substance, such as germanium or silicon, that conducts electricity with an efficiency between that of metals and insulators. Semiconductors can convert alternating current into direct current and amplify weak electric signals. Transistors, used in place of vacuum tubes in small radios, are made primarily of semiconductors. *n.*

RED LIGHT	YELLOW LIGHT	GREEN LIGHT
STOP	CAUTION	PROCEED

semaphore (def. 1)

sem i con scious (sem/i kon/shəs), half conscious; not fully conscious. *adj.* —**sem/i con/scious ness,** *n.*

sem i fi nal (sem/i fī/nl), 1 one of the two rounds, matches, etc., that settles who will play in the final one, which follows: *The team that will face the state champions defeated our team in the semifinal.* 2 designating or having to do with such a round, match, etc.: *Our team lost in the semifinal game.* 1 *n.,* 2 *adj.*

sem i liq uid (sem/i lik/wid), 1 partly liquid. 2 a partly liquid substance. 1 *adj.,* 2 *n.*

sem i month ly (sem/i munth/lē), 1 occurring or appearing twice a month.

2 twice a month. **3** magazine or newspaper published twice a month. **1** *adj.*, **2** *adv.*, **3** *n.*, *pl.* **sem i month lies.**

sem i nal (sem′ə nəl), **1** of or having to do with semen or seed. **2** like seed; having the possibility of future development: *a seminal idea. adj.*

sem i nar (sem′ə när), **1** group of students engaged in discussion and original research under the guidance of a professor. **2** meeting in class of such a group. *n.*

sem i nar y (sem′ə ner′ē), **1** school, especially one beyond high school. **2** academy or boarding school, especially for young women. **3** school or college for training students to be priests, ministers, rabbis, etc. *n.*, *pl.* **sem i nar ies.**

Sem i nole (sem′ə nōl), member of a tribe of North American Indians that settled in Florida. Most of this tribe now lives in Oklahoma. *n.*, *pl.* **Sem i nole** or **Sem i noles.**

sem i of fi cial (sem′ē ə fish′əl), partly official; having some degree of authority. *adj.*

sem i pre cious (sem′i presh′əs), having value, but not sufficient value to rank as gems. Amethysts and garnets are semiprecious stones; diamonds and rubies are precious stones. *adj.*

sem i skilled (sem′i skild′), partly skilled. *adj.*

sem i sol id (sem′i sol′id), **1** partly solid. **2** a partly solid substance. **1** *adj.*, **2** *n.*

Sem ite (sem′īt), member of a group of ancient and modern peoples speaking any of the Semitic languages. The ancient Hebrews, Phoenicians, and Assyrians were Semites. Arabs and Jews are sometimes called Semites. *n.*

Se mit ic (sə mit′ik), **1** of or having to do with the Semites or their languages. **2** group of languages including Hebrew, Arabic, Aramaic, Phoenician, and Assyrian. **1** *adj.*, **2** *n.*

sem i tone (sem′i tōn′), half step; half tone. *n.*

sem i trop i cal (sem′i trop′ə kəl), halfway between tropical and temperate: *Florida is a semitropical state. adj.*

sem i week ly (sem′i wēk′lē), **1** occurring or appearing twice a week. **2** twice a week. **3** newspaper or magazine published twice a week. **1** *adj.*, **2** *adv.*, **3** *n.*, *pl.* **sem i week lies.**

Sen., **1** Senate. **2** Senator.

sen ate (sen′it), **1** a governing or law-making assembly. The highest council of state in ancient Rome was called the senate. **2** the upper and smaller branch of an assembly that makes laws. **3** **Senate, a** the upper house of Congress or of a state legislature. **b** the upper house of the legislature of certain other countries, such as Canada and Australia. *n.*

sen a tor (sen′ə tər), member of a senate. *n.*

sen a to ri al (sen′ə tôr′ē əl), **1** of or befitting a senator or senators. **2** consisting of senators. **3** entitled to elect a senator: *a senatorial district. adj.*

sen a tor ship (sen′ə tər ship′), position, duties, etc., of a senator. *n.*

send (send), **1** cause to go from one place to another: *send a child on an errand, send someone for a doctor.* **2** cause to be carried: *send a letter, send news.* **3** cause to come, occur, or be: *Send help at once. May God send peace.* **4** drive; impel; throw: *send a ball. The volcano sent clouds of smoke into the air.* *v.*, **sent, send ing. —send′-er,** *n.*

send-off (send′ôf′), **1** a friendly demonstration in honor of a person setting out on a journey, course, career, etc. **2** INFORMAL. a start (favorable or unfavorable) given to a person or thing. *n.*

Sen e ca¹ (sen′ə kə), **Lucius Annaeus,** 4? B.C.-A.D. 65, Roman philosopher. He also wrote tragedies. *n.*

Sen e ca² (sen′ə kə), member of the largest tribe of Iroquois Indians, formerly living in western New York State. *n.*

Sen e gal (sen′ə gôl′), country in W Africa, on the Atlantic, a member of the French Community. *Capital:* Dakar. See **Upper Volta** for map. *n.*

sen es chal (sen′ə shəl), steward in charge of a royal palace or nobleman's estate in the Middle Ages. Seneschals often had the powers of judges or generals. *n.*

se nile (sē′nīl), **1** of old age. **2** showing the weakness of old age. **3** caused by old age. *adj.*

se nil i ty (sə nil′ə tē), **1** old age. **2** weakness of old age. *n.*

sen ior (sē′nyər), **1** the older (used of a father whose son has the same given name): *John Parker, Senior is the father of John Parker, Junior.* **2** older or elder: *a senior citizen.* **3** an older person: *She is her sister's senior by two years.* **4** of higher position or standing; higher in rank or longer in service: *a senior officer. Mr. Jones is the senior member of the firm of Jones and Brown.* **5** person of higher position or standing; person of higher rank or longer service. **6** student who is a member of the graduating class of a high school or college. **7** of or having to do with these students: *the senior class, the senior year.* **1,2,4,7** *adj.*, **3,5,6** *n.*

senior high school, school at-

---

tended after junior high school. It has grades 10, 11, and 12.

sen ior i ty (sē nyôr′ə tē), **1** superiority in age or standing; state or fact of being older: *He felt that two years' seniority gave him the right to advise his sister.* **2** priority or precedence in office or service. *n.*, *pl.* **sen ior i ties.**

sen na (sen′ə), **1** laxative made from the dried leaves or pods of any of several cassia plants. **2** the dried leaves of any of these plants. *n.*

Sen nach er ib (sə nak′ər ib), died 681 B.C., king of Assyria from 705 to 681 B.C. *n.*

se ñor (sā nyôr′), SPANISH. **1** Mr. or sir. **2** a gentleman. *n.*, *pl.* **se ño res** (sā nyō′rās).

se ño ra (sā nyôr′ä), SPANISH. **1** Mrs. or Madame. **2** a lady. *n.*, *pl.* **se ño ras.**

se ño ri ta (sā′nyō rē′tä), SPANISH. **1** Miss. **2** a young lady. *n.*, *pl.* **se ño ri tas.**

sen sa tion (sen sā′shən), **1** action of the senses; power to see, hear, feel, taste, smell, etc.: *A dead body is without sensation. Blindness is the loss of the sensation of sight.* **2** feeling: *Ice gives a sensation of coldness; sugar, of sweetness.* **3** strong or excited feeling: *The announcement of peace caused a sensation throughout the nation.* **4** cause of such feeling: *Atomic developments are the greatest sensations of the present age. n.*

sen sa tion al (sen sā′shə nəl), **1** arousing strong or excited feeling: *The outfielder's sensational catch made the crowd cheer wildly.* **2** trying to arouse strong or excited feeling: *a sensational newspaper story.* **3** of the senses; having to do with sensation. *adj.* **—sen sa′tion al ly,** *adv.*

sen sa tion al ism (sen sā′shə nə liz′əm), sensational methods, writing, language, etc., aimed at arousing strong or excited feeling. *n.*

sense (sens), **1** power of the mind to know what happens outside itself. Sight, hearing, touch, taste, and smell are the five senses. *A dog has a keen sense of smell.* **2** feeling: *The extra lock*

---

adj. adjective	*n.* noun
adv. adverb	*prep.* preposition
conj. conjunction	*pron.* pronoun
interj. interjection	*v.* verb
sing. singular	*pl.* plural

on the door gave him a sense of security. Duty well done brings a sense of pleasure. 3 be aware; feel; understand: *I sensed that he was tired.* 4 understanding; appreciation: *Everyone thinks he has a sense of humor.* 5 Usually, **senses,** *pl.* normal, sound condition of mind: *They must be out of their senses to act so.* 6 judgment; intelligence: *She had the good sense to keep out of foolish quarrels. Common sense would have prevented the accident.* 7 meaning: *He was a gentleman in every sense of the word.* 8 the general opinion: *The sense of the assembly was clear even before the vote.* 1,2,4-8 *n.,* 3 *v.,* **sensed, sens ing.**

in a sense, in some respects; to some degree.

make sense, have a meaning; be understandable; be reasonable: *The statement "Cow cat bless Monday" doesn't make sense.*

sense less (sens′lis), 1 unconscious: *A hard blow on the head knocked him senseless.* 2 foolish; stupid: *a senseless idea.* 3 meaningless: *senseless words. adj.* —**sense′less ly,** *adv.* —**sense′-less ness,** *n.*

sense organ, eye, ear, or other part of the body by which a person or an animal receives sensations of heat, colors, sounds, smells, etc.; receptor.

sen si bil i ty (sen′sə bil′ə tē), 1 ability to feel or perceive: *Some drugs lessen a person's sensibilities.* 2 sensitiveness: *a sensibility to the beauties of nature.* 3 fineness of feeling: *She has an unusual sensibility for colors.* 4 Usually, **sensibilities,** *pl.* sensitive feelings. 5 tendency to feel hurt or offended too easily. *n., pl.* **sen si bil i ties.**

sen si ble (sen′sə bəl), 1 having or showing good judgment; wise: *She is too sensible to do anything foolish.* 2 aware; conscious: *I am sensible of your kindness.* 3 that can be noticed: *There is a sensible difference between yellow and orange.* 4 that can be perceived by the senses. 5 sensitive. *adj.* —**sen′si ble ness,** *n.*

sen si bly (sen′sə blē), 1 in a sensible manner; with good sense. 2 so as to be felt. *adv.*

sen si tive (sen′sə tiv), 1 receiving impressions readily: *The eye is sensitive to*

light. 2 easily affected or influenced: *The mercury in the thermometer is sensitive to changes in temperature. Sensitive people are quickly touched by something beautiful or sad.* 3 easily hurt or offended: *be sensitive about one's weight. adj.* —**sen′si tive ly,** *adv.* —**sen′si tive ness,** *n.*

sen si tiv i ty (sen′sə tiv′ə tē), 1 condition or quality of being sensitive. 2 the degree of this. *n., pl.* **sen si tiv i ties.**

sen si tize (sen′sə tīz), make sensitive. *Camera films have been sensitized to light. v.,* **sen si tized, sen si tiz ing.**

sen sor y (sen′sər ē), of or having to do with sensation or the senses. *The eyes and ears are sensory organs. adj.*

sen su al (sen′shü əl), 1 having to do with the bodily senses rather than with the mind or soul: *Gluttons derive sensual pleasure from eating.* 2 caring too much for the pleasures of the senses. 3 lustful; lewd. *adj.* —**sen′su al ly,** *adv.*

sen su al i ty (sen′shü al′ə tē), 1 sensual nature. 2 excessive indulgence in the pleasures of the senses. 3 lewdness. *n., pl.* **sen su al i ties.**

sen su ous (sen′shü əs), 1 of or derived from the senses; having an effect on the senses; perceived by the senses: *the sensuous thrill of a warm bath, a sensuous love of color.* 2 enjoying the pleasures of the senses. *adj.* —**sen′su ous ly,** *adv.* —**sen′su ous ness,** *n.*

sent (sent), past tense and past participle of **send.** *They sent the trunks last week. She was sent on an errand. v.*

sen tence (sen′təns), 1 group of words that is grammatically complete and expresses a statement, request, command, exclamation, etc. "Boys and girls" is not a sentence. "The boys are here" is a sentence. 2 group of mathematical symbols that expresses a complete idea or a requirement. $4 + 2 = 6$ is a closed sentence expressing a complete idea. $X + 2 = 6$ is an open sentence expressing a requirement. 3 decision by a judge on the punishment of a criminal. 4 the punishment itself. 5 pronounce punishment on: *The judge sentenced her to a year in prison.* 1-4 *n.,* 5 *v.,* **sen tenced, sen tenc ing.**

sen ten tious (sen ten′shəs), 1 full of meaning; saying much in few words. 2 speaking as if one were a judge settling a question. 3 inclined to make

wise sayings; abounding in proverbs. *adj.* —**sen ten′tious ly,** *adv.*

sen tient (sen′shənt), that can feel; having feeling. *adj.*

sen ti ment (sen′tə mənt), 1 mixture of thought and feeling. Admiration, patriotism, and loyalty are sentiments. 2 feeling, especially refined or tender feeling: *a sentiment of pity.* 3 thought or saying that expresses feeling. 4 a mental attitude. 5 a personal opinion. *n.*

sen ti men tal (sen′tə men′tl), 1 having or showing much tender feeling: *sentimental poetry.* 2 likely to act from feelings rather than from logical thinking; having too much sentiment. 3 of sentiment; dependent on sentiment: *She values her mother's gift for sentimental reasons. adj.* —**sen′ti men′tal ly,** *adv.*

sen ti men tal ism (sen′tə men′tl iz′əm), 1 tendency to be influenced by sentiment rather than reason. 2 excessive indulgence in sentiment. 3 feeling expressed too openly or commonly or sentimentally. *n.*

sen ti men tal ist (sen′tə men′tl ist), a sentimental person; one who indulges in sentimentality. *n.*

sen ti men tal i ty (sen′tə men tal′ə tē), 1 tendency to be influenced by sentiment rather than reason. 2 excessive indulgence in sentiment. 3 feeling expressed too openly or sentimentally. *n., pl.* **sen ti men tal i ties.**

sen ti nel (sen′tə nəl), person stationed to keep watch and guard against surprise attacks. *n.*

stand sentinel, act as a sentinel; keep watch.

sen try (sen′trē), soldier stationed at a post to keep watch and guard against surprise attacks; sentinel. *n., pl.* **sentries.**

stand sentry, keep watch; guard: *We stood sentry over the sleepers.*

sentry box

sentry box, a small building for sheltering a sentry.

Seoul (sōl), capital of South Korea, in the NW part. *n.*

se pal (sē′pəl), one of the leaflike divisions of the calyx of a flower. The sepals are usually green and cover the unopened bud. In a carnation, the sepals make a green cup at the base of the flower. In a tulip, the sepals are colored in the same way as the petals. *n.*

sep a ra ble (sep′ər ə bəl), that can be separated. *adj.*

sep a rate (sep′ə rāt′ *for 1-4;* sep′ər it *for 5-7*), 1 be between; keep apart; divide: *The Atlantic Ocean separates America from Europe.* 2 divide into parts or groups: *separate a tangle of string.* 3 draw, come, or go apart: *After school the children separated in all directions. The rope separated under the strain.* 4 put apart; take away: *Separate your books from mine.* 5 apart from others: *in a separate room.* 6 divided; not joined: *separate seats, separate questions.* 7 individual; single: *The separate parts of a machine.* 1-4 *v.,* **sep a rat ed, sep a rat ing;** 5-7 *adj.* —**sep′ar ate ly,** *adv.*

sep a ra tion (sep′ə rā′shən), 1 a separating; dividing; taking apart. 2 a being apart; being separated: *The friends were glad to meet after so long a separation.* 3 line or point of separating: *We now come to the separation of the two branches of the river. n.*

sep a ra tist (sep′ər ə tist), member of a group that separates or withdraws from a larger group. *n.*

sep a ra tor (sep′ə rā′tər), person or thing that separates, especially a machine for separating the cream from milk, wheat from chaff or dirt, etc. *n.*

se pi a (sē′pē ə), 1 a dark-brown pigment prepared from the inky secretion of cuttlefish. 2 a dark brown. 3 dark-brown. 4 done in sepia: *a sepia print.* 1,2 *n., pl.* **se pi as;** 3,4 *adj.*

Sept., September.

Sep tem ber (sep tem′bər), the ninth month of the year. It has 30 days. *n.*

sep tic (sep′tik), 1 causing infection or putrefaction. 2 caused by infection or putrefaction. *adj.*

septic tank, tank in which sewage is decomposed by bacteria.

sep tum (sep′təm), a dividing wall; partition. There is a septum of bone and cartilage between the nostrils. The inside of a green pepper is divided into chambers by septa. *n., pl.* **sep ta** (sep′-tə).

sep ul cher (sep′əl kər), place of burial; tomb; grave. *n.* Also, **sepulchre.**

se pul chral (sə pul′krəl), 1 of sepulchers or burial: *sepulchral ceremonies.* 2 deep and gloomy; dismal; suggesting a tomb: *sepulchral darkness. adj.*

sep ul chre (sep′əl kər), sepulcher. *n.*

se quel (sē′kwəl), 1 something that follows as a result of some earlier happening; result of something; outcome: *Among the sequels of the party were many stomach aches.* 2 a complete story continuing an earlier one about

the same people: *Robert Louis Stevenson's "David Balfour" is a sequel to his "Kidnapped." n.*

se quence (sē′kwəns), 1 the coming of one thing after another; succession; order of succession: *Arrange the names in alphabetical sequence.* 2 a connected series: *a sequence of lessons on one subject.* 3 something that follows; result: *Crime has its sequence of misery. n.*

se quent (sē′kwənt), following: *a sequent king. adj.*

se ques ter (si kwes′tər), 1 remove or withdraw from public use or from public view: *The shy old lady sequestered herself from all strangers.* 2 take away (property) for a time from an owner until a debt is paid or some claim is satisfied. 3 seize by authority; take and keep: *The soldiers sequestered food from the people they conquered. v.*

se ques tra tion (sē′kwə strā′shən), 1 the seizing and holding of property until legal claims are satisfied. 2 forcible or authorized seizure; confiscation. 3 separation or withdrawal from others; seclusion. *n.*

se quin (sē′kwən), a small spangle used to ornament dresses, scarfs, etc. *n.*

se quoi a (si kwoi′ə), 1 the redwood. 2 the giant sequoia. *n., pl.* **se quoi as.** [from *Sequoya,* 1770?-1843, Cherokee Indian who invented an alphabet for his own language]

se ragl io (sə ral′yō), harem. *n., pl.* **se ragl ios.**

se ra pe (sə rä′pē), shawl or blanket, often having bright colors, worn by Spanish Americans. *n.* Also, **sara pe.**

ser aph (ser′əf), one of the highest order of angels. *n., pl.* **ser aphs** or **ser a phim.**

se raph ic (sə raf′ik), 1 of seraphs. 2 like a seraph; angelic. *adj.*

ser a phim (ser′ə fim), a plural of **seraph.** *n.*

Serb (sèrb), 1 person born or living in Serbia. 2 language of Serbia. 3 of Serbia, its people, or their language. 1,2 *n.,* 3 *adj.*

Ser bi a (sèr′bē ə), former kingdom in SE Europe, now part of Yugoslavia. *n.* —**Ser′bi an,** *adj., n.*

sere (sir), OLD USE. dried; withered. *adj.* Also, **sear.**

ser e nade (ser′ə nād′), 1 music played or sung outdoors at night, especially by a lover under his sweetheart's window. 2 piece of music suitable for such a performance. 3 sing or play a serenade (to). 1,2 *n.,* 3 *v.,* **ser e nad ed, ser e nad ing.**

se rene (sə rēn′), 1 peaceful; calm: *serene happiness, a serene smile.* 2 not

hat, āge, fär; let, ēqual, tèrm; it, īce; hot, ōpen, ôrder; oil, out; cup, pút, rüle; ch, child; ng, long; sh, she; th, thin; ₮H, then; zh, measure;

ə represents *a* in about, *e* in taken, *i* in pencil, *o* in lemon, *u* in circus.

cloudy; clear; bright: *a serene sky. adj.* —**se rene′ly,** *adv.*

se ren i ty (sə ren′ə tē), 1 peace and quiet; calmness. 2 clearness; brightness. *n., pl.* **se ren i ties.**

serf (sèrf), 1 (in the feudal system) slave who could not be sold off the land, but passed from one owner to another with the land. 2 person treated almost like a slave; person who is mistreated, underpaid, etc. *n.*

serf dom (sèrf′dəm), 1 condition of a serf. 2 custom of having serfs. Serfdom existed all over Europe in the Middle Ages and lasted in Russia till the middle of the 1800's. *n.*

serge (sèrj), kind of cloth woven with slanting ridges in it. *n.*

ser geant (sär′jənt), 1 (in the army and marine corps) a noncommissioned officer ranking next above a corporal. 2 (in the air force) a noncommissioned officer ranking above an airman. 3 a police officer ranking next above an ordinary policeman and next below a captain or lieutenant. *n.*

sergeant at arms, officer who keeps order in a legislature, court of law, etc. *pl.* **sergeants at arms.**

ser i al (sir′ē əl), 1 story published, broadcast, or televised one part at a time in a magazine or newspaper or on the radio or television. 2 of a series; arranged in a series; making a series: *Place volumes 1 to 5 on the shelf in serial order.* 1 *n.,* 2 *adj.*

ser i al ize (sir′ē ə līz), publish, broadcast, or televise in a series of installments. *v.,* **ser i al ized, ser i al iz ing.**

ser i al ly (sir′ē ə lē), in a series; as a serial. *adv.*

serial number, number given to one of a series of persons, articles, etc., as a means of easy identification. Every dollar bill has a serial number.

ser ies (sir′ēz), 1 number of similar things in a row: *A series of rooms opened off the long hall.* 2 number of things placed one after another: *Our names were listed in an alphabetical series.* 3 number of things or events coming one after the other: *A series of*

765

serious

adj.	adjective	n.	noun
adv.	adverb	prep.	preposition
conj.	conjunction	pron.	pronoun
interj.	interjection	v.	verb
sing.	singular	pl.	plural

rainy days spoiled their vacation. n., pl. **ser ies.**

ser i ous (sir′ē əs), 1 showing deep thought or purpose; thoughtful; grave; earnest: *a serious manner, a serious face.* 2 in earnest; not fooling; sincere: *Are you joking or are you serious?* 3 needing thought; important: *Choice of one's lifework is a serious matter.* 4 important because it may do much harm; dangerous: *The patient was in serious condition. adj.* —**ser′i ous ly,** *adv.* —**ser′i ous ness,** *n.*

ser mon (sėr′mən), 1 a public talk on religion or something connected with religion, usually given by a clergyman. 2 a serious talk about conduct or duty; moral lecture: *After the guests left, the children got a sermon on their bad table manners. n.*

Sermon on the Mount, (in the Bible) Christ's sermon to His disciples which presents His basic teachings.

ser ous (sir′əs), 1 of, having to do with, or producing serum. 2 like serum; watery. Tears are drops of a serous fluid. *adj.*

ser pent (sėr′pənt), 1 snake, especially a big snake. 2 a sly, treacherous person. 3 the devil; Satan. *n.*

ser pen tine (sėr′pən tēn′ *or* sėr′pən tīn *for 1-3;* sėr′pən tēn′ *for 4),* 1 of or like a serpent. 2 winding; twisting: *the serpentine course of a creek.* 3 cunning; sly; treacherous: *a serpentine suggestion.* 4 a greenish mineral with an oily luster, consisting chiefly of magnesium, and sometimes spotted like the skin of some serpents. 1-3 *adj.,* 4 *n.*

ser rate (ser′āt), notched like the edge of a saw; toothed. *adj.*

serrate leaf

ser rat ed (ser′ā tid), serrate. *adj.*
ser ried (ser′ēd), crowded closely together. *adj.*
ser um (sir′əm), 1 the clear, pale-yellow, watery part of the blood that separates from the clot when blood

coagulates. 2 a serous liquid used to prevent or cure a disease, usually obtained from the blood of an animal that has been made immune to the disease. Diphtheria antitoxin is a serum. 3 any watery liquid in animals. Lymph is a serum. *n., pl.* **ser ums, ser a** (sir′ə).

serv ant (sėr′vənt), 1 person employed in a household. Cooks and nursemaids are servants. 2 person employed by another. Policemen and firemen are public servants. 3 person devoted to any service: *a servant of God. n.*

serve (sėrv), 1 work for; give service to: *serve a worthwhile cause, serve customers in a store.* 2 give service; perform duties: *He served as a counselor. My cousin served three years in the navy.* 3 to honor and obey; worship: *serve God.* 4 wait on at table; bring food or drink to: *The waiter served us.* 5 put (food or drink) on the table: *Serve crackers with the soup. Dinner is served.* 6 supply with something needed; supply; furnish: *The dairy serves us with milk.* 7 supply enough for: *One pie will serve six persons.* 8 be useful; be what is needed; be used: *Boxes served as seats.* 9 be useful to; fulfill: *This will serve my purpose.* 10 be favorable or suitable; satisfy: *The ship will sail when the wind and tide serve.* 11 pass; spend: *The thief served a term in prison.* 12 deliver; present: *She was served with a notice to appear in court.* 13 in tennis, badminton, volleyball, etc.: **a** put (the ball or shuttlecock) in play by hitting it. **b** act or way of serving a ball or shuttlecock. **c** a player's turn to serve. 1-13a *v.,* **served, serv ing;** 13b,c *n.*

serve one right, be just what one deserves.

serv er (sėr′vər), 1 person who serves. 2 tray for dishes. *n.*

serv ice (sėr′vis), 1 helpful act or acts; aid; a being useful to others: *He performed many services for his friends.* 2 arrangements for supplying something useful or necessary: *Bus service was good.* 3 occupation or employment as a servant: *go into domestic service.* 4 Usually, **services,** *pl.* **a** performance of duties: *She no longer needs the services of a doctor.* **b** work in the service of others; useful labor: *We pay for services such as repairs, maintenance, and utilities.* 5 advantage; benefit; use: *This coat has given me great service. Every available vehicle was pressed into service.* 6 department of government or public employment, or the persons engaged in it: *the diplomatic service.* 7 the armed forces: *We entered the service together.* 8 duty in the armed forces: *He was on active service during the war.*

9 Often, **services,** *pl.* a religious meeting, ritual, or ceremony: *They attend services on Friday evening. The marriage service was performed at the home of the bride.* 10 manner of serving food or the food served: *The service in this restaurant is excellent.* 11 set of dishes, etc.: *a solid silver tea service.* 12 (in law) the serving of a process or writ upon a person. 13 make fit for service; keep fit for service: *The mechanic serviced our automobile.* 14 in tennis, badminton, volleyball, etc.: **a** act or manner of putting the ball or shuttlecock in play. **b** the ball or shuttlecock as put into play. 15 provide with a service of any kind: *Only two trains a day service the town.* 16 for use by household servants, tradesmen, etc.: *a service entrance.* 1-12,14 *n.,* 13,15 *v.,* **serv iced, serv ic ing;** 16 *adj.*

at one's service, ready to do what one wants.

of service, helpful; useful.

serv ice a ble (sėr′vi sə bəl), 1 useful for a long time; able to stand much use: *He wanted to buy a serviceable second-hand car.* 2 capable of giving good service; useful. *adj.*

serv ice man (sėr′vis man′), 1 member of the armed forces. 2 person who maintains or repairs machinery or some kind of equipment: *an automobile serviceman. n., pl.* **serv ice men.**

service station, filling station.

ser vile (sėr′vəl), 1 like that of slaves; fit for a slave; mean; base: *servile flattery.* 2 of or having to do with slaves: *a servile revolt, servile work. adj.*

ser vil i ty (sėr′vil′ə tē), attitude or behavior fit for a slave; servile yielding. *n., pl.* **ser vil i ties.**

serv ing (sėr′ving), portion of food served to a person at one time; helping. *n.*

ser vi tor (sėr′və tər), servant; attendant. *n.*

ser vi tude (sėr′və tüd *or* sėr′və tyüd), 1 slavery; bondage. 2 forced labor as punishment: *The criminal was sentenced to five years' servitude. n.*

ses a me (ses′ə mē), 1 the seeds of an Oriental plant, used to flavor bread, candy, and other foods, and in making an oil used in cooking. 2 plant producing these seeds. *n.*

ses sion (sesh′ən), 1 a sitting or meeting of a court, council, legislature, etc.: *a session of Congress.* 2 a series of such sittings. 3 term or period of such sittings: *This year's session of Congress was unusually long.* 4 a meeting: *an important session with some businessmen.* 5 a single, continuous course or a period of lessons: *Our school has two sessions, one in the morning and one in the afternoon. n.*

in session, meeting: *The teachers were in session all Saturday morning. Congress is now in session.*

set (set), 1 put in some place; put; place: *Set the box on its end.* 2 put in the right place, position, or condition; put in proper order; arrange: *The doctor set my broken leg. Set the clock. Set the table for dinner.* 3 cause to be; put in some condition or relation: *Their friendliness set me at ease. The prisoner was set free.* 4 fix; arrange; appoint: *set the rules of a contest. The teacher set a time limit for the examination.* 5 fixed or appointed beforehand; established: *a set time, set rules.* 6 prepared; ready: *They are all set to try again.* 7 provide for others to follow: *set a good example.* 8 put in a fixed, rigid, or settled state: *set one's teeth.* 9 fixed; rigid: *a set smile.* 10 make or become firm or hard: *Jelly sets as it cools.* 11 put in a frame or other thing that holds: *set a diamond in gold.* 12 go down; sink: *The sun sets in the west.* 13 number of things or persons belonging together; group; outfit: *a set of dishes.* 14 scenery of a play. 15 device for receiving or sending by radio, telephone, telegraph, etc. 16 way a thing is put or placed; form; shape: *His jaw had a stubborn set.* 17 direction; tendency; course; drift: *The set of opinion was toward building a new bridge.* 18 have a direction; tend: *The current sets to the south.* 19 turn in a particular direction; direct: *to set one's feet homeward.* 20 begin to move; start: *He set to work.* 21 (in music) adapt; fit: *set words of a poem to music.* 22 put (a hen) to sit on eggs to hatch them; place (eggs) under a hen to be hatched. 23 (of a hen) sit on eggs. 24 act or manner of setting. 25 INFORMAL. stubbornly fixed; obstinate. 26 group of games in tennis. One side must win six games and at least two more than the other side. 27 a young plant: *onion sets.* 28 (in mathematics) a group of numbers, points, objects, or other elements which are distinguished from all other elements by specific common properties. The numbers from 0 to 10 form a set, and any number in this set is a member of the set. 1-4,7,8,10-12,18-23 *v.,* **set, set ting;** 5,6,9,25 *adj.,* 13-17,24,26-28 *n.*

set about, start work upon; begin: *set about one's business.*

set against, 1 make unfriendly toward. 2 balance; compare.

set aside, 1 put to one side. 2 put by for later use. 3 discard, dismiss, or leave out; reject; annul: *Sometimes a higher court sets aside the decision in a lawsuit.*

set back, stop; hinder; check: *Road repairs were set back by bad weather.*

set down, 1 deposit or let alight; put down: *set down a suitcase. The bus set us down near town.* 2 put down in writing or printing. 3 consider; regard: *set a person down as a gossip.* 4 ascribe; attribute: *Your failure in the test can be set down to too much haste.*

set forth, 1 make known; express; declare: *set forth one's opinions on a subject.* 2 start to go: *set forth on a trip.*

set in, 1 begin: *Winter set in early.* 2 blow or flow towards the shore.

set off, 1 explode: *set off a string of firecrackers.* 2 start to go: *set off for home.* 3 increase or heighten by contrast: *The green dress set off her red hair.* 4 balance; compensate: *Our losses were set off by some gains.* 5 mark off; separate from the others: *One sentence was set off from the rest by quotation marks.*

set on or **set upon,** 1 attack: *The dog set on us.* 2 urge to attack.

set out, 1 start to go: *They set out on the hike with plenty of water.* 2 spread out to show, sell, or use: *set out a flag, set out goods for sale.* 3 to plant: *set out tomato plants in the spring.*

set to, 1 begin: *set to work.* 2 begin fighting: *The children set to.*

set up, 1 build: *set up a monument.* 2 begin; start. 3 put up; raise in place, position, power, pride, etc.: *They set him up above his rivals.* 4 claim; pretend: *set up to be honest.* 5 plan, prepare, or establish: *set up a business deal.*

set back (set′bak′), a check to progress; reverse. *n.*

set tee (se tē′), sofa or long bench with a back and, usually, arms. *n.*

setter (def. 2)—2 ft. high at shoulder

set ter (set′ər), 1 person or thing that sets: *a setter of type, a setter of jewels.* 2 a long-haired hunting dog, trained to stand motionless and point its nose toward the game that it scents. *n.*

set ting (set′ing), 1 frame or other thing in which something is set. The mounting of a jewel is its setting. 2 scenery of a play. 3 place, time, etc., of a play or story. 4 surroundings; background: *a scenic mountain setting.* 5 music composed to go with a story, poem, etc. 6 the eggs that a hen sets on for hatching. 7 act of a person or thing that sets. 8 dishes or cutlery required to set one place at a table: *a wedding present of six settings of china. n.*

set tle[1] (set′l), 1 determine; decide; agree (upon): *settle an argument. They*

hat, āge, fär; let, ēqual, tèrm;
it, īce; hot, ōpen, ôrder;
oil, out; cup, pùt, rüle; ch, child;
ng, long; sh, she; th, thin;
ᴛʜ, then; zh, measure;

ə represents *a* in about,
e in taken, *i* in pencil,
o in lemon, *u* in circus.

settled on a time for leaving. 2 put or be put in order; arrange: *I must settle all my affairs before going away for the winter.* 3 pay; arrange payment: *She settled a bill before leaving town. Let us settle up our expenses for the trip.* 4 take up residence (in a new country or place): *settle in New York.* 5 establish colonies in: *The English settled New England.* 6 set or be set in a fairly permanent position, place, or way of life: *We are settled in our new home.* 7 come to rest in a particular place; become set or fixed: *A heavy fog settled over the airport. My cold settled in my chest.* 8 place in or come to a desired or comfortable position: *The cat settled itself in the chair.* 9 make or become quiet: *A vacation will settle your nerves.* 10 go down; sink: *Our house has settled four inches since it was built.* 11 (of liquid) make or become clear: *A beaten egg or cold water will settle coffee. v.,* **set tled, set tling.** [Old English *setlan,* from *setl* a sitting place]

settle down, 1 live a more regular life. 2 direct steady effort or attention. 3 calm down; become quiet: *settle down for a nap.*

settle upon or **settle on,** give (property, etc.) to by law: *She settled one thousand dollars a year upon her housekeeper.*

set tle[2] (set′l), a long bench. *n.* [Old English *setl* a sitting place]

settle[2]

set tle ment (set′l mənt), 1 a settling or a being settled. 2 a putting in order; arrangement: *No settlement of the dispute is possible unless each side yields some point.* 3 payment: *Settlement of all claims against the company will be made shortly.* 4 the settling of persons in a new country: *The settlement of the English along the Atlantic coast gave England claim to that section.*

adj. adjective	*n.* noun
adv. adverb	*prep.* preposition
conj. conjunction	*pron.* pronoun
interj. interjection	*v.* verb
sing. singular	*pl.* plural

5 colony: *England had many settlements along the Atlantic coast.* 6 group of buildings and the people living in them: *Ships brought supplies to the scattered settlements of the colonists.* 7 place in a poor, neglected neighborhood where work for its improvement is carried on: *Hull House is a famous settlement on the west side of Chicago.* 8 the settling of property upon someone: *The will provided that each heir would get a settlement of $20,000.* *n.*

set tler (set′lər), 1 person who settles. 2 person who settles in a new country. *n.*

set up (set′up′), 1 arrangement of apparatus, machinery, etc. 2 arrangement of an organization. *n.*

sev en (sev′ən), one more than six; 7. *n., adj.*

sev en fold (sev′ən fōld′), 1 seven times as much or as many. 2 having seven parts. 3 seven times as much or as often. 1,3 *adv.,* 1,2 *adj.*

seven seas, all the seas and oceans of the world, traditionally believed to be the Arctic, Antarctic, N Atlantic, S Atlantic, N Pacific, S Pacific, and Indian oceans: *to sail the seven seas.*

sev en teen (sev′ən tēn′), seven more than ten; 17. *n., adj.*

sev en teenth (sev′ən tēnth′), 1 next after the 16th; last in a series of 17. 2 one of 17 equal parts. *adj., n.*

sev enth (sev′ənth), 1 next after the sixth; last in a series of 7. 2 one of 7 equal parts. *adj., n.*

sev en ti eth (sev′ən tē ith), 1 next after the 69th; last in a series of 70. 2 one of 70 equal parts. *adj., n.*

sev en ty (sev′ən tē), seven times ten; 70. *n., pl.* **sev en ties;** *adj.*

Seven Wonders of the World, the seven most remarkable structures of ancient times: the Pyramids of Egypt, the hanging gardens of Babylon, the 40-foot statue of Zeus by Phidias at Olympia, the temple of Artemis at Ephesus, the Colossus of Rhodes, the 140-foot high mausoleum at a city in southwestern Asia Minor, and the 400-foot high lighthouse at Alexandria.

sev er (sev′ər), 1 cut apart; cut off: *The sailor severed the rope with a knife.* 2 part; divide; separate: *The rope severed and the swing fell down.* 3 break

off: *The two countries severed friendly relations.* *v.*

sev er al (sev′ər əl), 1 more than two or three but not many; some; a few: *gain several pounds* (adj.). *Several have given their consent* (n.). 2 individual; different: *The boys went their several ways, each minding his own business.* 1,2 *adj.,* 1 *n.*

sev er al ly (sev′ər ə lē), 1 separately; singly; individually: *Consider these points, first severally and then collectively.* 2 respectively. *adv.*

sev er ance (sev′ər əns), 1 a severing or being severed; separation; division. 2 a breaking off: *the severance of diplomatic relations between two countries.* *n.*

se vere (sə vir′), 1 very strict; stern; harsh: *a severe reprimand.* 2 sharp or violent: *a severe headache, a severe storm.* 3 serious; grave: *a severe illness.* 4 very plain or simple; without ornament: *She wore a severe black dress.* 5 difficult: *a series of severe tests.* *adj.,* **se ver er, se ver est.** —**se vere′ly,** *adv.* —**se vere′ness,** *n.*

se ver i ty (sə ver′ə tē), 1 strictness; sternness; harshness: *The children feared their neighbor because of her severity.* 2 sharpness or violence: *the severity of storms, the severity of pain, the severity of grief.* 3 simplicity of style or taste; plainness: *the severity of a modern steel and glass building.* 4 seriousness. *n., pl.* **se ver i ties.**

Se ville (sə vil′), city in SW Spain. *n.*

sew (sō), 1 work with needle and thread. 2 fasten with stitches: *sew on a button, sew a hem on a sewing machine.* 3 close with stitches: *The doctor sewed up the wound.* *v.,* **sewed, sewed** or **sewn, sew ing.**

sew age (sü′ij), the waste matter that passes through sewers. *n.*

Sew ard (sü′ərd), **William Henry,** 1801-1872, American statesman. He was secretary of state from 1861 to 1869. *n.*

sew er¹ (sü′ər), an underground pipe or channel for carrying off waste water and refuse. *n.* [from French of the 1400's *seviere* sluice from a pond, from Latin *exaquaria,* from *ex-* out + *aqua* water]

sew er² (sō′ər), person or thing that sews. *n.* [*sew* + *-er¹*]

sew er age (sü′ər ij), 1 removal of waste matter by sewers. 2 system of sewers. 3 the waste matter that passes through sewers; sewage. *n.*

sew ing (sō′ing), 1 work done with a needle and thread. 2 something to be sewed. 3 for sewing; used in sewing: *a sewing room.* 1,2 *n.,* 3 *adj.*

sewing machine, machine for sewing or stitching cloth, etc.

sewn (sōn), sewed; a past participle of **sew.** *I've sewn on the buttons.* *v.*

sex (seks), 1 one of the two divisions of human beings or animals. Men, bulls, and roosters are of the male sex; women, cows, and hens are of the female sex. 2 the character of being male or female: *People were admitted without regard to age or sex.* *n., pl.* **sex es.**

sex chromosome, either of a pair of chromosomes, the X chromosome or the Y chromosome, which determine sex.

sex ism (sek′siz′əm), discrimination or prejudice against a sex or member of a sex, especially the female sex. *n.*

sex ist (sek′sist), of or having to do with sexism: *sexist attitudes.* *adj.*

sex tant (sek′stənt), instrument used by navigators, surveyors, etc., for measuring the angular distance between two objects. Sextants are used at sea to measure the altitude of the sun, a star, etc., in order to determine latitude and longitude. *n.*

sextant
A, mirror; B, mirror; C, telescope; D, handle; E, graduated arm

sex tet or **sex tette** (sek stet′), 1 piece of music for six voices or instruments. 2 group of six singers or players performing together. 3 any group of six. *n.*

sex ton (sek′stən), man who takes care of a church building, rings the church bell, arranges burials, etc. *n.*

sex u al (sek′shü əl), of or having to do with sex or the sexes. In sexual reproduction, animals and plants reproduce their own kind by the union of the male and female germ cells or gametes. *adj.* —**sex′u al ly,** *adv.*

sexual intercourse, the uniting of male and female sexual organs.

Sgt., Sergeant.

shab bi ly (shab′ə lē), in a shabby manner. *adv.*

shab bi ness (shab′ē nis), shabby condition or quality. *n.*

shab by (shab′ē), 1 much worn: *His old suit looks shabby.* 2 wearing old or much worn clothes: *She is always shabby.* 3 poor or neglected; run-down: *a shabby old house.* 4 not generous; mean; unfair: *a shabby way to treat a friend.* *adj.,* **shab bi er, shab bi est.**

shack (shak), 1 a roughly built hut or cabin: *The boys made a shack of old boards in the backyard.* 2 house in bad condition: *There are a lot of shacks in the run-down part of town near the railroad.* n.

shack le (shak′əl), 1 a metal band fastened around the ankle or wrist of a prisoner, slave, etc. Shackles are usually fastened to each other, the wall, floor, etc., by chains. 2 **shackles,** *pl.* fetters; chains. 3 link fastening together the two rings for the ankles and wrists of a prisoner. 4 put shackles on. 5 anything that prevents freedom of action, thought, etc. 6 restrain; hamper. 7 thing for fastening or coupling. 1-3,5,7 *n.,* 4,6 *v.,* **shack led, shackling.**

shackles (def. 1)

Shack le ton (shak′əl tən), Sir **Ernest**, 1874-1922, British antarctic explorer. *n.*

shad (shad), any of several saltwater fishes related to the herrings that ascend rivers in the spring to spawn. The shad common on the northern Atlantic coast is a valuable food fish. *n., pl.* **shad** or **shads.**

shade (shād), 1 a partly dark place, not in the sunshine: *We sat in the shade of a big tree.* 2 a slight darkness or coolness given by something that cuts off light: *Leafy trees cast shade.* 3 place or condition of comparative obscurity. 4 something that shuts out light: *Pull down the shades of the windows.* 5 keep light from: *A big hat shades the eyes.* 6 lightness or darkness of color: *silks in all shades of blue.* 7 the dark part of a picture. 8 make darker than the rest; use black or color to give the effect of shade in a picture. 9 a very small difference; little bit: *a shade too long.* 10 show very small differences; change little by little: *This scarf shades from deep rose to pale pink.* 11 ghost; spirit: *the shades of departed heroes.* 12 **the shades,** darkness of evening or night. 1-4,6,7,9,11,12 *n.,* 5,8,10 *v.,* **shad ed, shad ing.**

shad i ness (shā′dē nis), shady quality or condition. *n.*

shad ing (shā′ding), 1 a covering from the light. 2 use of black or color to give the effect of shade or depth in a picture. 3 a slight variation or difference of color, character, etc. *n.*

shad ow (shad′ō), 1 shade made by some person, animal, or thing. Sometimes a person's shadow is much longer than he is, and sometimes much shorter. 2 darkness; partial shade: *Don't turn on the light; we like to sit in the shadow.*

3 the dark part of a place or picture. 4 protect from light; shade: *The grass is shadowed by huge oaks.* 5 cast a shadow on. 6 a little bit; small degree; slight suggestion: *He is innocent beyond the shadow of a doubt.* 7 ghost. 8 a faint image: *She was worn to a shadow of her usual self.* 9 anything that is unreal or imaginary even though it seems to be real. 10 follow closely and secretly: *The detective shadowed the suspect.* 11 person who follows another closely and secretly. 12 a constant companion; follower. 13 sadness; gloom. 14 make sad or gloomy. 1-3, 6-9,11-13 *n.,* 4,5,10,14 *v.*

shad ow y (shad′ō ē), 1 having much shadow or shade; shady: *We are glad to leave the hot sun and come into the cool, shadowy room.* 2 like a shadow; dim, faint, or slight: *He saw a shadowy outline on the window curtain.* *adj.*

shad y (shād′ē), 1 in the shade; shaded. 2 giving shade. 3 INFORMAL. of doubtful honesty, character, etc.: *I hear they were involved in a shady business deal.* *adj.,* **shad i er, shad i est.**

shaft (def. 1)

shaft (shaft), 1 bar which supports turning parts in a machine or which transmits motion from one part of the machine to another. 2 a deep passage sunk in the earth. The entrance to a mine is called a shaft. 3 a passage that is like a well; long, narrow space: *an elevator shaft.* 4 the long, slender stem of an arrow, spear, etc. 5 arrow; spear. 6 something aimed at a person like an arrow or spear: *shafts of ridicule.* 7 ray or beam of light. 8 one of the two wooden poles between which a horse is harnessed to a carriage, etc. 9 the main part of a column. 10 the long, straight handle of a hammer, ax, golf club, etc. *n.* —**shaft′like′,** *adj.*

shag (shag), 1 rough, matted hair, wool, etc. 2 the long, rough nap of some kinds of cloth. 3 cloth having such a nap. *n.*

shag bark (shag′bärk′), kind of hickory tree whose rough bark peels off in long strips. *n.*

shag gy (shag′ē), 1 covered with a thick, rough mass of hair, wool, etc.: *a shaggy dog.* 2 long, thick, and rough: *shaggy eyebrows.* 3 unkempt in appearance, especially needing a haircut or shave. 4 having a long, rough nap; of

coarse texture: *a shaggy felt hat. adj.,* **shag gi er, shag gi est.**

Shah or **shah** (shä), a title of the ruler of Iran. *n.*

shake (shāk), 1 move quickly backward and forward, up and down, or from side to side: *shake a rug. The baby shook the rattle. The branches of the old tree shook in the wind.* 2 bring, throw, force, rouse, scatter, etc., by or as if by movement: *shake snow off one's clothes.* 3 clasp (hands) in greeting, congratulating, etc., another: *shake hands.* 4 tremble: *He is shaking with cold.* 5 make tremble: *The explosion shook the town.* 6 disturb; make less firm: *His lie shook my faith in his honesty.* 7 act or fact of shaking: *A shake of the head was her answer.* 8 **the shakes,** a trembling caused by chills or fear. 9 SLANG. get rid of: *Can't you shake her?* 1-6,9 *v.,* **shook, shak en, shak ing;** 7,8 *n.*

no great shakes, INFORMAL. not unusual, extraordinary, or important.

shake down, 1 bring or throw down by shaking. 2 cause to settle down. 3 bring into working order. 4 SLANG. get money from dishonestly.

shake off, get rid of.

shake up, 1 shake hard. 2 stir up. 3 to jar in body or nerves: *I was much shaken up by the experience.*

shak en (shā′kən), past participle of **shake.** *v.*

shak er (shā′kər), 1 person who shakes something. 2 machine or utensil used in shaking. 3 container for pepper, salt, etc., having a perforated top. 4 **Shaker,** member of an American religious sect, so called from movements of the body forming part of their worship. *n.*

Shake speare (shāk′spir), **William,** 1564-1616, English poet and dramatist. *n.*

Shake spear i an or **Shake-spear e an** (shāk spir′ē ən), of or having to do with Shakespeare or his works. *adj.*

shake-up (shāk′up′), a sudden and complete change: *The mayor resigned during a shake-up in the government.* n.

hat, āge, fär; let, ēqual, tėrm;
it, īce; hot, ōpen, ôrder;
oil, out; cup, pút, rüle; ch, child;
ng, long; sh, she; th, thin;
ᴛH, then; zh, measure;

ə represents *a* in about,
e in taken, *i* in pencil,
o in lemon, *u* in circus.

adj. adjective	*n.* noun
adv. adverb	*prep.* preposition
conj. conjunction	*pron.* pronoun
interj. interjection	*v.* verb
sing. singular	*pl.* plural

shak i ly (shā′kə lē), in a shaky manner. *adv.*

shak i ness (shā′kē nis), shaky condition. *n.*

shak o (shak′ō *or* shā′kō), a high, stiff military hat with a plume or other ornament. *n., pl.* **shak os.**

shako

shak y (shā′kē), 1 shaking: *a shaky voice.* 2 liable to break down; weak: *a shaky porch.* 3 not to be depended on; not reliable: *a shaky bank, a shaky knowledge of history, a shaky supporter of reform. adj.,* **shak i er, shak i est.**

shale (shāl), rock formed from hardened clay or mud in thin layers which split easily. *n.*

shall (shal; *unstressed* shəl). *Shall* is used to express future time, command, obligation, and necessity. *We shall come soon. You shall go to the party, I promise you. Shall I drink the milk? I shall miss you. v., past tense* **should.**

shal lop (shal′əp), a small, light, open boat with sail or oars. *n.*

shal lot (shə lot′), a small bulb much like an onion, often used for seasoning cooked foods. *n.*

shal low (shal′ō), 1 not deep: *shallow water, a shallow dish, a shallow mind.* 2 Usually, **shallows,** *pl.* a shallow place: *Children splashed in the shallows of the pond.* 3 become less deep. 1 *adj.,* 2 *n.,* 3 *v.* —**shal′low ly,** *adv.* —**shal′low ness,** *n.*

shalt (shalt), OLD USE. shall. "Thou shalt" means "You shall." *v.*

sham (sham), 1 pretense; fraud: *Her goodness is all a sham.* 2 false; pretended; imitation: *The soldiers fought a sham battle for practice.* 3 pretend: *He shammed sickness so he wouldn't have to work.* 4 person who is not what he pretends to be; fraud. 1,4 *n.,* 2 *adj.,* 3 *v.,* **shammed, sham ming.**

sha man (shä′mən, shā′mən, *or* sham′ən), priest with magic power over disease, spirits, etc.; medicine man. *n.*

sham ble (sham′bəl), 1 walk awkwardly or unsteadily: *The tired old man shambles.* 2 a shambling walk. 1 *v.,* **sham bled, sham bling;** 2 *n.*

sham bles (sham′bəlz), 1 confusion; mess; general disorder: *to make a shambles of a clean room.* 2 slaughterhouse. 3 place of butchery or of great bloodshed. *n. pl. or sing.*

shame (shām), 1 a painful feeling of having done something wrong, improper, or silly: *blush with shame.* 2 cause to feel shame: *My silly mistake shamed me.* 3 drive or force by shame: *be shamed into combing one's hair.* 4 a disgrace; dishonor: *bring shame to one's family.* 5 bring disgrace upon: *shame one's family.* 6 fact to be sorry about; a pity: *It is a shame to be so wasteful.* 7 person or thing to be ashamed of; cause of disgrace. 1,4,6, 7 *n.,* 2,3,5 *v.,* **shamed, sham ing. for shame!** shame on you!

put to shame, 1 disgrace; make ashamed. 2 surpass; make dim by comparison: *Your careful work has put the rest of us to shame.*

shame faced (shām′fāst′), 1 showing shame and embarrassment. 2 bashful; shy. *adj.*

shame ful (shām′fəl), causing shame; bringing disgrace. *adj.* —**shame′ful ly,** *adv.* —**shame′ful ness,** *n.*

shame less (shām′lis), 1 without shame. 2 not modest. *adj.* —**shame′less ly,** *adv.* —**shame′less ness,** *n.*

sham poo (sham pü′), 1 wash (the hair, the scalp, a rug, etc.) with a soapy or oily preparation. 2 a washing of the hair, the scalp, a rug, etc., with such a preparation. 3 the preparation used for shampooing. 1 *v.,* **sham pooed, sham poo ing;** 2,3 *n., pl.* **sham poos.**

shamrock (def. 1)

sham rock (sham′rok), 1 a bright-green leaf composed of three parts. The shamrock is the national emblem of Ireland. 2 any of various clovers that have leaves like this. *n.*

shang hai (shang′hī), 1 make unconscious by drugs, liquor, etc., and put on a ship to serve as a sailor. 2 force to do something by trickery or force. *v.,* **shang haied, shang hai ing.** [from *Shanghai* (from the practice of securing sailors by trickery or force for voyages to Shanghai)]

Shang hai (shang′hī′), seaport in E China. *n.*

shank (shangk), 1 the part of the leg between the knee and the ankle. 2 the corresponding part in animals. 3 cut of meat from the upper part of the leg of an animal. 4 the whole leg. 5 any part like a leg, stem, or shaft. The shank of a fishhook is the straight part between the hook and the loop. *n.*

Shan non (shan′ən), river flowing from N Republic of Ireland southwest into the Atlantic. It is the most important river in Ireland. *n.*

shan't (shant), shall not.

shan tung (shan′tung *or* shan tung′), 1 a rayon or cotton fabric similar to pongee and having a rough, uneven surface. 2 a heavy pongee. *n.* [from *Shantung*]

Shan tung (shan′tung′), 1 province in NE China. 2 peninsula in the E part of this province. *n.*

shan ty[1] (shan′tē), a roughly built hut or cabin. *n., pl.* **shan ties.** [from Canadian French *chantier* lumberjack's headquarters, from French *chantier* timber yard, from Latin *cantherius* framework]

shan ty[2] (shan′tē), chantey. *n., pl.* **shan ties.** [a different form of *chantey,* from French *chanter* sing]

shape (shāp), 1 the outward contour or outline; form; figure; appearance: *the shape of a triangle. A white shape stood at his bedside. A witch was supposed to take the shape of a cat or a bat.* 2 to form into a shape; mold: *The child shapes clay into balls. She shaped a clever reply.* 3 assume form; develop; take shape: *Her plan is shaping well.* 4 adapt in form: *That hat is shaped to your head.* 5 condition: *Athletes exercise to keep themselves in good shape.* 6 definite form; proper arrangement; order: *Take time to get your thoughts into shape.* 7 plan; devise; direct: *shape one's course in life.* 1,5,6 *n.,* 2-4,7 *v.,* **shaped, shap ing.**

shape up, 1 take on a certain form or appearance; develop. 2 show a certain tendency.

take shape, have or take on a definite form.

shape less (shāp′lis), 1 without definite shape: *He wore a shapeless old hat.* 2 having an unattractive shape: *a shapeless figure. adj.* —**shape′less ly,** *adv.* —**shape′less ness,** *n.*

shape li ness (shāp′lē nis), shapely condition. *n.*

shape ly (shāp′lē), having a pleasing shape; well-formed. *adj.,* **shape li er, shape li est.**

shap er (shā′pər), person or thing that shapes. *n.*

shard (shärd), piece of broken earthenware or pottery. *n.*

share[1] (sher *or* shar), 1 part belonging to one individual; portion; part: *Do your share of the work. Each of the heirs* was left an equal share of the property. 2 each of the equal parts into which the ownership of a company or corporation is divided: *The ownership of this railroad is divided into several million shares.* 3 use together; enjoy together; have in common: *The sisters share the same room.* 4 divide into parts, each taking a part: *The child shared his candy with his sister.* 5 have a share; take part: *Everyone shared in making the picnic a success.* 1,2 *n.*, 3-5 *v.*, **shared, shar ing.** [Old English *scearu* a cutting, shaving]

go shares, share in something.

share² (sher *or* shar), plowshare. *n.* [Old English *scear*]

share crop (sher′krop′ *or* shar′-krop′), farm as a sharecropper. *v.*, **share cropped, share crop ping.**

share crop per (sher′krop′ər *or* shar′krop′ər), person who farms land for the owner in return for part of the crops. *n.*

share hold er (sher′hōl′dər *or* shar′-hōl′dər), person owning shares of stock: *The railroad has many thousands of shareholders.* *n.*

shark¹—7½ to 12 ft. long

shark¹ (shärk), any of a group of fishes, mostly marine, certain kinds of which are large and ferocious, and destructive to other fishes and sometimes dangerous to man. *n.* [origin uncertain] —**shark′like′,** *adj.*

shark² (shärk), a dishonest person who preys on others. *n.* [probably from German *Schurke* scoundrel]

sharp (shärp), 1 having a thin cutting edge or a fine point: *a sharp knife, a sharp pencil.* 2 having a point; not rounded: *a sharp nose, a sharp corner on a box.* 3 with a sudden change of direction: *a sharp turn.* 4 very cold: *sharp weather, a sharp morning.* 5 severe; biting: *sharp words.* 6 feeling somewhat like a cut or prick; affecting the senses keenly: *a sharp taste, a sharp noise, a sharp pain.* 7 clear; distinct: *the sharp contrast between black and white.* 8 quick; brisk: *a sharp walk, a sharp run.* 9 fierce; violent: *a sharp struggle.* 10 keen; eager: *a sharp desire, a sharp appetite.* 11 being aware of things quickly: *a sharp eye, sharp ears.* 12 watchful; wide-awake: *keep a sharp watch.* 13 quick in mind; shrewd; clever: *a sharp boy, a sharp lawyer, sharp at a bargain.* 14 promptly; exactly: *Come at one o'clock sharp.* 15 high

in pitch; shrill. 16 above the true pitch in music: *sing sharp.* 17 one half step or half note above natural pitch in music. 18 such a tone or note: *music written in the key of F sharp.* 19 sign (♯) that shows such a tone in music. 20 in a sharp manner; in an alert manner; keenly: *Look sharp!* 21 suddenly: *pull a horse up sharp.* 22 make or become sharp. 1-13,15,17 *adj.*, 14,16,20,21 *adv.*, 18,19 *n.*, 22 *v.* —**sharp′ly,** *adv.* —**sharp′ness,** *n.*

sharp en (shär′pən), 1 make sharp: *sharpen a pencil. Sharpen your wits.* 2 become sharp. *v.* —**sharp′en er,** *n.*

sharp shoot er (shärp′shü′tər), person who shoots very well, especially with a rifle. *n.*

sharp-sight ed (shärp′sī′tid), 1 having sharp sight. 2 sharp-witted: *a sharp-sighted move.* *adj.*

sharp-wit ted (shärp′wit′id), having or showing a quick, keen mind. *adj.*

shat ter (shat′ər), 1 break into pieces: *A stone shattered the window. The glass shattered.* 2 disturb greatly; destroy: *Her hopes were shattered. The great mental strain shattered his mind.* 3 **shatters,** *pl.* fragments. 1,2 *v.*, 3 *n.*

shave (shāv), 1 remove hair with a razor; cut hair from (the face, chin, etc.) with a razor: *Father shaves every day. The actor shaved his head in order to portray a bald man.* 2 the cutting off of hair with a razor. 3 cut off (hair) with a razor. 4 cut off in thin slices: *She shaved the chocolate.* 5 cut very close. 6 come very close to; graze: *The car shaved the corner.* 7 a narrow miss or escape: *The car missed us, but it was a close shave.* 1,3-6 *v.*, **shaved, shaved** *or* **shav en, shav ing;** 2,7 *n.*

shav en (shā′vən), 1 shaved. 2 closely cut. 3 shaved; a past participle of **shave.** 1,2 *adj.*, 3 *v.*

shav er (shā′vər), 1 person who shaves. 2 instrument for shaving. 3 INFORMAL. youngster; small boy. *n.*

shav ing (shā′ving), 1 a very thin piece or slice. Shavings of wood are cut off by a plane. 2 act or process of cutting hair from the face, chin, etc., with a razor. *n.*

Shaw (shô), **George Bernard,** 1856-1950, British dramatist, critic, novelist, and social reformer, born in Ireland. *n.*

shawl (shôl), a square or oblong piece of cloth to be worn about the shoulders or head. *n.*

Shaw nee (shô nē′), member of a tribe of American Indians formerly living in eastern North America, especially Ohio, Tennessee, and South Carolina, and now living in Oklahoma. *n.*, *pl.* **Shaw nee** *or* **Shaw nees.**

shay (shā), INFORMAL. chaise, a light carriage. *n.*

hat, āge, fär; let, ēqual, tėrm; it, īce; hot, ōpen, ôrder; oil, out; cup, půt, rüle; ch, child; ng, long; sh, she; th, thin; ᴛʜ, then; zh, measure;

ə represents *a* in about, *e* in taken, *i* in pencil, *o* in lemon, *u* in circus.

Shays (shāz), **Daniel,** 1747-1825, American soldier in the Revolutionary War and leader of an uprising of farmers in Massachusetts against the state government. *n.*

she (shē), 1 girl, woman, or female animal spoken about or mentioned before: *My sister says she likes to read and her reading helps her in school.* 2 anything thought of as female and spoken about or mentioned before: *She was a fine old ship.* 3 a female: *Is the baby a he or a she?* 1,2 *pron.*, *pl.* **they;** 3 *n.*, *pl.* **shes.**

sheaf (shēf), bundle of things of the same sort: *a sheaf of wheat, a sheaf of arrows.* *n.*, *pl.* **sheaves.**

shear (shir), 1 cut with shears or scissors. 2 cut the wool or fleece from: *The farmer sheared his sheep.* 3 cut close; cut off; cut. 4 to strip or deprive as if by cutting: *The assembly had been shorn of its legislative powers.* *v.*, **sheared, sheared** *or* **shorn, shear ing.** —**shear′er,** *n.*

shears (shirz), 1 large scissors: *barber's shears.* 2 any cutting instrument resembling scissors: *grass shears, tin shears.* *n.pl.*

sheath (shēth), 1 case or covering for the blade of a sword, knife, etc. 2 any similar covering, especially on an animal or plant. 3 a narrow, tight-fitting dress with straight lines. *n.*, *pl.* **sheaths** (shēᴛʜz *or* shēths).

sheathe (shēᴛʜ), 1 put (a sword, etc.) into a sheath. 2 enclose in a case or covering: *a mummy sheathed in linen. The doors were sheathed in metal.* *v.*, **sheathed, sheath ing.**

sheath ing (shē′ᴛʜing), casing; covering. The first covering of boards on a house is sheathing. *n.*

sheave (shēv), gather and tie into a sheaf or sheaves. *v.*, **sheaved, sheaving.**

sheaves (shēvz), plural of **sheaf.** *n.*

She ba (shē′bə), 1 an ancient country in S Arabia. 2 **Queen of,** (in the Bible) a queen who visited Solomon to learn of his great wisdom. *n.*

shed¹ (shed), a building used for shelter, storage, etc., usually having only

adj.	adjective	*n.*	noun
adv.	adverb	*prep.*	preposition
conj.	conjunction	*pron.*	pronoun
interj.	interjection	*v.*	verb
sing.	singular	*pl.*	plural

one story: *a wagon shed, a train shed.* *n.* [Old English *scead* shelter]

shed[2] (shed), 1 pour out; let flow: *shed tears.* 2 cast off; let drop or fall: *The snake sheds its skin. The umbrella sheds water.* 3 get rid of: *shed one's worries, shed one's inhibitions.* 4 scatter abroad; give forth: *The sun sheds light. Flowers shed perfume.* *v.,* **shed, shed ding.** [Old English *scēadan*]

shed blood, destroy life; kill: *He will shed blood if he goes on driving like that.*

she'd (shed; *unstressed* shid), 1 she had. 2 she would.

sheen (shēn), brightness; luster. Satin and polished silver have a sheen. *n.*

sheep (def. 1)
about 3 ft. high
at the shoulder

sheep (shēp), 1 a cud-chewing mammal closely related to goats. Sheep are raised for wool, meat, and skin. 2 person who is timid, weak, or stupid. 3 leather made from the skin of sheep. *n., pl.* **sheep.** —**sheep′like′,** *adj.*

make sheep's eyes, give a longing, loving look.

sheep cote (shēp′kōt′), sheepfold. *n.*

sheep dog, collie or other dog trained to help a shepherd watch and tend sheep.

sheep fold (shēp′fōld′), pen or covered shelter for sheep. *n.*

sheep herd er (shēp′hėr′dər), person who watches and tends large numbers of sheep while they are grazing on unfenced land. *n.*

sheep ish (shē′pish), 1 awkwardly bashful or embarrassed: *a sheepish smile.* 2 like a sheep; timid; weak; stupid. *adj.* —**sheep′ish ly,** *adv.* —**sheep′ish ness,** *n.*

sheep skin (shēp′skin′), 1 skin of a sheep, especially with the wool on it. 2 leather or parchment made from the skin of a sheep. 3 INFORMAL. diploma. *n.*

sheer[1] (shir), 1 very thin; almost transparent: *She wore a sheer white dress.* 2 unmixed with anything else; complete: *sheer nonsense, sheer weariness.* 3 straight up and down; steep: *From the*

top of the wall it was a sheer drop of 100 feet to the water below. 4 completely; quite. 5 very steeply: *The cliff rose sheer from the river's edge.* 1-3 *adj.,* 4,5 *adv.* [Old English *scīr* bright] —**sheer′ness,** *n.*

sheer[2] (shir), 1 turn from a course; turn aside; swerve. 2 a turning of a ship from its course. 1 *v.,* 2 *n.* [probably from Dutch *scheren*]

sheer ly (shir′lē), absolutely; thoroughly; quite. *adv.*

sheet[1] (shēt), 1 a large piece of cotton, linen, or other cloth used to sleep on or under. 2 a broad, thin sheet of anything: *a sheet of glass.* 3 a single piece of paper. 4 newspaper. 5 a broad, flat surface: *a sheet of water.* 6 furnish or cover with a sheet. 1-5 *n.,* 6 *v.* [Old English *scēte*]

sheet[2] (shēt), rope that controls the angle at which a sail is set. *n.* [Old English *scēata* lower part of a sail]

sheet ing (shē′ting), cotton, linen, or other cloth for bed sheets.

sheet lightning, lightning in broad flashes. Sheet lightning is actually a reflection of lightning that occurs beyond the horizon.

sheet metal, metal in thin pieces or plates.

sheet music, music printed on unbound sheets of paper.

Shef field (shef′ēld), city in central England, famous for the manufacture of cutlery. *n.*

sheik or **sheikh** (shēk), 1 an Arab chief or head of a family, village, or tribe. 2 a Moslem religious leader. 3 title of respect used by Moslems. *n.*

shek el (shek′əl), 1 an ancient silver coin of the Hebrews that weighed about half an ounce. 2 an ancient unit of weight originating in Babylonia, equal to about half an ounce. *n.*

shel drake (shel′drāk′), 1 any of various large ducks of Europe and Asia. 2 merganser. *n., pl.* **shel drakes** or **shel drake.**

shelf (shelf), 1 a thin, flat piece of wood, metal, stone, etc., fastened to a wall or frame to hold things, such as books, dishes, etc. 2 anything like a shelf: *The ship hit a shelf of coral. n., pl.* **shelves.**

on the shelf, put aside as no longer useful or desirable.

shell (shel), 1 the hard outside covering of certain animals. Oysters, turtles, and beetles all have shells. 2 the hard outside covering of a nut, seed, fruit, etc. 3 the hard outside covering of an egg. 4 tortoise shell as used in combs or ornaments. 5 take out of a shell: *shell peas.* 6 separate (grains of corn) from the cob. 7 something like a shell. The framework of a house, a very light

racing boat, and a hollow case of pastry are called shells. 8 cartridge used in a rifle or shotgun. 9 a metal projectile filled with explosives that is fired by artillery and explodes on impact. 10 fire cannon at; bombard with shells: *The enemy shelled the town.* 1-4,7-9 *n.,* 5,6,10 *v.* —**shell′-like′,** *adj.*

come out of one's shell, stop being shy or reserved; join in conversation, etc., with others.

shell out, INFORMAL. 1 give something away: *shell out candy at Halloween.* 2 hand over (money); pay out: *He shelled out five dollars for the broken window.*

she'll (shel; *unstressed* shil), 1 she shall. 2 she will.

shel lac (shə lak′), 1 liquid that gives a smooth, shiny appearance to wood, metal, etc. Shellac is made from a resinous substance dissolved in alcohol. 2 put shellac on; cover with shellac. 3 INFORMAL. defeat completely. 1 *n.,* 2,3 *v.,* **shel lacked, shel lack ing.**

Shel ley (shel′ē), **Percy Bysshe,** 1792-1822, English poet. *n.*

shell fire (shel′fīr′), the firing of explosive shells or projectiles. *n.*

shell fish (shel′fish′), a water animal having a shell, especially a mollusk or a crustacean. Shellfish are very different from regular fish. Oysters, clams, crabs, and lobsters are shellfish. *n., pl.* **shell fish es** or **shell fish.**

shell proof (shel′prüf′), secure against shells, bombs, etc. *adj.*

shell shock, a nervous or mental disorder resulting from the strain of war.

shell work (shel′wėrk′), decorative work made of or made to look like sea shells. *n.*

shel ter (shel′tər), 1 something that covers or protects from weather, danger, or attack: *Trees are a shelter from the sun.* 2 protect; shield; hide: *shelter a fugitive.* 3 protection; refuge: *We took shelter from the storm in a barn.* 4 find shelter: *The sheep sheltered from the hot sun in the shade of the haystack.* 1,3 *n.,* 2,4 *v.*

shel ter less (shel′tər lis), having no shelter. *adj.*

shelve[1] (shelv), 1 put on a shelf. 2 lay aside: *Let us shelve that argument.* 3 furnish with shelves. *v.,* **shelved, shelv ing.** [from *shelf*]

shelve[2] (shelv), slope gradually. *v.,* **shelved, shelv ing.** [origin uncertain]

shelves (shelvz), plural of **shelf.** *n.*

shelv ing (shel′ving), 1 wood, metal, etc., for shelves: *The carpenter ordered 40 feet of pine shelving.* 2 shelves. *n.*

Shen an do ah (shen′ən dō′ə), river flowing through N Virginia into the Potomac River. *n.*

she nan i gans (shə nan′ə gənz), IN-

FORMAL. mischief or trickery. *n.pl.*

She ol (shē′ōl), a Hebrew name for the abode of the dead. *n.*

shep herd (shep′ərd), 1 man who takes care of sheep. 2 take care of: *He will shepherd his flock.* 3 guide; direct: *The teacher shepherded the children safely out of the burning building.* 4 person who cares for and protects. 5 a spiritual guide; pastor. 1,4,5 *n.,* 2,3 *v.*

shep herd ess (shep′ər dis), woman who takes care of sheep. *n., pl.* **shepherd ess es.**

sher bet (shėr′bət), 1 a frozen dessert made of fruit juice, sugar, and water or milk. 2 a cooling drink made of fruit juice, sugar, and water, popular in the Orient. *n.*

Sher i dan (sher′ə dən), **Philip Henry,** 1831-1888, Union general in the Civil War. *n.*

sher iff (sher′if), the most important law-enforcing officer of a county. A sheriff appoints deputies to help him keep order in the county. *n.*

Sher lock Holmes (shėr′lok). See **Holmes.**

Sher man (shėr′mən), **William Tecumseh,** 1820-1891, Union general in the Civil War. *n.*

sher ry (sher′ē), a strong wine. It varies in color from pale yellow to brown. *n., pl.* **sher ries.**

Sher wood Forest (shėr′wùd), a royal forest near Nottingham, where Robin Hood and his men are said to have lived.

she's (shēz; *unstressed* shiz), 1 she is. 2 she has.

Shet land Islands (shet′lənd), group of British islands northeast of Scotland.

Shetland pony
32 to 46 in. high at the shoulder

Shetland pony, a small, sturdy, rough-coated pony, originally from the Shetland Islands.

shew (shō), OLD USE. show. *v.,* **shewed, shew ing;** *n.*

shib bo leth (shib′ə lith), any test word, watchword, or pet phrase of a political party, a class, sect, etc. *n.* [from Hebrew *shibboleth* stream (mentioned in the Bible as the password used

to identify enemy troops who could not say *sh-* properly; Judges 12:4-6)]

shied (shīd), past tense and past participle of **shy.** *The horse shied and threw the rider. He had never shied like that before.* *v.*

shield (shēld), 1 piece of armor carried on the arm to protect the body in battle. 2 anything used to protect: *I turned up my collar as a shield against the cold wind.* 3 something shaped like a shield. 4 be a shield to; protect; defend: *They shielded me from unjust punishment.* 1-3 *n.,* 4 *v.* —**shield′like′,** *adj.*

shift (shift), 1 to move or change from one place, position, person, sound, etc., to another: *The wind has shifted to the southeast. I shifted the heavy bag from one hand to the other. She always tries to shift the blame to someone else.* 2 a change of direction, position, attitude, etc.: *a shift of the wind, a shift in policy.* 3 group of workmen who work during the same period of time: *They are on the night shift.* 4 time during which such a group works. 5 way of getting on; scheme; trick: *The child tried every shift to avoid going to bed.* 6 manage to get along; contrive: *I left home at an early age, and had to shift for myself.* 7 change the position of (the gears of an automobile). 1,6,7 *v.,* 2-5 *n.* —**shift′er,** *n.*

make shift, 1 manage to get along; do as well as one can. 2 manage with effort or difficulty.

shift i ly (shif′tə lē), in a shifty manner. *adv.*

shift i ness (shif′tē nis), character or quality of being shifty. *n.*

shift less (shift′lis), lazy; inefficient. *adj.* —**shift′less ly,** *adv.* —**shift′lessness,** *n.*

shift y (shif′tē), 1 full of shifts; quick-witted; inventive. 2 not straightforward; tricky: *shifty eyes, a shifty person.* *adj.,* **shift i er, shift i est.**

shil ling (shil′ing), 1 former unit of money in Great Britain equal to ¹/₂₀ of a pound and worth about 12 cents. 2 a British coin equal to one shilling. *n.*

shil ly-shal ly (shil′ē shal′ē), 1 vacillating; wavering; hesitating; undecided. 2 in a vacillating or hesitating manner. 3 be undecided; vacillate; hesitate. 4 inability to decide; hesitation. 1 *adj.,* 2 *adv.,* 3 *v.,* **shil ly-shal lied, shil ly-shal ly ing;** 4 *n.*

shim mer (shim′ər), 1 gleam faintly: *The satin shimmers.* 2 a faint gleam or shine: *The pearls have a beautiful shimmer.* 1 *v.,* 2 *n.*

shim mer y (shim′ər ē), shimmering; gleaming softly. *adj.*

shim my (shim′ē), 1 an unusual shaking or vibration: *a dangerous shimmy of a ladder.* 2 to shake; vibrate. 1 *n., pl.*

shim mies; 2 *v.,* **shim mied, shimmy ing.**

shin (shin), 1 the front part of the leg from the knee to the ankle. 2 climb by clasping or holding fast with the hands or arms and legs and drawing oneself up: *shin up a tree.* 1 *n.,* 2 *v.,* **shinned, shin ning.**

shin bone (shin′bōn′), the inner and thicker of the two bones of the leg between the knee and the ankle; tibia. *n.*

shin dig (shin′dig), INFORMAL. a merry, noisy dance, party, etc. *n.*

shine (shīn), 1 send out light; be bright with light; reflect light; glow: *The sun shines. His face is shining with soap and water.* 2 light; brightness: *the shine of a lamp.* 3 luster; polish. Silk has a shine. 4 fair weather; sunshine: *He goes to school rain or shine.* 5 do very well; be brilliant; excel: *She shines in school.* 6 make bright; polish: *shine shoes.* 7 polish; put on shoes. 8 cause to shine: *shine a light.* 1,5,6,8 *v.,* **shone** (or **shined** especially for 6), **shin ing;** 2-4,7 *n.*

shine up to, SLANG. try to please and get the friendship of.

take a shine to, SLANG. become fond of; like.

shin er (shī′nər), 1 person or thing that shines. 2 a small American freshwater fish with glistening scales. 3 SLANG. black eye. *n.*

shin gle¹ (shing′gəl), 1 a thin piece of wood, etc., used to cover roofs, walls, etc. Shingles are laid in overlapping rows with the thicker ends showing. 2 cover with shingles: *shingle a roof.* 3 a small signboard, especially one out-

shingle¹ (def. 1)—shingles on a roof

---

adj.	adjective	*n.*	noun
adv.	adverb	*prep.*	preposition
conj.	conjunction	*pron.*	pronoun
interj.	interjection	*v.*	verb
sing.	singular	*pl.*	plural

side a doctor's or lawyer's office. **4** cut (the hair) short. **5** a short haircut. 1,3,5 *n.*, 2,4 *v.*, **shin gled, shin gling.** [a different form of earlier *shindle*, from Latin *scindula*]

shin gle² (shing′gəl), loose stones or pebbles such as lie on the seashore; coarse gravel. *n.* [origin uncertain]

shin gles (shing′gəlz), a virus disease that causes pain in certain nerves and an outbreak of spots and blisters on the skin in the area of the affected nerves. *n. sing. or pl.*

shin gly (shing′glē), consisting of or covered with small, loose stones or pebbles: *a shingly beach. adj.*

shin i ness (shī′nē nis), shiny character or condition; sheen. *n.*

shin ing (shī′ning), that shines; brilliant; outstanding. *adj.*

shin ny¹ (shin′ē), **1** a simple kind of hockey, played with a ball or the like and clubs curved at one end. **2** play shinny. 1 *n., pl.* **shin nies;** 2 *v.*, **shinnied, shin ny ing.** [origin uncertain]

shin ny² (shin′ē), INFORMAL. to shin; climb. *v.*, **shin nied, shin ny ing.** [from *shin*]

Shin to (shin′tō), the native religion of Japan, primarily a system of nature worship and ancestor worship. *n.*

Shin to ism (shin′tō iz′əm), the Shinto religion. *n.*

shin y (shī′nē), **1** shining; bright: *a shiny new penny.* **2** worn to a glossy smoothness: *a coat shiny from hard wear. adj.*, **shin i er, shin i est.**

ship (ship), **1** any large vessel for travel on water, such as a steamship, frigate, or galley. **2** a large sailing vessel, especially one with three masts and a bowsprit. **3** an airship, airplane, spacecraft, etc. **4** officers and crew of a ship. **5** put or take on board a ship. **6** go on board a ship. **7** travel on a ship; sail. **8** send or carry from one place to another by a ship, train, truck, etc.: *Did you ship it by express or by freight?* **9** INFORMAL. send off; get rid of. **10** engage for service on a ship: *The captain is shipping a new crew.* **11** take a job on a ship: *He shipped as cook.* **12** take in (water) over the side, as a boat does when the waves break over it. **13** fix in a ship or boat in its proper

place for use: *ship a rudder.* 1-4 *n.*, 5-13 *v.*, **shipped, ship ping.**

when one's ship comes home or **when one's ship comes in,** when one's fortune is made; when one has money.

-ship, *suffix forming nouns from other nouns.* **1** office, position, or occupation of _____: *Governorship = office of governor. Authorship = occupation of an author.* **2** quality or condition of being _____: *Partnership = condition of being a partner.* **3** act, power, or skill of _____: *Craftsmanship = skill of a craftsman.* **4** relation between _____s: *Companionship = relation between companions.* [Old English *-scipe*]

ship biscuit, hardtack.

ship board (ship′bôrd′). **on shipboard,** on or inside a ship. *n.*

ship build er (ship′bil′dər), person who designs or constructs ships. *n.*

ship build ing (ship′bil′ding), **1** the building of ships. **2** the art of building ships. *n.*

ship load (ship′lōd′), a full load for a ship. *n.*

ship mas ter (ship′mas′tər), master, commander, or captain of a ship. *n.*

ship mate (ship′māt′), a fellow sailor on a ship. *n.*

ship ment (ship′mənt), **1** act of shipping goods: *A thousand boxes of oranges were ready for shipment.* **2** goods sent at one time to a person or company: *We received two shipments of boxes from the factory. n.*

ship own er (ship′ō′nər), person who owns a ship or ships. *n.*

ship per (ship′ər), person who ships goods. *n.*

ship ping (ship′ing), **1** the sending of goods by water, rail, etc. **2** ships: *Much of the world's shipping passes through the Panama Canal each year.* **3** their total tonnage. **4** the ships of a nation, city, or business: *British merchant shipping. n.*

ship shape (ship′shāp′), **1** in good order; trim. **2** in a trim, neat manner. **1** *adj.,* **2** *adv.*

ship worm (ship′wėrm′), any of various mollusks having long, wormlike bodies, which burrow into the timbers of ships, etc. *n.*

ship wreck (ship′rek′), **1** destruction or loss of a ship: *Only two people were saved from the shipwreck.* **2** a wrecked ship. **3** destruction; ruin: *The shipwreck of her plans discouraged her.* **4** wreck, ruin, or destroy. **5** suffer shipwreck. 1-3 *n.*, 4,5 *v.*

ship yard (ship′yärd′), place near the water where ships are built or repaired. *n.*

shire (shīr), one of the counties into which Great Britain is divided, es-

pecially one whose name ends in *-shire: Yorkshire. n.*

shirk (shėrk), **1** avoid or get out of doing (work, a duty, etc.): *He lost his job because he shirked his responsibilities.* **2** person who shirks or does not do his share. 1 *v.,* 2 *n.* **—shirk′er,** *n.*

shirr (shėr), **1** draw up or gather (cloth) on parallel threads. **2** a shirred arrangement of cloth, etc. **3** bake (eggs) in a shallow dish with butter, etc. 1,3 *v.,* 2 *n.*

shirr (def. 2)

shirt (shėrt), **1** garment for the upper part of the body. **2** undershirt. *n.* **—shirt′like′,** *adj.*

keep one's shirt on, SLANG. stay calm; keep one's temper.

shirt ing (shėr′ting), cloth for shirts. *n.*

shirt less (shėrt′lis), without a shirt or shirts. *adj.*

shirt waist (shėrt′wāst′), **1** a woman's or girl's loose waist or blouse, worn with a separate skirt. **2** a one-piece dress with a shirtlike top. **3** having a bodice that resembles a shirt. 1,2 *n.,* 3 *adj.*

shiv er¹ (shiv′ər), **1** shake with cold, fear, etc.: *I crept shivering into bed.* **2** a shaking from cold, fear, etc. 1 *v.,* 2 *n.* [Middle English *schiveren*] **—shiv′er er,** *n.*

shiv er² (shiv′ər), **1** break into small pieces: *He shivered the mirror with a hammer.* **2** a small piece; splinter: *There were shivers of glass on the floor.* 1 *v.,* 2 *n.* [origin uncertain]

shiv er y (shiv′ər ē), **1** quivering from cold, fear, etc.; shivering. **2** inclined to shiver from cold. **3** chilly. **4** causing shivers. *adj.*

shoal¹ (shōl), **1** place in a sea, lake, or stream where the water is shallow. **2** sandbank or sand bar that makes the water shallow, especially one which can be seen at low tide: *The ship was wrecked on the shoals.* **3** shallow. **4** become shallow. 1,2 *n.,* 3 *adj.,* 4 *v.* [Old English *sceald* shallow (*adj.*)]

shoal² (shōl), **1** a large number; crowd: *We saw a shoal of fish in the water.* **2** form into a shoal; crowd together. 1 *n.,* 2 *v.* [perhaps Old English *scolu* host (of people), school of fish]

shoat (shōt), a young pig that no longer suckles. *n.* Also, **shote.**

shock¹ (shok), **1** a sudden, violent shake, blow, or crash: *Earthquake* *shocks are often felt in Japan.* **2** a sudden, violent, or upsetting disturbance: *His death was a great shock to his family.* **3** cause to feel surprise, horror, or disgust: *That child's bad language shocks everyone.* **4** condition of physical collapse or depression, together with a sudden drop in blood pressure, often resulting in unconsciousness. Shock may set in after a severe injury, great loss of blood, or a sudden emotional disturbance. **5** disturbance produced by an electric current passing through the body. **6** give an electric shock to. **1,2,4,5** *n.,* **3,6** *v.* [probably from French *choc*] —**shock′er,** *n.*

shock² (shok), **1** group of cornstalks or bundles of grain set up on end together in order to dry. **2** make into shocks. **1** *n.,* **2** *v.* [Middle English *schokke*] —**shock′er,** *n.*

shock³ (shok), a thick, bushy mass: *a shock of red hair. n.* [origin uncertain]

shock ab sorb er (ab sôr′bər), **1** anything that absorbs or lessens shocks. **2** device consisting of springs, hydraulic pistons, etc., used on automobiles, airplanes, etc., to absorb the force of sudden impacts.

shock ing (shok′ing), **1** causing intense and painful surprise: *shocking news.* **2** offensive; disgusting; revolting: *a shocking sight.* **3** INFORMAL. very bad: *shocking manners. adj.* —**shock′ing ly,** *adv.*

shock troops, troops chosen and specially trained for making attacks.

shock wave, disturbance of the atmosphere created by the movement of an aircraft, rocket, etc., at a velocity greater than that of sound.

shod (shod), past tense and past participle of **shoe.** *The blacksmith shod the horses. They had never been shod before. v.*

shod di ly (shod′l ē), in a shoddy manner. *adv.*

shod di ness (shod′ē nis), shoddy quality or condition. *n.*

shod dy (shod′ē), **1** an inferior kind of wool made of woolen waste, old rags, yarn, etc. **2** made of woolen waste. **3** cloth made of woolen waste. **4** anything inferior made to look like what is better. **5** pretending to be better than it is: *a shoddy necklace.* **6** mean; shabby: *shoddy treatment, a shoddy trick.* **1,3,4** *n., pl.* **shod dies; 2,5,6** *adj.,* **shod di er, shod di est.**

shoe (shü), **1** an outer covering for a person's foot. Shoes are usually made of leather. **2** thing like a shoe in shape or use. **3** a horseshoe. **4** the part of a brake that presses on a wheel to slow it down or stop it. **5** furnish with a shoe or shoes: *A blacksmith shoes horses. Her feet were shod with silver slippers.*

6 protect or arm at the point; edge or face with metal: *a stick shod with steel.* **1-4** *n.,* **5,6** *v.,* **shod, shoe ing.**

in another's shoes, in another's place, situation, or circumstances.

shoe horn (shü′hôrn′), a curved piece of metal, horn, etc., used to help slip a shoe more easily over the heel. *n.*

shoe lace (shü′lās′), cord, braid, or leather strip for fastening a shoe. *n.*

shoe less (shü′lis), without a shoe or shoes. *adj.*

shoe mak er (shü′mā′kər), person who makes or mends shoes. *n.*

shoe string (shü′string′), **1** shoelace. **2** INFORMAL. a very small amount of money used to start or carry on a business, investment, etc.: *The company was formed on a shoestring. n.*

shoe tree, a shaped block inserted into a shoe to keep it in shape or to stretch it.

sho far (shō′fär *or* shō′fər), a ram's horn sounded during certain Jewish religious services, especially on Rosh Hashanah and Yom Kippur. *n., pl.* **sho froth** (shō′frōs *or* shō frōt′).

shone (shōn), a past tense and a past participle of **shine.** *The sun shone all last week. It has not shone since. v.*

shoo (shü), **1** an exclamation used to scare away hens, birds, etc. **2** scare or drive away by calling "Shoo!": *Shoo those flies away from the sugar.* **1** *interj.,* **2** *v.,* **shooed, shoo ing.**

shook (shuk), past tense of **shake.** *They shook hands. v.*

shoon (shün), OLD USE. a plural of **shoe.** *n.*

shoot (shüt), **1** hit, wound, or kill with a bullet, arrow, etc.: *He shot a rabbit.* **2** send swiftly: *A bow shoots an arrow. She shot question after question at us.* **3** fire or use (a gun, etc.): *shoot a rifle. They shot at the target.* **4** send a bullet: *This gun shoots straight.* **5** a trip, party, or contest for shooting. **6** move suddenly and swiftly: *A car shot by us. Flames shot up from the burning house.* **7** pass quickly along, through, over, or under: *Only a shallow boat can shoot this stretch of rapids.* **8** go sharply through part of the body: *Pain shot up her arm from her hurt finger.* **9** come forth from the ground; grow; grow rapidly: *Buds shoot forth in the spring. The corn is shooting up in the warm weather.* **10** a new part growing out; young branch: *The rosebush is putting out new shoots.* **11** take (a picture) with a camera; photograph. **12** project sharply: *a cape that shoots out into the sea.* **13** a sloping trough for conveying coal, grain, etc., to a lower level; chute. **14** propel (a marble) with the thumb and forefinger. **15** vary with some different color, etc.: *Her dress*

hat, āge, fär; let, ēqual, tèrm;
it, īce; hot, ōpen, ôrder;
oil, out; cup, pùt, rüle; ch, child;
ng, long; sh, she; th, thin;
ᴛʜ, then; zh, measure;

ə represents *a* in about,
e in taken, *i* in pencil,
o in lemon, *u* in circus.

was shot with threads of gold. **16** send (a ball, puck, etc.) toward the goal, pocket, etc. **1-4,6-9,11,12,14-16** *v.,* **shot, shoot ing; 5,10,13** *n.* —**shoot′er,** *n.*

shooting star, meteor.

shop (shop), **1** place where things are sold at retail; store: *a small dress shop.* **2** visit stores to look at or to buy things: *We shopped all morning for a coat.* **3** place where things are made or repaired: *He works in a carpenter's shop.* **4** place where a certain kind of work is done: *We got our hair cut at a barber shop.* **1,3,4** *n.,* **2** *v.,* **shopped, shop ping.**

set up shop, start work or business.

shut up shop, give up work or business.

talk shop, talk about one's work or occupation.

shop keep er (shop′kē′pər), person who owns or manages a shop or store. *n.*

shop lift er (shop′lif′tər), person who steals goods from a shop while pretending to be a customer. *n.*

shop lift ing (shop′lif′ting), a stealing goods from a shop while pretending to be a customer. *n.*

shop per (shop′ər), person who visits stores to look at or buy things. *n.*

shop ping (shop′ing), act of visiting stores to look at or to buy things: *We do our shopping on Saturday. n.*

go shopping, go to a store or stores in order to buy groceries, clothes, etc.: *Let's go shopping downtown.*

shopping center, group of stores built as a unit on or near a main road, especially in a suburban or new community. Most shopping centers have large areas for parking automobiles.

shop talk (shop′tôk′), talk about one's work or occupation, especially outside of working hours. *n.*

shop worn (shop′wôrn′), soiled by being displayed or handled in a store. *adj.*

shore¹ (shôr), **1** the land at the edge of a sea, lake, etc. **2** land near a sea. **3** land: *Our marines serve on both the*

shore

sea and shore. *n.* [Middle English *schore*]

off shore, in or on the water, not far from the shore.

shore² (shôr), 1 a prop placed against or beneath something to support it. 2 to prop up or support with shores. 1 *n.,* 2 *v.,* **shored, shor ing.** [Middle English *schore,* perhaps from Dutch of the 1300's *schore* a prop]

shore² (def. 1)
shores supporting
a ship frame

shore bird, any bird that frequents the shores of seas, inlets, lakes, etc.

shore line (shôr′lin′), line where shore and water meet. *n.*

shore ward (shôr′wərd), toward the shore: *The winds blew shoreward* (*adv.*). *We felt the shoreward breeze* (*adj.*). *adv., adj.*

shorn (shôrn), 1 a past participle of **shear.** *The sheep was shorn of his wool.* 2 sheared. 1 *v.,* 2 *adj.*

short (shôrt), 1 not long; of small extent from end to end: *a short distance, a short time, a short street.* 2 not tall: *a short man, short grass.* 3 not coming up to the right amount, measure, standard, etc.: *The cashier is short in her accounts.* 4 not having enough; scanty: *The prisoners were kept on short allowance of food.* 5 so brief as to be rude: *She was so short with me that I felt hurt.* 6 so as to be or make short. 7 in a short manner; abruptly; suddenly: *The horse stopped short.* 8 briefly. 9 breaking or crumbling easily; crisp or crumbly. Pastry is made short with butter or other shortening. 10 (of vowels or syllables) taking a comparatively short time to speak. The vowels are short in *fat, net, pin, not, up.* 11 something short. 12 **shorts,** *pl.* **a** short, loose trousers reaching to above the knees. Shorts are worn by men, women, or children in hot weather or when playing tennis, running races, etc. **b** a similar men's or boys' undergarment. 13 a short circuit. 14 to short-circuit. 1-5,9,10 *adj.,* 6-8 *adv.,* 11-13 *n.,* 14 *v.* —**short′ness,** *n.*

cut short, end suddenly; interrupt: *Sickness cut short my vacation.*

fall short, 1 fail to reach. 2 be insufficient.

for short, in order to make shorter: *Robert was called Rob for short.*

in short, briefly.

run short, 1 not have enough. 2 not be enough.

short for, a shortened form of: *The word "phone" is short for "telephone."*

short of, 1 not up to; less than: *Nothing short of your best work will satisfy me.* 2 not having enough of. 3 on the near side of.

short age (shôr′tij), too small an amount; lack; deficiency: *a shortage of grain due to poor crops.* *n.*

short bread (shôrt′bred′), a rich cake or cookie that crumbles easily. *n.*

short cake (shôrt′kāk′), 1 cake made of rich biscuit dough and shortening, covered or filled with berries or other fruit. 2 a sweet cake filled with fruit. *n.*

short-change (shôrt′chānj′), 1 give less than the right change to. 2 cheat. *v.,* **short-changed, short-chang ing.**

short circuit, an electrical circuit, usually formed accidentally by worn or faulty wiring, which has such low resistance that an excess of current flows through it, by-passing the main circuit. A short circuit may cause a fire unless it blows a fuse or activates a circuit breaker.

short-cir cuit (shôrt′sèr′kit), 1 make a short circuit in. 2 make a short circuit. *v.*

short com ing (shôrt′kum′ing), flaw in one's character or conduct; fault; defect: *Rudeness is a shortcoming.* *n.*

short cut (shôrt′kut′), a less distant or quicker way. *n.*

short en (shôrt′n), 1 make shorter; cut off: *The new highway shortens the trip. I've had my coat shortened.* 2 become shorter: *The days shorten in November in this country.* 3 make rich with butter, lard, etc.: *shorten a cake.* 4 take in (sail). *v.* —**short′en er,** *n.*

short en ing (shôrt′n ing), 1 butter, lard, or other fat, used to make pastry, cake, etc., crisp or crumbly. 2 act of a person or thing that shortens. *n.*

shorthand (def. 2) for "Your letter
was received today." (Gregg system)

short hand (shôrt′hand′), 1 method of rapid writing which uses symbols or abbreviations in place of letters, words, phrases, etc.; stenography. 2 writing in such symbols. *n.*

short-hand ed (shôrt′han′did), not

having enough workmen or helpers. *adj.*

short horn (shôrt′hôrn′), one of a breed of cattle with short horns, raised for beef. *n.*

short-lived (shôrt′līvd′ or shôrt′-livd′), living only a short time; lasting a short time. *adj.*

short ly (shôrt′lē), 1 in a short time; before long; soon: *I will be with you shortly.* 2 in a few words; briefly. 3 briefly and rudely; curtly. *adv.*

short-range (shôrt′rānj′), not reaching far in time or distance; not long-range: *a short-range forecast.* *adj.*

short shrift, little or no consideration, mercy, or delay in dealing with a person or problem: *Violators of these new regulations will get short shrift.*

short-sight ed (shôrt′si′tid), 1 near-sighted. 2 lacking in foresight; not prudent. *adj.* —**short′-sight′ed ness,** *n.*

short stop (shôrt′stop′), a baseball player stationed between second and third base. *n.*

short story, a prose story which usually describes a single event, has a limited number of characters, and is much shorter than a novel.

short-tem pered (shôrt′tem′pərd), easily made angry; quick-tempered. *adj.*

short wave (shôrt′wāv′), 1 a radio wave having a wavelength of 60 meters or less. 2 transmit by short waves: *The President's speech was shortwaved overseas.* 1 *n.,* 2 *v.,* **short waved, short wav ing.**

short-wind ed (shôrt′win′did), getting out of breath very easily or too quickly; having difficulty in breathing. *adj.*

Sho sho ne (shō shō′nē), member of a tribe of American Indians of Wyoming, Idaho, Utah, Colorado, and Nevada. *n., pl.* **Sho sho nes** or **Sho sho ne.**

Shos ta ko vich (shos′tə kō′vich), **Dimitri,** born 1906, Russian composer. *n.*

shot¹ (shot), 1 discharge of a gun or cannon: *We heard two shots.* 2 act of shooting. 3 tiny balls of lead, steel, etc.; bullets. 4 a single ball of lead, steel, etc., for a gun or cannon. 5 an attempt to hit by shooting: *That was a good shot, and it hit the mark.* 6 the distance a weapon can shoot; range: *We were within rifle shot of the fort.* 7 person who shoots: *He is a good shot.* 8 something like a shot. An aimed throw or stroke in a game is sometimes called a shot. 9 INFORMAL. injection of a vaccine or drug: *a polio shot, a tetanus shot.* 10 a remark aimed at some person or thing. 11 an attempt; try: *take a shot at the job.* 12 to attempt; try. 13 a heavy metal ball used in the shot-put.

14 picture taken with a camera; motion-picture record of a scene. 1-11,13,14 *n., pl.* **shots** (or **shot** or **shots** for 3); 12 *v.,* **shot ted, shotting.** [Old English *sceot,* from *scēotan* to shoot]

shot through with, full of: *a composition shot through with errors.*

shot[2] (shot), 1 past tense and past participle of **shoot.** *Many years ago he shot a rival and was himself shot in revenge.* 2 woven so as to show a play of colors: *blue silk shot with gold.* 3 SLANG. that has been used up, worn out, or ruined. 1 *v.,* 2,3 *adj.*

shote (shōt), shoat. *n.*

shotgun
above, double-barreled shotgun;
below, detail of gun opened for loading.

shot gun (shot′gun′), gun with no grooves in its barrel, for firing cartridges filled with small shot. *n.*

shot-put (shot′put′), contest in which a person sends a heavy metal ball through the air as far as he can with one push. *n.*

should (shud), 1 past tense of **shall.** "I said that I should come next week" means that I said, "I shall come next week." 2 ought to: *You should try to make fewer mistakes.* 3 *Should* is used to express uncertainty. *If it should rain, I should not go.* 4 *Should* is used in speaking of something which might have happened but did not. *I should have gone if you had asked me.* 5 *Should* is used to express a condition or reason for something. *He was pardoned on the condition that he should leave the country.* *v.*

shoul der (shōl′dər), 1 the part of the body to which an arm, foreleg, or wing is attached. 2 the part of a garment that covers a shoulder. 3 **shoulders,** *pl.* the two shoulders and the part of the back between them: *The man carried a trunk on his shoulders.* 4 cut of meat consisting of an upper foreleg and its adjoining parts. 5 take upon or support with the shoulder or shoulders: *shoulder a tray.* 6 bear (a burden, blame, etc.); assume (responsibility, expense, etc.): *She shouldered the responsibility of sending her niece to college.* 7 something that sticks out like a shoulder: *the shoulder of a hill.* 8 edge of a road, often unpaved. 9 push with the shoulders: *shoulder one's way through a crowd.* 1-4,7,8 *n.,* 5,6,9 *v.*

put one's shoulder to the wheel, make a great effort.

shoulder to shoulder, 1 side by side; together. 2 with united effort.

straight from the shoulder, frankly; directly.

turn a cold shoulder to, show dislike for; shun; avoid.

shoulder blade, the flat, triangular bone of either shoulder, in the upper back; scapula.

shoulder strap, 1 strap worn over the shoulder to hold a garment up. 2 an ornamental strip fastened on the shoulder of an officer's uniform to show his rank.

should n't (shud′nt), should not.

shouldst (shudst), OLD USE. should. "Thou shouldst" means "you should." *v.*

shout (shout), 1 call or cry loudly and vigorously: *I shouted for help when the boat sank. Somebody shouted, "Fire!" The crowd shouted with laughter.* 2 a loud, vigorous call or cry: *Shouts of joy rang through the halls.* 3 talk or laugh very loudly. 4 a loud outburst of laughter. 5 express by a shout or shouts. 1,3,5 *v.,* 2,4 *n.* —**shout′er,** *n.*

shout down, to silence by very loud talk.

shove (shuv), 1 move forward or along by the application of force from behind; push: *She shoved the bookcase into place.* 2 push roughly or rudely; jostle: *Someone shoved me out of the line. The people shoved to get on the crowded bus.* 3 a push: *We gave the boat a shove which sent it far out into the water.* 1,2 *v.,* **shoved, shov ing;** 3 *n.*

shove off, 1 push away from the shore; row away. 2 SLANG. leave a place; start on one's way.

shov el (shuv′əl), 1 tool with a broad blade or scoop attached to a long handle, used to lift and throw loose matter: *a coal shovel, a snow shovel.* 2 lift and throw with a shovel: *They shoveled the sand into the truck.* 3 make with a shovel: *They shoveled a path through the snow.* 4 a shovelful. 5 throw or lift as if with a shovel: *The hungry child greedily shoveled the food into her mouth.* 1,4 *n.,* 2,3,5 *v.*

shov el er (shuv′ə lər), 1 person or thing that shovels. 2 kind of freshwater duck with a broad, flat bill. *n.*

shov el ful (shuv′əl ful), as much as a shovel can hold. *n., pl.* **shov el fuls.**

show (shō), 1 let be seen; put in sight; display: *She showed me her rock collection. The dog showed its teeth.* 2 reveal; manifest; disclose: *show great energy, show signs of fear.* 3 be in sight; appear; be seen: *Anger showed in his face. The hole in her sock shows above her shoe.* 4 point out: *They showed us the way to town.* 5 direct;

hat, āge, fär; let, ēqual, tėrm;
it, īce; hot, ōpen, ôrder;
oil, out; cup, pùt, rüle; ch, child;
ng, long; sh, she; th, thin;
ŦH, then; zh, measure;

ə represents *a* in about,
e in taken, *i* in pencil,
o in lemon, *u* in circus.

guide: *Show them out.* 6 make clear; explain. 7 make clear to; explain to: *Show us how to do the problem.* 8 prove: *She showed that it was true.* 9 grant; give: *show mercy, show favor.* 10 a display: *The jewels made a fine show.* 11 a display for effect: *He put on a show of learning to impress us.* 12 any kind of public exhibition or display: *We are going to the flower show and to the automobile show.* 13 a play, motion picture, etc., or a performance of one of these: *The new show is a western. The late show starts at 11:00.* 14 a showing: *The club voted by a show of hands.* 15 appearance: *There is some show of truth in his excuse.* 16 false appearance; pretense: *hide one's dislike by a show of friendship.* 17 trace; indication: *a show of oil in a region.* 18 INFORMAL. entertainment. 19 object of scorn; something odd; queer sight: *Don't make a show of yourself.* 1-9 *v.,* **showed, shown** or **showed, showing;** 10-19 *n.*

for show, for effect; to attract attention.

show off, make a show (of); display (one's good points, etc.): *The toddler liked to show off his new shoes.*

show up, 1 expose. 2 stand out. 3 INFORMAL. put in an appearance.

show bill, poster, placard, or the like, advertising a show.

show boat (shō′bōt′), a river steamboat with a theater for plays. Showboats carry their own actors and make frequent stops to give performances. *n.*

show business, the industry or world of entertainment.

show case (shō′kās′), 1 a glass case to display and protect articles in a store, museum, etc. 2 any display or exhibit. *n.*

show down (shō′doun′), INFORMAL. a forced disclosure of facts, purposes, methods, etc. *n.*

show er (shou′ər), 1 a short fall of rain. 2 rain for a short time. 3 wet with a shower; spray; sprinkle. 4 anything like a fall of rain: *a shower of hail, a shower of tears, a shower of sparks from an engine.* 5 come in a shower. 6 send

adj.	adjective	*n.*	noun
adv.	adverb	*prep.*	preposition
conj.	conjunction	*pron.*	pronoun
interj.	interjection	*v.*	verb
sing.	singular	*pl.*	plural

in a shower; pour down: *Her rich aunt showered gifts upon her.* **7** party for giving presents to a woman about to be married or on some other special occasion. **8** shower bath. **9** take a shower bath. 1,4,7,8 *n.*, 2,3,5,6,9 *v.*

shower bath, 1 bath in which water pours down on the body from an overhead nozzle. 2 apparatus for such a bath.

show er y (shou′ər ē), 1 raining in showers. 2 having many showers. 3 like a shower. *adj.*

show i ly (shō′ə lē), in a showy manner. *adv.*

show i ness (shō′ē nis), quality of being showy; display. *n.*

show ing (shō′ing), 1 show; display; exhibition: *a current showing of paintings.* 2 manner of appearance or performance: *make a good showing. n.*

show man (shō′mən), 1 person who manages a show. 2 person skilled in presenting things in a dramatic and exciting way. *n., pl.* **show men.**

show man ship (shō′mən ship), skill or practice of a showman. *n.*

shown (shōn), a past participle of **show.** *We were shown many tricks by the magician. v.*

show-off (shō′ôf′), 1 a showing off. 2 INFORMAL. person who shows off by always calling attention to himself: *That athlete is a terrible show-off. n.*

show piece (shō′pēs′), anything displayed as an outstanding example of its kind. *n.*

show room (shō′rüm′ or shō′rum′), room used for the display of goods or merchandise. *n.*

show window, window in the front of a store, where things are shown for sale.

show y (shō′ē), 1 making a display; likely to attract attention; striking; conspicuous: *Peacocks are showy birds.* 2 too bright and gay to be in good taste. 3 ostentatious. *adj.,* **show i er, show i est.**

shrank (shrangk), a past tense of **shrink.** *My shirt shrank in the wash. v.*

shrap nel (shrap′nəl), 1 shell filled with fragments of metal and powder, set to explode in midair and scatter the fragments over a wide area. 2 fragments scattered by such a shell. *n.*

[from Henry *Shrapnel,* 1761-1842, a British army officer, who invented it]

shred (shred), 1 a very small piece torn off or cut off; very narrow strip; scrap: *The wind tore the sail to shreds.* 2 fragment; particle; bit: *There's not a shred of evidence that he took the money.* 3 tear or cut into small pieces: *Shredded paper is used in packing dishes.* 1,2 *n.*, 3 *v.*, **shred ded** or **shred, shred ding.**

shrew (shrü), 1 a bad-tempered, quarrelsome woman. 2 a mouselike mammal with a long snout and brownish fur. Shrews eat insects and worms. *n.*

shrew (def. 2)—6 in. long with tail

shrewd (shrüd), having a sharp mind; showing a keen wit; clever; keen; sharp: *She is a shrewd lawyer. adj.* —**shrewd′ly,** *adv.* —**shrewd′ness,** *n.*

shrew ish (shrü′ish), scolding or bad-tempered. *adj.* —**shrew′ish ly,** *adv.* —**shrew′ish ness,** *n.*

shriek (shrēk), 1 a loud, sharp, shrill sound: *We heard the shriek of the engine's whistle.* 2 make a loud, sharp, shrill sound. People sometimes shriek because of terror, anger, pain, or amusement. 3 utter loudly and shrilly. 1 *n.*, 2,3 *v.*

shrift (shrift), OLD USE. 1 confession to a priest, followed by the imposing of penance and the granting of absolution. 2 act of shriving. *n.*

shrike (shrīk), bird with a strong, hooked beak that feeds on large insects, frogs, and sometimes on other birds. *n.*

shrill (shril), 1 having a high pitch; high and sharp in sound; piercing: *Crickets, locusts, and katydids make shrill noises.* 2 make a shrill sound; sound sharply. 1 *adj.*, 2 *v.* —**shrill′ness,** *n.*

shril ly (shril′ē), in shrill tones. *adv.*

shrimp (shrimp), 1 a small, long-tailed shellfish. Some shrimps are used for food. 2 a small or insignificant person. *n., pl.* **shrimps** (or **shrimp** for 1). —**shrimp′like′,** *adj.*

shrine (shrīn), 1 a sacred place; place where sacred things are kept. A shrine may be the tomb of a saint, an altar in a church, or a box holding a holy object. 2 any place or object sacred because of its history; something sacred because of memories connected with it: *America sometimes is called freedom's shrine. Shakespeare's birthplace is visited as a shrine. n.*

shrink (shringk), 1 draw back: *The dog shrank from the whip. That shy girl*

shrinks from meeting strangers. 2 become smaller: *My wool sweater shrank when it was washed. When his influence began to shrink, his wealth also began to decrease.* 3 make smaller; cause to contract: *Hot water shrinks wool.* 4 SLANG. psychiatrist. 1-3 *v.*, **shrank** or **shrunk, shrunk** or **shrunk en, shrink ing;** 4 *n.* —**shrink′er,** *n.*

shrink age (shring′kij), 1 act or process of shrinking. 2 the amount or degree of shrinking: *a shrinkage of two inches in the length of a sleeve. n.*

shrive (shrīv), OLD USE. 1 hear the confession of, impose penance on, and grant absolution to. 2 make confession. *v.,* **shrove** or **shrived, shriv en** or **shrived, shriv ing.**

shriv el (shriv′əl), dry up; wither; shrink and wrinkle: *The hot sunshine shriveled the grass. v.*

shriv en (shriv′ən), OLD USE. a past participle of **shrive.** *v.*

shroud (shroud), 1 cloth or garment in which a dead person is wrapped or dressed for burial. 2 to wrap or dress for burial. 3 something that covers, conceals, or veils: *The fog was a shroud over the city.* 4 cover; conceal; veil: *plans shrouded in secrecy.* 5 a rope from a mast to the side of a ship. Shrouds help support the mast. 1,3,5 *n.*, 2,4 *v.*

SHROUDS

shrouds (def. 5)

shrove (shrōv), OLD USE. a past tense of **shrive.** *v.*

Shrove Tuesday, the day before Ash Wednesday; last day before Lent.

shrub (shrub), a woody plant smaller than a tree, usually with many separate stems starting from or near the ground; bush. A lilac bush is a shrub. *n.* —**shrub′like′,** *adj.*

shrub ber y (shrub′ər ē), 1 shrubs. 2 place planted with shrubs. *n., pl.* **shrub ber ies.**

shrub by (shrub′ē), 1 like shrubs. 2 covered with shrubs. 3 consisting of shrubs. *adj.,* **shrub bi er, shrub bi est.**

shrug (shrug), 1 raise (the shoulders) as an expression of dislike, doubt, indifference, or impatience: *He merely shrugged his shoulders in answer to our request for help. She shrugged and* walked away. **2** a raising of the shoulders in this way: *A shrug was her only reply.* **1** *v.*, **shrugged, shrug ging; 2** *n.*

shrunk (shrungk), a past tense and past participle of **shrink**. *His wool socks have shrunk so that he can't get them on.* *v.*

shrunk en (shrung′kən), **1** grown smaller; shriveled: *a shrunken fortune.* **2** shrunk; a past participle of **shrink**. **1** *adj.*, **2** *v.*

shuck (shuk), **1** a husk; pod. **2** remove the shucks from: *shuck corn.* **3** INFORMAL. take off; remove: *She likes to shuck her shoes when she's indoors.* **1** *n.*, **2,3** *v.* —**shuck′er,** *n.*

shud der (shud′ər), **1** tremble with horror, fear, cold, etc.: *shudder at a ghastly sight.* **2** a trembling; quivering. **1** *v.*, **2** *n.* —**shud′der ing ly,** *adv.*

shuf fle (shuf′əl), **1** walk without lifting the feet: *The old man shuffles feebly along.* **2** scrape or drag (the feet). **3** a scraping or dragging movement of the feet. **4** mix (cards, etc.) so as to change the order. **5** a shuffling of cards. **6** the right or turn to shuffle (cards). **7** push about; thrust or throw with clumsy haste: *He shuffled on his clothes and ran out of the house.* **8** move this way and that: *shuffle a stack of papers.* **9** movement this way and that: *After a hasty shuffle through his papers, the speaker began to talk.* **10** put or bring in a tricky way. **11** unfair act; trick: *Through some legal shuffle she secured a new trial.* **1,2,4,7,8,10** *v.*, **shuf fled, shuf fling; 3,5,6,9,11** *n.*
shuffle off, get rid of.

shuf fle board (shuf′əl bôrd′), game in which players use long sticks to push large disks along a flat surface to various numbered spaces. *n.*

shuf fler (shuf′lər), person or thing that shuffles. *n.*

shun (shun), keep away from; avoid: *She was lazy and shunned work.* *v.*, **shunned, shun ning.**

shunt (shunt), **1** move out of the way; turn aside. **2** a turning aside; shift. **3** sidetrack; put aside; get rid of. **4** switch (a train) from one track to another. **5** a railroad switch. **6** wire joining two points in an electric circuit and forming a path through which a part of the current may pass. Shunts are used to regulate the amount of current passing through the main circuit. **7** carry (a part of a current) by means of a shunt. **1,3,4,7** *v.*, **2,5,6** *n.*

shush (shush), hush. *v.*, *n.*, *pl.* **shush es;** *interj.*

shut (shut), **1** close (a container or opening) by pushing or pulling a lid, door, or some part into place: *shut a box, shut a door, shut a window.* **2** close (the eyes, a knife, a book, etc.)

by bringing parts together: *Shut your mouth.* **3** close tight; close securely; close doors or other openings of: *shut a house for the summer.* **4** become shut; be closed. **5** closed; fastened up; enclosed. **6** keep (from going out); enclose; confine: *The criminal was shut in prison.* **1-4,6** *v.*, **shut, shut ting; 5** *adj.*

shut down, 1 close by lowering. **2** close (a factory or the like) for a time; stop work. **3** settle down so as to cover or envelop. **4** INFORMAL. put a stop or check on.

shut in, keep from going out.

shut off, 1 turn off; close; obstruct; check; bar: *Shut off the radio.*

shut out, 1 keep from coming in: *The curtains shut out the light. Shut the dog out of this room.* **2** defeat (a team) without allowing it to score.

shut up, 1 shut the doors and windows of. **2** INFORMAL. stop talking. **3** keep from going out.

shut down (shut′doun′), a shutting down; closing of a factory, or the like, for a time. *n.*

shut-in (shut′in′), **1** kept in; held in; confined. **2** person who is kept from going out by sickness, weakness, etc. **1** *adj.*, **2** *n.*

shut out (shut′out′), the defeat of a team without allowing it to score. *n.*

shut ter (shut′ər), **1** a movable cover for a window. **2** a movable cover, slide, etc., for closing an opening. The device that opens and closes in front of the lens of a camera is the shutter. **3** put a shutter or shutters on or over: *As the hurricane approached, we hurried to shutter the windows.* **4** person or thing that shuts. **1,2,4** *n.*, **3** *v.*

shut tle (shut′l), **1** device that carries the thread from one side of the web to the other in weaving. **2** the sliding holder for the lower thread in a sewing machine, which moves back and forth once for each stitch. **3** move quickly to and fro. **4** bus, train, airplane, etc., that runs back and forth regularly over a short distance. **1,2,4** *n.*, **3** *v.*, **shut tled, shut tling.**

shut tle cock (shut′l kok′), a cork with feathers or, often, a light plastic webbing stuck in one end, hit back and forth in the game of badminton; bird. *n.*

shy[1] (shī), **1** uncomfortable in company; bashful: *He is shy and dislikes parties.* **2** easily frightened away; timid: *A deer is a shy animal.* **3** start back or aside suddenly: *The horse shied at the newspaper blowing along the ground.* **4** draw back; shrink: *I shied in fright when the dog snarled at me.* **5** not having enough; short; scant: *The store is shy on children's clothing.* **1,2,5** *adj.*, **shy er, shy est** or **shi er, shi est; 3,4**

v., **shied, shy ing.** [Old English *scēoh*] —**shy′ly,** *adv.* —**shy′ness,** *n.*

fight shy of, keep away from; avoid.

shy of, INFORMAL. **1** having little; short of: *I am shy of cash this week.* **2** not coming up to; lacking: *My sister is two months shy of voting age.*

shy[2] (shī), **1** to throw; fling: *The boy shied a stone at the tree.* **2** a throw; fling. **1** *v.*, **shied, shy ing; 2** *n.*, *pl.* **shies.** [origin unknown]

Shy lock (shī′lok), **1** the relentless and revengeful moneylender in Shakespeare's play *The Merchant of Venice.* **2** a greedy moneylender. *n.*

si (sē), ti. *n.*

Si am (sī am′), former name of **Thailand.** *n.*

Si a mese (sī ə mēz′), Thai. *adj.*, *n.*, *pl.* **Si a mese.**

Siamese cat, a short-haired, blue-eyed cat, usually with a light tan body and dark face, ears, feet, and tail.

Siamese twins, any twins who are born joined together. [from Eng and Chang, 1811-1874, twin Siamese boys who were so joined]

Si be li us (sə bā′lē əs), **Jean,** 1865-1957, Finnish composer. *n.*

Si ber i a (sī bir′ē ə), region in N Asia, extending from the Ural Mountains to the Pacific. It is part of the Soviet Union. *n.* —**Si ber′i an,** *adj.*, *n.*

sib i lant (sib′ə lənt), **1** hissing. **2** a hissing sound, letter, or symbol. *S* and *sh* are sibilants. **1** *adj.*, **2** *n.*

sib ling (sib′ling), brother or sister. An only child has no siblings. *n.*

sib yl (sib′əl), **1** any of several prophetesses that the ancient Greeks and Romans consulted about the future. **2** prophetess; fortuneteller; witch. *n.*

sic (sik), **1** set upon or attack (chiefly used as a command to a dog). **2** incite to set upon or attack: *sic a dog on a stranger.* *v.*, **sicked, sick ing.** Also, **sick.**

Si cil ian (sə sil′yən), **1** of or having to do with Sicily or its people. **2** person born or living in Sicily. **1** *adj.*, **2** *n.*

Sic i ly (sis′ə lē), island near the SW tip of Italy, belonging to Italy since 1860. It

hat, āge, fär; let, ēqual, tėrm;
it, īce; hot, ōpen, ôrder;
oil, out; cup, pūt, rüle; ch, child;
ng, long; sh, she; th, thin;
ŦH, then; zh, measure;

ə represents *a* in about,
e in taken, *i* in pencil,
o in lemon, *u* in circus.

adj. adjective	*n.* noun
adv. adverb	*prep.* preposition
conj. conjunction	*pron.* pronoun
interj. interjection	*v.* verb
sing. singular	*pl.* plural

is the largest island in the Mediterranean. *n.*

sick[1] (sik), 1 in poor health; having some disease; ill. 2 inclined to vomit; feeling nausea; vomiting. 3 for a sick person; connected with sickness: *sick pay.* 4 **the sick**, sick people: *The sick need special care.* 5 weary; tired: *I'm sick of school.* 6 disgusted. 7 affected with sorrow or longing: *sick at heart.* 1-3,5-7 *adj.,* 4 *n.* [Old English *sēoc*]

sick[2] (sik), sic. *v.* [perhaps a different form of *seek*]

sick bay, a place on a ship used as a hospital.

sick bed (sik′bed′), bed of a sick person. *n.*

sick en (sik′ən), 1 become sick: *The bird sickened when kept in the cage.* 2 make sick: *The sight of blood sickened him. v.*

sick en ing (sik′ə ning), making sick; causing nausea, faintness, disgust, or loathing. *adj.* —**sick′en ing ly,** *adv.*

sick ish (sik′ish), 1 somewhat sick. 2 somewhat sickening. *adj.* —**sick′-ish ly,** *adv.* —**sick′ish ness,** *n.*

sickle

sick le (sik′əl), tool consisting of a short, curved blade on a short handle, for cutting grass, etc. *n.*

sickle cell anemia, an inherited blood disease in which the normally round red blood cells become sickle-shaped. These cells prevent oxygen from getting to body tissues.

sick li ness (sik′lē nis), the state or fact of being sickly; ill health. *n.*

sick ly (sik′lē), 1 often sick; not strong; not healthy. 2 of or having to do with sickness: *Her skin is a sickly yellow.* 3 causing sickness: *That place has a sickly climate.* 4 faint; weak; pale: *a sickly glow. adj.,* **sick li er, sick li est.**

sick ness (sik′nis), 1 an abnormal, unhealthy condition; disease; illness. 2 nausea; vomiting. *n., pl.* **sick ness es.**

sick room (sik′rüm′ or sik′rùm′),

room in which a sick person is cared for. *n.*

side (sīd), 1 a surface or line bounding a thing: *the sides of a square, a side of a box.* 2 one of the two surfaces of an object that is not the front, back, top, or bottom: *There is a door at the side of the house.* 3 either of the two surfaces of paper, cloth, etc.: *Write only on one side of the paper.* 4 a particular surface: *the side of the moon turned toward the earth.* 5 the slope of a hill or bank. 6 either the right or the left part of a thing; either part or region beyond a central line: *the east side of a city, our side of the street, turn to one side.* 7 either the right or the left part of the body of a person or an animal: *I felt a sharp pain in my side.* 8 an aspect or view of someone or something: *the better side of one's nature, the bright side of a difficulty.* 9 group of persons who stand up for their beliefs, opinions, ways of doing things, etc., against another group: *Both sides are ready for the contest. The children chose sides for a game of softball.* 10 the position, course, or part of one person or party against another: *It is pleasant to be on the winning side.* 11 part of a family; line of descent: *The man is English on his mother's side.* 12 at one side; on one side: *the side aisles of a theater, a side door.* 13 from one side: *a side view.* 14 toward one side: *a side glance.* 15 less important: *a side issue.* 16 **side with,** take sides: *The sisters always side with each other.* 1-11 *n.,* 12-15 *adj.,* 16 *v.,* **sid ed, sid ing.**

by one's side, near one.

on the side, INFORMAL. in addition to one's ordinary duties.

side by side, beside one another.

take sides, place oneself with one person or group against another.

side arm (sīd′ärm′), throwing or thrown from the side with the arm at waist height; not overhand or underhand: *a sidearm pitcher, a sidearm pitch. adj.*

side arms, sword, revolver, bayonet, etc., carried at the side or in the belt.

side board (sīd′bôrd′), a low cabinet with drawers and shelves for holding silver and linen, and space on top for dishes; buffet. *n.*

side burns (sīd′bèrnz′), whiskers in front of the ears, especially when the

sideburns

chin is shaved. *n.pl.* [earlier *burnsides,* from Ambrose *Burnside,* 1824-1881, a Union general who wore such whiskers]

side light (sīd′līt′), 1 light coming from the side. 2 incidental information about a subject: *amusing sidelights in a biography. n.*

side line (sīd′līn′), 1 a line at the side of something. 2 line that marks the limit of play on the side of the field in football, etc. 3 **sidelines,** *pl.* space just outside these lines: *He watched the game from the sidelines.* 4 an additional line of goods or of business. *n.*

side long (sīd′lông′), to one side; toward the side: *a sidelong glance (adj.). He glanced sidelong at me (adv.). adj., adv.*

side piece (sīd′pēs′), piece forming a side or part of a side, or fixed by the side, of something. *n.*

si der e al (sī dir′ē əl), 1 of or having to do with the stars. 2 measured by the apparent motion of the stars: *sidereal time. adj.*

side sad dle (sīd′sad′l), 1 a woman's saddle so made that both of the rider's legs are on the same side of the horse. 2 with both legs on the same side of the horse: *ride sidesaddle.* 1 *n.,* 2 *adv.*

side show (sīd′shō′), a small show in connection with a principal one: *the sideshows of a circus. n.*

side step (sīd′step′), 1 step aside. 2 avoid by stepping aside; evade: *side-step a responsibility. v.,* **side stepped, side step ping.**

side swipe (sīd′swīp′), 1 hit with a sweeping blow along the side. 2 a sweeping blow along the side. 1 *v.,* **side-swiped, side swip ing;** 2 *n.*

side track (sīd′trak′), 1 a railroad siding. 2 switch (a train, etc.) to a sidetrack. 3 put aside; turn aside: *The teacher refused to be sidetracked by questions on other subjects.* 1 *n.,* 2,3 *v.*

side walk (sīd′wôk′), place to walk at the side of a street, usually paved. *n.*

side way (sīd′wā′), sideways. *adv., adj.*

side ways (sīd′wāz′), 1 to one side; toward one side: *walk sideways.* 2 from one side: *a sideways glimpse.* 3 with one side toward the front: *stand sideways, place a book sideways on a shelf. adv., adj.*

side wise (sīd′wīz′), sideways. *adv., adj.*

sid ing (sī′ding), 1 a short railroad track to which cars can be switched from a main track. 2 boards, shingles, etc., forming the outside walls of a wooden building. *n.*

si dle (sī′dl), 1 move sideways. 2 move sideways slowly so as not to attract attention: *The child shyly sidled up to the visitor. v.,* **si dled, si dling.**

siege (sēj), 1 the surrounding of a fortified place by an army trying to capture it; a besieging or a being besieged: *Troy was under a siege for ten years.* 2 any long or persistent effort to overcome resistance; any long-continued attack: *a siege of illness. n.*

lay siege to, 1 besiege: *The Greeks laid siege to Troy for ten years.* 2 attempt to win or get by long and persistent effort.

Sieg fried (sēg′frēd), (in German legends) a hero who killed a dragon, won a treasure, and rescued a maiden from an enchanted sleep. *n.*

si en na (sē en′ə), 1 any of various mixtures of clay and iron oxide, used as a pigment. In its natural state, it is yellowish-brown and is called **raw sienna.** After heating, it becomes reddish-brown and is called **burnt sienna.** 2 a yellowish brown or a reddish brown. *n.* [from earlier Italian *(terra di) Sienna* (earth from) Siena, city in Italy]

si er ra (sē er′ə), chain of hills or mountains whose peaks suggest the teeth of a saw. *n., pl.* **si er ras.** [from Spanish *sierra* a saw, from Latin *serra*]

Si er ra Le o ne (sē er′ə lē ō′nē), country on the W coast of Africa, a member of the Commonwealth of Nations.

Si er ra Ne vad a (sē er′ə nə vad′ə *or* sē er′ə nə vä′də), a mountain range in E California.

si es ta (sē es′tə), a nap or rest taken at noon or in the afternoon. *n., pl.* **si es tas.** [from Spanish *siesta*, from Latin *sexta (hora)* sixth (hour)]

sieve (siv), 1 utensil having holes that let liquids and smaller pieces pass through, but not the larger pieces: *Shaking flour through a sieve removes lumps.* 2 put through a sieve. 1 *n.*, 2 *v.*, **sieved, siev ing.**

sift (sift), 1 separate large pieces from small by shaking in a sieve: *Sift the gravel and put the larger stones in another pile.* 2 put through a sieve: *Sift sugar on the top of the cake.* 3 use a sieve. 4 fall through, or as if through, a sieve: *The snow sifted softly down.* 5 examine very carefully: *sift all available evidence. v.* **—sift′er,** *n.*

sigh (sī), 1 let out a very long, deep breath because one is sad, tired, relieved, etc.: *We heard her sigh.* 2 act or sound of sighing: *a sigh of regret, a sigh of relief.* 3 say or express with a sigh. 4 make a sound like a sigh: *The wind sighed in the treetops.* 5 wish very much; long: *He sighed for home and friends.* 6 lament with sighing: *sigh over one's unhappy fate.* 1,3-6 *v.*, 2 *n.*

sight (sīt), 1 power of seeing; vision: *Birds have better sight than dogs.* 2 act

or fact of seeing; look: *love at first sight.* 3 range of seeing: *Land was in sight.* 4 thing seen; view; glimpse: *I caught sight of him running around the corner.* 5 something worth seeing: *see the sights of the city. Niagara Falls is one of the sights of the world.* 6 something that looks bad or odd: *Your room is a sight.* 7 see: *At last Columbus sighted land.* 8 device to guide the eye in taking aim or observing: *the sights on a rifle.* 9 the aim or observation taken by such devices. 10 look at through sights; point to; aim at; aim: *I sighted carefully, then I fired at the target.* 11 way of looking or thinking; regard; opinion: *This is very important in my sight.* 1-6,8,9,11 *n.*, 7,10 *v.*

at sight or **on sight,** as soon as seen: *She reads music at sight.*

catch sight of, see: *I caught sight of him.*

in sight of, where one can see or be seen by: *We live in sight of the school.*

know by sight, know sufficiently to recognize when seen.

out of sight of, 1 where one cannot see: *Our ship was out of sight of land for several weeks.* 2 where one cannot be seen by: *out of sight of the neighbors.*

sight less (sīt′lis), 1 blind. 2 not in sight; invisible. *adj.*

sight ly (sīt′lē), 1 pleasing to the sight. 2 affording a fine view. *adj.*, **sight li er, sight li est.**

sight see ing (sīt′sē′ing), 1 a going around to see objects or places of interest: *a weekend of sightseeing.* 2 that goes around to see objects or places of interest: *a sightseeing tour.* 1 *n.*, 2 *adj.*

sight se er (sīt′sē′ər), person who goes around to see objects or places of interest. *n.*

sign (sīn), 1 any mark or thing used to mean, represent, or point out something: *The signs for addition, subtraction, multiplication, and division are +, −, ×, ÷.* 2 put one's name on; write one's name. A person signs a letter, a note promising to pay a debt, a check, etc. We sign for telegrams, parcels, etc. 3 write: *Sign your initials here.* 4 hire by a written agreement: *sign a new player.* 5 accept employment: *They signed for three years.* 6 motion or gesture used to mean, represent, or point out something: *A nod is a sign of agreement. We talked to the deaf man by signs. She made the sign of the cross. I gave the sign of the secret society.* 7 to mark with a sign. 8 an inscribed board, space, etc., serving for advertisement, information, etc.: *See the sign over the door. The sign reads, "Keep off the grass."* 9 indication: *There are no signs of life about the house.* 10 indication of a coming event; omen: *The*

hat, āge, fär; let, ēqual, tėrm; it, īce; hot, ōpen, ôrder; oil, out; cup, pùt, rüle; ch, child; ng, long; sh, she; th, thin; ᵺH, then; zh, measure;

ə represents *a* in about, *e* in taken, *i* in pencil, *o* in lemon, *u* in circus.

robin is a sign of spring. *Ancient peoples viewed comets as signs of evil.* 11 trace: *The hunter found signs of deer.* 12 any of the twelve divisions of the zodiac, each named for a constellation and each denoted by a special symbol. 1,6,8-12 *n.*, 2-5,7 *v.* **—sign′er,** *n.*

sign off, stop broadcasting.

sign up, enlist, join, etc., by written agreement: *sign up as a new member.*

sig nal (sig′nəl), 1 a sign giving notice, warning, or pointing out something: *A red light is a signal of danger. A siren is used as a fire signal. The raising of the flag was a signal to advance.* 2 a wave, current, impulse, etc., serving to convey sounds and images in communications by radio, television, etc. 3 make a signal or signals to: *She signaled the car to stop by raising her hand.* 4 make known by a signal or signals: *A bell signals the end of a school period.* 5 used as a signal or in signaling: *a signal flag.* 6 remarkable; striking; notable: *The airplane was a signal invention.* 1,2 *n.*, 3,4 *v.*, 5,6 *adj.*

sig nal ize (sig′nə līz), make stand out; make notable: *Many great inventions signalize the last 150 years. The year 1969 was signalized by man's landing on the moon. v.*, **sig nal ized, sig nal iz ing.**

sig nal ly (sig′nə lē), in a remarkable manner; strikingly; notably. *adv.*

sig nal man (sig′nəl mən *or* sig′nəl man′), man in charge of the signals on a railroad, in the army or navy, etc. *n., pl.* **sig nal men.**

sig na ture (sig′nə chər), 1 a person's name written by himself. 2 act of writing one's name. 3 signs printed at the beginning of a staff to show the key and time of a piece of music. 4 music, sound effects, etc., used to identify a radio or television program. *n.*

sign board (sīn′bôrd′), board having a sign, notice, advertisement, inscription, etc., on it. *n.*

sig net (sig′nit), 1 a small seal: *The order was sealed with the king's signet.* 2 the stamp or impression made by a signet. *n.*

adj.	adjective	n.	noun
adv.	adverb	prep.	preposition
conj.	conjunction	pron.	pronoun
interj.	interjection	v.	verb
sing.	singular	pl.	plural

sig nif i cance (sig nif′ə kəns), 1 importance; consequence: *The President wanted to see him on a matter of significance.* 2 meaning: *She did not understand the significance of my nod.* 3 significant quality; expressiveness: *the significance of her smile. n.*

sig nif i cant (sig nif′ə kənt), 1 full of meaning; important; of consequence: *July 4, 1776, is a significant date for Americans.* 2 having a meaning; expressive: *Smiles are significant of pleasure.* 3 having or expressing a hidden meaning: *A significant nod from his friend warned him to stop talking. adj.* —**sig nif′i cant ly,** *adv.*

sig ni fi ca tion (sig′nə fə kā′shən), a meaning; sense. *n.*

sig ni fy (sig′nə fī), 1 be a sign of; mean: *"Oh!" signifies surprise.* 2 make known by signs, words, or actions: *He signified his consent with a nod.* 3 have importance; be of consequence; matter: *What a fool says does not signify. v.,* **sig ni fied, sig ni fy ing.**

sign language, language in which motions, especially of the hands, stand for words, ideas, etc.

si gnor (sē′nyôr), ITALIAN. 1 Mr. or sir. 2 a gentleman. *n., pl.* **si gno ri** (sē nyôr′ē).

si gno ra (sē nyôr′ə), ITALIAN. 1 Mrs. or Madame. 2 a lady. *n., pl.* **si gno re** (sē nyôr′ā).

si gno ri na (sē′nyə rē′nə), ITALIAN. 1 Miss. 2 a young lady. *n., pl.* **si gno ri ne** (sē′nyə rē′nā).

sign post (sīn′pōst′), post having signs, notices, or directions on it; guidepost. *n.*

Sikh (sēk), member of a religious sect of northwestern India. Sikhs are famous as fighters. *n.*

Sik kim (sik′əm), small country in the Himalayas, between Tibet and India. It is a protectorate of India. *n.*

si lage (sī′lij), green fodder for winter feeding of farm animals, preserved and stored in a silo or other airtight chamber; ensilage. *n.*

si lence (sī′ləns), 1 absence of sound or noise; stillness: *The teacher asked for silence.* 2 a keeping still; not talking: *Silence gives consent.* 3 a not mentioning: *Mother passed over our foolish remarks in silence.* 4 stop the speech or noise of; make silent; quiet: *Please silence that barking dog.* 5 make silent by restraint or prohibition; repress: *to silence the press, to silence an uprising.* 6 keep still! be still! 1-3 *n.,* 4,5 *v.,* **si lenced, si lenc ing;** 6 *interj.*

si len cer (sī′lən sər), 1 person or thing that silences. 2 device which muffles the sound of a gun. *n.*

si lent (sī′lənt), 1 quiet; still; noiseless: *a silent house, the silent hills.* 2 not speaking; saying little or nothing: *The stranger was silent about his early life. Pupils must be silent during the study hour.* 3 not spoken; not said out loud: *a silent prayer. The "e" in "time" is a silent letter.* 4 not active; taking no open or active part. A silent partner in a business has no share in managing the business. 5 omitting mention of something, as in a narrative. *adj.* —**si′lent ly,** *adv.*

Si le sia (sə lē′shə *or* si lē′shə), region in central Europe most of which is now in Poland and Czechoslovakia. *n.* —**Si le′sian,** *adj., n.*

silhouette
(def. 1)

sil hou ette (sil′ü et′), 1 an outline portrait cut out of a black paper or filled in with some single color. 2 a dark image outlined against a lighter background. 3 show in outline: *The mountain was silhouetted against the sky.* 1,2 *n.,* 3 *v.,* **sil hou et ted, sil hou et ting.** [from Étienne de *Silhouette,* 1709-1767, French finance minister]

sil i ca (sil′ə kə), a hard, white or colorless substance. Flint, quartz, and sand are forms of silica. *n., pl.* **sil i cas.**

sil i cate (sil′ə kit *or* sil′ə kāt), compound containing silicon with oxygen and a metal. Mica, soapstone, asbestos, and feldspar are silicates. *n.*

sil i con (sil′ə kən), a nonmetallic element found only combined with other elements, chiefly with oxygen in silica. Next to oxygen, silicon is the most abundant element in nature. *n.*

sil i cone (sil′ə kōn), an organic compound in which silicon has replaced some of the carbon. Silicones are used for lubricants, varnishes, and insulators. *n.*

silk (silk), 1 a fine, soft fiber spun by silkworms to form their cocoons. 2 thread or cloth made from this fiber. 3 garment of such material. 4 fiber like silk, produced by spiders, etc. 5 anything like silk: *corn silk.* 6 of, like, or having to do with silk: *She sewed the silk dress with silk thread.* 1-5 *n.,* 6 *adj.* —**silk′like′,** *adj.*

silk en (sil′kən), 1 made of silk: *The king wore silken robes.* 2 like silk; smooth, soft, and glossy: *She has silken hair. adj.*

silk i ness (sil′kē nis), silky condition or quality. *n.*

SILKWORM

COCOON

silk worm (silk′wėrm′), caterpillar that spins silk to form a cocoon, especially the larva of a moth that feeds on mulberry leaves. *n.*

silk y (sil′kē), of or like silk; smooth, soft, and glossy; silken: *A kitten has silky fur. adj.,* **silk i er, silk i est.**

sill (sil), 1 piece of wood or stone across the bottom of a door or window frame. See **lintel** for picture. 2 a large, wooden beam on which the wall of a house, etc., rests. *n.*

sil li ness (sil′ē nis), 1 a being silly; foolishness. 2 a silly act, thing, etc. *n., pl.* **sil li ness es.**

sil ly (sil′ē), 1 without sense or reason; foolish; nonsensical: *Baby talk is silly.* 2 INFORMAL. stunned; dazed. 3 a silly or foolish person. 1,2 *adj.,* **sil li er, sil li est;** 3 *n., pl.* **sil lies.**

si lo (sī′lō), 1 an airtight building or pit in which green fodder for farm animals is preserved. 2 a vertical shaft built underground with facilities for housing and launching missiles, rockets, etc. *n., pl.* **si los.**

silo (def. 1)

silt (silt), 1 very fine particles of earth, sand, etc., carried by moving water and deposited as sediment: *The harbor is being choked up with silt.* 2 fill or choke up with silt. 1 *n.,* 2 *v.*

silt y (sil′tē), of silt; like silt; full of silt. *adj.,* **silt i er, silt i est.**

sil van (sil′vən), sylvan. *adj.*

sil ver (sil′vər), 1 a shining white, precious metallic element that can be hammered into very thin sheets or drawn out into very fine wire. Silver is superior to any other substance in its ability to conduct heat and electricity. It is used to make coins, jewelry, spoons, dishes, etc. 2 coins made from this or a similar metal: *a pocketful of silver.* 3 utensils or dishes made of or plated with silver; silverware: *table silver.* 4 something like silver. 5 made of or plated with silver: *a silver spoon.* 6 of or having to do with silver. 7 cover or coat with silver or something like silver: *a silver mirror.* 8 the color of silver. 9 having the color of silver: *a silver slipper.* 10 make the color of silver: *Moonlight silvered the lake.* 11 become the color of silver: *The old lady's hair had silvered.* 12 having a clear ringing sound like that of silver dropped on a hard surface. 1-4,8 *n.,* 5,6,9,12 *adj.,* 7,10,11 *v.*

silver lining, the brighter side of a sad or unfortunate situation.

sil ver smith (sil′vər smith′), person who makes articles of silver. *n.*

sil ver-tongued (sil′vər tungd′), eloquent. *adj.*

sil ver ware (sil′vər wer′ *or* sil′vər-war′), silver things; utensils or dishes made of or plated with silver. *n.*

sil ver y (sil′vər ē), like silver; like that of silver: *Moonbeams are silvery. The bell has a silvery sound. adj.*

sim i an (sim′ē ən), 1 apelike or monkeylike. 2 an ape; monkey. 1 *adj.,* 2 *n.*

sim i lar (sim′ə lər), 1 much the same; alike; like: *A creek and a brook are similar.* 2 (in geometry) having the same shape: *similar triangles. adj.* —**sim′i lar ly,** *adv.*

sim i lar i ty (sim′ə lar′ə tē), 1 a being similar; likeness; resemblance. 2 **similarities,** *pl.* points of resemblance. *n., pl.* **sim i lar i ties.**

sim i le (sim′ə lē′), a statement that one thing is like another. EXAMPLES: a face like marble, as brave as a lion. *n.*

si mil i tude (sə mil′ə tüd *or* sə mil′ə-tyüd), 1 a being similar; likeness; resemblance. 2 comparison: *She could think of no similitude to describe the sunset.* 3 a copy; image. *n.*

sim mer (sim′ər), 1 make a murmuring sound while boiling gently: *The kettle simmered on the stove.* 2 keep at or just below the boiling point; boil gently: *Simmer the milk, do not boil it. The soup should simmer for a few hours to improve its taste.* 3 process of cooking at or just below the boiling point: *Do not let the soup cook faster than at a simmer.* 4 be on the point of just breaking out: *simmering rebellion. He simmered with anger, but said nothing.* 1,2, 4 *v.,* 3 *n.*

simmer down, 1 cool off; calm down.

2 (of a liquid) be reduced in quantity through continued simmering.

Si mon Peter (sī′mən). See **Peter, Saint.**

si mo ny (sī′mə nē *or* sim′ə nē), act of buying and selling sacred things, especially positions or promotion in the church. *n.* [from *Simon,* a sorcerer described in the New Testament as trying to buy apostolic powers from the apostles Peter and John]

si moom (sə müm′), a hot, suffocating, sand-laden wind of the deserts of Arabia, Syria, and northern Africa. *n.*

si moon (sə mün′), simoom. *n.*

sim per (sim′pər), 1 smile in a silly, affected way. 2 express by a simper; say with a simper. 3 a silly, affected smile. 1,2 *v.,* 3 *n.*

sim ple (sim′pəl), 1 easy to do or understand: *a simple problem. This book is in simple language.* 2 not divided into parts; single; not compound. An oak leaf is a simple leaf. "John called his dog" is a simple sentence. 3 having few parts; not complex; not involved; elementary: *a simple one-celled animal.* 4 with nothing added; bare; mere: *My answer is the simple truth.* 5 without ornament; not rich or showy; plain: *He eats simple food and wears simple clothing.* 6 not affected; not showing off; natural: *She has a pleasant, simple manner.* 7 honest; sincere: *a simple heart.* 8 not subtle; not sophisticated; innocent; artless: *a simple child.* 9 common; ordinary: *a simple citizen.* 10 humble: *His parents were simple people.* 11 weak in mind; dull; stupid: *"Simple Simon met a pieman." adj.,* **sim pler, sim plest.** —**sim′ple ness,** *n.*

simple fraction, fraction having a whole number in both the numerator and the denominator. EXAMPLES: ¹/₃, ³/₄, ²¹⁹/₁₂₅.

sim ple-heart ed (sim′pəl här′tid), 1 having or showing a simple, unaffected nature. 2 guileless; sincere. *adj.*

simple machine, any of the basic mechanical devices which multiply or change the direction of force and on which more complex machines are based. The lever, wedge, pulley, wheel and axle, inclined plane, and screw are simple machines.

sim ple-mind ed (sim′pəl mīn′did), 1 without awareness of conventions; artless; inexperienced. 2 ignorant; foolish; stupid. 3 feeble-minded. *adj.*

simple sentence, sentence consisting of one main clause. EXAMPLE: The whistle blows.

sim ple ton (sim′pəl tən), a silly person; fool. *n.*

sim plic i ty (sim plis′ə tē), 1 a being simple. 2 freedom from difficulty;

hat, āge, fär; let, ēqual, tėrm;
it, īce; hot, ōpen, ôrder;
oil, out; cup, pùt, rüle; ch, child;
ng, long; sh, she; th, thin;
ŦH, then; zh, measure;

ə represents *a* in about,
e in taken, *i* in pencil,
o in lemon, *u* in circus.

clearness: *The simplicity of that book makes it suitable for children.* 3 plainness: *A room in a hospital should be furnished with simplicity.* 4 absence of show or pretense; sincerity. 5 lack of shrewdness; dullness: *Their simplicity made them easily fooled. n., pl.* **simplic i ties.**

sim pli fi ca tion (sim′plə fə kā′shən), 1 a making simpler or a being made simpler. 2 a change to a simpler form. *n.*

sim pli fi er (sim′plə fī′ər), person or thing that simplifies. *n.*

sim pli fy (sim′plə fī), make simple or simpler; make plainer or easier: *"Tho" is a simplified spelling of "though." v.,* **sim pli fied, sim pli fy ing.**

sim ply (sim′plē), 1 in a simple manner. 2 without much ornament; without pretense or affectation; plainly: *The nurse was simply dressed.* 3 merely; only: *The baby did not simply cry; he yelled.* 4 foolishly: *act as simply as an idiot.* 5 absolutely: *simply perfect, simply hopeless. adv.*

sim u late (sim′yə lāt), 1 put on a false appearance of; pretend; feign: *She simulated interest to please her friend.* 2 act like; look like; imitate: *Certain insects simulate flowers or leaves. v.,* **sim u-lat ed, sim u lat ing.**

sim u la tion (sim′yə lā′shən), 1 a putting on a false appearance; pretense; feigning. 2 an acting or looking like; imitation: *a harmless insect's simulation of a poisonous one. n.*

si mul cast (sī′məl kast′), transmit a program over radio and television simultaneously. *v.,* **si mul cast** *or* **si-mul cast ed, si mul cast ing.**

si mul ta ne ous (sī′məl tā′nē əs), existing, done, or happening at the same time: *The two simultaneous shots sounded like one. adj.*

si mul ta ne ous ly (sī′məl tā′nē əs-lē), at once; at the same time; together. *adv.*

sin (sin), 1 a breaking of the law of God on purpose. 2 break the law of God; be a sinner. 3 wrongdoing of any kind; immoral act. Lying, stealing, dishonesty, and cruelty are sins. 4 do

adj.	adjective	*n.*	noun
adv.	adverb	*prep.*	preposition
conj.	conjunction	*pron.*	pronoun
interj.	interjection	*v.*	verb
sing.	singular	*pl.*	plural

wrong. 1,3 *n.*, 2,4 *v.*, **sinned, sin ning.**

Si nai (sī′nī), **1 Mount,** (in the Bible) the mountain where God gave the Ten Commandments to Moses. It is thought to be located in the S part of the Sinai peninsula. **2** triangular peninsula in NE Egypt, between the Mediterranean Sea and the N end of the Red Sea. *n.*

Sin bad (sin′bad), sailor in *The Arabian Nights* who had seven extraordinary voyages. *n.*

since (sins), **1** from a past time till now: *The sun has been up since five.* **2** after the time that; from the time when: *He has been home only once since he went to New York.* **3** after: *She has worked hard since she left school.* **4** at any time between (some past time or event and the present): *We have not seen them since Saturday.* **5** from then till now: *He caught cold last Saturday and has been in bed ever since.* **6** at some time between then and now: *At first she refused the position, but since has accepted.* **7** before now; ago: *I heard that old joke long since.* **8** because: *Since you feel tired, you should rest.* 1,4 *prep.*, 2,3,8 *conj.*, 5-7 *adv.*

sin cere (sin sir′), free from pretense or deceit; genuine; real; honest: *sincere thanks. I made a sincere effort to pass my exams. adj.*, **sin cer er, sin cer est. —sin cere′ly,** *adv.*

sin cer i ty (sin ser′ə tē), freedom from pretense or deceit; honesty. *n., pl.* **sin cer i ties.**

sine of angle a = BC/AB;
sine of angle b = AC/AB.

sine (sin), length of the side opposite an acute angle of a right triangle divided by the length of the hypotenuse. *n.*

si ne cure (sī′nə kyùr *or* sin′ə kyùr), an extremely easy job; position requiring little or no work and usually paying well. *n.*

sin ew (sin′yü), **1** tendon: *You can see the sinews between muscle and bone in this cooked chicken leg.* **2** strength; energy. **3** means of strength; source of power: *Men and money are the sinews of war. n.*

sin ew y (sin′yü ē), **1** having strong sinews; strong; powerful: *A wrestler has sinewy arms.* **2** vigorous; forcible. **3** like sinews; having sinews; tough; stringy. *adj.*

sin ful (sin′fəl), full of sin; wicked; wrong; immoral; evil: *a sinful person, a sinful act. adj.* **—sin′ful ly,** *adv.* **—sin′ful ness,** *n.*

sing (sing), **1** make music with the voice: *She sings folk songs.* **2** make pleasant musical sounds: *Birds sing.* **3** utter musically: *He almost seemed to sing his lines from the play.* **4** bring, send, put, etc., with or by singing: *Sing the baby to sleep.* **5** tell in song or poetry: *Poets sang of Camelot.* **6** proclaim: *sing a person's praises.* **7** make a ringing, whistling, humming, or buzzing sound: *The teakettle sang on the stove.* **8** a singing, especially in a group: *We went to a community sing.* 1-7 *v.*, **sang** or **sung, sung, sing ing;** 8 *n.*

sing out, call loudly; shout.

sing., singular.

Sing a pore (sing′ə pôr), **1** island country off the S tip of the Malay Peninsula, a member of the Commonwealth of Nations. **2** its capital, on the S coast. *n.*

singe (sinj), **1** burn a little: *The chicken was singed to remove the fine hairs.* **2** a slight burn. **3** burn the ends or edges of: *The fire flared up and singed my hair.* **4** remove by a slight burning: *The cook singed the feathers from the chicken.* 1,3,4 *v.*, **singed, singe ing;** 2 *n.*

sing er (sing′ər), person or bird that sings: *Our canary is a fine singer. n.*

sin gle (sing′gəl), **1** one and no more; only one: *Please give me a single piece of paper.* **2** for only one; individual: *The sisters share one room with two single beds in it.* **3** not married: *a single man.* **4** having only one on each side: *The knights engaged in single combat.* **5 singles,** *pl.* game of tennis, etc., played with only one person on each side: *She likes to play singles rather than doubles.* **6** pick from among others: *The teacher singled us out for praise.* **7** a single thing or person. **8** in baseball: **a** a hit that allows the batter to reach first base only. **b** make such a hit. **9** having only one set of petals. Most cultivated roses have double flowers with many petals; wild roses have single flowers with five petals. **10** sincere; honest; genuine: *She showed single devotion to her work.* 1-4,9,10 *adj.*, 5,7,8a *n.*, 6,8b *v.*, **sin gled, sin gling. —sin′gle ness,** *n.*

sin gle-breast ed (sing′gəl bres′tid), overlapping across the breast just enough to fasten with one row of buttons: *a suit with a single-breasted jacket. adj.*

single file, line of persons or things arranged one behind another: *The Indians moved silently along the trail in single file.*

sin gle-hand ed (sing′gəl han′did), **1** without help from others; working alone. **2** using, requiring, or managed by only one hand or only one person: *a single-handed catch, a single-handed saw. adj.* **—sin′gle-hand′ed ly,** *adv.*

sin gle-heart ed (sing′gəl här′tid), **1** free from deceit; sincere. **2** having only one purpose. *adj.*

sin gle-mind ed (sing′gəl mīn′did), **1** having only one purpose in mind. **2** sincere; straightforward. *adj.* **—sin′gle-mind′ed ly,** *adv.* **—sin′gle-mind′ed ness,** *n.*

sin gle tree (sing′gəl trē′), whiffletree. *n.*

sin gly (sing′glē), **1** by itself; individually; separately: *Let us consider each point singly.* **2** one by one; one at a time: *Misfortunes never come singly.* **3** by one's own efforts; without help. *adv.*

sing song (sing′sông′), **1** a monotonous, up-and-down rhythm. **2** a monotonous tone or sound in speaking. **3** monotonous in rhythm: *a singsong recitation of the multiplication table.* 1,2 *n.*, 3 *adj.*

sin gu lar (sing′gyə lər), **1** extraordinary; unusual: *a person of singular ability, a story of singular interest.* **2** strange; queer; peculiar: *The detectives were greatly puzzled by the singular nature of the crime.* **3** being the only one of its kind: *an event singular in history.* **4** one in number. *Boy* is singular; *boys* is plural. **5** the singular number in grammar. *Ox* is the singular of *oxen.* **6** a word in the singular number. 1-4 *adj.*, 5,6 *n.* **—sin′gu lar ly,** *adv.*

sin gu lar i ty (sing′gyə lar′ə tē), **1** peculiarity; oddness; strangeness; unusualness: *The singularity of their speech and clothing attracted much attention.* **2** something singular; peculiarity; oddity: *One of the giraffe's singularities is the length of its neck. n., pl.* **sin gu lar i ties.**

sin is ter (sin′ə stər), **1** showing ill will; threatening: *a sinister rumor, a sinister look.* **2** bad; evil; dishonest: *a sinister plan. adj.*

sink (singk), **1** go down; fall slowly; go lower and lower: *sink to the floor in a faint. I sank into a chair.* **2** make go down; make fall: *Lack of rain sank the water level.* **3** go under: *The ship is sinking.* **4** make go under: *The submarine sank two ships.* **5** become lower or weaker: *The wind has sunk down.* **6** make lower; reduce: *Sink your voice to a whisper.* **7** pass gradually (into a state of sleep, silence, oblivion, etc.): *to* sink to rest. 8 go deeply: *Let the lesson sink into your mind.* 9 make go deep; dig: *The men are sinking a well.* 10 become worse: *My spirits sank.* 11 invest (money), especially unprofitably: *We sank $20 in a machine that we never used.* 12 a shallow basin or tub with a drainpipe: *The dishes are in the kitchen sink.* 13 place where dirty water or any filth collects. 14 a low-lying inland area where waters collect, or where they disappear by sinking downward or by evaporation. 1-11 *v.,* **sank** or **sunk, sunk, sink ing;** 12-14 *n.*

sink er (singk′kər), 1 person or thing that sinks. 2 a lead weight for sinking a fish line or net. *n.*

sink hole (singk′hōl′), 1 hole eroded in rock by running water and acting as a drain for surface water. 2 hole where water collects. *n.*

Sin kiang (sin′kyäng′), the westernmost province of China, northwest of Tibet. *n.*

sin less (sin′lis), without sin. *adj.*

sin ner (sin′ər), person who sins or does wrong. *n.*

sin u os i ty (sin′yü os′ə tē), 1 sinuous form or character; a winding. 2 curve; bend; turn. *n., pl.* **sin u os i ties.**

sin u ous (sin′yü əs), 1 having many curves or turns; winding: *The motion of a snake is sinuous.* 2 indirect; devious; morally crooked. *adj.* —**sin′u ous ly, adv.**

si nus (sī′nəs), cavity in a bone, especially one of the cavities in the bones of the skull that connect with the nasal cavity. *n., pl.* **si nus es.**

si nus i tis (sī′nə sī′tis), inflammation of one of the sinuses of the head. *n.*

Si on (sī′ən), Zion. *n.*

Sioux (sü), an American Indian tribe living on the plains of the northern United States and southern Canada. *n., pl.* **Sioux** (sü or süz).

Sioux City, city in W Iowa, on the Missouri River.

sip (sip), 1 drink little by little: *We sipped our tea.* 2 a very small drink: *She took a sip.* 3 a sipping. 1 *v.,* **sipped, sip ping;** 2,3 *n.*

si phon (sī′fən), 1 a bent tube through which liquid can be drawn over the edge of one container into another at a lower level by air pressure. 2 draw off or pass through a siphon: *They siphoned a gallon of gasoline from their car to ours.* 3 bottle for soda water with a tube through which the liquid is forced out by the pressure of the gas in the bottle. 4 a tube-shaped organ of some animals, such as certain shellfish, for drawing in and expelling water. 1,3,4 *n.,* 2 *v.* Also, **syphon.**

sir (sėr; *unstressed* sər), 1 title of respect or honor used to a man. A boy

calls an older man "sir." We begin business letters with "Dear Sir." 2 **Sir,** the title of a knight or baronet: *Sir Walter Scott.* 3 Mr. or Master: *You, sir, have no business here; get out. n.*

sire (sīr), 1 a male ancestor; forefather. 2 male parent; father: *Lightning was the sire of the race horse Danger.* 3 be the father of: *Lightning sired Danger.* 4 title of respect used formerly to a great noble and now to a king: *"I'm killed, Sire!" said the messenger to Napoleon.* 1,2,4 *n.,* 3 *v.,* **sired, sir ing.**

si ren (sī′rən), 1 kind of whistle that makes a loud, piercing sound: *We heard the sirens of the fire engines.* 2 (in Greek myths) any of a group of nymphs who, by their sweet singing, lured sailors to destruction upon the rocks. 3 woman who lures, tempts, or entices. 4 of a siren; tempting; charming. 1-3 *n.,* 4 *adj.* —**si′ren like′, adj.**

Sir i us (sir′ē əs), the brightest star in the sky; Dog Star. *n.*

sir loin (sėr′loin), cut of beef from the part of the loin in front of the rump. *n.*

si roc co (sə rok′ō), 1 a hot, dry, dust-laden wind blowing from northern Africa across the Mediterranean Sea and southern Europe. 2 any hot, unpleasant wind. *n., pl.* **si roc cos.**

sir rah (sir′ə), OLD USE. fellow, used to address men and boys when speaking contemptuously, angrily, impatiently, etc. *n.*

sir up (sir′əp *or* sėr′əp), syrup. *n.*

sis (sis), INFORMAL. sister. *n.*

sis al (sis′əl *or* sī′səl), 1 a strong, white fiber, used for making rope, twine, etc. 2 plant that it comes from. *n.* [from *Sisal,* former port in Yucatán, Mexico]

sis sy (sis′ē), INFORMAL. 1 sister. 2 boy or man who behaves too much like a girl. *n., pl.* **sis sies.**

siphon (def. 1)
The arrows show the direction of flow of the liquid.

sis ter (sis′tər), 1 daughter of the same parents. A girl is a sister to the other children of her parents. 2 a close friend or companion. 3 a female member of the same church, society, etc. 4 member of a religious order of women; nun: *Sisters of Charity. n.*

sis ter hood (sis′tər hùd), 1 bond between sisters; feeling of sister for sister. 2 persons joined as sisters; association of women with some common aim or characteristic. *n.*

hat, āge, fär; let, ēqual, tèrm;
it, īce; hot, ōpen, ôrder;
oil, out; cup, pùt, rüle; ch, child;
ng, long; sh, she; th, thin;
ŦH, then; zh, measure;

ə represents *a* in about,
e in taken, *i* in pencil,
o in lemon, *u* in circus.

sis ter-in-law (sis′tər in lô′), 1 sister of one's husband or wife. 2 wife of one's brother. *n., pl.* **sis ters-in-law.**

sis ter li ness (sis′tər lē nis), sisterly affection or sympathy. *n.*

sis ter ly (sis′tər lē), 1 of a sister: *sisterly traits.* 2 like a sister; very friendly; kindly: *sisterly interest. adj.*

Sis tine Chapel (sis′tēn′), chapel of the pope in the Vatican. It is decorated with frescoes by Michelangelo and other great artists.

Sis y phus (sis′ə fəs), (in Greek myths) a king condemned forever to roll a heavy stone up a steep hill in Hades, only to have it always roll down again. *n.*

sit (sit), 1 rest on the lower part of the body with the weight off the feet: *She sat in a chair.* 2 cause to sit; seat: *The woman sat the little boy in his stroller.* 3 sit on: *He sat his horse well.* 4 have place or position: *The clock has sat on that shelf for years.* 5 have a seat in an assembly, etc.; be a member of a council: *sit in Congress.* 6 hold a session: *The court sits next month.* 7 place oneself in a position for having one's picture made; pose: *sit for a portrait.* 8 be in a state of rest; remain inactive: *He did not join in the game; he just sat on the sidelines.* 9 press or weigh: *Care sat heavy on his brow.* 10 perch: *The birds were sitting on the fence rail.* 11 brood: *The hen will sit until the eggs are ready to hatch.* 12 baby-sit: *My sister sits for the woman next door when she goes shopping.* 13 to fit: *The coat sits well. v.,* **sat, sit ting.**

sit down, take a seat; put oneself in a sitting position.

sit in, 1 take part (in a game, conference, etc.). 2 take part in a sit-in.

sit on or **sit upon,** 1 sit in judgment or council on. 2 have a seat on (a jury, etc.).

sit out, 1 remain seated during (a dance). 2 stay through (a performance, etc.).

sit up, 1 raise the body to a sitting position. 2 keep such a position. 3 stay up instead of going to bed.

sit-down strike (sit′doun′), strike in

adj.	adjective	n.	noun
adv.	adverb	prep.	preposition
conj.	conjunction	pron.	pronoun
interj.	interjection	v.	verb
sing.	singular	pl.	plural

which the workers stay in the factory, store, etc., without working until their demands are met or an agreement is reached.

site (sīt), position or place (of anything); location: *This house has one of the best sites in town. The site for the new school has not yet been chosen.* *n.*

sit-in (sit′in′), form of protest in which a group of people enter and remain seated for a long period of time in a public place. Sit-ins are organized to protest racial discrimination, government policies, etc. *n.*

Sit ka (sit′kə), town in SE Alaska. *n.*

sit ter (sit′ər), 1 person who sits. 2 baby-sitter. 3 hen sitting on its eggs. *n.*

sit ting (sit′ing), 1 meeting or session of a court of law, legislature, etc. 2 time of remaining seated: *She read five chapters at one sitting.* 3 that sits or has to do with sitting: *to be in bed in a sitting position.* 1,2 *n.,* 3 *adj.*

Sitting Bull, 1834?-1890, Sioux Indian chief who defeated Custer in 1876.

sitting room, parlor; living room.

sit u ate (sich′ü āt), place or locate. *v.,* **sit u at ed, sit u at ing.**

sit u at ed (sich′ü ā′tid), 1 placed; located: *New York is a favorably situated city.* 2 in a certain financial or social position: *The doctor was quite well situated.* *adj.*

sit u a tion (sich′ü ā′shən), 1 circumstances; case; condition: *act calmly in a difficult situation.* 2 place to work; job; position: *She is trying to find a good situation.* 3 site; location; place: *Our house has a beautiful situation on a hill.* *n.*

sit-up (sit′up′), exercise in which a person lies on his back with his hands behind his head, legs extended, and then sits up without raising his feet. *n.*

six (siks), one more than five; 6. *n., pl.* **six es;** *adj.*

at sixes and sevens, 1 in confusion. 2 in disagreement.

six fold (siks′fōld′), 1 six times as much or as many. 2 having six parts. 1,2 *adj.,* 1 *adv.*

Six Nations, federation of Iroquois Indian tribes. The Tuscarora tribe of Iroquois in 1722 joined the original confederacy of Iroquois tribes called the Five Nations.

six-pack (siks′pak′), a cardboard container holding six bottle, cans, or other items sold as a unit. *n.*

six pence (siks′pəns), 1 six British pennies; six pence. 2 coin of this value. *n.*

six-shoot er (siks′shü′tər), INFORMAL. revolver that can fire six shots without being reloaded. *n.*

six teen (sik′stēn′), six more than ten; 16. *n., adj.*

six teenth (sik′stēnth′), 1 next after the 15th; last in a series of 16. 2 one of 16 equal parts. *adj., n.*

sixteenth note, (in music) a note played for one sixteenth as long a time as a whole note. See **note** for diagram.

sixth (siksth), 1 next after the fifth; last in a series of 6. 2 one of 6 equal parts. *adj., n.*

six ti eth (sik′stē ith), 1 next after the 59th; last in a series of 60. 2 one of 60 equal parts. *adj., n.*

six ty (sik′stē), six times ten; 60. *n., pl.* **six ties;** *adj.*

siz a ble (sī′zə bəl), fairly large. *adj.* Also, **sizeable.**

size¹ (sīz), 1 amount of surface or space a thing takes up: *The two boys are of the same size. The library contains books of all sizes, big and little. We need a house of larger size.* 2 extent; amount; magnitude: *the size of an industry.* 3 one of a series of measures: *His shoes are size 10. The size of card I want is 3 by 5 inches.* 4 arrange according to size or in sizes: *Will you size these nails?* 1-3 *n.,* 4 *v.,* **sized, siz ing.** [Middle English *sise* ordinance setting a fixed amount, shortened form of *assise* assizes, from French of the 1200's *assise* a sitting]

of a size, of the same size.

size up, INFORMAL. form an opinion of; estimate.

size² (sīz), 1 preparation made from glue, starch, or other sticky material. It is used to glaze paper, cover plastered walls, stiffen cloth, etc. 2 to coat or treat with size. 1 *n.,* 2 *v.,* **sized, siz ing.** [from French of the 1200's *assise* a sitting, fixing, layer, from *asseir* sit at, from Latin *assidere*]

size a ble (sī′zə bəl), sizable. *adj.*

siz zle (siz′əl), 1 make a hissing sound, as fat does when it is frying or burning. 2 a hissing sound. 1 *v.,* **siz zled, siz zling;** 2 *n.*

skate¹ (skāt), 1 a frame with a blade fixed to a shoe or that can be fastened to a shoe so that a person can glide over ice. 2 roller skate. 3 glide or move along on skates. 1,2 *n.,* 3 *v.,* **skat ed, skat ing.** [from Dutch *schaats,* from French of the 1400's *escache* stilt]

skate² (skāt), any of several broad, flat fishes, usually having a pointed snout. A skate is a kind of ray. *n., pl.* **skates** or **skate.** [from a Scandinavian word of the 1200's, such as Icelandic *skata*]

skate board (skāt′bôrd′), a narrow board resembling a surfboard, with roller-skate wheels attached to each end, used for gliding or moving on any hard surface. *n.*

skat er (skā′tər), person who skates. *n.*

skeet (skēt), kind of trapshooting in which clay pigeons are flung in the air at angles similar to those taken by a bird in flight. *n.*

skein of yarn

skein (skān), a small, coiled bundle of yarn or thread. There are 120 yards in a skein of cotton yarn. *n.*

skel e tal (skel′ə təl), of or like a skeleton; attached to a skeleton. *adj.*

skel e ton (skel′ə tən), 1 the bones of a body, fitted together in their natural places. The skeleton is a frame that supports the muscles, organs, etc. 2 frame: *the steel skeleton of a building.* 3 the basic features or elements; outline: *the skeleton of a poem.* *n.*

skeleton in the closet, a secret source of embarrassment, grief, or shame, especially to a family.

skeleton key, key made to open many locks.

skep tic (skep′tik), 1 person who questions the truth of theories or apparent facts; doubter. 2 person who doubts the truth of religious doctrines. *n.* Also, **sceptic.**

skep ti cal (skep′tə kəl), 1 of or like a skeptic; inclined to doubt; not believing easily. 2 questioning the truth of theories or apparent facts. *adj.* Also, **sceptical. —skep′ti cal ly,** *adv.*

skep ti cism (skep′tə siz′əm), skeptical attitude; doubt; unbelief. *n.* Also, **scepticism.**

sketch (skech), 1 a rough, quickly done drawing, painting, or design. 2 make a sketch of; draw roughly. 3 make sketches: *He sketches in his free time.* 4 outline; plan. 5 a short description, story, play, etc. 1,4,5 *n., pl.* **sketch es;** 2,3 *v.* **—sketch′er,** *n.*

sketch book (skech′bük′), 1 book to draw or paint sketches in. 2 book of short descriptions, stories, plays, etc. *n.*

sketch y (skech′ē), 1 like a sketch;

skate²
up to 5 ft. long

having or giving only outlines or main features. 2 incomplete; slight; imperfect: *a sketchy meal. adj.,* **sketch i er, sketch i est.**

skew (skyü), 1 twisted to one side; slanting. 2 a slant. 3 to slant. 1 *adj.,* 2 *n.,* 3 *v.*

skew er (skyü′ər), 1 a long pin of wood or metal stuck through meat to hold it together while it is cooking. 2 fasten with a skewer or skewers. 3 pierce with or as if with a skewer. 1 *n.,* 2,3 *v.*

skis (def. 1)

ski (skē), 1 one of a pair of long, slender pieces of hard wood, plastic, or metal fastened by straps or special harness to the shoes to enable a person to glide over snow. 2 glide over the snow on skis. 1 *n., pl.* **skis** or **ski;** 2 *v.,* **skied, ski ing. —ski′er,** *n.*

skid (skid), 1 to slip or slide sideways while moving: *The car skidded on the slippery road.* 2 a slip or slide while moving: *The car went into a skid on the icy road.* 3 piece of wood or metal to prevent a wheel from turning. 4 slide along without turning, as a wheel does when held by a skid. 5 timber, frame, etc., on which something rests, or on which something heavy may slide. 6 to slide along on a skid or skids. 1,4,6 *v.,* **skid ded, skid ding;** 2,3,5 *n.*

on the skids, SLANG. headed for dismissal, failure, or other disaster.

skies (skīz), plural of **sky.** *n.*

skiff (skif), 1 a light rowboat. 2 a small, light boat with a mast for a single triangular sail. *n.*

ski ing (skē′ing), act or sport of gliding over snow on skis. *n.*

skil ful (skil′fəl), skillful. *adj.* **—skil′-ful ly,** *adv.*

skill (skil), 1 ability gained by practice, knowledge, etc.; expertness: *The trained teacher managed the children with skill.* 2 ability to do things well with one's body or with tools: *It takes skill to tune a piano.* 3 an art or craft: *master the carpenter's skill. n.*

skilled (skild), 1 having skill; trained; experienced: *A carpenter is a skilled workman.* 2 showing skill; requiring skill: *Bricklaying is skilled labor. adj.*

skil let (skil′it), 1 a shallow pan with a long handle, used for frying. 2 saucepan with a long handle. *n.*

skill ful (skil′fəl), 1 having skill; expert: *a skillful surgeon.* 2 showing skill;

a skillful piece of bricklaying. adj. Also, **skilful. —skill′ful ly,** *adv.*

skim (skim), 1 remove from the top: *The cook skims the cream from the milk.* 2 take something from the top of: *skim milk by taking off the cream.* 3 move lightly over: *The pebble I threw skimmed the little waves. The skaters skimmed the ice.* 4 glide along: *The swallows were skimming by.* 5 send skimming: *We made a contest to see who could skim a flat stone over the water the farthest.* 6 read hastily or carelessly; read with omissions: *It took me an hour to skim the book. v.,* **skimmed, skim ming.**

skim mer (skim′ər), 1 one that skims. 2 a shallow ladle full of holes, with a long handle. It is used in skimming liquids. 3 kind of sea bird that skims along the surface of water to get food. *n.*

skim milk or **skimmed milk,** milk from which the cream has been removed.

skimp (skimp), 1 supply in too small an amount: *Don't skimp the butter in making a cake.* 2 be very saving or economical: *She had to skimp to send her son to college.* 3 do imperfectly: *The lazy man skimped his job. She is always skimping on her assignments. v.*

skimp y (skim′pē), 1 scanty; not enough: *She got hungry in the afternoon after a skimpy meal.* 2 too saving or economical. *adj.,* **skimp i er, skimp i est.**

skin (skin), 1 the outer layer of tissue of the body in persons and animals, especially when soft and flexible: *Cows have thick skins.* 2 a hide; pelt: *The skin of a calf makes soft leather.* 3 any outer surface layer, as the rind of a fruit, a sausage casing, etc. 4 take the skin off: *He skinned his knees when he fell. The hunter skinned the deer.* 5 container made of skin for holding liquids. 6 SLANG. to swindle of money, etc.; cheat. 1-3,5 *n.,* 4,6 *v.,* **skinned, skin ning. —skin′like′,** *adj.*

by the skin of one's teeth, very narrowly; barely.

save one's skin, escape without harm.

skin-deep (skin′dēp′), no deeper than the skin; shallow; slight. *adj.*

skin-dive (skin′dīv′), engage in skin diving. *v.,* **skin-dived, skin-div ing.**

skin diver, person engaged in skin diving.

skin diving, sport of swimming under water, sometimes at considerable depth and for long periods of time, equipped with a face mask, rubber flippers, and often a portable breathing device.

skin flint (skin′flint′), a mean, stingy person. *n.*

hat, āge, fär; let, ēqual, tėrm; it, īce; hot, ōpen, ôrder; oil, out; cup, put, rüle; ch, child; ng, long; sh, she; th, thin; ₮H, then; zh, measure;

ə represents *a* in about, *e* in taken, *i* in pencil, *o* in lemon, *u* in circus.

skin less (skin′lis), having no skin: *skinless frankfurters. adj.*

skin ner (skin′ər), 1 person who skins. 2 person who prepares or deals in skins, furs, etc. *n.*

skin ny (skin′ē), 1 very thin; very lean. 2 like skin. *adj.,* **skin ni er, skin ni est.**

skip (skip), 1 leap lightly; spring; jump: *Lambs skipped in the fields.* 2 leap lightly over: *children skipping rope.* 3 a light spring, jump, or leap: *The child gave a skip of joy.* 4 go or send bounding along a surface: *We liked to skip stones on the lake.* 5 pass over; omit; pass from one thing to another, disregarding what is between: *She skips the hard words. Answer the questions in order without skipping.* 6 a passing over; omission. 7 advance in school by being promoted one or more grades ahead of the next regular grade. 8 IN-FORMAL. leave in a hurry: *They skipped town to avoid paying their bills.* 1,2,4,5,7,8 *v.,* **skipped, skip ping;** 3,6 *n.*

skip jack (skip′jak′), any of various fishes that sometimes leap out of the water, such as a variety of tuna. *n., pl.* **skip jacks** or **skip jack.**

skip per (skip′ər), 1 captain of a ship, especially of a small trading or fishing boat. 2 any captain or leader. *n.*

skir mish (skėr′mish), 1 a slight fight between small groups: *The boys had a skirmish over who would wear the cowboy hat.* 2 a slight conflict, argument, contest, etc. 3 take part in a skirmish. 1,2 *n., pl.* **skir mish es;** 3 *v.*

skirt (skėrt), 1 the part of a dress that hangs from the waist. 2 a woman's or girl's garment that hangs from the waist. 3 something like a skirt: *the skirts of a*

skin diver

adj.	adjective	*n.*	noun
adv.	adverb	*prep.*	preposition
conj.	conjunction	*pron.*	pronoun
interj.	interjection	*v.*	verb
sing.	singular	*pl.*	plural

man's long coat. 4 border; edge: *The rabbits fed at the skirts of the field.* 5 the outer part of a place, group of people, etc. 6 pass along the border or edge; pass along the border or edge of: *We skirted the swamp.* 1-5 *n.,* 6 *v.*

skit (skit), a short sketch that contains humor or satire: *a television skit. When we graduated the school newspaper had skits about each one of us. n.*

skit ter (skit′ər), move lightly or quickly; skim or skip along a surface. *v.*

skit tish (skit′ish), 1 apt to start, jump, or run; easily frightened: *a skittish horse.* 2 fickle; changeable: *a skittish wind.* 3 shy and timid; coy: *a skittish young girl. adj.*

skit tles (skit′lz), game in which the players try to knock down nine wooden pins by rolling balls or throwing wooden disks at them. *n.*

skoal (skōl), a Scandinavian word used in drinking a health. It means "Hail" or "May you prosper." *n., interj.*

skul dug ger y (skul dug′ər ē), INFORMAL. trickery; dishonesty. *n.*

skulk (skulk), 1 keep out of sight to avoid danger, work, duty, etc.; hide or lurk in a cowardly way. 2 move in a stealthy, sneaking way: *The wolf was skulking near the sheep. v.*

skull (skul), the bony framework of the head and face in man and other animals with backbones. The skull encloses and protects the brain. *n.*

skull and crossbones, picture of a human skull above two crossed bones. It was often used on pirates' flags as a symbol of death, and it is now often used on labels of poisonous drugs, etc.

skull cap (skul′kap′), a close-fitting cap without a brim. *n.*

skunk (skungk), 1 a black, bushy-tailed mammal of North America, usually with white stripes along its back. It is about the size of a cat. When fright-

skunk (def. 1)
about 2 ft. long with the tail

ened or attacked it squirts a spray of liquid with a very unpleasant, strong smell produced by a pair of glands near its tail. 2 fur of this animal, used on coats, etc. 3 INFORMAL. a mean, contemptible person. *n.*

sky (skī), 1 the space high above the earth, appearing as a great arch or dome covering the world; the region of the clouds or the upper air; the heavens: *a cloudy sky.* 2 heaven. *n., pl.* **skies.**

out of a clear sky, suddenly; unexpectedly.

to the skies, very highly: *to praise someone to the skies.*

sky blue, a clear, soft blue.

sky-high (skī′hī′), very high. *adv., adj.*

sky jack (skī′jak′), 1 hijack (an airplane), especially to a foreign country. 2 a hijacking of an airplane. 1 *v.,* 2 *n.* —**sky′jack′er,** *n.*

Sky lab (skī′lab′), the first U.S. space station. It was launched May 14, 1973, and orbits the earth. *n.*

sky lark (skī′lärk′), 1 a common European lark, a small bird that sings very sweetly as it flies toward the sky. 2 play pranks; frolic. 1 *n.,* 2 *v.*

sky light (skī′līt′), window in a roof or ceiling. *n.*

sky line (skī′līn′), 1 line at which earth and sky seem to meet; horizon. 2 outline of buildings, mountains, trees, etc., as seen against the sky: *The tall buildings and towers of New York make a remarkable skyline. n.*

sky rock et (skī′rok′it), 1 firework that goes up high in the air and bursts into a shower of stars, sparks, etc. 2 act like a skyrocket; rise suddenly and make a brilliant show: *The movie star skyrocketed to fame.* 3 rise much and quickly: *The price of beef skyrocketed during the shortage.* 1 *n.,* 2,3 *v.*

sky scrap er (skī′skrā′pər), a very tall building. *n.*

sky ward (skī′wərd), toward the sky. *adv., adj.*

sky wards (skī′wərdz), skyward. *adv.*

sky writ ing (skī′rī′ting), the tracing of words, etc., against the sky from an airplane. Smoke or some similar substance is used. *n.*

slab (slab), 1 a broad, flat, thick piece (of stone, wood, meat, etc.): *a slab of cheese as big as my hand. This sidewalk is made of slabs of concrete.* 2 a rough outside piece cut from a log. *n.*

slack (slak), 1 not tight or firm; loose: *The rope hung slack.* 2 part that hangs loose: *He pulled in the slack of the rope.* 3 careless: *She is a slack housekeeper.* 4 slow: *The horse was moving at a slack pace.* 5 not active; not brisk; dull: *Business is slack at this season.* 6 a dull

season; quiet period. 7 make slack; let up on: *He slacked his pace so we could catch up.* 8 be or become slack; let up: *The breeze slacked.* 1,3-5 *adj.,* 2,6 *n.,* 7,8 *v.* —**slack′ly,** *adv.* —**slack′ness,** *n.*

slack off, 1 loosen. 2 lessen one's efforts.

slack up, slow down; go more slowly.

slack en (slak′ən), 1 make or become slower: *Don't slacken your efforts till the work is done. Their business always slackens in the winter.* 2 make or become looser: *Slacken the rope. The rope slackened as the wave sent the boat toward the pier. v.*

slack er (slak′ər), INFORMAL. person who shirks work or evades his duty. *n.*

slacks (slaks), trousers for casual wear. *n.pl.*

slag (slag), 1 the rough, hard waste left after metal is separated from ore by melting. 2 a light, spongy lava. *n.*

slain (slān), past participle of **slay.** *The sheep were slain by the wolves. v.*

slake (slāk), 1 satisfy (thirst, revenge, wrath, etc.): *We slaked our thirst at the spring.* 2 put out (a fire). 3 change lime to slaked lime by leaving it in the moist air or putting water on it. *v.,* **slaked, slak ing.**

slaked lime, a white powder obtained by exposing lime to moist air or by putting water on lime; calcium hydroxide. Plaster contains slaked lime and sand.

sla lom (slä′ləm *or* slal′əm), (in skiing) a zigzag race downhill. *n.*

slam (slam), 1 shut with force and noise; close with a bang: *She slammed the window down. The door slammed.* 2 throw, push, hit, or move hard with force: *He slammed himself down on his bed. That car slammed into a truck.* 3 a violent and noisy closing, striking, etc.; bang: *I threw my books down with a slam.* 4 INFORMAL. criticize harshly. 5 the winning of 12 (**little slam** or **small slam**) or all 13 (**grand slam**) tricks in the game of bridge. 1,2,4 *v.,* 3,5 *n.,* **slammed, slam ming.**

slan der (slan′dər), 1 a false spoken statement meant to do harm to the good name and reputation of another. 2 talk falsely about. 3 the spreading of false reports: *Malicious slander had caused some people to doubt the mayor's honesty.* 1,3 *n.,* 2 *v.* —**slan′der er,** *n.*

slan der ous (slan′dər əs), 1 containing a slander. 2 speaking or spreading slanders. *adj.*

slang (slang), 1 words, phrases, meanings, etc., not accepted as good English when speaking or writing formal English. Slang is often very vivid and expressive and is used in familiar talk between friends but is not usually appropriate in school themes. Slang is mostly made up of new words or meanings that are popular for only a short time. *Slob* and *on the skids* are slang. 2 special talk of a particular class of people. *Shake a leg* is a slang expression for *hurry up*. *n.*

slang y (slang′ē), 1 containing slang; full of slang. 2 using much slang. *adj.*, **slang i er, slang i est.**

slant (slant), 1 to slope: *Most handwriting slants to the right. The carpenters slanted the roof to allow water to run off.* 2 a slanting or oblique direction or position; slope: *Has your roof a sharp slant?* 3 sloping: *A lean-to has a slant roof.* 4 way of regarding something; mental attitude. 1 *v.*, 2,4 *n.*, 3 *adj.*

slant ing (slan′ting), sloping: *a slanting roof.* *adj.* —**slant′ing ly,** *adv.*

slant ways (slant′wāz′), slantwise. *adv.*

slant wise (slant′wīz′), 1 in a slanting manner; obliquely. 2 slanting; oblique. 1 *adv.*, 2 *adj.*

slap (slap), 1 a blow with the open hand or with something flat. 2 strike with the open hand or with something flat: *He slapped at the fly with a folded newspaper. I slapped the table with my hand.* 3 sound made by a slapping. 4 put, dash, or cast with force: *She slapped the book down on the table.* 1,3 *n.*, 2,4 *v.*, **slapped, slap ping.**

slap dash (slap′dash′), 1 hastily and carelessly. 2 hasty and careless. 3 hasty, careless action, methods, or work. 1 *adv.*, 2 *adj.*, 3 *n.*

slap stick (slap′stik′), 1 comedy full of rough play. 2 full of rough play. In slapstick comedy, the actors knock each other around, throw pies at each other, etc., to make people laugh. 1 *n.*, 2 *adj.*

slash (slash), 1 to cut with a sweeping stroke of a sword, knife, etc.; gash: *I slashed the bark off the tree with my knife.* 2 make a slashing stroke: *She slashed at the vines growing across the path with her knife.* 3 a sweeping, slashing stroke: *the slash of a sword, the slash of the rain.* 4 a cut or wound made by such a stroke. 5 to cut or slit to let a different cloth or color show through. 6 whip severely; lash. 7 criticize sharply, severely, or unkindly: *The critics slashed the new play in the next morning's papers.* 8 cut down sharply; reduce a great deal: *My salary was slashed when business became bad.* 9 a sharp cutting down; great reduction: *a slash in prices.* 1,2,5-8 *v.*, 3,4,9 *n.*, *pl.* **slash es.**

slat (slat), a long, thin, narrow piece of wood or metal. *n.*

slate (slāt), 1 a fine-grained, bluish-gray rock that splits easily into thin, smooth layers. Slate is used to cover roofs and for blackboards. 2 a thin piece of this rock. Children used to write on slates, but now they use paper. 3 to cover with slate. 4 a dark, bluish gray. 5 dark bluish-gray. 6 list of candidates, officers, etc., to be considered for appointment, nomination, election, etc. 7 put on such a list: *She is slated for nomination to the office of class president.* 1,2,4,6 *n.*, 3,7 *v.*, **slat ed, slat ing;** 5 *adj.*

a clean slate, a record not marred by mistakes or faults: *to start again with a clean slate.*

slat tern (slat′ərn), woman who is dirty, careless, or untidy in her dress, her ways, her housekeeping, etc. *n.*

slat tern ly (slat′ərn lē), like a slattern; slovenly; untidy. *adj.*

slat y (slā′tē), 1 of, like, or having to do with slate. 2 slate-colored. *adj.*, **slat i er, slat i est.**

slaugh ter (slô′tər), 1 the killing of an animal or animals for food; butchering: *the slaughter of a steer, to fatten hogs for slaughter.* 2 brutal killing; much or needless killing: *The battle resulted in a frightful slaughter.* 3 kill an animal or animals for food; butcher: *Millions of cattle are slaughtered every year in the stockyards.* 4 kill brutally; massacre. 1,2 *n.*, 3,4 *v.*

slaugh ter house (slô′tər hous′), place where animals are killed for food. *n.*, *pl.* **slaugh ter hous es** (slô′tər hou′ziz).

Slav (släv), 1 member of a group of peoples in eastern, southeastern, and central Europe whose languages are related. Russians, Poles, Czechs, Slovaks, Slovenes, Bulgarians, and Yugoslavs are Slavs. 2 of or having to do with Slavs; Slavic. 1 *n.*, 2 *adj.*

slave (slāv), 1 person who is the property of another. 2 person who is controlled or ruled by some desire, habit, or influence: *He became a slave to his emotions.* 3 person who works like a slave. 4 work like a slave: *We slaved all day long cleaning our house.* 5 of slaves; done by slaves: *slave labor.* 1-3 *n.*, 4 *v.*, **slaved, slav ing;** 5 *adj.* —**slave′- like′,** *adj.*

slave driver, 1 overseer of slaves. 2 an exacting taskmaster.

slave hold er (slāv′hōl′dər), owner of slaves. *n.*

slave hold ing (slāv′hōl′ding), 1 owning slaves. 2 the owning of slaves. 1 *adj.*, 2 *n.*

slav er¹ (slā′vər), 1 dealer in slaves. 2 ship used in the slave trade. *n.* [*slave* + *-er¹*]

slav er² (slav′ər), 1 let saliva run from

hat, āge, fär; let, ēqual, tėrm; it, īce; hot, ōpen, ôrder; oil, out; cup, pùt, rüle; ch, child; ng, long; sh, she; th, thin; ᴛʜ, then; zh, measure;

ə represents *a* in about, *e* in taken, *i* in pencil, *o* in lemon, *u* in circus.

the mouth. 2 saliva running from the mouth. 1 *v.*, 2 *n.* [from a Scandinavian word of the 1200's, such as Icelandic *slafra*]

slav er y (slā′vər ē), 1 condition of being a slave. Many African Negroes were captured and sold into slavery. 2 custom of owning slaves. Where slavery is permitted, certain people own other people. 3 condition like that of a slave. 4 hard work like that of a slave. *n.*

slave trade, the business of procuring and selling slaves.

Slav ic (slä′vik), 1 of or having to do with the Slavs or their languages. 2 language or group of languages spoken by the Slavs. 1 *adj.*, 2 *n.*

slav ish (slā′vish), 1 of or having to do with a slave or slaves. 2 mean; base. 3 weakly submitting; like slaves; fit for slaves: *their slavish obedience.* 4 lacking originality and independence: *a slavish reproduction. adj.* —**slav′ish- ly,** *adv.* —**slav′ish ness,** *n.*

slaw (slô), coleslaw. *n.*

slay (slā), kill with violence: *Jack slew the giant.* *v.*, **slew, slain, slay ing.** —**slay′er,** *n.*

slea zi ness (slē′zē nis), sleazy quality. *n.*

slea zy (slē′zē), 1 flimsy and poor: *sleazy cloth.* 2 disreputable: *a sleazy hotel. adj.*, **slea zi er, slea zi est.**

sled (sled), 1 framework mounted on runners for use on snow or ice. Sleds pulled by dogs are common in the Arctic. 2 ride on a sled. 3 carry on a sled. 1 *n.*, 2,3 *v.*, **sled ded, sled ding.**

sled ding (sled′ing), a riding or coasting on a sled: *two months of good sledding. n.*

hard sledding, unfavorable conditions; difficult going: *The bill will have hard sledding before the legislature passes it.*

sledge¹ (slej), 1 a heavy sled or sleigh, usually pulled by horses, etc. 2 carry on a sledge. 3 ride in a sledge. 1 *n.*, 2,3 *v.*, **sledged, sledg ing.** [from Dutch of the 1600's *sleedze*]

sledge² (slej), sledge hammer. *n.* [Old English *slecg*]

adj. adjective	*n.* noun
adv. adverb	*prep.* preposition
conj. conjunction	*pron.* pronoun
interj. interjection	*v.* verb
sing. singular	*pl.* plural

sledge ham mer (slej′ham′ər), a large, heavy hammer, usually swung with both hands. *n.*

sledgehammer

sleek (slēk), 1 soft and glossy; smooth: *sleek hair.* 2 having smooth, soft skin, hair, fur, etc.: *a sleek cat.* 3 smooth of manners and speech: *a sleek salesclerk.* 4 having clean lines; trim: *a sleek jet plane.* 5 to smooth or make smooth: *He sleeked down his hair.* 1-4 *adj.*, 5 *v.* —**sleek′ly,** *adv.*

sleep (slēp), 1 to rest body and mind; be without ordinary thought or movement: *We sleep at night.* 2 a rest of body and mind occurring naturally and regularly in animals: *Most people need eight hours of sleep a day.* 3 be in a condition like sleep: *The seeds sleep in the ground all winter.* 4 condition like sleep. The last sleep means death. 1,3 *v.,* **slept, sleep ing;** 2,4 *n.*

sleep away, pass or spend in sleeping: *I slept away the whole morning.*

sleep off, get rid of by sleeping: *She was sleeping off a headache.*

sleep er (slē′pər), 1 person or thing that sleeps: *The noise woke the sleepers.* 2 a railroad sleeping car. 3 a heavy horizontal beam used as a support. *n.*

sleep i ly (slē′pə lē), in a sleepy manner. *adv.*

sleep i ness (slē′pē nis), sleepy quality or condition. *n.*

sleep ing (slē′ping), 1 sleep. 2 that sleeps. 3 used for sleeping on or in: *sleeping quarters.* 1 *n.,* 2,3 *adj.*

sleeping bag, a canvas or waterproof bag, usually warmly lined, to sleep in out of doors.

sleeping car, a railroad car with berths for passengers to sleep in; Pullman.

sleeping sickness, 1 disease common in Africa and carried by the tsetse fly, causing fever, weakness, loss of weight, sleepiness, and usually death. 2 a virus disease marked by inflammation of the brain, weakness, and extreme drowsiness.

sleep less (slēp′lis), 1 without sleep; restless: *a hot, sleepless night.* 2 watchful; wide-awake. 3 always moving or acting. *adj.* —**sleep′less ly,** *adv.* —**sleep′less ness,** *n.*

sleep walk er (slēp′wô′kər), person who walks about while asleep. *n.*

sleep walk ing (slēp′wô′king), act of walking while asleep. *n.*

sleep y (slē′pē), 1 ready to go to sleep; inclined to sleep: *He never gets enough rest and is always sleepy.* 2 not active; quiet: *a sleepy little mountain town. adj.,* **sleep i er, sleep i est.**

sleep y head (slē′pē hed′), a sleepy, drowsy, or lazy person. *n.*

sleet (slēt), 1 partly frozen rain; snow or hail mixed with rain. Sleet forms when rain falls through a layer of cold air. 2 come down in sleet: *It sleeted; then it snowed; then it rained.* 1 *n.,* 2 *v.*

sleet y (slē′tē), of or like sleet; characterized by sleet: *a dismal and sleety morning. adj.,* **sleet i er, sleet i est.**

sleeve (slēv), 1 the part of a garment that covers the arm: *The sleeves of his coat were too long and hung down over his hands.* 2 tube into which a rod or another tube fits. *n.*

laugh up one's sleeve, be amused but not show it.

up one's sleeve, in reserve; ready for use when needed.

sleeve less (slēv′lis), without sleeves: *a sleeveless summer dress. adj.*

sleigh (def. 1)

sleigh (slā), 1 carriage or cart mounted on runners for use on ice or snow. In northern countries people use sleighs in the winter. 2 to travel or ride in a sleigh. 1 *n.,* 2 *v.*

sleight (slīt), 1 skill; dexterity. 2 a clever trick. *n.*

sleight of hand, 1 skill and quickness in moving the hands. 2 tricks or skill of a modern magician; juggling.

slen der (slen′dər), 1 long and thin; not big around; slim: *a slender child. A pencil is a slender piece of wood.* 2 slight; small; scanty: *a slender meal, a slender income, a slender hope. adj.* —**slen′der ness,** *n.*

slept (slept), past tense and past participle of **sleep.** *The child slept soundly. I haven't slept well for weeks. v.*

sleuth (slüth), 1 bloodhound. 2 INFORMAL. detective. *n.*

slew[1] (slü), past tense of **slay.** *Jack slew the giant. v.*

slew[2] (slü), 1 to turn; swing; twist: *She slewed the front wheels sharply to avoid hitting the dog. The car slewed to the left when she put the brakes on hard.* 2 a turn; swing; twist. 1 *v.,* 2 *n.* Also, **slue.** [origin unknown]

slew[3] (slü), INFORMAL. a lot; large number or amount: *The new girl quickly gained a slew of friends. n.* [from Irish *sluagh* crowd]

slice (slīs), 1 a thin, flat, broad piece cut from something: *a slice of bread, meat, or cake.* 2 cut into slices: *slice the bread. We ate sliced peaches.* 3 cut (off) as a slice. 4 cut through or across: *The boat sliced the waves.* 5 (in sports) hit (a ball) so that it curves to one's right if hit right-handed. 1 *n.,* 2-5 *v.,* **sliced, slicing.**

slic er (slī′sər), 1 tool or machine that slices: *a meat slicer.* 2 person who slices. *n.*

slick (slik), 1 soft and glossy; smooth: *slick hair.* 2 make sleek or smooth. 3 slippery; greasy: *a road slick with ice or mud.* 4 a smooth place or spot. Oil makes a slick on the surface of water. 5 INFORMAL. clever; ingenious. 6 sly; tricky. 7 smooth of speech, manners, etc. 1,3,5-7 *adj.,* 2 *v.,* 4 *n.* —**slick′ly,** *adv.* —**slick′ness,** *n.*

slick er (slik′ər), 1 a long, loose, waterproof coat, made of oilskin or the like. 2 INFORMAL. a sly, tricky person. *n.*

slid (slid), past tense and a past participle of **slide.** *The minutes slid rapidly by. v.*

slid den (slid′n), slid; a past participle of **slide.** *v.*

slide (slīd), 1 move smoothly along a surface: *The bureau drawers slide in and out.* 2 move easily, quietly, or secretly: *I hid by sliding behind the door.* 3 to slip as when losing one's foothold: *The car slid into the ditch.* 4 pass by degrees; slip: *They slid into bad habits.* 5 pass or put quietly or secretly: *He slid a gun into his pocket.* 6 act of sliding: *The children each take a slide in turn.* 7 a smooth surface for sliding on: *The frozen brook makes a good slide.* 8 track, rail, etc., on which something slides. 9 something that slides or that works by sliding. 10 mass of earth, snow, etc., sliding down: *The slide cut off the valley from the rest of the world.* 11 the sliding down of such a mass: *The slide was felt at the other end of the valley.* 12 a small, thin sheet of glass on which objects are placed in order to look at them under a microscope. 13 a small transparent photograph made of glass or film. Slides are put in a projector and shown on a screen. 1-5 *v.*, **slid, slid** or **slid den, slid ing;** 6-13 *n.*

let slide, neglect; not bother about: *They let their business slide until they were bankrupt.*

slide fastener, zipper.

slide projector, instrument for projecting onto a screen the images on photographic slides.

slide rule

slide rule, ruler with a sliding section in the center, both parts marked with logarithmic scales, used for making rapid mathematical calculations.

slight (slīt), 1 not much; not important; small: *I have a slight headache.* 2 not big around; slender: *She is a slight girl.* 3 treat as of little value; pay too little attention to; neglect: *They often slight their work. I felt slighted because I was not asked to the party.* 4 slighting treatment; act of neglect: *Cinderella suffered many slights from her stepsisters.* 1,2 *adj.*, 3 *v.*, 4 *n.* —**slight′ness,** *n.*

slight ing (slī′ting), that slights: *a slighting remark. adj.* —**slight′ing ly,** *adv.*

slight ly (slīt′lē), 1 in a slight manner. 2 to a slight degree; somewhat; a little: *I knew him slightly. adv.*

sli ly (slī′lē), slyly. *adv.*

slim (slim), 1 slender; thin: *He was very slim, being 6 feet tall and weighing only 130 pounds.* 2 small; slight; weak: *We had a slim attendance at the football game because of the rain. The invalid's chances for getting well were very slim.* 3 make or become slim or slender: *slim down one's weight with a rigid diet.* 1,2 *adj.*, **slim mer, slim mest;** 3 *v.*, **slimmed, slim ming.** —**slim′ly,** *adv.* —**slim′ness,** *n.*

slime (slīm), 1 soft, sticky mud or something like it: *Her shoes were covered with slime from the swamp.* 2 a sticky substance given off by snails, snakes, fish, etc. 3 disgusting filth. *n.*

slim y (slī′mē), 1 covered with slime: *The pond is too slimy to swim in.* 2 of or like slime. 3 disgusting; filthy. *adj.*, **slim i er, slim i est.**

sling (sling), 1 strip of leather with a string fastened to each end, for throwing stones. 2 a slingshot. 3 throw with a sling. 4 throw; cast; hurl; fling: *We slung some pebbles into the lake.* 5 a hanging loop of cloth fastened around the neck to support an injured arm. 6 loop of rope, band, chain, etc., by which heavy objects are lifted, carried,

or held: *We lowered the boxes into the cellar with a sling.* 7 raise, lower, etc., with a sling. 8 hang in a sling; hang so as to swing loosely: *I carried the bedroll slung over my shoulder.* 1,2,5,6 *n.*, 3,4,7,8 *v.*, **slung, sling ing.**

sling shot (sling′shot′), a Y-shaped stick with a band of rubber between its prongs, used to shoot pebbles, etc. *n.*

slink (slingk), move in a sneaking, guilty manner; sneak: *After stealing the meat, the dog slunk away. v.*, **slunk, slink ing.**

slip[1] (slip), 1 go or move smoothly, quietly, easily, or quickly: *She slipped out of the room. Time slips by. The ship slips through the waves. The drawer is slipping into place.* 2 slide; move out of place: *The knife slipped and cut his finger.* 3 slide suddenly without wanting to: *He slipped on the icy sidewalk.* 4 act or fact of slipping: *My broken leg resulted from a slip on a banana peel.* 5 cause to slip; put, pass, or draw smoothly, quietly, or secretly: *I slipped back the bolt on the door. I slipped the ring from my finger. Slip the note into her hand.* 6 put or take (something) easily or quickly: *Slip on your coat and come with us. Slip off your shoes.* 7 pillowcase. 8 a sleeveless garment worn under a dress. 9 pass without notice; pass through neglect; escape: *Don't let this opportunity slip.* 10 get loose from; get away from; escape from: *The dog has slipped its collar. Your name has slipped my mind.* 11 fall off; decline: *Sales are slipping.* 12 make a mistake or error: *I slipped when I mailed the wrong letter.* 13 mistake; error: *He makes slips in pronouncing words. That remark was a slip of the tongue.* 14 space for ships between wharves or in a dock. 1-3,5,6,9-12 *v.*, **slipped, slip ping;** 4,7,8,13,14 *n.* [perhaps from earlier German *slippen*]

let slip, tell without meaning to: *They talked too much and let the secret slip.*

slip one over on, INFORMAL. get the advantage of, especially by trickery: *The fox slipped one over on the hounds and got away.*

slip up, INFORMAL. make a mistake or error: *I must have slipped up somewhere when I did the problem, because my answer is wrong.*

slip[2] (slip), 1 a small, narrow strip of paper, wood, etc.: *The teacher passed out slips of paper for us to write our names on.* 2 a young, slender person:

sling (def. 6)

hat, āge, fär; let, ēqual, tėrm;
it, īce; hot, ōpen, ôrder;
oil, out; cup, pùt, rüle; ch, child;
ng, long; sh, she; th, thin;
ᵺH, then; zh, measure;

ə represents *a* in about,
e in taken, *i* in pencil,
o in lemon, *u* in circus.

He is just a slip of a boy. 3 a small branch or twig cut from a plant, used to grow a new plant: *She has promised us slips from her rosebush.* 4 cut branches from (a plant) to grow new plants; take (a part) from a plant. 1-3 *n.*, 4 *v.*, **slipped, slip ping.** [probably from earlier Dutch or German *slippen*]

slip cov er (slip′kuv′ər), a removable cloth cover for a chair, sofa, etc. *n.*

slip knot (slip′not′), knot made to slip along the rope or cord around which it is made; running knot. See **knot** for diagram. *n.*

slip per (slip′ər), a light, low shoe that is slipped on easily: *dancing slippers, bedroom slippers. n.*

slip pered (slip′ərd), wearing slippers. *adj.*

slip per i ness (slip′ər ē nis), slippery quality or condition. *n.*

slip per y (slip′ər ē), 1 causing or likely to cause slipping: *The steps are slippery with ice.* 2 slipping away easily: *Wet soap is slippery.* 3 not to be depended on; tricky. *adj.*, **slip per i er, slip per i est.**

slip shod (slip′shod′), careless in dress, habits, speech, etc.; untidy; slovenly. *adj.*

slip-up (slip′up′), INFORMAL. mistake; error: *I want this job done right, with no slip-ups. n.*

slit (slit), 1 cut or tear in a straight line; make a long, straight cut or tear in: *slit cloth into strips, slit a skirt to make a pocket.* 2 a straight, narrow cut, tear, or opening: *a slit in a bag, the slit in a letter box.* 1 *v.*, **slit, slit ting;** 2 *n.*

slith er (sliᵺ′ər), 1 slide down or along a surface, especially unsteadily: *Rocks slithered down the side of the hill.* 2 go with a sliding motion: *The snake slithered into the weeds.* 3 a slithering movement; a slide. 1,2 *v.*, 3 *n.*

sliv er (sliv′ər), 1 a long, thin piece that has been split off, broken off, or cut off; splinter. 2 split or break into slivers. 1 *n.*, 2 *v.*

slob (slob), SLANG. a stupid, untidy, or clumsy person. *n.*

slob ber (slob′ər), 1 let liquid run out from the mouth; drool. 2 saliva or other

adj. adjective	*n.* noun
adv. adverb	*prep.* preposition
conj. conjunction	*pron.* pronoun
interj. interjection	*v.* verb
sing. singular	*pl.* plural

liquid running out from the mouth. 3 speak in a silly, sentimental way. 1,3 *v.,* 2 *n.*

slob ber y (slob′ər ē), 1 slobbering. 2 disagreeably wet; sloppy. *adj.*

sloe (slō), 1 a dark-purple, plumlike fruit. 2 the thorny shrub that it grows on; blackthorn. *n.*

slo gan (slō′gən), 1 word or phrase used by a business, club, political party, etc., to advertise its purpose; motto: *"Service with a smile" was the store's slogan.* 2 a war cry; battle cry. *n.*

sloop (slüp), sailboat having one mast, a mainsail, a jib, and sometimes other sails. *n.*

sloop

slop (slop), 1 spill liquid upon; spill; splash: *She slopped water on me.* 2 liquid carelessly spilled or splashed about. 3 Often, **slops,** *pl.* dirty water; liquid garbage: *kitchen slops.* 4 a thin, liquid mud or slush. 5 splash through mud, slush, or water. 6 weak, liquid food, such as gruel. 1,5 *v.,* **slopped, slop ping;** 2-4,6 *n.*

slop over, SLANG. show too much feeling, enthusiasm, etc.

slope (slōp), 1 go up or down at an angle; slant: *a sloping roof. The land slopes toward the sea.* 2 any line, surface, land, etc., that goes up or down at an angle: *If you roll a ball up a slope, it will roll down again.* 3 amount of slope: *The floor of the theater has a slope of four feet from back to front.* 1 *v.,* **sloped, slop ing;** 2,3 *n.*

slop pi ly (slop′ə lē), in a sloppy manner. *adv.*

slop pi ness (slop′ē nis), sloppy quality or condition. *n.*

slop py (slop′ē), 1 very wet; slushy: *sloppy ground, sloppy weather.* 2 IN-FORMAL. careless; slovenly: *do sloppy work, use sloppy English.* 3 IN-

FORMAL. weak; silly: *sloppy sentiment. adj.,* **slop pi er, slop pi est.**

slosh (slosh), splash in slush, mud, or water: *He sloshed around in the bathtub and got the floor all wet. v.*

slot (slot), 1 a small, narrow opening or depression: *Put a penny in the slot to get a stick of gum from this machine.* 2 make a slot or slots in. 1 *n.,* 2 *v.,* **slot ted, slot ting.**

sloth (slôth *or* slōth), 1 unwillingness to work or exert oneself; laziness; idleness: *His sloth keeps him from engaging in sports.* 2 a very slow-moving mammal of South and Central America that lives in trees. Sloths hang upside down from tree branches. *n.*

sloth ful (slôth′fəl *or* slōth′fəl), unwilling to work or exert oneself; lazy; idle. *adj.* —**sloth′ful ly,** *adv.* —**sloth′ful ness,** *n.*

slot machine, machine that is worked by dropping a coin into a slot. Some slot machines sell peanuts, sticks of gum, etc.; others are used for gambling.

slouch (slouch), 1 stand, sit, walk, or move in an awkward, drooping manner: *The weary traveler slouched along.* 2 a bending forward of head and shoulders; awkward, drooping way of standing, sitting, or walking. 3 droop or bend downward: *I slouched my shoulders.* 4 an awkward, slovenly, or inefficient person. 1,3 *v.,* 2,4 *n., pl.* **slouch es.**

slouch hat, a soft hat, usually with a soft brim that bends down easily.

slouch y (slou′chē), slouching awkwardly; carelessly untidy. *adj.,* **slouch i er, slouch i est.**

slough¹ (slou *for 1;* slü *for 2),* 1 a soft, deep, muddy place. 2 a swampy place; marshy inlet; slue. *n.* [Old English *slōh*]

slough² (sluf), 1 the old skin shed or cast off by a snake. 2 drop off; throw off; shed or cast: *slough a heavy pack. I finally sloughed off my bad habits.* 3 be shed or cast; drop or fall: *A scab sloughs off when new skin takes its place.* 4 anything that has been shed or cast off: *As people become civilized, they cast off the slough of primitive ways, beliefs, etc.* 1,4 *n.,* 2,3 *v.* [Middle English *slouh*]

Slo vak (slō′vak), 1 member of a Slavic people living in Slovakia. The Slovaks are related to the Bohemians and the Moravians. 2 their language. 3 of or having to do with Slovakia, its people, or their language. 1,2 *n.,* 3 *adj.*

Slo va ki a (slō vä′kē ə), region in E Czechoslovakia. *n.* —**Slo va′ki an,** *adj., n.*

slov en (sluv′ən), 1 person who is untidy, dirty, or careless in dress, ap-

pearance, habits, work, etc. 2 untidy; dirty; careless. 1 *n.,* 2 *adj.*

Slo vene (slō′vēn′), 1 member of a Slavic people living in Slovenia. The Slovenes are related to the Croats and Serbians. 2 their language. *n.*

Slo ve ni a (slō vē′nē ə), region in NW Yugoslavia. *n.* —**Slo ve′ni an,** *adj., n.*

sloth (def. 2)
about 2 ft. long

slov en li ness (sluv′ən lē nis), lack of neatness; carelessness in appearance, dress, habits, work, etc. *n.*

slov en ly (sluv′ən lē), 1 untidy, dirty, or careless in dress, appearance, habits, work, etc. 2 in a slovenly manner. 1 *adj.,* **slov en li er, slov en li est;** 2 *adv.*

slow (slō), 1 taking a long time; taking longer than usual; not fast or quick: *a slow journey. She is slow to anger.* 2 behind time; running at less than proper speed: *a slow runner.* 3 indicating time earlier than the correct time: *a slow clock.* 4 causing a low or lower rate of speed: *slow ground, a slow track.* 5 make slow or slower; reduce the speed of: *slow down a car.* 6 become slow; go slower: *Slow up when you drive through a town.* 7 in a slow manner: *Drive slow past a school.* 8 sluggish; inactive: *Business is slow.* 9 dull; not interesting: *a slow party.* 10 not quick to understand: *a slow pupil.* 1-4,8-10 *adj.,* 5,6 *v.,* 7 *adv.* —**slow′ly,** *adv.* —**slow′ness,** *n.*

slow-mo tion (slō′mō′shən), showing action at much less than its actual speed: *slow-motion photography. adj.*

slow poke (slō′pōk′), INFORMAL. a very slow person or thing. *n.*

sludge (sluj), 1 soft mud; mire; slush. 2 a soft, thick, muddy mixture, deposit, sediment, etc. 3 small broken pieces of floating ice: *In winter there is sludge on the sea near the shore. n.*

slue¹ (slü), slew². *v.,* **slued, slu ing;** *n.* [a different form of *slew²*]

slue² (slü), slough¹ (def. 2). *n.* [a different form of *slough¹*]

slug¹ (slug), 1 a slow-moving animal like a snail, without a shell or with only a partially developed shell. Slugs live mostly in forests, gardens, and damp places feeding on plants. 2 caterpillar or larva that looks like a slug. 3 any slow-moving person, animal, wagon, etc. 4 piece of lead or other metal for firing from a gun. 5 a round metal piece or counterfeit coin inserted in a coin-operated machine instead of a genuine coin. 6 strip of metal used to space lines of type. A slug is more than $1/16$ of an inch in thickness. *n.* [Middle English *slugge* a slow person, from a Scandinavian word, such as Swedish *slogga* be sluggish]

slug² (slug), INFORMAL. 1 hit hard with the fist or with a baseball bat; hit hard. 2 a hard blow with the fist. 1 *v.*, **slugged, slug ging;** 2 *n.* [origin uncertain]

slug gard (slug′ərd), a lazy, idle person. *n.*

slug ger (slug′ər), INFORMAL. a person who slugs or hits hard, especially a boxer who punches very hard, or a home-run hitter in baseball. *n.*

slug gish (slug′ish), 1 slow-moving; not active; lacking energy or vigor: *When I stay up late, I am often sluggish the next day.* 2 moving slowly; having little motion: *The stream was so sluggish that I could hardly tell which way it flowed. adj.* —**slug′gish ly,** *adv.* —**slug′gish ness,** *n.*

sluice (slüs), 1 structure with a gate for holding back or controlling the water of a canal, river, or lake. 2 gate that holds back or controls the flow of water. When the water behind a dam gets too high, the sluices are opened. 3 let out or draw off (water) by opening a sluice. 4 flush or cleanse with a rush of water; pour or throw water over. 5 a long, sloping trough through which water flows, used to wash gold from sand, dirt, or gravel. 6 wash (gold) from sand, dirt, or gravel in a sluice. 7 channel for carrying off overflow or surplus water. 1,2,5,7 *n.*, 3,4,6 *v.*, **sluiced, sluic ing.**

slum (slum), 1 Often, **slums,** *pl.* a run-down, overcrowded part of a city or town. Poverty and disease are common in the slums. 2 go into or visit the slums. 1 *n.*, 2 *v.*, **slummed, slumming.**

slum ber (slum′bər), 1 to sleep lightly; doze. 2 a light sleep: *I awoke from my slumber.* 3 pass in sleep: *The baby slumbers away the hours.* 4 be inactive: *The volcano had slumbered for years.* 5 an inactive state or condition. 1,3,4 *v.*, 2,5 *n.* —**slum′ber er,** *n.*

slum ber ous (slum′bər əs), 1 sleepy; heavy with drowsiness: *slumberous eyelids.* 2 causing or inducing sleep. *adj.*

slum brous (slum′brəs), slumberous. *adj.*

slump (slump), 1 drop heavily; fall suddenly: *The thin air made me so faint that I slumped to the ground.* 2 move, walk, sit, etc., in a drooping manner; slouch: *The bored students slumped in their seats.* 3 a heavy or sudden fall; collapse. 4 a great or sudden decline: *a slump in prices.* 1,2 *v.*, 3,4 *n.*

slung (slung), past tense and past participle of **sling.** *They slung some stones and ran away. The girl had slung her laundry bag over her shoulder. v.*

slunk (slungk), past tense and past participle of **slink.** *The dog slunk away ashamed. v.*

slur (slėr), 1 pass lightly over; go through hurriedly or in a careless way. 2 pronounce indistinctly: *Many persons slur "how do you do."* 3 a slurred pronunciation, sound, etc. 4 sing or play (two or more tones of different pitch) without a break; run together in a smooth, connected manner. 5 a slurring of tones. 6 a curved mark (⌢) (⌣) indicating this. 7 a blot or stain (upon reputation); insulting or slighting remark: *a slur on a person's good name.* 8 harm the reputation of; insult; slight. 1,2,4,8 *v.*, **slurred, slur ring;** 3,5-7 *n.*

slush (slush), 1 partly melted snow; snow and water mixed. 2 soft mud. 3 silly, sentimental talk, writing, etc. *n.*

slush i ness (slush′ē nis), slushy condition or quality. *n.*

slush y (slush′ē), 1 having much slush. 2 of or like slush. *adj.*, **slush i er, slush i est.**

sluice (def. 5)—Grooves in the bottom of the sluice catch and hold the gold as the lighter material is washed away.

slut (slut), 1 a dirty, untidy woman. 2 woman of loose morals. *n.*

sly (slī), 1 able to fool, trick, or deceive; cunning; crafty; tricky; wily: *someone as sly as a fox. The sly cat stole the meat while the cook's back was turned.* 2 playfully mischievous or knowing: *a sly wink. Waiting for the surprise party to begin, the children exchanged many sly looks and smiles.* 3 acting secretly or stealthily. *adj.*, **sly er, sly est** or **sli er, sli est.** —**sly′ness,** *n.*

on the sly, in a sly way.

sly ly (slī′lē), in a sly manner. *adv.* Also, **slily.**

smack¹ (smak), 1 a slight taste or flavor: *The sauce had a smack of nutmeg.* 2 trace; suggestion: *The old sailor still had a smack of the sea about him.* 3 have a smack: *The immigrant talked in a way that smacked of the old country.* 1,2 *n.*, 3 *v.* [Old English *smæcc*]

smack² (smak), 1 open (the lips) quickly so as to make a sharp sound: *She smacked her lips at the thought of cake.* 2 a smacking movement of the lips.

hat, āge, fär; let, ēqual, tèrm; it, īce; hot, ōpen, ôrder; oil, out; cup, pùt, rüle; ch, child; ng, long; sh, she; th, thin; ᴛʜ, then; zh, measure;

ə represents *a* in about, *e* in taken, *i* in pencil, *o* in lemon, *u* in circus.

3 the sharp sound made in this way. 4 kiss loudly. 5 to slap: *She smacked the horse on its rump.* 6 crack (a whip, etc.). 7 a loud kiss, slap, or crack. 8 INFORMAL. directly; squarely: *He fell smack on his face.* 1,4-6 *v.*, 2,3,7 *n.*, 8 *adv.* [an imitation of the sound]

smack³ (smak), 1 a small sailboat with one mast. 2 a fishing boat with a well for keeping fish alive. *n.* [probably from Dutch *smak*]

small (smôl), 1 not large; little; not large as compared with other things of the same kind: *A cottage is a small house.* 2 not great in amount, degree, extent, duration, value, strength, etc.: *a small dose, small hope of success. The cent is our smallest coin.* 3 not important: *This is only a small matter.* 4 not prominent; of low social position; humble; poor: *Both great and small people mourned the President's death.* 5 having little land, capital, etc.; doing business on a limited scale: *a small farmer. They own a small business.* 6 having little strength; gentle; soft; low: *a small voice.* 7 mean: *A person with a small nature is not generous.* 8 (of letters) not capital. 9 that which is small; a small, slender, or narrow part: *the small of the back.* 1-8 *adj.*, 9 *n.* —**small′ness,** *n.*

feel small, be ashamed or humiliated.

small arms, weapons easily carried by a person, such as rifles or revolvers.

small change, 1 coins of small value, such as nickels, dimes, etc. 2 anything small and unimportant.

small fry, 1 babies or children; small or young creatures. 2 people or things having little importance.

small hours, the early hours in the morning.

small intestine, the slender part of the intestines, extending from the stomach to the large intestine. It is a long, winding tube that receives partly digested food from the stomach. The small intestine completes the digestion of food and sends it into the blood. See **intestine** for diagram.

small ish (smô′lish), rather small. *adj.*

adj. adjective	*n.* noun
adv. adverb	*prep.* preposition
conj. conjunction	*pron.* pronoun
interj. interjection	*v.* verb
sing. singular	*pl.* plural

small letter, an ordinary letter, not a capital.

small-mind ed (smôl′mīn′did), narrow-minded; petty; mean. *adj.*

small pox (smôl′poks′), a very contagious disease characterized by fever and eruptions like blisters on the skin that often leave permanent scars shaped like little pits. Vaccination prevents smallpox. *n.*

small talk, conversation about unimportant matters; chit-chat.

smart (smärt), 1 feel sharp pain: *Her eyes smarted.* 2 cause sharp pain: *The cut smarts.* 3 a sharp pain: *The smart of the wound kept me awake.* 4 feel distress or irritation: *I smarted from the scolding.* 5 sharp; severe: *He gave the horse a smart blow.* 6 keen; active; lively: *They walked home at a smart pace.* 7 clever; bright: *a smart student.* 8 fresh and neat; in good order: *the smart uniforms of the band members.* 9 stylish; fashionable: *some smart new clothes.* 10 in a smart manner; cleverly. 1,2,4 *v.,* 3 *n.,* 5-9 *adj.,* 10 *adv.* —**smart′ly,** *adv.* —**smart′ness,** *n.*

smart al eck (al′ik), a conceited, obnoxious person.

smart en (smärt′n), 1 improve in appearance; brighten. 2 make or become brisker. *v.*

smash (smash), 1 break into pieces with violence and noise: *smash a dish, smash a window with a stone.* 2 destroy; shatter; ruin: *smash an argument, smash a person's hopes.* 3 be broken to pieces: *The dishes smashed on the floor.* 4 become ruined. 5 rush violently; crash: *The car smashed into a tree.* 6 a violent crash or collision: *Two cars were involved in the smash.* 7 act or sound of smashing: *the smash of broken glass.* 8 a crushing defeat; disaster. 9 INFORMAL. a highly successful performance or production; great hit: *a theatrical smash.* 10 INFORMAL. highly successful: *a smash Broadway musical.* 1-5 *v.,* 6-9 *n., pl.* **smash es;** 10 *adj.*

smash-up (smash′up′), 1 a bad collision; wreck. 2 a great misfortune; disaster. *n.*

smat ter ing (smat′ər ing), slight or superficial knowledge: *a smattering of French. n.*

smear (smir), 1 cover or stain with anything sticky, greasy, or dirty: *I smeared my fingers with jam.* 2 rub or spread (oil, grease, paint, etc.). 3 a mark or stain left by smearing: *There are smears of paint on the wallpaper.* 4 receive a mark or stain; be smeared: *Wet paint smears easily.* 5 harm; soil; spoil: *smear a person's good reputation.* 6 act of smearing. 1,2,4,5 *v.,* 3,6 *n.*

smell (smel), 1 perceive by breathing in through the nose: *Can you smell the smoke?* 2 sense of smelling: *Smell is keener in dogs than in people.* 3 use this sense: *We smell with our noses.* 4 sniff at: *pick up a rose and smell it. The dog smelled the strange man's legs.* 5 quality in a thing that affects the sense of smell; odor: *The smell of burning rubber is not pleasant.* 6 give out a smell: *The garden smelled of roses.* 7 give out a bad smell; have a bad smell: *That dirty, wet dog smells.* 8 find a trace or suggestion of: *We smelled trouble.* 9 have the smell (of); have the trace (of): *The plan smells of trickery.* 10 act of smelling: *Have a smell of this rose.* 1,3,4,6-9 *v.,* **smelled** or **smelt, smell ing;** 2,5,10 *n.*

smelling salts, a form of ammonia inhaled to relieve faintness, headaches, etc.

smell y (smel′ē), having or giving out a strong or unpleasant smell: *Rotten fish are smelly. adj.,* **smell i er, smell i est.**

smelt[1] (smelt), 1 melt (ore) in order to get the metal out of it. 2 obtain (metal) from ore by melting. 3 refine (impure metal) by melting. *v.* [probably from earlier German *smelten*]

smelt[2] (smelt), a small, salt-water or fresh-water food fish with silvery scales. *n., pl.* **smelts** or **smelt.** [Old English]

smelt[3] (smelt), smelled; a past tense and a past participle of **smell.** *v.*

smelt er (smel′tər), 1 person whose work or business is smelting ores or metals. 2 place where ores or metals are smelted. 3 furnace for smelting ores. *n.*

smidg en (smij′ən), INFORMAL. a tiny bit: *There isn't a smidgen of truth in this rumor. n.*

smile (smīl), 1 look pleased or amused; show pleasure, favor, kindness, amusement, etc., by an upward curve of the mouth. 2 show scorn, disdain, etc., by a curve of the mouth: *She smiled bitterly.* 3 bring, put, drive, etc., by smiling: *Smile your tears away.* 4 give (a smile): *She smiled a sunny smile.* 5 express by a smile: *He smiled consent.* 6 act of smiling: *a friendly smile, a smile of pity.* 7 to look upon or regard with favor: *Good fortune always smiled at her.* 8 a favoring look or regard. 1-5,7 *v.,*

smiled, smil ing; 6,8 *n.* —**smil′ing ly,** *adv.*

smirch (smėrch), 1 make dirty; soil with soot, dirt, dust, dishonor, disgrace, etc. 2 a dirty mark; blot; stain. 1 *v.,* 2 *n., pl.* **smirch es.**

smirk (smėrk), 1 smile in an affected, silly, or self-satisfied way. 2 an affected, silly, or self-satisfied smile. 1 *v.,* 2 *n.*

smit (smit), 1 smitten; a past participle of **smite.** 2 NOT USED NOW. smote; a past tense of **smite.** *v.*

smite (smīt), strike hard; hit hard; strike: *The hero smote the giant with his sword. The sound of a blacksmith's hammer smote upon their ears. I was smitten with curiosity about the forbidden room. v.,* **smote, smit ten** or **smit, smit ing.**

smith (smith), 1 worker in metal, especially iron. 2 blacksmith. *n.*

Smith (smith), 1 Captain **John,** 1580-1631, English explorer and early settler in Virginia. 2 **Joseph,** 1805-1844, founder of the Mormon Church. *n.*

smith e reens (smiTH′ə rēnz′), INFORMAL. small pieces; bits: *smash a chair into smithereens. n.pl.*

smith y (smith′ē), workshop of a smith, especially a blacksmith: *"Under a spreading chestnut tree the village smithy stands." n., pl.* **smith ies.**

smit ten (smit′n), 1 hard hit; struck: *sudden sparks from smitten steel.* 2 a past participle of **smite.** *The country was smitten with a famine.* 1 *adj.,* 2 *v.*

smock (smok), 1 a loose outer garment worn to protect clothing. 2 ornament (a smock, dress, etc.) with a honeycomb pattern made of lines of stitches crossing each other diagonally. 1 *n.,* 2 *v.*

smocking

smock ing (smok′ing), a honeycomb pattern formed by lines of stitches crossing each other diagonally and gathering the material, used to ornament smocks, dresses, etc. *n.*

smog (smog), combination of smoke and fog in the air: *Automobile exhaust fumes were blamed as one of the major causes of smog. n.*

smoke (smōk), 1 the mixture of gases and particles of carbon that can be seen rising in a cloud from anything burning. 2 something like this. 3 give off smoke or steam, or something like it: *The fireplace smokes. The turkey was brought smoking hot to the table.* 4 draw the smoke from (a cigarette, cigar, pipe, etc.) into the mouth and puff it out again. **5** that which is smoked; cigarette, cigar, pipe, etc. **6** act or period of smoking tobacco. **7** cure (meat, fish, etc.) by smoking. People smoke fish to preserve them. 1,2,5,6 *n.*, 3,4,7 *v.*, **smoked, smok ing.**

smoke out, 1 drive out by smoke: *We tried to smoke the woodchuck out of its hole.* **2** find out and make known: *smoke out a plot.*

smoke house (smōk′hous′), building or place in which meat, fish, etc., are treated with smoke to keep them from spoiling. *n.*, *pl.* **smoke hous es** (smōk′hou′ziz).

smoke less (smōk′lis), making no smoke; having little smoke. *adj.*

smok er (smō′kər), **1** person who smokes tobacco. **2** a railroad car or a part of it where smoking is allowed. **3** an informal gathering of men for smoking and entertainment. *n.*

smoke screen, mass of thick smoke used to hide troops, ships, airplanes, etc., from the enemy.

smoke stack (smōk′stak′), **1** a tall chimney. **2** pipe that discharges smoke: *the smokestack of a steamship or locomotive. n.*

smok i ness (smō′kē nis), smoky condition. *n.*

smok y (smō′kē), **1** giving off much smoke: *a smoky fire.* **2** full of smoke. **3** darkened or stained with smoke. **4** like smoke or suggesting smoke: *a smoky gray, a smoky taste. adj.*, **smok i er, smok i est.**

smol der (smōl′dər), **1** burn and smoke without flame: *The campfire smoldered for hours after the blaze died down.* **2** a slow, smoky burning without flame; smoldering fire. **3** exist or continue in a suppressed condition: *The people's discontent smoldered for years before it broke out into open rebellion.* **4** show suppressed feeling: *I smoldered with anger and nearly shouted out that the charges against me were all lies.* 1,3,4 *v.*, 2 *n.* Also, **smoulder.**

smooth (smüᴛʜ), **1** having an even surface, like glass, silk, or still water; flat; level: *smooth stones.* **2** free from unevenness or roughness: *smooth sailing, a smooth voyage.* **3** without lumps: *smooth sauce.* **4** make smooth or smoother; make flat, even, or level: *Smooth this dress with a hot iron. He smoothed out the ball of crushed paper and read it.* **5** without trouble or difficulty; easy: *a smooth course of affairs.* **6** make easy: *Her tact smoothed the way to an agreement.* **7** calm; serene: *a smooth temper.* **8** polished; pleasant; polite: *That salesclerk is a smooth talker.* **9** not harsh in sound or taste: *smooth verses, smooth wine.* **10** make

less harsh or crude; polish or refine (writing, manners, etc.). **11** in a smooth manner. 1-3,5,7-9 *adj.*, 4,6,10 *v.*, 11 *adv.* —**smooth′ly,** *adv.* —**smooth′ness,** *n.*

smooth away, get rid of (troubles, difficulties, etc.): *He smoothed away all objections to the plan.*

smooth down, calm; soothe: *She smoothed down her friend's temper.*

smooth over, make (something) seem less wrong, unpleasant, or noticeable: *The teacher tried to smooth over the differences between the two students who always quarreled with each other.*

smooth bore (smüᴛʜ′bôr′), not rifled. A smoothbore gun has no grooves in its barrel. *adj.*

smooth en (smüᴛʜ′ən), make or become smooth or smoother. *v.*

smooth-faced (smüᴛʜ′fāst′), **1** having a smooth face or surface. **2** agreeable in speech and manner: *a smooth-faced hypocrite. adj.*

smooth-spo ken (smüᴛʜ′spō′kən), speaking easily and pleasantly; polished in speech. *adj.*

smooth-tongued (smüᴛʜ′tungd′), speaking smoothly; agreeable. *adj.*

smor gas bord (smôr′gəs bôrd′), a buffet meal featuring a large variety of meats, salads, hors d'oeuvres, etc. *n.*

smote (smōt), a past tense of **smite.** *The blacksmith smote the horseshoe with a hammer. v.*

smoth er (smuᴛʜ′ər), **1** make unable to get air; kill by depriving of air: *The gas almost smothered the coal miners but they got out in time.* **2** be unable to breathe freely; suffocate: *We are smothering in this stuffy room.* **3** cover thickly: *In the fall the grass is smothered with leaves.* **4** deaden or put out by covering thickly: *The fire is smothered by ashes.* **5** keep back; check; suppress: *He smothered a sharp reply. Her smothered anger finally broke out.* **6** cloud of dust, smoke, spray, etc. 1-5 *v.*, 6 *n.* —**smoth′er er,** *n.*

smoul der (smōl′dər), smolder. *v., n.*

smudge (smuj), **1** a dirty mark; smear. **2** mark with dirty streaks; smear: *The child's drawing was smudged.* **3** a smoky fire made to drive away insects or to protect fruit and plants from frost. 1,3 *n.*, 2 *v.*, **smudged, smudg ing.**

smudge pot, pot or stove in which oil or other fuel is burned to produce a smudge.

smudg y (smuj′ē), smudged; marked with smudges. *adj.*, **smudg i er, smudg i est.**

smug (smug), too pleased with one's own goodness, cleverness, respectability, etc.; self-satisfied; complacent: *Nothing disturbs the smug beliefs of some prim, narrow-minded people. adj.*,

smug ger, smug gest. —**smug′ly,** *adv.* —**smug′ness,** *n.*

smug gle (smug′əl), **1** bring into or take out of a country secretly and against the law, especially without payment of legal duties: *It is a crime to smuggle goods into the United States.* **2** bring, take, put, etc., secretly: *I tried to smuggle my puppy into the house. v.*, **smug gled, smug gling.**

smug gler (smug′lər), **1** person who smuggles. **2** ship used in smuggling. *n.*

smut (smut), **1** a bit or bits of soot, dirt, etc. **2** to soil or be soiled with smut: *smut one's hands with coal.* **3** a dirty mark; smudge. **4** indecent, obscene talk or writing. **5** a plant disease in which the ears of grain are replaced by black, dustlike spores. **6** fungus producing this disease. 1,3-6 *n.*, 2 *v.*, **smut ted, smut ting.**

smut ty (smut′ē), **1** soiled with smut; dirty or sooty. **2** indecent; nasty; obscene. **3** (of plants) having the disease smut. *adj.*, **smut ti er, smut ti est.**

Smyr na (smėr′nə), former name of **Izmir.** *n.*

snack (snak), a light meal, especially one eaten between meals: *She eats a snack before going to bed. n.*

snaf fle (snaf′əl), **1** a slender, jointed bit used on a bridle. **2** control or manage by a snaffle. 1 *n.*, 2 *v.*, **snaf fled, snaf fling.**

snag (snag), **1** tree or branch held fast in a river or lake. Snags are dangerous to boats. **2** any sharp or rough projecting point, such as the broken end of a branch. **3** run or catch on a snag: *He snagged his sweater on a nail.* **4** a tear made by snagging. **5** a hidden or unexpected obstacle: *Our plans hit a snag.* **6** hinder. 1,2,4,5 *n.*, 3,6 *v.*, **snagged, snag ging.**

snail (snāl), **1** a small, soft-bodied mol-

snail (def. 1)—about 2 in. long

adj. adjective	*n.* noun
adv. adverb	*prep.* preposition
conj. conjunction	*pron.* pronoun
interj. interjection	*v.* verb
sing. singular	*pl.* plural

---

lusk that crawls very slowly. Most snails have spiral shells on their backs into which they can withdraw for protection. **2** a lazy, slow-moving person. *n.*

snake (snāk), **1** a long, slender, crawling reptile without limbs. Some snakes are poisonous. **2** a sly, treacherous person. **3** a long, flexible, metal tool used by plumbers to clean out a drain. **4** move, wind, or curve like a snake: *The narrow road snaked through the mountains.* 1-3 *n.,* 4 *v.,* **snaked, snaking. —snake′like′,** *adj.*

snake skin (snāk′skin′), **1** skin of a snake. **2** leather made from it. *n.*

snak i ly (snā′kə lē), in a snaky manner. *adv.*

snak y (snā′kē), **1** of a snake or snakes. **2** like a snake; twisting; winding. **3** having many snakes. **4** sly; venomous; treacherous. *adj.,* **snaki er, snak i est.**

snap (snap), **1** make or cause to make a sudden, sharp sound: *This wood snaps as it burns. The teacher snapped her fingers to get our attention.* **2** a quick, sharp sound: *The box shut with a snap.* **3** move, shut, catch, etc., with a snap: *The latch snapped.* **4** break suddenly or sharply: *The violin string snapped because it was fastened too tight.* **5** a sudden breaking or the sound of breaking: *One snap made the knife useless.* **6** make a sudden, quick bite or snatch: *The turtle snapped at the child's hand. The dog snapped up the meat.* **7** seize suddenly: *to snap up a bargain. He snapped at the chance to visit his uncle.* **8** a quick, sudden bite or snatch: *The dog made a snap at a fly.* **9** speak quickly and sharply: *"Silence!" snapped the captain. Don't snap at him; he doesn't understand what you want.* **10** move quickly and sharply: *The soldiers snapped to attention. You better snap it up or you'll never get the job done.* **11** a quick, sharp way: *She moves with snap and energy.* **12** a short spell of cold weather. **13** made or done suddenly: *A snap judgment is likely to be wrong.* **14** fastener; clasp: *Several of the snaps of your dress are unfastened.* **15** a thin, crisp cooky: *a chocolate snap.* **16** snapshot. **17** take a snapshot of. **18** SLANG. an easy job, piece of work, etc. **19** SLANG. easy. 1,3,4, 6,7,9,10,17 *v.,* **snapped, snap ping;** 2,5,8,11,12,14-16,18 *n.,* 13,19 *adj.*

snap out of it, INFORMAL. change one's attitude or habit suddenly: *He was in a bad mood one minute, but then he snapped out of it and started to laugh.*

snap drag on (snap′drag′ən), a garden plant with spikes of showy flowers of crimson, purple, white, yellow, etc. *n.*

snap per (snap′ər), **1** person or thing that snaps. **2** snapping turtle. **3** any of several large fish of tropical seas used for food, especially the **red snapper** of the Gulf of Mexico. *n.*

snapping turtle, a large, savage turtle of American rivers and lakes that has powerful jaws with which it snaps at its prey.

snap pish (snap′ish), **1** apt to snap. **2** quick and sharp in speech or manner; impatient. *adj.* **—snap′pish ly,** *adv.* **—snap′pish ness,** *n.*

snap py (snap′ē), **1** snappish; sharp. **2** snapping or crackling in sound: *a snappy fire.* **3** INFORMAL. having snap, smartness, pungency, etc.; crispy; lively: *a snappy cheese, a snappy sports jacket. adj.,* **snap pi er, snap pi est.**

snap shot (snap′shot′), photograph taken quickly with a small camera. *n.*

snare[1] (def. 1)

snare[1] (sner *or* snar), **1** noose for catching small animals and birds: *They made snares to catch rabbits.* **2** catch with a snare: *One day they snared a skunk.* **3** a trap: *Flattery is a snare in which fools are caught.* **4** to trap. 1,3 *n.,* 2,4 *v.,* **snared, snar ing.** [probably from a Scandinavian word of the 1200's, such as Icelandic *snara*]

snare[2] (sner *or* snar), one of the strings of wire or gut stretched across the bottom of a snare drum. *n.* [probably from Dutch]

snare drum showing snares on bottom of drum

snare drum, a small drum with strings of wire or gut stretched across the bottom to make a rattling sound.

snarl[1] (snärl), **1** growl sharply and show one's teeth: *The dog snarled at the stranger.* **2** a sharp, angry growl. **3** say or express with a snarl; speak harshly in a sharp, angry tone: *snarl a nasty threat.* **4** a sharp, angry tone or remark: *A snarl was her only reply.* 1,3 *v.,* 2,4 *n.* [earlier *snar,* perhaps from Dutch *snarren* to rattle]

snarl[2] (snärl), **1** a tangle: *I combed the snarls out of my hair.* **2** confusion: *Her legal affairs were in a snarl.* **3** to tangle or become tangled: *The kitten snarled the yarn by playing with it. Her hair snarls easily.* **4** confuse. 1,2 *n.,* 3,4 *v.* [perhaps from *snare[1]*]

snatch (snach), **1** seize suddenly; grasp hastily: *The hawk snatched the chicken and flew away.* **2** act of snatching: *The boy made a snatch at the ball.* **3** take suddenly: *He snatched off his hat and bowed.* **4** a short time: *She had a snatch of sleep sitting in her chair.* **5** a small amount; bit; scrap: *We heard snatches of their conversation as they raised their voices from time to time.* 1,3 *v.,* 2,4,5 *n., pl.* **snatch es. —snatch′er,** *n.*

snatch at, **1** try to seize or grasp: *He snatched at the rail.* **2** take advantage of eagerly: *He snatched at the chance to travel.*

snaz zy (snaz′ē), SLANG. fancy; flashy: *a snazzy suit. adj.* **snaz zi er, snaz zi est.**

sneak (snēk), **1** move in a stealthy, sly way: *The man sneaked about the barn watching for a chance to steal the horse.* **2** get, put, pass, etc., in a stealthy, sly way: *The boys sneaked the puppy into the house.* **3** act like a thief or a person who is ashamed to be seen: *He sneaked in by the back way.* **4** person who sneaks; a sneaking, cowardly, or contemptible person. **5** stealthy; underhand; sneaking: *a sneak thief, a sneak attack.* 1-3 *v.,* 4 *n.,* 5 *adj.*

sneak er (snē′kər), **1** sneakers, *pl.* light canvas shoes with rubber soles, used for games, sports, etc. **2** person that sneaks; sneak. *n.*

sneak i ly (snē′kə lē), in a sneaky manner. *adv.*

sneak i ness (snē′kē nis), sneaky character or quality. *n.*

sneak ing (snē′king), **1** cowardly; underhand; concealed. **2** that one cannot justify or does not like to confess: *She had a sneaking suspicion that they knew she had broken the vase. adj.*

sneak y (snē′kē), cowardly, mean, or contemptible. *adj.,* **sneak i er, sneak i est.**

sneer (snir), **1** show scorn or contempt by looks or words: *The students sneered at the sentimentality of the poem.* **2** a look or words expressing scorn or contempt: *He feared sneers more than* *blows.* 3 say or express with scorn or contempt: *"Bah!" he sneered with a curl of his lip.* 1,3 *v.*, 2 *n.*

sneeze (snēz), 1 expel air suddenly and violently through the nose and mouth by an involuntary spasm. A person sneezes when he has a cold. *The pepper made her sneeze.* 2 a sudden, violent expelling of air through the nose and mouth. 1 *v.*, **sneezed, sneez ing;** 2 *n.*

sneeze at, INFORMAL. treat with contempt; despise; scorn: *Ten dollars is not a sum to be sneezed at.*

snick er (snik′ər), 1 a half-suppressed and often disrespectful laugh; sly or silly laugh; giggle. 2 laugh in this way. 1 *n.*, 2 *v.* Also, **snigger.**

snide (snīd), mean or spiteful in a sly way: *a snide remark. adj.*

sniff (snif), 1 draw air through the nose in short, quick breaths that can be heard: *The man who had a cold was sniffing.* 2 smell with sniffs: *The dog sniffed suspiciously at the stranger.* 3 try the smell of: *I sniffed the medicine before taking a spoonful of it.* 4 draw in through the nose with the breath: *He sniffed steam to clear his head.* 5 act or sound of sniffing: *He cleared his nose with a loud sniff.* 6 show contempt by sniffing: *sniff at an inexpensive gift.* 7 suspect; detect: *sniff a plot, sniff danger.* 8 a single breathing in of something; breath. 1-4,6,7 *v.*, 5,8 *n.*

snif fle (snif′əl), 1 sniff again and again as one does from a cold in the head or in trying to stop crying. 2 act or sound of sniffling. 3 **the sniffles,** a slight cold in the head. 1 *v.*, **snif fled, snif fling;** 2,3 *n.*

snig ger (snig′ər), snicker. *n., v.*

snip (snip), 1 cut with a small, quick stroke or series of strokes with scissors: *She snipped the thread.* 2 act of snipping: *With a few snips I cut out the picture.* 3 a small piece cut off: *Pick up the snips of cloth and thread from the floor.* 4 **snips,** *pl.* hand shears for cutting metal. 5 INFORMAL. a small or unimportant person. 1 *v.*, **snipped, snip ping;** 2-5 *n.*

snipe (snīp), 1 a marsh bird with a long bill. 2 hunt for snipe. 3 shoot from a concealed place at an enemy one at a time, as a sportsman shoots at game. 1 *n.*, *pl.* **snipes** or **snipe;** 2,3 *v.*, **sniped, snip ing.**

snip er (snī′pər), person who shoots at someone from a concealed place; a hidden sharpshooter. *n.*

snip pet (snip′it), a small piece snipped off; bit; scrap; fragment. *n.*

snip py (snip′ē), INFORMAL. 1 sharp; curt. 2 haughty; disdainful. *adj.*, **snip pi er, snip pi est.**

sniv el (sniv′əl), 1 cry with sniffling.

2 put on a show of grief; whine. 3 run at the nose; sniffle. *v.*

snob (snob), person who cares too much for rank, wealth, position, etc., and too little for real merit; person who tries too hard to please those above him and ignores those below him. *n.*

snob ber y (snob′ər ē), snobbishness. *n., pl.* **snob ber ies.**

snob bish (snob′ish), of or like a snob; looking down on those in a lower position. *adj.* —**snob′bish ly,** *adv.* —**snob′bish ness,** *n.*

snood (snüd), 1 net or bag worn over a woman's hair. A snood may be a part of a hat. 2 band or ribbon formerly worn around the hair by young unmarried women in Scotland and northern England. 3 bind (hair) with a snood. 1,2 *n.*, 3 *v.*

snoop (snüp), INFORMAL. 1 go about in a sneaking, prying way; prowl; pry: *Our neighbor snoops into everybody's business.* 2 person who snoops. 1 *v.*, 2 *n.* —**snoop′er,** *n.*

snoot y (snü′tē), INFORMAL. snobbish; conceited. *adj.*, **snoot i er, snoot i est.**

snooze (snüz), INFORMAL. 1 take a nap; sleep; doze: *The dog snoozed on the porch in the sun.* 2 a nap; doze. 1 *v.*, **snoozed, snooz ing;** 2 *n.*

snore (snôr), 1 breathe during sleep with a harsh rough sound: *The child had a stuffy nose and snored all night.* 2 sound made in snoring. 1 *v.*, **snored, snor ing;** 2 *n.*

snorkel (def. 2)

snor kel (snôr′kəl), 1 shaft for taking in air and discharging gases, which allows submarines to remain under water for a very long time. It is like a periscope in shape. 2 a curved tube which enables swimmers to breathe under water while swimming near the surface. *n.*

snort (snôrt), 1 force the breath violently through the nose with a loud, harsh sound: *The horse snorted.* 2 make a sound like this: *The engine snorted.* 3 act or sound of snorting. 4 show contempt, defiance, anger, etc., by snorting. 5 say or express with a snort: *"Indeed!" snorted my aunt.* 1,2,4,5 *v.*, 3 *n.*

snout (snout), 1 the projecting part of an animal's head that contains the nose, mouth, and jaws. Pigs, dogs, and crocodiles have snouts. 2 anything

like an animal's snout, such as a nozzle. *n.*

snow (snō), 1 water vapor frozen into crystals that fall to earth in soft, white flakes and often spread upon it as a white layer. Rain falls in summer; snow falls in winter. 2 a fall of snow. 3 fall as snow: *to snow all day.* 4 let fall or scatter as snow. 1,2 *n.*, 3,4 *v.*

snow in, shut in by snow: *The mountain village was snowed in for almost a week after the blizzard.*

snow under, 1 cover with snow: *The houses were snowed under by the blizzard.* 2 overwhelm: *He is snowed under with work.*

snow ball (snō′bôl′), 1 ball made of snow pressed together. 2 throw balls of snow at: *The children snowballed each other.* 3 shrub with white flowers in large clusters like balls. 4 increase rapidly by additions like a rolling snowball: *The number of signers of the petition for a new school snowballed.* 1,3 *n.*, 2, 4 *v.*

snow bank (snō′bangk′), large mass or drift of snow, especially at the side of a road. *n.*

snow bird (snō′bèrd′), 1 junco. 2 snow bunting. *n.*

snow-blind (snō′blīnd′), affected with snow blindness. *adj.*

snow blindness, temporary or partial blindness caused by the reflection of sunlight from snow or ice.

snow bound (snō′bound′), shut in by snow; snowed in. *adj.*

snow bunting, a small, white finch with black and brownish markings that lives in cold regions; snowbird.

snow capped (snō′kapt′), having its top covered with snow: *a snowcapped mountain. adj.*

snow drift (snō′drift′), 1 mass or bank of snow piled up by the wind. 2 snow driven before the wind. *n.*

snow drop (snō′drop′), a small plant with white flowers that blooms early in the spring. *n.*

snow fall (snō′fôl′), 1 a fall of snow. 2 amount of snow falling within a certain time and area: *The snowfall in that one storm was 16 inches. n.*

adj. adjective	*n.* noun
adv. adverb	*prep.* preposition
conj. conjunction	*pron.* pronoun
interj. interjection	*v.* verb
sing. singular	*pl.* plural

snowflakes

snow flake (snō'flāk'), a small, feathery crystal of snow. *n.*

snow i ness (snō'ē nis), 1 a being snowy. 2 whiteness. *n.*

snow line, line on mountains above which there is always snow.

snow man (snō'man'), mass of snow made into a figure somewhat like that of a man. *n., pl.* **snow men.**

snow mo bile (snō'mō bēl), tractor or other vehicle for use in snow, some having skis or runners in front. *n.*

snow plow (snō'plou'), machine for clearing away snow from streets, railroad tracks, etc. *n.*

snow shoe (snō'shü'), 1 a light, wooden frame with strips of leather stretched across it. Trappers in the far North wear snowshoes on their feet to keep from sinking in deep, soft snow. 2 walk or travel on snowshoes. 1 *n.,* 2 *v.,* **snow shoed, snow shoe ing.**

snow slide (snō'slīd'), the sliding down of a mass of snow on a steep slope. *n.*

snow storm (snō'stôrm'), storm with much snow. *n.*

snow-white (snō'hwīt'), white as snow. *adj.*

snow y (snō'ē), 1 having snow: *a snowy day.* 2 covered with snow: *a snowy roof.* 3 like snow; white as snow: *The old woman has snowy hair. adj.,* **snow i er, snow i est.**

snub (snub), 1 treat coldly, scornfully, or with contempt: *snub one's neighbors by ignoring them.* 2 cold, scornful, or disdainful treatment. 3 check or stop (a rope or cable running out) suddenly. 4 a sudden check or stop. 5 short and turned up at the tip: *a snub nose.* 1,3 *v.,* **snubbed, snub bing;** 2,4 *n.,* 5 *adj.*

snub-nosed (snub'nōzd'), having a snub nose. *adj.*

snuff[1] (snuf), 1 draw in through the nose; draw up into the nose. 2 sniff; smell: *The dog snuffed at the track of the fox.* 3 powdered tobacco taken into the nose. 1,2 *v.,* 3 *n.* [probably from Dutch *snuffen*]

up to snuff, 1 INFORMAL. in perfect order or condition; as good as expected. 2 SLANG. not easily deceived.

snuff[2] (snuf), 1 cut or pinch off the burned wick of. 2 put out (a candle); extinguish. *v.* [Middle English *snoffen*]

snuff out, put an end to suddenly and completely; wipe out: *The new dictator snuffed out the people's hopes for freedom.*

snuff box (snuf'boks'), a very small box for holding snuff. *n., pl.* **snuff-box es.**

snuff ers (snuf'ərz), small tongs for taking off burned wick or putting out the light of a candle. *n.pl.*

snuf fle (snuf'əl), 1 breathe noisily through the nose like a person with a cold in the head. 2 act or sound of snuffling. 3 **the snuffles,** a cold in the head. 1 *v.,* **snuf fled, snuf fling;** 2,3 *n.*

snug (snug), 1 comfortable and warm; sheltered; cozy: *The cat has found a snug corner behind the stove.* 2 neat; trim; compact: *The cabins on the boat are snug.* 3 fitting closely: *That coat is a little too snug.* 4 in a snug manner. 1-3 *adj.,* **snug ger, snug gest;** 4 *adv.* —**snug'ly,** *adv.* —**snug'ness,** *n.*

snowshoes (def. 1)

snug gle (snug'əl), lie or press closely for warmth or comfort or from affection; nestle; cuddle. *v.,* **snug gled, snug gling.**

so[1] (sō), 1 in that way; in the same way or degree; as stated; as shown: *Hold your pen so. The chair is broken and has been so for a long time. Do not walk so fast. He is not so tall as his brother. Is that really so?* 2 very: *You are so kind.* 3 very much: *My head aches so.* 4 for that reason; accordingly; therefore: *The dog seemed hungry; so we fed him.* 5 with the result that; in order that: *Go away so I can rest.* 6 with the purpose or intention that: *I did the work so he would not need to.* 7 likewise; also: *She likes dogs; so does he.* 8 So is sometimes used alone to ask a question or to exclaim: *So! late again! The train is late. So?* 9 more or less: *a pound or so.* 1-4,7 *adv.,* 5,6 *conj.,* 8 *interj.,* 9 *pron.* [Old English *swā*]

and so, 1 likewise; also: *He is here and so is she.* 2 accordingly: *I said I would go, and so I shall.*

so as, with the result or purpose: *go to bed early so as to get enough sleep.*

so that, with the result or purpose that:

The boy studies so that he will do well.

so[2] (sō), sol. *n.* [a different form of *sol*]

So., South.

soak (sōk), 1 make or become very wet; wet through: *The rain soaked my clothes.* 2 let remain in water or other liquid until wet clear through: *Soak the clothes all night before you wash them.* 3 make its way; enter; go: *Water will soak through the earth.* 4 act or process of soaking: *Give the clothes a long soak.* 5 INFORMAL. make pay too much; charge or tax heavily: *I was soaked in the deal.* 1-3,5 *v.,* 4 *n.*

soak up, 1 absorb: *The sponge soaked up the water.* 2 take into the mind: *soak up knowledge.*

so-and-so (sō'ən sō'), some person or thing not named. *n., pl.* **so-and-sos.**

soap (sōp), 1 substance used for washing, usually made of a fat and lye. 2 rub with soap: *Soap the dirty shirts well.* 1 *n.,* 2 *v.*

soap box (sōp'boks'), an empty box used as a temporary platform by speakers addressing gatherings on the street. *n., pl.* **soap box es.**

soap stone (sōp'stōn'), a soft rock that feels somewhat like soap, used for griddles, hearths, etc. *n.*

soap suds (sōp'sudz'), bubbles and foam made with soap and water. *n.pl.*

soap y (sō'pē), 1 covered with soap or soapsuds. 2 containing soap: *soapy water.* 3 of or like soap: *The water has a soapy taste. adj.,* **soap i er, soap i est.**

soar (sôr), 1 fly at a great height; fly upward: *The eagle soared without flapping its wings.* 2 rise beyond what is common and ordinary: *Prices are soaring. Her hope soared when she heard that she was a finalist in the contest.* *v.*

sob (sob), 1 cry or sigh with short, quick breaths: *"I have lost my penny," the child sobbed. She sobbed herself to sleep.* 2 a catching of short, quick breaths because of grief, etc. 3 make a sound like a sob: *The wind sobbed.* 4 a sound like a sob. 5 say or express with sobs: *sob out a sad story.* 1,3,5 *v.,* **sobbed, sob bing;** 2,4 *n.*

so ber (sō'bər), 1 not drunk. 2 temperate; moderate: *The Puritans led sober, hard-working lives.* 3 quiet; serious; solemn: *He looked sober at the thought of missing the picnic.* 4 calm; sensible; free from exaggeration: *sober facts. The judge's sober opinion was not influenced by prejudice or strong feeling.* 5 make or become sober: *Seeing the car accident sobered us all. The class sobered as the teacher came into the room.* 6 quiet in color: *dressed in sober gray.* 1-4,6 *adj.,* 5 *v.* —**so'ber ly,** *adv.* —**so'ber ness,** *n.*

so ber-mind ed (sō'bər mīn'did),

having or showing a sober mind; self-controlled; sensible. *adj.*

so bri e ty (sə brī′ə tē), 1 soberness. 2 temperance in the use of strong drink. 3 moderation. 4 quietness; seriousness. *n.*

so bri quet (sō′brə kā), nickname. *n.* Also, **soubriquet.**

so-called (sō′kôld′), called so, but really not so; called so improperly or incorrectly: *Her so-called friend hasn't even written to her. adj.*

soccer

soc cer (sok′ər), game played with a round ball between two teams of eleven players each. The players may strike the ball with any part of the body except the hands and arms. Only the goalkeeper may touch the ball with the hands and arms. *n.*

so cia bil i ty (sō′shə bil′ə tē), sociable disposition; friendly behavior. *n.*

so cia ble (sō′shə bəl), 1 liking company; friendly: *They are a sociable family and entertain a great deal.* 2 marked by conversation and companionship: *We had a sociable afternoon together.* 3 an informal social gathering. 1,2 *adj.,* 3 *n.*

so cia bly (sō′shə blē), in a sociable manner; familiarly. *adv.*

so cial (sō′shəl), 1 of or dealing with human beings in their relations to each other; having to do with the life of human beings in a community or society: *social conditions, social problems.* Schools and hospitals are social institutions. 2 living, or liking to live, with others: *Man is a social being.* 3 for companionship or friendliness; having to do with companionship or friendliness: *a social club.* 4 liking company: *She has a social nature.* 5 connected with fashionable society: *They are the social leaders in our town.* 6 a social gathering or party. 7 (of animals) living together in organized communities. Ants and bees are social insects. 1-5,7 *adj.,* 6 *n.*

so cial ism (sō′shə liz′əm), 1 theory or system of social organization by which the major means of production and distribution are owned, managed, or controlled by the government, by associations of workers, or by the community as a whole. 2 a political movement advocating or associated with this system. *n.*

so cial ist (sō′shə list), 1 person who favors or supports socialism. 2 socialistic. 3 **Socialist,** member of a Socialist Party. 4 **Socialist,** of or having to do with a Socialist Party. 1,3 *n.,* 2,4 *adj.*

so cial is tic (sō′shə lis′tik), 1 of or having to do with socialism or socialists. 2 favoring or supporting socialism. *adj.* —**so′cial is′ti cal ly,** *adv.*

Socialist Party, a political party which supports socialism.

so cial ite (sō′shə līt), member of the fashionable society of a community. *n.*

so cial i za tion (sō′shə lə zā′shən), a socializing or a being socialized. *n.*

so cial ize (sō′shə līz), 1 be social or sociable: *He has never learned to socialize with his fellow workers.* 2 establish or regulate in accordance with socialism. 3 make social; make fit for living with others. *v.,* **so cial ized, so cial iz ing.**

so cial ly (sō′shə lē), 1 in a social way or manner; in relation to other people. 2 as a member of society or of a social group: *He is an able man, but socially he is a failure. adv.*

social science, study of people, their activities, their customs, and their institutions in relationship to other people. History, sociology, economics, geography, and civics are social sciences. *n.*

social security, system of federal old-age pensions and medical care for retired persons and their dependents. The program is financed by compulsory contributions from the government, the employee, and the employer. *n.*

social studies, course of study in elementary schools and high schools that includes history, civics, economics, geography, and other subjects in the social sciences.

social work, work directed toward the betterment of social conditions in a community. Social work includes such services as free medical clinics, counseling for families, and recreational activities for underprivileged children.

social worker, person who does social work.

so ci e ty (sə sī′ə tē), 1 group of persons joined together for a common purpose or by a common interest: *a debating society, a legal society.* A club, a fraternity, a lodge, or an association may be called a society. 2 all the people; human beings living together as a group: *Gun-control laws have been enacted for the good of society.* 3 the people of any particular time or place: *20th-century society, American society, the lower and middle classes of industrial society.* 4 the activities and customs of society or of a particular society: *Magic plays an important part in primitive society.* 5 company; com-

hat, āge, fär; let, ēqual, tėrm;
it, īce; hot, ōpen, ôrder;
oil, out; cup, pủt, rüle; ch, child;
ng, long; sh, she; th, thin;
ŦH, then; zh, measure;

ə represents *a* in about,
e in taken, *i* in pencil,
o in lemon, *u* in circus.

panionship: *I enjoy his society.* 6 fashionable people or their doings: *Her parents are leaders in society. n., pl.* **so ci e ties.**

Society Islands, group of French islands in the S Pacific that includes Tahiti.

Society of Friends, the Quakers.

Society of Jesus, the religious order of the Jesuits.

so ci o log i cal (sō′sē ə loj′ə kəl), 1 of or having to do with human society or problems relating to it: *Care of the poor is a sociological problem.* 2 of sociology. *adj.* —**so′ci o log′i cal ly,** *adv.*

so ci ol o gist (sō′sē ol′ə jist), an expert in sociology. *n.*

so ci ol o gy (sō′sē ol′ə jē), study of the nature, origin, and development of human society and community life; science of society. Sociology deals with social conditions, such as crime and poverty, and social institutions, such as marriage and the church. *n.*

sock[1] (sok), a short, close-fitting, knitted covering for the foot and leg, especially one that reaches about half way to the knee. *n.* [Old English *socc,* from Latin *soccus*]

sock[2] (sok), SLANG. 1 strike or hit hard. 2 a hard blow. 3 squarely; right. 1 *v.,* 2 *n.,* 3 *adv.* [origin uncertain]

UPPER END OF THIGH BONE · PELVIC BONE · SOCKET · SOCKET

sock et (sok′it), a hollow part or piece for receiving and holding something. A candlestick has a socket in which to set a candle. A person's eyes are set in sockets. An electric lamp has a socket into which a bulb is screwed. *n.*

Soc ra tes (sok′rə tēz′), 469?-399 B.C., Athenian philosopher whose teachings were written down by his disciple Plato. *n.*

So crat ic (sō krat′ik), of or having to do with Socrates, his philosophy, followers, etc. *adj.*

adj.	adjective	*n.*	noun
adv.	adverb	*prep.*	preposition
conj.	conjunction	*pron.*	pronoun
interj.	interjection	*v.*	verb
sing.	singular	*pl.*	plural

sod (sod), 1 ground covered with grass. 2 piece or layer of this containing the grass and its roots. *Some pioneers built houses of sods.* 3 to cover with sods: *We had the bare spots of our lawn sodded.* 1,2 *n.,* 3 *v.,* **sod ded, sod ding. under the sod,** buried.

so da (sō′də), 1 any of several chemical substances containing sodium, such as sodium bicarbonate or baking soda, sodium carbonate or sal soda, and sodium hydroxide or caustic soda. 2 soda water. 3 soda water flavored with fruit juice or syrup, and often containing ice cream. *n., pl.* **so das.**

soda fountain, counter with places for holding soda water, flavored syrups, ice cream, etc.

so dal i ty (sō dal′ə tē), 1 fellowship; friendship. 2 (in the Roman Catholic Church) a lay society with religious or charitable purposes. *n., pl.* **so dal i ties.**

soda water, water charged with carbon dioxide to make it bubble and fizz, often served with the addition of syrup, ice cream, etc.

sod den (sod′n), 1 soaked through: *The girl's clothes were sodden with rain.* 2 heavy and moist: *This bread is sodden because it was not baked well. adj.*

so di um (sō′dē əm), a soft, silver-white, metallic element which reacts violently with water and occurs in nature only in combination with other elements. Salt and soda contain sodium. *n.*

sodium bicarbonate, a powdery, white, crystalline salt used in cooking, medicine, manufacturing, etc.; baking soda; bicarbonate of soda. Sodium bicarbonate soothes irritations of the skin and is a source of carbon dioxide.

sodium carbonate, a white crystalline powder or salt used for softening water, making soap and glass, and in medicine and photography; sal soda.

sodium chloride, salt (def. 1).

sodium fluoride, a crystalline salt used in the fluoridation of water and in treating certain forms of tooth decay.

sodium hydroxide, a white solid that is a strong, corrosive alkali; caustic soda. It is used in making soap and as a bleaching agent.

sodium nitrate, a colorless, crystalline compound used to produce other nitrates, such as potassium nitrate, and as a fertilizer; niter; saltpeter.

Sod om (sod′əm), (in the Bible) a wicked city destroyed, together with Gomorrah, by fire from heaven. *n.*

so fa (sō′fə), a long, upholstered seat or couch having a back and arms. *n., pl.* **so fas.**

So fi a (sō fē′ə), capital of Bulgaria, in the W part. *n.*

soft (sôft), 1 not hard; not stiff; yielding easily to touch: *a soft pillow. Feathers, cotton, and wool are soft.* 2 not hard compared with other things of the same sort: *Pine wood is softer than oak. Copper and lead are softer than steel.* 3 pleasant to the touch; not rough or coarse; smooth: *the soft hair of a kitten, soft silk.* 4 not loud: *a soft voice.* 5 quietly pleasant; mild; not harsh: *a soft spring morning, soft air, soft words, the soft light of candles.* 6 gentle; kind; tender: *a soft heart, soft eyes.* 7 weak; out of condition; not fit: *become soft from idleness and luxury.* 8 softly; quietly; gently. 9 free from mineral salts that keep soap from forming suds: *Soft water is easy to wash with.* 10 having a more or less hissing sound. The *c* is soft in *city* and hard in *corn; g* is soft in *gentle* and hard in *get.* 11 INFORMAL. easy; easy-going: *a soft job, a soft person.* 1-7,9-11 *adj.,* 8 *adv.* —**soft′ly,** *adv.* —**soft′ness,** *n.*

soft ball (sôft′bôl′), 1 a kind of baseball that uses a larger and softer ball and lighter bats. 2 the ball used in this game. *n.*

soft-boiled (sôft′boild′), (of an egg) boiled only a little so that the yolk is still soft. *adj.*

soft coal, bituminous coal.

soft drink, drink that does not contain alcohol.

soft en (sôf′ən), make or become soft: *Hand lotion softens the skin. Soap softens in water. v.* —**soft′en er,** *n.*

soft heart ed (sôft′här′tid), gentle; kind; tender. *adj.* —**soft′heart′ed ness,** *n.*

soft palate, the fleshy back part of the roof of the mouth.

soft-spo ken (sôft′spō′kən), 1 speaking with a soft voice. 2 spoken softly: *a soft-spoken reproof. adj.*

soft wood (sôft′wùd′), 1 any wood that is easily cut. 2 tree that has needles or does not have broad leaves. Pines and firs are softwoods; oaks and maples are hardwoods. 3 wood of such a tree. 4 having or made of such wood. 1-3 *n.,* 4 *adj.*

sog gi ness (sog′ē nis), soggy condition. *n.*

sog gy (sog′ē), 1 thoroughly wet; soaked: *The wash on the line was soggy from the rain.* 2 damp and heavy: *sog-*

sofa

gy bread. adj., **sog gi er, sog gi est.**

soil[1] (soil), 1 ground; earth; dirt. 2 land; country: *This is my native soil. n.* [from French of the 1300's *soil* one's piece of ground]

soil[2] (soil), 1 make or become dirty: *I soiled my clean clothes. White shirts soil easily.* 2 disgrace; dishonor: *False rumors have soiled his name.* 3 dirty or foul matter. 1,2 *v.,* 3 *n.* [from French of the 1200's *soillier*]

soil less (soil′lis), without soil. *adj.*

soi ree (swä rā′), an evening party or social gathering. *n., pl.* **soi rees.** [from French *soirée,* from *soir* evening]

soi rée (swä rā′), soiree. *n., pl.* **soi rées.**

so journ (sō′jėrn′ *or* sō jėrn′ *for 1;* sō′jėrn′ *for 2*), 1 stay for a time: *The Israelites sojourned in the land of Egypt.* 2 a brief stay; a stay that is not permanent: *During his sojourn in Africa he learned much about native customs.* 1 *v.,* 2 *n.* —**so journ′er,** *n.*

sol (sōl), the fifth tone of the musical scale. *n.* Also, **so.**

Sol (sol), 1 (in Roman myths) the god of the sun. The Greeks called him Helios. 2 sun. *n.*

sol ace (sol′is), 1 comfort or relief: *She found solace from her troubles in music.* 2 to comfort or relieve; cheer: *He solaced himself with a book.* 1 *n.,* 2 *v.,* **sol aced, sol ac ing.**

so lar (sō′lər), 1 of the sun: *a solar eclipse.* 2 measured or determined by the earth's motion in relation to the sun: *solar time.* 3 working by means of the sun's light or heat. A solar battery traps sunlight and converts it into electrical energy. *adj.*

so lar i um (sə ler′ē əm), room, porch, etc., where people can lie or sit in the sun. *n., pl.* **so lar i a** (sə ler′ē ə), **so lar i ums.**

solar plex us (plek′səs), network of nerves situated at the upper part of the abdomen, behind the stomach and in front of the aorta.

solar system, the sun and all the plan-

solar system

ets, satellites, comets, etc., that revolve around it.

solar year, the period of time required for the earth to make one revolution around the sun, which equals about 365¼ days.

sold (sōld), past tense and past participle of **sell.** *He sold it a week ago. She has sold her car.* *v.*

sol der (sod′ər), 1 metal or alloy that can be melted and used for joining or mending metal surfaces, parts, etc. 2 fasten, mend, or join with solder: *I soldered the broken wires together. I soldered a hole in the pan.* 1 *n.,* 2 *v.*

sol dier (sōl′jər), 1 person who serves in an army. 2 an enlisted man in the army, not a commissioned officer. 3 man having skill or experience in war. 4 person who serves in any cause: *Christian soldiers.* 5 act or serve as a soldier. 6 INFORMAL. pretend to work but do very little. 1-4 *n.,* 5,6 *v.*

sol dier ly (sōl′jər lē), like a soldier; like that of a soldier. *adj.*

soldier of fortune, man serving or ready to serve as a soldier under any government for money, adventure, or pleasure.

sol dier y (sōl′jər ē), 1 soldiers. 2 military training or knowledge. *n.*

sole[1] (sōl), 1 one and only; single: *He was the sole heir to the fortune when his aunt died.* 2 only: *We three were the sole survivors from the wreck.* 3 of or for only one person or group and not others; exclusive: *the sole right of use.* *adj.* [from French of the 1300's *soul,* from Latin *solus* alone]

sole[2] (sōl), 1 the bottom or under surface of the foot. 2 bottom of a shoe, slipper, boot, etc. 3 piece of leather, rubber, etc. cut in the same shape. 4 put a sole on: *I must have my shoes soled.* 1-3 *n.,* 4 *v.,* **soled, sol ing.** [from French of the 1300's *sole,* from Latin *solea* kind of sandal]

sole[3] (sōl), any of various flatfishes. European sole is valued highly as food. *n., pl.* **soles** or **sole.** [from *sole*[2] because of the flatness of the fish]

sol e cism (sol′ə siz′əm), 1 mistake in using words: *"I done it" is a solecism.* 2 mistake in social behavior; breach of good manners or etiquette. *n.*

sole ly (sōl′lē), 1 as the only one or ones; alone: *You will be solely responsible for providing the lunch.* 2 only: *Bananas grow outdoors solely in warm climates.* *adv.*

sol emn (sol′əm), 1 serious; grave; earnest: *I gave my solemn promise to do better. That minister speaks in a solemn voice.* 2 causing serious or grave thoughts: *The organ played solemn music.* 3 done with form and ceremony: *a solemn procession.* 4 con-

nected with religion; sacred. 5 gloomy, dark; somber in color. *adj.* —**sol′emn ly,** *adv.*

so lem ni ty (sə lem′nə tē), 1 solemn feeling; seriousness; impressiveness: *The solemnity of the occasion was felt even by the children.* 2 a solemn, formal ceremony: *Easter is observed with solemnities.* *n., pl.* **so lem ni ties.**

sol em nize (sol′əm nīz), 1 observe with ceremonies: *Christian churches solemnize the resurrection of Christ at Easter.* 2 hold or perform (a ceremony or service): *The marriage was solemnized in the temple.* 3 make serious or grave. *v.,* **sol em niz ed, sol em niz ing.**

so le noid (sō′lə noid), a spiral or cylindrical coil of wire that acts like a magnet when an electric current passes through it. It is used in circuit breakers, mechanical sorting devices, etc. *n.*

so lic it (sə lis′it), 1 ask earnestly; try to get: *The tailor sent around cards soliciting trade.* 2 make appeals or requests: *solicit for contributions to the Red Cross.* *v.*

so lic i ta tion (sə lis′ə tā′shən), a soliciting; earnest request; urging. *n.*

so lic i tor (sə lis′ə tər), 1 person who entreats or requests. 2 lawyer. In England a solicitor prepares a case, and a barrister pleads it. 3 lawyer for a town, city, state, etc. *n.*

so lic i tous (sə lis′ə təs), 1 showing care or concern; anxious; concerned: *Parents are solicitous for their children's progress in school.* 2 desirous; eager: *solicitous to please.* *adj.* —**so lic′i tous ly,** *adv.* —**so lic′i tous ness,** *n.*

so lic i tude (sə lis′ə tüd *or* sə lis′ə tyüd), anxious care; anxiety; concern. *n.*

sol id (sol′id), 1 not a liquid or a gas: *Water becomes solid when it freezes.* 2 substance that is not a liquid or a gas. Iron, wood, and ice are solids. 3 not hollow: *A bar of iron is solid; a pipe is hollow.* 4 strongly put together; hard; firm: *They were glad to leave the boat and put their feet on solid ground.* 5 alike throughout: *The cloth is a solid blue.* 6 firmly united: *The country was solid for peace.* 7 real; serious: *Chemistry and physics are solid subjects.* 8 that can be depended on: *He is a solid citizen.* 9 having good judgment; sound; sensible; intelligent: *a solid book by a solid thinker.* 10 whole; entire: *She spent a solid hour on her arithmetic.* 11 undivided; continuous: *a solid row of houses.* 12 having length, breadth, and thickness. 13 body that has length, breadth, and thickness. A cube is a solid. 1,3-12 *adj.,* 2,13 *n.* —**sol′id ly,** *adv.* —**sol′id ness,** *n.*

hat, āge, fär; let, ēqual, tėrm;
it, īce; hot, ōpen, ôrder;
oil, out; cup, pùt, rüle; ch, child;
ng, long; sh, she; th, thin;
ŦH, then; zh, measure;

ə represents *a* in about,
e in taken, *i* in pencil,
o in lemon, *u* in circus.

sol i dar i ty (sol′ə dar′ə tē), unity or fellowship arising from common responsibilities and interests. *n., pl.* **sol i dar i ties.**

solid geometry, branch of mathematics that deals with objects having the three dimensions of length, breadth, and thickness.

so lid i fi ca tion (sə lid′ə fə kā′shən), a solidifying or a being solidified. *n.*

so lid i fy (sə lid′ə fī), 1 make or become solid; harden: *Extreme cold will solidify water into ice. Jelly solidifies as it gets cold.* 2 unite firmly. *v.,* **so lid i fied, so lid i fy ing.**

so lid i ty (sə lid′ə tē), condition or quality of being solid; firmness or hardness; substantial quality: *the solidity of marble or steel, the solidity of Washington's character.* *n., pl.* **so lid i ties.**

so lil o quize (sə lil′ə kwīz), 1 talk to oneself. 2 speak a soliloquy. *v.,* **so lil o quized, so lil o quiz ing.**

so lil o quy (sə lil′ə kwē), 1 a talking to oneself. 2 speech made by an actor to himself. It reveals his thoughts and feelings to the audience, but not to the other characters in the play. *n., pl.* **so lil o quies.**

sol i taire (sol′ə ter *or* sol′ə tar), 1 any card game played by one person. 2 diamond or other gem set by itself. *n.*

sol i tar y (sol′ə ter′ē), 1 alone; single; only: *A solitary rider was seen in the distance.* 2 without companions; away from people; lonely: *She lead a solitary life in her hut in the mountains. The house is in a solitary spot miles from a town.* *adj.*

sol i tude (sol′ə tüd *or* sol′ə tyüd), 1 a being alone: *He likes company and hates solitude.* 2 a lonely place: *This forest is a solitude.* 3 loneliness. *n.*

so lo (sō′lō), 1 piece of music for one voice or instrument: *She sang three solos.* 2 arranged for and performed by one voice or instrument: *a solo part.* 3 without a partner, teacher, etc.; alone: *a solo flight across the ocean, a solo dance.* 4 anything done without a partner, teacher, etc. 5 make a solo flight in an airplane. 1,4 *n., pl.* **so los;** 2,3 *adj.,* 5 *v.,* **so loed, so lo ing.**

adj.	adjective	*n.*	noun
adv.	adverb	*prep.*	preposition
conj.	conjunction	*pron.*	pronoun
interj.	interjection	*v.*	verb
sing.	singular	*pl.*	plural

so lo ist (sō′lō ist), person who sings or plays a solo or solos. *n.*

Sol o mon (sol′ə mən), 1 king of Israel who lived in the 900's B.C. Solomon was a son of David and was famous for his wisdom, and for the great temple which he had built in Jerusalem. 2 man of great wisdom. *n.*

Solomon Islands, group of islands in the S Pacific, northeast of Australia.

So lon (sō′lən *or* sō′lon), 1 638?-558? B.C., wise Athenian lawgiver. 2 a wise man; sage. *n.*

so long, INFORMAL. good by; farewell.

sol stice (sol′stis), either of the two times in the year when the sun is at its greatest distance from the equator. In the Northern Hemisphere, June 21 or 22, the **summer solstice,** is the longest day of the year and December 21 or 22, the **winter solstice,** is the shortest. *n.*

sol u bil i ty (sol′yə bil′ə tē), quality that some substances have of dissolving or being dissolved easily: *Anyone can see the solubility of sugar in water. n.*

sol u ble (sol′yə bəl), 1 that can be dissolved: *Salt is soluble in water.* 2 that can be solved: *soluble puzzles. This problem is soluble. adj.*

so lu tion (sə lü′shən), 1 the solving of a problem: *That problem was hard; its solution required many hours.* 2 explanation: *The police are seeking a solution of the crime.* 3 process of dissolving; changing of a solid or gas to a liquid by mixing with a liquid: *The solution of gases in liquids is usually accompanied by heat.* 4 liquid or mixture formed by dissolving: *Every time you put sugar in lemonade you are making a solution.* 5 a separating into parts; dissolving. 6 a being dissolved: *Salt can be held in solution in water.* 7 any number which when substituted into an equation or inequality makes it a true statement. *n.*

solution set, the set which contains all the solutions of an equation or inequality.

solv a ble (sol′və bəl), capable of being solved. *adj.*

solve (solv), find the answer to; clear up; explain: *The detective solved the mystery. He has solved all the problems in the lesson. v.,* **solved, solv ing.**

sol ven cy (sol′vən sē), ability to pay

all one owes. *n., pl.* **sol ven cies.**

sol vent (sol′vənt), 1 able to pay all one owes: *A bankrupt firm is not solvent.* 2 able to dissolve: *Gasoline is a solvent liquid that removes grease spots.* 3 substance, usually a liquid, that can dissolve other substances: *Water is a solvent of sugar and salt.* 1,2 *adj.,* 3 *n.*

So ma lia (sə mä′lyə), country in E Africa. *n.*

so mat ic (sō mat′ik), of or having to do with the body. *adj.*

somatic cell, any cell of an animal or plant, except a germ cell.

som ber *or* **som bre** (som′bər), 1 having deep shadows; dark; gloomy: *A cloudy winter day is somber. It was a somber room with dark furniture and heavy black hangings.* 2 melancholy; dismal: *His losses made him very somber. adj.* —**som′ber ly,** *adv.*

sombrero

som brer o (som brer′ō), a broad-brimmed hat worn in the southwestern United States, Mexico, and Spain. *n., pl.* **som brer os.**

some (sum), 1 certain or particular, but not known or named: *Some dogs are large; some are small.* 2 a number of: *Ask some friends to help you. I left the city some years ago.* 3 a quantity of: *Drink some milk.* 4 a certain number or quantity: *She ate some and gave the rest away.* 5 a; any: *Can't you find some kind person who will help you?* 6 about: *Some twenty men asked for work.* 1-3,5,6 *adj.,* 4 *pron.*

-some[1], *suffix forming adjectives.* 1 (*added to verbs*) tending to _____: *Meddlesome = tending to meddle.* 2 (*added to nouns*) causing _____: *Troublesome = causing trouble.* 3 (*added to adjectives*) _____ to a considerable degree: *Lonesome = lone to a considerable degree.* [Middle English -*some*, Old English -*sum*]

-some[2], *suffix added to numbers.* group of _____: *Twosome = group of two. Foursome = group of four.* [Old English *sum* some]

some bod y (sum′bod′ē), 1 person not known or named; some person; someone: *Somebody has taken my pen.* 2 person of importance: *She acts as if she were somebody since she won the prize.* 1 *pron.,* 2 *n., pl.* **some bod ies.**

some day (sum′dā), at some future time. *adv.*

some how (sum′hou), in a way not

known or not stated; in one way or another: *I'll finish this work somehow. adv.*

some one (sum′wun), some person; somebody: *Someone is coming. pron.*

some place (sum′plās), in or to some place; somewhere. *adv.*

som er sault (sum′ər sôlt), 1 a roll or jump, turning the heels over the head. 2 roll or jump, turning the heels over the head. 1 *n.,* 2 *v.*

som er set (sum′ər set), somersault. *n., v.*

some thing (sum′thing), 1 some thing; a particular thing not named or known: *I'm sure I've forgotten something. He has something on his mind.* 2 a certain amount or quantity; a part; a little: *There is something of his father in his smile. Something yet of doubt remains.* 3 somewhat; to some extent or degree: *She is something like her father.* 4 thing or person of some value or importance: *He thinks he's something.* 1,2,4 *n.,* 3 *adv.*

some time (sum′tīm), 1 at one time or another: *Come to see me sometime.* 2 at an indefinite point of time: *It happened sometime last May.* 3 former: *a sometime pupil of our school.* 1,2 *adv.,* 3 *adj.*

some times (sum′tīmz), now and then; at times: *He comes to visit sometimes. adv.*

some way (sum′wā), in some way. *adv.*

some what (sum′hwot), 1 to some extent or degree; slightly: *My hat is somewhat like yours.* 2 some part; some amount: *A joke loses somewhat of its fun when you hear it the second time.* 1 *adv.,* 2 *n.*

some where (sum′hwer *or* sum′hwar), 1 in or to some place; in or to one place or another: *He lives somewhere in the neighborhood.* 2 at some time: *It happened somewhere in the last century. adv.*

som nam bu lism (som nam′byə liz′əm), sleepwalking. *n.*

som nam bu list (som nam′byə list), sleepwalker. *n.*

som no lence (som′nə ləns), sleepiness; drowsiness. *n.*

som no lent (som′nə lənt), 1 sleepy; drowsy. 2 tending to produce sleep: *The music had a somnolent effect. adj.*

son (sun), 1 a male child or person in relation to his parents or parent. A boy is the son of his father and mother. 2 male descendant. 3 boy or man attached to a country, cause, etc., as a child is to its parents: *sons of America, sons of liberty.* 4 **the Son,** Jesus Christ. *n.*

so nar (sō′när), device for detecting and locating objects under water by the reflection of sound waves. *n.* [formed

from *so(und) na(vigation) r(anging)*]

so na ta (sə näˊtə), piece of music for one or two instruments, having three or four movements in contrasted rhythms but related keys. *n., pl.* **so na tas.**

song (sông), 1 something to sing; a short poem set to music. 2 music to fit a poem; singing: *The canary burst into song.* 3 poetry that has a musical sound. 4 any sound like singing: *the cricket's song, the song of the teakettle. n.*

for a song, very cheap: *buy things for a song.*

song bird (sôngˊbėrdˊ), bird that sings. *n.*

Song of Solomon, The, book of the Old Testament.

Song of Songs, Song of Solomon.

song ster (sôngˊstər), 1 singer. 2 writer of songs or poems. 3 songbird. *n.*

song stress (sôngˊstris), 1 a woman singer. 2 a woman writer of songs or poems; poetess. 3 a female songbird. *n., pl.* **song stress es.**

son ic (sonˊik), 1 of, having to do with, or using sound waves. 2 having to do with the rate at which sound travels in air (1087 feet per second at sea level). *adj.*

sonic barrier, a sudden increase in air resistance met by an aircraft or projectile as it nears the speed of sound; sound barrier.

sonic boom, a loud noise caused by shock waves which are produced by an aircraft traveling at a rate greater than the speed of sound.

son-in-law (sunˊin lôˊ), husband of one's daughter. *n., pl.* **sons-in-law.**

son net (sonˊit), poem having 14 lines with a fixed measure and a formal arrangement of rhymes. *n.*

son net eer (sonˊə tirˊ), 1 writer of sonnets. 2 write sonnets. 3 an inferior poet. 1,3 *n.,* 2 *v.*

son ny (sunˊē), little son. *Sonny* is used as a pet name, or as a way of speaking to a little boy. *n., pl.* **son nies.**

so nor i ty (sə nôrˊə tē), sonorous quality or condition. *n., pl.* **so no ri ties.**

so no rous (sə nôrˊəs), 1 giving out or having a deep, loud sound: *a big, sonorous church bell.* 2 full and rich in sound. 3 having an impressive sound; high-sounding: *sonorous phrases, a sonorous style. adj.* **—so noˊrous ly,** *adv.*

soon (sün), 1 in a short time; before long: *I will see you again soon.* 2 before the usual or expected time; early: *Why have you come so soon?* 3 promptly; quickly: *As soon as I hear, I will let you know.* 4 readily; willingly: *I would as soon die as have to go through such a terrible experience again. adv.*

soot (sút *or* süt), a black substance in the smoke from burning coal, wood, oil,

etc. Soot makes smoke dark and collects on the inside of chimneys. *n.*

sooth (süth), OLD USE. truth. *n.*

soothe (süтн), 1 quiet; calm; comfort: *The mother soothed the crying child.* 2 make less painful; relieve; ease: *Heat soothes some aches; cold soothes others. v.,* **soothed, sooth ing.**

sooth ing (süˊтніng), that soothes: *soothing words, soothing syrup. adj.* **—soothˊing ly,** *adv.*

sooth say er (süthˊsāˊər), person who claims to foretell the future; person who makes prophecies or predictions. *n.*

sooth say ing (süthˊsāˊing), the foretelling of future events; prediction or prophecy. *n.*

soot y (sútˊē *or* süˊtē), 1 covered or blackened with soot. 2 dark-brown or black; dark-colored. *adj.,* **soot i er, soot i est.**

sop (sop), 1 piece of food dipped or soaked in milk, broth, etc. 2 dip or soak: *to sop bread in milk.* 3 something given to soothe or quiet; bribe. 4 take up (water, etc.); wipe; mop: *Please sop up that water with a cloth.* 5 soak thoroughly; drench. 1,3 *n.,* 2,4,5 *v.,* **sopped, sop ping.**

sopping wet, soaked; drenched.

soph ist (sofˊist), a clever but misleading reasoner. *n.*

so phis ti cate (sə fisˊtə kāt *for 1;* sə-fisˊtə kāt *or* sə fisˊtə kit *for 2*), 1 make experienced in worldly ways. 2 a sophisticated person. 1 *v.,* **so phis ti-cat ed, so phis ti cat ing;** 2 *n.*

so phis ti cat ed (sə fisˊtə kāˊtid), experienced in worldly ways; changed from natural simplicity. *adj.*

so phis ti ca tion (sə fisˊtə kāˊshən), a lessening or loss of naturalness, simplicity, or frankness; worldly experience or ideas; artificial ways. *n.*

soph ist ry (sofˊə strē), 1 unsound reasoning. 2 a clever but misleading argument. *n., pl.* **soph ist ries.**

Soph o cles (sofˊə klēzˊ), 495?-406? B.C., Greek writer of tragedies. *n.*

soph o more (sofˊə môr), student in the second year of high school or college. *n.*

soph o mor ic (sofˊə môrˊik), of, having to do with, or like a sophomore or sophomores. *adj.*

so po rif ic (sōˊpə rifˊik *or* sopˊə-rifˊik), 1 causing or tending to cause sleep. 2 sleepy; drowsy. 3 drug that causes sleep. 1,2 *adj.,* 3 *n.*

sop py (sopˊē), soaked; very wet; rainy: *soppy ground, soppy weather. adj.,* **sop pi er, sop pi est.**

so pran o (sə pranˊō), 1 the highest singing voice in women and boys. 2 singer with such a voice. 3 part for such a voice or for a corresponding

hat, āge, fär; let, ēqual, tėrm;
it, īce; hot, ōpen, ôrder;
oil, out; cup, pút, rüle; ch, child;
ng, long; sh, she; th, thin;
тн, then; zh, measure;

ə represents *a* in about,
e in taken, *i* in pencil,
o in lemon, *u* in circus.

instrument. 4 instrument playing such a part. 5 of, for, or having to do with the soprano. 1-4 *n., pl.* **so pran os;** 5 *adj.*

sor cer er (sôrˊsər ər), person who practices magic, especially with the supposed aid of evil spirits; wizard; magician. *n.*

sor cer ess (sôrˊsər is), woman who practices magic, especially with the supposed aid of evil spirits; witch. *n., pl.* **sor cer ess es.**

sor cer y (sôrˊsər ē), magic performed with the supposed aid of evil spirits; witchcraft: *The prince had been changed into a lion by sorcery. n., pl.* **sor cer ies.**

sor did (sôrˊdid), 1 dirty; filthy: *a sordid back street, a sordid shack.* 2 caring too much for money; meanly selfish; mean; low; base. *adj.* **—sorˊdid ly,** *adv.*

sore (sôr), 1 causing sharp or continuous pain; painful; aching; tender; smarting: *a sore throat, a sore finger.* 2 a painful place on the body where the skin or flesh is broken or bruised. 3 sad; distressed: *The suffering of her friend made her heart sore.* 4 INFORMAL. offended; angered; vexed: *He is sore at missing the game.* 5 causing misery, anger, or offense; vexing: *Their defeat is a sore subject with the members of the team.* 6 cause of pain, sorrow, sadness, anger, offense, etc. 7 severe; distressing: *Your going away is a sore grief to us.* 1,3-5,7 *adj.,* **sor er, sor est;** 2,6 *n.* **—soreˊly,** *adv.* **—soreˊness,** *n.*

sor ghum (sôrˊgəm), 1 any of a group of tall plants which resemble corn. One kind of sorghum has a sweet juice used for making molasses or syrup. Some kinds provide food for livestock either by their grain or as hay, and others

sorghum (def. 1)
up to 15 ft. high

803

adj. adjective	*n.* noun
adv. adverb	*prep.* preposition
conj. conjunction	*pron.* pronoun
interj. interjection	*v.* verb
sing. singular	*pl.* plural

furnish material for brushes or brooms. 2 molasses or syrup made from a sorghum plant. *n.*

so ro ri ty (sə rôr′ə tē), 1 a sisterhood. 2 club or society of women or girls, especially at a college. *n., pl.* **so ro ri ties.**

sor rel[1] (sôr′əl), 1 reddish-brown. 2 a reddish brown. 3 a horse having this color. 1 *adj.*, 2,3 *n.* [from French of the 1400's *sorel*, from *sor* yellowish-brown]

sor rel[2] (sôr′əl), any of several plants with sour leaves. *n.* [from French of the 1300's *surele*, from *sur* sour]

sor ri ly (sor′ə lē), in a sorry manner. *adv.*

sor ri ness (sor′ē nis), condition or feeling of being sorry. *n.*

sor row (sor′ō), 1 grief, sadness, or regret: *He felt sorrow at the loss of his kitten. He expressed sorrow at his mistake.* 2 cause of grief, sadness, or regret; trouble; suffering; misfortune: *Her sorrows have aged her.* 3 feel or show grief, sadness, or regret; be sad; feel sorry; grieve: *She sorrowed over the lost money.* 1,2 *n.*, 3 *v.*

sor row ful (sor′ə fəl), 1 full of sorrow; feeling sorrow; sad: *A funeral is a sorrowful occasion.* 2 showing sorrow. 3 causing sorrow. *adj.* **—sor′row ful ly,** *adv.*

sor ry (sor′ē), 1 feeling pity, regret, sympathy; sad: *I am sorry that you are sick. We are sorry that we cannot come to the party.* 2 wretched; poor; pitiful: *The ragged, hungry child was a sorry sight. adj.*, **sor ri er, sor ri est.**

sort (sôrt), 1 kind or class; type: *What sort of work does he do? I like this sort of candy best.* 2 character; quality; nature: *materials of an inferior sort.* 3 person or thing of a certain kind or quality: *He is a good sort.* 4 arrange by kinds or classes; arrange in order: *Sort these cards according to their colors.* 5 separate from others; put: *sort out the best apples for eating.* 1-3 *n.*, 4,5 *v.*

of sorts, of a poor or mediocre quality.

out of sorts, ill, cross, or uncomfortable.

sort of, INFORMAL. somewhat; rather: *In spite of her faults I sort of like her.*

sor tie (sôr′tē), 1 a sudden rushing forth of troops from a besieged fort, town, castle, etc., to attack the besiegers. 2 a single round trip of an aircraft against the enemy. *n.*

S O S (es′ō′es′), 1 signal of distress consisting of the letters *s o s* of the international Morse code (. . . --- . . .), used in wireless telegraphy by ships, aircraft, etc. 2 INFORMAL. any urgent call for help.

so-so (sō′sō′), 1 neither very good nor very bad; fairly good: *The speech was only so-so, but we enjoyed the singing that followed.* 2 in a passable or indifferent manner; tolerably: *"How is he doing his work?" "So-so."* 1 *adj.*, 2 *adv.*

sot (sot), person made stupid and foolish by drinking too much alcoholic liquor; drunkard. *n.*

sot tish (sot′ish), of or like a sot. *adj.*

sou (sü), a former French coin, worth 5 centimes or 1/20 of a franc. *n.*

sou bri quet (sü′brə kā), sobriquet. *n.*

souf flé (sü flā′), a frothy baked dish, usually made light by beaten eggs: *cheese soufflé. n., pl.* **souf flés.** [from French *soufflé* puffed up]

sough (suf *or* sou), 1 make a rustling or murmuring sound: *The pines soughed when the wind blew.* 2 a rustling or murmuring sound. 1 *v.*, 2 *n.*

sought (sôt), past tense and past participle of **seek.** *For days she sought a job. They were sought and found. v.*

soul (sōl), 1 the spiritual part of man, regarded as the source of thought, feeling, and action, and considered as separate from the body. Many religions believe that the soul and the body are separated in death and that the soul lives forever. 2 energy of mind or feelings; spirit: *She puts her whole soul into her work.* 3 cause of inspiration and energy: *Florence Nightingale was the soul of the movement to reform nursing.* 4 the essential part: *Brevity is the soul of wit.* 5 a distinctive emotional or spiritual quality associated with black American culture, especially as expressed through music. 6 person: *Don't tell a soul.* 7 embodiment: *the soul of grace. n.*

soul ful (sōl′fəl), 1 full of feeling; deeply emotional: *soulful music.* 2 expressing or suggesting deep feeling: *a soulful sigh. adj.* **—soul′ful ly,** *adv.* **—soul′ful ness,** *n.*

soul less (sōl′lis), having no soul; without spirit or noble feelings. *adj.* **—soul′less ly,** *adv.*

sound[1] (sound), 1 what is or can be heard; sensation produced in the organs of hearing by vibrations transmitted by the air or some other medium: *the sound of music, the sound of thunder.* 2 energy in the form of vibrations causing this sensation. Sound travels through air in waves about 1087 feet per second. 3 distance within which a noise may be heard. 4 one of the simple elements composing speech: *a vowel sound.* 5 make a sound or noise: *The trumpet sounds for battle. The wind sounds like an animal howling.* 6 pronounce: *Sound each syllable.* 7 be pronounced: *"Rough" and "ruff" sound just alike.* 8 cause to sound: *"Sound the trumpets; beat the drums."* 9 to test by noting sounds: *sound a person's lungs.* 10 to order or direct by a sound: *Sound the retreat.* 11 make known; announce; utter: *The trumpets sounded the call to battle. Everyone sounded his praises.* 12 seem: *That excuse sounds peculiar.* 13 effect produced on the mind by what is heard: *a warning sound, a queer sound.* 1-4,13 *n.*, 5-12 *v.* [Middle English *soun* (the -*d* is a later addition), from French of the 1200's *son*, from Latin *sonus*]

within sound, near enough to hear: *The incoming train was within sound when we reached the railroad station.*

sound[2] (sound), 1 free from disease; healthy: *a sound body and mind.* 2 free from injury, decay, or defect: *sound walls, a sound ship, sound fruit.* 3 strong; safe; secure: *a sound business firm.* 4 solid: *sound rock.* 5 correct; right; reasonable; reliable: *sound advice, sound arguments.* 6 morally good; honest; upright: *sound values.* 7 deep; heavy; profound: *a sound sleep.* 8 thorough; hearty: *a sound whipping.* 9 deeply; thoroughly: *sleep long and sound.* 1-8 *adj.*, 9 *adv.* [Old English *(ge)sund*]

sound[3] (sound), 1 to measure the depth of (water) by letting down a weight fastened on the end of a line. 2 examine or test (the bottom of the sea, etc.) by a line arranged to bring up a sample. 3 try to find out the views of; test; examine: *We sounded Mother on the subject of a picnic.* 4 go toward the bottom; dive: *The whale sounded. v.* [from French of the 1400's *sonder*]

sound[4] (sound), 1 a long, narrow strip of water, larger than a strait, joining two larger bodies of water or separating an island from the mainland: *Long Island Sound.* 2 inlet or arm of the sea: *Puget Sound.* 3 sac in fishes containing air or gas that helps them float. *n.* [partly Old English *sund* water, sea; partly from a Scandinavian word of the 1200's, such as Icelandic *sund* strait]

sound barrier, sonic barrier.

sound er[1] (soun′dər), person or thing that makes a sound. *n.* [*sound*[1] + -*er*[1]]

sound er[2] (soun′dər), person or thing that measures the depth of water. *n.* [*sound*[3] + -*er*[1]]

sound ing[1] (soun′ding), 1 that sounds. 2 resounding. *adj.* [*sound*[1] + -*ing*[2]]

sound ing[2] (soun′ding), 1 act of measuring the depth of water with a sounding line. 2 the depth of water found by this means. 3 **soundings,** *pl.* **a** depths of water found by using a sounding line. **b** water not more than 600 feet deep, which can be measured by an ordinary sounding line. *n.* [*sound³* + *-ing¹*]

sounding line, line having a weight fastened to the end, used to measure the depth of water.

sound less¹ (sound′lis), without sound; making no sound: *soundless steps, a soundless night. adj.* [*sound¹* + *-less*] —**sound′less ly,** *adv.*

sound less² (sound′lis), so deep that the bottom cannot be reached: *the soundless depths of the ocean. adj.* [*sound³* + *-less*]

sound ly (sound′lē), 1 deeply; heavily: *The tired child slept soundly.* 2 vigorously; heartily; thoroughly: *Father scolded us soundly.* 3 with good judgment: *to make a decision soundly. adv.*

sound ness (sound′nis), 1 good health: *soundness of body and mind.* 2 freedom from weakness or defect. 3 good judgment; correctness and reliability: *We have confidence in our doctor's soundness. n.*

sound proof (sound′prüf′), 1 not letting sound pass through: *a soundproof room or ceiling.* 2 make soundproof: *The halls at school are soundproofed.* 1 *adj.,* 2 *v.*

sound track, a recording of the sounds of words, music, etc., made along one edge of a motion-picture film.

soup (süp), a liquid food made by boiling meat, vegetables, fish, etc. *n.*

soup up, SLANG. to increase the horsepower of (an engine, automobile, etc.), especially by enriching the fuel mixture.

soup y (sü′pē), like soup. *adj.,* **soup i er, soup i est.**

sour (sour), 1 having a taste like vinegar or lemon juice; sharp and biting; acid: *This green fruit is sour.* 2 fermented; spoiled. Sour milk is healthful, but most foods are not good to eat when they become sour. 3 having a sour or rank smell. 4 disagreeable; bad-tempered; peevish: *a sour face, a sour remark.* 5 unusually acid: *sour soil.* 6 make or become sour; turn sour: *The milk soured while it stood in the hot sun.* 7 make or become peevish, bad-tempered, or disagreeable. 8 in a sour manner. 1-5 *adj.,* 6,7 *v.,* 8 *adv.* —**sour′ly,** *adv.* —**sour′ness,** *n.*

source (sôrs), 1 person or place from which anything comes or is obtained: *The newspaper gets news from many sources. Mines are the chief source of diamonds.* 2 beginning of a brook or river; fountain; spring. *n.*

sour dough (sour′dō′), 1 INFORMAL.

prospector or pioneer in Alaska or Canada. 2 fermented dough saved from one baking to start fermentation in the next. *n.*

Sou sa (sü′zə), **John Philip,** 1854-1932, American conductor and composer of band music. *n.*

souse (sous), 1 plunge into liquid; throw liquid over; soak in a liquid. 2 a plunging into a liquid; drenching. 3 soak in vinegar, brine, etc.; pickle. 4 liquid used for pickling. 5 something soaked or kept in pickle, especially the head, ears, and feet of a pig. 1,3 *v.,* **soused, sous ing;** 2,4,5 *n.*

south (south), 1 direction to the left as one faces the setting sun; direction just opposite north. 2 toward the south; farther toward the south: *drive south* (*adv.*), *the south side of town* (*adj.*). 3 from the south: *a south wind.* 4 in the south: *the south window.* 5 Also, **South.** the part of any country toward the south. 6 **South,** the southern part of the United States; the states south of Pennsylvania, the Ohio River, and Missouri, making up most of the states that formed the Confederate side in the Civil War. 1,5,6 *n.,* 2-4 *adj.,* 2 *adv.*

south of, further south than: *New York is south of Boston.*

South Africa, Republic of, country in S Africa, formerly called **Union of South Africa.** *Capitals:* Pretoria and Cape Town.

South African, 1 of or having to do with the Republic of South Africa. 2 person born or living in the Republic of South Africa.

South African Dutch, Afrikaans.

South America, continent in the Western Hemisphere southeast of North America.

South American, 1 of or having to do with South America or its people. 2 person born or living in South America.

South amp ton (sou thamp′tən), seaport in S England. *n.*

South Australia, state in S Australia. *Capital:* Adelaide.

South Bend, city in N Indiana.

south bound (south′bound′), going south. *adj.*

South Carolina, one of the south-

hat, āge, fär; let, ēqual, tėrm;
it, īce; hot, ōpen, ôrder;
oil, out; cup, pùt, rüle; ch, child;
ng, long; sh, she; th, thin;
ŦH, then; zh, measure;

ə represents *a* in about,
e in taken, *i* in pencil,
o in lemon, *u* in circus.

eastern states of the United States. *Capital:* Columbia.

South Dakota, one of the midwestern states of the United States. *Capital:* Pierre.

south east (south′ēst′), 1 halfway between south and east. 2 a southeast direction. 3 a place that is in the southeast part or direction. 4 toward the southeast. 5 from the southeast: *a southeast wind.* 6 in the southeast. 1,5,6 *adj.,* 2,3 *n.,* 4 *adv.*

south east er (south′ē′stər), wind or storm from the southeast. *n.*

south east er ly (south′ē′stər lē), 1 toward the southeast. 2 from the southeast. *adj., adv.*

south east ern (south′ē′stərn), 1 toward the southeast. 2 from the southeast. 3 of or in the southeast. *adj.*

south er ly (suŦH′ər lē), 1 toward the south: *a southerly exposure* (*adj.*). *The windows face southerly* (*adv.*). 2 from the south: *a southerly wind* (*adj.*). *The wind is southerly* (*adv.*). *adj., adv.*

south ern (suŦH′ərn), 1 toward the south: *a southern view.* 2 from the south: *a southern breeze.* 3 of or in the south: *southern countries.* 4 **Southern,** of or in the southern part of the United States. *adj.*

Southern Cross, group of four bright stars in the form of a cross, visible in the Southern Hemisphere and often used in finding the direction south.

south ern er (suŦH′ər nər), 1 person born or living in the south. 2 **Southerner,** person born or living in the southern part of the United States. *n.*

Southern Hemisphere, the half of the earth that is south of the equator.

south ern most (suŦH′ərn mōst), farthest south. *adj.*

Southern Yemen, country in SW Arabia. It was formerly the protectorate of Aden. Its official name is **People's Democratic Republic of Yemen.**

South Korea, country in the S part of the Korean peninsula. It is the area south of the 38th parallel. *Capital:* Seoul.

south land (south′lənd *or* south′-

adj.	adjective	*n.*	noun
adv.	adverb	*prep.*	preposition
conj.	conjunction	*pron.*	pronoun
interj.	interjection	*v.*	verb
sing.	singular	*pl.*	plural

land'), land in the south; southern part of a country. *n.*

south paw (south′pô′), SLANG. 1 a left-handed baseball pitcher. 2 any left-handed person. 3 left-handed. 1,2 *n.*, 3 *adj.*

South Pole, the southern end of the earth's axis. It was first reached in 1911 by Amundsen.

South Sea Islands, islands in the S Pacific.

South Vietnam, country in SE Asia, south of the 17th parallel. *Capital:* Saigon. See **Indochina** for map.

south ward (south′wərd), 1 toward the south; south: *She walked southward* (*adv.*). *The orchard is on the southward slope of the hill* (*adj.*). 2 a southward part, direction, or point. 1 *adv., adj.,* 2 *n.*

south wards (south′wərds), southward. *adv.*

south west (south′west′), 1 halfway between south and west. 2 a southwest direction. 3 a place that is in the southwest part or direction. 4 toward the southwest. 5 from the southwest: *a southwest wind.* 6 in the southwest. 1,5,6 *adj.,* 2,3 *n.,* 4 *adv.*

South-West Africa (south′west′), territory in SW Africa, under the supervision of the Republic of South Africa. See **South Africa** for map.

southwester
(def. 2)

south west er (south′wes′tər *for 1;* sou′wes′tər *for 2),* 1 wind or storm from the southwest. 2 a waterproof hat with a broad brim behind to protect the neck, worn especially by seamen. *n.* Also, **sou'wester.**

south west er ly (south′wes′tər lē), 1 toward the southwest. 2 from the southwest. *adj., adv.*

south west ern (south′wes′tərn), 1 toward the southwest. 2 from the southwest. 3 of or in the southwest. 4 **Southwestern,** of or in the southwestern part of the United States. *adj.*

sou ve nir (sü′və nir′ *or* sü′və nir), something given or kept for remem-

brance; a remembrance; keepsake: *She bought a pair of moccasins as a souvenir of her trip out West. n.*

sou'west er (sou′wes′tər), southwester. *n.*

sov er eign (sov′rən), 1 supreme ruler; king or queen; monarch. Queen Victoria was the sovereign of Great Britain from 1837 to 1901. 2 having the rank or power of a sovereign: *a sovereign prince.* 3 greatest in rank or power: *a sovereign court.* 4 independent of the control of other governments: *When the thirteen colonies won the Revolutionary War America became a sovereign nation.* 5 above all others; supreme; greatest: *Character is of sovereign importance.* 6 very excellent or powerful: *a sovereign cure for colds.* 7 a British gold coin, worth 20 shillings, or one pound. 1,7 *n.,* 2-6 *adj.*

sov er eign ty (sov′rən tē),1 supreme power or authority: *The French Revolution rejected the sovereignty of the king.* 2 freedom from outside control; independence in exercising power or authority: *Countries that are satellites lack full sovereignty.* 3 state, territory, community, etc., that is independent or sovereign. 4 the rank, power, or jurisdiction of a sovereign. 5 quality or condition of being sovereign. *n., pl.* **sov er eign ties.**

so vi et (sō′vē et), 1 any of the governing councils or assemblies of the Soviet Union, including town soviets and village soviets as well as the **Supreme Soviet,** the national legislative body. 2 of or having to do with soviets. 3 **Soviet,** of or having to do with the Soviet Union. 1 *n.,* 2,3 *adj.*

Soviet Russia, 1 the Russian Soviet Federated Socialist Republic, the largest republic in the Soviet Union. 2 Soviet Union.

Soviet Union, the Union of Soviet Socialist Republics, a union of fifteen republics in E Europe and W and N Asia, the largest of which is the Russian Soviet Federated Socialist Republic. The European part is often called Russia; Siberia comprises most of the Asian part. *Capital:* Moscow.

sow[1] (sō), 1 scatter (seed) on the ground; plant (seed): *He sows more wheat than oats.* 2 plant seed in: *The farmer sowed the field with oats.* 3 scatter (anything); spread abroad: *The enemy tried to sow discontent in our men. v.,* **sowed, sown** or **sowed, sow ing.** [Old English *sāwan*] —**sow′er,** *n.*

sow[2] (sou), a fully grown female pig. *n.* [Old English *sugu*]

sow bug (sou), wood louse. *n.*

sown (sōn), a past participle of **sow**[1]. *The field had been sown with oats. v.*

sox (soks), INFORMAL. socks (stockings). *n.pl.*

soy (soi), 1 a Chinese and Japanese sauce for fish, meat, etc., made from fermented soybeans. 2 soybean. *n.*

soy bean (soi′bēn′), 1 bean native to Asia, now grown in other parts of the world. Soybeans are used in making flour, oil, etc., and as a food. Soybean oil is used in making plastics, paint, linoleum, etc. 2 the plant that it grows on. *n.*

spa (spä), 1 a mineral spring. 2 town, locality, or resort where there is a mineral spring or springs. *n., pl.* **spas.** [from *Spa,* a Belgian resort]

space (spās), 1 the unlimited room or area which extends in all directions and in which all things exist: *The earth moves through space.* 2 limited place or room: *The brick will fill a space 2½ by 4 by 8 inches. Is there space in the car for another person?* 3 extent or area of ground, surface, etc.: *The trees covered acres of space.* 4 outer space: *the conquest and exploration of space, a rocket launched into space.* 5 of or having to do with outer space: *a space satellite, space flight, space vehicles, space medicine.* 6 distance: *The road is bad for a space of ten miles. The trees are set at equal spaces apart.* 7 length of time: *The flowers died in the space of a day. Many changes occur within the space of one person's life.* 8 OLD USE. an interval of time; a while. 9 (in music) one of the intervals between the lines of a staff. 10 fix the space or spaces of; divide into spaces. 11 separate by spaces: *Space your words evenly when you write.* 1-4, 6-9 *n.,* 5 *adj.,* 10,11 *v.,* **spaced, spac ing.**

spacecraft—partly cut away

space craft (spās′kraft′), vehicle used for flight in outer space. *n., pl.* **space craft.**

space man (spās′mən), astronaut. *n., pl.* **space men.**

space ship (spās′ship′), vehicle designed for travel between the planets or in outer space. *n.*

space station, an artificial earth satellite to be used as an observatory or a launching site for travel in outer space.

space suit (spās′süt′), an airtight, pressurized suit designed to protect travelers in outer space from radiation, heat, and lack of oxygen. *n.*

space walk (spās′wôk′), act of moving or floating in space while outside a spacecraft. *n.*

spac ing (spā′sing), 1 the fixing or arranging of spaces. 2 manner in which spaces are arranged: *even, close, or open spacing in printed matter.* 3 a space or spaces in printing or other work. *n.*

spa cious (spā′shəs), containing much space; with plenty of room; vast: *The rooms of the palace were spacious. adj.* —**spa′cious ly,** *adv.* —**spa′cious ness,** *n.*

spade¹ (def. 1)

spade¹ (spād), 1 tool for digging, having an iron blade which can be pressed into the ground with the foot, and a long handle with a grip or crosspiece at the top. 2 dig with a spade: *Spade up the garden.* 1 *n.,* 2 *v.,* **spad ed, spad ing.** [Old English *spadu*]

call a spade a spade, call a thing by its real name; speak plainly and frankly.

spade² (spād), 1 figure shaped like this: ♠. 2 a playing card marked with one or more black figures like this. 3 **spades,** *pl.* suit of such playing cards. *n.* [from Italian *spade,* from Latin *spatha,* from Greek *spathe* sword, broad blade]

←SPATHE
←SPADIX

spa dix (spā′diks), spike composed of minute flowers on a fleshy stem. A spadix is usually enclosed in a spathe, as in the jack-in-the-pulpit and the calla lily. *n., pl.* **spa dix es, spa di ces** (spā′di sēz′).

spa ghet ti (spə get′ē), long, slender sticks made of the same mixture of flour and water as macaroni. Spaghetti is thinner than macaroni and not hollow. It is cooked by boiling in water. *n.*

Spain (spān), country in SW Europe. *Capital:* Madrid. *n.*

spake (spāk), OLD USE. spoke; a past tense of **speak.** *v.*

span¹ (span), 1 part between two sup-

ports: *The bridge crossed the river in a single span.* 2 distance between two supports: *The arch had a fifty-foot span.* 3 a short space of time: *His span of life is nearly over.* 4 extend over: *A bridge spanned the river.* 5 measure by the hand spread out: *This post can be spanned by one's two hands.* 6 the distance between the tip of a man's thumb and the tip of his little finger when the hand is spread out; about 9 inches. 1-3,6 *n.,* 4,5 *v.,* **spanned, span ning.** [Old English *spann*]

span² (span), pair of horses or other animals harnessed and driven together. *n.* [probably from Dutch *span,* from *spannen* to stretch, yoke]

span gle (spang′gəl), 1 a small piece of glittering metal used for decoration: *The dress was covered with spangles.* 2 any small, bright bit: *This rock shows spangles of gold.* 3 decorate with spangles: *The dress was spangled with gold.* 4 sprinkle with small, bright bits: *The sky is spangled with stars.* 1,2 *n.,* 3,4 *v.,* **span gled, span gling.**

Span iard (span′yərd), person born or living in Spain. *n.*

span iel (span′yəl), 1 any of various breeds of dogs, usually of small or medium size, with long, silky hair and drooping ears. Spaniels are very gentle and affectionate. 2 person who yields too much to others. *n.*

Span ish (span′ish), 1 of or having to do with Spain, its people, or their language. 2 the people of Spain. 3 the language of Spain. It is also the language of most Latin-American countries. American Spanish is spoken in Mexico, Argentina, Cuba, Puerto Rico, Panama, etc., but not in Brazil. 1 *adj.,* 2 *n.pl.,* 3 *n.sing.*

Spanish America, countries and islands south and southeast of the United States, in which the principal language is Spanish.

Spanish American, person born or living in a Spanish-American country.

Span ish-A mer i can (span′ish ə mer′ə kən), 1 of or having to do with Spain and America, or with Spain and the United States. 2 of or having to do with the parts of America where Spanish is the principal language. *adj.*

Spanish-American War, war between Spain and the United States in 1898, fought chiefly in Cuba and the Philippines.

Spanish Main, 1 (formerly) the NW coast of South America, from which Spanish galleons used to sail with gold for Spain. 2 (in later use) the Caribbean Sea.

spank (spangk), 1 strike with the open hand, a slipper, etc.: *I spanked the*

hat, āge, fär; let, ēqual, tėrm;
it, īce; hot, ōpen, ôrder;
oil, out; cup, pùt, rüle; ch, child;
ng, long; sh, she; th, thin;
ŦH, then; zh, measure;

ə represents *a* in about,
e in taken, *i* in pencil,
o in lemon, *u* in circus.

naughty child. 2 a blow with the open hand, a slipper, etc.; slap. 1 *v.,* 2 *n.*

spank ing (spang′king), 1 a striking with the open hand, a slipper, etc. 2 blowing briskly: *a spanking breeze.* 3 INFORMAL. unusually fine, great, large, etc.: *a spanking team of horses.* 1 *n.,* 2,3 *adj.*

spaniel (def. 1)
about 18 in. high at the shoulder

spar¹ (spär), 1 a stout pole used to support or extend the sails of a ship; mast, yard, gaff, boom, etc., of a ship. 2 provide (a ship) with spars. 1 *n.,* 2 *v.,* **sparred, spar ring.** [Middle English *sparre* rafter]

spar² (spär), 1 make motions of attack and defense with the arms and fists; box. 2 a boxing match. 3 to dispute: *The two old men were sparring about who would win the election.* 4 a dispute. 1,3 *v.,* **sparred, spar ring;** 2,4 *n.* [Old English *sperran*]

spar³ (spär), any of various crystalline, shiny minerals that split into flakes easily. *n.* [from earlier German *spar,* related to Old English *spær(en)* of plaster]

spare (sper *or* spar), 1 show mercy to; refrain from harming or destroying: *spare a conquered enemy. Her quick wit spares nobody, not even herself.* 2 make (a person, etc.) free from labor, pain, etc.: *We walked up the hill to spare the horse. I did the work to spare you the trouble.* 3 get along without; do without: *Mother couldn't spare the car; so father and I had to take the bus. "Spare the rod and spoil the child."* 4 use in small quantities or not at all; be saving of: *to spare no expense.* 5 free for other use: *spare time.* 6 extra; in

adj. adjective	n. noun
adv. adverb	prep. preposition
conj. conjunction	pron. pronoun
interj. interjection	v. verb
sing. singular	pl. plural

reserve: *a spare tire.* **7** a spare thing, part, tire, etc. **8** thin; lean: *Lincoln was a tall, spare man.* **9** small in quantity; meager; scanty: *To get thin, one should live on a spare diet.* **10** the knocking down of all the pins with two rolls of a bowling ball. **1-4** *v.,* **spared, spar ing; 5,6,8,9** *adj.,* **spar er, spar est; 7,10** *n.* —**spare′ness,** *n.*

spare ly (sper′lē *or* spar′lē), not amply or fully; sparingly; scantily; sparsely. *adv.*

spare ribs (sper′ribs′ *or* spar′ribs′), ribs of pork having less meat than the ribs near the loins. *n.pl.*

spar ing (sper′ing *or* spar′ing), avoiding waste; economical; frugal: *a sparing use of sugar.* *adj.* —**spar′ing ly,** *adv.*

spark[1] (spärk), **1** a small bit of fire: *The burning wood threw off sparks.* **2** flash given off when electricity jumps across an open space. An electric spark explodes the gas in the engine of an automobile. **3** a bright flash; gleam; sparkle: *We saw a spark of light through the trees.* **4** to flash; gleam; sparkle. **5** a small amount: *I haven't a spark of interest in the plan.* **6** a glittering bit: *The moving sparks we saw were fireflies.* **7** send out small bits of fire; produce sparks. **8** make (one's friends, teammates, etc.) enthusiastic or determined. **9** stir to activity; stimulate: *spark a revolt, spark sales, etc.* **1-3,5,6** *n.,* **4,7-9** *v.* [Old English *spearca*]

spark[2] (spärk), **1** a gay and showy young man. **2** beau; lover. *n.* [perhaps special use of *spark*[1], or from a Scandinavian word of the 1200's, such as Icelandic *sparkr* lively]

spar kle (spär′kəl), **1** send out little sparks: *The fireworks sparkled.* **2** a little spark. **3** to shine; glitter; flash; gleam: *The diamonds sparkled.* **4** a shine; glitter; flash: *I like the sparkle of her eyes.* **5** be brilliant; be lively: *Wit sparkles.* **6** brilliance; liveliness. **7** bubble. Ginger ale and champagne sparkle. **1,3,5,7** *v.,* **spar kled, spar kling; 2,4,6** *n.*

spar kler (spär′klər), **1** person or thing that sparkles. **2** firework that sends out little sparks. **3** a sparkling gem, especially a diamond. *n.*

spar kling (spär′kling), **1** shining; glittering: *sparkling stars.* **2** brilliant: *She*

has a sparkling wit. **3** bubbling: *sparkling drinks.* *adj.*

spark plug, device in the cylinder of an internal-combustion engine by which the mixture of gasoline and air is exploded by an electric spark.

spar row (spar′ō), any of various small, usually brownish birds common in North and South America but also found in Europe, Asia, and Africa. English sparrows and some other kinds live near houses; others live in woods and fields. *n.*

sparrow hawk, a small hawk which feeds on birds, insects, and other small animals.

sparse (spärs), **1** thinly scattered; occurring here and there: *the sparse population of the country, sparse hair.* **2** scanty; meager: *a sparse diet.* *adj.,* **spars er, spars est.** —**sparse′ly,** *adv.* —**sparse′ness,** *n.*

spar si ty (spär′sə tē), sparse or scattered condition; sparseness. *n.*

(x indicates battlefield)
Mount Olympus
AEGEAN SEA
Thermopylae
Delphi
Thebes
Marathon
Corinth
Athens
• SPARTA
about 450 B.C.

Spar ta (spär′tə), one of the most important cities in ancient Greece, famous for its soldiers. *n.*

Spar tan (spärt′n), **1** of Sparta or its people. **2** person who was born or lived in Sparta. The Spartans were noted for living simply, saying little, being brave, and enduring pain without complaining. **3** like the Spartans; simple, frugal, and severe. **4** person who is like the Spartans. **1,3** *adj.,* **2,4** *n.*

spasm (spaz′əm), **1** a sudden, abnormal, involuntary contraction of a muscle or muscles. **2** any sudden, brief fit or spell of unusual energy or activity: *a spasm of temper, a spasm of industry.* *n.*

spas mod ic (spaz mod′ik), **1** having to do with spasms; resembling a spasm: *a spasmodic cough.* **2** occurring very irregularly: *a spasmodic interest in reading.* **3** having or showing bursts of excitement. *adj.* —**spas mod′i cal ly,** *adv.*

spas tic (spas′tik), **1** of, having to do with, or characterized by spasms. **2** person suffering from a form of paralysis marked by prolonged contraction of a muscle or muscles. **1** *adj.,* **2** *n.*

spat[1] (spat), **1** a slight quarrel. **2** IN-

FORMAL. quarrel slightly. **3** a light blow; slap. **4** slap lightly. **1,3** *n.,* **2,4** *v.,* **spat ted, spat ting.** [perhaps an imitation of the sound of slapping]

spat[2] (spat), a past tense and a past participle of **spit**[1]. *The cat spat at the dog.* *v.*

spat[3] (spat). Usually, **spats,** *pl.* a short gaiter covering the ankle. *n.* [shortened from earlier *spatterdash,* from *spatter* + *dash*]

spat[4] (spat), **1** the spawn of oysters or certain other shellfish. **2** a young oyster. **3** (of oysters and certain other shellfish) to spawn. **1,2** *n.,* **3** *v.,* **spatted, spat ting.** [origin uncertain]

spathe (spāŧH), a large bract or pair of bracts that encloses a flower cluster. The calla lily has a white spathe around a yellow flower cluster. See **spadix** for picture. *n.*

spa tial (spā′shəl), **1** of or having to do with space. **2** existing in space. *adj.*

spa tial ly (spā′shə lē), in spatial respects; so far as space is concerned; in space. *adv.*

spat ter (spat′ər), **1** to scatter or dash in drops or particles: *spatter mud.* **2** to fall in drops or particles: *Rain spatters on the sidewalk.* **3** to strike in a shower; strike in a number of places: *Bullets spattered the wall.* **4** a spattering: *a spatter of bullets.* **5** sound of spattering. **6** a splash or spot. **7** to splash or spot with mud, slander, disgrace, etc. **1-3,7** *v.,* **4-6** *n.*

spat u la (spach′ə lə), tool with a broad, flat, flexible blade, used for mixing drugs, spreading paints or frostings, etc. *n., pl.* **spat u las.**

spatulas

spav in (spav′ən), disease of horses in which a bony swelling forms at the hock, causing lameness. *n.*

spav ined (spav′ənd), having spavin; lame. *adj.*

spawn (spôn), **1** the eggs of fish, frogs, shellfish, etc. **2** the young newly hatched from such eggs. **3** (of fish, etc.) produce spawn. **4** bring forth; give birth to. **5** offspring, especially a large number of offspring. **1,2,5** *n.,* **3,4** *v.*

spay (spā), remove the ovaries of (a female animal). *v.*

S.P.C.A., Society for the Prevention of Cruelty to Animals.

speak (spēk), **1** say words; talk: *A person with a cold often has trouble speaking distinctly.* **2** make a speech:

Who is going to speak at the meeting?
3 make known; tell; express; say: *Speak the truth. Her eyes speak of suffering.* 4 use (a language): *Do you speak French?* 5 express an idea, feeling, etc.; communicate: *Actions speak louder than words.* 6 make sounds: *The cannon spoke. v.,* **spoke, spo ken, speak ing.**

so to speak, to speak in such a manner; to use that expression: *He has a chance to win the race; he is, so to speak, still in the running.*

speak for, 1 speak in the interest of; represent: *Why don't you speak for yourself instead of having others speak for you?* 2 ask or apply for: *We ought to speak for reserved seats ahead of time.*

speak of, refer to; mention: *He spoke of this matter to me. Speaking of school, how do you like the new gym? I have no complaints to speak of.*

speak out or **speak up,** speak loudly, clearly, or freely: *No one dared to speak out against the big bully. The children all spoke up in favor of the teacher's suggestion to have a party.*

speak well for, give a favorable idea of; be evidence in favor of: *Her behavior speaks well for her.*

speak er (spē′kər), 1 person who speaks. 2 Also, **Speaker.** person who presides over a legislative assembly. The Speaker of the House of Representatives is its presiding officer. 3 loudspeaker. *n.*

speak er ship (spē′kər ship), position of presiding officer. *n.*

speak ing (spē′king), 1 act, utterance, or discourse of a person who speaks. 2 that speaks; giving information as if by speech: *a speaking example of a thing.* 3 used in, suited to, or involving speech: *the speaking voice, within speaking distance, a speaking part in a play.* 4 permitting conversation: *a speaking acquaintance with a person.* 5 highly expressive: *speaking eyes.* 6 lifelike: *a speaking likeness.* 1 *n.,* 2-6 *adj.*

spear[1] (spir), 1 weapon with a long shaft and a sharp-pointed head. 2 pierce with a spear: *The Indian speared a fish.* 3 pierce or stab with anything sharp: *spear string beans with a fork.* 1 *n.,* 2,3 *v.* [Old English *spere*]

spear[2] (spir), sprout or shoot of a plant: *a spear of grass. n.* [a different form of *spire*[1]]

spear head (spir′hed′), 1 the sharppointed striking end of a spear. 2 part that is first in an attack, undertaking, etc. 3 lead or clear the way for; head: *He commanded the regiment which spearheaded the assault on the fort. The railway is spearheading a new system that will move goods more efficiently.* 1,2 *n.,* 3 *v.*

spear man (spir′mən), soldier armed with a spear. *n., pl.* **spear men.**

spear mint (spir′mint′), a fragrant herb much used for flavoring. It yields a fragrant oil. *n.*

spe cial (spesh′əl), 1 of a particular kind; distinct from others; not general: *This desk has a special lock. Have you any special color in mind for your new coat?* 2 more than ordinary; unusual; exceptional: *Today's topic is of special interest.* 3 for a particular person, thing, purpose, etc.: *The railroad ran special trains on holidays. Send the letter by a special messenger.* 4 a special train, car, bus, etc. 5 a specially featured product or service. 6 a television show produced especially for a single broadcast. 7 held in high regard; great; chief: *a special friend.* 1-3,7 *adj.,* 4-6 *n.*

special delivery, the delivery of a letter or package by a special messenger rather than by the regular mailman. Special delivery mail has much higher rates, but it is handled faster and delivered sooner than regular mail.

spe cial ist (spesh′ə list), 1 person who devotes himself to one particular branch of study, business, etc. A dentist is a specialist in the care of teeth. 2 (in the U.S. Army) a soldier with administrative or technical duties, ranking below a corporal and above a private. *n.*

spe cial i za tion (spesh′ə lə zā′shən), a specializing or a being specialized. *n.*

spe cial ize (spesh′ə līz), 1 pursue some special branch of study, work, etc.: *Some doctors specialize in treating heart disease.* 2 adapt to a special function or condition: *Lungs and gills are specialized for breathing.* 3 develop in a special way: *Animals and plants are specialized to fit their surroundings. v.,* **spe cial ized, spe cial iz ing.**

spe cial ly (spesh′ə lē), in a special manner or degree; particularly; unusually. *adv.*

spe cial ty (spesh′əl tē), 1 a special study, line of work, profession, trade, etc.: *Straightening teeth is that dentist's specialty. American history is the specialty of my social studies teacher.* 2 product, article, etc., to which special attention is given: *This store makes a specialty of children's clothes.* 3 special character or quality. 4 a special or particular characteristic; peculiarity. *n., pl.* **spe cial ties.**

spe cie (spē′shē), money in the form of coins; metal money. Silver dollars are specie. *n.*

spe cies (spē′shēz), 1 group of animals or plants that have certain permanent characteristics in common and are able to interbreed. A species ranks

hat, āge, fär; let, ēqual, tėrm;
it, īce; hot, ōpen, ôrder;
oil, out; cup, pùt, rüle; ch, child;
ng, long; sh, she; th, thin;
ŦH, then; zh, measure;

ə represents *a* in about,
e in taken, *i* in pencil,
o in lemon, *u* in circus.

next below a genus and may be divided into several varieties, races, or breeds. All species of apples belong in the same genus. Wheat is a species of grass. The domestic cat is one species of cat. 2 kind; sort; distinct kind or sort: *There are many species of advertisements.* 3 **the species,** the human race. *n., pl.* **spe cies.**

spe cif ic (spi sif′ik), 1 definite, precise, particular: *There was no specific reason for the quarrel.* 2 characteristic (of); peculiar (to): *Feathers are a feature specific to birds.* 3 curing some particular disease. 4 a cure for some particular disease: *Vitamin C is a specific for scurvy.* 5 produced by some special cause. 6 of or having to do with a species: *the specific name of a plant.* 1-3,5,6 *adj.,* 4 *n.*

spe cif i cal ly (spi sif′ik lē), in a specific manner; definitely; particularly: *The doctor told her specifically not to eat eggs. adv.*

spec i fi ca tion (spes′ə fə kā′shən), 1 act of specifying; definite mention; detailed statement of particulars: *She made careful specification as to the kinds of cake and candy for her party.* 2 Usually, **specifications,** *pl.* a detailed description of the dimensions, materials, etc., for a building, road, dam, boat, etc. 3 something specified; particular item, article, etc. *n.*

specific gravity, the ratio of the weight of a given volume of any substance to that of the same volume of some other substance taken as a standard, water being used for solids and liquids, and hydrogen or air for gases. The specific gravity of gold is 19 because any volume of gold weighs 19 times as much as the same volume of water. A hydrometer is often used to find the specific gravity of a liquid.

spec i fic i ty (spes′ə fis′ə tē), specific quality. *n.*

spec i fy (spes′ə fī), 1 mention or name definitely: *Did you specify any particular time for us to call?* 2 include in the specifications: *He delivered the paper as specified. v.,* **spec i fied, spec i fy ing.**

specimen

spec i men (spes/ə mən), one of a group or class taken to show what the others are like; sample: *He collects specimens of all kinds of rocks and minerals. The statue was a fine specimen of Greek sculpture. n.*

spe cious (spē/shəs), seeming desirable, reasonable, or probable, but not really so; apparently good or right, but without real merit: *The teacher saw through that specious excuse. adj.*

speck (spek), 1 a small spot; stain: *Can you clean the specks off this wallpaper?* 2 a tiny bit; particle: *I have a speck in my eye.* 3 mark with specks: *This fruit is badly specked.* 1,2 *n.,* 3 *v.*

speck le (spek/əl), 1 a small spot or mark: *This hen is gray with white speckles.* 2 mark with speckles: *The dog is speckled with paint.* 1 *n.,* 2 *v.,* **speckled, speck ling.**

spec ta cle (spek/tə kəl), 1 thing to look at; sight: *The children at play among the flowers made a charming spectacle. A quarrel is an unpleasant spectacle.* 2 a public show or display: *The big parade was a fine spectacle.* 3 **spectacles,** *pl.* eyeglasses. *n.*

spec tac u lar (spek tak/yə lər), 1 making a great display: *the spectacular eruption of a volcano.* 2 having to do with a spectacle or show. 3 a spectacular display. 4 a lengthy motion picture or television show, usually produced on a lavish scale. 1,2 *adj.,* 3,4 *n.*

spec tac u lar ly (spek tak/yə lər lē), 1 in a spectacular manner or degree. 2 as a spectacle. *adv.*

spec ta tor (spek/tā tər), person who looks on without taking part: *There were many spectators at the game. n.*

spec ter (spek/tər), 1 ghost. 2 thing causing terror or dread: *the grim specter of war. n.* Also, **spectre.**

spec tral (spek/trəl), 1 of or like a specter; ghostly: *the spectral form of a ship on a foggy sea.* 2 of or produced by the spectrum: *spectral colors. adj.*

spec tre (spek/tər), specter. *n.*

spec tro scope (spek/trə skōp), instrument for producing and examining the spectrum of a ray from any source. The spectrum produced by passing a light ray through a prism can be examined to determine the composition of the source of the ray. *n.*

spec trum (spek/trəm), the band of colors formed when a beam of light is broken up by being passed through a prism or by some other means. A rainbow has all the colors of the spectrum: red, orange, yellow, green, blue, indigo, and violet. *n., pl.* **spec tra** (spek/trə), **spec trums.**

spec u late (spek/yə lāt), 1 think carefully; reflect; meditate; consider: *The philosopher speculated about time and space.* 2 to guess; conjecture: *She refused to speculate about the possible winner.* 3 buy or sell when there is a large risk, with the hope of making a profit from future price changes: *He became poor after speculating in what turned out to be worthless oil wells. v.,* **spec u lat ed, spec u lat ing.**

spec u la tion (spek/yə lā/shən), 1 careful thought; reflection: *speculations about the nature of the universe.* 2 a guessing; conjecture: *Our estimates of the cost were based on speculation.* 3 a buying or selling when there is a large risk, with the hope of making a profit from future price changes: *Her speculations in the stock market cost her a thousand dollars. n.*

spec u la tive (spek/yə lā/tiv), 1 carefully thoughtful; reflective. 2 theoretical rather than practical. 3 of or involving buying or selling at a large risk. *adj.* —**spec/u la/tive ly,** *adv.* —**spec/u la/tive ness,** *n.*

spec u la tor (spek/yə lā/tər), person who speculates, usually in business. A ticket speculator buys tickets for shows, games, etc., in advance, hoping to sell them later at a higher price. *n.*

sped (sped), a past tense and a past participle of **speed.** *The police car sped down the road. v.*

speech (spēch), 1 act of speaking; talk. 2 power of speaking: *Animals lack speech.* 3 manner of speaking: *His speech showed that he was Southern.* 4 what is said; the words spoken: *We made the usual farewell speeches.* 5 a public talk: *Our Congresswoman gave a fine speech.* 6 language: *The native speech of most Americans is English. n., pl.* **speech es.**

speech less (spēch/lis), 1 not able to speak: *Animals are speechless. He was speechless with anger.* 2 silent: *Her frown gave a speechless message. adj.* —**speech/less ness,** *n.*

speech less ly (spēch/lis lē), 1 without speaking. 2 so as to be speechless. *adv.*

speed (spēd), 1 swift or rapid movement: *the amazing speed with which a cat jumps on a mouse.* 2 go fast: *The boat sped over the water.* 3 make go fast: *Let's all help speed the work.* 4 rate of movement: *The girls ran at full speed.* 5 go faster than is safe or lawful: *The car was caught speeding near the school zone.* 6 arrangement of gears to give a certain rate of movement. An automobile usually has three speeds forward and one backward. 7 help forward; promote: *speed an undertaking.* 8 OLD USE. good luck; success. 9 OLD USE. succeed. 10 OLD USE. give success to. 1,4,6,8 *n.,* 2,3,5,7,9,10 *v.,* **sped** or **speed ed, speed ing.**

speed up, go or cause to go faster; increase in speed.

speed boat (spēd/bōt/), motorboat built to go fast. *n.*

speed er (spē/dər), person or thing that speeds, especially a person who drives an automobile at a higher speed than is safe or lawful. *n.*

speed i ly (spē/də lē), quickly; with speed; soon. *adv.*

speed i ness (spē/dē nis), speedy quality; quickness; rapidity. *n.*

speed om e ter (spē dom/ə tər), instrument to indicate the speed of an automobile or other vehicle, and often the distance traveled. *n.*

speed up (spēd/up/), an increase in speed. *n.*

speed way (spēd/wā/), a road or track for fast driving. *n.*

speed well (spēd/wel), any of various low plants with small blue, purple, pink, or white flowers. *n.*

speed y (spē/dē), moving, going, or acting with speed; fast; rapid; quick; swift: *speedy workers, a speedy decision. adj.,* **speed i er, speed i est.**

spe le ol o gy (spē/lē ol/ə jē), the scientific study of caves. *n.*

spell[1] (spel), 1 write or say the letters of (a word) in order: *Some words are easy to spell.* 2 spell words: *We learn to spell in school.* 3 make up or form (a word): *C-a-t spells cat.* 4 mean: *These clouds spell a storm. Delay spells danger.* 5 read with difficulty: *If you have to spell out each sentence in the story, you'll never understand what it is about. v.,* **spelled** or **spelt, spell ing.** [from French of the 1400's *espeller*]

spell out, explain carefully, step by step, and in detail: *We asked him to spell out his plan for raising more money.*

spell[2] (spel), 1 word or set of words supposed to have magic power. 2 magic influence; fascination; charm: *A spell of mystery seemed to hang over the old castle. We were under the spell of the beautiful music. n.* [Old English *spell* story]

cast a spell on, put under the influence of a spell; fascinate.

under a spell, controlled by a spell; fascinated; spellbound: *The adventure story held the children under a spell.*

spell³ (spel), 1 period of work or duty: *The rower's spell at the oars was half an hour.* 2 period or time of anything: *The child has spells of coughing. There was a long spell of rainy weather in August.* 3 INFORMAL. a brief period: *rest for a spell.* 4 INFORMAL. to work in place of (another person) for a while: *I'll spell you at cutting the grass.* 5 give a time of rest to. 6 relief of one person by another in doing something. 1-3,6 *n.,* 4,5 *v.,* **spelled, spell ing.** [Old English *spelian, v.*]

sperm whale—up to 60 ft. long

spell bind (spel′bīnd′), make spellbound; fascinate; enchant. *v.,* **spellbound, spell bind ing.**

spell bind er (spel′bīn′dər), speaker who can hold his listeners spellbound. *n.*

spell bound (spel′bound′), too interested to move; fascinated; enchanted: *The children were spellbound by the circus performance. adj.*

spell er (spel′ər), 1 person who spells words. 2 book for teaching spelling. *n.*

spell ing (spel′ing), 1 the writing or saying of the letters of a word in order: *He is good at spelling.* 2 the way a word is spelled: *"Ax" has two spellings, "ax" and "axe." n.*

spelling bee, a spelling contest.

spelt (spelt), spelled; a past tense and a past participle of **spell¹.** *v.*

spe lunk er (spi lung′kər), person who explores and maps caves. *n.*

Spen cer (spen′sər), **Herbert,** 1820-1903, English philosopher. *n.*

spend (spend), 1 pay out: *She spent ten dollars shopping for food today.* 2 pay out money: *Earn before you spend.* 3 use; use up: *Don't spend any more time on that lesson.* 4 pass: *We spent last summer at the seashore.* 5 wear out: *The storm has spent its force.* 6 to waste; squander: *He spent his fortune on horse racing. v.,* **spent, spend ing.** —**spend′er,** *n.*

spend thrift (spend′thrift′), 1 person who wastes money. 2 extravagant with money; wasteful. 1 *n.,* 2 *adj.*

Spen ser (spen′sər), **Edmund,** 1552?-1599, English poet, author of *The Faerie Queene. n.*

spent (spent), 1 past tense and past participle of **spend.** *Saturday was spent in playing. How have you spent your time today?* 2 used up. 3 worn out; tired: *a spent swimmer, a spent horse.* 1 *v.,* 2,3 *adj.*

sperm (spėrm), 1 sperm cell. 2 semen. *n.*

sper ma cet i (spėr′mə set′ē or spėr′mə sē′tē), a whitish, waxy substance obtained from the oil in the head of the sperm whale and used in making fine candles, ointments, cosmetics, etc. *n.*

sperm cell, a male reproductive cell; sperm. A sperm cell unites with an ovum to fertilize it.

sperm whale, a large, square-headed, toothed whale that is valuable for its oil; cachalot.

spew (spyü), 1 throw out; cast forth; vomit. 2 something that is spewed; vomit. 1 *v.,* 2 *n.*

sp. gr., specific gravity.

sphere (sfir), 1 a round solid whose surface is at all points equally distant from the center. 2 ball or globe. The sun, moon, earth, and stars are spheres. A baseball is a sphere. 3 place or surroundings in which a person or thing exists, acts, works, etc.: *The woman's sphere today includes both home and business.* 4 range; extent; region: *England's sphere of influence.* 5 a place, position, or rank in society: *the sphere of the aristocracy.* 6 a supposed hollow globe, with the earth at its center, enclosing the stars, sun, and planets. 7 any one of a series of such globes, one inside another, in which the stars and planets were supposed by ancient astronomers to be set. Movement of the spheres was believed to cause the stars and planets to revolve around the earth. *n.*

spher i cal (sfir′ə kəl or sfer′ə kəl), 1 shaped like a sphere. 2 of or having to do with a sphere or spheres. *adj.*

spher i cal ly (sfir′ik lē or sfer′ik lē), 1 in the form of a sphere, or of part of a sphere. 2 so as to be spherical. *adv.*

spher oid (sfir′oid), body shaped somewhat like a sphere, but not perfectly round. *n.*

sphinc ter (sfingk′tər), a ringlike muscle that surrounds an opening or passage of the body, and can contract to close it. *n.*

sphinx (sfingks), 1 statue of a lion's body with the head of a man, ram, or hawk. There are many sphinxes in Egypt. The **Great Sphinx** is a huge statue with a man's head and a lion's body, near Cairo. 2 **Sphinx,** (in Greek myths) a monster with the head of a woman, the body of a lion, and wings. The Sphinx proposed a riddle to every passer-by and killed those unable to guess it. 3 a puzzling or mysterious person. *n., pl.* **sphinx es.**

spice (spīs), 1 any of various seasonings obtained from plants and used to flavor food. Pepper, cinnamon, cloves, ginger, and nutmeg are common spices. 2 put spice in; season: *spiced peaches.* 3 something that adds flavor or interest: *"Variety is the spice of life."* 4 add flavor or interest to: *The principal spiced her speech with stories and jokes.* 1,3 *n.,* 2,4 *v.,* **spiced, spic ing.**

Spice Islands, Moluccas.

spic i ness (spī′sē nis), spicy flavor or smell. *n.*

spick-and-span (spik′ən span′), neat and clean; spruce or smart; fresh; new: *a spick-and-span room. adj.*

spic ule (spik′yül), 1 a small, slender, sharp-pointed piece, usually bony or crystalline. 2 such a piece in a sponge. 3 a small spike of flowers. *n.*

spic y (spī′sē), 1 flavored with spice: *The cookies were rich and spicy.* 2 like spice: *Those apples have a spicy smell and taste.* 3 lively; keen: *spicy conversation full of gossip.* 4 somewhat improper. *adj.,* **spic i er, spic i est.**

spi der (spī′dər), 1 a small animal with eight legs and no wings. Spiders belong to the class of arachnids. Many spiders spin webs to catch insects for food. 2 something like or suggesting a spider. 3 a kind of frying pan with a handle. *n.* —**spi′der like′,** *adj.*

spider web, web spun by a spider.

spi der y (spī′dər ē), 1 long and thin like a spider's legs. 2 suggesting a spider web. *adj.*

spied (spīd), past tense and past participle of **spy.** *He spied his friend in the crowd. Who had spied on us? v.*

sphinx (def. 1)   sphinx (def. 2)

spig ot (spig′ət), 1 faucet. 2 peg or plug used to stop the small hole of a cask, barrel, or keg; bung. *n.*

spike¹ (spīk), 1 a large, strong nail.

spike

2 fasten with spikes: *The work crew laid the track by spiking the rails to the ties.* 3 a sharp-pointed piece or part: *Ballplayers wear shoes with spikes.* 4 provide with spikes: *Runners wear spiked shoes to keep from slipping.* 5 pierce or injure with a spike. 6 make (a cannon) useless by driving a spike into the opening where the powder is set off. 7 put an end or stop to; make useless; block: *The mayor spiked the talk of an increase in taxes.* 1,3 *n.,* 2,4-7 *v.,* **spiked, spik ing.** [from a Scandinavian word of the 1200's, such as Icelandic *spíkr*] —**spike′like′,** *adj.*

spike² (spīk), 1 ear of grain. 2 a long, pointed flower cluster. *n.* [from Latin *spica*]

spike²
(A, def. 1)
(B, def. 2)

A   B

spike nard (spīk′nərd *or* spīk′närd), 1 a sweet-smelling ointment used by the ancients. 2 the fragrant East Indian plant from which it was probably obtained. *n.*

spik y (spī′kē), 1 having spikes; set with sharp, projecting points. 2 having the shape of a spike. *adj.,* **spik i er, spik i est.**

spill¹ (spil), 1 let (liquid or any matter in loose pieces) run or fall: *spill milk or salt.* 2 fall or flow out: *Water spilled from the pail.* 3 shed (blood). 4 IN-FORMAL. cause to fall from a horse, car, boat, etc.: *The boat upset and spilled all of us into the water.* 5 act of spilling. 6 quantity spilled. 7 IN-FORMAL. a fall: *She got a bad spill trying to ride that horse.* 8 SLANG. make known; tell: *spill a secret.* 1-4,8 *v.,* **spilled** or **spilt, spill ing;** 5-7 *n.* [Old English *spillan* destroy, kill]

spill² (spil), a thin piece of wood, or a folded or twisted piece of paper, used to light a candle, pipe, etc. *n.* [Middle English *spille*]

spill way (spil′wā′), channel or passage for the escape of surplus water from a dam, river, etc. *n.*

spilt (spilt), spilled; a past tense and a past participle of **spill¹.** *v.*

spin (spin), 1 turn around rapidly: *The wheel spins round.* 2 make turn around rapidly: *The boy spins his top.* 3 feel as if one were whirling around; feel dizzy: *My head is spinning.* 4 draw out and twist (cotton, flax, wool, etc.) into thread. 5 make (thread, yarn, etc.) by drawing out and twisting cotton, wool, flax, etc. 6 make (a thread, web, cocoon, etc.) by giving out from the body sticky material that hardens in air. A spider spins a web. 7 draw out; produce; tell: *My grandparents often spin yarns about life on the farm.* 8 act of spinning. 9 a rapid run, ride, drive, etc.: *Get your bicycle and come for a spin with me.* 10 run, ride, drive, etc., rapidly. 11 a rapid turning around of an airplane as it falls. 1-7,10 *v.,* **spun, spin ning;** 8,9,11 *n.*

spin out, make long and slow; draw out; prolong.

spin ach (spin′ich), 1 plant whose green leaves are cooked and eaten as a vegetable, or used uncooked in a salad. 2 its leaves. *n.*

spi nal (spī′nl), of or having to do with the backbone. *adj.*

spinal column, backbone.

spinal cord, the thick, whitish cord of nerve tissue which extends from the brain down through most of the backbone and from which nerves to various parts of the body branch off.

spin dle (spin′dl), 1 the rod or pin used in spinning to twist, wind, and hold thread. See **distaff** for picture. 2 any rod or pin that turns around, or on which something turns. Axles and shafts are spindles. 3 something shaped like a spindle. 4 grow very long and thin. 1-3 *n.,* 4 *v.,* **spin dled, spin dling.**

spin dle-leg ged (spin′dl leg′id *or* spin′dl legd′), having long, thin legs. *adj.*

spin dle legs (spin′dl legz′), 1 long, thin legs. 2 INFORMAL. person with long, thin legs. *n.pl.*

spin dle shanks (spin′dl shangks′), spindlelegs. *n.pl.*

spin dling (spind′ling), very long and slender; too tall and thin: *a weak, spindling plant. adj.*

spin dly (spind′lē), spindling. *adj.,* **spin dli er, spin dli est.**

spin drift (spin′drift′), spray blown or dashed up from the waves. *n.* Also, **spoondrift.**

spine (spīn), 1 backbone. 2 anything like a backbone; long, narrow ridge or support. 3 a stiff, sharp-pointed growth on plants or animals; thorn or something like it. A cactus has spines; so has a porcupine. 4 the supporting back por-tion of a book cover. *n.* —**spine′like′,** *adj.*

spined (spīnd), having a spine or spines. *adj.*

spine less (spīn′lis), 1 having no backbone; invertebrate: *All insects are spineless.* 2 without courage; weak: *a spineless coward.* 3 having no spines: *a spineless cactus. adj.*

spin et (spin′it), 1 an old-fashioned musical instrument like a small harpsichord. 2 a compact upright piano. *n.*

spin na ker (spin′ə kər), a large, triangular sail carried by yachts on the side opposite the mainsail when running before the wind. *n.*

spin ner (spin′ər), person, animal, or thing that spins. *n.*

spin ner et (spin′ə ret′), organ by which spiders and certain insect larvae such as silkworms spin their threads. *n.*

spin ning (spin′ing), 1 that spins. 2 act of one that spins. 1 *adj.,* 2 *n.*

spinning jenny, an early type of spinning machine having more than one spindle, whereby one person could spin a number of threads at the same time; jenny.

spinning wheel

spinning wheel, a large wheel with a spindle, arranged for spinning cotton, flax, wool, etc., into thread or yarn.

Spi no za (spə nō′zə), **Baruch,** 1632-1677, Dutch philosopher. *n.*

spin ster (spin′stər), 1 an unmarried woman. 2 an elderly woman who has not married. *n.*

spin y (spī′nē), 1 covered with spines; having spines; thorny: *a spiny cactus, a spiny porcupine.* 2 stiff and sharp-pointed; spinelike: *the spiny quills of a porcupine. adj.,* **spin i er, spin i est.**

spi ra cle (spī′rə kəl *or* spir′ə kəl), a small opening for breathing. Insects take in air through tiny spiracles. A whale breathes through a spiracle in the top of its head. *n.*

spi rae a (spī rē′ə), a shrub that has clusters of small white, pink, or red flowers with five petals. *n.* Also, **spi rea.**

spi ral (spī′rəl), 1 a winding and gradually widening coil. A watch spring is a

spirals (def. 1)

spiral. The thread of a screw is a spiral. 2 coiled: *a spiral staircase. A snail's shell has a spiral shape.* 3 move in a spiral: *The flaming airplane spiraled to earth.* 4 form into a spiral. 1 *n.,* 2 *adj.,* 3,4 *v.* —**spi′ral ly,** *adv.*

SPIRE
STEEPLE **spire**[1] (def. 1)

spire[1] (spīr), 1 the top part of a tower or steeple that narrows to a point. 2 anything tapering and pointed. A blade of grass is sometimes called a spire of grass. *The sunset shone on the rocky spires of the mountains. n.* [Old English *spīr* spike, blade] —**spire′- like′,** *adj.*

spire[2] (spīr), a coil; spiral. *n.* [from Latin *spira,* from Greek *speira*]

spi re a (spī rē′ə), spiraea. *n.*

spi ril lum (spī ril′əm), any of a group of bacteria that have spirally twisted forms. *n., pl.* **spi ril la** (spī ril′ə).

spir it (spir′it), 1 the immaterial part of human beings; soul: *Some religions teach that at death the spirit leaves the body.* 2 a human being's moral, religious, or emotional nature: *a worthy spirit.* 3 a supernatural being. God is a spirit. Ghosts and fairies are spirits. 4 **the Spirit, a** God. **b** the Holy Ghost. 5 Often, **spirits,** *pl.* state of mind; disposition; temper: *She is in good spirits.* 6 person; personality: *She is a brave spirit. He was one of the more active spirits in our town.* 7 influence that stirs up and rouses: *people with a spirit of progress.* 8 courage; vigor; liveliness: *A race horse must have spirit.* 9 enthusiasm and loyalty. 10 what is really meant as opposed to what is said or written: *The spirit of a law is more important than its words.* 11 the prevailing character, quality, or tendency. 12 Often, **spirits,** *pl.* **a** solution of a volatile substance in alcohol: *spirits of camphor.* **b** strong alcoholic liquor. Whiskey or brandy is called spirits. 13 carry (away or off) secretly: *The child has been spirited away.* 14 of or having to do with spirits or spiritualism: *the spirit world.* 1-12 *n.,* 13 *v.,* 14 *adj.* **out of spirits,** sad or gloomy.

spir it ed (spir′ə tid), full of energy and spirit; lively; dashing; brave: *a spirited race horse. adj.* —**spir′it ed ly,** *adv.* —**spir′it ed ness,** *n.*

spir it less (spir′it lis), without spirit

or courage; depressed; tame. *adj.*

spir i tu al (spir′ə chü əl), 1 of or having to do with the spirit or spirits. 2 caring much for things of the spirit or soul. 3 having to do with the church: *spiritual lords.* 4 sacred; religious. 5 a religious song which originated among the Negroes of the southern United States. 1-4 *adj.,* 5 *n.* —**spir′i tu al ly,** *adv.*

spir i tu al ism (spir′ə chü ə liz′əm), 1 the belief that spirits of the dead communicate with the living, especially through persons called mediums. 2 spiritual quality. *n.*

spir i tu al ist (spir′ə chü ə list), person who believes that the dead communicate with the living. *n.*

spir i tu al is tic (spir′ə chü ə lis′tik), of or having to do with spiritualism or spiritualists. *adj.*

spir i tu al i ty (spir′ə chü al′ə tē), devotion to spiritual things; spiritual quality. *n., pl.* **spir i tu al i ties.**

spir i tu ous (spir′ə chü əs), 1 containing alcohol. 2 distilled, not fermented. *adj.*

spi ro chete (spī′rə kēt′), any of a group of bacteria that are slender, spiral, and very flexible. *n.*

spi ro gy ra (spī′rə jī′rə), any of a large group of green algae that grow in masses like scum in fresh-water ponds. *n., pl.* **spi ro gy ras.**

spirt (spėrt), spurt. *v., n.*

spit[1] (spit), 1 throw out saliva from the mouth. 2 throw out from the mouth. 3 throw out: *A gun spits fire. The crew spat curses.* 4 saliva. 5 sound or act of spitting. 6 make a spitting sound: *The cat spits when angry.* 7 a frothy secretion given off by some insects. 8 rain or snow slightly. 1-3,6,8 *v.,* **spat** or **spit, spit ting;** 4,5,7 *n.* [Old English *spit-tan*]

spit and image, spitting image.

spit[2] (def. 1)

spit[2] (spit), 1 a sharp-pointed, slender rod or bar on which meat is roasted. 2 run a spit through; pierce; stab: *The hunters spitted two rabbits.* 3 a narrow point of land running into the water. 1,3 *n.,* 2 *v.,* **spit ted, spit ting.** [Old English *spitu*]

spit ball (spit′bôl′), 1 a small ball of chewed-up paper, used as a missile. 2 (in baseball) an illegal curve pitched

hat, āge, fär; let, ēqual, tėrm; it, īce; hot, ōpen, ôrder; oil, out; cup, pút, rüle; ch, child; ng, long; sh, she; th, thin; ᴛʜ, then; zh, measure;

ə represents *a* in about, *e* in taken, *i* in pencil, *o* in lemon, *u* in circus.

by moistening one side of the ball with saliva. *n.*

spite (spīt), 1 ill will; grudge: *He broke my new radio out of spite.* 2 show ill will toward; annoy: *They left their yard dirty to spite the people who lived next door.* 1 *n.,* 2 *v.,* **spit ed, spit ing. in spite of,** not prevented by; notwithstanding: *The children went to school in spite of the rain.*

spite ful (spīt′fəl), full of spite; eager to annoy; behaving with ill will and malice: *My spiteful little cousin tore up all my drawings. adj.* —**spite′ful ly,** *adv.* —**spite′ful ness,** *n.*

spit fire (spit′fīr′), person, especially a woman or girl, who has a quick and fiery temper. *n.*

spitting image, INFORMAL. the exact likeness; spit and image: *She is the spitting image of her mother.*

spit tle (spit′l), saliva; spit. *n.*

spit toon (spi tün′), container to spit into; cuspidor. *n.*

spitz (spits), any of various sturdy, small dogs with long hair, pointed nose, and tail curled up over the back. *n., pl.* **spitz es.** [from German *Spitz,* from *spitz* pointed]

splash (splash), 1 cause (water, mud, etc.) to fly about. 2 dash liquid about: *The baby likes to splash in the tub.* 3 dash in scattered masses or drops: *The waves splashed on the beach.* 4 to wet, spatter, or soil: *Our car is all splashed with mud.* 5 act or sound of splashing; splashing: *The splash of the wave knocked him over. The boat upset with a loud splash.* 6 fall, move, or go with a splash or splashes: *He splashed across the brook.* 7 spot of liquid splashed upon a thing: *She had splashes of grease on her clothes.* 8 spot; patch: *The dog is white with brown splashes.* 1-4,6 *v.,* 5,7,8 *n., pl.* **splash es. make a splash,** INFORMAL. attract attention; cause excitement.

splash down (splash′doun′), the landing of a capsule or other spacecraft in the ocean after reentry. *n.*

splash er (splash′ər), 1 person or thing that splashes. 2 something that protects from splashes. *n.*

813

adj.	adjective	*n.*	noun
adv.	adverb	*prep.*	preposition
conj.	conjunction	*pron.*	pronoun
interj.	interjection	*v.*	verb
sing.	singular	*pl.*	plural

splash y (splash/ē), 1 making a splash. 2 full of irregular spots or streaks. 3 INFORMAL. attracting attention; causing excitement. *adj.,* **splash i er, splash i est.**

splat ter (splat/ər), 1 to splash or spatter. 2 a splash or spatter. 1 *v.,* 2 *n.*

splay (splā), 1 to spread out. 2 wide and flat: *splay feet.* 3 awkward; clumsy. 4 a slanting surface; surface which makes an oblique angle with another. 5 make slanting; bevel. 1,5 *v.,* 2,3 *adj.,* 4 *n.*

spleen (splēn), 1 a ductless, glandlike organ at the left of the stomach in human beings, and near the stomach or intestine in other vertebrates. The spleen stores blood and helps filter foreign substances from the blood. People used to think that the spleen caused low spirits, bad temper, and spite. 2 bad temper; spite; anger. 3 low spirits. *n.*

splen did (splen/did), 1 brilliant or glorious; magnificent; grand: *a splendid sunset, a splendid palace, splendid jewels, a splendid victory.* 2 very good; fine; excellent: *a splendid chance. adj.* —**splen/did ly,** *adv.* —**splen/did ness,** *n.*

splen dor (splen/dər), 1 great brightness; brilliant light: *The sun set in a golden splendor.* 2 magnificent show; pomp; glory. *n.*

sple net ic (spli net/ik), 1 having to do with the spleen. 2 bad-tempered; irritable; peevish. *adj.*

splice (splīs), 1 join together (ropes) by weaving together ends which have been untwisted. 2 join together (two pieces of timber) by overlapping. 3 join together (film, tape, wire, etc.) by gluing or cementing the ends. 4 a joining of ropes, timbers, film, etc., by splicing: *How neat a splice can you make?* 1-3 *v.,* **spliced, splic ing;** 4 *n.*

splic er (splī/sər), person or thing that splices. *n.*

splint (splint), 1 arrangement of wood, metal, or plaster to hold a broken or dislocated bone in place. 2 a thin strip of wood, such as is used in making baskets. 3 a thin metal strip or plate. Old armor often had overlapping splints to protect the elbow, knee, etc., and allow easy movement. *n.*

splin ter (splin/tər), 1 a thin, sharp piece of wood, bone, glass, etc.: *He got a splinter in his hand. The mirror broke into splinters.* 2 having to do with dissenting groups that break away from regular political groups, religious organizations, etc.: *the candidate of a splinter party.* 3 split or break into splinters: *splinter wood with an ax. The mirror splintered.* 1 *n.,* 2 *adj.,* 3 *v.*

splin ter y (splin/tər ē), 1 apt to splinter: *splintery wood.* 2 rough and jagged, as if from splintering. 3 full of splinters. *adj.*

split (split), 1 to break or cut from end to end, or in layers: *We are going to split the logs into firewood. I split the cake and filled it with jelly.* 2 separate into parts; divide: *The huge tree split when it was struck by lightning. We decided to split the cost of the dinner between us.* 3 divide into different groups, factions, parties, etc. 4 division in a group, party, etc.: *There was a split in the church for a time, but harmony was restored.* 5 a splitting; break; crack: *Frost caused the split in the rock.* 6 broken or cut from end to end; divided. 7 divide (a molecule, atom, or atomic nucleus) into two or more smaller parts. 8 an acrobatic trick of sinking to the floor with the legs spread far apart in opposite directions. 9 SLANG. go away; leave. 1-3,7, 9 *v.,* **split, split ting;** 4,5,8 *n.,* 6 *adj.*

split infinitive, infinitive having one or more words between *to* and the verb. EXAMPLE: *Last summer I learned to really enjoy swimming.*

split-lev el (split/lev/əl), house with two or more floor levels, each level about half a story above or below the adjacent level. *n.*

split ting (split/ing), 1 that splits. 2 very severe; extreme; violent: *a splitting headache. adj.*

splotch (sploch), 1 a large, irregular spot; splash. 2 make splotches on. 1 *n.,* *pl.* **splotch es;** 2 *v.*

splotch y (sploch/ē), marked with splotches. *adj.,* **splotch i er, splotch i est.**

splurge (splėrj), INFORMAL. 1 a showing off. 2 show off. 3 spend extravagantly. 1 *n.,* 2,3 *v.,* **splurged, splurg ing.**

splut ter (splut/ər), 1 talk in a hasty, confused way. People sometimes splutter when they are excited. 2 make spitting or popping noises; sputter: *The baked apples are spluttering in the oven.* 3 a spluttering. 1,2 *v.,* 3 *n.*

spoil (spoil), 1 damage or injure (something) so as to make it unfit or useless; ruin; destroy: *I spoiled two pieces of paper while trying to write a neat letter. The rain spoiled the picnic.* 2 be damaged; become bad or unfit for use: *The fruit spoiled because I kept it too long.* 3 injure the character or disposition of: *That child is being spoiled by too much attention.* 4 Often, **spoils,** *pl.* **a** things taken by force; things won: *The victors returned with the spoils of war.* **b** offices and positions filled by the political party that has won an election. 5 steal; take by force; plunder. 1-3,5 *v.,* **spoiled** or **spoilt, spoil ing;** 4 *n.* **be spoiling for,** INFORMAL. be longing for (a fight, etc.): *They are both spoiling for a fight.*

spoil a ble (spoi/lə bəl), that can be spoiled. *adj.*

spoil age (spoi/lij), 1 act of spoiling. 2 fact of being spoiled. 3 something spoiled. *n.*

spoil er (spoi/lər), 1 person or thing that spoils. 2 person who takes spoils. *n.*

spoils system, system or practice in which public offices with their salaries and advantages are awarded to supporters of the winning political party. *n.*

spoilt (spoilt), spoiled; a past tense and a past participle of **spoil.** *v.*

Spo kane (spō kan/), city in E Washington. *n.*

spoke[1] (spōk), 1 past tense of **speak.** *She spoke about that yesterday.* 2 OLD USE. spoken; a past participle of **speak.** *v.*

spoke[2] (spōk), 1 one of the bars from the center of a wheel to the rim. 2 rung of a ladder. *n.* [Old English *spāca*]

spo ken (spō/kən), 1 past participle of **speak.** *They have spoken about having a picnic.* 2 expressed with the mouth; uttered; told: *I usually understand a spoken direction better than a written one.* 3 speaking in a certain way: *a soft-spoken person.* 1 *v.,* 2,3 *adj.*

spoke shave (spōk/shāv/), a cutting tool having a blade with a handle at each end, used for smoothing and shaping curved surfaces. *n.*

spokes man (spōks/mən), person who speaks for another or others: *I am the spokesman for my class in the student council. n., pl.* **spokes men.**

spo li a tion (spō/lē ā/shən), a plundering; robbery. *n.*

sponge (spunj), 1 any of a group of water animals having a tough, elastic skeleton or framework. Most sponges live in large colonies on the bottom of the ocean, attached to stones, plants, etc. 2 the light, porous framework of any of these animals used for soaking up water in bathing, cleaning, etc. 3 a similar article made artificially of rubber, plastic, etc. 4 wipe or rub with a wet sponge; make clean or damp in this way: *Sponge up the spilled water. Sponge the mud spots off the car.* 5 absorb. 6 something like a sponge, such as a pad of gauze used by doctors, bread dough, a kind of cake, a kind of pudding, etc. 7 INFORMAL. live or profit at the expense of another in a mean way: *They are sponging on their parents instead of working.* 1-3,6 *n.,* 4,5,7 *v.,* **sponged, spong ing. —sponge'-like',** *adj.*

sponge cake, a light, spongy cake made with eggs, sugar, flour, etc., but no shortening.

spong er (spun'jər), 1 person or thing that sponges. 2 person or vessel engaged in gathering sponges. *n.*

spon gy (spun'jē), 1 like a sponge; soft, light, and full of holes: *spongy moss, spongy dough.* 2 full of holes: *a spongy rock. adj.,* **spon gi er, spon gi est.**

spon sor (spon'sər), 1 person or group that endorses, supports, or is responsible for a person or thing: *the sponsor of a law, the sponsor of a student applying for a scholarship.* 2 person who stands with the parents at an infant's baptism, agreeing to assist in the child's religious upbringing if necessary; godparent. 3 business firm or other organization that pays the costs of a radio or television program advertising its products or services. 4 act as sponsor for. 1-3 *n.,* 4 *v.*

spon sor ship (spon'sər ship), position and duties of a sponsor. *n.*

spon ta ne i ty (spon'tə nē'ə tē), quality, condition, or fact of being spontaneous. *n., pl.* **spon ta ne i ties.**

spon ta ne ous (spon tā'nē əs), 1 caused by natural impulse or desire; not forced or compelled; not planned beforehand: *Both sides burst into spontaneous cheers at the skillful play.* 2 taking place without external cause or help; caused entirely by inner forces: *The eruption of a volcano is spontaneous. adj.* **—spon ta'ne ous ly,** *adv.*

spontaneous combustion, the bursting into flame of a substance without anyone's having set it on fire. In spontaneous combustion, the heat produced by chemical action within the substance itself causes it to catch on fire.

spoof (spüf), INFORMAL. 1 a trick, hoax, or joke. 2 treat as a spoof; make fun of; ridicule. 1 *n.,* 2 *v.*

spook (spük), INFORMAL. ghost; specter. *n.*

spook y (spü'kē), INFORMAL. like a spook; suited to spooks; suggesting spooks. *adj.,* **spook i er, spook i est.**

spool (spül), 1 cylinder of wood or metal on which thread, wire, etc., is wound. 2 wind on a spool. 1 *n.,* 2 *v.*

spoon (spün), 1 utensil consisting of a small, shallow bowl at the end of a handle. Spoons are used to take up or stir food or drink. 2 take up in a spoon. 3 something shaped like a spoon. 1,3 *n.,* 2 *v.* **—spoon'like',** *adj.*

born with a silver spoon in one's mouth, born lucky or rich.

spoon bill (spün'bil'), a long-legged wading bird that has a long, flat bill with a spoon-shaped tip. *n.*

spoon ful (spün'fül), as much as a spoon can hold. *n., pl.* **spoon fuls.**

spoor (spur), trail of a wild animal; track. *n.*

spo rad ic (spə rad'ik), occurring in scattered cases; appearing here and there or now and then: *sporadic outbreaks of scarlet fever. adj.*

spo rad i cal ly (spə rad'ik lē), here and there; now and then. *adv.*

spo ran gi um (spə ran'jē əm), spore case. *n., pl.* **spo ran gi a** (spə ran'jē ə).

spore (spôr), 1 a single cell capable of growing into a new plant or animal. Ferns produce spores; mold grows from spores. 2 germ; seed. *n.*

spore case, receptacle containing spores; sporangium. The little brown spots on the underside of ferns are spore cases.

SPORRAN

spor ran (spôr'ən), a large purse, commonly of fur, hanging from the belt in front of a Scottish Highlands costume. *n.*

sport (spôrt), 1 game, contest, or other pastime requiring some skill and usually involving a certain amount of physical exercise. Baseball and fishing are outdoor sports; bowling and basketball are indoor sports. 2 any pastime or amusement: *He spends all his time in sport and play.* 3 amuse oneself; play: *Lambs sport in the fields. The kitten sports with its tail.* 4 of sports; suitable for sports. 5 playful joking; fun: *That was great sport.* 6 ridicule: *The fool's actions were a source of sport to the villagers.* 7 object of jokes and ridicule: *The awkward beginner was the sport of the experienced golfers.* 8 to jest. 9 sportsman. 10 INFORMAL. person who behaves in a sportsmanlike manner; good fellow: *be a sport.* 11 INFORMAL. to display: *sport a new*

hat, āge, fär; let, ēqual, tėrm;
it, īce; hot, ōpen, ôrder;
oil, out; cup, pùt, rüle; ch, child;
ng, long; sh, she; th, thin;
ᵺ, then; zh, measure;

ə represents *a* in about,
e in taken, *i* in pencil,
o in lemon, *u* in circus.

hat. 12 animal or plant that varies suddenly or in a marked manner from the normal type. A white blackbird would be a sport. 1,2,5-7,9,10,12 *n.,* 3,8,11 *v.,* 4 *adj.*

for sport or **in sport,** in fun; as a joke: *She teased her younger sister in sport.*

make sport of, make fun of; laugh at; ridicule: *Don't make sport of me.*

sport i ly (spôr'tə lē), INFORMAL. in a sporty fashion or manner. *adv.*

sport i ness (spôr'tē nis), INFORMAL. sporty quality or tendency. *n.*

sport ing (spôr'ting), 1 of, interested in, or engaging in sports. 2 playing fair; sportsmanlike: *The loser made a sporting gesture in shaking the winner's hand.* 3 willing to take a chance. 4 INFORMAL. involving risk; uncertain: *She took a sporting chance in climbing up the cliff. adj.* **—sport'ing ly,** *adv.*

spor tive (spôr'tiv), playful; merry: *The old dog seemed as sportive as the puppy. adj.*

sports (spôrts), of sports; suitable for sports: *sports clothes. adj.*

sports car, a small, low, fast car, usually with two seats and an open top.

sports man (spôrts'mən), 1 person who takes part in sports, especially hunting, fishing, or racing. 2 person who likes sports. 3 person who plays fair. *n., pl.* **sports men.**

sports man like (spôrts'mən līk'), like or suitable for a sportsman; fair and honorable. *adj.*

sports man ship (spôrts'mən ship), 1 qualities or conduct of a sportsman; fair play. 2 ability in sports. *n.*

sport y (spôr'tē), INFORMAL. 1 gay or fast; flashy. 2 smart in dress, appearance, manners, etc. 3 sportsmanlike; sporting. *adj.,* **sport i er, sport i est.**

spot (spot), 1 a small mark or stain that discolors or disfigures: *You have grease spots on your suit. That spot on her arm is a bruise.* 2 a blemish or flaw in character or reputation: *His record is without spot.* 3 a small part unlike the rest: *a blue tie with red spots.* 4 make spots on: *He has spotted the tablecloth. Rumors of bribery have spotted that judge's reputation.* 5 become spotted;

adj.	adjective	*n.*	noun
adv.	adverb	*prep.*	preposition
conj.	conjunction	*pron.*	pronoun
interj.	interjection	*v.*	verb
sing.	singular	*pl.*	plural

have spots: *This silk will spot.* 6 place: *From this spot you can see the ocean.* 7 to place in a certain spot; scatter in various spots: *Lookouts were spotted all along the coast.* 8 ready; on hand: *a spot answer.* 9 INFORMAL. pick out; find out; recognize: *I spotted my sister in the crowd. The teacher spotted every mistake.* 10 figure or dot on a playing card, domino, or die to show its kind and value. 1-3,6,10 *n.*, 4,5,7,9 *v.*, **spot ted, spot ting;** 8 *adj.*

hit the spot, INFORMAL. be just right; be satisfactory.

in a spot, in trouble or difficulty.

on the spot, 1 at that very place. 2 at once: *He expected his orders to be carried out on the spot.* 3 in an awkward or difficult position: *He put me on the spot by asking a question I could not answer.*

spot cash, money paid just as soon as the goods are delivered or the work is done.

spot check, 1 a brief, rough sampling. 2 a checkup made without warning.

spot less (spot′lis), without a spot: *She wore a spotless white smock. adj.* —**spot′less ly,** *adv.* —**spot′less ness,** *n.*

spot light (spot′līt′), 1 a spot or circle of bright light thrown upon a particular place or person. 2 lamp that gives such light: *a spotlight in a theater.* 3 light up with a spotlight or spotlights: *At night the baseball field is spotlighted.* 4 public notice; anything that directs attention on a person or thing: *Movie stars are often in the spotlight.* 5 call attention to; give public notice to: *The newspaper article will spotlight an industry that few Americans know anything about.* 1,2,4 *n.*, 3,5 *v.*

spot ted (spot′id), 1 stained with spots: *a spotted reputation.* 2 marked with spots: *a spotted dog. adj.*

spot ty (spot′ē), 1 having spots; spotted. 2 not of uniform quality; irregular: *Her work was spotty. adj.,* **spot ti er, spot ti est.**

spouse (spous), husband or wife: *Mr. Smith is Mrs. Smith's spouse, and she is his spouse. n.*

spout (spout), 1 throw out (a liquid) in a stream or spray: *The fountain spouted* up high. *A whale spouts water when it breathes.* 2 flow out with force: *Water spouted from a break in the pipe.* 3 stream; jet: *A spout of water shot up from the hole in the pipe.* 4 pipe for carrying off water: *Rain runs down a spout from our roof to the ground.* 5 tube or lip by which liquid is poured. A teakettle and a coffeepot have spouts. 6 INFORMAL. speak in loud and very emotional tones: *The old-fashioned actor used to spout his lines.* 1,2,6 *v.*, 3-5 *n.* —**spout′er,** *n.*

sprain (sprān), 1 injure (a joint or muscle) by a sudden twist or wrench. 2 injury caused by a sudden twist or wrench: *He got a bad sprain in his ankle when he missed the lower step.* 1 *v.,* 2 *n.*

sprang (sprang), a past tense of **spring.** *The hungry tiger sprang at the antelope. v.*

sprat (sprat), a small herring of the Atlantic coast of Europe. *n., pl.* **sprats** or **sprat.**

sprawl (sprôl), 1 toss or spread the limbs about, like an infant or animal lying on its back. 2 lie or sit with the limbs spread out, especially ungracefully: *The people sprawled on the beach in their bathing suits.* 3 spread out in an irregular or awkward manner: *He wrote in a large handwriting that sprawled across the page.* 4 act or position of sprawling. 1-3 *v.,* 4 *n.*

spray[1] (sprā), 1 liquid going through the air in small drops: *We were wet with the sea spray.* 2 something like this: *A spray of bullets hit the target.* 3 instrument that sends a liquid out as spray. 4 scatter spray on; sprinkle: *Spray this liquid on your throat. Spray the apple tree.* 1-3 *n.,* 4 *v.* [apparently from Dutch *sprayen*] —**spray′er,** *n.*

spray[2] (sprā), a small branch or piece of some plant with its leaves, flowers, or fruit: *a spray of lilacs, a spray of ivy, a spray of holly. n.* [apparently related to Danish *sprag*]

spray gun, device used to spray paint, insecticide, or other liquids.

spread (spred), 1 cover or cause to cover a large or larger area; stretch out; unfold; open out: *spread rugs on the floor, spread one's arms, a fan that spreads when shaken. The bird spread its wings.* 2 move farther apart: *Spread out your fingers. The rails of the tracks have spread.* 3 extend; lie: *Fields of corn spread out before us.* 4 scatter; distribute: *She spread the news. She spread grain for the chickens.* 5 cover with a thin layer: *She spread each slice with butter.* 6 put as a thin layer: *He spread jam on his bread.* 7 act of spreading: *fight the spread of infection,* encourage the spread of knowledge. 8 width; extent; amount of or capacity for spreading: *the spread of a bird's wings, the spread of elastic.* 9 a covering for a bed or table. 10 set or put food on (a table). 11 INFORMAL. food put on the table; feast. 12 something spread. Butter and jam are spreads. 13 advertisement, article, etc., occupying a number of adjoining columns or pages in a magazine or newspaper: *The advertisement was given a three-column spread.* 1-6,10 *v.*, **spread, spreading;** 7-9,11-13 *n.* —**spread′er,** *n.*

spread oneself, INFORMAL. 1 try hard to make a good impression. 2 display one's abilities fully. 3 brag.

spree (sprē), 1 a lively frolic; gay time. 2 a spell of drinking intoxicating liquor. *n.*

sprig (sprig), shoot, twig, or small branch: *a sprig of lilac. n.*

spright li ness (sprīt′lē nis), liveliness; gaiety. *n.*

spright ly (sprīt′lē), lively; gay: *a sprightly kitten. adj.,* **spright li er, spright li est.**

spring (def. 5)—four kinds of springs

spring (spring), 1 to leap or jump; rise or move suddenly and lightly: *I sprang to my feet. The dog sprang at the stranger.* 2 a leap or jump: *a spring over the fence.* 3 fly back or away as if by elastic force: *The door sprang shut.* 4 cause to spring; cause to act by a spring: *spring a trap.* 5 an elastic device that returns to its original shape after being pulled or held out of shape. Beds have wire springs. The spring in a clock makes it go. 6 elastic quality: *The old man's knees have lost their spring. There is no spring left in these old rubber bands.* 7 season after winter, when plants begin to grow. 8 of or having to do with spring or springs: *spring showers.* Spring wheat is wheat sown in the spring. 9 a small stream of water flowing naturally from the earth. 10 come from some source; arise; grow: *Plants spring from seeds. A wind has sprung up.* 11 source; beginning; cause. 12 begin to move, act, grow, etc., suddenly; burst forth: *Towns spring up where oil is discovered.* 13 bring out, produce, or make suddenly: *to spring a surprise on someone.* 14 to crack, split, warp, bend, strain, or break: *Frost has sprung the rock wall. Cracks all along the wall showed where it had sprung.* 1,3,4,10,12-14 *v.*, **sprang** or **sprung, sprung, spring-ing;** 2,5-7,9,11 *n.,* 8 *adj.*

springboard (def. 1) for diving

spring board (spring′bôrd′), 1 a flexible board used to give added spring in diving, jumping, and vaulting. 2 anything that serves as a way to get to something else: *Hard work was his springboard to success. n.*

spring bok (spring′bok′), a small antelope of South Africa. It leaps almost directly upward when excited or disturbed. *n., pl.* **spring boks** or **spring bok.**

Spring field (spring′fēld′), 1 capital of Illinois, in the central part. 2 city in S Massachusetts. *n.*

spring tide (spring′tīd′), springtime. *n.*

spring tide, 1 the exceptionally high and low tides which come at the time of the new moon or the full moon. 2 any great flood, swell, or rush.

spring time (spring′tīm′), the season of spring. *n.*

spring y (spring′ē), that springs; elastic: *Her step was springy. adj.,* **spring i er, spring i est.**

sprin kle (spring′kəl), 1 scatter in drops or tiny bits: *He sprinkled ashes on the icy sidewalk.* 2 spray or cover with small drops: *sprinkle flowers with water.* 3 a sprinkling; small quantity: *The cook put a sprinkle of nuts on the cake.* 4 rain a little. 5 a light rain. 1,2,4 *v.,* **sprinkled, sprin kling;** 3,5 *n.*

sprin kler (spring′klər), 1 person who sprinkles. 2 device or apparatus for sprinkling water. *n.*

sprin kling (spring′kling), a small quantity or number scattered here and there: *a sprinkling of gray hairs. n.*

sprint (sprint), 1 run at full speed, especially for a short distance. 2 a race or any short spell of running, rowing, etc., at top speed. 1 *v.,* 2 *n.* —**sprint′er,** *n.*

sprit (sprit), a small pole running diagonally from the foot of the mast to the top corner of a fore-and-aft sail, to support and stretch it. *n.*

sprite (sprīt), elf; fairy; goblin. *n.*

sprit sail (sprit′sāl′ *or* sprit′səl), sail supported and stretched by a sprit. *n.*

sprock et (sprok′it), 1 one of a set of

sprocket (def. 2)

projections on the rim of a wheel, arranged so as to fit into the links of a chain. The sprockets keep the chain from slipping. 2 Also, **sprocket wheel.** wheel made with sprockets. *n.*

sprout (sprout), 1 begin to grow; shoot forth: *Seeds sprout. Buds sprout in the spring. Weeds have sprouted in the garden.* 2 cause to grow: *The rain has sprouted the corn.* 3 a shoot of a plant: *The gardener was setting out sprouts.* 1,2 *v.,* 3 *n.*

spruce[1] (sprüs), 1 an evergreen tree with cones and needle-shaped leaves. The spruce is often used as a Christmas tree in America. 2 its wood. *n.* [Middle English *Spruce,* a different form of *Pruce* Prussia (perhaps because the trees first came from there)]

spruce[2] (sprüs), 1 neat; trim: *He looked very spruce in his new suit.* 2 make or become spruce: *Spruce up before you go back to school. She spruced herself before the mirror.* 1 *adj.,* **spruc er, spruc est;** 2 *v.,* **spruced, sprucing.** [perhaps special use of Middle English *Spruce* Prussia (that is, made in Prussia, therefore, smart-looking)] —**spruce′ly,** *adv.*

sprung (sprung), a past tense and the past participle of **spring.** *The trap was sprung. v.*

spry (sprī), active; lively; nimble: *The spry old lady traveled all over the country. adj.,* **spry er, spry est** *or* **spri er, spri est.** —**spry′ly,** *adv.*

spud (spud), 1 tool with a narrow blade for digging up or cutting the roots of weeds. 2 INFORMAL. potato. *n.*

spume (spyüm), 1 frothy matter; foam; froth. 2 to foam or froth. 1 *n.,* 2 *v.,* **spumed, spum ing.**

spun (spun), past tense and past participle of **spin.** *I spun all day yesterday. The thread was spun from silk. The car skidded and spun on the ice. v.*

spun glass, fiberglass.

SPRIT

spunk (spungk), INFORMAL. courage; pluck; spirit: *a little puppy full of spunk. n.*

spunk y (spung′kē), INFORMAL. courageous; plucky; spirited: *He is a spunky fellow. adj.,* **spunk i er, spunk i est.**

spun silk, silk waste spun into yarn.

spur (spér), 1 a pricking instrument consisting of a spike or a spiked wheel, worn on a horseman's heel for urging a

hat, āge, fär; let, ēqual, tèrm;
it, īce; hot, ōpen, ôrder;
oil, out; cup, pùt, rüle; ch, child;
ng, long; sh, she; th, thin;
ᵬH, then; zh, measure;

ə represents *a* in about,
e in taken, *i* in pencil,
o in lemon, *u* in circus.

horse on. 2 prick with spurs: *The rider spurred her horse on.* 3 ride quickly. 4 something like a spur; point sticking out. A cock has spurs on his legs. *A spur of rock stuck out from the hill.* 5 anything that urges on: *Ambition was the spur that made him work.* 6 urge on: *Anger spurred her unkind words.* 7 ridge sticking out from or smaller than the main body of a mountain or mountain range. 8 any short branch: *a spur of a railroad.* 1,4,5,7,8 *n.,* 2,3,6 *v.,* **spurred, spur ring.**

on the spur of the moment, on a sudden impulse or without previous thought or preparation.

win one's spurs, make a reputation for oneself or attain distinction.

spur i ous (spyùr′ē əs), not coming from the right source; not genuine; false; sham: *a spurious document, spurious anger. adj.* —**spur′i ous ly,** *adv.* —**spur′i ous ness,** *n.*

spurn (spèrn), 1 refuse with scorn; scorn: *The judge spurned the bribe.* 2 strike with the foot; kick away. *v.*

spurred (spèrd), having spurs or a spur: *a spurred boot, spurred feet. adj.*

spurt (spèrt), 1 flow suddenly in a stream or jet; gush out; squirt: *Blood spurted from the wound.* 2 a sudden rushing forth; jet: *Spurts of flame broke out all over the building.* 3 a great increase of effort or activity for a short time: *To win the race he put on a spurt of speed at the end.* 4 put forth great energy for a short time; show great activity for a short time: *The runners spurted near the end of the race.* 1,4 *v.,* 2,3 *n.* Also, **spirt.**

sput nik (sput′nik *or* spůt′nik), any of a group of earth satellites put into orbit by the Soviet Union. *n.* [from Russian *sputnik* satellite]

spur (def. 1)

sputter

adj. adjective		*n.* noun
adv. adverb		*prep.* preposition
conj. conjunction		*pron.* pronoun
interj. interjection		*v.* verb
sing. singular		*pl.* plural

sput ter (sput′ər), 1 make spitting or popping noises: *fat sputtering in the frying pan. The firecrackers sputtered.* 2 throw out (drops of saliva, bits of food, etc.) in excitement or in talking too fast. 3 say (words or sounds) in haste and confusion. 4 confused talk. 5 a sputtering; sputtering noise. 1-3 *v.*, 4,5 *n.* —**sput′ter er,** *n.*

spu tum (spyü′təm), 1 saliva; spit. 2 mixture of saliva and mucus coughed up and spat out. *n., pl.* **spu ta** (spyü′tə).

spy (spī), 1 person who keeps secret watch on the action of others. 2 person paid by a government to get secret information about another government or country, especially in time of war. A spy usually enters the territory he is spying on by disguising himself or his identity. 3 keep secret watch: *He saw two men spying on him from behind a tree.* 4 act as a spy; be a spy. The punishment for spying in wartime is death. 5 catch sight of; see: *He was the first to spy the rescue party in the distance.* 1,2 *n., pl.* **spies;** 3-5 *v.,* **spied, spy ing.**

spy out, find out by watching secretly or carefully: *They spy out everything that goes on in the neighborhood.*

spy glass (spī′glas′), a small telescope. *n., pl.* **spy glass es.**

sq., square.

squab (skwob), a very young bird, especially a young pigeon. *n.*

squab ble (skwob′əl), 1 a petty, noisy quarrel: *Children's squabbles annoy their parents.* 2 take part in a petty, noisy quarrel: *I won't squabble over a nickel.* 1 *n.,* 2 *v.,* **squab bled, squab bling.**

squad (skwod), 1 a military unit usually made up of ten to twelve men and composing the basic unit for drill, inspection, or work. It is usually commanded by a sergeant or a corporal and is the smallest tactical unit in an army. 2 any small group of persons working together: *A squad of children cleaned up the yard. n.*

squad car, automobile used by police which is equipped with a special radio to keep in communication with headquarters.

squad ron (skwod′rən), 1 part of a naval fleet used for special service: *a destroyer squadron.* 2 formation of eight or more airplanes that fly or fight together. 3 a military unit made up of two or more troops of cavalry, usually commanded by a major or a lieutenant colonel. A squadron corresponds to a battalion in other branches of the army. 4 any group or formation. *n.*

squal id (skwol′id), very dirty; degraded; wretched: *a squalid tenement. adj.* —**squal′id ly,** *adv.* —**squal′id ness,** *n.*

squall¹ (skwôl), 1 a sudden, violent gust of wind, often with rain, snow, or sleet. 2 undergo or give rise to a squall. 1 *n.,* 2 *v.* [apparently related to Swedish *skval* sudden rush of water]

squall² (skwôl), 1 cry out loudly; scream violently: *The baby squalled.* 2 a loud, harsh cry: *The parrot's squall was heard all over the house.* 1 *v.,* 2 *n.* [perhaps an imitation of the cry]

squall y (skwô′lē), having many sudden and violent gusts of wind: *squally weather. adj.,* **squall i er, squall i est.**

squal or (skwol′ər), misery and dirt; filth. *n.*

squan der (skwon′dər), spend foolishly; waste: *squander one's time and money in gambling. v.*

square (skwer *or* skwar), 1 a plane figure with four equal sides and four right angles (□). 2 having this shape: *a square box. A block of stone is usually square.* 3 anything having this shape or nearly this shape: *I gave the child a square of chocolate.* 4 make square; make rectangular; make cubical: *square a block of granite.* 5 mark out in squares: *The children squared the sidewalk to play hopscotch.* 6 space in a city or town bounded by streets on four sides: *The automobile factories fill several squares.* 7 distance along one side of such a space; block: *We lived three squares from the school.* 8 an open space in a city or town bounded by streets on four sides, often planted with grass, trees, etc.: *The library is in the square directly opposite the city hall.* 9 any similar open space, such as at the meeting of streets. 10 of a specified length on each side of a square: *a room ten feet square.* 11 forming a right angle: *a square corner.* 12 bring to the form of a right angle. 13 instrument shaped like a T or an L, used for drawing right angles and testing the squareness of anything. 14 straight; level; even. 15 make straight, level, or even: *square a picture on a wall.* 16 leaving no balance; even: *make accounts square.* 17 adjust; settle: *Let us square our accounts.* 18 agree; conform: *Her acts do not square with her promises.* 19 just; fair; honest: *You will get a square deal at this shop.* 20 IN-FORMAL. satisfying: *a square meal.* 21 product obtained when a number is multiplied by itself: *16 is the square of 4.* 22 multiply (a number) by itself: *25 squared makes 625.* 23 squared: *a square yard.* 24 SLANG. person who is too conventional or old-fashioned. 25 SLANG. too conventional or old-fashioned. 1,3,6-9,13,21,24 *n.,* 2, 10,11,14,16,19,20,23,25 *adj.,* **squar er, squar est;** 4,5,12,15,17,18,22 *v.,* **squared, squar ing.** —**square′ly,** *adv.* —**square′ness,** *n.*

on the square, 1 at right angles. 2 INFORMAL. justly; fairly; honestly.

square away, set the sails so that the ship will stay before the wind.

square off, INFORMAL. put oneself in a position of defense or attack.

square oneself, INFORMAL. 1 make up for something one has said or done. 2 get even.

square dance, dance performed by a set of couples arranged around a square space. The quadrille is one type of square dance.

square foot, measure of area one foot long and one foot wide; any area equal to that.

square inch, measure of area one inch long and one inch wide; any area equal to that.

square knot, knot firmly joining two loose ends of rope or cord. Each end is formed into a loop which both encloses and passes through the other. See **knot** for diagram.

square-rigged (skwer′rigd′ *or* skwar′rigd′), having the principal sails set at right angles across the masts. *adj.*

square-rigged sails on the foremast

square-rig ger (skwer′rig′ər *or* skwar′rig′ər), a square-rigged ship. *n.*

square root, number that produces a given number when multiplied by itself: *The square root of 16 is 4.*

squash¹ (skwosh), 1 press or be pressed until soft or flat; crush: *She squashed the bug. Carry the cream puffs carefully, for they squash easily.* 2 something squashed; a crushed mass: *The grapes are just a squash and not fit to eat.* 3 act, fact, or sound of squashing. 4 put an end to; stop by force: *The police quickly squashed the riot.* 5 to crowd; squeeze. 6 either of two games somewhat like handball and tennis, played in a walled court with rackets and a rubber ball. 1,4,5 *v.*, 2,3,6 *n.*, *pl.* **squash es.** [from French of the 1500's *esquasser,* from Latin *ex-*out + *quassare* press]

squash² (skwosh), 1 any of several vinelike plants belonging to the same family as the gourd. 2 its fruit, eaten as a vegetable and often used in pies. *n.*, *pl.* **squash** or **squash es.** [shortened from earlier *squantersquash,* from an Algonquian word]

squash i ness (skwosh′ē nis), a being squashy. *n.*

squash y (skwosh′ē), 1 easily squashed: *squashy cream puffs.* 2 soft and wet: *squashy ground. adj.,* **squash i er, squash i est.**

squat (skwot), 1 crouch on the heels. 2 sit on the ground or floor with the legs drawn up closely beneath or in front of the body: *The campers squatted around the fire.* 3 crouching: *A squat figure sat in front of the fire.* 4 act of squatting; squatting posture. 5 settle on another's land without title or right. 6 settle on public land to acquire ownership of it. 7 short and thick; low and broad: *a squat man, a squat teapot.* 1,2,5,6 *v.,* **squat ted** or **squat, squat ting;** 3,7 *adj.,* **squat ter, squat test;** 4 *n.*

squat ter (skwot′ər), 1 person who settles on another's land without right. 2 person who settles on public land to acquire ownership of it. 3 person or animal that crouches or squats. *n.*

squat ty (skwot′ē), short and thick; low and broad; squat. *adj.,* **squat ti er, squat ti est.**

squaw (skwô), a North American Indian woman (a term often considered offensive). *n.*

squaw fish (skwô′fish′), any of several large, slender carps, common in rivers of the Pacific coast of North America. *n., pl.* **squaw fish es** or **squaw fish.**

squawk (skwôk), 1 make a loud, harsh sound: *Hens and ducks squawk when frightened.* 2 such a sound. 3 SLANG. complain loudly. 4 SLANG. a loud complaint. 1,3 *v.,* 2,4 *n.*

squeak (skwēk), 1 make a short, sharp, shrill sound: *A mouse squeaks.* 2 such a sound: *We heard the squeak of the rocking chair.* 3 INFORMAL. get or pass (by or through) with difficulty: *The Senate will block the bill even if it squeaks through the House of Representatives.* 4 INFORMAL. a chance to get by or through; chance of escape: *a narrow squeak.* 1,3 *v.,* 2,4 *n.*

squeak i ly (skwē′kə lē), in a squeaky manner: *sing squeakily. adv.*

squeak i ness (skwē′kē nis), quality of being squeaky. *n.*

squeak y (skwē′kē), squeaking. *adj.,* **squeak i er, squeak i est.**

squeal (skwēl), 1 make a long, sharp, shrill cry: *A pig squeals when it is hurt.* 2 such a cry. 3 SLANG. turn informer. 1,3 *v.,* 2 *n.* —**squeal′er,** *n.*

squeam ish (skwē′mish), 1 too proper, modest, etc.; easily shocked. 2 too particular; too scrupulous. 3 slightly sick at one's stomach; nauseated. 4 easily affected with nausea; queasy. *adj.* —**squeam′ish ly,** *adv.* —**squeam′ish ness,** *n.*

squee gee (skwē′jē′), tool consisting of a blade of rubber and a handle, used for sweeping water from wet decks, removing water from windows after washing, etc. *n.*

squeeze (skwēz), 1 press hard; compress: *Don't squeeze the kitten; you'll hurt it.* 2 a squeezing; tight pressure: *a squeeze of the hand. She gave her sister's arm a squeeze.* 3 to hug: *She squeezed her child.* 4 force by pressing: *I can't squeeze another thing into my trunk.* 5 force out or extract by pressure: *squeeze juice from a lemon.* 6 get by pressure, force, or effort: *The dictator squeezed money from the people.* 7 yield to pressure: *Sponges squeeze easily.* 8 force a way: *squeeze through a crowd.* 9 crush; crowd: *Six people squeezed into the little car.* 1,3-9 *v.,* **squeezed, squeez ing;** 2 *n.*

squeez er (skwē′zər), person or thing that squeezes. *n.*

squelch (skwelch), cause to be silent; crush: *She squelched him with a look of contempt. v.*

squib (skwib), 1 a short, witty attack in speech or writing; sharp sarcasm. 2 a broken firecracker. 3 a small firework that burns with a hissing noise and finally explodes. *n.*

squid—body of this type to 18 ft. long

squid (skwid), a salt-water mollusk similar to a cuttlefish, but with a longer body and a pair of tail fins. Small squids are much used as bait. *n., pl.* **squids** or **squid.**

squig gle (skwig′əl), 1 a wriggly twist or curve. 2 make with twisting or curving lines. 3 twist and turn about; writhe; squirm; wriggle. 1 *n.,* 2,3 *v.,* **squiggled, squig gling.**

squint (skwint), 1 to look with the eyes partly closed. 2 a looking with partly closed eyes. 3 a sidelong look; hasty look. 4 to look sideways; look askance. 5 tendency to look sideways or askance. 6 looking sideways; looking

hat, āge, fär; let, ēqual, tėrm; it, īce; hot, ōpen, ôrder; oil, out; cup, pùt, rüle; ch, child; ng, long; sh, she; th, thin; ᵺH, then; zh, measure;

ə represents *a* in about, *e* in taken, *i* in pencil, *o* in lemon, *u* in circus.

askance. 7 be cross-eyed. 8 cross-eyed condition. 9 cross-eyed. 1,4,7 *v.,* 2,3,5,8 *n.,* 6,9 *adj.*

squire (skwīr), 1 (in Great Britain) a country gentleman, especially the chief landowner in a district. 2 (in the United States) a justice of the peace or a local judge. 3 a young man of noble family who attended a knight till he himself was made a knight. 4 attendant. 5 attend as squire. 6 a woman's escort. 7 escort (a woman). 1-4,6 *n.,* 5,7 *v.,* **squired, squir ing.**

squirm (skwėrm), 1 turn and twist; writhe: *The restless boy squirmed in his chair. The dog squirmed its way through the hole in the fence.* 2 a wriggle; twist. 3 show great embarrassment, annoyance, confusion, etc. 1,3 *v.,* 2 *n.*

squirm y (skwėr′mē), squirming; wriggling. *adj.,* **squirm i er, squirm i est.**

squir rel (skwėr′əl), 1 a small, bushy-tailed rodent that usually lives in trees. 2 its gray, reddish, or dark-brown fur. *n.*

squirt (skwėrt), 1 force out (liquid) through a narrow opening: *squirt water through a tube.* 2 come out in a jet or stream: *Water squirted from the hose.* 3 to wet or soak by shooting liquid in a jet or stream: *The elephant squirted me with its trunk.* 4 act of squirting. 5 jet of liquid, etc.: *I soaked her with squirts of water from the hose.* 6 something that squirts. 7 INFORMAL. an insignificant person who is impudent or conceited: *a little squirt of a man.* 1-3 *v.,* 4-7 *n.*

Sr., senior.

Sri Lan ka (srē′ lang′kə), official name of Ceylon.

SS or **S.S.,** steamship.

St., 1 Saint. 2 Street.

stab (stab), 1 pierce or wound with a pointed weapon. 2 to thrust with a pointed weapon; aim a blow. 3 a thrust or blow made with a pointed weapon. 4 any thrust or sudden, sharp blow. 5 wound made by stabbing. 6 wound sharply or deeply in the feelings: *The parents were stabbed to the heart by their son's ingratitude.* 7 injury to the feelings. 8 INFORMAL. an attempt. 1,

stabber

2,6 *v.*, **stabbed, stab bing;** 3-5,7,8 *n.*
stab ber (stab′ər), person or thing that stabs. *n.*

sta bil i ty (stə bil′ə tē), 1 being fixed in position; firmness: *A concrete wall has more stability than a light wooden fence.* 2 permanence. 3 steadfastness of character, purpose, etc.: *the stability of someone who helps a friend in need.* *n.*, *pl.* **sta bil i ties.**

sta bi li za tion (stā′bə lə zā′shən), a stabilizing or a being stabilized. *n.*

sta bi lize (stā′bə līz), 1 make stable or firm: *stabilize a government.* 2 prevent changes in; hold steady: *stabilize prices.* 3 keep well balanced. *v.*, **sta bilized, sta bi liz ing.**

sta bi liz er (stā′bə lī′zər), 1 person or thing that stabilizes. 2 device for keeping an airplane, ship, etc., steady. *n.*

sta ble[1] (stā′bəl), 1 building where horses or cattle are kept and fed: *I accompanied her to the stable where she took riding lessons.* 2 group of animals housed in such a building. 3 put or keep in a stable. 4 group of race horses belonging to one owner. 1,2,4 *n.*, 3 *v.*, **sta bled, sta bling.** [from French of the 1200's *estable*, from Latin *stabulum* a standing place]

sta ble[2] (stā′bəl), 1 not likely to move or change; steadfast; firm; steady: *Concrete reinforced with steel is stable. The whole world needs a stable peace.* 2 lasting without change; permanent. *adj.* [from French of the 1200's *estable*, from Latin *stabilis* able to stand]

stac ca to (stə kä′tō), in music: 1 with breaks between the successive tones; disconnected; abrupt. 2 in a staccato manner. 1 *adj.*, 2 *adv.*

stack (stak), 1 a large pile of hay, straw, etc. 2 pile of anything: *a stack of wood.* 3 group of three or more rifles arranged with their muzzles together to form a cone or pyramid. 4 pile or arrange in a stack: *stack hay, stack firewood, stack guns.* 5 arrange (playing cards) unfairly. 6 INFORMAL. a large number or quantity: *a stack of people, a stack of compliments.* 7 chimney. 8 rack with shelves for books: *the library stacks.* 1-3,6-8 *n.*, 4,5 *v.*

sta di um (stā′dē əm), structure shaped like an oval or U, consisting of tiers of seats for spectators around an arena or playing field: *The stadium was filled for the final baseball game of the series.* *n.*, *pl.* **sta di ums, sta di a** (stā′dē ə).

staff (staf), 1 a stick, pole, or rod used as a support, as an emblem of office, as a weapon, etc.: *The flag hangs on a staff. The woman leaned on her staff.* 2 something that supports or sustains. Bread is called the staff of life because it will support life. 3 group assisting a chief; group of employees: *Our school has a staff of twenty teachers.* 4 (in the armed forces) group of officers assisting a commanding officer with administration, planning, etc., but without command or combat duties. 5 provide with officers or employees. 6 set of five lines and the four spaces between them on which music is written; stave. 1-4,6 *n.*, *pl.* **staves** or **staffs** for 1 and 2, **staffs** for 3,4,6; 5 *v.*

stag (stag), 1 a full-grown male deer. 2 the male of various other animals. 3 attended by or for men only: *a stag dinner.* 1,2 *n.*, 3 *adj.*

stage (stāj), 1 one step or degree in a process; period of development. An insect passes through several stages before it is full-grown. Childhood, adolescence, and adulthood are stages in a person's life. 2 the raised platform in a theater on which the actors perform. 3 **the stage,** the theater; the drama; actor's profession: *Shakespeare wrote for the stage.* 4 scene of action: *Bunker Hill was the stage of a famous battle.* 5 put on a stage or arrange: *The play was very well staged. Mother had staged a surprise for the children's party by hiring a magician. The angry people staged a riot.* 6 section of a rocket or missile having its own engine and fuel. A three-stage rocket has three engines, one in each stage, which separate one after another from the rocket after the fuel is burned up. 7 stagecoach or bus. 8 place of rest on a journey; regular stopping place. 9 distance between two stopping places on a journey. 10 platform; flooring. 1-4,6-10 *n.*, 5 *v.*, **staged, stag ing.** —**stage′like′,** *adj.*
by easy stages, a little at a time; slowly; often stopping.
on the stage, being an actor or actress.

stage coach (stāj′kōch′), coach carrying passengers and parcels over a regular route. *n.*

stage fright, nervous fear of appearing before an audience.

stage hand (stāj′hand′), person whose work is moving scenery, arranging lights, etc., in a theater. *n.*

stage-struck (stāj′struk′), extremely interested in acting; wanting very much to become an actor or actress. *adj.*

stage whisper, a loud whisper on a stage meant for the audience to hear.

stag ger (stag′ər), 1 sway or reel (from weakness, a heavy load, or drunkenness): *The boy staggered and fell under the heavy load of books.* 2 make sway or reel: *The blow staggered me for the moment.* 3 a swaying or reeling. 4 become unsteady; waver: *The troops staggered under the severe gunfire.* 5 hesitate. 6 cause to hesitate or become confused: *The difficulty of the examination staggered her.* 7 confuse or astonish greatly: *He was staggered by the news of his friend's death.* 8 arrange in a zigzag order or way. 9 arrange to begin at different times: *Vacations were staggered so that only one person was away at a time.* 10 **staggers,** *pl.* in form, *sing.* in use. a nervous disease of horses, cattle, etc., that makes them stagger or fall suddenly. 1,2,4-9 *v.*, 3,10 *n.*

stag nant (stag′nənt), 1 not running or flowing: *stagnant air, stagnant water.* 2 foul from standing still: *a stagnant pool of water.* 3 not active; sluggish; dull: *During the summer, business is often stagnant.* *adj.*

stag nate (stag′nāt), 1 be stagnant; become stagnant. 2 make stagnant. *v.*, **stag nat ed, stag nat ing.**

stag na tion (stag nā′shən), becoming or making stagnant; stagnant condition. *n.*

staid (stād), 1 having a settled, quiet character; sober; sedate: *We think of the Puritans as staid people.* 2 OLD USE. stayed; a past tense and a past participle of **stay**[1]. 1 *adj.*, 2 *v.* —**staid′ly,** *adv.* —**staid′ness,** *n.*

stain (stān), 1 to discolor with streaks of dirt, blood, etc.; soil; spot: *Food that had been spilled stained the tablecloth.* 2 a discoloration made by soiling; a spot: *He has ink stains on his shirt.* 3 to spot by wrongdoing or disgrace; dishonor: *His crimes stained the family honor.* 4 mark of disgrace; dishonor: *Her character is without stain.* 5 color or dye: *He stained the chair green.* 6 a coloring or dye: *She painted the table with a brown stain.* 1,3,5 *v.*, 2,4,6 *n.* —**stain′er,** *n.*

stagecoach

stain less (stān′lis), without stain; spotless. *adj.*

stainless steel, steel containing a high percentage of chromium, making it very resistant to rust and corrosion.

stair (ster *or* star), 1 one of a series of

steps for going from one level or floor to another. 2 Also, **stairs**, *pl.* set of such steps; stairway: *the top of the stairs. We climbed the winding stair to the tower. n.*

stair case (ster′kās′ *or* star′kās′), flight of stairs with its framework; stairs. *n.*

stair way (ster′wā′ *or* star′wā′), way up and down by stairs; a flight or flights of stairs: *the back stairway. n.*

stair well (ster′wel′ *or* star′wel′), the vertical passage or open space containing the stairs of a building. *n.*

stake[1] (stāk), 1 a stick or post pointed at one end for driving into the ground. 2 **the stake, a** post to which a person was tied and then burned to death: *Joan of Arc was burned at the stake.* **b** death by being burned in this way. 3 fasten to a stake or with a stake: *stake down a tent.* 4 mark with stakes; mark the boundaries of: *stake out a mining claim.* 1,2 *n.,* 3,4 *v.,* **staked, stak ing.** [Old English *staca*]

pull up stakes, INFORMAL. move away: *Constant flooding of their land led the farmers to pull up stakes and leave the valley for the highlands.*

stake[2] (stāk), 1 risk (money or something valuable) on the result of a game or on any chance: *He staked all his money on the black horse.* 2 money risked; what is staked: *They played for high stakes.* 3 Often, **stakes,** *pl.* prize in a race or contest: *The stakes were divided up among the winners.* 4 something to gain or lose; interest; share in a property: *Each of us has a stake in the future of our country.* 5 INFORMAL. assist or back (a person) with money, etc.: *I'll stake you to a dinner if you'll come.* 1,5 *v.,* **staked, stak ing;** 2-4 *n.* [origin uncertain]

at stake, to be won or lost; risked: *Our friendship is at stake.*

sta lac tite (stə lak′tīt), a formation of lime, shaped like an icicle, hanging from the roof of a cave. It is formed by dripping water that contains lime. *n.*

STALACTITES

STALAGMITES

sta lag mite (stə lag′mīt), a formation of lime, shaped like a cone, built up on the floor of a cave. It is formed by water dripping from a stalactite. *n.*

stale (stāl), 1 not fresh: *stale bread.* 2 no longer new or interesting: *a stale*

joke. 3 out of condition: *The horse has gone stale from too much running.* 4 make stale. 5 become stale. 1-3 *adj.,* **stal er, stal est;** 4,5 *v.,* **staled, stal ing. —stale′ly,** *adv.* **—stale′ness,** *n.*

stale mate (stāl′māt′), 1 (in chess) a draw which results when a player cannot move any of his pieces without putting his own king in check. 2 any position in which no action can be taken; complete standstill. 3 put in such a position; bring to a complete standstill. 1,2 *n.,* 3 *v.,* **stale mat ed, stale mat ing.**

Sta lin (stä′lin), **Joseph,** 1879-1953, Soviet political leader, dictator of the Soviet Union from 1929 to 1953. *n.*

Sta lin grad (stä′lin grad), former name of **Volgograd.** *n.*

stalk[1] (stôk), 1 the main stem of a plant. 2 any slender, supporting part of a plant. A flower or a leaf blade may have a stalk. 3 any similar part of an animal. The eyes of a crayfish are on stalks. 4 a slender, upright support: *a wine glass with a tall stalk. n.* [Middle English *stalke*] **—stalk′like′,** *adj.*

stalk[2] (stôk), 1 approach or pursue without being seen or heard: *The hungry lion stalked a zebra.* 2 spread silently and steadily: *Disease stalked through the land.* 3 walk with slow, stiff, or haughty strides: *She became angry and stalked out of the room.* 4 a haughty gait. 5 act of stalking. 1-3 *v.,* 4,5 *n.* [Old English *(be)stealcian* steal along]

stalk ing-horse (stô′king hôrs′), 1 horse or figure of a horse, behind which a hunter conceals himself in stalking game. 2 anything used to hide plans or acts; pretext. *n.*

stall[1] (stôl), 1 place in a stable for one animal. 2 a small place for selling things: *At the public market different things were sold in different stalls under one big roof.* 3 seat in the choir of a church. 4 seat in the front part of a theater (a term used in Great Britain). 5 put or keep in a stall: *The horses were safely stalled.* 6 stop or bring to a standstill, usually against one's wish: *The engine stalled. We were stalled in the mud.* 7 a parking space. 1-4,7 *n.,* 5,6 *v.* [Old English *steall,* probably related to *stæl* a place]

stall[2] (stôl), INFORMAL. 1 pretext to prevent action, the accomplishment of a purpose, etc. 2 to delay. 3 pretend; evade; deceive: *Every time I ask for a raise my boss stalls.* 1 *n.,* 2,3 *v.* [earlier *stale* decoy, from French of the 1400's *estaler* to place, from *estal* a place]

stal lion (stal′yən), a male horse that can be used for breeding. *n.*

stal wart (stôl′wərt), 1 strongly built. 2 strong and brave: *a stalwart knight.*

hat, āge, fär; let, ēqual, tėrm;
it, īce; hot, ōpen, ôrder;
oil, out; cup, pút, rüle; ch, child;
ng, long; sh, she; th, thin;
ŦH, then; zh, measure;

ə represents *a* in about,
e in taken, *i* in pencil,
o in lemon, *u* in circus.

3 firm; steadfast: *a stalwart refusal.* 4 a stalwart person. 1-3 *adj.,* 4 *n.* **—stal′wart ly,** *adv.* **—stal′wart ness,** *n.*

sta men (stā′mən), the part of a flower that contains the pollen. The stamens are surrounded by the petals. A stamen consists of a slender stem or filament which supports the anther. *n.*

STAMEN | ANTHER
| FILAMENT

PETAL

stam i na (stam′ə nə), strength; endurance: *physical stamina, moral stamina. n.*

stam i nate (stam′ə nit *or* stam′ə nāt), having stamens but no pistils. *adj.*

stam mer (stam′ər), 1 hesitate in speaking; speak haltingly, as from nervousness, embarrassment, or fear. 2 utter in this manner: *stammer an excuse.* 3 a stammering; stuttering: *He has a nervous stammer.* 1,2 *v.,* 3 *n.* **—stam′mer er,** *n.* **—stam′mer ing ly,** *adv.*

stamp (stamp), 1 a small piece of paper with a sticky back, put on letters, papers, parcels, etc., to show that a charge for mailing has been paid; postage stamp. 2 a similar piece of paper given to customers as a bonus, to be exchanged for goods; trading stamp. 3 any official mark or label required by law to be affixed to a paper or item to show that a fee, duty, tax, etc., has been paid. 4 put a stamp on: *stamp an official document, stamp a letter.* 5 bring down (one's foot) with force: *He stamped on the spider. He stamped his foot in anger.* 6 act of stamping. 7 pound, crush, trample, or tread: *She stamped out the fire.* 8 fix firmly or deeply: *an event stamped on one's memory.* 9 instrument that cuts, shapes, or impresses a design on (paper, wax, metal, etc.); thing that puts a mark on: *The stamp had her name on it.* 10 to mark with such an

821

adj. adjective	*n.* noun
adv. adverb	*prep.* preposition
conj. conjunction	*pron.* pronoun
interj. interjection	*v.* verb
sing. singular	*pl.* plural

instrument: *She stamped the papers with the date.* **11** the mark made by such an instrument. **12** mill or machine that crushes rock, etc. **13** show to be of a certain quality or character; indicate: *Her speech stamps her as an educated woman.* **14** impression; marks: *a face bearing the stamp of suffering.* **15** kind; type: *Men of his stamp are rare.* 1-3, 6,9,11,12,14,15 *n.*, 4,5,7,8,10,13 *v.*

stam pede (stam pēd′), **1** a sudden scattering or headlong flight of a frightened herd of cattle, horses, etc. **2** any headlong flight of a large group: *a stampede of a panic-stricken crowd from a burning building.* **3** scatter or flee in a stampede. **4** a general rush: *a stampede to newly discovered gold fields.* **5** make a general rush. **6** cause to stampede. 1,2,4 *n.*, 3,5,6 *v.*, **stam ped ed, stam ped ing.**

stance (stans), **1** position of the feet of a player when making a stroke in golf or other games. **2** manner of standing; posture: *an erect stance. n.*

stanch[1] (stänch), **1** stop or check the flow of (blood, etc.). **2** stop the flow of blood from (a wound). **3** cease flowing. *v.* Also, **staunch.** [from French of the 1300's *estanchier* to stop, hinder] —**stanch′er,** *n.*

stanch[2] (stänch), staunch. *adj.* [from French of the 1400's *estanche,* from *estanchier* to stop, hinder] —**stanch′ly,** *adv.* —**stanch′ness,** *n.*

← STANCHION

stanchions for cattle. The closed one permits the cow to move her head but not to get away.

stan chion (stan′shən), an upright bar, post, or support (in a window, in a stall for cattle, on a ship, etc.). *n.*

stand (stand), **1** be upright on one's feet: *Don't stand if you are tired; sit down.* **2** have a certain height when

upright: *He stands six feet in his socks.* **3** rise to one's feet: *We stood when the guest entered the room. I stood to recite my poem.* **4** be set upright; be placed; be located: *The box stands over there. Some food stood on the table.* **5** set upright or in an indicated position, condition, etc.: *Stand the box here.* **6** be in a certain place, rank, scale, etc.: *He stood first in his class for service to the school.* **7** take or keep a certain position: *"Stand back!" called the policeman to the crowd.* **8** take a way of thinking or acting: *stand for fair play, stand on one's rights.* **9** be in a special condition: *She stands innocent of any wrong. The poor child stands in need of food and clothing. The door stood ajar.* **10** be unchanged; hold good; remain the same: *The rule against being late will stand.* **11** stay in place; last: *The old house has stood for a hundred years.* **12** be submitted to (a trial, test, ordeal, etc.); undergo: *stand a rigid examination.* **13** bear; endure; withstand: *cloth that will stand wear. Those plants cannot stand cold and die in winter.* **14** IN-FORMAL. bear the expense of: *I'll stand you a dinner.* **15** take a certain course: *The ship stood out to sea.* **16** stop moving; halt; stop: *The cars stood and waited for the light to change. "Stand!" cried the sentry.* **17** act of standing. **18** a halt; stop. **19** a stop for defense, resistance, etc.: *We made a last stand against the enemy.* **20** place where a person stands; position: *The policeman took his stand at the street corner.* **21** a moral position: *We took a strong stand against pumping sewage into the lake.* **22** Also, **stands,** *pl.* a raised place where people can sit or stand: *The mayor sat on the reviewing stand at the parade. The crowd in the stands cheered the winning team.* **23** something to put things on or in: *Leave your wet umbrella in the stand in the hall.* **24** stall, booth, table, etc., for a small business: *a newspaper stand.* **25** group of growing trees or plants: *stand of timber.* 1-16 *v.*, **stood, stand ing;** 17-25 *n.*

stand by, 1 be near. **2** help; support: *stand by a friend.* **3** be or get ready for use, action, etc.

stand for, 1 represent; mean: *What does the abbreviation St. stand for?* **2** be on the side of; take the part of; uphold: *Our school stands for fair play.* **3** INFORMAL. put up with: *The teacher said she would not stand for talking during class.*

stand off, keep off; keep away: *stand off an angry crowd.*

stand out, 1 project: *His ears stood out.* **2** be noticeable or prominent: *Certain facts stand out.* **3** refuse to yield:

stand out against popular opinion.

stand over, be left for later consideration, treatment, or settlement.

stand up, 1 get to one's feet: *I stood up and began to speak.* **2** endure; last.

stand up for, take the part of; defend; support: *stand up for a friend.*

stand up to, meet or face boldly.

stan dard (stan′dərd), **1** anything taken as a basis of comparison; model: *Your work is not up to the class standard.* **2** of the accepted or normal size, amount, power, quality, etc.: *the standard rate of pay, a standard gauge.* **3** used as a standard; according to rule: *standard spelling, standard pronunciation.* **4** having recognized excellence or authority: *Dickinson and Whitman are standard poets.* **5** flag, emblem, or symbol: *The dragon was the standard of China.* **6** an upright support: *The floor lamp has a long standard.* 1,5,6 *n.*, 2-4 *adj.*

stan dard i za tion (stan′dər də zā′shən), a standardizing or a being standardized. *n.*

stan dard ize (stan′dər dīz), **1** make standard in size, shape, weight, quality, strength, etc.: *Bicycle tires are standardized.* **2** regulate by a standard. **3** test by a standard. *v.*, **stan dard ized, stan dard iz ing.**

standard time, time officially adopted for a region or country.

stand by (stand′bī′), **1** person or thing that can be relied upon; chief support; ready resource. **2** person or thing held in reserve, especially as a possible replacement or substitute. *n.*, *pl.* **stand bys.**

stand-in (stand′in′), **1** person whose work is standing in the place of a motion-picture actor or actress while the lights, camera, etc., are being arranged, or during scenes in which dangerous action occurs. **2** person or thing that takes the place of another; substitute. *n.*

stand ing (stan′ding), **1** position; reputation: *a person of good standing.* **2** duration: *a family feud of long standing.* **3** straight up; erect: *standing timber.* **4** done from an erect position: *a standing jump.* **5** established; permanent: *a standing invitation, a standing army.* **6** not flowing; stagnant: *standing water.* **7** place of standing. 1,2,7 *n.*, 3-6 *adj.*

Stan dish (stan′dish), **Miles,** 1584?-1656, the military leader of the colony at Plymouth, Massachusetts. *n.*

stand pipe (stand′pīp′), a large, upright pipe or tower to hold water at a height great enough to provide pressure for a water system. *n.*

stand point (stand′point′), point of view; mental attitude. *n.*

stand still (stand′stil′), a complete stop; halt. *n.*

stank (stangk), a past tense of **stink**. *The dead fish stank. v.*

Stan ley (stan′lē), Sir Henry Morton, 1841-1904, British explorer in Africa. He found the Scottish missionary, David Livingstone, who had disappeared in Africa. *n.*

Stan ton (stan′tən), **Edwin M.**, 1814-1869, American statesman who was Secretary of War during the Civil War. *n.*

stan za (stan′zə), group of lines of poetry, usually four or more, arranged according to a fixed plan; verse of a poem: *They sang the first and last stanzas of "America." n., pl.* **stan zas.**

staph y lo coc cus (staf′ə lə kok′əs), any of a group of spherical bacteria that bunch together in irregular masses. *n., pl.* **staph y lo coc ci** (staf′ə lə kok′sī).

sta ple[1] (stā′pəl), 1 a U-shaped piece of metal with pointed ends. Staples are driven into doors, etc., to hold hooks, pins, or bolts. 2 a bent piece of wire used to hold together papers, parts of a book, etc. 3 fasten with a staple or staples. *1,2 n., 3 v.,* **sta pled, sta pling.** [Old English *stapol* post]

sta ple[2] (stā′pəl), 1 the most important or principal article grown or manufactured in a place: *Cotton is the staple in many Southern states.* 2 any major article of commerce or trade; something of recognized quality or in constant demand. 3 chief element or material. 4 most important; principal: *Bread is a staple food. The weather was their staple subject of conversation.* 5 a raw material. 6 fiber of cotton or wool. 7 regularly produced in large quantities for the market. *1-3,5,6 n., 4,7 adj.* [from French of the 1400's *estaple* mart]

sta pler (stā′plər), machine for fastening together papers, parts of a book, etc., with wire staples: *Many magazines are now bound by stapler. n.*

star (stär), 1 any of the heavenly bodies appearing as bright points in the sky at night. 2 any heavenly body that shines by its own light and is not a moon, planet, comet, or meteor. 3 a plane figure having five points, or sometimes six, like these: ☆✩. 4 thing having or suggesting this shape. 5 to set with stars; ornament with stars: *Her card was starred for perfect attendance.* 6 asterisk (*). 7 mark with an asterisk. 8 person having brilliant qualities: *an athletic star.* 9 a famous person in some art, profession, etc., especially one who plays the lead in a performance: *a movie star, an opera star.* 10 chief; best; leading; excellent: *the star player on the team.* 11 be prominent; be

a leading performer; excel: *She has starred in many motion pictures.* 12 to present as a star. 13 fate; fortune. *1-4,6,8,9,13 n., 5,7,11,12 v.,* **starred, star ring;** 10 *adj.*

star board (stär′bərd), 1 the right side of a ship, when facing forward. 2 on the right side of a ship. 3 turn (the helm) to the right side. *1 n., 2 adj., 3 v.*

starch (stärch), 1 a white, tasteless food substance. Potatoes, wheat, rice, and corn contain much starch. 2 preparation of this substance used to stiffen clothes, curtains, etc. 3 stiffen (clothes, curtains, etc.) with starch: *starch curtains.* 4 a stiff, formal manner; stiffness. *1,2,4 n., 3 v.* —**starch′-like′, adj.**

starch i ness (stär′chē nis), starchy condition or quality. *n.*

starch y (stär′chē), 1 like starch; containing starch. 2 stiffened with starch. 3 stiff in manner; formal. *adj.,* **starch i er, starch i est.**

star dom (stär′dəm), 1 a being a star actor or performer. 2 star actors or performers as a group. *n.*

stare (ster *or* star), 1 look long and directly with the eyes wide open. A person stares in wonder, surprise, stupidity, curiosity, or from mere rudeness. *The little girl stared at the toys in the window.* 2 a long and direct look with the eyes wide open: *The doll's eyes were set in an unwinking stare.* 3 be very striking or glaring: *His eyes stared with anger. 1,3 v.,* **stared, star ing;** 2 *n.*

stare down, confuse or embarrass by staring.

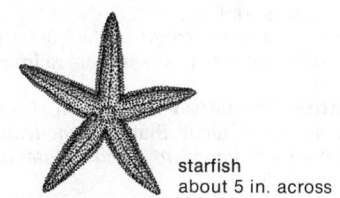

starfish
about 5 in. across

star fish (stär′fish′), any of a group of star-shaped sea animals with flattened bodies. Starfish are not fish. *n., pl.* **star fish es** or **star fish.**

stark (stärk), 1 downright; complete: *That fool is talking stark nonsense.* 2 entirely; completely: *The boys went swimming stark naked.* 3 stiff: *The dog lay stark in death.* 4 bare; barren; desolate: *a stark landscape. 1,3,4 adj., 2 adv.* —**stark′ly, adv.**

star less (stär′lis), without stars; without starlight. *adj.*

star let (stär′lit), 1 a young actress who is being trained for leading roles in motion pictures. 2 a little star. *n.*

star light (stär′līt′), 1 light from the

stars. 2 lighted by the stars. *1 n., 2 adj.*

star like (stär′līk′), 1 shaped like a star: *pattern of starlike snowflakes.* 2 shining like a star. *adj.*

star ling (stär′ling), a common European and American bird with glossy, greenish-black or brownish-black feathers. Starlings nest about buildings and fly in large flocks. *n.*

star lit (stär′lit′), lighted by the stars: *a starlit night. adj.*

star ry (stär′ē), 1 lighted by stars; containing many stars: *a starry sky.* 2 shining like stars: *starry eyes. adj.,* **star ri er, star ri est.**

Stars and Stripes, the flag of the United States.

star-span gled (stär′spang′gəld), sprinkled with stars. *adj.*

Star-Spangled Banner, 1 the national anthem of the United States. The words were composed by Francis Scott Key during the War of 1812. 2 flag of the United States; Stars and Stripes.

start (stärt), 1 begin to move, go, or act: *The train started on time.* 2 begin: *start reading a book, start in business, start at the beginning.* 3 set going; put into action: *start an automobile, start a fire.* 4 a setting in motion: *We pushed the car to give the motor a start.* 5 a beginning to move, go, or act: *see a race from start to finish.* 6 move suddenly: *He started in surprise.* 7 a sudden movement; jerk: *I awoke with a start. On seeing the snake, the man sprang up with a start.* 8 come, rise, or spring out suddenly: *Tears started from her eyes.* 9 a beginning ahead of others; advantage: *She got the start of her rivals.* 10 place, line, etc., where a race begins. 11 rouse: *start a rabbit.* 12 make or become loose: *The huge waves had started some of the ship's bolts. 1-3, 6,8,11,12 v., 4,5,7,9,10 n.*

start in, start out, or **start up,** begin to do something.

start er (stär′tər), 1 person or thing that starts. 2 person who gives the signal for starting. 3 the first in a series of things: *This request was only a starter. n.*

star tle (stär′tl), 1 frighten suddenly;

hat, āge, fär; let, ēqual, tėrm; it, īce; hot, ōpen, ôrder; oil, out; cup, pùt, rüle; ch, child; ng, long; sh, she; th, thin; ᵼн, then; zh, measure;

ə represents *a* in about, *e* in taken, *i* in pencil, *o* in lemon, *u* in circus.

adj. adjective	*n.* noun
adv. adverb	*prep.* preposition
conj. conjunction	*pron.* pronoun
interj. interjection	*v.* verb
sing. singular	*pl.* plural

surprise: *The dog jumped at the girl and startled her.* 2 a sudden shock of surprise or fright. 3 move suddenly in fear or surprise. 1,3 *v.*, **star tled, star tling;** 2 *n.*

star tling (stärt'ling), surprising; frightening: *startling tales. adj.* —**star tling ly,** *adv.*

star va tion (stär vā'shən), 1 a starving: *Starvation of prisoners is barbarous.* 2 suffering from extreme hunger; being starved: *Starvation caused his death. n.*

starve (stärv), 1 die because of hunger. 2 suffer severely because of hunger. 3 weaken or kill with hunger: *That cruel man half starves his horses. The enemy starved the men in the fort into surrendering.* 4 INFORMAL. feel very hungry. 5 have a strong desire or craving. *v.*, **starved, starv ing.**

starve for, suffer from lack of: *starve for news. That lonely child is starving for affection.*

starve ling (stärv'ling), 1 starving; hungry. 2 person or animal that is suffering from lack of food. 1 *adj.*, 2 *n.*

stash (stash), SLANG. hide or put away for safekeeping or future use. *v.*

state (stāt), 1 situation in which a person or thing is; condition of being: *The house is in a bad state of repair. He is in a state of poor health.* 2 a particular condition of mind or feeling: *a state of uncertainty, a state of excitement.* 3 the physical condition of a material with regard to its structure, composition, or form. A substance may exist in a solid, liquid, or gaseous state. Ice is water in a solid state. 4 group of people occupying a given area and organized under a government; commonwealth; nation. 5 Often, **State.** one of several organized political groups of people which together form a nation: *The state of Alaska is one of the United States.* 6 territory of a state. 7 the civil government; highest civil authority: *affairs of state.* 8 of or having to do with a state: *a state road, state police.* 9 position in life; rank: *a person of humble state.* 10 tell in speech or writing; express; say: *State your opinion of the new school rules.* 11 specify; fix; settle: *to state a price.* 12 high style of living; dignity; pomp: *Kings lived in great state.* 13 with ceremony; of ceremony: *state occasions, state robes.* 1-7,9,12 *n.*, 10, 11 *v.*, **stat ed, stat ing;** 8,13 *adj.*

lie in state, lie in a coffin so as to be seen formally and publicly before being buried: *The dead queen lay in state one day in the main hall of the royal palace.*

state craft (stāt'kraft'), skill in the management of public or national affairs; statesmanship. *n.*

stat ed (stā'tid), 1 put into words; said; told: *the stated facts of a case.* 2 specified; fixed; settled: *School begins daily at a stated time. adj.*

state hood (stāt'hůd), condition of being a state, especially a state of the United States. *n.*

state house or **State house** (stāt'hous'), building in which the legislature of a state meets; capitol of a state. *n.*

state less (stāt'lis), not belonging to any country; having no citizenship or nationality: *a stateless refugee. adj.*

state li ness (stāt'lē nis), stately quality or character. *n.*

state ly (stāt'lē), having dignity; imposing; grand; majestic: *The Capitol at Washington is a stately building. adj.*, **state li er, state li est.**

state ment (stāt'mənt), 1 something stated; report; account: *Her statement was correct.* 2 act of stating; manner of stating something: *The statement of an idea helps me to remember it.* 3 summary of an account, showing the amount owed or due: *a bank statement. n.*

Stat en Island (stat'n), island in New York Bay, south of Manhattan. It is part of New York City.

state room (stāt'rüm' *or* stāt'rům'), a private room on a ship or railroad train. *n.*

state side (stāt'sīd'), INFORMAL. from or in the United States: *Americans abroad are happy to receive stateside news. adj.*

states man (stāts'mən), person skilled in the management of public or national affairs. *n.*, *pl.* **states men.**

states man like (stāts'mən līk'), having the qualities of a statesman. *adj.*

states man ship (stāts'mən ship), the qualities of a statesman; skill in the management of public or national affairs. *n.*

states' rights, rights and powers considered as belonging to the individual states of the United States under the Constitution, especially those rights and powers which the Constitution does not specifically delegate to the federal government and does not specifically deny to the individual states.

states wom an (stāts'wům'ən), a woman skilled in the management of public or national affairs. *n.*, *pl.* **states wom en.**

state wide (stāt'wīd'), covering an entire state; over all of a state. *adj.*

stat ic (stat'ik), 1 at rest; standing still: *Civilization does not remain static, but changes constantly.* 2 having to do with bodies at rest or with forces that balance each other. 3 acting by weight without producing motion: *static pressure.* 4 having to do with stationary electrical charges that balance each other. Static electricity can be produced by rubbing a glass rod with a silk cloth. 5 electrical disturbances in the air caused by electrical storms, etc. 6 noises and other interference with radio and television reception caused by such electrical disturbances. 1-4 *adj.*, 5,6 *n.* —**stat'i cal ly,** *adv.*

stat ics (stat'iks), branch of mechanics that deals with bodies at rest or with forces that balance each other. *n.*

sta tion (stā'shən), 1 place to stand in; place which a person is appointed to occupy in the performance of some duty; assigned post: *The policeman took his station at the corner.* 2 building or place used for a definite purpose. A place where soldiers live, a harbor for ships, the police headquarters of a district, and a place for raising sheep or cattle are all called stations. 3 a regular stopping place: *She met her at the bus station.* 4 place or equipment for sending out or receiving programs, messages, etc., by radio or television. 5 assign a station to; place: *She stationed herself just outside the main doorway to collect tickets. The soldier was stationed at Fort Hays.* 6 social position; rank: *A serf was a person of humble station in life.* 1-4,6 *n.*, 5 *v.*

sta tion ar y (stā'shə ner'ē), 1 having a fixed station or place; not movable: *A factory engine is stationary.* 2 standing still; not moving: *A parked car is stationary.* 3 not changing in size, number, activity, etc.: *The population of this town has been stationary for ten years at about 5000 people. adj.*

sta tion er (stā'shə nər), person who sells paper, pens, pencils, ink, etc. *n.*

sta tion er y (stā'shə ner'ē), writing materials such as paper, cards, and envelopes. *n.*

sta tion mas ter (stā'shən mas'tər), person in charge of a railroad station. *n.*

station wagon, a closed automobile with a rear door for loading and unloading and seats in the rear that can be folded down, for use as a light truck.

sta tis tic (stə tis'tik), 1 statistical. 2 any value, item, etc., used in statistics: *an important statistic.* 1 *adj.*, 2 *n.*

sta tis ti cal (stə tis'tə kəl), of or having to do with statistics; consisting of or based on statistics. *adj.*

sta tis ti cal ly (stə tis′tik lē), in a statistical manner; according to statistics. *adv.*

stat is ti cian (stat′ə stish′ən), an expert in statistics; person who prepares statistics. *n.*

sta tis tics (stə tis′tiks), **1** *pl. in form and use.* numerical facts about people, the weather, business conditions, etc. Statistics are collected and classified systematically. **2** *pl. in form, sing. in use.* science of collecting and using such facts. *n.*

stat u ar y (stach′ü er′ē), **1** statues. **2** art of making statues. *n., pl.* **stat u ar ies.**

stat ue (stach′ü), image of a person or animal carved in stone or wood, cast in bronze, or modeled in clay or wax: *Nearly every city has a statue of some famous person. n.*

Statue of Liberty
The statue, not including the base, is about 152 ft. high.

Statue of Liberty, a huge statue of a woman holding aloft a lighted torch, given to the United States by France. It stands on an island in New York Bay.

stat u esque (stach′ü esk′), like a statue in dignity, formal grace, or classic beauty. *adj.*

stat u ette (stach′ü et′), a small statue. *n.*

stat ure (stach′ər), **1** height: *a young woman of average stature.* **2** physical, mental, or moral growth; accomplishment: *Thomas Jefferson was a man of great stature among his countrymen. n.*

sta tus (stā′təs *or* stat′əs), **1** social or professional standing; position; rank: *to lose status, to seek status. What is her status in the government?* **2** state; condition: *Diplomats are interested in the status of world affairs. n.*

status quo (kwō), the way things are; existing state of affairs. [from Latin *status quo* the state in which]

stat ute (stach′üt), **1** law enacted by a legislative body: *The statutes for the United States are made by Congress.* **2** a formally established rule; law; decree: *the statutes of a university. n.*

statute mile, mile (def.1).

stat u to ry (stach′ü tôr′ē), **1** having to do with a statute. **2** fixed by stat-

ute. **3** punishable by statute. *adj.*

St. Au gus tine (sānt ô′gə stēn′), seacoast city in NE Florida. It is the oldest city in the United States, founded by the Spanish in 1565.

staunch¹ (stônch), stanch¹. *v.* [from French of the 1300's *estanchier* to stop, hinder]

staunch² (stônch), **1** strong or firm: *staunch walls, a staunch defense.* **2** loyal; steadfast: *staunch friends, a staunch supporter of the law.* **3** watertight: *a staunch boat. adj.* Also, **stanch.** [from French of the 1400's *estanche,* from *estanchier* to stop, hinder] —**staunch′ly,** *adv.* —**staunch′ness,** *n.*

stave (stāv), **1** one of the curved pieces of wood that form the sides of a barrel, tub, etc. **2** stick or staff. **3** break a hole in (a barrel, boat, etc.). **4** become smashed or broken in. **5** verse or stanza of a poem or song. **6** the musical staff. **7** furnish with staves. **1,2,5,6** *n.,* **3,4,7** *v.,* **staved** *or* **stove, stav ing.**

stave off, put off; keep back; delay or prevent: *The lost campers ate birds' eggs to stave off starvation.*

staves (stāvz), **1** a plural of **staff** (defs. 1 and 2). **2** plural of **stave.** *n.*

stay¹ (stā), **1** continue to be as indicated; remain: *Stay still. Stay here till I tell you to move. The cat stayed out all night. Shall I go or stay?* **2** live for a while; dwell: *She is staying with her aunt for a few weeks.* **3** a staying; a stop; time spent: *a pleasant stay in the country.* **4** stop; halt: *We have no time to stay.* **5** pause; wait: *Time and tide stay for no man.* **6** put an end to for a while; satisfy: *He ate some bread and butter to stay his hunger till time for dinner.* **7** put off; hold back; delay; restrain: *The teacher stayed judgment till she could hear both sides.* **8** a check; restraint: *a stay on one's activity.* **9** a delay in carrying out the order of a court: *The judge granted the condemned man a stay for an appeal.* **10** to last; endure: *I was unable to stay to the end of the race.* **1,2,4-7,10** *v.,* **3,8,9** *n.* [from French of the 1400's *ester* to stand, from Latin *stare*] —**stay′er,** *n.*

stay² (stā), **1** a support; prop; brace: *The oldest child was the family's stay.* **2** strengthen mentally or spiritually; fix or rest in dependence or reliance; hold up; support; prop. **3 stays,** *pl.* corset, especially a stiffened one. **1,3** *n.,* **2** *v.* [probably from French of the 1500's *estayer*]

stay³ (stā), **1** a strong rope, often of wire, which supports the mast of a ship. **2** any rope or chain attached to something to steady it. **3** support or secure with stays. **1,2** *n.,* **3** *v.* [Old English *stæg*]

staying power, power to hold out and not give in even though weakened or tired; power or will to endure.

stay sail (stā′sāl′ *or* stā′səl), a sail fastened on a stay or rope. *n.*

stead (sted), place: *Our regular baby-sitter could not come, but sent her brother in her stead. n.*

stand in good stead, be of advantage or service to: *His ability to swim stood him in good stead when the boat upset.*

stead fast (sted′fast′), firmly fixed; constant; not moving or changing: *a steadfast friend, a steadfast defender of one's country. adj.* —**stead′fast′ly,** *adv.* —**stead′fast′ness,** *n.*

stead i ly (sted′l ē), in a steady manner; firmly; uniformly. *adv.*

stead i ness (sted′ē nis), steady character, quality, or condition. *n.*

stead y (sted′ē), **1** changing little; uniform; regular: *He is making steady progress at school.* **2** firmly fixed; firm; not swaying or shaking: *This post is steady as a rock. Hold the ladder steady.* **3** not easily excited; calm: *steady nerves.* **4** resolute; steadfast: *steady friendship.* **5** having good habits; reliable: *He is a steady young man.* **6** make steady; keep steady: *Steady the ladder while I climb to the roof.* **7** become steady: *Our sails filled as the wind steadied from the east.* **1-5** *adj.,* **stead i er, stead i est;** **6,7** *v.,* **stead ied, stead y ing.**

go steady, INFORMAL. be a boy's steady girl friend or a girl's steady boy friend.

steak (stāk), **1** slice of meat or fish for broiling or frying. *Steak often means beefsteak.* **2** finely ground meat shaped and cooked somewhat like a steak: *hamburger steak. n.*

steal (stēl), **1** take (something) that does not belong to one; take dishonestly: *Robbers stole the money.* **2** take, get, or do secretly: *She stole time from her lessons to read a story.* **3** take, get, or win by art, charm, etc.: *The baby stole our hearts.* **4** move secretly or quietly: *She stole softly out of the house.* **5** INFORMAL. act of stealing. **6** INFORMAL. something obtained at a very low cost or with very little effort:

stealth

This table is such a bargain it's a steal.
7 (in baseball) run to (second base, third base, or home plate) as the pitcher delivers the ball to the batter. A player steals a base when he reaches it without the help of a hit or an error. 1-4,7 *v.*, **stole, sto len, steal ing**; 5,6 *n.*

stealth (stelth), secret or sly action: *He obtained the letter by stealth, taking it while nobody was in the room. n.*

stealth i ly (stel′thə lē), by stealth. *adv.*

stealth i ness (stel′thē nis), condition of being stealthy. *n.*

stealth y (stel′thē), done in a secret manner; secret; sly: *The cat crept in a stealthy way toward the bird.* adj., **stealth i er, stealth i est.**

steam (stēm), 1 the invisible vapor or gas into which water is changed when heated to the boiling point. Steam is used to heat houses, run engines, etc. 2 the white cloud or mist formed by the condensation, when cooled, of the invisible vapor from boiling water. 3 give off steam: *The cup of coffee was steaming.* 4 become covered with steam: *The windshield had completely steamed up inside the heated car.* 5 rise in the form of steam. 6 move by steam: *The ship steamed off.* 7 cook, soften, or freshen by steam: *The cook steamed the plum pudding.* 8 INFORMAL. power; energy; force: *That old man still has a lot of steam left in him.* 9 of, having to do with, or consisting of steam: *steam power. Many large office buildings and apartments have steam heat.* 1,2,8 *n.*, 3-7 *v.*, 9 *adj.*

let off steam, INFORMAL. relieve one's feelings.

steam boat (stēm′bōt′), boat moved by steam. *n.*

steam engine, engine worked by the action of steam under pressure. The steam, generated in a boiler, expands so that it can push a piston in a cylinder. Locomotives, ships, and large machines may be driven by steam engines.

steam er (stē′mər), 1 steamboat; steamship. 2 engine run by steam. 3 container in which something is steamed or kept warm. *n.*

steam fitter, person who installs and repairs steam pipes, radiators, boilers, etc.

steam iron, an electric iron in which water is heated to produce steam which is released through holes in its undersurface to dampen cloth while pressing it.

steam roll er (stēm′rō′lər), 1 a heavy roller, formerly run by steam but now usually by an internal-combustion engine, used to crush and level materials in making roads. 2 INFORMAL. means of crushing opposition. 3 INFORMAL. to crush: *steamroller all political opposition.* 1,2 *n.*, 3 *v.*

steam ship (stēm′ship′), ship moved by steam. *n.*

steam shovel, a power shovel, especially one operated by steam power.

steam y (stē′mē), 1 of or like steam: *a steamy vapor.* 2 full of steam; giving off steam; rising in steam: *a steamy room.* adj., **steam i er, steam i est.**

steed (stēd), 1 horse, especially a riding horse. 2 a high-spirited horse. *n.*

steel (stēl), 1 an alloy of iron and carbon. Steel has greater hardness and flexibility than cast iron and is used for tools and machinery. 2 something made from steel; a sword or a piece of steel for making sparks; a rod of steel for sharpening knives. 3 made of steel. 4 to point, edge, or cover with steel. 5 make hard or strong like steel: *They steeled their hearts against the sufferings of the poor. I tried to steel myself against a possible failure.* 6 steellike hardness or strength: *nerves of steel.* 1,2,6 *n.*, 3 *adj.*, 4,5 *v.* **—steel′like′,** *adj.*

steel wool, mass of long, fine steel shavings, used in cleaning or polishing surfaces.

steel work er (stēl′wėr′kər), person who works in a place where steel is made. *n.*

steel works (stēl′wėrks′), place where steel is made. *n. pl. or sing.*

steam engine
above—Steam under pressure from boiler enters intake, driving piston to right. Used steam goes out exhaust at right.
below—Heavy flywheel keeps motion continuous and by attached gears changes valve positions in intake and exhaust. Steam now drives piston to left and used steam goes out exhaust at left.

steel y (stē′lē), 1 made of steel. 2 like steel in color, strength, or hardness. *adj.*, **steel i er, steel i est.**

steel yard (stēl′yärd *or* stil′yərd), scale for weighing, having arms of unequal length. The longer one has a movable weight and is marked in units of weight; the shorter one has a hook for holding the object to be weighed. *n.*

steelyard—When the arm is horizontal, the weight of any object hanging at the right is shown by a number where the movable weight at the left rests.

steep¹ (stēp), 1 having a sharp slope; almost straight up and down: *The hill is steep.* 2 unreasonable: *a steep price.* adj. [Old English *stēap*] **—steep′ly,** adv. **—steep′ness,** n.

steep² (stēp), 1 soak: *Let the tea steep in boiling water for five minutes. The knife was steeped in blood.* 2 immerse; imbue: *The professor steeps herself in Latin. v.* [Middle English *stepen*, probably related to Old English *stēap* bowl]

steeped in, filled with; permeated by: *ruins steeped in gloom, a mind steeped in hatred.*

steep en (stē′pən), make or become steep or steeper. *v.*

stee ple (stē′pəl), 1 a high tower on a church. Steeples usually have spires. See **spire¹** for picture. 2 spire on top of the tower or roof of a church or similar building. *n.*

stee ple chase (stē′pəl chās′), a horse race over a course having ditches, hedges, and other obstacles. *n.*

stee ple jack (stē′pəl jak′), person who climbs steeples, tall chimneys, or the like, to make repairs, etc. *n.*

steer¹ (stir), 1 guide the course of: *steer a ship, steer a sled, steer an automobile, steer an airplane.* 2 be guided: *This car steers easily.* 3 set and follow: *She steered a middle course during the debate, agreeing with speakers on both sides.* 4 direct one's way or course: *Steer away from trouble. Steer for the harbor. v.* [Old English *stēran*]

steer clear of, keep away from; avoid.

steer² (stir), 1 a young ox, usually two to four years old. 2 any male of beef cattle. *n.* [Old English *stēor*]

steer age (stir′ij), 1 the part of a passenger ship occupied by passengers traveling at the cheapest rate. 2 act of steering. *n.*

steering wheel, wheel that is turned to steer an automobile, ship, etc.

steers man (stirz/mən), person who steers a boat or ship. *n., pl.* **steers- men.**

steg o sau rus (steg/ə sôr/əs), an extinct reptile of great size, with heavy, bony armor. *n., pl.* **steg o sau ri** (steg/ə sôr/ī).

stegosaurus—about 18 ft. long

stein (stīn), a mug for beer. *n.*

Stein beck (stīn/bek), **John,** 1902- 1968, American novelist. *n.*

Stein metz (stīn/mets), **Charles P.,** 1865-1923, American scientist and engineer, born in Germany. *n.*

stel lar (stel/ər), 1 of or having to do with the stars or a star; like a star. 2 chief: *a stellar role. adj.*

St. El mo's fire (sānt el/mōz), ball of light due to a discharge of atmospheric electricity, often seen on masts of ships, towers, etc. [from *St. Elmo,* a Syrian martyr of the A.D. 200's who was considered a patron saint of sailors]

stem¹ (stem), 1 the main part of a plant, usually above the ground. The stem supports the branches, etc. The trunk of a tree and the stalks of corn are stems. 2 the part of a flower, a fruit, or a leaf that joins it to the plant or tree. 3 remove the stem from (a leaf, fruit, etc.). 4 anything like the stem of a plant: *the stem of a goblet, the stem of a pipe.* 5 line of descent of a family. 6 the part of a word to which endings are added and in which changes are made. *Run* is the stem of *running, runner, ran,* etc. 7 the bow or front end of a boat. 1,2,4-7 *n.,* 3 *v.,* **stemmed, stem ming.** [Old English *stemn*] —**stem/like/,** *adj.*

from stem to stern, from one end of a ship to the other.

stem from, come from; have as a source or cause: *The difficulty stems from their failure to plan properly.*

stem² (stem), 1 dam up (a stream, etc.); stop; check. 2 make headway or progress against: *When you swim upstream you have to stem the current. v.,* **stemmed, stem ming.** [perhaps from a Scandinavian word of the 1200's, such as Icelandic *stemma*]

stem less (stem/lis), having no stem or no visible stem. *adj.*

stemmed (stemd), 1 having a stem. 2 having the stem removed. *adj.*

stench (stench), a very bad smell; stink: *the stench of a pigsty, the stench of gas. n., pl.* **stench es.**

sten cil (sten/səl), 1 a thin sheet of metal, paper, etc., having letters or designs cut through it. When it is laid on a surface and ink or color is spread on, these letters or designs are made on the surface. 2 the letters or designs so made. 3 mark, paint, or make with a stencil: *The curtains have a stenciled border.* 1,2 *n.,* 3 *v.*

ste nog ra pher (stə nog/rə fər), person whose work is taking dictation in shorthand and transcribing it, usually with a typewriter. *n.*

sten o graph ic (sten/ə graf/ik), 1 of stenography. 2 made by stenography. 3 using stenography. *adj.*

ste nog ra phy (stə nog/rə fē), 1 method of rapid writing that uses symbols, abbreviations, etc.; shorthand. 2 act of writing in such symbols. *n.*

sten to ri an (sten tôr/ē ən), very loud or powerful in sound: *His stentorian voice rang through the valley. adj.* [from *Stentor,* a legendary Greek herald in the Trojan War whose voice was as loud as the voices of fifty men]

step (step), 1 a movement made by lifting the foot and putting it down again in a new position; one motion of the leg in walking, running, dancing, etc. 2 distance covered by one such movement: *We were three steps away when she called us back.* 3 move the legs as in walking, running, dancing, etc.: *Step lively!* 4 a short distance; little way: *The school is only a step from our house.* 5 walk a short distance: *Step this way.* 6 way of walking, dancing, etc.: *a quick step, a dance with fancy steps.* 7 measure (off) by taking steps: *Step off the distance from the door to the window.* 8 put the foot down: *He stepped on a bug.* 9 sound made by putting the foot down: *I hear steps upstairs.* 10 a place for the foot in going up or coming down. A stair or a rung of a ladder is a step. 11 footprint: *I see steps in the mud.* 12 a degree in a scale; a grade in rank: *A colonel is three steps above a captain.* 13 (in music) a degree of the staff or the scale. 14 part like a step; support, frame, etc., for holding the end of something upright: *the step of a mast.* 15 set (a mast) in place. 16 INFORMAL. go fast. 1,2,4,6,9-14 *n.,* 3,5,7,8,15,16 *v.,* **stepped, step ping.** —**step/like/,** *adj.*

in step, 1 making one's steps fit those of another person or persons; at a uniform pace with others or in time with music. 2 making one's actions or ideas agree with those of another person or

hat, āge, fär; let, ēqual, tèrm; it, īce; hot, ōpen, ôrder; oil, out; cup, pût, rüle; ch, child; ng, long; sh, she; th, thin; ₮H, then; zh, measure;

ə represents *a* in about, *e* in taken, *i* in pencil, *o* in lemon, *u* in circus.

persons; in harmony or agreement.

keep step, move the same leg at the same time that another person does.

out of step, not in step; not at a uniform pace or in harmony with another or others.

step by step, little by little; slowly.

step down, 1 surrender or resign from an office or position. 2 lower by steps or degrees; decrease.

step into, come into, acquire, or receive, especially without particular effort or by chance: *step into a fortune.*

step on it, INFORMAL. go faster; hurry up: *Please step on it or we'll be late.*

step up, raise by steps or degrees; go faster, higher, etc.; increase: *step up the production of automobiles, step up the pressure in a boiler.*

take steps, adopt, put into effect, or carry out measures considered to be necessary, desirable, etc.: *The principal took steps to stop needless absence from school.*

watch one's step, be careful: *Watch your step when you ride down that steep hill on the bicycle.*

step broth er (step/bru₮H/ər), a stepfather's or stepmother's son by a former marriage. *n.*

step child (step/chīld/), child of one's husband or wife by a former marriage. *n., pl.* **step chil dren** (step/chil/drən).

step daugh ter (step/dô/tər), daughter of one's husband or wife by a former marriage. *n.*

step fa ther (step/fä/₮Hər), man who has married one's mother after the death or divorce of one's real father. *n.*

step lad der (step/lad/ər), ladder with flat steps instead of rungs. *n.*

step moth er (step/mu₮H/ər), woman who has married one's father after the death or divorce of one's real mother. *n.*

step par ent (step/per/ənt *or* step/- par/ənt), stepfather or stepmother. *n.*

steppe (step), 1 one of the vast, treeless plains in southeastern Europe and in Asia, especially as found in Russia. 2 a vast, treeless plain. *n.*

stepping stone, 1 stone or one of a line of stones in shallow water, a

adj.	adjective	*n.*	noun
adv.	adverb	*prep.*	preposition
conj.	conjunction	*pron.*	pronoun
interj.	interjection	*v.*	verb
sing.	singular	*pl.*	plural

marshy place, or the like, used in crossing. 2 stone for use in mounting or ascending. 3 anything serving as a means of advancing or rising.

step sis ter (step′sis′tər), a stepfather's or stepmother's daughter by a former marriage. *n.*

step son (step′sun′), son of one's husband or wife by a former marriage. *n.*

ster e o (ster′ē ō *or* stir′ē ō), 1 stereophonic. 2 stereophonic equipment. 1 *adj.*, 2 *n., pl.* **ster e os.**

ster e o phon ic (ster′ē ə fon′ik *or* stir′ē ə fon′ik), giving the effect of lifelike sound by using two or more sets of equipment for recording or broadcasting and two or more sets of receiving equipment. Stereophonic sound has the same effects of depth and direction as the original sound. *adj.*

ster e op ti con (ster′ē op′tə kən *or* stir′ē op′tə kən), projector arranged to project two images upon a screen so that the image of one object or scene gradually passes into that of another with dissolving effect. *n.*

ster e o scope (ster′ē ə skōp′ *or* stir′ē ə skōp′), instrument through which two pictures of the same object or scene, taken from slightly different angles, are viewed, one by each eye. The object or scene thus viewed appears to have three dimensions. *n.*

stereoscope—The pictures are taken from two points a short distance apart, and the instrument contains lenses which make them appear to be one view.

ster e o scop ic (ster′ē ə skop′ik *or* stir′ē ə skop′ik), having to do with stereoscopes. *adj.*

ster e o type (ster′ē ə tīp′ *or* stir′ē ə tīp′), 1 a printing plate cast from a mold. 2 a fixed form, character, image, etc.; something stereotyped; conventional type. Long John Silver, in Stevenson's *Treasure Island,* is the stereotype of a pirate. 3 give a fixed or settled form to. 1,2 *n.,* 3 *v.,* **ster e o typed, ster e o typ ing.**

ster e o typed (ster′ē ə tīpt′ *or* stir′ē ə tīpt′), 1 cast in the form of, or printed from, a stereotype. 2 fixed or settled in form; conventional: *"It gives me great pleasure to be with you to-night"* is a stereotyped opening for a speech. *adj.*

ster ile (ster′əl), 1 free from living germs: *Bandages should always be kept sterile.* 2 not producing seed, offspring, crops, etc.; not fertile; barren: *sterile land, a sterile cow. adj.* **—ster′ile ly,** *adv.*

ste ril i ty (stə ril′ə tē), sterile condition or character; barrenness. *n.*

ster i li za tion (ster′ə lə zā′shən), a sterilizing or a being sterilized: *the sterilization of dishes by boiling them. n.*

ster i lize (ster′ə līz), 1 make free from living germs: *The water had to be sterilized by boiling to make it fit to drink.* 2 deprive of fertility. *v.,* **ster i lized, ster i liz ing.**

ster i liz er (ster′ə lī′zər), any device for killing germs. *n.*

ster ling (ster′ling), 1 of standard quality for silver; containing 92.5 per cent pure silver. *Sterling* is stamped on solid silver knives, forks, etc. 2 sterling silver or things made of it. 3 made of sterling silver. 4 genuine; excellent; dependable; reliable: *Everybody admired the statesman's sterling character.* 5 British money, especially the pound as the standard British monetary unit in international trade: *to pay in sterling.* 6 of British money; payable in British money. 1,3,4,6 *adj.,* 2,5 *n.*

sterling silver, solid silver; silver 92.5 per cent pure.

stern[1] (stern), 1 harshly firm; hard; strict: *a stern parent. A stern frown by our teacher silenced us.* 2 very severe; rigorous; harsh: *stern necessity. adj.* [Old English *styrne*] **—stern′ly,** *adv.* **—stern′ness,** *n.*

stern[2] (stern), the hind part of a ship or boat. *n.* [probably from a Scandinavian word of the 1200's, such as Icelandic *stjörn* steering]

ster nal (ster′nl), of or having to do with the breastbone or sternum. *adj.*

ster num (ster′nəm), breastbone. *n.*

steth o scope (steth′ə skōp), instrument used by doctors to hear the sounds produced in the lungs, heart, etc. *n.*

Steu ben (stü′bən *or* styü′bən), Baron **Friedrich Wilhelm von,** 1730-1794, Prussian general who aided the Americans in the Revolutionary War. *n.*

ste ve dore (stē′və dôr), person who loads and unloads ships. *n.*

Ste ven son (stē′vən sən), **Robert** **Louis,** 1850-1894, Scottish author of novels, poems, and essays. *n.*

stew (stü *or* styü), 1 cook by slow boiling: *The cook stewed the chicken for a long time.* 2 food cooked by slow boiling: *beef stew.* 3 INFORMAL. worry; fret. 4 INFORMAL. state of worry; fret: *They were in a stew over their lost luggage.* 1,3 *v.,* 2,4 *n.*

stew ard (stü′ərd *or* styü′ərd), 1 man who has charge of the food and table service for a club, ship, railroad train, airplane, etc. 2 servant on a ship: *A cabin steward waits on passengers in their staterooms.* 3 person who manages another's property: *My grandparents' banker is the steward of their large estate. n.*

stew ard ess (stü′ər dis *or* styü′ərdis), woman employed on an airplane, a ship, etc., to wait upon passengers. *n., pl.* **stew ard ess es.**

stew ard ship (stü′ərd ship *or* styü′ərd ship), position or work of a steward. *n.*

St. He le na (sānt hə lē′nə), British island in the S Atlantic. Napoleon I was exiled there from 1815 until his death in 1821.

stick[1] (stik), 1 a long, thin piece of wood: *Put some sticks on the fire.* 2 such a piece of wood shaped for a special use: *a walking stick.* 3 a slender branch or twig of a tree or shrub, especially when cut or broken off. 4 something like a stick in shape: *a stick of candy.* 5 INFORMAL. a stiff, awkward, or stupid person. *n.* [Old English *sticca* rod, twig, spoon]

stick[2] (stik), 1 pierce with a pointed instrument; thrust (a point) into; stab: *She stuck a fork into the potato.* 2 kill by stabbing or piercing. 3 fasten by thrusting the point or end into or through something: *He stuck a flower in his buttonhole.* 4 put into a position: *Don't stick your head out of the window.* 5 be thrust; extend (from, out, through, up, etc.): *My arms stick out of my coat sleeves.* 6 fasten; attach: *Stick a stamp on the letter.* 7 keep close: *The dog stuck to the little girl's heels.* 8 be or become fastened; become fixed; be at a standstill: *Our car stuck in the mud.*

stethoscope—Sounds are conveyed to the doctor's ears through two hollow tubes.

Two pages of the book stuck together. **9** bring to a stop: *Our work was stuck by the breakdown of the machinery.* **10** hold one's position; cling: *She stuck to the horse's back.* **11** INFORMAL. puzzle: *That problem in arithmetic stuck me.* **12** SLANG. impose upon; cheat. *v.,* **stuck, stick ing.** [Old English *stician*]

stick at, hesitate or stop for: *He sticks at nothing to get his own way.*

stick by or **stick to,** remain faithful or attached to; refuse to desert: *She sticks by her friends when they need her help.*

stick up, SLANG. hold up; rob.

stick up for, INFORMAL. stand up for; support; defend.

stigma (def. 3)

stick er (stik′ər), **1** person or thing that sticks. **2** a gummed label. *n.*

stick i ly (stik′ə lē), in a sticky manner. *adv.*

stick i ness (stik′ē nis), condition of being sticky. *n.*

stick le (stik′əl), make objections about trifles; contend or insist stubbornly. *v.,* **stick led, stick ling.**

stick le back (stik′əl bak′), a small, scaleless fish with a row of sharp spines on the back. The male builds an elaborate nest for the eggs. *n., pl.* **stick le backs** or **stick le back.**

stick ler (stik′lər), person who contends or insists stubbornly, sometimes over trifles: *a stickler for accuracy. n.*

stick pin (stik′pin′), pin worn in a necktie for ornament. *n.*

stick y (stik′ē), **1** that sticks: *sticky glue.* **2** that makes things stick; covered with adhesive matter: *sticky flypaper.* **3** hot and damp: *sticky weather. adj.,* **stick i er, stick i est.**

stiff (stif), **1** not easily bent; fixed; rigid: *a stiff collar.* **2** hard to move: *The old hinges on the barn door are stiff.* **3** not able to move easily: *a stiff neck.* **4** not fluid; firm: *The jelly is stiff enough to keep its shape.* **5** not easy or natural in manner; formal: *The magician made a stiff bow to the audience. The novelist writes in a stiff style.* **6** strong: *a stiff breeze.* **7** hard to deal with; hard: *The teacher gave us a stiff test.* **8** INFORMAL. more than seems suitable: *They are asking a stiff price for their house. adj.* —**stiff′ly,** *adv.* —**stiff′ness,** *n.*

stiff en (stif′ən), **1** make stiff: *stiffen an old shirt with starch.* **2** become stiff: *The jelly will stiffen as it cools. She*

stiffened with anger. *The wind was stiffening as the storm approached. v.* —**stiff′en er,** *n.*

stiff-necked (stif′nekt′), **1** having a stiff neck. **2** stubborn; obstinate. *adj.*

sti fle (stī′fəl), **1** stop the breath of; smother: *The smoke stifled the rescuers.* **2** be unable to breathe freely: *I am stifling in this close room.* **3** keep back; suppress; stop: *stifle a cry, stifle a yawn, stifle business activity, stifle a rebellion. v.,* **sti fled, sti fling.**

stig ma (stig′mə), **1** a mark of disgrace or shame; stain or reproach on one's reputation. **2** spot in the skin which bleeds or turns red. **3** the part of the pistil of a plant which receives the pollen. *n., pl.* **stig mas, stig ma ta** (stig′mə tə).

stig ma tize (stig′mə tīz), set some mark of disgrace upon; reproach; brand: *He always felt that his father's prison record stigmatized both of them. v.,* **stig ma tized, stig ma tiz ing.**

stile (stīl), **1** step or steps for getting over a fence or wall. **2** turnstile. *n.*

sti let to (stə let′ō), **1** dagger with a narrow blade. **2** a small, sharp-pointed instrument for making eyelet holes in embroidery. *n., pl.* **sti let tos** or **sti let toes.** *n.*

still[1] (stil), **1** staying in the same position or at rest; without motion; motionless: *to stand or lie still. Sit still. The lake is still today.* **2** without noise; quiet: *a still night. The room was so still that you could have heard a pin drop.* **3** make calm or quiet: *The father stilled the crying baby.* **4** become calm or quiet: *The people prayed that the storm might still.* **5** stillness; silence: *in the still of the night.* **6** even; yet: *You can read still better if you try.* **7** and yet; but yet; nevertheless: *Though she liked her other jobs, she still favors this one* (*adv.*). *He was hungry; still he would not eat* (*conj.*). **8** even to this time; even to that time: *Was the store still open?* **9** without moving; quietly. **10** OLD USE. always; ever. **1,2** *adj.,* **3,4** *v.,* **5** *n.,* **6-10** *adv.,* **7** *conj.* [Old English *stille*]

still[2] (def. 1)

still[2] (stil), **1** apparatus for distilling liquids, especially alcoholic liquors. **2** distillery. *n.* [shortened from *distill,* from Latin *distillare* drop down]

still born (stil′bôrn′), dead when born. *adj.*

hat, āge, fär; let, ēqual, tėrm;
it, īce; hot, ōpen, ôrder;
oil, out; cup, pùt, rüle; ch, child;
ng, long; sh, she; th, thin;
ᴛʜ, then; zh, measure;

ə represents *a* in about,
e in taken, *i* in pencil,
o in lemon, *u* in circus.

still life, **1** inanimate objects, such as fruit, flowers, pottery, dead animals, etc., shown in a picture. **2** picture of such objects.

still ness (stil′nis), **1** absence of noise; quiet; silence. **2** absence of motion; calm. *n.*

stilt (stilt), **1** one of a pair of poles, each with a support for the foot at some distance above the ground. Stilts are used in walking through shallow water, or by children for amusement. **2** a long post or pole used to support a house, shed, etc., above water, swampland, etc. **3** a wading bird with long, slender legs and bill that lives in marshes. *n., pl.* **stilts** (or **stilt** for 3). —**stilt′like′,** *adj.*

stilt ed (stil′tid), stiffly dignified or formal: *a stilted manner of speaking. adj.*

stim u lant (stim′yə lənt), **1** food, drug, medicine, etc., that temporarily increases the activity of the body or some part of the body. Tea and coffee are stimulants. **2** something that excites, stirs, or stimulates: *a stimulant to business.* **3** stimulating. **1,2** *n.,* **3** *adj.*

stim u late (stim′yə lāt), **1** spur on; stir up; rouse to action: *Praise stimulated her to work hard.* **2** act as a stimulant or a stimulus. *v.,* **stim u lat ed, stim u lat ing.**

stim u la tion (stim′yə lā′shən), a stimulating or a being stimulated: *This town needs new industries or some other stimulation to make it grow. n.*

stim u li (stim′yə lī), plural of **stimulus.** *n.*

stim u lus (stim′yə ləs), **1** something that stirs to action or effort: *Ambition is a great stimulus.* **2** something that excites the body or some part of the body to activity: *The doctor used mild electric shocks as a stimulus to keep the patient's heart beating. n., pl.* **stim u li.**

sting (sting), **1** to prick or wound with a sharp-pointed organ: *Bees, wasps, and hornets sting. A bee stung him.* **2** act of stinging. **3** a wound caused by stinging: *Put mud on the sting to take away the pain.* **4** the sharp-pointed organ of an insect, animal, or plant that pricks or wounds and often poisons. **5** pain sharp-

adj.	adjective	*n.*	noun
adv.	adverb	*prep.*	preposition
conj.	conjunction	*pron.*	pronoun
interj.	interjection	*v.*	verb
sing.	singular	*pl.*	plural

ly: *The actor was stung by the jeers of the audience.* **6** sharp pain: *The ball team felt the sting of defeat.* **7** cause a feeling like that of a sting: *Mustard stings. The electric spark stung her arm.* **8** drive or stir up as if by a sting: *Their ridicule stung him into making a sharp reply.* **9** SLANG. impose upon; charge too much. 1,5,7-9 *v.,* **stung, sting ing;** 2-4,6 *n.* —**sting′ing ly,** *adv.*

STIPULES

sting er (sting′ər), **1** the part of an insect or animal that stings. **2** anything that stings. *n.*

stin gi ly (stin′jə lē), in a stingy manner. *adv.*

stin gi ness (stin′jē nis), meanness about spending or giving money. *n.*

sting less (sting′lis), having no sting. *adj.*

sting ray (sting′rā′), a broad, flat fish that can inflict severe wounds with the sharp spines on its tail. *n.*

stingray—length up to 12 ft. with tail

stin gy (stin′jē), **1** mean about spending or giving money; not generous: *He tried to save money without being stingy.* **2** scanty; meager. *adj.,* **stin gi er, stin gi est.**

stink (stingk), **1** a very bad smell. **2** have a bad smell: *Decaying fish stink.* **3** cause to have a very bad smell. **4** have a very bad reputation; be in great disfavor. 1 *n.,* 2-4 *v.,* **stank** or **stunk, stunk, stink ing.** —**stink′er,** *n.*

stink y (sting′kē), that stinks; stinking. *adj.,* **stink i er, stink i est.**

stint (stint), **1** keep on short allowance; be saving or careful in using or spending; limit: *The parents stinted themselves of food to give it to their children.* **2** a limit; limitation: *a generous person who gives without stint.* **3** be saving; get along on very little. **4** amount or share set aside. **5** task assigned: *She did a stint as a reporter for the local newspaper.* 1,3 *v.,* 2,4,5 *n.*

sti pend (stī′pend), fixed or regular pay; salary: *The scholarship winner received a monthly stipend to cover her college expenses.* *n.*

stip ple (stip′əl), paint, draw, or engrave by using dots or small, light strokes. *v.,* **stip pled, stip pling.**

stip u late (stip′yə lāt), arrange definitely; demand as a condition of agreement: *He stipulated that he should receive a month's vacation every year if he took the job.* *v.,* **stip u lat ed, stip u lat ing.**

stip u la tion (stip′yə lā′shən), a definite arrangement; agreement; condition in an agreement or bargain: *We rented the house with the stipulation that certain rooms should be papered and painted.* *n.*

stip ule (stip′yül), one of the pair of little leaflike parts at the base of a leaf stem. *n.*

stir (stėr), **1** set in motion; move: *The wind stirred the leaves.* **2** move about: *No one was stirring in the house.* **3** mix by moving around with a spoon, fork, stick, etc.: *He stirs the sugar in his tea with his spoon.* **4** set going; affect strongly; excite: *She stirred up the other children to mischief.* **5** movement: *There was a stir in the bushes where the children were hiding.* **6** excitement: *The unexpected news caused a great stir.* **7** act of stirring: *She gave the mixture a hard stir.* 1-4 *v.,* **stirred, stir ring;** 5-7 *n.*

stir ring (stėr′ing), **1** moving, active, or lively: *stirring times.* **2** rousing; exciting: *a stirring speech.* *adj.* —**stir′ring ly,** *adv.*

stir rup (stėr′əp *or* stir′əp), loop or ring of metal or wood that hangs from a saddle to support a rider's foot: *The rider stood up in his stirrups.* *n.*

stirrup bone, the innermost of the three bones in the middle ear, resembling a stirrup.

stitch (stich), **1** one complete movement of a threaded needle through cloth in sewing: *Take short stitches.* **2** one complete movement in knitting, crocheting, embroidering, etc. **3** a particular method of taking stitches: *buttonhole stitch.* **4** loop of thread, etc., made by a stitch: *Rip out these long stitches. The doctor will take the stitches out of the wound tomorrow.* **5** make stitches in; fasten with stitches: *The tailor stitched a pocket on the new jacket. The doctor stitched the cut.* **6** sew. **7** INFORMAL. a small bit: *She wouldn't do a stitch of work.* **8** a sudden, sharp pain: *After running all the way home, I had a stitch in my side.* 1-4,7,8 *n., pl.* **stitch es;** 5,6 *v.* —**stitch′er,** *n.*

St. John's (sānt jonz′), capital of Newfoundland, in the SE part.

St. Lawrence, 1 river in SE Canada flowing northeast from Lake Ontario into the Gulf of St. Lawrence. **2 Gulf of,** arm of the Atlantic Ocean in E Canada.

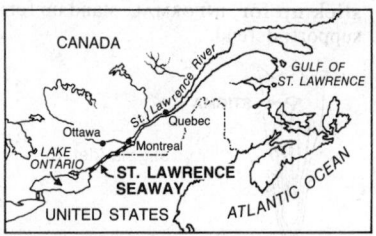

St. Lawrence Seaway, waterway that links the Great Lakes to the Atlantic Ocean by means of canals and the St. Lawrence River.

St. Lou is (sānt lü′is *or* sānt lü′ē), city in E Missouri, on the Mississippi River.

St.-Mo ritz (sānt mə rits′), winter resort in SE Switzerland. *n.*

stoat (stōt), **1** the ermine in its summer coat of brown. **2** weasel. *n.*

stock (stok), **1** things for use or for sale; supply used as it is needed: *This store keeps a large stock of toys.* **2** livestock: *The farm was sold with all its stock.* **3** furnish with stock; supply: *Our camp is well stocked with everything we need for a short stay.* **4** lay in a supply: *stock up for the winter.* **5** keep regularly for use or for sale: *A toy store stocks toys.* **6** kept on hand regularly: *stock sizes of dresses.* **7** in common use; commonplace; everyday: *The weather is a stock subject of conversation.* **8** shares in a company. The profits of a company are usually divided among the owners of stock. **9** race or family: *a person of aristocratic stock.* **10** race or other group of closely related animals or plants. **11** part used as a support or handle; part to which other parts are attached: *the wooden stock of a rifle.* **12** raw material: *Rags are used as a stock for making paper.* **13** water in which meat or fish has been cooked, used as a base for soups, sauces, etc. **14** an old-fashioned stiff necktie, used in place of the modern collar and tie. **15** something lifeless and stupid: *"You stocks and stones!"* **16** trunk or stump of a tree; main stem of a plant. **17** stem in which a graft is inserted. **18** furnish

the stocks
(def. 19)

with livestock: *stock a farm.* **19 the stocks,** an old instrument of punishment consisting of a heavy wooden frame with holes to put a person's feet and sometimes his hands through. 1,2,8-17,19 *n.,* 3-5,18 *v.,* 6,7 *adj.*

in stock, ready for use or sale; on hand.

out of stock, no longer on hand; lacking.

take stock, 1 find out how much stock one has on hand. **2** make an estimate or examination.

take stock in, INFORMAL. take an interest in; consider important; trust: *He took little stock in the story.*

stockade
(def. 1)

stock ade (sto kād′), **1** a defensive pen or barrier made of large, strong posts fixed upright in the ground: *A heavy stockade around the cabins protected the pioneers from attack.* **2** protect, fortify, or surround with a stockade. **1** *n.,* **2** *v.,* **stock ad ed, stock ad ing.**

stock bro ker (stok′brō′kər), person who buys and sells stocks and bonds for others for a commission. *n.*

stock company, 1 company whose capital is divided into shares. **2** a theatrical company employed more or less permanently under the same management, usually at one theater, to perform many different plays.

stock exchange, 1 place where stocks and bonds are bought and sold. **2** association of brokers and dealers in stocks and bonds.

stock hold er (stok′hōl′dər), owner of stocks or shares in a company. *n.*

Stock holm (stok′hōm *or* stok′hōlm), seaport and capital of Sweden, in the SE part. *n.*

stock ing (stok′ing), a close-fitting, knitted covering of wool, cotton, silk, nylon, etc., for the foot and leg. *n.*

stocking cap, a close-fitting, knitted cap with a long, pointed end that falls over the back or shoulder, worn for skiing, sledding, etc.

stock man (stok′mən), man who raises livestock. *n., pl.* **stock men.**

stock market, 1 place where stocks and bonds are bought and sold; stock exchange. **2** the buying and selling in such a place. **3** prices of stocks and bonds.

stock pile (stok′pīl′), **1** a supply of raw materials, essential items, etc., built up and held in reserve for use during a time of emergency or shortage. **2** such a reserve of weapons for warfare. **3** collect or bring together a stockpile. **1,2** *n.,* **3** *v.,* **stock piled, stock pil ing.**

stock room (stok′rüm′ *or* stok′-rům′), room where a stock is kept. *n.*

stock-still (stok′stil′), motionless. *adj.*

stock y (stok′ē), having a solid or sturdy form or build; thick for its height: *a stocky little child, a stocky building. adj.,* **stock i er, stock i est.**

stock yard (stok′yärd′), place with pens and sheds for cattle, sheep, hogs, and horses. A stockyard is often connected with a slaughterhouse, railroad, or market. *n.*

stodg y (stoj′ē), **1** dull or uninteresting; tediously commonplace: *a stodgy book.* **2** heavy: *stodgy food.* **3** stuffed full: *a stodgy bag. adj.,* **stodg i er, stodg i est.**

sto gie *or* **sto gy** (stō′gē), a long, slender, cheap cigar. *n., pl.* **sto gies.**

sto ic (stō′ik), **1** person who remains calm, represses his feelings, and is indifferent to pleasure and pain. **2** stoical. **1** *n.,* **2** *adj.*

sto i cal (stō′ə kəl), like a stoic; self-controlled; indifferent to pleasure and pain. *adj.* —**sto′i cal ly,** *adv.*

sto i cism (stō′ə siz′əm), patient endurance; indifference to pleasure and pain. *n.*

stoke (stōk), **1** stir up and feed (a fire); tend the fire of (a furnace). **2** tend a fire. *v.,* **stoked, stok ing.**

stoke hold (stōk′hōld′), place in a steamship where the furnaces and boilers are. *n.*

stoke hole (stōk′hōl′), **1** hole through which fuel is put into a furnace. **2** space in front of furnaces where men shovel in coal and take out ashes. *n.*

stok er (stō′kər), **1** worker who tends the fires of a furnace or boiler. **2** a mechanical device for putting coal in a furnace. *n.*

stole[1] (stōl), past tense of **steal.** *I stole some money years ago. v.*

stole[2] (stōl), **1** a narrow strip of silk or other material worn over the shoulders by a clergyman during certain church

stone

hat, āge, fär; let, ēqual, tėrm;
it, īce; hot, ōpen, ôrder;
oil, out; cup, půt, rüle; ch, child;
ng, long; sh, she; th, thin;
ŦH, then; zh, measure;

ə represents *a* in about,
e in taken, *i* in pencil,
o in lemon, *u* in circus.

functions. **2** a woman's collar or scarf of fur or cloth with ends hanging down in front. *n.* [Old English, from Latin *stola,* from Greek *stole* garment, equipment]

sto len (stō′lən), past participle of **steal.** *The money was not stolen; it was lost. v.*

stol id (stol′id), hard to arouse, not easily excited; showing no emotion; seeming dull. *adj.* —**stol′id ly,** *adv.*

sto lid i ty (stə lid′ə tē), stolid quality or condition. *n., pl.* **sto lid i ties.**

STOLON

sto lon (stō′lon), a slender branch that takes root at the tip or at a node and grows into a new plant. *n.*

sto ma (stō′mə), a small opening or pore in a plant or animal. A leaf contains many stomata which let water and gases in and out of the plant. *n., pl.* **sto ma ta** *or* **sto mas.**

stom ach (stum′ək), **1** the large muscular bag in the body which first receives the food, and digests some of it before passing it on to the intestines. **2** the part of the body containing the stomach; abdomen; belly: *I was hit in the stomach.* **3** appetite. **4** put up with; bear; endure: *She could not stomach such insults.* **5** desire; liking: *I have no stomach for killing harmless creatures.* **1-3,5** *n.,* **4** *v.*

stom ach er (stum′ə kər), an ornamental covering for the stomach and chest, formerly worn by women under the lacing of the bodice. *n.*

sto ma ta (stō′mə tə *or* stom′ə tə), a plural of **stoma.** *n.*

stomp (stomp), **1** to stamp with the foot. **2** a stomping. **1** *v.,* **2** *n.*

stone (stōn), **1** the hard, mineral material of which rocks consist; hard matter

Stone Age

that is not metal. Stone, such as granite and marble, is much used in building. 2 a small piece of rock: *They threw stones into the pond.* 3 piece of rock of definite size, shape, etc., used for a particular purpose: *His grave is marked by a fine stone.* 4 made of stone: *a stone wall, a stone house.* 5 having to do with stone. 6 put stone on; line with stone. 7 gem; jewel: *The queen's diamonds were very fine stones.* 8 something hard and rounded like a stone, which sometimes forms in the kidneys or gall bladder, causing sickness and pain. 9 throw stones at; drive by throwing stones. 10 kill by throwing stones: *The martyr was stoned as a heretic.* 11 a hard seed: *peach stones, plum stones.* 12 take stones or seeds out of: *to stone cherries or plums.* 13 made of stoneware or coarse clay. 14 a British measure of weight equal to 14 pounds. 1-3,7,8,11,14 *n., pl.* **stones** (but **stone** for 14); 4,5,13 *adj.,* 6,9,10,12 *v.,* **stoned, ston ing. —stone/like/,** *adj.*

Stone Age, the earliest known period of human culture, in which people used tools and weapons made from stone. It was followed by the Bronze Age.

stone-blind (stōn/blīnd/), totally blind. *adj.*

stone cut ter (stōn/kut/ər), 1 person who cuts or carves stones. 2 machine for cutting or dressing stone. *n.*

stone-deaf (stōn/def/), totally deaf. *adj.*

Stone henge (stōn/henj), a prehistoric ruin in southern England, consisting of huge slabs of roughly shaped stone in a circular arrangement. It may have been a kind of observatory used by astronomers. *n.*

stone ma son (stōn/mā/sn), person who cuts stone or builds walls, etc., of stone. *n.*

stone's throw, a short distance: *We live only a stone's throw from the school.*

stone ware (stōn/wer/ or stōn/war/), a coarse, hard, glazed pottery. *n.*

stone work (stōn/wèrk/), 1 wall, foundation, or other structure made of stone. 2 the part of a building made of stone. *n.*

ston i ly (stō/nə lē), in a stony manner; stiffly; harshly; coldly. *adv.*

ston y (stō/nē), 1 having many stones: *The beach is stony.* 2 hard like stone: *A cruel person has a stony heart.* 3 without expression or feeling: *a stony stare.* *adj.,* **ston i er, ston i est.**

stood (stůd), past tense and past participle of **stand.** *He stood in the corner for five minutes. I had stood in line all morning to buy tickets to the game.* *v.*

stooge (stüj), SLANG. 1 person on the stage who asks questions of a comedian and is the butt of the comedian's jokes. 2 person who follows and flatters another; hanger-on. *n.*

stool (stül), 1 seat without back or arms. 2 a similar article used to rest the feet on, or to kneel on. *n.* **—stool/like/,** *adj.*

stool pigeon, SLANG. a spy for the police; informer.

stoop[1] (stüp), 1 bend forward: *He stooped to pick up the money. She stoops over her desk.* 2 a forward bend: *My uncle walks with a stoop.* 3 carry head and shoulders bent forward: *The old man stoops.* 4 a forward bend of the head and shoulders. 5 lower oneself; descend: *He stooped to cheating.* 6 condescension. 1,3,5 *v.,* 2,4,6 *n.* [Old English *stūpian*]

stoop[2] (stüp), a porch or platform at the entrance of a house. *n.* [from Dutch *stoep*]

stop (stop), 1 keep from moving, acting, doing, being, working, etc.: *I stopped the children from teasing the cat. I stopped the clock.* 2 put an end to; interrupt; check: *stop a noise.* 3 stay; halt: *She stopped at the bank for a few minutes.* 4 leave off (moving, acting, doing, being, etc.); come to an end; cease: *The baby stopped crying. The rain is stopping.* 5 close (a hole or opening) by filling (it): *I will stop the rats' holes.* 6 close (a vessel) with a cork, plug, or the like; shut up (something) in a closed vessel or place: *stop a bottle.* 7 block (a way); obstruct: *A big box stops up the doorway.* 8 act of stopping; closing; filling up; blocking; hindering; checking; halting; cessation; stay: *Her sudden stop startled us. The singing came to a stop.* 9 a being stopped. 10 place where a stop is made: *a bus stop.* 11 thing that stops, such as a block, plug, etc.; obstacle. 12 a punctuation mark. The most used stops are ? ! . , ; : —. 13 a device that controls the pitch of a musical instrument. 14 (in organs) a graduated set of pipes of the same kind, or the knob or handle that controls them. 15 any piece or device that serves to check or control movement or action in a mechanism. 1-7 *v.,* **stopped, stop ping;** 8-15 *n.*

stop off, INFORMAL. stop for a short stay.

stop over, 1 make a short stay. 2 IN-FORMAL. stop in the course of a trip.

stop gap (stop/gap/), thing that fills the place of something lacking; a temporary substitute. *n.*

stop light (stop/līt/), 1 a red light on the rear end of a vehicle, that turns on automatically when the brakes are applied. 2 traffic light. *n.*

stop o ver (stop/ō/vər), a stopping over in the course of a journey, especially with the privilege of proceeding later on the ticket originally issued for the journey. *n.*

stop page (stop/ij), 1 act of stopping: *The foreman called for a stoppage of operations to oil the machinery.* 2 condition of being stopped: *During the work stoppage many workers looked for other jobs.* 3 a block; obstruction. *n.*

stop per (stop/ər), 1 plug or cork for closing a bottle, tube, etc. 2 close or fit with a stopper. 1 *n.,* 2 *v.*

stop ple (stop/əl), stopper for a bottle, etc. *n.*

stopt (stopt), OLD USE. stopped; past tense and a past participle of **stop.** *v.*

stop watch (stop/woch/ or stop/-wôch/), watch which has a hand that can be stopped or started at any instant. A stopwatch indicates fractions of a second and is used for timing races and contests. *n., pl.* **stop watch es.**

stor age (stôr/ij), 1 act or fact of storing goods: *The storage of storm windows in summertime.* 2 condition of being stored. Cold storage is used to keep eggs and meat from spoiling. 3 place for storing: *She has put her furniture in storage.* 4 price for storing: *She paid $30 storage on her furniture.* *n.*

storage battery, battery in which chemical energy is converted into direct-current electrical energy. When the cells of the battery have been discharged they may be charged again by passing a current through them in the direction opposite to that of the flow of current when discharging. *Our automobile needs a new storage battery.*

store (stôr), 1 place where goods are kept for sale: *a clothing store.* 2 something put away for use later; supply; stock: *We put up stores of preserves and jellies every year.* 3 to supply or stock. 4 put away for use later; lay up: *The squirrel stores away nuts. We stored our furs during the summer.* 5 place where supplies are kept for future use; storehouse. 6 put in a warehouse or place used for preserving. 7 OLD USE. quantity; abundance. 1,2,5,7 *n.,* 3,4,6 *v.,* **stored, stor ing.**

in store, on hand; in reserve; saved for the future.

set store by, to value; esteem: *She sets great store by her friend's opinions.*

store house (stôr′hous′), 1 place where things are stored; warehouse: *This factory has many storehouses for its products.* 2 person or thing resembling such a place: *A library is a storehouse of information.* n., pl. **store hous es** (stôr′hou′ziz).

store keep er (stôr′kē′pər), person who owns or manages a store or stores. n.

store room (stôr′rüm′ or stôr′rùm′), room where things are stored. n.

sto rey (stôr′ē), story[2]. n., pl. **sto reys.**

sto ried[1] (stôr′ēd), celebrated in story or history: *the storied Wild West.* adj. [story[1] + -ed[2]]

sto ried[2] (stôr′ēd), having stories or floors: *a storied tower, a two-storied house.* adj. [story[2] + -ed[2]]

stork
about 3 ft. high

stork (stôrk), a large, long-legged wading bird with a long neck and a long bill. Storks are found in most warm parts of the world. n. **—stork′like′,** adj.

storm (stôrm), 1 a strong wind often accompanied by rain, snow, hail, or thunder and lightning. A storm blows with a velocity of 64 to 72 miles per hour. In deserts there are storms of sand. 2 a heavy fall of rain, snow, or hail. 3 blow hard; rain; snow; hail. 4 anything like a storm: *a storm of arrows.* 5 a violent outburst or disturbance: *a storm of tears, a storm of angry words.* 6 be violent; rage. 7 rush violently: *He stormed out of the room.* 8 attack violently: *The troops stormed the city.* 9 a violent attack: *The castle was taken by storm.* 1,2,4,5,9 n., 3,6-8 v.

storm cellar, cellar for shelter during cyclones, tornadoes, etc.

storm center, 1 center of a cyclone, where there is very low air pressure and comparative calm. 2 any center of trouble, tumult, etc.

storm door, an extra door outside of an ordinary door, to keep out snow, cold winds, etc.

storm i ly (stôr′mə lē), in a stormy manner. adv.

storm i ness (stôr′mē nis), condition of being stormy. n.

storm petrel, any of several small,

black-and-white petrels, whose presence is supposed to give warning of a storm. See **petrel** for picture. Also, **stormy petrel.**

storm window, an extra window outside of an ordinary window, to keep out snow, cold winds, etc.

storm y (stôr′mē), 1 having storms; likely to have storms; troubled by storms: *a stormy sea, stormy weather, a stormy night.* 2 rough and disturbed; violent: *They had stormy quarrels.* adj., **storm i er, storm i est.**

stormy petrel, storm petrel.

sto ry[1] (stôr′ē), 1 an account of some happening or group of happenings: *Tell us the story of your life.* 2 such an account, either true or made up, intended to interest the reader or hearer; tale: *fairy stories, stories of adventure.* 3 INFORMAL. falsehood: *That's not true; you're telling stories.* n., pl. **sto ries.** [from French of the 1200's *estorie*, from Latin *historia* history, from Greek]

sto ry[2] (stôr′ē), set of rooms on the same level or floor of a building; one of the structural divisions in the height of a building: *That house has two stories.* n., pl. **stories.** Also, **storey.** [perhaps a special use of *story*[1] in the earlier sense of "row of historical statues across a building front"]

sto ry book (stôr′ē bùk′), 1 book containing one or more stories or tales, especially for children. 2 of or like that of a storybook; romantic; fictional: *a storybook hero, a storybook ending.* 1 n., 2 adj.

sto ry tell er (stôr′ē tel′ər), person who tells stories. n.

sto ry tell ing (stôr′ē tel′ing), 1 act or art of telling stories. 2 that tells stories. 1 n., 2 adj.

stoup (stüp), 1 a cup, flagon, tankard, or other drinking vessel. 2 amount it holds. 3 basin for holy water at the entrance to a church. n.

straddle (def. 3)
man straddling
a chair

stout (stout), 1 fat and large: *That boy could run faster if he weren't so stout.* 2 strongly built; firm; strong: *The fort has stout walls.* 3 brave; bold: *Robin Hood was a stout fellow.* 4 not yielding; stubborn: *stout resistance.* 5 a strong, dark-brown beer. 1-4 adj., 5 n.

hat, āge, fär; let, ēqual, tėrm; it, īce; hot, ōpen, ôrder; oil, out; cup, pùt, rüle; ch, child; ng, long; sh, she; th, thin; ᵺH, then; zh, measure;

ə represents *a* in about, *e* in taken, *i* in pencil, *o* in lemon, *u* in circus.

—stout′ly, adv. **—stout′ness,** n.

stout heart ed (stout′här′tid), having courage; brave; bold. adj. **—stout′-heart′ed ly,** adv.

stove[1] (stōv), apparatus for cooking and heating. There are wood, coal, gas, oil, and electric stoves. n. [probably from Dutch of the 1400's *stove* hot room, related to Old English *stofa* warm bathing room]

stove[2] (stōv), staved; a past tense and a past participle of **stave.** v.

stove pipe (stōv′pīp′), 1 a metal pipe that carries smoke and gases from a stove to a chimney. 2 INFORMAL. a tall silk hat. n.

stow (stō), 1 pack: *stow books in a trunk. The cargo was stowed in the ship's hold.* 2 pack things closely in; fill by packing: *stow a pantry with cans of food.* v.

stow away, hide on a ship, airplane, etc., to get a free passage or to escape secretly.

stow a way (stō′ə wā′), person who hides on a ship, train, etc., to get a free passage or to escape secretly. n.

Stowe (stō), Harriet Beecher, 1811-1896, American writer, author of *Uncle Tom's Cabin.* n.

St. Paul, capital of Minnesota, in the SE part, on the Mississippi River.

St. Pe ters burg (sānt pē′tərz bėrg′), 1 former capital of Russia, now called **Leningrad.** 2 city in W Florida.

strad dle (strad′l), 1 walk, stand, or sit with the legs wide apart. 2 spread (the legs) wide apart. 3 have a leg on each side of (a horse, bicycle, chair, ditch, etc.). 4 stand or lie across; be on both sides of: *A pair of field glasses straddled his nose.* 5 INFORMAL. avoid taking sides; attempt to favor both sides (of a question, etc.): *All three political candidates straddled on the tariff issue.* 6 a straddling. 1-5 v., **strad dled, strad dling;** 6 n.

strad dler (strad′lər), person or thing that straddles. n.

Strad i var i (strad′ə vär′ē), **Antonio,** 1644?-1737, Italian violin maker. His violins are famous for their beautiful tone and design. n.

adj. adjective	*n.* noun
adv. adverb	*prep.* preposition
conj. conjunction	*pron.* pronoun
interj. interjection	*v.* verb
sing. singular	*pl.* plural

Strad i var i us (strad/ə ver/ē əs), violin, viola, or cello made by Stradivari. *n.*

strafe (strāf), **1** (of aircraft) to fly low over enemy positions and attack with machine gun fire: *strafe a line of soldiers, strafe the deck of a ship.* **2** to shell or bombard heavily. *v.,* **strafed, strafing.**

strag gle (strag/əl), **1** wander in a scattered fashion: *Cows straggled along the lane.* **2** stray from the rest. **3** spread in an irregular, rambling manner: *Vines straggled over the yard. It was a straggling little town. v.,* **strag gled, straggling.**

strag gler (strag/lər), person or thing that straggles. *n.*

strag gly (strag/lē), spread out in an irregular, rambling way; straggling. *adj.*

straight (strāt), **1** without a bend or curve; not crooked or irregular: *a straight line, a straight path, a straight nose, straight hair.* **2** in a line; directly: *Walk straight. He went straight home.* **3** going in a line; direct: *a straight course, a straight aim or throw.* **4** frank; honest; upright: *straight conduct, a straight answer.* **5** frankly; honestly; uprightly: *Live straight.* **6** right; correct: *straight thinking, a straight thinker.* **7** in proper order or condition: *Keep your accounts straight. Set the room straight.* **8** showing no emotion, humor, etc.: *I kept a straight face, though I wanted to laugh.* **9** thoroughgoing or unreserved: *to vote a straight Republican ticket.* 1,3, 4,6-9 *adj.,* 2,5 *adv.* —**straight/ness,** *n.*

straight away or **straight off,** at once.

straight angle—ABC is a straight angle.

straight angle, angle of 180 degrees.

straight a way (strāt/ə wā/), **1** a straight course. **2** in a straight course. **3** straightway. 1 *n.,* 2 *adj.,* 3 *adv.*

straight edge (strāt/ej/), strip of wood or metal having one edge accurately straight, used in obtaining or testing straight lines and level surfaces. *n.*

straight en (strāt/n), **1** make straight: *He straightened the bent pin. Straighten your shoulders.* **2** become straight. **3** put in the proper order or condition: *Straighten up your room. We must straighten out our accounts and see how much we owe each other. v.* —**straight/en er,** *n.*

straight for ward (strāt/fôr/wərd), **1** honest; frank: *a straightforward answer.* **2** going straight ahead; direct. **3** directly. 1,2 *adj.,* 3 *adv.* —**straight/for/ward ly,** *adv.* —**straight/for/ward ness,** *n.*

straight way (strāt/wā/), at once; immediately: *The captain read the letter and burned it straightway. adv.*

strain¹ (strān), **1** draw tight; stretch: *The weight strained the rope.* **2** pull hard: *The dog strained at its leash.* **3** force or weight that stretches: *The strain on the rope made it break.* **4** stretch as much as possible: *She strained the truth in telling the story.* **5** use to the utmost: *He strained every muscle to lift the rock. She strained her eyes to see.* **6** injure by too much effort or by stretching: *I strained a muscle.* **7** injury caused by too much effort or by stretching: *The injury to his back was only a slight strain.* **8** any severe, trying, or wearing pressure: *the strain of worry. The strain of sleepless nights made her ill.* **9** effect of such pressure on the body or mind. **10** make a very great effort. **11** press or pour through a strainer: *Strain the soup before serving it. Babies eat strained foods.* **12** press closely; squeeze; hug: *She strained her child to her breast.* **13** part of a piece of music; melody; song. **14** manner or style of doing or speaking: *a playful strain, a poem in a melancholy strain.* 1,2,4-6,10-12 *v.,* 3,7-9,13,14 *n.* [from French of the 1200's *estreindre* bind tightly, from Latin *stringere* draw tight]

strain² (strān), **1** line of descent; race; stock: *My friend is of Spanish strain.* **2** group of animals or plants that form a part of a breed, race, or variety, and are distinguished from other members of the group by some feature. **3** an inherited quality: *There is a strain of musical talent in that family.* **4** trace or streak: *That horse has a mean strain.* n. [Old English *strēon* a gain, a begetting]

strained (strānd), forced; not natural: *Her greeting was cold and strained. adj.*

strain er (strā/nər), thing that strains. A filter, a sieve, and a colander are strainers. *n.*

strait (strāt), **1** a narrow channel connecting two larger bodies of water: *The Strait of Gibraltar connects the Mediterranean Sea and the Atlantic Ocean.* **2** OLD USE. narrow; limited; confining.

3 straits, *pl.* difficulty; need; distress: *be in desperate straits for money.* 1,3 *n.,* 2 *adj.*

strait en (strāt/n), limit by the lack of something; restrict. *v.*

in straitened circumstances, needing money badly.

strait jack et (strāt/jak/it), a strong, tight jacket or coat that binds the arms close to the sides. It keeps a violent person from harming himself or others.

strait-laced (strāt/lāst/), very strict in matters of conduct; prudish. *adj.*

strand¹ (strand), **1** bring or come into a helpless position: *She was stranded a thousand miles from home with no money.* **2** run aground; drive on the shore: *The ship was stranded on the rocks.* **3** shore; land bordering a sea, lake, or river. 1,2 *v.,* 3 *n.* [Old English]

strand² (strand), **1** one of the threads, strings, or wires that are twisted together to make a rope or cable: *This is a rope of three strands.* **2** thread or string: *a strand of pearls, a strand of hair. n.* [origin unknown]

strange (strānj), **1** unusual; queer; peculiar: *a strange accident, a strange experience. There was a strange quiet throughout the city.* **2** not known, seen, or heard of before; not familiar: *She is moving to a strange place. A strange cat is on our steps.* **3** not used to: *He is strange to the work but will soon learn.* **4** out of place; not at home: *The poor child felt strange in the palace. adj.,* **strang er, strang est.** —**strange/ly,** *adv.* —**strange/ness,** *n.*

stran ger (strān/jər), **1** person not known, seen, or heard of before: *She is a stranger to us.* **2** person or thing new to a place: *He is a stranger in New York.* **3** person who is out of place or not at home in something: *He is no stranger to hard work.* **4** person from another country: *The king received the strangers with kindness. n.*

stran gle (strang/gəl), **1** kill by squeezing the throat to stop the breath. **2** choke: *His high collar seemed to be strangling him. She almost strangled on a piece of meat that caught in her throat.* **3** choke down; suppress; keep back: *He strangled an impulse to cough. v.,* **stran gled, stran gling.**

stran gler (strang/glər), person or thing that strangles. *n.*

stran gu la tion (strang/gyə lā/shən), a strangling or a being strangled. *n.*

strap (strap), **1** a narrow strip of leather or other material that bends easily: *She has a strap around her books. Put a strap around the trunk.* **2** a narrow band or strip of cloth: *The general wore shoulder straps.* **3** a narrow strip for fastening things, holding things together, etc.: *The box was strengthened by straps of steel.* 4 fasten with a strap: *We strapped the trunk.* 5 beat with a strap. 6 a strop. 7 sharpen on a strap or strop. 1–3,6 *n.*, 4,5,7 *v.*, **strapped, strapping.**

strap less (strap′lis), having no strap or straps: *a strapless gown. adj.*

strap ping (strap′ing), INFORMAL. tall, strong, and healthy: *a fine, strapping girl. adj.*

Stras bourg (stras′bėrg′), city in NE France, on the Rhine River. *n.*

stra ta (strā′tə), a plural of **stratum.** *n.*

strat a gem (strat′ə jəm), scheme or trick for deceiving the enemy; trick; trickery: *The spy got into the castle by the stratagem of dressing as a royal guard. n.*

stra te gic (strə tē′jik), 1 of strategy; based on strategy; useful in strategy: *a strategic retreat.* 2 important in strategy: *The Panama Canal is a strategic link in our national defense. adj.* —**stra te′gi cal ly,** *adv.*

strat e gist (strat′ə jist), person trained or skilled in strategy: *a military strategist, a chess strategist, a football strategist. n.*

strat e gy (strat′ə jē), 1 science or art of war; planning and directing of large-scale military movements and operations. 2 the skillful planning and management of anything. 3 plan based on strategy: *We need some strategy to win this game. n., pl.* **strat e gies.**

Strat ford-on-A von (strat′fərd on ā′vən), town in central England on the Avon River. It is Shakespeare's birthplace and burial place. *n.*

strat i fi ca tion (strat′ə fə kā′shən), arrangement in layers or strata: *the stratification of society. n.*

strat i fy (strat′ə fī), arrange in layers or strata; form into layers or strata. *v.,* **strat i fied, strat i fy ing.**

strat o sphere (strat′ə sfir *or* strā′tə sfir), region of the atmosphere between the troposphere and the mesosphere, which begins about 10 miles above the earth. In the stratosphere, temperature varies little with changes in altitude, and the winds are chiefly horizontal. *n.*

strat o spher ic (strat′ə sfir′ik *or* strat′ə sfer′ik), of or having to do with the stratosphere. *adj.*

stra tum (strā′təm), 1 layer of material; especially, one of several parallel layers placed one upon another: *In digging the well, they first struck a stratum of sand, then several strata of rock.* 2 social level: *rise from a low stratum to a high stratum of society. n., pl.* **stra ta** *or* **stra tums.**

stra tus (strā′təs), a low, horizontal layer of gray cloud that spreads over a large area. *n., pl.* **stra ti** (strā′tī).

Strauss (strous), 1 **Johann,** 1804-1849, Austrian composer of dance music. 2 his son, **Johann,** 1825-1899, Austrian composer of dance music and light operas. 3 **Richard,** 1864-1949, German composer and conductor. *n.*

Stra vin sky (strə vin′skē), **Igor,** 1882-1971, American composer, born in Russia. *n.*

straw (strô), 1 the stalks or stems of grain after drying and threshing. Straw is used as bedding for horses and cows, for making hats, and for many other purposes. 2 one such stem or stalk. 3 tube made of waxed paper, plastic, or glass, used for sucking up drinks. 4 made of straw: *a straw hat.* 5 bit; trifle: *He doesn't care a straw.* 1–3,5 *n.,* 4 *adj.*

straw ber ry (strô′ber′ē), 1 a small, juicy, red fruit that is good to eat. It has many tiny, dry, yellow seeds on the skin. 2 plant that it grows on. *n., pl.* **straw ber ries.**

straw vote, an unofficial vote taken to find out general opinion.

stray (strā), 1 lose one's way; wander; roam: *Our dog has strayed off somewhere.* 2 wandering; lost: *A stray cat is crying at the door.* 3 wanderer; lost animal: *The cat is a stray that we took in.* 4 turn from the right course; go wrong. 5 scattered; here and there: *stray thoughts. There were a few stray cabins along the beach.* 1,4 *v.,* 2,5 *adj.,* 3 *n.* —**stray′er,** *n.*

streak (strēk), 1 a long, thin mark or line: *a streak of dirt on one's face. We saw a streak of lightning.* 2 layer: *Bacon has streaks of fat and streaks of lean.* 3 vein; strain; element: *He has a streak of humor, though he looks very serious.* 4 put long, thin marks or lines on: *The children streaked their faces with water colors.* 5 INFORMAL. a brief period; spell: *a streak of luck.* 6 INFORMAL. move very fast; go at full speed: *She streaked past the others and over the finish line.* 1–3,5 *n.,* 4,6 *v.*

like a streak, INFORMAL. very fast; at full speed: *When the dog saw its master it ran like a streak across the lawn to greet him.*

streak y (strē′kē), 1 marked with

strata (def. 1)

hat, āge, fär; let, ēqual, tėrm; it, īce; hot, ōpen, ôrder; oil, out; cup, pùt, rüle; ch, child; ng, long; sh, she; th, thin; ŦH, then; zh, measure;

ə represents *a* in about, *e* in taken, *i* in pencil, *o* in lemon, *u* in circus.

streaks. 2 occurring in streaks. 3 varying; uneven: *The dress has faded so much that the color is streaky. adj.,* **streak i er, streak i est.**

stream (strēm), 1 flow of water in a channel or bed. Small rivers and large brooks are both called streams. *Because of the lack of rain many streams dried up.* 2 any steady flow: *a stream of words, a stream of light, a stream of cars.* 3 to flow: *Tears streamed from her eyes.* 4 move steadily; move swiftly: *People streamed out of the theater.* 5 pour out: *The gash in his arm streamed blood.* 6 be so wet as to drip in a stream: *streaming eyes, a streaming umbrella.* 7 float or wave: *Flags streamed in the wind.* 1,2 *n.,* 3-7 *v.* —**stream′like′,** *adj.*

stream er (strē′mər), 1 any long, narrow, flowing thing: *Streamers of ribbon hung from the new boat.* 2 a long, narrow flag. *n.*

stream let (strēm′lit), a small stream. *n.*

stream line (strēm′līn′), 1 streamlined. 2 give a streamlined shape to. 3 bring up to date; make more efficient: *streamline an office.* 1 *adj.,* 2, 3 *v.,* **stream lined, stream lin ing.**

streamlined (def. 1)—streamlined bodies of racing car, submarine, and jet plane.

stream lined (strēm′līnd′), 1 having a shape that offers the least possible resistance to air or water. The fastest automobiles, airplanes, and trains have streamlined bodies. 2 brought up to date; made more efficient: *streamlined methods of production, a streamlined organization. adj.*

street (strēt), 1 road in a city or town, usually with buildings on both sides. 2 place or way for automobiles, wag-

adj. adjective	*n.* noun
adv. adverb	*prep.* preposition
conj. conjunction	*pron.* pronoun
interj. interjection	*v.* verb
sing. singular	*pl.* plural

ons, etc., to go: *Be careful in crossing the street.* 3 people who live in the buildings on a street: *The whole street planted new trees. n.*

street car (strēt/kär/), car that runs on rails in the streets and carries passengers; trolley car. *n.*

street piano, a small mechanical piano set on wheels and played by turning a handle.

strength (strengkth), 1 quality of being strong; power; force; vigor: *Because of his strength he could lift great weights. I did not have enough strength of mind to refuse. The strength of the dog's love for its master is well known.* 2 power to resist or endure: *the strength of a fort, the strength of a rope.* 3 military force measured in numbers of soldiers, warships, etc.: *an army at full strength.* 4 degree of strength; intensity: *the strength of a beverage, the strength of a sound. Some flavorings lose their strength in cooking.* 5 something that makes strong; support: *During those hard times, my friends were my refuge and strength. n.*

on the strength of, relying or depending on; with the support or help of: *They bought the dog on the strength of the children's promise to take care of it.*

strength en (strengk/thən), 1 make stronger: *Daily exercise strengthened my muscles.* 2 grow stronger. *v.* —**strength/en er,** *n.*

stren u ous (stren/yü əs), 1 very active: *We had a strenuous day moving into our new house.* 2 full of energy: *Beavers are strenuous workers.* 3 requiring much energy: *Running is strenuous exercise. adj.* —**stren/u ous ly,** *adv.* —**stren/u ous ness,** *n.*

strep to coc cus (strep/tə kok/əs), any of a group of spherical bacteria that multiply by dividing in only one direction, usually forming chains. Many serious infections and diseases, such as scarlet fever and erysipelas, are caused by streptococci. *n., pl.* **strep to coc ci** (strep/tə kok/sī).

strep to my cin (strep/tō mī/sn), a powerful antibiotic similar to penicillin, effective against tuberculosis, typhoid fever, and certain other bacterial infections. *n.*

stress (stres), 1 great pressure or force;

strain: *the stress of war. Under the stress of hunger the runaway stole some food.* 2 put pressure upon. 3 great effort. 4 emphasis; importance: *Our teacher lays stress upon punctuation and spelling.* 5 treat as important; emphasize: *Stress the important words of a sentence.* 6 the relative loudness in the pronunciation of syllables, words in a sentence, etc.; accent: *In "hero," the stress is on the first syllable.* 7 pronounce with stress: *"Accept" is stressed on the second syllable.* 1,3,4,6 *n., pl.* **stress es;** 2,5,7 *v.*

stress ful (stres/fəl), full of stress; subject to strain: *stressful conditions. adj.*

stretch (strech), 1 draw out; extend (one's body, arms, legs, wings, etc.) to full length: *The bird stretched its wings. She stretched herself out on the grass to rest.* 2 extend one's body or limbs: *I stretched out on the couch.* 3 continue over a distance; extend from one place to another; fill space; spread: *The forest stretches for miles. She stretched the hammock from a tree to a pole.* 4 reach out; hold out: *I stretched out my hand for the money.* 5 draw out to greater size: *Stretch the shoe a little.* 6 become longer or wider without breaking: *Rubber stretches.* 7 draw tight; strain: *stretch a guitar string until it breaks.* 8 extend beyond proper limits: *They stretched the law to suit their own purpose.* 9 INFORMAL. exaggerate: *stretch the truth.* 10 an unbroken length; extent: *A stretch of sand hills lay between the road and the ocean.* 11 a stretching or a being stretched: *With a sudden stretch he took the cap off the tall boy's head.* 12 capacity for being stretched; extent to which something can be stretched: *The stretch of that bird's wings is two feet.* 1-9 *v.,* 10-12 *n., pl.* **stretch es.**

stretch er (strech/ər), 1 person or thing that stretches. 2 canvas stretched on a frame for carrying the sick, wounded, or dead. *n.*

strew (strü), 1 scatter or sprinkle: *She strewed seeds in her garden.* 2 cover with something scattered or sprinkled: *The ground was strewn with leaves. v.,* **strewed, strewed** or **strewn, strewing.**

strewn (strün), strewed; a past participle of **strew.** *v.*

stri at ed (strī/ā tid), striped; streaked; furrowed. *adj.*

stri a tion (strī ā/shən), striated condition or appearance. *n.*

strick en (strik/ən), 1 hit, wounded, or affected by (a weapon, disease, trouble, sorrow, etc.): *a stricken deer. They fled from the stricken city. The stricken man was taken immediately to a hos-*

pital. 2 struck; a past participle of **strike.** 1 *adj.,* 2 *v.*

stricken in years, old.

strict (strikt), 1 very careful in following a rule or in making others follow it: *The teacher was strict but fair.* 2 harsh; severe: *a strict parent, strict discipline.* 3 exact; precise; accurate: *She told the strict truth.* 4 perfect; complete; absolute: *The secret was told in strict confidence. adj.* —**strict/ly,** *adv.* —**strict/ness,** *n.*

stric ture (strik/chər), 1 an unfavorable criticism; critical remark. 2 an unhealthy narrowing of some duct or tube of the body. 3 a binding restriction. *n.*

strid den (strid/n), past participle of **stride.** *She had stridden away angrily. v.*

stride (strīd), 1 walk with long steps: *She strides rapidly, as though always late. I strode the halls of the building, looking for the exit.* 2 pass with one long step: *She strode over the brook.* 3 a long step: *The child could not keep up with his father's stride.* 4 distance covered by a stride. 5 sit or stand with one leg on each side of: *stride a fence.* 1,2,5 *v.,* **strode, strid den, strid ing;** 3, 4 *n.*

hit one's stride, reach one's regular speed or normal activity.

take in one's stride, deal with in one's normal activity; do or take without difficulty, hesitation, or special effort.

stri dence (strīd/ns), a being strident. *n.*

stri den cy (strīd/n sē), stridence. *n.*

stri dent (strīd/nt), making or having a harsh sound; creaking; grating; shrill. *adj.* —**stri/dent ly,** *adv.*

strife (strīf), 1 a quarreling; fighting: *bitter strife between rivals.* 2 a quarrel; fight: *to find out the cause of a strife. n.*

strike (strīk), 1 hit: *strike a person in anger. Lightning struck the barn. The car struck a fence.* 2 give forth or out; deal: *strike a blow in self-defense.* 3 make by stamping, printing, etc.: *They will strike a medal in memory of the great victory.* 4 set or be set on fire by hitting or rubbing: *strike a match. The match wouldn't strike.* 5 have a strong effect on the mind or feeling of; impress: *The plan strikes me as silly.* 6 to sound: *The clock strikes twelve times at noon. This clock strikes the hour and the half hour.* 7 affect deeply; influence; overcome (by death, disease, suffering, fear, etc.): *They were struck with terror. The town was struck with a flu epidemic.* 8 to attack: *The enemy will strike at dawn. They struck the town by surprise.* 9 an attack: *a strike by bombers on a target.* 10 occur to: *An amusing thought struck her.* 11 find or come upon (ore, oil, water, etc.): *After years of prospecting, the old man finally struck gold.* **12** act or fact of finding rich ore in mining, oil in boring, etc.; sudden success: *He made a rich strike in the Yukon.* **13** stop work to get better pay, shorter hours, etc.: *The coal miners struck when the company refused to improve safety conditions in the mines.* **14** such a stopping of work: *The workers were home for six weeks during the strike last year.* **15** cross; rub: *Strike out the last word. Strike her name off the list.* **16** go; advance: *We struck into a gallop. We walked along the road a mile, then struck out across the fields.* **17** assume: *strike an amusing pose.* **18** send roots or take root: *Oaks strike deep.* **19** make; decide; enter upon: *The employer and the workers have struck an agreement.* **20** lower or take down (a sail, flag, tent, etc.): *The ship struck her flag as a sign of surrender.* **21** a striking. **22** (in baseball) failure of the batter to swing at a pitch in the strike zone, to hit a pitched ball at which he swings, or to hit a pitched ball into fair territory under the rules of the game. After three strikes, a batter is out. **23** (in bowling) an upsetting of all the pins with the first ball bowled. 1-8,10,11,13,15-20 *v.*, **struck, struck** or **strick en, striking;** 9,12,14,21-23 *n.*

on strike, stopping work to get more pay, shorter hours, etc.: *Most of the workers voted to go on strike.*

strike it rich, INFORMAL. **1** find rich ore, oil, etc. **2** have a sudden or unexpected great success.

strike out, 1 cross out; rub out. **2** (in baseball) put out or be put out by three strikes: *The batter struck out. The pitcher struck out six batters.*

strike up, begin: *The two girls struck up a friendship.*

strike break er (strīk′brā′kər), person who helps to break up a strike of workers by taking a striker's job or by furnishing persons who will do so. *n.*

strike break ing (strīk′brā′king), forceful measures taken to halt a strike. *n.*

strike out (strīk′out′), in baseball: **1** an out caused by three strikes. **2** a striking out. *n.*

strik er (strī′kər), **1** person or thing that strikes. **2** worker who is on strike: *The union won't accept any settlement that does not greatly improve the working conditions of the strikers.* *n.*

strike zone, (in baseball) zone or area above home plate, between the batter's knees and armpits, through which a pitch must be thrown to be called a strike.

strik ing (strī′king), **1** attracting attention; very noticeable: *a striking per-*

---

formance by an actor. **2** on strike: *The striking miners will soon return to work. adj.*

strik ing ly (strī′king lē), in a way that attracts attention: *strikingly handsome. adv.*

string (string), **1** a thick thread; small cord or wire; very thin rope: *The package is tied with red string.* **2** such a thread with things on it: *She wore a string of beads around her neck.* **3** put on a string: *The child is stringing beads.* **4** a special cord or wire for musical instruments, bows, etc.: *the strings of a violin.* **5** strings, *pl.* violins, cellos, and other stringed instruments. **6** furnish with strings: *He had his tennis racket strung.* **7** anything used for tying: *apron strings.* **8** tie with string or rope; hang with a string or rope: *We dry herbs by stringing them from the rafters in the barn.* **9** extend or stretch from one point to another: *string a cable.* **10** a cordlike part of plants. String beans have little strings connecting the two halves of a pod. **11** remove strings from: *String the beans.* **12** form into a string or strings. **13** number of things in a line or row: *A string of cars came down the street.* **14** INFORMAL. condition; proviso: *an offer with strings attached to it.* 1,2,4,5,7,10,13,14 *n.*, 3,6,8,9,11,12 *v.*, **strung, strung** or **stringed, string ing. —string′like′, adj.**

pull strings, 1 direct the actions of others secretly. **2** use secret influence.

string along, INFORMAL. **1** to fool; hoax. **2** go along (with); agree. **3** believe in or trust completely.

string out, INFORMAL. stretch; extend: *The program was strung out too long.*

string bean, 1 any of various bean plants bearing long, green or yellow pods with smooth, somewhat flat seeds. **2** the pod of any of these plants, eaten as a vegetable.

stringed instrument, a musical instrument having strings, played either with a bow or by plucking. A harp, a violin, and a guitar are stringed instruments.

strin gen cy (strin′jən sē), **1** strictness; severity. **2** tightness; lack of ready money. **3** convincing force: *stringency of an argument. n., pl.* **strin gen cies.**

strin gent (strin′jənt), **1** strict; severe: *stringent laws against speeding.* **2** lacking ready money; tight: *a stringent market for loans.* **3** convincing; forceful: *stringent arguments. adj.* **—strin′gent ly, adv.**

string er (string′ər), **1** person or thing that strings: *stringer of pearls.* **2** a long, horizontal timber in a building, bridge, railroad track, etc. *n.*

---

string i ness (string′ē nis), stringy quality or condition. *n.*

string y (string′ē), **1** like a string or strings. **2** forming strings: *a stringy syrup.* **3** having tough fibers: *stringy meat.* **4** lean and sinewy: *He is a boy of about sixteen, tall and stringy. adj.,* **string i er, string i est.**

strip¹ (strip), **1** make bare or naked; undress. **2** take off the covering of: *The boy stripped the banana by taking off the skin.* **3** remove; pull off: *The birds stripped the fruit from the trees.* **4** rob: *Thieves stripped the house of everything valuable.* **5** take away the titles, rights, etc., of (a person or thing). **6** tear off the teeth of (a gear, etc.). **7** break the thread of (a bolt, nut, etc.). *v.,* **stripped, strip ping.** [Old English *-strīepan*]

strip² (strip), a long, narrow, flat piece (of cloth, paper, bark, etc.). *n.* [apparently a different form of *strip¹*]

stripe¹ (strīp), **1** a long, narrow band of different color, material, etc. The stripes on a uniform show a person's rank. *A tiger has stripes. The American flag has thirteen stripes.* **2** mark with stripes. **3** sort; type: *A man of quite a different stripe.* 1,3 *n.,* 2 *v.,* **striped, strip ing.** [from Dutch *stripe*]

stripe² (strīp), a stroke or lash with a whip. *n.* [probably special use of *stripe¹*]

striped (strīpt *or* strī′pid), having stripes; marked with stripes: *Zebras are striped. adj.*

strip ling (strip′ling), boy just coming into manhood; youth; lad. *n.*

strip per (strip′ər), person or thing that strips. *n.*

strive (strīv), **1** try hard; work hard: *strive for self-control. Strive to succeed.* **2** struggle; fight: *The swimmer strove against the tide. v.,* **strove** or **strived, striv en, striv ing.**

striv en (striv′ən), past participle of **strive.** *She has striven hard to make the business a success. v.*

strode (strōd), past tense of **stride.** *I strode over the ditch. v.*

stroke¹ (strōk), **1** act of striking; blow: *drive in a nail with several strokes of a hammer. The house was hit by a*

stroke

adj. adjective	*n.* noun
adv. adverb	*prep.* preposition
conj. conjunction	*pron.* pronoun
interj. interjection	*v.* verb
sing. singular	*pl.* plural

stroke of lightning. **2** sound made by striking: *the stroke of a bell. We arrived at the stroke of three o'clock.* **3** piece of luck, fortune, etc.: *a stroke of bad luck.* **4** a single complete movement to be made again and again: *He rowed with a strong stroke of the oars. She swims a fast stroke.* **5** movement or mark made by a pen, pencil, brush, etc.: *I write with a heavy down stroke.* **6** a very successful effort; feat: *a stroke of genius.* **7** a single effort; act: *I felt lazy and didn't do a stroke of work all day.* **8** a sudden attack of illness, especially of apoplexy. **9** rower who sets the time for the other oarsmen. **10** be the stroke of: *Who stroked the Yale crew?* 1-9 *n.*, 10 *v.*, **stroked, strok ing.** [related to Old English *strīcan* to strike and *strācian* stroke²]

stroke² (strōk), **1** move the hand gently over: *She stroked the kitten.* **2** a stroking movement: *to brush away the crumbs with one stroke.* 1 *v.*, **stroked, strok ing;** 2 *n.* [Old English *strācian*]

stroll (strōl), **1** take a quiet walk for pleasure; walk. **2** a leisurely walk. **3** go from place to place: *strolling gypsies.* 1,3 *v.*, 2 *n.*

stroll er (strō′lər), **1** wanderer. **2** a strolling player or actor. **3** kind of light baby carriage in which a small child sits erect. *n.*

stroller
(def. 3)

strong (strông), **1** having much force or power: *A strong person can lift heavy things. A strong wind blew down the trees. A strong nation is one that has many able citizens and great resources.* **2** able to last, endure, resist, etc.: *a strong fort, a strong rope.* **3** not easily influenced or changed; firm: *a strong will.* **4** of great force or effectiveness: *strong arguments.* **5** having a certain number: *A group that is 100 strong has*

100 *members.* **6** having a particular quality or property in a high degree: *strong perfume, a strong acid. Strong tea has more flavor than weak tea.* **7** containing much alcohol: *a strong drink.* **8** with force; powerfully; vigorously; in a strong manner. 1-7 *adj.*, **strong er** (strông′gər), **strong est** (strông′gəst); 8 *adv.* —**strong′ly,** *adv.*

strong box (strông′boks′), a strongly made box to hold valuable things: *The diamonds were kept in a strongbox. n., pl.* **strong box es.**

strong hold (strông′hōld′), a strong place; safe place; fort; fortress: *The robbers have a stronghold in the mountains. n.*

stron ti um (stron′shē əm *or* stron′tē əm), a soft, silver-white, metallic element which occurs only in combination with other elements. It is used in making alloys and in fireworks and signal flares. *n.* [from *Strontian,* a mining locality in Scotland where the element was first found]

strontium 90, a radioactive isotope of strontium that occurs in the fallout from a hydrogen-bomb explosion. It is extremely dangerous because it is easily absorbed by the bones and tissues and may eventually replace the calcium in the body.

strop (strop), **1** a leather strap used for sharpening razors. **2** sharpen on a strop. 1 *n.*, 2 *v.*, **stropped, stropping.**

stro phe (strō′fē), group of lines of poetry; stanza. *n.*

strove (strōv), a past tense of **strive.** *They strove hard, but did not win the game. v.*

struck (struk), past tense and a past participle of **strike.** *The clock struck four. The barn was struck by lightning. v.*

struc tur al (struk′chər əl), **1** used in building. Structural steel is steel made into beams, girders, etc. **2** of or having to do with structure or structures: *The geologist showed the structural difference in rocks of different ages. adj.*

struc tur al ly (struk′chər ə lē), with regard to structure: *The new church is structurally perfect, but it is not beautiful. adv.*

struc ture (struk′chər), **1** something built; a building or construction. Dams, bridges, and tunnels are very large structures; apartment houses are smaller structures. **2** anything composed of parts arranged together: *The human body is a wonderful structure.* **3** manner of building; way parts are put together; construction: *The structure of the schoolhouse was excellent.* **4** arrangement of parts, elements, etc.: *the structure of a molecule, the structure of a flower,*

sentence structure, the structure of a story. **5** make into a structure; build; construct: *to structure a building, a sentence, etc.* 1-4 *n.*, 5 *v.*, **struc tured, struc tur ing.**

strug gle (strug′əl), **1** make great efforts with the body; try hard; work hard against difficulties: *The poor have to struggle for a living. The swimmer struggled against the tide. She struggled to keep back her anger.* **2** get, move, or make one's way with great effort: *The old horse struggled to its feet.* **3** great effort; hard work: *It was a struggle for the couple to send their six children to college. Making the baby eat his spinach is a struggle.* **4** to fight: *The brave dog struggled fiercely with the large wildcat.* **5** a fighting; conflict: *The struggle between the two enemy countries went on for years.* 1,2,4 *v.*, **strug gled, struggling;** 3,5 *n.*

strum (strum), **1** play by running the fingers lightly or carelessly across the strings or keys: *strum a guitar, strum on the piano.* **2** act of strumming. **3** sound of strumming. 1 *v.*, **strummed, strum ming;** 2,3 *n.*

strum mer (strum′ər), person who strums. *n.*

strum pet (strum′pit), prostitute. *n.*

strung (strung), past tense and a past participle of **string.** *The children strung along after the teacher. The vines had been strung on poles. v.*

strut¹ (strut), **1** walk in a vain, important manner: *The rooster struts about the barnyard.* **2** a strutting walk. 1 *v.*, **strut ted, strut ting;** 2 *n.* [Old English *strūtian* stand out stiffly]

strut² (strut), a supporting piece; brace. *n.* [related to *strut¹*]

strut²
struts
between beams

strych nine (strik′nən *or* strik′nīn), a poisonous drug used in medicine in small doses as a tonic or stimulant. *n.*

Stu art (stü′ərt *or* styü′ərt), **1** the royal family that ruled Scotland from 1371 to 1603, and England and Scotland for most of the period from 1603 to 1714. Charles I and Queen Anne belonged to the house of Stuart. **2 Gilbert,** 1755-1828, American portrait painter. **3 James E.B.,** 1833-1864, Confederate general. He was called "Jeb" Stuart. **4 Mary.** See **Mary, Queen of Scots.** *n.*

stub (stub), **1** a short piece that is left: *the stub of a pencil.* **2** the short piece of each leaf in a checkbook, etc., kept as a record. **3** something short and blunt; short, thick piece or part. **4** pen having a short, blunt point. **5** stump of a tree, a broken tooth, etc. **6** strike (one's toe) against something: *I stubbed my toe on a sharp rock.* 1-5 *n.,* 6 *v.,* **stubbed, stub bing.**

stub bi ness (stub′ē nis), stubby condition or form. *n.*

stub ble (stub′əl), **1** the lower ends of stalks of grain left in the ground after the grain is cut: *The stubble hurt the child's bare feet.* **2** any short, rough growth: *He had three days' stubble on his unshaven face. n.*

stub bly (stub′lē), **1** covered with stubble. **2** resembling stubble; bristly: *a stubbly mustache. adj.,* **stub bli er, stub bli est.**

stub born (stub′ərn), **1** fixed in purpose or opinion; not giving in to argument or requests: *The stubborn boy refused to listen to reasons for not going out in the rain.* **2** hard to deal with or manage: *a stubborn cough. adj.* —**stub′born ly,** *adv.* —**stub′born ness,** *n.*

stub by (stub′ē), **1** short and thick: *stubby fingers.* **2** short, thick, and stiff: *a stubby beard.* **3** having many stubs or stumps. *adj.,* **stub bi er, stub bi est.**

stuc co (stuk′ō), **1** plaster used for covering walls. One kind is used for covering the outer walls of buildings; another kind is used for cornices, moldings, and other interior decoration. **2** cover with stucco: *We had our house stuccoed last year.* 1 *n., pl.* **stuc coes** or **stuc cos;** 2 *v.*

stuck (stuk), past tense and past participle of **stick**². *She stuck out her tongue. We were stuck in the mud. v.*

stuck-up (stuk′up′), INFORMAL. too proud; conceited; haughty. *adj.*

stud¹ (stud), **1** head of a nail, knob, etc., sticking out from a surface, used especially for ornament: *Silver studs had been placed in the belt to form a design.* **2** to set with studs or something like studs: *The dagger handle was studded with jewels.* **3** be set or scattered over: *Little islands stud the harbor.* **4** to set like studs; scatter at intervals: *Shocks of corn were studded over the field.* **5** a kind of small button used in men's shirts. **6** an upright post to which boards or laths are nailed in making walls in houses. See **joist** for diagram. 1,5, 6 *n.,* 2-4 *v.,* **stud ded, stud ding.** [Old English *studu* pillar, post]

stud² (stud), **1** collection of horses kept for breeding, hunting, racing, etc. **2** a male horse kept for breeding; stallion. **3** any male animal kept for breeding. *n.* [Old English *stōd*]

stu dent (stüd′nt *or* styüd′nt), **1** person who studies: *She is a student of birds.* **2** person who is studying in a school, college, or university: *That high school has 3000 students. n.*

stud ied (stud′ēd), carefully planned; done on purpose; resulting from deliberate effort: *What she said to me was a studied insult. adj.* —**stud′ied ly,** *adv.*

stu di o (stü′dē ō *or* styü′dē ō), **1** workroom of a painter, sculptor, photographer, etc. **2** place where motion pictures are made. **3** place from which a radio or television program is broadcast. *n., pl.* **stu di os.**

studio couch, an upholstered couch, without a back or arms, that can be used as a bed.

stu di ous (stü′dē əs *or* styü′dē əs), **1** fond of study. **2** showing careful consideration; careful; thoughtful; zealous: *He is always studious of other peoples' comfort. The clerk made a studious effort to please customers. adj.* —**stu′di ous ly,** *adv.* —**stu′di ous ness,** *n.*

stud y (stud′ē), **1** effort to learn by reading or thinking: *After an hour's hard study, he knew his lesson.* **2** try to learn: *She studied her spelling lesson for half an hour. I am studying to be a doctor.* **3** a careful examination; investigation: *make a study of a person's life.* **4** examine carefully: *We studied the map to find the shortest road home.* **5** subject that is studied; branch of learning; thing investigated or to be investigated. History, music, and law are studies. **6** a room for study, reading, writing, etc.: *The author was at work in her study.* **7** piece of writing or work of art that deals in careful detail with one particular subject: *a study of art in Germany.* **8** sketch for a picture, story, etc. **9** consider with care; think out; plan: *The mayor studied ways to cut expenses.* **10** give care and thought to; try hard: *The grocer studies to please his customers.* **11** earnest effort, or the object of endeavor or effort: *Her constant study is to improve her English.* **12** deep thought; reverie: *The judge was absorbed in study about the case.* **13** étude. 1,3,5-8,11-13 *n., pl.* **stud ies;** 2,4,9,10 *v.,* **stud ied, stud y ing.**

stuff (stuf), **1** what a thing is made of; material. **2** any woven fabric, especially a woolen or worsted one: *She bought some white stuff for curtains.* **3** thing or things; substance: *The doctor rubbed some kind of stuff on the burn.* **4** goods; belongings: *He was told to move his stuff out of the room.* **5** worthless material; useless things: *Their attic is full of old stuff.* **6** silly words and thoughts: *a lot of stuff and nonsense.* **7** inward qualities; character: *That girl has good stuff in her.* **8** pack full; fill: *They stuffed the pillows with feathers.* **9** put fraudulent votes in (a ballot box). **10** stop up; block; choke up: *stuff one's ears with cotton. My head is stuffed up*

hat, āge, fär; let, ēqual, tėrm;
it, īce; hot, ōpen, ôrder;
oil, out; cup, pùt, rüle; ch, child;
ng, long; sh, she; th, thin;
ŦH, then; zh, measure;

ə represents *a* in about,
e in taken, *i* in pencil,
o in lemon, *u* in circus.

by a cold. **11** fill the skin of (a dead animal) to make it look as it did when alive. **12** fill (a chicken, turkey, etc.) with seasoned bread crumbs, etc., before cooking. **13** force; push; thrust: *She stuffed her clothes into the drawer.* **14** fill too much with food: *After I stuffed myself with candy, I felt sick.* 1-7 *n.,* 8-14 *v.*

stuffed shirt, SLANG. person who tries to seem more important than he really is.

stuff i ly (stuf′ə lē), in a stuffy manner. *adv.*

stuff i ness (stuf′ē nis), stuffy quality or condition. *n.*

stuff ing (stuf′ing), **1** material used to fill or pack something. **2** seasoned bread crumbs, etc., used to stuff a chicken, turkey, etc., before cooking. *n.*

stuff y (stuf′ē), **1** lacking fresh air: *a stuffy room.* **2** lacking freshness or interest; dull: *a stuffy conversation, a stuffy person.* **3** stopped up: *A cold makes one's head feel stuffy. adj.,* **stuff i er, stuff i est.**

stul ti fi ca tion (stul′tə fə kā′shən), a stultifying or a being stultified. *n.*

stul ti fy (stul′tə fī), to make useless, weak, or foolish; make futile or absurd; frustrate: *stultify a person's efforts or incentive. v.,* **stul ti fied, stul ti fy ing.**

stum ble (stum′bəl), **1** trip by striking the foot against something: *He stumbled over the stool in the dark kitchen.* **2** walk unsteadily: *The tired hikers stumbled along.* **3** speak, act, etc., in a clumsy or hesitating way: *The actors made many blunders as they stumbled through the play.* **4** make a mistake; do wrong. **5** a wrong act; mistake. **6** come by accident or chance: *While in the country, she stumbled upon some fine antiques.* **7** act of stumbling. 1-4,6 *v.,* **stum bled, stum bling;** 5,7 *n.*

stumbling block, **1** obstacle; hindrance. **2** something that makes a person stumble.

stum bling ly (stum′bling lē), in a clumsy or hesitating way; unsteadily. *adv.*

stump (stump), **1** the lower end of a tree or plant, left after the main part is

adj. adjective	*n.* noun
adv. adverb	*prep.* preposition
conj. conjunction	*pron.* pronoun
interj. interjection	*v.* verb
sing. singular	*pl.* plural

cut off: *We sat on top of a stump.* 2 anything left after the main or important part is removed: *the stump of a pencil, the stump of a candle.* The dog wagged its *stump of a tail.* 3 place where a political speech is made. 4 make political speeches in: *The candidates for governor will stump the state.* 5 walk in a stiff, clumsy way, as if one had a wooden leg. 6 INFORMAL. make unable to answer, do, etc.: *Nobody could think of anything to do —everybody was stumped.* 1-3 *n.,* 4-6 *v.* —**stump′like′,** *adj.*

stump y (stum′pē), 1 short and thick: *a stumpy person.* 2 having many stumps: *stumpy ground.* *adj.,* **stumpi er, stump i est.**

stun (stun), 1 make senseless; knock unconscious: *He was stunned by the fall.* 2 daze; bewilder; shock; overwhelm: *She was stunned by the news of her friend's death.* *v.,* **stunned, stunning.**

stung (stung), past tense and past participle of **sting.** *A wasp stung him. He had been stung on the neck.* *v.*

stunk (stungk), a past tense and past participle of **stink.** *The garbage dump stunk. The rotten eggs had stunk up the kitchen.* *v.*

stun ning (stun′ing), 1 INFORMAL. having striking excellence, beauty, etc.; very attractive; good-looking; pretty: *a stunning outfit.* 2 that stuns or dazes; bewildering: *a stunning blow, stunning news.* *adj.* —**stun′ning ly,** *adv.*

stunt¹ (stunt), to check in growth or development: *Lack of proper food stunts a child.* *v.* [earlier sense "to confound," from Middle English and Old English *stunt* foolish]

stunt² (stunt). INFORMAL. 1 feat to attract attention; act showing boldness or skill: *Circus riders perform stunts on horseback.* 2 perform stunts. 1 *n.,* 2 *v.* [perhaps a different form of *stint* a task]

stu pe fac tion (stü′pə fak′shən *or* styü′pə fak′shən), 1 dazed or senseless condition; stupor. 2 overwhelming amazement. *n.*

stu pe fy (stü′pə fī *or* styü′pə fī), 1 make stupid, dull, or senseless: *be stupefied by a drug.* 2 overwhelm with shock or amazement; astound: *They*

were *stupefied by the calamity.* *v.,* **stu pe fied, stu pe fy ing.**

stu pen dous (stü pen′dəs *or* styü pen′dəs), amazing; marvelous; immense: *Niagara Falls is a stupendous sight.* *adj.* —**stu pen′dous ly,** *adv.* —**stu pen′dous ness,** *n.*

stu pid (stü′pid *or* styü′pid), 1 not intelligent; dull: *a stupid person, a stupid remark.* 2 not interesting: *a stupid book.* 3 dazed; senseless. *adj.* —**stu′pid ly,** *adv.* —**stu′pid ness,** *n.*

stu pid i ty (stü pid′ə tē *or* styü pid′ə tē), 1 lack of intelligence; dullness. 2 a foolish act, idea, etc. *n., pl.* **stu pid i ties.**

stu por (stü′pər *or* styü′pər), a dazed condition; loss or lessening of the power to feel: *The injured man lay in a stupor, unable to tell what had happened to him.* *n.*

stur di ly (stėr′də lē), in a sturdy manner. *adv.*

stur di ness (stėr′dē nis), sturdy quality or condition; strength; firmness. *n.*

stur dy (stėr′dē), 1 strong; stout: *a sturdy child, a sturdy chair.* 2 not yielding; firm: *sturdy resistance, sturdy defenders.* *adj.,* **stur di er, stur di est.**

stur geon (stėr′jən), a large food fish whose long body has a tough skin with rows of bony plates. Caviar and isinglass are obtained from sturgeons. *n., pl.* **stur geons** *or* **stur geon.**

stut ter (stut′ər), 1 repeat (the same sound) in an effort to speak. Stuttering is the result of nervous spasms. 2 act or habit of stuttering. 1 *v.,* 2 *n.* —**stut′ter er,** *n.* —**stut′ter ing ly,** *adv.*

Stuy ve sant (stī′və sənt), **Peter,** 1592-1672, Dutch governor of the colony of New Netherland from 1646 to 1664. *n.*

St. Vi tus's dance (sānt vī′təs siz), a nervous disease, which usually affects children, characterized by involuntary twitching of the muscles; chorea. [from *St. Vitus,* Christian martyr of the A.D. 200's who was venerated for his gift of healing, especially by the custom of dancing before his image at his festival]

sty¹ (stī), 1 pen for pigs. 2 any filthy place. *n., pl.* **sties.** [Old English *stig* a building]

sty² (stī), a small, painful swelling on the edge of the eyelid. A sty is like a small boil. *n., pl.* **sties.** [probably from Middle English *styanye* (taken to mean "sty on eye"), from Old English *stīgend* rising + *ēage* eye]

Styg i an (stij′ē ən), 1 having to do with the river Styx or the lower world. 2 dark; gloomy: *a Stygian sky.* *adj.*

style (stīl), 1 fashion: *Several popular teen-agers set the style in dress at the*

school. *My clothes are out of style.* 2 manner; method; way: *The Gothic style of architecture. She learned several styles of swimming.* 3 way of writing or speaking: *Books for children should have a clear, easy style.* 4 good style: *She dresses in style.* 5 excellence of form or expression in literature, speech, art, etc.: *a model of style, a master of literary style.* 6 make in or conform to a given or accepted style; stylize: *Her poem is styled with care.* 7 to design according to a style or fashion: *His suits are styled by a famous designer.* 8 to name; call: *Joan of Arc was styled "the Maid of Orléans."* 9 stylus. 10 the stemlike part of the pistil of a flower containing the stigma at its top. 1-5, 9,10 *n.,* 6-8 *v.,* **styled, styl ing.**

style
(def. 10)

styl ish (stī′lish), having style; fashionable: *He wears stylish clothes.* *adj.* —**styl′ish ly,** *adv.* —**styl′ish ness,** *n.*

styl ist (stī′list), 1 writer, speaker, artist, etc., who is considered to be an expert or a master of style. 2 person who designs, arranges, or advises concerning interior decorations, clothes, hair styles, etc. *n.*

sty lis tic (stī lis′tik), of or having to do with style. *adj.*

sty lis ti cal ly (stī lis′tik lē), with regard to style; in matters of style. *adv.*

styl ize (stī′līz), make or design according to a particular or conventional style. *v.,* **styl ized, styl iz ing.**

stylus (def. 1)

sty lus (stī′ləs), 1 a pointed instrument for writing on wax; style. 2 a needlelike point used in making or playing phonograph records. *n., pl.* **sty lus es, sty li** (stī′lī).

sty mie (stī′mē), block completely; hinder; thwart: *to be stymied by a problem or by lack of money.* *v.,* **sty mied, sty mie ing.**

styp tic (stip′tik), 1 able to stop or check bleeding; astringent. 2 something that stops or checks bleeding by contracting the tissue. Alum is a common styptic. 1 *adj.,* 2 *n.*

Styx (stiks), (in Greek myths) a river in the lower world. The souls of the dead were ferried across it into Hades. *n.*

sua sion (swā′zhən), an advising or urging; persuasion. *n.*

suave (swäv), smoothly agreeable or polite. *adj.* —**suave′ly**, *adv.* —**suave′ness**, *n.*

sua vi ty (swä′və tē), smoothly agreeable quality of behavior; blandness; smooth politeness. *n.*

sub (sub), 1 substitute. 2 submarine. 3 act as a substitute. 1,2 *n.*, 3 *v.*, **subbed, sub bing.**

sub-, *prefix.* 1 under; below: *Subnormal = below normal.* 2 down; further; again: *Subdivide = divide again.* 3 near; nearly: *Subtropical = nearly tropical.* 4 lower; subordinate: *Subcommittee = a lower or subordinate committee.* 5 slightly; somewhat: *subacid = slightly acid.* [from Latin *sub* under, beneath]

sub., 1 subscription. 2 substitute.

sub com mit tee (sub′kə mit′ē), a small committee chosen from a larger general committee for some special duty. *n.*

sub com pact (sub′kom′pakt), automobile smaller than a compact, usually having a four-cylinder engine. *n.*

sub con scious (sub kon′shəs), 1 not wholly conscious; existing in the mind but not fully perceived or recognized: *Some students drop out of school not really because they have to go to work, but because of a subconscious fear of failure in school.* 2 thoughts, feelings, etc., that are present in the mind but not fully perceived or recognized. 1 *adj.*, 2 *n.* —**sub con′scious ly**, *adv.*

sub con ti nent (sub kon′tə nənt), a land mass or region that is very large, but smaller than a continent. *n.*

sub cu ta ne ous (sub′kyü tā′nē əs), 1 under the skin: *subcutaneous tissue.* 2 placed or performed under the skin: *a subcutaneous injection. adj.*

sub di vide (sub′də vīd′ *or* sub′də-vīd′), divide again; divide into smaller parts: *A real estate dealer bought the farm and subdivided it into building lots.* *v.*, **sub di vid ed, sub di vid ing.**

sub di vi sion (sub′də vizh′ən *or* sub′də vizh′ən), 1 division into smaller parts. 2 part of a part. 3 tract of land divided into building lots. *n.*

sub dom i nant (sub dom′ə nənt), the fourth note in a musical scale. F is the subdominant in the key of C. *n.*

sub due (səb dü′ *or* səb dyü′), 1 overcome by superior force; conquer: *The Spaniards subdued the Indian tribes in Mexico.* 2 keep down; hold back; suppress: *We subdued a desire to laugh.* 3 tone down; soften: *Pulling down the shades subdued the light in*

the room v., **sub dued, sub du ing.**

sub group (sub′grüp′), a subordinate group; division of a group.

sub head (sub′hed′), 1 a subordinate heading or title. 2 a subordinate division of a heading or title. *n.*

sub head ing (sub′hed′ing), subhead. *n.*

sub hu man (sub hyü′mən), 1 below the human race or type; less than human. 2 almost human. *adj.*

sub ject (sub′jikt *for 1-5,8,10-12;* səb jekt′ *for 6,7,9*), 1 something thought about, discussed, investigated, etc.: *The subject for our composition was "An Exciting Moment."* 2 something learned or taught; course of study in some branch of knowledge: *English, science, and arithmetic are some of the subjects we take up in school.* 3 person under the power, control, or influence of another: *The people are the subjects of the king.* 4 bound by loyalty or allegiance (to); obedient to some power or influence: *We are subject to our country's laws.* 5 under some power or influence: *the subject nations of an empire.* 6 bring under some power or influence: *Rome subjected all Italy to her rule.* 7 cause to undergo or experience something: *The school subjected new students to many tests.* 8 likely to have or receive; liable (to suffer from); prone (to): *I am subject to colds. Japan is subject to earthquakes. This play is subject to criticism.* 9 make liable (to have or receive); lay open (to); expose: *The location of the island in the middle of the ocean subjected it to frequent hurricanes.* 10 person or thing that undergoes or experiences something: *Rabbits and mice are often subjects for medical experiments.* 11 depending on; on the condition of: *I bought the car subject to your approval.* 12 (in grammar) a word or group of words about which something is said in a sentence. The subject is usually the performer of the action of an active verb or the receiver of the action of a passive verb. *I* is the subject of the following sentences: *I see the cat. I am seen by the cat. I can see.* 1-3,10,12 *n.*, 4,5,8,11 *adj.*, 6,7,9 *v.*

sub jec tion (səb jek′shən), 1 a bringing under some power or influence; conquering: *The subjection of the rebels took years.* 2 condition of being under some power or influence: *The peasants lived in subjection to the nobility. n.*

sub jec tive (səb jek′tiv), 1 existing in the mind; belonging to the person thinking rather than to the object thought of: *Base your subjective opinions on objective facts.* 2 about the thoughts and feelings of the speaker, writer, painter, etc.; personal: *a subjective poem.*

hat, āge, fär; let, ēqual, tėrm;
it, īce; hot, ōpen, ôrder;
oil, out; cup, pùt, rüle; ch, child;
ng, long; sh, she; th, thin;
ŦH, then; zh, measure;

ə represents *a* in about,
e in taken, *i* in pencil,
o in lemon, *u* in circus.

adj. —**sub jec′tive ly**, *adv.* —**sub jec′tive ness**, *n.*

subject matter, 1 something thought about, discussed, studied, written about, etc. 2 what a talk, book, etc., is about, as distinguished from its form or style: *The speaker's subject matter was better than her presentation.*

sub ju gate (sub′jə gāt), subdue; conquer. *v.*, **sub ju gat ed, sub ju gat ing.**

sub ju ga tion (sub′jə gā′shən), conquest; subjection. *n.*

sub junc tive (səb jungk′tiv), 1 (in grammar) having to do with a verb form which expresses a state, act, or event as possible, conditional, or dependent, rather than actual. 2 form of a verb which expresses this. In "I insist that he go" and "If I were you," *go* and *were* are subjunctives. 3 mood of such a verb. 1 *adj.*, 2,3 *n.*

sub lease (sub′lēs′ *for 1;* sub lēs′ *or* sub′les′ *for 2*), 1 a lease granted by a person on property which has been leased to himself. 2 grant or take a sublease of. 1 *n.*, 2 *v.*, **sub leased, sub leas ing.**

sub let (sub let′ *or* sub′let′), 1 rent to another (something which has been rented to oneself); give a sublease of: *We sublet our house for the summer.* 2 take a sublease of: *I have sublet an apartment whose tenants went away for the summer.* 3 give part of (a contract) to another: *The contractor for the whole building sublet the contract for the plumbing. v.*, **sub let, sub let ting.**

sub li mate (sub′lə māt *for 1-3;* sub′lə mit *or* sub′lə māt *for 4*), 1 purify; refine. 2 change (an undesirable impulse or trait) into a desirable activity. 3 to sublime (a solid substance). 4 material obtained when a substance is sublimed. 1-3 *v.*, **sub li mat ed, sub li mat ing;** 4 *n.*

sub li ma tion (sub′lə mā′shən), 1 purification; act or process of sublimating or subliming. 2 the resulting product or state. *n.*

sub lime (sə blīm′), 1 lofty or elevated in thought, feeling, language, etc.; noble; grand; exalted: *sublime devotion,*

sublimity

adj.	adjective	*n.*	noun
adv.	adverb	*prep.*	preposition
conj.	conjunction	*pron.*	pronoun
interj.	interjection	*v.*	verb
sing.	singular	*pl.*	plural

sublime poetry. *Mountain scenery is often sublime.* 2 that which is lofty, noble, exalted, etc.: *the sublime in literature and art.* 3 heat (a solid substance) and condense the vapor given off. 4 pass off as a vapor and condense as a solid without going through a liquid state; become purified. 1 *adj.*, 2 *n.*, 3,4 *v.*, **sub limed, sub lim ing. —sub lime′ly,** *adv.*

sub lim i ty (sə blim′ə tē), lofty excellence; grandeur; majesty; exalted state. *n.*, *pl.* **sub lim i ties.**

sub ma chine gun (sub′mə shēn′), a lightweight automatic or semi-automatic gun, designed to be fired from the shoulder or hip.

submarine (def. 1)

sub ma rine (sub′mə rēn′ *for 1*; sub′mə rēn′ *for 2*), 1 boat that can go under water. Submarines are used in warfare for attacking enemy ships with torpedoes and for launching missiles. 2 under the surface of the sea; underwater: *submarine plants, submarine warfare.* 1 *n.*, 2 *adj.*

sub merge (səb mėrj′), 1 put under water; cover with water: *A big wave submerged us. At high tide this path is submerged.* 2 cover; bury: *His talent was submerged by his shyness.* 3 sink under water; go below the surface: *The submarine submerged to escape enemy attack.* *v.*, **sub merged, sub merging.**

sub mer gence (səb mėr′jəns), a submerging or a being submerged. *n.*

sub merse (səb mėrs′), submerge. *v.*, **sub mersed, sub mers ing.**

sub mers i ble (səb mėr′sə bəl), 1 that can be submerged. 2 a submarine. 1 *adj.*, 2 *n.*

sub mer sion (səb mėr′zhən), a submerging or a being submerged. *n.*

sub mis sion (səb mish′ən), 1 a yielding to the power, control, or authority of another; submitting: *The defeated general showed his submission by giving up his sword.* 2 obedience; humbleness: *They all bowed in submission to the*

queen's order. 3 a referring or a being referred to the consideration or judgment of some person or group. *n.*

sub mis sive (səb mis′iv), yielding to the power, control, or authority of another; obedient; humble. *adj.* **—sub mis′sive ly,** *adv.* **—sub mis′sive ness,** *n.*

sub mit (səb mit′), 1 yield to the power, control, or authority of some person or group; surrender; yield: *The thief submitted to arrest by the police.* 2 refer to the consideration or judgment of some person or group: *The secretary submitted a report of the last meeting.* 3 suggest or urge respectfully: *I submit that more evidence is needed to support the case.* *v.*, **sub mit ted, sub mit ting.**

sub nor mal (sub nôr′məl), below normal; inferior to the normal: *a subnormal temperature, a subnormal person.* *adj.*

sub or di nate (sə bôrd′n it *for 1-3*; sə bôrd′n āt *for 4*), 1 lower in rank: *In the army, lieutenants are subordinate to captains.* 2 having less importance; secondary; dependent: *An errand boy has a subordinate position.* 3 a subordinate person or thing. 4 make subordinate: *A polite host subordinates his wishes to those of his guests.* 1,2 *adj.*, 3 *n.*, 4 *v.*, **sub or di nat ed, sub or di nat ing.**

subordinate clause, clause in a complex sentence that cannot act alone as a sentence; dependent clause. In "If I go home, my dog will follow me," *If I go home* is a subordinate clause.

sub or di na tion (sə bôrd′n ā′shən), 1 a subordinating or a being subordinated. 2 subordinate position or importance. 3 submission to authority; willingness to obey; obedience. *n.*

sub orn (sə bôrn′), 1 persuade, bribe, or cause (someone) to do an illegal or evil deed. 2 persuade or cause (a witness) to give false testimony in court. *v.*

sub pe na (sə pē′nə), subpoena. *n.*, *pl.* **sub pe nas;** *v.*

sub poe na (sə pē′nə), 1 an official written order commanding a person to appear in a court of law. 2 summon with such an order. 1 *n.*, *pl.* **sub poe nas;** 2 *v.*

sub scribe (səb skrīb′), 1 promise to give or pay (a sum of money): *She subscribed $15 to the hospital fund.* 2 promise to accept and pay for: *We subscribe to a few magazines.* 3 write (one's name) at the end of a document, etc.; show one's consent or approval by signing: *The men who subscribed to the Declaration of Independence are now famous.* 4 give one's consent or approval; agree: *She will not subscribe to anything unfair. I do not expect you to*

subscribe to my opinion. *v.*, **sub scribed, sub scrib ing.**

sub scrib er (səb skrī′bər), person who subscribes: *The magazines make a special offer to new subscribers.* *n.*

sub script (sub′skript), number, letter, etc., written underneath and to one side of a symbol. In H_2SO_4 the 2 and 4 are subscripts. *n.*

sub scrip tion (səb skrip′shən), 1 a subscribing. 2 money subscribed; contribution: *My subscription to the Fresh Air Fund was $5.* 3 the right to receive something, obtained by paying a certain sum: *Our subscription to the newspaper expires next week.* 4 sum of money raised by a number of persons: *We are raising a subscription for a new hospital.* *n.*

sub sec tion (sub′sek′shən), part of a section. *n.*

sub se quent (sub′sə kwənt), coming after; following; later: *Subsequent events proved that he was right. The story will be continued in subsequent chapters.* *adj.* **—sub′se quent ly,** *adv.*

sub serve (səb sėrv′), to help or assist (a purpose, action, etc.): *Chewing food well subserves digestion.* *v.*, **sub served, sub serv ing.**

sub ser vi ence (səb sėr′vē əns), tame submission; slavish politeness and obedience; servility. *n.*

sub ser vi ent (səb sėr′vē ənt), 1 tamely submissive; slavishly polite and obedient; servile. 2 useful as a means to help a purpose or end; serviceable. *adj.* **—sub ser′vi ent ly,** *adv.*

sub set (sub′set′), (in mathematics) a set, each of whose members is a member of a second set: *A subset of S is a set every element of which belongs to S.* *n.*

sub side (səb sīd′), 1 grow less; die down; become less active: *The storm finally subsided. Her fever subsided after she took the medicine.* 2 sink to a lower level: *Several days after the rain stopped, the flood waters subsided.* *v.*, **sub sid ed, sub sid ing.**

sub sid ence (səb sīd′ns *or* sub′sə dəns), act or process of subsiding: *the subsidence of a flood or a fever.* *n.*

sub sid i ar y (səb sid′ē er′ē), 1 useful to assist or supplement; auxiliary; supplementary: *The teacher sold books as a subsidiary occupation.* 2 thing or person that assists or supplements. 3 company having over half of its stock owned or controlled by another company: *The bus line was a subsidiary of the railroad.* 4 maintained by a subsidy. 1,4 *adj.*, 2,3 *n.*, *pl.* **sub sid i ar ies.**

sub si dize (sub′sə dīz), aid or assist

with a grant of money: *The government subsidizes airlines that carry mail.* v., **sub si dized, sub si diz ing.**

sub si diz er (sub′sə dī′zər), person or group that subsidizes. *n.*

sub si dy (sub′sə dē), grant or contribution of money, especially one made by a government: *a subsidy for education.* *n., pl.* **sub si dies.**

sub sist (səb sist′), 1 keep alive; live: *People in the far north subsist on fish and meat.* 2 continue to be; exist: *Many superstitions still subsist.* *v.*

sub sist ence (səb sis′təns), 1 a keeping alive; living: *Selling papers was his only means of subsistence.* 2 means of keeping alive; livelihood: *The sea provides a subsistence for fishermen.* 3 existence; continuance. *n.*

sub soil (sub′soil′), layer of earth that lies just under the surface soil. *n.*

sub son ic (sub son′ik), 1 of or having to do with speed which is less than the speed of sound (about 750 miles per hour). 2 that moves at a speed slower than the speed of sound: *a subsonic airplane.* *adj.*

sub stance (sub′stəns), 1 what a thing consists of; matter; material: *Ice and water are the same substance in different forms.* 2 the real, main, or important part of anything: *The substance of an education is its effect on your life, not just learning lessons.* 3 real meaning: *Give the substance of the speech in your own words.* 4 solid quality; body: *Pea soup has more substance than water.* 5 wealth; property: *a person of substance.* *n.*

sub stand ard (sub stan′dərd), below standard. *adj.*

sub stan tial (səb stan′shəl), 1 having substance; material; real; actual: *People and things are substantial; dreams and ghosts are not.* 2 strong; firm; solid: *The house is substantial enough to last a hundred years.* 3 large; important; ample: *He made a substantial improvement in health.* 4 providing ample or abundant nourishment: *Eat a substantial breakfast.* 5 in the main; in essentials: *The stories told by the two children were in substantial agreement.* 6 well-to-do; wealthy. *adj.*

sub stan tial ly (səb stan′shə lē), 1 essentially; mainly: *This report is substantially correct.* 2 really; actually. 3 strongly; solidly: *a substantially built house.* *adv.*

sub stan ti ate (səb stan′shē āt), establish by evidence; prove: *substantiate a rumor, substantiate a claim, substantiate a theory.* *v.,* **sub stan ti at ed, sub stan ti at ing.**

sub stan ti a tion (səb stan′shē ā′shən), a substantiating or a being substantiated; proof. *n.*

sub stan tive (sub′stən tiv), 1 noun or pronoun; the name of a person or thing. 2 used as a noun. 3 showing or expressing existence. The verb *to be* is the substantive verb. 4 independent. 5 real; actual. 6 substantial. 1 *n.,* 2-6 *adj.* —**sub′stan tive ly,** *adv.*

sub sta tion (sub′stā′shən), a branch station; subordinate station: *Besides the main post office in our city, there are six substations.* *n.*

sub sti tute (sub′stə tüt *or* sub′stə tyüt), 1 thing used instead of another; person taking the place of another: *Margarine is a common substitute for butter. A substitute taught us at school today.* 2 put in the place of another: *We substituted brown sugar for molasses in these cookies.* 3 take the place of another: *She substituted for our teacher, who is ill.* 4 put in or taking the place of another: *a substitute teacher.* 1 *n.,* 2,3 *v.,* **sub sti tut ed, sub sti tut ing;** 4 *adj.*

sub sti tu tion (sub′stə tü′shən *or* sub′stə tyü′shən), the use of one thing for another; a putting (one person or thing) in the place of another; a taking the place of another. *n.*

sub stra tum (sub strā′təm), 1 layer lying under another: *Beneath the sandy soil there was a substratum of clay ten feet thick.* 2 basis; foundation: *The story has a substratum of truth. n., pl.* **sub stra ta** (sub strā′tə), **sub stra tums.**

sub teen (sub′tēn′), boy or girl nearly thirteen years old. *n.*

sub ter fuge (sub′tər fyüj), trick, excuse, or expedient used to escape something unpleasant: *The child's headache was only a subterfuge to avoid going to school.* *n.*

sub ter ra ne an (sub′tə rā′nē ən), 1 underground: *A subterranean passage led from the castle to a cave.* 2 carried on secretly; hidden: *subterranean plotting.* *adj.*

sub ti tle (sub′tī′tl), 1 an additional or subordinate title of a book, article, etc. 2 word or words shown on a motion-picture screen, especially as the translation of the words spoken in a foreign-language film; caption. 3 give a subtitle to. 1,2 *n.,* 3 *v.,* **sub ti tled, sub ti tling.**

sub tle (sut′l), 1 delicate; thin; fine: *a subtle odor of perfume. Subtle humor is often hard to understand.* 2 faint; mysterious: *a subtle smile.* 3 discerning; acute: *a subtle mind, subtle reasoning. She is a subtle observer of slight differences in things.* 4 sly; crafty; tricky: *a subtle scheme to get some money.* 5 skillful; clever; expert: *a subtle worker in gold and silver. adj.,* **sub tler, sub tlest. —sub′tle ness,** *n.*

hat, āge, fär; let, ēqual, tėrm;
it, īce; hot, ōpen, ôrder;
oil, out; cup, pùt, rüle; ch, child;
ng, long; sh, she; th, thin;
ŦH, then; zh, measure;

ə represents *a* in about,
e in taken, *i* in pencil,
o in lemon, *u* in circus.

sub tle ty (sut′l tē), 1 subtle quality. 2 something subtle. *n., pl.* **sub tle ties.**

sub tly (sut′l ē), in a subtle manner. *adv.*

sub top ic (sub′top′ik), a subordinate or secondary topic. *n.*

sub tract (səb trakt′), take away: *Subtract 2 from 10 and you have 8.* *v.*

sub trac tion (səb trak′shən), act or process of subtracting one number or quantity from another; finding the difference between two numbers or quantities: $10-2 = 8$ *is a simple subtraction.* *n.*

sub trac tive (səb trak′tive), having to do with subtraction. *adj.*

sub tra hend (sub′trə hend), number or quantity to be subtracted from another: *In* $10-2 = 8,$ *the subtrahend is 2.* *n.*

sub trop i cal (sub trop′ə kəl), 1 bordering on the tropics. 2 nearly tropical. *adj.*

sub urb (sub′ėrb′), district, town, or village just outside or near a city: *Many people who work in the city live in the suburbs.* *n.*

sub ur ban (sə bėr′bən), 1 having to do with a suburb; in a suburb: *We have excellent suburban train service.* 2 characteristic of a suburb or its inhabitants. *adj.*

sub ur ban ite (sə bėr′bə nīt), person who lives in a suburb. *n.*

sub ver sion (səb vėr′zhən), a subverting or a being subverted; overthrow; destruction. *n.*

sub ver sive (səb vėr′siv), 1 tending to overthrow; destructive; causing ruin: *a subversive organization.* 2 person who seeks to overthrow or undermine (a government, etc.). 1 *adj.,* 2 *n.*

sub vert (səb vėrt′), 1 overthrow (something established or existing); cause the downfall, ruin, or destruction of: *Dictators subvert democracy.* 2 undermine the principles of; corrupt: *subvert a peaceful society.* *v.*

sub way (sub′wā′), 1 an electric railroad running beneath the surface of the streets in a city. 2 an underground passage. *n.*

suc ceed (sək sēd′), 1 turn out well;

adj. adjective	*n.* noun
adv. adverb	*prep.* preposition
conj. conjunction	*pron.* pronoun
interj. interjection	*v.* verb
sing. singular	*pl.* plural

do well; have success: *Her plans succeeded. The attack succeeded beyond all expectations.* 2 come next after; follow; take the place of: *John Adams succeeded Washington as President. Week succeeds week.* 3 come next after another; follow another; take the place of another: *When George VI died, Elizabeth II succeeded to the throne. v.*

suc cess (sək ses′), 1 a favorable result; wished-for ending; good fortune: *Success in school comes from intelligence and work.* 2 the gaining of wealth, position, etc.: *He has had little success in life.* 3 person or thing that succeeds: *The circus was a great success.* 4 result; outcome; fortune: *What success did you have in finding a new apartment? n.*

suc cess ful (sək ses′fəl), having success; ending in success; prosperous; fortunate: *a successful writer, a successful campaign. adj.* —**suc cess′ful ly,** *adv.*

suc ces sion (sək sesh′ən), 1 group of things happening one after another; series: *A succession of accidents spoiled our automobile trip.* 2 the coming of one person or thing after another. 3 right of succeeding to an office, property, or rank: *There was a dispute about the rightful succession to the throne.* 4 order or arrangement of persons having such a right of succeeding: *The king's oldest daughter is next in succession to the throne. n.*

in succession, one after another: *We visited our sick friend several days in succession.*

suc ces sive (sək ses′iv), coming one after another; following in order: *It rained for three successive days. adj.* —**suc ces′sive ly,** *adv.*

suc ces sor (sək ses′ər), one that follows or succeeds another in office, position, or ownership of property; thing that comes next after another in a series: *John Adams was Washington's successor as President. n.*

suc cinct (sək singkt′), expressed briefly and clearly; concise: *Her letter was succinct with all the main points on one page. adj.* —**suc cinct′ly,** *adv.* —**suc cinct′ness,** *n.*

suc cor (suk′ər), help; aid. *n., v.*

suc co tash (suk′ə tash), kernels of sweet corn and beans cooked together. *n.*

suc cu lence (suk′yə ləns), juiciness. *n.*

suc cu lent (suk′yə lənt), juicy: *a succulent peach. adj.*

suc cumb (sə kum′), 1 give way; yield: *She succumbed to temptation and stole the money.* 2 die: *She succumbed of old age. v.*

such (such), 1 of that kind; of the same kind or degree: *Such perfect diamonds as those are quite rare. The child had such a fever that she nearly died. The food, such as it was, was plentiful.* 2 of the kind already spoken of or suggested: *She did not like tea and coffee and such drinks.* 3 so great, so bad, so good, etc.: *He is such a liar. Such weather!* 4 some; certain: *The bank was robbed at such a time in such and such a town by such and such persons.* 5 such a person or thing: *Take from the blankets such as you need.* 1-4 *adj.,* 5 *pron.*

as such, as being what is indicated or implied: *A leader, as such, deserves obedience.*

such as, 1 similar to; like: *There are few writers such as Dickens.* 2 for example: *members of the dog family, such as the wolf and fox.*

suck (suk), 1 draw into the mouth by using the lips and tongue: *Lemonade can be sucked through a straw.* 2 draw liquid from with the mouth: *suck oranges.* 3 draw milk from the breast or a bottle. 4 draw or be drawn by sucking: *He sucked at his pipe.* 5 drink, take, or absorb: *Plants suck up moisture from the earth. A sponge sucks in water.* 6 hold in the mouth and lick: *The child sucked a lollipop.* 7 act of sucking: *The baby took one suck at the empty bottle and pushed it away.* 1-6 *v.,* 7 *n.*

suck er (suk′ər), 1 animal or thing that sucks. 2 any of various freshwater fishes that suck in food or have mouths that suggest sucking. 3 organ in some animals for sucking or holding fast by a sucking force. 4 shoot growing from an underground stem or root. 5 lump of hard candy, especially a lollipop. 6 SLANG. person easily deceived. *n.*

suck le (suk′əl), 1 feed with milk from the breast or udder: *The cat suckles her kittens.* 2 suck at the breast or udder. *v.,* **suck led, suck ling.**

suck ling (suk′ling), a very young animal or child, especially one not yet weaned. *n.*

Su cre (sü′krā), one of the two capitals of Bolivia, in the S part. La Paz is the other capital. *n.*

su crose (sü′krōs), ordinary sugar obtained from sugar cane, sugar beets, etc. *n.*

suc tion (suk′shən), 1 the production of a vacuum by removing all or part of the air in a space with the result that atmospheric pressure forces fluid or gas into the vacant space or causes surfaces to stick together. We draw lemonade through a straw by suction. Vacuum cleaners and some pumps work by suction. 2 the force caused by suction. 3 act or process of sucking. 4 causing a suction; working by suction: *a suction valve.* 1-3 *n.,* 4 *adj.*

Su dan (sü dan′), 1 country in NE Africa, formerly under the joint control of Great Britain and Egypt. *Capital:* Khartoum. 2 vast region in Africa, south of the Sahara Desert and extending from the Atlantic Ocean to the Red Sea. *n.*

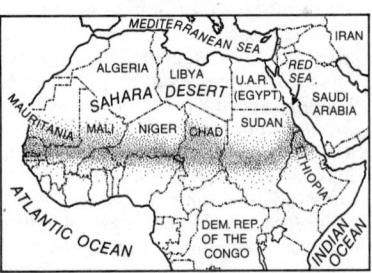

Sudan (def. 2)—the shaded area

Su da nese (süd′n ēz′), 1 of or having to do with the Sudan or its inhabitants. 2 person born or living in the Sudan. 1 *adj.,* 2 *n., pl.* **Su da nese.**

sud den (sud′n), 1 happening without warning or notice; not expected: *a sudden stop, a sudden rainstorm, a sudden rise to power.* 2 found or hit upon unexpectedly; abrupt: *There was a sudden turn in the road.* 3 quick; rapid: *The cat made a sudden jump at the mouse. adj.* —**sud′den ness,** *n.*

all of a sudden, in a sudden manner; unexpectedly or quickly.

sud den ly (sud′n lē), in a sudden manner. *adv.*

suds (sudz), 1 soapy water. 2 bubbles and foam on soapy water; soapsuds. *n.pl.*

suds y (sud′zē), full of soapsuds. *adj.,* **suds i er, suds i est.**

sue (sü), 1 start a lawsuit against: *He sued the railroad because his cow was killed by the engine.* 2 take action in law: *sue for damages.* 3 beg or ask (for); plead: *Messengers came suing for peace. v.,* **sued, su ing.**

suede or **suède** (swād), 1 a soft leather that has a velvety nap on one or both sides. 2 kind of cloth that has a similar appearance. 3 made of suede: *suede shoes, a suede jacket.* 1,2 *n.,*

3 *adj.* [from French (*gants de*) *Suède* (gloves from) Sweden]

su et (sü′it), the hard fat about the kidneys and loins of cattle and sheep. Suet is used in cooking and for making tallow. *n.*

Su ez (sü ez′), 1 city in NE Egypt, at the S end of the Suez Canal. 2 **Isthmus of,** the isthmus between Asia and Africa, in the NE part of Egypt. *n.*

Suez Canal, canal across the Isthmus of Suez, connecting the Mediterranean and Red seas. See **Nile** for map.

suf fer (suf′ər), 1 have pain, grief, injury, etc.: *Sick people suffer.* 2 have or feel (pain, grief, etc.): *I suffered sunburn from being at the beach all day.* 3 experience harm, loss, etc.: *His business suffered greatly during the war.* 4 allow; permit: *"Suffer the little children to come unto me."* 5 bear with patiently; endure: *I will not suffer such insults.* *v.* —**suf′fer er,** *n.*

suf fer ance (suf′ər əns), permission or consent given only by a failure to object or prevent. *n.*

on sufferance, allowed or tolerated, but not really wanted: *Pets were on sufferance in the apartment building.*

suf fer ing (suf′ər ing), 1 condition of being in pain: *Hunger causes suffering.* 2 the enduring of pain, trouble, or distress: *the suffering of a poor family.* *n.*

suf fice (sə fīs′), 1 be enough; be sufficient: *Fifty dollars will suffice to buy that coat.* 2 satisfy; make content: *A small amount of cake sufficed the baby.* *v.,* **suf ficed, suf fic ing.**

suf fi cien cy (sə fish′ən sē), 1 a sufficient amount; large enough supply: *The ship had a sufficiency of provisions for a voyage of two months.* 2 condition or fact of being sufficient; adequacy; ability. *n., pl.* **suf fi cien cies.**

suf fi cient (sə fish′ənt), as much as is needed; enough: *sufficient proof. The poor child did not have sufficient clothing for the winter. adj.* —**suf fi′cient ly,** *adv.*

suf fix (suf′iks *for 1;* sə fiks′ *or* suf′iks *for 2*), 1 syllable or syllables put at the end of a word to change its meaning or to make another word, as *-ly* in *badly, -ness* in *goodness, -ful* in *spoonful,* and *-ment* in *amazement.* 2 add at the end; put after. 1 *n., pl.* **suf fix es;** 2 *v.*

suf fo cate (suf′ə kāt), 1 kill by stopping the breath. 2 keep from breathing; hinder in breathing. 3 gasp for breath; choke. 4 die for lack of oxygen; be suffocated. 5 smother; suppress. *v.,* **suf fo cat ed, suf fo cat ing.**

suf fo ca tion (suf′ə kā′shən), a suffocating or a being suffocated. *n.*

Suf folk (suf′ək), county in SE Eng-

land, divided into **Suffolk East** and **Suffolk West.** *n.*

suf frage (suf′rij), 1 the right to vote; franchise: *The United States granted suffrage to women in 1920.* 2 a vote, usually in support of a proposal, candidate, etc. 3 a voting; casting of votes. *n.*

suf fra gette (suf′rə jet′), woman advocating suffrage for women. *n.*

suf fra gist (suf′rə jist), person who favors giving suffrage to more people, especially to women. *n.*

suf fuse (sə fyüz′), overspread (with a liquid, dye, etc.): *eyes suffused with tears. At twilight the sky was suffused with glorious color. v.,* **suf fused, suf fus ing.**

suf fu sion (sə fyü′zhən), 1 a suffusing or a being suffused. 2 that with which anything is overspread. 3 flush of color. *n.*

sug ar (shug′ər), 1 a sweet substance obtained chiefly from sugar cane or sugar beets and used extensively in food products; sucrose. 2 any of the class of carbohydrates to which this substance belongs. Glucose, lactose, and maltose are sugars. Most plants manufacture sugar. 3 put sugar in; sweeten with sugar: *She sugared her tea.* 4 cover with sugar; sprinkle with sugar: *to sugar doughnuts.* 5 form sugar crystals: *Honey sugars if kept too long.* 6 cause to seem pleasant or agreeable: *He sugared his criticism of the play with some praise for the performers.* 1,2 *n.,* 3-6 *v.*

sugar beet, a large beet with a white root that yields sugar.

sugar cane, a very tall grass with a strong, jointed stem and flat leaves, growing in warm regions. Sugar cane and sugar beets are the main sources of sugar.

sug ar-coat (shug′ər kōt′), 1 cover with sugar. 2 cause to seem more pleasant or agreeable: *to sugar-coat discipline with humor. v.*

sugar loaf, 1 a solid cone-shaped mass of molded sugar. 2 something shaped like a sugar loaf.

sugar maple, a maple tree of eastern North America, highly valued for its hard, tough wood and for its sweet sap, from which maple sugar and maple syrup are made.

sug ar plum (shug′ər plum′), piece of candy; bonbon. *n.*

sug ar y (shug′ər ē), 1 consisting of sugar; like sugar; sweet. 2 outwardly, but not sincerely, pleasant or agreeable: *a sugary greeting. adj.*

sug gest (səg jest′), 1 bring to mind; call up the thought of: *The thought of summer suggests swimming, tennis, and hot weather.* 2 put forward; propose:

She suggested a swim, and we all agreed. 3 show in an indirect way; hint: *His yawns suggest that he would like to go to bed. v.*

sug gest i bil i ty (səg jes′tə bil′ə tē), quality or condition of being suggestible. *n.*

sug gest i ble (səg jes′tə bəl), 1 capable of being influenced by suggestion. 2 that can be suggested. *adj.*

sug ges tion (səg jes′chən), 1 act of suggesting: *The suggestion of a swim made the children jump with joy.* 2 thing suggested; proposal: *The picnic was an excellent suggestion.* 3 a very small amount; slight trace: *She spoke with just a suggestion of a French accent. n.*

sug ges tive (səg jes′tiv), 1 tending to suggest ideas, acts, or feelings: *The teacher gave an interesting and suggestive list of composition subjects.* 2 tending to suggest something improper or indecent. *adj.* —**sug ges′tive ly,** *adv.* —**sug ges′tive ness,** *n.*

sugar cane
up to 15 ft. high

su i cid al (sü′ə sī′dl), 1 having to do with suicide; leading to suicide; causing suicide. 2 ruinous to one's own interests; disastrous to oneself: *It would be suicidal for a store to sell many things below cost. adj.*

su i cide (sü′ə sīd), 1 the killing of oneself on purpose. 2 person who kills himself on purpose. 3 destruction of one's own interests or prospects. *n.*

suit (süt), 1 set of clothes to be worn together. A man's suit consists of a coat, trousers, and sometimes a vest. A woman's suit consists of a coat and either a skirt or trousers. 2 case in a court of law; application to a court for justice: *He started a suit to collect damages for his injuries.* 3 make suita-

845

adj.	adjective	*n.*	noun
adv.	adverb	*prep.*	preposition
conj.	conjunction	*pron.*	pronoun
interj.	interjection	*v.*	verb
sing.	singular	*pl.*	plural

ble; make fit: *The teacher suited the punishment to the fault by making him sweep the room after he threw bits of paper on the floor.* 4 be suitable for; agree with: *A cold climate suits apples and wheat, but not oranges and tea.* 5 be agreeable, convenient, or acceptable to; please; satisfy: *Which date suits you best?* 6 be becoming to: *That blue sweater suits you.* 7 a request; asking; wooing: *King Arthur's suit was successful, and Guinevere married him.* 8 one of the four sets of cards (spades, hearts, diamonds, and clubs) making up a deck. 9 suite. 1,2,7-9 *n.*, 3-6 *v.*

follow suit, 1 play a card of the same suit as that first played. 2 follow the example of another.

suit oneself, do as one pleases.

suit a bil i ty (sü/tə bil/ə tē), a being suitable; fitness; appropriateness. *n.*

suit a ble (sü/tə bəl), right for the occasion; fitting; proper: *Plain clothes are suitable for school wear. The park gives the children a suitable playground. adj.*

suit a bly (sü/tə blē), in a suitable manner; fitly; appropriately. *adv.*

suit case (süt/kās/), a flat, rectangular traveling bag. *n.*

suite (swēt *for 1,3-5;* swēt *or* süt *for 2*), 1 set of connected rooms to be used by one person or family: *She has a suite of rooms at the hotel—a living room, bedroom, and bath.* 2 set of furniture that matches; suit. 3 any set or series of like things. 4 in music: a a series of connected instrumental movements: *suite for strings.* b a set of dance tunes. 5 group of attendants: *The queen traveled with a suite of twelve. n.*

sui tor (sü/tər), 1 man who is courting a woman: *The princess had many suitors.* 2 person bringing suit in a court of law. 3 anyone who sues or petitions. *n.*

su ki ya ki (sü/kē yä/kē *or* skē yä/kē), a Japanese dish consisting mainly of fried meat, onions, and other vegetables. *n.*

Su la we si (sü/lä wä/sē), Celebes. *n.*

sul fa (sul/fə), 1 of or having to do with a group of drugs derived from sulfanilamide, and used in treating various bacterial infections. 2 a sulfa drug. 1 *adj.,* 2 *n.*

sul fa nil a mide (sul/fə nil/ə mīd), a white, crystalline substance used

in treating various infections. *n.*

sul fate (sul/fāt), any salt of sulfuric acid. *n.* Also, **sulphate.**

sul fide (sul/fīd), any compound of sulfur with another element or radical. *n.* Also, **sulphide.**

sul fur (sul/fər), a yellow, highly flammable, nonmetallic element that burns with a blue flame and a stifling odor. Sulfur is found abundantly in volcanic regions, occurring in nature in both free and combined forms, and is also a constituent of proteins. It is used in making matches, gunpowder, paper pulp, fertilizers, insecticides, etc. *n.* Also, **sulphur.**

sul fur ic (sul fyür/ik), 1 of or having to do with sulfur. 2 containing sulfur. *adj.* Also, **sulphuric.**

sulfuric acid, a heavy, oily, colorless, and very corrosive acid derived from sulfur; oil of vitriol; vitriol. Sulfuric acid is used in making explosives and fertilizers, in refining petroleum, and in many other industrial processes.

sul fur ous (sul/fər əs *or* sul/fyər əs), 1 of or having to do with sulfur. 2 containing sulfur. 3 like sulfur; like burning sulfur. 4 of or like the fires of hell; hellish. *adj.* Also, **sulphurous.**

sulk (sulk), 1 hold aloof in a sullen manner; be sulky. 2 a sulking; a fit of sulking. 3 **the sulks,** bad humor shown by sulking: *The baby seems to have a fit of the sulks.* 1 *v.,* 2,3 *n.*

sulk i ly (sul/kə lē), in a sulky manner. *adv.*

sulk i ness (sul/kē nis), sulky behavior; sullenness. *n.*

sulk y (sul/kē), 1 silent and bad-humored because of resentment; sullen: *Some children become sulky when they cannot have their own way.* 2 a light one-horse carriage with two wheels, for one person, now commonly used in trotting races. 1 *adj.,* **sulk i er, sulk i est;** 2 *n., pl.* **sulk ies.**

sul len (sul/ən), 1 silent because of bad humor or anger: *The sullen child refused to answer my question.* 2 gloomy; dismal: *The sullen skies threatened rain. adj.* —**sul/len ly,** *adv.* —**sul/len ness,** *n.*

Sul li van (sul/ə vən), Sir **Arthur Seymour,** 1842-1900, English composer who wrote the music for comic operas for which Sir William Gilbert wrote the words. *n.*

sul ly (sul/ē), to soil, stain, or tarnish: *Malicious gossip sullied the lawyer's reputation. Smog sullied the usually attractive skyline of the city. v.,* **sul lied, sul ly ing.**

sul phate (sul/fāt), sulfate. *n.*

sul phide (sul/fīd), sulfide. *n.*

sul phur (sul/fər), sulfur. *n.*

sul phur ic (sul fyür/ik), sulfuric. *adj.*

sul phur ous (sul/fər əs *or* sul/fyər əs), sulfurous. *adj.*

sul tan (sul/tn), ruler of a Moslem country. Turkey was ruled by a sultan until 1922. *n.*

sul tan a (sul tan/ə), 1 wife of a sultan. 2 mother, sister, or daughter of a sultan. *n., pl.* **sul tan as.**

sul tan ate (sult/n āt), 1 position, authority, or period of rule of a sultan. 2 territory ruled over by a sultan. *n.*

sul tri ness (sul/trē nis), sultry condition or quality. *n.*

sul try (sul/trē), 1 hot, close, and moist: *We expect sultry weather during July.* 2 hot or fiery: *a sultry sun, a sultry glance. adj.,* **sul tri er, sul tri est.**

sum (sum), 1 amount of money: *We paid a large sum for the house.* 2 number or quantity obtained by adding two or more numbers or quantities together: *The sum of 2 and 3 and 4 is 9.* 3 problem in arithmetic: *He can do easy sums in his head, but he has to use pencil and paper for hard ones.* 4 the whole amount; total amount: *To win the prize seemed to her the sum of happiness.* 5 find the total of. 1-4 *n.,* 5 *v.,* **summed, sum ming.**

sum up, express or tell briefly: *Sum up the main points of the lesson in three sentences. The judge summed up the evidence.*

su mac *or* **su mach** (sü/mak *or* shü/mak), 1 shrub or small tree which has divided leaves that turn scarlet in the autumn and clusters of red or white fruit. 2 its dried leaves, used in tanning and dyeing. *n.*

sulky (def. 2)

Su ma tra (sù mä/trə), large island in Indonesia, off the SE coast of Asia. *n.*

Su mer (sü/mər), ancient region in the valley of the Euphrates River, north of its mouth. *n.*

Su mer i an (sü mir/ē ən), 1 of or having to do with the people of Sumer or their language. 2 person who was born or lived in Sumer. 3 their language. Sumerian is recorded in cuneiform inscriptions. 1 *adj.,* 2,3 *n.*

sum mar i ly (sə mer/ə lē *or* sum/ər ə lē), in a summary manner; briefly; without delay. *adv.*

sum ma rize (sum/ə rīz/), make a summary of; give only the main points of; express briefly: *summarize the story* *of a book.* *v.,* **sum ma rized, sum ma riz ing.**

sum mar y (sum′ər ē), 1 a brief statement giving the main points: *The history book had a summary at the end of each chapter.* 2 concise and comprehensive; brief; short. 3 direct and prompt; without delay or formality: *summary vengeance. The governor took summary action to aid the flood victims.* 1 *n.,* pl. **sum mar ies;** 2,3 *adj.*

sum ma tion (su mā′shən), 1 process of finding the sum or total; addition. 2 the total. 3 (in law) the final presentation of facts and arguments by the counsel for each side. *n.*

sum mer (sum′ər), 1 the warmest season of the year; season of the year between spring and autumn. 2 of or having to do with summer: *summer heat, summer clothes, summer holidays.* 3 pass the summer: *summer at the seashore.* 1 *n.,* 2 *adj.,* 3 *v.*

sum mer house (sum′ər hous′), building in a park or garden in which to sit in warm weather. Summerhouses often have no walls. *n.,* pl. **sum mer hous es** (sum′ər hou′ziz).

sum mer time (sum′ər tīm′), the summer season; summer. *n.*

sum mer y (sum′ər ē), 1 of summer: *summery heat.* 2 for summer: *a summery dress.* 3 like summer: *a summery day in spring. adj.*

sum mit (sum′it), the highest point; top: *the summit of a mountain. The summit of her ambition was to be a doctor. n.*

summit meeting, a meeting between heads of governments, especially for the purpose of settling disagreements.

sum mon (sum′ən), 1 to call with authority; order to come; send for: *I was summoned to the principal's office. A telegram summoned me home.* 2 to call together: *summon an assembly.* 3 to order or notify formally to appear before a court of law or judge, especially to answer a charge. 4 stir to action; rouse: *We summoned our courage and entered the deserted house. v.*

sunbonnet

sum mon er (sum′ə nər), person who summons. *n.*

sum mons (sum′ənz), 1 a formal order or notice to appear before a court of law or judge, especially to answer a charge: *receive a summons for fast driving.* 2 an urgent call; a summoning command, message, or signal: *I hurried*

in response to my friend's summons for help. n., pl. **sum mons es.**

sump (sump), 1 pit or reservoir for collecting water, oil, sewage, factory wastes, etc. 2 pool at the bottom of a mine, where water collects and from which it is pumped. *n.*

sump ter (sump′tər), horse or mule for carrying baggage. *n.*

sump tu ar y (sump′chü er ē), having to do with or regulating the spending of money, especially to control extravagance or waste. A law prohibiting any family from owning more than one car would be a sumptuary law. *adj.*

sump tu ous (sump′chü əs), involving great expense; lavish and costly; magnificent; rich: *sumptuous clothes. The king gave a sumptuous banquet. adj.* —**sump′tu ous ly,** *adv.*

Sum ter (sum′tər), **Fort,** fort in the harbor of Charleston, South Carolina. The Civil War began with a Confederate attack on this fort on April 12, 1861. *n.*

sun (sun), 1 the brightest heavenly body in the sky; the star around which the earth and planets revolve and which supplies them with light and heat. It is a glowing ball of hot gases and is about 93 million miles from the earth. 2 the light and warmth of the sun: *sit in the sun.* 3 expose to the sun's rays: *The swimmers sunned themselves on the beach.* 4 any heavenly body made up of burning gas and having satellites. Many stars are suns and have planets orbiting around them. 5 something like the sun in brightness or splendor; something that is a source of light, honor, glory, or prosperity. 1,2,4,5 *n.,* 3 *v.,* **sunned, sun ning.**

Sun., Sunday.

sun bath, exposure of the body to the sun's rays or to a sunlamp.

sun bathe (sun′bā᷉FH′), expose oneself to the sun's rays or to a sunlamp. *v.,* **sun bathed, sun bath ing.**

sun beam (sun′bēm′), ray of sunlight: *A sunbeam brightened the child's hair to gold. n.*

sun bon net (sun′bon′it), a large bonnet that shades the face and neck. *n.*

sun burn (sun′bėrn′), 1 a burning of the skin by the sun's rays or by a sunlamp. A sunburn is often red and painful. 2 burn the skin by the sun's rays or by a sunlamp. 3 become sunburned: *Her skin sunburns very quickly.* 1 *n.,* 2,3 *v.,* **sun burned** or **sun burnt, sun burn ing.**

sun burnt (sun′bėrnt′), sunburned; a past tense and a past participle of **sunburn.** *v.*

sun dae (sun′dē), dish of ice cream served with syrup, crushed fruits, nuts, etc., over it. *n.*

hat, āge, fär; let, ēqual, tėrm; it, īce; hot, ōpen, ôrder; oil, out; cup, pùt, rüle; ch, child; ng, long; sh, she; th, thin; ᴛ+H, then; zh, measure;

ə represents *a* in about, *e* in taken, *i* in pencil, *o* in lemon, *u* in circus.

Sun day (sun′dē), 1 the first day of the week. 2 the day of rest and worship among Christians. 3 of or on Sundays; not everyday or regular; occasional: *a Sunday driver, Sunday painters.* 1,2 *n.,* 3 *adj.*

Sunday school, 1 school held on Sunday for teaching religion. 2 its members.

sun der (sun′dər), put asunder; separate; part; sever; split: *Time often sunders friends. v.*

in sunder, apart: *Lightning tore the tree in sunder.*

sun dew (sun′dü′ *or* sun′dyü′), plant that grows in bogs and has hairy, sticky leaves with which it captures and absorbs insects. *n.*

sundial

sun di al (sun′dī′əl), instrument for telling the time of day by the position of a shadow cast by the sun; dial. *n.*

sun down (sun′doun′), sunset: *We'll be home by sundown. n.*

sun dries (sun′drēz), sundry things; items not named; odds and ends: *My expenses included $150.00 for room and board, $20.00 for clothing, $15.00 for books, and $10.50 for sundries. n.pl.*

sun dry (sun′drē), several; various: *From sundry hints, I guessed I was to be given a bicycle for my birthday. adj.*

sun fish (sun′fish′), 1 a large fish with tough flesh that lives in tropical or temperate seas. 2 a small freshwater fish of North America, used for food. Sunfish are related to perch. *n., pl.* **sun fish es** or **sun fish.**

sun flow er (sun′flou′ər), a tall plant of the same family as the aster, having large yellow flowers with brown centers. *n.*

sung (sung), a past tense and past participle of **sing.** *Many songs were sung at the concert. v.*

sun glass es (sun′glas′iz), spectacles to protect the eyes from the glare of the

adj. adjective	*n.* noun
adv. adverb	*prep.* preposition
conj. conjunction	*pron.* pronoun
interj. interjection	*v.* verb
sing. singular	*pl.* plural

sun. They are usually made of colored glass. *n.pl.*

sun god, god representing the sun. Many different peoples have worshiped sun gods. Apollo and Ra were sun gods.

sunk (sungk), a past tense and past participle of **sink**. *The ship had sunk to the bottom. v.*

sunk en (sung′kən), 1 that has sunk in water: *a sunken ship.* 2 submerged; underwater: *a sunken rock.* 3 situated below the general level: *a sunken garden.* 4 fallen in; hollow: *sunken eyes. adj.*

sun lamp (sun′lamp′), lamp for producing ultraviolet rays similar to those in sunlight. *n.*

sun less (sun′lis), without sun; without sunlight: *Most flowers will not grow in a sunless place. adj.*

sun light (sun′līt′), the light of the sun: *Outdoor sunlight is very good for the health. n.*

sun lit (sun′lit′), lighted by the sun. *adj.*

sun ni ly (sun′ə lē), in a sunny manner. *adv.*

sun ni ness (sun′ē nis), sunny condition or quality. *n.*

sun ny (sun′ē), 1 having much sunshine: *a sunny day.* 2 exposed to, lighted by, or warmed by the direct rays of the sun: *a sunny room.* 3 like the sun. 4 bright; cheerful; happy: *The baby gave a sunny smile. adj.,* **sun ni er, sun ni est.**

sun parlor, room with many windows to let in sunlight.

sun porch, porch enclosed largely by glass.

sun ray (sun′rā′), sunbeam. *n.*

sun rise (sun′rīz′), 1 the coming up of the sun; the first appearance of the sun in the morning. 2 the time when the sun comes up; the beginning of the day. 3 the display of light or color in the sky at this time. *n.*

sun room (sun′rüm′ *or* sun′rum′), room with many windows to let in sunlight. *n.*

sun set (sun′set′), 1 the going down of the sun; the last appearance of the sun in the evening. 2 the time when the sun goes down; the close of the day. 3 the display of light or color in the sky at this time. *n.*

sun shade (sun′shād′), an umbrella, parasol, awning, etc., used to provide protection against the sun.

sun shine (sun′shīn′), 1 the shining of the sun; light or rays of the sun. 2 the warmth, light, etc., deriving from the rays of the sun. 3 brightness; cheerfulness; happiness. *n.*

sun shin y (sun′shī′nē), 1 having much sunshine. 2 bright; cheerful; happy. *adj.,* **sun shin i er, sun shin i est.**

sun spot (sun′spot′), one of the dark spots that appear at regular intervals on the surface of the sun. Disturbances of the earth's magnetic field often occur when sunspots appear. *n.*

sun stroke (sun′strōk′), a sudden illness caused by overexposure to the sun's rays. Sunstroke results in extreme exhaustion and, often, loss of consciousness. *n.*

sun tan (sun′tan′), the reddish-brown color of a person's skin tanned by the sun or by a sunlamp. *n.*

sun up (sun′up′), sunrise. *n.*

sun ward (sun′wərd), toward the sun: *He glanced briefly sunward as the cloud cast its shadow (adv.). Apples grow larger on the sunward side of the tree (adj.). adv., adj.*

Sun Yat-sen (sün′ yät′sen′), 1866-1925, Chinese revolutionary leader and statesman, president of China from 1921 to 1922.

sup[1] (sup), eat the evening meal; take supper: *She supped alone on bread and milk. v.,* **supped, sup ping.** [from French of the 1200's *souper,* from *soupe* soup]

sup[2] (sup), sip. *v.,* **supped, sup ping;** *n.* [Old English *sūpan*]

su per (sü′pər), 1 INFORMAL. superintendent. 2 INFORMAL. a supernumerary. 3 SLANG. excellent. 1,2 *n.,* 3 *adj.*

super-, prefix. 1 over; above: *Superimpose = impose over or above.* 2 besides; further: *Superadd = add besides or further.* 3 in high proportion; to excess; exceedingly: *Superabundant = abundant to excess.* 4 surpassing: *Supernatural = surpassing the natural.* [from Latin *super* over, above]

su per a bun dance (sü′pər ə-bun′dəns), 1 very great abundance: *a superabundance of rain.* 2 a greater amount than is needed. *n.*

su per a bun dant (sü′pər ə-bun′dənt), 1 very abundant. 2 more than enough. *adj.*

su per add (sü′pər ad′), add besides; add further: *A toothache was superadded to her other troubles. v.*

su per an nu at ed (sü′pər an′yü-ā′tid), 1 retired on a pension. 2 too old for work, service, etc. *adj.*

su perb (su pėrb′), 1 grand and stately; majestic; magnificent; splendid: *Moun-tain scenery is superb. The queen's jewels were superb.* 2 rich; elegant; sumptuous: *a superb dinner.* 3 very fine; first-rate; excellent: *The actor gave a superb performance. adj.* —**su perb′ly,** *adv.*

su per car go (sü′pər kär′gō), officer on a merchant ship who represents the owner and has charge of the cargo and the business affairs of the voyage. *n., pl.* **su per car goes** *or* **su per car gos.**

su per charge (sü′pər chärj′), 1 increase the power of (an internal-combustion engine) by fitting it with a supercharger. 2 charge to excess with excitement, vigor, etc.: *The atmosphere at the trial was supercharged with tension. v.,* **su per charged, su per charg ing.**

su per charg er (sü′pər chär′jər), blower, pump, or similar device on an internal-combustion engine, by means of which a greater amount of the mixture of air and gasoline vapor is forced into the cylinders than the action of the pistons would draw. Superchargers are used especially on racing-car engines and on aircraft engines designed to operate at high altitudes. *n.*

su per cil i ous (sü′pər sil′ē əs), haughty, proud, and contemptuous; disdainful; showing scorn or indifference because of a feeling of superiority: *The duchess looked down at the workman with a supercilious stare. adj.* —**su per cil′i ous ly,** *adv.*

su per con duc tor (sü′pər kən-duk′tər), metal, such as lead or tin, that can conduct electric current with no resistance at temperatures near absolute zero. *n.*

su per e rog a to ry (sü′pər ə rog′ə-tôr′ē), 1 doing more than duty requires. 2 unnecessary; superfluous. *adj.*

su per fi cial (sü′pər fish′əl), 1 of the surface; on the surface; at the surface: *superficial measurement. His burns were superficial and soon healed.* 2 concerned with or understanding only what is on the surface; not thorough; shallow: *superficial knowledge, a superficial education.* 3 not real or genuine: *a superficial friendship. adj.*

su per fi ci al i ty (sü′pər fish′ē al′ə-tē), 1 superficial quality or condition; shallowness. 2 something superficial. *n., pl.* **su per fi ci al i ties.**

su per fi cial ly (sü′pər fish′ə lē), in a superficial manner; on the surface; not thoroughly: *superficially attractive. adv.*

su per fine (sü′pər fīn′), 1 very fine; extra fine. 2 too refined; too nice. *adj.*

su per flu i ty (sü′pər flü′ə tē), 1 a greater amount than is needed; excess: *Our orchard gives us a superfluity of apples.* 2 something not needed: *Lux-*

uries are superfluities. n., pl. **su per-
flu i ties.**

su per flu ous (sù per′flü əs), 1 more
than is needed; excessive; surplus: *In
writing telegrams it pays to omit superfluous words.* 2 needless; unnecessary:
A raincoat is superfluous on a clear day.
adj. —**su per′flu ous ly,** *adv.*

su per high way (sü′pər hī′wā),
highway for fast traveling. Superhigh-
ways are often very long and have
two or more lanes for traffic in each
direction. *n.*

su per hu man (sü′pər hyü′mən),
1 above or beyond what is human: *Angels are superhuman beings.* 2 above or
beyond ordinary human power, experience, etc.: *With a superhuman burst
of speed, the runner set a new Olympic
record.* *adj.*

su per im pose (sü′pər im pōz′), put
on top of something else. *v.,* **su per-
im posed, su per im pos ing.**

su per in tend (sü′pər in tend′), oversee and direct (work or workers); manage (a place, institution, etc.). *v.*

su per in tend ence (sü′pər in-
ten′dəns), guidance and direction; management. *n.*

su per in tend en cy (sü′pər in-
ten′dən sē), position, authority, or work
of a superintendent. *n., pl.* **su per intend en cies.**

su per in tend ent (sü′pər in ten′-
dənt), person who oversees, directs,
or manages; supervisor: *a superintendent of schools, a superintendent of a
factory or an apartment house.* *n.*

su per i or (sə pir′ē ər), 1 above the
average; very good; excellent: *superior
work in school.* 2 higher in quality; better; greater: *a superior blend of coffee.
We lost the baseball game to a superior
team.* 3 higher in position, rank, importance, etc.: *a superior officer.* 4 person
who is superior: *A captain is a lieutenant's superior.* 5 showing a feeling of
being above others; proud: *superior
airs, superior manners.* 6 head of
a monastery or convent. 1-3,5 *adj.,*
4,6 *n.*

superior to, 1 higher than; above:
*People consider themselves superior to
monkeys.* 2 better than; greater than:
superior to the enemy in weapons. 3 not
giving in to; above yielding to: *A wise
person is superior to flattery.*

Su per i or (sə pir′ē ər), **Lake,** the
largest of the five Great Lakes. It is
the largest body of fresh water in the
world. *n.*

su per i or i ty (sə pir′ē ôr′ə tē), superior state or quality: *No one doubts
the superiority of modern ways of traveling over those of olden times.* *n.*

su per la tive (sə pėr′lə tiv), 1 of the
highest kind; above all others; supreme:

King Solomon had superlative wisdom.
2 person or thing above all others; supreme example. 3 the highest degree of
comparison of an adjective or adverb.
Fairest and *most slowly* are the superlatives of *fair* and *slowly.* 4 showing the
highest degree of comparison of an
adjective or adverb. *Best* is the superlative form of *good.* 1,4 *adj.,* 2,3 *n.*
—**su per′la tive ness,** *n.*

talk in superlatives, exaggerate.

su per la tive ly (sə pėr′lə tiv lē), to
the highest degree; above all others;
supremely. *adv.*

su per man (sü′pər man′), person
having more than human powers. *n., pl.*
su per men.

su per mar ket (sü′pər mär′kit), a
large store for groceries and household
articles in which customers select their
purchases from open shelves and pay
for them just before leaving. *n.*

su per nal (sù pėr′nl), 1 heavenly;
divine. 2 lofty; exalted. *adj.*

su per nat ur al (sü′pər nach′ər əl),
1 above or beyond what is natural: *Angels and devils are supernatural beings.*
2 **the supernatural,** supernatural
agencies, influences, or phenomena.
1 *adj.,* 2 *n.*—**su′per nat′ur al ly,** *adv.*

su per nat ur al ism (sü′pər nach′-
ər ə liz′əm), 1 supernatural character or
agency. 2 belief in the supernatural. *n.*

su per nu me rar y (sü′pər nü′mə-
rer′ē *or* sü′pər nyü′mə rer′ē), 1 more
than the usual or necessary number;
extra. 2 an extra person or thing.
3 person who appears on the stage but
has no lines to speak: *In addition to the
regular actors, there were 20 super-
numeraries for the mob scene.* 1 *adj.,*
2,3 *n., pl.* **su per nu me rar ies.**

su per pow er (sü′pər pou′ər),
1 power on an extraordinary or extensive scale. 2 nation so great or strong
as a power that its actions and policies
greatly affect those of smaller, less powerful nations. The United States and
the Soviet Union are superpowers. *n.*

su per script (sü′pər skript), 1 written above. 2 number, letter, etc., written
above and to one side of a symbol.
In $a^3 = b^n$ the *3* and the *n* are super-
scripts. 1 *adj.,* 2 *n.*

su per scrip tion (sü′pər skrip′-
shən), 1 a writing above, on or outside of something. 2 something written above or on the outside, such as the
address on a letter or parcel. *n.*

su per sede (sü′pər sēd′), 1 take the
place of; cause to be set aside; displace:
*Electric lights have superseded gaslights
in American homes.* 2 fill the place of;
replace: *A new governor superseded the
old one.* *v.,* **su per sed ed, su persed ing.**

su per sen si tive (sü′pər sen′sə tiv),

hat, āge, fär; let, ēqual, tėrm;
it, īce; hot, ōpen, ôrder;
oil, out; cup, pùt, rüle; ch, child;
ng, long; sh, she; th, thin;
ŦH, then; zh, measure;

ə represents *a* in about,
e in taken, *i* in pencil,
o in lemon, *u* in circus.

extremely or abnormally sensitive. *adj.*

su per son ic (sü′pər son′ik), 1 of or
having to do with sound waves beyond
the limit of human audibility (above
frequencies of 20,000 cycles per second). 2 greater than the speed of sound
in air (about 741 miles per hour at sea
level). 3 capable of moving at a speed
greater than the speed of sound: *supersonic aircraft.* *adj.*

su per sti tion (sü′pər stish′ən), 1 an
unreasoning fear of what is unknown or
mysterious; unreasoning expectation.
2 belief or practice founded on ignorant
fear or mistaken reverence: *A common
superstition considers 13 an unlucky
number.* *n.*

su per sti tious (sü′pər stish′əs), full
of superstition; likely to believe superstitions; caused by superstition; having
to do with superstition: *a superstitious habit, a superstitious belief.* *adj.*
—**su′per sti′tious ly,** *adv.*

su per struc ture (sü′pər struk′-
chər), 1 structure built on something
else. 2 all of a building above the foundation. 3 parts of a ship above the main
deck. *n.*

SUPERSTRUCTURE

superstructure (def. 3)

su per tax (sü′pər taks′), tax in addition to a normal tax. *n., pl.* **su per-
tax es.**

su per vene (sü′pər vēn′), come as
something additional or interrupting. *v.,*
su per vened, su per ven ing.

su per vise (sü′pər vīz′), look after and
direct (work or workers, a process, etc.);
oversee; superintend; manage: *Study
halls are supervised by teachers.* *v.,*
su per vised, su per vis ing.

su per vi sion (sü′pər vizh′ən), management; direction; oversight: *The
house was built under the careful supervision of an architect.* *n.*

su per vi sor (sü′pər vī′zər), person
who supervises. *n.*

adj.	adjective	*n.*	noun
adv.	adverb	*prep.*	preposition
conj.	conjunction	*pron.*	pronoun
interj.	interjection	*v.*	verb
sing.	singular	*pl.*	plural

su per vi so ry (sü′pər vī′zər ē), 1 of a supervisor; having to do with supervision. 2 supervising. *adj.*

su pine (sü pīn′), 1 lying flat on the back: *a supine person.* 2 lazily inactive; listless. *adj.* —**su pine′ly**, *adv.*

sup per (sup′ər), the evening meal; meal eaten early in the evening if dinner is near noon, or late in the evening if dinner is at six or later. *n.*

sup per less (sup′ər lis), having no supper; going without supper: *The disobedient child was sent to bed supperless. adj.*

sup per time (sup′ər tīm′), the time at which supper is served. *n.*

sup plant (sə plant′), 1 take the place of; displace or set aside: *Machinery has supplanted hand labor in making shoes.* 2 take the place of by unfair methods or by treacherous means: *The prince plotted to supplant the king. v.*

sup ple (sup′əl), 1 bending or folding easily: *a supple birch tree, supple leather.* 2 capable of bending easily; moving easily or nimbly: *a supple dancer.* 3 readily adaptable to different ideas, circumstances, people, etc.; yielding: *a supple mind. She gets along well with people because of her supple nature. adj.*, **sup pler, sup plest.** —**sup′ple ness,** *n.*

sup ple ment (sup′lə mənt *for 1,3;* sup′lə ment *for 2*), 1 something added to complete a thing, or to make it larger or better. Many newspapers and periodicals have supplements that are usually of a special character and issued as an additional feature. 2 supply what is lacking in; add to; complete: *He supplements his diet with vitamin pills.* 3 something added to supply a deficiency: *a diet supplement.* 1,3 *n.,* 2 *v.*

sup ple men tal (sup′lə men′tl), supplementary. *adj.*

sup ple men tar y (sup′lə men′tər ē), added to supply what is lacking; additional: *a volume supplementary to the original set. The new members of the class received supplementary instruction. adj.*

supplementary angle, either of two angles which together form an angle of 180 degrees: *A 60-degree angle is the supplementary angle of a 120-degree angle.*

sup pli ance (sup′lē əns), supplication. *n.*

sup pli ant (sup′lē ənt), 1 asking humbly and earnestly: *He sent a suppliant message for help.* 2 person who asks humbly and earnestly: *I knelt as a suppliant before the queen.* 1 *adj.,* 2 *n.*

sup pli cant (sup′lə kənt), suppliant. *n., adj.*

sup pli cate (sup′lə kāt), 1 beg humbly and earnestly: *The parents supplicated the judge to spare their child.* 2 pray humbly. *v.,* **sup pli cat ed, sup pli cat ing.**

sup pli ca tion (sup′lə kā′shən), 1 a supplicating. 2 a humble and earnest request or prayer: *Supplications to God arose from many of the people in the besieged town. n.*

sup pli ca to ry (sup′lə kə tôr′ē), supplicating. *adj.*

sup pli er (sə plī′ər), person or thing that supplies. *n.*

sup ply (sə plī′), 1 provide (what is lacking); furnish: *Many cities supply books for children in school. He is supplying us with ice.* 2 quantity ready for use; stock; store: *The school gets its supplies of books, paper, pencils, chalk, etc., from the city. We have a large supply of milk in the refrigerator.* 3 quantity of an article in the market ready for purchase, especially at a given price: *a supply of coffee.* 4 **supplies,** *pl.* the food, equipment, etc., necessary for an army, expedition, or the like. 5 make up for (a loss, lack, absence, etc.); fill: *supply a deficiency. Rocks and stumps supplied the place of chairs at the picnic.* 6 satisfy (a want, need, etc.): *There was just enough to supply the demand.* 7 act of supplying. 1,5,6 *v.,* **sup plied, sup ply ing;** 2-4,7 *n., pl.* **sup plies.**

sup port (sə pôrt′), 1 keep from falling; hold up: *Walls support the roof.* 2 give strength or courage to; keep up; help: *Hope supported us during our troubles.* 3 provide for: *support a large family.* 4 maintain, keep up, or keep going: *This city supports two orchestras.* 5 be in favor of; back; second: *She supports the amendment.* 6 help prove; bear out: *The facts support his claim.* 7 put up with; bear; endure: *She couldn't support life without friends.* 8 act of supporting: *He spoke in support of the proposal.* 9 condition of being supported: *This argument lacks support.* 10 help or assistance: *He needs our financial support.* 11 means of livelihood: *That family lacks support.* 12 person or thing that supports; prop:

supplementary angles:
ABC and ABD

The neck is the support of the head. 13 provide a military unit with supplies, transportation, reserves, protection, etc. 14 part of a military unit which provides supplies, transportation, reserves, protection, etc., to the rest of the unit. 1-7,13 *v.,* 8-12,14 *n.*

sup port a ble (sə pôr′tə bəl), capable of being supported; bearable or endurable. *adj.*

sup port er (sə pôr′tər), person or thing that supports. *n.*

sup por tive (sə pôr′tiv), providing support; supporting: *supportive evidence. adj.*

sup pose (sə pōz′), 1 consider as possible; take for granted; assume: *Suppose you are late, what excuse will you make?* 2 believe, think, or imagine: *I suppose she will come at noon.* 3 involve as necessary; imply: *An invention supposes an inventor.* 4 expect: *I'm supposed to be there early. v.,* **sup posed, sup pos ing.**

sup posed (sə pōzd′), accepted as true; considered as possible or probable; assumed: *The supposed beggar was really a prince. adj.*

sup pos ed ly (sə pō′zid lē), according to what is supposed or was supposed. *adv.*

sup pos ing (sə pō′zing), in the event that; if: *Supposing it rains, shall we go? conj.*

sup po si tion (sup′ə zish′ən), 1 act of supposing. 2 thing supposed; belief; opinion: *The speaker planned her talk on the supposition that her listeners would be schoolchildren. n.*

sup pos i to ry (sə poz′ə tôr′ē), medicine in the form of a cone or cylinder to be put into the rectum or vagina. *n., adj.* **sup pos i to ries.**

sup press (sə pres′), 1 put an end to; stop by force; put down: *suppress a rebellion.* 2 keep in; hold back; keep from appearing: *suppress the news. She suppressed a yawn.* 3 subdue (a feeling, etc.): *suppress a desire.* 4 check the flow of; stop: *suppress bleeding. v.*

sup pres sion (sə presh′ən), 1 a putting down by force or authority; putting an end to: *Troops were used in the suppression of the revolt.* 2 a keeping in; holding back: *the suppression of a childish fear. The suppression of facts may be as dishonest as the telling of lies. n.*

sup pu rate (sup′yə rāt′), form or discharge pus; fester: *The wound suppurated badly. v.,* **sup pu rat ed, sup pu rat ing.**

sup pu ra tion (sup′yə rā′shən), 1 formation or discharge of pus; festering. 2 pus. *n.*

su pra re nal gland (sü′prə rē′nl), adrenal gland.

su prem a cy (sə prem′ə sē), 1 condition of being supreme. 2 supreme authority or power. *n., pl.* **su prem a cies.**

su preme (sə prēm′), 1 highest in rank or authority: *a supreme ruler.* 2 highest in degree or quality; greatest; utmost: *supreme disgust, supreme courage. People who die for their country make the supreme sacrifice. adj.* —**su preme′ly,** *adv.*

Supreme Being, God.

Supreme Court, 1 the highest court in the United States, which meets at Washington, D.C. It consists of a chief justice and eight associate justices. 2 the highest court in some states of the United States. 3 a similar court in other countries.

Supt., superintendent.

sur cease (sər sēs′), OLD USE. end; cessation. *n.*

sur charge (sėr′chärj′ *for 1,4;* sėr′chärj′ *or* sėr′chärj′ *for 2,3,5),* 1 an additional charge, load, or burden; extra charge: *The express company made a surcharge for delivering the trunk outside of the city limits.* 2 to charge extra. 3 overload; overburden: *The mourner's heart was surcharged with grief.* 4 an additional mark printed on a postage stamp to change its value, date, etc. 5 print a surcharge on (a postage stamp). 1,4 *n.,* 2,3,5 *v.,* **sur charged, sur charg ing.**

sur cin gle (sėr′sing gəl), strap or belt around a horse's body to keep a saddle, blanket, or pack in place. *n.*

surcoat

sur coat (sėr′kōt′), an outer coat; especially, such a garment worn by knights over their armor. *n.*

sure (shur), 1 free from doubt; certain; having ample reason for belief; confident; positive: *She is sure of success. I am quite sure of their guilt.* 2 to be trusted; safe; reliable: *a sure messenger.* 3 never missing, slipping, etc.; unfailing; unerring: *sure aim, a sure touch.* 4 admitting of no doubt or question: *sure proof.* 5 firm: *to stand on sure ground.* 6 INFORMAL. surely; certainly. 1-5 *adj.,* **sur er, sur est;** 6 *adv.* —**sure′ness,** *n.*

for sure, certainly; undoubtedly.

to be sure, of course; certainly: *The weather, to be sure, was unfavorable.*

sure-fire (shur′fīr′), INFORMAL. definite; certain: *a sure-fire success. adj.*

sure-foot ed (shur′fut′id), not liable to stumble, slip, or fall. *adj.*

sure ly (shur′lē), 1 undoubtedly; certainly: *Half a loaf is surely better than none.* 2 without mistake; without missing, slipping, etc.; firmly: *The goat leaped surely from rock to rock. adv.*

sur e ty (shur′ə tē), 1 security against loss, damage, or failure to do something: *An insurance company gives surety against loss by fire.* 2 person who agrees to be responsible for another: *She was surety for her sister's appearance in court on the day set.* 3 OLD USE. a sure thing; certainty. *n., pl.* **sur e ties.**

surf (sėrf), 1 waves or swell of the sea breaking in a foaming mass on the shore or upon shoals, reefs, etc. 2 the deep pounding or thundering sound of this. 3 travel or ride on the crest of a wave, especially with a surfboard. 1,2 *n.,* 3 *v.* —**surf′er,** *n.*

sur face (sėr′fis), 1 the outside of anything: *the surface of a golf ball, the surface of a mountain.* 2 any face or side of a thing: *A cube has six surfaces. The upper surface of the plate has pictures on it.* 3 the outward appearance: *He seems rough, but you will find him very kind below the surface.* 4 of the surface; on the surface; having to do with the surface: *a surface view.* 5 superficial; external: *surface emotions.* 6 put a surface on; make smooth: *surface a road.* 7 rise to the surface: *The submarine surfaced.* 1-3 *n.,* 4,5 *adj.,* 6,7 *v.,* **sur faced, sur fac ing.**

surf board (sėrf′bôrd′), a long, narrow board for riding the surf. *n.*

sur feit (sėr′fit), 1 too much; excess: *A surfeit of food makes one sick. A surfeit of advice annoys me.* 2 disgust or nausea caused by this. 3 to feed or supply to excess. 1,2 *n.,* 3 *v.*

surge (sėrj), 1 rise and fall; move like waves: *A great wave surged over us. The crowd surged through the streets.* 2 a swelling wave; sweep or rush of waves: *Our boat was upset by a surge.* 3 something like a wave: *A surge of anger swept over him.* 1 *v.,* **surged, surg ing;** 2,3 *n.*

sur geon (sėr′jən), doctor who performs operations: *A surgeon removed the boy's appendix. n.*

sur ger y (sėr′jər ē), 1 art and science of treating diseases, injuries, etc., by operations and instruments: *Malaria can be cured by medicine, but a ruptured appendix requires surgery.* 2 operating room or other area where surgical operations are performed. 3 the work performed by a surgeon. *n., pl.* **sur ger ies.**

sur gi cal (sėr′jə kəl), 1 of surgery;

having to do with surgery: *a surgical patient.* 2 used in surgery: *surgical instruments.* 3 performed by a surgeon: *a surgical operation. adj.*

Sur i nam (sur′ə nam), Dutch territory in N South America, on the Atlantic. *n.*

sur li ness (sėr′lē nis), surly condition or character. *n.*

sur ly (sėr′lē), bad-tempered and unfriendly; rude; gruff: *They got a surly answer from their grouchy neighbor. adj.,* **sur li er, sur li est.**

sur mise (sər mīz′ *for 1;* sər mīz′ *or* sėr′mīz *for 2),* 1 infer or guess: *We surmised that the delay was caused by some accident.* 2 formation of an idea with little or no evidence; a guessing: *Their guilt was a matter of surmise; there was no proof.* 1 *v.,* **sur mised, sur mis ing;** 2 *n.*

sur mount (sər mount′), 1 rise above: *That mountain surmounts all the peaks near it.* 2 be above or on top of: *A statue surmounts the monument.* 3 go up and across: *surmount a hill.* 4 overcome: *She surmounted many difficulties. v.*

sur name (sėr′nām′), 1 a last name; family name: *Smith is the surname of Jane Smith.* 2 name added to a person's real name: *William I of England had the surname "the Conqueror."* 3 give an added name to; call by a surname: *Simon was surnamed Peter.* 1,2 *n.,* 3 *v.,* **sur named, sur nam ing.**

sur pass (sər pas′), 1 do better than; be greater than; excel: *She surpasses her sister in arithmetic.* 2 be too much or too great for; go beyond; exceed: *The beauty of the sunset surpassed description. v.* —**sur pass′ing ly,** *adv.*

sur plice (sėr′plis), a broad-sleeved, white gown worn by clergymen

surplice

adj.	adjective	*n.*	noun
adv.	adverb	*prep.*	preposition
conj.	conjunction	*pron.*	pronoun
interj.	interjection	*v.*	verb
sing.	singular	*pl.*	plural

and choir singers over their other clothes. *n.*

sur plus (sėr′pləs *or* sėr′plus), 1 amount over and above what is needed; extra quantity left over; excess: *The bank keeps a large surplus of money in reserve.* 2 more than is needed; extra; excess: *Surplus wheat and cotton are shipped abroad.* 1 *n.,* 2 *adj.*

sur prise (sər prīz′), 1 the feeling caused by something happening suddenly or unexpectedly; astonishment; wonder: *His face showed surprise at the news.* 2 cause to feel surprised; astonish: *The victory surprised us.* 3 something unexpected: *Our grandparents always have a surprise for us on holidays.* 4 that is not expected; surprising: *a surprise party, a surprise visit.* 5 catch unprepared; come upon suddenly; attack suddenly: *The enemy surprised the fort.* 6 a catching unprepared; coming upon suddenly; sudden attack: *The fort was captured by surprise.* 7 lead or bring (a person, etc.) unawares: *The news surprised the visitor into tears.* 1,3,6 *n.,* 2,5,7 *v.,* **sur prised, sur pris ing;** 4 *adj.*

sur pris ing (sər prī′zing), causing surprise or wonder: *a surprising recovery. adj.* —**sur pris′ing ly,** *adv.*

sur re al ism (sə rē′ə liz′əm), a modern movement in painting, sculpture, literature, motion pictures, etc., that tries to show what takes place in dreams and in the subconscious mind. Surrealism is characterized by unusual and unexpected arrangements and distortions of images. *n.*

sur re al ist (sə rē′ə list), artist or writer who uses surrealism. *n.*

sur ren der (sə ren′dər), 1 give up; give (oneself or itself) up; yield: *The captain had to surrender to the enemy. As the storm increased, the castaways on the raft surrendered all hope. They surrendered themselves to bitter grief.* 2 act of surrendering: *The surrender of the fort saved it from bombardment.* 1 *v.,* 2 *n.*

sur rep ti tious (sėr′əp tish′əs), 1 stealthy: *a surreptitious look.* 2 secret and unauthorized: *surreptitious meetings. adj.* —**sur′rep ti′tious ly,** *adv.*

sur rey (sėr′ē), a light, four-wheeled carriage having two seats. *n., pl.* **sur-**

reys. [from *Surrey,* a county in England]

sur ro gate (sėr′ə gāt *or* sėr′ə git), 1 a deputy, especially the deputy of a bishop. 2 (in certain states of the United States) a judge having charge of the probate of wills, the administration of estates, etc. *n.*

sur round (sə round′), 1 shut in on all sides; be around; extend around: *A high fence surrounds the field.* 2 form an enclosure around; encircle: *They surrounded the invalid with every comfort. v.*

sur round ings (sə roun′dingz), surrounding things, conditions, etc.: *The family lived in poor but cheerful surroundings. n.pl.*

sur tax (sėr′taks′), 1 an additional or extra tax on something already taxed. The surtax on incomes usually increases in graded steps on the amount by which income exceeds a certain sum. 2 to subject to a surtax. 1 *n., pl.* **sur tax es;** 2 *v.*

sur veil lance (sər vā′ləns), 1 watch kept over a person: *The police kept the suspected criminal under close surveillance.* 2 supervision. *n.*

sur vey (sər vā′ *for 1,5;* sėr′vā *or* sər-vā′ *for 2-4,6,7*), 1 look over; view; examine: *The buyers surveyed the goods offered for sale.* 2 a general look; view; examination; inspection: *We were pleased with our first survey of the house.* 3 a comprehensive, literary examination, description, or discussion: *a survey of contemporary poetry.* 4 a formal or official inspection, study, poll, etc.: *a survey of public opinion.* 5 to measure for size, shape, position, boundaries, etc.: *They are surveying the land before it is divided into house lots.* 6 a careful measurement: *A survey showed that the northern boundary was not correct.* 7 plan or description of such a measurement: *She pointed out the route of the railroad on the government survey.* 1,5 *v.,* 2-4,6,7 *n., pl.* **sur veys.**

sur vey ing (sər vā′ing), 1 business or act of making surveys of land. 2 mathematical instruction in the principles of making surveys. *n.*

sur vey or (sər vā′ər), person who surveys, especially land. *n.*

sur viv al (sər vī′vəl), 1 act or fact of surviving; continuance of life; living or lasting longer than others. 2 person, thing, custom, belief, etc., that has lasted from an earlier time: *Belief in the evil*

eye is a survival of ancient magic. *n.*

sur vive (sər vīv′), 1 live longer than; remain alive after: *He survived his wife by three years. Only ten of the crew survived the shipwreck.* 2 sustain the effects of and continue to live: *The crops survived the drought.* 3 continue to exist; remain: *These cave paintings have survived for over 15,000 years. v.,* **sur vived, sur viv ing.**

sur vi vor (sər vī′vər), person, animal, or plant that remains alive; thing that continues to exist: *She is the only survivor of a family of nine. There were two survivors from the plane crash. n.*

sus cep ti bil i ty (sə sep′tə bil′ə tē), 1 quality or state of being susceptible; readiness to receive impressions; sensitiveness. 2 **susceptibilities,** *pl.* sensitive feelings. *n., pl.* **sus cep ti bil i ties.**

sus cep ti ble (sə sep′tə bəl), easily influenced by feelings or emotions; very sensitive: *Poetry appealed to his susceptible nature. adj.*

susceptible of, capable of receiving, undergoing, or being affected by: *Oak is susceptible of a high polish.*

susceptible to, easily affected by; liable to; open to: *Young children are susceptible to many diseases. Vain people are susceptible to flattery.*

sus pect (sə spekt′ *for 1-3;* sus′pekt *for 4;* sus′pekt *or* sə spekt′ *for 5*), 1 imagine to be so; think likely: *The old fox suspected danger and did not touch the trap. I suspect that some accident has delayed her.* 2 believe guilty, false, bad, etc., without proof: *The police suspected them of being shoplifters.* 3 feel no confidence in; doubt: *I suspected the truth of my guest's excuse.* 4 person suspected: *The police have arrested two suspects in connection with the bank robbery.* 5 open to or viewed with suspicion; suspected. 1-3 *v.,* 4 *n.,* 5 *adj.*

sus pend (sə spend′), 1 hang down by attaching to something above: *The lamp was suspended from the ceiling.* 2 hold in place as if by hanging: *We saw the smoke suspended in the still air.* 3 stop for a while: *We suspended building operations during the winter.* 4 cause (a law, etc.) to be for a time no longer in force. 5 remove or exclude for a while from some privilege or job: *They were suspended from school for a week for bad conduct.* 6 keep undecided; put off: *The court suspended judgment till next Monday. v.*

sus pend ers (sə spen′dərz), straps worn over the shoulders to hold up the trousers. *n.pl.*

sus pense (sə spens′), 1 condition of being uncertain: *The detective story kept me in suspense until the last chapter.*

surrey

2 anxious uncertainty; anxiety: *There was an air of suspense in the room as the teacher graded our tests.* *n.*

sus pen sion (sə spen′shən), 1 a suspending or a being suspended: *the suspension of a driver's license for speeding.* 2 support on which something is suspended. 3 arrangement of springs for supporting the body of an automobile, railroad car, etc. 4 mixture in which very small particles of a solid remain suspended without dissolving. *n.*

suspension bridge

suspension bridge, bridge having its roadway anchored at each end and suspended on cables or chains between towers.

sus pi cion (sə spish′ən), 1 state of mind of a person who suspects; act of suspecting: *The real thief tried to turn suspicion toward others.* 2 condition of being suspected. 3 a very small amount; slight trace; suggestion: *She spoke with a suspicion of humor.* *n.*

above suspicion, not to be suspected: *Don't blame my friend; he is above suspicion.*

on suspicion, because of being suspected: *They were arrested on suspicion of robbery.*

under suspicion, suspected.

sus pi cious (sə spish′əs), 1 causing one to suspect: *A man was hanging about the house in a suspicious manner.* 2 feeling suspicion; suspecting: *Our dog is suspicious of strangers.* 3 showing suspicion: *The dog gave a suspicious sniff at my leg.* *adj.* —**sus pi′ cious ly,** *adv.* —**sus pi′cious ness,** *n.*

Sus que han na (sus′kwə han′ə), river flowing from central New York State through Pennsylvania and Maryland into Chesapeake Bay. *n.*

Sus sex (sus′iks), county in SE England, divided into **Sussex East** and **Sussex West.** *n.*

sus tain (sə stān′), 1 keep up; keep going: *Hope sustains him in his misery. She eats barely enough to sustain life.* 2 supply with food, provisions, etc.: *sustain a family.* 3 hold up; support: *Arches sustain the weight of the roof.* 4 bear; endure: *The sea wall sustains the shock of the waves.* 5 suffer; experience: *She sustained a great loss in the death of her parents.* 6 allow; admit; favor: *The court sustained his suit.* 7 agree with; confirm: *The facts sustain her theory.* *v.*

sus te nance (sus′tə nəns), 1 means of sustaining life; food or provisions: *The lost campers went for two days without sustenance.* 2 means of living; support: *She gave money for the sustenance of the poor.* *n.*

sut ler (sut′lər), person who follows an army and sells provisions, etc., to the soldiers. *n.*

su ture (sü′chər), 1 the sewing together or joining of two surfaces, especially the edges of a cut or wound. 2 seam formed in sewing up a wound. 3 one of the stitches or fastenings used. 4 unite by suture or in a similar manner. 5 line where two bones, especially of the skull, join. 1-3,5 *n.,* 4 *v.,* **su tured, su tur ing.**

su zer ain (sü′zər in *or* sü′zə rān′), 1 a feudal lord. 2 state or government exercising political control over a dependent state. *n.*

su zer ain ty (sü′zər in tē *or* sü′zə rān′tē), position or authority of a suzerain. *n., pl.* **su zer ain ties.**

svelte (svelt), slender; lithe: *The countess was tall, svelte, and very pale.* *adj.*

SW or **S.W.,** 1 southwest. 2 southwestern.

swab (swob), 1 a mop for cleaning decks, floors, etc. 2 a bit of sponge, cloth, or cotton for cleansing some part of the body or for applying medicine to it. 3 a cleaner for the bore of a firearm. 4 clean with a swab; apply a swab to: *swab a person's throat.* 1-3 *n.,* 4 *v.,* **swabbed, swab bing.**

swad dle (swod′l), bind (a baby) with long, narrow strips of cloth; wrap tightly with clothes, bandages, etc. *v.,* **swad dled, swad dling.**

swaddling clothes (def. 1)

swaddling clothes, 1 long, narrow strips of cloth for wrapping a newborn infant. 2 long clothes for an infant.

swag (swag), SLANG. things stolen; booty; plunder; dishonest political gains. *n.*

swag ger (swag′ər), 1 walk with a bold, rude, or superior air; strut about or show off in a vain or insolent way: *The actor swaggered onto the stage.* 2 boast or brag noisily. 3 bluster; affect by bluster; bluff. 4 a swaggering way of walking, acting, or speaking. 1-3 *v.,* 4 *n.*

Swa hi li (swä hē′lē), a Bantu language containing many Arabic and other foreign words, spoken in much of east-

hat, āge, fär; let, ēqual, tėrm; it, īce; hot, ōpen, ôrder; oil, out; cup, pùt, rüle; ch, child; ng, long; sh, she; th, thin; ₮H, then; zh, measure;

ə represents *a* in about, *e* in taken, *i* in pencil, *o* in lemon, *u* in circus.

ern Africa and parts of Zaïre. *n.*

swain (swān), OLD USE. 1 lover. 2 a young man who lives in the country. *n.*

swale (swāl), a low, wet piece of land; low place. *n.*

swal low[1] (swol′ō), 1 take into the stomach through the throat: *We swallow all our food and drink.* 2 perform the act of swallowing: *I cannot swallow.* 3 take in; absorb: *The waves swallowed up the swimmer.* 4 INFORMAL. believe too easily; accept without question or suspicion: *He will swallow any story.* 5 put up with; take meekly; accept without opposing or resisting: *He had to swallow the insult.* 6 take back: *swallow words said in anger.* 7 keep back; keep from expressing: *She swallowed her displeasure and smiled.* 8 a swallowing: *He took the medicine at one swallow.* 9 amount swallowed at one time: *There are only about four swallows of water left in the bottle.* 1-7 *v.,* 8,9 *n.* [Old English *swelgan*]

swal low[2] (swol′ō), any of a large group of small, swift-flying birds with long, pointed wings and weak feet used only for perching. Swallows are noted for their regular flights or migrations, in large numbers and over very long distances, to avoid cold or find food. Some kinds have deeply forked tails. *n.* [Old English *swealwe*]

swal low tail (swol′ō tāl′), 1 a large butterfly having taillike extensions of the hind wings. 2 swallow-tailed coat. *n.*

swal low-tailed coat, (swol′ō-tāld′), a man's coat with tails, worn at formal evening parties.

swam (swam), past tense of **swim.** *When the boat sank, we swam to shore.* *v.*

swa mi (swä′mē), title of a Hindu religious teacher. *n., pl.* **swa mis.**

swamp (swomp), 1 wet, soft land; marsh: *We will drain the swamp on our farm so that we can plant crops there.* 2 plunge or sink in a swamp or in water: *The horses were swamped in the stream.* 3 fill with water and sink: *Their boat swamped. The wave swamped the boat.* 4 overwhelm or be overwhelmed as by a flood; make or become helpless:

adj. adjective	*n.* noun
adv. adverb	*prep.* preposition
conj. conjunction	*pron.* pronoun
interj. interjection	*v.* verb
sing. singular	*pl.* plural

swamped with work. *He was swamped with letters asking for money.* 1 *n.,* 2-4 *v.*

swamp land (swomp′land′), tract of land covered by swamps. *n.*

swamp y (swom′pē), 1 like a swamp; soft and wet: *The front yard is swampy from the heavy rain.* 2 containing swamps: *a swampy region.* 3 of swamps. *adj.,* **swamp i er, swamp i est.**

swan (swon), 1 a large, graceful water bird with a long, slender, curving neck. The adult is usually pure white. 2 a sweet singer; poet. *n.* —**swan′like′,** *adj.*

swan (def. 1) about 2½ ft. long

swank (swangk), SLANG. stylish; smart; dashing. *adj.*

swank y (swang′kē), SLANG. swank. *adj.,* **swank i er, swank i est.**

swan's-down (swonz′doun′), 1 the soft down of a swan, used for trimming, powder puffs, etc. 2 Also, **swansdown.** a fine, thick, soft cloth made from wool or cotton, used for babies' coats, bathrobes, etc. *n.*

swan song, 1 song which, according to fable, a swan sings as it is about to die. 2 a person's last piece of work.

swap (swop), INFORMAL. 1 to exchange, barter, or trade: *The children swapped books.* 2 an exchange, barter, or trade. 1 *v.,* **swapped, swap ping;** 2 *n.*

sward (swôrd), a grassy surface; turf. *n.*

sware (swer *or* swar), OLD USE. swore; a past tense of **swear.** *v.*

swarm (swôrm), 1 group of bees led by a queen that leave a hive and fly off together to start a new colony. 2 fly off together to start a new colony. 3 group of bees settled together in a hive. 4 a large group of insects, animals, people, etc., moving about together: *Swarms of children were playing in the park.* 5 fly or move about in great numbers; be in very great numbers: *The mosquitoes swarmed about us.* 6 be crowded;

crowd: *The swamp swarms with mosquitoes. Mosquitoes swarmed the open tent.* 1,3,4 *n.,* 2,5,6 *v.*

swart (swôrt), dark; swarthy. *adj.*

swarth y (swôr′THē *or* swôr′thē), having a dark skin: *The ship's crew was swarthy from the sun of the tropics.* *adj.,* **swarth i er, swarth i est.**

swash (swosh), 1 dash (water, etc.) about; splash. 2 a swashing action or sound: *the swash of waves against a boat.* 1 *v.,* 2 *n., pl.* **swash es.**

swash buck ler (swosh′buk′lər), a swaggering swordsman, bully, or boaster. *n.*

swash buck ling (swosh′buk′ling), swaggering; bullying; boasting: *military swashbuckling (n.), a swashbuckling adventurer (adj.).* *n., adj.*

swastikas
left, ancient symbol; right, Nazi symbol

swas ti ka (swos′tə kə), an ancient symbol or ornament like a cross with the arms bent. Swastikas were thought in early times to bring good luck. The swastika with arms turning clockwise was the symbol of the Nazis in Germany. *n., pl.* **swas ti kas.**

swat (swot), INFORMAL. 1 hit sharply or violently: *swat a fly.* 2 a sharp or violent blow. 1 *v.,* **swat ted, swat ting;** 2 *n.*

swatch (swoch), sample of cloth or other material. *n., pl.* **swatch es.**

swath (swoth), 1 the space covered by a single cut of a scythe or by one cut of a mowing machine. 2 row of grass, grain, etc., cut by a scythe or mowing machine. 3 a strip. *n.*

swathe (swāTH), 1 wrap up closely or fully: *swathed in a blanket.* 2 to bind, wrap, or bandage. 3 a wrapping or bandage. 4 envelop or surround like a wrapping: *White clouds swathed the mountain.* 1,2,4 *v.,* **swathed, swathing;** 3 *n.*

sway (swā), 1 swing back and forth; rock from side to side, or to one side: *We swayed across the ballroom. The pail swayed in her hands as she ran.* 2 make move; cause to sway: *The wind sways the grass.* 3 a swinging back and forth or from side to side: *The sway of the pail caused some milk to spill out.* 4 move to one side; turn aside: *The horse swayed left at the crossroads.* 5 to change in opinion or feeling: *Nothing could sway her after she had made up her mind.* 6 to influence, control, or rule: *The speaker's words swayed the audience.* 7 an influence, control, or rule: *a country under the sway of a dictator.* 1,2,4-6 *v.,* 3,7 *n.*

sway backed (swā′bakt′), having the

back sagged or hollowed to an unusual degree: *a swaybacked horse.* *adj.*

Swa zi land (swä′zē land′), country in SE Africa, a member of the Commonwealth of Nations. *n.*

swear (swer *or* swar), 1 make a solemn statement, appealing to God or some other sacred being or object: *A witness at a trial is asked, "Do you swear to tell the truth, the whole truth, and nothing but the truth, so help you God?"* 2 to promise on oath or solemnly (to observe or do something); vow; pledge: *to swear allegiance. The governor swore to uphold the constitution.* 3 bind by an oath; require to promise or pledge: *Members of the club were sworn to secrecy.* 4 use profane language; curse: *They raged and swore.* *v.,* **swore, sworn, swear ing.**

swear by, 1 name as one's witness in taking an oath. 2 have great confidence in.

swear in, admit to office or service by giving an oath: *to swear in a jury.*

swear off, promise to give up: *to swear off smoking.*

swear out, get by swearing that a certain charge is true: *He swore out a warrant for the arrest of the man who had hit him.*

sweat (swet), 1 moisture coming through the pores of the skin: *After mowing the lawn I wiped the sweat from my face.* 2 give out moisture through the pores of the skin: *We sweated because it was very hot.* 3 cause to sweat: *She sweated her horse by riding it too hard.* 4 get rid of by sweating or as if by sweating: *to sweat off excess weight, to sweat out a hard test.* 5 a fit or condition of sweating: *He was in a cold sweat from fear.* 6 INFORMAL. condition of anxiety, impatience, or anything that might make a person sweat: *We were all in a sweat over the big test we would get on Monday.* 7 moisture given out by something or gathered on its surface. 8 give out moisture; collect moisture from the air: *A pitcher of ice water sweats on a hot day.* 9 cause to work hard and under bad conditions: *a company that sweats its workers.* 10 INFORMAL. work very hard. 1, 5-7 *n.,* 2-4,8-10 *v.,* **sweat** or **sweat ed, sweat ing.**

sweat er (swet′ər), a knitted garment of wool, nylon, etc., worn for warmth on the upper part of the body. *n.*

sweat gland, one of the many small, coiled glands under the skin that secrete sweat. Human sweat glands are found in the deeper layer of the skin of most of the body, connecting with the surface through a tube or duct that ends in a pore.

sweat shirt, a heavy pullover with

long sleeves, sometimes with a fleece lining, worn especially by athletes to keep warm before and after exercise.

sweat shop (swet/shop/), place where workers are employed for long hours under very bad conditions of work and at very low wages. *n.*

sweat y (swet/ē), 1 covered or wet with sweat; sweating. 2 causing sweat. 3 laborious. *adj.,* **sweat i er, sweat i est.**

Swede (swēd), person born or living in Sweden. *n.*

Swe den (swēd/n), country in N Europe, east and south of Norway. *Capital:* Stockholm. *n.*

Swed ish (swē/dish), 1 of or having to do with Sweden, its people, or their language. 2 the people of Sweden. 3 language of Sweden. 1 *adj.,* 2 *n.pl.,* 3 *n.sing.*

sweep (swēp), 1 clean or clear (a floor, etc.) with a broom, brush, etc.; use a broom or something like one to remove dirt; brush: *The campers swept the floor of their cabin every morning.* 2 move, drive, or take away with or as with a broom, brush, etc.: *Please sweep the dust into a pan. The wind sweeps the snow into drifts.* 3 remove with a sweeping motion; carry along: *A flood swept away the bridge.* 4 act of sweeping; clearing away; removing: *I made a clean sweep of all my debts.* 5 pass over with a steady movement: *Her fingers swept the strings of the harp. His eyes swept the sky, searching for signs of rain.* 6 move swiftly; pass swiftly: *Bandits swept down on the town. The wind sweeps over the plain.* 7 a steady, driving motion or swift onward course of something: *The sweep of the wind kept the trees from growing tall.* 8 move with dignity: *The diplomat swept out of the room.* 9 move or extend in a long course or curve: *The shore sweeps to the south for miles.* 10 a curve; bend: *the sweep of a road.* 11 a swinging or curving motion: *cut a jungle path with strong sweeps of a machete.* 12 a continuous extent; stretch: *The house looks upon a wide sweep of farming country.* 13 a reach; range; extent: *The mountain is beyond the sweep of your eye.* 14 a winning of all the games in a series, match, contest, etc.; complete victory. 15 person who sweeps chimneys, streets, etc. 16 a long oar used to row or steer a boat. 17 a long pole which pivots on a high post and is used to raise or lower a bucket in a well. 1-3,5,6,8,9 *v.,* **swept, sweep ing;** 4,7,10-17 *n.*

sweep er (swē/pər), person or thing that sweeps: *a carpet sweeper. n.*

sweep ing (swē/ping), 1 passing over a wide space: *Her sweeping glance took in the whole room.* 2 having wide range:

a sweeping victory, a sweeping statement. adj. —**sweep/ing ly,** *adv.*

sweep ings (swē/pingz), dust, rubbish, scraps, etc., swept out or up. *n.pl.*

sweep stake (swēp/stāk/), sweepstakes. *n.*

sweep stakes (swēp/stāks/), 1 system of gambling on horse races, etc. People buy tickets, and the money they pay goes to the holder or holders of winning tickets. 2 the race or contest. 3 prize in such a race or contest. *n.*

sweet (swēt), 1 having a taste like sugar or honey: *Pears are much sweeter than lemons.* 2 having a pleasant taste or smell: *Perfume is sweet.* 3 pleasant; agreeable: *a sweet child, a sweet smile, sweet music.* 4 fresh; not sour, salty, bitter, or spoiled: *He drinks sweet milk and likes sweet butter better than salted butter.* 5 a dear; darling. 6 something sweet. 7 **sweets,** *pl.* candy or other sweet things. 8 in a sweet manner. 1-4 *adj.,* 5-7 *n.,* 8 *adv.* —**sweet/ly,** *adv.*

sweet bread (swēt/bred/), gland of a calf or other young animal, used for food. Neck sweetbread is the thymus gland; stomach sweetbread is the pancreas. *n.*

sweet bri er or **sweet bri ar** (swēt/brī/ər), a wild rose with a tall, prickly stem and single pink flowers; eglantine. *n.*

sweet corn, kind of corn which is eaten by people, usually when it is young and tender. It may be preserved by canning or freezing. *n.*

sweet en (swēt/n), 1 make sweet: *He sweetened his coffee with sugar.* 2 become sweet: *Those pears will sweeten as they ripen. v.* —**sweet/en er,** *n.*

sweet en ing (swēt/n ing), something that sweetens. Sugar is the most common sweetening. *n.*

sweet flag, 1 plant with long, sword-shaped leaves. 2 its fragrant root, used in perfumes and medicines. *n.*

sweet heart (swēt/härt/), a loved one; lover. *n.*

sweet ish (swē/tish), somewhat sweet. *adj.*

sweet meats (swēt/mēts/), candied fruits, sugar-covered nuts, etc.; candy; bonbons. *n.pl.*

sweet ness (swēt/nis), sweet quality: *He likes candy because of its sweetness. She played music that showed the sweetness of the violin's tone. n.*

sweet pea, 1 an annual climbing plant with delicate, fragrant flowers of various colors. 2 its flower.

sweet potato, 1 a creeping vine of warm regions. 2 its sweetish, thick, yellow or reddish root, much used as a vegetable.

sweet-tem pered (swēt/tem/pərd), having a gentle or pleasant nature. *adj.*

hat, āge, fär; let, ēqual, tėrm;
it, īce; hot, ōpen, ôrder;
oil, out; cup, pùt, rüle; ch, child;
ng, long; sh, she; th, thin;
₮H, then; zh, measure;

ə represents *a* in about,
e in taken, *i* in pencil,
o in lemon, *u* in circus.

sweet tooth, fondness for sweets.

sweet william or **sweet William,** plant with dense, rounded clusters of small flowers. It belongs to the same family as the pink.

swell (swel), 1 grow or make bigger: *Bread dough swells as it rises. The bee sting had swelled his finger.* 2 be larger or thicker in a particular place; stick out: *A barrel swells in the middle.* 3 increase in amount, degree, force, etc.: *Savings may swell into a fortune. Volunteers were swelling the ranks.* 4 act of swelling; an increase in amount, degree, force, etc. 5 condition of being swollen. 6 rise or cause to rise above the level: *Rounded hills swell gradually from the village plain. Rain swelled the river.* 7 part that rises or swells out. 8 piece of higher ground; rounded hill. 9 a long, unbroken wave or waves: *The boat rocked in the swell.* 10 grow or make louder: *The sound swelled from a murmur to a roar. All joined in to swell the chorus.* 11 become filled with emotion: *to swell with pride or indignation.* 12 a swelling tone or sound. 13 in music: **a** a gradual increase in sound followed by a decrease. **b** sign for this (<>). 14 INFORMAL. a fashionable person. 15 INFORMAL. stylish; grand. 16 SLANG. excellent; first-rate. 1-3, 6,10,11 *v.,* **swelled, swelled** or **swol len, swell ing;** 4,5,7-9,12-14 *n.,* 15,16 *adj.*

swell ing (swel/ing), an increase in size; swollen part: *There is a swelling on her head where she bumped it. n.*

swel ter (swel/tər), 1 suffer from heat. 2 perspire freely; sweat. 3 a sweltering condition. 1,2 *v.,* 3 *n.*

swept (swept), past tense and past participle of **sweep.** *I swept the room. It was swept clean. v.*

swept-back (swept/bak/), (of the wings of an aircraft) extending outward and sharply backward from the fuselage. *adj.*

swerve (swėrv), 1 turn aside: *The car swerved sharply to avoid hitting the truck. Nothing could swerve her from reaching her goal.* 2 a turning aside: *The swerve of the ball made it hard*

swift

adj.	adjective	*n.*	noun
adv.	adverb	*prep.*	preposition
conj.	conjunction	*pron.*	pronoun
interj.	interjection	*v.*	verb
sing.	singular	*pl.*	plural

to hit. 1 *v.*, **swerved, swerving;** 2 *n.*

swift (swift), 1 moving very fast: *a swift automobile.* 2 coming or happening quickly: *a swift response.* 3 quick, rapid, or prompt to act, etc.: *He is swift to repay a kindness.* 4 in a swift manner. 5 a small bird with long wings. It is related to the hummingbird but looks somewhat like a swallow. 1-3 *adj.*, 4 *adv.*, 5 *n.* —**swift′ly,** *adv.* —**swift′ness,** *n.*

Swift (swift), **Jonathan,** 1667-1745, English writer of satires, born in Ireland, author of *Gulliver's Travels. n.*

swift-foot ed (swift′fut′id), able to run swiftly. *adj.*

swig (swig), INFORMAL. 1 a big or hearty drink. 2 drink heartily or greedily. 1 *n.*, 2 *v.*, **swigged, swig ging.**

swill (swil), 1 kitchen refuse, especially when partly liquid; garbage; slops. Swill is sometimes fed to pigs. 2 drink greedily; drink too much. 1 *n.*, 2 *v.*

swim (swim), 1 move along on or in the water by using arms, legs, fins, etc.: *Fish swim. Most boys and girls like to swim.* 2 swim across: *She swam the river.* 3 make swim: *He swam his horse across the stream.* 4 float: *The roast lamb was swimming in gravy.* 5 be overflowed or flooded with: *Her eyes were swimming with tears.* 6 act, time, motion, or distance of swimming: *Her swim had tired her. She had had an hour's swim.* 7 **the swim,** the current of affairs, activities, etc.: *An active and sociable person likes to be in the swim.* 8 go smoothly; glide: *White clouds swam across the sky.* 9 be dizzy; whirl: *The heat and noise made my head swim.* 1-5,8,9 *v.*, **swam, swum, swim ming;** 6,7 *n.*

swim mer (swim′ər), person or animal that swims. *n.*

swim mer et (swim′ə ret′), an abdominal limb or appendage in many crustaceans, used for respiration, for carrying eggs, etc., and usually adapted for swimming. *n.*

swim ming (swim′ing), 1 practice or sport of swimming: *My friend is an expert at both swimming and diving. She is our teacher in swimming.* 2 act of swimming: *Can you reach the island by swimming?* 3 of or for swimming or

swimmers: *a swimming teacher, a swimming pool.* 4 that swims habitually: *a swimming bird or insect.* 5 dizzy: *a swimming sensation.* 1,2 *n.*, 3-5 *adj.*

swim ming ly (swim′ing lē), with great ease or success: *Everything went swimmingly at our party. adv.*

swim suit (swim′süt′), bathing suit. *n.*

Swin burne (swin′bèrn′), **Algernon Charles,** 1837-1909, English poet and critic. *n.*

swin dle (swin′dl), 1 cheat; defraud: *Honest merchants do not swindle their customers.* 2 get by fraud. 3 an act of swindling; fraud. 1,2 *v.*, **swin dled, swin dling;** 3 *n.*

swin dler (swin′dlər), person who cheats or defrauds. *n.*

swine (swīn), 1 hogs or pigs. 2 a hog. 3 a coarse or beastly person. *n., pl.* **swine.**

swine herd (swīn′hèrd′), person who tends pigs or hogs. *n.*

swing (swing), 1 move back and forth, especially with a regular motion: *The hammock swings. He swings his arms as he walks.* 2 move in a curve: *She swung the automobile around a corner.* 3 act or manner of swinging. 4 a swinging blow: *He brought the hammer down with a long swing.* 5 seat hung from ropes in which one may sit and swing. 6 hang: *We swung the hammock between two trees.* 7 move with a free, swaying motion: *The children came swinging down the street.* 8 a swinging gait or movement; steady, marked rhythm: *The song "Dixie" has a swing.* 9 movement; activity. 10 jazz music with a lively, steady rhythm, in which the players improvise freely on the original melody. 11 INFORMAL. manage successfully: *swing a business deal.* 1,2,6,7,11 *v.*, **swung, swing ing;** 3-5, 8-10 *n.*

in full swing, going on actively and completely; without restraint: *By five o'clock the party was in full swing.*

swin ish (swī′nish), 1 very selfish; greedy. 2 dirty; filthy; beastly. *adj.*

swipe (swīp), 1 INFORMAL. a sweeping stroke; hard blow: *He made two swipes at the golf ball without hitting it.* 2 INFORMAL. to strike with a sweeping blow. 3 SLANG. steal. 1 *n.*, 2,3 *v.*, **swiped, swip ing.**

swirl (swèrl), 1 move or drive along with a twisting motion; whirl: *dust swirling in the air, a stream swirling over rocks. The heat and noise made my head swirl.* 2 a swirling movement; whirl; eddy. 3 to twist or curl: *a lock of hair swirled against the neck.* 4 a twist or curl: *a swirl of whipped cream on top of a sundae. Swirls of crepe paper decorated the room.* 1,3 *v.*, 2,4 *n.*

swish (swish), 1 move with a thin,

light, hissing or brushing sound: *The whip swished through the air.* 2 make such a sound: *The long gown swished as she danced the floor.* 3 cause to swish: *He swished the stick.* 4 a swishing movement or sound: *the swish of little waves on the shore.* 1-3 *v.*, 4 *n., pl.* **swish es.**

Swiss (swis), 1 of or having to do with Switzerland or its people. 2 person born or living in Switzerland. 3 the people of Switzerland. 1 *adj.*, 2 *n.sing.*, 3 *n.pl.*

Swiss cheese, a firm, pale-yellow or whitish cheese with many large holes.

switch (def. 5)—two types of switches. Moving either lever as indicated turns the switch on.

switch (swich), 1 a slender stick used in whipping. 2 to whip or strike: *He switched the horse to make it gallop.* 3 a stroke or lash: *The big dog knocked a vase off the table with a switch of its tail.* 4 move or swing like a switch: *The horse switched its tail to drive off the flies.* 5 device for making or breaking a connection in an electric circuit. 6 pair of movable rails by which a train can shift from one track to another. 7 to shift or turn by using a switch: *to switch railroad cars from one track to another, switch the lights off or on.* 8 to change or shift: *switch places. They switched hats.* 9 a change or shift: *a last-minute switch of plans. He lost the election when his supporters made a switch of their votes to the other candidate.* 1,3,5,6,9 *n., pl.* **switch es;** 2,4,7,8 *v.*

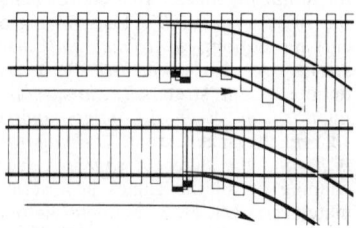

switch (def. 6) in two positions. Arrows show direction train will travel.

switch blade (swich′blād′), pocketknife with a blade that springs out at the push of a button or knob on the handle. *n.*

switch board (swich′bôrd′), panel containing the necessary switches, meters, and other devices for opening, closing, combining, or controlling electric circuits. A telephone switchboard has plugs for connecting one line to another. *n.*

switch-hit ter (swich′hit′ər), a baseball player who bats either right- or left-handed. *n.*

switch man (swich′mən), man in charge of one or more railroad switches. *n., pl.* **switch men.**

Swit zer land (swit′sər lənd), small country in central Europe, north of Italy. *Capital:* Bern. *n.*

swivel (def. 2)

swiv el (swiv′əl), 1 a fastening that allows the thing fastened to turn round freely upon it. 2 a chain link having two parts, one of which turns freely in the other. 3 support on which a gun can turn round. 4 turn on a swivel. 1-3 *n.,* 4 *v.*

swivel chair, chair having a seat that turns on a swivel.

swol len (swō′lən), 1 swelled: *a swollen ankle.* 2 swelled; a past participle of **swell.** 1 *adj.,* 2 *v.*

swoon (swün), 1 to faint: *swoon at the sight of blood.* 2 a faint: *Cold water may help to bring someone out of a swoon.* 1 *v.,* 2 *n.*

swoop (swüp), 1 come down with a rush, as a hawk does; sweep rapidly down upon in a sudden attack: *The pirates swooped down on the towns.* 2 a rapid downward sweep; sudden, swift descent or attack: *With one swoop the hawk seized the chicken and flew away.* 3 snatch: *The nurse rushed after the running child and swooped him up in her arms.* 1,3 *v.,* 2 *n.*

sword (sôrd), 1 weapon, usually metal, with a long, sharp blade fixed in a handle or hilt. 2 **the sword,** fighting, war, or military power: *Those that live by the sword shall perish by the sword.* *"The pen is mightier than the sword."* n. —**sword′like′,** *adj.*

at swords' points, very unfriendly.

cross swords, 1 fight. 2 quarrel; dispute.

swordfish—up to 15 ft. long

sword fish (sôrd′fish′), a very large saltwater food fish with a long, swordlike projection from its upper jaw. *n., pl.* **sword fish es** or **sword fish.**

sword play (sôrd′plā′), action, prac-

tice, or art of wielding a sword; fencing. *n.*

swords man (sôrdz′mən), 1 person skilled in using a sword. 2 person using a sword. *n., pl.* **swords men.**

swore (swôr), past tense of **swear.** *I swore not to tell anyone my friend's secret.* v.

sworn (swôrn), 1 past participle of **swear.** *A solemn oath of loyalty was sworn by all the knights.* 2 having taken an oath; bound by an oath: *There were ten sworn witnesses.* 3 declared, promised, etc., with an oath: *We have her sworn statement.* 1 *v.,* 2,3 *adj.*

swum (swum), past participle of **swim.** *He had never swum before.* v.

swung (swung), past tense and past participle of **swing.** *He swung his arms as he walked. The door had swung open.* v.

syb a rite (sib′ə rīt′), person who cares very much for luxury and pleasure. *n.*

syc a more (sik′ə môr), 1 a tall North American shade tree with broad leaves, small, round fruit, and bark that breaks or peels off in tiny scales; buttonwood; plane tree. 2 a large maple tree of Europe and Asia. 3 a fig tree of Egypt and Syria. *n.*

syc o phant (sik′ə fənt), a servile or self-seeking flatterer. *Great men are likely to be surrounded by sycophants who want favors.* *n.*

syc o phan tic (sik′ə fan′tik), having to do with, characteristic of, or acting as a sycophant. *adj.*

Syd ney (sid′nē), the largest city and most important seaport in Australia, in the SE part. *n.*

syl lab ic (sə lab′ik), 1 of, having to do with, or consisting of syllables. 2 forming a separate syllable by itself. The second *l* sound in *little* is syllabic. *adj.*

syl lab i cate (sə lab′ə kāt), syllabify. *v.,* **syl lab i cat ed, syl lab i cat ing.**

syl lab i ca tion (sə lab′ə kā′shən), division into syllables. *n.*

syl lab i fi ca tion (sə lab′ə fə kā′shən), syllabication. *n.*

syl lab i fy (sə lab′ə fī), divide into syllables. *v.,* **syl lab i fied, syl lab i fying.**

syl la ble (sil′ə bəl), 1 word or part of a word pronounced as a unit that usually consists of a vowel alone or a vowel with one or more consonants. The word *syllable* (sil′ə bəl), has three syllables. Certain consonant sounds may be used as a vowel sound in syllables, such as the (l) in *bottle* (bot′l) or the (n) in *hidden* (hid′n). 2 letter or group of letters representing a syllable in writing and printing. A syllable may be separated from other syllables of the word

hat, āge, fär; let, ēqual, tėrm;
it, īce; hot, ōpen, ôrder;
oil, out; cup, pu̇t, rüle; ch, child;
ng, long; sh, she; th, thin;
ᵺH, then; zh, measure;

ə represents *a* in about,
e in taken, *i* in pencil,
o in lemon, *u* in circus.

by a space, hyphen, or other mark to show where the word may be divided at the end of a line. *Strength* has only one syllable; *ap prox i mate* has four. *n.*

syl la bus (sil′ə bəs), a brief statement of the main points of a speech, a book, a course of study, etc. *n., pl.* **syl la bus es, syl la bi** (sil′ə bī).

syl lo gism (sil′ə jiz′əm), a form of argument or reasoning, consisting of two statements and a conclusion drawn from them. EXAMPLE: All trees have roots; an oak is a tree; therefore, an oak has roots. *n.*

sylph (silf), 1 a slender, graceful girl or woman. 2 an imaginary spirit of the air. *n.*

syl van (sil′vən), of the woods; in the woods; consisting of woods; having woods: *They lived in a sylvan retreat.* *adj.* Also, **silvan.**

sym bi o sis (sim′bē ō′sis), the association or living together of two unlike organisms for the benefit of each other. Most lichens, which are composed of an alga and a fungus, are examples of symbiosis; the alga provides the food, and the fungus provides water and protection. *n.*

sym bi ot ic (sim′bē ot′ik), having to do with symbiosis; living in symbiosis. *adj.*

sym bol (sim′bəl), something that stands for or represents something else: *The lion is the symbol of courage; the lamb, of meekness; the olive branch, of peace; the lily, of purity.* The marks +, −, ×, and ÷ are symbols for add, subtract, multiply, and divide. *n.*

sym bol ic (sim bol′ik), 1 used as a symbol: *A lily is symbolic of purity.* 2 of a symbol; expressed by a symbol or symbols; using symbols: *Writing is a symbolic form of expression.* *adj.* —**sym bol′i cal ly,** *adv.*

sym bol i cal (sim bol′ə kəl), symbolic. *adj.*

sym bol ism (sim′bə liz′əm), 1 use of symbols; representation by symbols. 2 system of symbols: *The cross, the crown, the lamb, and the lily are parts of Christian symbolism.* *n.*

sym bol i za tion (sim′bə lə zā′shən),

adj. adjective	*n.* noun
adv. adverb	*prep.* preposition
conj. conjunction	*pron.* pronoun
interj. interjection	*v.* verb
sing. singular	*pl.* plural

symbolizing; representation by symbols. *n.*

sym bol ize (sim′bə līz), 1 be a symbol of; stand for; represent: *A dove symbolizes peace.* 2 represent by a symbol or symbols: *The Indians and the settlers symbolized their friendship by smoking the peace pipe.* 3 use symbols. *v.,* **sym bol ized, sym bol iz ing.**

sym met ric (si met′rik), symmetrical. *adj.*

sym met ri cal (si met′rə kəl), having symmetry; well-proportioned: *symmetrical figures. adj.* —**sym met′ri cal ly,** *adv.*

symmetry (def. 1)
top, bilateral
bottom, radial

sym me try (sim′ə trē), 1 exact correspondence in size, shape, and arrangement of parts on opposite sides of a line or plane, or around a center or axis. 2 pleasing proportions between the parts of a whole; well-balanced arrangement of parts; harmony: *A swollen cheek spoiled the symmetry of his face. n., pl.* **sym me tries.**

sym pa thet ic (sim′pə thet′ik), 1 having or showing kind feelings toward others; sympathizing: *She is an unselfish and sympathetic friend.* 2 INFORMAL. approving; agreeing: *The teacher was sympathetic to the class's plan for a trip to the museum.* 3 enjoying the same things and getting along well together. 4 harmonious; agreeable: *a sympathetic environment. adj.*

sym pa thet i cal ly (sim′pə thet′ik lē), in a sympathetic way; with kindness: *The doctor spoke sympathetically while he bandaged my leg. adv.*

sym pa thize (sim′pə thīz), 1 feel or show sympathy: *The girl sympathized with her little brother who had hurt himself.* 2 share in or agree with a feeling or opinion: *My parents sympathize with my plan to be a painter. v.,* **sym pa thized, sym pa thiz ing.**

sym pa thiz er (sim′pə thī′zər), person who sympathizes; person who is favorably inclined toward a particular belief or person. *n.*

sym pa thy (sim′pə thē), 1 a sharing of another's sorrow or trouble: *We feel sympathy for a person who is ill.* 2 agreement in feeling; condition or fact of having the same feeling: *The sympathy between the twins was so great that they always smiled or cried at the same things.* 3 agreement; approval; favor: *I am in sympathy with your plan. n., pl.* **sym pa thies.**

sym phon ic (sim fon′ik), of, having to do with, or like a symphony: *symphonic music. adj.*

sym pho ny (sim′fə nē), 1 an elaborate musical composition for an orchestra. A symphony usually has three or more movements in different rhythms but related keys. 2 symphony orchestra: *the Chicago Symphony.* 3 harmony of sounds. 4 harmony of colors: *In autumn the woods are a symphony in red, brown, and yellow. n., pl.* **sym pho nies.**

symphony orchestra, a large orchestra for playing symphonies, made up of brass, woodwind, percussion, and stringed instruments.

sym po si um (sim pō′zē əm), 1 a meeting or conference for the discussion of some subject: *Our school will hold a symposium on science during Science Week.* 2 a collection of the opinions of several persons on some subject: *This magazine contains a sports symposium. n., pl.* **sym po si ums, sym po si a** (sim pō′zē ə).

symp tom (simp′təm), 1 a sign or indication: *Quaking knees and paleness are symptoms of fear.* 2 a noticeable change in the normal working of the body that indicates or accompanies disease, sickness, etc.: *The doctor made her diagnosis after studying the patient's symptoms. n.*

symp to mat ic (simp′tə mat′ik), being a sign or symptom: *Headaches are sometimes symptomatic of eyestrain. Riots are symptomatic of political or social unrest. adj.*

syn a gogue (sin′ə gôg), 1 building used by Jews for worship and religious instruction. 2 a Jewish congregation. *n.*

syn apse (si naps′ *or* sin′aps), place where a nerve impulse passes from one nerve cell to another. *n.*

syn chro nism (sing′krə niz′əm), occurrence at the same time; agreement in time. *n.*

syn chro ni za tion (sing′krə nə-zā′shən), act or process of synchronizing. *n.*

syn chro nize (sing′krə nīz), 1 occur at the same time; agree in time. 2 move or take place at the same rate and exactly together. 3 make agree in time: *synchronize all the clocks in a building. v.,* **syn chro nized, syn chro niz ing.**

syn chro niz er (sing′krə nī′zər), person or thing that synchronizes. *n.*

syn chro nous (sing′krə nəs), 1 occurring at the same time; simultaneous. 2 going on at the same rate and exactly together: *the synchronous movements of the two dancers. adj.*

syn co pate (sing′kə pāt), 1 shorten (a word) by omitting sounds from the middle: *Gloucester is usually syncopated to Gloster.* 2 (in music) begin (a tone) on an unaccented beat and hold it into an accented one. *v.,* **syn co pat ed, syn co pat ing.**

syn co pa tion (sing′kə pā′shən), a syncopating or a being syncopated. *n.*

syn di cate (sin′də kit *for 1,2;* sin′də-kāt *for 3-5*), 1 a combination of persons or companies formed to carry out some undertaking, especially one requiring a large capital investment. 2 agency that sells special articles, photographs, etc., to a large number of newspapers or magazines for publication at the same time. 3 combine into a syndicate. 4 manage by a syndicate. 5 publish through a syndicate. *1,2 n., 3-5 v.,* **syn di cat ed, syn di cat ing.**

syn di ca tion (sin′də kā′shən), a syndicating or a being syndicated. *n.*

syn drome (sin′drōm), group of symptoms considered together as characteristic of a particular disease. *n.*

Synge (sing), **John Millington,** 1871-1909, Irish dramatist and poet. *n.*

syn od (sin′əd), 1 assembly called together to discuss and decide church affairs; church council. 2 court of the Presbyterian Church ranking next above the presbytery. *n.*

syn o nym (sin′ə nim), word that means the same or nearly the same as another word. "Keen" is a synonym of "sharp." *n.*

syn on y mous (si non′ə məs), having the same or nearly the same meaning. "Little" and "small" are synonymous. *adj.*

syn op sis (si nop′sis), a brief statement giving a general view of some subject, book, play, etc.; summary: *Write a synopsis of "Treasure Island" in 200 words or less. n., pl.* **syn op ses** (si nop′sēz′).

syn tac tic (sin tak′tik), syntactical. *adj.*

syn tac ti cal (sin tak′tə kəl), of or having to do with syntax; in accordance with the rules of syntax. *adj.* —**syn tac′ti cal ly,** *adv.*

syn tax (sin′taks), 1 sentence structure; way in which the words and phrases of a sentence are arranged to

show how they relate to each other.
2 part of grammar dealing with this. *n.*

syn the sis (sin′thə sis), combination of parts or elements into a whole. A compound or complex substance may be produced by the chemical synthesis of various elements or simpler compounds. An idea or concept may be a synthesis of several other ideas. One speaks of a synthesis of good and bad qualities in a person, or a synthesis of various cultures in a nation. *Synthesis* is the opposite of *analysis. n., pl.* **syn the ses** (sin′thə sēz′).

syringe (def. 1)

syn the size (sin′thə sīz), 1 combine into a complex whole. 2 make up by combining parts or elements. 3 treat synthetically. *v.,* **syn the sized, syn the siz ing.**

syn thet ic (sin thet′ik), 1 having to do with synthesis: *synthetic chemistry.* 2 made artificially by chemical synthesis. Nylon is a synthetic fiber. Many kinds of fabrics, furs, dyes, rubbers, and drugs are synthetic products. 3 not real or genuine; artificial: *synthetic laughter.* 4 **synthetics,** *pl.* man-made substances formed by chemical synthesis. Plastics are synthetics. 1-3 *adj.,* 4 *n.* —**syn thet′i cal ly,** *adv.*

syph i lis (sif′ə lis), a contagious venereal disease that attacks the skin, internal organs, and finally the brain and spinal cord. *n.*

sy phon (sī′fən), siphon. *n., v.*
Syr a cuse (sir′ə kyüz), 1 city in central New York State. 2 city in SE Sicily, famous in ancient times. *n.*
Syr i a (sir′ē ə), country in W Asia, south of Turkey. *Capital:* Damascus. *n.* —**Syr′i an,** *adj., n.*
sy rin ga (sə ring′gə), shrub with fragrant white flowers blooming in early summer; mock orange. *n., pl.* **sy rin gas.**
sy ringe (sə rinj′), 1 a narrow tube fitted with a piston or rubber bulb for drawing in a quantity of fluid and then forcing it out in a stream. Syringes are used for cleaning wounds, injecting fluids into the body, etc. 2 hypodermic syringe. 3 clean, wash, inject, etc., by means of a syringe. 1,2 *n.,* 3 *v.,* **syringed, sy ring ing.**
syr up (sir′əp *or* sèr′əp), a sweet, thick liquid. Sugar boiled with water or fruit juices makes a syrup. A cough syrup contains medicine to relieve coughing. Maple syrup is made from the sap of maple trees. *n.* Also, **sirup.** —**syr′up like′,** *adj.*
syr up y (sir′ə pē *or* sèr′ə pē), like syrup in consistency or sweetness. *adj.*
sys tem (sis′təm), 1 set of things or parts forming a whole: *a mountain system, a railroad system, the digestive system, the nervous system.* 2 an ordered group of facts, principles, beliefs, etc.: *a system of government, a system of education.* 3 plan, scheme, or method: *a system of classification, a system for betting.* 4 an orderly way of getting things done: *He works by a system, not*

hat, āge, fär; let, ēqual, tėrm;
it, īce; hot, ōpen, ôrder;
oil, out; cup, pùt, rüle; ch, child;
ng, long; sh, she; th, thin;
ᵺH, then; zh, measure;

ə represents *a* in about,
e in taken, *i* in pencil,
o in lemon, *u* in circus.

by chance. 5 the body as a whole: *Exercise is good for your system. n.*
sys tem at ic (sis′tə mat′ik), 1 according to a system; having a system, method, or plan: *systematic work.* 2 orderly in arranging things or in getting things done: *a systematic person. adj.*
sys tem at i cal ly (sis′tə mat′ik lē), with system; according to some plan or method. *adv.*
sys tem a ti za tion (sis′tə mə tə zā′shən), act or process of systematizing. *n.*
sys tem a tize (sis′tə mə tīz), arrange according to a system; make into a system; make more systematic. *v.,* **sys tem a tized, sys tem a tiz ing.**
sys tem ic (si stem′ik), 1 having to do with or affecting a particular system of parts or organs of the body: *a systemic lesion, a systemic poison.* 2 having to do with or affecting the body as a whole: *systemic circulation. adj.*
sys to le (sis′tl ē), the normal rhythmical contraction of the heart. *n.*

Tt

T or **t** (tē), the 20th letter of the alphabet. *n., pl.* **T's** or **t's**.

to a T, exactly; perfectly: *That suits me to a T.*

T (tē), anything shaped like the letter T. *n., pl.* **T's.**

t., 1 teaspoon or teaspoons. 2 ton or tons.

T., tablespoon or tablespoons.

tab (tab), 1 a small flap, strap, loop, or piece: *a fur cap with tabs over the ears.* 2 a small extension of or attachment to a card, used for labeling, numbering, coding, etc., in filing. 3 INFORMAL. a bill or check: *pick up the tab.* *n.*

keep tab on or **keep tabs on,** INFORMAL. keep track of; keep watch on; check: *Please keep tabs on the children while I'm out.*

tab ard (tab′ərd), 1 a short, loose coat worn by heralds. 2 mantle worn over armor by knights. *n.*

tab by (tab′ē), 1 a gray or tawny cat with dark stripes. 2 a female cat. *n., pl.* **tab bies.**

tab er nac le (tab′ər nak′əl), 1 a temporary dwelling; tent. 2 the human body thought of as the temporary dwelling of the soul. 3 place of worship for a large congregation. 4 a Jewish temple. 5 **Tabernacle,** the covered, wooden framework carried by the Jews for use as a place of worship during their journey from Egypt to Palestine. 6 recess covered with a canopy and used as a shrine. 7 container for something holy or precious; container for the consecrated bread used in the Mass. *n.*

ta ble (tā′bəl), 1 piece of furniture having a smooth, flat top on legs. 2 food put on a table to be eaten: *Your mother sets a good table.* 3 the persons seated at a table, especially at a dinner or for informal discussion: *The whole table joined in the conversation.* 4 a flat surface; plateau. 5 information in a very brief, tabulated form; list: *a table of contents in the front of a book, the multiplication table.* 6 make a list or statement in tabulated form. 7 a thin, flat piece of wood, stone, metal, etc.; tablet: *The Ten Commandments were written on tables of stone.* 8 put on a table. 9 put off discussing (a bill, motion, etc.) until a future time. 1-5,7 *n.,* 6,8,9 *v.,* **ta bled, ta bling.**

turn the tables, reverse conditions or circumstances completely.

tab leau (tab′lō), 1 a striking scene; picture. 2 representation of a picture,

statue, scene, etc., by a person or group posing in appropriate costume: *Our school is going to present several tableaux from American history.* *n., pl.* **tab leaux** (tab′lōz), **tab leaus.**

ta ble cloth (tā′bəl klôth′), cloth for covering a table. *n., pl.* **ta ble cloths** (tā′bəl klôᴛʜz′ *or* tā′bəl klôths′).

ta ble land (tā′bəl land′), a high plain; plateau. *n.*

ta ble spoon (tā′bəl spün′), spoon larger than a teaspoon or dessert spoon, used to serve vegetables, etc. It holds the same amount as three teaspoons and is a standard unit of measurement in cookery. *n.*

ta ble spoon ful (tā′bəl spün′fùl), as much as a tablespoon holds. 1 tablespoon = 1/2 fluid ounce. *n., pl.* **ta ble spoon fuls.**

tab let (tab′lit), 1 a small flat sheet of stone, wood, ivory, etc., used to write or draw on. The ancient Romans used tablets as we use pads of paper. 2 number of sheets of writing paper fastened together at the edge. 3 a small, flat surface with an inscription: *The Hall of Fame is a building that has many tablets in memory of famous people.* 4 a small, flat piece of medicine, candy, etc.: *aspirin tablets.* *n.*

table tennis, game played on a large table marked somewhat like a tennis court, using small wooden rackets and a light, hollow ball.

ta ble ware (tā′bəl wer′ *or* tā′bəl war′), dishes, knives, forks, spoons, etc., used at meals. *n.*

tab loid (tab′loid), 1 a newspaper, usually having half the ordinary size newspaper page, that has many pictures and gives the news in short articles. 2 condensed. 1 *n.,* 2 *adj.*

ta boo (tə bü′), 1 forbidden by custom or tradition; prohibited; banned: *Marriage between brothers and sisters is taboo in most societies.* 2 make taboo; forbid; prohibit; ban. 3 system or act of setting things apart as forbidden; prohibition; ban. The Polynesians have many taboos under which certain things, places, and persons are set apart or prohibited as sacred, unclean, or cursed. 1 *adj.,* 2 *v.,* 3 *n., pl.* **ta boos.** Also, **tabu.**

ta bor (tā′bər), a small drum, used especially by a person playing a pipe or fife to accompany himself. *n.*

ta bu (tə bü′), taboo. *adj., v., n.*

tab u lar (tab′yə lər), 1 of tables or lists; arranged in lists; written or printed in columns.

EXAMPLE:

Book	Author	Type
Ivanhoe	Scott	Romantic novel
Macbeth	Shakespeare	Tragedy
Tales	Andersen	Fairy stories

2 flat like a table: *a tabular rock.* *adj.*

tab u late (tab′yə lāt), arrange (facts, figures, etc.) in tables or lists. *v.,* **tab u lat ed, tab u lat ing.**

tab u la tion (tab′yə lā′shən), arrangement in tables or lists. *n.*

tab u la tor (tab′yə lā′tər), person or thing that tabulates. *n.*

tac it (tas′it), 1 implied or understood without being openly expressed: *His eating the food was a tacit admission that he liked it.* 2 unspoken; silent: *a tacit prayer.* *adj.* —**tac′it ly,** *adv.*

tac i turn (tas′ə tėrn′), speaking very little; not fond of talking. *adj.*

tac i tur ni ty (tas′ə tėr′nə tē), habit of keeping silent; disinclination to talk much. *n.*

Tac i tus (tas′ə təs), A.D. 55?-120?, Roman historian. *n.*

tack (tak), 1 a short, sharp-pointed nail or pin having a broad, flat head: *carpet tacks.* 2 fasten with tacks: *She tacked mosquito netting over the windows.* 3 stitch used as a temporary fastening. 4 sew with temporary stitches. 5 attach; add: *He tacked a postscript to the end of the letter.* 6 sail in a zigzag course against the wind: *The ship was tacking, trying to make the harbor.* 7 a zigzag course against the wind. 8 a zigzag movement; one of the movements in a zigzag course. 9 direction in which a ship moves in regard to the position of her sails. When on port tack, a ship has the wind on her left. 10 act of zigzagging; a turn from one direction to the next. 11 course of action or conduct: *Ordering rather than asking her to help was the wrong tack to take.* 12 to change from one tack to another. 13 **a** rope to hold in place the outer lower corner of some sails. **b** corner to which this is fastened. 1,3,7-11,13 *n.,* 2,4-6,12 *v.*

tackle (def. 2)

tack le (tak′əl), 1 equipment; apparatus; gear. Fishing tackle means the rod, line, hooks, etc. 2 set of ropes and pulleys for lifting, lowering, or moving heavy things. The sails of a ship are raised and moved by tackle. 3 try to deal with: *We have a difficult problem to tackle.* 4 lay hold of; seize: *He tackled the thief and threw him.* 5 (in football) seize and stop, or throw to the ground (an opponent who has the ball). 6 act of tackling. **7** an offensive or defensive player between the guard and the end on either side of the line in football. **8** to harness. 1,2,6,7 *n.*, 3-5,8 *v.*, **tackled, tack ling.**

tack y¹ (tak′ē), sticky. *adj.* **tack i er, tack i est.** [*tack* + *-y¹*]

tack y² (tak′ē), INFORMAL. shabby; dowdy. *adj.*, **tack i er, tack i est.** [origin uncertain]

Ta co ma (tə kō′mə), seaport in W Washington, on Puget Sound. *n.*

tact (takt), ability to say and do the right things; skill in dealing with people or handling difficult situations: *Mother's tact kept her from talking about things likely to be unpleasant to her guests. n.*

tact ful (takt′fəl), **1** having tact: *a tactful person.* **2** showing tact: *a tactful reply. adj.* —**tact′ful ly,** *adv.* —**tact′ful ness,** *n.*

tac tic (tak′tik), **1** detail of military tactics; maneuver. **2** any skillful move; gambit. *n.*

tac ti cal (tak′tə kəl), **1** of tactics; concerning tactics. **2** having to do with the disposal of military or naval forces in action against an enemy. **3** characterized by skillful procedure, methods, or expedients. *adj.* —**tac′ti cal ly,** *adv.*

tac ti cian (tak tish′ən), an expert in tactics. *n.*

tac tics (tak′tiks), **1** *pl. in form, sing. in use.* art or science of disposing military or naval forces in action. **2** *pl. in form and use.* the operations themselves: *The tactics of pretending to cross the river and of making a retreat fooled the enemy.* **3** *pl. in form and use.* procedures to gain advantage or success; methods: *The child changed her tactics to crying when pleading failed. n.*

tac tile (tak′təl), **1** of or having to do with touch. **2** having the sense of touch. **3** that can be felt by touch. *adj.*

tact less (takt′lis), **1** without tact: *a tactless person.* **2** showing no tact: *a tactless reply. adj.* —**tact′less ly,** *adv.* —**tact′less ness,** *n.*

tadpole at different stages of growth

tad pole (tad′pōl′), a very young frog or toad in the larval stage when it lives in water and has gills, a long tail, and no limbs. *n.*

taf fe ta (taf′ə tə), **1** a light, stiff silk cloth with a smooth, glossy surface. **2** a

similar cloth of linen, rayon, etc. *n., pl.* **taf fe tas.**

taff rail (taf′rāl′), a rail around a ship's stern. *n.*

taf fy (taf′ē), **1** kind of chewy candy made of brown sugar or molasses boiled down, often with butter; toffee: *salt-water taffy.* **2** INFORMAL. flattery. *n., pl.* **taf fies.**

Taft (taft), **William Howard,** 1857-1930, the 27th president of the United States, from 1909 to 1913, and chief justice of the Supreme Court, from 1921 to 1930. *n.*

tag¹ (tag), **1** piece of card, paper, leather, etc., to be tied or fastened to something: *a price tag, a name tag.* **2** a small hanging piece; loosely attached piece; loose end: *I cut the tags off the frayed rug.* **3** a metal point at the end of a string. A shoelace has a tag on each end. **4** quotation, moral, etc., added for ornament or effect. **5** the last line or lines of a song, play, actor's speech, etc. **6** furnish with a tag or tags: *All his trunks and suitcases are tagged with his name and address.* **7** INFORMAL. follow closely: *The baby tagged after his sister.* 1-5 *n.*, 6,7 *v.*, **tagged, tag ging.** [origin uncertain]

tag² (tag), **1** a children's game in which the player who is "it" chases the others until he touches one. The one touched is then "it" and must chase the others. **2** touch or tap with the hand. **1** *n.*, **2** *v.*, **tagged, tag ging.** [origin uncertain]

Ta hi ti (tə hē′tē), one of the Society Islands in the S Pacific. See **Melanesia** for map. *n.*

Ta hi tian (tə hē′shən), **1** of or having to do with the island of Tahiti, its people, or their language. **2** person born or living in Tahiti. **3** the Polynesian language of Tahiti. **1** *adj.*, 2,3 *n.*

Ta hoe (tä′hō), **Lake,** mountain lake in NE California and W Nevada. *n.*

tail (tāl), **1** the part of an animal's body that sticks out beyond the back of the main part. Rabbits have very short tails. Mice have long tails. **2** something like an animal's tail: *the tail of a kite.* **3** the after portion of an airplane. **4** the hind part of anything; back; rear; conclusion: *the tail of a cart. A crowd of children formed the tail of the procession.* **5** tails, *pl.* **a** the reverse side of a coin. **b** INFORMAL. coat with long tails, worn on formal occasions. **6** furnish with a tail. **7** at the tail, back, or rear. **8** coming from behind: *a tail wind.* **9** follow close behind; form the tail of: *Children tailed after the parade.* **10** INFORMAL. follow closely and secretly, especially in order to watch or prevent escaping. 1-5 *n.*, 6,9,10 *v.*, 7,8 *adj.* —**tail′like′,** *adj.*

hat, āge, fär; let, ēqual, tėrm; it, īce; hot, ōpen, ôrder; oil, out; cup, pùt, rüle; ch, child; ng, long; sh, she; th, thin; ŦH, then; zh, measure;

ə represents *a* in about, *e* in taken, *i* in pencil, *o* in lemon, *u* in circus.

turn tail, run away from danger, trouble, etc.

with one's tail between one's legs, afraid, humiliated, or dejected.

tail board (tāl′bôrd′), tailgate of a truck or wagon. *n.*

tail gate (tāl′gāt′), **1** board at the back end of a wagon, truck, station wagon, etc., that can be let down or removed when loading or unloading. **2** drive a vehicle too close to the one ahead of it. **1** *n.*, **2** *v.*, **tail gat ed, tail gat ing.**

tail less (tāl′lis), having no tail: *An ape is a kind of tailless monkey. adj.*

tail light (tāl′līt′), a warning light, usually red, at the back end of a vehicle. *n.*

tai lor (tā′lər), **1** person whose business is making, altering, or mending clothes. **2** make by tailor's work: *The suit was well tailored.* **3** make or mend clothes. **4** make specially to fit; adjust; adapt. **1** *n.*, 2-4 *v.*

tai lor ing (tā′lər ing), business or work of a tailor. *n.*

tail piece (tāl′pēs′), piece added at or forming the end. *n.*

tail race (tāl′rās′), part of a millrace below the water wheel that leads the water away. *n.*

tail spin (tāl′spin′), a downward movement of an airplane with the nose first and the tail spinning in a circle above. *n.*

tail wind, wind blowing toward the direction in which a ship or aircraft is moving.

taint (tānt), **1** a stain or spot; trace of decay, corruption, or disgrace: *No taint of scandal ever touched the mayor.* **2** a cause of any such condition. **3** give a taint to; spoil: *Flies sometimes taint what they touch. Rumors that the judge had taken bribes tainted his reputation.* **4** become tainted; decay: *Meat will taint if it is left too long in a warm place.* 1,2 *n.*, 3,4 *v.*

Tai pei or **Tai peh** (tī′pā′), capital of Taiwan, in the N part. *n.*

Tai wan (tī′wän′), island off SE China, the seat after 1949 of the Chinese nationalist government. *Capital:* Taipei. *n.* Also, **Formosa.**

Taj Mahal

Taj Ma hal (täj´ mə häl´), a famous white marble mausoleum in northern India, built by a Mogul ruler in the 1600's.

take (tāk), 1 lay hold of; grasp: *I took her hand when we crossed the street.* 2 seize; catch; capture: *take a wild animal in a trap.* 3 catch hold; lay hold; have effect: *The fire has taken. The medicine seems to be taking; the fever is going away.* 4 accept: *Take my advice. The man won't take a cent less for the car.* 5 get; receive; assume the ownership or possession of: *She took the gifts and opened them.* 6 win: *He took first prize.* 7 get; have: *take a seat.* 8 obtain from a source: *Washington, D.C., takes its name from George Washington.* 9 absorb: *Marble takes a high polish.* 10 use; make use of: *take medicine. We took a train to go to Boston.* 11 receive into the body; swallow: *take food, take drink.* 12 submit to; put up with: *take hard punishment.* 13 need; require: *It takes time and patience to learn how to drive an automobile.* 14 choose; select: *Take the shortest way home.* 15 remove: *Please take the wastebasket away and empty it.* 16 subtract: *If you take 2 from 7, you have 5.* 17 go with; escort: *Take her home.* 18 lead: *Where will this road take me?* 19 carry: *Take your lunch along.* 20 do; make; obtain by some special method: *Take a walk. Please take my photograph.* 21 write down; record: *take dictation, take minutes at a meeting.* 22 form and hold in mind; feel: *She takes pride in her schoolwork.* 23 find out: *The doctor told her to take the child's temperature.* 24 understand or suppose: *How did you take his remark? I take it the train was late.* 25 regard; consider: *Let us take an example.* 26 engage; hire; lease: *We have taken a cottage for the summer.* 27 receive and pay for regularly; subscribe for: *take a newspaper.* 28 become affected by: *take cold.* 29 (in grammar) be used with: *A plural noun takes a plural verb.* 30 please; attract; charm: *The song took our fancy.* 31 become: *He took sick.* 32 SLANG. swindle; cheat. 33 amount taken: *a great take of fish.* 34 act of taking. 35 that which is taken. 1-32 *v.*, **took, tak en, tak ing;** 33-35 *n.*
take after, be like; resemble: *She takes after her mother.*

take back, withdraw; retract: *I apologized and took back my rude remark.*
take down, write down: *take down a speech.*
take for, suppose to be: *to be taken for a fool.*
take in, 1 receive; admit: *take in boarders.* 2 make smaller: *Please take in the waist of my pants.* 3 understand. 4 deceive; trick; cheat. 5 include; visit: *It's too late to take in her party now.*
take off, 1 leave the ground or water: *Three airplanes took off at the same time.* 2 rush away: *I took off at the first sign of trouble.* 3 INFORMAL. give an amusing imitation of; mimic.
take on, 1 engage; hire. 2 undertake to deal with: *take on an opponent.* 3 acquire: *take on the appearance of health.* 4 INFORMAL. show great excitement, grief, etc.
take over, take the ownership or control of.
take to, 1 form a liking for; become fond of: *Good students take to books.* 2 go to: *The cat took to the woods and became wild.*
take up, 1 soak up; absorb: *A sponge takes up liquid.* 2 make smaller: *The tailor took up the hem of the dress.* 3 begin; undertake: *He took up piano lessons in the summer.* 4 pay off. 5 lift.
take up with, INFORMAL. begin to associate or be friendly with.

tak en (tā´kən), past participle of **take.** *I have taken this toy from the shelf. v.*

take off (tāk´ôf´), 1 the leaving of the ground in leaping or in beginning a flight in an aircraft; taking off. 2 the place or point at which one takes off. 3 INFORMAL. an amusing imitation; mimicking. *n.*

take o ver (tāk´ō´vər), a taking over; seizure of ownership or control: *a takeover of a country by the military. n.*

tak er (tā´kər), person or thing that takes. *n.*

tak est (tā´kist), OLD USE. take. "Thou takest" means "you take." *v.*

tak eth (tā´kith), OLD USE. takes. *v.*

tak ing (tā´king), 1 attractive or pleasing; winning: *a taking smile.* 2 INFORMAL. infectious. 3 act of one who takes or condition of being taken. 4 that which is taken. 5 **takings,** *pl.* money taken in; receipts. 1,2 *adj.,* 3-5 *n.*

talc (talk), a soft, smooth mineral, used in making face powder, chalk, etc. *n.*

tal cum (tal´kəm), 1 talcum powder. 2 talc. *n.*

talcum powder, powder made of purified white talc, for use on the face and body.

tale (tāl), 1 story, especially a made-up story: *a tale about ghosts. She enjoys reading tales about life in fron-* tier days. 2 falsehood; lie. 3 piece of gossip or scandal. 4 number; count: *His tale of sheep amounted to over three hundred. n.*

tell tales, spread gossip or scandal.

tale bear er (tāl´ber´ər *or* tāl´bar´ər), person who spreads gossip or scandal. *n.*

tale bear ing (tāl´ber´ing *or* tāl´bar´ing), the spreading of gossip or scandal. *n.*

tal ent (tal´ənt), 1 a special natural ability: *She has a talent for music.* 2 person or persons with talent: *to introduce new talent on stage. That young singer is a real talent.* 3 an ancient unit of weight or money, varying with time and place. *n.*

tal ent ed (tal´ən tid), having natural ability; gifted: *a talented musician. adj.*

tal is man (tal´i smən), 1 stone, ring, etc., engraved with figures or characters supposed to have magic power; charm. 2 anything that acts as a charm. *n., pl.* **tal is mans.**

talk (tôk), 1 use words to express feelings or ideas; speak: *Baby is learning to talk.* 2 use in speaking: *talk sense. Can you talk French?* 3 exchange words; converse: *The two ministers talked for an hour.* 4 the use of words; spoken words; speech; conversation: *The old friends met for a good talk.* 5 an informal speech: *The coach gave the team a talk about the need for more team spirit.* 6 a way of talking: *baby talk.* 7 bring, put, drive, influence, etc., by talk: *We talked her into joining the club.* 8 discuss: *talk politics, talk business.* 9 consult; confer: *talk with one's doctor.* 10 conference; council: *summit talks.* 11 spread ideas by other means than speech: *talk by signs.* 12 spread rumors; gossip: *talk behind someone's back.* 13 gossip or rumor: *There is talk of a quarrel between them.* 14 a subject for talk or gossip: *be the talk of the town.* 1-3,7-9,11,12 *v.,* 4-6,10,13,14 *n.*

talk back, INFORMAL. answer rudely or disrespectfully.

talk down to, speak to in a superior tone.

talk a tive (tô´kə tiv), having the habit of talking a great deal; fond of talking: *He is a merry, talkative old man who knows everyone on our street. adj.*
—**talk´a tive ly,** *adv.* —**talk´a tive ness,** *n.*

talk er (tô´kər), 1 person who talks. 2 a talkative person. *n.*

talk ing-to (tô´king tü´), INFORMAL. a scolding. *n., pl.* **talk ing-tos.**

tall (tôl), 1 higher than the average; having great height: *a tall building.* 2 of the specified height: *six feet tall.* 3 INFORMAL. high or large in amount; extravagant: *a tall price, a tall order.*

4 INFORMAL. hard to believe; exaggerated: *a tall tale. adj.* —**tall′ness,** *n.*

Tal la has see (tal′ə has′ē), capital of Florida, in the N part. *n.*

tal low (tal′ō), the hard fat from sheep, cows, etc., used for making candles and soap. *n.*

tal ly (tal′ē), 1 stick of wood in which notches are cut to represent numbers. Tallies were formerly used to show the amount of a debt or payment. 2 anything on which a score or account is kept. 3 notch or mark made on a tally; mark made for a certain number of objects in keeping account. 4 mark on a tally; count up: *tally a score.* 5 account; reckoning; score: *a tally of a game.* 6 (in sports) make scoring points; score: *The hockey team tallied seven goals in their last game. The best scorer failed to tally in only one game all season.* 7 a distinguishing mark; label; tag. 8 mark with an identifying label; tag. 9 agree; correspond: *Your account tallies with mine.* 1-3,5,7 *n., pl.* **tal lies;** 4,6,8,9 *v.,* **tal lied, tal ly ing.**

tallyho (def. 1)

tal ly ho (tal′ē hō′ *for 1;* tal′ē hō′ or tal′ē hō′ *for 2*), 1 coach drawn by four horses. 2 a hunter's cry on catching sight of the fox. 1,2 *n., pl.* **tal ly hos;** 2 *interj.*

Tal mud (tal′məd), a collection of sixty-three volumes containing the Jewish civil and canonical law in the form of interpretation and expansion of the teachings of the Old Testament. *n.*

tal on (tal′ən), claw of an animal, especially a bird of prey: *The eagle seized a chicken with its talons. n.*

tam (tam), tam-o′-shanter. *n.*

tam a ble (tā′mə bəl), tameable. *adj.*

ta ma le (tə mä′lē), a Mexican food made of corn meal and minced meat, seasoned with red peppers, wrapped in cornhusks, and roasted or steamed. *n.*

tam a rack (tam′ə rak′), a North American larch tree which yields strong, heavy timber. *n.*

tam a rind (tam′ə rind′), 1 a tropical tree grown for its wood and fruit. 2 its fruit, a brown pod with juicy, acid pulp, used in foods, drinks, and medicine. *n.*

tam a risk (tam′ə risk′), an ornamental shrub or small tree with slender, feathery branches. *n.*

tam bou rine (tam′bə rēn′), a small drum with jingling metal disks around the side, played by striking it with the knuckles or by shaking it; timbrel. *n.*

tame (tām), 1 taken from the wild state and made obedient: *a tame bear.* 2 without fear; not wild; gentle: *The birds are so tame that they will eat from our hands.* 3 make tame; break in: *The lion was tamed for the circus.* 4 become tame: *White rats tame easily.* 5 deprive of courage; tone down; subdue: *News of our friend's automobile accident tamed our spirits.* 6 without spirit; dull: *a tame story. The party was tame because all the people were sleepy.* 1,2,6 *adj.,* **tam er, tam est;** 3-5 *v.,* **tamed, tam ing.** —**tame′ly,** *adv.* —**tame′ness,** *n.*

tame a ble (tā′mə bəl), that can be tamed or subdued. *adj.* Also, **tamable.**

tame less (tām′lis), that has never been tamed; that cannot be tamed. *adj.* —**tame′less ness,** *n.*

tam er (tā′mər), person who tames: *a lion tamer. n.*

tam-o′-shan ter (tam′ə shan′tər), a soft, woolen cap, originally of Scotland, with a flat, round crown and often with a tassel. *n.* Also, **tam.** [from *Tam o′ Shanter,* the hero of a poem by Robert Burns]

tamp (tamp), 1 pack down: *tamp the earth about a newly planted tree.* 2 (in blasting) fill (the hole containing explosive) with dirt, etc. *v.*

Tam pa (tam′pə), seaport in W Florida. *n.*

tam per (tam′pər), meddle improperly; meddle: *Do not tamper with the lock. v.*

tan (tan), 1 yellowish-brown: *He wore tan shoes.* 2 the brown color of a person's skin resulting from being in the sun and air: *Her arms and legs had a dark tan.* 3 make or become brown by exposure to sun and air: *Sun and wind had tanned the sailor's face. If you lie on the beach in the sun you will tan.* 4 make (a hide) into leather by soaking in a special liquid, especially one containing tannin. 5 tanbark. 6 INFORMAL. thrash or beat in punishment. 1 *adj.,* **tan ner, tan nest;** 2,5 *n.,* 3,4,6 *v.,* **tanned, tan ning.**

tan a ger (tan′ə jər), any of various small American birds related to the finches. The males are usually brilliantly colored. *n.*

tan bark (tan′bärk′), crushed bark used in tanning hides. Riding tracks and

tambourine

hat, āge, fär; let, ēqual, tèrm;
it, īce; hot, ōpen, ôrder;
oil, out; cup, pút, rüle; ch, child;
ng, long; sh, she; th, thin;
ŦH, then; zh, measure;

ə represents *a* in about,
e in taken, *i* in pencil,
o in lemon, *u* in circus.

circus rings are often covered with used tanbark. *n.*

tan dem (tan′dəm), 1 one behind the other: *drive horses tandem.* 2 having animals, seats, parts, etc., arranged one behind the other. 3 two horses harnessed tandem. 4 carriage drawn by two horses so harnessed. 5 bicycle with two seats, one behind the other. 6 truck or other vehicle with two attached parts, as a cab for pulling and a trailer to carry the load. 1 *adv.,* 2 *adj.,* 3-6 *n.*

tam-o′-shanter

tang (tang), 1 a strong taste or flavor: *the tang of mustard, the salt tang of sea air.* 2 a slight touch or suggestion; trace. 3 a long, slender projecting point, strip, or prong on a chisel, file, etc., that fits into the handle. *n.*

Tan gan yi ka (tang′gə nyē′kə), 1 former British trust territory in E Africa. It gained independence in 1961 and became part of Tanzania in 1964. 2 **Lake,** lake in central Africa. *n.*

tan gent (tan′jənt), 1 in contact; touching. 2 (in geometry) touching a curve or surface at one point but not intersecting. These circles are tangent: ∞. 3 a tangent line, curve, or surface. 4 (in trigonometry) the ratio of the length of the side opposite an acute angle in a right triangle to the length of the shorter of the other sides. 1,2 *adj.,* 3,4 *n.*

fly off at a tangent or **go off at a tangent,** change suddenly from one course of action or thought to another.

tan gen tial (tan jen′shəl), 1 of or having to do with a tangent. 2 diverging. 3 slightly connected. *adj.*

tan ge rine (tan′jə rēn′), a small, reddish-orange citrus fruit with a very loose peel and segments that separate easily. It is a kind of mandarin which is

863

adj. adjective	*n.* noun
adv. adverb	*prep.* preposition
conj. conjunction	*pron.* pronoun
interj. interjection	*v.* verb
sing. singular	*pl.* plural

widely grown in the United States. *n.*

tan gi bil i ty (tan′jə bil′ə tē), fact or quality of being tangible. *n.*

tan gi ble (tan′jə bəl), capable of being touched or felt by touch: *A chair is a tangible object.* 2 real; actual; definite: *The good will of a business is not as tangible as its buildings and stock.* adj.

tan gi bly (tan′jə blē), in a tangible manner. *adv.*

Tan gier (tan jir′), seaport in Morocco, on the Strait of Gibraltar. *n.*

tan gle (tang′gəl), 1 twist and twine together in a confused mass: *The kitten had tangled the ball of twine.* 2 a confused or tangled mass: *The climbing vines are all one tangle and need to be pruned and tied up.* 3 involve in something that hampers or obstructs. 4 a bewildering confusion; mess: *a tangle of contradictory statements.* 1,3 *v.,* **tan gled, tan gling;** 2,4 *n.*

tan go (tang′gō), 1 a Spanish-American dance with long, gliding steps and many figures and poses. 2 music for it. 3 dance the tango. 1,2 *n., pl.* **tan gos;** 3 *v.*

tang y (tang′ē), having a tang. *adj.*

tank (def. 3)

tank (tangk), 1 a large container for liquid or gas: *the gasoline tank of an automobile, a storage tank for water.* 2 put or store in a tank: *The plane tanked up on gas just before taking off.* 3 a heavily armored combat vehicle carrying machine guns and usually a cannon, moving on an endless track on each side. Tanks can travel over rough ground, fallen trees, and other obstacles. 1,3 *n.,* 2 *v.*

tank ard (tang′kərd), a large drinking mug with a handle and a hinged cover. *n.*

tank car, a railroad car with a tank for carrying liquids or gases.

tank er (tang′kər), ship, airplane, or truck with tanks for carrying oil or other liquid freight. *n.*

tank ful (tangk′fül), as much as a tank will hold. *n., pl.* **tank fuls.**

tan ner (tan′ər), person whose work is tanning hides. *n.*

tan ner y (tan′ər ē), place where hides are tanned. *n., pl.* **tan ner ies.**

tan nic acid (tan′ik), tannin.

tan nin (tan′ən), acid obtained from the bark or galls of oaks, etc., and from certain other plants. It is used in tanning, dyeing, making ink, and in medicine. *n.*

tan ning (tan′ing), the converting of hide or skins into leather. *n.*

tan sy (tan′zē), a coarse, strong-smelling, bitter-tasting plant with notched, divided leaves and clusters of small yellow flowers. Tansy was formerly much used in cooking and medicine. *n., pl.* **tan sies.**

tan ta lize (tan′tl īz), torment or tease by keeping something desired in sight but out of reach, or by holding out hopes that are repeatedly disappointed: *He tantalized the hungry dog by pretending to feed it.* *v.,* **tan ta lized, tan ta liz ing.** [from *Tantalus*] —**tan′ta liz′ing ly,** *adv.*

tan ta liz er (tan′tə lī′zər), person or thing that tantalizes. *n.*

tan ta lum (tan′tl əm), a hard, shiny, grayish-white metallic element occurring with niobium in certain rare minerals. It is very resistant to corrosion and is used as an alloy in nuclear reactors and in surgical and dental equipment. *n.* [from *Tantalus* (because it cannot absorb acid though immersed in it)]

Tan ta lus (tan′tl əs), (in Greek myths) a king punished in the lower world by having to stand up to his chin in water, under branches laden with fruit. Whenever he tried to drink or eat, the water or fruit withdrew from his reach. *n.*

tan ta mount (tan′tə mount), equivalent: *The withdrawal of his statement is tantamount to an apology.* adj.

tan trum (tan′trəm), INFORMAL. fit of bad temper or ill humor: *The spoiled child had a tantrum whenever she did not get her own way.* *n.*

Tan za ni a (tan′zə nē′ə), country in E Africa, a member of the Commonwealth of Nations. It was formed in 1964 by the union of Tanganyika and the adjacent islands of Zanzibar and Pemba. *Capital:* Dar es Salaam. See **Congo** for map. *n.*

Tao ism (tou′iz′əm), one of the main

tankard

religions of China. It teaches natural simplicity and humility as a way to peace and harmony in life. *n.*

Tao ist (tou′ist), 1 believer in Taoism. 2 of or belonging to Taoists or Taoism. 1 *n.,* 2 *adj.*

tap[1] (tap), 1 strike lightly: *tap on a window. Tap him on the shoulder.* 2 cause to strike lightly: *She tapped her foot to the music.* 3 a light blow: *There was a tap at the door.* 4 sound of a light blow. 5 make, put, etc., by light blows: *tap a rhythm, tap time, tap the ashes out of a pipe.* 1,2,5 *v.,* **tapped, tap ping;** 3,4 *n.* [from French of the 1200's *taper*]

tap² (def. 1)

tap[2] (tap), 1 stopper or plug to close a hole in a cask containing liquid. 2 faucet. 3 make a hole in to let out liquid: *They tapped the sugar maples when the sap began to flow.* 4 draw the plug from: *tap a cask.* 5 let out (liquid) by piercing or by drawing a plug. 6 make (resources, reserves, etc.) accessible; penetrate; open up: *This highway taps a large district.* 7 point in an electric circuit where a connection is or can be made. 8 make a connection on: *tap a telegraph wire to intercept the message.* 9 tool for cutting screw threads on the inner surface of a cylinder or opening. 1,2,7,9 *n.,* 3-6,8 *v.,* **tapped, tap ping.** [Old English *tæppa*]

on tap, 1 ready to be let out of a keg or barrel and served. 2 ready for use; on hand: *I try to keep an extra box of stationery on tap so that I won't run out of it unexpectedly.*

tap dance, dance in which the steps are accented by loud taps of the foot, toe, or heel.

tap-dance (tap′dans′), do a tap dance. *v.,* **tap-danced, tap-danc ing.**

tape (tāp), 1 a long, narrow woven strip of cotton, linen, etc. Tape is used to make loops and bind seams. 2 a long, narrow strip of other material. Surveyors measure with a steel tape. Stock quotations are printed on paper tape. Sounds and images are recorded on a kind of plastic tape. 3 fasten with tape; wrap with tape: *The doctor taped up the wound.* 4 measure with a tape measure. 5 to record on tape: *The President's arrival was taped to show on a television news program in the evening.* 6 strip, string, etc., stretched across a race track at the finish line. 1,2,6 *n.,* 3-5 *v.,* **taped, tap ing.**

tape line, tape measure.

tape measure, a long strip of cloth or

steel marked in inches, feet, etc., for measuring.

ta per (tā′pər), 1 make or become gradually smaller toward one end: *The carpenter slowly tapered the end of the fence post with an adz. The church spire tapers off to a point.* 2 grow less gradually; diminish: *Their business tapered to nothing as people moved away.* 3 becoming smaller toward one end. 4 a gradual decrease of force, capacity, etc. 5 a very slender candle; long wick coated with wax. 1,2 *v.,* 3 *adj.,* 4,5 *n.*

tape-re cord (tāp′ri kôrd′), record on a tape recorder. *v.*

tape recorder

tape recorder, machine that records sound magnetically on plastic tape and plays the sound back after it is recorded.

tape recording, 1 the recording of sound on a tape. 2 a tape on which sound has been recorded.

tap es try (tap′ə strē), 1 fabric with pictures or designs woven in it, used to hang on walls, cover furniture, etc. 2 cover with tapestry; cover with a pattern like that of tapestry. 1 *n., pl.* **tap es tries;** 2 *v.,* **tap es tried, tap es try ing.**

tape worm (tāp′wėrm′), a long, flat worm that lives during its adult stage as a parasite in the intestines of human beings and other vertebrates. *n.*

tap i o ca (tap′ē ō′kə), a starchy food obtained from the root of the cassava plant. It is used for puddings. *n.*

tapir—about 3 ft. high at the shoulder

ta pir (tā′pər), a large piglike mammal of tropical America and southern Asia, having hoofs and a flexible snout. It is related to the horse and rhinoceros. *n.*

tap room (tap′rüm′ *or* tap′rùm′), barroom. *n.*

tap root (tap′rüt′ *or* tap′rùt′), a main root growing downward. *n.*

taps (taps), signal on a bugle or drum to put out lights at night. Taps are also sounded when a member of the armed forces is buried. *n.pl.*

tar[1] (tär), 1 a thick, black, sticky substance obtained by the distillation of wood or coal. Tar is used to cover and patch roads and to keep telephone poles and other timber from rotting. 2 cover or smear with tar; soak in tar. Tarred paper is used on sheds to keep out water. *The street in front of our house is tarred.* 1 *n.,* 2 *v.,* **tarred, tar ring.** [Old English *teoru, teru*]

tar and feather, pour heated tar on and cover with feathers as a punishment.

tar[2] (tär), sailor. *n.* [probably shortened from *tarpaulin* (in early meaning) sailor]

tar an tel la (tar′ən tel′ə), 1 a rapid, whirling southern Italian dance in very quick rhythm, usually performed by a single couple. 2 music for this dance. *n., pl.* **tar an tel las.** [from Italian *tarantella,* from *Taranto,* town in Italy]

ta ran tu la (tə ran′chə lə), 1 a large spider of southern Europe, whose slightly poisonous bite was once imagined to cause an insane desire to dance. 2 any of a family of large, hairy spiders with a painful but not serious bite, especially a group of spiders in western America. *n., pl.* **ta ran tu las.** [from Latin *tarantula,* from *Taranto,* town in Italy where they were common]

tar di ly (tär′də lē), slowly; late; with delay. *adv.*

tar di ness (tär′dē nis), slowness; lateness. *n.*

tar dy (tär′dē), 1 behind time; late: *I was tardy for school four times last year.* 2 slow: *The old coach was tardier than ever. adj.,* **tar di er, tar di est.**

tare[1] (ter *or* tar), 1 vetch. 2 (in the Bible) an injurious weed, possibly the darnel: *Tares killed the wheat. n.* [probably related to Dutch of the 1300's *tarwe* wheat]

tare[2] (ter *or* tar), deduction made from the gross weight of goods to allow for the weight of the wrapper, box, or conveyance they are in. *n.* [from French of the 1400's *tare,* from Latin *tara* deduction, from Arabic *tarhah*]

tar get (tär′git), 1 mark for shooting at; thing aimed at. A target is often a circle, but anything may be used as a target. 2 object of abuse, scorn, criticism, etc.: *His crazy ideas made him the target of jokes.* 3 any aim one tries to achieve; goal; objective. 4 a small shield, especially a round shield. *n.*

tar iff (tar′if), 1 list of duties or taxes on imports or exports. 2 system of duties or taxes on imports or exports. 3 any duty or tax in such a list or system: *There is a very high tariff on imported jewelry.* 4 any table or scale of prices: *Our hotel's tariff ranges from $9 to $25 a day for a single room. n.*

hat, āge, fär; let, ēqual, tėrm;
it, īce; hot, ōpen, ôrder;
oil, out; cup, pùt, rüle; ch, child;
ng, long; sh, she; th, thin;
ŦH, then; zh, measure;

ə represents *a* in about,
e in taken, *i* in pencil,
o in lemon, *u* in circus.

tarn (tärn), a small lake or pool in the mountains. *n.*

tar nish (tär′nish), 1 dull the luster or brightness of: *The salt tarnished the silver saltcellar.* 2 lose luster or brightness: *The brass doorknobs tarnished.* 3 loss of luster or brightness. 4 a discolored coating, especially on silver. 5 bring disgrace upon (a reputation, one's honor, etc.); sully; taint. 1,2,5 *v.,* 3,4 *n.*

ta ro (tär′ō), 1 plant grown in the Pacific islands and other tropical regions for its starchy root which is used as food. 2 root of this plant. *n., pl.* **ta ros.**

tar pau lin (tär pô′lən), canvas or other strong cloth made waterproof by painting, tarring, etc., used as a protective covering. *n.*

tar pon (tär′pon *or* tär′pən), a large, silver-colored fish found in the warmer parts of the Atlantic Ocean. *n., pl.* **tar pons** or **tar pon.**

tar ry[1] (tar′ē), 1 to delay leaving; remain; stay: *We tarried another day to see all the sights.* 2 be tardy; hesitate: *Why do you tarry so long? v.,* **tar ried, tar ry ing.** [Middle English *tarien*]

tar ry[2] (tär′ē), 1 of tar; like tar: *a tarry smell.* 2 covered with tar: *a tarry road. adj.,* **tar ri er, tar ri est.** [*tar*[1] + -*y*[1]]

target (def. 1)
for archery,
scored (from center
out) as follows:
9, 7, 5, 3, 1

Tar ry town (tar′ē toun), village on the Hudson River, near New York City, mentioned often in the stories of Washington Irving. *n.*

tar sal (tär′səl), 1 of or having to do with the tarsus. 2 one of the bones or cartilages in the ankle. 1 *adj.,* 2 *n.*

tar sus (tär′səs), 1 the ankle. 2 the group of small bones composing it. *n., pl.* **tar si** (tär′sī).

Tar sus (tär′səs), city in S Turkey. It was the home of Saint Paul. *n.*

adj. adjective	*n.* noun
adv. adverb	*prep.* preposition
conj. conjunction	*pron.* pronoun
interj. interjection	*v.* verb
sing. singular	*pl.* plural

tart[1] (tärt), 1 having a sour but agreeable taste: *tart apples.* 2 sharp: *a tart reply. adj.* [Old English *teart* painful, sharp] —**tart′ly,** *adv.* —**tart′ness,** *n.*

tart[2] (tärt), pastry filled with cooked fruit, jam, etc. In the United States and Canada, a tart is small and the fruit shows; in England, any fruit pie is a tart. *n.* [from French of the 1300's *tarte*]

tar tan (tärt′n), 1 a plaid woolen cloth. Each Scottish Highland clan has its own pattern of tartan. 2 the pattern or design itself. 3 any similar plaid design or fabric of silk, cotton, etc. 4 made of tartan. 5 of, like, or having to do with tartan. 1-3 *n.,* 4,5 *adj.*

tartan
(def. 2)

tar tar (tär′tər), 1 an acid substance present in grape juice and deposited as a reddish crust on the inside of wine casks. After it is purified, this substance is called cream of tartar and is used with sodium bicarbonate to make baking powder. 2 a hard substance formed by the action of saliva on food and deposited as a crust on the teeth. *n.*

Tar tar (tär′tər), 1 member of a mixed horde of Mongolians and Turks who overran Asia and eastern Europe during the Middle Ages. Tartars now live in parts of the Soviet Union and central and western Asia. 2 **tartar,** person who has a bad temper. 3 of or having to do with a Tartar or Tartars. 1,2 *n.,* 3 *adj.* Also, **Tatar** for 1 and 3.

tar tar ic (tär tar′ik), of or having to do with tartar; containing tartar; derived from tartar. *adj.*

Tar tar us (tär′tər əs), in Greek myths: 1 a place of punishment below Hades. 2 the underworld; Hades. *n.*

Tar tar y (tär′tər ē), the ancient kingdom of the Tartars that included most of Russia and central and western Asia. *n.*

Tash kent (tash kent′), city in S central Soviet Union. It is the capital of the Uzbek. *n.*

task (task), 1 work to be done; piece of work; duty: *His task is to set the table.* 2 put work on; force to work: *The farmer tasked his horses beyond their strength.* 3 burden or strain: *Lifting that trunk tasked me beyond my strength.* 1 *n.,* 2,3 *v.*

take to task, blame; scold; reprove: *The teacher took him to task for not studying.*

task force, a temporary group of military units, especially naval units, assigned to one commander for carrying out a specific operation.

task mas ter (task′mas′tər), person who sets tasks for others to do. *n.*

Tas ma ni a (taz mā′nē ə), island off SE Australia. It is a state of the Commonwealth of Australia. *Capital:* Hobart. *n.* —**Tas ma′ni an,** *adj., n.*

tas sel (tas′əl), 1 a hanging bunch of threads, small cords, beads, etc., fastened together at one end. 2 something like this. Corn has tassels. 3 put tassels on. 4 take tassels from. 5 grow tassels: *Corn tassels just before the ears form.* 1,2 *n.,* 3-5 *v.*

Tas so (tas′ō), **Torquato,** 1544-1595, Italian poet. *n.*

taste (tāst), 1 what is special about (something) to the sense organs of the mouth; flavor. Sweet, sour, salt, and bitter are four important tastes. 2 try the flavor of (something) by taking a little into the mouth: *The cook tastes everything to see if it is right.* 3 the sense by which the flavor of things is perceived: *Her taste is unusually keen.* 4 get the flavor of by the sense of taste: *She tasted almond in the cake.* 5 have a particular flavor: *The soup tastes of onion.* 6 eat or drink a little bit of: *The children barely tasted their breakfast the day they went to the circus.* 7 a little bit; sample: *take a taste of a cake. The snowstorm will give you a taste of northern winter.* 8 experience; have: *taste freedom.* 9 a liking: *Suit your own taste.* 10 ability to perceive and enjoy what is beautiful and excellent: *Good books and pictures appeal to people of taste.* 11 manner or style that shows such ability: *Their house is furnished in excellent taste.* 1,3,7,9-11 *n.,* 2,4-6,8 *v.,* **tast ed, tast ing.**

taste bud, any of certain groups of cells, most of which are in the outer layer of the tongue, that are sense organs of taste.

taste ful (tāst′fəl), 1 having good taste; refined. 2 showing or done in good taste: *The room had tasteful furnishings in warm, inviting colors that went well together. adj.*

—**taste′ful ly,** *adv.* —**taste′ful ness,** *n.*

taste less (tāst′lis), 1 without taste: *Oatmeal is tasteless and unpleasant when it is allowed to stand and get cold.* 2 without good taste; in poor taste. *adj.* —**taste′less ly,** *adv.* —**taste′less ness,** *n.*

tast er (tā′stər), person who tastes, especially one whose work is judging the quality of wine, tea, coffee, etc., by the taste. *n.*

tast i ness (tā′stē nis), INFORMAL. tasty quality or condition. *n.*

tast y (tā′stē), INFORMAL. 1 tasting good; pleasing to the taste. 2 having or showing good taste. *adj.,* **tast i er, tast i est.**

tat (tat), make a kind of lace by looping and knotting (threads) with a shuttle. *v.,* **tat ted, tat ting.**

Ta tar (tä′tər), Tartar (defs. 1 and 3). *n., adj.*

tat ter (tat′ər), 1 a torn piece; rag: *After the storm the flag hung in tatters upon the mast.* 2 **tatters,** *pl.* torn or ragged clothing. 3 tear or wear to pieces; make ragged. 1,2 *n.,* 3 *v.*

tat tered (tat′ərd), 1 full of tatters; torn; ragged: *a tattered dress.* 2 wearing torn or ragged clothes. *adj.*

tat ting (tat′ing), 1 process or work of making a kind of lace by looping and knotting cotton or linen thread with a shuttle. 2 lace made in this way. *n.*

tat tle (tat′l), 1 tell tales or secrets. 2 talk or utter foolishly; gossip. 3 idle or foolish talk; gossip; telling tales or secrets. 1,2 *v.,* **tat tled, tat tling;** 3 *n.*

tat tler (tat′lər), a telltale. *n.*

tat tle tale (tat′l tāl′), INFORMAL. telltale. *n., adj.*

tat too[1] (ta tü′), 1 signal on a bugle, drum, etc., calling soldiers or sailors to their quarters at night. 2 series of raps, taps, etc.: *The hail beat a loud tattoo on the windowpane. n., pl.* **tat toos.** [from Dutch *taptoe,* from *tap* tap of a barrel + *toe* to pull to, shut]

tat too[2] (ta tü′), 1 mark (the skin) with designs or patterns by pricking it and putting in colors. 2 put such a design on the skin in this way: *The sailor had a ship tattooed on his arm.* 3 the mark or design made by tattooing. 1,2 *v.,* 3 *n., pl.* **tat toos.** [from Polynesian *tatu*] —**tat too′er,** *n.*

tattoo[2]
(defs. 1 and 3)

taught (tôt), past tense and past participle of **teach.** *That professor taught my mother. She has taught arithmetic for many years.* v.

taunt (tônt), 1 jeer at; mock; reproach: *My classmates taunted me for being teacher's pet.* 2 a bitter or insulting remark; mocking; jeering. 3 get or drive by taunts: *taunt someone into taking a dare.* 1,3 v., 2 n.

taupe (tōp), 1 a dark, brownish gray. 2 dark brownish-gray. 1 n., 2 adj.

Tau rus (tôr′əs), a northern constellation that was thought of as arranged in the shape of a bull. n.

taut (tôt), 1 tightly drawn; tense: *a taut rope.* 2 in neat condition; tidy: *a taut ship.* adj. —**taut′ly,** adv. —**taut′ness,** n.

tau tol o gy (tô tol′ə jē), a saying a thing over again in other words without adding clearness or force; useless repetition. EXAMPLE: the *modern* college student of *today.* n., pl. **tau tol o gies.**

tav ern (tav′ərn), 1 place where alcoholic drinks are sold and drunk; saloon. 2 inn. n.

taw (tô), 1 a fancy marble used for shooting. 2 game of marbles. 3 the line from which the players shoot their marbles. n.

taw dri ly (tô′drə lē), in a tawdry manner. adv.

taw dri ness (tô′drē nis), tawdry condition or quality. n.

taw dry (tô′drē), showy and cheap; gaudy. adj., **taw dri er, taw dri est.** [shortened from *(Sain)t Audrey('s lace),* sold at the fair of St. Audrey in England]

taw ny (tô′nē), brownish-yellow: *A lion has a tawny coat.* adj., **taw ni er, taw ni est.**

tax (taks), 1 money paid by people for the support of the government and the cost of public works and services; money regularly collected from citizens by their rulers: *Our parents pay taxes to the city, state, and federal government.* 2 put a tax on. People who own property are taxed in order to provide clean streets, good roads, protection against crime, and free education. 3 a burden, duty, or demand that oppresses; strain: *Climbing stairs is a tax on a weak heart.* 4 lay a heavy burden on; be hard for: *The work taxed my strength. Reading in a poor light taxes the eyes.* 5 reprove; accuse: *The teacher taxed him with having neglected his work.* 1,3 n., pl. **tax es** for 1; 2,4,5 v.

tax a ble (tak′sə bəl), liable to be taxed; subject to taxation: *a taxable income.* adj.

tax a tion (tak sā′shən), 1 a taxing: *Taxation is necessary to provide roads, schools, and police.* 2 amount people pay for the support of the government; taxes. n.

tax i (tak′sē), 1 taxicab. 2 ride in a taxi. 3 (of an aircraft) move across the ground or water under its own power. An airplane taxis into position before take-off or taxis off the field after landing. 1 n., pl. **tax is;** 2,3 v., **tax ied, tax i ing** or **tax y ing.**

tax i cab (tak′sē kab′), automobile for hire, usually with an automatic meter to record the amount to be paid. n.

tax i der mist (tak′sə dėr′mist), person who practices taxidermy. n.

tax i der my (tak′sə dėr′mē), art of preparing the skins of animals and stuffing and mounting them so that they look alive. n.

tax i me ter (tak′sē mē′tər), meter of a taxicab. n.

tax o nom ic (tak′sə nom′ik), of or having to do with taxonomy. adj.

tax on o my (tak son′ə mē), 1 classification, especially of plant and animal species. 2 branch of science dealing with classification. n.

tax pay er (taks′pā′ər), person who pays a tax or is required by law to do so. n.

Tay lor (tā′lər), Zachary, 1784-1850, the 12th president of the United States, from 1849 to 1850. n.

TB or **T.B.,** tuberculosis.

tbs. or **tbsp.,** tablespoon or tablespoons.

Tchai kov sky (chī kôf′skē), Peter Ilich, 1840-1893, Russian composer. n. Also, **Tschaikowsky** or **Tschaikovsky.**

TD, (in football) touchdown.

tea (tē), 1 a common drink made by pouring boiling water over the dried and prepared leaves of a certain shrub. Tea is served with milk or lemon, sugar, etc. 2 the dried and prepared leaves from which this drink is made. 3 the shrub on which these leaves grow. Tea is raised chiefly in China, Japan, and India. 4 a light meal in the late afternoon or early evening, at which tea is commonly served. The English have afternoon tea. 5 an afternoon reception at which tea is served. 6 something to drink prepared from some other thing named: *sage tea, senna tea, pepper tea.* **Beef tea** is a strong broth made from beef. n., pl. **teas.**

tea bag, tea leaves in a little bag of thin cloth or paper for easy removal from the cup or pot after use.

teach (tēch), 1 help to learn; show how to do; make understand: *He is teaching his dog tricks.* 2 give instruction to: *She teaches her classes well.* 3 give lessons in: *He teaches mathematics.* 4 give instruction; act as teacher: *She teaches for a living.* v., **taught, teach ing.**

teach a bil i ty (tē′chə bil′ə tē), fact or quality of being teachable. n.

teach a ble (tē′chə bəl), capable of being taught. adj.

teach er (tē′chər), person who teaches, especially one who teaches in a school. n. —**teach′er like′,** adj.

teach ing (tē′ching), 1 work or profession of a teacher. 2 act of a person who teaches. 3 what is taught; instruction; precept. n.

teaching machine, device that gives information in a series of units, usually with a gradual increase in difficulty, and checks how well the information has been learned by a set of questions which the pupil must answer correctly before going on to new material.

tea cup (tē′kup′), cup for drinking tea. n.

tea cup ful (tē′kup′fùl), as much as a teacup holds, usually four fluid ounces. n., pl. **tea cup fuls.**

tea house (tē′hous′), place where tea and other light refreshments are served. There are many teahouses in Japan and China. n., pl. **tea hous es** (tē′hou′ziz).

teak (tēk), 1 a large tree of the East Indies with a hard, durable, yellowish-brown wood. 2 this wood. Teak is used for shipbuilding, making fine furniture, etc. n.

tea ket tle (tē′ket′l), kettle for heating water to make tea, etc. n.

teal (tēl), any of several varieties of small ducks related to the mallard. n., pl. **teals** or **teal.**

team (tēm), 1 number of people working or acting together, especially one of the sides in a game or match: *a football team, a debating team.* 2 two or more horses or other animals harnessed together to work. 3 join together in a team: *Everybody teamed up to clean the classroom after the party.* 4 drive a team. 5 work, carry, haul, etc., with a team. 1,2 n., 3-5 v.

team mate (tēm′māt′), a fellow member of a team. n.

team ster (tēm′stər), man whose work is driving a team of horses or hauling things with a truck. n.

adj.	adjective	n.	noun
adv.	adverb	prep.	preposition
conj.	conjunction	pron.	pronoun
interj.	interjection	v.	verb
sing.	singular	pl.	plural

team work (tēm′wėrk′), the acting together of a number of people to make the work of the group successful and effective: *Football requires teamwork even more than individual skill.* n.

tea pot (tē′pot′), container with a handle and a spout for making and serving tea. n.

tear[1] (tir), 1 drop of salty liquid coming from the eye. 2 fill with tears; shed tears. 1 n., 2 v. [Old English *tēar*]
in tears, shedding tears; crying: *The baby is in tears because he is hungry.*

tear[2] (ter *or* tar), 1 pull apart by force: *tear a box open. I tore the letter into tiny pieces.* 2 make by pulling apart: *She tore a hole in her jeans.* 3 pull hard; pull violently: *Tear out the page.* 4 cut badly; wound: *The jagged stone tore his skin.* 5 rend; divide; split: *The party was torn by two factions.* 6 remove by effort; force away: *He could not tear himself from that spot.* 7 make miserable; distress: *She was torn by grief.* 8 become torn: *Lace tears easily.* 9 a torn place: *She has a tear in her jeans.* 10 act or process of tearing. 11 INFORMAL. move with great force or haste: *An automobile came tearing down the road.* 1-8,11 v., **tore, torn, tear ing;** 9,10 n. [Old English *teran*]
tear down, 1 pull down; raze; destroy: *The city tore down a whole block of apartment houses.* 2 bring about the wreck of; discredit; ruin: *tear down another's reputation.*
tear into, attack or criticize severely.

tear drop (tir′drop′), tear[1]. n.

tear ful (tir′fəl), 1 full of tears; weeping. 2 causing tears; sad. adj. **—tear′ful ly,** adv.

tear gas (tir), gas that irritates the eyes and temporarily blinds them with tears. It is used especially in dispersing rioters.

tear less (tir′lis), without tears; not crying. adj.

tea room (tē′rüm′ *or* tē′rùm′), room or shop where tea, coffee, and light meals are served. n.

tease (tēz), 1 vex or worry by jokes, questions, requests, etc.; annoy: *The children teased the dog until it bit them.* 2 beg: *The child teases for everything he sees.* 3 person who teases. 4 comb out; shred (wool). 5 raise nap on (cloth). 6 act of teasing or condition of being teased. 1,2,4,5 v., **teased, teas ing;** 3,6 n.

teas er (tē′zər), 1 person or thing that teases. 2 INFORMAL. an annoying problem; puzzling task. n.

teas ing ly (tē′zing lē), in a teasing way. adv.

tea spoon (tē′spün′), a spoon smaller than a tablespoon, commonly used to stir tea or coffee. It is a standard unit of measurement in cookery. n.

tea spoon ful (tē′spün fùl), as much as a teaspoon holds. 1 teaspoonful = ⅓ tablespoonful. n., pl. **tea spoonfuls.**

teat (tēt), nipple of a breast or udder, from which the young suck milk. n.

tech ne ti um (tek nē′shē əm), a radioactive metallic element produced artificially from uranium or molybdenum. n.

tech nic (tek′nik), 1 any technique. 2 technical. 1 n., 2 adj.

tech ni cal (tek′nə kəl), 1 of or having to do with a mechanical or industrial art or applied science: *This technical school trains engineers, chemists, and architects.* 2 of or having to do with the special facts of a science or art: *"Electrolysis," "tarsus," and "protein" are technical words.* 3 of or having to do with technique: *Her singing showed technical skill, but her voice was weak.* 4 by the rules of a certain science, art, game, etc.: *When the boxer was so badly hurt that the fight was stopped, his opponent won by a technical knockout.* adj.

tech ni cal i ty (tek′nə kal′ə tē), 1 a technical matter, point, detail, term, expression, etc.: *Books on engineering contain many technicalities which the ordinary reader does not understand.* 2 technical quality or character. n., pl. **tech ni cal i ties.**

tech ni cal ly (tek′nik lē), in a technical manner or respect; in technical terms; in a technical sense. adv.

tech ni cian (tek nish′ən), 1 person experienced in the technicalities of a subject. 2 person skilled in the technique of an art. n.

Tech ni col or (tek′nə kul′ər), trademark for a process of making colored motion pictures. n.

tech nique (tek nēk′), 1 method or ability of an artist's performance, execution, etc.; technical skill: *The pianist's technique was excellent, though his interpretation of the music was poor.* 2 a special method or system used to accomplish something. n.

tech noc ra cy (tek nok′rə sē), government by technical experts. n.

tech no log i cal (tek′nə loj′ə kəl), having to do with technology; used in technology. adj. **—tech′no log′i cal ly,** adv.

tech nol o gist (tek nol′ə jist), person skilled in technology. n.

tech nol o gy (tek nol′ə jē), science of the mechanical and industrial arts: *I studied engineering at a school of technology.* n.

Te cum seh (tə kum′sə), 1768?-1813, Shawnee Indian chief. n.

ted dy bear (ted′ē), a child's furry toy bear.

Te De um (tē dē′əm), 1 a hymn of praise and thanksgiving sung in Roman Catholic and Anglican churches at morning prayers or on special occasions. 2 music for this hymn. [from Latin *Te Deum (laudamus)* Thee God (we praise), the first words of the hymn]

te di ous (tē′dē əs *or* tē′jəs), long and tiring: *A long talk that you cannot understand is tedious.* adj. **—te′di ous ly,** adv. **—te′di ous ness,** n.

te di um (tē′dē əm), state of being wearisome; tiresomeness; tediousness. n.

tee (tē), 1 the mark aimed at in quoits, curling, and other games. 2 a mark or place from which a player starts in playing each hole in golf. 3 a short wooden or plastic peg with a concave top on which a golf ball is placed when a player drives. 4 put (a golf ball) on a tee. 1-3 n., 4 v., **teed, tee ing.**
tee off, drive (a golf ball) from a tee.

teem (tēm), be full (of); abound; swarm: *The swamp teemed with mosquitoes.* v.

teen (tēn), 1 teen-age: *teen fashions.* 2 teen-ager. 1 adj., 2 n.

-teen, suffix added to numbers. ten more than ____: *Sixteen = ten more than six.* [Old English *-tēne*, from *tēn* ten]

teen-age (tēn′āj′), 1 of or for a teenager or teen-agers: *a teen-age club.* 2 in one's teens; being a teen-ager: *a teen-age girl.* adj.

teen-aged (tēn′ājd′), in one's teens; being a teen-ager: *a teen-aged athlete.* adj.

teen-ag er (tēn′ā′jər), person in his or her teens. n.

teens (tēnz), the years of life from 13 to 19 inclusive. n.pl.

tee ny (tē′nē), INFORMAL. tiny. adj., **tee ni er, tee ni est.**

tee pee (tē′pē), tepee. n.

tee shirt, T-shirt.

tee ter (tē′tər), 1 rock unsteadily; sway. 2 balance on a seesaw. 3 seesaw. 1,2 v., 3 n.

tee ter-tot ter (tē′tər tot′ər), seesaw. n.

teeth (tēth), plural of **tooth.** n.
in the teeth of, 1 straight against; in the face of: *He advanced in the teeth of*

the wind. 2 in defiance of; in spite of.

teethe (tēᴛʜ), grow teeth; cut teeth; have teeth grow through the gums: *Babies teethe.* *v.*, **teethed, teeth ing.**

tee to tal er (tē tō′tl ər), person who never takes alcoholic liquor. *n.*

Te gu ci gal pa (tā gü′sē gäl′pä), capital of Honduras, in the S part. *n.*

teg u ment (teg′yə mənt), integument. *n.*

Te he ran or **Te hran** (te′ə ran′), capital of Iran, in the N part. *n.*

Tel A viv (tel′ ə vēv′), largest city of Israel, in the W part. *n.*

tel e cast (tel′ə kast′), 1 broadcast by television. 2 a television broadcast. 1 *v.*, **tel e cast** or **tel e cast ed, tel e cast ing;** 2 *n.* —**tel′e cast′er,** *n.*

tel e gram (tel′ə gram), message sent by telegraph: *receive a telegram.* *n.*

tel e graph (tel′ə graf), 1 apparatus, system, or process for sending coded messages over electric wires by means of electrical impulses. 2 send (a message) by telegraph. 3 send a message to (a person, etc.) by telegraph. 1 *n.*, 2,3 *v.*

te leg ra pher (tə leg′rə fər), person who sends and receives messages by telegraph. *n.*

tel e graph ic (tel′ə graf′ik), of or having to do with the telegraph; sent as a telegram. *adj.* —**tel′e graph′i cal ly,** *adv.*

te leg ra phy (tə leg′rə fē), the making or operating of telegraphs. *n.*

Te lem a chus (tə lem′ə kəs), (in Greek legends) the son of Ulysses and Penelope. When Ulysses returned from the Trojan War, Telemachus helped him slay Penelope's insolent suitors. *n.*

te lem e ter (tə lem′ə tər), 1 device for measuring heat, radiation, etc., and transmitting the information to a distant receiving station. 2 measure and transmit by telemeter. 1 *n.*, 2 *v.*

te lem e try (tə lem′ə trē), the use of telemeters for measuring and transmitting information. *n.*

tel e path ic (tel′ə path′ik), 1 of or having to do with telepathy. 2 by telepathy. *adj.*

tel e path i cal ly (tel′ə path′ik lē), by telepathy. *adv.*

te lep a thy (tə lep′ə thē), communication of one mind with another without using speech, hearing, sight, or any other sense used normally to communicate. *n.*

tel e phone (tel′ə fōn), 1 apparatus, system, or process for sending sound or speech to a distant point over wires by means of electrical impulses. 2 talk through a telephone; send (a message) by telephone. 3 make a telephone call to. 1 *n.*, 2,3 *v.*, **tel e phoned, tel e phon ing.**

telephone book or **telephone**

directory, list of names, addresses, and telephone numbers of people or businesses with telephones in a certain area.

tel e phon ic (tel′ə fon′ik), of or having to do with the telephone; by the telephone. *adj.*

te leph o ny (tə lef′ə nē), the making or operating of telephones. *n.*

tel e pho to lens (tel′ə fō′tō), lens used in a camera for producing an enlarged image of a distant object.

tel e scope (tel′ə skōp), 1 instrument for making distant objects appear nearer and larger. The stars are studied by means of telescopes. 2 force or be forced together one inside another like the sliding tubes of some telescopes: *When the two railroad trains crashed into each other, the cars were telescoped.* 3 shorten; condense. 1 *n.*, 2,3 *v.*, **tel e scoped, tel e scop ing.**

telescope
(def. 1)

tel e scop ic (tel′ə skop′ik), 1 of or having to do with a telescope. 2 obtained or seen by means of a telescope: *a telescopic view of the moon.* 3 visible only through a telescope. 4 far-seeing. 5 consisting of parts that slide one inside another like the tubes of some telescopes. *adj.*

tel e scop i cal ly (tel′ə skop′ik lē), by telescope. *adv.*

tel e type (tel′ə tīp), 1 **Teletype,** trademark for a teletypewriter. 2 system of sending signals by Teletype. 3 send (a message) by Teletype. 1,2 *n.*, 3 *v.*, **tel e typed, tel e typ ing.**

tel e type writ er (tel′ə tīp′rī′tər), a telegraphic device which resembles a typewriter, used in sending, receiving, and automatically printing out messages. *n.*

tel e view er (tel′ə vyü′ər), person who watches television. *n.*

tel e vise (tel′ə vīz), 1 send by television: *televise a baseball game.* 2 see by television. *v.*, **tel e vised, tel e vis ing.**

tel e vi sion (tel′ə vizh′ən), 1 process of sending the image of an object, scene, or event over wires or through the air by means of electrical impulses. In television, waves of light from an object are changed into electric waves which are sent to a receiving point where they are changed back into waves of

hat, āge, fär; let, ēqual, tėrm;
it, īce; hot, ōpen, ôrder;
oil, out; cup, pùt, rüle; ch, child;
ng, long; sh, she; th, thin;
ᴛʜ, then; zh, measure;

ə represents *a* in about,
e in taken, *i* in pencil,
o in lemon, *u* in circus.

light that produce an image of the object on a screen. The sound which accompanies the image is sent by radio at the same time. 2 the apparatus on which these pictures may be seen. 3 the business of television broadcasting; the television industry. 4 of, used in, or sent by television. 1-3 *n.*, 4 *adj.*

tell (tel), 1 put in words; say: *Tell the truth.* 2 tell to; inform: *Tell us about it.* 3 make known: *Don't tell where the money is.* 4 act as talebearer; reveal (something secret or private): *Promise not to tell.* 5 recognize; know; distinguish: *He couldn't tell which house it was.* 6 say to; order; command: *Tell her to stop!* 7 say to with force: *I don't like it, I tell you.* 8 count; count one by one: *The nun tells her beads.* 9 have effect or force: *Every blow told.* *v.*, **told, telling.**

tell off, 1 count off; count off and detach for some special duty. 2 strike back sharply in words; scold; reprove.

tell on, 1 inform on; tell tales about. 2 have a harmful effect on; break down: *The strain told on the man's health.*

Tell (tel), **William,** legendary hero in the Swiss struggle for independence against Austria. For refusing to salute the symbol of Austrian authority, a cap set up in the market place, he was condemned to death unless he could shoot an apple from his little son's head. He succeeded, and later started a revolt against Austria. *n.*

tell er (tel′ər), 1 person who tells. 2 person who counts. A teller in a bank takes in, gives out, and counts money. *n.*

tell ing (tel′ing), having effect or force; striking: *a telling blow.* *adj.*

tell ing ly (tel′ing lē), effectively; forcefully. *adv.*

tell tale (tel′tāl′), 1 person who tells tales on others; person who reveals private or secret matters from malice. 2 telling what is not supposed to be told; revealing: *a telltale fingerprint.* 1 *n.*, 2 *adj.*

tel lur i um (te lùr′ē əm), a silver-white nonmetallic element with some metallic properties. It usually occurs in

adj. adjective	*n.* noun
adv. adverb	*prep.* preposition
conj. conjunction	*pron.* pronoun
interj. interjection	*v.* verb
sing. singular	*pl.* plural

nature combined with various metals. *n.*

te mer i ty (tə merʹə tē), reckless boldness; rashness. *n.*

tem per (temʹpər), 1 state of mind; disposition; condition: *a sweet temper. She was in no temper to be kept waiting.* 2 angry state of mind: *fly into a temper at trifles. In his temper he slammed the door.* 3 calm state of mind: *I became angry and lost my temper.* 4 soften; moderate: *Temper justice with mercy.* 5 bring or be brought to a proper or desired condition of hardness, toughness, flexibility, etc., by mixing or preparing. A painter tempers his colors by mixing them with oil. Steel is tempered by heating it and cooling it under controlled conditions until it has the proper degree of hardness and flexibility. 6 the degree of hardness, toughness, flexibility, etc., of a substance given by tempering: *The temper of the clay was right for shaping.* 1-3,6 *n.,* 4,5 *v.*

tem per a ment (temʹpər ə mənt), 1 a person's nature or disposition: *That child has a nervous temperament.* 2 an easily irritated, sensitive nature. An artist, singer, or actor often has temperament. *n.*

tem per a men tal (temʹpər ə menʹtl), 1 subject to moods and whims; easily irritated; sensitive: *The young man was very temperamental about his haircut.* 2 showing a strongly marked individual temperament. 3 due to temperament; constitutional: *Cats have a temperamental dislike for water. adj.* —**temʹper a menʹtal ly**, *adv.*

tem per ance (temʹpər əns), 1 a being moderate in action, speech, habits, etc.; self-control: *Temperance should be applied not only to food and drink but also to work and play.* 2 a being moderate in the use of alcoholic drinks. 3 the principle and practice of not using alcoholic drinks at all. *n.*

tem per ate (temʹpər it), 1 not very hot and not very cold: *Seattle has a temperate climate.* 2 moderate; using self-control: *She spoke in a temperate manner, not favoring either side especially.* 3 moderate in using alcoholic drinks: *He is a temperate man, and never drinks too much. adj.* —**temʹper ate ly**, *adv.*

temperate zone or **Temperate Zone,** the part of the earth's surface between the tropic of Cancer and the arctic circle in the Northern Hemisphere, or the part between the tropic of Capricorn and the antarctic circle in the Southern Hemisphere.

tem per a ture (temʹpər ə chər), 1 degree of heat or cold. The temperature of freezing water is 32 degrees Fahrenheit. 2 a body temperature higher than normal (98.6 degrees Fahrenheit): *A sick person may have a temperature. n.*

tem pered (temʹpərd), 1 softened or moderated. 2 treated so as to become hard but not too brittle: *The sword was made of tempered steel. adj.*

tem pest (temʹpist), 1 a violent windstorm, usually accompanied by rain, hail, or snow: *The tempest drove the ship on the rocks.* 2 a violent disturbance: *The child burst into a tempest of anger. n.*

tem pes tu ous (tem pesʹchü əs), 1 stormy: *It was a tempestuous night.* 2 violent: *a tempestuous fit of anger. adj.* —**tem pesʹtu ous ly**, *adv.* —**tem pesʹtu ous ness**, *n.*

Tem plar (temʹplər), member of a religious and military order called Knights Templars, founded among the Crusaders about 1118 to protect the Holy Sepulcher and pilgrims to Palestine. *n.*

tem ple[1] (temʹpəl), 1 building used for the service of worship of a god or gods. 2 **Temple,** any of three temples in ancient Jerusalem built at different times by the Jews. Solomon built the first Temple. 3 building set apart for Christian worship; church. 4 synagogue. *n.* [Old English *tempel,* from Latin *templum*]

temple[2]

TEMPLE

tem ple[2] (temʹpəl), the flattened part on either side of the forehead. *n.* [from French of the 1300's *temple,* from Latin *tempora* the temples]

tem po (temʹpō), 1 (in music) the time or rate of movement; proper or characteristic speed of movement: *the correct tempo for a dance tune.* 2 rhythm; characteristic rhythm: *the fast tempo of modern life. n., pl.* **tem pos, tem pi** (temʹpē).

tem por al[1] (temʹpər əl), 1 of time. 2 lasting for a time only. 3 of this life only. 4 not religious or sacred; worldly. *adj.* [from Latin *temporalis,* from *tempus* time]

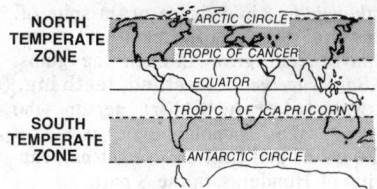

NORTH TEMPERATE ZONE
ARCTIC CIRCLE
TROPIC OF CANCER
EQUATOR
TROPIC OF CAPRICORN
SOUTH TEMPERATE ZONE
ANTARCTIC CIRCLE

tem por al[2] (temʹpər əl), of the temples or sides of the forehead. *adj.* [from Latin *temporalis,* from *tempora* the temples]

tem po rar i ly (temʹpə rerʹə lē), for a short time; for the present: *They are living in a hotel temporarily. The work is postponed temporarily. adv.*

tem po rar y (temʹpə rerʹē), lasting for a short time only; used for the time being; not permanent: *have a temporary job. adj.*

tem po rize (temʹpə rīzʹ), 1 evade immediate action or decision in order to gain time, avoid trouble, etc. 2 fit one's acts to the time or occasion. *v.,* **tem po rized, tem po riz ing.**

tempt (tempt), 1 make or try to make (a person) do something: *A person can be tempted by hunger to steal.* 2 appeal strongly to; attract: *That candy tempts me.* 3 provoke: *It is tempting fate to go sailing in that old boat.* 4 OLD USE. test. *v.*

temp ta tion (temp tāʹshən), 1 a tempting: *No temptation could make her break her promise.* 2 a being tempted: *"Lead us not into temptation."* 3 thing that tempts: *Money left carelessly about is a temptation. n.*

tempt er (tempʹtər), 1 person who tempts. 2 **the Tempter,** the Devil; Satan. *n.*

tempt ing (tempʹting), that tempts; alluring; inviting: *A nap is a tempting idea. adj.* —**temptʹing ly**, *adv.*

temp tress (tempʹtris), woman who tempts. *n., pl.* **temp tress es.**

ten (ten), 1 one more than nine; 10. 2 set of ten persons or things. 1,2 *n.,* 1 *adj.*

ten a ble (tenʹə bəl), that can be held or defended: *a tenable position, a tenable theory. adj.*

te na cious (ti nāʹshəs), 1 holding fast: *the tenacious jaws of a bulldog, a person tenacious of his rights, a tenacious memory.* 2 stubborn; persistent: *a tenacious salesman.* 3 holding fast together; not easily pulled apart. 4 sticky. *adj.* —**te naʹcious ly**, *adv.*

te nac i ty (ti nasʹə tē), 1 firmness in holding fast. 2 stubbornness; persistence. 3 firmness in holding together; toughness. 4 stickiness. *n.*

ten an cy (tenʹən sē), 1 condition of being a tenant; an occupying and paying rent for land or buildings. 2 property so held. **3** length of time a tenant occupies a property. *n., pl.* **ten an cies.**

ten ant (ten′ənt), **1** person paying rent for the temporary use of the land or buildings of another person: *That building has apartments for one hundred tenants.* **2** person or thing that occupies: *Birds are tenants of the trees.* **3** hold or occupy as a tenant; inhabit: *That old house has not been tenanted for many years.* 1,2 *n.,* 3 *v.*

tenant farmer, person who lives on and farms land belonging to another. The owner receives cash or a share of the crops as rent.

ten ant less (ten′ənt lis), without a tenant; vacant. *adj.*

ten ant ry (ten′ən trē), **1** all the tenants on an estate. **2** tenancy. *n., pl.* **ten ant ries.**

Ten Commandments, (in the Bible) the ten rules for living and for worship that God revealed to Moses on Mount Sinai.

tend[1] (tend), **1** be apt; be likely; incline (to): *Fruit tends to decay. Homes tend to use more mechanical appliances now.* **2** move; be directed: *The coastline tends to the south here. v.* [from French of the 1300's *tendre,* from Latin *tendere* stretch, extend]

tend[2] (tend), take care of; look after; attend to: *tend the sick. He tends shop for his parents. A shepherd tends his flock. v.* [shortened from *attend*]

tend en cy (ten′dən sē), inclination; leaning: *a tendency to fight. Wood has a tendency to swell if it gets wet. n., pl.* **tend en cies.**

ten den tious (ten den′shəs), having a tendency to take sides; one-sided: *a tendentious statement. adj.*

ten der[1] (ten′dər), **1** not hard or tough; soft: *The meat is tender. Stones hurt the little child's tender feet.* **2** not strong and hardy; delicate: *The leaves in spring are green and tender.* **3** kind; affectionate; loving: *She spoke tender words to the child.* **4** not rough or crude; gentle: *He patted the dog with tender hands. These young plants need tender care.* **5** young: *Two years old is a tender age.* **6** sensitive; painful; sore: *a tender wound. Automobiles are a tender subject with Dad since he wrecked his.* **7** feeling pain or grief easily: *a tender heart. adj.* [from French of the 1200's *tendre,* from Latin *tener*] —**ten′der ly,** *adv.*

ten der[2] (ten′dər), **1** offer formally: *He tendered his thanks.* **2** a formal offer: *She refused his tender of marriage.* **3** thing offered. Money that must be accepted as payment for a debt is called legal tender. **4** offer (money, goods, etc.) in payment of a debt. 1,4 *v.,* 2,3 *n.* [from French of the 1500's

tendre, from Latin *tendere* stretch, extend] —**ten′der er,** *n.*

tend er[3] (ten′dər), **1** person or thing that tends another: *a machine tender.* **2** a small boat carried or towed by a big one and used for landing passengers. **3** a small ship used for carrying supplies and passengers to and from larger ships. **4** the car that carries coal and water, attached behind a steam locomotive. *n.* [*tend*[2] + -*er*[1]]

ten der foot (ten′dər fut′), INFORMAL. **1** newcomer to the pioneer life of the western United States. **2** person not used to rough living and hardships. **3** an inexperienced person; beginner. **4** a beginning member of the Boy Scouts or Girl Scouts. *n., pl.* **ten der foots, ten der feet** (ten′dər fēt′).

ten der heart ed (ten′dər här′tid), kindly; sympathetic. *adj.*

ten der ize (ten′də rīz′), make soft or tender: *tenderize meat by pounding. v.,* **ten der ized, ten der iz ing.**

ten der loin (ten′dər loin′), a tender part of the loin of beef or pork. *n.*

ten der ness (ten′dər nis), **1** a being tender: *A steak is judged by its flavor and tenderness.* **2** tender feeling: *She has a tenderness for cats. n.*

TENDONS

ten don (ten′dən), a tough, strong band or cord of tissue that joins a muscle to a bone or some other part; sinew. *n.*

ten dril (ten′drəl), **1** a threadlike part of a climbing plant that attaches itself to something and helps support the plant. **2** something similar: *curly tendrils of hair. n.*

tendrils (def. 1) on a grapevine

ten e ment (ten′ə mənt), **1** a building, especially in a poor section of a city, divided into sets of rooms occupied by separate families. **2** a dwelling, or part of a dwelling, occupied by a tenant. *n.*

ten et (ten′it), doctrine, principle, belief, or opinion held as true. *n.*

ten fold (ten′fōld′), ten times as much or as many. *adj., adv.*

Tenn., Tennessee.

Ten nes see (ten′ə sē′), **1** one of the south central states of the United States. *Capital:* Nashville. **2** river flow-

ing from E Tennessee into the Ohio River. *n.*

ten nis (ten′is), game played by two or four players on a rectangular court, in which a ball is hit back and forth over a net with a racket. *n.*

Ten ny son (ten′ə sən), **Alfred,** Lord, 1809-1892, English poet. *n.*

ten on (ten′ən), **1** the end of a piece of wood cut so as to fit into the mortise in another piece and so form a joint. See **mortise** for diagram. **2** cut so as to form a tenon. **3** fit together with tenon and mortise. 1 *n.,* 2,3 *v.*

ten or (ten′ər), **1** the general tendency; course: *We found we enjoyed the even tenor of country life and didn't miss the city.* **2** the general meaning or drift: *I understand French well enough to get the tenor of her speech.* **3** the highest male voice in music. **4** singer with such a voice. **5** part to be sung by such a voice. **6** of or for a tenor. 1-5 *n.,* 6 *adj.*

tenor clef, the C clef when the clef symbol is placed on the fourth line of the staff. See **clef** for diagram.

ten pins (ten′pinz′), the game of bowling. *n.*

tense[1] (tens), **1** stretched tight; strained to stiffness: *a tense rope, a face tense with pain.* **2** stretch tight; stiffen: *She tensed her muscles for the leap.* **3** strained; keyed up: *tense nerves, a tense moment.* 1,3 *adj.,* **tens er, tensest;** 2 *v.,* **tensed, tens ing.** [from Latin *tensum,* from *tendere* stretch, extend] —**tense′ly,** *adv.* —**tense′ness,** *n.*

tense[2] (tens), **1** form of a verb that shows the time of the action or state expressed by the verb. *He obeys* is in the present tense. *He obeyed* is in the past tense. *He will obey* is in the future tense. **2** set of such forms for the various persons. The present tense of *obey* is: *I obey, you obey, he obeys, we obey, you obey, they obey. n.* [from French of the 1300's *tens* time, from Latin *tempus*]

ten sile (ten′səl), **1** of or having to do with tension: *Steel has great tensile strength.* **2** that can be stretched. *adj.*

ten sion (ten′shən), **1** a stretching. **2** a

adj. adjective	*n.* noun
adv. adverb	*prep.* preposition
conj. conjunction	*pron.* pronoun
interj. interjection	*v.* verb
sing. singular	*pl.* plural

stretched condition: *The tension of the bow gives speed to the arrow.* 3 mental strain: *tension brought on by overwork.* 4 strained condition: *political tension. n.*

tent (tent), 1 a movable shelter made of cloth or skins supported by a pole or poles. 2 live in a tent: *We sang "We are tenting tonight on the old campground."* 1 *n.,* 2 *v.* —**tent′like′,** *adj.*

ten ta cle (ten′tə kəl), 1 a long, slender, flexible growth on the head or around the mouth of an animal, used to touch, hold, or move; feeler: *An octopus has eight tentacles.* 2 a sensitive, hairlike growth on a plant. *n.*

ten ta tive (ten′tə tiv), 1 done as a trial or experiment; experimental: *a tentative plan.* 2 hesitating: *a tentative laugh.* *adj.* —**ten′ta tive ly,** *adv.* —**ten′ta tive ness,** *n.*

tent caterpillar, caterpillar that spins a tentlike, silken web in which it lives. Tent caterpillars feed on leaves and do great damage to fruit and forest trees.

ten ter (ten′tər), framework on which cloth is stretched so that it may set or dry evenly without shrinking. *n.*

ten ter hook (ten′tər hùk′), one of the hooks or bent nails that hold the cloth stretched on a tenter. *n.*

on tenterhooks, in painful suspense; anxious.

tenth (tenth), 1 next after the ninth; last in a series of 10. 2 one of 10 equal parts: *A dime is a tenth of a dollar. adj., n.*

ten u ous (ten′yü əs), 1 thin or slight; slender: *the tenuous thread of a spider's web.* 2 not dense: *The air ten miles above the earth is very tenuous.* 3 having slight importance; not substantial: *a tenuous claim. adj.* —**ten′u ous ly,** *adv.* —**ten′u ous ness,** *n.*

ten ure (ten′yər), 1 a holding or possessing. 2 length of time of holding or possessing: *The tenure of office of the president of our club is one year.* 3 manner of holding land, buildings, etc., from a feudal lord or superior. *n.*

te pee (tē′pē), tent used by the American Indians of the Great Plains, made of hides sewn together and stretched over poles arranged in the shape of a cone. *n.* Also, **teepee.**

tep id (tep′id), slightly warm; lukewarm. *adj.* —**tep′id ly,** *adv.* —**tep′id ness,** *n.*

ter bi um (tėr′bē əm), a metallic element which occurs in certain minerals with yttrium and ytterbium. *n.*

te re do (tə rē′dō), shipworm. *n., pl.* **te re dos.**

term (tėrm), 1 word or phrase used in connection with some special subject, science, art, or business: *medical terms. "Acid," "base," and "salt" are terms commonly used in chemistry.* 2 any particular word or expression: *a term of reproach, a foreign term.* 3 apply a term to; name; call: *He might be termed handsome.* 4 a set period of time; length of time that a thing lasts: *The President's term of office is four years.* 5 one of the periods into which the school year is divided: *Most schools have a fall term and a spring term.* **6 terms,** *pl.* **a** conditions: *The terms of the peace were very hard for the defeated nation.* **b** agreement: *The company and the union could not come to terms without someone acting as a mediator between them.* **c** way of speaking: *She talked about you in very flattering terms.* **d** personal relations: *We are on good terms with our neighbors.* 7 numerator or denominator in a fraction. 8 any part of an algebraic expression separated from the other parts by a plus or minus sign. In $13ax^2 - 2bxy + y$, $13ax^2$, $2bxy$, and y are the terms. 1,2,4-8 *n.,* 3 *v.*

ter ma gant (tėr′mə gənt), 1 a violent, quarreling, scolding woman. 2 violent quarreling, or scolding. 1 *n.,* 2 *adj.*

ter mi na ble (tėr′mə nə bəl), 1 that can be ended: *The contract was terminable by either party.* 2 coming to an end after a certain time: *a loan terminable in 10 years. adj.*

ter mi nal (tėr′mə nəl), 1 at the end; forming the end part. A terminal flower or bud is one growing at the end of a stem, branch, etc. 2 the end; the end part. A railroad terminal is the station, sheds, tracks, etc., at either end of the line. 3 resulting in death; fatal: *a terminal disease.* 4 device for making an electrical connection: *the terminals of a battery.* 1,3 *adj.,* 2,4 *n.*

ter mi nate (tėr′mə nāt), 1 bring to an end; put an end to: *The two lawyers terminated their partnership and each*

opened a separate office. 2 come to an end: *The contract terminates soon.* 3 form the end of; bound; limit. *v.,* **ter mi nat ed, ter mi nat ing.**

ter mi na tion (tėr′mə nā′shən), an ending; end: *Termination of the contract left both parties free to do business elsewhere. n.*

ter mi nol o gy (tėr′mə nol′ə jē), the special words or terms used in a science, art, business, etc.: *medical terminology, the terminology of engineering. n., pl.* **ter mi nol o gies.**

ter mi nus (tėr′mə nəs), 1 an end of a railroad line, bus line, etc. 2 boundary; goal; end. *n., pl.* **ter mi ni** (tėr′mə nī), **ter mi nus es.**

ter mite (tėr′mīt), any of a group of insects with soft, pale bodies that live in colonies somewhat like ants and eat wood, paper, and other material containing cellulose; white ant. Termites are very destructive to buildings, furniture, etc. *n.*

tern (tėrn), any of a group of sea birds related to the gulls but with a more slender body and bill and usually a long, forked tail. *n.*

ter race (ter′is), 1 a paved outdoor space adjoining a house, used for lounging, dining, etc. 2 the flat roof of a house, especially of an Oriental or Spanish house. 3 a row of houses or a short street running along the side or top of a slope: *She lives at 7 Oak Terrace.* 4 a flat, raised level of land with vertical or sloping sides, especially one of a series of such levels placed one above the other. 5 form into a terrace or terraces; furnish with terraces: *a terraced garden, a terraced apartment.* 1-4 *n.,* 5 *v.,* **ter raced, ter rac ing.**

terraces (def. 4)

ter ra cot ta (ter′ə kot′ə), 1 kind of hard, often unglazed, brownish-red earthenware, used for vases, statuettes, decorations on buildings, etc. 2 a dull brownish red. [from Italian *terra cotta* baked earth]

ter ra fir ma (ter′ə fėr′mə), solid earth; dry land. [from Latin]

ter rain (te rān′), tract of land, especially considered with respect to its extent and natural features: *the hilly, rocky terrain of parts of New England. n.*

ter ra pin (ter′ə pin), a North American turtle used for food. It lives in fresh water or tidewater. *n.*

tepees

ter rar i um (tə rer′ē əm), a glass enclosure in which plants or small land animals are kept. *n., pl.* **ter rar i ums, ter rar i a** (tə rer′ē ə).

ter res tri al (tə res′trē əl), 1 of the earth; not of the heavens: *this terrestrial globe.* 2 of land, not water: *Islands and continents make up the terrestrial parts of the earth.* 3 living on the ground, not in the air or water or in trees: *Cows, lions, and elephants are terrestrial animals.* 4 growing on land; growing in the ground: *terrestrial plants.* 5 worldly; earthly. *adj.*

ter ri ble (ter′ə bəl), 1 causing great fear; dreadful; awful: *The terrible storm destroyed many lives.* 2 distressing; severe: *the terrible suffering caused by war.* 3 INFORMAL. extremely bad; unpleasant: *She has a terrible temper. adj.*

ter ri bly (ter′ə blē), 1 in a terrible manner; dreadfully: *to be terribly afraid of lightning.* 2 INFORMAL. extremely: *I am terribly sorry I stepped on your toes. adv.*

ter ri er (ter′ē ər), any of various breeds of small, active, intelligent, and courageous dogs, formerly used to pursue prey into its burrow. Some well-known breeds are fox terriers, Irish terriers, and Scotch terriers. *n.*

ter rif ic (tə rif′ik), 1 causing great fear; terrifying: *A terrific earthquake shook Japan.* 2 INFORMAL. very unusual; remarkable; extraordinary: *A terrific hot spell ruined many of the crops.* 3 SLANG. very good; wonderful: *She is a terrific tennis player. The party was terrific. adj.*

ter rif i cal ly (tə rif′ik lē), in a terrific manner; to a terrific degree. *adv.*

ter ri fy (ter′ə fī), fill with great fear; frighten very much: *Terrified by the sight of the bear, he ran into the cabin. v.,* **ter ri fied, ter ri fy ing.**

ter ri to ri al (ter′ə tôr′ē əl), 1 of or having to do with territory: *The purchase of Louisiana was a valuable territorial addition to the United States.* 2 of a particular territory or district; restricted to a particular district: *a territorial governor. adj.*

ter ri to ry (ter′ə tôr′ē), 1 land; region: *Much territory in the northern part of Africa is desert.* 2 land belonging to a government; land under the rule of a distant government: *Gibraltar is British territory.* 3 region assigned to a salesman or agent. 4 a district not admitted as a state but having its own lawmaking body. Alaska was a territory of the United States until 1958. *n., pl.* **ter ri to ries.**

ter ror (ter′ər), 1 great fear: *The child has a terror of thunder.* 2 cause of great fear: *Pirates were once the terror of the sea. n.*

ter ror ism (ter′ə riz′əm), 1 a terrorizing; use of terror. 2 condition of fear and submission produced by frightening people. *n.*

ter ror ist (ter′ər ist), person who uses or favors terrorism. *n.*

ter ror is tic (ter′ə ris′tik), using or favoring methods that inspire terror. *adj.*

ter ror i za tion (ter′ər ə zā′shən), a terrorizing or a being terrorized; rule by terror. *n.*

ter ror ize (ter′ə rīz′), 1 fill with terror: *The sight of the growling dog terrorized the little child.* 2 rule or subdue by causing terror. *v.,* **ter ror ized, ter ror iz ing.**

ter ror-strick en (ter′ər strik′ən), terrified. *adj.*

ter ry (ter′ē), a rough cloth made of uncut looped yarn. *n., pl.* **ter ries.**

terry cloth, terry.

terse (tėrs), brief and to the point: *"No" was Father's terse reply when I asked to play after bedtime. adj.,* **ters er, ters est. —terse′ly,** *adv.* **—terse′ness,** *n.*

ter tian (tėr′shən), 1 fever or ague which recurs every other day. 2 recurring every other day. 1 *n.,* 2 *adj.*

ter ti ar y (tėr′shē er′ē), of the third order, rank, or formation. *adj.*

test (test), 1 examination or trial: *People who want a license to drive an automobile must pass a test. The teacher gave the class a test in arithmetic.* 2 means of trial: *Trouble is a test of character.* 3 examination of a substance to see what it is or what it contains: *A test showed that the water from our well was pure.* 4 put to a test of any kind; try out: *test a rope for strength. The doctor tested my eyes.* 5 to show a certain result on a test. 1-3 *n.,* 4,5 *v.* **—test′er,** *n.*

tes ta ment (tes′tə mənt), 1 written instructions telling what to do with a person's property after his death; will. 2 **Testament, a** a main division of the Bible; the Old Testament or the New Testament. **b** INFORMAL. the New Testament. *n.*

tes ta men tar y (tes′tə men′tər ē), 1 of or having to do with a testament or will. 2 given, done, or appointed by a testament or will. *adj.*

TEST TUBE

hat, āge, fär; let, ēqual, tėrm; it, īce; hot, ōpen, ôrder; oil, out; cup, pùt, rüle; ch, child; ng, long; sh, she; th, thin; ᵬH, then; zh, measure;

ə represents *a* in about, *e* in taken, *i* in pencil, *o* in lemon, *u* in circus.

tes tate (tes′tāt), having made and left a valid will. *adj.*

tes ta tor (tes′tā tər), 1 person who makes a will. 2 person who has died leaving a valid will. *n.*

tes ti cle (tes′tə kəl), gland in a male animal that produces the sperm; testis. *n.*

tes ti fy (tes′tə fī), 1 give evidence; bear witness: *The excellence of Shakespeare's plays testifies to his genius.* 2 declare or give evidence under oath in a court of law: *The witness testified that the speeding car had crashed into the truck. Other witnesses were unwilling to testify. v.,* **tes ti fied, tes ti fy ing.**

tes ti ly (tes′tə lē), in a testy manner. *adv.*

tes ti mo ni al (tes′tə mō′nē əl), 1 certificate of character, conduct, qualifications, value, etc.; recommendation: *a testimonial from a former employer. Advertisements of patent medicines often contain testimonials from people who have used them.* 2 something given or done to show esteem, admiration, gratitude, etc.: *The members of the church collected money for a testimonial to their retiring pastor.* 3 given or done as a testimonial. 1,2 *n.,* 3 *adj.*

tes ti mo ny (tes′tə mō′nē), 1 statement used for evidence or proof: *A witness gave testimony that the defendant was at home all day Sunday.* 2 evidence: *The pupils presented their teacher with a watch in testimony of their respect and affection.* 3 an open declaration or profession of one's faith. *n., pl.* **tes ti mo nies.**

tes ti ness (tes′tē nis), testy quality or condition. *n.*

tes tis (tes′tis), testicle. *n., pl.* **tes tes** (tes′tēz′).

test pilot, pilot employed to test new or experimental aircraft by subjecting them to greater than normal stress.

test tube, a thin glass tube closed at one end, used in making chemical tests.

tes ty (tes′tē), easily irritated; impatient: *a very unpleasant and testy old man. adj.,* **tes ti er, tes ti est.**

tet a nus (tet′n əs), disease caused by certain bacilli usually entering the body

tête-à-tête

|---|---|
adj. adjective	*n.* noun
adv. adverb	*prep.* preposition
conj. conjunction	*pron.* pronoun
interj. interjection	*v.* verb
sing. singular	*pl.* plural

through wounds, characterized by violent spasms and stiffness of many muscles, sometimes resulting in death. Tetanus of the jaw muscles is called lockjaw. You can be protected against it by inoculation. *n.*

tête-à-tête (tāt′ə tāt′), 1 two together in private: *They dined tête-à-tête.* 2 of or for two people in private: *a tête-à-tête conversation.* 3 a private conversation between two people. 1 *adv.*, 2 *adj.*, 3 *n.* [from French *tête-à-tête* head to head]

teth er (teᴛн′ər), 1 rope or chain for fastening an animal so that it can graze or move only within a certain limit: *The cow had broken her tether and was in the garden.* 2 fasten with a tether: *The horse is tethered to a stake.* 1 *n.*, 2 *v.*

at the end of one's tether, at the end of one's resources or endurance.

Teu ton (tüt′n *or* tyüt′n), 1 a German. 2 person belonging to the group of northern Europeans that speak Germanic languages. 3 member of an ancient Germanic tribe that threatened the Roman republic in the 100's B.C. 4 German. 1-3 *n.*, 4 *adj.*

Teu ton ic (tü ton′ik *or* tyü ton′ik), 1 of or having to do with the ancient Teutons or their language. 2 Germanic. 3 German. *adj.*

Tex., Texas.

Tex an (tek′sən), 1 of or having to do with Texas or its people. 2 person born or living in Texas. 1 *adj.*, 2 *n.*

Tex as (tek′səs), one of the southwestern states of the United States. *Capital:* Austin. *n.*

text (tekst), 1 the main body of reading matter in a book: *This history book contains 300 pages of text and about 50 pages of maps and pictures.* 2 the original words of a writer. A text is often changed here and there when it is copied. 3 a short passage in the Bible: *The minister preached on the text "Judge not, that ye be not judged."* 4 topic; subject: *Town improvement was the speaker's text.* 5 textbook. *n.*

text book (tekst′bůk′), book for regular study by pupils. Most books used in schools are textbooks. There are textbooks on arithmetic, grammar, social studies, science, and most other subjects. *n.*

tex tile (tek′stəl *or* tek′stīl), 1 woven: *Cloth is a textile fabric.* 2 a woven fabric; cloth: *Beautiful textiles are sold in Paris.* 3 suitable for weaving: *Linen, cotton, silk, nylon, and wool are common textile materials.* 4 material that can be woven. 5 of or having to do with the making, selling, etc., of textiles: *His father has been in the textile business for twenty years.* 1,3,5 *adj.*, 2,4 *n.*

tex tu al (teks′chü əl), of the text; having to do with the text: *A misprint is a textual error. adj.*

tex ture (teks′chər), 1 arrangement of threads in a woven fabric: *Homespun is cloth that has a loose texture. A piece of burlap has a much coarser texture than a linen handkerchief.* 2 arrangement of the parts of anything; structure; make-up: *Her skin has a fine texture. The texture of marble makes it take a polish. n.*

-th, *suffix added to numbers.* number ___ in order or position in a series: *Sixth = number six in order or position in a series.* [Old English *-tha, -the*]

Thack er ay (thak′ər ē), **William Makepeace,** 1811-1863, English novelist. *n.*

Thai (tī), 1 of Thailand, its people, or their language. 2 person born or living in Thailand. 3 language of Thailand. 1 *adj.*, 2,3 *n.*, *pl.* **Thais** for 2.

Thai land (tī′land), country in SE Asia. *Capital:* Bangkok. Formerly called **Siam.** *n.*

tha ler (tä′lər), a large silver coin formerly used in Germany. It was replaced by the mark. *n.*, *pl.* **tha ler.**

thal li um (thal′ē əm), a soft, bluish-white metallic element that occurs in iron and zinc ores and in various minerals. It is highly poisonous and its compounds are used to kill insects, rodents, etc. *n.*

thal lo phyte (thal′ə fīt), any of a large group of plants that have no leaves, stems, or roots. Bacteria, algae, fungi, and lichens are thallophytes. *n.*

thal lus (thal′əs), plant not divided into leaves, stem, and root. Mushrooms, toadstools, and lichens are thalli. *n.*, *pl.* **thal li** (thal′ī), **thal lus es.**

Thames (temz), river flowing from S England into the North Sea. London is on the Thames. See **Rhine** for map. *n.*

than (ᴛнan; *unstressed* ᴛнən), 1 in comparison with: *She is taller than her sister. This train is faster than that one.* 2 compared to that which: *You know better than I do.* 3 except; besides: *How else can we come than by train? conj.*

thane (thān), 1 man who ranked between an earl and an ordinary freeman in early England. Thanes held lands of the

king or lord and gave military service in return. 2 a Scottish baron or lord. *n.*

thank (thangk), 1 say that one is pleased and grateful for something given or done; express gratitude to: *She thanked her teacher for helping her.* 2 **thanks,** *pl.* **a** I thank you. **b** act of thanking; expression of gratitude and pleasure. **c** feeling of kindness received; gratitude: *You have our thanks for everything you have done.* 1 *v.*, 2 *n.*

have oneself to thank, be to blame: *You have yourself to thank if you eat too much.*

thanks to, owing to; because of: *Thanks to his efforts, the garden is a great success.*

thank ful (thangk′fəl), feeling or expressing thanks; grateful: *He is thankful for good health. adj.*

thank ful ly (thangk′fə lē), with thanks; gratefully. *adv.*

thank ful ness (thangk′fəl nis), thankful feeling; gratitude. *n.*

thank less (thangk′lis), 1 not feeling or expressing thanks; ungrateful: *The thankless child did not appreciate what we did for him.* 2 not likely to get thanks; not appreciated: *Giving advice is usually a thankless act. adj.* —**thank′less ly,** *adv.*

thanks giv ing (thangks giv′ing), 1 a giving of thanks. 2 expression of thanks: *They offered thanksgiving to God for their escape.* 3 **Thanksgiving,** Thanksgiving Day. *n.*

Thanksgiving Day, day set apart as a holiday on which to give thanks for God's kindness during the year. In the United States, Thanksgiving Day is the fourth Thursday in November. In Canada, it is the second Monday in October.

Thant (thänt), **U,** born 1909, Burmese diplomat, secretary-general of the United Nations from 1962 to 1971. *n.*

that (ᴛнat; *unstressed* ᴛнət), 1 *That* is used to point out some one person or thing or idea. We use *this* for the thing nearer us, and *that* for the thing farther away from us. *Do you know that boy? (adj.). Shall we buy this book or that one? (adj.). That is the right way (pron.). I like that better (pron.).* 2 *That* is also used to connect a group of words. *I know that 6 and 4 are 10.* 3 *That* is used to show purpose. *Study that you may learn.* 4 *That* is used to show result. *She ran so fast that she was five minutes early.* 5 who; whom; which: *Is he the man that sells dogs? She is the girl that you saw in school. Bring the box that will hold most.* 6 when; at or in which: *It was the day that school began. The year that we went to England was 1964.* 7 to that extent; to such a degree; so: *The baby cannot stay up that* long. 1 *adj.*, *pl.* **those;** 1,5,6 *pron.*, *pl.* **those;** 2-4 *conj.*, 7 *adv.*

in that, because: *I prefer his plan to yours, in that I think it is more practical.*

that's that, INFORMAL. that is settled or decided.

thatch (thach), 1 straw, rushes, palm leaves, etc., used as a roof or covering. 2 to roof or cover with thatch. 1 *n.*, 2 *v.*

thatch (def. 2)

that'll (ᴛнat′l), 1 that will. 2 that shall.

that's (ᴛнats), that is.

thaw (thô), 1 melt (ice, snow, or anything frozen); free from frost: *The sun at noon thaws the ice on the streets.* 2 weather above the freezing point (32 degrees Fahrenheit): *In January we usually have a thaw.* 3 become free of frost, ice, etc.: *Our sidewalk thawed yesterday. The pond freezes up in November and thaws out in April.* 4 make or become less stiff and formal in manner; soften: *His shyness thawed under the teacher's kindness.* 1,3,4 *v.*, 2 *n.*

the[1] (ᴛнə *or* ᴛнi; *stressed* ᴛнē), 1 that or those and no others; a certain; a particular: *The dog I saw had no tail. The girl driving the car is my sister.* 2 the well-known; the only: *the Alps.* 3 the best or most important: *the place to dine.* 4 any one of its kind; any: *The dog is a quadruped.* 5 that which is; those which are: *visit the sick, a love of the beautiful.* *definite article.* [Old English *thē, the*]

the[2] (ᴛнə *or* ᴛнē), in that degree; to that degree: *The longer you work, the more you get. The later I sit up, the sleepier I become.* *adv.* [Old English *thȳ, thē, thon*]

the a ter *or* **the a tre** (thē′ə tər), 1 place where plays are acted or motion pictures are shown. 2 place that looks like a theater in its arrangement of seats: *The surgeon performed an operation before the medical students in the operating theater.* 3 place of action: *France has been the theater for many wars.* 4 plays; writing, acting in, or producing plays; the drama: *She was interested in the theater and tried to write plays herself. n.*

the a tri cal (thē at′rə kəl), 1 of or having to do with the theater or actors:

theatrical performances, a theatrical company. 2 suggesting a theater or acting; for display or effect; artificial. 3 **theatricals,** *pl.* dramatic performances, especially as given by amateurs. 1,2 *adj.*, 3 *n.* —**the at′ri cal ly,** *adv.*

the a tri cal i ty (thē at′rə kal′ə tē), quality of being theatrical. *n.*

Thebes (thēbz), 1 important city in ancient Greece. 2 ancient city on the Nile, now in ruins, formerly a center of Egyptian civilization. *n.*

thee (ᴛнē), OLD USE. you. "Bless thee" means "bless you." *pron.*

theft (theft), stealing: *The prisoner was jailed for theft. The theft of the jewels caused much excitement. n.*

their (ᴛнer *or* ᴛнar), of them; belonging to them: *They like their fine, new school. adj.*

theirs (ᴛнerz *or* ᴛнarz), the one or ones belonging to them: *Our house is white; theirs is brown. Those books are theirs. not mine. pron.*

them (ᴛнem; *unstressed* ᴛнəm), the persons, animals, things or ideas spoken about: *The books are new; take care of them. pron.*

the mat ic (thē mat′ik), of a theme; having to do with themes. *adj.*

theme (thēm), 1 topic; subject: *The theme of her speech was equal rights for all Americans.* 2 a short written composition: *Our school themes must be written in ink and on white paper.* 3 the principal melody in a piece of music; short melody repeated in different forms. 4 melody used to identify a particular radio or television program. *n.*

The mis to cles (thə mis′tə klēz′), 527?-460? B.C., Athenian naval commander and statesman. *n.*

them selves (ᴛнem selvz′ *or* ᴛнəm-selvz′), 1 form of *they* or *them* used to make a statement stronger: *The teachers themselves said the test was too hard.* 2 form used instead of *them* in cases like: *They speak for themselves. They hurt themselves sledding down the hill.* 3 their normal or usual selves: *The children are restless and have not been themselves all morning. pron.*

then (ᴛнen), 1 at that time: *Father talked of his childhood, and recalled that prices were lower then.* 2 that time: *By then we shall know the result of the election.* 3 being at that time; existing then: *the then President.* 4 soon afterwards: *The noise stopped, and then began again.* 5 next in time or place: *First comes spring, then summer.* 6 at another time: *Now one team wins and then another.* 7 also; besides: *The circus was too good not to see, and then it costs very little.* 8 in that case; therefore: *If she painted the best pic-

hat, āge, fär; let, ēqual, tėrm;
it, īce; hot, ōpen, ôrder;
oil, out; cup, pùt, rüle; ch, child;
ng, long; sh, she; th, thin;
ᴛн, then; zh, measure;

ə represents *a* in about,
e in taken, *i* in pencil,
o in lemon, *u* in circus.

ture, then she should receive the first prize. 1,4-8 *adv.*, 2 *n.*, 3 *adj.*

thence (ᴛнens), 1 from that place; from there: *We went to Italy; thence we went to France.* 2 for that reason: *You didn't work, thence you will get no pay.* 3 from that time; from then: *a few years thence. adv.*

thence forth (ᴛнens′fôrth′), from then on; from that time forward: *Women won the same rights as men; thenceforth they could vote. adv.*

thence for ward (ᴛнens′fôr′wərd), thenceforth. *adv.*

the oc ra cy (thē ok′rə sē), 1 government in which God is recognized as the supreme civil ruler and in which religious authorities rule the state as God's representatives. 2 any government headed by religious authorities. 3 country or state governed by a theocracy. *n., pl.* **the oc ra cies.**

the o crat ic (thē′ə krat′ik), 1 of or having to do with theocracy. 2 having a theocracy. *adj.*

the od o lite (thē od′l īt), a surveying instrument for measuring horizontal and vertical angles. *n.*

the o lo gian (thē′ə lō′jən), an expert in theology. *n.*

the o log i cal (thē′ə loj′ə kəl), of theology; having to do with theology. A theological school trains people for the ministry. *adj.*

the o log i cal ly (thē′ə loj′ik lē), according to theology. *adv.*

the ol o gy (thē ol′ə jē), 1 doctrines concerning God and His relations to human beings and the universe. 2 study of religion and religious beliefs. 3 system of religious beliefs. *n., pl.* **the ol o gies.**

the o rem (thē′ər əm *or* thir′əm), 1 statement or rule in mathematics that has been or is to be proved. EXAMPLE: In an isosceles triangle the angles opposite the equal sides are equal. 2 any statement or rule that can be proved to be true. *n.*

the o ret ic (thē′ə ret′ik), theoretical. *adj.*

the o ret i cal (thē′ə ret′ə kəl), 1 planned or worked out in the mind,

theoretically

adj. adjective	*n.* noun
adv. adverb	*prep.* preposition
conj. conjunction	*pron.* pronoun
interj. interjection	*v.* verb
sing. singular	*pl.* plural

not from experience; based on theory, not on fact; limited to theory. 2 dealing with theory only; not practical: *City students can get a theoretical knowledge of farming from textbooks. adj.*

the o ret i cal ly (thē′ə ret′ik lē), in theory; according to theory; in a theoretical manner. *adv.*

the or e ti cian (thē′ər ə tish′ən), an expert in the theory of an art, science, etc. *n.*

the or ist (thē′ər ist), person who theorizes. *n.*

the o rize (thē′ə rīz′), form a theory or theories; speculate. *v.,* **the o rized, the o riz ing.**

the or y (thē′ər ē *or* thir′ē), 1 an explanation based on observation and reasoning, especially one that has been tested and confirmed as a general principle explaining a large number of related facts or occurrences: *Einstein's theory of relativity explains the motion of moving objects. According to one scientific theory of life, the more complicated animals developed from the simpler ones.* 2 the principles or methods of a science or art rather than its practice: *the theory of music.* 3 idea or opinion about something: *I think the fire was started by a careless smoker. What is your theory?* 4 thought or fancy as opposed to fact or practice: *He is right only in theory, because the facts contradict him. n., pl.* **the or ies.**

ther a peu tic (ther′ə pyü′tik), having to do with curing or therapy; curative: *Heat has therapeutic value. adj.*

ther a peu tics (ther′ə pyü′tiks), branch of medicine that deals with the treating or curing of disease. *n.*

ther a pist (ther′ə pist), person who specializes in some form of therapy. *n.*

ther a py (ther′ə pē), treatment of diseases or disorders. *n., pl.* **ther a pies.**

there (₸Her *or* ₸Har; *unstressed* ₸Hər), 1 in or at that place: *Sit there. Finish reading the page and stop there.* 2 to or into that place: *Have you seen the new house? We are going there tomorrow.* 3 that place: *We go to New York first and from there to Boston.* 4 in that matter: *You are mistaken there.* 5 There is also used in sentences in which the verb comes before its subject. *There are three new houses on our street. Is*

there a drugstore near here? 6 There is used to call attention to some person or thing. *There goes the bell.* 7 There is also used to express some feeling. *There, there! don't cry.* 1,2,4-6 *adv.,* 3 *n.,* 7 *interj.*

there a bout (₸Her′ə bout′ *or* ₸Har′-ə bout′), thereabouts. *adv.*

there a bouts (₸Her′ə bouts′ *or* ₸Har′ə bouts′), 1 near that place: *She lives downtown, on Main Street or thereabouts.* 2 near that time: *He went home in the late afternoon, at 5 o'clock or thereabouts.* 3 near that number or amount: *It was very cold and the temperature fell to zero or thereabouts. adv.*

there af ter (₸Her af′tər *or* ₸Har-af′tər), after that; afterward: *He was very ill as a child and was considered delicate thereafter. adv.*

there at (₸Her at′ *or* ₸Har at′), 1 when that happened; at that time. 2 because of that; because of it. 3 at that place; there. *adv.*

there by (₸Her bī′ *or* ₸Har bī′), 1 by means of that; in that way: *He wished to travel and thereby study the customs of other countries.* 2 in connection with that: *She won the game, and thereby hangs a tale.* 3 near there: *A farm lay thereby. adv.*

there'd (₸Herd *or* ₸Hard), 1 there had. 2 there would.

there for (₸Her fôr′ *or* ₸Har fôr′), for that; for this; for it: *They promised to give a building for a hospital and the land necessary therefor. adv.*

there fore (₸Her′fôr *or* ₸Har′fôr), for that reason; as a result of that: *She had to work last night and therefore had little time to study. adv.*

there from (₸Her from′, ₸Har from′, ₸Her frum′, *or* ₸Har frum′), from that; from this; from it: *He opened his bag and took therefrom an apple. adv.*

there in (₸Her in′ *or* ₸Har in′), 1 in that place; in it: *the oceans and all the creatures therein.* 2 in that matter; in that way: *The artist learned to devote long hours to study; therein lay her great success. adv.*

there'll (₸Herl *or* ₸Harl), 1 there will. 2 there shall.

there of (₸Her uv′, ₸Har uv′, ₸Her ov′, *or* ₸Har ov′), 1 of that; of it. 2 from it; from that source. *adv.*

there on (₸Her on′ *or* ₸Har on′), 1 on that; on it: *Before the window was a table. A huge book lay thereon.* 2 immediately after that: *Cinderella's fairy godmother cast a spell; thereon the pumpkin was changed into a coach. adv.*

there's (₸Herz *or* ₸Harz), there is.

The re sa (tə rē′sə), **Saint,** 1515-1582, Spanish nun and mystic. *n.*

there to (₸Her tü′ *or* ₸Har tü′), 1 to that; to it: *The castle stands on a hill,*

and the road thereto is steep and rough. 2 in addition to that; also: *The queen gave her faithful servant rich garments and added thereto a bag of gold. adv.*

there to fore (₸Her′tə fôr′ *or* ₸Har′-tə fôr′), before that time; until then. *adv.*

there un der (₸Her un′dər *or* ₸Har-un′dər), 1 under that; under it. 2 under the authority of that; according to that. *adv.*

there un to (₸Her un′tü *or* ₸Har-un′tü), to that; to it. *adv.*

there up on (₸Her′ə pon′ *or* ₸Har′-ə pon′), 1 immediately after that: *The clown appeared; thereupon the people clapped.* 2 because of that; therefore: *She planned to rent the old, abandoned house and thereupon remodeled it.* 3 on that; on it: *The knight carried a shield with a cross painted thereupon. adv.*

there with (₸Her wi₸H′, ₸Har wi₸H′, ₸Her with′, *or* ₸Har with′), 1 with that; with it: *She gave him a rose and a smile therewith.* 2 immediately after that; then: *"Avenge me!" said the ghost and therewith disappeared. adv.*

there with al (₸Her′wi ₸Hôl′, ₸Har′-wi ₸Hôl′, ₸Her′wi thôl′, *or* ₸Har′-wi thôl′), 1 with that; with this; with it. 2 in addition to that; also. *adv.*

ther mal (ther′məl), of or having to do with heat. *adj.*

ther mo dy nam ic (ther′mō dī-nam′ik), of or having to do with thermodynamics; using force due to heat or to the conversion of heat into other forms of energy. *adj.*

ther mo dy nam ics (ther′mō dī-nam′iks), branch of physics that deals with the relations between heat and other forms of energy, and of the conversion of one into the other. *n.*

ther mo e lec tric (ther′mō i lek′-trik), of or having to do with thermoelectricity. *adj.*

ther mo e lec tric i ty (ther′mō i lek-tris′ə tē), electricity produced directly by heat, especially that produced by a temperature difference between two different metals used as conductors in a circuit. *n.*

centigrade thermometer

ther mom e ter (thər mom′ə tər), instrument for measuring temperature. Most thermometers contain mercury or alcohol in a narrow tube. When the temperature outside the tube goes up, the liquid rises by expanding; when the temperature outside the tube goes down, the liquid drops by contracting. *n.*

ther mo nu cle ar (ther′mō nü′klē ər

or thẻr/mō nyü/klē ər), of or having to do with the fusion of atoms (as in the hydrogen bomb) through very high temperature: *a thermonuclear reaction.* adj.

Ther mop y lae (thər mop/ə lē), mountain pass in ancient Greece. In 480 B.C., a small force of Greeks defended it against an army of Persians until most of the Greeks, including all the Spartans, were killed. *n.*

ther mos bottle (thẻr/məs), vacuum bottle.

ther mo stat (thẻr/mə stat), an automatic device for regulating temperature. In most thermostats, the expansion and contraction of a metal, liquid, or gas opens and closes an electric circuit by which an appliance or device, such as an air conditioner or oil furnace, is made to work or to stop working. *n.*

the sau rus (thi sôr/əs), 1 dictionary in which synonyms, antonyms, and other related words are classified under certain headings. 2 any dictionary, encyclopedia, or other book filled with information. 3 treasury or storehouse. *n., pl.* **the sau ri** (thi sôr/ī).

these (ᴛʜēz). *These* is used to point out persons, things, or ideas. *These days are cold (adj.). These two problems are hard (adj.). These are my books (pron.).* *adj., pron.pl.* of **this.**

The se us (thē/sē əs *or* thē/süs), (in Greek legends) the chief hero of Athens. He killed the Minotaur and escaped from Crete with the help of Ariadne. *n.*

the sis (thē/sis), 1 proposition or statement to be proved or to be maintained against objections. 2 essay; essay presented by a candidate for a diploma or degree. *n., pl.* **the ses** (thē/sēz/).

Thes pi an (thes/pē ən), 1 having to do with the drama or tragedy. 2 actor or actress. 1 *adj.*, 2 *n.*

Thes pis (thes/pis), Greek tragic poet who lived about 534 B.C. Traditionally, he was the founder of Greek tragedy. *n.*

Thes sa lo ni ans (thes/ə lō/nē ənz), either of two books of the New Testament written by Saint Paul. *n.*

Thes sa ly (thes/ə lē), district in E Greece. *n.*

The tis (thē/tis), (in Greek legends) a sea nymph who was the mother of Achilles. *n.*

thews (thüz), 1 muscles. 2 sinews. 3 bodily force; might; strength. *n.pl.*

they (ᴛʜā), 1 the persons, animals, things, or ideas spoken about: *I had three books yesterday. Do you know where they are? They are on the table.* 2 INFORMAL. some people; any people; persons: *They say we should have a new school.* *pron. pl.*

they'd (ᴛʜād), 1 they had. 2 they would.

they'll (ᴛʜāl), 1 they will. 2 they shall.
they're (ᴛʜer), they are.
they've (ᴛʜāv), they have.

thi a min *or* **thi a mine** (thī/ə mən), vitamin B₁. *n.*

thick (thik), 1 with much space from one side to the opposite side; not thin: *The castle has thick stone walls.* 2 measuring between two opposite sides: *This brick is 8 inches long, 4 inches wide, and 2 1/2 inches thick.* 3 set close together: *She has thick hair. It is a thick forest.* 4 many and close together; abundant: *The troops were greeted by bullets thick as hail.* 5 like glue or syrup, not like water: *Thick liquids pour much more slowly than thin liquids.* 6 not clear; foggy: *The weather was thick and the airports were shut down.* 7 not clear in sound; hoarse: *She had a thick voice because of a cold.* 8 stupid; dull: *He has a thick head.* 9 thickly: *The field was planted so thick with corn that you could hide among the stalks. The cars came thick and fast.* 10 hardest part; place where there is the most danger, activity, etc.: *They were in the thick of the fight.* 11 very friendly; intimate. 1-8.11 *adj.*, 9 *adv.*, 10 *n.*

through thick and thin, in good times and bad.

thick en (thik/ən), 1 make or become thick or thicker: *The cook thickens the gravy with flour. The pudding will thicken as it cools.* 2 become more involved or complicated: *In the second act of the play the plot thickens.* *v.* **—thick/en er,** *n.*

thick et (thik/it), shrubs, bushes, or small trees growing close together: *We crawled into the thicket and hid.* *n.*

thick head ed (thik/hed/id), stupid; dull. *adj.* **—thick/head/ed ness,** *n.*

thick ly (thik/lē), 1 in a thick manner; closely; densely: *Most of New York City is thickly settled.* 2 in great numbers; in abundance: *Weeds grow thickly in the rich soil.* 3 frequently: *The houses came more thickly as we got closer to the city.* 4 in tones that are hoarse or hard to understand. *adv.*

thick ness (thik/nis), 1 quality or state of being thick: *The thickness of the walls shuts out all sounds.* 2 distance between two opposite sides; the third measurement of a solid, not length nor breadth: *The length of the board is 10 feet, the width 6 inches, the thickness 2 inches.* 3 thick part: *Turn the board so you can walk across on its thickness.* 4 layer: *The pad was made up of three thicknesses of cloth.* *n., pl.* **thick ness es.**

thick set (thik/set/), 1 thickly set: *a thickset hedge.* 2 thick in form or build: *a thickset opera singer.* adj.

thick-skinned (thik/skind/), 1 hav-

hat, āge, fär; let, ēqual, tẻrm;
it, īce; hot, ōpen, ôrder;
oil, out; cup, pùt, rüle; ch, child;
ng, long; sh, she; th, thin;
ᴛʜ, then; zh, measure;

ə represents *a* in about,
e in taken, *i* in pencil,
o in lemon, *u* in circus.

ing a thick skin. 2 not sensitive to criticism, rebuff, or the like. *adj.*

thief (thēf), person who steals, especially one who steals secretly and usually without using force: *A thief stole my bicycle from the yard.* *n., pl.* **thieves.**

thieve (thēv), steal: *She saw a student thieving at school today.* *v.,* **thieved, thiev ing.**

thiev er y (thē/vər ē), stealing; theft. *n., pl.* **thiev er ies.**

thieves (thēvz), plural of **thief.** *n.*

thiev ish (thē/vish), 1 having the habit of stealing; likely to steal. 2 like a thief; sly: *That cat has a thievish look.* adj.

thigh (thī), part of the leg between the hip and the knee. *n.*

thigh bone (thī/bōn/), bone of the leg between the hip and the knee; femur. *n.*

thim ble (thim/bəl), a small metal cap worn on the finger to protect it when pushing the needle in sewing. *n.*

thin (thin), 1 with little space from one side to the opposite side; not thick: *thin paper, thin wire. The ice on the pond is too thin for skating.* 2 having little flesh; slender; lean: *a thin person.* 3 not set close together; scanty: *He has thin hair.* 4 not dense: *The air on the top of high mountains is thin.* 5 few and far apart; not abundant: *The actors played to a thin audience.* 6 like water; not like glue or syrup: *This gravy is too thin.* 7 not deep or strong; having little depth, fullness, or intensity: *a thin color. They listened to a shrill, thin voice.* 8 easily seen through; flimsy: *It was a thin excuse that satisfied no one.* 9 make or become thin: *Hunger had thinned their cheeks.* 1-8 *adj.,* **thin ner, thin nest;** 9 *v.,* **thinned, thin ning.** **—thin/ly,** *adv.* **—thin/ness,** *n.*

thine (ᴛʜīn), OLD USE. 1 "yours." It is thine" means "it is yours." 2 your (used only before a vowel or *h*). "Thine eyes" means "your eyes." 1 *pron.,* 2 *adj.*

thing (thing), 1 any object or substance; what one can see or hear or touch or taste or smell: *All the things in the house were burned. Put these things away.* 2 **things,** *pl.* **a** personal belong-

think

adj. adjective	*n.* noun
adv. adverb	*prep.* preposition
conj. conjunction	*pron.* pronoun
interj. interjection	*v.* verb
sing. singular	*pl.* plural

ings. **b** clothes: *I packed my things and took the train.* **3** whatever is spoken or thought of; act; deed; fact; event; idea: *It was a good thing to do. A strange thing happened. That is a strange thing to think of.* **4** matter; affair: *Let's settle this thing between us. How are things going?* **5** person or creature: *I felt sorry for the poor thing. n.*

know a thing or two, INFORMAL. be experienced or wise.

make a good thing of, INFORMAL. profit from.

see things, have hallucinations.

think (thingk), **1** have ideas; use the mind: *You must learn to think clearly.* **2** have in the mind: *He thought that he would go.* **3** have an opinion; believe: *Do you think it will rain? We thought it might snow. Do what you think fit.* **4** reflect: *I want to think before answering that question.* **5** consider: *They think their teacher a genius.* **6** imagine: *You can't think how surprised I was.* **7** expect: *I did not think to find you here. v.,* **thought, think ing. —think/er,** *n.*

think of, 1 have in mind: *He thinks of her as an artist. I think of you often.* **2** imagine: *She doesn't like apple pie. Think of that!* **3** remember: *I can't think of his name.*

think out, 1 plan or discover by thinking. **2** solve or understand by thinking. **3** think through to the end.

think over, consider carefully.

think twice, think again before acting; hesitate.

think up, plan or discover by thinking.

thin-skinned (thin/skind/), **1** having a thin skin. **2** sensitive to criticism, reproach, rebuff, etc. *adj.*

third (thèrd), **1** next after the second; last in a series of three: *C is the third letter of the alphabet.* **2** one of three equal parts: *We divided the cake into thirds. adj., n.*

third degree, INFORMAL. use of severe treatment by the police to force a person to give information or make a confession.

third ly (thèrd/lē), in the third place. *adv.*

third person, form of a pronoun or verb used to refer to the person spoken

of. *He, she, it,* and *they* are pronouns of the third person.

third-rate (thèrd/rāt/), distinctly inferior. *adj.*

thirst (thèrst), **1** a dry, uncomfortable feeling in the mouth or throat caused by having had nothing to drink. **2** desire or need for drink: *She satisfied her thirst with a glass of water.* **3** feel thirst; be thirsty. **4** a strong desire: *Many young people have a thirst for adventure.* **5** have a strong desire. **1,2,4** *n.,* **3,5** *v.*

thirst i ly (thèr/stə lē), in a thirsty manner. *adv.*

thirst y (thèr/stē), **1** feeling thirst; having thirst: *The dog is thirsty; please give it some water.* **2** without water or moisture; dry: *The land seemed thirstier than a desert. adj.,* **thirst i er, thirst i est.**

thir teen (thèr/tēn/), three more than ten; 13. *n., adj.*

thir teenth (thèr/tēnth/), **1** next after the 12th; last in a series of 13. **2** one of 13 equal parts. *adj., n.*

thir ti eth (thèr/tē ith), **1** next after the 29th; last in a series of 30. **2** one of 30 equal parts: *A day is about one thirtieth of a month. adj., n.*

thir ty (thèr/tē), three times ten; 30. *n., pl.* **thir ties;** *adj.*

thir ty-sec ond note (thèr/tē sek/-ənd), (in music) a note played for one thirty-second (¹/₃₂) as long a time as a whole note. See **note** for diagram.

this (ᴛʜis), **1** *This* is used to point out some one person, thing, or idea as present, or near, or spoken of before. We use *that* for the thing farther away from us and *this* for the thing nearer us. *School begins at eight this year* (*adj.*). *This is my brother* (*pron.*). *Shall we buy this or that?* (*pron.*). **2** present; near; spoken of: *this minute, this child, this idea.* **3** to this degree or extent; so: *You can have this much.* **1,2** *adj., pl.* **these;** **1** *pron., pl.* **these;** **3** *adv.*

this tle (this/əl), any of various plants with prickly stalks and leaves and usually with purple flowers. One kind of purple thistle is the national flower of Scotland. *n.* **—this/tle like/,** *adj.*

this tle down (this/əl doun/), downy growth that forms on ripe thistle seeds. *n.*

thith er (thiᴛʜ/ər), to that place; toward that place; there. *adv.*

tho or **tho'** (ᴛʜō), though. *conj., adv.*

thole (thōl), peg or pin, often one of a

tholes

pair, on the side of a boat to hold an oar in rowing. *n.*

thole pin (thōl/pin/), thole. *n.*

Thom as (tom/əs), **1** one of Christ's twelve apostles. He at first doubted the Resurrection. **2 Dylan,** 1914-1953, Welsh poet. *n.*

thong (thông), **1** a narrow strip of leather, especially one used as a fastening: *The ancient Greeks laced their sandals with thongs.* **2** lash of a whip. *n.*

Thor (thôr), (in Scandinavian myths) the god of thunder. *n.*

tho rac ic (thô ras/ik), of or having to do with the thorax. The thoracic cavity contains the heart and lungs. *adj.*

thorax (def. 1)   thorax (def. 2)

tho rax (thôr/aks), **1** the part of the body between the neck and the abdomen; chest. **2** the second division of an insect's body, between the head and the abdomen. *n., pl.* **tho rax es, tho ra ces** (thôr/ə sēz/).

Tho reau (thə rō/), **Henry David,** 1817-1862, American author and naturalist. *n.*

tho ri um (thôr/ē əm), a dark-gray, radioactive, metallic element present in certain rare minerals. When thorium is bombarded with neutrons, it is used as into a form of uranium which is used as an atomic fuel. *n.* [from *Thor*]

thorn (thôrn), **1** stiff, sharp-pointed growth on a stem or branch of a tree or other plant: *Roses have thorns.* **2** tree or other plant with thorns: *Thorns sprang up and choked the wheat. n.*

thorn in the flesh or **thorn in the side,** a cause of trouble or annoyance.

thorn y (thôr/nē), **1** full of thorns: *He scratched his hand on the thorny bush.* **2** troublesome; annoying: *It took her a long time to solve the thorny problem. adj.,* **thorn i er, thorn i est.**

thor ough (thèr/ō), **1** being all that is needed; complete: *Please make a thorough search for the lost money. He is a thorough gentleman.* **2** doing all that should be done; very careful: *The doctor was very thorough in examining the patient. adj.* **—thor/ough ly,** *adv.* **—thor/ough ness,** *n.*

thor ough bred (thèr/ō bred/), **1** of pure breed or stock. **2** a thoroughbred animal. **3 Thoroughbred,** any race horse of a breed derived from a crossing of domestic English stock with Arabian stock. **4** well-bred; thoroughly trained. **5** a well-bred or thoroughly trained person. **1,4** *adj.,* **2,3,5** *n.*

thor ough fare (thèr′ō fer′ *or* thèr′- ō fär′), **1** passage, road, or street open at both ends: *A city street is a public thoroughfare.* **2** a main road; highway: *The new interstate highway is one of the main thoroughfares of the United States, extending from New York to San Francisco.* *n.*

no thoroughfare, people are forbidden to go through.

thor ough go ing (thèr′ō gō′ing), thorough; complete. *adj.*

those (ᴛʜōz). *Those* is used to point out several persons or things. *She owns that dog; the boys own those dogs (adj.). That is his book; those are my books (pron.).* *adj., pron.pl.* of **that.**

thou (ᴛʜou), OLD USE. you. God is sometimes addressed as Thou. *pron. sing.*

though (ᴛʜō), **1** in spite of the fact that: *We take our medicine, though we do not like it. Though it was pouring, the girls went to school.* **2** yet; still; nevertheless: *He is better, though not yet cured.* **3** even supposing that: *Though I fail, I shall try again.* **4** however: *I am sorry about our quarrel: you began it, though.* **1-3** *conj.,* **4** *adv.* Also, **tho** or **tho'.**

as though, as if; as it would be if: *You look as though you were tired.*

thought (thôt), **1** what one thinks; idea; notion: *Her thought was to have a picnic.* **2** thinking: *Thought helps us solve problems.* **3** care; attention; regard: *Show some thought for others than yourself.* **4** intention: *His thought was to avoid controversy.* **5** a little bit; trifle: *Be a thought more polite.* **6** the characteristic thinking of a particular person, time, or place: *20th-century scientific thought.* **7** past tense and past participle of **think.** *We thought it would snow yesterday.* **1-6** *n.,* **7** *v.*

thought ful (thôt′fəl), **1** full of thought; thinking: *He was thoughtful for a while and then replied, "No."* **2** careful of others; considerate: *She is always thoughtful of her parents.* **3** indicating thought: *a thoughtful expression. adj.* —**thought′ful ly,** *adv.* —**thought′ful ness,** *n.*

thought less (thôt′lis), **1** without thought; doing things without thinking; careless: *Thoughtless drivers cause many automobile accidents.* **2** showing little or no care or regard for others: *It is thoughtless of them to keep her waiting so long. adj.* —**thought′less ly,** *adv.* —**thought′less ness,** *n.*

thou sand (thou′znd), ten hundred; 1000. *n., adj.*

thou sandth (thou′zndth), **1** next after the 999th; last in a series of 1000.

2 one of 1000 equal parts. *adj., n.*

Thrace (thrās), region in the E part of the Balkan Peninsula. In ancient times it was first an independent country and later a Roman province. Today the region is in Bulgaria, Greece, and Turkey. *n.*

Thra cian (thrā′shən), **1** of or having to do with ancient Thrace or its people. **2** person who was born or lived in ancient Thrace. **1** *adj.,* **2** *n.*

thrall (thrôl), **1** person in bondage; slave: *The thralls did the work of the castle.* **2** bondage; slavery: *The witch's spell kept the princess in thrall.* *n.*

thrall dom *or* **thral dom** (thrôl′- dəm), bondage; slavery: *A sorcerer held the knight in thralldom.* *n.*

thrash (thrash), **1** beat as punishment; flog: *I'd like to thrash whoever broke my brand-new camera.* **2** move violently; toss: *Unable to sleep, the patient thrashed about in the bed.* **3** thresh (wheat, etc.). *v.*

thrash out, settle by thorough discussion.

thrash er (thrash′ər), **1** person or thing that thrashes. **2** any of several long-tailed North American birds related to the mockingbird. It is somewhat like a thrush. **3** thresher. *n.*

thread (thred), **1** cotton, silk, flax, etc., spun out into a fine cord. You sew with thread. **2** pass a thread through: *Can you thread a needle? I threaded beads onto a string.* **3** something long and slender like a thread: *Threads of gold could be seen in the ore. The spider hung by a thread.* **4** form into a thread: *Cook the syrup until it threads.* **5** the main thought that connects the parts of a story, speech, etc.: *Something distracted her and she lost the thread of their conversation.* **6** pass like a thread through; pervade. **7** make one's way through; make (one's way) carefully; go on a winding course: *He threaded his way through the crowd. The path threads through the forest.* **8** the sloping ridge that winds around a bolt, screw, pipe joint, etc. The thread of a nut interlocks with the thread of a bolt. **9** form a thread on (a bolt, screw, pipe joint, etc.). **1,3,5,8** *n.,* **2,4,6,7,9** *v.* —**thread′like′,** *adj.*

thread bare (thred′ber′ *or* thred′- bar′), **1** having the nap worn off; worn so much that the threads show: *a threadbare coat.* **2** wearing clothes worn to the threads; shabby: *a threadbare beggar.* **3** old and worn; stale: *Saying "I forgot" is a threadbare excuse. adj.*

thread y (thred′ē), **1** consisting of or resembling a thread. **2** fibrous; stringy or viscid. **3** (of the pulse) thin and feeble. **4** (of the voice, etc.) lacking in fullness. *adj.*

threat (thret), **1** statement of what will be done to hurt or punish someone: *I stopped buying firecrackers because of my parents' threats to take away my allowance.* **2** sign or cause of possible evil or harm: *Those black clouds are a threat of rain.* *n.*

threat en (thret′n), **1** make a threat against; say what will be done to hurt or punish: *threaten a person with imprisonment. The teacher threatened to fail all the students that did no homework.* **2** utter threats: *Do you mean to threaten? They threaten and scold too much.* **3** be a sign or warning of (possible evil or harm): *Black clouds threaten rain.* **4** be a cause of possible evil or harm to: *A flood threatened the city. v.* —**threat′en ing ly,** *adv.*

three (thrē), one more than two; 3. *n., adj.*

three fold (thrē′fōld′), **1** three times as much or as many. **2** having three parts. **1,2** *adj.,* **1** *adv.*

three pence (thrip′əns), **1** three British pennies; three pence. **2** coin of this value. *n.*

three pen ny (thrip′ə nē), **1** worth three pence. **2** of little worth; cheap; paltry. *adj.*

three score (thrē′skôr′), three times twenty; 60. *adj.*

thread (def. 8)

three some (thrē′səm), **1** group of three people. **2** game played by three people. **3** the players. *n.*

Three Wise Men, the Magi.

thren o dy (thren′ə dē), song of lamentation, especially at a person's death. *n., pl.* **thren o dies.**

thresh (thresh), **1** separate the grain or seeds from (wheat, etc.). Nowadays most farmers use a machine to thresh their wheat. **2** toss about; thrash. *v.*

thresh out, settle by thorough discussion.

thresh er (thresh′ər), **1** person or thing that threshes. **2** machine used for separating the grain or seeds from the stalks and other parts of wheat, oats,

adj.	adjective	*n.*	noun
adv.	adverb	*prep.*	preposition
conj.	conjunction	*pron.*	pronoun
interj.	interjection	*v.*	verb
sing.	singular	*pl.*	plural

etc. 3 a large shark with a very long tail; thrasher. *n.*

thresh old (thresh′ōld), 1 piece of wood or stone under a door. 2 doorway. 3 point of entering; beginning point: *The scientist was on the threshold of an important discovery. n.*

threw (thrü), past tense of **throw**. *She threw the ball to me. v.*

thrice (thrīs), three times: *He knocked thrice. adv.*

thrift (thrift), absence of waste; saving; economical management; habit of saving: *By thrift they managed to get along on their small income. A bank account encourages thrift. n.*

thrift i ly (thrif′tə lē), in a thrifty manner; with thrift; economically. *adv.*

thrift i ness (thrif′tē nis), the quality or condition of being thrifty. *n.*

thrift less (thrift′lis), without thrift; wasteful. *adj.*

thrift y (thrif′tē), 1 careful in spending; economical; saving: *a thrifty shopper.* 2 thriving; flourishing; prosperous: *The countryside had many fine, thrifty farms. adj.,* **thrift i er, thrift i est.**

thrill (thril), 1 a shivering, exciting feeling: *She gets a thrill whenever she sees a parade.* 2 give a shivering, exciting feeling to: *Stories of adventure thrilled him.* 3 have a shivering, exciting feeling: *The children thrilled with joy at the sight of the Christmas tree.* 4 quiver; tremble: *Her voice thrilled with excitement.* 1 *n.,* 2-4 *v.* —**thrill′ ing ly,** *adv.*

thrill er (thril′ər), 1 person or thing that thrills. 2 INFORMAL. story, play, or motion picture filled with excitement, suspense, etc. *n.*

thrive (thrīv), be successful; grow rich; grow strong; prosper: *Flowers will not thrive without sunshine. v.,* **throve** or **thrived, thrived** or **thriv en** (thriv′ən), **thriv ing.**

thro or **thro'** (thrü), through. *prep., adv., adj.*

throat (thrōt), 1 the front of the neck: *She had a muffler wrapped around her throat.* 2 the passage from the mouth to the stomach or the lungs: *A bone stuck in his throat.* 3 any narrow passage: *the throat of a mine. n.*

throat y (thrō′tē), 1 produced or modi-

fied in the throat; guttural: *The young girl had a throaty voice.* 2 low-pitched and resonant: *The engine started with a throaty roar. adj.,* **throat i er, throat i est.**

throb (throb), 1 beat rapidly or strongly: *The long climb up the hill made her heart throb. His wounded arm throbbed with pain.* 2 a rapid or strong beat: *A throb of pain shot through his head.* 3 beat steadily. 4 a steady beat: *the throb of a pulse.* 1,3 *v.,* **throbbed, throb bing;** 2,4 *n.*

throe (thrō), 1 a violent pang; great pain. 2 **throes,** *pl.* **a** anguish; agony. **b** a desperate struggle; violent disturbance. *n.*

throm bo sis (throm bō′sis), a coagulation of blood in a blood vessel or in the heart during life. *n., pl.* **throm bo ses** (throm bō′sēz′).

throne (thrōn), 1 chair on which a king, queen, bishop, or other person of high rank sits during ceremonies. 2 power or authority of a king, queen, etc.: *the throne of England.* 3 person who sits on a throne; sovereign. *n.*

throng (throng), 1 a crowd; multitude. 2 to crowd; fill with a crowd: *People thronged the theater to see the famous actress.* 3 come together in a crowd; go or press in large numbers: *The people thronged to see the king.* 1 *n.,* 2,3 *v.*

throt tle (throt′l), 1 valve regulating the flow of steam, gasoline vapor, etc., to an engine. 2 lever, pedal, etc., working such a valve. The throttle of a car is called an accelerator. 3 stop or lessen the speed of (an engine) by closing a throttle; to throttle a steam engine. 4 stop the breath of by pressure on the throat; choke; strangle: *The thief throttled the dog to keep it from barking.* 5 check or stop the flow of; suppress: *High tariffs throttle trade between countries.* 1,2 *n.,* 3-5 *v.,* **throt tled, throt tling.**

through (thrü), 1 from end to end of; from side to side of; between the parts of; from beginning to end of: *march through a town, cut a tunnel through a mountain, drive through a snowstorm.* 2 from end to end; from side to side; between the parts; from beginning to end: *The bullet hit the wall and went through. She read the book all the way through.* 3 here and there in; over; around: *We traveled through New England visiting many old towns.* 4 because of; by reason of: *The family refused help through pride.* 5 by means of: *She became rich through her wise investments.* 6 completely; thoroughly: *He walked home in the rain and was wet through.* 7 going all the way without change: *a through train from New York*

City to Chicago. 8 having reached the end of; finished with: *We are through school at three o'clock.* 9 having reached the end; finished: *I am almost through.* 1,3-5,8 *prep.,* 2,6 *adv.,* 7,9 *adj.* Also, **thro, thro',** or **thru.**

through out (thrü out′), 1 all the way through; through all; in every part of: *The Fourth of July is celebrated throughout the United States.* 2 in every part: *The house is well built throughout.* 1 *prep.,* 2 *adv.*

through way (thrü′wā′), thruway. *n.*

throve (thrōv), a past tense of **thrive.** *The plants throve in the rich soil. v.*

throw (thrō), 1 send through the air with force; cast; toss; hurl: *throw a ball. The man threw water on the fire.* 2 act of throwing; a cast, toss, or hurl: *That was a good throw from left field to the catcher.* 3 distance a thing is or may be thrown. 4 bring to the ground: *His horse threw him.* 5 put by force: *throw someone into jail.* 6 put carelessly or in haste: *I threw a coat over my shoulders.* 7 turn, direct, or move, especially quickly: *She threw a glance at each car that passed us.* 8 move (a lever, etc.) that connects or disconnects parts of a switch, clutch, or other mechanism. 9 INFORMAL. let an opponent win (a race, game, etc.), often for money. 1,4-9 *v.,* **threw, thrown, throw ing;** 2,3 *n.* —**throw′er,** *n.*

throw away, 1 get rid of; discard: *Throw away those old shoes.* 2 waste: *Don't throw away your opportunities.*

throw in, add as a gift: *Our grocer used to throw in an extra apple.*

throw off, 1 get rid of: *throw off a cold.* 2 give off; emit: *The burning oil threw off thick black smoke.*

throw out, 1 get rid of; discard. 2 reject. 3 (in baseball) put out (a base runner) by throwing the ball to a baseman.

throw over, give up; discard; abandon.

throw up, 1 INFORMAL. vomit. 2 give up; abandon. 3 build rapidly.

throw back (thrō′bak′), 1 a throwing back. 2 setback or check. 3 reversion to an ancestral type or character: *The white stallion was a throwback to an albino ancestor. n.*

thrown (thrōn), past participle of **throw.** *She has thrown her old toys away. v.*

thru (thrü), through. *prep., adv., adj.*

thrum (thrum), 1 play on a stringed instrument by plucking the strings, especially in an idle or careless way; strum: *thrum a guitar.* 2 drum or tap idly with the fingers: *thrum on a table.* 3 the sound made by thrumming. 1,2 *v.,* **thrummed, thrum ming;** 3 *n.*

thrush (thrush), any of a large group of

migratory songbirds that includes the robin, the bluebird, the wood thrush, etc. *n., pl.* **thrush es.**

thrust (thrust), 1 push with force: *He thrust his hands into his pockets.* 2 a push with force: *She hid the book behind the pillow with a quick thrust.* 3 stab; pierce: *thrust a knife into an apple.* 4 a stab: *A thrust with the pin broke the balloon.* 5 put forth; extend: *The tree thrust its roots deep into the ground.* 6 an attack. 7 the push exerted by the rotation of a propeller, that causes a ship, airplane, etc., to move. 8 the force driving a rocket or a jet engine forward as a reaction to the rearward discharge of gases, burning fuels, etc., through a nozzle or exhaust. 1,3,5 *v.,* **thrust, thrust ing;** 2,4, 6-8 *n.*

thru way (thrü/wā/), an express highway. *n.* Also, **throughway.**

Thu cyd i des (thü sid/ə dēz/), 460?-400? B.C., Greek historian. *n.*

thud (thud), 1 a dull sound. A heavy blow or fall may cause a thud. *The book hit the floor with a thud.* 2 hit, move, or strike with a thud: *The heavy box fell and thudded on the floor.* 1 *n.,* 2 *v.,* **thud ded, thud ding.**

thug (thug), ruffian; cutthroat. *n.*

thu li um (thü/lē əm), a metallic element found in various minerals. An isotope of thulium is used as the radiating element in portable X-ray units. *n.*

thumb (thum), 1 the short, thick finger of the human hand, next to the forefinger. 2 part that covers the thumb: *There was a hole in the thumb of my mitten.* 3 soil or wear by handling with the thumbs: *Some of the books were badly thumbed.* 4 turn pages of (a book, etc.) rapidly, reading only portions: *He thumbed the book and gave it back to me.* 5 handle awkwardly. 6 INFORMAL. ask for or get (a free ride) by holding up one's thumb to motorists going in one's direction. 1,2 *n.,* 3-6 *v.*

be all thumbs, be very clumsy, awkward, etc.

thumbs down, sign of disapproval or rejection.

thumbs up, sign of approval or acceptance.

twiddle one's thumbs, do nothing; be idle.

under one's thumb, under one's power or influence: *The bully tried to keep us all under his thumb but we outwitted him.*

thumb nail (thum/nāl/), 1 nail of the thumb. 2 something very small or short. 3 very small or short: *a thumbnail sketch.* 1,2 *n.,* 3 *adj.*

thumb screw (thum/skrü/), 1 screw made so that its head can be easily turned with the thumb and a finger. 2 an old instrument of torture that squeezed the thumbs. *n.*

thumb tack (thum/tak/), tack with a broad, flat head, that can be pressed into a wall, board, etc., with the thumb. *n.*

thump (thump), 1 strike with something thick and heavy; pound: *She thumped the table with her fist. He thumped on the piano.* 2 a blow with something thick and heavy; heavy knock: *He hit the thief a thump on the head.* 3 the dull sound made by a blow, knock, or fall: *We heard the thump as he fell.* 4 make a dull sound: *The hammer thumped as it struck the wood.* 5 beat violently: *My heart thumped.* 1,4,5 *v.,* 2,3 *n.* —**thump/er,** *n.*

thun der (thun/dər), 1 the loud noise that often follows a flash of lightning. It is caused by a disturbance of the air resulting from the discharge of electricity. 2 give forth thunder: *It thundered, but no rain fell.* 3 any noise like thunder: *the thunder of Niagara Falls, a thunder of applause.* 4 make a noise like thunder: *The cannon thundered.* 5 utter very loudly; roar: *thunder a reply.* 6 utter threats or denunciations. 1,3 *n.,* 2,4-6 *v.* —**thun/der er,** *n.*

thun der bolt (thun/dər bōlt/), 1 a flash of lightning and the thunder that follows it. 2 something sudden, startling, and terrible: *The news of his death came as a thunderbolt.* *n.*

thun der clap (thun/dər klap/), 1 a loud crash of thunder. 2 something sudden or startling. *n.*

thun der cloud (thun/dər kloud/), a dark, electrically charged cloud that brings thunder and lightning. *n.*

thun der head (thun/dər hed/), one of the round, swelling masses of cumulus clouds often appearing before thunderstorms and frequently developing into thunderclouds. *n.*

thun der ous (thun/dər əs), 1 producing thunder. 2 making a noise like thunder: *The congresswoman received a thunderous burst of applause at the end of her speech. adj.* —**thun/der ous ly,** *adv.*

thun der show er (thun/dər shou/-ər), shower with thunder and lightning. *n.*

thun der storm (thun/dər stôrm/), storm with thunder and lightning. *n.*

thun der struck (thun/dər struk/), overcome, as if hit by a thunderbolt; astonished; amazed: *We were thunderstruck by the news of the war. adj.*

Thurs. or **Thur.,** Thursday.

Thurs day (thèrz/dē), the fifth day of the week, following Wednesday. *n.* [Old English *Thuresdæg* Thor's day]

thus (FHus), 1 in this way; in the way just stated, indicated, etc.; in the following manner: *He spoke thus: "Friends, Romans, Countrymen."* 2 accordingly; consequently; therefore: *Thus we decided that you were wrong.* 3 to this extent or degree; so: *Thus far may you go and no farther. adv.*

thwack (thwak), 1 strike vigorously with a stick or something flat. 2 a sharp blow with a stick or something flat. 1 *v.,* 2 *n.*

thwart (thwôrt), 1 prevent from doing something, particularly by blocking the way; oppose and defeat: *Lack of money thwarted her plans for college.* 2 a seat across a boat, on which a rower sits. 3 a brace in a canoe. 4 lying across. 5 across; crosswise. 1 *v.,* 2,3 *n.,* 4 *adj.,* 5 *adv.*

thy (FHī), OLD USE. your. "Thy name" means "your name." *adj.*

thyme (tīm), any of several small plants related to the mints, with fragrant leaves. The leaves of the common garden thyme are used for seasoning. The common wild thyme is a creeping evergreen. *n.*

thy mus (thī/məs), a small ductless glandlike organ of uncertain function, found in young vertebrates near the base of the neck. In human beings it disappears or becomes rudimentary in the adult. The thymus of calves is used for food and is called sweetbread. *n.*

thy roid (thī/roid), 1 thyroid gland. 2 medicine made from the thyroid glands of animals, used to treat disorders caused by a deficiency in the thyroid gland. 3 thyroid cartilage. 4 of or having to do with the thyroid gland or thyroid cartilage. 1-3 *n.,* 4 *adj.*

thyroid cartilage, the principal cartilage of the larynx, which forms the lump called the Adam's apple.

thyroid gland, an important ductless gland in the neck of vertebrates that affects growth and metabolism. An enlargement of the thyroid gland is called a goiter.

thy rox in (thī rok/sən), thyroxine. *n.*

thy rox ine (thī rok/sēn), the principal secretion of the thyroid gland. *n.*

thy self (FHī self/), OLD USE. yourself. *pron.*

hat, āge, fär; let, ēqual, tèrm; it, īce; hot, ōpen, ôrder; oil, out; cup, put, rüle; ch, child; ng, long; sh, she; th, thin; ᴛH, then; zh, measure;

ə represents *a* in about, *e* in taken, *i* in pencil, *o* in lemon, *u* in circus.

adj. adjective	*n.* noun
adv. adverb	*prep.* preposition
conj. conjunction	*pron.* pronoun
interj. interjection	*v.* verb
sing. singular	*pl.* plural

ti (tē), the seventh tone of the musical scale; si. *n.*

ti ar a (tē er′ə *or* tē är′ə), 1 band of gold, jewels, flowers, etc., worn around the head as an ornament. 2 the triple crown worn by the pope as a symbol of his position . *n., pl.* **ti ar as.**

tiara (def. 1)   tiara (def. 2)

Ti ber (tī′bər), river flowing from central Italy through Rome into the Tyrrhenian Sea. *n.*

Ti bet (ti bet′), former country of central Asia, now under the control of the People's Republic of China. *Capital:* Lhasa. *n.*

Ti bet an (ti bet′n), 1 of or having to do with Tibet, its people, or their language. 2 person born or living in Tibet. 3 language of Tibet, related to Burmese and Thai. 1 *adj.*, 2,3 *n.*

tib i a (tib′ē ə), shinbone. *n., pl.* **tib i-ae** (tib′ē ē′), **tib i as.**

tic (tik), a habitual, involuntary twitching of the muscles, especially those of the face. *n.*

tick[1] (tik), 1 sound made by a clock or watch. 2 make such a sound: *The clock ticked.* 3 a sound like it: *the tick of a moth against a windowpane.* 4 mark off: *The clock ticked away the minutes.* 5 a small mark. We use ✓ or / as a tick. 6 mark with a tick; check: *He ticked off the items one by one.* 7 INFORMAL. to function, work, or go: *What makes that gadget tick?* 1,3,5 *n.*, 2,4,6,7 *v.* [probably an imitation of the sound]

tick[2] (tik), 1 a tiny eight-legged animal, related to the spider, that attaches itself to humans and animals and sucks blood. 2 a wingless insect that sucks blood of certain animals, such as sheep, cattle, or deer. *n.* [Middle English *tyke*]

tick[3] (tik), the cloth covering of a mattress or pillow. *n.* [probably from Dutch of the 1400's *tike*, from Latin *theca* case, from Greek *theke*]

tick er (tik′ər), 1 person or thing that ticks. 2 a telegraphic instrument that prints stock-market reports or news on a paper tape. 3 SLANG. the heart. *n.*

ticker tape, a paper tape on which a ticker prints stock-market reports or news.

tick et (tik′it), 1 card or piece of paper that gives its holder a right or privilege: *a ticket to the theater, a railroad ticket.* 2 INFORMAL. summons to appear in court given by a policeman to a person who has broken a traffic law: *a ticket for speeding, a parking ticket.* 3 INFORMAL. serve with such a summons. 4 card or piece of paper attached to something to show its price, etc. 5 put a ticket on; mark with a ticket: *All articles in the store are ticketed with the price.* 6 the list of candidates to be voted on that belong to one political party. 1,2,4,6 *n.*, 3,5 *v.*

tick ing (tik′ing), a strong cotton or linen cloth, used to cover mattresses and pillows and to make tents and awnings. *n.*

tick le (tik′əl), 1 touch lightly, causing little thrills, shivers, or wriggles: *He tickled the baby's feet and made her laugh.* 2 have a feeling like this; cause to have such a feeling: *My nose tickles.* 3 a tingling or itching feeling. 4 excite pleasantly; amuse: *The story tickled me. The child was tickled with her new toys.* 5 a tickling. 1,2,4 *v.*, **tick led, tick ling;** 3,5 *n.*

tick ler (tik′lər), person or thing that tickles, especially a small feather brush used to tickle the faces of others at a carnival, party, etc. *n.*

tick lish (tik′lish), 1 sensitive to tickling: *The bottoms of the feet are ticklish.* 2 requiring careful handling; delicate; risky: *the ticklish job of telling a person his faults.* 3 easily upset; unstable: *A canoe is a ticklish craft.* 4 easily offended: *be ticklish about one's weight.* *adj.*

```
 O | O | O
-----------
 O | X |      tick-tack-toe
-----------
 X | X |
```

tick-tack-toe (tik′tak tō′), game in which two players alternately put circles or crosses in a figure of nine squares, each player trying to be the first to fill three squares in a row with his mark. *n.*

Ti con de ro ga (tī′kon də rō′gə), village and old fort on Lake Champlain, in NE New York State. *n.*

tid al (tī′dl), of tides; having tides; caused by tides. A tidal river is affected by the ocean's tide. *adj.*

tidal wave, 1 a large wave or sudden increase in the level of water along a shore, caused by unusually strong winds. 2 an enormous, destructive ocean wave which is caused by an underwater earthquake. 3 any great movement or manifestation of feeling, opinion, or the like: *a tidal wave of popular indignation.*

tid bit (tid′bit′), a very pleasing bit of food, news, etc. *n.* Also, **titbit.**

tid dly winks (tid′lē wingks′), game in which the players try to make small colored disks jump from a flat surface into a cup by pressing on their edges with larger disks. *n.*

tide (tīd), 1 the rise and fall of the ocean about every twelve hours, caused by the attraction of the moon and the sun: *We go swimming at high tide; at low tide we dig clams.* 2 anything that rises and falls like the tide: *the tide of public opinion.* 3 a stream, current, or flood. 4 season; time. **5 tide over, a** help along for a time: *His savings will tide him over his illness.* **b** overcome (a difficulty, etc.). 1-4 *n.*, 5 *v.*, **tid ed, tid ing.**

turn the tide, change from one condition to the opposite: *A touchdown in the final minute of play turned the tide against us.*

tide land (tīd′land′), land flooded at high tide. *n.*

tide wa ter (tīd′wô′tər *or* tīd′wot′ər), 1 water in rivers, streams, etc., affected by the rise and fall of the tides. 2 low-lying land along a seacoast through which such waters flow. 3 of or along tidewater. Tidewater country is land along the seacoast. 1,2 *n.*, 3 *adj.*

ti di ly (tī′dl ē), in a tidy manner; neatly. *adv.*

ti di ness (tī′dē nis), neatness. *n.*

ti dings (tī′dingz), news; information: *joyful tidings.* *n.pl.*

ti dy (tī′dē), 1 neat and in order: *a tidy room.* 2 put in order; make neat: *I tidied the room. Be sure to tidy up before going out.* 3 INFORMAL. considerable; fairly large: *a tidy sum of money.* 4 a small cover to keep the back of a chair, etc., from becoming dirty or worn. 1,3 *adj.*, **ti di er, ti di est;** 2 *v.*, **ti died, ti dy ing;** 4 *n., pl.* **ti dies.**

tie (tī), 1 fasten with string or the like; bind: *Please tie this package.* 2 arrange to form a bow or knot: *We tied blue and white ribbons on the party favors.* 3 fasten; form a bow: *That ribbon doesn't tie well.* 4 tighten and fasten the string or strings of: *tie one's shoes.* 5 anything connecting or holding together two or more things or parts; link. 6 cord, chain, etc., used for tying. 7 necktie: *He always wears a shirt and tie.* 8 fasten, join, or connect in any way; make a bond or connection. 9 anything ties (def. 11)

that unites; bond; obligation: *family ties, ties of friendship, ties of duty.* 10 restrain; restrict; limit: *be tied to a steady job.* 11 a heavy piece of timber or iron placed crosswise to form a foundation or support. The rails of a railroad track are fastened to ties about a foot apart. 12 a connecting beam, rod, or the like. 13 equality in points, votes, etc.: *The game ended in a tie, 3 to 3.* 14 a match or contest in which this occurs. 15 make the same score; be equal in points: *The two teams tied.* 16 (in music) a curved line set above or below two notes of the same pitch, indicating that they are to be played or sung as one sustained tone. 1-4,8,10,15 *v.*, **tied, ty ing;** 5-7,9,11-14,16 *n.*

tie down, limit; confine; restrict: *She is tied down by her home and five children.*

tie in, make or have a connection; relate: *How does that statement tie in with what you said yesterday?*

tie up, 1 tie firmly or tightly. **2** wrap up. **3** hinder; stop: *The stalled truck tied up traffic for half an hour.* **4** invest (money) or place (property) in such a way as to make it unavailable for other uses: *Since his money was tied up in other investments, he was unable to buy the stocks and bonds.* **5** have one's program full; be very busy, etc.: *I can't go tomorrow; I'm all tied up.*

Tien tsin (tin′tsin′), port city in NE China, near Peking. *n.*

tier (tir), one of a series of rows arranged one above another: *tiers of seats in a football stadium. n.*

Tier ra del Fue go (tyer′ə del fwä′gō), group of islands at the S end of South America. Part belongs to Argentina, part to Chile. See **Patagonia** for map.

tie-up (tī′up′), **1** a stopping of work or action on account of a strike, storm, accident, etc.: *The heavy snowstorm caused a tie-up of traffic.* **2** INFORMAL. connection; relation. *n.*

tiff (tif), a little quarrel. *n.*

Tif lis (tif′lis), capital of the republic of Georgia, in SW Soviet Union. *n.*

ti ger (tī′gər), a large, fierce, flesh-eating mammal of Asia, that has dull-yellow fur striped with black. It belongs to the same family as the cat and the lion. *n.* —**ti′ger like′,** *adj.*

tiger beetle, an active, flying beetle that preys on other insects. Its larvae live in tunnels in sandy soil and catch insects that come near.

ti ger ish (tī′gər ish), like a tiger; fierce; cruel. *adj.*

tiger lily, lily that has dull-orange flowers spotted with black.

tiger moth, any of a group of moths having conspicuously spotted or striped wings.

tight (tīt), **1** packed or put together firmly; held firmly; firm: *a tight knot.* **2** closely; securely; firmly: *The rope was tied too tight.* **3** drawn; stretched: *a tight canvas.* **4** close; fitting closely or too closely: *tight clothing. This hat is too tight.* **5** not letting water, air, or gas in or out: *The tight roof kept rain from leaking in.* **6** hard to deal with or manage; difficult: *A lie got her into a tight spot.* **7** INFORMAL. almost even; close: *It was a tight race.* **8** hard to get; scarce: *Money is tight just now.* **9** strict; severe: *to rule with a tight hand.* **10** INFORMAL. stingy: *They are tight with their money.* 1,3-10 *adj.*, 2 *adv.* —**tight′ly,** *adv.* —**tight′ness,** *n.*

sit tight, INFORMAL. keep the same position, opinion, etc.

tie (def. 16)

tie (def. 16)

tight en (tīt′n), **1** make tight: *He tightened his belt.* **2** become tight: *The rope tightened as I pulled it. v.*

tight fist ed (tīt′fis′tid), stingy. *adj.*

tight-lipped (tīt′lipt′), **1** keeping the lips firmly together. **2** saying little or nothing. *adj.*

tight rope (tīt′rōp′), rope stretched tight on which acrobats perform. *n.*

tights (tīts), a close-fitting garment, usually covering the lower part of the body and the legs, worn by acrobats, dancers, etc. *n.pl.*

tight wad (tīt′wod′), SLANG. a stingy person. *n.*

ti gress (tī′gris), a female tiger. *n., pl.* **ti gress es.**

Ti gris (tī′gris), river flowing from SE Turkey through Iraq, where it joins the Euphrates River and empties into the Persian Gulf. See **Euphrates** for map. *n.*

tike (tīk), tyke. *n.*

til de (til′də), a diacritical mark (~) to indicate a special sound. It is used over *n* in Spanish when it is pronounced *ny*, as in *cañon* (kä nyōn′). It is used over certain vowels in Portuguese to

tiger—about 9 ft. long including tail

indicate that they are nasal, as in *São Paulo* (sou pou′lü). *n.*

tile (tīl), **1** a thin piece of baked clay, stone, etc. Tiles are used for covering roofs, paving floors, and ornamenting. **2** a baked clay pipe for draining land. **3** put tiles on or in: *to tile a bathroom floor.* 1,2 *n.*, 3 *v.*, **tiled, til ing.**

til ing (tī′ling), **1** tiles collectively. **2** the work of covering with tiles. **3** work consisting of tiles. *n.*

till[1] (til), **1** up to the time of; until: *The child played till eight.* **2** up to the time when; until: *Walk till you come to a white house.* **1** *prep.*, **2** *conj.* [Old English *til*]

till[2] (til), cultivate (land); plow: *Farmers till the land. v.* [Old English *tilian*]

till[3] (til), a small drawer for money under or behind a counter. *n.* [origin uncertain]

till age (til′ij), **1** cultivation of land. **2** tilled land. *n.*

till er[1] (til′ər), bar or handle used to turn the rudder in steering a boat. *n.* [from French of the 1400's *telier* weaver's beam, from Latin *tela* web, loom]

till er[2] (til′ər), person who tills land; farmer. *n.* [*till*[2] + *-er*[1]]

tilt (def. 4)

tilt (tilt), **1** tip or cause to tip; slope; slant; lean: *You tilt your head forward when you bow. You tilt your cup when you drink. This table tilts.* **2** a slope; sloping position; a slant: *This table is on a tilt.* **3** rush, charge, or fight with lances. Knights used to tilt on horseback. **4** a fight on horseback with lances. **5** any dispute or quarrel. 1,3 *v.*, 2,4,5 *n.*

full tilt, at full speed; with full force: *The car ran full tilt against the tree.*

tilth (tilth), **1** cultivation of land. **2** tilled land. *n.*

tim ber (tim′bər), **1** wood used for building and making things. Houses, ships, and furniture are made from tim-

hat, āge, fär; let, ēqual, tėrm;
it, īce; hot, ōpen, ôrder;
oil, out; cup, pùt, rüle; ch, child;
ng, long; sh, she; th, thin;
ŦH, then; zh, measure;

ə represents *a* in about,
e in taken, *i* in pencil,
o in lemon, *u* in circus.

adj. adjective	*n.* noun
adv. adverb	*prep.* preposition
conj. conjunction	*pron.* pronoun
interj. interjection	*v.* verb
sing. singular	*pl.* plural

ber. **2** a large piece of wood used in building. Beams and rafters are timbers. **3** growing trees, especially when used to provide wood for building. **4** cover, support, or furnish with timber. 1-3 *n.*, 4 *v.*

tim bered (tim′bərd), **1** made or furnished with timber. **2** covered with growing trees. *adj.*

tim ber land (tim′bər land′), land with trees that are, or will be, useful for timber. *n.*

tim ber line (tim′bər lin′), line on mountains and in polar regions beyond which trees will not grow because of the cold. *n.*

timber wolf, a large gray, black, or white wolf of northwestern North America.

tim bre (tim′bər), the quality in sounds, regardless of their pitch and volume, by which a certain voice, instrument, etc., can be distinguished from other voices, instruments, etc. Because of differences in timbre, identical notes played on a violin, an oboe, and a trumpet can be distinguished from one another. *n.*

tim brel (tim′brəl), tambourine. *n.*

time (tīm), **1** all the days there have been or ever will be; the past, present, and future. Time is measured in years, months, weeks, days, hours, minutes, and seconds. **2** a part of time: *A minute is a short time. A long time ago people lived in caves.* **3** period of time; epoch: *the time of the Stuarts in England.* **4** a long time: *What a time it took you!* **5** some point in time; a particular point in time: *What time is it? The time the game begins is 2 p.m., November 8.* **6** the right part or point of time: *It is time to eat.* **7** occasion: *This time we will succeed.* **8** way of reckoning time: *solar time.* **9** condition of life: *War brings hard times.* **10** an experience during a certain time: *He had a good time at the party.* **11** rate of movement in music or poetry; rhythm: *march time, waltz time, to beat time.* **12** amount of time that one has worked or should work: *Her normal time is 8 hours a day.* **13** the pay for a period of work. **14** leisure: *have time to read.* **15** measure the time of: *time a race.* **16** do at regular times; do in rhythm with; set the

time of: *The dancers timed their steps to the music.* **17** choose the moment or occasion for: *He timed his request for a raise so as to catch his boss in a good mood.* **18** of or having to do with time. **19** provided with a clocklike mechanism so that it will explode or ignite at a given moment: *a time bomb.* **20** times, *pl.* multiplied by. The sign for this in arithmetic is ×. *Four times three is twelve. Twenty is five times as much as four.* 1-14,20 *n.*, 15-17 *v.*, timed, tim ing; 18,19 *adj.*

against time, trying to finish before a certain time: *We are in a race against time in our efforts to rescue the trapped men.*

at the same time, however; nevertheless.

at times, now and then; once in a while.

behind the times, old-fashioned; out-of-date.

bide one's time, wait for a good chance.

for the time being, for the present; for now: *The baby is asleep for the time being.*

from time to time, now and then; once in a while: *From time to time we visit my grandparents.*

in no time, shortly; before long: *We hurried and arrived home in no time.*

in time, **1** after a while. **2** soon enough: *Will she arrive in time to have dinner with us?* **3** in the right rate of movement in music, dancing, marching, etc.

keep time, **1** (of a watch or clock) go correctly. **2** to measure or record time, rate of speed, etc.: *I kept time at the race with a stop watch.* **3** to sound or move at the right time: *The marchers kept time to the music.*

make time, go with speed.

mark time, **1** move the feet as in marching, but without advancing. **2** suspend progress temporarily. **3** go through motions without accomplishing anything.

on time, **1** at the right time; not late; punctual. **2** with time in which to pay; on credit: *She bought a car on time.*

tell time, know what time it is by the clock.

time after time or **time and again,** again and again.

time exposure, **1** exposure of a photographic film for a certain time, longer than a half second. **2** photograph taken in this way.

time-hon ored (tīm′on′ərd), honored because old and established: *Giving gifts at Christmas is a time-honored custom. adj.*

time keep er (tīm′kē′pər), measurer of time; person or thing that keeps time;

timer: *The factory timekeeper keeps account of the hours of work done. My watch is an excellent timekeeper. n.*

time less (tīm′lis), **1** never ending; eternal. **2** referring to no special time. *adj.*

time li ness (tīm′lē nis), condition of being timely. *n.*

time ly (tīm′lē), at the right time: *The timely arrival of the firemen prevented the fire from destroying the building. adj.,* **time li er, time li est.**

time piece (tīm′pēs′), clock or watch. *n.*

tim er (tī′mər), **1** person or thing that times; timekeeper. **2** device for indicating or recording intervals of time, such as a stopwatch. **3** a clockwork device for indicating when a certain period of time has elapsed: *Many stoves have timers for baking. n.*

time ta ble (tīm′tā′bəl), schedule showing the times when trains, boats, buses, airplanes, etc., arrive and depart. *n.*

time worn (tīm′wôrn′), worn by existence or use. *adj.*

time zone, a geographical region within which the same standard time is used. The world is divided into 24 time zones, beginning and ending at the International Date Line.

tim id (tim′id), easily frightened; shy: *The timid child was afraid of the dark. Deer are timid animals. adj.* —**tim′id ly,** *adv.* —**tim′id ness,** *n.*

ti mid i ty (tə mid′ə tē), a being timid; shyness. *n.*

tim ing (tī′ming), **1** arrangement or regulation of the time or speed of anything to get the greater effect: *the timing of a stroke in tennis, the timing of an actor in responding to a cue, the timing of the release of a new play.* **2** measurement of time: *the timing of a runner. n.*

tim or ous (tim′ər əs), easily frightened; timid: *The timorous rabbit ran away. adj.* —**tim′or ous ly,** *adv.*

tim o thy (tim′ə thē), kind of coarse grass with long, cylindrical spikes, often grown for hay. *n.* [from *Timothy Hanson,* a farmer who cultivated it in America around 1720]

Tim o thy (tim′ə thē), **1** a disciple of the apostle Paul. **2** either of the two books of the New Testament written as letters by Paul to Timothy. *n.*

tim pa ni (tim′pə nē), kettledrums. *n. pl.* [from Italian]

tim pa nist (tim′pə nist), person who plays the kettledrums. *n.*

tin (tin), **1** a soft, silver-white metallic element used in plating metals to prevent corrosion and in making alloys such as bronze and pewter. **2** tin plate. **3** made of tin or tin plate. **4** cover with

tin. 5 any can, box, pan, or other container made of or lined with tin; tinware: *a pie tin.* 1,2,5 *n.*, 3 *adj.*, 4 *v.*, **tinned, tin ning.**

tinc ture (tingk′chər), 1 solution of medicine in alcohol: *tincture of iodine.* 2 trace; tinge: *Her stern face showed for a moment a slight tincture of amusement.* 3 give a trace or tinge to: *Everything she says is tinctured with conceit.* 4 a color; tint: *The early dawn sky showed a faint tincture of pink.* 5 color; tint. 1,2,4 *n.*, 3,5 *v.*, **tinc tured, tinc tur ing.**

tin der (tin′dər), 1 anything that catches fire easily. 2 material used to catch fire from a spark. *n.*

tin der box (tin′dər boks′), 1 box for holding tinder, flint and steel for making a fire. 2 a very flammable thing. 3 a very excitable person. *n., pl.* **tin der box es.**

tine (tīn), a sharp projecting point or prong: *the tines of a fork. n.*

tin foil (tin′foil′), a very thin sheet of aluminum, tin, or tin and lead, used as a wrapping for candy, tobacco, etc. *n.*

ting (ting), 1 make or cause to make a clear, ringing sound. 2 such a sound. 1 *v.*, 2 *n.*

tinge (tinj), 1 color slightly: *A drop of ink will tinge a glass of water.* 2 a slight coloring or tint: *There is a tinge of red in those leaves.* 3 add a trace of some quality to; change slightly: *Sad memories tinged her present joy.* 4 a very small amount; trace: *She likes just a tinge of lemon in her tea.* 1,3 *v.*, **tinged, tinge ing** or **ting ing;** 2,4 *n.*

tin gle (ting′gəl), 1 have or cause a feeling of thrills or a pricking, stinging feeling: *He tingled with excitement on his first airplane trip. Shame tingled my cheeks.* 2 a pricking, stinging feeling: *The cold caused a tingle in my fingers.* 1 *v.*, **tin gled, tin gling;** 2 *n.*

tink er (ting′kər), 1 person who mends pots, pans, etc. 2 to mend; patch. 3 work or repair in an unskilled or clumsy way: *The children were tinkering with the clock and broke it.* 4 work or keep busy in a rather useless way: *tinker with a radio, tinker with a new idea.* 1 *n.*, 2-4 *v.*

tin kle (ting′kəl), 1 make short, light, ringing sounds: *Little bells tinkle.* 2 cause to tinkle. 3 series of short, light, ringing sounds: *the tinkle of sleigh bells.* 1,2 *v.*, **tin kled, tin kling;** 3 *n.*

tin ner (tin′ər), 1 person who works in a tin mine. 2 person who works with tin. *n.*

tin ny (tin′ē), 1 of tin; containing tin. 2 like tin in looks, sound, or taste: *These sardines have a tinny flavor. adj.*, **tin ni er, tin ni est.**

tin plate, thin sheets of iron or steel coated with tin. Ordinary tin cans are made of tin plate.

tin sel (tin′səl), 1 glittering material of metal, plastic, etc., in thin sheets, strips, or threads, used to trim Christmas trees, etc. 2 anything showy but having little value. 3 of or like tinsel; showy but not worth much. 4 trim with tinsel. 1,2 *n.*, 3 *adj.*, 4 *v.*

tin smith (tin′smith′), person who works with tin; maker of tinware. *n.*

tint (tint), 1 variety of a color: *The picture was painted in several tints of blue.* 2 a delicate or pale color. 3 put a tint on; color slightly: *The walls were tinted gray.* 1,2 *n.*, 3 *v.*

Tin to ret to (tin′tə ret′ō), 1518-1594, Venetian painter. *n.*

tin type (tin′tīp′), photograph taken on a sheet of enameled tin or iron. *n.*

tin ware (tin′wer′ or tin′war′), articles made of tin or tin plate. *n.*

ti ny (tī′nē), very small; wee: *a tiny baby chicken. adj.*, **ti ni er, ti ni est.**

-tion, *suffix added to verbs to form nouns.* 1 act or process of ____ing: *Addition = act or process of adding.* 2 condition of being ____ed: *Exhaustion = condition of being exhausted.* 3 result of ____ing: *Reflection = result of reflecting.* [from Latin -tionem]

tip¹ (tip), 1 the end part; end; point: *the tips of the fingers.* 2 a small piece put on the end of something: *Buy rubber tips to put on the legs of a stool.* 3 put a tip on; furnish with a tip: *spears tipped with steel.* 4 cover or adorn at the tip: *mountains tipped with snow. Sunlight tips the steeple.* 1,2 *n.*, 3,4 *v.*, **tipped, tip ping.** [from a Scandinavian word of the 1300's, such as Icelandic *typpa*]

tip² (tip), 1 slope; slant: *She tipped the table toward her.* 2 a slope; slant: *There is such a tip to that table that everything slips off it.* 3 upset; overturn: *He tipped over his glass of water.* 4 take off (a hat) in greeting: *The courtly old gentleman tipped his hat to a neighbor he met on the street.* 5 empty out; dump: *She tipped the money in her purse onto the table.* 1,3-5 *v.*, **tipped, tip ping;** 2 *n.* [Middle English *typpen*]

tip³ (tip), 1 a small present of money in return for service: *She gave the waiter a tip.* 2 give a small present of money to: *Did you tip the porter?* 3 piece of secret information: *He had a tip that the black horse would win the race.* 4 a useful hint, suggestion, etc.: *Someone gave me a helpful tip about pitching a tent where the trees would shade it.* 5 hit lightly and sharply; tap. 6 a light, sharp blow; tap. 1,3,4,6 *n.*, 2,5 *v.*, **tipped, tip ping.** [origin uncertain]

tip off, INFORMAL. 1 give secret information to: *They tipped me off about a*

hat, āge, fär; let, ēqual, tėrm;
it, īce; hot, ōpen, ôrder;
oil, out; cup, put, rüle; ch, child;
ng, long; sh, she; th, thin;
ŦH, then; zh, measure;

ə represents *a* in about,
e in taken, *i* in pencil,
o in lemon, *u* in circus.

good bargain. 2 warn: *Someone tipped off the criminals and they escaped before the police arrived.*

tip-off (tip′ôf′), INFORMAL. 1 piece of secret information. 2 a warning. *n.*

tip per (tip′ər), person who gives a tip or tips. *n.*

tip pet (tip′it), 1 scarf for the neck and shoulders with ends hanging down in front. 2 a long, narrow, hanging part of a hood, sleeve, or scarf. *n.*

tip ple (tip′əl), 1 drink (alcoholic liquor) often. 2 an alcoholic liquor. 1 *v.*, **tip pled, tip pling;** 2 *n.*

tip pler (tip′lər), a habitual drinker of alcoholic liquor. *n.*

tip si ly (tip′sə lē), in a tipsy manner. *adv.*

tip si ness (tip′sē nis), tipsy condition. *n.*

tip sy (tip′sē), 1 tipping easily; unsteady; tilted. 2 somewhat intoxicated but not thoroughly drunk. *adj.*, **tip si er, tip si est.**

tip toe (tip′tō′), 1 the tips of the toes. 2 walk on one's toes, without using the heels: *She tiptoed quietly up the stairs.* 1 *n.*, 2 *v.*, **tip toed, tip toe ing.**

on tiptoe, 1 walking on one's toes. 2 eager: *The children were on tiptoe for vacation to begin.* 3 in a secret manner.

tip top (tip′top′), 1 the very top; highest point. 2 at the very top or highest point. 3 INFORMAL. first-rate; excellent. 1 *n.*, 2,3 *adj.*

ti rade (tī′rād), 1 a long, vehement speech. 2 a long, scolding speech. *n.*

Ti ra na (ti rä′nə), capital of Albania, in the central part. *n.*

tire¹ (tīr), 1 to lower or use up the strength of; make weary: *The work tired him.* 2 become weary: *The old woman tired easily.* 3 wear down the patience, interest, or appreciation of because of dullness, excess, etc.: *Monotonous filing tired the office worker. v.*, **tired, tir ing.** [Old English *tēorian*]

tire² (tīr), 1 band of rubber or metal around a wheel. Some rubber tires hold air in an inner tube or in the tire itself; others are made of solid rubber. 2 furnish with a tire. 1 *n.*, 2 *v.*, **tired, tir ing.** [apparently shortened from

adj. adjective	*n.* noun
adv. adverb	*prep.* preposition
conj. conjunction	*pron.* pronoun
interj. interjection	*v.* verb
sing. singular	*pl.* plural

attire, in the sense of "a covering"]

tired (tīrd), weary; fatigued; exhausted: *I am tired, but I must get back to work. adj.* —**tired′ly,** *adv.* —**tired′ness,** *n.*

tire less (tīr′lis), 1 never becoming tired; requiring little rest: *a tireless worker.* 2 never stopping: *tireless efforts. adj.* —**tire′less ly,** *adv.* —**tire′less ness,** *n.*

tire some (tīr′səm), not interesting; tiring; boring: *a tiresome speech. adj.* —**tire′some ly,** *adv.* —**tire′some ness,** *n.*

Ti rol (tə rōl′ *or* tī′rōl), region in the Alps, partly in Austria and partly in Italy. *n.* Also, **Tyrol.**

'tis (tiz), it is.

tis sue (tish′ü), 1 substance forming the parts of animals and plants; mass of similar cells which performs a particular function: *brain tissue, muscular tissue, skin tissue.* 2 a thin, light cloth: *Her gown was of silk tissue.* 3 web; network: *The whole story was a tissue of lies.* 4 tissue paper. 5 a thin, soft paper that absorbs moisture easily. Tissue is used to wipe the face or the nose. *n.*

tissue paper, a very thin, soft paper, used for wrapping, covering things, making carbon copies of letters, etc.

tit[1] (tit), 1 titmouse. 2 any of certain other small birds. *n.* [related to Icelandic of the 1300's *tittr* titmouse]

tit[2] (tit), nipple; teat. *n.* [Old English *titt*]

Ti tan (tīt′n), 1 (in Greek myths) one of a family of giants who ruled the world before the gods of Mount Olympus. Prometheus and Atlas were Titans. 2 Also, **titan.** person or thing having enormous size, strength, power, etc.; giant. 3 of the Titans; gigantic; huge; very powerful. 1,2 *n.,* 3 *adj.*

Ti ta ni a (ti tā′nē ə), (in Shakespeare's *A Midsummer Night's Dream*) the queen of the fairies. *n.*

ti tan ic (tī tan′ik), having great size, strength, or power; gigantic; huge: *titanic energy. adj.*

ti ta ni um (tī tā′nē əm), a strong, lightweight, silver-gray metallic element occurring in various minerals. It is highly resistant to corrosion and is used in making steel and other alloys for missiles, jet engines, etc. *n.*

tit bit (tit′bit′), tidbit. *n.*

tit for tat, blow for blow; like for like.

tithe (tīᴛʜ), 1 one tenth. 2 tax of one tenth of the yearly produce of land, animals, and personal work, paid for the support of the church and the clergy. 3 put a tax of one tenth on. 4 pay a tithe on. 5 a very small part. 6 any small tax, levy, etc. 1,2,5,6 *n.,* 3,4 *v.,* **tithed, tith ing.**

Ti tian (tish′ən), 1477?-1576, Venetian painter. *n.*

tit il late (tit′l āt), 1 excite pleasantly; stimulate agreeably. 2 tickle. *v.,* **tit il lat ed, tit il lat ing.**

tit il la tion (tit′l ā′shən), 1 pleasant excitement; agreeable stimulation. 2 a tickling. *n.*

tit lark (tit′lärk′), pipit. *n.*

ti tle (tī′tl), 1 the name of a book, poem, picture, song, etc. 2 name showing rank, occupation, or condition in life. King, duke, lord, countess, captain, doctor, professor, Madame, and Miss are titles. 3 call by a title; name. 4 a first-place position; championship: *the tennis title.* 5 a legal right to the possession of property. 6 evidence, especially a document, showing such a right. When a house is sold, the seller gives title to the buyer. 7 a recognized right; claim: *What title does he have to my gratitude?* 1,2,4-7 *n.,* 3 *v.,* **ti tled, ti tling.**

ti tled (tī′tld), having a title: *a titled nobleman. adj.*

title page, page at the beginning of a book that contains the title, the name of the author and publisher, etc.

tit mouse (tit′mous′), any of certain small birds with short bills and dull-colored feathers. *n., pl.* **tit mice** (tit′mīs′).

Ti to (tē′tō), **Marshal,** born 1892, Yugoslav Communist leader, president of Yugoslavia since 1953. *n.*

tit ter (tit′ər), 1 laugh in a half-restrained manner; giggle. 2 a tittering laugh. 1 *v.,* 2 *n.*

tit tle (tit′l), 1 a very little bit; particle; whit. 2 a small stroke or mark over a letter in writing or printing. The dot over an *i* is a tittle. *n.*

tit tle-tat tle (tit′l tat′l), gossip. *n., v.,* **tit tle-tat tled, tit tle-tat tling.**

tit u lar (tich′ə lər), 1 in title or name only: *He is a titular prince without any power.* 2 having a title. 3 having to do with a title. *adj.*

Ti tus (tī′təs), A.D. 40?-81, Roman emperor from A.D. 79 to 81. *n.*

tiz zy (tiz′ē), SLANG. a very excited, confused state. *n., pl.* **tiz zies.**

TNT or **T.N.T.,** a pale yellow solid used as an explosive in hand grenades, torpedoes, etc.; trinitrotoluene.

to (tü; *unstressed* tu *or* tə), 1 in the direction of: *Go to the right.* 2 as far as;

until: *rotten to the core, faithful to the end.* 3 for the purpose of; for: *She came to the rescue.* 4 so as to produce, cause, or result in: *To their horror, the beast approached.* 5 into: *She tore the letter to pieces.* 6 along with; with: *We danced to the music.* 7 compared with: *The score was 9 to 5.* 8 in agreement or accordance with: *It is not to my liking.* 9 belonging with; of: *the key to my room.* 10 on; against: *Fasten it to the wall.* 11 about; concerning: *What did he say to that?* 12 in: *four apples to the pound.* 13 **To** is used to show action toward. *Give the book to me. Speak to her.* 14 **To** is used with the infinitive form of verbs. *He likes to read. The birds began to sing. "To err is human; to forgive, divine."* 15 forward: *He wore his cap wrong side to.* 16 together; touching; closed: *The door slammed to.* 17 to action or work: *We turned to gladly.* 1-14 *prep.,* 15-17 *adv.*

to and fro, first one way and then back again; back and forth.

toad—up to 5½ in. long

toad (tōd), a small, tailless amphibian somewhat like a frog, living most of the time on land rather than in water. Toads, which are found in gardens, have a rough, brown skin that suggests a lump of earth. *n.*

toad stool (tōd′stül′), mushroom, especially a poisonous mushroom. *n.*

toad y (tō′dē), 1 a fawning flatterer. 2 act like a toady. 3 fawn upon; flatter. 1 *n., pl.* **toad ies;** 2,3 *v.,* **toad ied, toad y ing.**

toad y ism (tō′dē iz′əm), the action or behavior of a toady; interested flattery; mean servility. *n.*

toast[1] (tōst), 1 slices of bread browned by heat. 2 brown by heat: *We toasted the bread.* 3 heat thoroughly: *He toasted his feet by the fire.* 1 *n.,* 2,3 *v.* [from French of the 1300's *toster* to dry by heat, from Latin *tostum* dried by heat]

toast[2] (tōst), 1 take a drink and wish good fortune to; drink to the health of: *We first toasted our hosts.* 2 person or thing whose health is proposed and drunk: *"The Queen" was the first toast drunk by the officers.* 3 a popular or celebrated person: *the toast of the town.* 4 act of drinking to the health of a person or thing. 1 *v.,* 2-4 *n.* [from *toast*[1] (from the custom of putting pieces of spiced toast into wine, etc., drunk to someone's health)]

toast er (tō′stər), 1 person who toasts something. 2 an electric appliance for toasting bread, etc. *n.*

toast mas ter (tōst′mas′tər), 1 person who presides at a dinner and introduces the speakers. 2 person who proposes toasts. *n.*

toga

to bac co (tə bak′ō), 1 the prepared leaves of certain plants, used for smoking or chewing or as snuff. 2 one of these plants. *n., pl.* **to bac cos** or **to bac coes.**

to bac co nist (tə bak′ə nist), dealer in tobacco. *n.*

To ba go (tə bā′gō), island in the West Indies, near Venezuela, part of the country of Trinidad and Tobago. *n.*

to bog gan (tə bog′ən), 1 a long, narrow, flat sled with its front end curved upward and without runners. 2 slide downhill on such a sled. 3 decline sharply and rapidly in value. 1 *n.,* 2,3 *v.*

toboggan (def. 1)

toc sin (tok′sən), 1 alarm sounded on a bell; warning signal. 2 bell used to sound an alarm. *n.*

to day or **to-day** (tə dā′), 1 this day; the present time: *Today is Wednesday.* 2 on or during this day: *What are you doing today?* 3 at the present time; now: *Pollution is a major problem today.* 1 *n.,* 2,3 *adv.*

tod dle (tod′l), walk with short, unsteady steps, as a baby does. *v.,* **toddled, tod dling.**

tod dler (tod′lər), child just learning to walk. *n.*

tod dy (tod′ē), drink made of whisky, brandy, etc., with hot water and sugar. *n., pl.* **tod dies.**

to-do (tə dü′), INFORMAL. fuss; bustle: *to make a great to-do over nothing. n., pl.* **to-dos.**

toe (tō), 1 one of the five end parts of the foot. 2 the part of a stocking, shoe, etc., that covers the toes: *have a hole in the toe of a sock.* 3 the forepart of a

foot or hoof. 4 anything like a toe: *the toe and heel of a golf club.* 5 touch or reach with the toes: *toe a line.* 1-4 *n.,* 5 *v.,* **toed, toe ing.**

on one's toes, ready for action; alert.

toe nail (tō′nāl′), the nail growing on a toe. *n.*

tof fee (tô′fē), taffy. *n.*

tof fy (tô′fē), toffee. *n., pl.* **tof fies.**

tog (tog), INFORMAL. 1 **togs,** *pl.* clothes. 2 to clothe; dress. 1 *n.,* 2 *v.,* **togged, tog ging.**

to ga (tō′gə), a loose, outer garment worn in public by citizens of ancient Rome. *n., pl.* **to gas.**

to geth er (tə geᴛH′ər), 1 with each other; in company: *They were standing together.* 2 with united action; in cooperation: *to work together for peace.* 3 into one gathering, company, mass, or body: *The principal called the school together. The tailor will sew these pieces together and make a suit.* 4 at the same time: *You cannot have day and night together.* 5 without a stop or break; continuously: *He worked for days together. adv.*

to geth er ness (tə geᴛH′ər nis), condition of being close together, especially in family or social activities. *n.*

toggle (def. 1)

tog gle (tog′əl), 1 pin, bolt, or rod put through a loop in a rope or a link of a chain to keep it in place, to hold two ropes together, to serve as a hold for the fingers, etc. 2 furnish with a toggle; fasten with a toggle. 1 *n.,* 2 *v.,* **toggled, tog gling.**

To go (tō′gō), country in W Africa, formerly a French trust territory. See **Upper Volta** for map. *n.*

toil[1] (toil), 1 hard work; labor: *to succeed after years of toil.* 2 work hard: *to toil with one's hands for a living.* 3 move with difficulty, pain, or weariness: *Carrying heavy loads, they toiled up the mountain.* 1 *n.,* 2,3 *v.* [from French of the 1200's *toeillier* drag about, from Latin *tudiculare* stir up, from *tudicula* olive press, from *tudes* mallet] —**toil′er.** *n.*

toil[2] (toil). Often, **toils,** *pl.* net or snare: *A lion was caught in the toils. The thief was caught in the toils of the law. n.* [from French of the 1500's *toile,* from Latin *tela* web]

toi let (toi′lit), 1 bathroom or lavatory. 2 a porcelain bowl with a seat attached and with a drain at the bottom connected to a water tank to flush the bowl clean. Waste matter from the body is disposed of in a toilet. 3 process of dressing. Bathing, combing the hair, and

hat, āge, fär; let, ēqual, tėrm;
it, īce; hot, ōpen, ôrder;
oil, out; cup, pùt, rüle; ch, child;
ng, long; sh, she; th, thin;
ᴛH, then; zh, measure;

ə represents *a* in about,
e in taken, *i* in pencil,
o in lemon, *u* in circus.

putting on one's clothes are all part of one's toilet. *I made a hurried toilet.* 4 of or for the toilet. Combs and brushes are toilet articles. 5 a person's dress; costume. 1-3,5 *n.,* 4 *adj.*

toi let ry (toi′lə trē), soap, face powder, perfumery, or other articles for the toilet. *n., pl.* **toi let ries.**

toilet water, a fragrant liquid not so strong as perfume, used after bathing, as a cologne in grooming, etc.

toil some (toil′səm), requiring hard work; laborious; wearisome: *a long, toilsome climb up the mountain. adj.*

to ken (tō′kən), 1 a mark or sign (of something): *Black is a token of mourning. His actions are a token of his sincerity.* 2 sign of friendship; keepsake: *She received many birthday tokens.* 3 piece of metal stamped for a higher value than the metal is worth and used for some special purpose, such as bus or subway fare. 4 piece of metal, plastic, etc., indicating a right or privilege: *This token will admit you to the swimming pool.* 5 having only the appearance of; serving as a symbol; nominal; partial: *a token payment, token resistance.* 1-4 *n.,* 5 *adj.*

by the same token, for the same reason; in the same way; moreover.

To ky o or **To ki o** (tō′kē ō), capital of Japan, in the central part. Tokyo is one of the largest cities in the world. *n.*

told (tōld), past tense and past participle of **tell.** *You told me that last week. We were told to wait. v.*

To le do (tə lē′dō), 1 city in NW Ohio. 2 city in central Spain. *n.*

tol er a ble (tol′ər ə bəl), 1 able to be borne or endured; bearable: *The pain has become tolerable.* 2 fairly good: *She is in tolerable health. adj.*

tol er a bly (tol′ər ə blē), 1 in a tolerable manner. 2 moderately. *adv.*

tol er ance (tol′ər əns), 1 a willingness to be tolerant; a putting up with people whose opinions or ways differ from one's own. 2 the power of enduring or resisting the action of a drug, poison, etc. 3 action of tolerating: *The principal's tolerance of their bad behavior surprised us. n.*

adj.	adjective	*n.*	noun
adv.	adverb	*prep.*	preposition
conj.	conjunction	*pron.*	pronoun
interj.	interjection	*v.*	verb
sing.	singular	*pl.*	plural

tol er ant (tol′ər ənt), 1 willing to let other people do as they think best; willing to endure beliefs and actions of which one does not approve: *The founders of the colony of Rhode Island were tolerant toward all religious beliefs.* 2 able to endure or resist the action of a drug, poison, etc. *adj.* —**tol′er ant ly,** *adv.*

tomahawk (def.1)—three types

tol e rate (tol′ə rāt′), 1 allow or permit: *The teacher won't tolerate any disorder. A nation at war will not tolerate treason.* 2 bear; endure; put up with: *They tolerated the grouchy old man only because he was their employer.* 3 endure or resist the action of (a drug, poison, etc.). *v.,* **tol e rat ed, tol e rat ing.**

tol e ra tion (tol′ə rā′shən), 1 willingness to put up with beliefs and actions of which one does not approve: *Toleration of dishonest officials encourages corruption.* 2 recognition of a person's right to worship as he thinks best without loss of civil rights or social privileges; freedom of worship. *n.*

toll[1] (tōl), 1 to sound with single strokes slowly and regularly repeated: *Bells were tolled all over the country at the President's death.* 2 stroke or sound of a bell being tolled. 3 act or fact of tolling. 4 call, announce, etc., by tolling. 1,4 *v.,* 2,3 *n.* [related to Old English *-tyllan* to draw]

toll[2] (tōl), 1 tax or fee paid for some right or privilege: *We pay a toll when we use the bridge.* 2 charge for a certain service. There is a toll on long-distance telephone calls. 3 something paid, lost, suffered, etc.: *Automobile accidents take a heavy toll of human lives.* n. [Old English *toll, toln,* from Latin *telonium,* from Greek *teloneion* toll house, from *telos* tax]

toll booth (tōl′büth′), booth or gate at which tolls are collected before or after going over a bridge, highway, etc. *n., pl.* **toll booths** (tōl′büᴛʜz′ *or* tōl′-büths′).

toll gate (tōl′gāt′), tollbooth. *n.*

toll road, road on which tolls are charged; turnpike.

Tol stoy (tol′stoi), **Leo,** 1828-1910, Russian novelist. *n.*

Tol tec (tol′tek), 1 member of an Indian people who lived in Mexico before the Aztecs and influenced their culture. 2 of or having to do with the Toltecs or their culture. 1 *n.,* 2 *adj.*

tol u ene (tol′yü ēn), a colorless, flammable liquid obtained from coal tar and petroleum. It is used as a solvent and for making explosives, dyes, etc. *n.*

tol u ol (tol′yü ōl), toluene. *n.*

tom or **Tom** (tom), 1 tomcat. 2 the male of various other animals: *Our Thanksgiving turkey was a tom. n.*

tom a hawk (tom′ə hôk), 1 a light ax used by North American Indians as a weapon and a tool. 2 strike or kill with a tomahawk. 1 *n.,* 2 *v.*

to ma to (tə mā′tō *or* tə mä′tō), 1 a spreading, strong-smelling plant with hairy leaves and stems, and small, yellow flowers. 2 its juicy, slightly acid fruit, eaten as a vegetable. Most tomatoes are red, but some kinds are yellow. *n., pl.* **to ma toes.**

tomb (tüm), grave, vault, mausoleum, etc., for a dead body, often above ground. *n.*

tom boy (tom′boi′), girl who likes to play games supposedly suited to boys; boisterous, romping girl. *n.*

tomb stone (tüm′stōn′), gravestone. *n.*

tom cat (tom′kat′), a male cat. *n.*

tome (tōm), a book, especially a large, heavy book. *n.*

tom fool er y (tom′fü′lər ē), silly behavior; nonsense. *n., pl.* **tom fool er ies.**

to mor row or **to-mor row** (tə-môr′ō), 1 the day after today. 2 the near future. 3 on the day after today. 4 very soon. 1,2 *n.,* 3,4 *adv.*

tom tit (tom′tit′), a small bird, especially a titmouse. *n.*

tom-tom (tom′tom′), a drum, usually

tongs
used to lift log

tom-tom

beaten with the hands, originally used in the East Indies. *n.*

ton (tun), measure of weight equal to 2000 pounds (**short ton**) in the United States and Canada, and 2240 pounds (**long ton**) in Great Britain. A **metric ton** is 1000 kilograms. *n.*

ton al (tō′nl), of or having to do with tone or tonality. *adj.*

to nal i ty (tō nal′ə tē), 1 in music: **a** sum of relations existing between the tones of a scale or musical system. **b** a key or system of tones. 2 the color scheme of a painting, etc. *n., pl.* **to nal i ties.**

tone (tōn), 1 any sound considered with reference to its quality, pitch, strength, source, etc.: *angry tones, gentle tones, the deep tone of an organ.* 2 quality of sound: *Her voice was silvery in tone.* 3 in music: **a** a sound of definite pitch and character. **b** whole step. C and D are one tone apart. 4 manner of speaking or writing: *a moral tone. We disliked the haughty tone of her letter.* 5 spirit; character; style: *A tone of quiet elegance prevails in their home.* 6 normal, healthy condition; vigor: *You must exercise regularly to keep your body in tone.* 7 effect of color and of light and shade in a picture: *I like the soft green tone of that painting.* 8 shade of color: *This room is furnished in tones of brown.* 9 harmonize: *This rug tones in well with the wallpaper and furniture.* 10 give a tone to. 1-8 *n.,* 9,10 *v.,* **toned, ton ing.**

tone down, soften: *Tone down your voice. Tone down the colors in that painting.*

tone up, give more sound, color, or vigor to; strengthen: *Bright curtains would tone up this dull room.*

tone less (tōn′lis), 1 without tone; without expression: *a toneless voice, a toneless reading.* 2 (of color) dull. *adj.*

Ton ga (tong′gə), island country in the S Pacific, northeast of New Zealand. It is a member of the Commonwealth of Nations. *n.*

tongs (tôngz), tool with two arms that are joined by a hinge, pivot, or spring, used for seizing, holding, or lifting. *n.pl.*

tongue (tung), 1 the movable fleshy

organ in the mouth. The tongue is used in tasting and, by people, for talking. 2 an animal's tongue used as food: *Father likes cold tongue and salad.* 3 power of speech: *Have you lost your tongue?* 4 way of speaking; speech; talk: *a flattering tongue.* 5 the language of a people: *the English tongue.* 6 something shaped or used like a tongue: *Tongues of flame leaped from the fire.* 7 the strip of leather under the laces of a shoe. 8 a narrow strip of land running out into water. 9 a movable piece inside a bell that swings against it, producing a sound. *n.*

hold one's tongue, keep silent: *"Hold your tongue while I'm speaking!"* she demanded.

on the tip of one's tongue, 1 almost spoken. 2 ready to be spoken.

with tongue in cheek, with sly humor; not to be taken seriously; in a mocking manner: *He spoke with tongue in cheek when he said he enjoyed doing all that homework.*

tongue less (tung′lis), 1 having no tongue. 2 unable to speak. *adj.*

tongue-tied (tung′tīd′), 1 having the motion of the tongue hindered. 2 unable to speak because of shyness, embarrassment, etc. *adj.*

tongue twister, phrase or sentence that is difficult to say quickly without a mistake. EXAMPLE: She sells seashells by the seashore.

ton ic (ton′ik), 1 anything that gives strength; medicine to give strength: *Cod-liver oil is a tonic.* 2 restoring to health and vigor; giving strength; bracing: *The mountain air is tonic.* 3 in music: **a** the first note of a scale; keynote. **b** having to do with tone or tones. **c** of or based on a keynote: *a tonic chord.* 1,3a *n.,* 2,3b,3c *adj.*

to night or **to-night** (tə nīt′), 1 the night of this day; this night: *I am going to bed early tonight.* 2 on or during this night: *Do you think it will snow tonight?* 1 *n.,* 2 *adv.*

ton nage (tun′ij), 1 the carrying capacity of a ship, expressed in units of 100 cubic feet per ton. A ship of 50,000 cubic feet of space or freight has a tonnage of 500 tons. 2 total amount of shipping in tons. 3 duty or tax on ships at so much a ton. 4 weight in tons. *n.*

ton sil (ton′səl), either of the two oval masses of lymphoid tissue on the sides of the throat, just back of the mouth. *n.*

ton sil lec to my (ton′sə lek′tə mē), the surgical removal of the tonsils. *n., pl.* **ton sil lec to mies.**

ton sil li tis (ton′sə lī′tis), inflammation of the tonsils. *n.*

ton so ri al (ton sôr′ē əl), of or having to do with a barber or the work of a barber. *adj.*

ton sure (ton′shər), 1 a clipping of the hair or shaving of a part or the whole of the head of a person entering the priesthood or an order of monks. 2 the shaved part of the head of a priest or monk. 3 shave the head of. 1,2 *n.,* 3 *v.,* **ton sured, ton sur ing.**

too (tü), 1 in addition; also; besides: *The dog is hungry, and thirsty too. We, too, are going away.* 2 beyond what is desirable, proper, or right; more than enough: *My dress is too long for you. He ate too much. The summer passed too quickly.* 3 very; exceedingly: *I am only too glad to help.* *adv.*

took (tuk), past tense of **take.** *She took the car an hour ago.* *v.*

tool (tül), 1 a knife, hammer, saw, shovel, or any instrument used in doing work: *Plumbers, mechanics, carpenters, and shoemakers need tools.* 2 person or thing used by another like a tool: *Books are a scholar's tools. He is a tool of the party boss.* 3 a part of a machine that cuts, bores, smooths, etc. 4 use a tool on; work or shape with a tool: *She tooled beautiful designs in the leather with a knife.* 5 ornament with a tool. 6 provide or equip (a factory, etc.) with tools. 1-3 *n.,* 4-6 *v.*

tool box (tül′boks′), box in which tools and sometimes small parts, accessories, etc., are kept. *n.*

tool mak er (tül′mā′kər), 1 machinist who makes, repairs, and maintains machine tools. 2 any maker of tools: *Prehistoric people were the first toolmakers.* *n.*

toot (tüt), 1 sound of a horn, whistle, etc. 2 give forth a short blast: *He heard the train whistle toot three times.* 3 sound (a horn, whistle, etc.) in short blasts. 1 *n.,* 2,3 *v.* —**toot′er,** *n.*

tooth (tüth), 1 one of the hard, bonelike parts in the mouth, used for biting and chewing. 2 something like a tooth. Each one of the projecting parts of a comb, rake, or saw is a tooth. 3 furnish with teeth; put teeth on. 4 cut teeth on the edge of; indent. 5 a taste; liking: *to have no tooth for fruit.* 1,2,5 *n., pl.* **teeth;** 3,4 *v.*

fight tooth and nail, fight fiercely, with all one's force.

tooth ache (tüth′āk′), pain in a tooth or the teeth. *n.*

TONSIL

UVULA

hat, āge, fär; let, ēqual, tėrm;
it, īce; hot, ōpen, ôrder;
oil, out; cup, pùt, rüle; ch, child;
ng, long; sh, she; th, thin;
ŦH, then; zh, measure;

ə represents *a* in about,
e in taken, *i* in pencil,
o in lemon, *u* in circus.

tooth brush (tüth′brush′), a small brush for cleaning the teeth. *n., pl.* **tooth brush es.**

toothed (tütht *or* tüŦHd), 1 having teeth. 2 notched: *the toothed surface of a gear. adj.*

tooth less (tüth′lis), without teeth. *adj.*

tooth paste (tüth′pāst′), paste used in cleaning the teeth. *n.*

tooth pick (tüth′pik′), a small, pointed piece of wood, plastic, etc., for removing bits of food from between the teeth. *n.*

tooth pow der (tüth′pou′dər), powder used in cleaning the teeth. *n.*

tooth some (tüth′səm), 1 pleasing to the taste; tasting good. 2 pleasing to the sight; pretty. *adj.*

top¹ (top), 1 the highest point or part: *the top of a mountain.* 2 the upper part, end, or surface: *the top of a table, a shoe top.* 3 the highest or leading place, rank, etc.: *She is at the top of her class.* 4 the highest point, pitch, or degree: *They were yelling at the top of their voices.* 5 the best or most important part: *top of the morning.* 6 part of a plant that grows above ground: *Beet tops are somewhat like spinach.* 7 the head: *The toddler was all bundled up from top to toe.* 8 the cover of an automobile, carriage, can, etc. 9 having to do with, situated at, or forming the top: *the top shelf of a cupboard.* 10 highest or greatest: *He received top honors at school. The runners set off at top speed.* 11 put a top on: *I will top the box.* 12 be on top of; be the top of: *A church tops the hill.* 13 reach the top of: *They topped the mountain.* 14 rise high; rise above: *The sun topped the horizon.* 15 be higher or greater than. 16 do better than; outdo; excel: *His story topped all the rest.* 17 remove the top of (a plant, tree, etc.). 18 platform around the upper part of a lower mast on a ship. It serves as a foothold for sailors and as a means of extending the upper rigging. 1-8,18 *n.,* 9,10 *adj.,* 11-17 *v.,* **topped, top ping.** [Old English *topp*]

on top, with success; with victory: *We*

top

have the best players so our team will come out on top.

top off, complete; finish; end.

top² (top), toy that spins on a point. *n.* [origin uncertain]

sleep like a top, sleep soundly.

to paz (tō′paz), a hard mineral that occurs in crystals of various forms and colors. It is a compound of aluminum, silica, and fluorine. Transparent yellow topaz is used as a gem. *n., pl.* **to paz es.**

top coat (top′kōt′), a lightweight overcoat. *n.*

To pe ka (tə pē′kə), capital of Kansas, in the NE part. *n.*

top gal lant (top′gal′ənt *or* tə-gal′ənt), 1 the mast or sail above the topmast; the third section of a mast above the deck. See **masthead** for picture. 2 next above the topmast. 1 *n.*, 2 *adj.*

top hat, a tall, black silk hat worn by men in formal clothes; high hat.

top-heav y (top′hev′ē), too heavy at the top. *adj.*

top ic (top′ik), subject that people think, write, or talk about: *Newspapers discuss the topics of the day. I chose women's rights as the topic for my report. n.*

top i cal (top′ə kəl), 1 having to do with topics of the day; of current or local interest. 2 of or having to do with a topic: *Some books have topical outlines for each chapter. adj.*

top knot (top′not′), a knot of hair or a tuft of feathers on the top of the head. *n.*

top mast (top′mast′ *or* top′məst), the second section of a mast above the deck. See **masthead** for picture. *n.*

top most (top′mōst), highest: *I need a ladder to reach the apples on the topmost branches. adj.*

top-notch (top′noch′), INFORMAL. first-rate; best possible. *adj.*

to pog ra pher (tə pog′rə fər), an expert in topography. *n.*

top o graph ic (top′ə graf′ik), topographical. *adj.*

top o graph i cal (top′ə graf′ə kəl), of or having to do with topography. A topographical map shows mountains, rivers, etc. *adj.*

to pog ra phy (tə pog′rə fē), 1 the accurate and detailed description or draw-

ing of places or their surface features. 2 the surface features of a place or region. The topography of a region includes hills, valleys, streams, lakes, bridges, tunnels, roads, etc. *n., pl.* **to pog ra phies.**

top ple (top′əl), 1 fall forward; tumble down: *The chimney toppled over on the roof.* 2 throw over or down; overturn: *The wrestler toppled his opponent. v.,* **top pled, top pling.**

tops (tops), SLANG. of the highest degree in quality, excellence, etc. *adj.*

top sail (top′sāl′ *or* top′səl), the second sail above the deck on a mast. *n.*

top side (top′sīd′), to or on the upper deck: *The captain ordered the crew topside. adv.*

top soil (top′soil′), the upper part of the soil; surface soil: *Farmers need rich topsoil for their crops. n.*

top sy-tur vy (top′sē tér′vē), 1 upside down. 2 in confusion or disorder: *On moving day everything in the house was topsy-turvy. adv., adj.*

toque

toque (tōk), hat without a brim or with a very little brim, formerly worn by men and women. *n.*

To rah (tôr′ə), 1 the entire body of Jewish law and tradition. 2 the Jewish Bible; Old Testament. 3 the Pentateuch. 4 scroll on which the Pentateuch is written. *n.* [from Hebrew *torah* teaching]

torch (tôrch), 1 light to be carried around or stuck in a holder on a wall. A piece of pine wood or anything that burns easily makes a good torch. The Statue of Liberty holds a torch. 2 device for producing a very hot flame, used especially to burn off paint, to solder metal, and to melt metal. 3 flashlight (a term used in Great Britain). 4 something thought of as a source of enlightenment: *the torch of civilization. n., pl.* **torch es.** —**torch′like′,** *adj.*

torch bear er (tôrch′ber′ər *or* tôrch′-bar′ər), person who carries a torch. *n.*

torch light (tôrch′līt′), light of a torch or torches. *n.*

tore (tôr), past tense of **tear²**. *She tore her dress on a nail yesterday. v.*

to re a dor (tôr′ē ə dôr), bullfighter. *n.* [from Spanish]

tor ment (tôr ment′ *for 1,5;* tôr′ment *for 2-4),* 1 cause very great pain to: *Headaches tormented him.* 2 a cause of very great pain: *A bad burn can be a*

torment. 3 very great pain: *She suffered torments from her toothache.* 4 a cause of very much worry or annoyance. 5 worry or annoy very much: *He torments everyone with silly questions.* 1,5 *v.,* 2-4 *n.*

tor men tor *or* **tor ment er** (tôr-men′tər), person or thing that torments. *n.*

torn (tôrn), past participle of **tear²**. *He has torn up the plant by the roots. Her coat was old and torn. v.*

tor na do (tôr nā′dō), an extremely violent and destructive whirlwind. A tornado extends down from a mass of dark clouds as a twisting funnel and moves over the land in a narrow path. *n., pl.* **tor na does** *or* **tor na dos.**

To ron to (tə ron′tō), city in SE Canada, on Lake Ontario. It is the capital of Ontario. *n.*

tor pe do (tôr pē′dō), 1 a large, cigarshaped metal tube that contains explosives and travels under water by its own power. Torpedoes may be fired from submarines or torpedo boats or launched from aircraft to blow up enemy ships. 2 attack or destroy with a torpedo. 3 an explosive put on a railroad track which makes a loud noise for a signal when a wheel of the engine runs over it. 4 a firework consisting of an explosive and gravel wrapped in tissue paper. It explodes when it is thrown against something hard. 1,3,4 *n., pl.* **tor pe does;** 2 *v.*

torpedo boat, a small, fast warship used for attacking with torpedoes. *n.*

tor pid (tôr′pid), 1 dull, inactive, or sluggish. 2 not moving or feeling. Animals that hibernate become torpid in winter. *adj.*

torch (def. 2)

tor pid i ty (tôr pid′ə tē), torpid condition. *n.*

tor por (tôr′pər), torpid condition. *n.*

torque (tôrk), force causing rotation. *n.*

tor rent (tôr′ənt), 1 a violent, rushing stream of water: *The mountain torrent dashed over the rock.* 2 a heavy downpour: *The rain came down in torrents during the thunderstorm.* 3 any violent, rushing stream; flood: *a torrent of abuse, a torrent of lava from the volcano. n.*

tor ren tial (tô ren′shəl), of, caused by, or like a torrent: *torrential rains, a* torrential flow of words. *adj.* **—torren′tial ly,** *adv.*

tor rid (tôr′id), very hot: *July is a torrid month. adj.*

Torrid Zone, the very warm region between the tropic of Cancer and the tropic of Capricorn; the tropics. The equator divides the Torrid Zone.

tor sion (tôr′shən), 1 act or process of twisting. 2 state of being twisted. 3 the twisting of a body by two equal and opposite forces. *n.*

tor so (tôr′sō), 1 the trunk of the human body. 2 the trunk or body of a statue without any head, arms, or legs. *n., pl.* **tor sos.**

tor til la (tôr tē′yə), a thin, flat, round cake made of corn meal, commonly eaten in Spanish America. It is baked on a flat surface and served hot. *n., pl.* **tor til las.** [from American Spanish]

tor toise (tôr′təs), 1 turtle living only on land, especially in dry regions. Tortoises have stumpy legs and a high, arched shell. 2 any turtle. *n., pl.* **tortois es** or **tor toise.**

tortoise shell, the mottled yellow-and-brown shell of some turtles. It is much used for combs and ornaments.

tor toise-shell (tôr′təs shel′), 1 made of tortoise shell. 2 mottled or colored like a tortoise shell. *adj.*

tor tu ous (tôr′chü əs), 1 full of twists, turns, or bends; twisting; winding; crooked: *We found the river's course very tortuous.* 2 mentally or morally crooked; not straightforward: *They used tortuous reasoning to trick me into joining their scheme. adj.* **—tor′tu ous ly,** *adv.*

tor ture (tôr′chər), 1 act of inflicting very severe pain. Torture was formerly used to make people give evidence about crimes, or to make them confess. 2 very severe pain; agony: *She suffered tortures from rheumatism.* 3 cause very severe pain to; torment: *It is cruel to torture animals.* 4 twist the meaning of. 5 twist or force out of its natural form: *Winds tortured the trees.* 1,2 *n.,* 3-5 *v.,* **tor tured, tor tur ing.**

tor tur er (tôr′chər ər), person or thing that tortures; tormentor. *n.*

tor tur ous (tôr′chər əs), full of, involving, or causing torture. *adj.*

To ry (tôr′ē), 1 member of the British political party that favored royal power and the established church and opposed change. Strictly speaking, there is no Tory party in modern Britain, although members of the Conservative party are often called Tories. 2 member of the Conservative party of Canada. 3 an American who favored British rule over the colonies at the time of the Revolutionary War. 4 Also, **tory.** a very conservative person. 5 of or having to do with Tories. 1-4 *n., pl.* **To ries;** 5 *adj.*

Tos ca ni ni (tos′kə nē′nē), **Arturo,** 1867-1957, American conductor, born in Italy. *n.*

toss (tôs), 1 throw lightly with the palm upward; cast; fling: *She tossed the ball to the baby.* 2 throw about; roll or pitch about: *The ship is tossed by the waves. He tossed on his bed all night.* 3 lift quickly; throw upward: *She tossed her head. The inexperienced bullfighter was tossed by the bull.* 4 shake up or about, especially to mix the ingredients: *toss a salad.* 5 throw a coin to decide something by the side that falls upward. 6 distance to which something is or can be tossed. 7 a throw; tossing: *A toss of a coin decided who should play first.* 1-5 *v.,* 6,7 *n., pl.* **toss es.**

toss off, 1 do or make quickly and easily: *He tossed off a poem.* 2 drink all at once: *He tossed off a glass of milk.*

toss up (tôs′up′), 1 a tossing of a coin to decide something. 2 INFORMAL. an even chance: *It's a tossup whether or not he'll accept. n.*

tot (tot), a little child. *n.*

to tal (tō′tl), 1 whole; entire: *The total cost of the house and land will be $25,000.* 2 the whole amount; sum: *Her expenses reached a total of $100.* 3 find the sum of; add: *Total that column of figures.* 4 reach an amount of; amount to: *The money spent yearly on chewing gum totals millions of dollars.* 5 complete; absolute; utter: *The play was a total failure. We were in total darkness.* 1,5 *adj.,* 2 *n.,* 3,4 *v.*

to tal i tar i an (tō tal′ə ter′ē ən), 1 of or having to do with a government controlled by one political group which suppresses all opposition, often with force, and which controls many aspects of people's lives. A totalitarian government usually regulates what goods are produced by industry, what radio or television programs are broadcast, what books the people may read, etc. Nazi Germany and fascist Italy had totalitarian systems of government. 2 person in favor of totalitarian principles. 1 *adj.,* 2 *n.*

to tal i tar i an ism (tō tal′ə ter′ē ə niz′əm), system, principles, or methods of a totalitarian government. *n.*

to tal i ty (tō tal′ə tē), the total amount; entirety. *n., pl.* **to tal i ties.**

to tal ly (tō′tl ē), wholly; entirely; completely: *We were totally unprepared. adv.*

tote (tōt), INFORMAL. carry; haul. *v.,* **tot ed, tot ing.**

to tem (tō′təm), 1 (among American Indians) a natural object, often an animal, taken as the emblem of a tribe, clan, or family. 2 image of such an object. Totems are often carved and painted on poles. *n.*

totem pole, pole carved and painted with representations of totems, erected by the Indians of the northwestern coast of North America, especially in front of their houses.

tot ter (tot′ər), 1 walk with shaky, unsteady steps: *The baby came tottering across the room.* 2 be unsteady; shake as if about to fall: *Babies totter as they walk. The old wall tottered in the gale and fell.* 3 shake; tremble. 4 a tottering. 1-3 *v.,* 4 *n.* **—tot′ter er,** *n.*

tou can (tü′kan), a bright-colored bird of tropical America, with an enormous beak. *n.*

touch (tuch), 1 put the hand or some other part of the body on or against: *She touched the pan to see whether it was still hot.* 2 put against; make contact with: *I touched the post with my umbrella.* 3 be against; come against: *Your sleeve is touching the butter.* 4 be in contact: *Our hands touched.* 5 a touching or a being touched: *A bubble bursts at a touch.* 6 the sense by which things are perceived by feeling, handling, or coming against them: *The blind develop a keen touch.* 7 communication or connection: *He always kept in touch with his family while he was overseas. She has been out of touch with events in her home town since she moved away.* 8 a slight amount; little bit: *We had a touch of frost. The child has a touch of fever.* 9 a light, delicate stroke with a brush, pencil, pen, etc.: *The artist finished my picture with a few touches.* 10 a detail in any artistic work: *a story with charming poetic touches.* 11 strike lightly or gently: *touch the strings of a harp.* 12 injure slightly: *The flowers were touched by the frost.* 13 affect with some feeling: *The sad story touched us.* 14 make slightly crazy. 15 have to do with; concern: *The matter touches your interest.* 16 speak of; deal with; refer to; treat lightly: *Our conversation touched many subjects.* 17 handle; use: *He won't touch liquor or tobacco.* 18 reach; come up to: *His head almost touches the ceiling. No-*

hat, āge, fär; let, ēqual, tėrm;
it, īce; hot, ōpen, ôrder;
oil, out; cup, pu̇t, rüle; ch, child;
ng, long; sh, she; th, thin;
ᵺ, then; zh, measure;

ə represents *a* in about,
e in taken, *i* in pencil,
o in lemon, *u* in circus.

adj. adjective	*n.* noun
adv. adverb	*prep.* preposition
conj. conjunction	*pron.* pronoun
interj. interjection	*v.* verb
sing. singular	*pl.* plural

body in our class can touch her in music. 19 make a brief stop: *Most ships touch at that port.* 20 act or manner of playing a musical instrument, especially an instrument with a keyboard: *The girl playing the piano has an excellent touch.* 21 a distinctive manner or quality: *The work showed an expert's touch.* 1-4,11-19 *v.,* 5-10,20,21 *n., pl.* **touch·es.**

touch down, land an aircraft: *The pilot touched down at a small country airfield.*

touch off, 1 represent exactly or cleverly. 2 cause to go off; fire.

touch on or **touch upon,** 1 mention; treat lightly: *Our conversation touched on many subjects.* 2 come close to.

touch up, change a little; improve: *touch up a photograph.*

touch-and-go (tuch′ən gō′), uncertain; risky. *adj.*

touch down (tuch′doun′), 1 in football: **a** act of a player in possessing the ball on or behind the opponent's goal line. **b** the score of six points made in this way. 2 the landing of an aircraft, especially the moment of first contact with the ground: *The pilot made an unexpected touchdown because of engine trouble. n.*

touched (tucht), 1 INFORMAL. slightly crazed. 2 stirred emotionally: *He was touched by our concern for his welfare. adj.*

touch football, game with rules similar to those of football except that the player carrying the ball is touched rather than tackled.

touch·ing (tuch′ing), 1 arousing tender feeling: *"A Christmas Carol" is a touching story.* 2 concerning; about: *The interviewer asked questions touching my home and school life.* 1 *adj.,* 2 *prep.* —**touch′ing ly,** *adv.*

touch·stone (tuch′stōn′), 1 a black stone used to test the purity of gold or silver by the color of the streak made on the stone by rubbing it with the metal. 2 any means of testing; a test: *Adversity is the touchstone of friendship. n.*

touch·y (tuch′ē), 1 apt to take offense at trifles; too sensitive: *He is tired and very touchy this afternoon.* 2 requiring skill in handling; ticklish; precarious: *Relations can be very touchy if one's*

friends are quarreling. *adj.,* **touch·i·er, touch·i·est.**

tough (tuf), 1 bending without breaking: *Leather is tough; cardboard is not.* 2 hard to cut, tear, or chew: *The steak was so tough I couldn't eat it.* 3 strong; hardy: *a tough plant. Donkeys are tough little animals and can carry big loads.* 4 hard; difficult: *Dragging the load uphill was tough work.* 5 hard to influence; stubborn: *a tough customer.* 6 rough; disorderly: *This is a tough neighborhood.* 7 a rough person: *A gang of toughs attacked him.* 1-6 *adj.,* 7 *n.* —**tough′ly,** *adv.* —**tough′ness,** *n.*

tough·en (tuf′ən), 1 make tough: *I toughened my muscles by doing exercises.* 2 become tough: *My muscles finally toughened. v.*

Tou·louse-Lau·trec (tü lüz′lō trek′), **Henri de,** 1864-1901, French painter, famous for his posters. *n.*

tou·pee (tü pā′), wig or patch of false hair worn to cover a bald spot. *n.*

tour (túr), 1 to travel from place to place: *Our Girl Scout troop toured by bus for a week.* 2 travel through: *Last year they toured Europe.* 3 a long journey: *The family made a European tour.* 4 a short journey; a walk around: *Our class made a tour of the old boat.* 5 walk around in: *The children will tour the museum.* 6 period or turn of military or other activity at a certain place or station: *a soldier away on a tour of duty overseas.* 1,2,5 *v.,* 3,4,6 *n.*

on tour, touring. A show on tour travels around the country giving performances in various places.

tour de force (túr′ də fôrs′), a notable feat of strength, skill, or ingenuity. *pl.* **tours de force** (túr′ də fôrs′). [from French]

tour·ism (túr′iz′əm), 1 a touring or traveling for pleasure. 2 the business of serving tourists. *n.*

tour·ist (túr′ist), 1 person traveling for pleasure. 2 of or for tourists: *tourist accommodations.* 1 *n.,* 2 *adj.*

tour·ma·line (túr′mə lən), a semiprecious colored mineral found in deposits of coarse granite. The transparent varieties of tourmaline are used in jewelry. *n.*

tour·na·ment (tėr′nə mənt *or* túr′nə mənt), 1 series of contests testing the skill of many persons in some sport: *a golf tournament.* 2 a medieval contest between two groups of knights on horseback who fought for a prize. *n.*

tour·ney (tėr′nē *or* túr′nē), 1 tournament. 2 take part in a tournament. 1 *n., pl.* **tour·neys;** 2 *v.,* **tour·neyed, tour·ney·ing.**

tour·ni·quet (túr′nə ket), device for stopping bleeding by compressing a

blood vessel, such as a bandage tightened by twisting with a stick, or a pad pressed down by a screw.

tou·sle (tou′zəl), put into disorder; make untidy; muss: *tousled hair.* *v.,* **tou·sled, tou·sling.**

tout (tout), INFORMAL. 1 try to get (customers, jobs, votes, etc.). 2 praise highly and insistently. 3 person who touts. 1,2 *v.,* 3 *n.*

tow[1] (tō), 1 pull by a rope, chain, etc.: *The tug is towing three barges.* 2 act of towing. 3 condition of being towed: *The launch had the sailboat in tow.* 4 that which is towed: *Each tug had a tow of three barges.* 5 the rope, chain, etc., used for towing. 1 *v.,* 2-5 *n.* [Old English *togian* to drag]

tow[2] (tō), the coarse, broken fibers of flax, hemp, etc., prepared for spinning. *n.* [Old English *tōw-* spinning, as in *tōwlīc* fit for spinning]

to·ward (tôrd *or* tə wôrd′), 1 in the direction of: *She walked toward the north.* 2 with respect to; regarding; about; concerning: *What is his attitude toward war?* 3 shortly before; near: *It must be toward four o'clock.* 4 as a help to; for: *Will you give something toward our new hospital? prep.*

to·wards (tôrdz *or* tə wôrdz′), toward. *prep.*

tow·boat (tō′bōt′), tugboat. *n.*

tow·el (tou′əl), piece of cloth or paper for wiping and drying something wet. We have hand towels, face towels, and bath towels. *n.*

tow·er (tou′ər), 1 a high structure, standing alone or forming part of a church, castle, or other building. Some towers are forts or prisons. 2 defense; protection. 3 rise high up: *The new skyscraper towers over the older buildings.* 1,2 *n.,* 3 *v.* —**tow′er like′,** *adj.*

tow·er·ing (tou′ər ing), 1 very high: *a towering mountain peak.* 2 very great: *Making electricity from atomic power is a towering achievement.* 3 very violent: *a towering rage. adj.*

Tower of London, an ancient palace-fortress of London. The present building dates back to William I. It has been used as a palace, prison, mint, and arsenal.

tow·head (tō′hed′), person having very light or pale-yellow hair. *n.*

tow·head·ed (tō′hed′id), having very light or pale-yellow hair. *adj.*

BLOOD VESSEL — ←TOURNIQUET

CUT —

tow hee (tou′hē *or* tō′hē), chewink or a bird like a chewink. *n.*

town (toun), **1** a large group of houses and buildings, smaller than a city but larger than a village: *Do you live in a town or in the country?* **2** any large place with many people living in it: *I hear that Boston is a fine town.* **3** the people of a town: *The whole town was having a holiday.* **4** the part of a town or city where the stores and office buildings are: *Let's go into town to see a show.* *n.*

town crier, (in former times) person who called out the news and made announcements in the streets of a city or town.

town hall, a building used for a town's business.

town meeting, **1** a general meeting of the inhabitants of a town. **2** (in New England) a meeting of the qualified voters of a town for the transaction of public business.

towns folk (tounz′fōk′), the people of a town. *n.pl.*

town ship (toun′ship), **1** part of a county in the United States and Canada having certain powers of government. **2** (in United States surveys of public land) a region or district six miles square, made up of 36 sections. *n.*

towns man (tounz′mən), **1** person who lives in a town. **2** person who lives in one's own town. *n., pl.* **towns men.**

towns peo ple (tounz′pē′pəl), the people of a town. *n.pl.*

tow path (tō′path′), path along the bank of a canal or river for use in towing boats. *n., pl.* **tow paths** (tō′paтнz′ *or* tō′paths′).

tox e mi a (tok sē′mē ə), blood poisoning caused by toxins. *n.*

tox ic (tok′sik), **1** of poison; caused by poison: *a toxic illness.* **2** poisonous: *toxic plants. adj.*

tox ic i ty (tok sis′ə tē), toxic or poisonous quality. *n.*

tox i col o gist (tok′sə kol′ə jist), an expert in toxicology. *n.*

tox i col o gy (tok′sə kol′ə jē), science that deals with poisons, their effects, antidotes, detection, etc. *n.*

tox in (tok′sən), any poison formed by an animal or plant organism as a product of its metabolism. Toxins formed by bacteria cause diseases such as diphtheria and scarlet fever. The body reacts to some toxins by producing antitoxins. *n.*

tox oid (tok′soid), toxin specially treated so that it will lose its poisonous quality but still cause antitoxins to be produced when injected into the body. *n.*

toy (toi), **1** something for a child to play with; plaything. **2** thing that has little value or importance. **3** of, made as, or like a toy. **4** small or miniature in size: *a toy poodle.* **5** amuse oneself; play; trifle: *She toyed with her string of beads.* **1,2** *n.,* **3,4** *adj.,* **5** *v.*

toy dog, a very small dog, especially one belonging to any of certain breeds. Some toy dogs are related to larger dogs, such as poodles or spaniels. Others belong to separate breeds, such as the Chihuahua.

trace[1] (trās), **1** a mark, sign, or evidence of the former existence, presence, or action of something: *Archaeologists found traces of an ancient city.* **2** footprint or other mark left; track; trail: *We saw traces of rabbits and squirrels on the snow.* **3** follow by means of marks, tracks, or signs: *trace deer.* **4** follow the course of: *We traced the river to its source. The Aldens trace their family back to John Alden, one of the Pilgrims.* **5** a very small amount; little bit: *There wasn't a trace of gray in her hair.* **6** mark out; draw: *She traced the plan of our new house.* **7** copy by following the lines of with a pencil or pen: *By putting thin paper over the map, he was able to trace it.* **1,2,5** *n.,* **3,4,6,7** *v.,* **traced, trac ing.** [from French of the 1200's *tracier,* from Latin *tractus* a drawing out, from *trahere* to drag]

trace[2] (trās), either of the two straps, ropes, or chains by which an animal pulls a wagon, carriage, etc. See **harness** for picture. *n.* [from French of the 1300's *traiz,* plural of *trait,* from Latin *tractus* a drawing out, from *trahere* to drag]

trace a ble (trā′sə bəl), that can be traced. *adj.*

trac er (trā′sər), **1** person or thing that traces. **2** inquiry sent from place to place to trace a missing person, letter, parcel, etc. **3** bullet with a substance in it that burns when the bullet is fired, leaving a trail that can be followed with the eye. **4** substance put in such a bullet to show its course. **5** a chemical element or atom of an element, usually radioactive, which can be traced and observed as it passes through a body, plant, or other system in order to study biological processes or chemical reactions within the system. *n.*

trac er y (trā′sər ē), ornamental work or designs consisting of lines. Stone-

tracery

hat, āge, fär; let, ēqual, tėrm; it, īce; hot, ōpen, ôrder; oil, out; cup, pùt, rüle; ch, child; ng, long; sh, she; th, thin; тн, then; zh, measure;

ə represents *a* in about, *e* in taken, *i* in pencil, *o* in lemon, *u* in circus.

work, carving, and embroidery often have tracery. *n., pl.* **trac er ies.**

tra che a (trā′kē ə), windpipe. *n., pl.* **tra che ae** (trā′kē ē′).

tra cho ma (trə kō′mə), a contagious inflammation of the eyelids. Trachoma is common in the Orient and sometimes causes blindness. *n.*

trac ing (trā′sing), copy of something made by marking or drawing over it. *n.*

track (trak), **1** line of metal rails for cars to run on. A railroad has tracks. **2** mark or pattern left: *The dirt road showed many automobile tracks.* **3** footprint: *We saw bear and deer tracks near the camp.* **4** follow by means of footprints, marks, smell, etc.: *We tracked the deer and photographed it.* **5** trace in any way: *I will track down her new address.* **6** make footprints or other marks on: *Don't track the floor.* **7** bring (snow or mud) into a place on one's feet: *He tracked mud into the house.* **8** path; trail; road: *A track runs through the woods to the farmhouse.* **9** a course for running or racing. **10** track and field. **11** one of the endless belts of linked steel plates on which a tank, bulldozer, etc., moves. **1-3,8-11** *n.,* **4-7** *v.* —**track′er,** *n.*

in one's tracks, INFORMAL. right where one is: *The squirrel froze in his tracks when he saw the boys.*

jump the track, leave the rails suddenly; derail without warning.

keep track of, keep within one's sight or attention: *The noise of the crowd made it difficult to keep track of what was going on.*

lose track of, fail to keep track of: *When on vacation, it is easy to lose track of what day it is.*

make tracks, INFORMAL. go very fast; run away: *We saw a bear and made tracks for home.*

off the track, off the subject; wrong. **on the track,** on the subject; right.

track and field, the sports or events of running, jumping, vaulting, throwing, etc., as a group. A track and field meet includes races around a track and the pole vault, shot-put, high jump, etc., on a field in the center of the track.

trackless

adj. adjective	*n.* noun
adv. adverb	*prep.* preposition
conj. conjunction	*pron.* pronoun
interj. interjection	*v.* verb
sing. singular	*pl.* plural

track less (trak′lis), 1 without a track. 2 without paths or trails: *The region near the South Pole is a trackless wilderness. adj.*

tract[1] (trakt), 1 stretch of land, water, etc.; extent; area: *A tract of desert land has little value to farmers.* 2 system of related parts or organs in the body. The stomach and intestines are part of the digestive tract. *n.* [from Latin *tractus* a drawing out, from *trahere* to drag]

tract[2] (trakt), 1 a little book or pamphlet on a religious or political subject. 2 any little book or pamphlet. *n.* [from Latin *tractatus* a handling, from *tractare* to handle]

trac ta ble (trak′tə bəl), 1 easily managed or controlled; easy to deal with; docile: *Dogs are more tractable than mules.* 2 easily handled or worked: *Tractable metals can be hammered and shaped or rolled out into thin sheets. adj.*

trac tion (trak′shən), 1 a drawing or pulling or a being drawn. 2 the drawing or pulling of loads along a road, track, etc. 3 kind of power used for this. Electric traction is used on subways and some railroads. 4 friction between a body and the surface on which it moves, enabling the body to move without slipping: *Wheels slip on ice because there is too little traction. n.*

trac tor (trak′tər), 1 a heavy, motor-driven vehicle which moves on wheels or on two endless tracks, used for pulling wagons, plows, etc. A tractor can do the work of many horses on a farm. 2 a powerful truck having a short body and a cab for the driver, used to pull a freight trailer along a highway. *n.*

tractor (def. 2)

trade (trād), 1 buying and selling; exchange of goods; commerce: *The United States has much trade with foreign countries.* 2 buy and sell; exchange goods; be in commerce: *Some American companies trade all over the world.* 3 an exchange: *an even trade.* 4 to exchange; make an exchange: *He traded* a stick of gum for a ride on her bicycle. *If you don't like your book, I'll trade with you.* 5 a bargain or deal: *I made a good trade.* 6 kind of work; business, especially one requiring skilled mechanical work: *He is learning the carpenter's trade.* 7 people in the same kind of work or business: *Carpenters, plumbers, and electricians are members of the building trade.* 8 INFORMAL. customers: *That store has a lot of trade.* 9 be a customer: *I have traded at the grocery store for years.* 10 **the trades,** the trade winds. 1,3,5-8,10 *n.,* 2,4,9 *v.,* **trad ed, trad ing.**

trade in, give (an automobile, refrigerator, etc.) as payment or part payment for something, especially for a newer model.

trade off, get rid of by trading.

trade on, take advantage of: *trade on one's wealth to gain political influence.*

trade-in (trād′in′), automobile, refrigerator, etc., given or accepted as payment or part payment for something, especially for a newer model. *n.*

trade mark (trād′märk′), 1 a mark, picture, name, word, symbol, or letters owned and used by a manufacturer or merchant to distinguish his goods from the goods of others. The registration and protection of trademarks are provided for by law. 2 register the trademark of. 1 *n.,* 2 *v.*

trade name, 1 name used by a manufacturer or merchant for some article that he sells. 2 a special name used for any thing by those who buy and sell it. 3 name under which a company does business.

trad er (trā′dər), 1 person who trades: *The trappers sold furs to traders.* 2 ship used in trading. *n.*

trade school, school where trades are taught.

trades man (trādz′mən), storekeeper; shopkeeper. *n., pl.* **trades men.**

trades peo ple (trādz′pē′pəl), storekeepers; shopkeepers. *n.pl.*

trade union, 1 association of workers in a trade or craft to protect and promote their interests. 2 any labor union.

trade wind, wind blowing steadily toward the equator from about 30 degrees north latitude and about 30 degrees south latitude. North of the equator, it blows from the northeast; south of the equator, from the southeast.

trading post, store or station of a trader, especially on the frontier or in unsettled country. Trading posts used to sell food, weapons, clothes, and other articles to Indians and trappers in exchange for hides and furs.

trading stamp, stamp (def. 2).

tra di tion (trə dish′ən), 1 the handing down of beliefs, opinions, customs, stories, etc., from parents to children. 2 what is handed down in this way: *According to the old tradition, Romulus was the founder of Rome. n.*

tra di tion al (trə dish′ə nəl), 1 of tradition. 2 handed down by tradition: *Tipping one's hat to a lady is a traditional custom.* 3 according to tradition: *traditional furniture.* 4 customary: *A Memorial Day parade is traditional in almost every town. adj.* —**tra di′tion al ly,** *adv.*

tra duce (trə düs′ *or* trə dyüs′), speak evil of (a person) falsely; slander. *v.,* **tra duced, tra duc ing.**

tra duc er (trə dü′sər *or* trə dyü′sər), person who traduces. *n.*

Tra fal gar (trə fal′gər), **Cape,** cape in SW Spain, on the Atlantic. In a naval battle near this cape in 1805, Napoleon's fleet was defeated by a British fleet under Nelson. *n.*

traf fic (traf′ik), 1 people, automobiles, wagons, ships, etc., coming and going along a way of travel: *Police control the traffic in large cities.* 2 buying and selling; commerce; trade. 3 carry on trade; buy; sell; exchange: *The men trafficked with the islanders for ivory.* 4 business done by a railroad line, steamship line, airline, etc.; number of passengers or amount of freight carried. 5 dealings; association: *Traffic with criminals is dangerous.* 6 have illicit dealings: *traffic in narcotics.* 1,2, 4,5 *n.,* 3,6 *v.,* **traf ficked, traf fick ing.**

traffic circle, junction of several roads at which the merging traffic goes around a central circle in one direction only; rotary.

traf fick er (traf′ə kər), person who buys and sells; trader. *n.*

traffic light, set of electric lights used for signaling at a corner or intersection to control traffic; stoplight. Usually a red light ("stop") and a green light ("go") are flashed automatically every so many seconds or minutes.

tra ge di an (trə jē′dē ən), 1 actor in tragedies. 2 writer of tragedies. *n.*

trag e dy (traj′ə dē), 1 a serious play having an unhappy ending. Shakespeare's *Hamlet* is a tragedy. 2 a very sad or terrible happening: *Her sudden death was a tragedy to her friends. n., pl.* **trag e dies.**

trag ic (traj′ik), 1 of tragedy; having to do with tragedy: *a tragic poet.* 2 very sad; dreadful: *a tragic event. adj.*

trag i cal (traj′ə kəl), tragic. *adj.*

trag i cal ly (traj′ik lē), in a tragic manner. *adv.*

trail (trāl), 1 path across a wild or unsettled region: *The hikers followed mountain trails for days.* 2 a track or smell: *The dogs found the trail of the rabbit.* 3 hunt by track or smell: *The dogs trailed the rabbit.* 4 anything that follows along behind: *The car left a trail of dust behind it.* 5 follow along behind; follow: *The dog trailed its master constantly.* 6 pull or be pulled along behind: *The bird trailed its broken wing. Her dress trails on the ground.* 7 grow along: *Poison ivy trailed by the road.* 8 go along slowly: *The children trailed to school.* 9 pass little by little: *Her voice trailed off into silence.* 1,2,4 *n.,* 3, 5-9 *v.*

trail blaz er (trāl′blā′zər), person or thing that pioneers or prepares the way to something new. *n.*

trail er (trā′lər), 1 person or animal that follows a trail. 2 vehicle, often large, designed to be pulled along the highway by a truck, etc., especially by a truck lacking a body of its own. See **tractor** for picture. 3 vehicle fitted up for people to live in and usually pulled by an automobile; house on wheels. *n.*

train (trān), 1 a connected line of railroad cars moving along together: *A very long freight train of 100 cars rolled by.* 2 line of people, animals, wagons, trucks, etc., moving along together: *The early settlers crossed the continent by wagon train.* 3 part that hangs down and drags along: *the train of a gown.* 4 group of followers: *the king and his train.* 5 series; succession: *A long train of misfortunes overcame them.* 6 order of succession; sequence: *Now where was I when you interrupted? I seem to have lost my train of thought.* 7 bring up; rear; teach: *They trained their child to be considerate of others.* 8 make skillful by teaching and practice: *train student nurses. Saint Bernard dogs were trained to hunt for travelers lost in the snow.* 9 make fit by exercise and diet: *Runners train for races.* 10 to point; aim: *train cannon upon a fort.* 11 bring into a particular position: *Train the vine around this post.* 12 line of gunpowder that acts as a fuse. 1-6,12 *n.,* 7-11 *v.*

train ee (trā nē′), person who is receiving training. *n.*

train er (trā′nər), person who trains: *He is an animal trainer for the circus. n.*

train ing (trā′ning), 1 practical education in some art, profession, etc.: *training for teachers.* 2 development of strength and endurance: *physical training.* 3 good condition maintained by exercise, diet, etc.: *The athlete kept in training by not overeating and not smoking. n.*

train load (trān′lōd′), as much as a train can hold or carry. *n.*

train man (trān′mən), brakeman or railroad worker in a train crew, of lower rank than a conductor. *n., pl.* **train-men.**

traipse (trāps), walk about aimlessly, carelessly, or needlessly: *The children went traipsing through the streets, looking for something exciting to do. v.,* **traipsed, traips ing.**

trait (trāt), quality of mind, character, etc.; distinguishing feature; characteristic: *Courage, love of fair play, and common sense are desirable traits. n.*

trai tor (trā′tər), 1 person who betrays his country or ruler: *Benedict Arnold became a traitor by helping the British during the Revolutionary War.* 2 person who betrays a trust, duty, friend, etc. *n.*

trai tor ous (trā′tər əs), like a traitor; treacherous; faithless. *adj.* —**trai′tor ous ly,** *adv.*

tra jec tor y (trə jek′tər ē), the curved path of a projectile, comet, or planet. *n., pl.* **tra jec tor ies.**

tram (tram), 1 streetcar (a term used in Great Britain). 2 truck or car on which loads are carried in mines. *n.*

tram mel (tram′əl), 1 Usually, **trammels,** *pl.* anything that hinders or restrains: *A large bequest freed the artist from the trammels of poverty.* 2 hinder; restrain. 3 a fine net to catch fish, birds, etc. 4 hook, bar, or chain in a fireplace to hold pots, kettles, etc., over the fire. 5 shackle for controlling the motions of a horse and making it amble. 1,3-5 *n.,* 2 *v.*

tramp (tramp), 1 walk heavily: *She tramped across the room in her heavy boots.* 2 step heavily (on): *He tramped on the flowers.* 3 sound of a heavy step: *We can hear the tramp of marching feet.* 4 go on foot; walk: *The hikers tramped through the mountains.* 5 a long, steady walk; hike: *The children went on a tramp through the woods.* 6 walk steadily; march: *The soldiers tramped mile after mile.* 7 person who travels from place to place on foot, living by doing odd jobs, begging, etc. 8 a freight ship that takes a cargo when and where it can. 1,2,4,6 *v.,* 3,5,7, 8 *n.*

tram ple (tram′pəl), 1 tread heavily on; crush: *The herd of wild cattle trampled the farmer's crops.* 2 treat cruelly, harshly, or scornfully: *The tyrant trampled his subjects and deprived them of all their rights.* 3 act or sound of trampling: *We heard the trample of many feet.* 1,2 *v.,* **tram pled, trampling;** 3 *n.*

trample on or **trample upon,** treat with scorn, harshness, or cruelty: *The dictator trampled on the rights of his people.*

tram po line (tram′pə lēn′), piece of canvas or other sturdy fabric stretched

hat, āge, fär; let, ēqual, tèrm; it, īce; hot, ōpen, ôrder; oil, out; cup, pùt, rüle; ch, child; ng, long; sh, she; th, thin; ₮H, then; zh, measure;

ə represents *a* in about, *e* in taken, *i* in pencil, *o* in lemon, *u* in circus.

on a metal frame, used for tumbling, acrobatics, etc., in gymnasiums and circuses. *n.*

tram way (tram′wā′), track for streetcars (a term used in Great Britain). *n.*

trance (trans), 1 state of unconsciousness somewhat like sleep. A person may fall into a trance from illness, from the influence of some other person, or from his own will. 2 a dreamy, absorbed condition that is like a trance: *The old man sat before the fire in a trance, thinking of his past life. n.* —**trance′like′,** *adj.*

tran quil (trang′kwəl), calm; peaceful; quiet: *the tranquil morning air. adj.* —**tran′quil ly,** *adv.*

tran quil ize (trang′kwə līz), 1 make calm, peaceful, or quiet. 2 become tranquil. *v.,* **tran quil ized, tran quil-iz ing.**

tran quil iz er (trang′kwə lī′zər), any of several drugs that relax muscles, reduce nervous tension, lower blood pressure, etc. *n.*

tran quil li ty or **tran quil i ty** (trang kwil′ə tē), tranquil condition; calmness; peacefulness; quiet. *n.*

trans-, *prefix.* 1 across; over; through; beyond: *Transcontinental = across the continent.* 2 to a different place, condition, etc.: *Transmigration = migration to another place.* [from Latin *trans* across]

trans act (tran zakt′), attend to; manage; do; carry on (business): *We transact business with stores all over the country. A lawyer will transact many affairs connected with the purchase of a home. v.*

trans ac tion (tran zak′shən), 1 the carrying on (of business): *He attends to the transaction of important matters*

trampoline

895

adj. adjective	*n.* noun
adv. adverb	*prep.* preposition
conj. conjunction	*pron.* pronoun
interj. interjection	*v.* verb
sing. singular	*pl.* plural

himself. **2** piece of business: *A record was kept of the firm's latest transaction with the bank.* **3 transactions,** *pl.* record of what was done at the meetings of a society, club, etc. *n.*

trans at lan tic (tran′sət lan′tik), **1** crossing the Atlantic: *a transatlantic liner, a transatlantic cable.* **2** on the other side of the Atlantic. *adj.*

tran scend (tran send′), **1** go beyond the limits or powers of; exceed; be above: *The grandeur of Niagara Falls transcends words.* **2** be higher or greater than; surpass; excel: *The speed of airplanes transcends that of any previous form of transportation.* *v.*

tran scend ence (tran sen′dəns), a being transcendent. *n.*

tran scend ent (tran sen′dənt), surpassing ordinary limits; excelling; superior; extraordinary. *adj.*

tran scen den tal (tran′sen den′tl), **1** transcendent. **2** supernatural. **3** explaining material things as products of the mind. *adj.*

trans con ti nen tal (tran′skon tə-nen′tl), **1** crossing a continent: *a transcontinental railroad.* **2** on the other side of a continent. *adj.*

tran scribe (tran skrīb′), **1** to copy in writing or in typewriting: *The account of the trial was transcribed from the stenographer's shorthand notes.* **2** make a recording or phonograph record for broadcasting. *v.,* **tran scribed, tran scrib ing.**

tran script (tran′skript), **1** a written or typewritten copy: *The club's secretary prepared several transcripts of the minutes of the meeting.* **2** copy or reproduction of anything: *The college wanted a transcript of the student's high-school record.* *n.*

tran scrip tion (tran skrip′shən), **1** a transcribing; copying. **2** a copy; transcript. **3** arrangement of music, etc., on a record for use in broadcasting. *n.*

trans duc er (trans dü′sər *or* trans-dyü′sər), any device which converts energy from one form to another. A microphone, which converts sound into electric energy, is a transducer. *n.*

tran sept (tran′sept), **1** the shorter part of a cross-shaped church. See **apse** for diagram. **2** either end of this part. *n.*

trans fer (tran sfėr′ *or* tran′sfėr′ for 1,2,5; tran′sfėr′ for 3,4,6,7), **1** convey or remove from one person or place to another; hand over: *The clerk was transferred to another department. Please have my trunks transferred to the Union Station.* **2** convey (a drawing, design, pattern) from one surface to another: *You transfer the embroidery design from the paper to cloth by pressing it with a warm iron.* **3** a transferring or a being transferred. **4** thing transferred; a drawing, pattern, etc., printed from one surface onto another. **5** change from one public vehicle, such as a bus, train, etc., to another. **6** ticket, given with or without an extra charge, allowing a passenger to continue his journey on another public vehicle. **7** point or place for transferring. 1,2,5 *v.,* **trans ferred, trans fer ring;** 3,4,6,7 *n.*

trans fer a ble (tran sfėr′ə bəl), that can be transferred. *adj.*

trans fer ence (tran sfėr′əns), a transferring or a being transferred. *n.*

trans fig u ra tion (tran sfig′yə rā′-shən), **1** a change in form or appearance; transformation. **2 Transfiguration, a** (in the Bible) the change in the appearance of Christ on the mountain. **b** the church festival on August 6 in honor of this. *n.*

trans fig ure (tran sfig′yər), **1** change in form or appearance; transform: *New paint and furnishings had transfigured the old house.* **2** change so as to glorify; exalt. *v.,* **trans fig ured, trans fig ur ing.**

trans fix (tran sfiks′), **1** pierce through: *The hunter transfixed the lion with a spear.* **2** make motionless (with amazement, terror, etc.). *v.*

trans form (tran sfôrm′), **1** change in form or appearance: *The blizzard transformed the bushes into mounds of white.* **2** change in condition, nature, or character: *The witch transformed men into pigs. A tadpole becomes transformed into a frog.* **3** change (one form of energy) into another. A dynamo transforms mechanical energy into electricity. **4** change (an electric current) to

a higher or lower voltage, from alternating to direct current, or from direct to alternating current. *v.*

trans for ma tion (tran′sfôr-mā′shən), a transforming or a being transformed: *the transformation of a caterpillar into a butterfly, the transformation of a brat into a sweet child.* *n.*

trans form er (tran sfôr′mər), **1** person or thing that transforms. **2** device for changing an alternating current into one of higher or lower voltage. *n.*

trans fuse (tran sfyüz′), **1** pour from one container into another. **2** transfer (blood) from one person or animal to another. **3** infuse; instill: *The speaker transfused her enthusiasm into the audience.* *v.,* **trans fused, trans fus ing.**

trans fu sion (tran sfyü′zhən), **1** a causing to pass from one container or holder to another. **2** transfer of blood from one person or animal to another: *The injured man had lost so much blood that he needed an immediate transfusion.* *n.*

trans gress (trans gres′), **1** break a law, command, etc.; sin. **2** go beyond (a limit): *Their manners transgress the bounds of good taste.* *v.*

trans gres sion (trans gresh′ən), a transgressing or a being transgressed: *the transgression of a law, to commit a grave transgression.* *n.*

trans gres sor (trans gres′ər), person who transgresses; sinner. *n.*

tran sient (tran′shənt), **1** passing soon; fleeting; not lasting: *Joy and sorrow are often transient.* **2** passing through and not staying long: *a transient guest in a hotel.* **3** visitor or boarder who stays for a short time. 1,2 *adj.,* 3 *n.* —**tran′sient ly,** *adv.*

tran sis tor (tran zis′tər), a small electronic device containing semiconductors such as germanium or silicon, which amplifies or controls the flow of electrons in an electric circuit. Transistors have replaced vacuum tubes in many radios, television sets, and electronic devices. *n.*

transistor radio, a usually small, battery-powered radio equipped with transistors.

tran sit (tran′sit *or* tran′zit), **1** a passing across or through. **2** a carrying or a being carried across or through: *The goods were damaged in transit.* **3** transportation by trains, buses, etc.: *All systems of transit are crowded during the rush hour.* **4** instrument used in surveying to measure angles. *n.*

transit (def. 4)

tran si tion (tran zish′ən), a change or passing from one condition, place, thing, activity, topic, etc., to another: *The time between two distinct periods of history, art, etc., is called a period of transition. The life of Lincoln illustrates* *a transition from poverty to power. Abrupt transitions in a book confuse the reader. n.*

tran si tion al (tran zish′ə nəl), of transition; of change from one more or less fixed condition to another. *adj.*

tran si tive (tran′sə tiv), taking a direct object. In "Bring me my coat" and "Raise the window," *bring* and *raise* are transitive verbs. *adj.* —**tran′si tive ly,** *adv.*

tran si to ry (tran′sə tôr′ē), passing soon or quickly; lasting only a short time: *We hope this hot weather will be transitory. adj.*

trans late (tran slāt′ *or* tran′slāt), 1 change from one language into another: *translate a book from French into English.* 2 express (one thing) in terms of another: *translate words into action.* 3 change from one place, position, or condition to another: *She was translated to the fairy palace by the story. v.,* **trans lat ed, trans lat ing.**

trans la tion (tran slā′shən), 1 a translating or a being translated: *the translation of the Bible from Hebrew into Latin, the translation of a promise into deed.* 2 result of translating; version. The Latin translation of the Bible is called the Vulgate. *n.*

trans la tor (tran slā′tər *or* tran′slā tər), person who translates. *n.*

trans lu cent (tran slü′snt), letting light through without being transparent: *Frosted glass is translucent. adj.* —**trans lu′cent ly,** *adv.*

trans mi gra tion (tran′smī grā′shən), 1 the passing of a soul at death into another body. Many people in India believe in the transmigration of souls. 2 the going from one place to another to settle there; migration. *n.*

trans mis sion (tran smish′ən), 1 a sending over; passing on; passing along; letting through: *Mosquitoes are the only means of transmission of malaria.* 2 the part of an automobile or other motor vehicle that transmits power from the engine to the rear axle or sometimes the front axle. 3 passage through space of electromagnetic waves from the transmitting station to the receiving station: *When transmission is good, even foreign radio stations can be heard.* 4 something transmitted. *n.*

trans mit (tran smit′), 1 send over; pass on; pass along; let through: *I will transmit the money by special messenger. Rats transmit disease.* 2 cause (light, heat, sound, etc.) to pass through a medium. 3 convey (force or movement) from one part of a body or mechanism to another. 4 send out (signals) by means of electromagnetic waves or by wire: *One or another broadcasting station is transmitting any hour of the*

day. 5 pass on through inheritance: *The physical characteristics of a person may be transmitted to his children. v.,* **trans mit ted, trans mit ting.**

trans mit ter (tran smit′ər), 1 person or thing that transmits something. 2 that part of a telegraph or telephone by which sound waves are converted to electrical impulses and sent to a receiver. 3 apparatus for sending out signals by means of electromagnetic waves. A transmitter used in broadcasting generates and modulates the radio waves and sends them to the antenna to be transmitted to a receiver. *n.*

trans mu ta tion (tran′smyə tā′shən), a change from one nature, substance, or form into another. *n.*

trans mute (tran smyüt′), change from one nature, substance, or form into another: *We can transmute water power into electrical power. v.,* **trans mut ed, trans mut ing.**

tran som (tran′səm), 1 window over a door or other window, usually hinged for opening. 2 a horizontal bar across a window; crossbar separating a door from the window over it. *n.*

tran son ic (tran son′ik), having to do with or moving at a speed immediately below or above the speed of sound, or between 600 and 900 miles per hour. *adj.* Also, **transsonic.**

trans pa cif ic (tran′spə sif′ik), 1 crossing the Pacific. 2 on the other side of the Pacific. *adj.*

trans par en cy (tran sper′ən sē *or* tran spar′ən sē), 1 transparent quality or condition. 2 something transparent. 3 picture, design, or the like, made visible by light shining through from behind. *n., pl.* **trans par en cies.**

trans par ent (tran sper′ənt *or* tran spar′ənt), 1 transmitting light so that bodies beyond or behind can be distinctly seen: *Window glass is transparent.* 2 easily seen through or detected: *a transparent excuse.* 3 frank; free from pretense or deceit: *a person of transparent honesty. adj.* —**trans par′ent ly,** *adv.*

tran spi ra tion (tran′spə rā′shən), a transpiring. *n.*

tran spire (tran spīr′), 1 take place; happen: *I heard later what transpired at the meeting.* 2 leak out; become known. 3 pass off or send off in the form of vapor through a wall or surface, as from the human body or from leaves. *v.,* **tran spired, tran spir ing.**

trans plant (tran splant′ *for* 1-3; tran′splant *for* 4,5), 1 plant again in a different place: *We grow the flowers indoors and then transplant them to the garden.* 2 remove from one place to another: *A group of farmers was transplanted to the island by the gov-*

hat, āge, fär; let, ēqual, tėrm; it, īce; hot, ōpen, ôrder; oil, out; cup, pùt, rüle; ch, child; ng, long; sh, she; th, thin; ₮H, then; zh, measure;

ə represents *a* in about, *e* in taken, *i* in pencil, *o* in lemon, *u* in circus.

ernment. 3 transfer (skin, an organ, etc.) from one person, animal, or part of the body to another: *transplant a kidney.* 4 the transfer of skin, an organ, etc., from one person, animal, or part of the body to another: *a heart transplant.* 5 something that has been transplanted. 1-3 *v.,* 4,5 *n.*

trans plan ta tion (tran′splan tā′shən), a transplanting or a being transplanted. *n.*

trans port (tran spôrt′ *for* 1,5,7; tran′spôrt *for* 2-4,6), 1 carry from one place to another: *Wheat is transported from the farms to the mills.* 2 a carrying from one place to another: *Trucks are much used for transport.* 3 ship used to carry men and supplies. 4 aircraft that transports passengers, mail, freight, etc. 5 carry away by strong feeling: *She was transported with joy by the good news.* 6 a strong feeling: *a transport of rage.* 7 send away to another country as a punishment: *Years ago, England transported many of her criminals to Australia.* 1,5,7 *v.,* 2-4,6 *n.*

trans por ta tion (tran′spər tā′shən), 1 a transporting: *The transportation for our trip was arranged by the travel bureau.* 2 a being transported. 3 the business of transporting people or goods: *Railroads, trucks, bus lines, and airlines are all engaged in transportation.* 4 Also, **Transportation.** department of the United States government in charge of transportation. It was established in 1966. 5 means of transport. 6 cost of transport; ticket for transport. 7 a sending away to another country as a punishment. *n.*

trans pose (tran spōz′), 1 change the position or order of; interchange: *Transpose the two colors to make a better design.* 2 change the usual order of (letters, words, or numbers): *I transposed the numbers and mistakenly wrote 19 for 91.* 3 (in music) change the key of. 4 transfer (a term) to the other side of an algebraic equation, changing plus to minus or minus to plus. *v.,* **trans posed, trans pos ing.**

trans po si tion (tran′spə zish′ən), 1 a transposing or a being transposed.

adj. adjective		*n.* noun	
adv. adverb		*prep.* preposition	
conj. conjunction		*pron.* pronoun	
interj. interjection		*v.* verb	
sing. singular		*pl.* plural	

2 piece of music transposed into a different key. *n.*

trans ship (tran ship′), transfer from one ship, train, car, etc., to another. *v.*, **trans shipped, trans ship ping.**

trans son ic (tran son′ik), transonic. *adj.*

tran sub stan ti a tion (tran′səb stan′shē ā′shən), **1** a changing of one substance into another. **2** in Christian theology: **a** the changing of the substance of the bread and wine of the Eucharist into the substance of the body and blood of Christ. **b** the doctrine that this change occurs, held by the Roman Catholic and Eastern churches. *n.*

Trans vaal (trans väl′), province of the Republic of South Africa, in the NE part. *n.*

trans ver sal (trans vėr′səl), **1** transverse. **2** line intersecting two or more other lines. **1** *adj.*, **2** *n.*

transversals (def. 2) AB and CD

trans verse (trans vėrs′), **1** lying across; placed crosswise; crossing from side to side: *transverse beams.* **2** something transverse. **1** *adj.*, **2** *n.*

trans verse ly (trans vėrs′lē), across; athwart; crosswise; from side to side. *adv.*

Tran syl van ia (tran′səl vā′nyə), region in central and W Romania, formerly part of Hungary. *n.*

trap (trap), **1** thing or means for catching animals. **2** trick or other means for catching someone off guard: *The lawyer set traps to make the witness contradict herself.* **3** catch in a trap: *The bear was trapped.* **4** set traps for animals. **5** trap door. **6** a bend in a drainpipe for holding a small amount of water to prevent the escape of air, sewer gas, etc. **7** a light, two-wheeled carriage. **8** device to throw clay pigeons, etc., into the air to be shot at. **9 traps,** *pl.* drums, cymbals, bells, gongs, etc., used especially in a small band or orchestra. **1,2,5-9** *n.*, **3,4** *v.*, **trapped, trap ping.**

trap door, door in a floor or roof.

tra peze (trə pēz′), a short horizontal bar hung by ropes like a swing, used in gymnasiums and circuses. *n.*

tra pe zi um (trə pē′zē əm), a four-sided plane figure having no sides parallel. *n., pl.* **tra pe zi ums, tra pe zi a** (trə pē′zē ə).

trap e zoid (trap′ə zoid), a four-sided plane figure having two sides parallel and two sides not parallel. *n.*

trap per (trap′ər), person who traps, especially one who traps wild animals for their furs. *n.*

trap pings (trap′ingz), **1** ornamental coverings for a horse. **2** things worn; ornaments: *trappings of a king and his court.* **3** outward appearances: *He had all the trappings of a cowboy, but he couldn't even ride a horse.* *n.pl.*

trap shoot er (trap′shü′tər), person who engages in trapshooting. *n.*

trap shoot ing (trap′shü′ting), sport of shooting at clay pigeons or other targets thrown or released from traps into the air. *n.*

trash (trash), **1** broken or torn bits, such as leaves, twigs, husks, etc.: *Rake up the trash in the yard and bag it.* **2** worthless stuff; rubbish: *That magazine is simply trash.* **3** disreputable people; riffraff. *n.*

trash y (trash′ē), like or containing trash; worthless. *adj.*, **trash i er, trash i est.**

trau ma (trô′mə *or* trou′mə), **1** a physical or psychic wound; injury. **2** the condition produced by it. *n.*

trau mat ic (trô mat′ik *or* trou-mat′ik), **1** of, having to do with, or produced by a wound, injury, or shock: *a traumatic experience.* **2** for or dealing with the treatment of wounds, injuries, or shock. *adj.*

tra vail (trə vāl′ *or* trav′āl), **1** toil; labor. **2** to toil; labor. **3** trouble; hardship: *It was a time of great travail.* **4** the pains of childbirth. **5** suffer the pains of childbirth. **1,3,4** *n.*, **2,5** *v.*

trav el (trav′əl), **1** go from one place to another; journey: *travel across the country. She is traveling to Europe this summer.* **2** a going in trains, ships, cars, etc., from one place to another; journeying: *She loves travel.* **3 travels,** *pl.* journeys: *"Gulliver's Travels."* **4** go from place to place selling things: *He travels for a large firm.* **5** move; proceed; pass: *Light and sound travel in waves.* **6** pass through or over: *travel a road.* **1,4-6** *v.*, **2,3** *n.*

trav eled or **trav elled** (trav′əld), **1** that has done much traveling: *Gulliver was a traveled man.* **2** much used by travelers: *a heavily traveled road. adj.*

trapezes

trapezium
trapezoids

trav el er or **trav el ler** (trav′ə lər), **1** person or thing that travels. **2** a traveling salesman. *n.*

trav e logue or **trav e log** (trav′ə-lôg), **1** lecture describing travel, usually accompanied by pictures or films. **2** motion picture depicting travel. *n.*

trav erse (trav′ərs *or* trə vėrs′ for 1; trav′ərs for 2,3), **1** pass across, over, or through: *We traversed the desert by truck.* **2** lying across; being across; transverse. **3** something put or lying across: *We walked over the traverse that lay across the gully.* **1** *v.*, **trav ersed, trav ers ing; 2** *adj.*, **3** *n.*

trav es ty (trav′ə stē), **1** an imitation of a serious literary work or subject, done in such a way as to make it seem ridiculous. **2** any treatment or imitation that makes a serious thing seem ridiculous: *The trial was a travesty of justice, since the judge and jury were prejudiced.* **3** make (a serious subject or matter) ridiculous; imitate in an absurd or grotesque way. **1,2** *n.*, *pl.* **trav es ties; 3** *v.*, **trav es tied, trav es ty ing.**

trawl (trôl), **1** a strong net dragged along the bottom of the sea. **2** to fish or catch fish with a net by dragging it along the bottom of the sea. **3** line supported by buoys and having many short lines with baited hooks attached to it. **4** to fish or catch fish with lines supported by buoys. **1,3** *n.*, **2,4** *v.*

trawl er (trô′lər), boat used in trawling. *n.*

tray (trā), **1** a flat, shallow holder or container with a low rim around it: *The waiter carries the dishes on a tray.* **2** tray with dishes of food on it: *a breakfast tray.* **3** a shallow box that fits into a trunk, cabinet, etc.: *Dentists keep many of their instruments in trays. n.*

treach er ous (trech′ər əs), **1** not to be trusted; not faithful; disloyal: *The treacherous soldier carried reports to the enemy.* **2** having a false appearance of strength, security, etc.; not reliable; deceiving: *This ice is treacherous. adj.* —**treach′er ous ly,** *adv.*

treach er y (trech′ər ē), **1** a breaking of faith; treacherous behavior; deceit. **2** treason. *n.*, *pl.* **treach er ies.**

trea cle (trē′kəl), molasses (a term used in Great Britain). *n.*

tread (tred), **1** set the foot down; walk;

step: *Don't tread on the flower beds. They trod through the meadow.* 2 set the feet on; walk on or through; step on: *tread the streets.* 3 press under the feet; trample on; crush: *tread grapes.* 4 make, form, or do by walking: *Cattle had trodden a path to the pond.* 5 act or sound of treading: *We heard the tread of marching feet.* 6 way of walking: *He walks with a heavy tread.* 7 the part of stairs or a ladder that a person steps on: *The stair treads were covered with rubber to prevent slipping.* 8 the part of a wheel or tire that presses against the ground, rail, etc. The treads of rubber tires are grooved to improve traction. 1-4 *v.,* **trod, trod den** or **trod, tread ing;** 5-8 *n.*

trea dle (tred′l), 1 lever or pedal worked by the foot to impart motion to a machine: *the treadle of a sewing machine.* 2 work a treadle. 1 *n.,* 2 *v.,* **trea dled, trea dling.**

treadmill (def. 1)

tread mill (tred′mil′), 1 apparatus for producing a turning motion by having a person or animal walk on the moving steps of a wheel or of a sloping, endless belt. 2 any wearisome or monotonous round of work or of life. *n.*

treas., 1 treasurer. 2 treasury.

trea son (trē′zn), betrayal of one's country or ruler. Helping the enemies of one's country is treason. *n.*

trea son a ble (trē′zn ə bəl), of treason; involving treason; traitorous. *adj.*

trea son ous (trē′zn əs), treasonable. *adj.*

treas ure (trezh′ər), 1 wealth or riches stored up; valuable things: *The pirates buried their treasure along the coast.* 2 any thing or person that is much loved or valued: *The silver teapot was the old couple's chief treasure.* 3 value highly: *She treasures her train more than all her other toys.* 4 put away for future use; store up. 1,2 *n.,* 3,4 *v.,* **treas ured, treas ur ing.**

treas ur er (trezh′ər ər), person in charge of money. The treasurer of a club pays its bills. *n.*

treas ur y (trezh′ər ē), 1 place where money is kept. 2 money owned; funds: *We voted to pay for the party out of the club treasury.* 3 Also, **Treasury.** department of the government that has charge of the income and expenses of a country. The Treasury of the United

States collects federal taxes, mints money, supervises national banks, enforces narcotics laws, and prevents counterfeiting. 4 place where treasure is kept. *n., pl.* **treas ur ies.**

treat (trēt), 1 act toward: *The driver treats his horses well.* 2 think of; consider; regard: *He treated his mistake as a joke.* 3 deal with to relieve or cure: *The dentist is treating my toothache.* 4 deal with to bring about some special result: *treat a metal plate with acid in engraving.* 5 deal with; discuss: *This magazine treats the progress of medicine.* 6 express in literature or art: *The author of these books always treats his themes realistically.* 7 discuss terms; arrange terms: *Messengers came to treat for peace.* 8 entertain with food, drink, or amusement: *treat some friends to ice cream.* 9 gift of food, drink, or amusement: *"This is my treat,"* she said. 10 anything that gives pleasure: *Being in the country is a treat to her.* 1-8 *v.,* 9,10 *n.*

treat of, deal with; discuss: *This issue of "The Medical Journal" treats of the progress of medicine.*

trea tise (trē′tis), a formal and systematic book or writing dealing with some subject. *n.*

treat ment (trēt′mənt), 1 act or process of treating: *My cold won't respond to treatment.* 2 way of treating: *This cat has suffered from bad treatment.* 3 thing done or used to treat something else, such as a disease. *n.*

trea ty (trē′tē), a formal agreement, especially one between nations, signed and approved by each nation: *The settlers broke many of the treaties the government made with the Indians.* *n., pl.* **trea ties.**

tre ble (treb′əl), 1 three times: *Her salary is treble mine.* 2 make or become three times as much: *He trebled his money by buying a dog for $25 and selling it for $75.* 3 the highest part in music; soprano. 4 voice, singer, or instrument that takes this part. 5 of or for the treble. 6 shrill; high-pitched. 7 a shrill, high-pitched voice or sound. 1,5,6 *adj.,* 2 *v.,* **tre bled, tre bling;** 3,4,7 *n.*

treble clef, symbol in music indicating that the pitch of the notes on a

trellis

staff is above middle C; G clef. See **clef** for diagram.

tre bly (treb′lē), three times. *adv.*

tree (trē), 1 a large perennial plant with a woody trunk and usually having branches and leaves at some distance from the ground. 2 any plant that resembles a tree in form or size. 3 piece or structure of wood for some special purpose: *a clothes tree.* 4 anything like a tree. A family tree is a diagram with branches showing how the members of a family are related. 5 chase up a tree: *The cat was treed by a dog.* 1-4 *n.,* 5 *v.,* **treed, tree ing.** —**tree′like′,** *adj.*

up a tree, INFORMAL. in a difficult position.

tree fern, fern that grows to the size of a tree and has a trunklike stem with fronds at the top.

tree frog, any of various small, tree-dwelling frogs with adhesive disks or suckers on their toes.

tree less (trē′lis), without trees: *a treeless plain. adj.*

tree toad, tree frog.

tree top (trē′top′), the top or uppermost part of a tree. *n.*

tre foil (trē′foil), 1 plant having three-fold leaves. Clover is a trefoil. 2 ornament like a threefold leaf. *n.*

trefoils
(def. 2)

trek (trek), 1 travel by ox wagon. 2 travel slowly by any means: *The pioneers trekked across the great western plains by covered wagon.* 3 a journey: *It was a long trek over the mountains.* 4 stage of a journey between one stopping place and the next. 1,2 *v.,* **trekked, trek king;** 3,4 *n.*

trel lis (trel′is), frame of light strips of wood or metal crossing one another with open spaces in between; lattice, especially one supporting growing vines. *n., pl.* **trel lis es.**

trel lis work (trel′is wėrk′), work made of crossed strips with open spaces in between; trellis or trellises. *n.*

adj.	adjective	*n.*	noun
adv.	adverb	*prep.*	preposition
conj.	conjunction	*pron.*	pronoun
interj.	interjection	*v.*	verb
sing.	singular	*pl.*	plural

trem a tode (trem′ə tōd), fluke³ (def. 2). *n.*

trem ble (trem′bəl), 1 shake because of fear, excitement, weakness, cold, etc.: *a voice trembling with fear. The patient's hands trembled from lack of strength.* 2 feel fear, anxiety, etc.: *We trembled for the safety of our lost dog.* 3 move gently: *The leaves trembled in the breeze.* 4 a trembling: *There was a tremble in her voice as she began to recite.* 1-3 *v.,* **trem bled, trem bling;** 4 *n.*

trem bly (trem′blē), trembling; tremulous. *adj.*

tre men dous (tri men′dəs), 1 very severe; dreadful; awful: *The army suffered a tremendous defeat.* 2 INFORMAL. very great; enormous: *That is a tremendous house for a family of three.* 3 INFORMAL. extraordinary: *We had a tremendous time at the party. adj.* —**tre men′dous ly,** *adv.*

trem o lo (trem′ə lō), 1 a rapid repetition of musical tones or a rapid alternation of tones, causing a trembling or vibrating effect. 2 device in an organ used to produce this effect. *n., pl.* **trem o los.** [from Italian]

trem or (trem′ər), 1 an involuntary shaking or trembling: *a nervous tremor in the voice.* 2 thrill of emotion or excitement. 3 a shaking or vibrating movement. An earthquake is sometimes called an earth tremor. *n.*

trem u lous (trem′yə ləs), 1 trembling; quivering: *The child's voice was tremulous with sobs.* 2 timid; fearful: *He was shy and tremulous in the presence of strangers. adj.* —**trem′u lous ly,** *adv.* —**trem′u lous ness,** *n.*

trestle (def. 2)

trench (trench), 1 a long, narrow ditch with earth thrown up in front to protect soldiers. 2 a deep furrow; ditch: *to dig a trench for a sewer pipe.* 3 dig a trench in. 1,2 *n., pl.* **trench es;** 3 *v.*

trench an cy (tren′chən sē), trenchant quality; sharpness. *n.*

trench ant (tren′chənt), 1 sharp; keen; cutting: *trenchant wit.* 2 vigorous; effective: *a trenchant policy. adj.* —**trench′ant ly,** *adv.*

trench coat, kind of belted raincoat with straps on the shoulders and cuffs.

trench er (tren′chər), a wooden platter on which meat was formerly served and carved. *n.*

trench er man (tren′chər mən), 1 person who has a hearty appetite; eater. 2 hanger-on; parasite. *n., pl.* **trench er men.**

trend (trend), 1 the general direction; course; tendency: *The hills have a western trend. The trend of modern living is away from many old customs.* 2 have a general direction; tend; run: *The road trends to the north.* 1 *n.,* 2 *v.*

triangles (def. 1)
A, equilateral; B, isosceles;
C, scalene; D, right; E, obtuse

Tren ton (tren′tən), capital of New Jersey, in the W part. *n.*

trep i da tion (trep′ə dā′shən), 1 nervous dread; fear; fright. 2 a trembling. *n.*

tres pass (tres′pəs), 1 go on somebody's property without any right: *The farmer put up "No Trespassing" signs to keep people off the farm.* 2 go beyond the limits of what is right, proper, or polite: *I won't trespass on your time any longer.* 3 act or fact of trespassing. 4 do wrong; sin. 5 a wrong; a sin: *"Forgive us our trespasses as we forgive those who trespass against us."* 6 an unlawful act done by force against the person, property, or rights of another. 1,2,4 *v.,* 3,5,6 *n., pl.* **tres pass es.** —**tres′pass er,** *n.*

tress (tres), 1 a lock, curl, or braid of hair. 2 **tresses,** *pl.* long, flowing hair: *golden tresses. n.*

tres tle (tres′əl), 1 framework similar to a sawhorse, used as a support for a table top, platform, etc. 2 a braced framework of timber, steel, etc., used as a bridge to support a road, railroad tracks, etc. *n.*

tres tle work (tres′əl wėrk′), 1 structure consisting of a trestle or trestles. 2 support, bridge, or the like, made of such structures. *n.*

tri-, *prefix.* 1 having three _____:

Triangle = (a figure) having three angles. 2 three _____s: *Trisect = divide into three parts.* 3 once every three _____: *Trimonthly = once every three months.* [from Latin or Greek *tri-,* from *tria* three]

tri ad (trī′ad), group of three, especially of three closely related persons or things. *n.*

tri al (trī′əl), 1 the examining and deciding of a case in court: *The suspect was caught and brought to trial.* 2 process of trying or testing the fitness, truth, strength, or other quality of anything: *The mechanic gave the motor another trial to see if it would start.* 3 for a try or test: *a trial trip, a trial model.* 4 condition of being tried or tested: *The new clerk is employed on trial.* 5 trouble; hardship: *The lives of the pioneers had many trials.* 6 cause of trouble or hardship: *be a trial to one's parents.* 7 an attempt to do something; effort. 1,2,4-7 *n.,* 3 *adj.*

trial and error, method of arriving at a desired result by repeated experiments until past errors are eliminated.

tri an gle (trī′ang′gəl), 1 a plane figure having three sides and three angles. 2 something shaped like a triangle. 3 a musical instrument consisting of a triangle of steel, open at one corner, that is struck with a steel rod. *n.*

triangle (def. 3)

tri an gu lar (trī ang′gyə lər), shaped like a triangle; three-cornered. *adj.*

trib al (trī′bəl), of a tribe: *tribal customs. adj.*

tribe (trīb), 1 group of people united by race and customs under the same leaders: *America was once the home of many Indian tribes.* 2 class or set of people: *the whole tribe of gossips.* 3 class, kind, or sort of animals, plants, or other things: *The feathered tribe is a name for birds. n.*

trestle
(def. 1)

tribes man (trībz/mən), member of a tribe. *n., pl.* **tribes men.**

trib u la tion (trib/yə lā/shən), great trouble; severe trial; affliction: *The castaways on the desert island suffered many tribulations. n.*

tri bu nal (tri byü/nl *or* trī byü/nl), 1 court of justice; place of judgment: *They were brought before the tribunal of seven judges for trial.* 2 place where judges sit in a court of law. 3 something by or in which judgment is given; deciding authority: *the tribunal of the polls, the tribunal of the press. n.*

trib une[1] (trib/yün), 1 official in ancient Rome chosen by the plebeians to protect their rights and interests. 2 defender of the people. *n.* [from Latin *tribunus,* from *tribus* tribe]

trib une[2] (trib/yün), a raised platform. *n.* [from Italian *tribuna* tribunal, from Latin *tribunus* tribune[1]]

trib u tar y (trib/yə ter/ē), 1 stream that flows into a larger stream or body of water: *The Ohio River is one of the tributaries of the Mississippi River.* 2 flowing into a larger stream or body of water. 3 paying tribute; required to pay tribute. 4 a person or country that pays tribute. 1,4 *n., pl.* **trib u tar ies;** 2,3 *adj.*

trib ute (trib/yüt), 1 money paid by one nation to another for peace or protection or because of some agreement. 2 any forced payment: *The pirates demanded tribute from passing ships.* 3 an acknowledgment of thanks or respect; compliment: *Labor Day is a tribute to workers. n.*

trice[1] (trīs), haul up and fasten with a rope: *trice up a sail. v.,* **triced, tricing.** [from Dutch of the 1400's *trisen* hoist, from *trise* pulley]

trice[2] (trīs), a very short time; moment; instant: *I'll open the gate in a trice. n.* [use of *trice*[1], from the phrase *at a trice* at a pull]

tri ceps (trī/seps), the large muscle at the back of the upper arm. It extends or straightens the arm. See **biceps** for diagram. *n., pl.* **tri ceps** *or* **tri cepses.**

tri chi na (tri kī/nə), a small, slender worm whose adult form lives in the intestines and whose larva lives in the muscles of human beings, pigs, and some other animals. Trichinae usually get into the human body from pork which is infected with the larvae and is not cooked long enough to destroy them. *n., pl.* **tri chi nae** (tri kī/nē).

trich i no sis (trik/ə nō/sis), disease due to the presence of trichinae in the intestines and muscular tissues. *n.*

trick (trik), 1 something done to deceive or cheat: *The false message was a trick to get her to leave.* 2 deceive;

cheat: *We were tricked into buying a stolen sailboat.* 3 feat of skill, as in juggling or sleight of hand; clever act: *We enjoyed the tricks of the trained animals.* 4 the best way of doing or dealing with something: *Mother certainly knows the trick of good driving.* 5 piece of mischief; prank: *Stealing his lunch was a mean trick.* 6 play tricks. 7 of, like, or done as a trick or stunt: *trick riding, trick shooting.* 8 a peculiar habit or way of acting: *He has a trick of pulling at his collar.* 9 the cards played in one round of a card game. 10 a turn or period of duty on a job, especially at steering a ship. 11 to dress: *The guests at the party were all tricked up in fancy clothes.* 1,3-5,8-10 *n.,* 2,6,11 *v.,* 7 *adj.*

do the trick *or* **turn the trick,** do what one wants done.

trick er y (trik/ər ē), use of tricks; deception; cheating. *n., pl.* **trick er ies.**

trick i ness (trik/ē nis), the quality of being tricky. *n.*

trick le (trik/əl), 1 flow or fall in drops or in a small stream: *Tears trickled down their cheeks. The brook trickled through the valley.* 2 cause to flow in drops or in a small stream: *He trickled the water into the container.* 3 a small flow or stream. 4 come, go, pass, etc., slowly and unevenly: *An hour before the show people began to trickle into the theater.* 1,2,4 *v.,* **trick led, trick ling;** 3 *n.*

trick ster (trik/stər), a cheat; deceiver. *n.*

trick y (trik/ē), 1 full of tricks; deceiving: *A fox is trickier than a sheep.* 2 not doing what is expected; dangerous or difficult to handle: *The back door has a tricky lock. adj.,* **trick i er, trick i est.**

tri col or (trī/kul/ər), 1 having three colors. 2 flag having three colors. The tricolor of France has three equal vertical sections of blue, white, and red. The tricolor of Italy is green, white, and red. 1 *adj.,* 2 *n.*

tri col ored (trī/kul/ərd), having three colors: *a tricolored flag. adj.*

tri cot (trē/kō), 1 a knitted fabric made by hand or machine. 2 a kind of woolen cloth. *n.*

tri cy cle (trī/sə kəl *or* trī/sik/əl), vehicle having three wheels, worked by pedals or handles. Children often ride tricycles before they are old enough for bicycles. *n.*

tri dent (trīd/nt), 1 a three-pronged spear, especially the spear carried by Neptune, or Poseidon, god of the sea. 2 three-pronged. 1 *n.,* 2 *adj.*

tried (trīd), 1 tested by experience or examination; proven: *a person of tried abilities.* 2 past tense and past par-

hat, āge, fär; let, ēqual, tėrm;
it, īce; hot, ōpen, ôrder;
oil, out; cup, pùt, rüle; ch, child;
ng, long; sh, she; th, thin;
ŦH, then; zh, measure;

ə represents *a* in about,
e in taken, *i* in pencil,
o in lemon, *u* in circus.

ticiple of **try.** *I tried to call you. Have you tried calling again?* 1 *adj.,* 2 *v.*

tri en ni al (trī en/ē əl), 1 lasting three years. 2 occurring every three years. 3 event that occurs every three years. 1,2 *adj.,* 3 *n.*

tri en ni al ly (trī en/ē ə lē), once every three years. *adv.*

tri er (trī/ər), person or thing that tries. *n.*

tries (trīz), 1 plural of **try.** 2 the present tense of **try.** *She always tries to do her best.* 1 *n.,* 2 *v.*

Tri este (trē est/), seaport in NE Italy. It was under administration of the United Nations from 1947 to 1954. *n.*

tri fle (trī/fəl), 1 thing having little value or importance. 2 a small amount; little bit: *He was a trifle late.* 3 a small amount of money: *The picture cost only a trifle.* 4 talk or act lightly, not seriously: *Don't trifle with serious matters.* 5 handle a thing idly; play or toy (with): *She trifled with her pencil and pen.* 6 spend (time, effort, money, etc.) on things having little value: *They trifled away the whole morning.* 1-3 *n.,* 4-6 *v.,* **tri fled, tri fling.**

tri fler (trī/flər), person who trifles; frivolous, shallow person. *n.*

tri fling (trī/fling), 1 having little value; not important; small: *The friends treated their quarrel as only a trifling matter.* 2 frivolous; shallow. *adj.*

trig ger (trig/ər), 1 the small lever pulled back by the finger in firing a gun. 2 lever pulled or pressed to release a spring or catch and set some mechanism in action. 3 set off (an explosion): *A spark triggered the explosion.* 4 initiate; start: *trigger an outburst of violence.* 5 anything that sets off or initiates something else. 1,2,5 *n.,* 3,4 *v.*

trig o no met ric (trig/ə nə met/rik), of or having to do with trigonometry. *adj.*

trig o nom e try (trig/ə nom/ə trē), branch of mathematics that deals with the relations between the sides and angles of triangles and the calculations based on these. *n.*

trill (tril), 1 sing, play, sound, or speak with a tremulous, vibrating sound:

adj.	adjective	*n.*	noun
adv.	adverb	*prep.*	preposition
conj.	conjunction	*pron.*	pronoun
interj.	interjection	*v.*	verb
sing.	singular	*pl.*	plural

Some birds trill their songs. 2 act or sound of trilling. 3 a quick alternation of two musical notes either a tone or a half tone apart. 4 in phonetics: **a** a rapid vibration of the lips, the tip of the tongue, or the uvula. **b** sound produced by such a vibration. 1 *v.*, 2-4 *n.*

tril lion (tril′yən), 1 (in the United States and France) 1 followed by 12 zeros; one thousand billions. 2 (in Great Britain) 1 followed by 18 zeros; one million billions. *n., adj.*

tril li um (tril′ē əm), plant with three leaves in a whorl from the center of which rises a single flower. *n.*

tri lo bite (trī′lə bīt), a small marine arthropod of the Paleozoic era, with a body divided into three vertical lobes and many horizontal segments. Fossil trilobites are widely found in various rocks. *n.*

tril o gy (tril′ə jē), group of three plays, operas, novels, etc., which together form a related series, although each is a complete work in itself. *n., pl.* **tril o gies.**

trim (trim), 1 put in good order; make neat by cutting away parts: *The gardener trimmed the hedge. Would you trim my hair?* 2 remove (parts that are not needed or not neat): *trim dead leaves off plants.* 3 neat; in good condition or order: *a trim room, a trim uniform, a trim athlete.* 4 well designed and maintained: *We saw a trim little sailboat out on the lake.* 5 good condition or order: *get in trim for a race.* 6 condition; order: *That ship is in poor trim for a voyage.* 7 trimming: *the trim on a dress.* 8 decorate: *The children trimmed the Christmas tree.* 9 balance (a boat, aircraft, etc.) by arranging the load carried. 10 such balance. 11 arrange (the sails) to fit wind and direction. 12 change (opinions, etc.) to suit circumstances. 13 the visible woodwork inside a building, especially that around doors, windows, and other openings. 14 INFORMAL. defeat; beat. 1,2,8,9,11,12,14 *v.*, **trimmed, trimming;** 3,4 *adj.*, **trim mer, trim mest;** 5-7,10,13 *n.* —**trim′ly.** —**trim′ness,** *n.*

trim mer (trim′ər), 1 person or thing that trims. 2 person who changes his

opinions, actions, etc., to suit the circumstances. *n.*

trim ming (trim′ing), 1 anything used to trim or decorate; decoration; ornament: *trimmings for a birthday party, trimming for a shirt.* 2 INFORMAL. a defeat; beating. 3 act of a person or thing that trims. 4 **trimmings,** *pl.* **a** parts cut away in trimming. **b** INFORMAL. everything needed to make something complete and festive: *turkey with all the trimmings.* *n.*

tri month ly (trī munth′lē), occurring every three months. *adj.*

Trin i dad (trin′ə dad), island in the West Indies, near Venezuela, part of the country of Trinidad and Tobago. *n.*

Trinidad and Tobago, country composed of two islands in the West Indies, a member of the Commonwealth of Nations. *Capital:* Port-of-Spain.

tri ni tro tol u ene (trī nī′trō tol′yü ēn′), TNT. *n.*

trin i ty (trin′ə tē), 1 group of three. 2 a being three. 3 **Trinity,** the union of Father, Son, and Holy Ghost in one divine nature. *n., pl.* **trin i ties.**

trin ket (tring′kit), 1 any small fancy article, bit of jewelry, or the like: *The baby played with the trinkets on the bracelet.* 2 a trifle. *n.*

tri o (trē′ō), 1 piece of music for three voices or instruments. 2 group of three singers or players performing together. 3 any group of three. *n., pl.* **tri os.**

trip (trip), 1 a traveling about; journey; voyage: *We took a trip to Europe.* 2 stumble: *He tripped on the stairs.* 3 a loss of footing; stumble; slip. 4 cause to stumble and fall: *The loose board on the stairs tripped her.* 5 act of catching a person's foot to throw him down. 6 make a mistake; do something wrong: *She tripped on that difficult question.* 7 a mistake; blunder. 8 cause to make a mistake or blunder: *The difficult question tripped him.* 9 take light, quick steps: *The children came tripping down the path to meet us.* 10 a light, quick tread; stepping lightly. 11 release or operate suddenly (a catch, clutch, etc.); operate, start, or set free (a mechanism, weight, etc.). 12 a projecting part, catch, or the like for starting or checking some movement. 1,3,5,7,10,12 *n.*, 2,4,6,8,9,11 *v.*, **tripped, trip ping.**

tri par tite (trī pär′tīt), 1 divided into three parts. 2 having three corresponding parts or copies. 3 made or shared by three parties: *a tripartite treaty between Great Britain, the United States, and France. adj.*

tripe (trīp), 1 the walls of the first and second stomachs of an ox, steer, or cow, used as food. 2 SLANG. something foolish, worthless, or offensive. *n.*

trip ham mer (trip′ham′ər), a heavy iron or steel block raised by machinery and then tripped by a mechanism and allowed to drop. *n.*

tri ple (trip′əl), 1 three times as much or as many: *a triple portion of cake, to get triple pay.* 2 number or amount that is three times as large: *Nine is the triple of three.* 3 having three parts: *a triple crown.* 4 make or become three times as much or as many: *My older brother has tripled the number of lawns he mows each week. Her savings have tripled in the past twenty years.* 5 hit by which a batter gets to third base in baseball. 6 make such a hit: *The batter tripled in the third inning.* 1,3 *adj.*, 2,5 *n.*, 4,6 *v.*, **tri pled, tri pling.**

trip let (trip′lit), 1 one of three children born at the same time from the same mother. 2 group of three. 3 (in music) group of three notes of equal value to be performed in the time of two. 4 three successive lines of poetry, usually rhyming and equal in length. *n.*

trip li cate (trip′lə kit *for 1,2;* trip′lə kāt *for 3*), 1 triple; threefold. 2 one of three things exactly alike. 3 make threefold; triple. 1 *adj.,* 2 *n.,* 3 *v.,* **trip li cat ed, trip li cat ing.**

in triplicate, in three copies exactly alike.

tri ply (trip′lē), in a triple manner; three times. *adv.*

tri pod (trī′pod), 1 a three-legged support or stand for a camera, telescope, etc. 2 stool or other article having three legs. *n.*

Trip o li (trip′ə lē), 1 region in N Africa. It was a Turkish province and later an Italian colony: it is now included in Libya. 2 seaport and one of the two capitals of Libya, in the NW part. The other is Benghazi. *n.*

trip ping (trip′ing), light and quick. *adj.* —**trip′ping ly,** *adv.*

trip tych (trip′tik), 1 set of three panels side by side, having pictures, carvings, or the like, on them. 2 a hinged, three-leaved writing tablet. *n.*

tri reme (trī′rēm′), (in ancient Greece and Rome) a ship, usually a warship, with three rows of oars, one above the other, on each side. *n.*

tri sect (trī sekt′), 1 divide into three parts. 2 divide into three equal parts. *v.*

trite (trīt), worn out by use; no longer interesting; commonplace: *"Cheeks like roses" is a trite expression. adj.,* **trit er, trit est.** —**trite′ly,** *adv.* —**trite′ness,** *n.*

Tri ton (trīt′n), (in Greek myths) a sea god having the head and body of a man and the tail of a fish. *n.*

tri umph (trī′umf), 1 victory; success: *final triumph over the enemy. The conquest of outer space is one of the great* triumphs of *modern science.* **2** gain victory; win success: *Our team triumphed over theirs.* **3** joy because of victory or success: *We welcomed the team home with cheers of triumph.* **4** rejoice because of victory or success. **5** a Roman procession in honor of a victorious general. 1,3,5 *n.,* 2,4 *v.*

tri um phal (trī um′fəl), of or for a triumph; celebrating a victory: *a triumphal march. adj.*

tri um phant (trī um′fənt), **1** victorious or successful: *a triumphant army.* **2** rejoicing because of victory or success: *The winners spoke in triumphant tones about their skillful play. adj.* —**tri um′phant ly,** *adv.*

tri um vir (trī um′vər), one of three men who shared the same public office in ancient Rome. *n., pl.* **tri um virs, tri um vi ri** (trī um′və rī′).

tri um vir ate (trī um′vər it), **1** government by three persons together. **2** any association of three in office or authority. **3** any group of three. *n.*

triv et (triv′it), a stand or support with three legs or feet. Trivets are used over fires and under platters. *n.*

triv i a (triv′ē ə), things of little or no importance; trifles; trivialities. *n.pl.*

triv i al (triv′ē əl), **1** not important; trifling; insignificant: *Your composition had only a few trivial mistakes.* **2** OLD USE. not new or interesting; ordinary. *adj.* —**triv′i al ly,** *adv.*

triv i al i ty (triv′ē al′ə tē), **1** trivial quality. **2** a trivial thing, remark, affair, etc.; trifle. *n., pl.* **triv i al i ties.**

trod (trod), past tense and a past participle of **tread.** *The path was trod by many feet. v.*

trod den (trod′n), a past participle of **tread.** *The cattle had trodden down the corn. v.*

Troi lus (troi′ləs *or* trō′i ləs), (in Greek legends) a son of King Priam of Troy. He was killed by Achilles. *n.*

Tro jan (trō′jən), **1** of or having to do with Troy or its people. **2** person who was born or lived in Troy. **3** person who shows courage or energy: *They all worked like Trojans.* 1 *adj.,* 2,3 *n.*

Trojan horse, 1 (in Greek legends) a huge wooden horse in which the Greeks concealed soldiers and brought them into Troy during the Trojan War. **2** an enemy group stationed inside a country to sabotage its industry and defense preparations.

Trojan War, (in Greek legends) a ten years' war carried on by the Greeks against Troy to get back Helen, wife of King Menelaus of Sparta, who was carried off by Paris, son of King Priam of Troy.

troll[1] (trōl), **1** sing in a full, rolling voice. **2** sing in succession. When three

people troll a round or catch, the soprano sings one line, the alto comes in next with the same line, and then the bass sings it, and so on, while the others keep on singing. **3** song whose parts are sung in succession; round: *"Three Blind Mice" is a well-known troll.* **4** to fish with a moving line, usually by trailing the line behind the boat near the surface: *I trolled for bass.* **5** a fishing lure or bait, especially one used for trolling. 1,2,4 *v.,* 3,5 *n.* [probably from French of the 1300's *troller* wander]

troll[2] (trōl), (in Scandinavian folklore) an ugly dwarf or giant living underground or in caves. *n.* [from a Scandinavian word, such as Swedish *troll*]

TROLLEY

trolley (def. 1)

trol ley (trol′ē), **1** pulley at the end of a pole which moves against a wire to carry electricity to a streetcar, trolley bus, electric engine, etc. **2** trolley car. **3** basket, carriage, etc., suspended from a pulley which runs on an overhead track. *n., pl.* **trol leys.**

trolley bus, a passenger bus drawing power from an overhead electric wire by means of a trolley.

trolley car, streetcar drawing power from an overhead electric wire by means of a trolley.

trom bone (trom′bōn), a large brass wind instrument with a loud tone, having a long, sliding piece for varying the length of the tube. *n.*

trombone

trom bon ist (trom′bō nist), person who plays the trombone. *n.*

troop (trüp), **1** group or band of persons: *a troop of boys.* **2** a herd, flock, or swarm: *a troop of deer.* **3** a military unit of cavalry, especially an armored cavalry unit, usually commanded by a captain. A troop corresponds to a company or battery in other branches of the army. **4 troops,** *pl.* soldiers: *The government sent troops to put down the revolt.* **5** unit of boy scouts or girl scouts made up of two to four patrols or 16 to 32 members. **6** gather in troops or bands; move together: *The children*

hat, āge, fär; let, ēqual, tèrm; it, īce; hot, ōpen, ôrder; oil, out; cup, pùt, rüle; ch, child; ng, long; sh, she; th, thin; ᵵʜ, then; zh, measure;

ə represents *a* in about, *e* in taken, *i* in pencil, *o* in lemon, *u* in circus.

trooped around the teacher. **7** walk; go; go away: *The younger girls trooped off after the older ones.* 1-5 *n.,* 6,7 *v.*

troop er (trü′pər), **1** soldier in a troop of cavalry. **2** a mounted policeman. The state police of some states are called troopers, because they were originally organized as mounted troops. **3** a cavalry horse. *n.*

troop ship (trüp′ship′), ship used to carry soldiers; transport. *n.*

trope (trōp), **1** the use of a word or phrase in a sense different from its ordinary meaning. **2** word or phrase so used. EXAMPLE:

"All in a hot and *copper* sky, The *bloody* sun at noon." *n.*

tro phy (trō′fē), **1** a spoil or prize of war, hunting, etc., especially if displayed as a memorial: *The hunter kept the lion's skin and head as trophies.* **2** any prize, cup, etc., awarded to a victorious person or team: *The champion kept her tennis trophy on the mantelpiece.* **3** (in ancient Greece and Rome) a structure consisting of the captured arms, flags, etc., of a defeated enemy, set up on the field of battle or elsewhere as a memorial of victory. **4** any similar monument or memorial. **5** anything serving as a remembrance. *n., pl.* **tro phies.**

trop ic (trop′ik), **1** either of two imaginary circles around the earth which represent the points farthest north and south at which the sun shines directly overhead. The **tropic of Cancer** is 23.45 degrees north of the equator; the **tropic of Capricorn** is 23.45 degrees south of the equator. **2 tropics** or **Tropics,** *pl.* the regions between these circles; the zone between latitudes 23.45 degrees north and south or between 30 degrees north and south; the Torrid Zone. The hottest part of the earth is in the tropics. **3** of the tropics; belonging to the Torrid Zone. 1,2 *n.,* 3 *adj.*

trop i cal (trop′ə kəl), of the tropics; having to do with the tropics: *Bananas are tropical fruit. adj.* —**trop′i cal ly,** *adv.*

tropical fish, any of certain small,

adj.	adjective	*n.*	noun
adv.	adverb	*prep.*	preposition
conj.	conjunction	*pron.*	pronoun
interj.	interjection	*v.*	verb
sing.	singular	*pl.*	plural

usually brightly colored fishes native to the tropics, commonly kept in home aquariums.

tro pism (trō′piz′əm), tendency of an animal or plant to turn or move in response to a stimulus. *n.*

trop o sphere (trop′ə sfir), region of the atmosphere between the earth and the stratosphere, extending to about 10 miles above the earth's surface. Within the troposphere, there is a steady fall of temperature with increasing altitude. Most cloud formations occur in the troposphere. *n.*

trot (trot), 1 go at a gait between a walk and a run by lifting the right forefoot and the left hind foot at about the same time and then the other two feet in the same way. Horses and some other four-legged animals trot. 2 the motion or gait of trotting. 3 ride or drive at a trot: *The rider trotted her horse down the road.* 4 run, but not fast: *The child trotted along after his father.* 5 a brisk, steady movement; a slow running. 1,3,4 *v.,* **trot ted, trot ting;** 2,5 *n.*

troth (trôth), 1 faithfulness or fidelity; loyalty. 2 to promise. 3 a promise. 4 truth. 5 betrothal. 1,3-5 *n., pl.* **troths** (trôths *or* trôᴛʜz); 2 *v.*

plight one's troth, 1 promise to marry. 2 promise to be faithful.

Trot sky (trot′skē), **Leon,** 1879-1940, leader in the Russian Revolution and Soviet minister of war from 1918 to 1925. He was later exiled and assassinated in Mexico. *n.*

trot ter (trot′ər), horse that trots, especially one bred and trained to trot in a race. *n.*

trou ba dour (trü′bə dôr), one of the lyric poets of southern France, eastern Spain, and northern Italy from the 1000's to the 1200's. The troubadours wrote mainly about love and chivalry. *n.*

trou ble (trub′əl), 1 pain and sorrow; distress; worry; difficulty: *The unruly students were a trouble to their teacher.* 2 cause trouble to; disturb: *The lack of business troubled the grocer. I am troubled by headaches.* 3 disturbance; disorder: *political troubles.* 4 extra work; bother; effort: *It is too much trouble to dust in this room every day. Take the trouble to do careful work.*

5 require extra work or effort of: *May I trouble you to pass the sugar?* 6 to cause oneself inconvenience: *Don't trouble to come to the door; I can let myself in.* 7 a cause of inconvenience: *Is helping me a trouble to you?* 8 ailment; disease: *The patient suffered from heart trouble.* 9 cause pain to; hurt; pain: *A toothache troubled me.* 10 agitate or ruffle (water, air, etc.). 1,3,4,7,8 *n.,* 2,5,6,9,10 *v.,* **trou bled, trou bling.**

trou ble mak er (trub′əl mā′kər), person who often causes trouble for others. *n.*

trou ble shoot er (trub′əl shü′tər), person who discovers and eliminates causes of trouble. *n.*

trou ble some (trub′əl səm), 1 causing trouble; disturbing; annoying: *noisy, troublesome neighbors.* 2 tiresome; difficult: *a troublesome process.* *adj.* —**trou′ble some ly,** *adv.*

trou blous (trub′ləs), 1 disturbed; unsettled. 2 troublesome. *adj.*

trough (trôf), 1 a long, narrow container for holding food or water: *He led the horses to the watering trough.* 2 something shaped like this: *The baker uses a trough for kneading dough.* 3 channel for carrying water; gutter: *The wooden trough under the eaves of the house carries off rain water.* 4 a long hollow between two ridges, etc.: *the trough between two waves.* *n.*

trounce (trouns), 1 beat or thrash. 2 INFORMAL. defeat in a contest or match: *The victors trounced the losing team.* *v.,* **trounced, trounc ing.**

troupe (trüp), troop, band, or company, especially a group of actors, singers, or acrobats. *n.*

troup er (trü′pər), 1 member of a theatrical troupe. 2 an experienced actor. *n.*

trou sers (trou′zərz), a two-legged outer garment reaching from the waist to the ankles; pants. *n.pl.*

trous seau (trü′sō *or* trü sō′), a bride's outfit of clothes, linen, etc. *n., pl.* **trous seaux** (trü′sōz *or* trü-sō′), **trous seaus.**

trout (trout), any of certain fresh-water food and game fishes of the same family as the salmon. *n., pl.* **trouts** *or* **trout.**

trow (trō), OLD USE. believe or think. *v.*

trow el (trou′əl), 1 tool with a broad, flat blade, used for spreading or smoothing plaster or mortar. 2 tool with a curved blade, used for taking up plants, loosening dirt, etc. *n.*

trowel (def. 1)   trowel (def. 2)

troy (troi), 1 in or by troy weight. 2 troy weight. 1 *adj.,* 2 *n.* [from *Troyes,* a city in northern France, former site of a fair at which this weight may have been used]

Troy (troi), 1 an ancient city in NW Asia Minor; Ilium. The Greeks laid siege to Troy for ten years. 2 city in E New York State, on the Hudson River. *n.*

Troy (def. 1)

troy weight, a standard system of weights used for gems and precious metals. One pound troy equals a little over four fifths of an ordinary pound. 12 troy ounces = 1 troy pound.

tru an cy (trü′ən sē), act or habit of playing truant; truant behavior. *n., pl.* **tru an cies.**

tru ant (trü′ənt), 1 student who stays away from school without permission. 2 staying away from school without permission. 3 person who neglects duty. 4 guilty of neglecting duty: *The truant factory worker left the machine running without watching it.* 5 lazy. 6 wandering: *That truant dog won't stay home.* 7 of or having to do with a truant or truants: *a truant report, a truant officer.* 1,3 *n.,* 2,4-7 *adj.*

play truant, 1 stay away from school without permission. 2 stay away from work or duties.

truce (trüs), 1 a stop in fighting; temporary peace: *A truce was declared between the two armies.* 2 a rest from trouble or pain: *The cough syrup gave me a short truce from coughing.* *n.*

truck[1] (truk), 1 a strongly built automobile, cart, wagon, etc., for carrying heavy loads: *Many trucks carry freight on the highways nowadays.* 2 carry on a truck: *truck freight to the warehouse.* 3 drive a truck. 4 frame on small wheels for moving trunks, etc. 5 frame with two or more pairs of wheels for supporting the end of a railroad car, locomotive, etc. 6 a small wheel. 1,4-6 *n.,* 2,3 *v.* [perhaps from Latin *trochus* iron hoop, from Greek *trochos* wheel]

truck[2] (truk), 1 vegetables raised for market. 2 small articles of little value; odds and ends. 3 INFORMAL. rubbish; trash. 4 INFORMAL. dealings: *She has no truck with peddlers.* 5 an exchange;

barter. **6** give in exchange; barter. 1-5 *n.*, 6 *v.* [from French of the 1200's *troquer* to barter, exchange, from Latin *trocare*]

truck er (truk′ər), **1** person who drives a truck. **2** person whose business is carrying goods, etc., by trucks. *n.*

truck farm, farm where vegetables are raised for market.

truck ing (truk′ing), act or business of carrying goods, etc., on a truck or trucks. *n.*

truck le (truk′əl), give up or submit tamely; be servile: *Some workers got promoted by truckling to superiors and flattering them.* *v.*, **truck led, truck ling.**

truckle bed, trundle bed.

truc u lence (truk′yə ləns), quality or condition of being truculent; fierceness; brutal harshness. *n.*

truc u lent (truk′yə lənt), **1** fierce, savage, or violent: *a truculent villain, be in a truculent mood, a truculent defense of one's rights.* **2** brutally harsh or scathing: *a truculent remark, a truculent satire.* *adj.* —**truc′u lent ly,** *adv.*

trudge (truj), **1** go on foot; walk. **2** walk wearily or with effort. **3** a hard or weary walk: *It was a long trudge up the hill.* 1,2 *v.*, **trudged, trudg ing;** 3 *n.*

true (trü), **1** agreeing with fact; not false: *It is true that 6 and 4 are 10. The story I told is true; I did not make it up.* **2** real; genuine: *true gold, true kindness.* **3** faithful; loyal: *a true patriot, true to your promises.* **4** agreeing with a standard; right; proper; correct; exact; accurate: *a true copy, a true voice, true to type.* **5** representative of the class named: *A sweet potato is not a true potato.* **6** rightful; lawful: *the true heir to the property.* **7** accurately formed, fitted, or placed: *a true angle.* **8** exact or accurate formation, position, or adjustment: *A slanting door is out of true.* **9** make true; shape, place, or make in the exact position, form, etc., required: *True up that slanting door.* **10** steady in direction, force, etc.; unchanging: *The arrow made a true course through the air.* **11** that which is true. **12** in a true manner; truly; exactly: *Your words ring true.* 1-7,10 *adj.*, **tru er, tru est;** 8,11 *n.*, 9 *v.*, **trued, tru ing** or **true ing;** 12 *adv.*

come true, happen as expected; become real.

true-blue (trü′blü′), staunch and unwavering in one's faith, beliefs, etc.; unchanging; loyal: *If you are true-blue, you'll keep the promise you've made.* *adj.*

truf fle (truf′əl), fungus that grows underground and is valued as a food. It resembles a potato in appearance. *n.*

tru ism (trü′iz′əm), statement that almost everybody knows is true, such as "Health is a blessing." *n.*

tru ly (trü′lē), **1** in a true manner; exactly; rightly; faithfully: *Tell me truly what you think.* **2** in fact; really: *It was truly a beautiful sight.* *adv.*

Tru man (trü′mən), **Harry S.,** 1884-1972, the 33rd president of the United States, from 1945 to 1953. *n.*

trump[1] (trump), **1** any playing card of a suit that during the play of a hand ranks higher than the other suits. **2** Often, **trumps,** *pl.* the suit itself. **3** take (a trick, card, etc.) with a trump. **4** play a card of the suit that is trump. 1,2 *n.*, 3,4 *v.* [a changed form of *triumph*, from French *triomphe*]

trump[2] (trump), OLD USE. trumpet. *n.* [from French of the 1200's *trompe*]

trump[3] (trump), make (up) to deceive: *trump up false charges against a person.* *v.* [perhaps a special use of *trump*[1]]

trump er y (trump′ər ē), **1** something showy but without value; worthless ornaments; useless stuff; rubbish; nonsense. **2** showy but without value; trifling; worthless; useless; nonsensical. 1 *n.*, *pl.* **trump er ies;** 2 *adj.*

trumpet (def. 1)

trum pet (trum′pit), **1** a brass wind instrument that has a powerful tone, commonly a curved tube with a flaring bell at one end. **2** thing shaped like a trumpet: *The deaf old woman had an ear trumpet to help her hearing.* **3** blow a trumpet. **4** a sound like that of a trumpet. **5** make a sound like a trumpet: *The elephant trumpeted in fright.* **6** proclaim loudly or widely: *trumpet a story all over town.* 1,2,4 *n.*, 3,5,6 *v.*

trumpet creeper, bignonia.

trum pet er (trum′pə tər), person who blows a trumpet. *n.*

trumpet vine, bignonia.

trun cate (trung′kāt), **1** cut off a part of. **2** cut off; blunt, as if cut off: *the truncate leaf of the tulip tree.* 1 *v.*, **trun cat ed, trun cat ing;** 2 *adj.*

trun cheon (trun′chən), **1** a stick cut and shaped for use as a weapon; club: *a policeman's truncheon.* **2** staff of office or authority: *a herald's truncheon.* *n.*

trun dle (trun′dl), **1** roll along; push along: *The workman trundled a wheelbarrow full of cement.* **2** a rolling; rolling along. **3** a small wheel; caster. **4** a trundle bed. **5** a low cart or wagon on small wheels. 1 *v.*, **trun dled, trun dling;** 2-5 *n.*

trundle bed, a low bed on small wheels; truckle bed. It can be pushed under a regular bed when not in use.

trunk (trungk), **1** the main stem of a tree, as distinct from the branches and the roots. **2** the main part of anything: *the trunk of a column.* **3** main; chief: *a trunk highway.* **4** a big box for holding clothes, etc., when traveling. **5** an enclosed compartment in an automobile for storing baggage, a spare tire, etc. **6** a human or animal body, not counting the head, arms, and legs. **7** an elephant's snout. **8** trunk line. **9 trunks,** *pl.* very short trousers or breeches worn by athletes, swimmers, acrobats, etc. 1,2,4-9 *n.*, 3 *adj.* —**trunk′like′,** *adj.*

trunk line, **1** the main line of a railroad, canal, etc. **2** any main line, such as the line between telephone exchanges.

truss (trus), **1** tie or fasten; bind: *truss up a prisoner hand and foot. The cook trussed up the chicken before roasting it.* **2** framework of beams or other supports, usually connected in a series of triangles and used to support a roof, bridge, etc. **3** support (a roof, bridge, etc.) with trusses. **4** bandage, pad, etc., attached to a belt, used to support a hernia. 1,3 *v.*, 2,4 *n.*, *pl.* **truss es.**

truss (def. 2)

TRUSS

trust (trust), **1** firm belief in the honesty, truthfulness, justice, or power of a person or thing; faith: *Children put trust in their parents.* **2** have faith; believe; rely: *Trust in their honesty.* **3** believe firmly in the honesty, truth, justice, or power of; have faith in: *a person you can trust.* **4** rely on; depend on: *If you can't trust your memory, write things down in a little notebook.* **5** person or thing trusted: *God is our trust.* **6** confident expectation or hope:

trust

hat, āge, fär; let, ēqual, tėrm; it, īce; hot, ōpen, ôrder; oil, out; cup, pút, rüle; ch, child; ng, long; sh, she; th, thin; ŦH, then; zh, measure;

ə represents *a* in about, *e* in taken, *i* in pencil, *o* in lemon, *u* in circus.

adj. adjective	n. noun
adv. adverb	prep. preposition
conj. conjunction	pron. pronoun
interj. interjection	v. verb
sing. singular	pl. plural

Our trust is that she will soon be well. **7** hope; believe: *I trust you will soon feel better.* **8** something managed for the benefit of another; something committed to one's care: *The house is a trust which she holds for her dead brother's children.* **9** obligation or responsibility imposed on one in whom confidence or authority is placed: *He will be faithful to his trust.* **10** keeping; care: *The will was left in my trust.* **11** managing for an owner. A trust company undertakes to manage property for anyone. **12** an illegal combination of companies to control the production and price of some commodity and to eliminate or reduce competition: *a steel trust.* **13** of or having to do with trust or trusts; held in trust. **14** commit to the care of; leave without fear: *Can I trust the keys to her?* **15** confidence in the ability or intention of a person to pay at some future time for goods, etc.; business credit. **16** give business credit to: *The butcher will trust us for the meat.* 1,5,6,8-10,12,15 *n.,* 2-4,7,14,16 *v.,* 11, 13 *adj.*

in trust, as a thing taken charge of for another.

trust to, rely on; depend on: *trust to luck.*

trus tee (tru stē′), person responsible for the property or affairs of another person, of a company, or of an institution: *A trustee will manage the children's property until they grow up. n.*

trus tee ship (tru stē′ship), **1** position of trustee. **2** administration by a country of a trust territory. **3** trust territory. *n.*

trust ful (trust′fəl), ready to confide; ready to have faith; trusting; believing: *The trustful boy would lend money to any of his friends. adj.* —**trust′ful ly,** *adv.* —**trust′ful ness,** *n.*

trust fund, money, property, or other valuables held in trust by one person for the benefit of another.

trust ing (trus′ting), that trusts; trustful. *adj.* —**trust′ing ly,** *adv.*

trust territory, any of various territories or regions administered by certain countries on behalf of the United Nations.

trust wor thi ness (trust′wėr′FHē-

nis), condition or character of being trustworthy. *n.*

trust wor thy (trust′wėr′FHē), that can be depended on; reliable: *The class chose a trustworthy student for treasurer. adj.*

trust y (trus′tē), **1** that can be depended on; reliable: *She left her new car with a trusty friend.* **2** a convict who is given special privileges because of his good behavior. 1 *adj.,* **trust i er, trust i est;** 2 *n., pl.* **trust ies.**

truth (trüth), **1** that which is true: *Tell the truth.* **2** a fixed or established principle, law, etc.; proven doctrine: *a basic scientific truth.* **3** quality or nature of being true, exact, honest, sincere, or loyal. *n., pl.* **truths** (trüFHz *or* trüths). **in truth,** truly; really; in fact: *It was in truth a beautiful scene.*

truth ful (trüth′fəl), **1** telling the truth: *He is a truthful boy and will tell exactly what really happened.* **2** conforming to truth; agreeing with the facts: *You can count on her for a truthful report of the accident. adj.* —**truth′ful ly,** *adv.* —**truth′ful ness,** *n.*

try (trī), **1** make an effort; attempt: *I tried to do the work. Try harder if you wish to succeed.* **2** attempt to do or accomplish: *It seems easy until you try it.* **3** experiment on or with; make trial of: *Try this candy and see if you like it.* **4** find out about; test: *We try each car before we sell it.* **5** an attempt; test; experiment: *Each girl had three tries at the high jump.* **6** investigate in a court of law: *The man was tried and found guilty.* **7** to subject to trials; afflict: *Job was greatly tried.* **8** put to severe test; strain: *Her carelessness tries my patience.* **9** make pure by melting or boiling: *The lard was tried in a big kettle.* 1-4,6-9 *v.,* **tried, try ing;** 5 *n., pl.* **tries.**

try on, put on to test the fit, looks, etc.: *I tried on several coats.*

try out, 1 test or sample: *Try out this new recipe for apple pie.* **2** undergo a test or trial to determine fitness: *He tried out for the baseball team.*

try ing (trī′ing), hard to endure; annoying: *a trying day, a trying person. adj.*

try out (trī′out′), INFORMAL. test or trial made to determine fitness for a specific purpose: *Tryouts for the swimming team will start a week after school opens. n.*

tryp sin (trip′sən), enzyme in the pancreatic juice that aids in the digestion of proteins. *n.*

tryst (trist), **1** appointment to meet at a certain time and place. **2** place of meeting. *n.*

tsar (zär), czar. *n.*

tsa ri na (zä rē′nə), czarina. *n., pl.* **tsa ri nas.**

Tschai kow sky or **Tschai kov sky** (chī kôf′skē), Tchaikovsky. *n.*

tset se (tset′sē), tsetse fly. *n.* Also, **tzetze.**

tsetse fly, any of a group of African flies that suck the blood of mammals and transmit disease. One kind transmits the germ that causes sleeping sickness.

T-shirt (tē′shėrt′), **1** a light, close-fitting knitted shirt with short sleeves and no collar, worn for sports. **2** an undershirt resembling this. *n.* Also, **tee shirt.**

tsp., teaspoon or teaspoons.

T square

T square, a T-shaped ruler used for making parallel lines, etc. The shorter arm slides along the edge of the drawing board, which serves as a guide.

tub (tub), **1** a large, open container for washing or bathing. **2** bathtub. **3** INFORMAL. bath: *He takes a cold tub every morning.* **4** wash or bathe in a tub. **5** a round, wooden container for holding butter, lard, etc. **6** as much as a tub can hold. **7** INFORMAL. a clumsy, slow boat or ship. 1-3,5-7 *n.,* 4 *v.,* **tubbed, tub bing.**

tu ba (tü′bə *or* tyü′bə), a large brass wind instrument of low pitch. *n., pl.* **tu bas.**

tuba

tub by (tub′ē), **1** shaped like a tub; short and fat. **2** having a sound like that of an empty tub when struck. *adj.,* **tub bi er, tub bi est.**

tube (tüb *or* tyüb), **1** a long pipe of metal, glass, rubber, etc., mostly used to hold or carry liquids or gases. **2** a small cylinder of thin, easily bent metal with a cap that screws on the open end, used for holding toothpaste, paint, etc. **3** inner tube. **4** pipe or tunnel through which something travels: *The railroad runs under the river in a tube.* **5** anything like a tube: *the bronchial tubes.*

6 an electron or vacuum tube. 7 **the tube,** INFORMAL. television. *n.* —**tube′like′,** *adj.*

tube less (tüb′lis *or* tyüb′lis), having no inner tube or tubes: *a tubeless tire.* *adj.*

tu ber (tü′bər *or* tyü′bər), the thick part of an underground stem. A potato is a tuber. *n.*

tu ber cle (tü′bər kəl *or* tyü′bər kəl), 1 a small, rounded swelling or knob on an animal or plant. 2 a swelling caused by tuberculosis. *n.*

tu ber cu lar (tü bėr′kyə lər *or* tyü- bėr′kyə lər), 1 having tubercles. 2 having to do with tubercles. 3 having tuberculosis. 4 having to do with tuberculosis: *tubercular symptoms.* *adj.*

tu ber cu lin (tü bėr′kyə lən *or* tyü- bėr′kyə lən), a liquid substance pre- pared from the germ that causes tuberculosis. Tuberculin is used in the diagnosis and treatment of tubercu- losis. *n.*

tu ber cu lo sis (tü bėr′kyə lō′sis *or* tyü bėr′kyə lō′sis), an infectious dis- ease affecting various tissues of the body, but most often the lungs. Tuber- culosis of the lungs is often called con- sumption. *n.*

tu ber cu lous (tü bėr′kyə ləs *or* tyü- bėr′kyə ləs), tubercular. *adj.*

tube rose (tüb′rōz′ *or* tyüb′rōz′), plant with a spike of fragrant white flowers. It grows from a tuber. *n.*

tu ber ous (tü′bər əs *or* tyü′bər əs), 1 bearing tubers. 2 of or like tubers: *a tuberous root.* 3 covered with rounded knobs or swellings. *adj.*

tub ing (tü′bing *or* tyü′bing), 1 ma- terial in the form of a tube: *rubber tubing.* 2 tubes collectively. 3 a piece of tube. *n.*

tu bu lar (tü′byə lər *or* tyü′byə lər), 1 shaped like a tube; round and hollow. 2 of or having to do with a tube or tubes. 3 constructed with or consisting of a number of tubes: *a tubular boiler.* *adj.*

tu bule (tü′byül *or* tyü′byül), a small tube. *n.*

tuck (tuk), 1 thrust into some narrow space or into some out-of-the-way place: *She tucked the book under her arm. He tucked the letter into his pocket.* 2 thrust the edge or end of (a garment, covering, etc.) closely into place: *Tuck your shirt in. He tucked a napkin under his chin.* 3 cover snugly: *Tuck the chil- dren in bed.* 4 pull or gather in a fold or folds: *We tucked up the legs of our jeans and waded across the stream.* 5 a fold sewed in a garment: *The pants were big, so the tailor put a tuck in them.* 6 sew a fold in (a garment) for trimming or to make it shorter or tighter: *The baby's dress was beautifully tucked with tiny*

hand-sewn stitches. 1-4,6 *v.,* 5 *n.*

tuck er[1] (tuk′ər), piece of muslin, lace, etc., worn around the neck or over the chest. *n.* [*tuck* + *-er*[1]]

tuck er[2] (tuk′ər), INFORMAL. tire; weary; exhaust: *She was all tuckered out after the long trip.* *v.* [origin uncertain]

Tuc son (tü′son), city in S Arizona, famous as a health resort. *n.*

Tu dor (tü′dər *or* tyü′dər), 1 the royal family that ruled England from 1485 to 1603. Henry VIII and Elizabeth I be- longed to the house of Tudor. 2 of or having to do with the English Gothic style of architecture prevailing during the reign of the Tudor family. It was characterized by flat arches, shallow moldings, and elaborate paneling. 1 *n.,* 2 *adj.*

Tues., Tuesday.

Tues day (tüz′dē *or* tyüz′dē), the third day of the week, following Mon- day. *n.* [Old English *Tīwesdæg,* from *Tīw,* the Germanic god of war + *dæg* day]

tu fa (tü′fə *or* tyü′fə), any of various porous rocks, especially a form of lime- stone deposited by springs, etc. *n., pl.* **tu fas.**

tuft (tuft), 1 bunch of feathers, hair, grass, etc., held together at one end: *The goat had a tuft of hair on its chin.* 2 clump of bushes, trees, etc. 3 cluster of threads sewn tightly through a mat- tress, comforter, etc., so as to keep the padding in place. 4 put tufts on; furnish with tufts; divide into tufts. 5 form a tuft or tufts; grow in tufts. 1-3 *n.,* 4,5 *v.*

tuft ed (tuf′tid), 1 furnished with a tuft or tufts. 2 formed into a tuft or tufts. *adj.*

tug (tug), 1 pull with force or effort; pull hard: *We tugged the boat in to shore. The child tugged at his mother's hand.* 2 a hard pull: *The baby gave a tug at my hair.* 3 strive hard; toil. 4 a hard strain, struggle, effort, or contest. 5 tugboat. 6 tow by a tugboat. 7 trace[2]. 1,3,6 *v.,* **tugged, tug ging;** 2,4,5,7 *n.*

tug boat (tug′bōt′), a small, powerful boat used to tow or push other boats; towboat. *n.*

tug-of-war (tug′əv wôr′ *or* tug′ə- wôr′), 1 contest between two teams pulling at the ends of a rope, each trying to drag the other over a line marked between them. 2 any hard struggle. *n., pl.* **tugs-of-war.**

Tui ler ies (twē′lər ēz), former royal palace in Paris. It was burned in 1871. *n.*

tu i tion (tü ish′ən *or* tyü ish′ən), 1 teaching or instruction: *She is busy with the tuition of slow learners.* 2 money paid for instruction: *a $300 increase in college tuition.* *n.*

tu lip (tü′lip *or* tyü′lip), 1 any of cer-

hat, āge, fär; let, ēqual, tèrm; it, īce; hot, ōpen, ôrder; oil, out; cup, pùt, rüle; ch, child; ng, long; sh, she; th, thin; ŦH, then; zh, measure;

ə represents *a* in about, *e* in taken, *i* in pencil, *o* in lemon, *u* in circus.

tain plants of the same family as the lily, that grow from bulbs and have large cup-shaped flowers of various colors. Most tulips bloom in the spring. 2 the flower or bulb of any of these plants. *n.*

tulle (tül), a thin, fine net, usually of silk, used for veils, etc. *n.* [from *Tulle,* a town in France, where it was first made]

Tul sa (tul′sə), city in NE Oklahoma, on the Arkansas River. *n.*

tum ble (tum′bəl), 1 to fall headlong or in a helpless way: *The child tumbled down the stairs.* 2 a fall by tumbling: *The tumble hurt him badly.* 3 throw over or down; cause to fall: *The strong winds tumbled a tree in our yard.* 4 roll or toss about: *The sick child tumbled restlessly in the bed.* 5 move in a hurried or awkward way: *I tumbled out of bed.* 6 perform leaps, springs, somer- saults, etc. 7 turn over; rumple; muss: *to tumble bedclothes.* 8 confusion; disor- der: *Her desk was a complete tumble of papers.* 1,3-7 *v.,* **tum bled, tum bling;** 2,8 *n.*

tum ble-down (tum′bəl doun′), ready to fall down; not in good con- dition; dilapidated: *a tumble-down shack in the mountains.* *adj.*

tum bler (tum′blər), 1 person who performs leaps, springs, etc.; acrobat. 2 a drinking glass without a stem and with a heavy, flat bottom. 3 the con- tents of a tumbler. 4 part in the lock that must be moved from a certain position in order to release the bolt. *n.*

tum ble weed (tum′bəl wēd′), plant growing in the western United States that breaks off from its roots in autumn and is blown about by the wind. *n.*

tum brel *or* **tum bril** (tum′brəl), 1 any of various two-wheeled carts, especially one used on a farm for haul- ing and dumping manure. 2 cart that carried prisoners to be executed during the French Revolution. *n.*

tu mes cence (tü mes′ns *or* tyü- mes′ns), a swelling; a swollen con- dition. *n.*

tu mes cent (tü mes′nt *or* tyü- mes′nt), becoming swollen; swelling. *adj.*

adj.	adjective	*n.*	noun
adv.	adverb	*prep.*	preposition
conj.	conjunction	*pron.*	pronoun
interj.	interjection	*v.*	verb
sing.	singular	*pl.*	plural

tu mid (tü′mid *or* tyü′mid), 1 swollen. 2 swollen with big words; pompous. *adj.*

tum my (tum′ē), INFORMAL. stomach. *n., pl.* **tum mies.**

tu mor (tü′mər *or* tyü′mər), 1 a swollen part; swelling. 2 an abnormal growth in or on some part of the body. *n.*

tu mult (tü′mult *or* tyü′mult), 1 noise or uproar; commotion: *The sailors' voices could not be heard above the tumult of the storm.* 2 a violent disturbance or disorder: *The cry of "Fire! Fire!" caused a tumult in the theater.* 3 a violent disturbance of mind or feeling; confusion or excitement: *The quarrel left her in a tumult. n.*

tu mul tu ous (tü mul′chü əs *or* tyü mul′chü əs), 1 characterized by tumult; very noisy or disorderly; violent: *a tumultuous celebration.* 2 greatly disturbed: *tumultuous emotion.* 3 rough; stormy: *Tumultuous ocean waves. adj.*

tun (tun), 1 a large cask for holding liquids. 2 (in former times) a measure of capacity of liquor, equal to 252 gallons. *n.*

tu na (tü′nə), 1 a large sea fish closely related to the mackerel, having coarse, oily flesh that is widely used as food; tunny. It is also valued as a game fish. 2 the flesh of the tuna. *n., pl.* **tu nas** *or* **tu na.**

tuna fish, tuna.

tun dra (tun′drə), a vast, level, treeless plain in the arctic regions. The ground beneath the surface of the tundras is frozen even in summer. Much of Alaska and northern Canada is tundra. *n., pl.* **tun dras.**

tuning fork

tune (tün *or* tyün), 1 piece of music; an air or melody: *hymn tunes.* 2 the proper pitch: *The piano is out of tune. I can't sing in tune.* 3 mood or manner; tone: *She'll soon change her tune.* 4 agreement; harmony: *A person out of tune with his surroundings is unhappy.* 5 be in tune; be in harmony. 6 adjust to the proper pitch; put in tune: *tune a piano.* 1-4 *n.,* 5,6 *v.,* **tuned, tun ing.**

to the tune of, INFORMAL. to the amount or sum of.

tune in, adjust a radio or television set to hear (what is wanted).

tune out, adjust a radio or television set to get rid of (a signal or interference that is unwanted).

tune up, 1 bring (musical instruments) to the same pitch; put in tune. 2 put (a motor or engine) into the best working order.

tune ful (tün′fəl *or* tyün′fəl), musical; melodious: *a tuneful song. adj.* —**tune′ful ly,** *adv.* —**tune′ful ness,** *n.*

tune less (tün′lis *or* tyün′lis), without tune; not musical. *adj.* —**tune′less ly,** *adv.*

tun er (tü′nər *or* tyü′nər), 1 person who tunes pianos, organs, or other musical instruments. 2 device for adjusting a radio receiver to accept a given frequency and reject other frequencies. *n.*

tune-up (tün′up′ *or* tyün′up′), series of checks and adjustments and replacement of certain parts of an engine or motor to keep it running well. *n.*

tung sten (tung′stən), a heavy, hard, steel-gray, metallic element found only in certain rare minerals; wolfram. Tungsten has the highest melting point of all metals. It is added to steel to make it harder, stronger, and more elastic. It is also used in making electric-lamp filaments, surgical instruments, automobile parts, etc. *n.*

DYNAMO

TURBINE

tu nic (tü′nik *or* tyü′nik), 1 garment like a shirt or gown, worn by the ancient Greeks and Romans. 2 any garment like this. 3 a woman's garment extending below the waist or over the skirt. 4 a short, close-fitting coat worn by soldiers, policemen, etc. *n.*

tuning fork, a small, two-pronged steel instrument used in tuning musical instruments. When struck, it vibrates at a fixed, constant, known rate and so makes a musical tone of a certain pitch.

Tu nis (tü′nis *or* tyü′nis), seaport and capital of Tunisia, in the NE part. *n.*

Tu ni sia (tü nē′zhə *or* tyü nē′zhə), country in N Africa. *Capital:* Tunis. See **Algeria** for map. *n.* —**Tu ni′sian,** *adj., n.*

tun nel (tun′l), 1 any underground passage, such as an underground roadway for a railroad, a passage in a mine, or an animal's burrow: *Motor traffic passes under the river through a tunnel.* 2 make a tunnel: *The mole tunneled in the ground. The workmen are tunneling through the mountain.* 1 *n.,* 2 *v.*

tun ny (tun′ē), tuna. *n., pl.* **tun nies** *or* **tun ny.**

tu pe lo (tü′pə lō *or* tyü′pə lō), 1 a large North American tree whose flowers are used for honey. 2 its strong, tough wood. *n., pl.* **tu pe los.**

tup pence (tup′əns), twopence. *n.*

turban (def. 1)

tur ban (tér′bən), 1 scarf wound around the head or around a cap, worn by men in parts of India and in some other countries of Asia. 2 any headdress like this, such as a big handkerchief tied around the head. 3 a small hat with little or no brim, worn by women and children. *n.*

tur baned (tér′bənd), wearing a turban. *adj.*

tur bid (tér′bid), 1 not clear; muddy; thick: *a turbid river.* 2 confused; disordered: *a turbid imagination. adj.*

tur bine (tér′bən *or* tér′bīn), engine or motor consisting of a wheel with vanes which is made to revolve by the force of water, steam, or air. Turbines are often used to turn dynamos that produce electric power. *n.*

tur bo jet (tér′bō jet′), 1 jet engine having a turbine-driven air compressor which supplies a continuous, high-pressure flow of air to the burners. 2 aircraft having such an engine. *n.*

tur bo prop (tér′bō prop′), 1 adaptation of the turbojet in which a propeller, driven by a shaft from the turbine, provides most of the thrust. Some additional thrust is provided by the ejection of exhaust gases from the rear. 2 aircraft having such an engine. *n.*

tur bot (tér′bət), 1 a large European flatfish, much valued as food. 2 any of various similar fishes, such as certain flounders. *n., pl.* **tur bots** *or* **tur bot.**

tur bu lence (tér′byə ləns), turbulent condition; disorder; tumult; commotion. *n.*

tur bu lent (tér′byə lənt), 1 causing disturbance; disorderly; unruly; violent: *a turbulent mob.* 2 stormy; tem-

pestuous: *turbulent weather. adj.*
—tur′bu lent ly, *adv.*

tu reen (tə rēn′), a deep, covered dish for serving soup, etc. *n.*

turf (tèrf), 1 the upper surface of the soil covered with grass and other small plants, including their roots and the soil clinging to them; sod. 2 piece of this. 3 cover with turf. 4 peat. 5 Usually, **the turf. a** a race track for horses. **b** horse racing. 1,2,4,5 *n., pl.* **turfs;** 3 *v.*

Tur ge nev (tür gā′nyef), **Ivan,** 1818-1883, Russian novelist. *n.*

tur gid (tèr′jid), 1 puffed out; swollen; bloated. 2 using big words and elaborate comparisons; pompous. *adj.*

Turk (tèrk), person born or living in Turkey. *n.*

Tur ke stan (tèr′kə stan′), region in W and central Asia. Part of Turkestan belongs to China, part to the Soviet Union, and part to Afghanistan. *n.*

tur key (tèr′kē), 1 a large wild or domesticated American bird related to the pheasants. 2 its flesh, used for food. *n., pl.* **tur keys.** [from *Turkey* (apparently from confusion with a guinea fowl originally imported by way of Turkey)]

Tur key (tèr′kē), country in W Asia and SE Europe. *Capital:* Ankara. *n.*

turkey buzzard, vulture of South and Central America and southern United States, having a bare, reddish head and dark plumage.

Turk ish (tèr′kish), 1 of Turkey or the Turks. 2 language of the Turks. 1 *adj.,* 2 *n.*

Turkish Empire, Ottoman Empire.

turkish towel, a thick, cotton towel with a long nap made of uncut loops.

tur mer ic (tèr′mər ik), 1 a yellow powder prepared from the root of an East Indian plant, used as a seasoning, as a yellow dye, in medicine, etc. 2 the plant itself. 3 its root. *n.*

tur moil (tèr′moil), state of agitation or commotion; disturbance; tumult: *Unexpected guests put us in a turmoil. n.*

turn (tèrn), 1 move round as a wheel does; rotate: *The merry-go-round turned.* 2 cause to move round as a wheel does: *I turned the crank twice.* 3 a motion like that of a wheel: *At each turn the screw goes in further.* 4 move part way around; change from one side to the other: *Turn over on your back.* 5 do by turning; open, close, make lower, higher, tighter, looser, etc., by moving around: *She turned the key in the lock.* 6 take a new direction: *The road turns to the north here.* 7 give a new direction to: *We turned our steps to the north.* 8 a change of direction: *a turn to the left.* 9 place where there is a change in direction: *a turn in the road.* 10 change in direction or position; in-

vert; reverse: *turn a page.* 11 change or transform so as to be; become: *She turned pale.* 12 change for or to a worse condition; make or become sour or spoiled: *Warm weather turns milk.* 13 a change in affairs, conditions, or circumstances: *Matters have taken a turn for the worse. The sick child took a turn for the better.* 14 the time at which such a change takes place: *the turn of the year, the turn of a fever.* 15 give form to; make: *He can turn pretty compliments.* 16 change from one language into another: *Turn this sentence into Latin.* 17 a form; style: *a happy turn of expression.* 18 put out of order; unsettle: *Too much praise turns his head.* 19 depend: *The success of the picnic turns on the weather.* 20 direct (one's thoughts or attention): *He turned his thoughts toward home.* 21 direct thought, eyes, etc.: *turn to God for help.* 22 move to the other side of; go round; get beyond: *turn the corner.* 23 pass or get beyond (a particular age, time, or amount): *a man turning sixty.* 24 a twist; bend: *Give that rope a few more turns around the tree.* 25 time or chance to do something; opportunity: *My turn comes after yours.* 26 deed; act: *One good turn deserves another.* 27 performance. 28 make antagonistic; prejudice: *turn friends against friends.* 29 a walk, drive, or ride: *a turn in the park.* 30 form, work, or make by means of a lathe. 31 make sick; become sick: *The sight of blood turns my stomach.* 32 become dizzy: *The height made my head turn.* 33 INFORMAL. a nervous shock: *give someone a bad turn.* 1,2,4-7,10-12,15,16,18-23,28,30-32 *v.,* 3,8,9,13,14,17,24-27,29,33 *n.*

at every turn, on every occasion; without exception; constantly.

by turns, one after another.

in turn, in proper order.

out of turn, not in proper order.

take turns, act one after another in proper order.

to a turn, to just the right degree: *meat done to a turn.*

turn about or **turn and turn about,** one after another in proper order.

turn down, 1 fold down: *turn down the covers on the bed.* 2 bend downward. 3 place with face downward. 4 refuse: *turn down a plan.* 5 lower by turning something: *turn down the gas.*

turn in, 1 turn and go in. 2 point (toes) inward. 3 INFORMAL. go to bed: *It's late and I'm going to turn in now.* 4 give back. 5 exchange: *turn in an old appliance for a new model.*

turn off, 1 stop the flow of; shut off: *Is the water tap turned off?* 2 put out (a light). 3 turn aside. 4 SLANG. cause (a person) to feel displeasure or dis-

hat, āge, fär; let, ēqual, tèrm;
it, īce; hot, ōpen, ôrder;
oil, out; cup, pùt, rüle; ch, child;
ng, long; sh, she; th, thin;
ŦH, then; zh, measure;

ə represents *a* in about,
e in taken, *i* in pencil,
o in lemon, *u* in circus.

like: *She turns me off with her bragging.*

turn on, 1 start the flow of; put on. 2 put on (a light). 3 attack; resist; oppose: *The dog turned on its pursuer.* 4 SLANG. **a** take or use an intoxicating drug. **b** cause (a person) to feel pleasure or liking: *That music turns me on.*

turn out, 1 put out; shut off. 2 let go out: *turn the cows out.* 3 drive out. 4 come or go out: *Everyone turned out for the circus.* 5 make; produce. 6 result: *How did the game turn out?* 7 come to be; become: *She turned out a successful lawyer.* 8 equip; fit out: *be smartly turned out in a new suit.*

turn over, 1 give; hand over; transfer: *turn over a job to someone.* 2 think carefully about; consider in different ways: *turn over an idea in the mind.*

turn to, 1 go to for help. 2 get busy; set to work.

turn up, 1 fold up or over, especially so as to shorten; give upward turn to; bring underside up. 2 make (a lamp, etc.) burn stronger. 3 make (a radio, television set, etc.) louder. 4 turn and go up. 5 be directed upward. 6 appear: *An old friend has turned up.*

turn buck le (tèrn′buk′əl), a short, hollow piece turning on a screw, used to unite and tighten two parts. *n.*

turn coat (tèrn′kōt′), person who changes his party or principles; renegade. *n.*

tur nip (tèr′nəp), 1 plant with a large, fleshy, roundish root. 2 its root, eaten as a vegetable. *n.*

turn key (tèrn′kē′), person in charge of the keys of a prison; keeper of a prison. *n., pl.* **turn keys.**

turn off (tèrn′ôf′ or tèrn′of′), 1 place at which a road, path, etc., turns off to another. 2 SLANG. thing that causes displeasure or dislike: *Final exams are a real turnoff. n.*

turn-on (tèrn′ôn′ or tèrn′on′), SLANG. thing that is pleasurably exciting: *Music can be a real turn-on. n.*

turn out (tèrn′out′), 1 a gathering of people. 2 output. 3 a wide place in the road, where vehicles can pass. 4 way in which somebody or something is equipped; equipment. *n.*

adj.	adjective	*n.*	noun
adv.	adverb	*prep.*	preposition
conj.	conjunction	*pron.*	pronoun
interj.	interjection	*v.*	verb
sing.	singular	*pl.*	plural

turn o ver (tėrn′ō′vər), 1 a turning upside down; an overturn; upset. 2 the amount of changing from one job to another: *Employers wish to reduce labor turnover.* 3 the paying out and getting back of the money involved in a business transaction: *The store reduced prices to make a quick turnover.* 4 the total amount of business done in a given time: *She made a profit of $6000 on a turnover of $90,000.* 5 a small pie made by folding half the crust over the filling and upon the other half. 6 having a part that turns over: *a turnover collar.* 1-5 *n.,* 6 *adj.*

turn pike (tėrn′pīk′), 1 toll road. 2 gate where toll is paid. 3 road that has, or used to have, a gate where toll is paid. *n.*

turn spit (tėrn′spit′), person or thing that turns a roast of meat on a spit. *n.*

turnstile

turn stile (tėrn′stīl′), post with bars that turn, set in an entrance or an exit. Only one person at a time can pass through a turnstile. *n.*

turn ta ble (tėrn′tā′bəl), 1 a revolving platform with a track for turning locomotives around. 2 the round, revolving platform of a phonograph upon which records are placed. *n.*

tur pen tine (tėr′pən tīn), 1 mixture of oil and resin obtained from various cone-bearing trees. 2 a volatile oil distilled from this mixture. Turpentine is used in mixing paints and varnishes, in medicine, etc. *n.*

tur pi tude (tėr′pə tüd *or* tėr′pə tyüd), shameful wickedness; baseness. *n.*

tur quoise (tėr′koiz *or* tėr′kwoiz), 1 a sky-blue or greenish-blue mineral which is valued as a gem. 2 a sky blue or greenish blue, like that of the turquoise. 3 sky-blue; greenish-blue. 1,2 *n.,* 3 *adj.*

tur ret (tėr′it), 1 a small tower, often on the corner of a building. 2 any of various low, rotating armored structures within which guns are mounted. The big guns of warships are mounted in turrets. The heavy gun of an armored tank is mounted in a turret which makes up the entire upper portion of the tank. 3 a plastic bubble on the fuselage of some bombers, for machine guns and a gunner. 4 an attachment on a lathe, drill, etc., to hold cutting tools. *n.*

tur ret ed (tėr′ə tid), having a turret or turrets. *adj.*

tur tle (tėr′tl), reptile whose body is enclosed in a shell from which the head, tail, and four legs protrude. Turtles live in fresh water, salt water, or on land; those living on the land are often called tortoises. *n.*

turn turtle, turn bottom side up.

tur tle dove (tėr′tl duv′), kind of small, slender dove, noted for its soft cooing and the affection that the mates seem to have for each other. *n.*

tur tle neck (tėr′tl nek′), 1 a round, high, closely fitting collar on a sweater, etc., usually turned down over itself when the garment is worn. 2 sweater, etc., with such a collar. 3 (of a sweater, etc.) having such a collar. 1,2 *n.,* 3 *adj.*

Tus can (tus′kən), 1 of or having to do with Tuscany or its people. 2 person born or living in Tuscany. 3 dialect of Tuscany, regarded as the classical and standard form of Italian. *n.*

Tus ca ny (tus′kə nē), district in central Italy. Florence is its chief city. *n.*

Tus ca ro ra (tus′kə rôr′ə), member of a tribe of Iroquois Indians that lived in colonial North Carolina and now live in New York State and Ontario. *n., pl.* **Tus ca ro ra** *or* **Tus ca ro ras.**

tusk (tusk), a very long, pointed, projecting tooth. Elephants, walruses, and wild boars have tusks. *n.*

tusk er (tus′kər), animal with well developed tusks, such as a mature elephant, walrus, or wild boar. *n.*

tus sah (tus′ə), 1 a coarse, tan, Asian silk. 2 the silkworm that makes it. *n.*

tus sle (tus′əl), 1 struggle or wrestle; scuffle: *The boys tussled over the hat.* 2 a vigorous or disorderly conflict; severe struggle or hard contest. 1 *v.,* **tus sled, tus sling;** 2 *n.*

tus sock (tus′ək), a tuft of growing grass or the like. *n.*

tut (tut), exclamation of impatience, contempt, or rebuke. *interj., n.*

tu te lage (tü′tl ij *or* tyü′tl ij), 1 the office or function of a guardian; guardianship; protection. 2 instruction. *n.*

tu te lar (tü′tl ər *or* tyü′tl ər), tutelary. *adj.*

tu te lar y (tü′tl er′ē *or* tyü′tl er′ē), 1 having the position of guardian; protecting; guardian: *a tutelary saint.* 2 of a guardian; used as a guardian; protective: *a tutelary charm. adj.*

tu tor (tü′tər *or* tyü′tər), 1 a private teacher: *A tutor comes once a week to help me with mathematics.* 2 teach; instruct, especially individually or privately: *She was tutored at home during her long illness.* 3 INFORMAL. be taught by a tutor: *He is tutoring in algebra.* 1 *n.,* 2,3 *v.*

tu to ri al (tü tôr′ē əl *or* tyü tôr′ē əl), 1 of or having to do with a tutor: *tutorial authority.* 2 using tutors: *the tutorial system. adj.*

tut ti-frut ti (tü′tē frü′tē), 1 a preserve of mixed fruits. 2 ice cream containing a variety of fruits or fruit flavorings. 3 flavored by mixed fruits. 1,2 *n.,* 3 *adj.* [from Italian *tutti frutti* all fruits]

tux (tuks), INFORMAL. tuxedo. *n., pl.* **tux es.**

tux e do (tuk sē′dō), 1 a man's coat for evening wear, made without tails, usually black with satin lapels. 2 the suit to which such a coat belongs. *n., pl.* **tux e dos** *or* **tux e does.**

TURRETS

TURRETS

turret (def. 1, left; def. 2, right)

tusks
of a walrus

TV, television.

TVA, Tennessee Valley Authority (a United States government organization for developing the resources of the region of the Tennessee River valley, started in 1933).

twad dle (twod′l), 1 silly, feeble, tiresome talk or writing. 2 talk or write in a silly, feeble, tiresome way. 1 *n.,* 2 *v.,* **twad dled, twad dling.**

twain (twān), OLD USE. two. *n., adj.*

Twain (twān), **Mark,** 1835-1910, American writer, author of *Tom Sawyer* and *Huckleberry Finn.* His real name was **Samuel Langhorne Clemens.** *n.*

twang (twang), 1 a sharp, ringing

sound: *The bow made a twang when I shot the arrow.* 2 make or cause to make a sharp, ringing sound: *The banjos twanged.* 3 a sharp, nasal tone: *the twang of a Yankee farmer.* 4 speak with a sharp, nasal tone. 1,3 *n.,* 2,4 *v.*

'twas (twoz *or* twuz), it was: *" 'Twas the night before Christmas."*

tweak (twēk), 1 seize and pull with a sharp jerk and twist: *tweak a person's ear.* 2 a sharp pull and twist. 1 *v.,* 2 *n.*

tweed (twēd), 1 a woolen cloth with a rough surface. Tweed is sometimes made of wool and cotton, and usually has two or more colors. 2 suit, etc., made of this cloth. 3 **tweeds,** *pl.* clothes made of tweed. *n.*

tweet (twēt), 1 the note of a young bird: *We heard the "tweet, tweet" from a nest in the tree.* 2 utter a tweet or tweets. 1 *n., interj.,* 2 *v.*

 tweezers

tweez ers (twē′zərz), small pincers for pulling out hairs, picking up small objects, etc. *n.pl.*

twelfth (twelfth), 1 next after the 11th; last in a series of 12. 2 one of 12 equal parts. *adj., n.*

twelve (twelv), one more than 11; 12. A year has twelve months. *n., adj.*

twelve month (twelv′munth′), twelve months; a year. *n.*

twen ti eth (twen′tē ith), 1 next after the 19th; last in a series of 20. 2 one of 20 equal parts. *adj., n.*

twen ty (twen′tē), two times ten; 20. *n., pl.* **twen ties;** *adj.*

'twere (twėr), it were.

twice (twīs), 1 two times: *twice a day.* 2 doubly: *twice as much. adv.*

twice-told (twīs′tōld′), 1 told twice. 2 told many times before; trite. *adj.*

twid dle (twid′l), 1 twirl: *twiddle one's pencil.* 2 play with idly. 3 a twirl. 1,2 *v.,* **twid dled, twid dling;** 3 *n.*

twig (twig), a slender shoot of a tree or other plant; very small branch: *Dry twigs are good to start a fire with. n.*

twi light (twī′līt′), 1 the faint light reflected from the sky before the sun rises and after it sets. 2 the period during which this prevails, especially from sunset to dark night. 3 condition or period after or before full development, glory, etc. 4 of twilight; like that of twilight: *the twilight hour.* 1-3 *n.,* 4 *adj.*

twill (twil), 1 cloth woven in raised diagonal lines. Serge is a twill. 2 weave (cloth) in this way. 3 a diagonal line or pattern formed by such weaving. 1,3 *n.,* 2 *v.*

'twill (twil), it will.

twilled (twild), woven in raised diagonal lines. *adj.*

twin (twin), 1 one of two children or animals born at the same time from the same mother. Twins sometimes look just alike. 2 being a twin: *twin sisters.* 3 one of two persons or things exactly alike. 4 being one of two things very much or exactly alike: *twin beds. Twin candlesticks stood on the shelf.* 5 having two like parts. 1,3 *n.,* 2,4,5 *adj.*

twine (twīn), 1 a strong thread or string made of two or more strands twisted together. 2 twist together: *She twined holly into wreaths.* 3 wind or wrap around: *The vine twines around the tree.* 4 extend or proceed in a winding manner; meander. 5 a twisting; twisting together. 6 a twist; twisted thing. 1,5,6 *n.,* 2-4 *v.,* **twined, twin ing.**

twinge (twinj), 1 a sudden, sharp pain: *a twinge of rheumatism, a twinge of remorse.* 2 feel or affect with such a pain. 1 *n.,* 2 *v.,* **twinged, twing ing.**

twin kle (twing′kəl), 1 shine with quick little gleams: *The stars twinkled. His eyes twinkled when he laughed.* 2 a twinkling; sparkle; gleam: *He has a merry twinkle in his eye.* 3 move quickly: *The dancer's feet twinkled.* 4 a quick motion of the eye; wink; blink. 5 time required for a wink: *in the twinkle of an eye.* 1,3 *v.,* **twin kled, twin kling;** 2,4,5 *n.*

twin kling (twing′kling), 1 a little, quick gleam. 2 a very brief period; an instant. *n.*

twirl (twėrl), 1 revolve rapidly; spin; whirl. 2 turn round and round idly: *He twirled his umbrella as he walked.* 3 a twirling; spin; whirl; turn: *a twirl in a dance.* 4 a twist; curl; flourish: *He signed his name with many twirls.* 1,2 *v.,* 3,4 *n.* —**twirl′er,** *n.*

twist (twist), 1 turn with a winding motion; wind: *She twisted her ring on her finger.* 2 wind together: *This rope is twisted from many threads. She twisted flowers into a wreath.* 3 turn around: *She twisted in her seat to see what was happening behind her.* 4 give a spiral form to. 5 curve; crook; bend: *to twist a piece of wire into a loop. The path twists in and out among the rocks.* 6 a curve; crook; bend: *It is full of twists.* 7 force out of shape or place: *twist an ankle. His face was twisted with pain.* 8 give a wrong meaning to; distort the meaning of: *twist an opposing candidate's words to get votes.* 9 a twisting or a being twisted. 10 anything made by twisting: *a twist of bread.* 11 a thread, cord, or rope made of two or more strands twisted together. 12 a peculiar bias or inclination: *His answer showed a mental twist.* 13 an unexpected variation: *A new twist in the plot kept*

---

hat, āge, fär; let, ēqual, tėrm;
it, īce; hot, ōpen, ôrder;
oil, out; cup, pùt, rüle; ch, child;
ng, long; sh, she; th, thin;
ᵺH, then; zh, measure;

ə represents *a* in about,
e in taken, *i* in pencil,
o in lemon, *u* in circus.

---

the audience in suspense. 1-5,7,8 *v.,* 6,9-13 *n.*

twist er (twis′tər), 1 person or thing that twists. 2 INFORMAL. whirlwind; tornado; cyclone. *n.*

twit (twit), 1 jeer at; reproach; taunt; tease: *The boys twitted me because I would not fight.* 2 a reproach; taunt. 1 *v.,* **twit ted, twit ting;** 2 *n.*

twitch (twich), 1 move with a quick jerk: *The child's mouth twitched as if she were about to cry.* 2 a quick, jerky movement of some part of the body. 3 pull with a sudden tug or jerk; pull (at): *She twitched the curtain aside.* 4 a short, sudden pull or jerk: *I felt a twitch at my shirt tail.* 1,3 *v.,* 2,4 *n., pl.* **twitch es.**

twit ter (twit′ər), 1 sound made by birds; chirping. 2 make such a sound: *Birds begin to twitter just before sunrise.* 3 to titter; giggle. 4 a brief or muffled giggle; titter. 5 an excited condition: *My nerves are in a twitter when I have to speak in public.* 6 tremble with excitement. 1,4,5 *n.,* 2,3,6 *v.*

'twixt (twikst), betwixt; between. *prep.*

two (tü), one more than one; 2. *n., pl.* **twos;** *adj.*

in two, in two parts or pieces.

two-by-four (tü′bī fôr′), 1 measuring two inches, feet, etc., by four inches, feet, etc. 2 piece of lumber four inches wide and two inches thick. Two-by-fours are much used in building. 3 INFORMAL. small; narrow; limited. 1,3 *adj.,* 2 *n.*

two-edged (tü′ejd′), 1 having two edges; cutting both ways: *a two-edged sword.* 2 effective either way. *adj.*

two-faced (tü′fāst′), deceitful; hypocritical. *adj.*

two-fist ed (tü′fis′tid), INFORMAL. strong; vigorous. *adj.*

two fold (tü′fōld′), 1 two times as much or as many; double. 2 having two parts: *a twofold shipment, part coming now and the rest later.* 1,2 *adj.,* 1 *adv.*

two pence (tup′əns), 1 two British pennies; two pence. 2 coin of this value. *n.* Also, **tuppence.**

two pen ny (tup′ə nē), 1 worth twopence. 2 trifling; worthless. *adj.*

two-ply

adj. adjective	*n.* noun
adv. adverb	*prep.* preposition
conj. conjunction	*pron.* pronoun
interj. interjection	*v.* verb
sing. singular	*pl.* plural

two-ply (tü/plī/), having two thicknesses, folds, layers, or strands. *adj.*

two some (tü/səm), 1 group of two people. 2 game played by two people. 3 the players. *n.*

two-step (tü/step/), 1 a dance in march or polka rhythm, performed with sliding steps. 2 music for it. *n.*

two-time (tü/tīm/), SLANG. betray or be disloyal to; double-cross. *v.*, **two-timed, two-tim ing.**

'twould (twůd), it would.

two-way (tü/wā/), 1 moving or allowing movement in two directions: *a two-way street.* 2 used in two ways or for two purposes: *a two-way radio for receiving and transmitting messages.* *adj.*

-ty¹, *suffix added to numbers.* _____ tens; _____ times ten: *Seventy = seven tens, or seven times ten.* [Old English *-tig*]

-ty², *suffix added to adjectives to form nouns.* quality, condition, or fact of being _____: *Safety = condition or quality of being safe.* Also, **-ity.** [from French before 1400 *-te,* from Latin *-tatem*]

ty coon (tī kün/), INFORMAL. an important businessman. *n.*

ty ing (tī/ing), present participle of **tie.** *He is tying his shoes.* *v.*

tyke (tīk), 1 INFORMAL. a mischievous or troublesome child. 2 a mongrel dog; cur. *n.* Also, **tike.**

Ty ler (tī/lər), **John,** 1790-1862, tenth president of the United States, from 1841 to 1845. *n.*

tym pan ic (tim pan/ik), of the eardrum or the middle ear. *adj.*

tympanic membrane, eardrum.

tym pa num (tim/pə nəm), 1 the eardrum. 2 the middle ear. *n., pl.* **tym pa nums, tym pa na** (tim/pə nə).

Tyne (tīn), river in N England, flowing into the North Sea. *n.*

type (tīp), 1 a kind, class, or group having common characteristics: *three types of local government. She is the type of person I like, kind and considerate of others.* 2 person or thing having the characteristics of a kind, class, or group; example; illustration; model; representative; symbol: *He is a fine type of schoolboy.* 3 the general form, style, or character of some kind,

class, or group: *She is above the ordinary type of student.* 4 be a type or symbol of; symbolize; typify. 5 piece of metal or wood having on its upper surface a raised letter for use in printing. 6 collection of such pieces: *set the manuscript for a book in type.* 7 printed letters; typewritten letters: *small or large type.* 8 write with a typewriter; typewrite: *type a letter asking for a job.* 9 find out the type of; classify: *type a person's blood.* 1-3,5-7 *n.,* 4,8,9 *v.,* **typed, typ ing.**

type script (tīp/skript/), a typewritten manuscript. *n.*

type set ter (tīp/set/ər), person or machine that sets type for printing. *n.*

type set ting (tīp/set/ing), 1 act of setting type for printing. 2 used or adapted for setting type: *a typesetting machine.* 1 *n.,* 2 *adj.*

type write (tīp/rīt/), write with a typewriter; type: *to typewrite a letter, to know how to typewrite.* *v.,* **type wrote** (tīp/rōt/), **type writ ten, type writ ing.**

type writ er (tīp/rī/tər), 1 machine for writing which reproduces letters, figures, etc., similar to printed ones. 2 typist. *n.*

type writ ing (tīp/rī/ting), 1 act or art of using a typewriter: *to study typewriting.* 2 work done on a typewriter: *Your typewriting is very accurate.* *n.*

type writ ten (tīp/rit/n), 1 written with a typewriter: *a typewritten letter.* 2 past participle of **typewrite.** *Your letter was typewritten and mailed yesterday.* 1 *adj.,* 2 *v.*

ty phoid (tī/foid), 1 of or having to do with typhoid fever. 2 typhoid fever. 3 like typhus. 1,3 *adj.,* 2 *n.*

typhoid fever, an infectious, often fatal, fever with intestinal inflammation, caused by a germ taken into the body with food or drink. People can be inoculated against typhoid fever.

ty phoon (tī fün/), 1 violent storm or tempest occurring in India. 2 violent cyclone or hurricane occurring in the western Pacific, chiefly during the period from July to October. *n.*

ty phus (tī/fəs), an acute, infectious

tyrannosaurus—about 19 ft. tall

disease characterized by high fever, extreme weakness, and dark-red spots on the skin. It is caused by germs carried by fleas, lice, ticks, or mites. *n.*

typ i cal (tip/ə kəl), 1 being a type; representative: *The typical Thanksgiving dinner consists of turkey, cranberry sauce, several vegetables, and mince or pumpkin pie.* 2 of or having to do with a type; characteristic: *the hospitality typical of frontier people.* *adj.*

typ i cal ly (tip/ik lē), 1 in a typical manner. 2 to a typical degree. 3 ordinarily. *adv.*

typ i fy (tip/ə fī), 1 be a symbol of: *The Statue of Liberty typifies the American tradition of freedom.* 2 have the common characteristics of: *Daniel Boone typifies the pioneer.* *v.,* **typ i fied, typ i fy ing.**

typ ist (tī/pist), person operating a typewriter, especially one who does typewriting as a regular occupation. *n.*

ty pog ra pher (tī pog/rə fər), printer. *n.*

ty po graph ic (tī/pə graf/ik), typographical. *adj.*

ty po graph i cal (tī/pə graf/ə kəl), of or having to do with printing or typing: *"Catt" and "hoRse" contain typographical errors.* *adj.*

ty pog ra phy (tī pog/rə fē), 1 art or process of printing with type; work of setting and arranging type and of printing from it. 2 arrangement, appearance, or style of printed matter. *n.*

Tyr (tir), (in Scandinavian myths) the god of war and victory, son of Odin. *n.*

ty ran nic (tə ran/ik), tyrannical. *adj.*

ty ran ni cal (tə ran/ə kəl), of a tyrant; like a tyrant; arbitrary; cruel; unjust: *a tyrannical government.* *adj.* **—ty ran/ni cal ly,** *adv.*

tyr an nize (tir/ə nīz), 1 use power cruelly or unjustly; oppress: *Those who are strong should not tyrannize over those who are weaker. The feudal lord tyrannized the peasants who farmed his land.* 2 rule as a tyrant. *v.,* **tyr an nized, tyr an niz ing.**

ty ran no sau rus (ti ran/ə sôr/əs), a huge, prehistoric, flesh-eating dinosaur that lived in North America and walked erect on its two hind limbs. *n., pl.* **ty ran no sau rus es.**

tyr an nous (tir/ə nəs), acting like a tyrant; cruel or unjust; arbitrary; tyrannical: *The Stamp Act seemed tyrannous to the colonists.* *adj.*

tyr an ny (tir/ə nē), 1 cruel or unjust use of power: *Cinderella escaped the tyranny of her stepsisters.* 2 a tyrannical act: *The colonists rebelled against the king's tyrannies.* 3 government by an absolute ruler. *n., pl.* **tyr an nies.**

ty rant (tī/rənt), 1 person who uses his

power cruelly or unjustly. **2** a cruel or unjust ruler; cruel master. **3** an absolute ruler, as in ancient Greece, owing his office to usurpation. Some tyrants of Greek cities were mild and just rulers. *n.*

Tyre (tīr), ancient seaport in S Phoenicia. It was noted for its wealth and wickedness. *n.*

Tyr i an (tir′ē ən), **1** of or having to do with Tyre. **2** person who was born or lived in Tyre. **1** *adj.*, **2** *n.*

Tyrian purple, **1** a crimson or purple dye used by the ancient Greeks and Romans. **2** bluish red.

ty ro (tī′rō), beginner in learning anything; novice: *Much practice changed the tyro into an expert.* *n., pl.* **ty ros.**

Ty rol (tə rōl′ *or* tī′rōl), Tirol. *n.*

Tyr rhe ni an Sea (tə rē′nē ən), part of the Mediterranean Sea lying between Italy, Sicily, Sardinia, and Corsica.

tzar (zär), czar. *n.*

tza ri na (zä rē′nə), czarina. *n., pl.* **tza ri nas.**

tzet ze (tset′sē), tsetse. *n.*

U u

U or **u** (yü), 1 the 21st letter of the alphabet. 2 anything shaped like a U. *n., pl.* **U's** or **u's**.

U.A.R., United Arab Republic.

u biq ui tous (yü bik′wə təs), that is everywhere at the same time; present everywhere. *adj.* **—u biq′ui tous ly,** *adv.*

u biq ui ty (yü bik′wə tē), a being everywhere at the same time. *n.*

U-boat (yü′bōt′), a German submarine. U-boats were first used to torpedo enemy ships during World War I. *n.* [shortened from German *Unterseeboot* undersea boat]

ud der (ud′ər), the downward-hanging bag of a cow, female goat, etc., which contains the milk-producing glands and the protruding teats through which milk can be drawn. *n.*

UFO or **U.F.O.,** unidentified flying object (a flying saucer).

U gan da (ü gan′də *or* yü gan′də), country in E Africa, a member of the Commonwealth of Nations. See **Congo** for map. *n.*

ugh (ug *or* u), exclamation expressing disgust or horror. *interj.*

ug li ness (ug′lē nis), ugly quality or appearance; a being ugly. *n.*

ug ly (ug′lē), 1 very unpleasant to look at: *an ugly house.* 2 bad; disagreeable; offensive: *an ugly smell, ugly language.* 3 morally low or offensive; base: *an ugly act of treason.* 4 likely to cause trouble; threatening; dangerous: *an ugly wound, ugly clouds.* 5 INFORMAL. bad-tempered; quarrelsome; cross: *an ugly dog. adj.,* **ug li er, ug li est.**

U.K., United Kingdom.

u kase (yü kās′), 1 (in former times) an official decree having the force of law, issued by a Russian czar or his government. 2 any official proclamation or order. *n.*

U kraine (yü krān′), republic in SW Soviet Union. *Capital:* Kiev. *n.* **—U krain′i an,** *adj., n.*

u ku le le (yü′kə lā′lē), a small guitar having four strings. *n.*

ul cer (ul′sər), 1 an open sore on the skin or, within the body, on a mucous membrane. It sometimes discharges pus. 2 a moral sore spot; corrupting influence. *n.*

ul ce rate (ul′sə rāt′), 1 affect or be affected with an ulcer: *An ulcerated stomach may be very painful.* 2 form or be formed into an ulcer. *v.,* **ul ce rat ed, ul ce rat ing.**

ul ce ra tion (ul′sə rā′shən), 1 an ulcerating or a being ulcerated. 2 an ulcer. *n.*

ul cer ous (ul′sər əs), 1 having or affected with an ulcer or ulcers. 2 having the nature of an ulcer; like an ulcer. *adj.*

ul na (ul′nə), the thinner, longer bone of the forearm, on the side opposite the thumb. *n., pl.* **ul nae** (ul′nē), **ul nas.**

ul ster (ul′stər), a long, loose, heavy overcoat, often belted at the waist. *n.* [from *Ulster*]

Ul ster (ul′stər), former province of Ireland, now forming all of Northern Ireland and part of the Republic of Ireland. *n.*

ult., of the past month: *your order of the 14th ult.* [abbreviation of Latin *ultimo* (*mense*) last (month)]

ul te ri or (ul tir′ē ər), 1 beyond what is seen or expressed; hidden: *an ulterior motive, an ulterior purpose.* 2 more distant; on the farther side. 3 further; later. *adj.*

umbel

ul ti mate (ul′tə mit), 1 coming at the end; last; final: *Most people who drive too fast never consider that the ultimate result of their action might be a serious accident.* 2 that is an extremity; beyond which there is nothing at all; extreme: *the ultimate limits of the universe.* 3 fundamental; basic: *The brain is the ultimate source of ideas.* 4 greatest possible: *He gave his life and thereby paid the ultimate price.* 5 an ultimate point, result, fact, etc. 1-4 *adj.,* 5 *n.*

ul ti mate ly (ul′tə mit lē), in the end; finally. *adv.*

ul ti ma tum (ul′tə mā′təm), a final proposal or statement of conditions, acceptance of which is required under penalty of ending a relationship, negotiations, etc. *n., pl.* **ul ti ma tums, ul ti ma ta** (ul′tə mā′tə).

ul tra (ul′trə), beyond what is usual; very; excessive; extreme. *adj.*

ultra-, *prefix.* 1 beyond the _____:

Ultraviolet = beyond the violet. 2 extremely _____: *Ultramodern = extremely modern.* [from Latin, from *ultra* beyond]

ul tra ma rine (ul′trə mə rēn′), 1 a deep blue. 2 deep-blue. 3 a blue pigment made from powdered lapis lazuli. 4 imitation of this. 1,3,4 *n.,* 2 *adj.*

ul tra mod ern (ul′trə mod′ərn), extremely modern: *ultramodern furniture. adj.*

ul tra son ic (ul′trə son′ik), of or having to do with sound waves beyond the limit of human hearing. *adj.*

ul tra vi o let (ul′trə vī′ə lit), of the invisible part of the spectrum whose rays have wavelengths shorter than those of the violet end of the visible spectrum. Ultraviolet rays are present in sunlight and are important in healing, forming vitamins, etc. *adj.*

U lys ses (yü lis′ēz), (in Greek legends) a king of Ithaca and hero of the Trojan War, known for his wisdom and shrewdness. Ulysses is the hero of Homer's *Odyssey,* which tells about his adventures. The Greeks called him Odysseus. *n.*

um bel (um′bəl), a flower cluster in which stalks nearly equal in length spring from a common center, as in parsley. *n.*

um ber (um′bər), 1 any of various mixtures of clay and iron oxide. In its natural state it is a brown pigment called **raw umber.** After heating it becomes dark reddish brown and is called **burnt umber.** 2 a brown or reddish brown. 3 brown or reddish-brown. 1,2 *n.,* 3 *adj.*

um bil i cal cord (um bil′ə kəl), a cordlike structure that connects the navel of an embryo or fetus with the placenta of the mother. It carries nourishment to the fetus and carries away waste.

um bra (um′brə), 1 the completely dark shadow cast by the earth, moon, etc., during an eclipse. See **eclipse** for diagram. 2 the dark inner part of a sunspot. 3 shade; shadow. *n., pl.* **um brae** (um′brē), **um bras.**

um brage (um′brij), suspicion that one has been slighted or injured; feeling offended; resentment. *n.*

take umbrage, take offense; feel insulted or offended: *take umbrage at the slightest criticism.*

um brel la (um brel/ə), a light, folding frame covered with cloth, used as a protection against rain or sun. *n., pl.* **um brel las.** —**um brel/la like/,** *adj.*

u mi ak (ü/mē ak), an open Eskimo boat made of skins covering a wooden frame and worked with paddles. It is very much broader and usually longer than a kayak. *n.*

umiak

um pire (um/pīr), **1** person who rules on the plays in a game: *The umpire called the ball a foul.* **2** person chosen to settle a dispute. **3** act as an umpire in (a game, dispute, etc.). **4** act as an umpire. **1,2** *n.,* **3,4** *v.,* **um pired, um pir ing.**

un-, *prefix.* **1** not _____: *Unchanged = not changed. Unjust = not just.* **2** do the opposite of _____: *Unfasten = do the opposite of fasten. Uncover = do the opposite of cover.* [Old English]

UN or **U.N.,** United Nations.

un a bashed (un/ə basht/), not embarrassed, ashamed, or awed. *adj.*

un a ble (un ā/bəl), not able: *A newborn baby is unable to walk or talk. adj.*

un a bridged (un/ə brijd/), not shortened or condensed; complete: *an unabridged book. adj.*

un ac cent ed (un ak/sen tid), not pronounced with force; not accented. *adj.*

un ac com pa nied (un/ə kum/pə nēd), **1** not accompanied; alone. **2** (in music) without instrumental accompaniment. *adj.*

un ac count a ble (un/ə koun/tə bəl), **1** that cannot be accounted for or explained. **2** not responsible: *be unaccountable for one's actions. adj.*

un ac count a bly (un/ə koun/tə blē), in a manner that cannot be accounted for; strangely. *adv.*

un ac count ed-for (un/ə koun/tid

fôr/), not accounted for or explained. *adj.*

un ac cus tomed (un/ə kus/təmd), **1** not accustomed: *Polar bears are unaccustomed to hot weather.* **2** not familiar; unusual; strange: *unaccustomed surroundings. adj.*

un ac quaint ed (un/ə kwān/tid), not acquainted. *adj.*

un a dul te rat ed (un/ə dul/tə rā/tid), not adulterated; pure: *unadulterated flour. adj.*

un ad vis ed ly (un/əd vī/zid lē), in an indiscreet manner; without careful consideration; rashly. *adv.*

un af fect ed[1] (un/ə fek/tid), not affected; not influenced. *adj.* [*un-* + *affected*[1]]

un af fect ed[2] (un/ə fek/tid), simple and natural; straightforward; sincere. *adj.* [*un-* + *affected*[2]] —**un/af fect/ed ly,** *adv.*

un aid ed (un ā/did), not aided; without help. *adj.*

un al ien a ble (un ā/lyə nə bəl), inalienable. *adj.*

un al ter a ble (un ôl/tər ə bəl), that cannot be altered; not changeable. *adj.*

un al ter a bly (un ôl/tər ə blē), in a way that cannot be changed; permanently. *adv.*

un al tered (un ôl/tərd), not altered; unchanged. *adj.*

un-A mer i can (un/ə mer/ə kən), not characteristic of or proper to America or the United States; foreign or opposed to the American character, people, government, etc. *adj.*

u na nim i ty (yü/nə nim/ə tē), complete accord or agreement. *n.*

u nan i mous (yü nan/ə məs), **1** in complete accord or agreement; agreed: *The children were unanimous in their wish to go to the beach.* **2** characterized by or showing complete accord: *She was elected president of her class by a unanimous vote. adj.*

u nan i mous ly (yü nan/ə məs lē), with complete agreement; without a single opposing vote. *adv.*

un an swer a ble (un an/sər ə bəl), **1** that cannot be answered. **2** that cannot be disproved. *adj.*

un ap proach a ble (un/ə prō/chə

hat, āge, fär; let, ēqual, tėrm;
it, īce; hot, ōpen, ôrder;
oil, out; cup, pùt, rüle; ch, child;
ng, long; sh, she; th, thin;
ŦH, then; zh, measure;

ə represents *a* in about,
e in taken, *i* in pencil,
o in lemon, *u* in circus.

bəl), **1** very hard to approach; distant. **2** without an equal; unrivaled. *adj.*

un arm (un ärm/), disarm. *v.*

un armed (un ärmd/), without weapons; without armor: *an unarmed robber. adj.*

un as sum ing (un/ə sü/ming), modest; not putting on airs: *The people of the village were delighted with the duke's unassuming manner. adj.* —**un/as sum/ing ly,** *adv.*

un at tached (un/ə tacht/), **1** not attached. **2** not engaged or married. *adj.*

un at tend ed (un/ə ten/did), **1** without attendants; alone. **2** not accompanied. **3** not taken care of; not attended to. *adj.*

un a vail ing (un/ə vā/ling), not successful; useless: *The dog kept jumping at the high fence but its efforts to get out of the pen were unavailing. adj.*

un a void a ble (un/ə voi/də bəl), that cannot be avoided: *an unavoidable delay. adj.*

un a void a bly (un/ə voi/də blē), because of something that cannot or could not be avoided or prevented; inevitably. *adv.*

un a ware (un/ə wer/ or un/ə war/), **1** not aware; unconscious: *We were unaware of the approaching storm.* **2** unawares. **1** *adj.,* **2** *adv.* —**un/a ware/ness,** *n.*

un a wares (un/ə werz/ or un/ə warz/), **1** without being expected; by surprise: *The police caught the burglar unawares.* **2** without knowing; unintentionally: *approach danger unawares. adv.*

un bal anced (un bal/ənst), **1** not bal-

In each of the words below **un** means not.

un/a bat/ed	un/am big/u ous	un/ap proached/	un/at tempt/ed
un/ab solved/	un/am bi/tious	un/ap pro/pri at/ed	un/at trac/tive
un/ac a dem/ic	un a/mi a ble	un/ap proved/	un/au then/tic
un/ac cept/a ble	un an/i mat/ed	un/ar rest/ed	un/au then/ti cat/ed
un/ac cli/mat ed	un/an nounced/	un/ar tis/tic	un au/thor ized
un/ac cli/ma tized	un an/swered	un/a shamed/	un/a vail/a ble
un/ac com/mo dat/ing	un/ap peal/ing	un asked/	un/a venged/
un/ac com/plished	un/ap peased/	un/as sail/a ble	un/a vowed/
un/ac cred/it ed	un ap/pe tiz/ing	un/as signed/	un baked/
un/ac knowl/edged	un/ap pre/ci at/ed	un/as sist/ed	
	un/ap pre/ci a/tive	un/at tain/a ble	

adj. adjective	*n.* noun
adv. adverb	*prep.* preposition
conj. conjunction	*pron.* pronoun
interj. interjection	*v.* verb
sing. singular	*pl.* plural

anced. 2 not entirely sane: *an unbalanced mind. adj.*

un bar (un bär′), remove the bars from; unlock. *v.,* **un barred, un barring.**

un bear a ble (un ber′ə bəl *or* unbar′ə bəl), that cannot be endured; intolerable: *The pain from a severe toothache is almost unbearable. adj.*

un bear a bly (un ber′ə blē *or* unbar′ə blē), in an unbearable manner; intolerably. *adv.*

un beat a ble (un bē′tə bəl), that cannot be beaten, overcome, or surpassed. *adj.*

un beat en (un bēt′n), 1 not defeated or surpassed. 2 not trodden; not traveled: *unbeaten paths.* 3 not struck, pounded, or whipped: *unbeaten metal, unbeaten eggs. adj.*

un be com ing (un′bi kum′ing), 1 not becoming; not appropriate: *unbecoming clothes.* 2 not fitting; not proper: *unbecoming behavior. adj.* —**un′be com′ing ly,** *adv.*

un be known (un′bi nōn′), not known: *He arrived unbeknown to anyone. adj.*

un be knownst (un′bi nōnst′), unbeknown. *adj.*

un be lief (un′bi lēf′), lack of belief; lack of faith. *n.*

un be liev a ble (un′bi lē′və bəl), not believable; incredible: *an unbelievable lie. adj.*

un be liev a bly (un′bi lē′və blē), beyond belief; incredibly: *The pottery we found at the archaeological site was unbelievably old. adv.*

un be liev er (un′bi lē′vər), 1 person who does not believe. 2 person who does not believe in a particular religion. *n.*

un be liev ing (un′bi lē′ving), not believing; doubting. *adj.*

un bend (un bend′), 1 make or become straight; straighten: *unbend the fingers. The wire was hard and would*

not unbend. 2 release from strain: *unbend a bow.* 3 relax: *Sitting and listening to music helps me unbend after a hard day of work.* 4 unfasten: *to unbend a sail. v.,* **un bent** *or* **un bend ed, un bend ing.**

un bend ing (un ben′ding), 1 not bending or curving; rigid. 2 not yielding; stubborn; firm: *an unbending attitude.* 3 relaxation. 1,2 *adj.,* 3 *n.*

un bent (un bent′), a past tense and a past participle of **unbend.** *v.*

un bi ased (un bī′əst), not prejudiced; impartial; fair: *Each member of a jury should have an unbiased mind when listening to the testimony of a trial. adj.*

un bid den (un bid′n), 1 not invited: *an unbidden guest.* 2 not commanded. *adj.*

un bind (un bīnd′), release from bonds or restraint; let loose; untie; unfasten. *v.,* **un bound, un bind ing.**

un bleached (un blēcht′), not bleached; not made white by bleaching: *unbleached linen. adj.*

un blem ished (un blem′isht), not blemished; spotless; flawless. *adj.*

un blessed *or* **un blest** (un blest′), 1 not blessed. 2 evil. 3 unhappy. *adj.*

un blush ing (un blush′ing), 1 not blushing. 2 unabashed; shameless. *adj.* —**un blush′ing ly,** *adv.*

un bolt (un bōlt′), draw back the bolts of (a door, etc.). *v.*

un bolt ed (un bōl′tid), not bolted or fastened: *an unbolted door. adj.*

un born (un bôrn′), not yet born; still to come; of the future: *unborn generations. adj.*

un bos om (un búz′əm *or* un bü′zəm), reveal; disclose. *v.*

unbosom oneself, tell or reveal one's thoughts, feelings, secrets, etc.

un bound (un bound′), 1 not bound: *Unbound sheets of music were scattered about the room.* 2 past tense and past participle of **unbind.** 1 *adj.,* 2 *v.*

un bound ed (un boun′did), 1 not limited; very great; boundless: *the unbounded reaches of the universe.* 2 not kept within limits; not controlled. *adj.*

un break a ble (un brā′kə bəl), not breakable; not easily broken: *Some plastic phonograph records are unbreakable. adj.*

un bri dled (un brī′dld), 1 not having a bridle on. 2 not controlled; not restrained: *unbridled anger. adj.*

un bro ken (un brō′kən), 1 not broken; whole: *an unbroken dish.* 2 not interrupted; continuous: *I had eight hours of unbroken sleep.* 3 not tamed: *an unbroken colt. adj.*

un buck le (un buk′əl), 1 unfasten the buckle or buckles of. 2 unfasten; detach. *v.,* **un buck led, un buckling.**

un bur den (un bėrd′n), 1 free from a burden. 2 relieve (one's mind or heart) by talking. *v.*

un but ton (un but′n), unfasten the button or buttons of. *v.*

un called-for (un kôld′fôr′), 1 unnecessary and improper: *an uncalled-for remark.* 2 not called for; not requested. *adj.*

un can ni ly (un kan′ə lē), in an uncanny manner. *adv.*

un can ny (un kan′ē), 1 strange and mysterious; weird: *The trees took uncanny shapes in the half darkness.* 2 so far beyond what is normal or expected as to have some special power: *an uncanny knack for solving math problems in her head. adj.*

un cap (un kap′), take the cap, top, or covering off of: *uncap a bottle. v.,* **un capped, un cap ping.**

un cared-for (un kerd′fôr′ *or* unkard′fôr′), not cared for or looked after; neglected. *adj.*

un cer e mo ni ous (un′ser ə mō′nē-əs), 1 not ceremonious; informal. 2 not as courteous as would be expected. *adj.* —**un′cer e mo′ni ous ly,** *adv.*

un cer tain (un sėrt′n), 1 not certain; doubtful: *The election results were still uncertain. She came so late that she was uncertain of her welcome.* 2 likely to change; not to be depended on: *This dog has an uncertain temper.* 3 vague; indefinite: *an uncertain shape. adj.*

un cer tain ly (un sėrt′n lē), in an uncertain manner: *He spoke slowly and uncertainly. adv.*

un cer tain ty (un sėrt′n tē), 1 uncertain state or condition; doubt. 2 something uncertain. *n., pl.* **un certain ties.**

un chain (un chān′), let loose; set free. *v.*

un change a ble (un chān′jə bəl), not changeable; that cannot be changed. *adj.*

un changed (un chānjd′), not changed; the same: *unchanged tradition. adj.*

In each of the words below **un** *means not.*

un band′aged	**un blam′a ble**	**un bowed′**	**un brushed′**	**un caught′**
un′bap tized′	**un blamed′**	**un braced′**	**un bur′ied**	**un ceas′ing**
un barbed′	**un blink′ing**	**un branched′**	**un burned′**	**un cen′sored**
un′be fit′ting	**un blurred′**	**un brand′ed**	**un burnt′**	**un cen′sured**
un′be trothed′	**un bought′**	**un broth′er ly**	**un can′celed**	**un chal′lenged**
		un bruised′	**un cap′i tal ized**	

un char i ta ble (un char′ə tə bəl), not generous; not charitable; severe; harsh. *adj.*

un chart ed (un chär′tid), not mapped; not marked on a chart. *adj.*

un chaste (un chāst′), not chaste; not virtuous. *adj.*

un checked (un chekt′), not checked; not restrained. *adj.*

un chris tian (un kris′chən), 1 not Christian. 2 unworthy of Christians. *adj.*

un civ il (un siv′əl), not civil; rude; impolite. *adj.* —**un civ′il ly,** *adv.*

un civ i lized (un siv′ə līzd), not civilized; barbarous; savage: *The Germanic barbarians who captured Rome were uncivilized. adj.*

un clad (un klad′), not dressed; not clothed; naked. *adj.*

un clasp (un klasp′), 1 unfasten. 2 release or be released from a clasp or grasp. *v.*

un cle (ung′kəl), 1 brother of one's father or mother. 2 husband of one's aunt. *n.*

un clean (un klēn′), 1 not clean; dirty; filthy. 2 not pure morally; evil. 3 not ceremonially clean. *adj.* —**un clean′ness,** *n.*

un clean li ness (un klen′lē nis), lack of cleanliness; dirtiness; filthiness. *n.*

un clean ly[1] (un klen′lē), not cleanly; unclean. *adj.* [*un-* + *cleanly*[1]]

un clean ly[2] (un klēn′lē), in an unclean manner. *adv.* [*un-* + *cleanly*[2]]

un clench (un klench′), open or become opened from a clenched state: *unclench one's fists. v.*

Uncle Sam, the government or people of the United States. Uncle Sam is usually drawn in pictures as a tall, thin man with white chin whiskers, wearing a high hat, a blue swallow-tailed coat, and red-and-white striped pants.

un cloak (un klōk′), 1 remove the coat from. 2 reveal; expose. *v.*

un clothed (un klōᵺd′), not clothed; naked; bare. *adj.*

un coil (un koil′), unwind. *v.*

un com fort a ble (un kum′fər tə bəl), 1 not comfortable. 2 uneasy.

3 causing discomfort; disagreeable. *adj.*

un com fort a bly (un kum′fər tə blē), in a way that is not comfortable; with discomfort and uneasiness; disagreeably. *adv.*

un com mon (un kom′ən), 1 rare; unusual. 2 remarkable. *adj.* —**un com′mon ness,** *n.*

un com mon ly (un kom′ən lē), 1 rarely; unusually. 2 remarkably; especially: *She is an uncommonly good cook. adv.*

un com mu ni ca tive (un′kə myü′nə kā′tiv), not giving out any information, opinions, etc.; talking little; reserved; reticent. *adj.*

un com pro mis ing (un kom′prə mī′zing), unyielding; firm: *His uncompromising attitude makes him very hard to deal with. adj.* —**un com′pro mis′ing ly,** *adv.*

un con cern (un′kən sėrn′), lack of concern; lack of interest; freedom from care or anxiety; indifference. *n.*

un con cerned (un′kən sėrnd′), not concerned; not interested; free from care or anxiety; indifferent. *adj.*

un con cern ed ly (un′kən sėr′nid lē), in an unconcerned manner; without concern or anxiety. *adv.*

un con di tion al (un′kən dish′ə nəl), without conditions; absolute: *The victorious general demanded the unconditional surrender of the enemy. adj.*

un con di tion al ly (un′kən dish′ə nə lē), without any conditions. *adv.*

un con nect ed (un′kə nek′tid), separated; disconnected. *adj.*

un con quer a ble (un kong′kər ə bəl), that cannot be conquered. *adj.*

un con scion a ble (un kon′shə nə bəl), 1 not influenced or guided by conscience: *an unconscionable liar.* 2 very great; unreasonable: *an unconscionable delay. adj.*

un con scious (un kon′shəs), 1 not conscious; not able to feel or think: *knock unconscious, unconscious from anesthetic.* 2 not aware: *unconscious of being followed, unconscious of the time.* 3 not done or felt consciously; not purposeful: *unconscious neglect,*

unconscious resentment. 4 the part of the mind containing thoughts, feelings, etc., that one is not directly or fully aware of; one's unconscious thoughts, feelings, etc.; subconscious. 1-3 *adj.,* 4 *n.* —**un con′scious ly,** *adv.* —**un con′scious ness,** *n.*

un con sti tu tion al (un′kon stə tü′shə nəl *or* un′kon stə tyü′shə nəl), contrary to the constitution; not constitutional. *adj.* —**un′con sti tu′tion al ly,** *adv.*

un con sti tu tion al i ty (un′kon stə tü′shə nal′ə tē *or* un′kon stə tyü′shə nal′ə tē), a being contrary to the constitution. *n.*

un con trol la ble (un′kən trō′lə bəl), that cannot be controlled; not able to be checked or restrained: *an uncontrollable temper. adj.*

un con trolled (un′kən trōld′), not controlled; not restrained. *adj.*

un con ven tion al (un′kən ven′shə nəl), not bound by or conforming to convention, rule, or precedent; free from conventionality. *adj.*

un cork (un kôrk′), pull the cork from. *v.*

un count a ble (un koun′tə bəl), that cannot be counted; innumerable: *an uncountable number of stars. adj.*

un count ed (un koun′tid), 1 not counted; not reckoned. 2 very many; innumerable. *adj.*

un cou ple (un kup′əl), disconnect; unfasten: *They uncoupled two freight cars. The last two freight cars uncoupled and rolled to a stop. v.,* **un cou pled, un cou pling.**

hat, āge, fär; let, ēqual, tėrm;
it, īce; hot, ōpen, ôrder;
oil, out; cup, pùt, rüle; ch, child;
ng, long; sh, she; th, thin;
ᵺ, then; zh, measure;

ə represents *a* in about,
e in taken, *i* in pencil,
o in lemon, *u* in circus.

In each of the words below **un** *means not.*

un chang′ing	un cleared′	un com′fort ed	un′con fined′	un′con tra dict′ed
un chap′e roned′	un closed′	un′com mit′ted	un′con firmed′	un′con vert′ed
un charged′	un cloud′ed	un′com pan′ion a ble	un′con gealed′	un′con vinced′
un chas′tened	un clut′tered	un′com plain′ing	un′con gen′ial	un′con vinc′ing
un chewed′	un coat′ed	un′com plai′sant	un′con gest′ed	un cooked′
un chiv′al rous	un cocked′	un′com plet′ed	un con′quered	un′co op′e ra′tive
un chris′tened	un′col lect′ed	un′com′pli cat′ed	un′con se crat′ed	un′co or′di nat′ed
un claimed′	un col′ored	un′com pli men′tar y	un con sid′ered	un cor′dial
un clas′si fied	un combed′	un′com pound′ed	un′con strained′	un corked′
un cleaned′	un′com bined′	un′com pre hend′ing	un′con sumed′	un′cor rect′ed
un clear′	un come′ly	un′com′pro mised	un′con tam′i nat′ed	un′cor rob′o rat′ed
		un′con cealed′	un′con test′ed	un′cor rupt′ed

uncourteous

adj.	adjective	*n.*	noun
adv.	adverb	*prep.*	preposition
conj.	conjunction	*pron.*	pronoun
interj.	interjection	*v.*	verb
sing.	singular	*pl.*	plural

un cour te ous (un kėr′tē əs), not courteous; impolite; rude. *adj.*

un couth (un küth′), 1 not refined; awkward; clumsy; crude: *uncouth manners, an uncouth person.* 2 unusual and unpleasant; strange: *the eerie and uncouth noises of the jungle. adj.* —**uncouth′ly,** *adv.* —**un couth′ness,** *n.*

un cov er (un kuv′ər), 1 remove the cover from. 2 make known; reveal; expose. 3 remove one's hat or cap in respect: *The men uncovered as the flag passed by. v.*

un crowned (un kround′), 1 not crowned; not having yet assumed the crown. 2 having royal power without being king, queen, etc. *adj.*

unc tion (ungk′shən), 1 an anointing with oil, ointment, etc., for medical purposes or as a religious rite. 2 the oil, ointment, or the like, used for anointing. 3 something soothing or comforting: *the unction of flattery.* 4 fervor; earnestness. 5 affected earnestness. *n.*

unc tu ous (ungk′chu əs), 1 like an oil or ointment in texture; oily; greasy. 2 soothing, sympathetic, and persuasive. 3 too smooth and oily: *the hypocrite's unctuous manner. adj.* —**unc′tu ous ly,** *adv.* —**unc′tu ous ness,** *n.*

un cul ti vat ed (un kul′tə vā′tid), not cultivated; wild; undeveloped. *adj.*

un curl (un kėrl′), straighten out. *v.*

un daunt ed (un dôn′tid), not afraid; not discouraged; fearless: *an undaunted leader. The skier was undaunted by the bad fall she suffered in the first race. adj.*

un de ceive (un′di sēv′), free (a person) from error, mistake, or deception. *v.,* **un de ceived, un de ceiving.**

un de cid ed (un′di sī′did), 1 not decided; not settled. 2 not having one's mind made up. *adj.* —**un′de cid′ed ly,** *adv.*

un de filed (un′di fīld′), not defiled; pure. *adj.*

un de fined (un′di fīnd′), 1 not defined or explained. 2 indefinite. *adj.*

un de ni a ble (un′di nī′ə bəl), 1 that cannot be denied or disputed; certain. 2 unquestionably good; excellent. *adj.*

un de ni a bly (un′di nī′ə blē), beyond denial or dispute; certainly. *adv.*

un der (un′dər), 1 below; beneath: *The book fell under the table* (prep.). *The swimmer went under* (adv.). 2 below the surface of: *under the sea.* 3 in or to a lower place or condition. 4 lower in position, rank, degree, amount, price, etc.: *the under lip.* 5 lower than; lower down than; not so high as: *He hit me under the belt.* 6 less than: *It will cost under ten dollars.* 7 during the rule or time of: *England under King John.* 8 in the position or condition of being affected by: *under the new rules.* 9 because of: *We cannot join your club under these conditions.* 10 according to: *under the law. The soldiers acted under orders.* 11 represented by: *under a new name.* 12 required or bound by: *You are not under any obligation to pay for merchandise that arrives damaged.* 13 included in a particular group, category, or class: *In this library, books on stamp collecting are listed under philately.* 1,2,5-13 *prep.,* 1,3 *adv.,* 4 *adj.*

under-, *prefix.* 1 below; beneath: *Underline = draw a line below. Underground = beneath the ground.* 2 being beneath; worn beneath: *Underclothes = clothes worn beneath one's outer clothes.* 3 lower in rank; subordinate: *Undersecretary = secretary that is lower in rank.* 4 lower than: *Underbid = bid lower than.* 5 not enough; not sufficiently: *Undernourished = not sufficiently nourished.* 6 below normal: *Underweight = below normal weight.* [from *under*]

un der age (un′dər āj′), not of full age; less than the usual or required age. *adj.*

un der arm (un′dər ärm′), 1 situated or placed under the arm; found in or near the armpit: *an underarm scar, an underarm deodorant.* 2 armpit. 3 underhand: *an underarm pitcher* (adj.). *In softball a pitcher must throw underarm* (adv.). 1,3 *adj.,* 2 *n.,* 3 *adv.*

un der bid (un′dər bid′), make a lower bid than (another): *to underbid a*

competitor in seeking a contract to be awarded to the lowest bidder. *v.,* **under bid, un der bid ding.**

un der brush (un′dər brush′), shrubs, bushes, and small trees growing under large trees in woods or forests. *n.*

un der clothes (un′dər klōz′ *or* un′dər klōŦHz′), underwear. *n.pl.*

un der cloth ing (un′dər klō′ŦHing), underwear. *n.*

un der cov er (un′dər kuv′ər), working or done in secret: *The jeweler was an undercover agent of the police. adj.*

un der cur rent (un′dər kėr′ənt), 1 current below the upper currents, or below the surface, of a body of water, air, etc. 2 an underlying tendency: *There was an undercurrent of sadness in her laugh. n.*

un der cut (un′dər kut′ *for 1,3;* un′dər kut′ *for 2*), 1 cut under or beneath; cut away material from so as to leave a portion overhanging. 2 a cut, or a cutting away, underneath. 3 sell or work for less than (another). 1,3 *v.,* **un der cut, un der cut ting;** 2 *n.*

un der de vel oped (un′dər di vel′əpt), 1 not normally developed: *an underdeveloped limb.* 2 poorly or insufficiently developed in production, technology, medicine, standard of living, etc.: *The underdeveloped countries need trained personnel. adj.*

un der dog (un′dər dôg′), 1 person having the worst of any struggle; person in an inferior position: *The senator's early experience of poverty made him a champion of the underdog.* 2 contestant considered unlikely to win. *n.*

un der done (un′dər dun′ *or* un′dər dun′), not cooked enough; cooked very little. *adj.*

un der es ti mate (un′dər es′tə māt *for 1;* un′dər es′tə mit *or* un′dər es′tə māt *for 2*), 1 to estimate at too low a value, amount, rate, etc. 2 an estimate that is too low. 1 *v.,* **un der es ti mat ed, un der es ti mat ing;** 2 *n.*

un der ex po sure (un′dər ek spō′zhər), too little or too short an exposure. Underexposure to light makes a photograph look dim. *n.*

un der feed (un′dər fēd′), feed too little. *v.,* **un der fed** (un′dər fed′), **un der feed ing.**

un der foot (un′dər fůt′), 1 under one's foot or feet; on the ground; un-

---

In each of the words below **un** *means not.*

un′cre at′ed	**un′curbed′**	**un′dat′ed**	**un′dec′o rat′ed**	**un′de mon′stra ble**
un cred′it ed	**un cured′**	**un daz′zled**	**un′de feat′ed**	**un′de mon′stra tive**
un crit′i cal	**un′cur′tained**	**un′de bat′a ble**	**un′de fend′ed**	**un′de pend′a ble**
un crowd′ed	**un′cut′**	**un′de cayed′**	**un′de fen′si ble**	
un crys′tal lized	**un dam′aged**	**un′de ceived′**	**un′de layed′**	
un cul′tured	**un damped′**	**un′de ci′phered**	**un′de liv′ered**	
		un′de clared′	**un dem o crat′ic**	

918

derneath. **2** in the way: *The cat is always underfoot when I'm cooking a meal.* *adv.*

un der gar ment (un/dər gär/mənt), garment worn under an outer garment, especially next to the skin. *n.*

un der go (un/dər gō/), **1** go through; pass through; be subjected to: *The town is undergoing many changes as more and more people are moving in.* **2** endure; suffer: *The poor undergo many hardships.* *v.*, **un der went, un der gone, un der go ing.**

un der gone (un/dər gôn/), past participle of **undergo.** *The town has undergone many changes.* *v.*

un der grad u ate (un/dər graj/ü it), **1** student in a college or university who has not yet received a degree. **2** of, for, or having to do with undergraduates. **1** *n.*, **2** *adj.*

un der ground (un/dər ground/ *for 1,5;* un/dər ground/ *for 2-4,6,7*), **1** beneath the surface of the ground: *The mole burrowed underground.* **2** being, working, or used beneath the surface of the ground: *an underground passage.* **3** a place or space beneath the surface of the ground. **4** subway (a term used in Great Britain). **5** in or into secrecy or concealment: *The thief went underground after the robbery.* **6** secret: *an underground plot.* **7** a secret organization working against an unpopular government, especially during military occupation: *the French underground during World War II.* **1,5** *adv.*, **2,6** *adj.*, **3,4,7** *n.*

un der growth (un/dər grōth/), underbrush. *n.*

un der hand (un/dər hand/), **1** not open or honest; secret; sly. **2** secretly; slyly. **3** with the hand below the level of the shoulder: *an underhand pitch (adj.), throw a ball underhand (adv.).* **1,3** *adj.*, **2,3** *adv.*

underpinning
(def. 1)

un der hand ed (un/dər han/did), underhand; secret; sly: *an underhanded trick.* *adj.* —**un/der hand/ed ly,** *adv.* —**un/der hand/ed ness,** *n.*

un der lie (un/dər lī/), **1** lie under; be beneath. **2** be at the basis of; form the foundation of. *v.*, **un der lay** (un/dər lā/), **un der lain** (un/dər lān/), **un der ly ing.**

un der line (un/dər līn/ *or* un/dər līn/), **1** draw a line or lines under: *In writing, we underline titles of books.* **2** make emphatic or more emphatic; emphasize. *v.*, **un der lined, un der lin ing.**

un der ling (un/dər ling), person of lower rank or position; inferior. *n.*

un der ly ing (un/dər lī/ing), **1** lying under or beneath. **2** fundamental; basic; essential. **3** present participle of **underlie.** **1,2** *adj.*, **3** *v.*

un der mine (un/dər mīn/ *or* un/dər mīn/), **1** make a passage or hole under; dig under: *undermine a foundation. The soldiers undermined the wall.* **2** wear away the foundations of: *The waves had undermined the cliff.* **3** weaken by secret or unfair means: *Some people tried to undermine the chairman's influence by spreading lies about him.* **4** weaken or destroy gradually: *Many severe colds had undermined her health.* *v.*, **un der mined, un der min ing.**

un der most (un/dər mōst), lowest. *adj.*, *adv.*

un der neath (un/dər nēth/), beneath; below; under: *They sat underneath a tree (prep.). Someone was pushing from underneath (adv.).* *prep.*, *adv.*

un der nour ished (un/dər nėr/isht), not sufficiently nourished. *adj.*

un der nour ish ment (un/dər nėr/ish mənt), lack of nourishment; not having enough food. *n.*

un der pants (un/dər pants/), pants worn as an undergarment; drawers. *n.pl.*

un der part (un/dər pärt/), the part of an object, animal, etc., that lies below or underneath. *n.*

un der pass (un/dər pas/), passageway underneath; road under railroad tracks or under another road. *n.*, *pl.* **un der pass es.**

un der pay (un/dər pā/), pay too little. *v.*, **un der paid** (un/dər pād/), **un der pay ing.**

un der pin ning (un/dər pin/ing), **1** the materials or structure that give support from beneath to a building, wall, etc. **2** a support; prop. *n.*

un der priv i leged (un/dər priv/ə lijd), having fewer advantages than most have, especially because of poor economic or social status: *an underprivileged nation, underprivileged children.* *adj.*

un der rate (un/dər rāt/), to rate or estimate too low; put too low a value on. *v.*, **un der rat ed, un der rat ing.**

un der score (un/dər skôr/ *or* un/dər skôr/), underline. *v.*, **un der scored, un der scor ing.**

un der sea (un/dər sē/ *for 1;* un/dər sē/ *for 2*), **1** being, working, or used beneath the surface of the sea: *an un-*

dersea cable, undersea exploration. **2** underseas. **1** *adj.*, **2** *adv.*

un der seas (un/dər sēz/), beneath the surface of the sea: *Submarines go underseas.* *adv.*

un der sec re tar y (un/dər sek/rə ter/ē), an assistant secretary, especially of a government department. *n.*, *pl.* **un der sec re tar ies.**

un der sell (un/dər sel/), sell things at a lower price than (another): *This store can undersell other stores because it sells in great volume.* *v.*, **un der sold** (un/dər sōld/), **un der sell ing.**

un der shirt (un/dər shėrt/), shirt worn next to the skin under other clothing. *n.*

undershot
(def. 2)
undershot
water wheel

WATER NOZZLE

un der shot (un/dər shot/), **1** having the lower jaw projecting beyond the upper. **2** driven by water passing beneath: *an undershot water wheel.* *adj.*

un der side (un/dər sīd/), surface lying underneath; bottom side: *The underside of the stone was covered with ants.* *n.*

un der signed (un/dər sīnd/), **1** signed, or having signed at the end of a letter or document. **2 the undersigned,** person or persons signing a letter or document. **1** *adj.*, **2** *n.*

un der sized (un/dər sīzd/), smaller than the usual size: *an undersized fish.* *adj.*

un der skirt (un/dər skėrt/), skirt worn under an outer skirt. *n.*

un der stand (un/dər stand/), **1** get the meaning of: *Now I understand the teacher's question.* **2** get the meaning: *I have told her three times, but she still doesn't understand.* **3** know how to deal

understandable

adj.	adjective	*n.*	noun
adv.	adverb	*prep.*	preposition
conj.	conjunction	*pron.*	pronoun
interj.	interjection	*v.*	verb
sing.	singular	*pl.*	plural

with; know well; know: *A good teacher understands children.* 4 be informed; learn: *I understand that she bought a house.* 5 take as a fact; believe: *It is understood that you will come.* 6 take as meaning; interpret: *I understood your comment as approval of the plan.* 7 supply in the mind. In "He hit the tree harder than I," the word *did* is understood after *I.* *v.*, **un der stood, un der stand ing.**

un der stand a ble (un/dər stan/də-bəl), able to be understood. *adj.*

un der stand a bly (un/dər stan/də-blē), in a manner that can be understood. *adv.*

un der stand ing (un/dər stan/ding), 1 comprehension; knowledge: *a clear understanding of the problem.* 2 ability to learn and know; intelligence: *That scholar is a man of great understanding.* 3 that understands; intelligent and sympathetic: *an understanding reply.* 4 knowledge of each other's meaning and wishes: *True friendship is based on understanding.* 5 a mutual arrangement or agreement: *We have an understanding about the use of the car on Saturdays.* 1,2,4,5 *n.*, 3 *adj.* —**un/der stand/ing-ly,** *adv.*

un der state (un/dər stāt/), 1 state too weakly. 2 say less than the full truth about. *v.*, **un der stat ed, un der stat ing.**

un der state ment (un/dər stāt/-mənt), 1 statement that expresses a fact too weakly. 2 statement that says less than could be said truly. *n.*

un der stood (un/dər stud/), past tense and past participle of **understand.** *Have all of you understood today's lesson? I understood what she said.* *v.*

un der stud y (un/dər stud/ē), 1 person who can act as a substitute for an actor, actress, or any other regular performer. 2 learn (a part) in order to replace the regular performer when

necessary. 3 to act as an understudy to. 1 *n., pl.* **un der stud ies;** 2,3 *v.*, **un der stud ied, un der stud y ing.**

un der sur face (un/dər sėr/fis), underside: *the undersurface of a leaf.* *n.*

un der take (un/dər tāk/), 1 set about; try; attempt: *undertake to reach home before dark.* 2 agree to do; take upon oneself: *I will undertake the feeding of your dogs while you are away.* 3 to promise; guarantee. *v.*, **un der took, un der tak en, un der tak ing.**

un der tak er (un/dər tā/kər *for 1;* un/dər tā/kər *for 2),* 1 person whose business is preparing the dead for burial and arranging funerals; mortician. 2 person who undertakes something. *n.*

un der tak ing (un/dər tā/king *for 1,2;* un/dər tā/king *for 3),* 1 something undertaken; task; enterprise. 2 a promise; guarantee. 3 business of preparing the dead for burial and arranging funerals. *n.*

un der tone (un/dər tōn/), 1 a low or very quiet tone: *talk in undertones.* 2 a subdued color; color seen through other colors: *There was an undertone of brown beneath all the gold and crimson of autumn.* 3 something beneath the surface; an underlying quality, condition, or element: *an undertone of sadness in her gaiety.* *n.*

un der took (un/dər tuk/), past tense of **undertake.** *He failed because he undertook more than he could do.* *v.*

un der tow (un/dər tō/), 1 any strong current below the surface of the water, moving in a direction different from that of the surface current. 2 the backward flow from waves breaking on a beach. *n.*

un der val ue (un/dər val/yü), put too low a value on. *v.*, **un der val ued, un der val u ing.**

un der waist (un/dər wāst/), waist worn under another waist. *n.*

un der wa ter (un/dər wô/tər *or* un/dər wot/ər), 1 below the surface of the water. 2 made for use under the water: *A submarine is an underwater boat.* *adj.*

un der way (un/dər wā/), going on; in motion; in progress: *The drive to raise money for the new library is finally underway.* *adv.*

un der wear (un/dər wer/ *or* un/dər-war/), clothing worn under one's outer clothes, especially next to the skin; underclothes; underclothing. *n.*

un der weight (un/dər wāt/), 1 having too little weight; below the normal or required weight. 2 weight that is not up to standard. 1 *adj.*, 2 *n.*

un der went (un/dər went/), past tense of **undergo.** *Transportation underwent a great change with the development of the automobile.* *v.*

un der wood (un/dər wud/), underbrush. *n.*

un der world (un/dər wėrld/), 1 the criminal part of human society. 2 the lower world; Hades. *n.*

un der write (un/dər rīt/ *or* un/dər-rīt/), 1 insure (property) against loss. 2 sign (an insurance policy), thereby accepting the risk of insuring something against loss. 3 write under (other written matter); sign one's name to (a document, etc.). 4 agree to buy (all the stocks or bonds of a certain issue that are not bought by the public): *The bankers underwrote the steel company's bonds.* *v.*, **un der wrote** (un/dər rōt/ *or* un/dər rōt/), **un der writ ten** (un/-dər rit/n *or* un/dər rit/n), **un der writ-ing.**

un der writ er (un/dər rī/tər), 1 person who underwrites an insurance policy or carries on an insurance business. 2 person who underwrites (usually with others) an issue or issues of stocks or bonds. *n.*

un de sir a ble (un/di zī/rə bəl), 1 objectionable; disagreeable: *The drug was taken off the market because it had undesirable effects on persons who used it.* 2 an undesirable person or thing: *a gathering of criminals and other undesirables.* 1 *adj.*, 2 *n.*

un de sir a bly (un/di zī/rə blē), in an undesirable manner. *adv.*

un de vel oped (un/di vel/əpt), 1 not fully grown; immature. 2 not put to full use: *undeveloped natural resources of a country.* *adj.*

un did (un did/), past tense of **undo.** *The fire in the artist's studio undid many years of work.* *v.*

un dis ci plined (un dis/ə plind), not disciplined; without proper control; untrained. *adj.*

un dis guised (un/dis gīzd/), 1 not disguised. 2 unconcealed; open; plain; frank: *undisguised delight.* *adj.*

un dis mayed (un/dis mād/), not dismayed; undaunted. *adj.*

un dis put ed (un/dis pyü/tid), not disputed; not doubted. *adj.*

In each of the words below **un** *means not.*

un/de served/	un/de tach/a ble	un/dif fe ren/ti at/ed	un/dip lo mat/ic	un/dis cov/ered
un/de serv/ing	un/de tect/ed	un/di gest/ed	un/dis cern/i ble	un/dis crim/i nat/ing
un des/ig nat/ed	un/de ter/mined	un dig/ni fied	un/dis cern/ing	un/dis so/ci at/ed
un/de sired/	un/de terred/	un/di lut/ed	un/dis charged/	un/dis solved/
un/de spair/ing	un/de vout/	un/di min/ished	un/dis closed/	
		un dimmed/	un/dis cour/aged	

un dis tin guish a ble (un′dis-
ting′gwi shə bəl), that cannot be distinguished. *adj.*

un dis tin guished (un′dis ting′-
gwisht), not distinguished; commonplace. *adj.*

un dis turbed (un′dis tėrbd′), not
disturbed; not troubled; calm. *adj.*

un di vid ed (un′də vī′did), not divided; not separated into parts; complete:
*The teacher asked for our undivided
attention. adj.*

un do (un dü′), 1 unfasten; untie:
*Please undo the package. I undid the
string.* 2 do away with the effect of; cause
to be as if never done; cancel or reverse:
*The workers mended the road, but a
heavy storm undid their work.* 3 bring
to ruin; spoil; destroy. *v.*, **un did,
un done, un do ing.**

un do ing (un dü′ing), 1 a bringing to
ruin; spoiling; destroying. 2 cause of
destruction or ruin: *Gambling was this
man's undoing.* 3 a canceling or reversing the effect of something. 4 an untying; unfastening. *n.*

un done (un dun′), 1 not done; not
finished. 2 ruined. 3 untied; unfastened. 4 past participle of **undo.** 1-3
adj., 4 *v.*

un doubt ed (un dou′tid), not doubted; accepted as true. *adj.*

un doubt ed ly (un dou′tid lē), beyond doubt; certainly. *adv.*

un draw (un drô′), draw back or away:
She undrew the curtain. *v.*, **un drew**
(un drü′), **un drawn** (un drôn′), **un-
draw ing.**

un dreamed-of (un drēmd′uv′ or un-
drēmd′ov′), never thought of, even in
the imagination: *undreamed-of advances in medicine. adj.*

un dreamt-of (un dremt′uv′ or un-
dremt′ov′), undreamed-of. *adj.*

un dress (un dres′ for 1,2; un′-
dres′ or un dres′ for 3), 1 take the
clothes off; strip. 2 take off one's
clothes. 3 loose, informal dress. 1,2 *v.*,
3 *n.*

un due (un dü′ or un dyü′), 1 not fitting; not right; improper: *make rude,
undue remarks to someone, undue actions.* 2 too great; too much; excessive:

*undue praise, give undue importance to
money. adj.*

un du lant (un′jə lənt), waving; wavy.
adj.

un du late (un′jə lāt), 1 move or
cause to move in waves: *undulating
water.* 2 have a wavy form or surface:
undulating hair, an undulating prairie.
v., **un du lat ed, un du lat ing.**

un du la tion (un′jə lā′shən), 1 a
wavelike motion; undulating. 2 a wavy
form. 3 one of a series of wavelike
bends, curves, swellings, etc. *n.*

un du ly (un dü′lē or un dyü′lē), 1 in
an undue manner; improperly. 2 too
much; excessively: *unduly harsh, unduly optimistic. adv.*

un dy ing (un dī′ing), that never dies;
deathless; immortal; eternal: *undying
beauty, a dog's undying love for its
master. adj.*

un earned (un ėrnd′), 1 not earned:
an unearned gift of nature. 2 not deserved: *unearned punishment. adj.*

un earth (un ėrth′), 1 dig up: *unearth
a buried city.* 2 find out; discover: *unearth a plot. v.*

un earth ly (un ėrth′lē), 1 not of this
world; supernatural. 2 strange; weird;
ghostly. *adj.*

un eas i ly (un ē′zə lē), in an uneasy
manner; restlessly. *adv.*

un eas i ness (un ē′zē nis), a being
uneasy; restlessness. *n.*

un eas y (un ē′zē), 1 restless; disturbed; anxious. 2 not comfortable.
3 not easy in manner; awkward. *adj.*,
un eas i er, un eas i est.

un ed u cat ed (un ej′ə kā′tid), not
educated; not taught or trained. *adj.*

un em ployed (un′em ploid′), 1 not
employed; not in use: *an unemployed
skill.* 2 not having a job; having no
work: *an unemployed person.* 3 **the
unemployed,** people out of work: *The
unemployed sought aid from the government.* 1,2 *adj.*, 3 *n.*

un em ploy ment (un′em ploi′mənt),
lack of employment; being out of
work. *n.*

un e qual (un ē′kwəl), 1 not the same
in amount, size, number, value, degree,
or rank: *unequal sums of money.* 2 not

hat, āge, fär; let, ēqual, tėrm;
it, īce; hot, ōpen, ôrder;
oil, out; cup, put, rüle; ch, child;
ng, long; sh, she; th, thin;
ᴛʜ, then; zh, measure;

ə represents *a* in about,
e in taken, *i* in pencil,
o in lemon, *u* in circus.

fair; one-sided: *an unequal contest.*
3 not enough; not adequate: *Their
strength was unequal to the task.* 4 not
regular; not even: *unequal vibrations.*
adj. —**un e′qual ly,** *adv.*

un e qualed (un ē′kwəld), that has no
equal or superior; matchless: *unequaled
beauty, unequaled speed. adj.*

un e quiv o cal (un′i kwiv′ə kəl),
clear; plain: *an unequivocal refusal. adj.*
—**un′e quiv′o cal ly,** *adv.*

un err ing (un ėr′ing or un er′ing),
making no mistakes; exactly right: *unerring aim. adj.* —**un err′ing ly,** *adv.*

U NES CO or **U nes co** (yü nes′kō),
United Nations Educational, Scientific,
and Cultural Organization. *n.*

un e ven (un ē′vən), 1 not even; not
level, flat, or smooth: *uneven ground.*
2 not equal: *an uneven contest.* 3 not
uniform or regular; changeable; inconsistent: *Her work is of uneven quality.*
4 leaving a remainder of 1 when divided
by 2; odd: *1, 3, 5, 7, and 9 are uneven
numbers. adj.* —**un e′ven ly,** *adv.*
—**un e′ven ness,** *n.*

un e vent ful (un′i vent′fəl), without
important or striking occurrences: *a
quiet, uneventful day in the country.*
adj. —**un′e vent′ful ly,** *adv.*

un ex am pled (un′eg zam′pəld),
having no equal or like; without precedent or parallel; without anything like
it: *This man's run of 100 yards in 9
seconds is unexampled. adj.*

un ex cep tion a ble (un′ek sep′shə-
nə bəl), beyond criticism; wholly admirable. *adj.*

un ex pect ed (un′ek spek′tid), not

In each of the words below **un** *means not.*

un′dis tin′guish ing	un draped′	un ed′i fy′ing	un′en dur′ing	un′e quipped′
un′dis tort′ed	un dreamed′	un′e lim′i nat′ed	un′en force′a ble	un′es sen′tial
un′dis tract′ed	un dreamt′	un′em bar′rassed	un′en forced′	un es′ti mat′ed
un′dis trib′ut ed	un dressed′	un′em bel′lished	un′en gaged′	un eth′i cal
un′di ver′si fied	un drilled′	un′e mo′tion al	un′en joy′a ble	un′ex ag′ge rat′ed
un′di vulged′	un du′ti ful	un′em phat′ic	un′en light′ened	un′ex celled′
un′do mes′ti cat′ed	un dyed′	un′en closed′	un′en ter pris′ing	un′ex cep′tion al
un dou′bled	un eat′a ble	un′en cum′bered	un′en ter tain′ing	un′ex cit′ed
un doubt′ing	un eat′en	un′en dan′gered	un′en thu′si as′tic	un′ex cit′ing
un drained′	un′e co nom′ic	un end′ing	un en′vi a ble	un′ex cused′
un′dra mat′ic	un′e co nom′i cal	un′en dorsed′	un en′vied	un ex′e cut′ed
		un′en dur′a ble	un en′vi ous	un′ex haust′ed

---

adj. adjective	*n.* noun
adv. adverb	*prep.* preposition
conj. conjunction	*pron.* pronoun
interj. interjection	*v.* verb
sing. singular	*pl.* plural

expected: *an unexpected difficulty, an unexpected change in the weather. The President made an unexpected visit to the city. adj.* —**un'ex pect'ed ness,** *n.*

un ex pect ed ly (un'ek spek'tid lē), without being expected; in a way that is not expected; suddenly. *adv.*

un ex per i enced (un'ek spir'ē- ənst), inexperienced. *adj.*

un fail ing (un fā'ling), 1 never fail- ing; always ready when needed; loyal: *an unfailing friend.* 2 never running short; endless: *an unfailing supply of water.* 3 sure; certain: *an unfailing proof. adj.*

un fail ing ly (un fā'ling lē), without fail; always. *adv.*

un fair (un fer' or un far'), not fair; unjust: *an unfair decision by an umpire. It was unfair of you to trick your little sister into giving you all the candy. adj.* —**un fair'ly,** *adv.* —**un fair'- ness,** *n.*

un faith ful (un fāth'fəl), 1 not faith- ful; not true to duty or one's promises; faithless. 2 not accurate; not exact: *an unfaithful translation. adj.* —**un- faith'ful ly,** *adv.* —**un faith'ful- ness,** *n.*

un fal ter ing (un fôl'tər ing), not hes- itating; firm; steadfast. *adj.*

un fa mil iar (un'fə mil'yər), 1 not well known; unusual; strange: *That face is unfamiliar to me.* 2 not acquainted: *She is unfamiliar with the Greek lan- guage. adj.*

un fa mil iar i ty (un'fə mil'yar'ə- tē), lack of familiarity. *n.*

un fas ten (un fas'n), undo; untie; loosen; open. *v.*

un fath om a ble (un faтн'ə mə bəl),

1 too deep to be measured. 2 too mys- terious to be understood. *adj.*

un fath omed (un faтн'əmd), 1 not measured. 2 not understood. *adj.*

un fa vor a ble (un fā'vər ə bəl), not favorable; adverse; harmful. *adj.*

un fa vor a bly (un fā'vər ə blē), in an unfavorable manner. *adv.*

un feel ing (un fē'ling), 1 hard- hearted; cruel: *a cold, unfeeling person.* 2 not able to feel. *adj.* —**un feel'ing- ly,** *adv.*

un feigned (un fānd'), not feigned; sincere; real: *unfeigned anger, unfeigned joy. adj.*

un fet ter (un fet'ər), remove fetters from; make free; unchain. *v.*

un fin ished (un fin'isht), 1 not fin- ished; not complete: *unfinished home- work, an unfinished symphony.* 2 with- out some special finish; not polished or painted: *unfinished furniture. adj.*

un fit (un fit'), 1 not fit; not suitable. 2 not good enough; unqualified. 3 make unfit; spoil. 1,2 *adj.,* 3 *v.,* **un fit ted, un fit ting.** —**un fit'ness,** *n.*

un flag ging (un flag'ing), not weak- ening or failing: *unflagging strength, unflagging efforts. adj.*

un fledged (un flejd'), 1 too young to fly; not having full-grown feathers: *an unfledged crow.* 2 undeveloped; imma- ture; inexperienced. *adj.*

un flinch ing (un flin'ching), not drawing back from difficulty, danger, or pain; firm; resolute: *unflinching cour- age. adj.*

un fold (un fōld'), 1 open the folds of; open up; spread out: *unfold a napkin.* 2 reveal; show; explain: *unfold the plot of a story.* 3 open; develop: *Buds un- fold into flowers. v.*

un forced (un fôrst'), 1 not forced; not compelled; willing. 2 natural; spon- taneous. *adj.*

un fore seen (un'fôr sēn'), not known beforehand; unexpected. *adj.*

un for get ta ble (un'fər get'ə bəl), that can never be forgotten. *adj.*

un for get ta bly (un'fər get'ə blē), in an unforgettable manner. *adv.*

un formed (un fôrmd'), 1 without definite or regular form; shapeless: *an*

unformed ball of clay. 2 unde- veloped: *an unformed mind. adj.*

un for tu nate (un fôr'chə nit), 1 not lucky; having bad luck. 2 not suitable; not fitting: *an unfortunate choice of words. The child's display of temper was an unfortunate thing for the guest to see.* 3 an unfortunate person. 1,2 *adj.,* 3 *n.* —**un for'tu nate ly,** *adv.*

un found ed (un foun'did), without foundation; without reason; baseless: *an unfounded complaint. adj.*

un fre quent ed (un'frē kwen'tid), not frequented; seldom visited; rarely used. *adj.*

un friend li ness (un frend'lē nis), a being unfriendly. *n.*

un friend ly (un frend'lē), 1 not friendly; hostile. 2 not favorable. *adj.*

un fruit ful (un früt'fəl), not fruitful; not productive; barren. *adj.*

un furl (un fèrl'), spread out; shake out; unfold: *Unfurl the sail. The flag unfurled. v.*

un fur nished (un fèr'nisht), not fur- nished; without furniture. *adj.*

un gain li ness (un gān'lē nis), a being ungainly; awkwardness; clumsi- ness. *n.*

un gain ly (un gān'lē), awkward; clum- sy: *The boy's long arms and large hands give him an ungainly appearance. adj.*

un gen er ous (un jen'ər əs), not gen- erous; mean. *adj.*

un god li ness (un god'lē nis), lack of godliness; wickedness; sinfulness. *n.*

un god ly (un god'lē), 1 not devout; not religious; impious. 2 wicked; sinful. 3 INFORMAL. very annoying; out- rageous; shocking: *an ungodly noise, pay an ungodly price. adj.*

un gov ern a ble (un guv'ər nə bəl), impossible to control; very hard to con- trol or rule; unruly. *adj.*

un grace ful (un grās'fəl), not grace- ful; not elegant or beautiful; clumsy; awkward. *adj.* —**un grace'ful ly,** *adv.*

un gra cious (un grā'shəs), 1 not po- lite; discourteous; rude. 2 unpleasant; disagreeable; displeasing. *adj.* —**un- gra'cious ly,** *adv.*

un grate ful (un grāt'fəl), 1 not grateful; not thankful. 2 unpleasant;

In each of the words below **un** *means not.*

un'ex pend'ed	un fad'ed	un'fer ment'ed	un'for giv'en	un gen'tle
un'ex pired'	un fad'ing	un fer'ti lized	un'for giv'ing	un gen'tle man ly
un'ex plain'a ble	un fash'ion a ble	un fet'tered	un'for got'ten	un gift'ed
un'ex plained'	un fas'tened	un fil'i al	un for'mu lat'ed	un glam'or ous
un'ex plod'ed	un fazed'	un filled'	un for'ti fied	un glazed'
un'ex plored'	un fea'si ble	un fil'tered	un framed'	un gov'erned
un'ex posed'	un fed'	un fit'ting	un fre'quent	un grad'ed
un'ex pressed'	un fed'e rat'ed	un fixed'	un'ful filled'	un'gram mat'i cal
un'ex pres'sive	un felt'	un flat'ter ing	un fun'ny	
un ex'pur gat'ed	un fem'i nine	un fla'vored	un gal'lant	
un'ex tin'guished	un fenced'	un'for get'ting	un gar'nished	
		un'for giv'a ble	un gath'ered	

disagreeable: *an ungrateful task. adj.*
—**un grate′ful ly,** *adv.* —**un grate′-ful ness,** *n.*

un ground ed (un groun′did), without foundation; without reasons; unfounded. *adj.*

un grudg ing (un gruj′ing), not grudging; willing; hearty; liberal. *adj.*

un guard ed (un gär′did), 1 not protected: *an unguarded camp.* 2 careless: *In an unguarded moment she gave away the secret. adj.*

un guent (ung′gwənt), ointment for sores, burns, etc.; salve. *n.*

un gu late (ung′gyə lit), 1 having hoofs; belonging to the group of animals having hoofs. 2 animal that has hoofs. Horses, cows, sheep, and deer are ungulates. 1 *adj.*, 2 *n.*

un hal lowed (un hal′ōd), 1 not made holy; not sacred. 2 wicked; sinful; evil. *adj.*

un hand (un hand′), let go; take the hands from; release. *v.*

un hand y (un han′dē), 1 not easy to handle: *an unhandy tool.* 2 not skillful: *an unhandy worker. adj.*

un hap pi ly (un hap′ə lē), 1 not happily: *to live unhappily.* 2 unfortunately: *Unhappily I missed seeing him.* 3 unsuitably. *adv.*

un hap pi ness (un hap′ē nis), 1 a being unhappy; sadness; sorrow. 2 bad luck; ill fortune. *n.*

un hap py (un hap′ē), 1 without gladness; sad; sorrowful: *an unhappy face.* 2 unlucky: *an unhappy accident.* 3 not suitable: *an unhappy selection of colors. adj.,* **un hap pi er, un hap pi est.**

un har ness (un här′nis), 1 take harness off from (a horse, etc.). 2 take (armor) off from a person. *v.*

un health ful (un helth′fəl), bad for the health. *adj.*

un health i ly (un hel′thə lē), in an unhealthy manner. *adv.*

un health i ness (un hel′thē nis), 1 lack of health; sickness. 2 condition causing disease or harmful to health. *n.*

un health y (un hel′thē), 1 not possessing good health; not well: *an unhealthy child.* 2 coming from or showing poor health: *an unhealthy paleness.* 3 hurtful to health; unwholesome: *an unhealthy climate.* 4 morally or spiritually harmful. *adj.,* **un health i er, un health i est.**

un heard (un hėrd′), 1 not listened to;

not heard: *unheard melodies.* 2 not given a hearing: *condemn a person unheard. adj.*

un heard-of (un hėrd′uv′ *or* un-hėrd′ov′), 1 that was never heard of; unknown: *Electric stoves were unheard-of 200 years ago.* 2 such as was never known before; unprecedented: *unheard-of prices, an unheard-of scandal involving top government officials. adj.*

un heed ed (un hē′did), not heeded; disregarded; unnoticed. *adj.*

un hes i tat ing (un hez′ə tā′ting), prompt; ready. *adj.* —**un hes′i tat′-ing ly,** *adv.*

un hinge (un hinj′), 1 take (a door, etc.) off its hinges. 2 remove the hinges from. 3 separate from something; detach. 4 unsettle; upset: *a mind unhinged by shock. v.,* **un hinged, un-hing ing.**

unicorn

un hitch (un hich′), to free from being hitched; unfasten: *unhitch horses from a wagon. We unhitched the trailer from the car. v.*

un hol i ness (un hō′lē nis), a being unholy; lack of holiness. *n.*

un ho ly (un hō′lē), not holy; wicked; sinful. *adj.,* **un ho li er, un ho li est.**

un hook (un húk′), 1 loosen from a hook. 2 undo by loosening a hook or hooks. 3 become unhooked; become undone. *v.*

un hoped-for (un hōpt′fôr′), not expected; in addition to or beyond what is anticipated: *an unhoped-for blessing. adj.*

un horse (un hôrs′), throw from a horse's back; cause to fall from a horse. *v.,* **un horsed, un hors ing.**

un hur ried (un hėr′ēd), not hurried; without haste; leisurely. *adj.* —**un-hur′ried ly,** *adv.*

un hurt (un hėrt′), not hurt; not harmed. *adj.*

u ni cam er al (yü′nə kam′ər əl), having only one house in a lawmaking

body. Nebraska has a unicameral legislature. *adj.*

U NI CEF *or* **U ni cef** (yü′nə sef), United Nations Children's Fund. *n.*

u ni cel lu lar (yü′nə sel′yə lər), having one cell only. The amoeba is a unicellular animal. *adj.*

u ni corn (yü′nə kôrn), an imaginary animal like a horse, but having a single, long horn in the middle of its forehead. *n.*

u ni fi ca tion (yü′nə fə kā′shən), 1 formation into one unit; union: *the unification of many states into one nation.* 2 a making or a being made more alike: *The traffic laws of the different states need unification. n.*

u ni form (yü′nə fôrm), 1 always the same; not changing: *The earth turns at a uniform rate.* 2 all alike; not varying: *All the bricks have a uniform size.* 3 the distinctive clothes worn by the members of a group when on duty, by which they may be recognized as belonging to that group. Soldiers, policemen, and nurses wear uniforms. 4 clothe or furnish with a uniform. 1,2 *adj.,* 3 *n.,* 4 *v.*

u ni formed (yü′nə fôrmd), wearing a uniform; in uniform: *a uniformed soldier, a uniformed schoolgirl. adj.*

u ni form i ty (yü′nə fôr′mə tē), uniform condition or character; sameness throughout. *n., pl.* **u ni form i ties.**

u ni form ly (yü′nə fôrm′lē), without variation; always; regularly. *adv.*

u ni fy (yü′nə fī), make or form into one; unite: *Several small states were unified into one nation. v.,* **u ni fied, u ni fy ing.**

u ni lat er al (yü′nə lat′ər əl), of, on, or affecting one side only: *unilateral disarmament. adj.* —**u′ni lat′er al ly,** *adv.*

un i mag i na ble (un′i maj′ə nə bəl),

In each of the words below **un** *means not.*

un grat′i fied	un hanged′	un hatched′	un′he ro′ic	un′id i o mat′ic
un′guar an teed′	un har′assed	un healed′	un hes′i tant	un′il lu′mi nat′ed
un guid′ed	un hard′ened	un heat′ed	un hin′dered	un′i mag′i na tive
un ham′pered	un harmed′	un heed′ful	un hon′ored	un′im paired′
un hand′i capped	un′har mo′ni ous	un heed′ing	un housed′	un′im pas′sioned
un hand′some	un har′nessed	un help′ful	un′hy gi en′ic	
		un her′ald ed	un′i den′ti fied	

unimpeachable

abbr		abbr	
adj.	adjective	*n.*	noun
adv.	adverb	*prep.*	preposition
conj.	conjunction	*pron.*	pronoun
interj.	interjection	*v.*	verb
sing.	singular	*pl.*	plural

that cannot be imagined or thought of; inconceivable. *adj.*

un im peach a ble (un′im pē′chə bəl), free from fault, flaw, or error; not to be doubted or questioned: *an unimpeachable fact, an unimpeachable reputation. adj.*

un im por tance (un′im pôrt′ns), unimportant nature or quality. *n.*

un im por tant (un′im pôrt′nt), not important; insignificant; trifling. *adj.*

un in hab it ed (un′in hab′ə tid), not lived in; without inhabitants: *an uninhabited wilderness. adj.*

un in jured (un in′jərd), not hurt; not damaged. *adj.*

un in spired (un′in spīrd′), not inspired; dull; tiresome: *uninspired writing. adj.*

un in tel li gi ble (un′in tel′ə jə bəl), not intelligible; not able to be understood: *unintelligible handwriting. adj.*

un in ten tion al (un′in ten′shə nəl), not intentional; not done purposely. *adj.* —**un′in ten′tion al ly,** *adv.*

un in ter est ed (un in′tər ə stid *or* un in′tə res′tid), not interested; showing or having no interest. *adj.*

un in ter rupt ed (un′in tə rup′tid), without interruption; continuous. *adj.* —**un′in ter rupt′ed ly,** *adv.*

un in vit ed (un′in vī′tid), not invited; without an invitation. *adj.*

un ion (yü′nyən), **1** a uniting or a being united: *The United States was formed by the union of thirteen former British colonies.* **2** group of people, states, etc., united for some special purpose: *The ten provinces of Canada form a union.* **3 the Union, a** the United States of America. **b** those states that supported the federal government of the United States during the Civil War. **4** group of workers joined together to protect and promote their interests; labor union or trade union. **5** marriage. **6** device for connecting parts of machinery or apparatus, especially a piece to join pipes

or tubes together; coupling. **7** (in mathematics) a set including all the elements which belong to either or both of two sets. EXAMPLE: If set A = {1,2,3,4} and set B = {4,5,6}, then the union of the two sets is {1,2,3,4,5,6}. *n.*

un ion ism (yü′nyə niz′əm), **1** principle of union. **2** system, principles, or methods of labor unions. *n.*

un ion ist (yü′nyə nist), **1** person who promotes or advocates union. **2 Unionist,** supporter of the federal government of the United States during the Civil War. **3** member of a labor union. *n.*

un ion i za tion (yü′nyə nə za′shən), a unionizing or a being unionized. *n.*

un ion ize (yü′nyə nīz), **1** form into a labor union. **2** organize under a labor union. *v.,* **un ion ized, un ion iz ing.**

union jack, **1** a small flag which shows the symbol of union of a national flag. The United States union jack has 50 white stars against a blue background. **2 Union Jack,** the flag of the United Kingdom.

Union of South Africa, former name of the **Republic of South Africa.**

Union of Soviet Socialist Republics, the Soviet Union.

u nique (yü nēk′), **1** having no like or equal; being the only one of its kind: *a unique specimen of rock, a unique experience.* **2** INFORMAL. very uncommon or unusual; rare; remarkable: *a rather unique idea. adj.* —**u nique′ly,** *adv.* —**u nique′ness,** *n.*

u ni son (yü′nə sən), **1** agreement: *The marchers' feet moved in unison. We spoke in unison.* **2** agreement in pitch of two or more tones, voices, etc.; a sounding together at the same pitch. *n.*

u nit (yü′nit), **1** a single thing or person. **2** any group of things or persons considered as one: *The family is a social unit.* **3** one of the individuals or groups of which a whole is composed: *The body consists of units called cells.* **4** a standard quantity or amount, used as a basis for measuring: *A foot is a unit of length; a pound is a unit of weight.* **5** a part of a machine or other apparatus that has one specific purpose: *the storage unit in an electronic computer.* **6** the smallest whole number; 1. *n.*

U ni tar i an (yü′nə ter′ē ən *or* yü′nə tar′ē ən), **1** person who accepts the moral teachings of Jesus, but does not

union (def. 6)
pipe union

believe that He was divine. **2** of or having to do with Unitarians. **1** *n.,* **2** *adj.*

u nite (yü nīt′), join together; make one; become one; combine: *We united in song. The firms were united to form one company. v.,* **u nit ed, u nit ing.**

u nit ed (yü nī′tid), **1** made one; joined; combined. **2** having to do with or produced by two or more. **3** that harmonizes or agrees; in concord. *adj.*

United Arab E mir ates (ə mir′-its), country in E Arabia.

United Arab Republic, official name of **Egypt.** In 1958 Egypt and Syria joined together in the United Arab Republic and invited other Arab nations to join. Syria withdrew in 1961.

United Kingdom, **1** country in NW Europe composed of Great Britain and Northern Ireland. It is a member of the Commonwealth of Nations. *Capital:* London. **2** Great Britain and Ireland from 1801 to 1922.

United Kingdom (def. 1)—the shaded area

United Nations, **1** a worldwide organization established in 1945 to promote world peace and economic and social welfare. It has over 120 members. Its headquarters are in New York City. **2** the nations that belong to this organization.

United States, country in North America composed of 50 states and the District of Columbia. It extends from the Atlantic to the Pacific and from the Gulf of Mexico to Canada. Alaska, the 49th state, lies west and northwest of Canada, and Hawaii, the 50th state, is an island group in the Pacific. *Capital:* Washington, D.C.

United States of America, United States.

In each of the words below **un** *means not.*

un′im ped′ed	un′im proved′	un′in flu enced	un′in struc′tive	un′in ven′tive
un′im pos′ing	un′in cor′po rat ed	un′in formed′	un′in sured′	un′in vit′ing
un′im pressed′	un′in cum′bered	un′in hab′it a ble	un in′te grat ed	un′in volved′
un′im pres′sion a ble	un′in fect′ed	un′in hib′it ed	un′in tel′li gent	un is′sued
un′im pres′sive	un′in flect′ed	un′i ni′ti at ed	un′in tend′ed	
		un′in struct′ed	un in′ter est ing	

u ni ty (yü/nə tē), 1 a being united; oneness: *A circle has unity; scattered dots do not. A nation has more unity than a group of tribes.* 2 harmony: *Brothers and sisters should live together in unity.* 3 the number one. 4 oneness of effect; choice and arrangement of material (for a composition, book, picture, statue, etc.) to secure a single effect. *n., pl.* **u ni ties.**

u ni valve (yü/nə valv/), any mollusk whose shell consists of one piece. Snails are univalves. See **bivalve** for picture. *n.*

u ni ver sal (yü/nə vėr/səl), 1 of all; belonging to all; concerning all: *Food is a universal need.* 2 existing everywhere: *The law of gravity is universal. adj.*

U ni ver sal ist (yü/nə vėr/sə list), member of a Christian church holding the belief that all people will finally be saved. *n.*

u ni ver sal i ty (yü/nə vər sal/ə tē), a being universal. *n., pl.* **u ni ver sal i ties.**

universal joint, joint or coupling between two shafts that allows or provides for movement in almost any direction. In an automobile, power is transmitted from the transmission to the drive shaft through a universal joint.

u ni ver sal ly (yü/nə vėr/sə lē), 1 in every instance; without exception. 2 everywhere. *adv.*

u ni verse (yü/nə vėrs/), 1 the whole of existing things; everything there is, including all space and matter; the cosmos. Our world is but a small part of the universe. 2 (in mathematics and logic) the set of all objects being considered at any one time. The universe might be the set of all natural numbers, the numbers from 0 through 10, all animals, the animals on a farm, etc. *n.*

u ni ver si ty (yü/nə vėr/sə tē), institution of learning of the highest grade. A university usually has schools of law, medicine, teaching, business, etc., as well as a college of liberal arts and a graduate school. *n., pl.* **u ni ver si ties.**

un just (un just/), not just; not fair. *adj.* —**un just/ly,** *adv.*

un jus ti fi a ble (un jus/tə fī/ə bəl), that cannot be justified. *adj.*

un kempt (un kempt/), 1 not combed. 2 not properly cared for; neglected; untidy: *unkempt clothes, an unkempt house. adj.*

un kind (un kīnd/), not kind; harsh; cruel. *adj.* —**un kind/ness,** *n.*

un kind ly (un kīnd/lē), 1 harsh; unkind. 2 in an unkind way; harshly. 1 *adj.,* 2 *adv.*

un know a ble (un nō/ə bəl), that cannot be known. *adj.*

un known (un nōn/), 1 not known; not familiar; strange: *Most of Antarctica was once unknown land.* 2 person or thing that is unknown: *a political unknown. The diver descended into the unknown.* 1 *adj.,* 2 *n.*

un lace (un lās/), undo the laces of. *v.,* **un laced, un lac ing.**

un latch (un lach/), unfasten or open by lifting a latch. *v.*

un law ful (un lô/fəl), contrary to the law; against the law; forbidden; illegal. *adj.* —**un law/ful ly,** *adv.*

un learn (un lėrn/), get rid of (ideas, habits, or tendencies); give up knowledge of; forget. *v.*

universal joint

un learn ed (un lėr/nid *for 1;* un-lėrnd/ *for 2*), 1 not educated; ignorant: *They were unlearned and could not read or write.* 2 not learned; known without being learned: *Swallowing is an unlearned part of the process of eating. adj.*

un leash (un lēsh/), 1 release from a leash: *She unleashed the dog.* 2 let loose: *unleash one's temper. v.*

un leav ened (un lev/ənd), not leavened. Unleavened bread is made without yeast. *adj.*

un less (ən les/ *or* un les/), if it were not that; if not: *We shall go unless it rains. conj.*

un let tered (un let/ərd), 1 not educated. 2 not able to read or write; illiterate. *adj.*

un like (un līk/), 1 not like; different: *The two problems are quite unlike.* 2 different from: *to act unlike others.* 1 *adj.,* 2 *prep.*

un like li hood (un līk/lē hůd), improbability. *n.*

un like li ness (un līk/lē nis), a being unlikely; improbability. *n.*

un like ly (un līk/lē), 1 not likely; not probable: *He is unlikely to win the race.*

hat, āge, fär; let, ēqual, tėrm; it, īce; hot, ōpen, ôrder; oil, out; cup, půt, rüle; ch, child; ng, long; sh, she; th, thin; ŦH, then; zh, measure;

ə represents *a* in about, *e* in taken, *i* in pencil, *o* in lemon, *u* in circus.

2 not likely to succeed: *an unlikely undertaking. adj.*

un like ness (un līk/nis), a being unlike; difference. *n.*

un lim it ed (un lim/ə tid), 1 without limits; boundless. 2 not restrained; not restricted: *a government of unlimited power. adj.*

un load (un lōd/), 1 remove (a load). 2 take the load from. 3 get rid of: *They tried to unload their problems on us.* 4 remove powder, shot, bullets, or shells from (a gun). 5 discharge a cargo: *The ship is unloading. v.*

un lock (un lok/), 1 open the lock of; open (anything firmly closed). 2 disclose; reveal: *Science has unlocked the mystery of the atom. v.*

un looked-for (un lůkt/fôr/), unexpected; unforeseen. *adj.*

un loose (un lüs/), let loose; set free; release. *v.,* **un loosed, un loos ing.**

un loos en (un lü/sn), unloose; loosen. *v.*

un love ly (un luv/lē), without beauty or charm; unpleasing in appearance; unpleasant; objectionable; disagreeable. *adj.*

un luck i ly (un luk/ə lē), in an unlucky manner; unfortunately. *adv.*

un luck i ness (un luk/ē nis), a being unlucky. *n.*

un luck y (un luk/ē), not lucky; bringing bad luck; unfortunate. *adj.,* **un luck i er, un luck i est.**

un man (un man/), deprive of the qualities of a man; weaken or break down the spirit of: *They were unmanned by fear. v.,* **un manned, un man ning.**

un manned (un mand/), without a crew: *an unmanned space flight. adj.*

un man ner ly (un man/ər lē), 1 having bad manners; rude; discourteous. 2 with bad manners; rudely. 1 *adj.,* 2 *adv.*

---

adj.	adjective	*n.*	noun
adv.	adverb	*prep.*	preposition
conj.	conjunction	*pron.*	pronoun
interj.	interjection	*v.*	verb
sing.	singular	*pl.*	plural

un mar ried (un mar′ēd), not married; single. *adj.*

un mask (un mask′), 1 remove a mask or disguise: *The guests unmasked at midnight.* 2 take off a mask or disguise from. 3 expose the true character of: *unmask a hypocrite, unmask a conspiracy.* *v.*

un match a ble (un mach′ə bəl), that cannot be matched or equaled. *adj.*

un mean ing (un mē′ning), 1 without meaning or significance; meaningless: *unmeaning words.* 2 empty of feeling or thought; without sense or expression; vacant: *an unmeaning stare.* *adj.*

un meas ured (un mezh′ərd), 1 not measured; unlimited; measureless. 2 not restrained; excessive. *adj.*

un meet (un mēt′), not fit; not proper; unsuitable. *adj.*

un men tion a ble (un men′shə nə bəl), that cannot be mentioned; not fit to be spoken about. *adj.*

un mer ci ful (un mèr′si fəl), having no mercy; showing no mercy; cruel. *adj.*

un mind ful (un mīnd′fəl), not mindful; heedless; careless: *He went ahead despite our warning and unmindful of the results.* *adj.*

un mis tak a ble (un′mə stā′kə bəl), that cannot be mistaken or misunderstood; clear; plain; evident. *adj.*

un mis tak a bly (un′mə stā′kə blē), in an unmistakable manner. *adv.*

un mit i gat ed (un mit′ə gā′tid), 1 not softened or lessened: *unmitigated harshness, the unmitigated glare of sun or snow.* 2 unqualified or absolute: *an unmitigated fraud.* *adj.*

un mixed (un mikst′), not mixed; pure. *adj.*

un mo lest ed (un′mə les′tid), not molested; undisturbed. *adj.*

un mo ral (un môr′əl), neither moral nor immoral; not perceiving or involving right and wrong. *adj.*

un moved (un müvd′), 1 not moved; firm. 2 not disturbed; indifferent. *adj.*

un named (un nāmd′), 1 having no name; nameless. 2 not mentioned by name. *adj.*

un nat ur al (un nach′ər əl), 1 not natural; not normal. 2 shocking; horrible. 3 artificial. *adj.* —**un nat′ur al ly,** *adv.* —**un nat′ur al ness,** *n.*

un nec es sar i ly (un nes′ə ser′ə lē), in an unnecessary manner; needlessly. *adv.*

un nec es sar y (un nes′ə ser′ē), not necessary; needless. *adj.*

un nerve (un nèrv′), deprive of nerve, firmness, or self-control: *The sight of blood unnerved the new nurse's aide.* *v.,* **un nerved, un nerv ing.**

un no ticed (un nō′tist), not noticed; not observed; not receiving any attention. *adj.*

un num bered (un num′bərd), 1 not numbered; not counted. 2 too many to count; innumerable: *There are unnumbered fish in the ocean.* *adj.*

un ob served (un′əb zèrvd′), not observed; not noticed; disregarded. *adj.*

un ob tru sive (un′əb trü′siv), modest; inconspicuous. *adj.* —**un′ob tru′sive ly,** *adv.*

un oc cu pied (un ok′yə pīd), 1 not occupied; vacant: *The driver pulled her car into the unoccupied parking space.* 2 not in action or use; idle: *an unoccupied mind.* *adj.*

un of fend ing (un′ə fen′ding), not offending; inoffensive. *adj.*

un of fi cial (un′ə fish′əl), not official. *adj.* —**un′of fi′cial ly,** *adv.*

un or gan ized (un ôr′gə nīzd), 1 not formed into an organized or systematized whole. 2 not organized into labor unions. *adj.*

un pack (un pak′), 1 take out (things packed in a box, trunk, etc): *I unpacked my clothes from the suitcase.* 2 take things out of: *unpack a trunk.* 3 take out things packed: *start unpacking.* *v.*

un paid (un pād′), not paid: *Our unpaid bills amounted to $200.* *adj.*

un pal at a ble (un pal′ə tə bəl), not agreeable to the taste; distasteful; unpleasant. *adj.*

un par al leled (un par′ə leld), having no parallel; unequaled; matchless: *an unparalleled achievement.* *adj.*

un pin (un pin′), take out a pin or pins from; unfasten: *I unpinned the baby's bib.* *v.,* **un pinned, un pin ning.**

un pleas ant (un plez′nt), not pleasant; disagreeable. *adj.* —**un pleas′ant ly,** *adv.*

un pleas ant ness (un plez′nt nis), 1 unpleasant quality. 2 something unpleasant. 3 a quarrel. *n.*

un plug (un plug′), 1 remove the plug or stopper from. 2 disconnect by removing the plug from an electric outlet. *v.,* **un plugged, un plug ging.**

un pop u lar (un pop′yə lər), not popular; not generally liked; disliked. *adj.*

un pop u lar i ty (un′pop yə lar′ə tē), lack of popularity; being unpopular. *n.*

un prac ticed or **un prac tised** (un prak′tist), 1 not skilled; not expert. 2 not put into practice; not used. *adj.*

un prec e dent ed (un pres′ə den′tid), having no precedent; never done before; never known before: *An unprecedented event in history took place in 1961, when a human being*

In each of the words below **un** *means not.*

un mar′riage a ble	**un mov′a ble**	**un′ob struct′ed**	**un paved′**	**un planned′**
un mas′tered	**un mov′ing**	**un′ob tain′a ble**	**un peace′a ble**	**un plant′ed**
un matched′	**un mu′si cal**	**un of′fered**	**un peo′pled**	**un played′**
un meant′	**un muz′zled**	**un o′pened**	**un′per ceived′**	**un pleased′**
un′me chan′i cal	**un nat′ur al ized**	**un′op posed′**	**un′per ceiv′ing**	**un pleas′ing**
un melt′ed	**un nav′i ga ble**	**un′or dained′**	**un′per fect′ed**	**un pledged′**
un men′tioned	**un need′ed**	**un or′dered**	**un′per plexed′**	**un pli′ant**
un mer′it ed	**un neigh′bor ly**	**un′o rig′i nal**	**un′per suad′ed**	**un plowed′**
un′me thod′i cal	**un not′ed**	**un or′tho dox**	**un′per sua′sive**	**un plumbed′**
un mil′i tar′y	**un no′tice a ble**	**un′os ten ta′tious**	**un′per turbed′**	**un′po et′ic**
un min′gled	**un′o beyed′**	**un owned′**	**un′phil o soph′ic**	**un′po et′i cal**
un′mis tak′en	**un′ob jec′tion a ble**	**un paint′ed**	**un′phil o soph′i cal**	**un poised′**
un mod′i fied	**un′o blig′ing**	**un paired′**	**un picked′**	**un′po liced′**
un mod′u lat′ed	**un′ob scured′**	**un par′don a ble**	**un pierced′**	**un pol′ished**
un mo′ti vat′ed	**un′ob serv′a ble**	**un par′doned**	**un pit′ied**	**un pol lut′ed**
un mount′ed	**un′ob serv′ant**	**un′par lia men′tar y**	**un pit′y ing**	**un pop′u lat′ed**
un mourned′	**un′ob serv′ing**	**un pas′teur ized**	**un placed′**	
		un′pa tri ot′ic	**un plagued′**	

traveled for the first time in outer space. *adj.*

un pre dict a ble (un′pri dik′tə bəl), that cannot be predicted; uncertain or changeable. *adj.*

un pre dict a bly (un′pri dik′tə blē), in an unpredictable manner. *adv.*

un prej u diced (un prej′ə dist), without prejudice; fair; impartial. *adj.*

un pre med i tat ed (un′prē med′ə tā′tid), not premeditated; not planned in advance. *adj.*

un pre pared (un′pri perd′ *or* un′pri-pard′), 1 not made ready; not worked out ahead: *an unprepared speech.* 2 not ready: *a person unprepared to answer.* *adj.*

un pre par ed ness (un′pri per′id-nis *or* un′pri par′id nis), a being unprepared. *n.*

un pre tend ing (un′pri ten′ding), unpretentious. *adj.*

un pre ten tious (un′pri ten′shəs), not given to or characterized by pretension; modest. *adj.*

un prin ci pled (un prin′sə pəld), lacking good moral principles; bad. *adj.*

un print a ble (un prin′tə bəl), not fit or proper to be printed. *adj.*

un pro fes sion al (un′prə fesh′ə-nəl), contrary to professional etiquette; unbecoming in members of a profession: *It would be unprofessional for doctors to speak publicly of their patients' personal problems. adj.*

un prof it a ble (un prof′ə tə bəl), not profitable; producing no gain or advantage. *adj.*

un prof it a bly (un prof′ə tə blē), in an unprofitable manner; without profit, gain, benefit, advantage, or use. *adv.*

un pro nounce a ble (un′prə noun′-sə bəl), that cannot be pronounced. *adj.*

un pro voked (un′prə vōkt′), not provoked; without provocation. *adj.*

un qual i fied (un kwol′ə fīd), 1 not qualified; not fitted: *They are unquali-*
fied for this job. 2 not modified, limited, or restricted in any way: *unqualified praise.* 3 complete; absolute: *an un-qualified failure. adj.*

un quench a ble (un kwen′chə-bəl), that cannot be quenched or extinguished: *an unquenchable thirst, unquenchable zeal. adj.*

un ques tion a ble (un kwes′chə-nə bəl), beyond dispute or doubt; certain: *Having a school diploma is an unquestionable advantage to a person who is looking for a good job. adj.*

un ques tion a bly (un kwes′chə nə-blē), beyond dispute or doubt; certainly. *adv.*

un ques tioned (un kwes′chənd), not questioned; not disputed. *adj.*

un quote (un kwōt′), to mark the end of a quotation. *v.,* **un quot ed, un quot ing.**

un rav el (un rav′əl), 1 separate the threads of; pull apart: *The kitten un-raveled the string of yarn.* 2 come apart: *This sweater is unraveling at the elbow.* 3 bring or come out of a tangled state: *The detective unraveled the mystery. v.*

un read (un red′), 1 not read: *an un-read book.* 2 not instructed by reading; not having read much: *an unread person. adj.*

un read y (un red′ē), 1 not ready; not prepared. 2 not prompt or quick; slow. *adj.*

un re al (un rē′əl), not real; imaginary; fanciful. *adj.*

un re al i ty (un′rē al′ə tē), 1 lack of reality; imaginary or fanciful quality. 2 impractical or visionary character or tendency; impracticality. 3 something without reality; something unreal. *n., pl.* **un re al i ties.**

un rea son a ble (un rē′zn ə bəl), 1 not reasonable: *The little child had an unreasonable fear of the dark.* 2 not moderate; excessive: *$50 is an un-reasonable price for a pair of shoes. adj.* **—un rea′son a ble ness,** *n.*

hat, āge, fär; let, ēqual, tėrm; it, īce; hot, ōpen, ôrder; oil, out; cup, pùt, rüle; ch, child; ng, long; sh, she; th, thin; ŦH, then; zh, measure;

ə represents *a* in about, *e* in taken, *i* in pencil, *o* in lemon, *u* in circus.

un rea son a bly (un rē′zn ə blē), 1 in a way that is not reasonable; contrary to reason; foolishly. 2 extremely: *Au-gust often has some unreasonably hot days. adv.*

un rea son ing (un rē′zn ing), not reasoning; not using reason; irrational. *adj.*

un re flect ing (un′ri flek′ting), not thinking; thoughtless. *adj.*

un re gard ed (un′ri gär′did), not heeded or noticed; disregarded. *adj.*

un re gen er ate (un′ri jen′ər it), 1 not born again spiritually; not turned to the love of God. 2 wicked; bad. *adj.*

un re lent ing (un′ri len′ting), 1 not yielding to feelings of kindness or compassion; merciless; cruel: *an unrelent-ing enemy.* 2 not slackening or relaxing: *unrelenting anger, an unrelenting pace. adj.* **—un′re lent′ing ly,** *adv.*

un re li a ble (un′ri lī′ə bəl), not reliable; not to be depended on; irresponsible. *adj.*

un re mit ting (un′ri mit′ing), never stopping; not slackening; maintained steadily: *Driving in heavy traffic re-quires unremitting attention. adj.*

un re served (un′ri zėrvd′), 1 not restrained in action or speech; frank; open. 2 not restricted, limited, or qualified; without reservation. *adj.*

un re serv ed ly (un′ri zėr′vid lē), in an unreserved manner. *adv.*

un rest (un rest′), 1 lack of ease and

---

un′pre pos sess′ing	un′pro test′ed	un quot′a ble	un′re fined′	un′re pealed′
un pressed′	un proved′	un raised′	un′re formed′	un′re pent′ant
un′pre vail′ing	un prov′en	un ran′somed	un reg′is tered	un′re pent′ing
un′pre vent′a ble	un′pro vid′ed	un rat′i fied	un reg′u lat′ed	un′re port′ed
un print′ed	un′pro vok′ing	un read′a ble	un′re lat′ed	un′rep re sent′a tive
un priv′i leged	un pruned′	un′re al is′tic	un′re laxed′	un′rep re sent′ed
un′pro duc′tive	un pub′li cized	un re′al ized	un′re lax′ing	un′re pressed′
un′pro faned′	un pub′lished	un rea′soned	un′re lieved′	un′re proved′
un′pro gres′sive	un punc′tu al	un′re ceived′	un′re mem′bered	un′re quit′ed
un prom′is ing	un pun′ished	un′re claimed′	un′re mit′ted	un′re signed′
un prompt′ed	un pur′chas a ble	un rec′og niz′a ble	un′re mu′ne ra′tive	un′re sist′ed
un′pro nounced′	un quail′ing	un rec′og nized	un′re nowned′	un′re sist′ing
un′pro pi′tious	un quenched′	un rec′om pensed	un rent′ed	un′re solved′
un′pro por′tioned	un ques′tion ing	un rec′on ciled	un′re paid′	un′re spon′sive
un′pro tect′ed	un qui′et	un′re cord′ed	un′re paired′	
		un′re deemed′		

927

adj. adjective	*n.* noun
adv. adverb	*prep.* preposition
conj. conjunction	*pron.* pronoun
interj. interjection	*v.* verb
sing. singular	*pl.* plural

quiet; restlessness. 2 agitation or disturbance amounting almost to rebellion. *n.*

un re strained (un′ri strānd′), not restrained; not held back; not checked: *unrestrained laughter, unrestrained freedom. adj.*

un re straint (un′ri strānt′), lack of restraint. *n.*

un right eous (un rī′chəs), not righteous; wicked; sinful; unjust. *adj.* —**un right′eous ly,** *adv.* —**un right′eous ness,** *n.*

un ripe (un rīp′), not ripe; not fully developed; immature. *adj.*

un ri valed or **un ri valled** (un rī′vəld), having no rival; without an equal. *adj.*

un roll (un rōl′), 1 to open or spread out (something rolled). 2 become opened or spread out. 3 lay open; display. *v.*

un ruf fled (un ruf′əld), 1 not ruffled; smooth. 2 not disturbed; calm. *adj.*

un ruled (un rüld′), 1 not kept under control; not governed. 2 not marked with lines: *unruled paper. adj.*

un rul i ness (un rü′lē nis), a being unruly. *n.*

un rul y (un rü′lē), hard to rule or control; ungovernable; disorderly: *an unruly horse, a disobedient and unruly child, an unruly mob, an unruly section of a country. adj.*

un sad dle (un sad′l), 1 take the saddle off (a horse). 2 cause to fall from a horse; unhorse. *v.,* **un sad dled, un sad dling.**

un safe (un sāf′), not safe; dangerous. *adj.*

un said (un sed′), 1 not said: *Everything I had meant to say remained un-*

said. 2 past tense and past participle of **unsay.** 1 *adj.,* 2 *v.*

un san i tar y (un san′ə ter′ē), not sanitary; bad for the health; unhealthful. *adj.*

un sat is fac tor i ly (un′sat i sfak′tər ə lē), in an unsatisfactory manner. *adv.*

un sat is fac tor y (un′sat i sfak′tər ē), not satisfactory; not good enough to satisfy; inadequate. *adj.*

un sat is fied (un sat′i sfīd), not satisfied; not contented. *adj.*

un sa vor y (un sā′vər ē), 1 tasteless. 2 unpleasant in taste or smell; distasteful: *an unsavory medicine.* 3 morally unpleasant; offensive: *an unsavory companion. adj.*

un say (un sā′), take back (something said). *v.,* **un said, un say ing.**

un scathed (un skāŦHd′), not harmed; uninjured: *She escaped unscathed from the car wreck. adj.*

un schooled (un sküld′), not schooled; not taught; not disciplined. *adj.*

un sci en tif ic (un′sī ən tif′ik), 1 not in accordance with the facts or principles of science: *an unscientific notion.* 2 not acting in accordance with the facts or principles of science: *an unscientific farmer. adj.* —**un′sci en tif′i cal ly,** *adv.*

un scram ble (un skram′bəl), change from confusion to order; bring out of a scrambled condition: *After the wind died down, she unscrambled the papers that had blown on the floor. v.,* **un scram bled, un scram bling.**

un screw (un skrü′), 1 take out the screw or screws from. 2 loosen or take off by turning: *unscrew an electric light bulb. v.*

un scru pu lous (un skrü′pyə ləs), not careful about right and wrong; without principles or conscience: *The unscrupulous student cheated on the test. adj.* —**un scru′pu lous ly,** *adv.* —**un scru′pu lous ness,** *n.*

un seal (un sēl′), 1 break or remove the seal of: *unseal a letter.* 2 open: *The threat of punishment unsealed their lips. v.*

un search a ble (un sėr′chə bəl), not to be searched into; that cannot be understood by searching; mysterious. *adj.*

un sea son a ble (un sē′zn ə bəl), 1 not suitable to or characteristic of the season: *an unseasonable heat wave.* 2 coming at the wrong time; not timely: *an unseasonable suggestion. adj.*

un sea son a bly (un sē′zn ə blē), in an unseasonable manner. *adv.*

un seat (un sēt′), 1 displace from a seat. 2 throw (a rider) from a saddle. 3 remove from office: *unseat a congressman, unseat a government. v.*

un seem ly (un sēm′lē), 1 not seemly; not suitable; improper: *unseemly haste. Laughter is often unseemly in a courtroom.* 2 improperly; unsuitably. 1 *adj.,* **un seem li er, un seem li est;** 2 *adv.*

un seen (un sēn′), 1 not seen; unnoticed: *an unseen error.* 2 not able to be seen; invisible: *an unseen spirit. adj.*

un self ish (un sel′fish), not selfish; considerate of others; generous. *adj.* —**un self′ish ly,** *adv.* —**un self′ish ness,** *n.*

un set tle (un set′l), make or become unstable; disturb; shake; weaken: *The shock unsettled his mind. v.,* **un set tled, un set tling.**

un set tled (un set′ld), 1 not in proper condition or order; disordered; disturbed: *an unsettled mind. Our house is still unsettled.* 2 not fixed or firmly established; unstable: *an unsettled government.* 3 liable to change; uncertain: *The weather is unsettled.* 4 not adjusted or disposed of: *an unsettled estate, an unsettled bill.* 5 not determined or decided: *an unsettled question.* 6 not populated; uninhabited: *Some parts of the world are still unsettled. adj.*

un shak a ble (un shā′kə bəl), that cannot be shaken; firm. *adj.*

un shak en (un shā′kən), not shaken; firm: *unshaken courage, an unshaken belief in liberty. adj.*

un sheathe (un shēŦH′), draw (a sword, knife, etc.) from a sheath. *v.,* **un sheathed, un sheath ing.**

un shod (un shod′), without shoes. *adj.*

In each of the words below **un** *means not.*

un′re strict′ed	un rip′ened	un sat′u rat′ed	un sea′soned	un set′
un′re ten′tive	un′ro man′tic	un saved′	un sea′wor′thy	un shad′ed
un′re trieved′	un saint′ly	un scaled′	un sec′ond ed	un shad′owed
un′re turned′	un sal′a ble	un scarred′	un′se cured′	un shaped′
un′re vealed′	un sal′ar ied	un scent′ed	un seed′ed	un shape′ly
un′re venged′	un salt′ed	un sched′uled	un see′ing	un sharp′ened
un′re voked′	un sanc′ti fied	un schol′ar ly	un seg′ment ed	un shav′en
un′re ward′ed	un sanc′tioned	un scorched′	un seg′re gat′ed	un shed′
un′re ward′ing	un sat′ed	un scratched′	un′se lec′tive	un shelled′
un rhymed′	un sa′ti at′ed	un screened′	un′self-con′scious	un shel′tered
un right′ful	un sat′is fy′ing	un scrip′tur al	un′sen ti men′tal	un shield′ed
		un sealed′	un serv′ice a ble	

un sight li ness (un sīt′lē nis), a being unsightly; ugliness. *n.*

un sight ly (un sīt′lē), ugly or unpleasant to look at: *an unsightly old shack. adj.*

un skilled (un skild′), 1 not skilled; not trained; not expert: *unskilled workers, an unskilled athlete.* 2 not requiring special skills or training: *unskilled labor. adj.*

un skill ful or **un skil ful** (un-skil′fəl), not skillful; lacking in skill; awkward; clumsy. *adj.* —**un skill′ful ly, un skil′ful ly,** *adv.*

un smil ing (un smī′ling), not smiling; grave; serious. *adj.* —**un smil′ing ly,** *adv.*

un snap (un snap′), unfasten the snap or snaps of. *v.,* **un snapped, un snap ping.**

un snarl (un snärl′), remove the snarls from; untangle. *v.*

un so cia ble (un sō′shə bəl), not sociable; not associating easily with others: *unsociable behavior, an unsociable hermit. adj.*

un so phis ti cat ed (un′sə fis′tə-kā′tid), not sophisticated; simple; natural; artless. *adj.*

un sought (un sôt′), not sought; not looked for; not asked for: *unsought advice, an unsought compliment. adj.*

un sound (un sound′), 1 not in good condition; not sound: *unsound walls, an unsound business. A diseased mind is unsound.* 2 not based on truth or fact; not valid: *an unsound doctrine, an unsound theory.* 3 not deep; not restful; disturbed: *an unsound sleep. adj.* —**un sound′ly,** *adv.* —**un sound′ness,** *n.*

un spar ing (un sper′ing or un-spar′ing), 1 not sparing; very generous; liberal. 2 not merciful; severe. *adj.* —**un spar′ing ly,** *adv.*

un speak a ble (un spē′kə bəl), 1 that cannot be expressed in words; beyond description; indescribable: *unspeakable joy, an unspeakable loss.*

2 extremely bad; bad or objectionable beyond description. *adj.*

un speak a bly (un spē′kə blē), beyond words; extremely: *unspeakably rude. adv.*

un spot ted (un spot′id), not spotted; without spot or stain; pure: *an unspotted reputation. adj.*

un sta ble (un stā′bəl), 1 not firmly fixed; easily moved, shaken, or overthrown. 2 not constant; variable: *an unstable nature.* 3 (of a chemical compound) easily decomposed; readily changing into other compounds. *adj.*

un stained (un stānd′), not stained; without stain or spot. *adj.*

un stead i ly (un sted′ə lē), in an unsteady manner; without steadiness. *adv.*

un stead y (un sted′ē), 1 not steady; shaky: *an unsteady voice, an unsteady flame.* 2 likely to change; not reliable: *an unsteady mind, unsteady winds. adj.,* **un stead i er, un stead i est.**

un strap (un strap′), take off or loosen the strap or straps of (a trunk, box, etc.). *v.,* **un strapped, un strap ping.**

un stressed (un strest′), not stressed; unaccented. In *upward,* the second syllable is unstressed. *adj.*

un strung (un strung′), 1 weakened in the nerves; nervous. 2 with strings loose, broken, or missing: *an unstrung guitar. adj.*

un sub stan tial (un′səb stan′shəl), not substantial; flimsy; slight; unreal. *adj.*

un suc cess ful (un′sək ses′fəl), not successful; without success. *adj.* —**un′suc cess′ful ly,** *adv.*

un suit a ble (un sü′tə bəl), not suitable; unfit. *adj.*

un suit a bly (un sü′tə blē), in an unsuitable manner. *adv.*

un suit ed (un sü′tid), not suited; unfit. *adj.*

un sul lied (un sul′ēd), not sullied; spotless; stainless; pure. *adj.*

un sung (un sung′), 1 not sung: *an*

hat, āge, fär; let, ēqual, tėrm;
it, īce; hot, ōpen, ôrder;
oil, out; cup, pu̇t, rüle; ch, child;
ng, long; sh, she; th, thin;
ᴛʜ, then; zh, measure;

ə represents *a* in about,
e in taken, *i* in pencil,
o in lemon, *u* in circus.

unsung note. 2 not honored or celebrated, especially by song or poetry: *unsung heroes. adj.*

un sup port a ble (un′sə pôr′tə bəl), insupportable. *adj.*

un sur mount a ble (un′sər-moun′tə bəl), insurmountable. *adj.*

un sus pect ed (un′sə spek′tid), 1 not suspected. 2 not thought of: *an unsuspected danger. adj.*

un tan gle (un tang′gəl), 1 take the tangles out of; disentangle. 2 straighten out or clear up (anything confused or perplexing). *v.,* **un tan gled, un tan gling.**

un taught (un tôt′), 1 not taught; not educated: *an untaught child.* 2 known without being taught; learned naturally: *untaught wisdom. adj.*

un thank ful (un thangk′fəl), 1 ungrateful. 2 not appreciated; thankless. *adj.*

un think a ble (un thing′kə bəl), that cannot be imagined; inconceivable. *adj.*

un think ing (un thing′king), 1 not thinking; thoughtless; heedless; careless. 2 showing little or no thought: *blind, unthinking anger. adj.* —**un think′ing ly,** *adv.*

un thought-of (un thôt′uv′ or un-thôt′ov′), not imagined or considered. *adj.*

un ti di ly (un tī′dl ē), in an untidy manner. *adv.*

In each of the words below **un** *means not.*

un shorn′	un sound′ed	un ster′i lized	un′ sus pi′cious	un tast′ed
un shrink′ing	un sown′	un stint′ed	un′sus tained′	un taxed′
un sift′ed	un spe′cial ized	un stint′ing	un swayed′	un teach′a ble
un sight′ed	un′spe cif′ic	un stitched′	un sweet′ened	un tech′ni cal
un signed′	un spec′i fied	un stopped′	un swept′	un tem′pered
un sized′	un′spec tac′u lar	un strained′	un swerv′ing	un ten′a ble
un slacked′	un spec′u la′tive	un strat′i fied	un′sym met′ri cal	un ten′ant ed
un slaked′	un spent′	un stud′ied	un′sym pa thet′ic	un tend′ed
un so′cial	un spir′i tu al	un′sub dued′	un sym′pa thiz′ing	un ter′ri fied
un soiled′	un spoiled′	un′sub mis′sive	un′sys tem at′ic	un test′ed
un sold′	un spoilt′	un′sub stan′ti at ed	un tact′ful	un thanked′
un sol′dier ly	un spo′ken	un′sug ges′tive	un taint′ed	un thought′
un′so lic′it ed	un sports′man like′	un sup port′ed	un tak′en	un thought′ful
un solv′a ble	un stamped′	un′sup pressed′	un tal′ent ed	un thrift′y
un solved′	un stat′ed	un sure′	un tamed′	
un sort′ed	un states′man like′	un′sur passed′	un tanned′	
		un′sus pect′ing	un tar′nished	

adj. adjective	n. noun
adv. adverb	prep. preposition
conj. conjunction	pron. pronoun
interj. interjection	v. verb
sing. singular	pl. plural

un ti di ness (un tī'dē nis), a being untidy. *n.*

un ti dy (un tī'dē), not in order; not neat; slovenly: *an untidy house. adj.,* **un ti di er, un ti di est.**

un tie (un tī'), 1 loosen; unfasten; undo: *untie a knot. She was untying bundles.* 2 make free; release: *untie a horse. v.,* **un tied, un ty ing.**

un til (un til'), 1 up to the time of: *It was cold from December until April.* 2 up to the time when: *We waited until the sun had set.* 3 before: *She did not leave until morning (prep.). He did not come until the meeting was almost over (conj.).* 4 to the degree or place that: *She worked until she was too tired to do more.* 1,3 *prep.,* 2-4 *conj.*

un time li ness (un tīm'lē nis), a being untimely. *n.*

un time ly (un tīm'lē), 1 at a wrong time or season; unseasonable: *an untimely refusal. Snow in May is untimely.* 2 too early; too soon: *his untimely death at the age of 18.* 1,2 *adj.,* 2 *adv.*

un tir ing (un tī'ring), that does not tire; tireless: *an untiring runner, untiring efforts to succeed. adj.* —**un tir'ing ly,** *adv.*

un to (un'tü), to: *be faithful unto death. prep.*

un told (un tōld'), 1 not told; not revealed: *an untold story, untold heroism.* 2 too many to be counted or numbered; innumerable; countless: *There are untold stars in the sky.* 3 very great; immense: *untold wealth. The tornado did untold damage. adj.*

un touch a ble (un tuch'ə bəl), 1 that cannot be touched; out of reach. 2 that must not be touched. 3 person of the lowest caste in India, whose touch supposedly defiled members of higher castes. 1,2 *adj.,* 3 *n.*

un touched (un tucht'), not touched:

The cat left the milk untouched. The miser was untouched by the poor man's story. The last topic remained untouched. adj.

un to ward (un tôrd' or un'tə wôrd'), 1 unfavorable; unfortunate; *an untoward wind, an untoward accident.* 2 perverse; stubborn; willful: *The untoward child was very hard to manage. adj.*

un trained (un trānd'), not trained; without discipline or education: *The new recruits were completely untrained. adj.*

un tram meled (un tram'əld), not hindered; not restrained; free. *adj.*

un tried (un trīd'), not tried; not tested: *an untried plan. adj.*

un trod (un trod'), not trodden. *adj.*

un true (un trü'), 1 not true to the facts; false. 2 not faithful; disloyal. 3 not true to a standard or rule; not exact; inaccurate. *adj.*

un tru ly (un trü'lē), in an untrue manner; falsely. *adv.*

un truth (un trüth'), 1 lack of truth; falsity. 2 a lie; falsehood. *n., pl.* **un truths** (un trüᴛʜz' or un trüths').

un truth ful (un trüth'fəl), 1 not truthful; contrary to the truth: *an untruthful rumor.* 2 not telling the truth: *an untruthful person. adj.* —**un truth'ful ly,** *adv.* —**un truth'ful ness,** *n.*

un tu tored (un tü'tərd or un tyü'tərd), not tutored; not educated; untaught. *adj.*

un twine (un twīn'), untwist. *v.,* **un twined, un twin ing.**

un twist (un twist'), 1 undo or loosen (something twisted); unravel. 2 become untwisted. *v.*

un used (un yüzd' for 1,2; for 3, before the word "to" usually, un yüst'), 1 not in use; not being used: *an unused room.* 2 never having been used: *unused drinking cups.* 3 not accustomed: *The actor's hands were unused to labor. adj.*

un u su al (un yü'zhü əl), not usual; not ordinary; not in common use; uncommon; rare. *adj.* —**un u'su al ness,** *n.*

un u su al ly (un yü'zhü ə lē), in an unusual manner; uncommonly; rarely. *adv.*

un ut ter a ble (un ut'ər ə bəl), 1 that cannot be expressed in words; un-

speakable. 2 that cannot be pronounced. *adj.*

un ut ter a bly (un ut'ər ə blē), in an unutterable manner; to a degree that cannot be expressed in words; unspeakably. *adv.*

un var nished (un vär'nisht), 1 not varnished. 2 plain; unadorned: *the unvarnished truth. adj.*

un var y ing (un ver'ē ing or un var'ē ing), steady; constant. *adj.*

un veil (un vāl'), 1 remove a veil from; disclose; reveal: *The statue was unveiled the day the graduating class presented it to the school.* 2 become unveiled; remove one's veil; reveal oneself: *The princess unveiled. v.*

un war i ness (un wer'ē nis or un war'ē nis), a being unwary. *n.*

un war rant a ble (un wôr'ən tə bəl), not justifiable or defensible; improper. *adj.*

un war rant ed (un wôr'ən tid), not authorized or justified: *unwarranted interference. adj.*

un war y (un wer'ē or un war'ē), not wary; not cautious; careless; unguarded. *adj.,* **un war i er, un war i est.**

un wear ied (un wir'ēd), 1 not weary; not tired. 2 never growing weary; tireless. *adj.*

un wel come (un wel'kəm), not welcome; not wanted: *The bees were unwelcome guests at our picnic. adj.*

un well (un wel'), not in good health; ailing; ill; sick. *adj.*

un wept (un wept'), 1 not wept for; not mourned. 2 not shed: *unwept tears. adj.*

un whole some (un hōl'səm), not wholesome; bad for the body or the mind; unhealthy: *a damp, unwholesome climate. A diet consisting mainly of candy is unwholesome. adj.*

un wield i ness (un wēl'dē nis), a being unwieldy. *n.*

un wield y (un wēl'dē), hard to handle or manage because of size, shape, or weight; bulky and clumsy: *a large, unwieldy package, a fat, unwieldy man. adj.,* **un wield i er, un wield i est.**

un will ing (un wil'ing), 1 not willing; not consenting. 2 not freely or willingly granted or done: *an unwilling acceptance of necessity. adj.* —**un will'ing ly,** *adv.* —**un will'ing ness,** *n.*

In each of the words below **un** *means not.*

un tilled'	un trav'ersed	un us'a ble	un versed'	un wa'ver ing
un trace'a ble	un trimmed'	un ut'tered	un vexed'	un weaned'
un traced'	un trod'den	un vac'ci nat'ed	un vis'it ed	un wear'y ing
un tracked'	un trou'bled	un val'ued	un voiced'	un weath'ered
un'trans fer'a ble	un trust'wor'thy	un van'quished	un want'ed	un wed'
un'trans lat'ed	un turned'	un var'ied	un war'like'	un wed'ded
un trav'eled	un twist'ed	un veiled'	un washed'	un weed'ed
un trav'elled	un typ'i cal	un ven'ti lat'ed	un wast'ed	un wife'ly
		un ver'i fied	un watched'	

un wind (un wīnd′), 1 wind off or uncoil; take from a spool, ball, etc. 2 become unwound. 3 relax: *unwind after a hard day.* *v.,* **un wound, un wind ing.**

un wise (un wīz′), not wise; not showing good judgment; foolish: *It is unwise to delay going to the doctor if you are sick.* *adj.* —**un wise′ly,** *adv.*

un wit ting (un wit′ing), not knowing; unaware; unconscious; unintentional. *adj.*

un wit ting ly (un wit′ing lē), not knowingly; not intentionally; unconsciously. *adv.*

un wont ed (un wun′tid), not customary; not usual: *unwonted anger.* *adj.*

un world ly (un wèrld′lē), not caring much for the things of this world, such as money, pleasure, and power. *adj.*

un wor thi ly (un wèr′ŦHə lē), 1 in a way that is not worthy or honorable; shamefully. 2 not according to one's merits. *adv.*

un wor thi ness (un wèr′ŦHē nis), a being unworthy. *n.*

un wor thy (un wèr′ŦHē), 1 not worthy; not deserving: *Such a silly story is unworthy of belief.* 2 unsuitable; unfit; unbecoming: *a gift unworthy of a king.* 3 base; shameful: *unworthy conduct. adj.,* **un wor thi er, un wor thi est.**

un wound (un wound′), past tense and past participle of **unwind.** *v.*

un wrap (un rap′), 1 remove the wrapping from; open. 2 become opened. *v.,* **un wrapped, un wrap ping.**

un writ ten (un rit′n), 1 not written: *an unwritten order.* 2 understood or customary, but not actually expressed in writing: *an unwritten law. adj.*

un yield ing (un yēl′ding), not yielding; not giving way; firm: *succeed because of unyielding determination. adj.*

un yoke (un yōk′), 1 to free from a yoke: *Unyoke the oxen.* 2 to separate; disconnect. 3 remove a yoke. *v.,* **un yoked, un yok ing.**

up (up), 1 from a lower to a higher place or condition: *The bird flew up. Prices have gone up.* 2 in a higher place or condition: *We stayed up in the mountains several days* (*adv.*). *The sun is up* (*adj.*). 3 up along, through, in, or into: *The cat ran up the tree. She walked up the street. We sailed up the river.* 4 going or pointed upward: *an up trend.* 5 piece of good luck: *Life has its ups and downs.* 6 out of bed: *Please get up or you will be late* (*adv.*). *On Christmas morning the children were up at dawn* (*adj.*). 7 thoroughly; completely; entirely: *The house burned up.* 8 at an end; over: *The time is up now.* 9 in or into being or action: *Don't stir up trouble.* 10 to or in an even position; not behind: *catch up in a race, keep up with the times.* 11 into storage or a safe place: *Squirrels lay up nuts for the winter.* 12 at bat in baseball: *She was up four times in the game.* 13 for each one; apiece; each: *The score at the half was ten up.* 14 INFORMAL. put, lift, or get up. 15 INFORMAL. to increase: *They upped the price of eggs.* 1,2,6-11,13 *adv.,* 2,4,6,12 *adj.,* 3 *prep.,* 5 *n.,* 14,15 *v.,* **upped, up ping.**

up against, INFORMAL. facing as a thing to be dealt with.

up for, 1 a candidate for: *be up for senator, be up for reelection.* 2 on trial in a court of law for: *be up for robbery.*

up to, 1 about to do; doing: *She is up to some mischief.* 2 equal to; capable of doing: *Do you feel up to going out so soon after being sick?* 3 before (a person) as a duty or task to be done: *It's up to the judge to decide if he is guilty.*

up-and-com ing (up′ən kum′ing), on the way to prominence or success; promising: *an up-and-coming young scientist. adj.*

up braid (up brād′), find fault with; blame; reprove: *The captain upbraided the guards for falling asleep. v.*

up bring ing (up′bring′ing), care and training given to a child while growing up; bringing-up. *n.*

up com ing (up′kum′ing), forthcoming: *the upcoming semester. adj.*

up coun try (up′kun′trē), in the interior of a country: *an upcountry village* (*adj.*). *We went fishing upcountry* (*adv.*). *adj., adv.*

up date (up dāt′), bring up to date. *v.,* **up dat ed, up dat ing.**

up draft (up′draft′), an upward movement of air, wind, gas, etc. *n.*

up end (up end′), to set on end; stand on end: *If you upend the box it will take up less space. v.*

up grade (up′grād′), 1 an upward slope or incline. 2 raise to a higher position, status, rating, etc.: *upgrade a job, upgrade an employee.* 1 *n.,* 2 *v.,* **up grad ed, up grad ing.**

on the upgrade, rising; improving.

up heav al (up hē′vəl), 1 a heaving up or a being heaved up. 2 a sudden or violent agitation; great turmoil: *a flood, earthquake, or other upheaval. n.*

hat, āge, fär; let, ēqual, tèrm; it, īce; hot, ōpen, ôrder; oil, out; cup, pùt, rüle; ch, child; ng, long; sh, she; th, thin; ŦH, then; zh, measure;

ə represents *a* in about, *e* in taken, *i* in pencil, *o* in lemon, *u* in circus.

up heave (up hēv′), heave up; lift up: *land upheaved by volcanic forces. v.,* **up heaved, up heav ing.**

up held (up held′), past tense and past participle of **uphold.** *The higher court upheld the lower court's decision. v.*

up hill (up′hil′ *for 1,3;* up′hil′ *for 2*), 1 up the slope of a hill; upward: *It is an uphill road all the way.* 2 upward: *We walked a mile uphill.* 3 difficult: *an uphill fight.* 1,3 *adj.,* 2 *adv.*

up hold (up hōld′), 1 give support to; confirm: *The principal upheld the teacher's decision.* 2 hold up; not let down; support: *Walls uphold the roof. We uphold the good name of our school. v.,* **up held, up hold ing.** —**up hold′-er,** *n.*

up hol ster (up hōl′stər), provide (furniture) with coverings, cushions, springs, stuffing, etc. *v.*

up hol ster er (up hōl′stər ər), person whose business is upholstering. *n.*

up hol ster y (up hōl′stər ē), 1 coverings for furniture; curtains, cushions, carpets, and hangings. 2 business of upholstering. *n., pl.* **up hol ster ies.**

up keep (up′kēp′), 1 maintenance: *the upkeep of a house.* 2 cost of operating and repair: *The upkeep of a yacht is very expensive. n.*

up land (up′lənd), 1 high land. 2 of high land; living or growing on high land: *upland meadows, upland flowers.* 1 *n.,* 2 *adj.*

up lift (up lift′ *for 1,3;* up′lift′ *for 2,4*), 1 lift up; raise; elevate. 2 act of lifting up. 3 raise socially or morally. 4 social or moral improvement or effort toward it. 1,3 *v.,* 2,4 *n.*

up most (up′mōst), uppermost. *adj.*

up on (ə pôn′ *or* ə pon′), on. *prep.*

up per (up′ər), 1 higher: *the upper lip, the upper floors of an office building.* 2 farther from the sea: *the upper reaches of a river.* 3 the part of a shoe or boot above the sole. 1,2 *adj.,* 3 *n.*

In each of the words below **un** *means not.*

un wink′ing	**un work′man like′**	**un wound′ed**	**un wrought′**
un wit′nessed	**un wom′an ly**	**un worn′**	**un wo′ven**
	un work′a ble	**un wor′ried**	**un wrin′kled**

adj.	adjective	*n.*	noun
adv.	adverb	*prep.*	preposition
conj.	conjunction	*pron.*	pronoun
interj.	interjection	*v.*	verb
sing.	singular	*pl.*	plural

uppercut delivered by boxer on right

up per cut (up′ər kut′), (in boxing) a swinging blow directed upward from beneath. *n.*

upper hand, advantage; control: *Do what the doctor says or that cold may get the upper hand.*

Upper House or **upper house,** the smaller and less representative branch of a lawmaking body that has two branches. The House of Lords is the Upper House of the British Parliament.

up per most (up′ər mōst), 1 highest; topmost. 2 having the most force or influence; most prominent. 3 in, at, or near the top. 4 first: *The safety of the passengers was uppermost in the pilot's mind.* 1,2 *adj.,* 3,4 *adv.*

Upper Vol ta (vol′tə), country in W Africa, north of Ghana.

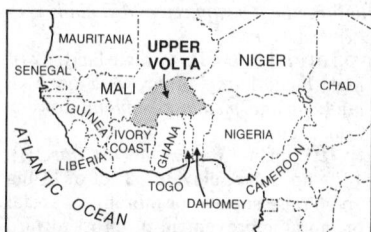

up raise (up rāz′), lift up; raise. *v.,* **up raised, up rais ing.**

up right (up′rīt′), 1 standing up straight; erect: *an upright post.* 2 straight up; in a vertical position: *Hold yourself upright.* 3 something standing erect; vertical part or piece. 4 an upright piano. 5 good; honest; righteous: *an upright citizen.* 1,5 *adj.,* 2 *adv.,* 3,4 *n.* —**up′right′ly,** *adv.* —**up′right′ness,** *n.*

upright piano, a rectangular piano

having vertical strings behind the keyboard.

up rise (up rīz′), 1 rise up. 2 to slope upward; ascend. *v.,* **up rose, up ris en, up ris ing.**

up ris en (up riz′n), past participle of **uprise.** *v.*

up ris ing (up′rī′zing), 1 a revolt; rebellion: *There were many Indian uprisings in the area.* 2 a rising up. *n.*

up roar (up′rôr′), 1 a noisy or violent disturbance: *The town was in an uproar when a lion escaped from the circus.* 2 a loud or confused noise: *the uproar following a last-minute touchdown.* *n.*

up roar i ous (up rôr′ē əs), 1 making an uproar; noisy and disorderly: *an uproarious crowd.* 2 loud and confused: *uproarious laughter. adj.* —**up roar′i ous ly,** *adv.*

up root (up rüt′ *or* up rùt′), 1 tear up by the roots: *The storm uprooted many trees.* 2 tear away, remove, or displace completely: *Famine uprooted many families from their homes in Ireland during the 1840's. v.*

up rose (up rōz′), past tense of **uprise.** *v.*

ups-and-downs (ups′ən dounz′), changes in fortune; successes and failures: *Her career has had many ups-and-downs. n.pl.*

up set (up set′ *for* 1,4,7; up′set′ *for* 2,5,8; up set′ *or* up′set′ *for* 3,6), 1 tip over; overturn: *She upset the milk pitcher. Moving about in a boat may upset it.* 2 a tipping over; overturn. 3 tipped over; overturned. 4 disturb greatly; disorder: *Rain upset our plans for a picnic. The shock upset my nerves.* 5 a great disturbance; disorder. 6 greatly disturbed; disordered: *an upset stomach.* 7 defeat unexpectedly in a contest: *The independent candidate upset the mayor in the election.* 8 an unexpected defeat: *The hockey team suffered an upset.* 1,4,7 *v.,* **up set, up set ting;** 2,5,8 *n.,* 3,6 *adj.*

up shot (up′shot′), 1 conclusion; result: *The upshot of the scandal was that he resigned from office.* 2 the essential facts. *n.*

up side (up′sīd′), the upper side. *n.*

upside down, 1 having what should be on top at the bottom: *The slice of bread and butter fell upside down on the floor.* 2 in or into complete disorder: *The room was upside down. The children turned the house upside down.*

up side-down cake (up′sīd′doun′), a cake made of batter poured over fruit, baked, and served bottom up.

up stage (up′stāj′), 1 toward or at the back of the stage: *walk upstage (adv.), upstage furniture (adj.).* 2 draw attention away from (an actor) by standing upstage or in back of him or by forcing

him to face away from the audience. 1 *adv., adj.,* 2 *v.,* **up staged, up staging.**

up stairs (up′sterz′ *or* up′starz′), 1 up the stairs: *The boy ran upstairs.* 2 on or to an upper floor: *She lives upstairs (adv.). He is waiting in an upstairs hall (adj.).* 3 the upper floor or floors: *That small cottage has no upstairs.* 4 INFORMAL. in the mind; mentally: *Something's wrong with him upstairs.* 1,2,4 *adv.,* 2 *adj.,* 3 *n.*

kick upstairs, INFORMAL. promote (a person) to a higher but less powerful or important position.

up stand ing (up stan′ding), 1 standing up; erect: *short, upstanding hair.* 2 honorable: *a fine, upstanding young woman. adj.*

up start (up′stärt′), 1 person who has suddenly risen from a humble position to wealth, power, or importance. 2 an unpleasant and conceited person who puts himself forward too much. *n.*

up state (up′stāt′), of the part of a state away from and usually north of the principal city: *upstate New York. adj.*

up stream (up′strēm′), against the current of a stream; up a stream: *He swam upstream (adv.). They stopped at an upstream camping site (adj.). adv., adj.*

up surge (up′sėrj′), a rising upward; rise; upturn. *n.*

up swing (up′swing′), 1 an upward swing; movement upward. 2 a marked improvement; strong advance. *n.*

up-to-date (up′tə dāt′), 1 extending to the present time: *an up-to-date record of sales.* 2 keeping up with the times in style, ideas, etc.; modern: *an up-to-date store. adj.*

up town (up′toun′), to or in the upper part or away from the main business section of a town or city: *go uptown (adv.), an uptown store (adj.). adv., adj.*

up turn (up tėrn′ *for* 1; up′tėrn′ *for* 2,3), 1 turn up. 2 an upward turn: *The airplane made a sudden upturn to avoid the mountain.* 3 an improvement: *As business improved, his income took an upturn.* 1 *v.,* 2,3 *n.*

up turned (up tėrnd′), turned upward. *adj.*

up ward (up′wərd), 1 toward a higher place: *fly upward. I climbed upward until I reached the apple.* 2 directed or moving toward a higher place; in a higher position: *an upward course, an upward flight.* 3 toward a higher or greater rank, amount, age, etc.: *From ten years of age upward, she had studied French.* 4 above; more: *Children of five years and upward must pay the full fare.* 5 toward the source: *We traced*

the brook upward. *1,3-5 adv., 2 adj.*
upward of, more than: *Repairs to the car will cost upward of $100.*

up wards (up′wərdz), upward. *adv.*

upwards of, more than; upward of.

Ur (ėr), city in ancient Sumer, on the Euphrates River. *n.*

Ur al Mountains (yur′əl), mountain range in W Soviet Union, between Europe and Asia.

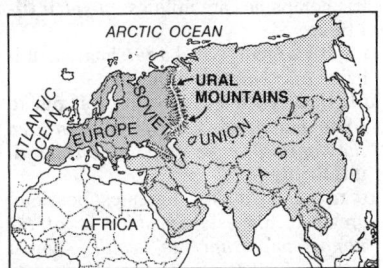

Ural Mountains—Mainland Europe is shaded area to west of Ural Mountains; mainland Asia is shaded area to east.

Ural River, river flowing south from the Ural Mountains into the Caspian Sea.

Ur als (yur′əlz), Ural Mountains. *n.pl.*

u ra ni um (yu rā′nē əm), a white, radioactive metallic element that weighs more than any other element found in nature. Uranium occurs naturally in pitchblende. Certain isotopes of uranium are used as sources of atomic energy. *n.* [from *Uranus*]

Ur a nus (yur′ə nəs), 1 (in Greek myths) a god who represented heaven. Uranus was the father of the Titans and the Cyclopes. 2 the third largest planet in the solar system and the seventh in distance from the sun. *n.*

ur ban (ėr′bən), 1 of or having to do with cities or towns: *an urban district, urban planning.* 2 living in a city or cities: *the urban population. Most people who live in large apartment houses are urban dwellers.* 3 characteristic of cities: *urban life. adj.*

ur bane (ėr bān′), 1 courteous, refined, or elegant: *urbane manners.* 2 smoothly polite: *an urbane scoundrel. adj.* —**ur′bane′ly,** *adv.*

ur ban i ty (ėr′ban′ə tē), 1 courtesy, refinement, or elegance. 2 smooth politeness. *n., pl.* **ur ban i ties.**

ur ban i za tion (ėr′bə nə zā′shən), a making or becoming urban. *n.*

ur ban ize (ėr′bə nīz), make or become urban: *urbanize an area. v.,* **urban ized, ur ban iz ing.**

ur chin (ėr′chən), 1 a small child. 2 a mischievous child. 3 a poor, ragged child: *Urchins played in the streets.* 4 sea urchin. *n.*

-ure, *suffix added to verbs to form nouns.* 1 act or fact of _____ing:

Failure = act of failing. 2 state of being _____ed: *Pleasure = state of being pleased.* 3 result of being _____ed: *Exposure = result of being exposed.* 4 something that _____s: *Legislature = something that legislates.* 5 thing that is _____ed: *Disclosure = thing that is disclosed.* [from French, from Latin *-ura*]

u re a (yu rē′ə), substance present in the urine of mammals, and also produced synthetically. Urea is used in making adhesives and plastics, in fertilizers, in medicine, etc. *n.*

u re ter (yu rē′tər), duct that carries urine from a kidney to the bladder. *n.*

u re thra (yu rē′thrə), duct through which urine is discharged from the bladder. *n., pl.* **u re thras, u re thrae** (yu rē′thrē).

urge (ėrj), 1 push, force, or drive forward or onward: *The rider urged on his horse with whip and spurs. Hunger urged her to steal.* 2 a driving force or impulse: *The urge of hunger led him to beg.* 3 try to persuade with arguments; ask earnestly: *We urged them to stay.* 4 plead or argue earnestly for; recommend strongly: *The doctor urged a change of climate.* *1,3,4 v.,* **urged, urg ing; 2 n.**

ur gen cy (ėr′jən sē), 1 urgent character; need for immediate action or attention: *A house on fire is a matter of great urgency.* 2 insistence. *n., pl.* **ur gen cies.**

ur gent (ėr′jənt), 1 demanding immediate action or attention; pressing; important: *an urgent duty, an urgent message.* 2 insistent. *adj.* —**ur′gently,** *adv.*

ur i nal (yur′ə nəl), 1 container for urine. 2 place for urinating. *n.*

ur i nal y sis (yur′ə nal′ə sis), a chemical analysis of a sample of urine. By means of urinalysis doctors can detect certain diseases, such as diabetes. *n., pl.* **ur i nal y ses** (yur′ə nal′ə sēz′).

ur i nar y (yur′ə ner′ē), 1 of or having to do with urine. 2 of or having to do with the organs that secrete and discharge urine. *adj.*

ur i nate (yur′ə nāt), discharge urine from the body. *v.,* **ur i nat ed, ur i nat ing.**

ur ine (yur′ən), the fluid that is secreted by the kidneys as a waste product of the body. Urine passes through the ureters into the bladder, and is then discharged through the urethra from the body. *n.*

urn (ėrn), 1 vase with a foot or pedestal. Urns were used in ancient Greece and Rome to hold the ashes of the dead. 2 a coffeepot or teapot with a faucet, used for making or serving coffee or tea at the table. *n.*

hat, āge, fär; let, ēqual, tėrm;
it, īce; hot, ōpen, ôrder;
oil, out; cup, put, rüle; ch, child;
ng, long; sh, she; th, thin;
ŦH, then; zh, measure;

ə represents *a* in about,
e in taken, *i* in pencil,
o in lemon, *u* in circus.

Ur sa Major (ėr′sə), the most prominent northern constellation, shaped somewhat like a bear, and including the stars of the Big Dipper; Great Bear.

Ur sa Minor (ėr′sə), a northern constellation, shaped somewhat like a bear, that includes the stars of the Little Dipper; Little Bear.

Ur u guay (yur′ə gwä *or* yur′ə gwī), country in the SE part of South America. *Capital:* Montevideo. *n.* —**Ur′u guay′an,** *adj., n.*

us (us; *unstressed* əs). We and us mean the person speaking plus the person or persons addressed or spoken about: *We learn when our teacher helps us. Mother went with us to the theater.* *pron.*

U.S., the United States.

U.S.A. or **USA,** 1 the United States of America. 2 United States Army.

us a ble (yü′zə bəl), that can be used; fit for use. *adj.* Also, **useable.**

USAF or **U.S.A.F.,** United States Air Force.

us age (yü′sij *or* yü′zij), 1 way or manner of using or of being used; treatment: *The car has had rough usage.* 2 a long-continued practice; customary use; habit; custom: *Travelers should learn many of the usages of the countries they visit.* 3 the customary way of using words: *The usage of the best speakers and writers determines what is good English. n.*

USCG or **U.S.C.G.,** United States Coast Guard.

use (yüz *for* 1-4; yüs *for* 5-12), 1 put into action or service: *use a knife to cut the meat. We use our legs in walking.* 2 act toward; treat: *She used us well.* 3 consume or expend by using: *We have*

urn (def. 1)   urn (def. 2)

933

adj.	adjective	*n.*	noun
adv.	adverb	*prep.*	preposition
conj.	conjunction	*pron.*	pronoun
interj.	interjection	*v.*	verb
sing.	singular	*pl.*	plural

used most of the money. He uses tobacco. **4** avail oneself of; put to one's own purposes: *May I use your telephone?* **5** a using: *the use of tools.* **6** a being used: *methods long out of use.* **7** usefulness: *a thing of no practical use. There is no use crying over spilled milk.* **8** purpose that a thing is used for: *find a new use for something.* **9** way of using: *a proper use of one's time, poor use of a material.* **10** need or occasion for using; necessity; demand: *A camper has use for a hatchet. I had no further use for it.* **11** power or capacity of using; ability to use: *lose the use of an arm.* **12** right or privilege of using: *have the use of a friend's boat for the summer.* 1-4 *v.,* **used, us ing;** 5-12 *n.*

have no use for, 1 not need or want. 2 INFORMAL. dislike.

in use, being used.

make use of, use; utilize: *She made use of her Spanish while in Mexico.*

put to use, use: *If you can put to use that old bicycle, you may have it.*

used to (yüst′tü *or* yü′stə), 1 accustomed to: *used to hardships. Eskimos are used to cold weather.* 2 formerly did: *He used to come at ten o'clock, but now he comes at noon.*

use up, consume or expend entirely: *use up the available funds. We have used up our sugar.*

use a ble (yü′zə bəl), usable. *adj.*

used (yüzd), not new; that has belonged to another or others: *a used car. adj.*

use ful (yüs′fəl), of use; giving service; helpful: *a useful suggestion. He made himself useful about the house. adj.* —**use′ful ly,** *adv.* —**use′ful ness,** *n.*

use less (yüs′lis), of no use; worthless: *A television set would be useless in a house without electricity. adj.* —**use′less ly,** *adv.* —**use′less ness,** *n.*

us er (yü′zər), person or thing that uses. *n.*

ush er (ush′ər), 1 person who shows people to their seats in a theater, church, etc. 2 to conduct; escort; show:

We ushered the visitors to the door. 1 *n.,* 2 *v.*

usher in, inaugurate; introduce: *a winter ushered in by cold rains.*

ush er ette (ush′ə ret′), a girl or woman usher. *n.*

USMC *or* **U.S.M.C.,** United States Marine Corps.

USN *or* **U.S.N.,** United States Navy.

U.S.S.R. *or* **USSR,** Union of Soviet Socialist Republics.

u su al (yü′zhü əl), commonly seen, found, or happening; ordinary; customary: *This is our usual spring weather. Her usual bedtime is 8 p.m. adj.*

as usual, in the usual manner; as is customary: *My friend and I met, as usual, on the way to school.*

u su al ly (yü′zhü ə lē), according to what is usual; commonly; ordinarily; customarily: *We usually eat dinner at 6. adv.*

u sur er (yü′zhər ər), person who lends money at an extremely high or unlawful rate of interest. *n.*

u sur i ous (yü zhùr′ē əs), 1 taking extremely high or unlawful interest for the use of money. 2 of or having to do with usury: *Fifty per cent is a usurious rate of interest. adj.*

u surp (yü zėrp′), seize and hold (power, position, or authority) by force or without right: *The queen's younger sister tried to usurp the throne. v.* —**u surp′er,** *n.*

u sur pa tion (yü′zər pā′shən), a usurping; the seizing and holding of the place or power of another by force or without right: *the usurpation of the throne by a pretender. n.*

u sur y (yü′zhər ē), 1 the lending of money at an extremely high or unlawful rate of interest. 2 an extremely high or unlawful interest. *n., pl.* **u sur ies.**

Ut., Utah.

U tah (yü′tô *or* yü′tä), one of the western states of the United States. *Capital:* Salt Lake City. *n.* —**U′tah an,** *adj., n.*

u ten sil (yü ten′səl), 1 container or implement used for practical purposes. Pots, pans, kettles, and mops are kitchen utensils. 2 instrument or tool used for some special purpose. Pens and pencils are writing utensils. *n.*

u ter us (yü′tər əs), the part of the body in mammals that holds and nourishes the young till birth; womb. *n., pl.* **u ter i** (yü′tər ī).

U ti ca (yü′tə kə), city in central New York State. *n.*

u til i tar i an (yü til′ə ter′ē ən), 1 of or having to do with utility. 2 aiming at usefulness rather than beauty, style, etc. *adj.*

u til i ty (yü til′ə tē), 1 power to satisfy people's needs; usefulness: *A fur coat has more utility in winter than in summer.* 2 a useful thing. 3 company that performs a public service; public utility. Railroads, bus lines, and gas and electric companies are utilities. *n., pl.* **u til i ties.**

u ti li za tion (yü′tl ə zā′shən), a utilizing or a being utilized. *n.*

u ti lize (yü′tl īz), make use of; put to some practical use: *The cook utilized the bones to make soup. v.,* **u ti lized, u ti liz ing.**

ut most (ut′mōst), 1 greatest possible; greatest; highest: *Sunshine is of the utmost importance to health.* 2 most distant; farthest; extreme: *She walked to the utmost edge of the cliff.* 3 the most that is possible; extreme limit: *He enjoyed himself to the utmost at the circus.* 1,2 *adj.,* 3 *n.*

u to pi a *or* **U to pi a** (yü tō′pē ə), 1 an ideal place or state with perfect laws. 2 a visionary, impractical system of political or social perfection. *n.*

u to pi an *or* **U to pi an** (yü tō′pē-ən), 1 of or like a utopia. 2 visionary; impractical. 3 an ardent but impractical reformer; idealist. 1,2 *adj.,* 3 *n.*

ut ter[1] (ut′ər), complete; total; absolute: *utter surprise, utter darkness, utter defeat. adj.* [Old English *ūterra* outer]

ut ter[2] (ut′ər), 1 make known; speak; express: *the last words he uttered, utter one's thoughts.* 2 give forth; give out: *He uttered a cry of pain. v.* [Middle English *utteren,* from Old English *ūt* out] —**ut′ter er,** *n.*

ut ter ance (ut′ər əns), 1 an uttering; expression in words or sounds: *The child gave utterance to her grief.* 2 way or manner of speaking. 3 something uttered; a spoken word or words. *n.*

ut ter ly (ut′ər lē), completely; totally; absolutely. *adv.*

ut ter most (ut′ər mōst), utmost. *adj., n.*

u vu la (yü′vyə lə), the small piece of flesh hanging down from the soft palate in the back of the mouth. See **tonsil** for diagram. *n., pl.* **u vu las, u vu lae** (yü′vyə lē).

Uz bek (üz′bek), republic of the Soviet Union, in central Asia. *Capital:* Tashkent. *n.*

V v

V or **v** (vē), 1 the 22nd letter of the alphabet. 2 anything shaped like a V. 3 the Roman numeral for 5. *n., pl.* **V's** or **v's.**

v., 1 verb. 2 versus.

Va., Virginia.

va can cy (vā′kən sē), 1 a being vacant; emptiness. 2 an unoccupied position: *The retirement of two bookkeepers made two vacancies in our office.* 3 a room, space, or apartment for rent; empty space: *There was a vacancy in the motel. There was a vacancy in the parking lot.* 4 emptiness of mind. *n., pl.* **va can cies.**

va cant (vā′kənt), 1 not occupied: *a vacant chair, a vacant house.* 2 empty; not filled: *a vacant space.* 3 empty of thought or intelligence: *a vacant smile.* 4 free from work, business, etc.: *vacant time. adj.* —**va′cant ly,** *adv.*

va cate (vā′kāt), go away from and leave empty or unoccupied; make vacant: *They will vacate the house at the end of the month. v.,* **va cat ed, va cat ing.**

va ca tion (vā kā′shən), 1 freedom from school, business, or other duties: *There is a vacation from school every summer.* 2 take a vacation. 1 *n.,* 2 *v.* —**va ca′tion er,** *n.*

vac ci nate (vak′sə nāt), inoculate with vaccine. Children who are vaccinated against measles, smallpox, whooping cough, diphtheria, and tetanus are made immune to these diseases. *v.,* **vac ci nat ed, vac ci nat ing.**

vacuum tube

vac ci na tion (vak′sə nā′shən), 1 act or process of vaccinating: *Vaccination has made smallpox a very rare disease.* 2 scar where vaccine was injected. *n.*

vac cine (vak′sēn′ *or* vak sēn′), a mildly toxic preparation of dead or weakened bacteria or viruses of a particular disease, used to inoculate a person in order to prevent or lessen the effects of that disease. Vaccines work by causing the body to develop antibodies against the disease germs. The Salk vaccine is used against polio. Inoculation with cowpox vaccine prevents smallpox. *n.*

vac il late (vas′ə lāt), 1 waver in mind or opinion: *A vacillating person finds it hard to make up his mind.* 2 move first one way and then another; waver. *v.,* **vac il lat ed, vac il lat ing.**

vac il la tion (vas′ə lā′shən), 1 a wavering in mind or opinion. 2 unsteadiness; swaying. *n.*

va cu i ty (va kyü′ə tē), 1 emptiness. 2 an empty space; vacuum. 3 emptiness of mind; lack of ideas or intelligence. *n., pl.* **va cu i ties.**

vac u ole (vak′yü ōl), a tiny cavity in the protoplasm of a living cell, containing fluid. *n.*

vac u ous (vak′yü əs), 1 showing no intelligence; stupid. 2 empty. *adj.* —**vac′u ous ly,** *adv.*

vac u um (vak′yü əm *or* vak′yùm), 1 an empty space without even air in it. 2 an enclosed space from which almost all air or gas has been removed. 3 an empty space; void: *Their child's death left a vacuum in their lives.* 4 vacuum cleaner. 5 clean with a vacuum cleaner: *We vacuum the rugs every week or two.* 1-4 *n., pl.* **vac u ums** or (except for def. 4) **vac u a** (vak′yü ə); 5 *v.*

vacuum bottle, bottle made with a vacuum between its inner and outer walls so that its contents remain hot or cold for long periods of time. A thermos bottle is a kind of vacuum bottle.

vacuum cleaner, apparatus for cleaning carpets, curtains, floors, etc., by suction.

vac u um-packed (vak′yü əm pakt′ *or* vak′yùm pakt′), 1 packed in an airtight container to keep fresh: *vacuum-packed coffee.* 2 having had all or most of the air removed before sealing: *vacuum-packed cans. adj.*

vacuum tube, a sealed tube from which most of the air has been removed. It is used in radio and television sets, photoelectric cells, radar, electron microscopes, and other devices to control the flow of electric currents.

vag a bond (vag′ə bond), 1 an idle wanderer; wanderer; tramp. 2 wandering: *The gypsies lead a vagabond life.* 3 a disreputable person; rascal. 1,3 *n.,* 2 *adj.*

va gar y (və ger′ē *or* vā′gər ē), 1 an odd fancy; extravagant notion: *the vagaries of a dream.* 2 odd action; caprice: *the vagaries of today's fashions. n., pl.* **va gar ies.**

va gi na (və jī′nə), the passage in female mammals that leads from the uterus to the external genital organs. *n., pl.* **va gi nas.**

va gran cy (vā′grən sē), a wandering idly from place to place without proper means or ability to earn a living: *The tramp was arrested for vagrancy. n., pl.* **va gran cies.**

va grant (vā′grənt), 1 an idle wanderer; tramp. 2 moving in no definite direction or course; wandering. 3 wandering without proper means of earning a living. 1 *n.,* 2,3 *adj.*

vague (vāg), not definite; not clear; not distinct: *In a fog everything looks vague. His vague statement confused them. adj.,* **va guer, va guest.** —**vague′-ly,** *adv.* —**vague′ness,** *n.*

vain (vān), 1 having too much pride in one's looks, ability, etc.: *vain of one's good looks.* 2 of no use; unsuccessful: *I made vain attempts to reach her by telephone.* 3 of no value; empty; worthless: *a vain boast. adj.*

in vain, 1 without effect or success: *My shout for help was in vain, for no one was near enough to hear me.* 2 in a disrespectful manner; lightly or irreverently: *The Bible says that one must not take God's name in vain.*

vain glo ri ous (vān′glôr′ē əs), excessively proud or boastful; extremely vain. *adj.* —**vain′glo′ri ous ly,** *adv.* —**vain′glo′ri ous ness,** *n.*

vain glo ry (vān′glôr′ē), 1 an extreme pride in oneself; boastful vanity. 2 worthless pomp or show. *n.*

vain ly (vān′lē), 1 in vain. 2 with conceit. *adv.*

valance (def. 1) valance (def. 2)

val ance (val′əns), 1 a short drapery over the top of a window. 2 a short curtain hanging from the frame or canopy of a bed. *n.*

vale (vāl), valley. *n.*

val e dic tion (val′ə dik′shən), a bidding farewell. *n.*

adj. adjective	*n.* noun
adv. adverb	*prep.* preposition
conj. conjunction	*pron.* pronoun
interj. interjection	*v.* verb
sing. singular	*pl.* plural

val e dic to ri an (val′ə dik tôr′ē ən), student who gives the farewell address at the graduating exercises. The valedictorian is usually the student who ranks highest in the class. *n.*

val e dic tor y (val′ə dik′tər ē), 1 a farewell address, especially at the graduating exercises of a school or college. 2 bidding farewell. 1 *n., pl.* **val e dic tor ies**; 2 *adj.*

va lence (vā′ləns), the combining capacity of an atom or radical, determined by the number of electrons that an atom will lose, add, or share when it reacts with other atoms. Elements whose atoms lose electrons, such as hydrogen and the metals, have a positive valence. Elements whose atoms add electrons, such as oxygen and other nonmetals, have a negative valence. Oxygen has a negative valence of 2; hydrogen has a positive valence of 1; one atom of oxygen combines with two of hydrogen to form a molecule of water. *n.*

Va len cia (və len′shə), seaport in E Spain. *n.*

Va len ci ennes (və len′sē enz′), a fine lace in which the pattern and background are made together of the same threads. *n.* [from *Valenciennes,* city in northern France, where it was originally made]

val en tine (val′ən tīn), 1 a greeting card or small gift sent on Saint Valentine's Day, February 14. 2 a sweetheart chosen on this day. *n.*

Val en tine (val′ən tīn), **Saint,** Christian martyr of the A.D. 200's. He was beheaded by the Romans on February 14. *n.*

va ler i an (və lir′ē ən), 1 a strong-smelling drug used to quiet the nerves. 2 plant from whose root it is made. Valerian has small pinkish or white flowers and is often grown in gardens. *n.*

val et (val′it *or* val′ā), 1 servant who takes care of a man's clothes and gives him personal service. 2 worker in a hotel who cleans or presses clothes. 3 serve as a valet. 1,2 *n.,* 3 *v.*

Val hal la (val hal′ə), (in Scandinavian myths) the hall where the souls of heroes slain in battle feast with the god Odin. *n.*

val iant (val′yənt), brave; courageous: a valiant soldier, a valiant deed. *adj.* —**val′iant ly,** *adv.*

val id (val′id), 1 supported by facts or authority; sound or true: *a valid argument.* 2 having legal force; legally binding: *A contract made by an insane person is not valid.* 3 having force; holding good; effective: *Illness is a valid excuse for being absent from school. adj.* —**val′id ly,** *adv.*

val i date (val′ə dāt), 1 make valid; give legal force to: *The farmer's deed validated his claim to the land.* 2 support by facts or authority; confirm. *v.,* **val i dat ed, val i dat ing.**

va lid i ty (və lid′ə tē), 1 truth or soundness: *the validity of an argument, the validity of an excuse.* 2 legal soundness or force: *the validity of a contract. n., pl.* **va lid i ties.**

va lise (və lēs′), a traveling bag to hold clothes, etc. *n.*

Val kyr ie (val kir′ē), (in Scandinavian myths) one of the goddesses sent by Odin to ride through the air and hover over battlefields, choosing the heroes who would die in battle and afterward leading them to Valhalla. *n.*

val ley (val′ē), 1 low land between hills or mountains: *Most large valleys have rivers running through them.* 2 a wide region drained by a great river system: *the Mississippi valley. n., pl.* **val leys.**

Valley Forge, village in SE Pennsylvania, in which Washington and his army spent the winter of 1777-1778.

val or (val′ər), bravery; courage. *n.*

val or ous (val′ər əs), valiant; brave; courageous. *adj.* —**val′or ous ly,** *adv.*

Val pa rai so (val′pə ri′zō), chief seaport of Chile, in the central part. *n.*

val u a ble (val′yü ə bəl *or* val′yə bəl), 1 having value; being worth something: *valuable information, a valuable friend.* 2 worth much money: *a valuable ring. He has a valuable stamp collection.* 3 Usually, **valuables,** *pl.* articles of value: *She keeps her jewelry and other valuables in a safe.* 1,2 *adj.,* 3 *n.*

val u a tion (val′yü ā′shən), 1 value estimated or determined: *The jeweler's valuation of the necklace was $10,000.* 2 an estimating or determining of the value of something. *n.*

val ue (val′yü), 1 the real worth; proper price: *We bought the house for less than its value.* 2 high worth; excellence, usefulness, or importance: *the value of education, the value of milk as a food.* 3 power to buy: *The value of the dollar lessened from 1930 to 1970.* 4 rate at a certain value or price; estimate the value of: *The land is valued at $5000.* 5 estimated worth: *We placed a value on our furniture.* 6 think highly of: regard highly: *We all value our teacher's opin-* ion of our work. 7 meaning, effect, or force: *the value of a symbol.* 8 number or amount represented by a symbol: *The value of XIV is fourteen.* 9 the relative length of a tone in music indicated by a note. 1-3,5,7-9 *n.,* 4,6 *v.,* **val ued, val u ing.**

val ued (val′yüd), 1 having its value estimated or determined. 2 regarded highly. *adj.*

val ue less (val′yə lis), without value; worthless. *adj.*

VALVE valve (def. 1)

valve (valv), 1 a movable part that controls the flow of a liquid, gas, etc., through a pipe by opening and closing the passage. A faucet contains a valve. 2 part of the body that works like a valve. The valves of the heart are membranes that control the flow of blood into and out of the heart. 3 one of the parts of hinged shells like those of oysters and clams. 4 device in certain brass wind instruments, such as trumpets, French horns, etc., for changing the pitch of the tone by changing the direction and length of the column of air. *n.*

valve less (valv′lis), having no valve. *adj.*

VAMP vamp (def. 1)

vamp (vamp), 1 the upper front part of a shoe or boot. 2 furnish with a vamp; repair with a new vamp. 3 piece or patch added to an old thing to make it look new. 4 patch up; make (an old thing) look new. 1,3 *n.,* 2,4 *v.*

vam pire (vam′pīr), 1 corpse supposed to come to life at night and suck the blood of people while they sleep. 2 person who preys ruthlessly on others. 3 vampire bat. *n.*

vampire bat, 1 any of various bats of South and Central America that pierce the skin of animals with their sharp teeth and drink their blood. 2 of various other bats incorrectly supposed to drink blood.

van[1] (van), the front part of an army, fleet, or other advancing group. *n.* [shortened from *vanguard*]

van[2] (van), a covered truck or wagon for moving furniture, etc. *n.* [shortened from *caravan*]

va na di um (və nā′dē əm), a very

hard, silver-white metallic element used in making various strong alloys of steel. *n.* [from *Vanadis*, Scandinavian goddess of love (because it was discovered in Sweden)]

Van Al len radiation belt (van al′ən), either of two broad bands of intense radiation surrounding the earth, consisting of charged particles which are apparently held by the earth's magnetic field. [from James A. *Van Allen*, 1914-1966, American physicist who discovered them in 1958]

Van Bur en (van byür′ən), **Martin,** 1782-1862, the eighth president of the United States, from 1837 to 1841.

Van cou ver (van kü′vər), 1 seaport in SW Canada. 2 island in the Pacific Ocean, just off the SW coast of Canada. It is part of British Columbia. *n.*

van dal (van′dl), 1 person who destroys or damages beautiful or valuable things on purpose. 2 **Vandal,** member of a Germanic tribe that ravaged Gaul, Spain, and northern Africa. In A.D. 455 the Vandals took Rome. *n.*

van dal ism (van′dl iz′əm), the destroying or damaging of beautiful or valuable things on purpose. *n.*

Van Dyck (van dīk′), Vandyke.

vandyke (def. 2)

Van dyke (van dīk′), 1 Sir **Anthony,** 1599-1641, Flemish painter who lived for some years in England. 2 **vandyke,** a short, pointed beard. *n.*

vane (vān), 1 a flat piece of metal, or some other device, fixed upon a spire or some other high object in such a way as to move with the wind and indicate its direction; weather vane; weathercock. 2 blade of a windmill, a ship's propeller, etc. 3 blade, wing, or similar part attached to an axis, wheel, etc., so as to be acted upon by a current of air or liquid or to produce a current by rotation. 4 the flat, soft part of a feather. *n.*

Van Gogh (van gō′), **Vincent,** 1853-1890, Dutch painter.

van guard (van′gärd′), 1 the front part of an army; soldiers marching ahead of the main part of an army to clear the way and guard against surprise. 2 the foremost or leading position. 3 leaders of a movement. *n.*

va nil la (və nil′ə), 1 a flavoring extract made from the vanilla bean, used in candy, ice cream, etc. 2 the tropical climbing plant that yields vanilla beans. 3 vanilla bean. *n.*

vanilla bean, the long pod of the vanilla plant.

van ish (van′ish), 1 disappear, especially suddenly: *The sun vanished behind a cloud.* 2 pass away; cease to be: *Dinosaurs have vanished from the earth.* *v.*

van i ty (van′ə tē), 1 too much pride in one's looks, ability, etc. 2 lack of real value: *the vanity of wealth.* 3 worthless pleasure or display. *n., pl.* **van i ties.**

van quish (vang′kwish), conquer; defeat; overcome. *v.* —**van′quish er,** *n.*

van tage (van′tij), a better position or condition; advantage. *n.*

vap id (vap′id), without much life or flavor; tasteless; dull. *adj.* —**vap′id ly,** *adv.*

va por (vā′pər), 1 moisture in the air that can be seen, such as steam, fog, mist, etc., usually due to the effect of heat upon a liquid. 2 gas formed from a substance that is usually a liquid or a solid; the gaseous form of a liquid or solid. *n.*

va por i za tion (vā′pər ə zā′shən), a changing or a being changed into vapor. *n.*

va por ize (vā′pə rīz′), change into vapor: *Heat vaporizes water.* *v.,* **va por ized, va por iz ing.**

va por iz er (vā′pə rī′zər), device for converting a liquid into vapor, such as an apparatus that releases steam into a room for medicinal purposes. *n.*

va por ous (vā′pər əs), 1 full of vapor; misty. 2 like vapor. 3 soon passing; worthless. *adj.*

vane (def. 1)

va por y (vā′pər ē), vaporous. *adj.*

va quer o (vä ker′ō), (in the southwestern United States) a cowboy, herdsman, or cattle driver. *n., pl.* **va quer os.** [from Spanish *vaquero* cowherd]

var i a bil i ty (ver′ē ə bil′ə tē *or* var′ē ə bil′ə tē), 1 changeableness. 2 tendency to vary. *n.*

var i a ble (ver′ē ə bəl *or* var′ē ə bəl), 1 apt to change; changeable; uncertain: *variable winds. The weather is more variable in New York than it is in California.* 2 that can be varied: *These adjustable curtain rods are of variable length.* 3 thing or quantity that varies. 4 **a** quantity that can assume any of a given set of values. **b** symbol repre-

hat, āge, fär; let, ēqual, tėrm;
it, īce; hot, ōpen, ôrder;
oil, out; cup, pùt, rüle; ch, child;
ng, long; sh, she; th, thin;
ŦH, then; zh, measure;

ə represents *a* in about,
e in taken, *i* in pencil,
o in lemon, *u* in circus.

senting this quantity. 1,2 *adj.,* 3,4 *n.* —**var′i a ble ness,** *n.*

var i a bly (ver′ē ə blē *or* var′ē ə blē), in a variable manner; changeably. *adv.*

var i ance (ver′ē əns *or* var′ē əns), 1 difference; disagreement. 2 a varying; change. *n.*

at variance, in disagreement: *His actions are at variance with his promises.*

var i ant (ver′ē ənt *or* var′ē ənt), 1 varying; different: *"Rime" is a variant spelling of "rhyme."* 2 a different form; a different pronunciation or spelling of the same word. 1 *adj.,* 2 *n.*

var i a tion (ver′ē ā′shən *or* var′ē ā′shən), 1 a varying: *There was a variation of 30 degrees in the temperature yesterday.* 2 a varied or changed form. 3 (in music) a tune or theme repeated with changes in rhythm, harmony, etc. *n.*

var i col ored (ver′ē kul′ərd *or* var′ē kul′ərd), having various colors. *adj.*

var i cose (var′ə kōs), abnormally swollen or enlarged: *legs covered with varicose veins. adj.*

var ied (ver′ēd *or* var′ēd), 1 of different kinds; having variety: *a varied assortment of candies.* 2 changed; altered. *adj.*

var i e gat ed (ver′ē ə gā′tid *or* var′ē ə gā′tid), 1 varied in appearance; marked with different colors: *variegated pansies.* 2 having variety. *adj.*

var i e ga tion (ver′ē ə gā′shən *or* var′ē ə gā′shən), a variegating or a being variegated; varied coloring. *n.*

va ri e ty (və rī′ə tē), 1 lack of sameness; difference or change: *Variety is the spice of life.* 2 number of different kinds: *This shop has a variety of toys.* 3 kind or sort: *Which varieties of cake did you buy?* 4 division of a species. *n., pl.* **va ri e ties.**

variety show, entertainment featuring different kinds of acts, such as songs, dances, acrobatic feats, and comic skits.

var i ous (ver′ē əs *or* var′ē əs), 1 differing from one another; different: *There have been various opinions as to the best way to raise children.* 2 sev-

varlet

adj. adjective	*n.* noun
adv. adverb	*prep.* preposition
conj. conjunction	*pron.* pronoun
interj. interjection	*v.* verb
sing. singular	*pl.* plural

eral; many: *We have looked at various houses, but have decided to buy this one. adj.* —**var′i ous ly**, *adv.*

var let (vär′lit), a low fellow; rascal. *n.*

var mint (vär′mənt), DIALECT. vermin. *n.*

var nish (vär′nish), **1** a liquid that gives a smooth, glossy appearance to wood, metal, etc. Varnish is often made from substances like resin dissolved in oil or turpentine. **2** the smooth, hard surface made by this liquid when it dries: *The varnish on the table was scratched.* **3** put varnish on. **4** a glossy appearance. **5** a false or deceiving appearance; pretense: *cover one's selfishness with a varnish of good manners.* **6** give a false or deceiving appearance to: *to varnish over the truth with a lie.* 1,2,4,5 *n., pl.* **var nish es;** 3,6 *v.*

var si ty (vär′sə tē), the most important team in a given sport in a university, college, or school. *n., pl.* **var si ties.**

var y (ver′ē *or* var′ē), **1** make or become different; change: *The driver can vary the speed of an automobile. The weather varies.* **2** be different; differ: *Stars vary in brightness. v.,* **var ied, var y ing.**

vas cu lar (vas′kyə lər), having to do with, made of, or provided with vessels that carry blood, sap, etc. *adj.*

vase

vase (vās), holder or container used for ornament or for holding flowers. *n.* —**vase′like′,** *adj.*

Vas e line (vas′ə lēn′), trademark for a soft, greasy, yellow or whitish substance made from petroleum, used as a healing ointment or as a lubricant. *n.*

vas sal (vas′əl), **1** (in the feudal system) a person who held land from a lord or superior, to whom in return he gave help in war or some other service. A great noble could be a vassal of the king and have many other men as his vassals. **2** like a vassal; like that of

a vassal: *a vassal nation.* **3** servant. 1,3 *n.,* 2 *adj.*

vas sal age (vas′ə lij), **1** condition of being a vassal. **2** the homage or service due from a vassal to his lord or superior. **3** dependence; servitude. *n.*

vast (vast), very great; immense: *Texas and Alaska cover vast territories. A billion dollars is a vast amount of money. adj.* —**vast′ness,** *n.*

vast ly (vast′lē), very greatly; to a vast extent or degree. *adv.*

vat (vat), a large container for liquids; tank: *a vat of dye. n.*

Vat i can (vat′ə kən), **1** the collection of buildings grouped about the palace of the pope in Rome. **2** the government, office, or authority of the pope. *n.*

Vatican City, an independent state inside the city of Rome. It is ruled by the pope and includes Saint Peter's Church and the Vatican.

vau de ville (vô′də vil *or* vôd′vil), theatrical entertainment featuring a variety of acts. Vaudeville consists of songs, dances, acrobatic feats, short plays, trained animals, etc. *n.*

vault[1] (def. 1)—different types

vault[1] (vôlt), **1** an arched roof or ceiling; series of arches. **2** an arched space or passage. **3** something like an arched roof. The vault of heaven means the sky. **4** make in the form of a vault: *The roof was vaulted.* **5** cover with a vault. **6** an underground cellar or storehouse. **7** place for storing valuable things and keeping them safe. Vaults are often made of steel. **8** place for burial. 1-3,6-8 *n.,* 4,5 *v.* [from French of the 1300's *voulte,* from Latin *volutum* rolled] —**vault′like′,** *adj.*

vault[2] (vôlt), **1** jump or leap over by using the hands or a pole: *She vaulted the fence.* **2** act of vaulting. **3** to jump; to

vault[2] (def. 1)
pole vault

leap: *He vaulted over the wall.* 1,3 *v.,* 2 *n.* [from French of the 1500's *volter,* from Italian *voltare,* from *volta* roll, from Latin *volutum* rolled]

vaunt (vônt), boast. *v., n.*

veal (vēl), flesh of a calf, used for food. *n.*

vector (def. 1)
DA and DC are vectors; DB is resultant.

vec tor (vek′tər), **1** quantity involving direction as well as magnitude, represented by an arrow which shows the direction of the force. The length of the arrow indicates the magnitude of the force. **2** organism that transmits disease germs, such as a mosquito or a tick. *n.*

veer (vir), **1** change in direction; shift; turn: *The wind veered to the south. The talk veered to ghosts.* **2** change the direction of: *We veered our boat.* **3** a shift; turn: *The car made a sudden veer to the left.* 1,2 *v.,* 3 *n.*

veer y (vir′ē), thrush of eastern North America with tawny head, back, and tail and a faintly spotted white breast. *n., pl.* **veer ies.**

Ve ga (vē′gə), a bluish-white star, the brightest star in the constellation Lyra. *n.*

veg e ta ble (vej′ə tə bəl), **1** plant whose fruit, shoots or stems, leaves, roots, or other parts are used for food. Peas, corn, lettuce, tomatoes, and beets are vegetables. **2** the part of such a plant which is used for food. **3** any plant. **4** of, having to do with, or like plants: *the vegetable kingdom, vegetable life.* **5** consisting of or made from vegetables: *vegetable soup.* 1-3 *n.,* 4,5 *adj.*

veg e tar i an (vej′ə ter′ē ən), **1** person who eats only vegetable foods and abstains from meat, fish, or other animal products. **2** eating vegetable foods only. **3** containing no meat: *a vegetarian diet.* **4** serving no meat: *a vegetarian restaurant.* 1 *n.,* 2-4 *adj.*

veg e tar i an ism (vej′ə ter′ē ə niz′əm), practice or principle of eating only vegetable foods and abstaining from meat, fish, or other animal products. *n.*

veg e tate (vej′ə tāt), **1** grow as plants do. **2** live with very little action, thought, or feeling. *v.,* **veg e tat ed, veg e tat ing.**

veg e ta tion (vej′ə tā′shən), **1** plant

life; growing plants: *There is not much vegetation in deserts.* 2 act or process of vegetating; growth of plants. *n.*

veg e ta tive (vej′ə tā′tiv), 1 growing as plants do. 2 of plants or plant life. 3 having very little action, thought, or feeling. *adj.*

ve he mence (vē′ə məns), vehement quality or nature; strong feeling; forcefulness; violence: *The two brothers argued loudly and with vehemence. n.*

ve he ment (vē′ə mənt), 1 having or showing strong feeling; caused by strong feeling; eager; passionate. 2 forceful; violent: *He finished the job with a vehement burst of energy. adj.* —**ve′he ment ly,** *adv.*

ve hi cle (vē′ə kəl), 1 any means of carrying, conveying, or transporting, such as a car, carriage, cart, wagon, sled, etc. Automobiles and trucks are motor vehicles. Rockets and satellites are space vehicles. 2 a means or medium by which something is communicated, shown, done, etc.: *Language is the vehicle of thought.* 3 (in painting) a liquid into which pigment is mixed to apply color to a surface: *Linseed oil is a vehicle for paint. n.*

ve hic u lar (vi hik′yə lər), of or having to do with vehicles: *vehicular traffic. adj.*

veil (vāl), 1 piece of very thin material worn to protect or hide the face, or as an ornament. 2 piece of material worn so as to fall over the head and shoulders. 3 cover with a veil: *Some Moslem women veil their faces before going into public.* 4 anything that screens or hides: *a veil of clouds, a veil of deception.* 5 to cover, screen, or hide: *Fog veiled the shore. They veiled their plans in secrecy.* 1,2,4 *n.,* 3,5 *v.* —**veil′like′,** *adj.*

take the veil, become a nun.

veins
(def. 2, above;
def. 3, below)

vein (vān), 1 one of the blood vessels or tubes that carry blood to the heart from all parts of the body. 2 one of the strands or bundles of vascular tissue forming the principal framework of a leaf. 3 one of the ribs that strengthen the wing of an insect. 4 a crack or seam in rock filled with a deposit, especially of metallic ore: *a vein of copper.* 5 any streak or marking of a different shade or color in wood, marble, etc. 6 a special character or disposition; state of mind; mood: *a vein of cruelty, a joking vein.* 7 cover with veins; mark with veins:

veined marble. 1-6 *n.,* 7 *v.* —**vein′-like′,** *adj.*

veld or **veldt** (velt), open country in South Africa, having grass or bushes but few trees. *n.* [from Afrikaans *veld,* from Dutch *veld, veldt* field]

vel lum (vel′əm), 1 the finest kind of parchment, usually prepared from the skins of calves and lambs, once used instead of paper for books. Some very expensive books are still bound with vellum. 2 paper or cloth imitating such parchment. A college diploma is usually made of vellum. *n.*

ve loc i pede (və los′ə pēd′), 1 a child's tricycle. 2 an early kind of bicycle or tricycle. *n.*

ve loc i ty (və los′ə tē), 1 quickness of motion; speed; swiftness; rapidity: *fly with the velocity of a bird. The velocity of light is about 186,000 miles per second.* 2 rate of motion in a particular direction. *n., pl.* **ve loc i ties.**

ve lour or **ve lours** (və lür′), fabric like velvet, usually made of silk, wool, cotton, or rayon. Velours is used for clothing, draperies, upholstery, etc. *n.*

veil (def. 2)
two styles

vel vet (vel′vit), 1 cloth with a thick, soft pile, made of silk, rayon, cotton, etc. 2 made of velvet: *a velvet jacket.* 3 like velvet: *Our kitten has soft velvet paws.* 1 *n.,* 2,3 *adj.* —**vel′vet like′,** *adj.*

vel vet een (vel′və tēn′), a cotton fabric resembling velvet. *n.*

vel vet y (vel′və tē), smooth and soft like velvet. *adj.*

ve na ca va (vē′nə kā′və), either of two large veins that empty blood from the upper and lower halves of the body into the right auricle of the heart. *pl.* **ve nae ca vae** (vē′nē kā′vē). [from Latin *vena cava* hollow vein]

ve nal (vē′nl), 1 willing to sell one's services or influence basely; open to bribes; corrupt: *Venal judges are a disgrace to a country.* 2 influenced or obtained by bribery: *venal conduct. adj.*

ve nal i ty (vē nal′ə tē), quality of being venal. *n.*

ve na tion (vē nā′shən), 1 arrangement of veins in a leaf, in an insect's wing, etc. 2 these veins. *n.*

vend (vend), sell; peddle: *He vends fruit from a cart. v.*

vend er (ven′dər), vendor. *n.*

ven det ta (ven det′ə), feud in which a

murdered person's relatives try to kill the slayer or his relatives. *n., pl.* **ven det tas.**

vending machine, machine from which one obtains candy, stamps, etc., when a coin is dropped in.

ven dor (ven′dər), seller; peddler. *n.* Also, **vender.**

ve neer (və nir′), 1 cover (wood) with a thin layer of finer wood or other material: *The pine desk is veneered with mahogany.* 2 a thin layer of wood or other material used in veneering: *The panel had a veneer of gold and ivory.* 3 cover (anything) with a layer of something else to give an appearance of superior quality. 4 surface appearance or show: *Their treachery was hidden by a veneer of friendship.* 1,3 *v.,* 2,4 *n.*

ven er a ble (ven′ər ə bəl), worthy of reverence; deserving respect because of age, character, or importance: *a venerable teacher, venerable customs. adj.*

ven e rate (ven′ə rāt′), regard with deep respect; revere: *He venerates his father's memory. v.,* **ven e rat ed, ven e rat ing.**

ven e ra tion (ven′ə rā′shən), deep respect; reverence. *n.*

ve ner e al (və nir′ē əl), having to do with or transmitted by sexual intercourse. Syphilis is a venereal disease. *adj.*

Ve ne tian (və nē′shən), 1 of Venice or its people. 2 person born or living in Venice. 1 *adj.,* 2 *n.*

Venetian blind, a window blind made of many horizontal wooden, steel, or aluminum slats. The blind can be raised and lowered, or the slats can be tilted so that they overlap, to regulate the light that is allowed in.

Ven e zue la (ven′ə zwā′lə or ven′ə-zwē′lə), country in the N part of South America. *Capital:* Caracas. *n.* —**Ven′-e zue′lan,** *adj., n.*

venge ance (ven′jəns), punishment in return for a wrong; revenge: *She swore vengeance against her hateful enemies. n.*

with a vengeance, 1 with great force or violence: *By six o'clock it was rain-*

vengeful

ing with a vengeance. 2 extremely. 3 much more than expected.

venge ful (venj′fəl), feeling or showing a strong desire for vengeance. *adj.* —**venge′ful ly,** *adv.* —**venge′ful ness,** *n.*

ve ni al (vē′nē əl), that can be forgiven; not very wrong; wrong but pardonable. *adj.*

Ven ice (ven′is), city on the NE coast of Italy. Venice has many canals in place of streets. *n.*

ven i son (ven′ə sən), the flesh of a deer, used for food; deer meat. *n.*

ven om (ven′əm), 1 the poison of snakes, spiders, etc. 2 spite; malice: *They spoke of their enemies with venom. n.*

ven om ous (ven′ə məs), 1 poisonous: *a venomous snake.* 2 spiteful; malicious. *adj.* —**ven′om ous ly,** *adv.* —**ven′om ous ness,** *n.*

ve nous (vē′nəs), of, in, or having to do with veins: *venous blood. adj.*

vent[1] (vent), 1 hole or opening, especially one serving as an outlet: *He used a pencil to make air vents in the box so the frog could breathe.* 2 outlet; way out; free expression: *Her great energy found vent in hard work. We gave vent to our grief in tears.* 3 let out; express freely: *I vented my anger on the dog.* 4 make a vent in. 1,2 *n.,* 3,4 *v.* [from French of the 1300's *vent* wind and *évent* vent, both from Latin *ventus* wind]

vent[2] (vent), slit in a garment. *n.* [from French of the 1400's *fente,* from *fendre* to split, from Latin *findere*]

ven ti late (ven′tl āt), 1 change the air in: *We ventilate a room by opening windows.* 2 purify by fresh air: *The lungs ventilate the blood.* 3 make known publicly; discuss openly. *v.,* **ven ti lat ed, ven ti lat ing.**

ven ti la tion (ven′tl ā′shən), 1 change of air; act or process of supplying with fresh air. 2 means of supplying fresh air: *Air conditioning provides ventilation in the summer.* 3 an open discussion in public. *n.*

ven ti la tor (ven′tl ā′tər), any apparatus or means, such as an opening, an air conditioner, or a fan, for changing or improving the air in an enclosed space. *n.*

ven tral (ven′trəl), abdominal. We call the side of any animal where its belly is the ventral side. *adj.*

ven tri cle (ven′trə kəl), one of the two chambers of the heart that receive the blood from the auricles and force it into the arteries. See **heart** for diagram. *n.*

ven tril o quism (ven tril′ə kwiz′əm), art or practice of speaking or uttering sounds with the lips shut or nearly shut so that the voice may seem to come from some source other than the speaker. *n.*

ven tril o quist (ven tril′ə kwist), person skilled in ventriloquism. *n.*

ven ture (ven′chər), 1 a risky or daring undertaking: *Our courage was equal to any venture. A lucky venture in oil stock made her rich.* 2 expose to risk or danger: *She ventured her life to rescue me.* 3 dare: *No one ventured to interrupt the speaker.* 4 dare to come or go: *We ventured out on the thin ice and fell through.* 5 dare to say or make: *He ventured an objection.* 1 *n.,* 2-5 *v.,* **ven tured, ven tur ing.**

ven ture some (ven′chər səm), 1 inclined to take risks; rash; daring. 2 risky. *adj.*

ven tur ous (ven′chər əs), 1 bold; daring; adventurous. 2 risky. *adj.*

Ve nus (vē′nəs), 1 (in Roman myths) the goddess of love and beauty. The Greeks called her Aphrodite. 2 a very beautiful woman. 3 the sixth largest planet in the solar system and the second in distance from the sun. It is the most brilliant planet in the solar system, and the one that comes closest to the earth. *n.*

ve ra cious (və rā′shəs), 1 truthful. 2 true. *adj.* —**ve ra′cious ly,** *adv.* —**ve ra′cious ness,** *n.*

ve rac i ty (və ras′ə tē), 1 truthfulness. 2 truth. 3 correctness; accuracy. *n., pl.* **ve rac i ties.**

Ver a cruz (ver′ə krüz′), seaport city in SE Mexico. *n.*

Vera Cruz, Veracruz.

ve ran da (və ran′də), a large porch along one or more sides of a house. *n., pl.* **ve ran das.**

ve ran dah (və ran′də), veranda. *n.*

verb (vėrb), word that tells what is or what is done; the part of speech that expresses action or being. *Do, go, come, be, sit, think, know,* and *eat* are verbs. *n.*

ver bal (vėr′bəl), 1 in words; of words: *A description is a verbal picture.* 2 expressed in spoken words; oral: *a verbal message, a verbal promise.* 3 word for word; literal: *a verbal translation from the French.* 4 having to do with a verb. Two common verbal endings are *-ed* and *-ing.* 5 derived

from a verb: *a verbal noun.* 6 a noun, adjective, or other word derived from a verb. 1-5 *adj.,* 6 *n.*

ver bal ly (vėr′bə lē), 1 in spoken words; orally: *Instead of replying verbally, I answered with a nod of my head.* 2 word for word: *The witness reported the conversation verbally.* 3 as a verb: *"Breast" is used verbally in "The boat breasts the wave." adv.*

ver ba tim (vər bā′tim), word for word; in exactly the same words: *His speech was printed verbatim in the newspaper* (*adv.*). *The newspaper gave a verbatim report of the speech* (*adj.*). *adv., adj.*

ver be na (vər bē′nə), any of certain garden plants with elongated or flattened spikes of flowers having various colors. *n., pl.* **ver be nas.**

ver bi age (vėr′bē ij), use of too many words; abundance of useless words. *n.*

ver bose (vər bōs′), using too many words; wordy. *adj.* —**ver bose′ly,** *adv.*

ver bos i ty (vər bos′ə tē), use of too many words; wordiness. *n.*

ver bo ten (fer bōt′n), a German word meaning absolutely forbidden by authority. *adj.*

ver dant (vėr′dnt), green: *The fields are covered with verdant grass. adj.* —**ver′dant ly,** *adv.*

Verde (vėrd), **Cape,** the most western point of Africa, in Senegal. *n.*

Ver di (ver′dē), **Giuseppe,** 1813-1901, Italian composer of operas. *n.*

ver dict (vėr′dikt), 1 the decision of a jury: *The jury returned a verdict of "Not guilty."* 2 any decision or judgment: *the public's verdict, the verdict of history. n.*

ver di gris (vėr′də grēs′), 1 a green or bluish coating that forms on brass, copper, or bronze when exposed to the air for long periods of time. 2 a green or bluish-green poisonous compound used in paints and insecticides. *n.*

ver dure (vėr′jər), 1 fresh greenness. 2 a fresh growth of green grass, plants, or leaves. *n.*

verge[1] (vėrj), 1 the point at which something begins or happens; brink: *The country is on the verge of a civil war. Our business is on the verge of ruin.* 2 be on the verge; border: *The speech was so poorly prepared that it verged on the ridiculous.* 1 *n.,* 2 *v.,* **verged, verg ing.** [from French of the 1300's *verge,* from Latin *virga* staff, rod]

verge[2] (vėrj), tend; incline: *The cook was plump, verging toward fatness. v.,* **verged, verg ing.** [from Latin *vergere*]

Ver gil (vėr′jəl), 70-19 B.C., Roman

poet, author of *The Aeneid*. n. Also, **Virgil**.

ver i fi a ble (ver′ə fī′ə bəl), that can be verified. *adj.*

ver i fi ca tion (ver′ə fə kā′shən), proof by evidence or testimony; confirmation. *n.*

ver i fy (ver′ə fī), **1** prove to be true; confirm: *The driver's report of the accident was verified by two women who had seen it happen.* **2** test the correctness of; check for accuracy: *You can verify the spelling of a word by looking in a dictionary.* *v.,* **ver i fied, ver i fy ing.**

ver i ly (ver′ə lē), OLD USE. in truth; truly; really. *adv.*

ver i si mil i tude (ver′ə sə mil′ə tüd *or* ver′ə sə mil′ə tyüd), an appearance of truth; resemblance to reality; closeness to fact. *n.*

ver i ta ble (ver′ə tə bəl), true; real; actual. *adj.*

ver i ta bly (ver′ə tə blē), in truth; truly; really; actually. *adv.*

ver i ty (ver′ə tē), **1** truth. **2** a true statement or fact. **3** reality. *n., pl.* **ver i ties.**

ver mi cel li (ver′mə sel′ē), a mixture of flour and water like spaghetti but thinner. *n.* [from Italian *vermicelli* little worms]

ver mi form (ver′mə fôrm), shaped like a worm. *adj.*

vermiform appendix, a slender tube, closed at one end, growing out of the large intestine in the lower right-hand part of the abdomen; appendix. Appendicitis is inflammation of the vermiform appendix.

ver mil ion (vər mil′yən), **1** a bright red. **2** bright-red. **3** a bright-red coloring matter. **1,3** *n.,* **2** *adj.*

ver min (ver′mən), **1** small animals that are troublesome or destructive. Fleas, lice, bedbugs, rats, and mice are vermin. **2** very unpleasant or vile person or persons. *n. pl. or sing.*

Ver mont (vər mont′), one of the northeastern states of the United States. *Capital:* Montpelier. *n.*

ver mouth (vər müth′), a white wine flavored with wormwood or other herbs and used as a liqueur or in cocktails. *n.*

ver nac u lar (vər nak′yə lər), **1** a native language; language used by the people of a certain country or place. **2** of or in the native language, rather than a literary or learned language. **3** everyday language; informal speech. **4** language of a profession, trade, etc.: *There are many technical words in the vernacular of lawyers.* **1,3,4** *n.,* **2** *adj.*

ver nal (ver′nl), **1** of spring; coming in spring: *vernal green, vernal flowers, vernal months.* **2** youthful: *The old couple*

liked to talk of memories from their vernal days. *adj.*

Verne (vern), **Jules,** 1828-1905, French writer of science fiction and adventure stories. *n.*

Ve ro na (və rō′nə), city in N Italy. The story of *Romeo and Juliet* takes place in Verona. *n.*

Ver sailles (ver sī′), **1** city in N France, near Paris. A treaty of peace between the Allies and Germany was signed there after World War I, on June 28, 1919. **2** a large palace there. *n.*

ver sa tile (ver′sə təl), able to do many things well: *She is a versatile student; she is skilled at science, art, mathematics, English, German, and history. adj.*

ver sa til i ty (ver′sə til′ə tē), ability to do many things well. *n.*

verse (vers), **1** lines of words with a regularly repeated accent and often with rhyme. Poetry is usually composed in verse. **2** a single line of verse. **3** group of such lines: *Sing the first verse of "America."* **4** type of verse; meter: *blank verse, iambic verse.* **5** a short division of a chapter in the Bible. *n.*

versed (verst), experienced; practiced; skilled: *Our doctor is well versed in medicine. adj.*

ver si fi ca tion (ver′sə fə kā′shən), **1** the making of verses. **2** art or theory of making verses. **3** form or style of poetry; metrical structure. *n.*

ver si fi er (ver′sə fī′ər), person who makes verses. *n.*

ver si fy (ver′sə fī), **1** write verses. **2** tell in verse. **3** turn (prose) into poetry. *v.,* **ver si fied, ver si fy ing.**

ver sion (ver′zhən), **1** a translation from one language to another: *a version of the Bible.* **2** one particular statement, account, or description: *Each of the three boys gave his own version of the quarrel.* **3** a special form or variant of something: *a Scottish version of the Christmas tree. n.*

ver sus (ver′səs), against: *The most exciting game was Harvard versus Yale. prep.*

ver te bra (ver′tə brə), one of the bones of the backbone. *n., pl.* **ver te brae** (ver′tə brē), **ver te bras.**

vertebra
Detail below shows
three vertebrae.

SIDE
VIEW

BACK
VIEW

hat, āge, fär; let, ēqual, tėrm;
it, īce; hot, ōpen, ôrder;
oil, out; cup, pùt, rüle; ch, child;
ng, long; sh, she; th, thin;
ᵺ, then; zh, measure;

ə represents *a* in about,
e in taken, *i* in pencil,
o in lemon, *u* in circus.

ver te bral (ver′tə brəl), of or having to do with a vertebra or the vertebrae. *adj.*

ver te brate (ver′tə brit *or* ver′tə-brāt), **1** animal that has a backbone. Fishes, amphibians, reptiles, birds, and mammals are vertebrates. **2** having a backbone. **1** *n.,* **2** *adj.*

ver tex (ver′teks), **1** the highest point; top. **2 a** point opposite the base of a triangle, pyramid, etc. **b** the point where the two sides of an angle meet. *n., pl.* **ver tex es, ver ti ces** (ver′tə-sēz′).

ver ti cal (ver′tə kəl), **1** straight up and down; perpendicular to a level surface. A person standing up straight is in a vertical position. **2** a vertical line, plane, direction, position, etc. **1** *adj.,* **2** *n.* —**ver′ti cal ly,** *adv.*

ver ti go (ver′tə gō), dizziness; giddiness. *n., pl.* **ver ti goes.**

verve (verv), enthusiasm; energy; vigor; spirit; liveliness. *n.*

ver y (ver′ē), **1** much; greatly; extremely: *The sunshine is very hot in July.* **2** absolutely; exactly: *He stood in the very same place for an hour.* **3** same; identical: *The very people who supported the plan are against it now.* **4** even; mere; sheer: *The very thought of blood makes me sick. We wept from very joy.* **5** real; true; genuine: *Your kindness makes you a very saint.* **6** actual: *caught in the very act of stealing.* **1,2** *adv.,* **3-6** *adj.,* **ver i er, ver i est.**

ves i cle (ves′ə kəl), a small bladder, cavity, sac, or cyst. A blister is a vesicle in the skin. *n.*

ve sic u lar (və sik′yə lər), of or having to do with a vesicle or vesicles. *adj.*

ves per (ves′pər), **1** evening. **2 Vesper,** the planet Venus, when it appears as the evening star. **3** of evening. **4** an evening prayer, hymn, or service. **5 vespers** or **Vespers,** *pl.* a church service held in the late afternoon or in the evening; evensong. **6** of or having to do with vespers. **1,2,4,5** *n.,* **3,6** *adj.*

Ves puc ci (ve spü′chē), **Amerigo,** 1451-1512, Italian merchant, adventurer, and explorer. America is named after him. *n.*

adj.	adjective	n.	noun
adv.	adverb	prep.	preposition
conj.	conjunction	pron.	pronoun
interj.	interjection	v.	verb
sing.	singular	pl.	plural

ves sel (ves′əl), 1 a large boat; ship: *Ocean liners and other vessels are usually docked by tugboats.* 2 a hollow holder or container. Cups, bowls, pitchers, bottles, barrels, and tubs are vessels. 3 tube carrying blood or other fluid. Veins and arteries are blood vessels. *n.*

vest (vest), 1 a short, sleeveless garment worn by men or boys under the coat. 2 garment like this worn by women. 3 clothe or robe: *The vested priest stood before the altar.* 4 furnish with powers, authority, rights, etc.: *Congress is vested with the power to declare war.* 5 put in the possession or control of a person or persons: *The management of the hospital is vested in a board of trustees.* 1,2 *n.*, 3-5 *v.*

Ves ta (ves′tə), (in Roman myths) the goddess of the hearth. A sacred fire was always kept burning in the temple of Vesta. *n.*

ves tal (ves′tl), 1 one of the vestal virgins. 2 virgin. *n.*

vestal virgin, priestess of the Roman goddess Vesta. Six vestal virgins tended an undying fire in honor of Vesta at her temple in Rome.

vest ed (ves′tid), 1 placed in the possession or control of a person or persons; fixed: *vested rights.* 2 clothed or robed, especially in church garments: *a vested choir. adj.*

ves ti bule (ves′tə byül), 1 passage or hall between the outer door and the inside of a building. 2 the enclosed space at the end of a railroad passenger car. *n.*

ves tige (ves′tij), a slight remnant; trace; mark: *A blackened, charred stump was a vestige of the fire. Ghost stories are vestiges of a former widespread belief in ghosts. n.*

ves tig i al (ve stij′ē əl), remaining as a vestige of something that has disappeared. *adj.*

vest ment (vest′mənt), 1 garment worn by a clergyman in performing sacred duties. 2 garment, especially a robe or gown, worn by an official on a ceremonial occasion. *n.*

ves try (ves′trē), 1 room in a church, where vestments are kept. 2 room in a church or an attached building, used for Sunday school, prayer meetings, etc. 3 (in the Church of England and the Protestant Episcopal Church of America) a committee that helps manage church business. 4 (in parishes of the Church of England) a meeting of parishioners on church business. *n., pl.* **ves tries.**

ves try man (ves′trē mən), member of a committee that helps manage church business. *n., pl.* **ves try men.**

ves ture (ves′chər), clothing; garments. *n.*

Ve su vi us (və sü′vē əs), **Mount,** an active volcano near Naples, Italy. During an eruption in A.D. 79 its lava buried the ancient city of Pompeii. *n.*

vet (vet), INFORMAL. 1 veterinarian. 2 veteran. *n.*

vetch (vech), vine of the same family as the pea, grown as food for cattle and sheep; tare. *n., pl.* **vetch es.**

vet er an (vet′ər ən), 1 person who has had much experience in war; an old soldier, sailor, airman, etc. 2 having had much experience in war: *Veteran troops fought side by side with the young soldiers.* 3 person who has served in the armed forces: *There are millions of American veterans from World War II and the Korean and Vietnam wars.* 4 person who has had much experience in some position, occupation, etc. 5 grown old in service; experienced: *a veteran farmer.* 1,3,4 *n.*, 2,5 *adj.*

Veterans Day, November 11, formerly Armistice Day. In most states it is observed as a legal holiday on the fourth Monday in October. The name was changed by act of Congress in 1954.

vet er i nar i an (vet′ər ə ner′ē ən), doctor or surgeon who treats animals. *n.*

vet er i nar y (vet′ər ə ner′ē), 1 having to do with the medical or surgical treatment of animals. 2 veterinarian. 1 *adj.*, 2 *n., pl.* **vet er i nar ies.**

ve to (vē′tō), 1 the right of the president, governor, etc., to reject bills passed by a lawmaking body: *The President has the power of veto over most bills passed in Congress.* 2 having to do with a veto: *veto power.* 3 the use of this right: *The governor's veto kept the bill from becoming a law.* 4 statement of the reasons for disapproval of a bill passed by the legislature. 5 reject by a veto. 6 refusal of consent; prohibition: *Our plan met with a veto from the boss.* 7 refuse to consent to: *Her parents vetoed her plan to buy a car.* 1,3,4, 6 *n., pl.* **ve toes;** 2 *adj.*, 5-7 *v.* [from Latin *veto* I forbid] —**ve′to er,** *n.*

vex (veks), 1 anger by trifles; annoy; provoke: *The student's rudeness vexed the teacher. It is vexing to have to wait for somebody.* 2 disturb; trouble: *The island is much vexed by storms. v.*

vex a tion (vek sā′shən), 1 a vexing or a being vexed: *His face showed his vexation at the delay.* 2 thing that vexes: *Rain on Saturday was a vexation to the children. n.*

vex a tious (vek sā′shəs), vexing; annoying. *adj.*

V.I., Virgin Islands.

vi a (vī′ə *or* vē′ə), by way of; by a route that passes through: *She is going from New York to Paris via London. prep.*

vi a bil i ty (vī′ə bil′ə tē), quality or condition of being viable. *n.*

vi a ble (vī′ə bəl), 1 able to keep alive: *a viable animal or plant.* 2 fit to live in; livable: *a viable community.* 3 that can work or be put to use; workable: *a viable program, a viable economy. adj.*

vi a duct (vī′ə dukt), bridge for carrying a road or railroad over a valley, a part of a city, etc. *n.*

vi al (vī′əl), a small glass or plastic bottle for holding medicines or the like; phial. *n.*

vi and (vī′ənd), 1 article of food. 2 **viands,** *pl.* articles of choice food. *n.*

vi bran cy (vī′brən sē), quality or condition of being vibrant. *n.*

vi brant (vī′brənt), 1 vibrating. 2 resounding; resonant. 3 throbbing with vitality, enthusiasm, etc.: *a vibrant personality. adj.* —**vi′brant ly,** *adv.*

vi brate (vī′brāt), 1 move rapidly to and fro: *A snake's tongue vibrates. A piano string vibrates and makes a sound when a key is struck.* 2 cause to swing to and fro; set in motion. 3 be moved; quiver. 4 thrill: *Their hearts vibrated to the speaker's stirring appeal.* 5 resound: *The clanging vibrated in her ears. v.,* **vi brat ed, vi brat ing.**

vi bra tion (vī brā′shən), 1 a rapid movement to and fro; quivering motion; vibrating: *The buses shake the house so much that we feel the vibration.* 2 motion back and forth across a position of equilibrium. *n.*

vi bra tor (vī′brā tər), 1 thing that vibrates. 2 instrument causing a vibrating motion or action, such as an electrical device used to massage a part of the body: *Electric vibrators are used on the scalp to stimulate circulation. n.*

vi bra to ry (vī′brə tôr′ē), of, having to do with, or causing vibration. *adj.*

vi bur num (vī bėr′nəm), any of several shrubs or small trees of the same family as the honeysuckle, having showy clusters of white or pinkish flowers. *n.*

vic ar (vik′ər), 1 (in the Church of England) the minister of a parish, who is paid a salary by the person who receives the tithes. 2 (in the Protestant Episcopal Church) a clergyman who

has charge of one chapel in a parish.
3 (in the Roman Catholic Church) a
clergyman who represents the pope or a
bishop. 4 person acting in place of
another; representative. Roman Catholics sometimes refer to the pope as the
vicar of Christ. *n.*

vic ar age (vik′ər ij), 1 residence of a
vicar. 2 position or duties of a vicar.
3 salary paid to a vicar. *n.*

vi car i ous (vī ker′ē əs), 1 done or
suffered for others: *vicarious work.*
2 felt by sharing in others' experience: *The invalid received vicarious
pleasure from reading travel stories.*
3 taking the place of another; doing
the work of another: *a vicarious
agent.* *adj.* —**vi car′i ous ly,** *adv.*
—**vi car′i ous ness,** *n.*

vice¹ (vīs), 1 an evil habit or tendency:
Lying and cruelty are vices. 2 evil;
wickedness. 3 a moral fault or defect:
They admitted that gambling was a vice.
n. [from French of the 1200's *vice,*
from Latin *vitium*]

vice² (vīs), vise. *n.* [from French of the
1300's *vis* screw, from Latin *vitis* ten-
dril of a vine]

victoria

vice-, *prefix.* person who acts in place
of another; substitute; deputy: *Vice-
president = person who acts in place of
the president.* [from Latin *vice* instead
of]

vice-ad mir al (vīs′ad′mər əl), a
naval officer ranking next below an admiral and next above a rear admiral. *n.*

vice-pres i den cy (vīs′prez′ə dən-
sē), position of vice-president. *n., pl.*
vice-pres i den cies.

vice-pres i dent (vīs′prez′ə dənt),
officer next in rank to the president,
who takes the president's place when
necessary. If the President of the United States dies, the Vice-President becomes President. *n.*

vice roy (vīs′roi), person ruling a country or province as the deputy of the
sovereign. *n.*

vi ce ver sa (vī′sə vėr′sə), the other
way round; conversely: *John blamed
Mary, and vice versa (Mary blamed
John).*

Vich y (vē′shē), city in central France.
It was the German-controlled capital of
France from 1940 to 1944. *n.*

vi cin i ty (və sin′ə tē), 1 region near
or about a place; neighborhood; surrounding district: *I know many people
in New York and its vicinity.* 2 nearness

in place; being close. *n., pl.* **vi cin i-
ties.**

vi cious (vish′əs), 1 evil; wicked: *The
criminal led a vicious life.* 2 having bad
habits or a bad disposition; fierce; savage: *a vicious animal, a person with a
vicious temper.* 3 spiteful; malicious: *I
won't listen to such vicious gossip.*
4 INFORMAL. unpleasantly severe: *a
vicious headache.* 5 not correct; having
faults: *This argument contains vicious
reasoning.* *adj.* —**vi′cious ly,** *adv.*
—**vi′cious ness,** *n.*

vicious circle, two or more undesirable things each of which keeps
causing the other.

vi cis si tude (və sis′ə tüd *or* və sis′ə-
tyüd), change in circumstances, fortune, etc.: *The vicissitudes of life may
suddenly make a rich person poor.* *n.*

vic tim (vik′təm), 1 person or animal
sacrificed, injured, or destroyed: *victims of war, victims of an accident.*
2 person badly treated or taken advantage of; dupe: *the victim of a swindler.*
3 person or animal killed as a sacrifice
to a god. *n.*

vic tim ize (vik′tə mīz), 1 make a victim of; cause to suffer. 2 cheat; swindle. *v.,* **vic tim ized, vic tim iz ing.**

vic tor (vik′tər), 1 winner; conqueror.
2 victorious. 1 *n.,* 2 *adj.*

vic to ri a (vik tôr′ē ə), a low, four-
wheeled carriage with a folding top and
a seat for two passengers. A victoria
has a raised seat in front for the driver.
n., pl. **vic to ri as.** [from Queen *Victoria*]

Vic to ri a (vik tôr′ē ə), 1 1819-1901,
queen of Great Britain from 1837 to
1901. 2 capital of British Columbia, in
the SW part. 3 state in SE Australia.
4 **Lake,** lake in E Africa. *n.*

Vic to ri an (vik tôr′ē ən), 1 of or having to do with the time of Queen Victoria. 2 person, especially an author,
who lived during the reign of Queen
Victoria. 3 having characteristics
considered typical of Victorians. 1,3
adj., 2 *n.*

vic to ri ous (vik tôr′ē əs), 1 having
won a victory; conquering: *a victorious
team.* 2 having to do with victory;
ending in victory: *a victorious war.* *adj.*
—**vic to′ri ous ly,** *adv.*

vic tor y (vik′tər ē), defeat of an
enemy or opponent; success in a contest: *The game ended in a victory for our
school.* *n., pl.* **vic tor ies.**

vict ual (vit′l), 1 **victuals,** *pl.* food
or provisions. 2 supply with food or provisions: *The crew victualed their ship
for the voyage.* 3 take on a supply of
food or provisions: *The ship will victual
before sailing.* 1 *n.,* 2,3 *v.*

vict ual er (vit′l ər), 1 person who
supplies food or provisions to a ship, an

hat, āge, fär; let, ēqual, tėrm;
it, īce; hot, ōpen, ôrder;
oil, out; cup, pùt, rüle; ch, child;
ng, long; sh, she; th, thin;
ᵺ, then; zh, measure;

ə represents *a* in about,
e in taken, *i* in pencil,
o in lemon, *u* in circus.

army, etc. 2 keeper of an inn, tavern,
saloon, etc. *n.*

vi cu ña (vi kü′nə), 1 a wild mammal
of South America, related to and resembling a llama, having a soft, delicate
wool. 2 cloth made from this wool, or
from some substitute. *n., pl.* **vi cu ñas.**
[from Spanish]

vicuña (def. 1)
about 2½ ft. high at the shoulder

vid e o (vid′ē ō), 1 of or used in the
transmission or reception of images in
television. 2 television. 1 *adj.,* 2 *n.*
[from Latin *video* I see]

vid e o tape (vid′ē ō tāp′), 1 a wide,
magnetized tape that records and reproduces both sound and picture for
television. 2 to record on videotape.
1 *n.,* 2 *v.,* **vid e o taped, vid e o tap-
ing.**

vie (vī), strive for superiority; contend
in rivalry; compete. *v.,* **vied, vy ing.**

Vi en na (vē en′ə), capital of Austria,
in the NE part, on the Danube River. *n.*

Vi en nese (vē′ə nēz′), 1 of or having
to do with Vienna or its people. 2 person born or living in Vienna. 1 *adj.,*
2 *n., pl.* **Vi en nese.**

Vien tiane (vyen tyän′), administrative capital of Laos, in the NW
part. *n.*

Vi et cong (vē et′kông′), 1 the Communist guerrilla force in Vietnam.
2 member of this force. *n., pl.* **Viet cong.**

Vi et minh (vē et′min′), the Communist party in Indochina, in power in
North Vietnam. *n.*

Viet Minh, Vietminh.

Vi et nam (vē et′näm′), country in SE

adj.	adjective	*n.*	noun
adv.	adverb	*prep.*	preposition
conj.	conjunction	*pron.*	pronoun
interj.	interjection	*v.*	verb
sing.	singular	*pl.*	plural

Asia. Since 1954 it has been divided into two countries, North Vietnam and South Vietnam. Prior to 1954, Vietnam was part of French Indochina. See **Indochina** for map. *n.*

Viet Nam, Vietnam.

Vi et nam ese (vē et/nä mēz/), 1 of or having to do with Vietnam or its people. 2 person born or living in Vietnam. 3 language of Vietnam. 1 *adj.*, 2,3 *n.*, *pl.* **Vi et nam ese.**

Vietnam War, war between South Vietnam, the United States, and their allies on the one side, and the Vietcong, North Vietnam, and their allies on the other side. The war began about 1957. The United States withdrew from the war in 1973.

view (vyü), 1 act of seeing; sight: *It was our first view of the ocean.* 2 power of seeing; range of the eye: *A ship came into view.* 3 see; look at: *They viewed the scene with pleasure.* 4 look at carefully; inspect. 5 thing seen; scene: *The view from our house is beautiful.* 6 picture of some scene: *Various views of the coast hung on the walls.* 7 a mental picture; an idea: *This book will give you a general view of the way the pioneers lived.* 8 way of looking at or considering a matter; opinion: *Children take a different view of school from that of their teachers.* 9 consider; regard: *The plan for having classes on Saturdays was not viewed with favor by the students.* 1,2,5-8 *n.*, 3,4,9 *v.*

in view, 1 in sight: *As the noise grew louder, the airplane came in view.* 2 under consideration: *Keep the teacher's advice in view as you try to improve your work.* 3 as a purpose or intention. 4 as a hope; as an expectation.

in view of, considering; because of.

on view, to be seen; open for people to see: *The exhibit is on view from 9 a.m. to 5 p.m.*

with a view to, 1 with the purpose or intention of: *She worked hard after school with a view to earning money for a new bicycle.* 2 with a hope of; expecting to.

view er (vyü/ər), person who views, especially one who views television. *n.*

view less (vyü/lis), 1 that cannot be seen. 2 without views or opinions. *adj.*

view point (vyü/point/), point of

view: *A heavy rain that is good from the viewpoint of farmers may be bad from the viewpoint of tourists.* *n.*

vig il (vij/əl), 1 a staying awake for some purpose; act of watching; watch: *All night the parents kept vigil over the sick child.* 2 **vigils,** *pl.* prayers, services, etc., on the night before a religious festival. 3 the day and night before a solemn religious festival. *n.*

vig i lance (vij/ə ləns), watchfulness; alertness; caution: *Constant vigilance is necessary in order to avoid accidents in driving.* *n.*

vig i lant (vij/ə lənt), watchful; alert; wide-awake: *The dog kept vigilant guard.* *adj.* —**vig/i lant ly,** *adv.*

vig i lan te (vij/ə lan/tē), member of a group of citizens organized to maintain order and punish criminals. In the 1800's, committees of vigilantes were common in frontier territories of the United States. *n.* [from Spanish *vigilante* watchman]

vi gnette (vin yet/), 1 a decorative design on a page of a book, especially on the title page or at the beginning or end of a chapter. 2 a literary sketch; short verbal description. *n.*

vig or (vig/ər), 1 active strength or force: *The principal argued with vigor that the new school should have a library.* 2 healthy energy or power: *A person's vigor lessens with old age.* *n.*

vig or ous (vig/ər əs), full of vigor; strong and active; energetic; forceful: *The old man is still vigorous and lively. Doctors wage a vigorous war against disease.* *adj.* —**vig/or ous ly,** *adv.*

vi king or **Vi king** (vī/king), one of the daring Scandinavian seamen who raided the coasts of Europe during the A.D. 700's, 800's, and 900's. The vikings were great warriors and explorers who conquered parts of England, France, Russia, and other countries and explored distant lands that may have included North America. *n.*

vile (vīl), 1 very bad: *The weather today was vile—rainy, windy, and cold.* 2 foul; disgusting: *A vile smell hung in the air around the garbage dump.* 3 evil; immoral: *The criminal used vile language.* 4 poor; mean; lowly: *I worked long and hard at a vile job for low wages.* *adj.*, **vil er, vil est.** —**vile/ly,** *adv.* —**vile/ness,** *n.*

vil i fi ca tion (vil/ə fə kā/shən), a vilifying or a being vilified. *n.*

vil i fy (vil/ə fī), speak evil of; revile; slander. *v.*, **vil i fied, vil i fy ing.**

vil la (vil/ə), a house in the country or suburbs, sometimes at the seashore. A villa is usually a large and elegant residence. *n.*, *pl.* **vil las.**

vil lage (vil/ij), 1 group of houses, usually smaller than a town. 2 the peo-

ple of a village: *The whole village was out to see the fire.* *n.*

vil lag er (vil/i jər), person who lives in a village. *n.*

vil lain (vil/ən), 1 a very wicked person: *The villain stole the money and cast the blame on a friend.* 2 villein. *n.*

vil lain ous (vil/ə nəs), 1 very wicked. 2 extremely bad; vile. *adj.* —**vil/lain ous ly,** *adv.*

vil lain y (vil/ə nē), 1 great wickedness. 2 a wicked act; a crime. *n.*, *pl.* **vil lain ies.**

vil lein (vil/ən), one of a class of half-free peasants in the Middle Ages. A villein was under the control of his lord, but in his relations with other persons had the rights of a freeman. *n.*

vil li (vil/ī), tiny, hairlike parts growing out of the membrane of the small intestine. The villi aid in absorbing certain substances. *n.pl.* of **vil lus** (vil/əs).

vim (vim), force; energy; vigor: *The campers were full of vim after a good night's sleep.* *n.*

Vin ci (vin/chē), **Leonardo da.** See **da Vinci.** *n.*

vin di cate (vin/də kāt), 1 clear from suspicion, dishonor, or any charge of wrongdoing: *The verdict of "Not guilty" vindicated them.* 2 defend successfully against opposition; uphold; justify: *The heir vindicated her claim to the fortune.* *v.*, **vin di cat ed, vin di cat ing.**

vin di ca tion (vin/də kā/shən), a vindicating or a being vindicated; defense; justification. *n.*

vin dic tive (vin dik/tiv), 1 bearing a grudge; wanting revenge: *He is so vindictive that he never forgives anybody.* 2 showing a strong tendency toward revenge: *Vindictive acts rarely do much good.* *adj.* —**vin dic/tive ly,** *adv.* —**vin dic/tive ness,** *n.*

vine (vīn), 1 plant with a long, slender stem, that grows along the ground or that climbs by attaching itself to a wall, tree, or other support. Melons and pumpkins grow on vines. Ivy is a vine. 2 grapevine. *n.* —**vine/like/,** *adj.*

vin e gar (vin/ə gər), a sour liquid produced by the fermentation of cider, wine, malt, etc. Vinegar is used in salad dressing and in flavoring or preserving food. *n.*

vin e gar y (vin/ə gər ē), of or like vinegar; sour: *a vinegary taste, a vinegary disposition.* *adj.*

villa

vine yard (vīn′yərd), a place planted with grapevines. *n.*

vi nous (vī′nəs), of, like, or having to do with wine. *adj.*

vin tage (vin′tij), 1 the wine from a certain crop of grapes: *The finest vintages cost much more than others.* 2 a year's crop of grapes. 3 the season of gathering grapes and making wine. 4 of outstanding quality; choice: *vintage wines.* 5 type of thing fashionable or popular during an earlier season: *a hat of the vintage of 1940.* 1-3,5 *n.,* 4 *adj.*

violin (def. 1)

vint ner (vint′nər), dealer in wine; wine merchant. *n.*

vi nyl (vī′nl), any of various tough synthetic plastics or resins used in floor coverings, toys, molded articles, phonograph records, etc. *n.*

vi ol (vī′əl), 1 any of several stringed musical instruments played with a bow and usually held either on or between the knees while they are played. Viols, used chiefly in the 1500's and 1600's, have been superseded by instruments of the violin type. 2 double bass. *n.*

vi o la (vē ō′lə), a stringed musical instrument like a violin, but somewhat larger and lower in pitch. *n., pl.* **vi o las.**

vi o late (vī′ə lāt), 1 break (a law, rule, agreement, promise, etc.); act contrary to; fail to perform: *She violated the law and was arrested by the police.* 2 break in upon; disturb: *to violate someone's privacy. The sound of automobile horns violated the usual calm of Sunday morning.* 3 treat with disrespect or contempt: *Vandals violated several grave sites by overturning the tombstones.* *v.,* **vi o lat ed, vi o lat ing.**

vi o la tion (vī′ə lā′shən), 1 a breaking (of a law, rule, agreement, promise, etc.): *He was fined $10 for his violation of the traffic law.* 2 a breaking in upon; interruption or disturbance. 3 treatment (of a holy thing) with disrespect or contempt. *n.*

vi o la tor (vī′ə lā′tər), person who violates something. *n.*

vi o lence (vī′ə ləns), 1 rough force in action: *She slammed the door with violence.* 2 rough or harmful action or treatment: *The policeman had to use violence in arresting the murderer.* 3 harm; injury: *It would do violence to her principles to work on Sunday.* 4 strength of action, feeling, etc. *n.*

vi o lent (vī′ə lənt), 1 acting or done with strong, rough force: *a violent blow.* 2 caused by strong, rough force: *a violent death.* 3 showing or caused by very strong feeling, action, etc.: *violent language, a violent rage.* 4 very great; extreme; severe: *a violent pain, violent heat. adj.* —**vi′o lent ly,** *adv.*

vi o let (vī′ə lit), 1 a small plant with purple, blue, yellow, or white flowers. Many common violets grow wild and bloom in the spring. 2 its flower. Some violets are very fragrant. 3 a bluish purple. Violet is red and blue mixed. 4 bluish-purple. 1-3 *n.,* 4 *adj.*

vi o lin (vī′ə lin′), 1 a musical instrument with four strings played with a bow. The violin has the highest pitch of the stringed instruments. 2 person who plays the violin in an orchestra. *n.*

vi o lin ist (vī′ə lin′ist), person who plays the violin. *n.*

vi ol ist (vē ō′list), person who plays the viola. *n.*

vi o lon cel list (vī′ə lən chel′ist), cellist. *n.*

vi o lon cel lo (vī′ə lən chel′ō), cello. *n., pl.* **vi o lon cel los.**

VIP or **V.I.P.,** INFORMAL. very important person.

vi per (vī′pər), 1 any of various poisonous snakes with a pair of large, hollow fangs and often having a thick, heavy body. Rattlesnakes are vipers. 2 a spiteful, treacherous person. *n.*

vi per ous (vī′pər əs), 1 of, like, or having to do with a viper or vipers. 2 spiteful; treacherous. *adj.*

vi ra go (və rā′gō), a violent, bad-tempered, or scolding woman. *n., pl.* **vi ra goes** or **vi ra gos.**

vir e o (vir′ē ō), a small, olive-green, North American songbird that eats insects. *n., pl.* **vir e os.**

Vir gil (vėr′jəl), Vergil. *n.*

vir gin (vėr′jən), 1 person who has not had sexual intercourse. 2 an unmarried woman; maiden. 3 **the Virgin,** Virgin Mary. 4 of or having to do with a virgin; suitable for a virgin: *virgin modesty.* 5 pure; spotless. Virgin snow is newly fallen snow. 6 not yet used: *virgin soil, a virgin forest.* 1-3 *n.,* 4-6 *adj.*

vir gin al (vėr′jə nəl), 1 of or suitable for a virgin; maidenly. 2 a small harpsichord set in a rectangular box without legs. It was much used in the 1500's and 1600's. 1 *adj.,* 2 *n.*

Vir gin ia (vėr jin′yə), one of the southeastern states of the United States. *Capital:* Richmond. *n.* —**Virgin′ian,** *adj., n.*

Virginia creeper, an American climbing plant having leaves with five leaflets and bluish-black berries that are not good to eat; woodbine.

hat, āge, fär; let, ēqual, tėrm;
it, īce; hot, ōpen, ôrder;
oil, out; cup, pùt, rüle; ch, child;
ng, long; sh, she; th, thin;
ŦH, then; zh, measure;

ə represents *a* in about,
e in taken, *i* in pencil,
o in lemon, *u* in circus.

Virginia reel, an American folk dance in which the partners form two lines facing each other and perform a number of dance steps.

Virgin Islands, group of islands in the West Indies, east of Puerto Rico. Several of these islands belong to the United States and the rest (**British Virgin Islands**) are a British territory.

vir gin i ty (vər jin′ə tē), virgin condition; maidenhood. *n.*

Virgin Mary, the mother of Jesus.

vir ile (vir′əl), 1 of, belonging to, or characteristic of a man; manly; masculine. 2 full of strength or vigor; vigorous; forceful. *adj.*

vi ril i ty (və ril′ə tē), 1 manhood. 2 strength; vigor; forcefulness. *n., pl.* **vi ril i ties.**

vi rol o gist (vī rol′ə jist), an expert in virology. *n.*

vi rol o gy (vī rol′ə jē), science that deals with viruses and virus diseases. *n.*

vir tu al (vėr′chü əl), being something in effect, though not so in name; for all practical purposes; actual; real: *The battle was won with so great a loss of soldiers that it was a virtual defeat. He is the virtual president, though his title is secretary. adj.*

vir tu al ly (vėr′chü ə lē), in effect, though not in name; practically: *If you travel by jet plane, New York and Los Angeles are virtually neighbors. adv.*

virginal (def. 2)

vir tue (vėr′chü), 1 moral excellence; goodness: *They are people of the highest virtue.* 2 a particular moral excellence: *Justice and kindness are virtues.* 3 a good quality: *She praised the virtues of the car.* 4 chastity; purity. 5 power to produce good results: *There is little virtue in that medicine. n.*

945

adj. adjective	*n.* noun
adv. adverb	*prep.* preposition
conj. conjunction	*pron.* pronoun
interj. interjection	*v.* verb
sing. singular	*pl.* plural

by virtue of or **in virtue of,** because of; on account of.

vir tu os i ty (vėr´chü os´ə tē), character or skill of a virtuoso. *n., pl.* **vir tu os i ties.**

vir tu o so (vėr´chü ō´sō), 1 person skilled in the techniques of an art, especially in playing a musical instrument. 2 person who has a cultivated appreciation of artistic excellence. 3 student or collector of objects of art, curios, antiquities, etc. *n., pl.* **vir tu o sos, vir tu o si** (vėr´chü ō´sē). [from Italian]

vir tu ous (vėr´chü əs), 1 good; moral; righteous: *virtuous conduct, a virtuous life.* 2 chaste; pure: *a virtuous maiden.* *adj.* —**vir´tu ous ly,** *adv.* —**vir´tu ous ness,** *n.*

vir u lence (vir´yə ləns), 1 quality of being very poisonous or harmful; deadliness: *the virulence of a rattlesnake's bite.* 2 intense bitterness or spite; violent hostility. *n.*

vir u lent (vir´yə lənt), 1 very poisonous or harmful; deadly: *a virulent form of a disease.* 2 intensely bitter or spiteful; violently hostile: *virulent abuse.* *adj.* —**vir´u lent ly,** *adv.*

vi rus (vī´rəs), 1 any of a group of disease-producing agents composed of protein and nucleic acid. Viruses are smaller than any known bacteria and depend on the living tissue of larger cells for their reproduction and growth. Viruses cause such diseases in man as rabies, polio, chicken pox, and the common cold. They are so small that they cannot be seen through most microscopes. 2 something that poisons the mind or morals; corrupting influence: *the virus of prejudice. n., pl.* **vi rus es.**

vi sa (vē´zə), an official signature or endorsement upon a passport, showing that it has been examined and approved. A visa is granted by the consul or other representative of the country to which a person wishes to travel. *n., pl.* **vi sas.**

vis age (viz´ij), face or appearance: *a dark visage, a grim visage, a visage of despair. n.*

vis-à-vis (vē´zə vē´), 1 face to face; opposite: *We sat vis-à-vis.* 2 in relation to; in comparison with; over against: *He looked poor and shabby vis-à-vis his* *well-dressed companion.* 1 *adv.,* 2 *prep.* [from French]

vis cer a (vis´ər ə), the soft internal organs of the body. The heart, stomach, liver, intestines, kidneys, etc., are viscera. *n.pl.*

vis cer al (vis´ər əl), of or having to do with the viscera. *adj.*

vis cid (vis´id), thick like heavy syrup or glue; sticky. *adj.*

vis cose (vis´kōs), a thick, sticky substance made by treating cellulose with caustic soda and other chemicals. It is used in manufacturing rayon, cellophane, etc. *n.*

vis cos i ty (vi skos´ə tē), condition or quality of being viscous. *n., pl.* **vis cos i ties.**

vis count (vī´kount), nobleman ranking next below an earl or count and next above a baron. *n.*

vis count ess (vī´koun tis), 1 wife or widow of a viscount. 2 woman whose rank is equal to that of a viscount. *n., pl.* **vis count ess es.**

vis cous (vis´kəs), thick like heavy syrup or glue; sticky. *adj.*

vise (vīs), tool having two jaws opened and closed by a screw, used to hold an object firmly while work is being done on it. *n.* Also, **vice.**

vise

vis i bil i ty (viz´ə bil´ə tē), 1 condition or quality of being visible: *In a fog the visibility is very poor.* 2 distance at which things are visible: *Fog and rain decreased visibility to about 50 feet. n.*

vis i ble (viz´ə bəl), 1 that can be seen: *The shore was barely visible through the fog.* 2 readily evident; apparent; obvious: *The vagrant had no visible means of support. adj.*

vis i bly (viz´ə blē), so as to be visible; plainly; evidently: *After the hike over the mountain the children were visibly weary. adv.*

Vis i goth (viz´ə goth), member of the western division of the Goths. The Visigoths sacked Rome in A.D. 410 and eventually settled in France and Spain. *n.*

vi sion (vizh´ən), 1 power of seeing; sense of sight: *I have to wear glasses because my vision is poor.* 2 act or fact of seeing; sight: *The vision of the table loaded with food made our mouths water.* 3 power of perceiving by the imagination or by clear thinking: *the vision of a prophet, a person of great* *vision.* 4 something seen in the imagination, in a dream, in one's thoughts, etc.: *The gambler had visions of great wealth.* 5 a very beautiful person, scene, etc. *n.*

vi sion ar y (vizh´ə ner´ē), 1 person given to imagining or dreaming; person whose ideas are not practical; dreamer: *Many great scientists have been visionaries.* 2 not practical; dreamy: *He is a visionary child; he spends hours day-dreaming.* 3 not practicable; fanciful: *Not too many years ago people would have regarded plans for an atomic power plant as visionary.* 4 of or belonging to a vision; seen in a vision; imaginary: *The visionary scene faded, and she awoke.* 5 person who sees visions. 1,5 *n., pl.* **vi sion ar ies;** 2-4 *adj.*

vis it (viz´it), 1 go to see; come to see: *He visited New York.* 2 make a call on or stay with; be a guest of: *She is visiting her aunt.* 3 go or come to see in order to inspect, examine officially, give professional service or treatment to, etc.: *The doctor visited her patients at the hospital every weekday morning. The inspector visits the factory once a month.* 4 a visiting; a call from friendship, for purpose of inspection, examination, professional treatment, etc.: *pay a visit to a friend, a visit to the dentist.* 5 come upon; afflict: *Job was visited by many troubles.* 6 send upon; inflict: *visit one's anger on someone.* 7 INFORMAL. to talk or chat. 1-3,5-7 *v.,* 4 *n.*

vis it ant (viz´ə tənt), visitor; guest. *n.*

vis i ta tion (viz´ə tā´shən), 1 act of visiting. 2 a visit for the purpose of making an official inspection or examination. A nation at war has the right of visitation of neutral ships; that is, the right to inspect their cargoes. 3 punishment or reward sent by God. *n.*

vis i tor (viz´ə tər), person who visits or is visiting; guest. *n.*

VISOR

visor (def. 1)

vi sor (vī´zər), 1 the movable front part of a helmet, covering the face. 2 the brim of a cap, projecting in front to shade the eyes. 3 a shade that can be lowered from above to the inside of a car windshield to shield the eyes from the sun. *n.* Also, **vizor.**

vis ta (vis´tə), 1 view seen through a narrow opening or passage: *The opening between the two rows of trees afforded a vista of the lake.* 2 such an opening or passage itself: *a shady vista of elms.* **3** a mental view: *Education should open up new vistas.* *n., pl.* **vis tas.**

Vis tu la (vis′chə lə), river flowing through Poland to the Baltic Sea. *n.*

vis u al (vizh′ü əl), **1** of, having to do with, or used in sight or vision: *Being near-sighted is a visual defect. The teacher often used visual aids such as large charts and photographic slides.* **2** received through the sense of sight: *visual sensations or impressions.* **3** that can be seen; visible: *the visual parts of the spectrum.* *adj.* **—vis′u al ly,** *adv.*

vis u al i za tion (vizh′ü ə lə zā′-shən), **1** a visualizing or a being visualized. **2** thing visualized. *n.*

vis u al ize (vizh′ü ə līz), **1** form a mental picture of: *visualize the scene of a battle, visualize a friend's face when he is away.* **2** make visible. *v.,* **vis u al ized, vis u al iz ing.**

vi tal (vī′tl), **1** of life; having to do with life. Vital statistics give facts about births, deaths, marriages, etc. *Growth and decay are vital processes.* **2** necessary to life: *Eating is a vital function. The heart is a vital organ.* **3** **vitals,** *pl.* **a** parts or organs necessary to life. The brain, heart, lungs, and stomach are vitals. **b** essential parts or features. **4** very important; basic: *a vital question. Pure water is vital to the welfare of a community.* **5** causing death, failure, or ruin: *a vital wound, a vital blow to an industry.* **6** full of life and spirit; lively: *What a vital person she is—never idle, never dull!* **1,2,4-6** *adj.,* **3** *n.* **—vi′tal ly,** *adv.*

vi tal i ty (vī tal′ə tē), **1** vital force; power to live: *Her vitality was lessened by illness.* **2** power to endure and be active: *Poetry of great vitality is read hundreds of years after it was written.* **3** strength; energy; vigor: *There is little vitality in his weak efforts to cope with his problems.* *n., pl.* **vi tal i ties.**

vi tal ize (vī′tl īz), **1** give life to. **2** put vitality into; make more energetic, lively, or enterprising. *v.,* **vi tal ized, vi tal iz ing.**

vi ta min (vī′tə mən), **1** any of certain special substances required for the normal growth and proper nourishment of the body, found especially in milk, butter, raw fruits and vegetables, cod-liver oil, and the outside part of wheat and other grains. Vitamins are also obtained in the form of tablets, injections, etc., prescribed by doctors for people suffering from vitamin deficiency. Lack of essential vitamins causes such diseases as rickets and scurvy, as well as generally poor health. **2** of or containing vitamins: *a vitamin tablet, a vitamin deficiency.* **1** *n.,* **2** *adj.*

vitamin A, vitamin found in milk, butter, cod-liver oil, egg yolk, liver, green and yellow vegetables, etc. Vitamin A increases the resistance of the body to infection and prevents night blindness.

vitamin B₁, vitamin found in yeast, meats, whole-grain cereals, and certain vegetables, thiamin. It promotes growth, gives energy, and prevents beriberi.

vitamin B₂, riboflavin.

vitamin B complex, group of vitamins including vitamin B₁, vitamin B₂, nicotinic acid, etc., found in high concentration in yeast and liver.

vitamin C, vitamin found in citrus fruits, tomatoes, leafy green vegetables, etc.; ascorbic acid. Vitamin C prevents and cures scurvy.

vitamin D, vitamin found in cod-liver oil, milk, and egg yolk, that is necessary for the growth and health of bones and teeth. Vitamin D prevents rickets.

vitamin E, vitamin found in wheat germ oil, whole grain cereals, lettuce, etc. Vitamin E prevents sterility.

vitamin G, riboflavin.

vitamin K, vitamin found in certain vegetables, egg yolk, etc., that promotes clotting of the blood.

vi ti ate (vish′ē āt), **1** impair or injure the quality of; spoil: *Pollution from smoke and dust vitiates the air. His illness vitiated his chances of success.* **2** destroy the legal force or authority of: *The contract was vitiated because one person signed under compulsion.* *v.,* **vi ti at ed, vi ti at ing.**

vi ti a tion (vish′ē ā′shən), a vitiating or a being vitiated. *n.*

vit re ous (vit′rē əs), of or like glass; made from glass: *vitreous china, vitreous tableware.* *adj.*

vitreous humor, the transparent, jellylike substance that fills the eyeball behind the lens.

vit ri fy (vit′rə fī), to change into glass or something like glass, especially by fusion through heat. *v.,* **vit ri fied, vit ri fy ing.**

vit ri ol (vit′rē əl), **1** sulfuric acid. **2** any of certain sulfates of metals, such as **blue vitriol,** a sulfate of copper, **green vitriol,** a sulfate of iron, or **white vitriol,** a sulfate of zinc. Vitriols are characterized by a glassy appearance. **3** very sharp speech or severe criticism. *n.*

vit ri ol ic (vit′rē ol′ik), **1** of, like, or containing vitriol. **2** bitterly severe; sharp: *vitriolic criticism.* *adj.*

vi tu pe rate (vī tü′pə rāt′ *or* vī-tyü′pə rāt′), scold very severely; find fault with in abusive words; revile. *v.,* **vi tu pe rat ed, vi tu pe rat ing.**

vi tu pe ra tion (vī tü′pə rā′shən

hat, āge, fär; let, ēqual, tėrm;
it, īce; hot, ōpen, ôrder;
oil, out; cup, pùt, rüle; ch, child;
ng, long; sh, she; th, thin;
ŦH, then; zh, measure;

ə represents *a* in about,
e in taken, *i* in pencil,
o in lemon, *u* in circus.

or vī tyü′pə rā′shən), bitter abuse in words; very severe scolding. *n.*

vi tu pe ra tive (vī tü′pə rā′tiv *or* vī-tyü′pə rā′tiv), abusive; reviling. *adj.* **—vi tu′pe ra′tive ly,** *adv.*

vi va (vē′və), a Spanish or Italian exclamation of approval, meaning (long) live (the person or thing named). *interj.*

vi va cious (vī vā′shəs *or* vi vā′shəs), lively; sprightly; animated; gay: *a vivacious manner, a vivacious puppy.* *adj.* **—vi va′cious ly,** *adv.* **—vi va′cious-ness,** *n.*

vi vac i ty (vī vas′ə tē *or* vi vas′ə tē), liveliness; sprightliness; animation; gaiety. *n., pl.* **vi vac i ties.**

vive (vēv), a French exclamation of approval, meaning (long) live (the person or thing named). *interj.*

viv id (viv′id), **1** strikingly bright; strong and clear; brilliant: *Dandelions are a vivid yellow.* **2** full of life; lively: *a vivid description of an experience.* **3** strong and distinct: *I have a vivid memory of the fire.* **4** very active or intense: *a vivid imagination.* *adj.* **—viv′id ly,** *adv.* **—viv′id ness,** *n.*

viv i fy (viv′ə fī), **1** give life or vigor to: *vivify the desert by irrigation.* **2** make vivid; enliven: *vivify an idea with wit.* *v.,* **viv i fied, viv i fy ing.**

vi vip ar ous (vī vip′ər əs), bringing forth living young, rather than eggs. Dogs, cats, cows, and human beings are viviparous. *adj.*

viv i sec tion (viv′ə sek′shən), act or practice of dissecting or operating on living animals for scientific study or experimentation. *n.*

vix en (vik′sən), **1** a female fox. **2** a quarrelsome or malicious woman. *n.*

viz., that is to say; namely: *There are four seasons, viz., spring, summer, fall, and winter.* [abbreviation of Latin *videlicet,* from *videre licet* it is permissible to see]

vi zier or **vi zir** (vi zir′), (in Moslem countries) a high official, such as a minister of state. *n.*

vi zor (vī′zər), visor. *n.*

Vlad i vos tok (vlad′ə vos′tok), seaport on the Sea of Japan in SE Soviet Union. *n.*

vocabulary

adj. adjective	*n.* noun
adv. adverb	*prep.* preposition
conj. conjunction	*pron.* pronoun
interj. interjection	*v.* verb
sing. singular	*pl.* plural

vo cab u lar y (vō kab′yə ler′ē), 1 the stock of words used by a person or group of people: *Reading will increase your vocabulary. The vocabulary of science has grown tremendously in the past 20 years.* 2 collection or list of words, usually in alphabetical order, with their translations or meanings: *There is a vocabulary in the back of our French book. n., pl.* **vo cab u lar ies.**

vo cal (vō′kəl), 1 of or having to do with the voice: *The tongue is a vocal organ.* 2 made with the voice: *I like vocal music better than instrumental.* 3 having a voice; giving forth sound: *Humans are vocal beings. The zoo was vocal with the roar of the lions.* 4 aroused to speech; inclined to talk freely: *become vocal with indignation.* 5 of a vowel. 6 a vocal sound. All vowels are vocals. 1-5 *adj.,* 6 *n.* —**vo′cal ly,** *adv.*

vocal cords, two pairs of membranes in the throat, projecting into the cavity of the larynx. The lower pair can be pulled tight and the passage of breath between them then causes them to vibrate, which produces the sound of the voice.

vo cal ic (vō kal′ik), 1 of or like a vowel. 2 having many vowel sounds. *adj.*

vo cal ist (vō′kə list), singer. *n.*

vo cal i za tion (vō′kə lə zā′shən), a vocalizing or a being vocalized. *n.*

vo cal ize (vō′kə līz), 1 use the voice; speak, sing, shout, etc. 2 make vocal; utter: *The dog vocalized his pain in a series of long howls.* 3 change into a vowel; use as a vowel. Some speakers of English vocalize the *r* in *four. v.,* **vo cal ized, vo cal iz ing.**

vo ca tion (vō kā′shən), 1 occupation, business, profession, or trade: *Teaching is her vocation.* 2 an inner call or summons. *n.*

vo ca tion al (vō kā′shə nəl), having to do with some occupation, business, profession, or trade. A vocational school trains boys and girls for special trades, such as printing, stenography, or mechanics. *adj.* —**vo ca′tion al ly,** *adv.*

vo cif er ous (vō sif′ər əs), loud and noisy; shouting; clamoring: *a vociferous person, vociferous cheers. adj.* —**vo-**

cif′er ous ly, *adv.* —**vo cif′er ous-ness,** *n.*

vod ka (vod′kə), an alcoholic drink distilled from potatoes, rye, barley, or corn. *n., pl.* **vod kas.**

vogue (vōg), 1 the fashion: *Hoop skirts were in vogue many years ago.* 2 popularity or acceptance: *That song had a great vogue at one time. n.*

voice (vois), 1 sound made through the mouth, especially by people in speaking, singing, shouting, etc.: *The voices of the children could be heard coming from the playground.* 2 power to make sounds through the mouth: *His voice was gone because of a sore throat.* 3 anything like speech or song: *the voice of the wind, the voice of bells.* 4 ability as a singer: *She knew she had no voice.* 5 singer: *a choir of fifty voices.* 6 part of a piece of music for one kind of singer or instrument. 7 express; utter: *They voiced their approval of the plan.* 8 expression: *They gave voice to their joy.* 9 an expressed opinion or choice: *His voice was for compromise.* 10 the right to express an opinion or choice: *We have no voice in the matter.* 11 form of a verb that shows whether its subject is active or passive. 12 utter with a sound made by vibration of the vocal cords. *Z* and *v* are voiced; *s* and *f* are not. 1-6,8-11 *n.,* 7,12 *v.,* **voiced, voic ing.**

voice box, larynx.

voice less (vois′lis), 1 having no voice; dumb; silent. 2 not voiced. The consonants *p, t,* and *k* are voiceless. *adj.*

void (void), 1 an empty space: *The death of his dog left an aching void in the boy's heart.* 2 empty; vacant: *a void space.* 3 without legal force or effect; not binding in law: *A contract made by a twelve-year-old is void.* 4 make of no force or effect in law. 5 to empty out. 1 *n.,* 2,3 *adj.,* 4,5 *v.*

void a ble (voi′də bəl), capable of being voided or given up: *The contract was voidable by either party after twelve months. adj.*

voile (voil), a very thin cloth with an open weave, used for dresses. *n.*

vol., volume.

vol a tile (vol′ə təl), 1 evaporating rapidly; changing into vapor easily: *Gasoline is volatile.* 2 changing rapidly from one mood or interest to another; fickle: *Flighty people often have volatile dispositions. adj.*

vol a til i ty (vol′ə til′ə tē), volatile quality or condition. *n.*

vol can ic (vol kan′ik), 1 of or caused by a volcano; having to do with volcanoes: *a volcanic eruption.* 2 like a volcano; liable to break out violently: *a volcanic temper. adj.*

vol ca no (vol kā′nō), 1 an opening in the earth's crust through which steam, ashes, and lava are forced out in periods of activity. 2 a cone-shaped hill or mountain around this opening, built up of the material that is forced out. *n., pl.* **vol ca noes** or **vol ca nos.**

vole (vōl), rodent belonging to the same family as rats and mice, usually of heavier build and having short limbs and tail. *n.*

vole
about 5½ in.
long with tail

Vol ga (vol′gə), river in the W Soviet Union, flowing into the Caspian Sea. *n.*

Vol go grad (vol′gə grad), city in SW Soviet Union, on the Volga River. Formerly, **Stalingrad.** *n.*

vo li tion (vō lish′ən), 1 act of willing: *She took on extra work of her own volition.* 2 power of willing: *The use of drugs weakens volition. n.*

vol ley (vol′ē), 1 shower of stones, bullets, words, oaths, etc.: *A volley of arrows rained down from the walls upon the attacking troops.* 2 the discharge of a number of guns at once. 3 discharge or be discharged in a volley: *Cannon volleyed on all sides.* 4 the hitting or return of a tennis ball before it touches the ground. 5 hit or return (a tennis ball) before it touches the ground. 1,2,4 *n., pl.* **vol leys;** 3,5 *v.*

vol ley ball (vol′ē bôl′), 1 game played by two teams of players with a large ball and a high net. The players must hit the ball back and forth over the net with their hands without letting it touch the ground. 2 ball used in this game. *n.*

volt (vōlt), measure of electrical force, equal to the amount of energy needed to cause a current of one ampere to flow through a resistance of one ohm. *n.* [from Alessandro *Volta,* 1745-1827, an Italian physicist]

volt age (vōl′tij), strength of electrical force, measured in volts. A current of high voltage is used in transmitting electric power over long distances. *n.*

vol ta ic cell (vol tā′ik), an electric cell consisting of two electrodes, each of a different metal, immersed in an electrolyte. An electric current is produced by a chemical reaction between the electrolyte and one of the electrodes.

Vol taire (vol ter′ *or* vol tar′), 1694-1778, French writer and philosopher. *n.*

volt me ter (vōlt′mē′tər), instrument for measuring the number of volts between any two points in an electric circuit. *n.*

vol u bil i ty (vol′yə bil′ə tē), tendency to talk much; fondness for talking. *n.*

vol u ble (vol′yə bəl), tending to talk much; fond of talking; talkative: *a voluble speaker. adj.*

vol u bly (vol′yə blē), in a voluble manner. *adv.*

vol ume (vol′yəm), 1 book: *We own a library of five hundred volumes.* 2 book forming part of a set or series: *You can find what you want to know in the ninth volume of this encyclopedia.* 3 space occupied: *The storeroom has a volume of 800 cubic feet.* 4 amount; quantity: *the volume of business at a store. Volumes of smoke poured from the chimneys of the factory.* 5 amount of sound; fullness of tone: *A pipe organ has more volume than a flute. n.*

vol u met ric (vol′yə met′rik), of or having to do with measurement by volume. *adj.* **—vol′u met′ri cal ly,** *adv.*

vol u mi nous (və lü′mə nəs), 1 forming or filling a large book or many books: *a voluminous report.* 2 writing much: *a voluminous author.* 3 of great size; very bulky; large: *A voluminous cloak covered him from head to foot. adj.*

vol un tar i ly (vol′ən ter′ə lē), of one's own free will; without force or compulsion. *adv.*

vol un tar y (vol′ən ter′ē), 1 done, made, or given of one's own free will; not forced or compelled: *The thief's confession was voluntary. The state is supported by taxes, the church by voluntary contributions.* 2 acting of one's own free will or choice: *Voluntary workers built a road to the scout camp.* 3 done on purpose; intended: *voluntary manslaughter. Voluntary disobedience will be punished.* 4 controlled by the will: *voluntary muscles. Talking is voluntary; breathing is only partly so. adj.*

vol un teer (vol′ən tir′), 1 person who enters any service by his own choice; one who is not drafted. Some soldiers are volunteers. 2 person who serves without pay. In some towns, the firemen are volunteers. 3 offer one's services: *After graduating from college she volunteered for the Peace Corps.* 4 to offer of one's own free will: *He volunteered to carry the water.* 5 of or made up of volunteers: *Our village has a volunteer fire department.* 6 serving as a volunteer: *a volunteer fireman.* 7 tell or say voluntarily: *She volunteered the information.* 1,2 *n.,* 3,4,7 *v.,* 5,6 *adj.*

vo lup tu ar y (və lup′chü er′ē), person who cares much for luxurious or sensual pleasures. *n., pl.* **vo lup tu ar ies.**

vo lup tu ous (və lup′chü əs), 1 caring much for the pleasures of the senses. 2 giving pleasure to the senses: *voluptuous music, voluptuous beauty. adj.* **—vo lup′tu ous ly,** *adv.* **—vo lup′tu ous ness,** *n.*

vom it (vom′it), 1 expel the contents of the stomach through the mouth; throw up what has been eaten. 2 the substance thrown up from the stomach. 3 throw out with force: *The chimneys vomited forth smoke.* 4 come out with force or violence. 1,3,4 *v.,* 2 *n.*

voo doo (vü′dü), 1 religion that came from Africa, made up of mysterious rites and practices that include the use of sorcery, magic, and conjuration. Belief in voodoo still prevails in many parts of the West Indies and some parts of the southern United States. 2 person who practices voodoo. *n., pl.* **voodoos.**

voo doo ism (vü′dü iz′əm), voodoo rites or practices. *n.*

vo ra cious (və rā′shəs), 1 eating much; greedy in eating; ravenous: *voracious sharks.* 2 very eager; unable to be satisfied: *He is a voracious reader of history. adj.* **—vo ra′cious ly,** *adv.*

vo rac i ty (və ras′ə tē), a being voracious. *n.*

vor tex (vôr′teks), a whirling mass or movement of water, air, etc., that sucks everything near it toward its center; whirlpool; whirlwind. *n., pl.* **vor tex es, vor ti ces** (vôr′tə sēz′).

vo tar y (vō′tər ē), 1 person bound by vows to a religious life; monk or nun. 2 person devoted to something; devotee: *She is a votary of golf. n., pl.* **vo tar ies.**

vote (vōt), 1 a formal expression of a wish or choice on a proposal, motion, candidate for office, etc. A vote can be cast by a ballot or indicated by saying "aye" or "nay," holding up the hand, standing up, or otherwise. In an election the person receiving the most votes is elected. 2 the right to cast or indicate a vote. Children do not have the vote, and adults can lose it by being convicted of certain crimes. 3 ballot or other means by which a vote is cast or indicated: *More than a million votes were counted.* 4 what is expressed or granted by a majority of voters: *a vote of confidence.* 5 votes considered together: *the labor vote, the vote of the people.* 6 give or cast a vote: *He voted for the Democrats.* 7 support by one's vote: *vote the Republican ticket.* 8 pass, determine, or grant by a vote: *Money for a new school was voted by the board.* 9 declare: *The children all voted the trip a great success.* 1-5 *v.,* 6-9 *v.,* **vot ed, vot ing.**

vot er (vō′tər), 1 person who votes. 2 person who has the right to vote:

hat, āge, fär; let, ēqual, tèrm;
it, īce; hot, ōpen, ôrder;
oil, out; cup, pùt, rüle; ch, child;
ng, long; sh, she; th, thin;
ŦH, then; zh, measure;

ə represents *a* in about,
e in taken, *i* in pencil,
o in lemon, *u* in circus.

Women have been voters in the United States only since 1920. n.

voting machine, machine which records and counts votes in political elections.

vo tive (vō′tiv), promised by a vow; done, given, etc., because of a vow: *votive offerings to the gods, a knight on a votive quest. adj.* **—vo′tive ly,** *adv.*

vouch (vouch), be responsible; give a guarantee (for): *I can vouch for the truth of the story. The principal vouched for the girl's honesty. v.*

vouch er (vou′chər), 1 person or thing that vouches for something. 2 written evidence of payment; receipt. Canceled checks returned from one's bank are vouchers. *n.*

vouch safe (vouch sāf′), be willing to grant or give; deign (to do or give): *She vouchsafed no reply to their rude, prying questions. v.,* **vouch safed, vouch saf ing.**

vow (vou), 1 a solemn promise: *a vow of secrecy, marriage vows.* 2 a promise made to God: *a nun's vows.* 3 make a vow: *I vowed never to leave home again.* 4 make a vow to do, give, get, etc.: *vow revenge. The knight vowed loyalty to the king.* 1,2 *n.,* 3,4 *v.*

vow el (vou′əl), 1 a voiced speech sound produced by not blocking the breath with the lips, teeth, or tongue. A vowel can form a syllable by itself, as the first syllable of *awful* (ô′fəl). 2 letter that stands for such a sound. *A, e, i, o,* and *u* are vowels. *Y* is sometimes a vowel, as in *bicycle.* 3 of or having to do with a vowel. *Voluntary* has four vowel sounds; *strength* has only one. 1,2 *n.,* 3 *adj.*

voy age (voi′ij), 1 a journey or travel by water; cruise: *We had a pleasant voyage to England.* 2 a journey or travel through the air or through space: *an airplane voyage, the earth's voyage around the sun.* 3 make or take a voyage; go by sea or air: *Columbus voyaged across unknown seas.* 1,2 *n.,* 3 *v.,* **voy aged, voy ag ing.**

voy ag er (voi′i jər), person who makes a voyage; traveler. *n.*

vo ya geur (vwä yä zhèr′), a French

adj.	adjective	*n.*	noun
adv.	adverb	*prep.*	preposition
conj.	conjunction	*pron.*	pronoun
interj.	interjection	*v.*	verb
sing.	singular	*pl.*	plural

Canadian worker for the early fur-trading companies who transported men and supplies to and from remote places, especially by boat. *n., pl.* **vo ya geurs** (vwä yä zhèrz′).

VP or **V.P.**, Vice-President.

vs., versus.

Vt., Vermont.

Vul can (vul′kən), (in Roman myths) the god of fire and metalworking. *n.*

vul can ite (vul′kə nīt), a hard, black substance made by heating rubber with a large quantity of sulfur; ebonite. Vulcanite is used in making combs, buttons, electric insulation, etc. *n.*

vul can i za tion (vul′kə nə zā′shən), act or process of vulcanizing. *n.*

vul can ize (vul′kə nīz), treat (rubber) with sulfur and heat to make it more elastic and durable. *v.,* **vul can ized,**

vul can iz ing. [from *Vulcan* + *-ize*]

vul gar (vul′gər), 1 showing a lack of good breeding, manners, taste, etc.; not refined; coarse; low: *use vulgar language.* 2 of the common people. *adj.* —**vul′gar ly,** *adv.*

vul gar ism (vul′gə riz′əm), word, phrase, or expression used only in ignorant or coarse speech. In "I disrecollect his name," *disrecollect* is a vulgarism. *n.*

vul gar i ty (vul gar′ə tē), 1 lack of refinement; lack of good breeding, manners, taste, etc.; coarseness. 2 thing done or said that shows vulgarity; vulgar act or word: *Their vulgarities made them unwelcome in our home. n., pl.* **vul gar i ties.**

vul gar ize (vul′gə rīz′), make vulgar: *Signs and advertisements often vulgarize the countryside. v.,* **vul gar ized, vul gar iz ing.**

Vul gate (vul′gāt), the Latin translation of the Bible, made about A.D. 405 by Saint Jerome. It is the Bible used by the Roman Catholic Church. *n.*

vul ner a bil i ty (vul′nər ə bil′ə tē), vulnerable quality or condition; a being open to attack or injury. *n.*

vul ner a ble (vul′nər ə bəl), 1 capable of being wounded or injured; open to attack: *The army's retreat left the city vulnerable to attack by the enemy.* 2 sensitive to criticism, temptations, influences, etc.: *Most people are vulnerable to ridicule. adj.*

vul ner a bly (vul′nər ə blē), in a vulnerable manner. *adv.*

vul pine (vul′pin), of or like a fox. *adj.*

vulture (def. 1)
about 2½ ft. long

vul ture (vul′chər), 1 a large bird of prey related to eagles, falcons, and hawks, that eats the flesh of dead animals. Vultures usually have featherless heads and necks. 2 person who preys upon another; greedy, ruthless person. *n.*

vy ing (vī′ing), present participle of **vie.** *Members of the class were vying with each other for a position on the student council. v.*

W w

W or **w** (dub′əl yü), the 23rd letter of the alphabet. *n., pl.* **W's** or **w's.**

w, watt or watts.

W, 1 west. 2 western.

Wa bash (wô′bash), river flowing from W Ohio southwest across Indiana into the Ohio River. *n.*

wab ble (wob′əl), wobble. *v.,* **wab bled, wab bling;** *n.*

wab bly (wob′lē), wobbly. *adj.*

WAC or **Wac** (wak), woman in the United States Army other than a nurse. *n.* [from abbreviation of *Women's Army Corps*]

wad (wod), 1 a small, soft mass: *I plugged my ears with wads of cotton.* 2 a tight roll; compact bundle or mass: *a wad of chewing gum.* 3 make into a wad; press into a wad: *I wadded up the paper and threw it away.* 4 a round plug of felt, cardboard, etc., used to hold powder and shot in place in a gun or cartridge. 5 stuff with a wad. 6 hold in place by a wad. 7 fill out with padding; pad. 1,2,4 *n.,* 3,5-7 *v.,* **wad ded, wad ding.**

wad dle (wod′l), 1 walk with short steps and an awkward, swaying motion, as a duck does: *The toddler waddled from the house bundled in his snowsuit.* 2 act of waddling: *He made us laugh by imitating the waddle of a duck.* 3 an awkward, swaying gait. 1 *v.,* **wad dled, wad dling;** 2,3 *n.*

wad dler (wod′lər), person or animal that waddles. *n.*

wade (wād), 1 walk through water, snow, sand, mud, or anything that hinders free motion. 2 make one's way with difficulty: *Must I wade through that dull book?* 3 cross or pass through by wading: *wade a stream.* *v.,* **wad ed, wad ing.**

wade into, INFORMAL. attack or go to work upon vigorously.

wad er (wā′dər), 1 person or thing that wades. 2 a long-legged bird that wades about in shallow water, searching for food. Cranes, herons, storks, and sandpipers are waders. 3 a high, waterproof boot. *n.*

WAF or **Waf** (waf), woman in the United States Air Force other than a nurse. *n.* [from abbreviation of *Women in the Air Force*]

wa fer (wā′fər), 1 a very thin cake or biscuit, sometimes flavored or sweetened. 2 the thin, round piece of unleavened bread used in Holy Communion in the Roman Catholic Church.

3 a thin piece of candy, chocolate, medicine, etc. 4 piece of sticky paper, dried paste, etc., used as a seal or fastening. *n.*

waf fle (wof′əl *or* wô′fəl), a batter cake cooked in a waffle iron until brown and crisp, usually eaten while hot with butter, syrup, etc. *n.*

waffle iron, utensil in which waffles are cooked, consisting of two hinged parts having on the inside projections that make the cakes very thin in places.

waft (waft), 1 carry over water or through air: *The waves wafted the boat to shore.* 2 a breath or puff of air, wind, scent, etc.: *A waft of fresh air came through the open window.* 3 a waving movement: *A waft of the hand was her only farewell.* 1 *v.,* 2,3 *n.*

wag (wag), 1 move from side to side or up and down, especially rapidly and repeatedly: *The dog wagged its tail. Its tail wagged back and forth.* 2 a wagging motion: *She refused with a wag of her head.* 3 person who is fond of making jokes. 1 *v.,* **wagged, wag ging;** 2,3 *n.*

wage (wāj), 1 Usually, **wages,** *pl.* **a** amount paid for work: *wages of $200 a week.* **b** something given in return: *"The wages of sin is death."* 2 carry on: *Doctors wage war against disease.* 1 *n.,* 2 *v.,* **waged, wag ing.**

wage earner, person who works for wages.

wa ger (wā′jər), 1 make a bet; bet; gamble: *I'll wager the black horse will win the race. He doesn't often wager.* 2 act of betting; bet: *The wager of $10 was promptly paid.* 1 *v.,* 2 *n.* —**wa′-ger er,** *n.*

wag ger y (wag′ər ē), 1 act or habit of joking. 2 a joke. *n., pl.* **wag ger ies.**

wag gish (wag′ish), 1 fond of making jokes. 2 characteristic of a wag; funny; humorous: *a waggish remark. adj.*

wag gle (wag′əl), 1 move quickly and repeatedly from side to side; wag. 2 a waggling motion. 1 *v.,* **wag gled, wag gling;** 2 *n.*

Wag ner (väg′nər), **Richard,** 1813-1883, German composer. *n.*

wag on (wag′ən), a four-wheeled vehicle, especially one for carrying loads: *a milk wagon. n.*

wag on er (wag′ə nər), person who drives a wagon. *n.*

wag on load (wag′ən lōd′), amount that a wagon can hold or carry. *n.*

waif (wāf), 1 person without home or friends, especially a homeless or neglected child. 2 anything without an owner; stray thing, animal, etc. *n.*

wail (wāl), 1 cry loud and long because of grief or pain: *The baby wailed.* 2 a long cry of grief or pain. 3 a sound like such a cry: *the wail of a hungry coyote.*

hat, āge, fär; let, ē qual, tėrm;
it, īce; hot, ō pen, ôr der;
oil, out; cup, pût, rüle; ch, child;
ng, long; sh, she; th, thin;
ŦH, then; zh, measure;

ə represents *a* in about,
e in taken, *i* in pencil,
o in lemon, *u* in circus.

4 make a mournful sound: *The wind wailed around the old house.* 5 lament; mourn. 1,4,5 *v.,* 2,3 *n.* —**wail′er,** *n.*

wain (wān), OLD USE. wagon. *n.*

wain scot (wān′skōt *or* wān′skət), 1 a lining of wood, usually in panels, on the walls of a room. 2 line with wood: *a room wainscoted in oak.* 3 the lower part of the wall of a room when it is decorated differently from the upper part. 1,3 *n.,* 2 *v.*

wainscot (def. 3)

wain scot ing (wān′skō ting *or* wān′skə ting), 1 wainscot. 2 material used for wainscots. *n.*

waist (wāst), 1 the part of the human body between the ribs and the hips. 2 waistline. 3 garment or part of a garment covering the body from the neck or shoulders to the waistline; blouse or bodice. 4 the middle part: *the waist of a ship. n.*

waist band (wāst′band′), a band around the waist: *the waistband of a skirt or of a pair of trousers. n.*

waist coat (wāst′kōt *or* wes′kət), a man's vest (a term used in Great Britain). *n.*

waist line (wāst′līn′), 1 line around the body at the smallest part of the waist. 2 place of smallest width in a woman's dress between the arms and the knees. 3 line where the waist and skirt of a dress join. *n.*

wait (wāt), 1 stay or stop doing something until someone comes or something happens: *Let's wait in the shade.* 2 act or time of waiting: *I had a long wait at the doctor's office.* 3 look forward; be expecting or ready: *The children wait impatiently for vacation.* 4 be left undone; be put off: *That matter can wait until tomorrow.* 5 INFORMAL. delay or put off: *Wait dinner for me.* 6 act as a

adj.	adjective	*n.*	noun
adv.	adverb	*prep.*	preposition
conj.	conjunction	*pron.*	pronoun
interj.	interjection	*v.*	verb
sing.	singular	*pl.*	plural

servant; change plates, pass food, etc., at table. **7 waits,** *pl.* group of singers and musicians who go about the streets singing and playing at Christmas time. 1,3-6 *v.*, 2,7 *n.*

lie in wait, stay hidden ready to attack: *Robbers lay in wait for the caravan.*

wait on or **wait upon, 1** be a servant to; serve, especially at the table: *wait on hotel guests.* **2** call on (a superior) to pay a respectful visit: *The victorious general waited upon the king.*

wait er (wā′tər), **1** person who waits. **2** man who waits on table in a hotel, restaurant, etc. *n.*

wait ing (wā′ting), **1** that waits: *The waiting crowd rushed to the train as soon as it was ready.* **2** time that one waits. 1 *adj.*, 2 *n.*

in waiting, in attendance on a king, queen, prince, princess, etc.

waiting room, room at a railroad station, doctor's office, etc., for people to wait in.

wai tress (wā′tris), woman who waits on table in a hotel, restaurant, etc. *n.*, *pl.* **wai tress es.**

waive (wāv), **1** give up (a right, claim, etc.); refrain from claiming or pressing; do without; relinquish: *The lawyer waived the privilege of cross-examining the witness.* **2** put aside; defer. *v.*, **waived, waiv ing.**

waiv er (wā′vər), **1** a giving up of a right, claim, etc.; a waiving. **2** a written statement of this: *For $100, the injured man signed a waiver of all claims against the railroad. n.*

wake[1] (wāk), **1** stop sleeping: *I usually wake at dawn. She wakes up at seven every morning.* **2** cause to stop sleeping: *The noise of the traffic always wakes the baby. Wake me up early.* **3** be awake; stay awake: *all her waking hours.* **4** become alive or active: *The flowers wake in the spring.* **5** make alive or active: *He needs some interest to wake him up.* **6** a watching. **7** an all-night watch kept beside the body of a dead person before its burial. **8** keep watch. 1-5,8 *v.*, **waked** or **woke, waked** or **wo ken, wak ing;** 6,7 *n.* [Old English *wacian* become awake and *wacan* to awake]

wake[2] (wāk), **1** track left behind a moving ship. **2** track left behind any moving thing. *n.* [probably from Dutch of the 1500's *wak*]

in the wake of, behind; after: *floods coming in the wake of a hurricane, a dog following in the wake of its master.*

wake ful (wāk′fəl), **1** not able to sleep. **2** without sleep. **3** watchful. *adj.* —**wake′ful ness,** *n.*

Wake Island, small island in the N Pacific, about 2000 miles west of Hawaii, belonging to the United States.

wak en (wā′kən), wake. *v.*

wale (wāl), **1** a streak or ridge made on the skin by a stick or whip; welt. **2** to mark with wales; raise wales on. **3** a ridge in the weave of cloth. **4** to weave with ridges. 1,3 *n.*, 2,4 *v.*, **waled, wal ing.**

Wales (wālz), division of Great Britain west of England; the land of the Welsh. *Capital:* Cardiff. *n.*

walk (wôk), **1** go on foot. In walking, a person always has one foot on the ground. *Walk down to the post office with me.* **2** go over, on, or through: *walk the length of a trail.* **3** cause to walk; make go step by step: *The rider walked the horse up the hill.* **4** act of walking, especially for pleasure or exercise: *We went for a walk in the country.* **5** accompany or escort in walking; conduct on foot: *walk a guest to the door.* **6** distance to walk: *It is a long walk from here.* **7** manner or way of walking; gait: *We could tell she was happy from her lively walk.* **8** place for walking; path: *There are many pretty walks in the park.* **9** way of living: *A doctor and a street cleaner are in different walks of life.* **10** in baseball: **a** go to first base after the pitcher has thrown four balls. **b** a going to first base after four balls. **c** allow a batter to reach first base by pitching four balls. 1-3,5,10a,10c *v.*, 4,6-9,10b *n.* —**walk′er,** *n.*

walk ie-talk ie (wô′kē tô′kē), a small, portable receiving and transmitting radio set. It is powered by a battery and has a collapsible antenna. *n.*, *pl.* **walk ie-talk ies.**

walking stick, 1 cane. **2** any of various insects having a body like a stick or twig.

walk out (wôk′out′), INFORMAL. **1** strike of workers. **2** a sudden departure from a room, meeting, etc., usually as a form of protest. *n.*

walk o ver (wôk′ō′vər), INFORMAL. an easy victory. *n.*

walk-up (wôk′up′), an apartment house or building having no elevator. *n.*

walk way (wôk′wā′), **1** structure for walking: *an overhead steel walkway.* **2** path; walk. *n.*

wall (wôl), **1** side of a house, room, or other hollow thing. **2** structure of stone, brick, or other material built up to en-close, divide, support, or protect. Cities used to be surrounded by high walls to keep out enemies. **3** something like a wall in looks or use: *a wall of water ten feet high, a wall of ignorance. The mayor met a solid wall of protesters.* **4** enclose, divide, protect, or fill with a wall, or as if with a wall: *wall a garden, wall out the noise of the city, wall up a doorway.* 1-3 *n.*, 4 *v.* —**wall′-like′,** *adj.*

drive to the wall, make desperate or helpless: *Poverty drove the family to the wall.*

go to the wall, 1 give way; be defeated. **2** fail in business.

wal la by (wol′ə bē), any of various small kangaroos. Some wallabies are no larger than rabbits. *n.*, *pl.* **wal la bies** or **wal la by.**

Wal lace (wol′is or wô′lis), Sir **William,** 1272?-1305, Scottish leader and general. *n.*

wall board (wôl′bôrd′), any of various building materials, such as plasterboard or fiberboard, made by pressing wood pulp, plaster, etc., into large, flat sheets. Wallboard is used instead of wood or plaster to make or cover inside walls. *n.*

wal let (wol′it or wô′lit), **1** a small, flat, leather case for carrying paper money, cards, etc., in one's pocket; folding pocketbook; billfold. **2** bag for carrying food and small articles for personal use when on a journey. *n.*

wall eye (wôl′ī′), any of various fishes with large, staring eyes. *n.*

wall eyed (wôl′īd′), **1** having eyes that show much white and little color. **2** having one or both eyes turned away from the nose, so as to show much white. **3** having large, staring eyes, as a fish. *adj.*

wall flow er (wôl′flou′ər), **1** IN-FORMAL. person who sits by the wall at a dance instead of dancing. **2** a perennial plant with sweet-smelling yellow, orange, or red flowers, found growing on walls, cliffs, etc. *n.*

wal lop (wol′əp), INFORMAL. **1** beat soundly; thrash. **2** hit very hard; strike with a vigorous blow. **3** a very hard blow: *The wallop knocked him down.* **4** power to hit very hard blows. **5** defeat thoroughly, as in a game. 1,2,5 *v.*, 3,4 *n.*

wal low (wol′ō), **1** roll about; flounder: *The pigs wallowed in the mud. The boat wallowed helplessly in the stormy sea.* **2** live contentedly in filth, wickedness, etc., like a beast. **3** live or delight self-indulgently or luxuriously in some form of pleasure, manner of life, etc.: *wallow in wealth, wallow in sentimentality.* **4** act of wallowing. **5** place where an animal wallows: *There used to be* *many buffalo wallows on the prairies.* 1-3 *v.,* 4,5 *n.*

wall pa per (wôl´pā´pər), 1 paper, commonly with printed decorative patterns in color, for pasting on and covering walls. 2 put wallpaper on. 1 *n.,* 2 *v.*

Wall Street, 1 street in downtown New York City that is the chief financial center of the United States. 2 the money market or the financiers of the United States.

wal nut (wôl´nut), 1 a rather large, almost round nut with a hard, ridged shell and a division between its two halves. The meat of the walnut is eaten by itself, used in cakes, etc. 2 the tree that it grows on. 3 the wood of a walnut tree. Some kinds of walnut are used in making furniture. *n.*

wal rus (wôl´rəs *or* wol´rəs), a large sea mammal of the arctic regions, resembling a seal but having long tusks. Walrus hide is made into leather for suitcases, bags, etc. *n., pl.* **wal rus es** *or* **wal rus.**

waltz (wôlts), 1 a smooth, even, gliding dance with three beats to a measure, in which a complete turn is made to each measure. 2 music for it. 3 dance a waltz. 1,2 *n., pl.* **waltz es;** 3 *v.*

wampum—a string of seven pieces

wam pum (wom´pəm *or* wôm´pəm), beads made from shells, formerly used by North American Indians as money and for ornament. *n.*

wan (won), 1 lacking natural color; pale: *Her face looked wan after her long illness.* 2 looking worn or tired; faint; weak: *The sick boy gave the doctor a wan smile. adj.,* **wan ner, wan nest.** —**wan´ly,** *adv.* —**wan´ness,** *n.*

wand (wond), a slender stick or rod: *a magician's wand.*

wan der (won´dər), 1 move here and there without any special purpose: *We wandered by stores, window-shopping.* 2 follow an uncertain or irregular course; meander: *a driver who wanders all over the road.* 3 go from the right way; stray: *The dog wandered off and got lost. The speaker wandered away from the subject.* 4 not be able to think sensibly; be delirious or incoherent: *His mind wandered when he had a very high fever. v.* —**wan´der er,** *n.*

wan der lust (won´dər lust´), a strong desire to wander: *Her wanderlust led her all over the world. n.*

wane (wān), 1 lose size; become smaller gradually: *The moon wanes after it has become full.* 2 lose power, influence, or importance: *Many great empires have waned.* 3 lose strength or intensity: *The light of day wanes in the*

evening. 4 draw to a close: *Summer wanes as autumn approaches.* 5 a waning. 1-4 *v.,* **waned, wan ing;** 5 *n.* **on the wane,** growing less; waning.

wan gle (wang´gəl), INFORMAL. 1 manage to get by schemes, tricks, persuasion, etc.: *wangle an interview with the president.* 2 make one's way through difficulties. *v.,* **wan gled, wan gling.**

Wan kel engine (wong´kəl), an internal-combustion engine with few moving parts. It produces power by the spinning of (usually) two triangular rotors in an oval combustion chamber. [from Felix *Wankel,* born 1902, the German inventor of the engine]

want (wont *or* wônt), 1 wish for; wish: *We want a new car. I want to become an engineer.* 2 thing desired or needed; desire: *a person having few wants.* 3 be without; lack: *The fund wants half of the sum needed.* 4 condition of being without something desired or needed; a lack: *The plant died from want of water.* 5 to need; require: *Your hands want washing. Plants want water.* 6 a need: *supply a long-felt want.* 7 a lack of food, clothing, or shelter; great poverty: *The old couple is now in want.* 8 need food, clothing, and shelter; be very poor. 9 wish to see, speak to, or use (a person): *Call me if you want me. He is the man we want for the job.* 10 seek after to catch or arrest: *wanted by the police.* 1,3,5,8-10 *v.,* 2,4,6,7 *n.*

want ad, INFORMAL. a small notice in a newspaper stating that an employee, an apartment, etc., is wanted.

want ing (won´ting *or* wôn´ting), 1 not found or in evidence; lacking; missing: *One volume of the set is wanting.* 2 without; less; minus: *a year wanting three days.* 3 not satisfactory; not coming up to a standard or need: *The vegetables were weighed and found wanting.* 1,3 *adj.,* 2 *prep.*

wan ton (won´tən), 1 done in a reckless, heartless, or malicious way; done without reason or excuse: *a wanton attack, wanton mischief, wanton cruelty.* 2 not moral; not chaste. 3 not restrained; frolicsome; playful: *a wanton breeze, a wanton child, a wanton mood.* 4 a wanton person. 5 act in a wanton manner: *The wind wantoned with the leaves.* 1-3 *adj.,* 4 *n.,* 5 *v.* —**wan´ton ly,** *adv.* —**wan´ton ness,** *n.*

wap i ti (wop´ə tē), the elk of North America, a large, reddish deer with long, slender antlers. *n., pl.* **wap i tis** *or* **wap i ti.**

war (wôr), 1 fighting carried on by armed force between nations or parts of a nation. 2 any fighting or struggle; strife; conflict: *Doctors carry on war against disease.* 3 the occupation or art

hat, āge, fär; let, ēqual, tèrm;
it, īce; hot, ōpen, ôrder;
oil, out; cup, pùt, rüle; ch, child;
ng, long; sh, she; th, thin;
ᵀH, then; zh, measure;

ə represents *a* in about,
e in taken, *i* in pencil,
o in lemon, *u* in circus.

of fighting with weapons: *Soldiers are trained for war.* 4 make war; fight: *to war with an aggressor, to war against poverty.* 5 having to do with war; used in war; caused by war: *war weapons, war crimes, war casualties.* 1-3 *n.,* 4 *v.,* **warred, war ring;** 5 *adj.*

War Between the States, the American Civil War.

war ble (wôr´bəl), 1 sing with trills, quavers, or melodious turns: *Birds warbled in the trees.* 2 make a sound like that of a bird warbling: *The brook warbled over its rocky bed.* 3 a bird's song or a sound like it. 1,2 *v.,* **war bled, war bling;** 3 *n.*

war bler (wôr´blər), 1 person, bird, etc., that warbles. 2 any of a large group of small songbirds, often brightly colored. *n.*

war bonnet, a ceremonial headdress set with feathers and often a long trailing piece with feathers, worn by certain North American Indians.

war cry, battle cry.

ward (wôrd), 1 a division of a hospital or prison. 2 district of a city or town. 3 person under the care of a guardian or of a court. 4 guard: *keep watch and ward over the royal jewels. n.*

ward off, keep away; turn aside: *ward off a blow, ward off an illness.*

-ward, *suffix forming adverbs.* in the direction of _____; toward _____: *Homeward = in the direction of home. Backward = toward the back.* Also, **-wards.** [Old English *-weard*]

ward en (wôrd´n), 1 the official in charge of a prison. 2 any official who enforces certain laws and regulations: *an air-raid warden, a fire warden.* 3 game warden. 4 the head of certain schools or colleges in Great Britain. 5 churchwarden. 6 keeper, guard, or custodian. *n.*

ward er (wôr´dər), 1 guard or watchman. 2 warden or jailer (a term used in Great Britain). *n.*

ward robe (wôrd´rōb´), 1 stock of clothes: *She is shopping for her spring wardrobe.* 2 room, closet, or piece of furniture for holding clothes. *n.*

-wards, *suffix forming adverbs.* in the

ware

direction of _____; toward _____: *Backwards = in the direction of or toward the back.* Also, **-ward.** [Old English *-weardes*]

ware (wer *or* war), 1 Usually, **wares,** *pl.* a manufactured thing; article for sale: *The peddler sold his wares cheap.* 2 earthenware; pottery: *porcelain ware. Mother bought some lovely blue-and-white ware in Canada last summer. n.*

ware house (wer′hous′ *or* war′hous′), place where goods are kept; storehouse. *n., pl.* **ware hous es** (wer′hou′ziz *or* war′hou′ziz).

war fare (wôr′fer′ *or* wôr′far′), war; fighting. *n.*

war head (wôr′hed′), the forward part of a torpedo, missile, etc., that contains the explosive. *n.*

war horse, 1 horse used in war; charger. 2 INFORMAL. person who has taken part in many battles, struggles, etc.; veteran.

war i ly (wer′ə lē *or* war′ə lē), in a wary manner; cautiously; carefully: *The hikers climbed warily up the dangerous path. adv.*

war i ness (wer′ē nis *or* war′ē nis), caution; care. *n.*

war like (wôr′līk′), 1 fit for war; ready for war; fond of war: *a warlike nation.* 2 threatening war: *a warlike speech.* 3 of or having to do with war; martial: *warlike music. adj.*

war lock (wôr′lok), a male witch; wizard. *n.*

warm (wôrm), 1 more hot than cold; having some heat; giving forth moderate or gentle heat: *a warm fire. She sat in the warm sunshine.* 2 having a feeling of heat: *be warm from running.* 3 that makes or keeps warm: *a warm coat.* 4 having or showing affection, enthusiasm, or zeal: *a warm welcome, a warm friend, a warm heart.* 5 easily excited: *a warm temper.* 6 exciting; lively: *a warm dispute.* 7 fresh and strong: *a warm scent.* 8 (in games, treasure hunts, etc.) near what one is searching for. 9 suggesting heat. Red, orange, and yellow are called warm colors. 10 make or become warm: *warm a room.* 11 make or become cheered, interested, friendly, or sympathetic: *Her happiness warms my heart. The speaker warmed to his sub-*

ject. 1-9 *adj.,* 10,11 *v.* —**warm′ly,** *adv.* —**warm′ness,** *n.*

warm up, 1 heat or cook again. 2 make or become more interested, friendly, etc. 3 to practice or exercise for a few minutes before entering a game, contest, etc. 4 run (a machine) before using it until it reaches its normal working condition.

warm-blood ed (wôrm′blud′id), 1 having blood that stays about the same temperature regardless of the air or water around the animal. Birds and mammals are warm-blooded; reptiles, turtles, fishes, etc., are cold-blooded. 2 with much feeling; eager; ardent. *adj.*

warm front, the advancing edge of a warm air mass as it passes over and displaces a cooler one.

warm-heart ed (wôrm′här′tid), kind; sympathetic; friendly. *adj.*

warming pan, a covered pan with a long handle for holding hot coals, formerly used to warm beds.

war mon ger (wôr′mong′gər), person who is in favor of war or attempts to bring about war. *n.*

warmth (wôrmth), 1 a being warm: *the warmth of the open fire.* 2 warm or friendly feeling: *the warmth of our host's welcome.* 3 liveliness of feelings or emotions; fervor: *She spoke with warmth of the natural beauty of the country. n.*

warm-up (wôrm′up′), 1 practice or exercise taken for a few minutes before entering a game, contest, etc. 2 period of running required for a machine to reach normal working condition before use. *n.*

warn (wôrn), 1 give notice to in advance; put on guard (against danger, evil, harm, etc.): *The clouds warned us that a storm was coming.* 2 give notice to; inform: *The whistle warned visitors that the ship was ready to sail. v.*

warn ing (wôr′ning), something that warns; notice given in advance. *n.* —**warn′ing ly,** *adv.*

War of 1812, war between the United States and Great Britain. It lasted from 1812 to 1815.

War of Independence, Revolutionary War.

warp (wôrp), 1 bend or twist out of shape: *This floor has warped so that it is not level.* 2 mislead; pervert: *Prejudice warped her judgment.* 3 a bend or twist; distortion. 4 move (a ship, etc.) by ropes fastened to something fixed. 5 rope used in moving a ship. 6 the threads running lengthwise in a fabric. The warp is crossed by the woof. 1,2,4 *v.,* 3,5,6 *n.*

war paint, paint put on the face or body by American Indians, members of

some African tribes, etc., before going to war.

war path (wôr′path′), the way taken by a fighting expedition of North American Indians. *n., pl.* **war paths** (wôr′paᴛнz′ *or* wôr′paths′).

on the warpath, 1 ready for war. 2 looking for a fight; angry.

war plane (wôr′plān′), airplane used in war. *n.*

war rant (wôr′ənt *or* wor′ənt), 1 that which gives a right; authority: *He had no warrant for his action.* 2 a written order giving authority for something: *a warrant to search the house, a warrant for the payment of money.* 3 authorize: *The law warrants his arrest.* 4 a good and sufficient reason; promise; guarantee: *He had no warrant for his hopes.* 5 justify: *Nothing can warrant such rudeness.* 6 give one's word for; guarantee; promise: *The storekeeper warranted the quality of the eggs.* 7 INFORMAL. declare positively; certify: *I'll warrant they won't try that again.* 1,2,4 *n.,* 3,5-7 *v.*

warrant officer, (in the armed forces) an officer who has received a certificate of appointment, but not a commission, ranking between commissioned officers and enlisted men.

war ran ty (wôr′ən tē *or* wor′ən tē), 1 warrant or authorization. 2 a promise or pledge that something is what it is claimed to be; guarantee: *a warranty of the quality of the goods sold. n., pl.* **war ran ties.**

war ren (wôr′ən *or* wor′ən), 1 piece of ground filled with burrows, where rabbits live or are raised. 2 a crowded district or building. *n.*

War ren (wôr′ən *or* wor′ən), **Earl,** born 1891, chief justice of the United States Supreme Court from 1953 to 1969. *n.*

war ri or (wôr′ē ər *or* wor′ē ər), a fighting man; experienced soldier. *n.*

War saw (wôr′sô), capital and largest city of Poland, in the E part. *n.*

war ship (wôr′ship′), ship armed and manned for war. *n.*

wart (wôrt), 1 a small, hard lump on the skin. 2 a similar lump on a plant. *n.* —**wart′like′,** *adj.*

wart hog, a wild hog of Africa that has two large tusks and large, wartlike growths on each side of its face.

war time (wôr′tīm′), 1 a time of war. 2 of or having to do with a time of war. 1 *n.,* 2 *adj.*

warp
(def. 6)

wart y (wôr′tē), 1 having warts. 2 covered with lumps like warts. 3 of or like a wart. *adj.*, **wart i er, wart i est.**

war y (wer′ē *or* war′ē), 1 on one's guard against danger, deception, etc.: *a wary fox.* 2 cautious or careful: *give wary answers to a stranger's questions. adj.*, **war i er, war i est.**

wary of, cautious or careful about: *Be wary of gossip.*

was (woz *or* wuz; *unstressed* wəz), form of the verb **be** used with *I, he, she, it,* or any singular noun to indicate the past tense. *Once there was a king. I was late to school. The candy was eaten. v.*

wash (wosh *or* wôsh), 1 clean with water or other liquid: *wash one's face, wash clothes, wash dishes.* 2 remove (dirt, stains, paint, etc.) by or as by scrubbing with soap and water: *Can you wash that spot out?* 3 wash oneself: *I washed before eating dinner.* 4 wash clothes: *I have to wash today.* 5 make clean or free from guilt, corruption, etc.; purify: *washed from sin.* 6 a washing or a being washed: *This floor needs a good wash.* 7 quantity of clothes washed or to be washed: *Take the wash from the dryer.* 8 undergo washing without damage: *That cloth washes well.* 9 that can be washed without damage: *a wash dress.* 10 carry or be carried along or away by water or other liquid: *Wood is often washed ashore by the waves. The road washed out during the storm.* 11 material carried along by moving water and then deposited as sediment. A delta is formed by the wash of a river. 12 wear (by water or any liquid): *The cliffs are being washed away by the waves.* 13 to flow or beat with a lapping sound: *The waves washed upon the rocks.* 14 motion, rush, or sound of water: *We listened to the wash of the waves against the boat.* 15 make wet: *The flowers are washed with dew.* 16 tract of land sometimes overflowed with water and sometimes left dry; tract of shallow water; fen, marsh, or bog. 17 liquid for a special use: *a hair wash.* 18 waste liquid matter; liquid garbage: *The kitchen wash is given to the pigs.* 19 a thin coating of color or metal. 20 cover with a thin coating of color or of metal: *walls washed with blue, silver washed with gold.* 21 sift (earth, ore, etc.) by action of water to separate. 22 the rough or broken water left behind a moving ship. 23 disturbance in air made by an airplane or any of its parts. 1-5,8,10,12,13,15,20,21 *v.,* 6,7,11,14, 16-19,22,23 *n., pl.* **wash es;** 9 *adj.*

wash down, 1 wash from top to bottom or from end to end: *wash down the walls of a kitchen.* 2 drink some liquid along with or after solid food to help in swallowing.

wash up, wash one's hands and face, as before eating.

Wash., the state of Washington.

wash a ble (wosh′ə bəl *or* wô′shə-bəl), that can be washed without damage: *washable silk. adj.*

wash ba sin (wosh′bā′sn *or* wôsh′-bā′sn), basin for holding water to wash one's face and hands. *n.*

wash board (wosh′bôrd′ *or* wôsh′-bôrd′), a board having ridges on it, used for rubbing the dirt out of clothes. *n.*

wash bowl (wosh′bōl′ *or* wôsh′bōl′), bowl for holding water to wash one's hands and face. *n.*

wash cloth (wosh′klôth′ *or* wôsh′-klôth′), a small cloth for washing oneself. *n., pl.* **wash cloths** (wosh′-klôᴛʜz′, wosh′klôths′, wôsh′klôᴛʜz′, *or* wôsh′klôths′).

washed-out (wosht′out′ *or* wôsht′-out′), 1 lacking color; faded. 2 IN-FORMAL. lacking life, spirit, etc. *adj.*

wash er (wosh′ər *or* wô′shər), 1 person who washes. 2 machine that washes. 3 a flat ring of metal, rubber, leather, etc., used with bolts or nuts, to make joints tight. *n.*

WASHER

washer (def. 3)

wash er wom an (wosh′ər wùm′ən *or* wô′shər wum′ən), woman whose work is washing clothes. *n., pl.* **wash-er wom en.**

wash ing (wosh′ing *or* wô′shing), 1 a cleaning with water. 2 clothes, etc., washed or to be washed: *hang washing out today, send washing to the laundry.* 3 liquid that has been used to wash something. 4 matter removed in washing something: *washings of gold obtained from earth. n.*

washing machine, machine that washes clothes.

Wash ing ton (wosh′ing tən *or* wô′shing tən), 1 capital of the United States, covering the entire District of Columbia. Washington is situated along the Potomac River between Maryland and Virginia. 2 one of the Pacific states of the United States. *Capital:* Olympia. 3 **Mount,** the highest mountain in New England, in N New Hampshire. 4 **Booker T.,** 1856-1915, American Negro writer and educator. 5 **George,** 1732-1799, commander in chief of the American army in the Revolutionary War and the first president of the United States, from 1789 to 1797. 6 **Martha,** 1731-1802, wife of George Washington. *n.*

hat, āge, fär; let, ēqual, tėrm; it, īce; hot, ōpen, ôrder; oil, out; cup, pùt, rüle; ch, child; ng, long; sh, she; th, thin; ᴛʜ, then; zh, measure;

ə represents *a* in about, *e* in taken, *i* in pencil, *o* in lemon, *u* in circus.

wash out (wosh′out′ *or* wôsh′out′), 1 a washing away of earth, a road, etc., by water. 2 the hole or break made by it. 3 SLANG. failure; disappointment: *The party was a complete washout. n.*

wash room (wosh′rüm′, wosh′rùm′, wôsh′rüm′, *or* wôsh′rùm′), room where toilet facilities are provided; lavatory. *n.*

wash stand (wosh′stand′ *or* wôsh′-stand′), 1 bowl with pipes and faucets for running water to wash one's hands and face. 2 stand for holding a basin, pitcher, etc., for washing. *n.*

wash tub (wosh′tub′ *or* wôsh′tub′), tub used to wash or soak clothes in. *n.*

was n't (woz′nt *or* wuz′nt), was not.

wasp (wosp *or* wôsp), insect related to the ants and the bees, having a slender body, two pairs of wings, and a powerful sting. Hornets and yellow jackets are kinds of wasps. *n.*

wasp ish (wos′pish *or* wô′spish), 1 like a wasp; like that of a wasp. 2 bad-tempered; irritable. *adj.*—**wasp′ish ly,** *adv.* —**wasp′ish ness,** *n.*

was sail (wos′əl), 1 a drinking party; revelry with drinking of healths. 2 take part in a wassail; revel. 3 spiced ale or other liquor drunk at a wassail. 4 salutation wishing good health or good luck to a person, used especially in England in former times when drinking a toast. 5 to drink to the health of. 1,3,4 *n.,* 2,5 *v.,* 4 *interj.*

was sail er (wos′ə lər), 1 reveler. 2 drinker of healths. *n.*

wast (wost), OLD USE. were. "Thou wast" means "you were." *v.*

wast age (wā′stij), 1 loss by use, wear, decay, leakage, etc.; waste. 2 amount wasted. *n.*

waste (wāst), 1 make poor use of; spend uselessly; fail to get full value or benefit from: *Though I had much work to do, I wasted my time doing nothing.* 2 poor use; useless spending; failure to get the most out of something: *Buying that suit was a waste of money; it is already starting to wear out.* 3 thrown away as useless or worthless: *waste products, a pile of waste lumber.* 4 useless or worthless material; stuff to

adj.	adjective	*n.*	noun
adv.	adverb	*prep.*	preposition
conj.	conjunction	*pron.*	pronoun
interj.	interjection	*v.*	verb
sing.	singular	*pl.*	plural

be thrown away; refuse: *Garbage or sewage is waste.* 5 carrying off or holding refuse: *a waste drain.* 6 left over; not used: *waste food.* 7 stuff that is left over. Bunches of cotton waste are used to clean machinery. 8 bare or wild land; desert; wilderness: *We traveled through treeless wastes. Before us stretched a waste of snow and ice.* 9 not cultivated; that is a desert or wilderness; bare; wild. 10 wear down little by little; destroy or lose gradually: *The sick man was wasted by disease.* 11 a wearing down little by little; gradual destruction or loss: *Both waste and repair are constantly going on in our bodies.* 12 damage greatly; destroy; spoil; ruin: *The soldiers wasted the enemy's fields.* 1,10,12 *v.*, **wast ed, wast ing;** 2,4,7, 8,11 *n.*, 3,5,6,9 *adj.*

go to waste, be wasted.

lay waste, damage greatly; destroy; ravage.

waste bas ket (wāst′bas′kit), basket or other container for wastepaper. *n.*

waste ful (wāst′fəl), using or spending too much: *be wasteful of water. adj.* —**waste′ful ly,** *adv.* —**waste′ful ness,** *n.*

waste land (wāst′land′), barren, uncultivated land. *n.*

waste pa per (wāst′pā′pər), paper thrown away or to be thrown away as useless or worthless. *n.*

wast er (wā′stər), person or thing that wastes; squanderer; spendthrift. *n.*

wast rel (wā′strəl), 1 waster. 2 good-for-nothing. *n.*

watch (woch *or* wôch), 1 look attentively or carefully: *The medical students watched while the surgeon performed the operation.* 2 look at; observe; view: *Are you watching that show on television? We watched the kittens play.* 3 look or wait with care and attention; be very careful: *I watched for a chance to cross the street.* 4 a careful looking; attitude of attention: *Be on the watch for automobiles when you cross the street.* 5 keep guard: *The sentry watched throughout the night.* 6 keep guard over: *The police watched the prisoner.* 7 a protecting; guarding: *A man keeps watch over the bank at night.* 8 person or persons kept to guard and protect: *A call for help aroused the*

night watch. 9 period of time for guarding: *a watch in the night.* 10 stay awake for some purpose: *The nurse watches with the sick.* 11 a staying awake for some purpose. 12 device for telling time, small enough to be carried in a pocket or worn on the wrist. 13 the time of duty of one part of a ship's crew. A watch usually lasts four hours. 14 the part of a ship's crew on duty at the same time. 1-3,5,6,10 *v.*, 4,7-9,11-14 *n.*, *pl.* **watch es.**

watch out, be careful; be on guard: *Watch out for cars when you cross the street.*

watch dog (woch′dôg′ *or* wôch′-dôg′), dog kept to guard property. *n.*

watch er (woch′ər *or* wô′chər), a person who watches. *n.*

watch ful (woch′fəl *or* wôch′fəl), watching carefully; on the lookout; wide-awake: *He is watchful of his health. You should always be watchful for cars when you cross the street. adj.* —**watch′ful ly,** *adv.* —**watch′ful ness,** *n.*

watch mak er (woch′mā′kər *or* wôch′mā′kər), person who makes and repairs watches. *n.*

watch man (woch′mən *or* wôch′-mən), man who keeps watch; guard: *A watchman guards the bank at night. n., pl.* **watch men.**

watch tow er (woch′tou′ər *or* wôch′-tou′ər), tower from which a man watches for enemies, fires, ships, etc. *n.*

watch word (woch′wėrd′ *or* wôch′-wėrd′), 1 password: *We gave the watchword, and the sentinel let us pass.* 2 motto; slogan: *"Forward" is our watchword. n.*

wa ter (wô′tər *or* wot′ər), 1 the liquid that fills the oceans, rivers, lakes, and ponds, and falls from the sky as rain. We use water for drinking and washing. Perfectly pure water is a transparent, colorless, tasteless, and odorless compound of hydrogen and oxygen, freezing at 32 degrees Fahrenheit or 0 degrees centigrade, and boiling at 212 degrees Fahrenheit or 100 degrees centigrade. 2 any of various watery

water clock—Water is piped through the funnel into the reservoir. As the water level in the reservoir rises, the float and rod move up. Cogs on the rod and cogs on the wheel mesh, moving the hand around the dial.

substances occurring in or discharged from the body, such as tears, sweat, saliva, urine, serum, etc. 3 any liquid preparation that suggests water: *lavender water.* 4 body of water; sea, lake, river, etc.: *cross the water on a ferry.* 5 to sprinkle or wet with water: *water grass.* 6 supply with water: *Our valley is well watered by rivers and brooks.* 7 weaken by adding water: *It is against the law to sell watered milk.* 8 get or take in a supply of water: *A ship waters before sailing.* 9 fill with water; discharge water: *Her eyes watered. The cake made the boy's mouth water.* 10 of water; holding, storing, or conveying water: *a water jug, a water pipe, a water system.* 11 done or used in or on water: *water sports.* 12 growing or living in or near water: *water plants, water insects.* 13 degree of clearness and brilliance of a precious stone: *a diamond of excellent water.* 14 a wavy marking on silk, metal, etc. 15 make a wavy marking on. 16 **waters,** *pl.* **a** flowing water. **b** water moving in waves; the sea; the high sea. **c** mineral water. 1-4,13,14,16 *n.*, 5-9,15 *v.*, 10-12 *adj.*

above water, out of trouble or difficulty, especially out of financial trouble or difficulty.

by water, on a ship or boat: *ship by water.*

hold water, stand the test; be true, dependable, effective, etc.

of the first water, of the highest degree.

throw cold water on, discourage: *My parents threw cold water on my plan to camp in the mountains by myself.*

tread water, keep oneself from sinking by moving the feet up and down.

water bed, bed with a mattress consisting of a vinyl bag filled with water.

water bird, bird that swims or wades in water.

wa ter buck (wô′tər buk′ *or* wot′ər-buk′), any of various African antelopes that frequent rivers, marshes, etc. *n., pl.* **wa ter bucks** *or* **wa ter buck.**

water buffalo, buffalo of Asia, commonly used as a draft animal. See **buffalo** for picture.

Wa ter bur y (wô′tər ber′ē *or* wot′ər-ber′ē), city in W Connecticut. *n.*

water clock, instrument for measuring time by the flow of water.

water closet, toilet flushed by water.

wa ter col or (wô′tər kul′ər *or* wot′-ər kul′ər), 1 paint mixed with water instead of oil. 2 art of painting with watercolors. 3 picture made with watercolors. *n.*

water cooler, any device for cooling water, or for cooling something by means of water.

wa ter course (wô′tər kôrs′ *or* wot′-ər kôrs′), 1 stream of water; river; brook. 2 channel or bed of a stream of water: *In the summer many water-courses dry up.* *n.*

wa ter cress (wô′tər kres′ *or* wot′ər-kres′), 1 plant that grows in water and has crisp, pungent leaves. 2 its leaves, used for salad and as a garnish. *n.*

wa ter fall (wô′tər fôl′ *or* wot′ər-fôl′), fall of water from a high place; cascade or cataract. *n.*

wa ter fowl (wô′tər foul′ *or* wot′ər-foul′), a water bird, especially one that swims. *n., pl.* **wa ter fowls** or **wa ter-fowl.**

wa ter front (wô′tər frunt′ *or* wot′ər-frunt′), land at the water's edge, especially the part of a city beside a river, lake, or harbor. *n.*

Wa ter gate (wô′tər gāt *or* wo′tər-gāt), 1 **the Watergate,** set of buildings in Washington, D.C., site of Democratic Party headquarters in 1972. 2 a burglary of this office, followed by a series of illegal actions related to the presidential campaign of 1972, and attempts to obstruct justice during subsequent investigations by the Senate and the Justice Department. *n.*

water hole, hole in the ground where water collects; small pond; pool.

watering place, 1 resort with springs of mineral water. 2 resort where there is bathing, boating, etc. 3 place where water may be obtained.

wa ter less (wô′tər lis *or* wot′ər lis), using or containing little or no water. *adj.*

water level, the surface level of a body of water: *The water level of the pond rose after the heavy rains.*

water lily, 1 a water plant having flat, floating leaves and showy, fragrant flowers. The flowers of the common American water lily are white, or sometimes pink. 2 its flower.

water line, 1 line where the surface of the water touches the side of a ship or boat. 2 any of several lines marked on a ship's hull to show the depth to which it sinks when unloaded, partly loaded, or fully loaded.

wa ter-logged (wô′tər lôgd′ *or* wot′ər lôgd′), so full of water that it will barely float. *adj.*

Wa ter loo (wô′tər lü *or* wot′ər lü), 1 small town in Belgium, near Brussels, the site of the battle in which Napoleon I was finally defeated in 1815. 2 any decisive or crushing defeat. *n., pl.* **Wa ter loos** for 2.

water main, a large or main pipe for carrying water.

wa ter man (wô′tər mən *or* wot′ər-mən), 1 boatman. 2 oarsman. *n., pl.* **wa ter men.**

wa ter mark (wô′tər märk′ *or* wot′ər märk′), 1 a mark showing how high water has risen or how low it has fallen: *the high watermark of a river.* 2 a faint distinguishing design made in some kinds of paper. 3 put a watermark in. Some letter paper is watermarked. 1,2 *n.,* 3 *v.*

wa ter mel on (wô′tər mel′ən *or* wot′ər mel′ən), 1 a large, juicy melon with red or pink pulp and a hard, green rind. 2 vine bearing these melons. *n.*

water moccasin, a large, poisonous snake of the southern United States that lives in swamps and along streams; cottonmouth.

water pistol, a toy pistol that shoots water taken in by suction.

water polo, game played in a swimming pool by two teams of seven swimmers who try to throw or push an inflated ball into the opponent's goal.

water power, the power from flowing or falling water. It can be used to drive machinery and generate electricity.

wa ter proof (wô′tər prüf′ *or* wot′ər-prüf′), 1 that will not let water through; resistant to water: *An umbrella should be waterproof.* 2 a waterproof material. 3 a waterproof coat; raincoat. 4 make waterproof: *These hiking shoes have been waterproofed.* 1 *adj.,* 2,3 *n.,* 4 *v.*

water rat, 1 rodent that lives on the banks of streams or lakes. 2 muskrat.

wa ter shed (wô′tər shed′ *or* wot′ər-shed′), 1 ridge between the regions drained by two different river systems. On one side of a watershed, rivers and streams flow in one direction; on the other side, they flow in the opposite direction. 2 the region drained by one river system. *n.*

wa ter side (wô′tər sīd′ *or* wot′ər-sīd′), the land along the sea, a lake, a river, etc. *n.*

water ski, one of a pair of skis for gliding over water while being towed at the end of a rope by a motorboat.

wa ter-ski (wô′tər skē′ *or* wot′ər-skē′), glide over the water on water skis. *v.,* **wa ter-skied, wa ter-ski ing. —wa′ter-ski′er,** *n.*

wa ter spout (wô′tər spout′ *or* wot′ər spout′), 1 pipe which takes away or discharges water, especially one used to drain water from a roof. 2 a rapidly spinning column or cone of mist, spray, and water, produced by the action of a whirlwind over the ocean or a lake. *n.*

water table, the level below which the ground is saturated with water.

wa ter tight (wô′tər tīt′ *or* wot′ər-tīt′), 1 so tight that no water can get in

hat, āge, fär; let, ēqual, tėrm;
it, īce; hot, ōpen, ôrder;
oil, out; cup, pút, rüle; ch, child;
ng, long; sh, she; th, thin;
₮H, then; zh, measure;

ə represents *a* in about,
e in taken, *i* in pencil,
o in lemon, *u* in circus.

or out. Large ships are often divided into watertight compartments by watertight partitions. 2 leaving no opening for misunderstanding, criticism, etc.; perfect: *a watertight argument. adj.*

water vapor, water in a gaseous state, especially when fairly diffused, as it is in the air, and below the boiling point, as distinguished from steam.

wa ter way (wô′tər wā′ *or* wot′ər-wā′), 1 river, canal, or other body of water that ships can go on. 2 channel for water. *n.*

water wheel, wheel turned by water and used to do work. The grindstones of grain mills used to be run by water wheels. See **undershot** for picture.

wa ter works (wô′tər wėrks′ *or* wot′ər wėrks′), 1 system of pipes, reservoirs, pumps, etc., for supplying a city or town with water. 2 building with machinery for pumping water. *n. pl. or sing.*

wa ter y (wô′tər ē *or* wot′ər ē), 1 of water; connected with water. 2 full of water; wet: *watery soil.* 3 indicating rain: *a watery sky.* 4 full of tears; tearful: *watery eyes.* 5 containing too much water: *watery soup.* 6 like water: *a watery discharge.* 7 weak; thin; poor; pale: *a watery blue. adj.,* **wa ter i er, wa ter i est.**

watt (wot), measure of electric power, equal to the flow of one ampere under the pressure of one volt: *My lamp uses 60 watts; my toaster uses 1000 watts. n.* [from James *Watt*]

Watt (wot), **James,** 1736-1819, Scottish engineer and inventor. Watt perfected the steam engine. *n.*

watt age (wot′ij), amount of electric power, measured in watts, especially kilowatts. *n.*

watt-hour (wot′our′), measure of electrical energy, equal to the work done by one watt acting for one hour. *n.*

wat tle¹ (wot′l), 1 sticks interwoven with twigs or branches; framework of wicker: *a hut built of wattle.* 2 make (a fence, wall, roof, hut, etc.) of wattle. 3 twist or weave together (twigs, branches, etc.). 1 *n.,* 2,3 *v.,* **wattled, wat tling.** [Old English *watol*]

957

wattle

WATTLE wattle² of a turkey

wat tle² (wot′l), the red flesh hanging down from the throat of a chicken, turkey, etc. *n.* [origin uncertain]

wave (wāv), 1 a moving ridge or swell of water: *The raft rose and fell on the waves.* 2 any movement like this, especially a movement of particles, by which energy is transferred from one place to another. Light, heat, and sound travel in waves. Waves are usually measured by their length, amplitude, velocity, and frequency. 3 a swell or sudden increase in some condition, emotion, etc.: *A wave of cold weather is sweeping over the country. The announcement brought a wave of enthusiasm.* 4 move as waves do; move up and down; sway: *The tall grass waved in the breeze.* 5 move back and forth: *wave a flag. Wave your hand.* 6 to signal or direct by waving: *The stranded motorist waved a passing driver to the side of the road.* 7 a waving: *a wave of the hand.* 8 a curve or series of curves: *waves in a boy's hair.* 9 have a wavelike form: *Her hair waves naturally.* 10 give a wavelike form to: *wave one's hair.* 1-3,7, 8 *n.,* 4-6,9,10 *v.,* **waved, wav ing.** —**wave′like′,** *adj.*

Wave or **WAVE** (wāv), woman in the United States Navy other than a nurse. *n.* [from *WAVES,* abbreviation for *Women Accepted for Volunteer Emergency Service*]

wave length (wāv′lengkth′ *or* wāv′-length′), distance between one peak or crest of a wave of light, sound, etc., and the next corresponding peak or crest. The wavelengths of radio waves are measured in meters; the wavelengths of X rays are measured in billionths of an inch. *n.*

wave let (wāv′lit), a little wave. *n.*

wa ver (wā′vər), 1 move to and fro; flutter: *a wavering voice.* 2 vary in intensity; flicker: *a wavering light.* 3 be undecided; hesitate: *She is still wavering between staying for another week and having us visit her in town for a*

week. 4 become unsteady; begin to give way: *My determination began to waver.* 5 act of wavering. 1-4 *v.,* 5 *n.* —**wa′ver er,** *n.* —**wa′ver ing ly,** *adv.*

wav i ness (wā′vē nis), condition of being wavy. *n.*

wav y (wā′vē), having waves or curves: *wavy hair, a wavy line. adj.,* **wav i er, wav i est.**

wax¹ (waks), 1 a yellowish substance made by bees for constructing their honeycomb. Wax is hard when cold, but can be easily shaped when warm. 2 any substance like this. Most of the wax used for candles, for keeping air from jelly, etc., is really paraffin. Sealing wax and shoemaker's wax are other common waxes. 3 rub, stiffen, polish, etc., with wax or something like wax: *We wax the floor once a month.* 1,2 *n.,* pl. **wax es** for 2; 3 *v.* [Old English *weax*] —**wax′like′,** *adj.*

wax² (waks), 1 grow bigger and greater; increase: *The moon waxes till it becomes full, and then wanes.* 2 become: *The party waxed merry. v.* [Old English *weaxan*]

wax bean, a yellow string bean.

wax en (wak′sən), 1 made of wax. 2 like wax; smooth, soft, and pale: *Her skin was waxen. adj.*

wax i ness (wak′sē nis), condition of being waxy; waxy appearance. *n.*

wax myrtle, any of various shrubs or trees whose small berries are coated with wax. The bayberry is a wax myrtle.

wax paper, paper coated with paraffin.

wax wing (waks′wing′), a small bird with a showy crest and red markings at the tips of the wings. *n.*

wax work (waks′wėrk′), 1 figure or figures made of wax. 2 **waxworks,** pl. exhibition of figures made of wax. *n.*

wax y (wak′sē), 1 like wax. 2 made of wax; containing wax. *adj.,* **wax i er, wax i est.**

way (wā), 1 form or mode of doing; manner; style: *a new way of wearing one's hair.* 2 method; means: *Doctors are using new ways of preventing disease.* 3 point; feature; respect; detail: *This plan is bad in several ways.* 4 direction: *Look this way.* 5 a coming or going; moving along a course: *Our guide led the way through the museum.* 6 distance: *The sun is a long way off.* 7 means of moving along a course; road; path: *The children found a way through the forest.* 8 space for passing or going ahead: *Automobiles must make way for a fire engine.* 9 habit; custom: *Don't mind his teasing; it's just his way.* 10 one's wish; will: *A spoiled child wants his own way all the time.* 11 INFORMAL. condition; state: *The patient was in a bad way.* 12 movement; for-

ward motion: *The ship slowly gathered way.* 13 INFORMAL. district; area; region: *He lives out our way.* 14 **ways,** pl. timbers on which a ship is built and launched. 15 INFORMAL. at or to a (great) distance; far: *The cloud of smoke stretched way out to the pier.* 1-14 *n.,* 15 *adv.*

by the way, 1 while coming or going. 2 in that connection; incidentally.

by way of, 1 by the route of; through. 2 as; for: *By way of an answer he just nodded.*

give way, 1 make way; retreat; yield. 2 break down or fall. 3 abandon oneself to emotion: *give way to despair.*

in the way, being an obstacle, hindrance, etc.

make one's way, 1 go. 2 get ahead; succeed.

out of the way, 1 so as not to be an obstacle, hindrance, etc. 2 far from where most people live or go. 3 unusual; strange.

under way, going on; in motion, in progress.

way far er (wā′fer′ər *or* wā′far′ər), traveler. *n.*

way far ing (wā′fer′ing *or* wā′far′-ing), traveling. *adj.*

way laid (wā′lād′ *or* wā′lād′), past tense and past participle of **waylay.** *I waylaid her when she entered the meeting. v.*

way lay (wā′lā′ *or* wā′lā′), 1 lie in wait for; attack on the way: *Robin Hood waylaid travelers and robbed them.* 2 stop (a person) on his way: *Newspaper reporters waylaid the famous actor and asked him many questions. v.,* **way laid, way lay ing.** —**way′lay′er,** *n.*

Wayne (wān), **Anthony,** 1745-1796, American general in the Revolutionary War. *n.*

-ways, *suffix forming adverbs.* 1 in the direction or position of the _____: *Lengthways = in the direction of the length.* 2 in _____ manner: *Anyways = in any manner.* [*way* + *-s,* suffix used to form some adverbs]

way side (wā′sīd′), 1 edge of a road or path: *We ate lunch on the wayside.* 2 along the edge of a road or path: *We slept in a wayside inn.* 1 *n.,* 2 *adj.*

way ward (wā′wərd), 1 turning from the right way; disobedient; willful: *In a wayward mood, the boy ran away from home.* 2 irregular; unsteady. *adj.* —**way′ward ly,** *adv.* —**way′ward ness,** *n.*

we (wē), 1 the persons speaking: *We are glad to see you.* 2 the person speaking. An author, an editor, a king, or a judge sometimes uses *we* to mean *I. pron. pl.*

weak (wēk), 1 that can easily be broken, crushed, overcome, torn, etc.; not strong: *a weak board in the floor, a weak foundation, weak defenses.* 2 not having bodily strength or health: *The weak old man tottered as he walked.* 3 lacking power, authority, force, etc.: *a weak law.* 4 lacking moral strength or firmness: *a weak character.* 5 lacking mental power: *A weak mind is a feeble one.* 6 lacking or poor in amount, volume, loudness, taste, intensity, etc.: *Weak tea has less flavor than strong tea. A weak acid solution contains much water and little acid.* 7 lacking or poor in something specified: *She is still a little weak in spelling. adj.*

weak en (wē/kən), 1 make weak or weaker: *You can weaken tea by adding water.* 2 become weak or weaker: *We are almost to the top of the mountain; let's not weaken now. v.*

weak fish (wēk/fish/), a spiny-finned saltwater food fish with a tender mouth. *n., pl.* **weak fish es** or **weak fish.**

weak ling (wēk/ling), 1 a weak person or animal. 2 weak. 1 *n.,* 2 *adj.*

weak ly (wēk/lē), 1 in a weak manner. 2 weak; feeble; sickly. 1 *adv.,* 2 *adj.,* **weak li er, weak li est.**

weak-mind ed (wēk/mīn/did), 1 having or showing little intelligence; feeble-minded. 2 lacking firmness of mind. *adj.*

weak ness (wēk/nis), 1 a being weak; lack of power, force, or vigor: *Weakness kept him in bed.* 2 a weak point; slight fault: *Putting things off is her weakness.* 3 a liking that one is a little ashamed of; fondness: *She has a weakness for sweets. n., pl.* **weak ness es.**

weal[1] (wēl), well-being; prosperity: *Good citizens act for the public weal. n.* [Old English *wela* wealth, welfare]

weal[2] (wēl), streak or ridge on the skin made by a stick or whip; welt; wale; wheal. *n.* [Old English *walu*]

wealth (welth), 1 many valuable possessions; property; riches: *a man of wealth, the wealth of a city.* 2 all things that have money value; resources: *The wealth of our country includes its mines and forests as well as its factories.* 3 a large quantity; abundance: *a wealth of hair, a wealth of words. n.*

wealth y (wel/thē), having wealth; rich. *adj.,* **wealth i er, wealth i est.**

wean (wēn), 1 accustom (a child or young animal) to food other than its mother's milk. 2 accustom (a person) to do without something; cause to turn away: *wean someone from a bad habit. v.*

weap on (wep/ən), 1 any object or instrument used in fighting. Swords, spears, arrows, clubs, guns, cannons, and shields are man-made weapons. Animals use claws, horns, teeth, and stings as weapons. 2 any means of attack

or defense: *Drugs are effective weapons against many diseases. n.*

weap on less (wep/ən lis), having no weapon; unarmed. *adj.*

weap on ry (wep/ən rē), 1 the developing and producing of weapons. 2 weapons. *n.*

wear (wer *or* war), 1 have on the body: *wear a coat, wear a beard, wear black, wear a ring.* 2 have or show: *The empty old house wore an air of sadness.* 3 a wearing or a being worn: *Clothing for summer wear is being shown in the shops. This suit has been in constant wear for two years.* 4 things worn or to be worn; clothing: *The store sells children's wear.* 5 last long; give good service: *This material wears well. Their friendship wore well.* 6 lasting quality; good service: *There is still much wear in these shoes.* 7 use up; be used up: *The pencil is worn to a stub. The paint wears off the house.* 8 damage from use: *The rug shows wear.* 9 make by rubbing, scraping, washing away, etc.: *Walking wore a hole in my shoe.* 10 to tire; weary: *She was worn with toil and care.* 11 pass or go gradually: *It became hotter as the day wore on.* 1,2,5,7,9-11 *v.,* **wore, worn, wear ing;** 3,4,6,8 *n.* —**wear/er,** *n.*

wear down, 1 overcome by persistent effort. 2 reduce in height.

wear off, become less.

wear out, 1 wear until no longer fit for use. 2 use up. 3 tire out; weary: *They are worn out by too much work.*

wear i ly (wir/ə lē), in a weary manner: *The tired hikers walked slowly and wearily along the road. adv.*

wear i ness (wir/ē nis), weary condition; tired feeling: *After tramping all day the hikers were overcome with weariness. n.*

wear ing (wer/ing *or* war/ing), exhausting; tiring: *a very wearing trip, a wearing conversation. adj.*

wear i some (wir/ē səm), wearying; tiring; tiresome: *a long, boring, and wearisome tale. adj.*

wear y (wir/ē), 1 worn out; tired: *weary feet, a weary brain.* 2 causing tiredness; tiring: *a weary wait.* 3 having one's patience, tolerance, or liking exhausted. 4 make weary; tire: *Walking all day wearied the sightseers.* 5 become weary. 1-3 *adj.,* **wear i er, wear i est;** 4,5 *v.,* **wear ied, wear y ing.**

wea sel (wē/zəl), a small, flesh-eating mammal related to the mink and skunk,

weasel—about 16 in. long with tail

hat, āge, fär; let, ēqual, tėrm; it, īce; hot, ōpen, ôrder; oil, out; cup, půt, rüle; ch, child; ng, long; sh, she; th, thin; ᴛʜ, then; zh, measure;

ə represents *a* in about, *e* in taken, *i* in pencil, *o* in lemon, *u* in circus.

with a long, slender, furry body and short legs. Weasels have keen sight and smell and are known for their quickness and slyness. They feed on rats, mice, birds, other small animals, and eggs. *n.*

weath er (weᴛʜ/ər), 1 condition of the atmosphere with respect to temperature, moisture, cloudiness, etc.: *hot weather. The weather is very windy today in Chicago.* 2 windy, rainy, or stormy weather: *damage done by the weather.* 3 expose to the weather; wear or discolor by sun, rain, frost, etc.: *Wood turns gray if weathered for a long time.* 4 become discolored or worn by air, rain, sun, frost, etc. 5 go or come through safely: *The ship weathered the storm.* 6 sail to the windward of: *The ship weathered the cape.* 7 toward the wind; windward; of the side exposed to the wind: *It was very cold on the weather side of the ship.* 1,2 *n.,* 3-6 *v.,* 7 *adj.*

under the weather, INFORMAL. sick; ailing.

weath er-beat en (weᴛʜ/ər bēt/n), worn or hardened by the wind, rain, and other forces of the weather: *a seaman's weather-beaten face, a weather-beaten old barn. adj.*

weathercock

weath er cock (weᴛʜ/ər kok/), vane to show which way the wind is blowing, especially one in the shape of a rooster. *n.*

weath er glass (weᴛʜ/ər glas/), any of several instruments used to show the state of the atmosphere or predict the weather. A barometer is a weatherglass. *n., pl.* **weath er glass es.**

weath er ing (weᴛʜ/ər ing), destructive or discoloring action of air, water, frost, etc., especially on rocks. *n.*

weath er man (weᴛʜ/ər man/), ɪɴ-

adj. adjective	*n.* noun
adv. adverb	*prep.* preposition
conj. conjunction	*pron.* pronoun
interj. interjection	*v.* verb
sing. singular	*pl.* plural

FORMAL. man who forecasts the weather. *n., pl.* **weath er men.**

weath er proof (weŦH′ər prüf′), protected against rain, snow, or wind; able to stand exposure to all kinds of weather. *adj.*

weather strip, a narrow strip of cloth or metal to fill or cover the space between the door or window and the casing, so as to keep out rain, snow, and wind.

weather vane, vane.

weave (def. 4)—the three basic types: A, plain; B, twill; C, satin

weave (wēv), 1 form (threads or strips) into a thing or fabric. People weave thread into cloth, straw into hats, and reeds into baskets. 2 make out of thread, strips, etc. A spider weaves a web. *She is weaving a rug.* 3 work with a loom. 4 method or pattern of weaving: *Homespun is a cloth of coarse weave.* 5 combine into a whole: *The author wove three plots together into one story.* 6 make by combining parts: *The author wove a story from three plots.* 7 go by twisting and turning; move with a rocking or swaying motion: *The car ahead was weaving in and out of traffic.* 1-3, 5-7 *v.,* **wove, wo ven** or **wove, weaving;** 4 *n.*

weav er (wē′vər), 1 person who weaves. 2 person whose work is weaving. *n.*

web (web), 1 something woven. The fabric of delicate, silken threads spun by a spider is a web. 2 a whole piece of cloth while being woven or after being taken from the loom. 3 anything like a web, especially something that ensnares or entangles: *a web of lies.* 4 the skin joining the toes of swimming birds and certain other water animals. *n.*—**web′like′, adj.**

webbed (webd), 1 formed like a web or with a web. 2 having the toes joined by a web. Ducks have webbed feet. *adj.*

web bing (web′ing), 1 cloth woven into strong strips, used in upholstery

and for belts. 2 skin joining the toes, as in a duck's feet. *n.*

web foot (web′fut′), foot in which the toes are joined by a web. *n., pl.* **web-feet** (web′fēt′).

web-foot ed (web′fut′id), having the toes joined by a web. *adj.*

Web ster (web′stər), 1 **Daniel,** 1782-1852, American statesman and orator. 2 **Noah,** 1758-1843, American author and lexicographer. *n.*

wed (wed), 1 marry. 2 unite. *v.,* **wedded, wed ded** or **wed, wed ding.**

we'd (wēd), 1 we had. 2 we should. 3 we would.

Wed., Wednesday.

wed ded (wed′id), 1 married. 2 of marriage: *wedded bliss.* 3 united. 4 devoted. *adj.*

wed ding (wed′ing), 1 the marriage ceremony. 2 an anniversary of it. A golden wedding is the fiftieth anniversary of a marriage. *n.*

wedge (wej), 1 piece of wood or metal in the form of an inclined plane, thick at one end and tapering to a thin edge at the other, used in splitting logs, etc. It is a simple machine. 2 something shaped like a wedge or used like a wedge: *Wild geese fly in a wedge. Their grand party was an entering wedge into society.* 3 split or separate with a wedge. 4 fasten or tighten with a wedge. 5 thrust or pack in tightly; squeeze: *He wedged himself through the narrow window. The man's foot was wedged between the rocks.* 1,2 *n.,* 3-5 *v.,* **wedged, wedging.**

Wedg wood (wej′wud′), **Josiah,** 1730-1795, famous English potter. *n.*

wed lock (wed′lok), married life; marriage. *n.*

Wednes day (wenz′dē), the fourth day of the week, following Tuesday. *n.* [Old English *Wodnesdæg* Woden's day, from *Woden* + *dæg* day]

wee (wē), very small; tiny. *adj.,* **we er, we est.**

weed[1] (wēd), 1 a useless or troublesome plant: *Weeds choked out the vegetables and flowers in the garden.* 2 take weeds out of: *Please weed the garden now.* 3 take out weeds. 1 *n.,* 2,3 *v.* [Old English *wēod*] —**weed′like′, adj.**

weed out, 1 free from what is useless, or worthless. 2 remove as useless or worthless.

weed[2] (wēd), 1 **weeds,** *pl.* mourning garments: *a widow's weeds.* 2 OLD USE. garment. *n.* [Old English *wǣd*]

weed er (wē′dər), 1 person who

webbed (def. 2) webbed foot of a duck

weeds. 2 tool or machine for digging up weeds. *n.*

weed y (wē′dē), 1 full of weeds: *a weedy garden.* 2 of or like weeds. 3 thin and lanky; weak. *adj.,* **weed i er, weed i est.**

week (wēk), 1 seven days, one after another. 2 the time from Sunday through Saturday: *She is away most of the week but comes home on Sunday.* 3 the working days of a seven-day period: *A school week is usually five days. n.*

week day (wēk′dā′), any day of the week except Sunday or (now often) Saturday. *n.*

week end (wēk′end′), 1 Saturday and Sunday as a time for recreation, visiting, etc.: *a weekend in the country.* 2 spend a weekend. 1 *n.,* 2 *v.*

EFFORT

RESISTANCE   RESISTANCE

MOTION

wedge (def. 1)

week ly (wēk′lē), 1 of a week; for a week; lasting a week: *a weekly wage of $150.* 2 done or happening once a week: *She writes a weekly letter to her grandmother.* 3 once each week; every week. 4 newspaper or magazine published once a week. 1,2 *adj.,* 3 *adv.,* 4 *n., pl.* **week lies.**

ween (wēn), OLD USE. think; suppose; believe; expect. *v.*

weep (wēp), 1 shed tears; cry: *She wept for joy when she won the award.* 2 shed tears for; mourn: *No one wept him when he died.* 3 let fall or flow in drops; shed: *weep bitter tears.* 4 be very damp; drip. *v.,* **wept, weep ing.** —**weep′er, n.**

weep ing (wē′ping), 1 that weeps. 2 having thin, drooping branches: *a weeping willow. adj.*

wee vil (wē′vəl), any of a group of small beetles that have long snouts and feed on plants. The larvae of the weevil feed on and destroy grain, nuts, cotton, fruit, etc. *n.*

weft (weft), woof. *n.*

weigh (wā), 1 find out how heavy a thing is. We weigh persons, cattle, coal, and many other things. 2 measure by weight: *The grocer weighed out five pounds of potatoes.* 3 have as a measure by weight: *I weigh 110 pounds.* 4 bend by weight; burden: *The boughs of the apple tree are weighed down with fruit. She is weighed down with many troubles.*

960

5 bear down; be a burden: *Don't let the mistake weigh on your mind.* 6 have importance or influence: *Your excuses will not weigh with us.* 7 balance in the mind; consider carefully: *weigh both sides of an argument. She weighed her words before speaking.* 8 lift up (an anchor): *The ship weighed anchor and sailed away.* v. —**weigh′er,** n.

weigh in, find out one's weight before a contest.

weight (wāt), 1 how heavy a thing is; the amount a thing weighs: *The dog's weight is 50 pounds.* 2 quality that makes all things tend toward the center of the earth; heaviness: *Gas has hardly any weight.* 3 system of units for expressing weight: *avoirdupois weight.* 4 unit of such a system. 5 piece of metal used in weighing things: *a pound weight.* 6 quantity that has a certain weight: *a half-ounce weight of gold dust.* 7 a heavy thing or mass: *A weight keeps the papers in place.* 8 load; burden: *The pillars support the weight of the roof. Your good news has taken a weight off my mind.* 9 load down; burden: *weighted with troubles.* 10 add weight to; put weight on: *The elevator is weighted too heavily.* 11 influence; importance; value: *the weight of public opinion.* 1-8,11 n., 9,10 v.

weight i ly (wā′tl ē), in a weighty manner; heavily. *adv.*

weight less (wāt′lis), 1 having little or no weight: *weightless snow.* 2 being free from the pull of gravity: *Astronauts know what it is like to float in space while in a weightless condition.* *adj.* —**weight′less ly,** *adv.* —**weight′less ness,** n.

weight y (wā′tē), 1 heavy. 2 too heavy; burdensome: *weighty cares of state.* 3 important; influential: *a weighty speaker.* *adj.,* **weight i er, weight i est.**

weir (wir), 1 dam in a river. 2 fence of stakes or broken branches put in a stream or channel to catch fish. *n.*

weird (wird), 1 unearthly or mysterious; wild; strange: *They were awakened by a weird shriek.* 2 IN-FORMAL. odd; fantastic; queer: *The shadows made weird figures on the wall.* *adj.* —**weird′ly,** *adv.*

wel come (wel′kəm), 1 greet kindly; give a friendly reception to: *We always welcome guests at our house.* 2 a kind or friendly reception: *You will always have a welcome here.* 3 receive gladly: *We welcome new ideas and suggestions.* 4 gladly received: *a welcome letter, a welcome visitor, a welcome rest.* 5 gladly or freely permitted: *You are welcome to pick the flowers.* 6 free to enjoy courtesies, etc., without obligation (said in response to thanks): *You*

are *quite welcome.* 7 exclamation of friendly greeting: *Welcome, everyone!* 1,3 *v.,* **wel comed, wel com ing;** 2 *n.,* 4-6 *adj.,* 7 *interj.*

wear out one's welcome, visit a person too often or too long.

weld (weld), 1 join (pieces of metal) together by heating the parts that touch to the melting point, so that they can be hammered or pressed together or flow together and become one piece: *She welded the broken rod.* 2 a welded joint. 3 act of welding. 4 unite closely: *Working together for a month welded them into a strong team.* 5 be welded or be capable of being welded: *Steel welds; wood does not. Copper welds easily.* 1,4,5 *v.,* 2,3 *n.* —**weld′er,** n.

wel fare (wel′fer′ or wel′far′), health, happiness, and prosperity; condition of being or doing well: *My uncle asked about the welfare of everyone in our family.* n.

on welfare, receiving aid from the government because of hardship or need.

welfare state, state whose government provides for the welfare of its citizens through social security, unemployment insurance, free medical treatment, etc.

welfare work, work done to improve the conditions of people who need help, carried on by government, private organizations, or individuals.

wel kin (wel′kən), OLD USE. the sky. *n.*

well[1] (wel), 1 in a satisfactory, favorable, or good manner; all right: *The job was well done. Is everything going well at school?* 2 satisfactory; good; right: *It is well you came along.* 3 thoroughly: *Shake the medicine well before taking it. He knew the lesson well.* 4 to a considerable degree; much: *The fair brought in well over a hundred dollars.* 5 fairly; reasonably: *You can't well argue today for what you were against yesterday.* 6 in good health: *I am very well.* 7 expression used to show mild surprise or merely to fill in: *Well! Well! Here he is. Well, I'm not sure.* 1,3-5 *adv.,* **better, best;** 2,6 *adj.,* 7 *interj.* [Old English *wel*]

as well, 1 also; besides. 2 equally.

as well as, 1 in addition to; besides. 2 as much as.

well[2] (wel), 1 hole dug or bored in the ground to get water, oil, gas, etc.: *I pumped a bucket of water from the well.* 2 spring, fountain, or source: *This book is a well of ideas.* 3 something like a well in shape or use. The reservoir of a fountain pen is a well. 4 shaft for stairs or elevator, extending vertically through the floors of a building. 5 to spring, rise, or gush: *Tears welled up in her eyes. Water wells from a spring*

hat, āge, fär; let, ēqual, tėrm;
it, īce; hot, ōpen, ôrder;
oil, out; cup, pùt, rüle; ch, child;
ng, long; sh, she; th, thin;
ŦH, then; zh, measure;

ə represents *a* in about,
e in taken, *i* in pencil,
o in lemon, *u* in circus.

beneath the rock. 1-4 *n.,* 5 *v.* [Old English *welle,* stem of *weallan* to boil]

we'll (wēl), 1 we shall. 2 we will.

well a day (wel′ə dā′), OLD USE. alas! *interj.*

well a way (wel′ə wā′), OLD USE. alas! *interj.*

well-bal anced (wel′bal′ənst), 1 rightly balanced, adjusted, or regulated: *A well-balanced diet includes plenty of fruit and vegetables.* 2 sensible; sane: *She has a well-balanced outlook on life.* *adj.*

well-be haved (wel′bi hāvd′), showing good manners or conduct. *adj.*

well-be ing (wel′bē′ing), health and happiness; welfare. *n.*

well born (wel′bôrn′), belonging to a good family. *adj.*

well-bred (wel′bred′), well brought up; having or showing good manners. *adj.*

well-de fined (wel′di fīnd′), rightly, properly, or definitely marked. *adj.*

well-de vel oped (wel′di vel′əpt), 1 developed or worked out well: *a well-developed plan.* 2 showing good development: *The athlete had a well-developed body.* *adj.*

well-done (wel′dun′), 1 performed well; skillfully done: *a well-done job, a well-done translation.* 2 (of meat) thoroughly cooked: *a well-done steak.* *adj.*

well-fed (wel′fed′), showing the result of good feeding; fat; plump. *adj.*

well-formed (wel′fôrmd′), rightly or finely formed; shapely. *adj.*

well-found ed (wel′foun′did), rightly or justly founded: *a well-founded faith in education.* *adj.*

well-groomed (wel′grümd′ or wel′-grümd′), well cared for; neat and trim. *adj.*

well-ground ed (wel′groun′did), 1 based on good reasons. 2 thoroughly instructed in the fundamental principles of a subject. *adj.*

well-in formed (wel′in fôrmd′), 1 having reliable or full information on a subject. 2 having information on a wide variety of subjects. *adj.*

Wel ling ton (wel′ing tən), 1 first Duke of, 1769-1852, British general

adj. adjective	*n.* noun
adv. adverb	*prep.* preposition
conj. conjunction	*pron.* pronoun
interj. interjection	*v.* verb
sing. singular	*pl.* plural

who defeated Napoleon I at Waterloo in 1815. 2 capital of New Zealand, on the S coast of North Island. *n.*

well-kept (wel′kept′), well cared for; carefully tended. *adj.*

well-known (wel′nōn′), 1 clearly or fully known. 2 familiar. 3 generally or widely known. *adj.*

well-made (wel′mād′), skillfully made; sturdily built: *a well-made old desk. adj.*

well-man nered (wel′man′ərd), having good manners; polite; courteous: *The well-mannered boy always remembered to say "please" and "thank you." adj.*

well-mean ing (wel′mē′ning), 1 having good intentions. 2 caused by good intentions. *adj.*

well-nigh (wel′nī′), very nearly; almost. *adv.*

well-off (wel′ôf′), 1 in a good condition or position. 2 fairly rich. *adj.*

well-pre served (wel′pri zėrvd′), showing few signs of age. *adj.*

well-read (wel′red′), having read much; knowing a great deal about books and literature. *adj.*

Wells (welz), H(erbert) G(eorge), 1866-1946, English writer of science fiction, history, and essays. *n.*

well spring (wel′spring′), 1 fountainhead. 2 source of supply that never fails; source. *n.*

well-thought-of (wel′thôt′uv′ or wel′thôt′ov′), highly respected; esteemed. *adj.*

well-timed (wel′tīmd′), at the right time; timely. *adj.*

well-to-do (wel′tə dü′), having enough money to live well; prosperous. *adj.*

well-wish er (wel′wish′ər), person who wishes well to a person, cause, etc. *n.*

well-worn (wel′wôrn′), 1 much worn by use. 2 used too much; trite; stale. *adj.*

Welsh (welsh *or* welch), 1 of or having to do with Wales, its people, or their Celtic language. 2 the people of Wales. 3 their language. 1 *adj.*, 2 *n.pl.*, 3 *n.sing.*

Welsh man (welsh′mən *or* welch′mən), man born or living in Wales. *n., pl.* **Welsh men.**

Welsh rabbit or **Welsh rarebit,** dish of cheese melted and cooked with milk, egg, etc., and poured over toast or crackers; rarebit.

welt (welt), 1 a strip of leather between the upper part and the sole of a shoe. 2 put a welt on. 3 a raised streak or ridge made on the skin by a stick or whip. 4 INFORMAL. beat severely. 1,3 *n.*, 2,4 *v.*

wel ter (wel′tər), 1 roll or tumble about; wallow. 2 a rolling or tumbling about. 3 a surging or confused mass: *All we saw was a welter of arms, legs, and bodies.* 4 confusion; commotion. 5 be drenched. 1,5 *v.*, 2-4 *n.*

wel ter weight (wel′tər wāt′), boxer who weighs more than 135 and less than 147 pounds. *n.*

wen (wen), a harmless tumor of the skin. *n.*

wench (wench), 1 girl or young woman. 2 a woman servant. *n., pl.* **wenches.**

wend (wend), 1 direct (one's way): *We wended our way home.* 2 go. *v.*

went (went), past tense of **go.** *I went home promptly after school. v.*

wept (wept), past tense and past participle of **weep.** *The children wept over the loss of their dog. v.*

were (wėr), 1 form of the verb **be** used with *you, we, they* or any plural noun to indicate the past tense. *The officer's orders were obeyed.* 2 form of **be** used to express something as possible or as a condition but not as an actual thing. *If I were rich, I would help the poor. Would you, if you were rich? v.*

we're (wir), we are.

weren't (wėrnt), were not.

were wolf (wir′wulf′), (in folklore) a person who has been changed into a wolf or one who can change himself into a wolf. *n., pl.* **were wolves** (wir′-wulvz′). Also, **werwolf.**

wert (wėrt), OLD USE. were. "Thou wert" means "you were." *v.*

wer wolf (wir′wulf′), werewolf. *n., pl.* **wer wolves** (wir′wulvz′).

Wes ley (wes′lē), 1 **John,** 1703-1791, English clergyman who founded the Methodist Church. 2 his brother, **Charles,** 1707-1788, English clergyman and helper of John. He wrote many hymns. *n.*

Wes ley an (wes′lē ən), member of the church founded by John Wesley; Methodist. *n.*

Wes sex (wes′iks), ancient kingdom in S England from A.D. 500? to 886. *n.*

west (west), 1 direction of the sunset. 2 toward the west; farther toward the west: *We took the west road (adj.). Walk west three blocks (adv.).* 3 from the west: *a warm, west wind.* 4 in the west: *the west wing of a house.* 5 Also, **West.** the part of any country toward the west. 6 **West, a** the western part of the United States. **b** the countries in Europe and America as distinguished from those in Asia. 1,5,6 *n.*, 2-4 *adj.*, 2 *adv.*

west of, farther west than: *Kansas is west of Pennsylvania.*

West Berlin, the W part of Berlin belonging to West Germany. It is located in East Germany and separated from East Berlin by a wall.

west bound (west′bound′), going west. *adj.*

west er ly (wes′tər lē), 1 toward the west. 2 from the west: *a westerly wind.* 3 wind that blows from the west. 1,2 *adj., adv.*, 3 *n., pl.* **west er lies.**

west ern (wes′tərn), 1 toward the west. 2 from the west. 3 of or in the west. 4 INFORMAL. story, motion picture, or television show dealing with life in the western part of the United States, especially cowboy life. 5 **Western, a** of or in the western part of the United States. **b** of or in the countries of Europe and America. 1-3,5 *adj.*, 4 *n.*

Western Australia, state in W Australia. *Capital:* Perth.

west ern er (wes′tər nər), 1 person born or living in the west. 2 **Westerner,** person born or living in the western part of the United States. *n.*

Western Hemisphere, the half of the world that includes North and South America.

west ern most (wes′tərn mōst), farthest west. *adj.*

West Germany, country in central Europe, consisting of the part of Germany which came under American, British, and French control at the end of World War II. *Capital:* Bonn.

West Indian, 1 of or having to do with the West Indies. 2 person born or living in the West Indies.

West Indies, long chain of islands between Florida and South America; Greater Antilles, Lesser Antilles, and the Bahama Islands. See **Caribbean Sea** for map.

West ing house (wes′ting hous), **George,** 1846-1914, American inventor. *n.*

West Ir i an (ir′ē än), W part of New Guinea, belonging to Indonesia.

West min ster Abbey (west′min′-stər), church in London where the kings and queens of Great Britain are crowned and in which many English monarchs and famous men are buried.

West Point, college for training cadets to become officers in the United States Army. It is located on the Hudson River in SE New York State.

West Virginia, one of the southeastern states of the United States. *Capital:* Charleston.

west ward (west′wərd), 1 toward the

west; west: *We walked westward (adv.). The orchard is on the westward slope of the hill (adj.).* 2 a westward part, direc-/tion, or point. 1 *adv., adj.,* 2 *n.*

west wards (west/wərdz), westward. *adv.*

wet (wet), 1 covered or soaked with water or other liquid: *wet hands, a wet sponge.* 2 watery: *eyes wet with tears.* 3 not yet dry: *The paint is wet; don't touch it.* 4 make or become wet: *Wet the cloth before you wipe off the window. Your good suit will wet in the rain.* 5 water or other liquid. 6 rainy: *wet weather.* 7 wetness; rain: *Come in out of the wet.* 8 INFORMAL. permitting the sale of alcoholic drinks: *a wet town or district.* 1-3,6,8 *adj.,* **wet ter, wet test;** 4 *v.,* **wet** or **wet ted, wet ting;** 5,7 *n.* —**wet/ly,** *adv.* —**wet/ness,** *n.*

wet blanket, person or thing that has a discouraging or depressing effect.

wet ter (wet/ər), person or thing that wets. *n.*

we've (wēv), we have.

whack (hwak), 1 INFORMAL. a sharp, resounding blow. 2 INFORMAL. to strike with such a blow: *The batter whacked at the ball and hit it out of the park.* 3 SLANG. trial or attempt: *I'd like to have a whack at flying in a glider to see what it's like.* 1,3 *n.,* 2 *v.*

whale[1] (hwāl), 1 mammal shaped like a huge fish and living in the sea. Men get oil and whalebone from whales. 2 hunt and catch whales. 1 *n., pl.* **whales** or **whale;** 2 *v.,* **whaled, whal ing.** [Old English *hwæl*]

a whale of, INFORMAL. a very excellent, big, or impressive kind of: *a whale of a good time, a whale of a party.*

whale[2] (hwāl), INFORMAL. whip severely; beat; thrash. *v.,* **whaled, whal ing.** [apparently a different form of *wale,* Old English *walu* mark of a lash, weal]

whale boat (hwāl/bōt/), a long, narrow rowboat, pointed at both ends, formerly much used in whaling. *n.*

whale bone (hwāl/bōn/), an elastic, horny substance growing in place of teeth in the upper jaw of certain whales; baleen. Thin strips of whalebone were formerly used for stiffening corsets and dresses. *n.*

whal er (hwā/lər), 1 hunter of whales. 2 ship used for hunting and catching whales. *n.*

whal ing (hwā/ling), the hunting and catching of whales. *n.*

wharf (hwôrf), platform built on the shore or out from the shore, beside which ships can load and unload. *n., pl.* **wharves** or **wharfs.**

wharves (hwôrvz), a plural of **wharf.** *n.*

what (hwot or hwut; *unstressed* hwət), 1 *What* is used in asking questions about persons or things. *What is your name? (pron.). What time is it? (adj.).* 2 that which: *I know what you mean (pron.). Put back what money is left (adj.).* 3 whatever; anything that; any that: *Do what you please (pron.). Take what supplies you will need (adj.).* 4 how much; how: *What does it matter?* 5 partly: *What with the wind and what with the rain, our walk was spoiled.* 6 *What* is often used to show surprise, doubt, anger, liking, etc., or to add emphasis. *What a pity! (adj.). What happy times! (adv.). What! are you late again? (interj.).* 1-3 *pron.,* 1-3,6 *adj.,* 4-6 *adv.,* 6 *interj.*

and what not, and all kinds of other things: *She collects buttons, beads, and what not.*

what if, what would happen if: *What if it rains on the day of the game?*

what's what, INFORMAL. the true state of affairs: *to know what's what.*

what e'er (hwot er/ or hwut er/), whatever. *pron., adj.*

what ev er (hwot ev/ər or hwut-ev/ər), 1 anything that: *Do whatever you like.* 2 any that: *Take whatever books you need.* 3 no matter who; at all: *Any person whatever can tell you the way.* 4 no matter what: *Whatever happens, she is safe (pron.). Whatever excuse he makes will not be believed (adj.).* 5 *Whatever* is used for emphasis instead of *what. Whatever do you mean?* 1,4,5 *pron.,* 2-4 *adj.*

what not (hwot/not/ or hwut/not/), a stand with several shelves for books, ornaments, etc. *n.*

what's (hwots or hwuts), 1 what is: *What's the latest news?* 2 what has: *What's been going on here lately?*

what so ev er (hwot/sō ev/ər or hwut/sō ev/ər), whatever. *pron., adj.*

wheal (hwēl), weal; welt. *n.*

wheat (hwēt), 1 the grain of a common cereal grass, used to make flour. 2 the plant yielding this grain. *n.*

wheat en (hwēt/n), made of wheat: *wheaten flour. adj.*

wheat germ, the tiny germ or embryo of the wheat kernel, separated in the milling of flour and used as a cereal, etc. It is rich in vitamins.

whee dle (hwē/dl), 1 persuade by flattery, smooth words, caresses, etc.; coax: *The children wheedled their parents into letting them go to the picnic.*

wharf

hat, āge, fär; let, ēqual, tėrm; it, īce; hot, ōpen, ôrder; oil, out; cup, pùt, rüle; ch, child; ng, long; sh, she; th, thin; ᵺH, then; zh, measure;

ə represents *a* in about, *e* in taken, *i* in pencil, *o* in lemon, *u* in circus.

2 get by wheedling: *They finally wheedled the secret out of me. v.,* **wheedled, whee dling.**

wheel (hwēl), 1 a round frame turning on a pin or shaft in the center. 2 any instrument, machine, apparatus, etc., shaped or moving like a wheel. A bicycle is often called a wheel. A ship's wheel is used in steering. Clay is shaped into dishes on a potter's wheel. 3 any force thought of as moving or propelling: *the wheels of government.* 4 turn: *The rider wheeled his horse about. I wheeled around suddenly.* 5 move on wheels: *The workman was wheeling a load of bricks on a wheelbarrow.* 6 INFORMAL. ride a bicycle. 1-3 *n.,* 4-6 *v.*

at the wheel, 1 at the steering wheel of an automobile. 2 at the wheel of a ship. 3 in control.

wheel and axle

WHEEL
AXLE
EFFORT
RESISTANCE
MOTION

wheel and axle, axle on which a wheel is fastened, used to lift weights by winding a rope onto the axle as the wheel is turned. It is a simple machine.

wheel bar row (hwēl/bar/ō), a small vehicle which has one wheel and two handles. A wheelbarrow holds a small load which one man can push. *n.*

wheel chair (hwēl/cher/ or hwēl/-char/), chair mounted on wheels, used especially by invalids. It can be propelled by the person who is sitting in the chair. *n.*

wheeled (hwēld), having a wheel or wheels. *adj.*

wheel house (hwēl/hous/), pilothouse. *n., pl.* **wheel hous es** (hwēl/-hou/ziz).

wheel wright (hwēl/rīt/), man whose work is making or repairing wheels, carriages, and wagons. *n.*

wheeze (hwēz), 1 breathe with difficulty and a whistling sound. 2 a whis-

wheezy

tling sound caused by difficult breathing. **3** make a sound like this: *The old engine wheezed.* 1,3 *v.,* **wheezed, wheez ing;** 2 *n.*

wheez y (hwē′zē), wheezing: *The old dog was fat and wheezy. adj.,* **wheez i-er, wheez i est.**

whelk (hwelk), a sea mollusk with a spiral shell, used for food in Europe. *n.*

whelk—shell,
2 to 3 in. long

whelm (hwelm), overwhelm. *v.*

whelp (hwelp), **1** puppy or cub; young dog, wolf, bear, lion, tiger, etc. **2** give birth to whelps. **3** a good-for-nothing boy or young man. 1,3 *n.,* 2 *v.*

when (hwen), **1** at what time: *When does school close?* **2** at the time that: *Stand up when your name is called.* **3** at any time that: *The dog comes when it is called.* **4** at which time; and then: *We had just decided to go out for a walk, when it began to rain.* **5** although: *We have only three books when we need five.* **6** what time; which time: *Since when have they had a new car?* **7** the time or occasion: *the when and where of an act.* 1 *adv.,* 2-5 *conj.,* 6 *pron.,* 7 *n.*

whence (hwens), from what place, source, or cause; from where: *Whence do you come?* (*adv.*). *Whence has he learned so much about our affairs?* (*adv.*). *They returned to the country whence they came* (*conj.*). *adv., conj.*

whence so ev er (hwens′sō ev′ər), from whatever place, source, or cause. *conj.*

when e'er (hwen er′), whenever. *conj., adv.*

when ev er (hwen ev′ər), when; at whatever time; at any time that: *Please come whenever you wish* (*conj.*). *You may come whenever possible* (*adv.*). *conj., adv.*

when so ev er (hwen′sō ev′ər), whenever; at whatever time. *conj., adv.*

where (hwer *or* hwar), **1** in what place; at what place: *Where do you live? Where is he?* **2** to what place: *Where are you going?* **3** from what place: *Where did you get that story?* **4** what place: *Where did it come from?* **5** in which; at

which: *That is the house where I was born.* **6** to which: *the place where he is going.* **7** in what way; in what respect: *Where is the harm in trying?* **8** in the place in which; at the place at which: *Your coat is where you left it.* **9** in any place in which; at any place at which: *Use the salve where the pain is felt.* **10** any place to which: *I will go where you go.* **11** in or at which place: *They came to the town, where they stayed for the night.* **12** place or scene. 1-3,5-7 *adv.,* 4,12 *n.,* 8-11 *conj.*

where a bouts (hwer′ə bouts′ *or* hwar′ə bouts′), **1** where; near what place: *Whereabouts can I find a doctor?* (*adv.*). *We did not know whereabouts we were* (*conj.*). **2** place where a person or thing is: *Do you know the whereabouts of the cottage?* 1 *adv., conj.,* 2 *n.*

where as (hwer az′ *or* hwar az′), **1** on the contrary; but; while: *Some children like school, whereas others do not.* **2** considering that; since: *"Whereas the people of the colonies have been grieved and burdened with taxes. . . ." conj.*

where at (hwer at′ *or* hwar at′), at what; at which. *adv., conj.*

where by (hwer bī′ *or* hwar bī′), by what; by which: *There is no other way whereby she can do it. adv., conj.*

where fore (hwer′fôr *or* hwar′fôr), **1** for what reason? why? **2** for which reason; therefore; so. **3** for what reason; why. **4** reason: *I don't want to hear all the whys and wherefores.* 1,2 *adv.,* 3 *conj.,* 4 *n.*

where in (hwer in′ *or* hwar in′), in what; in which; how. *adv., conj.*

where of (hwer uv′, hwar uv′, hwer-ov′, *or* hwar ov′), of what; of which; of whom: *Solomon knew whereof he spoke. adv., conj.*

where on (hwer ôn′, hwar ôn′, hwer-on′, *or* hwar on′), on which; on what: *Summer cottages occupy the land whereon the old farmhouse stood. adv., conj.*

where so ev er (hwer′sō ev′ər *or* hwar′sō ev′ər), wherever. *conj., adv.*

where to (hwer tü′ *or* hwar tü′), **1** to what; to which; where: *He went to that place whereto he had been sent.* **2** for what purpose; why: *Whereto do you lay up riches? adv., conj.*

where up on (hwer′ə pôn′, hwar′ə-pôn′, hwer′ə pon′, *or* hwar′ə pon′), **1** upon what; upon which. **2** at which; after which. *adv., conj.*

wher ev er (hwer ev′ər *or* hwar-ev′ər), where; to whatever place; in whatever place: *Sit wherever you like* (*conj.*). *Wherever are you going?* (*adv.*). *conj., adv.*

where with (hwer wiŦн′, hwar-wiŦн′, hwer with′, *or* hwar with′), with

what; with which: *Wherewith shall we be fed? adv., conj.*

where with al (hwer′wi Ŧнôl *or* hwar′wi Ŧнôl *for 1;* hwer′wi Ŧнôl′ *or* hwar′wi Ŧнôl′ *for 2*), **1** means, supplies, or money needed: *Has she the wherewithal to pay for the trip?* **2** OLD USE. wherewith. 1 *n.,* 2 *adv., conj.*

wher ry (hwer′ē), a light, shallow row-boat for carrying passengers and goods on rivers. *n., pl.* **wher ries.**

whet (hwet), **1** sharpen by rubbing: *whet a knife.* **2** make keen or eager; stimulate: *The smell of food whetted my appetite.* **3** act of whetting. 1,2 *v.,* **whet ted, whet ting;** 3 *n.*

wheth er (hweŦн′ər), **1** *Whether* is used in expressing a choice or an alternative. *It matters little whether we go or stay. I do not know whether to work or rest.* **2** either: *Whether sick or well, she is always cheerful.* **3** if: *I asked whether I should finish the work. conj.*

whet stone (hwet′stōn′), stone for sharpening knives or tools. *n.*

whew (hwyü), exclamation of surprise, dismay, etc.: *Whew! it's cold! interj., n.*

whey (hwā), the watery part of milk that separates from the curd when milk sours and becomes coagulated or when cheese is made. *n.*

which (hwich), **1** *Which* is used in asking questions about persons or things. *Which is the best plan?* (*pron.*). *Which book do you want to read?* (*adj.*). **2** *Which* is also used in connecting a group of words with some word in the sentence. *Read the book which you have* (*pron.*). *Be careful which way you turn* (*adj.*). **3** the one that; any that: *Here are three boxes. Choose which you like best.* 1-3 *pron.,* 1,2 *adj.*

which ev er (hwich ev′ər), **1** any one; any that: *Take whichever you want* (*pron.*). *Buy whichever hat you like* (*adj.*). **2** no matter which: *Whichever you take will be becoming* (*pron.*). *Whichever side wins, I shall be satisfied* (*adj.*). *pron., adj.*

which so ev er (hwich′sō ev′ər), whichever. *pron., adj.*

whiff (hwif), **1** a slight gust; puff; breath: *A whiff of smoke blew in my face. A whiff of fresh air cleared my head.* **2** to blow or puff. 1 *n.,* 2 *v.*

whif fle tree (hwif′əl trē′), the hori-zontal crossbar of a carriage or wagon, to which the traces of a harness are fastened; singletree. *n.* Also, **whipple-tree.**

Whig (hwig), **1** member of a former political party in Great Britain that fa-vored reforms and opposed the Tory party. The Whig party became the Lib-eral party of Great Britain. **2** an Ameri-can who opposed British rule over the colonies at the time of the Revolutionary War. 3 member of a political party in the United States that was formed about 1834 in opposition to the Democratic Party. It was succeeded by the Republican Party about 1855. 4 of or having to do with Whigs. 1-3 *n.*, 4 *adj.*

while (hwīl), 1 time; space of time: *He kept us waiting a long while. The postman came a while ago.* 2 **the while,** during the time: *They danced and sang the while.* 3 during the time that; in the time that: *While I was speaking he said nothing. Summer is pleasant while it lasts.* 4 although: *While I like the color of the hat, I do not like its shape.* 5 pass or spend in some easy, pleasant manner: *The children while away many afternoons on the beach.* 1,2 *n.*, 3,4 *conj.*, 5 *v.*, **whiled, whil ing.**

worth one's while, worth one's time, attention, or effort: *If you help me with the painting, I'll make it worth your while—I'll pay you ten dollars.*

whi lom (hwī′ləm), OLD USE. 1 former. 2 formerly; once. 1 *adj.*, 2 *adv.*

whilst (hwīlst), while. *conj.*

whim (hwim), a sudden fancy or notion; freakish or capricious idea or desire: *I had a whim for gardening, but it didn't last.* *n.*

whim per (hwim′pər), 1 cry with low, broken sounds, in the way that a sick child or dog does. 2 a whimpering cry. 3 complain in a peevish, childish way; whine. 1,3 *v.*, 2 *n.*

whim sey (hwim′zē), whimsy. *n.*, *pl.* **whim seys.**

whim si cal (hwim′zə kəl), having many odd notions or fancies; fanciful; odd. *adj.* —**whim′si cal ly,** *adv.*

whim si cal i ty (hwim′zə kal′ə tē), 1 whimsical character or quality. 2 a whimsical notion, speech, act, etc. *n.*, *pl.* **whim si cal i ties.**

whim sy (hwim′zē), 1 an odd or fanciful notion. 2 odd or fanciful humor; quaintness: *"Alice in Wonderland" is full of whimsy. n., pl.* **whim sies.** Also, **whimsey.**

whine (hwīn), 1 make a low, complaining cry or sound: *The dog whined to go out with us.* 2 a low, complaining cry or sound. 3 complain in a peevish, childish way: *Some people are always whining about trifles.* 4 say with a whine. 1,3,4 *v.*, **whined, whining;** 2 *n.*

whin ny (hwin′ē), 1 the sound that a horse makes. 2 make such a sound. 1 *n.*, *pl.* **whin nies;** 2 *v.*, **whin nied, whin ny ing.**

whip (hwip), 1 thing to strike or beat with, usually a stick or handle with a flexible cord at the end. Lawbreakers used to be punished with a whip. 2 strike or beat with or as with a whip;

lash: *whip a horse to make it gallop. Rain whipped the pavement.* 3 a blow or stroke with or as with a whip. 4 move, put, or pull quickly and suddenly: *whip off a coat, whip out a knife. The child whipped behind the tree to hide from us.* 5 INFORMAL. defeat in a fight, contest, etc.: *The mayor whipped his opponent in the election.* 6 beat (cream, eggs, etc.) to a froth. 7 dessert made by beating cream, eggs, etc., into a froth. 8 rouse; incite: *whip up some enthusiasm.* 1,3,7 *n.*, 2,4-6,8 *v.*, **whipped** or **whipt, whip ping.** —**whip′like′,** *adj.*

whip hand, 1 the hand that holds the whip in driving. 2 position of control; advantage: *A clever person often gets the whip hand over others.*

whip lash (hwip′lash′), lash of a whip. *n.*, *pl.* **whip lash es.**

whip per-snap per (hwip′ər-snap′ər), an insignificant person who thinks he is smart or important. *n.*

whip pet (hwip′it), a very swift dog that looks somewhat like a small greyhound, often used in racing. *n.*

whip ple tree (hwip′əl trē′), whiffletree. *n.*

whip poor will (hwip′ər wil′ or hwip′ər wil), a North American bird whose call sounds somewhat like its name. It is active at night or twilight. *n.*

whir (hwėr), 1 noise that sounds like whir-r-r: *the whir of machinery.* 2 operate or move with such a noise: *The motor whirs.* 1 *n.*, 2 *v.*, **whirred, whir ring.** Also, **whirr.**

whirl (hwėrl), 1 turn or swing round and round; spin: *The leaves whirled in the wind.* 2 move round and round: *whirl a lasso. We whirled about the room.* 3 move or carry quickly: *We were whirled away in an airplane.* 4 a whirling movement: *The dancer suddenly made a whirl.* 5 feel dizzy or confused. 6 dizzy or confused condition: *My thoughts are in a whirl.* 7 a rapid round of happenings, parties, etc. 1-3,5 *v.*, 4,6,7 *n.*

whirligig
(def. 1)

whirl i gig (hwėr′lē gig′), 1 toy that whirls or spins. 2 merry-go-round. 3 anything that whirls. *n.*

whirl pool (hwėrl′pül′), current of water whirling round and round rapidly and violently; eddy or vortex of water. *n.*

whirl wind (hwėrl′wind′), current of

air whirling violently round and round; whirling windstorm; vortex of air. *n.*

whirr (hwėr), whir. *n.*, *v.*

whisk (hwisk), 1 sweep or brush from a surface: *I whisked the crumbs from the table.* 2 a quick sweep: *I brushed away the dirt with a few whisks of a broom.* 3 move quickly: *The mouse whisked into its hole. She whisked the letter out of sight.* 4 a light, quick movement. 5 beat or whip to a froth. 6 a wire beater for eggs, cream, etc. 1,3,5 *v.*, 2,4,6 *n.*

whisk broom, a small broom for brushing clothes, etc.

whisk er (hwis′kər), 1 one of the hairs growing on a man's face. 2 **whiskers,** *pl.* the hair or part of a beard that grows on a man's cheeks. 3 a long, stiff hair growing near the mouth of a cat, rat, etc. *n.*

whisk ered (hwis′kərd), having whiskers. *adj.*

whis key (hwis′kē), a strong, intoxicating liquor made from grain. Some kinds of whiskey contain as much as one half alcohol. *n.*, *pl.* **whis keys.**

whis ky (hwis′kē), whiskey. *n.*, *pl.* **whis kies.**

whis per (hwis′pər), 1 speak very softly and low. 2 a very soft, low, spoken sound. 3 speak to in a whisper. 4 tell secretly or privately: *It is whispered that the business is failing.* 5 something told secretly or privately: *No whisper about having a new teacher has come to our ears.* 6 make a soft, rustling sound: *The wind whispered in the pines.* 7 a soft, rustling sound: *The wind was so gentle that we could hear the whisper of the leaves.* 1,3,4,6 *v.*, 2,5,7 *n.* —**whis′per-er,** *n.*

whist (hwist), a card game somewhat like bridge for two pairs of players. *n.*

whis tle (hwis′əl), 1 make a clear, shrill sound by forcing breath through one's teeth or pursing one's lips: *The girl whistled and her dog ran to her quickly.* 2 the sound made by whistling. 3 instrument for making whistling sounds. The whistles used by factories, ships, and trains to signal or to warn are tubes through which air or steam is

hat, āge, fär; let, ēqual, tėrm; it, īce; hot, ōpen, ôrder; oil, out; cup, pùt, rüle; ch, child; ng, long; sh, she; th, thin; ŦH, then; zh, measure;

ə represents *a* in about, *e* in taken, *i* in pencil, *o* in lemon, *u* in circus.

adj.	adjective	*n.*	noun
adv.	adverb	*prep.*	preposition
conj.	conjunction	*pron.*	pronoun
interj.	interjection	*v.*	verb
sing.	singular	*pl.*	plural

blown.   4 blow a whistle: *The traffic officer whistled for the cars to stop. The engineer whistled to warn the people at the train crossing.* 5 produce or utter by whistling: *whistle a tune.* 6 move with a shrill sound: *The wind whistled around the house.* 1,4-6 *v.*, **whis tled, whis tling;** 2,3 *n.*

whis tler (hwis′lər), person or thing that whistles. *n.*

Whis tler (hwis′lər), **James Abbott McNeill,** 1834-1903, American painter and etcher. *n.*

whit (hwit), a very small bit: *I don't care a whit what we do. n.*

white (hwīt), 1 the color of snow, salt, or the paper on which this book is printed.   2 having this color.   3 approaching this color: *Grandmother has white hair.* 4 white coloring matter. 5 white clothing.   6 part that is white or whitish, such as the albumen surrounding the yolk of an egg or the white part of the eyeball.   7 pale: *They all turned white with fear.* 8 light-colored: *white meat, a white wine.* 9 having a light-colored skin; Caucasian.   10 a white person; Caucasian.   11 silvery; gray. 12 snowy.   13 spotless; pure; innocent. 1,4-6,10 *n.*, 2,3,7-9,11-13 *adj.*, **whit er, whit est. —white′ness,** *n.*

White (hwīt), **E(lwyn) B(rooks),** born 1899, American writer of essays, children's stories, and poems. *n.*

white ant, termite.

white blood cell, a colorless cell in the blood, formed chiefly in bone marrow, that destroys disease germs; white corpuscle; leucocyte.

white cap (hwīt′kap′), wave with a foaming white crest. *n.*

white-col lar (hwīt′kol′ər), of or having to do with clerical, professional, or business work or workers. *adj.*

white corpuscle, white blood cell.

white elephant, anything that is expensive and troublesome to keep and take care of.

white feather, symbol of cowardice.

white fish (hwīt′fish′), a food fish with white or silvery sides, found in lakes and streams. *n.*, *pl.* **white fish es** or **white fish.**

white flag, a plain white flag displayed as a sign of truce or surrender.

white frost, hoarfrost.

white gold, alloy of gold and nickel or platinum, sometimes with copper and zinc. White gold looks much like platinum and is used for jewelry.

White hall (hwīt′hôl′),   1 street in London, where many government offices are located.   2 the British government or its policies. *n.*

White horse (hwīt′hôrs), capital of Yukon territory, in NW Canada. *n.*

white-hot (hwīt′hot′),   1 white with heat; extremely hot.   2 extremely angry; passionate, violent, etc. *adj.*

White House, 1 the official residence of the President of the United States, in Washington, D.C.   2 office, authority, opinion, etc., of the President of the United States.

white lie, a lie about some small matter; polite or harmless lie.

white matter, the tissue in the brain and spinal cord that consists chiefly of nerve fibers.

White Mountains, range of the Appalachian Mountains in New Hampshire. The highest mountain is Mount Washington.

whit en (hwīt′n), make or become white: *Sunshine helps to whiten clothes. They whitened when they heard the bad news. v.*

white oak,   1 an oak tree of eastern North America having light-gray or whitish bark and hard wood.   2 wood of this tree.

white potato, another name for the potato.

White Russia, Byelorussia.

White Sea, arm of the Arctic Ocean, in NW Soviet Union.

white wash (hwīt′wosh′ or hwīt′-wôsh′),   1 liquid for whitening walls, woodwork, etc. Whitewash is usually made of lime and water.   2 whiten with whitewash.   3 cover up the faults or mistakes of.   4 a covering up of faults or mistakes.   5 INFORMAL. to defeat in a game without a score for the loser. 1,4 *n.*, 2,3,5 *v.*

whith er (hwiᴛʜ′ər), to what place; to which place; where. *adv., conj.*

whit ing[1] (hwī′ting), 1 a common European sea fish related to the cod, used for food.   2 any of several fishes found along the Atlantic coast of the United States, used for food. *n., pl.* **whit ings** or **whit ing.** [probably from Dutch of the 1400's *wijting*]

whit ing[2] (hwī′ting), a powdered white chalk. Whiting is used in making putty, whitewash, and silver polish. *n.* [apparently *white* + *-ing*[1]]

whit ish (hwī′tish), somewhat white. *adj.*

Whit man (hwit′mən), **Walt,** 1819-1892, American poet. *n.*

Whit ney (hwit′nē),   1 **Eli,** 1765-1825,

American who invented the cotton gin. 2 **Mount,** peak of the Sierra Nevada mountains, in E California, the highest mountain in the United States outside Alaska. *n.*

Whit sun day (hwit′sun′dē), the seventh Sunday after Easter; Pentecost. *n.*

Whit sun tide (hwit′sən tīd′), the week beginning with Whitsunday, especially the first three days. *n.*

Whit ti er (hwit′ē ər), **John Greenleaf,** 1807-1892, American poet. *n.*

whit tle (hwit′l),   1 to cut shavings or chips from (wood, etc.) with a knife, usually for fun.   2 shape by whittling; carve: *The students learned how to whittle animals from wood. v.,* **whit tled, whit tling.**

whittle down, cut down little by little: *whittle down expenses.*

whiz or **whizz** (hwiz),   1 a humming or hissing sound.   2 move or rush with such a sound: *An arrow whizzed past his head.*   1 *n., pl.* **whiz zes;** 2 *v.,* **whizzed, whiz zing.**

who (hü),   1 *Who* is used in asking questions about a person or persons. *Who goes there? Who is your friend? Who told you?* 2 *Who* is also used in connecting a group of words with some previous word in the sentence. *The girl who spoke is my best friend. We saw people who were working in the fields.* 3 the person that; any person that; one that: *Who is not for us is against us. pron.*

whoa (hwō or wō), stop! "*Whoa there!*" *said the cowgirl to her horse. interj.*

who'd (hüd),   1 who would.   2 who had.

who ev er (hü ev′ər),   1 who; any person that: *Whoever wants the book may have it.*   2 no matter who: *Whoever else goes hungry, he won't. pron.*

whole (hōl),   1 having all its parts; complete: *They gave us a whole set of dishes.*   2 full; entire: *She worked the whole day. He ate the whole melon.* 3 all of a thing; the total: *Three thirds make a whole.*   4 thing complete in itself; a system.   5 not injured, broken, or defective: *I came out of the fight with a whole skin.*   6 in one piece; undivided: *The dog swallowed the meat whole.*   7 well; healthy.   1,2,5-7 *adj.,* 3,4 *n.* **—whole′-ness,** *n.*

on the whole,   1 considering everything.   2 for the most part.

whole heart ed (hōl′här′tid), earnest; sincere; hearty; cordial: *The school gave the team its wholehearted support. adj.* **—whole′heart′ed ly,** *adv.*

whole milk, milk from which none of the natural elements have been removed.

whole note, (in music) note to be

played four times as long as one quarter note. See **note** for diagram.

whole number, 1 a positive integer or zero. The set of whole numbers is usually {0, 1, 2, 3, . . . }; 0 is sometimes excluded. 2 number denoting one or more whole things or units; integer.

whorl (def. 1) whorl (def. 2)
whorl of leaves shell with whorls

whole sale (hōl/sāl/), 1 sale of goods in large quantities at a time, usually to storekeepers or others who will in turn sell them to users: *We buy at wholesale and sell at retail.* 2 in large lots or quantities: *buy something wholesale* (adv.). *The wholesale price of this coat is $30; the retail price is $50* (adj.). 3 selling in large quantities: *a wholesale fruit business.* 4 sell or be sold in large quantities: *They wholesale these jackets at $10 each. Such jackets usually wholesale for much less.* 5 general; extensive: *Avoid wholesale condemnation.* 1 *n.,* 2,3,5 *adj.,* 2 *adv.,* 4 *v.,* **whole saled, whole sal ing.**

whole sal er (hōl/sā/lər), a wholesale merchant. *n.*

whole some (hōl/səm), 1 good for the health; healthful: *Milk is a wholesome food.* 2 healthy-looking; suggesting health: *a clean, wholesome face.* 3 good for the mind or morals; beneficial: *The students had a wholesome interest in learning. adj.* —**whole/some ness,** *n.*

whole step, (in music) an interval of two half steps, such as D to E, or F to G.

whole tone, whole step.

whole-wheat (hōl/hwēt/), 1 made of the entire wheat kernel: *whole-wheat flour.* 2 made from whole-wheat flour: *whole-wheat bread. adj.*

who'll (hül), 1 who will. 2 who shall.

whol ly (hō/lē), to the whole amount or extent; completely; entirely; totally: *The patient was wholly cured. adv.*

whom (hüm), what person; which person: *Whom do you like best? He does not know whom to believe. The girl to whom I spoke is my cousin. pron.*

whom ev er (hüm/ev/ər), 1 whom; any person whom. 2 no matter whom. *pron.*

whom so ev er (hüm/sō ev/ər), any person whom. *pron.*

whoop (hüp, húp, hwüp, *or* hwúp), 1 a loud cry or shout: *The winner gave a whoop of joy.* 2 shout loudly. 3 the loud, gasping sound a person with whooping cough makes after a fit of coughing. 4 make this noise. 1,3 *n.,* 2,4 *v.*

whooping cough, an infectious disease of children, and rarely of adults, that causes fits of coughing that end with a loud, gasping sound.

whooping crane, a large, white, North American crane having a loud, raucous cry. It is nearly extinct.

whop per (hwop/ər), INFORMAL. 1 something very large. 2 a big lie. *n.*

whore (hôr), prostitute. *n.*

whorl (hwèrl), 1 circle of leaves or flowers round a stem of a plant. 2 one of the turns of a spiral shell. 3 anything that circles or turns on or around something else. People can be identified by the whorls of their fingerprints. *n.*

wicket
(def. 3, left)
(def. 4, right)

who's (hüz), 1 who is. 2 who has.

whose (hüz), of whom; of which: *The girl whose work got the prize is the youngest in her class. Whose book is this? pron.*

who so ev er (hü/sō ev/ər), whoever. *pron.*

why (hwī), 1 for what reason: *Why did the baby cry? He does not know why he lost.* 2 for which; because of which: *That is the reason why I left.* 3 the reason for which: *That is why she raised the question.* 4 reason: *I tried to find out the whys and wherefores of their strange behavior.* 5 *Why* is sometimes used to show surprise, doubt, etc., or just to fill in, without adding any important meaning to what is said. *Why it's all gone! Why, yes, I will if you wish.* 1-3 *adv.,* 4 *n., pl.* **whys;** 5 *interj.*

Wich i ta (wich/ə tô), city in S Kansas. *n.*

Wichita Falls, city in N Texas.

wick (wik), the part of a candle or oil lamp that is lighted. It is usually a cord or tape of loosely twisted or woven cotton through which oil or melted wax is drawn up and burned. *n.*

wick ed (wik/id), 1 bad; evil; sinful: *a wicked person, a wicked heart, wicked deeds.* 2 mischievous; playfully sly: *a wicked smile.* 3 INFORMAL. unpleasant; severe: *A wicked snowstorm swept through the northern part of the state. adj.* —**wick/ed ly,** *adv.*

wick ed ness (wik/id nis), 1 quality of being wicked. 2 a wicked thing or act. *n., pl.* **wick ed ness es.**

wick er (wik/ər), 1 a slender, easily bent branch or twig. 2 twigs or branches woven together. Wicker is used in making baskets and furniture.

hat, āge, fär; let, ēqual, tėrm;
it, īce; hot, ōpen, ôrder;
oil, out; cup, pùt, rüle; ch, child;
ng, long; sh, she; th, thin;
ŦH, then; zh, measure;

ə represents *a* in about,
e in taken, *i* in pencil,
o in lemon, *u* in circus.

3 made of wicker. 1,2 *n.,* 3 *adj.*

wick er work (wik/ər wėrk/), 1 twigs or branches woven together. 2 objects made of wicker. *n.*

wick et (wik/it), 1 a small door or gate: *The big door has a wicket in it.* 2 a small window: *Buy your tickets at this wicket.* 3 (in croquet) a wire arch stuck in the ground to knock the ball through. 4 (in cricket) either of the two sets of sticks that one side tries to hit with the ball. *n.*

wide (wīd), 1 filling much space from side to side; not narrow; broad: *a wide street. The ship sailed across the wide ocean. They went forth into the wide world.* 2 extending a certain distance from side to side: *The door is three feet wide.* 3 over an extensive space or region: *travel far and wide.* 4 having great range; including many different things: *A trip around the world gives wide experience. Wide reading gives wider understanding of other times and places.* 5 far open: *The child stared with wide eyes.* 6 to the full extent; fully: *Open your mouth wide. The gates stand wide open.* 7 far from a named point or object: *His guess was wide of the truth. The shot was wide of the mark.* 1,2,4,5,7 *adj.,* **wid er, wid est;** 3,6 *adv.*

wide-a wake (wīd/ə wāk/), 1 with the eyes wide open; fully awake. 2 alert; keen; knowing: *A watchdog must be a wide-awake guard against danger. adj.*

wide-eyed (wīd/īd/), with the eyes wide open: *The children watched the rabbits with wide-eyed interest. adj.*

wide ly (wīd/lē), to a wide extent: *a person who is widely known, to be widely read, widely opened eyes, two widely different accounts of a quarrel. adv.*

wid en (wīd/n), 1 make wide or wider: *We widened the path through the forest.* 2 become wide or wider: *The river widens as it flows. v.*

wide spread (wīd/spred/), 1 spread widely: *widespread wings.* 2 spread over a wide space: *a widespread flood.* 3 occurring in many places or among many persons far apart: *a widespread belief. adj.*

adj. adjective	*n.* noun
adv. adverb	*prep.* preposition
conj. conjunction	*pron.* pronoun
interj. interjection	*v.* verb
sing. singular	*pl.* plural

widg eon (wij'ən), any of several kinds of wild ducks of fresh waters. *n., pl.* **widg eons** or **widg eon.**

wid ow (wid'ō), 1 woman whose husband is dead and who has not married again. 2 make a widow of: *She was widowed when she was only thirty years old.* 1 *n.,* 2 *v.*

wid ow er (wid'ō ər), man whose wife is dead and who has not married again. *n.*

wid ow hood (wid'ō hud), condition or time of being a widow. *n.*

width (width), 1 how wide a thing is; distance across; breadth: *The room is 12 feet in width.* 2 piece of a certain width: *Two widths of cloth will make the curtains. n.*

wield (wēld), hold and use; manage; control: *The worker wielded a hammer. A writer wields the pen. The people wield the power in a democracy. v.*

wie ner (wē'nər), frankfurter. *n.* [from German *Wiener* (*Würstchen*) Viennese (sausages)]

wife (wīf), woman who has a husband; a married woman. *n., pl.* **wives.**

wife ly (wīf'lē), of a wife; like a wife; suitable for a wife. *adj.,* **wife li er, wife li est.**

wig (wig), an artificial covering of natural or false hair for the head: *The bald man wore a wig. n.*

wig gle (wig'əl), 1 move with short, quick movements from side to side; wriggle: *The restless child wiggled in the chair.* 2 such a movement. 1 *v.,* **wiggled, wig gling;** 2 *n.*

wig gler (wig'lər), 1 person or thing that wiggles. 2 the larva or pupa of a mosquito. *n.*

wig gly (wig'lē), 1 wiggling. 2 wavy. *adj.,* **wig gli er, wig gli est.**

wight (wīt), OLD USE. a human being; person. *n.*

wig wag (wig'wag'), 1 move to and fro. 2 signal by movements of arms, flags, or lights, according to a code.

wigwag (def. 2)
girl scout
wigwagging

3 such signaling. 1,2 *v.,* **wig wagged, wig wag ging;** 3 *n.*

wig wam (wig'wom *or* wig'wôm), hut made of bark or mats laid over a dome-shaped frame of poles, used by the Algonquian Indians of the eastern woodlands of North America. *n.*

wild (wīld), 1 living or growing in the forests or fields; not tamed; not cultivated: *The tiger is a wild animal. The daisy is a wild flower.* 2 with no people living in it: *Airplanes now fly from California to Europe over the wild region of the far north.* 3 **wilds,** *pl.* wild country. 4 not civilized; savage: *He is reading about the wild tribes of ancient times in Europe.* 5 not checked; not restrained: *a wild rush for the ball.* 6 not in proper control or order: *wild hair.* 7 violently excited; frantic: *The injured animal was wild with rage.* 8 violent: *Wild waves came roaring onto the shore.* 9 rash; crazy: *a wild scheme.* 10 far from the mark. 11 in a wild manner; to a wild degree. 1,2,4-10 *adj.,* 3 *n.,* 11 *adv.* **—wild'ly,** *adv.* **—wild'ness,** *n.*

run wild, live or grow without restraint.

wild and woolly, rough and uncivilized.

wild boar, a wild hog of Europe, southern Asia, and northern Africa.

wild cat (wīld'kat'), 1 any of several wild animals related to the common cat and similar to it in appearance, but larger. A lynx is one kind of wildcat. 2 not safe; reckless: *We lost all of our money by investing in wildcat stocks.* 3 a fierce fighter. 4 a well drilled for oil or gas in a region where none has been found before. 5 not authorized by proper union officials; precipitated by small groups or local unions: *a wildcat strike.* 1,3,4 *n.,* 2,5 *adj.*

Wilde (wīld), **Oscar,** 1854-1900, British playwright, poet, and novelist, born in Ireland. *n.*

Wil der (wil'dər), **Thornton,** born 1897, American playwright and novelist. *n.*

wil der ness (wil'dər nis), a wild, uncultivated, or desolate region with no people living in it. *n., pl.* **wil der ness es.**

wild fire (wīld'fīr'), any of certain substances easily set on fire whose flames could not be put out by water, formerly used in warfare. *n.*

like wildfire, very rapidly: *The news spread like wildfire.*

wild flower, 1 any uncultivated flowering plant that grows in the woods, fields, etc. 2 flower of such a plant.

wild fowl, birds ordinarily hunted, such as wild ducks or geese, partridges, quail, and pheasants.

wigwam

wild-goose chase (wīld'güs'), a useless search or attempt; foolish or hopeless quest.

wild life (wīld'līf'), wild animals: *The campers saw many kinds of wildlife. n.*

wild West, the western United States during pioneer days.

wile (wīl), 1 a trick to deceive; cunning way: *The automobile dealer used many wiles to make a sale.* 2 coax; lure; entice: *The sunshine wiled me away from my work.* 1 *n.,* 2 *v.,* **wiled, wil ing.**

wil ful (wil'fəl), willful. *adj.* **—wil'ful ness,** *n.*

wil ful ly (wil'fə lē), willfully. *adv.*

Wil helm II (vil'helm), 1859-1941, last emperor of Germany, known as Kaiser Wilhelm. He abdicated the throne in 1918.

wil i ness (wī'lē nis), wily quality; craftiness; slyness. *n.*

will[1] (wil), 1 am going to; is going to; are going to: *I will go shopping tomorrow; he will too, and I hope you will join us.* 2 am willing to; is willing to; willing to: *I will help clean the house if you do.* 3 wish; desire: *We cannot always do as we will.* 4 be able to; can: *The pail will hold four gallons.* 5 must: *Don't argue with me; you will do it at once!* 6 do often or usually: *She will read for hours at a time. v., past tense* **would.** [Old English *willan*]

will[2] (wil), 1 power of the mind to decide and do: *A good leader must have a strong will.* 2 decide by using this power; use the will: *I willed to keep awake.* 3 influence or try to influence by deliberate control over thought and action: *She willed the person in front of her to turn around.* 4 determine; decide: *Fate has willed it otherwise.* 5 purpose or determination: *the will to live.* 6 wish; desire: *"Thy will be done."* 7 a legal statement of a person's wishes about what shall be done with his property after he is dead. 8 document containing such a statement. 9 give by such a statement: *They willed all their property to their children.* 10 feeling toward another: *Most of us feel good will toward people we like and ill will toward people we dislike.* 1,5-8,10 *n.,* 2-4,9 *v.* [Old English *willa*]

at will, whenever one wishes.

will ful (wil'fəl), 1 wanting or taking one's own way; stubborn: *The willful child would not follow orders.* 2 done on purpose; intended: *willful murder,*

willful waste. *adj.* Also, **wilful.**
—will'ful ness, *n.*

will ful ly (wil'fə lē), 1 by choice; voluntarily. 2 by design; intentionally. 3 selfishly; perversely; obstinately; stubbornly. *adv.* Also, **wilfully.**

Wil liam I (wil'yəm), 1027?-1087, duke of Normandy who conquered England at the battle of Hastings in 1066 and was king of England from 1066 to 1087. He was called "William the Conqueror."

wimple
(def. 1)

Wil liams (wil'yəmz), 1 **Roger,** 1604?-1683, English clergyman who founded Rhode Island. 2 **Tennessee,** born 1911, American playwright. *n.*
Wil liams burg (wil'yəmz bèrg'), city in SE Virginia. It has been restored to look as it did before the Revolutionary War. *n.*

wil lies (wil'ēz), INFORMAL. spell of nervousness. *n.*

will ing (wil'ing), 1 ready; consenting: *He is willing to wait.* 2 cheerfully ready: *willing obedience. adj.* **—will'ing ly,** *adv.* **—will'ing ness,** *n.*

will-o'-the-wisp (wil'ə ŦHə wisp'), 1 a flickering light appearing at night over marshy places. It is thought to be caused by combustion of marsh gas. 2 thing that deceives or misleads by luring on: *Any scheme to get rich quickly is likely to be a will-o'-the-wisp. n.*

wil low (wil'ō), 1 tree or shrub with tough, slender branches and narrow leaves. The branches of most willows bend easily and are used to make furniture, baskets, etc. 2 its wood. *n.*

wil low y (wil'ō ē), 1 like a willow; slender; supple; graceful. 2 having many willows. *adj.,* **wil low i er, wil low i est.**

wil ly-nil ly (wil'ē nil'ē), willingly or not; with or against one's wishes. *adv.*

Wil ming ton (wil'ming tən), city in N Delaware, on the Delaware River. *n.*

Wil son (wil'sən), 1 **Harold,** born 1916, British statesman, prime minister from 1964 to 1970 and since 1974. 2 (**Thomas**) **Woodrow,** 1856-1924, the 28th president of the United States, from 1913 to 1921. 3 **Mount,** peak in SW California. One of the largest telescopes in the world is in the observatory on top of Mount Wilson. *n.*

wilt¹ (wilt), 1 become limp and drooping; wither. 2 lose strength, vigor, assurance, etc. 3 cause to wilt. 4 any of various plant diseases that cause leaves to wilt. 1-3 *v.,* 4 *n.* [a changed form of *welk,* an old word meaning to wither, probably from Dutch of the 1200's *welkeń*]

wilt² (wilt), OLD USE. will¹. "Thou wilt" means "you will." *v.*

wil y (wī'lē), using subtle tricks to deceive; crafty; cunning; sly: *a wily thief. The wily fox got away. adj.,* **wil i er, wil i est.**

wim ble (wim'bəl), tool for boring. *n.*

wim ple (wim'pəl), 1 cloth for the head arranged in folds about the head, cheeks, chin, and neck, worn by nuns and formerly by other women. 2 to cover with a wimple. 3 to ripple. 1 *n.,* 2,3 *v.,* **wim pled, wim pling.**

win (win), 1 be successful over others; get victory or success: *The tortoise won over the hare in the end. We all hope our team will win.* 2 get victory or success in: *He won the race.* 3 INFORMAL. success; victory: *We had four wins and no defeats.* 4 get by effort, ability, or skill; gain: *win fame, win a prize.* 5 gain the favor of; persuade: *The speaker soon won his audience. She has completely won the other scientists over to her theory.* 6 get to; reach, often by effort: *win the summit of a mountain.* 1,2,4-6 *v.,* **won, win ning;** 3 *n.*

wince (wins), 1 draw back suddenly; flinch slightly: *I winced when the dentist's drill touched my tooth.* 2 act of wincing: *Seeing the wince, the dentist stopped drilling for a moment.* 1 *v.,* **winced, winc ing;** 2 *n.*

winch (def. 1)

winch (winch), 1 machine for lifting or pulling, turned by hand with a crank or by an engine. The crank is attached to a drum around which rope for hoisting or hauling is wound. 2 crank of a revolving machine. 3 lift or pull by using a winch. 1,2 *n., pl.* **winch es;** 3 *v.*

wind¹ (wind), 1 air in motion. The wind varies in force from a slight breeze to a strong gale. *The wind bends the branches.* 2 a strong wind; gale: *Winds blowing at ninety miles an hour toppled a tree on our roof.* 3 air filled with some smell: *The deer caught the wind of us and ran off.* 4 follow by scent; smell. 5 power of breathing; breath: *A runner needs good wind.* 6 put out of breath; cause difficulty in breathing: *The hiker*

hat, āge, fär; let, ēqual, tèrm;
it, īce; hot, ōpen, ôrder;
oil, out; cup, pùt, rüle; ch, child;
ng, long; sh, she; th, thin;
ŦH, then; zh, measure;

ə represents *a* in about,
e in taken, *i* in pencil,
o in lemon, *u* in circus.

was winded by walking up the steep hill. 7 **winds,** *pl.* wind instruments. 1-3,5,7 *n.,* 4,6 *v.,* **wind ed, wind ing.** [Old English]

get wind of, find out about; get a hint of: *Don't let Mother get wind of our plans to have a surprise party on her birthday.*

in the wind, happening; about to happen.

take the wind out of one's sails, take away one's advantage, argument, etc., suddenly or unexpectedly.

wind² (wīnd), 1 move this way and that; go in a crooked way; change direction; turn: *A brook winds through the woods. We wound our way through the narrow streets.* 2 to fold, wrap, or place about something: *She wound her arms around her new puppy.* 3 to cover with something put, wrapped, or folded around: *The patient's arm is wound with bandages.* 4 roll into a ball or on a spool: *We took turns winding yarn. Thread comes wound on spools.* 5 a bend; turn; twist. 6 twist or turn around something: *The vine winds around a pole.* 7 make (some machine) go by turning some part of it: *wind a clock.* 8 be wound: *This clock winds easily.* 1-4,6-8 *v.,* **wound, wind ing;** 5 *n.* [Old English *windan*]

wind up, 1 end; settle; conclude. 2 (in baseball) make swinging and twisting movements of the arm and body just before pitching the ball.

wind³ (wīnd), blow: *wind a fanfare on a trumpet. v.,* **wind ed** or **wound, wind ing.** [special use of *wind¹*]

wind bag (wind'bag'), SLANG. person who talks a great deal but does not say much. *n.*

wind break (wind'brāk'), a shelter from the wind: *The campers pitched their tent next to the stone wall, so that it would serve as a windbreak. n.*

wind fall (wind'fôl'), 1 fruit blown down by the wind. 2 an unexpected piece of good luck. *n.*

wind flow er (wind'flou'ər), anemone. *n.*

wind i ly (win'də lē), in a windy manner. *adv.*

windiness

wind i ness (win′dē nis), a being windy. *n.*

wind ing (wīn′ding), 1 act of one that winds. 2 a bend; turn. 3 bending; turning. 4 something that is wound or coiled. 1,2,4 *n.*, 3 *adj.*

wind instrument (wind), a musical instrument sounded by blowing air into it. French horns, flutes, and trombones are wind instruments.

wind jam mer (wind′jam′ər), INFORMAL. 1 a sailing ship. 2 member of its crew. *n.*

wind lass (wind′ləs), machine for pulling or lifting things. The windlass is a kind of winch used to hoist water from a well or an anchor out of the water. *n.*, *pl.* **wind lass es.**

wind less (wind′lis), free from wind; calm. *adj.*

windmill

wind mill (wind′mil′), a mill or machine worked by the action of the wind upon a wheel of vanes or sails mounted on a tower. Windmills are mostly used to pump water. *n.*

win dow (win′dō), 1 an opening in a wall or roof to let in light or air. 2 such an opening with its frame and glass. *n.*

window box, container of wood, metal, or plastic, set on or fastened to a window sill, in which small plants may be grown.

win dow less (win′dō lis), without windows: *a windowless wall. adj.*

win dow pane (win′dō pān′), piece of glass in a window. *n.*

win dow-shop (win′dō shop′), look at articles in store windows without going in to buy anything. *v.*, **win dow-shopped, win dow-shop ping.**

win dow sill (win′dō sil′), piece of wood or stone across the bottom of a window. *n.*

wind pipe (wind′pīp′), the passage by which air is carried from the throat to the lungs; trachea. *n.*

wind row (wind′rō′), row of hay raked together to dry before being made into heaps. *n.*

wind shield (wind′shēld′), sheet of glass, etc., to keep off the wind. Automobiles and locomotives have windshields. *n.*

Wind sor (win′zər), 1 town in S England, where **Windsor Castle,** chief residence of the British sovereign, is located. 2 the family name of the royal house of Great Britain since 1917. *n.*

wind storm (wind′stôrm′), storm with much wind but little or no rain. *n.*

wind tunnel (wind), tunnel for testing the effects of wind and air pressure on aircraft, missiles, etc., with air forced through at high speeds.

wind up (wīnd′up′), 1 a winding up; end; close; conclusion. 2 series of swinging and twisting movements of the arm and body made by a baseball pitcher just before pitching the ball. *n.*

wind ward (wind′wərd), 1 on the side toward the wind. 2 the side toward the wind. 3 in the direction from which the wind is blowing. 1,3 *adj., adv.*, 2 *n.*

Wind ward Islands (wind′wərd), the S part of the Lesser Antilles in the West Indies.

wind y (win′dē), 1 having much wind: *a windy day, the windy deck of a ship, windy weather.* 2 made of wind; empty: *windy talk.* 3 talking a great deal; voluble. *adj.*, **wind i er, wind i est.**

wine (wīn), 1 the juice of grapes after it has fermented and contains alcohol. 2 the fermented juice of other fruits or plants: *currant wine, dandelion wine.* 3 entertain with wine. 1,2 *n.*, 3 *v.*, **wined, win ing.**

wine press, machine for pressing the juice from grapes in making wine.

wing (wing), 1 one of the movable parts of a bird, insect, or bat used in flying, or a corresponding part of a bird or insect that does not fly. Birds have one pair of wings; insects have usually two pairs. 2 anything like a wing in shape or use: *the wings of an airplane.* 3 part that sticks out from the main part or body, especially the part of a building that sticks out sideways from the main part. 4 either of the side portions of an army or fleet ready for battle. 5 either of the spaces to the right or left of the stage in a theater. 6 part of an organization; faction. The liberals or radicals of a political group are often called the left wing. 7 an air force unit composed of two or more groups. 8 fly: *The bird wings its way to the south.* 9 supply with wings. 10 make able to fly; give speed to: *Terror winged our steps as the bear drew nearer.* 11 to wound in the wing or arm: *The bullet winged the bird but did not kill it.* 1-7 *n.*, 8-11 *v.* **—wing′like′,** *adj.*

on the wing, in flight.

take wing, fly away: *The bird took wing when the cat came near.*

under the wing of, under the protection of.

wing case, either of the pair of thickened front wings that form a protective covering for the hind pair in certain insects. Beetles have wing cases.

winged (wingd *or* wing′id), 1 having wings. 2 swift; rapid: *winged messenger. adj.*

wing less (wing′lis), having no wings. *adj.*

wing spread (wing′spred′), distance between the tips of the wings when they are spread. *n.*

wink (wingk), 1 close the eyes and open them again quickly: *The bright light made him wink.* 2 close and open one eye on purpose as a hint or signal: *I winked at my sister to keep still.* 3 a winking. 4 a hint or signal given by winking. 5 twinkle: *The stars winked.* 6 a very short time: *I didn't sleep a wink.* 1,2,5 *v.*, 3,4,6 *n.*

wink at, pretend not to see: *My parents knew I came home past my bedtime last night, but they winked at it.*

win ner (win′ər), person or thing that wins: *The winner of the contest got a prize. n.*

win ning (win′ing), 1 that wins: *a winning team.* 2 charming; attractive: *a very winning smile.* 3 **winnings,** *pl.* what is won; money won: *The gamblers pocketed their winnings.* 1,2 *adj.*, 3 *n.* **—win′ning ly,** *adv.*

Win ni peg (win′ə peg), 1 city in S Canada, capital of Manitoba. 2 **Lake,** lake in S Canada. *n.*

win now (win′ō), 1 blow off the chaff from (grain); drive or blow away (chaff). 2 sort out; separate; sift: *winnow truth from lies. v.*

win some (win′səm), charming; attractive; pleasing: *a winsome young couple, a winsome smile. adj.* **—win′some ly,** *adv.* **—win′some ness,** *n.*

win ter (win′tər), 1 the coldest of the four seasons; time of the year between autumn and spring. 2 of or having to do with winter: *winter clothes, winter weather.* 3 pass the winter: *Robins winter in the south.* 4 keep or feed during winter: *We wintered our cattle in the warm valley.* 1 *n.*, 2 *adj.*, 3,4 *v.*

win ter green (win′tər grēn′), 1 a small evergreen plant of North America with bright-red berries and aromatic leaves. An oil made from its leaves is used in medicine and as a flavoring. 2 this oil. 3 its flavor. *n.*

win ter ize (win′tə rīz′), make (an automobile, etc.) ready for operation or use during the winter. *v.,* **win ter ized, win ter iz ing.**

win ter time (win′tər tīm′), the season of winter. *n.*

win try (win′trē), **1** of winter; like that of winter: *wintry weather, a wintry sky.* **2** not warm or friendly; chilly: *a wintry manner, a wintry smile, a wintry greeting. adj.,* **win tri er, win tri est.**

wipe (wīp), **1** rub in order to clean or dry: *We wipe our shoes on the mat. We wiped the dishes with a towel.* **2** take (away, off, or out) by rubbing: *Wipe away your tears. I wiped off the dust.* **3** remove: *The rain wiped away all the footprints.* **4** rub or draw (something) over a surface. **5** act of wiping: *He gave his face a hasty wipe.* **1-4** *v.,* **wiped, wip ing; 5** *n.*

wipe out, destroy completely: *Whole cities were wiped out by the barbarians that swept over Europe.*

wip er (wī′pər), **1** person who wipes. **2** thing used for wiping: *a windshield wiper. n.*

wire (wīr), **1** metal drawn out into a thin, flexible rod or fine thread. **2** a long piece of such metal used for electrical transmission, as in electric lighting, telephones, and telegraphs. **3** made of or consisting of wire: *a wire fence, wire netting.* **4** furnish with wire: *wire a house for electricity.* **5** fasten with wire: *She wired the two pieces together.* **6** telegraph: *I sent a message by wire.* **7** to telegraph: *He wired a birthday greeting.* **8** INFORMAL. telegram: *The news of his arrival came in a wire.* **1,2,6,8** *n.,* **3** *adj.,* **4,5,7** *v.,* **wired, wir ing.**

pull wires, INFORMAL. use secret influence to accomplish one's purposes: *She pulled wires to get her son a job.*

wire-haired (wīr′herd′ *or* wīr′hard′), having coarse, stiff hair: *a wire-haired fox terrier. adj.*

wire less (wīr′lis), **1** using no wires; transmitting by radio waves instead of by electric wires: *wireless telegraphy.* **2** system of transmission by radio waves without the use of wires. **3** radio (a term used in Great Britain). **4** message sent by radio; radiogram. **1** *adj.,* **2-4** *n., pl.* **wire less es.**

wire tap ping (wīr′tap′ing), the making of a secret connection with telephone or telegraph wires to listen to or record the messages sent over them. Wiretapping is forbidden by law in many countries and states. *n.*

wire worm (wīr′wėrm′), the slender, hard-bodied larva of certain beetles. Wireworms feed on the roots of plants and do much damage to crops. *n.*

wir i ness (wī′rē nis), a being wiry. *n.*

wir ing (wī′ring), system of wires to carry an electric current. *n.*

wir y (wī′rē), **1** made of wire. **2** like wire. **3** lean, strong, and tough. *adj.,* **wir i er, wir i est.**

Wis. *or* **Wisc.,** Wisconsin.

Wis con sin (wi skon′sən), one of the north central states of the United States. *Capital:* Madison. *n.*

wis dom (wiz′dəm), **1** knowledge and good judgment based on experience; being wise. **2** wise conduct; wise words: *Her wisdom guided us.* **3** scholarly knowledge. *n.*

wisdom tooth, the back tooth on either side of each jaw, ordinarily appearing between the ages of 17 and 25.

wise[1] (wīz), **1** having or showing knowledge and good judgment: *a wise judge, wise plans.* **2** having knowledge or information: *We are none the wiser for his explanations. adj.,* **wis er, wis est.** [Old English *wīs*] —**wise′ly,** *adv.*

wise[2] (wīz), way; manner: *He is in no wise a bad boy, but he is often a little mischievous. n.* [Old English *wīse*]

-wise, suffix forming adverbs. **1** in _____ manner: *Likewise = in a like manner.* **2** in a _____ing manner: *Slantwise = in a slanting manner.* **3** in the characteristic way of a _____: *Clockwise = in the way the hands of a clock go.* **4** in the direction of the _____: *Lengthwise = in the direction of the length.* [from *wise*[2]]

wise a cre (wī′zā′kər), person who thinks he knows everything. *n.*

wise crack (wīz′krak′), SLANG. **1** a snappy comeback; smart remark. **2** make wisecracks. **1** *n.,* **2** *v.*

wise guy, SLANG. person who pretends to know more than he really does; impudent or conceited fellow.

wish (wish), **1** have a need or longing for; want; desire: *What is it that you wish? They wish to see you urgently.* **2** have a desire; express a hope: *I wish that I had enough money to buy that model boat. She wished for a telescope.* **3** a wishing or wanting; desire; longing: *What is your wish? He had no wish to be king.* **4** expression of a wish: *Please give her my best wishes for a happy New Year.* **5** to desire (something) for someone; have or express a hope for: *I wish you a happy New Year. He wished her good night.* **6** to request or command: *Do you wish me to come over now?* **7** a request or command: *grant someone's slightest wish.* **8** thing wished for: *She got her wish.* **1,2,5,6** *v.,* **3,4,7,8** *n., pl.* **wish es. —wish′er,** *n.*

wish bone (wish′bōn′), the forked bone in the front of the breastbone in poultry and other birds. *n.*

wish ful (wish′fəl), having or expressing a wish; desiring; desirous: *His boast about winning the race was only wishful thinking. adj.*

wish y-wash y (wish′ē wosh′ē *or* wish′ē wôsh′ē), **1** thin and weak: *wishy-washy soup with no flavor.* **2** feeble; weak; poor: *a wishy-washy story. adj.*

wisp (wisp), **1** a small bundle; small bunch: *a wisp of hay.* **2** a small tuft, lock, or portion of anything; slight bit: *a wisp of hair, a wisp of smoke.* **3** a little thing: *a wisp of a girl. n.*

wisp y (wis′pē), like a wisp; thin; slight. *adj.,* **wisp i er, wisp i est.**

wist (wist), OLD USE. knew. *v.*

wis tar i a (wi ster′ē ə), wisteria. *n., pl.* **wis tar i as.**

wis ter i a (wi stir′ē ə), a climbing shrub with large, drooping clusters of purple, blue, or white flowers. *n., pl.* **wis ter i as.** [from Caspar *Wistar,* 1761-1818, an American physician]

wist ful (wist′fəl), longing; yearning: *A child stood looking with wistful eyes at the toys in the window. adj.* —**wist′ful ly,** *adv.* —**wist′ful ness,** *n.*

wit (wit), **1** the power to perceive quickly and express cleverly ideas that are unusual, striking, and amusing: *Her wit made even troubles seem amusing.* **2** person with such power: *Mark Twain and Oliver Wendell Holmes were two famous wits.* **3** power of understanding; mind or sense: *People with quick wits learn easily. The child was out of his wits with fright. That poor man hasn't wit enough to earn a living.* **4** OLD USE. know. **1-3** *n.,* **4** *v.,* **wist, wit ting.**

to wit, that is to say; namely: *To my daughter I leave all I own—to wit: my house, what is in it, and the land on which it stands.*

witch (wich), **1** woman supposed to be under the influence of supernatural spirits and to have magic powers which she generally uses to do evil. **2** an ugly old woman. **3** INFORMAL. a charming or fascinating girl or woman. *n., pl.* **witch es.**

witch craft (wich′kraft′), what a witch does or can do; magic power or influence. *n.*

witch doctor, medicine man, especially in certain primitive societies.

witch er y (wich′ər ē), **1** witchcraft;

adj.	adjective	*n.*	noun
adv.	adverb	*prep.*	preposition
conj.	conjunction	*pron.*	pronoun
interj.	interjection	*v.*	verb
sing.	singular	*pl.*	plural

magic. 2 charm; fascination. *n., pl.* **witch er ies.**

witch hazel, 1 shrub or small tree of eastern North America that has yellow flowers in the fall or winter after the leaves have fallen. 2 lotion for cooling and soothing the skin, made from the bark and leaves of this shrub.

witch ing (wich′ing), bewitching; magical; enchanting. *adj.*

with (wiŦH *or* with). *With* shows that persons or things are taken together in some way. 1 in the company of: *Come with me.* 2 among: *They will mix with the crowd.* 3 having, wearing, carrying, etc.: *He is a man with brains. She received a telegram with good news.* 4 by means of: *The man cut the meat with a knife.* 5 using; showing: *Work with care.* 6 added to: *Do you want sugar with your tea?* 7 in relation to: *They are friendly with us.* 8 in regard to: *We are pleased with the house.* 9 in proportion to: *Her pay increased with her responsibilities.* 10 because of: *The man almost died with thirst. The child is shaking with cold.* 11 in the keeping or service of: *Leave the dog with me.* 12 in the region, sphere, experience, opinion, or view of: *It is day with us while it is night with the Chinese. High taxes are unpopular with many people.* 13 at the same time as: *With this battle the war ended.* 14 in the same direction as: *The boat floated along with the current.* 15 on the side of; for: *They are with us in our plan.* 16 from: *I hate to part with my favorite things.* 17 against: *The English fought with the Germans.* 18 receiving; having: *I went with his permission.* 19 in spite of: *With all his weight he was not a strong man. prep.*

with al (wi ŦHôl′ *or* wi thôl′), 1 with it all; as well; besides; also: *The lady is rich and fair and wise withal.* 2 OLD USE. with. 1 *adv.,* 2 *prep.*

with draw (wiŦH drô′ *or* with drô′), 1 draw back; draw away: *The child quickly withdrew his hand from the hot stove. I withdrew from the discussion before it became an argument.* 2 take back; remove: *The owner of the store agreed to withdraw the charge of theft if the robbers returned the money. She withdrew all of her savings from the bank.* 3 go away: *She withdrew from the*

room. *v.,* **with drew, with drawn, with draw ing.**

with draw al (wiŦH drô′əl *or* with-drô′əl), a withdrawing or a being withdrawn. *n.*

with drawn (wiŦH drôn′ *or* with-drôn′), past participle of **withdraw.** *The goalie was withdrawn from the game because of an injury. v.*

with drew (wiŦH drü′ *or* with drü′), past tense of **withdraw.** *The coach withdrew the player from the game when he was hurt. v.*

withe (wiŦH *or* with), 1 a willow twig. 2 any tough, easily bent twig suitable for binding things together. *n., pl.* **withes** (wiŦHz *or* withs).

with er (wiŦH′ər), 1 lose or cause to lose freshness; make or become dry and lifeless; dry up; fade; shrivel: *The hot sun withers the grass. Flowers wither after they are cut. Age had withered the old woman's face.* 2 cause to feel ashamed or confused: *be withered by a scornful look. v.*

with ers (wiŦH′ərz), the highest part of a horse's or other animal's back, behind the neck. See **horse** for diagram. *n.pl.*

with held (with held′ *or* wiŦH held′), past tense and past participle of **withhold.** *The witness withheld information from the police. Because information had been withheld, the wrong person was charged with the crime. v.*

with hold (with hōld′ *or* wiŦH hōld′), 1 refrain from giving or granting: *There will be no school play if the principal withholds his consent.* 2 hold back; keep back: *The general withheld two regiments from the attack. v.,* **with-held, with hold ing.**

withholding tax, the part of a person's income tax that is deducted from his salary or wages by his employer on behalf of the government.

with in (wiŦH in′ *or* with in′), 1 inside the limits of; not beyond: *The task was within my power. I will guess your weight within five pounds.* 2 in or into the inner part of; inside of: *By the use of X rays, doctors can see within the body.* 3 in or into the inner part; inside: *The house has been painted within and without. The curtains were white without and green within.* 1,2 *prep.,* 3 *adv.*

with out (wiŦH out′ *or* with out′), 1 with no; not having; free from; lacking: *A cat walks without noise. I drink tea without sugar.* 2 so as to leave out, avoid, or neglect: *She walked past without noticing us.* 3 outside of; beyond: *Children were playing within and without the house.* 4 on the outside; outside: *The house is painted without and within.* 1-3 *prep.,* 4 *adv.*

with stand (with stand′ *or* wiŦH-stand′), stand against; hold out against;

resist; oppose, especially successfully; endure: *withstand hardships. These heavy shoes will withstand much hard wear. v.,* **with stood, with stand-ing.**

with stood (with stud′ *or* wiŦH stud′), past tense and past participle of **with-stand.** *The family withstood many hard-ships. These shoes have withstood three years of hard wear. v.*

wit less (wit′lis), lacking sense; stupid; foolish: *Crossing the street without looking in both directions is a witless thing to do. adj.*

wit ness (wit′nis), 1 person who saw something happen; spectator; eyewit-ness: *There were several witnesses to the accident.* 2 be a witness of; see: *He witnessed the accident.* 3 person who gives evidence or testifies under oath in a court of law. 4 evidence; testimony: *A person who gives false witness in court is guilty of perjury.* 5 testify to; give evidence of: *Her whole manner witnessed her surprise.* 6 person who writes his name on a document to show that he saw the maker sign it. 7 sign (a document) as a witness: *The lawyer asked two secretaries to witness his client's will.* 1,3,4,6 *n., pl.* **wit ness es;** 2,5,7 *v.*

bear witness, be evidence; give evi-dence; testify: *The woman's finger-prints bore witness to her guilt. His blushes bore witness to his great embarrassment.*

wit ti cism (wit′ə siz′əm), a witty remark. *n.*

wit ti ly (wit′ə lē), in a witty manner; with wit. *adv.*

wit ti ness (wit′ē nis), quality or char-acter of being witty. *n.*

wit ting ly (wit′ing lē), knowingly; in-tentionally. *adv.*

wit ty (wit′ē), full of wit; clever and amusing: *A witty person makes witty remarks. adj.,* **wit ti er, wit ti est.**

wive (wīv), 1 marry a woman. 2 take as a wife. *v.,* **wived, wiv ing.**

wives (wīvz), plural of **wife.** *n.*

wiz ard (wiz′ərd), 1 man supposed to have magic power; magician; sorcerer. 2 INFORMAL. a very clever person; ex-pert: *She is a wizard at mathemat-ics. n.*

wiz ard ry (wiz′ər drē), magic skill; magic. *n.*

wiz ened (wiz′nd), dried up; withered; shriveled: *a wizened apple, a wizened face. adj.*

wk., week. *pl.* **wks.**

wo (wō), woe. *n., interj.*

wob ble (wob′əl), 1 move unsteadily from side to side; shake; tremble: *A baby wobbles when it begins to walk alone.* 2 be uncertain, unsteady, or in-constant; waver. 3 a wobbling motion.

1,2 *v.*, **wob bled, wob bling; 3** *n.*
Also, **wabble.**

wob bly (wob′lē), unsteady; shaky;
wavering. *adj.*, **wob bli er, wob bli
est.** Also, **wabbly.**

wo be gone (wō′bi gôn′), woebegone.
adj.

Wo den (wōd′n), (in Anglo-Saxon
myths) the chief god. The Scandinavians
called him Odin. *n.*

wolverine—about 3½ ft. long with tail

woe (wō), 1 great grief, trouble, or
distress: *Sickness and poverty are common woes.* 2 an exclamation of grief,
trouble, or distress: *"Woe! woe is me!"*
1 *n.*, 2 *interj.* Also, **wo.**

woe be gone (wō′bi gôn′), looking
sad, sorrowful, or wretched. *adj.*

woe ful (wō′fəl), 1 full of woe; sad;
sorrowful; wretched: *The lost child had
a woeful expression.* 2 pitiful. *adj.*
—**woe′ful ly,** *adv.*

wo ful (wō′fəl), woeful. *adj.* —**wo′-
ful ly,** *adv.*

woke (wōk), waked; a past tense of
wake[1]. *She woke before we did.* *v.*

wo ken (wō′kən), waked; a past participle of **wake**[1]. *He was woken by the
sound of bells.* *v.*

wold (wōld), high, rolling country, bare
of woods. *n.*

wolf (def. 1)
up to 3 ft. high at the shoulder

wolf (wùlf), 1 a carnivorous wild mammal somewhat like and related to the
dog. Wolves usually hunt in packs and
sometimes kill livestock. They are now
very rare in the United States. 2 a
cruel, greedy person. 3 eat greedily:
The starving man wolfed down the food.
1,2 *n.*, *pl.* **wolves; 3** *v.* —**wolf′like′,**
adj.

cry wolf, give a false alarm.

keep the wolf from the door, keep
safe from hunger or poverty.

Wolfe (wùlf), 1 **James,** 1727-1759,
British general who was killed at the
battle of Quebec, in which he defeated
the French. 2 **Thomas,** 1900-1938,
American novelist. *n.*

wolf hound (wùlf′hound′), a large

dog of any of various breeds once used
in hunting wolves. *n.*

wolf ish (wùl′fish), 1 like a wolf; savage: *wolfish cruelty.* 2 greedy: *a wolfish
appetite.* *adj.* —**wolf′ish ly,** *adv.*
—**wolf′ish ness,** *n.*

wolf ram (wùl′frəm), tungsten. *n.*

wol ve rine or **wol ve rene** (wùl-
və rēn′), a heavily built, carnivorous mammal living in the northern
regions of North America. It is related
to the weasel and badger. *n.*

wolves (wùlvz), plural of **wolf.** *n.*

wom an (wùm′ən), 1 an adult female
person. When a girl grows up, she becomes a woman. 2 women as a group;
womankind. 3 a female servant: *The
princess told her woman to wait outside.*
n., pl. **wom en.**

wom an hood (wùm′ən hùd), 1 condition or time of being a woman: *The girl
was entering womanhood.* 2 character
or qualities of a woman. 3 women as a
group: *the womanhood of America.* *n.*

wom an ish (wùm′ə nish), 1 characteristic of a woman: *a womanish way of
walking.* 2 suitable for a woman rather
than for a man: *womanish clothing.* *adj.*

wom an kind (wùm′ən kīnd′), wom-
en as a group. *n.*

wom an like (wùm′ən līk′), 1 like a
woman. 2 suitable for a woman. *adj.*

wom an li ness (wùm′ən lē nis),
womanly quality or behavior. *n.*

wom an ly (wùm′ən lē), 1 having
qualities traditionally admired in a
woman: *a womanly expression of sympathy.* 2 suitable for a woman: *Tennis
is as much a womanly as it is a manly
sport.* *adj.*

woman's rights, social, political,
and legal rights for women, equal to
those of men.

woman suffrage, 1 the political right
of women to vote. 2 women's votes.

womb (wüm), the part of the body in
mammals that holds and nourishes the
young till birth; uterus. *n.*

wom bat (wom′bat), a burrowing Australian mammal that looks like a small
bear. A female wombat has a pouch for
carrying her young. *n.*

wom en (wim′ən), plural of
woman. *n.*

wom en folk (wim′ən fōk′), women.
n.pl.

wom en folks (wim′ən fōks′), wom-
en. *n.pl.*

Women's Liberation, movement
of women calling for liberation from
male discrimination and dominance.

won (wun), past tense and past participle of **win.** *Which side won yesterday? We have won four games.* *v.*

won der (wun′dər), 1 a strange and
surprising thing or event: *The Grand
Canyon is one of the wonders of the*

*world. It is a wonder that he refused
such a good offer.* 2 the feeling caused
by what is strange and surprising: *The
baby looked with wonder at the snow.*
3 feel wonder: *We wonder at the splendor of the stars.* 4 be surprised or
astonished: *I shouldn't wonder if she
wins the prize.* 5 be curious; be curious
about; wish to know: *I wonder where
she has gone.* 1,2 *n.*, 3-5 *v.* —**won′der-
ing ly,** *adv.*

won der ful (wun′dər fəl), 1 causing
wonder; marvelous; remarkable: *The
explorer had wonderful adventures.*
2 excellent; splendid; fine: *We had a
wonderful time at the party.* *adj.*
—**won′der ful ly,** *adv.* —**won′der-
ful ness,** *n.*

won der land (wun′dər land′), a land
full of wonders. *n.*

won der ment (wun′dər mənt), wonder; surprise: *He stared at the huge bear
in wonderment.* *n.*

won drous (wun′drəs), 1 wonderful.
2 wonderfully. 1 *adj.*, 2 *adv.* —**won′-
drous ly,** *adv.*

wombat—2 to 4 ft. long

wont (wunt), 1 accustomed: *He was
wont to read the paper at breakfast.*
2 custom; habit: *He rose early, as was
his wont.* 1 *adj.*, 2 *n.*

won't (wōnt *or* wunt), will not.

wont ed (wun′tid), accustomed; customary; usual: *The cat was in its wonted
place by the stove.* *adj.*

woo (wü), 1 make love to; seek to
marry. 2 seek to win; try to get: *Some
people woo fame; some woo wealth.*
3 try to persuade; urge. *v.*

wood (wùd), 1 the hard substance beneath the bark of trees and shrubs.
2 trees or parts of trees cut up for use in
building houses, making boats and furniture, etc.: *The carpenter brought*

adj.	adjective	*n.*	noun
adv.	adverb	*prep.*	preposition
conj.	conjunction	*pron.*	pronoun
interj.	interjection	*v.*	verb
sing.	singular	*pl.*	plural

wood to build a playhouse. *Put some wood on the fire.* **3** made of wood; wooden: *a wood house.* **4** Often, **woods,** *pl.* **a** a large number of growing trees; small forest: *The children go to the woods behind the farm for wild flowers and for nuts.* **1,2,4** *n.*, **3** *adj.* **b** area covered by a forest or forests: *Many campers go to the Maine woods.* **1,2,4** *n.*, **3** *adj.*
out of the woods, out of danger or difficulty.

wood alcohol, a colorless, poisonous, flammable liquid made by distilling wood; methyl alcohol. It is used as a solvent, fuel, etc., and to make formaldehyde.

wood bine (wud′bīn), **1** honeysuckle. **2** Virginia creeper. *n.*

wood carv er (wud′kär′vər), person who carves figures or other objects from wood. *n.*

wood chuck (wud′chuk′), a small, thick-bodied North American mammal with short legs and a bushy tail; ground hog. It is a kind of marmot. Woodchucks grow fat in summer and sleep in their holes in the ground all winter. *n.*

woodchuck—about 2 ft. long with tail

wood cock (wud′kok′), a small game bird with short legs and a long bill used to probe the ground for worms. *n., pl.* **wood cocks** or **wood cock.**

wood craft (wud′kraft′), **1** knowledge about how to get food and shelter in the woods; skill in hunting, trapping, finding one's way, etc. **2** skill in working with wood. *n.*

wood cut (wud′kut′), **1** an engraved block of wood to print from. **2** a print from such a block. *n.*

wood cut ter (wud′kut′ər), person who cuts down trees or chops wood. *n.*

wood ed (wud′id), covered with trees: *The house stood on a wooded hill.* *adj.*

wood en (wud′n), **1** made of wood. **2** stiff as wood; awkward. **3** dull;

stupid. *adj.* **—wood′en ly,** *adv.* **—wood′en ness,** *n.*

wooden horse, Trojan horse.

wood i ness (wud′ē nis), woody condition or quality. *n.*

wood land (wud′lənd), **1** land covered with trees. **2** of, having to do with, or living in the woods: *woodland sounds, woodland animals.* **1** *n.*, **2** *adj.*

wood louse, a small crustacean with a flat, oval body that lives in decaying wood, damp soil, etc.; sow bug.

wood man (wud′mən), **1** man who cuts down trees. **2** person who lives in the woods. *n., pl.* **wood men.**

wood nymph, nymph that lives in the woods; dryad.

wood peck er (wud′pek′ər), bird with a hard, pointed bill for pecking holes in trees to get insects. The flicker is one kind of woodpecker. *n.*

wood pile (wud′pīl′), pile of wood, especially wood for fuel. *n.*

wood shed (wud′shed′), shed for storing wood. *n.*

woods man (wudz′mən), **1** person used to life in the woods and skilled in hunting, fishing, trapping, etc. **2** lumberjack. *n., pl.* **woods men.**

woods y (wud′zē), of, having to do with, or like the woods. *adj.,* **woods i er, woods i est.**

wood tar, tar obtained by the distillation of wood, and containing resins, turpentine, etc. It is used as a preservative on wood, rope, etc.

wood thrush, thrush with a white, spotted breast, common in the thickets and woods of eastern North America.

wood wind (wud′wind′), **1** any of a group of wind instruments which were originally made of wood, but are now often made of metal. Clarinets, flutes, oboes, and bassoons are woodwinds. **2** of or having to do with woodwinds: *Flutes are in the woodwind section of an orchestra.* **1** *n.*, **2** *adj.*

wood work (wud′werk′), things made of wood; wooden parts inside a house, such as doors, stairs, moldings, and the like. *n.*

wood work ing (wud′wer′king), **1** making or shaping things of wood: *She is skilled in woodworking.* **2** of or for woodworking: *woodworking tools.* **1** *n.*, **2** *adj.*

wood y (wud′ē), **1** having many trees; covered with trees: *a woody hillside.* **2** consisting of wood: *the woody parts of a shrub.* **3** like wood: *Turnips become woody when they are old.* *adj.,* **wood i er, wood i est.**

woo er (wü′ər), one that woos; suitor. *n.*

woof (wüf), **1** the threads running from side to side across a woven fabric. The woof crosses the warp. See **warp** for

picture. **2** fabric; cloth; texture. *n.*

wool (wul), **1** the soft curly hair or fur of sheep and some other animals. **2** short, thick, curly hair. **3** something like wool. **4** yarn, cloth, or garments made of wool: *wear wool in winter.* **5** made of wool. **1-4** *n.*, **5** *adj.* **—wool′-like′,** *adj.*
pull the wool over one's eyes, INFORMAL. deceive or trick one.

wool en (wul′ən), **1** made of wool: *a woolen suit.* **2** yarn or cloth made of wool. **3** **woolens,** *pl.* cloth or clothing made of wool: *I put my woolens in a plastic bag every summer to protect them against moths.* **4** of or having to do with wool or cloth made of wool: *a woolen mill.* **1,4** *adj.,* **2,3** *n.*

wool gath er ing (wul′gaŦH′ər ing), **1** absorption in thinking or daydreaming; absent-mindedness. **2** inattentive; absent-minded; dreamy. **1** *n.*, **2** *adj.*

wool len (wul′ən), woolen. *adj., n.*

wool ly (wul′ē), **1** consisting of wool: *the woolly coat of a sheep.* **2** like wool. **3** covered with wool or something like it. **4** not clear; confused; muddled: *Both his thinking and his writing are woolly. adj.,* **wool li er, wool li est.**

wool y (wul′ē), woolly. *adj.,* **wool i er, wool i est.**

wooz y (wü′zē or wuz′ē), SLANG. muddled; confused. *adj.,* **wooz i er, wooz i est.**

Worces ter (wus′tər), city in central Massachusetts. *n.*

word (werd), **1** a sound or a group of sounds that has meaning and is a unit of speech. We speak words when we talk. **2** the writing or printing that stands for a word: *This page is filled with words.* **3** a short talk: *May I have a word with you?* **4** speech: *He is honest in word and deed.* **5** a brief expression: *The teacher gave us a word of advice.* **6** command; order: *The tyrant's word was law.* **7 the Word,** the Bible. **8** signal: *The word for tonight is "the King."* **9** promise: *She kept her word. He is a man of his word.* **10** news: *No word has come from the battle front.* **11 words,** *pl.* angry talk; quarrel; dispute. **12** put into words: *She worded her message clearly.* **1-11** *n.*, **12** *v.*

be as good as one's word, keep one's promise.

by word of mouth, by spoken words; orally.

eat one's words, take back what one has said; retract.

in a word, briefly.

take one at his word, take one's words seriously and act accordingly.

take the words out of one's mouth, say exactly what one was just going to say.

upon my word, 1 I promise. **2** expression of surprise.

word for word, in the exact words.

word book (wėrd′bùk′), list of words, usually with explanations, etc.; dictionary. *n.*

word i ness (wėr′dē nis), a being wordy; verbosity. *n.*

word ing (wėr′ding), way of saying a thing; choice and use of words: *Careful wording helps you make clear to others what you really mean. n.*

word less (wėrd′lis), **1** without words; speechless. **2** not put into words, unexpressed. *adj.* —**word′less ly,** *adv.*

word of honor, a solemn promise.

Words worth (wėrdz′wėrth′), **William,** 1770-1850, English poet. *n.*

word y (wėr′dē), using too many words; verbose. *adj.,* **word i er, word i est.**

wore (wôr), past tense of **wear.** *He wore out his shoes in two months. v.*

work (wėrk), **1** effort in doing or making something: *Some people like hard work.* **2** something to do; occupation; employment: *My friend is out of work.* **3** something made or done; result of effort: *The artist considers that picture to be his greatest work.* **4** that on which effort is put: *We carried our work out onto the front porch.* **5** works, *pl.* **a** factory or other place for doing some kind of work. **b** the moving parts of a machine: *the works of a watch.* **c** buildings, bridges, docks, etc. **d** actions: *good works.* **6** do work; labor: *Most people must work to earn money.* **7** work for pay; be employed: *She works at an airplane factory.* **8** put effort on: *He worked his farm with success.* **9** act; operate: *This pump will not work. The plan worked well.* **10** cause to do work: *He works his employees hard.* **11** make, get, do or bring about by effort: *The injured man worked his way across the room on his hands and knees. She worked her way through college.* **12** move as if with effort: *His face worked as he tried to keep back the tears.* **13** bring about; cause; do: *The plan worked harm.* **14** go slowly or with effort: *The ship worked to windward.* **15** become (up, round, loose, etc.): *The window catch has worked loose.* **16** to form; shape: *He worked a piece of copper into a tray.* **17** move; stir; excite: *Don't work yourself into a temper.* 1-5 *n.,* 6-17 *v.,* **worked, work ing.**

make short work of, deal with quickly.

out of work, having no job.

work in, put in.

work off, get rid of: *work off a debt.*

work on or **work upon,** try to persuade or influence.

work out, 1 plan; develop. **2** solve; find out. **3** give exercise to; practice. **4** result.

work up, plan; develop.

work a ble (wėr′kə bəl), that can be worked. *adj.*

work a day (wėr′kə dā′), of working days; practical; commonplace; ordinary. Also, **workday.** *adj.*

work bench (wėrk′bench′), table at which a mechanic or artisan works. *n.,* *pl.* **work bench es.**

work book (wėrk′bùk′), book containing outlines for the study of some subject, questions to be answered, etc.; book in which a student does parts of his written work. *n.*

work day (wėrk′dā′), **1** day for work; day that is not Sunday or a holiday. **2** part of a day during which work is done. **3** workaday. 1,2 *n.,* 3 *adj.*

work er (wėr′kər), **1** person or thing that works. **2** bee, ant, wasp, or other insect that works for its community and usually does not produce offspring. *n.*

work horse (wėrk′hôrs′), **1** horse used for labor, and not for showing, racing, or hunting. **2** a very hard worker. *n.*

work house (wėrk′hous′), **1** house of correction where petty criminals are kept and made to work. **2** (in Great Britain) a house where very poor people are lodged and set to work. *n., pl.* **work hous es** (wėrk′hou′ziz).

work ing (wėr′king), **1** method or manner of work; operation; action: *Do you understand the working of this machine?* **2** that works: *The class constructed a working model of a helicopter.* **3** of, for, or used in working: *working hours, working clothes.* **4** used to operate with or by: *a working majority.* **5** workings, *pl.* parts of a mine, quarry, tunnel, etc., where work is being done. 1,5 *n.,* 2-4 *adj.*

work ing man (wėr′king man′), **1** man who works. **2** man who works with his hands or with machines. *n., pl.* **work ing men.**

work man (wėrk′mən), **1** worker. **2** person who works with his hands or with machines. *n., pl.* **work men.**

work man like (wėrk′mən līk′), skillful; well-done: *a workmanlike job. adj.*

work man ship (wėrk′mən ship), **1** the art or skill in a worker or his work: *Good workmanship requires long practice.* **2** quality or manner of work. **3** the work done. *n.*

work out (wėrk′out′), INFORMAL. **1** exercise; practice: *She had a good workout running around the track before breakfast.* **2** trial; test: *The mechanic gave the car a thorough workout after repairing it. n.*

work room (wėrk′rüm′ or wėrk′-

hat, āge, fär; let, ēqual, tėrm; it, īce; hot, ōpen, ôrder; oil, out; cup, pùt, rüle; ch, child; ng, long; sh, she; th, thin; ₮H, then; zh, measure;

ə represents *a* in about, *e* in taken, *i* in pencil, *o* in lemon, *u* in circus.

rüm′), room where work is done. *n.*

work shop (wėrk′shop′), **1** shop or building where work is done. **2** group of people working on a special project or study. *n.*

work ta ble (wėrk′tā′bəl), table to work at. *n.*

world (wėrld), **1** the earth: *Ships can sail around the world.* **2** all of certain parts, people, or things of the earth: *the insect world, the world of books, the world of fashion, the ancient world.* **3** all people; the public: *The whole world knows it.* **4** the things of this life and the people devoted to them: *Monks and nuns live apart from the world.* **5** any planet, especially when considered as inhabited: *"The War of the Worlds" is about the creatures from Mars who want to conquer Earth.* **6** any time, condition, or place of life: *the next world, a better world.* **7** all things; everything; the universe. **8** a great deal; very much; large amount: *Sunshine does children a world of good. n.*

for all the world, 1 for any reason, no matter how great. **2** in every respect; exactly.

world li ness (wėrld′lē nis), worldly ideas, ways, or conduct. *n.*

world ly (wėrld′lē), **1** of this world; not of heaven: *worldly wealth.* **2** caring much for the interests and pleasures of this world. **3** worldly-wise. *adj.,* **world li er, world li est.**

world ly-wise (wėrld′lē wīz′), wise about the ways and affairs of this world. *adj.*

World Series, series of baseball games played each fall between the winners of the two major league championships, to decide the professional championship of the United States.

world's fair, an international exposition with exhibits of arts, crafts, products, etc., from various countries.

World War I, war fought mainly in Europe and the Middle East, from July 28, 1914, to November 11, 1918. The United States, Great Britain, France, Russia, and their allies were on one side; Germany, Austria-Hungary, and their allies were on the other side.

adj.	adjective		n.	noun
adv.	adverb		prep.	preposition
conj.	conjunction		pron.	pronoun
interj.	interjection		v.	verb
sing.	singular		pl.	plural

World War II, war fought in Europe, Asia, Africa, and elsewhere, from September 1, 1939, to August 14, 1945. The chief conflict was between Great Britain, the United States, France, and the Soviet Union on one side and Germany, Italy, and Japan on the other.

world-wear y (wèrld′wir′ē), weary of this world; tired of living. *adj.*

world wide (wèrld′wīd′), spread throughout the world: *Gasoline now has worldwide use. adj.*

worms (def. 1)—A, earthworm; B, leech; C, hookworm; D, tapeworm

worm (wèrm), 1 a small, slender, crawling or creeping animal. Most worms have soft bodies and no legs. 2 something like a worm in shape or movement, such as the thread of a screw. 3 move like a worm; crawl or creep like a worm: *The soldier wormed his way through the grass. We wormed under the fence.* 4 get by persistent and secret means: *worm information out of someone, worm the truth from a person. He wormed himself into our confidence.* 5 person who deserves contempt or pity. **6 worms,** *pl.* disease caused by parasitic worms in the body, especially in the intestines. 1,2,5,6 *n.,* 3,4 *v.* **—worm′like′,** *adj.*

worm-eat en (wèrm′ēt′n), 1 eaten into by worms: *worm-eaten timbers.* 2 worn-out; worthless; out-of-date. *adj.*

worm i ness (wèr′mē nis), a being wormy. *n.*

worm wood (wèrm′wùd′), 1 a bitter plant used in medicine and in certain liquors. 2 something bitter or extremely unpleasant. *n.*

worm y (wèr′mē), 1 having worms; containing many worms: *wormy apples.* 2 damaged by worms: *wormy wood. adj.,* **worm i er, worm i est.**

worn (wôrn), 1 past participle of **wear.** *I have worn these jeans for two years.* 2 damaged by use: *worn rugs.* 3 tired; wearied: *a worn face.* 1 *v.,* 2,3 *adj.*

worn-out (wôrn′out′), 1 used until no longer fit for use. 2 very tired; exhausted. *adj.*

wor ri er (wèr′ē ər), person who worries. *n.*

wor ri some (wèr′ē səm), 1 causing worry. 2 inclined to worry. *adj.*

wor ry (wèr′ē), 1 feel anxious; be uneasy: *Don't worry about little things. She will worry if we are late.* 2 make anxious; trouble: *The problem worried him.* 3 anxiety; uneasiness; trouble; care: *Worry kept me awake.* 4 cause of trouble or care: *Parents of a sick child have many worries.* 5 annoy; bother; vex: *Don't worry me right now with so many questions.* 6 seize and shake with the teeth; bite at; snap at: *The cat worried the mouse.* 1,2,5,6 *v.,* **wor ried, wor ry ing;** 3,4 *n., pl.* **wor ries.**

worse (wèrs), 1 less well; more ill: *The patient seems even worse today.* 2 less good; more evil: *He is bad enough, but his sister is much worse.* 3 in a more severe or evil manner or degree: *It is raining worse than ever today.* 4 that which is worse: *Loss of her property was bad enough, but worse followed.* 1,2 *adj.,* 3 *adv.,* 4 *n.*

wors en (wèr′sən), make or become worse. *v.*

wor ship (wèr′ship), 1 great honor and reverence paid to someone or something regarded as sacred: *the worship of God, idol worship, fire worship.* 2 pay great honor and reverence to: *People go to church to worship God.* 3 religious ceremonies or services in which one expresses such honor and reverence. Prayers and hymns are part of worship. 4 take part in a religious service. 5 great love and admiration; adoration: *hero worship, the worship of wealth and power.* 6 consider extremely precious; hold very dear; adore: *She worships her mother. A miser worships money.* 7 title used in Great Britain in addressing certain magistrates: *"Yes, your worship," she said to the judge.* 1,3,5,7 *n.,* 2,4,6 *v.* **—wor′ship er, n.**

wor ship ful (wèr′ship fəl), 1 honorable: *We beg you, worshipful gentlemen, to grant our request.* 2 worshiping: *the worshipful eyes of a dog watching its master. adj.*

worst (wèrst), 1 least well; most ill: *This is the worst I've been since I got sick.* 2 least good; most evil: *It is the worst movie I've seen.* 3 in the worst manner or degree: *He acts worst when he's tired.* 4 that which is worst: *Yesterday was bad, but the worst is yet to come.* 5 beat; defeat: *worst one's enemies.* 1,2 *adj.,* 3 *adv.,* 4 *n.,* 5 *v.*

at worst, under the least favorable circumstances.

if worst comes to worst, if the very worst thing happens.

wor sted (wùs′tid *or* wèr′stid), 1 a firmly twisted woolen thread or yarn. 2 made of worsted. 3 cloth made from such thread or yarn. 1,3 *n.,* 2 *adj.* [from *Worsted* (now *Worstead*), town in England, where it was originally made]

worth (wèrth), 1 good or important enough for; deserving of: *That book is worth reading. New York is a city worth visiting.* 2 merit; usefulness; importance: *We should read books of real worth.* 3 value: *She got her money's worth out of that coat.* 4 quantity that a certain amount will buy: *I bought a dollar's worth of stamps.* 5 equal in value to: *That book is worth $5.* 6 having property that amounts to: *That man is worth a million dollars.* 1,5,6 *adj.,* 2-4 *n.*

wor thi ly (wèr′ŦHə lē), in a worthy manner. *adv.*

wor thi ness (wèr′ŦHē nis), quality or condition of being worthy; merit; worth; excellence. *n.*

worth less (wèrth′lis), without worth; good-for-nothing; useless: *Throw those worthless, broken toys away. Don't read that worthless book. adj.* **—worth′less ly,** *adv.* **—worth′less ness,** *n.*

worth while (wèrth′hwīl′), worth time, attention, or effort; having real merit: *This is a worthwhile book; you should read it. adj.*

wor thy (wèr′ŦHē), 1 having worth or merit: *Helping the poor is a worthy cause.* 2 deserving; meriting: *Her courage was worthy of high praise. Bad acts are worthy of punishment.* 3 person of great merit; admirable person: *The Wright brothers stand high among American worthies.* 1,2 *adj.,* **wor thi er, wor thi est;** 3 *n., pl.* **wor thies.**

wot (wot), OLD USE. know. "I wot" means "I know." "He wot" means "He knows." *v.*

would (wùd), 1 past tense of **will**[1]. *He said that he would come. He would go in spite of our warning.* 2 *Would* is also used: **a** to express future time: *Would she never go?* **b** to express action done again and again in the past time: *The children would play for hours on the beach.* **c** to express a wish: *I would I were rich.* **d** to make a statement or question sound more polite than *will* sounds: *Would you help us, please?* **e** to express conditions: *If you would only try, you could do it. v.*

would-be (wùd′bē′), 1 wishing or pretending to be. 2 intended to be. *adj.*

would n't (wùd′nt), would not.

wouldst (wùdst), OLD USE. would. "Thou wouldst" means "you would." *v.*

wound[1] (wünd), 1 a hurt or injury

caused by cutting, stabbing, shooting, etc.: *a knife wound, a bullet wound.* **2** injure by cutting, stabbing, shooting, etc.; hurt: *The hunter wounded the deer.* **3** any hurt or injury to feelings, reputation, etc.: *The loss of his job was a wound to his pride.* **4** injure in feelings, reputation, etc.: *Her unkind words wounded me.* 1,3 *n.,* 2,4 *v.* [Old English *wund*]

wound² (wound), past tense and past participle of **wind²**. *I wound the yarn into a ball. The yarn is wound too tightly. v.*

wound³ (wound), winded; a past tense and a past participle of **wind³**. *v.*

wove (wōv), past tense and a past participle of **weave**. *The spider wove a new web after the first was destroyed. v.*

wo ven (wō′vən), a past participle of **weave**. *This cloth is closely woven. v.*

wow (wou), exclamation of surprise, joy, etc. *interj.*

wrack (rak), **1** wreckage. **2** ruin; destruction. **3** seaweed cast ashore. *n.*

wraith (rāth), **1** ghost of a person seen shortly before or soon after his death. **2** specter; ghost. *n.*

wran gle (rang′gəl), **1** argue or dispute in a noisy or angry way: *The children wrangled about who should sit in the front seat of the car.* **2** a noisy dispute; angry quarrel. **3** (in the western United States and Canada) to herd or tend (horses, cattle, etc.) on the range. 1,3 *v.,* **wran gled, wran gling;** 2 *n.*

wran gler (rang′glər), **1** person who wrangles. **2** (in the western United States and Canada) a herder in charge of horses, cattle, etc. *n.*

wrap (rap), **1** to cover by winding or folding something around: *She wrapped herself in a shawl.* **2** to wind or fold as a covering: *Wrap a shawl around yourself.* **3** to cover with paper and tie up or fasten: *Have you wrapped her birthday present yet?* **4** to envelop; veil: *The mountain peak is wrapped in clouds. She sat wrapped in thought.* **5** an outer covering. *Shawls, scarfs, coats, and furs are wraps.* 1-4 *v.,* **wrapped** or **wrapt, wrap ping;** 5 *n.*

wrapped up in, devoted to; thinking mainly of: *She is so wrapped up in her work that she never sees her old friends any more.*

wrap per (rap′ər), **1** person or thing that wraps. **2** a covering or cover: *Some magazines are mailed in paper wrappers.* **3** a woman's long, loose garment to wear in the house. *n.*

wrap ping (rap′ing), paper, cloth, etc., in which something is wrapped. *n.*

wrapt (rapt), wrapped; a past tense and a past participle of **wrap**. *v.*

wrath (rath), very great anger; rage. *n.*

wrath ful (rath′fəl), very angry; showing wrath: *The wrathful lion turned on the hunters. Its wrathful eyes flashed.* *adj.* —**wrath′ful ly,** *adv.*

wreak (rēk), **1** give expression to; work off (feelings, desires, etc.): *I wreaked my anger on my sister by screaming at her.* **2** inflict (vengeance, punishment, etc.). *v.*

wreath (rēth), **1** a ring of flowers or leaves twisted together: *We hang wreaths in the windows at Christmas.* **2** something suggesting a wreath: *a wreath of smoke. n., pl.* **wreaths** (rēᵬHz).

wreathe (rēᵬH), **1** make into a wreath: *The children wreathed flowers to put on the soldiers' graves.* **2** decorate or adorn with wreaths: *The doors of the houses we passed were wreathed with greens.* **3** make a ring around; encircle: *Mist wreathed the hills. v.,* **wreathed, wreath ing.**

wreathed in smiles, smiling greatly.

wreck (rek), **1** destruction of a motor vehicle, ship, building, train, or aircraft: *The hurricane caused many wrecks. Reckless driving causes many wrecks on the highway.* **2** any destruction or serious injury: *Heavy rains caused the wreck of many crops.* **3** what is left of anything that has been destroyed or much injured: *The waves cast the wreck of a ship upon the shore.* **4** cause the wreck of; destroy; ruin: *Raccoons wrecked our campsite looking for food.* **5** person who has lost his health or money: *She is a wreck from overwork.* 1-3,5 *n.,* 4 *v.*

wreck age (rek′ij), **1** what is left by a wreck or wrecks: *The shore was covered with the wreckage of ships.* **2** a wrecking or a being wrecked: *She wept at the wreckage of her hopes. n.*

wreck er (rek′ər), **1** person who causes wrecks. **2** person whose work is tearing down buildings. **3** person, car, train, or machine that removes wrecks. **4** person or ship that recovers wrecked or disabled ships or their cargoes. **5** person who causes shipwrecks by showing false lights on shore so as to plunder the wrecks. *n.*

wren (ren), any of a group of small songbirds with slender bills and short tails, often held erect. Wrens often build their nests near houses. *n.*

Wren (ren), Sir **Christopher,** 1632-1723, English architect. *n.*

wrench (rench), **1** a violent twist or twisting pull: *He broke the branch off with a sudden wrench. I gave my ankle a wrench when I jumped from the tree.* **2** twist or pull violently: *He wrenched the knob off when he was trying to open the door. The policeman wrenched the gun out of the man's hand.* **3** injure by

hat, āge, fär; let, ēqual, tėrm;
it, īce; hot, ōpen, ôrder;
oil, out; cup, pùt, rüle; ch, child;
ng, long; sh, she; th, thin;
ᵬH, then; zh, measure;

ə represents *a* in about,
e in taken, *i* in pencil,
o in lemon, *u* in circus.

wrench (def. 6)
pipe wrench

twisting: *She wrenched her back doing acrobatics.* **4** injury caused by twisting. **5** source of grief or sorrow: *It was a wrench to leave our old home.* **6** tool for turning nuts, bolts, etc. 1,4-6 *n., pl.* **wrench es;** 2,3 *v.*

wrest (rest), **1** twist, pull, or tear away with force; wrench away: *He bravely wrested the knife from his attacker.* **2** take by force: *An enemy wrested the power from the duke.* **3** twist or turn from the proper meaning, use, etc.: *You wrest my words from their real meanings.* **4** obtain by persistence or persuasion; wring: *wrest a secret from someone. v.*

wres tle (res′əl), **1** try to throw or force (an opponent) to the ground. **2** a wrestling match. **3** contend with in wrestling, or as if in wrestling. **4** struggle: *wrestle with temptation. I have been wrestling with this problem for over an hour.* 1,3,4 *v.,* **wres tled, wres tling;** 2 *n.*

wres tler (res′lər), person who wrestles, especially as a sport. *n.*

wres tling (res′ling), sport or contest in which each of two opponents tries to throw or force the other to the ground. The rules for wrestling do not allow using the fists or certain holds on the body. *n.*

wretch (rech), **1** a very unfortunate or unhappy person. **2** a very bad person. *n., pl.* **wretch es.**

wretch ed (rech′id), **1** very unfortunate or unhappy. **2** very unsatisfactory; miserable: *a wretched hut.* **3** very bad: *a wretched traitor. adj.* —**wretch′ed ly,** *adv.* —**wretch′ed ness,** *n.*

wrig gle (rig′əl), **1** twist and turn: *Children wriggle when they are restless.* **2** move by twisting and turning: *The worm wriggled out of my hand when I*

adj.	adjective	*n.*	noun
adv.	adverb	*prep.*	preposition
conj.	conjunction	*pron.*	pronoun
interj.	interjection	*v.*	verb
sing.	singular	*pl.*	plural

tried to put it on the hook. **3** make one's way by shifts and tricks: *wriggle out of a difficulty.* **4** a wriggling. 1-3 *v.*, **wriggled, wrig gling;** 4 *n.*

wrig gler (rig′lər), **1** person who wriggles. **2** larva of a mosquito. *n.*

Wright (rīt), **1 Frank Lloyd,** 1869-1959, American architect. **2 Orville,** 1871-1948, and his brother **Wilbur,** 1867-1912, American inventors, who perfected the airplane and made the world's first flight in a motor-powered plane, in 1903. *n.*

wring (ring), **1** twist with force; squeeze hard: *wring clothes. Wring out your wet bathing suits and hang them up.* **2** get by twisting or squeezing; force out: *The boy wrung water from his wet bathing suit.* **3** get by force, effort, or persuasion: *wring a secret from someone.* **4** clasp and hold firmly; press: *She wrung her old friend's hand.* **5** cause pain or pity in: *Their poverty wrung his heart.* **6** twist violently; wrench: *wring a chicken's neck.* **7** a twist or squeeze. 1-6 *v.*, **wrung, wring ing;** 7 *n.*

wring er (ring′ər), machine for squeezing water from wet clothes. *n.*

wrin kle (ring′kəl), **1** an irregular ridge or fold; crease: *The old man's face has wrinkles. I must press out the wrinkles in this dress.* **2** make a wrinkle or wrinkles in: *She wrinkled her forehead.* **3** have wrinkles; acquire wrinkles: *This shirt will not wrinkle.* **4** INFORMAL. useful hint or idea; clever trick: *He knows all the latest wrinkles in style.* 1,4 *n.*, 2,3 *v.*, **wrin kled, wrin kling.**

wrist (rist), the joint connecting hand and arm. *n.*

wrist band (rist′band′), the band of a sleeve fitting around the wrist. *n.*

wrist watch (rist′woch′ *or* rist′-wôch′), a small watch worn on a strap around the wrist. *n., pl.* **wrist watch es.**

writ (rit), **1** something written; piece of writing. *The Bible is Holy Writ.* **2** formal order directing a person to do or not to do something: *A writ from the*

judge ordered the man's release from jail. **3** OLD USE. written. 1,2 *n.*, 3 *v.*

write (rīt), **1** make letters or words with pen, pencil, or chalk: *You can read and write.* **2** mark with letters or words: *Please write on both sides of the paper.* **3** put down the letters or words of: *Write your name and address.* **4** make up stories, books, etc.; compose: *He writes for the magazines.* **5** be a writer: *Her ambition was to write.* **6** write a letter: *I write to my family every week.* **7** write a letter to: *She wrote her parents that she would be home for New Year's.* **8** show plainly: *Amusement was written on her face.* *v.*, **wrote, writ ten, writ ing.**

write down, 1 put into writing. **2** put a lower value on.

write off, cancel.

write out, 1 put into writing. **2** write in full.

write up, 1 write a description or account of. **2** write in detail. **3** put a higher value on.

writ er (rī′tər), **1** person who writes. **2** person whose occupation is writing; author. *n.*

write-up (rīt′up′), INFORMAL. a written description or account. *n.*

writhe (rīᴛʜ), **1** twist and turn; twist about: *writhe with pain, writhe with laughter. The snake writhed along the branch.* **2** suffer mentally; be very uncomfortable. *v.*, **writhed, writh ing.**

WRINGER

writ ing (rī′ting), **1** act of making letters or words with pen, pencil, chalk, etc. **2** written form: *Put your ideas in writing.* **3** handwriting: *Your writing is hard to read.* **4** something written; a letter, paper, document, etc. **5** literary work; a book or other literary production: *the writings of Benjamin Franklin.* **6** profession or business of a person who writes. *n.*

writ ten (rit′n), past participle of **write.** *He has written a letter. v.*

wrong (rông *or* rong), **1** not right; bad: *It is wrong to tell lies.* **2** not true; not correct; not what it should be: *give a wrong answer.* **3** not proper; not fit; unsuitable: *Heavy boots would be the*

wrong thing to wear for tennis. **4** out of order: *Something is wrong with the car.* **5** in a wrong manner; badly: *She did her homework wrong and had to do it over.* **6** anything not right; wrong thing or action: *know right from wrong.* **7** injustice; injury; harm: *You do an honest man wrong to call him a liar.* **8** do wrong to; treat unfairly; injure: *forgive someone who has wronged you.* **9** not meant to be seen; least important: *the wrong side of cloth.* 1-4,9 *adj.*, 5 *adv.*, 6,7 *n.*, 8 *v.* **—wrong′ly,** *adv.* **—wrong′ness,** *n.*

go wrong, 1 turn out badly: *Everything went wrong today.* **2** stop being good and become bad.

in the wrong, at fault; guilty.

wrong do er (rông′dü′ər *or* rong′-dü′ər), person who does wrong. *n.*

wrong do ing (rông′dü′ing *or* rong′dü′ing), a doing wrong; bad acts: *The thief was guilty of wrongdoing. n.*

wrong ful (rông′fəl *or* rong′fəl), **1** wrong. **2** unlawful. *adj.* **—wrong′ful ly,** *adv.*

wrong head ed (rông′hed′id *or* rong′hed′id), **1** wrong in judgment or opinion. **2** stubborn even when wrong. *adj.*

wrote (rōt), past tense of **write.** *He wrote his mother a long letter last week. v.*

wroth (rôth *or* roth), angry. *adj.*

wrought (rôt), **1** OLD USE. worked; a past tense and a past participle of **work. 2** made: *The gate was wrought with great skill.* **3** (of metals) formed by hammering. 1 *v.*, 2,3 *adj.*

wrought iron, a tough, durable form of iron with little carbon in it. Wrought iron is soft enough to be forged and welded easily, but it will not break as easily as cast iron.

wrung (rung), past tense and past participle of **wring.** *I wrung out the wet cloth and hung it up. Her heart is wrung with pity for the poor.*

wry (rī), **1** turned to one side; twisted: *She made a wry face to show her disgust.* **2** ironic: *wry humor. adj.*, **wri er, wri est. —wry′ly,** *adv.*

wt., weight.

W. Va., West Virginia.

Wyc liffe (wik′lif), **John,** 1320?-1384, English religious reformer who translated the Bible into English. *n.*

Wy eth (wī′əth), **Andrew N.,** born 1917, American painter. *n.*

Wyo., Wyoming.

Wy o ming (wī ō′ming), one of the western states of the United States. *Capital:* Cheyenne. *n.*

X x

X or **x** (eks), 1 the 24th letter of the alphabet. 2 an unknown quantity. 3 anything shaped like an X. 4 the Roman numeral for 10. *n.*, *pl.* **X's** or **x's.**

Xan thip pe (zan tip′ē), 1 the wife of Socrates, famous as a scold. 2 a scolding woman; shrew. *n.*

Xa vi er (zā′vē ər *or* zav′ē ər), **Saint Francis,** 1506-1552, Spanish Jesuit missionary in the Far East. *n.*

X chromosome, one of the two chromosomes that determine sex. A fertilized egg cell containing two X chromosomes, one from each parent, develops into a female.

xe bec (zē′bek), a small, three-masted vessel of the Mediterranean. *n.*

xe non (zē′non), a colorless, odorless, inert gas, forming a very small part of

X ray (def. 2) of an abscessed tooth. The abscess is shown by the dark area around the roots of the tooth.

the air. It is a chemical element. Xenon is used in filling flashbulbs, vacuum tubes, etc. It forms compounds with fluorine and oxygen. *n.*

xen o pho bi a (zen′ə fō′bē ə), hatred or fear of foreigners. *n.*

Xen o phon (zen′ə fən), 434?-355? B.C., Greek historian and military leader. *n.*

Xer ox (zir′oks), trademark for a dry process of making copies of letters, etc., by using electrically charged particles instead of ink and pressure to transfer the original copy from a metal plate to paper. *n.*

Xerx es (zėrk′sēz′), 519?-465 B.C., king of ancient Persia from 486? to 465 B.C. He tried to conquer Greece but was defeated in 480 B.C. *n.*

Xmas (kris′məs), Christmas. *n.*

X ray, 1 an electromagnetic ray having an extremely short wavelength, that can go through substances that ordinary rays of light cannot penetrate; Roentgen ray. X rays are formed when a high-speed stream of electrons strikes a target, usually of metal, in a special kind of vacuum tube. X rays are used to locate breaks in bones, bullets lodged in the body, etc., and to diagnose and treat certain diseases. 2 picture made by means of X rays.

X-ray (eks′rā′), 1 examine, photograph, or treat with X rays: *The doctor X-rayed my knee to find out if any bones had been broken by my fall.* 2 of, by, or having to do with X rays: *an X-ray examination of one's teeth.* 1 *v.*, 2 *adj.*

hat, āge, fär; let, ēqual, tėrm;
it, īce; hot, ōpen, ôrder;
oil, out; cup, pùt, rüle; ch, child;
ng, long; sh, she; th, thin;
₮H, then; zh, measure;

ə represents *a* in about,
e in taken, *i* in pencil,
o in lemon, *u* in circus.

xy lem (zī′lem), the woody part of plants. It consists of tissue that conveys upward the water and dissolved minerals absorbed by the roots. *n.*

xylophone

xy lo phone (zī′lə fōn), a musical instrument consisting of two rows of wooden bars of varying lengths, which are sounded by striking with wooden hammers. *n.*

xy lo phon ist (zī′lə fō′nist), person who plays on a xylophone. *n.*

Y y

Y or **y** (wī), 1 the 25th letter of the alphabet. 2 anything shaped like a Y. *n., pl.* **Y's** or **y's.**

y., 1 yard or yards. 2 year.

-y[1], *suffix forming adjectives.* 1 (*added to nouns*) full of _____: *Bumpy = full of bumps.* 2 (*added to nouns*) containing _____: *Salty = containing salt.* 3 (*added to nouns*) having _____: *Cloudy = having clouds.* 4 (*added to nouns*) characterized by _____: *Funny = characterized by fun.* 5 (*added to adjectives*) somewhat _____: *Chilly = somewhat chill.* 6 (*added to verbs*) inclined to _____: *Sleepy = inclined to sleep.* [Old English *-ig*]

-y[2], *suffix added to nouns to form nouns.* 1 small _____: *Dolly = a small doll.* 2 dear _____: *Daddy = dear dad.* [Middle English]

-y[3], *suffix forming nouns.* 1 (*added to adjectives*) _____ condition or quality: *Jealousy = a jealous condition or quality.* 2 (*added to nouns*) condition or quality of being _____: *Victory = condition or quality of being a victor.* 3 (*added to verbs*) activity of _____ing: *Delivery = activity of delivering. Entreaty = activity of entreating.* [from French before the 1400's *-ie*, from Latin *-ia*, from Greek]

yacht (yot), 1 boat for pleasure trips or for racing. 2 to sail or race on a yacht. 1 *n.*, 2 *v.*

yacht ing (yot′ing), 1 art of sailing a yacht. 2 pastime of sailing on a yacht. *n.*

yachts man (yots′mən), person who owns or sails a yacht. *n., pl.* **yachtsmen.**

yak—5 to 6 ft. high at the shoulder

yak (yak), a long-haired ox of Tibet and central Asia. The domesticated yak is raised for its meat, milk, and hair and is used as a beast of burden. *n.*

Yal ta (yôl′tə), seaport and winter resort in S Crimea, on the Black Sea. *n.*

Ya lu (yä′lü), river in E Asia, between Manchuria and Korea. *n.*

yam (yam), 1 a vine of warm regions with a starchy root much like the sweet potato. 2 its root, eaten as a vegetable.

3 the sweet potato: *We often have candied yams with ham.* *n.*

Yang tze (yang′sē′), river flowing from Tibet through China. It is the longest river in China. *n.*

yank (yangk), INFORMAL. 1 to pull with a sudden motion; jerk; tug: *The dentist yanked the tooth.* 2 a sudden pull; jerk; tug: *She gave the door a yank.* 1 *v.*, 2 *n.*

Yan kee (yang′kē), 1 a native of New England. 2 a native of any part of the northern United States. 3 person born or living in the United States; American. 4 of or having to do with Yankees: *Yankee shrewdness.* 1-3 *n.*, 4 *adj.*

Yankee Doo dle (dü′dl), an American song, probably of English origin and taken over by the American soldiers in the Revolutionary War.

yap (yap), 1 a snappish bark; yelp. 2 bark snappishly; yelp: *The little dog yapped at every strange person who came to the door.* 3 SLANG. snappish, noisy, or foolish talk. 4 SLANG. talk snappishly, noisily, or foolishly. 1,3 *n.*, 2,4 *v.*, **yapped, yap ping.**

yard[1] (yärd), 1 piece of ground near or around a house, barn, school, etc.: *You can play outside, but you must not leave the yard.* 2 piece of enclosed ground for some special purpose or business: *a chicken yard.* 3 space with tracks where railroad cars are stored, shifted around, etc.: *My cousin works in the railroad yards.* *n.* [Old English *geard* enclosure]

yard[2] (yärd), 1 measure of length equal to 36 inches; 3 feet: *I bought three yards of blue cloth for curtains. Whoever runs 50 yards the fastest will be the winner.* 2 a beam or pole fastened across a mast, used to support a sail. *n.* [Old English *gerd* rod]

yard age (yär′dij), 1 length in yards. 2 amount measured in yards. *n.*

yard arm (yärd′ärm′), either end of the beam or pole used to support a square sail. *n.*

yard goods, cloth cut to measure and sold by the yard.

yard mas ter (yärd′mas′tər), person in charge of a railroad yard. *n.*

yard stick (yärd′stik′), 1 a stick one yard long, used for measuring. 2 standard of judgment or comparison: *What yardstick do you use to decide whether your conduct is right or wrong?* *n.*

yarn (yärn), 1 any spun thread, especially that prepared for weaving or knitting: *I know how to knit a scarf from yarn.* 2 INFORMAL. tale; story: *We took turns making up yarns and telling them.* 3 INFORMAL. tell stories. 1,2 *n.*, 3 *v.*

yar row (yar′ō), a common plant with

finely divided leaves and flat clusters of white or pink flowers. *n.*

yaw (yô), 1 to turn from a straight course; go unsteadily. 2 (of an aircraft) to turn from a straight course by a motion about its vertical axis. 3 movement from a straight course. 1,2 *v.*, 3 *n.*

yawl (yôl), 1 boat with a large mast near the bow and a small mast near the stern. 2 a ship's boat rowed by four or six oars. *n.*

yawn (yôn), 1 open the mouth wide because one is sleepy, tired, or bored. 2 act of doing so. 3 open wide: *The canyon yawned beneath our feet.* 1,3 *v.*, 2 *n.*

yaws (yôz), a contagious disease of the tropics, characterized by sores on the skin. *n.*

Y chromosome, one of the two chromosomes that determine sex. A fertilized egg cell containing a Y chromosome develops into a male.

yard[2] (def. 2)
mast with
two yards

y clept or **y cleped** (i klept′), OLD USE. called; named. *adj.*

yd., yard. *pl.* **yd.** or **yds.**

ye[1] (yē; *unstressed* yi), OLD USE. you. *pron.pl.* [Old English *gē*]

ye[2] (ŦHē; *incorrectly* yē), an old way of writing the definite article "the." *definite article.* [from the fact that the letter *y* was used by printers instead of the Old English letter Þ, which stood for the sound *th*]

yea (yā), 1 yes (used in agreeing with or assenting to something). 2 indeed; truly (used to introduce a sentence or clause). 3 a vote or voter in favor of something. 1,2 *adv.*, 3 *n., pl.* **yeas.**

year (yir), 1 12 months or 365 days; January 1 to December 31. Leap year has 366 days. 2 12 months reckoned from any point: *I will see you again a year from today.* 3 the part of a year spent in a certain activity: *Our school year is 9 months.* 4 period of the earth's revolution around the sun. **5 years**, *pl.* age: *Young in years but old in experience. I hope to live to your years. n.*

year after year, every year.

year by year, with each succeeding year; as years go by.

year in, year out, always; continuously.

year book (yir/bùk/), book or report published every year. Yearbooks often report facts of the year. The graduating class of a school or college usually publishes a yearbook, with pictures of its members. *n.*

year ling (yir/ling), 1 animal one year old. 2 one year old: *a yearling colt.* 1 *n.,* 2 *adj.*

year long (yir/lông/), 1 lasting for a year. 2 lasting for years. *adj.*

year ly (yir/lē) 1 once a year; in every year: *He takes a yearly trip to New York* (*adj.*). *That company sends out new calendars to its customers yearly* (*adv.*). 2 lasting a year: *The earth makes a yearly revolution around the sun.* 3 for a year: *She is paid $1000 a month, or a yearly salary of $12,000.* 1-3 *adj.,* 1 *adv.*

yearn (yèrn), 1 feel a longing or desire; desire earnestly: *I yearned for home.* 2 feel pity; have tender feelings: *Our hearts yearned for the homeless victims of the flood. v.*

yearn ing (yèr/ning), earnest or strong desire; longing. *n.* —**yearn/ing ly**, *adv.*

year-round (yir/round/), throughout the year: *year-round residents. adj., adv.*

yeast (yēst), 1 the substance that causes dough for bread to rise and beer to ferment. It is a yellowish froth made up of masses of certain tiny fungi which grow quickly in a liquid containing sugar. 2 any of the fungi which form yeast. 3 yeast cake. 4 foam; froth. *n.*

yeast cake, a small block or cake of compressed yeast.

yeast y (yē/stē), 1 of, containing, or resembling yeast. 2 frothy or foamy: *yeasty waves.* 3 light or trifling; frivolous. *adj.*

Yeats (yāts), **William Butler,** 1865-1939, Irish writer of poems, plays, and essays. *n.*

yell (yel), 1 cry out with a strong, loud sound: *I yelled with pain.* 2 a strong, loud cry. 3 say with a yell: *We yelled our good-bys to our friends as the bus moved away.* 4 a special shout or cheer used by a school or college to encourage its sports teams. 1,3 *v.,* 2,4 *n.*

yel low (yel/ō), 1 the color of gold,

---

butter, or ripe lemons. 2 having this color. 3 become yellow: *Paper yellows with age.* 4 make yellow: *Buttercups yellowed the field.* 5 having a yellowish skin. 6 the yolk of an egg, or other thing that is yellow. 7 INFORMAL. cowardly. 1,6 *n.,* 2,5,7 *adj.,* 3,4 *v.* —**yel/low ness,** *n.*

yel low bird (yel/ō bėrd/), 1 the goldfinch of America. 2 yellow warbler. 3 any of various other yellow birds. *n.*

yellow fever, a dangerous, infectious disease of warm climates, transmitted by the bite of a certain kind of mosquito; yellow jack. Yellow fever was once common in some southern parts of the United States.

yel low ham mer (yel/ō ham/ər), a European bunting with a bright-yellow head, neck, and breast. *n.*

yel low ish (yel/ō ish), somewhat yellow. *adj.*

yellow jack, 1 yellow fever. 2 a yellow flag used as a signal of quarantine.

yellow jacket, wasp marked with bright yellow.

Yellow River, Hwang Ho.

Yellow Sea, part of the Pacific Ocean between NE China and Korea.

Yel low stone (yel/ō stōn/), Yellowstone National Park. *n.*

Yellowstone National Park, a large, national park, mostly in NW Wyoming, famous for its scenery, hot springs, and geysers.

yellow warbler, a small, American warbler; yellowbird. The male has yellow plumage, streaked with brown.

yelp (yelp), 1 the quick, sharp bark or cry of a dog, fox, etc. 2 make such a bark or cry. 3 utter with a yelp. 1 *n.,* 2,3 *v.*

Yem en (yem/ən), country in SW Arabia. *n.*

yen[1] (yen), unit of money of Japan, worth about one third of a cent. *n., pl.* **yen.** [from Japanese *yen*, from Chinese *yüan* round object]

yen[2] (yen), INFORMAL. 1 a sharp desire or hunger; urgent fancy: *a yen for ice cream, a sudden yen to leave.* 2 have a yen; desire sharply or urgently. 1 *n.,* 2 *v.,* **yenned, yen ning.** [perhaps from a local pronunciation of *yearn*]

yeo man (yō/mən), 1 (in the United States Navy) a petty officer who performs clerical duties. 2 (formerly, in Great Britain) a person who owned land, but not a large amount, and usually farmed it himself. 3 OLD USE. servant or attendant in a royal or noble household. *n., pl.* **yeo men.**

yeo man ry (yō/mən rē), yeomen. *n.*

yes (yes), 1 word used to indicate that one can or will, or that something is so; word used to affirm, accept, or agree:

---

hat, āge, fär; let, ēqual, tèrm;
it, īce; hot, ōpen, ôrder;
oil, out; cup, pùt, rüle; ch, child;
ng, long; sh, she; th, thin;
ŦH, then; zh, measure;

ə represents *a* in about,
e in taken, *i* in pencil,
o in lemon, *u* in circus.

"Yes, five and two are seven," he said. *Will you go? Yes.* 2 agreement; acceptance; consent: *You have my yes to that.* 3 and what is more; in addition to that: *"Your work is good, yes, very good,"* said the teacher. 4 a vote for; person voting in favor of something: *The yeses won.* 1,3 *adv.,* 2,4 *n., pl.* **yes es** or **yes ses.**

Ye shi va (yə shē/və), 1 a Jewish school for higher studies, often a rabbinical seminary. 2 a Jewish elementary school or high school in which both religious and secular subjects are taught. *n., pl.* **Ye shi vas.** [from Hebrew]

yes ter day (yes/tər dē), 1 the day before today: *Yesterday was cold and rainy.* 2 on the day before today. 3 the recent past: *We are often amused by the fashions of yesterday.* 4 recently. 1,3 *n.,* 2,4 *adv.*

yes ter night (yes/tər nīt/), OLD USE. last night; the night before today. *n., adv.*

yes ter year (yes/tər yir/), OLD USE. last year; the year before this. *n., adv.*

yet (yet), 1 up to the present time; thus far: *The work is not yet finished.* 2 at this time; now: *Don't go yet.* 3 at that time; then: *It was not yet dark.* 4 even now; still: *She is doing her homework yet. It is yet light.* 5 sometime: *I may yet get rich.* 6 also; again: *Yet once more I forbid you to go.* 7 moreover: *They won't do it for you nor yet for me.* 8 even: *The judge spoke yet more harshly to the lawbreaker.* 9 nevertheless; however; but: *The story was strange, yet true* (*adv.*). *The work is good, yet it could be better* (*conj.*). 1-9 *adv.,* 9 *conj.*

as yet, up to now.

yew (yü), 1 an evergreen tree native to Europe and Asia. Some kinds of yew are now widely grown in the United States as shrubs. 2 the wood of this tree. Bows for archery used to be made of a kind of yew that grows in England. *n.*

Yid dish (yid/ish), 1 language which developed from a dialect of German. Yiddish contains many Hebrew expressions and is written in Hebrew characters. It is spoken mainly by Jews of

adj.	adjective	*n.*	noun
adv.	adverb	*prep.*	preposition
conj.	conjunction	*pron.*	pronoun
interj.	interjection	*v.*	verb
sing.	singular	*pl.*	plural

eastern and central Europe, and their descendants. 2 having to do with Yiddish. 1 *n.,* 2 *adj.*

yield (yēld), 1 produce: *This land yields good crops. Mines yield ore.* 2 amount yielded; product: *This year's yield from the silver mine was very large.* 3 give in return; bring in: *an investment which yielded a large profit.* 4 give; grant: *Her parents yielded their consent to the plan.* 5 give up; surrender: *The enemy yielded to our soldiers.* 6 give way: *The door yielded to his touch.* 7 give place: *We yield to nobody in love of freedom.* 1,3-7 *v.,* 2 *n.*

yield ing (yēl′ding), not resisting; submissive: *a person with a humble and yielding nature. adj.*

yip (yip), INFORMAL. 1 (especially of dogs) bark or yelp briskly. 2 a sharp, barking sound. 1 *v.,* **yipped, yip ping;** 2 *n.*

Y.M.C.A., Young Men's Christian Association.

Y.M.H.A., Young Men's Hebrew Association.

yo del (yō′dl), 1 sing with frequent changes from the ordinary voice to a forced shrill voice or falsetto and back again, in the manner of mountaineers of Switzerland and the Tirol. 2 act or sound of yodeling. 1 *v.,* 2 *n.* —**yo′del er,** *n.*

yo dle (yō′dl), yodel. *v.,* **yo dled, yo dling;** *n.*

yo ga or **Yo ga** (yō′gə), 1 system of Hindu religious philosophy that requires intense mental and physical discipline as a means of attaining a state of union with the universal spirit. 2 system of physical exercises and positions used in yoga. *n.*

yo gi (yō′gē), person who practices or follows yoga. *n., pl.* **yo gis.**

yo gurt (yō′gərt), kind of thickened, slightly fermented liquid food made from milk acted upon by bacteria. *n.*

yoke (yōk), 1 a wooden frame which fits around the necks of two work ani-

yoke
(def. 1)

YOKE

mals to fasten them together for pulling a plow or vehicle. 2 pair fastened together by a yoke: *The plow was drawn by a yoke of oxen.* 3 any frame connecting two other parts: *I tried to carry two buckets on a yoke, one at each end.* 4 put a yoke on; fasten with a yoke. 5 harness or fasten a work animal or animals to: *The farmer yoked the plow.* 6 part of a garment fitting the neck and shoulders closely. 7 a top piece to a skirt, fitting the hips. 8 something that binds together; bond; tie: *the yoke of marriage.* 9 join; unite: *They are yoked in marriage.* 10 something that holds people in slavery or submission: *Throw off your yoke and be free.* 11 rule; dominion: *The country was under the yoke of a dictator.* 1-3,6-8,10,11 *n.,* 4,5,9 *v.,* **yoked, yok ing.**

yoke fel low (yōk′fel′ō), 1 person associated with another in a task; partner. 2 husband or wife. *n.*

yo kel (yō′kəl), a country fellow. *n.*

Yo ko ha ma (yō′kə hä′mə), large seaport in central Japan, near Tokyo. *n.*

yolk (yōk), 1 the yellow part of an egg. 2 fat or grease in sheep's wool. *n.*

Yom Kip pur (yom kip′ər), a Jewish fast day of atonement for sins; Day of Atonement. It occurs ten days after Rosh Hashanah, the Jewish New Year.

yon (yon), OLD USE. yonder. *adj., adv.*

yond (yond), OLD USE. yonder. *adj., adv.*

yon der (yon′dər), 1 within sight, but not near; over there: *Look at that wild duck yonder! The sky is getting black yonder in the west.* 2 being within sight, but not near; situated over there: *On yonder hill stands a ruined castle.* 3 farther; more distant: *Look at the snow on yonder mountains.* 1 *adv.,* 2,3 *adj.*

Yon kers (yong′kərz), city just north of New York City. *n.*

yore (yôr). **of yore,** now long since gone; long past: *She told us an old tale about days of yore. adv.*

York (yôrk), 1 city in NE England. 2 Yorkshire. 3 the English royal house from 1461 to 1485. Its emblem was a white rose. 4 industrial city in SE Pennsylvania. *n.*

York shire (yôrk′shər), county in NE England. *n.*

Yorkshire pudding, a batter cake often served with roast beef.

Yorkshire terrier, one of an English breed of small, shaggy dogs with a steel-blue coat, weighing 4 to 8 pounds.

York town (yôrk′toun′), town in SE Virginia, where Lord Cornwallis surrendered to George Washington in 1781. *n.*

Yo sem i te (yō sem′ə tē), 1 Yosemite National Park. 2 a very deep valley in

this park, famous for its lofty, beautiful waterfalls. *n.*

Yosemite National Park, large national park in E California.

you (yü; *unstressed* yü), 1 the person or persons spoken to: *Are you ready? Then you may go.* 2 one; anybody: *You never can tell. You push this button to get a light. pron. sing. or pl.*

you'd (yüd; *unstressed* yůd), 1 you had. 2 you would.

you'll (yül; *unstressed* yůl), 1 you will. 2 you shall.

young (yung), 1 in the early part of life or growth; not old: *A puppy is a young dog.* 2 young offspring: *An animal will fight to protect its young.* 3 **the young,** young people. 4 having the looks or qualities of youth or a young person: *She looks and acts young for her age.* 5 of youth; early: *one's young days.* 6 not so old as another or the other: *Young Mr. Jones worked for his father.* 7 in an early stage; not far advanced: *The night was still young when they left the party.* 8 without much experience or practice: *I was too young in the trade to be successful.* 1,4-8 *adj.,* **young er** (yung′gər), **young est** (yung′gist), 2,3 *n.*

with young, pregnant.

Young (yung), **Brigham,** 1801-1877, American Mormon leader. *n.*

young ish (yung′ish), rather young. *adj.*

young ling (yung′ling), 1 a young person, animal, or plant. 2 young; youthful. 1 *n.,* 2 *adj.*

young ster (yung′stər), 1 child: *He is a lively youngster.* 2 a young person: *The old woman was as spry as a youngster. n.*

Youngs town (yungz′toun′), city in NE Ohio. *n.*

your (yůr; *unstressed* yər), 1 belonging to you: *Wash your hands.* 2 having to do with you: *We enjoyed your visit.* 3 that you know; well-known; that you speak of; that is spoken of: *your real lover of music, your average voter.* 4 *Your* is used as part of a title. *Your Lordship, Your Ladyship, Your Highness, Your Honor. adj.*

you're (yůr; *unstressed* yər), you are.

yours (yůrz), 1 the one or ones belonging to you: *This pencil is yours. My hands are clean; yours are dirty.* 2 at your service: *I am yours to command.* 3 *Yours* is used in closing a letter, just before the signature. *Yours truly, Sincerely yours, Yours, as ever. pron. sing. or pl.*

your self (yůr self′ or yər self′), 1 form of *you* used to make a statement stronger: *You yourself know the story is not true.* 2 form used instead of *you* in cases like: *Did you hurt yourself? Ask* *yourself what you really want. Try to do it by yourself.* **3** your real or true self: *Now that your cold is better, you'll feel like yourself again.* *pron., pl.* **yourselves.**

your selves (yùr selvz′ *or* yər selvz′), plural of **yourself.** *You can all see for yourselves that the jar is full.* *pron.*

youth (yüth), **1** fact or quality of being young: *She has all the vigor of youth.* **2** the time between childhood and adulthood. **3** a young man. **4** young people. **5** the first or early stage of anything: *Many of our beliefs go back to the youth of this country.* *n., pl.* **youths** (yüths *or* yüꟘHz), **youth.**

youth ful (yüth′fəl), **1** young. **2** of or suitable for youth: *youthful faults, youthful energy, youthful clothing.* **3** having the looks or qualities of youth; fresh; lively: *The old man had a very gay and youthful spirit.* *adj.* —**youth′ful ness,** *n.*

youth ful ly (yüth′fə lē), in a youthful manner. *adv.*

you've (yüv; *unstressed* yùv), you have.

yowl (youl), **1** a long, distressful, or dismal cry; howl. **2** to howl: *That dog is always yowling.* **1** *n.,* **2** *v.*

yo yo (yō′yō), a small toy consisting of a deeply grooved disk which is spun out and reeled in by means of an attached string. *n., pl.* **yo yos.**

Y pres (ē′prə), town in W Belgium. Many battles of World War I were fought there. *n.*

yr., year. *pl.* **yr.** *or* **yrs.**

yt ter bi um (i tèr′bē əm), a metallic

element which occurs in certain minerals and is used in making special alloys. *n.* [from *Ytterby,* a town in Sweden, where it was first discovered]

yt tri um (it′rē əm), a metallic element which occurs in various minerals. It is used in making iron alloys and to remove impurities from metals. *n.* [from a changed form of *Ytterby,* a town in Sweden]

Yu ca tán (yü′kə tan′), **1** peninsula of SE Mexico and N Central America. **2** state in SE Mexico. *n.*

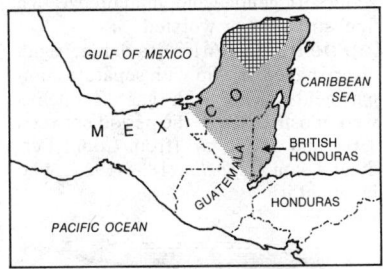

Yucatán (def. 1, entire shaded area)
(def. 2, upper shaded area only)

yuc ca (yuk′ə), **1** plant found in dry, warm regions of North and Central America, having stiff, narrow leaves at its base and an upright cluster of white, bell-shaped flowers. **2** its flower. *n., pl.* **yuc cas.**

Yu go slav (yü′gō släv′), **1** person born or living in Yugoslavia. **2** of or having to do with Yugoslavia or its people. **1** *n.,* **2** *adj.* Also, **Jugoslav.**

hat, āge, fär; let, ēqual, tèrm;
it, īce; hot, ōpen, ôrder;
oil, out; cup, pùt, rüle; ch, child;
ng, long; sh, she; th, thin;
ꟘH, then; zh, measure;

ə represents *a* in about,
e in taken, *i* in pencil,
o in lemon, *u* in circus.

Yu go sla vi a (yü′gō slä′vē ə), country in SE Europe, on the Adriatic. *Capital:* Belgrade. *n.* Also, **Jugoslavia.** —**Yu′go sla′vi an,** *adj., n.*

Yu kon (yü′kon), **1** river in Canada and flowing through Alaska into the Bering Sea. **2** territory in NW Canada. *Capital:* Whitehorse. *n.*

yule or **Yule** (yül), **1** Christmas. **2** yuletide. *n.*

Yule log, a large log burned at Christmas.

yule tide or **Yule tide** (yül′tīd′), Christmastide; the Christmas season. *n.*

yum my (yum′ē), SLANG. very pleasing to the senses; delicious; delightful. *adj.,* **yum mi er, yum mi est.**

Y.W.C.A., Young Women's Christian Association.

Y.W.H.A., Young Women's Hebrew Association.

y wis (i wis′), OLD USE. certainly; indeed. *adv.*

Z z

Z or **z** (zē), the 26th and last letter of the alphabet. *n., pl.* **Z's** or **z's.**

Zach a ri ah (zak′ə rī′ə), in the Bible: 1 the father of John the Baptist. 2 a man mentioned as a martyr in the New Testament. *n.*

Za greb (zä′greb), city in NW Yugoslavia. *n.*

Za ïre (zä ir′ *or* zar), 1 country in central Africa. It was formerly called **Democratic Republic of the Congo.** *Capital:* Kinshasa. See **Congo** for map. 2 Congo (def. 1). *n.*

Zam be zi (zam bē′zē), river flowing through S Africa into the Indian Ocean. *n.*

Zam bi a (zam′bē ə), country in S Africa, a member of the British Commonwealth. See **South Africa** for map. *n.* —**Zam′bi an,** *adj., n.*

za ny (zā′nē), 1 a fool. 2 a clown. 3 clownish; foolish; idiotic. 1,2 *n., pl.* **za nies;** 3 *adj.,* **za ni er, za ni est.**

Zan zi bar (zan′zə bär), island near the E coast of Africa. It is part of Tanzania. *n.*

zeal (zēl), eager desire or effort; earnest enthusiasm: *work with zeal. n.*

Zea land (zē′lənd), the largest island in Denmark, in the E part. Copenhagen is located on it. *n.*

zeal ot (zel′ət), person who shows too much zeal; fanatic. *n.*

zeal ous (zel′əs), full of zeal; eager; earnest; enthusiastic: *They seem very zealous to please. We made zealous efforts to clean up the house. adj.* —**zeal′ous ly,** *adv.* —**zeal′ous ness,** *n.*

Zeb e dee (zeb′ə dē′), (in the Bible) the father of the apostles James and John. *n.*

ze bra (zē′brə), a wild mammal of Africa, related to the horse or donkey but striped with dark bands on white. *n., pl.* **ze bras** or **ze bra.**

zebu—up to 5 ft. high at the shoulder

ze bu (zē′byü), mammal like an ox but with a large hump. The zebu is a domestic animal in Asia and eastern Africa. *n.*

Zech a ri ah (zek′ə rī′ə), 1 a Hebrew prophet of the 500's B.C. 2 book of the Old Testament. *n.*

Zen Buddhism (zen), a Japanese form of Buddhism that emphasizes meditation and introspection.

ze nith (zē′nith), 1 the point in the heavens directly overhead; point where a vertical line would pierce the sky. To an observer at the North Pole, the North Star would be about at his zenith. 2 the highest point: *At the zenith of its power Rome dominated the world. n.*

Ze no (zē′nō), 336?-264? B.C., Greek philosopher. *n.*

zeph yr (zef′ər), 1 the west wind. 2 any soft, gentle wind; mild breeze. 3 a fine, soft yarn or worsted. *n.*

Zep pe lin (zep′ə lən), a large, rigid, cigar-shaped airship with separate compartments filled with gas. Zeppelins were mostly used in the period between 1914 and 1937. *n.* [from Count Ferdinand von *Zeppelin,* 1838-1917, who invented it]

Zeppelin moored

zer o (zir′ō), 1 the figure or digit 0; naught. Zero shows the absence of quantity. 2 point marked with a zero on the scale of a thermometer, etc. 3 temperature that corresponds to zero on the scale of a thermometer. 4 of or at zero: *The other team's score was zero.* 5 complete absence of quantity; nothing. 6 not any; none at all: *zero visibility in dense fog.* 7 a very low point: *The team's spirit sank to zero after its fifth straight defeat.* 1-3,5,7 *n., pl.* **zer os** or **zer oes;** 4,6 *adj.*

zero in on, 1 get the range of (a target) by adjusting the sights of a firearm, etc. 2 to aim with precision toward (a target).

zero g or **zero gravity,** condition in which the effects of gravity are not felt. In an orbiting spacecraft, zero g is experienced as weightlessness.

zero hour, 1 time set for beginning an attack or other military operation. 2 time set for any important action to begin; crucial moment.

zest (zest), 1 keen enjoyment; relish: *The hungry man ate with zest.* 2 a pleasant or exciting quality, flavor, etc.: *Wit gives zest to conversation. n.*

zest ful (zest′fəl), characterized by zest. *adj.* —**zest′ful ly,** *adv.* —**zest′ful ness,** *n.*

zest y (zes′tē), having much zest; full of zest; zestful. *adj.,* **zest i er, zest i est.**

Zeus (züs), (in Greek myths) the chief

zenith (def. 1)
Observer A has zenith Z_1 and nadir N_1;
Observer B has zenith Z_2 and nadir N_2.

god, ruler of gods and human beings. The Romans called him Jupiter. *n.*

zig gu rat (zig′ù rat), an ancient Assyrian and Babylonian temple in the form of a great pyramid having stories each smaller than that below it, so as to leave a terrace at each level. *n.*

zig zag (zig′zag′), 1 with short, sharp turns from one side to the other: *to go in a zigzag direction* (adj.). *The path ran zigzag up the hill* (adv.). 2 move in a zigzag way: *Lightning zigzagged across the sky.* 3 a zigzag line or course. 4 one of the short, sharp turns of a zigzag. 1 *adj., adv.,* 2 *v.,* **zig zagged, zig zagging;** 3,4 *n.*

zigzag (def. 1)—zigzag design

zinc (zingk), a bluish-white metallic element that is little affected by air and moisture at ordinary temperatures, but at high temperatures it burns in air with a bright, blue-green flame. Zinc is used as a coating for iron, in alloys such as brass, as a roofing material, in electric batteries, in paint, and in medicine. *n.*

zinc oxide, compound of zinc and oxygen, used in making paint, rubber, glass, cosmetics, and ointments.

zing (zing), 1 a sharp, humming sound. 2 SLANG. liveliness; spirit; zest: *a story without zing.* 1,2 *n.,* 1 *interj.*

zin ni a (zin′ē ə), 1 a garden plant grown for its showy flowers of many colors. 2 its flower. *n., pl.* **zin ni as.** [from Johann *Zinn,* 1727-1759, a German botanist]

Zi on (zī′ən), 1 hill in Jerusalem on which the royal palace and the Temple were built. 2 Israel or the Israelites; the people of Israel. 3 heaven, as the final home of those who are virtuous. 4 the Christian church of God. *n.*

984

Zi on ism (zī′ə niz′əm), movement that started in the 1800's to set up a Jewish national state in Palestine and that now seeks to help maintain and develop the state of Israel. *n.*

Zi on ist (zī′ə nist), person who supports or favors Zionism. *n.*

Zion National Park, a national park in SW Utah.

FRIGID ZONE *N*

TEMPERATE ZONE

EQUATOR

TORRID ZONE

TEMPERATE ZONE

FRIGID ZONE *s*

zone (def. 1)

zip (zip), 1 fasten or close with a zipper: *zip up one's jacket before going out.* 2 a sudden, brief, hissing sound, as of a flying bullet. 3 make such a sound. 4 INFORMAL. energy or vim. 5 INFORMAL. proceed with energy. 1,3,5 *v.*, **zipped, zip ping;** 2,4 *n.*

Zip Code, 1 Zone Improvement Plan Code (system of numbers, each number of which identifies one of the postal delivery areas into which the United States and its larger cities have been divided). 2 a number in this system.

zip per (zip′ər), 1 a sliding fastener for clothing, shoes, etc.: *a zipper on a jacket.* 2 fasten or close with a zipper: *Zipper up your jacket before you go out in the cold.* 1 *n.*, 2 *v.*

zip py (zip′ē), INFORMAL. full of energy; lively; gay. *adj.*, **zip pi er, zip pi est.**

zir con (zėr′kon), a crystalline mineral that occurs in various forms and colors. Transparent zircon is used as a gem. *n.*

zir co ni um (zėr′kō′nē əm), a white metallic element obtained from zircon. Zirconium is used in alloys for wires, filaments, etc., in making steel, and in atomic reactors. *n.*

zith er (zith′ər *or* zĭтн′ər), a musical instrument having 30 to 40 strings, played with the fingers and a plectrum. *n.*

zo di ac (zō′dē ak), 1 an imaginary belt of the heavens extending on both sides of the apparent yearly path of the sun and including the apparent path of the major planets and the moon. The zodiac is divided into 12 equal parts, called signs, named after 12 groups of stars. 2 diagram representing the zodiac, used in astrology. *n.*

zo di a cal (zō dī′ə kəl), 1 of or having to do with the zodiac. 2 situated in the zodiac. *adj.*

Zo la (zō′lə), Émile, 1840-1902, French novelist. *n.*

zom bi (zom′bē), zombie. *n., pl.* **zom bis.**

zom bie (zom′bē), 1 corpse supposedly brought to a trancelike condition resembling life by a supernatural power. People who practice voodoo believe in zombies. 2 a supernatural power or force that supposedly makes the dead move and act. *n., pl.* **zombies.**

zon al (zō′nl), 1 of a zone; having to do with zones. 2 divided into zones. *adj.*

zone (zōn), 1 any of the five great divisions of the earth's surface, bounded by imaginary lines going around the earth parallel to the equator. 2 any region or area especially considered or set off. A combat zone is a district where fighting is going on. 3 area or district in a city or town under special restrictions as to building. 4 one of the numbered sections into which a large city or metropolitan area is divided in order to speed the sorting and delivery of mail. 5 a circular area or district within which the same rate of postage is charged for parcel post shipments from a particular point. 6 divide into zones: *The city was zoned for factories and residences.* 7 be formed into zones. 8 OLD USE. belt; girdle. 9 surround like a belt or girdle. 10 surround with a belt or girdle. 1-5,8 *n.*, 6,7,9,10 *v.*, **zoned, zon ing.**

zoo (zü), place where animals are kept and shown; zoological garden: *Father takes us to the zoo every summer. We saw lions and tigers in the zoo. There are often many tame animals in a children's zoo. n., pl.* **zoos.**

zither

zo o log i cal (zō′ə loj′ə kəl), 1 of animals and animal life. 2 having to do with zoology. *adj.* —**zo′o log′i cal ly,** *adv.*

zoological garden, zoo.

zo ol o gist (zō ol′ə jist), an expert in zoology. *n.*

zo ol o gy (zō ol′ə jē), 1 the science of animals; the study of animals and animal life. Zoology is a branch of biology.

hat, āge, fär; let, ēqual, tėrm;
it, īce; hot, ōpen, ôrder;
oil, out; cup, pùt, rüle; ch, child;
ng, long; sh, she; th, thin;
тн, then; zh, measure;

ə represents *a* in about,
e in taken, *i* in pencil,
o in lemon, *u* in circus.

2 the animals inhabiting a certain area. *n.*

zoom (züm), 1 move suddenly upward: *The airplane zoomed.* 2 an act of zooming; sudden upward flight: *The airplane made a zoom and left the mountain far below.* 3 move or travel with a humming or buzzing sound. 1,3 *v.*, 2 *n.*

Zo ro as ter (zôr′ō as′tər), famous Persian religious teacher who lived about 600 B.C. *n.*

Zo ro as tri an (zôr′ō as′trē ən), 1 of or having to do with Zoroaster or the religion founded by him. 2 person believing in the teachings of Zoroaster. 1 *adj.*, 2 *n.*

Zo ro as tri an ism (zôr′ō as′trē ə niz′əm), religion founded by Zoroaster and practiced in ancient Persia. Zoroastrianism taught that there is an eternal struggle between the powers of light and the powers of darkness. *n.*

zounds (zoundz), OLD USE. oath expressing surprise or anger. *interj.*

zuc chi ni (zü kē′nē), 1 kind of dark-green squash shaped like a cucumber. It is eaten as a vegetable. 2 plant it grows on. *n., pl.* **zuc chi ni** or **zuc chi nis.**

Zui der Zee (zī′dər zē′), a shallow gulf in central Netherlands. It is now closed off from the North Sea by a dike. Also, **Zuyder Zee.**

Zu lu (zü′lü), 1 member of a large, formerly warlike, Bantu people of Africa. 2 their language. 3 of this people or their language. 1,2 *n., pl.* **Zu lus** or **Zu lu;** 3 *adj.*

Zu lu land (zü′lü land), territory in NE Natal, in the Republic of South Africa. Zululand is the home of the Zulus. *n.*

Zu ñi (zü′nyē), member of a tribe of Pueblo Indians living in western New Mexico. *n., pl.* **Zu ñis** or **Zu ñi.**

Zur ich (zür′ik), city in N Switzerland. *n.*

Zuy der Zee (zī′dər zē′), Zuider Zee.

zwie back (swī′bak′ *or* zwī′bak′), kind of bread or cake cut into slices and toasted dry in an oven. *n.*

zy gote (zī′gōt), the cell formed by the union of two germ cells or gametes. A fertilized egg is a zygote. *n.*